DIRECT

MARKETING

MARKET PLACE®

The Networking Source of the Direct Marketing Industry

DMMP
2013

DIRECT

MARKETING

MARKET PLACE®

The Networking Source of the Direct Marketing Industry

DMMP
2013

National Register Publishing
A division of Marquis Who's Who LLC

Berkeley Heights, New Jersey

National Register Publishing
A division of Marquis Who's Who LLC

Chairman	James A. Finkelstein
Chief Executive Officer	Fred Marks
Chief Technology Officer	Ariel Spivakovsky
Publisher	Robert Docherty

Editorial

Managing Editor	Eileen Fanning
Content Manager	Rachel S. Pattabhi
Editors	Linda Hummer
	Elizabeth Melillo
	Mary Whitehouse

Editorial Services

Production Manager	David Lubanski

Marketing

Business Analyst & Forecasting Manager	Kim Pappas
Creative Services Manager	Kathleen F. Stein

Marketing Analysts:	Abhijeet Atalia
	Jeff Fitzgerald

Sales

Director of Sales	Kelli MacKinnon
Wholesale Account Representative	Gina Marie Delia

Information Technology

Director of IT Development	Jeff Rooney
Director of Web Operations	Ben McCullough
Composition Programmer	Tom Haggerty
Manager of Web Development	Orlando Freda
Database Programmer	Latha Shankar

Published by Marquis Who's Who LLC.

For information, contact:
  Marquis Who's Who
  300 Connell Drive, Suite 2000
  Berkeley Heights, New Jersey 07922
  1-908-673-1000
  www.marquiswhoswho.com

DIRECT MARKETING MARKET PLACE ® is a trademark of Marquis Who's Who LLC.

Library of Congress Catalog Card Number   79-649244
International Standard Book Number   978-0-87217-015-5

Manufactured in the United States of America.

Contents

SERVICE FIRMS & SUPPLIERS (Continued)

CREATIVE SERVICES (35-39)

ASSOCIATIONS, COURSES, & EVENTS (40-42)

BIBLIOGRAPHY (43)

INDEXES

Preface

Since 1980, National Register Publishing's *Direct Marketing Market Place* (DMMP) has been the one-stop source for all of your direct marketing needs. DMMP encompasses each segment of the industry, from companies who use direct marketing to the companies that supply them.

CONTENT AND COVERAGE

At your fingertips are approximately 9,300 organizations in the direct marketing industry, with over 17,300 key personnel listed. To keep pace with the changing industry, we enhanced this directory to include e-mail and web site addresses when provided by the entrant. A company's listing will note whether a catalog is available online and if its products and services are available online.

Entries generally include the company name, address, phone and fax numbers, and at least one key executive. Some companies provide gross sales or billings, number of employees, countries in which they conduct business, whether they market primarily to consumers or businesses, and information about their direct marketing budget. A THE DMA symbol to the left of a company's name denotes the company's membership in The Direct Marketing Association.

ARRANGEMENT AND INDEXES

DMMP is comprised of 43 sections divided into five chapters representing key segments of the direct marketing industry: Direct Marketers (1-19); Service Firms & Suppliers (20-34); Creative Services (35-39); Associations, Courses & Events (40-42); Bibliography (43).

DMMP features a cumulative Alphabetical Index to Companies & Individuals, which references all companies and personnel by section number. The company entries in this index feature the name, city and state or province, telephone and fax numbers, as well as e-mail and web site addresses. The individual entries in this index reference each company's name, city and state or province, telephone and fax numbers. Companies and individuals are listed together in an alphabetical format.

The Direct Marketers chapter includes a geographic index listing all companies contained in the chapter by state or province. Two additional indexes identify direct marketers by their market: business or consumer. Geographic indexes precede each section in both the Service Firms and Suppliers and Creative Services chapters. These indexes allow the user to easily locate a company providing a particular service in his or her local area.

COMPILATION METHOD

The *Direct Marketing Market Place* is compiled and updated from information supplied by the organizations themselves. Every organization is sent a questionnaire prior to inclusion in each edition. Wherever possible, entrants not responding to the questionnaires are verified by our research department.

RELATED SERVICES

Mailing lists or database tapes in raw data format compiled from information contained in the *Direct Marketing Market Place* may be ordered from Agnes Orlowska, 300 Connell Dr., Suite 2000, Berkeley Heights, NJ

07922, telephone (800) 473-7020, ext. 1206.

ACKNOWLEDGEMENTS

Thanks to the thousands of organizations throughout the United States and Canada who took the time to provide us with the information necessary to compile an accurate, comprehensive *Direct Marketing Market Place.*

In addition to keeping information in our directory as up to date as possible, we are constantly trying to improve the design and add features, which our subscribers will find useful. If you have a question about your company's listing or would like to offer any comments or suggestions, please call the NRP/Marquis Editorial Staff at (800) 473-7020, or write to us at: National Register Publishing, DMMP Editorial, 300 Connell Drive, Suite 2000, Berkeley Heights, NJ 07922.

Direct Marketing Association

The Direct Marketing Association (www.the-dma.org) is the world's largest trade association of businesses and nonprofit organizations using and supporting multichannel direct marketing techniques. DMA advocates standards for responsible marketing, promotes relevance as the key to reaching consumers with desirable offers, and provides cutting-edge research, education, and networking opportunities to improve results throughout the end-to-end direct marketing process. Founded in 1917, DMA today represents companies from dozens of vertical industries in the US and 48 other nations, including half of the Fortune 100 companies.

DMA represents its members' interests in each of the 50 states as well as on Capitol Hill, at the Federal TradeCommission, the Federal Communications Commission, and other agencies such as the United States PostalService (USPS). Each year, DMA tracks thousands of proposed laws and regulations in Washington, DC, and across the nation. We address key federal and state policy issues that affect the direct marketing community, including self-regulation, behavioral marketing, data security, privacy, postal reform, and many others.

DMA believes the best way to honor consumer choices in the ever-expanding digital marketplace is through self-regulation. DMA has maintained the preeminent marketing self-regulatory programs in the United States for the past 35years. The DMA self-regulatory initiative covers all marketing channels, including mobile, online (behavioral advertising), mail, and social media. DMA is the only trade association that covers and lobbies on legislation in all 50 US states, protecting direct marketing and fundraising.

In 2011, DMA partnered with other associations to launch the Self-Regulatory Program for Online Behavioral Advertising, which gives consumers a better understanding of and greater control over ads that are customized based on their online behavior. In 2012, during a special White House event, DMA and our partners in the Digital Advertising Alliance (DAA) were recognized by the Obama Administration for our work on data protection and self-regulation. In addition, the Administration indicated that they want us to play a critical role as the privacy discussion moves to the standardization of processes at the browser level.

DMA conferences and events arm marketers with a rich array of specialized skills built on a strong foundation of data and analytics – focusing on cross-channel marketing techniques that engage customers in real time and deliver measurable results. DMA conferences present the best classic and current marketing techniques across all industry segments. DMA hosts a wide range of conferences and events, including the DMA Annual Conference & Exhibition, the Global Event for Integrated Marketing. This global event for real-time marketers delivers everything marketers need to know about data, customer engagement, and accountable marketing.

DMA is recognized throughout the marketing community as a definitive source for leading-edge education —providing cutting-edge professional training and seminars. From one-off workshops to comprehensive certification programs and webinars, we address virtually every aspect of direct and digital marketing. In 2012, DMA launched the Institute for Marketing Data Governance and Certification, a comprehensive course and certification for marketers who use, access, and live in the world of data and information. The course details the most current information on the public policy debate about data and information, covering all facets of marketing data governance.

DMA research highlights and analyzes the latest industry trends, helping DMA member companies and the marketing community at-large maintain profitability in changing economic times. The DMA research department is committed to staying ahead of marketing advancements, tracking marketing trends and providing actionable benchmarks for the marketing community. Our studies provide detailed, far-reaching coverage of all marketing channels. In 2012, marketers — commercial and nonprofit —will spend $168.5 billion on direct marketing, which accounts for 52.7 percent of all ad expenditures in the United States. Measured against total US sales, these advertising expenditures will generate approximately $2.05 trillion in incremental sales. In 2012, direct marketing accounts for 8.7 percent of total US gross domestic product and produces 1.3 million direct marketing employees in the US. Their collective sales efforts directly support 7.9 million other jobs, accounting for a total of 9.2 million US jobs.

Canadian Marketing Association

The Canadian Marketing Association (CMA) embraces Canada's major business sectors and all marketing disciplines, channels and technologies. Our programs help shape the future of marketing in Canada by building talented marketers and exceptional business leaders and by demonstrating marketing's strategic role as a key driver of business success. Our members make a major contribution to the Canadian economy through the sale of goods and services, investments in media and new marketing technologies and employment for Canadians.

CMA is the marketing community's leading advocate on the key public policy issues which impact marketing. Current threats include Canada's new anti-spam law and its impact on ecommerce, restrictions on online interest-based advertising and tighter consumer privacy laws. CMA also leads the marketing community by developing self-regulatory policies and marketing best practices to protect the marketplace against unwarranted government intervention. Compliance with the Association's Code of Ethics and Standards of Practice is compulsory for our members. We also offer a Do Not Contact Service, whereby consumers register without charge to have their names and addresses removed from marketing lists held by CMA Member organizations; and a customer complaint resolution program known as Operation Integrity.

The Association promotes industry growth, development and education through its network of nine marketing councils. These multi-disciplined groups provide a forum for members to exchange marketing intelligence through research, case studies, white papers, articles and guidelines. Supporting this activity is the Association's website – www.the-cma.org — an important information resource on the key issues facing the marketing community.

CMA professional development programs are designed to help marketers sharpen their skill set and acquire new skills. We offer marketing certificate courses on research and analytics, integrated branding, e-marketing, advertising and media, direct marketing and strategic promotions and provide in-house training and seminars. And we feature an education platform that includes webinars, conferences, the CMA Summit and the CMA Awards program.

The Canadian Marketing Association was established in 1967. Headquartered in Toronto, CMA is a national not-for-profit corporation with affiliated organizations in Quebec, Ontario, Manitoba, Alberta and British Columbia. An elected Board of Directors nominated from the Association membership determines CMA policies. The Association is managed by a full-time professional staff.

Summary of DM Advertising Expenditures
(BILLIONS OF DOLLARS)

	2006	2010	2011	2012	2016	COMPOUND ANNUAL GROWTH	
						2006-11	2011-16
TOTAL DM ADVERTISING EXPENDITURES	$170.8	$154.4	$163.0	$168.5	$196.0	-0.9%	3.8%

	2006	2010	2011	2012	2016	COMPOUND ANNUAL GROWTH	
DM ADVERTISING EXPENDITURES BY MEDIUM						2006-11	2011-16
DIRECT MAIL (TOTAL)	$53.1	$47.8	$50.1	$51.1	$57.6	-1.2%	2.8%
DIRECT MAIL (NON-CATALOG)	33.0	31.5	32.8	33.4	37.1	-0.1%	2.5%
DIRECT MAIL (CATALOG)	20.1	16.4	17.3	17.7	20.5	-3.0%	3.5%
TELEPHONE MARKETING	44.8	36.3	36.6	36.9	38.1	-3.9%	0.8%
INTERNET MARKETING (NON-EMAIL)	15.9	24.2	28.8	32.5	48.4	12.7%	10.9%
INTERNET DISPLAY	5.0	7.2	8.5	9.5	14.1	11.3%	10.6%
INTERNET SEARCH	8.4	11.8	13.9	15.6	22.4	10.6%	9.9%
SOCIAL NETWORKING	0.6	2.0	2.5	3.0	6.1	34.4%	19.4%
INTERNET OTHER	1.9	3.2	3.9	4.4	5.9	15.7%	8.8%
MOBILE	0.1	0.6	0.9	1.2	3.1	75.2%	28.7%
COMMERCIAL EMAIL	0.8	1.4	1.6	1.7	2.3	13.8%	8.6%
DR NEWSPAPER	16.1	8.4	7.8	7.0	4.9	-13.6%	-9.0%
DR TELEVISION	22.0	20.8	22.1	22.9	25.9	0.1%	3.2%
DR MAGAZINE	8.4	6.9	7.0	6.9	7.2	-3.7%	0.6%
DR RADIO	4.9	3.9	3.9	3.8	3.9	-4.4%	-0.2%
INSERT MEDIA	1.9	2.1	2.1	2.2	2.3	2.4%	1.7%
OTHER	2.8	2.0	2.1	2.1	2.3	-5.2%	1.4%

Summary of DM-Driven Sales

(BILLIONS OF DOLLARS)

	2006	2010	2011	2012	2016	COMPOUND ANNUAL GROWTH 2006-11	COMPOUND ANNUAL GROWTH 2011-16
TOTAL DM SALES	$1,948.4	$1,830.7	$1,960.5	$2,052.3	$2,489.8	0.1%	4.9%

DM SALES BY MEDIUM	2006	2010	2011	2012	2016	COMPOUND ANNUAL GROWTH 2006-11	COMPOUND ANNUAL GROWTH 2011-16
DIRECT MAIL (TOTAL)	$654.9	$604.6	$630.5	$642.4	$724.1	-0.8%	2.8%
DIRECT MAIL (NON-CATALOG)	510.4	484.6	504.5	513.8	577.4	-0.2%	2.7%
DIRECT MAIL (CATALOG)	144.5	120.0	126.1	128.6	146.7	-2.7%	3.1%
TELEPHONE MARKETING	379.2	303.6	303.6	305.1	310.0	-4.3%	0.4%
INTERNET MARKETING (NON-EMAIL)	338.7	480.0	576.0	651.8	970.3	11.2%	11.0%
INTERNET DISPLAY	103.5	141.9	168.1	186.9	279.2	10.2%	10.7%
INTERNET SEARCH	197.1	259.3	309.7	350.2	506.1	9.5%	10.3%
SOCIAL NETWORKING	7.1	24.7	31.9	38.8	81.8	34.9%	20.7%
INTERNET OTHER	30.9	54.1	66.2	76.0	103.3	16.4%	9.3%
MOBILE	0.3	6.0	9.4	14.0	39.1	98.3%	33.1%
COMMERCIAL EMAIL	42.7	57.8	63.1	67.8	82.2	8.2%	5.4%
DR NEWSPAPER	212.6	103.0	94.1	84.5	58.3	-15.0%	-9.1%
DR TELEVISION	150.6	136.6	143.3	147.6	163.4	-1.0%	2.7%
DR MAGAZINE	86.2	69.3	69.6	68.6	70.3	-4.2%	0.2%
DR RADIO	41.9	31.9	31.9	31.2	30.6	-5.3%	-0.8%
INSERT MEDIA	22.1	23.9	24.4	24.7	26.1	1.9%	1.4%
OTHER	19.3	14.0	14.6	14.6	15.5	-5.4%	1.2%

Association, Membership & Fundraising Organizations (1)

Listed in this section are associations, membership and fundraising organizations that use direct marketing. These may include, but are not limited to non-profit, religious, service or professional organizations. Direct marketing related organizations can be found in the section on Direct Marketing Associations, Clubs & Organizations (40).

AAA AUTO CLUB SOUTH
Subs. of American Automobile Association
1515 N Westshore Blvd
Tampa, FL 33607-4505
Telephone: (813) 289-1344, FAX: (813) 289-1340, Web Site: www.aaa.com
Pres: Robert Sharp
VP, Mktg & Publg: John Counter
Conducts Business: U.S.
Employees: 2,000
Primary Market Served: Business & Consumer
Founded: 1936

AAA membership, insurance & travel services.

AAA-CHICAGO MOTOR CLUB
Affiliate of American Automobile Association
975 Meridian Lake Dr
Aurora, IL 60504-4904
Telephone: (847) 390-9000, (866) 968-7222, FAX: (847) 390-7738, Web Site: www.aaa.com
VP Mktg & Travel Svcs: Jim Thompson
Mng Dir Membership Mktg: Ray Saathoff
Conducts Business: U.S.
Employees: 525
Primary Market Served: Business & Consumer
Catalog available online
Indirect online sales
Advertising/Marketing Budget Related to Direct Marketing: 26-50%
Founded: 1906

Membership, travel, insurance & financial services.

AAA SOUTHERN NEW ENGLAND
Div. of American Automobile Association
110 Royal Little Dr
Providence, RI 02904-1860
Telephone: (401) 868-2005, FAX: (401) 868-2085, Web Site: www.aaa.com
Sr VP Corp Affairs, AAA Southern New England: Robert P. Murray
VP, Mktg: Mary Wyatt
VP Travel: William Southerland
Car Doctor: John Paul
Conducts Business: U.S.
Employees: 1,900
Primary Market Served: Consumer
Catalog available online
Advertising/Marketing Budget Related to Direct Marketing: 26-50%
Direct Marketing ad budget:
Direct Mail: 74%
Magazines: 2%
TV/Radio: 24%
Gross sales or billing: $100,000,000

Tax-paying, not-for-profit organization offering a wide range of member services: automotive, travel agency, insurance & financial.

AAAS/SCIENCE
1200 New York Ave NW (fl 9)
Washington, DC 20005-3928
Telephone: (202) 326-6400, FAX: (202) 371-9526, E-Mail: webmaster@aaas.org, Web Site: www.aaas.org
Chmn: John Holden Dr.
Pres: David Baltimore Dr.
CEO: Alan I. Leshner Dr.
Treas: David E. Shaw
Conducts Business: U.S.
Employees: 210
Catalog available online
Direct online sales
Founded: 1848
Gross sales or billing: $85,000,000

Membership organization with some 137,000 individual members who are scientists, engineers & others interested in science. Publish Science, a weekly journal; Science Books & Films, a critical review of books, films, video cassettes & filmstrips & numerous other books. Also conduct various meetings each year.

AARP
THE DMA
601 E St NW
Washington, DC 20049-0003
Telephone: (202) 434-2277, Web Site: www.aarp.org
Sr VP Membership Devel/ Member Experience: Lynn Mento

ACBL
6575 Windchase Dr
Horn Lake, MS 38637-1523
Telephone: (901) 332-5586, FAX: (901) 398-7754, E-Mail: service@acbl.org, Web Site: www.acbl.org
CEO: Jay Baum
CFO: Jack Zdancewicz
COO: Gary Blaiss
Human Resources Dir: Barbara Varner
Acctg: Stan Katz
Conducts Business: U.S., Canada, Mexico, Bermuda
Employees: 85
Primary Market Served: Business & Consumer

Membership service organization for bridge players in North America.

ACN USA
THE DMA
725 Leonard St
Brooklyn, NY 11222-2350
Telephone: (212) 334-5340, Web Site: www.churchinneed.org
Natl Dir: Sarkis Boghjalian

Gift store selling religious items in support of the Church in Need

ADRA INTERNATIONAL
THE DMA
12501 Old Columbia Pike
Silver Spring, MD 20904-6601
Telephone: (301) 680-6373, Web Site: www.adra.org
Bureau Chief, Mktg & Devel: Julio Munoz

Agency that helps those in need

THE DMA ADRFCO
1612 K St NW (Suite 510)
Washington, DC 20006-2849
Telephone: (202) 293-9640, Web Site:
www.adrfco.org
Primary Market Served: Business &
Consumer

AFL-CIO
815 16th St NW (5th fl)
Washington, DC 20006
Telephone: (202) 637-5000, FAX:
(202) 637-5058, (202) 637-5323,
Web Site: www.aflcio.org
Sec & Treas: Richard Trumka
Exec VP: Arlene Holt Baker
Dir, Corp Affairs: Ron Blackwell
Employees: 380
Primary Market Served: Business &
Consumer
Founded: 1955

Association federation of approximately 80 international unions.

AIIM INTERNATIONAL
1100 Wayne Ave (Suite 1100)
Silver Spring, MD 20910-5616
Telephone: (301) 587-8202, (800) 477-2446, FAX: (301) 587-2711, E-Mail:
aiim@aiim.org, Web Site: www.aiim.
org
Chair: Jan Anderson
Vice Chmn: Robert W. Zagami
Pres: John Mancini
VP, Membership: Karen Carey
Mktg Dir: Meg Golberg
Conducts Business: Worldwide
Employees: 27
Primary Market Served: Business
Catalog available online
Direct online sales
Direct Marketing ad budget:
Direct Mail: 90%
Magazines: 5%
Newspapers: 1%
TV/Radio: 2%
Telephone: 2%

Global industry association that connects the users and suppliers of information management technologies; focuses on the technologies that are enablers of e-business; and produces events, provides industry research, education & information.

THE DMA ALSAC - ST. JUDE
501 Saint Jude Pl
Memphis, TN 38105-1905
Telephone: (901) 495-3300, FAX:
(901) 495-3103, Web Site: www.
stjude.org
COO: David McKee
Dir Mktg: Tabitha Glenne
Dir Fin Mktg & Analysis: Cynthia
Vanelli

Employees: 3,000
Primary Market Served: Consumer
Catalog available online
Indirect online sales
Founded: 1957

An international resource in the battle against childhood cancers. Conducts basic & clinical research into catastrophic childhood diseases, primarily childhood cancer & provides the necessary medical care for patients admitted to its research programs. Admission is based solely on medical criteria: children must be under 18 years of age with a physician referral, an illness relevant to studies at St Jude & have had no extensive treatment elsewhere. No family is turned away because of inability to pay. The hospital relies on donations from fundraising throughout the U.S.. The family & patient's domiciliary care is fully paid by St Jude.

**THE DMA AMVETS NATIONAL
SERVICE FOUNDATION**
Div. of AMVETS
4647 Forbes Blvd
Lanham, MD 20706
Telephone: (301) 459-6181, (877) 726-8387, FAX: (301) 459-5578, Web
Site: www.amvets.org
Controller: Robert Thompson
Exec Dir: Joe F. Ramsey Jr
Fin Mgr: Robert Gujral
Conducts Business: U.S.
Employees: 2,000
Primary Market Served: Consumer
Direct Marketing ad budget:
Direct Mail: $10,000,000
Gross sales or billing: $23,000,000

Fundraising through direct mail for parent organization.

ARE PRESS
Div. of Association for Research &
Enlightenment
215 67th St
Virginia Beach, VA 23451-2061
Telephone: (757) 491-0689, (888) 273-3400, FAX: (757) 491-0689, Web
Site: www.arepress.com
Pres: Charles Thomas Cayce
Conducts Business: Worldwide
Primary Market Served: Business &
Consumer
Advertising/Marketing Budget Related
to Direct Marketing: 51-75%
Direct Marketing ad budget:
Direct Mail: $300,000
Founded: 1931

Non-profit open membership organization interested in spiritual growth, holistic healing & parapsychology through the Edgar Cayce readings.

ASM INTERNATIONAL
9639 Kinsman Rd
Materials Park, OH 44073-0002
Telephone: (440) 338-5151, (800) 336-5152, FAX: (440) 338-4634, E-Mail:
customerservice@asminternational.
org, Web Site: www.
asminternational.org
Pres & CEO: Stanley C. Theobald
Pres & Bd Trustees: Dr. Diane Chong
Trustee: Sue S. Baik-Kromalic
VP: Roger J. Fabian
Treas: Paul L. Herber
Mktg & Commun Officer: Rego Giovanetti
Conducts Business: Worldwide
Employees: 125
Primary Market Served: Consumer
Catalog available online
Direct online sales
Advertising/Marketing Budget Related
to Direct Marketing: 76-100%
Direct Marketing ad budget:
Direct Mail: $2,000,000
Magazines: $10,000
Founded: 1913
Gross sales or billing: $16,000,000

Society of professionals in applications & research of metals & materials, supplying technical publications & educators.

THE DMA ASPCA
520 8th Ave (fl 7)
New York, NY 10018-4195
Telephone: (212) 876-7700, Web Site:
www.aspca.org
Sr VP, Devel: Todd Hendricks

ASTM INTERNATIONAL
100 Barr Harbor Dr
West Conshohocken, PA 19428-2959
Telephone: (610) 832-9500, FAX:
(610) 832-9555, E-Mail: service@
astm.org, Web Site: www.astm.org
Pres: James Thomas
Sr VP: Kenneth Pearson
VP: Teresa Cendrowska
Dir: Jim Olshefsky
Dir: Robert Morgan
Conducts Business: Worldwide
Employees: 200
Primary Market Served: Business
Catalog available online
Indirect online sales
Advertising/Marketing Budget Related
to Direct Marketing: 51-75%
Direct Marketing ad budget:
$1,500,000
Direct Mail: 98%
Magazines: 2%
Founded: 1898

Developer of voluntary consensus standards for materials, products, systems & services. Branch offices in Washington, DC & Hertfordshire, England.

ABBEY OF GETHSEMANI
3642 Monks Rd
New Haven, KY 40051-6152
Telephone: (502) 549-3117, FAX:
(502) 549-4124, Web Site: www.
monks.org
Mgr: Brother Anselm Brown
Friar: Peter Tong
Friar: Anton Rusnak
Conducts Business: U.S.
Employees: 85
Primary Market Served: Business &
Consumer
Advertising/Marketing Budget Related
to Direct Marketing: 76-100%
Founded: 1848

Monastery. Markets cheese, fruitcakes
& fudge.

ACCURACY IN MEDIA INC
4455 Connecticut Ave NW (Suite 330)
Washington, DC 20008-2372
Telephone: (202) 364-4401, FAX:
(202) 364-4098, E-Mail: info@aim.
org, Web Site: www.aim.org
Chmn: Donald Irvine
Pres: Gene Schaerr
VP: Joan Hueter
Exec Sec: Roger Aronoff
Opers Mgr: Heidi Barnes
Conducts Business: U.S.
Employees: 16
Primary Market Served: Business &
Consumer
Catalog available online
Direct online sales
Advertising/Marketing Budget Related
to Direct Marketing: 0-25%
Direct Marketing ad budget: $50,000
Direct Mail: 10%
Magazines: 60%
Online: 20%
TV/Radio: 10%
Founded: 1969

Newsletter about news media bias,
error & distortion - target audience is
news media consumers.

ACTIONAID
1420 K St NW (Suite 900)
Washington, DC 20005-2507
Telephone: (202) 835-1240, Web Site:
www.actionaidusa.org
Chief Devel Officer: Randi Hogan

THE ADVERTISING COUNCIL INC
815 2nd Ave (Bsmt 815 2nd Ave)
New York, NY 10017-4511
Telephone: (212) 922-1500, FAX:
(212) 922-1676, E-Mail: info@
adcouncil.org, Web Site: www.
adcouncil.org
Pres & CEO: Peggy Conlon
Sr VP: Donna Feiner

Exec VP: Paula Veale
Exec VP Media: Timothy Davis
Exec VP Devel: Barbara Leshinsky
Conducts Business: U.S.
Employees: 45
Primary Market Served: Business &
Consumer
Catalog available online
Advertising/Marketing Budget Related
to Direct Marketing: 51-75%
Founded: 1942
Gross sales or billing: $1,000,000,000

Non-profit organization that works to
create, produce, & distribute public
service announcements to the media, to
increase public awareness of critical
issues in education, environment, substance abuse, community service,
health & public safety.

AFFINITY FEDERAL CREDIT UNION
73 Mountain Rd
Basking Ridge, NJ 07920
Telephone: (908) 860-7306, Web Site:
www.affinityfcu.org
Sr Mktg Officer: Katharine Farrington
Primary Market Served: Consumer

AFRICAN MEDICAL & RESEARCH FOUNDATION INC (AMREF USA)
4 W 43rd St (fl 2)
New York, NY 10036-7408
Telephone: (212) 768-2440, Web Site:
www.amref.org
CEO: Lisa Meadowcroft

THE DMA AFRICAN WILDLIFE FOUNDATION
1400 16th St NW (Suite 120)
Washington, DC 20036-2249
Telephone: (202) 939-3333, Web Site:
www.awf.org
Dir Membership: Kate Mathews

AIR FORCE SERGEANTS ASSOCIATION
5211 Auth Rd
Suitland, MD 20746-4339
Telephone: (301) 899-3500, (800) 638-
0594, FAX: (301) 899-8136, E-Mail:
staff@hqafsa.org, Web Site: www.
hqafsa.org
CEO: Richard M. Dean
Dir Member & Field Rels: Lorinda F.
Tromblee
Conducts Business: U.S. & Europe
Employees: 25
Primary Market Served: Consumer
Catalog available online
Direct online sales
Advertising/Marketing Budget Related
to Direct Marketing: 76-100%

Founded: 1961
Gross sales or billing: $3,800,000

Non-profit association for Air Force
Active Duty, Air National Guard, Air
Force Reserve & personnel in active
retired and veteran status. Legislation
& lobbying for Air Force enlisted
personnel. Also group insurance &
service policies for members.

THE DMA AIRCRAFT OWNERS & PILOTS ASSOCIATION
421 Aviation Way
Frederick, MD 21701-4756
Telephone: (301) 695-2000, (800) 872-
2672, FAX: (301) 695-2375, E-Mail:
aopahq@aopa.org, Web Site: www.
aopa.org
Pres: Phil Boyer
VP, Prods & Svcs: Michelle Peterson
Sr VP, Products & Svcs: Karen Geb-
hart
Conducts Business: U.S.
Employees: 180
Primary Market Served: Consumer
Direct Marketing ad budget:
Direct Mail: 90%
Magazines: 3%
Telephone: 7%
Founded: 1939

Membership solicitation, aviation
safety seminars & courses promoted by
mail. Also offer merchandise & special
services to members.

ALEXIAN BROTHERS BONAVENTURE HOUSE
825 W Wellington Ave
Chicago, IL 60657
Telephone: (773) 327-9921, FAX:
(773) 327-9113, E-Mail: info@abam.
org, Web Site: www.
bonaventurehouse.org
CEO: Bart Winters
Dir, Programs & Svcs: Marty Hansen
Bus Mgr: Rufus Davis
Bus Mgr: Marjorie Orr
Asst Bus Mgr: Joyce Towner
Primary Market Served: Consumer

Non-profit housing project for men &
women living with AIDS.

THE DMA ALLIANCE DEFENSE FUND
15100 N 90th St
Scottsdale, AZ 85260-2901
Telephone: (480) 444-0020, Web Site:
www.telladf.org
Direct Mktg Analyst: Candace Duncan
Primary Market Served: Consumer

ALLIANCE FOR THE ARTS
330 W 42nd St (Suite 1701)
New York, NY 10036-6902

Telephone: (212) 947-6340, FAX: (212) 947-6416, E-Mail: info@ allianceforarts.org, Web Site: www. nyc-arts.org
Pres: Randall Bourscheidt
Dir of Devel: Lane Harwell
Conducts Business: U.S.
Employees: 7
Primary Market Served: Business & Consumer

Events clearing house calendar, a registry of special events & fund-raising activities sold to non-profit, special event planners & suppliers.

ALLIANCE OF AREA BUSINESS PUBLICATIONS

1970 E Grand Ave (Suite 300)
El Segundo, CA 90245-5038
Telephone: (323) 937-5514, FAX: (323) 937-0959, E-Mail: info@ bizpubs.org, Web Site: www.bizpubs. org
Pres: David Blake
VP: Jane Larkin
Sec & Treas: Grady Johnson
Exec Dir: C. James Dowden
Dir: Chris Eddings
Conducts Business: U.S., Canada
Employees: 3
Primary Market Served: Business
Founded: 1979
Gross sales or billing: $500,000

Products include a database of 2500 privately held companies & "The Newsmaker's Guide to Local Business Publications."

ALPHA DOG MARKETING INC

9060 Andermatt Dr Ste 101
Lincoln, NE 68526-9644
Telephone: (402) 486-0668, Web Site: www.alphadogmktg.com
CEO: Mike Monk

Full service direct marketing agency serving non-profit organizations

ALZHEIMER SOCIETY OF CANADA

20 Eglinton Ave W (Suite 1200)
Toronto, ON, Canada M4R 1K8
Telephone: (416) 488-8772, (800) 616-8816, FAX: (416) 488-3778, E-Mail: gpage@alzheimer.ca, Web Site: www.alzheimer.ca
Chief Commun & Devel: Graeme Page
Conducts Business: Canada
Employees: 25
Primary Market Served: Business & Consumer
Founded: 1977

Conduct sustaining campaign throughout the year utilizing direct marketing for collecting contributions.

ᴛʜᴇ ᴅᴍᴀ ALZHEIMER'S ASSOCIATION

225 N Michigan Ave
Chicago, IL 60601-7757
Telephone: (312) 335-8700, Web Site: www.alz.org
Dir Direct Mktg: Robert Beatty
Primary Market Served: Consumer

ᴛʜᴇ ᴅᴍᴀ AMERGENT

9 Centennial Dr Unit 201
Peabody, MA 01960-7940
Telephone: (800) 370-7500, Web Site: www.amergent.com
Pres: Jack Doyle

ᴛʜᴇ ᴅᴍᴀ AMERICAN ACADEMY OF NEUROLOGY

1080 Montreal Ave Ste 100
Saint Paul, MN 55116-2387
Telephone: (651) 695-2793, Web Site: www.aan.com
Strategic Mktg Mgr: Arlene Sanchez

AMERICAN ARBITRATION ASSOCIATION

1633 Broadway Lowr 2C01
New York, NY 10019-6707
Telephone: (212) 716-5800, (800) 778-7879, FAX: (212) 716-5905, E-Mail: kesslerw@adr.org, Web Site: www.adr.org
Chmn: James H. Carter
Pres, CEO: William K. Slate
Sr VP, CFO, Treas: Franceso Rossi
Conducts Business: U.S., Europe, Asia
Employees: 65
Primary Market Served: Business & Consumer
Catalog available online
Direct online sales
Gross sales or billing: $125,000,000

The American Arbitration Association (AAA) is available to resolve a wide range of disputes through mediation, arbitration, elections and other out-of-court settlement procedures. AAA offers ADR (alternative dispute resolution), systems design, educational seminars and publications.

AMERICAN ASSOCIATION FOR JUSTICE

777 6th St NW (Suite 200), The Leonard M Ring Law Center
Washington, DC 20001-3707
Telephone: (202) 965-3500, (800) 424-2725, FAX: (202) 625-7313, Web Site: www.justice.org
CEO: Jon Haber
Pres: Kathleen Flynn Peterson

Pres Elect: Les Weisbrod
VP: Anthony Tarricone
Sec: C. Gibson
Treas: Gary Paul
Conducts Business: U.S., Canada
Employees: 160
Primary Market Served: Business
Direct Marketing ad budget: $40,000
Direct Mail: 60%
Magazines: 40%
Founded: 2006

Membership association for trial lawyers. Market membership lists of trial attorneys.

AMERICAN ASSOCIATION OF CRITICAL-CARE NURSES

101 Columbia
Aliso Viejo, CA 92656-4109
Telephone: (949) 362-2000, (800) 809-CARE, FAX: (949) 362-2020, E-Mail: info@aacn.com, Web Site: www.aacn.org
Chair: Judy Verger
Pres: Debbie Brinker
Sr VP Chief Nurse Exec: Donna M. Herrin
Mktg Dir: Dana Woods
Conducts Business: Worldwide
Employees: 110
Primary Market Served: Consumer
Catalog available online
Direct online sales
Advertising/Marketing Budget Related to Direct Marketing: 51-75%
Direct Marketing ad budget:
Direct Mail: 50%
Magazines: 50%
Founded: 1969

Specialty nursing organization with over 76,000 members. The Association now has more than 270 chapters worldwide & is working toward a healthcare system driven by patients' needs where critical care nurses make their optimal contribution.

AMERICAN ASSOCIATION OF INDIVIDUAL INVESTORS

625 N Michigan Ave
Chicago, IL 60611-3110
Telephone: (312) 280-0170, FAX: (312) 280-9883, E-Mail: adam@aaii. com, Web Site: www.aaii.com
Chmn: James B. Cloonan
VP Mktg: Adam B. Pfeffer
Pres: John D. Markese
VP, Opers: Harry Madorin
Conducts Business: U.S.
Employees: 21
Primary Market Served: Consumer
Catalog available online
Direct online sales

Direct Marketing ad budget:
$2,000,000
Direct Mail: 96%
Online: 4%
Founded: 1978
Gross sales or billing: $5,000,000

Membership organization for serious
individuals managing own assets. Publish journal & other educational
materials.

AMERICAN ASSOCIATION OF UNIVERSITY WOMEN

1111 16th St NW Ste Mailrm
Washington, DC 20036-4809
Telephone: (202) 725-7611, Web Site:
www.aauw.org
Mgr Individual Giving: Tremayne Par-
quet

AMERICAN BANKERS ASSOCIATION

1120 Connecticut Ave NW
Washington, DC 20036-3959
Telephone: (202) 789-0300, (800)
BANKERS, FAX: (202) 296-9258,
Web Site: www.aba.com
Pres & CEO: Edward L. Yingling
Chmn: Bradley E. Rock
Dir Mktg: Maggie Kelly
Conducts Business: U.S.
Employees: 400
Primary Market Served: Business
Catalog available online
Direct online sales
Advertising/Marketing Budget Related
to Direct Marketing: 51-75%
Direct Marketing ad budget:
Direct Mail: 70%
Magazines: 5%
Newspapers: 20%
TV/Radio: 5%
Founded: 1875
Gross sales or billing: $83,700,000

Non-profit organization of American
Bankers.

THE DMA AMERICAN BAR ASSOCIATION

321 N Clark St (fl 16)
Chicago, IL 60654-4740
Telephone: (312) 988-5435, FAX:
(312) 988-5455, Web Site: www.
abanet.org
Dir Database: Rick Van Gundy
Primary Market Served: Business &
Consumer

Professional organization with over
380,000 members. All lists available
for rental.

AMERICAN BASEBALL COACHES ASSOCIATION

108 S University (Suite 3)
Mount Pleasant, MI 48858-2327
Telephone: (989) 775-3300, FAX:
(989) 775-3600, E-Mail: abca@abca.
org, Web Site: www.abca.org
Exec Dir: Dave Keilitz
Asst to Exec Dir: Betty Rulong
Admin Asst: Nick Phillips
Admin Asst: John Clark
Conducts Business: U.S.
Employees: 4
Catalog available online
Advertising/Marketing Budget Related
to Direct Marketing: 0-25%
Founded: 1945

National organization of amateur baseball coaches.

THE DMA AMERICAN BIBLE SOCIETY

1865 Broadway
New York, NY 10023-7505
Telephone: (212) 408-1200, FAX:
(212) 408-1264, Web Site: www.
americanbible.org
Dir Donor Cultivation: Lee Manis
Pres: Dr. Paul Irwin
EVP & COO: Richard B. Stewart Jr
EVP: Dr. Lamar Vest
EVP: Simon Barnes
Conducts Business: Worldwide
Employees: 300
Primary Market Served: Consumer
Advertising/Marketing Budget Related
to Direct Marketing: 76-100%
Founded: 1816

Translate, publish & distribute
scriptures.

AMERICAN BREAST CANCER FOUNDATION

1220B E Joppa Rd (Suite 332)
Baltimore, MD 21286-5823
Telephone: (410) 825-9388, Web Site:
www.abcf.org
VP: Tammy Wagner
Primary Market Served: Consumer

THE DMA AMERICAN CANCER SOCIETY

250 Williams St NW Ste 6000
Atlanta, GA 30303-1034
Telephone: (404) 471-5852, (800)
ACS-2345, FAX: (404) 982-3677,
Web Site: www.cancer.org
Chair: Marion E. Morra
CEO: John R. Sefrin
Pres & Dir: Elmer E. Huerta
Opers Dir: Margie Asburn
Gross sales or billing: $1,000,000,000

Nationwide volunteer health organization dedicated to eliminating cancer as
a major health problem through research, education & service.

THE DMA AMERICAN CATALOG MAILERS ASSOCIATION

188 Briarwood Dr
Somers, NY 10589-1810
Telephone: (914) 669-8391, Web Site:
www.catalogmailers.org
Primary Market Served: Consumer

THE DMA AMERICAN CHEMICAL SOCIETY

1155 16th St NW
Washington, DC 20036-4839
Telephone: (202) 872-4600, (800) 227-
5558, FAX: (202) 833-7716, E-Mail:
service@acs.org, Web Site: www.
acs.org
Pres: Catherine T. Hunt
Exec Dir: John K. Crum
Membership Dir: Nancy R. Gray
Sec: Halley A. Merrell
Conducts Business: Worldwide
Employees: 1,800
Founded: 1876

Scientific society providing chemical
knowledge for chemists & chemical
engineers, through journals, books,
professional development courses &
national meetings.

AMERICAN CIVIL LIBERTIES UNION FOUNDATION

125 Broad St (fl 18)
New York, NY 10004-2454
Telephone: (212) 549-2600, Web Site:
www.aclu.org
Deputy Dir Devel: Geraldine Engel
Primary Market Served: Consumer

THE DMA AMERICAN COLLEGE OF CARDIOLOGY

2400 N St NW
Washington, DC 20037-1153
Telephone: (202) 375-6426, Web Site:
www.acc.org
Sr Dir Mktg Commun: Catherine Ort-
Mabry
Primary Market Served: Consumer

THE DMA AMERICAN COLLEGE OF EMERGENCY PHYSICIANS

1125 Executive Cir
Irving, TX 75038-2522
Telephone: (972) 550-0911, Web Site:
www..acep.org
Primary Market Served: Consumer

AMERICAN COLLEGE OF PHYSICIAN EXECUTIVES

400 N Ashley Dr (Suite 400)
Tampa, FL 33602-4322
Telephone: (813) 287-2000, (800) 562-8088, FAX: (813) 287-8993, E-Mail: acpe@acpe.org, Web Site: www.acpe.org
Exec VP: Roger Schenke
Art Dir: Jill Howell Fasnacht
Conducts Business: U.S.
Employees: 20
Primary Market Served: Consumer
Founded: 1974

Provide medical business management education to physician executives.

AMERICAN COUNCIL ON EXERCISE

4851 Paramount Dr
San Diego, CA 92123
Telephone: (858) 279-8227, (888) 825-3636, FAX: (858) 279-8064, E-Mail: kristie.spalding@acefitness.org, Web Site: www.acefitness.org
Pres: Scott Goudeseune
VP Mktg: Rachelle Deal
Corp Commun Dir: Kristie Spalding
Primary Market Served: Consumer
Catalog available online
Direct online sales

Non-profit fitness education & certification organization.

AMERICAN COUNSELING ASSOCIATION

305 N Beech Cir
Broken Arrow, OK 74012-2293
Telephone: (703) 823-6862, FAX: (703) 823-0252, E-Mail: webmaster@counseling.org, Web Site: www.counseling.org
Exec Dir: Richard Yep
Pres: Judy Lewis
Conducts Business: U.S.
Employees: 60
Primary Market Served: Business & Consumer
Catalog available online
Direct online sales
Advertising/Marketing Budget Related to Direct Marketing: 51-75%
Founded: 1942
Gross sales or billing: $9,000,000

Non-profit membership organization with a growing membership of over 52,000 counselors & human development specialists.

THE DMA AMERICAN DIABETES ASSOCIATION

1701 N Beauregard St
Alexandria, VA 22311-1733

Telephone: (703) 549-1500, Web Site: www.diabetes.org
Exec VP Income Devel: Vaneeda Bennett
Primary Market Served: Consumer

AMERICAN FEDERATION OF ASTROLOGERS

6535 S Rural Rd
Tempe, AZ 85283-3746
Telephone: (480) 838-1751, (888) 301-7630, FAX: (480) 838-8293, E-Mail: afa@msn.com, Web Site: www.astrologers.com
Exec Dir: Kris Brandt Riske
Opers Mgr: Jack Cipolla
Conducts Business: Worldwide
Employees: 3
Primary Market Served: Business & Consumer
Catalog available online
Direct online sales
Direct Marketing ad budget:
Online: 100%
Founded: 1938

Membership, educational, astrology.

THE AMERICAN FILM INSTITUTE

2021 N Western Ave
Los Angeles, CA 90027-1657
Telephone: (323) 856-7600, FAX: (323) 467-4578, Web Site: www.afi.com
Pres & CEO: Bob Gazzale
Founding Dir: George Stevens Jr.
Chair: Jon Avet
Vice Chair: Mark Canton
Honorary Trustee: Al Pacino
Conducts Business: U.S.
Employees: 115
Primary Market Served: Consumer
Catalog available online

A national trust dedicated to preserving the heritage of film & television; to identifying, developing & training creative individuals; and to presenting the moving image as an art form. Offices in Los Angeles.

AMERICAN FORESTS

734 15th St NW (Suite 800)
Washington, DC 20005-1016
Telephone: (202) 737-1944, FAX: (202) 737-2457, E-Mail: info@amfor.org, Web Site: www.americanforests.org
Exec Dir: Deborah Gangloff
Sr VP: Gary Moll
VP: Gerald Gray
VP: Gregory Meyer
VP: Cheryl Kollin
Conducts Business: U.S., Canada
Employees: 20

Primary Market Served: Business & Consumer
Direct Marketing ad budget: $250,000
Direct Mail: 98%
Magazines: 2%
Founded: 1875
Gross sales or billing: $4,000,000

All members, 30,000+, receive a quarterly highlighting our Global ReLeaf projects, involving treeplanting and reforestation projects aimed at repairing damaged ecosystems.

AMERICAN FOUNDATION FOR THE BLIND INC

2 Penn Plaza Rm 1102
New York, NY 10121-1100
Telephone: (212) 502-7600, FAX: (212) 502-7777, E-Mail: afbinfo@afb.org, Web Site: www.afb.org/afb
Pres: Carl Augusto
Commun: Katlyn McFeely
Conducts Business: U.S.
Employees: 125
Primary Market Served: Business & Consumer
Catalog available online
Direct online sales
Gross sales or billing: $20,500,000

Individual and family services for people who are blind or visually impaired. Taking a national leadership role in public policy & legislation, information & education programs, and diversified products & services.

THE DMA AMERICAN HEALTH ASSISTANCE FOUNDATION

22512 Gateway Ctr Dr
Clarksburg, MD 20871-2005
Telephone: (301) 948-3224
CEO & Pres: Stacy Pagos Haller

AMERICAN HEALTH INFORMATION MANAGEMENT ASSOCIATION

233 N Michigan Ave (21st fl)
Chicago, IL 60601-5519
Telephone: (312) 233-1100, FAX: (312) 233-1090, E-Mail: info@ahima.org, Web Site: www.ahima.org
CEO: Linda L. Kloss
VP: Donald Mon
Dir: Daniel Barron
Conducts Business: Worldwide
Primary Market Served: Business & Consumer
Catalog available online
Direct online sales
Advertising/Marketing Budget Related to Direct Marketing: 76-100%
Founded: 1928
Gross sales or billing: $7,500,000

THE DMA AMERICAN HEART ASSOCIATION

7272 Greenville Ave
Dallas, TX 75231-5129
Telephone: (214) 373-6300, (800) AHA-USA-1, FAX: (214) 373-3406, Web Site: www.americanheart.org
CEO: M. Cass Wheeler
Chmn, Natl Sec & Treas: Andrew B. Buroker
Pres: Raymond J. Gibbons
VP, Devel: Gordon McCullough
Dir, Direct Response: Sherry Minton
Conducts Business: Worldwide
Employees: 550
Primary Market Served: Consumer

Association dedicated to the reduction of death & disability due to cardiovascular disease & stroke. Affiliates nationwide.

THE DMA AMERICAN HUMANE ASSOCIATION

1400 16th St NW Ste 360
Washington, DC 20036-2215
Telephone: (303) 925-9497, Web Site: www.americanhumane.org
Sr Devel Officer Direct Mktg: De Ann Acosta

THE DMA AMERICAN INDIAN COLLEGE FUND

8333 Greenwood Blvd Ste 120
Denver, CO 80221-4483
Telephone: (303) 426-8900, Web Site: www.collegefund.org
CFO & COO: Tamela Miller-Carlson
Primary Market Served: Consumer

THE DMA AMERICAN INSTITUTE FOR CANCER RESEARCH

1759 R St NW
Washington, DC 20009-2570
Telephone: (202) 328-7744, (800) 843-8114, FAX: (202) 328-7226, E-Mail: aicrweb@aicr.org, Web Site: www.aicr.org
Pres: Marilyn Gentry
Exec VP: Kelly B. Browning
Conducts Business: U.S.
Employees: 35
Catalog available online
Direct online sales
Founded: 1982
Gross sales or billing: $40,000,000

Funding support for research into prevention of cancer through nutrition & diet.

AMERICAN INSTITUTE FOR ECONOMIC RESEARCH

250 Division St
Great Barrington, MA 01230-1198
Telephone: (413) 528-1216, (888) 528-1216, E-Mail: info@aier.org, Web Site: www.aier.org
Dir Commun: Ryan Goodenough
Dir Devel: Declan J Sheehy
Employees: 22
Founded: 1933

AMERICAN INSTITUTE OF CHEMICAL ENGINEERS

3 Park Ave
New York, NY 10016-5991
Telephone: (203) 702-7660, (800) 242-4363, FAX: (203) 775-5177, E-Mail: xpress@aiche.org, Web Site: www.aiche.org
Sr Dir Pubns & Info Tech Sys: Stephen R. Smith
Mktg Dir: Tim McCreight
Employees: 52
Primary Market Served: Business & Consumer
Catalog available online
Indirect online sales
Advertising/Marketing Budget Related to Direct Marketing: 76-100%
Founded: 1908
Gross sales or billing: $18,000,000

Individual professional organization of chemical engineers, dedicated to continually improving service to members, employees, the chemical engineering profession & society.

AMERICAN INSTITUTE OF CPAS

1211 Avenue Of The Americas Ste 1900
New York, NY 10036-8702
Telephone: (212) 596-6200, (888) 777-7077, FAX: (212) 596-6213, Web Site: www.aicpa.org
Pres: Barry C. Melancon
Sr VP Member Competency & Devel: Arleen R. Thomas
VP Conferences & Sls: John Toman
Dir Membership Mktg: Joseph Syrowiik
Conducts Business: U.S.
Employees: 400
Primary Market Served: Business & Consumer
Advertising/Marketing Budget Related to Direct Marketing: 76-100%
Founded: 1887

Non-profit membership organization for CPAs.

THE DMA AMERICAN KIDNEY FUND

6110 Executive Blvd (Suite 1010)
Rockville, MD 20852-3914
Telephone: (301) 881-3052, Web Site: www.kidneyfund.org
Dir Devel Svcs: Chris Hines

THE DMA THE AMERICAN LEGION NATIONAL HEADQUARTERS

5745 Lee Rd
Indianapolis, IN 46216-2063
Telephone: (317) 630-1247, FAX: (317) 630-1369, E-Mail: acy@legion.org, Web Site: www.legion.org
Membership Dir: Billy R. Johnson
Mktg Dir: Ronald E. Brooks
Exec Dir: Jeffrey Brown
Conducts Business: U.S., Canada
Primary Market Served: Consumer
Direct Marketing ad budget:
Direct Mail: 90%
TV/Radio: 10%

Non-profit service organization serving the needs of wartime veterans.

AMERICAN LIBRARY ASSOCIATION-PUBLISHING SERVICES

50 E Huron St
Chicago, IL 60611
Telephone: (312) 944-6780, (800) 545-2433, FAX: (312) 280-4380, Web Site: www.ala.org
Publg Dir: Donald Chatham
Opers Mgr: Robert Hershman
Rights & Permissions Mgr: Eve Cotton
Mktg Mgr: Catherine English
Conducts Business: Worldwide
Employees: 70
Primary Market Served: Business & Consumer
Direct online sales
Advertising/Marketing Budget Related to Direct Marketing: 26-50%
Direct Marketing ad budget:
Direct Mail: 90%
Magazines: 10%
Founded: 1894
Gross sales or billing: $7,000,000

Publish & market books & periodicals (advertising & subscriptions) for librarians, information specialists & educators.

THE DMA AMERICAN LUNG ASSOCIATION

21 W 38th St (fl 3)
New York, NY 10018-2254
Telephone: (212) 889-3370, (800) LUNGUSA, FAX: (212) 889-3375, E-Mail: info@alany.org, Web Site: www.lungusa.org
Chmn: H James Gooden
Chmn Elect: Albert A Rizzo
Pres & CEO: Scott Santarella
Sec & Treas: Christine L Bryant
Commun Mgr: Kathleen O'Neill
Conducts Business: U.S.
Employees: 500
Primary Market Served: Consumer

Founded: 1904
Gross sales or billing: $50,300,000

Non-profit health organization whose mission is to prevent lung disease and promote lung health. Uses direct mail to raise funds from the general public.

THE DMA **AMERICAN MANAGEMENT ASSOCIATION**
1601 Broadway
New York, NY 10019-7434
Telephone: (212) 586-8100, FAX: (212) 903-8186, Web Site: www. amanet.org
Pres: Barry Williams
VP, Mktg: Larry Geiger
Sr VP Mktg & Membership: Robert Smith
Conducts Business: U.S., Canada, Mexico, Japan, Belgium
Employees: 800
Primary Market Served: Business
Advertising/Marketing Budget Related to Direct Marketing: 76-100%
Direct Marketing ad budget:
Direct Mail: 90%
Telephone: 10%
Founded: 1923
Gross sales or billing: $200,000,000

Business management seminars and publishing to business professionals.

THE DMA **AMERICAN MEDICAL ASSOCIATION**
Div. of Data Base Products & Licensing
515 N State St
Chicago, IL 60610
Telephone: (312) 464-5000, (800) 621-8335, FAX: (312) 464-4184, Web Site: www.ama-assn.org
Data Base Products & Licensing Dir: Mark Frankel
Data Base Licensing Svcs Dir: Jean Dixon
Conducts Business: Worldwide
Employees: 1,000
Primary Market Served: Business
Advertising/Marketing Budget Related to Direct Marketing: 26-50%
Gross sales or billing: $260,000,000

Non-profit organization promoting the science & art of medicine.

AMERICAN NATIONAL STANDARDS INSTITUTE
24 W 43rd St (fl 4)
New York, NY 10036-7422
Telephone: (212) 642-4900, Web Site: www.ansi.org
Dir Online Mktg: Robert Russotti

AMERICAN NICARAGUAN FOUNDATION
1000 NW 57th Ct Ste 770
Miami, FL 33126-3288
Telephone: (305) 374-3391, Web Site: www.aidnicaragua.org
Dir/ Sr Consultant: Angela Hirsch
Primary Market Served: Consumer

THE DMA **AMERICAN NUMISMATIC ASSOCIATION**
818 N Cascade Ave
Colorado Springs, CO 80903-3279
Telephone: (719) 632-2646, Web Site: www.money.org
Enterprise Mgr: Cary Hardy

AMERICAN NURSES' ASSOCIATION
8515 Georgia Ave (Suite 400)
Silver Spring, MD 20006-4105
Telephone: (301) 628-5000, (800) 284-2378, (800) 274-4262, FAX: (301) 628-5001, Web Site: www. nursingworld.org
Mktg Dir Commns/Mktg Cluster: Leo Schargorodski
Conducts Business: U.S.
Employees: 150
Primary Market Served: Consumer

National, professional association for registered nurses.

THE AMERICAN PHYTOPATHOLOGICAL SOCIETY
3340 Pilot Knob Rd
Saint Paul, MN 55121-2055
Telephone: (651) 454-7250, Web Site: www.apsnet.org
Publications Mktg Mgr: Ashley Armstrong

AMERICAN PSYCHOLOGICAL ASSOCIATION
750 First St NE
Washington, DC 20002-4242
Telephone: (202) 336-5500, (800) 374-2721, FAX: (202) 336-5568, E-Mail: order@apa.org, Web Site: www.apa.org
Pres & Dir: Sharon Stevens Brehm
CEO, Exec VP & Dir: Norma B. Anderson
COO, Deputy CEO, Exec Dir: L. Michael Honaker
Pubns & Commun Exec Dir: Gary VandenBos
Conducts Business: Worldwide
Employees: 650
Primary Market Served: Business & Consumer
Catalog available online

Direct online sales
Direct Marketing ad budget: $600,000
Direct Mail: $400,000
Magazines: $200,000
Founded: 1892
Gross sales or billing: $5,500,000

Publish scientific, scholarly journals, psychology books, computer tapes & CD-ROMs.

THE DMA **AMERICAN RADIO RELAY LEAGUE**
225 Main St
Newington, CT 06111-1494
Telephone: (860) 594-0200, Web Site: www.arrl.org
Mktg Mgr: Robert Inderbitzen
Primary Market Served: Consumer

AMERICAN RED CROSS
2025 E St NW, National HQ
Washington, DC 20006-5009
Telephone: (703) 303-5000 X5, (800) RED-CROSS, Web Site: www. redcross.org
VP, Devel: Jennifer Dunlad
Integrated Dir Response Program Mgr: Janet Shinsky
Conducts Business: U.S.
Employees: 25,000
Primary Market Served: Business & Consumer

Non-profit organization providing disaster relief, blood collection & health & safety education.

AMERICAN RUNNING ASSOCIATION
dba American Medical Athletic Association
4405 East-West Hwy (#405)
Bethesda, MD 20814-4522
Telephone: (301) 913-9517, (800) 776-2732, FAX: (301) 913-9520, E-Mail: run@americanrunning.org, Web Site: www.americanrunning.org
Exec Dir: David Watt
Editor Running & FitNews: Jeffrey Venables
Proj Cons: Barbara Baldwin
Conducts Business: U.S.
Employees: 3
Primary Market Served: Business & Consumer
Catalog available online
Direct online sales
Advertising/Marketing Budget Related to Direct Marketing: 51-75%
Direct Marketing ad budget: $10,000
Direct Mail: 70%
Magazines: 10%
Online: 20%
Founded: 1968
Gross sales or billing: $400,000

Non-profit educational association of athletes & sports medicine professionals, dedicated to enhancing the physical & mental well-being of runners from youth to adult through the promotion of exercise.

AMERICAN SOCIETY FOR QUALITY-ASQ

600 N Plankinton Ave
Milwaukee, WI 53203
Telephone: (414) 272-8575, (800) 248-1946, FAX: (414) 272-1734, E-Mail: help@asq.org, Web Site: www.asq.org
Exec Dir: Paul E. Borawski
Pres: Ron Atkinson
Mgr, Mktg Svcs: Michele Luebke
Employees: 220
Primary Market Served: Business & Consumer
Catalog available online
Direct online sales
Founded: 1946
Gross sales or billing: $10,000,000

Identify, communicate & promote the use of quality principles, concepts & technologies through membership in a professional society; also has a substantial book publishing operation; offers training, conferences & a series of professional certifications in the field of quality.

AMERICAN SOCIETY FOR TRAINING & DEVELOPMENT

1640 King St, PO Box 1443
Alexandria, VA 22313-2043
Telephone: (703) 683-8100, (800) NAT-ASTD, FAX: (703) 683-8103, Web Site: www.astd.org
Pres & CEO: Tina Sung
Reg Pres: Jill McCormack
Reg VP: Diane Dvoskin
Reg VP Fin: Nelson Howell
Primary Market Served: Business & Consumer
Catalog available online
Direct online sales
Founded: 1944

A professional society in the field of workplace learning & performance offering membership, conferences & publications.

AMERICAN SOCIETY OF CIVIL ENGINEERS

1801 Alexander Bell Dr Ste 100
Reston, VA 20191-4382
Telephone: (703) 295-6000, (800) 548-2723, FAX: (703) 295-6343, Web Site: www.asce.org
Pres: David G. Morgan

Exec Dir: Patrick J. Natale
Deputy Exec Dir: Lawrence H. Roth
Dir: Allan M. Beene
Dir: Kathy J. Caldwell
Catalog available online

Non-profit professional association for civil engineers.

AMERICAN SOCIETY OF INTERIOR DESIGNERS

608 Massachusetts Ave NE
Washington, DC 20002-6006
Telephone: (202) 546-3480, FAX: (202) 546-3240, E-Mail: asid@asid.org, Web Site: www.asid.org
Exec Dir: Michael Alin
Dir Mktg Commun & Creative Svcs: Eric Hansen
Mktg Support Mgr: Lizzie Hanner
Conducts Business: U.S., Canada, U.K.
Employees: 45
Primary Market Served: Business & Consumer
Catalog available online
Indirect online sales
Founded: 1975

Mailing list rentals to firms that promote products or services to the interior design profession.

AMERICAN SOCIETY OF RADIOLOGIC TECHNOLOGISTS

15000 Central Ave SE
Albuquerque, NM 87123-3909
Telephone: (505) 298-4500, Web Site: www.asrt.org
Promos Mgr: Anthony Acree
Primary Market Served: Consumer

AMERICAN SOCIETY ON AGING

71 Stevenson St (Suite 1450)
San Francisco, CA 94105-2938
Telephone: (415) 974-9600, (800) 537-9728, FAX: (415) 974-0300, E-Mail: info@asaging.org, Web Site: www.asaging.org
Pres & CEO: Robert G. Stein
VP Education: Carole A Anderson
Sr Dir Opers & IT: Robert R Lowe
Sr Dir Diversity & Member Inclusion: Anne R Ornela de Lemos
Conducts Business: U.S., Canada
Employees: 30
Primary Market Served: Business & Consumer
Catalog available online
Direct online sales
Advertising/Marketing Budget Related to Direct Marketing: 76-100%
Direct Marketing ad budget: $750,000
Direct Mail: 100%
Founded: 1954

Gross sales or billing: $2,500,000

Market membership, subscriptions, conferences, advertising & mailing lists, trade shows & videos to professionals in the field of aging & those who want to reach it.

THE DMA AMERICAN SPEECH-LANGUAGE-HEARING ASSOCIATION

2200 Research Blvd
Rockville, MD 20850-3289
Telephone: (301) 897-5700, (800) 638-8255, E-Mail: productsales@asha.org, Web Site: www.asha.org
Exec Dir: Arlene Pietranton
Dir Assets & Corp Alliances: Barb Lecker
Mktg Dir: Rick Henderson
Dir Brand Mktg: Leslie Katz
List Mktg Mgr: Leah Byndon
Conducts Business: Worldwide
Employees: 250
Primary Market Served: Business & Consumer
Catalog available online
Indirect online sales
Advertising/Marketing Budget Related to Direct Marketing: 0-25%
Founded: 1925
Gross sales or billing: $46,000,000

National professional & scientific association for speech-language pathologists, audiologists & speech, language & hearing scientists concerned with communication behavior & disorders. Market products, mailing list, journals, advertising & conferences to membership & interested parties.

AMERICAN STUDENT ASSISTANCE

100 Cambridge St (Suite 1600)
Boston, MA 02114-2567
Telephone: (800) 999-9000, Web Site: www.amsa.com
Mgr Mkt Res & Analysis: John Lane
Primary Market Served: Business & Consumer

AMERICAN TRUCKING ASSOCIATION

950 N Glebe Rd (Suite 210)
Arlington, VA 22203-4181
Telephone: (703) 838-1700, FAX: (800) 254-2571, E-Mail: atamembership@trucking.org, Web Site: www.truckline.com
Pres & CEO: Bill Graves
Chmn Bd: Ray Kuntz
Vice Chmn: Barbara Windsor
First Vice Chmn: Charles L. Whittington

Second Vice Chmn: G. Tommy
  Hodges
VP, Prod Mktg: Eric Wolfe
Conducts Business: Worldwide
Employees: 300
Primary Market Served: Business
Catalog available online
Indirect online sales

Trade association offering publications
& services to the trucking industry.

AMERICANS FOR PEACE NOW

2100 M St NW Ste 619
Washington, DC 20037-1269
Telephone: (202) 408-9898, FAX:
  (202) 728-1895, E-Mail: apndc@
  peacenow.org
CEO: Debra DeLee
CFO: Mark Bilisky
Conducts Business: U.S.
Primary Market Served: Business &
  Consumer

Raise funds in support of Middle East
peace.

THE DMA AMERICARES

88 Hamilton Ave
Stamford, CT 06902-3100
Telephone: (203) 658-9500, Web Site:
  www.americares.org
VP Dir Response Mktg: Lee Weiner

THE DMA AMNESTY INTERNATIONAL USA

Five Penn Plaza (fl 16)
New York, NY 10001-1823
Telephone: (212) 807-8400, FAX:
  (212) 989-5478, E-Mail: vpotter@
  aiusa.org, Web Site: www.
  amnestyusa.org
Mng Dir, Direct Response: Vivanne
  Potter

AMPLIFY FEDERAL CREDIT UNION

PO Box 85300
Austin, TX 78708-5300
Telephone: (512) 834-6519, Web Site:
  www.goamplify.com
Bus Intelligence Analyst: Sheryl Will-
  iams
Primary Market Served: Consumer

THE DMA MD ANDERSON CANCER CENTER - CHILDREN'S ART PROJECT

6900 Fannin St (Suite FHB 1.1000)
Houston, TX 77030-3800
Telephone: (713) 745-2575, (800) 231-
  1580, FAX: (713) 794-1950, E-Mail:
  krenner@mdanderson.org, Web Site:
  www.childrensart.org

Mgr Sls & Mktg - Direct Mail: Kelly
  Renner
Exec Dir: Shannon Murray
Assoc Dir Mktg: Angela Cheves
Conducts Business: USA
Employees: 26
Primary Market Served: Consumer
Catalog available online
Direct online sales
Advertising/Marketing Budget Related
  to Direct Marketing: 0-25%
Founded: 1973
Gross sales or billing: $2,500,000

ANGLICANS UNITED & LATIMER PRESS

904 Forest Hill Ct
Cedar Hill, TX 75104-5712
Telephone: (972) 293-7443, (800) 553-
  3645, FAX: (972) 293-7559, E-Mail:
  anglicansunited@sbcglobal.net, Web
  Site: www.anglicansunited.com,
  www.latimerpress.com
Exec Dir: Rev Todd H. Wetzel
Admin: Cheryl M. Wetzel
Conducts Business: U.S. & Canada
Employees: 2
Primary Market Served: Business &
  Consumer
Catalog available online
Indirect online sales
Advertising/Marketing Budget Related
  to Direct Marketing: 0-25%
Direct Marketing ad budget: $1,400
Magazines: $1,000
Online: $400
Founded: 1986

Provide bi-monthly newspaper & resources for church members & pro-
spective members to educate the laity
to fight liberal trends to keep the Episcopal church orthodox.

ANSAR INC

6651 Bethesda Arno Rd
Thompsons Station, TN 37179-9216
Telephone: (615) 368-2025, Web Site:
  www.ansarinc.com
Pres: Patricia Hinton

Provides print & mail services to non-
profit organizations, universities & corporations

ANTI-DEFAMATION LEAGUE

605 3rd Ave (fl 9)
New York, NY 10158-0102
Telephone: (212) 885-5870, Web Site:
  www.adl.org
Deputy Dir Mktg & Commun: Bonnie
  Mitelman

ANTIQUARIAN BOOKSELLERS ASSOCIATION OF AMERICA INC

20 W 44th St
New York, NY 10036
Telephone: (212) 944-8291, FAX:
  (212) 944-8293, E-Mail: sbenne@
  abaa.org, Web Site: www.abaa.org
Exec Dir: Susan Benne
Primary Market Served: Business &
  Consumer
Catalog available online
Founded: 1949

Non-profit trade organization for antiquarian book dealers.

THE DMA APPALACHIAN MOUNTAIN CLUB

5 Joy St
Boston, MA 02108-1490
Telephone: (617) 523-0655, Web Site:
  www.outdoors.com
Dir Membership: Teri Morrow

APPRAISAL INSTITUTE

200 W Madison St Ste 1500
Chicago, IL 60606-3515
Telephone: (312) 335-4100, FAX:
  (312) 335-4400, E-Mail: info@
  appraisalinstitute.org, Web Site:
  www.appraisalinstitute.org
Exec VP: John Ross
Dir Mktg & Pub Rels: Hope Atvel
Conducts Business: U.S.
Employees: 100
Primary Market Served: Business &
  Consumer
Catalog available online
Indirect online sales
Advertising/Marketing Budget Related
  to Direct Marketing: 0-25%
Direct Marketing ad budget:
Direct Mail: 40%
Magazines: 50%
Newspapers: 5%
TV/Radio: 5%
Founded: 1991

Professional association of real estate
appraisers, engaged in marketing
books, videotapes, periodicals & educational functions.

THE DMA ARBOR DAY FOUNDATION

211 N 12th St (Suite 501)
Lincoln, NE 68508-1411
Telephone: (402) 474-5655, Web Site:
  www.arborday.org
Dir Direct Mktg: Glen A Beasley
Primary Market Served: Consumer
Founded: 1972

THE DMA ARTHRITIS FOUNDATION
1330 W Peachtree St NW (Suite 100)
Atlanta, GA 30309-2922
Telephone: (404) 872-7100, FAX:
(404) 872-0457, Web Site: www.
arthritis.org
Pres & CEO: John H. Klippel
COO: Roberta K. Byrum
Exec VP, Strategy Mngmt & CIO:
Marla Davidson
Dir Year Round Program: Deborah
Scotti
Sr VP: Angie Moore
Conducts Business: U.S.
Employees: 160
Primary Market Served: Business &
Consumer
Founded: 1948
Gross sales or billing: $748,000,000

Voluntary health agency using direct
marketing to raise funds to distribute
educational information about the prevention, control & cure of arthritis.

THE DMA ASHLAND UNIVERSITY
224 Andrews Hall
Ashland, OH 44805
Telephone: (419) 289-5063, Web Site:
www.ashland.edu
Primary Market Served: Consumer
Founded: 1878

College

ASSOCIATION FOR COMPUTING MACHINERY (ACM)
2 Penn Plaza (Rm 701)
New York, NY 10121-0799
Telephone: (212) 869-7440, FAX:
(212) 944-1318, Web Site: www.
acm.org
Membership Dir: Lillian Israel
Mktg & Comm: Brian Hebert
Mktg Coord: Steven Geringer
Conducts Business: Worldwide
Employees: 94
Primary Market Served: Business &
Consumer

Non-profit international educational &
scientific society serving the computing
community.

ASSOCIATION FOR FACILITIES ENGINEERING
12801 Worldgate Dr (Suite 500)
Herndon, VA 20170
Telephone: (571) 203-7171, FAX:
(571) 766-2142, E-Mail: info@afe.
org, Web Site: www.afe.org
Chmn: Alex Keller
CEO: Laurence Gration
Conducts Business: U.S.
Employees: 8

Primary Market Served: Business &
Consumer
Catalog available online
Indirect online sales
Direct Marketing ad budget:
Direct Mail: 10%
Online: 90%
Founded: 1954

Membership organization.

THE DMA ASSOCIATION OF AMERICAN PUBLISHERS
455 Massachusetts Ave NW
Washington, DC 20001-2777
Telephone: (202) 347-3375, FAX:
(202) 347-3690, Web Site: www.
publishers.org
VP, Legal & Govt Affairs: Allan Adler
Conducts Business: Worldwide
Employees: 25
Primary Market Served: Business &
Consumer
Catalog available online
Indirect online sales
Founded: 1970

Trade association of publishing
companies.

ASSOCIATION OF BRIDAL CONSULTANTS
56 Danbury Rd (Suite 11)
New Milford, CT 06776-2521
Telephone: (860) 355-0464, FAX:
(860) 354-1404, E-Mail: office@
bridalassn.com, Web Site: www.
bridalassn.com
Pres: David Wood
Conducts Business: Worldwide
Employees: 7
Primary Market Served: Business &
Consumer
Catalog available online
Indirect online sales
Advertising/Marketing Budget Related
to Direct Marketing: 0-25%
Founded: 1955
Gross sales or billing: $900,000

Professional services for Wedding
Planner worldwide.

THE ASSOCIATION OF FUNDRAISING PROFESSIONALS
4300 Wilson Blvd (Suite 300)
Arlington, VA 22203-4179
Telephone: (800) 666-3863, Web Site:
www.afpnet.org
Mktg Dir: Todd McLaughlin

THE DMA ASSOCIATION OF MARIAN HELPERS
Eden Hill
Stockbridge, MA 01263

Telephone: (413) 298-3691, Web Site:
www.marian.org
Prog Planner: James G. Morrison
Gen Mgr: Fran Borden
Conducts Business: U.S., Canada
Employees: 90
Primary Market Served: Business &
Consumer
Advertising/Marketing Budget Related
to Direct Marketing: 0-25%

Catholic fund raising organization.

THE DMA ASSOCIATION OF THE MIRACULOUS MEDAL
Subs. of Congregation of the Mission
Province
1811 W Saint Joseph St
Perryville, MO 63775-1598
Telephone: (573) 547-8343, (800) 264-
6279, FAX: (573) 547-1389, E-Mail:
amm1@amm.org, Web Site: www.
amm.org
Finance Dir: Wesley Sparkman
Opers Dir: Renee Brueckner
Conducts Business: U.S.
Employees: 50
Primary Market Served: Consumer
Catalog available online
Direct online sales
Advertising/Marketing Budget Related
to Direct Marketing: 76-100%
Direct Marketing ad budget:
Direct Mail: 99%
Online: 1%
Founded: 1918
Gross sales or billing: $8,000,000

Non-profit direct mail evangelization &
fund-raising organization to national
Catholic mailing lists.

ASTRONOMICAL SOCIETY OF THE PACIFIC
390 Ashton Ave
San Francisco, CA 94112-1722
Telephone: (415) 337-1100, (800) 335-
2624, FAX: (415) 337-5205, E-Mail:
service@astrosociety.org, Web Site:
www.astrosociety.org
Mgr, Sls & Mktg: Joycelin Craig
Editor: Paula Szkody
Exec Dir: James Manning
Mng Dir: J. Ward Moody
Publication Mgr: Lisa Roper
Chief Advancement Officer: Michael
Gibbs
Conducts Business: Worldwide
Employees: 15
Primary Market Served: Business &
Consumer
Catalog available online
Direct online sales
Advertising/Marketing Budget Related
to Direct Marketing: 0-25%
Direct Marketing ad budget:
Direct Mail: 90%

Magazines: 10%
Founded: 1889
Gross sales or billing: $1,800,000

Non-profit society. Online store sells materials in astronomy including slides, CD-ROMS, prints, posters, video & audio tapes, books, maps, globes & charts. Wholesale products also available.

AUDIO-DIGEST FOUNDATION
Affiliate of Calif Medical Assn
1577 E Chevy Chase Dr
Glendale, CA 91206-4107
Telephone: (818) 240-7500, (800) 423-2308, FAX: (818) 240-7379, Web Site: www.audio-digest.org
VP, Mktg: George Groveman
Pres: Allen Stamey
Conducts Business: Worldwide
Employees: 135
Primary Market Served: Business & Consumer
Direct Marketing ad budget:
Direct Mail: 80%
Magazines: 20%
Founded: 1953

Involved in continuing postgraduate medical education. Publish medical education on audio & video cassette recordings sold to health care profession via direct mail.

AVMED HEALTH PLAN INC
9400 S Dadeland Blvd
Miami, FL 33156-2823
Telephone: (305) 671-5437, Web Site: www.avmed.org
VP: Javier Mendoza

THE AYN RAND INSTITUTE
2121 Alton Pkwy (Suite 250)
Irvine, CA 92606-4926
Telephone: (949) 222-6550, FAX: (949) 222-6558, E-Mail: mail@aynrand.org, Web Site: www.aynrand.org
Exec Dir: Yaron Brook
Employees: 33
Primary Market Served: Business
Catalog available online
Advertising/Marketing Budget Related to Direct Marketing: 76-100%
Founded: 1985
Gross sales or billing: $5,900,000

Non-profit fundraiser for academia & publishers.

THE DMA BBS & ASSOCIATES
130 Springside Dr (Suite 200)
Akron, OH 44333-4553
Telephone: (330) 665-5227, Web Site: www.servantheart.com

Project Asst: Suzanne Ludwick
Primary Market Served: Consumer

Consulting firm serving ministries

BMI
10 Music Sq E
Nashville, TN 37203-4321
Telephone: (615) 401-2000, (800) 925-8451, FAX: (615) 401-2812, E-Mail: genlic@bmi.com, Web Site: www.bmi.com
Chmn Bd: Kenneth J. Elkins
VP, Gen Licensing: Tom Annastas
Pres & CEO: Del R. Bryant
Asst VP, Bus & Indus Devel: Michele Reynolds
Primary Market Served: Business
Catalog available online
Direct online sales
Founded: 1939

Performing rights organization. Market music property rights of songwriters.

BATON ROUGE CONVENTIONS & VISITORS BUREAU
359 3rd St Ste A
Baton Rouge, LA 70801-1310
Telephone: (225) 383-1825, (800) LA-ROUGE, FAX: (225) 346-1253, E-Mail: br@bracvb.com, Web Site: www.bracvb.com
Pres & CEO: Paul J. Arrigo
Exec VP, Sls & Mktg: Renee Arang
Dir, Destination Svcs: Philipa Bkir
Dir, Destination Sls: Geraldine Bordelon
Controller: Sid Jackson
Conducts Business: U.S.
Employees: 15
Primary Market Served: Business & Consumer
Catalog available online

Promote Baton Rouge to tourists & conventions.

BENET ACADEMY
2200 Maple Ave
Lisle, IL 60532-2393
Telephone: (630) 719-2794, Web Site: www.benet.org

BERKEY BRENDEL SHELINE
130 Springside Dr (Suite 200)
Akron, OH 44333-3755
Telephone: (330) 665-5227, FAX: (330) 665-5055, Web Site: www.servantheart.com
Primary Market Served: Business

THE DMA BEST FRIENDS ANIMAL SOCIETY
5001 Angel Canyon Rd
Kanab, UT 84741-5000
Telephone: (435) 644-2001, Web Site: www.bestfriends.org

Animal society for abused & abandoned animals

BETHESDA HOSPITAL FOUNDATION
2815 S Seacrest Blvd
Boynton Beach, FL 33435-7934
Telephone: (561) 737-7733
Pub Rels & Annual Giving: Kristin Calder

BIG BROTHERS BIG SISTERS OF GREATER KANSAS CITY
3908 Washington St
Kansas City, MO 64111-2925
Telephone: (816) 561-5269, Web Site: www.bigbrothersbigsisterskc.org
Dir Communs: Kristi Hutchison

B'NAI B'RITH INTERNATIONAL
2020 K St NW (7th fl)
Washington, DC 20006
Telephone: (202) 857-6600, FAX: (202) 857-6609, E-Mail: internet@bnaibrith.org, Web Site: www.bnaibrith.org
Deputy Exec VP: Daniel H. Heckelman
Pres: Joel S. Kaplan
Primary Market Served: Business
Founded: 1843

Jewish non-profit organization.

BORN FREE USA
United with Animal Protection Institute
1122 S St
Sacramento, CA 95811-6525
Telephone: (916) 447-3085, FAX: (916) 447-3070, E-Mail: info@bornfreeusa.org, Web Site: www.bornfreeusa.org
CEO: Will Travers
VP Devel: Tracy Lesperance
Media Rels: Zibby Wilder
Online Store & Campaign Matls: Steve Wyckoff
Conducts Business: U.S.
Employees: 21
Primary Market Served: Consumer
Catalog available online
Direct online sales
Advertising/Marketing Budget Related to Direct Marketing: 76-100%
Direct Marketing ad budget:
Direct Mail: 100%
Founded: 1968

Gross sales or billing: $1,500,000

National non-profit organization for the protection & welfare of animals.

THE BOWERY MISSION
132 Madison Ave
New York, NY 10016-7004
Telephone: (212) 684-2800, Web Site:
    www.bowery.org
Primary Market Served: Consumer
Founded: 1879

Gospel mission

BOY SCOUTS OF AMERICA/ NATIONAL SUPPLY GROUP
2109 Westinghouse Blvd
Charlotte, NC 28273-6310
Telephone: (972) 580-2161, (800) 323-
    0736, E-Mail: customerservice@
    scoutstuff.org, Web Site: www.
    scoutstuff.org
Natl Commissioner: Donald D. Belcher
Chief Scout Exec: Robert Mazzuca
Dir Mktg: Arlene Harris
Pres: John C. Cushman III
VP, HR: James R. Turley
Primary Market Served: Consumer
Catalog available online
Direct online sales

Provide uniforms, equipment & literature for the Boy Scouts of America.

BOYS & GIRLS CLUBS OF AMERICA NATIONAL HEADQUARTERS
1275 Peachtree St NE
Atlanta, GA 30309-3506
Telephone: (404) 487-5700, FAX:
    (404) 487-5757, (404) 815-5757,
    E-Mail: info@bgca.org, Web Site:
    www.bgca.org
SVP Mktg & Commun: Evan McElroy
Conducts Business: U.S.
Primary Market Served: Consumer

Non-profit organization with over 2000 Boys & Girls Clubs facilities nationwide. Solicit funds through direct mail.

BRONX COUNCIL ON THE ARTS
1738 Hone Ave
Bronx, NY 10461-1486
Telephone: (718) 931-9500, FAX:
    (718) 409-6445, E-Mail: info@
    bronxarts.org, Web Site: www.
    bronxarts.org
Exec Dir: Deirdre Scott
Bus Mgr: Lorraine Pizarro
Employees: 21
Primary Market Served: Business &
    Consumer
Founded: 1962

Non-profit organization. Official cultural agency of Bronx county.

BROOKFIELD ZOO
Chicago Zoological Society
3300 Golf Rd
Brookfield, IL 60513-1060
Telephone: (708) 485-0263, (800) 201-
    0784, FAX: (708) 485-3532, Web
    Site: www.brookfieldzoo.org
Pres & CEO: Dr. Stuart D. Strahl
Sr VP Mktg: Amy Walgren
Employees: 500
Primary Market Served: Consumer
Founded: 1934
Gross sales or billing: $64,100,000

Uses direct mail to recruit members & animal adoption parents.

CAA AUTO CLUB & TRAVEL AGENCY INC
60 Commerce Valley Dr E
Thornhill, ON, Canada L3T 7P9
Telephone: (519) 255-1212, (800) 564-
    6222, FAX: (519) 255-7379, E-Mail:
    info@caasco.ca, Web Site: www.
    central.on.caa.ca
Chmn: Bill Graham
Mgr: Paolo Morassut
Conducts Business: Canada
Employees: 200
Primary Market Served: Business &
    Consumer
Advertising/Marketing Budget Related
    to Direct Marketing: 51-75%
Founded: 1903

Auto club services.

CCIM INSTITUTE
Div. of National Association of Realtors
430 N Michigan Ave (Suite 800)
Chicago, IL 60611-4011
Telephone: (312) 321-4460, (800) 621-
    7027, FAX: (312) 321-4530, Web
    Site: www.ccim.com
CEO: Jonathan Salk
Pres: Tim Hatlestad
Pres-Elect: Charles McClure
First VP: Richard E. Juge
Treas: Stephen Perfit
Conducts Business: U.S., Canada,
    China, Mexico, U.K.
Employees: 40
Primary Market Served: Business
Catalog available online
Direct online sales
Advertising/Marketing Budget Related
    to Direct Marketing: 51-75%
Direct Marketing ad budget:
Direct Mail: 85%
Magazines: 5%
Newspapers: 5%
Telephone: 5%
Founded: 1969

National trade association specializing in education & business development programs for commercial investment real estate practitioners.

CDMI INC
711 Pacific Coast Hwy (Unit 118)
Huntington Beach, CA 92648-5051
Telephone: (714) 969-4064
Pres: Phillip F. Sheats
Primary Market Served: Consumer

CDR FUNDRAISING GROUP
16900 Science Dr (Suite 210)
Bowie, MD 20715-4412
Telephone: (301) 858-1500, FAX:
    (301) 858-0107, Web Site: www.cdr-nfl.com
Pres & CEO: Geoffrey Peters

CMS LLC
1900 Campus Commons Dr (Suite 450)
Reston, VA 20191-1559
Telephone: (703) 258-0000, Web Site:
    www.craveronline.com
Principal & CEO: Ellen Church

Direct response fundraising

CALENDAR MARKETING ASSOCIATION
214 N Hale St
Wheaton, IL 60187-5115
Telephone: (630) 510-4500, FAX:
    (630) 510-4501, E-Mail: info@
    calendarassociation.org, Web Site:
    www.calendarassociation.org
Exec Dir: Michael Hansen
Employees: 6
Primary Market Served: Business &
    Consumer
Advertising/Marketing Budget Related
    to Direct Marketing: 26-50%
Founded: 1989

Involved in all aspects of the calendar industry including publishing, printing & manufacturing.

CALIFORNIA CHAMBER OF COMMERCE
1332 N Market Blvd
Sacramento, CA 95834-1912
Telephone: (800) 331-8877, Web Site:
    www.calbizcentral.com
Mktg Mgr: Lisa Hein
Primary Market Served: Business

CALIFORNIA SOCIETY OF CPA'S
1800 Gateway Dr (Suite 200)
San Mateo, CA 94404-4072

Telephone: (800) 922-5272, FAX: (650) 522-3009, E-Mail: info@ culcpa.org, Web Site: www.calcpa. org
CEO: John Dunleavy
PR Dir: Bill Spaniel
Mktg Dir: Patricia Kilner
Publications: Aldo Marogni
Adv: Bobbi Petrov
Mktg Mgr: Laura Toland
Conducts Business: U.S.
Employees: 120
Primary Market Served: Business & Consumer
Catalog available online
Direct online sales

Association representing 30,000 California CPA's.

CANADIAN BLOOD SERVICES

1800 Alta Vista Dr
Ottawa, ON, Canada K1G 4J5
Telephone: (613) 739-2300, Web Site: www.blood.ca
Natl Dir, Sls & Mktg: Jeff Moat
Primary Market Served: Consumer

ᵀᴴᴱ_ᴅᴹᴬ CANADIAN INSTITUTE OF CHARTERED ACCOUNTANTS

277 Wellington St W
Toronto, ON, Canada M5V 3H2
Telephone: (416) 977-3222, Web Site: www.cica.ca
VP, Member Svcs: Cairine Wilson
Primary Market Served: Business

CANCER FUND OF AMERICA INC

2901 Breezewood Ln
Knoxville, TN 37921-1099
Telephone: (865) 938-5281, (800) 578-5284, FAX: (865) 938-2968, Web Site: www.cfoa.org
Pres: James T. Reynolds
Hospice Coord: Brenda Clarke
Patient Svc Dir: Joshua Loveless
Fundraiser: Michael Reynolds
Primary Market Served: Business & Consumer
Catalog available online
Gross sales or billing: $26,000,000

Non-profit national health agency; direct aid to cancer patients, hospices, and other healthcare providers nationwide. Provider of emergency supplies to third world countries. Program Services 72%; Fundraising 26%; Administration 2%.

CANCER RESEARCH SOCIETY

625 President Kennedy Ave (Suite 402)
Montreal, PQ, Canada H3A 3S5
Telephone: (514) 861-9227, (888) 766-2262, FAX: (514) 861-9220, Web Site: www.CancerResearchSociety.ca
Dir Fin: Alain Laurendeau
Exec Dir: Andy Chabot
Deputy Exec Dir: Nathalie Giroux
Admin Asst: Helene Boucher
Conducts Business: Canada
Employees: 23
Primary Market Served: Business & Consumer
Founded: 1945
Gross sales or billing: $18,500,000

Raise funds nationally for the exclusive purpose of supporting cancer research.

CARE2

1100 15th S NW (Suite 600)
Washington, DC 20005-1759
Telephone: (650) 622-0860, Web Site: www.care2.com
VP, Bus Devel: Clinton O'Brien
Primary Market Served: Business & Consumer
Founded: 1998

Online community focusing on green living. Connects individuals with non-profit organizations

ᵀᴴᴱ_ᴅᴹᴬ CARE USA

151 Ellis St NE
Atlanta, GA 30303-2420
Telephone: (404) 979-9255, (800) 521-CARE, FAX: (404) 589-2600, E-Mail: info@care.org, Web Site: www.careusa.org
Dir Direct Response Mktg: Jennifer Jones
Pres & CEO: Helene D. Gayle M.D., M.P.H.
COO: Steve Hollingworth
Sr VP: Susan Farnsworth
Sr VP: Joe Iarocci
Sec Bd: Carol Hudson
Conducts Business: Worldwide
Employees: 7,000
Primary Market Served: Business & Consumer
Catalog available online
Founded: 1945
Gross sales or billing: $646,000,000

International development & relief organization.

ᵀᴴᴱ_ᴅᴹᴬ CAREER EDUCATION CORP

231 N Martingale Rd Ste 100
Schaumburg, IL 60173-2007

Telephone: (847) 781-3600, Web Site: www.careered.com
Sr VP: Paul Misniak
Primary Market Served: Consumer
Founded: 1999

Educational services company

ᵀᴴᴱ_ᴅᴹᴬ CATHOLIC CHARITIES - BROOKLYN & QUEENS

191 Joralemon St
Brooklyn, NY 11201-4306
Telephone: (718) 722-6000, Web Site: www.ccbq.org
Primary Market Served: Consumer

Service agency promoting unity among all persons

CATHOLIC CHURCH EXTENSION SOCIETY

150 S Wacker Dr (fl 20)
Chicago, IL 60606-4103
Telephone: (312) 795-6076, Web Site: www.catholicextension.org

CATHOLIC HEALTH EAST

3805 West Chester (#100)
Newtown Square, PA 19073-2329
Telephone: (610) 355-2000, (877) 424-3001, FAX: (610) 271-9600, Web Site: www.che.org
VP: Kay Miller

ᵀᴴᴱ_ᴅᴹᴬ CATHOLIC RELIEF SERVICES

228 Lexington St
Baltimore, MD 21201-3443
Telephone: (410) 951-7491, Web Site: www.catholicrelief.org
Dir, Direct Response Fundraising: Jean Simmons
Primary Market Served: Consumer

ᵀᴴᴱ_ᴅᴹᴬ BRAD CECIL & ASSOCIATES

2700 W Park Row
Arlington, TX 76013-2258
Telephone: (817) 795-8808
Pres: Brad Cecil

Direct response fundraising

THE CENTER FOR EBUSINESS & ADVANCED IT

5340 Fryling Rd (Suite 201)
Erie, PA 16510-4672
Telephone: (814) 898-6500, Web Site: www.ebizitpa.org
Dir EMarketing: Catherine Von Birgelen

CENTER FOR SCIENCE IN THE PUBLIC INTEREST
dba Nutrition Action Healthletter
1220 L St NW Ste 300
Washington, DC 20005-4053
Telephone: (202) 332-9110, FAX: (202) 265-4954, E-Mail: circ@cspinet.org, Web Site: www.cspinet.org
Exec Dir: Michael Jacobson
Mktg Dir: Cecilia Saad
Deputy Dir: Dennis Bass
Conducts Business: U.S., Canada
Employees: 65
Primary Market Served: Consumer
Catalog available online
Direct online sales
Direct Marketing ad budget:
Direct Mail: 98%
Newspapers: 2%
Founded: 1971
Gross sales or billing: $17,052,338

Also publishes the Nutrition Action Healthletter.

CHARITY DYNAMICS
3420 Executive Center Dr Ste G100
Austin, TX 78731-1692
Telephone: (512) 241-0561, Web Site: www.charitydynamics.com
Pres: Donna Wilkins

CHARLOTTE CHAMBER OF COMMERCE
330 S Tryon St (Suite 200)
Charlotte, NC 28202-1923
Telephone: (704) 378-1300, Web Site: www.boomcharlotte.com
Primary Market Served: Consumer

CHERRY BROTHERS LLC/ CHERRYDALE
1900 Am Dr (Suite 203)
Quakertown, PA 18951-6403
Telephone: (800) 570-6010, Web Site: www.cherrydale.com
Exec Asst: Kim Snyder

Fundraising ideas & products for school fundraising

CHESAPEAKE BAY FOUNDATION
6 Herndon Ave
Annapolis, MD 21403-4503
Telephone: (410) 268-8816, Web Site: www.savethebay.cbf.org
Dir Membership: Amelia Koch

CHICAGO CONVENTION & TOURISM BUREAU
301 E Cermak Rd
Chicago, IL 60616-1578
Telephone: (312) 567-8500, Web Site: www.choosechicago.com
Mktg Dir: Harvey Morris
Primary Market Served: Consumer

CHILDFUND INTERNATIONAL
2821 Emerywood Pkwy
Richmond, VA 23294-3726
Telephone: (804) 756-2700, Web Site: www.ChildFund.org
Dir Mktg: Mary Arnold
Primary Market Served: Consumer

CHILDREN INTERNATIONAL
2000 E Red Bridge Rd
Kansas City, MO 64131-3694
Telephone: (816) 942-2000, FAX: (816) 942-3714, E-Mail: RobS@cikc.org, Web Site: www.children.org
VP Mktg: Robert Saint Thomas
Dir, Mktg Children Intl: Carole Spencer

CHILDREN OF THE NIGHT
14530 Sylvan St
Van Nuys, CA 91411
Telephone: (818) 908-4474, (800) 551-1300, FAX: (818) 908-1468, E-Mail: llee@childrenofthenight.com, Web Site: www.childrenofthenight.org
Exec Dir: Dr. Lois Lee
Primary Market Served: Business & Consumer
Catalog available online
Advertising/Marketing Budget Related to Direct Marketing: 0-25%
Founded: 1979

Children's shelter dealing with youths ages 11-17 involved in prostitution and/or pornography. A 24-bed licensed shelter.

CHILDREN'S AID SOCIETY
105 E 22nd St (Rm 504)
New York, NY 10010-5453
Telephone: (212) 949-4945, Web Site: www.childrensaidsociety.org
Dir Mktg & Special Events: Kathy Gallagher de Meij
Employees: 1,000
Primary Market Served: Consumer
Founded: 1853

CHILDREN'S BETTER HEALTH INSTITUTE
1100 Waterway Blvd
Indianapolis, IN 46202
Telephone: (317) 634-1100, FAX: (317) 684-8094, E-Mail: gjoray@tcon.net, Web Site: www.cbhi.org
Pres: Joan Servaas
Circ Dir: Gregory M. Joray
Conducts Business: Worldwide

Employees: 40
Primary Market Served: Consumer
Catalog available online
Direct online sales
Founded: 1976
Gross sales or billing: $5,000,000

A non-profit organization providing information & encouragement to parents, teachers & health professionals to educate on the fundamentals of good health.

CHILDREN'S HOSPITAL FOUNDATION
111 Michigan Ave NW, Children's Hospital Foundation
Washington, DC 20010-2916
Telephone: (202) 476-3000, (800) 884-LIFE, FAX: (202) 884-5999, Web Site: www.dcchildrens.com
Pres & CEO: Edwin K. Zechman Jr.
COO & VP: Jody M. Burdell
VP, Devel: John Thomas
VP & Chief of Governmental Affairs: Jaqueline D. Bowens
Dir, Corp & Foundation Devel: Barbara Schroeder
Conducts Business: U.S.
Employees: 3,500
Primary Market Served: Business & Consumer
Catalog available online
Founded: 1870
Gross sales or billing: $574,000,000

Pediatric hospital.

CHILDREN'S HOSPITAL OF PITTSBURGH
4401 Penn Ave.
Pittsburgh, PA 15224
Telephone: (412) 692-5325, FAX: (412) 692-7140, Web Site: www.chp.edu
Devel Dir Giving: Carol Ashby
Primary Market Served: Consumer

Various fund-raising projects.

CHRISTIAN APPALACHIAN PROJECT
PO Box 55911
Lexington, KY 40555-5911
Telephone: (859) 792-3051, (866) 270-4CAP, FAX: (859) 792-6560, E-Mail: capinfo@chrisapp.org, Web Site: www.christianapp.org
Pres: Mike Sanders
Treas: Jack Hamm
Sec: Bob Boduch
Exec VP: Sue Sword
Conducts Business: U.S.
Employees: 40
Primary Market Served: Consumer

Charitable, non-profit fund-raising organization. Also, catalog sales of Christmas season wreaths.

THE DMA CHRISTIAN BROADCASTING NETWORK INC

977 Centerville Tpke
Virginia Beach, VA 23463-1001
Telephone: (757) 226-3542, FAX: (757) 226-2017, Web Site: www.cbn. org
Pres, COO & Dir: Michael D. Little
Chmn: M. G. Robertson
VP Devel Integration: Edie Wasserberg
Controller: Jim Barr
DM Dir: Kathy Pollack
Employees: 941
Primary Market Served: Business & Consumer
Gross sales or billing: $18,600,000

Christian services.

CHRISTIAN CHILDREN'S FUND INC

2821 Emerywood Pkwy
Richmond, VA 23294
Telephone: (804) 756-2700, (800) 776-6767, FAX: (804) 756-2718, Web Site: www.christianchildrensfund.org
VP, Mktg: Betty Forbes
Dir, Mktg: Mary Arnold
Employees: 130
Primary Market Served: Consumer
Founded: 1938

International non-profit & non-sectarian humanitarian organization dedicated to serving the needs of children worldwide, primarily through person-to-person assistance programs.

CHRISTIAN HERALD ASSOCIATION

132 Madison Ave
New York, NY 10016-7004
Telephone: (212) 684-2800, (800) BOWERY-1, FAX: (212) 684-3740, E-Mail: info@chaonline.org, Web Site: www.bowery.org
Chmn Bd: Jan Nagel
Pres: Edward H. Morgan
Dir: Douglas John
Dir: Donald Kolowsky
Dir: Miguel Sanchez
Conducts Business: U.S.
Employees: 75
Primary Market Served: Consumer
Founded: 1879
Gross sales or billing: $12,000,000

Ministry encompassing Bowery mission, women's mission & summer camp for kids.

THE DMA CHRISTIAN RELIEF SERVICES CHARITIES INC

2550 Huntington Ave (Suite 200)
Alexandria, VA 22303-1400
Telephone: (703) 317-9086, Web Site: www.christianrelief.org
Gen Counsel: Paul Krizek
Primary Market Served: Consumer

THE DMA CHURCH PENSION FUND

445 5th Ave
New York, NY 07652-1461
Telephone: (866) 802-6333, Web Site: www.cpg.org
VP: Joyce Wade
Primary Market Served: Business

CITIZENS AGAINST GOVERNMENT WASTE

1301 Pennsylvania Ave NW Ste 1075
Washington, DC 20004-1707
Telephone: (202) 467-5300, (800) USA-DEBT, FAX: (202) 467-4253, E-Mail: membership@cagw.org, Web Site: www.cagw.org
Pres: Thomas A. Schatz
Sr VP: Robert J. Tedeschi
VP, Devel: Ariane E. Sweeney
VP: David E. Williams
VP: Elizabeth L. Wright
Employees: 16
Primary Market Served: Business & Consumer
Founded: 1984
Gross sales or billing: $5,501,194

Non-profit, non-partisan taxpayer watchdog.

THE DMA CITY OF CERRITOS

PO Box 3130
Cerritos, CA 90703-3130
Telephone: (562) 916-1319, Web Site: www.ci.cerritos.ca.us
City & Theatre Mktg Mgr: Annie Hylton
Primary Market Served: Consumer

THE DMA CITY OF HOPE CANCER CENTER

1055 Wilshire Blvd
Los Angeles, CA 90017-2431
Telephone: (626) 256-4673, Web Site: www.cityofhope.org
Dir Devel: Noel De Leon
Primary Market Served: Consumer

CITY OF LAGRANGE

200 Ridley Ave, PO Box 430
LaGrange, GA 30240
Telephone: (706) 883-2010, FAX: (706) 883-2062, Web Site: www.lagrange-ga.org
City Mgr: Tom Hall

Deputy City Mgr - Admin & Fin: Meg Kelsey
Primary Market Served: Business & Consumer

Municipal government.

CIVIL WAR PRESERVATION TRUST

1156 15th St NW (Suite 900)
Washington, DC 20005-4761
Telephone: (202) 367-1861, Web Site: www.civilwar.org
Dir Membership & Devel: David Duncan

THE DMA CLEVELAND CLINIC FOUNDATION

9500 Euclid Ave (AC311)
Cleveland, OH 44195-0001
Telephone: (216) 444-2200, Web Site: www.clevelandclinic.org
Dir Database Mktg: Sylvia Morrison

THE DMA THE CLEVELAND ORCHESTRA

The Musical Arts Association
11001 Euclid Ave
Cleveland, OH 44106-1796
Telephone: (216) 231-7441, FAX: (216) 231-4038, Web Site: www. clevelandorchestra.com
Exec Dir: Thomas W. Morris
Mktg Dir: Ross Binnie
Conducts Business: U.S.
Primary Market Served: Consumer
Direct Marketing ad budget:
Direct Mail: 25%
Newspapers: 25%
TV/Radio: 25%
Telephone: 25%

Perform 26 concert weekends per year at Severance Hall & ten weekends at Blossom Music Center.

COAST TO COAST INC

Div. of Affinity Group AGI
PO Box 6574
Englewood, CO 80155-6574
Telephone: (303) 728-2267, Web Site: www.coastresorts.com
Chmn Bd: Kenneth R. Jensen
Pres, CEO & Dir: Michael A. Schneider
Sr VP & CFO: Thomas F. Wolfe
Primary Market Served: Consumer
Catalog available online
Direct online sales

Membership camping.

COASTAL HOTEL GROUP

18525 36th Ave S
Seattle, WA 98188-4967

Telephone: (206) 388-0400, FAX: (206) 388-0401, E-Mail: info@coastalhotel.com, Web Site: www.coastalhotels.com
Pres & CEO: Yogi Hutsen
CFO: Peter LaFemina
Sr VP Sls & Mktg: Ed Schwitsky
Corp Dir Sls: Janelle Cornett
Natl Dir Sls: Laura Kroth
Primary Market Served: Business
Catalog available online
Direct online sales

Hotel management company.

COIN LAUNDRY ASSOCIATION
1S660 Midwest Rd Ste 205
Oakbrook Terrace, IL 60181-4738
Telephone: (630) 963-5547, FAX: (630) 963-5864, Web Site: www.coinlaundry.org
Pres & CEO: Brian Wallace
Chair: Jeff Hooper
Conducts Business: U.S., Canada
Employees: 8
Primary Market Served: Business
Catalog available online
Direct online sales
Advertising/Marketing Budget Related to Direct Marketing: 51-75%
Direct Marketing ad budget: $75,000
Direct Mail: 75%
Magazines: 10%
Telephone: 15%
Founded: 1960

National trade association to coin laundry/dry cleaning industry offering membership to qualified business owners, manufacturers & distributors.

THE COLLEGE BOARD
45 Columbus Ave
New York, NY 10023-6917
Telephone: (212) 713-8000, FAX: (212) 713-8143, Web Site: www.collegeboard.com
Pres: W. Gaston Caperton III
Sr VP & CFO: Thomas Higgins
Conducts Business: U.S., Canada, Europe
Employees: 598
Primary Market Served: Consumer
Founded: 1900
Gross sales or billing: $484,900,000

Non-profit education association. Offer services & programs for the transition between high school & college.

COLLEGEAMERICA
4021 S 700 E (Suite 300)
Salt Lake City, UT 84107-2184
Telephone: (801) 284-7553
Primary Market Served: Consumer
Founded: 1964

College programs

THE COLONIAL WILLIAMSBURG FOUNDATION
DMA
PO Box 1776
Williamsburg, VA 23187-1776
Telephone: (757) 229-1000, (757) 220-7275, (800) 761-8331, Web Site: www.williamsburgmarketplace.com
Chmn, Pres & CEO: Colin G. Campbell
Sr VP, Fin & Admin: Robert Taylor
Vice Chair: Robert G. Tilghman
Dir, Direct Mktg Oper: Tammy Kersey
Conducts Business: U.S.
Employees: 3,100
Primary Market Served: Consumer
Catalog available online
Indirect online sales
Gross sales or billing: $235,000,000

Non-profit educational foundation.

COMMUNITY FOOD BANK
THE DMA
3003 S Country Club Rd (Ste 221)
Tucson, AZ 85713-4084
Telephone: (520) 622-0525, Web Site: www.communityfoodbank.org
Dir Mktg Mgr: Melanie Morgan

COMPASSION INTERNATIONAL
THE DMA
12290 Voyager Pkwy
Colorado Springs, CO 80921-3694
Telephone: (800) 336-7676, Web Site: www.compassion.com
Agency Print Prod Mgr: Michelle Dana

COMPUTERS FOR EDUCATION
180 Freedom Ave
Murfreesboro, TN 37129-6926
Telephone: (615) 896-3800, FAX: (615) 895-9041
CEO: Tom Crook
Conducts Business: U.S.
Employees: 150
Primary Market Served: Business & Consumer
Advertising/Marketing Budget Related to Direct Marketing: 0-25%
Direct Marketing ad budget:
Direct Mail: 20%
Telephone: 80%
Founded: 1981
Gross sales or billing: $5,000,000

School fund-raising.

CONCERN WORLDWIDE
THE DMA
355 Lexington Ave Fl 19
New York, NY 10017-6603
Telephone: (212) 557-8000, Web Site: /www.concernusa.org

Devel Officer: Aine Doddy

CM CONNOLLY
9545 Coney Island Cir
Elk Grove, CA 95758-3646
Telephone: (916) 897-8095, Web Site: www.cmconnolly.com
Proprietor: Catherine Connolly

Direct marketing for non-profit organizations

CONSERVATION INTERNATIONAL
2011 Crystal Dr (Suite 500)
Arlington, VA 22202-3787
Telephone: (202) 912-1285
VP Digital Mktg: Beth Wallace
Primary Market Served: Consumer

CONTINUING EDUCATION OF THE BAR (CEB)
2100 Franklin St Ste 500
Oakland, CA 94612-3098
Telephone: (510) 302-2000, (800) 232-3444, FAX: (510) 302-2001, Web Site: www.ceb.com
Dir Mktg: Michael Taylor
Consultant: Diane Kretschmer
Employees: 210
Primary Market Served: Business
Catalog available online
Direct online sales
Advertising/Marketing Budget Related to Direct Marketing: 76-100%
Founded: 1947
Gross sales or billing: $22,375,068

Provide tools for legal continuing education. Also publish legal publications & CD ROM's in print and online.

CORNELL LAB OF ORNITHOLOGY
THE DMA
Div. of Cornell University
159 Sapsucker Woods Rd
Ithaca, NY 14850-1923
Telephone: (607) 254-2157, (800) 843-BIRD, FAX: (607) 254-2415, E-Mail: birdslides@cornell.edu, Web Site: www.birds.cornell.edu
Exec Dir: Scott Sutcliffe
Sr Dir: Paul Miller
Dir Mktg: Mary Guthrie
Dir: John Fitzpatrick
Admin: Nora Ettinger
Conducts Business: U.S., Canada
Employees: 60
Primary Market Served: Business & Consumer
Catalog available online
Direct online sales
Advertising/Marketing Budget Related to Direct Marketing: 76-100%
Direct Marketing ad budget:

Direct Mail: 90%
Magazines: 10%
Founded: 1954
Gross sales or billing: $1,000,000

All supplies for birding. Books, binoculars, bird song recordings, etc.

CORPUS CHRISTI MUSEUM OF SCIENCE & HISTORY

1900 N Chaparral St
Corpus Christi, TX 78401-1114
Telephone: (361) 826-4667, FAX: (361) 884-7392, Web Site: www.ccmuseum.com
Opers & Pub Rels: Bonnie Laya
Dir: Richard Stryker
Dev Dir: Patricia Drolet
Conducts Business: U.S.
Employees: 30
Primary Market Served: Business & Consumer
Advertising/Marketing Budget Related to Direct Marketing: 0-25%
Founded: 1957

Sell membership in the Corpus Christi Museum of Science & History.

THE DMA COUNCIL FOR ADVANCEMENT AND SUPPORT OF EDUCATION (CASE)

1307 New York Ave NW (Suite 100)
Washington, DC 20005
Telephone: (202) 328-2273, Web Site: www.case.org
Primary Market Served: Business & Consumer

COUNCIL OF BETTER BUSINESS BUREAUS - BBBONLINE

3033 Wilson Blvd Ste 600
Arlington, VA 22201-3863
Telephone: (703) 276-0100, FAX: (703) 525-8277, Web Site: www.bbb.org
Pres & CEO: Steven Cole
Sr VP & COO: Russell Bodoff
Exec VP: Charles Underhill
VP Membership Mktg: Sallly Munn
Conducts Business: U.S., Canada
Employees: 113
Primary Market Served: Business & Consumer
Catalog available online
Advertising/Marketing Budget Related to Direct Marketing: 26-50%
Direct Marketing ad budget:
Direct Mail: $25,000
Founded: 1975
Gross sales or billing: $21,900,000

Supported by 350 companies & 138 local Better Business Bureaus operated autonomously in the United States, which are in turn supported by 230,000 local business members. Seeks to promote & foster the highest ethical relationship between businesses & the public through voluntary self-regulation, consumer & business education and service excellence.

COUNCIL OF SMALLER ENTERPRISES (COSE)

100 Public Square (Suite 210), The Higbee Building
Cleveland, OH 44113-2227
Telephone: (216) 621-3300, Web Site: www.cose.org
Mktg Commun: Rose DiPietro

COUNTRY DANCE AND SONG SOCIETY

132 Main St
Haydenville, MA 01039-0338
Telephone: (413) 268-7426, FAX: (413) 268-7471, E-Mail: office@cdss.org, Web Site: www.cdss.org
Pres: Bruce Hamilton
Exec Dir: Bradley R. Foster
VP: Sandy Rotenberg
Opers Mgr: Carol Compton
Sec: Alisa Dodson
Conducts Business: U.S., Canada, Western Europe
Employees: 8
Primary Market Served: Business & Consumer
Catalog available online
Advertising/Marketing Budget Related to Direct Marketing: 0-25%
Founded: 1915
Gross sales or billing: $110,000

Non-profit organization dedicated to the preservation, study, teaching & enjoyment of our English & American dance, music & song heritage.

THE DMA COURAGE CARDS & GIFTS

3915 Golden Valley Rd Courage Ctr
Golden Valley, MN 55422-4249
Telephone: (763) 588-081, Web Site: www.couragecards.org
Dir Mktg: Wayne Mikos
Primary Market Served: Business & Consumer

THE DMA COVENANT HOUSE INTERNATIONAL HEADQUARTERS

5 Penn Plaza
New York, NY 10001-1810
Telephone: (212) 727-4000, (800) 999-9999, FAX: (212) 727-4992, Web Site: www.covenanthouse.org

Pres: Sr. Patricia A. Cruise S.C.
Sr VP, Program Devel: Thomas Kennedy
Sr VP, Devel: Judith E. Nichols Ph.D
Conducts Business: U.S., Canada, Guatamala, Honduras, Mexico
Employees: 180
Primary Market Served: Consumer
Founded: 1972
Gross sales or billing: $34,000,000

Crisis intervention for runaway & homeless children who are under 21.

THE BEN CRAIG CENTER

8701 Mallard Creek Rd # 106
Charlotte, NC 28262-6007
Telephone: (704) 548-9113, Web Site: www.bencraigcenter.com
Primary Market Served: Business

CRAIG/VARTORELLA INTERNATIONAL MARKETING & ADVERTISING INC

277 Peckwood Rd
Camden, SC 29020
Telephone: (803) 432-4353, FAX: (803) 432-4353, E-Mail: globebiz@juno.com, Web Site: www.colasc.com/Marketing_&_Fundraising
Pres: Joanna B. Craig
Exec VP: William F. Vartorella
Conducts Business: Worldwide
Primary Market Served: Business & Consumer
Catalog available online
Indirect online sales
Advertising/Marketing Budget Related to Direct Marketing: 26-50%
Direct Marketing ad budget:
Direct Mail: 25%
Magazines: 50%
Online: 25%
Founded: 1985

CRAVER MATHEWS SMITH & CO

1900 Campus Commons Dr (Suite 450)
Reston, VA 20191-1559
Telephone: (703) 258-0000, FAX: (703) 258-0001, Web Site: www.craveronline.com
Pres: Rosemary Amatetti
Conducts Business: U.S.
Employees: 100
Primary Market Served: Business
Gross sales or billing: $4,000,000

Represent 40 non-profit organizations engaged in direct mail fund-raising & membership development efforts. Provide a full range of services from creative to production to management. Services include telephone marketing.

CREDICORP
PO Box 569001
Dallas, TX 75356-9001
Telephone: (214) 915-7200, FAX:
   (214) 915-7415, E-Mail: support@
   credicorp.net, Web Site: www.
   credicorp.net
Pres: Randy Walls
Sec: Victoria Jensen
Conducts Business: U.S.
Employees: 9
Primary Market Served: Consumer
Catalog available online
Indirect online sales
Advertising/Marketing Budget Related
   to Direct Marketing: 76-100%
Direct Marketing ad budget:
Direct Mail: 100%
Founded: 1990
Gross sales or billing: $1,000,000

Membership services including general
merchandise with financing available
to retail customers; and various other
discounts/benefits.

**CREDIT UNION EXECUTIVES
   SOCIETY**
5510 Research Park Dr
Madison, WI 53711-5377
Telephone: (608) 271-2664, Web Site:
   www.cues.org
VP Mktg: Jessica Hrubes
Primary Market Served: Consumer

**THE DMA CROHN'S & COLITIS
   FOUNDATION OF AMERICA
   (CCFA)**
386 Park Ave S (fl 17)
New York, NY 10016-8804
Telephone: (212) 685-3440, Web Site:
   www.ccfa.org
Mgr Donor Svcs: Alicia Kozma
Primary Market Served: Consumer

CUNA - TRADE ASSOCIATION
5710 Mineral Point Rd
Madison, WI 53705-4454
Telephone: (608) 231-4215, Web Site:
   www.cuna.org
Corp Mktg Dir: Bonnie Bailey
Primary Market Served: Consumer

**THE DMA CYSTIC FIBROSIS
   FOUNDATION**
6931 Arlington Rd
Bethesda, MD 20814-5231
Telephone: (301) 951-4422, Web Site:
   www.cff.org
Dir, Direct Mail Opers: Keith Hinnant
Primary Market Served: Consumer

THE DMA DEI
401 N 3rd St (Suite 370)
Minneapolis, MN 55401-1350

Telephone: (612) 677-1505, Web Site:
   www.deiworksite.org
Dir, Mktg Communs: Virginia Dambach

Assists local public radio stations with
fundraising activities

**D/FW GROCERS
   ASSOCIATION**
Associated with Texas Grocery & Con-
   venience Association
3044 Old Denton Rd (Suite 111)
Carrollton, TX 75007-5074
Telephone: (972) 353-5885, FAX:
   (469) 574-5252, Web Site: www.
   dfwga.net
Conducts Business: U.S.
Primary Market Served: Business
Advertising/Marketing Budget Related
   to Direct Marketing: 0-25%
Direct Marketing ad budget:
Direct Mail: 60%
Telephone: 40%
Founded: 1906

Trade association & trade journal representing grocers, convenience store
owners & suppliers in 50 counties of
the Dallas/Fort Worth metroplex area,
north central Texas and east Texas.

**DAIRY COUNCIL OF
   CALIFORNIA**
2151 Michelson Ave (Suite 235)
Irvine, CA 92612-1339
Telephone: (949) 756-7896, Web Site:
   www.dairycouncilofca.org
Schools Supvr: Sarah Mathot
Primary Market Served: Business &
   Consumer

DAIRY MANAGEMENT INC
dba National Dairy Council
10255 W Higgins Rd (Suite 900)
Rosemont, IL 60018
Telephone: (847) 803-2000, FAX:
   (847) 803-2077, Web Site: www.
   nationaldairycouncil.org
Employees: 80
Primary Market Served: Business &
   Consumer
Founded: 1970
Gross sales or billing: $5,200,000

Educational material on health.

**DANA-FARBER CANCER
   INSTITUTE**
44 Binney St
Boston, MA 02215-6013
Telephone: (617) 632-3000, FAX:
   (617) 632-4070, E-Mail:
   suzanne_fountain@dfci.harvard.edu,
   Web Site: www.dana-farber.org
Pres & CEO: Edward J. Benz, Jr MD
Sr VP Communs: Steven R. Singer

VP Devel: Susan S. Paresky
Assoc Dir Devel: Suzanne Fountain
Employees: 3,000
Primary Market Served: Consumer
Direct online sales
Founded: 1947
Gross sales or billing: $616,000,000

Comprehensive cancer center.

**DARDEN SCHOOL
   FOUNDATION EXECUTIVE
   FOUNDATION**
PO Box 7186
Charlottesville, VA 22906-7186
Telephone: (434) 924-3904, Web Site:
   www.darden.virginia.edu/execed
Dir Mktg: Susian Brooks
Primary Market Served: Consumer

THE DMA DARTMOUTH-HITCHCOCK
Hinman Box 7070, One Medical Cen-
   ter Dr
Lebanon, NH 03756-1000
Telephone: (603) 653-0700, Web Site:
   www.dmsnet.org
Primary Market Served: Consumer

THE DMA DA VINCI DIRECT
36 Cordage Park Cir (Suite 339)
Plymouth, MA 02360-7320
Telephone: (508) 746-2555, FAX:
   (815) 301-9884, Web Site: www.
   davinci-direct.com
CEO: Anthony Genovese
Pres & CCO: Steven J. Maggio
Conducts Business: U.S.
Employees: 5
Primary Market Served: Consumer
Advertising/Marketing Budget Related
   to Direct Marketing: 76-100%
Direct Marketing ad budget: $20,000
Direct Mail: 10%
Magazines: 90%
Founded: 2005
Gross sales or billing: $2,000,000

Strategy: Creative production and
analysis for non-profit and consumer
direct marketing campaigns.

THE DMA DEFENDERS OF WILDLIFE
1130 17th St NW
Washington, DC 20036-4604
Telephone: (202) 682-9400, Web Site:
   www.defenders.org
VP, Membership+: Karin Kirchoff

**DEMOCRATIC
   CONGRESSIONAL
   CAMPAIGN COMMITTEE**
430 S Capitol St SE
Washington, DC 20003
Telephone: (202) 863-1500, FAX:
   (202) 485-3436, Web Site: www.
   dccc.com

Chmn: Chris Van Hollen
Deputy Dir Direct Mktg: Angela Guzman
Conducts Business: U.S.
Employees: 65
Primary Market Served: Business & Consumer
Direct Marketing ad budget:
Direct Mail: 75%
Telephone: 25%

National political party committee.

DENVER METRO CONVENTION & VISITORS BUREAU

1555 California St (Suite 300)
Denver, CO 80202
Telephone: (303) 892-1112, FAX: (303) 892-1636, Web Site: www.denver.org
Pres & CEO: Richard Scharf
VP Fin & Admin: Lauren Arnold
HR Dir: Kim Lorenza Marshall
Sr Pr Mgr: Angela Berardino
Acctg Mgr: Tinisha Manns
Conducts Business: U.S.
Employees: 43
Primary Market Served: Business & Consumer
Catalog available online
Indirect online sales
Advertising/Marketing Budget Related to Direct Marketing: 51-75%
Direct Marketing ad budget:
Magazines: 30%
Newspapers: 70%
Founded: 1944
Gross sales or billing: $900,000

A private non-profit corporation organized in 1908 to promote Denver as a convention & leisure travel destination.

DIAKON LUTHERAN SOCIAL MINISTRIES

798 Hausman Rd (Suite 300)
Allentown, PA 18104-9108
Telephone: (610) 682-2145, (888) 582-2230, FAX: (610) 682-1055, E-Mail: swangerb@diakon.org, Web Site: www.diakon.org
Pres & CEO: Rev. Daun McKee
VP, Commun: William Swanger
Exec Matls Mngmt: Richard Benjamin
Sr VP, Advancement: Kenneth Feinour
Employees: 3,100
Primary Market Served: Consumer
Founded: 1868

Adoption, foster care, retirement communities, and social sciences.

DIRECT MARKETING ASSOCIATION

1120 Ave of the Americas
New York, NY 10036-6713
Telephone: (212) 768-7277, Web Site: www.the-dma.org
Interim CEO: Robert Allen
Employees: 300
Primary Market Served: Business
Founded: 1917

THE DIRECT MARKETING CLUB OF NEW YORK INC

54 Adams St
Garden City, NY 11530-3918
Telephone: (516) 746-6700, FAX: (516) 294-8141, E-Mail: info@dmcny.org, Web Site: www.dmcny.org
Pres: Pegg Nadler
Past Pres: Regina Brady
First VP: Pam Haas
Second VP: Cyndi Lee
Exec Dir: Stuart Boysen
Treas: Arthur Blumenfield
Conducts Business: U.S.
Employees: 1
Primary Market Served: Business
Indirect online sales
Advertising/Marketing Budget Related to Direct Marketing: 76-100%
Direct Marketing ad budget:
Direct Mail: 20%
Online: 80%
Founded: 1926

Non-profit association serving the direct marketing interests of its members who are primarily located in the New York City metropolitan area. Membership is available to individuals and or companies who use direct marketing in their business or who create, manage or provide services to such businesses. Holds monthly meetings.

DIRECTBUY INC

Subs. of United Consumers Club Franchising Corp
PO Box 13006
Merrillville, IN 46410-3006
Telephone: (219) 736-1100, FAX: (219) 755-6208, Web Site: www.ucctotalhome.com
Pres: Scott M. Powell
Chief Mktg Officer: Mark Gonsalves
Mktg Dir: Kristy Hughes
Sr Commun Coord: Sara Shragal
Conducts Business: U.S.
Primary Market Served: Consumer
Catalog available online
Founded: 1970

Private buying service offering furniture, furnishings, carpeting, electronics & appliances to members.

THE DMA DISABLED AMERICAN VETERANS

PO Box 14301
Cincinnati, OH 45250-0301
Telephone: (859) 441-7300, FAX: (859) 442-2084, E-Mail: feedback@davmail.org, Web Site: www.dav.org
Exec Dir: Rick Patterson
Mgr Planned Giving: Judy Sweeney
Dir, Fundraising: Susan M. Loth
Direct Mktg Mgr: Tracey Burguon
Asst Dir, Fundraising: Jim Walding
Conducts Business: U.S.
Primary Market Served: Consumer
Catalog available online
Direct online sales
Advertising/Marketing Budget Related to Direct Marketing: 0-25%
Founded: 1921

Veterans' membership service organization with approximately one million disabled veterans. Funds are raised from the general public to support service programs for disabled veterans & their dependents.

THE DMA DIVINE WORD MISSIONARIES

1835 Waukegan Rd
Techny, IL 60082
Telephone: (847) 412-7233, Web Site: www.svdmissions.org
Devel Officer: Carmelita Linden
Primary Market Served: Business & Consumer

THE DMA DOCTORS WITHOUT BORDERS

333 7th Ave (fl 2)
New York, NY 10001-5089
Telephone: (212) 655-3767, Web Site: www.doctorswithoutborders.org
Dir Mktg: Melanie West
Primary Market Served: Consumer

DONOR SERVICES GROUP

6715 W Sunset Blvd
Los Angeles, CA 90028-7107
Telephone: (310) 788-9000, (888) 474-1900, Web Site: www.donorservicesgroup.com
Dir of Bus Devel: Colin Bickley

THE DMA DOUGLAS SHAW & ASSOCIATES

1717 Park St Ste 300
Naperville, IL 60563-4864
Telephone: (630) 562-1321, Web Site: www.douglasshaw.com
Chmn Bd & CEO: Douglas Shaw

Full service fundraising counsel for non-profit organizations

DRUG INFORMATION ASSOCIATION

800 Enterprise Rd (Suite 200)
Horsham, PA 19044-3595

Telephone: (215) 442-6124, Web Site:
www.diahome.org
Mktg Dir: Lisa Zoks
Primary Market Served: Consumer

DRUG POLICY ALLIANCE
131 W 33 St (fl 15)
New York, NY 10001-2938
Telephone: (212) 613-8020, FAX:
(212) 613-8021, E-Mail: nyc@
drugpolicy.org, Web Site: www.
drugpolicy.org
Exec Dir: Ethan Nadelmann
Donor Dir: Bill North-Rudin
Primary Market Served: Business &
Consumer
Founded: 1986

Non-profit organization.

THE DMA **DUCKS UNLIMITED**
1 Waterfowl Way
Memphis, TN 38120-2351
Telephone: (901) 758-3825, (800)
45DUCKS, FAX: (901) 758-3850,
Web Site: www.ducks.org
Creative Dir: Kevin Carpenter
Art Dir: Doug Barnes
Mgr Acquisition Campaign: Pamela
Miles
Conducts Business: U.S., Canada,
Mexico
Employees: 500
Primary Market Served: Business &
Consumer
Catalog available online
Direct online sales
Advertising/Marketing Budget Related
to Direct Marketing: 0-25%
Direct Marketing ad budget:
$1,100,000
Direct Mail: 20%
Magazines: 60%
Newspapers: 5%
Online: 15%
Founded: 1937
Gross sales or billing: $198,400,000

Sportsman & environmentalist supported non-profit organization, dedicated to preserving & restoring North
America's wetland wildlife habitat.

DUNHAM & CO
2400 Dallas Pkwy (Suite 400)
Plano, TX 75093-4381
Telephone: (469) 454-0100
Pres & CEO: Rick Dunham

Strategic consulting company working
with non-profit organizations

THE DMA **EASTER SEALS**
223 S Wacker Dr (Suite 2400)
Chicago, IL 60606-6410

Telephone: (312) 726-6200, FAX:
(312) 726-1494, Web Site: www.
easter-seals.org
Sr VP & DM: Chris Cleghorn
VP, Devel Svcs: Maureen Haller
Conducts Business: U.S., Canada
Employees: 80
Primary Market Served: Consumer
Advertising/Marketing Budget Related
to Direct Marketing: 51-75%
Founded: 1919

National agency serving the needs of
people with disabilities.

EBERLE & ASSOCIATES INC
Subs. of Eberle Communications
Group Inc
1420 Spring Hill Rd (Suite 490)
McLean, VA 22102-3006
Telephone: (703) 821-1550, FAX:
(703) 821-0920, E-Mail: info@
eberle1.com, Web Site: www.
eberleassociates.com
Chmn: Bruce W. Eberle
Pres: M. Declan Bransfield
CFO: William D. Griffiths
Conducts Business: U.S.
Employees: 33
Primary Market Served: Consumer
Founded: 1974
Gross sales or billing: $3,000,000

Create, consult & implement direct
mail fundraising campaigns for conser-
vative political organizations, candi-
dates & charitable organizations.

EDISON ELECTRIC INSTITUTE
701 Pennsylvania Ave NW
Washington, DC 20004-2696
Telephone: (202) 508-5000, FAX:
(202) 508-5096, Web Site: www.eei.
org
Sr VP External Affairs: Brian Wolff
Admin Asst: Suzette Herchig
Conducts Business: Worldwide
Employees: 197
Primary Market Served: Business
Catalog available online
Founded: 1933

Trade association for shareholder-
owned electric utilities.

THE DMA **EDUCATION MANAGEMENT CORP**
210 6th Ave Ste 3300
Pittsburgh, PA 15222-2603
Telephone: (412) 995-7627, Web Site:
www.edmc.edu
Sr VP Mktg & Admissions: Anthony
Digiovanni

EDUCATIONAL FIRST STEPS
2800 Swiss Ave
Dallas, TX 75204-5926
Telephone: (214) 824-7940), Web Site:
educationalfirststeps.org
Pres & CEO: Merriott Terry

Non-profit organization dedicated to
improving the quality and availability
of early childhood education for economically disadvantaged children between the ages of birth to five.

ELDERHOSTEL INC
11 Ave de Lafayette
Boston, MA 02111-1736
Telephone: (617) 426-7788, (800) 454-
5678, FAX: (617) 426-2166, Web
Site: www.elderhostel.org
Pres & CEO: James Moses
VP, Mktg: Peter Spiers
VP Devel: Linda Chernick
Assoc VP Devel Annual Giving: Ann
Simanis
Conducts Business: Worldwide
Employees: 100
Primary Market Served: Consumer
Catalog available online
Direct online sales
Founded: 1975
Gross sales or billing: $190,000,000

Provide educational programs for
adults over 55.

ENVELOPE MANUFACTURERS ASSOCIATION
500 Montgomery St (Suite 550)
Alexandria, VA 22314-1581
Telephone: (703) 739-2200, FAX:
(703) 739-2209, Web Site: www.
envelope.org
Pres & CEO: Maynard H. Benjamin
Dir Member Svcs: Killian Cousins
Asst Dir, Indus Res & Acctg: Barbara
M. Monson
Asst to Pres: Jacqueline E. Jordan
Conducts Business: Worldwide
Employees: 7
Primary Market Served: Business &
Consumer
Indirect online sales
Founded: 1933

Trade association of commercial envelope manufacturers.

THE DMA **ENVIRONMENTAL DEFENSE FUND**
1875 Connecticut Ave NW (# 600)
Washington, DC 20009-5739
Telephone: (202) 387-3500
Dir Membership Analytics & Opers:
Bill Bond

EPILEPSY FOUNDATION

8301 Professional Pl
Landover, MD 20785-2267
Telephone: (301) 459-3700, (800) 332-1000, FAX: (301) 577-9056, E-Mail: postmaster@efa.org, Web Site: www.efa.org
CEO & Pres: Eric Hargis
DM Dir: Ms. Danielle Griffin
Conducts Business: U.S.
Employees: 80
Primary Market Served: Consumer
Catalog available online
Direct online sales
Advertising/Marketing Budget Related to Direct Marketing: 76-100%
Direct Marketing ad budget: $2,700,000
Direct Mail: 100%
Founded: 1988
Gross sales or billing: $16,000,000

Non-profit health organization dedicated to the welfare of people with epilepsy.

THE DMA EPISCOPAL RELIEF & DEVELOPMENT

815 2nd Ave (fl 7)
New York, NY 10017-4503
Telephone: (212) 922-5129, Web Site: www.er-d.org
Primary Market Served: Consumer

EVENT 360 INC

205 N Michigan Ave (Suite 2640)
Chicago, IL 60601-5944
Telephone: (773) 247-5360, Web Site: www.event360.com
Mktg Specialist: Lindsey Von Weller

THE DMA FIU ONLINE

11200 SW 8th St (Marc 210)
Miami, FL 33199
Telephone: (305) 348-8489
Primary Market Served: Business & Consumer

THE DMA FALLON COMMUNITY HEALTH PLAN

10 Chestnut St
Worcester, MA 01608-2898
Telephone: (800) 333-2535, Web Site: www.fchp.org
Dir Sls & Svc Commun: Melissa Cordial
Primary Market Served: Business & Consumer

FASHION INSTITUTE OF TECHNOLOGY LIBRARY

227 W 27th St, Library Room (E619)
New York, NY 10001-5902
Telephone: (212) 217-4346, Web Site: www.fitnyc.edu

Head Acquisitions, Library: Leslie Preston

FATHER FLANAGAN'S BOY'S HOME

234 Monsky Dr
Boys Town, NE 68010-7550
Telephone: (402) 498-1934, FAX: (402) 498-1969, Web Site: www.boystown.org
PR Dir: John Melingagio APR
Assoc Exec Dir: Robert Pick
Dir, Annual Giving: Mike Vcelik
Conducts Business: U.S.
Primary Market Served: Business & Consumer
Founded: 1921

Non-profit children's home.

FATHERS OF ST EDMUND SOUTHERN MISSIONS INC

1428 Broad St
Selma, AL 36701
Telephone: (334) 872-2359, FAX: (334) 875-8189, E-Mail: jm1428@aol.com, Web Site: www.edmunditemissions.org
Pres & Missions Dir: Father Roger J. La Charite
Office Mgr: Joyce L. Mott
Conducts Business: U.S.
Employees: 21
Primary Market Served: Consumer
Gross sales or billing: $3,400,000

Direct fund-raising for Fathers of St. Edmund's mission, a sponsor for the Edmundite missions in Alabama & New Orleans.

THE DMA FEED THE CHILDREN

PO Box 36
Oklahoma City, OK 73101-0036
Telephone: (800) 627-4556, Web Site: www.feedthechildren.org
Mgr Web Svcs: Wendy Schreffler
Primary Market Served: Consumer

THE DMA FEEDING AMERICA

35 E Wacker Dr (Suite 2000)
Chicago, IL 60601-2200
Telephone: (312) 263-2303, Web Site: www.secondharvest.org
Dir Direct Response: Suzanne Joiner

THE FIELD MUSEUM

1400 S Lake Shore Dr
Chicago, IL 60605-2827
Telephone: (312) 665-7909, FAX: (312) 665-7101, Web Site: www.fieldmuseum.org
Chmn: Miles D. White
Pres & CEO: John W. McCarter Jr.
Exec VP: James Croft
VP, Opers: Diane White

Provost: Neil L. Shubin
Employees: 400
Primary Market Served: Business & Consumer
Catalog available online
Direct online sales
Advertising/Marketing Budget Related to Direct Marketing: 76-100%
Gross sales or billing: $30,000,000

Non-profit membership organization using direct response for marketing, development & fund-raising.

FIFTH AVENUE COMMITTEE

621 DeGraw St
Brooklyn, NY 11217
FAX: (718) 237-5366, Web Site: www.fifthave.org
Exec Dir: Michelle de la Uz
Dir Asset & Property Mgmnt: Haleema Ahmed
Project Mgr: Elizabeth Ferber
Project Mgr: Ann Solomon
Project Mgr: Sheilah Gibbs
Conducts Business: U.S.
Employees: 3
Primary Market Served: Business & Consumer
Catalog available online
Founded: 1977

Commercial revitalization & community support organization.

FINANCIAL EXECUTIVES INTERNATIONAL

125 Headquarters Plaza (fl 7)
Morristown, NJ 07960
Telephone: (973) 765-1000, FAX: (973) 765-1018, Web Site: www.financialexecutives.org
Pres & CEO: Michael Cangemi
CFO: Paul Chase
VP & Chief Mktg Officer: Christopher Allen
Conducts Business: Worldwide
Employees: 40
Primary Market Served: Business
Direct online sales
Founded: 1931

Publisher of Financial Executive Magazine.

FITTER INTERNATIONAL INC

dba Fitter First
3050 - 2600 Portland St SE
Calgary, AB, Canada T2G 4M6
Telephone: (800) 348-8371, FAX: (866) 250-8824, E-Mail: sales2@filler1.com, Web Site: www.fitter1.com
Founder & CEO: Louis Stack
Conducts Business: U.S., Canada, Europe

Employees: 21
Primary Market Served: Business &
  Consumer
Catalog available online
Direct online sales
Founded: 1985

We promote "Balance and Fitness for
Life", globally, through education and
the use of functional products. We sell
retail & wholesale - quality products.

FLORIDA GIFT FRUIT SHIPPERS ASSOCIATION

5500 W Concord Ave
Orlando, FL 32808-7700
Telephone: (407) 295-1491, FAX:
  (407) 290-0918, Web Site: www.
  fgfsa.com
Pres: George Scales
VP: Don Wright
Conducts Business: U.S., Canada, Europe
Employees: 18
Primary Market Served: Business &
  Consumer
Founded: 1946
Gross sales or billing: $9,600,000

Members use direct mail to obtain orders for gift fruit packages. Packages
are packed at members' packing
houses & picked up by association
trucks where they are brought to the
association terminal for routing &
shipping.

FLORIDA INSTITUTE OF CPA'S

325 W College Ave
Tallahassee, FL 32301
Telephone: (850) 224-2727, (800) 342-
  3197 (FL), FAX: (850) 222-8190,
  E-Mail: msc@ficpa.org, Web Site:
  www.ficpa.org
Exec Dir: Kathy Anderson
Sr Dir Commun: Jan Dobson
Conducts Business: U.S.
Employees: 56
Primary Market Served: Business
Catalog available online
Founded: 1905

Dedicated to the advancement of public accounting.

THE DMA FOOD & WATER WATCH

1616 P St NW (Suite 300)
Washington, DC 20036-1408
Telephone: (202) 683-2500, Web Site:
  www.foodandwaterwatch.org
COO: Lane Brooks

THE DMA FOOD FOR THE HUNGRY INC

1224 E Washington St
Phoenix, AZ 85034-1365

Telephone: (480) 998-3100, (800) 248-
  6437, FAX: (480) 998-4806, E-Mail:
  hunger@fh.org, Web Site: www.fh.
  org
Pres & CEO: Benjamin Homan
VP, Strategic Svcs & CFO: Gary St.
  John
VP, Ministry Partnerships &
  Resources: Matthew Panos
VP, Govts & Gifts-in-Kind Resources:
  David Evans
Sr Dir, Volunteer & Team Ministry:
  Alisa Smitz
Conducts Business: Worldwide
Employees: 50
Primary Market Served: Consumer
Catalog available online
Direct online sales
Advertising/Marketing Budget Related
  to Direct Marketing: 76-100%
Direct Marketing ad budget:
  $1,851,045
Direct Mail: 95%
Online: 2%
Telephone: 3%
Founded: 1971
Gross sales or billing: $10,000,000

Non-profit, charitable organization offering both disaster & long range self-
help assistance.

THE DMA FOOD FOR THE POOR INC

6401 Lyons Rd
Coconut Creek, FL 33073-3602
Telephone: (954) 427-2222, Web Site:
  www.foodforthepoor.com
Web Mktg Dir: Jennifer Vogt
Primary Market Served: Consumer

FOOTE, FRANCISCO & CO

19 Beverly Rd
West Caldwell, NJ 07006-6501
Telephone: (973) 226-1212, FAX:
  (973) 226-3409
Pres: Peter W. Francisco
Conducts Business: U.S.
Employees: 15
Primary Market Served: Business

Full-service direct mail fund-raising
consultants. Work with all production
& data preparation configurations including in-house programs.

THE DMA FOUNDATION FIGHTING BLINDNESS

7168 Columbia Gateway Dr Ste 100
Columbia, MD 21046-3256
Telephone: (410) 423-0600, Web Site:
  www.fightblindness.org
Dir Membership: Anastasia Staten

FOUNDATION FOR CHIROPRACTIC EDUCATION & RESEARCH

PO Box 400
Norwalk, IA 50211-0400
Telephone: (515) 282-7118
Exec Dir: DeAnna Beck
Conducts Business: U.S.
Primary Market Served: Business &
  Consumer

Foundation that promotes research and
education to further the chiropractic
profession.

THE DMA FOUNDATION OF FIRSTHEALTH

150 Applecross Rd
Pinehurst, NC 28374-8520
Telephone: (910) 695-7500, Web Site:
  www.firsthealth.org/foundation
Dir Program Devel: Carrie Driver
Primary Market Served: Consumer

THE DMA FOX CHASE CANCER CENTER

333 Cottman Ave
Philadelphia, PA 19111-2497
Telephone: (215) 728-6900, (888)
  FOXCHASE, FAX: (215) 728-2594,
  Web Site: www.fccc.edu
Pres: Michael V. Seiden MD, Ph.D.
VP, Communs: Christine Wilson
VP, Institutional Advancements: Sandra
  Weckesser
Dir PR: Diana Quattrone
Dir Annual Programs: Linda Lowe
Conducts Business: U.S.
Employees: 1,800
Primary Market Served: Business &
  Consumer
Catalog available online
Indirect online sales
Advertising/Marketing Budget Related
  to Direct Marketing: 0-25%
Direct Marketing ad budget:
Direct Mail: 10%
Magazines: 15%
Newspapers: 15%
TV/Radio: 60%
Founded: 1974

Hospital & institute for cancer
research.

THE DMA RICH FOX & ASSOCIATES INC

175 Chaparral Rd
Carmel Valley, CA 93924-9634
Telephone: (831) 659-1123
Chmn & CEO: Rich Fox

FRANCISCAN FRIARS OF THE ATONEMENT - GRAYMOOR

Rte Nine
Garrison, NY 10524

Telephone: (845) 424-3671, FAX: (845) 424-2168, E-Mail: info@atonementfriars.org, Web Site: www.atonementfriars.org
Assoc Dir Devel: Raymond Morrissey
Exec Dir Community Devel: Andrew Rivers
Conducts Business: U.S., Canada, England, Italy & Japan
Employees: 300
Primary Market Served: Consumer
Founded: 1898

Ecumenical & missionary religious order.

THE DMA FRANCISCAN MISSION ASSOCIATES
274-280 W Lincoln Ave
Mount Vernon, NY 10550-2509
Telephone: (914) 664-5604, FAX: (914) 664-3017, E-Mail: admin@franciscanmissionassoc.org, Web Site: www.franciscanmissionassoc.org
Exec Dir: Madeline Bonnici
Dir Opers: Theresa Federici
Conducts Business: U.S., Canada
Employees: 34
Primary Market Served: Consumer
Indirect online sales
Advertising/Marketing Budget Related to Direct Marketing: 0-25%
Direct Marketing ad budget: $100,000
Direct Mail: 95%
Magazines: 1%
Newspapers: 4%
Founded: 1961

Religious non-profit organization.

THE DMA FRENCH TRADE OFFICE EMBASSY OF FRANCE
1700 Broadway Ste 3201
New York, NY 10019-5925
Telephone: (212) 400-2167, Web Site: www.missioneco.org
Trade Counselor: Cecile Delettre

FUND FOR PUBLIC INTEREST RESEARCH
218 D St SE Fl 2
Washington, DC 20003-1900
Telephone: (202) 546-3965, Web Site: www.ffpir.org
Assoc Dir Partnership Prog: David Wyman
Primary Market Served: Consumer

FUNDAMENTALS CO INC
411 Euclid Ave
Bristol, VA 24201
Telephone: (800) 303-8861 (Fax), (800) 303-8861
Pres: Bud Cooper

Conducts Business: U.S., Canada, Mexico
Employees: 8
Primary Market Served: Business & Consumer
Advertising/Marketing Budget Related to Direct Marketing: 26-50%
Direct Marketing ad budget:
Direct Mail: 30%
Telephone: 70%
Founded: 1983

Fund-raising products - candy, cookies, citrus fruits, first aid kits, flower bulbs, fire extinguishers, greeting cards & gift wrap to schools, leagues, churches, businesses (executive gifts) & groups.

GALLUP INTER-TRIBAL INDIAN CEREMONIAL
202 W Coal Ave
Gallup, NM 87301-6306
Telephone: (505) 863-3896, FAX: (505) 863-9168, E-Mail: ceremonial@cnetco.com, Web Site: www.indianceremonial.com
Office Mgr: Gary Holtsoi
Conducts Business: U.S.
Employees: 4
Primary Market Served: Business & Consumer
Catalog available online
Direct online sales
Advertising/Marketing Budget Related to Direct Marketing: 0-25%
Founded: 1922

Nonprofit organization presenting Indian culture to tourists in the form of tribal dances, rodeos, arts & crafts displays, food & performing arts. Year-round wholesale & retail of posters, prints & stationery of American Indian design.

GALVESTON BAY FOUNDATION
17330 Hwy 3
Webster, TX 77598-4133
Telephone: (281) 332-3381, Web Site: www.galvbay.org
Mktg & Membership Dir: Vicki Conley

GAY MEN'S HEALTH CRISIS
446 W 33rd St
New York, NY 10001-2601
Telephone: (212) 367-1000, FAX: (212) 367-1220, E-Mail: webmaster@gmhc.org, Web Site: www.gmhc.org
CEO: Dr. Marjorie Hill
Dir Media & Mktg: Noel Alicea
Primary Market Served: Consumer

Non-profit AIDS service organization.

GEORGETOWN UNIVERSITY MCDONOUGH SCHOOL OF BUSINESS
37th & O Streets, NW, 211 Hariri Bldg
Washington, DC 20057
Telephone: (202) 687-4591, Web Site: www.msb.edu
Primary Market Served: Business & Consumer

GEORGIA INSTITUTE OF TECHNOLOGY
84 5th St NW Distance Learning & Profess
Atlanta, GA 30308-1031
Telephone: (404) 385-3500, Web Site: www.dlpe.gatech.edu

THE DMA GILLETTE CHILDREN'S SPECIALTY HEALTHCARE
200 University Ave E
Saint Paul, MN 55101-2507
Telephone: (651) 229-1726, Web Site: www.gillettechildrens.org
Sr Annual Giving Officer: Jenny Floria
Primary Market Served: Business & Consumer
Founded: 1897

GIRL SCOUTS OF THE USA
420 Fifth Ave
New York, NY 10018-2729
Telephone: (212) 852-8009, Web Site: www.girlscouts.org
Primary Market Served: Consumer

GLENS FALLS HOSPITAL FOUNDATION
126 South St
Glens Falls, NY 12801-4321
FAX: (518) 926-7012, Web Site: www.glensfallshospital.org
Pres & CEO: David G. Kruczlnicki
Annual Fund Mgr: Christine A. Hoard
Devel Commun Coord: Kelly J. Meader
Primary Market Served: Consumer

Non-profit healthcare organization.

THE DMA GOLDEN KEY INTERNATIONAL HONOUR SOCIETY
1040 Crown Pointe Pkwy Ste 900
Atlanta, GA 30338-4724
Telephone: (404) 377-2400, Web Site: www.goldenkey.org
Dir Mktg: Melissa Leitzell

GOLF CARD INTERNATIONAL
Subs. of Affinity Group Inc
64 Inverness Dr E
Englewood, CO 80112

Telephone: (800) 321-8269, FAX: (303) 792-7332, Web Site: www. golfcard.com
Chmn: Stephen Adams
Pres, CEO & Dir: Michael A. Schneider
Sr VP & CFO: Thomas F. Wolfe
Sr VP HR: Laura A. James
Primary Market Served: Consumer
Catalog available online
Direct online sales

Golf memberships providing savings at over 3500 courses.

THE JANE GOODALL INSTITUTE

4245 N Fairfax Dr (Suite 600)
Arlington, VA 22203-1698
Telephone: (703) 682-9220, Web Site: www.janegoodall.org

Non profit institute whose goal is to improve the global understanding & treatment of great apes through research, public education & advocacy

GOODWILL INDUSTRIES OF SAN FRANCISCO

Subs. Goodwill Industries International
1500 Mission St
San Francisco, CA 94103-2513
Telephone: (415) 575-2101, FAX: (415) 575-2170, Web Site: www. sfgoodwill.org
Devel Mgr: Richard Martin
Conducts Business: U.S.
Employees: 450
Primary Market Served: Consumer
Advertising/Marketing Budget Related to Direct Marketing: 76-100%
Direct Marketing ad budget: $30,000
Direct Mail: 100%
Gross sales or billing: $60,000

Raise money for successful vocational rehabilitation & job training for adults with disabling or disadvantaging conditions.

GOVERNMENT OF INDIA TOURIST OFFICE

1270 Ave of the Americas (Suite 1808)
New York, NY 10020-1700
Telephone: (212) 586-4901, (800) 953-9399, FAX: (212) 582-3274, Web Site: www.incredibleindia.org
Dir: T. Balakrishan
Conducts Business: U.S., Canada, S. America
Employees: 8
Primary Market Served: Business & Consumer
Advertising/Marketing Budget Related to Direct Marketing: 76-100%
Founded: 1952

Publicity & promotion of tourism.

THE DMA GRADUATE SCHOOL USDA

US Dept. of Agriculture
600 Maryland Ave SW
Washington, DC 20024
Telephone: (202) 314-3300, FAX: (202) 690-6577, E-Mail: pubaffairs@ grad.usda.gov, Web Site: www.grad. usda.gov
Dir: Philip Hudson
Conducts Business: Worldwide
Employees: 235
Primary Market Served: Consumer
Catalog available online
Indirect online sales
Advertising/Marketing Budget Related to Direct Marketing: 0-25%
Direct Marketing ad budget:
Direct Mail: $200,000
Magazines: $10,000
Newspapers: $20,000
TV/Radio: $5,000
Telephone: $20,000
Founded: 1921
Gross sales or billing: $45,000,000

Provide continuing education for adults with focus on government job skills.

THE DMA BILLY GRAHAM EVANGELISTIC ASSOCIATION

1 Billy Graham Pkwy
Charlotte, NC 28201-0001
Telephone: (704) 401-2491, (877) 2-GRAHAM, Web Site: www. billygraham.org
Chmn: Billy Graham
Pres, First Vice Chmn & CEO: Franklin Graham
Program Dir: Cliff Barrows
Conducts Business: U.S., Canada, U.K., France, Australia, Germany
Employees: 500
Primary Market Served: Consumer
Catalog available online
Direct online sales

Religious evangelistic organization.

GRAND CANYON ASSOCIATION

1824 S Thompson St (Suite 205)
Flagstaff, AZ 86001-2694
Telephone: (928) 863-3876, Web Site: www.grandcanyon.org
Dir Devel: Bonnie O'Donnell

THE GREAT BOOKS FOUNDATION

35 E Wacker Dr (Suite 400)
Chicago, IL 60601-2298
Telephone: (312) 332-5870, Web Site: www.greatbooks.org
VP: Mary Kent

GREATER FORT WORTH BUILDERS ASSOCIATION

100 E 15th St Ste 600
Fort Worth, TX 76102-6569
Telephone: (817) 284-3566, FAX: (817) 284-6465, E-Mail: info@ fortworthbuilders.org, Web Site: www.forthworthbuilders.org
Pres: Danny Moss
First VP: Cary Clarke
Office Mgr: Bobby Lovelets
VP: Jay Brown
VP: Jerry Thomas
Sec: Shane Goldem
Conducts Business: U.S.
Employees: 6
Primary Market Served: Business & Consumer
Advertising/Marketing Budget Related to Direct Marketing: 0-25%
Direct Marketing ad budget: $150,000
Direct Mail: 5%
Newspapers: 45%
TV/Radio: 45%
Telephone: 5%
Founded: 1945
Gross sales or billing: $1,000,000

Trade association promoting housing. Sell memberships to builder, supplier & subcontractor companies.

VAN GROESBECK & CO

2124 Hanover Ave.
Richmond, VA 23220
Telephone: (804) 285-3176, Web Site: www.vangroesbeckco.com
Pres: Stefani Fisher

THE DMA GUIDEPOSTS

39 Old Ridgebury Rd Ste 2AB
Danbury, CT 06810-5122
Telephone: (845) 225-3681, FAX: (845) 228-2056, Web Site: www. guideposts.org
Sr VP: Rocco Martino
Pres & CEO: Richard V. Hopple
CFO & Sr VP: David Teitler
Conducts Business: U.S., Canada
Employees: 300
Primary Market Served: Consumer
Direct online sales
Advertising/Marketing Budget Related to Direct Marketing: 76-100%
Founded: 1945

A non-profit organization & publisher of inspirational magazines, books, audio/video & related products. Guideposts magazine circulation 4,000,000.

THE DMA HSP DIRECT

13755 Sunrise Valley Dr (Suite 450)
Herndon, VA 20171-4682
Telephone: (703) 793-3220, FAX: (703) 793-3221, Web Site: www. hspdirect.com

CEO: Matthew Hafer
Partner: James Hogan
Partner: Amy Paul
Partner: Matthew Schenk
Conducts Business: U.S.
Employees: 30
Primary Market Served: Business
Founded: 2001

Direct mail fundraising.

HABITAT FOR HUMANITY INTERNATIONAL
121 Habitat St
Americus, GA 31709-3423
Telephone: (229) 924-6935, FAX:
(229) 924-6541, Web Site: www.
habitat.org
Pres: Millard Fuller
Sr Dir Direct Mktg: Tim Daugherty
VP, Commun & Devel: Sandra Byrd
Direct Mail Dir: Linda Fuller
Primary Market Served: Business &
Consumer
Gross sales or billing: $19,500,000

Non-profit ecumenical Christian housing ministry which works in partnership with families in need of housing.

HARPER COLLEGE
1200 W Algonquin Rd
Palatine, IL 60067-7373
Telephone: (847) 925-6000, Web Site:
www.harpercollege.com
Dir Mktg Svcs: Mike Barzacchini

HARRIS CONNECT LLC
1511 Route 22 (Suite C25)
Brewster, NY 19047-1706
Telephone: (800) 326-6600, Web Site:
www.harrisconnect.com
Sr VP Opers & Admin: Susan
D'Agostino

Directory publishers serving non-profit organizations including educational institutions, associations & organizations

HARRIS DIRECT
6800 Owensmouth Ave (Suite 200)
Canoga Park, CA 91303-3170
Telephone: (818) 222-3470 x102, Web
Site: www.harris-direct.org

Telefundraising

HARVARD BUSINESS SCHOOL - EXECUTIVE EDUCATION
Soldiers Field, Teele Hall
Boston, MA 02163-1000
Telephone: (617) 496-2193, Web Site:
www.exed.hbs.edu
Mgr Direct Mktg Opers: Daniel Sears
Primary Market Served: Consumer

HEALTHRIGHT INTERNATIONAL
80 Maiden Ln
New York, NY 10038-4811
Telephone: (212) 226-9890, Web Site:
www.healthright.org
Exec Dir: Thomas Dougherty
Primary Market Served: Consumer

HEBRON ACADEMY
PO Box 309 (Rte 119)
Hebron, ME 04238-0309
Telephone: (207) 966-2100, Web Site:
www.habronacademy.org
Asst Head of School: Dr Robert Caldwell

JAMES J HILL REFERENCE LIBRARY
80 4th St W
Saint Paul, MN 55102-1605
Telephone: (651) 265-5500, Web Site:
www.jjhill.org
Collection Coord: Karolyn MacAskill
Primary Market Served: Consumer

Private non-profit business library

CONRAD N HILTON COLLEGE OF HOTEL & RESTAURANT MANAGEMENT UNIVERSITY OF HOUSTON
229 CN Hilton Hotel College
Houston, TX 77204-3028
Telephone: (713) 743-0209
Dean: John Bowden
Primary Market Served: Consumer

HIMSS
33 W Monroe St Ste 1700
Chicago, IL 60603-5616
Telephone: (312) 664-4467, Web Site:
www.himss.org

US not-for-profit organization dedicated to promoting a better understanding of health care information & management systems

THE HUMANE SOCIETY OF THE US
700 Professional Dr
Gaithersburg, MD 20879-3418
Telephone: (202) 452-1100, Web Site:
www.hsus.org
Dir, Direct Mktg: Nancy Campbell
Primary Market Served: Consumer

IDC, LTD
2500 Paseo Verde Pkwy
Henderson, NV 89074

Telephone: (702) 450-1000, FAX:
(702) 450-1020, E-Mail: info@
goidc.com, Web Site: www.goidc.
com
Founder: William Freyd
Chmn Bd & CEO: L. Gregg Carlson
Pres: Bradley S. Carlson
VP Client Svcs & Sr Consultant:
Bruce Wenger
Conducts Business: U.S., Canada, Australia, U.K.
Employees: 300
Primary Market Served: Consumer
Founded: 1974

Fund-raising consultants. Specialists in mail & phone solicitation.

ISA-THE INSTRUMENTATION SYSTEMS & AUTOMATION SOCIETY
67 Alexander Dr
Research Triangle Park, NC 27709
Telephone: (919) 549-8411, FAX:
(919) 549-8288, E-Mail: info@isa.
org, Web Site: www.isa.org
Exec Dir & CEO: Patrick Gouhin
Assoc Exec Dir: Fred Gebarowski
Dir, Education: Dale Lee
Conducts Business: Worldwide
Employees: 120
Primary Market Served: Business &
Consumer
Catalog available online
Direct online sales
Advertising/Marketing Budget Related
to Direct Marketing: 26-50%
Direct Marketing ad budget:
Direct Mail: 70%
Magazines: 20%
Telephone: 10%
Founded: 1945
Gross sales or billing: $20,000,000

Technical magazines, books, trade shows & training centers.

IN TOUCH MINISTRIES
3836 DeKalb Technology Pkwy
Atlanta, GA 30340-3604
Telephone: (770) 451-1001), Web Site:
www.intouch.org
Dir, Strategy: Andy Maddocks
Primary Market Served: Consumer

INDEPENDENT INSURANCE AGENTS & BROKERS OF AMERICA
127 S Peyton St
Alexandria, VA 22314
Telephone: (703) 683-4422, (800) 221-7917, FAX: (703) 683-7556, E-Mail:
info@iiaba.org, Web Site: www.
iiaba.org
CEO: Robert A. Rusbuldt
Pres: Thomas Grau

Sr VP: Charles E. Symington Jr.
Conducts Business: U.S.
Employees: 65
Primary Market Served: Business
Catalog available online
Direct online sales
Founded: 1896
Gross sales or billing: $20,000,000

Trade association of insurance agents.

INDIAN ARTS & CRAFTS ASSOCIATION

4010 Carlisle NE (Suite C)
Albuquerque, NM 87107
Telephone: (505) 265-9149, FAX:
　(505) 265-8251, E-Mail: info@iaca.
　com, Web Site: www.iaca.com
Exec Dir: Susan McGuire
Mgr: Gail E. Chehak
Fin Coord: Lois Begay
Admin: Thomas Ormsby
Conducts Business: U.S., U.K., Austra-
　lia, Canada, Germany, Italy, Japan,
　New Zealand
Employees: 3
Primary Market Served: Business
Catalog available online
Indirect online sales
Advertising/Marketing Budget Related
　to Direct Marketing: 0-25%
Direct Marketing ad budget:
Direct Mail: $10,000
Magazines: $63,000
Founded: 1974

Trade association promoting, protecting
& preserving handmade native American arts & crafts.

THE INSPIRATION NETWORKS

3000 World Reach Dr
Indian Land, SC 29707-6542
Telephone: (704) 561-7872, Web Site:
　www.insptoday.com
Exec VP: Ossie Mills

INSTITUTE FOR STUDENT ACHIEVEMENT

1 Old Country Rd Ste 250
Carle Place, NY 11514-1818
Telephone: (516) 812-6700, Web Site:
　www.studentachievement.org
VP & Chief Devel Officer: Gena Davis
　Watkins

INSTITUTE OF BUSINESS FORECASTING

350 Northern Blvd (Suite 203)
Great Neck, NY 11021-4809
Telephone: (516) 504-7576, Web Site:
　www.ibf.org
Mktg Coord: Jonathan Tafarella

THE DMA INSTITUTE OF MANAGEMENT ACCOUNTANTS INC

Ten Paragon Dr
Montvale, NJ 07645-1718
Telephone: (201) 573-9000, (800) 638-
　4427, FAX: (201) 474-1600, E-Mail:
　ima@imanet.org, Web Site: www.
　imanet.org
Pres: Paul Sharman
VP Certification: Dennis Whitney
Dir Mktg: Maureen Walsh
Conducts Business: U.S.
Employees: 60
Primary Market Served: Business &
　Consumer
Catalog available online
Direct online sales
Advertising/Marketing Budget Related
　to Direct Marketing: 0-25%
Direct Marketing ad budget:
Direct Mail: 20%
Magazines: 70%
Online: 10%
Founded: 1919
Gross sales or billing: $2,500,000

A non-profit membership organization.
Develop practices for measurement,
control & reporting of accounting &
business financial results. List rental
available on conditional basis. Provide
educational programs for member continuing education needs. Publish magazines & books.

INSTITUTE OF READING DEVELOPMENT

Five Commercial Blvd
Novato, CA 94949
Telephone: (415) 884-8100, (800) 964-
　8888, FAX: (415) 382-0760, E-Mail:
　contactus@readingprograms.org,
　Web Site: www.readingprograms.org
Pres: Paul Copperman
Dir: David Soloway
Curriculum Dir: Jared Namenson
Design & Production Dir: Maureen
　McDonald
Editor: Lisa Fink
Primary Market Served: Business &
　Consumer

Private reading enrichment school.

INSTITUTE OF REAL ESTATE MANAGEMENT

430 N Michigan Ave
Chicago, IL 60611-4090
Telephone: (312) 329-6000, (800) 837-
　0706, FAX: (800) 338-4736, E-Mail:
　custserv@irem.org, Web Site: www.
　irem.org
CEO & Exec VP: Russ Salzman
VP, Fin: Kenneth M. Paul
VP, Res: Charles A. Achilles
VP, Mktg: Lynn M. Disbrow

VP, Education: Jane McDonald
Conducts Business: U.S.
Employees: 80
Primary Market Served: Business
Catalog available online
Direct online sales
Advertising/Marketing Budget Related
　to Direct Marketing: 76-100%
Direct Marketing ad budget:
Direct Mail: 90%
Magazines: 10%
Founded: 1933
Gross sales or billing: $11,000,000

Real estate management education,
designations & public policy advocacy.

INSTITUTIONAL ADVANCEMENT PROGRAMS INC

35 Park View Ave (Suite 4A)
Bronxville, NY 10708-2953
Telephone: (914) 779-4092, FAX:
　(914) 961-4202
Pres: Bernard Brecher
Conducts Business: Worldwide
Employees: 3
Primary Market Served: Business &
　Consumer
Founded: 1979
Gross sales or billing: $240,000

Strategic planners for not for profit
organizations, board retreats, governance consulting, feasibility studies &
institutional managers.

INTEGRATED PRODUCT DEVELOPMENT GROUP

30 S Wacker Dr (Suite 2200), Chicago
　Mercantile Exchange
Chicago, IL 60606-7452
Web Site: www.integratedpdg.com
Pres: Scott Miller

Help companies market products

THE INTERFAITH ALLIANCE

1212 New York Ave NW (#7)
Washington, DC 20005-3905
Telephone: (202) 639-6370, Web Site:
　www.interfaithalliance.org
Deputy Dir Devel: Julieanne Simitz
Primary Market Served: Consumer

INTERFAITH COMMUNITY CARE

PO Box 8450
Surprise, AZ 85374-0124
Telephone: (623) 584-4999, Web Site:
　www.interfaithcommunitycare.org
Mktg Mgr: Mary Chou-Thompson
Primary Market Served: Consumer

INTERNATIONAL ACADEMY - COMPOUNDING PHARMACISTS

4638 Riverstone Blvd Ste 100
Missouri City, TX 77459-6157
Telephone: (281) 933-8400, Web Site:
www.iacprx.org
Dir Devel: Elizabeth Proctor
Primary Market Served: Business

INTERNATIONAL ADVERTISING ASSOCIATION

275 Madison Ave (Suite 2102), World
Service Center
New York, NY 10016-1118
Telephone: (212) 557-1133, FAX:
(212) 983-0455, E-Mail:
membership@iaaglobal.com, Web
Site: www.iaaglobal.org
Dir Membership Svcs: Marie Scotti
Mgr Info Sys: Karl Kam
Mgr Mktg Commun: Mateja Simic
Exec Dir: Michael Lee
Education Admin: Nubia Martinez
Conducts Business: Worldwide
Employees: 5
Primary Market Served: Business &
Consumer
Founded: 1938

International trade association for marketing communications/advertising industry.

INTERNATIONAL BIBLE SOCIETY

1820 Jet Stream Dr
Colorado Springs, CO 80921-3696
Telephone: (719) 488-9200, FAX:
(719) 867-2812, Web Site: www.ibs.
org
Interim Pres & CEO: Mike Richards
VP, Pubns: Dean Merrill
VP, Translation: Dr. Eugene Rubingh
Mktg Dir: Paul Moede
Sls Dir: Bob Swales
Conducts Business: Worldwide
Employees: 1,000
Primary Market Served: Business &
Consumer
Catalog available online
Direct online sales
Advertising/Marketing Budget Related
to Direct Marketing: 26-50%
Direct Marketing ad budget:
$2,500,000
Direct Mail: 80%
Magazines: 5%
Newspapers: 1%
TV/Radio: 7%
Telephone: 7%
Founded: 1809
Gross sales or billing: $30,000,000

Not-for-profit ministry services.

INTERNATIONAL CITY/ COUNTY MANAGEMENT ASSOCIATION

777 N Capitol St NE (Suite 500)
Washington, DC 20002-4201
Telephone: (202) 289-ICMA, FAX:
(202) 962-3500, E-Mail:
customerservice@icma.org, Web
Site: www.icma.org
Exec Dir: Robert J. O'Neil
Exec Dir: Scott A. Hancock
City Mgr: Michael C. Van Milligen
City Admin: Peter J. Herlofsky
City Mgr: Michael C. Walker
Conducts Business: Worldwide
Employees: 123
Primary Market Served: Business
Catalog available online
Indirect online sales
Advertising/Marketing Budget Related
to Direct Marketing: 51-75%
Founded: 1914

Professional & educational organization for over 7500 appointed local government administrators.

THE DMA **INTERNATIONAL FELLOWSHIP OF CHRISTIANS AND JEWS**

30 N La Salle St Ste 4300
Chicago, IL 60602-2584
Telephone: (312) 641-7200, Web Site:
www.ifcj.org
Sr VP: Chris Cleghorn

THE DMA **INTERNATIONAL FOUNDATION OF EMPLOYEE BENEFIT PLANS**

18700 W Bluemound Rd
Brookfield, WI 53045-2936
Telephone: (262) 373-7758, FAX:
(262) 786-8670, Web Site: www.
ifebp.org
CEO: Michael Wilson
Pres: Nicholas Counter
Sr Dir Mktg, Membership & Pub Rels:
Terry Davidson
Conducts Business: U.S. & Canada
Employees: 130
Primary Market Served: Business &
Consumer
Catalog available online
Direct online sales
Advertising/Marketing Budget Related
to Direct Marketing: 51-75%
Gross sales or billing: $25,800,000

Nonprofit educational association providing information to the employee benefits and compensation industry through seminars and conferences, books, an information center, online resources, distance learning, a job and resume posting service. Certified Employee Benefits Specialist (CEBS) and Certificate Series courses. Visit www. ifebp.org for more information.

THE DMA **INTERNATIONAL FUND FOR ANIMAL WELFARE**

290 Summer St
Yarmouth Port, MA 02675-1734
Telephone: (508) 744-2000, Web Site:
www.ifaw.org
Dir Direct Mktg: Nancy Noble
Primary Market Served: Consumer

INTERNATIONAL PLANNED PARENTHOOD FEDERATION WESTERN HEMISPHERE REGION INC

125 Maiden Ln (9th Fl)
New York, NY 10038-5063
Telephone: (212) 248-6400, (866) IP-
PFWHR, FAX: (212) 248-2441,
E-Mail: info@ippfwhr.org, Web Site:
www.ippfwhr.org
Direct Response Mgr: Lloyd Alexander
Dir Devel & Pub Affairs: Dr. Pierre M.
LaRamee
Deputy Dir Devel: Dana Rogers
Conducts Business: U.S.
Employees: 62
Primary Market Served: Consumer
Advertising/Marketing Budget Related
to Direct Marketing: 76-100%
Direct Marketing ad budget: $580,000
Direct Mail: 100%
Founded: 1954
Gross sales or billing: $21,000,000

Global service provider & a leading advocate of sexual & reproductive health and rights for all

THE DMA **INTERNATIONAL SOCIETY FOR TECHNOLOGY IN EDUCATION**

175 W Broadway (Suite 300)
Eugene, OR 97401-2916
Telephone: (541) 349-7575, Web Site:
www.iste.org
Sr Dir Mktg & Commun: Steve Abbott
Primary Market Served: Consumer

INVESTORS ALLIANCE INC

PO Box 10136
Pompano Beach, FL 33061-6136
Telephone: (800) 490-6627, E-Mail:
info@powerinvestor.com, Web Site:
www.powerinvestor.com
Dir: Frank Lardino

Conducts Business: U.S.
Employees: 10
Primary Market Served: Business &
  Consumer
Catalog available online
Direct online sales
Advertising/Marketing Budget Related
  to Direct Marketing: 76-100%
Direct Marketing ad budget:
Direct Mail: 95%
Online: 5%
Founded: 1987
Gross sales or billing: $2,000,000

Investment education & research
publications. Computer software, investment models & research databases
for individual investors.

INVOLVE SOCIAL
44288 Fremont Blvd
Fremont, CA 94538-6000
Telephone: (510) 396-3941, Web Site:
  www.involvesocial.com
Opers Mgr: Mush Ahmad

IOWA MEDICAL SOCIETY
aka IMS
1001 Grand Ave
West Des Moines, IA 50265
Telephone: (515) 223-1401, FAX:
  (515) 223-0590, Web Site: www.
  iowamedical.org
Exec Dir: Mike Abrams
VP Communs: Lucinda Stephenson
  APR
Conducts Business: U.S., Canada
Employees: 22
Primary Market Served: Business &
  Consumer
Founded: 1850

Raises money through private donations for political action.

IOWA STUDENT LOAN
LIQUIDITY CORP
6805 Vista Dr, Ashford I Bldg
West Des Moines, IA 50266-9362
Telephone: (515) 243-5626, Web Site:
  www.studentloan.org
Mktg Dir: Suzanne Lowman
Primary Market Served: Consumer

THE JACKSON
LABORATORY JAX
RESEARCH SYSTEMS
600 Main St
Bar Harbor, ME 04609-1523
Telephone: (800) 422-6423, Web Site:
  www.jax.org/jaxmice
Database Mktg: Christian Gilbert

Non-profit organization focusing on
mammalian genetics research to advance human health

THE JEWISH FEDERATION
OF GREATER
WASHINGTON
6101 Montrose Rd Ste 400
Rockville, MD 20852-4816
Telephone: (301) 230-7261, Web Site:
  www.shalomdc.org
Dir Mktg: Marsha Sussman
Primary Market Served: Consumer

THE DMA JOINT COMMISSION
1 Renaissance Blvd
Oakbrook Terrace, IL 60181-4805
Telephone: (630) 792-5000, Web Site:
  www.jcaho.org
Assoc Dir: Donna Rutkowski
Primary Market Served: Consumer

THE DMA JUVENILE DIABETES
RESEARCH FOUNDATION
26 Broadway (fl 14)
New York, NY 10004-1838
Telephone: (212) 785-9500, (800) 533-
  CURE, FAX: (212) 785-9595,
  E-Mail: info@jdrf.org, Web Site:
  www.jdrf.org
Dir, Individual Gift Programs: Shawn
  McKenna
Pres & CEO: Arnold Donald
VP & COO: Robin Harding
VP: Richard A. Insel
VP: Benita Shobe
VP: Paul Burn
Primary Market Served: Business &
  Consumer
Founded: 1970
Gross sales or billing: $196,727,000

Raises money to fund research in the
search for a cure for diabetes & its
complications.

THE DMA KCEOC COMMUNITY
ACTION PARTNERSHIP INC
PO Box 490
Barbourville, KY 40906-0490
Telephone: (606) 546-3152, Web Site:
  kceoc.com
Pres & CEO: Paul Dole

KCET
4401 W Sunset Blvd
Los Angeles, CA 90027-6017
Telephone: (323) 666-6500, FAX:
  (323) 953-5661, E-Mail:
  viewerservices@kcet.org, Web Site:
  www.kcet.org
Pres & CEO: Al Jerome
Chair: Scott A. Edelman
VP, Membership Mktg: Renee Will-
  iams
Vice Chmn: Ann Ehringer
Sr VP, Devel & Mktg: Nancy
  Rishagen
Treas: W. Scott Sanford

Sec: Vicki Reynolds
Conducts Business: U.S.
Employees: 260
Primary Market Served: Business &
  Consumer
Catalog available online
Advertising/Marketing Budget Related
  to Direct Marketing: 51-75%
Gross sales or billing: $52,400,000

Viewer-supported public television station broadcasting alternative entertainment & educational programs for
southern & central California.

KMA DIRECT
COMMUNICATIONS
5151 Belt Line Rd Ste 900
Dallas, TX 75254-6757
Telephone: (972) 244-1900, FAX:
  (972) 244-1901, E-Mail: sales@kma.
  com, Web Site: www.kma.com
CEO: Tom McCabe
Exec Officer: Tony Santoro
Exec Officer: Darrel Dahlke
Conducts Business: Worldwide
Employees: 60
Primary Market Served: Business &
  Consumer
Advertising/Marketing Budget Related
  to Direct Marketing: 76-100%
Founded: 1980
Gross sales or billing: $19,000,000

Full service agency specializing in direct response communications fund-
raising for non-profit organizations.

THE DMA KPBS FM/TV
5200 Campanile Dr San Diego State
  Univ
San Diego, CA 92182-1901
Telephone: (619) 594-1515, Web Site:
  www.kpbs.org
Dir Mktg & Corp Support: Charlotte
  Albergetis
Commun Mgr: Julie Schauble
Employees: 100
Primary Market Served: Consumer
Advertising/Marketing Budget Related
  to Direct Marketing: 0-25%
Founded: 1960

KAISER FOUNDATION
HEALTH PLAN OF THE
MID-ATLANTIC STATES
INC
2101 E Jefferson St
Rockville, MD 20852-4908
Telephone: (301) 816-5641, Web Site:
  kp.org
Dir Mktg: Keith Montgomery

KANSAS STATE UNIVERSITY DIVISION OF CONTINUING EDUCATION
13 College Ct Bldg
Manhattan, KS 66506-6005
Telephone: (785) 532-5888, Web Site: www.dce.ksu.edu
Pub Info Coord: Melinda Sinn
Primary Market Served: Business & Consumer

THE DMA **KAPLAN TEST PREP & ADMISSIONS**
395 Hudson St.
New York, NY 10014
Telephone: (212) 997-5800, Web Site: www.kaptest.com
Primary Market Served: Consumer

KENTUCKY BANKERS ASSOCIATION
600 W Main St (Suite 400)
Louisville, KY 40202-2998
Telephone: (502) 582-2453, FAX: (502) 584-6390, Web Site: www.kybanks.com
Pres: Luther Deaton
VP Spec Projects, Opers & Member Svcs Dir: Selina Parrish
Conducts Business: U.S.
Primary Market Served: Business

Vendors, banking & financial institution products.

THE KIDNEY FOUNDATION OF CANADA/GREATER ONTARIO BRANCH
35 Goderich Rd (Unit 9)
Hamilton, ON, Canada L8E 4P2
Telephone: (800) 414-3484, FAX: (905) 318-8491, E-Mail: kidneyfoundation@bellnet.ca, Web Site: www.kidney.on.ca
Natl Dir: Niloufer Bhesania
Nat'l Exec Dir: Gavin Turley
Pres - Greate Ontario Branch: Maria Carnahan
Conducts Business: Canada
Primary Market Served: Business & Consumer
Founded: 1964
Gross sales or billing: $13,000,000

National non-profit health organization dedicated to the eradication of kidney diseases & related disorders.

THE DMA **SUSAN G KOMEN FOR THE CURE**
5005 Lyndon B Johnson Fwy (Suite 250)
Dallas, TX 75244-6125
Telephone: (972) 855-1600, Web Site: www.komen.org
Dir, Direct Mktg: Tabetha Leinweber

Primary Market Served: Business & Consumer

LIM COLLEGE
12 E 53rd St
New York, NY 10022-5268
Telephone: (212) 752-1530, Web Site: www.limcollege.edu
Professor Mktg Dept: Sally Shapiro

LIMRA INTERNATIONAL
300 Day Hill Rd
Windsor, CT 06095-1783
Telephone: (860) 688-3358, Web Site: www.limra.com
Primary Market Served: Consumer

THE DMA **LAHEY CLINIC**
41 Mall Rd
Burlington, MA 01805-0002
Telephone: (781) 744-5100, Web Site: www.lahey.org
Annual Fund Prog Dir: David Pearson
Primary Market Served: Consumer

Physician-led non-profit group medical practice

THE DMA **LARKWOOD GROUP LLC**
4096 Piedmont Ave (Suite 214)
Oakland, CA 94611-5221
Telephone: (510) 444-7766
Principal: Ann Thompson-Hass

LAUTMAN MASKA NEILL & CO
1730 Rhode Island Ave NW (Suite 301)
Washington, DC 20036-3120
Telephone: (202) 296-9660, Web Site: www.lautmandc.com
Partner: Tiffany Neill
Partner: Lisa Maska
VP: Amy Sukol
Primary Market Served: Business

Consulting firm specializing in direct response fundraising for non-profit organizations

LEAGUE OF AMERICAN ORCHESTRAS
33 W 60th St (5th fl)
New York, NY 10023-7905
Telephone: (212) 262-5161, FAX: (212) 262-5198, Web Site: www.symphony.org; www.americanorchestras.org
Pres & CEO: Henry Fogel
Exec VP & Mng Dir: Jesse Rosen
VP Devel: Stacey Weston
VP Mktg & Member Devel: Russell Jones
Conducts Business: U.S.
Employees: 38

Primary Market Served: Business
Founded: 1973
Gross sales or billing: $5,600,000

National service association chartered by Congress to ensure artistic excellence & administrative effectiveness of symphony orchestras in North America.

LEGAL DEFENSE FOUNDATION INC
8001 Braddock Rd
Springfield, VA 22160-2115
Telephone: (703) 321-8501, (800) 336-3600, FAX: (703) 321-9613, E-Mail: info@nrtw.org, Web Site: www.nrtw.org
Chmn Bd: Charles R. Serio
Pres: Mark A. Mix
VP & Treas: Douglass A. Stafford
VP: Stephen O. Goodrick
Sec: Anne M. Coulter
Conducts Business: U.S.
Employees: 50
Primary Market Served: Business & Consumer
Catalog available online
Direct Marketing ad budget:
Direct Mail: $3,500,000
Gross sales or billing: $6,500,000

Organization of citizens dedicated to the principle of the right to work. Conducts nationwide educational & lobbying activities in Congress & state legislatures.

THE LEGAL STUDIES FORUM
PO Box 6130 University Ave
Morgantown, WV 26506-6130
Telephone: (304) 293-7354, FAX: (304) 293-6891, E-Mail: jelkins@labs.net
Ed: James Elkins
Conducts Business: U.S., Canada
Employees: 4
Primary Market Served: Business
Advertising/Marketing Budget Related to Direct Marketing: 76-100%
Direct Marketing ad budget: $1,500
Direct Mail: 90%
Telephone: 10%
Gross sales or billing: $14,000

Professional quarterly journal for professionals & scholars in legal studies.

THE DMA **THE LEUKEMIA & LYMPHOMA SOCIETY**
1311 Mamaroneck Ave
White Plains, NY 10605-5228
Telephone: (914) 949-5213
Natl Dir, Direct Response: Brunny Lynch
Primary Market Served: Consumer

THE DMA LIBERTY FUND INC

8335 Allison Pointe Trail (Suite 300)
Indianapolis, IN 46250-1684
Telephone: (317) 842-0880, Web Site:
   www.libertyfund.org
VP Publishing: Patricia Gallagher
Primary Market Served: Consumer

LIFEWAY CHRISTIAN RESOURCES

1 Lifeway Plaza
Nashville, TN 37234-1002
Telephone: (615) 251-5822, Web Site:
   www.lifeway.com
Mktg Mgr: Ben Harbin

LIFT OUTREACH

7370 Dogwood Pk
Richland Hills, TX 76118-6403
Telephone: (817) 658-2980
Principal: Gary Lawrence

LINCOLN PARK ZOO

2100 N Clark St
Chicago, IL 60614
Telephone: (312) 742-2000, FAX:
   (312) 742-2137, E-Mail:
   webmaster@lpzoo.com, Web Site:
   www.lpzoo.com
Pres, CEO & Dir: Kevin Bell
Mktg Dir: Ann Carson
Membership Dir: Michelle Clayton
Conducts Business: U.S.
Employees: 240
Primary Market Served: Consumer
Catalog available online
Direct online sales
Advertising/Marketing Budget Related
   to Direct Marketing: 0-25%
Direct Marketing ad budget: $150,000
Direct Mail: 70%
Telephone: 30%
Founded: 1868
Gross sales or billing: $8,000,000

Regional fund-raisers through direct
mail & telemarketing.

LORMAN EDUCATION SERVICES

2510 Alpine Rd
Eau Claire, WI 54703-9560
Telephone: (715) 833-3940
CEO: John Busch

LOUISIANA STATE MUSEUM

Div. of Dept of Culture Recreation &
   Tourism State of Louisiana
751 Chartres St
New Orleans, LA 70116-3205
Telephone: (504) 568-6968, (800) 568-
   6968, FAX: (504) 568-4995, Web
   Site: www.lsm.crt.state.la.us
Deputy Dir: Bob Martin
PR Dir: Lawrence L. Lovell III

Dir, Curatorial Svcs: Tamra Carboni
Museum Dir: Sam Rykels
Dir: James F. Sefcik
Res Historian: Alecia Long
Conducts Business: U.S.
Employees: 100
Primary Market Served: Consumer
Catalog available online
Advertising/Marketing Budget Related
   to Direct Marketing: 0-25%
Founded: 1912

State museum system comprised of
nine landmarks & permanent collections of artifacts, documents & works
of art.

LOYOLA UNIVERSITY CHICAGO

820 N Michigan Ave
Chicago, IL 60611-2147
Telephone: (312) 915-8900, Web Site:
   www.luc.edu

LUTHERAN CHURCH EXTENSION FUND - MISSOURI SYNOD

10733 Sunset Office Dr (Suite 300),
   Sunset Corporate Center
Saint Louis, MO 63127-1020
Telephone: (800) 843-5233, FAX:
   (314) 996-1131, Web Site: www.lcef.
   org
Pres, Missouri Synod: Rev. Ray Mirly
Conducts Business: U.S.
Employees: 50
Primary Market Served: Business &
   Consumer

Provides funds for church construction.

THE DMA MSU FEDERAL CREDIT UNION

3777 West Rd
East Lansing, MI 48823-8029
Telephone: (517) 333-2254, Web Site:
   www.msufcu.org
VP, Mktg Ecommerce: April Clobes

MAILORDER GARDENING ASSOCIATION

5836 Rockburn Woods Way
Elkridge, MD 21075-7302
Telephone: (410) 540-9830, FAX:
   (410) 540-9827, Web Site: www.
   mailordergardening.com
Exec Dir: Camille G. Cimino
Primary Market Served: Business &
   Consumer
Founded: 1933

Trade association representing mail
order gardening industry.

MAILWORKS INC

PO Box M
Freeport, ME 04032-0919
Telephone: (207) 865-1477, FAX:
   (207) 865-1479, E-Mail: mailwks@
   aol.com, Web Site: www.mailworks.
   net
Pres: Joan Fields
Conducts Business: U.S.
Employees: 3
Primary Market Served: Consumer
Advertising/Marketing Budget Related
   to Direct Marketing: 76-100%
Founded: 1981
Gross sales or billing: $1,000,000

Provides non-profit organizations with
fundraising and membership
campaigns.

MAINE POTATO BOARD

744 Main St (Rm 1)
Presque Isle, ME 04769
Telephone: (207) 769-5061, FAX:
   (207) 764-4148, E-Mail:
   mainepotatoes@mainepotatoes.com,
   Web Site: www.mainepotatoes.com
Pres: Thomas Qualey
Exec Dir: Michael P. Corey
Asst Exec Dir: Donald Flannery
Employees: 4
Primary Market Served: Business &
   Consumer

State agency promoting Maine
potatoes.

THE DMA MAKE-A-WISH FOUNDATION OF AMERICA

4742 N 24th St Ste 400
Phoenix, AZ 85016-4862
Telephone: (602) 279-9474, FAX:
   (602) 279-0855, Web Site: www.
   wish.org
CEO & Pres: Paula Vanness
Direct Response Mgr: Gigi Schmidt
Pres & CEO: David Williams
Primary Market Served: Consumer
Founded: 1980

Fund-raising organization that grants
wishes for children with life-
threatening illnesses.

THE DMA MANHATTAN COLLEGE

Manhattan College Pkwy
Bronx, NY 10471-3915
Telephone: (718) 862-7285, Web Site:
   www.manhattan.edu
Primary Market Served: Consumer

MAP INTERNATIONAL

2200 Glynco Pkwy
Brunswick, GA 31521
Telephone: (912) 265-6010, (800) 225-
   8550, FAX: (912) 265-6170, Web
   Site: www.map.org

Pres: Michael Nyenauis
Primary Market Served: Business &
Consumer
Founded: 1954

Non-profit Christian global
organization.

MARCH OF DIMES BIRTH DEFECTS FOUNDATION

1275 Mamaroneck Ave
White Plains, NY 10605
Telephone: (914) 428-7100, FAX:
(914) 428-8203, Web Site: www.
modimes.org
Pres: Jennifer Howse
VP, Donor Devel: Carol Portale
Conducts Business: Worldwide
Primary Market Served: Business &
Consumer

Not-for-profit health agency.

MARIAN HELPERS CENTER

Subs. of Congregation of Marians
Eden Hill
Stockbridge, MA 01263-0001
Telephone: (413) 298-3691, (800) 462-
7426, FAX: (413) 298-3583, Web
Site: www.marian.org
Dir: Father Joseph
Gen Mgr: Francis Bourdon
Info Svcs Mgr: Kevin Dougherty
Donor Devel Mgr: Suzanne Zavatter
Mgr Editorial: David Came
Mgr Special Gifts: Ellen Miller
Mgr Intl: Maciej Talar
Conducts Business: Worldwide
Employees: 95
Primary Market Served: Consumer
Advertising/Marketing Budget Related
to Direct Marketing: 0-25%
Direct Marketing ad budget:
Direct Mail: $400,000
Founded: 1945

Non-profit Catholic religious fund-
raising & publishing organization.

MARKET DEVELOPMENT GROUP INC

5151 Wisconsin Ave NW (Suite 400)
Washington, DC 20016-4124
Telephone: (202) 298-8030, FAX:
(202) 244-4999, Web Site: www.
mdginc.org
Pres: W. Michael Gretschel
Employees: 50
Founded: 1978

MARYKNOLL FATHERS & BROTHERS

PO Box 304
Maryknoll, NY 10545-0304
Telephone: (914) 941-7590, (888) 627-
9566, FAX: (914) 944-3613, E-Mail:
mkweb@maryknoll.org, Web Site:
www.maryknoll.org
Creative Svcs & Gift Plng Dir: Edward
Hayde
Conducts Business: Worldwide
Employees: 429
Primary Market Served: Consumer
Catalog available online
Indirect online sales
Advertising/Marketing Budget Related
to Direct Marketing: 76-100%
Founded: 1911

Recruit, train, send & support American missionaries working in 38 foreign
countries.

GEORGE MASON UNIVERSITY SCHOOL OF MANAGEMENT

4400 University Dr (MS 1B1)
Fairfax, VA 22030-4422
Telephone: (703) 993-1871
Primary Market Served: Consumer

Business school

MASSACHUSETTS HORTICULTURAL SOCIETY

900 Washington St (Rte 16)
Wellesley, MA 02482
Telephone: (617) 933-4929, (617) 933-
4900, FAX: (617) 933-4901, E-Mail:
hort_line@masshort.org, Web Site:
www.masshort.org
Exec Dir: Bob Feige
Dir Mktg & Commun: Jeanne
O'Rourke
Dir Horticulture Education &
Outreach: Trish Wesley Umbrell
Dir Flower Show & Special Events:
Carolyn H. Weston
Gardens Curator: David Fiske
Conducts Business: U.S.
Employees: 26
Primary Market Served: Business &
Consumer
Catalog available online
Direct online sales
Advertising/Marketing Budget Related
to Direct Marketing: 0-25%
Direct Marketing ad budget:
Direct Mail: $20,000
Founded: 1829

Non-profit educational organization
specializing in horticultural books,
prints, shows & instructional classes.

MASTERWORKS

19462 Powder Hill Pl NE Ste 100
Poulsbo, WA 98370-7472
Telephone: (360) 394-4300, Web Site:
www.masterworks.com
Sr VP Fin & Admin: Thomas Behrens
Pres: Stephen Woodworth

Marketing firm for non-profit fundraising Christian ministries

MATT & KUMPANY KUZINS

68 Aiken Way
Sacramento, CA 95819-2118
Telephone: (916) 446-2008, FAX:
(916) 446-5302, E-Mail: matt@
kuzins.com
Pres: Matt Kuzins
Conducts Business: U.S.
Employees: 5
Primary Market Served: Consumer
Catalog available online
Advertising/Marketing Budget Related
to Direct Marketing: 76-100%
Direct Marketing ad budget:
Direct Mail: 100%
Founded: 1983
Gross sales or billing: $400,000

Direct mail fund-raising consultants.

MCPHERSON ASSOCIATES INC

312 E King St
Malvern, PA 19355-2520
Telephone: (610) 640-1555, Web Site:
www.mcphersonassociates.com
Pres & Creative Dir: Richard McPher-
son

Fundraising consulting

MEDIC ALERT FOUNDATION

2323 Colorado Ave
Turlock, CA 95382
Telephone: (209) 668-3333, (888) 633-
4298, FAX: (209) 669-2495, Web
Site: www.medicalert.org
Pres: Tonya Glazebrook
Exec Asst: Jana Rhine-Patrick
VP: Effie Debow
Primary Market Served: Consumer
Founded: 1956

Provides medical emergency information to emergency responders via a
body-worn emblem (bracelet or neck-
lace) with critical information tied to a
medical hotline.

MEDICAL GROUP MANAGEMENT ASSOCIATION (MGMA)

104 Inverness Terr Dr E
Englewood, CO 80112-5306
Telephone: (303) 799-1111, FAX:
(303) 643-4439, E-Mail: marketing@
mgma.com, Web Site: www.mgma.
com
COO: James Paxton
Primary Market Served: Business

Medical group administration professional association.

MEDICAL LETTER INC
145 Huguenot St (Suite 312)
New Rochelle, NY 10801-7537
Telephone: (914) 235-0500, Web Site:
www.medicalletter.org
Dir Mktg: Joanne Valentino
Primary Market Served: Business
Direct online sales
Advertising/Marketing Budget Related
to Direct Marketing: 76-100%
Founded: 1959

MEDILL IMC/ NORTHWESTERN UNIVERSITY
1870 Campus Dr
Evanston, IL 60208-0885
Telephone: (847) 467-3433
Assoc Dean: Tom Collinger
Primary Market Served: Consumer

MEMORIAL SLOAN KETTERING CANCER CENTER
633 3rd Ave
New York, NY 10017-6706
Telephone: (646) 227-3528, Web Site:
www.mskcc.org
Dir Direct Mail: Kim Walker
Primary Market Served: Consumer

THE MENNINGER FOUNDATION
2801 Gessner Dr, Menninger Clinic
Houston, TX 77280
Telephone: (713) 275-5000, (800) 351-
9058, FAX: (713) 275-5107, Web
Site: www.menningerclinic.com
Pres & CEO: Ian Aitken
Sr Bus Devel Rep: Alan Altman
PRN Nurse: Andrea Adams
Charge Nurse: Claudia Blakemore
Conducts Business: U.S.
Employees: 1,100
Primary Market Served: Business &
Consumer
Catalog available online
Advertising/Marketing Budget Related
to Direct Marketing: 26-50%
Direct Marketing ad budget:
Direct Mail: $400,000
Newspapers: $200,000
Telephone: $50,000
Founded: 1926
Gross sales or billing: $60,000,000

Psychiatric institute providing care &
treatment. Also involved in research,
education & the promotion of mental
health.

MERCY HOME FOR BOYS & GIRLS
1140 W Jackson Blvd
Chicago, IL 60607-2906

Telephone: (312) 738-7560, Web Site:
www.mercyhome.org
Dir, Direct Mktg: James Mantz

THE METROPOLITAN OPERA
3 Lincoln Center, Metropolitan Opera
House
New York, NY 10023-7230
Telephone: (212) 799-3100, (212) 362-
6000, FAX: (212) 870-7695, Web
Site: www.metopera.org
Chmn: Christine F. Hunter
Vice Chmn: Mercedes T. Bass
Music Dir: James Levine
Assoc Dir, Membership & Promos:
Debra Reich
Primary Market Served: Consumer
Catalog available online
Direct online sales
Founded: 1883

Performing arts association.

JOYCE MEYER MINISTRIES
700 Grace Pkwy
Fenton, MO 63026-5390
Telephone: (636) 349-0303, Web Site:
www.joycemeyer.org
Division Mgr, Mktg Dir: Paul Huse

MEYER PARTNERS
1701 E Woodfield Rd (Suite 425)
Schaumburg, IL 60173-5313
Telephone: (630) 339-3930, (800) 676-
4176, FAX: (630) 339-3939, E-Mail:
info@meyerpartners.com, Web Site:
www.meyerpartners.com
Pres: Dennis L. Meyer

Full service integrated fundraising &
marketing communications agency
serving non-profit organizations

MICHIGAN APPLE COMMITTEE
13750 S Sedona Pkwy Ste 3
Lansing, MI 48906-8101
Telephone: (517) 669-8353, (800) 456-
2753, FAX: (517) 669-9506, E-Mail:
staff@michiganapples.com, Web
Site: www.michiganapples.com
Dir, Fin: Diane Smith
Sec & Mgr: Mark Arney
Mktg & Communs: Patrick O'Connor
Member: Dr. Donald Ricks
Conducts Business: U.S., Europe
Employees: 6
Primary Market Served: Business &
Consumer

Management of marketing & promotional programs for apple growers located in Michigan.

MILITARY OFFICERS ASSOCIATION OF AMERICA
201 N Washington St
Alexandria, VA 22314-2539
Telephone: (703) 838-8144, Web Site:
www.moaa.org
Deputy Dir Contract Svcs & Mktg:
Katherine Partain
Primary Market Served: Business &
Consumer

MILITARY ORDER OF THE PURPLE HEART SVC
PO Box 49
Annandale, VA 22003-0049
Telephone: (703) 256-6139
Primary Market Served: Business &
Consumer

MINDSET DIRECT
1700 N Jefferson St
Arlington, VA 22205-2817
Telephone: (703) 538-6463, Web Site:
www.mindsetdirect.com
Principal: Kristin McCurry

MINNESOTA MULTI HOUSING ASSOCIATION
1600 W 82nd St (Suite 110)
Bloomington, MN 55431-1411
Telephone: (952) 854-8500, FAX:
(952) 854-3810, E-Mail: mha@
mmha.com, Web Site: www.mmha.
com
Pres: Mary Rippe
MHS Mng Dir: Tom Cassidy
Mktg & Membership Dir: Connie Kin-
grey
Conducts Business: U.S.
Employees: 11
Primary Market Served: Business
Catalog available online
Direct online sales
Advertising/Marketing Budget Related
to Direct Marketing: 26-50%
Direct Marketing ad budget:
Direct Mail: 75%
Newspapers: 15%
Telephone: 10%
Founded: 1967
Gross sales or billing: $450,000

Membership - apartment owners association, owners & vendors. Forms,
leases, legal handbooks. Exhibit space
in one trade show.

MINNESOTA PUBLIC RADIO
480 Cedar St
Saint Paul, MN 55101-2230
Telephone: (651) 290-1500, (800) 228-
7123, FAX: (651) 290-1260, E-Mail:
mail@mpr.org, Web Site: www.mpr.
org

VP, Devel: Jon Gossett
Dir, Membership Mktg: Al Anderson
Employees: 450
Primary Market Served: Business &
   Consumer
Catalog available online
Direct online sales
Advertising/Marketing Budget Related
   to Direct Marketing: 0-25%
Founded: 1967
Gross sales or billing: $46,000,000

Public Radio.

MISSIONARY SOCIETY OF ST COLUMBAN

PO Box 10
Saint Columbans, NE 68056-0010
Telephone: (402) 291-1920, Web Site:
   www.columban.org
COO: Jeff Norton

MISSOURI LANDSCAPE & NURSERY ASSOCIATION

PO Box 81
Bowling Green, MO 63334
Telephone: (636) 542-1234, E-Mail:
   admin@mlng.org, Web Site: www.
   mlna.org
Pres: Rob Johnson
VP: Kim Lovelace-Young
Dir: Anne McKinstry
Coord: Mary Ann Fink
Treas: Bryan Stringer
Conducts Business: U.S.
Employees: 250
Primary Market Served: Business
Catalog available online
Direct Marketing ad budget: $10,000
Direct Mail: 90%
Magazines: 10%
Gross sales or billing: $40,000

Professional trade association representing the nursery, landscape & garden center industry in the state of MO.

MITSUBISHI MOTOR SALES OF AMERICA INC

6400 W Katella Ave
Cypress, CA 90630
Telephone: (714) 372-6000, FAX:
   (714) 373-1736, Web Site: www.
   mitsubishicars.com
Pres & CEO: Jeff Young
VP, Mktg Svcs: Frances Oda
Dir, Mktg & Sls: Gene Cook
Brand Mgr: Shannon Kalunian
Conducts Business: U.S.
Primary Market Served: Consumer
Catalog available online
Indirect online sales
Advertising/Marketing Budget Related
   to Direct Marketing: 0-25%
Direct Marketing ad budget: $500,000
Direct Mail: 1%
Magazines: 8%

Newspapers: 5%
TV/Radio: 85%
Telephone: 1%
Founded: 1981

Automobile distributor to franchisees.

THE MORTON ARBORETUM
THE DMA

4100 Illinois (Route 53)
Lisle, IL 60532-1293
Telephone: (630) 968-0074, Web Site:
   www.mortonarb.org
Asst Dir, Membership: Karin Jaros

MOTION PICTURE & TELEVISION FUND FOUNDATION

23388 Mulholland Dr
Woodland Hills, CA 91364-2733
Telephone: (818) 876-1888, Web Site:
   www.mptvfund.org
CEO, MPTF Foundation: Ken Scherer
Gift Plng Specialist: Marcia Braunstein
Pres & CEO: David Tillman M.D.
Chmn Bd: Jeffrey Katzenberg
Primary Market Served: Business &
   Consumer
Founded: 1921

Fund-raising for hospital & health-care
for anyone in motion picture & television industry.

MULTI-LEVEL MARKETING INTERNATIONAL ASSOCIATION (MLMIA)

119 Stanford Ct
Irvine, CA 92612-1671
Telephone: (949) 854-0484, FAX:
   (949) 854-7687, E-Mail: info@
   mlmia.com, Web Site: www.mlmia.
   com/
Chmn: Doris Wood
Co-Founder: Michael L. Sheffield
Exec Dir: Del Hickman
Conducts Business: U.S., Canada, Ma-
   laysia, U.K., Australia, Hong Kong
Employees: 2
Primary Market Served: Business &
   Consumer
Indirect online sales
Advertising/Marketing Budget Related
   to Direct Marketing: 51-75%
Direct Marketing ad budget:
Newspapers: 100%
Founded: 1985

MLMIA is a non-profit association
representing the Network Marketing
Industry. The three major categories of
membership are: Network Marketing
Companies, Independent Network Marketing Distributors or Representatives
& Support Companies - those companies who provide products or services
to MLM companies or distributors.

MULTIPLE SCLEROSIS ASSOCIATION OF AMERICA
THE DMA

706 Haddonfield Rd
Cherry Hill, NJ 08002-2652
Telephone: (856) 488-4500, Web Site:
   www.msaa.com
VP Fin & Admin: Gary Wallace

MULTIVIEW
THE DMA

7701 Las Colinas Ridge (Suite 800)
Irving, TX 75063-7555
Telephone: (972) 402-7056
VP Sls: Michael Scheevel
Catalog available online

MURDER BY MAIL

PO Box 789
West Tisbury, MA 02575
Telephone: (617) 670-9400, (508) 693-
   5205, FAX: (508) 693-7997, E-Mail:
   info@murderbymail.com, Web Site:
   www.murderbymail.com
Pres: Janice Sparks
Conducts Business: U.S., U.K., S.
   America, Canada
Employees: 3
Primary Market Served: Business &
   Consumer
Catalog available online
Indirect online sales
Advertising/Marketing Budget Related
   to Direct Marketing: 51-75%
Direct Marketing ad budget:
Magazines: 75%
Newspapers: 25%
Founded: 1980
Gross sales or billing: $125,000

Interactive murder mystery parties &
events. Used for social events, incentive groups, fund raisers, private parties, T & E, used professionally by
restaurants, hotels, inns & event
planners. Package includes: custom
materials, complete scenario, props,
storyline & assistance in planning.
Done on a reasonable per person fee.
Package is customized by size &
theme.

MUSCULAR DYSTROPHY ASSOCIATION
THE DMA

3300 E Sunrise Dr
Tucson, AZ 85718-3299
Telephone: (520) 529-2000, (800) 344-
   4863, FAX: (520) 529-5300, Web
   Site: www.mdausa.org
Chmn: Lori R. West
Pres & CEO: Gerald Weinberg
Treas: Victor R. Wright
VP, Direct Mktg: Brenda Davis
Conducts Business: U.S.
Employees: 1,500
Primary Market Served: Business &
   Consumer

Advertising/Marketing Budget Related
to Direct Marketing: 0-25%
Direct Marketing ad budget:
Direct Mail: $10,000,000
Online: $10,000
TV/Radio: $6,000,000
Founded: 1950
Gross sales or billing: $187,000,000

Voluntary national health agency dedicated to conquering neuromuscular diseases.

NAACP (NATIONAL ASSOCIATION FOR THE ADVANCEMENT OF COLORED PEOPLE)

4805 Mount Hope Dr
Baltimore, MD 21215-3206
Telephone: (410) 580-5617, Web Site:
www.naacp.org
National Dir Annual Funds: Scott Melton
Primary Market Served: Consumer

NARAL PRO-CHOICE AMERICA

1156 15th St NW
Washington, DC 20005-1704
Telephone: (202) 973-3000, Web Site:
www.naral.com
Membership Mgr: Heidi Combs

THE DMA NASA FEDERAL CREDIT UNION

500 Prince Georges Blvd.
Upper Marlboro, MD 20774-8732
Telephone: (301) 249-1800, Web Site:
www.nasafcu.com

NASW ASSURANCE SERVICES INC

Subs. of National Association of Social
Workers Inc
50 Citizens Way (Suite 304)
Frederick, MD 21701
Telephone: (800) 668-4274, E-Mail:
zxi@naswasi.org, Web Site: www.
naswinsurancetrust.org
Exec VP: Tony Benedetto
Sr Mktg Assoc: Lucinda Branaman
Prod Mgr: Mike Auth
Mgr Reporting & Analysis: Stacy
Hammond
Conducts Business: U.S.
Employees: 6
Primary Market Served: Consumer
Catalog available online
Indirect online sales
Direct Marketing ad budget:
$3,000,000
Direct Mail: 85%
Magazines: 5%
Online: 5%
Telephone: 5%

Founded: 2007
Gross sales or billing: $6,000,000

Sell group and professional liability
insurance to National Association of
Social Workers members.

THE DMA NBI INC

PO Box 3067
Eau Claire, WI 54702-3067
Telephone: (715) 835-8525, Web Site:
www.nbi-sems.com
Dir Mktg: Tia Embke
Primary Market Served: Consumer

Provides continuing legal education

THE DMA NEA'S MEMBER BENEFITS CORP

900 Clopper Rd
Gaithersburg, MD 20878-1360
Telephone: (301) 251-9600, FAX:
(301) 527-8210, Web Site: www.
neamb.com
VP Mktg: Steve Levy
Primary Market Served: Consumer
Founded: 1941

Market to NEA members & family.

NFIB - NATIONAL FEDERATION OF INDEPENDENT BUSINESS

53 Century Blvd (Suite 250)
Nashville, TN 37214-4618
Telephone: (615) 872-5800, Web Site:
www.nfib.com
Mktg Res Mgr: Deidre Popovich

THE DMA NNE MARKETING

105 Paul Revere Rd
Concord, MA 01742-4817
Telephone: (617) 429-7999, Web Site:
www.nnemarketing.com
Principal: Craig Zelstar

Direct marketing agency focusing on
fundraising & membership programs

NTL INSTITUTE

1901 S Bell St (Suite 300)
Arlington, VA 22202-4503
Telephone: (703) 548-8840, (800) 277-
4685, FAX: (703) 684-1256, E-Mail:
info@ntl.org, Web Site: www.ntl.org
Pres: Diane Porter
Conducts Business: Worldwide
Employees: 20
Primary Market Served: Business &
Consumer
Catalog available online
Indirect online sales
Advertising/Marketing Budget Related
to Direct Marketing: 0-25%
Founded: 1947
Gross sales or billing: $5,000,000

Conducts programs in the areas of human relations training, diversity, management development, organizational development & training of facilitators & consultants; also run a joint Masters program with The American University in OD & with Cleveland State University in Diversity.

NYSARC, INC

393 Delaware Ave
Delmar, NY 12054
Telephone: (518) 439-8311, FAX:
(518) 439-1893, E-Mail: info@
nysarc.org, Web Site: www.nysarc.
org
Primary Market Served: Consumer

Family-based organization working
with and for people with intellectual &
other developmental disabilities

NATIONAL ACTIVE & RETIRED FEDERAL EMPLOYEES ASSOCIATION

606 N Washington St
Alexandria, VA 22314-1914
Telephone: (703) 838-7760, (800) 456-
8410, FAX: (703) 838-7785, Web
Site: www.narfe.org
Natl Pres & CEO: Frank G. Atwater
VP: Margaret Baptiste
Treas: Charles Fallis
Sec: David Sullivan
Primary Market Served: Business &
Consumer
Direct online sales
Founded: 1921

Association for retired federal
employees. Alternate toll free number:
(800) 627-3394.

NATIONAL ALLIANCE OF BUSINESS

1455 Pennsylvania Ave NW (Suite
375)
Washington, DC 20004
Telephone: (202) 289-2888, (800) 787-
2448
Pres & CEO: Robert T. Jones
Conducts Business: U.S.
Employees: 130
Primary Market Served: Business
Direct Marketing ad budget: $500,000
Direct Mail: $150,000
Magazines: $75,000
Newspapers: $75,000
TV/Radio: $150,000
Telephone: $50,000
Founded: 1968
Gross sales or billing: $10,000,000

Non-profit corporation, supported by business, to promote employer leadership in education reform, private sector training & job opportunities for the economically disadvantaged & long-term unemployed.

NATIONAL ASSOCIATION FOR FEMALE EXECUTIVES (NAFE)

Div. of Working Mother Media
2 Park Ave Fl 10
New York, NY 10016-5604
Telephone: (800) 927-6233, E-Mail: info@nafe.com, Web Site: www. nafe.com
Pres: Dr Betty Spence
Editor: Paula Damiano
Conducts Business: U.S.
Employees: 32
Primary Market Served: Business & Consumer
Catalog available online
Direct online sales
Advertising/Marketing Budget Related to Direct Marketing: 76-100%
Founded: 1972
Gross sales or billing: $9,000

Woman's organization & publisher of a magazine for career-oriented women.

NATIONAL ASSOCIATION FOR PRINTING LEADERSHIP

1 Meadowlands Plz (Suite 1511)
East Rutherford, NJ 07073-2167
Telephone: (201) 634-9600, (800) 642-6275, FAX: (201) 634-0324, Web Site: www.napl.org
Pres & CEO: Joseph Truncali
EVP & COO: Timothy Fischer
VP: Joan Kasper
VP: Andrew D. Paparozzi
Employees: 36
Primary Market Served: Business
Founded: 1933
Gross sales or billing: $2,700,000

Non-profit printing association.

NATIONAL ASSOCIATION OF PROFESSIONAL INSURANCE AGENTS

400 N Washington St
Alexandria, VA 22314-2353
Telephone: (703) 836-9340, FAX: (703) 836-1279, E-Mail: web@pianet.org, Web Site: www.pianet.com
Exec VP: Leonard Brevik
Sr VP: Patricia A. Borowski
Dir State Affairs: David Epstein
VP: Ted Besesparis
Mgr: Anelda Peters
Primary Market Served: Consumer

Catalog available online
Founded: 1931

Consumer not-for-profit association.

NATIONAL ASSOCIATION OF REALTORS

430 N Michigan Ave
Chicago, IL 60611-4088
Telephone: (312) 329-8526, Web Site: www.realtors.org
Mgr Mktg Res: Lisa Herceg
Primary Market Served: Business & Consumer

NATIONAL AUTOMATED CLEARING HOUSE ASSOCIATION

13450 Sunrise Valley Dr (Suite 100)
Herndon, VA 20171
Telephone: (703) 561-1100, FAX: (703) 787-0996, Web Site: www. nacha.org
Pres: Elliott C. McEntee
Membership Mktg & Commun Dir: Robin Reeder
Conducts Business: U.S.
Employees: 21
Primary Market Served: Business & Consumer
Founded: 1974

Electronic payments network association.

NATIONAL BASKETBALL ASSOCIATION

100 Plaza Dr Fl 3
Secaucus, NJ 07094-3677
Telephone: (212) 407-8000, FAX: (212) 826-0579, Web Site: www.nba.com
Commissioner: David Stern
Conducts Business: U.S., Italy, Germany, Australia, Mexico
Employees: 400
Primary Market Served: Consumer
Advertising/Marketing Budget Related to Direct Marketing: 0-25%
Direct Marketing ad budget:
Magazines: 90%
TV/Radio: 10%
Gross sales or billing: $500,000

Promotes the association and catalog.

NATIONAL COMMITTEE TO PRESERVE SOCIAL SECURITY & MEDICARE

10 "G" St NE (Suite 600)
Washington, DC 20002-4215
Telephone: (202) 216-0420, (800) 966-1935, FAX: (202) 216-0446, E-Mail: kreard@ncpssm.org, Web Site: www. ncpssm.org
Chair: Carroll L. Estes Ph.D.

Exec VP: Max Richtman
Dir Mktg: J. David Krear
Sec: Sandra J. Wagenfeld
Conducts Business: U.S.
Employees: 43
Primary Market Served: Consumer
Catalog available online
Direct online sales
Advertising/Marketing Budget Related to Direct Marketing: 76-100%
Direct Marketing ad budget:
$18,000,000
Direct Mail: 100%
Founded: 1982
Gross sales or billing: $25,000,000

Non-profit organization.

NATIONAL COMMUNITY PHARMACISTS ASSOCIATION

100 Daingerfield Rd
Alexandria, VA 22314
Telephone: (703) 683-8200, (800) 544-7447, FAX: (703) 683-3619, E-Mail: info@ncpanet.org, Web Site: www. ncpanet.org
Pres: Stephen L. Giroux
Pres Elect: Holly W. Henry
Sec & Treas: Bradley J. Arthur
First VP: Mark Riley
Second VP: Keith Hodges
Conducts Business: U.S.
Employees: 40
Primary Market Served: Business & Consumer
Catalog available online
Direct online sales
Advertising/Marketing Budget Related to Direct Marketing: 51-75%
Direct Marketing ad budget:
Direct Mail: 35%
Magazines: 30%
Telephone: 35%
Founded: 1898

Provide professional services, co-sponsored continuing education & promotional programs to the owners of over 30,000 pharmacies.

NATIONAL CONTRACT MANAGEMENT ASSOCIATION

21740 Beaumeade Cir (Suite 125)
Ashburn, VA 20147-6237
Telephone: (571) 382-1134, (800) 344-8096, E-Mail: memberservices@ncmghq.org, Web Site: www. ncmahq.org
Exec Dir: Neal J Couture
Mktg Specialist: Danielle Johnson
Dir Commun: Eileen Moore
Primary Market Served: Business & Consumer

NATIONAL COUNCIL ON COMPENSATION INSURANCE INC (NCCI)

901 Peninsula Corp Cir
Boca Raton, FL 33487
Telephone: (561) 893-1000, (800) 622-4123, FAX: (561) 893-1191, Web Site: www.ncci.com
Pres & CEO: Stephen J. Klingel
Mktg: Diane Clifton
Employees: 950
Primary Market Served: Business
Founded: 1919

Data products for insurance companies.

NATIONAL COURT REPORTERS ASSOCIATION

8224 Old Courthouse Rd
Vienna, VA 22182-3808
Telephone: (703) 556-6272, (800) 272-6272, FAX: (703) 556-6291, E-Mail: msic@ncrahg.org, Web Site: www.ncraonline.org
Pres: Kathleen DiLorenzo
Pres Elect: Karen Yates
VP: Sue Lynn Morgan
Sec Treas: R. Douglas Friend
Dir: Richard Greenspan
Conducts Business: U.S., Canada
Employees: 45
Primary Market Served: Business & Consumer
Catalog available online
Direct online sales
Advertising/Marketing Budget Related to Direct Marketing: 0-25%
Direct Marketing ad budget:
Direct Mail: 85%
Magazines: 10%
Telephone: 5%
Founded: 1899
Gross sales or billing: $300,000

Memberships, programs & services to court reporters, court reporting students, and other members of the legal system.

NATIONAL DEFENSE INDUSTRIAL ASSOCIATION

2111 Wilson Blvd (Suite 400)
Arlington, VA 22201-3061
Telephone: (703) 522-1820, FAX: (703) 522-1885, Web Site: www.ndia.org
Conducts Business: U.S.
Employees: 60
Primary Market Served: Consumer
Direct online sales
Advertising/Marketing Budget Related to Direct Marketing: 26-50%
Founded: 1919

Non-profit membership association that represents the concerns & business interests of nearly 1,000 companies & their one million employees, & over 28,000 individual members from both government & industry. Members come from a broad range of commercial, research & development, legal & educational entities & individuals from the United States & countries that have reciprocal procurement agreements with the U.S. Department of Defense & educational entities from U.S. Department of Defense. Our basic mission is to foster awareness of and support for a technological/industrial infrastructure that is capable of responding to any global challenge. Sponsors more than fifty technical symposia & exhibitions annually. The journal, National Defense, is published twelve times a year.

THE DMA NATIONAL FIRE PROTECTION ASSOCIATION

1 Batterymarch Park Bsmt
Quincy, MA 02169-7484
Telephone: (617) 770-3000, FAX: (617) 770-0700, Web Site: www.nfpa.org
Pres: Jim Shannon
Division Dir Mktg: Andrew Wandell
VP DM: Paul G. Crossman
Conducts Business: Worldwide
Employees: 300
Primary Market Served: Business
Catalog available online
Advertising/Marketing Budget Related to Direct Marketing: 76-100%
Direct Marketing ad budget:
Direct Mail: 95%
Magazines: 2%
Telephone: 3%
Founded: 1896

Non-profit membership association. Produce & distribute a variety of publications, films, A/V, seminar/training material for both members & non-members. Markets served include: fire service, government, health care, schools, architects, engineers & industry.

NATIONAL FOUNDATION FOR CANCER RESEARCH

4600 E West Hwy (Suite 525)
Bethesda, MD 20814-6900
Telephone: (301) 654-1250, (800) 321-CURE, FAX: (301) 654-5824, E-Mail: info@nfcr.org, Web Site: www.nfcr.org
Pres: Franklin C. Salisbury
Exec VP: Tamara Salisbury
COO: Sujuan Ba

Dir Direct Resources: Joseph Mosinski
VP Comm & Mktg: Silas Deane
Conducts Business: U.S.
Employees: 21
Primary Market Served: Business & Consumer
Direct online sales
Advertising/Marketing Budget Related to Direct Marketing: 26-50%
Direct Marketing ad budget: $1,500,000
Direct Mail: $8,400,000
Telephone: $100,000
Founded: 1973
Gross sales or billing: $7,090,000

Not-for-profit organization conducting basic cancer research.

THE DMA NATIONAL GOLF FOUNDATION

1150 S US Hwy One (Suite 401)
Jupiter, FL 33477
Telephone: (561) 744-6006, FAX: (561) 744-6107, E-Mail: ngf@ngf.org, Web Site: www.ngf.org
Pres: Joseph Beditz
VP & Gen Mgr: Richard Norton
Conducts Business: Worldwide
Employees: 47
Primary Market Served: Business
Catalog available online
Indirect online sales
Founded: 1936

Unparalleled clearinghouse of industry information, provided in the form of research, reports, seminars, consulting services & more

NATIONAL HUMANE EDUCATION SOCIETY

PO Box 340
Charles Town, WV 25414-0340
Telephone: (304) 725-0506, FAX: (304) 725-1523, E-Mail: nhesinformation@nhes.org, Web Site: www.nhes.org
Pres: James D. Taylor
Founder & VP: Anna C. Briggs
VP: Cynthia L. Taylor
Sec: Christina B. Fernandez
Treas: Virginia B Dungan
Employees: 38
Primary Market Served: Consumer
Founded: 1948
Gross sales or billing: $4,188,634

Non-profit humane education service on rescue services for animals.

THE DMA NATIONAL INSTITUTE FOR TRIAL ADVOCACY (NITA)

1685 38th St
Boulder, CO 80301-2735
Telephone: (800) 225-6482, Web Site: www.nita.org

Dir Programs Sls & Mktg: Daniel McHugh

THE DMA NATIONAL JEWISH HEALTH
1400 Jackson St
Denver, CO 80206-2761
Telephone: (303) 398-1070, (800) 222-LUNG, (800) 423, FAX: (303) 398-1663, E-Mail: trubeyp@njhealth.org, Web Site: www.njhealth.org
VP Devel: Carol Gibson
Dir Direct Mktg: Paulette Trubey
Conducts Business: Worldwide
Employees: 1,200
Primary Market Served: Consumer
Direct Marketing ad budget:
Direct Mail: $1,500,000
Telephone: $35,000
Founded: 1899

National direct mail fund-raising program for medical research center.

THE DMA NATIONAL LAW ENFORCEMENT OFFICERS MEMORIAL FUND
901 E St NW Ste 100
Washington, DC 20004-2025
Telephone: (202) 737-3400, Web Site: www.nleomf.com
Chairman & CEO: Craig Floyd
Primary Market Served: Business & Consumer

NATIONAL LEAGUE FOR NURSING
61 Broadway (fl 33)
New York, NY 10006-2800
Telephone: (212) 363-5555, (800) 669-1656, FAX: (212) 812-0391, E-Mail: generalinfo@nln.org, Web Site: www.nln.org
CEO: Dr Beverly Malone
Mgr, Mktg Communs: Stacy Heatherington
Conducts Business: U.S.
Employees: 50
Primary Market Served: Business & Consumer
Founded: 1893
Gross sales or billing: $9,500,000

As the voice for nursing education, the National League for Nursing is the premier organization for nurse faculty and leaders in nursing education offering faculty development, networking opportunities, testing services, nursing research grants, and public policy initiatives to more than 30,000 individual and 1,100 education and associate members.

NATIONAL LUGGAGE DEALERS ASSOCIATION
Div. of NLDA Associates Inc
1817 Elmdale Ave
Glenview, IL 60625-1355
Telephone: (847) 998-6869, FAX: (847) 998-6884, E-Mail: inquiry@nlda.com, Web Site: www.nlda.com
Exec Dir: Marilyn Murray
Conducts Business: U.S.
Employees: 10
Primary Market Served: Business & Consumer
Catalog available online
Advertising/Marketing Budget Related to Direct Marketing: 0-25%
Founded: 1925
Gross sales or billing: $10,000,000

National Association of 300 stores selling luggage, small leather goods, gifts & handbags. Produce various consumer catalogs & import merchandise for stores.

NATIONAL MEDICAL FELLOWSHIPS
347 5th Ave (Suite 510)
New York, NY 10016-5007
Telephone: (212) 483-8880, FAX: (212) 483-8897, Web Site: www.nfm-online.org
Pres & CEO: Esther R. Dyer
Exec VP: Paula Madison
Sec & Treas: Stephen N. Keith MD
Primary Market Served: Business & Consumer
Advertising/Marketing Budget Related to Direct Marketing: 0-25%
Founded: 1946

Non-profit organization that provides financial & other assistance to under represented minority medical students.

NATIONAL MOTOR CLUB OF AMERICA INC
130 E John Carpenter Fwy
Irving, TX 75062-2708
Telephone: (972) 999-4400, (800) 523-4582, FAX: (972) 999-4405, Web Site: www.nmca.com
Pres: Jeffrey J. Jensen
VP, Corp Sls: Brian Joseph
Conducts Business: U.S., Canada, Mexico
Employees: 400
Primary Market Served: Business & Consumer
Catalog available online
Founded: 1956

Motor club membership organization.

THE DMA NATIONAL MULTIPLE SCLEROSIS SOCIETY
900 S Broadway Ste 210
Denver, CO 80209-4269

Telephone: (303) 813-1052, Web Site: www.nmss.org
Assoc VP, Individual Giving: Krista Byers

THE DMA NATIONAL OSTEOPOROSIS FOUNDATION
1150 17th St NW (Suite 850)
Washington, DC 20037-1216
Telephone: (202) 721-6346, Web Site: www.nof.org
Exec Dir/CEO: Amy Porter
Primary Market Served: Consumer

NATIONAL PARKINSON FOUNDATION
1501 NW 9th Ave
Miami, FL 33136-1407
Telephone: (800) 937-4545, Web Site: www.parkinson.org
VP & Chief Devel Officer: Kathleen Wiedemer

THE DMA NATIONAL RELIEF CHARITIES
13318 Airport Dr
Elkwood, VA 22718-1760
Telephone: (540) 825-5950
Dir Fundraising: Chuck Smith

THE DMA NATIONAL RESEARCH CENTER FOR COLLEGE & UNIVERSITY ADMISSIONS
3651 NE Ralph Powell Rd
Lees Summit, MO 64064-2357
Telephone: (816) 525-2201, Web Site: www.nrccua.org
Pres: Don Munce

THE DMA THE NATIONAL RESTAURANT ASSOCIATION EDUCATIONAL FOUNDATION
175 W Jackson Blvd
Chicago, IL 60604
Telephone: (312) 715-1010, FAX: (312) 583-9767
Sr Dir Brand Mktg: Cheryl Lynn-Shiflett
Primary Market Served: Business & Consumer

Educational arm of the national restaurant association.

NATIONAL RETAIL FEDERATION INC
325 Seventh St NW (Suite 1100)
Washington, DC 20004
Telephone: (202) 783-7971, (800) 673-4692, FAX: (202) 737-2849, E-Mail: webmaster@nrf.com, Web Site: www.nrf.com

Pres & CEO: Tracy Mullen
Sr VP Gen Counsel: Mallory Duncan
Sr VP & CIO: David Hogan
Sr VP, Member Svcs: Karen Knobloch
Sr VP & CFO: Carleen Kohut
Employees: 96
Primary Market Served: Business &
  Consumer
Direct online sales
Gross sales or billing: $30,600,000

Industry services.

NATIONAL RIFLE ASSOCIATION OF AMERICA
11250 Waples Mill Rd
Fairfax, VA 22030-7400
Telephone: (703) 267-1000, (800) 672-
  3888, FAX: (703) 267-3957, E-Mail:
  nra.contact@nra.org, Web Site:
  www.nra.org
Pres: Charlton Heston
Exec VP: Wayne LaPierre
Membership Dir: Robert W. Marcario
Mgr, Fiscal Opers: Lisa Whited
Conducts Business: U.S.
Employees: 360
Primary Market Served: Consumer
Founded: 1871

National membership association. Pub-
lish The American Rifleman, The
American Hunter, InSights & The
American Guardian.

NATIONAL RURAL ELECTRIC COOPERATIVE ASSOCIATION
4301 Wilson Blvd
Arlington, VA 22203-1860
Telephone: (703) 907-5500, FAX:
  (703) 907-5528, Web Site: www.
  nreca.org
CEO: Glenn English
Media & PR Dir: Patrick Levigne
Assoc Membership Mgr: Nancy Mc-
  Mahen
Conducts Business: U.S.
Employees: 900
Primary Market Served: Business
Founded: 1942
Gross sales or billing: $139,400,000

A service organization that represents
the nation's 1000 non-profit, consumer-
owned electric cooperatives which provide service to more than 25 million
people in 46 states.

NATIONAL SCHOOL BOARDS ASSOCIATION INC
1680 Duke St
Alexandria, VA 22314
Telephone: (703) 838-6722, FAX:
  (703) 683-7590, E-Mail: info@nsba.
  org, Web Site: www.nsba.org

Exec Dir: Anne Bryant
Pres: Norman D. Wooten
Conducts Business: United States
Employees: 150
Primary Market Served: Business
Indirect online sales
Advertising/Marketing Budget Related
  to Direct Marketing: 0-25%
Founded: 1940
Gross sales or billing: $23,500,000

Non-profit organization aiming to advance the quality of education in public schools, providing up-to-date information & training for educators &
strengthening local support for schools.

NATIONAL SOCIETY OF COLLEGIATE SCHOLARS
2000 M St NW Ste 600
Washington, DC 20036-3328
Telephone: (202) 265-9000, Web Site:
  www.nscs.org
Exec Dir & Founder: Stephen Loflin
Primary Market Served: Business &
  Consumer

NATIONAL TRUST FOR HISTORIC PRESERVATION
1785 Massachusetts Ave NW
Washington, DC 20036-2189
Telephone: (202) 588-6124, Web Site:
  www.nationaltrust.org
Mgr Recruitment & Outreach: David
  Field

NATIONAL UNIVERSITY
11355 N Torrey Pines Rd
La Jolla, CA 92037-1013
Telephone: (800) 628-8648, Web Site:
  www.nu.edu
Dir Media & Markets: Kendra Losee
Primary Market Served: Consumer

NATIONAL WILDLIFE FEDERATION
11100 Wildlife Center Dr
Reston, VA 20190-5362
Telephone: (703) 438-6000, Web Site:
  www.nwf.org
Sr Dir Membership: Anne Senft
Primary Market Served: Consumer

NATIVE AMERICAN HERITAGE ASSOCIATIONS
830 John Marshall Hwy (Suite F)
Front Royal, VA 22630-3743
Telephone: (540) 636-1020, Web Site:
  www.naha-inc.org
VP: Pam Pullen

NATIVE AMERICAN RIGHTS FUND
1506 Broadway
Boulder, CO 80302-6217
Telephone: (303) 447-8760, Web Site:
  www.narf.org
Devel Projects Mgr: Mereille Martinez

THE NATURE CONSERVANCY
4245 N Fairfax Dr (Suite 100)
Arlington, VA 22203-1650
Telephone: (703) 841-5300, (800) 628-
  6860, FAX: (703) 841-1283, E-Mail:
  magazine@tnc.org, Web Site: www.
  nature.org
Pres, CEO & Dir: Steven J. McCor-
  mick
Dir Membership: Begona Vazquez
  Santos
CFO: Stephen Howell
CIO: John-Louis Echohard
Conducts Business: Worldwide
Employees: 230
Primary Market Served: Business &
  Consumer
Founded: 1951

A non-profit organization that preserves plants, animals & natural communities that represent the diversity of
life on earth by protecting the lands &
water they need to survive in.

NEIGHBORHOOD CLEANERS ASSOCIATION INTERNATIONAL
252 W 29th St
New York, NY 10001
Telephone: (212) 967-3002, (800) 888-
  1622, FAX: (212) 967-2240, E-Mail:
  info@nca-i.com, Web Site: www.
  nca-i.com
Exec Dir: Nora Nealis
Pres: Joseph Halleak Jr.
VP: Ted Aveni
VP: John Fehlner
Adv & Mktg: Anne Hargrove
Conducts Business: Worldwide
Employees: 12
Primary Market Served: Business
Advertising/Marketing Budget Related
  to Direct Marketing: 0-25%
Founded: 1946
Gross sales or billing: $900,000

Advertising & promotional services,
educational material & customer relations insurance to members. A cleaning
industry trade association.

NETWORK FOR GOOD
7920 Norfolk Ave (Suite 520)
Bethesda, MD 20814-2571
Telephone: (240) 482-3211, Web Site:
  www.networkforgood.org

Mktg Assoc: Rebecca Higman

NEVADA COMMISSION ON TOURISM

401 N Carson St
Carson City, NV 89701-4221
Telephone: (775) 687-4322, (800) NE-
VADA 8, FAX: (775) 687-6779,
Web Site: www.travelnevada.com
Dir: Tim Maland
Chair: Lorraine Hunt
Exec Dir: Bruce C. Bommarito
Conducts Business: U.S.
Employees: 35
Primary Market Served: Consumer

State tourism promotion agency.

ᵀᴴᴱ NEW JERSEY INSTITUTE FOR CONTINUING LEGAL EDUCATION

1 Constitution Sq
New Brunswick, NJ 08901-1587
Telephone: (732) 249-5100, Web Site:
www.njicle.com
Exec Dir: Lawrence Maron Esq.
Primary Market Served: Business &
Consumer

ᵀᴴᴱ NEW YORK BLOOD CENTER INC

310 E 67th St
New York, NY 10021
Telephone: (212) 570-3000, (800) 933-
2566, FAX: (212) 570-3195, Web
Site: www.nybloodcenter.org
Pres & CEO: Dr. Robert Jones
VP & CFO: Lawrence Hannigan
VP, Strategic Plng & Mktg: Margie
Gandolfi
VP, Gen Counsel: Miriam Sparrow
VP, Chief Medical Officer: Robert Re-
iss
Conducts Business: U.S.
Employees: 1,500
Primary Market Served: Business &
Consumer
Catalog available online
Advertising/Marketing Budget Related
to Direct Marketing: 0-25%
Direct Marketing ad budget:
$2,000,000
Direct Mail: 50%
Newspapers: 25%
Telephone: 25%
Founded: 1964
Gross sales or billing: $327,600,000

Blood products and services: Rely on
volunteer blood donations & financial
contributions.

NEW YORK EASTER SEAL SOCIETY

40th W 37th St (Suite 503)
New York, NY 10018-7345

Telephone: (312) 726-6200, (212) 943-
4364, (800) 221-6827, FAX: (212)
695-4807, (312) 726-4258, Web Site:
ny.easterseals.com
Pres: Larry Gammon
Sr VP: Jeremy Kohomvan
Mgr: Allen Beaufort
Conducts Business: U.S.
Employees: 70
Primary Market Served: Business &
Consumer
Indirect online sales
Advertising/Marketing Budget Related
to Direct Marketing: 76-100%
Founded: 1923
Gross sales or billing: $20,200,000

Fund-raising, and other health and human services.

NEW YORK FOUNDATION FOR THE ARTS

20 Jay St Ste 740
Brooklyn, NY 11201-8352
Telephone: (212) 366-6900, FAX:
(212) 366-1778, E-Mail: deleget@
nyfa.org, Web Site: www.nyfa.org
Exec Dir: Theodore S. Berger
Conducts Business: U.S.
Employees: 20
Primary Market Served: Business
Advertising/Marketing Budget Related
to Direct Marketing: 0-25%

Foundation working with New York
State artists.

NEW YORK LANDMARKS CONSERVANCY

One Whitehall St
New York, NY 10004
Telephone: (212) 995-5260, FAX:
(212) 995-5268, Web Site: www.
nylandmarks.org
Pres: Peg Breen
Chair: Frank J. Sciame Jr.
Vice Chair: Allison Simmons Prouty
Esq.
Treas: Lloyd P. Zuckerberg
Dir: Justin Abelow
Conducts Business: U.S.
Employees: 17
Primary Market Served: Business &
Consumer
Advertising/Marketing Budget Related
to Direct Marketing: 0-25%

Non-profit organization preserving historic buildings.

ᵀᴴᴱ NEW YORK PHILHARMONIC

10 Lincoln Ctr Plaza, Avery Fisher
Hall
New York, NY 10023-6970
Telephone: (212) 875-5691, Web Site:
www.newyorkphilharmonic.org
Dir Individual Giving: Judith Helf

Primary Market Served: Consumer

NEW YORK UNIVERSITY

11 W 42nd St (Rm 431)
New York, NY 10036-8083
Telephone: (212) 992-3221, Web Site:
www.scps.nyu.edu
Academic Dir, Professor: Dr. Marjorie
Kalter

NEW YORK UNIVERSITY MEDICAL CENTER

550 First Ave
New York, NY 10016
Telephone: (212) 263-7800, FAX:
(212) 263-8426, Web Site: www.
med.nyu.edu
Dean & CEO, NYU Medical Ctr: Rob-
ert I. Grossman M.D.
Exec VP, Vice Dean & Chief of Staff:
Andrew W. Litt M.D.
Conducts Business: U.S., Canada
Primary Market Served: Business &
Consumer

Non-profit medical organization.

ᵀᴴᴱ NEWPORT CREATIVE COMMUNICATIONS

33 Railroad Ave
Duxbury, MA 02332-3884
Telephone: (781) 934-1414, Web Site:
www.newportcreative.com
Acct Mgr: Allie Moore

Direct marketing fundraising agency
that assists non-profit charitable organizations

ᵀᴴᴱ NEWSPAPER ASSOCIATION OF AMERICA

4401 Wilson Blvd (Suite 900)
Arlington, VA 22203-4195
Telephone: (703) 902-1600, FAX:
(571) 366-1195, Web Site: www.naa.
org
Pres & CEO: John Sturm
VP, Circulation Mktg: John Murray
Sr VP: Paul Doyle
Sr VP: Thomas Croteu
Sr VP: John Kimball
Sr VP: Su-Liu Nichols
Primary Market Served: Business &
Consumer
Catalog available online
Direct online sales
Founded: 1992
Gross sales or billing: $31,100,000

Provide help for member newspapers.

ᵀᴴᴱ NORTH POINT RESOURCES

4400 North Point Pkwy (Suite 152)
Alpharetta, GA 30022-2429
Telephone: (678) 892-5000, Web Site:
www.northpointstore.org

Assoc Dir Ministry: Daniel Stonaker

Provide Christian resources

THE DMA NORTH SHORE ANIMAL LEAGUE AMERICA INC
750 Port Washington Blvd
Port Washington, NY 11050-3720
Telephone: (516) 883-7900, FAX: (516) 883-8256, E-Mail: donorservices@nsalamerica.org, Web Site: www.nsalamerica.org
Pres: J. John Stevenson
VP Devel: Glen Bonderenko
List Mgr: Lori Murray
VP Devel: Alesia Sottanpanah
Sr Dir & List Mgr: Danielle Griffin
Conducts Business: U.S.
Employees: 250
Primary Market Served: Consumer
Catalog available online
Direct online sales
Advertising/Marketing Budget Related to Direct Marketing: 0-25%
Founded: 1944

Direct mail sweepstakes for fundraising purposes.

NOVA SOUTHEASTERN UNIVERSITY - FSEHS
1750 NE 167th St
North Miami Beach, FL 33162-3017
Telephone: (954) 262-8651, Web Site: www.schoolofed.nova.edu
Exec Dir Creative Devel & Innovation: Brian Croswhite
Primary Market Served: Consumer

OMP
1133 19th St NW (Suite 300)
Washington, DC 20036-3610
Telephone: (202) 467-0048, Web Site: www.ompdirect.com
COO: Anita Pearson

Full service fundraising & communications agency

OMSI INC
9480 N Demazenod Dr
Belleville, IL 62223-1159
Telephone: (618) 398-7640, Web Site: www.oblatesusa.org

Missionaries

OBLATE MISSIONS
323 Oblate Dr, PO Box 659432
San Antonio, TX 78265-9432
Telephone: (210) 736-1685, FAX: (210) 736-1314
Mktg: Ken Amerson

THE DMA OCEAN CONSERVANCY
1300 19th St NW
Washington, DC 20036

Telephone: (202) 429-5609, Web Site: www.oceanconservancy.org
Primary Market Served: Business & Consumer

OKLAHOMA DEPT OF COMMERCE
900 N Stiles Ave
Oklahoma City, OK 73104-3234
Telephone: (405) 815-6552, (800) 879-6552, FAX: (405) 815-5344, Web Site: www.okcommerce.com
Exec Dir: Ron Bussert
Sec: Russell Perry
Sec Commerce & Tourism: Kathy Taylor
Employees: 1,007
Primary Market Served: Business

An economic developer in Oklahoma.

THE DMA OPERATION SMILE INC
6435 Tidewater Dr
Norfolk, VA 23509-1600
Telephone: (757) 321-7645, Web Site: www.operationsmile.org
Sr VP Response Mktg & Devel: Kyla Shawyer

ORAL ROBERTS UNIVERSITY
Graduate Ctr (7th fl), 7777 S Lewis Ave
Tulsa, OK 74171
Telephone: (918) 495-6161, FAX: (918) 495-6222, E-Mail: admissions@oru.edu, Web Site: www.oru.edu
Pres: Richard Roberts
Dean: Dr. Debbie Sowell
VP, Devel: George Fisher
Conducts Business: Worldwide
Primary Market Served: Consumer
Catalog available online

Non-profit religious organization.

ORANGE LEAP
13800 Montfort Dr (Suite 220)
Dallas, TX 75240-4347
Telephone: (972) 220-0341, Web Site: www.orangeleap.com
CEO: Randy McCabe
Office Mgr: Leslie McCabe

Provides software-based solutions to non-profit organizations

THE DMA ORION
33926 9th Ave S
Federal Way, WA 98003-6708
Telephone: (253) 661-7805, Web Site: www.orionworks.org
Dir, Teleservices: Mathew Van De Voorde

Orion provides job assessment, training, placement and support services to individuals with disabilities & barriers to employment

OUR LADY OF VICTORY HOMES OF CHARITY
780 Ridge Rd
Lackawanna, NY 14218-1682
Telephone: (716) 828-9648, FAX: (716) 828-9643, E-Mail: rheist@olv-bvs.org, Web Site: www.ourladyofvictory.org
Exec VP & Treas: Rev. Msgr Paul J.E. Burkarel
Exec Dir: Richard L. Heist
Conducts Business: U.S., Canada
Employees: 65
Primary Market Served: Consumer
Advertising/Marketing Budget Related to Direct Marketing: 0-25%
Direct Marketing ad budget:
Direct Mail: 100%
Founded: 1854

Raise funds to subsidize the programs of Baker Victory Services, a therapeutic program for children with emotional disturbances & mental illnesses, children with physical & mental disabilities & unwed mothers.

THE DMA OXFAM AMERICA
226 Causeway St (5th fl)
Boston, MA 02114-2155
Telephone: (617) 482-1211, (800) 776-9326, FAX: (617) 728-2594, E-Mail: kmallette@oxfamamerica.org, Web Site: www.oxfamamerica.org
Dir Annual Fund: Ken Mallette

International relief & development organization

PC ONTARIO FUND
401-19 Duncan St
Toronto, ON, Canada M5H 3H1
Telephone: (416) 861-3085, (416) 861-0020, (800) 903-6453, FAX: (416) 861-1760, (416) 861-9593, E-Mail: comments@ontariopc.net, Web Site: www.ontariopc.com
Party Leader: Tim Hudak
Conducts Business: Canada
Primary Market Served: Business & Consumer
Advertising/Marketing Budget Related to Direct Marketing: 51-75%

Political fund-raising.

PALLOTTINE CENTER FOR APOSTOLIC CAUSES INC/ ST JUDE SHRINE
Div. of Catholic Church of the US
512 W Saratoga St
Baltimore, MD 21201-1896

Telephone: (410) 685-6026, (877) 278-5833, FAX: (410) 234-1459, E-Mail: info@stjudeshrine.org, Web Site: www.stjudeshrine.org
Pastoral Dir: Father Louis Micca
Asst Pastoral Dir: Father Joseph Kochar
Pastor: Father Frank Donio
Pastor: Father Peter Sticco
Conducts Business: U.S.
Employees: 19
Primary Market Served: Consumer
Catalog available online
Indirect online sales
Direct Marketing ad budget:
Direct Mail: 100%
Founded: 1953
Gross sales or billing: $600,000

Social services religious fund-raising organization promoting devotions to St. Jude.

THE DMA PARALYZED VETERANS OF AMERICA

801 18th St NW
Washington, DC 20006-3517
Telephone: (202) 416-7636, (800) 424-8200, FAX: (202) 416-7643, E-Mail: info@pva.org, Web Site: www.pva.org
Pres: Randy L. Pleva
Natl Sr VP: Gene A. Crayton
Natl VP: Jack Franklin
Assoc Exec Dir: Mark Dowis
Natl VP: John T. Jackson
Natl VP: Richard C. Glotfelty
Conducts Business: U.S.
Employees: 300
Primary Market Served: Consumer
Catalog available online
Direct online sales
Advertising/Marketing Budget Related to Direct Marketing: 76-100%
Direct Marketing ad budget:
Direct Mail: $20,000,000
Founded: 1946
Gross sales or billing: $111,000,000

Advocate for appropriate health care & benefits for veterans. Promotes medical research to cure spinal cord dysfunction & educates society about the abilities of the disabled.

PARKINSON'S DISEASE FOUNDATION

710 West 168th St.
New York, NY 10032
Telephone: (212) 923-4700, (800) 457-6676, FAX: (212) 923-4778, Web Site: www.pdf.org
Exec Dir: Robin Elliot

THE DMA PENN STATE HAZLETON

76 University Dr
Hazleton, PA 18202-8025

Telephone: (570) 450-3175, Web Site: www.hn.psu.edu
Dir Institutional Advancement: Kevin Salaway
Primary Market Served: Consumer

PEOPLE FOR THE AMERICAN WAY

1101 15th St NW Ste 600
Washington, DC 20005-5023
Telephone: (202) 467-2352, Web Site: www.pfaw.org
Membership Dir: Steve Kaufman

PHARMACEUTICAL CARE MANAGEMENT ASSOCIATION

601 Pennsylvania Ave NW Ste 740S
Washington, DC 20004-2699
Telephone: (202) 207-3610, FAX: (202) 207-3623, E-Mail: info@pcmanet.org, Web Site: www.pcmanet.org
Pres & CEO: Mark Merritt
Asst VP, Pub Affairs & Policy: Timothy Brogan
Dir, Indus Rels & Policy: Kristen Pumphrey
Mgr, Indus Rels & Policy: John Stelmachowicz
Employees: 16
Primary Market Served: Business
Founded: 1975

Represents managed care pharmacy & healthcare partners in pharmaceutical care: managed healthcare organizations, PBMs, HMOs, PPOs, third party administrators & community pharmacy networks. Serves its members & America's healthcare system by promoting education, legislation, practice standards & research that foster quality, & affordable pharmaceutical care. Members serve more than 150 million.

PHILADELPHIA MUSEUM OF ART

PO Box 7646
Philadelphia, PA 19101-7646
Telephone: (215) 684-7840, Web Site: www.philamuseum.org
Dir Membership & Visitor Svcs: Suzette Sherman

PHONE BANK SYSTEMS INC

4990 Northwind Dr (Suite 235)
East Lansing, MI 48823-5091
Telephone: (517) 332-1500, FAX: (517) 332-1514, E-Mail: rusha@phonebanks.com, Web Site: www.phonebanks.com
Pres: Sarah Shaw

THE DMA PITTSBURGH PARKS CONSERVANCY

2000 Technology Dr (Suite 300)
Pittsburgh, PA 15219-3137
Telephone: (412) 682-7275, Web Site: www.pittsburghparks.org
Pres & CEO: Meg Cheever

PLAN USA

US Member of Plan International
155 Plan Way
Warwick, RI 02886-1099
Telephone: (401) 737-5770, (800) 556-7918, FAX: (401) 738-5608, Web Site: www.planusa.org
Mktg Mgr: Patte Brown
Mng Dir Opers & Commun: Carol Donelly
Youth Education & Action Asst: Laura Breeze
Plan Intl Press Officer: Jon Slater
Exec Dir: Thomas Miller
Conducts Business: Worldwide
Employees: 80
Primary Market Served: Consumer
Advertising/Marketing Budget Related to Direct Marketing: 76-100%
Direct Marketing ad budget:
Direct Mail: $1,600,000
Newspapers: $50,000
TV/Radio: $1,000,000
Telephone: $100,000
Founded: 1937
Gross sales or billing: $30,000,000

Recruit sponsors for needy children overseas. The cost to the sponsor is $22 per month.

THE DMA PLANNED PARENTHOOD FEDERATION OF AMERICA

434 W 33rd St
New York, NY 10001-2600
Telephone: (212) 261-4686, Web Site: www.plannedparenthood.org
Dir Response Mgr: Paul Vogel
Primary Market Served: Consumer

PLANNED PARENTHOOD MAR MONTE

Affiliate of Planned Parenthood Federation
1691 The Alameda
San Jose, CA 95126-2203
Telephone: (408) 287-7532, FAX: (408) 971-6935, Web Site: www.plannedparenthood.org
CEO: Linda Williams
CFO: John Giambruno
VP, Clinic Svcs: Lynn Fielder
Conducts Business: U.S.
Employees: 250
Primary Market Served: Consumer
Advertising/Marketing Budget Related to Direct Marketing: 0-25%
Founded: 1916

Reproductive health care provider in Santa Clara, San Benito, Santa Cruz, Sacramento Valley, San Joaquin Valley, the Central Valley including Fresno & Bakersfield, Reno & Monterey counties, including all of northern Nevada with 35 clinic sites. Extensive community education, training programs & family planning services provided to women, teens & men.

THE DMA PONTIFICAL MISSION SOCIETIES IN THE US

70 W 36th St (fl 8)
New York, NY 10018-1256
Telephone: (212) 563-8700, Web Site:
www.onefamilyinmission.org
Dir Devel & Programs, Editor,
Mission: Monica Yehle

POPULATION CONNECTION

2120 L St NW (Suite 500)
Washington, DC 20037-1534
Telephone: (202) 332-2200, Web Site:
www.populationconnection.net
Dir Mktg & Info Svcs: Ray Huber
Primary Market Served: Consumer

Grassroots population organization. Educate grades K-12 about unsustainable population growth

THE DMA RICHARD M PORDES LLC

99 Dolphin Cove Quay
Stamford, CT 06902-7716
Telephone: (203) 316-9190
Pres: Richard Pordes

PORTLAND CEMENT ASSOCIATION

5420 Old Orchard Rd
Skokie, IL 60077-1083
Telephone: (847) 966-6200, FAX:
(847) 966-9781, Web Site: www.
cement.org
Pres: John P. Gleason
Sr VP, Mktg Devel & Tech Svcs
Admin: George B. Barney
Staff VP, Mktg Promo: Mark A. Justman
Staff VP, Commun: Bruce D. McIntosh
Sr VP, Fin & Admin: James F. Rappel
Primary Market Served: Business & Consumer
Founded: 1917

Trade association.

THE DMA PORTLAND RESCUE MISSION

PO Box 3713
Portland, OR 97208-3713
Telephone: (503) 906-7605, Web Site:
www.portlandrescuemission.org
Dir Devel: Bill Miller

PREVENT BLINDNESS AMERICA

211 W Wacker Dr (Suite 1700)
Chicago, IL 60606-1375
Telephone: (800) 331-2020, Web Site:
www.preventblindness.org

THE DMA PRIESTS OF THE SACRED HEART

6889 S Lovers Ln Rd
Hales Corners, WI 53130-0900
Telephone: (414) 425-3383, FAX:
(414) 425-5719, Web Site: www.
poshusa.org
Exec Dir: William B. Rondeau
Assoc Dir: John Cain
Primary Market Served: Consumer

Solicit donations for the education of priests.

PRINT SERVICES DISTRIBUTION ASSOCIATION

401 N Michigan Ave Ste 2200
Chicago, IL 60611-4245
Telephone: (703) 836-6232, (800) 336-4641, FAX: (703) 836-2241, E-Mail:
psda@psda.org, Web Site: www.
psda.org
Pres: Robert O'Connell
VP: Michael Fisher
Treas: Joel Chyke
Exec VP: Peter Colainni
Bd Member: George Crump
Conducts Business: Worldwide
Employees: 48
Primary Market Served: Business
Catalog available online
Indirect online sales
Advertising/Marketing Budget Related to Direct Marketing: 0-25%
Founded: 1946

Trade association organized for promoting & encouraging the independent concept of business printed products distribution.

THE DMA THE PROFESSIONAL GOLFERS' ASSOCIATION OF AMERICA

100 Avenue of the Champions
Palm Beach Gardens, FL 33410-9601
Telephone: (561) 624-8400, Web Site:
www.pga.com
Dir, Consumer Mktg, Player Devel & Res: Paul Metzler
Primary Market Served: Consumer

THE PROFESSIONAL PUTTERS ASSOCIATION

Subs. of Putt-Putt Golf Courses of America Inc
300 S Liberty St (Suite 100)
Winston Salem, NC 27101-5279

Telephone: (336) 714-3950, (866)
PUTT-PUTT, FAX: (336) 714-3955,
Web Site: www.putt-putt.com
CEO: David Callahan
Mktg Dir: Sheri Shaw
Conducts Business: U.S., Canada, Japan, Lebanon, Indonesia, Australia
Employees: 300
Primary Market Served: Business & Consumer
Catalog available online
Indirect online sales
Advertising/Marketing Budget Related to Direct Marketing: 26-50%
Direct Marketing ad budget:
Direct Mail: 40%
Newspapers: 10%
TV/Radio: 40%
Telephone: 10%
Founded: 1960

Sports organization that rewards the nation's best putters cash prizes & awards through local, state, regional & national tournament competition on Putt-Putt Golf Courses.

PROFIT POTENTIALS INC

Div. of The Foreign Candy Co. Inc
1 Foreign Candy Dr
Hull, IA 51239-7719
Telephone: (712) 439-1496, (800) 543-5480, FAX: (712) 439-1434, Web
Site: www.profitpotentials.com
Pres: Peter W. De Yager
Mktg Mgr Fundraising: Barb Bentele
Conducts Business: U.S.
Employees: 50
Primary Market Served: Business & Consumer
Advertising/Marketing Budget Related to Direct Marketing: 26-50%
Direct Marketing ad budget: $400,000
Direct Mail: 20%
Magazines: 60%
Newspapers: 10%
Telephone: 10%
Gross sales or billing: $18,000,000

Sell fund-raising products to community groups, schools, churches, scouts & all other groups involved in fundraising activities.

THE DMA PROJECT HOPE

255 Carter Hall Ln
Millwood, VA 22646-0255
Telephone: (540) 837-2100, Web Site:
www.projecthope.org
Mgr Direct Mail: Dorothy Combs
Primary Market Served: Consumer

PROMOTION MARKETING ASSOCIATION (PMA) INC

650 1st Ave Fl 2
New York, NY 10016-3207

Telephone: (212) 420-1100, FAX: (212) 533-7622, E-Mail: pma@pmalink.org, Web Site: www.pmalink.org
Pres: Bonnie J. Carlson
Interim VP Mktg: Kathleen Mulcahy
Conducts Business: Worldwide
Primary Market Served: Business & Consumer
Catalog available online
Direct online sales
Founded: 1911

A not-for-profit organization and resource for research, education and collaboration for marketing professionals.

PROMOTIONAL PRODUCT PROFESSIONALS OF CANADA

6700 Cote-de-Liesse (Suite 100)
Saint-Laurent, PQ, Canada H4T 2B5
Telephone: (514) 489-5359, FAX: (514) 489-7760, (800) 489-8741, E-Mail: gladys@pppc.ca, Web Site: www.pppc.ca
Customer Svc Specialist: Claire Martin
Dir Communs: Carol Phillips
Dir Professional Devel: Chantal Fontaine
Dir Membership: Debbie Pinkerton
Dir, Info Tech: Marc C. Phillips
Events Mgr: Linda Sloan
Mktg Mgr: Gladys Kasp
Pres & CEO: Edward Ahad
Employees: 10
Primary Market Served: Business
Catalog available online
Indirect online sales
Founded: 1956

A major show & exposition of the Promotional Products Association of Canada, of interest to promotional products distributors & open only to members of the association.

RMA-THE RISK MANAGEMENT ASSOCIATION

1801 Market St (Suite 300)
Philadelphia, PA 19103-1628
Telephone: (215) 446-4000, FAX: (215) 446-4101, E-Mail: customers@rmahq.org, Web Site: www.rmahq.org
CEO: Allen Sanborn
Mktg & Commun Dir: Paul Kushner
Conducts Business: U.S., Canada, Puerto Rico
Employees: 80
Primary Market Served: Business
Direct Marketing ad budget:
Direct Mail: $350,000
Magazines: $5,000
Newspapers: $5,000
Founded: 1914

Association of bank loan & credit officers.

THE DMA RAPPAHANNOCK ELECTRIC COOPERATIVE

247 Industrial Ct
Fredericksburg, VA 22408-2443
Telephone: (540) 898-8500, Web Site: www.myrec.coop
Dir Mkt Devel: Todd Jordan

REDSTONE FEDERAL CREDIT UNION

220 Wynn Dr NW
Huntsville, AL 35893-0001
Telephone: (256) 837-6110, Web Site: www.redfcu.org
Adv VP Mktg: Kenneth Jost

REFEREE ENTERPRISES

PO Box 161
Franksville, WI 53126-0161
Telephone: (262) 632-8855, FAX: (262) 632-5460, E-Mail: questions@referee.com, Web Site: www.referee.com
Pres: Barry Mano
Mktg & Mngmt Dir: Tom Herre
Conducts Business: U.S., Canada
Employees: 21
Primary Market Served: Business & Consumer
Catalog available online
Direct online sales
Advertising/Marketing Budget Related to Direct Marketing: 76-100%
Direct Marketing ad budget:
Direct Mail: 100%

Manage the National Association of Sports Officials. Publish Referee magazine & two monthly newsletters.

RESEARCH TO PREVENT BLINDNESS INC

645 Madison Ave (fl 21)
New York, NY 10022-1010
Telephone: (212) 752-4333, (800) 621-0026, FAX: (212) 688-6231, E-Mail: inforequest@rpbusa.org, Web Site: www.rpbusa.org
Chmn: David F. Weeks
Pres: Diane S. Swift
Dir, Commun & Mktg: Matthew Levine
COO: James V. Romano
Conducts Business: U.S.
Employees: 10
Primary Market Served: Business & Consumer
Founded: 1960

Non-profit voluntary health agency funding research into the causes & treatment of blinding diseases.

ROSE RESNICK LIGHTHOUSE FOR THE BLIND & VISUALLY IMPAIRED

214 Van Ness Ave
San Francisco, CA 94102
Telephone: (415) 431-1481, FAX: (415) 863-7568, E-Mail: executive@lighthouse-sf.org, Web Site: www.lighthouse-sf.org
Exec Dir: Anita S. Baldwin
Chief Devel Officer: George L. Clark
CFO: Howard Maull
Sr Dir Svcs: Kathy Abrahamson
Devel & Mktg Assoc: Andrea Ogarrio
Conducts Business: U.S.
Employees: 12
Primary Market Served: Business & Consumer
Founded: 1993

Develop & deliver services to people who are blind or visually impaired.

THE DMA LW ROBBINS ASSOCIATES

201 Summer St
Holliston, MA 01746-2258
Telephone: (508) 893-0210, (800) 229-5972, FAX: (508) 893-0212, E-Mail: ppapsador@lwra.com, Web Site: www.lwra.com
Pres: Lynn S. Edmonds
Dir Mktg: Polly Papsadore
Primary Market Served: Consumer
Advertising/Marketing Budget Related to Direct Marketing: 76-100%
Founded: 1970

Strategic fundraising specialists serving non-profit organizations.

THE DMA ROCHESTER INSTITUTE OF TECHNOLOGY

55 Lomb Memorial Dr
Rochester, NY 14623-5602
Telephone: (585) 475-7436, Web Site: www.rit.edu
Mng Editor, Print in the Mix: Liz Dopp

ROSICRUCIAN ORDER AMORC

1342 Naglee Ave
San Jose, CA 95191
Telephone: (408) 947-3600, FAX: (408) 947-3677, E-Mail: rosicrucian@amorcmail.org, Web Site: www.rosicrucian.org
Pres: Julie Scott
Conducts Business: U.S., Canada, Europe, Central America, S. America, Africa, Asia, Australia, Mexico.
Employees: 65
Primary Market Served: Business & Consumer
Advertising/Marketing Budget Related

to Direct Marketing: 0-25%
Founded: 1915
Gross sales or billing: $10,000,000

Books, audio & video cassettes, miscellaneous, to members & the public. Study course to members.

RURAL ALASKA COMMUNITY ACTION PROGRAM INC
aka RurAL CAP
731 E 8th Ave
Anchorage, AK 99501-3772
Telephone: (907) 279-2511, FAX: (907) 278-2309, Web Site: www. ruralcap.com
Exec Dir: David Hardenbergh
Employees: 500
Primary Market Served: Business & Consumer
Gross sales or billing: $20,000,000

Non-profit community action program.

ᴛʜᴇ ᴅᴍᴀ SCA DIRECT
11200 Waples Mill Rd (Suite 150)
Fairfax, VA 22030-7418
Telephone: (703) 293-6339, Web Site: www.scadirect.com
VP Mktg: Katie Oakes

Provides marketing to non-profit organizations.

SIFMA
120 Broadway (fl 35)
New York, NY 10271-0080
Telephone: (212) 313-1200, FAX: (212) 313-1301, E-Mail: inquiry@ sifma.org, Web Site: www.sifma.org
Pres & CEO: T. Timothy Ryan Jr
Employees: 70
Primary Market Served: Business
Catalog available online
Founded: 1976

Trade association.

SOS CHILDREN'S VILLAGES - USA
1001 Connecticut Ave NW Ste 1250
Washington, DC 20036-5520
Telephone: (202) 347-7920, Web Site: www.sos-usa.org
Comptroller: David Stinson

THE SAINT FRANCIS ACADEMY INC
509 E Elm St
Salina, KS 67401
Telephone: (785) 825-0541, (800) 423-1342, FAX: (785) 825-2940, Web Site: www.st-francis.org
Pres & CEO: Philip J. Rapp
Sr VP & COO: John A. Cosco
VP Fin Svcs: David G. Schatz

VP Care Svcs: Joan Shirley
VP Mngmt Svcs: Joseph Stratton
Conducts Business: U.S.
Employees: 400
Primary Market Served: Business & Consumer
Catalog available online
Advertising/Marketing Budget Related to Direct Marketing: 0-25%
Direct Marketing ad budget:
Direct Mail: 60%
Magazines: 20%
Newspapers: 20%
Founded: 1945

Fund-raising for community-based treatment programs for boys & girls. A system of behavioral, healthcare, non-profit hospitals & programs treating at-risk youth ages 10-18. Located in Indianapolis, IN; Salina, Ellsworth, & Atchison, KS; Picayune & Pascaguola, MS; Santa Fe, Espanola, NM; Lake Placid, NY; Philadelphia, PA & Cincinnati, OH.

ST JOSEPH'S COLLEGE
245 Clinton Ave
Brooklyn, NY 11205-3602
Telephone: (718) 399-1223, Web Site: www.sjcny.edu
Coord Recruitment & Mktg: Robert Napolitano
Primary Market Served: Consumer

ᴛʜᴇ ᴅᴍᴀ ST JOSEPH'S INDIAN SCHOOL
1301 N Main St
Chamberlain, SD 57325-1656
Telephone: (605) 734-3300, Web Site: www.stjo.org
Exec Dir Devel: Kory Christianson

ᴛʜᴇ ᴅᴍᴀ ST LABRE INDIAN SCHOOL
PO Box 77
Ashland, MT 59003-0077
Telephone: (406) 784-4500, Web Site: www.stlabre.org
Devel Assoc: Rachel Earl
Advertising/Marketing Budget Related to Direct Marketing: 26-50%
Direct Marketing ad budget:
Direct Mail: 97%
Online: 2%
Telephone: 1%
Founded: 1884

ST PETERSBURG/ CLEARWATER AREA CVB
13805 58th St N (Suite 2-200)
Clearwater, FL 33760-3716
Telephone: (727) 464-7200, Web Site: www.floridasbeach.com
Internet Mktg Mgr: Deborah Holland
Primary Market Served: Business & Consumer

ᴛʜᴇ ᴅᴍᴀ SALESIAN MISSIONS
2 Lefevre Ln
New Rochelle, NY 10801-5710
Telephone: (914) 633-8344, FAX: (914) 633-7404, E-Mail: info@ salesianmissions.org, Web Site: www.salesianmissions.org.
Production Coord: Jennifer Blum
Conducts Business: U.S.
Employees: 80
Primary Market Served: Business & Consumer
Catalog available online
Direct online sales
Advertising/Marketing Budget Related to Direct Marketing: 0-25%
Founded: 1962
Gross sales or billing: $40,000,000

Fundraising association supporting seminaries and missionaries at home and abroad who provide services to poor youth.

ᴛʜᴇ ᴅᴍᴀ THE SALVATION ARMY NATIONAL HEADQUARTERS
615 Slaters Ln
Alexandria, VA 22314-1112
Telephone: (703) 684-5500, Web Site: www.salvationarmyusa.org
National Community Rels & Devel Sec: George Hood

SANKY COMMUNICATIONS INC
599 11th Ave Fl 6
New York, NY 10036-2110
Telephone: (212) 868-4300, Web Site: www.sankyinc.com
Pres: Judy Maneval

Direct mail & website fundraising for non-profits

ᴛʜᴇ ᴅᴍᴀ SAVE THE CHILDREN FEDERATION INC
54 Wilton Rd
Westport, CT 06880-3108
Telephone: (203) 221-4000, (800) 728-3843, FAX: (203) 222-1067, E-Mail: twebster@savethechildren.org, Web Site: www.savethechildren.org
Pres & CEO: Charles MacCormack
VP & Mng Dir Devel: Diana Myers
Assoc Dir Mktg: Gail Arcamone
Conducts Business: Worldwide
Employees: 276
Primary Market Served: Business & Consumer
Advertising/Marketing Budget Related to Direct Marketing: 0-25%
Founded: 1932
Gross sales or billing: $332,400,000

Child assistance agency.

SCHOOL OF MANAGEMENT, THE UNIVERSITY OF TEXAS AT DALLAS
800 W Campbell Rd (SM 32)
Richardson, TX 75080-3021
Telephone: (972) 883-4421, Web Site: www.utdallas.edu
Primary Market Served: Consumer

College

SCHOOLCRAFT COLLEGE
18600 Haggerty Rd
Livonia, MI 48152-2696
Telephone: (734) 462-4417, Web Site: www.schoolcraft.edu
Dir Mktg: Marty Heator

THE DMA SCHULTZ & WILLIAMS INC
325 Chestnut St (Suite 700)
Philadelphia, PA 19106-2616
Telephone: (215) 625-9955, FAX: (215) 625-2701, E-Mail: mail@schultzwilliams.com, Web Site: www.sw-inc.com
Pres: L. Scott Schultz
Principal: M. Jane Williams
VP Direct Response: Jessica Harrington
VP: Rick Biddle
VP: Cathy Card Sterling
Conducts Business: U.S.
Employees: 9
Primary Market Served: Business
Founded: 1987

Consulting services to non-profit organizations in marketing & fund-raising. Creative through production, fulfillment & analysis of direct-mail.

SESAME WORKSHOP
1 Lincoln Plaza
New York, NY 10023-7163
Telephone: (212) 875-6677, Web Site: www.sesameworkshop.org
Primary Market Served: Consumer

SETON HALL UNIVERSITY
400 South Orange Ave
South Orange, NJ 07079-2646
Telephone: (973) 378-2650, Web Site: www.shu.edu
Dir Strategy Multi-Channel Mktg: Erin Weaver
Primary Market Served: Consumer

SICKKIDS FOUNDATION
525 University Ave (fl 14)
Toronto, ON, Canada M5G 2L3
Telephone: (416) 813-6166, Web Site: www.sickkidsfoundation.com
Dir Acquisitions: Biekke De La Mothe

THE DMA SIERRA CLUB BOOKS
Subs. of Sierra Club
85 Second St
San Francisco, CA 94105-3488
Telephone: (415) 977-5500, FAX: (415) 977-5792, E-Mail: books. publishing@sierraclub.org, Web Site: www.sierraclub.org
Publr: Helen Sweetland
COO & Chief Devel Officer: Deborah Sorondo
Conducts Business: Worldwide
Primary Market Served: Consumer
Catalog available online
Direct online sales
Advertising/Marketing Budget Related to Direct Marketing: 0-25%
Gross sales or billing: $85,000,000

Retailer of books, calendars & t-shirts on nature & the outdoors. Co-Publisher/Distributor: University of California Press

SIMMONS COLLEGE
300 Fenway
Boston, MA 02115-5898
Telephone: (617) 521-2027, Web Site: www.simmons.edu
Dir Online Mktg: Jake Berry

SMALL BUSINESS SERVICE BUREAU INC
554 Main St, PO Box 15014
Worcester, MA 01615-2014
Telephone: (508) 756-3513, (800) 343-0939, FAX: (508) 770-0528, E-Mail: membership@sbsb.com, Web Site: www.sbsb.com
Media Svcs Dir: Vincent J. Tynan
CEO: Francis R. Carroll
Conducts Business: U.S., China
Employees: 140
Primary Market Served: Business
Founded: 1968
Gross sales or billing: $12,500,000

National membership organization for small businesses.

THE DMA THE SMILE TRAIN
41 Madison Ave Rm 2801
New York, NY 10010-2325
Telephone: (212) 689-9199, Web Site: www.smiletrain.org
VP Mktg: Priscilla Ma
Primary Market Served: Consumer

SOCIETY FOR HUMAN RESOURCE MANAGEMENT
1800 Duke St (Suite 100)
Alexandria, VA 22314-3499
Telephone: (703) 548-3440, (800) 283-SHRM, FAX: (703) 535-6490, E-Mail: shrmstore@shrm.org, Web Site: www.shrm.org
Chair: Janet N. Parker
Treas: Robb E. Van Cleave
Pres & CEO: Laurence O'Neil
Sec: Nancy L. Volpe
Primary Market Served: Business & Consumer
Catalog available online
Direct online sales
Founded: 1948
Gross sales or billing: $88,000,000

S.H.R.M. is the voice of the human resource professionals, representing the interest of more than 77,000 professionals & student members from around the world.

THE DMA SOCIETY FOR NEUROSCIENCE
1121 14th St NW (Suite 1010)
Washington, DC 20005-5642
Telephone: (202) 962-4000
Dir, Membership & Mktg: Wendy Sturley

SOCIETY OF AMERICAN MAGICIANS INC
PO Box 505
Parker, CO 80134-0505
E-Mail: rmblowers@aol.com, Web Site: www.magicsam.com
Pres: Maria Ibanez
Natl Admin: Richard Blowers
Treas: Richard Dooley
Admin: Manon Rodriguez
Conducts Business: Worldwide
Employees: 6,000
Primary Market Served: Consumer
Catalog available online
Direct online sales
Direct Marketing ad budget:
Direct Mail: 30%
Magazines: 70%
Gross sales or billing: $150,000

Non-profit association of amateur & professional magicians & magic hobbyists. More than 200 local "Assemblies" throughout U.S. & foreign countries. Publish monthly magazine, M-U-M.

SOCIETY OF FINANCIAL SERVICE PROFESSIONALS
19 Campus Blvd (Suite 100)
Newtown Square, PA 19073-3239
Telephone: (610) 526-2500, FAX: (610) 527-1499, Web Site: www.financialpro.org
CEO: Joseph Frack
Conducts Business: U.S.
Employees: 53
Primary Market Served: Business
Advertising/Marketing Budget Related to Direct Marketing: 0-25%
Founded: 1928
Gross sales or billing: $7,000,000

Professional membership association. Services include continuing education programs & public relations tools sold to members & others in life insurance & financial services.

SOCIETY OF MANUFACTURING ENGINEERS

One SME Dr, PO Box 930
Dearborn, MI 48121
Telephone: (313) 425-3000, (800) 733-4763, FAX: (313) 425-3400, E-Mail: communications@sme.org, Web Site: www.sme.org
Exec Dir: Mark Tomilson
Dir, Expositions: Gary Mikola
Dir, HR: Jim Spilos
Dir, Fin: Bob Harris
Conducts Business: Worldwide
Employees: 300
Primary Market Served: Business
Catalog available online
Direct online sales
Founded: 1932

Technical training, technical books & videotapes. Also rent mailing lists from 570,000 name database.

THE DMA SOCIETY OF PETROLEUM ENGINEERS

222 Palisades Creek Dr
Richardson, TX 75080-2040
Telephone: (972) 952-9393, Web Site: www.spe.org
Mktg Mgr: Dana Otillio
Primary Market Served: Consumer

SOCIETY OF THE DIVINE SAVIOR

1303 Milwaukee Dr
New Holstein, WI 53061-1443
Telephone: (920) 898-4201
Production Svcs Mgr: Jean Keuler
Primary Market Served: Consumer

SOUTHERN CALIFORNIA GAS CO

1919 S State College Blvd
Anaheim, CA 92806-6114
Telephone: (714) 634-3054, (800) 427-2200, FAX: (714) 937-7712, E-Mail: Tjavid@socalgas.com, Web Site: www.socalgas.com
Pres & CEO: Debra L. Reed
COO: Michael R. Niggli
Sr VP & CFO: Dennis Arriola
VP Customer Opers: Pamela J. Fair
Pub Affairs Mgr: Tina Javid
Primary Market Served: Business & Consumer
Catalog available online
Indirect online sales
Advertising/Marketing Budget Related to Direct Marketing: 26-50%
Direct Marketing ad budget:
Direct Mail: $1,000,000

Public utilities company.

THE DMA SOUTHERN POVERTY LAW CENTER

400 Washington Ave
Montgomery, AL 36104-4344
Telephone: (334) 956-8200, FAX: (334) 956-8483, Web Site: www.splcenter.org
Chmn & Exec Committee: Morris Dees
Pres: Joseph J. Levin Jr.
Legal Dir: Rhonda Brownstein
Controller: Teeni Hutchinson
Dir, Membership: Wendy Via
Employees: 113
Primary Market Served: Consumer
Advertising/Marketing Budget Related to Direct Marketing: 76-100%
Direct Marketing ad budget:
Direct Mail: 80%
Telephone: 20%
Founded: 1971

Non profit organizations that combats hate, intolerance and discrimination through education and litigation.

THE DMA SPECIAL OLYMPICS INTERNATIONAL

1133 19th St NW Ste 1200
Washington, DC 20036-3645
Telephone: (202) 628-3630, FAX: (202) 824-0200, Web Site: www.specialolympics.org
VP Donor Devel: Joan Wheatley
Chmn Bd: Timothy Shrivers
Sr VP, Constituent Svcs & Support: Dr. Stephen B. Corbin
COO: John Dow
CIO: Andre Mendes
VP HR: Don Laing

Consumer/non-profit organization.

THE DMA SPECIALIZED ASSOCIATION SERVICES

130 E John Carpenter Fwy
Irving, TX 75062-2708
Telephone: (469) 524-5122, E-Mail: hvincent@1sas.com, Web Site: www.1sas.com
Pres: Jeff Jensen
Mktg Dir: Heidi Vincent
Conducts Business: U.S.
Employees: 100
Primary Market Served: Business
Catalog available online
Founded: 1986
Gross sales or billing: $3,500,000

Association management company, membership marketing and retention.

THE DMA SPECIALIZED INFORMATION PUBLISHERS ASSOCIATION (SIPA)

8229 Boone Blvd (Suite 260)
Vienna, VA 22182-2661
Telephone: (703) 992-9339, (800) 356-9302, FAX: (703) 610-9005, E-Mail: info@sipaonline.org, Web Site: www.sipaonline.com
Pres: Richard M. Ossoff
VP: Wayne Cooper
Exec Dir: Henry Greene
VP, Publications: Andy McLaughlin
Treas: Guy Cecala
Conducts Business: Worldwide
Primary Market Served: Business & Consumer
Catalog available online
Indirect online sales
Direct Marketing ad budget:
Direct Mail: 100%
Founded: 1977

International trade association of subscription newsletter publishers & information services.

SPECIALTY EQUIPMENT MARKET ASSOCIATION

1575 S Valley Vista Dr
Diamond Bar, CA 91765-3914
Telephone: (909) 396-0289, Web Site: www.sema.org
VP Mktg & Member Svcs: Tom Myroniak
Primary Market Served: Consumer

DON STEWART ASSOCIATION

PO Box 21004
Tulsa, OK 74121-1004
Telephone: (602) 678-3280, FAX: (602) 678-3288, Web Site: www.donstewartassociation.com
Pres: Don Stewart
Conducts Business: Worldwide
Employees: 30
Primary Market Served: Consumer
Catalog available online
Direct online sales

Non-profit religious organization involved in humanitarian causes.

THE DMA STRATEGIC FUNDRAISING INC

7591 9th St N
Saint Paul, MN 55128-6626
Telephone: (651) 649-0404, Web Site: www.strategicfundraising.com
Dir Bus Devel: Paul Wilson

THE DMA STRATMARK

855 E Collins Blvd
Richardson, TX 75081-2251

Telephone: (800) 222-6070, Web Site: www.stratmark.com

Sr VP: Max Bunch

Direct marketing & non-profit fund-raising

STUDENT UNION AT SJSU

211 S 9th St
San Jose, CA 95192-0001
Telephone: (408) 924-6353, Web Site: www.union.sjsu.edu
Mktg & Info Svcs: Gloria Robertson

THE DMA SUSTAINABLE FORESTRY INITIATIVE INC

900 17th St NW Ste 700
Washington, DC 20006-2515
Telephone: (202) 596-3450, FAX: (202) 596-3451, E-Mail: info@sfiprogram.org, Web Site: www.sfiprogram.org
Office Mgr: Julia Hershberger

JIMMY SWAGGART MINISTRIES

8919 World Ministry Ave Ste B
Baton Rouge, LA 70810-9007
Telephone: (225) 768-8300, (800) 288-8350, FAX: (225) 769-2244, Web Site: www.jsm.org
Owner: Rev Jimmy Swaggart
Conducts Business: Worldwide
Primary Market Served: Consumer
Catalog available online
Direct online sales

Spread the gospel.

SYRACUSE UNIVERSITY

820 Comstock Ave
Syracuse, NY 13244-0001
Telephone: (315) 443-4944, Web Site: syr.edu
Exec Dir, Devel Communs: Veronica Hotaling

TAPPI (TECHNICAL ASSOCIATION OF THE PULP & PAPER INDUSTRY)

15 Technology Pkwy S
Norcross, GA 30092-2923
Telephone: (678) 642-66, (800) 332-8686, FAX: (770) 446-6947, E-Mail: webmaster@tappi.org, Web Site: www.tappi.org
Chmn: Mark R. McCollister
Vice Chmn: Jeffrey J. Siegel
Pres: Larry N. Montague
Dir: Katherine Gibson
Dir: Charles E. Hodges
Conducts Business: Worldwide
Employees: 91
Primary Market Served: Business
Catalog available online
Direct online sales

Advertising/Marketing Budget Related to Direct Marketing: 51-75%
Direct Marketing ad budget:
Direct Mail: $400,000

Association serving the pulp & paper, packaging & converting, non-wovens & allied industries. Membership includes over 30,000 industry professionals from over 80 countries.

TECHBA - FUMEC

1737 1st St (Suite 110)
San Jose, CA 95112-4522
Telephone: (408) 821-6297, Web Site: www.techba.com

THE DMA THD INC

80 Hayden Ave (Suite 300)
Lexington, MA 02421-7962
Telephone: (781) 859-1400), Web Site: www.thdinc.com
Co-Founder & EVP: Jay Denison

Full service non-profit agency

TAYMARK INC

dba M&N International; Parent is Taylor Corp
4875 White Bear Pkwy
White Bear Lake, MN 55110
Telephone: (651) 426-1667, (800) 479-2043, FAX: (651) 426-0275, Web Site: www.mninternational.com
Pres: Troy Ethen
Mktg Mgr: David Larson
Employees: 350
Primary Market Served: Business & Consumer
Catalog available online
Indirect online sales
Founded: 1970
Gross sales or billing: $59,200,000

Sell goods for holidays & theme parties, as well as novelty promotional items to businesses & consumers.

THE DMA TEACHERS CREDIT UNION

110 S Main St
South Bend, IN 46601-1833
Telephone: (574) 284-6455, Web Site: www.tcunet.com
Res Analyst: Julie Sisco

THE DMA TEXAS CHILDREN'S HOSPITAL

1919 S Braeswood
Houston, TX 77030-4412
Telephone: (832) 824-2936, Web Site: www.texaschildrenshospital.org
Dir Annual Giving: Christine Paust
Primary Market Served: Consumer

THE DMA TEXAS FARM BUREAU INSURANCE COMPANIES

1200 Sycamore St
Waxahachie, TX 75165-2397
Telephone: (972) 825-4842, Web Site: www.sagu.edu
Dir Mktg: Ryan McElhany

TEXAS PARKS & WILDLIFE DEPT

4200 Smith School Rd
Austin, TX 78744
Telephone: (512) 389-4800, (800) 792-1112, FAX: (512) 389-8029, Web Site: www.tpwd.state.tx.us
Dir: Peter P. Flores
Project Mgr: Walter Moldenhauer
Division Attorney: Boyd Kennedy
Budget/Purchasing: Brenda Braune
Primary Market Served: Business & Consumer

State agency.

THEATRE DEVELOPMENT FUND INC

520 8th Ave (Suite 801)
New York, NY 10018-6507
Telephone: (212) 912-9770, E-Mail: info@tdf.org, Web Site: www.tdf.org
Chmn Bd: Earl D. Weiner
Exec Dir: Victoria Bailey
Mng Dir: Veronica Claypool
Commun Dir: David LeShay
Devel Mgr: Patty Allen
Conducts Business: U.S.
Employees: 77
Primary Market Served: Business & Consumer
Founded: 1968

Promote marketing services for commercial & non-profit theatre, dance & music. Mailing list owner of TKTS Times Square ticket booth purchasers list.

THIRTEEN/WNET

450 W 33rd St
New York, NY 10001
FAX: (212) 560-1314, Web Site: www.thirteen.org
Gen Counsel: Eleanor Applewhaite
Commun Dir: Stella Giammasi
Conducts Business: U.S.
Primary Market Served: Business & Consumer

Public television station soliciting membership contributions by direct mail.

STEPHEN THOMAS

184 Front St E (Suite 501)
Toronto, ON, Canada M5A 4N3

Telephone: (416) 690-8801, FAX: (416) 690-7256, E-Mail: mail@stephenthomas.ca, Web Site: www.stephenthomas.ca
Chmn & Creative Dir: Steve Thomas
Pres: Marie Sauve Lloyd
VP, Client Svcs: Mary Attfield
Conducts Business: U.S., Canada, Australia, W. Europe
Employees: 30
Primary Market Served: Business & Consumer
Founded: 1980
Gross sales or billing: $2,000,000

Direct marketing consultant specializing in fund-raising. Clients include charities, causes, political campaigns, educational institutions, PBS stations, universities & hospitals.

TORONTO HYDRO-ELECTRIC SYSTEM

14 Carlton St
Toronto, ON, Canada M5B 1K5
Telephone: (416) 542-2743, Web Site: www.torontohydro.com
Mktg & Communs: Marina Tomasone
Primary Market Served: Business

Provides municipal electric distribution utility service

THE DMA TRANSITCENTER INC

1065 Avenue of the Americas
New York, NY 10018-1878
Telephone: (212) 329-2000, Web Site: www.transitcenter.com
VP Mktg: Susan Ginsberg O'Sullivan
Primary Market Served: Consumer

TRAVEL INDUSTRY ASSOCIATION

1100 New York Ave NW Ste 450W
Washington, DC 20005-6130
Telephone: (202) 408-8422, FAX: (202) 408-1255, E-Mail: feedback@tia.org, Web Site: www.tia.org
Pres & CEO: Roger Dow
Sr VP, Mktg & Prod Devel: Adam Vance
Sr VP, Bus Devel: Gary Oster
Dir Mktg: Rebecca Pearson
Conducts Business: U.S., Canada, Mexico, Europe
Employees: 54
Primary Market Served: Business & Consumer
Advertising/Marketing Budget Related to Direct Marketing: 76-100%
Founded: 1973

National non-profit center for travel & tourism research. Produce reports on demographics & trip characteristics of U.S. travelers.

THE DMA TROUT UNLIMITED

1300 17th St N (Suite 500)
Arlington, VA 22209-3800
Telephone: (703) 522-0200, Web Site: www.tu.org
Membership Mktg Dir: Lori Held
Primary Market Served: Business

THE DMA UCEA

910 Commonwealth Ave
Boston, MA 02215-1204
Telephone: (617) 738-6410, FAX: (617) 734-1452, Web Site: www.revike.org
DM Project Mgr: Carolyn Jackson
Project Coord: Linda Norman
Conducts Business: U.S., Canada
Primary Market Served: Consumer

Fund-raising organization.

THE DMA UJA/FEDERATION OF NEW YORK

130 E 59th St
New York, NY 10022-1302
Telephone: (212) 980-1000, FAX: (212) 785-9321, Web Site: www.ujafedny.org
Dir Telegiving: Mary Ellen Murphy
Mng Dir: Leslie Lichter
Conducts Business: Worldwide
Employees: 550
Primary Market Served: Consumer

Raise funds for social & human services programs for 130 agencies in New York, Long Island, Westchester, Israel & worldwide.

ULI-THE URBAN LAND INSTITUTE

1025 Thomas Jefferson St NW (Suite 500W)
Washington, DC 20007-5201
Telephone: (202) 624-7000, FAX: (202) 624-7140, Web Site: www.uli.org
Pres: Rick Rosan
Sr VP, Policy & Practice: Rachelle Levitt
Sr VP, Leadership & Outreach: Ann Oliveri
Sr Adv Mgr: Carmela Acampora
Conducts Business: Worldwide
Employees: 90
Primary Market Served: Business
Advertising/Marketing Budget Related to Direct Marketing: 76-100%
Direct Marketing ad budget:
Direct Mail: $800,000
Telephone: $100,000
Founded: 1936

Non-profit real estate development research & educational organization. Publish & sell books through direct mail.

THE DMA UNICEF

3 United Nations Plaza
New York, NY 10017-4486
Telephone: (212) 326-7000, Web Site: www.unicef.org
Intl Sls & Mktg Officer: Laura Colassano
Primary Market Served: Business & Consumer

UNICEF CANADA

2200 Yonge St (Suite 1100)
Toronto, ON, Canada M4S 2C6
Telephone: (416) 482-4444, (800) 567-4483, FAX: (416) 487-8875, E-Mail: on.secretary@unicef.ca, Web Site: www.unicef.ca
Chmn: Alan Ely
Vice Chmn: Christopher Lee-Fong
Sec: Dale Doan
Treas: Amy Tong
Pres & CEO: Nigel Fisher
Conducts Business: Canada
Employees: 60
Primary Market Served: Business & Consumer
Catalog available online
Advertising/Marketing Budget Related to Direct Marketing: 26-50%
Direct Marketing ad budget:
Direct Mail: 10%
Magazines: 75%
Online: 5%
Founded: 1955
Gross sales or billing: $6,500,000

Use direct marketing techniques to solicit donations & sell UNICEF greeting cards to individuals & corporations.

THE DMA UPMC HEALTH PLAN

Washington Pl (fl 9), 1 Chatham Ctr
Pittsburgh, PA 15219-3441
Telephone: (412) 454-3469, Web Site: www.upmchealthplan.com
Mgr Medicare Mktg: Alicia McVey

USC VITERBI SCHOOL OF ENGINEERING

3650 McClintock Ave, Olin Hall (Suite 5)
Los Angeles, CA 90089-1451
Telephone: (213) 740-2502, Web Site: http://viterbi.usc.edu/
Exec Dir Mktg & Communs: Leslie DaCruz
Dean: Yannis C Yortsos

USO INC

2111 Wilson Blvd Ste 1200
Arlington, VA 22201-3052
Telephone: (703) 908-6400, Web Site: www.usa.org
Primary Market Served: Consumer

Private, non-profit & non-political organization that aids troops & their families

THE DMA UMASS DARTMOUTH
285 Old Westport Rd
North Dartmouth, MA 02747-2356
Telephone: (508) 999-8403, Web Site: www.umassd.edu
Primary Market Served: Business & Consumer

THE DMA UNION PRIVILEGE, AFL-CIO
1125 15th St NW (Suite 300)
Washington, DC 20005-2707
Telephone: (202) 293-5330, FAX: (202) 293-5311, Web Site: www.unionplus.org
Pres: Leslie Tolf
Intl Pres: Samuel A. Cabral
VP Direct Mktg: Karol Olson
Exec VP: Linda Chavez-Thompson
Gen Sec & Treas: Vincent J. Bollon
Sec & Treas: Richard L. Trumka
Primary Market Served: Consumer
Catalog available online
Indirect online sales
Founded: 1986
Gross sales or billing: $4,500,000

Labor union organization.

UNITED CHURCH HOMES
170 E Center St
Marion, OH 43302-3815
Telephone: (740) 382-4885, (800) 750-0750, FAX: (740) 382-4884, Web Site: www.unitedchurchhomes.org
Pres & CEO: Brian Allen
Branch Mgr: Susan Chambers
Primary Market Served: Business & Consumer
Catalog available online

Provides older adults with Christian caring and quality services

THE DMA UNITED FARM WORKERS OF AMERICA, AFL-CIO
29700 Woodford-Tehachapi Rd
Keene, CA 93531
Telephone: (661) 823-6158, FAX: (661) 823-6177, E-Mail: execoffice@ufw.org, Web Site: www.ufw.org
Pres: Arturo Rodriguez
Sec & Treas: Sergio Guzman
Conducts Business: U.S.
Employees: 75
Primary Market Served: Consumer
Catalog available online
Direct online sales
Advertising/Marketing Budget Related to Direct Marketing: 51-75%
Founded: 1962

Labor Union supported through donations.

THE DMA UNITED JEWISH COMMUNITIES
25 Broadway Fl 17
New York, NY 10004-1015
Telephone: (212) 284-6500, Web Site: www.ujc.org
Mgr Direct Mktg Analysis: David Semler
Primary Market Served: Consumer

THE DMA UNITED NATIONS FEDERAL CREDIT UNION
2401 44th Rd (fl 7) Ct Sq Pl
Long Island City, NY 11101-4605
Telephone: (347) 686-6000, Web Site: www.unfcu.org
VP Mktg: Debra I. Da Costa
Primary Market Served: Consumer

UNITED NATIONS FOUNDATION
1800 Massachusetts Ave NW (Suite 400)
Washington, DC 20036-1218
Telephone: (202) 778-3539, Web Site: www.unfoundation.org
Dir Annual Giving: Denise Dolan

THE DMA UNITED SPINAL ASSOCIATION
7520 Astoria Blvd
East Elmhurst, NY 11370-1138
Telephone: (718) 803-3782, Web Site: www.unitedspinal.org
Sr VP Devel & Commun: Cary Castle
Primary Market Served: Business & Consumer

UNITED STATES BRONZE SIGN CO INC
811 Second Ave
New Hyde Park, NY 11040
Telephone: (516) 352-5155, FAX: (516) 352-1761, Web Site: www.usbronze.com
Pres: George T. Barbeosch
VP NY: Alan Kasten
Gen Mgr NY: Peter Kasten
Conducts Business: U.S.
Employees: 30
Primary Market Served: Business & Consumer
Advertising/Marketing Budget Related to Direct Marketing: 0-25%
Founded: 1933
Gross sales or billing: $2,000,000

Sell to churches, temples, organizations & commercial accounts. Trees of life, donor tablets, honor rolls, dedicatory tablets, memorial plaques & metal letters.

US CHAMBER OF COMMERCE
1615 "H" St NW
Washington, DC 20062-0001
Telephone: (202) 778-6063, (800) 638-6582, FAX: (202) 887-3430, Web Site: www.uschamber.com
Pres & CEO: Thomas J. Donohue
Exec VP & COO: David C. Chavern
Dir Opers: Rita Perlman
Exec VP, Congressional Rels: Bruce Josten
Sr VP, Communs: Carl Grant
Sr VP: Thomas Collamore
Conducts Business: Worldwide
Employees: 1,200
Primary Market Served: Business
Catalog available online
Direct online sales
Advertising/Marketing Budget Related to Direct Marketing: 76-100%
Founded: 1912
Gross sales or billing: $70,000,000

Publisher of Nation's Business & The Business Advocate. Produce TV programs. Lobbyist for business on economic legislative issues. Regional Offices: San Mateo, CA; Alpharetta, GA; Oak Brook, IL; Rockville, MD & Dallas, TX.

THE DMA US DEPARTMENT OF COMMERCE
Intl Trade Admin (Rm H-1124)
Washington, DC 20230-0001
Telephone: (202) 482-4582
Intl Trade Specialist: Bruce Harsh
Primary Market Served: Business & Consumer

US PHARMACOPEIA
5645 Fisher Ln
Rockville, MD 20852
Telephone: (301) 881-0666, FAX: (301) 816-8236
Sls & Mktg: Maureen Rawson
Primary Market Served: Business

Sets the drug standard for the U.S.

THE DMA UNITED STATES TENNIS ASSOCIATION
70 W Red Oak Ln
White Plains, NY 10604-3610
Telephone: (914) 696-7156, Web Site: www.usta.com
Dir Mktg: Sherry Elinsky

UNITED WAY OF GREATER TORONTO
26 Wellington St E (11th fl)
Toronto, ON, Canada M5E 1W9
Telephone: (416) 777-2001, FAX: (416) 777-0962, Web Site: www.unitedwaytoronto.com

Pres & CEO: Frances Lankin
COO & VP Fin: Catherine Smith
VP Resource Devel: Susan McIsaac
VP Mktg & Commun: Lyn Witham
Conducts Business: Canada
Primary Market Served: Business &
Consumer
Direct Marketing ad budget:
Direct Mail: 80%
Telephone: 20%
Gross sales or billing: $61,000,000

Help over 1.2 million people in Toronto through 205 agencies. The direct
marketing arm is responsible for soliciting donations outside of the traditional employee campaigns.

THE DMA UNITED WAY WORLDWIDE
701 N Fairfax St
Alexandria, VA 22314-2058
Telephone: (703) 836-7100, Web Site:
www.liveunited.org
Dir, Strategic Prods: Stephanie Brady

THE DMA UNIVERSITY OF AKRON
Business Admin Bldg 312
Akron, OH 44325-0001
Telephone: (330) 972-5758
Exec Dir: Dale Lewison
Primary Market Served: Business &
Consumer

THE DMA UNIVERSITY OF CALIFORNIA IRVINE EXTENSION
PO Box 6050
Irvine, CA 92616-6050
Telephone: (949) 824-5413, Web Site:
extension.uci.edu
Strategic Mktg Mgr: Michelle Mador-
sky
Primary Market Served: Consumer

UNIVERSITY OF CHICAGO GSB
450 N Cityfront Plaza Dr
Chicago, IL 60611-5500
Telephone: (312) 464-8733, Web Site:
www.chicagoexec.net
Assoc Dean: Steven LaCivita
Primary Market Served: Consumer

UNIVERSITY OF ILLINOIS COLLEGE OF LAS, OFFICE OF ADVANCEMENT
2111 S Oak St (Suite 100)
Champaign, IL 61820-0908
Telephone: (217) 333-7108, Web Site:
www.las.uiuc.edu
Sr Dir Commun: Holly Korab

UNIVERSITY OF ILLINOIS FOUNDATION
1305 W Green St (MC-386)
Urbana, IL 61801-2962
Telephone: (217) 333-0810, FAX:
(217) 333-5577, E-Mail: uif@
uillinois.edu, Web Site: www.uif.
uillinois.edu
Sr Reg Dir of Gift Devel: Stephen H.
Bell
Dir Mktg & Commun: Jim Gobberdiel
Dir of Principal Gifts: Margaret A.
Cline
Asst Dir of Annual Giving: Amy L.
Braghini
Gift Plng Advisor: Lynn Bennett
Conducts Business: U.S.
Employees: 125
Primary Market Served: Business &
Consumer
Advertising/Marketing Budget Related
to Direct Marketing: 51-75%
Direct Marketing ad budget:
Direct Mail: 50%
Telephone: 50%
Founded: 1935

Fund-raising arm of the University of
Illinois campuses at Chicago, Springfield & Urbana-Champaign.

THE DMA UNIVERSITY OF MINNESOTA
1420 Eckles Ave 340 Coffee Hall
Saint Paul, MN 55108-1030
Telephone: (612) 625-0256, Web Site:
www.cce.umn.edu
Mktg Mgr: Sheila Flatz
Primary Market Served: Consumer

UNIVERSITY OF MINNESOTA ALUMNI ASSOCIATION
Div. of University of Minnesota
200 Oak St SE (Suite 200)
Minneapolis, MN 55455-2040
Telephone: (612) 624-2323, (800) UM-
ALUMS, FAX: (612) 626-8167,
E-Mail: umalumni@umn.edu, Web
Site: www.umaa.umn.edu
Chair: Anthony R. Baraga
Vice Chair: Patricia S. Simmons
Pres: Robert H. Pruiniks
Sr VP, Academic Affairs & Provost: E.
Thomas Sullivan
Vice Provost & Dean: Craig Swan
Employees: 35
Primary Market Served: Consumer
Catalog available online
Direct online sales
Founded: 1904
Gross sales or billing: $1,500,000,000

Membership organization for alumni &
friends of the University of Minnesota.

THE DMA UNIVERSITY OF NORTH TEXAS
PO Box 311460
Denton, TX 76203-1460

Telephone: (940) 565-2205, Web Site:
www.unt.edu/journalism
Regents Professor: Roy Busby

UNIVERSITY OF PENNSYLVANIA
3451 Walnut St, 601 Franklin Bldg
Philadelphia, PA 19104-6285
Telephone: (215) 898-5000, FAX:
(215) 898-9659, Web Site: www.
upenn.edu
Pres: Amy Gutman
VP Devel & Alumni Rels: John H.
Zeller
Provost: Ronald J. Daniels
Dept Chair: Chuck Snow
Dept Chair: Lee A. Fleischer
DM Dir: Jean Findley
Conducts Business: U.S.
Primary Market Served: Consumer
Catalog available online
Founded: 1751

UNIVERSITY OF PENNSYLVANIA - VETERINARY MEDICINE (DEVELOPMENT)
3800 Spruce St (Suite 172E)
Philadelphia, PA 19104-4192
Telephone: (215) 898-1480, Web Site:
www.vet.upenn.edu
Dir Annual Giving: Mary Berger

UNIVERSITY OF SOUTHERN MISSISSIPPI
118 College Dr (Box 5016)
Hattiesburg, MS 39406-0001
Telephone: (601) 266-4734, Web Site:
www.usm.edu
Mktg Mgr: Melanie Gardner
Primary Market Served: Consumer

THE DMA UNIVERSITY OF TEXAS SCHOOL OF LAW
727 E Dean Keeton St, Continuing
Legal Education
Austin, TX 78705-3224
Telephone: (512) 232-1174, Web Site:
www.utcle.org
Primary Market Served: Consumer

UNIVERSITY OF WASHINGTON EDUCATIONAL OUTREACH
Box 359480
Seattle, WA 98195-9480
Telephone: (206) 685-6566, Web Site:
www.pce.uw.edu

Professional & continuing education

UNIVERSITY OF WISCONSIN-MADISON SCHOOL OF BUSINESS EXECUTIVE EDUCATION

601 University Ave Fluno Ctr for Exec Ed
Madison, WI 53715-1035
Telephone: (608) 441-7357
Dir Exec Mktg Education: Linda Gorchels
Primary Market Served: Consumer

VEGETARIAN AWARENESS NETWORK/VEGANET

PO Box 3545
Washington, DC 20027-0045
Telephone: (800) USA-VEGE, (800) 872-8343, FAX: (877) 329-8343
Pres: Lige Weill
Mktg Dir: Sean Anderson
Conducts Business: U.S., Canada
Primary Market Served: Business & Consumer
Advertising/Marketing Budget Related to Direct Marketing: 51-75%
Direct Marketing ad budget:
Direct Mail: 10%
Magazines: 20%
Newspapers: 30%
Telephone: 40%
Founded: 1980

THE DMA VERIDIAN CREDIT UNION

1827 Ansborough Ave
Waterloo, IA 50701-3629
Telephone: (319) 236-5692, (800) 235-3228, FAX: (319) 833-1185, E-Mail: sarahma@veridiancu.org, Web Site: www.veridiancu.org
VP Commun: Ann Longseth
Mgr Commun: Eric Kinman
Project Specialist: Amela Cejvanovic
Res Specialist: Sarah Austin
Conducts Business: U.S.
Employees: 400
Primary Market Served: Business & Consumer
Indirect online sales
Advertising/Marketing Budget Related to Direct Marketing: 0-25%
Direct Marketing ad budget: $40,000
Direct Mail: 100%
Founded: 1924

Financial services, members and non-members.

VERMONT SKI AREAS ASSOCIATION

26 State St Ste 12
Montpelier, VT 05602-2943
Telephone: (802) 223-2439, FAX: (802) 229-6917, E-Mail: info@skivermont.com, Web Site: www.skivermont.com
Pres: David Dillon

Mktg Dir: Molly Mahar Kerr
Conducts Business: U.S.
Primary Market Served: Consumer
Advertising/Marketing Budget Related to Direct Marketing: 0-25%
Founded: 1960

Trade association promoting skiing in the state of Vermont.

THE DMA VETERANS OF FOREIGN WARS (VFW) OF THE US-NATIONAL HEADQUARTERS

406 W 34th St Fl 11
Kansas City, MO 64111-2736
Telephone: (816) 756-3390, FAX: (816) 968-1149, E-Mail: info@vfw.org, Web Site: www.vfw.org
Chmn: Gary L. Kurpius
Pres: Allan F. Kent
Sec Treas: Lawrence M. Maher
Commander in Chief: George Lisicki
Sr Programs Coord: Rebecca Curtis
Primary Market Served: Business & Consumer
Catalog available online
Founded: 1899
Gross sales or billing: $86,300,000

Non-profit organization helping to meet the needs of veterans & their families.

THE DMA VIETNAM VETERANS OF AMERICA

8719 Colesville Rd (Suite 100)
Silver Spring, MD 20910-3710
Telephone: (301) 585-4000, Web Site: www.clothingdonations.org
Bus Mgr: Quentin Butcher
Primary Market Served: Consumer

VIRGINIA HOME FOR BOYS

8716 W Broad St
Richmond, VA 23294
Telephone: (804) 270-6566, FAX: (804) 270-6574, Web Site: www.boyshome.org
Exec Dir: Tod Balsbaugh
Conducts Business: U.S.
Employees: 50
Primary Market Served: Business & Consumer

Non-profit children's home providing residential care & services to disadvantaged young people.

THE DMA VOLUNTEERS OF AMERICA

1660 Duke St Ste 100
Alexandria, VA 22314-3427
Telephone: (703) 341-5000, Web Site: www.volunteersofamerica.org
Dir, Direct Mktg & Devel Info: Richard Frazier
Primary Market Served: Consumer

WGBH EDUCATIONAL FOUNDATION

1 Guest St
Brighton, MA 02135-2016
Telephone: (617) 300-5400, FAX: (617) 300-1026, Web Site: www.wgbh.org
Chmn Bd Trustees: Amos B. Hostetter Jr.
Pres & Chmn Bd: Henry P. Becton Jr.
Exec VP & COO: Jonathan C. Abbot
Employees: 1,100
Primary Market Served: Consumer
Catalog available online
Gross sales or billing: $198,000,000

Commercial activities including selling books, videos & gifts.

THE DMA WAKE FOREST UNIVERSITY BAPTIST MEDICAL CENTER

Medical Center Blvd
Winston Salem, NC 27157-0001
Telephone: (336) 716-4665, Web Site: www.wfubmc.edu
Dir PR & Mktg: Susan McBurney
Primary Market Served: Consumer

WALK THRU THE BIBLE MINISTRIES INC

4201 N Peachtree Rd
Atlanta, GA 30341-1207
Telephone: (770) 458-9300, Web Site: www.walkthru.org
CEO: Chip Ingram
Primary Market Served: Consumer

THE DMA MAL WARWICK ASSOCIATES

2550 9th St (Suite 103)
Berkeley, CA 94710-2551
Telephone: (510) 843-8888, FAX: (510) 843-0142, E-Mail: info@malwarwick.com, Web Site: www.malwarwick.com
Pres & CEO: Daniel S. Doyle

Develops direct marketing programs for non-profit causes

WASHINGTON MARKETING GROUP

5155 N 37th St
Arlington, VA 22207
Telephone: (703) 534-9331, FAX: (703) 534-0242, E-Mail: william.shaker@twmg.com, Web Site: www.twmg.com
CEO & Creative Dir: William Shaker
Conducts Business: U.S.
Employees: 4
Primary Market Served: Business & Consumer
Catalog available online
Indirect online sales
Advertising/Marketing Budget Related

to Direct Marketing: 76-100%
Direct Marketing ad budget:
Direct Mail: 100%
Founded: 1987
Gross sales or billing: $3,000,000

Full-service production, printing & creative organization, serving both non-profit & commercial clients.

THE DMA WASHINGTON UNIVERSITY
1 Brookings Dr
Saint Louis, MO 63130-4899
Telephone: (314) 935-4623, (800) 638-0700, FAX: (314) 935-7088, Web Site: www.wustl.edu
Chmn: David W. Kemper
Chancellor: Mark S. Wrighton
Exec VP Chancellor, Alumni & Devel Programs: David T. Blasingame
Mktg & Strategic Planning: Annette Unsur
Conducts Business: United States
Employees: 9,600
Primary Market Served: Consumer
Catalog available online
Gross sales or billing: $1,700,000,000

Fund-raising, development, alumnae resources.

WELLNESS COUNCILS OF AMERICA
17002 Marcy St (Suite 140)
Omaha, NE 68118-2933
Telephone: (402) 827-3590, FAX: (402) 827-3594, E-Mail: wellworkplace@welcoa.org, Web Site: www.welcoa.org
Pres: David Hunnicutt
Dir Membership: M.Ed. David K. Steurer
Conducts Business: U.S.
Employees: 8
Primary Market Served: Business
Advertising/Marketing Budget Related to Direct Marketing: 51-75%
Direct Marketing ad budget:
Direct Mail: 75%
Telephone: 25%
Founded: 1987

Books, manuals & videotapes for business owners & health promotion planners in companies on corporate health promotion. Mailing list for rent. Also, newsletters & brochures.

THE DMA WESTERN PENNSYLVANIA CONSERVANCY
800 Waterfront Dr Fl 2
Pittsburgh, PA 15222-4718
Telephone: (412) 288-2777, Web Site: www.paconserve.org
Dir Annual Fund: Pamela Geary
Primary Market Served: Business & Consumer

Non-profit conservation organization

SIMON WIESENTHAL CENTER
1399 Roxbury Dr Ste 100
Los Angeles, CA 90035-4709
Telephone: (310) 553-9036, Web Site: wiesenthal.com
Dir Membership Devel: Marlene Hier

THE DMA WIN-WIN GIVING
429 Waltham St
West Newton, MA 02465-1939
Telephone: (617) 645-5479
Pres: Mary Beth McIntyre

WINNIPEG ART GALLERY
300 Memorial Blvd
Winnipeg, MB, Canada R3C 1V1
Telephone: (204) 786-6641, FAX: (204) 788-4998, E-Mail: inquiries@wag.mb.ca, Web Site: www.wag.mb.ca
Adv: Heather Mousseau
Exec Asst: Sandra Udell
Mgr: Crystal Hiebert
Deputy Dir: Claire Whelan
Graphic Design: Lisa Frisen
Conducts Business: U.S., Canada
Employees: 60
Primary Market Served: Consumer
Founded: 1912

Public art gallery using direct mail for fund-raising & to sell art books, exhibition catalogs, reproductions & gift items.

WISCONSIN HISTORICAL FOUNDATION
368 Park Ave
Sun Prairie, WI 53590-3014
Telephone: (608) 318-1044
Dir Membership & Annual Giving: Martha Truby

WOMEN'S SPORTS FOUNDATION
Eisenhower Park 1899 Hemstead Turnpike
East Meadow, NY 11554-1099
Telephone: (516) 542-4700, Web Site: www.womenssportsfoundation.org
Annual Giving & Membership: Nicole Pawlak

WORLD FUTURE SOCIETY
7910 Woodmont Ave (Suite 450)
Bethesda, MD 20814
Telephone: (301) 656-8274, (800) 989-8274, FAX: (301) 951-0394, E-Mail: info@wfs.org, Web Site: www.wfs.org
Pres: Timothy C. Mack

Bus Mgr: Jefferson Cornish
Dir Commun: Patrick Tucker
Founder: Edward Cornish
Conducts Business: U.S., Canada, Australia, Western Europe
Employees: 13
Primary Market Served: Business & Consumer
Catalog available online
Indirect online sales
Advertising/Marketing Budget Related to Direct Marketing: 76-100%
Direct Marketing ad budget:
Direct Mail: $300,000
Founded: 1966
Gross sales or billing: $900,000

Membership association & publisher of periodicals & books dealing with social & technological change.

WORLD VILLAGES FOR CHILDREN
180 Admiral Cochrane Dr Ste 240
Annapolis, MD 21401-7367
Telephone: (301) 779-4141, Web Site: www.worldvillages.org
CEO: Joseph Vita
Primary Market Served: Business & Consumer

THE DMA WORLD VISION CANADA
One World Dr
Mississauga, ON, Canada L5T 2Y4
Telephone: (905) 565-6200 X2173, Web Site: www.worldvision.ca
Dir Bus Process Improvement: Dennis Ivancic

WORLD VISION INC
PO Box 9716
Federal Way, WA 98063-9716
Telephone: (253) 815-1000, (888) 511-6548, FAX: (253) 815-3140, E-Mail: info@worldvision.org, Web Site: www.worldvision.org
Pres & CEO: Richard Stearns
VP & Mktg Dir: Marty Lonsdale
CFO: Ken Cassey
Employees: 1,500
Primary Market Served: Consumer
Catalog available online
Direct online sales
Founded: 1953
Gross sales or billing: $274,600,000

Christian world relief and non-profit community development organization.

THE DMA WORLD WILDLIFE FUND
1250 24th St NW (fl4)
Washington, DC 20037-1145
Telephone: (202) 293-4800, Web Site: www.worldwildlife.org
Chief Mktg Officer: Terry Macko

YWCA OF THE USA
2025 M St NW (Suite 550)
Washington, DC 20036-3320
Telephone: (202) 467-0801, FAX:
(202) 467-0802, E-Mail: info@ywca.
org, Web Site: www.ywca.org
CEO: Lorraine Cole PhD
Employees: 53
Primary Market Served: Consumer
Founded: 1855
Gross sales or billing: $7,944,131

**THE DMA YELLOW PAGES
ASSOCIATION**
400 Connell Dr (Suite 1100), Connell
Corp Park
Berkeley Heights, NJ 07922-2818
Telephone: (908) 286-2380, (800) 336-
0440, FAX: (908) 286-0620, Web
Site: www.yellowpagesima.org
Pres: Negley Norton
VP, Commun: Stephanie Hobbs
Dir, Pub Policy: Amy Perlik Healy
Dir Res: Larry Small
CFO: Donna Borowicz
Conducts Business: Worldwide
Employees: 50
Primary Market Served: Business &
Consumer
Catalog available online
Direct online sales
Founded: 1988

Trade association representing the Yellow Pages industry.

**YOUNG AMERICA'S
FOUNDATION**
110 Elden St
Herndon, VA 20170-4891
Telephone: (800) USA-1776, Web Site:
www.yaf.org
Primary Market Served: Consumer

Principal outreach program of the con-
servative movement

**ZOOLOGICAL SOCIETY OF
SAN DIEGO**
2920 Zoo Dr, PO Box 120551
San Diego, CA 92112
Telephone: (619) 231-1515, FAX:
(619) 557-3937, Web Site: www.
sandiegozoo.org
Pres: Berit N. Durler
VP: Frederick A. Frye
Exec Dir: Douglas G. Myers
Treas: Frank C. Alexander
Sec: Rick Gulley
Primary Market Served: Business &
Consumer
Catalog available online
Founded: 1916

A-T SURGICAL MANUFACTURING CO

115 Clemente St
Holyoke, MA 01040-5644
Telephone: (413) 532-4551, (800) 225-2023, FAX: (413) 532-0826, E-Mail: atsmci@a-surgical.com, Web Site: www.atsurgical.com
Pres: Eugene P. Kirejczyk
VP: Cynthia F. Kirejczyk
Sls Mgr: Jim Puhala
Conducts Business: U.S.
Employees: 38
Primary Market Served: Business
Catalog available online
Direct online sales
Advertising/Marketing Budget Related to Direct Marketing: 0-25%
Founded: 1969
Gross sales or billing: $3,100,000

Health products & elastic supports.

AMC INC

Div. of The Portman Cos
240 Peachtree St NW (Suite 2200)
Atlanta, GA 30303-1327
Telephone: (404) 220-2000, FAX: (404) 220-3030
CFO: Hank Almquist
Exec VP, Sls & Mktg: Jeff Portman
Sr VP, Opers: Virginia Gorday
Mktg Mgr: Mike Turnbull
Conducts Business: Worldwide
Employees: 300
Primary Market Served: Business

Home accents & furnishings, holiday & floral, decorative garden accessories & area rugs. General gifts - table top, linens, fashion accessories, jewelry & gourmet.

THE DMA AEROSOLES

201 Meadow Rd
Edison, NJ 08817-6030
Telephone: (732) 985-6900, FAX: (732) 985-3697, E-Mail: bgarris@aerosoles.com, Web Site: www.aerosoles.com
Dir Catalog & Internet Opers: Robert Garris
VP Direct Mktg: Magnus Gustafsson

AMAZON DRYGOODS

411 Brady St
Davenport, IA 52801-1518
Telephone: (800) 798-7979, FAX: (563) 322-4003, E-Mail: info@amazondrygoods.com, Web Site: www.amazondrygoods.com
Pres: Janet Burgess
Conducts Business: Worldwide
Employees: 10

Primary Market Served: Business & Consumer
Indirect online sales
Advertising/Marketing Budget Related to Direct Marketing: 76-100%
Direct Marketing ad budget:
Magazines: 100%
Founded: 1982
Gross sales or billing: $1,000,000

Historic reproductions of 3,300 items in four catalogs. Clothing, shoes, hats, sewing patterns, books & much more.

THE DMA AMERICAN EAGLE OUTFITTERS

77 Hot Metal St
Pittsburgh, PA 15203-2382
Telephone: (412) 432-3382, Web Site: www.ae.com
Dir CRM: David Slavick
Mgr CRM: Casey Cassioli

HANNA ANDERSSON CORP

1010 NW Flanders
Portland, OR 97209
Telephone: (503) 242-0920, (800) 222-0544, FAX: (503) 321-5289, Web Site: www.hannaandersson.com
Pres & CEO: Phil Iosca
VP & CFO: Laura McCue
VP, HR: Gretchen Peterson
Conducts Business: U.S., Canada
Employees: 270
Primary Market Served: Business & Consumer
Gross sales or billing: $45,200,000

Mail order catalog of 100% cotton children's clothing.

THE DMA ARAMARK UNIFORM SERVICES

115 N First St
Burbank, CA 91502-1856
Telephone: (818) 953-2022, Web Site: www.aramark-uniform.com
Sr Dir, Base Bus Growth: Tom Maloney

BACHRACH CLOTHING INC

Div. of Sun Capital
323 W 39th St (Fl 11)
New York, NY 10018
Telephone: (630) 523-5035, Web Site: www.bachrach.com
Conducts Business: U.S.
Employees: 300
Primary Market Served: Consumer
Catalog available online
Direct online sales

Retail chain. Produce & mail catalogs featuring clothing for men.

MAURICE BADLER FINE JEWELRY LTD

578 Fifth Ave
New York, NY 10036
Telephone: (212) 575-9632, (800) M-BADLER, FAX: (212) 575-9205, E-Mail: info@badler.com, Web Site: www.badler.com
Pres: Jeffrey P. Badler
Primary Market Served: Consumer
Catalog available online
Indirect online sales
Advertising/Marketing Budget Related to Direct Marketing: 76-100%

Retailing & cataloging fine jewelry.

BANANA REPUBLIC

Div. of The Gap Inc
5900 N Meadows Dr
Grove City, OH 43123-9541
Telephone: (888) 277-8953, FAX: (888) 906-2465, Web Site: www.bananarepublic.com
Sr VP: Kay Isaacson
Conducts Business: U.S.
Primary Market Served: Consumer

Authentic, classic, travel & safari clothing in natural fabrics for men & women sold in retail stores.

JOSEPH A BANK CLOTHIERS INC

500 Hanover Pike
Hampstead, MD 21074-2002
Telephone: (410) 239-2700, (800) 285-2265, FAX: (410) 239-5911, E-Mail: service@jos-a-bank.com, Web Site: www.josbank.com
Pres, Chmn & CEO: Robert N. Wildrick
Exec VP: Robert Hensley
CFO & Exec VP, Admin: Dave Ullman
Mktg Mgr: Jerry Deboer
Conducts Business: U.S.
Employees: 2,000
Primary Market Served: Consumer
Catalog available online
Founded: 1905
Gross sales or billing: $500,000,000

Manufacturers & merchants of fine traditional clothing for men through own retail stores & catalog. Stores located throughout U.S.

BARELY NOTHINGS LINGERIE

560 W Tefft St.
Nipomo, CA 93444

Telephone: (805) 489-5591, (800) 422-7359, FAX: (888) 489-5987, E-Mail: lingerie@barelynothings.com, Web Site: www.getpassionhere.com
Co-Owner: Sandi Spinelli
Co-Owner: Ozzie Spinelli
Conducts Business: U.S.
Primary Market Served: Consumer
Catalog available online
Direct online sales
Advertising/Marketing Budget Related to Direct Marketing: 0-25%
Founded: 1991
Gross sales or billing: $600,000

Lingerie for sizes 4 to 14 & another catalog for sizes 16 to 26.

RG BARRY CORP
13405 Yarmouth Rd NW
Pickerington, OH 43147-8493
FAX: (614) 866-9787, E-Mail: sales@rgbarry.com, Web Site: www.rgbarry.com
Pres & CEO: Greg A. Tunney
Sr VP & CFO: Daniel D. Viren
Sr VP, Sls: Pam Gentile
Sr VP: Glenn Evans
Sr VP: Lee Evans
Conducts Business: U.S.
Employees: 2,500
Primary Market Served: Business & Consumer
Catalog available online
Direct online sales
Gross sales or billing: $108,900,000

Footwear manufacturer.

EDDIE BAUER
Div. of Spiegel
PO Box 7001
Groveport, OH 43125-7001
Telephone: (425) 882-6100, (800) 426-8020, FAX: (425) 556-7696, Web Site: www.eddiebauer.com
VP, Mktg: Bill Michel
Conducts Business: U.S., Canada
Primary Market Served: Consumer

Sell sportswear, footwear, home furnishings & accessories.

LL BEAN INC
Casco St
Freeport, ME 04033-0001
Telephone: (207) 865-4761, (800) 441-5713, FAX: (207) 552-3080, Web Site: www.llbean.com
Chmn: Leon Gorman
Pres: Christopher McCormick
Sr VP & COO: Bob Peixotto
Co-Spokesperson: Rich Donaldson
Chief Mktg Officer: Steve Fuller
Conducts Business: U.S.
Employees: 5,300
Primary Market Served: Business & Consumer

Catalog available online
Direct online sales
Advertising/Marketing Budget Related to Direct Marketing: 76-100%
Founded: 1912
Gross sales or billing: $1,400,000,000

Direct mail catalog featuring active & casual apparel for men, women & children, footwear, sporting equipment, luggage, furnishings & accessories for home & camp.

BENCONE UNIFORM CONNECTION
1855 Runnymede Rd
Winston Salem, NC 27104-3109
Telephone: (800) 326-3261, FAX: (866) 311-8254, E-Mail: bencone1@bellsouth.net, Web Site: www.bencone.com
Pres & CEO: Sanders Mosley
VP & Mktg Dir: Ben Mosley
Conducts Business: U.S.
Employees: 15
Primary Market Served: Business & Consumer
Catalog available online
Direct online sales

Sell professional uniforms & accessories to nurses, doctors, dentists, hospitals, restaurants & hotels. Also sell white professional shoes, hosiery, maternity uniforms, watches & novelty tops.

BENETTON USA
601 Fifth Ave
New York, NY 10017-1024
Telephone: (212) 593-0290, (800) 274-7192, FAX: (212) 371-1438, E-Mail: mtaylor@bennettonusa.com, Web Site: www.benetton.com
CEO: Carlo Tunioli
VP & Controller: Dian Marvoak
Conducts Business: Worldwide
Employees: 3,700
Primary Market Served: Business
Advertising/Marketing Budget Related to Direct Marketing: 0-25%
Gross sales or billing: $2,000,000,000

Marketer of men's, women's & children's clothing, including Nautica and Prince clothing.

BERGDORF GOODMAN
754 Fifth Ave
New York, NY 10019-2503
Telephone: (212) 753-7300, (800) 967-3788, (800) 218-4918, FAX: (212) 872-8677, E-Mail: clientservices@bergdorfgoodman.com, Web Site: www.bergdorfgoodman.com
VP: Linda Fargo
Conducts Business: U.S.

Primary Market Served: Consumer
Founded: 1901

Retail ladies' & men's apparel & decorative housewares.

THE BLACK DOG TAVERN CO INC
PO Box 2219, 20 Beach St Extension
Vineyard Haven, MA 02568
Telephone: (508) 696-8182, (800) 626-1991, Web Site: www.theblackdog.com; www.theblackdogtshirt.com
CEO: Robert S. Douglas
Dir Retail Opers: Jaime Douglas
Primary Market Served: Consumer
Founded: 1971

Restaurant-bakery, general store, & catalog on Martha's Vineyard for 25 years. Catalog features casual clothing & outerwear with Black Dog logo. Packaged foods prepared by the bakery: cookies, scotties, bread & jellies.

BLAIR CORP
220 Hickory St
Warren, PA 16366-0001
Telephone: (814) 723-3600, (800) 458-6057, FAX: (814) 726-6123, E-Mail: blair@blair.com, Web Site: www.blair.com
Pres & CEO: Adelmo S. Lopez
Conducts Business: U.S.
Employees: 900
Primary Market Served: Consumer
Direct Marketing ad budget:
Direct Mail: $67,300,000
Founded: 1910
Gross sales or billing: $433,000,000

Sell low to medium-priced men's and women's apparel and home furnishings, primarily by mail.

BLUBLOCKER CORP
3350 Palm Ctr Dr
Las Vegas, NV 89103-5668
Telephone: (702) 597-2000, (800) BLUBLOCKER, FAX: (702) 597-2002, Web Site: www.blublocker.com
Treas: Joseph Sugarman

BODYSCAPES INC
115 W 30th St (Rm 1202)
New York, NY 10001-4041
Telephone: (212) 243-2414, FAX: (212) 239-9058
Pres: Henrietta Drewes
VP: William Drewes
VP: Alyssa Drewes
Conducts Business: U.S.
Employees: 2
Primary Market Served: Consumer
Advertising/Marketing Budget Related

to Direct Marketing: 0-25%
Gross sales or billing: $100,000

Manufacturer & retailer of custom-made clothing for infants, children, and women.

BOSTON APPAREL GROUP
42 Thomas Patten Dr
Randolph, MA 02368-3902
Telephone: (508) 583-8110, Web Site:
www.bostonapparel.com
Sr Dir Catalog Mktg: Robert Bergdoll

VERA BRADLEY
2208 Production Rd
Fort Wayne, IN 46808-3660
Telephone: (800) 823-8372, Web Site:
www.verabradley.com
Dir Mktg: Stephanie Scheele
Primary Market Served: Business & Consumer

BROOKS BROTHERS
346 Madison Ave (fl 10
New York, NY 10017-3788
Telephone: (212) 682-8800, (800) 274-1815, FAX: (212) 309-7273, Web Site: www.brooksbrothers.com
Pres: Claudio Del Vecchio
CFO: Brian Baumann
Sr VP: Debra Del Vecchio
Dir, Adv & Pub Rels: Arthur Wayne
Dir CRM: Jan Cantler
Conducts Business: United States, Japan, China, Italy, United Kingdom
Employees: 3,500
Primary Market Served: Consumer
Catalog available online
Direct online sales
Founded: 1818
Gross sales or billing: $260,000,000

Men's, women's & boys' retail & mail order clothing.

ROBERT BRYAN LTD
909 Caroline St
Port Royal, VA 22535
Telephone: (804) 742-5555, (800) 742-8883, FAX: (804) 742-5220, E-Mail: customerservice@robertbryanltd.com, Web Site: www.robertbryanltd.com
Pres & CEO: Robert Bryan
Primary Market Served: Business
Catalog available online
Indirect online sales
Founded: 1993

Sell fine men's & women's shirts to high end retail stores, golf pro shops, exclusives shops & boutiques.

BRYLANE
Subs. of Pinault Printemps Redoute
Div. of Redcats
PO Box 8320
Indianapolis, IN 46283-8320
Telephone: (800) 677-0339, Web Site:
www.brylanehome.com
Chmn & CEO: Russell Stravitz
Pres Apparel Grp: Sheila Garelick
CFO & Sr VP: Pascal Cesbron Lavau
Exec VP Mktg Brylane: Jules Silbert
VP, Mktg & Circ: Philip Hoffman
Conducts Business: U.S.
Employees: 8,000
Primary Market Served: Consumer
Catalog available online
Advertising/Marketing Budget Related to Direct Marketing: 0-25%
Direct Marketing ad budget:
Direct Mail: 100%
Founded: 1924
Gross sales or billing: $2,000,000,000

Publish Lane Bryant, Roaman's, Lerner, Chadwicks, Jessica London, King Size, Brylane Home

BURBERRY
444 Madison Ave
New York, NY 10022-6903
Telephone: (212) 707-6508, Web Site:
www.burberry.com
Dir Media: Geri Moran
Primary Market Served: Business & Consumer

CABLE CAR CLOTHIERS/ ROBERT KIRK LTD
200 Bush St
San Francisco, CA 94104-3500
Telephone: (415) 397-4740, FAX: (415) 616-8998, E-Mail: info@cablecarclothiers.com, Web Site: www.cablecarclothiers.com
Pres: Charles Pivnick
VP: Janice Pivnick
Mktg Mgr: Harry Siewort
Conducts Business: Worldwide
Employees: 7
Primary Market Served: Consumer
Catalog available online
Direct online sales
Advertising/Marketing Budget Related to Direct Marketing: 76-100%
Direct Marketing ad budget:
Direct Mail: 80%
Magazines: 15%
Newspapers: 5%
Founded: 1939

Mail order & retail clothing store specializing in traditional clothing for men.

CARABELLA COLLECTION
Div. of Carabella Corp
17662 Armstrong Ave

Irvine, CA 92614
Telephone: (949) 263-2300, (800) 227-2235, FAX: (949) 263-2323, Web Site: www.carabella.com
Pres: Houshang Jalili
VP: Monir Jalili
Conducts Business: U.S.
Employees: 150
Primary Market Served: Consumer
Catalog available online
Direct online sales
Advertising/Marketing Budget Related to Direct Marketing: 76-100%
Direct Marketing ad budget: $500,000
Magazines: $100,000
Online: $400,000
Founded: 1983
Gross sales or billing: $20,000,000

Women's swim, sports & evening wear & accessories.

CASUAL MALE RETAIL GROUP
555 Turnpike St
Canton, MA 02021-2724
Telephone: (781) 828-9300, (800) 767-0319, E-Mail: info@casualmale.com, Web Site: www.casualmale.com
Chief Mktg Officer: Ric Della Bernarda
Conducts Business: U.S.
Employees: 4,000
Primary Market Served: Business & Consumer
Catalog available online
Direct online sales
Advertising/Marketing Budget Related to Direct Marketing: 0-25%
Gross sales or billing: $700,000,000

Men's apparel. Retail clothing.

CATTLE KATE
6701 W State St
Boise, ID 83714-7412
Telephone: (208) 377-5283, (800) 332-5283, FAX: (208) 375-3827, E-Mail: cattlekate@rmisp.com, Web Site: www.cattlekate.com
Owner & Pres: Michelle Oster
Conducts Business: U.S., Canada, Japan, Germany, France, Switzerland
Employees: 10
Primary Market Served: Business & Consumer
Catalog available online
Indirect online sales
Advertising/Marketing Budget Related to Direct Marketing: 76-100%
Direct Marketing ad budget:
Direct Mail: 50%
Magazines: 50%
Founded: 1981

Manufacture and design Old West style clothing for men & women. High quality specialty line.

CHADWICK'S OF BOSTON INC

Owned by Redcats USA; part of PPR
35 United Dr
West Bridgewater, MA 02379-1027
Telephone: (508) 583-8110, FAX: (508) 587-3345, Web Site: www. chadwicks.com
Chmn & CEO: Eric Faintreny
Conducts Business: U.S.
Employees: 805
Primary Market Served: Consumer
Founded: 1983
Gross sales or billing: $139,200,000

Consumer catalog offering women's name brand off-price fashions & casual apparel.

CHARMING SHOPPERS

3750 State Rd
Bensalem, PA 19020-5903
Telephone: (215) 245-9100, Web Site: www.charmingshoppers.com
Pres: Bill Bass
Primary Market Served: Consumer

CHEAP APRONS

Div. of Catalog Sales Cos
55 Crystal Ave (#265)
Derry, NH 03038-1702
Telephone: (978) 689-0694, (800) 367-2374, FAX: (978) 689-2483, E-Mail: rkurman@cheapaprons.com, Web Site: www.cheapaprons.com
VP: Rick Kurman
Conducts Business: U.S.
Primary Market Served: Business & Consumer
Catalog available online
Indirect online sales
Advertising/Marketing Budget Related to Direct Marketing: 76-100%
Founded: 1989

Corporate apparel: tees, polos, etc. Sell to the business & food service industry.

THE DMA CHICO'S FAS INC

11215 Metro Pkwy
Fort Myers, FL 33966-1206
Telephone: (239) 277-6200, Web Site: www.chicos.com
VP, CRM: Charlie White
Primary Market Served: Business & Consumer

CLOTHING SOLUTIONS

aka Enhanced Lifestyle Inc
5405 Alton Pkwy (Suite A)
Irvine, CA 92604-3718
Telephone: (800) 336-2660, (800) 465-1981, FAX: (800) 336-6510, Web Site: www.clothingsolutions.com
Pres: James E. Lechner

Primary Market Served: Business
Manufactures dresses, tops & slacks for nursing homes.

THE DMA COACH

516 W 34th St
New York, NY 10001-1394
Telephone: (212) 594-1850, (800) 444-3611, FAX: (212) 594-1682, Web Site: www.coach.com
Pres & CEO: Lou Frankfort
CFO: Richard Randall
Divisional VP: Nancy Cohen Chhahira
Conducts Business: Worldwide
Employees: 7,500
Primary Market Served: Consumer
Catalog available online
Direct online sales
Advertising/Marketing Budget Related to Direct Marketing: 51-75%

Marketer of quality leather goods & accessories.

COCKPIT USA INC

15 W 39th St (#12)
New York, NY 10018-0628
Telephone: (212) 575-1616, FAX: (212) 575-1636, E-Mail: jacky@cockpitusa.com, Web Site: www.cockpitusa.com
CEO: Jeff Clyman
Exec VP: Jacky R. Clyman
Conducts Business: Worldwide
Employees: 37
Primary Market Served: Business & Consumer
Catalog available online
Indirect online sales
Advertising/Marketing Budget Related to Direct Marketing: 0-25%
Direct Marketing ad budget:
Magazines: 75%
Newspapers: 5%
TV/Radio: 10%
Founded: 1975

Catalog featuring leather jackets, apparel, accessories, gifts & collectibles made famous by heroes & legends from aviation & military heritage. Also, updated sportswear for active men.

COLDWATER CREEK

751 W Hanley Ave
Coeur D Alene, ID 83815
Telephone: (800) 787-9196, FAX: (800) 262-0080, Web Site: www.coldwatercreek.com
Chmn Internet Sls & Pres: Dennis Pence
CFO: Don Robson
Conducts Business: U.S.
Primary Market Served: Business & Consumer

Sells nature related items.

COLUMBIA SPORTSWEAR

14375 NW Science Park Dr
Portland, OR 97229-5418
Telephone: (503) 985-4203, Web Site: www.columbia.com
Ecommerce Mktg Mgr: Kristina Zlateff

CRITTER MOUNTAIN WEAR

PO Box 975, 86 Jacqueline Lane
Crested Butte, CO 81224-0975
Telephone: (970) 349-9326, (800) 686-9327, FAX: (978) 389-5900, E-Mail: critter@crestedbutte.net, Web Site: www.crittermountainwear.com
Pres: Richard Kocurek
Conducts Business: U.S.
Employees: 8
Primary Market Served: Business & Consumer
Indirect online sales
Advertising/Marketing Budget Related to Direct Marketing: 0-25%
Founded: 1986
Gross sales or billing: $500,000

Outdoor clothing for skiing, hiking & mountain biking.

CROSSTOWN TRADERS INC

7840 E Broadway Blvd Ste 224
Tucson, AZ 85710-3908
Telephone: (520) 745-4500
Pres: Steve Lightman
Primary Market Served: Consumer

Swaps clothing & footwear across the country through catalogs & e-commerce sites

DEGRADO INC

PO Box 1211
Mandeville, LA 70470
Telephone: (504) 626-5291, (800) 433-6849, FAX: (504) 626-7379, Web Site: www.orleansjewels.com
Pres: Joseph De Grado
Conducts Business: U.S.
Employees: 20
Primary Market Served: Consumer
Catalog available online
Direct online sales
Advertising/Marketing Budget Related to Direct Marketing: 76-100%

Retail jeweler.

THE DMA DESTINATION MATERNITY CORP

456 N Fifth St
Philadelphia, PA 19123-4007
Telephone: (215) 873-2200, Web Site: www.motherswork.com
Mgr Mktg Partnerships: Dan Vogel

DHARMA TRADING CO

1805 S McDowell Boulevard Ext Ste D
Petaluma, CA 94954-6945
Telephone: (415) 456-7657, (800) 542-5227, FAX: (415) 456-8747, E-Mail: service@dharmatrading.com, Web Site: www.dharmatrading.com
Owner & Pres: Isaac Goff
Gen Mgr: Sharon Lang
Conducts Business: Worldwide
Employees: 50
Primary Market Served: Business & Consumer
Catalog available online
Direct online sales
Direct Marketing ad budget:
Magazines: 5%
Online: 95%
Founded: 1969

Catalog marketer of natural cotton & silk clothing & fabric, dyes, paints & related supplies.

DIAMOND ESSENCE

3906 Cricket Cir
Edison, NJ 08820
Telephone: (800) 909-2525, E-Mail: info@diamondessence.com, Web Site: www.diamond-essence.com
Pres: Ranjit Singh
VP: Shri Singh
Conducts Business: U.S.
Primary Market Served: Consumer
Advertising/Marketing Budget Related to Direct Marketing: 76-100%
Direct Marketing ad budget:
Direct Mail: 100%
Founded: 1978

A leading designer and marketer of the high-quality 14 karat solid gold cubic zirconia and other simulated gem jewelry. Sold through catalog (70%), retail stores (10%) & department & jewelry stores (10%).

DRS FOSTER & SMITH INC

PO Box 100
Rhinelander, WI 54501-0100
Telephone: (715) 369-3305, Web Site: www.drsfostersmith.com
Mktg: Ann Mapes
Primary Market Served: Consumer

Pet supplies & pet medications

THE DMA DR JAYS

853 Broadway (Suite 1900)
New York, NY 10003-4703
Telephone: (212) 334-7999, Web Site: drjays.com
Primary Market Served: Consumer

Sells apparel & accessories

DRAPER'S & DAMON'S

Subs. of Orchard Brands
Nine Pasteur (Suite 200)
Irvine, CA 92618-3804
Telephone: (949) 784-3000, (800) 843-1174, FAX: (949) 784-3400, E-Mail: jilld@drapers.com, Web Site: www.drapers.com
Sr Circulation Mgr: Jill Medina
Retail Adv Mgr: Colleen Drew
Dir E-commerce: Jim Collins
VP Direct: Dennis Diemer
Conducts Business: U.S.
Employees: 200
Primary Market Served: Consumer
Catalog available online
Direct online sales
Advertising/Marketing Budget Related to Direct Marketing: 0-25%
Direct Marketing ad budget:
Direct Mail: 90%
Magazines: 2%
Newspapers: 8%
Founded: 1927

Ready-to-wear clothing for women.

EASTBAY RUNNING STORE INC

Div. of Woolworth's Corp
111 S First Ave
Wausau, WI 54401
Telephone: (715) 845-5538, (800) 826-2205, FAX: (715) 261-9500, Web Site: www.eastbay.com
Pres: Dick Johnson
CFO: Mike Zawoysky
VP: Jeff Penn
Mktg Mgr: Tod Meerdink
Conducts Business: U.S.
Primary Market Served: Business & Consumer

Catalog & retail sales for athletic footwear & sportswear.

EBBETS FIELD FLANNELS INC

dba Stall & Dean
562 First Ave S (Suite 200)
Seattle, WA 98104
Telephone: (206) 382-7249, FAX: (206) 382-4411, E-Mail: clubhouse@ebbets.com, Web Site: www.ebbets.com
Pres & CEO: Jerry P. Cohen
VP: Lisa Cooper
Primary Market Served: Business & Consumer
Founded: 1987

Vintage athletic apparel sold through mail order catalogs & retail store.

ELITE SPORTSWEAR LP

2136 N 13th St (Ste A)
Reading, PA 19604-1213

Telephone: (610) 921-1469, (800) 345-4087, FAX: (610) 921-0208, E-Mail: gkelite@gkelite.com, Web Site: www.gk-elitesportswear.com
Owner & Pres: Sallie Weaver
VP Mktg: Birgitte Sorensen
Conducts Business: Worldwide
Primary Market Served: Business & Consumer
Catalog available online
Direct online sales
Founded: 1981

Sells men's & women's gymnastics apparel (workout wear & competitive wear) direct to individuals, gyms, dance schools, YMCAs, public schools, colleges, universities & specialty stores.

ELKHART CASES

dba Sprunger Engineering, Sprunger Parts Company Inc
3605 Cooper Dr
Elkhart, IN 46514
Telephone: (574) 295-7700, (800) 582-0319, FAX: (574) 295-7761, E-Mail: elkcases@aol.com
Pres: Dale D. Fahlbeck
Conducts Business: U.S.
Employees: 30
Primary Market Served: Business & Consumer
Advertising/Marketing Budget Related to Direct Marketing: 26-50%
Direct Marketing ad budget: $260,000
Direct Mail: 60%
Magazines: 20%
Newspapers: 5%
Telephone: 15%
Founded: 1964
Gross sales or billing: $2,000,000

Manufactures briefcases, attache cases, catalog cases, all types of custom carrying cases & musical instrument cases.

THE DMA EXPRESS LLC

1 Limited Pkwy
Columbus, OH 43230-1498
Telephone: (614) 415-4282, Web Site: www.expressfashion.com
Dir Customer Mktg: James Wright

EYEGLASS SERVICE INDUSTRIES

dba Vision World
481 Sunrise Hwy
Lynbrook, NY 11563-3017
Telephone: (516) 599-1135, FAX: (516) 599-4825
Pres: Bruce Topol
VP: Leonard Baritz
Conducts Business: U.S.
Employees: 75
Primary Market Served: Consumer

Advertising/Marketing Budget Related
to Direct Marketing: 76-100%
Direct Marketing ad budget:
Direct Mail: 80%
Newspapers: 20%
Founded: 1958
Gross sales or billing: $4,900,000

Sells Ray-Ban sunglasses at low
prices.

FAIR INDIGO
579 Donofrio Dr Ste 1
Madison, WI 53719-2838
Telephone: (608) 824-8974, Web Site:
www.fairindigo.com
Pres & CEO: Bill Bass
Pres: Rob Behnke

THE DMA FORMAL APPROACH
281 W Old Andrew Johnson Hwy
Jefferson City, TN 37760-1805
Telephone: (865) 475-8641, Web Site:
www.formalapproach.com
Owner: Mike Denton
Primary Market Served: Consumer

THE DMA FOSSIL
2323 N Central Expy
Richardson, TX 75080-2712
Telephone: (469) 587-2628, Web Site:
www.fossil.com
Primary Market Served: Consumer

FREDERICK'S OF HOLLYWOOD GROUP INC
6255 Sunset Blvd (fl 6)
Los Angeles, CA 90028-7403
Telephone: (323) 466-5151, (800) 323-
9525, FAX: (323) 464-5149, Web
Site: www.fredericks.com
CEO: Linda LoRe
Sr VP, Mktg: Yolanda Dunbar
Sr VP: Denise Marsicano
Sr VP: John Schulman
VP Direct Mktg: Tracy Rhyan
PR Mgr: Jennifer Lowitz
Conducts Business: U.S., Canada
Employees: 1,000
Primary Market Served: Consumer
Catalog available online
Direct online sales
Direct Marketing ad budget:
$8,800,000
Direct Mail: $7,000,000
Magazines: $1,000,000
Newspapers: $800,000
Founded: 1946
Gross sales or billing: $57,000,000

Mail order company specializing in
ladies' & men's apparel & accessories.
Sells direct to the public through catalogs & approximately 206 retail stores.

PAUL FREDRICK MENSTYLE
223 W Poplar St
Fleetwood, PA 19522
Telephone: (610) 944-0909, (800) 247-
1417, FAX: (610) 944-6452, E-Mail:
custserv@menstyle.com, Web Site:
www.paulfredricks.com
Pres: Paul Sacher
COO & Exec VP: Allen Abbott
VP Mktg: Scott Drayer
Opers Mgr: Ross Alaimo
Conducts Business: U.S., Japan
Employees: 85
Primary Market Served: Business &
Consumer
Catalog available online
Direct online sales
Gross sales or billing: $32,000,000

Design & manufacture men's shirts,
sell through catalog & retail sales.
Catalog co. for men's clothing.

FRENCH CREEK SHEEP & WOOL CO INC
600 Pines Swamp Rd, PO Box 110
Elverson, PA 19520-8917
Telephone: (610) 286-5700, (800) 977-
4337, FAX: (610) 286-0324, E-Mail:
info@frenchcreeksw.com, Web Site:
www.frenchcreeksw.com
Pres: Jean Flaxenburg
Co Owner: Eric Flaxenburg
Conducts Business: Worldwide
Employees: 50
Primary Market Served: Consumer
Catalog available online
Direct online sales

Mail order catalog company specializing in the manufacture & retailing of
sheepskin coats, leather & suede fashions & sweaters.

ALAN FURMAN & CO
12250 Rockville Pike (Suite 270)
Rockville, MD 20852
Telephone: (202) 397-8463, (800) 654-
7184, FAX: (301) 881-0810, E-Mail:
watches@alanfurman.com, Web Site:
www.alanfurman.com
Pres & CEO: Alan Furman
Conducts Business: U.S.
Employees: 8
Primary Market Served: Consumer
Catalog available online
Indirect online sales
Advertising/Marketing Budget Related
to Direct Marketing: 76-100%
Founded: 1985
Gross sales or billing: $9,000,000

Direct marketing of jewelry &
watches. 85% mail order.

THE DMA GTM SPORTSWEAR
PO Box 8
Manhattan, KS 66505-0008

Telephone: (800) 336-4486, Web Site:
www.gtmsportswear.com
VP Mktg: Nikki Miller

GARNET HILL INC
231 Main St
Franconia, NH 03580
Telephone: (603) 823-5545, FAX:
(603) 823-7034, Web Site: www.
garnethill.com
Pres: Russ Gateskill
Mktg Dir: Jim Alden
Conducts Business: U.S.
Employees: 85
Primary Market Served: Consumer
Advertising/Marketing Budget Related
to Direct Marketing: 76-100%

All natural fiber apparel, beddings &
furnishings.

GENESCO INC
1415 Murfeesboro Rd (Suite 190)
Nashville, TN 37217-2895
Telephone: (615) 367-7000, (888) 324-
6189, FAX: (615) 367-8278, Web
Site: www.genesco.com
CEO: Hal Pennington
COO & Dir: Robert J. Dennis
Sr VP, Fin & CFO: James S. Gulmi
Corp Media Contact: Claire S. McCall
Employees: 12,450
Primary Market Served: Business &
Consumer
Catalog available online
Direct online sales
Gross sales or billing: $1,400,000,000

Retail & wholesale men's footwear.
High-end or up-scale.

WL GORE & ASSOCIATES INC
555 Paper Mill Rd
Newark, DE 19711
Telephone: (410) 506-7787, (888) 914-
4673, E-Mail: info@wlgore.com,
Web Site: www.wlgore.com
Assoc: Mary Ellen Panousis
Conducts Business: U.S.
Primary Market Served: Business &
Consumer

Manufacture fabrics for catalog & retail sales.

GORSUCH LTD
263 E Gore Creek Dr
Vail, CO 81657
Telephone: (970) 476-2294, (800) 525-
9808, FAX: (970) 476-4323, Web
Site: www.gorsuchltd.com
Pres: David Gorsuch
Owner: Renie Gorsuch
Catalog Consultant: Jane Imber
Conducts Business: U.S.
Employees: 100

Primary Market Served: Consumer
Catalog available online
Direct online sales
Advertising/Marketing Budget Related
  to Direct Marketing: 51-75%
Direct Marketing ad budget:
Direct Mail: $2,500,000
Founded: 1966
Gross sales or billing: $20,000,000

Retail and catalog marketer. Offer
products from designer casual wear to
furnishings & gifts. Specialize in ski
wear. Eight locations.

GOULD & GOODRICH

709 E McNeil St
Lillington, NC 27546
Telephone: (910) 893-2071, (800) 277-
  0732, FAX: (910) 893-4742, E-Mail:
  service@gouldusa.com, Web Site:
  www.gouldusa.com
Mktg & Cust Svc Mgr: Phyllis Gould
Pres: Robert Gould
Co Owner: Jon E. Goodrich
Conducts Business: Worldwide
Primary Market Served: Business
Catalog available online
Indirect online sales

Holsters, belts & accessories of leather
& nylon. Full line for law enforcement
& sporting.

THE GREEN POND CO

3179 Maple Dr NE (Suite 11)
Atlanta, GA 30305-2511
Telephone: (404) 233-6343, (800) 827-
  7663, FAX: (404) 233-6340, E-Mail:
  sales@greenpond.com, Web Site:
  www.greenpond.com
Pres: Louise Bohannon
Conducts Business: U.S.
Employees: 5
Primary Market Served: Consumer

Sells apparel through direct mail &
catalogs.

THE GYMBOREE CORP

500 Howard St
San Francisco, CA 94105-3000
Telephone: (877) 449-6932, Web Site:
  www.gymboree.com
Dir Mktg: Marc Laven

HABAND CO INC

110 Bauer Dr
Oakland, NJ 07436-3105
Telephone: (201) 651-1000, FAX:
  (201) 405-7777, Web Site: www.
  haband.com
Dir Mktg: Steve Schlumpf
Conducts Business: U.S.
Employees: 349
Primary Market Served: Consumer
Catalog available online

Direct online sales
Founded: 1925
Gross sales or billing: $59,100,000

Retail mail order catalog for men's &
women's clothing.

HANESBRANDS INC

1000 E Hanes Mill Rd
Winston Salem, NC 27105-1384
Telephone: (336) 519-7460, Web Site:
  www.hanesbrands.com
VP, Direct to Consumer: Carol Davis
Primary Market Served: Consumer

HERMES OF PARIS

55 E 59th St (front 2)
New York, NY 10022
Telephone: (212) 759-7585, (800) 441-
  4488, FAX: (212) 644-2132
Pres & CEO: Robert Chavez
CFO & VP: Virginie Costa
Exec VP: Melissa Parker
Conducts Business: U.S.
Employees: 140
Primary Market Served: Business
Catalog available online
Direct online sales

Manufacturer & retailer of leather
goods, perfume, ready-to-wear &
porcelain.

THE DMA TOMMY HILFIGER

601 W 26th St Rm 500
New York, NY 10001-1142
Telephone: (212) 548-1368, Web Site:
  www.tommy.com

HITCHCOCK SHOES INC

225 Beal St
Hingham, MA 02043-1543
Telephone: (781) 749-3260, (888) 599-
  9433, FAX: (781) 749-3576, E-Mail:
  hitchcock@wideshoes.com, Web
  Site: www.wideshoes.com
Pres & CEO: Thomas R. Bright
Gen Mgr: Shirley A. Mortland
Conducts Business: U.S.
Employees: 20
Primary Market Served: Consumer
Catalog available online
Direct online sales
Founded: 1951
Gross sales or billing: $7,000,000

Catalog marketer of men's shoes in
widths EEE to EEEEEE only.

HOOVER'S MFG CO

4133 Progress Blvd
Peru, IL 61354-1125
Telephone: (815) 223-1159, (888) 333-
  1499, FAX: (815) 223-1499, Web
  Site: www.hmchonors.com
Pres & CFO: David R. Hoover
Conducts Business: U.S., Europe, Asia

Employees: 18
Primary Market Served: Business &
  Consumer
Catalog available online
Direct online sales
Advertising/Marketing Budget Related
  to Direct Marketing: 0-25%
Founded: 1963
Gross sales or billing: $2,000,000

Advertising specialties such as hats,
military & political pins & belt
buckles.

HOT TOPIC INC

18305 E San Jose Ave
City of Industry, CA 91748
Telephone: (626) 839-4681, (800) 275-
  9169, FAX: (626) 839-4686, Web
  Site: www.hottopic.com
Chmn: Bruce A. Quinnell
CEO & Dir: Elizabeth M. McLaughlin
Pres: Gerald A. Cook
CFO: James J. McGinty
Sr VP & CIO: Thomas Beauchamp
Employees: 9,794
Primary Market Served: Consumer
Catalog available online
Direct online sales
Founded: 1989
Gross sales or billing: $751,000,000

Specialty retail company selling apparel & accessories through mall-based
stores.

HOUSE OF EYES II

2222 Patterson St Ste A
Greensboro, NC 27407-2539
Telephone: (336) 852-7107, FAX:
  (336) 854-0311
Pres: Clay Hoff
VP: Jeff Hoff
Sec & Treas: Tammy Hoff
Mktg Mgr: Ricky Sheldon
Conducts Business: U.S.
Employees: 10
Primary Market Served: Business &
  Consumer
Advertising/Marketing Budget Related
  to Direct Marketing: 0-25%
Direct Marketing ad budget: $20,000
Newspapers: 30%
TV/Radio: 30%
Telephone: 40%
Founded: 1980
Gross sales or billing: $1,000,000

Repair shop for sunglasses, frames &
accessories.

HOUSE OF ORANGE

PO Box 444
Brentwood Bay, BC, Canada V8M
  1R3

Telephone: (866) 401-9174, FAX: (250) 652-8673, E-Mail: houseoforange@shaw.ca, Web Site: www.houseoforange.biz
Mgr: Ed Johnson
Conducts Business: U.S., Canada
Employees: 3
Primary Market Served: Business & Consumer
Advertising/Marketing Budget Related to Direct Marketing: 0-25%
Direct Marketing ad budget: $20,000
Magazines: 50%
Telephone: 50%
Founded: 1968
Gross sales or billing: $500,000

Beads & findings for costume jewelry manufacturers & bead stores. Also wholesales hobby supplies.

HYMAN'S
5809 N Rhett Ave
Hanahan, SC 29410-2510
Telephone: (843) 571-7870, (800) 354-9626, FAX: (843) 571-7575, E-Mail: support@hymans.com, Web Site: www.hymans.com
Owner, Pres & CEO: David Odle
VP: Mier Hyme
Conducts Business: U.S., Canada
Primary Market Served: Business & Consumer
Catalog available online
Direct online sales
Advertising/Marketing Budget Related to Direct Marketing: 0-25%
Direct Marketing ad budget:
Direct Mail: 50%
Magazines: 25%
Telephone: 25%
Founded: 1890

Uniforms & corporate apparel.

ICIS INC
1908 Ringing Rock Rd
Upper Black Eddy, PA 18912
Telephone: (610) 982-0429, E-Mail: icis@ptdprolog.net, Web Site: www.icisjewelry.com
Pres: Lisa Schwartz
Primary Market Served: Business & Consumer
Catalog available online
Indirect online sales

Manufactures fashion accessories. Market through wholesale & catalogs.

INDUSTRIAL UNIFORM CO INC
902 E Indianapolis St
Wichita, KS 67211-2407

Telephone: (316) 264-2871, (800) 333-3666, FAX: (316) 264-2708, E-Mail: uniform@industrialuniform.com, Web Site: www.industrialuniform.com
Pres: Tony Taravella
Pur Dir: Elaine Stull
Conducts Business: U.S.
Employees: 21
Primary Market Served: Business & Consumer
Advertising/Marketing Budget Related to Direct Marketing: 76-100%
Founded: 1938
Gross sales or billing: $2,500,000

Working apparel to industrial customers & franchisers. Corporate embroidered apparel & accessories.

INSTRUCTOR'S CHOICE DANCEWEAR
5020 Sunrise Hwy
Massapequa Park, NY 11762-2913
Telephone: (516) 799-7010, FAX: (516) 799-7993, E-Mail: customerservice@instructorschoice.com, Web Site: www.instructorschoice.com
Owner: Felicia Marino
Conducts Business: Worldwide
Employees: 1
Primary Market Served: Business & Consumer
Catalog available online
Direct online sales
Advertising/Marketing Budget Related to Direct Marketing: 76-100%
Direct Marketing ad budget: $20,000
Direct Mail: 80%
Magazines: 20%
Founded: 1980
Gross sales or billing: $200,000

Ladies' & girls' dancewear & shoes.

THE DMA JOS A BANK CLOTHIERS INC
500 Hanover Pike
Hampstead, MD 21074-2002
Telephone: (410) 239-2700, Web Site: www.josbank.com
Dir Retail Mktg: Patricia Collingwood

JAZZERCISE INC
2460 Impala Dr
Carlsbad, CA 92008
Telephone: (760) 476-1750, (800) FIT IS IT, FAX: (760) 602-7180, E-Mail: info@jazzercise.com, Web Site: www.jazzercise.com
CEO: Judi Shepphard Missett
COO & CFO: Sally Baldridge
Exec VP: Shana Missett Nelson
VP, Mktg: Kathy Missett
VP, Tech: Brad Jones
Conducts Business: Worldwide
Employees: 80

Primary Market Served: Consumer
Catalog available online
Direct online sales
Advertising/Marketing Budget Related to Direct Marketing: 0-25%
Direct Marketing ad budget:
Direct Mail: 80%
Magazines: 5%
Newspapers: 5%
TV/Radio: 5%
Telephone: 5%
Founded: 1982
Gross sales or billing: $5,000,000

Fitness related products. Fitness wear & accessories, fitness videos, exercise mats, weights, etc.

J JILL GROUP, INC
Subs. of Talbots
Four Batterymarch Park
Quincy, MA 02169
Telephone: (617) 376-4300, (800) 642-9989, FAX: (617) 769-0177, Web Site: www.jjillgroup.com
Pres: Philip Konalczyk
CFO: Olga Conley
Sr VP & Chief Mktg Coord: Hillary Chasing
Mgr, Pub Rels: Lauren Cooke
Conducts Business: U.S.
Employees: 3,041
Primary Market Served: Consumer
Catalog available online
Direct online sales
Gross sales or billing: $532,000,000

Publisher of the "J. Jill Catalog," a catalog featuring apparel in the 4-20 size range.

THE DMA JOCKEY INTERNATIONAL GLOBAL INC
2300 60th St
Kenosha, WI 53140-3822
Telephone: (262) 658-8111
VP, E-Commerce & Catalog: Christopher Smith
Primary Market Served: Business & Consumer

JOHNNY APPLESEED'S INC
30 Tozer Rd
Beverly, MA 01915-5510
Telephone: (978) 922-2040, (800) 767-6666, FAX: (978) 922-7001, Web Site: www.appleseeds.com
Chmn & CEO: Neale Attenborough
Pres: Brenda Koskinen
CFO: Dave Walde
VP, Database Mktg: Richard Hodges
VP Opers: John Civali
Conducts Business: U.S.
Employees: 450
Primary Market Served: Consumer
Catalog available online
Direct online sales

Direct Marketing ad budget:
Direct Mail: 100%
Founded: 1946
Gross sales or billing: $50,000,000

Women's ready-to-wear & gifts. Catalog sales to consumers.

JOURNEYS
Div. of Genesco Inc
1415 Murfreesboro Pike Ste 181, Genesco Park
Nashville, TN 37217-2829
Telephone: (615) 367-8000, (888) 324-6356, FAX: (615) 367-8123, Web Site: www.journeys.com
Pres, Journeys: Jim Estepa
Mktg Dir: Susan Joy
Conducts Business: U.S., Puerto Rico, US Virgin Islands
Employees: 360
Primary Market Served: Consumer
Catalog available online
Direct online sales
Advertising/Marketing Budget Related to Direct Marketing: 0-25%
Direct Marketing ad budget:
Direct Mail: 33%
Magazines: 33%
Online: 33%
Founded: 1925
Gross sales or billing: $593,516

Marketer of cutting edge footwear products & accessories for young men & women, ages 12-24, and shoes for women early 20's to mid-30 years old. Retailer & wholesaler of shoes.

JOYS SA INC
PO Box 98
Hatillo, PR 00659-0098
Telephone: (954) 426-9100, (800) 526-7148, FAX: (800) 232-9569, E-Mail: info@joyssa.com
VP Sls: Roy Blumhos
Conducts Business: Worldwide
Employees: 21
Primary Market Served: Business & Consumer
Advertising/Marketing Budget Related to Direct Marketing: 0-25%
Founded: 1979

Embroidery & heat applied lettering/personalization.

JUSTIN DISCOUNT BOOTS & COWBOY OUTFITTERS
101 N Hwy 156, PO Box 67
Justin, TX 76247
Telephone: (940) 648-2797, FAX: (940) 648-3282, Web Site: www.justinboots.com
Pres & CEO: Randy Watson
VP & CFO: Rick Savitz
Conducts Business: U.S.

Employees: 25
Primary Market Served: Consumer
Catalog available online
Advertising/Marketing Budget Related to Direct Marketing: 26-50%
Founded: 1954

Western clothing & boots retail store.

KAPPLER PROTECTIVE APPAREL & FABRICS
55 Grimes Dr
Guntersville, AL 35976
Telephone: (256) 505-4005, (800) 600-4019, FAX: (256) 505-4151, E-Mail: usa@kappler.com, Web Site: www.kappler.com
Pres: George Kappler
Sr VP, Sls & Mktg: Craig Woodward
Sr VP & Dir: Jerry Jones
VP & CFO: Chuck Strader
VP: Mike Willis
Conducts Business: U.S., Canada
Employees: 1,400
Primary Market Served: Business & Consumer
Catalog available online
Indirect online sales
Advertising/Marketing Budget Related to Direct Marketing: 0-25%
Direct Marketing ad budget: $200,000
Direct Mail: 40%
Magazines: 50%
Telephone: 10%
Founded: 1976
Gross sales or billing: $85,000,000

Manufacturer of protective clothing, selling everything from coveralls to fully encapsulated suits through distributors.

KAYSER-ROTH CORP INC
Div. of Kayser Roth Corp
102 Corporate Center Blvd
Greensboro, NC 27408
Telephone: (800) 575-3497, Web Site: www.nononsense.com
VP, Mktg & Gen Mgr: Carol Burke
Opers Dir: Tom Shank
Conducts Business: U.S.
Employees: 85
Primary Market Served: Consumer
Advertising/Marketing Budget Related to Direct Marketing: 76-100%
Direct Marketing ad budget:
Direct Mail: 100%
Founded: 1985
Gross sales or billing: $10,000,000

Manufacture & market men's & women's hosiery & leg wear.

KELLY'S KIDS
391 Liberty Rd
Natchez, MS 39120-4344

Telephone: (601) 442-5332, (800) 837-2066, FAX: (601) 442-4399, E-Mail: customerservice@kellyskids.com, Web Site: www.kellyskids.com
Founder: Lynn James
CEO: Ashton James
Mktg Dir: Meg Payment
CFO: Serge Boldyrev
Conducts Business: U.S.
Employees: 50
Primary Market Served: Consumer
Catalog available online
Direct online sales
Advertising/Marketing Budget Related to Direct Marketing: 51-75%
Direct Marketing ad budget:
Direct Mail: 80%
Newspapers: 2%
Online: 18%
Founded: 1983

High quality, classic clothing for girls, boys & the entire family.

KROPP ENTERPRISES
232 Longview Ave
Kissimmee, FL 34747-5042
Telephone: (407) 566-9276, FAX: (407) 566-9276
Pres: Mike Kropp
Conducts Business: Worldwide
Employees: 1
Primary Market Served: Business & Consumer
Advertising/Marketing Budget Related to Direct Marketing: 0-25%
Founded: 1980
Gross sales or billing: $100,000

Designs & manufactures leather name plates for wholesalers & retailers.

PATRICIA KUTZA CO
PO Box 4127
Vallejo, CA 94590
Telephone: (707) 552-0442, E-Mail: pkutza@pacbell.net
Owner & Pres: Patricia Kutza
Employees: 1
Primary Market Served: Business & Consumer
Advertising/Marketing Budget Related to Direct Marketing: 26-50%
Founded: 1999
Gross sales or billing: $200,000

Retail & wholesale.

AB LAMBDIN INC
1134 56 St
Hampton, VA 23630-4000
Telephone: (800) 528-9817, FAX: (800) 221-9231, E-Mail: service@ablambdin.com
VP: Adrienne Cote
Pres: Carl Tott
List Mgr: Kelly McDowell
Conducts Business: U.S.

Primary Market Served: Consumer
Advertising/Marketing Budget Related
  to Direct Marketing: 76-100%
Direct Marketing ad budget:
Direct Mail: 5%
Magazines: 90%
Newspapers: 5%

Mail order catalog company featuring
women's designer swim & resort
apparel.

LANDS' END INC

One Lands' End Ln
Dodgeville, WI 53595
Telephone: (608) 935-9341, (800) 963-
  4816, FAX: (680) 935-4831, Web
  Site: www.landsend.com
Pres & CEO: David McCreight
SVP, Employee Svcs: Kelly A. Richie
CMO: Gerard Cunningham
Conducts Business: United Kingdom,
  Japan, Ireland, France, Italy
Employees: 8,400
Primary Market Served: Business &
  Consumer
Catalog available online
Direct online sales
Founded: 1963
Gross sales or billing: $1,300,000,000

Direct marketer of casual, dress & active clothing for the family.

LEATHER UNLIMITED CORP

PO Box 342
Belgium, WI 53004-0342
Telephone: (920) 994-9464, (800) 993-
  2889, FAX: (920) 994-4099, E-Mail:
  leatherunltd@yahoo.com, Web Site:
  www.leatherunltd.com
Pres: Joseph M. O'Connell
Treas: Patricia C. O'Connell
Conducts Business: U.S.
Employees: 12
Primary Market Served: Business &
  Consumer
Catalog available online
Indirect online sales
Advertising/Marketing Budget Related
  to Direct Marketing: 51-75%
Direct Marketing ad budget:
Direct Mail: 80%
Online: 20%
Founded: 1970
Gross sales or billing: $1,000,000

Manufacturer & distributor of leather
accessories & leathercraft supplies.
Also, steel cutting dies & centrifically
cast buckles & other small accessories.

LESLIE JORDAN

1930 NW 24th Ave
Portland, OR 97210
Telephone: (503) 295-1987, (800) 935-
  3343, FAX: (503) 295-1989, E-Mail:
  sales@lesliejordan.com, Web Site:
  www.lesliejordan.com
Pres & Owner: Leslie Jordan
Mktg & Sls: Vicky Hartwig
Mktg & Sls: Dickie Christensen
Mktg & Sls: Craig Lamar
Conducts Business: U.S.
Employees: 50
Primary Market Served: Business
Advertising/Marketing Budget Related
  to Direct Marketing: 26-50%

Manufacture jackets, bags, aprons &
apparel out of Dupont Tyvek.

LESLIE SHOE CO INC

dba sexyshoes.com
480 N Second St
Rogers City, MI 49779-1367
Telephone: (989) 734-4030, (800) 716-
  8617, E-Mail: info@sexyshoes.com,
  Web Site: www.sexyshoes.com
CEO: Jeffrey Hopp
COO: Sandra Ruttan
Conducts Business: U.S., Canada
Employees: 10
Primary Market Served: Consumer
Catalog available online
Direct online sales
Advertising/Marketing Budget Related
  to Direct Marketing: 76-100%
Direct Marketing ad budget:
Direct Mail: 100%
Founded: 1984
Gross sales or billing: $1,400,000

Catalog marketer of ladies' tall-heeled
shoes.

THE LIMITED STORES INC

Subs. of The Limited Inc
Three Limited Pkwy
Columbus, OH 43230
Telephone: (614) 415-2000, FAX:
  (614) 415-2057, Web Site: www.
  limited.com
Pres & CEO: Robert Bernard
VP, Mktg: Wanda Gierhart
Asst to Exec VP: Judy Ballenger
Conducts Business: U.S.
Employees: 13
Primary Market Served: Consumer
Advertising/Marketing Budget Related
  to Direct Marketing: 76-100%

Women's fashion specialty stores.

LION APPAREL

7200 Poe Ave # 400
Dayton, OH 45414-2547
Telephone: (937) 898-1949, (800) 548-
  6614, FAX: (937) 913-5667, Web
  Site: www.lionapparel.com
Chmn Bd: Richard Lapedes
CEO: Steve Schwartz
VP, Sls & Mktg Mgr: Steve Allison

Dir Sls: Cliff Gallarneau
Conducts Business: U.S.
Employees: 700
Primary Market Served: Business &
  Consumer
Gross sales or billing: $25,700,000

Uniforms, identity apparel, protective
fire & safety clothing.

THE DMA LOEHMANN'S

2500 Halsey St
Bronx, NY 10461-3637
Telephone: (718) 409-2000, Web Site:
  www.loehmanns.com
VP Database Mktg & Sls: Mara Kelly
Primary Market Served: Consumer

LOTIONS & LACE

3960 Garner Rd
Riverside, CA 92501
Telephone: (909) 686-5223, FAX:
  (909) 686-5765, E-Mail: linda@ez-
  access.com, Web Site: www.
  sexyvideos.com
Pres: Ray Hargreaves
VP & Treas: Linda Hargreaves
Conducts Business: U.S., Australia,
  Canada, Europe, Japan, S. America
Employees: 30
Primary Market Served: Business &
  Consumer
Catalog available online
Direct online sales
Advertising/Marketing Budget Related
  to Direct Marketing: 51-75%
Direct Marketing ad budget: $100,000
Direct Mail: 50%
Magazines: 45%
Newspapers: 5%
Founded: 1981
Gross sales or billing: $2,000,000

Ladies & men's exotic lingerie, swimwear, costumes, hosiery, day/evening
wear, massage lotions, adult games,
books, videos & novelties.

LUXOTTICA RETAIL

4000 Luxottica Pl
Mason, OH 45040-8114
Telephone: (513) 765-6956, Web Site:
  www.luxottica.com
Dir CRM - Database/Analytics: Greg
  Branch

M&M HEALTH CARE APPAREL CO

1541 60th St
Brooklyn, NY 11219-5023
Telephone: (800) 221-8929, E-Mail:
  fashionease@aol.com
CEO: Abraham M Klein
Conducts Business: U.S.
Employees: 17

Primary Market Served: Business & Consumer
Catalog available online
Direct online sales
Advertising/Marketing Budget Related to Direct Marketing: 0-25%
Founded: 1973

Specialized clothing & footwear for the disabled.

THE DMA MAIDENFORM INC
485-F US Hwy 1S
Iselin, NJ 08830-3055
Telephone: (732) 621-2281, Web Site: www.maidenform.com
Primary Market Served: Consumer

MAKING IT BIG
525 Portal St
Cotati, CA 94931-3023
Telephone: (707) 795-1995, (877) 644-1995, FAX: (707) 795-4874, E-Mail: mib@makingitbig.com, Web Site: www.makingitbig.com
Pres: Tracy Amiral
Mktg Mgr: Leila Van Meter
Conducts Business: U.S., Canada, Europe, Asia, Australia, Russia
Employees: 20
Primary Market Served: Consumer
Direct online sales
Advertising/Marketing Budget Related to Direct Marketing: 51-75%
Founded: 1984
Gross sales or billing: $5,000,000

Retail and Mail order clothing for plus size women sizes 1X - 8X.

THE MARK GROUP
6500 Park of Commerce Blvd
Boca Raton, FL 33487-8293
Telephone: (561) 241-1700, (800) 637-0152, FAX: (561) 241-1055, Web Site: www.bostonproper.com
Pres & CEO: Michael W. Tiernan
CFO & Exec VP: Seth L. Miller
Exec VP, Chief Creative & Internet Officer: Skip Hartzell
VP, Opers: Scott Bryant
Conducts Business: U.S.
Primary Market Served: Consumer
Catalog available online
Direct online sales
Founded: 1951

A multi-brand, multi-channel, direct-to-consumer marketer of apparel and home accessories, The Mark Group consists of three dynamic brands: Boston Proper, Charles Keath, and Mark, Fore & Strike. The company, founded in 1951, is headquartered in Boca Raton, Fla., and mails more than 60 million catalogs annually. Additionally, the company operates 18 retail and outlet stores along the eastern seaboard of the United States in coastal, resort communities and three e-commerce Web sites. The company's annual sales for the year 2000 exceeded $118 million.

THE DMA MASON COMPANIES INC
1251 First Ave
Chippewa Falls, WI 54729-1408
Telephone: (715) 723-1871, (800) 826-7030, FAX: (715) 720-4247, Web Site: www.masoncompaniesinc.com
Chmn: William Scobie
Pres: John Lubs
VP Mktg: Darin Schemenauer
Exec VP: Dan Hunt
VP, Info Sys: Carl Lijewski
Coord: Clark Woznicki
Conducts Business: U.S.
Employees: 550
Primary Market Served: Business & Consumer
Advertising/Marketing Budget Related to Direct Marketing: 51-75%
Direct Marketing ad budget:
Direct Mail: $5,000,000
Magazines: $50,000
Newspapers: $5,000
Founded: 1904

Manufacturer & marketer of men's & women's shoes through independent representatives.

MAUS & HOFFMAN INC
225 S Federal Hwy
Fort Lauderdale, FL 33301-1938
Telephone: (954) 463-1200, Web Site: www.mausandhoffman.com
Catalog Dir: Greg Goodwin

MERCURY INTERNATIONAL TRADING
20 Alice Agnew Dr
North Attleboro, MA 02763-1036
Telephone: (508) 699-9000, FAX: (508) 699-9088, Web Site: www.mercuryfootwear.com
Chmn & Founder: Irwin Wiseman
CEO: Howard Wisemen
Pres: Gary Gorsuch
Primary Market Served: Business
Founded: 1979
Gross sales or billing: $15,000,000

Athletic & men's casual footwear for the mass market.

METROPOLIS MAGAZINE
Part of Bellerophon Publications, Inc
61 W 23rd St (4th fl)
New York, NY 10010
Telephone: (212) 627-9977, (800) 334-3046, FAX: (212) 627-9988, E-Mail: edit@metropolismag.com, Web Site: www.metropolismag.com
Publr: Horace Hauemeyer III
Mktg Mgr: Kimberly Taylor
Mktg Mgr: Allison R. Carroll
Adv Mgr: Tamara Costa
Conducts Business: U.S., Canada
Employees: 35
Primary Market Served: Consumer
Advertising/Marketing Budget Related to Direct Marketing: 76-100%
Gross sales or billing: $3,600,000

Examines contemporary life through design architecture, interior design, product design, graphic design, crafts, planning, and preservation.

MILLER STOCKMAN
Div. of Rocky Mountain Clothing Co
8500 Zuni St
Denver, CO 80260-5007
Telephone: (303) 428-5696, FAX: (303) 430-1130
Pres: Les Ball
CFO & VP: Larry Hagen
MO Dir: Joyce Hunter
Primary Market Served: Consumer

Western apparel.

MINNETONKA BY MAIL
229 City Island Ave.
Bronx, NY 10464
FAX: (718) 885-3500, E-Mail: eileenlwagner@email.msn.com
Pres: Eileen Wagner
Treas & Computer Adviser: Ellen Wagner
Conducts Business: U.S., Australia, Canada, Europe, Hong Kong, Israel, Japan, Mexico, Singapore
Employees: 4
Primary Market Served: Business & Consumer
Catalog available online
Direct online sales
Advertising/Marketing Budget Related to Direct Marketing: 0-25%
Direct Marketing ad budget:
Direct Mail: 80%
Magazines: 20%
Founded: 1984

Leather moccasins & casual shoes for infants, children, ladies & men. Ankle-high, knee-high & driving moccasins, some lined.

THE DMA MOBY WRAP INC
PO Box 1066
Chico, CA 95927-1066

Telephone: (530) 898-8200
CEO: David Beerman

MOTHERWEAR
110 Lyman St
Holyoke, MA 01040-4653
Telephone: (413) 586-1978, (800) 950-2500, FAX: (413) 532-4058, E-Mail: customerservice@motherwear.com, Web Site: www.motherwear.com
Co-Owner & Pres: Jodi Wright
Co-Owner & CEO: Prakash Laufer
CFO: Holly Smith-Bove
Mktg Dir: Stephanie Ferres
Primary Market Served: Consumer

Mail order catalog & web site for nursing mothers.

THE DMA NATIONAL WHOLESALE CO INC
400 National Blvd
Lexington, NC 27292-2631
Telephone: (336) 248-5904, (800) 480-4673, FAX: (336) 248-2880, E-Mail: customerservice@shopnational.com, Web Site: www.shopnational.com
Pres: E.C. Smith Sr.
CFO: Mike Tate
VP, Adv & DM: Betty Allred
Mktg Mgr: Ian Silverdides
Admin Sec: Cathy Reich
Primary Market Served: Consumer
Catalog available online
Direct online sales
Founded: 1952
Gross sales or billing: $32,355,890

Catalog apparel, lingerie & hosiery sales.

THE DMA NEW YORK & CO
450 W 33rd St (fl 5)
New York, NY 10001-2632
Telephone: (212) 884-2169, Web Site: www.nyandcompany.com
Dir CRM: Evan Rubin

NEWPORT NEWS
Div. of Signature Styles & Artemiss LLC
110 William St (11th Fl)
New York, NY 10038-3945
Telephone: (800) 759-3950, Web Site: www.newport-news.com
Pres & CEO: George Ittner
CFO: James Brewster
VP, Mktg: Martin Smith
Conducts Business: U.S.
Employees: 2,000
Primary Market Served: Consumer
Catalog available online
Direct online sales
Advertising/Marketing Budget Related to Direct Marketing: 76-100%
Founded: 1973

Sell women's fashions by mail nationwide; also home textiles.

NIKE INC
1 SW Bowerman Dr
Beaverton, OR 97005-0979
Telephone: (503) 671-4565, (800) 344-6543, FAX: (503) 671-6300, Web Site: www.nike.com
Co-Founder & Chmn: Phil Knight
CEO: Mark Parker
Consultant: P.J. Santoro
Pres: Charles D. Denson
Pres Global Opers: Gary M. DeStefano
VP & CFO: Donald W. Blair
Employees: 30,000
Primary Market Served: Consumer
Catalog available online
Direct online sales
Gross sales or billing: $16,300,000,000

Manufacturer & retailer of athletic footwear & apparel.

NORDSTROM INC
1700 7th Ave Ste 1000
Seattle, WA 98101-4407
Telephone: (206) 303-2301, FAX: (206) 373-3198
VP, Sls Promos: Linda Finn
Dir, Consumer Insights/Database Mktg: Jay Long
Admin Mgr & Corp Advisor: Jean McDonald
Primary Market Served: Consumer

Retail children's, men's & women's apparel, accessories & shoes. Also, catalog sales.

NU-PARR SWIMWEAR
929 E Indian School Rd
Phoenix, AZ 85014-4745
Telephone: (602) 279-4044, (800) 230-7277, FAX: (602) 212-2636, E-Mail: info@nu-parr.com, Web Site: www.nu-parr.com
Owner: Kim Dye
Conducts Business: U.S., Canada
Primary Market Served: Business & Consumer
Advertising/Marketing Budget Related to Direct Marketing: 0-25%

European men's bikinis, underbriefs & low-rise shorts; tights, short tights & tank tops. Women's custom bikinis & activewear.

THE DMA OAKLEY INC
1 Icon
Foothill Ranch, CA 92610-3000
Telephone: (949) 829-0991, Web Site: www.oakley.com
Direct Mktg Coord: Cale Thompson
Primary Market Served: Business & Consumer

Sunglasses, goggles & apparel

OKUN BROTHERS SHOES INC
179 Portage Rd
Kalamazoo, MI 49007-4801
Telephone: (269) 342-1536, (800) 433-6344, FAX: (269) 383-3401
Mgr: Dan Nawrot
Conducts Business: U.S., Canada
Primary Market Served: Consumer

Catalog mail order company offering famous brand footwear at discount prices.

OLSEN'S MILL DIRECT
1641 S Main St
Oshkosh, WI 54902-6913
Telephone: (800) 537-4979, (800) 452-3699, FAX: (920) 426-6369, E-Mail: sales@olsensmilldirect.com
Pres: Paul Olsen
Conducts Business: Worldwide
Primary Market Served: Consumer
Catalog available online
Advertising/Marketing Budget Related to Direct Marketing: 0-25%
Founded: 1986

Sells clothing via internet and mail order for the entire family.

ONE HANES PLACE CATALOG
Div. of Sara Lee Corp
450 W Hanes Mill Rd
Winston Salem, NC 27105
Telephone: (336) 519-4400, (800) 300-2600, FAX: (336) 519-0655, Web Site: www.onehanesplace.com
VP & Gen Mgr: John Craig
Customer & Electronic Mktg Dir: Carol Davis
Conducts Business: U.S.
Primary Market Served: Consumer
Catalog available online
Direct online sales
Advertising/Marketing Budget Related to Direct Marketing: 76-100%

Apparel.

ORIENT EXPRESSED IMPORTS INC
3905 Magazine St
New Orleans, LA 70115
Telephone: (888) 856-3948, FAX: (504) 899-5566, E-Mail: orient@orientexpressed.com, Web Site: www.orientexpressed.com
Owner: Dabney Jacob
Owner: Bea Fitzpatrick
Catalogue Dir: Mary Malone
Employees: 22
Primary Market Served: Consumer
Catalog available online

Direct online sales
Founded: 1978
Gross sales or billing: $4,000,000

Catalogue company specializing in children's clothes and antiques.

PFI WESTERN STORES INC

2816 S Ingram Mill Rd
Springfield, MO 65804
Telephone: (417) 889-2668, (800) 222-4734, FAX: (417) 889-7204, E-Mail: pfi.@pfiwestern.com, Web Site: www.pfiwestern.com
Owner & Mgr: Randy Little
Employees: 250
Primary Market Served: Business & Consumer
Catalog available online
Direct online sales
Advertising/Marketing Budget Related to Direct Marketing: 51-75%
Direct Marketing ad budget:
Direct Mail: 20%
Magazines: 15%
Newspapers: 5%
TV/Radio: 50%
Telephone: 10%
Founded: 1974

Retail seller of western clothes, boots & gifts.

PANGO PANGO SWIMWEAR CORP

1909 E Atlantic Blvd
Pompano Beach, FL 33060-6562
Telephone: (954) 786-0255, (800) 858-9431, FAX: (954) 786-7745, E-Mail: pango_swimwear@bellsouth.net, Web Site: www.pango-pangoswimwear.com
Pres & CEO: Joan Ashby
Mgr: Meere Sahadeo
Conducts Business: U.S.
Employees: 6
Primary Market Served: Business & Consumer
Catalog available online
Direct online sales
Advertising/Marketing Budget Related to Direct Marketing: 26-50%
Direct Marketing ad budget:
Direct Mail: 45%
Magazines: 5%
Newspapers: 5%
Online: 35%
TV/Radio: 5%
Telephone: 5%
Gross sales or billing: $300,000

Sell mix & match swimwear separates in all sizes from XS to XXL.

PARENTING CONCEPTS INC

25060 Hancock Ave (Suite 103-124)
Murrieta, CA 92562

Telephone: (951) 672-1131, (800) 727-3683, E-Mail: babyslings@aol.com, Web Site: www.parentingconcepts.com
Pres & CEO: Tracy Urban
VP: Norman Urbin
Conducts Business: U.S., Canada
Employees: 5
Primary Market Served: Business & Consumer
Catalog available online
Direct online sales
Advertising/Marketing Budget Related to Direct Marketing: 0-25%
Direct Marketing ad budget:
Direct Mail: 70%
Magazines: 30%
Founded: 1987
Gross sales or billing: $300,000

Baby products, parenting books & children's books.

PASSPORT INTERNATIONAL LTD

4838 Jenkins Ave
North Charleston, SC 29405-4816
Telephone: (843) 881-8690, (800) 606-1383, FAX: (843) 881-6247, E-Mail: csv@passportintl.com, Web Site: www.passportintl.com
Pres: Mike Fewell
VP, Opers: Cindy Williams
Conducts Business: U.S., Canada
Primary Market Served: Business & Consumer
Catalog available online
Direct online sales
Advertising/Marketing Budget Related to Direct Marketing: 76-100%
Founded: 1983
Gross sales or billing: $4,000,000

Personalized clothing company. Direct mail clothing catalog sales.

THE DMA PATAGONIA

259 W Santa Clara St
Ventura, CA 93001-2545
Telephone: (805) 643-8616, Web Site: www.patagonia.com
Mgr: Ken Storey
Primary Market Served: Consumer

PATAGONIA MAIL ORDER INC

Subs. of Patagonia Inc
8550 White Fir St
Reno, NV 89523-2050
Telephone: (775) 747-1992, (800) 638-6464, FAX: (775) 747-6159, Web Site: www.patagonia.com
Pres: Yvon Chouinard
CFO: Dave Abeloe
Mktg Dir Patagonia Inc: Bill Kulczycki
Mktg Mgr: Marlee Griswald

Circ Mgr Catalog Div: Jeff Wogoman
Conducts Business: Worldwide
Employees: 50
Primary Market Served: Consumer
Catalog available online
Direct online sales
Advertising/Marketing Budget Related to Direct Marketing: 0-25%
Direct Marketing ad budget:
Magazines: 90%
Newspapers: 10%
Founded: 1982

Mail order retail & wholesale distributor of outdoor clothing.

THE DMA PAYLESS SHOESOURCE INC

3231 SE 6th Ave
Topeka, KS 66607-2260
Telephone: (785) 233-5171, Web Site: www.payless.com
Dir CRM: Brent Cooke

THE DMA PERUVIAN CONNECTION LTD

24535 McLouth Rd
Tonganoxie, KS 66086-3132
Telephone: (913) 845-2450, Web Site: www.peruvianconnection.com
CFO: Lori Green

Men's & women's luxury alpaca sweaters. Peruvian pima knitwear & jewelry

PHILLIPS-VAN HEUSEN CORP

200 Madison Ave (Bsmt 1)
New York, NY 10016-3913
Telephone: (212) 381-3500, (800) 388-9122, FAX: (212) 381-3950, Web Site: www.pvh.com
Chmn & CEO: Emanuel Chirico
Pres & COO: Mark Weber
Exec VP: Michael Shaffer
VP: Lynn Spindell
Primary Market Served: Business & Consumer
Catalog available online
Indirect online sales

Manufacturers of men's & women's apparel & footwear, mainly shirts.

PILANI'S LIVE IN STYLE

Div. of Overseas Manufacturing Inc
284 Steelmanville Rd
Egg Harbor Township, NJ 08234-7806
Telephone: (609) 927-4686, (800) 537-1832, FAX: (609) 927-5686, E-Mail: sihart@aol.com
Dir: Sanjay Aggarwal
Dir: Bharat Aggarwal
Conducts Business: U.S.
Employees: 6
Primary Market Served: Business & Consumer

Advertising/Marketing Budget Related
to Direct Marketing: 76-100%
Direct Marketing ad budget:
Direct Mail: 75%
Magazines: 25%
Founded: 1985
Gross sales or billing: $700,000

Fashion jewelry & accessories. Sell
mainly to wholesalers.

PLANET COTTON

8001 Cessna Ave
Gaithersburg, MD 20879-4116
Telephone: (301) 948-0400, FAX:
(301) 948-9031, Web Site: www.
planetcotton.com
Mktg Dir: Jim Hickey
Dir Sls & Mktg: Sherry Ramburg
VP: Lorraine Downs
Sr Accountant: Cindy Snow
Sls: Kenny Singer
Conducts Business: U.S.
Employees: 18
Primary Market Served: Business &
Consumer
Catalog available online
Indirect online sales
Direct Marketing ad budget: $300,000
Direct Mail: 80%
Magazines: 20%
Gross sales or billing: $10,000,000

Custom printing of T-shirts, sweat
shirts & other accessories.

THE DMA POLO RALPH LAUREN

9 Polito Ave (fl 5)
Lyndhurst, NJ 07071-3406
Telephone: (212) 531-6537, (800) 377-
7656, FAX: (212) 318-7690, Web
Site: www.ralphlauren.com
Chmn Bd & CEO: Ralph Lauren
Pres, COO & Dir: Rogen N. Farah
Sr VP, HR Legal Dept: Mitchell A.
Kosh
Exec VP: Charles E. Fagan
VP, Mktg: Liz Morris
Sr Dir, Database Mktg Sys: Eli Cohen
Conducts Business: Worldwide
Employees: 14,000
Primary Market Served: Business &
Consumer
Catalog available online
Direct online sales
Advertising/Marketing Budget Related
to Direct Marketing: 0-25%
Direct Marketing ad budget:
Direct Mail: 3%
Magazines: 90%
Newspapers: 5%
TV/Radio: 1%
Telephone: 1%
Founded: 1967
Gross sales or billing: $4,200,000,000

Designer & manufacturer of men's,
women's & children's apparel, footwear, accessories & home furnishings.

QUARTERMASTER UNIFORM & EQUIPMENT CO

PO Box 4147
Cerritos, CA 90703-4147
Telephone: (562) 304-7300, (800) 444-
8643, FAX: (562) 304-7335, Web
Site: www.qmuniforms.com
Pres: James R. DiRosa
Conducts Business: Worldwide
Primary Market Served: Business &
Consumer
Catalog available online
Direct online sales

Sells military clothing--flight jackets,
wearing apparel, insignias, security
uniforms & equipment. Law enforcement uniforms & equipment.

RANGER JOE'S INTERNATIONAL MILITARY SUPPLY

325 Farr Rd
Columbus, GA 31907
Telephone: (706) 689-0082, (800) 247-
4541, FAX: (706) 682-8840, E-Mail:
customerservice@rangerjoes.com,
Web Site: www.rangerjoes.com
Owner: Janice Voorhees
Owner: Paul Voorhees
VP & Office Mgr: Gladys Arroyo
COO: Janet Morris
Adv Dir: Julie Buice
Employees: 85
Primary Market Served: Business &
Consumer
Catalog available online
Advertising/Marketing Budget Related
to Direct Marketing: 26-50%
Founded: 1963

Military and law enforcement gear.

REDCATS USA

463 Fashing Ave (Rm 1603)
New York, NY 10018-7421
Telephone: (212) 613-9500, Web Site:
www.brylane.com
VP: Milton Pappas
Primary Market Served: Consumer

REEBOK INTERNATIONAL LTD

1895 JW Foster Blvd
Canton, MA 02021
Telephone: (781) 401-5000, (800) 843-
4444, FAX: (781) 401-4402, Web
Site: www.reebok.com
Pres & CEO: Paul Harrington
Sr VP & Chief Commun Officer: Den-
ise Kaigler
Employees: 400

Primary Market Served: Consumer
Gross sales or billing: $310,800,000

Retail sales manufacturer of athletic
footwear & apparel.

ROCKETWEAR

Div. of the P'nena Group Inc
101 W 57th St (#15 D)
New York, NY 10019
Telephone: (212) 977-9227, Web Site:
www.rocketwear.net
CEO: P.J. Frishman
Conducts Business: U.S.
Primary Market Served: Business &
Consumer
Catalog available online
Indirect online sales
Founded: 1994

Mail order business offering sleepwear
and loungewear in conversational
prints.

ROD'S WESTERN PALACE

3099 Silver Dr D
Columbus, OH 43224-3945
Telephone: (614) 268-8200, (800) 325-
8508, FAX: (800) 330-7637, E-Mail:
rods@rods.com, Web Site: www.
rods.com
Pres: Scott Hartle
VP: Charles Hartle
Employees: 100
Primary Market Served: Business &
Consumer
Founded: 1976
Gross sales or billing: $14,000,000

Western clothing store.

ROMAN RESEARCH INC/ SIMPLY WHISPERS EARRING

800 Franklin St
Hanson, MA 02341
Telephone: (781) 447-3411, (800) 451-
5700, FAX: (781) 447-0995, Web
Site: www.simplywhispers.com
Pres: Dale Southworth
Mktg Dir: Bill Russell
Conducts Business: U.S.
Employees: 100
Primary Market Served: Business &
Consumer
Catalog available online
Direct online sales
Advertising/Marketing Budget Related
to Direct Marketing: 76-100%
Direct Marketing ad budget: $400,000
Magazines: 100%
Founded: 1970
Gross sales or billing: $5,000,000

Fashion earrings.

SC DIRECT

Div. of Specialty Catalog
400 Manley St Ste 1
West Bridgewater, MA 02379-1085
Telephone: (800) 343-9695, Web Site:
  www.scdirect.com
Pres & CEO: Ron Fabbro
CFO: Peter Tulp
VP Adv & E Commerce: Scott Moore
Employees: 359
Primary Market Served: Business &
  Consumer
Catalog available online
Direct online sales
Advertising/Marketing Budget Related
  to Direct Marketing: 51-75%
Founded: 1978
Gross sales or billing: $60,800,000

Sell women's wigs & fashion apparel
to the Caucasian & African American
market.

DONNA SALYERS' FABULOUS-FURS

25 W Robbins St
Covington, KY 41011-3005
Telephone: (859) 291-3300, (800) 848-
  4650, E-Mail: abell@fabulousfurs.
  com, Web Site: fabulousfurs.com
CEO: Guy van Rooyen
Pres: Ms. Donna Salyers
Dir Opers: Diane Combs
Mktg Dir: John D. Engel
Sr Mktg Mgr: Allison Bell
Conducts Business: U.S., Canada
Employees: 16
Primary Market Served: Consumer
Catalog available online
Direct online sales
Advertising/Marketing Budget Related
  to Direct Marketing: 76-100%
Founded: 1989
Gross sales or billing: $5,800,000

High quality faux fur fashion.

SANSEGAL SPORTSWEAR (HQ)

611 W 9560 S
Sandy, UT 84070-2587
Telephone: (801) 566-3248, (800) 338-
  6048, FAX: (801) 566-3350, E-Mail:
  sansegal@sansegal.com, Web Site:
  www.sansegal.com
Pres: Macon Rudick
CFO: Dale Payne
Natl Sls Mgr: Jim Moore
Employees: 260
Primary Market Served: Business
Gross sales or billing: $18,000,000

Sell T-shirt imprints & sportswear.

SARA LEE DIRECT HOME SHOPPING

Div. of Sara Lee Corp
450 W Hanes Mill Rd
Winston-Salem, NC 27105
Telephone: (336) 519-4400, (800) 671-
  5056, E-Mail: ohp.managor@
  onehanesplace.com, Web Site: www.
  onehanesplace.com
CEO: Charles Chambers
VP, One Hanes Place: John Craig
Dir, Just My Size: Jennifer Akers
Dir, New Ventures: Cindy Sutton
Conducts Business: U.S.
Employees: 3,000
Primary Market Served: Consumer
Catalog available online
Direct online sales
Advertising/Marketing Budget Related
  to Direct Marketing: 76-100%
Direct Marketing ad budget:
Direct Mail: $40,000,000
Founded: 1978
Gross sales or billing: $200,000,000

Direct sales of Sara Lee apparel.

SARA LEE HOSIERY

1000 E Hanes Mill Rd
Winston Salem, NC 27105-1384
Telephone: (336) 519-2711/2369, FAX:
  (336) 519-3254, Web Site: www.
  leggs.com
Pres & CEO L'eggs Div: Mike Flatow
VP: Vicki Chancellor
VP Mktg: Howard Upchurch
Mktg Dir: Dave McBride
Primary Market Served: Consumer

Textile company that retails underwear
& hosiery.

THE DMA SCULPTZ

1150 Northbrook Dr Ste 300
Feasterville Trevose, PA 19053-8443
Telephone: (215) 494-2900, E-Mail:
  sdudek@sculptz.com, Web Site:
  www.silkies.com
Sr Dir Mktg: Sue Dudek
Natl Sls Rep: Amanda Bird
Conducts Business: United States,
  Canada, United Kingdom, Germany
Primary Market Served: Consumer
Founded: 1974

SHEPLERS CATALOG SALES INC

Div. of Sheplers Westernwear Inc
6501 W Kellogg
Wichita, KS 67209
Telephone: (316) 946-3838, (800) 835-
  4004, FAX: (316) 946-3729, Web
  Site: www.sheplers.com
Pres: Mike Anop
CFO: John Mosley
VP, Catalog Mktg: Mark Hampton
VP, Mdsg: Tom Tongue
VP, Adv & Promo: John Wilcox
Conducts Business: Worldwide
Employees: 300
Primary Market Served: Consumer

Advertising/Marketing Budget Related
  to Direct Marketing: 26-50%
Direct Marketing ad budget:
  $10,000,000
Direct Mail: 100%
Gross sales or billing: $100,000,000

Sell western apparel for the entire family through catalog & retail. Merchandise is geared to leisure living in the
western manner. Assortments include a
variety of gifts for all ages. Stores in
20 cities.

SHORT SIZES INC

907 Spicers Ln
Northfield, OH 44067-2235
Telephone: (440) 605-1000, (800) 272-
  9000, FAX: (440) 605-1065, E-Mail:
  orders@shortsizesinc.com, Web Site:
  www.shortsizesinc.com
Pres: Robert Stern
VP: Tom Schwab
Bookkeeper: Susan Murray
Conducts Business: U.S., Japan, Eu-
  rope
Employees: 12
Primary Market Served: Consumer
Catalog available online
Indirect online sales
Advertising/Marketing Budget Related
  to Direct Marketing: 51-75%
Direct Marketing ad budget:
Direct Mail: 70%
Magazines: 10%
Newspapers: 15%
TV/Radio: 5%
Founded: 1972

Distinctive apparel for men & young
men under five feet, eight inches.

SICKAFUS SHEEPSKINS

8373 Rte 183
Strausstown, PA 19559
Telephone: (610) 488-1782, (888) 751-
  1300, FAX: (610) 488-1576, E-Mail:
  pat@patgarrett.com, Web Site: www.
  sheepcoat.com
Pres: Patrick Garrett
Conducts Business: U.S., Canada
Primary Market Served: Consumer
Catalog available online
Indirect online sales
Founded: 1966

Sell sheepskin coats, vests, slippers &
car, truck, airplane & motorcycle seat
covers both wholesale & retail.

THE DMA SIERRA TRADING POST

5025 Campstool Rd
Cheyenne, WY 82007-1816
Telephone: (307) 775-8050, (800) 713-
  4534, FAX: (307) 775-8089, Web
  Site: www.sierratradingpost.com
Pres: Keith Richardson
CFO: Gary Imig

Pur Mgr: Ken Walter
Mktg Coord: T.J. Croissant
Catalog Mgr: Sheila Russell
Employees: 500
Primary Market Served: Consumer
Catalog available online
Direct online sales
Founded: 1986

Sell name brand clothing, footwear, and outdoor gear.

SIGNATURE STYLES LLC
110 Wiliam St (11th Fl)
New York, NY 10038-3945
Telephone: (800) 443-4856, FAX:
    (902) 862-5063
VP Acctg: Patty Lyon
Primary Market Served: Consumer

THE DMA SOFT SURROUNDINGS
1100 N Lindbergh Blvd
Saint Louis, MO 63132-2914
Telephone: (314) 812-5200, Web Site:
    www.softsurroundings.com
CEO: Thomas Wilcher
Primary Market Served: Consumer

SPIEGEL BRANDS INC
Div. of Signature Styles & Artemiss
    LLC
110 William St (11th Fl)
New York, NY 10038-3945
Telephone: (800) 222-5680, Web Site:
    www.spiegel.com
SVP Mktg: Tony Chivari
Primary Market Served: Consumer

SPORTIF MAIL ORDER INC
Div. of Sportif USA Inc
1415 Greg St (Suite 101)
Sparks, NV 89431
Telephone: (775) 359-6400, (800) 776-
    7843, FAX: (800) 776-3291, Web
    Site: www.sportif.com
Controller: Doug Moir
Inventory Mgr & Buyer: Kim Radzik
MIS Mgr: Mike Youngblood
Circ Mgr: Matt Glerum
Conducts Business: Worldwide
Employees: 29
Primary Market Served: Business &
    Consumer
Catalog available online
Advertising/Marketing Budget Related
    to Direct Marketing: 76-100%
Direct Marketing ad budget:
    $2,500,000
Direct Mail: 100%
Founded: 1965
Gross sales or billing: $4,500,000

Specialty active apparel for the outdoor enthusiast & comfortable casual wear for business & pleasure.

STAR SILKSCREEEN DESIGN INC
2281 Hubbard Ave
Decatur, IL 62526-2149
Telephone: (217) 877-0804, FAX:
    (217) 877-0843
Pres: Jon Kozeliski
VP: Karen Rajee
Employees: 5
Primary Market Served: Consumer
Gross sales or billing: $600,000

Silk screen & embroidery on fabric articles.

PAUL STUART
Madison Ave & 45th St
New York, NY 10017
Telephone: (212) 682-0320, FAX:
    (212) 983-5871, E-Mail: info@
    paulstuart.com, Web Site: www.
    paulstuart.com
Pres: Clifford Grodd
Brand Mgr: Jack Freedman
Catalog Opers Dir: Mona Reilly
Conducts Business: U.S.
Employees: 250
Primary Market Served: Consumer
Direct online sales
Advertising/Marketing Budget Related
    to Direct Marketing: 51-75%
Direct Marketing ad budget:
Direct Mail: 60%
Newspapers: 35%
Online: 5%

Retail & catalog sales of men's & women's apparel.

STULLER, INC
302 Rue Louis XIV, PO Box 87777
Lafayette, LA 70508
Telephone: (337) 262-7700, (800) 877-
    7777, FAX: (337) 981-1655, E-Mail:
    info@stuller.com, Web Site: www.
    stuller.com
Chmn & CEO: Matthew G. Stuller
Pres & COO: Chuck Lein
Exec VP & CFO: Linus Cortez
VP, Mktg: Ray Stroup Jr.
Employees: 1,500
Primary Market Served: Consumer
Catalog available online
Direct online sales
Advertising/Marketing Budget Related
    to Direct Marketing: 26-50%
Founded: 1970
Gross sales or billing: $112,000,000

Jewelry items.

TCJC
40 W 37th St Ph A
New York, NY 10018-7415
Telephone: (212) 268-4100, FAX:
    (212) 268-4209
Pres: Martin P. Krasner

Conducts Business: U.S., Canada
Primary Market Served: Business &
    Consumer
Advertising/Marketing Budget Related
    to Direct Marketing: 76-100%
Direct Marketing ad budget:
Direct Mail: 50%
Magazines: 50%

Women's costume jewelry, apparel & accessories.

TAFFORD UNIFORMS
104 Park Dr
Montgomeryville, PA 18936-9612
Telephone: (215) 643-9666, E-Mail:
    customerservice@tafford.com, Web
    Site: www.tafford.com
VP Mktg: David Kaplan
Conducts Business: U.S., Canada
Primary Market Served: Consumer
Catalog available online
Direct online sales
Advertising/Marketing Budget Related
    to Direct Marketing: 76-100%

Nursing uniforms, scrubs, stethoscopes, nursing shoes and medical accessories sold to nurses, doctors, dentists, hygienists and veterinarians.

THE DMA TALBOTS
Div. of Jusco Co Ltd/AEON Group
One Talbots Dr
Hingham, MA 02043-1583
Telephone: (781) 749-7600, (800) 825-
    2687, FAX: (781) 741-4369, Web
    Site: www.talbots.com
Pres & CEO: Trudy Sullivan
CFO: Edward Larsen
Exec VP & Chief Mktg Officer: Lori
    Wagner
Sr VP Dir Mktg & Customer Svc:
    Bruce Prescott
Conducts Business: Worldwide
Employees: 10,000
Primary Market Served: Consumer
Catalog available online

Specialty retailer, cataloger and e-tailer of women's classic apparel, shoes and accessories. Also offers children's and men's clothing.

THE DMA TAMRAC INC
9240 Jordan Ave
Chatsworth, CA 91311-5769
Telephone: (818) 407-9500, Web Site:
    www.tamrac.com
VP & CFO: Russell Kantor
Primary Market Served: Business &
    Consumer

Camera carrying systems, such as camera bags, camera cases, photo daypacks & photo backpacks

ANN TAYLOR INC
Subs. of Macy's
7 Times Square Tower (Fl 14)
New York, NY 10036
Telephone: (212) 457-2075, (800)
FAX-ANN, FAX: (800) DIAL-ANN,
Web Site: www.anninc.com
Pres & CEO, Macy's: Terry J.
Lundgren
Pres & CEO: Kay Krill
Exec VP & CFO: Karen M. Hoquest
Conducts Business: U.S.
Employees: 2,000
Primary Market Served: Business &
Consumer
Catalog available online
Direct online sales

Marketer of contemporary women's
fashions.

TEAM CHEER
131 Main St Ste 2
Geneseo, NY 14454-1242
Telephone: (585) 243-8400, (585) 243-
0841, (877) 243-5268, FAX: (800)
350-1562, E-Mail: custserv@
teamcheer.com, Web Site: www.
teamcheer.com
Pres & CEO: Randy Cofield
VP Creative Svcs: Linda Cofield
Dir Sls & Mktg: Cindy Sobieraj
Fulfillment Mgr: Dan Johnson
Mktg Mgr: Sherry Paddon
Conducts Business: U.S.
Employees: 25
Primary Market Served: Business &
Consumer
Catalog available online
Direct online sales
Advertising/Marketing Budget Related
to Direct Marketing: 76-100%
Founded: 1991
Gross sales or billing: $2,800,000

Provides cheer and dance apparel and
accessories.

**NORM THOMPSON
OUTFITTERS INC**
3188 NW Aloclek Dr
Hillsboro, OR 97124
Telephone: (503) 614-4600, (800) 547-
1160, FAX: (503) 614-4599, Web
Site: www.normthompson.com
Chmn: John Emrick
Pres: Neale Attenborough
CEO: Shelley Nandkeolyar
Conducts Business: U.S.
Employees: 500
Primary Market Served: Consumer
Advertising/Marketing Budget Related
to Direct Marketing: 0-25%
Founded: 1949
Gross sales or billing: $200,000,000

Mail order firm selling high quality
clothing by direct mail to the general
public. Also, footwear, foods & gifts.

THE TOG SHOP INC
Subsidiary of Appleseed's
30 Tozer Rd
Beverly, MA 01915
Telephone: (800) 342-6789, FAX:
(800) 755-7557, Web Site: www.
togshop.com
CEO & Pres: Paula Bennett
CIO: Jane Pendergast
Dir: Margaret Donohue
Conducts Business: U.S.
Employees: 350
Primary Market Served: Consumer
Catalog available online
Direct online sales
Advertising/Marketing Budget Related
to Direct Marketing: 76-100%
Direct Marketing ad budget:
Direct Mail: 100%

Retail & mail order sales of ladies
clothing & footwear.

TUTTLE
23 Village Ln
Wallingford, CT 06492-2426
Telephone: (203) 949-4290, (800) 882-
7511, FAX: (203) 949-4288, Web
Site: www.tuttlecatalog.com
Pres: Ben Mosher
Co-Owner: Adam Mosher
Conducts Business: Worldwide
Primary Market Served: Business &
Consumer
Catalog available online
Direct online sales
Advertising/Marketing Budget Related
to Direct Marketing: 76-100%
Founded: 1990

Consumer mail order products. Sports
apparel for golf & tennis.

UNDERCOVERWEAR INC
30 Commerce Way (Unit 2)
Tewksbury, MA 01876
Telephone: (978) 851-8580, FAX:
(978) 640-2882, E-Mail: jamiej@
undercoverwear.com, Web Site:
www.undercoverwear.com
Pres: Walter James
CEO: Tiffany James
VP: Adrian Canto
VP: Jamie Jamitkowski
Sls Dir: Nancy Cosimini
Conducts Business: U.S., Canada
Employees: 140
Primary Market Served: Consumer
Catalog available online
Direct online sales
Advertising/Marketing Budget Related
to Direct Marketing: 26-50%
Founded: 1977

Gross sales or billing: $100,000,000
Distributes Lingerie - Home Party
Planning.

UNDERGEAR.COM
455 Park Plz Dr
La Crosse, WI 54601
Telephone: (717) 633-3413, (800) 853-
8555, FAX: (717) 633-3214, Web
Site: www.undergear.com
Primary Market Served: Business &
Consumer

Men's fashion.

UNIFIRST CORP
2801 UniFirst Dr
Owensboro, KY 42301-7701
Telephone: (270) 683-5250 X523, Web
Site: www.unifirst.com
Catalog Mgr: Sherry Cecil
Primary Market Served: Consumer

UNITED RETAIL INC
365 W Passaic St (Suite 230)
Rochelle Park, NJ 07662-3017
Telephone: (201) 845-0880, Web Site:
www.avenue.com
VP Mktg: Brad Orloff
Primary Market Served: Consumer

VF IMAGEWEAR
Div. of VF Workwear
545 Marriott Dr (Ste 200)
Nashville, TN 37214-5077
Telephone: (615) 565-5000, (800) 733-
5271, Web Site: www.
vfimagewear.com
COO: Robert Gates
VP, Direct Sls: Ronald O. Pate Sr
VP, Indirect Sls: Jim Tewmey
Mdsg & Prod Devel Dir: Dave Neimer
Mktg Svcs Dir: Elaine Wilber
Conducts Business: Worldwide
Employees: 1,500
Primary Market Served: Business
Catalog available online
Advertising/Marketing Budget Related
to Direct Marketing: 26-50%
Founded: 1972
Gross sales or billing: $218,400,000

Complete uniform & accessory programs for government & law enforcement agencies & private industry. Apparel manufacturing company.

VENATOR GROUP
Subs. of Woolworth Corp
112 W 34th St
New York, NY 10020
Telephone: (212) 720-3700, FAX:
(212) 720-4689
Pres & COO: Matt Serra
Conducts Business: U.S., Europe
Primary Market Served: Consumer

Retail shoe stores.

THE DMA VENUS FASHION, INC
11711 Mario Beach Dr
Jacksonville, FL 32224
Telephone: (904) 645-6000, Web Site:
www.venus.com
Primary Market Served: Business &
Consumer

**VICTORIA'S SECRET
CATALOGUE**
Subs. of Limited Inc & Div. of Inti-
mate Brands Inc
PO Box 16589
Columbus, OH 43216-6589
FAX: (614) 337-5075, Web Site: www.
victoriassecret.com
VP, Circ: Sue Horn
Conducts Business: U.S., Canada
Employees: 3,000
Primary Market Served: Consumer
Catalog available online
Direct online sales
Advertising/Marketing Budget Related
to Direct Marketing: 76-100%
Direct Marketing ad budget:
Magazines: 100%
Founded: 1982

Catalog marketer of designer lingerie
& fine quality sportswear.

WARNACO
501 Fashion Ave Fl 14
New York, NY 10018-5942
Telephone: (212) 287-8207, FAX:
(212) 682-7368, E-Mail: contactus@
warnaco.com, Web Site: www.
warnaco.com
CEO: Joseph Gromek
Primary Market Served: Business &
Consumer

Men's & women's apparel products.

WASSERMAN UNIFORM CO
700 NW 57th Pl
Fort Lauderdale, FL 33309
Telephone: (614) 279-8888, (614) 279-
7000, (800) 848-3576, FAX: (614)
464-0416, (800) 204-0416, E-Mail:
custserv@wassermanuniform.com,
Web Site: www.wassermanuniform.
com
CEO, CFO & Gen Mgr: Joel Luck
Postal Sls Mgr: Ted McCord
Conducts Business: U.S.
Employees: 105
Primary Market Served: Business &
Consumer
Founded: 1971
Gross sales or billing: $5,500,000

Uniform apparel & shoes: postal, fire
& industrial.

WATHNE LTD
156 W 56 St
New York, NY 10019
Telephone: (212) 757-3001, FAX:
(212) 757-2448
Pres: Ron Senkirk
VP: Andrea Dubrow
Mktg Dir: Steve Izoz
Primary Market Served: Business &
Consumer

Handbag manufacturer.

WEARGUARD CORP
141 Longwater Dr
Norwell, MA 02061-1683
Telephone: (781) 871-4100, (800) 388-
3300, FAX: (781) 871-2639, Web
Site: www.wearguard.com
Chmn & Pres: David Gold
CFO: Bill Glass
Conducts Business: U.S.
Employees: 1,200
Primary Market Served: Business &
Consumer
Catalog available online
Direct online sales

Catalog & mail order house selling
work clothing, footwear & accessories.

**THE WEXNER COMPANIES
INC**
418 S Grove Park Rd
Memphis, TN 38117-3518
Telephone: (901) 763-3925, (800) 890-
5470, FAX: (901) 763-3736, E-Mail:
info@JosephStores.com, Web Site:
www.josephstores.com
Pres: Alfred B. Wexner
Adv Coord: Nancy Sewell
Asst Adv Coord: Lee Thompson
Conducts Business: U.S.
Employees: 60
Primary Market Served: Consumer
Catalog available online
Direct online sales
Gross sales or billing: $12,800,000

Retailer of high fashion ladies shoes &
related products, apparel & accessories.
Manufacturer, wholesale & retail shoe
stores.

THE WIG CO
Div. of Vincent James Co Inc
1391 McLaughlin Run Rd
Pittsburgh, PA 15241
Telephone: (412) 221-4790, (800) 456-
1788, FAX: (412) 257-8181, E-Mail:
custserv@twcwigs.com
Owner & Pres: Vincent James DeCar-
lucci
Co-Owner: Karen DeCarlucci
Controller: Jim McCassney
Conducts Business: U.S., Canada
Employees: 40

Primary Market Served: Consumer

Catalog shopping service featuring Eva
Gabor brand of ladies' synthetic wigs
& hairpieces. Mail or Customer Service available for wigs.

**WILLIAMSON-DICKIE
MANUFACTURING CO**
509 W Vickery Blvd
Fort Worth, TX 76104
Telephone: (800) 336-7201, FAX:
(817) 877-5027, E-Mail:
customerservice@dickies.com, Web
Site: www.dickies.com
Chmn, CEO & Pres: Phillip C. Will-
iamson
CFO: Britt Ingebritson
VP, Mktg Svcs: John Ragsdale
Primary Market Served: Business
Catalog available online
Direct online sales

A garment manufacturing company.

WILSONS LEATHER
7401 Boone Ave N
Brooklyn Park, MN 55428
Telephone: (763) 391-4000, (866) 305-
4704, FAX: (763) 391-4906, Web
Site: www.wilsonsleather.com
CEO: Michael M. Searles
VP Store Sls & Real Estate: M. Adam
Boucher
Mktg Mgr: Lisa Kummer
Employees: 3,461
Primary Market Served: Consumer
Founded: 1899
Gross sales or billing: $321,300,000

Sells leather goods.

WINTERSILKS LLC
100 Murray Dr
Warren, PA 16368-0001
Telephone: (904) 645-6000, Web Site:
www.wintersilks.com
Pres: Chris Vig
VP, Mdsg: Jay Saftchick
Mgr: Kimberly During
Conducts Business: U.S., Canada
Employees: 10
Primary Market Served: Consumer
Catalog available online
Direct online sales
Advertising/Marketing Budget Related
to Direct Marketing: 76-100%

Catalog marketer of silk clothing for
winter warmth. Mail order catalog
company.

THE DMA WOOLRICH INC
2 Mill St
Woolrich, PA 17779
Telephone: (570) 769-6464, Web Site:
www.woolrich.com
Special Projects Mgr: Lisa Smith

Primary Market Served: Consumer

ZAPPOS.COM
2280 Corporate Cir (Suite 100)
Henderson, NV 89074-6382
Telephone: (702) 943-7832, Web Site:
  www.zappos.com
Brand Mktg Mgr: Michelle Thomas

Electronics, Audio, Computer & Video Catalogs (3)

ACE COMMUNICATIONS
625 Locust St Ste 300
Garden City, NY 11530-6557
Telephone: (718) 458-3800, (800) 468-7667, FAX: (516) 872-8156, Web Site: www.aceav.com
Chmn & CEO: Matt O'Reilly
VP & CFO: Neil Seiden
Mktg Mgr: Younjee Kim
Mktg Mgr: Nyoto Wallace
Conducts Business: U.S.
Employees: 30
Primary Market Served: Business
Catalog available online
Indirect online sales
Advertising/Marketing Budget Related to Direct Marketing: 0-25%
Direct Marketing ad budget:
Direct Mail: 80%
Telephone: 20%

Sale, rental & service of audiovisual & video equipment.

AEROGRAPHICS
1725 N Lexington Ave
DeLand, FL 32724
Telephone: (386) 736-4793, FAX: (386) 736-9786, Web Site: www.skydivingmagazine.com
Publr: Michael F. Truffer
Editor: Sue Clifton
Adv: Sandy Bobo
Conducts Business: U.S.
Employees: 6
Primary Market Served: Business & Consumer
Founded: 1979

Books & videos.

AMERICAN MEGATRENDS INC
5555 Oakbrook Pkwy (Suite 200)
Norcross, GA 30093-2286
Telephone: (770) 246-8600, (800) 828-9264, FAX: (770) 246-8790, Web Site: www.ami.com
Pres & CEO: Subromanian Shankar
CFO: Victor Kannan
Sls Dir: Howard Johnston
Dir Engrng: Carl Sheadoker
Conducts Business: U.S., Germany, India, Japan, Taiwan, U.K.
Employees: 500
Primary Market Served: Business & Consumer
Catalog available online
Direct online sales
Advertising/Marketing Budget Related to Direct Marketing: 0-25%
Founded: 1985

Core technology provider of RAID, BIOS, motherboard and utilities.

AMERICAN POWER CONVERSION CORP
132 Fairgrounds Rd
West Kingston, RI 02889
Telephone: (401) 789-5735, (800) 788-2208, FAX: (401) 789-3710, E-Mail: public.relations@apcc.com, Web Site: www.apcc.com
Chmn, Pres & CEO: Rodger B. Dowdell Jr
Sr VP & CTO: Neil E. Ramussen
Sr VP, Fin & CFO: Richard J. Thompson
Conducts Business: Worldwide
Employees: 1,200
Primary Market Served: Business & Consumer
Catalog available online
Advertising/Marketing Budget Related to Direct Marketing: 0-25%
Direct Marketing ad budget: $1,500,000
Direct Mail: 100%
Founded: 1981
Gross sales or billing: $2,000,000,000

Designs, develops, manufactures & markets a line of uninterruptible power supply products (UPS) for use with computers & other sensitive electronic devices. Markets its products worldwide through computer distributor & dealers, mass merchandisers, catalog merchandisers & private label accounts.

AMERICAN RESEARCH CORP
11581 Federal Rd
El Monte, CA 91731
Telephone: (626) 284-1904, (800) FIND-ARC, (800) 346-3272, FAX: (626) 284-4213, E-Mail: arcinfo@800findarc.com, Web Site: www.800findarc.com
Pres: Alex Hou
Employees: 40
Primary Market Served: Business & Consumer
Founded: 1985

Computer systems, components, peripherals & software.

ANGEL RECORDS
150 Fifth Ave
New York, NY 10011
Telephone: (212) 786-8600, FAX: (212) 253-3119, Web Site: www.angelrecords.com
Sr VP & Gen Mgr: Gilbert Hegtherwick
Primary Market Served: Consumer

Market music.

ANTIQUE ELECTRONIC SUPPLY
6221 S Maple Ave
Tempe, AZ 85283
Telephone: (480) 820-5411, (800) 706-6789, FAX: (480) 820-4643, E-Mail: info@tubesandmore.com, Web Site: www.tubesandmore.com
Pres, Opers: Noreen Cravener
VP, Tech Svcs: Greg Cravener
Conducts Business: Worldwide
Employees: 24
Primary Market Served: Business & Consumer
Catalog available online
Indirect online sales
Founded: 1982

Electron tubes (vacuum tubes) & other electronic parts, supplies & books.

AREA ELECTRONICS SYSTEMS INC
1247 N Lakeview Ave Ste C
Anaheim, CA 92807-1833
Telephone: (714) 993-0300, (800) 796-1580, FAX: (714) 993-0987, E-Mail: areasales@areasys.com, Web Site: www.areasys.com
Mktg Mgr: Hao Zhang
Conducts Business: Worldwide
Primary Market Served: Business
Founded: 1987
Gross sales or billing: $15,000,000

Manufacturer of computers & multimedia systems.

ARKLINE COMPUTERS & SUPPLY
Div. of Arkline Inc
14524 Orchard Park Ave
Cleveland, OH 44111
Telephone: (216) 252-6560, (800) 695-1441, FAX: (216) 671-2037, Web Site: www.geocities.com
Pres: Ray W. Tapajna
Conducts Business: U.S., Canada
Primary Market Served: Business & Consumer
Advertising/Marketing Budget Related to Direct Marketing: 26-50%
Direct Marketing ad budget:
Direct Mail: 40%
Magazines: 20%
Newspapers: 10%
Telephone: 30%
Founded: 1976
Gross sales or billing: $250,000

Computer warranty programs & repair, keyboards & toner cartridges for printers & copiers. Internet online business.

ARROW ADVANTAGE

Div. of Arrow Electronics Inc
7627 Anagram Dr
Eden Prairie, MN 55344-7310
Telephone: (952) 906-7100, (800) 833-3557, FAX: (952) 906-7135, Web Site: www.arrow.com
Chmn, Pres & CEO: William E. Mitchell
Conducts Business: U.S.
Employees: 26
Primary Market Served: Business & Consumer
Advertising/Marketing Budget Related to Direct Marketing: 0-25%

Distributor of electronic components.

ASSISTED ACCESS- NFSS

PO Box 230
Lake Villa, IL 60046
Telephone: (847) 265-8022, (800) 950-9655, FAX: (888) 552-1708, E-Mail: sales@nfss.com, Web Site: www.nfss.com
Pres: Diane Tischler
Conducts Business: U.S., Canada
Employees: 4
Primary Market Served: Business & Consumer
Catalog available online
Direct online sales
Advertising/Marketing Budget Related to Direct Marketing: 26-50%
Founded: 1976

Sales & repair service of products for the hearing-impaired such as telecommunication devices & visual alerting signalers.

AUDIO CLASSICS LTD

3501 Vestal Rd
Vestal, NY 13850-2244
Telephone: (607) 766-3501, FAX: (607) 766-3502, E-Mail: steve@audioclassics.com, Web Site: www.audioclassics.com
Pres: Steve Rowell
VP: Mike Sastra
Retail Sls Mgr: Brian Smith
Sls Rep: Frank Gow
Sls Rep: Ernie Schleider
Conducts Business: Worldwide
Primary Market Served: Business & Consumer
Catalog available online
Indirect online sales
Advertising/Marketing Budget Related to Direct Marketing: 51-75%
Direct Marketing ad budget: $90,000
Direct Mail: 65%
Magazines: 25%
Newspapers: 10%
Founded: 1979
Gross sales or billing: $2,600,000

High-end stereo equipment.

AUDIO EDITIONS BOOKS-ON-CASSETTE & CD

Div. of The Audio Partners Inc
PO Box 6930
Auburn, CA 95604-6930
Telephone: (800) 231-4261, FAX: (800) 882-1840, E-Mail: info@audioeditions.com, Web Site: www.audioeditions.com
CEO: Grady Hesters
Catalog Mgr: Hazel Guse
Dir Sls & Mktg: Frank Gianopulos
Conducts Business: U.S.
Employees: 35
Primary Market Served: Consumer
Catalog available online
Direct online sales
Advertising/Marketing Budget Related to Direct Marketing: 76-100%
Direct Marketing ad budget:
Direct Mail: 80%
Online: 20%
Founded: 1987

Complete AudioBook source. Over 19,000 titles including bestsellers, mysteries and more.

BBC WORLDWIDE AMERICAS INC

1120 Ave of the Americas (Fl 5)
New York, NY 10036-6700
Telephone: (212) 705-9300, (800) 898-4921, FAX: (212) 888-0576, Web Site: www.bbcamerica.com
Pres: Herb Scannell
COO: Ann Sarnoff
CFO: Andrew Bott
Conducts Business: U.S.
Primary Market Served: Consumer
Catalog available online
Direct online sales

Offers the U.S. British programming through its website & catalog. Markets DVDs, books, audiobooks, music, home decor & collectibles developed for BBC & British brands.

BDL HOMEWARE

PO Box 11744
Glendale, AZ 85318-1744
Telephone: (623) 572-5038, (800) BDL-4BDL, FAX: (623) 572-5082
Pres: Bette Laswell
Conducts Business: U.S., Canada
Employees: 1
Primary Market Served: Consumer
Founded: 1983

Developer of small business software.

BARNES & NOBLE DIRECT

Div. of Barnes & Noble Bookstores Inc
76 9th Ave Fl 9
New York, NY 10011-4962
Telephone: (212) 414-6000, FAX: (212) 414-6171, Web Site: www.barnesandnoble.com
VP, Catalog Mktg: Greg Oviatt
Conducts Business: Worldwide
Employees: 200
Primary Market Served: Consumer
Advertising/Marketing Budget Related to Direct Marketing: 76-100%
Direct Marketing ad budget: $10,000,000
Direct Mail: 95%
Magazines: 5%
Gross sales or billing: $33,000,000

Book video catalog sold primarily to consumers & some institutional marketing, schools & libraries.

BELTONE

2601 Patriot Blvd
Glenview, IL 60026-8023
Telephone: (800) 235-8663, FAX: (847) 832-3300, E-Mail: info@beltone.com, Web Site: www.beltone.com
Pres: Alan Dozier
VP, Bus Communs: Barbara Van Someren
Conducts Business: Worldwide
Employees: 1,000
Primary Market Served: Business & Consumer
Advertising/Marketing Budget Related to Direct Marketing: 76-100%

In-house agency for Beltone Electronics Corp, manufacturer of hearing aids & hearing test instruments distributed through 3,000 authorized dispenser offices in the U.S., Canada & 47 countries worldwide.

BENNETT MARINE VIDEO

2321 Abbot Kinney Blvd Ste 201
Venice, CA 90291-4876
Telephone: (310) 827-8064, (800) 733-8862, FAX: (310) 827-8074, E-Mail: questions@bennettmarine.com, Web Site: www.bennettmarine.com
Pres: Michael Bennett
Catalog available online
Direct online sales
Gross sales or billing: $100,000

BERKSHIRE RECORD OUTLET INC

461 Pleasant St
Lee, MA 01238-9804
Telephone: (413) 243-4080, FAX: (413) 243-4340, E-Mail: broinc@berkshirerecordoutlet.com, Web Site: www2.broinc.com
Mgr: Steve Nikitas
Conducts Business: U.S., Japan
Employees: 15

Primary Market Served: Business & Consumer
Catalog available online
Direct online sales
Advertising/Marketing Budget Related to Direct Marketing: 0-25%
Founded: 1974

Deleted & overstocked classical compact discs, tapes, LPs & videos, as well as books on classical music.

BERWAY VISUAL PRODUCTS INC

668 Main St (Suite 10)
Wilmington, MA 01887-3377
Telephone: (978) 694-9195, (800) 452-0410, FAX: (978) 694-9212, E-Mail: sales@berway.com, Web Site: www.berway.com
Pres: Bernadette Gerald
Opers & Sls Mgr: Michael Gerald
Office Mgr: Terri Amaral
Conducts Business: U.S.
Employees: 7
Primary Market Served: Business & Consumer
Catalog available online
Indirect online sales
Advertising/Marketing Budget Related to Direct Marketing: 0-25%
Direct Marketing ad budget: $10,000
Direct Mail: 60%
Magazines: 15%
Telephone: 25%
Founded: 1996
Gross sales or billing: $1,300,000

AV sales, design & installation.

THE DMA BEST BUY

7601 Penn Ave S
Richfield, MN 55423-3683
Telephone: (612) 291-1000, Web Site: www.bestbuy.com
Dir Customer Loyalty Mktg: Mark Juba
Primary Market Served: Consumer

BIGELOW ELECTRONICS

186 E Jefferson St
Bluffton, OH 45817-0125
Telephone: (419) 358-7851
Owner: C. Bigelow
Conducts Business: U.S.
Primary Market Served: Business & Consumer
Advertising/Marketing Budget Related to Direct Marketing: 76-100%
Founded: 1954

Sell electronic parts, tools & kits to factories, schools, repair shops & hobbyists.

BLACK BOX CORP

1000 Park Dr
Lawrence, PA 15055-1018
Telephone: (412) 873-6795, (877) 877-2269, FAX: (800) 321-0746, E-Mail: brian.kutchma@blackbox.com, Web Site: www.blackbox.com
CEO & Pres: Terry Blakemore
Dir Mktg: Brian Kutchma
Conducts Business: Worldwide
Employees: 4,384
Primary Market Served: Business
Catalog available online
Direct online sales
Founded: 1976
Gross sales or billing: $999,458,000

Providers of voice communications, data infrastructure & 118,000 networking products, dedicated to designing & building & maintaining today's integrated voice & data communications systems.

BLUE RAVEN TECHNOLOGY

110 Fordham Rd
Wilmington, MA 01887-2165
Telephone: (781) 778-4600, (800) 274-5343, (800) 20RAVEN, FAX: (781) 778-4848, E-Mail: sales@blueraven.com, Web Site: www.blueraven.com
VP: Charles H. Kouyoumjian
Dir Bus Opers: Jeffrey S. Harrison
Exec VP Sls Mktg: Barry Yates
Conducts Business: United States
Employees: 200
Primary Market Served: Business & Consumer
Catalog available online
Direct online sales
Advertising/Marketing Budget Related to Direct Marketing: 0-25%
Direct Marketing ad budget:
Online: 25%
Telephone: 75%
Founded: 1985
Gross sales or billing: $100,000

Remanufacturer of brand personal computers (Compaq, H-P, IBM, Apple) and repair parts. Sell through catalogs.

BOSE CORP

Div. of The Bose Corp
The Mountain
Framingham, MA 01701-9168
Telephone: (508) 879-7330, FAX: (508) 766-7543
CEO & Chm: Amar G. Bose
Conducts Business: Worldwide
Primary Market Served: Consumer
Stereo equipment.

BRIM ELECTRONICS INC

120 Home Pl
Lodi, NJ 07644

Telephone: (201) 796-2886, FAX: (973) 778-2792, E-Mail: info@brimelectronics.com, Web Site: www.brimelectronics.com
Pres: B. Danziger
Gen Mgr: B. Brown
Sls: M. Aaron
Conducts Business: U.S., Canada, Europe, Asia, Africa
Employees: 45
Primary Market Served: Business
Catalog available online
Indirect online sales
Advertising/Marketing Budget Related to Direct Marketing: 0-25%
Direct Marketing ad budget:
Direct Mail: 25%
Magazines: 60%
Telephone: 15%
Founded: 1975

Sell electronic wires & cables, tubings & sleevings, fastening devices & ceramic insulators to OEMs, government, institutions, distributors & supply houses.

BROADCAST ELECTRONICS INC

4100 N 24th St
Quincy, IL 62305
Telephone: (217) 224-9600, FAX: (217) 224-9607, E-Mail: bdcast@bdcast.com, Web Site: www.bdcast.com
Pres & CEO: John Pedlow
VP Strategic Mktg: Neil Glassman
VP RF Engrng: Richard Hinkle
Mktg Svcs Mgr: Kim Winking
VP RF Products: Tim Bealor
VP Studio Sys: Ray Miklius
Conducts Business: Worldwide
Employees: 150
Primary Market Served: Business
Catalog available online
Advertising/Marketing Budget Related to Direct Marketing: 0-25%
Direct Marketing ad budget: $35,000
Direct Mail: 7%
Magazines: 93%
Founded: 1959
Gross sales or billing: $20,000

Radio broadcast equipment.

BROOKE DISTRIBUTORS INC

16250 NW 52nd Ave
Miami, FL 33014
Telephone: (305) 624-9752, (800) 275-8792, FAX: (305) 620-3988, E-Mail: sales@brookedms.com, Web Site: www.brooke.com
Pres: David Rutter
VP Opers Mdsg Sls: Mark Cohen
Conducts Business: U.S., Caribbean Basin, Latin America
Employees: 30

Primary Market Served: Business
Indirect online sales
Advertising/Marketing Budget Related
   to Direct Marketing: 26-50%
Direct Marketing ad budget:
Direct Mail: 50%
Magazines: 15%
Newspapers: 5%
Telephone: 30%
Founded: 1949
Gross sales or billing: $7,700,000

Wholesale distributor of consumer
electronics, specialty gift items, computers & computer peripherals.

BROOKSTONE CO

1 Innovation Way
Merrimack, NH 03054-4873
Telephone: (603) 880-9500, (800) 846-
   3000, FAX: (603) 577-8005, E-Mail:
   customerservice@brookstone.com,
   Web Site: www.brookstone.com
Interim Pres & CEO: Philip W. Rozin
Exec VP, Store Opers: George Suther-
   land
VP, Distr & Logistics & CIO: Steven
   P. Brigham
VP, HR: Carole A. Lambert
VP, Fin: Thomas F. Moynihan
VP, Mktg: Steven C. Strickland
VP & Gen Mgr Dir Mktg: Gregory
   Sweeney
VP, Mdsg: M. Rufus Woodard Jr
Conducts Business: U.S.
Employees: 3,278
Primary Market Served: Consumer
Catalog available online
Direct online sales
Advertising/Marketing Budget Related
   to Direct Marketing: 76-100%
Founded: 1965
Gross sales or billing: $511,900,000

Sell hard-to-find products to consumers
& business firms through catalog mailings & retail stores.

BUENA VISTA HOME ENTERTAINMENT

Div. of Walt Disney Co
500 S Buena Vista St
Burbank, CA 91521
Telephone: (818) 560-1000, FAX:
   (818) 845-8728, Web Site: www.
   bvhe.com
Pres: Robert Chapek
Sr VP, Gen Mgr: Lori MacPherson
Sr VP: William Segill
Exec VP, Sls: Patrick Fitzgerald
Conducts Business: Worldwide
Employees: 100
Primary Market Served: Business &
   Consumer
Catalog available online
Direct online sales
Founded: 1982

Gross sales or billing: $20,000,000

Marketer of Disney, Touchstone, Hollywood Pictures, Buena Vista, Jim
Henson & Miramax home video
products.

BUTLER DISTRIBUTING CO

Subs. of B&W Printing Co Inc
730 Fairfield Ave
Kenilworth, NJ 07033-2012
Telephone: (908) 241-3060, FAX:
   (908) 298-9248, E-Mail:
   bwprinting@worldnet.att.net, Web
   Site: www.bwprinting.com
Pres: Gary L. Butler
Conducts Business: U.S.
Employees: 4
Primary Market Served: Business &
   Consumer
Catalog available online
Direct online sales
Advertising/Marketing Budget Related
   to Direct Marketing: 0-25%
Direct Marketing ad budget:
Direct Mail: 70%
Magazines: 10%
Telephone: 20%
Founded: 1979
Gross sales or billing: $500,000

Manufacturer of ideal self inking and
handle rubber stamps. Order on-line at
bwprinting.com.

CDW COMPUTER CENTERS INC

200 N Milwaukee Ave
Vernon Hills, IL 60061
Telephone: (847) 465-6000, (800) 800-
   4239, FAX: (847) 465-3444, Web
   Site: www.cdw.com
VP, Adv: Don Gordon
Conducts Business: U.S.
Employees: 2,700
Primary Market Served: Business &
   Consumer
Catalog available online
Direct online sales
Founded: 1984
Gross sales or billing: $1,700,000,000

Over 20,000 hardware, peripheral &
software products at discount prices.

CABLE CONNECTION

1035 Mission Ct
Fremont, CA 94539-8203
Telephone: (408) 395-6700, FAX:
   (408) 354-3980, E-Mail: cables4u@
   cable-connection.com, Web Site:
   www.cable-connection.com
Chmn: Jim Johnson
Pres: Greg Gaches
Employees: 100
Primary Market Served: Business &
   Consumer

Founded: 1985
Gross sales or billing: $14,000,000

Manufacturer of cable products and
accessories serving the electronics,
communications and medical
industries.

CABLE FILMS & VIDEO

Div. of HMS Ltd
2026 West 63rd St
Mission Hills, KS 66208-1975
Telephone: (913) 362-2804, (800) 514-
   2804, FAX: (913) 362-2864, E-Mail:
   cablefilms@kc.rr.com, Web Site:
   www.onlineworld.com/movies
Pres: Herbert Miller
VP: Todd Randall
Conducts Business: Worldwide
Employees: 2
Primary Market Served: Business &
   Consumer
Catalog available online
Direct online sales
Advertising/Marketing Budget Related
   to Direct Marketing: 51-75%
Direct Marketing ad budget:
Direct Mail: 75%
Magazines: 25%
Founded: 1976
Gross sales or billing: $250,000

Produce over 300 classic motion pictures on VHS, SVHS, U-Matic, DVD,
One-Inch & Beta SP for duplication to
the retail & consumer markets. In-
house marketing/duplication; provide
master tapes for others to produce under their own VHS cassette and DVD
labels. All programs available to
broadcast stations and CATV
worldwide. Tokyo, Rome & Seoul representative offices.

CABLES TO GO

Subs of Lastar, Inc
3555 Kettering Blvd
Moraine, OH 45439
Telephone: (937) 224-8646, (800) 506-
   9607, FAX: (800) 331-2841, (937)
   496-2666, Web Site: www.
   cablestogo.com
Pres: Bill Diedrich
Dir Sls: Brian Minchew
VP Mktg: Gregory Billhardt
Dir Mktg: Sonia Williams
Employees: 217
Primary Market Served: Business
Catalog available online
Direct online sales
Gross sales or billing: $68,400,000

Connectivity products distributor.

CALUMET PHOTOGRAPHIC INC

890 Supreme Dr
Bensenville, IL 60106-1107

Telephone: (630) 860-7447, (800) 453-2550, FAX: (800) 577-3686, E-Mail: custserv@calumetphoto.com, Web Site: www.calumetphoto.com
CEO: Gary Shapiro
Adv & Mktg Dir: Don Earnest
Conducts Business: Worldwide
Employees: 100
Primary Market Served: Business & Consumer
Catalog available online
Direct online sales

Marketer of still photographic equipment. Sell to professional photographers, industry, business, schools & government agencies.

CATALOG MUSIC CORP
4301 Hillsboro Rd (Suite 320), PO Box 159297
Nashville, TN 37215
Telephone: (615) 298-4338, (800) 992-4487, FAX: (615) 298-4628, Web Site: www.purecountrymusic.com
Mng Dir: Martin D. Davis
Conducts Business: U.S., Canada
Primary Market Served: Consumer
Advertising/Marketing Budget Related to Direct Marketing: 76-100%
Founded: 1988

Old time country music greats on cassette, CD & video.

CHAMPS SOFTWARE INC
1255 N Vantage Point Dr
Crystal River, FL 34429
Telephone: (352) 795-2362, FAX: (352) 795-9100, E-Mail: champs@champsinc.com, Web Site: www.champsinc.com
COO: Bruce Black
Sls Dir: Brian Gay
Bus Devel Dir: Mike Meifi
Conducts Business: Worldwide
Employees: 50
Primary Market Served: Business
Catalog available online
Direct online sales
Advertising/Marketing Budget Related to Direct Marketing: 0-25%
Founded: 1979
Gross sales or billing: $5,000,000

Business solutions.

COMP USA, INC
Div. of Systemax
14951 N Dallas Pkwy
Miami, FL 33144
Telephone: (972) 982-4000, (800) COMP-USA, FAX: (972) 982-4030, Web Site: www.compusa.com
Exec VP, Sls & Opers: Gabriella Villalobos
Pres: Richard Leeds
VP, Mdsg: Brian Woods

VP, Bus Svcs: Jim Loden
Primary Market Served: Business
Catalog available online
Direct online sales

Direct source for PC products.

COMPUSTAR
250 D Jericho Tpke
Mineola, NY 11501
Telephone: (516) 747-2510, FAX: (516) 747-4349, E-Mail: compustar@hotmail.com, Web Site: www.compustar-usa.com
Pres: Henry Bai
Employees: 14
Primary Market Served: Business & Consumer
Catalog available online
Advertising/Marketing Budget Related to Direct Marketing: 0-25%
Founded: 1985

Build Compustar computer systems.

COMPUTER DYNAMICS INC
Subs. of GE Fanuc
7640 Pelham Rd
Greenville, SC 29615
Telephone: (864) 627-8800, FAX: (864) 675-0106, E-Mail: CDIsales@gefanuc.com, Web Site: www.cdynamics.com
Catalog available online
Founded: 1981

COMPUTER STATION CORP
6611 Bissonnet (Suite 107)
Houston, TX 77074
Telephone: (713) 777-6860, FAX: (713) 777-3431, E-Mail: csc@computerstationcorp.com, Web Site: www.computerstationcorp.com
Pres: Tsong (Jeff) Jow
Gen Mgr: Annie Jow
Employees: 15
Primary Market Served: Business & Consumer
Catalog available online
Founded: 1983

Computer hardware, software, sales & service.

CONCURRENT COMPUTER CORP
4375 River Green Pkwy
Duluth, GA 30096-2572
Telephone: (678) 228-4000, (877) 978-7363, FAX: (954) 977-5580, Web Site: www.ccur.com
Pres & CEO: Jack Bryant
VP & CFO: Steve Norton
VP Mktg: Del Kunert
Conducts Business: U.S., Canada
Primary Market Served: Business

Sales of computer supplies & accessories, spare parts for Concurrent Computer Corporation OS/32 & RT Series Computer Systems.

CONSOLIDATED ELECTRONICS INC
705 Watervliet Ave
Dayton, OH 45420
Telephone: (800) 543-3568, FAX: (937) 252-4066, E-Mail: scoy@ceitron.com, Web Site: www.ceitron.com
Pres: Steven S. Coy
Conducts Business: Worldwide
Employees: 1
Primary Market Served: Business & Consumer
Catalog available online
Indirect online sales
Advertising/Marketing Budget Related to Direct Marketing: 51-75%
Direct Marketing ad budget: $5,000
Online: 40%
Telephone: 60%
Founded: 1979
Gross sales or billing: $500,000

Electronic parts & equipment.

THE DMA CRUTCHFIELD CORP
1 Crutchfield Pk
Charlottesville, VA 22911-9097
Telephone: (434) 817-1000, (800) 955-9091, FAX: (804) 817-1010, E-Mail: administration@crutchfield.com, Web Site: www.crutchfield.com
Pres: William G. Crutchfield
Exec VP, Mdsg: Rick Sounder
Sr VP, Mdsg: Daniel Hodgson
Sr VP, Mktg & Creative Svcs: John Haydock
Sr VP, Fin: Richard L. Stavitski
VP, HR: Mark Maynard
VP, Direct Mktg: Brendan Edgerton
Conducts Business: U.S.
Employees: 500
Primary Market Served: Consumer
Catalog available online
Direct online sales
Founded: 1974

Mail order catalog of consumer electronics.

CRYSTAL RECORDS INC
28818 NE Hancock Rd
Camas, WA 98607
Telephone: (360) 834-7022, FAX: (360) 834-9680, E-Mail: info@crystalrecords.com, Web Site: www.crystalrecords.com
Pres: Peter Christ
Conducts Business: U.S., Asia, Australia, Canada, Europe, New Zealand
Employees: 4

Primary Market Served: Business &
  Consumer
Catalog available online
Indirect online sales
Advertising/Marketing Budget Related
  to Direct Marketing: 0-25%
Direct Marketing ad budget:
Direct Mail: 20%
Magazines: 80%
Founded: 1966
Gross sales or billing: $140,000

Sell compact discs, classical only.

DA VINCI TECHNOLOGIES LLC

PO Box 3637
Auburn, AL 36831
Telephone: (334) 502-8925, (877) 334-
  4731, FAX: (208) 485-7749, E-Mail:
  sales@davinci.aero, Web Site: www.
  davincitechnologies.com
Pres & CEO: Megha Shyam
Webmaster: Shawn Bretta
Conducts Business: U.S.
Employees: 28
Primary Market Served: Business &
  Consumer
Catalog available online
Indirect online sales
Advertising/Marketing Budget Related
  to Direct Marketing: 51-75%
Direct Marketing ad budget: $450,000
Direct Mail: 85%
Magazines: 10%
Newspapers: 5%
Founded: 1976
Gross sales or billing: $12,000,000

Calculators, palmtops & laptops &
their related accessories & peripherals.

DALCO ELECTRONICS

425 S Pioneer Blvd
Springboro, OH 45066-1180
Telephone: (937) 743-8042, (800) 445-
  5342, FAX: (937) 743-9251, Web
  Site: www.dalco.com
Owner: Dale Ditmer
Conducts Business: Worldwide
Employees: 20
Primary Market Served: Business &
  Consumer
Catalog available online
Indirect online sales
Advertising/Marketing Budget Related
  to Direct Marketing: 51-75%
Direct Marketing ad budget: $250,000
Direct Mail: 25%
Online: 75%
Founded: 1986

IBM compatible computer components
& accessories sold to end users & re-
sellers, corporate & individual
consumers.

DATA DIRECT NETWORKS (HQ)

9351 Deering Ave
Chatsworth, CA 91311
Telephone: (818) 700-7607, (800) 837-
  2298, FAX: (818) 700-7601, E-Mail:
  info@ddn.com, Web Site: www.
  datadirectnet.com
CEO: Alex Bouzari
Pres: Paul Bloch
Sr VP Sls & Support: Scott Genereaux
VP Prod Mktg: Josh Goldstein
Primary Market Served: Business
Founded: 1988

Catalogs & brochures of computer related items.

DELORME MAPPING

Two DeLorme Dr
Yarmouth, ME 04096
Telephone: (207) 846-7000, (800) 561-
  5105, FAX: (207) 846-7051, E-Mail:
  caleb.mason@delorme.com, Web
  Site: www.delorme.com
Chmn & CEO: David Delorme
Pres: Gordon Pow
VP, Sls & Mktg: David Eshelman
VP Sls: Jim Skillings
Mktg Dir: Caleb Mason
Conducts Business: U.S.
Primary Market Served: Consumer
Catalog available online
Indirect online sales

Maps, atlases & mapping software for
consumers.

DIGI INTERNATIONAL

11001 Bren Rd E
Minnetonka, MN 55343-4410
Telephone: (952) 912-3444, (877) 912-
  3444, FAX: (952) 912-4953, Web
  Site: www.digi.com
Chmn, Pres & CEO: Joe Dunsmore
VP: Sven A. Wehrwein
VP, Mktg: Burk Murray
VP, Global Sls & Mktg: Larry Kraft
Conducts Business: Worldwide
Employees: 50
Primary Market Served: Business &
  Consumer
Catalog available online
Indirect online sales
Advertising/Marketing Budget Related
  to Direct Marketing: 0-25%
Direct Marketing ad budget: $200,000
Direct Mail: 40%
Magazines: 30%
Telephone: 30%
Founded: 1983

PC connectivity products.

DIGI-KEY CORP

701 Brooks Ave S, Box 677
Thief River Falls, MN 56701

Telephone: (218) 681-6674, (800) 344-
  4539, FAX: (218) 681-3380, Web
  Site: www.digikey.com
Pres: Mark A. Larson
VP, Mktg: Steven G. Tsukichi
Conducts Business: U.S., Canada
Employees: 1,900
Primary Market Served: Business &
  Consumer
Catalog available online
Advertising/Marketing Budget Related
  to Direct Marketing: 76-100%
Founded: 1972
Gross sales or billing: $236,000,000

Catalog marketer of electronic parts.

DIGITAL SPEECH SYSTEMS

1241 N Glenville Dr
Richardson, TX 75081-2412
Telephone: (972) 235-2999, FAX:
  (972) 235-3036, Web Site: www.
  digitalspeech.com
Pres: Lev Frenkel
Primary Market Served: Business
Catalog available online
Founded: 1983

Voice mail systems.

DIRECT SAT TV LLC

1930 N Poplar St (Suite 21)
Southern Pines, NC 28387-7092
Telephone: (910) 693-3042, (800) 595-
  4101, FAX: (866) 935-4097, Web
  Site: www.directsattv.com
Mgr: Steven Baldelli
Primary Market Served: Business &
  Consumer

DISC MAKERS

7905 N Route 130
Pennsauken, NJ 08110-1402
Telephone: (800) 237-6666, Web Site:
  www.discmakers.com
Pres: Tony Van Veen

DOORGUARD SYSTEMS INC

8970 D Route 108
Columbia, MD 21045-2145
Telephone: (410) 992-5600, (800) 442-
  6247, FAX: (410) 992-5694, Web
  Site: www.doorguardsystems.com
Pres: Sonny Croson
Conducts Business: U.S. and Canada
Primary Market Served: Business
Founded: 1985

Manufacturer of time-delay electro-
magnetic locks for fire emergency
doors.

DYNAMIC ENGINEERING

150 Dubois St Ste C
Santa Cruz, CA 95060-2114

Telephone: (831) 457-8891, FAX: (831) 457-4793, E-Mail: contact@penguinparty.com, Web Site: www.dyneng.com
Sls Mgr: Joyce Boncato
Office Mgr, Sls & Mktg Mgr: Dedra Lakely
Conducts Business: Worldwide
Employees: 6
Primary Market Served: Business & Consumer
Catalog available online
Direct online sales
Advertising/Marketing Budget Related to Direct Marketing: 0-25%
Direct Marketing ad budget:
Direct Mail: 20%
Magazines: 60%
Newspapers: 5%
Telephone: 15%
Founded: 1988

Full service engineering & computer company & embedded hardware specialist.

EBA WHOLESALE CORP
2361 Nostrand Ave
Brooklyn, NY 11210
Telephone: (718) 253-4700, (866) 2 ASK EBA, FAX: (718) 253-9232, Web Site: www.shopeba.com
Pres: Tony Tesoriero
Conducts Business: U.S.
Employees: 25
Primary Market Served: Business & Consumer
Catalog available online
Direct online sales
Advertising/Marketing Budget Related to Direct Marketing: 0-25%
Direct Marketing ad budget: $100,000
Direct Mail: 75%
Telephone: 25%
Founded: 1980

Sell electronics, appliances & bedding products to the public & discount to businesses & members of various organizations.

EDUCATIONAL RESOURCES
1550 Executive Dr
Elgin, IL 60121-1900
Telephone: (800) 860-7004, FAX: (800) 610-5005, E-Mail: sales@edresources.com, Web Site: www.educationalresources.com
CEO: Dan Figurski
Pres: Michael DiMino
Conducts Business: U.S., Canada
Employees: 125
Primary Market Served: Business & Consumer
Indirect online sales
Advertising/Marketing Budget Related to Direct Marketing: 76-100%

Direct Marketing ad budget:
Direct Mail: 90%
Magazines: 10%
Founded: 1985
Gross sales or billing: $9,800,000

Distributor of educational computer software & CD-ROM's. Primary market is K-12 schools & professional development training.

EFSTONSCIENCE INC
3350 Dufferin St
Toronto, ON, Canada M6A 3A4
Telephone: (416) 787-4581, (888) 777-5255, FAX: (416) 787-5140, E-Mail: info@escience.ca, Web Site: www.e-sci.com
Pres: Nick Efston
VP, Mktg: Irene Efston
Conducts Business: Canada
Employees: 12
Primary Market Served: Business & Consumer
Catalog available online
Direct online sales
Advertising/Marketing Budget Related to Direct Marketing: 26-50%
Direct Marketing ad budget: $250,000
Direct Mail: 70%
Magazines: 10%
Newspapers: 5%
TV/Radio: 10%
Telephone: 5%
Founded: 1970

Sell today's technology products: optics, specialty tools, electronic instruments, telescopes, microscopes & consumer electronics.

ELECTRONIC ARTS INC
209 Redwood Shores Pkwy
Redwood City, CA 94065-1175
Telephone: (650) 628-1500, Web Site: www.ea.com
CEO: John Riccitiello
CFO: Eric Brown
Dir, Direct to Consumer Mktg: Caroline Sheu
Primary Market Served: Consumer

Video game maker.

FILMS MEDIA GROUP
aka FMG; Div. of Primedia, Inc
132 W 31st St Fl 17
New York, NY 10001-3406
Telephone: (609) 671-1000, (800) 257-5126, FAX: (609) 671-0266, E-Mail: custserv@films.com, Web Site: www.filmsmediagroup.com
Sr VP Sls & Direct Mktg: Vincent Vezza
Exec VP, Gen Mgr: Amy Bevilacqua
Pres & CEO: Judy L. Harris
Conducts Business: Worldwide
Employees: 50

Primary Market Served: Business
Catalog available online
Direct online sales
Founded: 1981

Educational software, videos, books, posters, CD-ROMs to junior high through college age markets, libraries, prisons, DOD schools, etc.

FRY INC
650 Avis Dr
Ann Arbor, MI 48108-9649
Telephone: (415) 896-5300 X221, FAX: (741) 741-0906, E-Mail: mbriggs@frymulti.com, Web Site: www.fry.com
Assoc: Amy Tsai

GBH COMMUNICATIONS
1309 S Myrtle Ave
Monrovia, CA 91016-4150
Telephone: (818) 246-9900, (800) 222-5424, FAX: (818) 246-5850, E-Mail: customerservice@gbh.com, Web Site: www.gbh.com
Pres & CEO: Von Bedikian
Mktg Mgr: Hans Matthes
Mgr: Randy Lee
Primary Market Served: Business
Catalog available online
Direct online sales
Founded: 1986

Wireless headsets, teleconferencing & video conferencing products.

GMG PRODUCTIONS INC
346 Baltustrol Cir
Roslyn, NY 11576-3058
Telephone: (516) 482-0022, FAX: (516) 482-0097, Web Site: www.gmgproductions.com
VP, Sls & Mktg: Arthur Gurtman
Pres: Bernard Gurtman
Employees: 5
Primary Market Served: Business & Consumer
Catalog available online
Indirect online sales
Founded: 1987

Video marketing firm.

GATEWAY INC
7565 Irvine Center Dr
Irvine, CA 92618
Telephone: (949) 471-7000, (800) 369-1409, FAX: (949) 471-7041, Web Site: www.gateway.com
Chmn: Richard D. Snyder
CEO: Rudi Schmidleithner
Sr VP & CFO: John P. Goldsberry
Sr VP, Mktg: Bart R. Brown
Sr VP: James R. Burdick
Conducts Business: Worldwide
Employees: 1,700

Primary Market Served: Business & Consumer
Catalog available online
Direct online sales
Advertising/Marketing Budget Related to Direct Marketing: 76-100%
Direct Marketing ad budget:
Magazines: 100%
Gross sales or billing: $3,900,000,000

One of the largest manufacturers of PC's for home & office. Sell a full line of PC's in the U.S. & abroad to large corporations & home users.

GLOBAL COMPUTER CORP

Div. of Systemax
11 Harbor Park Dr
Port Washington, NY 11050-4602
Telephone: (516) 625-4300, (888) 845-6225, FAX: (516) 625-4072, Web Site: www.globalcomputer.com
Pres: Richard Leeds
Exec VP & CFO: Lawrence P. Reinhold
VP, Indus Div: Gilbert Rothenberg
VP, Mktg: Robert Dooley
Dir HR: Natasha Ward
Conducts Business: U.S., Canada, U.K., France
Employees: 1,000
Primary Market Served: Business
Catalog available online
Direct online sales
Direct Marketing ad budget:
Direct Mail: 90%
Magazines: 5%
Telephone: 5%
Gross sales or billing: $500,000,000

Sell industrial, office & computer products to business & institutional firms. Branch offices in Compton, CA; Suwanee, GA; Addison, IL; France & Scotland

GOLD LINE CONNECTOR INC

PO Box 500
West Redding, CT 06896
Telephone: (203) 938-2588, FAX: (203) 938-8740, E-Mail: sales@gold-line.com, Web Site: www.gold-line.com
Pres: Martin Miller
VP, Sls: Marj Miller
Natl Sls Mgr: Greg Miller
Conducts Business: Worldwide
Employees: 30
Primary Market Served: Business
Catalog available online
Direct online sales
Founded: 1961
Gross sales or billing: $2,000,000

Manufacturer of professional audio products, marine & CB accessories & connectors for radio communications.

GULF COAST DATA SUPPLY INC

5455 Rowe Trl
Milton, FL 32571-9556
Telephone: (850) 994-7042, (800) 226-DISK, FAX: (850) 479-4441, Web Site: www.gulfdata.com
Pres: Alan Johnson
Primary Market Served: Business & Consumer
Founded: 2003

Authorized media distributor of computer supplies, video & audio supplies, custom forms & 3M media supplies.

HARVARD SQUARE RECORDS

dba as lpnow
PO Box 2525
Round Rock, TX 78680-2525
Telephone: (877) 465-7669, E-Mail: LPnow@yahoo.com, Web Site: www.lpnow.com
Pres: Barry D. Mayer
Conducts Business: U.S.
Employees: 1
Primary Market Served: Consumer
Catalog available online
Direct online sales
Advertising/Marketing Budget Related to Direct Marketing: 76-100%
Direct Marketing ad budget:
Online: 100%
Founded: 1985

Sell in print & out-of-print rare LP's to people worldwide. All products are new & unplayed.

HAVE INC

350 Power Ave
Hudson, NY 12534-2448
Telephone: (518) 828-2000, (800) 999-HAVE (4283), FAX: (518) 828-2008, E-Mail: kstein@haveinc.com, Web Site: www.haveinc.com
Pres: Nancy Gordon
Mktg Mgr: Kevin Stein
Conducts Business: Worldwide
Employees: 35
Primary Market Served: Business
Catalog available online
Direct online sales
Advertising/Marketing Budget Related to Direct Marketing: 26-50%
Direct Marketing ad budget:
Direct Mail: 25%
Magazines: 10%
Online: 25%
TV/Radio: 5%
Telephone: 35%
Founded: 1977

Complete Multimedia duplication & replication services including CD-Rom & DVD presentation development, authoring & mastering, CD, DVD & Video Duplication & Replication, packaging and graphic design services, and web-based order fulfillment services. Manufacture of professional audio, video & data cable assemblies & distribution of cable-connected products & blank professional media.

HEAR MUSIC

Subs. of Starbux Corp.
545 Bellevue Sq
Bellevue, WA 98004
Telephone: (425) 452-5534, E-Mail: gail@hearmusic.com, Web Site: www.hearmusic.com
Pres & CEO Starbucks: Jim Donald
Pres Hear Music: Don MacKinnon
Dir: Barbara Bass
Dir: Howard Behar
Mktg Mgr: Gail Countryman
Conducts Business: U.S.
Primary Market Served: Consumer
Catalog available online
Direct online sales
Founded: 1990

Retail CD & tape store.

HEARTLAND AMERICA

8085 Century Blvd
Chaska, MN 55318
Telephone: (952) 361-3640, (800) 229-2901, FAX: (952) 368-3452, E-Mail: info@heartlandamerica.com, Web Site: www.heartlandamerica.com
CEO: Bruce Brekke
Pres: Mark Platt
VP, Opers & Mfg: Thomas Bulver
Conducts Business: U.S.
Employees: 100
Primary Market Served: Business & Consumer
Catalog available online
Direct online sales
Advertising/Marketing Budget Related to Direct Marketing: 100%%
Direct Marketing ad budget: $8,000,000
Direct Mail: 75%
Newspapers: 25%
Founded: 1985
Gross sales or billing: $40,000,000

Auto, cameras, electronics, furniture, tools, housewares, lighting, luggage, phones, sporting goods, TV/VCR, video & stereo.

HEATH KIT CO

2024 Hawthorne Ave
Saint Joseph, MI 49085

Telephone: (269) 925-6000, (800) 253-0570, FAX: (269) 925-2898, E-Mail: info@heathkit.com, Web Site: www.heathkit.com
Pres & CEO: Lori Marciniak
Mktg Mgr: Kristan Kusek
Conducts Business: Worldwide
Employees: 30
Primary Market Served: Consumer
Catalog available online

Market innovative electronic home automation & education products to individuals & educators.

HOMESPUN TAPES MUSIC INSTRUCTION
dba Homespun Video
PO Box 340
Woodstock, NY 12498-0340
Telephone: (845) 246-2550, (800) 338-2737, FAX: (845) 246-5282, E-Mail: info@homespuntapes.com, Web Site: www.homespuntapes.com
Pres: Happy Traum
VP: Jane Traum
Office Mgr: Susan Robinson
Adv Dept: Scott Steyer
Conducts Business: Worldwide
Employees: 12
Primary Market Served: Business & Consumer
Catalog available online
Direct online sales
Founded: 1967
Gross sales or billing: $1,300,000

Retail Mail order musical instruments. Video & audio tapes to teach people to play musical instruments. Hundreds of tapes of all levels & styles. Wide variety of instruments.

HOOLEON CORP
304 W Denby Ave
Melrose, NM 88124
Telephone: (928) 634-7515, (800) 937-1337, E-Mail: sales@hooleon.com, Web Site: www.hooleon.com
Pres: Joan Crozier
VP: Robert F. Crozier
Opers: Bill Whitney
Gen Mgr: Barry Green
Conducts Business: Canada, Europe, Middle East, Far East, S. America, Mexico
Employees: 14
Primary Market Served: Business & Consumer
Catalog available online
Direct online sales
Advertising/Marketing Budget Related to Direct Marketing: 0-25%
Direct Marketing ad budget: $30,000
Direct Mail: 10%
Telephone: 90%
Founded: 1982

Gross sales or billing: $55,000,000

Customized computer keyboard keys, keyboard covers, labels, templates & keyboard accessories.

ICS AUDIO VIDEO SUPPLY INC
6721 N Black Canyon Hwy
Phoenix, AZ 85069-5489
Telephone: (602) 242-9207
Pres: Ruben Vejar
VP: Alma Vejar
Conducts Business: U.S.
Employees: 2
Primary Market Served: Business & Consumer
Advertising/Marketing Budget Related to Direct Marketing: 76-100%
Direct Marketing ad budget: $20,000
Direct Mail: 100%
Founded: 1967
Gross sales or billing: $450,000

Audio/video supplies, equipment & accessories.

IMPULSE INC
8238 W Charleston Blvd
Las Vegas, NV 89117
Telephone: (702) 948-1100, (800) 328-0184, FAX: (702) 948-1104
Pres: Michael Halvorson
VP: Larry R. Halvorson
Conducts Business: U.S., Canada
Employees: 8
Primary Market Served: Business & Consumer
Advertising/Marketing Budget Related to Direct Marketing: 0-25%
Founded: 1987

Computer software, 3D animation to businesses & consumers.

INDIAN HOUSE RECORDS & TAPES
PO Box 472
Taos, NM 87571-0472
Telephone: (575) 776-2953, (800) 748-0522, FAX: (575) 776-2804, E-Mail: music@indianhouse.com, Web Site: www.indianhouse.com
Owner: Tony Isaacs
Conducts Business: Worldwide
Employees: 1
Primary Market Served: Business & Consumer
Catalog available online
Direct online sales
Advertising/Marketing Budget Related to Direct Marketing: 0-25%
Founded: 1966

Catalog marketer of high fidelity recordings of traditional American Indian music.

INFOSOURCE INC
1300 City View Ctr
Oviedo, FL 32755-5530
Telephone: (407) 796-5200, (800) 393-4636, FAX: (407) 796-5190, E-Mail: isisale@howtomaster.com, Web Site: www.infosourcelearning.com
CEO: Michael Werner
Pres: Thomas Warrner
Acct Exec Fin & Insurance: Lisa McGovern
Acct Exec: Chris Niemir
Acct Exec: Dylan Punter
Conducts Business: U.S., United Kingdom
Employees: 105
Primary Market Served: Business
Catalog available online
Direct online sales
Advertising/Marketing Budget Related to Direct Marketing: 0-25%
Founded: 1983

Training company that develops & sells computer-based training tutorials, instructor-led training materials & skills assessment software on all of today's popular PC applications, MCSE certification & A+ certification.

INTER7 INTERNET TECHNOLOGIES INC
219 S Prospect St
Galena, IL 61036-2119
Telephone: (815) 776-9465, Web Site: www.inter7.com
CFO: Catherine Kouzmanoff
Primary Market Served: Business

J&R MUSIC/J&R COMPUTER WORLD
23 Park Row
New York, NY 10038-2302
Telephone: (212) 238-9000, (800) 806-1115, FAX: (212) 238-9191, Web Site: www.jandr.com
Co-CEO: Joseph Freidman
Co-CEO: Rachelle Freidman
Mktg Mgr: Phil Tudanger
Adv/Mktg Coord: Abe Brown
Sls Mgr: Marty Singer
Primary Market Served: Business & Consumer
Catalog available online
Direct online sales

Corporate electronic sales.

JDR MICRODEVICES
229 Polaris Ave Ste 17
Mountain View, CA 94043-4579
Telephone: (408) 494-1400, (800) 538-5000, FAX: (800) 538-5005, E-Mail: sales@jdr.com, Web Site: www.jdr.com
Pres & CEO: Jeffrey D. Rose
VP, MIS: Matthew Smith

Mktg Mgr: George Zenos
Conducts Business: Worldwide
Employees: 150
Primary Market Served: Business &
  Consumer
Catalog available online
Direct online sales
Advertising/Marketing Budget Related
  to Direct Marketing: 76-100%
Direct Marketing ad budget:
Direct Mail: 70%
Newspapers: 10%
TV/Radio: 20%
Founded: 1979
Gross sales or billing: $10,000,000

Manufactures & sells PC related products, including systems, components,
peripherals & software nationally &
internationally via direct market & web
advertising.

JAMECO ELECTRONICS

1355 Shoreway Rd
Belmont, CA 94002
Telephone: (650) 592-8097, (800) 831-
  4242, FAX: (650) 592-2503, (800)
  237-6948, E-Mail: domestic@
  jameco.com, Web Site: www.jameco.
  com
CEO & Pres: Bob Croshaw
VP Mktg: Ray Bellantoni
Employees: 100
Primary Market Served: Business &
  Consumer
Catalog available online
Direct online sales
Advertising/Marketing Budget Related
  to Direct Marketing: 26-50%
Founded: 1974
Gross sales or billing: $14,800,000

Mail order electronic & computer parts
& components.

MARLIN P JONES &
ASSOCIATES INC

PO Box 530400
Lake Park, FL 33403
Telephone: (561) 848-8236, (800) 652-
  6733, FAX: (561) 844-8764, E-Mail:
  mpja@mpja.com, Web Site: www.
  mpja.com
Pres: Marlin P. Jones
VP: David A. Jones
VP: Marlin L. Jones
Conducts Business: U.S.
Employees: 17
Primary Market Served: Business &
  Consumer
Catalog available online
Direct online sales
Advertising/Marketing Budget Related
  to Direct Marketing: 0-25%
Direct Marketing ad budget:
Direct Mail: 90%
Magazines: 10%

Founded: 1973
Sell electronic parts for industrial,
commercial & educational electronics.

KIKUCALL

14 Wall St Fl 15
New York, NY 10005-2139
Telephone: (646) 747-1078, Web Site:
  www.kikucall.com
Dir Premium Svcs: Brian Hecht

Mobile services company

LDS TEST & MEASUREMENT

19 Bartlett St
Marlborough, MA 01752-3014
Telephone: (608) 821-6600, FAX:
  (608) 821-6691, E-Mail: info-us@
  lds.spx.com, Web Site: www.lds-
  group.com
Dir MIS: Fred Decker
Dir Mktg: Krista Tweed
Conducts Business: U.S., Canada,
  U.K., France, Germany, Japan
Employees: 75
Primary Market Served: Consumer
Direct Marketing ad budget: $2,000
Direct Mail: 20%
Magazines: 80%
Founded: 1937
Gross sales or billing: $7,100,000

Manufacturer & supplier of test &
measurement systems. High quality
vibration test systems & integrated
solutions for the physical test & measurement market.

LAPLINK SOFTWARE INC

600 108th Ave NE Ste 610
Bellevue, WA 98004-5125
Telephone: (425) 952-6000, (800) 527-
  5465, FAX: (425) 952-6002, E-Mail:
  marketing@laplink.com, Web Site:
  www.laplink.com
Sr VP Corp Sls & Bus Devel: Mark
  Chestnut
Mktg Mgr: Neil Minetto
CEO: Thomas Koll
Conducts Business: Worldwide
Employees: 90
Primary Market Served: Business &
  Consumer
Founded: 1982

Developer of communications & remote access software.

LEARNING SEED

641 W Lake St (Suite 301)
Chicago, IL 60661-1308
Telephone: (800) 634-4941, Web Site:
  www.learningseed.com
VP: Kari McCarthy
Primary Market Served: Consumer

Publishes educational videotapes &
CD-ROMS

LENOVO

1009 Think Pl
Morrisville, NC 27560-9002
Telephone: (919) 257-6315, Web Site:
  www.uslenovo.com
Dir Mktg: Ajay Kaul

Maker of personal computers

LISTENING LIBRARY INC,
RANDOM HOUSE AUDIO

Div. of Random House Audio Publish-
  ing Group
1745 Broadway
New York, NY 10019
Telephone: (800) 726-0600, FAX:
  (800) 454-0606, Web Site: www.
  randomhouse.com/audio
Pres: Peter Olsen
Conducts Business: U.S., Canada
Employees: 20
Primary Market Served: Consumer
Catalog available online
Indirect online sales
Advertising/Marketing Budget Related
  to Direct Marketing: 26-50%
Direct Marketing ad budget:
Direct Mail: 100%
Founded: 1956

Audio books - literature based media
for children & adults. Sell to schools,
libraries, individuals & distributors.

LOCATION SOUND CORP

10639 Riverside Dr
North Hollywood, CA 91602-2355
Telephone: (818) 980-9891, (800) 228-
  4429, FAX: (818) 980-9911, E-Mail:
  information@locationsound.com,
  Web Site: www.locationsound.com
Pres & CEO: David Panfili
Conducts Business: Worldwide
Employees: 50
Primary Market Served: Business
Catalog available online
Indirect online sales
Direct Marketing ad budget:
Direct Mail: 10%
Magazines: 90%
Founded: 1977

Professional audio equipment for film
& video production, broadcast & live
sound. Consulting, sales, service &
rental.

LONG'S ELECTRONICS INC

2630 S Fifth Ave
Irondale, AL 35210-1209
Telephone: (205) 956-6767, (800) 633-
  3410, FAX: (800) 633-2530, E-Mail:
  info@longselectronics.com, Web
  Site: www.longselectronics.com

E-Commerce Dept Mgr: Blanche Beardon
Pres: Roy Long
Conducts Business: U.S.
Employees: 126
Primary Market Served: Business
Catalog available online
Direct online sales
Advertising/Marketing Budget Related to Direct Marketing: 76-100%
Direct Marketing ad budget: $960,000
Direct Mail: 100%
Founded: 1969
Gross sales or billing: $27,500,000

Sell audio-visual equipment & accessories to churches & schools. Major manufacturers: Sony, Panasonic, 3M, Magnavox, Sharp, JVC, Elmo, TEAC, Tascam, Bogen, Shure & Telex.

LUCENT DIRECT CATALOG
Div. of Lucent Technologies
600 Mountain Ave
New Providence, NJ 07974
Telephone: (908) 582-8500, (908) 582-3000, (800) 4-LUCENT, E-Mail: execoffice@alcatel-lucent.com, Web Site: www.alcatel-lucent.com
VP, Mktg: John Leonard
Employees: 79,000

MCA/UNIVERSAL STUDIOS INC
Subs. of NBC Universal Inc
111 Universal Hollywood Dr Ste 890
Universal City, CA 91608-1138
Telephone: (818) 777-1000, FAX: (818) 866-3330, Web Site: www.universalstudios.com
Pres & COO: Ron Meyer
Exec VP & CFO: Christy Rupert Shibata
Exec VP & Gen Counsel: Maren Christensen
Exec VP: Michael J. Connor
Sr VP, Tech Opers: Michael Daruty
Employees: 15,000
Primary Market Served: Business & Consumer
Gross sales or billing: $2,100,000,000

Home video production, sales & marketing.

MRV COMMUNICATIONS
20415 Nordhoff St
Chatsworth, CA 91311
Telephone: (818) 773-0900, FAX: (818) 773-0906, Web Site: www.mrv.com
Chmn & CEO: Shlomo Margalit
Pres, CEO & Dir: Noam Lotan
CFO: Guy Avitan
VP, Tech: Eli Laufer
VP, Tech: Sergio Rotenstein
Employees: 1,450

Primary Market Served: Business & Consumer
Gross sales or billing: $356,000,000

Manufacture computer networking devices.

MANHEIM STEAMROLLER
9130 Mormon Bridge Rd
Omaha, NE 68152-1937
Telephone: (402) 457-4341, FAX: (402) 457-4332, E-Mail: mailbox@amgram.com, Web Site: www.manheimsteamroller.com
Co-Founder: Jackson Barkley
Co-Founder: Chip Davis
Conducts Business: U.S.
Employees: 40
Primary Market Served: Business & Consumer
Catalog available online
Direct online sales
Advertising/Marketing Budget Related to Direct Marketing: 0-25%
Direct Marketing ad budget: $500,000
Direct Mail: 55%
Magazines: 15%
TV/Radio: 30%

Sells music to distributors, retailers & consumers.

MARKERTEK VIDEO SUPPLY
Div. of Tower Products Inc
One Tower Dr, PO Box 397
Saugerties, NY 12477-4386
Telephone: (845) 246-3036, (800) 522-2025, FAX: (847) 246-1757, E-Mail: sales@markertek.com, Web Site: www.markertek.com
VP, Gen Mgr: Erick Krein
Head Mktg Coord: Vince Morano
Conducts Business: Worldwide
Employees: 110
Primary Market Served: Consumer
Catalog available online
Direct online sales
Gross sales or billing: $18,400,000

Pro Audio-IAV Supplies & Accessories.

MEDIA MANAGEMENT & MAGNETICS INC
N93 W14636 Whitaker Way
Menomonee Falls, WI 53051
Telephone: (262) 251-5511, (800) 242-2090, FAX: (262) 251-4737, E-Mail: medmgt@computersupplypeople.com, Web Site: www.computersupplypeople.com
Pres: John Schimberg
Sls Mgr: Jim Noonan
Conducts Business: U.S., Canada, Europe, S. America
Employees: 9

Primary Market Served: Business & Consumer
Founded: 1974

Sell complete line of computer supplies & accessories.

MERIKS INC
822 Guilford Ave (#1700)
Baltimore, MD 21202-3707
Telephone: (787) 721-0000
Pres: Voleen Ashtin

MERIKS MARKETERS
2200 W 66th St (#190)
Richfield, MN 55423-2196
Telephone: (787) 721-0000
Pres: Shawna Clara

MICRO CENTER
4119 Leap Rd
Hilliard, OH 43026
Telephone: (800) 634-3478, FAX: (614) 777-2620, E-Mail: csrs@microcenterorder.com, Web Site: www.microcenter.com
Chmn, Pres & CEO: Richard M. Mershad
COO: Peggy Wolfe
CFO: James Koehler
CIO: Misty Kuamoo
VP, Retail Sls: Robert Demme
Conducts Business: U.S.
Primary Market Served: Business & Consumer
Catalog available online
Direct online sales
Advertising/Marketing Budget Related to Direct Marketing: 0-25%
Direct Marketing ad budget:
Direct Mail: 95%
Magazines: 5%
Founded: 1986

Computers & computer related supplies sold to businesses & consumers.

MICROBIZ CORP
Div. of CAM Commerce Solutions
17075 Newhope St (Suite A)
Fountain Valley, CA 92708-4299
Telephone: (201) 785-1311, (800) 726-3282, FAX: (201) 758-1568, E-Mail: info@microbiz.com, Web Site: www.microbiz.com
Pres: Andy Pauker
VP: Dina Puccio
CFO: Sheri McMillan
Conducts Business: International
Employees: 24
Primary Market Served: Business
Catalog available online
Direct online sales
Advertising/Marketing Budget Related to Direct Marketing: 0-25%
Founded: 1987

MICROVIDEO LEARNING SYSTEMS, INC
208 E 51st St (#273)
New York, NY 10022-6500
Telephone: (403) 233-9411, (800) 231-4021, FAX: (800) 879-6857, E-Mail: info@microvideo.com, Web Site: www.microvideo.com
Pres: Walter Schoustal
Mktg Mgr: Jeff Popovich
Employees: 8
Primary Market Served: Business
Founded: 1982

Video-based training for software applications.

MITSUBISHI DIGITAL ELECTRONICS AMERICA INC
9351 Geronimo Rd
Irvine, CA 92618
Telephone: (949) 465-6000, FAX: (949) 859-4770, Web Site: www.mitsubishi-tv.com
Pres: Ikuo Morisada
Sr VP: Masato Sakui
Sr VP, Sls & Mktg: Aki Ninomiya
Primary Market Served: Consumer
Catalog available online
Indirect online sales

Manufacture of audio & video equipment.

MODULAR DEVICES, LLC
35-D Wilson Dr
Sparta, NJ 07871
Telephone: (973) 579-7220, (800) 292-2201, FAX: (973) 579-1820, E-Mail: modulardevices@optonline.net, Web Site: www.modulardevices.biz
Gen Mgr: Dennis Dignardi
Sls Dir: Patricia Murphy
Employees: 8
Primary Market Served: Business & Consumer
Advertising/Marketing Budget Related to Direct Marketing: 0-25%
Founded: 1984

Telephone & computer accessories & networking.

MOTO FRANCHISE CORP
dba Moto Photo and Portrait Avenue
7086 Corporate Way
Dayton, OH 45459
Telephone: (937) 291-1900, (800) 733-6686, FAX: (937) 291-2005, E-Mail: expert@motophoto.com, Web Site: www.motophoto.com; www.portraitavenue.com
Pres & CEO: Harry D. Loyle
VP Opers: Ron A. Mohney
VP Franchise Sls: Joseph M. O'Hara
Dir Mktg: Ashley Breidenbach

Employees: 52
Primary Market Served: Consumer
Gross sales or billing: $4,600,000

Franchises about 90 photo development stores in nearly 20 US states and the District of Columbia offering one-hour processing and other services such as enlargements and digital reproductions.

MOTOWN RECORDS
Sub. of Universal Music Group
1755 Broadway (fl 6)
New York, NY 10019-3768
Telephone: (212) 373-0750, FAX: (212) 489-9096, Web Site: www.motown.com
Pres, Universal Music Enterprises: Bruce Resnikoff
Chmn & CEO: Mel Lewinter
Primary Market Served: Business & Consumer

Record Producer.

MOUNTAIN WEST SUPPLY CO
5116 E Charter Oak
Scottsdale, AZ 85254
Telephone: (602) 971-1200, (800) 528-6169, FAX: (602) 996-5077
Pres: Faye Towns
Intl Opers Mgr: Erlene Lan
Conducts Business: Worldwide
Employees: 10
Primary Market Served: Business & Consumer
Advertising/Marketing Budget Related to Direct Marketing: 76-100%
Direct Marketing ad budget:
Direct Mail: $100,000
Magazines: $10,000
Telephone: $25,000
Gross sales or billing: $1,700,000

One-hundred page direct mail catalog, representing 200 manufacturers & offering security products. Includes burglar & fire alarm systems & supplies, as well as closed circuit television, personal protection products, access control devices, bugging & debugging equipment, intercoms, vacuum systems (built in) & voice stress analysis.

MUSTEK INC
14751 Franklin Ave Ste B
Tustin, CA 92780-7272
Telephone: (949) 790-3800, FAX: (949) 788-3670, Web Site: www.mustek.com
CEO: David Kan
Prod & Mktg Mgr: Michael Todd
Acct Mgr: Mel Fouse
Primary Market Served: Business & Consumer

Catalog available online
Indirect online sales
Advertising/Marketing Budget Related to Direct Marketing: 0-25%
Founded: 1988

Scanners & digital cameras.

NESTFAMILY.COM
1461 S Beltline Rd (Suite 500)
Coppell, TX 75019-4939
Telephone: (972) 402-7100, (800) 596-7386, FAX: (972) 629-7181, Web Site: www.nestfamily.com
Pres & CEO: Ernie Frausto
VP: Charles Len
VP: Donna McManus
Primary Market Served: Consumer
Catalog available online
Direct online sales

Family video distribution.

NEW & UNIQUE VIDEOS
Subs. of Crystal Pyramid Inc.
7323 Rondel Ct
San Diego, CA 92119
Telephone: (619) 644-3001, (619) 644-3000, E-Mail: info@newuniquevideos.com, Web Site: www.newuniquevideos.com
CEO: Mark Schulze
COO: Patricia Mooney
Conducts Business: U.S., Europe
Employees: 5
Primary Market Served: Business & Consumer
Catalog available online
Indirect online sales
Advertising/Marketing Budget Related to Direct Marketing: 0-25%
Founded: 1981
Gross sales or billing: $500,000

Television shows & home video titles to the general public (via distributors & mail-order marketing). Extensive stock footage, library & custom shots. One-stop video production house.

NEWARK ELECTRONICS
Div. of Premier Farnell p/c
4801 Ravenswood Ave
Chicago, IL 60640-4496
Telephone: (773) 784-5100, (800) 4-Newark, FAX: (888) 551-4801, E-Mail: webmaster@newark.com, Web Site: www.newark.com
VP: Scott Leichtling
VP: Tom Walkowiak
VP: Doug Witt
VP: Chuck Yurko
Conducts Business: Worldwide
Employees: 2,000
Primary Market Served: Business & Consumer
Catalog available online
Direct online sales

Founded: 1934

Electronic component parts, data & accessories.

THE NEWMAN GROUP
2577 Newport Rd
Ann Arbor, MI 48103-2274
Telephone: (734) 426-3200, FAX: (734) 426-0777, E-Mail: anewman@ newman.com
Pres: Allan Newman
VP, Mktg: Mark Morton
VP, Messaging Svcs: Anthony J. Co- mazzi
Treas: Rob Havens
Acct Mgr: Andy Hood
Conducts Business: Worldwide
Employees: 95
Primary Market Served: Business & Consumer
Catalog available online
Indirect online sales
Direct Marketing ad budget: $100,000
Direct Mail: 15%
Telephone: 85%
Founded: 1971

Sell used DEC, HP, Sun and Cisco minicomputers & peripherals.

PBS DISTRIBUTION
2100 Crystal Dr
Arlington, VA 22202-3784
Telephone: (703) 739-5085, Web Site: shoppbs.org
Primary Market Served: Consumer

Online shopping that supports PBS public television

PC MALL
2555 W 190 St
Torrance, CA 90504
Telephone: (310) 225-2600, (800) 555- MALL, Web Site: www.pcmall.com
Chmn, Pres & CEO: Frank Khulusi
Exec VP, Mktg: Daniel J. DeVries
Exec VP, Sls: Kristin M. Rogers
Gen Counsel: Robert I. Newton
Primary Market Served: Business & Consumer
Catalog available online
Direct online sales

Computer catalog company with four stores.

THE DMA PARTS EXPRESS
725 Pleasant Valley Dr
Springboro, OH 45066-1158
Telephone: (937) 743-3000, (800) 338- 0531, FAX: (937) 743-1677, E-Mail: sales@parts-express.com, Web Site: www.partsexpress.com
Pres: Jeffrey Stahl
Primary Market Served: Business & Consumer

Catalog available online
Direct online sales
Founded: 1986

Electronics distributor catalog.

POLYLINE LLC
845 N Church St
Elmhurst, IL 60126
Telephone: (630) 993-2700, (800) 701- 3865, FAX: (800) 816-3330, Web Site: www.polylinecorp.com
Pres: Ed Kaiser
Mktg: Ray Kaiser
Employees: 40
Primary Market Served: Business
Catalog available online
Direct online sales
Advertising/Marketing Budget Related to Direct Marketing: 76-100%
Direct Marketing ad budget:
Direct Mail: 95%
Magazines: 5%
Founded: 1972
Gross sales or billing: $4,700,000

Catalog audio, video & CD production packaging & mailing supply.

PORTER'S CAMERA STORE INC
411 Viking Rd
Cedar Falls, IA 50613-6930
Telephone: (319) 266-0303, (800) 553- 2001, FAX: (800) 221-5329, E-Mail: bcondra@porters.com, Web Site: www.porters.com
Pres: Jeff Schmitt
Head Adv: Bob Condra
Conducts Business: U.S.
Employees: 25
Primary Market Served: Business & Consumer
Catalog available online
Direct online sales
Advertising/Marketing Budget Related to Direct Marketing: 0-25%
Direct Marketing ad budget:
Direct Mail: 90%
TV/Radio: 10%
Founded: 1914
Gross sales or billing: $7,000,000

Sell photographic & video equipment supplies to advanced amateurs, schools & industry through catalog.

PROJECTOR-RECORDER BELT CORP
Div. of Russell Industries Inc
3375 Royal Ave
Oceanside, NY 11572-4812
Telephone: (516) 536-5000, (800) 645- 2202, FAX: (516) 764-5747, (800) 645-2200, E-Mail: sales@russellind. com, Web Site: www.russellind.com
Pres: Adam Russell

Sls Mgr: Neil Eiger
Conducts Business: Worldwide
Employees: 9
Primary Market Served: Business & Consumer
Catalog available online
Advertising/Marketing Budget Related to Direct Marketing: 0-25%
Founded: 1956
Gross sales or billing: $3,000,000

Wholesale electronic components

PSION TEKLOGIX INC
2100 Meadowvale Blvd
Mississauga, ON, Canada L5N 719
Telephone: (905) 813-9900, (800) 322- 3437, E-Mail: ptinfo@psion.com, Web Site: www.psionteklogix.com
VP HR: Louise Martin
Pres & CEO: I.D. McElroy
CFO: Bill Jessup
COO: Michael Homer
Conducts Business: Worldwide
Employees: 1,100
Primary Market Served: Business
Catalog available online
Indirect online sales
Founded: 1967
Gross sales or billing: $190,000,000

Manufacturer of hand-held computing products.

THE DMA RADIOSHACK CORP
300 Radioshack Cir (MS CF7-331)
Fort Worth, TX 76102-1964
Telephone: (817) 415-2010, FAX: (817) 415-2647, Web Site: www. radioshack.com
Dir Customer Mktg: Tom Levey
Primary Market Served: Consumer

Retail stores-consumer electronics.

RECYCLED SOFTWARE INC
3764 Serenity Trl
Palm Springs, CA 92262-9774
Telephone: (760) 655-5666, (800) 851- 2425, FAX: (702) 323-5333, E-Mail: diane@recycledsoftware.com, Web Site: www.recycledsoftware.com
Pres: Diane M. Hathaway
Conducts Business: Worldwide
Employees: 2
Primary Market Served: Business & Consumer
Catalog available online
Direct online sales
Advertising/Marketing Budget Related to Direct Marketing: 0-25%
Direct Marketing ad budget: $6,000
Direct Mail: 50%
Magazines: 50%
Founded: 1992
Gross sales or billing: $170,000

Mail order computer software.

REDISCOVER MUSIC CATALOGUE

Div. of Aztec Corp
705 S Washington St Ste 3
Naperville, IL 60540-6697
Telephone: (630) 305-0770, (800) 232-7328, FAX: (630) 305-0782, E-Mail: rediscovermusic@rediscovermusic.com, Web Site: www.rediscovermusic.com
Pres: Allan Shaw
Admin Asst: Karen Rumaner
Conducts Business: Worldwide
Employees: 4
Primary Market Served: Consumer
Catalog available online
Direct online sales
Advertising/Marketing Budget Related to Direct Marketing: 76-100%
Direct Marketing ad budget: $135,000
Direct Mail: 100%
Founded: 1989
Gross sales or billing: $800,000

Sell pre-recorded music (compact discs) to general public.

RESUMATE INC

2500 Packard (Suite 200)
Ann Arbor, MI 48104
Telephone: (734) 477-9402, (800) 530-9310, FAX: (734) 477-9415, E-Mail: info@resumate.com, Web Site: www.resumate.com
Pres: C.L. Schaldenbrand
Conducts Business: U.S., Canada
Employees: 5
Primary Market Served: Business
Catalog available online
Direct online sales
Advertising/Marketing Budget Related to Direct Marketing: 76-100%
Direct Marketing ad budget:
Telephone: 100%
Gross sales or billing: $500,000

Sell software for human resource professionals. Several versions include a candidate search & match program; an integrated multiple database for candidate, client & job order searching & matching - both available for networks or single users.

RIGHT ON COMPUTER SOFTWARE

Div. of Computeam Inc
27 Bowdon Rd
Greenlawn, NY 11740-1901
E-Mail: riteonsoft@aol.com, Web Site: rightonprograms.com
Pres: Barbara Feinstein
Exec VP: Don Feinstein
VP: David Farren
Conducts Business: U.S., Europe
Employees: 16

Primary Market Served: Business & Consumer
Catalog available online
Indirect online sales
Advertising/Marketing Budget Related to Direct Marketing: 76-100%
Direct Marketing ad budget:
Direct Mail: 80%
Magazines: 10%
Telephone: 10%
Founded: 1980

Computer software for offices, libraries & homes, including commercial, academic, medical & law organizations.

ROSE ELECTRONICS

10707 Stancliff Rd
Houston, TX 77099
Telephone: (281) 933-7673, (800) 333-9343, FAX: (281) 933-0044, E-Mail: sales@rose.com, Web Site: www.rose.com
Partner: Peter Macourek
Partner: David Rahvar
VP, Mktg: Sande Olson
VP, Mktg: Brenda Munson
Primary Market Served: Business & Consumer
Catalog available online
Indirect online sales

Computer peripherals, printers and data switches.

ROUNDER MAIL ORDER

Div. of Rounder Records
One Rounder Way
Burlington, MA 01803
Telephone: (617) 354-0700, (800) 768-6337, FAX: (617) 868-8769, E-Mail: info@rounder.com, Web Site: www.rounder.com
Opers Mgr: Mike Annis
Conducts Business: Worldwide
Employees: 60
Primary Market Served: Consumer
Catalog available online
Direct online sales
Founded: 1970
Gross sales or billing: $10,900,000

Retail & mail order cassettes, compact discs & videos.

SF VIDEO INC

1000 Sansome St (Suite 280)
San Francisco, CA 94111
Telephone: (415) 288-9400, (800) 545-5865, FAX: (415) 288-9410, E-Mail: selfservice@sfvideo.com, Web Site: www.sfvideo.com
CEO: Dawn Tognoli
Pres: Steven Feinberg
Exec VP: Michael Brandon
VP: Stan Feinberg
Conducts Business: Canada, Israel
Employees: 10

Primary Market Served: Business
Catalog available online
Direct online sales
Founded: 1990

SEASTROM MANUFACTURING CO INC

456 Seastrom St
Twin Falls, ID 83301
Telephone: (208) 737-4300, (800) 634-2356, FAX: (208) 734-7222, E-Mail: info@seastrom-mfg.com, Web Site: www.seastrom-mfg.com
Pres: Robert A. Seastrom
Dir: Diane Mueke
Catalog available online
Direct online sales
Gross sales or billing: $7,000,000

Manufacture electronic parts & brackets.

SECURITY MICRO SYSTEMS INC

Div. of Luckit
19135 N 94th St
Scottsdale, AZ 85255
Web Site: www.luckit.com
Primary Market Served: Business & Consumer

SHAPE LLC

2105 Corporate Dr
Addison, IL 60101
Telephone: (630) 620-8394, (800) 367-5811, FAX: (630) 620-0784, E-Mail: sales@shapellc.com, Web Site: www.shapellc.com
Pres: Ted Maka
Sls: Scott Wood
Primary Market Served: Business & Consumer

Manufacture OEM electrical transformers.

SIERRA INC

558 State St
Racine, WI 53402-5132
Telephone: (262) 638-1851, FAX: (414) 638-1852, E-Mail: support@sierrainc.com, Web Site: www.sierra.com
Pres, CEO: Jim Andrews
Primary Market Served: Business & Consumer
Catalog available online
Advertising/Marketing Budget Related to Direct Marketing: 0-25%

Computer builders.

SMARTERVILLE PRODUCTIONS LLC

1550 Executive Dr
Elgin, IL 60123-9311

Telephone: (800) 861-6531, FAX: (410) 843-8318, E-Mail: tom. callahan@smartville.com, Web Site: www.hooked-on-phonics.com
EVP Consumer Products: Tom Callahan

SOFTWARE AG USA
Div. of Software AG
11700 Plaza America Dr (Suite 700)
Reston, VA 20190
Telephone: (703) 860-5050, (877) 724-4965, FAX: (703) 391-6975, E-Mail: info@softwareagusa.com, Web Site: www.softwareagusa.com
Pres, CEO: Gary Voight
Head of N America Mktg: Christina Cravens
Primary Market Served: Business

Enterprise software company.

SOFTWARE ASSISTANCE INTERNATIONAL LTD (SAIL)
85 Moraine Rd
Morris Plains, NJ 07950
Telephone: (973) 285 1400, FAX: (201) 539-3253
Mgr: John Smith
Employees: 2
Primary Market Served: Business & Consumer
Gross sales or billing: $100,000

Market electronic commerce hybrid solutions that run on CD ROM & the Internet.

THE SOFTWARE LABS INC
3824 140th Ave NE
Bellevue, WA 98005
Telephone: (425) 653-2432, FAX: (425) 643-8090, Web Site: www.softwarelabs.com
Mktg Dir: Paul J. O'Dell
Conducts Business: Worldwide
Employees: 10
Primary Market Served: Business & Consumer
Catalog available online
Direct online sales
Advertising/Marketing Budget Related to Direct Marketing: 76-100%
Founded: 1986

Publishers of graphics & wireless software.

THE
DMA **SONY DADC**
555 Madison Ave (#1810)
New York, NY 10022-3301
Telephone: (212) 833-8000, Web Site: www.sonydadc.com
Dir Bus Devel: John MacDonald

SONY MEDIA SOFTWARE
8215 Greenway Blvd
Middleton, WI 53562-3685
Telephone: (608) 256-3133
VP Mktg: David Chaimson

SPRINT NEXTEL CORP
12502 Sunrise Valley Dr
Reston, VA 20191-3438
Telephone: (703) 433-4000, FAX: (703) 433-4343, Web Site: www.nextel.com
Sr VP Corp Commun: Bill White
Primary Market Served: Business

Wireless communication products.

THE SUPPLIES GUYS
268 Greenwood Ave
Midland Park, NJ 07432-1445
Telephone: (201) 493-8433, Web Site: www.suppliesguys.com
Primary Market Served: Consumer

Sells computer ink, toner & printers

SUPPORT SYSTEMS INTERNATIONAL CORP
136 S Second St
Richmond, CA 94804
Telephone: (510) 234-9090, (800) 777-6269, FAX: (510) 233-8888, E-Mail: info@support-systems-intl.com, Web Site: www.support-systems-intl.com
Pres: Ben Parsons
VP, Mktg: Richard St John
Conducts Business: Worldwide
Employees: 65
Primary Market Served: Business
Advertising/Marketing Budget Related to Direct Marketing: 26-50%
Direct Marketing ad budget:
Direct Mail: 50%
Magazines: 50%
Founded: 1976
Gross sales or billing: $5,000,000

Manufacturer of computer & PC data switching & sharing devices. Produces custom cable and assemblies.

TWL KNOWLEDGE GROUP
Div. of Trinity Workplace Learning
4101 International Pkwy
Carrollton, TX 75007
Telephone: (972) 309-4000, (800) 624-2272, FAX: (972) 309-5105, Web Site: www.twlk.com
CEO: Dennis J. Cagan
CFO & COO: Pat Quinn
VP & CIO: Andrew Lechner
Sr VP & CMO: Thomas E. Morris
Exec VP: Douglas D. Cole
Primary Market Served: Business
Catalog available online
Advertising/Marketing Budget Related to Direct Marketing: 0-25%

Founded: 1986
Gross sales or billing: $43,000,000

TIGER DIRECT INC
Div. of Systemax Inc
7795 W Flagler St (Suite 35)
Miami, FL 33144-2367
Telephone: (305) 415-2200, (800) 800-8300, FAX: (305) 415-2202, Web Site: biz.tigerdirect.com
Chmn & CEO: Richard Leeds
Vice Chmn: Bruce Leeds
Vice Chmn: Robert Leeds
Mgr: Yzes Bayol
Mgr: Paul Beirne
Conducts Business: Worldwide
Employees: 140
Primary Market Served: Business
Catalog available online
Direct online sales
Advertising/Marketing Budget Related to Direct Marketing: 0-25%
Direct Marketing ad budget:
Direct Mail: 20%
Online: 15%
Telephone: 65%
Founded: 1978

Catalog marketer of computer supplies & accessories.

TIGERDIRECT.CA
Div. of Systemax
55 E Beaver Creek Rd (Unit G)
Richmond Hill, ON, Canada L4B 1E5
Telephone: (888) 771-9999, (800) 800-8300, FAX: (905) 482-3134, Web Site: www.tigerdirect.ca
VP: Joseph Dunne
Corp Acct Mgr: David McGregor
Conducts Business: Canada
Employees: 23
Primary Market Served: Business & Consumer
Catalog available online
Direct online sales
Advertising/Marketing Budget Related to Direct Marketing: 76-100%
Direct Marketing ad budget: $950,000
Direct Mail: 95%
Magazines: 5%
Gross sales or billing: $11,000,000

Trade in computer supplies & accessories, networking & data communications products.

THE
DMA **THE TOWNSEND GROUP**
616 W 207th St (Suite 4E)
New York, NY 10034-2638
Telephone: (212) 304-9069, Web Site: livemusicguide.com
Primary Market Served: Consumer

TUCKER ELECTRONICS CO

1717 Reserve St
Garland, TX 75042
Telephone: (214) 348-8800, (887) 667-
6044, FAX: (214) 348-0367, E-Mail:
sales@tucker.com, Web Site: www.
tucker.com
Pres: James Tucker
Dir: Duanne Harvey
Adv Mgr: Lynn Cage
Conducts Business: Worldwide
Employees: 65
Primary Market Served: Business &
Consumer
Catalog available online
Direct online sales
Advertising/Marketing Budget Related
to Direct Marketing: 76-100%
Direct Marketing ad budget:
$1,000,000
Direct Mail: 100%
Founded: 1967
Gross sales or billing: $13,000,000

Sells new & re-conditioned electronic
test equipment to businesses, schools
& individuals. Authorized Tektronics
distributor.

VCOM INTERNATIONAL MULTI-MEDIA CORP

55 Ruta Ct, PO Box 3171
South Hackensack, NJ 07606
Telephone: (201) 229-9800, (800) 425-
4268, FAX: (800) 453-6338, E-Mail:
sales@800VALIANT.com, Web Site:
www.800VALIANT.com
Pres: Sheldon Goldstein
VP: Vincent Bruno
Conducts Business: U.S., Canada
Employees: 30
Primary Market Served: Business &
Consumer
Founded: 1963

Video, audio & audio/visual presentation equipment.

VENTURE ENTERTAINMENT GROUP

PO Box 55113
Sherman Oaks, CA 91413
Telephone: (800) 981-8433, FAX:
(818) 981-3466, E-Mail:
venture818@aol.com, Web Site:
www.venture818.com
Pres: Leigh Leshner
Conducts Business: U.S., Canada
Primary Market Served: Business &
Consumer
Catalog available online
Direct online sales
Advertising/Marketing Budget Related
to Direct Marketing: 51-75%
Direct Marketing ad budget:
Direct Mail: 40%
Magazines: 5%

Newspapers: 40%
Telephone: 15%
Founded: 1991

Full service video/film/TV production
company producing in-house as well as
providing services to businesses &
consumers. Also, a line of videos that
are marketed directly to consumers.

VERIZON COMMUNICATIONS INC

140 West St LBBY 1
New York, NY 10007-2123
Telephone: (212) 395-1000, (800) 621-
9900, FAX: (212) 571-1897, Web
Site: www.verizon.com
Chmn & CEO: Ivan Seidenberg
Pres & COO: Dennis F. Strigl
Exec VP & CFO: Doreen F. Toben
Exec VP & CIO: Shaygan Kheradpir
Exec VP & CMO: John G. Stratton
Employees: 242,000
Primary Market Served: Business &
Consumer
Catalog available online
Direct online sales
Founded: 1983
Gross sales or billing: $6,100,000,000

VIDEO ARTISTS INTERNATIONAL

109 Wheeler Ave
Pleasantville, NY 10570
Telephone: (914) 769-3691, (800) 477-
7146, FAX: (914) 769-5407, E-Mail:
orders@vaimusic.com, Web Site:
www.vaimusic.com
Pres: Ernest Gilbert
Gen Mgr: Edward Cardona
Prod Devel Mgr: Allan Altman
Mgr, Sls: Foster Grimm
Customer Rep: Jeff Mclancon
Conducts Business: Worldwide
Employees: 8
Primary Market Served: Business &
Consumer
Catalog available online
Direct online sales
Advertising/Marketing Budget Related
to Direct Marketing: 0-25%
Direct Marketing ad budget: $10,000
Magazines: 100%
Founded: 1983

Video Artists produces, manufactures
and distributes DVDs for the home
video market focusing on classical music performances of orchestral, instru-
mental, opera and dance. VAI also produces and distributes compact discs of
classical music.

VILLAGE SOFTWARE INC

76 Summer St (Suite 600)
Boston, MA 02110-1267

Telephone: (617) 695-9332, (800) 724-
9332, FAX: (617) 695-1935, E-Mail:
requests@villagesoft.com, Web Site:
www.villagesoft.com
Pres: Ford D. Cavallari
Mktg Mgr: An-Chian Kao
Assoc Mktg Mgr: Jay Saleh
Conducts Business: U.S., Canada, Eu-
rope, Far East
Primary Market Served: Business &
Consumer
Catalog available online
Direct online sales
Advertising/Marketing Budget Related
to Direct Marketing: 76-100%
Direct Marketing ad budget:
Direct Mail: 65%
Magazines: 20%
Telephone: 15%
Founded: 1991

Microsoft Excel, Lotus 1-2-3 & Quatro
Pro spreadsheet add-ons as well as
Microsoft Office, Lotus Smart-Suite &
Perfect Office add-ons, solving most
common business problems for small
businesses & individuals.

WARNER BROS

Div. of Time-Warner
4000 Warner Blvd
Burbank, CA 91522-0001
Telephone: (818) 954-6000, Web Site:
www.warnerbros.com
Pres: Barry M. Meyer
Pres & COO: Alan F. Horn
Exec VP Corp Commun: Susan Nahley
Fleishman
Exec VP, Opers: Peter Lynch
Conducts Business: U.S.
Primary Market Served: Consumer
Advertising/Marketing Budget Related
to Direct Marketing: 0-25%
Founded: 1923
Gross sales or billing: $11,850,000,000

Distributes videos, DVDs, apparel &
gifts.

ZTEK CO

PO Box 967
Lexington, KY 40588-0967
Telephone: (859) 281-1611, (800) 247-
1603, FAX: (859) 281-1521, E-Mail:
cs@ztek.com, Web Site: www.ztek.
com
Pres: Max Kurtz
Catalog available online
Indirect online sales

Multi media for physics education.

ZONES INC

1102 15th St SW (Suite 102)
Auburn, WA 98001-6509

Telephone: (253) 205-3000, (800) 408-
9663, FAX: (425) 430-3626, E-Mail:
corpsales@zones.com, Web Site:
www.zones.com
Pres & CEO: Firoz Lalji
Pres & COO: Christina Corley
Exec VP Sls: Sean Hobday
Exec VP Bus Devel: Tom Ducatelli
Sr VP & CFO: Ronald McFadden
Primary Market Served: Business
Catalog available online
Direct online sales

Hardware, software & services provider for small to medium businesses.

THE DMA 02KL
800 Westchester Ave (Suite S440)
Rye Brook, NY 10573-1329
Telephone: (914) 253-4500, Web Site:
www.illyusa.com
VP Mktg: Beverly Stotz
Primary Market Served: Business &
Consumer

ATLANTIC SPICE CO
PO Box 205
North Truro, MA 02652
Telephone: (508) 487-6100, (800) 316-
7965, FAX: (508) 487-2550, E-Mail:
mark@atlanticspice.com, Web Site:
www.atlanticspice.com
Owner & Pres: Mark Irving
Co-Owner: Neil Hanscomb
Mgr: Linnet Hultin
Conducts Business: U.S.
Employees: 8
Primary Market Served: Business &
Consumer
Catalog available online
Direct online sales
Advertising/Marketing Budget Related
to Direct Marketing: 0-25%
Founded: 1994
Gross sales or billing: $1,000,000

Bulk herbs, spices, teas & potpourri
ingredients.

THE DMA RC BIGELOW INC
201 Black Rock Tpke
Fairfield, CT 06825-5512
Telephone: (203) 334-1212, Web Site:
www.bigelowtea.com
Direct Mktg Mgr: Renee Walker
Employees: 330
Primary Market Served: Consumer
Catalog available online
Direct online sales
Advertising/Marketing Budget Related
to Direct Marketing: 26-50%
Founded: 1945

BISSINGER FRENCH
CONFECTIONS
3983 Gratiot St
Saint Louis, MO 63110-1723
Telephone: (314) 534-2401, (800) 325-
8881, FAX: (314) 534-2419, Web
Site: www.bissingers.com
Pres: Ken Kellerhals
Sr VP, Gen Mgr: Dana R. Whiter
Sr VP, Catalog & Internet: Dana James
Corp Sls Mgr: Maureen Bassett-Baran
Conducts Business: U.S.
Employees: 55
Primary Market Served: Business &
Consumer
Catalog available online

Direct online sales
Advertising/Marketing Budget Related
to Direct Marketing: 51-75%
Founded: 1668

Manufacture & sell gourmet confections through direct mail catalog, retail
stores & website.

BLAND FARMS
1126 Raymond Bland Rd
Glennville, GA 30427
Telephone: (912) 654-1426, (800) 843-
2542, FAX: (912) 654-1330, Web
Site: www.blandfarms.com
Media Dir: Susan Lynah
Owner: Delbert Bland
Conducts Business: U.S.
Primary Market Served: Business &
Consumer
Catalog available online
Indirect online sales
Founded: 1984

Vidalia sweet onions, by-products,
cakes, pies, candies, meats, frozen
vidalia bits & southern produce.

BOCA JAVA
200 S Biscayne Blvd Ste 1818
Miami, FL 33131-2329
Telephone: (954) 949-2010, Web Site:
www.bocajava.com
Pres: Kevin Holbrook

BRAND NEW PRODUCTS LLC
2506 N Clark St (#280)
Chicago, IL 60614-1848
Telephone: (773) 486-8813, Web Site:
www.brandnewllc.com
CEO: Steven Faso
Primary Market Served: Business &
Consumer

Confections

BROWN & JENKINS
TRADING CO
287 Old Route 15
Cambridge, VT 05444-9772
Telephone: (802) 862-2395, (800) 456-
JAVA, FAX: (802) 863-4009, Web
Site: www.brownjenkins.com
Pres: Jay Michaud
Conducts Business: U.S.
Employees: 4
Primary Market Served: Consumer
Catalog available online
Direct online sales
Advertising/Marketing Budget Related
to Direct Marketing: 76-100%
Direct Marketing ad budget:
Direct Mail: 100%
Founded: 1984

Gross sales or billing: $5,000,000
Gourmet coffees.

BURGER'S OZARK COUNTRY
CURED HAMS INC
32819 Hwy 87
California, MO 65018
Telephone: (573) 796-3134, (800) 345-
5185, FAX: (573) 796-3137, E-Mail:
burgers@smokehouse.com, Web
Site: www.smokehouse.com
Pres: Steve Burger
Catalog Dir: Lisa Parry
Order Fulfillment: Chris Mouse
VP: Phil Burger
Conducts Business: U.S.
Employees: 250
Primary Market Served: Business &
Consumer
Catalog available online
Direct online sales
Advertising/Marketing Budget Related
to Direct Marketing: 51-75%
Direct Marketing ad budget:
Direct Mail: 95%
Magazines: 3%
TV/Radio: 2%
Founded: 1952

Smoked meats, primarily country cured
hams via direct mail, food services,
distributors & warehouses.

BUTTERFIELD FARMS INC
904 Silver Spur Rd (Suite 485)
Rolling Hills Estates, CA 90274-3800
Telephone: (310) 750-6160, (800) 633-
2767, E-Mail: dave@gifttrading.com,
Web Site: www.butterfieldfarms.com
Pres, Gen Mgr: David Mayer
Conducts Business: U.S.
Employees: 10
Primary Market Served: Business &
Consumer
Catalog available online
Advertising/Marketing Budget Related
to Direct Marketing: 0-25%

Catalog marketer of gourmet foods.
Provide fulfillment of goods or services for outside companies. Shrink
wrapping & special packaging. Also
provide fruit cakes.

BYRON PLANTATION
Div. of Holland Investments Inc
PO Box 60
Vidalia, GA 30475-0060
Telephone: (800) 356-0171, E-Mail:
greenline/byron@bellsouth.net, Web
Site: www.byronplantation.com
Pres, Owner: Mike Holland
Conducts Business: U.S., Europe,
Canada

Employees: 4
Primary Market Served: Business &
  Consumer
Catalog available online
Direct online sales
Advertising/Marketing Budget Related
  to Direct Marketing: 76-100%
Direct Marketing ad budget:
Direct Mail: $50,000
Magazines: $30,000
Gross sales or billing: $500,000

Specializes in Southern gourmet foods,
both fresh & processed, packaged for
gifts & home use.

THE CANDY FACTORY
1020 Saratoga St
Newport, KY 41071-2129
Telephone: (859) 581-4663, FAX:
  (859) 581-1979
Pres: Robert Schneider
Office Mgr: Judy Bedwell
Conducts Business: U.S.
Primary Market Served: Consumer

Sell boxed chocolates.

CARVEL CORP
200 Glenridge Point Pkwy NE Ste 200
Atlanta, GA 30342-1450
Telephone: (404) 255-3250, (800) 227-
  8353, FAX: (404) 255-4978, Web
  Site: www.carvel.com
Pres: Gary Bales
Conducts Business: U.S.
Employees: 599
Primary Market Served: Business &
  Consumer
Advertising/Marketing Budget Related
  to Direct Marketing: 0-25%
Direct Marketing ad budget:
  $7,000,000
Direct Mail: 20%
TV/Radio: 80%
Founded: 1936
Gross sales or billing: $181,200,000

Ice cream - both soft-serve ice cream
fountain & bakery style desserts, (ice
cream cakes & novelties). Sold
through retail outlets & via direct
response.

CAVIARTERIA NEW YORK INC
2584 Steinway St Ste A
Astoria, NY 11103-3706
Telephone: (212) 759-7410, (800) 422-
  8427, FAX: (212) 750-0358, E-Mail:
  info@caviarteria.com, Web Site:
  www.caviarteria.com
Mgr: John Drobenko
Conducts Business: U.S., S. America,
  Asia, EEC
Primary Market Served: Business &
  Consumer

Catalog available online
Indirect online sales
Advertising/Marketing Budget Related
  to Direct Marketing: 26-50%
Direct Marketing ad budget:
Direct Mail: 40%
Magazines: 25%
Newspapers: 25%
TV/Radio: 10%
Founded: 1950

Russian & American Caviar, smoked
Scottish salmon, French Foie Gras -
gourmet specialty foods & accessories.

COLLIN STREET BAKERY
401 W Seventh Ave
Corsicana, TX 75110-6362
Telephone: (800) 292-7400, Web Site:
  www.collinstreetbakery.com
CEO: L. William McNutt
VP Fin: R. Scott Hollomon
VP Opers: Jerry Grimmett
Pres: Robert P. McNutt
VP, Sls: John Crawford
Conducts Business: Worldwide
Employees: 60
Primary Market Served: Business &
  Consumer
Catalog available online
Direct online sales
Advertising/Marketing Budget Related
  to Direct Marketing: 76-100%
Founded: 1896
Gross sales or billing: $30,000,000

Sells the Deluxe Fruitcake through
catalog sales.

COMMUNITY COFFEE CO
3332 Partridge Ln (Bldg A)
Baton Rouge, LA 70809-2413
Telephone: (225) 291-3900, (800) 525-
  5583, FAX: (800) 643-8199, E-Mail:
  ccc@communitycoffee.com, Web
  Site: www.communitycoffee.com
Pres & CEO: K. Randall Russ
VP, Sls: David Belanger
VP: Matthew C. Saurage
Conducts Business: U.S.
Employees: 30
Primary Market Served: Business &
  Consumer
Catalog available online
Direct online sales

Sell coffees, teas & other gourmet food
items.

CORONA-LOTUS INC
Subs. of Gourmet Center
465 Green St
San Francisco, CA 94133-4001
Telephone: (415) 956-8956, (800) 422-
  2924, FAX: (415) 956-4922, E-Mail:
  customerservice@biscoff.com, Web
  Site: www.biscoff.com
Chmn Bd & CEO: Matthew Boone

Pres: Michael McGuire
VP & Treas: Jan Boone
Mng Dir: Jan Vander Stichele
HR Dir: Jos Destrooper
Conducts Business: U.S.
Employees: 20
Primary Market Served: Business &
  Consumer
Catalog available online
Direct online sales
Advertising/Marketing Budget Related
  to Direct Marketing: 76-100%
Direct Marketing ad budget: $100,000
Direct Mail: 100%
Founded: 1990
Gross sales or billing: $3,000,000

Sell imported gourmet cookies - individually wrapped in tins & gift boxes -
via catalog.

CRABTREE & EVELYN LTD
102 Peake Brook Rd
Woodstock, CT 06281-3429
Telephone: (860) 928-2761, (800)
  CRABTREE, FAX: (860) 928-0452,
  Web Site: www.crabtree-evelyn.com
Mktg Dir: Alison Orme
CEO: Michael Stromberg
VP Opers: Stephen Bestwick
VP Retail: Scott Sincerbeaux
Dir Consumer Mktg: Catie Briscoe
Conducts Business: U.S.
Employees: 150
Primary Market Served: Consumer
Catalog available online
Direct online sales
Gross sales or billing: $100,000,000

Sell imported toiletries & gourmet
foods from England, France &
Switzerland.

CREST FRUIT INC
4000 E Goodwin Rd
Mission, TX 78574-9525
Telephone: (956) 205-7300, Web Site:
  www.redcooper.com
Pres: John Launer
Primary Market Served: Consumer

CUBA CHEESE SHOPPE
53 Genesee St
Cuba, NY 14727-1199
Telephone: (585) 968-3949, FAX:
  (716) 968-1746, Web Site: www.
  cubacheese.com
Pres & Owner: Jeff Bradley
VP: Bill Bradley
Primary Market Served: Business &
  Consumer
Catalog available online
Direct online sales
Gross sales or billing: $1,000,000

Retail & wholesale cheese products;
NY state cheddar cheese.

CUSHMAN FRUIT CO INC
3325 Forest Hill Blvd
West Palm Beach, FL 33406-5812
Telephone: (561) 965-3535, (800) 776-
2295, FAX: (561) 968-7263, E-Mail:
info@honeybell.com, Web Site:
www.honeybell.com
CEO: Allen Cushman
Pres: Don Wright
Sec & Treas: John Cushman
Dir Mktg: Eileen Schlagerhapt
Conducts Business: U.S. & Canada
Employees: 50
Primary Market Served: Business &
Consumer
Catalog available online
Direct online sales
Advertising/Marketing Budget Related
to Direct Marketing: 76-100%
Direct Marketing ad budget: $500,000
Direct Mail: 75%
Newspapers: 24%
Online: 1%
Founded: 1945

Citrus gifts.

CUVAISON INC
4550 Silverado Trail
Calistoga, CA 94515
Telephone: (707) 942-6266, FAX:
(707) 942-5732, E-Mail:
jschuppert@cuvaison.com, Web Site:
www.cuvaison.com
Pres: Jay Schuppert
CFO: Tory Britton Sims
Asst Mgr Mktg Sls: Marie Derr
Mgr Tasting Room: Jean Varner
Assoc Winemaker: Todd Heth
Primary Market Served: Business &
Consumer
Catalog available online
Direct online sales

Winery.

**DS WATERS OF NORTH
AMERICA LP**
4170 Tanners Creek Dr
Flowery Branch, GA 30542
Telephone: (626) 585-1000, (800) 669-
3402, FAX: (626) 585-8563, E-Mail:
customerservice@water.com, Web
Site: www.water.com
Pres: John Bilbrey
VP, Mktg: Conrad Smits
Primary Market Served: Business &
Consumer

Manufacturer & distributor of bottled
water.

DAKIN FARM
5797 Rte Seven
Ferrisburgh, VT 05456-9798

Telephone: (802) 425-3971, (800) 993-
2546, FAX: (802) 425-2765, E-Mail:
scutting@dakinfarm.com, Web Site:
www.dakinfarm.com
Pres: Sam Cutting IV
Conducts Business: U.S.
Employees: 50
Primary Market Served: Business &
Consumer
Catalog available online
Indirect online sales
Advertising/Marketing Budget Related
to Direct Marketing: 76-100%
Direct Marketing ad budget: $340,000
Direct Mail: $225,000
Magazines: $10,000
Newspapers: $30,000
Online: $65,000
TV/Radio: $20,000
Founded: 1960
Gross sales or billing: $5,000,000

Vermont specialty foods: cob-smoked
meats, aged Vermont cheddar cheese &
pure Vermont maple syrup.

**DEAN & DELUCA BRANDS
INC**
2402 E 37th St N
Wichita, KS 67219-3538
Telephone: (316) 683-1255, Web Site:
www.deandeluca.com
VP Mktg: Deb Stockman
VP Ecommerce: Tiena Manypenny
Primary Market Served: Consumer

DECKO PRODUCTS INC
2105 Superior St
Sandusky, OH 44870
Telephone: (419) 626-5757, FAX:
(419) 626-3135
Owner: W.F. Niggemeyer
VP & Gen Mgr: Bob Vance
Conducts Business: U.S., Canada
Employees: 70
Primary Market Served: Business &
Consumer
Gross sales or billing: $5,000,000

Manufacturer of candy cake decorations & lay-ons for candy
manufacturing.

DELICIOUS ORCHARDS
36 Rte 34
Colts Neck, NJ 07722-1987
Telephone: (732) 462-1989, FAX:
(732) 542-2111, E-Mail: info@
deliciousorchardsnj.com, Web Site:
www.deliciousorchardsnj.com
Pres: Thomas A. Gesualdo
MO Div Mgr: Frederick J. Walsifer
Conducts Business: U.S.
Employees: 300
Primary Market Served: Consumer
Founded: 1911
Gross sales or billing: $16,500,000

Catalog marketer of quality fruit baskets & bakery products.

DINEWISE
500 Bi-County Blvd (Suite 400)
Farmingdale, NY 11735-3996
Telephone: (631) 694-1111, (800) 749-
1170, FAX: (631) 694-4064, E-Mail:
info@dinewise.com, Web Site: www.
dinewise.com
CEO: Paul Roman
VP & CFO: Thomas McNeil
VP Mktg: Craig Livernoche
Conducts Business: U.S.
Primary Market Served: Business &
Consumer
Catalog available online
Founded: 1959

Marketer & distributor of fully prepared gourmet & nutritional meals.

**DUCKTRAP RIVER FISH
FARM**
57 Little River Dr
Belfast, ME 04915
Telephone: (207) 338-6280, (800) 828-
3825, FAX: (207) 338-9020, E-Mail:
smoked@ducktrap.com, Web Site:
www.ducktrap.com
Mktg Dir: Michael Hollandbaek
Employees: 150
Primary Market Served: Business &
Consumer
Catalog available online
Direct online sales
Advertising/Marketing Budget Related
to Direct Marketing: 76-100%
Founded: 1979

Gourmet smoked seafood.

**DUDLEY'S COUNTRY
KITCHEN**
2230 Viar Rd
Dyersburg, TN 38024-9802
Telephone: (901) 285-3681, (800) 242-
8066, FAX: (901) 285-3638, Web
Site: www.dckitchen.com
Pres: Dudley Davis
Conducts Business: U.S.
Primary Market Served: Business &
Consumer
Catalog available online
Indirect online sales
Advertising/Marketing Budget Related
to Direct Marketing: 0-25%
Founded: 1985
Gross sales or billing: $150,000

Southern foods, gift boxes & baskets.

**DUREY-LIBBY EDIBLE NUTS
INC**
100 Industrial Rd
Carlstadt, NJ 07072

Telephone: (201) 939-2775, (800) 332-6887, FAX: (201) 939-0386, E-Mail: info@dureylibby.com, Web Site: www.dureylibby.com
Pres: Wendy Dicker
VP: William Dicker
Conducts Business: U.S.
Primary Market Served: Business & Consumer
Founded: 1950
Gross sales or billing: $5,000,000

Processor & distributor of nuts, seeds, dried fruit & candy.

THE DMA S WALLACE EDWARDS & SONS INC
PO Box 25
Surry, VA 23883-0025
Telephone: (757) 294-3121, (800) 290-9213, FAX: (757) 294-5378, E-Mail: info@virginiatraditions.com, Web Site: www.virginiatraditions.com
Pres: Samuel W. Edwards III
Primary Market Served: Consumer
Founded: 1926

Sell specialty meats, Virginia seafood, smoked poultry & desserts.

EICHTEN'S HIDDEN ACRES
16809 310th St, PO Box 216
Center City, MN 55012
Telephone: (651) 257-4752, FAX: (651) 257-6286, E-Mail: eichtens@frontiernet.net, Web Site: www.specialtycheese.com
Mgr: Ed Eichten
Mgr: Eileen Eichten-Carlson
Conducts Business: U.S.
Employees: 7
Primary Market Served: Business & Consumer
Catalog available online
Direct online sales
Advertising/Marketing Budget Related to Direct Marketing: 0-25%
Founded: 1976

Producers of European style cheeses & American Bison. Retail & wholesale gift packages containing cheese & bison to the general public, grocery stores, co-ops & farm markets.

EILENBERGER'S BAKERY INC
512 N John St
Palestine, TX 75801-2725
Telephone: (903) 729-2253, (800) 831-2544, FAX: (903) 723-2915, Web Site: www.eilenbergerbakery.com
Pres: Terresa Smith
Co-Owner: Stephen Smith
Conducts Business: Worldwide
Employees: 70

Primary Market Served: Business & Consumer
Catalog available online
Direct online sales
Advertising/Marketing Budget Related to Direct Marketing: 26-50%
Founded: 1898
Gross sales or billing: $4,000,000

Mail order of fruit cake, pecan apple cake, pecan apricot cake & Texas fudge pecan pie.

EMPIRE COFFEE & TEA CO
568 9th Ave Frnt 1
New York, NY 10036-3726
Telephone: (212) 268-1220, (800) 262-5908, E-Mail: owners@empirecoffeetea.com, Web Site: www.empirecoffeetea.com
Pres: Paul Shaytin
Conducts Business: U.S.
Primary Market Served: Business & Consumer
Catalog available online
Direct online sales
Founded: 1908

Retailer of gourmet coffee & tea. Appliances & accessories available.

ETHEL M CHOCOLATES INC
Div. of M&M/Mars
One Sunset Way
Henderson, NV 89014
Telephone: (702) 458-8864, (800) 471-0352, FAX: (800) 392-2587, E-Mail: chocolatier@ethelm.com, Web Site: www.ethelm.com
Pres: Lynn Moran
Pub Rels Mgr: Phil Levine
E-commerce Mgr: Tari Huddelston
Conducts Business: U.S.
Employees: 450
Primary Market Served: Business & Consumer
Catalog available online
Direct online sales
Founded: 1984

Fine boxed chocolate confections.

THE FX MATT BREWING CO
830 Varick St
Utica, NY 13502
Telephone: (315) 732-0022, (800) 765-6288, FAX: (315) 624-2401, E-Mail: info@saranac.com, Web Site: www.saranac.com
Pres: Nicolas O. Matt
Dir Production: Dave Campbell
Dir Opers: Jim Kuhr
Packaging Mgr: Frank Vlossak
VP: Fred Matt
Controller: Bob Cooley
Conducts Business: U.S.
Employees: 150
Primary Market Served: Business

Founded: 1853
Brewers.

FAIRYTALE BROWNIES
4610 E Cotton Center Blvd (Suite 100)
Phoenix, AZ 85040-8898
Telephone: (800) 324-7982, FAX: (602) 489-5122, E-Mail: service@brownies.com, Web Site: www.brownies.com
Co-Owner, Sls & Mktg Team Leader: Eileen Spitalny
Corp Sls: Brandie Davenport
VP: David Kravetz
Conducts Business: Worldwide
Employees: 26
Primary Market Served: Business & Consumer
Catalog available online
Direct online sales
Advertising/Marketing Budget Related to Direct Marketing: 51-75%
Direct Marketing ad budget: $13,000
Direct Mail: 80%
Online: 20%
Founded: 1992
Gross sales or billing: $7,800,000

Mail order gourmet Belgian chocolate brownie gifts.

FERRARA BAKERY & CAFE INC
195 Grand St
New York, NY 10013
Telephone: (212) 226-6150, FAX: (212) 226-0667, E-Mail: information@ferraracafe.com, Web Site: www.ferraracafe.com
Pres: Peter Lepore
Conducts Business: U.S., Canada, Italy
Employees: 110
Primary Market Served: Business & Consumer
Catalog available online
Direct online sales
Founded: 1892

Mail order & retail outlets for Italian specialty foods & confections.

FIGI'S INC
Subs. of Fingerhut Corp
3200 S Maple Ave
Marshfield, WI 54404-2000
Telephone: (715) 387-1771, (800) 422-3444, FAX: (715) 384-1129, Web Site: www.figis.com
Pres: Jim Krueger
Dir Mktg: Sheri Dick
Conducts Business: U.S.
Employees: 150
Primary Market Served: Business & Consumer
Catalog available online
Direct online sales

Gross sales or billing: $24,800,000

Produce seasonal mail order catalogs featuring decorative gift packages of aged cheeses, sausages, smoked meats, nuts, cookies, jams & other gift ideas.

FOWLER'S CHOCOLATES INC

100 River Rock Dr (Suite 102)
Buffalo, NY 14207-2163
Telephone: (716) 877-9983, (800) 824-2263, FAX: (716) 877-9959, E-Mail: customerservice@fowlerschocolates.com, Web Site: www.fowlerschocolates.com
Pres: Ted Marks
Mgr: Dana Reynolds
Mgr: Richard Eince
Conducts Business: U.S.
Employees: 19
Primary Market Served: Business
Catalog available online
Direct online sales
Founded: 1910

Manufacturer & distributor of chocolates & related products.

FRAN'S GIFTS TO GO

3700 Clay Pond Rd
Myrtle Beach, SC 29577
Telephone: (843) 445-2625, (800) 476-6887, E-Mail: customerservice@fransgiftstogo.com, Web Site: www.fransgiftstogo.com
Pres: Mike McNabb
Acctg: Bill Rollins
Conducts Business: U.S., Canada, Europe
Primary Market Served: Business & Consumer
Catalog available online
Direct online sales
Advertising/Marketing Budget Related to Direct Marketing: 76-100%
Direct Marketing ad budget:
Direct Mail: 90%
Magazines: 10%

Direct marketing of pecans for retail, gift & home use. Also, market candy coated pecans.

GODIVA CHOCOLATIER

333 W 34th St Fl 6
New York, NY 10001-2566
Telephone: (212) 984-5977, Web Site: www.godiva.com
Sr Mgr CRM: Benjamin Rotnicki
Primary Market Served: Consumer

GOLDEN BISON LLC

dba Highplains Bison
1395 S Platte River Dr
Denver, CO 80223-3467
Telephone: (303) 962-0100, Web Site: www.highplainsbison.com
SVP Mktg & CMO: Ronald Bruggeman
Primary Market Served: Consumer

GOLDEN RIVER FRUIT CO

505 66th Ave SW, PO Box 2090
Vero Beach, FL 32961-2090
Telephone: (772) 562-4502, FAX: (772) 562-9747
Pres: George S. Lambeth Jr.
Primary Market Served: Business
Gross sales or billing: $3,400,000

Packer & exporter of citrus. Grower of Indian River citrus.

GOLDEN TROPHY

Div. of The Bruss Co
3548 N Kostner Ave
Chicago, IL 60641
Telephone: (800) 835-6607, FAX: (800) 835-6601, E-Mail: goldentrophy@bruss.com, Web Site: www.giftsteaksonline.com
Sr VP, Intl Sls: Roel G.M. Andriessen
Sr VP, Beef Production Opers: Dan Brook
Sr VP, Beef Margin Mngmt: Chris Daniel
Conducts Business: U.S.
Primary Market Served: Business & Consumer
Catalog available online
Direct online sales
Advertising/Marketing Budget Related to Direct Marketing: 51-75%
Direct Marketing ad budget:
Direct Mail: 80%
Magazines: 10%
Telephone: 10%
Founded: 1975

Supplier of gourmet cuisine for gifts & incentives.

GRACEWOOD FRUIT CO

PO Box 370
Vero Beach, FL 32961-0370
Telephone: (772) 567-1154, E-Mail: info@gracewoodgroves.com, Web Site: www.gracewoodgroves.com
Pres & CEO: John M. Luther
VP, Gift Fruit Div: Don Wright
Mktg Coord: Lisa DiMauro
Telemktg Mgr: Sandra Koosha
Conducts Business: U.S., Europe, Japan
Employees: 850
Primary Market Served: Business & Consumer
Catalog available online
Direct online sales
Advertising/Marketing Budget Related to Direct Marketing: 76-100%
Founded: 1938

Gross sales or billing: $14,000,000

Marketer of gift fruits, gourmet baskets & foods, plants & flowers.

GRANDMA BROWN'S BEANS INC

5837 Scenic Ave
Mexico, NY 13114
Telephone: (315) 963-7221, FAX: (315) 963-4072
Pres: Sandra L. Brown
Conducts Business: U.S.
Employees: 15
Primary Market Served: Business & Consumer
Advertising/Marketing Budget Related to Direct Marketing: 0-25%
Founded: 1938

Canned food specialties, including baked beans & soups, sold to wholesale & retail accounts as well as to individual consumers.

THE DMA GREEN MOUNTAIN COFFEE ROASTERS, INC

33 Coffee Ln
Waterbury, VT 05676
Telephone: (802) 244-5621, (800) 545-2326, FAX: (802) 244-5436, Web Site: www.gmcr.com
Pres: Larry Blanford
VP Mktg: T. J. Whalen
Conducts Business: U.S.
Employees: 849
Primary Market Served: Business & Consumer
Catalog available online
Direct online sales
Advertising/Marketing Budget Related to Direct Marketing: 0-25%
Founded: 1981
Gross sales or billing: $342,000,000

Manufacture & sell gourmet coffees.

HADLEY FRUIT ORCHARDS INC

50130 Main St
Cabazon, CA 92230-3218
Telephone: (951) 849-4668, FAX: (951) 849-5255, Web Site: www.hadleys.com
Mgr: Wayne Dickson
Mgr: Shawn Latimer
Conducts Business: Worldwide
Employees: 86
Primary Market Served: Business & Consumer
Catalog available online
Direct online sales
Advertising/Marketing Budget Related to Direct Marketing: 26-50%
Founded: 1931
Gross sales or billing: $16,800,000

Sell dried fruit, nuts, dates, honey, vitamins, natural foods & gifts. Offer a complete mail order catalog featuring a wide range of products. Also operate retail stores. 800 # available Mon.-Fri. 8:00 AM - 4:40 PM.

HARMAN'S CHEESE & COUNTRY STORE INC
1400 Rte 117
Sugar Hill, NH 03586
Telephone: (603) 823-8000, E-Mail: cheese@harmanscheese.com, Web Site: www.HarmansCheese.com
Owner & Pres: Maxine Aldrich
Mgr & Owner: Brenda Aldrich
Conducts Business: U.S.
Employees: 5
Primary Market Served: Business & Consumer
Catalog available online
Advertising/Marketing Budget Related to Direct Marketing: 0-25%
Direct Marketing ad budget: $20,000
Direct Mail: 30%
Magazines: 10%
Newspapers: 20%
Founded: 1955
Gross sales or billing: $300,000

Retail mail order of aged cheddar (over 2 years), maple products, preserves, condiments & gourmet food items.

THE DMA HARRINGTON'S OF VERMONT INC
210 E Main St
Richmond, VT 05477-7721
Telephone: (802) 434-7500, FAX: (802) 434-3166, E-Mail: info@harringtonham.com, Web Site: www.harringtonham.com
COO: R.B. Klinkenberg
DM Mgr: Carol Wisley
Conducts Business: U.S.
Employees: 50
Primary Market Served: Consumer
Catalog available online
Direct online sales
Founded: 1873
Gross sales or billing: $16,600,000

Sell specialty foods & smoked meats through direct mail & retail shops.

HARRY & DAVID HOLDINGS INC
2500 S Pacific Hwy
Medford, OR 97501-8724
Telephone: (541) 864-2500, (800) 345-5655, FAX: (541) 864-2742
Pres & CEO: Bill Williams
Conducts Business: U.S., Canada
Employees: 900
Primary Market Served: Business & Consumer

Catalog available online
Direct online sales
Advertising/Marketing Budget Related to Direct Marketing: 76-100%
Founded: 1934

Grower, processor & marketer of fine fruit, gift baskets, bakery delicacies & gourmet foods; specialize in mail-order distribution.

THE DMA HAWAIIAN HOST INC
500 Alakawa St (Suite 111)
Honolulu, HI 96817-4576
Telephone: (808) 848-0500, Web Site: www.hawaiianhost.com
Direct Sls Mgr: Carolyn Hara

HERSHEY FOODS CORP
100 Crystal A Dr
Hershey, PA 17033
Telephone: (800) 454-7737, FAX: (717) 534-5204, Web Site: www.hersheygifts.com
Chmn: James Nevels
Pres, CEO & Dir: John Bilbrey
Sr VP & CIO: George Davis
Conducts Business: U.S.
Employees: 250
Primary Market Served: Business & Consumer
Catalog available online
Direct online sales
Advertising/Marketing Budget Related to Direct Marketing: 0-25%

Provides unique and personalized chocolate gifts for the holidays and special occasions.

HERSHEY'S MAIL ORDER
Div. of Hershey Foods Corp
200 E Hersheypark Dr, PO Box 801
Hershey, PA 17033-0801
Telephone: (717) 534-7381, (800) 544-1347, FAX: (717) 534-7947, E-Mail: hersheygiftsinfo@hersheys.com, Web Site: www.hersheygifts.com
Gen Mgr: Donald Papson
Mktg Mgr: Chriss Albe
Conducts Business: U.S.
Primary Market Served: Business & Consumer
Advertising/Marketing Budget Related to Direct Marketing: 76-100%
Founded: 1982
Gross sales or billing: $7,000,000

Fine chocolate gifts through mail order.

HICKORY FARMS
1505 Holland Rd, PO Box 219
Maumee, OH 43537-0219
Telephone: (419) 893-7611, (800) 822-4438, FAX: (419) 893-0164, Web Site: www.hickoryfarms.com

Chmn, Pres & CEO: John J. Langdon
Sr VP Bus Devel: Ike Herb
VP & CFO: Mark J. Wagner
Conducts Business: U.S.
Employees: 250
Primary Market Served: Business & Consumer
Catalog available online
Direct online sales
Advertising/Marketing Budget Related to Direct Marketing: 76-100%
Gross sales or billing: $16,300,000

Specialty foods.

THE DMA THE HONEYBAKED HAM CO
aka The Original HoneyBaked Ham Co of Georgia, Inc
6145 Merger Dr
Holland, OH 43528-8430
Telephone: (419) 868-6400, E-Mail: info@honeybaked.com, Web Site: www.honeybaked.com
Chmn Bd: Linda F. Van Rees
Pres: George J. Kurz
Mktg Mgr: Kathleen Regan
Conducts Business: U.S., Canada
Employees: 650
Primary Market Served: Business & Consumer
Catalog available online
Direct online sales
Founded: 1957
Gross sales or billing: $58,000,000

Full line gourmet food catalog, featuring the authentic honeybaked ham & gift packages.

HOT SAUCE HARRY'S
1077 Innovation Ave Unit 109
North Port, FL 34289-9345
Telephone: (214) 902-8552, (800) 588-8979, FAX: (214) 956-9885, E-Mail: info@hotsauceharrys.com, Web Site: www.hotsauceharrys.com
VP: Bob Harris

HYATT FRUIT CO
PO Box 639
Vero Beach, FL 32961-0639
Telephone: (772) 567-3766, (866) 991-8889, FAX: (772) 567-0973, Web Site: www.hyattfruitco.com
Pres: Tom R. Jones
Adv Mgr: Jennifer Jones
Conducts Business: U.S. Canada
Employees: 25
Primary Market Served: Business & Consumer
Catalog available online
Advertising/Marketing Budget Related to Direct Marketing: 76-100%
Direct Marketing ad budget:
Direct Mail: 70%
Online: 25%
TV/Radio: 5%

Founded: 1946
Gross sales or billing: $5,200,000

Catalog & retail sales of Indian River citrus gift cartons & baskets for individuals, businesses & fund-raising. Also, tropical jellies & candy. Packing & retail located in Vero Beach, FL.

INTERNATIONAL WINE ACCESSORIES INC

Subs. of Dean & DeLuca
4115 E Harry
Wichita, KS 67218
Telephone: (214) 349-6097, (800) 527-4072, FAX: (214) 349-8712, E-Mail: customerservice@iwawine.com, Web Site: www.iwawine.com
Pres: Robert Orenstein
Conducts Business: U.S., Canada, Spain, Mexico, Japan
Employees: 17
Primary Market Served: Business & Consumer
Catalog available online
Direct online sales
Advertising/Marketing Budget Related to Direct Marketing: 76-100%
Founded: 1983
Gross sales or billing: $9,000,000

Cataloger of wine accessory products. Everything for the wine lover, including wine storage systems, racking systems, stemware, corkscrews, books & videos.

JAFFE BROTHERS NATURAL FOODS

28560 Lilac Rd
Valley Center, CA 92082
Telephone: (760) 749-1133, (800) 548-1886, FAX: (760) 749-1282, E-Mail: jb54@worldnet.att.net, Web Site: www.organicfruitsandnuts.com
Pres: Dean Bibler
Exec Sec: S. Wentz
Conducts Business: U.S., Canada, Japan, Hong Kong, Singapore, Germany
Employees: 9
Primary Market Served: Business & Consumer
Catalog available online
Direct online sales
Advertising/Marketing Budget Related to Direct Marketing: 0-25%
Founded: 1948

Mail order dried fruits, nuts, seeds, grains, beans, oils, nut butters, & other natural foods. Specialize in organically grown foods. Sell to stores, co-ops & individuals.

KNOLLWOOD GROVES AT CUSHMAN'S

Sub. of Cushman's Fruit Co
3325 Forest Hill Blvd
West Palm Beach, FL 33406
Telephone: (561) 734-4800, (800) 222-9696, FAX: (800) 776-4329, E-Mail: sales@knollwoodgroves.com, Web Site: www.knollwoodgroves.com
Owner & Mgr: Barbara Dwyer
Conducts Business: U.S., Canada
Employees: 60
Primary Market Served: Business & Consumer
Catalog available online
Indirect online sales
Advertising/Marketing Budget Related to Direct Marketing: 26-50%
Founded: 1930
Gross sales or billing: $2,000,000

Citrus fruit grower & shipper.

KNOTT'S BERRY FARM FOODS

Div. of ConAgra Foods
8039 Beach Blvd
Buena Park, CA 90620-3200
Telephone: (714) 220-5200, (800) 877-6887, FAX: (714) 220-5150, Web Site: www.knotts.com
Mktg Mgr: Cindy Gevorkian
Conducts Business: U.S.
Employees: 200
Primary Market Served: Business & Consumer

Manufacturer & marketer of jams, jellies, preserves, salad dressings, fruit syrups and cookies.

EC KRAUS HOME WINE & BEER MAKING SUPPLIES

733 S Northern Blvd, PO Box 7850
Independence, MO 64054
Telephone: (816) 254-7448, (800) 353-1906, FAX: (816) 254-7051, E-Mail: customerservice@eckraus.com, Web Site: www.eckraus.com
Owner: Ed Kraus
Conducts Business: U.S.
Primary Market Served: Consumer
Catalog available online
Direct online sales
Founded: 1966

Sell home wine & beer making supplies.

THE KROGER CO

1014 Vine St (Suite 1000)
Cincinnati, OH 45202-1100
Telephone: (513) 762-4000, Web Site: www.kroger.com
Primary Market Served: Business & Consumer

LAPREFERIDA INC

3400 W 35th St
Chicago, IL 60632
Telephone: (773) 254-7200, (800) 621-5422, FAX: (773) 254-8546, Web Site: www.lapreferida.com
Pres: Rich Steinbarth
VP, Mktg & Adv: David A. Steinbarth
VP: Jeff Belski
VP: Robert R. Gouwens
Sls Mgr: Bill Nash
Conducts Business: U.S., Canada
Primary Market Served: Business & Consumer
Catalog available online
Direct online sales

Manufacturers & distributors of Mexican food.

LEGAL SEA FOODS INC

One Seafood Way
Boston, MA 02210-2702
Telephone: (617) 530-9000, (800) 343-5804, FAX: (617) 530-9649, Web Site: www.legalseafoods.com
Pres & CEO: Roger Berkowitz
COO: Chip Wade
Dir Mktg: Ann Flannery
Dir Mail Order: Lisa Landry
Conducts Business: Worldwide
Employees: 3,000
Primary Market Served: Business & Consumer
Catalog available online
Direct online sales
Founded: 1950
Gross sales or billing: $65,100,000

Catalog marketer of fresh seafood products for personal gifts, corporate premiums & incentives.

MAGIC SEASONINGS MAIL ORDER

Subs. of Magic Seasoning Blends
720 Distributors Row
New Orleans, LA 70183-3208
Telephone: (504) 731-3590, (800) 457-2857, FAX: (504) 731-3576, E-Mail: jlm@chefpaul.com, Web Site: www.chefpaul.com
Pres & CEO: Shawn McBride
CFO: Paula LaCour
VP, Sls & Mktg: John L. McBride
Office Coord: Anna Zuniga
Conducts Business: Worldwide
Employees: 70
Primary Market Served: Consumer
Catalog available online
Direct online sales
Advertising/Marketing Budget Related to Direct Marketing: 0-25%
Founded: 1985

Mail order featuring Louisiana foods, cookbook gift packs, gift packages & Chef Paul Prudhomme's Magic Seasoning Blends(R).

MAISON GLASS DELICACIES
2321 John F Kennedy Blvd.
Jersey City, NJ 07304
Telephone: (212) 755-3316, (800) 822-
5564, E-Mail: info@maisonglass.
com, Web Site: www.maisonglass.
com
Consultant: Vincent Lampariello
Conducts Business: Worldwide
Employees: 10
Primary Market Served: Business &
Consumer
Advertising/Marketing Budget Related
to Direct Marketing: 51-75%
Direct Marketing ad budget: $75,000
Direct Mail: 80%
Magazines: 5%
Newspapers: 5%
Telephone: 10%
Founded: 1902

Selling & worldwide shipping of imported & domestic delicacies: caviar,
foie gras, truffles, smoked salmon,
cheeses, chocolates, freshly-roasted
nuts, oils, vinegars, coffees, teas, candies, Smithfield Hams, mustards, honeys, preserves, Spanish, French & Italian specialties & gift baskets.

MANCHESTER FARMS INC
8126 Garners Ferry Rd
Columbia, SC 29209-9402
Telephone: (803) 469-2588, (800) 845-
0421, FAX: (803) 469-8637, E-Mail:
customerservice@manchesterfarms.
com, Web Site: www.
manchesterfarms.com
Pres: Bill Odom
Natl Acct Rep: Brittney Miller
Acct Rep: Michael Kurtz
Acct Rep: Jim Lenox
Acct Rep: Steve Odom
Primary Market Served: Business &
Consumer
Catalog available online
Gross sales or billing: $5,500,000

MAPLE GROVE FARMS OF VERMONT INC
1052 Portland St
Saint Johnsbury, VT 05819-2815
Telephone: (802) 748-5141, FAX:
(802) 748-9647, E-Mail: maple@
maplegrove.com, Web Site: www.
maplegrove.com
VP, Sls & Mktg: Steve Jones
Conducts Business: U.S., Canada, Eu-
rope
Employees: 75
Primary Market Served: Business &
Consumer

Catalog featuring pure maple syrup,
meat, cheese, candy, preserves & other
gifts.

T MARZETTI CO INC
1105 Schrock Rd (3rd fl)
Columbus, OH 43229-1146
Telephone: (614) 846-2232, FAX:
(614) 848-8330, Web Site: www.
marzetti.com
Pres: Larry Noble
VP, Mktg: A. Richard Anderson
Employees: 8
Primary Market Served: Business &
Consumer
Direct Marketing ad budget:
Direct Mail: 40%
Magazines: 20%
Newspapers: 20%
Telephone: 20%
Founded: 1952

Importers & packers of all varieties of
caviar, both fresh & pasteurized.

MATTHEWS 1812 HOUSE INC
250 Kent Rd
Cornwall Bridge, CT 06754
Telephone: (860) 672-0149, (800) 662-
1812, FAX: (860) 672-1812, E-Mail:
info@matthews1812house.com, Web
Site: www.matthews1812house.com
Pres: Deanna Matthews
Sec: Blaine Matthews
Conducts Business: U.S.
Employees: 14
Primary Market Served: Consumer
Catalog available online
Direct online sales
Advertising/Marketing Budget Related
to Direct Marketing: 76-100%
Direct Marketing ad budget:
Direct Mail: 100%
Founded: 1979

Mail-order gourmet foods to
consumers.

MCCORMICK & CO INC
211 Schilling Cir
Hunt Valley, MD 21031
Telephone: (410) 771-7301, (800) 474-
7742, FAX: (410) 527-6337, Web
Site: www.mccormick.com
Chmn: Robert J. Lawless
Conducts Business: Worldwide
Employees: 8,000
Primary Market Served: Business &
Consumer
Catalog available online
Direct online sales
Founded: 1889

Manufacture specialty food products,
spices, seasonings, flavorings & decorations for cakes.

MEDIFAST INC
11445 Cronhill Dr Ste 200
Owings Mills, MD 21117-2270
Telephone: (410) 504-8222, Web Site:
www.medifastdiet.com

Primary Market Served: Consumer

THE DMA MELITTA USA
13925 58th St
Clearwater, FL 33760-3721
Telephone: (727) 535-2111, Web Site:
www.melitta.com
Dir ECommerce: Donna Gray

MILLERCOORS LLC
250 S Wacker Dr Ste 800
Chicago, IL 60606-5888
Telephone: (800) 645-5376, Web Site:
www.millercoors.com
CEO: Leo Kiely
Pres & Chief Comml Officer: Tom
Long
CFO: Gavin Hattersly
Chief Mktg Officer: Andrew J. En-
gland
Primary Market Served: Consumer

MOON SHINE TRADING CO
Div. of Z Specialty Food Co LLC
1250A Harter Ave
Woodland, CA 95776
Telephone: (530) 668-0660, (800) 678-
1226, FAX: (530) 668-6061, E-Mail:
store@moonshinetrading.com, Web
Site: www.moonshinetrading.com
Owner: Amina Harris
Owner: Ishai Zeldner
Sls Mgr: Wedy Twichell-O'Neal
Conducts Business: U.S.
Employees: 6
Primary Market Served: Business &
Consumer
Catalog available online
Direct online sales
Advertising/Marketing Budget Related
to Direct Marketing: 0-25%
Direct Marketing ad budget:
Direct Mail: 95%
Magazines: 5%
Founded: 1979
Gross sales or billing: $1,000,000

Varietal honeys, comb honey, nut butters, honey fruit spreads, gift boxes,
honey straws, all items Kosher, Judaica
Goodies (food gifts).

MORKES CHOCOLATES
aka Morkes Inc
1890 N Rand Rd
Palatine, IL 60074
Telephone: (847) 359-3454, FAX:
(847) 359-3553, E-Mail: yummy@
morkeschocolates.com, Web Site:
www.morkeschocolates.com
Pres: Rhonda Morkes
Conducts Business: U.S.
Employees: 10
Primary Market Served: Business &
Consumer
Catalog available online

Direct online sales
Advertising/Marketing Budget Related
  to Direct Marketing: 0-25%
Direct Marketing ad budget: $14,000
Direct Mail: 30%
Newspapers: 10%
TV/Radio: 40%
Telephone: 20%
Founded: 1920

Marketer of gourmet chocolates, cara-
mel apples & specialty items.

MRS BEASLEY'S & MISS GRACE LEMON CAKE CO

Div. of KA Industries
PO Box 25575
Los Angeles, CA 90025-0575
Telephone: (800) 710-7742, FAX:
  (310) 668-2148, E-Mail: general@
  mrsbeasleys.com, Web Site: www.
  mrsbeasleys.com
Pres & CEO: Ken Harris
VP, Mktg: Bea Sharif
Employees: 50
Primary Market Served: Business &
  Consumer
Catalog available online
Direct online sales
Advertising/Marketing Budget Related
  to Direct Marketing: 76-100%
Founded: 1979

Provide gourmet bakery goods, baskets
& corporate gift items.

NELSON CRAB INC

3088 Kindred Ave
Tokeland, WA 98590
Telephone: (360) 267-2911, (800) 262-
  0069, FAX: (360) 267-2921, E-Mail:
  seatreats@techline.com, Web Site:
  www.nelsoncrab.com
Pres: Kristi Nelson
Sec & Treas: Melvin Preston
Canned & Gift Sls: Cathy Davis
Conducts Business: U.S.
Employees: 30
Primary Market Served: Business &
  Consumer
Catalog available online
Indirect online sales
Advertising/Marketing Budget Related
  to Direct Marketing: 0-25%
Direct Marketing ad budget: $5,000
Direct Mail: 50%
Magazines: 10%
Newspapers: 5%
TV/Radio: 10%
Telephone: 25%
Founded: 1934
Gross sales or billing: $2,700,000

Retail & mail order wholesale seafood:
fresh, frozen & canned.

NESTLE USA

800 N Brand Blvd
Glendale, CA 91203-1216
Telephone: (818) 549-6000, (800) 225-
  2270, FAX: (818) 549-6952, Web
  Site: www.nestleusa.com
Chmn & CEO: Brad Alford
VP & CFO: Dan Stroud
CIO: Kimberly Lund
Sr VP, HR: Judy Cascapera
Sr VP, Mktg: Doreen Ida
Primary Market Served: Business
Catalog available online
Indirect online sales
Founded: 1985

Food service manufacturer.

NEW ENGLAND CHEESEMAKING SUPPLY CO

54 Whately Rd Ste B
South Deerfield, MA 01373-9608
Telephone: (413) 628-3808, FAX:
  (413) 628-4061, E-Mail: info@
  cheesemaking.com, Web Site: www.
  cheesemaking.com
Owner: Ricki Carroll
Conducts Business: Worldwide
Employees: 4
Primary Market Served: Business &
  Consumer
Catalog available online
Direct online sales
Advertising/Marketing Budget Related
  to Direct Marketing: 0-25%
Founded: 1978
Gross sales or billing: $425,000

Cheese making & dairy supplies to
individuals & businesses.

NODINE'S SMOKEHOUSE

65 Fowler Ave
Torrington, CT 06790-6529
Telephone: (860) 489-3213, (800) 222-
  2059, FAX: (860) 496-9787, E-Mail:
  nodinesmoke@optonline.net, Web
  Site: www.nodinesmokehouse.com
Pres: Ronald Nodine
Sls Mgr: Ken Cherry
Primary Market Served: Business &
  Consumer
Founded: 1969

Smoked foods such as hams, bacon,
poultry, whole birds, cheese, fish &
sausage.

THE DMA OMAHA CREATIVE GROUP INC

11030 O St
Omaha, NE 68137-2346
Telephone: (800) 228-2778, Web Site:
  www.omahasteaks.com
VP Gen Mgr: Vickie Hagen
Primary Market Served: Consumer

OMAHA STEAKS INC

11030 "O" St
Omaha, NE 68137-2346
Telephone: (402) 597-3000, FAX:
  (402) 597-8252, E-Mail: info@
  omahasteaks.com, Web Site: www.
  omahasteaks.com
Pres & CEO: Bruce A. Simon
Chmn Bd: Alan Simon
Exec VP: Frederick J. Simon
Sr VP: Todd Simon
VP Mktg: Vickie Hagen
Online Dir: Julie Evans
Opers Dir: Ron Eike
Corp Commun Dir: Beth Weiss
Conducts Business: U.S.
Employees: 1,800
Primary Market Served: Business &
  Consumer
Catalog available online
Direct online sales
Advertising/Marketing Budget Related
  to Direct Marketing: 76-100%
Direct Marketing ad budget:
Direct Mail: 60%
Magazines: 10%
Newspapers: 10%
Online: 13%
TV/Radio: 2%
Telephone: 5%
Founded: 1917
Gross sales or billing: $457,000,000

Sell steaks & frozen gourmet foods to
businesses & consumers for gifts
and/or personal use. Sales are made
through direct mail, space ads online,
telephone marketing & retail stores.

OREGON FREEZE DRY INC

525 W 25th Ave SE
Albany, OR 97321-3900
Telephone: (541) 926-6001, FAX:
  (541) 967-6527, Web Site: www.ofd.
  com
Pres: Herbert Aschkenasy
Employees: 250
Primary Market Served: Business
Advertising/Marketing Budget Related
  to Direct Marketing: 0-25%
Founded: 1963
Gross sales or billing: $106,000,000

Sell freeze-dried products.

THE ORIGINAL HONEY BAKED HAM CO OF THE EAST

105 Green St
Marblehead, MA 01945-1439
Telephone: (781) 639-2200, Web Site:
  www.honeybakedmailorder.com
Pres: Stephen McHugh
Primary Market Served: Consumer

PJT INC

dba River Street Sweets
PO Box 1265

Savannah, GA 31402-1265
Telephone: (912) 233-6220, Web Site:
www.riverstreetsweets.com
Dir Mail Order & Corp Sls: Kelley
Cale

Gourmet homemade southern candy

PAPA JOHN'S
  INTERNATIONAL
2002 Papa John's Blvd
Louisville, KY 40299-2333
Telephone: (502) 261-7272, Web Site:
www.papajohns.com
Dir Database Mktg: Susan Poulsen
Primary Market Served: Business &
Consumer

PECAN PRODUCERS
  INTERNATIONAL
2131 E State Hwy 31
Corsicana, TX 75151-1301
Telephone: (903) 872-1337, (800) 732-
2648, FAX: (903) 874-7143
Mgr: Linda Garza
Primary Market Served: Business &
Consumer

Mail order pecans & candy.

PEET'S COFFEE & TEA INC
PO Box 12509
Berkeley, CA 94712-3509
Telephone: (510) 594-2100, (800) 999-
2132, FAX: (510) 594-2180, E-Mail:
mailorder@peets.com, Web Site:
www.peets.com
Chmn: Jean-Michel Valette
Pres, CEO & Dir: Patrick J. O'Dea
VP, CFO & Sec: Thomas P. Cawley
Mktg Dir: Felicia Chan
Employees: 3,000
Primary Market Served: Business &
Consumer
Catalog available online
Direct online sales
Advertising/Marketing Budget Related
to Direct Marketing: 0-25%
Founded: 1966
Gross sales or billing: $210,000,000

PINNACLE ORCHARDS
Subs. of Hickory Farms
1505 Holland Rd
Maumee, OH 43537
Telephone: (419) 893-7611, (800) 442-
5671, FAX: (419) 893-0164, Web
Site: www.pinnacleorchards.com
Pres, Chmn & CEO: John J. Langdon
Sr VP, Bus Devel: Ike Herb
VP & CFO: Mark Wagner
VP, Sls & Mktg: Erik Long
VP & HR: Amy Eaton
Primary Market Served: Business &
Consumer
Catalog available online

Direct online sales
Fruit seller.

PIONEER HI-BRED
  INTERNATIONAL INC
7100 NW 62nd Ave, PO Box 1000
Johnston, IA 50131-1000
Telephone: (515) 270-3200, FAX:
(515) 270-3581, E-Mail: web.
editor@pioneer.com, Web Site:
www.pioneer.com
VP & CFO: Jeff Austin
VP: Dennis Byron
VP: Grant Ian
Mktg: Jerry Harrington
Conducts Business: Worldwide
Employees: 6,500
Primary Market Served: Business &
Consumer

Distribute catalog sales of corn, soy-
bean, wheat & alfalfa seeds.

PITTMAN & DAVIS INC
801 N Expressway 77
Harlingen, TX 78552
Telephone: (956) 423-2154, (800) 289-
7829, FAX: (866) 329-7829, E-Mail:
fruit@pittmandavis.com, Web Site:
www.pittmandavis.com
CEO: Edward Davis Sr
Pres: Frank E. Davis
Sec: Kathy Yarborough
Conducts Business: U.S.
Employees: 50
Primary Market Served: Business &
Consumer
Catalog available online
Direct online sales
Advertising/Marketing Budget Related
to Direct Marketing: 76-100%
Direct Marketing ad budget:
Direct Mail: 95%
Magazines: 5%
Founded: 1926
Gross sales or billing: $18,000,000

Specializes in the sale of gift packages
of fresh fruit, smoked meat, cheese,
pastries, candy & nuts.

THE POPCORN FACTORY
13970 W Laurel Dr
Lake Forest, IL 60045-4533
Telephone: (847) 362-0028, (888) 216-
0235, FAX: (888) 333-4595, E-Mail:
service@thepopcornfactory.com,
Web Site: www.thepopcornfactory.
com
Pres: Kent Arett
Opers Dir: Glenn Gazzolo
Mdsg Dir: Ann Bromley
Mktg Dir: Cheryl Zatz
Sls & Svc Dir: Julie Kaufman
Controller: Gary Jeffery
Conducts Business: Worldwide

Employees: 80
Primary Market Served: Business &
Consumer
Catalog available online
Indirect online sales
Advertising/Marketing Budget Related
to Direct Marketing: 76-100%
Direct Marketing ad budget:
Direct Mail: 99%
Magazines: 1%
Founded: 1979

Specialty gift catalog featuring exclusively designed baskets, gift assortments & popcorn cans, fresh-packed &
shipped for gift giving. Also features
other confectionery, snack & non-food
gift items. Offers both consumer &
corporate catalogs.

PRESQUE ISLE WINE
  CELLARS INC
9440 W Main Rd
North East, PA 16428
Telephone: (814) 725-1314, (800) 488-
7492, FAX: (814) 725-2092, E-Mail:
info@piwine.com, Web Site: www.
piwine.com
Dir Opers: Marc Boettcher
Pres & Owner: Douglas P. Moorhead
Conducts Business: U.S., Canada
Employees: 11
Primary Market Served: Business &
Consumer
Catalog available online
Direct online sales
Advertising/Marketing Budget Related
to Direct Marketing: 51-75%
Direct Marketing ad budget:
Direct Mail: $16,000
Magazines: $3,000
Newspapers: $1,500
Founded: 1964
Gross sales or billing: $3,600,000

Sell supplies to amateur winemakers &
small commercial wineries.

PRIESTER PECAN CO INC
208 E Old Fort Rd
Fort Deposit, AL 36032-4012
Telephone: (334) 227-4301, Web Site:
www.priesters.com
Pres: Thomas Ellis
Primary Market Served: Consumer

PROFESSIONAL CUTLERY
  DIRECT
242 Branford Rd
North Branford, CT 06471
Telephone: (203) 871-1000, FAX:
(203) 871-1010, E-Mail: terri@
cutlery.com, Web Site: www.cutlery.
com
Pres: Jacob Alpert
CEO: Terri S. Alpert
Mktg Dir: Greg Ellal

Conducts Business: U.S., Canada
Employees: 52
Primary Market Served: Consumer
Catalog available online
Direct online sales
Advertising/Marketing Budget Related
    to Direct Marketing: 0-25%
Direct Marketing ad budget:
Direct Mail: 95%
Magazines: 3%
Newspapers: 2%
Founded: 1993
Gross sales or billing: $9,000,000

Culinary tools.

QUEEN BEE GARDENS
1863 Lane 11 1/2
Lovell, WY 82431-9751
Telephone: (307) 548-2543, (800) 225-
    7553, FAX: (307) 548-6721, E-Mail:
    queenbee@tctwest.net, Web Site:
    queenbeegardens.com
Exec Sec: Bessie Zeller
Mktg Dir: Peggy Fowler
Mktg Dir: Ben Zeller
Conducts Business: U.S.
Employees: 12
Primary Market Served: Business &
    Consumer
Catalog available online
Indirect online sales
Advertising/Marketing Budget Related
    to Direct Marketing: 0-25%
Direct Marketing ad budget:
Direct Mail: 50%
Magazines: 20%
Newspapers: 20%
Telephone: 10%
Founded: 1976
Gross sales or billing: $350,000

Sell honey candy, truffles, turtles, English toffee & pralines to health food
stores, gourmet shops & consumers.

RANCH HOUSE MEAT CO
PO Box 977
Menard, TX 76859-0977
Telephone: (800) 749-6329, FAX:
    (888) 917-6328, E-Mail: sales@
    brisket.net, Web Site: www.brisket.
    net
Owner: Max Stabel
Mail Order Mgr: Marsha Stabel
Conducts Business: U.S.
Employees: 15
Primary Market Served: Business &
    Consumer
Catalog available online
Direct online sales
Advertising/Marketing Budget Related
    to Direct Marketing: 0-25%
Direct Marketing ad budget: $75,000
Direct Mail: 60%
Online: 40%
Founded: 1978

Gross sales or billing: $2,173,708

Mail order marketer of meat products
including smoked brisket, turkey, ham
& bacon.

RED COOPER
PO Box 3089
Mission, TX 78573-0052
Telephone: (800) 825-8531, FAX:
    (956) 205-7331, Web Site: www.
    redcooper.com
Pres: John Launer
Primary Market Served: Consumer
Catalog available online
Direct online sales

Mail order gifts.

RENT MOTHER NATURE
PO Box 380193
Cambridge, MA 02238-0193
Telephone: (617) 868-5059, (800) 232-
    4048, FAX: (617) 868-5861, Web
    Site: www.rentmothernature.com
Sr Advisor: Richard Hill
Conducts Business: U.S.
Primary Market Served: Business &
    Consumer
Advertising/Marketing Budget Related
    to Direct Marketing: 76-100%
Founded: 1979
Gross sales or billing: $2,000,000

Foods & gifts.

THE DMA RIVER STREET SWEETS
13 E River St
Savannah, GA 31401-1295
Telephone: (912) 234-4608, (800) 793-
    3876, FAX: (912) 234-1584, E-Mail:
    randerson@riverstreetsweets.com,
    Web Site: www.riverstreetsweets.
    com
Owner & VP: Jennifer Strickland
Owner: Tim Strickland
Mgr: Megan Fisher
Owner & Pres: Pam Strickland
Dir Corp Sls: Kelley Cale
Conducts Business: U.S.
Primary Market Served: Business &
    Consumer
Catalog available online
Direct online sales
Advertising/Marketing Budget Related
    to Direct Marketing: 76-100%
Direct Marketing ad budget:
Direct Mail: 97%
Magazines: 1%
Newspapers: 1%
TV/Radio: 1%
Founded: 1973

Gourmet Southern candies and gifts.

ROCKY MOUNTAIN CHOCOLATE FACTORY
265 Turner Dr
Durango, CO 81303-7941
Telephone: (970) 259-0554, (888) 525-
    2462, FAX: (970) 259-5895, E-Mail:
    customerservice@rmcfusa.com, Web
    Site: www.rmcf.com
Pres: Frank Crail
Conducts Business: U.S., Canada, Tai-
    wan, UAE
Employees: 450
Primary Market Served: Business &
    Consumer
Catalog available online
Direct online sales
Advertising/Marketing Budget Related
    to Direct Marketing: 0-25%
Founded: 1981
Gross sales or billing: $27,000,000

Retail candy manufacturer.

SAN FRANCISCO HERB & NATURAL FOOD CO
47444 Kato Rd
Fremont, CA 94538-7319
Telephone: (510) 770-1215, (800) 227-
    2830, FAX: (510) 770-9021, E-Mail:
    customerservice@herbspicetea.com,
    Web Site: www.herbspicetea.com
CEO, Pres & Owner: Barry Meltzer
Adv Mgr: Tiffany Nguyen
Conducts Business: U.S.
Employees: 80
Primary Market Served: Business &
    Consumer
Catalog available online
Direct online sales
Advertising/Marketing Budget Related
    to Direct Marketing: 0-25%
Direct Marketing ad budget:
Direct Mail: 75%
Magazines: 25%
Founded: 1969
Gross sales or billing: $16,000,000

Sell herbal teas, bulk herbs & spices to
pharmaceutical companies, retailers &
herbal tea manufacturers.

SANTA FE SCHOOL OF COOKING
116 W San Francisco St
Santa Fe, NM 87501
Telephone: (505) 983-4511, FAX:
    (505) 983-7540, Web Site: www.
    santafeschoolofcooking.com
Owner & Dir: Susan Curtis
Conducts Business: U.S.
Employees: 7
Primary Market Served: Consumer
Catalog available online
Direct online sales
Founded: 1989

Regional cooking ingredients and
products.

SAUCE CO
aka Mellon Corp
11525 Cantrell Rd (Suite 910)
Little Rock, AR 72212-1721
Telephone: (501) 663-3338, (800) 43-Sauce, FAX: (501) 663-0956, Web Site: www.sauceco.net
Owner: Melissa Rowland
Owner: Jay Rowland
Employees: 3
Primary Market Served: Business
Catalog available online
Direct online sales
Advertising/Marketing Budget Related to Direct Marketing: 76-100%
Direct Marketing ad budget:
Newspapers: 35%
Online: 30%
TV/Radio: 35%
Founded: 1992

Gourmet retail & mail order Southern sauce & related items.

THE SAUSAGE MAKER INC
1500 Clinton St (Suite 123)
Buffalo, NY 14206-3099
Telephone: (716) 824-5814, (888) 490-8525, FAX: (716) 824-6465, E-Mail: customerservice@sausagemaker.com, Web Site: www.sausagemaker.com
Pres: Kris Stanuscek
Conducts Business: U.S., Canada
Employees: 24
Primary Market Served: Business & Consumer
Catalog available online
Direct online sales
Advertising/Marketing Budget Related to Direct Marketing: 76-100%
Direct Marketing ad budget:
Direct Mail: $115,000
Magazines: $28,000
Founded: 1976
Gross sales or billing: $4,000,000

Equipment & supply catalog for sausage-making, meat-curing & food smoking.

SCHERMER PECANS
PO Box 399
Glennville, GA 30427
Telephone: (800) 841-3403, E-Mail: information@schermerpecans.com, Web Site: www.pecantreats.com
Office Mgr: Melita Humphries
Conducts Business: U.S.
Employees: 50
Primary Market Served: Business & Consumer
Advertising/Marketing Budget Related to Direct Marketing: 76-100%
Founded: 1946

Processor & marketer of pecans for fund-raising purposes.

THE DMA SEE'S CANDIES INC
20600 S Alameda St
Carson, CA 90810-1105
Telephone: (800) 347-7337, Web Site: www.sees.com
Sr Admin Asst: Carol Lowe
Primary Market Served: Consumer

THE DMA THE JM SMUCKER CO
1 Strawberry Ln
Orrville, OH 44667-1298
Telephone: (330) 682-3000, Web Site: www.smucker.com
Primary Market Served: Business & Consumer

STARBUCKS CORP
2401 Utah Ave S, PO Box 34067
Seattle, WA 98134
Telephone: (206) 447-1575, (800) 344-1575, FAX: (206) 447-0828, Web Site: www.starbucks.com
Chmn: Howard D. Schultz
Pres, CEO & Dir: James L. Donald
Exec VP, Partner Resources: David A. Pace
Dir: Barbara Bass
Dir: Howard P. Behar
Conducts Business: U.S., Canada
Employees: 145,000
Primary Market Served: Business & Consumer
Catalog available online
Direct online sales
Founded: 1985
Gross sales or billing: $7,700,000,000

Coffee roaster & retail distributor.

THE STASH TEA CATALOG
7204 SW Durham Rd (Suite 200)
Tigard, OR 97224
Telephone: (800) 547-1514, FAX: (503) 684-4424, E-Mail: stash@stashtea.com, Web Site: www.stashtea.com
Pres & CEO: Thomas D. Lisicki
VP Mktg: Dorothy Arnold
Community Rels Mgr: Jan Acker
Conducts Business: U.S.
Employees: 49
Primary Market Served: Consumer
Catalog available online
Indirect online sales
Founded: 1972
Gross sales or billing: $9,900,000

A full line of premium specialty teas.

STEW LEONARD'S
100 Westport Ave
Norwalk, CT 06851
Telephone: (203) 847-7214, FAX: (203) 847-1488, Web Site: www.stewleonards.com
Pres: Stew Leonards Jr.

Art Dir: Richard Lung
Employees: 30
Primary Market Served: Business & Consumer
Advertising/Marketing Budget Related to Direct Marketing: 0-25%
Founded: 1990
Gross sales or billing: $5,000,000

Grocery store, dairy & gifts catalog.

STOCK YARDS PACKING CO INC
340 N Oakley Blvd
Chicago, IL 60612
Telephone: (312) 733-6050, (877) STK-YARD, FAX: (312) 733-1746, E-Mail: customerservice@stockyards.com, Web Site: www.stockyards.com
CEO: Daniel Pollack
Pres: Mark Saviski
VP, Fin: Ross Bridge
Conducts Business: U.S.
Primary Market Served: Business & Consumer
Catalog available online
Direct online sales
Advertising/Marketing Budget Related to Direct Marketing: 76-100%

Marketers of U.S. prime meats & gourmet foods to consumers & businesses via catalogs, direct mail & space ads.

SUGARBUSH FARM INC
591 Sugarbush Farm Rd
Woodstock, VT 05091
Telephone: (802) 457-1757, (800) 281-1757, FAX: (802) 457-3269, E-Mail: contact@sugarbushfarm.com, Web Site: www.sugarbushfarm.com
Pres: Elizabeth Luce
Conducts Business: U.S.
Employees: 20
Primary Market Served: Business & Consumer
Catalog available online
Direct online sales
Advertising/Marketing Budget Related to Direct Marketing: 51-75%
Direct Marketing ad budget:
Direct Mail: 90%
Magazines: 10%
Founded: 1945

Sell natural & aged Vermont cheeses in waxed cracker sized sticks & maple syrup.

SULLIVAN-VICTORY GROVES
PO Box 10
Cocoa, FL 32923-0010

Telephone: (321) 632-0550, (800) 672-6431, FAX: (321) 639-4069, E-Mail: citrus@sullivanvictorygroves.net, Web Site: www. sullivanvictorygroves.net
Gen Mgr: Frank E. Sullivan
President: Jeanette Sullivan
Office Mgr: Carol Wham
Conducts Business: U.S., Canada, Europe
Employees: 6
Primary Market Served: Business & Consumer
Indirect online sales
Direct Marketing ad budget: $50,000
Direct Mail: 80%
Newspapers: 20%
Founded: 1952

Gift order citrus. Sell citrus fruit gifts.

THE DMA SUNNYLAND FARMS INC
PO Box 1275
Albany, GA 31702-1275
Telephone: (229) 436-5654, (800) 999-2488, FAX: (229) 888-8332, Web Site: www.sunnylandfarms.com
Pres: Jane Willson
VP: Larry Willson
VP: Frankye Lemay
Conducts Business: U.S.
Employees: 100
Primary Market Served: Business & Consumer
Catalog available online
Direct online sales
Advertising/Marketing Budget Related to Direct Marketing: 76-100%
Founded: 1948

Sell pecans, nuts, candies, cakes & dried fruits through catalogs to the general public.

THE SWISS COLONY INC
1112 7th Ave
Monroe, WI 53566-1364
Telephone: (608) 328-8400, FAX: (608) 328-8457, Web Site: www. swisscolony.com
Pres: John Baumann
Conducts Business: U.S.
Employees: 4,000
Primary Market Served: Business & Consumer

Mail order company specializing in corporate & individual food gifts.

TILLAMOOK COUNTY CREAMERY ASSOCIATION
4185 Hwy 101 N
Tillamook, OR 97141-7770
Telephone: (503) 842-4481, (800) 542-7290, FAX: (503) 842-6039, Web Site: www.tillamookcheese.com
Chmn: George Allen

Interim CEO: Cliff Brady
Pres: James Mcmullen
Mgr: Harold Schild
Retail Sls Mgr: Judith Hill
Conducts Business: U.S.
Employees: 650
Primary Market Served: Business & Consumer
Direct Marketing ad budget: $900,000
Direct Mail: $50,000
Magazines: $100,000
Newspapers: $650,000
TV/Radio: $100,000
Founded: 1909
Gross sales or billing: $326,000,000

Sell natural cheddar cheese in gift packs. Gift packs may also contain canned seafood, smoked meats, local jams & jellies.

TODARO BROTHERS MAIL ORDER CO
Div. of Todaro Brothers
555 Second Ave
New York, NY 10016
Telephone: (877) 472-2767, FAX: (212) 689-1679, E-Mail: eat@todarobros.com, Web Site: www.todarobros.com
Pres & Treas: Luciano Todaro
Store Mgr: Michael Spano
Conducts Business: U.S.
Employees: 50
Primary Market Served: Business & Consumer
Catalog available online
Direct online sales
Advertising/Marketing Budget Related to Direct Marketing: 0-25%
Direct Marketing ad budget:
Online: 100%
Founded: 1917
Gross sales or billing: $5,000,000

Catalog marketer of imported & domestic gourmet specialty foods.

UNCLE BEN'S INC
Div. of Mars Food US, LLC
1098 N Broadway St
Greenville, MS 38701-2004
Telephone: (662) 335-8000, (800) 548-6253, (800) 54-UNCLE, FAX: (662) 378-4370, E-Mail: info@unclebens.com, Web Site: www.unclebens.com
Dir Corp Commun: Alice Nathanson
VP Mktg, Masterfoods USA: Michelle Kessler
Conducts Business: Worldwide.
Employees: 150
Primary Market Served: Business
Catalog available online
Indirect online sales
Founded: 1943
Gross sales or billing: $500,000

Manufacture & sell rice products.

US FOODSERVICE
9399 W Higgins Rd Ste 500
Rosemont, IL 60018-4992
Telephone: (410) 312-7100, FAX: (410) 312-7167, Web Site: www. usfoodservice.com
Pres & CEO: Robert Aiken
Exec VP Bus Devel: David Schreibman
Sr VP Info Sys: Rod Harris
Employees: 27,630
Primary Market Served: Business
Gross sales or billing: $25,356,900,000

Food service distributor.

URBANI TRUFFLES USA CORP
Div. of Urbani-Italy
10 West End Ave
New York, NY 10023
Telephone: (212) 247-8800, FAX: (212) 247-8900, E-Mail: info@urbani.com, Web Site: www. urbanitartufi.com
VP: John A. Natale Jr.
Consultant: Paul A. Urbani
Conducts Business: Worldwide
Employees: 3
Primary Market Served: Business & Consumer
Advertising/Marketing Budget Related to Direct Marketing: 0-25%

Market white & black truffles packed in tins, jars & tubes. Also fresh truffles in season & flash frozen truffles.

THE VIRGINIA DINER INC
322 W Main St
Wakefield, VA 23888-2940
Telephone: (757) 899-6213, (888) 823-4637, FAX: (757) 899-2281, E-Mail: vadiner@vadiner.com, Web Site: www.vadiner.com
Chmn: Mary Galloway
Pres: Christine Epperson
VP & CEO: William B. Jones
Conducts Business: Worldwide
Employees: 100
Primary Market Served: Business & Consumer
Catalog available online
Indirect online sales
Advertising/Marketing Budget Related to Direct Marketing: 51-75%
Direct Marketing ad budget:
Direct Mail: 77%
Newspapers: 8%
TV/Radio: 15%
Founded: 1929

Restaurant, gift shop & mail order business.

WAKEFIELD PEANUT CO
Subs. of Wakefield Peanut Co LLC
11253 General Mahone Hwy (Rte 460)

Wakefield, VA 23888
Telephone: (757) 899-5481, (800) 803-1309, FAX: (757) 899-7604, Web Site: www.wakefieldpeanutco.com
Gen Mgr: Jimmy Laine
Conducts Business: U.S., Worldwide
Employees: 20
Primary Market Served: Consumer
Catalog available online
Direct online sales
Founded: 1965

Sell peanuts wholesale & retail to customers, other peanut businesses, to farmers, mail order, and fundraising activities.

WHOLE FOODS MARKET INC

550 Bowie St Ste 99
Austin, TX 78703-4644
Telephone: (512) 477-4455, FAX: (512) 482-7000, Web Site: www.wholefoodsmarket.com
Global VP Growth & Bus Devel: Betsy Foster

THE DMA WILD FLAVORS INC

1261 Pacific Ave
Erlanger, KY 41018-1260
Telephone: (859) 342-3600, Web Site: www.wildflavors.com
Sr Dir Mktg: Donna Hansee
Primary Market Served: Business & Consumer

WIMMER'S MEAT PRODUCTS INC

126 W Grant St, PO Box 286
West Point, NE 68788-0286
Telephone: (402) 372-2437, (800) 358-0761, FAX: (402) 372-5659, Web Site: www.wimmersmeats.com
Chmn, CEO & Pres: Dave Wimmer
VP, Sls & Mktg: Terry Maul
VP: Dean Hughson
Conducts Business: U.S.
Primary Market Served: Business & Consumer
Catalog available online
Indirect online sales
Founded: 1934

Ethnic & European-style sausage & cured meat products.

WINE ENTHUSIAST COS

333 N Bedford Rd
Mount Kisco, NY 10523-1158
Telephone: (914) 345-9463, (800) 356-8466, FAX: (914) 345-3129, Web Site: www.wineenthusiast.com
Chmn & Owner: Adam M. Strum
Sr Dir Online Mktg & Mdsg: Glenn Edelman
COO: Sybil N. Strum

Conducts Business: Worldwide
Primary Market Served: Business & Consumer
Catalog available online
Direct online sales
Founded: 1979

Source for wine accessories, storage, information, education, events and travel.

WINETASTING.COM

2545 Napa Valley Corporate Dr
Napa, CA 94558-6275
Telephone: (800) 435-2225, FAX: (707) 252-0268, Web Site: www.geerwade.com
Gen Mgr: Chris Edwards
Conducts Business: U.S.
Employees: 105
Primary Market Served: Consumer
Catalog available online
Direct online sales
Advertising/Marketing Budget Related to Direct Marketing: 0-25%
Founded: 1986
Gross sales or billing: $30,000,000

Wine & wine accessories.

THE WISCONSIN CHEESEMAN

301 Broadway Dr
Sun Prairie, WI 53590-1742
Telephone: (608) 837-5166, (800) 698-1721, FAX: (608) 837-5493, Web Site: www.wisconsincheeseman.com
Pres: Holly Cremer
CEO: John Jeffrey
CFO: Jerry Stinger
VP: Paul Esser
VP: Francis S. Cremer
Dir, Mktg: Doug First
Conducts Business: U.S.
Primary Market Served: Consumer
Catalog available online
Direct online sales
Advertising/Marketing Budget Related to Direct Marketing: 76-100%
Direct Marketing ad budget:
Direct Mail: 95%
Magazines: 5%
Founded: 1947

Sell gift boxes of cheese, candy & related items by mail order.

YOUNG PECAN CO

Subs. of King Ranch, Inc
1200 Pecan St
Florence, SC 29501-2827
Telephone: (843) 662-8591, (800) 829-6864, FAX: (843) 664-2344, E-Mail: sales@youngpecan.com, Web Site: www.youngpecan.com
Pres & CEO: James Swink
Exec VP: Helen Watts

VP, Fin: Kimberly Griffith
Conducts Business: U.S.
Employees: 183
Primary Market Served: Business & Consumer
Advertising/Marketing Budget Related to Direct Marketing: 26-50%
Direct Marketing ad budget:
Direct Mail: 100%
Founded: 1923
Gross sales or billing: $98,800,000

Sell fresh pecans & pecan gift items.

Telephone: (212) 560-2000, FAX: (212) 582-3297, Web Site: www.thirteen.org
CEO & Dir: William F. Baker
Pres: Neal B. Shapiro
VP Natl Mktg & Content Devel: Don Rogosin
Dir Mktg Commun: Barbara Bantivoglio
Dir Online Fund Raising: Ben Smith
Conducts Business: US
Employees: 500
Primary Market Served: Business & Consumer
Catalog available online
Direct online sales
Founded: 1962
Gross sales or billing: $167,900,000

Premiums offered to Channel 13 members and online donations.

CLARIN BY HUSSEY SEATING

Div. of Greenwich Industries
38 Dyer St Ext
North Berwick, ME 03906-6763
Telephone: (207) 676-2271, Web Site: www.husseyseating.com
VP, Adv: Wilson Troup
Employees: 100
Primary Market Served: Business & Consumer
Advertising/Marketing Budget Related to Direct Marketing: 0-25%
Founded: 1925
Gross sales or billing: $7,000,000

Manufacture & distribute portable seating products.

THE DMA CLARKSON EYECARE

217 Clarkson Rd
Ellisville, MO 63011-2219
Telephone: (636) 227-2600
Primary Market Served: Consumer

COLUMBIA UNIVERSITY, ANNUAL FUND PROGRAMS

622 W 113th St (MC4520)
New York, NY 10025-7982
Telephone: (212) 851-7956, Web Site: http://giving.columbia.edu
Primary Market Served: Consumer

THE DMA CORNERSTONE BRANDS INC

PO Box 1308
West Chester, OH 45071-1308
Telephone: (513) 603-1400, Web Site: www.cornerstonebrands.com
CFO: Jim Pekarek
Primary Market Served: Consumer

Comprised of home & apparel lifestyle brands, such as Frontgate, Ballard Designs & Garnet Hill

CORONA CIGAR CO

7792 W Sand Lake Rd
Orlando, FL 32819
Telephone: (407) 248-1212, (888) 702-4427, FAX: (407) 248-1211, E-Mail: info@coronacigar.com, Web Site: www.coronacigar.com
Pres & Founder: Jeff Borysiewicz
Conducts Business: U.S.
Employees: 42
Primary Market Served: Consumer
Catalog available online
Direct online sales
Founded: 1996
Gross sales or billing: $4,000,000

Cigars, humidors & cigar accessories.

CORTZ INC

320 Industrial Dr
West Chicago, IL 60185-1817
Telephone: (630) 876-1080, Web Site: www.intheswim.com
Pres: Barry Pace
Primary Market Served: Business & Consumer
Founded: 1982

Pool supplies

CUSTOM TOLL FREE

914 164th St SE (#1670)
Mill Creek, WA 98012-6385
Telephone: (800) 933-3030, Web Site: www.customtollfree.com
VP Sls & Mktg: Christy Brugger

Provides customized toll free numbers for businesses

DFS GROUP LIMITED

Subs. of LVMH Moet Hennessy Louis Vuitton
525 Market St, First Market Tower
San Francisco, CA 94105-2708
Telephone: (415) 977-2700, FAX: (415) 977-2970, Web Site: www.dfsgalleria.com
DM Dir: Audrey A. Gerber

Operates more than 180 duty free & general merchandise stores throughout the Pacific Rim. DFS Direct manages the company's database of international customers and all direct marketing initiatives.

DOM CORP

4305 Redwood Ave
Marina Del Rey, CA 90292
Telephone: (310) 578-1164
Pres: Richard L. James
Primary Market Served: Consumer

DAEDALUS BOOKS INC

9645 Gerwig Ln
Columbia, MD 21046-1520

Telephone: (410) 309-2700, (800) 395-2665, FAX: (410) 309-2701, Web Site: www.salebooks.com
Pres: Robin Moody
VP: Helaine Harris
Conducts Business: Worldwide
Employees: 100
Primary Market Served: Business & Consumer
Catalog available online
Direct online sales
Advertising/Marketing Budget Related to Direct Marketing: 26-50%
Direct Marketing ad budget:
Direct Mail: 100%
Founded: 1980

Literary sale books & classical, jazz & world compact discs to direct consumers & wholesale customers.

DAVE'S SODA & PET CITY

151 Springfield St
Agawam, MA 01001-1553
Telephone: (413) 789-2259, Web Site: www.daveratner.com
Pres: Dave Ratner

Pet supplies

DECK THE WALLS INC

221 First Executive Ave
Saint Peters, MO 63376-1697
Telephone: (314) 719-8200, (866) 719-8200, FAX: (314) 719-8290, Web Site: www.deckthewalls.com
Pres & CEO: John W. Jones
COO & VP: Connie Williams
Dir, Mktg: Melinda Riley
Spokeswoman: Jane Seymour
Primary Market Served: Consumer
Catalog available online

Franchisor of antique & custom framing specialty store.

DIAPERS.COM

PO Box 483
Jersey City, NJ 07303
Telephone: (800) 342-7377, Web Site: www.diapers.com
CEO & Chmn: Marc Lore
COO & Bd Dir: Vinit Bharara
EVP Opers: Scott Hilton
CIO: Eugene Hertz

Online baby care specialty site

THE DMA DREAM PRODUCTS INC

9754 Deering Ave
Chatsworth, CA 91311-4301
Telephone: (818) 773-4233, Web Site: www.dreamproducts.net
Pres: Rick Goldman
Primary Market Served: Consumer

Sells a variety of products through direct mail

EOS INTERNATIONAL INC
2292 Faraday Ave Frnt
Carlsbad, CA 92008-7237
Telephone: (760) 431-8400, (800) 876-5484, FAX: (760) 431-8448, Web Site: www.eosintl.com
CFO: Tony Saadat
VP Global Sls & Mktg: Salvatore Provenza
Res & Devel Dir: Jeff Goodwin
Conducts Business: U.S., Canada
Employees: 125
Primary Market Served: Business & Consumer
Advertising/Marketing Budget Related to Direct Marketing: 26-50%
Gross sales or billing: $25,000,000

Personal development, seminars & tape programs.

THE DMA ESPN
77 W 66th St (FL 4)
New York, NY 10023-6201
Telephone: (212) 456-4995
Primary Market Served: Consumer

Provides comprehensive sports coverage

ELDERLY INSTRUMENTS
1100 N Washington, Box 14210
Lansing, MI 48901
Telephone: (517) 372-7890, (888) 473-5810, FAX: (517) 372-5155, E-Mail: elderly@elderly.com, Web Site: www.elderly.com
Pres: Stanley R. Werbin
Mktg Dir: Steve Szilagyi
Conducts Business: U.S.
Employees: 86
Primary Market Served: Consumer
Catalog available online
Direct online sales
Founded: 1972
Gross sales or billing: $16,700,000

Sell vintage & new musical instruments, compact discs, instruction books & accessories.

THE DMA EXCELLIGENCE LEARNING CORP
2 Lower Ragsdale Dr (Suite 125)
Monterey, CA 93940-7810
Telephone: (831) 333-2000, Web Site: www.excelligencelearning.com
Dir, Direct Mktg: Kevin Kiper
Primary Market Served: Business & Consumer

Developer, manufacturer & retailer of educational products, which are sold to child care programs, preschools, elementary schools & consumers

FAIRE HARBOUR LIMITED
44 Captain Pierce Rd
Scituate, MA 02066-2644
Telephone: (781) 545-2465, FAX: (781) 545-2465
Pres: Irving R. Versoy Jr.
VP: Mary J. Versoy
Conducts Business: U.S., Canada
Employees: 6
Primary Market Served: Business & Consumer
Catalog available online
Indirect online sales
Advertising/Marketing Budget Related to Direct Marketing: 51-75%
Founded: 1960
Gross sales or billing: $200,000

Catalog sales of kerosene lamps, cooking devices & marine supplies.

FAMILY CHRISTIAN STORES
5300 Patterson Ave SE
Grand Rapids, MI 49530
Telephone: (616) 554-8700, (888) 319-0319, FAX: (616) 554-8694, E-Mail: info@fcsdirect.familychristian.com, Web Site: www.familychristian.com
Chmn: David Browne
Pres: Leslie E. Dietzman
Sr VP, HR: Hal Bailey
Mktg & Promo Dir: David Austin
Conducts Business: U.S., Canada, Korea, Taiwan
Employees: 5,000
Primary Market Served: Business & Consumer
Catalog available online
Direct online sales
Founded: 1999
Gross sales or billing: $360,300,000

Sell Christian products to the public & to the CBA market.

FEDERAL CITIZEN INFORMATION CENTER
Consumer Information Catalog
Pueblo, CO 81009
Telephone: (888) 8-PUEBLO, FAX: (719) 948-9724, E-Mail: catalog.pueblo@gsa.gov, Web Site: www.pueblo.gsa.gov
Exec VP: Mark Simon
Dir: Teresa S. Nasif
Dir, Publications & Media: Mark Levy
Consumer Education Specialist: Samantha Donaldson
Consumer Education Specialist: Shantae Goodloe
Conducts Business: U.S.
Employees: 48
Primary Market Served: Consumer
Catalog available online
Direct online sales
Advertising/Marketing Budget Related to Direct Marketing: 0-25%

Founded: 1970
Consumer information catalog listing 200+ free & low cost federal publications.

FINCK CIGAR CO
6100 West Ave, PO Box 831007
San Antonio, TX 78213
Telephone: (210) 341-8888, (800) 221-0638, FAX: (210) 341-8890, E-Mail: info@finckcigar.com, Web Site: www.finckcigar.com
Pres: Bill Finck
VP: Bill Finck Jr
Mktg Mgr: Lynn Rangel
Conducts Business: U.S.
Employees: 80
Primary Market Served: Consumer
Catalog available online
Direct online sales
Advertising/Marketing Budget Related to Direct Marketing: 76-100%
Direct Marketing ad budget:
Direct Mail: 85%
Magazines: 5%
Online: 10%
Founded: 1893

Sell cigars, pipes, pipe tobacco, cigarette tobacco & accessories direct to consumers.

FLAGHOUSE INC
601 Flaghouse Dr
Hasbrouck Heights, NJ 07604
Telephone: (201) 288-7600, (800) 793-7900, FAX: (800) 793-7922, E-Mail: sales@flaghouse.com, Web Site: www.flaghouse.com
CEO & Pres: George Carmel
COO: Douglas Carmel
VP, Sls & Mktg: Veronica Bolcik
Mgr: Keith Gold
Art Dir: John Onuschak
Conducts Business: Worldwide
Employees: 100
Primary Market Served: Business
Catalog available online
Direct online sales
Advertising/Marketing Budget Related to Direct Marketing: 76-100%
Direct Marketing ad budget: $3,000,000
Direct Mail: 99%
Magazines: 1%
Founded: 1954
Gross sales or billing: $29,000,000

Mail order & catalog firm selling furniture, athletic equipment, recreational, special needs & rehabilitation supplies to schools & institutions.

FORD FOUNDATION OFFICE OF COMMUNICATIONS
320 E 43rd St
New York, NY 10017-4816

Telephone: (212) 573-5169, E-Mail: office-of-communications@ fordfound.org, Web Site: www. fordfound.org
Dissemination & Admin Mgr: Carolee E. Iltis
Conducts Business: Worldwide
Primary Market Served: Business & Consumer
Catalog available online
Founded: 1936

Publishes and distributes free publications covering Foundation programs.

THE DMA FREESTYLE PHOTOGRAPHIC SUPPLIES
5124 Sunset Blvd
Los Angeles, CA 90027-9897
Telephone: (323) 660-3640, Web Site: www.freestylephoto.biz
Pres & COO: Gerald Karmele
Primary Market Served: Consumer
Founded: 1946

Photographic supplies

THE DMA FRESHDIRECT
23-30 Borden Ave
Long Island City, NY 11101-4515
Telephone: (718) 928-1531
Primary Market Served: Consumer

Online grocer

THE FULLER BRUSH CO
One Fuller Way
Great Bend, KS 67530
Telephone: (800) 522-0499, FAX: (620) 792-1906, E-Mail: info@fuller. com, Web Site: www.fuller.com
Pres: Norbert Schneider
Conducts Business: U.S.
Primary Market Served: Business
Catalog available online
Direct online sales
Advertising/Marketing Budget Related to Direct Marketing: 26-50%
Direct Marketing ad budget:
Direct Mail: 100%
Founded: 1991

Cleaning products, including cleaning brushes & boar bristle hair brushes, for consumers & businesses.

GENERAL GROWTH PROPERTIES
110 N Wacker
Chicago, IL 60606-1511
Telephone: (312) 960-5413, Web Site: www.generalgrowth.com
Dir CIM: Betsy Alperstein

Real estate investment trust that owns, develops & operates regional shopping malls

GO PROMOS
Div. of EGI
PO Box 272
Gloversville, NY 12078
Telephone: (800) 523-9909, FAX: (800) 523-3292, E-Mail: customerservice@gopromos.com, Web Site: www.gopromos.com
Pres: Kevin Kirby
Primary Market Served: Business & Consumer
Catalog available online
Indirect online sales

Print promotional products, logos & slogans & provide samples as needed.

GOHN BROTHERS
PO Box 1110
Middlebury, IN 46540
Telephone: (219) 825-2400, (800) 595-0031, Web Site: www.gohnbrothers. com
Pres: John S. Swartzentruber
Conducts Business: U.S.
Employees: 10
Primary Market Served: Business & Consumer

Sell Amish work clothing: hats, hosiery & underwear. Also, quilting supplies, yard goods, notions & Red Wing shoes.

HSN INC
Subs. of IAC
One HSN Dr
Saint Petersburg, FL 33729
Telephone: (727) 872-1000, (800) 284-3100, Web Site: www.hsn.com
Chmn Bd: Barry Diller
CEO: Mindy Grossman
Exec VP Mdsg: Lynne Ronon
Conducts Business: U.S.
Employees: 4,000
Primary Market Served: Consumer
Catalog available online
Direct online sales
Founded: 1977
Gross sales or billing: $3,290,000,000

Mail order shoes, clothing & hard goods sold through catalogs, package inserts, solo direct mail & space advertising offers.

THE DMA HALLELUJAH ACRES
900 S Post Rd
Shelby, NC 28152-7423
Telephone: (704) 481-1700, Web Site: www.hacres.com
Primary Market Served: Consumer

Vegan raw food diet

HAMAKOR JUDAICA INC
7777 Merrimac
Niles, IL 60714

Telephone: (847) 966-4040, (800) 426-2567, FAX: (847) 966-4033, E-Mail: service@ewishource.com, Web Site: www.jewishsource.com
Pres: Herschel Strauss
VP & List Mgr: Naomi Strauss
Conducts Business: U.S.
Employees: 25
Primary Market Served: Consumer
Catalog available online
Direct online sales
Advertising/Marketing Budget Related to Direct Marketing: 76-100%
Founded: 1975

Producers of several catalogs including the Source for Everything Jewish which contains collectibles, fine art, festival & ritual products, books, cassettes, videos, jewelry & children's items.

HANOVER DIRECT INC
1500 Harbor Blvd
Weehawken, NJ 07086-6768
Telephone: (201) 863-7300, FAX: (201) 272-3280, Web Site: www. hanoverdirect.com
Pres & CEO: Wayne Garten
Corp Legal Administrator: Sherran Turner
Conducts Business: U.S.
Employees: 2,500
Primary Market Served: Consumer
Advertising/Marketing Budget Related to Direct Marketing: 76-100%
Direct Marketing ad budget:
Direct Mail: 80%
Magazines: 10%
Telephone: 10%
Founded: 1952
Gross sales or billing: $550,000,000

Sell ladies ready-to-wear, shoes, gifts, household items, home furnishings, electronics & garden products through catalogs & space ads.

THE DMA HEALTHFEST
100 Nixon Ln
Edison, NJ 08837-3804
Telephone: (732) 225-0100

HEAVEN & EARTH
1255 Fordham Dr (Suite 120)
Virginia Beach, VA 23464
Telephone: (757) 420-3576, E-Mail: teamkr8@heavenandearth.hrcoxmail. com, Web Site: www. heavenandearth.com
Mgr: Nathan Quade
Primary Market Served: Consumer

Specialty Christian store.

HERSCHEND FAMILY ENTERTAINMENT
399 Indian Point Rd
Branson, MO 65616
Telephone: (417) 338-3810, FAX:
(417) 338-8144, Web Site: www.
silverdollarcity.com
Corp VP Mktg: Rick Baker
Mktg Mgr: Janet Oller
Conducts Business: U.S.
Employees: 2,500
Primary Market Served: Business &
Consumer
Direct online sales
Direct Marketing ad budget: $250,000
Direct Mail: 75%
TV/Radio: 15%
Telephone: 10%
Founded: 1960
Gross sales or billing: $50,000,000

Theme park/crafts marketer. Sell season passes, crafts products & classes directly to consumers & tickets through companies, associations, etc.

DIANA HILS
700 Milam
Houston, TX 77002-2806
Telephone: (713) 546-4550
Primary Market Served: Consumer

HORN PACKAGING CORP
580 Fort Pond Rd
Lancaster, MA 01523-3224
Telephone: (978) 772-0290, (800) 832-
7020, FAX: (978) 772-4611, E-Mail:
mccarthy@horncorp.com, Web Site:
www.hornpackaging.com
Chmn: Lawrence Udell
Mktg Dir: Jerry Slim
VP, Bus Devel: David Shipps
Dir, Nextgen Broadband: Robert Zack
Conducts Business: U.S.
Employees: 125
Primary Market Served: Business &
Consumer
Catalog available online
Indirect online sales
Advertising/Marketing Budget Related
to Direct Marketing: 0-25%
Founded: 1940
Gross sales or billing: $20,000,000

Fabricated foam & corrugated shipping room supplies sold to manufacturers.

INTELISPEND PREPAID SOLUTIONS
1400 S Highway Dr
Fenton, MO 63026-2281
Telephone: (636) 226-2000, Web Site:
www.aeis.com
Primary Market Served: Consumer

THE DMA J&J COMMERCE
PO Box 1517
Galesburg, IL 61402-1517
Telephone: (309) 344-2950, Web Site:
www.jjdog.com
Chmn: Mark Godsil
Primary Market Served: Business &
Consumer
Founded: 1965

Pet supplies

JC PENNEY INC
6501 Legacy Dr
Plano, TX 75024-3612
Telephone: (972) 431-1000, FAX:
(972) 431-1977, Web Site: www.
jcpenney.com
Chmn & CEO: Myron Ullman III
Pres & CMO: Kenneth Hicks
Exec VP & CFO: Robert B. Ca-
vanaugh
DVP & Dir Customer File Mktg: Rob-
ert DiRienzo
Conducts Business: Brazil & Mexico
Employees: 155,000
Primary Market Served: Consumer
Catalog available online
Direct online sales
Founded: 1902
Gross sales or billing: $19,000,000,000

Retail department store.

JR TOBACCO/800-JR CIGAR INC
800-JR Cigar Inc
2589 Eric Ln
Burlington, NC 27215
Telephone: (800) 572-4427, FAX:
(800) 457-3299, Web Site: www.
jrcigars.com
Pres & CEO: Lew Rothman
CFO: Michael E. Colleton
VP: LaVonda Rothman
VP: Jane Vargas
Employees: 1,100
Primary Market Served: Business &
Consumer
Advertising/Marketing Budget Related
to Direct Marketing: 76-100%
Direct Marketing ad budget: $250,000
Direct Mail: 100%
Founded: 1970
Gross sales or billing: $285,000,000

Sell cigars & related products mail order, retail & wholesale.

JEFFERS & CO
Subs. of Jeffers Inc
310 W Saunders Rd
Dothan, AL 36302-8622
Telephone: (334) 793-6257, (800) 533-
3377, FAX: (334) 793-5179, Web
Site: www.1800jeffers.com
Pres & Owner: Dorothy Jeffers

Mktg Svcs Mgr: Ruth Jeffers
Primary Market Served: Business &
Consumer
Founded: 1975

Livestock, veterinary & pet care products.

JEFFREY LANT ASSOCIATES INC
50 Follen St (Suite 507)
Cambridge, MA 02138
Telephone: (617) 547-6372, FAX:
(617) 547-0061, E-Mail: drjlant@
worldprofit.com, Web Site: www.
worldprofit.com
Pres: Jeffrey Lant
Conducts Business: Worldwide
Employees: 5
Primary Market Served: Business &
Consumer
Catalog available online
Direct online sales
Founded: 1979

Extensive product line focused on assisting businesses prosper on and offline. For details go to www. worldprofit.com/autoresponse, www. worldprofit.com, www.trafficcenter.com & www.worldbannerexchange.com. For dealer details go to www. trafficcenter.com.

JOHNSON SMITH CO
4514 19th St Ct E
Bradenton, FL 34203-3709
Telephone: (941) 747-5566, Web Site:
www.johnsonsmith.com
Pres: Ralph Hoenle
Founded: 1914

Catalog company

KV VET SUPPLY CO, INC
3190 N Rd (#245)
David City, NE 68632-5142
Telephone: (402) 367-6047, Web Site:
www.kvvet.com
Pres: Raymond Metzner
Gen Mgr: Tracie Lloyd
Mktg: Deb Lensch
Conducts Business: U.S.
Employees: 100
Primary Market Served: Business &
Consumer
Catalog available online
Direct online sales
Advertising/Marketing Budget Related
to Direct Marketing: 76-100%
Founded: 1979

Pet & equine animal health supplies & equipment to pet owners and retailers.

LAB SAFETY SUPPLY INC
Subs. of W W Grainger Inc
401 S Wright Rd, Box 1368

Janesville, WI 53547-1368
Telephone: (608) 754-2345, (800) 356-
    2855, FAX: (800) 543-9910, Web
    Site: www.labsafety.com
Pres: Larry Loizzo
VP, Mktg: Rob Malewicki
VP, Fin: Tom Drury
Copywriter: Cindy Joyce
VP, Opers: Bill Stroner
Conducts Business: Worldwide
Employees: 800
Primary Market Served: Business
Catalog available online
Direct online sales
Advertising/Marketing Budget Related
    to Direct Marketing: 76-100%
Direct Marketing ad budget:
Direct Mail: 90%
Magazines: 10%
Founded: 1978

Catalog distributor of safety & industrial products.

LARK IN THE MORNING

PO Box 1176
Mendocino, CA 95460
Telephone: (707) 964-5569, FAX:
    (707) 964-1979, E-Mail: info@
    larkinam.com, Web Site: www.
    larkinthemorning.com
Gen Mgr: William Taylor
Conducts Business: Worldwide
Employees: 35
Primary Market Served: Business &
    Consumer
Catalog available online
Indirect online sales
Advertising/Marketing Budget Related
    to Direct Marketing: 76-100%
Founded: 1974
Gross sales or billing: $3,100,000

Sell world musical instruments, recordings, instructional videos & books to
individuals, music stores & book
stores. From over 60 cultures.

ᴛʜᴇ ᴅᴍᴀ LEVENGER

420 S Congress Ave Ste 101
Delray Beach, FL 33445-4696
Telephone: (561) 276-2436, (800) 677-
    8034, FAX: (561) 266-2181, E-Mail:
    orders@levenger.com, Web Site:
    www.levenger.com
Pres & CEO: Steve Leveen
COO & CFO: Larry Jenkins
VP, HR: Vincent G. Dunn
Exec VP & Co-Owner: Lori Leveen
Employees: 350
Primary Market Served: Business &
    Consumer
Catalog available online
Direct online sales
Advertising/Marketing Budget Related
    to Direct Marketing: 76-100%
Founded: 1987

Gross sales or billing: $59,200,000
Mail order catalog & retail store.

LIBERTY TREE NETWORK

The Independent Institute
100 Swan Way
Oakland, CA 94621-1428
Telephone: (510) 568-6047, (800) 927-
    8733, FAX: (510) 568-6040, E-Mail:
    info@liberty-tree.com, Web Site:
    www.liberty-tree.org
Pres: David J. Theroux
Customer Svc Dir: Nichelle Beardsley
Conducts Business: U.S.
Employees: 12
Primary Market Served: Business &
    Consumer
Catalog available online
Direct online sales
Advertising/Marketing Budget Related
    to Direct Marketing: 76-100%
Direct Marketing ad budget:
Direct Mail: 90%
Magazines: 10%
Founded: 1986

Mail order catalog featuring books,
tapes & collectibles on the history &
pursuit of liberty.

LIGONIER MINISTRIES

400 Technology Park
Lake Mary, FL 32746
Telephone: (407) 333-4244, (800) 435-
    4343, FAX: (407) 333-4377, Web
    Site: www.ligonier.org
Founder & Owner: Dr. R. C. Sproul
Dir: Vesta Sproul
Mktg Dir: Alan Yardis
Dir Devel: John Peterson
Creative Dir: Chris Larson
Primary Market Served: Business &
    Consumer
Catalog available online
Direct online sales
Founded: 1971
Gross sales or billing: $12,500,000

Christian education materials.

LOVE TO LEARN INC

741 N State Rd 198
Salem, UT 84653
Telephone: (801) 423-2009, (888) 771-
    1034, FAX: (801) 423-9188, E-Mail:
    customerservice@lovetolearn.net,
    Web Site: www.lovetolearn.net
Pres: Rick Hopkins
Primary Market Served: Consumer
Catalog available online
Direct online sales

Educational products for parents with
children under five years old.

ᴛʜᴇ ᴅᴍᴀ LOVES TRAVEL STOPS & COUNTRY STORES

10601 N Pennsylvania
Oklahoma City, OK 73120-4198
Telephone: (405) 242-2490, Web Site:
    www.loves.com
Primary Market Served: Consumer

Chain of travel stops & country stores
located across the USA

ᴛʜᴇ ᴅᴍᴀ MMS EDUCATION

105 Terry Dr (Suite 120)
Newtown, PA 18940-1872
Telephone: (215) 579-8590
Primary Market Served: Consumer

Education data, marketing & consulting

MACY'S

Div. of Federated Co
15541 Gale Ave
City Of Industry, CA 91745-1512
Telephone: (323) 227-2000, FAX:
    (323) 227-2774, Web Site: www.
    federated-fds.com
VP, Direct Mktg: Gary Ostrager
Primary Market Served: Business &
    Consumer

Retail department stores-complete
clothing & home store products
catalogs.

ᴛʜᴇ ᴅᴍᴀ MAGELLAN'S CATALOG

110 W Sola St
Santa Barbara, CA 93101-3007
Telephone: (800) 962-4943, FAX:
    (800) 962-4940, E-Mail: sales@
    magellans.com, Web Site: www.
    magellans.com
Pres & CEO: Mark Gallo
Mktg Dir: Lynn Staneff
Conducts Business: U.S., Canada, Ja-
    pan, Europe
Employees: 100
Primary Market Served: Business &
    Consumer
Catalog available online
Direct online sales
Advertising/Marketing Budget Related
    to Direct Marketing: 76-100%
Direct Marketing ad budget:
Direct Mail: 75%
Online: 25%
Founded: 1989
Gross sales or billing: $35,000,000

Travel gear including security wallets,
electrical converters, water purifiers,
packing aids, luggage, etc.

MAGNA-TEL INC

775 S Kings Hwy St
Cape Girardeau, MO 63703

Telephone: (573) 334-3096, FAX: (573) 335-1715, Web Site: www.magna.tel.com
Pres: Maryann Farmer
Mktg Dir: Kathy Peters
Conducts Business: U.S.
Primary Market Served: Business
Catalog available online
Indirect online sales
Advertising/Marketing Budget Related to Direct Marketing: 26-50%

Advertising specialty firm specializing in custom magnetic products.

MARKETPLACE OF THE MASTER INC
4790 Colt Rd
Rockford, IL 61109-2635
Telephone: (815) 874-1733, (800) 621-1255, FAX: (815) 874-4351, E-Mail: marketplace@marketplaceofthemaster.com, Web Site: www.marketplaceofthemaster.com
Pres: Richard C. Krause
Gen Mgr: Dorothy L. Krause
Conducts Business: U.S.
Primary Market Served: Business & Consumer
Catalog available online
Direct online sales

Sell church & school supplies, gifts, jewelry, wall plaques & name badges.

MARSHALL DOMESTICS LLC
12 Factory St, PO Box 107
West Warwick, RI 02893
Telephone: (401) 821-8760, (800) 556-7440, FAX: (401) 821-2230, E-Mail: marshalldomestics@verizon.net, Web Site: www.marshalldomestics.com
Pres: David Greenstein
Conducts Business: U.S.
Employees: 20
Primary Market Served: Business
Advertising/Marketing Budget Related to Direct Marketing: 51-75%
Founded: 1970

Sheets, towels, bedding & table linens to motels, hotels, nursing homes & banquet facilities.

MARSHALL FIELDS DEPT STORES
Subs. of Target Corp
7235 France Ave S
Minneapolis, MN 55435-4337
Telephone: (612) 375-3004, Web Site: www.fields.com
Print Buying Mgr: Barbara DiBlasi
Project Mngmt Mgr: Linda Stokes
Sr Analyst Mktg Effectiveness: Jill Hungsberg
Direct Mail Specialist: Kevin Bonthius

Conducts Business: U.S.
Primary Market Served: Consumer
Direct online sales
Advertising/Marketing Budget Related to Direct Marketing: 26-50%
Gross sales or billing: $3,000,000,000

Department store retailer with 64 stores.

MAVERICK VENTURES PRODUCT LINE
Maverick Ventures Inc
15698 Ferncreek Dr
Chesterfield, MO 63017-0702
Telephone: (636) 537-4656, (800) 467-4656, FAX: (636) 537-4657, E-Mail: hang10cd@aol.com, Web Site: www.hang10cd.com
Pres: Ronald Kuczer
Conducts Business: U.S., Australia, Canada
Employees: 3
Primary Market Served: Business
Catalog available online
Direct online sales
Advertising/Marketing Budget Related to Direct Marketing: 0-25%
Founded: 1984
Gross sales or billing: $1,000,000

Innovative gadgets.

MEDIBADGE INC
PO Box 12307
Omaha, NE 68112-0307
Telephone: (402) 571-1800, (800) 228-0040, FAX: (800) 546-1072, E-Mail: stan@medibadge.com, Web Site: www.medibadge.com
CEO: Stanley Teutsch
Pres: Teri A. Teutsch
Conducts Business: Ireland, Japan, Australia
Employees: 46
Primary Market Served: Business & Consumer
Catalog available online
Direct online sales
Advertising/Marketing Budget Related to Direct Marketing: 51-75%
Direct Marketing ad budget:
Direct Mail: 100%
Founded: 1980
Gross sales or billing: $8,500,000

Motivational stickers, character licensed stickers and awards catalog.

THE MILLER GROUP
1610 Design Way
Dupo, IL 62239-1820
Telephone: (636) 343-5700, (800) 325-3350, FAX: (618) 286-6202, E-Mail: info@miller-group.com, Web Site: www.multiplexdisplays.com
Pres: Randy Castle

Mktg Dir: Kathy Webster
VP Sls & Mktg: Tom Grzywa
Conducts Business: Worldwide
Employees: 100
Primary Market Served: Business
Catalog available online
Direct online sales
Founded: 1903

Display systems for schools, libraries, hotels, real estate, printers, gift & retail stores, etc. Assortment of swinging panels, freestanding & portable panels, plus book displays & art displays. Catalogs available for floorcovering products, fabric, wallpaper, trim & custom production.

MOVADA MEDIA INC
3-16 Mazenod Rd
Winnipeg, MB, Canada R2J 4H2
Telephone: (204) 284-9000, Web Site: www.movadamedia.com
VP: Cameron Saltel

THE MUSEUM OF MODERN ART
11 W 53rd St
New York, NY 10019-5497
Telephone: (212) 708-9400, FAX: (212) 333-1123, E-Mail: info@moma.org, Web Site: www.moma.org
Chmn Bd: Jerry I. Speyer
Pres: Marie Josee Kravis
Pres, Emerita: Agnes Gund
Pres, Emeritus: Donald B. Marron
Dir: Glen D. Lowry
Conducts Business: U.S.
Primary Market Served: Business & Consumer
Catalog available online

Mail order catalog of books & objects of industrial design.

MUSICIAN'S FRIEND
PO Box 5111
Westlake Village, CA 91359-5111
Telephone: (541) 772-5173, Web Site: www.musiciansfriend.com
CEO: Craig Johnson
Founded: 1983

Direct marketer of music gear

THE DMA NASCO
Div. of Nasco International Inc
901 Janesville Ave
Fort Atkinson, WI 53538-2497
Telephone: (920) 563-2446, FAX: (920) 563-8296, E-Mail: info@nasco.com, Web Site: www.enasco.com
Pres: W. Phil Niemeyer
Dir Mktg & Commun: Bob Meier
Adv Dir: Kent Parks

Conducts Business: Worldwide
Employees: 400
Primary Market Served: Business &
　Consumer
Catalog available online
Gross sales or billing: $200,000,000

Mail order supplier of products for
education, agriculture & industry.

THE DMA NETC
50 Franklin St
Boston, MA 02110-1308
Telephone: (617) 725-0044

NATURAL ESSENTIALS INC
1800 Miller Pkwy
Streetsboro, OH 44241-5067
Telephone: (330) 562-8022, (888) 968-
　7220, FAX: (330) 562-8022, E-Mail:
　questions@naturalessentials.com,
　Web Site: www.naturalessentials.com
CEO: Gary Pellegrino
Conducts Business: Worldwide
Employees: 50
Primary Market Served: Business &
　Consumer
Catalog available online
Indirect online sales
Advertising/Marketing Budget Related
　to Direct Marketing: 51-75%
Direct Marketing ad budget:
Direct Mail: 65%
Magazines: 5%
Newspapers: 10%
TV/Radio: 10%
Telephone: 10%
Founded: 1992

Consumer products to retail cosmetic
products via catalog & in home demos.

NEW WAVE MEDIA INC
dba AdoTube
915 Broadway (Suite 1301)
New York, NY 10010
Telephone: (646) 723-4681, FAX:
　(212) 982-1060, Web Site: www.
　adotube.com
Primary Market Served: Consumer

NORSCOT GROUP
1000 W Donges Bay Rd
Mequon, WI 53092
Telephone: (262) 241-3313, (800) 653-
　3313, FAX: (262) 241-4904, Web
　Site: www.norscot.com
Pres & CEO: Scott Stern
Chmn Bd: Norm Stern
Conducts Business: Worldwide
Employees: 80
Primary Market Served: Business &
　Consumer
Founded: 1970
Gross sales or billing: $35,000,000

Develops turn-key marketing, promotional product and brand identity programs for Fortune 500 companies.

OKEEFE
408 Woodstone W Dr.
Marietta, GA 30068-4083
Telephone: (973) 632-7630
VP: Neil Christopher

THE DMA ORIENTAL TRADING CO INC
5455 S 90th St
Omaha, NE 68127-3501
Telephone: (402) 596-1200, (800) 875-
　8480, FAX: (402) 331-3873, Web
　Site: www.oriental.com
Pres & CEO: Stephen R. Frary
CFO: Steven Mendlik
Exec VP, Opers: Rodger Jensen
Mktg Dir: Robert Goldsmith
Corp HR Mgr: Stacy Young
VP Mktg: Sr. Dave Goldsmith
Employees: 4,000
Primary Market Served: Business &
　Consumer
Catalog available online
Direct online sales
Advertising/Marketing Budget Related
　to Direct Marketing: 76-100%
Direct Marketing ad budget:
Direct Mail: 97%
Magazines: 2.5%
Telephone: .5%
Founded: 1932
Gross sales or billing: $166,400,000

Mail order catalog.

THE DMA PHE INC
PO Box 8200
Hillsborough, NC 27278-8200
Telephone: (919) 644-8100, (800) 293-
　4654, FAX: (919) 644-8150, E-Mail:
　custserv@adameve.com
VP: David Groves
Conducts Business: U.S.
Employees: 325
Primary Market Served: Consumer
Catalog available online
Advertising/Marketing Budget Related
　to Direct Marketing: 76-100%
Founded: 1970
Gross sales or billing: $88,000,000

Books, condoms, lingerie, adult videos
& marital aids.

**PACIFIC SPORTSWEAR CO
INC**
dba Pacific Sportswear & Emblem Co
6160 Fairmount Ave (Suite F)
San Diego, CA 92120-3427
Telephone: (619) 281-6688, (800)
　USA-8778, FAX: (619) 281-6687,
　E-Mail: info@pacsport.com, Web
　Site: www.pacsport.com

Pres: Rich C. Soergel
Controller: Cathy Caine
Conducts Business: U.S., Japan, Eu-
　rope
Employees: 12
Primary Market Served: Business
Catalog available online
Advertising/Marketing Budget Related
　to Direct Marketing: 0-25%
Founded: 1984
Gross sales or billing: $3,000,000

Licensee & founder of Class of
2000(TM) brand caps, jackets, count-
down clocks, pins & keychains. Custom, private label headwear, patches &
rubber products.

PAPYRUS
500 Chadbourne Rd
Fairfield, CA 94534-9656
Telephone: (707) 428-0200, Web Site:
　www.papyrusonline.com
VP Info Svcs: Bob Jellison
Primary Market Served: Business &
　Consumer

Stationery, greeting cards, gifts, wrap
& ribbons

PENGUIN PARTY PRODUCTS
PO Box 1434
Campbell, CA 95009-1434
Telephone: (408) 377-1303, FAX:
　(408) 377-6319, Web Site: www.
　penguinparty.com
Owner: Vaughn Meyers
Primary Market Served: Business
Advertising/Marketing Budget Related
　to Direct Marketing: 76-100%
Founded: 1978

Party goods & decorations for hotels,
restaurants, nightclubs, stores &
offices.

PETCO ANIMAL SUPPLIES
9125 Rehco Rd
San Diego, CA 92121-2270
Telephone: (858) 453-7845, (877) 738-
　6742, FAX: (858) 453-6585, Web
　Site: www.petco.com
Chmn Bd: Brian K. Devine
CEO & Dir: James M. Myers
Pres & COO: Bruce C. Hall
VP Mktg & Adv: Neil Guliano
Dir Database Relationship: Heather
　McGhee
Conducts Business: U.S.
Employees: 17,900
Primary Market Served: Consumer
Gross sales or billing: $1,161,000,000

Retail pet supplies stores.

J PETERMAN CO
Subs. of Paul Harris Stores Inc
400 Old Vine St Ste 200

Lexington, KY 40507-1910
Telephone: (888) 647-2555, FAX:
 (859) 254-0869, Web Site: www.
 jpeterman.com
Pres: Glenn S. Lyon
VP, Fin, Controller & Corp Sec: Keith
 L. Himmel Jr.
VP, Mdsg Accessories: Terri L. Erick-
 son
Primary Market Served: Business &
 Consumer

Catalog sales.

PETS UNITED LLC

One Maplewood Dr
Hazleton, PA 18202-9790
Telephone: (570) 384-5555, (800) 738-
 7877, FAX: (570) 384-2500, E-Mail:
 customerservice@petsupplies.com,
 Web Site: www.allpets.com
VP, Mdsg: Judith Patterson
Conducts Business: Worldwide
Employees: 96
Primary Market Served: Business &
 Consumer
Indirect online sales
Advertising/Marketing Budget Related
 to Direct Marketing: 76-100%
Founded: 1969

International mail order company that
publishes four titles-The Dog Outfitters
(business to business pet supply
catalog). Discount Master Animal Care
(consumer pet product catalog). Maplewood Crafts (institutional & consumer
craft catalog). Home Pet Shop (consumer pet product catalog).

THE DMA PETSMART INC

Div. of Pet's Mart Direct
19601 N 27th Ave
Phoenix, AZ 85027-4010
Telephone: (623) 587-2009, (800) 738-
 1385, FAX: (623) 580-6183, Web
 Site: www.petsmart.com
Chmn & CEO: Philip L. Francis
Pres & COO: Robert F. Moran
Sr VP & CFO: Lawrence Molloy
Sr VP & CIO: Donald E. Beaver
Sr VP & CMO: Mary L. Miller
VP, Cust Rel Mktg: Erica Thompson
Employees: 38,400
Primary Market Served: Consumer
Catalog available online
Direct online sales
Founded: 1986
Gross sales or billing: $4,233,900,000

Complete line of pet supplies & services (engraving, tags, etc).

PHOTOSTAMPS.COM

12959 Coral Tree Pl
Los Angeles, CA 90066-7020
Telephone: (310) 482-5800, Web Site:
 www.photostamps.com

Primary Market Served: Business
Personalized stamps

PRAISES, PRIZES & PRESENTS

3822 Richmond St NW
Grand Rapids, MI 49534-2300
Telephone: (361) 851-9663, FAX:
 (361) 851-9663, Web Site: www.
 praisesprizespresents.com
Owner: Judy Bottum
Owner: Sylvia Chambers
Employees: 2
Primary Market Served: Business &
 Consumer
Founded: 1998
Gross sales or billing: $130,000

School & teaching supplies, rewards,
incentives & religious novelties.

PROFESSIONAL CREATIONS

1220 Church St
New Castle, IN 47362
Telephone: (765) 529-1590, (800) 428-
 8855, E-Mail: sales@professional-
 creations.com, Web Site: www.
 professional-creations.com
Pres & CEO: Pam Brake
Conducts Business: U.S.
Primary Market Served: Business
Catalog available online

Market a wide variety of promotional
products to professionals - orthodon-
tists, dentists, chiropractors, medical
doctors, optometrists, veterinarians,
teachers & podiatrists. The focus of the
product line is practice promotion.
Also carry a line of office apparel &
sportswear geared to each individual
profession.

PROGRESSIVE ENERGY CORP

650 Corte Raquel
San Marcos, CA 92069-7320
Telephone: (760) 727-2906, (800) 525-
 8624, FAX: (760) 727-0947, E-Mail:
 patrickkilleen@cox.net
Pres: Patrick Killeen
Catalog Prod Mgr: Judith Trevaskis
Conducts Business: Worldwide
Employees: 3
Primary Market Served: Business &
 Consumer
Advertising/Marketing Budget Related
 to Direct Marketing: 51-75%
Direct Marketing ad budget:
Direct Mail: 40%
Magazines: 60%
Founded: 1980

Market automotive aftermarket products & home security products through
catalogs, space ads & export.

PROSING KARAOKE

Subs. of Jesco
PO Box 7
Nederland, CO 80466-0007
Telephone: (800) 776-7464, FAX:
 (888) 388-9741, E-Mail: jack@
 prosing.com, Web Site: www.
 prosing.com
Pres: Jack Strauser
Primary Market Served: Business

Distributor of karaoke catalogs.

PUTNAM ROLLING LADDER CO INC

32 Howard St
New York, NY 10013-3112
Telephone: (212) 226-5147, FAX:
 (212) 941-1836, E-Mail:
 putnam1905@aol.com, Web Site:
 www.putnamrollingladder.com
Owner Pres: Gregg Peters Monsees
Conducts Business: Worldwide
Employees: 16
Primary Market Served: Business &
 Consumer
Catalog available online
Direct online sales
Advertising/Marketing Budget Related
 to Direct Marketing: 26-50%
Direct Marketing ad budget:
Magazines: 75%
Online: 25%
Founded: 1905
Gross sales or billing: $3,500,000

Sell custom-made solid hardwood rolling ladders for homes, home libraries,
businesses, lofts & stores; step stools
& library carts; step & extension ladders in wood, aluminum & fiberglass;
steel warehouse ladders, oak telephone
ladders.

REAL GOODS TRADING CORP

Subs. of Gaiam Inc
27 Simms St
San Rafael, CA 94901
Telephone: (707) 542-2600, (888) 567-
 6527, Web Site: www.realgoods.com
Pres & CEO: John Schaeffer
CFO & Treas: Vilia Valentine
VP: John Jackson
Employees: 102
Primary Market Served: Consumer
Catalog available online
Direct online sales
Advertising/Marketing Budget Related
 to Direct Marketing: 0-25%
Founded: 1978

Renewable energy & conservation
products.

RELIAPON POLICE PRODUCTS

4620 Calimesa St # 1D
Las Vegas, NV 89115-2364

Telephone: (805) 289-0145, (888) 263-4482, FAX: (805) 735-4276, E-Mail: info@reliapon.com, Web Site: www.reliapon.com
Pres: Vincent Zucchero
Conducts Business: Worldwide
Employees: 4
Primary Market Served: Business & Consumer
Catalog available online
Indirect online sales
Advertising/Marketing Budget Related to Direct Marketing: 26-50%
Founded: 1985

Market pepper sprays, videos & books & other non lethal law enforcement products.

RENAISSANCE GREETING CARDS INC
Subs. of FTD Inc
PO Box 845
Springvale, ME 04083
Telephone: (207) 324-4153, (800) 688-9998, FAX: (207) 324-9564, E-Mail: rencards@rencards.com
Pres: Randy Kleinrock
VP: Bill Grabin
Mktg Commun Dir: Ken Caitlin
Mktg Dir: Margaret Kleinrock
Natl Sls Mgr: Scott Lovejoy
Conducts Business: Worldwide
Employees: 65
Primary Market Served: Business
Indirect online sales
Advertising/Marketing Budget Related to Direct Marketing: 0-25%
Direct Marketing ad budget:
Direct Mail: $100,000
Magazines: $50,000
Telephone: $100,000
Founded: 1977

Greeting cards for all occasions to small businesses for resale to consumers. Customers are primarily card & gift shops, grocery stores, drug stores, hospital gift shops & florists.

RENAISSANCE LEARNING
2911 Peach St, PO Box 8036
Wisconsin Rapids, WI 54495-8036
Telephone: (715) 424-3636, (800) 338-4204, FAX: (715) 424-4242, E-Mail: answers@renlearn.com, Web Site: www.renlearn.com
CEO: Glenn James
Pres & COO: Steven A. Schmidt
VP Mktg: Jeff Walker
Conducts Business: Worldwide
Employees: 893
Primary Market Served: Business & Consumer
Catalog available online
Direct online sales
Advertising/Marketing Budget Related

to Direct Marketing: 51-75%
Founded: 1986
Gross sales or billing: $130,094,000

Publish & market Accelerated Reader, STAR Reading, STAR Math & NEO laptops. School improvement & student assessment programs for K-12 schools.

THE RIGHT START INC
3000 E Third Ave (#15)
Denver, CO 80206
Telephone: (303) 320-8312, Web Site: www.rightstart.com
VP Opers & HR: Gigi Healy
Dir Mdsg: Mary Ellen Currie
Conducts Business: U.S.
Primary Market Served: Consumer
Advertising/Marketing Budget Related to Direct Marketing: 76-100%
Direct Marketing ad budget:
Direct Mail: 100%
Founded: 1985

Sell quality juvenile & preschool products to upscale families through catalogs & retail stores.

ROBERT MARKETING INC
17 The Court of Island Point
Northbrook, IL 60062-3210
Telephone: (847) 564-3550, FAX: (847) 564-3551
Pres: Lewis Robert
VP: Jeff Robert
Conducts Business: U.S., Mexico, S. America, Caribbean
Employees: 5
Primary Market Served: Business
Catalog available online
Direct online sales
Advertising/Marketing Budget Related to Direct Marketing: 0-25%
Direct Marketing ad budget:
Direct Mail: 100%
Founded: 1987
Gross sales or billing: $5,000,000

Find new products for introduction to direct mail catalogs & export items.

THE KEN ROBERTS CO
435 Village Dr
Daphne, AL 36526-4003
Telephone: (541) 955-2867, FAX: (541) 955-2730, Web Site: www.kenroberts.com
Asst Mktg Dir: Melody Joakins
Founder & CEO: Kenneth Roberts
Primary Market Served: Business
Gross sales or billing: $2,500,000

Sell education course catalogs.

RONELL CLOCK CO
Div. of Roland V Tapp Imports
5001 Jerome Prairie Rd

Grants Pass, OR 97527
Telephone: (541) 471-0194, (800) 334-0135, FAX: (541) 471-0099, Web Site: www.ronellclock.com
Owner: Roland V. Tapp
Bus Mgr: Lucia M. Foxx
Office Mgr: Lynell L. Tapp
Conducts Business: U.S., Australia, U.K.
Employees: 3
Primary Market Served: Business & Consumer
Catalog available online
Direct online sales
Advertising/Marketing Budget Related to Direct Marketing: 76-100%
Direct Marketing ad budget: $250,000
Direct Mail: 50%
Magazines: 20%
Newspapers: 5%
Telephone: 25%
Founded: 1972
Gross sales or billing: $1,000,000

Clock-related supplies, parts & tools to the clock, watch & jewelry industry. Also, cleaning solutions & ultrasonic tanks.

SAVEOLOGY.COM
1 Cragwood Rd Ste 3
South Plainfield, NJ 07080-2448
Telephone: (866) 755-9008, Web Site: www.elephantgroup.com
Primary Market Served: Consumer

Comparison shopping for service providers

JACQUES C SCHIFF JR INC
195 Main St
Ridgefield Park, NJ 07660-1620
Telephone: (201) 641-5566, FAX: (201) 641-5705
Pres: Jacques C. Schiff Jr
Conducts Business: Worldwide
Employees: 7
Primary Market Served: Business & Consumer
Advertising/Marketing Budget Related to Direct Marketing: 76-100%
Direct Marketing ad budget:
Direct Mail: 50%
Magazines: 20%
Newspapers: 20%
Telephone: 10%
Founded: 1947
Gross sales or billing: $600,000

Philatelic auctioneers selling U.S. & worldwide postage stamps & postal history to collectors, dealers & investors throughout the world.

THE SCHOLAR'S BOOKSHELF
21 Palmer Sq W Apt A
Princeton, NJ 08542-3726

Telephone: (609) 395-6933, FAX: (609) 395-0755, E-Mail: books@scholarsbookshelf.com, Web Site: www.scholarsbookshelf.com
Pres: Abbot Friedland
Conducts Business: Worldwide
Employees: 25
Primary Market Served: Consumer
Catalog available online
Direct online sales
Advertising/Marketing Budget Related to Direct Marketing: 76-100%
Direct Marketing ad budget: $150,000,000
Direct Mail: 80%
Online: 20%
Founded: 1974
Gross sales or billing: $2,700,000

Sell books & videos on military history, history, literature, fine arts, philosophy, religion, music & baseball through 20 catalogs.

SCHWAN'S HOME SERVICE INC
115 W College Dr
Marshall, MN 56258-1747
Telephone: (507) 532-3274

SEARS CANADA INC
222 Jarvis St
Toronto, ON, Canada M5B 2B8
Telephone: (416) 362-1711, (888) 473-2772, FAX: (613) 391-3047, E-Mail: home@sears.ca, Web Site: www.sears.ca
Chmn Bd: William Crowley
Pres & CEO: Dene L. Rogers
Exec VP, Sls & Svc: Brent Hollister
Sr VP & CFO: John Butcher
Sr VP & CFO: David B. Merkley
Conducts Business: Canada
Employees: 41,000
Primary Market Served: Consumer
Catalog available online
Direct online sales
Founded: 1953
Gross sales or billing: $6,000,000,000

Mass merchandiser selling to consumers through retail stores & catalogs.

SETA CORP OF BOCA INC
6400 E Rogers Cir
Boca Raton, FL 33499-0002
Telephone: (561) 994-2660, FAX: (561) 997-2881, Web Site: www.setacorporatin.com
Pres: Joe D. Seta
VP: Angie Seta
Conducts Business: U.S.
Primary Market Served: Consumer
Catalog available online
Indirect online sales
Advertising/Marketing Budget Related to Direct Marketing: 76-100%

Gross sales or billing: $14,800,000

Mail order marketer of costume jewelry, cosmetics, health care products & general merchandise.

SHEEP SHOP
222 N High St (Rte 302)
Bridgton, ME 04009-9400
Telephone: (207) 647-3548, FAX: (207) 647-3172
Pres: Richard A. Darry
Owner: Gloria Darry
Conducts Business: U.S.
Employees: 2
Primary Market Served: Consumer
Advertising/Marketing Budget Related to Direct Marketing: 0-25%
Direct Marketing ad budget: $3,000
Direct Mail: 20%
Magazines: 5%
Newspapers: 75%
Founded: 1982
Gross sales or billing: $100,000

Wool & sheepskin products - gift items, yarns, handknits, sheepskin rugs, slippers, gloves, mitts & vests. Anything wool &/or sheep related.

SHORTAGE CONTROL INC & SC VIDEO
22643 Ascoa Ct
Strongsville, OH 44149-4700
Telephone: (440) 238-5432, (800) 332-2288, FAX: (440) 238-8687, E-Mail: sales@shortagecontrol.com, Web Site: www.shortagecontrol.com
Pres: Joseph Young
Dir Mktg Adv: Mark Young
Employees: 16
Primary Market Served: Business
Catalog available online
Direct online sales
Gross sales or billing: $1,800,000

Sell closed circuit television equipment & accessories through dealer division to resellers in NA & WW. CCTV systems, consulting services to major retailers, manufacturers & entertainment users in the US.

SIEGEL DISPLAY PRODUCTS
Affiliate of Ebsco Industries, Inc.
300 Sixth Ave N (Suite 200)
Minneapolis, MN 55401-1212
Telephone: (612) 340-1493, (800) 626-0322, FAX: (800) 230-5598, E-Mail: mwendel@siegeldisplay.com, Web Site: www.siegeldisplay.com
Gen Mgr: Bernie Bauhof
Mktg Mgr: Mary Wendel
Conducts Business: U.S., Canada
Employees: 20
Primary Market Served: Business
Catalog available online

Direct online sales
Advertising/Marketing Budget Related to Direct Marketing: 76-100%
Direct Marketing ad budget: $1,500,000
Direct Mail: 80%
Online: 20%
Founded: 1969

In-stock selection of P.O.P. materials, specializing in literature displays.

THE DMA SIPCAMADVAN
2520 Meridian Pkwy (Suite 525)
Durham, NC 27713-4210
Telephone: (919) 226-1287
Primary Market Served: Consumer

SKYLINE DISPLAYS
3355 Discovery Rd
Saint Paul, MN 55121-2098
Telephone: (651) 234-6634, Web Site: www.skyline.com
Dir, Prod Mktg: Julie Heck
Primary Market Served: Business & Consumer

Trade show exhibits & portable displays

SOLAR CINE PRODUCTS INC
4247 S Kedzie Ave
Chicago, IL 60632
Telephone: (773) 254-8310, (800) 621-8796, FAX: (773) 254-4124
Conducts Business: U.S.
Primary Market Served: Business & Consumer
Advertising/Marketing Budget Related to Direct Marketing: 51-75%
Founded: 1940

SOUTHERN EMBLEM CO
PO Box 8
Toast, NC 27049
Telephone: (336) 789-3348, (800) 927-0526, FAX: (336) 789-6547, Web Site: www.southernemblemco.com
Treas: Jim Buck
VP, Sls: Nancy Buck
Conducts Business: Worldwide
Employees: 4
Primary Market Served: Business & Consumer
Catalog available online
Indirect online sales
Advertising/Marketing Budget Related to Direct Marketing: 76-100%
Direct Marketing ad budget:
Direct Mail: 50%
Magazines: 45%
Newspapers: 5%
Founded: 1970

Advertising specialties, custom embroidered emblems, decals, bumper stickers & emblematic jewelry. Complete screen printing, caps, shirts, jackets & license plates. Direct embroidery.

SPORTY'S PREFERRED LIVING

Div. of Sportsman's Market Inc
2001 Sportys Dr, Clermont County Airport
Batavia, OH 45103-9719
Telephone: (513) 735-9000, (800) 776-7897, FAX: (800) 543-8633, Web Site: www.sportys.com
Chmn: Hal Shevers Jr.
VP, Mktg: Howard W. Law
Primary Market Served: Consumer
Catalog available online
Direct online sales
Advertising/Marketing Budget Related to Direct Marketing: 76-100%
Founded: 1962

Consumer catalog.

STAGESTEP INC

4701 Bath St (# 46)
Philadelphia, PA 19137
Telephone: (267) 672-2900, (800) 523-0961, FAX: (267) 672-2914, E-Mail: stagestep@stagestep.com, Web Site: www.stagestep.com
Pres: Randy Swartz
VP, Opers: David Bock
Acctg: Christina Crozzoli
Conducts Business: Worldwide
Employees: 20
Primary Market Served: Business & Consumer
Catalog available online
Direct online sales
Advertising/Marketing Budget Related to Direct Marketing: 51-75%
Direct Marketing ad budget: $400,000
Direct Mail: 45%
Magazines: 45%
Online: 10%
Founded: 1969

Catalog of performing arts merchandise including books, CDs, video tapes & services directed to universities, professionals, libraries, schools & individuals & health & fitness including books, CDs, videos, CD-ROMs & equipment. Sell a complete line of dance & theatrical stage flooring, plus aerobic & weight room floors. Carry tapes, adhesives & other floor care products.

STICK-EM UP INC

PO Box 5445
Pleasanton, CA 94566-1445

Telephone: (925) 426-1040, FAX: (925) 426-1085, E-Mail: stickemup@trivalley.com, Web Site: www.stickemup.com
Gen Mgr: Cea Jay Johnson
Conducts Business: U.S., Australia, U.K., France, Guam, Japan, Puerto Rico
Primary Market Served: Business & Consumer
Catalog available online
Indirect online sales
Founded: 1972

Distributor of pressure-sensitive stickers for decoration of home, boat, car & bike.

STOCK DRIVE PRODUCTS

2101 Jericho Tpke
New Hyde Park, NY 11040
Telephone: (516) 328-3300, FAX: (516) 326-8827, E-Mail: sdp-sisupport@sdp-si.com, Web Site: www.sdp.si.com
Pres: Frank Buchsbaum
Gen Mgr: Robert E. Lindemann
Mktg Mgr: Herbert R. Arum
Conducts Business: U.S.
Employees: 180
Primary Market Served: Business
Catalog available online
Advertising/Marketing Budget Related to Direct Marketing: 26-50%
Direct Marketing ad budget: $220,000
Direct Mail: 50%
Magazines: 50%
Founded: 1969
Gross sales or billing: $12,000,000

Publish a 2,400-page catalog for machinists, mechanics, inventors & hobbyists. Feature over 53,000 electromechanical components.

THE DMA SUAREZ CORP INDUSTRIES

7800 Whipple Ave NW
North Canton, OH 44767-0001
Telephone: (330) 494-5504, FAX: (330) 497-6837, E-Mail: suarez@suarez.com, Web Site: www.suarez.com
Pres: Benjamin Suarez
CFO & Gen Mgr: Michael R. Giorgio
Dir Media Svcs: Lorraine Kamp
Print Dir: Kim Clark
Opers Dir: Doug Heck
Intl Commun Dir: Paul Klingaman
Conducts Business: U.S., Canada
Employees: 965
Primary Market Served: Consumer
Direct online sales
Advertising/Marketing Budget Related to Direct Marketing: 76-100%
Direct Marketing ad budget: $66,500,000
Direct Mail: $61,000,000

Magazines: $550,000
Newspapers: $553,000
TV/Radio: $420,000
Telephone: $4,000,000
Founded: 1968
Gross sales or billing: $112,000,000

Catalog, TV & direct mail sales of consumer items. Also, online computer services & magazine publisher.

SUMMIT INDUSTRIES INC

839 Pickens Industrial Dr
Marietta, GA 30062
Telephone: (770) 590-0600, (800) 241-6996, FAX: (770) 590-0714, E-Mail: info@summitinds.com, Web Site: www.summitinds.com
Chmn: Arthur Howell
Pres: Michael Franchot
VP, Sls: Phil Meyers
Conducts Business: U.S. & 40 other countries
Employees: 30
Primary Market Served: Business & Consumer
Catalog available online
Direct online sales
Advertising/Marketing Budget Related to Direct Marketing: 0-25%
Direct Marketing ad budget:
Direct Mail: 25%
Magazines: 75%
Founded: 1920

Sell leather care products to owners of high-end cars with leather seats. Sell skincare products to nursing homes, home health care & hospitals. Also sell over-the-counter cough/cold & animal health products.

SVOBODA COLLINS LLC

One North Franklin (Suite 1500)
Chicago, IL 60606
Telephone: (312) 267-8750, FAX: (312) 267-6025, E-Mail: info@svoco.com, Web Site: www.svoco.com
Sr Mng Dir: John A. Svoboda
Mng Dir: Alex R. Miller
Mng Dir & Oper Partner: Andrew B. Albert
Conducts Business: U.S.
Employees: 180
Primary Market Served: Business & Consumer
Catalog available online
Direct online sales
Advertising/Marketing Budget Related to Direct Marketing: 0-25%
Founded: 1998
Gross sales or billing: $80,000,000

Pool supplies & used printer parts.

TEACHERS' DISCOVERY

Div. of American Eagle Co Inc
2741 Paldan Dr
Auburn Hills, MI 48326-1827
Telephone: (248) 340-7220, FAX:
(248) 340-7212
Chmn: Bruce McWilliams
Opers Mgr: Julie Hart
Conducts Business: U.S.
Primary Market Served: Business

Direct mail marketer to schools & hospitals including supplies to aid teachers in English, social studies & foreign languages.

THE DMA TERUMO CARDIOVASCULAR SYSTEMS CORP

6200 Jackson Rd
Ann Arbor, MI 48103-9586
Telephone: (734) 663-4145, Web Site:
www.terumo-cvs.com
Dir, Corp Communs: Barbara Schmid

Develop, manufacture & distribute medical devices for cardiac & vascular surgery

THE DMA 3D MAIL RESULTS

6205 S 231st St
Kent, WA 98032-3208
FAX: (853) 859-7300
Pres: Keith Lee
VP, Mktg: Gerri Norris
Conducts Business: U.S.
Employees: 32
Primary Market Served: Business
Advertising/Marketing Budget Related
to Direct Marketing: 51-75%
Direct Marketing ad budget: $500,000
Direct Mail: 30%
Telephone: 70%
Founded: 1970
Gross sales or billing: $6,000,000

Supplies & fixtures for retail stores.
Marking, packaging display products & computer systems.

TORAH UMESORAH PUBLICATIONS

Div. of Torah Umesorah-National Society for Hebrew Day Schools
1090 Coney Island Ave (Suite 4)
Brooklyn, NY 11203-2341
Telephone: (212) 227-1000, E-Mail:
umesorah@aol.com, Web Site: torah-umesorah.com
Natl Dir: Rabbi Dovid Nojowitz
Conducts Business: Worldwide
Employees: 6
Primary Market Served: Business &
Consumer
Catalog available online
Advertising/Marketing Budget Related
to Direct Marketing: 0-25%
Founded: 1945

Learning material to be used by Hebrew teachers & Hebrew day schools students & parents.

TOTAL TRAINING SOLUTIONS LLC

PO Box 310
Waunakee, WI 53597-0310
Telephone: (608) 849-5563, (800) 831-0678, FAX: (608) 849-5605, (800)
831-3776, E-Mail: kbennett@ttstrain.
com, Web Site: www.ttstrain.com
Pres: Mark D. Bennett
Conducts Business: U.S.
Employees: 5
Primary Market Served: Business
Catalog available online
Indirect online sales
Advertising/Marketing Budget Related
to Direct Marketing: 51-75%

Provide quality videos, software, furniture displays, & coin handling materials to financial organizations. Fax line for orders: (800) 845-2262.

TRACTOR SUPPLY CO

200 Powell Pl
Brentwood, TN 37027
Telephone: (615) 366-4600, (877) 872-7721, FAX: (615) 227-4608, Web
Site: www.mytscstore.com
Chmn & CEO: Joe Scarlett
VP, Fin: Cal Massmann
VP, Mktg & Mdse: Jerry Brase
Conducts Business: U.S.
Employees: 1,400
Primary Market Served: Consumer
Direct Marketing ad budget:
Direct Mail: $800,000
Newspapers: $3,900,000
TV/Radio: $100,000
Gross sales or billing: $216,000,000

Retail chain of 206 farm supply stores.

TROPHYLAND USA INC

7001 W 20th Ave
Hialeah, FL 33014
Telephone: (305) 823-4830, (800) 327-5820, FAX: (305) 823-4836, E-Mail:
info@trophyland.com, Web Site:
www.trophyland.com
Pres: Anthony Mendez
Mgr: Jackie Moran
Conducts Business: Worldwide
Employees: 75
Primary Market Served: Business &
Consumer
Catalog available online
Indirect online sales
Advertising/Marketing Budget Related
to Direct Marketing: 51-75%
Direct Marketing ad budget: $40,000
Direct Mail: 45%
Magazines: 15%
Telephone: 40%

Founded: 1969
Gross sales or billing: $3,000,000

Sell trophies, plaques, medals, desk sets, display cases & laminations.

THE DMA ULINE

12575 Uline Dr
Pleasant Prairie, WI 53158-3686
Telephone: (847) 473-3000, FAX:
(800) 295-5571, E-Mail: ulinecs@
uline.com, Web Site: www.uline.com
Chmn: Richard Uihlein
Pres: Elizabeth Uihlein
Govt Cust Svcs: Trish Schultz
Conducts Business: U.S., Canada, Puerto Rico, Mexico
Employees: 2,000
Primary Market Served: Business
Catalog available online
Direct online sales
Advertising/Marketing Budget Related
to Direct Marketing: 76-100%
Direct Marketing ad budget:
Direct Mail: 100%
Founded: 1980

Industrial mail order firm selling shipping & packaging supplies.

UNION PEN CO

PO Box 220
Hagaman, NY 12086-0220
Telephone: (800) 846-6600, FAX:
(518) 770-7018, Web Site: www.
unionpen.com
Pres: Robert Rosenthal
Plant Mgr: Luis Andrade
VP: Maria Coyle
Conducts Business: U.S., Canada,
U.K., Germany
Employees: 165
Primary Market Served: Business
Catalog available online
Direct online sales
Advertising/Marketing Budget Related
to Direct Marketing: 76-100%
Direct Marketing ad budget:
$5,000,000
Direct Mail: 75%
Magazines: 5%
Telephone: 20%
Founded: 1904
Gross sales or billing: $22,000,000

Imprinted promotional products, advertising specialties, office products & business gifts.

UNIVERSITY AT BUFFALO CENTER FOR ENTREPRENEURIAL LEADERSHIP

672 Delaware Ave
Buffalo, NY 14209-2202

Telephone: (716) 885-5715, Web Site: http://mgt.buffalo.edu/entrepreneurship/cel
Primary Market Served: Consumer

THE DMA VECTOR MARKETING CORP
Subs. of Atlas Corp
1116 E State St
Olean, NY 14760-3814
Telephone: (716) 373-6141, FAX: (716) 373-6145, Web Site: www.cutco.com
Production Coord: Michele Oakley
Mktg Mgr: Steve Pokrzyk
Mktg Web Coord: Charles LaBorde
Conducts Business: U.S., Canada, Korea
Primary Market Served: Consumer
Founded: 1985

Marketer of consumer products including cutlery & sporting knives.

THE DMA VEHICLE ASSURANCE
2747 W Clay
Saint Charles, MO 63301-2557
Telephone: (636) 925-7800
Primary Market Served: Consumer

THE DMA THE VERMONT COUNTRY STORE
5650 Main St
Manchester Center, VT 05255-9711
Telephone: (802) 362-8200, Web Site: www.vermontcountrystore.com
Dir Mktg: Lori Vilbrin

General store

WHAT ON EARTH
Div. of Universal Direct Fulfillment Corp
5581 Hudson Industrial Pkwy
Hudson, OH 44236-5019
Telephone: (330) 963-6554, (800) 945-2552, FAX: (800) 950-9569, Web Site: www.whatonearthcatalog.com
Pres & CEO: Jared Florian
Primary Market Served: Consumer
Catalog available online
Direct online sales

Mail order catalog.

WHIRLEY DRINK WORKS
618 Fourth Ave
Warren, PA 16365
Telephone: (814) 723-7600, (800) 825-5575, FAX: (814) 723-3245, E-Mail: info@whirleydrinkworks.com, Web Site: www.whirleydrinkworks.com
Pres: Lincoln Sokolski
VP: Andrew Sokolski
VP, Mktg & Natl Accts Sls Mgr: Bill Turner
HR Mgr: Rita Bevevino
Employees: 300

Primary Market Served: Business
Catalog available online
Direct online sales
Advertising/Marketing Budget Related to Direct Marketing: 0-25%

Custom decorated plastic beverage containers including Thermo Mugs and sports bottles.

WIKCO INDUSTRIES INC
1467 N Grant Ave
Casa Grande, AZ 85222
Telephone: (520) 316-0446, FAX: (520) 316-0446, E-Mail: sales@wikco.com, Web Site: www.wikco.com
Co-Owner: Mary Jo Hussey
Pres: Mike Hussey
Conducts Business: U.S.
Employees: 5
Primary Market Served: Business & Consumer
Catalog available online
Indirect online sales
Advertising/Marketing Budget Related to Direct Marketing: 76-100%
Direct Marketing ad budget:
Direct Mail: 80%
Magazines: 20%
Founded: 1976

Catalog marketers of grounds maintenance equipment, physical therapy equipment.

WIN CRAFT INC
1124 W Fifth St, PO Box 888
Winona, MN 55987
Telephone: (507) 454-5510, (800) 533-8100, FAX: (507) 454-6403, Web Site: www.wincraftschool.com
Pres: Richard Pope
Sr VP: Robert Flom
VP, Sls: Don Trandem
VP, Mktg: Eric Johnson
VP: John Killen
Conducts Business: U.S.
Employees: 300
Primary Market Served: Consumer
Catalog available online
Direct online sales
Direct Marketing ad budget: $300,000
Direct Mail: 100%

Sell school related novelty items (personalized with school colors) & cheerleader related products by mail order catalog. Used for fund-raising purposes.

THE DMA WIRELESS IDEA
1213 Calle Luchetti (Apt 2), Condado Mansions
San Juan, PR 00907-1850
Telephone: (787) 925-7000
Primary Market Served: Consumer

Mobile entertainment & distribution network

WOODWIND & BRASSWIND INC
6625 Network Way Ste 200
Indianapolis, IN 46278-1683
Telephone: (574) 251-3500, (800) 348-5003, FAX: (574) 251-3501, Web Site: www.wwbw.com
Pres: Dennis Bamber
Gen Mgr: Joe Hickner
Adv: Rona Palmer
Conducts Business: Worldwide
Employees: 170
Primary Market Served: Business & Consumer
Catalog available online
Indirect online sales
Advertising/Marketing Budget Related to Direct Marketing: 76-100%
Direct Marketing ad budget:
Direct Mail: 90%
Newspapers: 10%
Founded: 1978

Sell musical instruments & supplies.

THE DMA XCEL ENERGY
414 Nicollet Mall (GO 6)
Minneapolis, MN 55401-1927
Telephone: (612) 330-6783, Web Site: xcelenergy.com
Primary Market Served: Consumer

THE DMA DAVID YURMAN
24 Vestry St
New York, NY 10013-1903
Telephone: (212) 896-1550, Web Site: davidyurman.com
Primary Market Served: Consumer

Jewelry, timepieces & gift items

Gifts & Collectibles Catalogs (6)

ABBEY PRESS
Subs. of St Meinrad Archabbey
One Hill Dr
Saint Meinrad, IN 47577-1004
Telephone: (812) 357-8011, FAX:
(812) 357-8388, Web Site: www.
abbeypress.com
Prod Mngmt Dir: Sharon Lueken
CEO: Gerald Wilhite
DataBase Analyst: Linda Altman
Conducts Business: U.S.
Employees: 280
Primary Market Served: Business &
Consumer
Advertising/Marketing Budget Related
to Direct Marketing: 76-100%

Direct mail marketing company specializing in publishing The Abbey Press Christian Family Gift Catalog. Seventeen catalogs are mailed each year to over 25 million families.

AMERICA
21 Enterprise Ct
Fredericksburg, VA 22405
Telephone: (540) 658-3388, (800) 927-8277, FAX: (540) 658-3389, Web
Site: www.americastore.com
Pres: Jane Crawford
Catalog Opers Mgr: Rick Lovisone
Conducts Business: U.S.
Employees: 40
Primary Market Served: Consumer
Catalog available online
Direct online sales
Advertising/Marketing Budget Related
to Direct Marketing: 76-100%
Direct Marketing ad budget:
Direct Mail: 100%
Founded: 1988

American themed gifts, clothing & flags.

THE DMA AMERICAN GIRL BRANDS LLC
8400 Fairway Pl
Middleton, WI 53562-2548
Telephone: (608) 836-4848, Web Site:
www.americangirl.com
Pres: Ellen Brothers
Primary Market Served: Consumer

THE DMA AMERICAN MINT LLC
5020 Louise Dr (Suite 300)
Mechanicsburg, PA 17055-4927
Telephone: (717) 458-9200, (877) 807-MINT, FAX: (717) 458-9211,
E-Mail: contact@americanmint.com,
Web Site: www.americanmint.com
Owner: Michael Goede
Accts Payable: Lorri Dietz
Conducts Business: U.S.

Primary Market Served: Consumer
Catalog available online
Direct online sales
Advertising/Marketing Budget Related
to Direct Marketing: 76-100%
Direct Marketing ad budget:
$5,000,000
Direct Mail: 70%
Magazines: 5%
Newspapers: 10%
Online: 5%
TV/Radio: 5%
Telephone: 5%
Founded: 1999
Gross sales or billing: $10,000,000

Consumer mail order products and continuity offers.

ANCIENT CIRCLES
Div. of Open Circle Distributors
190 North St
Willits, CA 95490-3420
Telephone: (800) 726-8032, FAX:
(707) 459-0261, E-Mail: ancient@pacific.net, Web Site: www.
ancientcircles.com
Owner & Adv: Ann Weller
Conducts Business: U.S., U.K., Germany, Canada
Employees: 5
Primary Market Served: Business &
Consumer
Catalog available online
Indirect online sales
Advertising/Marketing Budget Related
to Direct Marketing: 26-50%
Direct Marketing ad budget: $4,000
Magazines: 90%
Telephone: 10%
Founded: 1986

Celtic & symbolic jewelry, scarves, masks, textiles & drums to the pagan, Celtic & metaphysical market.

ANHEUSER-BUSCH INC PROMOTIONAL PRODUCTS GROUP
Anheuser-Busch Co Inc
20 Constitution Blvd S
Shelton, CT 06484
Telephone: (800) 742-5283, Web Site:
www.budshop.com
Prod Promos Dir: Mary Houlihan
Mdsg Mgr: Ann Gast
Category Mgr: Regina Garofalo
Category Mgr: Tami Bafaro
Category Mgr: Beth Schlegel
Category Mgr: Melissa Toennies
Conducts Business: U.S.
Employees: 140
Primary Market Served: Business &
Consumer

Advertising/Marketing Budget Related
to Direct Marketing: 0-25%

Direct to consumer & business-to-business catalog marketers of Anheuser-Busch Inc logo merchandise.

ANYTHING GOES
dba Heavenly Treasures
321 Main St
Allenhurst, NJ 07711-1037
Telephone: (732) 531-8040, Web Site:
www.heavenlytreasures.com
Pres: Abraham Ades
Primary Market Served: Consumer

ARCTIC TRADING CO INC
Kelsey & Bernier Sts Box 910
Churchill, MB, Canada R0B 0E0
Telephone: (204) 675-8804, (800) 665-0431, FAX: (204) 675-2164, E-Mail:
atcpenny@mts.net, Web Site: www.
arctictradingco.com
Governess: Penny Rawlings
Sls Assoc Computer Skills: Susie
Bunka
Conducts Business: U.S., Canada, Japan, France, U.K.
Employees: 9
Primary Market Served: Business &
Consumer
Catalog available online
Direct online sales
Advertising/Marketing Budget Related
to Direct Marketing: 0-25%
Direct Marketing ad budget: $50,000
Direct Mail: 66%
Magazines: 5%
Newspapers: 3%
TV/Radio: 2%
Telephone: 24%
Founded: 1978
Gross sales or billing: $850,000

Native arts & crafts. Manufacturing mittens, moccasins, mukluks, gauntlets, caribou hair sculptures, tuftings & jewelry. Native Inuit & Indian carvings, tools & other handcrafts. Sell to tourists, businesses on the wholesale level & mail order catalog sales.

WENDELL AUGUST FORGE INC
390 Lincoln Ave
Grove City, PA 16127
Telephone: (724) 458-8360, (800) 923-1390, FAX: (724) 458-0906, E-Mail:
info@wendell.com, Web Site: www.
wendellaugust.com
Pres: Jim Colleran
Mgr: Karl Hart
Artisan: David Bruck
Artisan: Leonard Youngo

Primary Market Served: Business &
Consumer
Catalog available online
Direct online sales
Advertising/Marketing Budget Related
to Direct Marketing: 76-100%
Direct Marketing ad budget: $425,000
Direct Mail: 94%
Magazines: 6%
Founded: 1923

Creators & merchandisers of artistic
hand wrought metal gifts.

AWARD CO OF AMERICA
Div. of Randall Publishing Co Inc
3200 Rice Mine Rd
Tuscaloosa, AL 35406-1510
Telephone: (205) 349-2990, FAX:
(205) 752-0930, Web Site: www.
randallpub.com
Pres: Mike Reilly
Conducts Business: U.S.
Primary Market Served: Business &
Consumer

Sell laminated & do-it-yourself award
plaques & advertising specialties
through direct mail.

BABYSHOE.COM
306 Hebron St
Hendersonville, NC 28739-5210
Telephone: (828) 697-5811, (800) 543-
8566, FAX: (828) 697-5815, E-Mail:
info@babyshoe.com, Web Site:
www.babyshoe.com
Pres: Michael Schwartz
Opers Dir: Joy Keifer
Sr Baby Gift Specialist: Connie Medlin
Employees: 6
Primary Market Served: Business &
Consumer
Catalog available online
Advertising/Marketing Budget Related
to Direct Marketing: 76-100%
Direct Marketing ad budget:
Direct Mail: 90%
Magazines: 10%
Founded: 1950

Infant products.

BATTLEGROUND ANTIQUES
INC
3910 US Hwy 70 E
New Bern, NC 28560
Telephone: (252) 636-3039, FAX:
(252) 637-1862, E-Mail:
tarheelrebel2000@aol.com, Web
Site: www.civilwarantiques.com
Sec: William D. Gorges
Textiles Specialist: Lynn Gorges
Conducts Business: Worldwide
Employees: 6
Primary Market Served: Business &
Consumer

Catalog available online
Indirect online sales
Advertising/Marketing Budget Related
to Direct Marketing: 51-75%
Direct Marketing ad budget: $30,000
Direct Mail: 10%
Magazines: 70%
Newspapers: 10%
Telephone: 10%
Founded: 1983
Gross sales or billing: $600,000

Antique militaria, primarily Civil War
era, sports collectibles, gold & silver
coins, quilts & fine art.

BICK INTERNATIONAL
dba "International Coin & Stamp Col-
lectors Society"
PO Box 854
Van Nuys, CA 91408-0854
Telephone: (818) 997-6496, FAX:
(818) 988-4337, E-Mail: iibick@
sbcglobal.net, Web Site: www.
bickinternational.com
Pres: Israel Bick
Conducts Business: Worldwide
Employees: 6
Primary Market Served: Business &
Consumer
Catalog available online
Direct online sales
Advertising/Marketing Budget Related
to Direct Marketing: 0-25%
Founded: 1952

Wholesale & retail collectibles.

BIRTHDAY KEEPSAKES
1323 S Garfield Ave
Loveland, CO 80537-6334
Telephone: (970) 669-5506, Web Site:
www.bkeepsakes.com
Gen Mgr: Karin Delaney

BIZZARO RUBBER STAMPS
PO Box 292
Greenville, RI 02828-0292
Telephone: (401) 231-8777, FAX:
(401) 231-4770, E-Mail:
bizzaroinc@earthlink.net, Web Site:
www.bizzaro.com
Pres: Doreen Tirocchi
Mktg Mgr: Bob Tirocchi
Conducts Business: U.S., Canada
Employees: 5
Primary Market Served: Business &
Consumer
Catalog available online
Indirect online sales
Advertising/Marketing Budget Related
to Direct Marketing: 0-25%
Direct Marketing ad budget: $5,000
Direct Mail: 20%
Magazines: 40%
Online: 40%
Founded: 1971

Gross sales or billing: $80,000
Artistic rubber stamps & supplies sold
retail & wholesale.

BEVERLY BREMER SILVER
SHOP
3164 Peachtree Rd NE
Atlanta, GA 30305-1853
Telephone: (404) 261-4009, (800) 270-
4009, E-Mail: sterlingsilver@
worldnet.att.net, Web Site: www.
beverlybremer.com
Pres: Beverly H. Bremer
Employees: 22
Primary Market Served: Consumer
Founded: 1975

Retailer of sterling silver products,
flatware, hollowware & gifts.

THE DMA BRONNER'S CHRISTMAS
WONDERLAND
25 Christmas Ln
Frankenmuth, MI 48734-1807
Telephone: (989) 652-9931, Web Site:
www.bronners.com
Pres & CEO: Wayne Bronner
Primary Market Served: Consumer

BROWNELL HOLLY FARMS
17251 S Clackamas River Dr
Oregon City, OR 97045-9493
Telephone: (503) 631-7475, FAX:
(503) 631-7481, E-Mail: sales@
brownellhollyfarms.com, Web Site:
www.brownellhollyfarms.com
Owner: Granville R. Lee
Assoc: Lauren Lee
Assoc: Jenny Lee
Conducts Business: U.S.
Employees: 10
Primary Market Served: Business &
Consumer
Catalog available online
Advertising/Marketing Budget Related
to Direct Marketing: 76-100%
Direct Marketing ad budget:
Direct Mail: 80%
Magazines: 10%
Newspapers: 5%
Telephone: 5%
Founded: 1918
Gross sales or billing: $200,000

Grower & shipper of Christmas holly
& wreaths directly to the consumer or
as gifts. Supplier to florists, fund raisers & businesses.

BUNKER HILL AUCTIONS
10251 Fox River Dr
Newark, IL 60541-9657
Telephone: (630) 770-7132, E-Mail:
bunkerhillauctions@joimail.com,
Web Site: www.bunkerhillauctions.
com

Owner: Kaye Kerekes
Co-Owner & Sls: Nick Bruscato
Conducts Business: U.S.
Employees: 2
Primary Market Served: Business &
   Consumer
Catalog available online
Indirect online sales
Advertising/Marketing Budget Related
   to Direct Marketing: 0-25%
Founded: 1985
Gross sales or billing: $35,000

Close-out & discounted name brand
holiday decorations & collectibles.

CARIBE DIRECT INC
107 Tres Hermanos
San Juan, PR 00907-2306
Telephone: (787) 722-5188, FAX:
   (787) 723-6165, E-Mail: islaonline@
   prw.net, Web Site: www.islaonline.
   com
Pres: Elizabeth Parker
VP, Opers: Gerardo Cumpiano
Conducts Business: U.S.
Employees: 8
Primary Market Served: Business &
   Consumer
Catalog available online
Indirect online sales
Advertising/Marketing Budget Related
   to Direct Marketing: 76-100%
Direct Marketing ad budget:
Direct Mail: 100%
Founded: 1994
Gross sales or billing: $1,000,000

Mail order catalog of products from
Puerto Rico.

HARRIET CARTER GIFTS
INC
PO Box 427
Montgomeryville, PA 18936-0427
Telephone: (215) 361-5100, FAX:
   (215) 361-1127, Web Site: www.
   harrietcarter.com
Pres: Ronald P. Lassin
VP: Gary Lassin
Dir Circulation: Linda Mallory
Conducts Business: U.S.
Primary Market Served: Consumer
Catalog available online
Direct online sales

Sell gifts & decorative accessories direct to the consumer.

CARTOUCHE LTD
100 S Early St
Alexandria, VA 22304
Telephone: (703) 823-7904, (800) AT-
   EGYPT, FAX: (888) 283-4978,
   E-Mail: sales@egyptianimports.com,
   Web Site: www.egyptianimports.com
Owner: Eileen S. Cox

Employees: 5
Primary Market Served: Business &
   Consumer
Catalog available online
Direct online sales
Advertising/Marketing Budget Related
   to Direct Marketing: 76-100%
Direct Marketing ad budget:
Direct Mail: 40%
Magazines: 60%
Founded: 1980

Gold importers; personalized hiero-
glyphic jewelry.

CASUAL LIVING USA
The Thompson Group
5401 Hangar Ct
Tampa, FL 33634-5341
Telephone: (813) 884-6955, (800) 652-
   2948, FAX: (813) 882-4605, Web
   Site: www.casuallivingusa.com
Pres: Robert Franzblau
Conducts Business: U.S., Puerto Rico,
   Guam, Virgin Islands, Canada
Employees: 75
Primary Market Served: Consumer
Catalog available online
Direct online sales
Founded: 1960

Sell giftware through direct mail/
catalogs.

CHARISMA BRANDS LLC
23482 Peralta Dr Ste A
Laguna Hills, CA 92653-1733
Telephone: (949) 788-8803, Web Site:
   www.charismabrands.com
Pres & CEO: Anthony Shutts
Primary Market Served: Business &
   Consumer

CHARTIFACTS
3221 Marlboro Ct
Richmond, VA 23225-0654
Telephone: (804) 272-7120
VP: Susan Auburn
Conducts Business: U.S.
Employees: 1
Primary Market Served: Business &
   Consumer
Indirect online sales
Advertising/Marketing Budget Related
   to Direct Marketing: 76-100%
Direct Marketing ad budget: $2,000
Direct Mail: 20%
Magazines: 80%
Founded: 1987
Gross sales or billing: $50,000

Antique nautical maps & reproductions
to general public.

CHELSEA CLOCK CO INC
284 Everett Ave
Chelsea, MA 02150-1598

Telephone: (617) 884-0250, (800) 284-
   1778, FAX: (617) 830-0599, Web
   Site: www.chelseaclock.com
Pres: J. K. Nicholas
Mktg Commun Mgr: Rosanne Spinali
Conducts Business: Worldwide
Employees: 41
Primary Market Served: Business
Advertising/Marketing Budget Related
   to Direct Marketing: 0-25%
Direct Marketing ad budget:
Online: 100%
Founded: 1897

Sell wall clocks: marine, striking &
non-striking, 8 day spring wound,
quartz crystal, tide & time &
barometers. Also carry an assortment
of jeweler's clocks.

CHIASSO
1440 N Dayton St (Suite 307)
Chicago, IL 60642-2645
Telephone: (877) CHIASSO, FAX:
   (312) 477-3827, Web Site: www.
   chiasso.com
Pres: David Marshall
VP, Mktg: Linda Spellman
Conducts Business: U.S.
Employees: 10
Primary Market Served: Business &
   Consumer
Catalog available online
Direct online sales

Sell contemporary accessories for the
home & office.

THE DMA CHILDREN'S MIRACLE
NETWORK
205 W 700 S
Salt Lake City, UT 84101-2726
Telephone: (801) 214-7400, Web Site:
   www.cmn.org
Sr VP: Robert Banner
Primary Market Served: Consumer

CLUBS OF AMERICA
426 Scotland Rd
Lakemoor, IL 60051
Telephone: (815) 363-4000, (800)
   CLUB-USA, FAX: (815) 363-4677,
   E-Mail: info@greatclubs.com, Web
   Site: www.clubsofamerica.com
Pres: Douglas M. Doretti
VP: Dirk J. Doretti
Conducts Business: U.S.
Employees: 30
Primary Market Served: Business &
   Consumer
Catalog available online
Direct online sales
Founded: 1994

Continuity mail order company. Eight gift-of-the-month clubs in beer, wine, flowers, coffee, cigars, pizza, fruit & chocolate. Customers have the option to join any or all clubs. Different selections are delivered each month. No minimum membership time. Corporate discount plans available.

COLLECTOR'S ARMOURY LTD

PO Box 2948
McDonough, GA 30253-1743
Telephone: (703) 493-9120, FAX: (703) 493-9424, Web Site: www.collectorsarmoury.com
VP: Scott Nelson
CEO: Tom Nelson
Pres: Jim Kemp
Conducts Business: U.S., Canada, Australia, Belgium, France, U.K., Germany, S. America, Scandinavia
Employees: 15
Primary Market Served: Business & Consumer
Catalog available online
Advertising/Marketing Budget Related to Direct Marketing: 0-25%
Direct Marketing ad budget:
Direct Mail: 55%
Magazines: 45%
Founded: 1968
Gross sales or billing: $4,000,000

Provide non-firing replicas of famous guns & other military memorabilia to the general public through mail order catalogs, retail store & wholesale operations.

COLLECTOR'S TEAPOT

Subs. of Bailey Pottery Corp
PO Box 1577
Kingston, NY 12402-1577
Telephone: (845) 339-1109, (800) 724-3306, FAX: (845) 339-5530, Web Site: www.collectorsteapot.com
CEO: Anne Bailey
CEO: Jim Bailey
Conducts Business: U.S.
Employees: 20
Primary Market Served: Business & Consumer
Advertising/Marketing Budget Related to Direct Marketing: 0-25%
Direct Marketing ad budget:
Direct Mail: 75%
Magazines: 25%
Founded: 1978

Full-color catalog direct mail to retail consumers selling food & collectible giftware.

THE DMA THE COUNTRY HOUSE INC

805 E Main St
Salisbury, MD 21804-5024
Telephone: (410) 749-1959, (800) 331-3602, FAX: (410) 548-3224, E-Mail: web@thecountryhouse.com, Web Site: www.thecountryhouse.com
Pres: Michael Delano
Employees: 30
Primary Market Served: Consumer
Catalog available online
Direct online sales
Advertising/Marketing Budget Related to Direct Marketing: 51-75%
Founded: 1985

Gifts, accessories & mail order catalogs.

CREATIVE CATALOGS CORP

19W661 101st St
Lemont, IL 60439-9642
Telephone: (630) 783-2400, Web Site: www.personalcreations.com
Dir Mktg: Judy Nelson
Primary Market Served: Consumer

CREATIVE IRISH GIFTS

3801 Woodland Heights Rd Ste 100
Little Rock, AR 72212-2410
Telephone: (330) 954-1200, FAX: (330) 650-8888, E-Mail: gifts@shopirish.com, Web Site: www.shopirish.com
Pres: Diane O'Connor
COO: Robert O'Connor
Conducts Business: Worldwide
Employees: 50
Primary Market Served: Consumer
Catalog available online
Direct online sales
Advertising/Marketing Budget Related to Direct Marketing: 0-25%
Founded: 1982
Gross sales or billing: $8,000,000

Irish items & gifts.

CURRENT USA INC

Subs. of Deluxe Corp
1025 E Woodmen Rd
Colorado Springs, CO 80920-3181
Telephone: (719) 594-4100, (877) 665-4458, FAX: (719) 531-2283, Web Site: www.currentinc.com
Pres: Dave Humbert
VP, Mktg: Wendy Huxta
CFO: Kirby Heck
Dir, IT: Mickey Gardner
Dir, HR: Paul Andersen
Conducts Business: U.S.
Employees: 1,600
Primary Market Served: Consumer
Catalog available online
Direct online sales
Advertising/Marketing Budget Related to Direct Marketing: 76-100%
Founded: 1950
Gross sales or billing: $208,000,000

Sell greeting cards, stationery, calendars, gift wrapping paper, gift items, personal & business checks via catalog.

CUSTOM MINIATURES

19 Winnhaven Dr
Hudson, NH 03051-4748
Telephone: (603) 882-6392
Owner: Al Chandronnait
Conducts Business: U.S.
Employees: 1
Primary Market Served: Business & Consumer
Advertising/Marketing Budget Related to Direct Marketing: 0-25%
Direct Marketing ad budget: $3,000
Direct Mail: 80%
Magazines: 20%
Gross sales or billing: $50,000

Custom dollhouse miniatures sold to miniature shops & retail customers throughout the country.

DAVIDOFF OF GENEVA INC

Subs. of Davidoff of Geneva of Switzerland
3001 Gateway Centre Pkwy N
Pinellas Park, FL 33782-6124
Telephone: (203) 323-5811, (800) 328-4365, FAX: (203) 975-0090
Pres, US Division: Peter Banninger
VP, Opers: Eva Baurenfeind
Sr Mktg Mgr: Samuel Russel
Mktg Mgr: Sam Russell
Gen Mgr: Michael Herklots
Conducts Business: Worldwide
Employees: 90
Primary Market Served: Business & Consumer
Catalog available online
Advertising/Marketing Budget Related to Direct Marketing: 0-25%
Founded: 1906

Catalog marketer of cigars, smoker's & men's accessories.

DESIGN TOSCANO, INC

1400 Morse Ave
Elk Grove Village, IL 60007-5722
Telephone: (847) 952-0100, (800) 525-5141, FAX: (847) 952-8992, Web Site: www.designtoscano.com
Pres: Michael Stopka
Primary Market Served: Consumer
Gross sales or billing: $17,000,000

Sells classic European reproductions & French tapestry. Catalog & mail-order houses.

DIAMONDS BY RENNIE ELLEN

15 W 47th St (Rm 503)
New York, NY 10036

Telephone: (212) 869-5525, FAX: (212) 869-5526, Web Site: www. rennieellen.com
Owner: Rennie Ellen
Conducts Business: U.S.
Primary Market Served: Business & Consumer
Catalog available online
Founded: 1965

Diamonds sold direct to the public.

DRUMBEAT INDIAN ARTS INC
4143 N 16th St (Suite 1)
Phoenix, AZ 85016-5351
Telephone: (602) 266-4823, (800) 895-4859, FAX: (602) 265-2402, E-Mail: info@drumbeatindianarts.com, Web Site: www.drumbeatindianarts.com
Pres: Robert L. Nuss
Conducts Business: Worldwide
Employees: 8
Primary Market Served: Business & Consumer
Catalog available online
Advertising/Marketing Budget Related to Direct Marketing: 51-75%
Direct Marketing ad budget:
Direct Mail: 40%
Magazines: 35%
Newspapers: 20%
TV/Radio: 5%
Founded: 1984
Gross sales or billing: $3,000,000

American Indian music recordings-cassettes, compact discs, DVDs, books & craft supplies. Sell to anyone interested in American Indian music. Wholesale & retail.

EMBLEM & BADGE INC
16 Sunnyside Ave
Johnston, RI 02919-5318
Telephone: (401) 365-1265, (800) 875-5444, FAX: (401) 365-1263, E-Mail: sales@recognition.com, Web Site: www.recognition.com
Pres: David A. Resnik
Conducts Business: U.S.
Employees: 35
Primary Market Served: Business & Consumer
Catalog available online
Indirect online sales
Advertising/Marketing Budget Related to Direct Marketing: 26-50%
Founded: 1932

Awards & recognition products.

FAMILY ALBUM
4887 Newport Rd
Kinzers, PA 17535-9793

Telephone: (717) 442-0220, FAX: (717) 442-7904, E-Mail: rarebooks@pobox.com
Dir: Ron Lieberman
Conducts Business: U.S., Canada, Europe
Employees: 2
Primary Market Served: Business & Consumer
Catalog available online
Indirect online sales
Advertising/Marketing Budget Related to Direct Marketing: 26-50%
Direct Marketing ad budget:
Direct Mail: 60%
Magazines: 30%
Telephone: 10%
Founded: 1969
Gross sales or billing: $250,000

Antiquarian books & library supplies.

MICHAEL C FINA
545 5th Ave Frnt
New York, NY 10017-3616
Telephone: (212) 557-2500, Web Site: www.michaelcfina.com
Pres: George Fina

GAELSONG
PO Box 15356
Seattle, WA 98115-0356
Telephone: (206) 526-8350, Web Site: www.gaelsong.com
Pres: Colleen Connell

GALLERY OF CATS
26136 Galvez Ct
Valencia, CA 91355-3349
Telephone: (818) 782-6264, E-Mail: helpdesk@galleryofcats.com, Web Site: www.galleryofcats.com
Pres: Neil L. Kleeger
Conducts Business: U.S., Canada, Hong Kong
Primary Market Served: Consumer
Catalog available online
Indirect online sales
Advertising/Marketing Budget Related to Direct Marketing: 0-25%
Founded: 1987

Sell gifts & collectibles of cats to wholesale & consumer outlets.

THE GALLERY SHOP
1285 Elmwood Ave, Albright-Knox Art Gallery
Buffalo, NY 14222-1096
Telephone: (716) 882-8700 X258, FAX: (716) 882-1958, E-Mail: gallshop@albrightknox.org, Web Site: www.albrightknox.org
Dir: Louis Granchos
Dir Advancement: Elaine Pyne
Dep Dir: Karen Lee Spaulding

CFO: Patrick Kilcullen
Sr Curator: Douglas Dreishpoon Ph.D.
Conducts Business: U.S., Canada, Europe, Asia
Employees: 8
Primary Market Served: Business & Consumer
Catalog available online
Advertising/Marketing Budget Related to Direct Marketing: 0-25%

Sell publications & reproductions from the permanent collection of the Albright-Knox Art Gallery. Art objects, educational toys & stationery designed & created by contemporary artists commissioned by the Gallery Shop.

GEARY'S OF BEVERLY HILLS
aka Tjb Geary's LLC
351 N Beverly Dr
Beverly Hills, CA 90210-4794
Telephone: (310) 273-4741, (800) 793-6670, FAX: (310) 858-7555, Web Site: www.gearys.com
Pres: Tom Blumental
Conducts Business: U.S.
Employees: 65
Primary Market Served: Consumer
Advertising/Marketing Budget Related to Direct Marketing: 26-50%
Founded: 1930
Gross sales or billing: $5,000,000

Catalog & retail sales of fine china, crystal, silver, gifts, table linens, tabletop items & accessories.

GERSTNER WOODWORKS
Div of H. Gerstner & Sons, Inc.
20 Gerstner Way
Dayton, OH 45402-8408
Telephone: (937) 228-1662, FAX: (937) 228-8557, E-Mail: info@gerstnerusa.com, Web Site: www.gerstnerusa.com
Pres: Jack Campbell
Conducts Business: U.S.
Employees: 10
Primary Market Served: Business & Consumer
Catalog available online
Indirect online sales
Advertising/Marketing Budget Related to Direct Marketing: 0-25%
Founded: 1906
Gross sales or billing: $1,500,000

Manufacturer of wooden tool chests, jewelry chests & other fine wood products to industrial & retail markets.

GIFT SERVICES INC
Div. of Gifttree
1800 W Fourth Plain Blvd (Suite 120B)

Vancouver, WA 98660-1367
Telephone: (800) 379-4065, FAX:
   (360) 699-0597, E-Mail: corpsales@
   gifttree.com, Web Site: www.gifttree.
   com
Mktg Dir: Bonny Elder
Pres & CEO: Craig Bowen
Reg VP Sls: David Kresser
Conducts Business: U.S.
Employees: 40
Primary Market Served: Business &
   Consumer
Catalog available online
Direct online sales
Direct Marketing ad budget:
Direct Mail: 95%
Telephone: 5%
Founded: 1997
Gross sales or billing: $11,000,000

Retail ecommerce website. Hand
crafted gift baskets, fresh flowers, balloons, fruit baskets, corporate &
unique gifts.

GIFTS CORP

130 Bell Farm Rd (Unit 2)
Barrie, ON, Canada L4M 6J4
Telephone: (905) 670-1126, (800) 565-
   3130, FAX: (905) 670-1127, E-Mail:
   customerservice@regal.ca, Web Site:
   www.regalgreetings.com
CEO & Sr VP Fin: Kevin Watkinson
Pres: Greg Neanth
Exec VP & COO: Gregory W. Dunn
Dir Mktg: Brian Lucas
Conducts Business: Canada
Employees: 1,100
Primary Market Served: Consumer
Catalog available online
Direct online sales
Advertising/Marketing Budget Related
   to Direct Marketing: 26-50%
Founded: 1928
Gross sales or billing: $100,000,000

Manufacturer of greeting cards, gift
wrap & novelties sold via seasonal
catalogs.

GIMBELS OF MAINE INC

14 Commercial St
Boothbay Harbor, ME 04538-1821
Telephone: (207) 633-5088, FAX:
   (207) 633-5128, Web Site: www.
   gimbelscollectibles.com
Pres: Mark S. Gimbel
CEO: Diane Gimbel
Conducts Business: U.S.
Employees: 28
Primary Market Served: Consumer
Advertising/Marketing Budget Related
   to Direct Marketing: 76-100%
Direct Marketing ad budget:
Direct Mail: 100%
Gross sales or billing: $2,500,000

By mail-collectors thimbles, dolls &
figurines.

GRACELAND

Div. of Elvis Presley Entertainment
3734 Elvis Presley Blvd
Memphis, TN 38116-4106
Telephone: (901) 332-3322, (800) 238-
   2010, FAX: (901) 344-3120, Web
   Site: www.elvis.com
Dir Mdsg: Danny Hiltenbrand
Conducts Business: U.S., Canada
Employees: 250
Primary Market Served: Consumer
Catalog available online
Direct online sales
Founded: 1981
Gross sales or billing: $12,600,000

Print two catalogs per year, offering
Elvis Presley memorabilia.

GREAT CHEFS TELEVISION PUBLISHING

Div. of GCI Inc
747 Magazine St
New Orleans, LA 70130
Telephone: (504) 581-5000, (800) 321-
   1499, FAX: (504) 581-1188, E-Mail:
   info@greatchefs.com, Web Site:
   www.greatchefs.com
COO & Exec Producer: John Shoup
Admin Asst: Cybil Curtis
Conducts Business: U.S., Europe, Far
   East, South America
Employees: 10
Primary Market Served: Business &
   Consumer
Catalog available online
Direct online sales
Advertising/Marketing Budget Related
   to Direct Marketing: 0-25%
Direct Marketing ad budget:
Direct Mail: $100,000
Magazines: $25,000
TV/Radio: $200,000
Telephone: $25,000
Founded: 1979
Gross sales or billing: $1,000,000

Publisher & marketer of cookbooks,
video & audio cassettes & CD's.

GUMP'S BY MAIL INC

Subs. of Hanover Direct
135 Post St
San Francisco, CA 94108
Telephone: (415) 982-1616, (800) 882-
   8055, FAX: (800) 984-9361, Web
   Site: www.gumpsbymail.com
Pres: John Di Francesco
CEO: Rakesh J. Paul
VP: Farley Nachemin
VP: Edward J. O'Brien
Media Mgr: Shirley Wilson
Conducts Business: U.S.
Employees: 150

Primary Market Served: Consumer
Catalog available online
Direct online sales
Advertising/Marketing Budget Related
   to Direct Marketing: 76-100%
Gross sales or billing: $5,500,000

Retail store & mail order operation
selling jewelry, jade, silver, china,
crystal, interior design, Asian & contemporary gifts & stationery. Store is
located in San Francisco.

THE HAMILTON COLLECTION

Div of The Bradford Exchange
7018 A C Skinner Pkwy (Suite 300)
Jacksonville, FL 32256-6975
Telephone: (904) 279-1300, (866) 323-
   5577, FAX: (904) 279-1495, Web
   Site: www.hamiltoncollection.com
Mktg Dir: Marianne Graham
Conducts Business: Worldwide
Employees: 400
Primary Market Served: Consumer
Advertising/Marketing Budget Related
   to Direct Marketing: 76-100%

Direct mail marketer of collectible
products.

HAMPSHIRE PEWTER CO

43 Mill St
Wolfeboro, NH 03894
Telephone: (603) 569-4944, (800) 639-
   7704, FAX: (603) 569-4524, E-Mail:
   gifts@hampshirepewter.com, Web
   Site: www.hampshirepewter.com
Pres & Owner: Robert S. Steele
Co-Owner: Jenine Steele
Conducts Business: U.S., Canada
Employees: 15
Primary Market Served: Business &
   Consumer
Catalog available online
Direct online sales
Advertising/Marketing Budget Related
   to Direct Marketing: 0-25%
Founded: 1974
Gross sales or billing: $750,000

Handcast pewter tableware &
ornaments.

HOFFMAN MINT

1400 NW 65th Pl
Fort Lauderdale, FL 33309-1902
Telephone: (831) 625-5333, (800) 227-
   5813, FAX: (831) 649-3318, E-Mail:
   sales@hoffmanmint.com, Web Site:
   www.hoffmanmint.com
Pres & CEO: Michael Hoffman
VP: Terry Spaight
Conducts Business: Worldwide
Primary Market Served: Business &
   Consumer
Catalog available online

Indirect online sales
Founded: 1980

Manufacturer of medals, tokens, name-plates & special coins.

HOUSE OF OLDIES

35 Carmine St Frnt 1
New York, NY 10014-4429
Telephone: (212) 243-0500, FAX:
   (212) 989-1697, E-Mail:
   rabramson@houseofoldies.com, Web
   Site: www.houseofoldies.com
Pres: Robert Abramson
Conducts Business: Worldwide
Primary Market Served: Business &
   Consumer

Sell 45s & LPs. Feature collectors' items & out-of-print records.

HOUSE OF ONYX, INC

120 N Main St, The Aaron Bldg
Greenville, KY 42345-1504
Telephone: (270) 338-2363, (800) 844-3100, FAX: (270) 338-9605, E-Mail:
   sales@houseofonyx.com, Web Site:
   www.houseofonyx.com
VP & Mgr: Charlotte Lewis
Graduate Gemologist: Betsy Smith
Conducts Business: U.S.
Employees: 20
Primary Market Served: Business &
   Consumer
Catalog available online
Direct online sales
Advertising/Marketing Budget Related
   to Direct Marketing: 76-100%
Direct Marketing ad budget: $500,000
Direct Mail: 90%
Magazines: 10%
Founded: 1967
Gross sales or billing: $2,000,000

Fine gemstones, gold jewelry & GIA diamonds.

THE IEI CORP

Subs. of Imperial Enterprises Inc
29 Emmons Dr Ste A30
Princeton, NJ 08540-5994
Telephone: (609) 987-2700, FAX:
   (609) 987-2703
Pres: Yuko Shaub
Conducts Business: Japan
Primary Market Served: Consumer
Founded: 1985

Sell collectibles & luxury merchandise through catalogs to consumers in Japan.

INTERNATIONAL COINS & CURRENCY INC

62 Ridge St
Montpelier, VT 05602

Telephone: (802) 223-6331, FAX:
   (800) 229-3239, Web Site: www.
   iccoin.com
Pres: Michael Boardman
VP, Mktg: John Devitt
Conducts Business: Worldwide
Employees: 20
Primary Market Served: Consumer
Catalog available online
Direct online sales
Advertising/Marketing Budget Related
   to Direct Marketing: 76-100%
Direct Marketing ad budget:
Direct Mail: 60%
Magazines: 20%
Newspapers: 5%
Telephone: 15%
Founded: 1974
Gross sales or billing: $3,500,000

Offer U.S. & world coins & other fine collectibles.

INTERNATIONAL COLLECTORS SOCIETY

Div. of Mystic Stamp Co.
9700 Mill St
Camden, NY 13316-6109
Telephone: (800) 606-3490, FAX:
   (410) 998-9707, E-Mail: info@
   mysticstamp.com, Web Site: www.
   icsnow.com
Pres: Don Sundman
Conducts Business: U.S., Canada
Primary Market Served: Consumer
Advertising/Marketing Budget Related
   to Direct Marketing: 76-100%

Sell rare coins & stamps.

ISLANDS TROPICALS

PO Box 1989
Keaau, HI 96749-1989
Telephone: (808) 961-0606, (800) 367-5155, FAX: (808) 966-7684, Web
   Site: www.islandtropicals.com
Pres & Treas: Mike Goldstein
Mgr: Sharon Cann
Conducts Business: U.S.
Employees: 4
Primary Market Served: Business &
   Consumer
Catalog available online
Direct online sales
Advertising/Marketing Budget Related
   to Direct Marketing: 76-100%
Direct Marketing ad budget: $100,000
Direct Mail: 70%
Magazines: 30%
Founded: 1967
Gross sales or billing: $750,000

Flowers by mail order.

MICHAEL JAFFE STAMPS INC/BROOKMAN STAMP CO

PO Box 61484
Vancouver, WA 98666-1484

Telephone: (360) 695-6161, (800) 782-6770, FAX: (360) 695-1616, E-Mail:
   mjaffe@brookmanstamps.com, Web
   Site: www.brookmanstamps.com
Pres: Michael Jaffe
Conducts Business: U.S., Canada
Employees: 5
Primary Market Served: Consumer
Catalog available online
Direct online sales
Advertising/Marketing Budget Related
   to Direct Marketing: 26-50%
Direct Marketing ad budget: $30,000
Direct Mail: 40%
Magazines: 5%
Newspapers: 47%
Telephone: 8%
Founded: 1975
Gross sales or billing: $1,000,000

Federal, state & foreign duck stamps by subscription at $1.75 over issue price.

BRIAN JENNER INC

PO Box 2466
Pasco, WA 99302
Telephone: (509) 735-2172, FAX:
   (509) 783-8042
Pres: Brian Jenner
Conducts Business: U.S., Canada
Primary Market Served: Consumer

Mail order marketer of rare coins & precious metals.

JONES SCHOOL SUPPLY CO INC

PO Box 2909
Irmo, SC 29063-4009
Telephone: (803) 772-3796, FAX:
   (800) 942-5921, Web Site: www.
   jonesawards.com
Pres: Sarah Jones
Mktg Dir: Shelly O'Quinn-Humphries
Conducts Business: U.S.
Employees: 8
Primary Market Served: Business
Advertising/Marketing Budget Related
   to Direct Marketing: 76-100%
Direct Marketing ad budget:
Direct Mail: 100%
Gross sales or billing: $1,500,000

Academic awards, certificates, medals & pins.

KENMORE STAMP CO

119 West St, PO Box 331
Milford, NH 03055-4855
Telephone: (603) 673-1745, (800) 225-5059, FAX: (603) 673-3222, Web
   Site: www.kenmorestamp.com
Owner: Henry E. Harris Jr.
Conducts Business: United States
Employees: 40
Primary Market Served: Consumer

Catalog available online
Direct online sales
Advertising/Marketing Budget Related
  to Direct Marketing: 76-100%
Direct Marketing ad budget:
Direct Mail: 15%
Magazines: 10%
Newspapers: 50%
Online: 25%
Founded: 1952
Gross sales or billing: $4,800,000

Deals in all aspects of stamp collecting.

MILES KIMBALL CO

PO Box 3600
Oshkosh, WI 54903-3600
Telephone: (920) 231-3800, FAX:
  (920) 231-0422, Web Site: www.
  mileskimball.com
Circulation Mgr: Ryan Hennig
VP Catalog Mktg: Vicki Updike
Primary Market Served: Business &
  Consumer
Advertising/Marketing Budget Related
  to Direct Marketing: 76-100%

Giftwares, housewares, toys & greeting cards.

KING'S CHANDELIER CO

729 S Van Buren Rd (Hwy 14 S)
Eden, NC 27288-5321
Telephone: (336) 623-6188, FAX:
  (336) 627-9935, E-Mail: crystal@
  chandelier.com, Web Site: www.
  chandelier.com
Pres: Franklin K. Ricks
Asst Mgr & Mktg Dir: Nancy Talbert
Conducts Business: Worldwide
Employees: 10
Primary Market Served: Business &
  Consumer
Catalog available online
Direct online sales
Advertising/Marketing Budget Related
  to Direct Marketing: 0-25%
Founded: 1933

Sell chandeliers of imported crystal in original designs. Also wired Victorian gas reproductions of hand polished brass with Victorian crystals. Publish a yearly illustrated catalog of showline chandeliers & sconces.

WILL KIRKPATRICK
SHOREBIRD DECOYS INC

124 Forest Ave
Hudson, MA 01749-2840
Telephone: (978) 562-7841, FAX:
  (978) 562-3514, E-Mail:
  wekdecoys@aol.com, Web Site:
  www.kirkpatrickdecoys.com
Owner: Will Kirkpatrick
Conducts Business: U.S., Canada

Primary Market Served: Business &
  Consumer
Catalog available online
Direct online sales
Founded: 1979

Handmade reproductions of antique decoys & folk art carvings of other whimsical animals - songbirds, cows, fish, frogs, chickens & more. Sell to museum shops, fine galleries & direct mail (retail).

KLAHOWYA NATIVE
AMERICAN & NATURE
GIFT SHOP

4055 Royal Ave SPC 71
Bandon, OR 97402-6823
Telephone: (541) 347-5099, FAX:
  (541) 347-4132
Owner & Mgr: Dianne Galbraith
Gen Mgr: Lynn Elbert
Employees: 3
Primary Market Served: Consumer
Advertising/Marketing Budget Related
  to Direct Marketing: 76-100%
Direct Marketing ad budget:
Newspapers: 100%
Founded: 1994

Gifts related to Native American or Nature theme.

KLITZNER INDUSTRIES

44 Warren St
Providence, RI 02907
Telephone: (401) 751-7500, (800) 556-
  6860, FAX: (800) 556-3199, E-Mail:
  info@klitzner.com, Web Site: www.
  klitzner.com; www.providenceline.
  com
Chmn: Alan Klitzner
COO: Dean Klitzner
Pres: Hank Riccitelli
Conducts Business: U.S., Canada
Employees: 200
Primary Market Served: Consumer
Catalog available online
Direct online sales
Founded: 1907
Gross sales or billing: $10,000,000

Manufacturing emblematic jewelry through direct mail.

KLOCKIT

Div. of Primex
PO Box 636, N3211 Country Rd H
Lake Geneva, WI 53147-0636
Telephone: (262) 248-7000, (800) 556-
  2548, FAX: (262) 248-9899, E-Mail:
  klockit@klockit.com, Web Site:
  www.klockit.com
Mktg Coord: Tammy Roath
Mktg Dir: Barb Heath
Conducts Business: U.S., Canada
Employees: 120

Primary Market Served: Business &
  Consumer
Founded: 1971

Sell clock movements, dials, hands & accessories. Also, clock & toy kits, wood & lamp parts & tools. Books, weather instruments, mini-fit-ups. Retail outlet store in Lake Geneva, WI. Free catalog. Quantity discounts.

LEANIN' TREE INC

6055 Longbow Dr, Box 9800
Boulder, CO 80301
Telephone: (303) 530-7768, (800) 525-
  0656, FAX: (303) 530-5124, E-Mail:
  info@leanintree.com, Web Site:
  www.leanintree.com
Founder & Chmn Bd: Ed Trumble
Pres: Tom Trumble
Sr VP: Jane Trumble
VP: Tim Trumble
Mktg Mgr: Pat Wallace
Conducts Business: U.S., Canada
Employees: 200
Primary Market Served: Business &
  Consumer
Catalog available online
Indirect online sales
Gross sales or billing: $20,000,000

Manufacture & sell Christmas cards, all occasion cards, poster prints & related products through direct mail to consumers & wholesale through dealers.

LEFTY'S CORNER

601 Nichols St, PO Box 615
Clarks Summit, PA 18411-1487
Telephone: (570) 586-LEFT, (570)
  586-5338, FAX: (570) 585-2906,
  E-Mail: info@leftyscorner.com, Web
  Site: www.leftyscorner.com
Owner: Dale Hersh
Co-Owner: Bob Hersh
Conducts Business: U.S.
Employees: 1
Primary Market Served: Business &
  Consumer
Catalog available online
Direct online sales
Advertising/Marketing Budget Related
  to Direct Marketing: 0-25%
Direct Marketing ad budget:
Direct Mail: 25%
Magazines: 25%
Newspapers: 25%
Online: 25%
Founded: 1988
Gross sales or billing: $100,000

Products for lefthanders. Retail & wholesale.

THE DMA LENOX GROUP INC

1414 Radcliffe St
Bristol, PA 19007-5413

Telephone: (267) 525-7800, (800) 223-4311, Web Site: www.lenox.com
Primary Market Served: Business

LILLIAN VERNON CORP
PO Box 35980
Colorado Springs, CO 80935-3598
Telephone: (757) 427-7923, FAX: (757) 427-7819, E-Mail: publicrelations@lillianvernon.com, Web Site: www.lillianvernon.com
Chief Mktg Officer: Kevin Green
Pres & CEO: Michael Muoio
Chief Mktg Officer: Alyce Goodman
VP Fin: Jane Lee
Pub Rels: Phillip Read
Conducts Business: U.S.
Employees: 3,500
Primary Market Served: Consumer
Catalog available online
Direct online sales
Advertising/Marketing Budget Related to Direct Marketing: 76-100%
Direct Marketing ad budget:
Direct Mail: 90%
Newspapers: 5%
TV/Radio: 5%
Founded: 1951

Gift catalogs & website for customers. Publish catalog titles selling 6,000 products.

LIN TERRY
185 6th Ave Ste 4
Paterson, NJ 07524-1247
Telephone: (973) 345-6677, FAX: (973) 345-5551, E-Mail: linterry@aol.com, Web Site: www.linterry.com
Pres: Dan Neufeld
Conducts Business: U.S.
Employees: 5
Primary Market Served: Business & Consumer
Catalog available online
Direct online sales
Advertising/Marketing Budget Related to Direct Marketing: 51-75%
Founded: 1984
Gross sales or billing: $1,000,000

Sports card supplies, acrylic cases for collectibles, custom cases & point of purchases cases, mail order to consumers as well as businesses. Others include, restaurant table tents, acrylic wall mountable menu holders, sign holders, and custom acrylic displays.

LITTLETON COIN CO INC
1309 Mt Eustis Rd
Littleton, NH 03561
Telephone: (603) 444-5386, FAX: (603) 444-0121, E-Mail: jhennessey@littletoncoin.com, Web Site: www.littletoncoin.com
Pres: David Sundman

CFO: Edward Hennessey
COO: Michael Morelli
Mktg Dir: Jeffrey Marsh
Employees: 350
Primary Market Served: Consumer
Catalog available online
Direct online sales
Advertising/Marketing Budget Related to Direct Marketing: 76-100%
Founded: 1945

Sell coins, paper money & ancient coins & supplies to collectors by mail.

MADISONAVEGIFTS.COM
325 Barben Ave
Watertown, NY 13601-4503
Telephone: (315) 779-9228, (866) 421-1744, E-Mail: magsales@madisonavegifts.com, Web Site: www.madisonavegifts.com
Owner: Joan A. Smith
Conducts Business: U.S.
Employees: 5
Primary Market Served: Consumer
Catalog available online
Direct online sales
Advertising/Marketing Budget Related to Direct Marketing: 26-50%
Direct Marketing ad budget: $5,000
Direct Mail: 15%
Magazines: 5%
Newspapers: 5%
Online: 75%
Founded: 2000
Gross sales or billing: $200,000

Upscale online gift store featuring latest products in the gift market today; offering corporate gifts, bridal registry and home decor.

BRUCE MCGAW GRAPHICS
PO Box 1528
Manchester Center, VT 05255-1528
Telephone: (845) 353-8600, (888) 4BMCGAW, FAX: (845) 353-3155, E-Mail: sales@bmcgaw.com, Web Site: www.bmcgaw.com
Pres: Nancy McGaw
CEO: Gyr King
Mgr, Mktg: Alissa Passoff
VP, Sls & Design: Amy Wessan
Supvr Cust Svc: Ursula Carioscia
Conducts Business: U.S., Australia, Canada, Europe, Japan, South Africa, South America
Employees: 100
Primary Market Served: Business
Catalog available online
Direct online sales
Advertising/Marketing Budget Related to Direct Marketing: 51-75%
Direct Marketing ad budget:
Direct Mail: 50%
Magazines: 50%
Founded: 1978

Publisher & distributor of American & European fine art posters.

MEDALS OF AMERICA
114 Southchase Blvd
Fountain Inn, SC 29644-9019
Telephone: (864) 862-0635, (800) 308-0849, FAX: (800) 407-8640, E-Mail: medals@usmedals.com, Web Site: www.usmedals.com
Pres: Linda Foster
Dir: Frank Foster
Conducts Business: U.S.
Employees: 30
Primary Market Served: Consumer
Catalog available online
Direct online sales
Advertising/Marketing Budget Related to Direct Marketing: 76-100%
Direct Marketing ad budget:
Direct Mail: 20%
Magazines: 80%
Founded: 1976

U.S. military medals, display cases & all military insignia.

MERIKS GIFTS
1380 Garnet Ave (Suite E-278)
San Diego, CA 92109-3081
Telephone: (787) 721-0000
Pres: Rey Amble

MUSIC BARN INC
PO Box 1083
Niagara Falls, NY 14304-0383
Telephone: (800) 984-0047, FAX: (905) 513-6918, E-Mail: info@themusicbarn.com, Web Site: www.themusicbarn.com
Pres: Robert Bell
Conducts Business: U.S., Canada
Primary Market Served: Consumer
Catalog available online
Direct online sales
Advertising/Marketing Budget Related to Direct Marketing: 26-50%
Founded: 1985

MUSIC TREASURES CO
Div. of Technical Marketing Inc
PO Box 9138
Richmond, VA 23227-0138
Telephone: (804) 730-8800, (800) 666-7565, FAX: (888) MUSIC-TC, E-Mail: musict@musictreasures.com, Web Site: www.musictreasures.com
Pres & CEO: Daniel J. Tuszynski Jr.
VP Opers: Leslie Radock
Conducts Business: U.S., Canada
Employees: 10
Primary Market Served: Business & Consumer
Catalog available online
Indirect online sales
Advertising/Marketing Budget Related

to Direct Marketing: 51-75%
Direct Marketing ad budget: $480,000
Direct Mail: 90%
Magazines: 10%
Founded: 1985
Gross sales or billing: $2,000,000

Music & dance gift and educational resource items, fund-raising to qualified groups. Over 9000 custom imprinted products, such as totes, mugs, stationery, T's & candy, teaching resources, awards, trophies, certificates, stationery, videos & CDs.

MYSTIC SEAPORT MUSEUM STORES

75 Greenmanville Ave
Mystic, CT 06355-0990
Telephone: (860) 572-5315, (860) 572-0711, FAX: (860) 572-5324, Web Site: www.mysticseaport.org
Mdsg Dir: Jane Wilkins
Conducts Business: Worldwide
Employees: 75
Primary Market Served: Business & Consumer
Direct Marketing ad budget:
Direct Mail: 90%
Magazines: 8%
Newspapers: 2%

Sells nautical merchandise.

NARROW WAY

712 Moraga Rd
Lafayette, CA 94549-4916
Telephone: (925) 283-4074
Mgr: Olajire Idowu
Conducts Business: U.S.
Employees: 2
Primary Market Served: Consumer
Advertising/Marketing Budget Related to Direct Marketing: 26-50%
Founded: 1993
Gross sales or billing: $110,000

Egg yolk separator, skirt printing, bumper stickers, mugs, flyers & logos.

NATIONAL PEN CORP

12121 Scripps Summit Dr (Suite 200)
San Diego, CA 92131-4609
Telephone: (858) 675-3000, FAX: (858) 675-3030, Web Site: www.pens.com
Pres: Tom Liguory
Sr VP, Direct Mktg: Ron Childs
VP Mktg: Mike Delaney
Conducts Business: Worldwide
Employees: 1,000
Primary Market Served: Business
Catalog available online
Direct online sales
Advertising/Marketing Budget Related to Direct Marketing: 76-100%
Founded: 1966

Gross sales or billing: $100,000,000
Manufacturer & distributor of imprinted products, ball point pens, key tags & calendars.

NEW YORK FINDINGS

17625 Union Tpke, PMB 402
Fresh Meadows, NY 11366-1515
Telephone: (212) 925-5745, FAX: (212) 925-5870, E-Mail: nyfindings@aol.com, Web Site: www.newyorkfindings.com
Pres: Cheryl Kerber
Conducts Business: U.S., Canada
Primary Market Served: Business
Advertising/Marketing Budget Related to Direct Marketing: 76-100%

Sells "findings."

NOWETAH'S AMERICAN INDIAN STORE & MUSEUM

2 Colegrove Rd
New Portland, ME 04961-3821
Telephone: (207) 628-4991, Web Site: www.nowetahs.webs.com
Pres, Owner & Purchaser: Mrs. Nowetah Cyr
Purchaser: Mr. Tom Cyr
Artist: Wahleyah Black
Conducts Business: U.S., Canada, U.K., Japan, Italy, Germany, France
Employees: 2
Primary Market Served: Consumer
Advertising/Marketing Budget Related to Direct Marketing: 0-25%
Direct Marketing ad budget:
Magazines: 10%
Newspapers: 85%
TV/Radio: 5%
Founded: 1968
Gross sales or billing: $60,000

American Indian art, gifts, and collectibles. Mail order & retail store selling & manufacturing hand-woven Indian rugs, baskets, pottery, bead jewelry, leather goods & gifts. Receive a free brochure listing the 12 different catalogs available by sending a S.A.S.E. Educational classes on history, wild plants and herbs as food and medicines are also conducted for schools and scouts.

ONE WORLD PROJECTS

43 Ellicott Ave
Batavia, NY 14020-2010
Telephone: (585) 343-4490, FAX: (585) 344-3551, E-Mail: sales@oneworldprojects.com, Web Site: www.oneworldprojects.com
Owner, Pres: Phil Smith
Employees: 7
Primary Market Served: Business
Catalog available online

Direct online sales
Founded: 1992
Gross sales or billing: $800,000

Wholesale distribution of forest harvest material products & forest preservation products.

OOMINGMAK MUSK OX PRODUCERS COOPERATIVE

604 "H" St
Anchorage, AK 99501
Telephone: (907) 272-9225, (888) 360-9665, FAX: (907) 258-4225, E-Mail: oomingmak@qiviut.com, Web Site: www.qiviut.com
Pres: Mesonga Atkinson
Exec Dir: Ms. Sigrun C. Robertson
Conducts Business: U.S.
Employees: 7
Primary Market Served: Consumer
Catalog available online
Indirect online sales
Founded: 1969
Gross sales or billing: $1,000,000

Hand-knitted hats & scarves from the underwool of the Musk Ox. Made by cooperative members & Eskimo women from remote Alaskan villages.

PACIFIC SPIRIT CORP

1334 Pacific Ave
Forest Grove, OR 97116-2315
Telephone: (503) 357-1566, (800) 634-9057, FAX: (503) 357-1699, Web Site: www.pacificspiritcatalogs.com
Pres: Mark Kenzer
Conducts Business: U.S.
Employees: 15
Primary Market Served: Consumer
Direct online sales
Advertising/Marketing Budget Related to Direct Marketing: 76-100%
Direct Marketing ad budget:
Direct Mail: 98%
Magazines: 2%
Founded: 1984

Mail order gifts & collectibles.

PARADISE GALLERIES

PO Box 57086
Irvine, CA 92619-7086
Telephone: (858) 793-4000, FAX: (858) 793-3425, E-Mail: omancinelli@paradisegalleries.com, Web Site: www.paradisegalleries.com
Pres: David Brownlee
VP New Mkts & Wholesale: Ozzie Mancinelli
Primary Market Served: Consumer

Porcelain dolls.

PARMER BOOKS
7644 Forrestal Rd
San Diego, CA 92120-2203
Telephone: (619) 287-0693, E-Mail:
    parmerbook@aol.com, Web Site:
    www.parmerbook.com
Owner: Jean Marie Parmer
Conducts Business: Worldwide
Employees: 3
Primary Market Served: Consumer
Catalog available online
Direct online sales
Advertising/Marketing Budget Related
    to Direct Marketing: 76-100%
Direct Marketing ad budget:
Direct Mail: 15%
Online: 85%
Founded: 1983

Rare & out of print books to collectors
& libraries.

**PARTY KITS & EQUESTRIAN
    GIFTS**
10920 Plantside Dr Ste C
Louisville, KY 40299-6113
Telephone: (502) 425-2126, (800) 99-
    DERBY, FAX: (502) 425-5230,
    E-Mail: info@partykits.com, Web
    Site: www.derbygifts.com
Pres: Becky Biesel
Conducts Business: Worldwide
Employees: 10
Primary Market Served: Business &
    Consumer
Catalog available online
Direct online sales
Advertising/Marketing Budget Related
    to Direct Marketing: 76-100%
Direct Marketing ad budget:
Direct Mail: 90%
Magazines: 5%
Newspapers: 3%
TV/Radio: 2%
Founded: 1979
Gross sales or billing: $1,000,000

Equestrian party supplies, fine equine
gifts & Kentucky delicacies for horse
lovers, party supply stores & tack
shops.

PERSONAL CREATIONS
1005 101st St Ste A
Lemont, IL 60439-9628
Telephone: (630) 783-2400, (866) 834-
    7695, Web Site: www.
    personalcreations.com
Dir, Mktg: Judy Nelson
Primary Market Served: Consumer

Mail order personalized gifts.

PHARMART
Div. of Healthcare Logistics
PO Box 400
Circleville, OH 43113-0400
Telephone: (860) 932-8588, (800) 848-
    1633, FAX: (800) 477-2923, Web
    Site: www.healthcarelogistics.com/
    Pharmart
Owner: Gary Sharp
Owner: Bethany Reid
Conducts Business: U.S., Canada
Employees: 3
Primary Market Served: Business &
    Consumer
Catalog available online
Direct online sales
Advertising/Marketing Budget Related
    to Direct Marketing: 76-100%
Direct Marketing ad budget: $150,000
Direct Mail: 90%
Telephone: 10%
Founded: 1990
Gross sales or billing: $700,000

Gifts & collectibles to the pharmacy
profession.

**BUD PLANT ILLUSTRATED
    BOOKS**
3809 Laguna Ave
Palo Alto, CA 94306-2629
Telephone: (650) 493-1191, FAX:
    (650) 493-1145, E-Mail: jim@bpib.
    com, Web Site: www.bpib.com
Owner: Jim Vadeboncoeur Jr.
Conducts Business: Worldwide
Employees: 3
Primary Market Served: Business &
    Consumer
Catalog available online
Indirect online sales
Advertising/Marketing Budget Related
    to Direct Marketing: 0-25%
Founded: 1987

Out-of-print illustrated books to collectors, artists & libraries.

POSH PAPERS
73 Terrace Ave
Riverside, RI 02915-4726
Telephone: (401) 331-9873, FAX:
    (401) 331-2229, E-Mail: info@
    poshpapersonline.com, Web Site:
    www.poshpapersonline.com
Owner: Judi Boren
Conducts Business: U.S.
Employees: 2
Primary Market Served: Business &
    Consumer
Catalog available online
Direct online sales
Advertising/Marketing Budget Related
    to Direct Marketing: 0-25%
Direct Marketing ad budget:
Direct Mail: 75%
Magazines: 25%
Founded: 1983
Gross sales or billing: $100,000

Personalized handcrafted note cards by
mail order - over 50 gift boxed
assortments.

THE DMA POTPOURRI GROUP INC
222 Mill Rd
Chelmsford, MA 01824-4127
Telephone: (978) 256-4100, FAX:
    (978) 256-1961/0344, Web Site:
    www.potpourrigroup.com
Buyer (Nature's Jewelry): Gwen House
Buyer (The Stitchery): Donna Saiia
Buyer (Potpourri): Peter Maloney
Buyer (Expressions): Doug Star
Sr VP Mktg: Bob Webb
Buyer (Back In The Saddle): Mikako
    Fukagawa
Buyer (In The Company of Dogs):
    Kim Kavanagh
Buyer (Serengeti): Peri Siegel
Buyer (The Pyramid Collection): Terry
    Renwick
Circulation Dir: David Wilson
Buyer (Catalog Favorites): Kathy Har-
    vey
Buyer (NorthStyle): Caitlin Palange
Buyer (Whatever Works): Mark Fair-
    man
Buyer (Young Explorers): Clarisse
    Cowdery
Buyer (Country Store): Katy Halligan
CEO: John Fleischmann
Employees: 700
Primary Market Served: Consumer
Direct online sales
Advertising/Marketing Budget Related
    to Direct Marketing: 76-100%

Nature, wildlife and gift catalogs.
Spiritual, ethnic & self-help. Affiliates:
Nature's Jewelry; The Stitchery; Pot-
pourri; Expressions: Back in the
Saddle; In The Company of Dogs;
Serengeti; The Pyramid Collection;
Catalog Favorites; NorthStyle; What-
ever Works; Young Explorers; Country
Store.

REDENVELOPE INC
4840 Eastgate Mall
San Diego, CA 92121-1977
Telephone: (619) 528-4888, (877) 733-
    3683, Web Site: www.redenvelope.
    com
Pres & CEO: Alison May
Circulation Dir: Steve Fleming
Dir Online Mktg: Myles Felsing
Conducts Business: U.S.
Primary Market Served: Business &
    Consumer
Catalog available online
Advertising/Marketing Budget Related
    to Direct Marketing: 76-100%
Founded: 1999

Gifts for major gift giving and everyday occasions, decorative items for the home, jewelry, plants and flowers, and baby gifts.

ROGERS & ROSENTHAL INC

2150 Center Ave Apt 21E
Fort Lee, NJ 07024-5805
Telephone: (201) 346-1862, FAX: (201) 947-5812
Pres: Gerald Rosenthal
Conducts Business: U.S.
Employees: 1
Primary Market Served: Consumer
Advertising/Marketing Budget Related to Direct Marketing: 0-25%
Direct Marketing ad budget:
Direct Mail: 50%
Telephone: 50%
Founded: 1940
Gross sales or billing: $400,000

Silver, china, crystal, pewter & stainless table top items.

THE DMA ROSS-SIMONS

9 Ross Simons Dr
Cranston, RI 02920-4475
Telephone: (401) 463-3100, (800) 835-0919, FAX: (401) 463-8599, Web Site: www.ross-simons.com
Pres & CEO: Darrell S. Ross
VP Mktg: Larry Davis
Exec VP & COO: Robert Simone
Internet Mktg Dir: Mario Protano
VP HR: Tom Gibson
Conducts Business: U.S., Japan
Employees: 500
Primary Market Served: Business & Consumer
Catalog available online
Direct online sales
Advertising/Marketing Budget Related to Direct Marketing: 76-100%
Founded: 1952
Gross sales or billing: $166,000,000

Sells fine jewelry, china, silver, crystal, giftware & home decor.

RUBBER STAMPS OF AMERICA

1110 Main St
Dublin, NH 03444
Telephone: (800) 553-5031, FAX: (603) 563-8102, E-Mail: stampusa@verizon.net, Web Site: www.stampusa.com
Partner: Laurie Indenbaum
Partner: Andy Toepfer
Conducts Business: Worldwide
Employees: 4
Primary Market Served: Business & Consumer
Advertising/Marketing Budget Related to Direct Marketing: 76-100%

Manufactures & sells pictorial rubber stamps used to make artwork out of stationery, invitations & to decorate paperwork.

THE DMA SAE INTERNATIONAL

400 Commonwealth Dr
Warrendale, PA 15086-7511
Telephone: (724) 776-4841, Web Site: www.sae.org
Mktg Mgr: Marcy Estok

ST LAWRENCE ISLAND ORIGINAL IVORY COOPERATIVE

PO Box 189
Gambell, AK 99742
Telephone: (907) 985-5707, FAX: (907) 985-5927
Mgr: William Soonagrook Jr.
Conducts Business: U.S.
Employees: 1
Primary Market Served: Business & Consumer
Founded: 1982

Original Ivory carvings made from walrus & whale bone.

ST LOUIS SLOT MACHINE CO

9617 Dielman Rock Island Industrial Dr
Saint Louis, MO 63132-2149
Telephone: (314) 432-1699, E-Mail: stlslot@earthlink.net, Web Site: www.stlouisslot.com
Pres: Tom Kolbrener
Mgr: Marty Wilke
Conducts Business: U.S.
Employees: 4
Primary Market Served: Business & Consumer
Advertising/Marketing Budget Related to Direct Marketing: 0-25%
Founded: 1979

Antique slot machines, neon signs & decoratives, old soda machines & jukeboxes.

SAUNDERS MILITARY INSIGNIA

PO Box 1831
Naples, FL 34106-1831
Telephone: (239) 298-8228, (800) 442-3133, FAX: (239) 774-3323, E-Mail: info@saundersinsignia.com, Web Site: www.saundersinsignia.com
Mgr: Earl Keaton
Conducts Business: U.S.
Primary Market Served: Business & Consumer
Catalog available online
Direct online sales
Advertising/Marketing Budget Related

to Direct Marketing: 0-25%
Founded: 1968

A large retail insignia company with over 14,000 different patches, badges, wings, ribbons & medals plus 100 different publications on insignia. Sell to veterans & collectors.

SCHWARTZ & CO

524 Bloomfield Ave
Verona, NJ 07044
Telephone: (973) 571-2160, (800) 526-1440, FAX: (973) 571-2165, E-Mail: swartzandcompany@gmail.com, Web Site: www.natschwartz.com
Pres: Rose Schwartz
VP: Larry Schwartz
Gen Mgr: Marilyn Schwartz
Conducts Business: U.S.
Employees: 25
Primary Market Served: Consumer
Direct online sales
Advertising/Marketing Budget Related to Direct Marketing: 76-100%
Direct Marketing ad budget:
Direct Mail: 75%
Magazines: 20%
Newspapers: 5%
Founded: 1979

China, crystal, flatware, gifts, collectibles & housewares (most major manufacturers). Also maintains a national bridal registry service.

L.H. SELMAN LTD

410 S Michigan Ave Ste 207
Chicago, IL 60605-1448
Telephone: (831) 427-1177, (800) 538-0766, FAX: (831) 427-0111
Pres: L.H. Selman
Conducts Business: Worldwide
Employees: 13
Primary Market Served: Business & Consumer

Catalog marketer of paperweights and art glass sold mainly to collectors & retail gift shops.

B SHACKMAN & CO INC

9964 W Miller Dr
Galesburg, MI 49053
Telephone: (269) 484-1000, (800) 221-7656, FAX: (269) 484-1010, Web Site: www.shackman.com
Pres: Dan Durrett
Mgr: Johanna Durrett
Mgr: Jason Durrett
Conducts Business: U.S., Canada, England, Germany
Employees: 35
Primary Market Served: Business & Consumer
Catalog available online
Direct online sales
Direct Marketing ad budget:

Direct Mail: 85%
TV/Radio: 5%
Telephone: 10%
Founded: 1898
Gross sales or billing: $5,000,000

Turn of the century paper novelties: greeting cards, children's picture books, stickers, favors, toys, tree trims, etc. Sells to gift shops, boutiques & stationery shops.

THE SHARPER IMAGE
1450 Broadway Fl 4
New York, NY 10018-2204
Telephone: (415) 445-6000, (800) 344-5555, FAX: (800) 552-2525, E-Mail: info@sharperimage.com, Web Site: www.sharperimage.com
CEO: Richard Thalheimer
COO: Tracy Wan
Pub Rels: Molly Madrigal
Conducts Business: U.S., Japan, Saudi Arabia, Switzerland
Employees: 1,500
Primary Market Served: Consumer
Catalog available online
Direct online sales
Advertising/Marketing Budget Related to Direct Marketing: 76-100%
Founded: 1977
Gross sales or billing: $217,000,000

Develop, introduce & sell original gifts & products through stores, catalogs & other marketing channels.

SMITHSONIAN INSTITUTION
Div. of Smithsonian Institution
PO Box 37012, SI Bldg, Room 153 MRC 010
Washington, DC 20013-7012
Telephone: (202) 357-2700, Web Site: www.si.edu
CEO: Tom Oh
VP: Jeanny Kim
Dir: Era C. Marshall
Conducts Business: U.S.
Catalog available online
Indirect online sales

Gift items based primarily on reproductions & adaptations of objects in the Smithsonian collection.

ALBERT S SMYTH CO INC
Smyth Jewelers
2020 York Rd
Timonium, MD 21093
Telephone: (410) 252-6666, (800) 638-3333, FAX: (410) 252-2355, E-Mail: smyth@albertsmyth.com, Web Site: www.albertsmyth.com
Mktg Pres: Tom Smyth
Mktg Dir: Ruth Ann Carroll
Conducts Business: U.S.
Employees: 180
Primary Market Served: Consumer

Catalog available online
Direct online sales
Founded: 1914

Retail store marketing nationally through catalogs. Products include china, crystal, silver, watches, clocks, jewelry & diamonds at discounted prices. Showroom located at company address.

SOITENLY STOOGES
Subs. of C3 Entertainment Inc
1415 Gardena Ave
Glendale, CA 91204-2709
Telephone: (818) 543-0778, (800) 543-0778, FAX: (818) 543-0779, E-Mail: custserv@threestooges.com, Web Site: www.soitenlystooges.com
Pres: Earl Benjamin
Dir, Mktg: Eric Lamond
VP, Licensing: Ani Khachoian
Conducts Business: U.S.
Primary Market Served: Consumer
Catalog available online
Direct online sales
Founded: 1989

Soitenly Stooges is licensed by Comedy III Productions to sell and market official "Three Stooges" products nationally through the mail order operation.

SOTHEBY'S
1334 York Ave at 72nd St
New York, NY 10021-4806
Telephone: (212) 606-7000, FAX: (212) 606-7107, Web Site: www.sothebys.com
Chmn: Michael I. Sovern
Pres & CEO: William F. Rupricht
Pres Sotheby's Fin Svcs & Sotheby's Ventures Intl: Mitchell Zuckerman
Exec VP & CFO: William Sheridan
Exec VP & CEO Sotheby's Intl: Robin G. Woodhead
Conducts Business: Worldwide
Employees: 1,497
Primary Market Served: Business & Consumer
Catalog available online
Indirect online sales
Gross sales or billing: $664,800,000

Provides auction catalogs & art books, covering a complete range of art & collectibles to galleries, dealers & individual collectors.

SOUNDPRINTS
Div. of Trudy Corp
353 Main Ave
Norwalk, CT 06851-1552
Telephone: (800) 228-7839, FAX: (203) 846-1776, E-Mail: soundprints@soundprints.com, Web Site: www.soundprints.com

Pres: William Burnham
Conducts Business: U.S., Canada
Employees: 16
Primary Market Served: Business & Consumer
Catalog available online
Indirect online sales
Founded: 1947
Gross sales or billing: $6,000,000

Children's storybooks, audio cassettes, dolls & stuffed animals sold to retailers, wholesalers & direct mail consumers.

THE SPERRY & HUTCHINSON CO INC
S&H Green Points
1625 S Congress Ave
Delray Beach, FL 33445
Telephone: (561) 454-7621, FAX: (561) 265-2493, E-Mail: mediarelations@shsolutions.com, Web Site: www.greenpoints.com
Sr Mgr: Dianne Morris
Conducts Business: U.S.
Employees: 1,300
Primary Market Served: Business

Electronic incentive promotions.

STEUBEN GLASS
Div. of Corning Inc
667 Madison Ave Lowr Level
New York, NY 10065-8029
Telephone: (607) 974-8659, (800) STEUBEN, FAX: (607) 974-8441, E-Mail: info@steuben.com, Web Site: www.steuben.com
Chmn: Wendell P. Weaks
Pres & CEO: Marie McKee
Sr VP: Dr. Jean-Fierre Mazeau
Gen Mgr: Peter J. Aagaard
Conducts Business: U.S.
Employees: 210
Primary Market Served: Business & Consumer
Catalog available online
Direct online sales
Advertising/Marketing Budget Related to Direct Marketing: 51-75%
Founded: 1903

Decorative crystal accessories for home & office.

STICKERS 'N' STUFF INC
245 W Sycamore Ln
Louisville, CO 80027-2235
Telephone: (303) 661-0200, E-Mail: sales@stickersnstuff.com, Web Site: www.stickersnstuff.biz
Pres: Marilyn McVoy
Conducts Business: U.S., Belgium, Japan
Employees: 1
Primary Market Served: Consumer

Catalog available online
Direct online sales
Advertising/Marketing Budget Related
  to Direct Marketing: 0-25%
Direct Marketing ad budget: $20,000
Direct Mail: 50%
Magazines: 50%
Founded: 1980
Gross sales or billing: $50,000

Prism, glitter, holographic, fuzzy, flowers, butterflies, hummingbirds, teddy bears, unicorn & other assorted stickers. Send $2 for samples & catalog.

SUN HARVEST CITRUS

14810 Metro Pkwy
Fort Myers, FL 33912-4307
Telephone: (239) 768-2686, (800) 743-1480, FAX: (239) 768-9255, E-Mail: info@sunharvestcitrus.com, Web Site: www.SunHarvestCitrus.com
Pres: David McKenzie
Co-Owner & Mgr: Sandy McKenzie
VP: Jr. Robert Edsall
Mktg Mgr: Tina Giufre
Primary Market Served: Business & Consumer
Catalog available online
Direct online sales
Founded: 1940

Mail order gifts & fruit.

SUNDANCE CATALOG CO

3865 W 2400 S
Salt Lake City, UT 84120-7212
Telephone: (801) 973-2711, (800) 422-2770, FAX: (801) 973-4989, E-Mail: jessica.bassin@sundance.net, Web Site: www.sundancecatalog.com
Pres & CEO: Bruce Willard
Primary Market Served: Consumer
Catalog available online
Direct online sales

Gift items, jewelry, clothing & home furnishings.

TVC ENTERPRISES AND THE TV COLLECTOR MAGAZINE

6704 Fruit Flower Ave
Las Vegas, NV 89130
Telephone: (760) 495-7956, E-Mail: tvcinquiries@happyretrogirl.com, Web Site: www.angelfire.com/ma/tvcollector/home.html
Owner: Diane Albert
Conducts Business: U.S., Canada
Employees: 2
Primary Market Served: Business & Consumer
Catalog available online
Indirect online sales
Advertising/Marketing Budget Related

to Direct Marketing: 0-25%
Founded: 1980

TV, movie & rock 'n roll memorabilia catalog. Memorabilia catalog is online only; no hard copies available. TV nostalgia magazine "The TV Collector" no longer published, but all back issues still available.

TAILWINDS INC

775 E Blithedale (#166)
Mill Valley, CA 94941-1554
Telephone: (415) 927-4242, (800) TAILWIND, FAX: (415) 927-0199, E-Mail: service@tailwinds.com, Web Site: www.tailwinds.com
Owner: Nancy Palozola
Conducts Business: U.S.
Primary Market Served: Business & Consumer
Catalog available online
Direct online sales
Founded: 1986

Aviation gifts & software.

TENDER HEART TREASURES

Subs. of Synergy4 Enterprises, Inc.
11005 E Cir
Omaha, NE 68137-1228
Telephone: (402) 593-1313, (800) 443-1367, FAX: (402) 593-1316, E-Mail: bcamenzind@thtdesigns.com
Pres & CEO: Mimi Quinn
Controller: Maureen Smallwood
Dir Mktg & Creative: Betty Camenzind
Dir Inventory Mngmt & Contact Center: Christi Bowling Karschner
Dir Fulfillment Center: Scott Gerdes
Conducts Business: US, Canada
Primary Market Served: Consumer
Direct online sales
Advertising/Marketing Budget Related
  to Direct Marketing: 76-100%
Founded: 1987

Consumer mail order products, sold through catalogs & online.

THINGS DECO

130 E 18th St (Suite 8F)
New York, NY 10003-2416
Telephone: (212) 362-8961, E-Mail: thingsdeco@hotmail.com, Web Site: www.thingsdeco.com
Owner, Pres: Harriet Seltzer
Creative: Bob Josen
Conducts Business: U.S., Canada, U.K., Australia, New Zealand, Europe
Employees: 2
Primary Market Served: Business & Consumer
Catalog available online
Indirect online sales
Advertising/Marketing Budget Related

to Direct Marketing: 76-100%
Direct Marketing ad budget:
Direct Mail: 90%
Magazines: 5%
Newspapers: 2%
Online: 3%
Founded: 1994

Consumer gift catalog with products of Art Deco and early 20th century design.

THINGS REMEMBERED

Subs. of Cole National Corp
5500 Avion Park Dr
Highland Heights, OH 44143-1992
Telephone: (440) 473-2000, (866) 902-4438, FAX: (440) 473-2018, E-Mail: customerservice@thingsremembered.com, Web Site: www.thingsremembered.com
Chmn, Pres & CEO: Michael F. Anthony
Sr VP Store Sls & Opers: Ron Batts
VP HR: Alice Guiney
Mktg Dir: Michael Bargas
Sr VP Mktg: Tony Chivari
Employees: 4,000
Primary Market Served: Business & Consumer
Advertising/Marketing Budget Related
  to Direct Marketing: 0-25%
Direct Marketing ad budget:
Direct Mail: 100%
Founded: 1945
Gross sales or billing: $300,000,000

Retailer of personalized gifts.

THOMPSON CIGAR CO

5401 Hangar Ct
Tampa, FL 33634
Telephone: (813) 884-6344, (800) 237-2559, FAX: (813) 882-4605, Web Site: www.thompsoncigar.com
Pres: R.M. Franzblau
Conducts Business: U.S.
Employees: 400
Primary Market Served: Consumer
Catalog available online
Indirect online sales
Advertising/Marketing Budget Related
  to Direct Marketing: 76-100%

Sells cigars, pipes, tobacco & gift items through direct mail.

TIFFANY & CO

600 Madison Ave Fl 4
New York, NY 10022-1689
Telephone: (212) 755-8000, FAX: (212) 320-7550, Web Site: www.tiffany.com
Pres: Mike Kowolaski
CFO: James Fernandez
Sr VP Mktg: Caroline Naggiar
VP Direct Mktg: Kevin O'Halloran
Primary Market Served: Consumer

Retail jeweler.

THE DMA TRUMBLE GREETINGS
6055 Longbow Dr
Boulder, CO 80301-3203
Telephone: (800) 525-0656, FAX:
(303) 530-5124, E-Mail: info@
leanintree.com, Web Site: www.
leanintree.com
Dir Consumer Svcs: Dana Pauley
Direct Mktg Analyst: Jean-Marie
Peirce
CFO & COO: Pete Mahlstedt
Mgr Order Entry & Customer Svc:
Marcia Soderberg
Conducts Business: U.S., Canada
Primary Market Served: Business &
Consumer
Catalog available online
Direct online sales
Advertising/Marketing Budget Related
to Direct Marketing: 76-100%
Direct Marketing ad budget:
Direct Mail: 80%
Online: 20%
Founded: 1949

Fine-art greeting cards and gifts for
consumers and businesses.

TURNCRAFT CLOCKS INC
4310 Shoreline Dr
Spring Park, MN 55384-9722
Telephone: (952) 471-9573, (800) 544-
1711, FAX: (952) 471-8579, E-Mail:
office@meiselwoodhobby.com, Web
Site: www.meiselwoodhobby.com
Owner & Mgr: Eric Meisel
Owner: Greg Meisel
Pres: Paul Meisel
Conducts Business: U.S.
Primary Market Served: Business &
Consumer
Catalog available online
Direct online sales
Advertising/Marketing Budget Related
to Direct Marketing: 26-50%
Direct Marketing ad budget:
Direct Mail: 100%
Founded: 1972

Clock plans, kits, movements, dials,
hardware & fit-ups (inserts).

THE DMA UNICOVER CORP
1 Unicover Ctr
Cheyenne, WY 82008-0001
Telephone: (307) 771-3000, (800) 443-
3232, FAX: (307) 771-3134, E-Mail:
qands@unicover.com, Web Site:
www.unicover.com
Pres & CEO: James A. Willms
VP, Client Svcs: Larry Schoeler
Conducts Business: U.S., Canada
Primary Market Served: Business &
Consumer
Catalog available online

Direct online sales
Advertising/Marketing Budget Related
to Direct Marketing: 76-100%
Founded: 1968

Marketer of postage stamps and original art. Supplier of services including
advertising agency and packaging.

US CAVALRY
2855 Centennial Ave
Radcliff, KY 40160-9000
Telephone: (270) 351-1164, FAX:
(270) 352-0266, E-Mail: hq@
uscavalry.com, Web Site: www.
uscavalry.com
Pres: Randy Acton
Opers Dir: Ron Miller
Conducts Business: Worldwide
Employees: 300
Primary Market Served: Consumer
Indirect online sales
Advertising/Marketing Budget Related
to Direct Marketing: 51-75%
Direct Marketing ad budget:
$7,000,000
Direct Mail: $6,880,000
Magazines: $100,000
Newspapers: $20,000
Founded: 1973
Gross sales or billing: $45,000,000

Sells to civilian, military & law enforcement markets: gifts, jewelry,
books, boots, shoes, military equipment, uniforms, police equipment, martial arts & adventure equipment. Stores
located in Radcliff, Louisville & Oak
Grove, KY, Fayetteville, NC, Columbus, GA & Kileen, TX.

US FUND FOR UNICEF
125 Maiden Ln
New York, NY 10038-4912
Telephone: (212) 686-5522, FAX:
(212) 779-1679, Web Site: www.
unicefusa.org
Dir: Wendy Miller
Mng Dir: Christine Squires
Mng Dir, Direct Mktg: Helene
Vallone-Raffaele
Conducts Business: U.S.
Employees: 200
Primary Market Served: Business &
Consumer
Catalog available online
Founded: 1947

Sells UNICEF cards & gifts to consumers & businesses through catalogs.

VERMONT TEDDY BEAR CO
6655 Shelburne Rd
Shelburne, VT 05482

Telephone: (802) 985-3001, (800) 829-
BEAR, (800) 282-3131, FAX: (802)
985-1304, E-Mail: info@vtbear.com,
Web Site: www.vermontteddybear.
com
Pres & CEO: Elisabeth Robert
Conducts Business: U.S.
Employees: 289
Primary Market Served: Business &
Consumer
Catalog available online
Advertising/Marketing Budget Related
to Direct Marketing: 76-100%
Direct Marketing ad budget:
$5,000,000
Direct Mail: 36%
Magazines: 2%
Newspapers: 2%
TV/Radio: 60%
Founded: 1984
Gross sales or billing: $7,200,000

Manufactures custom teddy bears and
sells them as gifts & collectibles. Sells
other merchandise with the teddy bear
theme.

VILLAGE COIN SHOP
Div. of USG Inc
51C Plaistow Rd
Plaistow, NH 03865
Telephone: (603) 382-5492/7151, FAX:
(603) 382-5682, E-Mail: don@
villagecoin.com, Web Site: www.
villagecoin.com
Owner & Pres: Domenic J. Mangano
Conducts Business: U.S., Canada
Employees: 5
Primary Market Served: Business &
Consumer
Catalog available online
Indirect online sales
Advertising/Marketing Budget Related
to Direct Marketing: 76-100%
Direct Marketing ad budget: $110,000
Direct Mail: 40%
Magazines: 5%
Newspapers: 10%
TV/Radio: 5%
Telephone: 40%
Founded: 1959
Gross sales or billing: $2,000,000

Sell coin and coin supplies to the individual collector.

**WINTERTHUR MUSEUM &
COUNTRY ESTATE**
5105 Kennett Pike
Wilmington, DE 19735
Telephone: (302) 888-4600, (800) 448-
3883, FAX: (302) 888-4730, E-Mail:
tourinfo@winterthur.org, Web Site:
www.winterthur.org
CEO & Dir: Leslie Greene Bowman
DM Gen Mgr: Bonnie Maradonna

Dir of Mktg Commun: Lynn Davis-
  Trier
Media Rels Mgr: Hillary K. Holland
Sr Mgr Adv & Mktg: Lynne Boyle
Conducts Business: U.S.
Employees: 200
Direct online sales
Gross sales or billing: $60,000,000

Collection of American decorative arts
- 175 display rooms; galleries &
changing exhibitions; naturalistic
garden. Direct mail catalog sells reproductions, gifts, home accessories &
plants.

ZALE CORP

901 W Walnut Hill Ln
Irving, TX 75038-1001
Telephone: (972) 580-4376, Web Site:
  www.zalecorp.com
VP E-Commerce: Vicki Spencer
Primary Market Served: Business &
  Consumer

ABBOTT
100 Abbott Park Rd
North Chicago, IL 60064-3502
Telephone: (847) 937-8641, FAX:
(847) 937-9555, Web Site: www.
abbott.com
Chmn Bd & CEO: Miles White
Dir Corp Mktg: Mitchell West
Exec VP, Corp Devel: Richard W. Ashley
Conducts Business: Worldwide
Employees: 65,000
Primary Market Served: Business &
Consumer
Founded: 1888
Gross sales or billing: $22,500,000,000

Healthcare company.

ACURIAN
2 Walnut Grove (Suite 375)
Horsham, PA 19044-2286
Telephone: (215) 323-9000, Web Site:
www.acurian.com
VP Mktg: Scott Connor
Primary Market Served: Consumer

ADVANCED MEDICAL NUTRITION INC
Subs. of HVL, LLC
600 Boyce Rd
Pittsburgh, PA 15205-9742
Telephone: (412) 494-0100, (800) 879-
2664, (800) 437-8888, FAX: (888)
245-4440, Web Site: www.
douglaslabs.com
Pres: Douglas L. Lioon
SVP Sls Mktg: Anthony Wasson
Conducts Business: Worldwide
Employees: 275
Primary Market Served: Business &
Consumer
Catalog available online
Direct online sales
Advertising/Marketing Budget Related
to Direct Marketing: 76-100%
Direct Marketing ad budget:
Direct Mail: 85%
Telephone: 15%
Gross sales or billing: $500,000

Manufacturer & wholesale distributor
of vitamins & nutritional supplements
to Gaines Nutrition & Vitamin Shoppe
Inc.

ALIMED INC
297 High St
Dedham, MA 02026-2898
Telephone: (781) 329-2900, (800) 225-
2610, FAX: (781) 329-8392, (800)
437-2966, E-Mail: info@alimed.com,
Web Site: www.alimed.info
Pres: Julian Cherubini

Conducts Business: U.S.
Employees: 150
Primary Market Served: Business &
Consumer
Catalog available online
Direct online sales
Founded: 1972

Orthopedic, occupational & physical
therapy products. Products for Alzheimer's, wound management, speech
therapy & ergonomics.

THE DMA ALLSTATE MOTOR CLUB, INC
302 Wilmot Rd Ste 101
Deerfield, IL 60015-4618
Telephone: (847) 914-2972, FAX:
(847) 914-2804, Web Site: www.
walgreens.com
Chmn & CEO: Jeffrey A. Rein
Pres & COO: Gregory D. Wasson
Sr VP & CFO: William A. Rudolphsen
VP & CIO: Denise K. Wong
Exec VP, Mktg: George J. Riedl
Mgr Direct Mktg: John Schmidtke
Employees: 200,000
Primary Market Served: Consumer
Catalog available online
Direct online sales
Gross sales or billing: $53,000,000,000

Drug store chain.

ALMORE INTERNATIONAL INC
PO Box 25214
Portland, OR 97298-0214
Telephone: (503) 643-6633, (800) 547-
1511, FAX: (503) 643-9748, E-Mail:
info@almore.com, Web Site: www.
almore.com
Pres & Owner: Davy Dupon
Employees: 15
Primary Market Served: Business &
Consumer
Catalog available online
Direct online sales
Advertising/Marketing Budget Related
to Direct Marketing: 76-100%
Direct Marketing ad budget:
Direct Mail: 90%
Magazines: 10%
Founded: 1946
Gross sales or billing: $2,000,000

Dental manufacturer & distributor
(hand instruments, optical aids, registration wax & waxing units).

AMBIENT SHAPES INC
856 21st Street Dr SE
Hickory, NC 28602-8376

Telephone: (800) 438-2244, FAX:
(800) 872-2005, E-Mail: sales@
ambientshapes.com, Web Site: www.
ambientshapes.com
Pres: Christoph Klingspor
VP: Rosemarie Klingspor
Conducts Business: U.S., Germany
Employees: 4
Primary Market Served: Business &
Consumer
Catalog available online
Direct online sales
Direct Marketing ad budget:
Direct Mail: $250,000
Magazines: $250,000

Sells health aids, tinnitus maskers &
white noise generators.

AMERICAN PRINTING HOUSE FOR THE BLIND
1839 Frankfort Ave
Louisville, KY 40206-0085
Telephone: (502) 895-2405, (800) 223-
1839, FAX: (502) 899-2274, E-Mail:
info@aph.org, Web Site: www.aph.
org
Pres: Tuck Tinsley III
VP: William Beavin
VP, Production: Jack Decker
VP, Devel: Donald J. Keefe
VP, Prods & Svcs: Robert P. Brasher
Conducts Business: Worldwide
Employees: 320
Primary Market Served: Business &
Consumer
Catalog available online
Indirect online sales
Advertising/Marketing Budget Related
to Direct Marketing: 76-100%
Founded: 1858
Gross sales or billing: $17,000,000

A not-for-profit manufacturer of products for blind people. Offers books in
large type, Braille, recorded & computer disk form. Also offers instructional aids, tools, supplies, computer
products & on-line database accessible
books.

AMERICANSOURCE BERGAN
1300 Morris Ave
Chesterbrook, PA 19087-5559
Telephone: (610) 727-7000, (800) 829-
3132, E-Mail: info@
amerisourcebergan.com, Web Site:
www.amerisourcebergan.com
Chmn of Bd & CEO: Robert Martini
VP Mktg: David New
Media Rels Mgr: Barbara Proni
Conducts Business: U.S.
Employees: 4,000
Primary Market Served: Consumer
Founded: 2001

Distributor of pharmaceuticals, health & beauty aids, over-the-counter medicine, consumer electronics & video software.

AMMED DIRECT
5720 Crossings Blvd
Antioch, TN 37013-3144
Telephone: (615) 941-3900, Web Site:
www.ammeddirect.com
VP Mktg: John Mills
Primary Market Served: Business & Consumer

THE DMA AMWAY GLOBAL
7575 Fulton Rd SE
Ada, MI 49355-0001
Telephone: (616) 787-6000, Web Site:
www.amwayglobal.com
Sr CRM Mgr: Karen Bezemek

ANATOMICAL CHART CO
Div. of Wolters Kluwer Health
4025 W Peterson Ave
Chicago, IL 60646-6069
Telephone: (847) 679-4700, (800) 621-7500, FAX: (847) 674-0211, E-Mail:
service@anatomical.com, Web Site:
www.anatomical.com
Gen Mgr: William Demas
Sls Rep: Marily Lack
Conducts Business: Worldwide
Primary Market Served: Business & Consumer
Catalog available online
Direct online sales
Founded: 1971

Anatomical charts & models, medical & nursing training aids, medical books & pamphlets.

ANDA INC
2915 Weston Rd
Weston, FL 33331-3627
Telephone: (954) 217-4144, Web Site:
www.andanet.com
Sr Mktg Mgr: Pamela Ossa
Primary Market Served: Business & Consumer

APOTHECARY PRODUCTS INC
11750 12th Ave S
Burnsville, MN 55337-1297
Telephone: (952) 890-1940, (800) 328-2742, FAX: (800) 328-1584, Web
Site: www.apothecaryproducts.com
Pres & COO: John Creel
CEO: Terry Noble
Sr VP Sls: David Polfliet
Sr VP & CFO: Ron Barg
Sr VP Global Sls & Mktg: James Koeppl
Conducts Business: Worldwide

Employees: 240
Primary Market Served: Business & Consumer
Catalog available online
Direct online sales
Advertising/Marketing Budget Related to Direct Marketing: 76-100%
Founded: 1975
Gross sales or billing: $29,500,000

Manufacture & distribute health related products sold in any pharmacy. Sales are made via telemarketing, personal sales force, key representatives & by catalog.

ARNET PHARMACEUTICAL
2525 Davie Rd
Davie, FL 33317
Telephone: (954) 236-9053, (800) 968-6673, FAX: (954) 370-2508, E-Mail:
arnet@arnetusa.com, Web Site:
www.arnetusa.com
Pres: Jose Tabacinic
VP Sls: Mark Tabacinic
VP Opers: Manuel Tabacinic
Conducts Business: Worldwide
Employees: 100
Primary Market Served: Business
Catalog available online
Advertising/Marketing Budget Related to Direct Marketing: 76-100%
Direct Marketing ad budget:
Direct Mail: 10%
TV/Radio: 90%
Founded: 1972

Manufacturer of nutritional supplements.

AS WE CHANGE
250 City Center
Oshkosh, WI 54901
Telephone: (619) 213-2200, (800) 993-0192, FAX: (619) 213-2253, E-Mail:
help@aswechange.com, Web Site:
www.aswechange.com
Pres & CEO: John Dullea
Employees: 45
Primary Market Served: Consumer
Catalog available online
Direct online sales
Advertising/Marketing Budget Related to Direct Marketing: 76-100%
Direct Marketing ad budget:
$5,000,000
Direct Mail: 80%
Online: 20%
Founded: 1996

Main Demographics: Peri-Menopausal/ Menopausal Women, Sell Vitamins/ Supplements, Activewear/Activegear, Pampering Items (Body/Hair Care).

ASTRAL BRANDS LLC
4900 Highlands Pkwy SE
Smyrna, GA 30082-5132

Telephone: (678) 303-3088, Web Site:
www.astralbrands.com
Exec VP Mktg Astral Direct: David Brown
Primary Market Served: Business & Consumer

ASTRAZENECA
1800 Concord Pike A3C-122
Wilmington, DE 19850
Telephone: (302) 866-1482, Web Site:
www.astrazeneca-us.com
Dir IS Mktg: Doug Caldwell
Primary Market Served: Consumer

AT LAST NATURALS
PO Box 338
North Salem, NY 10560-0338
Telephone: (800) 527-8123, FAX:
(914) 747-3791, E-Mail: info@
atlastnaturals.com, Web Site: www.
atlastnaturals.com
Pres: Bruce Last
Sr VP: Zane Last
Gen Mgr VP: Ray Last
Conducts Business: Worldwide
Employees: 60
Primary Market Served: Business & Consumer
Catalog available online
Direct online sales
Advertising/Marketing Budget Related to Direct Marketing: 0-25%
Founded: 1967
Gross sales or billing: $6,000,000

Health & beauty aids to wholesalers, retailers, catalogs, consumers & private labels.

AVEDA CORP
4000 Pheasant Ridge Dr
Minneapolis, MN 55449-7106
Telephone: (763) 951-4201, Web Site:
www.aveda.com
Dir Consumer Mktg: Rachael Ostrom

AVON PRODUCTS INC
1345 Ave of the Americas
New York, NY 10105-0302
Telephone: (212) 282-7000, (800) 367-2866, FAX: (212) 282-6225, Web
Site: www.avon.com
Sr VP, Gen Counsel & Sec: Ward Miller
Conducts Business: Worldwide
Employees: 30,000
Primary Market Served: Consumer
Advertising/Marketing Budget Related to Direct Marketing: 0-25%
Gross sales or billing: $3,500,000,000

Sells cosmetics, fragrances, toiletries, jewelry & gift items to consumers via direct marketing.

BACK DESIGNS INC

PO Box 2810
Novato, CA 94948-2810
Telephone: (415) 883-4683, FAX: (510) 549-0837, E-Mail: info@ backdesigns.com, Web Site: www. backdesigns.com
Pres & Founder: Eileen Vollowitz
Conducts Business: U.S.
Employees: 20
Primary Market Served: Business & Consumer
Catalog available online
Direct online sales
Advertising/Marketing Budget Related to Direct Marketing: 0-25%
Direct Marketing ad budget:
Direct Mail: 50%
Magazines: 25%
Newspapers: 25%
Founded: 1984
Gross sales or billing: $2,000,000

Ergonomic & orthopedic products & furniture for office, home & travel. Marketed to clinics, businesses & individuals.

BASIC RESEARCH

5742 Harold Gatty Dr
Salt Lake City, UT 84116-3762
Telephone: (801) 234-7000, Web Site: www.silversage.com
Dir Mktg & Adv: Gina Daines

BAXTER HEALTHCARE, RENAL DIVISION

1620 Waukegan Rd
Waukegan, IL 60085
Telephone: (847) 473-6586

BEAUTY NATURALLY

850 Stanton Rd
Burlingame, CA 94010-1404
Telephone: (650) 697-1845, (800) 432-4323, FAX: (650) 697-1970, E-Mail: sales@beautynaturally.com, Web Site: www.beautynaturally.com
Pres: Frederick K. Wong
Co Owner: Janet Wong
Co Owner: Karen Barnes
Conducts Business: U.S., Canada, Mexico, New Zealand
Employees: 4
Primary Market Served: Business & Consumer
Catalog available online
Direct online sales
Founded: 1981
Gross sales or billing: $200,000

Catalog marketer of unique cosmetics. Also, hair & skin products.

J&H BERGE/THE LAB MART

4111 S Clinton Ave
South Plainfield, NJ 07080
Telephone: (908) 561-1234, FAX: (908) 561-3002, E-Mail: rgardner@ labmart.com, Web Site: www. labmart.com
Pres: Steven Krupp
VP, Sls & Mktg: Robert Gardner
Mktg Mgr: James Thomson
Graphic Designer: Mark Chua
Conducts Business: U.S.
Employees: 30
Primary Market Served: Business
Catalog available online
Direct online sales
Advertising/Marketing Budget Related to Direct Marketing: 51-75%
Founded: 1850

Marketer of laboratory equipment to research scientists.

BIOMERICA INC

17571 Von Karman Ave
Irvine, CA 92614-6207
Telephone: (949) 645-2111, FAX: (949) 722-6674, E-Mail: bmra@ biomerica.com, Web Site: www. biomerica.com
Pres: Fran Capitanio
CEO: Zack Irani
Intl Mktg: Mark Fisher
Quality Control: Joe Rink
Cust Svc: Dar Barber
Cust Svc: Connie Trahan
Conducts Business: Worldwide
Employees: 150
Primary Market Served: Business & Consumer
Catalog available online
Direct online sales
Advertising/Marketing Budget Related to Direct Marketing: 0-25%
Direct Marketing ad budget:
Direct Mail: $30,000
Magazines: $25,000
Newspapers: $20,000
TV/Radio: $10,000
Telephone: $15,000
Founded: 1971

Medical home test kits, such as pregnancy, stool, blood, urine, etc, sold in AARP, pharmacies & catalogs.

THE BODY SHOP INC

5036 One World Way
Wake Forest, NC 27587-7732
Telephone: (919) 554-4900, (800) BODYSHOP, FAX: (919) 554-4361, Web Site: www.thebodyshop.com
CEO: Sophie Gasperment
Employees: 15,000
Primary Market Served: Consumer
Catalog available online
Direct online sales

Advertising/Marketing Budget Related to Direct Marketing: 76-100%
Gross sales or billing: $849,000,000

Naturally based skin & hair care preparations.

CAROL BOND HEALTH FOODS

334 N Main St
Liberty, TX 77575
Telephone: (800) 833-8282, Web Site: www.carolbond.com
CEO: Carol Bond
Conducts Business: U.S.
Employees: 8
Primary Market Served: Consumer
Catalog available online
Direct online sales
Advertising/Marketing Budget Related to Direct Marketing: 76-100%
Direct Marketing ad budget:
Direct Mail: $60,000
Magazines: $135,000
Newspapers: $7,000
TV/Radio: $250,000
Founded: 1978
Gross sales or billing: $2,000,000

Mail-order marketer of vitamin supplements.

BOSOM BUDDY BREAST FORMS

aka B & B Lingerie Co, Inc
2417 Bank Dr (Suite 201)
Boise, ID 83705-0731
Telephone: (208) 343-9696, (800) 262-2789, FAX: (208) 343-9266, E-Mail: custserv@bosombuddy.com, Web Site: www.bosombuddy.com
Pres: Stacie Neely
Conducts Business: Worldwide
Employees: 10
Primary Market Served: Business & Consumer
Catalog available online
Indirect online sales
Advertising/Marketing Budget Related to Direct Marketing: 76-100%
Founded: 1976

Manufacture & distribute internationally an all-fabric, weight-adjustable external breast prosthesis for women who have had mastectomies.

THE DMA BRONSON NUTRITIONALS LLC

70 Commerce St
Hauppauge, NY 11788-3962
Telephone: (631) 750-0000, Web Site: www.bronsonnutritionals.com
Mktg Dir: Sheri Taubes
Primary Market Served: Business & Consumer

BRUCE MEDICAL SUPPLY

411 Waverly Oaks Rd
Waltham, MA 02452-8494
Telephone: (781) 894-6262, (800) 225-8446, FAX: (781) 894-9519, E-Mail: sales@brucemedial.com, Web Site: www.brucemedical.com
Conducts Business: U.S., Canada
Primary Market Served: Business & Consumer
Catalog available online
Direct online sales

Sells medical supplies by mail.

CHG

6440 S Millrock Dr
Salt Lake City, UT 84121
Telephone: (801) 930-3000, (800) 453-3030, Web Site: www.comphealth.com
COO: Scott Beck
Primary Market Served: Business & Consumer

CVS CAREMARK

1 CVS Dr
Woonsocket, RI 02895-6146
Telephone: (401) 765-1500, FAX: (401) 769-4488, Web Site: www.cvs.com
CEO: Thomas M. Ryan
VP: Chris Badin
VP: Larry J. Merlo
Dir, Mktg Intelligence: Adrian Sosa
Conducts Business: U.S.
Primary Market Served: Consumer
Catalog available online
Direct online sales
Advertising/Marketing Budget Related to Direct Marketing: 0-25%
Direct Marketing ad budget: $5,000,000
Direct Mail: 100%
Founded: 1963
Gross sales or billing: $43,800,000,000

Prescriptions, health & beauty aids.

CALIFORNIA COSMETICS CORP

dba Silkskin
18757 Burbank Blvd (Suite 110)
Tarzana, CA 91356-3345
Telephone: (818) 225-2999, (800) 366-8243, FAX: (800) 345-7763, E-Mail: calcos@silkskin.com, Web Site: www.silkskin.com
Pres: Bob Sidell
Conducts Business: U.S., Canada
Employees: 19
Primary Market Served: Consumer
Founded: 1985
Gross sales or billing: $2,600,000

Skin care & cosmetics via mail order & catalog sales.

CALIFORNIA PACIFIC RESEARCH & NEW GENERATION

300 Brinkby Ave (Suite 200)
Reno, NV 89509-4359
Telephone: (775) 829-5600, (800) 541-5703, FAX: (775) 829-5619, E-Mail: sales@newgen2000.com, Web Site: www.newgen2000.com
Pres: Robert E. Murphy
Conducts Business: Worldwide
Primary Market Served: Consumer
Catalog available online
Direct online sales

Sells hair preparations for male pattern baldness. Also, health care products.

CANYON MARKETING

43 Hunting Hollow Ct
Dix Hills, NY 11746-6166
Telephone: (516) 316-7090
Primary Market Served: Consumer

THE DMA CAREINGTON INTERNATIONAL

7400 Gaylord Pkwy (fl 3)
Frisco, TX 75034-9463
Telephone: (972) 335-6970, Web Site: www.careington.com
Dir Mktg: Ed Cline
Primary Market Served: Consumer

CARESTREAM HEALTH INC

150 Verona St
Rochester, NY 14608
Telephone: (585) 627-1800, (888) 777-2072, Web Site: www.carestreamhealth.com
Vice Chmn: Eliot Siegel M.D.
Primary Market Served: Business & Consumer

CASWELL-MASSEY CO LTD

121 Fieldcrest Ave Ste A
Edison, NJ 08837-3658
Telephone: (732) 225-2181, (800) 326-0500, FAX: (732) 225-2385, E-Mail: info@caswellmasseyltd.com, Web Site: www.caswellmassey.com
Pres & CEO: Anne E. Robinson
COO: Anthony Nichtawitz
Dir, Consumer Bus: Sally Rue
Conducts Business: U.S., Canada, Hong Kong, Philippines
Employees: 71
Primary Market Served: Consumer
Catalog available online
Direct online sales
Founded: 1752
Gross sales or billing: $22,500,000

Fine personal care products for men & women.

CLAIROL INC

Div. of P&G
One Blachley Rd
Stamford, CT 06922-0003
Telephone: (203) 357-5000, (800) 252-4765, FAX: (203) 357-5003, Web Site: www.clairol.com
Global Mktg Officer: Jim Stengel
Primary Market Served: Consumer

Hair care company.

COASTAL HEALTH TRAIN

500 Studio Dr
Virginia Beach, VA 23452-1175
Telephone: (757) 631-3142, Web Site: www.coastalhealth.com
Dir Mktg: Lori Stanley

COLLIS CURVE CATALOG SALES

Subs. of Collis Curve Inc
6110 California Rd
Brownsville, TX 78521
Telephone: (210) 576-4818, (800) 298-4818, FAX: (800) 298-4818, E-Mail: brushteeth@aol.com, Web Site: www.colliscurve.com
Pres: David Collis
VP: Jane Gonzalez
Conducts Business: U.S.
Employees: 3
Primary Market Served: Business & Consumer
Catalog available online
Indirect online sales
Advertising/Marketing Budget Related to Direct Marketing: 51-75%
Direct Marketing ad budget: $5,000
Online: 60%
Founded: 1981

Toothbrushes with curved bristles & dental home care products to consumers, handicapped individuals & institutions.

CONNEY SAFETY PRODUCTS LLC

Owned by Caxton-Iseman Capital
3202 Latham Dr
Madison, WI 53713-4614
Telephone: (608) 271-3300, (800) 356-9100, FAX: (608) 271-3322, (800) 845-9095, E-Mail: safety@conney.com, Web Site: www.conney.com
VP Mktg: Chuck Moyer
CEO: Mike Wessner
VP Sls: Joe Scime
Conducts Business: U.S.
Employees: 175
Primary Market Served: Business & Consumer
Catalog available online
Direct online sales
Advertising/Marketing Budget Related to Direct Marketing: 76-100%

Direct Marketing ad budget:
Direct Mail: 90%
Telephone: 10%
Founded: 1946
Gross sales or billing: $30,300,000

Sells first-aid & personal safety supplies directly to industry, schools, utilities, contractors & government.

COOPER SURGICAL INC

95 Corporate Dr
Trumbull, CT 06611
Telephone: (203) 601-5200, (800) 645-3670, FAX: (203) 601-1007, Web Site: www.coopersurgical.com
Chmn Bd: A. Thomas Bender
CEO: Nicholas J. Pichotta
Pres & COO: Paul L. Reumell
CFO & VP: Steven M. Neil
Pres & COO, Coopervision: Gregory A. Fryling
Employees: 500
Primary Market Served: Business
Catalog available online
Indirect online sales
Gross sales or billing: $125,000,000

Manufacturer of Ob-Gyn products.

COOPER VISION

370 Woodcliff Dr (Suite 200)
Fairport, NY 14450
Telephone: (585) 385-6810, (800) 341-2020, Web Site: www.coopervision.com
VP, Sls & Mktg: David Fancher
Mktg Dir: Thomas Shone
Mktg Mgr: Joan Martt
Sls Admin Mgr: Lorraine LaGona
Primary Market Served: Business

Manufactures soft contact lenses, Preference & PreferenceToric Planned Replacement lenses, Hydrasoft & Custom Toric lenses.

COVIDIEN INTERNATIONAL

15 Hampshire St
Mansfield, MA 02048-1113
Telephone: (508) 261-8000, (800) 962-9888, FAX: (508) 261-8105, Web Site: www.covidien.com
Pres: Richard J. Meelia
Sr VP Corp Commun: Eric A. Kraus
Exec: K.J. Gould
Adv & Convention Coord: Deborah McDermott
Corp Media Adv: David Young
Conducts Business: Worldwide
Employees: 43,000
Primary Market Served: Business & Consumer
Catalog available online
Indirect online sales
Advertising/Marketing Budget Related to Direct Marketing: 0-25%
Gross sales or billing: $9,600,000,000

Manufactures, markets, and distributes disposable medical supplies and devices.

D&E PHARMACEUTICALS INC

700 Central Ave
Farmingdale, NJ 07727-3787
Telephone: (973) 838-8300, (800) 221-1833, FAX: (877) 838-0560, E-Mail: customerservice@dnepharm.com, Web Site: www.dnepharm.com
Pres: Eric Organ
CEO: Denise Organ
VP, Mktg: Richard Quine
Sls Mgr: Todd Weller
Pur Mgr: Ted Weller
Conducts Business: U.S.
Primary Market Served: Business & Consumer
Catalog available online
Direct online sales
Founded: 1979

Mail order pharmaceuticals.

THE DMA DENTSPLY INTERNATIONAL

570 W College Ave
York, PA 17401-3880
Telephone: (800) 877-0020, Web Site: www.dentsply.com
Corp Commun: Michele Mummert
Primary Market Served: Consumer

CHRISTIAN DIOR PERFUMES

21 E 57th St
New York, NY 10022-2506
Telephone: (212) 931-2200, FAX: (212) 931-2954, Web Site: www.dior.com
Pres: Bernard Potier
Sr VP Mktg, Sls & Edn: Terry Darland
Chmn Bd: Bernard Armault
CEO: Sidney Toledano
Conducts Business: Worldwide
Primary Market Served: Consumer

Retail cosmetic, fragrance & skin care products to consumers.

DR LEONARD'S HEALTHCARE CORP

100 Nixon Ln
Edison, NJ 08837-3804
Telephone: (732) 225-0100, FAX: (732) 225-0302, Web Site: www.doctorleonard.com
Pres & CEO: Tom McIntyre
Exec VP, Mdse & Mktg: Susan Metcalfe
Mktg Dir: Susan Pizzano
Mdse Dir: Gina Van Der Veer
Primary Market Served: Consumer

Healthcare catalog-Dr. Leonard's product buyers are active, mature individuals who purchase high quality attractively priced products to enhance their lifestyles.

E-Z-EM INC

532 Broadhollow Rd Ste 126
Melville, NY 11747-3625
Telephone: (516) 333-8230, (800) 544-4624, FAX: (516) 333-8278, E-Mail: webmaster@ezem.com, Web Site: www.ezem.com
Pres, CEO & Dir: Anthony A. Lombardo
Sr VP, Global Sls Mktg Engrng: Brad S. Schreck
VP NA Imaging Sls: Tom McLaughlin
Dir Corp & Mktg Commun: Tom Johnson
Conducts Business: Worldwide
Employees: 611
Primary Market Served: Business
Catalog available online
Founded: 1962
Gross sales or billing: $137,800,000

CT Imaging, virtual colonoscopy, speech pathology, gastrointestinal devices & accessories & Healthcare decontaminants. Leading manufacturer of contrast agents for gastrointestinal radiology.

ETS INC

6270 Corporate Dr
Indianapolis, IN 46278-2900
Telephone: (317) 290-8982, (800) 228-6292, FAX: (317) 329-4630, E-Mail: info@etstsan.com, Web Site: www.etstans.com
Pres: Trevor Gray
Exec VP: Edna Gray
VP Mktg: Leslie Hartlieb
Exec Dir Bus Devel: John Keiffner
Conducts Business: U.S., Canada, S. America, Pacific Rim, Europe
Employees: 300
Primary Market Served: Business & Consumer
Catalog available online
Advertising/Marketing Budget Related to Direct Marketing: 26-50%
Founded: 1984
Gross sales or billing: $65,000,000

Suntanning equipment & supplies. Lotions, apparel & accessories.

THE DMA EMERSON ECOLOGICS

7 Commerce Dr
Bedford, NH 03110-6835
Telephone: (603) 656-9778
Primary Market Served: Consumer

Distributor of natural & herbal health care products to healthcare professionals

ESSENTIAL PRODUCTS CO INC

90 Water St.
New York, NY 10005-3511
Telephone: (212) 344-4288
Pres: Barry Striem
Conducts Business: U.S.
Primary Market Served: Business &
Consumer
Founded: 1895

Offer discount versions of designer fragrances. Offer 68-72 perfumes & men's colognes as recommended on TV, radio & shopping guides. Request free scent cards & list.

EYE CARE CENTERS OF AMERICA

dba Stein Optical, Eyemasters, EyeDr
Rx and more
175 E Houston St (6th Fl)
San Antonio, TX 78205-2210
Telephone: (210) 340-3531, (800) 669-
1183, FAX: (210) 340-0123, E-Mail:
customerservice@visionworks.com,
Web Site: www.ecca.com
Pres & COO: James J. Denny
Integrated Mktg Mgr: Rebecca Gidish
Exec VP Msdg & Managed Vision
Care: George E. Gebhardt
Conducts Business: U.S.
Employees: 4,800
Primary Market Served: Consumer
Advertising/Marketing Budget Related
to Direct Marketing: 26-50%
Direct Marketing ad budget:
Direct Mail: $100,000
Newspapers: $110,000
Gross sales or billing: $301,900,000

Operates or manages over 400 optical retail stores in 37 states and the District of Columbia through 11 store names that are leaders in eye care service in each of their respective markets. Vision insurance & contact lenses by mail.

FAMILY FOOT CARE

530 Lakehurst Rd (Suite 205)
Toms River, NJ 08755
Telephone: (732) 341-3355
Owner: Kimberly Daley
Primary Market Served: Consumer

Podiatry.

FIRST TO THE FINISH INC

1325 N Broad St
Carlinville, IL 62626-9770
Telephone: (217) 854-8305, Web Site:
www.firsttothefinish.com
Gen Mgr: John Costello
Primary Market Served: Consumer

FITNESS SYSTEMS MANUFACTURING CORP

104 Evans Ave
Sinking Spring, PA 19608-1318
Telephone: (610) 670-0135, (800) 822-
9995, E-Mail: vitaminout@aol.com,
Web Site: www.fitness-systems.net
Pres: David Hoffman
Conducts Business: Worldwide
Primary Market Served: Business &
Consumer
Catalog available online
Direct online sales
Advertising/Marketing Budget Related
to Direct Marketing: 0-25%
Founded: 1985

Athletic, body building & weight loss vitamin supplements such as human growth hormones, creatine, andros, proteins & vitamin packs at wholesale prices.

FRONTIER NATURAL PRODUCTS CO-OP

Div. of Frontier Cooperative Herbs
3021 78th St, PO Box 299
Norway, IA 52318
Telephone: (319) 227-7996, (800) 669-
3275, FAX: (319) 227-7966, (800)
717-4372, E-Mail: info@
frontiercoop.com, Web Site: www.
frontiercoop.com
CEO: Tony Bedard
Chief Mktg Officer: Clint Landis
VP Sls: Dan Lloyd
Conducts Business: U.S.
Employees: 225
Primary Market Served: Business &
Consumer
Advertising/Marketing Budget Related
to Direct Marketing: 0-25%
Founded: 1976
Gross sales or billing: $48,000,000

Bulk herbs, spices, teas, bottled spices, baking flavors; essential oils, fragrances, soaps, shampoos, homeopathics, extracts, encapsuled herbs, salves & cough syrups, bulk & packaged coffee & teas.

GARDEN BOTANIKA INC

Div. of Schroeder & Tremayne
8500 Valcour Ave
Saint Louis, MO 63123
Telephone: (425) 881-9603, (800) 968-
7842, FAX: (425) 869-6235, Web
Site: www.gardenbotanika.com
Dir Mktg: Mary Holmes
Pres: Jamie Wilmsen
Primary Market Served: Consumer
Founded: 1989

Retail & catalog selling botanically based skin care products & cosmetics.

GENERAL NUTRITION CORP

300 6th Ave Fl 2
Pittsburgh, PA 15222-2511
Telephone: (412) 288-4600, (877)
GNC-4700, FAX: (412) 402-7218,
Web Site: www.gnc.com
Pres & CEO: Joseph Fortunato
VP Mktg: Rich Oprison
Conducts Business: U.S.
Employees: 12,707
Primary Market Served: Consumer
Direct Marketing ad budget:
Direct Mail: 5%
Magazines: 10%
Newspapers: 3%
TV/Radio: 80%
Telephone: 2%
Founded: 1935
Gross sales or billing: $1,490,000,000

A national retail chain of vitamins, health foods & cosmetics which direct markets to an internal mail file with various promotions.

GENERAL WIG MANUFACTURERS INC

Div. of Tressallure/General Wig
1480 SW 3rd St (Suite 3)
Pompano Beach, FL 33069-3225
Telephone: (305) 823-0600, (800) 268-
7210, FAX: (314) 785-0224, E-Mail:
4service@beautytrends.com, Web
Site: www.beautytrends.com
VP: Christopher Prior
Mktg Dir: Sarah Berke
Conducts Business: U.S.
Primary Market Served: Consumer
Catalog available online
Direct online sales
Advertising/Marketing Budget Related
to Direct Marketing: 0-25%
Founded: 1988
Gross sales or billing: $10,300,000

Wigs via mail order catalogs to women.

GIBSON AUER LLC

dba GA Labs
PO Box 228
Victor, ID 83455-0228
Telephone: (208) 787-2153, E-Mail:
helpdesk@galabs.com, Web Site:
www.galabs.com
Owner: Rebecca Franklin
Conducts Business: U.S., Canada
Primary Market Served: Business &
Consumer
Catalog available online
Indirect online sales
Advertising/Marketing Budget Related
to Direct Marketing: 0-25%
Direct Marketing ad budget:
Direct Mail: 90%
Magazines: 10%
Founded: 2003

Gross sales or billing: $80,000

Mail order company selling proprietary medicines & cosmetics.

GOLD MEDAL HAIR PRODUCTS INC

104 Allen Blvd Ste H
Farmingdale, NY 11735-5627
Telephone: (516) 378-6900, (800) 324-7136, FAX: (516) 378-0168, E-Mail: customerservice@goldmedalhair.com, Web Site: www.goldmedalhair.com
Pres: Rick Laban
Art Dir: Ray Wallace
Conducts Business: U.S., U.K.
Employees: 6
Primary Market Served: Business & Consumer
Catalog available online
Direct online sales
Advertising/Marketing Budget Related to Direct Marketing: 76-100%
Direct Marketing ad budget: $50,000
Direct Mail: 100%
Founded: 1942
Gross sales or billing: $1,000,000

Mail order company specializing in sales to black clientele.

GRAHAM FIELD HEALTH PRODUCTS INC

2935 Northeast Pkwy
Atlanta, GA 30360-2808
Telephone: (800) 347-5678, FAX: (800) 726-0601, E-Mail: ics@grahamfield.com, Web Site: www.lumiscope.net
Pres: Marc Bernstein
VP, Natl Sls: Harvey Cohen
Export Dir: Ed Roark
Conducts Business: U.S., Canada, Europe, S. America, Asia
Employees: 100
Primary Market Served: Business & Consumer
Advertising/Marketing Budget Related to Direct Marketing: 0-25%

Health care products, fitness & personal care products & medical instruments. Sells to professional, retail & premium markets.

HMI MARKETING

8000 85th Ave N
Brooklyn Park, MN 55445
Telephone: (800) 468-4144, FAX: (800) 468-8814, Web Site: www.hmimarketing.com
CEO: Terri Abraham
Conducts Business: U.S.
Employees: 60
Primary Market Served: Business
Founded: 1981

Marketing eye care, dental materials & veterinary products direct to doctors, dentists, optometrists & chiropractors.

HANDI-RAMP INC

510 North Ave
Libertyville, IL 60048-2025
Telephone: (847) 680-7700, (800) 876-RAMP, FAX: (847) 816-7689, E-Mail: info@handiramp.com, Web Site: www.handiramp.com
Pres: Thomas R. Disch
Conducts Business: U.S., Canada
Employees: 8
Primary Market Served: Business & Consumer
Catalog available online
Direct online sales
Advertising/Marketing Budget Related to Direct Marketing: 26-50%
Direct Marketing ad budget:
Direct Mail: 25%
Magazines: 75%
Founded: 1958

Ramps for the handicapped & for hotels etc.

THE DMA HARVARD PILGRIM HEALTH CARE

93 Worcester St
Wellesley, MA 02481-3609
Telephone: (617) 509-1000, FAX: (617) 509-7590, Web Site: www.harvardpilgrim.org
Pres & CEO: Charles D. Baker
CFO: Joseph C. Capezza
COO: Bruce M. Bullen
VP HR: Deborah A. Hicks
VP Customer Svc: Lynn A. Bowman
Sr Mktg Mgr: Tim Walsh
Conducts Business: U.S.
Employees: 1,350
Primary Market Served: Business & Consumer
Catalog available online
Advertising/Marketing Budget Related to Direct Marketing: 0-25%
Direct Marketing ad budget:
Direct Mail: 15%
Newspapers: 40%
TV/Radio: 45%
Founded: 1969

Healthcare/Insurance.

THE DMA HAVEL'S INC

3726 Lonsdale St
Cincinnati, OH 45227-3651
Telephone: (800) 638-4770
Primary Market Served: Consumer

Specialty medical supplies distributor

HAZELDEN

Div. of Hazelden Foundation
CO 3 PO Box 11

Center City, MN 55012-0011
Telephone: (651) 213-4200, (800) 257-7810, FAX: (651) 213-4411, E-Mail: info@hazelden.org, Web Site: www.hazelden.org
VP, Publr: Nick Moto
Conducts Business: Worldwide
Employees: 140
Primary Market Served: Business & Consumer
Catalog available online
Direct online sales
Advertising/Marketing Budget Related to Direct Marketing: 76-100%
Direct Marketing ad budget:
Direct Mail: 80%
Magazines: 5%
Newspapers: 5%
TV/Radio: 10%
Founded: 1954
Gross sales or billing: $24,000,000

Educational programs of videos, workbooks, pamphlets & other media for substance abuse treatment.

HEALTH FREEDOM NUTRITION LLC

255 Bell St (2nd fl)
Reno, NV 89503-5352
Telephone: (775) 324-2050, Web Site: www.hfn-usa.com
CEO & Mgr: Dale Fowkes
Primary Market Served: Consumer

HERBALIFE INTERNATIONAL OF AMERICA INC

PO Box 80210
Los Angeles, CA 90080-0210
Telephone: (310) 410-9600, (866) 617-4273, FAX: (310) 258-7019, Web Site: www.herbalife.com
Chmn & CEO: Michael O. Johnson
Pres & COO: Gregory Probert
CFO: Richard Goudis
VP, Corp Mktg: Doug Braun
Employees: 3,600
Primary Market Served: Business
Catalog available online
Gross sales or billing: $1,885,500,000

Health & nutrition company & personal care products.

HOPKINS MEDICAL PRODUCTS

Div. of Hopkins Uniform Co Inc.
Five Greenwood Pl
Baltimore, MD 21208-2763
Telephone: (410) 484-2036, (800) 835-1995, FAX: (410) 484-4036, E-Mail: customerservice@hopkinsmedical.net, Web Site: www.hopkinsmedicalproducts.com
Pres: Philip M. Kenney

Conducts Business: U.S.
Employees: 11
Primary Market Served: Business &
Consumer
Catalog available online
Direct online sales
Founded: 1945
Gross sales or billing: $1,800,000

Medical supplies, devices and hospital
equipment for the medical profession.

THE DMA HUMANA INC
1951 Bishop Ln
Louisville, KY 40218-1930
Telephone: (502) 580-5005, FAX:
(502) 580-3141, Web Site: www.
humana.com
Sr VP, Sls, Mktg & Bus Devel: Ken
Fasola
Assoc Dir, Response Mktg: Stacy A.
Wilson
Mgr, Database Market & Modeling:
Angie Weigel
Conducts Business: U.S., England,
Switzerland
Employees: 30,000
Primary Market Served: Business &
Consumer

Provides health coverage through Humana Health Care Plans.

INDEPENDENT LIVING AIDS
200 Robbins Ln (Unit A)
Jericho, NY 11753-2341
Telephone: (516) 937-1848, (800) 537-
2118, FAX: (516) 937-3906, E-Mail:
techsupport@independentliving.com,
Web Site: www.independentliving.
com
Pres: Marvin Sandler
VP & Owner: Mimi Berman
Conducts Business: U.S., Europe, Asia
Employees: 25
Primary Market Served: Business &
Consumer
Catalog available online
Direct online sales
Advertising/Marketing Budget Related
to Direct Marketing: 0-25%
Founded: 1977
Gross sales or billing: $2,200,000

Catalog of aids for visually, audibly &
physically disabled.

**JAFRA COSMETICS
INTERNATIONAL INC**
Subs of Vorwerk & Co KG
2451 Townsgate Rd
Westlake Village, CA 91361
Telephone: (805) 557-1889, (800) 551-
2345, Web Site: www.jafra.com
CEO & Pres: Frank P. Mineo
Pres Jafra Worldwide Holdings:
Gonzalo R. Rubio

Sr VP & Chief Global Mktg Officer:
Beatrice Gutai
Pres Jafra USA: Dyan Lucero
Conducts Business: Worldwide
Employees: 1,016
Primary Market Served: Consumer
Founded: 1956
Gross sales or billing: $90,500,000

Direct selling & marketing company
specializing in cosmetics, toiletries,
fragrances & related products &
skincare.

**JAMES MEDICAL RENTS &
SALES INC**
7821 Coldwater Rd Ste A
Fort Wayne, IN 46825-8412
Telephone: (260) 423-9571, E-Mail:
sales@jamesmedical.com, Web Site:
www.jamesmedical.net
Pres & Treas: Sandra James
VP: Mike James
Mgr: Jeff Castator
Sls Mgr: Mark Church
Consultant: Dave Ponder
Primary Market Served: Business
Catalog available online

Healthcare.

JAN ASSOCIATES
7001 Exeter Dr
Oakland, CA 94611
Telephone: (510) 530-6180
Conducts Business: U.S., Canada
Employees: 1
Primary Market Served: Business &
Consumer
Advertising/Marketing Budget Related
to Direct Marketing: 0-25%
Direct Marketing ad budget:
Direct Mail: 92%
Magazines: 5%
Newspapers: 1%
Telephone: 2%
Founded: 1972

Distributor of Rexall Showcase Intl.
Natural preventive supplements.

**JASON NATURAL PERSONAL
CARE PRODUCTS**
Part of Hain Celestial Group
4600 Sleepytime Dr
Boulder, CO 80301-3284
Telephone: (877) 527-6601, Web Site:
www.jason-natural.com
Chmn, Pres & CEO: Irwin David Si-
mon
Exec VP, CFO & Sec: Ira J. Lamel
Exec VP: John Carroll
Sr VP, Sls & Mktg: James R. Lemsky
Dir: Melanie Brown
Conducts Business: U.S., Canada,
Mexico, Europe, Korea
Employees: 39

Primary Market Served: Business &
Consumer
Catalog available online
Direct online sales
Advertising/Marketing Budget Related
to Direct Marketing: 0-25%

Manufactures & sellsprivate label natural cosmetics.

**KALMED DENTAL
PRODUCTS INC**
3048 Alberta Dr
Marietta, GA 30062-1513
Telephone: (770) 971-8815, (800) 322-
8815, FAX: (770) 509-8823, E-Mail:
sales@kalmed.com, Web Site: www.
kalmed.com
Pres: Leonard Jacobs
Conducts Business: U.S.
Employees: 2
Primary Market Served: Business
Catalog available online
Direct online sales
Advertising/Marketing Budget Related
to Direct Marketing: 76-100%
Direct Marketing ad budget:
Direct Mail: 100%
Founded: 1984
Gross sales or billing: $500,000

Dental consumables & small instruments to general & some specialty
dentists.

**KING PHARMACEUTICALS,
INC**
501 Fifth St
Bristol, TN 37620
Telephone: (423) 989-8000, (888) 840-
5370, FAX: (423) 274-8677, Web
Site: www.kingpharm.com
Chmn, Pres & CEO: Brian A. Markin-
son
CFO: Joseph Squicciarino
CCO: Steve Andrzejewski
Primary Market Served: Consumer
Catalog available online
Gross sales or billing: $2,000,000,000

Specializes in critical care
pharmaceuticals.

**CALVIN KLEIN COSMETICS
CO**
Subs. of Calvin Klein Inc
205 W 39th St
New York, NY 10018-3102
Telephone: (212) 759-8888, FAX:
(212) 479-4399
CEO, Calvin Klein: Gaetano Sal-
lorenzo
Pres: Paulanne Mancuso
VP, Mktg: Lori Singer
Primary Market Served: Consumer

Fragrances.

KRAMES - STAYWELL
780 Township Line Rd
Yardley, PA 19067-4200
Telephone: (267) 685-2500, Web Site:
www.krames.com
Pres & CEO: George Parker

LATEST PRODUCTS CORP
36 Orchard Dr
Woodbury, NY 11797-2830
Telephone: (516) 367-4700, (800) 288-
3547, FAX: (516) 367-4714, E-Mail:
info@latestprod.com, Web Site:
www.latestprod.com
Pres: Steven E. Spaeth
Sr VP: Aaron M. Herman
Conducts Business: U.S.
Employees: 4
Primary Market Served: Business
Catalog available online
Indirect online sales
Advertising/Marketing Budget Related
to Direct Marketing: 76-100%
Direct Marketing ad budget:
Direct Mail: 80%
Online: 20%
Founded: 1972
Gross sales or billing: $2,000,000

Distributor & direct marketer of specialty items to hospitals & nursing
homes, government agencies, VAMC's,
prisons, correctional facilities & other
institutions.

THE DMA LIFE EXTENSION FOUNDATION
3600 W Commercial Blvd Ste 100
Fort Lauderdale, FL 33309-3324
Telephone: (954) 766-8433, (800) 678-
8989, FAX: (954) 771-2827, E-Mail:
info@lef.org, Web Site: www.lef.org
CEO: Paul Gilner
Dir Mktg & Sls: Rey Searles
Conducts Business: U.S.
Employees: 100
Primary Market Served: Business &
Consumer
Catalog available online
Direct online sales
Advertising/Marketing Budget Related
to Direct Marketing: 76-100%
Founded: 1980
Gross sales or billing: $55,000,000

Sells top quality dietary supplements to
consumers and re-sellers. Also funds
anti-aging research.

THE DMA LIFE LINE SCREENING
6150 Oak Tree Blvd (Suite 200)
Independence, OH 44131-2569
Telephone: (216) 581-6556, Web Site:
www.lifelinescreening.com
VP Mktg: Eric Greenburg
Primary Market Served: Consumer

LIFESCRIPT
26001 Pala
Mission Viejo, CA 92691-7955
Telephone: (949) 454-0422, Web Site:
www.lifescript.com
COO: Jack Hogan

LONGEVITY NETWORK LTD
5 Longevity Dr
Henderson, NV 89014-2048
Telephone: (702) 454-7000, (800) 242-
1000, FAX: (702) 435-4786, Web
Site: www.longevitynetwork.com
Chmn Bd: Adi Song
CEO: Jim Song
Chmn Bd: Yoan Kim
CIO: Kirk Johnsong
Conducts Business: U.S.
Employees: 55
Primary Market Served: Consumer
Founded: 1993

Makes over 45 nutritional supplements,
weight loss, skin, hair & body-care
products.

LONGEVITY PURE MEDICINE
Subs. of Lacausa Inc
611 S Palm Canyon Dr (Suite 7522)
Palm Springs, CA 92264
Telephone: (800) 327-5519, FAX:
(760) 329-3651, E-Mail: info@
longetivtypuremedicine.com, Web
Site: www.longevitypuremedicine.
com
Mng Dir: Reni Chase
Conducts Business: U.S., S. America,
Central America, Asia, Europe
Employees: 11
Primary Market Served: Business &
Consumer
Catalog available online
Direct online sales
Advertising/Marketing Budget Related
to Direct Marketing: 26-50%
Direct Marketing ad budget: $150,000
Direct Mail: 45%
Magazines: 5%
Newspapers: 5%
TV/Radio: 20%
Telephone: 25%
Founded: 1984
Gross sales or billing: $1,000,000

14 natural homeopathic medicines for
colds & flu, PMS, stress, sinus, hay
fever, insomnia, cough & sore throat.

LUCKY HEART COSMETICS INC
390 Mulberry St
Memphis, TN 38103-4212
Telephone: (901) 526-7658, (800) 283-
1014, FAX: (901) 526-7660, Web
Site: www.luckyheart.com
Pres: Tom Colturi

VP: Chandra Miller
Conducts Business: U.S.
Employees: 20
Primary Market Served: Consumer
Catalog available online
Indirect online sales
Advertising/Marketing Budget Related
to Direct Marketing: 76-100%
Direct Marketing ad budget:
Direct Mail: 35%
Magazines: 65%
Founded: 1935
Gross sales or billing: $2,000,000

Manufactures & sells cosmetics to independent sales representatives. Also
carries an ethnic line which includes
hair & skin products.

LUZIER PERSONALIZED COSMETICS
7910-7912 Troost Ave
Kansas City, MO 64131-1920
Telephone: (816) 531-8338, (800) 821-
6632, FAX: (816) 531-6979, Web
Site: www.luzier.com
Pres: Kathleen Grissom
VP: Michelle Walters
Primary Market Served: Consumer
Catalog available online
Indirect online sales

Cosmetics.

MDR
14101 NW Fourth St
Sunrise, FL 33325-6209
Telephone: (954) 845-9500, (800) 327-
4660, FAX: (954) 845-9505, E-Mail:
customerservice@mdr.org, Web Site:
www.mdr.org
Pres & CEO: Patricia Riley
Conducts Business: U.S.
Employees: 60
Primary Market Served: Consumer
Catalog available online
Direct online sales
Advertising/Marketing Budget Related
to Direct Marketing: 0-25%
Direct Marketing ad budget:
Direct Mail: $100,000
Magazines: $1,000,000
TV/Radio: $1,000,000

Catalog marketer of cosmetics & skin
care products.

MJA INTERNATIONAL
9 Roslyn Dr
Glen Head, NY 11545
Telephone: (516) 759-1000, FAX:
(516) 674-3309
VP: Jay Berliner
Conducts Business: U.S.
Primary Market Served: Business
Advertising/Marketing Budget Related
to Direct Marketing: 0-25%

Founded: 1988
Medical equipment.

ROBERT J MATTHEWS CO
dba PBS Animal Health
2780 Richville Dr SE
Massillon, OH 44646-8396
Telephone: (330) 834-3000, (800) 321-0235, FAX: (330) 830-2762, Web Site: www.pbsanimalhealth.com
Pres: J. Daniel Matthews
Mktg Production Supvr: Bridget Gillogly
Conducts Business: U.S.
Primary Market Served: Business & Consumer
Catalog available online
Indirect online sales
Advertising/Marketing Budget Related to Direct Marketing: 76-100%
Founded: 1941

Distributor of animal health products & livestock pharmaceuticals.

THE DMA MCKESSON CORP
Div. of Red Line Medical Supply
1 Post St
San Francisco, CA 94104-5203
Telephone: (415) 983-8300, FAX: (415) 983-7160, Web Site: www.mckesson.com
Chmn, Pres & CEO: John H. Hammergren
Exec VP & Grp Pres: Paul C. Julian
Exec VP & CFO: Jeffrey C. Campbell
Conducts Business: U.S.
Employees: 31,800
Primary Market Served: Business & Consumer
Advertising/Marketing Budget Related to Direct Marketing: 0-25%
Gross sales or billing: $93,000,000,000

National distributor of medical supplies.

THE DMA MEAD JOHNSON CO
2400 W Lloyd Expwy
Evansville, IN 47721-0001
Telephone: (812) 429-5204, Web Site: www.MeadJohnson.com
Dir: Andrew Mosier
Primary Market Served: Business & Consumer

THE DMA MEDCO HEALTH SOLUTIONS INC
100 Parsons Pond Dr
Franklin Lakes, NJ 07417-2604
Telephone: (201) 269-3400, FAX: (201) 269-6400, Web Site: www.medco.com
VP Prod & Channel Generics Strategy: Kenneth Malley
Pres & CEO: David Snow

Chmn: Richard Clark
Dir: Boris Fainstein
Primary Market Served: Business
Catalog available online
Direct online sales
Gross sales or billing: $42,000,000,000

Leading pharmacy benefit management company providing benefits to more than 53 million Americans, including more than 14 million retirees. Merck-Medco subsidiary National Rx Services Inc serves patients through 12 state of the art mail service facilities, and its paid prescription subsidiary manages prescriptions dispensed at 52,000 community pharmacies worldwide.

MEDCO SUPPLY CO INC
500 Fillmore Ave
Tonawanda, NY 14150
Telephone: (716) 695-3244, (800) 556-3326, FAX: (800) 222-1934, E-Mail: sales@medcosupply.com, Web Site: www.medcosupply.com
Sr Prod Mgr: Karen Blaha
Pres: Mark Ladouceur
VP, Sls: Paul DeMartins
Dir, Mktg: Don Laux
Conducts Business: United States
Employees: 120
Primary Market Served: Business
Catalog available online
Direct online sales
Advertising/Marketing Budget Related to Direct Marketing: 76-100%
Direct Marketing ad budget:
Direct Mail: 90%
Magazines: 10%
Founded: 1955

National distributor of first aid, safety sports medicine and podiatry products for athletic physical therapy, chiropractic, school nurse and podiatry markets.

MIDWEST CENTER FOR STRESS & ANXIETY INC
106 N Church St (Suite 200), PO Box 205
Oak Harbor, OH 43449
Telephone: (419) 898-4357, (800) 611-0857, FAX: (419) 898-0669, Web Site: www.stresscenter.com
Pres & CEO: Lucinda Bassett
VP: David Bassett
Conducts Business: U.S., Canada
Employees: 15
Primary Market Served: Business & Consumer
Indirect online sales
Advertising/Marketing Budget Related to Direct Marketing: 51-75%
Direct Marketing ad budget:
$5,000,000
Direct Mail: 1%
TV/Radio: 99%

Gross sales or billing: $8,000,000

Self help program for anxiety & panic disorder to professionals & lay individuals. (Attacking Anxiety).

MIRACLE OF ALOE
PO Box 612688
Dallas, TX 75261-2688
Telephone: (800) 966-2563, FAX: (800) 859-9881, E-Mail: LJohnson@miracleofaloe.com, Web Site: www.miracleofaloe.com
Founder: Jess F. Clarke Jr.
Pres: Jess F. Clarke III
Creative Dir: Chris Sykes
New Products Mgr: Chris Clarke
CFO: Jennifer Babiak
Conducts Business: U.S., Nigeria, Taiwan, U.K., Finland, Argentina, China, Canada, Japan
Employees: 20
Primary Market Served: Business & Consumer
Catalog available online
Direct online sales
Advertising/Marketing Budget Related to Direct Marketing: 76-100%
Direct Marketing ad budget:
$1,000,000
Direct Mail: 70%
Magazines: 20%
Newspapers: 10%
Founded: 1986
Gross sales or billing: $7,000,000

Mail order catalog specializing in health & beauty aids made with pure aloe vera gel.

THE DMA MOORE MEDICAL LLC
Subs. of McKesson Corp
1690 New Britain Ave Ste A
Farmington, CT 06032-3361
Telephone: (860) 826-3600, FAX: (860) 223-2382, Web Site: www.mooremedical.com
VP, Mktg: Lori Steinberg
VP, Direct Mktg & Market Mgr: Tim Bidwell
Conducts Business: U.S.
Employees: 305
Primary Market Served: Business
Catalog available online
Direct online sales
Advertising/Marketing Budget Related to Direct Marketing: 76-100%
Direct Marketing ad budget:
Direct Mail: 90%
Magazines: 2%
Telephone: 8%
Founded: 1965
Gross sales or billing: $46,000,000

Medical supply distributor to alternate care facilities.

MURAD INC

2121 Rosecrans Ave 5th Fl
El Segundo, CA 90245-4744
Telephone: (310) 726-0600, Web Site:
www.murad.com
Exec VP Direct to Consumer: Carey
Grange
Primary Market Served: Consumer

NBTY INC

2100 Smithtown Ave
Ronkonkoma, NY 11779-7347
Telephone: (631) 200-2000, FAX:
(631) 567-7148, Web Site: www.
nbty.com
Chmn Bd & CEO: Scott Rudolph
Sr VP, Adv & Mktg: Jim Flaherty
Conducts Business: Worldwide
Employees: 10,900
Primary Market Served: Business &
Consumer
Catalog available online
Direct online sales
Advertising/Marketing Budget Related
to Direct Marketing: 26-50%
Founded: 1971
Gross sales or billing: $1,880,222,000

Manufacturer, marketer & distributor
of nutritional supplements including
vitamins, minerals, herbs & sports
drinks to pharmacies, wholesalers, supermarkets, health food stores & consumers via mail order and online.

NATURMED

dba Institute of Vibrant Living
PO Box 1270
Camp Verde, AZ 86322
Telephone: (800) 218-1378, Web Site:
www.ivlproducts.com

NEWMARK LABORATORIES

164 Northfield Ave
Edison, NJ 08837
Telephone: (732) 417-1870, (800) 338-
8079, FAX: (732) 225-0066, E-Mail:
newmark@injersey.com
Pres: Pat Lonergan
VP, Mktg: Moaiz Daya
VP, Sls: Lou Sullivan
Primary Market Served: Consumer

Sells over-the-counter pharmaceuticals,
health & beauty aids.

NOEVIR DIRECT MARKETING INC

Subs. of Noevie Ltd Japan
200 W Grand Ave
Montvale, NJ 07645-1716
Telephone: (201) 391-0001, (800) 872-
8888, FAX: (201) 391-1740, E-Mail:
marketing@noevirusa.com, Web
Site: www.noevir.com
Pres: Hitoshi Moritani

Primary Market Served: Business &
Consumer
Founded: 1978

Direct selling of skin care products &
cosmetics to consultants.

NOVARTIS PHARMACEUTICALS CORP

1 Health Plaza (Bldg 701 Rm 060)
East Hanover, NJ 07936-1016
Telephone: (862) 778-6914, FAX:
(973) 781-8119, Web Site: www.
pharma.us.novartis.com
COO & VP Mktg: David Epstein
Dir Head Relationship Mktg: Marc
Schwartz
Primary Market Served: Business &
Consumer

Ethical & over-the-counter
pharmaceuticals.

NUTRAORIGIN

1983 Marcus Ave (Suite 206)
Lake Success, NY 11042-1016
Telephone: (516) 858-0301, Web Site:
www.nutraorigin.com
VP Mktg: Timothy Peterson

NUTRI-HEALTH SUPPLEMENTS

260 Justin Dr
Cottonwood, AZ 86326
Telephone: (928) 340-5400

NUTRISYSTEM INC

600 Office Center Dr
Fort Washington, PA 19034-3232
Telephone: (215) 706-5300, (800) 321-
THIN, FAX: (215) 706-5388, Web
Site: www.nutrisystem.com
Chmn & CEO: Michael J. Hagan
Pres & COO: Joseph Redling
Dir Database Mktg: Donna Lamber-
tucci
CFO: David D. Clark
Exec VP & CMO: Thomas F. Connerty
Sr VP, Opers: Bruce Blair
Conducts Business: Worldwide
Primary Market Served: Consumer
Catalog available online
Direct online sales
Advertising/Marketing Budget Related
to Direct Marketing: 51-75%
Direct Marketing ad budget:
Direct Mail: 25%
Newspapers: 25%
TV/Radio: 50%
Founded: 1971
Gross sales or billing: $568,000,000

National weight loss company.

1-800-CONTACTS

51 W Center St
Orem, UT 84057-4605
Telephone: (800) CONTACTS, FAX:
(801) 924-9000, Web Site: www.
1800contacts.com
Primary Market Served: Business &
Consumer

PPN INC

275 Center St (Suite 3)
Holbrook, MA 02343-1079
Telephone: (781) 767-5776, (800) 289-
4776, FAX: (781) 767-4776, E-Mail:
customer.service@ppninc.com, Web
Site: www.ppninc.com
Pres & CEO: William F. Shaffer
Exec VP: Michael L. Shaffer
Conducts Business: U.S.
Employees: 25
Primary Market Served: Consumer
Founded: 1972
Gross sales or billing: $4,300,000

Clothing to health care industry.

PACIFIC BOTANICALS LLC

4840 Fish Hatchery Rd
Grants Pass, OR 97527-9547
Telephone: (541) 479-7777, FAX:
(541) 479-7780, E-Mail: pacbot1@
earthlink.net, Web Site: www.
pacificbotanicals.com
Founder: Mark Wheeler
COO: Toni Corrente-Evans
Farm Mgr: Dave Metzger
Mill Mgr: Bruce Fain
QC Mgr: Dori Moran
Conducts Business: Worldwide
Employees: 15
Primary Market Served: Consumer
Catalog available online
Advertising/Marketing Budget Related
to Direct Marketing: 0-25%
Founded: 1979

Certified organic bulk herbs & spices.

PARIS PRESENTS INC

3800 Swanson Ct
Gurnee, IL 60031-1226
Telephone: (847) 263-5500, (800) 431-
5723, FAX: (847) 263-5191, Web
Site: www.parispresents.com
VP Mktg: Beth Cassiday
Conducts Business: U.S., Canada,
Mexico, Sweden, Europe, Far East
Employees: 75
Primary Market Served: Business
Direct online sales
Founded: 1947
Gross sales or billing: $9,800,000

Distributor of cosmetics, bath, beauty
& travel accessories.

PENN HERB CO LTD

dba Nature's Wonderland
10601 Decatur Rd (Suite 2)
Philadelphia, PA 19154-3293
Telephone: (215) 632-6100, (800) 523-9971, FAX: (215) 632-7945, E-Mail: information@pennherb.com, Web Site: www.pennherb.com
Pres & CEO: Ronald Betz
VP: William P. Betz Jr
Gen Mgr: Jerome Hannah
Conducts Business: U.S.
Employees: 26
Primary Market Served: Business & Consumer
Founded: 1924
Gross sales or billing: $3,500,000

Sell dried herbs, herbal products, capsules, books, essential oils, homeopathic remedies, vitamins, health food items, herbal extracts & Olbas products.

THE DMA PHILIPS LIFELINE

111 Lawrence St
Framingham, MA 01702-8156
Telephone: (508) 988-1533, Web Site: www.lifelinesys.com
Dir Direct Mktg: Brenda Vere
Primary Market Served: Consumer

POCKET NURSE ENTERPRISES INC

610 Frankfort Rd
Monaca, PA 15061-2218
Telephone: (800) 225-1600, FAX: (800) 763-0237, E-Mail: info@pocketnurse.com, Web Site: www.pocketnurse.com
Primary Market Served: Consumer
Founded: 1992

Medical supplies & equipment for health care educators

THE DMA PURITAN'S PRIDE

2100 Smithtown Ave
Ronkonkoma, NY 11779-7347
Telephone: (631) 567-9500, FAX: (631) 471-5693, E-Mail: info@puritan.com, Web Site: www.puritan.com
Pres & CFO: Harvey Kamil
Sr VP, Puritan Direct Response: Sabir Somerkamp
Conducts Business: Worldwide
Employees: 100
Primary Market Served: Consumer
Catalog available online
Direct online sales
Advertising/Marketing Budget Related to Direct Marketing: 76-100%
Gross sales or billing: $1,900,000

Manufactures & distributes top quality natural vitamins, minerals, herbs & other nutritional supplements by mail order & online.

RASCAL

591 Mantua Blvd
Sewell, NJ 08080
Telephone: (856) 468-1000, (800) 662-4548, FAX: (856) 468-3426, Web Site: www.electricmobility.com
Pres: Michael Flowers
Mktg: Dan Rowan
Conducts Business: U.S., Canada, U.K.
Employees: 200
Primary Market Served: Business & Consumer
Indirect online sales
Advertising/Marketing Budget Related to Direct Marketing: 26-50%
Direct Marketing ad budget:
Direct Mail: 10%
Magazines: 70%
TV/Radio: 20%
Founded: 1974
Gross sales or billing: $24,000,000

Compact portable electric wheelchairs & scooters for the elderly & disabled.

RAVEN'S NEST HERBALS, LLC

PO Box 370
Duluth, GA 30096
Telephone: (678) 642-6691, (678) 584-0830, E-Mail: info@ravensnestherbals.com, Web Site: www.ravensnestherbals.com
Owner, Master Herbalist & Sls: Terry Cochran
Seasonal Mgr: Mark Gravitt
Conducts Business: U.S., Canada, Caribbean, Japan, U.K., S. Africa
Employees: 1
Primary Market Served: Consumer
Catalog available online
Direct online sales
Advertising/Marketing Budget Related to Direct Marketing: 0-25%
Direct Marketing ad budget: $1,500
Direct Mail: 50%
Magazines: 5%
Newspapers: 45%
Founded: 1985
Gross sales or billing: $30,000

Herbs, spices, teas, essential oils, fragrances, potpourri, dried flowers & incense to health food/vitamin stores, herb shops, crafters & individuals.

RELAXO-BAK INC

PO Box 2613
Anderson, IN 46018-2613
Telephone: (765) 643-2934, (800) 527-5496, FAX: (765) 641-7448, Web Site: www.relaxobak.com

Pres: Diane Cameron
Conducts Business: U.S.
Employees: 3
Primary Market Served: Business & Consumer
Catalog available online
Direct online sales
Direct Marketing ad budget: $10,000
Direct Mail: 25%
Magazines: 75%
Founded: 1963
Gross sales or billing: $200,000

Thin form-fitting plastic auxiliary seat. Used on any over-soft seat to give it firmness. Contoured for better weight distribution & greater comfort. Recessed at the spine's end to shield the tailbone. Used in office chairs, autos, trucks, buses & airplanes.

ROCHE DIAGNOSTICS CORP

9115 Hague Rd
Indianapolis, IN 46256-1045
Telephone: (317) 521-2000, Web Site: www.accu-chek.com
Group Mgr Prof Mktg: Angie Nelis
Primary Market Served: Consumer

ROCHE PHARMACEUTICALS

Div. of Hoffmann-La Roche Inc
340 Kingsland St
Nutley, NJ 07110-1150
Telephone: (973) 235-5000, FAX: (973) 235-7605, Web Site: www.rocheusa.com
Pres, HLR: George Abercrombie
Dir Integrated Promo Plan: Linda Parisi
VP, Specialty Mktg: Patrick Higgins
VP, Sls & Mktg: Barbara Senich
Conducts Business: Worldwide
Primary Market Served: Business & Consumer

Market pharmaceutical products through general advertising, direct mail & personal representation.

SALLY BEAUTY SUPPLY LLC

3001 Colorado Blvd
Denton, TX 76210
Telephone: (940) 898-7500, (800) 275-7255, Web Site: www.sallybeauty.com
Pres: Michael Spinozzi
CEO: Gary Winterhaltee
Commun Specialist: Shana Tyler
Adv Dir Sally Stores: Christy Ehlers
Conducts Business: U.S., Canada, UK, Germany, Japan, Ireland, Spain, Mexico
Employees: 5,500
Primary Market Served: Business & Consumer
Catalog available online
Direct online sales

Advertising/Marketing Budget Related
to Direct Marketing: 76-100%
Direct Marketing ad budget:
$10,000,000
Direct Mail: 86%
Magazines: 5%
Newspapers: 7%
TV/Radio: 2%
Founded: 1969
Gross sales or billing: $1,300,000,000

Professional beauty products to salons,
hairdressers & consumers. Over 2700
store locations.

THE SCOOTER STORE

PO Box 310709
New Braunfels, TX 78131-0709
Telephone: (830) 608-9200
Exec VP Mktg: Dan Gibbens
Primary Market Served: Business &
Consumer

SECURITEC PUBLICATIONS

W175N11117 Stonewood Dr (Suite
110)
Germantown, WI 53022-6505
Telephone: (262) 532-4000, (800) 783-
2145, FAX: (262) 532-4001, E-Mail:
securitec@securitec.com
VP Mktg: Jean Kahl

SENSORY CONSUMER
SCIENCE

300 North St
Teterboro, NJ 07608-1204
Telephone: (201) 462-2389, Web Site:
www.symrise.com
VP, Mktg & Sensory Consumer
Science: Emmanuel Laroche
Primary Market Served: Business

SHIELD HEALTHCARE

Div. of Kobayashi Pharmaceuticals Inc
(Japan)
27911B Franklin Pkwy
Valencia, CA 91355-4110
Telephone: (661) 294-4200, (800) 228-
7150, FAX: (661) 294-1043, Web
Site: www.shieldhealthcare.com
Pres: Jim Snell
Info Sys Mgr: Tillman Lindsay
Mktg Mgr: Todd Smith
Catalog Mgr: Tim Baker
Conducts Business: U.S.
Employees: 187
Primary Market Served: Business &
Consumer
Advertising/Marketing Budget Related
to Direct Marketing: 76-100%
Direct Marketing ad budget:
Direct Mail: 60%
Magazines: 5%
Telephone: 35%
Founded: 1955
Gross sales or billing: $30,000,000

National wholesaler of disposable
medical products. Ostomy, Diabetes,
incontinence, urology, airway &
internal. Retailer with reimbursement
capabilities in California, Colorado &
Illinois. Managed Care Division, Retail
Catalog Division.

SHISEIDO COSMETICS
AMERICA

900 Third Ave (15th fl)
New York, NY 10022
Telephone: (212) 805-2300, FAX:
(212) 688-0109, Web Site: www.sca.
shiseido.com
CEO: Heidi Manheimer
VP, Mktg: Anne Marino
VP, Mktg: Tomoko Yamagishi
VP: Seiji Nishimori
Primary Market Served: Consumer
Catalog available online
Founded: 1965

Market cosmetics & skincare.

ᴛʜᴇ DMA SIMPLY BATTERIES INC

PO Box 948
Dekalb, IL 60115-0948
Telephone: (815) 756-1473, Web Site:
www.simplybatteries.com
Pres: Laura Stuebing
Primary Market Served: Consumer

THE SOAP FACTORY

3 Burlington Rd
Bedford, MA 01730-1305
Telephone: (781) 275-8363, E-Mail:
soapfac@verizon.net, Web Site:
www.alcasoft.com/soapfact/
Pres & Owner: Marietta Ellis
VP: Arthur Ellis
Conducts Business: U.S.
Employees: 2
Primary Market Served: Business &
Consumer
Catalog available online
Indirect online sales
Advertising/Marketing Budget Related
to Direct Marketing: 76-100%
Direct Marketing ad budget:
Direct Mail: 80%
Magazines: 10%
Newspapers: 10%
Founded: 1989
Gross sales or billing: $25,000

Handcrafted castile toilet soap. Sell our
handmade soaps direct to the retail
consumer at craft shows & direct mail
to our customer lists. Sell to owners of
herb & gift shops.

SONGBIRD HEARING INC

1 Penbrook Ct
Princeton Junction, NJ 08550-1805

Telephone: (732) 828-8300, Web Site:
www.songbirdhearing.com
VP Mktg: Jennifer Haus
Primary Market Served: Consumer

SPA-FINDER INC

257 Park Ave S (10th fl)
New York, NY 10010
Telephone: (212) 924-6800, (800)
ALL-SPAS, FAX: (212) 924-7240,
Web Site: www.spafinder.com
Chmn Bd & CEO: Pete Ellis
Pres: Susie Ellis
COO: Sallie Fraenkel
VP Grp Publr: Sara Greenwood
VP: Milana Knowles
Conducts Business: U.S., Canada, Eu-
rope, Japan
Employees: 25
Primary Market Served: Business &
Consumer
Catalog available online
Direct online sales
Direct Marketing ad budget: $875,000
Direct Mail: $500,000
Magazines: $300,000
Newspapers: $75,000
Gross sales or billing: $10,000,000

Marketer of spa vacations worldwide
through 140-page catalog.

SPALDING LABORATORIES
INC

760 Printz Rd
Arroyo Grande, CA 93420-5022
Telephone: (805) 489-5946, (888) 880-
1579, FAX: (866) 738-9632, Web
Site: www.spalding-labs.com
Pres & Owner: Tom Spalding
VP: Jake Blehm
Sec: Lee Ann Merrill
Treas: Glen Scriven
Conducts Business: U.S.
Primary Market Served: Business &
Consumer
Catalog available online
Indirect online sales
Advertising/Marketing Budget Related
to Direct Marketing: 26-50%
Direct Marketing ad budget:
Direct Mail: 70%
Magazines: 25%
Newspapers: 5%
Founded: 1976

Beneficial insects called fly predators.
Sell to dairies, chicken farms, horse
ranches & anyone who has a pest fly
problem.

ᴛʜᴇ DMA SUN HOPE NUTRITIONAL
HEALTH

1158 26th St (#566)
Santa Monica, CA 90403-4698
Telephone: (888) 553-5476, Web Site:
www.sunhope.net

Dir: Jim Chen
Primary Market Served: Business & Consumer

SUPPORT PLUS
Div. of Surgical Products
5581 Hudson Industrial Pkwy, PO Box 500
Hudson, OH 44236-5019
Telephone: (508) 359-2910, (800) 229-2910, FAX: (508) 359-0139, E-Mail: cs@supportplus.com, Web Site: www.supportplus.com
Pres: Edward H. Janos
VP: Eloise Janos
Conducts Business: U.S., Canada, Asia, Europe
Employees: 47
Primary Market Served: Consumer
Catalog available online
Indirect online sales
Advertising/Marketing Budget Related to Direct Marketing: 76-100%
Direct Marketing ad budget:
Direct Mail: 99%
Magazines: 1%
Founded: 1972

Sells home health care products directly to consumer.

TEVA PHARMACEUTICALS USA
1090 Horsham Rd, Box 1090
North Wales, PA 19454-1090
Telephone: (215) 591-3000, (888) TEVAUSA, FAX: (215) 591-8600, Web Site: www.tevausa.com
Pres & CEO: William Marth
VP, Generic Sls: Larry Rosenthal
CFO: Dan Suesskind
Dir Investor Rels: Dorit Meltzer
COO: George Barnett
Conducts Business: Worldwide
Employees: 1,025
Primary Market Served: Business
Catalog available online
Indirect online sales
Advertising/Marketing Budget Related to Direct Marketing: 0-25%
Direct Marketing ad budget:
Direct Mail: 35%
Magazines: 30%
Telephone: 35%
Founded: 1945
Gross sales or billing: $2,100,000,000

Sell generic pharmaceutical products through direct mail, personal & general sales.

TOOLS FOR WELLNESS
638 Lindero Canyon Rd (Suite 128)
Oak Park, CA 91377-5457

Telephone: (800) 456-9887, FAX: (818) 532-1775, E-Mail: info@toolsforwellness.com, Web Site: www.toolsforwellness.com
Pres: Kenneth Chane
VP: Andrew Chane
Conducts Business: Worldwide
Employees: 13
Primary Market Served: Consumer
Catalog available online
Direct online sales
Advertising/Marketing Budget Related to Direct Marketing: 0-25%
Direct Marketing ad budget: $300,000
Direct Mail: 40%
Online: 60%
Founded: 1989
Gross sales or billing: $5,000,000

Consciousness technologies, peak performance, optimum wellness & cognitive enhancement products.

TOTAL CARE
Div. of Total Medical Systems Inc
PO Box 1661
Rockville, MD 20849-1661
Telephone: (301) 251-2061, (800) 334-3802, FAX: (301) 251-5891, E-Mail: totalcare@sprintmail.com, Web Site: www.totalmedinc.com
Pres: Michael J. Hanik
Conducts Business: U.S., Canada
Employees: 12
Primary Market Served: Business
Catalog available online
Direct online sales
Advertising/Marketing Budget Related to Direct Marketing: 51-75%
Direct Marketing ad budget:
Direct Mail: 75%
Online: 25%
Founded: 1976

Direct mail marketing to hospitals, nursing homes & E.C.F. facilities. Specialized line of medical soft goods & disposables.

TOVA CORP
1200 Wilson Dr, Studio Park
West Chester, PA 19380
Telephone: (484) 701-1000, Web Site: www.beautybytova.com
Chmn: Tova Borgnine
Mktg Dir: David Johnson
Conducts Business: U.S.
Employees: 50
Primary Market Served: Consumer

Market skin care, bath & fragrance products for men & women through mail order.

TROY BIOLOGICALS INC
1238 Rankin
Troy, MI 48083

Telephone: (800) 521-0445, FAX: (248) 585-2490, E-Mail: info@troybio.com, Web Site: www.troybio.com
Pres: Robert Ricketts
Supvr: Lynn Michaud
Opers Mgr: Tom Ricketts
Mktg Dir: Janine Deighan
Conducts Business: U.S.
Employees: 25
Primary Market Served: Business
Catalog available online
Direct online sales
Advertising/Marketing Budget Related to Direct Marketing: 76-100%
Direct Marketing ad budget:
Direct Mail: 100%
Founded: 1976
Gross sales or billing: $10,000,000

Distribute microbiology supplies & rapid diagnostic kits to surgical supply houses nationwide.

UDL LABORATORIES INC
Subs. of Mylan Laboratories, Inc
12720 Darry Ashford
Sugar Land, TX 77478
Telephone: (281) 240-1000, (800) 231-3052, FAX: (281) 240-0002, Web Site: www.udllabs.com
Chmn Bd & CEO: Robert J. Coury
COO: Heather Bresch
Exec VP & Gen Mgr: Vincent Mancelli
VP, Corp Controller: Daniel C. Rizzo Jr.
Head of Global Tech Opers: Rajiv Malik
Prod Mgr: Ross Whitfield
Conducts Business: U.S.
Employees: 230
Primary Market Served: Business
Catalog available online
Direct Marketing ad budget: $70,000
Direct Mail: 20%
Magazines: 70%
Telephone: 10%
Gross sales or billing: $30,000,000

Manufacturer & marketer of wound care products for chronic & burn related wounds.

THE DMA ULTA SALON COSMETICS FRAGRANCE
1135 Arbor Dr
Romeoville, IL 60446-1174
Telephone: (630) 226-0020
Dir CRM: Andrew McGarry

ULTRADENT PRODUCTS INC
505 W 10200 S
South Jordan, UT 84095-3935
Telephone: (801) 572-4200, Web Site: www.ultradent.com
CRM Dir: Mary Lou Lettig

Primary Market Served: Consumer

UNIFORMS & SCRUBS.COM
910 Kehrs Mill Rd (Suite 106)
Ballwin, MO 63011-2404
Telephone: (636) 391-9200, FAX:
(636) 391-9205, E-Mail: questions@
uniformsandscrubs.com, Web Site:
www.whiteswanscrubs.com
Pres: David Huelsbeck
VP, Mktg: Bob Fogel
Conducts Business: U.S.
Employees: 450
Primary Market Served: Business
Advertising/Marketing Budget Related
to Direct Marketing: 51-75%
Founded: 1896
Gross sales or billing: $30,000,000

Identity & image apparel for healthcare
(nursing) industry.

THE DMA UNITED SYSTEMS C/O BIOMED
2354 Stanwell Dr
Concord, CA 94520-4822
Telephone: (925) 609-2820
Pres: Richard Colman
VP: Deborah Cheung
Primary Market Served: Business &
Consumer

VGH SOLUTIONS
145 Anderson Ave
Markham, ON, Canada L6E 1A4
Telephone: (905) 471-4735, FAX:
(905) 471-2608
Pres: Vincent Ho
Primary Market Served: Consumer

VAXSERVE
111 N Washington Ave Fl 1
Scranton, PA 18503-1841
Telephone: (800) 752-9338, Web Site:
www.vaxserve.com
E-Commerce/Mktg Analysis: Edward
Russo
Primary Market Served: Business

VEMMA NUTRITION CO
8322 E Hartford Dr
Scottsdale, AZ 85255
Telephone: (800) 577-0777, FAX:
(888) 314-9827, E-Mail: ms@
vemma.com, Web Site: www.vemma.
com
Founder: Glen Halverson
Pres & CEO: B.K. Boreyko
Co-CEO: Jason Boreyko
Sls & Mktg Dir: Laurie Prondzinski
Primary Market Served: Business &
Consumer
Catalog available online
Indirect online sales

Nutritional liquid antioxidants

VITAMIN POWER INC
73 Commerce Dr
Hauppauge, NY 11788-3902
Telephone: (516) 378-0900, (800) 645-
6567, FAX: (516) 378-0919, E-Mail:
vitpower@aol.com, Web Site: www.
vitaminpower.com
Chmn: Edward Friedlander
Pres: David H. Friedlander
Conducts Business: Worldwide
Employees: 42
Primary Market Served: Business &
Consumer
Catalog available online
Direct online sales
Advertising/Marketing Budget Related
to Direct Marketing: 76-100%
Direct Marketing ad budget: $300,000
Direct Mail: $230,000
Magazines: $60,000
Newspapers: $10,000
Founded: 1975
Gross sales or billing: $6,000,000

Manufacturer & marketer of health &
fitness products including nutritional
supplements & skin care products.

VITAMIN RESEARCH PRODUCTS
4610 Arrowhead Dr
Carson City, NV 89706-2017
Telephone: (775) 884-8205, Web Site:
www.vrp.com
VP Mktg: Staci Glovsky
Primary Market Served: Business &
Consumer

VITAMIN SPECIALTIES CO
IVC Industries
500 Halls Mill Rd
Freehold, NJ 07728
Telephone: (732) 308-3000, FAX:
(732) 683-1622, Web Site: www.
ivcinc.com
VP, Mktg: Rich Meyers
Conducts Business: U.S.
Primary Market Served: Consumer

Mail order sales of vitamins & other
health items. Operate retail outlets in
PA & NJ.

WRS GROUP LTD
5045 Franklin Ave
Waco, TX 76710-6919
Telephone: (254) 776-6461, (800) 299-
3366, FAX: (888) 977-7653, E-Mail:
sales@wrsgroup.com, Web Site:
www.wrsgroup.com
CEO: Scott J. Salmans
Pres & COO: Gary Hutchinson
VP: Cathi Davis
VP: Tom Kaylor
VP: Cynthia Peterson
Primary Market Served: Business &
Consumer

Catalog available online
Direct online sales
Founded: 1969
Gross sales or billing: $18,949,955

Provider of health education materials.
Available online or via catalog.

THE DMA WELLPOINT
201 N Westshore Dr (Apt 1801)
Chicago, IL 60601-7265
Telephone: (312) 533-9779, Web Site:
www.wellpoint.com

WINNING SOLUTIONS INC
4401 Diplomacy Rd
Fort Worth, TX 76155-2665
Telephone: (972) 986-5355, (866) 494-
6765, E-Mail: winninginc@aol.com
Pres: Jess F. Clarke III
VP: Jess F. Clarke Jr
Creative Dir: Chris Sykes
Primary Market Served: Business &
Consumer
Catalog available online
Advertising/Marketing Budget Related
to Direct Marketing: 0-25%
Founded: 1984

Makers & distributors of Aloe Vera
self, healthcare products brand name
Miracle of Aloe Westport, CT & Dallas, TX.

WYSONG CORP
7550 Eastman Ave
Midland, MI 48642-7779
Telephone: (989) 631-0009, (800) 748-
0188, FAX: (989) 631-8801, E-Mail:
wysong@wysong.net, Web Site:
www.wysong.net
Pres: Randy L. Wysong
Mktg Dir: Christine Johnsten
Conducts Business: Worldwide
Employees: 30
Primary Market Served: Business &
Consumer
Catalog available online
Direct online sales
Advertising/Marketing Budget Related
to Direct Marketing: 0-25%
Founded: 1979

Full line of nutritional foods, natural
vitamins, pet foods, pet supplements,
cat litter to veterinarians, consumers,
etc.

THE DMA YVES ROCHER NORTH AMERICA INC
2199 Boul Fernaud LaFontaine
Longueuil, PQ, Canada J4G2V7
Telephone: (450) 442-9555, Web Site:
www.yvesrocherusa.com
Dir Sls: Philippe Hervieu
Primary Market Served: Business &
Consumer

ABC CARPET & HOME
888 Broadway at E 19th St
New York, NY 10003-1280
Telephone: (212) 473-3000, (800) 888-RUGS, FAX: (212) 777-3713, Web Site: www.abccarpet.com
Mktg: Grace Kim
Conducts Business: Worldwide
Employees: 300
Primary Market Served: Business & Consumer
Founded: 1897

Direct marketer & retailer of broadloom rugs, antique & fine reproduction furniture, handmade oriental rugs, bed, bath & linen, gifts & accessories.

ACME TOOLS
1603 12th Ave N
Grand Forks, ND 58203-2304
Telephone: (701) 746-2881, Web Site: www.acmetoolcrib.com
VP: Paul Kuhlman
Primary Market Served: Consumer

AMARYLLIS INC
1452 Glenmore Ave
Baton Rouge, LA 70808-1225
Telephone: (225) 924-5560
Owner: Ed Beckham
Conducts Business: Worldwide
Employees: 1
Primary Market Served: Business & Consumer

Amaryllis bulbs wholesale & retail.

AMERICAN MEADOWS INC & VERMONT WILD FLOWERS FARM
Subs. of Foster & Gallagher Inc
223 Ave D (#30)
Williston, VT 05495-7139
Telephone: (802) 985-9455, (877) 309-7333, FAX: (802) 985-9268, E-Mail: erin@americanmeadows.com, Web Site: www.americanmeadows.com
Founder: Charlotte Allen
Pres: Ray Allen
VP: Chy Allen
Sls Mgr: Mike Lizotte
Conducts Business: U.S., Canada
Employees: 15
Primary Market Served: Business & Consumer
Catalog available online
Advertising/Marketing Budget Related to Direct Marketing: 76-100%
Direct Marketing ad budget:
Direct Mail: 90%
Magazines: 10%
Founded: 1981

Sell wildflower seed mixes & individual species of wildflower seeds to consumer home gardeners & landscapers, states, municipalities & commercial accounts.

AMERICAN PERIOD LIGHTING INC
3004 Columbia Ave
Lancaster, PA 17603-4001
Telephone: (717) 392-5649, FAX: (717) 509-3127, E-Mail: conygham@yahoo.com, Web Site: www.americanperiod.com
Pres: Jack Cunningham
Conducts Business: U.S., Canada
Employees: 3
Primary Market Served: Business & Consumer
Catalog available online
Indirect online sales
Advertising/Marketing Budget Related to Direct Marketing: 51-75%
Direct Marketing ad budget: $40,000
Magazines: 50%
Online: 50%
Founded: 1969
Gross sales or billing: $300,000

Manufactures retail & wholesale traditional, period & historical hand crafted lighting fixtures for home & garden.

AMES-TRU-TEMPER
465 Railroad Ave
Camp Hill, PA 17011-5611
Telephone: (304) 424-3000, FAX: (304) 424-3330
Category Mgr: Karen Richwine
Category Mgr: Jackie Smalley
Conducts Business: U.S., Canada
Employees: 1,400
Primary Market Served: Consumer
Advertising/Marketing Budget Related to Direct Marketing: 0-25%
Direct Marketing ad budget:
Direct Mail: 15%
Telephone: 85%
Gross sales or billing: $300,000,000

Manufacturer of lawn & garden products.

AMVAC CHEMICAL CORP
Div. of American Vanguard Corp
4100 E Washington Blvd
Los Angeles, CA 90023-4406
Telephone: (323) 264-3910, FAX: (323) 268-1028, Web Site: www.amvac-chemical.com
Exec VP: David Cassidy
VP & Mfg Dir: Doug Ashmore
Tech Dir: William Feiler
Conducts Business: Worldwide

Employees: 126
Primary Market Served: Business
Advertising/Marketing Budget Related to Direct Marketing: 0-25%
Direct Marketing ad budget:
Direct Mail: 20%
Magazines: 80%
Founded: 1948
Gross sales or billing: $50,000,000

Agricultural chemical manufacturer selling insecticides, molluscicides, pheromones, herbicides, plant growth regulators & fungicides to licensed pesticide distributors.

ANTIQUE ROSE EMPORIUM
9300 Lueckemeyer Rd
Brenham, TX 77833-6453
Telephone: (800) 441-0002, FAX: (979) 836-0928, E-Mail: roses@industyinet.com, Web Site: www.weareroses.com
Pres: Mike Shoup
MO Mgr: Alison Duckworth
Conducts Business: U.S.
Primary Market Served: Consumer
Catalog available online
Direct online sales
Advertising/Marketing Budget Related to Direct Marketing: 51-75%
Direct Marketing ad budget:
Direct Mail: 75%
Magazines: 10%
Newspapers: 2%
TV/Radio: 3%
Telephone: 10%
Founded: 1982

APPALACHIAN NURSERIES, INC
Div. of Appalachian Nurseries
1724 Clay Hill Rd
Chambersburg, PA 17201
Telephone: (717) 597-0066, (877) 743-4733, E-Mail: info@appnursery.com, Web Site: www.appnursery.com
Owner & Pres: Tom McCloud
Admin Asst: Fern McCloud
Conducts Business: U.S.
Employees: 3
Primary Market Served: Business
Advertising/Marketing Budget Related to Direct Marketing: 76-100%
Direct Marketing ad budget:
Direct Mail: 75%
Magazines: 20%
Newspapers: 5%
Founded: 1985
Gross sales or billing: $56,000

Sell potted, hardy ornamental trees & shrubs.

ART.COM
2100 Powell St 10th Fl
Emeryville, CA 94608-1893
Telephone: (510) 879-4700, Web Site:
www.art.com
Dir Catalog Mktg: Christopher Inman
CEO: Michael Heinstein
Primary Market Served: Consumer

ARTISANAL LLC
PO Box 625
Holicong, PA 18928-0625
Telephone: (215) 862-8000, FAX:
(215) 862-8008, E-Mail: info@
artisanaldesign.com, Web Site: www.
artisanaldesign.com
Pres: Christine Soderman
Mgr: Kenneth Patrick
Conducts Business: U.S.
Employees: 2
Primary Market Served: Consumer
Catalog available online
Direct online sales
Advertising/Marketing Budget Related
to Direct Marketing: 76-100%
Direct Marketing ad budget:
Magazines: 100%
Founded: 2004

Provide distinctive hand-crafted decorative art objects & home decor products to upscale clientele.

ASSOCIATED MATERIALS
3773 State Rd
Cuyahoga Falls, OH 44223-2603
Telephone: (330) 922-2182, Web Site:
www.alside.com
Dir Mktg, Siding: Mike Kemper

AUTHENTIC DESIGNS COLONIAL AND EARLY AMERICAN LIGHTING FIXTURES INC
The Mill Rd
West Rupert, VT 05776-9716
Telephone: (802) 394-7713, (800) 844-9416, FAX: (802) 394-2422, E-Mail:
mail@authenticdesigns.com, Web
Site: www.authenticdesigns.com
Pres: Michael Krauss
VP: Maria Peragine-Krauss
Conducts Business: U.S., Canada
Employees: 10
Primary Market Served: Business &
Consumer
Catalog available online
Indirect online sales
Advertising/Marketing Budget Related
to Direct Marketing: 26-50%
Founded: 1971
Gross sales or billing: $1,000,000

Makers of colonial & early American
reproduction chandeliers, sconces,
lanterns. Custom work. 64 page catalog available for $3.

BACKYARD GARDENING
PO Box 8
Tiger, GA 30576-0008
Telephone: (706) 782-4224, (800) 681-3962, FAX: (800) 311-9539, E-Mail:
info@yardzone.com, Web Site:
www.yardzone.com
VP: Emmett Krivsky
Primary Market Served: Consumer

Mail order catalog for gardeners including garden tools and bird houses.

BALLARD DESIGNS
1670 Defoor Ave
Atlanta, GA 30318-7528
Telephone: (404) 352-8486, (800) 367-2775, FAX: (404) 352-1660, Web
Site: www.ballarddesigns.com
Acting CEO: Mark Fasolv
Conducts Business: U.S.
Employees: 70
Primary Market Served: Business &
Consumer

Unique direct mail catalog of decorative furnishings & accessories for the
home; garden statuary, plaques, pedestals, glass tops & gifts.

BAMBOO SOURCERY
666 Wagnon Rd
Sebastopol, CA 95472-9546
Telephone: (707) 823-5866, FAX:
(707) 829-8106, E-Mail:
bamboosource@earthlink.net, Web
Site: www.bamboosourcery.com
Owner: Jennifer York
Employees: 4
Primary Market Served: Business &
Consumer
Catalog available online
Direct online sales
Advertising/Marketing Budget Related
to Direct Marketing: 0-25%
Founded: 1980

Specialty nursery with nearly 300 species of bamboo from around the world.
Offer expert consultation services &
extensive demonstration gardens as
well as rhizome barriers, books &
bamboo poles.

BATHROOM MACHINERIES
495 Main St
Murphys, CA 95247
Telephone: (209) 728-3860, FAX:
(209) 728-2320, E-Mail: info@
deabath.com, Web Site: www.
deabath.com
Pres: Tom Scheller
Conducts Business: U.S., Canada, Japan
Employees: 11
Primary Market Served: Business &
Consumer
Catalog available online

Direct online sales
Advertising/Marketing Budget Related
to Direct Marketing: 76-100%
Direct Marketing ad budget:
Direct Mail: $20,000
Magazines: $5,000
Founded: 1976
Gross sales or billing: $700,000

Antique or reproduction plumbing,
hardware & lighting.

BED BATH & BEYOND
110 Bi County Blvd (Suite 114)
Farmingdale, NY 11735-3923
Telephone: (631) 420-7050
VP Mktg: Rita Little
Primary Market Served: Consumer

BELLACOR
2425 Enterprise Dr (Suite 900)
Mendota Heights, MN 55120
Telephone: (651) 294-2500, (877) 723-5522, FAX: (651) 294-2595, E-Mail:
customerservice@bellacor.com, Web
Site: www.bellacor.com
Pres: Jan Andersen
VP, Fin & CFO: Jim Lawrence
Conducts Business: Worldwide
Primary Market Served: Business &
Consumer
Catalog available online
Direct online sales
Founded: 1926

Sell lighting fixtures, ceiling fans &
lamps online at Bellacor.com

BERGER'S TABLE PAD CO
1501 W Market St
Indianapolis, IN 46222
Telephone: (317) 631-2577, (800) 428-4567, FAX: (317) 631-2584, Web
Site: www.bergerstablepads.net
Pres: Dave Berger
Conducts Business: Worldwide
Employees: 27
Primary Market Served: Business &
Consumer
Catalog available online
Direct online sales
Advertising/Marketing Budget Related
to Direct Marketing: 26-50%
Direct Marketing ad budget:
$1,000,000
Direct Mail: 50%
Magazines: 25%
Newspapers: 25%
Founded: 1981

Manufacture custom made table pads
as well as custom made tablecloths.

BERRY HILL LTD
75 Burwell Rd
Saint Thomas, ON, Canada N5P 3R5

Telephone: (519) 631-0480, (800) 668-3072, FAX: (519) 631-8935, E-Mail: info@berryhilllimited.com, Web Site: www.berryhilllimited.com
Gen Mgr: Ken Fox
Conducts Business: Canada
Employees: 10
Primary Market Served: Business & Consumer
Advertising/Marketing Budget Related to Direct Marketing: 76-100%
Direct Marketing ad budget: $50,000
Direct Mail: 50%
Magazines: 30%
Newspapers: 10%
TV/Radio: 10%
Founded: 1946
Gross sales or billing: $1,160,000

Mail order company selling hobby farm equipment, country living products & hobby garden equipment.

BLISSLIVING HOME

5515 Security Ln (Suite 1100)
Rockville, MD 20852-5009
Telephone: (301) 816-4224, Web Site: www.blisslivinghome.com
Bus Mgr: Sarah Constantyn

BLUESTONE PERENNIALS INC

7211 Middle Ridge Rd
Madison, OH 44057-3050
Telephone: (440) 428-7535, (800) 852-5243, FAX: (440) 428-7198, E-Mail: bluestone@bluestoneperennials.com, Web Site: www.bluestoneperennials.com
Pres: William N. Boonstra
Corp Sec & Treas: Sarah Boonstra
Conducts Business: U.S.
Primary Market Served: Business & Consumer
Catalog available online
Direct online sales
Advertising/Marketing Budget Related to Direct Marketing: 76-100%
Founded: 1972

Over 900 varieties of perennials & ornamental shrubs shipped Spring & Fall.

THE BOMBAY CO

3389 Steeles Ave E
Brampton, ON, Canada L6T 5W4
Telephone: (877) 326-6229, E-Mail: customerservice@bombay.ca, Web Site: www.bombay.com
Chmn, Pres & CEO: Carmie Mehrlander
Sr VP, Mktg: Steve Farley
Dir, Mktg: Laura Stein
Conducts Business: U.S., Canada
Primary Market Served: Consumer

Catalog marketer & specialty retailer of antique reproductions & accessories for the home. Operates 415 retail stores in Canada & the U.S. Traditional & classic home style furnishings.

BORBELETA GARDENS

15980 Canby Ave
Fairbault, MN 55021
Telephone: (507) 334-2807, FAX: (507) 332-0365
Pres: Dave Campbell
Mktg: Jack Campbell
Conducts Business: U.S., Canada
Employees: 4
Primary Market Served: Business & Consumer
Advertising/Marketing Budget Related to Direct Marketing: 0-25%
Direct Marketing ad budget:
Direct Mail: 90%
Magazines: 10%
Founded: 1971
Gross sales or billing: $200,000

Sell perennial flowers such as lilies, daylilies, median bearded iris & Siberian Iris.

BOUNTIFUL GARDENS

Div. of Ecology Action Inc
18001 Shafer Ranch Rd
Willits, CA 95490-9626
Telephone: (707) 459-6410, FAX: (707) 459-1925, E-Mail: bountiful@sonic.net, Web Site: www.bountifulgardens.org
Mktg Mgr: Bill Bruneau
Conducts Business: Worldwide
Employees: 7
Primary Market Served: Business & Consumer
Catalog available online
Advertising/Marketing Budget Related to Direct Marketing: 0-25%
Founded: 1983

Training materials for sustainable high-yield organic gardening & untreated heirloom seeds. Specializes in unusual vegetables, herbs, grains, compost crops & organic controls & supplies.

BRADLEY DIRECT

WC Bradley Co
PO Box 1240
Columbus, GA 31902-1240
Telephone: (706) 565-2100, (866) 239-6774, (800) 241-8981, FAX: (706) 565-2132, (888) 224-7455, E-Mail: customerservice@grilllovers.com, Web Site: www.grilllovers.com
Pres: Connie Warner
Mgr, New Bus Devel: Andrew Lichter
VP, Opers: Nick McNair
Conducts Business: Worldwide

Employees: 550
Primary Market Served: Consumer
Catalog available online
Direct online sales
Advertising/Marketing Budget Related to Direct Marketing: 76-100%

Full service, direct response marketing, order processing and fulfillment. Sells grill parts & accessories through Grill Lover's catalog.

BRECK'S BULBS

Subs. of Foster & Gallagher
5700 Schenley Pl
Lawrenceburg, IN 47025-2191
Telephone: (309) 693-8600, FAX: (309) 691-9693
Chmn Foster & Gallagher: Melvyn R. Regal
Vice Chmn Foster & Gallagher: A. Robert Pellegrino
Mktg Dir: Mike Vandervliet
VP HR Foster & Gallagher: Terry Cole
Conducts Business: U.S.
Primary Market Served: Consumer

Market European flower bulbs, roses & domestically grown garden plants.

BROWN & CO

8527 Semiahmoo Dr
Blaine, WA 98230
Telephone: (360) 371-2489
Owner: Ed Brown
Owner: Barbara Brown
Conducts Business: U.S.
Employees: 2
Primary Market Served: Business & Consumer
Advertising/Marketing Budget Related to Direct Marketing: 0-25%
Founded: 1985

Plants wholesale & retail.

BROWN'S OMAHA PLANT FARMS

110 McLean Ave
Omaha, TX 75571
Telephone: (903) 884-2421, FAX: (903) 884-2423, E-Mail: mail@bopf.com, Web Site: www.bopf.com
VP: Greg Brown
Conducts Business: U.S.
Employees: 2
Primary Market Served: Business & Consumer
Catalog available online
Direct online sales
Advertising/Marketing Budget Related to Direct Marketing: 0-25%
Direct Marketing ad budget: $10,000
Direct Mail: 100%
Founded: 1938
Gross sales or billing: $350,000

Vegetable plants for the home gardener.

W ATLEE BURPEE CO
300 Park Ave
Warminster, PA 18974-4860
Telephone: (215) 674-4900, (800) 333-5808, FAX: (215) 674-4170, Web Site: www.burpee.com
Pres & Owner: George Ball
Exec VP: Chris Romas
DM Mgr: Donald Zeidler
Mgr Sls: Rick Troja
Conducts Business: U.S.
Primary Market Served: Consumer
Catalog available online
Direct online sales
Advertising/Marketing Budget Related to Direct Marketing: 51-75%
Founded: 1876

Sell garden products, flower & vegetable seeds, nursery stock, bulbs & roots, plus general garden aids to the home gardener. Commercial seed sales & retail seed distribution. Catalogs mailed to homeowners.

DV BURRELL SEED GROWERS CO
405 N Main St
Rocky Ford, CO 81067
Telephone: (719) 254-3318, (866) 254-7333, FAX: (719) 254-3319, E-Mail: burrellseeds@centurytel.net, Web Site: www.burrellseeds.us
Pres: Bill Burrell
Conducts Business: U.S., Canada
Employees: 8
Primary Market Served: Business & Consumer
Catalog available online
Advertising/Marketing Budget Related to Direct Marketing: 0-25%
Founded: 1898

Sell vegetable, flower & herb seed, both wholesale & retail.

CAS DESIGN CENTER
Div. of Thomas McDowell Inc
7205 Boulevard 26
North Richland Hills, TX 76180
Telephone: (817) 788-1782
Pres: Tom F. McDowell
VP: Shirley A. McDowell
Conducts Business: U.S., Canada, Australia, Caribbean, Singapore
Employees: 32
Primary Market Served: Business & Consumer
Catalog available online
Advertising/Marketing Budget Related to Direct Marketing: 26-50%
Direct Marketing ad budget: $60,000
Direct Mail: 67%
Magazines: 5%

Newspapers: 1%
Online: 25%
TV/Radio: 1%
Telephone: 1%
Founded: 1979
Gross sales or billing: $2,000,000

Two showrooms & corporate headquarters/distribution center in Dallas/Fort Worth metroplex selling uncommon architectural ornamentation to builders, designers, architects & the general public. Sell nationwide/worldwide via catalogue & the internet. Accept Visa, MasterCard & American Express.

CAMELLIA FOREST NURSERY
626 Hwy 54 W
Chapel Hill, NC 27516-7911
Telephone: (919) 968-0504, FAX: (919) 929-8971, E-Mail: camforest@aol.com, Web Site: www.camforest.com
Treas: Kai-Mei Parks
Pres: David Parks
Conducts Business: U.S.
Employees: 4
Primary Market Served: Consumer
Catalog available online
Indirect online sales
Advertising/Marketing Budget Related to Direct Marketing: 0-25%
Direct Marketing ad budget:
Direct Mail: 90%
Magazines: 10%
Founded: 1979

Plants.

CANE & BASKET SUPPLY CO
1283 S Cochran Ave
Los Angeles, CA 90019-2846
Telephone: (323) 939-9644, FAX: (323) 939-7237, E-Mail: info@canebasket.com, Web Site: www.canebasket.com
Pres: William L. Fimpler
VP: William Fimpler Jr.
Conducts Business: U.S.
Employees: 10
Primary Market Served: Business & Consumer
Catalog available online
Indirect online sales
Advertising/Marketing Budget Related to Direct Marketing: 0-25%
Founded: 1934

Catalog marketer of caning & basketry supplies.

CAPE COD CUPOLA CO INC
78 State Rd
North Dartmouth, MA 02747-2994

Telephone: (508) 994-2119, FAX: (508) 997-2511, Web Site: www.capcodcupola.com
Pres: John E. Bernier
Mgr: Brian Chabot
Conducts Business: U.S., Canada
Employees: 5
Primary Market Served: Business & Consumer
Founded: 1939

Specialize in custom cupolas & weathervanes.

CARINO NURSERIES
PO Box 538
Indiana, PA 15701
Telephone: (800) 223-7075, FAX: (724) 463-3050, E-Mail: carino@carinonurseries.com, Web Site: www.carinonurseries.com
Chmn: James L. Carino
Gen Mgr: Douglas Wilhide
Office Mgr: Grace Mihoerck
Nursery Mgr: Ronald Sensebaugh
VP: Laura Carino
Asst Nursery Mgr: Mark Longwell
Conducts Business: U.S., Canada
Employees: 65
Primary Market Served: Business & Consumer
Catalog available online
Direct online sales
Advertising/Marketing Budget Related to Direct Marketing: 26-50%
Direct Marketing ad budget: $100,000
Direct Mail: 60%
Magazines: 25%
Newspapers: 10%
Telephone: 5%
Founded: 1946
Gross sales or billing: $2,000,000

Evergreen & deciduous seedlings & transplants for nurserymen, Christmas tree growers, landowners & homeowners.

CARLSON'S GARDENS
74 Brightenback Ln
Waitsfield, VT 05673-6090
Telephone: (914) 763-5958, E-Mail: bob@carlsonsgardens.com, Web Site: www.carlsonsgardens.com
Owner: Bob Carlson
Conducts Business: U.S.
Employees: 3
Primary Market Served: Business & Consumer
Catalog available online
Direct online sales
Founded: 1973

Sell super-hardy, landscape-size azaleas & rhododendrons.

CAROLINA EXOTIC GARDENS/CEG NURSERY

Div. of Minton Enterprises
2237 Sunnyside Rd
Greenville, NC 27834
Telephone: (252) 758-2600, FAX:
   (252) 758-3252, E-Mail:
   cegnursery@aol.com, Web Site:
   www.cegnursery.com
Owner: D.R. Minton
Conducts Business: Worldwide
Employees: 10
Primary Market Served: Business &
   Consumer
Catalog available online
Direct online sales
Advertising/Marketing Budget Related
   to Direct Marketing: 0-25%
Direct Marketing ad budget:
Direct Mail: 50%
Magazines: 50%
Founded: 1973

Grower & supplier of carnivorous
plants & seeds to seed companies, individuals & research facilities.

CARTER & HOLMES INC

629 Mendenhall Rd
Newberry, SC 29108
Telephone: (803) 276-0579, FAX:
   (803) 276-0588, E-Mail: orchids@
   carterandholmes.com, Web Site:
   www.carterandholmes.com
Pres: Owen M. Holmes IV
VP & Gen Mgr: Gene Crocker
Conducts Business: Worldwide
Employees: 35
Primary Market Served: Business &
   Consumer
Catalog available online
Direct online sales
Advertising/Marketing Budget Related
   to Direct Marketing: 76-100%
Founded: 1945
Gross sales or billing: $1,000,000

Orchid plants, house plants.

CASCADE FOREST NURSERY

Div. of Cascade Forestry Service Inc
36460 333rd Ave
Bellevue, IA 52031-9691
Telephone: (563) 872-3025, (800) 596-
   9437, FAX: (563) 872-5003, Web
   Site: www.cascadeforestry.com
Pres: Leo H. Fruech
Conducts Business: U.S.
Employees: 50
Primary Market Served: Business &
   Consumer
Advertising/Marketing Budget Related
   to Direct Marketing: 0-25%
Direct Marketing ad budget: $20,000
Magazines: 40%
Newspapers: 25%
TV/Radio: 25%

Telephone: 10%
Founded: 1974

Seedling shrubs & trees, evergreen
transplants. Full range of reforestation
services, tree planting & timber stand
improvement.

CHADSWORTH'S 1-800-COLUMNS

277 N Front St
Wilmington, NC 28401-3907
Telephone: (910) 763-7600, (800) 486-
   2118, FAX: (910) 763-3191, E-Mail:
   sales@columns.com, Web Site:
   www.columns.com
Mktg Dir: Amy Osborne
CEO: Jeffrey L. Davis
Sr VP, Opers: Raye Jackson Frazelle
Conducts Business: Worldwide
Employees: 15
Primary Market Served: Business &
   Consumer
Catalog available online
Advertising/Marketing Budget Related
   to Direct Marketing: 0-25%
Direct Marketing ad budget:
Direct Mail: 25%
Magazines: 75%
Founded: 1987

Columns to consumers, builders, architects & designers.

CHAR-BROIL GRILL LOVER'S CATALOG

Div. of Char-Broil/WC Bradley Co
PO Box 2737
Louisville, KY 40201-2737
Telephone: (706) 565-2100, (800) 241-
   8981, FAX: (706) 565-2121, Web
   Site: www.grilllovers.com
VP & Dir: Connie Warner
Catalog Mgr: Lynn Wright
Conducts Business: U.S.
Employees: 250
Primary Market Served: Consumer
Catalog available online
Indirect online sales
Advertising/Marketing Budget Related
   to Direct Marketing: 76-100%
Founded: 1885
Gross sales or billing: $20,000,000

Offer casual living & barbecue grill
accessories to gas, charcoal & electric
grill owners.

CHARMASTER PRODUCTS INC

2307 W US Hwy 2
Grand Rapids, MN 55744-2152
Telephone: (218) 326-6786, FAX:
   (218) 326-1065, E-Mail: info@
   charmaster.com, Web Site: www.
   charmaster.com
Pres: Larry Lessin

VP: Carol Lessin
Conducts Business: U.S. and Canada
Primary Market Served: Business &
   Consumer
Catalog available online
Indirect online sales
Advertising/Marketing Budget Related
   to Direct Marketing: 76-100%

Manufacture solid-fuel furnaces for
central forced-air heating & boiler
models.

CHEFS CATALOG

5070 Centennial Blvd
Colorado Springs, CO 80919-2402
Telephone: (719) 272-2600, Web Site:
   www.chefscatalog.com
Pres & CEO: Tim Littleton
Primary Market Served: Consumer

CHILDREACH US MEMBER OF PLAN INTERNATIONAL

Div. of Strong Enterprises
155 Plan Way
Warwick, RI 02886
Telephone: (916) 797-8707, (800) 556-
   7918, FAX: (916) 797-1056, Web
   Site: www.planusa.org
Owner: Tom Strong
Conducts Business: Worldwide
Employees: 1
Primary Market Served: Business &
   Consumer
Catalog available online
Direct online sales
Advertising/Marketing Budget Related
   to Direct Marketing: 26-50%
Direct Marketing ad budget: $2,500
Direct Mail: 50%
Magazines: 40%
Online: 10%
Founded: 1969
Gross sales or billing: $250,000

Distribute quality drip irrigation products to homeowners, landscape contractors, and commercial growers. Feature the Add-It and Green Machine Pro
proportioning fertilizer injectors for
drip and conventional sprinkler irrigation systems. Product catalog and design guide available online.

CINMAR LP

dba "Frontgate"; Parent "Cornerstone
   Brands, Inc (CBI)"
5566 West Chester Rd
West Chester, OH 45069-2914
Telephone: (513) 603-1000, FAX:
   (513) 603-1020, Web Site: www.
   frontgate.com
Pres: Paul Tarvin
Dir Fin: Jeffrey Scalf
Conducts Business: U.S.
Employees: 130
Primary Market Served: Consumer

Founded: 1991
Gross sales or billing: $20,200,000
General merchandise for the homeowner.

COHASSET COLONIALS

PO Box 0548
Ashburnham, MA 01430-0548
Telephone: (978) 827-3001, (800) 288-2389, FAX: (978) 827-3227, E-Mail: cohasset@cohassetcolonials.com, Web Site: www.cohassetcolonials.com
Pres & Treas: Richard Dabrowski
Conducts Business: U.S., Canada
Employees: 10
Primary Market Served: Consumer
Catalog available online
Direct online sales
Advertising/Marketing Budget Related to Direct Marketing: 76-100%
Founded: 1949
Gross sales or billing: $4,800,000

Reproduction of American Colonial furniture, lighting, and decorative accessories.

COLD STREAM FARM

8585 N Stephens Rd
Free Soil, MI 49411
Telephone: (231) 464-5809, E-Mail: info@coldstreamfarm.net, Web Site: www.coldstreamfarm.net
Owner: Craig Hradel
Conducts Business: US & Canada
Employees: 40
Primary Market Served: Business & Consumer
Catalog available online
Direct online sales
Direct Marketing ad budget:
Direct Mail: 10%
Online: 90%
Founded: 1978
Gross sales or billing: $240,000

Cash sales of trees & shrubs.

COLE'S APPLIANCE & FURNITURE CO

4026 Lincoln Ave
Chicago, IL 60618-3097
Telephone: (773) 525-1797, FAX: (773) 525-0728
Pres: Barry Krasney
Conducts Business: U.S.
Employees: 11
Primary Market Served: Consumer
Advertising/Marketing Budget Related to Direct Marketing: 0-25%
Founded: 1957
Gross sales or billing: $1,500,000

Sell all major appliances & furniture for every room to consumers in the U.S.

COMPANION PLANTS

7247 N Coolville Ridge Rd
Athens, OH 45701
Telephone: (740) 592-4643, FAX: (740) 593-3092, E-Mail: complants@frognet.net, Web Site: www.companionplants.com
Pres: Peter Borchard
Conducts Business: U.S.
Employees: 10
Primary Market Served: Business & Consumer
Catalog available online
Direct online sales
Advertising/Marketing Budget Related to Direct Marketing: 76-100%
Direct Marketing ad budget:
Direct Mail: 80%
Magazines: 20%
Founded: 1982
Gross sales or billing: $120,000

Sell herb plants & seeds to the industry & the consumer. Over 600 varieties of live herb plants & seeds.

THE CONTAINER STORE

THE DMA
500 Freeport Pkwy Ste 100
Coppell, TX 75019-3998
Telephone: (214) 654-2000, Web Site: www.containerstore.com
Dir Direct Mktg: Catherine Davis

COPPA WOODWORKING, INC

1231 Paraiso Ave
San Pedro, CA 90731
Telephone: (310) 548-4142, FAX: (310) 548-6740, E-Mail: ciro@earthlink.net, Web Site: www.coppawoodworking.com
Pres: Ciro C. Coppa
VP: Carol Coppa
Conducts Business: U.S.
Employees: 10
Primary Market Served: Business & Consumer
Advertising/Marketing Budget Related to Direct Marketing: 0-25%
Direct Marketing ad budget: $25,000
Magazines: 75%
Newspapers: 25%
Founded: 1980
Gross sales or billing: $800,000

Wood screen doors & lawn chairs.

COPPER ART BY MORSE

PO Box 1220
Claremont, NH 03743-1220
Telephone: (603) 542-2324
Dir: Stephen Morse
Conducts Business: U.S.
Employees: 1
Primary Market Served: Business & Consumer
Advertising/Marketing Budget Related to Direct Marketing: 0-25%%

Founded: 1986

Custom made copper & brass, weathervanes, sculptures & windowsill trays for potted plants.

JOSIAH R COPPERSMYTHE

10 Mill Pond Rd
Harwich, MA 02645
Telephone: (508) 432-8590, (800) 426-8249, FAX: (508) 432-8587, E-Mail: kethompson@jrcoppersmythe.com, Web Site: www.jrcoppersmythe.com
CEO: Karen E. Thompson
Conducts Business: U.S.
Employees: 1
Primary Market Served: Business & Consumer
Catalog available online
Indirect online sales
Advertising/Marketing Budget Related to Direct Marketing: 76-100%
Founded: 1984
Gross sales or billing: $100,000

Colonial reproduction lighting, post lights, exterior house lights, onion lights, interior sconces, chandeliers in tubular wrought & turned wood styles, wooden posts, table & floor lamps.

COUNTRY CURTAINS INC

THE DMA
705 Pleasant St
Lee, MA 01238-9323
Telephone: (413) 243-1474, (800) 456-0321, FAX: (413) 243-1067, Web Site: www.countrycurtains.com
Owner & Chm Bd: Jane Fitzpatrick
CEO: William Booth
Conducts Business: U.S., Canada, U.K., Japan
Primary Market Served: Consumer
Founded: 1956

Sell curtains, bed ensembles & home decorating accessories. 68-page color mail order catalog available. Retail shops in New England, Mid-Atlantic & Mid-West.

CRATE & BARREL

1250 Techny Rd
Northbrook, IL 60062-5419
Telephone: (847) 272-2888, Web Site: www.crateandbarrel.com
Sr Mgr Direct Mktg: Diane Lonis

CUDDLEDOWN INC

THE DMA
Subs of Bush Equities, Inc
312 Canco Rd
Portland, ME 04103-4281
Telephone: (207) 761-0201, (800) 323-6793, FAX: (207) 761-1948, Web Site: www.cuddledown.com
CEO: Christopher W. Bradley
Mgr: Colleen Carter
Mktg Dir: Deb Dyer

Conducts Business: U.S.
Employees: 70
Primary Market Served: Consumer
Founded: 1973
Gross sales or billing: $13,400,000

Marketer of down comforters, pillows, flannel sheets, fine linens & bath products.

CUMBERLAND GENERAL STORE INC

PO Box 4468
Alpharetta, GA 30023-4468
Telephone: (800) 334-4640, FAX: (678) 240-0410, E-Mail: info@cumberlandgerneral.com, Web Site: www.cumberlandgeneral.com
Pres: Ann Ebert
Mgr: Sharon Hassler
Conducts Business: Worldwide
Employees: 10
Primary Market Served: Consumer
Catalog available online
Indirect online sales

Old-time country provisions, housewares, furniture, hardware, buggies, implements, remedies, farm & garden supplies.

CUMBERLAND WOODCRAFT CO INC

PO Drawer 609
Carlisle, PA 17013-0609
Telephone: (717) 243-0063, (800) 367-1884, FAX: (717) 243-6502, E-Mail: sales@cumberlandwoodcraft.com, Web Site: www.cumberlandwoodcraft.com
Pres: Don Stevens
Conducts Business: U.S.
Primary Market Served: Business & Consumer
Catalog available online
Direct online sales
Direct Marketing ad budget:
Direct Mail: 20%
Magazines: 15%
Newspapers: 5%
Online: 60%
Founded: 1975

Manufacturer of solid oak & poplar Victorian millwork & architectural woodwork & accessories. Sell to designers, decorators, architects, builders & homeowners. Standard line plus custom design & manufacturing.

D'LIGHTS

2107 Chico Ave
South El Monte, CA 91733
Telephone: (818) 956-5656, FAX: (818) 956-5657, Web Site: www.dlights.com
Gen Mgr: Christine Labonowski

Conducts Business: U.S., Canada
Employees: 14
Primary Market Served: Business
Advertising/Marketing Budget Related to Direct Marketing: 0-25%
Direct Marketing ad budget:
Direct Mail: 40%
Magazines: 20%
Telephone: 40%
Founded: 1974
Gross sales or billing: $1,500,000

Custom light manufacturing.

DAVIS INSTRUMENTS CORP

3465 Diablo Ave
Hayward, CA 94545-2746
Telephone: (510) 732-9229, (510) 670-0589, E-Mail: info@davisnet.com, Web Site: www.davisnet.com
Chmn: James S. Acquistapace
Pres: Bob Selig
VP, Mktg: Joan Peterson
Mktg Communs: John Hansen
Cust Svc Mgr: Kim DeRespini
Conducts Business: Worldwide
Primary Market Served: Business & Consumer
Catalog available online
Indirect online sales
Advertising/Marketing Budget Related to Direct Marketing: 51-75%
Founded: 1963
Gross sales or billing: $7,700,000

Distributes marine products, weather instruments & driving monitors.

DOLE FRESH FLOWERS

Subs. of Dole Food Co
2200 NW 70th Ave
Miami, FL 33122-1816
Telephone: (305) 925-7900, Web Site: www.dole.com
DM Mgr: Larry Achtman
Primary Market Served: Business & Consumer
Founded: 1998

Mail order catalog selling fresh cut floral bouquets.

DOROTHY BIDDLE SERVICE

348 Greeley Lake Rd
Greeley, PA 18425-9799
Telephone: (570) 226-3239, FAX: (570) 226-0349, E-Mail: info@dorothybiddle.com, Web Site: www.dorothybiddle.com
Owner: Lynne Dodson
Mgr: Amy Conklin
Office Mgr: Amy Keane
Conducts Business: U.S., Canada
Employees: 6
Primary Market Served: Business & Consumer
Catalog available online
Indirect online sales

Advertising/Marketing Budget Related to Direct Marketing: 0-25%
Direct Marketing ad budget:
Magazines: 100%
Founded: 1936
Gross sales or billing: $900,000

Sell flower arranging equipment & gardening accessories to garden centers, gift shops & florists.

DOROTHY'S RUFFLED ORIGINALS INC

6721 Market St
Wilmington, NC 28405-3703
Telephone: (910) 686-8087, (800) 367-6849, FAX: (910) 686-2958, E-Mail: curtains@dorothysoriginals.com, Web Site: www.dorothysoriginals.com
Pres: Dorothy C. Noe
CEO: James B. Noe
Mktg Mgr: Becky Wright
Conducts Business: U.S., Canada
Employees: 40
Primary Market Served: Business & Consumer
Catalog available online
Indirect online sales
Advertising/Marketing Budget Related to Direct Marketing: 0-25%
Founded: 1978
Gross sales or billing: $1,200,000

Mail order, retail & wholesale sales of original design ruffled curtains & accessories & traditional curtains & accessories.

DOWN HOME COMFORTS

128 Woodland St
Windsor, CT 06095-3454
Telephone: (860) 830-0606, (860) 688-3780, Web Site: downhomecomforts.com
Owner: Elizabeth Eisenhauer
Conducts Business: U.S.
Employees: 1
Primary Market Served: Consumer
Catalog available online
Indirect online sales
Advertising/Marketing Budget Related to Direct Marketing: 0-25%
Direct Marketing ad budget:
Online: 100%
Founded: 1981

New & remade to order comforters, pillows & featherbeds.

DROLL YANKEES INC

27 Mill Rd
Foster, RI 02825
Telephone: (860) 799-8980, (800) 352-9164, FAX: (860) 779-8938, E-Mail: jen@drollyankees.com, Web Site: www.drollyankees.com

Pres: Betsy Puckett
Mktg Mgr: Jennifer Masiello
Conducts Business: U.S., Canada
Employees: 30
Primary Market Served: Business &
  Consumer
Catalog available online
Advertising/Marketing Budget Related
  to Direct Marketing: 0-25%
Founded: 1960

Sell bird feeders & accessories.

DULUTH TRADING CO INC

Div. of Kempler
170 Countryside Dr, PO Box 200
Belleville, WI 53508-0200
Telephone: (800) 505-8888, FAX:
  (888) 950-3199, E-Mail:
  customerservice@duluthtrading.com,
  Web Site: www.duluthtrading.com
Founder & CEO: Steven Schlecht
Exec VP: Carol Mueller
VP Prod Mngmt: Mike Hollenstein
Primary Market Served: Consumer
Catalog available online
Direct online sales

Tool carriers, parts, organizers & accessories catalogs.

DUTCH GARDENS

144 Intervale Rd
Burlington, VT 05401
Telephone: (802) 660-3500, (800) 950-
  4470, FAX: (800) 551-6712, E-Mail:
  info@dutchgardens.com, Web Site:
  www.dutchgardens.com
Mktg Mgr: Michael Allen
Primary Market Served: Consumer

Mail order company selling perennials
& flower bulbs at close to wholesale
prices shipped directly from Holland.

E-Z BOWZ INC

PO Box 1597
Gatlinburg, TN 37738-1597
Telephone: (865) 453-3060, FAX:
  (865) 429-3743, Web Site: www.
  ezbows.com
Pres: Lea Cavender
COO: Art Cavender
Conducts Business: U.S., Canada
Employees: 18
Primary Market Served: Business &
  Consumer
Direct online sales
Advertising/Marketing Budget Related
  to Direct Marketing: 0-25%
Direct Marketing ad budget: $175,000
Direct Mail: 30%
Magazines: 30%
TV/Radio: 40%
Founded: 1993
Gross sales or billing: $4,000,000

E-Z Craft supplies, bowmaker with
spool holder, rose & flower maker,
memory items & other products that
make craft projects easy.

EDIBLE LANDSCAPING

361 Spirit Ridge Ln
Afton, VA 22920
Telephone: (434) 361-9134, (800) 524-
  4156, FAX: (434) 361-1916, E-Mail:
  info@ediblelandscaping.com, Web
  Site: www.eat-it.com
Office Mgr: Janet Anderson
Conducts Business: Worldwide
Employees: 5
Primary Market Served: Business &
  Consumer
Catalog available online
Direct online sales
Advertising/Marketing Budget Related
  to Direct Marketing: 0-25%
Founded: 1983
Gross sales or billing: $360,000

Mail order potted plants, shipped
throughout the year.

ELECTROWARMTH
PRODUCTS LLC

PO Box A
Danville, OH 43014-4601
Telephone: (740) 599-7222, (800) 990-
  4622, FAX: (740) 599-6848, E-Mail:
  sales@electrowarmth.com, Web Site:
  www.electrowarmth.com
Consultant: Larry Grindle
Owner/Pres: Dan Grindle
Conducts Business: U.S., Canada
Employees: 6
Primary Market Served: Business &
  Consumer
Indirect online sales
Advertising/Marketing Budget Related
  to Direct Marketing: 51-75%
Direct Marketing ad budget:
Direct Mail: 25%
Magazines: 75%
Founded: 1939
Gross sales or billing: $750,000

Manufacturers of Electro-Warmth 12
volt RV & truck & 115 volt automatic
mattress warming pads.

EVERFAST INC

dba Calico Corners
203 Gale Ln
Kennett Square, PA 19348-1735
Telephone: (610) 444-9700, Web Site:
  www.calicocorners.com
Mktg Mgr: Linda Emmons

EVERGREEN ENTERPRISES
INC

5915 Midlothian Tpke
Richmond, VA 23225-5917

Telephone: (804) 231-1800, Web Site:
  www.myevergreen.com
Pres: Ting Xu
Primary Market Served: Business

FANCY FRONDS

PO Box 1090
Gold Bar, WA 98251
Telephone: (360) 793-1472, FAX:
  (360) 793-4243, E-Mail: judith@
  fancyfronds.com, Web Site: www.
  fancyfronds.com
Pres: Judith Jones
Mktg Mgr & Webmaster: Benjamin
  Jones
Pub Rels: Kathryn Reith
Conducts Business: U.S.
Employees: 1
Primary Market Served: Consumer
Catalog available online
Direct online sales
Advertising/Marketing Budget Related
  to Direct Marketing: 0-25%
Direct Marketing ad budget: $7,000
Direct Mail: $2,000
Founded: 1977
Gross sales or billing: $45,000

Mail order sales of temperate, tree &
desert ferns.

FIELDER'S CHOICE DIRECT

Subs. of Landec Ag Inc
306 N Main St
Monticello, IN 47960
Telephone: (574) 583-2741 X107,
  (800) 321-3177, FAX: (574) 583-
  CORN, Web Site: www.
  fielderschoicedirect.com
Pres: Tom Crowley
VP, Sls: Dennis Schlott
Mktg Mgr: Linda Waymire
VP, Mktg & New Bus Devel: Bill
  Gass
Conducts Business: U.S. & Canada
Employees: 100
Catalog available online
Direct online sales
Founded: 1983

Agricultural products to farmers.

FIELDSTONE GARDENS INC

55 Quaker Ln
Vassalboro, ME 04989-3816
Telephone: (207) 923-3836, FAX:
  (207) 923-3836, E-Mail: info@
  fieldstonegardens.com, Web Site:
  www.fieldstonegardens.com
Owner: Steven D. Jones
Conducts Business: U.S.
Employees: 6
Primary Market Served: Business &
  Consumer
Catalog available online
Indirect online sales
Advertising/Marketing Budget Related

to Direct Marketing: 26-50%
Direct Marketing ad budget:
Direct Mail: 50%
Magazines: 20%
Newspapers: 30%
Founded: 1985

Variety of hardy northern grown perennials.

FLICKINGER'S NURSERY

Rte 85
Sagamore, PA 16250
Telephone: (800) 368-7381, FAX: (724) 783-6528, Web Site: www.flicknursery.com
Owner & Pres: Richard Flickinger
Mgr: Thomas Flickinger
Conducts Business: U.S.
Employees: 20
Primary Market Served: Business & Consumer
Catalog available online
Indirect online sales
Advertising/Marketing Budget Related to Direct Marketing: 0-25%
Founded: 1947

Bare root seedlings & transplants at wholesale prices: Pine, Spruce, Fir, Hemlock & Myrtle.

FLORIAN TOOLS

157 Water St
Southington, CT 06489-3018
Telephone: (860) 628-9643, (800) 275-3618, FAX: (860) 628-6036, E-Mail: sales@floriantools.com, Web Site: www.floriantools.com
CEO: Nathaniel Florian
Treas & Bus Mgr: Beth Florian
Pres & COO: Sean E. Florian
Sec: Judy Florian
Accts Payable: Linsey Rivers
Conducts Business: U.S., Europe, S. America
Employees: 35
Primary Market Served: Business & Consumer
Catalog available online
Direct online sales
Advertising/Marketing Budget Related to Direct Marketing: 0-25%
Founded: 1937
Gross sales or billing: $4,000,000

FOUR SEASONS SUNROOMS

Subs. of Four Seasons Solar Products Corp
5005 Veterans Memorial Hwy
Holbrook, NY 11741
Telephone: (631) 563-4000, FAX: (631) 563-4010
Pres: Chris Esposito
VP: Joe Esposito
Franchise Opers Dir: Tony Ruso
Conducts Business: U.S., Canada,
U.K., Germany, France, Switzerland
Employees: 250
Primary Market Served: Business & Consumer

Manufacturer & distributor of passive solar greenhouses & sunrooms.

FRAN'S BASKET HOUSE, INC

295 Rte 10 E
Succasunna, NJ 07876
Telephone: (973) 584-2230, (800) 372-6799, FAX: (973) 584-7446, E-Mail: inquiry@franswicker.com, Web Site: www.franswicker.com
Pres: David Gruber
Dir & Mktg Mgr: Louis Kaplan
Conducts Business: U.S.
Employees: 50
Primary Market Served: Consumer
Founded: 1967
Gross sales or billing: $3,200,000

Wicker furniture & accessories.

GALLOWAY FARMS

7790 SW 87th Ave
Miami, FL 33173
Telephone: (305) 274-7472, FAX: (305) 274-3233, E-Mail: galloway_inc@bellsouth.net, Web Site: www.gallowayform.com
VP, DM: Jim Lawrence
Conducts Business: U.S.
Employees: 20
Primary Market Served: Consumer
Advertising/Marketing Budget Related to Direct Marketing: 0-25%
Direct Marketing ad budget:
Direct Mail: 15%
Magazines: 10%
Newspapers: 70%
Telephone: 5%
Founded: 1888
Gross sales or billing: $500,000

Market orchids & other rare collector's plants such as aroids, bromeliads & ferns.

GARDEN PERENNIALS

85261 Hwy 15
Wayne, NE 68787
Telephone: (402) 375-3615, (888) 375-3615, Web Site: www.gardenperennials.net
Owner: Gail Korn
Conducts Business: U.S.
Employees: 4
Primary Market Served: Consumer
Advertising/Marketing Budget Related to Direct Marketing: 76-100%
Direct Marketing ad budget:
Direct Mail: 75%
Magazines: 10%
Newspapers: 5%
TV/Radio: 10%
Founded: 1981

Gross sales or billing: $50,000

Specialize in flowering perennials.

GARDENER'S EDEN

Div. of Brookstone Inc
One Innovation Way
Merrimack, NH 03054
Telephone: (603) 888-9500, (800) 822-9600, FAX: (603) 577-8005, E-Mail: gsweeney@brookstone.com
DM Dir: Mark Anthony
Buyer: Christine Bogusky
VP & Gen Mgr Direct Mktg: Greg Sweeney
Buyer: Lenny Parrella
Conducts Business: U.S.
Primary Market Served: Consumer
Catalog available online
Direct online sales
Advertising/Marketing Budget Related to Direct Marketing: 76-100%
Direct Marketing ad budget: $12,000,000
Direct Mail: 100%
Gross sales or billing: $21,000,000

Garden tools, fittings, furnishings, decorative plantings, accessories & gifts.

THE DMA GARDENER'S SUPPLY CO

128 Intervale Rd
Burlington, VT 05401-2804
Telephone: (802) 660-3500, (888) 833-1412, FAX: (802) 660-3501, E-Mail: info@gardeners.com, Web Site: www.gardeners.com
Pres: Jim Feinson
CEO: William Raap
COO: Cindy Turcot
Employees: 220
Primary Market Served: Consumer
Founded: 1983
Gross sales or billing: $36,400,000

Gardening mail order company.

GARDENIMPORT INC

135 W Beaver Creek Rd, PO Box 760
Richmond Hill, ON, Canada L4B 1C6
Telephone: (905) 731-1950, (800) 339-8314, FAX: (905) 731-3093, E-Mail: flower@gardenimport.com, Web Site: www.gardenimport.com
Pres: Dugald Cameron
Conducts Business: U.S., Canada
Primary Market Served: Consumer
Catalog available online
Direct online sales
Advertising/Marketing Budget Related to Direct Marketing: 76-100%
Direct Marketing ad budget:
Magazines: 100%
Founded: 1982
Gross sales or billing: $1,000,000

Sell unusual & hard-to-find plants, bulbs & seeds for the hobby gardener.

THE DMA GARDENS ALIVE! INC
5100 Schenley Pl
Lawrenceburg, IN 47025-2100
Telephone: (812) 537-8665, FAX: (812) 537-5108, E-Mail: service@gardensalive.com, Web Site: www.gardens-alive.com
Chmn: Niles Kinerk
Pres: Phil Bontrager
Conducts Business: U.S.
Employees: 150
Primary Market Served: Consumer
Founded: 1991

Sell organic garden supplies.

GARDENS OF THE BLUE RIDGE INC
Subs. of Fletcher Enterprises
PO Box 10, 9056 Pittman Gap Rd
Pineola, NC 28662
Telephone: (828) 733-2417, FAX: (828) 733-8894, E-Mail: gardensblueridge@boone.net, Web Site: www.gardensoftheblueridge.com
Pres: Katy R. Fletcher
CEO: Paul H. Fletcher
Sec & Treas: Robyn P. Fletcher
Conducts Business: Worldwide
Employees: 7
Primary Market Served: Business & Consumer
Catalog available online
Direct online sales
Advertising/Marketing Budget Related to Direct Marketing: 0-25%
Direct Marketing ad budget: $3,000
Direct Mail: 30%
Magazines: 50%
Newspapers: 10%
Telephone: 10%
Founded: 1892
Gross sales or billing: $260,000

Wildflowers, ferns & native plants.

GARY'S PERENNIALS, LLC
Subs. of perennialmarket.com
1122 E Welsh Rd
Maple Glen, PA 19002-2224
Telephone: (215) 628-4070, (800) 898-6653, FAX: (215) 628-0216, E-Mail: roots@garysperennials.com, Web Site: www.garysperennials.com; www.perennialmarket.com
Partner: Gary Steinberg
Partner: Andrea Steinberg
Office Mgr: Phyllis Chandler
Conducts Business: U.S., Canada
Employees: 4
Primary Market Served: Business
Catalog available online
Indirect online sales

Advertising/Marketing Budget Related to Direct Marketing: 76-100%
Direct Marketing ad budget: $35,000
Direct Mail: 55%
Magazines: 10%
Online: 15%
Telephone: 20%
Founded: 1984
Gross sales or billing: $800,000

Large bare root & cell pack perennials: Astilbe, Hemerocallis, Hosta, Geranium, Ferns, Ornamental Grasses, Natives, etc. Sell to nurseries, landscapers, garden centers, organizations, fundraising & arboreta.

GENADA IMPORTS
PO Box 204 (Dept 2)
Teaneck, NJ 07666
Telephone: (973) 569-9660, FAX: (973) 569-9660
Pres: Gerald Hertz
Conducts Business: U.S., Canada
Employees: 3
Primary Market Served: Consumer
Advertising/Marketing Budget Related to Direct Marketing: 0-25%
Direct Marketing ad budget: $10,000
Direct Mail: 50%
Magazines: 50%
Founded: 1968
Gross sales or billing: $100,000

Danish styled furniture.

GENERAL MILLS INC
One General Mills Blvd
Minneapolis, MN 55426
Telephone: (763) 764-7600, FAX: (763) 764-7384, Web Site: www.generalmills.com
Chmn: Stephen W. Sanger
Pres, CEO & Dir: Kendall J. Powell
Exec VP & COO: Ian R. Friendly
Exec VP: Roderick Palmore
VP: Christina L. Shea
Conducts Business: U.S.
Primary Market Served: Consumer
Catalog available online
Indirect online sales
Advertising/Marketing Budget Related to Direct Marketing: 76-100%
Gross sales or billing: $12,400,000,000

Marketer of housewares & food-related merchandise available from the Betty Crocker catalog.

GILLIOM MANUFACTURING INC
500 Boonslick Rd
Saint Charles, MO 63301-2437
Telephone: (636) 724-1812, FAX: (314) 723-0080
Conducts Business: Worldwide
Employees: 5

Primary Market Served: Consumer
Direct Marketing ad budget:
Magazines: $15,000
Gross sales or billing: $200,000

Sell metal parts kits for home woodworking.

GODDARD MANUFACTURING CO
107 Mill
Logan, KS 67646
Telephone: (785) 689-4341, (800) 536-4341, E-Mail: jerry@spiral-staircases.com, Web Site: www.spiral-staircases.com
Pres: Jerry Goddard
Sec: Christina Rundle
Conducts Business: U.S.
Employees: 9
Primary Market Served: Business & Consumer
Catalog available online
Advertising/Marketing Budget Related to Direct Marketing: 76-100%
Founded: 1978

Custom-built spiral steel & wood stairs. Extra railings, balusters & newels. Wholesale prices.

GOOD DIRECTIONS CO INC
20 Commerce Dr
Danbury, CT 06810
Telephone: (203) 743-3775, FAX: (203) 743-5226, E-Mail: sales@good-directions.com, Web Site: www.good-directions.com
Primary Market Served: Business & Consumer

Imports & sells weathervanes.

GOSSLER FARMS NURSERY
1200 Weaver Rd
Springfield, OR 97478-9691
Telephone: (541) 746-3922, FAX: (541) 744-7924, Web Site: www.gosslerfarms.com
Partner: Marjory Gossler
Partner: Roger Gossler
Partner: Eric Gossler
Conducts Business: U.S.
Primary Market Served: Business & Consumer
Catalog available online
Advertising/Marketing Budget Related to Direct Marketing: 0-25%
Founded: 1969

Sell ornamental trees & shrubs wholesale & retail.

GOTHIC ARCH GREENHOUSES INC
PO Box 1564
Mobile, AL 36633

Telephone: (251) 432-7529, (800) 531-4769, FAX: (251) 432-2655, E-Mail: gothicarch@comcast.net, Web Site: www.GothicArchGreenhouses.com
Pres: William H. Sierke Jr.
VP: Paul C. Sierke
Admin Sls Assoc: Tasha DeMouy
Sls Assoc: Zack Sierke
Conducts Business: Worldwide
Employees: 5
Primary Market Served: Business & Consumer
Catalog available online
Direct online sales
Advertising/Marketing Budget Related to Direct Marketing: 76-100%
Direct Marketing ad budget:
Direct Mail: 20%
Magazines: 80%
Founded: 1946
Gross sales or billing: $500,000

Sell pre-fab greenhouse kits manufactured from top grade redwood & western cedar, warrantied fiberglass & polycarbonate. Also market a complete line of horticultural accessories.

GREEN RIVER TRADING CO
578 Boston Corners Rd
Millerton, NY 12546
Telephone: (518) 789-3311
Pres: Art Kerber
Conducts Business: U.S., Canada, Worldwide
Employees: 3
Primary Market Served: Business & Consumer
Advertising/Marketing Budget Related to Direct Marketing: 51-75%
Founded: 1975

Manufacturer of quality log homes. Provide log packages & lumber products. Also publish & sell (retail & wholesale) limited edition prints of fine art. Specializing in Western-Americana art.

GREER GARDENS
1280 Goodpasture Island Rd
Eugene, OR 97401-1755
Telephone: (541) 686-8266, (800) 548-0111, FAX: (541) 686-0910, E-Mail: orders@greergardens.com, Web Site: www.greergardens.com
Pres: Harold Greer
Conducts Business: U.S., Canada, Europe, Australia, New Zealand, Pacific Rim countries
Employees: 10
Primary Market Served: Business & Consumer
Catalog available online
Direct online sales
Advertising/Marketing Budget Related to Direct Marketing: 0-25%

Founded: 1968

Sell unusual trees, shrubs, vines & perennials with emphasis on rhododendrons, maples, conifers & magnolias. Also bonsai materials, tools, pots, horticultural books & horticultural photographs.

GRIMES SEEDS AND PLANTS
11335 Concord Hambden Rd
Concord, OH 44077-0640
Telephone: (800) 241-7333, FAX: (440) 352-1800, Web Site: www.grimesseeds.com
Pres: Gary S. Grimes
Conducts Business: Worldwide
Employees: 40
Primary Market Served: Business
Catalog available online
Indirect online sales
Advertising/Marketing Budget Related to Direct Marketing: 0-25%
Direct Marketing ad budget:
Direct Mail: 10%
Telephone: 90%
Founded: 1925

Wholesale seeds and plants to greenhouses.

GROWER'S SUPPLY CO
PO Box 219
Dexter, MI 48130-0219
Telephone: (734) 426-5852, FAX: (734) 426-5750, E-Mail: growers@grower-supply.com, Web Site: www.growerssupplycompany.com
Pres: Donald Plusterer
Conducts Business: U.S.
Employees: 8
Primary Market Served: Business
Catalog available online
Advertising/Marketing Budget Related to Direct Marketing: 0-25%
Direct Marketing ad budget:
Direct Mail: 100%
Founded: 1954
Gross sales or billing: $1,000,000

Indoor gardening supplies.

THE GUILD INC
931 E Main St (Suite 9)
Madison, WI 53703-2956
Telephone: (608) 257-2590, Web Site: www.guild.com
Pres: Michael Baum
VP Mktg: Terry Nelson

HANDY STORE FIXTURES INC
337 Sherman Ave
Newark, NJ 07114-1592
Telephone: (973) 242-1600, (800) 631-4280, FAX: (973) 642-6222, Web Site: www.handystorefixtures.com

VP, Mktg: Walter Pincus
Conducts Business: U.S., Canada
Employees: 200
Direct Marketing ad budget:
Direct Mail: 60%
Magazines: 20%
Newspapers: 20%
Founded: 1952
Gross sales or billing: $21,000,000

Wall units, display cases, gondolas & counters.

HISTORICAL REPLICATIONS INC
3908 N State St
Jackson, MS 39206-5752
Telephone: (601) 981-8743, (800) 426-5628, FAX: (601) 981-8185, E-Mail: info@historicaldesigns.com, Web Site: www.historicaldesigns.com
Co-Owner: Cecilia Reese Bullock
Co-Owner: Mike Stephens
Conducts Business: U.S.
Employees: 2
Primary Market Served: Consumer
Catalog available online
Direct online sales
Advertising/Marketing Budget Related to Direct Marketing: 76-100%
Direct Marketing ad budget: $30,000
Online: 100%
Founded: 1977
Gross sales or billing: $200,000

House plans that specialize in historic facades with updated interiors.

HOLLAND WILDFLOWER FARM
PO Box 328, 290 O'Neil Lane
Elkins, AR 72727
Telephone: (501) 643-2622, (800) 684-3734, FAX: (501) 643-2249, E-Mail: hwildflowerfarm@yahoo.com, Web Site: www.hwildflower.com
Pres: Julie Holland
Conducts Business: U.S.
Employees: 5
Primary Market Served: Business & Consumer
Catalog available online
Direct online sales
Advertising/Marketing Budget Related to Direct Marketing: 26-50%
Direct Marketing ad budget: $4,000
Direct Mail: 50%
Magazines: 30%
Newspapers: 10%
TV/Radio: 10%
Founded: 1985
Gross sales or billing: $40,000

Mail order wildflower seeds & seed mixtures in small & large quantities; unique wildflower collections; displays available to retail businesses.

HOME DECORATORS COLLECTION INC

8920 Pershall Rd
Hazelwood, MO 63042-2809
Telephone: (314) 993-1516, FAX: (314) 521-5780, Web Site: www. homedecoratorscollection.com
Chmn Bd: W. Grant Williams III
Pres, Home Decorating Catalogue: Gil Kemp
Pres, Soft Surroundings: Robin Sheldon
VP & Creative Prodn Dir: Lisa Brougham
VP, Opers: Steve Kessler
Conducts Business: U.S.
Employees: 180
Primary Market Served: Consumer
Catalog available online
Direct online sales
Direct Marketing ad budget:
Direct Mail: $8,500,000
Gross sales or billing: $44,000,000

Mail order catalogs: three featuring women's personal items & apparel & one featuring home decorating items & beddings.

HOMECRAFT VENEER & WOODWORKER SUPPLY

PO Box 776
Youngstown, PA 15696-0776
Telephone: (724) 537-8435, (800) 796-6348, FAX: (724) 537-0543, E-Mail: woodman@homecraftveneer.com, Web Site: www.homecraftveneer.com
Owner: Alan J. McCullough
Conducts Business: U.S., Canada
Primary Market Served: Business & Consumer
Advertising/Marketing Budget Related to Direct Marketing: 0-25%

Sell domestic & imported veneers. Also veneering tools, woodworking supplies, flexible veneers, lumber & plywood.

MARTHA M HOUSE FURNITURE

House Furniture Market Inc
1022 S Decatur St.
Montgomery, AL 36104-5116
Telephone: (334) 264-3558, (800) 225-4195, FAX: (334) 262-2610, Web Site: www.marthahouse.com
Pres: William C. House
CEO: Martha M. House
Sec & Treas: Laurie House
Conducts Business: Worldwide
Primary Market Served: Consumer
Catalog available online
Founded: 1954

Victorian & French reproductions, furniture, lamps, pictures & accessories.

HOUSE OF WESLEY INC

1700 Morrissey Dr
Bloomington, IL 61704
Telephone: (309) 663-9551, FAX: (309) 663-6691, Web Site: www. houseofwesley.com
Pres: Richard Owen
Conducts Business: U.S.
Employees: 100
Primary Market Served: Consumer
Founded: 1954

Sell horticultural products through mail order space advertising.

IMPROVEMENTS

Subs. of Home Shopping Network
5566 West Chester Rd
West Chester, OH 45069-2914
Telephone: (216) 591-9148, (800) 634-9484, FAX: (216) 831-4026, Web Site: www.improvementscatalog.com
Pres & CEO, HSN: Mindy F. Grossman
COO, HSN: Mark Ethier
Exec VP, Gen Counsel: Steve Armstrong
VP, Mktg: Bill Buchler
Conducts Business: U.S.
Employees: 150
Primary Market Served: Business & Consumer
Catalog available online
Direct online sales
Advertising/Marketing Budget Related to Direct Marketing: 76-100%
Direct Marketing ad budget:
Direct Mail: 95%
Magazines: 5%

Marketer of home repair & improvement items.

INDOOR GARDENING SUPPLIES

PO Box 527
Dexter, MI 48130
Telephone: (734) 426-9080, (800) 823-5740, FAX: (866) 823-4978, Web Site: www.indoorgardensupplies.com
Pres: Tina Havro
Conducts Business: U.S.
Employees: 3
Primary Market Served: Consumer
Catalog available online
Direct online sales

Marketer of indoor gardening equipment. Specialize in plant stands, plant lights, trays, meters & lamps.

INTERNATIONAL IRRIGATION SYSTEMS

Div. of Regional Leasing Corp Ltd
1755 Factory Outlet Blvd, PO Box 163
Niagara Falls, NY 14304-0163

Telephone: (905) 688-4090, (877) IR-RIGRO, FAX: (905) 688-4093, E-Mail: info@irrigro.com, Web Site: www.irrigro.com
Pres: R.L. Neff
Conducts Business: Worldwide
Employees: 5
Primary Market Served: Business & Consumer
Catalog available online
Direct online sales
Advertising/Marketing Budget Related to Direct Marketing: 76-100%
Direct Marketing ad budget:
Direct Mail: 10%
Magazines: 90%
Founded: 1975
Gross sales or billing: $300,000

Manufacture & market micro-porous drip irrigation systems to home gardeners & commercial growers worldwide. Also "Treegro" tubes for growth acceleration & protection of young saplings.

INTERNATIONAL MANUFACTURING CO

Div. of Textile Enterprises Inc
216 Main St, Box 154
Whitesburg, GA 30185
Telephone: (770) 834-2094, FAX: (770) 834-2096, E-Mail: textilenterprise@aol.net
Pres: Martha G. Arnold
Conducts Business: U.S.
Primary Market Served: Business & Consumer
Catalog available online
Direct online sales
Founded: 1973

Sell all types of dried floral items including wreaths, excelsior, Spanish moss, macrame cord & all the accessories.

INTERWOOD DIRECT

50 Staples Ave - Richmond Hill
Toronto, ON, Canada L4B O47
Telephone: (888) 275-5205, Web Site: www.interwood.com
Pres: Robert G. Woodrooffe
Web Mgr: Allyson Woodrooffe
Conducts Business: Worldwide
Employees: 60
Primary Market Served: Consumer
Advertising/Marketing Budget Related to Direct Marketing: 76-100%

Housewares, exercise equipment, music & jewelry.

JANICE'S LLC

30 Arbor St S
Hartford, CT 06106

Telephone: (860) 523-4479, FAX: (860) 523-4178, E-Mail: dlerner@janices.com, Web Site: www.janices.com
Pres: David Lerner
Conducts Business: U.S., Europe, Japan, Canada, Mexico
Employees: 20
Primary Market Served: Consumer
Catalog available online
Direct online sales
Advertising/Marketing Budget Related to Direct Marketing: 76-100%
Founded: 1980
Gross sales or billing: $1,000,000

Manufacturer & catalog marketer of bedding, linens & cotton clothing; specializing in hypo-allergenic mattress sets.

THE DMA JW JUNG SEED CO
335 S High St
Randolph, WI 53957-0001
Telephone: (920) 326-3121, (800) 297-3123, FAX: (920) 326-5769, E-Mail: info@jungseed.com, Web Site: www.jungseed.com
Pres: Richard Zondag
Controller: Patrick Gavin
Conducts Business: U.S.
Employees: 150
Primary Market Served: Consumer
Catalog available online
Direct online sales
Founded: 1907

Seed & nursery company supplying complete line of vegetable & flower seeds, nursery stock & gardening accessories for the home gardener.

THE DMA K-LOG
1224 27th St
Zion, IL 60099-2673
Telephone: (847) 872-6611, Web Site: www.k-log.com
Pres: Tim Klebe

KAR GRAPHICS
31 Highland St, PO Box 2430
Mashpee, MA 02649
Telephone: (508) 539-9270, (800) 760-5192, FAX: (508) 539-1108, E-Mail: hoop@cape.com, Web Site: www.hoophouse.com
Conducts Business: U.S., Canada, Bermuda, Argentina
Employees: 4
Primary Market Served: Business & Consumer
Catalog available online
Direct online sales
Advertising/Marketing Budget Related to Direct Marketing: 76-100%
Direct Marketing ad budget: $20,000
Magazines: 100%

Founded: 1985
Gross sales or billing: $500,000

Hoop house, green house kits sold to commercial & hobby garden growers.

KAYNE & SON CUSTOM HARDWARE INC
100 Daniel Ridge Rd
Candler, NC 28715-9434
Telephone: (828) 667-8868, FAX: (828) 665-8303, E-Mail: kaynehdwe@charter.net, Web Site: www.customforgedhardware.com
Owner: Steve Kayne
VP & Asst Mgr: David Kayne
Mgr: Shirley Kayne
Office Mgr: Catherine Kayne
Conducts Business: U.S., Canada, Japan
Employees: 4
Primary Market Served: Business & Consumer
Founded: 1971

Custom-forged steel & cast brass interior/exterior door, window, cabinet, drawer, fireplace & furniture hardware for individuals as well as builders, architects, museums & antique dealers. Repairs, restorations & reproductions.

KESTER'S WILD GAME FOOD NURSERIES INC
4582 Hwy 116 E
Omro, WI 54963
Telephone: (920) 685-2929, (800) 558-8815, FAX: (920) 685-6727, E-Mail: pkester@vbe.com, Web Site: www.kestersnursery.com
Pres: David Kester
Owner: Patricia Kester
Conducts Business: U.S., Canada
Employees: 4
Primary Market Served: Business & Consumer
Advertising/Marketing Budget Related to Direct Marketing: 0-25%
Founded: 1903

Sell aquatic plants & various seeds for planting to attract & provide food for wildlife.

THE DMA KING RANCH SADDLE SHOP
Subs. of King Ranch Inc
PO Box 1594
Kingsville, TX 78364-1594
Telephone: (361) 595-1424, (800) 282-KING, FAX: (361) 595-1011, E-Mail: krsaddleshop@king-ranch.com, Web Site: www.krsaddleshop.com
Gen Mgr: Rose Morales
Asst Mktg Mgr: Robin Rocha
Conducts Business: U.S.

Primary Market Served: Business & Consumer
Catalog available online
Direct online sales
Founded: 1926

Leather goods and home furnishings.

KITCHEN KOMPACT INC
PO Box 868
Jeffersonville, IN 47131-0868
Telephone: (812) 282-6681, FAX: (812) 282-7880, E-Mail: webmaster@kitchenkompact.com, Web Site: www.kitchenkompact.com
Dir: Phillip Gahm
VP, Prodn: Walter Gahm
VP, Sls: Gordon Gahm
Conducts Business: U.S., Canada, Mexico
Employees: 260
Primary Market Served: Business
Catalog available online
Advertising/Marketing Budget Related to Direct Marketing: 0-25%
Direct Marketing ad budget: $400,000
Magazines: 100%
Founded: 1937
Gross sales or billing: $87,000,000

Kitchen & bath cabinets.

THE LADYBUG CO
12857 Oroville Quincy Hwy
Berry Creek, CA 95916-9754
Telephone: (530) 589-5227, FAX: (530) 589-4639
Owner: Julie Steele
Conducts Business: U.S., Canada
Primary Market Served: Business & Consumer
Direct Marketing ad budget:
Magazines: 75%
Newspapers: 25%

Sell beneficial insects: ladybugs, green lacewings, fly control parasites, praying mantis, trichogramma wasps & predatory mites.

LE JARDIN DU GOURMET
PO Box 75 (Dept DM)
Saint Johnsbury Center, VT 05863-0075
Telephone: (802) 748-1446, FAX: (802) 748-9592, E-Mail: orderdesk@artisticgardens.com, Web Site: www.artisticgardens.com
Owner: Paul Taylor
Conducts Business: U.S.
Employees: 3
Primary Market Served: Consumer
Catalog available online
Direct online sales
Advertising/Marketing Budget Related to Direct Marketing: 26-50%
Direct Marketing ad budget:
Direct Mail: 50%

Magazines: 50%
Founded: 1954
Gross sales or billing: $320,000

Retail seeds sold in 30 cent sample packets. Garlic, herbs, shallots & perennials.

LEE'S NURSERY

233 Lee's Dr
McMinnville, TN 37110-6939
Telephone: (931) 668-4870, FAX: (931) 668-4870, E-Mail: leesnursery@blomand.net, Web Site: stores.ebay.com/Lees-Nursery
Proprietor: Malinda L. Brown
Conducts Business: U.S.
Employees: 2
Advertising/Marketing Budget Related to Direct Marketing: 76-100%
Direct Marketing ad budget:
Direct Mail: 40%
Online: 60%
Founded: 1968
Gross sales or billing: $100,000

Sell over 200 varieties of plants to home gardeners & businesses, including flowering shrubs, shade & flowering trees, fruit & nut trees, evergreens, perennials, berry & hedge plants, vines & ground covers. Free full color catalog.

LEHMAN'S

aka Lehman Hardware & Appliances, Inc
289 N Kurzen Rd
Dalton, OH 44618
Telephone: (330) 857-5757, (877) 438-5346, FAX: (330) 857-5785, E-Mail: info@lehmans.com, Web Site: www.lehmans.com
Founder: Jay Lehman
Pres: Galen Lehman
VP Mktg: Glenda Lehman
Conducts Business: Worldwide
Employees: 8
Primary Market Served: Business & Consumer
Catalog available online
Direct online sales
Founded: 1955

Sell non-electric appliances, tools, kitchenware & wood stoves.

LEMEE'S INC

Subs. of Lemee's Fireplace Equipment
815 Bedford St, Rtes 18 & 28
Bridgewater, MA 02324-3007
Telephone: (508) 697-2672, E-Mail: slemeephot@aol.com, Web Site: www.lemeesfireplace.com
Pres: Ruth E. Lemee
Treas & Dir: Brian D. Lemee
VP: Susan Lemee
Conducts Business: U.S.

Employees: 4
Primary Market Served: Consumer
Catalog available online
Direct online sales
Founded: 1954

Sell fireplace screens, toolsets, irons, grates, wood baskets & other fireplace accessories. Also, brass items, cabinet hardware, bathroom fixtures, lamps & lampshades. Mail orders through ads & catalog.

AM LEONARD INC

241 Fox Dr, PO Box 816
Piqua, OH 45356-0816
Telephone: (937) 773-2694, (800) 543-8955, FAX: (800) 433-0633, (937) 773-9993, E-Mail: info@amleo.com, Web Site: www.amleo.com
Pres: Gregory Stephens
Mktg Mgr: Beth Marshall
Conducts Business: U.S.
Employees: 90
Primary Market Served: Business & Consumer
Catalog available online
Founded: 1885

Sell horticulture supplies and hardware to growers, landscapers, ground management professionals, arborists & contractors.

LIFETIME BRANDS INC

1000 Stewart Ave
Garden City, NY 11530
Telephone: (516) 683-6000, FAX: (516) 683-6161, E-Mail: postmaster@brands.com, Web Site: www.lifetimebrands.com
Pres & CEO: Jeffrey Siegel
VP Mktg: Heather Schall
Direct to Consumer Div: Bill Marquilis
Conducts Business: U.S., Eastern Europe, S. America, Mexico, Canada
Employees: 1,199
Primary Market Served: Business
Catalog available online
Advertising/Marketing Budget Related to Direct Marketing: 0-25%
Direct Marketing ad budget:
Magazines: 100%
Founded: 1945
Gross sales or billing: $457,400,000

Kitchenware, Tabletop, Cutlery, Cutting boards, Bakeware, Pantryware, Spices, BBQ & Bar accessories, indoor-outdoor thermometers & gadgets sold to other direct marketers.

LILYPONS WATER GARDENS

6800 Lilypons Rd, PO Box 10
Adamstown, MD 21710
Telephone: (301) 874-3763, (800) 999-5459, FAX: (301) 874-2959, Web Site: www.lilypons.com

Pres: Margaret Koogle
Conducts Business: U.S.
Primary Market Served: Business & Consumer
Catalog available online
Direct online sales
Founded: 1917

Aquatic plants, water lilies & garden pools to gardeners.

LINDUSTRIES INC

21 Shady Hill Rd
Weston, MA 02493-1407
Telephone: (781) 237-8177
Pres: Willard H. Lind
Co-Owner & VP: Louise T. Lind
Conducts Business: Worldwide
Primary Market Served: Business & Consumer
Catalog available online
Indirect online sales
Advertising/Marketing Budget Related to Direct Marketing: 0-25%
Direct Marketing ad budget:
Magazines: 75%
Telephone: 25%
Founded: 1983
Gross sales or billing: $210,000

Leveron, door knob lever adaptor. ADA compliant for access in public buildings & private homes.

LINENS N' THINGS

Div. of Linens Holding Co.
80 E State Rte 4 Ste 290
Paramus, NJ 07652-2661
Telephone: (973) 778-1300, FAX: (973) 778-0822, (973) 815-2990, Web Site: www.lnt.com
Chmn, Pres & CEO: Robert J. Di Nicola
Sr VP Mktg: Michael Larkey
Conducts Business: US, Canada
Employees: 18,500
Primary Market Served: Business & Consumer
Direct online sales
Founded: 1975
Gross sales or billing: $2,534,400,000

Linens, towels & bedding.

LOUISIANA NURSERY

5853 Hwy 182
Opelousas, LA 70570
Telephone: (337) 948-3696, FAX: (337) 942-6404, Web Site: www.dvrionursery.com
Pres: Ken Durio
VP: Dalton Durio
Sec: Belle Durio
Conducts Business: Worldwide
Employees: 10
Primary Market Served: Consumer
Catalog available online
Advertising/Marketing Budget Related

to Direct Marketing: 76-100%
Founded: 1950

Sell plants.

LOWE'S COMPANIES INC
1000 Lowes Blvd
Mooresville, NC 28117-8520
Telephone: (704) 758-1000, FAX:
   (336) 651-4766, Web Site: www.
   lowes.com
Chmn & CEO: Robert Tillman
Sr Exec VP Mdsg & Mktg: Dale C.
   Pond
Sr VP Mktg & Adv: Robert J. Gfeller
Pres: Robert A. Niblock
Project Leader: Mark Malone
Conducts Business: U.S.
Employees: 130,000
Primary Market Served: Business &
   Consumer
Direct online sales
Founded: 1946
Gross sales or billing: $6,117,814

Home center chain with over 850
stores.

MAGNOLIA HALL
138 Emerald Creek Dr
Jasper, GA 30143
Telephone: (404) 351-1910, (866) 410-
   2755, FAX: (404) 351-2151, E-Mail:
   belvedere@magnoliahall.com, Web
   Site: www.magnoliahall.com
Pres: David Rosinger
Conducts Business: U.S., Canada,
   Mexico, Puerto Rico, Caribbean Is-
   lands
Employees: 4
Primary Market Served: Consumer
Catalog available online
Direct online sales
Founded: 1962

Sell yesteryear furniture & accessories.

MARIMAC INC
6395 Cote-de-Liesse
Montreal, PQ, Canada H4T 1E5
Telephone: (514) 725-7600, FAX:
   (514) 376-0801, Web Site: www.
   marimac.com
Pres: Paul Nassar
CFO & VP, Fin: Christine Valleaux
VP, Mktg & Mdse: Mara Piccolo
Conducts Business: Worldwide
Employees: 200
Primary Market Served: Business &
   Consumer

Sell juvenile bedding.

MARY'S PLANT FARM &
   LANDSCAPING
2410 Lanes Mill Rd
Hamilton, OH 45013-9181

Telephone: (513) 894-0022, FAX:
   (513) 892-2053, E-Mail:
   marysplantfarm@zoomtown.com,
   Web Site: www.marysplantfarm.com
Pres & Owner: Mary E. Harrison
Mgr: Sherri Berger
Conducts Business: U.S.
Employees: 4
Primary Market Served: Business &
   Consumer
Catalog available online
Direct online sales
Advertising/Marketing Budget Related
   to Direct Marketing: 26-50%
Direct Marketing ad budget:
Direct Mail: 50%
Newspapers: 25%
Online: 25%
Founded: 1976

Nursery stock.

MCCLURE & ZIMMERMAN
Subs of J. W. Jung Seed Co
335 S High St
Randolph, WI 53956-1425
Telephone: (800) 883-6998, FAX:
   (800) 374-6120, Web Site: www.
   mzbulb.com
Pres: Richard Zondag
Conducts Business: U.S.
Primary Market Served: Business &
   Consumer
Catalog available online
Indirect online sales

Flower bulbs, corns & rootstocks for
the bulb enthusiast.

MCFAYDEN/MCCONNELL
Div. of A E McKenzie Co Ltd
30 Ninth St
Brandon, MB, Canada R7A 6E1
Telephone: (800) 205-7111, FAX:
   (877) 625-1888, Web Site: www.
   mcfayden.com
VP, DM: Lawrence Grodecki
Employees: 250
Primary Market Served: Business &
   Consumer
Gross sales or billing: $20,000,000

Garden seeds & nursery stock.

MELANIPHY & ASSOCIATES,
   INC
6333 N Milwaukee Ave (Suite 106)
Chicago, IL 60646-3744
Telephone: (773) 467-1212, FAX:
   (773) 774-0454, E-Mail:
   jmelaniphy@melaniphy.com, Web
   Site: www.melaniphy.com
Pres: John Melaniphy Sr
VP: John Melaniphy Jr
Mktg Consultant: Patty Talbot
Primary Market Served: Business &
   Consumer

Catalog available online

Publish books about food & beverages,
in both the fast-food & restaurant
industries. Real estate consultants.

METROPOLITAN MUSEUM
   OF ART
6 E 82nd St
New York, NY 10028-0304
Telephone: (212) 879-5500, FAX:
   (718) 628-5485, Web Site: www.
   metmuseum.org/store
Gen Mgr, Mktg & Publicity: Jody
   Malordy
Conducts Business: Worldwide
Primary Market Served: Business &
   Consumer

Sell museum reproductions, adaptations & books.

MEYER DECORATIVE
   SURFACES INC
PO Box 43765
Atlanta, GA 30336-0765
Telephone: (404) 699-3900, (800) 776-
   3900, FAX: (404) 699-3914, Web
   Site: www.meyerdeco.com
CEO: David Sullivan
Dir: Sandy Herb
Dir: Bob Sweat
Employees: 249
Primary Market Served: Business &
   Consumer
Catalog available online
Gross sales or billing: $45,500,000

Wholesale cabinet hardware.

JE MILLER NURSERIES INC
5060 W Lake Rd
Canandaigua, NY 14424-8952
Telephone: (585) 396-2647, (800) 836-
   9630, FAX: (585) 396-2154, E-Mail:
   jmiller@millernurseries.com, Web
   Site: www.millernurseries.com
Pres: John E. Miller
VP: David J. Miller
Treas: George R. Miller
Conducts Business: U.S.
Employees: 25
Primary Market Served: Consumer
Catalog available online
Indirect online sales
Advertising/Marketing Budget Related
   to Direct Marketing: 0-25%
Direct Marketing ad budget: $900,000
Direct Mail: 90%
Magazines: 10%
Founded: 1936
Gross sales or billing: $6,000,000

Sell mostly dwarf fruits & small fruits
to the backyard gardener.

BOB MORGAN WOODWORKING SUPPLIES INC

6521 Jacob Dr
Westport, KY 40077
Telephone: (502) 265-0954, E-Mail:
    bmorgan@insightbb.com, Web Site:
    www.morganwood.com
Owner: Bob Morgan
Conducts Business: U.S.
Primary Market Served: Business &
    Consumer
Catalog available online
Direct online sales
Advertising/Marketing Budget Related
    to Direct Marketing: 0-25%
Direct Marketing ad budget:
Direct Mail: 100%
Founded: 1974

Sell hardwood veneers, raised panel
cabinet doors, inlays, exotic hardwoods, cane, dowels, carving blocks.

MOULTRIE MANUFACTURING CO

1403 Georgia Hwy
Moultrie, GA 31776-2948
Telephone: (229) 985-1312, (800) 841-
    8674, FAX: (229) 890-7245, Web
    Site: www.moultriemanufacturing.
    com
Natl Sls Mgr: Jerrold L. Becker
CEO: Peter Dillard
Assoc: Wayne Perry
Conducts Business: U.S., Canada
Employees: 75
Primary Market Served: Consumer
Catalog available online
Direct online sales
Direct Marketing ad budget:
Magazines: 90%
Newspapers: 5%
TV/Radio: 5%
Founded: 1952

Traditional cast aluminum furniture,
fountains, urns, plaques & mailboxes
sold direct to customers & interior designers under the Old South brand
name.

MURPHY BED CO INC

42 Central Ave
Farmingdale, NY 11735
Telephone: (631) 420-4330, (800) 845-
    2337, FAX: (631) 420-4337, E-Mail:
    info@murphybedcompany.com, Web
    Site: www.murphybedcompany.com
Pres: Clark W. Murphy
VP: Gene Kolakowski
Conducts Business: U.S., Canada
Employees: 10
Primary Market Served: Business &
    Consumer
Catalog available online
Direct online sales

Advertising/Marketing Budget Related
    to Direct Marketing: 0-25%
Direct Marketing ad budget: $20,000
Direct Mail: 40%
Magazines: 20%
Newspapers: 10%
Telephone: 30%
Founded: 1908
Gross sales or billing: $1,000,000

Market wall beds (beds that store in an
upright position when not in use) to
general public, hospitals, firehouses,
hotels, motels, apartments &
condominiums.

NEIMAN-MARCUS GROUP

1618 Main St
Dallas, TX 75201
Telephone: (214) 743-7600, (888) 888-
    4757, FAX: (214) 573-5320, Web
    Site: www.neimanmarcus.com
Chmn, Pres & CEO: Burton M. Tan-
    sky
Pres & CEO, Bergdorf Goodman:
    James J Gold
CFO: James E. Skinner
Pres & CEO, Neiman Marcus Direct:
    Gerald A Barnes
Exec VP, Mktg: Karen Katz
Primary Market Served: Consumer
Catalog available online
Direct online sales

Sell hard goods, soft goods & apparel.

NOR'EAST MINIATURE ROSES INC

PO Box 440
Arroyo Grande, CA 93421
Telephone: (805) 426-6485, (800) 426-
    6485, FAX: (805) 481-7374, E-Mail:
    noreast@greenheartfarms.com, Web
    Site: www.noreast-miniroses.com
Pres & Treas: John M. Saville
Office Mgr & Clerk: Barbara S. Black-
    hall
Conducts Business: U.S.
Employees: 14
Primary Market Served: Business &
    Consumer
Catalog available online
Direct online sales
Advertising/Marketing Budget Related
    to Direct Marketing: 26-50%
Direct Marketing ad budget:
Direct Mail: 15%
Magazines: 50%
Newspapers: 25%
Telephone: 10%
Founded: 1971

Miniature rose plants.

NORTHERN GREENHOUSE SALES

PO Box 42
Neche, ND 58265-0042

Telephone: (204) 327-5540, FAX:
    (204) 327-5527, E-Mail: info@
    northerngreenhouse.com, Web Site:
    www.northerngreenhouse.com
Partner: Bob Davis
Partner: Margaret Davis
Conducts Business: U.S., Canada
Primary Market Served: Business &
    Consumer
Catalog available online
Indirect online sales
Advertising/Marketing Budget Related
    to Direct Marketing: 76-100%
Founded: 1979

Pond liners, greenhouse plastics &
supplies.

NOURSE FARMS

41 River Rd
South Deerfield, MA 01373
Telephone: (413) 665-2658, FAX:
    (413) 665-7888, E-Mail: info@
    noursefarms.com, Web Site: www.
    noursefarms.com
VP & Adv Dir: Sylvia Robertson
Sls Mgr: Nathan Norse
Conducts Business: U.S.
Employees: 100
Primary Market Served: Business &
    Consumer
Catalog available online
Direct online sales
Advertising/Marketing Budget Related
    to Direct Marketing: 76-100%
Direct Marketing ad budget: $35,000
Direct Mail: 75%
Magazines: 24%
Newspapers: 1%
Founded: 1932

Sell berry plants to gardeners &
farmers.

NOWELL'S INC

615 Irwin St
San Rafael, CA 94901-3940
Telephone: (415) 332-4933, FAX:
    (415) 332-4936, E-Mail: contact@
    nowellslighting.com, Web Site:
    www.nowellslighting.com
Pres: Jim Artz
VP: Lennart Sandin
Conducts Business: U.S., Canada,
    U.K., Australia, Hong Kong, Taiwan
Employees: 10
Primary Market Served: Business &
    Consumer
Catalog available online
Indirect online sales
Advertising/Marketing Budget Related
    to Direct Marketing: 0-25%
Founded: 1954

Manufacturer & marketer of antique &
traditional-style light fixtures & custom
lighting; restorations of Victorian
fixtures.

OFFICEFURNITURE.COM

A National Bus Furniture, Inc
company. Subs of K&K America,
LLC
735 N Water (#400)
Milwaukee, WI 53202-4103
Telephone: (414) 272-6080, (800) 933-
0053, FAX: (414) 272-0248, (800)
468-1526, Web Site: www.
officefurniture.com
Pres: Kent Anderson
Dir Mktg: Steve Twining
Conducts Business: U.S.
Employees: 70
Primary Market Served: Business
Catalog available online
Direct online sales
Gross sales or billing: $24,800,000

Sell office furniture through catalogs &
showroom. Offers 15 year guarantee
on most products.

OMAHA FIXTURE INTERNATIONAL

10320 "J" St
Omaha, NE 68127-1092
Telephone: (402) 592-3720, (800) 531-
6627, FAX: (402) 593-5716, (800)
531-6627, Web Site: www.
omahafixture.com
Pres: Joel Alperson
Sls Mgr: Pete Sirotkin
Primary Market Served: Business

Catalogs featuring retail store fixtures.

OPUS INC

69 N Locust St
Lititz, PA 17543
Telephone: (717) 626-2125, (800) 800-
1819, FAX: (717) 626-1912, E-Mail:
opususa@woodstream.com, Web
Site: www.opususa.com
Mktg Devel: Elaine Gorlenkova
Conducts Business: Worldwide
Employees: 30
Primary Market Served: Business &
Consumer
Catalog available online
Indirect online sales
Gross sales or billing: $1,900,000

Manufacturer of wild bird feeders &
indoor & outdoor garden products.

GEORGE W PARK SEED CO INC

One Parkton Ave
Greenwood, SC 29647
Telephone: (864) 223-8555, (864) 223-
7333, FAX: (864) 941-4206, E-Mail:
info@parkseed.com, Web Site: www.
parkseed.com
Pres & CEO: Karen Jennings
VP DM: Ray Moore
Conducts Business: U.S., Canada

Employees: 600
Primary Market Served: Business &
Consumer
Catalog available online
Direct online sales
Founded: 1868

Sell flower, garden & vegetable seeds,
bulbs, plants & gardening accessories
to consumers by mail order.

PARTYLITE GIFTS INC

59 Armstrong Rd
Plymouth, MA 02360-4840
Telephone: (508) 830-3100, FAX:
(508) 830-0026, Web Site: www.
partylite.com
Dir New Category Devel: Donna
Baker Schwenk
Mgr Mktg Commun: Paul Katz

THE PATIO

36298 Toulon Dr, PO Box 1042
Murrieta, CA 92564
Telephone: (909) 304-0460
Pres: James Hoffman
Conducts Business: Worldwide
Primary Market Served: Consumer
Gross sales or billing: $100,000

Sell outdoor furniture & accessories to
consumers via mail order catalog &
space ads.

PENNSYLVANIA FIREBACKS

Div. of Pennsylvania Firebacks Inc
2237 Bethel Rd
Lansdale, PA 19446-6003
Telephone: (215) 699-0805, (888) 349-
30002, FAX: (215) 699-3332,
E-Mail: info@fireback.com, Web
Site: www.fireback.com
Pres: J. Del Conner
VP: Gerald Crowe
Conducts Business: U.S.
Employees: 2
Primary Market Served: Consumer
Advertising/Marketing Budget Related
to Direct Marketing: 0-25%
Direct Marketing ad budget:
Magazines: $1,500
Gross sales or billing: $250,000

Sell fireplace accessories.

PERENNIAL PLEASURES NURSERY

63 Brickhouse Rd
East Hardwick, VT 05836
Telephone: (802) 472-5104, FAX:
(802) 472-6572, E-Mail: annex@
perennialpleasures.net, Web Site:
www.antiqueplants.com
Proprietor: Rachel Kane
Conducts Business: U.S.
Employees: 4
Primary Market Served: Consumer

Catalog available online
Indirect online sales
Advertising/Marketing Budget Related
to Direct Marketing: 0-25%
Direct Marketing ad budget:
Direct Mail: 70%
Magazines: 30%
Founded: 1981
Gross sales or billing: $120,000

Sell heirloom flowers & herbs from the
17th, 18th & 19th centuries, both
plants & seeds, also garden books to
householders, historical societies, museums & garden restorationists.

PETER PAULS NURSERIES

4665 Chapin Rd
Canandaigua, NY 14424-8720
Telephone: (716) 394-7397, FAX:
(716) 394-4122, E-Mail: ippnurse@
eznet.net
Gen Mgr: Jay Miller
Conducts Business: Worldwide
Primary Market Served: Business &
Consumer
Catalog available online
Direct online sales
Advertising/Marketing Budget Related
to Direct Marketing: 26-50%
Founded: 1955

Sell carnivorous plants, seeds, books &
supplies.

PFALTZGRAFF CO

Subs. of Susquehanna Pf
140 E Market St
York, PA 17401-1219
Telephone: (717) 852-2211, (800) 999-
2811, FAX: (800) 717-2481, E-Mail:
service@pfaltzgraff.com, Web Site:
www.pfaltzgraff.com
Pres & CEO: Marsha Everton
Commun Dir: Floyd Sullivan
Consumer Dir: Barb Grafton
Conducts Business: Worldwide
Employees: 2,000
Primary Market Served: Business &
Consumer
Catalog available online
Founded: 1811
Gross sales or billing: $23,700,000

Manufacturer & marketer of tabletop
products.

PIER 1 IMPORTS INC

100 Pier 1 Pl
Fort Worth, TX 76102-2600
Telephone: (817) 252-8000, Web Site:
www.pier1.com
Sr Mgr, Direct Mktg: Susan Rodgers

THE PLOW & HEARTH INC

Subs. of 1-800-FLOWERS
7021 Wolftown-Hood Rd, PO Box 5000
Madison, VA 22727
Telephone: (540) 948-2272, (800) 494-7544, FAX: (540) 948-2273, Web Site: www.plowhearth.com
Pres & CEO: Peter G. Rice
VP, Mktg: Peter Rice Jr.
Conducts Business: U.S., Canada, Japan
Employees: 150
Primary Market Served: Consumer
Catalog available online
Direct online sales
Direct Marketing ad budget:
Direct Mail: 100%
Founded: 1980
Gross sales or billing: $100,000,000

Mail order catalog selling "products for country living" to retail customers throughout the nation.

PRAIRIE NURSERY

W5875 Dyke Ave, PO Box 306
Westfield, WI 53964
Telephone: (608) 296-3679, (800) 476-9453, FAX: (608) 296-2741, E-Mail: webcs@prairienursery.com, Web Site: www.prairienursery.com
Pres: Neil Diboll
Mktg Dir: Sharon Dahlke
Conducts Business: U.S., Canada
Employees: 26
Primary Market Served: Business & Consumer
Catalog available online
Direct online sales
Founded: 1972

Sell native grasses & wild flowers, plants & seeds.

ST PRESTON & SON INC

102 Main St Wharf
Greenport, NY 11944-1422
Telephone: (631) 477-1990, (800) 836-1165, FAX: (631) 477-8541, E-Mail: andrew@prestons.com, Web Site: www.prestons.com
Pres: George H. Rowsom
VP: Peter Rowsom
Mktg Mgr: Andrew Rowsom
Conducts Business: U.S., Canada, Europe
Employees: 16
Primary Market Served: Business & Consumer
Catalog available online
Direct online sales
Advertising/Marketing Budget Related to Direct Marketing: 51-75%
Direct Marketing ad budget:
Direct Mail: 60%
Magazines: 5%

Online: 35%
Publisher of catalogs featuring ships models, marine prints, books & nautical gifts.

QUALCO, INC

225 Passaic St
Passaic, NJ 07055-6414
Telephone: (973) 473-1222, (800) 289-2567, FAX: (973) 473-0535, E-Mail: feedback@qualco.com, Web Site: www.qualco.com
Pres: John Ferentinos
VP, Sls & Mktg: Thomas Ferentinos
Pur Dir: Ed Solla
Conducts Business: Worldwide
Employees: 30
Primary Market Served: Business
Direct Marketing ad budget:
Direct Mail: $25,000
Magazines: $25,000
Newspapers: $100,000
TV/Radio: $50,000
Telephone: $50,000
Founded: 1986
Gross sales or billing: $5,000,000

Sales of swimming pool chemicals & accessories through mass merchant & individual retailers.

REDWOOD CITY SEED CO

PO Box 361
Redwood City, CA 94064-0361
Telephone: (650) 325-7333, FAX: (650) 325-4056, Web Site: www.ecoseeds.com
Co-Owner, Sales & Res: Craig C. Dremann
Co-Owner & Mgr: Sue Dremann
Sales & Svcs: Alex Dremann
Conducts Business: Wordwide
Primary Market Served: Business & Consumer
Catalog available online
Indirect online sales
Advertising/Marketing Budget Related to Direct Marketing: 100%
Direct Marketing ad budget:
Direct Mail: 90%
Magazines: 5%
Online: 5%
Founded: 1971

Garden seeds, principally old fashioned vegetable & herb seeds for home gardeners.

THE REGGIO REGISTER CO INC

31 Jytek Rd
Leominster, MA 01453-5934
Telephone: (978) 870-1020, (800) 880-3090, FAX: (978) 870-1030, E-Mail: reggio@reggioregister.com, Web Site: www.reggioregister.com

Pres: Michael Reggio
Exec Asst: Sue Sheeler
Exec Asst: Shelley Maldonado
Conducts Business: U.S., Canada, U.K.
Employees: 13
Primary Market Served: Business & Consumer
Catalog available online
Direct online sales
Advertising/Marketing Budget Related to Direct Marketing: 0-25%
Direct Marketing ad budget:
Direct Mail: 67%
Magazines: 33%
Founded: 1978

Manufacturer of solid brass & cast iron, aluminum & wood floor registers & grilles.

REPLACEMENTS LTD

1089 Knox Rd
Greensboro, NC 27420-6029
Telephone: (336) 697-3000, (800) RE-PLACE, FAX: (336) 697-3100, E-Mail: mark.donahue@replacements.com, Web Site: www.replacements.com
CEO & Pres: Bob Page
CIO: Kelly Smith
Sr VP: Jack Whitley
Exec VP: Scott Fleming
Media Buyer: Mark Donahue
Conducts Business: U.S.
Employees: 450
Primary Market Served: Business & Consumer
Catalog available online
Direct online sales
Advertising/Marketing Budget Related to Direct Marketing: 51-75%
Direct Marketing ad budget:
Direct Mail: 40%
Magazines: 55%
Newspapers: 5%
Founded: 1981
Gross sales or billing: $75,000,000

Discontinued & active china, crystal, silver & collectibles.

RINFRET LTD

354 Greenwich Ave
Greenwich, CT 06830-6522
Telephone: (203) 622-0000, Web Site: www.rinfretltd.com
CFO: Jo Ann Zawalski
Primary Market Served: Consumer

ROCKLER WOODWORKING & HARDWARE

Div. of Rockler Cos Inc
4365 Willow Dr
Medina, MN 55340

Telephone: (763) 478-8201, (800) 279-4441, FAX: (763) 478-8393, E-Mail: info@rockler.com, Web Site: www.rockler.com
CEO: Ann Jackson
DM Mgr: Ro Finnegan
List Mgr: Ellen Manderfield
Conducts Business: Worldwide
Employees: 300
Primary Market Served: Business & Consumer
Catalog available online
Direct online sales
Advertising/Marketing Budget Related to Direct Marketing: 0-25%
Direct Marketing ad budget:
Direct Mail: 75%
Magazines: 25%
Founded: 1954

Retailer of specialty hardware, hardwoods, tools & other wood working supplies. 80% of sales are to private individuals, 20% commercial & institutional.

RUBBERMAID INC

3320 W Market St
Fairlawn, OH 44333
Telephone: (888) 895-2110, (866) 271-9249, E-Mail: info@rubbermaid.com, Web Site: www.rubbermaid.com
Communs: Jim Miller
Conducts Business: Worldwide
Employees: 7,500
Primary Market Served: Business & Consumer
Indirect online sales
Advertising/Marketing Budget Related to Direct Marketing: 0-25%
Founded: 1920
Gross sales or billing: $2,200,000,000

Plastic housewares.

SANDY MUSH HERB NURSERY

316 Surrett Cove Rd
Leicester, NC 28748
Telephone: (828) 683-2014, E-Mail: info@sandymushherbs.com, Web Site: www.sandymushherbs.com
Owner: Fairman Jayne
Owner: Kate Jayne
Conducts Business: U.S.
Primary Market Served: Consumer
Catalog available online
Founded: 1976

Catalog featuring over 1700 items: tea, culinary, decorative & fragrant herbs plus books, seeds, garden plants & growing instructions. Catalog $5.

SANTA BARBARA GREENHOUSES

721 Richmond Ave
Oxnard, CA 93030
Telephone: (805) 483-4288, (800) 544-5276, E-Mail: robsbg@aol.com, Web Site: www.sbgreenhouse.com
Pres: V. Solakian
Conducts Business: U.S.
Employees: 6
Primary Market Served: Business & Consumer
Catalog available online
Advertising/Marketing Budget Related to Direct Marketing: 76-100%
Founded: 1972

Sell greenhouses in kit form to home gardeners, commercial growers & schools.

THE SCOTTS CO DIV OF LAWN SERVICE

Div. of North American Consumer
14111 Scottslawn Rd
Marysville, OH 43041
Telephone: (937) 644-0011, FAX: (937) 644-7261, Web Site: www.scotts.com
Chmn & CEO: Charles Berger
Pres & CEO: James Hagedorn
Sr Mktg Mgr: Dan Adams
VP, HR: Hadia Lefavre
Mgr Partnership & Dir Mktg: Carol Edwards Holmes
Conducts Business: U.S., Canada, Germany
Employees: 850
Primary Market Served: Business & Consumer
Advertising/Marketing Budget Related to Direct Marketing: 0-25%
Gross sales or billing: $390,000,000

Manufacturer of lawn fertilizers & control products, grass seed & mechanical lawn & garden equipment.

SEEDBURO EQUIPMENT CO

2293 S Mount Prospect Rd
Des Plaines, IL 60018-1810
Telephone: (312) 738-3700, (800) 284-5779, FAX: (312) 738-5329, E-Mail: sales@seedburo.com, Web Site: www.seedburo.com
CEO: Gordon B. Phillips
Pres: Thomas E. Runyon
VP, Sls: Katherine A. Reading
Mktg & Sls Mgr: Timothy G. Snader
Conducts Business: Worldwide
Employees: 17
Primary Market Served: Business & Consumer
Catalog available online
Indirect online sales
Advertising/Marketing Budget Related to Direct Marketing: 51-75%
Direct Marketing ad budget:
Direct Mail: 2%
Magazines: 80%
Online: 10%
Telephone: 8%
Founded: 1912

Worldwide sales & distribution of handling, testing & inspection equipment for the agricultural (grain, feed & seed) industry.

SEQUOIA NURSERY

9133 N Stoneridge Ln
Fresno, CA 93720-0843
Telephone: (559) 732-0309, FAX: (559) 732-0192, E-Mail: seqnursery@aol.com, Web Site: www.sequoianursery.com
Pres: Ralph S. Moore
Conducts Business: U.S.
Employees: 10
Primary Market Served: Business & Consumer
Catalog available online
Indirect online sales
Founded: 1937

Breeders & growers of miniature rose plants.

THE DMA SERVICEMASTER CO

860 Ridge Lake Blvd
Memphis, TN 38120-9434
Telephone: (901) 766-1400, (901) 597-8502, (888) 937-3783, (866) 782-6787, FAX: (901) 766-1491, Web Site: www.servicemaster.com
Chmn Bd ServiceMaster Global Holdings: George W. Tamke
CEO ServiceMaster & ServiceMaster Global Holdings: J. Patrick Spainhour
VP Direct Mktg Group: Mark Allen
CIO: Dan Marks
Sr VP Corp Strategy & Mktg: Jim Kunihiro
SVP & CFO: Steven Martin
Employees: 32,000
Primary Market Served: Consumer
Catalog available online
Direct online sales
Founded: 2007
Gross sales or billing: $3,429,100,000

Lawn care & landscape maintenance, termite & pest control, home warranties, home inspection, house cleaning & furniture repair, disaster response & reconstruction, cleaning & disaster restoration.

SHADES OF LIGHT

4924 W Broad St
Richmond, VA 23230
Telephone: (804) 288-3235, (877) 288-5029, FAX: (804) 288-5029, E-Mail: visitor@shadesoflight.com, Web Site: www.shadesoflight.com
Pres: Ashton Harrison
Catalog Mgr: Suellen Wexler

Primary Market Served: Business &
Consumer
Gross sales or billing: $14,500,000

Lighting store retailer. Catalog to decorators, designers & consumers.

SHADY OAKS NURSERY, LLC
PO Box 708, 1601 Fifth St SE
Waseca, MN 56093-0708
Telephone: (507) 835-5033, FAX:
(507) 835-8772, E-Mail:
shadyoaks@shadyoaks.com, Web
Site: www.shadyoaks.com
Pres: Gordon J. Oslund
Conducts Business: Worldwide
Employees: 35
Primary Market Served: Business
Catalog available online
Indirect online sales
Advertising/Marketing Budget Related
to Direct Marketing: 0-25%
Direct Marketing ad budget:
Direct Mail: 80%
Magazines: 20%
Founded: 1982

Perennial plants & liners.

SHAKER WORKSHOPS
PO Box 8001
Ashburnham, MA 01430-8001
Telephone: (978) 827-9900, FAX:
(978) 827-6554, E-Mail:
shaker9973@shakerworkshops.com,
Web Site: www.shakerworkshops.
com
Pres: Richard C. Dabrowski
Conducts Business: U.S., Canada, Denmark, Germany, Japan, U.K., Ireland, Italy
Primary Market Served: Consumer
Catalog available online
Direct online sales
Advertising/Marketing Budget Related
to Direct Marketing: 76-100%
Direct Marketing ad budget:
Direct Mail: 85%
Magazines: 10%
Online: 5%
Founded: 1970

Manufacture Shaker furniture reproductions & decorative accessories for sale, both as kits & custom-finished direct to consumers.

SHELBURNE CO
3617 Old Taneytown Rd
Taneytown, MD 21787-2723
Telephone: (410) 876-5902, FAX:
(410) 876-4612, Web Site: www.
zoysiafarms.com
Pres: Richard Friedberg
Opers: Julie Simermeyer
Exec VP Sls & Mkrg: John Ridgway
Conducts Business: U.S.
Employees: 15

Primary Market Served: Consumer
Catalog available online
Direct online sales
Advertising/Marketing Budget Related
to Direct Marketing: 76-100%
Direct Marketing ad budget:
Direct Mail: 30%
Magazines: 30%
Newspapers: 30%
Online: 10%
Founded: 1953

Sell Zoysia grass/lawn care products.

THE SILO INC
44 Upland Rd
New Milford, CT 06776
Telephone: (860) 355-0300, (800) 353-
SILO, FAX: (860) 350-5495,
E-Mail: info@hunthillfarmtrust.org,
Web Site: www.thesilo.com
Pres: Ruth Henderson
VP, Fin & Admin: Susan E. York
Cooking School Dir: Debbe Christensen
Store Mgr: Renee Fitch
Conducts Business: U.S.
Employees: 7
Primary Market Served: Consumer
Direct online sales
Advertising/Marketing Budget Related
to Direct Marketing: 0-25%
Founded: 1972

A country kitchen store, gallery & cooking school filled with culinary tools & equipment: gourmet, nonperishable foods, table & cookware & gifts for kitchen & home & also cooking instruction for adults and young children by professional chefs.

SIMPLICITY PATTERN CO INC/STYLE PATTERNS LTD/ NEW LOOK ENGLISH PATTERN CO LTD
Subs. Conso Products Co
261 Madison Ave (fl 4)
New York, NY 10016-3906
Telephone: (212) 372-0500, (888) 588-
2700, FAX: (212) 372-0628, E-Mail:
info@simplicitypatt.com, Web Site:
www.simplicitypatt.com
Pres: Frank J. Rizzo
Sr VP, Sls: Louis S. Ottman
CFO: Richard Zonin
Conducts Business: U.S., Australia,
New Zealand, Canada, U.K.
Employees: 200
Primary Market Served: Business &
Consumer
Catalog available online
Advertising/Marketing Budget Related
to Direct Marketing: 0-25%
Founded: 1927

Publisher of home sewing, fashion, home decorating, craft patterns, catalogs & instruction booklets for quilters & crafters.

SLOCUM WATER GARDENS
921 Ave S SE
Winter Haven, FL 33880-4639
Telephone: (863) 293-7151, FAX:
(800) 322-1896, Web Site: www.
slocumwatergardens.com
Pres: Peter D. Slocum
Conducts Business: U.S.
Employees: 8
Primary Market Served: Business &
Consumer
Indirect online sales
Advertising/Marketing Budget Related
to Direct Marketing: 0-25%
Direct Marketing ad budget:
Magazines: 100%
Founded: 1938
Gross sales or billing: $300,000

Water lilies, aquarium plants & supplies.

SMITH & HAWKEN LTD
Subs. of The Scotts Miracle-Gro Co
4 Hamilton Landing Ste 100
Novato, CA 94949-8247
Telephone: (415) 506-3700, (800) 940-
1170, FAX: (415) 506-3900, Web
Site: www.smithandhawken.com
CEO: Gordon M. Erikson
CFO: Rob Walter
Sr VP, HR: Nori Kricensky
Pub Rels Mgr: Noelle Smith
Gen Mgr: Felix Carbullido
Conducts Business: U.S.
Employees: 300
Primary Market Served: Business &
Consumer
Catalog available online
Direct online sales
Advertising/Marketing Budget Related
to Direct Marketing: 76-100%
Direct Marketing ad budget:
Direct Mail: 90%
Magazines: 10%
Founded: 1979
Gross sales or billing: $103,000,000

Garden tools & supplies, outdoor furniture, durable work & casual clothing.

SMITH & NOBLE
1181 California Ave
Corona, CA 92881
Telephone: (909) 734-4444, (800) 248-
8888, FAX: (800) 426-7780, E-Mail:
contactus@smithnoble.com, Web
Site: www.smithandnoble.com
Founder: Fred Kamgar
COO: Stephen Christie
VP, Creative: David Fruge
VP, Mdse: Stephen Hall

Mktg Coord: Shareen Romig
Conducts Business: U.S.
Employees: 150
Primary Market Served: Consumer
Catalog available online
Direct online sales
Founded: 1986

Sell custom-crafted window coverings, rugs & fabric decor to consumers nationwide.

SPATES THE FLORIST

20 Elm St
Newport, VT 05855
Telephone: (802) 334-8330, (800) 473-3688, FAX: (802) 334-1751, E-Mail: spates@sover.net, Web Site: www.spatestheflorist.com
Pres & Co-Owner: Douglas Spates
Co-Owner: Vivian Spates
Conducts Business: U.S., Canada
Employees: 30
Primary Market Served: Business & Consumer
Catalog available online
Direct online sales
Founded: 1945

Flower shop, greenhouse & landscaping service plus mail order division.

STANLEY HOME PRODUCTS

Fuller Brush Co
1 Fuller Way
Great Bend, KS 67530
Telephone: (620) 792-1711, (800) 628-9032, Web Site: www.shponline.com
Pres: Robert C Isaacs
Conducts Business: U.S.
Primary Market Served: Consumer
Founded: 1931

Direct sale of household & personal brushes, mops, cleaners, polishes, cosmetics & giftware.

STARK BROTHERS FULFILLMENT SERVICES

Subs. of Foster & Gallagher Inc
PO Box 1800
Louisiana, MO 63353-7800
Telephone: (573) 754-5511, (800) 325-4180, FAX: (573) 754-5290, E-Mail: info@starkbros.com, Web Site: www.starkbros.com
Chmn & CEO: Stephen Kahn
VP, Opers & Fulfillment Svcs & Gen Mgr: Jack Alexander
Mng Dir: Frank Stark
Conducts Business: U.S.
Employees: 450
Primary Market Served: Business & Consumer
Catalog available online
Direct online sales
Advertising/Marketing Budget Related

to Direct Marketing: 76-100%
Direct Marketing ad budget: $1,925,000
Direct Mail: $1,500,000
Magazines: $375,000
Telephone: $50,000
Founded: 1816

Market fruit trees, other nursery stock & related gardening products retail to the home gardener & commercial orchardists. Also perform full-service fulfillment work for outside companies.

THE DMA STARK BROTHERS NURSERIES & ORCHARDS

PO Box 1800
Louisiana, MO 63353
Telephone: (573) 754-8800, (800) 325-4180, E-Mail: info@starkbros.com, Web Site: www.starkbros.com
Dir Mktg Mgr: Christine Mantych
Primary Market Served: Business & Consumer

STEPTOE & WIFE ANTIQUES LTD

90 Tycos Dr
Toronto, ON, Canada M6B 1V9
Telephone: (416) 780-1707, (800) 461-0060, FAX: (416) 780-1814, E-Mail: info@steptoewife.com, Web Site: www.steptoewife.com
Pres: Bernard Snitman
Co-Owner: Marna Snitman
Conducts Business: Worldwide
Employees: 35
Primary Market Served: Business & Consumer
Catalog available online
Advertising/Marketing Budget Related to Direct Marketing: 76-100%
Direct Marketing ad budget:
Direct Mail: 25%
Magazines: 75%
Founded: 1972
Gross sales or billing: $5,000,000

Architectural products, metalwork & drapery hardware.

STOKES SEEDS INC

PO Box 548
Buffalo, NY 14240-0548
Telephone: (716) 695-6980, (800) 396-9238, FAX: (888) 834-3334, Web Site: www.stokeseeds.com
Pres: Wayne Gale
VP: Thelma Anderson
Adv Coord: Joan Adam
Conducts Business: U.S., Canada
Employees: 200
Primary Market Served: Consumer
Catalog available online
Direct online sales
Advertising/Marketing Budget Related to Direct Marketing: 76-100%

Founded: 1886
Mail order sales of flower & vegetable seed & gardening accessories.

SUNBILT CREATIVE SUNROOMS

Div. of J Sussman Inc
109-10 180th St
Jamaica, NY 11433-2622
Telephone: (718) 297-6040, FAX: (718) 297-3090, E-Mail: info@sunbilt.com, Web Site: www.sunbilt.com
Pres: Steve Sussman
VP: David Sussman
Mktg Dir: Mel Wachsstock
Conducts Business: U.S., Europe
Employees: 55
Primary Market Served: Business & Consumer
Catalog available online
Indirect online sales
Advertising/Marketing Budget Related to Direct Marketing: 0-25%
Direct Marketing ad budget:
Direct Mail: 25%
Magazines: 75%
Founded: 1984
Gross sales or billing: $1,000,000

Aluminum & glass sunrooms through a dealer network & factory direct to consumers.

SUNPORCH STRUCTURES INC

495 Post Rd E
Westport, CT 06880-4433
Telephone: (203) 454-0040, (866) 919-9620, FAX: (203) 454-0020, E-Mail: leo@sunporch.com, Web Site: www.sunporch.com
Mktg Mgr: Leo Mueller
Gen Mgr: Dean A. Schwartz
Conducts Business: U.S., Canada
Employees: 36
Primary Market Served: Consumer
Catalog available online
Direct online sales
Advertising/Marketing Budget Related to Direct Marketing: 76-100%
Direct Marketing ad budget: $800,000
Direct Mail: 20%
Magazines: 60%
Online: 20%
Founded: 1974
Gross sales or billing: $4,500,000

Manufacturer sun-porches, sunrooms & screen rooms.

SUNSHINE FARM & GARDENS

HC 67 Box 539B
Renick, WV 24966

Telephone: (304) 497-2208, FAX: (304) 497-2698, E-Mail: barry@sunfarm.com, Web Site: www.sunfarm.com
Pres: Barry Glick
VP: Abbey Glick
Sec & Treas: Angie Glick
Mgr: Zak Glick
Conducts Business: Worldwide
Employees: 27
Primary Market Served: Business & Consumer
Catalog available online
Direct online sales
Advertising/Marketing Budget Related to Direct Marketing: 26-50%
Direct Marketing ad budget:
Direct Mail: 25%
Magazines: 50%
Newspapers: 10%
Telephone: 15%
Founded: 1972
Gross sales or billing: $400,000

Grower of rare and unusual perennial plants. Sells retail & wholesale worldwide.

SUR LA TABLE
5701 Sixth Ave S (Suite 486)
Seattle, WA 98108
Telephone: (206) 682-7175, FAX: (206) 682-1026
PR & Mktg Mgr: Suzanna Lindsey
Employees: 250
Primary Market Served: Business & Consumer
Advertising/Marketing Budget Related to Direct Marketing: 76-100%
Founded: 1972

Gifts & fine equipment for domestic & professional kitchens.

SURE FIT INC
8000 Quarry Rd (Suite C)
Alburtis, PA 18011-9599
Telephone: (610) 264-7300, Web Site: www.surefit.com
Dir Mktg: Laura Hilburt

TAYLOR GIFTS INC
600 Cedar Hollow Rd
Paoli, PA 19301
Telephone: (610) 725-1122, FAX: (610) 725-1144, Web Site: www.taylorgifts.com
Pres: B. Loyall Taylor Jr
Exec VP: J. Reed Taylor
VP, Opers: Joseph Falcone
Mktg Dir: Frank Ruthkosky
Conducts Business: U.S.
Employees: 150
Primary Market Served: Consumer
Catalog available online
Direct online sales
Founded: 1952

Nationwide mail order gift catalog. Three editions yearly (spring, summer & fall).

THOMPSON & MORGAN INC
Div. of Thompson & Morgan of England
110 W Elm St
Tipp City, OH 45371-1655
Telephone: (732) 363-2225, (800) 274-7333, FAX: (888) 466-4769, E-Mail: tminc@thompson-morgan.com, Web Site: www.tmseeds.com
VP: Claire Watson
Conducts Business: U.S., Worldwide
Employees: 15
Primary Market Served: Consumer
Catalog available online
Direct online sales
Founded: 1855

Flower & vegetable seeds, bulbs & plants.

TIDEWATER WORKSHOP
Div. of Modern Boatworks Inc
1515 Grant St
Egg Harbor City, NJ 08215-2730
Telephone: (609) 965-4000, (800) 666-8433, FAX: (609) 965-8212, Web Site: www.tidewaterworkshop.com
CEO: Peter Caporilli
Dir, Mktg: Janet Magley
Employees: 35
Primary Market Served: Consumer
Catalog available online
Direct online sales
Advertising/Marketing Budget Related to Direct Marketing: 76-100%
Founded: 1991

Garden furniture catalog.

TIMBERLINE GEODESICS
2015 Blake St
Berkeley, CA 94704
Telephone: (510) 849-4481, (800) 366-3466, FAX: (510) 849-3265, E-Mail: info@domehome.com, Web Site: www.domehome.com
Pres: Robert M. Singer
Conducts Business: U.S., Canada, Pacific Rim
Employees: 5
Primary Market Served: Business & Consumer
Direct online sales
Advertising/Marketing Budget Related to Direct Marketing: 0-25%
Direct Marketing ad budget:
Direct Mail: 25%
Magazines: 75%
Founded: 1969

Sell geodesic dome houses in kit form.

THE DMA TOUCH OF CLASS CATALOG
Div. of Parke-Bell Ltd Inc
709 W 12th St
Huntingburg, IN 47542-8915
Telephone: (812) 683-3707, (800) 457-7456, FAX: (812) 683-5921, Web Site: www.touchofclasscatalog.com
Chmn: Carla Parke-Bell
Pres & CEO: Frederick Bell
Admin Asst: Chris Schlachter
Conducts Business: Worldwide
Employees: 225
Primary Market Served: Consumer
Catalog available online
Direct online sales

Mail-order catalog house featuring bed linens, down comforters & custom monogramming.

TURNER GREENHOUSES
Div. of Turner Equipment Co Inc
1500 US Hwy 117 S
Goldsboro, NC 27530-8587
Telephone: (919) 734-8345, (800) 672-4770, FAX: (919) 736-4550, E-Mail: sales@turnergreenhouses.com, Web Site: www.turnergreenhouses.com
Pres: Gary Smithwick
Mktg Mgr: Duffy Smithwick Fleming
Conducts Business: U.S.
Employees: 9
Primary Market Served: Consumer
Catalog available online
Direct online sales
Advertising/Marketing Budget Related to Direct Marketing: 76-100%
Founded: 1957
Gross sales or billing: $900,000

Manufacture & sell by direct mail prefabricated hobby greenhouses & related equipment & accessories in fiberglass & polyethylene.

U-BILD
Div. of U-Build Inc
821 S Tremont St Ste B, PO Box 2383
Oceanside, CA 92054-4158
Telephone: (818) 785-6368, (800) 828-2453, FAX: (818) 785-3229, Web Site: www.ubild.com
Pres: Kevin Taylor
Conducts Business: U.S.
Employees: 7
Primary Market Served: Business & Consumer
Catalog available online
Indirect online sales
Advertising/Marketing Budget Related to Direct Marketing: 0-25%
Direct Marketing ad budget:
Direct Mail: 20%
Newspapers: 80%
Founded: 1948

Do-it-yourself plans for home improvement & recreation. Sell to amateur & experienced do-it-yourselfers.

VAN BOURGONDIEN BROS

Div. of K. Van Bourgondien of VA, Inc.
2820 Crusader Cir
Virginia Beach, VA 23453-3134
Telephone: (800) 327-4268, E-Mail: blooms@dutchbulbs.com, Web Site: www.dutchbulbs.com
VP Mktg: Fred Van Bourgondien
Conducts Business: U.S.
Employees: 300
Primary Market Served: Business & Consumer
Catalog available online
Direct online sales
Advertising/Marketing Budget Related to Direct Marketing: 76-100%
Direct Marketing ad budget:
Direct Mail: 75%
Magazines: 25%
Founded: 1919
Gross sales or billing: $5,000,000

Wholesale & retail catalog of Dutch bulbs & perennials.

VERMONT TUBBS

87 Brown St
Whitefield, NH 03598-3024
Telephone: (603) 837-2547, E-Mail: dogurkis@vermonttubbs.com, Web Site: www.vermonttubbs.com
Plant Mgr: Harold Anderson
Conducts Business: U.S.
Employees: 50
Primary Market Served: Business & Consumer
Gross sales or billing: $4,000,000

Manufacture contemporary bentwood furniture & accessories: tables, beds & chests.

VESEY'S SEEDS LTD

PO Box 9000
Charlottetown, PE, Canada C1A 8K6
Telephone: (902) 368-7333, (800) 363-7333, FAX: (800) 686-0329, E-Mail: customerservice@veseys.com, Web Site: www.veseys.com
Pres: B.E. Simpson
Dir, Sls, Mktg & Devel: John Barrett
VP: Gerry Simpson
Conducts Business: U.S., Canada
Employees: 60
Primary Market Served: Consumer
Catalog available online
Direct online sales
Advertising/Marketing Budget Related to Direct Marketing: 51-75%
Direct Marketing ad budget:
Direct Mail: 75%
Magazines: 10%

Newspapers: 5%
TV/Radio: 10%
Founded: 1939
Gross sales or billing: $4,400,000

Mail order seed company offering vegetable & flower seeds. Specializing in "seeds for short seasons."

VILLAGE INTERIORS CARPET ONE

3203 Hwy 70 SE
Newton, NC 28658
Telephone: (828) 465-6818, FAX: (828) 465-1864, E-Mail: sales@carpet-one.net, Web Site: www.carpetone.com/village
Pres: Robert E. Norris
VP: Patsy Norris
Conducts Business: U.S.
Employees: 10
Primary Market Served: Business & Consumer
Advertising/Marketing Budget Related to Direct Marketing: 0-25%
Founded: 1989
Gross sales or billing: $1,000,000

Retail carpet, vinyl, ceramic, wood & laminate flooring.

VINTAGE WOOD WORKS

Hwy 34 S
Quinlan, TX 75474
Telephone: (903) 356-2158, FAX: (903) 356-3023, E-Mail: mail@vintagewoodworks.com, Web Site: www.vintagewoodworks.com
Pres: Gregory Tatsch
VP, Mktg: Holly Tatsch
Conducts Business: U.S., Canada
Employees: 50
Primary Market Served: Business & Consumer
Catalog available online
Direct online sales
Advertising/Marketing Budget Related to Direct Marketing: 76-100%
Direct Marketing ad budget: $400,000
Direct Mail: 5%
Magazines: 95%
Gross sales or billing: $2,500,000

Victorian house trim.

WEST SHORE DISTRIBUTORS

Div. of Curatolo Enterprises Inc
31060 Clemens Rd
Westlake, OH 44145-1005
Telephone: (440) 835-5600, (800) 344-8141, FAX: (440) 835-8654, E-Mail: westshore@ameritech.net, Web Site: www.westshoreframes.com
Pres: B.L. Curatolo
Conducts Business: U.S.
Employees: 5
Primary Market Served: Business

Catalog available online
Direct online sales
Advertising/Marketing Budget Related to Direct Marketing: 76-100%
Founded: 1985

Wholesale picture framing supplies, commercial framing services, and fine art giclee printing.

THE DMA WHITE FLOWER FARM

30 Irene St
Torrington, CT 06790-6657
Telephone: (860) 496-9624, (800) 503-9624, FAX: (860) 496-1418, Web Site: www.whiteflowerfarm.com
Owner: Eliot Wadsworth II
Pres: Lorraine Calder
Conducts Business: U.S.
Employees: 250
Primary Market Served: Business & Consumer
Catalog available online
Direct online sales
Advertising/Marketing Budget Related to Direct Marketing: 0-25%
Founded: 1950

Nursery marketer of perennials, shrubs, annuals, tools & garden decor.

GILBERT H WILD & SON INC

2944 State Hwy 37
Reeds, MO 64859
Telephone: (417) 548-3514, FAX: (417) 548-6831, Web Site: www.gilberthwild.com
Pres: Gregory P. Jones
Conducts Business: U.S.
Primary Market Served: Consumer
Catalog available online
Direct online sales
Advertising/Marketing Budget Related to Direct Marketing: 76-100%
Founded: 1885

Plants: daylilies & peonies.

WILDSEED FARMS

100 Legacy Dr, PO Box 3000
Fredericksburg, TX 78624
Telephone: (830) 990-8080, (800) 848-0078, FAX: (830) 990-8090, E-Mail: orders1@wildseedfarms.com, Web Site: www.wildseedfarms.com
Pres: John Thomas
COO & Mktg Dir: Tom Kramer
Primary Market Served: Business & Consumer
Catalog available online
Advertising/Marketing Budget Related to Direct Marketing: 26-50%
Founded: 1983
Gross sales or billing: $5,718,407

Seed company. Branch office in Eagle Lake, TX.

THE DMA WILLIAMS-SONOMA INC

3250 Van Ness Ave
San Francisco, CA 94109-1012
Telephone: (415) 421-7900, FAX:
(415) 983-9887, Web Site: www.
williams-sonomainc.com
Chmn & CEO: W. Howard Lester
Pres: Laura J. Alber
Exec VP, Chief Mktg Officer: Patrick
J. Connolly
Conducts Business: U.S.
Employees: 38,800
Primary Market Served: Consumer
Catalog available online
Direct online sales
Advertising/Marketing Budget Related
to Direct Marketing: 0-25%
Founded: 1956
Gross sales or billing: $3,727,500,000

Retail & mail order sales of cooking &
serving equipment, tabletop accessories
& bed/bath products.

WILLIAMSBURG BLACKSMITHS INC

26 Williams St
Williamsburg, MA 01096
Telephone: (413) 268-7341, (800) 248-
1776, FAX: (413) 268-9317, Web
Site: www.williamsburgblacksmiths.
com
Owner: Liz Tilley
Conducts Business: U.S., Canada
Primary Market Served: Business &
Consumer
Founded: 1840

Reproductions of early American
wrought iron hardware.

WINDOW COVERINGS EXCHANGE

855 Rte 22
North Plainfield, NJ 07060-3619
Telephone: (908) 755-4700
Member: Bruce Heyman

Ready-made designer curtains, drapes,
shades & window treatments

WINSTON MARKETING GROUP

2521 Busse Rd
Elk Grove Village, IL 60007-6118
Telephone: (847) 350-5800
Pres: Todd Lustbader
Primary Market Served: Consumer

WRISCO INDUSTRIES INC

355 Hiatt Dr (Suite B)
Palm Beach Gardens, FL 33418-7106
Telephone: (561) 626-5700, (800) 627-
2646, FAX: (561) 627-3574, E-Mail:
sales.staff@wrisco.com, Web Site:
www.wrisco.com
Owner: A.J. Monastra

Owner: Steve Monastra
Pres: Mark Davidson
Division Mgr: Roman Bender
Conducts Business: Worldwide
Employees: 95
Primary Market Served: Business &
Consumer
Catalog available online
Indirect online sales
Advertising/Marketing Budget Related
to Direct Marketing: 0-25%
Direct Marketing ad budget: $100,000
Direct Mail: $70,000
Magazines: $10,000
Telephone: $20,000
Founded: 1916

Window coverings, patio enclosures &
carport awnings to dealers & consumers, coatings to businesses, prefinished
aluminum to sign companies, architectural firms & racers.

AGCO INC
2782 Simpson Cir
Norcross, GA 30071
Telephone: (770) 447-6990, FAX:
(770) 446-2102, Web Site: www.
agcomarble.com
Pres: Larry Pulliam
Primary Market Served: Business &
Consumer
Catalog available online

Manufacturer of bath tiles.

ABBEON CAL INC
123 Gray Ave
Santa Barbara, CA 93101-1809
Telephone: (805) 966-0810, (800) 922-
0977, FAX: (805) 966-7659, E-Mail:
abbeoncal@abbeon.com, Web Site:
www.abbeon.com
Pres: A.J. Wertheim
Conducts Business: U.S.
Employees: 11
Primary Market Served: Business
Catalog available online
Direct online sales
Advertising/Marketing Budget Related
to Direct Marketing: 76-100%
Direct Marketing ad budget:
$1,000,000
Direct Mail: 100%
Founded: 1970
Gross sales or billing: $2,000,000

Marketer of industrial products through
350 page catalog.

ACTIVE WEB GROUP
Subs. of Lab Safety Supply
30 Oser Ave (Suite 500)
Hauppauge, NY 11788
Telephone: (800) 978-3417, FAX:
(800) 719-4402, E-Mail: info@
activewebgroup.com, Web Site:
www.activewebgroup.com
Pres: Pat Norton
Sr SEO & Dir Bus Devel: David Mon-
talvo
Conducts Business: U.S., Canada
Primary Market Served: Business
Catalog available online
Direct online sales

Full-service web marketing agency
specializing in website design and development, search engine optimization,
pay per click management,
e-commerce solutions, and email
marketing.

**ADAMS MANUFACTURING
CO**
9790 Midwest Ave
Cleveland, OH 44125-2497

Telephone: (216) 587-6801, FAX:
(216) 587-6807, E-Mail: adamsx@
att.net, Web Site: www.
adamsmanufacturing.com
Pres: Marty Schonberger Sr.
VP: Ruth Schonberger
VP Pur: M. Schonberger Jr.
Sls Mgr: J. Dubasek
Primary Market Served: Business
Founded: 1945

Manufacture heating equipment & sell
to wholesale distributors. Gas & oil
residential & commercial warm air
furnaces, gas & oil burners, air cleaners & gas conversion heaters.

ADVANCED MACHINERY
PO Box 430
New Castle, DE 19720
Telephone: (302) 322-2226, (800) 727-
6553, FAX: (866) 686-1615, E-Mail:
jean@advmachinery.com, Web Site:
www.advmachinery.com
Pres: Wolfgang Derke
VP, Sls & Mktg: Hanns Derke
Conducts Business: U.S., Canada
Employees: 10
Primary Market Served: Business &
Consumer
Catalog available online
Direct online sales
Advertising/Marketing Budget Related
to Direct Marketing: 76-100%
Direct Marketing ad budget:
Direct Mail: 45%
Magazines: 40%
Telephone: 15%
Founded: 1975
Gross sales or billing: $1,600,000

Specialty woodcrafting & woodworking equipment for upscale hobbyists &
professionals.

AGRI DRAIN CORP
1462 340th St
Adair, IA 50002
Telephone: (641) 742-5211, (800) 232-
4742, FAX: (641) 742-5222, (800)
282-3353, E-Mail: info@agridrain.
com, Web Site: www.agridrain.com
Pres: Charlie Schafer
Sls & Mktg Mgr: Lisa Newby
Employees: 54
Primary Market Served: Business
Gross sales or billing: $4,600,000

Manufacturer of water management
products.

AIR CHEK INC
PO Box 2000
Naples, NC 28760-5000

Telephone: (828) 684-0893, (800) AIR-
CHEK, FAX: (828) 684-8498, Web
Site: www.radon.com
Cust Svc Mgr: Nancy Fairchild
Conducts Business: U.S.
Employees: 12
Primary Market Served: Business &
Consumer
Advertising/Marketing Budget Related
to Direct Marketing: 0-25%
Direct Marketing ad budget:
Direct Mail: 30%
Magazines: 15%
Newspapers: 15%
Telephone: 40%
Founded: 1985

Manufactures & analyzes radon test
kits. Sell to the National Safety Council, State & Federal agencies, as well
as private citizens & major
corporations. Radon kits are used to
determine the radon levels in schools,
workplaces & homes all over the U.S.

AIRLINES REPORTING CORP
3000 Wilson Blvd Ste 300
Arlington, VA 22201-3862
Telephone: (703) 816-8135, Web Site:
www.arccorp.com
Primary Market Served: Consumer

**ALFA AESAR-A JOHNSON
MATTHEY CO**
Div. of Johnson Matthey
26 Partridge Rd
Ward Hill, MA 01835-8099
Telephone: (800) 343-0660, FAX:
(800) 322-4757, E-Mail: info@alfa.
com, Web Site: www.alfa.com
Controller: Kimberly Keniston
Gen Mgr: Barry Singelais
Bulk & Specialty Sls Dir: Gwilym
Clarke
Mktg Mgr & Catalog Sls Mgr: John
Shirley
Prod Mgr: Aaron Frederick
Acctg Supv: Rosalie Berard
Mktg Specialist: Pamela Poulin
Credit Analyst: Allison Corcoran
Conducts Business: Worldwide
Employees: 79
Primary Market Served: Business
Catalog available online
Indirect online sales
Advertising/Marketing Budget Related
to Direct Marketing: 26-50%
Direct Marketing ad budget:
Direct Mail: $250,000
Magazines: $30,000
Telephone: $20,000
Founded: 1991

Catalog sales operation featuring research chemicals & materials for the worldwide research community.

AMERICAN SCIENCE & SURPLUS
7410 N Lehigh Ave
Niles, IL 60714-4024
Telephone: (847) 647-0020, (800) SCI-PLUS, FAX: (847) 647-5010, E-Mail: info@sciplus.com, Web Site: www.sciplus.com
Pres: Philip E. Cable
Conducts Business: U.S.
Employees: 70
Primary Market Served: Business & Consumer
Catalog available online
Direct online sales
Advertising/Marketing Budget Related to Direct Marketing: 76-100%
Direct Marketing ad budget:
Direct Mail: 90%
Magazines: 10%
Founded: 1937

Unusual surplus items at 50-90% discount from original price.

AMERICAN TRIM
Div. of American Trim
1005 W Grand Ave
Lima, OH 45801
Telephone: (419) 228-1145, FAX: (419) 996-4850, E-Mail: sales@amtrim.com, Web Site: www.amtrim.com
CEO: Jeffrey A. Hawk
Pres: Rick Pfeifer
VP, HR: Bob Stead
Conducts Business: U.S. & Mexico
Employees: 90
Primary Market Served: Business
Catalog available online
Founded: 1970
Gross sales or billing: $230,000,000

Plastic injected molded parts.

AMES TAPING TOOL SYSTEM INC
Subs. of AXIA Enterprise Inc
1380 Beverage Dr Ste W
Stone Mountain, GA 30083-2133
Telephone: (770) 243-2647, FAX: (770) 243-2658, Web Site: www.amestools.com
Pres: Robert G. Zdravecky
Sr VP, Sls & Mktg: Carol R. Winn
Mktg Mgr: Ford Owen
Conducts Business: U.S., Canada
Primary Market Served: Business
Advertising/Marketing Budget Related to Direct Marketing: 76-100%

Feature quality tools & accessories in 22 page catalog to meet the needs of both worker & contractor in the drywall field.

ANALYTICAL MEASUREMENTS
22 Mountain View Dr
Chester, NJ 07930-3104
Telephone: (800) 635-5580, FAX: (973) 399-1446, E-Mail: phmeter@bellatlantic.net, Web Site: www.analyticalmeasurements.com
Pres: W. Richard Adey
Conducts Business: U.S., Canada, S. America, Singapore
Employees: 7
Primary Market Served: Business
Catalog available online
Indirect online sales
Advertising/Marketing Budget Related to Direct Marketing: 76-100%
Direct Marketing ad budget: $100,000
Direct Mail: 40%
Magazines: 40%
Online: 20%
Founded: 1948
Gross sales or billing: $1,000,000

Manufacture pH & ORP meters, recorders & controllers which are then sold to plants, schools & laboratories.

ARBILL SAFETY PRODUCTS
aka Arbill Industries, Inc
10450 Drummond Rd
Philadelphia, PA 19154
Telephone: (215) 632-2000, (800) 523-5367, FAX: (800) 426-5808, E-Mail: orders@arbill.com, Web Site: www.arbill.com
Chmn Bd: Barry Bickman
Pres & CEO: Julie Bickman Copeland
CFO: Sharon Miller
Conducts Business: U.S.
Employees: 75
Primary Market Served: Business
Catalog available online
Direct online sales
Advertising/Marketing Budget Related to Direct Marketing: 0-25%
Direct Marketing ad budget:
Direct Mail: 40%
Magazines: 10%
Telephone: 50%
Founded: 1945
Gross sales or billing: $4,000,000

Safety products to businesses: gloves, respirators, hearing, head, eye & face protection & clothing, safety compliance, training & services.

THE DMA ARENT FOX LLP
1050 Connecticut Ave NW
Washington, DC 20036

Telephone: (202) 715-8582, Web Site: www.arentfox.com
Primary Market Served: Business & Consumer

ASTRO AIR, LP
Subs. of Luvata
1653 N Fulton
Jacksonville, TX 75766
Telephone: (903) 586-3691, FAX: (903) 589-8094, E-Mail: sales@astroair.com, Web Site: www.astroair.com
Pres & CEO (Luvata): John-Peter Leesi
VP, Mktg: Pavlos Pavlides
VP: Warren Bartel
VP: Eric Tate
Conducts Business: U.S., Canada
Employees: 195
Primary Market Served: Business & Consumer
Catalog available online
Advertising/Marketing Budget Related to Direct Marketing: 0-25%
Direct Marketing ad budget: $20,000
Direct Mail: 20%
Magazines: 80%
Founded: 1972
Gross sales or billing: $20,000,000

Manufacturer of condensers, heating and cooling coils (tube & finishing) for HVACR industry.

ATRINSIC INC
469 7th Ave (fl 10)
New York, NY 10018-7640
Telephone: (212) 716-1977, Web Site: www.atrinsic.com
Primary Market Served: Consumer

THE DMA BAILEY'S INC
PO Box 550
Laytonville, CA 95454-0550
Telephone: (707) 984-6133, (800) 322-4539, FAX: (707) 984-8115, E-Mail: baileys@bbaileys.com, Web Site: www.baileys-online.com
Pres: Nik Bailey

BASIC ADHESIVES INC
Also dba Dritac
60 Webro Rd
Clifton, NJ 07012
Telephone: (718) 497-5200, (800) 394-9310, FAX: (718) 366-1425, E-Mail: info@basicadhesives.com, Web Site: www.basicadhesives.com
Pres: Yale Block
Exec VP: Myrna Block
Conducts Business: Worldwide
Employees: 60
Primary Market Served: Business
Catalog available online
Founded: 1960

Gross sales or billing: $11,000,000

Industrial, water-based & solvent adhesives: laminating, pressure sensitive, cohesive, heat activated, remoistenable, etc.

BATTERY PROS INC

dba Pro Battery
PO Box 54
Horseshoe Beach, FL 32648-0054
Telephone: (352) 498-2477, (800) 451-7171, FAX: (352) 498-2482, E-Mail: sales@probattery.com, Web Site: www.probattery.com
Pres & CEO: Patty Novak
Admin Asst: Maria Arce
Conducts Business: U.S., Canada
Employees: 25
Primary Market Served: Business
Advertising/Marketing Budget Related to Direct Marketing: 76-100%
Direct Marketing ad budget:
Magazines: 100%
Founded: 1980
Gross sales or billing: $3,500,000

Batteries & battery assemblies.

THE DMA BELL & HOWELL LTD

Subs. of Bell & Howell Co
5650 Young St (Suite 1802)
North York, ON, Canada M2M 4G3
Telephone: (416) 746-2200, FAX: (416) 228-2439, Web Site: www. bellhowell.com
CFO: Leader Wong
Sls Dir & Mktg Mgr: Eric Pascoe
Conducts Business: U.S.
Primary Market Served: Business & Consumer

Business equipment manufacturer of Phillipsburg inserters & Documail sorting systems.

BELL PERFORMANCE INC

1340 Bennett Dr
Longwood, FL 32750-7623
Telephone: (407) 831-5021, (800) 659-2355, FAX: (407) 767-8685, E-Mail: info@bellperformance.net, Web Site: www.bellperformance.net
VP Gen Mgr: Glenn Williams
Intl Mktg: Fene Rumley
Sls Rep: Richard Morin
Sls Rep: Bob Kress
Conducts Business: U.S., Canada, Europe, Asia, Pacific Rim
Primary Market Served: Business & Consumer
Catalog available online
Direct online sales
Advertising/Marketing Budget Related to Direct Marketing: 0-25%
Direct Marketing ad budget:
Direct Mail: 25%
Magazines: 15%

Telephone: 60%
Founded: 1909

Fuel conditioners for gasoline, diesel & fuel oil. All purpose grease, oil enhancer for motors, gearboxes, transmissions, bearings & compressors.

BETTER TOOLS FOR INDUSTRY

9525 Pathway St
Santee, CA 92071
Telephone: (619) 562-3071, FAX: (619) 562-0592, Web Site: www.bti-tool.com
Pres: Jim Barnhill
VP, Sls & Mktg: Chris Barnhill
Conducts Business: U.S.
Employees: 24
Primary Market Served: Business & Consumer
Catalog available online
Direct online sales
Founded: 1967

Manufacturer of specialty & contract tooling & hand tools & pneumatic shop vacuums & stainless hex wrenches.

BLAINE WINDOW HARDWARE INC

17319 Blaine Dr
Hagerstown, MD 21740
Telephone: (301) 797-6500, (800) 678-1919, FAX: (888) 250-3960, E-Mail: info@blainewindow.com, Web Site: www.blainewindow.com
Pres: Magreth Blaine
Adv & Mktg Mgr: Elaine Swartz
Conducts Business: U.S.
Employees: 55
Primary Market Served: Business & Consumer
Catalog available online
Founded: 1954

Obsolete, hard-to-find & current replacement hardware for windows, doors, patio doors, lockers. Also custom made screens, toilet partitions & components.

BRIDGE CITY TOOL WORKS INC

Div. of Fine Tools, LLC
2545 SW Spring Garden St (Suite 120)
Portland, OR 97219-3942
Telephone: (503) 282-6997, (800) 253-3332, FAX: (503) 287-1085, E-Mail: jjeconomaki@comcast.net, Web Site: www.bridgecitytools.com
Pres: John Economaki
Mktg Mgr: Ming Sok
Conducts Business: Worldwide
Employees: 25
Primary Market Served: Consumer

Catalog available online
Indirect online sales
Advertising/Marketing Budget Related to Direct Marketing: 26-50%
Founded: 1983

Manufacturer of precision layout tools & distributor of high quality woodworking layout tools.

BROOKS EQUIPMENT CO

10926 David Taylor Dr (Suite 300)
Charlotte, NC 28262
Telephone: (704) 596-9438, (800) 826-3473, FAX: (704) 596-1096, Web Site: www.brooksequipment.com
VP, Commun: Kathryn Mahan
Mktg Coord: Carole Seagle
Conducts Business: U.S.
Employees: 400
Primary Market Served: Business & Consumer
Catalog available online
Direct online sales
Advertising/Marketing Budget Related to Direct Marketing: 51-75%
Founded: 1941
Gross sales or billing: $90,000,000

Wholesaler in the fire equipment district market, supply chain management in fire and police equipment to municipalities and individuals.

BURDEN SALES CO

1015 W "O" St
Lincoln, NE 68528-1322
Telephone: (402) 474-4055, (800) 488-3407, FAX: (402) 474-5198, E-Mail: ccole@surpluscenter.com
Pres: Dave Burden
VP, Sls & Mktg: Chris Cole
Sls Mgr: Jeff Atkinson
Conducts Business: U.S.
Employees: 40
Primary Market Served: Business & Consumer
Catalog available online
Indirect online sales
Advertising/Marketing Budget Related to Direct Marketing: 76-100%
Founded: 1933

Mail order sales of hydraulics, air compressors, winches, chemical spraying equipment & alarm systems.

C&H DISTRIBUTORS LLC

770 S 70th St, PO Box 14770
Milwaukee, WI 53214-0770
Telephone: (414) 443-1700, (888) 316-2223, FAX: (414) 443-9213, E-Mail: customerservice@chdist.com, Web Site: www.chdist.com
Pres & CEO: David McKeon
CFO: Dan Paruzynski
VP, Catalog & Creative: Marvin D. Mason

VP, Mdsg: Steve J. Preiss
VP, Customer Svc: Anita Kowalski
Conducts Business: U.S., Canada
Employees: 175
Primary Market Served: Business & Consumer
Catalog available online
Direct online sales
Gross sales or billing: $158,000,000

Mail order distributor of industrial products to warehouses, offices, stores, factories, institutions. Products include storage shelving, shop furniture, parts bins, dock equipment, hoists, winches, iron handlers, hand trucks, office equipment & safety aids. Branches in Reno, NV; Dallas, TX; Atlanta, GA; Dayton, NJ; Milwaukee, WI.

C&S SALES INC
150 Carpenter Ave
Wheeling, IL 60090
Telephone: (847) 541-0710, (800) 292-7711, FAX: (847) 541-9904, E-Mail: sales@cs-sales.com, Web Site: www.cs_sales.com
Pres: James Cecchin
Gen Mgr: Dave Jonesi
Asst Gen Mgr: Paula Asher
Conducts Business: U.S., Canada
Employees: 5
Primary Market Served: Business & Consumer
Catalog available online
Advertising/Marketing Budget Related to Direct Marketing: 0-25%
Founded: 1985
Gross sales or billing: $2,000,000

Electronic testing equipment & educational material.

CAIG LABORATORIES INC
12200 Thatcher Ct
Poway, CA 92064
Telephone: (858) 486-8388, FAX: (858) 486-8398, E-Mail: caig123@caig.com, Web Site: www.caig.com
Pres: Mark Lohkemper
Corp Sls: Diane James
Mktg Mgr: Susan Prenatt
Conducts Business: Worldwide
Employees: 12
Primary Market Served: Business & Consumer
Catalog available online
Direct online sales
Advertising/Marketing Budget Related to Direct Marketing: 26-50%
Direct Marketing ad budget:
Direct Mail: 10%
Magazines: 90%
Founded: 1956

Manufacturer of high quality, environmentally-safe, electronic chemicals & soldering apparatus. Products include: gold conditioners, lubricants, preservatives, deoxidizers, anti-static sprays, degreasers, solder pots & controls. Products sold to a variety of industries requiring clean electrical connections.

CALBIOCHEM-NOVABIOCHEM CORP
Div. of EM Industrial & Subs. of Merck
10394 Pacific Ctr Ct
San Diego, CA 92121-4340
Telephone: (858) 450-9600, (800) 854-3417, FAX: (858) 453-3552, E-Mail: customerservice@emdbioscience.com, Web Site: www.calbiochem.com
Pres, CEO & Chmn: Richard T. Clark
Sr VP: Willie A. Deese
Sr VP, HR: Mirian Graddick Weir
Dir: Douglas Brown
Conducts Business: U.S., Germany, U.K., Switzerland, Australia, Japan
Employees: 260
Primary Market Served: Business & Consumer
Catalog available online
Direct online sales
Advertising/Marketing Budget Related to Direct Marketing: 0-25%
Direct Marketing ad budget:
Direct Mail: 80%
Magazines: 15%
Telephone: 5%
Founded: 1952
Gross sales or billing: $50,000,000

Four brands (CALBIOCHEM, NOVA-BIOCHEM, Oncogene Research Products & Novagen) encompass over 10,000 reagents & tools for the life sciences academic research, biotechnology, pharmaceutical & industrial markets. Niche catalogs with in-depth technical information, reviews, structures & references are offered in Signal Transduction, Apoptosis, Neuroscience/Drug Discovery, Glycobiology, Combinatorial Chemistry & Molecular Biology.

CAMELOT ENTERPRISES
8234 199th Ave
Bristol, WI 53104-9701
Telephone: (262) 857-2695
Pres: James R. Zinkel
VP: Sandra L. Zinkel
Conducts Business: U.S.
Employees: 4
Primary Market Served: Business & Consumer
Advertising/Marketing Budget Related to Direct Marketing: 76-100%

Direct Marketing ad budget: $4,000
Direct Mail: 10%
Magazines: 80%
Newspapers: 5%
Telephone: 5%
Founded: 1983

Industrial & automotive fasteners & tools.

CAMPBELL TOOLS CO
125 N Tecumseh Rd
Springfield, OH 45504-3404
Telephone: (937) 882-6716, FAX: (937) 882-6648, E-Mail: campbell@campbelltools.com, Web Site: www.campbelltools.com
Pres: Leo Foster
Member: Renee Morningstar
Conducts Business: U.S., Canada
Employees: 6
Primary Market Served: Business & Consumer
Catalog available online
Indirect online sales

Sell machinery, precision tools & shop supplies.

CAROLINA BIOLOGICAL SUPPLY CO
2700 York Rd
Burlington, NC 27215-3387
Telephone: (800) 334-5551, (800) 222-7112, E-Mail: carolina@carolina.com, Web Site: www.carolina.com
Pres: Larry Gross
VP, Fulfillment: Ray Gladden
VP: Daniel E. James
VP, HR: Leon Joyce
Adv Dir: Harry L. Shoffner
Conducts Business: Worldwide
Employees: 435
Primary Market Served: Business
Catalog available online
Direct online sales
Advertising/Marketing Budget Related to Direct Marketing: 76-100%
Direct Marketing ad budget:
Direct Mail: 90%
Magazines: 5%
Online: 5%
Founded: 1927

Direct marketer of science teaching materials & supplies to schools.

CENTAUR FORGE LLC
117 N Spring St
Burlington, WI 53105-1532
Telephone: (262) 763-9175, (800) 666-9175, FAX: (262) 763-8350, E-Mail: info@centaurforge.com, Web Site: www.centaurforge.com
Pres: Maj Ernest Lifynski
Gen Mgr: Tom Riddle
Conducts Business: Worldwide

Employees: 9
Primary Market Served: Business
Founded: 1960

Blacksmith's & horseshoer's equipment & supplies, including books & videos.

CHEM-TAINER INDUSTRIES INC

361 Neptune Ave
North Babylon, NY 11704
Telephone: (631) 661-8300, (800) ASK-CHEM, (800) 275-2436, FAX: (631) 661-8209, E-Mail: sales@chemtainer.com, Web Site: www.chemtainer.com
Pres: Robert Devine
VP: Anthony Lamb
Conducts Business: U.S., Europe, South America
Employees: 256
Primary Market Served: Business & Consumer
Catalog available online
Indirect online sales
Advertising/Marketing Budget Related to Direct Marketing: 26-50%
Direct Marketing ad budget: $150,000
Direct Mail: 5%
Magazines: 70%
Online: 15%
TV/Radio: 10%
Founded: 1958
Gross sales or billing: $32,000,000

Manufacturer of wholesale roto-molded plastic industrial containers and products.

CLINGZ INC

541 Laser Dr NE
Rio Rancho, NM 87124-4518
Telephone: (505) 892-2500, Web Site: www.clingz.com
Primary Market Served: Consumer

COLLIDER MEDIA

619 Congress Ave Ste B
Austin, TX 78701-3024
Telephone: (512) 745-8070, Web Site: collidermedia.com
Primary Market Served: Consumer

WM F COMLY & SON INC

1825 E Boston St
Philadelphia, PA 19125-1201
Telephone: (215) 634-2500, Web Site: www.comly.com
Primary Market Served: Consumer

COMPASS ELECTRONICS

397 SW Stringtown Rd
Forest Grove, OR 97116
Telephone: (503) 357-2111, FAX: (503) 357-2111

Pres: Steve Garriss
Primary Market Served: Business & Consumer

Manufacture & repair electronic metal detectors.

CONSOLIDATED PLASTICS CO INC

4700 Prosper Rd
Stow, OH 44224-1068
Telephone: (330) 425-3900, (800) 362-1000, FAX: (330) 425-3333, Web Site: www.consolidatedplastics.com
Pres: Brent Harland
Sr VP, Mktg: Gregg Gilkey
Conducts Business: U.S.
Employees: 100
Primary Market Served: Business & Consumer
Catalog available online
Direct online sales
Advertising/Marketing Budget Related to Direct Marketing: 76-100%

Business-to-business catalog marketer of plastic products for industry & laboratories including bottles, containers, bags & commercial matting & carpeting.

CONTINENTAL SUPPLY INC

PO Box 33663
Cleveland, OH 44133
Telephone: (440) 864-6231, (800) 672-0321, FAX: (888) 672-9808
Pres: Bruce Abbott
Primary Market Served: Business & Consumer
Advertising/Marketing Budget Related to Direct Marketing: 76-100%
Direct Marketing ad budget:
Direct Mail: 95%
Magazines: 5%

Janitorial & safety supply company.

CORONIS BUILDING SYSTEMS INC

2305 Rancocas Rd.
Burlington, NJ 08016-4113
Telephone: (609) 723-2600, FAX: (609) 723-6700, E-Mail: coronis@trussframe.com, Web Site: www.trussframe.com
Pres: Emanuel A. Coronis Jr
Sec & Treas: Magdalene P. Coronis
Conducts Business: Worldwide
Employees: 21
Primary Market Served: Business & Consumer
Direct Marketing ad budget:
Magazines: 50%
Telephone: 50%
Founded: 1956
Gross sales or billing: $2,000,000

Trussframes pre-engineered structural steel building framing for commercial, industrial, agricultural & recreational projects.

THE DMA COUNCIL OF SMALLER ENTERPRISES (COSE)

2535 Spring Grove Ave
Cincinnati, OH 45214-1729
Telephone: (512) 455-5432, Web Site: kaobrands.com
Primary Market Served: Consumer

THE DMA CREATIVE BANNER ASSEMBLIES

2730 Nevada Ave
New Hope, MN 55427-2807
Telephone: (763) 278-6515, Web Site: www.creativebanner.com
Primary Market Served: Consumer

CREATIVE LEARNING SYSTEMS INC

1140 Boston Ave (Unit A)
Longmont, CO 80501-5890
Telephone: (800) 458-2880, FAX: (760) 546-1490, Web Site: www.clsinc.com
CEO: Robert McIntosh
Pres: Brick Kani
VP, Opers: Bret Vedder
Mktg Dir: Kyle Hudson
Primary Market Served: Business

Cutting edge technology products, especially for schools.

CRYSTEK CORP

12730 Commonwealth Dr
Fort Myers, FL 33913
Telephone: (239) 561-3311, (800) 237-3061, FAX: (239) 561-1025, E-Mail: sales@crystek.com, Web Site: www.crystek.com
Pres & CEO: Anthony Mastropole
VP: Mark S. Stearns
Dir Sls, West Coast: Daniel Loomis
Dir Sls, Miami: Maria Guerra
Sls Mgr: Jim Carrasco
Conducts Business: U.S.
Employees: 25
Primary Market Served: Business
Catalog available online
Direct online sales
Advertising/Marketing Budget Related to Direct Marketing: 76-100%
Founded: 1958
Gross sales or billing: $5,000,000

Manufacture crystals & crystal oscillators.

DARCO INTERNATIONAL INC

810 Memorial Blvd
Huntington, WV 25701-7002

Telephone: (304) 522-4883, Web Site: www.darcointernational.com

DATUM TIMING, TEST & MEASUREMENT

34 Tozer Rd
Beverly, MA 01915
Telephone: (978) 927-8220, FAX: (978) 927-4099, E-Mail: wriley@ datum.com, Web Site: www.datum. com
Pres: Paul E. Baia
VP Sls & Mktg: David Briggs
Tech Svc Mgr: Greg Handley
Prod Mgr Components & Space: Ed Bryant
Prod Mgr Instruments: Karl Reuning
Prod Mgr Instruments: Fred Zwart
Mktg Mgr: Doug Lowrie
Conducts Business: Worldwide
Employees: 100
Primary Market Served: Business
Catalog available online
Indirect online sales
Advertising/Marketing Budget Related to Direct Marketing: 51-75%
Direct Marketing ad budget:
Direct Mail: 40%
Magazines: 50%
Telephone: 10%
Founded: 1970
Gross sales or billing: $33,000,000

Electronic instruments-precision clocks (atomic, space & hi-Rel), frequency sources, quartz oscillators & military electronics. Active hydrogen masers & atomic clocks (cesium-subidium).

DIAMOND MACHINING TECHNOLOGY

85 Hayes Memorial Dr
Marlborough, MA 01752-1831
Telephone: (508) 481-5944, (800) 666-4368, FAX: (508) 485-3924, Web Site: www.dmtsharp.com
VP, Mktg & Sls: William E. Fletcher
VP Sls: Daniel Ekberg
Conducts Business: Worldwide
Employees: 45
Primary Market Served: Consumer
Catalog available online
Direct online sales
Advertising/Marketing Budget Related to Direct Marketing: 0-25%
Founded: 1976
Gross sales or billing: $4,000,000

Manufacturer of handheld diamond and unbreakable ceramic sharpeners sold to distributors & retailers in gourmet, hardware, skiing, hunting, fishing, woodworking, industrial & commercial markets.

DINYARI INC

500 Phelan Ave
San Jose, CA 95112-2506

Telephone: (408) 289-5400, Web Site: www.dinyari.com
Pres: Farbod Dinyari

THE DMA DISCOVERY

12 Christopher Way Ste 202
Eatontown, NJ 07724-3331
Telephone: (732) 933-1899, Web Site: www.discoveryco.com
Primary Market Served: Consumer

DO-IT CORP

PO Box 592
South Haven, MI 49090-0592
Telephone: (269) 637-1121, (800) 426-4822, FAX: (269) 637-7223, E-Mail: sales@do-it.com, Web Site: www.do-it.com
Pres: Mark McClendon
Sls Mgr: Ron MacIntyre
Conducts Business: U.S., Canada, UK, Mexico, Hong Kong
Employees: 70
Primary Market Served: Business & Consumer
Catalog available online
Direct online sales
Advertising/Marketing Budget Related to Direct Marketing: 0-25%
Founded: 1973
Gross sales or billing: $10,000,000

Manufacturer of plastic hang tabs.

DOUBLEVERIFY

575 8th Ave (fl 7)
New York, NY 10018-3186
Telephone: (212) 631-2111, Web Site: www.doubleverify.com
Primary Market Served: Consumer

DOZIER EQUIPMENT INTERNATIONAL

770 S 70th St, PO Box 88031
Milwaukee, WI 53288
Telephone: (800) 251-1234, FAX: (800) 336-6608, Web Site: www.dozierequip.com
Pres: David Stark
Mktg Mgr: Amy Tartarsky
Conducts Business: Worldwide
Primary Market Served: Business & Consumer
Advertising/Marketing Budget Related to Direct Marketing: 76-100%
Direct Marketing ad budget:
Direct Mail: 80%
Magazines: 10%
Telephone: 10%
Founded: 1952

Headquartered in Nashville, TN with over 1800 distributors selling dumpers, drum handlers, hoist & crane attachments & all material handling products.

E-PIPECONNECTION

Div. of PVC Plastics Co Inc
4406 E Morgan Ave
Evansville, IN 47715-2254
Telephone: (812) 474-4529, (800) 262-4300, FAX: (812) 474-4531, E-Mail: sales@e-pipeconnection.com, Web Site: www.e-pipeconnection.com
Pres & Gen Mgr: William D. Smith
Sls Mgr: Jeff Mullis
VP: Jeff Eckels
Catalog Mgr: Mark Moore
Conducts Business: U.S.
Employees: 50
Primary Market Served: Business & Consumer
Catalog available online
Indirect online sales
Advertising/Marketing Budget Related to Direct Marketing: 51-75%
Direct Marketing ad budget:
Direct Mail: 90%
Telephone: 10%
Founded: 1990
Gross sales or billing: $12,000,000

Industrial plastic distribution, such as plastic pipe valves, fittings & related products.

THE DMA EDMUND OPTICS INC

101 E Gloucester Pike
Barrington, NJ 08007-1331
Telephone: (856) 573-6250, (800) 363-1992, FAX: (856) 573-6295, E-Mail: sales@edmundoptic.com, Web Site: www.edmundoptics.com
Pres: John Stack
CEO: Robert M. Edmund
Dir Sls: Wallace Latimer
Chief Scientist: Jim Michalski
VP, HR & Mktg: Marisa Edmund
Conducts Business: Worldwide
Employees: 300
Primary Market Served: Business & Consumer
Catalog available online
Direct online sales
Advertising/Marketing Budget Related to Direct Marketing: 51-75%
Founded: 1942

Optics & optical instruments for industry & research.

THE DMA 89 DEGREES

25 Burlington Mall Rd (Suite 610)
Burlington, MA 01803-4100
Telephone: (781) 221-5400, Web Site: www.89degrees.com
Primary Market Served: Business & Consumer

ELEMENTAL SCIENTIFIC LLC

Storefront is Galaxy Science & Hobby Center, Inc
1607 N Richmond St

Appleton, WI 54911-3553
Telephone: (920) 882-1277, E-Mail:
    info@elementalscientific.net
Pres: Wade Van Ryzin
Conducts Business: U.S.
Employees: 3
Primary Market Served: Business &
    Consumer
Indirect online sales
Gross sales or billing: $500,000

Scientific chemicals & apparatus.

ELLERBUSCH INSTRUMENT CO

4505 Vine St
Cincinnati, OH 45217-1617
Telephone: (513) 641-1800, (800) 582-
    2644, FAX: (513) 641-4360, E-Mail:
    info@ellerbusch.com, Web Site:
    www.ellerbusch.com
Pres: Michael Ellerbusch
Sls Rep: Jim Henson
Conducts Business: U.S.
Employees: 5
Primary Market Served: Business
Advertising/Marketing Budget Related
    to Direct Marketing: 51-75%
Direct Marketing ad budget: $10,000
Direct Mail: 90%
Magazines: 5%
Telephone: 5%
Founded: 1955
Gross sales or billing: $1,000,000

Sales & service of surveying equipment to builders, contractors, surveyors
& engineers.

ELLIS SYSTEMS CORP

28457 N Ballard Dr Ste F
Lake Forest, IL 60045-4545
Telephone: (847) 371-0200, (800) 253-
    5547, FAX: (847) 371-0202, E-Mail:
    tom@ellisfiling.com, Web Site:
    www.ellismh.com
CEO & Sls mgr: Tom Hynes
Primary Market Served: Business
Founded: 1962

Distributor of high density storage systems including high density shelving,
vertical carousels, rotary files & vertical lift modules.

ENCO MANUFACTURING CO

400 Nevada Pacific Hwy
Fernley, NV 89408
Telephone: (775) 788-7175, (800) 873-
    3626, FAX: (800) 965-5857, E-Mail:
    milanesp@use-enco.com, Web Site:
    www.use-enco.com
Catalog Mgr: Jack Rayher
Gen Mgr Mktg & Mdse: Perry Mi-
    lanesi
Opers Mgr: Doug Styes

Conducts Business: U.S., Canada,
    Mexico
Employees: 100
Primary Market Served: Business &
    Consumer
Catalog available online
Indirect online sales
Advertising/Marketing Budget Related
    to Direct Marketing: 76-100%
Direct Marketing ad budget:
Direct Mail: 95%
Magazines: 2%
Online: 3%
Founded: 1940
Gross sales or billing: $45,000,000

Machinery and industrial tools.

ENGINEERING SERVICES & PRODUCTS CO

FarmTek & TekSupply
1395 John Fitch Blvd
South Windsor, CT 06074-1029
Telephone: (860) 528-1119, (800) 835-
    7877, FAX: (800) 457-8887, Web
    Site: www.teksupply.com
Pres: Barry Goldsher
Sls & Mktg Dir: Matt Niaura
Pur Mgr: Jack Jordan
Employees: 199
Primary Market Served: Business &
    Consumer
Catalog available online
Direct online sales
Founded: 1981
Gross sales or billing: $87,200,000

Supplier of industrial, construction,
maintenance, lighting and plumbing
products.

ENMAX CORP

141 - 50 Ave SE
Calgary, AB, Canada T2G 4S7
Telephone: (403) 514-3122, Web Site:
    www.enmax.com
Primary Market Served: Business &
    Consumer

FLIGHT FORM CASES INC

6543 S Laramie Ave
Bedford Park, IL 60638
Telephone: (708) 458-8989, (800) 657-
    1199, FAX: (708) 458-9023, E-Mail:
    info@caseguys.net, Web Site: www.
    flightform.com
Pres: Edward Ostrusina
Conducts Business: U.S.
Employees: 40
Primary Market Served: Business &
    Consumer
Catalog available online
Advertising/Marketing Budget Related
    to Direct Marketing: 0-25%
Founded: 1966
Gross sales or billing: $2,000,000

Carrying & reusable shipping cases.
Also a major guitar case company
serving the music products industry
through distributors.

THE DMA FORESTRY SUPPLIERS INC

205 W Rankin St, PO Box 8397
Jackson, MS 39284-6126
Telephone: (601) 354-3565, (800) 543-
    4203, FAX: (601) 292-0165, E-Mail:
    fsi@forestry-suppliers.com, Web
    Site: www.forestry-suppliers.com
Sr VP Mktg: Ray Hansen
VP Mktg: Ken Peacock
Admin Asst: Deborah Barlow
Prod & Mktg Mgr: Clay Walker
Pres: John Gwaltney
Conducts Business: Worldwide
Employees: 100
Primary Market Served: Business
Catalog available online
Direct online sales
Founded: 1949

Mail order catalog featuring forestry,
engineering & environmental
equipment.

FOSTORIA INDUSTRIES INC

Div. of TPI
PO Box 4973
Johnson City, TN 37502-4973
Telephone: (419) 435-9201, (800) 495-
    4525, FAX: (419) 435-0842, E-Mail:
    email@fostoriaindustries.com, Web
    Site: www.fostoriaindustries.com
Pres & CEO: Larry E. Dunlap
CFO: Jerry L. Donaldson
VP & Mktg Mgr: Steve Fruth
Conducts Business: U.S., Canada, Ja-
    pan, England, Korea, China, Brazil,
    Peru, Poland
Employees: 120
Primary Market Served: Business &
    Consumer
Catalog available online
Founded: 1917
Gross sales or billing: $9,400,000

Manufacturer of electric & gas process
infrared equipment. Comfort heating &
machine tool lighting. Products include
gas & electric infrared and convection
process heating systems, gas & electric
infrared comfort heating systems, electric infrared snow & ice control systems, maritime tool lighting, portable
industrial lighting, loading area lighting, and critical work area lighting.

FOX LITE, INC

8300 Dayton Rd
Fairborn, OH 45324
Telephone: (937) 864-1966, FAX:
    (937) 864-7010, E-Mail: doug@
    foxlite.com, Web Site: www.foxlite.
    com

Pres: Douglas Hoy
VP, Sls: Mark Hopkins
Conducts Business: Worldwide
Employees: 30
Primary Market Served: Business &
   Consumer
Advertising/Marketing Budget Related
   to Direct Marketing: 0-25%
Gross sales or billing: $4,000,000

Manufacture vacuum & thermal
formed plastic parts; in particular, sky-
lights, plastic & glass, to wholesalers
of building products.

FOX VALLEY SYSTEMS INC
640 Industrial Dr
Cary, IL 60013
Telephone: (847) 639-5744, (800) 323-
   4770, FAX: (847) 639-8190, Web
   Site: www.foxpaint.com
Pres: Thomas Smrt
Conducts Business: U.S.
Primary Market Served: Business
Catalog available online
Direct online sales

Manufacturer & direct mail marketer
of aerosol paints, striping & marking
equipment.

FRESNO OXYGEN
Div. of RRAM Sales
2825 S Elm Ave (#101)
Fresno, CA 93706-5460
Telephone: (559) 233-6684, (800) 404-
   9353, FAX: (559) 233-4206, E-Mail:
   info@fresnooxygen.com, Web Site:
   www.fresnooxygen.com
Chmn Bd: Red Barnes
Pres: Mike Barnes
CFO: Todd Rayburn
VP, Opers & Mktg Dir: David Barnes
Primary Market Served: Business &
   Consumer
Catalog available online
Direct online sales
Founded: 1949
Gross sales or billing: $20,000,000

Welding & industrial distributor.

GE CANADA
Subs. of General Electric Co
2300 Meadowvale Blvd
Mississauga, ON, Canada L5N 5P9
Telephone: (905) 858-5100, Web Site:
   www.ge.com/canada
Pres & CEO: Elyse Allan
Conducts Business: Canada
Primary Market Served: Business &
   Consumer

Industrial manufacturer & service
organization. Manufacture & service
electrical appliances

GAIAM INC
PO Box 3095
Boulder, CO 80307-3095
Telephone: (877) 989-6321, Web Site:
   life.gaiam.com
Pres & Founder: John Schaeffer
Conducts Business: U.S., Canada,
   Mexico, Africa, Papua-New Guinea
Employees: 4
Primary Market Served: Business &
   Consumer
Catalog available online
Direct online sales
Advertising/Marketing Budget Related
   to Direct Marketing: 76-100%
Direct Marketing ad budget: $15,000
Direct Mail: 95%
Magazines: 3%
Newspapers: 2%
Founded: 2006
Gross sales or billing: $500,000

Appropriate technology products sold
mail-order worldwide.

GATES CORP
1551 Wewatta St
Denver, CO 80202
Telephone: (303) 744-1911, FAX:
   (303) 744-4000, Web Site: www.
   gates.com
CEO: Richard Bell
Grp Pres: Ralph Rivera
VP: Brian Harris
Dir: Greg Vigil
Conducts Business: Worldwide
Primary Market Served: Business &
   Consumer
Catalog available online
Indirect online sales

Manufacturer of industrial rubber
products: automotive & industrial
v-belts & hoses & power transmission
belting.

GEMS SENSORS & CONTROLS
Div. of Danaker Corp
One Cowles Rd
Plainville, CT 06062-1198
Telephone: (860) 747-3000, (800) 378-
   1600, FAX: (860) 747-4244, E-Mail:
   info@gemssensors.com, Web Site:
   www.gemssensors.com
Pres: Muriel Bras-Jorge
VP Opers: Bill Vincelette
Dir Sls: John Mauer
Dir Mktg: Patrick Murphy
Conducts Business: Worldwide
Employees: 299
Primary Market Served: Business
Catalog available online
Direct online sales
Advertising/Marketing Budget Related
   to Direct Marketing: 0-25%
Direct Marketing ad budget:

Direct Mail: 10%
Magazines: 60%
Online: 30%
Founded: 1955
Gross sales or billing: $21,400,000

Manufacturer & marketer of fluid sensors & controls.

GILSON CO INC
PO Box 200
Lewis Center, OH 43035-0200
Telephone: (740) 548-7298, (800) 444-
   1508, FAX: (740) 548-5314, E-Mail:
   sales@gilsonco.com, Web Site:
   www.globalgilson.com
Principal: Tamara Felshman
Mktg Mgr: Carl Kramer
Conducts Business: Worldwide
Employees: 40
Primary Market Served: Business &
   Consumer
Catalog available online
Direct online sales
Advertising/Marketing Budget Related
   to Direct Marketing: 26-50%
Direct Marketing ad budget: $350,000
Direct Mail: 25%
Magazines: 65%
Telephone: 10%
Founded: 1939
Gross sales or billing: $12,000,000

Laboratory equipment for materials
testing asphalt, concrete, soils & general laboratory equipment for particle
sizing, sampling, etc.

GLOBAL EQUIPMENT CO INC
Div. of Systemax
11 Harbor Park Dr
Port Washington, NY 11050
Telephone: (516) 484-3100, (888) 978-
   7759, FAX: (516) 608-7111, Web
   Site: www.globalindustrial.com
Chmn & CEO: Richard Leeds
Vice Chmn: Bob Leeds
Vice Chmn: Bruce Leeds
VP, Controller: Thomas Axmacher
Dir Mktg: Sean Aryai
Conducts Business: U.S.
Employees: 400
Primary Market Served: Business &
   Consumer
Catalog available online
Direct online sales
Advertising/Marketing Budget Related
   to Direct Marketing: 76-100%
Direct Marketing ad budget:
   $2,000,000
Direct Mail: 75%
Magazines: 5%
Telephone: 20%
Founded: 1949
Gross sales or billing: $15,000,000

Material handling equipment, office furniture & products, computer furniture, safety products, shop equipment.

THE DMA WW GRAINGER INC
14441 W II Route 60
Lake Forest, IL 60045-5203
Telephone: (847) 535-1000, (888) 361-8649, FAX: (847) 535-9122, Web Site: www.grainger.com
Chmn Bd & CEO: Richard L. Keyser
Pres & COO: James T. Ryan
Pres US Branch-based Bus: Y. C. Chen
VP Mktg: Laura Brown
Dir, Mktg Communs: Robert Finn
Conducts Business: U.S.
Employees: 17,074
Primary Market Served: Business
Founded: 1927
Gross sales or billing: $5,900,000,000

Sell tools & equipment.

GRAVES LAPIDARY CO
Subs. of Vee Enterprises Inc.
1800 N Andrews Ave
Pompano Beach, FL 33069-1421
Telephone: (954) 960-0300, (800) 327-9103, FAX: (954) 960-0301, E-Mail: sales@gravescompany.com, Web Site: www.gravescompany.com
Pres: Peter Erdo
Mktg Mgr: Victoria Erdo
Conducts Business: U.S., Europe, Asia, Australia
Employees: 10
Primary Market Served: Business & Consumer
Catalog available online
Direct online sales
Direct Marketing ad budget: $30,000
Direct Mail: $15,000
Magazines: $15,000
Founded: 1957
Gross sales or billing: $800,000

Manufacture machines & supplies used to cut gemstones. Also, optical machinery & deburring equipment. Supplier of loose, natural & rough gemstones.

GRIZZLY INDUSTRIAL INC
PO Box 2069
Bellingham, WA 98227
Telephone: (360) 647-0801, (800) 523-4777, FAX: (360) 671-8375, E-Mail: csr@grizzly.com, Web Site: www.grizzly.com
VP: Don Osterloh
Primary Market Served: Consumer
Catalog available online
Direct online sales
Advertising/Marketing Budget Related to Direct Marketing: 76-100%
Founded: 1983

Mail order company for woodworking & metalworking tools.

HAGIE MANUFACTURING CO
721 Central Ave W, PO Box 273
Clarion, IA 50525
Telephone: (515) 532-2861, (800) 247-4885, FAX: (515) 532-3553, E-Mail: info@hagie.com, Web Site: www.hagie.com
Pres: John Hagie
Sls Mgr: Shane Williams
Conducts Business: Worldwide
Employees: 120
Primary Market Served: Business & Consumer
Catalog available online
Direct online sales
Advertising/Marketing Budget Related to Direct Marketing: 0-25%
Founded: 1947
Gross sales or billing: $8,900,000

Manufacturer of high clearance self-propelled sprayers & detasseler equipment. Factory direct sales.

HARBOR FREIGHT TOOLS
3491 Mission Oaks Blvd
Camarillo, CA 93012-5034
Telephone: (805) 445-4791, (800) 423-2567, FAX: (800) 445-4925, Web Site: www.harborfreight.com
Chmn: Alan Smidt
Pres: Eric Smidt
CFO: Bob Glickman
VP Mktg: David Martel
Conducts Business: U.S.
Employees: 1,600
Primary Market Served: Business & Consumer
Catalog available online
Direct online sales
Advertising/Marketing Budget Related to Direct Marketing: 0-25%
Founded: 1968
Gross sales or billing: $278,000,000

Mail order sales of tools & equipment.

HARWIL CORP
541 Kinetic Dr
Oxnard, CA 93030
Telephone: (805) 988-6800, FAX: (805) 988-6804, E-Mail: harwil@harwil.com, Web Site: www.harwil.com
Mktg Mgr: Bruce Bowman
Pres & CEO: Harold Hutchinson
Founded: 1956

Designer, manufacturer & marketer of fluid flow and liquid level switches.

HERBACH & RADEMAN CO
353 Crider Ave
Moorestown, NJ 08057
Telephone: (856) 802-0422, (800) 848-8001, FAX: (856) 802-0465, E-Mail: sales@herbach.com, Web Site: www.herbach.com
Pres: Frank Lobascio
Admin Asst: Diane Devine
Conducts Business: Worldwide
Employees: 20
Primary Market Served: Business & Consumer
Catalog available online
Indirect online sales
Direct Marketing ad budget:
Direct Mail: $250,000
Founded: 1936
Gross sales or billing: $1,000,000

Electronic, electro-mechanical & optical mail order catalog to industry, universities, labs, institutions & hobbyists.

HILLSIDE WIRE CLOTH CO
PO Box 1190
Bloomfield, NJ 07003-1190
Telephone: (973) 751-3131, (800) 826-7395, FAX: (973) 470-8183, E-Mail: info@hillsidewirecloth.com, Web Site: www.hillsidewirecloth.com
Pres: William Messinger
Conducts Business: Worldwide
Employees: 12
Primary Market Served: Business
Catalog available online
Indirect online sales
Advertising/Marketing Budget Related to Direct Marketing: 0-25%
Direct Marketing ad budget:
Direct Mail: 35%
Magazines: 50%
Telephone: 15%
Founded: 1986
Gross sales or billing: $3,000,000

Wire cloth & wire cloth fabrications.

HOME SAFEGUARD INDUSTRIES
29706 Baden Pl
Malibu, CA 90265
Telephone: (310) 457-5813, FAX: (310) 457-4862, E-Mail: expert@homesafeguard.com, Web Site: www.homesafeguard.com
Pres: Leon Cooper
Conducts Business: Worldwide
Employees: 4
Primary Market Served: Business
Catalog available online
Indirect online sales
Advertising/Marketing Budget Related to Direct Marketing: 0-25%
Direct Marketing ad budget: $60,000
Direct Mail: 15%
Magazines: 85%
Founded: 1979
Gross sales or billing: $1,500,000

Fire safety devices allowing user to test smoke & heat & carbon monoxide detectors.

HYDRA GROUP LLC

10940 Wilshire Blvd (Fl 11)
Los Angeles, CA 90024
Telephone: (310) 526-6680, FAX: (310) 526-6682, Web Site: www. hydragroup.com
Sr VP Mktg: Mason Wiley

IDEAL INDUSTRIES (CANADA) CORP

33 Fuller Rd
Ajax, ON, Canada L1S 2E1
Telephone: (905) 683-3400, (800) 824-3325, FAX: (905) 683-0209, E-Mail: nick.shkordoff@idealindustries.com, Web Site: www.idealindustries.com
Gen Mgr: Nick Shkordoff
Fin Dir: Rob Ackford
Deputy Minister: Richard Dicerni
Sr Assoc Deputy Minister: Paul Boothe
Conducts Business: Canada
Primary Market Served: Business
Catalog available online

Annual catalog of industrial & institutional items (18,000) mailed directly to national accounts throughout Canada.

INDUSTRIAL INSTRUMENTS & SUPPLIES INC

125 Countyline Indus Park
Southampton, PA 18966
Telephone: (215) 396-0822, (800) 523-6079, FAX: (215) 396-0833, E-Mail: customerservice@iisusa.com, Web Site: www.iisusa.com
Pres: Charles Walter
Mktg Mgr: Christine Walter
Conducts Business: Worldwide
Employees: 15
Primary Market Served: Business
Catalog available online
Direct online sales
Advertising/Marketing Budget Related to Direct Marketing: 76-100%
Direct Marketing ad budget:
Direct Mail: 70%
Magazines: 20%
Telephone: 10%
Founded: 1989
Gross sales or billing: $1,000,000

Tools & test equipment, industrial instrumentation & safety supplies to government & industrial manufacturers.

THE DMA INTELLIGENT DIRECT

10 1st St
Wellsboro, PA 16901-8167
Telephone: (570) 724-7355, Web Site: www.marketmaps.com
Natl Client Svcs Mgr: Theresa Bordas

J&L INDUSTRIAL SUPPLY

20921 Lahser Rd
Southfield, MI 48034-4432
Telephone: (734) 458-7000, (800) 521-9520, FAX: (734) 261-0352, Web Site: www.jlindustrial.com
Adv Mgr: Therese Snow
Conducts Business: U.S., Europe & U.K.
Employees: 300
Primary Market Served: Business & Consumer

Distributors of tools & machinery. Mail order industrial supply company specializing in high speed cutting tools & machine shop accessories.

JANTZ SUPPLY KOVAL KNIVES

309 W Main, PO Box 584
Davis, OK 73030
Telephone: (580) 369-2316, (800) 351-8900, FAX: (580) 369-3082, Web Site: www.knifemaking.com
Pres: Mick Koval
VP: Judy Koval
Primary Market Served: Business & Consumer
Catalog available online
Direct online sales

Catalogs for knife making & knife accessories. Knifemaking supplies and equipment.

KAO BRANDS

2535 Spring Grove Ave
Cincinnati, OH 45214
Telephone: (512) 455-5432, Web Site: www.kaobrands.com
Primary Market Served: Business

KETT TOOL CO

5055 Madison Rd
Cincinnati, OH 45227
Telephone: (513) 271-0333, FAX: (513) 271-5318, E-Mail: info@kett-tool.com, Web Site: www.kett-tool.com
CEO: Rowe Hoffman
Pres: Kathy Conlon
VP Sls: Rick Fowkes
Conducts Business: Worldwide
Employees: 31
Primary Market Served: Business & Consumer
Catalog available online
Advertising/Marketing Budget Related to Direct Marketing: 51-75%
Direct Marketing ad budget:
Direct Mail: 5%
Magazines: 95%
Founded: 1940

Portable power saws, shears & nibblers.

KLINGSPOR'S WOODWORKING SHOP

Div. of Klingspor Corp
856 21st St Dr SE
Hickory, NC 28602
Telephone: (828) 326-WOOD, (800) 228-0000, FAX: (828) 327-4634, E-Mail: sales@woodworkingshop.com, Web Site: www.woodworkingshop.com
Pres: Christoph Klingspor
VP, Mktg: Peter Spuller
Gen Mgr: Coleman Fourshee
Conducts Business: U.S., Canada, Mexico
Employees: 25
Primary Market Served: Business & Consumer
Catalog available online
Direct online sales
Advertising/Marketing Budget Related to Direct Marketing: 76-100%
Direct Marketing ad budget: $1,500,000
Direct Mail: 96%
Magazines: 1%
TV/Radio: 3%
Founded: 1989
Gross sales or billing: $4,000,000

Sanding & finishing equipment, abrasives & power tools for home hobbyists, small to medium sized woodworking shops & custom woodworkers.

LAFFERTY EQUIPMENT MANUFACTURING INC

5614 Oak Grove Rd
North Little Rock, AR 72118
Telephone: (501) 851-2820, (800) 999-2820, FAX: (501) 851-3719, E-Mail: webmaster@laffertyequipment.com, Web Site: www.laffertyequipment.com
Pres: Drew Lafferty
VP: Alex Lafferty
Primary Market Served: Business
Catalog available online

Manufacture chemical applicators.

LESMAN INSTRUMENT CO

135 Bernice Dr
Bensenville, IL 60106-3366
Telephone: (630) 595-8400, (800) 953-7626, FAX: (630) 595-2386, E-Mail: sales@lesman.com, Web Site: www.lesman.com
Pres: Mike De Lacluyse
Mktg Mgr: Beth Rose
Sls: George Maumee
Conducts Business: U.S.
Employees: 33
Primary Market Served: Business
Direct Marketing ad budget: $200,000
Direct Mail: 95%
Telephone: 5%

Founded: 1962
Gross sales or billing: $12,500,000

Catalog sales of process control instrumentation to industry. Distributor for instrumentation.

LIFE TECHNOLOGIES
Subs. of Invitrogen Corp
3175 Staley Rd
Grand Island, NY 14072-2028
Telephone: (800) 955-6288, FAX: (800) 331-2286, E-Mail: catalog@lifetech.com, Web Site: www.lifetechnologies.com
Conducts Business: Worldwide
Primary Market Served: Business
Catalog available online
Direct online sales
Founded: 1982
Gross sales or billing: $500,000,000

Sell biotechnical products for research.

LOCKHART INDUSTRIES INC
9610 Skillman St
Dallas, TX 75243-8202
Telephone: (214) 348-1422, Web Site: www.lockhartadvantage.com

MFE INSTRUMENTS
Div. of Stocker & Yale Inc
32 Hampshire Rd
Salem, NH 03079
Telephone: (603) 893-8778, (800) 843-8011, FAX: (603) 893-8851, Web Site: www.stockeryale.com
Chmn: M.W. Blodgett
Pres: Alain Beauregard
VP, Fin: Gary Godin
Sls & Mktg Mgr: Joe Diruzza
Mfg Mgr: Jim Sullivan
Conducts Business: Worldwide
Primary Market Served: Business

Manufacturer of oscillographic strip chart recorders, thermal printers & galvano-meters for OEM & End User medical & industrial test & measurement applications.

MI-T-M CORP
8650 Enterprise Dr
Peosta, IA 52068-9433
Telephone: (863) 556-7484, Web Site: www.mitm.com
Mktg Mgr: Karen Anderson
Primary Market Served: Business & Consumer

THE MR GROUP INC
2042 Dogwood Rd
Charleston, SC 29414
Telephone: (843) 402-0566, FAX: (843) 852-9051, E-Mail: mgm@themrgroup.com, Web Site: www.themrgroup.com

Pres: Mike Murray
Conducts Business: U.S.
Employees: 5
Primary Market Served: Business
Catalog available online
Indirect online sales
Founded: 1995

Consultant marketing, direct mail/interact/telemarketing. Mostly industrial, also consumer startups.

MSC INDUSTRIAL SUPPLY CO
75 Maxess Rd
Melville, NY 11747-3151
Telephone: (516) 812-2000, (800) 645-7270, FAX: (800) 255-5067, E-Mail: executive@mscdirect.com, Web Site: www.mscdirect.com
Chmn: Mitchell Jacobson
CEO: David Sandler
VP: Steve Armstrong
Conducts Business: Worldwide
Employees: 4,500
Primary Market Served: Business
Catalog available online
Indirect online sales
Advertising/Marketing Budget Related to Direct Marketing: 51-75%
Direct Marketing ad budget:
Direct Mail: 80%
Magazines: 5%
Telephone: 15%
Founded: 1941
Gross sales or billing: $1,700,000,000

International distributor of industrial supplies.

MAGNA VISUAL INC
9400 Watson Rd
Saint Louis, MO 63126
Telephone: (314) 843-9000, (800) 843-3399, FAX: (314) 843-0000, E-Mail: magna@magnavisual.com, Web Site: www.magnavisual.com
CEO: William R. Cady
COO: Diane L. Crews
Dir, Sls & Mktg: Frank J. Venturella
Conducts Business: U.S.
Employees: 50
Primary Market Served: Business
Catalog available online
Advertising/Marketing Budget Related to Direct Marketing: 0-25%
Direct Marketing ad budget: $200,000
Direct Mail: 70%
Magazines: 10%
Online: 10%
Telephone: 10%
Founded: 1961
Gross sales or billing: $5,500,000

Sell magnetic dry erase white boards & accessories through dealers. Custom boards available.

MARKSON SCIENTIFIC LLC
dba Markson LabSales
336 E Montgomery St
Henderson, NC 27536
Telephone: (808) 791-0490, (800) 528-5114, FAX: (800) 858-2243, E-Mail: sales@markson.com, Web Site: www.markson.com
Gen Mgr: John W. Marlowe
Customer Svc Rep: Trevor Barnes
Conducts Business: Worldwide
Employees: 7
Primary Market Served: Business
Catalog available online
Indirect online sales
Advertising/Marketing Budget Related to Direct Marketing: 76-100%
Direct Marketing ad budget:
Direct Mail: 80%
Magazines: 5%
Newspapers: 5%
Telephone: 10%
Founded: 1968

Catalog marketer of laboratory equipment, sell to food industry, universities & labs.

MCMASTER-CARR SUPPLY CO (HQ)
600 County Line Rd
Elmhurst, IL 60126-2081
Telephone: (630) 600-3600, FAX: (630) 834-9427, E-Mail: chi.sales@mcmaster.com, Web Site: www.mcmaster.com
Pres & CEO: Jay Delaney
Dir Sls & Mktg: Jim Friedland
Employees: 800
Primary Market Served: Business
Catalog available online
Direct online sales

Sell industrial equipment via catalog.

METHODE ELECTRONICS INC
7401 W Wilson Ave
Chicago, IL 60706
Telephone: (708) 867-6777, FAX: (708) 867-6999, E-Mail: info@methode.com, Web Site: www.methode.com
Chmn: William T. Jensen
Pres & CEO Stratos Lightware, Inc: James W. McGinley
Pres: Donald Duda
CFO & EVP: Dale W. Phillips
Dir: Kevin Hayes
Mktg Mgr: Ken Mitsui
Conducts Business: Worldwide
Employees: 3,400
Primary Market Served: Business & Consumer
Advertising/Marketing Budget Related to Direct Marketing: 26-50%
Founded: 1946

Gross sales or billing: $422,000,000

Interconnection devices including one & two piece printed circuit board connectors, chip carrier sockets, emulator cables & adapters, P.C. boards, fiber optic products, computer I/O terminators, automotive connectors/controls/ switches & sensors, power wiring harnesses, battery cables, electronic chemicals, electronic & related materials testing, & testing & fixturing services. Sell to OEM's & distributors.

MEYLAN CORP

543 Valley Rd (Suite 1)
Montclair, NJ 07043-1844
Telephone: (973) 744-6400, (888) 769-9667, FAX: (973) 744-1011, E-Mail: meylan1@aol.com, Web Site: www.meylan.com/home.html
Sls Mgr: Alex Prinaris
Conducts Business: U.S., Canada, S. America
Employees: 6
Primary Market Served: Business & Consumer
Catalog available online
Indirect online sales
Advertising/Marketing Budget Related to Direct Marketing: 76-100%
Direct Marketing ad budget:
Direct Mail: 90%
Magazines: 5%
Online: 5%
Founded: 1921
Gross sales or billing: $1,000,000

Serve industry, labs & schools with all types of measuring and timing devices. Digital & mechanical stopwatches, counters, loggers & timers.

MIDWEST TECHNOLOGY PRODUCTS & SERVICES

aka Midwest Shop Supplies, Inc
PO Box 3717
Sioux City, IA 51102
Telephone: (712) 252-3601, (800) 831-5904, FAX: (800) 258-7054, E-Mail: web@midwesttechnology.com, Web Site: www.midwesttechnology.com
CEO: Linda Karlstad Flom
VP: Robin Peterson
Mktg Mgr: Rick Oldenkamp
Conducts Business: U.S., Guam, China, Germany, West Africa, Saudi Arabia
Employees: 26
Primary Market Served: Business & Consumer
Catalog available online
Direct online sales
Gross sales or billing: $7,900,000

Industrial arts supplier & technology education.

MILLIPORE CORP

75 Wiggins Ave
Bedford, MA 01730-2337
Telephone: (781) 533-6000, FAX: (781) 533-3110, Web Site: www.millipore.com
CFO & Corp VP: Kathleen Allen
VP Mktg: Edward Graham Brown
Conducts Business: Worldwide
Employees: 6,100
Primary Market Served: Business
Catalog available online
Direct online sales
Advertising/Marketing Budget Related to Direct Marketing: 0-25%
Founded: 1954
Gross sales or billing: $1,260,000,000

Filtration products for lab researchers, biopharmaceutical & microelectronics manufacturers.

MOHAWK LIFTS

Div. of Mohawk Resources
65 Vrooman Ave, PO Box 110
Amsterdam, NY 12010
Telephone: (518) 842-1431, (800) 833-2006, FAX: (518) 842-1289, E-Mail: rwells@mohawklifts.com, Web Site: www.mohawklifts.com
Pres: Rick Wells
Mgr, Sls & Mktg: Steve Perlstein
Mgr, Govt Sls: Ray Pedrick
Asst Sls Mgr: Tim Malone
Conducts Business: U.S., Canada
Employees: 70
Primary Market Served: Business
Catalog available online
Advertising/Marketing Budget Related to Direct Marketing: 76-100%
Direct Marketing ad budget:
Direct Mail: 20%
Magazines: 60%
Telephone: 20%
Founded: 1981
Gross sales or billing: $7,400,000

Vehicle service lifts sold to public or private sector businesses/agencies with fleet of cars and/or trucks.

MORCON INDUSTRIAL SPECIALTY INC

658 Hardy Way (Suite 2)
Mesquite, NV 89027-3914
Telephone: (702) 346-3447, (888) 842-7953, Web Site: www.morcon-ind.com
Pres: Scott Siemers
Mgr: John Collom
Employees: 15
Primary Market Served: Business & Consumer
Catalog available online
Indirect online sales
Advertising/Marketing Budget Related to Direct Marketing: 0-25%

Founded: 1987
Gross sales or billing: $2,700,000

Big industry supplies & equipment, power tools, hand tools, pipe fitting hoses, generators & water pumps.

NSA TECHNOLOGIES LLC

3867 W Market St (Suite 256)
Akron, OH 44333
Telephone: (330) 576-4600
CFO & Gen Counsel: Victor Bierman
Primary Market Served: Business & Consumer

NELSON-JAMESON INC

2400 E Fifth St, PO Box 647
Marshfield, WI 54449-0647
Telephone: (715) 387-1151, (800) 826-8302, FAX: (715) 387-8746, E-Mail: sales@nelsonjameson.com, Web Site: www.nelsonjameson.com
Dir Sls & Mktg: Murray Smith
Chmn Bd: John Nelson
Pres: Jerry Lippert
Conducts Business: U.S., Canada
Employees: 83
Primary Market Served: Business
Catalog available online
Indirect online sales
Founded: 1947
Gross sales or billing: $11,300,000

Products, equipment & supplies used in food processing.

NEOPOST

1335 Valwood Pkwy (Suite 111)
Carrollton, TX 75006-6881
Telephone: (510) 489-6800, (800) 636-7678, FAX: (510) 475-6317, (510) 487-6704, Web Site: www.neopostinc.com
Pres & CEO: Tony Atkins
CFO: Steve Dickerson
Mktg Commun Mgr: Kris Wagner
VP Mktg: Carl Amacker
Primary Market Served: Business

Sell postage machines and shipping equipment.

NEW PIG CORP

1 Pork Ave
Tipton, PA 16684
Telephone: (814) 684-0101, (800) 468-4647, FAX: (814) 684-0961, E-Mail: hothogs@newpig.com, Web Site: www.newpig.com
Chmn & CEO: Ben Stapelfeld
Pres: Nino Vella
CFO: Rebecca Cowan
Exec VP: Douglas Hershey
VP, Mktg: Mark DeYulis
Conducts Business: Worldwide
Employees: 320

Primary Market Served: Business & Consumer
Catalog available online
Direct online sales
Advertising/Marketing Budget Related to Direct Marketing: 0-25%
Founded: 1985

Industrial maintenance industry provider of innovative solutions & technical expertise to customers to help maintain a cleaner, safer workplace.

NORTHEAST HINGE DISTRIBUTORS INC
261 Proctor Hill Rd
Hollis, NH 03049
Telephone: (603) 465-3244, (800) 882-0120, FAX: (603) 465-3313, E-Mail: nehinge@nehinge.com, Web Site: www.nehinge.com
Pres: Martha Myers
Conducts Business: U.S.
Employees: 5
Primary Market Served: Business & Consumer
Catalog available online
Advertising/Marketing Budget Related to Direct Marketing: 0-25%
Founded: 1983
Gross sales or billing: $1,000,000

We sell all types of hinges and their related products.

NORTHWEST LABORATORIES
241 S Holden St
Seattle, WA 98108
Telephone: (206) 763-6252, FAX: (206) 763-3949, Web Site: www.nwlabs.net
Pres & CEO: Patrick Tessier
Primary Market Served: Business

Full-service testing & research laboratory

O'BRIEN MANUFACTURING
Subs. of Hi-Vac
117 Industry Rd
Marietta, OH 45750-9355
Telephone: (740) 374-2306, (800) 638-1901, FAX: (740) 374-5447, Web Site: www.obrienmfg.com
Pres: Tom Bonnell
Primary Market Served: Business & Consumer
Catalog available online
Direct online sales
Founded: 1950

Sewer Equipment: Sewer cleaning tools and accessories.

OLD WORLD MOULDINGS INC
821 Lincoln Ave
Bohemia, NY 11716
Telephone: (631) 563-8660, FAX: (631) 563-8815, E-Mail: mouldings@optonline.com, Web Site: www.oldworldmouldings.com
Pres: Alan D. Havranek
Mgr: Michael Diers
Conducts Business: U.S., Canada
Employees: 5
Primary Market Served: Business & Consumer
Indirect online sales
Advertising/Marketing Budget Related to Direct Marketing: 51-75%
Direct Marketing ad budget:
Direct Mail: 10%
Magazines: 20%
Telephone: 70%
Founded: 1975
Gross sales or billing: $700,000

Sell interior wood moulding, both wholesale & retail.

ORBIT MANUFACTURING CO
1507 W Park Ave
Perkasie, PA 18944
Telephone: (215) 453-9228, (888) 895-0958, FAX: (215) 257-7399, Web Site: www.orbitmfg.com
Pres & CEO: Norman Shriver
VP, Sls & Mktg Mgr: Terry Allen
Conducts Business: U.S.
Employees: 26
Primary Market Served: Business
Catalog available online
Direct Marketing ad budget:
Magazines: 100%
Founded: 1961

Electric in-floor heating cables, gutter ice & snow melting cables & commercial electric heating products.

PPC
aka PPC BEST
PO Box 246
Johnston, IA 50131
Telephone: (515) 986-5070, E-Mail: sales@ppcbest.com, Web Site: www.ppcbest.com
Pres: Dean Bibler
Mktg Mgr: James Hauge
Primary Market Served: Business & Consumer
Catalog available online
Indirect online sales
Founded: 1981

Surface care products for exterior & interior. Whenever feasible, incorporates ag-based chemistry into formulations, avoiding the use of hazardous or questionable ingredients that potentially could damage the environment.

PARKER HANNIFIN CORP
6035 Parkland Blvd
Cleveland, OH 44124-4186
Telephone: (216) 896-2490, Web Site: www.parker.com
Primary Market Served: Consumer

PHOTOGRAPHER'S FORMULARY INC
7079 Hwy 83 N
Condon, MT 59826
Telephone: (406) 754-2891, (800) 922-5255, FAX: (406) 754-2896, E-Mail: formulary@blackfoot.net, Web Site: www.photoformulary.com
Pres: Bud Wilson
VP: Lynn Wilson
Conducts Business: Worldwide
Employees: 4
Primary Market Served: Business & Consumer
Catalog available online
Direct online sales
Advertising/Marketing Budget Related to Direct Marketing: 26-50%
Direct Marketing ad budget:
Direct Mail: 20%
Magazines: 80%
Founded: 1977

Sell photographic chemicals for the amateur & professional darkroom enthusiast.

PLAS-TANKS INDUSTRIES INC
39 Standen Dr
Hamilton, OH 45015
Telephone: (513) 942-3800, FAX: (513) 942-3993, E-Mail: info@plastanks.com, Web Site: www.plastanks.com
Pres: J. Kent Covey
Mktg Mgr: Dave Alarie
CFO: Connie Royse
Conducts Business: U.S., Canada
Employees: 39
Primary Market Served: Business
Founded: 1976
Gross sales or billing: $6,500,000

Fiberglass reinforced plastic vessels to business & government.

PLASTIC VIEW ATC
4585 Runway (Suite B)
Simi Valley, CA 93063
Telephone: (805) 520-9390, (800) 468-6301, FAX: (805) 520-0260, E-Mail: info@pvatc.com, Web Site: www.pvatc.com
Pres: Sonny Voges
Gen Mgr: Ryan Voges
VP: Chris Voges
Conducts Business: Worldwide
Employees: 8

Primary Market Served: Business &
Consumer
Indirect online sales
Advertising/Marketing Budget Related
to Direct Marketing: 51-75%
Direct Marketing ad budget:
Direct Mail: 80%
Magazines: 5%
Online: 15%
Founded: 1947
Gross sales or billing: $700,000

Manufacture & distribute "See Thru"
(transparent) window shades.

POLYAIR PACKAGING
808 E 113th St
Chicago, IL 60628
Telephone: (773) 995-1818, (888)
POLYAIR X444, FAX: (773) 995-
7725, E-Mail: marketing@polyair.
com, Web Site: www.polyair.com
Pres: Alan Castle
Interim CEO: Victor D'Souza
VP, Opers: Lew C. Coffin
Dir, Fin: Michael Freel
Sec: Louis Manetti
Conducts Business: U.S., Canada
Employees: 400
Primary Market Served: Business &
Consumer
Catalog available online
Advertising/Marketing Budget Related
to Direct Marketing: 0-25%
Founded: 1987

Sell protective packaging products
such as bubble wrap, courier envelopes, foam & foam-in-place systems
through distributors.

THE DMA POWR-FLITE, A TACONY CO
3101 Wichita Ct
Fort Worth, TX 76140-1755
Telephone: (800) 880-2913, Web Site:
www.powrflite.com
VP Mktg: Rob Godlewski

PRINT PRODUCTS INTERNATIONAL
Subs. of Pace Inc
9030 Junction Dr
Annapolis Junction, MD 20701
Telephone: (910) 695-7223, FAX:
(910) 944-1724, Web Site: www.
paceworldwide.com
Opers Mgr: Keith Rice
Mktg Mgr: Tracey Stanley
Sls Mgr: Scott MacDonald
Conducts Business: Worldwide
Employees: 9
Primary Market Served: Business &
Consumer
Indirect online sales
Advertising/Marketing Budget Related
to Direct Marketing: 51-75%
Direct Marketing ad budget:

Direct Mail: 75%
Magazines: 25%
Founded: 1978
Gross sales or billing: $5,000,000

Distributor of electronic test
equipment.

QUICK DRAW CLIP SYSTEMS INC
4869 McGrath St (Suite 130)
Ventura, CA 93003-7767
Telephone: (805) 644-6888, (888) 254-
7797, FAX: (805) 644-7320, E-Mail:
ron@clipsystems.com, Web Site:
www.clipsystems.com
Pres: Terry Ward-Llewellyn
Dir Opers: Ron Boyd
Mktg Mgr: Linda Luce
Conducts Business: Worldwide
Employees: 15
Primary Market Served: Business &
Consumer
Catalog available online
Direct online sales
Advertising/Marketing Budget Related
to Direct Marketing: 51-75%
Direct Marketing ad budget: $30,000
Direct Mail: $5,000
Online: $25,000
Founded: 1953
Gross sales or billing: $2,000,000

The clip system is designed for anyone
who carries a cellular phone, pager,
tools or any of the portable music
systems. Most cameras can also be
carried by any of the stainless units
with the simple addition of the camera
bolt.

REB STORAGE SYSTEMS INTERNATIONAL
4556 W Grand Ave
Chicago, IL 60639-4734
Telephone: (773) 252-0400, (800) 252-
5955, FAX: (773) 252-0303, E-Mail:
sales@rebsteel.com, Web Site: www.
industrialebuy.com
Pres: Tom Lesko
Co-Founder: Edward Lesko
VP, Sys: Mike Bailey
Conducts Business: U.S.
Employees: 10
Primary Market Served: Business &
Consumer
Catalog available online
Direct online sales
Direct Marketing ad budget:
$1,200,000
Direct Mail: 100%
Gross sales or billing: $12,000,000

Wholesale catalog of material handling
industrial products.

REGITAR USA INC
Subs. of Mobiletron Electronics Co
Ltd
2575 Container Dr
Montgomery, AL 36109
Telephone: (334) 244-1885, (877) 734-
4827, FAX: (334) 244-1901, E-Mail:
info@regitar.com, Web Site: www.
regitar.com
CEO: Y.T. Tsai
VP: Chau Lee
Conducts Business: U.S., Canada,
South America
Primary Market Served: Business
Catalog available online
Indirect online sales
Advertising/Marketing Budget Related
to Direct Marketing: 0-25%
Direct Marketing ad budget:
Direct Mail: 5%
Magazines: 10%
Newspapers: 10%
Telephone: 75%
Founded: 1987
Gross sales or billing: $21,000,000

Auto parts & ignition components for
domestic & import autos, power tools,
fastening systems, tackers & cordless
tools.

RELIANCE ELECTRIC
Div. of Rockwell Automation
5711 RS Boreham Jr St
Fort Smith, AR 72901-8301
Telephone: (479) 646-4711, FAX:
(479) 648-5792, E-Mail: smtraylor@
powersystems.rockwell.com, Web
Site: www.reliance.com
Pres: Joe Swann
VP, Fin Svcs: Tom Mascari
Mgr: Shawn Traylor
Info Technologist: Elaine Durrah
Conducts Business: U.S., Europe, Asia,
Latin America
Primary Market Served: Business
Catalog available online
Advertising/Marketing Budget Related
to Direct Marketing: 0-25%

Industrial electrical motors, variable
speed drives, motor controls, mechanical power transmission products &
telecommunications equipment.

THE RENOVATOR'S SUPPLY INC
Renovator's Old Mill
Millers Falls, MA 01349
Telephone: (413) 423-3300, (800) 659-
2211, FAX: (413) 423-3800, E-Mail:
customercare@rensup.com, Web
Site: www.rensup.com
Pres: Claude Jenloz
Conducts Business: Worldwide
Primary Market Served: Business &
Consumer

Catalog available online
Direct online sales
Gross sales or billing: $5,000,000

Manufacture & sell hardware, lighting & plumbing supplies for residential & commercial applications. 2000 item catalog available.

RETAWMATIC CORP

14911 41st Ave
Flushing, NY 11355-1025
Telephone: (718) 886-0502
Pres: Charles J. Hsu
Conducts Business: U.S.
Primary Market Served: Business & Consumer

Sell surface water & oil detectors, water-in-oil detectors & water separators.

ROCK-TRED CORP

405 N Oakwood Ave
Waukegan, IL 60085
Telephone: (847) 673-8200, (800) 762-8733, FAX: (847) 679-6665, Web Site: www.rocktred.com
Pres: Dan Moran
Conducts Business: Worldwide
Employees: 35
Primary Market Served: Business
Advertising/Marketing Budget Related to Direct Marketing: 0-25%
Founded: 1939
Gross sales or billing: $3,100,000

Floor coatings marketed to qualified applicators.

RUUD LIGHTING INC

9201 Washington Ave
Racine, WI 53406-3772
Telephone: (262) 886-1900, (800) 236-7000, FAX: (800) 236-7500, E-Mail: sales@ruudlighting.com, Web Site: www.ruudlighting.com
Pres: Alan Ruud
VP, Mktg: Stephen Morelli
Direct Mktg Mgr: Gianna O'Keefe
Dev: Troy Rosengarten
VP Opers: Wayne Gillien
Conducts Business: Worldwide
Employees: 475
Primary Market Served: Business
Catalog available online
Indirect online sales
Advertising/Marketing Budget Related to Direct Marketing: 76-100%
Direct Marketing ad budget:
Direct Mail: 90%
Magazines: 10%
Founded: 1982

Lighting fixtures directly marketed to electrical contractors.

SSHC INC/RADIANT HEATING COMMERCIAL APPLICATIONS

Four Custom Dr
Old Saybrook, CT 06475-4008
Telephone: (860) 399-5434, (800) 544-5182, FAX: (860) 399-6460, (877) 675-4968, E-Mail: info@sshcinc.com, Web Site: www.sshcinc.com
Pres, CEO & CFO: Richard Watson
Mktg Mgr: Susan Delise
Conducts Business: U.S., Canada
Employees: 10
Primary Market Served: Business & Consumer
Catalog available online
Advertising/Marketing Budget Related to Direct Marketing: 26-50%
Founded: 1989
Gross sales or billing: $5,000,000

Manufacturer of energy efficient electric radiant heat modules.

SAN FRANCISCO VICTORIANA INC

2070 Newcomb Ave
San Francisco, CA 94124
Telephone: (415) 648-0313, FAX: (415) 648-2812, Web Site: www.sfvictoriana.com
Pres: Gary Root
Conducts Business: U.S.
Employees: 12
Primary Market Served: Business & Consumer
Catalog available online
Indirect online sales
Gross sales or billing: $500,000

Manufacture & supply architectural moldings & castings for restoration & new construction.

SEDGWICK MORAN DETERT & ARNOLD LLP

1 N Wacker Dr (Suite 4200)
Chicago, IL 60606-2862
Telephone: (312) 849-1985, Web Site: www.michaelbest.com

SIERRA SCIENTIFIC INC

dba Value-Tek
1005 N 50th St (Suite 150)
Phoenix, AZ 85008-0117
Telephone: (602) 256-0540, FAX: (602) 252-1972, Web Site: www.value-tek.com
Pres: Greg Heiland
VP: George Heiland
Dir Sls: Chris Heiland
Dir Mktg: David Ducic
Mktg e-Commerce: Joshua Guild
Employees: 25
Primary Market Served: Business
Catalog available online

Direct online sales
Advertising/Marketing Budget Related to Direct Marketing: 0-25%
Direct Marketing ad budget:
Online: 100%
Gross sales or billing: $8,000,000

Clean room products. Distributor of critical environment products.

SNAP-ON INC

2801 80th St
Kenosha, WI 53141-1410
Telephone: (262) 656-5200, (800) 866-5748, (800) 786-6600, FAX: (262) 656-5577, Web Site: www.snapon.com
Pres & CEO: Nicholas T. Pinchuk
VP, Chief Mktg Ofcr: Andrew R. Ginger
Conducts Business: Worldwide
Employees: 12,400
Primary Market Served: Business & Consumer
Gross sales or billing: $2,840,000,000

Direct marketer of hand tools & related equipment for professional mechanics.

SOLAR COMPONENTS CORP

121 Valley St
Manchester, NH 03103-0237
Telephone: (603) 668-8186, FAX: (603) 668-1783, Web Site: www.solar-components.com
Mktg Mgr: Mark Miville
Pres: Scott Keller
Conducts Business: Worldwide
Employees: 5
Primary Market Served: Business & Consumer
Catalog available online
Direct online sales
Advertising/Marketing Budget Related to Direct Marketing: 0-25%
Direct Marketing ad budget:
Direct Mail: 10%
Magazines: 75%
Telephone: 15%
Founded: 1972
Gross sales or billing: $500,000

Energy saving, energy producing photovoltaics, aquaculture tanks & greenhouse kits. Complete catalog available, also check our website.

SPECTRONICS CORP

956 Brush Hollow Rd
Westbury, NY 11590-1731
Telephone: (800) 274-8888, FAX: (800) 491-6868, E-Mail: vscherer@spectroline.com, Web Site: www.spectroline.com
Pres: Jonathan Cooper
VP, Sls & Mktg: Gary Fixel
VP Opers: John Duerr

Mktg Commun Mgr: Bob Savasta
Customer Svc Mgr: Gloria Blusk
Publicist: Valerie Scherer
Conducts Business: U.S., Canada
Employees: 200
Primary Market Served: Business
Catalog available online
Advertising/Marketing Budget Related
    to Direct Marketing: 0-25%
Direct Marketing ad budget:
Direct Mail: 75%
Magazines: 20%
Online: 5%
Founded: 1955
Gross sales or billing: $25,000,000

Wide variety of products based on
ultra-violet technology: laboratory
equipment, security, banking, forensics,
NDT, air conditioning & refrigeration
& vehicle leak detectors.

STANDARD TOOLS & EQUIPMENT CO
4810 Clover Rd
Greensboro, NC 27405-9607
Telephone: (336) 697-7177, Web Site:
    www.toolsusa.com
Pres & CEO: Bob Shepley

STAR SPRINKLER INC
Subs. of Tyco International Ltd
1400 Pennbrook Pkwy
Lansdale, PA 19446-3840
Telephone: (414) 570-5000, (800) 558-
    5236, FAX: (414) 570-5010, Web
    Site: www.starsprinkler.com
Exec VP: Jim Smyrl
Mktg Mgr: John Corcorah
Conducts Business: Worldwide
Employees: 150
Primary Market Served: Business &
    Consumer
Catalog available online
Advertising/Marketing Budget Related
    to Direct Marketing: 26-50%
Direct Marketing ad budget: $20,000
Direct Mail: 70%
Magazines: 30%
Founded: 1894

Fire sprinklers & accessories. Branches
in West Springfield, MA; Nashville,
TN; Dardanelle, AR & Oakland, CA.

START INTERNATIONAL
4270 Airborn Dr
Addison, TX 75001-5182
Telephone: (972) 248-1999, (800) 259-
    1986, FAX: (972) 248-1991, E-Mail:
    info@startinternational.com, Web
    Site: www.startinternational.com
Pres: Todd Sternbert
Conducts Business: U.S., Canada, Eu-
    rope, Asia
Employees: 15
Primary Market Served: Business

Catalog available online
Advertising/Marketing Budget Related
    to Direct Marketing: 51-75%
Founded: 1981

Industrial tape and label dispensers.
Optical inspection devices and
magnifiers.

STATSOFT INC
2300 E 14th St
Tulsa, OK 74104
Telephone: (918) 749-1119, FAX:
    (918) 749-2217, E-Mail: info@
    statsoft.com, Web Site: www.statsoft.
    com
CFO: Elizabeth Paszkiewic
Mgr: John Hillis
Sls: Gary Miner
Mktg Coord: Sarah Beaumont
Conducts Business: Worldwide
Primary Market Served: Business &
    Consumer
Catalog available online
Indirect online sales
Founded: 1984

Statistical software called STATIS-
TICA, sells worldwide.

STELLAR TECHNOLOGY INC
237 Commerce Dr
Amherst, NY 14228-2302
Telephone: (800) 274-1846, FAX:
    (716) 250-1909, E-Mail: info@
    stellartech.com, Web Site: www.
    stellartech.com
Pres: Bob Haefner
Sls Mgr: James Borkowski
Employees: 35
Primary Market Served: Business
Catalog available online

Manufacture pressure transducers.

STILE-TILE LIKE METAL ROOFING
Metal Sales Manufacturing Corp
7800 State Rd (#60)
Sellersburg, IN 47172
Telephone: (812) 246-1866, (800) 999-
    7777, FAX: (800) 477-9318, (800)
    944-6884, Web Site: www.mtsales.
    com
Mktg Dir: Don Durs
Pres & CEO: Tom Morris
Primary Market Served: Business &
    Consumer
Founded: 1963

Manufacture metal roofing products.

STRONGWELL
400 Commonwealth Ave
Bristol, VA 24201-3800

Telephone: (276) 645-8000, FAX:
    (276) 645-8132, E-Mail: gbarefoot@
    strongwell.com, Web Site: www.
    strongwell.com
Pres: John Tickle
COO & Exec VP: Keith Liskey
Corp Mktg Mgr: Glenn P. Barefoot
Natl Sls Mgr: Dave Faulkner
Conducts Business: Worldwide
Employees: 800
Primary Market Served: Business &
    Consumer
Catalog available online
Advertising/Marketing Budget Related
    to Direct Marketing: 0-25%
Direct Marketing ad budget: $150,000
Direct Mail: 45%
Magazines: 50%
Online: 5%
Founded: 1971
Gross sales or billing: $120,000,000

Fiberglass structural shapes & grating.
Precast polymer concrete.

SUNSHINE UNLIMITED INC
Box 71
Lindsborg, KS 67456-0071
Telephone: (785) 227-3880, FAX:
    (785) 227-3880, E-Mail: cpeterjr@
    aol.com, Web Site: www.sunshine-
    unlimited.com
Pres: Chester Peterson Jr.
Conducts Business: Worldwide
Primary Market Served: Business &
    Consumer
Catalog available online
Indirect online sales
Advertising/Marketing Budget Related
    to Direct Marketing: 76-100%
Founded: 1976

Computer software.

SURPLUS CENTER
Div. of Burden Sales Co
1015 W "O" St
Lincoln, NE 68528-1322
Telephone: (402) 474-4055, (800) 488-
    3407, FAX: (402) 474-5198, E-Mail:
    customerservice1@surpluscenter.
    com, Web Site: www.surpluscenter.
    com
Pres: David Burden
VP, Sls: Chris Cole
Sls Mgr: Jeff Atkinson
Conducts Business: U.S.
Employees: 40
Primary Market Served: Business &
    Consumer
Catalog available online
Direct online sales
Advertising/Marketing Budget Related
    to Direct Marketing: 76-100%
Direct Marketing ad budget: $350,000
Direct Mail: 67%
Magazines: 33%

Founded: 1933
Gross sales or billing: $16,000,000

Hydraulic equipment, motors, pumps, etc. Customer base of farmers, contractors & small fabrication shops.

TECRA TOOLS INC
2925 S Umatilla St
Englewood, CO 80110-1217
Telephone: (303) 338-9224, (800) 284-0808, FAX: (303) 338-9289, E-Mail: info@tecratools.com, Web Site: www.tecratools.com
Pres: Terry Tautz
VP: Nicole Tautz
Catalog available online
Direct online sales

TELPRO INC
7251 S 42nd St
Grand Forks, ND 58201
Telephone: (701) 775-0551, FAX: (701) 775-0629
Pres: Rolland Young
VP Mktg: Dana Young
Sls Mgr Mktg: Mark Haaland
Primary Market Served: Business

Manufacturer of construction equipment.

TEMPCO ELECTRIC HEATER CORP
607 N Central Ave
Wood Dale, IL 60191-1452
Telephone: (630) 350-2252, (800) 323-6859, FAX: (630) 350-0232, E-Mail: dpadlo@tempco.com, Web Site: www.tempco.com
Pres: Fermin Adames
VP Sls: William Kilberry
Dept Mgr: Dennis C. Padlo
Conducts Business: U.S., Canada, Mexico, Japan, Netherlands
Employees: 325
Primary Market Served: Business
Catalog available online
Indirect online sales
Advertising/Marketing Budget Related to Direct Marketing: 0-25%
Founded: 1972
Gross sales or billing: $15,000,000

Manufacturer of electric heating elements for commercial & industrial heating of liquids, solids & process air. From stock or made to specifications.

TEXAS REFINERY CORP
840 N Main St
Fort Worth, TX 76106-9419
Telephone: (817) 332-1161, FAX: (817) 336-8441, E-Mail: jhopkins@texasrefinery.com, Web Site: www.texasrefinery.com
Owner & Chmn Bd: A.M. Pate

Pres: Jerry Hopkins
VP: Jim Peel
VP, Pur: Barbara Main
Conducts Business: U.S., Canada, Europe, Mexico
Employees: 125
Primary Market Served: Business
Catalog available online
Indirect online sales
Founded: 1922

Marketer of building maintenance products & heavy duty lubricants to business & industry.

THERMO FISHER SCIENTIFIC I
81 Wyman St
Waltham, MA 02451-1223
Telephone: (781) 622-1000, (800) 678-5599, FAX: (781) 622-1207, Web Site: www.thermofisher.com
Chmn: Jim P. Manzi
Pres, CEO & Dir: Marijn E. Dekkers
Sr VP & CFO: Peter M. Wilver
Sr VP, HR: Stephen G. Sheehan
VP & CIO: Ina B. Kamenz
Conducts Business: Worldwide
Primary Market Served: Business & Consumer
Catalog available online
Direct online sales
Founded: 1950
Gross sales or billing: $3,700,000,000

Manufacturing of lab equipment.

THE DMA THERMO FISHER SCIENTIFIC SID
5225 Verona Rd
Madison, WI 53711-4497
Telephone: (608) 276-6100, Web Site: www.thermo.com
Mgr, Marcom Opers: Cliff Wolcott
Primary Market Served: Business

THOMAS SCIENTIFIC
1654 High Hill Rd
Swedesboro, NJ 08085
Telephone: (800) 345-2100, FAX: (856) 467-3087, E-Mail: value@thomassci.com, Web Site: www.thomassci.com
Chm Bd: R. Patterson
Pres: G. Wesner
VP, Mktg & Sls: Ed Pierzynski
Conducts Business: U.S., Canada, Europe, S. America, Asia
Employees: 100
Primary Market Served: Business
Catalog available online
Indirect online sales
Advertising/Marketing Budget Related to Direct Marketing: 51-75%
Direct Marketing ad budget:
Direct Mail: 75%
Magazines: 20%

Telephone: 5%
Founded: 1900

Lab & scientific equipment & supplies.

THREEFOLD
5151 N Shadeland Ave
Indianapolis, IN 46226-2603
Telephone: (317) 607-1995, Web Site: www.certaindy.com
Primary Market Served: Consumer

TIME MOTION TOOLS
Div. of WASSCO
12778 Brookprinter Pl
Poway, CA 92064
Telephone: (800) 779-8170, FAX: (800) 779-8171, Web Site: www.timemotion.com
CEO: Ward Leber
VP: Al Rios
Conducts Business: U.S., Canada
Employees: 50
Primary Market Served: Business
Catalog available online
Direct online sales
Advertising/Marketing Budget Related to Direct Marketing: 76-100%
Direct Marketing ad budget:
Direct Mail: 100%
Founded: 1985

Service tools to the service & repair industry.

TINSLEY TOOL SUPPLY INC
8038 Canter Ln
Powell, TN 37849-3143
Telephone: (865) 681-9633, FAX: (865) 982-1655, E-Mail: gene@tinsleytool.com, Web Site: www.tinsleytool.com
Pres & Owner: Ellen Sapp
Inside Sls Mgr: Paula Snyder
Office Mgr: Gene Sapp
Sls Mgr: Michael Sapp
Sls: Charlie Pepper
Primary Market Served: Business
Catalog available online

Distributor of metal cutting tools & cutting tool machinery.

TORQMASTER INTERNATIONAL
200 Harvard Ave
Stamford, CT 06902-6230
Telephone: (203) 326-5945, (888) 414-4643, FAX: (203) 326-5944, E-Mail: info@torqmaster.com, Web Site: www.torqmaster.com
Pres: Garrett Bebell
Exec VP: Steven Rubin
Fin Controller & HR Dir: Nisley Montes
Dir Sls: Douglas Collins
Dir Mktg: Van Valkenburgh

Conducts Business: Worldwide
Employees: 70
Primary Market Served: Business
Catalog available online
Indirect online sales
Advertising/Marketing Budget Related
to Direct Marketing: 0-25%
Founded: 1979
Gross sales or billing: $6,000,000

Friction hinges & torque producing
devices.

TRICOR DIRECT INC/SETON

20 Thompson Rd
Branford, CT 06405-2842
Telephone: (800) 243-6624, E-Mail:
custsvc_setonus@seton.com, Web
Site: www.seton.com
Database Mktg Assoc: Donna J.
Canestri
Employees: 250
Primary Market Served: Business
Catalog available online
Direct online sales
Founded: 1956

Seton Identification products is a
manufacturer of all types of identification products including signs, tags,
labels, pipe & valve markers & much
more.

THE DMA TRIDIUM INC

3951 Westerre Pkwy
Richmond, VA 23233-1317
Telephone: (804) 525-1648, Web Site:
www.tridium.com

UNITRON LTD

73 Mall Dr
Commack, NY 11725-5703
Telephone: (631) 589-6666, FAX:
(631) 589-6795, E-Mail: johnc@
unitronusa.com, Web Site: www.
unitronusa.com
Pres: Jay Berliner
Sr VP: Brian Taub
VP: Peter I. Indrigo
Consultant: John D. Coyle
Conducts Business: U.S., Canada
Employees: 20
Primary Market Served: Business &
Consumer
Catalog available online
Indirect online sales
Advertising/Marketing Budget Related
to Direct Marketing: 51-75%
Founded: 1952
Gross sales or billing: $4,000,000

Service & market a full line of microscopes, telescopes, & binoculars to the
industrial, medical, educational & retail
markets.

UPBEAT INC

211 N Lindbergh Blvd (fl 2)
Saint Louis, MO 63141-7838
Telephone: (314) 535-5005, (800) 325-
3047, FAX: (314) 535-4419, E-Mail:
custservice@upbeat.com, Web Site:
www.upbeat.com
Pres: Terry Knoplol
Dir Mktg: Eric Gilbert
Dir Mdsg: Nancy Mills
Natl Sales: Carl van der Horst
Conducts Business: U.S.
Employees: 70
Primary Market Served: Business &
Consumer
Catalog available online
Direct online sales
Advertising/Marketing Budget Related
to Direct Marketing: 76-100%
Founded: 1982

Institutional catalog company.

VARIAN MEDICAL SYSTEMS

3100 Hansen Way
Palo Alto, CA 94304
Telephone: (650) 493-4000, FAX:
(650) 842-5196, Web Site: www.
varian.com
Chmn Bd: Richard Levy
VP Pub Rels: Spencer Sias
VP Gen Counsel & Sec: John W. Kuo
Pres & CEO: Timothy E. Guertin
Dir: John Seely Brown
Employees: 3,900
Primary Market Served: Business
Catalog available online
Gross sales or billing: $1,600,000,000

Medical equipment.

VICTOR MACHINERY EXCHANGE

56 Bogart St
Brooklyn, NY 11206-3817
Telephone: (800) 723-5359, E-Mail:
sales@victornet.com, Web Site:
www.victornet.com
Pres: Marc Freidus
Conducts Business: U.S.
Employees: 10
Primary Market Served: Business &
Consumer
Catalog available online
Indirect online sales
Advertising/Marketing Budget Related
to Direct Marketing: 76-100%
Direct Marketing ad budget:
Direct Mail: 50%
Magazines: 10%
Online: 40%
Founded: 1918

Industrial & metalworking supplies to
machine shops, manufacturers &
hobbyists.

WATTS RADIANT

Subs. of DBA
4500 E Progress Pl
Springfield, MO 65803
Telephone: (417) 864-6108, (800) 276-
2419, FAX: (417) 864-8161, Web
Site: www.wattsheatway.com
Pres & CEO: Mike Chiles
VP: Dan Chiles
VP, Sls: Russ Rose
Engr Design Asst: Tony Ledford
Conducts Business: U.S., Canada, New
Zealand
Employees: 51
Primary Market Served: Business &
Consumer
Catalog available online
Indirect online sales
Advertising/Marketing Budget Related
to Direct Marketing: 0-25%
Founded: 1981
Gross sales or billing: $7,900,000

Radiant floor heating & snow melting.

WELCH ALLYN, INC

4341 State Street Rd
Skaneateles Falls, NY 13153-5300
Telephone: (315) 685-4100, Web Site:
www.welchallyn.com
Pres: William F Allyn
Primary Market Served: Consumer

THE DMA WELCOMEMAT SERVICES INC

3348 Peachtree Rd (Suite 1095)
Atlanta, GA 30326-1400
Telephone: (404) 841-2226, Web Site:
www.welcomematservices.com
Primary Market Served: Business &
Consumer

WESTHOFF MACHINE CO

9462 Watson Industrial Park
Saint Louis, MO 63126
Telephone: (314) 963-7130, (800) 364-
0280, FAX: (800) 324-1942, E-Mail:
mail@westhoffinc.com, Web Site:
www.westhoffinc.com
CEO: Allen Johnson
Pres: Janice Westhoff Johnson
Conducts Business: U.S.
Employees: 12
Primary Market Served: Business &
Consumer
Catalog available online
Direct online sales
Advertising/Marketing Budget Related
to Direct Marketing: 76-100%
Direct Marketing ad budget:
Direct Mail: 85%
Magazines: 10%
Telephone: 5%
Founded: 1967
Gross sales or billing: $2,750

Sell small industrial magnetic products, hand tools & die casting supplies through direct mail to the metal working industries.

WHOLESALE TOOL CO

12155 Stephens Dr
Warren, MI 48089
Telephone: (800) 521-3420, FAX: (800) 521-3661, E-Mail: wtmich@aol.com, Web Site: www.wttool.com
Pres: Mark Dowdy
Adv Dir: Matthew Decker
Conducts Business: U.S., Canada, Mexico
Employees: 45
Primary Market Served: Business & Consumer
Catalog available online
Direct online sales
Direct Marketing ad budget: $1,600,000
Direct Mail: 75%
Magazines: 8%
Newspapers: 2%
Telephone: 15%
Founded: 1960
Gross sales or billing: $20,000,000

Industrial tooling, hand, power, & cutting tools, precision, machinery, abrasives, material handling equipment.

WIRE WORKS

200 Keystone Rd (Suite 1)
Chester, PA 19013
Telephone: (610) 485-1981, (800) 292-1940, Web Site: www.wire-works.com
Pres & Chmn Bd: Ron Francis
Conducts Business: Worldwide
Employees: 14
Primary Market Served: Business & Consumer
Catalog available online
Direct online sales
Founded: 1974

Sell wiring harnesses for auto, marine & industrial use.

WOOD CARVERS SUPPLY INC

PO Box 7500
Englewood, FL 34295-7500
Telephone: (941) 698-0123, (800) 284-6229, FAX: (941) 698-0329, E-Mail: info@woodcarverssupply.com, Web Site: www.woodcarverssupply.com
Pres: Timothy Effrem
VP: Debbie Effrem
Primary Market Served: Business & Consumer
Founded: 1955

Complete line of tools, equipment & supplies for woodcarving.

THE DMA WOODCRAFT SUPPLY CORP LLC

Subs. of SBR Inc
1177 Rosemar Rd
Parkersburg, WV 26105-8272
Telephone: (304) 422-5412, (800) 344-3348, FAX: (304) 422-5417, Web Site: www.woodcraft.com
Pres: Bryan J. Katchur
CEO: Sam Ross
Controller: Larry Gerrard
Catalog Mktg Dir: Ken Kupshe
Store Opers Dir: Gary Lombard
Conducts Business: U.S., Canada
Employees: 300
Primary Market Served: Business & Consumer
Advertising/Marketing Budget Related to Direct Marketing: 76-100%
Founded: 1928

Sells woodworking hand tools, books & related equipment & supplies to industrial, vocational & consumer markets. Retail locations in 29 major cities from coast to coast.

WOODCRAFTERS LUMBER SALES INC

212 NE Sixth Ave
Portland, OR 97232-2976
Telephone: (503) 231-0226, (800) 777-3709, FAX: (503) 232-0511, E-Mail: spen@worldnet.att.net, Web Site: www.woodcrafters.us
Pres: Stephen Penberthy
Sls Mgr: Carl Paasche
Conducts Business: U.S.
Employees: 25
Primary Market Served: Business & Consumer
Advertising/Marketing Budget Related to Direct Marketing: 51-75%
Direct Marketing ad budget: $114,000
Direct Mail: 10%
Magazines: 10%
Newspapers: 10%
TV/Radio: 70%
Founded: 1973
Gross sales or billing: $5,000,000

Sell hardware, tools, books & stair cast woodwork. Catalogs for carving, tools, millwork & books related to woodworking.

ZORO TOOLS INC

1445 Armour Blvd
Mundelein, IL 60060-4403
Web Site: www.zorotools.com

ACCOUNTANTS EDUCATION GROUP

8111 Lyndon B Johnson Fwy Ste 1345
Dallas, TX 75251-1354
Telephone: (214) 373-3486, (800) 627-7310, FAX: (800) 627-7310, E-Mail: customerservice@accountantsed.com, Web Site: www.accountantsed.com
Pres: Marc C. Pinelli
Primary Market Served: Business & Consumer
Catalog available online
Direct online sales

Business/industrial mail order & books: catalogs, printed & recorded materials.

ACCOUNTANTS' SUPPLY HOUSE

Div. of Histacount Corp
PO Box 1186
Lancaster, CA 93584-1186
Telephone: (856) 384-1144, (800) 342-5274, FAX: (800) 468-4446, Web Site: www.rapidforms.com
Pres: John Fairbanks
VP, Mktg: Tom Jule
VP, Fin: Tim Broadhead
Mktg Mgr: Kent Fegley
Mgr, Circulation Svcs: Christopher Gordon
Conducts Business: Worldwide
Employees: 300
Primary Market Served: Business & Consumer
Advertising/Marketing Budget Related to Direct Marketing: 76-100%
Direct Marketing ad budget:
Direct Mail: 98%
Magazines: 2%
Founded: 1952
Gross sales or billing: $3,000,000

Manufacture & sell office, accounting supplies, printers, medical & dental stationeries.

AD-LIB ADVERTISING INC

109 White Oak Ln (Suite 72A)
Old Bridge, NJ 08857
Telephone: (732) 679-9226, (800) 622-3542, FAX: (732) 679-9511, E-Mail: info@adlibadvertising.com, Web Site: www.adlibadvertising.com
Pres: Don Cogland
Customer Svc: Victoria DeLuca
Conducts Business: U.S.
Employees: 4
Primary Market Served: Business
Advertising/Marketing Budget Related to Direct Marketing: 0-25%
Founded: 1968
Gross sales or billing: $1,000,000

Custom printed post-it note pads, calendars & specialty advertising products.

ADIRONDACK DIRECT

Div. of Adirondack Chair Co Inc
3040 48th Ave
Long Island City, NY 11101
Telephone: (718) 932-4003, (800) 221-2444, FAX: (800) 477-1330, E-Mail: info@adirondackdirect.com, Web Site: www.adirondackdirect.com
Pres: Syl Cangero
Mktg Dir: Margaret Haggerty
Adv Dir: Marianna Lokis
Conducts Business: Worldwide
Employees: 100
Primary Market Served: Business
Catalog available online
Direct online sales
Founded: 1926

Catalog offering business & institutional furniture distributed to business firms, churches, schools, clubs & organizations.

ADMORE INC

Subs. of Ennis Business Forms
24707 Wood Ct
Macomb, MI 48042-5378
Telephone: (810) 949-8200, (800) 523-6673, FAX: (800) 215-2664, Web Site: www.admoreonline.com
Gen Mgr: Bill Tignanelli
Natl Acct Rep: John Andersen
Customer Svc: Brenda Barozzini
Primary Market Served: Business
Catalog available online
Indirect online sales
Founded: 1947

Manufacture paper presentation products through distributors.

ALFA CTP SYSTEMS

554 Clark Rd # 2
Tewksbury, MA 01876-1631
Telephone: (603) 689-1101, FAX: (603) 689-1197, Web Site: www.alfactp.com
Gen Mgr: Tony Ford
Primary Market Served: Business & Consumer

AMERICAN STATIONERY CO INC

100 N Park Ave, Box 207
Peru, IN 46970
Telephone: (765) 473-4438, (800) 822-2577, FAX: (800) 253-9054, Web Site: www.americanstationery.com
VP Mktg: Kathy Calderbank
Pres: Michael Bakehorn

Controller: Joyce McCarty
Conducts Business: U.S.
Employees: 250
Primary Market Served: Consumer
Catalog available online
Direct online sales
Advertising/Marketing Budget Related to Direct Marketing: 26-50%
Founded: 1919

Quality personalized paper products & accessories for home or office. Complete line of wedding stationery & accessories.

ARMBRUST PAPER TUBES INC

6255 S Harlem Ave
Chicago, IL 60638-3990
Telephone: (773) 586-3232, FAX: (773) 586-8997, E-Mail: tubesrus@corecomm.net, Web Site: www.tubesrus.com
Pres: Bernerd Armbrust
CFO: Jack Slattery
VP: Marc Armbrust
Conducts Business: U.S., Canada
Employees: 30
Primary Market Served: Business & Consumer
Catalog available online
Direct online sales
Advertising/Marketing Budget Related to Direct Marketing: 51-75%
Direct Marketing ad budget: $50,000
Telephone: $25,000
Founded: 1938
Gross sales or billing: $3,200,000

Manufacturer of paper tubes, cores & cans for packaging & shipping.

ASSOCIATED BAG CO

400 W Boden St
Milwaukee, WI 53207-7120
Telephone: (414) 769-1000, (800) 926-6100, FAX: (800) 926-4610, E-Mail: customerservice@associatedbag.com, Web Site: www.associatedbag.com
Pres: Herb Rubenstein
*Mktg Designer: Kay Beavers

THE DMA AVERY DENNISON CORP

50 Pointe Dr
Brea, CA 92821-3699
Telephone: (714) 674-8500, (800) 462-8379, FAX: (714) 674-6929, Web Site: www.avery.com
Pres & CEO: Dean A. Scarborough
Sr VP Corp Commun & Adv: Diane B. Dixon
Mgr Email Opers & Analytics: Hossein Hosseini
Conducts Business: U.S., Canada

Employees: 22,700
Primary Market Served: Business &
  Consumer
Catalog available online
Advertising/Marketing Budget Related
  to Direct Marketing: 0-25%
Direct Marketing ad budget:
Direct Mail: 70%
Online: 30%
Founded: 1935
Gross sales or billing: $5,575,900,000

Company specializing in office
products.

BROOKHOLLOW CARDS

Div. of Taylor Corp
1 Stationary Pl
Rexburg, ID 83440-3567
Telephone: (800) 822-0256, FAX:
  (800) 443-8847, E-Mail: service@
  brookhollowcards.com, Web Site:
  www.brookhollowcards.com
Mktg Rep: Jamie Eckman
Conducts Business: U.S.
Primary Market Served: Business &
  Consumer
Direct Marketing ad budget:
Direct Mail: 100%

Sell imprinted greeting cards & calendars for business-to-business use.

ARTHUR BROWN & BRO INC

2 W 45th St Frnt 1
New York, NY 10036-4214
Telephone: (212) 575-5555, (800) 772-
  PENS, FAX: (212) 575-5825,
  E-Mail: penshop@artbrown.com,
  Web Site: www.artbrown.com
Owner: B. Warren Brown
Pres: J. Powell Brown
Mgr: Marilyn Brown
Conducts Business: U.S.
Employees: 30
Primary Market Served: Business &
  Consumer
Catalog available online
Direct online sales
Founded: 1924

Fine art, commercial art & drafting
supplies, fine writing instruments -
wholesale & retail. Publishers of pen
catalogs & dealer imprint programs.

CABLEXPRESS
TECHNOLOGIES

5404 S Bay Rd
Syracuse, NY 13212-3801
Telephone: (315) 476-3000, (800) 913-
  9467, FAX: (315) 455-1800, E-Mail:
  info@cablexpress.com, Web Site:
  www.CXTec.com
Pres: William G. Pomeroy
VP: Frank Kobuszewski Jr.
VP, Opers & Acctg: Al Gough

VP, Bus Devel: Peter Belyea
Corp Affairs Dir: Paula Miller
Conducts Business: U.S., Canada, Eu-
  rope, Pacific Rim
Employees: 160
Primary Market Served: Business &
  Consumer
Catalog available online
Indirect online sales
Advertising/Marketing Budget Related
  to Direct Marketing: 51-75%
Founded: 1978
Gross sales or billing: $116,000,000

Reseller of connectivity solutions for
IBM & compatible mainframe,
midrange & LAN environments. Free
catalog.

CENTURY PHOTO

Div. of Centis Inc
10425 Slusher Dr
Santa Fe Springs, CA 90670-3750
Telephone: (800) 767-0777, FAX:
  (714) 441-4550, Web Site: www.
  centuryphoto.com
Circ Dir: Bill Martin
Conducts Business: U.S.
Employees: 480
Primary Market Served: Business &
  Consumer
Catalog available online
Direct online sales
Advertising/Marketing Budget Related
  to Direct Marketing: 51-75%
Direct Marketing ad budget:
  $5,000,000
Direct Mail: 75%
Telephone: 25%
Founded: 1950

Manufacture & sell via mail order
business products that protect, organize
& display office paper work & photographic materials.

CHAMPION AMERICA INC

PO Box 3092
Branford, CT 06405-1692
Telephone: (203) 315-1181, (877) 242-
  6709, FAX: (800) 336-3707, E-Mail:
  teamca@champion-america.com,
  Web Site: www.championamerica.
  com
Pres & Gen Mgr: Cynthia Czyz
Dir, Mktg Admin: Donna J. Canestri
Conducts Business: U.S.
Employees: 250
Primary Market Served: Business
Catalog available online
Direct online sales
Advertising/Marketing Budget Related
  to Direct Marketing: 76-100%
Direct Marketing ad budget:
Direct Mail: 100%
Founded: 1989

Safety signs & identification products.

CLASSIC
THERMOGRAPHERS

1680 Roe Crest Dr
North Mankato, MN 56003-2658
Telephone: (623) 582-0002, (800) 727-
  4200, FAX: (800) 727-4202
Pres: Shannin Hustad
Mktg Mgr: Tiffany Bennett
Conducts Business: U.S.
Primary Market Served: Business &
  Consumer
Founded: 1976

Printer of wedding invitations.

COLONIAL REDI-RECORD
CORP

1225 36th St
Brooklyn, NY 11218-2023
Telephone: (718) 972-7433, (800) 637-
  0040, FAX: (718) 972-7438, Web
  Site: www.asisupplier.com/81110
Pres: Joe Berkobits
Conducts Business: U.S.
Employees: 8
Primary Market Served: Business
Catalog available online
Direct online sales
Founded: 1948

Sell business forms to stationers.

COMMUNICATION
INDUSTRIES CORP

117 J L H Memorial Dr.
Grafton, VT 05146-0116
Telephone: (802) 869-6500, FAX:
  (802) 869-6565, E-Mail: info@
  cicmail.com, Web Site: www.
  careersatcic.com
Pres: Scott Heller
VP & Gen Mgr: Bob Singleton
Mktg Supvr: Paula Ryan
Web Mktg Coord: Nathan Schmidt
Employees: 36
Primary Market Served: Business
Catalog available online
Direct online sales
Advertising/Marketing Budget Related
  to Direct Marketing: 76-100%
Direct Marketing ad budget:
  $2,000,000
Direct Mail: $2,000,000
Founded: 1976

Product distributor of audio visual
equipment to schools, hospitals & government agencies & corporations.

DATABAZAAR.COM

12070 Miramar Pkwy
Miramar, FL 33025
Telephone: (954) 843-0483, (888) 335-
  3282, FAX: (954) 843-0429, E-Mail:
  rudy@databazaar.com, Web Site:
  www.databazaar.com
VP Mktg: David L. Cohen

CEO: Oney Seal
Conducts Business: U.S.
Employees: 55
Primary Market Served: Business &
Consumer
Catalog available online
Direct online sales
Advertising/Marketing Budget Related
to Direct Marketing: 0-25%
Direct Marketing ad budget:
Direct Mail: 1%
Magazines: 1%
Newspapers: 1%
Online: 95%
TV/Radio: 1%
Telephone: 1%
Founded: 1999
Gross sales or billing: $50,000,000

Discount original & value priced compatible ink and toner, specialty paper, backup tapes, flash memory & cables.

DAY RUNNER DIRECT
Subs. of Day Runner Inc
101 Oneil Rd
Sidney, NY 13838-1055
Telephone: (800) 643-9923, FAX:
(800) 643-9927, Web Site: www.
dayrunner.com
Mgr: Nancy Lloyd
Primary Market Served: Business &
Consumer

Personal organizers, planners, calendars, refills & accessories.

DECAL SHOP
1849 Foster Dr
Jacksonville, FL 32216
Telephone: (904) 721-3177, (800) 634-
1889
Pres: Jerry Walsh
Conducts Business: U.S.
Employees: 6
Primary Market Served: Business &
Consumer

Manufacture decals & bumper strips.

DELFORTGROUP
T.S.P., Inc.
1530 Dunwoody Village Pkwy (Suite
130)
Atlanta, GA 30338
Telephone: (678) 325-5751, Web Site:
www.paperisbetter.com

THE DMA DEMCO INC
4810 Forest Run Rd
Madison, WI 53704-7338
Telephone: (608) 241-1201, FAX:
(608) 241-1799, E-Mail: custserv@
demco.com, Web Site: www.demco.
com
Chmn: John Wall
Pres: Bill Stroner

VP, Mktg: Michael Snapper
VP, Fin: Donald Rogers
Dir Consumer Mktg: Stephanie Mueller
VP, Opers: Mike Goethel
VP, IS: Mark Anderson
Conducts Business: U.S.
Employees: 250
Primary Market Served: Business
Advertising/Marketing Budget Related
to Direct Marketing: 76-100%
Direct Marketing ad budget:
Direct Mail: 95%
Magazines: 5%
Founded: 1905
Gross sales or billing: $50,000,000

Supplies & equipment for libraries, schools, business & professional offices.

DIVERSIFIED PHOTO SUPPLY CORP
333 W Alondra Blvd (Suite C)
Gardena, CA 90248-2428
Telephone: (310) 328-8577, (800) 544-
1609, FAX: (310) 328-8518, Web
Site: www.diversifiedphoto.com
Pres: Darrell Benton
Conducts Business: U.S.
Employees: 32
Primary Market Served: Business &
Consumer
Catalog available online
Indirect online sales
Advertising/Marketing Budget Related
to Direct Marketing: 51-75%
Direct Marketing ad budget:
Direct Mail: 20%
Magazines: 5%
Telephone: 75%
Founded: 1989

Distributor of all major brands of photographic amateur & professional film, papers, chemicals, lab supplies, equipment & graphic arts. Sales are conducted via telemarketing & direct mail.

EGGS BY BYRD
HC 3 Box 3653
Wappapello, MO 63966-9727
Telephone: (573) 222-7999, (800) 235-
EGGS, FAX: (573) 222-8009,
E-Mail: eggsbybyrd@dishmail.net
Owner: Kim Allen
Conducts Business: Worldwide
Employees: 3
Primary Market Served: Consumer
Catalog available online
Indirect online sales
Advertising/Marketing Budget Related
to Direct Marketing: 0-25%
Founded: 1979

Sell complete line of egg art supplies, ten varieties of eggshells, instruction books & miniatures. 80 page catalog $4.50.

EPSON AMERICA
3840 Kilroy Airport Way
Long Beach, CA 90806-2469
Telephone: (562) 981-3840, (800) 873-
7766, FAX: (562) 290-5220, Web
Site: www.epson.com
Pres & CEO: John Lang
Sr VP & CFO: Alan Pound Sr.
Sr VP: James Marshall Sr.
VP, Legal Affairs: Judith S. Bain
VP, Mktg: Keith Krutzberg
Conducts Business: U.S.
Primary Market Served: Business &
Consumer
Catalog available online
Direct online sales
Advertising/Marketing Budget Related
to Direct Marketing: 0-25%
Direct Marketing ad budget:
Direct Mail: $1,000,000
Founded: 1988

Provide accessories & supplies for Epson imaging products.

FARM HOME OFFICES
Div. of Sylvette Corp
6739 12th Ave S
Richfield, MN 55423
Telephone: (612) 920-0907, (800) 788-
7218, FAX: (866) 404-0257, Web
Site: www.sylvette.com
Pres: Jim Halbur
Conducts Business: U.S.
Employees: 3
Primary Market Served: Business &
Consumer
Advertising/Marketing Budget Related
to Direct Marketing: 76-100%
Direct Marketing ad budget: $40,000
Direct Mail: 75%
Magazines: 25%
Founded: 1980
Gross sales or billing: $250,000

Farm & agricultural business forms & business management products.

A I FRIEDMAN INC
44 W 18th St
New York, NY 10011
Telephone: (212) 243-9000, (800) 204-
6352, FAX: (212) 929-7320, Web
Site: www.aifriedman.com
VP: Jeff Goldfarb
Conducts Business: U.S.
Employees: 150
Primary Market Served: Business &
Consumer
Catalog available online
Direct online sales
Advertising/Marketing Budget Related
to Direct Marketing: 0-25%
Founded: 1929

Art supplies.

G-NEIL DIRECT MAIL
Subs. of Taylor Corp.
720 International Pkwy, PO Box 450939
Sunrise, FL 33345-0939
Telephone: (800) 999-9111, FAX: (954) 851-1264, E-Mail: tcs@gneil.com, Web Site: www.gneil.com
Pres: Joe Hilger
Former Pres: Terry Tukes
VP: Steve Singer
Conducts Business: U.S., U.K.
Employees: 275
Primary Market Served: Business
Catalog available online
Direct online sales
Advertising/Marketing Budget Related to Direct Marketing: 51-75%
Founded: 1987

Provide human resource products to over 800,000 business professionals. Also, labor law forms, software quality tools, manuals, videos, testing & motivational products. Free catalog.

GCC PRINTERS
209 Burlington Rd
Bedford, MA 01730
Telephone: (781) 275-5800, (800) 422-7777, FAX: (781) 275-1115, (800) 442-2329, E-Mail: sales@gccprinters.com, Web Site: www.gcctech.com
Pres, CEO: Kevin Curran
US Sls Dir: Andrew Droutman
Conducts Business: Worldwide
Employees: 7
Primary Market Served: Business & Consumer
Catalog available online
Direct online sales
Direct Marketing ad budget:
Direct Mail: 40%
Magazines: 60%
Founded: 1981

Printer consumables.

GENERAL BINDING CORP
One GBC Plaza
Northbrook, IL 60062
Telephone: (800) 723-4000, FAX: (800) 952-1166, (847) 272-1389, Web Site: www.gbc.com
Sr VP, Americas: Elliot Smith
Sr VP, Strategic Plng & Corp Communs: Walter Hebb
Corp Commun Dir: Sally Folkes
Conducts Business: Worldwide
Employees: 1,000
Primary Market Served: Business & Consumer
Advertising/Marketing Budget Related to Direct Marketing: 0-25%
Direct Marketing ad budget: $300,000
Direct Mail: 40%

Magazines: 60%
Founded: 1947
Gross sales or billing: $600,000,000

Specializing in document finishing systems including binding & laminating, paper shredders & visual communications products.

GHENT MANUFACTURING INC
US Partner - The Millennium Group
2999 Henkle Dr
Lebanon, OH 45036-9260
Telephone: (513) 932-3445, (800) 543-0550, FAX: (513) 932-9252, E-Mail: customer_service@!ghent.com, Web Site: www.ghent.com
Pres: George Leasure
Sr VP: John Rouse
Exec VP: G. Mark Leasure
Dir of Res & Mdsg: Scott Bowers
Conducts Business: U.S.
Employees: 160
Primary Market Served: Business & Consumer
Catalog available online
Founded: 1977
Gross sales or billing: $10,200,000

Sell visual communication aids such as markerboards, chalkboards, bulletin boards, directory boards, easels & glass enclosed boards to dealers, distributors & wholesalers.

HR DIRECT
Div. of Executive Greetings Inc
PO Box 452049
Sunrise, FL 33345-2049
Telephone: (800) 346-1231, FAX: (800) 350-7760, Web Site: www.hrdirect.com
Pres: Lee Bracken
Conducts Business: U.S.
Employees: 12
Primary Market Served: Business & Consumer
Advertising/Marketing Budget Related to Direct Marketing: 76-100%

Direct marketer of personal & career development products.

HISTACOUNT & EXPRESSIONS
Div. of Rapidforms
PO Box 1186
Lancaster, CA 93584-4486
Telephone: (800) 645-5220, FAX: (800) 332-5502, E-Mail: service@rapidforms.com, Web Site: www.rapidforms.com
Pres: Richard Riley
Mktg Svcs Mgr: Tim Broadhead
Conducts Business: U.S.
Employees: 250

Primary Market Served: Business
Direct Marketing ad budget: $1,000,000
Direct Mail: 90%
Magazines: 5%
Telephone: 5%
Gross sales or billing: $20,000,000

Engraving, stationery, forms, office supplies & business systems to doctors, dentists, lawyers & accountants (business-to-business).

INNOVATIVE CLIP ART
4772 Betty Davis Rd
York, SC 29745
Telephone: (803) 831-6727, FAX: (704) 290-2069, E-Mail: sales@innovativeclipart.com, Web Site: innovativeclipart.com
Owner: David Dachs
Conducts Business: U.S.
Employees: 5
Primary Market Served: Business & Consumer
Advertising/Marketing Budget Related to Direct Marketing: 0-25%
Direct Marketing ad budget:
Direct Mail: 15%
Magazines: 85%
Founded: 1986

Seller of computer software and electronic clip art.

INTUIT
2632 Marine Way
Mountain View, CA 94043
Telephone: (650) 944-6000, Web Site: www.inuit.com
Chmn: Scott Cook
Chmn Bd: Bill Campbell
Pres & CEO: Brad Smith
Primary Market Served: Business & Consumer

Develop, manufacture & market financial software.

IROQUOIS PRODUCTS
Div. of Iroquois Industries Corp
2220 W 56th St
Chicago, IL 60636-3900
Telephone: (773) 436-3900, (800) 453-3355, FAX: (773) 436-4908, E-Mail: sales@iroquoisproducts.com, Web Site: www.iroquoisproducts.com
Pres: Alan R. Gordon
Mktg Dir: Casey Scuoc
Conducts Business: U.S.
Primary Market Served: Business
Advertising/Marketing Budget Related to Direct Marketing: 76-100%

Direct mail marketer of discount-priced office, information processing, shipping supplies & disposable wipers. Printer of business forms, envelopes, stationery, shipping & mailing labels.

ROBERT JAMES CO INC

PO Box 520
Moody, AL 35004
Telephone: (205) 640-7081, (800) 633-8296, FAX: (205) 640-7087
Chmn: James A. Abele Jr.
Conducts Business: U.S.
Primary Market Served: Business
Founded: 1935

Printing, graphic arts & receipt books to businesses & dealers.

JERRY'S ARTARAMA

PO Box 58638J
Raleigh, NC 27658-8638
Telephone: (919) 878-8478, (800) U-ARTIST, FAX: (919) 873-9565, E-Mail: micah@jerrysartarama.com, Web Site: www.jerrysartarama.com
Pres: Ira Goldstein
CEO: David Goldstein
Mktg: Micah Mullen
Conducts Business: U.S., Canada
Employees: 200
Primary Market Served: Business & Consumer
Catalog available online
Direct online sales
Advertising/Marketing Budget Related to Direct Marketing: 76-100%
Direct Marketing ad budget:
Direct Mail: 70%
Magazines: 30%
Founded: 1968
Gross sales or billing: $50,000,000

Artist supplies & picture frames at near wholesale prices. Market to artists, schools, students & advertising agencies.

KRAFTBILT

Div. of Corporate Express DPM
6504 E 44th St
Tulsa, OK 74145-4614
Telephone: (918) 628-1260, (800) 331-7290, FAX: (918) 632-7371, Web Site: www.kraftbilt.com
Asst Mktg Mgr: Carolyn Hartman
Conducts Business: U.S., Canada
Employees: 12
Primary Market Served: Business & Consumer
Catalog available online
Direct online sales
Advertising/Marketing Budget Related to Direct Marketing: 76-100%
Direct Marketing ad budget: $300,000
Direct Mail: $295,000
Telephone: $5,000

Founded: 1951
Gross sales or billing: $1,400,000

Catalog marketer of office products, stationery, analysis & writing pads & all-weather marking tags.

LASER LABEL TECHNOLOGIES INC

Div. of Bemis Co
4560 Darrow Rd
Stow, OH 44224-1888
Telephone: (800) 882-4050, FAX: (800) 395-4721, E-Mail: sales@lltproducts.com, Web Site: www.lltproducts.com
Mgr: Kathy Altenpohl
Conducts Business: U.S., Canada
Employees: 33
Primary Market Served: Business
Catalog available online
Direct online sales
Advertising/Marketing Budget Related to Direct Marketing: 0-25%
Direct Marketing ad budget:
Direct Mail: 90%
Newspapers: 5%
Telephone: 5%
Founded: 1991
Gross sales or billing: $6,300,000

Labels, ribbons, equipment & supplies for bar code systems.

MAGNAPLAN CORP

dba Visual Planning Group
1320 State Rte 9 (#3314)
Champlain, NY 12919-5412
Telephone: (518) 298-8404, (800) 361-1192, FAX: (518) 298-2368, E-Mail: info@visualplanning.com, Web Site: www.visualplanning.com
Pres: Joseph P. Josephson
Sls Mgr: Carl Maurice
Conducts Business: U.S., Canada
Employees: 20
Primary Market Served: Business & Consumer
Catalog available online
Indirect online sales
Founded: 1958

Magnetic & perforated scheduling boards, t-cards & accessories. Graphic Arts materials: lettering, precision knives, etc. Audio-Visual equipment & supplies: easels & pads, lecterns, bulletin boards, projectors, screens, markers & signs.

MAXON FURNITURE INC

505 Ford Ave
Muscatine, IA 52761-5662
Telephone: (253) 395-4139, Web Site: www.maxonfurniture.com
Bus Devel: Bill Duncan

Primary Market Served: Business & Consumer

Manufactures office furniture

MCBEE

Subs. of New England Business Service Inc
PO Box 1186
Lancaster, CA 93584-1186
Telephone: (973) 263-3225, (800) 878-9443, (800) 662-2331, FAX: (973) 263-8165, E-Mail: info@mcbeeinc.com, Web Site: www.mcbeeweb.com
VP, Sls: Bob Kane
VP, Mktg: Dave Poles
Pres: John Fairbanks
Adv & Commun Dir: Elaine Dunnes
VP, Finance: Tim Broadhead
Mktg: Barbara Volpe
Conducts Business: U.S., Canada
Employees: 580
Primary Market Served: Business
Catalog available online
Advertising/Marketing Budget Related to Direct Marketing: 26-50%
Direct Marketing ad budget:
Direct Mail: $650,000
Magazines: $150,000
Founded: 1906
Gross sales or billing: $75,000,000

Supplies businesses with computer checks & forms, folders, labels, cards & other office supplies.

MEAD WESTVACO CONSUMER & OFFICE PRODUCTS

Div. of Mead Corp
PO Box 290001
Dayton, OH 45429-1290
Telephone: (937) 222-6323, (800) 345-6323, FAX: (937) 495-3192, Web Site: www.mead.com
Pres Consumer & Office Prods: Neil McLachlan
VP Prodn Div: John Draper
Chmn: Jerome Tater
Primary Market Served: Business & Consumer
Founded: 1846

Make paper products. Sell office & school supplies.

MERIKS PARTNERS

2509 N Campbell St (#311)
Tucson, AZ 85719-3362
Telephone: (413) 243-0857
Pres: Tillian Montepaula

MERRIMADE STATIONERY CO LLC

200 Main St (Suite 100)
Ansonia, CT 06401

Telephone: (800) 344-4256, FAX: (800) 883-6515, E-Mail: custserv@merrimadestationery.com, Web Site: www.merrimade.com
Pres: Mike Brakehorn
Conducts Business: U.S.
Employees: 15
Primary Market Served: Consumer
Catalog available online
Direct online sales
Advertising/Marketing Budget Related to Direct Marketing: 76-100%
Founded: 1919

Sell personalized stationery, paper goods & gifts primarily through catalog.

THE DMA MODERN POSTCARD

1675 Faraday Ave
Carlsbad, CA 92008-7314
Telephone: (800) 959-8365, Web Site: www.modernpostcard.com
Mktg Mgr: Fred Hernandez
Primary Market Served: Business

NEBS

500 Main St
Groton, MA 01471-0001
Telephone: (978) 448-6111, (888) 823-6327, (800) 225-6380, FAX: (800) 234-4324, (978) 448-3653, E-Mail: customerservice@nebs.com, Web Site: www.nebs.com
Chmn, Pres & CEO: Robert J. Murray
Pres, Chiswick Div: John F. Fairbanks
Pres, Rapid Forms Div: Richard T. Riley
Pres, NEBS Direct Mktg & Sr VP: Edward M. Bolesky
Sr VP & CFO: Daniel M. Junius
VP, Investor Rels: Timothy D. Althof
Conducts Business: U.S., Canada, U.K., France
Employees: 3,800
Primary Market Served: Business
Catalog available online
Indirect online sales
Advertising/Marketing Budget Related to Direct Marketing: 76-100%
Founded: 1952
Gross sales or billing: $470,477

Supplier of personalized business products for small businesses.

NATIONAL BUSINESS FURNITURE INC

735 N Water St Ste 440
Milwaukee, WI 53202-4103
Telephone: (414) 276-8511, (800) 558-1010, FAX: (414) 276-8371, Web Site: www.nationalbusinessfurniture.com
Pres: Kent Anderson
CIO & VP: John McCormick
Sr Sls Rep: Mary McCormick

Sr Graphic Designer: Mary Odland
Conducts Business: U.S.
Employees: 150
Primary Market Served: Business & Consumer
Catalog available online
Direct online sales
Advertising/Marketing Budget Related to Direct Marketing: 76-100%
Direct Marketing ad budget: $10,000,000
Direct Mail: 100%
Founded: 1975
Gross sales or billing: $24,800,000

Sells office furniture by catalog throughout the U.S. Branches in Atlanta, Dallas, Los Angeles, New York & Chicago.

THE DMA OFFICEMAX INC

263 Shuman Blvd
Naperville, IL 60563-8147
Telephone: (630) 864-5809, (800) 661-5931, Web Site: www.officemax.com
Mgr Customer Acq: Maureen Gilroy
Employees: 30,000
Primary Market Served: Business & Consumer
Catalog available online
Direct online sales
Gross sales or billing: $2,620,500,000

Office supplies & furniture.

ONE POINT

101 Poplar St Unit 2
Scranton, PA 18509-2745
Telephone: (570) 342-0737, (800) 526-4460, FAX: (570) 343-6361, Web Site: www.opoffice.com
Owner: Pat McMahon
Conducts Business: U.S.
Primary Market Served: Business

Sell examination & office forms, pegboard systems, office desk accessories to physicians, dentists & other health professionals.

PTI PYRAMID TECHNOLOGIES LLC

45 Gracey Ave
Meriden, CT 06451-2284
Telephone: (203) 238-0550, (888) 479-7264, FAX: (203) 634-1696, Web Site: www.pyramid-technologies.com
Sls & Mktg Mgr: Bob Cooper
Primary Market Served: Business

Manufacturer of time clocks, ribbons and inks.

PAASCHE AIRBRUSH CO

4311 N Normandy Ave
Chicago, IL 60634-1395

Telephone: (773) 867-9191, FAX: (773) 867-9198, E-Mail: info@paascheairbrush.com, Web Site: www.paascheairbrush.com
VP: Brian Pettersen
VP & Sls Mgr: John Lagerlof
Asst Sls Mgr: Patricia Lagerlof
Employees: 95
Primary Market Served: Business & Consumer
Catalog available online
Direct online sales
Advertising/Marketing Budget Related to Direct Marketing: 0-25%
Founded: 1904

Manufacturer of the most complete line of artist's airbrushes, industrial, manual & automatic spray guns, paint spray booths & special coating equipment.

PATTERSON DENTAL

1031 Mendota Heights Rd
Saint Paul, MN 55120-1419
Telephone: (651) 686-1600, (800) 328-5536, FAX: (651) 686-9331, Web Site: www.pattersondental.com
Chmn: Peter L. Frechette
Pres, CEO & Dir: James W. Wiltz
Exec VP, CFO & Treas: R. Stephen Armstrong
VP, Opers: Gary D. Johnson
VP: Lynn E. Askew
Mktg Dir: Julie Heck
Conducts Business: U.S.
Primary Market Served: Business
Catalog available online
Direct online sales
Direct Marketing ad budget:
Direct Mail: 90%
Magazines: 3%
Telephone: 7%

Sell practice management supplies (bookkeeping systems, appointment logs, stationery, filing supplies) to the medical & dental industry. Also, business forms, stationery & computer supplies for small businesses & attorneys.

PENNY WISE OFFICE PRODUCTS

6911 Laurel Bowie Rd (Suite 209)
Bowie, MD 20715-1712
Telephone: (301) 805-7733, (800) 942-3311, FAX: (800) 622-4411, Web Site: www.penny-wise.com
VP, Mktg: Kathryn Peffers
Employees: 80
Primary Market Served: Business
Catalog available online
Direct online sales
Advertising/Marketing Budget Related to Direct Marketing: 76-100%
Gross sales or billing: $7,600,000

Sell office products via catalog & the internet.

THE DMA PITNEY BOWES
Div. of Pitney Bowes Americas
1 Elmcroft Rd
Stamford, CT 06926-0700
Telephone: (203) 356-5000, (800) MR-BOWES, Web Site: www.pitneybowes.com
Exec VP & Pres, Mailing Solutions Mngmt: Leslie Abi-Karam
Conducts Business: Worldwide
Employees: 34,454
Primary Market Served: Business
Advertising/Marketing Budget Related to Direct Marketing: 51-75%
Gross sales or billing: $4,213,000

Manufacture mailing systems, including addressing, inserting, weighing, and postage.

PRO CHEMICAL & DYE INC
126 Shove St
Fall River, MA 02724-2039
Telephone: (508) 676-3838, FAX: (508) 676-3980, Web Site: www.prochemicalanddye.com
Pres: Adelle S. Wiener
VP: Donald Wiener
Gen Mgr: Steve Grunebach
Conducts Business: Worldwide
Primary Market Served: Consumer
Catalog available online
Direct online sales
Advertising/Marketing Budget Related to Direct Marketing: 51-75%
Founded: 1970

Sell dyes, chemicals & supplies for batik, silkscreen & dyeing. Suppliers of Pebeo products & PROfab Textile Inks for painting, stenciling & silkscreening, marbling colors & supplies.

THE DMA QUADRIGA ART INC
30 E 33rd St
New York, NY 10016-5317
Telephone: (212) 685-0751
CEO: Tom Schulhof
Primary Market Served: Business & Consumer

QUALITY PRODUCTS INC
2415 Hwy 45 N, PO Box 564
Columbus, MS 39703
Telephone: (662) 328-1477, (800) 647-1057, FAX: (800) 824-8510, E-Mail: kshep@classroomsupply.com, Web Site: www.classroomsupply.com
Pres: Fred Jones
Conducts Business: U.S.
Employees: 14
Primary Market Served: Business
Catalog available online

Direct online sales
Advertising/Marketing Budget Related to Direct Marketing: 76-100%
Direct Marketing ad budget:
Direct Mail: 90%
Online: 10%
Founded: 1964

Sell school items.

RENTON'S INC
6551 S Revere Pkwy (Suite 205)
Centennial, CO 80111-6411
Telephone: (303) 865-7025, (800) 365-6644, E-Mail: info@rentons.com, Web Site: www.rentons.com
Owner: Dawn Goldwasser
Employees: 4
Primary Market Served: Business
Catalog available online
Direct online sales
Founded: 1989

Mail order business-to-business labels.

THE RYTEX CO
CD Bakehorn Inc/The Rytex Co
100 N Park Ave
Peru, IN 46970-1701
Telephone: (317) 872-8553, (800) 277-5458, FAX: (317) 872-8535, (800) 329-1669, Web Site: www.rytex.com
Pres & Owner: Mike Bakehorn
Gen Mgr: Bob Ellett
Primary Market Served: Consumer
Advertising/Marketing Budget Related to Direct Marketing: 76-100%
Direct Marketing ad budget:
Direct Mail: 100%
Founded: 1929

Catalog & retail sales of personalized stationery.

SAX ARTS & CRAFTS
Div. of School Specialty, Inc
PO Box 1579
Appleton, WI 54912-1579
Telephone: (800) 558-6696, FAX: (800) 328-4729, E-Mail: info@saxarts.com, Web Site: www.saxarts.com
Sls Mgr: Mary Reilly
Exec VP: John Thoreson
Exec VP Dir Mktg - School Specialty: David Johnson
Conducts Business: U.S.
Employees: 160
Primary Market Served: Business
Advertising/Marketing Budget Related to Direct Marketing: 0-25%
Founded: 1945

Full line of art supplies to schools.

DANIEL SMITH INC
4150 First Ave S
Seattle, WA 98134

Telephone: (206) 223-9599, (800) 426-6740, FAX: (800) 238-4065, E-Mail: sales@danielsmith.com, Web Site: www.danielsmith.com
Owner: Daniel Smith
CEO: John Cogley
VP, Mktg & Sls: Debra Kehoe
Conducts Business: Worldwide
Employees: 150
Primary Market Served: Consumer
Catalog available online
Direct online sales
Founded: 1976

Cataloger/retailer of fine artists' materials.

THE DMA STANDARD REGISTER
600 Albany St
Dayton, OH 45417-3405
Telephone: (937) 221-1000, (800) 755-6405, FAX: (937) 221-1239, E-Mail: julie.mcewan@standardregister.com, Web Site: www.standardregister.com
Pres & CEO: Dennis L. Rediker
Exec VP & COO: Peter A. Dorsman
Sr VP, Treas & CFO: Craig J. Brown
Sr VP, HR: M. Jay Romans
Pub Rels Mgr: Julie McEwan
Pres & CEO SMARTworks: Joe Morgan
VP, Sls: Charlie Simmons
Dir, Mktg: Kathy Harper
Conducts Business: U.S.
Employees: 5,200
Primary Market Served: Business
Direct online sales
Founded: 1912
Gross sales or billing: $1,100,000,000

An information solutions company that helps businesses make the most of their information. Focused on understanding and meeting customers' unique challenges with complete solutions ranging from electronic and paper-based business communications to compliance and bar-code labeling to document-management systems and integration services to workflow consulting.

THE DMA STAPLES INC
500 Staples Dr
Framingham, MA 01702-4474
Telephone: (508) 253-5000, FAX: (508) 253-7803, Web Site: www.staples.com
Sr VP: Peter Howard
Conducts Business: U.S., Canada
Employees: 50,000
Primary Market Served: Business & Consumer
Founded: 1986
Gross sales or billing: $3,000,000,000

Sell discount office supplies to small & mid-sized businesses & to home offices.

STRATFORD HALL

1680 Roe Crest Dr
North Mankato, MN 56003-2658
Telephone: (708) 496-4908, (800) 628-9028, FAX: (708) 496-8058, E-Mail: stratfordhall@myprinter.com, Web Site: www.stratfordhall.com
VP, Opers: Tom Kleen
Mktg Dir: Dolores Milam
Conducts Business: U.S.
Employees: 300
Primary Market Served: Business & Consumer

Sell personalized Christmas cards.

SUNRISE BUSINESS PRODUCTS

69 E Jericho Tpke
Mineola, NY 11501
Telephone: (800) 222-7367, FAX: (631) 588-3900
Pres: Joseph Caldwell
Conducts Business: U.S., Canada
Employees: 21
Primary Market Served: Business
Catalog available online
Indirect online sales
Advertising/Marketing Budget Related to Direct Marketing: 0-25%
Direct Marketing ad budget: $300,000
Direct Mail: $200,000
Magazines: $50,000
Telephone: $50,000
Founded: 1945
Gross sales or billing: $4,500,000

Supplier of office products, industrial products and restaurant supplies.

SUPERIOR REAL ESTATE SUPPLY

8373 W Troy St
Phoenix, AZ 85382-8095
Telephone: (623) 516-9202, (800) 234-0095, FAX: (623) 516-9209, E-Mail: sales@superiorrealestatesupply.com, Web Site: www.superiorrealestate.com
Pres: Peggy Nystrom
Primary Market Served: Business
Direct Marketing ad budget:
Online: 100%
Founded: 1989

Real estate marketing supplies.

TALAS

330 Morgan Ave
Brooklyn, NY 11211
Telephone: (212) 219-0770, FAX: (212) 219-0735, E-Mail: info@talasonline.com, Web Site: www.talasonline.com
CEO: Jacob Salic
Employees: 25
Primary Market Served: Business & Consumer
Catalog available online
Founded: 2006

THINK INK

9709 Riverbend Dr
Bothell, WA 98011-4030
Telephone: (425) 778-1935, (800) 778-1935, E-Mail: jean.lewis1@comcast.net, Web Site: www.thinkink.net
Owner: Jean Lewis
Primary Market Served: Business & Consumer
Catalog available online
Direct online sales
Founded: 1981

Hand-operated printers & embossing powder.

TUTTLE PRINTING & ENGRAVING

414 Quality Ln
Rutland, VT 05702
Telephone: (802) 773-9171, (800) 776-7682, FAX: (802) 773-5785, E-Mail: info@tuttleprinting.com, Web Site: www.tuttleprinting.com
Chmn: Deva M. Bolgioni
Pres: Joanne Cillo
VP, Plant Opers: Paul Bishop
VP, Telesls: Eugenia Cooke
Dir, Mktg: Patrick J. McMorrow
Conducts Business: U.S.
Employees: 61
Primary Market Served: Business
Catalog available online
Direct online sales
Advertising/Marketing Budget Related to Direct Marketing: 76-100%
Direct Marketing ad budget:
Direct Mail: 80%
Magazines: 15%
Online: 5%
Founded: 1912

Professional stationery and professional office supplies & services.

UTRETCH ART SUPPLIES

6 Corporate Dr Ste 1
Cranbury, NJ 08512-3616
Telephone: (609) 409-8001, (800) 223-9132, FAX: (800) 382-1979, Web Site: www.utrechtart.com
Web Content Mgr: Don Rodriguez
Primary Market Served: Business & Consumer

VAGABOND CREATIONS INC

2560 Lance Dr
Dayton, OH 45409-1581
Telephone: (937) 298-1124, (800) 738-7237, FAX: (937) 298-1124, E-Mail: sales@vagabondcreations.net, Web Site: www.vagabondcreations.net
Pres: George F. Stanley Jr.
Conducts Business: U.S., Canada, Japan
Employees: 5
Primary Market Served: Business
Catalog available online
Direct online sales
Advertising/Marketing Budget Related to Direct Marketing: 76-100%
Direct Marketing ad budget: $2,000
Direct Mail: 20%
Online: 60%
Telephone: 20%
Founded: 1955
Gross sales or billing: $110,000

Illustrated stationery tablets with assorted pages. Sell to all types of retail outlets.

APSCO

7994 CR Ten
Davenport Center, NY 13751
Telephone: (607) 278-6218, FAX:
(607) 278-6218, E-Mail:
webmaster@antiquephono.com, Web
Site: www.antiquephono.com
Owner: Dennis J. Valente
Owner: Patricia F. Valente
Conducts Business: Worldwide
Employees: 2
Primary Market Served: Business &
Consumer
Catalog available online
Indirect online sales
Direct Marketing ad budget: $800
Magazines: 5%
Newspapers: 95%
Founded: 1976
Gross sales or billing: $125,000

Repairs, parts & service for antique &
wind-up phonographs. Steel needles,
record sleeves, steel mainsprings &
decals. Sell to dealers, hobbyists &
collectors. Supply catalog is $3.

ACTION DIRECT INC

513 NW 72nd St
Miami, FL 33150-3731
Telephone: (305) 969-0056, E-Mail:
info@action-direct.com, Web Site:
www.action-direct.com
Pres: J.O. Flores
VP: Eliezer Flores
Treas: Omar Flores
Conducts Business: US
Employees: 9
Primary Market Served: Business &
Consumer
Catalog available online
Direct online sales
Advertising/Marketing Budget Related
to Direct Marketing: 76-100%
Direct Marketing ad budget: $500,000
Direct Mail: 35%
Magazines: 5%
Online: 60%
Founded: 1981

Publisher of camping, hunting, self
defense & outdoor merchandise
catalogs.

ACUSPORT CORP

1 Hunter Pl
Bellefontaine, OH 43311-3001
Telephone: (937) 593-7010, FAX:
(937) 592-5625, E-Mail: mwsales@
acusport.com, Web Site: www.
acusport.com
Chmn & CEO: William L. Fraim
Pres & COO: James A. Broering
Dir, IT: Deb Ward
Prod Mgr: Rick Robinson
Conducts Business: U.S.
Employees: 150
Primary Market Served: Business
Direct online sales
Advertising/Marketing Budget Related
to Direct Marketing: 76-100%
Founded: 1965
Gross sales or billing: $142,000,000

Distributor of hunting & shooting
sports products.

AKERS SKI INC

51 Akers Way
Andover, ME 04216
Telephone: (207) 392-4582, FAX:
(207) 392-1225, E-Mail: sales@
akers-ski.com, Web Site: www.akers-
ski.com
Pres: Leon Akers
Conducts Business: U.S.
Employees: 5
Primary Market Served: Consumer
Catalog available online
Direct online sales
Advertising/Marketing Budget Related
to Direct Marketing: 76-100%
Founded: 1958

Sell cross-country ski equipment &
accessories via mail order.

ALLBRANDS.COM SEWING MACHINE SUPERSTORE

20415 Highland Rd
Baton Rouge, LA 70817-7348
Telephone: (225) 923-1285, (866) 255-
2726, FAX: (225) 923-1261, E-Mail:
info@allbrands.com, Web Site:
www.allbrands.com
Owner & Teacher: Annette Douthat
Owner & Technician: John M. Douthat
VP, Opers: Warren Sagen
Conducts Business: Worldwide
Employees: 20
Primary Market Served: Business &
Consumer
Catalog available online
Direct online sales
Advertising/Marketing Budget Related
to Direct Marketing: 0-25%
Direct Marketing ad budget: $250,000
Magazines: $50,000
Newspapers: $50,000
Online: $100,000
Telephone: $50,000
Founded: 1976
Gross sales or billing: $12,000,000

Sewing, embroidery, serger, knitting, &
industrial machines for home &
industry. Also, vacuum cleaners and
small appliances.

AMERICAN HORSE PRODUCTS

Div. of Interfab Corp
31896 Plaza Dr (Suite C4)
San Juan Capistrano, CA 92675
Telephone: (949) 248-5300, (800) 500-
0799, FAX: (949) 248-5305, E-Mail:
zjim@sbcglobal.net, Web Site: www.
americanhorseproducts.com
Pres: James Carter
Mktg: Diane Carter
Office Mgr: Mary Weinik
Sls: Lori Melville
Buyer: Lorinda Engelhorn
Conducts Business: U.S.
Employees: 12
Primary Market Served: Consumer
Catalog available online
Direct online sales
Advertising/Marketing Budget Related
to Direct Marketing: 51-75%
Direct Marketing ad budget: $200,000
Direct Mail: 75%
Magazines: 15%
Online: 10%
Founded: 1998
Gross sales or billing: $2,500,000

Products for horses including saddles,
boots, supplements, topicals, hoof care,
grooming & leather care products,
books, music & trail accessories.

AMERICAN RECREATION PRODUCTS INC

Div. of Kellwood Corp
1224 Fern Ridge Pkwy
Saint Louis, MO 63141-4404
Telephone: (314) 576-8000, FAX:
(314) 576-8072
Chmn: Hal Upbin
VP Fin: Len Klonowski
VP, Opers: Tim Hinds
Mktg & Sls Mgr: Eric Reinsfelder
Conducts Business: U.S., Canada
Employees: 750
Primary Market Served: Business

Manufacturer of outdoor recreational
gear: tents, sleeping bags, backpacks &
sleep systems. Retail stores & catalogs.

AMPERSAND PRESS

750 Lake St
Port Townsend, WA 98368-2216
Telephone: (360) 379-5187, (800) 624-
4263, FAX: (360) 379-0324, E-Mail:
info@ampersandpress.com, Web
Site: www.ampersandpress.com
Pres: Lou Haller
Conducts Business: U.S., Canada, Aus-
tralia
Employees: 6
Primary Market Served: Business

Catalog available online
Direct online sales
Advertising/Marketing Budget Related
to Direct Marketing: 0-25%
Direct Marketing ad budget: $500
Magazines: 100%
Founded: 1973
Gross sales or billing: $1,000,000

Nature & science games, rubber
stamps & educational materials &
supplies.

ANGLER'S CATALOG CO
3551 W Deerfield Dr
Eagle, ID 83616
Telephone: (208) 378-9536, (800) 657-
8040, FAX: (208) 735-8758, E-Mail:
sales@anglers-catalog.com, Web
Site: www.anglers-catalog.com
Owner: John Meyer
Conducts Business: Worldwide
Employees: 4
Primary Market Served: Business &
Consumer
Catalog available online
Direct online sales
Founded: 1976
Gross sales or billing: $600,000

Unique gift ideas for the fly fisherman.

THE ANGLER'S DEN
11 W Main St (Suite 4)
Pawling, NY 12564-1341
Telephone: (845) 855-5182, E-Mail:
flyfish@anglersden.net, Web Site:
www.anglersden.net
Partner: Rob O'Neill
Conducts Business: U.S., Canada
Employees: 2
Primary Market Served: Consumer
Catalog available online
Indirect online sales
Advertising/Marketing Budget Related
to Direct Marketing: 51-75%
Direct Marketing ad budget: $15,000
Direct Mail: 30%
Magazines: 70%
Founded: 1984
Gross sales or billing: $100,000

High quality fly tying materials. Specialize in natural & hard-to-find. Catalogs upon request ($2.50 a piece).

ANNIE'S ATTIC LLC
111 Corporate Dr
Big Sandy, TX 75755-2446
Telephone: (903) 636-4303, FAX:
(903) 636-4088, Web Site: www.
anniesattic.com
CEO & Pres: David McKee
Partner: Arthur K. Muselman
VP, Sls & Mktg: Marge Evans
VP: Dan Kennedy
Conducts Business: U.S., Canada
Employees: 150

Primary Market Served: Business &
Consumer
Catalog available online
Direct online sales
Advertising/Marketing Budget Related
to Direct Marketing: 76-100%

Mail order needlecraft company specializing in crochet & needlecraft
patterns.

ANTIQUE & COLLECTIBLE TOOLS INC
27 Fickett Rd
Pownal, ME 04069
Telephone: (207) 688-4962, FAX:
(207) 688-4831, E-Mail: ceb@
finetoolj.com, Web Site: www.
finetoolj.com
Pres: Clarence Blanchard
Conducts Business: Worldwide
Employees: 4
Primary Market Served: Business &
Consumer
Catalog available online
Direct online sales
Advertising/Marketing Budget Related
to Direct Marketing: 76-100%
Direct Marketing ad budget:
Direct Mail: $10,000
Magazines: $4,000
Founded: 1970

Market antique, obsolete & vintage
hand tools through "The Fine Tool
Journal" for collectors & craftsmen.
Also market books on antique tools
and sell advertising in "Fine Tool
Journal." Direct sales of vintage, high
quality hand tools. Quarterly absentee
auction of antique tools.

ATLANTA CUTLERY CORP
2147 Gees Mill Rd
Conyers, GA 30013-1333
Telephone: (770) 922-3700, (800) 833-
8838, FAX: (770) 760-8993, E-Mail:
webmaster@atlantacutlery.com, Web
Site: www.atlantacutlery.com
CEO: Pradeep Windlass
Pres: Sudhir Windlass
VP: Robin Chauduri
VP: Dave DiPietro
VP: Bruce Brookhurt
Conducts Business: Worldwide
Employees: 45
Primary Market Served: Business &
Consumer
Catalog available online
Direct online sales
Advertising/Marketing Budget Related
to Direct Marketing: 76-100%
Direct Marketing ad budget:
$1,200,000
Direct Mail: 60%
Magazines: 10%
Online: 30%

Founded: 1971
Gross sales or billing: $9,000,000

Hunting, survival & military issue
knives plus finished blades, handle
materials & books for knifemakers.

BARON/BARCLAY BRIDGE SUPPLIES
Div. of Devyn Press
3600 Chamberlain Ln (Suite 206)
Louisville, KY 40241
Telephone: (502) 426-0410, (800) 274-
2221, FAX: (502) 426-2044, E-Mail:
baronbarclay@baronbarclay.com,
Web Site: www.baronbarclay.com
Founder: Randall Baron
Pres: Jim Maier
VP: Mary Baron
Conducts Business: Worldwide
Employees: 12
Primary Market Served: Business &
Consumer
Catalog available online
Direct online sales
Advertising/Marketing Budget Related
to Direct Marketing: 51-75%
Founded: 1942

Everything on the game of bridge.

BART'S WATERSPORTS
7581 E 800th N
North Webster, IN 46555-9604
Telephone: (574) 834-7666, (800) 348-
5016, FAX: (574) 834-4246, E-Mail:
info@barts.com, Web Site: www.
bartswatersports.com
Pres: J. Bart Culver
CEO: Bringier McConnell
Art Dir: Judy Wagner
Mgr: Michael Wilson
Conducts Business: Worldwide
Employees: 45
Primary Market Served: Business &
Consumer
Catalog available online
Direct online sales
Advertising/Marketing Budget Related
to Direct Marketing: 76-100%
Founded: 1971

Discount marketer of water sports
equipment & accessories.

BASS PRO SHOPS
2500 E Kearney
Springfield, MO 65898-0001
Telephone: (417) 873-5000, FAX:
(417) 873-5882, Web Site: www.
basspro.com
Founder: John Morris
COO: Jim Hagale
Dir, Corp Database Mktg: Carl Ken-
drick
Dir, Database Mktg: Timothy Scott
Conducts Business: Worldwide

Employees: 4,000
Primary Market Served: Business &
Consumer
Catalog available online
Direct online sales
Founded: 1969

Catalog & retail marketer of fishing,
hunting & outdoor recreational
products.

BEAR WOODS SUPPLY CO INC

PO Box 275
Cornwallis, NS, Canada B0S 1H0
Telephone: (902) 638-8622, (800) 565-
5066, FAX: (902) 638-8637, Web
Site: www.bearwood.com, www.
woodparts.ca
Pres: Victor Schneweiss
VP-Mktg: Shela Breau
Conducts Business: Canada, U.S.,
U.K., Hong Kong, Iceland, New
Zealand
Employees: 10
Primary Market Served: Business &
Consumer
Catalog available online
Direct online sales
Advertising/Marketing Budget Related
to Direct Marketing: 76-100%
Direct Marketing ad budget:
Magazines: 100%
Founded: 1987

Mail order wood turnings, hardware &
craft supplies.

BEEMAN PRECISION AIRGUNS

SR Industries Inc
10652 Bloomfield Ave
Santa Fe Springs, CA 90670-3912
Telephone: (714) 890-4800, FAX:
(714) 890-4808, E-Mail: sales@
beeman.com, Web Site: www.
beeman.com
Pres: Robert Eck
Conducts Business: Worldwide
Employees: 20
Primary Market Served: Business &
Consumer
Founded: 1971

Importer & distributor of precision
adult air rifles, pistols, pellets & related accessories. Sell through jobbers,
dealers, mail-order & export.

BETTER HEALTH FITNESS

5302 New Utrecht Ave
Brooklyn, NY 11219-4139
Telephone: (718) 436-4693, FAX:
(718) 854-3381, Web Site: www.
betterhealthfitness.com
Pres & Owner: Rita Gottehrer
Gen Mgr: Marvin Friedman

Conducts Business: U.S.
Employees: 9
Primary Market Served: Business &
Consumer
Catalog available online
Direct online sales
Advertising/Marketing Budget Related
to Direct Marketing: 0-25%
Direct Marketing ad budget:
Direct Mail: 10%
Magazines: 70%
Newspapers: 10%
Telephone: 10%
Founded: 1977
Gross sales or billing: $180,000

Fitness & recreation equipment.

BIKE NASHBAR

Div. of Nashbar & Associates Inc
PO Box 1455
Crab Orchard, WV 25827-1455
Telephone: (800) NAS-HBAR, FAX:
(877) 778-9456, E-Mail: custserv@
nashbar.com, Web Site: www.
bikenashbar.com
Pres: Gary Snook
CFO: David Prvitt
VP: Bob Martin
VP, Mktg: Stewart Westland
Conducts Business: U.S., Canada
Employees: 240
Primary Market Served: Consumer
Catalog available online
Direct online sales
Advertising/Marketing Budget Related
to Direct Marketing: 76-100%
Direct Marketing ad budget:
Direct Mail: 80%
Magazines: 20%
Founded: 1974
Gross sales or billing: $30,000,000

Catalog sales of high-tech bicycles,
parts, accessories & apparel.

BITS & PIECES INC

PO Box 4150
Lawrenceburg, IN 47025
Telephone: (866) 503-6395, FAX:
(513) 354-1290, Web Site: www.
bitsandpieces.com
Pres: Alan Segal
Conducts Business: Worldwide
Primary Market Served: Consumer
Catalog available online
Direct online sales
Advertising/Marketing Budget Related
to Direct Marketing: 26-50%
Founded: 1983

Mail order marketer of jigsaw puzzles.

BRIGADE QUARTERMASTERS LTD

177 Georgia Ave
Providence, RI 02905-4422

Telephone: (770) 428-1248, (800) 338-
4327, FAX: (800) 892-2992, Web
Site: www.actiongear.com
Pres: Mitchell L. WerBell IV
CFO: Geoffrey WerBell
Mktg Dir: Wendy Abney
Conducts Business: Worldwide
Employees: 80
Primary Market Served: Business &
Consumer
Advertising/Marketing Budget Related
to Direct Marketing: 76-100%
Founded: 1978
Gross sales or billing: $40,500,000

Sell products for camping, hunting,
survival, military & police use.

BUSHNELL CORPORATION

Owned by Worldwide Sports & Recre-
ation
9200 Cody
Overland Park, KS 66214-1734
Telephone: (913) 752-3400, (800) 423-
3537, FAX: (913) 752-3561, Web
Site: www.bushnell.com
VP, Sls: Mark Welsch
Conducts Business: Worldwide
Employees: 150
Primary Market Served: Business &
Consumer
Founded: 1947

Sell Bushnell, Bausch & Lomb & Jason binoculars, telescopes, riflescopes
& rangefinders.

C&T BRIDGE SUPPLIES

3532 Katella Ave (Suite 103)
Los Alamitos, CA 90720-3138
Telephone: (562) 598-7010, (800) 525-
4718, FAX: (562) 430-8309, E-Mail:
tedinlosal@aol.com
VP: Chris Brown
Conducts Business: Worldwide
Employees: 2
Primary Market Served: Business &
Consumer
Catalog available online
Direct online sales
Advertising/Marketing Budget Related
to Direct Marketing: 51-75%
Direct Marketing ad budget: $10,000
Newspapers: 70%
Telephone: 30%
Founded: 1982
Gross sales or billing: $200,000

Books & supplies about the game of
bridge distributed to individuals &
bridge clubs.

CJ HUMMUL CO

PO Box 522, 422 Third St
Nescapeck, PA 18635-0522

Telephone: (570) 752-0936, (800) 762-0235, FAX: (570) 752-0938, E-Mail: mail@hummul.com, Web Site: www.hummul.com
Pres: Raymond Zajac
Conducts Business: U.S., Canada, Japan, U.K.
Employees: 3
Primary Market Served: Consumer
Catalog available online
Direct online sales
Advertising/Marketing Budget Related to Direct Marketing: 76-100%
Direct Marketing ad budget:
Direct Mail: 98%
Magazines: 2%
Founded: 1977

Woodcarving supplies.

CPM DELTA 1, INC
10830 Sanden Dr
Dallas, TX 75238
Telephone: (214) 349-6886, (800) 627-0252, FAX: (214) 503-1557, Web Site: www.cpmdelta1.com
Adv Mgr & Sls: Teresa Dingus
Dir: Larry Long
Sls: Rick Wait
Conducts Business: Worldwide
Employees: 30
Primary Market Served: Business & Consumer
Advertising/Marketing Budget Related to Direct Marketing: 26-50%
Direct Marketing ad budget: $100,000
Magazines: 100%
Founded: 1972
Gross sales or billing: $2,000,000

Manufacture photographic, darkroom & studio equipment. Sell direct through catalogs to distributors.

THE DMA CABELA'S INC
1 Cabela Dr
Sidney, NE 69160-1001
Telephone: (308) 254-5505, (800) 237-4444, FAX: (308) 254-4800, Web Site: www.cabelas.com
Chmn & Dir: Richard Cabela
Vice Chmn & Dir: James Cabela
Pres & CEO: Dennis Highby
Sr VP of Mdsg Mktg & Retail Opers: Patrick A. Snyder
Sr VP of Bus Devel & Intl Opers: Michael Callahan
Dir, Direct Mktg: Ryan Watchorn
Conducts Business: Worldwide
Employees: 12,000
Primary Market Served: Business & Consumer
Catalog available online
Direct online sales
Founded: 1961
Gross sales or billing: $2,000,000,000

Catalog marketer of outdoor products for fishing, camping, hunting, archery & gift items for the outdoor enthusiasts.

CAMPING WORLD INC
Box 90018
Bowling Green, KY 42102-9018
Telephone: (270) 781-2718, (800) 626-6189, FAX: (270) 796-8991, Web Site: www.campingworld.com
Pres & CEO: Marcus Lemonis
Sr VP, Fin & Info: Kenneth Marshall
VP & Mktg Dir: Murray S. Coker
Retail Mktg Mgr: Cathy Beard
Mail Order Opers Mgr: Jane Browning
Conducts Business: U.S., Canada
Employees: 675
Primary Market Served: Consumer
Catalog available online
Direct online sales
Direct Marketing ad budget: $7,500,000
Direct Mail: $7,250,000
Magazines: $200,000
Newspapers: $30,000
TV/Radio: $20,000
Gross sales or billing: $250,000,000

Mass merchandiser & mail order catalog house for recreational vehicle accessories.

THE CANING SHOP
926 Gilman St
Berkeley, CA 94710
Telephone: (510) 527-5010, (800) 544-3373, FAX: (510) 527-7718, Web Site: www.caning.com
Owner: Jim Widess
Conducts Business: Worldwide
Primary Market Served: Business & Consumer
Catalog available online
Direct online sales
Advertising/Marketing Budget Related to Direct Marketing: 51-75%
Direct Marketing ad budget:
Direct Mail: 100%
Founded: 1969

Complete selection of basketry, chair caning & gourd embellishment supplies, books & tools.

CASCADE OUTFITTERS
604 E 45th St
Boise, ID 83714-4848
Telephone: (208) 322-4411, (800) 223-7328, FAX: (208) 322-5016, E-Mail: mail@cascadeoutfitters.com, Web Site: www.cascadeoutfitters.com
VP: Gary Scott
Conducts Business: U.S., Canada, Japan, Chile, Mexico, Israel, Australia, New Zealand
Employees: 7

Primary Market Served: Consumer
Direct Marketing ad budget: $15,000
Magazines: 100%
Gross sales or billing: $950,000

Sell quality whitewater & outdoor equipment through 80 page catalog.

CATCH THE WIND KITE SHOP
PO Box 973
Lincoln City, OR 97367-0973
Telephone: (541) 994-9500, (800) 227-7878, FAX: (541) 994-4766, E-Mail: catchthewindkites@yahoo.com, Web Site: www.catchthewind.com
Sls Mgr: Lisa M. Herndon
Mgr: Keith Mcneil
Employees: 5
Primary Market Served: Consumer
Founded: 1979

Sells kites, windsocks, banners & fun wind-related items through catalogs & stores.

CHAMPS CORP
311 Manatee Ave W
Bradenton, FL 34205
Telephone: (941) 748-0577, (800) 991-6813, E-Mail: customer_service@champssports.com, Web Site: www.champssports.com
Chmn, Pres & CEO: Matthew D. Serra
Sr VP: Gary M. Bahler
Sr VP: Peter D. Brown
Sr VP: Lauren B. Peters
CFO & Sr VP: Robert W. Mc Hugh
Primary Market Served: Consumer

All types sporting goods. Corp Headquarters (212) 720-3700.

CHAROLETTE FORD TRUNKS
PO Box 495
Dumas, TX 79029
Telephone: (806) 934-8477, (800) 659-5614, FAX: (806) 372-3061, E-Mail: charolette@charolettefordtrunks.com, Web Site: www.charolettefordtrunks.com
Pres: Charolette Ford
Conducts Business: U.S., Canada
Primary Market Served: Business & Consumer
Catalog available online
Direct online sales
Advertising/Marketing Budget Related to Direct Marketing: 51-75%
Direct Marketing ad budget:
Magazines: $30,000
Founded: 1977

Publish trunk parts catalog, how-to-restore trunks & trunk talk.

CHERRY TREE TOYS INC

12446 W State Rd 81
Beloit, WI 53511-8049
Telephone: (608) 314-3090, (800) 848-4363, FAX: (608) 314-3097, E-Mail: sales@cherrytreetoys.com, Web Site: www.cherrytreetoys.com
VP: Matt Simon
Principal: Karen Cooper
Conducts Business: Worldwide
Primary Market Served: Business & Consumer
Catalog available online
Direct online sales

Supply plans, parts, kits, tools, books, supplies & accessories for making wooden toys, whirligigs, doll houses, door harps, clocks & weather instruments.

CHICK HARNESS & SUPPLY INC

dba Chick's Discount Saddlery & Equine Wholesalers
18011 S Dupont Hwy
Harrington, DE 19952-2135
Telephone: (302) 398-4630, (800) 444-2441, FAX: (302) 398-3920, E-Mail: saddles@chicksaddlery.com, Web Site: www.chicksaddlery.com
Pres: Robert L. Fleming
Conducts Business: U.S., Canada, Middle East, Europe
Employees: 55
Primary Market Served: Business & Consumer
Catalog available online
Direct online sales
Advertising/Marketing Budget Related to Direct Marketing: 76-100%
Founded: 1975
Gross sales or billing: $4,100,000

Retailer & wholesaler of products for horse owners.

CON-COR INTERNATIONAL

Div. of James M Conway Corp
8101 E Research Ct Ste 101
Tucson, AZ 85710-6758
Telephone: (520) 721-8939, (888) 255-7688, FAX: (520) 721-8940, Web Site: www.con-cor.com
Pres: James Conway
Conducts Business: U.S., Canada
Employees: 15
Primary Market Served: Consumer
Catalog available online
Direct online sales
Founded: 1959

Sell a large selection of model trains & railroad books & videos.

CRAZY CROW TRADING POST

1801 Airport Rd, PO Box 847
Pottsboro, TX 75076-3094
Telephone: (903) 786-2287, (800) 786-6210, FAX: (903) 786-9059, E-Mail: info@crazycrow.com, Web Site: www.crazycrow.com
Owner: J. Rex Reddick
Mktg Dir: Jessica Reddick
Conducts Business: U.S., Canada, Europe
Employees: 35
Primary Market Served: Business & Consumer
Catalog available online
Direct online sales
Advertising/Marketing Budget Related to Direct Marketing: 26-50%
Direct Marketing ad budget: $100,000
Direct Mail: 85%
Magazines: 10%
Telephone: 5%
Founded: 1970
Gross sales or billing: $5,000,000

American Indian craft supplies & muzzleloading supplies to Indians, hobbyists, crafts people, muzzleloaders & buckskinners.

CUSTOM ACCESSORIES

6440 W Howard St
Niles, IL 60714-3391
Telephone: (847) 966-6900, (800) 962-6676, FAX: (847) 966-9650, Web Site: www.causa.com
Chmn Bd: Abe Matthew
Pres: Ken Matthew
Sr Exec VP: Norman Matthew
Conducts Business: U.S.
Employees: 30
Primary Market Served: Business
Catalog available online
Indirect online sales
Advertising/Marketing Budget Related to Direct Marketing: 0-25%

Auto compasses, Sherrill compasses, private labels & automotive accessories.

DIMMOCK HILL GOLF COURSE PRO SHOP

638 Dimmock Hill Rd
Binghamton, NY 13905-9801
Telephone: (607) 729-5511, (800) 727-5511, FAX: (607) 797-7434, Web Site: www.dimmockhill.com
Owner: Michael Senio
Conducts Business: U.S.
Employees: 8
Primary Market Served: Business & Consumer
Catalog available online
Indirect online sales
Advertising/Marketing Budget Related to Direct Marketing: 51-75%
Direct Marketing ad budget: $50,000
Direct Mail: 10%
Magazines: 40%
Newspapers: 40%
TV/Radio: 10%
Founded: 1970
Gross sales or billing: $1,500,000

Professional golf equipment to golfers.

DIRECT SPORTS SUPPLY

Eastern Gun & Supply Co Inc
1720 Curve Rd
Pearisburg, VA 24134
Telephone: (540) 921-1243, (800) 456-0072, FAX: (540) 921-1475, Web Site: www.directsports.com
VP & CEO: Mike Lively
Pres: Paul V. Wagner
Sec & Treas: Charlotte Wagner
Conducts Business: U.S., England, Germany
Employees: 10
Primary Market Served: Consumer
Advertising/Marketing Budget Related to Direct Marketing: 76-100%
Direct Marketing ad budget:
Direct Mail: $15,000
Newspapers: $6,000
Gross sales or billing: $2,000,000

Sell softball & baseball supplies to consumers.

DOVER SADDLERY

525 Great Rd
Littleton, MA 01460-6221
Telephone: (978) 952-8062, (800) 406-8204, Web Site: www.doversaddlery.com
VP: Lorelle Carpenter
Founded: 1975

Saddlery shop

E HILLE, ANGLER'S SUPPLY HOUSE

441 William St
Williamsport, PA 17701-6103
Telephone: (570) 323-7564, (800) 326-6612, FAX: (570) 323-9995, Web Site: www.anglersupplyhouse.com
Owner: Ken Beane
Owner: Cindi Beane
Store Mgr: Chris Beane
Conducts Business: Worldwide
Employees: 2
Primary Market Served: Business & Consumer
Catalog available online
Direct online sales
Advertising/Marketing Budget Related to Direct Marketing: 76-100%
Direct Marketing ad budget:
Direct Mail: 50%
Online: 50%
Founded: 1932
Gross sales or billing: $200,000

Sell materials for making fishing flies & lures. Also rod kits & fishing tackle.

EWA & MINIATURE CARS USA INC

369 Springfield Ave., P.O. Box 188
Berkeley Heights, NJ 07922-0188
Telephone: (732) 424-7811, (800) 392-
4454, FAX: (732) 424-7814, E-Mail:
ewa@ewacars.com
Pres: Eric Waiter
VP: Carl Pflanzer
Conducts Business: U.S., Canada
Employees: 12
Primary Market Served: Business &
Consumer
Founded: 1981

Sell model cars, auto books, auto videos & magazines to consumers &
businesses.

EAGLE CLAW FISHING TACKLE

Privately owned by Wright/McGill Co
4245 E 46th Ave
Denver, CO 80216-3219
Telephone: (303) 321-1481, FAX:
(303) 321-4750, E-Mail: info@
eagleclaw.com, Web Site: www.
eagleclaw.com
Owner & Chmn: Lee McGill
Vice Chmn: Bill Miller
Pres: John Jilling
Sr VP, Sls: Tenny Mount
Programmer: Jackie Hock
Conducts Business: Worldwide
Primary Market Served: Business &
Consumer
Catalog available online
Direct online sales
Advertising/Marketing Budget Related
to Direct Marketing: 0-25%
Founded: 1925

Manufacturer of Eagle Claw fish
hooks, rods, reels & fishing apparel.

EBERSOLE LAPIDARY SUPPLY INC

5830 W Hendryx St
Wichita, KS 67209-1234
Telephone: (316) 945-4771, (877)
EBERSOLE, FAX: (316) 945-4773,
E-Mail: ebersolerocks@sbcglobal.
net, Web Site: www.ebersolelapidary.
com
Pres: Del Ebersole
VP: Len Ebersole
Treas: Carolyn Hendryx
Conducts Business: U.S.
Employees: 4
Primary Market Served: Business &
Consumer
Catalog available online
Direct online sales
Direct Marketing ad budget: $35,000
TV/Radio: 100%

Complete lapidary line: jewelry mount-
ings, equipment, tools & supplies for
the hobbyist. Shells, rough rock cabs
& books. Arts & crafts, casting & sil-
versmithing supplies & equipment.
Complete art supplies: brushes, paints,
canvas, paper, pens, inks, solvents,
mediums, books & pastels. Wood
forms & plaques.

EDWIN WATTS GOLF

20 Hill Ave
Fort Walton Beach, FL 32548
Telephone: (850) 244-2066, (800) 874-
0146, FAX: (850) 244-5217, Web
Site: www.edwinwatts.com
CEO & Pres: Edwin Watts
VP Catalog & Online: John Watts
VP Mktg & Adv: Lincoln Cox
Conducts Business: Worldwide
Primary Market Served: Consumer
Catalog available online
Direct online sales
Founded: 1968

Retailer of golf equipment: clubs, bags,
balls & shoes.

ESTES INDUSTRIES

aka Estes-Cox Corp
1295 "H" St
Penrose, CO 81240
Telephone: (719) 372-6565, FAX:
(719) 372-3419, Web Site: www.
estesrockets.com
Pres: Barry Tunick
CFO: James Mauss
Mktg Dir: Mike Fritz
Conducts Business: U.S.
Employees: 200
Primary Market Served: Business &
Consumer
Advertising/Marketing Budget Related
to Direct Marketing: 0-25%
Founded: 1958
Gross sales or billing: $17,000,000

Manufacturer of flying model rockets
& airplanes, engines & accessory products sold to the public through retail
distribution throughout the U.S.

ETCHWORLD

176-180 Fifth Ave
Hawthorne, NJ 07506
Telephone: (973) 423-4002, (800) 872-
3458, FAX: (973) 427-8823, Web
Site: www.etchworld.com
Pres: Terrence Picone
VP: Sydney St. James
Primary Market Served: Consumer
Catalog available online
Direct online sales
Advertising/Marketing Budget Related
to Direct Marketing: 0-25%
Founded: 1975

Glass etching & mirror decorating
supplies.

FAO SCHWARZ

767 Fifth Ave
New York, NY 10153
Telephone: (212) 644-9400, (800) 426-
TOYS, FAX: (212) 688-6053, Web
Site: www.fao.com
Chmn & CEO: Bud Johnson
VP: Michelle Geshkovich
CEO: Edward Schmultz
Pres & CMO: David Niggli
Exec VP: Kim Richmond
Sr VP: Claudia Sandoval
Conducts Business: U.S.
Employees: 2,000
Primary Market Served: Consumer
Catalog available online
Direct online sales
Advertising/Marketing Budget Related
to Direct Marketing: 76-100%
Founded: 1862

Retail toy stores, on-line store & mail-
order catalog.

FAUNTLEROY SUPPLY CO/ WING SUPPLY

PO Box 368
Greenville, KY 42345
Telephone: (270) 338-5866, (800) 388-
9464, FAX: (270) 338-0057, Web
Site: www.wingsupply.com
Pres: Walter Fauntleroy
Gen Mgr: Joey Steele
Conducts Business: U.S.
Employees: 75
Primary Market Served: Consumer
Catalog available online
Direct online sales
Direct Marketing ad budget:
Direct Mail: 5%
Online: 95%
Founded: 1975

Sell hunting & sports clothing.

FREEPORT MUSIC INC

65 Clove Ave
Farmingville, NY 11738-1630
Telephone: (631) 549-4108, (888) 549-
4108, E-Mail: sales@
musicalinstruments.com; sales@
freeportmusic.com, Web Site: www.
musicalinstruments.com
Pres: Steve Interrante
Conducts Business: Worldwide
Primary Market Served: Business &
Consumer
Catalog available online
Direct online sales
Advertising/Marketing Budget Related
to Direct Marketing: 76-100%
Founded: 1921

Sell name brand & hard-to-find musical instruments & accessories at discount prices.

FROG TOOL CO LTD
2169 IL Rte 26
Dixon, IL 61021-9217
Telephone: (815) 288-3811, E-Mail: info@frogwoodtools.com, Web Site: www.frogwoodtools.com
Pres: Richard Watkins
Conducts Business: Worldwide
Employees: 4
Primary Market Served: Business & Consumer
Catalog available online
Indirect online sales
Advertising/Marketing Budget Related to Direct Marketing: 76-100%
Direct Marketing ad budget:
Direct Mail: $10,000
Magazines: $11,000
Online: $1,000
Founded: 1961
Gross sales or billing: $1,900,000

Catalog sales of hand woodworking tools, books on woodworking & wood finishing materials.

GAMETIME INC
Subs. of Playcore Wisconsin
150 Playcore Dr
Fort Payne, AL 35967
Telephone: (256) 845-5610, (800) 633-2394, FAX: (256) 845-9361/2649, Web Site: www.gametime.com
Pres & CEO: Bob Fansworth
Sr VP Opers: Spencer Cheak
Mktg Coord: Matt Meeks
VP, Sls & Mktg: Tom Norquist
VP HR: David H. Hammelman
Conducts Business: Worldwide
Employees: 1,000
Primary Market Served: Business & Consumer
Catalog available online
Indirect online sales
Advertising/Marketing Budget Related to Direct Marketing: 0-25%
Gross sales or billing: $30,000,000

Park, playground, site furnishings & sports equipment.

GILMAN'S LAPIDARY SUPPLY
726 Durham St
Hellertown, PA 18055-1926
Telephone: (610) 838-8767, FAX: (610) 838-2961, E-Mail: info@ lostcave.com, Web Site: www. lostcave.com
Partner: Robert Gilman
Conducts Business: Worldwide
Employees: 15

Primary Market Served: Business & Consumer
Advertising/Marketing Budget Related to Direct Marketing: 0-25%
Gross sales or billing: $500,000

Products for all aspects of jewelry making including findings, cut & rough gem stones, metals, small tools, saws, grinders & polishers, lapidary & lapidary equipment & metal detectors

GOLF HAUS
700 N Pennsylvania Ave
Lansing, MI 48906-5319
Telephone: (517) 482-8842, FAX: (517) 482-8843
Owner: Jim Hornberger
Employees: 3
Primary Market Served: Consumer
Advertising/Marketing Budget Related to Direct Marketing: 0-25%
Founded: 1973

Pro-Line golf clubs, bags & balls.

GOLFSMITH INTERNATIONAL INC
11000 N IH-35
Austin, TX 78753-3152
Telephone: (512) 821-4050, (800) 813-6897, FAX: (512) 837-9347, E-Mail: comments@golfsmith.com, Web Site: www.golfsmith.com
Pres & Co-Owner: Carl F. Paul
VP & Co-Owner: Frank C. Paul
VP & Gen Mgr: Ken Brugh
VP Mktg: Barry Rinke
VP Opers: Curt Young
VP DM: Steve Jones
Conducts Business: Worldwide
Employees: 1,400
Primary Market Served: Consumer
Catalog available online
Direct online sales
Advertising/Marketing Budget Related to Direct Marketing: 76-100%
Direct Marketing ad budget:
Direct Mail: 75%
Magazines: 10%
Newspapers: 15%
Founded: 1967

Golf club components, tools, supplies & accessories.

GUN VIDEO CATALOG/LMP
4585 Murphy Canyon Rd
San Diego, CA 92123-4318
Telephone: (858) 569-4000, (800) 942-8273, FAX: (858) 569-0505, Web Site: www.gunvideo.com; www. glockstore.com
Owner & Pres: Lenny Magill
Exec Asst: Stacy Eckstein
Bus Mgr: Chad Casper
Conducts Business: Worldwide

Employees: 40
Primary Market Served: Business & Consumer
Catalog available online
Direct online sales
Advertising/Marketing Budget Related to Direct Marketing: 0-25%
Direct Marketing ad budget:
Direct Mail: 80%
Magazines: 20%
Founded: 1983

Sell self-defense/firearms instructional videos to consumers, dealers, gun stores, sporting goods stores & the military.

HAPPY JACK INC
PO Box 475
Snow Hill, NC 28580
Telephone: (252) 747-2911, (800) 326-5225, FAX: (252) 747-4111, E-Mail: happyjack@happyjackinc.com, Web Site: www.happyjackinc.com
Co-Owner: Ashe B. Exum
Co-Owner: Joe Exum
Conducts Business: U.S.
Employees: 10
Advertising/Marketing Budget Related to Direct Marketing: 0-25%
Founded: 1946
Gross sales or billing: $3,900,000

Sell animal health products for dogs, cats & horses. Also, sportswear & gifts for the outdoorsman.

THE DMA HASBRO INC
1027 Newport Ave
Pawtucket, RI 02861-2500
Telephone: (401) 727-5000, (800) 242-7276, FAX: (401) 727-5121, Web Site: www.hasbro.com
Chmn & CEO: Alan Hassenfeld
Sr VP Mktg Svcs: Edward Kriete
Pres US Toy Grp & COO: Alfred Verrecchia
Conducts Business: Worldwide
Primary Market Served: Consumer

Manufacturer of toys for U.S. & international sales. Utilize direct marketing via package inserts & direct mail.

HEARTHSIDE QUILTS & SUPPLIES
90 Mechanicsville Rd, PO Box 610
Hinesburg, VT 05461
Telephone: (802) 482-7800, (800) 451-3533, FAX: (802) 482-7803, E-Mail: hearthsidequilts@att.net, Web Site: www.hearthsidequilts.com
Pres: George Wachob
Conducts Business: U.S., Canada, Europe, Australia, Japan, New Zealand
Employees: 14

Primary Market Served: Business & Consumer
Catalog available online
Direct online sales
Direct Marketing ad budget: $120,000
Direct Mail: 20%
Magazines: 60%
Telephone: 20%
Founded: 1981
Gross sales or billing: $950,000

Sell full line of pre-cut quilt kits & sewing supplies. Also, custom die-cutting of fabric shapes.

HERRSCHNERS INC
2800 Hoover Rd
Stevens Point, WI 54492-0001
Telephone: (715) 341-4554, (800) 441-0838, FAX: (715) 341-2250, E-Mail: customerservice@herrschners.com, Web Site: www.herrschners.com
Pres: Ted Hesemann
VP Mktg: John Gritzmacher
Conducts Business: U.S., Canada
Employees: 200
Primary Market Served: Consumer
Advertising/Marketing Budget Related to Direct Marketing: 76-100%
Gross sales or billing: $33,700,000

Catalog sales operation selling needle-craft kits & supplies to the consumer.

HIREKO GOLF
16185 Stephens St
City of Industry, CA 91745
Telephone: (800) 367-8912, FAX: (888) 367-8912, E-Mail: support@hirekogolf.com, Web Site: www.hireko.com
Primary Market Served: Business & Consumer

HOBBY BUILDERS SUPPLY
2388 Pleasantdale Rd
Atlanta, GA 30340
Telephone: (770) 242-1498, (800) 223-7171, FAX: (770) 242-1497, (800) 926-6464, Web Site: www.miniatures.com
Mktg Mgr: Sue Johnson
Primary Market Served: Consumer

World supplier of doll houses & miniature supplies.

HOBBY SURPLUS SALES
Sub. of Amato's Enterprises, LLC
287 Main St
New Britain, CT 06050-2202
Telephone: (860) 223-0600, (800) 233-0872, FAX: (860) 225-5316, E-Mail: amatohobby@sbcglobal.net, Web Site: www.hobbysurplus.com
Owner: Vincent Amato
Owner & Principal: Sheri L. Amato

Owner: Steven Amato
Conducts Business: U.S., Canada
Employees: 18
Primary Market Served: Consumer
Catalog available online
Direct online sales
Advertising/Marketing Budget Related to Direct Marketing: 76-100%
Direct Marketing ad budget:
Direct Mail: 75%
Magazines: 25%
Founded: 1940
Gross sales or billing: $260,000

Sell hobby items: model trains, airplanes, cars, tools, books & miniatures.

HOME-SEW INC
1825 W Market St, PO Box 4099
Bethlehem, PA 18018-0099
Telephone: (610) 867-3833, (800) 344-4739, FAX: (610) 867-9717, Web Site: www.homesew.com
Partner: Edward Perusse
Partner: Lucy Perusse
Conducts Business: Worldwide
Employees: 25
Primary Market Served: Consumer
Catalog available online
Direct online sales
Advertising/Marketing Budget Related to Direct Marketing: 76-100%
Direct Marketing ad budget:
Direct Mail: 90%
Magazines: 1%
Online: 9%
Founded: 1960
Gross sales or billing: $3,000,000

Mail order sewing supplies.

HOOK & HACKLE CO INC
607 Ann St Rear
Homestead, PA 15120
Telephone: (800) 652-8342, FAX: (412) 476-8639, E-Mail: ron@hookhack.com, Web Site: www.hookhack.com
Pres: Robert K. Ellsworth
Conducts Business: Worldwide
Employees: 13
Primary Market Served: Business & Consumer
Catalog available online
Direct online sales
Advertising/Marketing Budget Related to Direct Marketing: 0-25%
Founded: 1975

Mail order marketer of fly fishing equipment/supplies.

WILLIAM B HUGG ENTERPRISE INC SWIM WEAR & ACCESSORIES
44 1/2 E Butler Ave
Ambler, PA 19002-4517

Telephone: (215) 646-5544, (800) 255-7946, FAX: (215) 646-1280, E-Mail: wbhswim@aol.com, Web Site: www.800allswim.com
Pres: Bill Hugg
Conducts Business: Worldwide
Primary Market Served: Business & Consumer
Catalog available online
Direct online sales
Advertising/Marketing Budget Related to Direct Marketing: 51-75%
Founded: 1975

Racing swimwear, accessories & swimwear for mature people.

THE DMA INFORMAL EDUCATION PRODUCTS
dba Museum Tour Catalog
2517 SE Mailwell Dr
Milwaukie, OR 97222-7329
Telephone: (503) 794-7100, (888) 444-5500, FAX: (503) 794-7111, E-Mail: sales@museumtour.com, Web Site: www.museumtour.com
Pres: Marilynne Eichinger
Mktg: Barbara Lund
Operations Mgr: Linda Woytke
Design Dir: Macia Mantz
Conducts Business: U.S.
Primary Market Served: Consumer
Catalog available online
Direct online sales
Advertising/Marketing Budget Related to Direct Marketing: 51-75%
Direct Marketing ad budget: $1,800,000
Direct Mail: 80%
Online: 20%
Founded: 1995

Children's educational products.

INFORMATION UNLIMITED INC
PO Box 716
Amherst, NH 03031-0716
Telephone: (603) 673-4730, (800) 221-1705, FAX: (603) 672-5406, E-Mail: wako2@xtdl.com, Web Site: www.amazing1.com
Pres & Owner: Robert E. Iannini
Conducts Business: Worldwide
Employees: 15
Primary Market Served: Business & Consumer
Direct online sales
Direct Marketing ad budget: $120,000
Magazines: 100%
Founded: 1974
Gross sales or billing: $1,750,000

Marketer of scientific products & kits for the home hobbyist, school education & laboratory.

INTERNATIONAL CURRENCY LLC
8725 Eastex Fwy
Beaumont, TX 77708-1307
Telephone: (409) 866-0588
Partner: Jeff Knight

Coin collections, jewelry & paper currency

JAYPRO SPORTS
976 Hartford Tpke
Waterford, CT 06385-4044
Telephone: (860) 447-3001, (800) 243-0533, FAX: (800) 988-3363, E-Mail: info@jaypro.com, Web Site: www.jaypro.com
Graphic Designer & Mktg Asst: Doreen Fratoni
Exec VP: Bill Wild
VP Sls & Mktg: Michael Gullickson
Conducts Business: U.S.
Employees: 40
Primary Market Served: Business & Consumer
Catalog available online
Direct online sales
Advertising/Marketing Budget Related to Direct Marketing: 51-75%
Direct Marketing ad budget:
Direct Mail: 50%
Magazines: 50%
Founded: 1953
Gross sales or billing: $3,500,000

Manufacturer & distributor of athletic, physical education, recreation & special education equipment.

KELLYCO METAL DETECTOR DISTRIBUTORS
1085 Belle Ave
Winter Springs, FL 32708
Telephone: (407) 699-8700, (800) 327-9697, FAX: (407) 695-6671, E-Mail: customerservice@kellycodetectors.com, Web Site: www.kellycodetectors.com
CEO: Stuart Auerbach
VP: Carolyn Auerbach
VP: John Fetner
Conducts Business: Worldwide
Employees: 50
Primary Market Served: Business & Consumer
Catalog available online
Direct online sales
Advertising/Marketing Budget Related to Direct Marketing: 26-50%
Direct Marketing ad budget: $500,000
Direct Mail: 5%
Magazines: 2%
Online: 90%
Telephone: 3%
Founded: 1953
Gross sales or billing: $26,000,000

Wholesale & retail sales of all major lines of metal detecting equipment, including gold detector, d.p. radar & security detectors.

KENNEL VET
PO Box 523
Laurel, DE 19956
Telephone: (302) 875-7111, (800) 782-0627, FAX: (302) 269-3986, E-Mail: info@petmarket.com, Web Site: www.kennelvet.com
CEO: Fred Kretschmann
Pres: Meryl Kretschmann
Sls & Mktg Dir: Nancy Lynn
Conducts Business: Worldwide
Employees: 14
Primary Market Served: Business & Consumer
Catalog available online
Direct online sales
Advertising/Marketing Budget Related to Direct Marketing: 26-50%
Direct Marketing ad budget:
Direct Mail: 80%
Magazines: 10%
Newspapers: 5%
Telephone: 5%
Founded: 1971

Dog & cat supplies at discount prices, such as cages, vaccines, flea & tick products, show needs, health needs, vitamins, grooming supplies, toys, & bones shipped worldwide.

KINGSLEY NORTH INC
910 Brown St, PO Box 216
Norway, MI 49870
Telephone: (906) 563-9228, (800) 338-9280, FAX: (906) 563-7143, E-Mail: sales@kingsleynorth.com, Web Site: www.kingsleynorth.com
Pres, Sec & Treas: Daniel Paupore
VP: Mark Paupore
Conducts Business: Worldwide
Employees: 8
Primary Market Served: Business & Consumer
Advertising/Marketing Budget Related to Direct Marketing: 0-25%
Founded: 1939

Sell tools, supplies, equipment, gemstones & accessories for the jewelry-lapidary trade, hobbyist & craftsman.

LAKEWOOD PRODUCTS LLC
Div of Midwest Textile Mfg Corp
3188 Bowling Green Ln
Suamico, WI 54173
Telephone: (920) 361-7717, (800) 872-8458, FAX: (920) 361-7719, E-Mail: info@lakewoodproducts.com, Web Site: www.lakewoodproducts.com
Pres: Steve Wagnitz
Conducts Business: Worldwide

Primary Market Served: Business
Catalog available online
Advertising/Marketing Budget Related to Direct Marketing: 0-25%
Founded: 1992

Manufacture sporting goods & specialty cases, such as gun/bow, tackle boxes & convenience cases.

LAMKIN CORP
6530 Gateway Park Dr
San Diego, CA 92154-7510
Telephone: (619) 661-7090, (800) 642-7755, FAX: (619) 661-0014, E-Mail: info@lamkingrips.com, Web Site: www.lamkingrips.com
Pres & CEO: Bob Lamkin
Dir Mktg: Kim Dorew

Sell golf grips.

LEGO DIRECT MARKETING
555 Taylor Rd
Enfield, CT 06082-2372
Telephone: (860) 749-2291, FAX: (860) FAX-LEGO, Web Site: www.lego.com
OE Supv: Carlene Smith
VP, Direct-to-Consumer: Skip Kodak
DM Mgr: Steven Hawco
Conducts Business: Worldwide
Employees: 250
Primary Market Served: Consumer

Mail order catalog services.

LIBERTYVILLE SADDLE SHOP INC
306 Peterson Rd, Box M
Libertyville, IL 60048
Telephone: (847) 362-0570, FAX: (847) 680-3200, E-Mail: info@saddleshop.com, Web Site: www.saddleshop.com
Pres: Jack L. Martin
Mdse Mgr: Beverly Martin
Opers Mgr: James A. Holland
Prod Mgr: Greg Martin
Mdse: Steve Martin
Conducts Business: U.S.
Employees: 110
Primary Market Served: Consumer
Catalog available online
Direct online sales
Advertising/Marketing Budget Related to Direct Marketing: 76-100%
Direct Marketing ad budget:
Direct Mail: 98%
Magazines: 2%
Founded: 1962

Equestrian English, Western, show, performance & pleasure items.

LIFE FITNESS
Div. of Brunswick Corp
5100 N River Rd

Schiller Park, IL 60176
Telephone: (847) 288-3300, (800) 735-3867, FAX: (847) 288-3703, E-Mail: webmaster@lifefitness.com, Web Site: www.lifefitness.com
Exec VP Global Sls: Jay Megna
Pres: John E. Stransky
Sr Dir Prod Mngmt: Bob Quast
Conducts Business: Worldwide
Employees: 1,400
Primary Market Served: Business & Consumer
Catalog available online
Founded: 1977
Gross sales or billing: $145,700,000

Fitness products manufacturer & marketer.

THE LOS ANGELES LAKERS INC

555 N Nash St
El Segundo, CA 90245
Telephone: (310) 426-6000, FAX: (310) 426-6115, E-Mail: vlawlor@la-lakers.com, Web Site: www.nba.com/lakers
Dir, Ticket Sls & Opers: Veronica Lawler
Conducts Business: U.S.
Primary Market Served: Business & Consumer
Catalog available online

LOWRANCE ELECTRONICS

Subs. of Navico Holdings AS
12000 E Skelly Dr
Tulsa, OK 74128
Telephone: (918) 437-6881, FAX: (918) 234-1707, Web Site: www.lowrance.com
Dir: Darrell Lowrance
CIO & CTO: Ronald Weber
Mfg: David Craig
Conducts Business: U.S., Canada
Employees: 5
Primary Market Served: Consumer
Catalog available online
Indirect online sales
Gross sales or billing: $1,000,000

Sell accessory parts for Lowrance & Eagle Fish Locators to the consumer.

LURE-CRAFT

513 W Central
Lagrange, IN 46761
Telephone: (260) 463-2687, (800) 925-9088, FAX: (260) 463-8383, E-Mail: kimstraley@lurecraft.com, Web Site: www.lurecraft.com
Owner: Shawn Straley
Mgr: Kim Straley
Conducts Business: U.S.
Employees: 3
Primary Market Served: Business & Consumer

Catalog available online
Direct online sales
Advertising/Marketing Budget Related to Direct Marketing: 76-100%
Direct Marketing ad budget: $20,000
Direct Mail: 80%
Magazines: 20%
Founded: 1970
Gross sales or billing: $500,000

Manufacturing & sales of fishing lure components, especially plastics & coloring for plastic worm production. Specialize in production & custom molds.

MARDIRON OPTICS

Dept DMP
Four Spartan Cir
Stoneham, MA 02180
Telephone: (781) 938-8339, FAX: (781) 938-8339, Web Site: www.mardironooptics.com
Proprietor: K. Greg Mardirosian
Conducts Business: U.S.
Employees: 2
Primary Market Served: Business & Consumer
Catalog available online
Indirect online sales
Advertising/Marketing Budget Related to Direct Marketing: 0-25%
Direct Marketing ad budget:
Direct Mail: 5%
Magazines: 95%
Founded: 1983
Gross sales or billing: $300,000

Provides binoculars, telescopes, opera-glasses, range finders, nightvision & microscopes to consumers.

THE MARYLAND SADDLERY INC

14924 Falls Rd
Butler, MD 21023
Telephone: (410) 771-4135, (800) 428-5077, FAX: (410) 472-9722, E-Mail: mdsaddle@aol.com, Web Site: www.marylandsaddlery.com
Pres & Natl Sls Dir: Hope Birsh
Conducts Business: U.S.
Primary Market Served: Business & Consumer
Catalog available online
Direct online sales
Founded: 1989

Specialize in children's riding apparel & ponies.

MASTERGRIP INC

3410 Century Cir
Irving, TX 75062-4904
Telephone: (972) 554-4450, (800) 275-1100, FAX: (972) 554-1109, Web Site: www.mastergrip.com

Pres: Richard Card
Conducts Business: U.S.
Employees: 60
Primary Market Served: Consumer
Catalog available online
Direct online sales
Direct Marketing ad budget: $100
Direct Mail: 100%
Founded: 1979
Gross sales or billing: $7,500,000

Mail order sales of golf equipment, clubs, shirts, sweaters & gloves.

MARY MAXIM INC

2001 Holland Ave
Port Huron, MI 48061-5019
Telephone: (810) 987-2000, (800) 962-9504, FAX: (810) 987-5056, E-Mail: info@marymaxim.com, Web Site: www.marymaxim.com
Pres: Rusty McPhedrain
VP, Mktg: Brian Harris
VP, Opers: Chuck Cowley
Comptroller: Donna Hietikko
Conducts Business: U.S., Canada
Employees: 225
Primary Market Served: Consumer
Catalog available online
Direct online sales
Advertising/Marketing Budget Related to Direct Marketing: 51-75%
Founded: 1956
Gross sales or billing: $20,000,000

Sell needlecraft kits to make sweaters, afghans, baby items, needlepoint, counted cross-stitch & Christmas ornaments.

MEMPHIS NET & TWINE CO INC

2481 Matthews Ave
Memphis, TN 38108
Telephone: (901) 458-2656, (888) 674-7638, FAX: (901) 458-1601, E-Mail: fishinfo@memphisnet.net, Web Site: www.memphisnet.net
Pres: Albert Carruthers
VP, Sls & Mktg: Peter Cowen
Mktg Mgr: William Raiford
Gen Mgr: Frank A. Gibson
Conducts Business: Worldwide
Employees: 36
Primary Market Served: Business & Consumer
Catalog available online
Direct online sales
Advertising/Marketing Budget Related to Direct Marketing: 76-100%
Direct Marketing ad budget: $213,000
Direct Mail: $150,000
Magazines: $3,000
Telephone: $60,000
Founded: 1962
Gross sales or billing: $5,000,000

Catalog sales of commercial fishing supplies, netting, nets, seines, twine & rope to commercial fishermen, fish farmers, hatcheries, state & federal institutions. Also, baseball & other sport nets.

METRO SPEEDGEAR
Div. of F1 Marketing
70 Okner Pkwy (Suite A)
Livingston, NJ 07039
Telephone: (908) 286-1886, (800) 777-4453, FAX: (908) 286-0002, E-Mail: info@speedgear.com, Web Site: www.speedgear.com
Pres: Gary M. Low
Mktg Dir: Fred Ritter
Conducts Business: Worldwide
Employees: 50
Primary Market Served: Business & Consumer
Catalog available online
Direct online sales
Advertising/Marketing Budget Related to Direct Marketing: 76-100%
Direct Marketing ad budget:
Direct Mail: 25%
Magazines: 25%
TV/Radio: 50%
Founded: 1987
Gross sales or billing: $7,000,000

Car racing apparel.

MICHAEL'S
8000 Bent Branch
Irving, TX 75063-6023
Telephone: (972) 409-1300, FAX: (972) 409-1551, Web Site: www.michaels.com
Sr VP, Mktg: Stuart Aitken
Conducts Business: U.S.
Employees: 2,000
Primary Market Served: Consumer
Catalog available online
Direct online sales

Specialty retailing chain selling arts, crafts, needlework, framing & floral supplies.

MILLER HARNESS CO
PO Box 406
Westford, MA 01886-0406
Telephone: (800) 784-5831, E-Mail: customerservice@millerharness.com, Web Site: www.millerharness.com
Pres: Gary Dunbart
VP, Sls: Sharon Wick
Mktg & Adv Dir: Patti Leonhardt
Conducts Business: Worldwide
Employees: 100
Primary Market Served: Consumer
Direct online sales
Advertising/Marketing Budget Related to Direct Marketing: 51-75%
Founded: 1912

Distributor of English saddlery & apparel.

FRANK MITTERMEIER INC
PO Box 2
Bronx, NY 10465-0001
Telephone: (718) 828-3843, (800) 360-3843, FAX: (718) 518-7233, E-Mail: info@dastrausa.com, Web Site: www.dastrausa.com
Owner: Angelo Morales
Primary Market Served: Business & Consumer
Advertising/Marketing Budget Related to Direct Marketing: 0-25%
Founded: 1936

Sell wood carving tools to consumers, businesses, clubs, schools that sell or teach woodcarving.

MOUNTAIN CRAFT SHOP CO
RR1 Box 122
Proctor, WV 26055
Telephone: (304) 455-3570, (877) 365-5869, (800) FOLK-TOY, FAX: (304) 455-1740, (866) FOLK-TOY, E-Mail: info@folktoys.com, Web Site: www.folktoys.com
Pres: E. T. Conlon
Sec: S. A. Conlon
Conducts Business: U.S.
Employees: 3
Primary Market Served: Business & Consumer
Catalog available online
Indirect online sales
Advertising/Marketing Budget Related to Direct Marketing: 0-25%
Founded: 1963
Gross sales or billing: $100,000

American folk toys, including games, puzzles, dolls & curios. Most made of hardwood, all authentic reproductions.

NRS
1410 S Fm 51
Decatur, TX 76234-2416
Telephone: (940) 393-7009, Web Site: www.nrsworld.com
Gen Mgr: Jim Lamirand

Specializing in products for ropers, including tack for barrel racing, calf & ranch roping. Western clothing, cowboy boots, cowboy hats, gifts & home decor

THE DMA NANCY'S NOTIONS LLC
A Tacony Co
333 Beichl Ave
Beaver Dam, WI 53916-0683
Telephone: (920) 887-0391, (800) 833-0690, FAX: (800) 255-8119, E-Mail: comments@nancysnotions.com, Web Site: www.nancysnotions.com

Pres & Gen Mgr: Mike Schuster
VP, Mdsg: Chris Stam
VP, Info Sys: Scott Stanton
VP Creative Svcs: Kathleen Gittus
VP HR & Fulfillment: Lori Bartruff
Conducts Business: U.S., Canada, Australia
Employees: 110
Primary Market Served: Business & Consumer
Catalog available online
Indirect online sales
Advertising/Marketing Budget Related to Direct Marketing: 76-100%
Direct Marketing ad budget: $2,800,000
Direct Mail: 75%
Magazines: 1%
Online: 20%
TV/Radio: 4%
Founded: 1979
Gross sales or billing: $14,000,000

Multi-channel direct marketer of sewing supplies.

THE DMA NAUTILUS INC
16400 SE Nautilus Dr
Vancouver, WA 98683-5535
Telephone: (360) 859-2900, (800) 675-0171, FAX: (360) 694-2755, Web Site: www.nautilus.com
VP/ Gen Mgr Bowflex: Bill McMahon
Chmn, CEO & Pres: Robert S. Falcone
CFO, VP & Treas: William D. Meadowcroft
Pres Intl Equipment Bus: Darryl K. Thomas
Pres Fitness Apparel: Juergen Eckmann
Employees: 1,500
Primary Market Served: Business & Consumer
Catalog available online
Direct online sales
Gross sales or billing: $680,000,000

Manufacture exercise equipment marketed by infomercial & catalogs.

NO FAULT SPORTS PRODUCTS
2101 Briarglen Dr
Houston, TX 77027-3711
Telephone: (713) 683-7101, (800) 462-7766, FAX: (713) 683-7103, E-Mail: nofaultsports@comcast.net, Web Site: www.nofaultsports.com
Owner: Alfredo Trullenque
Conducts Business: U.S., Canada
Employees: 4
Primary Market Served: Business
Catalog available online
Indirect online sales
Advertising/Marketing Budget Related to Direct Marketing: 0-25%
Founded: 1982

Tennis court equipment & accessories.

NOMADICS TIPI MAKERS
17671 Snow Creek Rd
Bend, OR 97701-9149
Telephone: (541) 389-3980, FAX:
(541) 389-3980, Web Site: www.tipi.
com
Pres & Owner: Jeb Barton
Bus Mgr: Harry Janicki
Conducts Business: Worldwide
Employees: 2
Primary Market Served: Business &
Consumer
Catalog available online
Advertising/Marketing Budget Related
to Direct Marketing: 0-25%
Founded: 1970

Market authentic Native American Indian tipis for adults & children.

NYLON NET CO
PO Box 592
Memphis, TN 38101-0592
Telephone: (901) 526-6500, (877) 893-
6535, (800) 238-7529, FAX: (901)
526-6538, E-Mail: nylonnet@
nylonnet.com, Web Site: www.
nylonnet.com
Pres: Stephen Christides
Conducts Business: U.S., Canada,
Mexico
Employees: 100
Primary Market Served: Business &
Consumer
Catalog available online
Direct online sales
Founded: 1953

Mail order catalog marketer of sports related items such as nets.

OPTRONICS INC
401 S 41st St E
Muskogee, OK 74403
Telephone: (918) 683-9514, (800) 364-
5483, FAX: (918) 683-9517, E-Mail:
sales@optronicsinc.com, Web Site:
www.optronicsinc.com
CEO: Greg G. Bland
VP OEM Sls & Mktg: Brett Johnson
Purchasing Mgr: Richard Tracy
Conducts Business: Worldwide
Employees: 40
Primary Market Served: Business &
Consumer
Catalog available online
Indirect online sales
Advertising/Marketing Budget Related
to Direct Marketing: 0-25%
Direct Marketing ad budget: $200,000
Direct Mail: 10%
Magazines: 45%
Newspapers: 40%
Telephone: 5%
Founded: 1972
Gross sales or billing: $16,000,000

Twelve-volt vehicular & recreational lighting equipment & accessories sold to consumers & specialized end-users via direct mail, mail order, telephone, distributors, warehouse clubs, mass merchandisers & specialty chains.

ORION TELESCOPES & BINOCULARS
89 Hangar Way
Watsonville, CA 95076
Telephone: (831) 763-7000, (800) 447-
1001, FAX: (408) 763-7017, E-Mail:
sales@telescope.com, Web Site:
www.telescope.com
CEO: Tim J. Gieseler
VP: Cynthia Phinn
Mktg VP: Terry D'Auray
Conducts Business: U.S., Canada
Employees: 50
Primary Market Served: Business &
Consumer
Catalog available online
Direct online sales
Advertising/Marketing Budget Related
to Direct Marketing: 76-100%
Founded: 1975

Manufacturer & distributor of recreational telescopes, binoculars & other optical products.

THE ORVIS CO INC
Historic Rte Seven A
Manchester, VT 05254
Telephone: (802) 362-3622, FAX:
(802) 362-3525, Web Site: www.
orvis.com
Chmn: Leigh H. Perkins
Pres & CEO: Perk Perkins
VP, Fin: Thomas Vaccaro
VP, Internet Sls & Mktg: Joseph
Cassidy
Catalog Mktg Dir: Eric Johnson
Fishing & Hunting Catalog Mgr: Tom
Rosenbauer
Conducts Business: Worldwide
Employees: 400
Primary Market Served: Consumer
Founded: 1856

Offer seasonal catalogs displaying hunting & fishing items, as well as country clothes & gifts for the sporting family.

OUTDOOR RESEARCH
2203 First Ave S (Suite 700)
Seattle, WA 98134-1424
Telephone: (206) 467-8197, (888) 467-
4327, FAX: (206) 467-0374, Web
Site: www.outdoorresearch.com
Pres & CEO: Daniel J. Nordstrom
VP: Dan Gulden
Mktg Mgr: Candace Springstead
Copywriter, Mktg Assoc: Teresa
Bruffey

Conducts Business: U.S.
Primary Market Served: Business
Catalog available online
Direct online sales
Advertising/Marketing Budget Related
to Direct Marketing: 0-25%
Gross sales or billing: $11,000,000

Manufacturers of innovative accessories for the outdoors.

OVERTON'S INC
111 Red Banks Rd
Greenville, NC 27858-5702
Telephone: (252) 355-7600, (800) 334-
6541, FAX: (252) 355-2923, E-Mail:
service@overtons.com, Web Site:
www.overtons.com
CFO: John Daigle
Mgr: Richard Finlaysonitsj
Mfg: Mark Metcalfe
Conducts Business: U.S.
Employees: 231
Primary Market Served: Consumer
Catalog available online
Direct online sales
Advertising/Marketing Budget Related
to Direct Marketing: 76-100%
Founded: 1976
Gross sales or billing: $38,300,000

Watersports & marine equipment & accessories dealer featuring ten catalogs yearly.

PACHMAYR LTD
Subs. of Lyman Products Corp
475 Smith St
Middletown, CT 06457-1529
Telephone: (800) 225-9626, FAX:
(860) 632-1699, Web Site: www.
lymanproducts.com
Pres: Mace Thompson
Conducts Business: Worldwide
Employees: 80
Primary Market Served: Business &
Consumer

Manufacturer & catalog marketer of gun accessories.

PARTNERS VILLAGE STORE
865 Main Rd
Westport, MA 02790-4315
Telephone: (508) 636-2572, FAX:
(508) 636-2529, E-Mail: info@
partnersvillagestore.com, Web Site:
www.partnersvillagestore.com
Partner: Nancy C. Crosby
Partner: Jan Hall
Store Opers: Dorri Legge
Conducts Business: U.S.
Employees: 9
Primary Market Served: Business &
Consumer
Catalog available online
Direct online sales

Sell books, gifts, cards, toys, gourmet foods & garden supplies.

PLAY FAIR TOYS

3043 Walnut St
Boulder, CO 80301-2509
Telephone: (303) 444-7502, (800) 824-7255, FAX: (303) 440-3393, E-Mail: service@playfairtoys.com, Web Site: www.playfairtoys.com
Pres: Susan S. Lounsbury
VP: Jon B. Lounsbury
Conducts Business: U.S.
Employees: 22
Primary Market Served: Consumer
Catalog available online
Direct online sales
Advertising/Marketing Budget Related to Direct Marketing: 76-100%
Founded: 1983

National mail order catalog & retail operation specializing in quality non-sexist, non-violent toys for children.

PLAYER PIANO CO INC

300 N Mead St (Suite 200)
Wichita, KS 67202-2745
Telephone: (316) 263-3241, FAX: (316) 263-5480, Web Site: www.playerpianocompany.com
Pres: Durrell Armstrong
Conducts Business: Worldwide
Employees: 6
Primary Market Served: Business & Consumer
Catalog available online
Advertising/Marketing Budget Related to Direct Marketing: 0-25%
Founded: 1951
Gross sales or billing: $700,000

Player piano restoration supplies, rolls & accessories.

PLEASANT COMPANY

Div. of Mattel Inc
PO Box 620497
Middleton, WI 53562-0497
Telephone: (608) 836-4848, (800) 845-0005, FAX: (608) 836-1999, Web Site: www.americangirl.com
VP, Catalogue Mktg: Mike Grasee
Pres: Ellen Brothers
VP Brand Mktg: Kathy Monetti
Conducts Business: U.S.
Employees: 1,500
Primary Market Served: Consumer
Catalog available online
Direct online sales
Advertising/Marketing Budget Related to Direct Marketing: 76-100%
Founded: 1986

Direct mail marketer of books, dolls & toys to girls 7-12. Products include The American Girls Collection, American Girl Magazine, American Girl Today, American Girl Library, American Girl Gear & Bitty Baby.

PORTA-BOTE INTERNATIONAL

Div. of Sandy Kaye Enterprises
1074 Independence Ave
Mountain View, CA 94043-1602
Telephone: (650) 961-5334, (800) 227-8882, Web Site: www.porta-bote.com
Pres: Sandy Kaye
Sales Exec: Paul Mintz
VP Mktg Commun: Carl Blackwell
Conducts Business: Worldwide
Primary Market Served: Business & Consumer
Catalog available online
Direct online sales
Advertising/Marketing Budget Related to Direct Marketing: 51-75%
Founded: 1973

Sell portable folding boats, accessories, jewelry & gifts to dealers & end users.

REI-RECREATIONAL EQUIPMENT INC

6750 S 228th St
Kent, WA 98032
Telephone: (253) 891-2500, (800) 426-4840, FAX: (253) 891-2523, Web Site: www.rei.com
Mktg Mgr: Cindy Huffman
Mkt Opers: Karen Avletta
Conducts Business: Worldwide
Employees: 6,000
Primary Market Served: Consumer
Catalog available online
Direct online sales
Advertising/Marketing Budget Related to Direct Marketing: 26-50%
Founded: 1938
Gross sales or billing: $460,000,000

Outdoor gear & clothing for muscle-power activities.

RAINBOW GROUP LLC

dba Beacon Athletics
8233 Forsythia St Ste 120
Middleton, WI 53562-1496
Telephone: (608) 824-0068, Web Site: www.beaconathletics.com
Primary Market Served: Business & Consumer

THE DMA RECREATIONAL EQUIPMENT INC

6750 S 228th St
Kent, WA 98032-4803
Telephone: (253) 395-4803, Web Site: www.rei.com

Dir, Direct Mktg & Analysis: Michael Bowcut
Primary Market Served: Consumer

RELIABLE RACING SUPPLY

643 Upper Glen St (Suite B)
Queensbury, NY 12804-2014
Telephone: (518) 793-5677, FAX: (518) 793-6491, Web Site: www.reliableracing.com
Pres: Tom Jacobs
Commun Dir: Mike Sylvia
Conducts Business: U.S., Canada
Employees: 40
Primary Market Served: Business & Consumer
Catalog available online
Indirect online sales
Advertising/Marketing Budget Related to Direct Marketing: 51-75%
Direct Marketing ad budget: $350,000
Direct Mail: 70%
Magazines: 30%
Founded: 1965
Gross sales or billing: $6,000,000

Snow skiing products, golf course & event supplies & timing equipment.

RHYTHM BAND INC

1316 E Lancaster Ave
Fort Worth, TX 76102-6634
Telephone: (817) 335-2561, (800) 424-4724, FAX: (800) 784-9401, E-Mail: sales@rhythmband.com, Web Site: www.rhythmband.com
Pres: Brad Kirkpatrick
VP, Sls: Laura Bergin
VP, Opers: Flora Brewer
Conducts Business: U.S.
Employees: 25
Primary Market Served: Business & Consumer
Catalog available online
Direct online sales
Advertising/Marketing Budget Related to Direct Marketing: 51-75%
Direct Marketing ad budget:
Direct Mail: 95%
Newspapers: 5%
Founded: 1961

Musical instruments geared to the early childhood & elementary school market.

PETE RICKARD INC

115 Roy Walsh Rd
Cobleskill, NY 12043-4422
Telephone: (518) 234-2731, (800) 282-5663, FAX: (518) 234-2454, E-Mail: info@peterickard.com, Web Site: www.peterickard.com
Staff Shooter: John Johnston Jr.
Staff Shooter: Scott Alkinburgh
Staff Shooter: John Haynes
Conducts Business: Worldwide
Employees: 8

Primary Market Served: Business &
Consumer
Catalog available online
Direct online sales
Advertising/Marketing Budget Related
to Direct Marketing: 0-25%
Direct Marketing ad budget:
Direct Mail: 1%
Magazines: 20%
Newspapers: 1%
Online: 25%
TV/Radio: 30%
Telephone: 23%
Founded: 1934

Deer hunting scents & lures, accessories, gun dog training scents & trapping lures. Scotch game calls & gear.

ROAD RUNNER SPORTS INC
5549 Copley Dr
San Diego, CA 92111-7904
Telephone: (858) 974-4200, (800) 636-3560, FAX: (800) 453-5443, Web
Site: www.roadrunnersports.com
Pres & CEO: Mike Gotfredson
Dir E-Commerce: Peter Taylor
Conducts Business: U.S., Canada
Employees: 280
Primary Market Served: Consumer
Direct online sales
Founded: 1983
Gross sales or billing: $105,000,000

Sell athletic shoes, fitness apparel & accessories to sports enthusiasts ranging from the triathlete, marathoner & team sport player to the weekend fitness enthusiast.

AG RUSSELL KNIVES INC
2900 S 26th St
Rogers, AR 72758-8571
Telephone: (479) 631-0130, (800) 255-9034, FAX: (479) 631-8493, E-Mail:
ag@agrussell.com, Web Site: www.agrussell.com
Pres: Goldie Russell
Co-Owner: A.G. Russell
Conducts Business: Worldwide
Employees: 13
Primary Market Served: Consumer
Catalog available online
Direct online sales
Advertising/Marketing Budget Related
to Direct Marketing: 76-100%
Direct Marketing ad budget:
Direct Mail: $1,000,000
Magazines: $100,000
Founded: 1964

Sell high quality & handmade knives.

S&S WORLDWIDE
75 Mill St
Colchester, CT 06415-0513

Telephone: (860) 537-3451, (800) 288-9941, FAX: (860) 537-2866, E-Mail:
cservice@ssww.com, Web Site:
www.ssww.com
Co-Pres: Hy Schwartz
Co-Pres: Adam Schwartz
Dir Mktg: Greg Hilbert
Database Dir: Kathy Knapp
Conducts Business: U.S., Canada, International
Employees: 300
Primary Market Served: Business &
Consumer
Catalog available online
Direct online sales
Advertising/Marketing Budget Related
to Direct Marketing: 26-50%
Direct Marketing ad budget:
Direct Mail: 80%
Online: 10%
Telephone: 10%
Founded: 1906
Gross sales or billing: $40,000,000

Catalog sales of arts, crafts, games & adaptive equipment. Manufacturers of arts, crafts & small wood products.

SAFE PUBLICATIONS INC
PO Box 263
Southampton, PA 18966
Telephone: (215) 357-9049, FAX:
(215) 357-5202, E-Mail: sales@safepub.com, Web Site: www.safepub.com
Pres: Axel J. Braun
Conducts Business: U.S., Canada
Employees: 4
Primary Market Served: Business &
Consumer
Catalog available online
Indirect online sales
Advertising/Marketing Budget Related
to Direct Marketing: 0-25%
Direct Marketing ad budget:
Direct Mail: 30%
Newspapers: 70%
Founded: 1974
Gross sales or billing: $500,000

Catalog marketer of German made stamp & coin albums & supplies.

SAILRITE ENTERPRISES, INC
2390 E 100 S
Columbia City, IN 46725-8751
Telephone: (260) 693-2242, (800) 348-2769, FAX: (260) 693-2246, E-Mail:
sailrite@sailrite.com, Web Site:
www.sailrite.com
VP: Matthew Grant
VP: Hallie Grant
Conducts Business: Worldwide
Employees: 13
Primary Market Served: Consumer
Catalog available online
Direct online sales

Direct Marketing ad budget:
Direct Mail: 20%
Magazines: 80%
Founded: 1969
Gross sales or billing: $1,500,000

Sell sailmaking supplies & instructions & offer a home study program in sailmaking. Also, sewing machines for sailmaking.

SCHNEIDER SADDLERY
8255 E Washington St
Chagrin Falls, OH 44023
Telephone: (440) 543-2700, (800) 365-1311, FAX: (440) 543-2710, Web
Site: www.sstack.com
Pres: Donald Schneider
VP: Stan Schneider
Conducts Business: U.S., Canada, Europe, Australia, S. America, Middle
East, Japan
Employees: 35
Primary Market Served: Business &
Consumer
Catalog available online
Direct online sales
Advertising/Marketing Budget Related
to Direct Marketing: 76-100%
Direct Marketing ad budget:
Direct Mail: 75%
Magazines: 20%
Newspapers: 5%

Equestrian riding equipment, apparel & supplies-private label lines.

SCOTT'S DOG SUPPLY INC
PO Box 34302
Indianapolis, IN 46234-0302
Telephone: (317) 222-5382, (800) 966-3647, FAX: (317) 298-7284, E-Mail:
cmurphy154@aol.com, Web Site:
www.scottsdog.com
Pres: C. Joe Murphy
Conducts Business: U.S., Canada
Primary Market Served: Business &
Consumer
Catalog available online
Direct online sales
Advertising/Marketing Budget Related
to Direct Marketing: 0-25%
Direct Marketing ad budget:
Direct Mail: 20%
Magazines: 80%
Founded: 1982
Gross sales or billing: $500,000

Hunter & hunting dog supplies.

SHAKESPEARE CO
Div. of K/2 Inc
7 Science Ct
Columbia, SC 29203-9344
Telephone: (803) 754-7000, (800) 347-3759, FAX: (803) 754-7342, Web
Site: www.shakespeare-fishing.com
Pres, K/2: Rich Rodstein

VP, Sls & Gen Mgr: Scott Hogsett
Conducts Business: U.S., Canada
Primary Market Served: Business &
Consumer

Fishing rods, reels, kits, combos &
lines.

SIMS STOVES

PO Box 21405
Billings, MT 59104
Telephone: (406) 259-5644, (800) 736-
5259, Web Site: www.simsstoves.
com
Owner: Wyatt Sims
Conducts Business: U.S., Canada
Employees: 4
Primary Market Served: Business &
Consumer
Catalog available online
Indirect online sales
Advertising/Marketing Budget Related
to Direct Marketing: 51-75%
Direct Marketing ad budget:
Magazines: 80%
Telephone: 20%
Founded: 1946
Gross sales or billing: $50,000

Manufacturer & catalog marketer of
folding, wood burning campstoves &
related sporting goods such as pack-
saddles & tents.

SMART DOG PRODUCTS

1009 S College St
Winchester, TN 37398
Telephone: (931) 967-7482, (800) 264-
3647, FAX: (931) 967-7483, E-Mail:
sales@shopsmartdog.com
Pres & Treas: Michael Rudder
Conducts Business: U.S.
Employees: 10
Primary Market Served: Business &
Consumer

Quality accessories for house pets.

SOAR INFLATABLES

20 Healdsburg Ave
Healdsburg, CA 95448
Telephone: (707) 433-5599, FAX:
(707) 433-4499, E-Mail: sales@
soar1.com, Web Site: www.soar1.
com
Pres: Larry Laba
Conducts Business: Worldwide
Employees: 3
Primary Market Served: Business &
Consumer
Catalog available online
Indirect online sales
Direct Marketing ad budget:
Direct Mail: 38%
Magazines: 40%
Newspapers: 2%
Telephone: 20%
Founded: 1993

SPILSBURY PUZZLE CO

70 W Madison St (Suite 2300)
Chicago, IL 60602-4250
Telephone: (800) 722-1760, FAX:
(630) 575-0857, E-Mail: service@
spilsbury.com, Web Site: www.
spilsbury.com
Pres: Jerry Schillinger
Conducts Business: U.S.
Employees: 5
Primary Market Served: Consumer
Catalog available online
Direct online sales
Advertising/Marketing Budget Related
to Direct Marketing: 76-100%
Direct Marketing ad budget:
Direct Mail: 100%
Founded: 1995

Puzzles, games & gifts.

SPORT SUPPLY GROUP

1901 Diplomat Dr
Dallas, TX 75234
Telephone: (972) 484-9484, FAX:
(972) 247-0650, Web Site: www.
sportsupplygroup.com
Pres: John Walker
VP, Opers: Douglas Pryor
Mktg Dir: Bob Parks
Investor Rels: Peggy Rozelle
Primary Market Served: Business
Catalog available online
Indirect online sales

Manufacturer of sports gear &
equipment. Sell via catalog.

SPORTIME INTERNATIONAL

Subs. of School Specialty Inc
3155 Northwoods Pkwy
Norcross, GA 30071
Telephone: (770) 449-5700, (800) 283-
5700, FAX: (770) 510-7290, E-Mail:
orders@sportime.com, Web Site:
www.sportime.com
VP, Sls: Duane Puckett
Mktg Info Mgr: Greg Bayer
Mktg Dir: Tom Jones
Sportime Catalog Dir: Mark Dresser
Conducts Business: U.S., Japan, New
Zealand, Australia
Employees: 120
Primary Market Served: Business
Indirect online sales
Advertising/Marketing Budget Related
to Direct Marketing: 76-100%
Direct Marketing ad budget:
Direct Mail: 98%
Magazines: 2%
Founded: 1967

Two mail order catalogs featuring
movement & physical education equipment for elementary grade, secondary
& therapy markets.

THE SPORTSMAN'S GUIDE INC

411 Farwell Ave
South Saint Paul, MN 55075-2428
Telephone: (651) 451-3030, (800) 882-
2962, FAX: (651) 450-6130, E-Mail:
custserv@sportsmansguide.com, Web
Site: www.sportsmansguide.com
Pres & CEO: Gregory R. Binkley
Exec VP Mdsg, Mktg & Creative
Svcs: John M. Casler
Conducts Business: U.S., Canada
Employees: 754
Primary Market Served: Consumer
Catalog available online
Direct online sales
Founded: 1970
Gross sales or billing: $130,200,000

Sporting goods, accessories & clothing
sold primarily to hunters, wild life enthusiasts, fishermen, campers & RV
owners.

SPORTSMITH LLC

5925 S 118th Ave
Tulsa, OK 74146-6827
Telephone: (918) 307-2446, Web Site:
www.sportsmith.net
Mktg Mgr: Troy Mosley
Primary Market Served: Consumer

SUNSHINE DISCOUNT CRAFTS

12335 62nd St N
Largo, FL 33773
Telephone: (727) 530-9572, (800) 729-
2878, FAX: (727) 531-2739, E-Mail:
webmaster@sunshinecrafts.com, Web
Site: www.sunshinecrafts.com
Pres: David Rothschild
Conducts Business: U.S.
Employees: 12
Primary Market Served: Business &
Consumer
Catalog available online
Direct online sales
Advertising/Marketing Budget Related
to Direct Marketing: 76-100%
Direct Marketing ad budget:
Direct Mail: 90%
Magazines: 10%
Founded: 1980
Gross sales or billing: $1,000,000

Offer discounts on 14,000 craft supply
items. Doll making, jewelry, muslin
animals, wood, paints, glass painting &
etching.

SUNSHINE GLASSWORKS LTD

111 Industrial Pkwy
Buffalo, NY 14227-2712

Telephone: (716) 668-2918, (800) 828-7159, FAX: (716) 668-2932, E-Mail: info23@sunshineglass.com, Web Site: www.sunshineglass.com
Pres: Scott G. Emslie
Conducts Business: U.S.
Employees: 10
Primary Market Served: Business & Consumer
Catalog available online
Direct online sales
Advertising/Marketing Budget Related to Direct Marketing: 76-100%
Direct Marketing ad budget: $35,000
Direct Mail: 90%
Magazines: 10%
Founded: 1979
Gross sales or billing: $1,250,000

Sell stained glass supplies: sheet glass, lead, foil, tools, solder & accessories.

TACKLE CRAFT

W5043 480th Ave
Ellsworth, WI 54011-5209
Telephone: (715) 273-5300, E-Mail: tacklecr@aol.com
Pres: Alan M. Woll
Partner: Linda J. Woll
Conducts Business: Worldwide
Primary Market Served: Business & Consumer
Advertising/Marketing Budget Related to Direct Marketing: 76-100%
Direct Marketing ad budget:
Magazines: 100%
Founded: 1970

Fly & lure making materials.

TANDY LEATHER CO

1900 SE Loop 820
Fort Worth, TX 76140-1003
Telephone: (817) 872-3200, FAX: (817) 496-7859, E-Mail: tlfhelp@tandyleather.com, Web Site: www.tandyleatherfactory.com
Mktg Mgr: Dana Jones
Conducts Business: U.S., Canada, Australia, U.K., Japan
Employees: 125
Primary Market Served: Business & Consumer
Indirect online sales
Advertising/Marketing Budget Related to Direct Marketing: 76-100%
Founded: 1919
Gross sales or billing: $7,500,000

Retail & mail-order sales with over 25 company-owned leathercraft stores nationwide.

TOWER HOBBIES/HOBBICO

2904 Research Rd
Champaign, IL 61822
Telephone: (217) 398-3636, (800) 637-6050, FAX: (217) 398-1104, Web Site: www.towerhobbies.com
Pres: Clint Atkins
CFO: Willard Muirheid
VP, Admin: Sue Ciolli
VP, Sls: Ken Cutler
VP, Mktg: Rick Priester
Conducts Business: Worldwide
Primary Market Served: Consumer
Catalog available online
Direct online sales
Advertising/Marketing Budget Related to Direct Marketing: 76-100%

Supplier of radio controlled model cars, planes, boats, parts & accessories.

THE DMA TOYS "R" US

1 Geoffrey Way
Wayne, NJ 07470-2066
Telephone: (973) 617-5879, FAX: (973) 617-4006, Web Site: www.toysrus.com
Chmn & CEO: Gerald L. Storch
Exec VP & CFO: F. Clay Creasey Jr.
Exec VP HR: Daniel Caspersen
Sr VP, Adv & Mktg: Ernest V. Speranza
Dir CRM & Loyalty: Barbara Canning Brown
Conducts Business: Worldwide
Employees: 59,000
Primary Market Served: Consumer
Catalog available online
Direct online sales
Gross sales or billing: $13,000,000,000

Toy specialty retailing chain.

TOYS TO GROW ON

Div. of Lakeshore Learning Materials
2695 E Dominguez St
Carson, CA 90895
Telephone: (310) 537-8600, (800) 874-4242, FAX: (800) 537-5403, E-Mail: toyinfo@toystogrowon.com, Web Site: www.ttgo.com
Pres: Bo Kaplan
CEO: Michael Kaplan
VP, Mdsg: Charles Kaplan
Conducts Business: U.S.
Employees: 78
Primary Market Served: Consumer
Catalog available online
Direct online sales

Produce & distribute catalogs of quality, educator-approved toys for children aged one month to 12 years.

US GAMES SYSTEMS INC

179 Ludlow St
Stamford, CT 06902
Telephone: (203) 353-8400, (800) 544-2637, FAX: (203) 353-8431, Web Site: www.usgamesinc.com
Chmn: Stuart R. Kaplan
Owner: Rhianna Mirabello
Conducts Business: Worldwide
Employees: 40
Primary Market Served: Business & Consumer
Catalog available online
Direct online sales
Advertising/Marketing Budget Related to Direct Marketing: 0-25%
Founded: 1968

Publish playing cards, tarot cards & new age books from around the world. Also, reproductions of antique & museum playing cards, historical cards, plus adult card games & award winning children's card games.

UNIVERSAL HOVERCRAFT

1204 Third St
Cordova, IL 61242
Telephone: (309) 654-2588, FAX: (309) 654-2588, Web Site: www.hovercraft.com
Owner: R.J. Windt
Pres: Bill Zang
Conducts Business: Worldwide
Employees: 3
Primary Market Served: Business & Consumer
Catalog available online
Direct online sales
Advertising/Marketing Budget Related to Direct Marketing: 0-25%
Founded: 1971

Sell Hovercraft plans, props & fans.

UNIVERSAL VINTAGE TIRE CO

2994 Elizabethtown Rd
Hershey, PA 17033
Telephone: (717) 534-0175, (800) 233-3827, FAX: (717) 534-0719, E-Mail: sales@universaltire.com, Web Site: www.universaltire.com
Pres: Joseph Coker
Mgr: John Northeimer
Conducts Business: U.S.
Employees: 3
Primary Market Served: Business & Consumer
Catalog available online
Direct online sales
Advertising/Marketing Budget Related to Direct Marketing: 26-50%
Direct Marketing ad budget:
Direct Mail: 5%
Magazines: 95%
Founded: 1968
Gross sales or billing: $1,500,000

Classic automobile tires for vehicles made between 1900-1970.

VET VAX

1203 E Hwy 24-40
Tonganoxie, KS 66086-9507

Telephone: (913) 845-3760, (800) 369-8297, FAX: (913) 845-9472, E-Mail: sales@vetvax.com
Pres: Bud Moomau
Conducts Business: U.S.
Employees: 8
Primary Market Served: Business & Consumer
Catalog available online
Advertising/Marketing Budget Related to Direct Marketing: 26-50%
Direct Marketing ad budget: $50,000
Direct Mail: 70%
Magazines: 20%
Newspapers: 10%
Founded: 1969
Gross sales or billing: $1,800,000

Animal health & hunting supplies for dogs, horses & cats.

VOYAGEUR INC

Div. of Mad River Canoe Co
111 Kayaker Way
Easley, SC 29642-2433
Telephone: (802) 496-3127, (800) 311-7245, FAX: (802) 496-6247
VP, Mfg & Prodn Mgr: Ken Beauchemin
Paddle Sport Equip Dir: Gordon Colby
Foreman: Scott Griffith
Conducts Business: U.S., Canada, Germany, Japan, England, Finland, The Netherlands, Norway, France
Employees: 7
Primary Market Served: Business & Consumer
Direct Marketing ad budget:
Direct Mail: 15%
Magazines: 85%
Gross sales or billing: $350,000

Manufacturer of waterproof gear storage bags, flotation, & accessories for canoeing & kayaking.

WM. K. WALTHERS INC

5601 W Florist Ave
Milwaukee, WI 53218
Telephone: (414) 527-0770, FAX: (414) 527-4423, Web Site: www.walthers.com
Pres: Phil Walthers
VP Mktg & Sls: John Sanheim
Dir: Chris Schaenzer
Conducts Business: U.S.
Employees: 187
Primary Market Served: Business & Consumer
Catalog available online
Direct online sales

Catalog marketer of model railroad kits & accessories.

THE DMA WARRIOR CUSTOM GOLF INC

15 Mason (Suite A)
Irvine, CA 92618-2707

Telephone: (949) 699-2499, Web Site: www.warriorcustomgolf.com
Pres: Brendan Flaherty

WE-NO-NAH CANOE INC

1252 Bundy Blvd, Box 247
Winona, MN 55987-4872
Telephone: (507) 454-5430, FAX: (507) 454-5448, E-Mail: info@wenonah.com, Web Site: www.wenonah.com
Pres: Mike Cichanowski
Conducts Business: U.S., Canada, Germany
Employees: 50
Primary Market Served: Business & Consumer
Catalog available online
Indirect online sales
Advertising/Marketing Budget Related to Direct Marketing: 0-25%
Founded: 1966
Gross sales or billing: $5,000,000

Manufacturer of canoes, kayaks and accessories.

THE DMA WEST MARINE INC

500 Westridge Dr
Watsonville, CA 95076-4171
Telephone: (831) 761-4825, (800) BOATING, (800) 262-8464, FAX: (831) 768-5000, E-Mail: customercare@westmarine.com, Web Site: www.westmarine.com
Pres, CEO & Dir: Geoffrey A. Eisenberg
Sr VP & CFO: Thomas Moran
Exec VP Mdsg: Ronald Japinga
Dir Database & Loyalty: Craig Ajeska
Conducts Business: US, Puerto Rico & Canada
Employees: 5,026
Primary Market Served: Business & Consumer
Catalog available online
Direct online sales
Advertising/Marketing Budget Related to Direct Marketing: 76-100%
Direct Marketing ad budget:
Direct Mail: 80%
Newspapers: 10%
TV/Radio: 10%
Founded: 1968
Gross sales or billing: $716,600,000

Sell retail boating equipment to pleasure boaters. Produce 12 catalogs yearly. 4.5 million total pieces mailed.

WHITEHORSE GEAR

107 E Conway Rd
Center Conway, NH 03813-4012

Telephone: (603) 356-6556, FAX: (603) 356-6590, E-Mail: customerservice@whitehorsepress.com, Web Site: www.whitehorsepress.com
Pres: Daniel W. Kennedy
Co-Owner: Judith M. Kennedy
Primary Market Served: Business & Consumer
Catalog available online
Direct online sales
Advertising/Marketing Budget Related to Direct Marketing: 76-100%
Founded: 1989

Publishers of books & a catalog for motorcycle enthusiasts.

WIND IN THE RIGGING

Div. of Port Publications, Inc
PO Box 249
Port Washington, WI 53074-0249
Telephone: (262) 284-3494, (800) 236-7444, FAX: (262) 284-0067, E-Mail: info@windintherigging.com, Web Site: www.windintherigging.com
Pres: William F. Schanen III
Mgr: Jean Schanen
Conducts Business: U.S., Canada, Europe, Australia, Japan, Puerto Rico
Employees: 50
Primary Market Served: Consumer
Catalog available online
Direct online sales
Advertising/Marketing Budget Related to Direct Marketing: 76-100%
Founded: 1970
Gross sales or billing: $3,500,000

Sell nautical gifts, clothing, personalized products & specialty items relating to sailing & cruising.

SYLVIA WOODS HARP CENTER

Div. of Woods Music & Books Inc
PO Box 816
Montrose, CA 91021
Telephone: (800) 272-4277, FAX: (818) 247-5212, E-Mail: info@harpcenter.com, Web Site: www.harpcenter.com
Pres: Sylvia Woods
Conducts Business: U.S.
Primary Market Served: Consumer
Catalog available online
Direct online sales
Advertising/Marketing Budget Related to Direct Marketing: 76-100%

Sell harps, harp music books & accessories.

WOODWORKER'S SUPPLY INC

1108 N Glenn Rd
Casper, WY 82601

Telephone: (307) 237-5528, (800) 645-9292, FAX: (307) 57-5272, E-Mail: kenp@woodworker.com, Web Site: www.woodworker.com
Pres: John Wirth Jr
Dept Mgr: Ken Pollitt
Conducts Business: U.S.
Employees: 150
Primary Market Served: Business & Consumer
Advertising/Marketing Budget Related to Direct Marketing: 76-100%
Founded: 1972

Market woodworking machinery, tools, accessories, & supplies to advanced amateur & professional woodworkers.

YOUR MOVE CHESS & GAMES

Div. of ICD Corp
832 N Broadway
North Massapequa, NY 11758
Telephone: (516) 882-9800, (800) 645-4710, FAX: (631) 424-3405, E-Mail: icd@icdchess.com, Web Site: www.icdchess.com
Gen Mgr: Steven A. Schwartz
Conducts Business: Worldwide
Employees: 18
Primary Market Served: Business & Consumer
Catalog available online
Direct online sales
Advertising/Marketing Budget Related to Direct Marketing: 0-25%
Founded: 1978
Gross sales or billing: $5,000,000

Sell chess & other games.

Transportation Catalogs (12)

AW DIRECT INC
1125 Deming Way
Madison, WI 53717-1953
Telephone: (860) 828-7800, (800) 243-3194, FAX: (800) 828-9678, E-Mail: contactus@awdirect.com, Web Site: www.awdirect.com
VP: Richard Thibadeau
Pres: Larry Loizzo
Conducts Business: Worldwide
Employees: 85
Primary Market Served: Consumer
Founded: 2005
Gross sales or billing: $28,000,000

Sell accessories for tow trucks, recovery and service vehicles.

ACCELLOS INC
90 S Cascade Ave (Suite 1200)
Colorado Springs, CO 80903-1678
Telephone: (719) 433-7000, Web Site: www.accellos.com
Mktg: Christopher O'Shea

AIR POWER USA
Div. of Multitech Industries Ltd
8366 Isis Ave
Los Angeles, CA 90045
Telephone: (310) 641-0830, (888) 888-8231, FAX: (310) 641-8515, Web Site: www.airpowerusa.com
Pres: Robert Go
Import Mgr: Amanda Yee
Export Mgr: Samuel Moon
Controller: Sheila Liao
Conducts Business: U.S.
Employees: 30
Primary Market Served: Business & Consumer
Catalog available online
Advertising/Marketing Budget Related to Direct Marketing: 25-50%
Founded: 1995
Gross sales or billing: $3,000,000

Global air & ocean freight, logistics, transportation, insurance warehousing, distribution & customs.

AIRCRAFT SPRUCE & SPECIALTY CO
Div. of Irwin International
225 Airport Cir
Corona, CA 92880-2527
Telephone: (909) 372-9555, (877) 4-Spruce, FAX: (909) 372-0555, E-Mail: info@aircraft-spruce.com, Web Site: www.aircraft-spruce.com
Pres: Jim Irwin
VP, Fin: Nanci Irwin
Gen Mgr: Tom Marrachi
Conducts Business: Worldwide
Employees: 100

Primary Market Served: Business & Consumer
Catalog available online
Direct online sales
Founded: 1965
Gross sales or billing: $25,000,000

Distributor of aircraft supplies for home-built & certified aircraft. Over 30,000 parts sold through a 600 page catalog.

AMERICAN AIRLINES
AMR Corp
4333 Amon Carter Blvd
Fort Worth, TX 76155-2605
Telephone: (817) 963-1234
Exec VP: Robert W. Reding
Primary Market Served: Consumer

AUTOMOD
3353 W Hospital Ave
Atlanta, GA 30341-3419
Telephone: (770) 457-9663, (800) 241-1832, FAX: (770) 457-6089, Web Site: www.automod.net
Pres: Earl Rogers
Conducts Business: U.S.
Employees: 5
Primary Market Served: Business & Consumer
Founded: 1972

Distributor & retailer of high-end automotive accessories, racing & restoration products.

BUGGIES UNLIMITED
3510 Port Jacksonville Pkwy
Jacksonville, FL 32226
Telephone: (888) 444-6364, E-Mail: support@buggiesunlimited.com, Web Site: www.buggiesunlimited.com
Founder & CEO: Bart Mahan
Primary Market Served: Consumer

Golf cart parts & accessories

CAMBRIDGE EDUCATIONAL
Imprint of Films Media Group - a div. of Primedia, Inc
132 W 31st St Fl 17
New York, NY 10001-3406
Telephone: (800) 257-5126, FAX: (917) 339-0325, Web Site: www.filmsmediagroup.com
CFO: James Housley
Conducts Business: U.S., Canada, U.K., Australia, New Zealand, Hong Kong
Primary Market Served: Business & Consumer
Catalog available online
Indirect online sales

Founded: 1985

Market videocassettes, CD-Rom books & posters to guidance counselors, home economists, coaches, business, social studies, vocational, science, art & music & physical education teachers, librarians, corporations & government programs.

CARFAX INC
5860 Trinity Pkwy (Suite 600)
Centreville, VA 20120-1998
Telephone: (703) 934-2664, Web Site: www.carfax.com
Dealer Mktg Coord: Derek Legendre
Primary Market Served: Business & Consumer

CLARK'S CORVAIR PARTS, INC
400 Mohawk Trl
Shelburne Falls, MA 01370-8503
Telephone: (413) 625-9776, FAX: (413) 625-8498, E-Mail: clarks@corvair.com, Web Site: www.corvair.com
Pres: Calvin Clark Jr.
VP: Joan Clark
Conducts Business: U.S., Canada
Employees: 25
Primary Market Served: Consumer
Catalog available online
Direct online sales
Advertising/Marketing Budget Related to Direct Marketing: 76-100%
Direct Marketing ad budget:
Direct Mail: 10%
Magazines: 80%
Newspapers: 10%
Founded: 1973

Over 14,000 restoration parts for the Chevy Corvair automobile.

CON-WAY FREIGHT
2211 Old Earhart Rd Ste 100
Ann Arbor, MI 48105-2963
Telephone: (734) 994-6600
Direct Mktg Mgr: Tanya Koziara

CON-WAY TRUCKLOAD
4701 E 32nd St
Joplin, MO 64804
Telephone: (417) 623-5229, (800) CFI-DRIVE, FAX: (417) 623-8939, E-Mail: gnichols@cfi-us.com, Web Site: www.cfi-us.com
Pres & CEO: Herbert Schmidt
Exec VP & CFO: Angelo Ianoello
VP, Opers: Saul Gonzalez
VP, IT: Mark Swab
Conducts Business: U.S., Canada, Mexico

Employees: 2,400
Primary Market Served: Business
Catalog available online
Indirect online sales
Advertising/Marketing Budget Related
to Direct Marketing: 0-25%
Founded: 1951
Gross sales or billing: $272,400,000

Trucking, specializing in transportation
of high value & time sensitive equipment & products throughout North
America.

DAIMLERCHRYSLER CORP
1000 Chrysler Dr (CIMS 485-06-73)
Auburn Hills, MI 48326-2766
Telephone: (248) 512-1879, Web Site:
www.daimlerchrysler.com
Information Architect: J.J. Schultz II
Primary Market Served: Business &
Consumer

DAKOTA DIGITAL
4510 W 61st St N
Sioux Falls, SD 57107-0639
Telephone: (605) 332-6513, (800) 593-
4160, FAX: (605) 339-4106, E-Mail:
sales@dakotadigital.com, Web Site:
www.dakotadigital.com
Pres: Ross Ortman
Sls Exec: Scott Johnson
Conducts Business: U.S.
Employees: 30
Primary Market Served: Business &
Consumer
Catalog available online
Direct online sales
Advertising/Marketing Budget Related
to Direct Marketing: 51-75%
Direct Marketing ad budget: $250,000
Direct Mail: 20%
Magazines: 70%
Telephone: 10%
Founded: 1985
Gross sales or billing: $3,000,000

Electronic automotive instrumentation
& remote vehicle entry systems sold
directly to auto enthusiasts & through
dealer network.

DELTA TECH INDUSTRIES
1901 S Vineyard Ave # 7
Ontario, CA 91761-7747
Telephone: (714) 577-8028, FAX:
(714) 577-0140, E-Mail: sales@
deltatechindustries.com, Web Site:
www.deltatechindustries.com
Pres: Bogdan Durian
Customer Svcs Mgr: Matt Tsernal
Natl Sales Mgr: Paul Barnaby
Conducts Business: U.S., U.K., S. Af-
rica, Australia, Canada, Germany,
Italy, Korea, Poland, Taiwan, China,
Indonesia, Russia
Employees: 15

Primary Market Served: Business &
Consumer
Catalog available online
Indirect online sales
Advertising/Marketing Budget Related
to Direct Marketing: 0-25%
Direct Marketing ad budget:
Direct Mail: 40%
Magazines: 30%
Telephone: 30%
Founded: 1978

Manufacturing of auxiliary automobile
lighting to distributors & consumers.

**DESERT RAT TRUCK
CENTERS**
3705 S Palo Verde St
Tucson, AZ 85713-5401
Telephone: (520) 790-8502, (866) 444-
5337, FAX: (520) 750-1918, Web
Site: www.desertrat.com
Chmn: Jack Furrier
Pres: Mike Furrier
Conducts Business: Worldwide
Employees: 15
Primary Market Served: Consumer
Advertising/Marketing Budget Related
to Direct Marketing: 0-25%
Gross sales or billing: $4,200,000

Sell tires & accessories for RV &
4-wheel drive pick-ups.

**DYNAMIC DEVELOPMENT
CO**
25512 Pampero Cir
Mission Viejo, CA 92691-5436
Telephone: (949) 768-5798, E-Mail:
antiwear@dynamicdevelopment.com,
Web Site: www.
dynamicdevelopment.com
Pres: Eugene F. Lally
Conducts Business: U.S., Canada, Eu-
rope
Employees: 2
Primary Market Served: Business &
Consumer
Catalog available online
Indirect online sales
Advertising/Marketing Budget Related
to Direct Marketing: 26-50%
Founded: 1962

Chemical oil additive that reduces
metal parts wear 90% & increases auto
engine compression, performance, and
fuel mileage. The additive is also used
in industrial and aerospace mechanical
equipment to reduce maintenance costs
and improve equipment efficiency.

EASTHILL GROUP INC
dba The Eastwood Co
263 Shoemaker Rd
Pottstown, PA 19464-6433

Telephone: (610) 323-9099, (610) 323-
9063, (610) 323-2200, (888) 869-
4433, (800) 345-1178, FAX: (610)
323-6268, Web Site: www.
eastwoodcompany.com
Founder & Chmn: Curt Strohacker
Circulation Coord: Diane Short
Affiliate Mktg: John Schell
Conducts Business: Worldwide
Employees: 40
Primary Market Served: Business &
Consumer
Catalog available online
Direct online sales
Advertising/Marketing Budget Related
to Direct Marketing: 51-75%
Direct Marketing ad budget: $500,000
Magazines: 100%
Founded: 1978

Automotive tools.

ECKLERS
5200 S Washington Ave
Titusville, FL 32780-7316
Telephone: (888) 787-3626, (800) 284-
3906, E-Mail: custsvc@ecklers.net,
Web Site: www.ecklers.com
Primary Market Served: Business &
Consumer

**FARRINGTON
TRANSPORTATION**
553 S Joliet Rd (Suite B)
Bolingbrook, IL 60440-3631
Telephone: (630) 783-9200
VP Sls & Mktg: James Reifenberg
Primary Market Served: Business

FIRSTGROUP AMERICA
600 Vine St (Suite 1400)
Cincinnati, OH 45202-2426
Telephone: (513) 419-8635, Web Site:
www.firstgroupamerica.com
Dir Customer Mktg: Bobbie Hartman
Employees: 95,000
Primary Market Served: Business
Advertising/Marketing Budget Related
to Direct Marketing: 0-25%

**FOUR WHEEL DRIVE
HARDWARE LLC**
44488 State Rte 14
Columbiana, OH 44408-9540
Telephone: (330) 482-4733, FAX:
(330) 482-5035, E-Mail: info@4wd.
com, Web Site: www.4wd.com
Pres: Barry Ryan
IT Mgr: Ed Peters
Conducts Business: Worldwide
Employees: 155
Primary Market Served: Business &
Consumer
Catalog available online
Indirect online sales
Advertising/Marketing Budget Related

to Direct Marketing: 76-100%
Founded: 1977
Gross sales or billing: $14,900,000

Automotive retail catalogs specializing in Jeep products.

HARLEY-DAVIDSON INC
3700 W Juneau Ave
Milwaukee, WI 53208-2865
Telephone: (414) 343-7286, FAX:
 (414) 343-4806, Web Site: www.
 harley-davidson.com
Pres & CEO: James L. Ziemer
Mktg Mgr: Susan McBeth
VP Communs: Kathleen A. Lawler
VP Licensing & Special Events:
 Joanne M. Bischmann
VP Core Cust Mktg: Bill Davidson
VP No Am Sls: Jeff Merton
Employees: 9,704
Primary Market Served: Business
Advertising/Marketing Budget Related
 to Direct Marketing: 26-50%
Founded: 1903
Gross sales or billing: $6,185,000,000

Manufacture motorcycles, recreational vehicles, specialized commercial vehicles, motorcycle fashions & clothing & liquid fueled target drone rocket engines for the military.

HISTORIC AVIATION
Div. of Sky Media LLC
640 Taft St NE
Minneapolis, MN 55413-2815
Telephone: (651) 635-0100, (800) 225-
 5575, FAX: (651) 635-0700, E-Mail:
 info@historicaviation.com, Web Site:
 www.historicaviation.com
Pres: Dave Wood
Member: Gregory Herrick
Conducts Business: Worldwide
Employees: 9
Primary Market Served: Consumer
Catalog available online
Direct online sales
Direct Marketing ad budget: $250,000
Magazines: $20,000
Founded: 1970

Catalog marketer of aviation books, video cassettes & art.

IPD CO INC
11744 NE Ainsworth Cir
Portland, OR 97220
Telephone: (503) 257-7500, (800) 444-
 6473, FAX: (503) 257-7596, E-Mail:
 info@ipdusa.com, Web Site: www.
 ipdusa.com
CEO: Sue Hart
COO: David Precechtil
Conducts Business: U.S., Canada, Japan
Employees: 24

Primary Market Served: Business & Consumer
Catalog available online
Indirect online sales
Advertising/Marketing Budget Related
 to Direct Marketing: 26-50%
Direct Marketing ad budget: $150,000
Direct Mail: $80,000
Magazines: $39,000
Telephone: $31,000
Founded: 1963
Gross sales or billing: $7,000,000

Sell parts & accessories for Volvo and Subaru to both retail & wholesale markets.

INDUS-TOOL
Div. of Bird-X Inc
300 N Oakley Blvd
Chicago, IL 60612
Telephone: (312) 226-2473, (800) 662-
 5021, FAX: (312) 226-2480, E-Mail:
 sales@indus-tool.com, Web Site:
 www.indus-tool.com
Pres: Ronald Schwarcz
Export Sls: Luisa Ramirez
Conducts Business: Worldwide
Employees: 28
Primary Market Served: Business & Consumer
Catalog available online
Direct online sales
Founded: 1962

Vehicle warning lights & backup alarms, dock loading lights & electric footwarmers.

INTERNATIONAL AUTO PARTS
PO Box 9036, Rte 29 North
Charlottesville, VA 22906-9036
Telephone: (804) 974-7118, (800) 726-
 0555, FAX: (804) 973-2368, E-Mail:
 iap1@international-auto.com, Web
 Site: www.international-auto.com
Pres: Paul Opiela
Creative: Mike Brobhy
Conducts Business: U.S.
Employees: 45
Primary Market Served: Consumer
Advertising/Marketing Budget Related
 to Direct Marketing: 76-100%
Direct Marketing ad budget:
Direct Mail: 100%
Founded: 1971

Auto accessories & travel products.

J&P CYCLES
13225 Circle Dr
Anamosa, IA 52205-7321
Telephone: (319) 462-4819, Web Site:
 www.j-pcycles.com
Pres: John Parham

Motorcycle parts & accessories

JC WHITNEY
225 N Michigan Ave (Suite 9)
Chicago, IL 60601-7757
Telephone: (312) 431-6000, FAX:
 (312) 431-5650, Web Site: www.
 jcwhitney.com
CFO: Tim Ford
Mktg Dir: Bob Sebastian
List Buyer: Michael McCarthy
Conducts Business: U.S., Canada
Primary Market Served: Business & Consumer
Catalog available online
Direct online sales
Advertising/Marketing Budget Related
 to Direct Marketing: 76-100%
Direct Marketing ad budget:
Direct Mail: 95%
Magazines: 5%
Founded: 1915

Sell auto parts & accessories direct to consumers.

K-D LAMP CO
Div. of Advanced Technology Corp
101 Parker Dr
Andover, OH 44003-9456
Telephone: (440) 293-4064, FAX:
 (440) 293-4591, E-Mail: admin@atc-
 lighting-plastics.com, Web Site:
 www.k-dlamp.com
Pres & CEO: Seymour S. Stein
Dir Opers: Kevin Kirby
Conducts Business: Worldwide
Employees: 261
Primary Market Served: Business
Catalog available online
Direct online sales
Advertising/Marketing Budget Related
 to Direct Marketing: 51-75%
Direct Marketing ad budget:
Direct Mail: 60%
Magazines: 40%
Founded: 1914
Gross sales or billing: $45,000,000

O.E.M. vehicle lighting includes but not limited to: heavy duty truck, school/transit/coach buses, emergency, automobile, military, motorcycle, and agricultural applications. Products provided are headlights, in H.I.D., halogen and composite. Other light products in L.E.D. and incandescent are: interior, tail, marker, clearance, back-up, license, and signal lights. Mirrors and custom wiring harnesses also available.

LAZYDAYS RV CENTER
6131 Lazydays Blvd
Seffner, FL 33584-2968
Telephone: (813) 246-4333, Web Site:
 www.lazydays.com
Chief Mktg Officer: Stewart Schaffer
Primary Market Served: Consumer

Motorhomes

THE
DMA **LEXUS DIVISION OF TOYOTA**
19001 S Western Ave (Suite L100)
Torrance, CA 90501-1106
Telephone: (213) 328-2075
Customer Info Mgr: Paul Nieberding
Primary Market Served: Business & Consumer

THE
DMA **LITHIA MOTORS INC**
360 E Jackson St
Medford, OR 97501-5892
Telephone: (541) 774-7602
Direct Mktg Coord: Sandy Stack
Primary Market Served: Business & Consumer

MID AMERICA DESIGNS INC
Div. of Mid America Direct
17082 N US Hwy 45
Effingham, IL 62401-6764
Telephone: (217) 540-4200, (800) 350-4543, FAX: (217) 540-4800, E-Mail: mail@mamotorworks.com, Web Site: www.mamotorworks.com
Pres: Michael Yager
VP, PR Events: Stephen Wiedman
VP, Opers: Lori Worman
VP: Perrie Richards
Dir Mktg: Cheryl Habing
Dir: Ed Baumgarten
Conducts Business: Worldwide
Employees: 130
Primary Market Served: Business & Consumer
Catalog available online
Indirect online sales
Advertising/Marketing Budget Related to Direct Marketing: 76-100%
Direct Marketing ad budget: $1,500,000
Direct Mail: $13,000
Magazines: $500,000
Newspapers: $1,000
Online: $5,000
TV/Radio: $150,000
Founded: 1972
Gross sales or billing: $13,900,000

Parts & accessories for the Chevrolet Corvette, Porsche & air-cooled Volkswagen.

MID AMERICA MOTORWORKS
Subs. of Mid America Direct
17082 N US Hwy 45
Effingham, IL 62401-7107
Telephone: (217) 347-5591, (800) 500-1500, FAX: (217) 347-2952, E-Mail: mail@mamotorworks.com, Web Site: www.mamotorworks.com
Pres: Mike Yager
Dir Procurement: Tim Curtis
VP Mktg: Henk vanDongen
VP Events: Lori Worman

Conducts Business: Worldwide
Employees: 100
Primary Market Served: Business & Consumer
Catalog available online
Direct online sales
Advertising/Marketing Budget Related to Direct Marketing: 51-75%
Direct Marketing ad budget: $10,000,000
Direct Mail: 70%
Magazines: 15%
Newspapers: 5%
Online: 5%
TV/Radio: 5%
Founded: 1974
Gross sales or billing: $35,000,000

Mail order catalog for restoration, accessories & performance parts for Corvette & Air-Cooled Volkswagen.

MINI CITY LTD
799 Holt Rd Ste 170
Webster, NY 14580-9188
Telephone: (716) 872-6560, FAX: (716) 872-4094, E-Mail: minicityus@aol.com, Web Site: www.minicityltd.com
Mgr: Laurie Blue
Conducts Business: Worldwide
Employees: 9
Primary Market Served: Business & Consumer
Catalog available online
Indirect online sales
Advertising/Marketing Budget Related to Direct Marketing: 51-75%
Direct Marketing ad budget:
Direct Mail: 75%
Magazines: 25%
Founded: 1967

Parts & accessories for British automobiles including Austin & Morris Minis, Morris Minors, MG 1100s & 1300s, & Austin Americas

OMEGA RESEARCH & DEVELOPMENT
981 N Burnt Hickory Rd
Douglasville, GA 30134
Telephone: (770) 942-9876, (800) 554-4053, Web Site: www.caralarm.com
Pres: Kenneth E. Flick
Employees: 30
Founded: 1971
Gross sales or billing: $3,300,000

Keyless vehicle entry & security.

PARTS PLACE INC
2300 N Opdyke Rd
Auburn Hills, MI 48326
Telephone: (248) 373-2300, (888) 432-3548, FAX: (248) 373-5950, Web Site: www.partsplaceinc.com

Primary Market Served: Business & Consumer
Catalog available online
Mail order Volkswagen parts.

PEGASUS AUTO RACING SUPPLIES INC
2475 S 179th St
New Berlin, WI 53146-2150
Telephone: (262) 317-1234, (800) 688-6946, FAX: (262) 317-1201, E-Mail: info@pegasusautoracing.com, Web Site: www.pegasusautoracing.com
Co-Owner: Christopher J. Heitman
Conducts Business: Worldwide
Employees: 15
Primary Market Served: Business & Consumer
Catalog available online
Direct online sales
Advertising/Marketing Budget Related to Direct Marketing: 26-50%
Direct Marketing ad budget: $100,000
Direct Mail: 40%
Magazines: 5%
Online: 55%
Founded: 1980
Gross sales or billing: $5,800,000

Auto racing parts, components & accessories.

RACER WALSH CO
1849 Foster Dr
Jacksonville, FL 32216-3104
Telephone: (904) 721-2289, FAX: (904) 721-2935, Web Site: www.racerwalsh.com
Pres: Jerry Walsh
Conducts Business: U.S., Canada, Europe, South America, Australia
Employees: 5
Primary Market Served: Business & Consumer
Direct Marketing ad budget:
Magazines: 100%
Gross sales or billing: $600,000

Sell auto parts. Specialize in Ford performance cars.

RAYBUCK AUTOBODY PARTS
2829 Saint John Rd
Punxsutawney, PA 15767-8501
Telephone: (814) 938-5248, FAX: (814) 938-4250, E-Mail: service@raybuck.com, Web Site: www.raybuck.com
Owner: Randy Raybuck
Office Mgr: Lisa Raybuck
Sls Mgr: Deb Macko
Employees: 6
Primary Market Served: Business & Consumer
Catalog available online

Indirect online sales
Direct Marketing ad budget: $65,000
Direct Mail: 10%
Magazines: 70%
Newspapers: 10%
TV/Radio: 10%
Founded: 1985

Post market truck & car body parts and accessories to shops and do-it-yourselfers.

THE DMA **SPEEDWAY**

Speedway Motors Inc
PO Box 81906
Lincoln, NE 68501-1906
Telephone: (402) 323-3100, FAX: (402) 477-7476
Gen Partner: Clay Smith

STORAGE BATTERY SYSTEMS INC

dba SBS
N 56 W 16665 Ridgewood Dr
Menomonee Falls, WI 53051
Telephone: (262) 703-5800, (800) 554-2243, FAX: (262) 703-3073, E-Mail: sbs@sbsbattery.com, Web Site: www.sbsbattery.com
Pres: Scott Rubenzer
VP: Robert Rubenzer
VP Sls & Mktg: Bill Rubenzer
Employees: 46
Founded: 1915
Gross sales or billing: $22,900,000

Batteries.

THE DMA **SUMMIT RACING EQUIPMENT**

1200 Southeast Ave
Tallmadge, OH 44278-3161
Telephone: (330) 630-0270, FAX: (330) 630-5330, Web Site: www.summitracing.com
Pres: Raymond J. Tatko
Pur Mgr: Frank Kremer
Sls Mgr: Rob Collova
Opers Mgr: Scott Peterson
Conducts Business: Worldwide
Primary Market Served: Business & Consumer
Catalog available online
Direct online sales
Advertising/Marketing Budget Related to Direct Marketing: 76-100%
Founded: 1968

Sell specialty automotive performance equipment & truck accessories by direct mail.

TIME LOGISTICS INC

115 Dyer St (Suite 2)
Columbia, TN 38401-4551
Telephone: (931) 540-2801, (866) 293-8463, FAX: (931) 540-2995, Web Site: www.timelogisticsinc.com
Owner & Pres: Laura Shorette
VP, Fin & Sls: Ken Shorette
VP Opers: Scott Coble

TRANSIT TREASURE INC

311 E 38th St (Suite 19B)
New York, NY 10016
Telephone: (646) 706-1001, Web Site: www.transittreasure.com
Founder & CEO: Dan Miller
Primary Market Served: Business & Consumer

Clubs, Continuities & Correspondence Schools (13)

This section contains listings for clubs, continuities and correspondence schools that utilize direct marketing and direct response services.

AMS DIRECT
7020 High Grove Blvd
Burr Ridge, IL 60527-7637
Telephone: (630) 382-1000, FAX: (630) 325-0825, Web Site: www. amsdirect.com
Chmn: Mark S. Holecek
Vice Chmn: Donald R. Strumillo
Pres: Michael E. Hussey
Conducts Business: U.S.
Employees: 100
Primary Market Served: Business & Consumer
Advertising/Marketing Budget Related to Direct Marketing: 76-100%

Sell home study courses in finance, real estate & investment.

ALLSTATE MOTOR CLUB
Subs. of Allstate Insurance
51 W Higgins Rd (Suite RGA)
South Barrington, IL 60010-9300
Telephone: (847) 551-2300, (800) 998-8697
VP, Mktg: Garry Ballek
Pres: Jim Ejupi
Dir Bus Acq: Karen Burns
Conducts Business: U.S.
Employees: 250
Primary Market Served: Consumer
Founded: 1961

Teleservices.

ART INSTRUCTION SCHOOLS
Div. of Bureau of Engraving
3400 Technology Dr
Minneapolis, MN 55418-6000
Telephone: (612) 362-5075, FAX: (612) 362-5260, Web Site: www. artinstructionschools.edu
Pres & CEO: Tom Stuart
Mktg Dir: Steve Unverzagt
Conducts Business: U.S., Canada, Puerto Rico
Employees: 30
Primary Market Served: Consumer
Advertising/Marketing Budget Related to Direct Marketing: 76-100%
Direct Marketing ad budget:
Magazines: 5%
Online: 85%
TV/Radio: 10%
Founded: 1914

Distance education art instruction.

ASHEVILLE COMPASSIONATE COMMUNICATION CENTER
150 E Chestnut St (#1)
Asheville, NC 28801-2337
Telephone: (828) 252-0538, E-Mail: jerry@ashevilleccc.com, Web Site: ashevilleccc.com
Pres: Jerry Donoghue
Primary Market Served: Business

Video training.

ASHWORTH UNIVERSITY
430 Technology Pkwy
Norcross, GA 30092-3406
Telephone: (770) 729-8400, (800) 957-5412, FAX: (770) 729-9294, E-Mail: info@ashworthuniversity.edu, Web Site: www.ashworthuniversity.edu
Natl Dir Education: F. Milton Miller
Dean, Undergraduate Studies: John Graves
Dir, Curriculum: Karl Freedman
Registrar: Renee Mason
Primary Market Served: Business & Consumer
Catalog available online
Direct online sales
Founded: 1987

Home study course-work.

BJ'S WHOLESALE CLUB INC
PO Box 5230
Westborough, MA 01581-5230
Telephone: (508) 651-7400, FAX: (508) 651-6167, Web Site: www.bjs. com
Pres: Jack Nugent
Sr VP, Mktg: Edward Gillooly
VP Mktg Opers: Steven Germain
VP, Adv: Carol Wilgus
Conducts Business: U.S.
Employees: 300
Primary Market Served: Business & Consumer
Founded: 1984
Gross sales or billing: $4,000,000,000

Wholesale club for cash & carry members only. Offer name brand & general merchandise. Credit cards accepted.

BMG COLUMBIA HOUSE
1 Penn Plaza
New York, NY 10119-0002
Telephone: (212) 287-0081, E-Mail: cs1@bmgmusicservice.com
Sr VP, Commun: Paula Batson
Conducts Business: U.S.
Primary Market Served: Consumer
Advertising/Marketing Budget Related to Direct Marketing: 26-50%

Direct marketers of music, CDs & other entertainment products.

BENTLEY COLLEGE
Center for Executive and Professional Education
175 Forest St
Waltham, MA 02452-4705
Telephone: (781) 891-2800, FAX: (781) 891-3449, Web Site: www. bentley.edu
Dean: Pat Flynn
Assoc Dean & Dir: Karen Seibinico
VP, Mktg: Andre Le Bell
Conducts Business: U.S.
Employees: 800
Primary Market Served: Business & Consumer
Catalog available online
Indirect online sales
Advertising/Marketing Budget Related to Direct Marketing: 51-75%
Founded: 1917

Offer a comprehensive information age marketing certificate professional development program for those working in or aspiring to the field of direct response marketing.

THE DMA BERKELEY COLLEGE
64 E Midland Ave
Paramus, NJ 07652-2947
Telephone: (201) 291-1111
Primary Market Served: Business & Consumer

BOOKSPAN
Subs. of Bertelsmann and AOL Time Warner
501 Franklin Ave
Garden City, NY 11530
Telephone: (516) 490-4561, FAX: (516) 490-4856
Pres: Markus Wilhelm
Exec VP, Mktg: Lucia Coffey
Sr VP HR: William A. Gatti
VP & CFO: John Vlachos
Conducts Business: U.S., Canada
Employees: 1,200
Primary Market Served: Consumer
Catalog available online
Direct online sales
Advertising/Marketing Budget Related to Direct Marketing: 76-100%
Founded: 1928

Operate approximately 50 book clubs including The Literary Guild & The Doubleday Book Club plus specialty clubs (Mystery Guild, Science Fiction, International Collector's Guild and Book of the Month Club). Sell to the general public through a combination of print, direct mail & other advertising vehicles.

CENTER FOR PROFESSIONAL ADVANCEMENT

25 Kennedy Blvd (Suite 400)
East Brunswick, NJ 08816-1258
Telephone: (732) 238-1600, FAX: (732) 238-9113, E-Mail: info@cfpa. com, Web Site: www.cfpa.com
Pres: Charles W. Bendel Jr
Conducts Business: U.S., Amsterdam, Holland
Employees: 41
Primary Market Served: Business
Catalog available online
Direct online sales
Founded: 1967
Gross sales or billing: $8,685,000

Sell technical short courses to professional engineers in chemical processing, pharmaceutical technology & mechanical engineering.

CLEVELAND INSTITUTE OF ELECTRONICS

1776 E 17th St
Cleveland, OH 44114-3636
Telephone: (216) 781-9400, FAX: (216) 781-0331, E-Mail: instruct@ cie-wc.edu, Web Site: www.cie-wc. edu
Pres: J. Randall Drinko
Controller: Paul Valvoda
Asst Mgr: Ted Sheroke
Conducts Business: Worldwide
Employees: 65
Primary Market Served: Business & Consumer
Catalog available online
Direct online sales
Advertising/Marketing Budget Related to Direct Marketing: 26-50%
Direct Marketing ad budget:
Direct Mail: $250,000
Magazines: $100,000
Newspapers: $200,000
TV/Radio: $360,000
Founded: 1934

Correspondence school in electronic technology & engineering.

COSMETIQUE, INC

dba Cosmetique Beauty Club Inc
200 Corporate Woods Pkwy
Vernon Hills, IL 60061-3167
Telephone: (847) 913-9099, (800) 621-8822, Web Site: www.cosmetique. com
Pres: June Giugni
Mktg Mgr: Patti Venturini
VP: Aaron Horowitz
Conducts Business: U.S.
Primary Market Served: Consumer
Advertising/Marketing Budget Related to Direct Marketing: 0-25%
Founded: 1974

Gross sales or billing: $13,000,000

Marketer of name-brand cosmetics via continuity club. Distribute over 3 million kits annually. Direct marketing programs include: lists rental, package inserts & statement stuffers.

THE CROSS COUNTRY GROUP LLC

1 Cabot Rd
Medford, MA 02155-5117
Telephone: (781) 396-3700, Web Site: www.ccgroup.com
Exec VP: Jeffrey Wolk
Conducts Business: U.S., Canada, Mexico
Employees: 1,500
Primary Market Served: Business
Advertising/Marketing Budget Related to Direct Marketing: 76-100%
Founded: 1972
Gross sales or billing: $250,000,000

Specialty marketing organization.

DAY-TIMERS

Div. of Acco Brands Corp
5700 Lower Macungie Rd
Macungie, PA 18046
Telephone: (610) 398-1151, (800) 457-5702, (800) 225-5005, FAX: (800) 452-7398, E-Mail: connie@ lomottastrategic.com, Web Site: www.daytimer.com
VP Mktg: Brian Huck
Mgr: Art Gross
Conducts Business: Worldwide
Employees: 510
Primary Market Served: Business & Consumer
Catalog available online
Direct online sales
Founded: 1947
Gross sales or billing: $49,900,000

Retail store for Day-Timer time management planners & organizers & business accessories.

THE DMA DIRECT BRANDS INC

W 34th St (fl 5), 1 Penn Plaza
New York, NY 10119-0002
Telephone: (212) 930-4949, Web Site: www.bmgmusic.com

DOUBLEDAY DIRECT

Div. of Doubleday Canada Ltd
5900 Finch Ave E
Scarborough, ON, Canada M1B 0A2
Telephone: (416) 977-7891, FAX: (416) 977-8707
VP: Carmela Porco
Conducts Business: Canada
Employees: 128
Primary Market Served: Consumer
Advertising/Marketing Budget Related

to Direct Marketing: 76-100%
Gross sales or billing: $17,000,000

Operates book clubs: Doubleday Book Club, Crossing Book Club, Mystery Guild & Science Fiction Book Club. Mailing lists available through Watts List Brokerage, Toronto, ON.

GEORGETOWN UNIVERSITY LAW CENTER/CONTINUING LEGAL EDUCATION DIV

600 New Jersey Ave NW, Georgetown CLE
Washington, DC 20001
Telephone: (202) 662-9890, FAX: (202) 662-9891, E-Mail: nds25@law. georgetown.edu, Web Site: www. georgetowncle.org
Mktg Mgr: Nicole Steckman
Bus Opers Mgr: Mark Dizon
Conducts Business: U.S.
Primary Market Served: Business & Consumer

Legal educational programs for attorneys.

GRAND CANYON UNIVERSITY

3300 W Camelback Rd
Phoenix, AZ 85017-1097
Telephone: (602) 639-6277, Web Site: www.gcu.edu
Exec Dir Mktg: Eric McHaney
Primary Market Served: Business & Consumer

THE HISTORY BOOK CLUB INC

Subs. of Time Warner
1225 S Market St
Mechanicsburg, PA 17055
Telephone: (718) 918-2665, E-Mail: paula.batson@dgna.com, Web Site: www.historybookclub.com
Pres & CEO: George Artandi
Sr VP Club Mngmt: Juanita James
Sr VP Commun: Paula Batson
Conducts Business: U.S., Canada
Primary Market Served: Consumer
Catalog available online
Direct online sales
Advertising/Marketing Budget Related to Direct Marketing: 76-100%
Direct Marketing ad budget:
Direct Mail: 40%
Magazines: 40%
Newspapers: 20%
Founded: 1947

Offer club memberships to history buffs, sell history & children's books at discounts.

IVY TECH STATE COLLEGE
50 W Fall Creek Pkwy N Dr
Indianapolis, IN 46208-5752
Telephone: (317) 921-4800, (888) IVY-
   LINE, FAX: (317) 921-4753, Web
   Site: www.ivytech.edu/indianapolis
Pres: Tom Snyder
Sr VP, Provost: Donald S. Doucette
Dean: Todd Roswarski
PR & Adv: Lisa Butt
Primary Market Served: Consumer
Catalog available online

Public Education.

THE LIBRARY OF AMERICA
14 E 60th St Ste 1101
New York, NY 10022-7115
Telephone: (212) 308-3360, (800) 964-
   5778, FAX: (212) 750-8352, E-Mail:
   info@loa.org, Web Site: www.loa.org
Pres: Cheryl Hurley
Publr: Max Rudin
Conducts Business: U.S.
Employees: 15
Primary Market Served: Business &
   Consumer
Founded: 1979

Publish deluxe hardcover collections of
America's greatest writers.

LINCOLN EDUCATIONAL
SERVICES
200 Executive Dr Ste 340
West Orange, NJ 07052-3303
Telephone: (973) 736-9340
Chief Mktg Officer: Piper Jameson
Primary Market Served: Business &
   Consumer

MARASTAR
COMMUNICATIONS
11 West Ave (Suite 220)
Wayne, PA 19087-3224
Telephone: (610) 902-0080, FAX:
   (610) 902-0600, E-Mail: info@
   marastar.com, Web Site: www.
   marastar.com
Chmn & CEO: Raymond Hansell
Pres & COO: Marysue Lucci
VP: Ken Sachar
Conducts Business: U.S.
Employees: 15
Catalog available online
Direct online sales
Advertising/Marketing Budget Related
   to Direct Marketing: 0-25%
Founded: 1998

Web-based training.

MOVIE/ENTERTAINMENT
BOOK CLUB
Div. of Eagle Book Clubs Inc
One Massachusetts Ave
Washington, DC 20001

Telephone: (800) 879-3270, FAX:
   (202) 216-0614, E-Mail: meb@
   eaglepub.com
Pres: Brian Lewis
Editor: Jeff Rubin
Conducts Business: Worldwide
Primary Market Served: Consumer
Advertising/Marketing Budget Related
   to Direct Marketing: 0-25%
Direct Marketing ad budget:
Direct Mail: 5%
Magazines: 90%
Newspapers: 5%
Founded: 1973

Sell books to club members.

NEW YORK ROAD RUNNERS
CLUB, INC
Nine E 89th St
New York, NY 10128-0602
Telephone: (212) 860-4455, (800) 405-
   2288, FAX: (212) 369-4704, E-Mail:
   webmaster@nyrr.org, Web Site:
   www.nyrrc.org
Mdse Dir: Beth Creighton
Primary Market Served: Consumer
Founded: 1958

Running organization.

THE DMA NORTH AMERICAN
MEMBERSHIP GROUP INC
12301 Whitewater Dr
Minnetonka, MN 55343-9447
Telephone: (952) 936-9333, FAX:
   (952) 936-9755, Web Site: www.
   namginc.com
Pres & CEO: Nancy Evensen
VP, Grp Publr: Russ Nolan
Sr VP: Tony DeFrance
VP, Fin & Opers: Kate Pope
VP, Membership Devel: Laura
   Burkholder
Conducts Business: U.S., Canada
Employees: 400
Primary Market Served: Consumer
Direct online sales
Advertising/Marketing Budget Related
   to Direct Marketing: 76-100%
Founded: 1978

Membership organization serving hunt-
ing, fishing, gardening, cooking, golf
& do-it-yourself health and wellness,
home arts enthusiasts through the
North American Hunting Club, the
North American Fishing Club, the
Handyman Club of America, the Na-
tional Home Gardening Club, the
Cooking Club of America, the PGA
Tour Partners Club, National Health &
Wellness Club & the Creative Home
Arts Club.

RANDOM HOUSE
CHILDREN'S BOOKS
Div. of Random House, Inc.
1745 Broadway

New York, NY 10019
Telephone: (212) 782-9000, (800) 726-
   0600, Web Site: www.randomhouse.
   com/kids
Mktg Mgr: Barry O'Donovan
Conducts Business: U.S., Canada
Primary Market Served: Consumer

One of the largest English-language
children's trade book publishers. Creates books for preschool children
through young adult readers, in all formats from board books to activity
books to picture books and novels.
Brings together award-winning authors
and illustrators, world-famous franchise characters, and multimillion-copy
series.

REMINGTON COLLEGE
500 International Pkwy (Suite 200)
Heathrow, FL 32746-5627
Telephone: (407) 562-5691, Web Site:
   www.remingtoncollege.edu
Direct Mail Coord: Julie Pappas

STABENFELDT INC
457 N. Main St (#3C)
Danbury, CT 06811-4700
Telephone: (203) 730-2178
Controller: Matthew Sganga
Primary Market Served: Consumer

TRUMP UNIVERSITY
40 Wall St Ste 3200
New York, NY 10005-1332
Web Site: www.trumpuniversity.com
VP Mktg: Josef Katz

UNIVERSAL
COMMUNICATION
ENTERPRISE
66 Elmora Ave
Elizabeth, NJ 07202-1630
Telephone: (908) 355-2299, FAX:
   (908) 352-2931
Pres: Julio Sabater
Conducts Business: U.S.
Employees: 49
Primary Market Served: Business &
   Consumer
Founded: 1985
Gross sales or billing: $1,800,000

School for people whose second language is English. Also offers computer
& word processing classes.

UNIVERSITY OF ALABAMA
College of Continuing Studies, Box
   870388
Tuscaloosa, AL 35487-0388
Telephone: (205) 348-6010, FAX:
   (205) 348-0249, Web Site: www.ua.
   edu
Dean: John Snider

Pres: Dr Robert E. Witt
Conducts Business: U.S.
Primary Market Served: Business &
  Consumer
Founded: 1831

Provides correspondence school, weekend seminars & workshops. Evening &
weekend programs in credit course.

ᵀᴴᴱ UNIVERSITY OF PHOENIX
4025 S Riverpoint Pkwy
Phoenix, AZ 85040-0723
Telephone: (480) 557-1662, Web Site:
  www.phoenix.edu
Mktg Mgr: Sadie Braune

VERTRUE INC
20 Glover Ave
Norwalk, CT 06850-1219
Telephone: (203) 324-7635, FAX:
  (203) 674-7080, Web Site: www.
  vertrue.com
Pres: Gary Johnson
Exec VP, Client Svcs: William Olson
Exec VP, CFO & COO: James P.
  Duffy
Exec VP Bus Devel: David Schechne
VP Creative Sls: Kip Finch
Conducts Business: U.S.
Employees: 2,400
Primary Market Served: Business &
  Consumer
Advertising/Marketing Budget Related
  to Direct Marketing: 76-100%
Direct Marketing ad budget:
Direct Mail: 25%
Telephone: 75%
Founded: 1988
Gross sales or billing: $800,000,000

Credit card enhancement services.

ᵀᴴᴱ WESTON DISTANCE LEARNING
2001 Lowe St
Fort Collins, CO 80525-3474
Telephone: (970) 282-6322
Adv Dir: Debbie Thomson
Primary Market Served: Business &
  Consumer

Financial Services (14)

ACADEMIC MANAGEMENT SERVICES
P.O. Box 55807
Boston, MA 02205-8507
Telephone: (508) 235-2900, (800) 891-4203, FAX: (508) 235-2991, E-Mail: info@amsweb.com, Web Site: www.amsweb.com
Pres & CEO: William Hastings
Mktg Mgr: Laura Redmond
Conducts Business: U.S.
Employees: 125
Primary Market Served: Business & Consumer
Advertising/Marketing Budget Related to Direct Marketing: 51-75%
Founded: 1970

Tuition payment plans, loans & credit lines for education. Sell to colleges & prep schools, direct mail to parents.

ACCOUNTING WITH DEBITS AND CREDITS WITH COATES & HUTCHINSON PC
PO Box 561
Odenton, MD 21113
Telephone: (800) 833-5933, FAX: (301) 912-3364, E-Mail: info@awdc.org
VP: Theresa Hutchinson
Pres: Doreen Coates
Conducts Business: U.S.
Employees: 4
Primary Market Served: Business
Advertising/Marketing Budget Related to Direct Marketing: 0-25%
Founded: 1989
Gross sales or billing: $290,000

Charitable solicitation filings. Tax & bookkeeping services.

ACCUTRADE INC
Sub. of Ameritrade Holding Corp
1005 Ameritrade Pl, PO Box 68103-2227
Bellevue, NE 68005
Telephone: (800) 882-4887, FAX: (816) 243-3762, E-Mail: info@accutrade.com
Pres: Mark Gibson
Conducts Business: U.S.
Primary Market Served: Business & Consumer

Discount stock brokerage firm.

ADVANCED FINANCIAL SERVICES
25 Enterprise Ctr
Middletown, RI 02842-7233

Telephone: (401) 846-3100, Web Site: www.afsfitfinance.com
Mktg Dir: Dana Fortin
Primary Market Served: Consumer

THE DMA ADVANCEME INC
2015 Vaughn Rd NW (Suite 500)
Kennesaw, GA 30144-7831
Telephone: (888) 700-8181, Web Site: www.advanceme.com
VP, Direct Mktg: Christopher Rabbu

ADVANTA CORP
Welsh & McKean Rd
Spring House, PA 19477
Telephone: (215) 657-4000, (800) 255-0022, Web Site: www.advanta.com
CEO & Chmn: Dennis Alter
VP Mktg & Acquisition: Meredith Hein

AEGON CORP
400 W Market St
Louisville, KY 40202-4000
Telephone: (502) 560-2000, FAX: (502) 560-2611, Web Site: www.aegonins.com
Pres, CEO: Donald Shepard
Conducts Business: U.S.
Employees: 60
Primary Market Served: Consumer

Reverse mortgages to over 2,000 homeowners whose homes are worth at least $75,000.

THE DMA AETNA - MARKETING PRODUCT & COMMUNICATION
151 Farmington Ave
Hartford, CT 06156
Telephone: (860) 273-0123, (800) 872-3862, FAX: (860) 273-3971, Web Site: www.aetna.com
Chmn & CEO: Ronald A. Williams
Pres: Mark T. Bertolini
Sr VP & CIO: Margaret McCarthy
Sr VP Strategic Mktg & Communs: Robert M Mead
VP Mktg: Frank McCauley
Conducts Business: U.S.
Employees: 34,024
Primary Market Served: Business & Consumer
Catalog available online
Gross sales or billing: $25,100,000,000

Direct marketing of mutual funds to business & consumer.

THE DMA AGILIS CO
2380 Crossroads Blvd
Albert Lea, MN 56007-4001

Telephone: (507) 377-5028
Pres: Patty Tewes
Primary Market Served: Business & Consumer

ALERUS FINANCIAL
401 Demers Ave Ste 100
Grand Forks, ND 58201-4574
Telephone: (701) 795-3200, (800) 279-3200, Web Site: www2.alerusfinancial.com
Primary Market Served: Consumer

ALLIANCE BERNSTEIN
1345 Ave of the Americas
New York, NY 10105-0302
Telephone: (212) 969-1000, (800) 962-2134, FAX: (212) 969-2229, Web Site: www.alliancebernstein.com
Chmn & CEO: Lewis A. Sanders
Pres, COO & Dir: Gerald M. Lieberman
Exec VP & CTO: Lawrence H. Cohen
Sr VP & CFO: Robert H. Joseph Jr.
CIO: Sharen E. Fay
Employees: 5,580
Primary Market Served: Business & Consumer
Founded: 1987
Gross sales or billing: $4,700,000,000

AMERICAN APPRAISAL ASSOCIATES
411 E Wisconsin Ave (Suite 1900)
Milwaukee, WI 53202-4466
Telephone: (414) 271-7240, (800) 558-8650, FAX: (414) 225-1271, Web Site: www.american-appraisal.com
Mktg Mgr: Laura Brophy
Chm & CEO: Joseph Zvesper
Natl Mng Dir & Sr VP: Herb Sanders
Mktg Specialist: Paul Perez
Conducts Business: U.S., Canada, Europe, Asia
Employees: 850
Primary Market Served: Business
Advertising/Marketing Budget Related to Direct Marketing: 51-75%
Founded: 1896

Valuation consulting services.

AMERICAN CENTURY INVESTMENTS
4500 Main St, Box 418210
Kansas City, MO 64111
Telephone: (816) 531-5575, (800) 345-2021, FAX: (816) 340-7962, Web Site: www.americancentury.com
Chmn: James E. Stowers III
Pres & CEO: Jonathan Thomas
Exec VP & COO: Barry Fink
Sr VP: Glen Foggle

Conducts Business: U.S.
Employees: 1,837
Primary Market Served: Business & Consumer
Catalog available online
Indirect online sales
Gross sales or billing: $249,000,000

Mutual fund company serving retail & institutional markets.

THE DMA AMERICAN EXPRESS CO
Div. of American Express Co
200 Vesey St (fl 47
New York, NY 10285-0002
Telephone: (212) 640-2000, FAX: (212) 619-9802, Web Site: www. americanexpress.com
CEO: Kenneth I. Chenault
Grp VP: Edward Gilligan
VP Mktg, Consumer Tvl: Audrey Hendley
Dir, Brand Mngmt: Lisa Drapkin
Conducts Business: Worldwide
Employees: 58,400
Primary Market Served: Business & Consumer
Gross sales or billing: $24,300,000

Promotes traveler's cheques & card products. Engaged in acquisition of new cardmembers & cross-selling of various services.

AMERIPRISE FINANCIAL SERVICES INC
2324 Ameriprise Financial Center
Minneapolis, MN 55474-0023
Telephone: (651) 671-3434, (612) 671-3131, (800) 386-2042, Web Site: www.ameriprise.com
Chm & CEO: James Cracchiolo
Client Acquisition Direct Mktg Mgr: Cid Rode

ARBOR CAPITAL 1
1414 Harney St (Suite 400)
Omaha, NE 68102-2255
Telephone: (402) 991-4962
Mng Partner: Susan Henricks
Primary Market Served: Consumer

THE DMA ARBOR COMMERCIAL MORTGAGE
333 Earle Ovington Blvd
Uniondale, NY 11553-3610
Telephone: (516) 229-6615, Web Site: www.thearbornet.com
Sr VP Mktg: Bonnie Habyan

ASSOCIATION FOR FINANCIAL PROFESSIONALS
4520 East West Hwy (Suite 750)
Bethesda, MD 20814-3574

Telephone: (301) 907-2862, FAX: (301) 907-2864, Web Site: www. afponline.org
Pres & CEO: James A. Kaitz
VP & COO: Thomas W. Derry
Primary Market Served: Business

Serves financial professionals with products, education and training for treasury and corporate finance.

THE DMA ASTORIA FEDERAL SAVINGS
1 Astoria Federal Plaza
Lake Success, NY 11042-1076
Telephone: (516) 327-7000, Web Site: www.astoriafederal.com

THE DMA AVIVA USA CORP
611 Fifth Ave
Des Moines, IA 50309
Telephone: (515) 362-3600, FAX: (800) 531-0038, Web Site: www. avivausa.com
Sr VP Corp Communs: Jonna LaToure
Pres & CEO: Thomas C. Godlasky
Primary Market Served: Consumer
Advertising/Marketing Budget Related to Direct Marketing: 0-25%
Founded: 1896
Gross sales or billing: $101,400,000

Holding company for banks, realty, investment & mortgage companies.

AXIS CAPITAL
430 Park Ave (fl 2)
New York, NY 10022-3539
Telephone: (212) 500-7743
Primary Market Served: Consumer

BNY MELLON
1 Wall St
New York, NY 10286
Telephone: (412) 234-5000, (212) 495-1784, FAX: (412) 234-1928, Web Site: www.bnymellon.com
Mktg Analysis & Reporting Dir: John Ragusa
Conducts Business: Worldwide
Employees: 16,000
Primary Market Served: Business & Consumer

Retail bank.

BT ALEX BROWN INC
Subs. of Bankers Trust NY Corp
1 South St
Baltimore, MD 21202-3298
Telephone: (410) 727-1700, (800) 638-2956, Web Site: www.dbalexbrown. com
Conducts Business: Worldwide
Employees: 2,575
Primary Market Served: Business & Consumer
Founded: 1800

Investment banking subsidiary providing financial services.

BANK BOSTON
1075 Main St
Waltham, MA 02451-7424
Telephone: (781) 788-7795, FAX: (781) 788-2513, Web Site: www. bankboston.com
Consumer Prod Mngmt Dir: Tisha Capello
Conducts Business: U.S.
Employees: 2,000
Primary Market Served: Business & Consumer

Full-service bank.

BANK OF AMERICA
100 N Tryon St Ste 220, Bank America Corp Ctr
Charlotte, NC 28202-4031
Telephone: (704) 386-5681, (800) 841-4000, FAX: (704) 386-6699, Web Site: www.bankofamerica.com
Chmn, Pres & CEO: Kenneth D. Lewis
COO for Office of CFO: Milton H. Jones Jr
CFO: Joe Price
Chief Admin Officer: J. Steele Alphin
Global Risk Exec: Amy Woods Brinkley
Conducts Business: U.S.
Employees: 203,000
Primary Market Served: Business & Consumer
Catalog available online
Gross sales or billing: $117,000,000,000

Full-service bank.

THE DMA BANK OF HAWAII
Subs. of Bank of Hawaii Corporate
PO Box 2900
Honolulu, HI 96846-0001
Telephone: (808) 537-8398, FAX: (808) 536-9433, Web Site: www.boh. com
Exec VP & Mgr Mktg & Commun Grp: Laurie McCarney
CEO: Michael O'Neil
VP & Mgr: Margaret Dang
VP, DM & Collateral: June Kaneshiro
Sr VP: Cindy Thomas
Conducts Business: U.S.
Employees: 4,000
Primary Market Served: Business & Consumer
Advertising/Marketing Budget Related to Direct Marketing: 0-25%

Full-service bank.

THE BANK OF NEW YORK/ DELAWARE

Subs. of The Bank of New York Corp
PO Box 6995
Newark, DE 19714-6995
Telephone: (302) 451-2500, (800) 942-1977, FAX: (302) 451-2537, Web Site: www.bankofny.com
Conducts Business: U.S.
Employees: 850
Primary Market Served: Business & Consumer

Lending company.

ᵀᴴᴱ_ᴰᴹᴬ BANK OF THE WEST

300 S Grand Ave
Los Angeles, CA 90071-3109
Telephone: (509) 736-0131, Web Site: www.bankofthewest.com
Sr VP: David Covert

BANK ONE

One Bank One Plaza
Chicago, IL 60670
Telephone: (888) 963-4000, (866) 265-1727, (800) 452-3141, Web Site: www.bankone.com
Pres: Verne Istock
Primary Market Served: Business & Consumer

User of direct marketing to sell financial services.

THE BAUMAN GROUP

50 Main St
Ashland, MA 01721-3113
Telephone: (508) 879-3009, (800) 876-3009, FAX: (508) 875-3751, E-Mail: info@bauman.com, Web Site: www.bauman.com
Pres & Owner: Marcia Bauman
Primary Market Served: Business & Consumer
Founded: 1987

Credit card marketing firm.

BEARINGPOINT INC

50 Chestnut Ridge Rd
Montvale, NJ 07645-1814
Telephone: (201) 307-7000, FAX: (201) 505-3765, Web Site: www.bearingpoint.com
Pres & CEO: Ed Harbach
Exec VP & CFO: Judy A. Ethell
Exec VP & CMO: Connie K. Weaver
Exec VP & CIO: Eric Goldfarb
Exec VP: Rick Martino
Conducts Business: Worldwide
Employees: 40,000
Primary Market Served: Business
Advertising/Marketing Budget Related to Direct Marketing: 0-25%

Accounting, audit & tax consulting firm.

BILL ME LATER INC

9690 Deereco Rd (Suite 705)
Timonium, MD 21093-6936
Telephone: (443) 921-1184, Web Site: www.coporate.billmelater.com
Mktg & Events: Melissa Foreman

WILLIAM BLAIR & CO LLC

222 W Adams St
Chicago, IL 60606-5312
Telephone: (312) 236-1600, (800) 621-0687, FAX: (312) 368-9418, E-Mail: info@williamblair.com, Web Site: www.williamblair.com
Chmn: Edgar D. Jannotta
Pres & CEO: John R. Ettelson
CIO: W. George Greig
Head Corp Fin: Richard P. Kiphart
Dir, Res: Robert D. Newman
Primary Market Served: Business & Consumer
Catalog available online
Founded: 1935

Investment banking firm.

THE BOSTON CO

Subs. of Mellon Corp
1 Boston Pl
Boston, MA 02108-4407
Telephone: (617) 722-7000, FAX: (617) 722-7569
Chmn & CEO: David Lamere
Conducts Business: U.S., England
Primary Market Served: Business & Consumer

Multi-faceted investment management & banking organization.

ᵀᴴᴱ_ᴰᴹᴬ BRAINTREE PAYMENT SOLUTIONS LLC

833 W Jackson Blvd (Suite 500)
Chicago, IL 60607-5400
Telephone: (773) 489-9539, Web Site: www.braintreepaymentsolutions.com

BRANCH BANKING & TRUST CO

Subs. of BB&T Financial Corp
223 W Nash St
Wilson, NC 27893-3801
Telephone: (252) 399-4111, FAX: (252) 246-4030
Sr Exec VP: W. Ken Chalk
Sr Exec VP: Scott E. Reed
COO: Henry G. Williamson Jr
BB&T Network Mgr: Kelly S. King
Conducts Business: U.S.
Employees: 3,000
Primary Market Served: Business & Consumer
Gross sales or billing: $6,500,000,000

Financial institution.

CIT

Change of control 2002
1 CIT Dr
Livingston, NJ 07039-5703
Telephone: (973) 422-6040, FAX: (973) 740-5383, Web Site: www.cit.com
Exec VP: Omar Farooq
Dir Mktg Communs: Gia Porto-Lenza
Conducts Business: U.S.
Employees: 5,620
Primary Market Served: Business
Direct Marketing ad budget:
Direct Mail: 50%
Magazines: 25%
Newspapers: 25%
Founded: 2002
Gross sales or billing: $3,036,400

Financial service corporation specializing in equipment financing & leasing for business firms. Financing of office products, manufactured housing & recreational vehicles.

CMS INC

2650 Pilgrim Ct
Winston Salem, NC 27106-5238
Telephone: (336) 631-2524, Web Site: www.promotionslogistics.com
Dir Mktg: Matthew Tilley
Primary Market Served: Consumer

CARDFLEX FINANCIAL SERVICES

2900 Bristol Ave Suite F-206
Costa Mesa, CA 92626-7911
Telephone: (866) 634-3044, Web Site: www.flex1.com
Sr VP Bus Devel: Leo Daboub

CASHNETUSA

200 W Jackson Blvd (Suite 2400)
Chicago, IL 60606-6941
Telephone: (312) 676-1583, Web Site: www.cashnetusa.com
Traditional Mktg Mgr: Tesha Strom

CENTRAL PACIFIC BANK

220 S King St
Honolulu, HI 96813-4530
Telephone: (808) 544-0500, (800) 544-0500, (800) 342-8422, FAX: (808) 531-2875, Web Site: www.centralpacificbank.com
Chmn Bd & CEO: Joichi Saito
Employees: 850
Primary Market Served: Business & Consumer
Founded: 1982
Gross sales or billing: $320,400,000

Operates 40 branch locations in the Hawaiian Islands. Targets individuals & local businesses. Checking, savings, money market accounts & CDs, commercial real-estate loans including residential mortgages, business, construction, & consumer loans.

CHARTER ONE BANK
Subs. of Citizens Financial Group
1215 Superior Ave
Cleveland, OH 44114-3299
Telephone: (216) 566-5300, (877) CHARTER, (877) 242-7837, FAX: (216) 566-1465, Web Site: www.charterone.com
CEO & Pres: Edward O' Handy III
Mktg: Gail Hanisko
Primary Market Served: Business & Consumer
Catalog available online
Indirect online sales
Founded: 2004
Gross sales or billing: $8,255,000,000

Full service bank.

CHECKS BY PHONE/CHECKS BY WEB
9770 S Military Trail (Suite 380)
Boynton Beach, FL 33436
Telephone: (561) 737-8700, FAX: (561) 737-5800, E-Mail: LarrySchwartz@checksbyphone.com, Web Site: www.checksbyphone.com
Pres, CEO & Founder: Larry Schwartz
Founder & Dir: Pearl Sax
Natl Sls Mgr: Leslie Adams
Conducts Business: Worldwide
Employees: 20
Primary Market Served: Business
Catalog available online
Direct online sales
Advertising/Marketing Budget Related to Direct Marketing: 76-100%
Direct Marketing ad budget: $100,000
Direct Mail: 25%
Magazines: 25%
Online: 25%
Telephone: 25%
Founded: 1982
Gross sales or billing: $20,000,000

Worldwide processor of check transactions received by merchants via phone, fax, modem, e-mail & the internet.

CHECKVANTAGE
1908 Parkside Ln
Austin, TX 78745-3615
Telephone: (512) 442-2332, (877) 243-2501, FAX: (512) 442-5515, E-Mail: marya@checkvantage.com, Web Site: www.checkvantage.com
CFO: Mary Anderson
VP: Nann Orina
Conducts Business: U.S.

Employees: 3
Primary Market Served: Business
Catalog available online
Advertising/Marketing Budget Related to Direct Marketing: 0-25%
Founded: 1999

Electronic check processing.

CHURCH EXTENSION PLAN
4070 27th Ct SE (Suite 210)
Salem, OR 97302-1359
Telephone: (800) 821-1112, Web Site: www.cepnet.com
Primary Market Served: Consumer

Ministry providing financial & administrative services to the churches & districts to the Assemblies of God

THE DMA CITI CARDS / CITICORP CREDIT SERVICES
1 Court Sq
Long Island City, NY 11120-0001
Telephone: (718) 248-5400
Sr VP Dir of Adv: Jennifer Lindauer
Primary Market Served: Business

CITIBANK
Subs. of Citigroup Inc
399 Park Ave
New York, NY 10022-4699
Telephone: (212) 559-9425, (800) 285-3000, FAX: (212) 527-2318, Web Site: www.citibank.com
Pres: Vikram Pandit
Conducts Business: U.S.
Primary Market Served: Business & Consumer
Advertising/Marketing Budget Related to Direct Marketing: 51-75%

Personal & credit card banking.

CITIFINANCIAL
Subs. of Citigroup Inc
300 Saint Paul St Fl 3
Baltimore, MD 21202-2120
Telephone: (410) 332-3000, (800) 995-2274, (800) 922-6235, FAX: (410) 332-3489, Web Site: www.citifinancial.com
Sr VP Mktg: Jim Ryan
Mktg: Terry Mitchell
Conducts Business: U.S., CA
Employees: 18,500
Primary Market Served: Consumer
Founded: 1998
Gross sales or billing: $2,147,500,000

Consumer lending subsidiary of Citigroup offering bill consolidation, debt refinancing, home equity, home improvement, auto and other personal loans.

CITIGROUP INC
399 Park Ave
New York, NY 10043-0001
Telephone: (212) 559-1000, (800) 285-3000, FAX: (212) 793-3946, Web Site: www.citigroup.com
Chmn: Winfried F.W. Bischoff
Vice Chmn: Stephen R. Volk
CEO, Dir: Vikram S. Pandit
COO: Robert Druskin
Chief Auditor: Bonnie Howard
Conducts Business: U.S., Canada, Australia, U.K.
Employees: 6,000
Primary Market Served: Consumer
Catalog available online
Advertising/Marketing Budget Related to Direct Marketing: 76-100%

Financial services company specializing in consumer loans.

CITIZENS BANK
770 Legacy Pl (Stop MLP250), Mail Stop MLP250
Dedham, MA 02026-6837
Telephone: (603) 634-7000, FAX: (603) 634-7191, Web Site: www.citizensbank.com
Pres: Thomas Metzger
Dir Mktg: Theresa McLaughlin
Conducts Business: U.S.
Employees: 400
Primary Market Served: Business & Consumer
Gross sales or billing: $529,100,000

A full-service state commercial bank.

CITIZENS REPUBLIC BANK
328 S Saginaw St
Flint, MI 48502-1923
Telephone: (810) 766-7651, Web Site: www.citizensbanking.com

CLEARONE ADVANTAGE
7125 Thomas Edison Dr (Suite 203)
Columbia, MD 21046-2976
Telephone: (443) 996-1889, Web Site: www.clearoneadvantage.com

CLIENTS & PROFITS WORLDWIDE
4755 Oceanside Blvd (#200)
Oceanside, CA 92056-3056
Telephone: (760) 945-4334, Web Site: www.clientsandprofits.com
Pres: Mark Robillard
Primary Market Served: Business

COMDATA CORP
5301 Maryland Way
Brentwood, TN 37027
Telephone: (615) 370-7000, (800) 266-3282, Web Site: www.comdata.com
Pres: Gary Krow

VP Mktg & Corp Commun: Kedran Whitten
Primary Market Served: Business & Consumer

Provider of transaction and information services offering information management, credit and debit transaction, processing and reporting, telecommunications, fuel management & travel plaza products and services.

COMERICA INC
1717 Main St
Dallas, TX 75201-4612
Telephone: (800) 521-1190, FAX: (925) 941-1999, Web Site: www. comerica.com
Chmn, Pres & CEO: Ralph W. Babb Jr.
Vice-Chmn: Joseph J. Buttigeg III
Exec VP & CFO: Elizabeth S. Acton
Exec VP & CIO: John R. Beran
Exec VP: Timothy P. Ashley
Conducts Business: U.S.
Employees: 11,200
Primary Market Served: Business & Consumer
Catalog available online
Gross sales or billing: $4,200,000,000

Bank holding company. Comerica Banks in Michigan, California, Florida, & Texas.

THE DMA COMMERCE BANCSHARES INC
8000 Forsyth Blvd (CBIR-1)
Saint Louis, MO 63105-1707
Telephone: (800) 453-2265, Web Site: www.commercebank.com
Corp Mktg Dir: Eric Steinhouse
Primary Market Served: Business

COMMERCIAL FEDERAL BANK
Commercial Federal Corp
13220 California St
Omaha, NE 68154-5228
Telephone: (402) 554-9200, FAX: (402) 514-5304
Pres & COO: Frederick R Kulikowski
Mktg Dir: Roger Lewis
Conducts Business: U.S.
Employees: 850
Primary Market Served: Business & Consumer

Full-service financial institution.

COMPASS BANK
15 20th St S Ste 100
Birmingham, AL 35233-2011
Telephone: (205) 933-4848, (800) 239-4357, FAX: (205) 933-3702, Web Site: www.compassbank.com

VP, Adv & Mktg Res: Eleanor Strickland
VP & Mktg Mgr: Mark Gibson
Conducts Business: U.S.
Primary Market Served: Business & Consumer

Sell retail, commercial & correspondent banking services to individuals, corporations & financial institutions.

THE DMA COPILEVITZ & CANTER, LLC
310 W 20th St (Suite 300)
Kansas City, MO 64108-2025
Telephone: (816) 472-9000, FAX: (816) 472-5000, Web Site: www. copilevitz-canter.com
Sr Partner: Errol Copilevitz

COSGROVE ASSOCIATES
747 Third Ave (16th fl)
New York, NY 10017-2803
Telephone: (212) 888-7202, FAX: (212) 888-7201, Web Site: www. cosgrovejuro.com
Pres: Jerry Cosgrove
Conducts Business: U.S.
Employees: 35
Primary Market Served: Business & Consumer
Advertising/Marketing Budget Related to Direct Marketing: 76-100%

Direct response & marketing communications firm for financial institutions & health-related firms.

COUGAR MOUNTAIN SOFTWARE
7180 Potomac Dr (Suite D)
Boise, ID 83704
Telephone: (208) 375-4455, (800) 388-3038, FAX: (208) 375-4460, E-Mail: sales@cougarmtn.com, Web Site: www.cougarmtn.com
Pres: David Bassiri
Mktg Mgr: Graham Paterson
Conducts Business: U.S., Canada
Employees: 40
Primary Market Served: Business
Catalog available online
Direct online sales
Advertising/Marketing Budget Related to Direct Marketing: 0-25%
Direct Marketing ad budget: $500,000
Direct Mail: 50%
Magazines: 45%
Newspapers: 5%
Founded: 1982
Gross sales or billing: $5,000,000

Full featured accounting, fund-accounting & point of sale software for small to mid-sized businesses.

COUNTRYWIDE FINANCIAL CORP
4500 Park Granada
Calabasas, CA 91302
Telephone: (818) 225-3000, FAX: (818) 225-4051, Web Site: www. countrywide.com
Chmn Bd & CEO: Angelo R. Mozillo
Sr Mng Dir Mktg: Andrew S. Bielanski
Employees: 54,655
Primary Market Served: Business & Consumer
Founded: 1969
Gross sales or billing: $2,675,000,000

Mortgage bankers.

DMB FINANCIAL
152 Conant St Ste 4
Beverly, MA 01915-1659
Telephone: (866) 810-3210, Web Site: www.dmbfinancial.com
Mktg Mgr: Terry Ward

DWS INVESTMENTS SERVICE CO
Division of Deutsche Bank
PO Box 219151, Attn: General Correspondence
Kansas City, MO 64121-9151
Telephone: (800) 543-5776, Web Site: www.dws-investments.com
CFO: Harold D. Kahn
COO DWS Investments America: Alban Miranda
COO Mutual Fund Grp: Lorie O'Malley
VP: Jeffrey M. Smith
Conducts Business: U.S.
Primary Market Served: Business & Consumer
Catalog available online
Direct online sales

Direct marketing of mutual funds & other financial products to the public & to AARP members.

DAIN RAUSCHER INC
60 S Sixth St
Minneapolis, MN 55402-4422
Telephone: (612) 371-2711, FAX: (612) 373-1627, Web Site: www. dainrauscher.com
Pres: Irving Weiser
VP & Mktg Dir: Peter Furuseth
Primary Market Served: Business & Consumer

Brokerage firm.

DALRADA FINANCIAL CORP
11956 Bernardo Plaza Dr (Suite 516)
San Diego, CA 92128-2538

Telephone: (858) 427-8716, (877) 325-7232, FAX: (858) 277-3448, E-Mail: inquiries@dalrada.com, Web Site: www.dalrada.com
Chmn: Richard Green
Pres: John Capezzuto
CFO: David Lieberman
Primary Market Served: Business & Consumer
Catalog available online
Founded: 1982
Gross sales or billing: $70,400,000

Manufacture computer printers.

DEALERTRACK
1111 Marcus Ave (Suite M04)
New Hyde Park, NY 11042-1034
Telephone: (866) 339-5723, Web Site: www.dealertract.com
Sr Prod Mktg Mgr: Jason Barrie
Primary Market Served: Business

DELAWARE INVESTMENTS
Subs. of Lincoln National Corp
2005 Market St
Philadelphia, PA 19103
Telephone: (215) 255-1200, E-Mail: service@delinvest.com, Web Site: www.delawareinvestments.com
Conducts Business: U.S., U.K.
Employees: 550
Primary Market Served: Business
Advertising/Marketing Budget Related to Direct Marketing: 0-25%
Founded: 1929

Investment advisory company & provider of mutual funds to individual & institutional investors.

DELOITTE & TOUCHE
200 Berkeley St
Boston, MA 02116
Telephone: (617) 437-2000, FAX: (617) 437-2111, Web Site: www.deloitte.com
United States CEO: Barry Salzberg
Global CEO: James H. Quigley
Sr Partner: William G. Parrett
Global Svc Line Leader Intl Tax: Peter N. Corcoran
European Leader Intl Tax Svc Line: Jan Roels
Primary Market Served: Business
Catalog available online
Founded: 1891

Accounting firm offering auditing & tax services.

DEUTSCHE BANK ALEX BROWN INC
60 Wall St
New York, NY 10005

Telephone: (212) 250-2500, FAX: (212) 469-5315, Web Site: www.db.com
CEO: Seth Waugh
Primary Market Served: Business

Merchant/retail investment.

THE DIME SAVINGS BANK OF NEW YORK FSB
209 Havemeyer St
Brooklyn, NY 11211
Telephone: (800) 321-3463, Web Site: www.dimewill.com
Chmn & CEO: Vincent F. Palagiano
Pres & COO: Michael Philip Devine
Conducts Business: U.S.
Primary Market Served: Business & Consumer

Full-service savings bank.

THE DMA DISCOVER FINANCIAL SERVICES
2500 Lake Cook Rd
Riverwoods, IL 60015-1838
Telephone: (224) 405-3373
VP: Karin Giffney
Primary Market Served: Business

DIVERSIFIED INVESTMENT ADVISORS
PO Box 1000
Harrison, NY 10528-7000
Telephone: (914) 697-8967, FAX: (914) 697-3743, Web Site: www.divinvest.com
Pres: Peter Kunkel
CFO: Mark Mufflin
Mktg Dir: Wendy Daniels
VP West Coast Client Relationship Devel Team: Lisa Steinberg
Employees: 900
Primary Market Served: Business
Catalog available online
Founded: 1963

Pension investment firm.

DOMESTIC BANK
15 Park Row W
Providence, RI 02903-1104
Telephone: (401) 943-1600, (800) 566-6600, FAX: (401) 943-6708, Web Site: www.domesticbank.com
Pres: Nathaniel Baker
CFO: Walter H. Braillard II
Exec VP: Craig A. Baker
Sr VP: Joseph LaPlume
VP: Jeff Baker
Primary Market Served: Business & Consumer
Catalog available online

Full service banking institution for businesses & consumers, specializing in loans & long term investments.

THE DREYFUS CORP
Subs. of Mellon Bank NA
200 Park Ave
New York, NY 10166
Telephone: (212) 922-6000, FAX: (212) 922-8165
Pres, CEO & COO: Christopher Condron
VP, Fulfillment: Evelyn Garrett
Corp Commun Dir: Patrice Koslowski
Direct Mail Mgr: Karin Waldman
Conducts Business: U.S.
Employees: 1,864
Primary Market Served: Business & Consumer
Founded: 1951

Investment advisor & manager of mutual funds.

ECHO - ELECTRONIC CLEARING HOUSE INC
21215 Burbank Blvd (#100)
Woodland Hills, CA 91367-6607
Telephone: (805) 419-8700, Web Site: www.echo-inc.com
Sr VP: Jack Wilson
Primary Market Served: Consumer

ESL FEDERAL CREDIT UNION
PO Box 92714
Rochester, NY 14692-8814
Telephone: (585) 336-1000, (800) 848-2265, FAX: (585) 336-1138, Web Site: www.esl.org
Vice Chmn: Gary P. Van Graafeiland
Pres, CEO, Dir: David L. Fieldler
COO: Michael Armbuster
CFO: Walter Rusnak
Sr VP: Donald Aldred
Sr VP & Marketplace Mgr: Faheem Masood
Conducts Business: Canada
Employees: 560
Primary Market Served: Business & Consumer
Catalog available online
Gross sales or billing: $189,900,000

EAGLE ASSET MANAGEMENT INC
Subs. of Raymond James Financial Corp
PO Box 10520
Saint Petersburg, FL 33733-0520
Telephone: (727) 573-2453, FAX: (727) 573-8020, Web Site: www.eagleasset.com
Pres: Steven Hill
Exec VP, Mktg: Richard Rossi
Conducts Business: Worldwide
Employees: 85
Primary Market Served: Consumer

Professionally managed investment portfolios including individual retirement plans, endowments & trusts with assets exceeding $100M.

EASTERN BANK
195 Market St
Lynn, MA 01901-1517
Telephone: (800) EASTERN, Web
  Site: www.easternbank.com
Asst VP: Erin Silva
Primary Market Served: Business

ELITE DEBIT
11450 Sheldon St
Sun Valley, CA 91352-1121
Telephone: (435) 688-0634 X302, Web
  Site: www.elitedebit.com

THE DMA EMBRACE HOME LOANS
25 Enterprise Ctr
Middletown, RI 02842-7233
Telephone: (401) 846-3100, Web Site:
  www.afsfitfinance.com
Mktg Dir: Dana Fortin
Primary Market Served: Business &
  Consumer

EMIGRANT SAVINGS BANK
5 E 42nd St
New York, NY 10017-6904
Telephone: (212) 850-4521, (800)
  EMIGRANT, FAX: (212) 850-4372,
  Web Site: www.emigrant.com
Chmn & CEO: Howard P. Milstein
Sr VP & Mktg Dir: Ted Morehouse
Sr VP, Chief Credit Officer: Patricia
  Goldstein
Mng Dir: David Feingold
Mng Dir: Chris Grey
Conducts Business: U.S.
Employees: 1,600
Primary Market Served: Consumer
Catalog available online
Gross sales or billing: $639,000,000
Retail bank.

ENCIRCLE
1691 NW 107th Ave
Miami, FL 33172
Telephone: (305) 592-7800, FAX:
  (305) 470-2660, E-Mail:
  merchantservices@encirclepayments.
  com, Web Site: www.insta-check.
  com
Conducts Business: U.S.
Primary Market Served: Business

Provide financial/cash payment systems services to retailers.

ENTREPRENEUR PARTNERS
2000 Market St Ste 720
Philadelphia, PA 19103-3214

Telephone: (267) 322-7000, Web Site:
  www.epfunds.com
Mng Partner: Salem Shuchman
Primary Market Served: Business &
  Consumer

THE DMA ESIGNAL
3955 Point Eden Way
Hayward, CA 94545-3720
Telephone: (510) 266-6000, Web Site:
  www.esignal.com
VP Mktg: Julie Craig
Primary Market Served: Business

FNC INC
1214 Office Park Dr
Oxford, MS 38655-3597
Telephone: (662) 236-8254, Web Site:
  www.fncinc.com
CEO: William Rayburn
Primary Market Served: Business &
  Consumer

FANNIE MAE
3900 Wisconsin Ave NW
Washington, DC 20016-2806
Telephone: (202) 752-7000, FAX:
  (202) 752-3808, Web Site: www.
  fanniemae.com
Chmn & CEO: Franklin D. Raines
Vice Chmn & COO: Daniel H. Mudd
Vice Chmn: Jamie S. Gorelick
Mktg Dir: Edith Bollard
Conducts Business: U.S.
Employees: 2,500
Primary Market Served: Business &
  Consumer

Congressionally chartered & shareholder owned supplier of home mortgage funds.

FATWALLET
100 E Grand Ave
Beloit, WI 53511-6255
Telephone: (815) 877-8992, Web Site:
  www.fatwallet.com
Dir Mktg: Brent Shelton
Primary Market Served: Business &
  Consumer

FEDERAL HOME LOAN MORTGAGE CORP (FREDDIE MAC)
8200 Jones Branch Dr
McLean, VA 22102-3110
Telephone: (703) 903-2000, (800) 424-
  5401, Web Site: www.freddiemac.
  com
Chmn & CEO: Richard F. Syron
Pres, COO & Dir: Eugene M. Mc-
  Quade
Exec VP & CFO: Anthony S. Piszel
Sr VP & COO: Michael C. May
Mktg Commun Dir: Sara E. Leonard

Sr VP & CIO: Robert Lux
Conducts Business: Worldwide
Employees: 5,500
Primary Market Served: Business
Catalog available online
Indirect online sales
Gross sales or billing: $43,000,000,000

Purchase pools of home loans & package into securities for resale to investors.

FEDERATED INVESTORS CO
Corporate Communications
1001 Liberty Ave, Federated Investors
  Tower
Pittsburgh, PA 15222-3779
Telephone: (412) 288-1900, (800) 341-
  7400, FAX: (412) 288-1171, Web
  Site: www.federatedinvestors.com
Pres & CEO: J. Christopher Donahue
Conducts Business: U.S.
Employees: 1,243
Primary Market Served: Business &
  Consumer
Catalog available online
Direct online sales
Founded: 1955
Gross sales or billing: $978,900,000

Mutual fund investment company dealing with institutions & individuals.

THE DMA FIDELITY INVESTMENTS
Subs. of FMR Corp
82 Devonshire St
Boston, MA 02109-3605
Telephone: (617) 563-7000, (800) 343-
  3548, FAX: (617) 476-6150, Web
  Site: www.fidelity.com
Chmn & CEO: Edward C. Johnson
Pres: Roger Allan Lawson
Pres, Fidelity Strategic New Bus
  Devel: Roger T. Servison
VP, Customer Programs: Henry Wellott
Pres, Fidelity Shared Svcs: Marvin
  Adams
Exec VP & CFO: Claire S. Richer
Conducts Business: Worldwide
Employees: 30,000
Primary Market Served: Business &
  Consumer
Direct online sales
Founded: 1946
Gross sales or billing: $12,800,000,000

Mutual fund manager serving as an investment advisor to the Fidelity Group of Funds.

THE DMA FIFTH THIRD BANK
38 Fountain Square Plz
Cincinnati, OH 45202-3102
Telephone: (800) 972-3030, FAX:
  (231) 922-4060, Web Site: www.53.
  com
Chmn: George A. Schaefer Jr
Pres & CEO: Kevin T. Kabat

EVP & COO: Greg D. Carmichael
EVP: Charles Drucker
EVP: Bruce K. Lee
Conducts Business: U.S.
Employees: 4,000
Primary Market Served: Business & Consumer
Advertising/Marketing Budget Related to Direct Marketing: 26-50%
Direct Marketing ad budget: $1,000,000
Direct Mail: 30%
Magazines: 10%
Newspapers: 20%
TV/Radio: 30%
Telephone: 10%

Financial services & banking.

FINANCIAL SERVICES INTERNATIONAL CORP
701 Fifth Ave (Suite 6870)
Seattle, WA 98104
Telephone: (206) 386-5475, FAX: (206) 654-0499
Principal: Joe Maas
Conducts Business: U.S., Canada, Brazil
Employees: 7
Primary Market Served: Business & Consumer
Advertising/Marketing Budget Related to Direct Marketing: 76-100%
Direct Marketing ad budget:
Direct Mail: $10,000
Magazines: $10,000
Newspapers: $10,000
TV/Radio: $20,000
Telephone: $100,000
Founded: 1992
Gross sales or billing: $2,000,000

Brokerage firm.

THE DMA FIREMAN'S FUND INSURANCE CO
Subs. of Allianz A G
777 San Marin Dr
Novato, CA 94998-0002
Telephone: (415) 899-2000, FAX: (415) 899-3600, Web Site: www.firemansfund.com
Chmn Bd: John Carendi
Pres & COO: Joseph J. Beneducci
Pres Cmml Bus: Gary C. Bhojwani
Bd Member: Charles Kravitsky
Pres Specialty Insurance: Art Moosmann
Conducts Business: U.S., Canada
Employees: 8,000
Primary Market Served: Business & Consumer
Advertising/Marketing Budget Related to Direct Marketing: 0-25%
Founded: 1991

Insurance - property, casualty, workers' compensation & homeowners.

FIRST ADVANTAGE MEMBERSHIP SERVICES
12395 First American Way
Poway, CA 92064-6897
Telephone: (619) 938-6803
Sr VP, FAMS: Scott Hermann
Primary Market Served: Consumer

FIRST BANKS INC
600 McDonnell Blvd
Hazelwood, MO 63042
Telephone: (314) 592-5000, (800) 760-2265, Web Site: www.firstbanks.com
Chmn: James F. Dierberg
Pres, CEO & Dir: Terrance M. McCarthy
Mktg Mgr: Nancy Barnes
Employees: 3,500
Primary Market Served: Business & Consumer
Catalog available online
Founded: 1906

Credit card processing.

FIRST DATA MERCHANT SERVICES
6200 S Quebec St Ste 1
Greenwood Village, CO 80111-4733
Telephone: (303) 488-8000, (800) 735-3362, Web Site: www.firstdata.com
Chmn & CEO: Michael D. Capellas
Exec VP & CFO: Kimberly S. Patmore
Exec VP & CTO: David E. Dibble
Sr Exec VP: David P. Bailis
Sr Exec VP: Edward A. Labry III
Conducts Business: Worldwide
Employees: 900
Primary Market Served: Business & Consumer
Catalog available online
Gross sales or billing: $7,000,000,000

Full service card processing featuring Direct Solutions to maximize card approvals & Citi Profiles, targeted marketing information to increase sales.

THE DMA FIRST HAWAIIAN BANK
Div. of BancWest Corp
999 Bishop St Ste 3200
Honolulu, HI 96813-4424
Telephone: (808) 525-6273, (888) 844-4444, FAX: (808) 525-5798, E-Mail: bfarias@fhb.com, Web Site: www.fhb.com
EVP, Corp Commun: Gerald J. Keir
VP: Susan Soken
Conducts Business: HI, Guam, Saipan, British W Indies, Japan
Employees: 2,100
Primary Market Served: Business & Consumer
Founded: 1974
Gross sales or billing: $596,300,000

Traditional deposit and lending services, commercial equipment and vehicle leasing, money management for individual and institutional investors.

FIRST MERIT BANK (HQ)
aka First Merit Corp
III Cascade Plaza (7 fl)
Akron, OH 44308-1124
Telephone: (330) 996-6300, (888) 554-4362, Web Site: www.firstmerit.com
Chmn, Pres & CEO: Paul G. Greig
Conducts Business: U.S.
Employees: 2,755
Primary Market Served: Business & Consumer
Founded: 1981
Gross sales or billing: $799,000,000

A diversified financial services company that provides a complete range of banking & financial services. Serves individuals & businesses through approx 160 branches in 25 northeastern & central OH counties & PA's Lawrence County.

FIRST TENNESSEE BANK
165 Madison Ave Ste Mezz1
Memphis, TN 38103-2725
Telephone: (901) 523-4547, Web Site: www.firsttennessee.com
Direct Mktg Specialist: Katharine Hopkins
Primary Market Served: Business

THE DMA FISERV
4411 E Jones Bridge Rd
Norcross, GA 30092-1615
Telephone: (678) 375-3000, Web Site: www.checkfreecorp.com
Dir, Channel Mktg: Kim Sergent
Primary Market Served: Business

FISHER INVESTMENTS
13100 Skyline Blvd
Woodside, CA 94062-4542
Telephone: (650) 851-3334, Web Site: www.fi.com
Group VP: Tommy Romero
Primary Market Served: Business & Consumer

CAIMIN FLANNERY & ASSOCIATES
4275 Stableford Ln
Naperville, IL 60564-9768
Telephone: (630) 236-1955
Partner: Caimin Flannery
Primary Market Served: Consumer

FLEET ONE LLC
613 Bakertown Rd
Antioch, TN 37013-2657

Telephone: (615) 523-6465, Web Site:
www.fleetone.com
VP Mktg: Stacey Bright
Primary Market Served: Business

THE DMA FLORIDA CREDIT UNION
PO Box 5549
Gainesville, FL 32627
Telephone: (352) 377-4141, Web Site:
www.flcu.org
Primary Market Served: Business &
Consumer

**FORECASTER PUBLISHING
CO INC**
19623 Ventura Blvd
Tarzana, CA 91356
Telephone: (818) 345-4421
Pres: John V. Kamin
Bookkeeper: Regina Lawrence
Conducts Business: Worldwide
Employees: 4
Primary Market Served: Business &
Consumer
Advertising/Marketing Budget Related
to Direct Marketing: 0-25%
Founded: 1962

Publish a speculator's weekly money
letter that predicts economic trends,
money movements, gold, silver & rare
coin trends, interest rates & distressed
property speculation. Also business
forecasts & management consulting.

FROST BANK
100 W Houston St (Ste 100)
San Antonio, TX 78205-1400
Telephone: (210) 220-5155, Web Site:
www.frostbank.com
Sr VP: Ericka Pullin
Primary Market Served: Business

THE DMA GE MONEY
4125 Windward Plaza Dr
Alpharetta, GA 30005-8738
Telephone: (678) 518-2403
Direct Mktg Opers Execution Leader:
Patrick Blankman
Primary Market Served: Business

**GE PARTNERSHIP
MARKETING GROUP**
200 N Martingale Rd
Schaumburg, IL 60173
Telephone: (847) 605-3000, FAX:
(847) 605-7368, Web Site: www.
gepmg.com
Chmn & CEO: Jeffrey R. Immelt
Vice Chmn: Michael A. Neal
Vice Chmn: John G. Rice
Conducts Business: Worldwide
Employees: 300
Primary Market Served: Business &
Consumer

Catalog available online
Advertising/Marketing Budget Related
to Direct Marketing: 76-100%

Provider of credit card enhancement
services & fee-generating continuity
programs.

GRP FUNDING LLC
1350 Main St (fl 4)
Springfield, MA 01103-1664
Telephone: (877) 571-7999, Web Site:
www.grpfunding.com
Dir Opers: Gary Emond
Primary Market Served: Business &
Consumer

**GWR WEALTH
MANAGEMENT**
14301 First National Bank Pkwy
Omaha, NE 68154-5213
Telephone: (402) 496-7200, FAX:
(402) 496-0378, Web Site: www.
gwrwealth.com
Founder & CEO: Gail Werner-
Robinson
PR Mgr: Bridget Hannon
Primary Market Served: Business

Investment bankers.

GATEWAY BANK AND TRUST
2235 Gateway Access Point (Suite
200)
Raleigh, NC 27607-3076
Telephone: (919) 865-3869, Web Site:
www.gatewaybankandtrust.com
Primary Market Served: Consumer

GENWORTH FINANCIAL INC
6620 W Broad St
Richmond, VA 23230
Telephone: (804) 281-6000, (888) 436-
9678, FAX: (804) 662-2414, Web
Site: www.genworth.com
Chmn, Pres & CEO: Michael D.
Fraizer
Sr VP & CFO: Patrick Kelleher
Sr VP & CIO: Scott J. McKay
Conducts Business: U.S.
Employees: 7,200
Primary Market Served: Business &
Consumer
Catalog available online
Gross sales or billing: $11,000,000,000

Securities & annuities.

**THE DMA GLENVIEW CAPITAL
MANAGEMENT**
767 Fifth Ave (fl 44)
New York, NY 10153-0023
Telephone: (212) 812-4700
Primary Market Served: Consumer

GLENVIEW STATE BANK
800 Waukegan Rd
Glenview, IL 60025-4300
Telephone: (847) 729-1900, FAX:
(847) 729-5847, E-Mail: info@gsb.
com, Web Site: www.gsb.com
Exec VP: Bill Campbell
VP, Mktg: David Kreiman
Conducts Business: U.S.
Employees: 210
Primary Market Served: Business &
Consumer
Catalog available online
Indirect online sales
Advertising/Marketing Budget Related
to Direct Marketing: 0-25%
Direct Marketing ad budget:
Direct Mail: 15%
Magazines: 10%
Newspapers: 70%
Online: 2%
Telephone: 3%
Gross sales or billing: $42,800,000

State commercial bank & user of direct
marketing for financial services.

GOLDLINE INTERNATIONAL
1601 Cloverfield Blvd (Suite 100S)
Santa Monica, CA 90404-4162
Telephone: (310) 587-1420, (800) 827-
4653, FAX: (310) 319-0265, E-Mail:
president@goldlinecoins.com, Web
Site: www.goldlinecoins.com
VP: Robert Fazio
Mktg Dir: Charles Sorasky
Conducts Business: U.S., Canada,
Hong Kong, U.K.
Primary Market Served: Consumer
Advertising/Marketing Budget Related
to Direct Marketing: 0-25%
Direct Marketing ad budget:
Direct Mail: 20%
TV/Radio: 40%
Telephone: 40%

Buyer & seller of gold, silver & other
precious metals.

GOLDSMITH AGIO HELMS
225 S 6th St Ste 4600
Minneapolis, MN 55402-5611
Telephone: (612) 339-0500, FAX:
(612) 339-0507, Web Site: www.
agio.com
Chmn: Jack P. Helms
Co-CEO: Michael F. McFadden
Co-CEO: David J. Solomon
COO & Mng Dir: William Sharpe III
Mng Dir: Terry A. Lynner
Mng Dir: Gerald M. Caruso Jr.
Mng Dir: David L. Hallett
Mng Dir & Partner: Kevin Jach
Mng Dir: Robert I. Burns Jr.
Mng Dir: Joseph M. Conte
Mng Dir: David M. Santoni
Man Dir: Brooks D. Myhran

Mng Dir: William S. Jarrett Jr.
Mng Dir: Barry D. Freeman
Mng Dir: James R. Clancy
Mng Dir: Lars Ekstrom
Mng Dir: Edward W. Villeneuve
Conducts Business: U.S., Canada, Europe, Pacific Rim
Employees: 110
Primary Market Served: Business
Direct online sales
Founded: 1979

Provides financial advisory services to middle market businesses. Services include mergers and acquisitions, distressed advisory and restructuring, valuations and fairness opinions, and private placements of debt and equity. The firm operates internationally from offices in Minneapolis, New York, Chicago, Los Angeles, and London. Member of the National Association of Securities Dealers (NASD).

THE GRAPH CO
PO Box 961
Vineland, NJ 08362-0961
Telephone: (856) 825-9199, FAX: (856) 825-5573, E-Mail: graphco2@verizon.net
Primary Market Served: Consumer
Indirect online sales
Founded: 1986

THE DMA GREAT WESTERN BANK
100 N Phillips Ave
Sioux Falls, SD 57104-6715
Telephone: (605) 334-2545, Web Site: greatwesternbank.com
Primary Market Served: Consumer

THE DMA GRIDLEY & CO LLC
10 E 53rd St (fl 24)
New York, NY 10022-5070
Telephone: (212) 400-9720, Web Site: www.gridleyco.com
Pres & CEO: Linda Gridley
Primary Market Served: Consumer

GRUPPO LEVEY & CO
122 E 42nd St (fl 46)
New York, NY 10168-0002
Telephone: (212) 697-5753, FAX: (212) 949-7294, E-Mail: info@glconline.com, Web Site: www.glconline.com
Chmn & Mng Dir: Hugh Levey
Pres & Mng Dir: Claire Gruppo
VP: Antonia Ness
Sr VP: Edward McCabe
Primary Market Served: Business
Catalog available online
Indirect online sales
Founded: 1992

Investment banking for the direct marketing industry.

GUARANTY BANK
4000 W Brown Deer Rd
Brown Deer, WI 53209
Telephone: (414) 362-4636, (800) 235-4636, Web Site: www.guarantybank.com
Chmn, Pres & CEO: Kenneth Debuque
Sr VP Mktg: Bruce McCall
Primary Market Served: Business & Consumer
Advertising/Marketing Budget Related to Direct Marketing: 26-50%

Full-service financial institution.

H&R BLOCK INC
1 H&R Block Way
Kansas City, MO 64105-1905
Telephone: (816) 572-6446, (800) 472-5625, FAX: (816) 854-8500, Web Site: www.hrblock.com
Dir Mktg Svcs: Steven Harris
Chmn Bd: Henry W. Bloch
Interim CEO: Alan Bennett
Exec VP & Gen Counsel: Carol Graebner
Grp Pres, Retail Tax Svcs: Tim Gokey
Grp Pres, Digital Tax Solutions: Tom Allanson
Employees: 136,000
Primary Market Served: Business & Consumer
Advertising/Marketing Budget Related to Direct Marketing: 0-25%
Founded: 1955
Gross sales or billing: $4,000,000,000

Nationwide tax, financial and mortgage service.

HSBC BANK USA, NA
PO Box 643
Buffalo, NY 14240-0643
Telephone: (716) 841-2424, FAX: (716) 841-5391, Web Site: www.banking.us.hsbc.com
Sr VP Mktg Communs: Carlos M. Alves
Primary Market Served: Business & Consumer

Full service financial institution.

HAMPSHIRE AGENCY
Hampshire Planning Inc
33 Great Neck Rd (#7)
Great Neck, NY 11021-3335
Telephone: (516) 466-3814, FAX: (516) 466-0910
Pres: Stanley R. Goldberg
Owner & Mgr: Pat Giordano
Conducts Business: U.S.
Employees: 11

Primary Market Served: Business & Consumer
Advertising/Marketing Budget Related to Direct Marketing: 51-75%
Direct Marketing ad budget:
Direct Mail: 60%
Magazines: 20%
Newspapers: 10%
Telephone: 10%
Founded: 1954

Financial management & turn-around services for failing companies, as well as tax, financial planning, insurance & estate planning for small businesses & individuals. Elder-plan meets needs of seniors with long term care insurance. General agents for life insurance and annuities, qualified retail agents are welcome.

HARRIS BANCORP INC
111 W Monroe St (fl 21W)
Chicago, IL 60603-4096
Telephone: (312) 461-7961, (888) 340-BANK, FAX: (312) 461-7869, E-Mail: onlineservices@harrisbank.com, Web Site: www.harrisbank.com
Vice-Chmn: Peter B. McNitt
Vice-Chmn: Charles R. Tonge
CEO: Ellen M. Costello
Pres, Community Banking: Timothy Crane
Sr VP: Thomas Kesman
VP: Tim Franzen
Conducts Business: U.S.
Employees: 6,595
Primary Market Served: Business & Consumer
Catalog available online
Advertising/Marketing Budget Related to Direct Marketing: 51-75%
Direct Marketing ad budget:
Direct Mail: 75%
Telephone: 25%
Founded: 1875

Provide all phases of consumer banking services to consumers.

HELLER FINANCIAL
Div. of Heller Financial
500 W Monroe St
Chicago, IL 60661-3671
Telephone: (312) 441-7000, FAX: (312) 441-7367, Web Site: www.hellerfin.com
Pres: Scott Miller
VP, Mktg: Paul Puryear
Primary Market Served: Business

Provide asset based financing to middle market companies.

HOME LOAN INVESTMENT BANK
One Home Loan Plaza (Suite 3)
Warwick, RI 02886

Telephone: (800) 223-1700 X278,
  E-Mail: contactus@homeloanbank.
  com, Web Site: www.homeloanbank.
  com
Pres: John M. Murphy
VP: Kurt Lauth
Mktg Mgr: Frank Conway
Conducts Business: U.S.
Primary Market Served: Consumer
Catalog available online
Indirect online sales
Advertising/Marketing Budget Related
  to Direct Marketing: 76-100%
Founded: 1959

Mortgage banking company soliciting
loans & mortgages through the mail.

HOME 123 MORTGAGE
2033 Milwaukee Ave (Suite 237)
Riverwoods, IL 60015
Telephone: (888) 215-0080, E-Mail:
  info@home123.com, Web Site:
  www.home123.com

HOULIHAN LOKEY HOWARD & ZUKIN
1930 Century Park W
Los Angeles, CA 90067
Telephone: (310) 553-8871, (800) 788-
  5300, FAX: (310) 553-2173, Web
  Site: www.hlhz.com
Co-CEO: Scott L. Beiser
Co-CEO: Jeffrey Werbalowsky
CFO: Gary E. Meek
Dir: Richard Philips
Conducts Business: Worldwide
Primary Market Served: Business
Catalog available online
Founded: 1970

Investment banking services.

HOWARD RICE NEMEROVSKI CANADY FALK & RABKIN
3 Embarcadero Ctr (fl 7)
San Francisco, CA 94111-4078
Telephone: (415) 464-1000, Web Site:
  www.howardrice.com
Client & Relationship Mktg: Jessamy
  Field
Primary Market Served: Business &
  Consumer

HUNTINGTON BANCSHARES
41 S High St Fl 1
Columbus, OH 43215-6167
Telephone: (614) 480-8300, (800) 480-
  BANK, FAX: (614) 480-5284, Web
  Site: www.huntington.com
CEO: Tom Hoaglin
VP, Treas & Dir: Thomas P. Reed
VP & Dir: Richard A. Cheap
VP & Dir: R. Larry Hoover
Primary Market Served: Business

Catalog available online
Indirect online sales
Gross sales or billing: $338,000,000
Financial institution.

ICMA RETIREMENT CORP
777 N Capitol St NE (Suite 500)
Washington, DC 20002
Telephone: (202) 962-4600, (800) 669-
  7400, FAX: (202) 962-4601, E-Mail:
  investorservices@icmarc.org, Web
  Site: www.icmarc.org
Pres & CEO: Joan McCallen
Sr VP Mktg: Gregory Dyson
Sr VP New Bus Devel: Chris Matzke
Employees: 600
Catalog available online
Indirect online sales
Founded: 1914
Gross sales or billing: $132,500,000

Offers pension funds for city government employees.

IPS - SENDERO CORP
Subs. of Fiserv Inc
107 Technology Pkwy
Norcross, GA 30092-2909
Telephone: (770) 409-0047, (800) 879-
  1996, FAX: (770) 409-1735, E-Mail:
  sales@ips-sendero.com, Web Site:
  www.ips-sendero.com
Pres: Dave Ulrich
Mktg Dir: Kirk Gunther
Conducts Business: Worldwide
Employees: 200
Primary Market Served: Business
Founded: 1982

Provides a suite of integrated products
which comprise "Sendero Vision," a
comprehensive strategic management
solution for financial institutions.
These products include a centralized
data management system, asset/liability
management systems, funds transfer
pricing & profitability measurement
systems.

INMAR
2650 Pilgrim Ct
Winston-Salem, NC 27106-5238
Telephone: (336) 631-2524, FAX:
  (336) 770-3470, E-Mail: ibizdev@
  inmar.com, Web Site: www.
  promotionslogistics.com
Dir Mktg: Matthew Tilley
Chmn & CEO: John C. Whitaker Jr.
HR: Perry Wiles
Customer Svc: Ashley Kerman
Conducts Business: U.S.
Catalog available online
Direct online sales

Clearing house for retailers.

THE DMA INTERSECTIONS
3901 Stonecroft Blvd
Chantilly, VA 20151-1032
Telephone: (703) 488-6100, Web Site:
  www.charteredmarketing.com
Exec VP: Steven Schwartz
Primary Market Served: Business &
  Consumer

INVESTORS MARKETING SERVICES
168 Centre St
Danvers, MA 01923-1321
Telephone: (978) 774-2990, (800) 462-
  2551, FAX: (978) 774-4249, Web
  Site: www.investorsmarketing.com
Pres: Janice Charles
VP, Mktg: Jennifer Gallo
Conducts Business: U.S.
Employees: 15
Primary Market Served: Business
Advertising/Marketing Budget Related
  to Direct Marketing: 51-75%
Founded: 1987

Provides insurance products & fixed
annuities to financial planners & insurance agents.

JP MORGAN CHASE & CO
270 Park Ave (10th fl)
New York, NY 10017-2070
Telephone: (212) 270-6000, E-Mail:
  jpmcinvestorrelations@jpmchase.
  com, Web Site: www.jpmorgan.com
Chmn & CEO: James Dimon
Bd Member: Crandall C. Bowles
Pres Asset Mngmt: Paul T. Bateman
Pres Investment Bank: Anthony J. Best
HR Dir: John F. Bradley
Conducts Business: Worldwide
Primary Market Served: Consumer
Catalog available online

Investment services.

THE DMA JEFFERSON NATIONAL
9920 Corporate Campus Dr (Suite
  1000)
Louisville, KY 40223-4051
Telephone: (502) 587-3853, Web Site:
  www.jeffnat.com
Mktg Mgr: Amber Mullaney
Primary Market Served: Business &
  Consumer

JOHN DEERE CREDIT USA
6400 NW 86th St, PO Box 6600
Johnston, IA 50131-6600
Telephone: (515) 267-3000, FAX:
  (515) 267-3292, Web Site: www.
  deere.com/en_US/jdc/index.html
Pres: James A. Israel
Commun Mgr: David Patterson
eBus Mktg Mgr: Steve Brubaker
Employees: 1,494

Primary Market Served: Business & Consumer
Gross sales or billing: $194,400,000

One of the largest equipment finance companies in the United States and has operations in 17 countries. It provides retail, wholesale and lease financing, and offers revolving credit and operating loans.

JOHN HANCOCK RETIREMENT PLAN SERVICES
200 Bloor St W - ET6
Toronto, ON, Canada M4W1E5
Telephone: (416) 852-1035, Web Site: www.jhancock.com
Primary Market Served: Business

EDWARD JONES
12555 Manchester Rd
Des Peres, MO 63131-3710
Telephone: (314) 515-2000, Web Site: www.edwardjones.com
Dir Direct Mktg: Sean Ebeling
Primary Market Served: Business

THE JORDAN EDMISTON GROUP INC
150 E 52nd St (18th fl)
New York, NY 10022-6260
Telephone: (212) 754-0710, Web Site: www.jegi.com
VP Mktg: Adam Gross
Primary Market Served: Consumer

KEY BANK
800 Superior Ave E Ste 1000
Cleveland, OH 44114-2601
Telephone: (216) 689-3000, (888) 539-2968, FAX: (207) 874-7044, Web Site: www.key.com
Pres: Michael McNamera
Chmn & CEO: Henry L. Meyer III
Vice Chmn & Chief Admin Officer: Thomas Stevens
Exec VP: Michael P. Barnum
Chief Mktg & Commun Officer: Karen Haefling
Exec VP: Susan P. Brockett
Vice Chair: Thomas W. Bunn
Conducts Business: Worldwide
Employees: 1,110
Primary Market Served: Business & Consumer
Catalog available online
Founded: 1825
Gross sales or billing: $4,800,000

Full-service commercial bank with 96 branch offices statewide.

KEY BANK NATIONAL ASSOCIATION
Affiliate of KeyCorp
19 Corporate Woods Blvd
Albany, NY 12211-2345
Telephone: (518) 434-4871, (800) 539-2968, Web Site: www.keybank.com
Chmn, Pres & CEO: Henry L. Miller III
Vice Chmn: Beth E. Mooney
Vice Chmn: Thomas W. Bunn
Sr Exec VP & CFO: Jeffrey B. Weeden
Sr VP: Charles Miller
Conducts Business: U.S.
Employees: 3,900
Primary Market Served: Business & Consumer
Catalog available online
Indirect online sales
Founded: 1825

State commercial bank. Consumer banking & finance, investment management & trust, corporate & investment banking, securities brokerage, private banking & customized financial services within 38 states & more than 1300 branch & affiliates offices.

L6 HOLDINGS CORP
6555 Sugarloaf Pkwy (Suite 307)
Duluth, GA 30097-4934
Telephone: (678) 957-0511
Mng Partner: Daniel Lonergan
Primary Market Served: Business & Consumer

THE LAW OFFICES OF JAMES SOKOLOVE
93 Worcester St # 101
Wellesley Hills, MA 02481-3609
Telephone: (617) 742-0696, Web Site: www.jimsokolove.com
Exec Asst: Randi Donovan

LEADFLASH
6700 Broken Sound Pkwy NW
Boca Raton, FL 33487-5701
Telephone: (561) 499-3329, Web Site: www.leadflash.com
Dir Bus Devel: John Dalton
Primary Market Served: Business & Consumer

LENDING TREE/HOME LOAN CENTER
11115 Rushmore Dr
Charlotte, NC 28277-3442
Telephone: (704) 541-5351, Web Site: www.lendingtree.com
Dir Direct Mktg: Tracy Jenkins
Primary Market Served: Consumer

LEUCADIA NATIONAL CORP
315 Park Ave S (20th fl)
New York, NY 10010
Telephone: (212) 460-1900, FAX: (212) 598-4869, Web Site: www.leucadia.com
Exec VP: Thomas Mara
Chmn: Ian M. Cumming
VP & CFO: Joseph A. Orlando
Pres & Dir: Joseph S. Steinberg
Conducts Business: U.S.
Employees: 1,300
Primary Market Served: Business & Consumer
Gross sales or billing: $862,000,000

Investment holding company for businesses & consumers.

LIBERTY TAX SERVICE
1716 Corporate Landing Pkwy
Virginia Beach, VA 53454-5681
Telephone: (757) 493-8855 X8115
Primary Market Served: Consumer

Income Tax Preparation

LIFE INVESTORS INSURANCE CO OF AMERICA
Member of Aegon Insurance Group
4333 Edgewood Rd NE
Cedar Rapids, IA 52499
Telephone: (319) 398-8511, (800) 231-7220, FAX: (319) 369-2188, Web Site: www.lifeinvestors.com
Exec VP & COO: Brenda K. Clancy
Chmn Bd: Ronald F. Wagley
Pres: Tim Kneeland
Employees: 1,953
Primary Market Served: Consumer
Gross sales or billing: $1,123,800,000

Provides financial services, life insurance, annuities & mutual funds.

LITLE & CO
900 Chelmsford St
Lowell, MA 01851-8100
Telephone: (978) 275-6500, Web Site: www.litle.com
Chmn: Tim Litle
Mktg Dir: Krishne Wood
Primary Market Served: Consumer

LOCAL GOVERNMENT FEDERAL CREDIT UNION
323 W Jones St (Suite 600)
Raleigh, NC 27603-1369
Telephone: (919) 755-0534, Web Site: www.lgfcu.org
Dir Mktg Mgr: Karen Mantica
Primary Market Served: Consumer

LOTSOLUTIONS
10151 Deerwood Park Blvd Ste 200-330
Jacksonville, FL 32256-0564
Telephone: (904) 350-9660, Web Site: www.lotsolutions.com
Pres: Robert Fullington
Primary Market Served: Business & Consumer

THE DMA MCCS
Div. of Mayc's Inc.
9111 Duke Blvd
Mason, OH 45040-8999
Telephone: (513) 573-2284, FAX: (513) 573-2197, Web Site: www.federated.com
VP, Opers & Credit Mktg: Jan Rosenbaum
Credit Mktg Dir: Maya Wadleigh
Dir Mktg: Robyn Wentzel
Conducts Business: U.S.
Primary Market Served: Consumer
Advertising/Marketing Budget Related to Direct Marketing: 76-100%

New credit accounts of Macy's Inc.

MFS INVESTMENT MANAGEMENT
500 Boylston St
Boston, MA 02116-3740
Telephone: (617) 954-6249, Web Site: www.mfs.com
VP Electronic Commun: William Pluckhahn
Primary Market Served: Consumer

MXT CARD SERVICES, LLC
2 Penns Way (Suite 201)
New Castle, DE 19720-2407
Telephone: (302) 323-6203, FAX: (302) 323-6219, Web Site: www.mxtcs.com
Chief Mktg Officer: Mark Chronister
Dir Sls: Steve Cochran
Primary Market Served: Consumer

MARSHALL & ILSLEY CORP
Parent to M & I Marshall & Ilsley Bank
770 N Water St
Milwaukee, WI 53202
Telephone: (414) 765-7801, FAX: (414) 765-7899, Web Site: www.micorp.com
Chmn Bd: Dennis J. Kuester
Pres & CEO: Mark F. Furlong
Sr VP & Dir Corp Mktg: Brent J. Kelly
Conducts Business: U.S.
Employees: 14,699
Primary Market Served: Consumer
Founded: 1847
Gross sales or billing: $5,146,400,000

Financial institution.

MASTERCARD WORLDWIDE
2000 Purchase St
Purchase, NY 10577
Telephone: (914) 249-2000, (800) 622-7747, FAX: (914) 249-4220, Web Site: www.mastercard.com
Sr VP-Group Head Global Brand Strategy & Devel: Courtney Gibbons
Conducts Business: Worldwide
Employees: 5,000
Primary Market Served: Business & Consumer
Founded: 1966
Gross sales or billing: $3,000,000,000

Credit-debit products for consumers; transaction processing & settlement services, as well as business-building cooperative marketing programs for businesses.

MAX FEDERAL CREDIT UNION
PO Box 244040
Montgomery, AL 36124-4040
Telephone: (334) 260-2600, (800) 776-6776, FAX: (334) 270-0921, Web Site: www.mymax.com
Pres & CEO: Greg McClellan
Mktg Dir: D.G. Markwell
Mgr: Lois Woodard
Mgr: Will Epperson
Mgr: Patricia Taylor
Conducts Business: U.S.
Employees: 235
Primary Market Served: Consumer
Catalog available online
Indirect online sales
Advertising/Marketing Budget Related to Direct Marketing: 26-50%
Founded: 1955
Gross sales or billing: $3,500,000

Financial services including: savings, investments & loans.

MECHANICAL BREAKDOWN ADMINISTRATORS INC
Subs. of MBA Holdings Inc
PO Box 6545
Scottsdale, AZ 85261-6545
Telephone: (480) 860-2288, FAX: (480) 860-0425, E-Mail: gaylenb@mbadirect.com, Web Site: www.mbadirect.com
Pres: Gaylen M. Brotherson
Conducts Business: U.S.
Employees: 60
Primary Market Served: Business & Consumer
Catalog available online
Indirect online sales
Advertising/Marketing Budget Related to Direct Marketing: 26-50%
Direct Marketing ad budget:

Direct Mail: $3,500,000
Magazines: $20,000
Newspapers: $10,000
TV/Radio: $250,000
Telephone: $500,000
Founded: 1984
Gross sales or billing: $30,000,000

General financial & marketing services.

MERCHANT E-SOLUTIONS
3400 Bridge Pkwy Ste 100
Redwood City, CA 94065-1195
Telephone: (678) 493-8853
Gen Mgr E-Commerce: Kevin Gallagher

MERGENT INC
Div. of Financial Information Corp
580 Kingslet Park Dr
Fort Mill, SC 29715-6403
Telephone: (800) 342-5647, Web Site: www.mergent.com
Sr VP, Mktg: Joe Emanuelli
Conducts Business: U.S.
Primary Market Served: Business
Catalog available online
Direct online sales
Advertising/Marketing Budget Related to Direct Marketing: 0-25%
Founded: 1900

Offer business & financial information on public domestic & foreign companies.

THE DMA MERRICK BANK
10705 S Jordan Gtwy (Suite 200)
South Jordan, UT 84095-3977
Telephone: (801) 545-6647, Web Site: www.merrickbank.com
Sr VP: Kellie Harper
Primary Market Served: Business & Consumer

MERRILL LYNCH
250 Vesey St (4th fl), Four World Financial Center
New York, NY 10080-0002
Telephone: (212) 449-1000, (800) 637-7455, FAX: (212) 449-9418, Web Site: www.ml.com
Chmn & CEO: John A. Thain
Vice Chmn, Pub Markets: Paul W. Critchlow
Vice Chmn, Gen Counsel: Rosemary T. Berkery
Exec VP & CFO: Nelson Chai
Media Contact: Michael O'Looney
Conducts Business: U.S.
Employees: 56,000
Primary Market Served: Business & Consumer
Catalog available online
Founded: 1820

Gross sales or billing: $62,000,000,000

Financial service & investment firm dealing in stocks, investments & other financial services. Sell to the public & to institutions.

MIDCONTINENT FINANCIAL CENTER INC

2614 Calvert Dr # B
Columbia, MO 65202-2321
Telephone: (573) 443-6002, Web Site: www.americanmutualloans.com
Pres: J. Schulte
Primary Market Served: Business & Consumer

MONEX DEPOSIT CO

4910 Birch St Ste 103
Newport Beach, CA 92660-2188
Telephone: (949) 752-1400, (800) 444-8317, FAX: (949) 752-7214, E-Mail: info@monex.com, Web Site: www.monex.com
Founder: Louis E. Carabini
Pres: Michael Carabini
Dir: Christina Carabini
VP, Sls: William A. Nelles
Conducts Business: U.S., Canada, Mexico
Employees: 250
Primary Market Served: Consumer
Catalog available online
Indirect online sales
Founded: 1967
Gross sales or billing: $9,600,000

Brokerage firm specializing in marketing precious metals for investment purposes to the general public.

THE DMA MONEYGRAM INTERNATIONAL

2828 N Harwood (fl 15)
Dallas, TX 75201
Telephone: (800) 666-3947, Web Site: www.moneygram.com
Dir Loyalty & Database Mktg: Brent Carter
Primary Market Served: Consumer

MONTAG & CALDWELL INC

Alleghany Corp
3455 Peachtree Rd NE (Suite 1200)
Atlanta, GA 30326-3248
Telephone: (404) 836-7100, (800) 458-5868, FAX: (404) 836-7230, Web Site: www.montag.com
Chmn: Solon P. Patterson
Pres, Investments: Ronald Canakaris
Conducts Business: U.S.
Employees: 35
Primary Market Served: Business & Consumer
Founded: 1945

Investment counseling firm.

MORGAN STANLEY

1585 Broadway
New York, NY 10036
Telephone: (212) 761-4000, FAX: (212) 761-0096
Chmn & CEO: John J. Mack
Co-Pres: Walid Chammah
COO: Jim Rosenthal
Co-Pres: James P. Gorman
Dir: Robert Scully
Conducts Business: Worldwide
Primary Market Served: Business & Consumer
Catalog available online
Gross sales or billing: $76,500,000,000

Provide managed commodity trading programs for corporate & individual clients.

MORNINGSTAR INC

22 W Washington St
Chicago, IL 60602
Telephone: (312) 696-6000, Web Site: www.morningstar.com
Chmn & CEO: Joe Mansueto
Pres Software Div: Chris Boruff
Pres Global Investment: Peng Chen
Pres Intl Opers & Global HR: Bevin Desmond
CFO: Scott Cooley
Pres Equity Research: Catherine Gillis Odelbo
Pres Data Div: Elizabeth Kirscher
Pres Fund Research: Don Phillips
Primary Market Served: Consumer

THE MOTLEY FOOL

2000 Duke St (fl 4)
Alexandria, VA 22314
FAX: (703) 254-1999, E-Mail: cs@fool.com, Web Site: www.Fool.com
Partner: David Gardner
Partner: Tom Gardner
Conducts Business: U.S., UK
Employees: 200
Primary Market Served: Business & Consumer
Founded: 1993

Provider of investment advice and financial information.

MUTUAL OF AMERICA LIFE INSURANCE CO

320 Park Ave
New York, NY 10022-6839
Telephone: (212) 224-1600, (800) 468-3785, FAX: (212) 224-2539, Web Site: www.mutualofamerica.com
Chmn Bd: William J. Flynn
Pres & CEO: Thomas J. Moran
Sr VP, Corp Commun: Thomas A. Harwood
Exec VP: Manfred Altstadt
Exec VP, Mktg & Corp Commun: William S. Conway

Conducts Business: U.S.
Employees: 1,100
Primary Market Served: Business
Catalog available online
Advertising/Marketing Budget Related to Direct Marketing: 76-100%
Founded: 1945
Gross sales or billing: $1,700,000,000

Employee retirement plans.

NATIONAL ASSOCIATION OF FEDERAL CREDIT UNIONS

3138 10th St N
Arlington, VA 22201-2160
Telephone: (800) 336-4644, Web Site: www.nafcu.org
Assoc Dir Mktg: Jessa Foor

NATIONAL CITY BANK

Subs. of National City Corp
1900 E Ninth St
Cleveland, OH 44114
Telephone: (216) 222-2000, (800) 622-8100, FAX: (216) 222-9359, Web Site: www.nationalcity.com
Sr VP, Corp Mktg: Karin Stone
Conducts Business: U.S.
Employees: 3,300
Primary Market Served: Business & Consumer
Direct online sales

Commercial bank.

NATIONAL PENSION SERVICE INC

40 Main St (Suite 300)
Burlington, VT 05401-8433
Telephone: (802) 862-3994, FAX: (802) 865-2861, E-Mail: retirementservices@people.com, Web Site: www.peoples.com/retirementservices/
Pres: S. Tracy Braun
Conducts Business: U.S.
Employees: 140
Primary Market Served: Business & Consumer
Founded: 1976

Design & administer pension plans for corporations.

THE DMA NAVY FEDERAL CREDIT UNION

820 Follin Ln SE
Vienna, VA 22180-4907
Telephone: (703) 206-4245, Web Site: www.navyfederal.org
Primary Market Served: Business

THE DMA NETSPEND

901 Mariners Island Blvd Ste 300
San Mateo, CA 94404-5025
Web Site: www.netspend.com

Dir Bus Devel: Preet Chhokar
Primary Market Served: Consumer

NEUBERGER & BERMAN MANAGEMENT
605 3rd Ave (fl 21)
New York, NY 10158-3698
Telephone: (212) 476-8800, (800) 877-9700, FAX: (212) 476-9090, Web Site: www.nb.com
Pres: Peter Sundman
Global Head: Eric Johnson
VP: Kenneth J. Turek
VP: Sajjad S. Ladiuala
VP: David H. Burshtan
Conducts Business: U.S.
Employees: 1,247
Primary Market Served: Business & Consumer
Catalog available online

Mutual fund management firm.

NISSAN MOTOR ACCEPTANCE CORP
8900 Freeport Pkwy
Irving, TX 75063
Telephone: (800) 647-7261, Web Site: www.nissanusa.com
CEO: Steve Lambert
Pres: Mark Kaczynski
VP, Sls,: Mike McConnell
Employees: 670
Primary Market Served: Business
Founded: 1982
Gross sales or billing: $2,000,000,000

Financial products.

NO LOAD FUND INVESTOR
PO Box 3029
Brentwood, TN 37024-3029
Telephone: (800) 706-6364, FAX: (800) 785-9212, E-Mail: NoLoad@ mleesmith.com, Web Site: www. noloadfundinvestor.com
Editor: Sheldon Jacobs
Publr: Mark Salzinger
Assoc Ed: Layne Aurand
Conducts Business: U.S.
Employees: 5
Primary Market Served: Consumer
Catalog available online
Direct online sales
Advertising/Marketing Budget Related to Direct Marketing: 76-100%
Direct Marketing ad budget:
Direct Mail: 80%
Online: 20%
Founded: 1979

Mutual fund & exchange traded fund investment newsletter & book.

NO LOAD FUND*X
235 Montgomery St (Suite 1049)
San Francisco, CA 94104-2994

Telephone: (415) 986-7979, (800) 763-8639, FAX: (415) 986-1595, Web Site: www.noloadfundx.com
Publr & Mng Ed: Janet Brown
Publr: Burt Berry
Conducts Business: U.S.
Employees: 12
Primary Market Served: Business & Consumer
Catalog available online
Direct online sales
Advertising/Marketing Budget Related to Direct Marketing: 0-25%
Direct Marketing ad budget: $400,000
Direct Mail: 92%
Magazines: 2%
Newspapers: 2%
TV/Radio: 4%
Founded: 1979
Gross sales or billing: $1,000,000

A monthly newsletter that monitors the performance of over 730 no-load mutual funds for sophisticated fund investors. Also, CAP - Mid-month report & shorter version of newsletter & update of monthly report.

THE NORTHERN TRUST CO
50 S LaSalle St
Chicago, IL 60675
Telephone: (312) 630-6000, (888) 289-6542, FAX: (312) 630-1512, Web Site: www.ntrs.com
Chmn: William Osborne
Pres, CEO & Dir: Frederick H. Waddell
Exec VP & CFO: Steven L. Fradkin
Exec VP: William R. Dodds Jr.
CIO: Steven A. Schoenfield
Primary Market Served: Business
Catalog available online

Full service financial institution.

NORTHWESTERN MUTUAL
720 E Wisconsin Ave
Milwaukee, WI 53202-4703
Telephone: (414) 271-1444, Web Site: www.northwesternmutual.com
Primary Market Served: Business & Consumer

NUVEEN INVESTMENTS
333 W Wacker Dr
Chicago, IL 60606
Telephone: (312) 917-7700, (800) 257-8787, FAX: (312) 917-8049, Web Site: www.nuveen.com
CEO & Dir: John P. Amboian
Pres & Exec Dir, Investment Svcs: Mark J.P. Anson
Exec VP & CAO: Glenn R. Richter
CIO, Asset Mngmt: John P. Waterman
CIO: John D. Bosse
Primary Market Served: Business & Consumer

Catalog available online
Gross sales or billing: $709,000,000

Investment services.

OLESUK FINANCIAL SERVICES
Affiliated with SagePoint Financial Inc
5206 W Elm St (Route 120)
McHenry, IL 60050-4000
Telephone: (815) 363-0808, FAX: (815) 363-0843, E-Mail: folesuk@ sagepointadvisor.com, Web Site: www.olesukfinancialservices.com
Pres & Owner: Frank D. Olesuk
Admin Asst: Patricia S. Olesuk
Admin Asst: Karlene M. Olesuk
Conducts Business: U.S.
Employees: 3
Primary Market Served: Business & Consumer
Direct Marketing ad budget:
Direct Mail: 20%
Online: 5%
Telephone: 75%
Founded: 1985
Gross sales or billing: $4,500,000

Mutual funds, insurance products, tax preparation, investment products & services, stocks & bonds, Investment Management.

OLIVER WYMAN
1166 Avenue of the Americas
New York, NY 10036-2726
Telephone: (212) 541-8100, (212) 345-8000, Web Site: www.oliverwyman. com

OPPENHEIMER FUNDS
225 Liberty St (fl 11), 2 World Financial Ctr
New York, NY 10281-1005
Telephone: (212) 323-0200, FAX: (212) 323-0493, Web Site: www. oppenheimerfunds.com
Sr VP, Prod Mngmt: Thomas Keffer
VP, Dir Investor Mktg: Lisa Lamentino
Primary Market Served: Business

Market & sell mutual funds.

OVERSEAS PRIVATE INVESTMENT CORP (OPIC)
1100 New York Ave NW
Washington, DC 20527
Telephone: (202) 336-8400, FAX: (202) 336-7949, E-Mail: info@opic. gov, Web Site: www.opic.gov
Pres & CEO: Robert Mosbacher Jr.
Chief of Staff: Dulce A. Zahniser
VP & CFO: Howard L. Burris
Exec VP: John A. Simon
Dir: Samuel E. Ebbesen
Employees: 140
Primary Market Served: Business

Catalog available online
Indirect online sales
Founded: 1971

Self-sustaining U.S. government agency. Developing countries & emerging economies.

PNC BANK CORP

249 5th Ave Ste 1200, One PNC Plaza
Pittsburgh, PA 15222-2707
Telephone: (412) 762-2000/3514, (800) 422-6537, FAX: (412) 762-4482
Chmn: Tom O'Brien
VP, Mktg Svc: Tim Doering
Direct Mktg Mgr: Gregg Fink
Primary Market Served: Business & Consumer

Provide a variety of financial services for consumers & commercial corporation.

PNC GLOBAL INVESTMENT SERVICING

66 Broadway Ste 3
Lynnfield, MA 01940-2369
Telephone: (781) 477-4124, Web Site: www.pnc.com
VP: Mark Stranberg
Primary Market Served: Business & Consumer

ᵀᴴᴱ_ᴅᴹᴬ PACNET SERVICES LTD

595 Howe St (fl 4)
Vancouver, BC, Canada V6C 2T5
Telephone: (604) 689-0399, FAX: (604) 689-0313, E-Mail: info@pacnetservices.com, Web Site: www.pacnetservices.com
Mng Dir: Rosanne Day
Commun Specialist: Joy Wood
Dir Mktg: Renee Frappier
Bus Devel Mgr: Brendan Mahar
Mktg Asst: Melody Buchwitz
Conducts Business: U.S., Canada
Primary Market Served: Business
Indirect online sales
Founded: 1994

Offering a wide range of international payment processing services including multi currency cheque cashing, cheque issuing, electronic cheque conversion, credit card processing, direct debit & transfer collection.

PAYMENTECH

Four Northeastern Blvd
Salem, NH 03079
Telephone: (603) 896-6000, FAX: (603) 896-8717, Web Site: www.paymentech.com
Pres, CEO: Pam Patsley
COO: Michael Duffy
Sls: James Hebert
Employees: 300

Primary Market Served: Business
Indirect online sales

Payment processing service provider dedicated to the direct response industry - process merchant payment transactions covering a broad range of marketing channels. Support authorization & settlement for all major credit cards, consumer bank account (electronic check) debit processing, private-label & purchasing cards & international currencies.

ᵀᴴᴱ_ᴅᴹᴬ PAYPAL INC

9690 Deereco Rd (Suite 705)
Timonium, MD 21093-6936
Telephone: (443) 921-1184, Web Site: www.corporate.billmelater.com
Mktg & Events: Melissa Foreman
Primary Market Served: Consumer

PEAK IMPACT INC

2 Beaverbrook Rd (Suite 204)
Ottawa, ON, Canada K2K 1L2
Telephone: (613) 592-3100, Web Site: www.peakimpact.com
Mktg Dir: David Lipson
Primary Market Served: Business & Consumer

ᵀᴴᴱ_ᴅᴹᴬ PEOPLE'S UNITED BANK

850 Main St
Bridgeport, CT 06604-4917
Telephone: (203) 338-7171, Web Site: www.peoples.com
VP: Jeff Lee
Primary Market Served: Consumer

ᵀᴴᴱ_ᴅᴹᴬ PETSKY PRUNIER LLC

60 Broad St Ste 3810
New York, NY 10004-2329
Telephone: (212) 842-6001, FAX: (212) 842-6039, Web Site: www.petskyprunier.com
Partner: Michael Petsky
Pres: John Prunier
Mng Dir: Sanjay Chadda
Mktg Mgr: Elizabeh Ehmann
Conducts Business: U.S.
Primary Market Served: Business
Advertising/Marketing Budget Related to Direct Marketing: 76-100%

An investment bank providing merger and acquisition and private placement advisory services for clients in direct marketing, marketing services & technology, advertising & promotion and information industries.

ᵀᴴᴱ_ᴅᴹᴬ PIPER JAFFRAY

800 Nicollet Mall
Minneapolis, MN 55402-7000
Telephone: (612) 303-0000, Web Site: www.pjc.com

POWERPAY

320 Cumberland Ave
Portland, ME 04101
Telephone: (207) 775-6900, (877) 877-3737, FAX: (888) 204-4040, Web Site: www.powerpay.biz
Mktg Mgr: Lisa Valentine

PRICEWATERHOUSECOOPERS LLP

300 Madison Ave (fl 24)
New York, NY 10017
Telephone: (646) 471-4000, FAX: (646) 471-4444, Web Site: www.pwc.com
CEO: Sam DiPiazza
Global Co Leader, People: Richard L. Baird
Global Co Leader, Human Capital: Marie-Jeanne Chevremont-Lorenzini
Dir Commun: Mike Davies
Employees: 146,000
Primary Market Served: Business
Founded: 1849
Gross sales or billing: $21,900,000,000

Professional services, including accounting, taxes, management & human resources consulting & outsourcing.

PROPAY

3400 N Ashton Blvd (Suite 200)
Lehi, UT 84043-5310
Telephone: (801) 341-5647, Web Site: www.propay.com
Dir Strategic Devel: Michael McClellan

ᵀᴴᴱ_ᴅᴹᴬ PRUDENTIAL FINANCIAL

751 Broad St
Newark, NJ 07102-2195
Telephone: (973) 802-2195, Web Site: www.prudential.com
VP eBusiness Devel Group: James Brett
Primary Market Served: Business

PUTNAM INVESTMENTS

Div. of Marsh & McLennan Cos Inc
30 Dan Rd
Canton, MA 02021-2809
Telephone: (617) 292-1000, (800) 225-1581, FAX: (617) 292-1683, Web Site: www.putnam.com
Mng Dir: Mark McKenna
Conducts Business: U.S., Japan, U.K.
Employees: 2,000
Primary Market Served: Business & Consumer

Investment firm managing assets for individual shareholders & institutional clients.

RBC DAIN RAUSCHER
One Beacon St
Boston, MA 02108
Telephone: (617) 725-2000, FAX:
(617) 725-1393, Web Site: www.
rbcdainrauscher.com
CEO: Gordon Nixon
COO: Barbara Stymiest
CFO: Jancie R. Fukakusa
Grp Head Global Tech Opers: Martin
J. Lipper
Grp Head Capital Markets: Charles M.
Winograd
Conducts Business: U.S., London,
Paris
Primary Market Served: Business &
Consumer
Catalog available online
Gross sales or billing: $17,000,000

Brokerage firm.

RBC FUNDS
Div. of RBC Global Asset Manage-
ment (US) Inc
PO Box 702
Milwaukee, WI 53201-0701
Telephone: (800) 422-2766, Web Site:
us.rbcgam.com
Pres: Jennifer Lammers
VP & Dir: David P. Lux
Mng Dir & Chief Compliance Officer:
Kathleen A. Gorman
Sec & Chief Legal Officer: Monica V.
Ballard
Mgr, Mutual Fund Admin: Martin A.
Cramer
Conducts Business: U.S., Canada, Eu-
rope
Employees: 3
Primary Market Served: Consumer
Catalog available online
Indirect online sales
Gross sales or billing: $100,000

Direct marketing of 100%, no load
mutual funds.

RBS CITIZENS FINANCIAL
GROUP INC
770 Legacy Pl (MLP 250)
Dedham, MA 02026-6837
Telephone: (781) 471-1565, Web Site:
www.citizensbank.com
Sr VP: Pete Constant
Primary Market Served: Business &
Consumer

REGIONS
1900 5th Ave N Ste 300
Birmingham, AL 35203-2669
Telephone: (205) 326-5262, FAX:
(205) 326-4072, Web Site: www.
regions.com
Pres & CEO: C. Dowd Ritter
CFO: Alton E. Yother

Sr Exec VP, Chief Mktg Officer: Scott
Peters
Sr Exec VP, Gen Banking Grp: O. B.
Grayson Hall Jr
Sr VP: Leigh Anne Kelley
Employees: 35,900
Primary Market Served: Consumer
Gross sales or billing: $7,756,400,000

Commercial bank.

RESEARCH INSTITUTE
AMERICA
2395 Midway Rd
Carrollton, TX 75006-2521
Telephone: (972) 250-7000, (800) 950-
1216, Web Site: www.ria.thompson.
com
CEO: Bob Scharin
Tax Analyst: Richard O' Donnell
Conducts Business: Worldwide
Employees: 400
Primary Market Served: Business
Catalog available online
Direct online sales
Advertising/Marketing Budget Related
to Direct Marketing: 26-50%
Direct Marketing ad budget:
Direct Mail: 35%
Magazines: 65%
Founded: 1965
Gross sales or billing: $111,000,000

In-house tax return preparation systems
for corporations. Services include software, equipment, training & complete
support from a single source. Offices
located in major cities throughout the
U.S.

ROLLYSON FINANCIAL
GROUP
150 Oak Dr
Pasadena, MD 21122-4421
Telephone: (410) 437-5596
Dir & CEO: Richard V. Rollyson
Conducts Business: U.S.
Employees: 3
Primary Market Served: Business &
Consumer
Advertising/Marketing Budget Related
to Direct Marketing: 76-100%
Direct Marketing ad budget: $150,000
Direct Mail: 10%
Newspapers: 10%
Telephone: 80%
Gross sales or billing: $400,000

Investment, annuities & retirement services & college funding to small businesses & individuals.

THE DMA ROSLAND CAPITAL LLC
429 Santa Monica Blvd (Suite 450)
Santa Monica, CA 90401-3401
Telephone: (800) 891-2341, Web Site:
www.roslandcapital.com

CEO & Mgr: Marin Aleksov
Primary Market Served: Business &
Consumer

ROYAL BANK OF CANADA
200 Bay St, Royal Bank Plaza
Toronto, ON, Canada M5J 2J5
Telephone: (416) 974-5151, FAX:
(416) 974-0365, Web Site: www.
royalbank.com
Sr VP: Jane Broderick
Conducts Business: U.S., Canada
Primary Market Served: Business &
Consumer

Markets financial data to promote investment opportunities.

RUSSELL INVESTMENTS
1301 Second Ave (18th Fl)
Seattle, WA 98101
Telephone: (206) 505-7877, (800) 426-
7969, Web Site: www.russell.com

SDI MARKETING
65 International Blvd (Suite 200)
Toronto, ON, Canada M9W 6L9
Telephone: (949) 718-4800, (877) SDI-
TEAM, FAX: (416) 674-9011,
E-Mail: info@sdicapital.com, Web
Site: www.sdimarketing.com
Pres & CEO: Scott Daniels
VP: Ted Wagstaff
Conducts Business: U.S.
Employees: 70
Primary Market Served: Business
Direct online sales
Advertising/Marketing Budget Related
to Direct Marketing: 26-50%
Direct Marketing ad budget: $800,000
Direct Mail: 28%
Magazines: 10%
Newspapers: 8%
Telephone: 54%
Founded: 1993
Gross sales or billing: $45,000,000

Commercial financing source offering
programs for equipment leasing, working capital, acquisition, expansion &
sale & lease back transactions.

SEI
100 Cider Mill Rd.
Oaks, PA 19456-9989
Telephone: (610) 676-1000, E-Mail:
webmaster@seic.com, Web Site:
www.seic.com
Dir Mktg: Judy Arnold
Primary Market Served: Business &
Consumer

THE DMA SW CAGING CORP
5342 NW 25th St
Topeka, KS 66618-3738

Telephone: (785) 232-0061, Web Site: www.swcaging.com
Pres: Thomas Bender
Primary Market Served: Consumer

SWBC
9311 San Pedro Ave (Suite 600)
San Antonio, TX 78216-4459
Telephone: (210) 525-1241, Web Site: www.swbc.com
VP Mktg: Julie Ring
Primary Market Served: Business & Consumer

SAGE FINANCIAL GROUP
300 Barr Harbor Dr (Suite 200), Five Tower Bridge
West Conshohocken, PA 19428
Telephone: (484) 342-4400, FAX: (484) 537-0550, E-Mail: sage@ sagefinancial.com, Web Site: www. sagefinancial.com
CEO: David Cohn
Co-Pres & VP Mktg: Stephen Cohn
Co-Pres & VP Mktg: Alan J. Cohn
VP Principal: Mitchell E. Bednoff
VP Principal: John J. Sion
Conducts Business: U.S.
Employees: 10
Primary Market Served: Business & Consumer
Catalog available online
Advertising/Marketing Budget Related to Direct Marketing: 76-100%
Direct Marketing ad budget: $80,000
Direct Mail: 100%
Gross sales or billing: $1,000,000
Financial planning for individuals.

CHARLES SCHWAB & CO INC
211 Main St
San Francisco, CA 94105-1905
Telephone: (415) 627-7000, (800) 648-5300, FAX: (415) 421-0810, Web Site: www.schwab.com
Exec VP & Chief Mktg Officer: Rebecca Saeger
Pres & CEO: Walter W. Bettinger II
Conducts Business: U.S.
Employees: 5,000
Primary Market Served: Consumer
Gross sales or billing: $1,000,000,000
Provide discount securities brokerage & related financial services to individual investors.

SHESHUNOFF INFORMATION SERVICES INC
Div. of Thompson Publishing Group
4120 Friedrich Ln (Suite 100)
Austin, TX 78744-1003
Telephone: (800) 456-2340, Web Site: www.sheshunoff.com

CEO: Gabrielle Sheshunoff
Mgr: John Kimbrough
VP, Production: Pat Ximenes
Conducts Business: Worldwide
Primary Market Served: Business
Catalog available online
Direct online sales
Manuals, reports & data for bank markets.

SKINDER-STRAUSS ASSOCIATES
240 Mulberry St
Newark, NJ 07102-3528
Telephone: (973) 642-1440, Web Site: www.elaw.com
Publr & CEO: Ed Denne
Primary Market Served: Business & Consumer

PETER J SOLOMON CO
520 Madison Ave (fl 29)
New York, NY 10022-4385
Telephone: (212) 508-1600, Web Site: www.pjsc.com
Mng Dir: Cathy Leonhardt

SOVEREIGN BANK NEW ENGLAND
140 Hebron Ave
Glastonbury, CT 06033-4239
Telephone: (877) 768-2265, FAX: (860) 727-6517
Chmn Bd: John Hamil
Pres & CEO: Joe Campanelli
CPA & CFO: Marc R. McCollom
Chief of Staff & Dir of Admin: Salvatore J. Rinaldi
Conducts Business: U.S.
Employees: 1,100
Primary Market Served: Business & Consumer
Catalog available online
Regional banking institution.

SPOKANE TEACHERS CREDIT UNION
1620 N Signal Dr
Liberty Lake, WA 99019-9517
Telephone: (509) 326-1954, Web Site: www.stcu.org
Sr Res Analyst: Renee Taylor
Primary Market Served: Business & Consumer

ROBERT A STANGER & CO INC
1129 Broad St
Shrewsbury, NJ 07702
Telephone: (732) 389-3600, FAX: (732) 389-1751, E-Mail: info@ rastanger.com, Web Site: www. rastanger.com
Pres & CEO: Robert Stanger

Principal: Kevin T. Gannon
Conducts Business: U.S., Canada, Europe
Employees: 25
Primary Market Served: Business
Advertising/Marketing Budget Related to Direct Marketing: 0-25%
Direct Marketing ad budget:
Direct Mail: 15%
Magazines: 25%
Telephone: 60%
Founded: 1978
Gross sales or billing: $1,400,000
Investment banking, research & publishing firm serving real estate industry & financial intermediaries.

STATE STREET GLOBAL ADVISORS
1 Lincoln St (fl 30)
Boston, MA 02111-2901
Telephone: (617) 664-2618, Web Site: www.ssga.com
Mktg Mgr: Katie McClain
Primary Market Served: Consumer

THE SUBURBAN CHAMBER OF COMMERCE
71 Summit Ave Ste 1
Summit, NJ 07901-3690
Telephone: (908) 522-1700, FAX: (908) 522-9252, E-Mail: info@ suburbanchambers.org, Web Site: www.suburbanchambers.org
Exec Dir: Maureen C. Kelly
Adv & Sls: Judy Holloway
Adv & Sls: Renee Del Mauro
Conducts Business: U.S.
Employees: 31
Primary Market Served: Consumer
Catalog available online
Founded: 1917
Gross sales or billing: $1,200
NJ Chamber of Commerce representing Summit, New Providence & Berkeley Heights

SUNSHINE MINTING INC
7600 N Mineral Dr (Suite 700)
Coeur D'Alene, ID 83815-9170
Telephone: (208) 772-9592, (800) 274-5837, FAX: (208) 772-9739, E-Mail: sunshine@sunshinemint.com, Web Site: www.sunshinemint.com
Owner: Tom Powers
Dir Bus Devel: Tony Williams
Conducts Business: U.S., U.K., Asia
Employees: 95
Primary Market Served: Business & Consumer
Advertising/Marketing Budget Related to Direct Marketing: 0-25%
Founded: 1979
Gross sales or billing: $51,500,000

Provide investment grade silver & gold bullion to the dealer market & handle custom minting.

SUNTRUST BANKS INC
303 Peachtree Center Ave NE (Suite 320)
Atlanta, GA 30303-1280
Telephone: (404) 588-7914, (800) 786-8787, FAX: (404) 532-0550, E-Mail: emmett.harmon@suntrust.com, Web Site: www.suntrust.com
Grp VP DM: Emmett Harmon
VP DM: Angela Holland
VP Direct Mktg: Christine Farrell
VP DM: Terri Hawkins
Asst VP DM: Allyson Barrington
Asst VP DM: Tracy Kennedy
Asst VP DM: Kathleen Tucker
Employees: 28,000
Primary Market Served: Business & Consumer
Catalog available online
Indirect online sales
Advertising/Marketing Budget Related to Direct Marketing: 0-25%
Direct Marketing ad budget: $10,000,000
Direct Mail: $8,000,000
Online: $2,000,000
Founded: 1891

Financial services.

T ROWE PRICE ASSOCIATES INC
Subs. of T. Rowe Price Group Inc.
100 E Pratt St (fl 4)
Baltimore, MD 21202-1081
Telephone: (410) 345-2000, (800) 638-7890, FAX: (410) 986-3618, E-Mail: info@troweprice.com, Web Site: www.troweprice.com
Vice Chmn: Edward C. Bernard
CEO, Dir & Pres: James A.C. Kennedy
Pres: George J. Collins
Conducts Business: U.S.
Employees: 4,100
Primary Market Served: Business & Consumer
Founded: 1937
Gross sales or billing: $462,100,000

Investment research & counsel firm with $36 billion in assets under management. Direct marketer of mutual funds.

TAB BOARDS INTERNATIONAL INC
11031 Sheridan Blvd
Westminster, CO 80020-3201
Telephone: (303) 839-1200, FAX: (303) 839-0012, Web Site: www.tabboards.com
Sr Mktg Dir: Jeffrey Pederson

Primary Market Served: Business
Founded: 1990

THE DMA TD BANK NA
70 Gray Rd
Falmouth, ME 04105-2019
Telephone: (207) 770-2196, Web Site: www.tdbanknorth.com
VP Direct Mktg: Maria Michaud
Primary Market Served: Consumer

TAX REDUCTION INSTITUTE
13200 Executive Park Terr
Germantown, MD 20874-5313
Telephone: (301) 972-3600, (800) TRI-0-TAX, FAX: (301) 972-0819, E-Mail: info@taxreductioninstitute.com, Web Site: www.taxreductioninstitute.com
Pres: Sanford Botkin
Conducts Business: U.S.
Employees: 5
Primary Market Served: Business & Consumer
Catalog available online
Direct online sales
Founded: 1989

Provide speakers to lecture on tax strategies.

TAYLOR CAPITAL GROUP, INC
dba Cole Taylor Bank
9550 W Higgins Rd
Rosemont, IL 60018-4906
Telephone: (847) 653-7978, FAX: (847) 653-7890, E-Mail: investor.relations@coletaylor.com, Web Site: www.taylorcapitalgroup.com
Chmn Bd, Pres & CEO: Bruce W. Taylor
CFO: Robin Van Castle
Exec Mng Dir, Mktg Devel & New Ventures: Jeffrey W. Taylor
Mktg Dir: Kathy Kaporis
Employees: 421
Primary Market Served: Business & Consumer
Gross sales or billing: $46,200,000

User of direct marketing for financial services.

THE DMA TEXADA CAPITAL CORP
62 Greenwood Shoals
Grasonville, MD 21638-9659
Telephone: (866) 595-6224, Web Site: www.texada.com

THOMA CRESSEY BRAVO
300 N La Salle Dr (Suite 4300)
Chicago, IL 60654-3422
Telephone: (312) 777-4444, FAX: (312) 777-4445, Web Site: www.tcb.com

Partner: Lee Mitchell
Partner: Carl Thoma
CFO: Scott A. Maskalunas
VP: Seth J. Boro
IT Mgr: Damian McIntosh
Conducts Business: U.S.
Primary Market Served: Business

Private equity investor. Capital source for direct marketing & other service businesses. Existing or past investments in direct mail, telemarketing, newspaper, trade magazines & trade show businesses. Provider of growth & acquisition equity & recapitalization financing.

THOMSON RESEARCH
Div. of Thomson Financial
22 Thompson Pl
Boston, MA 02210
Telephone: (617) 856-2000, Web Site: www.thomson.com/solutions/financial
Exec VP & COO for Global Sls, Mktg & Svcs: Warren Breakstone
Conducts Business: Worldwide
Employees: 9,300
Primary Market Served: Business
Catalog available online
Direct online sales
Gross sales or billing: $2,000,000,000

Provides businesses with an electronic collection of company, industry & product research & analysis.

THOMSON REUTERS LPC
Subs. of Reuters
3 Times Sq
New York, NY 10036
Telephone: (646) 223-6890, E-Mail: lpc.americas@reuters.com, Web Site: www.loanpricing.com
Pres: Jim Davis
Conducts Business: Worldwide
Employees: 105
Primary Market Served: Business
Catalog available online
Direct online sales
Advertising/Marketing Budget Related to Direct Marketing: 26-50%

Business & industrial financial services.

THRIVENT FINANCIAL FOR LUTHERANS
4321 N Ballard Rd
Appleton, WI 54919-0001
Telephone: (920) 734-5721, (800) 847-4836, FAX: (920) 730-4781, E-Mail: mail@thrivent.com, Web Site: www.thrivent.com
Exec VP, Mktg & Prods: Pam Moret
Strategic Mktg: Beth Larsen
Sr VP Mktg: Timothy J. Lehman

Sr VP Communs: Marie A. Uhrich
Conducts Business: U.S.
Employees: 2,676
Primary Market Served: Consumer
Founded: 1902
Gross sales or billing: $6,086,200,000

Fortune 500 national fraternal benefit society. Provides insurance and financial products as well as educational and volunteer opportunities.

TRANS UNION CORP
555 W Adams St
Chicago, IL 60661-3614
Telephone: (312) 258-1717, (800) 335-9888, FAX: (312) 466-8385, Web Site: www.transunion.com
CEO & Pres: Bobby Mehta
Pres US Info Svcs: Jeff Hellinga
Exec VP Global Analytics & Decision Svcs: Wilbert Noronha
Exec VP Fin Svcs Group: Steve Sassaman
VP Sls Strategy & Thought Leadership Fin Svcs Group: F. J. Guarrera
Conducts Business: U.S.
Employees: 4,100
Primary Market Served: Business
Founded: 1968
Gross sales or billing: $1,200,000,000

Sell credit & non-credit promotional listings to various industries.

TRANSFIRST EPAYMENT SERVICES
13220 Birch Dr (Suite 110)
Omaha, NE 68164-5434
Telephone: (888) 541-9800, Web Site: epay.transfirst.com
Pres: Mike Phelan
Primary Market Served: Consumer

THE DMA TRANSFIRST HOLDINGS INC
5400 Lyndon B Johnson Fwy (Suite 900)
Dallas, TX 75240-1054
Telephone: (214) 453-7700, (888) 254-4137, FAX: (214) 453-7739, Web Site: www.transfirst.com
Sr VP & CFO: Mark Travis
Sr VP & CIO: John Peterson
Sr VP, Corp Devel: Andrew Rueff
VP, Client Svcs: Alea Brim
Conducts Business: U.S.
Employees: 20
Primary Market Served: Business
Catalog available online
Indirect online sales
Founded: 1991
Gross sales or billing: $10,000,000

Provide payment processing solutions designed for the direct marketing/electronic retailing industry. Offer credit card processing, electronic check drafting & ACH payment services. Complete data management facilities accommodate monthly management needs such as installment and/or continuity billing. Offer seamless interface between the order taking & fulfillment facilities and/or new payment methods.

TRAVELEX AMERICA INC
Subs. of Travelex
1152 15th St NW (fl 7)
Washington, DC 20005
Telephone: (202) 408-1200, FAX: (202) 513-5215, Web Site: business.travelex.com/us
Pres: Larry D. Taylor
Sr VP & Head of Sls, Bus Svcs Div: Tom Tucker
Conducts Business: U.S., Canada
Employees: 428
Primary Market Served: Consumer
Gross sales or billing: $112,000,000

THE DMA TULLY & HOLLAND INC
20 William St Ste 135
Wellesley, MA 02481-4133
Telephone: (781) 239-2900, FAX: (781) 239-2901, E-Mail: info@tullyandholland.com, Web Site: www.tullyandholland.com
Pres: Timothy Tully
Sr VP: Elizabeth Richards Tulley
Mng Dir: Chris Kaupe
Mng Dir: Andrew Crain
Mng Dir: Russ Robb
Mng Dir: Elizabeth Napier
Mng Dir: Donald O'Connor
Mng Dir: Stuart Rose
Mng Dir: Alfred Rossou
Employees: 10
Primary Market Served: Business
Founded: 1992

Investment banking.

UBS WEALTH MANAGEMENT US
1200 Harbor Blvd
Weehawken, NJ 07086-6728
Telephone: (201) 352-3000, (888) 279-3343, FAX: (201) 617-8589, Web Site: www.ubs.com/financialservicesinc
Chmn & CEO: Joseph Grano
Conducts Business: U.S.
Primary Market Served: Business & Consumer

Brokerage firm using direct marketing techniques to gain qualified prospects for investment brokers.

USAA ALLIANCE SERVICES MARKETING
Subs. of United Services Automobile Association (USAA)
9800 Fredericksburg Rd
San Antonio, TX 78288-0141
Telephone: (210) 456-9857, FAX: (210) 498-4542, Web Site: www.usaa.com
Pres USAA Alliance Svcs Inc: Janice Marshall
CEO USAA: Robert T. Herres
ASC Mktg Dir: William Choate
ASC Mktg Sys Dir: Dawnelle Gozenbach
Sr Mktg Specialist: Ginny Alexander
Conducts Business: Worldwide
Employees: 200
Primary Market Served: Consumer
Catalog available online
Direct online sales
Advertising/Marketing Budget Related to Direct Marketing: 76-100%
Direct Marketing ad budget: $6,600,000
Direct Mail: 100%
Founded: 1922
Gross sales or billing: $65,200,000

Member merchandise buying & cruise travel services. Alliance services include long distance telephone service, home security, internet service provider, rental cars, the USAA/Sprint program, USAA Choice Ride & USAA Floral Service.

UNION FEDERAL SAVINGS BANK
1565 Mineral Spring Ave
North Providence, RI 02904
Telephone: (401) 353-8900, (800) 992-0278, FAX: (401) 353-8938, Web Site: www.unionfsb.com
Pres & Treas: William F. Sullivan
Primary Market Served: Business & Consumer
Catalog available online
Gross sales or billing: $4,800,000,000

Financial services.

THE DMA UNITED COMMUNITY BANK
63 Hwy 51 S
Blairsville, GA 30512
Telephone: (706) 745-0911, Web Site: www.ucbi.com
VP Direct Mktg: Tricia Stoeckig
Primary Market Served: Business & Consumer

US BANCORP
Div. of US Bancorp Minneapolis
800 Nicollet Mall
Minneapolis, MN 55402-7014

Telephone: (651) 466-3000, (800) 872-2657, FAX: (612) 303-0782, Web Site: www.usbank.com
Chmn, Pres & CEO: Richard K. Davis
Vice Chmn: Richard C. Hartnack
Vice Chmn: Joseph M. Otting
Sr VP Mktg: Jenny Powell
Conducts Business: U.S.
Employees: 50,000
Primary Market Served: Business & Consumer
Catalog available online
Indirect online sales
Advertising/Marketing Budget Related to Direct Marketing: 0-25%
Gross sales or billing: $19,109,000,000

Full-service commercial & retail bank serving the Colorado market.

THE DMA US BANK
200 S 6th St
Minneapolis, MN 55402-1403
Telephone: (612) 973-1111, Web Site: www.usbank.com
Direct Mktg Mgr, Co-branded Credit Cards: Joan Forde
Primary Market Served: Business & Consumer

US DIGITAL TRANSACTIONS CORPORATION
228 Park Ave S
New York, NY 10003-1502
Telephone: (800) 728-1190, Web Site: www.usdtcorp.com
Primary Market Served: Consumer

THE DMA US TAX SHIELD
17328 Ventura Blvd
Encino, CA 91316-3904
Telephone: (877) 929-3535, Web Site: www.ustaxshield.com
Mktg Mgr: Andy Klein
Conducts Business: USA
Primary Market Served: Consumer
Advertising/Marketing Budget Related to Direct Marketing: 51-75%

UNIVERSAL FIDELITY CORP
1445 Langham Creek Dr
Houston, TX 77084
Telephone: (281) 550-1444, (800) 580-8887, FAX: (281) 647-4207, Web Site: www.ufccorp.com
CEO: Terry Simonds
VP, Mktg: Ken Sebek
Primary Market Served: Business
Advertising/Marketing Budget Related to Direct Marketing: 0-25%

Collection agency.

UNIVERSITY BANK
2015 Washtenaw Ave
Ann Arbor, MI 48104

Telephone: (734) 741-5858, FAX: (734) 741-5859, E-Mail: ranzini@university-bank.com, Web Site: www.university-bank.com
Pres: Stephen Lange Ranzini
Employees: 4
Primary Market Served: Business
Founded: 1993

Business investment development for corporations & financing.

THE DMA UWHARRIE CAPITAL CORP
PO Box 338
Albemarle, NC 28002-0338
Telephone: (704) 991-1181, Web Site: www.uwharriecapitalcorp.com
Primary Market Served: Consumer

VW CREDIT
2200 Ferdinand Porsche Dr
Herndon, VA 20171-5884
Telephone: (703) 364-7755
Gen Mgr, Mktg & Bus Devel: Joanna Sherry
Primary Market Served: Consumer

VANDERBILT ADVERTISING
Div. of Value Line Publishing Inc
220 E 42nd St
New York, NY 10017-5806
Telephone: (212) 907-1500, FAX: (212) 907-1914, Web Site: www.valueline.com
Direct Mail Mgr: Marla Newell
Adv Dir: Lawrence Freeman
Media Supvr: Gloria Rodriguez
Conducts Business: U.S., Canada
Employees: 6
Primary Market Served: Business & Consumer
Catalog available online
Advertising/Marketing Budget Related to Direct Marketing: 26-50%

Value Line Investment Survey (weekly advisory service) & related financial investment information to individual investors.

VANGUARD
PO Box 2600
Valley Forge, PA 19482-2600
Telephone: (610) 648-6000, Web Site: www.vanguard.com
Mgr: Patricia Jacona
Primary Market Served: Business & Consumer

THE VANTAGE GROUP INC
90 Canal St
Boston, MA 02114
Telephone: (617) 878-6000, FAX: (617) 878-6156, Web Site: www.vantagetravel.com
Exec VP: Harry Melikian

Conducts Business: Worldwide
Primary Market Served: Consumer
Catalog available online
Founded: 1983
Gross sales or billing: $140,000,000

Consumer financial services & mail order products.

THE DMA VERONIS SUHLER STEVENSON LLC
55 E 52nd St (fl 33)
New York, NY 10055-0007
Telephone: (212) 935-4990, FAX: (212) 381-8168, E-Mail: stevensonj@vss.com, Web Site: www.vss.com
Chmn: John J. Veronis
Pres & Founding Gen Partner: John S. Suhler
Partner: Marco Sodi
Partner: Jeffrey T. Stevenson
Exec VP: James P. Rutherford
Conducts Business: Worldwide
Employees: 114
Primary Market Served: Business
Catalog available online
Indirect online sales
Founded: 1981
Gross sales or billing: $203,000,000

Investment bankers to the direct marketing, media, communications & information industries.

VISA USA
800 Metro Center Blvd
Foster City, CA 94404-4252
Telephone: (650) 432-3200, FAX: (650) 432-2875, Web Site: www.visa.com
Sr VP, Mktg: Robert Pifke
VP, Mktg: Kelly Krug
Sr Bus Leader: Jessica Graham
Primary Market Served: Business & Consumer

WACHOVIA BANK, NATIONAL ASSOCIATION
1 Wachovia Center, 301 S College St
Charlotte, NC 28228-0206
Telephone: (704) 590-0000, (800) WACHOVIA, FAX: (704) 427-6748
CEO & Chmn: Ken Thompson
CFO: Thomas J. Wurtz
Sr Exec VP & CMO: Ranjana Clark
Sr Exec VP: Steve Cummings
Vice Chmn & Pres of Natl Bank: Ben Jenkins
Primary Market Served: Business
Catalog available online
Indirect online sales

Full service bank.

WASHINGTON MUTUAL HOME LOAN, INC

3050 Highland Pkwy (Suite 100)
Downers Grove, IL 60515-5565
Telephone: (847) 549-6500, FAX:
(847) 549-2975
Chmn & CEO: Kerry Killinger
Pres & COO: Stephen Rotella
Exec VP & CFO: Thomas W. Casey
Exec VP & CIO: Deborah Horvath
Conducts Business: U.S.
Employees: 2,500
Primary Market Served: Business
Catalog available online
Indirect online sales
Direct Marketing ad budget:
Direct Mail: 45%
Magazines: 5%
Newspapers: 5%
Telephone: 45%

Direct marketing of mortgage loan
products through mail & telemarketing.

WEBSTER BANK

Subs. of Webster Financial Corp
145 Bank St Fl 1
Waterbury, CT 06702-2211
Telephone: (203) 578-2460, FAX:
(203) 754-5939, Web Site: www.
websterbank.com
Chmn & CEO: James C. Smith
VP, Mktg Database: Patty Murphy
Primary Market Served: Business &
Consumer

Savings & loan bank.

THE DMA WEICHERT CO

1625 State Route 10
Morris Plains, NJ 07950-2905
Telephone: (973) 397-8516, Web Site:
www.weichert.com
VP Info Svcs: George La Penta
Primary Market Served: Business &
Consumer

RICHARD WEINER CONSULTANT

1814 NE Miami Gardens Dr (Suite
904)
North Miami Beach, FL 33179-5043
Telephone: (305) 441-6470
Consultant: Richard Weiner
Primary Market Served: Consumer

WELLS FARGO

420 Montgomery St
San Francisco, CA 94163
Telephone: (866) 878-5865, (800) 869-
3557, FAX: (626) 312-3015, Web
Site: www.wellsfargo.com
Chmn: Richard Kuvacevich
Pres & CEO: John Stumpf
Exec VP & CFO: Howard I. Atkins
Sr VP, Mktg & Adv: Charles Preston

Mng Dir: Kevin Brogan
Conducts Business: U.S.
Employees: 160,000
Primary Market Served: Business &
Consumer
Catalog available online
Direct online sales
Founded: 1872
Gross sales or billing: $31,000,000,000

Financial services & bank holding
company.

WINMILL & CO

11 Hanover Sq
New York, NY 10005-2818
Telephone: (212) 785-0900, (800) 400-
MIDAS, FAX: (212) 363-1100,
E-Mail: info@midasfunds.com, Web
Site: www.midasfunds.com
Pres: Thomas Winmill
Fund Dir: Bruce B. Harber
Dir: James E. Hunt
Dir: Peter K. Werner
Dir & Vice Chair: Robert D. Anderson
Conducts Business: Worldwide
Employees: 33
Primary Market Served: Business &
Consumer
Catalog available online
Indirect online sales
Gross sales or billing: $17,000,000

No-load mutual fund & discount brokerage service.

THE DMA XCELERATED INVESTMENTS INC

2940 Hebron Park Dr (Suite 307)
Hebron, KY 41048-9573
Telephone: (877) 489-3347, Web Site:
www.xcelerated.com

A-MARK INC
715 Twining Rd (Suite 118)
Dresher, PA 19025-1832
Telephone: (215) 886-4740, FAX:
(215) 886-4749
Pres & CEO: John Myers
Conducts Business: U.S.
Employees: 2

Financial Services

AAA MID-ATLANTIC INSURANCE GROUPS
Div. of AAA Midatlantic
1 River Pl
Wilmington, DE 19801-5125
Telephone: (302) 299-4700, (800) 451-5921, FAX: (215) 864-5486, Web
Site: www.aaamidatlantic.com
Pres: Allen DeWalle
Reg VP: Nick Eppinger
Mng Dir Mktg: Bill Harris
Primary Market Served: Consumer

Property, casualty, accident & health
insurance.

AEGON DIRECT MARKETING SERVICES INC
Aegon USA Inc
100 Light St Fl B1
Baltimore, MD 21202-1098
Telephone: (410) 209-5617, FAX:
(410) 209-5932, Web Site: www.
aegondms.com
Pres, CEO: Merlin Carp
Dir, Mktg: Dien Sapp
Pub Rels Mgr: Veronica Mouring
Primary Market Served: Consumer
Advertising/Marketing Budget Related
to Direct Marketing: 76-100%

Insurance.

THE DMA AFLAC
1932 Wynnton Rd
Columbus, GA 31999
Telephone: (706) 243-5428, Web Site:
www.aflac.com

AGIA INSURANCE SERVICES
1155 Eugenia Pl
Carpinteria, CA 93013-2061
Telephone: (805) 566-9191, FAX:
(805) 566-1887, Web Site: www.
agia.com
VP, Mktg: Kimberly Gonzales
VP Mktg: Susan Roe
Conducts Business: U.S.
Employees: 200
Primary Market Served: Consumer
Founded: 1964

Broker/administrator of group insurance programs.

AIG ACCIDENT & HEALTH
Div. of AIG
70 Pine St (50th fl)
New York, NY 10270
Telephone: (212) 770-7000, (877) 638-4244, FAX: (212) 509-9705, Web
Site: www.aig.com
VP, Accident Health Div: Jeff Kestenbaum
Chmn: Rob B. Willumstad
Pres, CEO & Dir: Martin J. Sullivan
Exec VP & CFO: Steven J. Bensinger
Primary Market Served: Business &
Consumer
Catalog available online
Indirect online sales
Founded: 1919

Provide insurance products worldwide.

AIG MARKETING
Div. of American International Group
70 Pine St (40th fl)
New York, NY 10270-0002
Telephone: (212) 770-7000, (212) 770-2237, Web Site: www.agac.com
Sr VP, New Bus: John G. Colona
VP, Sls: Mark Duchene
EVP & Chief Direct Mktg Officer: Eugene Raitt
Conducts Business: International
Employees: 400
Primary Market Served: Consumer

Marketer of property, casualty, health
& life insurance products to affinity
groups.

AMA INSURANCE AGENCY INC
Subs. of American Medical Association
515 N State St
Chicago, IL 60601
Telephone: (312) 464-2425, (800) 458-5736, FAX: (312) 419-5096, Web
Site: www.amainsure.com
Asst VP, Direct Response Sls: Cynthia
K. Warden
VP, Sls: Denise S. Friday
Conducts Business: U.S.
Employees: 135
Primary Market Served: Business &
Consumer
Catalog available online
Indirect online sales
Advertising/Marketing Budget Related
to Direct Marketing: 76-100%
Founded: 1988

Provide insurance for medical students,
physicians, other health care professionals & other professional
associations.

AON CENTER
200 E Randolph St
Chicago, IL 60601-6436
Telephone: (312) 381-1000, FAX:
(312) 381-6032, Web Site: www.aon.
com
Exec Chm: Pat Ryan
Pres & CEO: Greg Case
Sr Exec VP: Michael O'Halleran
Global CIO: Baljit Dail
Chief Diversity Officer: Corbette Doyle
Conducts Business: U.S., Canada
Employees: 43,000
Primary Market Served: Business &
Consumer
Catalog available online
Direct Marketing ad budget:
$1,800,000
Direct Mail: 90%
Magazines: 4%
Newspapers: 4%
Telephone: 2%
Founded: 1982
Gross sales or billing: $9,000,000,000

Sell group life & health insurance by
mail through sponsoring organizations
& through an agency sales force. Also,
sell life & health products through
mail on a broad market basis.

AON CONSULTING NEW YORK
Aon Corp
199 Water St (fl 12)
New York, NY 10038-3541
Telephone: (212) 792-9759, (212) 792-9700, (212) 441-2000, FAX: (212)
792-9720, E-Mail: garry_sullivan@
aoncons.com
VP, Mktg: Frank J. Fimmano
Conducts Business: Worldwide
Employees: 50,000
Primary Market Served: Business &
Consumer
Advertising/Marketing Budget Related
to Direct Marketing: 0-25%

Provide sales, service & administration
of insurance services to associations,
financial institutions & other membership organizations.

THE DMA ARAG
400 Locust St (Suite 480)
Des Moines, IA 50309
Telephone: (800) 247-4184, FAX:
(515) 246-8710, E-Mail: service@
ARAGgroup.com, Web Site: www.
araggroup.com
Chief Mktg Officer: Ann Dieleman
Primary Market Served: Business &
Consumer

AXA EQUITABLE
1290 Ave of the Americas (fl 7)
New York, NY 10104-0101
Telephone: (212) 554-1234, (212) 314-2956, Web Site: www.axaonline.com
AVP: Lisa Mahaffey
AVP Mktg: Santo Loporto

AFFINION GROUP
400 Duke Dr (Suite 200)
Franklin, TN 37067-2700
Telephone: (800) 251-2148, Web Site:
www.progenymarketing.com
VP Mktg: Barry Starr

JOHN ALDEN LIFE INSURANCE CO/NORTH STAR MARKETING
Div. of Fortis Health
11465 Johns Creek Pkwy (Suite 160)
Duluth, GA 30097-1573
Telephone: (678) 473-1211, (800) 768-6288, FAX: (678) 473-9573, Web
Site: www.nstarmarketing.com
CEO: Kae Groshong Wagner
Exec VP: Bowen Smith
VP: Bob Bartlett
VP: Amy Neary
Mgr: Joe McLaughlin
Conducts Business: U.S., Canada
Primary Market Served: Business &
Consumer
Catalog available online

Sell life, accident & health insurance.

THE DMA ALFA INSURANCE
PO Box 11000
Montgomery, AL 36191-0001
Telephone: (334) 288-3900, Web Site:
www.alfains.com
VP Mktg Communs: Christy Cantrell
Primary Market Served: Consumer

ALLIANZ LIFE INSURANCE CO OF NORTH AMERICA
5701 Golden Hills Dr, PO Box 1344
Minneapolis, MN 55416-1297
Telephone: (763) 765-6500, (800) 950-5872, Web Site: www.allianzlife.com
CEO: Gary C. Bhojwani
Exec VP: Jill Paterson
Sr VP: Tom Burns
VP, HR: Cary Brinkley
Bus Fin Officer: Giulio Terzariol
Conducts Business: U.S.
Employees: 1,800
Primary Market Served: Business &
Consumer
Catalog available online
Founded: 1896

Sell life insurance.

AMERICAN CAPITAL
aka American Capital Strategies Ltd
2 Bethesda Metro Ctr Ste 1400
Bethesda, MD 20814-5390
Telephone: (301) 951-6122, FAX:
(301) 654-6714, E-Mail: info@
americancapital.com, Web Site:
www.americancapital.com
Chmn, Pres & CEO: Malon Wilkus
Exec VP & COO: Ira J. Wagner
Exec VP & CFO: John R. Erikson
Conducts Business: U.S.
Employees: 484
Primary Market Served: Business &
Consumer
Advertising/Marketing Budget Related
to Direct Marketing: 26-50%
Direct Marketing ad budget: $10,000
Direct Mail: 75%
Telephone: 25%
Gross sales or billing: $1,330,000,000

AMERICAN FAMILY INSURANCE GROUP
6000 American Pkwy
Madison, WI 53783-0001
Telephone: (608) 249-2111, FAX:
(608) 243-6525, E-Mail: akin1@
amfam.com, Web Site: www.amfam.
com
DM Mgr: Andy King
DM Specialist: Christina Parrott
DM Specialist: Justin Miller
DM Specialist: Erik Busse
DM Specialist: Cynthia Mochalski
Conducts Business: U.S.
Employees: 7,000
Primary Market Served: Business &
Consumer
Indirect online sales
Direct Marketing ad budget:
Direct Mail: 70%
Online: 10%
Telephone: 20%
Founded: 1927
Gross sales or billing: $4,000,000,000

Multi-line captive agent insurance
company.

AMERICAN FAMILY LIFE ASSURANCE CO OF COLUMBUS (AFLAC)
1932 Wynnton Rd
Columbus, GA 31999-0001
Telephone: (706) 323-3431, (800) 992-3522, FAX: (706) 660-7446, Web
Site: www.aflac.com
CEO, AFLAC Inc: Daniel P. Amos
CFO & Exec VP: Kriss Cloninger III
Dir: Sheryl Manville
Mgr Investor Rels: Delia Moore
Sr VP: Ronald E. Kirkland
Conducts Business: U.S. & Japan
Employees: 7,400

Primary Market Served: Business &
Consumer
Catalog available online
Indirect online sales
Founded: 1955
Gross sales or billing: $14,600,000,000

Market supplemental health insurance
to consumers & businesses.

AMERICAN FIDELITY ASSURANCE CO
2000 Classen Blvd, PO Box 73125
Oklahoma City, OK 73106
Telephone: (405) 525-6900, FAX:
(405) 523-5215, Web Site: www.
afadvantage.com
Asst VP Mktg: Mike Carroll
Team Leader Direct Mktg: Kim Hood
Conducts Business: Worldwide
Employees: 1,400
Primary Market Served: Business &
Consumer
Catalog available online
Advertising/Marketing Budget Related
to Direct Marketing: 0-25%
Founded: 1960

Insurance for trade associations,
groups, employers & educators.

AMERICAN GENERAL CO
Subs. of American International Group
Inc
AIG Benefit Solutions
3600 State Rte 66
Neptune, NJ 07753
Telephone: (732) 922-7000, FAX:
(732) 922-7595
Pres: Jim Weakley
VP: John Penko
Sr VP: Mike Witwer
Sr VP: David Armstrong
Sr VP: Chris Calos
Dir, Mktg Commun: Kathy Nisivocci
Conducts Business: U.S.
Employees: 700
Primary Market Served: Business
Advertising/Marketing Budget Related
to Direct Marketing: 0-25%
Direct Marketing ad budget: $125,000
Magazines: 100%

Designs, develops, and manufactures a variety of group insurance products and services for the Employer-Paid, Voluntary, Worksite, Association and Financial Institution markets. Products include life, disability, dental, vision, mortgage, credit account protector, traditional loan, debt protection, voluntary and worksite products which are distributed nationwide through multiple channels including general agents, brokers and independent agents, third party administrators, benefit consultants or financial institutions. Product flexibility exists to accommodate all size groups on a national or international basis.

AMERICAN GENERAL LIFE & ACCIDENT INSURANCE

Div. of American International Group, Inc
American General Ctr
Nashville, TN 37250
Telephone: (615) 749-1000, (800) 888-2452, Web Site: www.agla.com
Pres & CEO: Matthew Winter
Exec VP: David O'Leary
DM Mgr: Steven Doster
Employees: 5,000
Primary Market Served: Consumer
Catalog available online
Gross sales or billing: $2,100,000,000

Provider of life & health insurance.

AMERICAN GENERAL LIFE INSURANCE CO

2929 Allen Pkwy
Houston, TX 77019-2155
Telephone: (713) 522-1111, FAX: (713) 522-8531, Web Site: www.aglife.com
Chmn: Rodney O. Martin Jr.
Pres & CEO: Matthew E. Winter
Sr VP, Strategic Mktg & Bus Devel: Erik Baden
VP, Branding & Media Svcs: Susan Howard
Employees: 11,000
Primary Market Served: Business & Consumer
Catalog available online

Life insurance.

AMERICAN HEALTH & LIFE INSURANCE CO

Div. of Citigroup
3001 Meacham Blvd (Suite 200)
Fort Worth, TX 76137
Telephone: (817) 348-7500, (800) 995-2274, FAX: (817) 348-7553, Web Site: www.citifinancial.com
Chmn & CEO: Charles Prince
Vice Chmn: Peter Dahlberg
Pres & COO: Robert Williumstad

CFO: Gary Crittenden
Sr VP, Corp Citizenship: Pamela M. Flaherty
Conducts Business: U.S.
Employees: 75
Primary Market Served: Business & Consumer

Health & life insurance company.

AMERICAN INSURANCE ADMINISTRATORS INC

3070 Riverside Dr
Columbus, OH 43221
Telephone: (614) 486-5388, FAX: (614) 486-2728
Pres: Alan E. Zink
Sr VP, Sls: Philip Super
VP, Admin: Nancy Tiburzio
VP, Direct Mktg: Jeff Roedel
Conducts Business: U.S.
Employees: 32
Primary Market Served: Business & Consumer
Advertising/Marketing Budget Related to Direct Marketing: 76-100%
Founded: 1967

Marketer & administrator of life & health insurance products to constituents of affinity associations.

AMERICAN INTERNATIONAL GROUP

Div. of AIG
70 Pine St (fl 50)
New York, NY 10270
Telephone: (212) 770-7000, (877) 638-4244, FAX: (212) 742-8692, Web Site: www.aig.com
CEO & Pres: Martin J. Sullivan
Conducts Business: 138 Countries worldwide
Employees: 5,700
Primary Market Served: Business & Consumer
Founded: 1919

International division handles life, accident, and health insurance direct marketing outside the USA in 138 countries worldwide.

THE DMA AMERICAN MODERN INSURANCE GROUP

Subs. of The Midland Co
7000 Midland Blvd
Amelia, OH 45102-2607
Telephone: (513) 943-7200, (800) 759-9008, FAX: (513) 947-4779, (800) 217-5150, E-Mail: customer_care@amig.com, Web Site: www.amig.com
Pres & CEO: John Hayden
VP Mktg Strategy & Devel: Jenny Hodge
Dir, Natl Life Sls: Larry Compton
Employees: 900

Primary Market Served: Business
Property & casualty insurance.

AMERICAN SECURITIES CAPITAL PARTNERS

666 3rd Ave (fl 29)
New York, NY 10017-4030
Telephone: (212) 476-8000, Web Site: www.american-securities.com
Dir of Strategic Initiatives: Lee Dranikoff
Primary Market Served: Consumer

AMERISURE INSURANCE COS

26777 Halsted Rd
Farmington Hills, MI 48331-3586
Telephone: (248) 615-9000, (800) 257-1900, FAX: (248) 615-8224, Web Site: www.amerisure.com
Chmn: James B. Nicholson
Pres & CEO: Richard F. Russell
Mgr Corp Commun & Adv: Linda S. DeSimone
Sr VP, CFO & Treas: R. Douglas Kinnan
Exec VP & COO: Thomas E. Hoeg
VP, IT: Frank L. Petersmark
Conducts Business: U.S.
Employees: 815
Primary Market Served: Business
Advertising/Marketing Budget Related to Direct Marketing: 0-25%
Founded: 1912
Gross sales or billing: $430,000,000

Commercial property casualty insurance.

THE DMA AMICA INSURANCE

100 Amica Way
Lincoln, RI 02865-1158
Telephone: (401) 334-6000, (800) 652-6422, FAX: (401) 334-4241, Web Site: www.amica.com
Exec VP & Gen Mgr: Carl R. Neal
Sr Asst VP: Bruce Maynard
VP: James E. McDermott Jr.
Sr Asst VP: Craig Phelps
Pres & CEO: Robert A. DiMuccio
Sr VP HR: Patricia A. Talin
Primary Market Served: Business & Consumer
Catalog available online
Indirect online sales
Founded: 1907

Life insurance.

ANTHEM BLUE CROSS

Formerly Blue Cross of California
1 Wellpoint Way
Westlake Village, CA 91362-3893
Telephone: (805) 557-6655, (800) 333-0912, FAX: (800) 557-6872, Web Site: www.bluecrossca.com

VP Mktg & Brand Strategy: Kate
Quinn
Pres & Gen Mgr: Leslie Margolin
Sr VP Individual & Grp Svcs: Deborah
F. Lachman
Sr VP & CIO: Elinor Mackinnon
VP Cust Svc: Bob Novelli
Employees: 7,000
Primary Market Served: Business &
Consumer
Founded: 1937

Insurance sales.

ANTHEM BLUE CROSS BLUE SHIELD
370 Bassett Rd
North Haven, CT 06473
Telephone: (203) 239-8381, (800) 545-
0948, FAX: (203) 985-7918, Web
Site: www.anthem.com
Pres: Marjorie Dorr
Reg Pub Rels Mgr: Carol Pompano
Primary Market Served: Consumer

Provide health insurance to Connecticut, Maine & New Hampshire
residents.

ANTHEM BLUE CROSS BLUE SHIELD
1831 Chestnut St (#1)
Saint Louis, MO 63103-2275
Telephone: (314) 923-4444, (888) 877-
9125, FAX: (314) 923-5151, E-Mail:
moreinfo@bcbsmo.com, Web Site:
www.bcbsmo.com
Pres, Anthem Blue Cross/Blue Shield
Missouri: Dennis Matheis
Exec VP & CIO: Mark Boxer
Dir, HR: Morry Berger
Employees: 2,300
Primary Market Served: Business &
Consumer
Catalog available online

Healthcare insurance.

ANTHEM CORPORATE COMMUNICATIONS
Div. of Anthem Inc
120 Monument Cir
Indianapolis, IN 46204
Telephone: (207) 822-7000, FAX:
(207) 822-7741, Web Site: www.
anthem.com
Chmn, Pres & CEO: Larry C. Glass-
cock
Primary Market Served: Business &
Consumer
Founded: 1938

A managed-care insurance company.

AON'S AFFINITY INSURANCE SERVICES INC
159 E County Line Rd
Hatboro, PA 19040-1218

Telephone: (215) 773-4600, Web Site:
www.aon.com
Sr VP Corp Mktg & Commun: Sharon
Cohen
Primary Market Served: Business &
Consumer

ASSURANT GROUP
Parent Co of Fortis Inc
1 Chase Manhattan Plaza
New York, NY 10005-1401
Telephone: (305) 253-2244, FAX:
(305) 252-6987, Web Site: www.
assurant.com
Chmn & CEO: Rob Pollock
Pres & COO: Bruce Comancho
Exec VP Sls & Mktg: Kevin Clotz
Conducts Business: U.S., Canada, U.K.
Primary Market Served: Business &
Consumer
Founded: 1999

Insurance services for financial institutions & business. Provide specialty
insurance, membership and extended
services program. Typically serving
segments of the population under-
served by other mainstream insurance
agencies.

ᴛʜᴇ ᴅᴍᴀ ASSURANT HEALTH
Bus seg of Assurant, Inc.
501 W Michigan St
Milwaukee, WI 53203-2706
Telephone: (414) 244-0658, (800) 800-
1212, FAX: (414) 224-0472, Web
Site: www.assuranthealth.com
Pres & CEO: Don Hamm
Dir Online Mktg & Ecommerce:
Steven Keller
VP Sls Strategy: Mike Norderhaug
Sr VP Strategic Devel: Mike Kellen
Conducts Business: Worldwide
Employees: 3,000
Primary Market Served: Business &
Consumer
Founded: 1892
Gross sales or billing: $634,500,000

Health insurance.

ASSURANT SOLUTIONS PRENEED DIVISION
260 Interstate North Cir SE
Atlanta, GA 30339-2110
Telephone: (770) 763-1000, (800) PRE
NEED, FAX: (770) 859-4325, Web
Site: www.assurantpreneed.com
Pres & CEO: Craig Lemasters
Exec VP & CFO: Phillip Bruce Cama-
cho
Sr VP: Christopher Reznyk
Employees: 13,400
Primary Market Served: Business
Catalog available online

Preneed insurance.

BALBOA LIFE & CASUALTY
3349 Michelson (Suite 200)
Irvine, CA 92623-9702
Telephone: (949) 222-8000, (800) 854-
6115, FAX: (949) 222-8777, Web
Site: www.balboainsurance.com
Pres, CEO & Sr Mng Dir: Robert
James
Exec VP & COO: Doreen DeLaney
Exec VP & CFO: Kenneth Mertzel
Exec VP: Ron Closser
Conducts Business: U.S., U.K.,
Canada, Australia
Employees: 1,980
Primary Market Served: Business &
Consumer
Advertising/Marketing Budget Related
to Direct Marketing: 51-75%
Direct Marketing ad budget:
Direct Mail: $50,000
Telephone: $100,000
Gross sales or billing: $1,710,000,000

Creditor & lender related insurance
programs & services for financial institutions & their customers.

BANKERS LIFE & CASUALTY CO
Subs. of Conseco
600 W Chicago Ave
Chicago, IL 60654-2800
Telephone: (312) 396-6000, (800) 231-
9150, Web Site: www.bankerslife.
com
CEO: C. James Prieur
Pres: Scott Perry
Sr VP, Sls & Distr: David Nelson
VP, Strategy & Mktg: Scott L. Gold-
berg
VP, Bankers Long Lerm Care: Gerardo
Monroy
VP, Underwriting & New Bus: Gary
Brown
Conducts Business: U.S.
Primary Market Served: Consumer
Catalog available online
Indirect online sales
Direct Marketing ad budget:
Direct Mail: 100%
Founded: 1880
Gross sales or billing: $2,800,000,000

Sell life & health insurance through
agents who are provided with leads
obtained through direct response
promotions.

ᴛʜᴇ ᴅᴍᴀ BENEFITMALL
485 Lyndon B Johnson Fwy (Suite
1100)
Dallas, TX 75244-6025
Telephone: (469) 791-3355, Web Site:
www.benefitmall.com
VP Mktg: Laura Clenney
Primary Market Served: Business &
Consumer

BLUE CROSS & BLUE SHIELD COBALT

Subs. of United Wisconsin Services Inc
North 17 W 24340 Riverwood Dr
Waukesha, WI 53188
Telephone: (262) 523-4020, Web Site: www.bcbsuw.org
Mktg Dir: Anna Marie Anderson
Primary Market Served: Business & Consumer

Group & individual life insurance & managed care products.

BLUE CROSS & BLUE SHIELD OF FLORIDA

4800 Deerwood Corporate Campus Pkwy
Jacksonville, FL 32246
Telephone: (904) 791-6111, (800) 477-3736, FAX: (904) 905-6638, E-Mail: katie.magee@bcbsfl.com, Web Site: www.bcbsfl.com
Chmn & CEO: Robert I. Lufrano
Exec VP, CAO, & CFO: R. Chris Doerr
Exec VP & COO: Arnold Livermore
Sr VP: Fred Ryder
Conducts Business: U.S.
Employees: 9,500
Primary Market Served: Business & Consumer
Indirect online sales
Direct Marketing ad budget:
Direct Mail: 80%
Newspapers: 20%
Founded: 1944
Gross sales or billing: $2,147,500,000

Marketer of individual & group healthcare insurance coverage.

BLUE CROSS & BLUE SHIELD OF OKLAHOMA

1215 Boulder Ave
Tulsa, OK 74119-2827
Telephone: (918) 560-3500, (800) 942-5837, E-Mail: info@bcbsok.com, Web Site: www.bcbsok.com
Pres: Rodney Huey
Dir: Dr. Joseph Cunningham
CIO & VP: Jerry D. Scherer
VP, Plng: Jon Polcha
Conducts Business: U.S.
Employees: 1,000
Primary Market Served: Business & Consumer
Catalog available online

Marketer of health & life insurance products.

BLUE CROSS & BLUE SHIELD OF SOUTH CAROLINA

I-20 E at Alpine Rd
Columbia, SC 29219
Telephone: (803) 788-0222, (800) 288-2227, FAX: (803) 736-4516, Web Site: www.bcbssc.com
Pres: Ed Sellers
VP, DM: Jim Deyling
VP Info: Wayne Roberts
VP Chief Medical Officers: John Little
Asst VP: Fred Rowell
Employees: 7,000
Primary Market Served: Business & Consumer
Catalog available online
Indirect online sales
Advertising/Marketing Budget Related to Direct Marketing: 0-25%
Founded: 1946
Gross sales or billing: $4,000,000,000

Health insurance marketer.

BLUE CROSS/BLUE SHIELD OF ILLINOIS

300 E Randolph
Chicago, IL 60601
Telephone: (312) 938-6000, FAX: (312) 938-5722, Web Site: www.bcbsil.com
Pres: Raymond McCaskey
Sr VP, Mktg: Paula Steiner
Acct Exec: Cary Goldstein
Acct Exec: Dan MacKenzie
Acct Exec: Dave Gieselman
Primary Market Served: Business & Consumer
Catalog available online

Healthcare insurance.

BLUE CROSS BLUE SHIELD OF LOUISIANA

5525 Reitz Ave
Baton Rouge, LA 70809-3802
Telephone: (225) 295-3307, (800) 599-2583, FAX: (225) 295-2054, E-Mail: help@bcbsla.com, Web Site: www.bcbsla.com
VP, Corp Commun: John Maginnis
Reg Dir: Larry Blackman
Reg Dir: James Bustillo
Reg Dir: Dan Wagner
Reg Mgr: Merle Francis
Conducts Business: U.S.
Employees: 1,500
Primary Market Served: Business & Consumer
Catalog available online
Advertising/Marketing Budget Related to Direct Marketing: 76-100%
Direct Marketing ad budget: $2,000,000
Direct Mail: 90%
Newspapers: 5%
TV/Radio: 5%
Founded: 1934
Gross sales or billing: $500,000,000

Health insurance.

BLUE CROSS BLUE SHIELD OF NORTH CAROLINA

PO Box 2291
Durham, NC 27702-2291
Telephone: (800) 250-3630, Web Site: www.bcbsnc.com
SEM Mgr: Marc Moore

BLUE SHIELD LIFE

Subs. of Blue Shield of California
50 Beale St
San Francisco, CA 94105-1813
Telephone: (888) 800-2742, FAX: (800) 329-2742, Web Site: www.blueshieldca.com
Chmn, Pres & CEO: Bruce Bodaken
Exec VP & CFO: Heidi Kunz
Exec VP Customer Svcs & Corp Mktg: Bob Novelli
Sr VP Chief Actuary: Ed Cymerys
Sr VP HR: Marianne Jackson
Conducts Business: U.S.
Employees: 40
Primary Market Served: Business & Consumer
Catalog available online
Advertising/Marketing Budget Related to Direct Marketing: 0-25%
Founded: 1953
Gross sales or billing: $39,000,000

Life & health insurance.

BLUE SHIELD OF CALIFORNIA

50 Beale St
San Francisco, CA 94105-1808
Telephone: (415) 229-5000, FAX: (415) 229-5056, Web Site: www.blueshieldca.com
Chmn, Pres & CEO: Bruce Bodaken
VP Corp Mktg: Doug Biehn
Conducts Business: U.S.
Employees: 750
Primary Market Served: Business & Consumer
Founded: 1939
Gross sales or billing: $8,150,000,000

Healthcare insurance.

BRITISH COLUMBIA AUTOMOBILE ASSOCIATION

dba BCAA
4567 Canada Way
Burnaby, BC, Canada V5G 4T1
Telephone: (604) 268-5000, (800) 564-6222, FAX: (604) 268-5585, Web Site: www.bcaa.com
Pres & CEO: William Bullis
VP HR & Corp Communs: John Evans
Dir, Customer Mngmt: Liliana Daminato
Conducts Business: Canada

Primary Market Served: Business &
Consumer
Gross sales or billing: $115,000,000

Full service agency providing auto,
travel & insurance services.

BROKERS/CONSULTANTS INC

1332 Dartmouth Rd
Flossmoor, IL 60422-1905
Telephone: (708) 957-2900, FAX:
(708) 957-4155
Pres: J.S. Tiernan
Conducts Business: U.S.
Employees: 4
Primary Market Served: Business &
Consumer
Advertising/Marketing Budget Related
to Direct Marketing: 0-25%
Direct Marketing ad budget:
Direct Mail: 95%
Magazines: 5%
Founded: 1964

Marketers of term life & group health
insurance.

BUSINESS PLANNERS & CONSULTANTS INC

370 Lexington Ave (Suite 909)
New York, NY 10017-6503
Telephone: (212) 972-1970, FAX:
(212) 972-1126
Pres: Kevin S. Foley
Conducts Business: U.S.
Employees: 20
Primary Market Served: Business &
Consumer
Advertising/Marketing Budget Related
to Direct Marketing: 0-25%
Direct Marketing ad budget:
Direct Mail: 10%
Newspapers: 20%
Telephone: 70%
Gross sales or billing: $1,200,000

Insurance administration (TPA); basi-
cally short term disability (Statutory
NY). Broker, property casualty, life &
health.

CMI DIRECT

2349 B Honolulu Ave
Montrose, CA 91020-2513
Telephone: (951) 300-1700, FAX:
(866) 723-5433, Web Site: www.
cmidirect.net
Pres: Charles F. Murray
CFO: Jim Aeling
Mktg Dir: Dana Kelley
Conducts Business: U.S.
Employees: 33
Primary Market Served: Consumer
Advertising/Marketing Budget Related
to Direct Marketing: 76-100%
Founded: 1979

Direct marketing services company.
Specializes in telemarketer insurance
products through financial institutions,
& other organizations.

CNA

333 S Wabash Ave
Chicago, IL 60604-4107
Telephone: (312) 822-5000, (800) 262-
2000, E-Mail: cna_help@cna.com,
Web Site: www.cna.com
Chmn Bd & CEO: Stephen Lilienthal
Exec VP & CFO: D. Craig Mense
Exec VP & CIO: John Golden
Chief Risk Officer: John Beckman
Underwriting Dir: Katherine Fenwick
Conducts Business: U.S.
Employees: 16,000
Primary Market Served: Business &
Consumer
Catalog available online
Gross sales or billing: $10,000,000,000

Insurance carrier.

CANADA BROKERLINK INSURANCE

Subs. of ING Canada
17520 111th Ave
Edmonton, AB, Canada T55 OA2
Telephone: (780) 474-8911, FAX:
(780) 479-0573, Web Site: www.
brokerlink.ca
Mktg: Chris Miller
Conducts Business: Canada
Primary Market Served: Consumer
Direct Marketing ad budget: $25,000
Direct Mail: 30%
Magazines: 5%
Newspapers: 20%
TV/Radio: 45%
Founded: 1960

Sell general insurance by mail to homeowners, business owners & auto
owners on a mass merchandising basis.

CAPITAL INSURANCE GROUP (CIG)

2300 Garden Rd
Monterey, CA 93940-5326
Telephone: (831) 233-5500, Web Site:
www.ciginsurance.com
Mktg Mgr: Sandie Borthwick

CAREFIRST BLUE CROSS BLUE SHIELD

840 First St NE
Washington, DC 20002-8046
Telephone: (202) 479-8000, FAX:
(301) 470-8049, Web Site: www.
carefirst.com
Pres & CEO: Chet Burrell
VP: Daniel Winn MD
Vice Chmn: Edward J. Basan
COO: Michael L. Daly

Pub Rels: Michael Sullivan
Conducts Business: Worldwide
Employees: 5,400
Primary Market Served: Business &
Consumer
Catalog available online
Indirect online sales

Health insurance marketer.

CARHILL ENTERPRISES INC

1232 Washington Ave (Suite 300)
Saint Louis, MO 63103-1983
Telephone: (314) 621-7646, Web Site:
www.cahillinsight.com
Owner: Andrew Hillin

CATERPILLAR INSURANCE SERVICES CORP

Subs. of Caterpillar Inc
2120 West End Ave
Nashville, TN 37203
Telephone: (615) 386-5800, Web Site:
www.cat.com
Pres: Linda D. Turner
Pres, Fin Svcs & VP: James S. Beard
Primary Market Served: Business &
Consumer
Founded: 1981

Insurance company providing insurance to business & consumers using
Caterpillar machinery.

CELTIC LIFE INSURANCE CO

233 S Wacker Dr (Suite 700)
Chicago, IL 60606-6300
Telephone: (312) 332-5401, FAX:
(312) 441-0341, E-Mail: info@
celtic-net.com, Web Site: www.
celtic-net.com
Chmn, Pres & CEO: Frederick J. Man-
ning
Sr VP & CFO: Lewis R. Marszalek
Sr VP, Admin: Blake A. Westerfield
COO: James P. Daly
VP, HR: Barbara Basham
Primary Market Served: Business &
Consumer
Catalog available online

Group health insurance.

CENTRAL STATES HEALTH & LIFE CO OF OMAHA

1212 N 96th St
Omaha, NE 68114
Telephone: (402) 397-1111, (800) 826-
6587, FAX: (402) 391-3772, Web
Site: www.cso.com
Chmn: Richard T. Kizer
Pres: T. Edward Kizer
Sr VP, Opers: Jeffrey J. Wanning
Sr VP & CFO: Leonard A. Pacer
VP & CIO: David W. Dibben
Employees: 650

Primary Market Served: Consumer
Catalog available online
Advertising/Marketing Budget Related
to Direct Marketing: 26-50%
Founded: 1932
Gross sales or billing: $78,900,000

Sell credit card insurance.

CENTRAL STATES INDEMNITY
Subs. of Berkshire Hathaway Inc
1212 N 96th St
Omaha, NE 68114-2274
Telephone: (402) 997-8000, (402) 397-1111, (800) 445-6500, Web Site: www.csi-omaha.com
Pres: John Kizer
Exec VP: Kevin Moran
VP Mktg: Mike Hoody
Asst VP: Mark Spack
Conducts Business: U.S.
Employees: 450
Primary Market Served: Business & Consumer
Advertising/Marketing Budget Related to Direct Marketing: 76-100%
Direct Marketing ad budget:
Direct Mail: 50%
Telephone: 50%
Founded: 1977
Gross sales or billing: $54,000,000

Provider of payment protection insurance: Life, disability, involuntary unemployment & family leave insurance.

THE DMA CHAIRMAN'S MARKETING GROUP LLC
8 Lafayette Rd W
Princeton, NJ 08540-2428
Telephone: (732) 745-4700
Primary Market Served: Consumer

CHARTIS
70 Pine St (fl 22)
New York, NY 10270-0001
Telephone: (212) 770-8013, Web Site: www.chartisinsurance.com/pcg
Primary Market Served: Consumer

THE DMA CIGNA INTERNATIONAL
1601 Chestnut St, 2 Liberty Pl (fl 53)
Philadelphia, PA 19192-0003
Telephone: (215) 761-1741, FAX: (215) 761-5515, Web Site: www.cigna.com
Chmn & CEO CIGNA Corp: H. Edward Hanway
Exec VP & CFO: Michael W. Bell
Exec VP HR & Svcs CIGNA Corp: John M. Murabito
Sr VP Bus Devel: Michael Ross
Exec VP & Gen Counsel CIGNA Corp: Carol Ann Petren

Employees: 27,000
Primary Market Served: Consumer
Founded: 1792
Gross sales or billing: $1,200,000,000

Discount brokerage services.

CIVIL SERVICE EMPLOYEES INSURANCE GROUP
2121 N California Blvd (Suite 555)
Walnut Creek, CA 94596-3501
Telephone: (925) 817-6300, (415) 274-7803, (800) 282-6848, Web Site: www.cseinsurance.com
Sr VP: John Adiletti
Conducts Business: U.S.
Employees: 300
Primary Market Served: Business & Consumer
Catalog available online
Indirect online sales
Founded: 1949
Gross sales or billing: $74,000,000

Market personal lines, small commercial & life insurance products through independent agents & financial institutions to both public & non-public employees.

COLONIAL LIFE INSURANCE CO TEXAS
2600 West Freeway
Fort Worth, TX 76113
Telephone: (817) 390-2350, (888) 227-5119, FAX: (817) 390-2209, E-Mail: insurance@colonialinsurance.com, Web Site: www.colonialinsurance.com
Pres: Edwin Dubose
VP: William B. Hampton
Conducts Business: U.S.
Primary Market Served: Consumer
Catalog available online
Founded: 1978

Insurance underwriters for individual life insurance policies.

COLUMBIAN MUTUAL LIFE INSURANCE CO
Vestal Pkwy E
Binghamton, NY 13902-4600
Telephone: (607) 724-2472, (800) 423-9765
Pres & CEO: Thomas E. Rattmann
Conducts Business: U.S.
Employees: 292
Primary Market Served: Business & Consumer
Catalog available online
Advertising/Marketing Budget Related to Direct Marketing: 0-25%
Founded: 1903

Mutual life insurance company licensed in 50 states, the District of Columbia, the Commonwealth of Puerto Rico & the Virgin Islands. Products sold directly include life insurance, guaranteed issue senior life, annuity & IRA products.

THE DMA COMBINED INSURANCE CO OF AMERICA
1000 Milwaukee Ave Fl 1
Glenview, IL 60025-2424
Telephone: (847) 953-8116, (800) 490-1322, FAX: (847) 953-8070, Web Site: www.combinedinsurance.com
VP Mktg: Rebecca Mills
Chmn & CEO: Doug Wendt
Primary Market Served: Consumer

COMMERCIAL TRAVELERS MUTUAL INSURANCE CO
70 Genesee St
Utica, NY 13502-3503
Telephone: (315) 797-5200, (800) 422-6200, FAX: (315) 797-3198, E-Mail: comtravl@commercialtravelers.com, Web Site: www.commercialtravelers.com
Chmn Bd: Richard Griffith
Pres & CEO: Herbert E. Trevvett
VP: Paul H. Trevvett
Conducts Business: U.S.
Employees: 97
Primary Market Served: Business & Consumer
Catalog available online
Advertising/Marketing Budget Related to Direct Marketing: 0-25%
Direct Marketing ad budget:
Direct Mail: 100%
Founded: 1883
Gross sales or billing: $34,800,000

Student accident insurance pre-school through college, life & disability income insurance for small employers.

CONSECO INC
11825 N Pennsylvania Ave
Carmel, IN 46032-4555
Telephone: (317) 817-6100, FAX: (317) 817-2847, Web Site: www.conseco.com
CEO: C. James Prieur
Pres: Dan R. Bardin
VP Bus Devel: Mark A Cecil
Exec VP: Brad Corbin
Sr VP Strategic Plng: Barbara S. Stewart
Conducts Business: U.S.
Employees: 4,000
Primary Market Served: Consumer
Advertising/Marketing Budget Related to Direct Marketing: 76-100%
Founded: 1979
Gross sales or billing: $4,467,400,000

Life insurance for the 50+ market. Medicare supplement & term insurance.

CONTINENTAL WESTERN GROUP

aka CWG. Operating Unit of W.R. Berkley Corp
11201 Douglas Ave
Des Moines, IA 50322
Telephone: (515) 473-3000, (800) 533-0303, FAX: (515) 473-3015, Web Site: www.cwgins.com
Pres & CEO: Bradley S. Kuster
VP Prod Mngmt: Aaron M. Larson
AVP Agency Sls: Mike Elam
Conducts Business: U.S.
Primary Market Served: Consumer
Founded: 1925

Sell insurance to owners of antique & collectible automobiles.

COUNTRY FINANCIAL

PO Box 2020
Bloomington, IL 61702-2020
Telephone: (309) 821-3000
Mgr, Agency Promos: Jennifer Manning
Primary Market Served: Business & Consumer

COVERDELL & CO INC

Subsidiary of Vertrue Inc.
8770 W Bryn Mawr Ave (Suite 1000)
Chicago, IL 60631-3515
Telephone: (404) 881-2227, (800) 992-2196, FAX: (404) 881-2222, Web Site: www.coverdell.com
Pres: Michael Owens
VP, Client & Mktg Svc: Susan Pavloff
Conducts Business: U.S.
Primary Market Served: Business & Consumer
Catalog available online
Founded: 1963
Gross sales or billing: $4,700,000

Sell insurance through magazine coupon advertising & direct mail solicitation, primarily within the rural & financial institution markets.

CUNA MUTUAL GROUP

5910 Mineral Point Rd
Madison, WI 53705-4498
Telephone: (608) 238-5851, (800) 356-2644, FAX: (608) 231-8839, Web Site: www.cunamutual.com
Chmn: Loretta M. Burd
Pres, CEO & Dir: Jeff Post
Exec VP & CFO: Jeffrey D. Holley
Bus Mngmt & Analysis Leader: Chris Kennedy
Conducts Business: Worldwide
Employees: 5,500

Primary Market Served: Business & Consumer
Catalog available online
Indirect online sales
Founded: 1926
Gross sales or billing: $2,800,000,000

Insurance company serving credit unions & their members. Handle life, health & casualty policies.

CUNNINGHAM GROUP

7234 W North Ave (Suite 101)
Elmwood Park, IL 60707-4200
Telephone: (708) 848-2300, (800) 962-1224, FAX: (708) 848-2174, E-Mail: cunngroup@cg-ins.com, Web Site: www.cg-ins.com
Pres: James H. Cunningham
Employees: 25
Primary Market Served: Business & Consumer
Advertising/Marketing Budget Related to Direct Marketing: 76-100%
Founded: 1947
Gross sales or billing: $2,900,000

User of direct marketing for insurance.

DESJARDINS FINANCIAL SECURITIES

Div. of La Societe Financiere Des Caisses Desjardins Inc
200 Ave des Commandeurs
Levis, PQ, Canada G6V 6R2
Telephone: (418) 838-7870, FAX: (418) 833-5985, Web Site: www.desjardinsfinancialsecurity.com
VP, Adv: Daniel Roussel
Sr VP, HR & Advisory Svcs: Lise Bordeleau
Conducts Business: Canada
Employees: 1,215
Primary Market Served: Business & Consumer
Gross sales or billing: $745,000,000

Sell life & disability insurance, annuities & pension funds to individuals, groups & credit unions.

DIRECT AUTO INSURANCE

1281 Murfreesboro Pike Ste 150
Nashville, TN 37217-2437
Telephone: (615) 399-4859, Web Site: www.directgeneral.com
Dir Mktg: Tara Harrington
Primary Market Served: Consumer

DIRECTORY OF AMERICAN BUSINESS & INSURANCE ATTORNEYS

130 Church St (#303)
New York, NY 10007-2906

Telephone: (732) 458-7788, (800) 445-7995, FAX: (732) 458-7710, E-Mail: staff@abialaw.com, Web Site: www.abialaw.com
Pres: George Wilson
Asst: Donald Simpson
Conducts Business: U.S.
Primary Market Served: Business & Consumer

Association of insurance & business attorneys.

DIVERSIFIED HEALTHCARE SERVICES

800 E Campbell Rd (Suite 399)
Richardson, TX 75081
Telephone: (972) 238-1492, FAX: (972) 907-8283, Web Site: www.dhscorp.com
Owner & Pres: Jerry O'Connor
Conducts Business: U.S.
Primary Market Served: Business & Consumer

Medical billing & collection agency.

THE DOCTOR'S CO

185 Greenwood Rd
Napa, CA 94558
Telephone: (707) 226-0176, E-Mail: info@thedoctors.com, Web Site: www.thedoctors.com
Pres: R. Anderson
Primary Market Served: Business
Founded: 1976

Medical malpractice insurance for doctors.

ELECTRIC INSURANCE CO

75 Sam Fonzo Dr
Beverly, MA 01915-1000
Telephone: (978) 921-2080, (800) 227-2757, FAX: (978) 524-5583, E-Mail: sales@electricinsurance.com, Web Site: www.electricinsurance.com
Mktg Coord: Jennifer Fielding
Mktg Mgr: Mike Sullivan
Conducts Business: U.S.
Primary Market Served: Business & Consumer
Founded: 1966

Auto & home insurance.

EMPIRE BLUE CROSS & BLUE SHIELD

1 Liberty Plz (Suite 1300)
New York, NY 10006-1419
Telephone: (212) 476-1000, (877) 476-7111, FAX: (212) 476-1281, Web Site: www.empireblue.com
CMO: Jack Smith
Pres: Mark Wagner
Primary Market Served: Business & Consumer

Health insurance provider.

EMPLOYERS INSURANCE
10375 Professional Cir
Reno, NV 89521-4802
Telephone: (775) 327-2677, Web Site:
www.employers.com
VP Corp Mktg: Ty Vukelich

**EQUITABLE LIFE &
CASUALTY INSURANCE CO**
Three Triad Ctr
Salt Lake City, UT 84180-1200
Telephone: (801) 579-3400, FAX:
(801) 579-3789, Web Site: www.
equilife.com
Pres & CEO: E. Rod Ross
Chief Mktg Officer: Larry Thomas
Actuary: Rick Klar
Treas: Kristine S. Christensen
Mktg Svcs Dir: Louis Trani
Legal Counsel: Ken Surfass
Conducts Business: U.S.
Employees: 140
Primary Market Served: Consumer
Founded: 1935
Gross sales or billing: $125,719,941

Life & health insurance for the elderly.

FCIA MANAGEMENT CO INC
Great American Insurance Co
125 Park Ave (fl 14)
New York, NY 10017-5529
Telephone: (212) 885-1500, FAX:
(212) 885-1535, E-Mail: service@
fcia.com, Web Site: www.fcia.com
Pres: Lindley Franklin
Conducts Business: U.S.
Employees: 120
Primary Market Served: Business
Catalog available online
Direct Marketing ad budget:
Direct Mail: $12,000
Founded: 1991

Manage & administer credit & political
risk insurance policies.

FARM BUREAU INSURANCE
7373 W Saginaw Hwy, Box 30400
Lansing, MI 48917
Telephone: (517) 323-7000, (800) 292-
2680, FAX: (517) 327-0208, Web
Site: www.farmbureauinsurance-mi.
com
Pres: Wayne Wood
Dir: Greg Waldie
Exec VP: Jim Robinson
VP, Mktg: Kevin P. Kelly
Conducts Business: U.S.
Employees: 700
Primary Market Served: Business &
Consumer
Catalog available online
Direct Marketing ad budget: $500,000

Newspapers: 90%
TV/Radio: 10%
Marketer of multiple line insurance
products.

FARMERS INSURANCE
4680 Wilshire Blvd
Los Angeles, CA 90010
Telephone: (410) 366-1000, (410) 338-
1633, (800) 327-6377, FAX: (410)
554-1926, Web Site: www.farmers.
com
Dir Mktg: John Ingersoll
Employees: 18,000
Primary Market Served: Consumer
Founded: 1928

Personal insurance including auto &
homeowners.

**FIDELITY SECURITY LIFE
INSURANCE CO**
3130 Broadway
Kansas City, MO 64111-2406
Telephone: (816) 756-1060, (800) 648-
8624, FAX: (816) 968-0580, E-Mail:
info@fslins.com, Web Site: www.
fslins.com
Pres & Treas: Richard F. Jones
Sr VP, Mktg: David Smith
Exec VP: Michael E. Hall
VP: Mark L. Burley
Asst VP: Dana L. Hamilton
Conducts Business: U.S.
Employees: 300
Primary Market Served: Business &
Consumer
Catalog available online
Advertising/Marketing Budget Related
to Direct Marketing: 30%
Founded: 1969

Third party endorsement & broad market insurance.

**FOREMOST INSURANCE
GROUP**
Div. of Farmers Insurance Co
PO Box 2450
Grand Rapids, MI 49501-2450
Telephone: (616) 956-8241, (800) 527-
3905, FAX: (800) 325-1507, Web
Site: www.foremost.com
Pres: Steve Boshoven
VP, Mktg: Nancy Treul
Claims Dir: Dennis Squibb
VP, Fin: Jeff Pepper
VP, Commun: John Kalinka
Dir, Mktg: Mike Cok
Dir, Direct Mktg: Randy Slotten
Mgr, List Mngmt/Direct Mail: David
Simmonds
Conducts Business: U.S., Canada
Employees: 2,300
Primary Market Served: Consumer
Gross sales or billing: $1,500,000,000

Insurer of auto, homeowners, mobile
homes & recreational vehicles. Complete turnkey marketing programs.

FORESTERS
789 Don Mills Rd
Toronto, ON, Canada M3C 1T9
Telephone: (416) 467-2544, Web Site:
www.foresters.com
Primary Market Served: Business

**FORETHOUGHT FINANCIAL
SERVICES INC**
Subs. of Hillenbrand Industries
1 Forethought Ctr
Batesville, IN 47006-1279
Telephone: (812) 934-7139, (800) 331-
8853, FAX: (812) 934-8564, Web
Site: www.forethought.com
Sr VP: John Prentice
Conducts Business: U.S.
Employees: 160
Primary Market Served: Business &
Consumer
Founded: 1985

Sell pre-need funeral insurance through
independent funeral homes.

GEICO DIRECT
Subs. of GEICO Corp
1 GEICO Plaza
Washington, DC 20076-0005
Telephone: (301) 986-2842, (800) 841-
3000, FAX: (301) 986-2068, Web
Site: www.geico.com
Pres & CEO: Olza M. Nicely
VP, Mktg: Ted Ward
Conducts Business: U.S.
Employees: 18,400
Primary Market Served: Consumer
Advertising/Marketing Budget Related
to Direct Marketing: 76-100%
Gross sales or billing: $4,324,200,000

Market auto insurance.

GMAC INSURANCE
Div. of General Motors
1000 Abernathy Rd NE, 400 Northpark
(Suite 275)
Atlanta, GA 30328-5606
Telephone: (314) 493-8000, (800)
GMAC-123, FAX: (314) 493-8114,
Web Site: www.gmacinsurance.com
Chmn, GM Acceptance Corp: Eric A.
Feldstein
Pres: William F. Muir
Pres, Work Site Div: Scott Miller
VP, HR: John C. Beattie
VP Direct Mktg: Danny Villa
Conducts Business: U.S.
Employees: 417
Primary Market Served: Consumer
Catalog available online
Indirect online sales

Sell auto & home insurance.

GERBER LIFE INSURANCE CO
Subs. of Gerber Products Co
1311 Mamaroneck Ave
White Plains, NY 10605-5221
Telephone: (914) 272-4000, (800) 704-2180, FAX: (914) 272-4099, Web Site: www.gerberlife.com
CEO: Wesley Protheroe
Sr VP, Mktg: Peter Mendelson
Mktg Mgr: Andrea Borgelt
Dir, Creative Svcs: Sharon Langel
Conducts Business: U.S., Puerto Rico, and Canada
Employees: 200
Primary Market Served: Consumer
Advertising/Marketing Budget Related to Direct Marketing: 76-100%
Direct Marketing ad budget:
Direct Mail: 50%
Magazines: 15%
Newspapers: 10%
Online: 10%
TV/Radio: 15%
Founded: 1967
Gross sales or billing: $148,000,000

Supplementary life & health insurance policies sold using various direct response techniques to budget-minded people of all ages.

GOLDEN RULE INSURANCE CO
7440 Woodland Dr, Golden Rule Bldg
Indianapolis, IN 46278-1719
Telephone: (317) 297-4123, FAX: (317) 297-0908, Web Site: www.goldenrule.com
Sr VP: Richard Merril
Media Svcs Mgr: Joanne Robinson
Conducts Business: U.S.
Primary Market Served: Business & Consumer

Health & life insurance company.

GREAT-WEST LIFE
8515 E Orchard Rd
Greenwood Village, CO 80111
Telephone: (800) 537-2033, Web Site: www.greatwest.com
Pres & CEO: Raymond L. McFeetors
Mktg: Michelle Buckalew
Conducts Business: U.S.
Employees: 6,600
Primary Market Served: Business

Pension insurance.

GUARANTEE TRUST LIFE INSURANCE CO
1275 Milwaukee Ave (Suite 100)
Glenview, IL 60025-2489

Telephone: (847) 298-0670, FAX: (847) 298-1215, E-Mail: pr@gtlic.com, Web Site: www.gtlic.com
Pres: Richard S. Holson Jr.
Sr VP Mktg: B. Montgomery Edson
VP, Direct Mktg: Mike Haas
VP: Jeff Burman
Conducts Business: U.S.
Employees: 274
Primary Market Served: Consumer
Founded: 1936
Gross sales or billing: $279,000,000

Marketer of life insurance.

THE GUARDIAN LIFE INSURANCE CO
7 Hanover Sq (fl 14)
New York, NY 10004-4013
Telephone: (212) 598-8000, Web Site: www.guardianlife.com
Interim Exec VP: Brad Thomas
Primary Market Served: Business & Consumer

GUIDEONE INSURANCE
1111 Ashworth Rd
West Des Moines, IA 50265-3537
Telephone: (877) 448-4331, Web Site: www.guideone.com
Mktg Specialist: Jason Darrah
Primary Market Served: Business

THE HARTFORD FINANCIAL SERVICES INC
Div. of Hartford Life Insurance Co
200 Executive Blvd
Southington, CT 06489-1058
Telephone: (860) 843-8070, (860) 547-5000, FAX: (860) 547-2680, Web Site: www.thehartford.com
Chmn & CEO: Ramani Ayer
Pres, COO & Dir: Thomas M. Marra
Exec VP & Gen Counsel: Alan J. Kreczko
AVP Mktg: Daniel Lavoie
Exec VP & CFO: David M. Johnson
Exec VP Grp Benefits Division: Ronald R. Gendreau
Employees: 31,000
Primary Market Served: Consumer
Catalog available online
Advertising/Marketing Budget Related to Direct Marketing: 76-100%
Founded: 1994
Gross sales or billing: $26,000,000,000

Life insurance.

HEALTH ALLIANCE PLAN
2850 W Grand Blvd
Detroit, MI 48202-2692
Telephone: (248) 443-1075, FAX: (248) 443-8851, E-Mail: alandin1@hapcorp.org, Web Site: www.hapcorp.org

Dir Adv, Commun & Direct Mktg: Anita Landino

HEALTHPLAN SERVICES
3501 E Frontage Rd
Tampa, FL 33607
Telephone: (813) 289-1000, (800) 545-6441, Web Site: www.healthplan.com
Sr VP Sls: Jay McLauchlin
Conducts Business: U.S.
Employees: 600
Primary Market Served: Business & Consumer
Founded: 1970

Manage & administer small group and individual benefit health plan.

HIGH POINT INSURANCE
PO Box 906
Lincroft, NJ 07738-0906
Telephone: (732) 978-6255, Web Site: www.highpointins.com
Admin: Donna Diehl
Primary Market Served: Business & Consumer

HIGHMARK BLUE CROSS BLUE SHIELD
120 Fifth Ave (Suite 1044)
Pittsburgh, PA 15222-3099
Telephone: (412) 544-7000, FAX: (412) 544-5350, Web Site: www.highmark.com
Chmn: J. Robert Baum
Pres & CEO: Kenneth R. Melani
EVP: S. Tyrone Alexander
EVP, CFO, & Treas: Nanette P. De Turk
EVP: Robert C. Gray
Primary Market Served: Business & Consumer
Founded: 1996

Individual & group health insurance.

HOMESTEADERS LIFE CO
5700 Westown Pkwy
West Des Moines, IA 50266-8214
Telephone: (515) 440-7777, (800) 477-3633, E-Mail: service@homesteaderslife.com, Web Site: www.homesteaderslife.com
Mktg Mgr: Karen King
VP Mktg: Dean Lambert
Direct Mail: Pam Davis
Conducts Business: U.S.
Primary Market Served: Business
Advertising/Marketing Budget Related to Direct Marketing: 0-25%
Direct Marketing ad budget: $1,000,000
Direct Mail: 100%
Founded: 1906

Pre-need insurance marketer.

HORACE MANN EDUCATORS CORP

1 Horace Mann Plaza
Springfield, IL 62715-0002
Telephone: (217) 789-2500, FAX: (217) 788-5161, Web Site: www. horacemann.com
Chmn: Joseph J. Malone
Pres, CEO, Dir: Louis G. Lower II
Exec VP, CFO: Peter H. Heckman
Exec VP: Douglas W. Reynolds
Sr VP Mktg: Robert B. Joyner
VP & CIO: Mark Hansen
Conducts Business: U.S.
Employees: 2,400
Primary Market Served: Consumer
Catalog available online
Founded: 1945
Gross sales or billing: $873,800,000

Multi-line insurance company that targets teachers & other school employees in the U.S. Homeowners auto, individual & group life insurance & retirement annuities.

ING

dba Relia Star Insurance Co
20 Washington Ave S
Minneapolis, MN 55401-1908
Telephone: (612) 342-7061, (800) 333-6965, FAX: (612) 372-5339, Web Site: www.ing.com
Chmn: Michael Tilmant
Chmn: Eric Boyer de la Giroday
Chmn: Henk Breukink
Chmn: Peter Elverding
Chmn: Luella Gross-Goldberg
Employees: 118,000
Primary Market Served: Business & Consumer
Gross sales or billing: $163,000,000

Sell insurance plans through brokers including all financial services.

ING USA ANNUITY & LIFE INS CO

Div. of ING
909 Locust St
Des Moines, IA 50309-2899
Telephone: (515) 698-7100, FAX: (515) 698-2001, Web Site: www.ing-usa.com
Strategic Plng & Commun: Michele Burkholder
Corp Commun: Cynthia M. Schaus
COO: Christopher Welp
Employees: 900
Primary Market Served: Business & Consumer

Insurance equities, annuities & life.

ᴛʜᴇ ᴅᴍᴀ INFINITY INSURANCE CO

3700 Colonnade Pkwy (Suite 600)
Birmingham, AL 35243-3219
Telephone: (800) 527-5412, Web Site: www.infinityauto.com
AVP Natl Mktg: Greg Fasking
Primary Market Served: Business

INSURANCE.COM

29000 Aurora Rd
Solon, OH 44139-1843
Telephone: (440) 715-0075, Web Site: www.insurance.com
Customer Commun Mgr: Karen Imbrogno
Primary Market Served: Business

INTELLIQUOTE INSURANCE SERVICES

5170 Golden Foothill Pkwy
El Dorado Hills, CA 95762-9658
Telephone: (800) 543-3467, Web Site: www.intelliquote.com
Mktg Program Mgr: Shawn Trumbull
Primary Market Served: Business

HERBERT L JAMISON & CO LLC

100 Executive Dr (Suite 200)
West Orange, NJ 07052-3362
Telephone: (973) 731-0806, (800) JAMISON, (800) 526-4766, FAX: (973) 731-3035, Web Site: www.jamisongroup.com
SVP Sls Mktg: Christopher J. Serreino
VP Sls Mktg: Anthony F. Bavaro
Conducts Business: Worldwide
Employees: 100
Primary Market Served: Business & Consumer
Catalog available online
Indirect online sales
Advertising/Marketing Budget Related to Direct Marketing: 51-75%
Founded: 1938

Insurance brokerage.

JOHN HANCOCK FINANCIAL SERVICES INC

Subs. of Manulife Financial
601 Congress St, Box 111
Boston, MA 02117
Telephone: (617) 572-6000, (800) 732-5543, FAX: (617) 572-6451, Web Site: www.johnhancock.com
Pres & CEO: Dominic D'Alessandro
PR Coord: Melissa Salmon
Pres, CEO & Dir: John D. Des Prez III
Sr VP Bus Devel & Gen Counsel: Jean-Paul Bisnaire
Chmn Bd: Arthur R. Sawchuck
Dir: John M. Cassaday
Conducts Business: U.S., Canada, Europe
Employees: 21,287
Primary Market Served: Business & Consumer

Founded: 1862

Life insurance company with several subsidiaries.

KELSEY NATIONAL CORP

3030 S Bundy Dr
Los Angeles, CA 90066
Telephone: (310) 390-1000, (800) 366-5656, FAX: (310) 390-3158, E-Mail: info@kelsey.com, Web Site: www.kelsey.com
Chmn & CEO: Van Kelsey
Pres: Mark Kelsey
VP, Sls: Warren Blumberg
VP, Mktg & Administration: Van Kelsey III
Controller: Brian K. Buhler
Conducts Business: U.S.
Primary Market Served: Business & Consumer
Catalog available online
Advertising/Marketing Budget Related to Direct Marketing: 76-100%
Founded: 1964

Insurance TPA (Third Party Administrator) & marketer specializing in small business & association group employee benefits nationwide.

LANCER INSURANCE CO

Div. of Lancer Financial Group
PO Box 9004
Long Beach, NY 11561-9004
Telephone: (516) 431-4441, (800) 782-8902, FAX: (516) 889-5111, E-Mail: roneill@lancer-ins.com, Web Site: www.lancer-ins.com
Pres & CEO: David P. Delaney Jr.
VP, Safety & Engrng: Bob Crescenzo
Exec VP: Timothy D. Delaney
Exec VP: Thomas Theiler
Sr VP, Customer Svc: Randy O'Neill
Conducts Business: U.S.
Employees: 475
Primary Market Served: Business
Catalog available online
Indirect online sales
Advertising/Marketing Budget Related to Direct Marketing: 51-75%
Direct Marketing ad budget: $100,000
Direct Mail: 60%
Magazines: 25%
Telephone: 15%
Founded: 1945
Gross sales or billing: $275,000,000

Provides commercial automobile & physical damage insurance coverage to motor coaches, municipal & school buses, vanpools, limousines, long-haul truck owner/operations, oil heat distributors in Northeast U.S. Complete drug testing services. Also provides commercial automobile & physical damage insurance coverage to the car rental industry & personal auto and umbrella coverage to active & retired teachers & school administrators in NJ.

L'ENTRAIDE ASSURANCE

520 Charest Blvd E (fl1), Quebec-Centre Station
Quebec, PQ, Canada G2J 0A2
Telephone: (418) 658-0663, FAX: (418) 658-5065, E-Mail: service@ lentraide.com, Web Site: www. lentraide.com
Chmn, Pres & CEO: Gaetan Gagne
Primary Market Served: Business

LIBERTY LIFE INSURANCE CO

Subs. of Liberty Corp.
2000 Wade Hampton Blvd
Greenville, SC 29615-1064
Telephone: (864) 609-8111, (800) 344-5834 (Mktg), FAX: (864) 609-4411, Web Site: www.libertycorp.com
Pres: Robert Evans
Sr VP: Judith Tshibangu
Primary Market Served: Consumer

Life insurance.

THE DMA LIBERTY MUTUAL GROUP, INC

Subs. of Liberty Mutual Holding Company, Inc
175 Berkeley St
Boston, MA 02116-5066
Telephone: (617) 357-9500, (800) 837-5274, Web Site: www.libertymutual. com
Chmn Bd, Pres & CEO: Edmund F. Kelly
Exec VP & CIO: A. Alexander Fontanes
Exec VP, Personal Markets: J. Paul Condrin III
Exec VP, Comml Markets: David H. Long
VP Direct Mktg: Debra Shear
Conducts Business: South America, East Asia, Spain, Portugal, Poland, Turkey
Employees: 40,000
Primary Market Served: Consumer
Catalog available online
Indirect online sales
Gross sales or billing: $390,000,000

Direct writing insurance company.

LINCOLN FINANCIAL GROUP

aka Lincoln Financial Corp
150 N Radnor Chester Rd (Suite A305)
Radnor, PA 19087
Telephone: (215) 448-1400, (877) 275-5462, FAX: (215) 448-3962, Web Site: www.lfg.com
CEO & Pres: Dennis R. Glass
Dir: William J. Avery
CFO: Randal J. Freitaq
Conducts Business: Worldwide
Employees: 10,744
Primary Market Served: Business & Consumer
Direct online sales
Advertising/Marketing Budget Related to Direct Marketing: 0-25%
Founded: 1905
Gross sales or billing: $1,316,000,000

Market life insurance products & investment services. Mutual funds & financial planning.

LONG & FOSTER INSURANCE

14501 George Carter Way
Chantilly, VA 20151-1770
Telephone: (703) 278-1426
Pres: James Maiden
Primary Market Served: Business

THE DMA MANULIFE FINANCIAL INC

2 Queen St E
Toronto, ON, Canada M5C 3G7
Telephone: (416) 229-4515, (800) 387-0990, FAX: (416) 229-3028, Web Site: www.manulife.com
Admin Asst: Josephine Villanueva
Conducts Business: Canada, U.S.
Primary Market Served: Business & Consumer
Founded: 1887
Gross sales or billing: $1,000,000,000

Market life & health insurance & annuity to credit card holders & members of associations through direct mail & agency sales force.

MARSH AFFINITY GROUP SERVICES

500 W Monroe St (Suite 2400)
Chicago, IL 60661
Telephone: (800) 621-3008, Web Site: www.seaburychicago.com
Sr VP, Mktg: Joan O'Sullivan
Primary Market Served: Business & Consumer
Founded: 1949

Life, health & professional liability insurance, through association sponsorship, for healthcare professionals, accountants & retired persons.

THE DMA MARSH US CONSUMER

12421 Meredith Dr
Urbandale, IA 50398-9001
Telephone: (515) 365-6102
Mng Dir: Mark M. Poole
CEO: Liz Flynn
Primary Market Served: Business

THE DMA MASSMUTUAL FINANCIAL GROUP

1295 State St
Springfield, MA 01111-0001
Telephone: (413) 788-8411, FAX: (413) 744-8889, E-Mail: name@ www.massmutual.com, Web Site: www.massmutual.com
Pres & CEO: Stuart Reese
Dir of Media & PR: James Lacey
Dir Distr Mktg: David Vermette
Conducts Business: U.S., Chile, Argentina, Bermuda, Luxembourg, Hong Kong, Japan, Taiwan & Macal
Employees: 28,000
Primary Market Served: Business & Consumer
Advertising/Marketing Budget Related to Direct Marketing: 0-25%
Founded: 1851

Diversified insurance & financial services organization.

MEDCO INSURANCE CO

1515 S 75th St
Omaha, NE 68124-1618
Telephone: (800) 228-6080, E-Mail: clientservices@gomedico.com, Web Site: www.gomedico.com
Primary Market Served: Business

THE DMA MEEMIC INSURANCE CO

1685 N Opdyke Rd
Auburn Hills, MI 48326-2656
Telephone: (888) 463-3642, Web Site: www.meemic.com

MERASTAR INSURANCE CO

Subsidiary of Unitrin
5600 Brainard Rd (Suite 1A)
Chattanooga, TN 37411-5336
Telephone: (800) 637-2782, FAX: (800) 369-1430, E-Mail: merastar. assist.team@unitrindirect.com, Web Site: www.merastar.com
CEO: Tim Brunn
Mktg Dir: Don Smith
Mktg Mgr: Allyson Bowman
Acct Rep: Paul A. Boyles
Acct Rep: William J. Capone
VP Sys: Ken Lytle
Conducts Business: U.S.
Employees: 250
Primary Market Served: Business & Consumer
Catalog available online
Indirect online sales

Advertising/Marketing Budget Related to Direct Marketing: 76-100%
Direct Marketing ad budget: $1,500,000
Direct Mail: $1,500,000
Founded: 1974
Gross sales or billing: $30,000,000

Marketer of personal lines of insurance products through employer-sponsored payroll deduction.

THE DMA METLIFE INTERNATIONAL
2701 Queens Plaza N (#4E-148)
Long Island City, NY 11101-4020
Telephone: (212) 578-3128
VP Direct Mktg: Hallie Harenski

THE DMA METROPOLITAN PROPERTY & CASUALTY INS
700 Quaker Ln
Warwick, RI 02886-6681
Telephone: (401) 827-2104
Dir: Kevin Raymond
Primary Market Served: Business

THE MIDLAND CO
7000 Midland Blvd
Amelia, OH 45102-2608
Telephone: (513) 943-7200
VP Mktg: Joe David
Primary Market Served: Business & Consumer

MILLER'S FIRST INSURANCE COMPANIES
111 E Fourth St, PO Box 220
Alton, IL 62002
Telephone: (618) 463-3636, (800) 558-0500, FAX: (618) 463-3614, Web Site: www.millersfirst.com
Pres & CEO: George Milnor
Conducts Business: U.S.
Primary Market Served: Consumer
Catalog available online
Founded: 1888

Homeowner and auto insurance.

MINNESOTA LIFE
Subs of Securian Financial Group, Inc
400 Robert St N
Saint Paul, MN 55101
Telephone: (651) 665-3500, (888) 237-1838, FAX: (651) 665-4488, Web Site: www.minnesotalife.com; www.securian.com
Chairman & CEO: Robert L. Senkler
Pres & Dir: Randy F. Wallake
Mktg Dir: David F. Steppat
Dir Mktg: Paula Bilitz
Conducts Business: U.S., Puerto Rico
Employees: 5,000
Primary Market Served: Business & Consumer
Gross sales or billing: $2,093,664,000

Provider of insurance, annuities & mutual funds.

THE DMA MUTUAL OF OMAHA
Mutual of Omaha Plaza (fl 7)
Omaha, NE 68175-0001
Telephone: (402) 342-7600, (800) 775-6000, FAX: (402) 351-2775, Web Site: www.mutualofomaha.com
Chmn & CEO: Daniel P. Neary
Exec VP & CFO: David A. Diamond
Exec VP, Info Svcs: James L. Hanson
Sr VP: Tom Graham
Sr VP DTC Mktg: Stephen Abels
Conducts Business: Worldwide
Employees: 4,867
Primary Market Served: Business & Consumer
Catalog available online
Founded: 1909
Gross sales or billing: $4,200,000,000

Insurance & financial services.

NGL INSURANCE GROUP
Subs. of National Guardian Life
Two E Gilman St (Stop 1)
Madison, WI 53703-1494
Telephone: (608) 257-5611, (800) 548-2962, FAX: (608) 257-9340, Web Site: www.nationalguardian.com
Chm & CEO: John Larson
Pres & COO: Mark L. Solverud
Treas, Dir Corp Svcs: Robert A. Mucci
VP & Dir Mktg: Steven M. Phelps
VP, Gen Counsel & Asst Sec: Matthew J. Dew III
Employees: 177
Primary Market Served: Business & Consumer
Catalog available online
Indirect online sales
Founded: 1984
Gross sales or billing: $253,000,000

Life insurance.

NATIONWIDE MUTUAL INSURANCE CO
1 Nationwide Plaza
Columbus, OH 43215-2220
Telephone: (614) 249-7111, (800) 882-2822, FAX: (614) 854-3676, Web Site: www.nationwide.com
Chmn: Arden L. Shisler
Vice Chmn: James F. Patterson
CEO: Jerry G. Jurgensen
CIO: Gail G. Synder
CFO: Lawrence A. Hilsheimer
Conducts Business: U.S., Puerto Rico, Virgin Islands, Germany
Employees: 36,000
Primary Market Served: Business & Consumer
Catalog available online
Gross sales or billing: $22,000,000,000

Market automobile, fire, life, health & casualty insurance for the individual, family & business. Involved in providing associated financial services such as mutual funds.

NEW ENGLAND LIFE INSURANCE CO
Subsidiary of Metlife
501 Boylston St
Boston, MA 02110
Telephone: (617) 578-2000, FAX: (617) 536-2393, Web Site: www.nefn.metlife.com
Sr VP, Mktg: George Maloof
Dir Computer Opers: Thomas Yang
Pres: C. Robert Henricson
Conducts Business: U.S.
Employees: 4,000
Primary Market Served: Business & Consumer
Catalog available online
Founded: 1835
Gross sales or billing: $162,000,000

Insurance & financial services organization.

THE DMA NEW YORK LIFE INSURANCE CO/AARP
5505 W Cypress St (Suite 300)
Tampa, FL 33607-1707
Telephone: (813) 288-5500, FAX: (813) 288-5256, Web Site: www.nylaarp.com
Sr VP: Thomas Kelly
VP, Mktg: Ralph Cohen
Corp VP, Mktg: Victoria Buhrow
First VP Mktg: Victoria Vilaret
Conducts Business: Worldwide
Employees: 10,000
Primary Market Served: Consumer
Direct online sales
Advertising/Marketing Budget Related to Direct Marketing: 76-100%

Financial service company. Provide individual & group life & long term care insurance.

NORTH AMERICA LIFE INSURANCE CO
1300 Guadalupe St Ste 200
Austin, TX 78701-1630
Telephone: (512) 347-1835, Web Site: www.nagrp.com
Primary Market Served: Consumer

NORTH AMERICAN CO FOR LIFE & HEALTH INSURANCE
525 W Van Buren St Ste 1200
Chicago, IL 60607-3820
Telephone: (312) 648-7600, (800) 800-3656, FAX: (614) 365-9209, Web Site: www.nacolah.com

CEO: Ihor Hron
Adv Dir: Dan Miller
Mktg: Evelyn Pletch
Conducts Business: U.S.
Primary Market Served: Business &
   Consumer
Advertising/Marketing Budget Related
   to Direct Marketing: 0-25%
Founded: 1905

Life & health insurance & annuities.

OXFORD HEALTH PLANS, INC

48 Monroe Turnpike
Trumbull, CT 06611
Telephone: (800) 889-7658, FAX:
   (203) 459-6464, E-Mail: info@
   speedmat.com, Web Site: www.oxhp.
   com
CEO: Michael Turpin
Primary Market Served: Business &
   Consumer

Healthcare insurance.

PPI BENEFIT SOLUTIONS

10 Research Pkwy
Wallingford, CT 06492-1963
Telephone: (888) 674-0046, FAX:
   (203) 468-9886, E-Mail:
   clientservices@ppibenefits.com, Web
   Site: www.ppibenefits.com
Pres: Luis Nunes
Conducts Business: U.S.
Employees: 52
Primary Market Served: Business

Sell pension plans & group insurance
to associations & individual employers.

PARCEL INSURANCE PLAN INC

Subs. of Brown & Brown Insurance
9666 Olive Blvd (Suite 200)
Saint Louis, MO 63132-3012
Telephone: (314) 692-0300, (800) 325-
   7390, FAX: (314) 692-7598, E-Mail:
   office@pipinsure.com, Web Site:
   www.pipinsure.com
Pres: Charles Smith Jr.
VP: Ric Victores
Mktg Dir: Scott Gehner
Conducts Business: U.S.
Employees: 15
Primary Market Served: Business
Indirect online sales
Advertising/Marketing Budget Related
   to Direct Marketing: 0-25%
Direct Marketing ad budget:
Direct Mail: 25%
Magazines: 5%
Telephone: 70%
Founded: 1966

Sell UPS, parcel post & air cargo insurance at low cost. Offer reduced
record-keeping. Sell direct to high volume small parcel shippers. Mailing
address: PO Box 66708, Saint Louis,
MO 63166-6708.

PARTNERS HEALTH

901 Market St (Suite 500)
Philadelphia, PA 19107
Telephone: (215) 849-9600, (800) 553-
   0784, E-Mail: sroberts@healthpart.
   com, Web Site: www.healthpart.com
Pres & CEO: William George
Sr VP Bus Developer: Judy B. Har-
   rington
Sr VP Resources Mngmt &
   Compliance: Vicki Sessoms
Sr VP Chief Medical Officer: Mary K.
   Stom MD
Sr VP Opers: Debra R. Kirches
Conducts Business: U.S.
Employees: 550
Primary Market Served: Business &
   Consumer
Founded: 1985

HMO.

THE DMA PEARL INSURANCE GROUP LLC

1200 E Glen Ave
Peoria Heights, IL 61616-5325
Telephone: (309) 688-9000, Web Site:
   www.pearlinsurance.com
Exec VP, Chief Sls & Mktg Officer:
   Michael Murphy
Primary Market Served: Business

PEMCO INSURANCE COS

325 Eastlake Ave E
Seattle, WA 98109-5466
Telephone: (206) 628-4000, (800) 467-
   3626, FAX: (206) 628-5886, Web
   Site: www.pemco.com
CEO: Stanley W. McNaughton
Sr VP & COO: Steve Miller
VP Chief Mktg Officer: Rod Brooks
Commun Mgr: Jon Osterberg
Conducts Business: U.S.
Employees: 1,150
Primary Market Served: Consumer
Founded: 1949
Gross sales or billing: $232,000,000

Group of insurance companies offering
auto, home, boat, excess personal liability & life insurance to the general
public & the educational industry in
Washington.

THE DMA PENN MUTUAL

600 Dresher Rd
Horsham, PA 19044-2204

Telephone: (215) 956-8083, FAX:
   (215) 956-8368, Web Site: www.
   pennmutual.com
Chmn & CEO: Robert E. Chappell
Pres & COO: Daniel J. Toran
Mktg Support Grp Mgr: Wendy A.
   Madonna
Mktg Support Grp Mgr: Judy Nigro
Dir Prog Mktg: Tracy Marrocco
Conducts Business: U.S.
Employees: 600
Primary Market Served: Business &
   Consumer
Advertising/Marketing Budget Related
   to Direct Marketing: 0-25%
Founded: 1847
Gross sales or billing: $250,000,000

Life insurance & financial services.

PEOPLES BENEFIT LIFE INSURANCE CO

Div. of Aegon USA
300 Eagleview Blvd
Exton, PA 19341-1155
Telephone: (610) 648-5000, FAX:
   (610) 648-5348
Mktg Dir: Lou Whalen
Conducts Business: U.S.
Employees: 2,000
Primary Market Served: Consumer

Market life & health insurance & related financial services through multimedia direct response to the general
public, credit card files, credit unions,
veterans & other affinity groups, customer lists & association members.

THE PHILADELPHIA CONTRIBUTORSHIP INSURANCE CO

212 S Fourth St
Philadelphia, PA 19106-3787
Telephone: (215) 627-1752, (800) 346-
   9229, E-Mail: info@contributorship.
   com, Web Site: www.contributorship.
   com
VP, Mktg: Joan Saracino
Primary Market Served: Consumer
Catalog available online
Founded: 1752

Homeowners insurance.

THE DMA PHYSICIANS MUTUAL INSURANCE CO

2600 Dodge St
Omaha, NE 68131
Telephone: (402) 633-1604, (888) 932-
   7642, FAX: (402) 633-1604, Web
   Site: www.physiciansmutual.com
Chmn: William R. Hamsa
Pres & CEO: Robert A. Reed
Exec VP & COO: Edward W. Graycar
Mgr: Mike Story
Conducts Business: U.S.

Employees: 1,000
Primary Market Served: Consumer
Catalog available online
Advertising/Marketing Budget Related
   to Direct Marketing: 76-100%
Founded: 1902

Individual health & accident supplementary insurance. Individual life
insurance.

PREMERA BLUE CROSS
3900 E Sprague Ave (Bldg 1)
Spokane, WA 99202-4847
Telephone: (425) 670-4000, (800) 422-
   0032, FAX: (425) 670-5853, Web
   Site: www.premera.com
Chief Mktg Officer & Exec VP Sls: C.
   Marion Butler
DM: Chris Wickizer
Sr Mgr Producer Rels & Mktg: Kelly
   Jones
Conducts Business: U.S.
Primary Market Served: Business &
   Consumer

Marketer of health insurance products.

THE PRINCIPAL FINANCIAL
GROUP
711 High St
Des Moines, IA 50392-0330
Telephone: (515) 247-5111, (800) 986-
   3343, FAX: (515) 246-5475, Web
   Site: www.principal.com
Chmn & CEO: J. Barry Griswell
Pres, COO & Dir: Larry D. Zimple-
   man
Exec VP & CFO: Michael H. Gersie
VP, Mktg: Mike Beer
Conducts Business: Worldwide
Employees: 15,200
Primary Market Served: Business &
   Consumer
Catalog available online
Gross sales or billing: $9,800,000,000

Insurance.

PROFILE COVERAGE CORP
PO Box 9081
Melville, NY 11747-9081
Telephone: (631) 981-7600, FAX:
   (631) 981-7681, E-Mail: info@
   profileinsure.com, Web Site: www.
   profileinsure.com
Pres: Louis Pellegrino
Conducts Business: U.S.
Employees: 28
Primary Market Served: Business
Advertising/Marketing Budget Related
   to Direct Marketing: 0-25%
Gross sales or billing: $3,600,000

Full service insurance agency selling
personal, commercial & health
insurance.

THE PROGRESSIVE CORP
6300 Wilson Mills Rd
Mayfield Village, OH 44143-2182
Telephone: (440) 461-5000, (800)
   PROGRESSIVE, (800) 776-4737,
   FAX: (800) 456-6590, Web Site:
   www.progressive.com
Chmn: Peter B. Lewis
Pres & CEO: Glen M. Renwick
CFO: Brian C. Domeck
CIO: Raymond M. Voelker
VP: Jeffrey W. Basch
Employees: 27,778
Primary Market Served: Business &
   Consumer
Catalog available online
Direct online sales
Advertising/Marketing Budget Related
   to Direct Marketing: 26-50%
Founded: 1965
Gross sales or billing: $14,786,400,000

Leader in nonstandard, high-risk personal auto insurance. Standard-risk and
preferred auto insurance, personal use
coverage (motorcycles, recreational
vehicles & snowmobiles), collateral
insurance for auto lenders, directors' &
officers' insurance & employee mis-
conduct insurance.

PROTECTIVE LIFE CORP
PO Box 770
Deerfield, IL 60015-0770
Telephone: (847) 948-8988, (800) 323-
   5771, FAX: (847) 948-1156, Web
   Site: www.protective.com
Chmn, Pres & CEO: John D. Johns
Vice Chmn & CFO: Richard J. Bielen
Exec VP & COO: Carolyn M. Johnson
Sr VP: Brent Griggs
Sr VP: Thomas D. Keyes
Conducts Business: U.S.
Employees: 180
Primary Market Served: Business
Catalog available online
Direct Marketing ad budget:
Magazines: $500,000
Gross sales or billing: $150,000,000

Sell credit insurance via direct
marketing.

PROTECTIVE LIFE
INSURANCE CO
Div. of Protective Life Corp
2801 Hwy 280 S
Birmingham, AL 35223-2488
Telephone: (205) 268-1000, (800) 866-
   3555, FAX: (205) 868-3086, Web
   Site: www.protective.com
Pres: John E. Johns
CEO: Drayton Nabers Jr
Sr VP, Fin Institutions Insurance Div:
   Steven A. Schultz
Conducts Business: U.S., Guam
Employees: 1,000

Primary Market Served: Business &
   Consumer
Founded: 1907

Sell life, accidental death, accident,
health (disability) & investment products through direct marketing methods.

REASSURE AMERICA LIFE
INSURANCE CO
Affiliate of Swiss Re
1275 Sandusky Rd
Jacksonville, IL 62650
Telephone: (800) 637-4475, FAX:
   (217) 291-2398, Web Site: www.
   swissre.com
Pres: W. Weldon Wilson
Conducts Business: U.S.
Employees: 128
Primary Market Served: Consumer
Founded: 1950
Gross sales or billing: $52,200,000

Sell life, accident & health insurance
to consumers by direct response
techniques.

REGIT INC
1200 Roosevelt Rd (Suite 115)
Glen Ellyn, IL 60137
Telephone: (630) 495-1500, (800) 537-
   9786, FAX: (630) 495-1611, E-Mail:
   regit@regitinc.com, Web Site: www.
   regitinc.com
Pres: Donna Freestate
Mktg Dir: Marilyn Smaron
Conducts Business: U.S.
Primary Market Served: Consumer

Market health insurance to real estate
professionals.

REMARK USA
Subs. of Reinsurers Marketing BV
   Amstelveen Holland
301 Carlson Pkwy (Suite 305)
Minnetonka, MN 55305
Telephone: (952) 938-4699, FAX:
   (952) 988-8500, E-Mail: jessica.
   sbragia@remarkgroup.com, Web
   Site: www.remarkamericas.com
CEO: Michael Levison
Pres: Brad Smith
Chief Mktg Officer: Jessica Sbragia
Conducts Business: U.S., Canada,
   U.K., Holland, Australia
Primary Market Served: Consumer
Advertising/Marketing Budget Related
   to Direct Marketing: 76-100%
Direct Marketing ad budget:
Direct Mail: 100%
Gross sales or billing: $2,700,000

Design & implement direct marketing
programs which provide life & accident insurance offers to customers of
financial institutions, insurance companies & banks.

THE DMA RESERVE NATIONAL INSURANCE CO

PO Box 138801
Oklahoma City, OK 73113-8801
Telephone: (405) 848-7931, Web Site:
www.reservenational.com
Sr VP Opers: Orin Crossley

RESPONSE INSURANCE

PO Box 4079
Scranton, PA 18505-6079
Telephone: (203) 634-7255, (800) 518-
2984, FAX: (203) 634-7319, E-Mail:
webcs@response.com, Web Site:
www.response.com
Pres: Mory Katz
Exec VP & COO: John Ammendola
VP & Gen Counsel: Susan Stonebill
Clafin
VP, Fin: George Kowalsky
VP, Customer Svc & Sls: Kathleen A.
Gleeson
Primary Market Served: Consumer
Founded: 1995

Direct writer of auto insurance.

SCA PROMOTIONS INC

3030 LBJ Fwy (Suite 300)
Dallas, TX 75234
Telephone: (214) 860-3700, (888) 860-
3700, FAX: (214) 860-3723, E-Mail:
scainfo@scapromo.com, Web Site:
www.scapromo.com
Pres & Founder: Robert Hamman
Sr VP: Sheila Murphy Brian
Mktg Coord: Nancy Rodriguez
Conducts Business: U.S., Canada
Employees: 40
Primary Market Served: Business
Catalog available online
Advertising/Marketing Budget Related
to Direct Marketing: 0-25%
Founded: 1986

Offers fixed fee solutions for jumbo
prize funding, conditional prize fulfillment & over redemption protection, to
eliminate risk in promotional programs
such as contests, internet games and
telecards.

THE DMA SAFECO INSURANCE CO

4333 Brooklyn NE
Seattle, WA 98185-0001
Telephone: (206) 545-5000, (800) 332-
3226, FAX: (206) 545-5767/5651,
Web Site: www.safeco.com
Pres & CEO: Paula Rosput Reynolds
Exec VP & Chief Legal Officer: Arthur
Chong
Exec VP, Insurance Opers: Mike
Hughes
AVP Mktg: DeAnna Kerrick
Exec VP & CFO: Ross Kari
CIO: William Jenks
Conducts Business: U.S.

Employees: 7,000
Primary Market Served: Business &
Consumer
Catalog available online
Indirect online sales
Advertising/Marketing Budget Related
to Direct Marketing: 26-50%
Founded: 1923
Gross sales or billing: $6,200,000,000

Insurance & financial products sold to
consumers.

SAFEWARE, THE INSURANCE AGENCY INC

6500 Busch Blvd (Suite 233)
Columbus, OH 43229
Telephone: (614) 781-1492, (800) 800-
1492, FAX: (614) 781-0559, E-Mail:
service@safeware.com, Web Site:
www.safeware.com
Pres: James Johnson
Dir: Arthur Heggen
Conducts Business: Worldwide
Employees: 24
Primary Market Served: Business &
Consumer
Catalog available online
Indirect online sales
Advertising/Marketing Budget Related
to Direct Marketing: 76-100%
Direct Marketing ad budget: $250,000
Magazines: 10%
Telephone: 90%
Founded: 1982
Gross sales or billing: $3,000,000

Insurance for computer owners for
business & personal uses. Covers computers against theft, fire, power surges,
natural disasters & while in transit.

THE DMA SAVINGS BANK LIFE INSURANCE CO OF MA (SBLI)

1 Linscott Rd
Woburn, MA 01801-2001
Telephone: (781) 938-3500, Web Site:
www.sbli.com
VP, Dir: Rose Cahill
Primary Market Served: Consumer

SELMAN & CO

6110 Parkland Blvd
Cleveland, OH 44124-4187
Telephone: (440) 646-9336, (800) 735-
6262, FAX: (440) 646-9339, E-Mail:
ldenning@selmaninsurance.com,
Web Site: www.sel-co.com
Chmn: John L. Selman
Pres: David L. Selman
Mktg Dir: Laura Denning
Conducts Business: U.S.
Employees: 100
Primary Market Served: Consumer
Catalog available online
Direct online sales

Advertising/Marketing Budget Related
to Direct Marketing: 51-75%
Founded: 1905

Insurance agency/third-party administration specializing in direct marketing
of life & health, property & casualty
insurance to professional associations
& financial institutions.

SENTRY LIFE INSURANCE CO

Subs. of Sentry Insurance Co
1800 Northpoint Dr
Stevens Point, WI 54481
Telephone: (715) 346-6000, FAX:
(715) 346-7028, E-Mail: infoctr@
coredcs.com, Web Site: www.sentry.
com
Pres & CEO: Dale Schuh
VP & COO: Bob Recko
Conducts Business: U.S.
Primary Market Served: Business &
Consumer

Sell life, health, auto, home, commercial, group & individual insurance, also
retirement planning.

SHELBY INSURANCE COMPANIES

300 Riverhills Business Park
Birmingham, AL 35242-5037
Telephone: (800) 443-1573, FAX:
(877) 837-8203, Web Site: www.
vesta.com
Pres Vesta Ins Grp, Inc: Norman W.
Gayle III
Sr VP, CFO & Treas: W. Perry Cronin
VP Mktg: Howard Barber
Primary Market Served: Business &
Consumer

Property casualty insurance company;
markets through independent agents.
Providing homeowners, automobile,
dwelling fire, umbrella (personal
catastrophe). Non-standard automobile
and other insurance needs.

SPECTRUM ECOMMERCE

26023 Acero (Suite 100)
Mission Viejo, CA 92691-7942
Telephone: (949) 600-7900, Web Site:
elifemarketers.com
Pres: Sy Alter
Primary Market Served: Consumer

STANDARD LIFE

1245 Sherbrooke St W
Montreal, PQ, Canada H3G 1G3
Telephone: (514) 499-8855, (877) 499-
9555, FAX: (514) 499-4908, Web
Site: www.standardlife.ca
Pres & CEO: Joseph Iacinelli
Sr VP Retail Markets: Dennis Berthi-
aume

Sr VP Grp Savings & Retirement: Anthony Cardone
Sr VP Fin: Christian Martineau
Sr VP Legal & Compliance: Penny Westman
Conducts Business: U.S., Canada
Primary Market Served: Business & Consumer
Catalog available online
Gross sales or billing: $30,000,000

Direct marketer to promote healthcare insurance coverage through mailings.

STARMOUNT LIFE INSURANCE CO

8485 Goodwood Blvd
Baton Rouge, LA 70806-7878
Telephone: (225) 926-2888, (888) 729-7827, (888) 729-5433, E-Mail: info@starmountlife.com, Web Site: www.starmountlife.com
Chmn: Hans J. Sternberg
Pres: Erich Sternberg
Exec VP: Donna Sternberg
Mktg Coord: Julie Andre
VP: Deborah Sternberg
Conducts Business: U.S.
Employees: 160
Primary Market Served: Consumer
Catalog available online
Direct online sales
Advertising/Marketing Budget Related to Direct Marketing: 76-100%
Direct Marketing ad budget:
Direct Mail: 95%
Newspapers: 5%
Founded: 1983
Gross sales or billing: $40,000,000

Life, accident & health insurance.

STATE FARM INSURANCE COS

1 State Farm Plaza
Bloomington, IL 61710-0001
Telephone: (309) 766-2311, FAX: (309) 766-3621, Web Site: www.statefarm.com
Chmn & CEO: Edward B. Rust Jr.
Vice Chmn, CFO & Treas: Michael L. Tipsord
Vice Chmn & CMO: Michael C. Davidson
Vice Chmn & CAO: James E. Rutrough
Sr Exec VP: Jack W. North
Dir, Database Mktg: Don Lynn
Conducts Business: U.S., Canada
Employees: 57,000
Primary Market Served: Business & Consumer
Catalog available online
Indirect online sales
Advertising/Marketing Budget Related to Direct Marketing: 51-75%
Direct Marketing ad budget:

Direct Mail: $7,000,000
Founded: 1922

STATE MUTUAL INSURANCE CO

PO Box 153
Rome, GA 30162-0153
Telephone: (706) 291-1054, FAX: (706) 291-9459
VP: J. Gary Barton
Employees: 11
Primary Market Served: Business & Consumer
Gross sales or billing: $19,600,000

Sells all forms of insurance.

SUNLIFE OF CANADA

1 Sunlife Executive Park
Wellesley Hills, MA 02481
Telephone: (781) 237-6030, (800) SUNLIFE, FAX: (781) 446-1779, Web Site: www.sunlife-usa.com
Chmn Bd: Ronald W. Osbourne
CEO: Donald A. Stewart
Corp Dir: Krystyna T. Hoeg
Corp Dir: David Kerr
Conducts Business: Worldwide
Primary Market Served: Business & Consumer
Catalog available online
Gross sales or billing: $6,100,000,000

Group individuals & annuities.

JOHN SUTHERLAND & ASSOCIATES

6275 Lusk Blvd
San Diego, CA 92121-2731
Telephone: (858) 535-1139, (800) 545-9591, FAX: (858) 535-9124
CEO: Smokey Sutherland
Dir: Joanne Garcia
Conducts Business: U.S.
Employees: 10
Primary Market Served: Consumer
Gross sales or billing: $900,000

Water bed insurance.

SYMETRA FINANCIAL

777 108th Ave (Suite 1200)
Bellevue, WA 98004-5135
Telephone: (425) 256-8000, (800) 426-7355, FAX: (425) 256-5737, Web Site: www.symetra.com
Chmn: David T. Foy
Pres, CEO & Dir: Randall H. Talbot
Dir, Commun: Colin Johnson
Exec VP & COO: Roger F. Harbin
Sr VP, Mktg: Allyn D. Close
Conducts Business: U.S.
Employees: 1,200
Primary Market Served: Business & Consumer
Founded: 1923
Gross sales or billing: $1,500,000,000

Life insurance company selling through independent agents & financial planners. Regional offices: Atlanta, GA; Chicago, IL; Fountain Valley, CA; Redmond, WA.

TIAA-CREF

730 Third Ave
New York, NY 10017
Telephone: (212) 490-9000, FAX: (212) 916-6505, Web Site: www.tiaa-cref.org
Head Mktg: Jamie Depeau
Conducts Business: U.S., Canada
Employees: 3,800
Primary Market Served: Business & Consumer

Sell pensions & insurance to education market.

TEXAS FARM BUREAU INSURANCE COS

7420 Fish Pond Rd
Waco, TX 76710-1010
Telephone: (254) 751-2688, Web Site: www.txfb-ins.com
VP Mktg: Kimberly Kemper
Primary Market Served: Consumer

TRANSAMERICA LIFE & PROTECTION

520 Park Ave
Baltimore, MD 21201-4500
Telephone: (410) 209-5617, Web Site: www.aegondms.com

TRANSAMERICA LIFE INSURANCE CO

Subs. of Aegon
4333 Edgewood Rd NE
Cedar Rapids, IA 52499
Telephone: (319) 398-8511, (800) 558-9011, FAX: (319) 369-2825, Web Site: www.transamerica.com
Chmn & Pres: Larry M. Norman
Exec VP, COO & Dir: Brenda K. Clancey
Sr VP & CFO: Darryl D. Button
Conducts Business: U.S.
Employees: 300
Primary Market Served: Consumer
Indirect online sales
Direct Marketing ad budget:
Direct Mail: $25,000
Gross sales or billing: $139,000,000

Sell life insurance.

TRANSAMERICA OCCIDENTAL LIFE CO

Subs. of Aegon USA
1150 S Olive St (T-24)
Los Angeles, CA 90015

Telephone: (213) 742-3111, FAX: (213) 741-6623, Web Site: www. transamerica.com
Pres & Chmn: Ron Wagley
Sr VP & CIO: Eric Goodman
VP & COO: Paul Realburn
VP, Counsel & Sec: Craig D. Vermie
Conducts Business: U.S., Canada, Europe, Hong Kong, Puerto Rico, Guam, Virgin Islands
Employees: 3,700
Primary Market Served: Business & Consumer
Direct Marketing ad budget:
Direct Mail: $1,000,000
Founded: 1911
Gross sales or billing: $2,100,000,000

Promote the sale of life insurance & related financial services to the general public.

THE DMA TRANSAMERICA RETIREMENT SERVICES
1150 S Olive St (#T-9-10)
Los Angeles, CA 90015-2211
Telephone: (213) 742-3363, Web Site: www.ta-retirement.com
VP Mktg: Dave Shute

Provides companies with retirement plan benefits for their employees. Services include turn-key retirement plans, profit sharing, defined benefit & new comparability plans for clients & third party administrators

THE TRAVELERS INSURANCE COS
1 Tower Sq (#9PB-B)
Hartford, CT 06183-0001
Telephone: (860) 277-8252, (651) 317-2685, FAX: (860) 954-7691, Web Site: www.travelers.com
Corp Commun Adv: Joan Palm
Mktg Mgr: Patrick Todd
Primary Market Served: Business & Consumer
Founded: 1864

Insurance & financial services.

TRIGON BLUE CROSS/BLUE SHIELD
602 S Jefferson St, PO Box 13047
Roanoke, VA 24011
Telephone: (540) 853-5000, (800) 553-3164, FAX: (540) 853-3053, Web Site: www.trigon.com
CEO: Tom Snead
Mktg Dir: James Hicks
Direct Response Mgr: Lora Lee Hart
Primary Market Served: Business & Consumer
Advertising/Marketing Budget Related to Direct Marketing: 51-75%

Health insurance.

21ST CENTURY INSURANCE
Owned by AIG
6301 Owensmouth Ave
Woodland Hills, CA 91367
Telephone: (818) 704-3700, FAX: (818) 226-1198, E-Mail: executiveoffice@21st.com, Web Site: www.21st.com
Chmn: Robert M. Sandler
Pres & CEO: Bruce W. Marlow
Mktg Mgr: Bernarda Durate
Employees: 2,500
Primary Market Served: Consumer
Founded: 1958
Gross sales or billing: $1,375,300,000

Insurance company.

2-10 HOME BUYERS WARRANTY
10375 E Harvard Ave, 1 Denver Highlands (Suite 100)
Denver, CO 80231-3966
Telephone: (720) 747-6000, Web Site: www.2-10.com
Gen Mgr Direct Sls: Frederick Diehl

THE DMA USAA
Subs. of United Services Automobile Assn (USAA)
9800 Fredericksburg Rd, USAA Building
San Antonio, TX 78240-4100
Telephone: (512) 498-6524, FAX: (512) 498-8000
Chmn: Gen Herres
Pres: Edwin L. Rosane
Sr VP Mktg: Kenneth A. McClure
VP Sales: Art Settles
Exec Dir, Mktg Svcs: Barbara Shields
Conducts Business: Worldwide
Primary Market Served: Business & Consumer
Direct Marketing ad budget: $2,700,000
Telephone: 100%

Offer a complete line of life & health insurance & annuities.

USI AFFINITY
Subs. of USI Holdings Corp
1 International Plz (Suite 400)
Philadelphia, PA 19113-1535
Telephone: (610) 833-2876, (800) 625-2876, FAX: (610) 265-2876, E-Mail: info@usiaffinity.com, Web Site: www.brcorp.com
Pres & CEO: Alan Zink
VP, Mktg: Anne Keenan
VP: James A. Young
VP: Jose Rivera
Sr VP: Joseph B. Kaiser
Conducts Business: U.S.
Employees: 115
Primary Market Served: Consumer
Direct Marketing ad budget:

Direct Mail: $800,000
Magazines: $30,000
Founded: 1944

Insurance administrators. Branch Offices: Chicago, IL, Boston, MA & Washington, DC.

THE DMA USI AFFINITY COLLEGIATE INSURANCE RESOURCES
3070 Riverside Dr
Columbus, OH 43221-2547
Telephone: (614) 486-5388, Web Site: www.collegiateinsuranceresources.com
COO: Jeff Roedel

UNIFORMED SERVICES BENEFIT ASSOCIATION
10895 Grandview Dr (Suite 350)
Overland Park, KS 66210
Telephone: (800) 368-7021, Web Site: www.usba.com
Pres, CEO: Jerry V. Patton
Conducts Business: U.S.
Employees: 68
Primary Market Served: Consumer
Catalog available online
Indirect online sales
Advertising/Marketing Budget Related to Direct Marketing: 76-100%
Direct Marketing ad budget: $1,100,000
Direct Mail: 30%
Magazines: 40%
Newspapers: 30%
Founded: 1959
Gross sales or billing: $25,000,000

Sell life insurance, health insurance & financial services to military veterans & federal employees.

THE DMA THE UNION LABOR LIFE INSURANCE CO
Div. of Ullico Inc
8403 Colesville Rd
Silver Spring, MD 20910-6331
Telephone: (202) 962-2945, FAX: (202) 962-8429, E-Mail: info@ullico.com, Web Site: www.unioncare.com
Chmn, Pres & CEO: Mark E. Singleton
Mktg Mgr, Direct Mktg: Tammi Leathers
Dir Mktg Indus Life Insurance & Illustration Actuary: Blaine Barham
Conducts Business: U.S., Canada
Employees: 1,520
Primary Market Served: Consumer
Advertising/Marketing Budget Related to Direct Marketing: 76-100%
Direct Marketing ad budget: $2,400,000
Direct Mail: 100%
Founded: 1925

Gross sales or billing: $539,000,000

Insurance programs for third party clients.

UNITED INVESTORS LIFE INSURANCE CO

Div. of Torchmark Corp
2001 3rd Ave S Bsmt, Box 10207
Birmingham, AL 35233-2196
Telephone: (205) 325-4300, (800) 288-2722, FAX: (205) 325-4157, Web Site: www.uilic.com
Pres & CEO: Anthony McWhorter
Sr VP, Chief Actuary: Thomas Aycock
VP, Mktg: Ross Stagner
VP, Controller: James L. Mayton Jr.
Conducts Business: U.S.
Employees: 100
Primary Market Served: Business & Consumer
Gross sales or billing: $339,000,000

Sell life insurance to consumers.

UNITRIN

1 E Wacker Dr
Chicago, IL 60601-1883
Telephone: (312) 661-4600, (800) 733-7366, FAX: (312) 494-6995, Web Site: www.unitrin.com
Chmn: Richard C. Vie
Pres, CEO & Dir: Donald G. Southwell
Exec VP, CFO & Dir: Eric J. Draught
Sr VP: Scott Renwick
VP, Chief Acctg Officer: Richard Roeske
Conducts Business: U.S.
Employees: 700
Primary Market Served: Business & Consumer
Catalog available online
Advertising/Marketing Budget Related to Direct Marketing: 0-25%
Gross sales or billing: $3,000,000,000

Mid-west multiple line insurer.

UNUM CORP

2211 Congress St (Suite B118)
Portland, ME 04122
Telephone: (207) 770-2211, (800) 421-0344, FAX: (207) 770-4510, Web Site: www.unum.com
Pres & CEO: Thomas R. Watjen
Exec VP, CFO & Chief Actuary: Robert C. Greving
Exec VP & Gen Counsel: Charles Glick
Pres Unum US: Kevin P. McCarthy
COO Unum US: Robert O. Best
Conducts Business: U.S., Canada, U.K., France
Employees: 4,000
Primary Market Served: Business & Consumer

Gross sales or billing: $1,500,000,000

Insurance marketer.

WELLMARK BLUE CROSS & BLUE SHIELD OF IOWA

PO Box 9232, 636 Grand Ave
Des Moines, IA 50309-2565
Telephone: (515) 245-4500, FAX: (515) 323-7722, Web Site: www.wellmark.com
Pres: John Forsyth
Primary Market Served: Business & Consumer

Health insurance & financial service.

THE DMA WESTERN-SOUTHERN LIFE

400 Broadway
Cincinnati, OH 45202-3312
Telephone: (513) 629-1800, Web Site: www.westernsouthernlife.com
Mktg Officer: Jim DeLuca
Primary Market Served: Consumer

XL ENVIRONMENTAL

Div. of Capital Ltd
505 Eagleview Blvd
Exton, PA 19341-1119
Telephone: (610) 968-9500, (800) 327-1414, FAX: (610) 458-9109, E-Mail: webinfo.xli@xlgroup.com, Web Site: www.xlenvironmental.com
Reg Mgr Mktg & Commun NA: Sarah German
COO: David Du Clos
Conducts Business: U.S.
Employees: 468
Primary Market Served: Business
Advertising/Marketing Budget Related to Direct Marketing: 0-25%
Founded: 1985
Gross sales or billing: $32,200,000

Insurance for hazardous waste companies.

ZURICH

1400 American Ln
Schaumburg, IL 60196-5452
Telephone: (847) 605-3712, (800) 382-2150, FAX: (847) 605-6403, Web Site: www.zurichna.com
CEO: James J. Schiro
CFO: Louis J. Mannello Jr.
CAO: Tina Mallie
VP, Direct Mktg: Kathleen Trautmann
Exec VP: Barry J. Gilany
Exec VP: Jane Tutoki
Employees: 1,200
Primary Market Served: Business & Consumer
Catalog available online
Founded: 1996
Gross sales or billing: $19,800,000,000

Sell life insurance & annuities.

A&B EQUIPMENT CO
2101 Riverside Dr
Fort Worth, TX 76103-2120
Telephone: (817) 332-8361, (800) 426-0683, FAX: (817) 332-8430, Web Site: www.abequipmentcompany.com
Gen Mgr: Holly Hughes
Conducts Business: U.S.
Employees: 25
Primary Market Served: Business
Advertising/Marketing Budget Related to Direct Marketing: 26-50%
Direct Marketing ad budget: $50,000
Direct Mail: 100%

Sell construction equipment to construction companies.

A&P
2 Paragon Dr
Montvale, NJ 07645
Telephone: (201) 573-9700, (866) 44 FRESH, FAX: (201) 505-3054, E-Mail: apcustomerrel@aptea.com, Web Site: www.aptea.com
CEO: Christian Haub
Exec VP: John Metzger
Sr VP & CFO: Brenda Galgano
Sr VP Mdsg: Stephen Slade
Consumer Mktg Svcs Dir: Susan Hamilton
Employees: 38,000
Primary Market Served: Consumer
Gross sales or billing: $6,800,000,000

Retail supermarket chain.

A LA CARTE
Div. of David Scott Industries
5610 W Bloomingdale Rd
Chicago, IL 60639
Telephone: (773) 745-5900, (800) 723-2370, FAX: (773) 237-3075, E-Mail: info@alacarteline.com, Web Site: www.alacarteline.com
Pres: Anna Robins
Dir: Nancy Goldstein
Conducts Business: U.S.
Employees: 25
Primary Market Served: Business & Consumer
Catalog available online
Indirect online sales
Gross sales or billing: $1,000,000

Direct mail marketer of incentives, executive gifts & gourmet foods. Decorator of all types of cans & tins. Manufacturer of private label microwave popcorn & candies.

AAA UMBRELLA CO INC
230 Pegasus Ave
Northvale, NJ 07647-1904
Telephone: (201) 784-3242, (800) 426-7446, FAX: (201) 226-0041, Web Site: www.aaaumbrella.com
Pres: Jeff Nanus
Conducts Business: U.S., Canada
Employees: 18
Primary Market Served: Business

Umbrellas as premium items.

ACCO NORTH AMERICA
Div. of ACCO World Corp
300 Tower Pkwy
Lincolnshire, IL 60069
Telephone: (847) 541-9500, (800) 222-6462, FAX: (847) 478-0073, Web Site: www.acco.com
Pres: David Campbell
Conducts Business: US, Canada, Europe
Employees: 500
Primary Market Served: Business & Consumer

Manufacturer of office, school & computer supplies & furniture sold through commercial & mass market retailers. Branches in Wheeling, IL; Los Angeles, CA & Ogdensburg, NY.

ACP - AUTOMATION CONTROL PRODUCTS
4080 McGinnis Ferry Rd (Suite 801)
Alpharetta, GA 30005
Telephone: (678) 990-0945, FAX: (678) 990-0951, E-Mail: info@thinmanager.com, Web Site: www.thinmanager.com
Pres: Matt Crandell
Chief Tech Officer: Tim Caine
Conducts Business: U.S.
Employees: 50
Primary Market Served: Business & Consumer

Makers of Thin Client management software.

ADM PRODUCTIONS INC
40 Seaview Blvd
Port Washington, NY 11050-4618
Telephone: (516) 484-6900, (800) ADM-DIAL, FAX: (516) 621-2531, Web Site: www.admpro.com
Pres & CEO: Anthony DeMartino
VP & CFO: Angelo DeMartino
Producer: John Dunn
Employees: 50
Primary Market Served: Business
Advertising/Marketing Budget Related to Direct Marketing: 26-50%
Direct Marketing ad budget:
Direct Mail: 20%
Magazines: 20%
Newspapers: 20%
TV/Radio: 20%
Telephone: 20%
Founded: 1981
Gross sales or billing: $16,000,000

Specialize in creating & producing dynamic corporate image, sales/marketing & training films & videos. Majority of clients are corporate.

ADP INC
aka Automatic Data Processing, Inc
1 ADP Blvd
Roseland, NJ 07068-1728
Telephone: (973) 974-5000, (800) 225-5237, FAX: (973) 974-3334, Web Site: www.adp.com
Pres & CEO: Gary C. Butler
CFO: Christopher R. Reidy
COO: S. Michael Martone
VP Mktg & Bus Devel: Greg Secord
Sr VP Direct Mktg: Sandy Angevine
Conducts Business: U.S.
Employees: 46,000
Primary Market Served: Business
Founded: 1949
Gross sales or billing: $7,800,000,000

Leading provider of payroll & employer related services in U.S.

ADT WORLDWIDE
1 Town Center Rd
Boca Raton, FL 33486
Telephone: (561) 988-3600, FAX: (561) 988-3673, Web Site: www.tycofireandsecurity.com
Pres: Naren K. Gurshaney
VP, HR: Rich Lovely
VP, Gen Mgr: John McStravick
VP: Donald Lyman
Dir, Sls & Mktg: Greg Gatlin
Primary Market Served: Business & Consumer
Catalog available online
Gross sales or billing: $11,000,000,000

Manufacture of anti-theft devices.

AFA SERVICE CORP
3495 Piedmont Rd NE 11
Atlanta, GA 30305
Telephone: (404) 262-2729, (404) 237-2964, Web Site: www.arbys.com
Pres & Chief Mktg Officer: Debbie Pike
Primary Market Served: Business

Create & produce all creative materials for Arby's Roast Beef Restaurants.

AIN PLASTICS INC
Div. of Thyssen Kruup Materials NA, Inc
60 Fullerton Ave

Yonkers, NY 10704
Telephone: (914) 668-6800, (800) 431-2451, FAX: (914) 668-8820, Web Site: www.ainplastics.com
Sls Mgr: John Colleluori
Conducts Business: U.S., Canada
Employees: 250
Primary Market Served: Business & Consumer
Catalog available online
Direct online sales
Advertising/Marketing Budget Related to Direct Marketing: 51-75%
Founded: 1970
Gross sales or billing: $10,000,000

Plastic, sheet, rod, tube, film & accessories.

ALCO CHEMICAL

Div. of National Starch & Chemical Co
909 Mueller Dr
Chattanooga, TN 37406-1334
Telephone: (423) 629-1405, FAX: (423) 698-8723, Web Site: www.alcochemical.com
VP, Opers: George Arabea
Div VP: Win Cooke
Natl Sls Mgr: John Cate
Intl Bus Mgr: Chet Kawa
Mktg Mgr: Wayne Kibble
Mktg Mgr: Mike Standish
Conducts Business: Worldwide
Employees: 145
Primary Market Served: Business
Advertising/Marketing Budget Related to Direct Marketing: 0-25%
Direct Marketing ad budget:
Direct Mail: 70%
Magazines: 30%
Founded: 1960

Offer a wide variety of specialty chemicals to industrial companies. Sell rheology modifiers, microbiocides, wetting agents, dispersants, metal precipitants, scale inhibitors, thickeners & anti-stats.

AON INNOVATIVE SOLUTIONS

175 W Jackson Blvd Ste 1100
Chicago, IL 60604-2709
Telephone: (303) 279-2900, FAX: (303) 216-1732, Web Site: www.aon.com
Adv Mgr: Tammi Mayfield
Primary Market Served: Business

Provider of customer services & technology support solutions for Fortune 500 companies.

APW-WRIGHT LINE

Div. of Applied Power Inc
160 Gold Star Blvd

Worcester, MA 01606
Telephone: (508) 852-4300, (800) 225-7348, FAX: (508) 852-3060, Web Site: www.wrightline.com
Mktg Commun Dir: Sandy Flanagan
Conducts Business: Worldwide
Employees: 850
Primary Market Served: Business
Advertising/Marketing Budget Related to Direct Marketing: 0-25%

Manufacturer of specialty filing systems & office furnishings. Manufacturer of LAN management, engineering environment, multi-media environment & technical furniture solutions.

ARI

2523 S McDonough Rd
Orchard Hill, GA 30266
Telephone: (770) 227-8222, (800) 241-5064, FAX: (770) 227-9190, Web Site: www.halt.com
Pres: J. Gordon Dixon
Conducts Business: U.S.
Employees: 35
Primary Market Served: Business
Catalog available online

Aerosol manufacturer.

ASE TECHNOLOGIES INC

226 Lowell St
Wilmington, MA 01887-3074
Telephone: (978) 658-0009, FAX: (978) 658-9990, E-Mail: info@ase-tech.com, Web Site: www.ase-tech.com
Pres: Jay Baumgarten
Primary Market Served: Business

Sell software & services for high speed laser printers, data conversion, open printing.

ᴛʜᴇ ᴅᴍᴀ AT&T

1 ATT Way
Bedminster, NJ 07921-2694
Telephone: (800) 222-0300, FAX: (908) 532-1675, Web Site: www.att.com
Chmn & CEO: David Dorman
Conducts Business: Worldwide
Primary Market Served: Business & Consumer

Promote international long distance telecommunications services & equipment.

ABBOTT PRODUCTS

86 Finnell Dr
Weymouth, MA 02188-1126
Telephone: (781) 331-2030, (800) 392-7700, FAX: (781) 331-2030, Web Site: www.abbottproducts.com
Conducts Business: U.S., Canada

Primary Market Served: Business & Consumer
Direct Marketing ad budget: $200,000
Direct Mail: 100%
Gross sales or billing: $50,000,000

Sell bingo equipment & supplies to distributors & organizations for fundraising. Branches throughout the U.S. & Canada.

ACCOONA CORP

101 Hudson St (Suite 3606)
Jersey City, NJ 07302-3915
Telephone: (201) 557-9388, Web Site: www.accoona.com
VP: Shelley Rochester
Primary Market Served: Consumer

ACCOUNTEMPS

Div. of Robert Half International Inc
2884 Sand Hill Rd
Menlo Park, CA 94025-7059
Telephone: (650) 234-6000, (800) 803-8367, FAX: (650) 234-6998, Web Site: www.accountemps.com
Pres: Max Messmer
Conducts Business: U.S., Canada, U.K., Israel, Europe
Primary Market Served: Business
Advertising/Marketing Budget Related to Direct Marketing: 0-25%

Provides professional accountants & financial executives to industry on a temporary basis. Use direct mail to sell temporary employment services to corporate controllers & financial executives.

ACCUSPLIT INC

3090 Independence Dr Ste 150
Livermore, CA 94551-9423
Telephone: (925) 226-0888, (800) 935-1996, FAX: (925) 463-0147, E-Mail: sales@accusplit.com, Web Site: www.accusplit.com
Pres: W. Ron Sutton
VP, Natl Team Sls Div: Steve Simmons
Conducts Business: Worldwide
Employees: 14
Primary Market Served: Business & Consumer
Catalog available online
Direct online sales
Advertising/Marketing Budget Related to Direct Marketing: 76-100%
Direct Marketing ad budget: $160,000
Direct Mail: $50,000
Magazines: $60,000
Newspapers: $10,000
TV/Radio: $5,000
Telephone: $20,000
Founded: 1972

Manufacture stopwatches, sports watches, cycle computers & pedometers for sports, industry, auto racing, horse racing & sailing. Also, import & distribute fitness products.

ACE HARDWARE CORP
2200 Kensington Ct
Oak Brook, IL 60523-2100
Telephone: (630) 990-6600, FAX:
(630) 990-6838, Web Site: www.
acehardware.com
Chmn: J. Thomas Glenn
Pres & CEO: Ray A. Griffith
Consumer Mktg Specialist: Dana
Larsen
Exec VP: Rita D. Kahle
VP, Fin: Ronald J. Knutson
VP, IT: Michael G. Elmore
Primary Market Served: Business &
Consumer
Catalog available online
Direct online sales

Distribute power tools & hardware.

ACHIEVE GLOBAL
Subs. of Times Mirror
8875 Hidden River Pkwy (Suite 400)
Tampa, FL 33637
Telephone: (813) 631-5500, (800) 566-
0630, FAX: (813) 631-5796, Web
Site: www.achieveglobal.com
CEO: Sharon Daniels
Conducts Business: Worldwide
Employees: 1,850
Primary Market Served: Business
Founded: 1972

Marketer of training programs to business organizations designed to strengthen sales, customer service & management.

ACTIVISION VALUE
7800 Equitable Dr (Suite 200)
Eden Prairie, MN 55344
Telephone: (952) 918-9400, FAX:
(952) 918-9560
Gen Mgr: Dave Oxford
Conducts Business: U.S.
Primary Market Served: Business &
Consumer

Computer software & services for both business & personal use.

ACTIVSTYLE
3100 Pacific St
Minneapolis, MN 55411
Telephone: (612) 520-9333, (800) 651-
6223, FAX: (612) 520-9300, Web
Site: www.activstyle.com
Pres: Keith Trowbridge
Conducts Business: U.S., Canada
Primary Market Served: Business &
Consumer

Catalog available online
Indirect online sales

Manufacturer of healthcare products for incontinence & medical supplies.

AD INFINITUM BOOKS
7 N MacQuesten Pkwy
Mount Vernon, NY 10550-1811
Telephone: (914) 664-5930, (800) 697-
0402, FAX: (914) 664-2642, E-Mail:
aibservice@adinfinitumbooks.com,
Web Site: www.
adinfinitumbooks.com
Pres: William Brandon

ADNET USA
909 N Forrest Ave
Arlington Heights, IL 60004-5814
Telephone: (847) 483-5300, FAX:
(773) 304-2700, Web Site: www.
adnet.us
Pres: Kent Kirby
Conducts Business: U.S.
Employees: 3
Primary Market Served: Business &
Consumer
Catalog available online
Indirect online sales
Advertising/Marketing Budget Related
to Direct Marketing: 51-75%

Real estate related products & services.

ADVENTURE CREATIONS INC
2077 Harbor Blvd (#B)
Costa Mesa, CA 92625-2630
Telephone: (949) 515-3600, FAX:
(949) 515-3933, E-Mail: sales@adv-
creations.com, Web Site: www.adv-
creations.com
Pres: Dale Frankhouse
Conducts Business: Worldwide
Employees: 6
Primary Market Served: Business
Catalog available online
Indirect online sales
Advertising/Marketing Budget Related
to Direct Marketing: 0-25%
Founded: 1981

Large inflatables used for advertising; helium & cold air inflatables in stock & custom made.

AEROVOX INC
167 John Vertente Blvd
New Bedford, MA 02745-1221
Telephone: (508) 994-9661, (888)
AEROVOX, FAX: (508) 995-3000,
E-Mail: sales1@aerovox.com, Web
Site: www.aerovox.com
Pres & COO: Bob Elliott
Sr VP: F. Randal Hunt
Mktg Mgr: Al Sembos
Mktg Mgr: Dan Filkins

Mktg Mgr: Enrique Sanches Jr
Conducts Business: Worldwide
Employees: 1,500
Primary Market Served: Business &
Consumer
Catalog available online
Indirect online sales
Advertising/Marketing Budget Related
to Direct Marketing: 0-25%
Founded: 1922
Gross sales or billing: $111,600,000

AC & power DC capacitors, DC film capacitors, aluminum electrolytic capacitors, power factor correction capacitors & EMI filters.

AFFINION GROUP INC
6 High Ridge Park
Stamford, CT 06905-1327
Telephone: (203) 956-1176, Web Site:
www.affiniongroup.com
VP Legal Mktg/Adv Review: Lynn
Doonan

AFFINITY EXPRESS
2200 Point Blvd (Suite 130)
Elgin, IL 60123
Telephone: (847) 930-3200, FAX:
(847) 930-3299, E-Mail: kellyg@
affinityexpress.com, Web Site: www.
affinityexpress.com
VP Mktg: Kelly Glass
Conducts Business: U.S., Canada
Employees: 300
Primary Market Served: Business &
Consumer
Catalog available online
Direct online sales
Advertising/Marketing Budget Related
to Direct Marketing: 76-100%
Direct Marketing ad budget:
Direct Mail: 15%
Online: 70%
Telephone: 15%
Founded: 2000

Builds online identity programs for corporations, colleges, retail organizations and service organizations. Full service product fulfillment company.

AFFINITY4
999 Waterside Dr (Suite 1910)
Norfolk, VA 23510-3319
Telephone: (757) 465-4602, Web Site:
www.affinity4.com
VP Mktg: Charles Jamieson
Primary Market Served: Business &
Consumer

AGCO SPRA-COUP
Div. of Willknight Inc
4205 River Green Pkwy
Duluth, GA 30096

Telephone: (320) 231-9400, FAX: (320) 231-9413, Web Site: www.agcocorp.com
Pres: Dale Jones
HR Mgr: Paulette Hagen
Conducts Business: U.S., Canada
Primary Market Served: Business & Consumer
Direct Marketing ad budget:
Magazines: 99%
Newspapers: 1%

Manufacturer of liquid & granular fertilizing application equipment.

AHRENSDORF & ASSOCIATES
PO Box 7494
Saint Davids, PA 19087-7494
Telephone: (610) 971-0500, FAX: (610) 971-9530, E-Mail: leeahrensdorf@att.net
Pres: Lee Ahrensdorf
Primary Market Served: Business

Executive search consultant.

AIR AMBULANCE NETWORK INC
3607 Alt 19 Ste A
Palm Harbor, FL 34683-1412
Telephone: (727) 934-3999, (800) 327-1966, FAX: (727) 937-0276, Web Site: www.airambulancenetwork.com
Chmn & Pres: Richard Hunter
Dir: Barbara Hunter
Sr Flight Coord: Sherry Gincel
Conducts Business: Worldwide
Employees: 8
Primary Market Served: Business & Consumer
Direct Marketing ad budget:
Direct Mail: $250,000
Telephone: $500,000
Founded: 1991
Gross sales or billing: $650,000

Toll-free, 24-hour air ambulance service.

AIR FRANCE
125 W 55th St
New York, NY 10019
Telephone: (212) 830-4000, FAX: (212) 830-4244, Web Site: www.airfrance.fr.com
Mktg Mgr US: Natalie Grabczak
Conducts Business: U.S., Canada
Primary Market Served: Business & Consumer

Full-service marketer to generate sales of Air France Airlines.

AIR-LEC INDUSTRIES INC
3300 Commercial Ave
Madison, WI 53714-1458

Telephone: (608) 244-4754, FAX: (608) 246-7676, E-Mail: info@air-lec.com, Web Site: www.air-lec.com
Pres: John T. Lunenschloss
Sls & Svc: Harold Clute
Conducts Business: Worldwide
Employees: 8
Primary Market Served: Business
Founded: 1921

Heavy duty automatic industrial door operating equipment & aquatic weed cutters sold direct to users.

AIR-SCENT INTERNATIONAL
290 Alpha Dr, RIDC Industrial Park
Pittsburgh, PA 15238-2906
Telephone: (800) 247-0770, FAX: (412) 252-2000, E-Mail: laura@aromaresource.com, Web Site: www.airscent.com
Pres: A. Zlotnik
Gen Mgr: A. Howard
Conducts Business: U.S., Canada
Employees: 50
Primary Market Served: Business
Catalog available online
Indirect online sales
Advertising/Marketing Budget Related to Direct Marketing: 0-25%
Direct Marketing ad budget:
Direct Mail: 10%
Magazines: 80%
Telephone: 10%
Founded: 1946

Manufacturer of air freshener products & systems. Scented specialty items.

AIRLINES REPORTING CORP
3000 Wilson Blvd Ste 300
Arlington, VA 22201-3862
Telephone: (703) 816-8135, FAX: (703) 816-8104, E-Mail: corpcom@arccorp.com, Web Site: www.arccorp.com
VP & CFO: Alfred Altschul
Campaign Mktg Database Analyst: Arthur Redman
VP & Gen Counsel: Kathleen O. Agiropolous
VP Tech Svcs: Randy Black
VP HR: Mike Gilliland
Primary Market Served: Business
Catalog available online
Indirect online sales

Accredit & maintain a list of travel agencies based in U.S.A.

AIROMAT CORP
2916 Engle Rd
Fort Wayne, IN 46809-1198
Telephone: (260) 747-7408, (800) 348-4905, FAX: (260) 747-7409, E-Mail: airomat@airomat.com, Web Site: www.mymatting.com
Pres, CEO & Mktg Dir: Joanne Feasel

Opers Mgr: Pam Peters

THE AKADINE PRESS INC
120 Bloomingdale Rd (Suite 100)
White Plains, NY 10605-1522
Telephone: (914) 747-0777, FAX: (914) 747-0778, Web Site: www.commonreader.com
Pres: James Mustich Jr
Mktg Dir: Lisa Camilly
Conducts Business: Worldwide
Primary Market Served: Business & Consumer
Catalog available online
Direct online sales

Sell books.

ALAMO RENT A CAR
Subs. of Republic Industries
6929 N Lakewood Ave (Suite 100)
Tulsa, OK 74117
Telephone: (918) 401-6000, Web Site: www.alamo.com
Pres & CEO: William Lobeck
Exec VP & COO: Jerry F. Parrell
Exec VP & CFO: Thomas C. Kennedy
Sr VP & CIO: Tyler A. Best
Conducts Business: U.S.
Employees: 6,000
Primary Market Served: Business & Consumer
Catalog available online
Gross sales or billing: $539,000,000

Rental car company.

ALARMINGYOU.COM
One Town Center Rd.
Boca Raton, FL 33486-1002
Telephone: (714) 981-2900, Web Site: www.alarmingyou.com
Mng Partner: Dave Saenz

ALL STAR CARTS & VEHICLES
1565-D Fifth Industrial Ct
Bay Shore, NY 11706-3434
Telephone: (631) 666-5252, (800) 831-3166, FAX: (631) 666-1319, Web Site: www.allstarcarts.com
Pres: Stephen Kronrad
VP: Robert Kronrad
Sls: Robert Smith
Conducts Business: Worldwide
Employees: 51
Primary Market Served: Business
Catalog available online
Indirect online sales
Advertising/Marketing Budget Related to Direct Marketing: 0-25%
Direct Marketing ad budget:
Direct Mail: 5%
Magazines: 20%
Online: 75%
Founded: 1978

Gross sales or billing: $4,400,000

Ice cream, hot dog & hot food push-carts, trailers, trucks & kiosks for food & merchandising. Sell to individuals & companies.

ALL-STATE LEGAL

All-State International Inc
1 Commerce Dr
Cranford, NJ 07016-3508
Telephone: (908) 272-0800, (800) 222-0510, FAX: (800) 634-5184, E-Mail: sjacobs@aslegal.com, Web Site: www.aslegal.com
CEO: Robert Busch
Conducts Business: US
Employees: 230
Primary Market Served: Business
Catalog available online
Indirect online sales
Advertising/Marketing Budget Related to Direct Marketing: 26-50%
Founded: 1954
Gross sales or billing: $47,000,000

Serve the legal profession & corporations with engraving, printing, office products, legal specialty products & corporate outfits. Branch offices in Fort Wayne, IN & Los Angeles.

ALLERGAN INC

2525 DuPont Dr
Irvine, CA 92612-1531
Telephone: (714) 246-4500, (800) 433-8871, FAX: (714) 246-4971, Web Site: www.allergan.com
Chmn & CEO: David Pyott
Vice Chmn: Herbert W. Boyer
Pres: F. Michael Ball
Exec VP: Raymond Diradoorian
Media Contact: Heather Katt
Conducts Business: Worldwide
Employees: 6,770
Primary Market Served: Business & Consumer
Catalog available online
Founded: 1948
Gross sales or billing: $3,000,000,000

Provider of specialty therapeutic products.

ALLOYD BRANDS

SBU of Tegrant Corp
1401 Pleasant St
Dekalb, IL 60115-2663
Telephone: (815) 756-8451, (800) 756-7639, FAX: (815) 756-5187/9192, Web Site: www.alloyd.com
Pres: William M. Kelly
Sls & Mktg Mgr: Rob Van Gilse
Conducts Business: Worldwide
Employees: 560
Primary Market Served: Business
Founded: 1961
Gross sales or billing: $41,900,000

A custom thermoformer & manufacturer of packaging machinery.

ALLTEL

1 Allied Dr
Little Rock, AR 72202
Telephone: (501) 905-2590, (877) 446-3628, FAX: (501) 905-5444, Web Site: www.alltel.com
Pres & CEO: Scott T. Ford
Grp Pres Opers: Keven L. Beebe
Grp Pres Opers: Jeffrey H. Fox
Exec VP & CFO: Sharilyn Gasaway
Exec VP: Richard Massey
Employees: 15,000
Primary Market Served: Business & Consumer
Catalog available online
Direct online sales
Gross sales or billing: $8,000,000,000

User of direct marketing to sell telecommunications products & services.

ALMOST HEAVEN GROUP

HC 67 Box 539 BB
Renick, WV 24966
Telephone: (304) 645-2310, FAX: (304) 497-2698, E-Mail: art@almostheaven.net, Web Site: www.almostheaven.net
Mktg Dir: Art Glick
Conducts Business: Worldwide
Employees: 232
Primary Market Served: Business & Consumer
Catalog available online
Indirect online sales
Direct Marketing ad budget: $372,000
Direct Mail: 50%
Magazines: 50%
Founded: 1976
Gross sales or billing: $28,700,000

Leisure & computer related companies.

ALPHA SUPPLY INC

1225 Hollis
Bremerton, WA 98310-3611
Telephone: (360) 373-3302, (800) 257-4211, FAX: (360) 377-9235
Pres: Tom Orme
Mgr: Al Clever
Conducts Business: Worldwide
Employees: 10
Primary Market Served: Business & Consumer
Catalog available online
Advertising/Marketing Budget Related to Direct Marketing: 76-100%
Direct Marketing ad budget:
Direct Mail: 60%
Magazines: 35%
Telephone: 5%
Founded: 1968
Gross sales or billing: $4,000,000

Sell jewelers' supplies, equipment & lapidary supplies.

ALSTOM SIGNALING INC

1025 John St
West Henrietta, NY 14586-9781
Telephone: (585) 279-2228, Web Site: www.alstomsignalingsolutions.com
Mktg Commun/Graphics Specialist: James Heinlein
Primary Market Served: Business & Consumer

AMANET

dba American Manufacturing Network
7001 Eton Ave # B
Canoga Park, CA 91303-2112
Telephone: (818) 786-1113, FAX: (818) 786-5736, E-Mail: info@amanet-usa.com, Web Site: www.amanet.com
Pres: Sandip Desai
Gen Mgr: Leonor Towell
Sls Mgr: Lorene Tremblay
Conducts Business: U.S.
Employees: 20
Primary Market Served: Business
Indirect online sales
Advertising/Marketing Budget Related to Direct Marketing: 0-25%
Gross sales or billing: $2,800,000

Custom component manufacturer of all types of machining including CNC mills, lathes, metal stamping & sheet metal parts for industrial & aerospace applications.

AMATEUR ELECTRONIC SUPPLY LLC

5710 W Good Hope Rd
Milwaukee, WI 53223
Telephone: (414) 558-0333, (800) 558-0411, FAX: (414) 358-3337, Web Site: www.aesham.com
Dir: Mike Hansen
Mgr: Bruce Lapointe
Mgr: Ben Taeusch
Branch Mgr: Dale Porray
Conducts Business: U.S.
Primary Market Served: Business & Consumer
Catalog available online
Direct online sales

Provide electronics for amateur radio buffs.

THE DMA AMAZON.COM

126 C St NW Fl 2
Washington, DC 20001-2132
Telephone: (202) 347-7390
VP, Global Pub Policy: Paul Misener

AMCAT TELEPROFIT INC

300 Johnny Bench Dr (# 120)
Oklahoma City, OK 73104-2476
Telephone: (405) 216-8080, (800) 364-5518, FAX: (405) 216-8063, E-Mail: smart@amcat.com, Web Site: www.amcat.com
Pres: Richard Costello
Chmn: Mark Costello
Primary Market Served: Business & Consumer
Founded: 1990

Affordable, predictive dialing systems for small & medium size business.

THE DMA AMERICAN AUTOMOBILE ASSOCIATION

1000 AAA Dr MS-74
Heathrow, FL 32746-5063
Telephone: (407) 444-7282, Web Site: www.aaa.com
Mgr MRM Action Center: Sue Beaupre

AMERICAN BRONZING CO

Div. of Bronze Shoe Co
1313 Alum Creek Dr
Columbus, OH 43209-2706
Telephone: (614) 252-7388, (800) 423-5678, FAX: (614) 252-4602, E-Mail: bronzeinfo@bronshoe.com, Web Site: www.abcbronze.com
Pres: Robert Kaynes Jr.
VP, Mktg & Sls: Diane Taylor
Sls Dir: John Falor
Conducts Business: U.S.
Employees: 90
Primary Market Served: Consumer
Catalog available online
Direct online sales
Advertising/Marketing Budget Related to Direct Marketing: 51-75%
Direct Marketing ad budget:
Direct Mail: 95%
Magazines: 5%
Founded: 1934
Gross sales or billing: $1,500,000

Bronzed baby shoes for consumers.

AMERICAN CIVIL DEFENSE ASSOCIATION

11576 S State St (Suite 502)
Draper, UT 84020-7111
Telephone: (800) 501-0077, FAX: (800) 403-1369, E-Mail: info@tacda.org, Web Site: www.tacda.org
Exec Dir: Sharon Packer
Pres Board: Jay Whimpey
Conducts Business: U.S.
Employees: 3
Primary Market Served: Business & Consumer
Catalog available online
Indirect online sales
Founded: 1962

Sell medical emergency triage tags to civil defense directors, hospitals, rescue, fire departments & large industry.

AMERICAN CRANE & EQUIPMENT CORP

531 Old Swede Rd
Douglassville, PA 19518-1205
Telephone: (610) 385-6061, (877) 877-6778, FAX: (610) 385-3191/4876, E-Mail: info@americancrane.com, Web Site: www.americancrane.com
Pres: Oddvar Norheim
VP & CFO: Dave Hope
Sls Engr: Paul Smyk
Sls Engr: Bruce Seiz
Sls Engr: Jami Rubendall
Conducts Business: Worldwide
Employees: 105
Primary Market Served: Business & Consumer
Catalog available online
Advertising/Marketing Budget Related to Direct Marketing: 0-25%
Founded: 1972
Gross sales or billing: $15,000,000

Manufacturer of electric overhead cranes & hoists.

AMERICAN DERMATOLOGICAL CORP

PO Box 565014
Miami, FL 33256-5014
Telephone: (305) 573-0763, (888) 573-0763, FAX: (305) 573-1704, E-Mail: info@dermatique.com, Web Site: www.dermatique.com
Pres: William J. O'Malley
VP: Thomas O'Malley
Conducts Business: Worldwide
Employees: 10
Primary Market Served: Consumer
Catalog available online
Direct online sales
Advertising/Marketing Budget Related to Direct Marketing: 0-25%

Sell skin care products to women.

AMERICAN GREETINGS CORP

1 American Rd
Cleveland, OH 44144
Telephone: (216) 252-7300, FAX: (216) 252-6777
Chmn & CEO: Morry Weiss
Sr VP & Gen Sls Mgr: William R. Mason
Primary Market Served: Business & Consumer
Advertising/Marketing Budget Related to Direct Marketing: 76-100%

Import greeting cards & gift items.

AMERICAN HEALTH & SAFETY INC

Div. of LabSource
325 Industrial Cir
Stoughton, WI 53589
Telephone: (630) 413-5662, (800) 522-7554, FAX: (800) 326-3245, Web Site: www.ahsafety.com
Pres & CEO: David Gust
Conducts Business: U.S.
Employees: 34
Primary Market Served: Business
Catalog available online
Founded: 1980

Nationwide distributor of personal safety equipment & supplies.

AMERICAN HEALTHWAYS

701 Cool Springs Blvd
Franklin, TN 37067-2697
Telephone: (615) 665-7716, FAX: (615) 665-7697, Web Site: www.americanhealthways.com
Info Tech: Regina Seider
Primary Market Served: Business & Consumer
Advertising/Marketing Budget Related to Direct Marketing: 26-50%

For-profit health care company with 70 diabetes, cardiac & respiratory disease management treatment centers across the country.

AMERICAN LOCKER SECURITY SYSTEMS INC

Subs. of American Locker Group Inc
PO Box 169
Coppell, TX 75019-0169
Telephone: (817) 329-1600, (800) 828-9118, E-Mail: info@americanlocker.com, Web Site: www.americanlocker.com
Pres, COO & Treas: Roy J. Glosser
CFO: Paul M. Zadins
VP, Mktg: Jonathan M. Ruttenberg
VP, Mfg: Jim Panho
VP & Gen Mgr: David L. Henderson
Conducts Business: Worldwide
Employees: 88
Primary Market Served: Business & Consumer
Catalog available online
Indirect online sales
Advertising/Marketing Budget Related to Direct Marketing: 0-25%
Direct Marketing ad budget: $80,000
Direct Mail: 15%
Magazines: 85%
Founded: 1931
Gross sales or billing: $24,000,000

Manufacture coin & key operated lockers which are marketed through direct salesmen & distributors nationwide to municipalities, private sectors & industrial corporations.

AMERICAN MOVIE CLASSICS HOLDING CORP

Div. of Rainbow Programming
220 Jericho Quadrangle
Jericho, NY 11753
Telephone: (516) 803-3000, FAX:
(516) 803-3003, Web Site: www.
amctv.com
Pres: Ed Carroll
VP: Theana Apostolou
VP: Joshua Berger
VP, Production: Mary Conlon
VP, Res: Sean Fassett
Conducts Business: U.S.
Primary Market Served: Business &
Consumer

Cable television programmer offering a
channel of classic American films to
cable television companies.

AMERICAN OSTOMY SUPPLY

13400 Lakefront Dr
Earth City, MO 63045-1516
Telephone: (314) 291-2900, (800) 858-
5858, FAX: (800) 545-0065
Opers Mgr: Lisa Juenger
Conducts Business: U.S., Asia, Europe
Employees: 28
Primary Market Served: Business &
Consumer
Advertising/Marketing Budget Related
to Direct Marketing: 76-100%

Mail order marketer of medical
supplies.

THE DMA AMERICAN 3B SCIENTIFIC

2189 Flintstone Dr (Suite O)
Tucker, GA 30084-5023
Telephone: (770) 492-9111, Web Site:
www.a3bs.com
Mktg Mgr: Mark Dresser
Conducts Business: U.S., Canada, Bra-
zil
Primary Market Served: Business
Catalog available online
Direct online sales
Advertising/Marketing Budget Related
to Direct Marketing: 0-25%
Direct Marketing ad budget:
Direct Mail: 75%
Online: 25%

AMERICA'S FINEST PET DOORS

Patio Pacific Inc
202 Tank Farm Rd (Suite F1)
San Luis Obispo, CA 93401-7520
Telephone: (805) 781-7700 X201,
(800) 826-2871, FAX: (805) 781-
9734, E-Mail: alan@petdoors.com,
Web Site: www.petdoors.com
Pres: Alan Lethers
Opers Mgr: Cheri Segovia
Conducts Business: U.S., Canada

Employees: 10
Primary Market Served: Business &
Consumer
Catalog available online
Indirect online sales
Advertising/Marketing Budget Related
to Direct Marketing: 0-25%
Direct Marketing ad budget:
Magazines: 40%
Online: 60%
Founded: 1973
Gross sales or billing: $3,500,000

Pet doors.

AMERICRAFT - THE GIFT BROKERS INC

210 Lockes Village Rd
Wendell, MA 01379
Telephone: (978) 544-7330, (800) 866-
2723, FAX: (978) 544-2771, E-Mail:
info@americraft.us, Web Site: www.
americraft.us
Pres: Robert M. Cabral Jr
Project Mgr: Patricia J. Mitchell
Employees: 2
Primary Market Served: Business
Advertising/Marketing Budget Related
to Direct Marketing: 0-25%
Founded: 1978
Gross sales or billing: $5,000,000

Product sourcing & development for
mail order merchants. Provide innovative niche specific merchandise & reliable, personalized drop shipped items.

AMERITECH SERVICES INC

Div. of Ameritech
722 N Broadway (fl 13)
Milwaukee, WI 53202-4303
Telephone: (800) 924-1000, Web Site:
www.ameritech.com
Sr Mgr Mktg Commun: Mary Shully
Conducts Business: US
Primary Market Served: Business &
Consumer

A communications company marketing
services with direct response programs.

AMIGO MOBILITY INTERNATIONAL INC

6693 Dixie Hwy
Bridgeport, MI 48722-9725
Telephone: (989) 777-0910, (800) 692-
6446, FAX: (989) 777-8184, E-Mail:
info@myamigo.com, Web Site:
www.myamigo.com
Founder & Pres: Alan Thieme
Mktg Commun Mgr: Janet Princing
Opers Mgr: Mike Labrake
Dir Fin & Admin: Mike Galer
Dir New Bus: Janet Hausbeck
Mktg Mgr: Frances E. Hetzuer
VP: Beth Thieme
Conducts Business: Worldwide

Employees: 50
Primary Market Served: Business &
Consumer
Founded: 1968

Power operated vehicles.

AMREL

3445 Fletcher Ave
El Monte, CA 91731
Telephone: (626) 443-6818, (800) 654-
9838, FAX: (626) 443-8600, E-Mail:
amrel@amrel.com, Web Site: www.
amrel.com
CEO: Edward Chen
Mktg Coord: Alice Chang
Conducts Business: Worldwide
Employees: 100
Primary Market Served: Business &
Consumer
Catalog available online
Indirect online sales
Advertising/Marketing Budget Related
to Direct Marketing: 76-100%
Founded: 1989
Gross sales or billing: $25,000,000

Rugged mobile computer, program-
mable power supplies, and electronic
loads manufacturer.

AMSTERDAM PRINTING

Div. of Holland USA, Inc
166 Wallins Corners Rd
Amsterdam, NY 12010-1899
Telephone: (518) 842-6000, (800) 203-
9917, FAX: (518) 843-5204, E-Mail:
customerservice@amsterdamprinting.
com, Web Site: www.
amsterdamprinting.com
Chmn & CEO: Glenn Taylor
Pres: Kevin Kirbey
Conducts Business: U.S., Canada, Eu-
rope
Employees: 585
Primary Market Served: Business
Catalog available online
Direct online sales
Advertising/Marketing Budget Related
to Direct Marketing: 76-100%
Founded: 1898
Gross sales or billing: $10,000,000

Direct mail marketer of business
forms, imprinted promotional items, &
human resources products.

AMTELCO

4800 Curtin Dr
McFarland, WI 53558
Telephone: (608) 838-4194, (800) 356-
9148, FAX: (608) 838-8367, E-Mail:
info@amtelco.com, Web Site: www.
amtelco.com
CEO: Joseph W. Everly
Reg Sls Mgr: Mike Friedel
Mgr: Greg Beale
Conducts Business: Worldwide

Employees: 110
Primary Market Served: Business
Catalog available online
Founded: 1977

Manufacture & develop telemessaging equipment.

ANDREA ELECTRONICS CORP

65 Orville Dr (Suite 1)
Bohemia, NY 11716-2517
Telephone: (631) 719-1800, (800) 442-7787, FAX: (631) 719-1950, Web Site: www.andreaelectronics.com
Chmn & CEO: Frank A.D. Andrea Jr
Co-Pres & COO: John Andrea
Co-Pres: Douglas Andrea
VP, Pub Rels: Molly Jankey
Employees: 80
Primary Market Served: Business
Founded: 1934
Gross sales or billing: $6,000,000

Airborne intercom & telecommunication products sold to the government & to industry.

ANDREW WIRELESS SOLUTIONS

Subs of Comscope
3 Westbrook Corporate Ctr (Suite 900)
Westchester, IL 60154-5765
Telephone: (800) 349-5444, Web Site: www.andrew.com
Pres, CEO & Dir: Ralph E. Faison
Conducts Business: Worldwide
Employees: 11,251
Primary Market Served: Business
Advertising/Marketing Budget Related to Direct Marketing: 0-25%
Founded: 1937
Gross sales or billing: $2,195,100,000

A global designer, manufacturer, and supplier of communications equipment, services, and systems

ANGELICA IMAGE APPAREL

Div. of Angelica Corp
7700 Forsyth Blvd (Suite 1010)
Saint Louis, MO 63105-1821
Telephone: (314) 854-3800, (800) 235-8410, Web Site: www.angelica.com
Chm, CEO & Pres: Stephen M. O'Hara
VP & CEO: James W. Shaffer
Conducts Business: U.S.
Employees: 5,000
Primary Market Served: Business & Consumer

Manufacturer of uniforms & career apparel for healthcare, hospitality, retail & industrial applications.

THE ANIMAL MEDICAL CENTER

510 E 62nd St
New York, NY 10065-8314
Telephone: (212) 838-8100, FAX: (212) 832-9630, Web Site: www.amcny.org
Pub Rels Dir & Devel: Karen Aiken
CEO: Cynthia Phipps
Conducts Business: U.S.
Primary Market Served: Consumer

Non-profit veterinary hospital, research institute & educational center.

ANNE KLEIN

1411 Broadway Rm 2002
New York, NY 10018-3762
Telephone: (212) 536-9000, FAX: (212) 536-9000
CEO: Arthur Levine
Sr Dir of Mktg Ann Klein: Eileen McMaster
Mktg Dir: Dee Salomon
Conducts Business: U.S., Canada
Primary Market Served: Business & Consumer

Retailer of women's clothing.

ANRITSU CO

Div. of Anritsu Corp
490 Jarvis Dr
Morgan Hill, CA 95037
Telephone: (408) 778-2000, (800) 267-4878, FAX: (408) 776-1744, Web Site: www.us.anritsu.com
VP, Telecommuns: Don Mulder
VP, Engrng Dir & Gen Mgr: Frank Tiernan
VP & Gen Mgr Americas Sls Region: Wade Hulon
Conducts Business: Worldwide
Employees: 4,000
Primary Market Served: Business
Advertising/Marketing Budget Related to Direct Marketing: 0-25%
Direct Marketing ad budget:
Direct Mail: $30,000
Magazines: $90,000
Founded: 1895
Gross sales or billing: $80,000,000

Microwave & telecommunications test & measurement equipment to commercial, government, domestic & international markets.

APPLE COMPUTER INC

1 Infinite Loop
Cupertino, CA 95014-2083
Telephone: (408) 996-1010, FAX: (408) 996-0275, Web Site: www.apple.com
Pres: Steve Jobs
Conducts Business: Worldwide
Employees: 14,000

Primary Market Served: Business & Consumer

Manufacturer of personal computers for business, home & education.

ARBUS CAPITAL LTD

1320 Tower Rd
Schaumburg, IL 60173
Telephone: (847) 290-9600, FAX: (847) 290-9601
Owner: Stephen Jauzapaitis
Conducts Business: U.S.
Employees: 5
Primary Market Served: Business

Business brokerage firm.

ARCELOR MITTAL

139 Modena Rd
Coatesville, PA 19320-4036
Telephone: (610) 383-2000, FAX: (610) 383-5036, Web Site: www.arcelormittal.com
Gen Mgr: Edward Frey
Dir Prod Control: Bob Insetta
Primary Market Served: Business
Advertising/Marketing Budget Related to Direct Marketing: 76-100%
Direct Marketing ad budget:
Direct Mail: $100,000
Magazines: $200,000

Producer of carbon, alloy & clad plate & sheet steels.

ARCELORMITTAL

1 S Dearborn St
Chicago, IL 60603-2302
Telephone: (312) 899-3440, FAX: (312) 899-3504, Web Site: www.mittalsteel.com
CEO: Louis Schorsch
Primary Market Served: Business & Consumer
Catalog available online
Gross sales or billing: $12,900,000,000

Manufacturers of steel & steel products.

ARCH TELECOM INC

210 Barton Springs (Suite 275)
Austin, TX 78704
Telephone: (512) 492-0735, (800) 890-7575, FAX: (512) 495-7101, Web Site: www.archtelecom.com
Pres: Charles Russo
Dir: John Llorens
Mktg Dir: Steve Cortez
Mgr: Randy Rice
Conducts Business: U.S.
Primary Market Served: Business & Consumer
Catalog available online
Indirect online sales

Provides 800 line services.

ARGENT TRADING LLC
521 5th Ave Rm 2200
New York, NY 10175-2900
Telephone: (212) 697-8800, FAX:
(212) 697-8606, Web Site: www.
Argenttrading.com
Chmn Bd: Jose Canino
CEO & Pres: Rafael Corral
COO & Pres: John Ende
Exec VP & Gen Counsel: Gregg
Young
Exec VP Acq: Bill Levitz
Sls Coord: Kiki Mosterion
Primary Market Served: Business
Catalog available online
Advertising/Marketing Budget Related
to Direct Marketing: 0-25%
Founded: 1958

Marketing services.

ARISTOKRAFT INC
Div. of Fortune Brands
1 Masterbrand Cabinets Dr
Jasper, IN 47547-0420
Telephone: (812) 482-2527, FAX:
(812) 482-9872, Web Site: www.
aristokraft.com
Pres: Greg Stoner
Sr VP & CFO: Steve Svetik
Exec VP, Sls: Gary G. Lautzenhiser
Exec VP, Mktg: Neil P. Lynch
Exec VP, HR: Rick Mullis
Conducts Business: U.S.
Employees: 2,300
Primary Market Served: Business &
Consumer
Catalog available online
Advertising/Marketing Budget Related
to Direct Marketing: 0-25%
Founded: 1954
Gross sales or billing: $250,000,000

Manufacturer of kitchen & bath cabinets & vanities.

ARNAUD'S
813 Bienville St
New Orleans, LA 70112-3121
Telephone: (504) 523-0611, (866) 230-
8895, FAX: (504) 581-7908, Web
Site: www.arnauds.com
Owner: Jane Casbarian
Owner: Archie Casbarian
Sls & Mktg Dir: Lisa Sins
Assoc Sls Dir: Debbie Ryall
Conducts Business: U.S.
Employees: 50
Primary Market Served: Consumer
Catalog available online
Indirect online sales

Restaurant featuring French Creole
cuisine.

ARQUEST INC
14 Scotto Farm Ln.
Millstone Twp, NJ 08535-9426
Telephone: (609) 395-9500, (888) AR-
QUEST, (888) 270-8378, FAX:
(609) 395-9778, Web Site: www.
arquest.com
Pres & COO: Matthew J. Rinaldi
VP, Sls & Mktg: M. Reid Macfarlan
Mktg & Bus Devel: Scott Traister
Conducts Business: U.S., Canada,
Mexico, Russia
Employees: 500
Primary Market Served: Business
Advertising/Marketing Budget Related
to Direct Marketing: 0-25%
Founded: 2004
Gross sales or billing: $63,100,000

Private label disposable diapers, training & swim pants for infants.

ARROW CO
Div. of Cabot Corp
5457 W 79th St
Indianapolis, IN 46268-1675
Telephone: (317) 692-6666, FAX:
(317) 692-6769, Web Site: www.
aearo.com
Mktg Dir: Susan Chaille
Conducts Business: Worldwide
Primary Market Served: Business &
Consumer

Manufacturer of hearing protection &
noise abatement products.

ARROWHEAD MOUNTAIN SPRING WATER
Div. of Perrier Group of America
PO Box 628
Wilkes Barre, PA 18703-0628
Telephone: (800) 873-7775, Web Site:
www.arrowheadwater.com
Pres & CEO: Donald W. Wood
VP: Russel Rogers
Corp Sec Dir Bd: Ross Drysdale
Dir Bd: Patty McGinley
Dir Bd: Michael Nicolichuk
Conducts Business: U.S.
Employees: 1,500
Primary Market Served: Business &
Consumer
Catalog available online
Direct online sales
Founded: 1894

Sell coffee & coffee equipment, bottled
drinking water & water filtration
equipment to both residential & commercial customers.

ARTS & ENTERTAINMENT TELEVISION NETWORK
235 E 45th St
New York, NY 10017
Telephone: (212) 210-1400, FAX:
(212) 210-1326, Web Site: www.
aetv.com
CEO: Abbie Raven
Conducts Business: US, Canada
Primary Market Served: Consumer
Catalog available online
Direct online sales

Broadcast A&E Network History
Channels; publish Biography Magazine; sell A&E Home Videos.

ASHLAND INC
50 E Rivercenter Blvd (Suite 1600)
Covington, KY 41011-1678
Telephone: (859) 815-3333, Web Site:
www.ashland.com
Chmn & CEO: James J. O'Brien
Sr VP & CFO: Lamar M. Chambers
Sr VP & Gen Counsel: David L.
Hausrath
VP & Pres Ashland Distr: Robert M.
Craycraft
VP HR & Communs: Susan B. Esler
Conducts Business: Worldwide
Primary Market Served: Business
Advertising/Marketing Budget Related
to Direct Marketing: 0-25%

Manufactures chemical specialty products for a variety of markets.

ASIAEXP
1835 NE Miami Gardens Dr
Miami, FL 33179-5035
Telephone: (305) 675-5969, Web Site:
www.asiaexp.com
Sr VP: Richard Goldberg

THE DMA ASSET MARKETING SERVICES INC
14101 Southcross Dr W
Burnsville, MN 55337-6902
Telephone: (952) 707-7000, Web Site:
www.amsi-corp.com
VP Mktg: Richard Bauer
Primary Market Served: Consumer
Catalog available online
Direct online sales

ASSOCIATED PHOTO
PO Box 817
Florence, KY 41022-0817
Telephone: (859) 344-1460, (800) 727-
2580, FAX: (859) 282-0032
Pres: Fred Mosher
VP: Carla Steinbrunner
Conducts Business: U.S.
Employees: 4
Primary Market Served: Business &
Consumer
Direct Marketing ad budget:
Direct Mail: 90%
Magazines: 5%
Telephone: 5%
Founded: 1912
Gross sales or billing: $685,000

Replacement photo lamps & specialty
photo cards.

ASSOCIATED TEXTILE RENTAL SERVICES

548 Saint Paul St
Rochester, NY 14605-1735
Telephone: (585) 454-5988, (800) 639-4624, Web Site: www.associatedtextile.com
Pres: David Abelove
Sr VP: Anthony Barbato
Conducts Business: U.S.
Employees: 175
Primary Market Served: Business
Catalog available online
Gross sales or billing: $13,000,000

Linens & uniform sales & rentals.
Mailing address: PO Box 6510, Utica, NY 13504.

ASTROLOGER'S FUND INC

Subs. of New York Astrology Center
7913 Bay Pkwy (#A7)
Brooklyn, NY 11214
Telephone: (212) 949-7275, FAX: (212) 608-6964, E-Mail: books@afund.com, Web Site: www.afund.com
Dir: Henry Weingarten
Conducts Business: Worldwide
Employees: 4
Primary Market Served: Consumer
Catalog available online
Direct online sales
Founded: 1968

Mail order sales of books & audio & video tapes. Specialize in astrology, multi-dimensional healing & new age consciousness.

AUDIO & VIDEO LABS INC

Div. of Audio & Video Labs Inc
7905 N Route 130
Pennsauken, NJ 08110-1402
Telephone: (856) 663-9030, (800) 468-9353, FAX: (856) 661-3450, E-Mail: info@discmakers.com, Web Site: www.discmakers.com
Chmn: Morris Ballen
Dir, Mktg & E-Commerce: Lee Sowers
Conducts Business: Worldwide
Primary Market Served: Business & Consumer
Catalog available online
Indirect online sales
Advertising/Marketing Budget Related to Direct Marketing: 26-50%
Direct Marketing ad budget: $1,000,000
Direct Mail: 60%
Magazines: 20%
Telephone: 20%
Founded: 1946

Manufacturer of CD-Rom, CD-audio & cassettes. Complete printing & packaging.

AUDIOVOX

150 Marcus Blvd
Hauppauge, NY 11788-3794
Telephone: (631) 231-7750, (800) 645-4994, FAX: (631) 434-3995, Web Site: www.audiovox.com
Chief Mktg Officer: Ann M. Boutcher
PR Mgr: Jeremy Stoehr
Conducts Business: U.S., Canada, Mexico, Europe, Far East, S America
Employees: 940
Primary Market Served: Business & Consumer
Direct Marketing ad budget:
Direct Mail: 20%
Magazines: 50%
Newspapers: 20%
Telephone: 10%
Founded: 1960
Gross sales or billing: $456,700,000

Mobile & consumer electronics & accessories

AUSTRALIAN TOURIST COMMISSION

6100 Center Drive
Los Angeles, CA 90045
Telephone: (310) 695-3200, Web Site: www.australia.com
Consumer Mktg Dir: Bob Monfrini
Primary Market Served: Consumer
Catalog available online
Direct online sales
Advertising/Marketing Budget Related to Direct Marketing: 0-25%
Gross sales or billing: $200,000

Promotes travel to Australia to U.S. & Canadian citizens.

AUTODESK INC

111 McInnis Pkwy
San Rafael, CA 94903
Telephone: (415) 507-5000, FAX: (415) 507-5100, Web Site: www.autodesk.com
Chmn Bd: Carol Bartz
Pres & CEO: Carl Bass
Sr VP, CFO: Alfred Castino
Exec VP, Worldwide Sls: Ken Bado
VP, Investor Rels: Sue Pirri
Conducts Business: Worldwide
Primary Market Served: Business
Catalog available online
Direct online sales

Software manufacturer.

AUTOMATION MAILING & SHIPPING SOLUTIONS INC

Subs. of Automated Fastening Inc
1138 W Ninth St
Cleveland, OH 44113-1060
Telephone: (216) 241-4487, (800) 883-7935, FAX: (216) 241-5918, E-Mail: service@mailshipsolutions.com, Web Site: www.mailshipsolutions.com
CEO & Pres: James W. Johnson
Conducts Business: U.S.
Employees: 15
Primary Market Served: Business
Catalog available online
Direct online sales
Advertising/Marketing Budget Related to Direct Marketing: 26-50%
Direct Marketing ad budget:
Direct Mail: 50%
Online: 50%
Founded: 1941
Gross sales or billing: $2,000,000

Mailroom equipment & accessories, shipping supplies, postage meters, folders, inserters & bar code printers (postal discounts).

AUTOMOTIVE FORMS

Div. of Keary Advertising Company Inc
7215 Rolling Mill Rd
Baltimore, MD 21224-2033
Telephone: (410) 285-3700, FAX: (410) 284-8418, E-Mail: sales@autoforms.com, Web Site: www.autoforms.com
Owner: Wayne Keary
VP: Shari McLaughlin
Conducts Business: U.S.
Primary Market Served: Business
Catalog available online

Mail marketer of forms to new & used car dealers in the U.S. Also provide mailing lists.

AUTOMOTIVE HEADPHONES

44648 Mound Rd (# 161)
Sterling Heights, MI 48314-1322
Telephone: (586) 292-6166
Asst: Kim Jankowski
Primary Market Served: Business & Consumer

AVNET INC

2211 S 47th St
Phoenix, AZ 85034
Telephone: (480) 643-2000, FAX: (480) 643-7240, Web Site: www.avnet.com
Chmn & CEO: Roy Vallee
Pres, Avnet Electronics Mktg, Global: Harley Feldberg
Chief Commun Officer: Alan Maag
Employees: 11,800
Primary Market Served: Business
Catalog available online
Direct online sales
Founded: 1921
Gross sales or billing: $15,681,000,000

Distributors of semi-conductors, electromechanical components & production tools.

B&G LIEBERMAN CO INC
2420 Distribution St
Charlotte, NC 28203
Telephone: (704) 376-0717, (800) 438-0346, FAX: (800) 248-2696, E-Mail: bgl@bglieberman.com, Web Site: www.bglieberman.com
Pres: Gerald Lieberman
VP: Larry Lieberman
Conducts Business: U.S., Canada
Employees: 40
Founded: 1949

Sell tailoring supplies & equipment to department stores, clothiers, dry cleaners & tailors. Uniform rentals.

B BUNCH CO INC
9619 N 21st Dr
Phoenix, AZ 85021-1895
Telephone: (602) 997-6452, FAX: (602) 997-7266, E-Mail: sales@bbunch.com, Web Site: www.bbunch.com
COO: Ed Bunch
Primary Market Served: Business & Consumer
Founded: 1968

Pre & post paper equipment processing.

BFS CREDIT SERVICES CO
Div. of Bridgestone/Firestone Inc
6275 Eastland Rd
Brook Park, OH 44142-1301
Telephone: (216) 362-5094, FAX: (216) 362-5236, E-Mail: lupinettijim@bfsusa.com
Pres: L.A. Ehmke
Sls Promo Mgr: Jim Lupinetti
Conducts Business: U.S.
Primary Market Served: Consumer

Conduct the direct marketing sales of merchandise, credit offerings, clubs & services to account holder base & new account prospects.

BGE HOME PRODUCTS & SERVICES INC
1409 Tangiere Dr (Suite A)
Baltimore, MD 21220-2878
Telephone: (888) 243-4663, Web Site: www.bgehome.com
VP Mktg: Catherine M. Davenport
Primary Market Served: Business & Consumer

BMI HOME DECORATING
Div. of BMI Group Inc
6917 Catalpa Ct
Spring Grove, IL 60081
Telephone: (815) 675-3703, FAX: (815) 675-3703, E-Mail: bmigroup@aol.com
Owner: Betty Meyn
Owner: George Meyn
Conducts Business: U.S., Canada
Employees: 3
Primary Market Served: Business & Consumer
Advertising/Marketing Budget Related to Direct Marketing: 26-50%
Direct Marketing ad budget: $10,000
Magazines: 100%
Founded: 1978
Gross sales or billing: $150,000

Sell fabrics & wallpaper at discount prices.

BOC GASES
Div. of BOC Group
575 Mountain Ave
Murray Hill, NJ 07974
Telephone: (908) 464-8100, (800) 262-4273, FAX: (410) 749-4073, E-Mail: info@linde.com, Web Site: www.boc-gases.com
Mktg: Grace Mauro
Conducts Business: U.S.
Primary Market Served: Business & Consumer

Principal products sold through Welding Supply Distributors: oxygen, acetylene, nitrogen, argon, helium, hydrogen, carbon dioxide, MAPP, medical gases, special gases, food gases, cylinders & liquid cylinders.

BP
4101 Winfield Rd (Suite 100)
Warrenville, IL 60555-3522
Telephone: (630) 821-3000, (800) 638-5672, Web Site: www.bp.com
Employees: 11,000
Primary Market Served: Business & Consumer

Marketing, refining & transportation.

BYK-GARDNER USA
9104 Guilford Rd
Columbia, MD 21046-2677
Telephone: (310) 483-6500, Web Site: www.byk.com
VP & Gen Mgr: Michael Gogoel
Primary Market Served: Business & Consumer

BADGE-A-MINIT
345 N Lewis Ave
Oglesby, IL 61348-9776
Telephone: (815) 883-8822, (800) 223-4103, FAX: (815) 883-9696, Web Site: www.badgeaminit.com
Chmn Bd & Treas: Malcom Roebuck
Conducts Business: U.S.

Employees: 105
Primary Market Served: Business & Consumer
Catalog available online
Direct online sales
Advertising/Marketing Budget Related to Direct Marketing: 76-100%
Direct Marketing ad budget:
Magazines: 100%

Manufacturer of badge making equipment.

BAKER & TAYLOR INC
2550 W Tyvola Rd (#300)
Charlotte, NC 28217-4579
Telephone: (704) 998-3100, (800) 775-1800, FAX: (704) 998-3316, E-Mail: btinfo@btol.com, Web Site: www.btol.com
VP, Mktg: Conny Koury
Mktg Dir: Joanne Young
Chmn, Pres & CEO: Richard Wills
Exec VP & COO: Marshall A. Wright
Exec VP & CFO: James C. Melton
Conducts Business: Worldwide
Employees: 3,750
Primary Market Served: Business
Catalog available online
Direct online sales
Advertising/Marketing Budget Related to Direct Marketing: 26-50%
Founded: 1828
Gross sales or billing: $2,200,000,000

Distributor of books, video & music to retailers & libraries worldwide.

THE DMA BAKER CORP
3020 Old Ranch Pkwy (Suite 220)
Seal Beach, CA 90740-8805
Telephone: (562) 430-6262
Mktg Mgr: Lore McKenna

BALDUCCI ENTERPRISES INC
12920 Cloverleaf Center Dr (Suite B)
Germantown, MD 20874
Telephone: (240) 403-2440, FAX: (240) 403-2520
CEO: Barbara Parasco
Primary Market Served: Business & Consumer

Sell gourmet food.

BALDWIN FILTERS
A CLARCOR Co
4400 E Hwy 30
Kearney, NE 68848-6010
Telephone: (308) 234-1951, (800) 822-5394, FAX: (800) 828-4453, E-Mail: info@baldwinfilter.com, Web Site: www.baldwinfilter.com
Pres: Sam Ferrise
VP, Branded Sls: Jay Hussey
HR: Mike Sandgeroth

Sls: Julie Sheckler
Conducts Business: U.S., Europe, Australia, Mexico
Employees: 850
Primary Market Served: Business & Consumer
Catalog available online
Indirect online sales
Founded: 1936
Gross sales or billing: $100,000,000

Manufacturer of filters.

BALE CO
222 Public St
Providence, RI 02940
Telephone: (800) 822-5350, FAX: (401) 831-5500, Web Site: www. bale.com
Mktg Mgr: Jane Byrne
Conducts Business: U.S.
Primary Market Served: Business & Consumer
Catalog available online
Direct online sales
Advertising/Marketing Budget Related to Direct Marketing: 76-100%

Manufacturer of jewelry & award products - customized pins, trophy & plaque services. Also, honor awards for schools, hospitals, industry & government.

BALFOUR
Div. of Commemorative Brands Inc
PO Box 149107
Austin, TX 78714-9107
Telephone: (512) 444-0571, FAX: (512) 440-1138, Web Site: www. artcarved.com
Pres: Dave Fiore
VP, Mktg: Dennis Reed
Conducts Business: Worldwide
Employees: 1,000
Primary Market Served: Business & Consumer
Advertising/Marketing Budget Related to Direct Marketing: 0-25%
Founded: 1914

Markets sports accessories & jewelry to retailers & manufactures class rings.

BANKERS WARRANTY GROUP
11101 Roosevelt Blvd N
Saint Petersburg, FL 33716-2340
Telephone: (800) 431-5843, E-Mail: info@bankerswarrantygroup.com, Web Site: www. bankerswarrantygroup.com
CEO: Kevin Rupkey
Conducts Business: U.S, Canada, Caribbean
Employees: 300
Primary Market Served: Business

Advertising/Marketing Budget Related to Direct Marketing: 0-25%
Direct Marketing ad budget:
Direct Mail: 40%
Telephone: 60%
Founded: 1981

Extended warranties, telemarketing, parts distribution, product fulfillment.

BARNESANDNOBLE.COM
76 Ninth Ave (fl 9)
New York, NY 10011
Telephone: (212) 414-6000, (800) THE-BOOK, FAX: (212) 414-6140, E-Mail: service@barnesandnoble. com, Web Site: www. barnesandnoble.com
Chmn: Leonard S. Riggio
CEO: Marie J. Toulantis
VP & CFO: Kevin M. Frain
VP, Interactive Mktg: Andreas Schmidt
Conducts Business: Worldwide
Primary Market Served: Business & Consumer
Catalog available online
Direct online sales
Advertising/Marketing Budget Related to Direct Marketing: 76-100%
Gross sales or billing: $419,800,000

Mail order division of Barnes & Noble.

THE DMA BARTON-COTTON
3030 Waterview Ave (Suite 100)
Baltimore, MD 21230-3520
Telephone: (410) 247-4800, (800) 348-1102, FAX: (410) 536-0491, E-Mail: info@bartoncotton.com, Web Site: www.bartoncotton.com
CEO: Rob Dragonette
VP: Dawn Brelsford
Dir, Client Svcs: Rosemarie Carlyle
Primary Market Served: Business
Founded: 1928

Manufacture greeting cards.

BAUDVILLE INC
5380 52nd St SE
Grand Rapids, MI 49512-9702
Telephone: (616) 698-0889, (800) 728-0888, FAX: (616) 698-0554, E-Mail: service@baudville.com, Web Site: www.baudville.com
Pres: Debra Sikanas
CEO: Bill Darooge
Employees: 64
Primary Market Served: Business & Consumer
Founded: 1983
Gross sales or billing: $4,100,000

Computer software; specialty paper & accessories for award certificates & badges.

BAUSCH & LOMB INC
1 Bausch & Lomb Pl
Rochester, NY 14604-2701
Telephone: (585) 338-6000, (800) 344-8815, FAX: (585) 338-6007, Web Site: www.bausch.com
Chmn & CEO: Gerald M. Ostrov
Sr VP, Opers: Gerhard Bauer
VP, Pres, US Vision Care: Robert J. Moore
Dir Sls, Retinal Prods, US: Edward Kennedy
Corp VP Commun & Investor Rels: Barbara M. Kelley
Sr Mgr Publicity & Prof Mtgs: Tor Constantino
Employees: 13,000
Primary Market Served: Business & Consumer
Catalog available online
Founded: 2007
Gross sales or billing: $2,292,400,000

Healthcare & optic company.

BAY MANUFACTURING
Div. of Hemco Inc
PO Box 1250
Milan, OH 44846-1250
Telephone: (419) 499-4602, FAX: (419) 499-4603, Web Site: www. baymfg.com
Pres: M.J. McGuire
Adv Mgr: Cheryl Graziani
Sec & Treas: Deb McGuire
Conducts Business: Worldwide
Employees: 8
Primary Market Served: Business & Consumer
Catalog available online
Direct Marketing ad budget:
Magazines: 100%
Founded: 1939
Gross sales or billing: $300,000

Sell specialty boating accessories, outboard long shaft kits, swim platforms, outboard motor brackets & replacement skegs.

BAYER CORP CONSUMER CARE DIVISION
36 Columbia Rd
Morristown, NJ 07962
Telephone: (973) 254-5000, FAX: (973) 408-8215, Web Site: www. bayercare.com
VP, Mktg: Jay Kolpon
Gen Mgr: Gary Balkema
PR Mgr: Anne Coiley
Conducts Business: Worldwide
Primary Market Served: Business & Consumer

Diversified pharmaceutical company with worldwide operations. Manufacturer & marketer of prescription & over-the-counter medicines.

BAYLOR HEALTH CARE SYSTEM

2001 Bryan St (Suite 2300)
Dallas, TX 75201-3063
Telephone: (214) 820-4901, (800) 4Baylor, FAX: (214) 820-7499, Web Site: www.baylorhealth.com
Pres & CEO: Boone Powell Jr
VP Mktg: Steve Tatum
Creative Svcs Dir: Lauren Law
Dir, Health Svcs: Dana Choate
Employees: 13,000
Primary Market Served: Business & Consumer
Catalog available online
Advertising/Marketing Budget Related to Direct Marketing: 26-50%
Founded: 1903

Provide healthcare services.

BEACON SHOE CO INC

11 Worthington Access Dr Stop 1
Maryland Heights, MO 63043-3804
Telephone: (636) 488-5444, FAX: (636) 488-3103
Pres: Robert Tucker
Conducts Business: U.S.
Primary Market Served: Consumer

Warehouse of women's footwear.

BEAR COMPUTER SYSTEMS INC

PO Box 559001
Dallas, TX 75355
Telephone: (818) 509-0459, (800) 252-1691, FAX: (818) 769-3055, E-Mail: info@bearcom.com, Web Site: www.bearcom.com
Pres: Larry Robertson
Conducts Business: U.S., Canada, Europe, Asia
Employees: 10
Primary Market Served: Business
Catalog available online
Direct online sales
Advertising/Marketing Budget Related to Direct Marketing: 0-25%
Founded: 1982
Gross sales or billing: $1,000,000

Software & integrated print solutions.

BEAUTICONTROL COSMETICS INC

2121 Midway Rd
Carrollton, TX 75006-5039
Telephone: (972) 458-0601, (800) BEAUTI-1, FAX: (972) 458-6904, E-Mail: clientservices@beauticontrol.com, Web Site: www.beauticontrol.com
CEO & Co-Founder: Jinger L. Heath
Pres: Kristi Hubbard
COO & Exec VP: J. Robert Ward-Burns

Sr VP, Mktg: Jo-Anne C. Jaeger
Conducts Business: U.S., Canada, Taiwan, Hong Kong
Employees: 275
Primary Market Served: Consumer
Catalog available online
Indirect online sales
Founded: 1981
Gross sales or billing: $120,000,000

Direct sales cosmetics company.

BECKMAN COULTER INC

250 S Kraemer Blvd.
Brea, CA 92821-6232
Telephone: (714) 993-5321, (800) 526-3821, FAX: (800) 232-3828, Web Site: www.beckmancoulter.com
Pres & CEO: Scott Garrett
Pres: Tom Joyce
Conducts Business: Worldwide
Employees: 6,900
Primary Market Served: Business
Gross sales or billing: $857,000,000

Develops, manufactures & markets automated systems & supplies for life science research & clinical diagnostic laboratories which advance biological discovery & diagnosis of disease. Products include instruments, accessories, software & consumables for sample preparation, separation, detection, measurement & data handling.

BECKMANN CONVERTING INC

14 Park Dr, PO Box 390
Amsterdam, NY 12010-5340
Telephone: (518) 842-0073, FAX: (518) 842-0282, E-Mail: ppiusz@beckmannconverting.com, Web Site: www.beckmannconverting.com
CEO: Klaus Beckmann
VP Sls & Mktg: Scott Ayers
Gen Mgr: Peter Piusz
Conducts Business: Worldwide
Employees: 35
Primary Market Served: Business
Advertising/Marketing Budget Related to Direct Marketing: 76-100%
Founded: 2006
Gross sales or billing: $5,100,000

Contract ultrasonic & hot melt gravure laminating processes to manufacture precision laminates of non-woven films & fabrics.

BEEMAK PLASTICS INC

Subs of Jordan Industries Inc
16711 Knott Ave
La Mirada, CA 90638-6013
Telephone: (310) 886-5880, (800) 421-4393, FAX: (310) 764-0330, E-Mail: info@beemak.com, Web Site: www.beemak.com

Pres: Chris Braun
VP Mktg: Dwight Lewis
VP Sls: Julia Alty
Conducts Business: U.S., Canada
Employees: 100
Primary Market Served: Business
Catalog available online
Direct online sales
Founded: 1951
Gross sales or billing: $8,200,000

Manufacturer of plastic holders & racks to display brochures, pamphlets, books, magazines, forms or "take one" purposes. Custom injection molding, acrylic fabrication & in-house imprinting & fulfillment services. We also produce all of our holders in almost any PMS color.

BEHLEN MANUFACTURING CO

4025 E 23rd St
Columbus, NE 68601-3448
Telephone: (402) 564-3111, FAX: (402) 563-7405, E-Mail: behlen@megavision.com, Web Site: www.behlenmfg.com
Chmn & CEO: Tony F. Raimondo
VP, Sls: John Bowes
Gen Mgr: John Underwood
Conducts Business: U.S.
Employees: 800
Primary Market Served: Business
Founded: 1936
Gross sales or billing: $68,000,000

Pre-engineered metal buildings, grain bins & agriculturally related products, animal confinement & livestock equipment.

BELK STORES SERVICES INC

Div. of Belk Inc.
2801 W Tyvola Rd
Charlotte, NC 28217-4500
Telephone: (704) 357-1000, FAX: (704) 357-1782, Web Site: www.belk.com
Chmn: John M. Belk
Pres, Mktg: H. McKay Belk
Primary Market Served: Consumer
Catalog available online
Direct online sales
Advertising/Marketing Budget Related to Direct Marketing: 0-25%

Retail.

BERMAN GROUP

18 Tarleton Rd
Newton Center, MA 02459-1733
Telephone: (617) 426-0870, FAX: (617) 719-1505, E-Mail: rob@bermanusa.com, Web Site: www.bermanusa.com
Pres: Robert S. Berman

Conducts Business: Worldwide
Employees: 10
Primary Market Served: Business
Advertising/Marketing Budget Related
    to Direct Marketing: 76-100%
Founded: 1905
Gross sales or billing: $5,000,000

Manufacturer of genuine leather wallets, diaries & notebooks for stationery, luggage & promotional product gift trades. Manufacture & distribute Encore(REG) tools for leathercrafting (tools, kits, hardware, books, supplies). Also, importer & wholesaler of belt buckles & garment leather hides.

BIC CORP
1 BIC Way (Suite 1)
Shelton, CT 06484-6223
Telephone: (203) 783-2000, FAX:
    (203) 783-2081, Web Site: www.
    bicworld.com
Pres: Mario Guevara
Global Brand Design Mgr: Daniel Dittmar
Conducts Business: Worldwide
Employees: 1,500
Primary Market Served: Business &
    Consumer
Gross sales or billing: $300,000,000

Manufacturer of disposable lighters, shavers, writing instruments & White Out.

BIJOUX TERNER
6950 NW 77th Ct
Miami, FL 33126-2714
Telephone: (305) 500-7500, (800) 262-3614, FAX: (305) 262-9286, E-Mail:
    customerservice@bijouxterner.com,
    Web Site: www.bijouxterner.com
Pres & CEO: Moni Terner
VP: Rosa Terner
Conducts Business: Worldwide
Employees: 250
Primary Market Served: Business &
    Consumer

Sell high fashion custom jewelry.

THE BIL-RAY ALUMINUM SIDING CORP OF QUEENS INC
The Bil-Ray Group
102 Jericho Tpke
New Hyde Park, NY 11040-4507
Telephone: (516) 616-4200, (800) 474-4415, FAX: (516) 616-4030, Web
    Site: www.homeclub.com
Chmn: Ferdinando L. Assinin
CEO: Charles G. Le Poin
Mktg Dir: Robert Silverman
Mktg Mgr: Tom Langon
Employees: 32
Primary Market Served: Consumer

Founded: 1949

General home improvement contractors.

BIOSCIENCES-AMERSHAM
Subs. of GE Healthcare
800 Centennial Ave, PO Box 1327
Piscataway, NJ 08855-1327
Telephone: (732) 457-8000, FAX:
    (732) 457-0557, Web Site: www.
    amersham.com
CEO & Sr VP: Joe Hogan
Exec VP & CIO: Russel P. Mayer
Exec VP & CFO: Kathryn McCarthy
CTO: Michael J. Barber
Gen Mgr, Opers: Raphael Strosin
Primary Market Served: Business
Catalog available online

Sell labeling detection & analysis of biological molecules for the life science research community.

BLACK & DECKER (US) INC
701 E Joppa Rd
Towson, MD 21286-5559
Telephone: (410) 239-5000, (800) 544-6986, FAX: (410) 239-5227, Web
    Site: www.blackanddecker.com
Pres & CEO: Nolan Archibald
Conducts Business: U.S.
Employees: 25,500
Primary Market Served: Business &
    Consumer
Founded: 1910

Manufacturer of power tool accessories & replacement service parts for all Black & Decker household products.

BLACK ENTERTAINMENT TELEVISION INC
1900 "W" Pl NE
Washington, DC 20018-1211
Telephone: (202) 608-2000/2006, (800)
    766-0053, FAX: (202) 608-2599,
    Web Site: www.bet.com
Sr VP, Corp Mktg & Communs: Kelli
    Richardson
VP, Adv & Res Dir: Cheryl Holmes
Conducts Business: U.S.
Employees: 100
Primary Market Served: Business &
    Consumer

Producer of music videos, black college sports, news & family entertainment.

BLANCHARD & CO INC
909 Poydras St (Suite 1900)
New Orleans, LA 70112
Telephone: (504) 837-3010, (800) 880-4653, FAX: (504) 837-4884, Web
    Site: www.blanchardonline.com
CEO: Donald W. Doyle Jr.
COO: Michael McGoey

CFO: Debra L. Cash
Sr VP Sls: L. Craig Baudot
Conducts Business: Worldwide
Employees: 85
Primary Market Served: Consumer
Catalog available online
Direct online sales
Advertising/Marketing Budget Related
    to Direct Marketing: 51-75%
Direct Marketing ad budget:
Direct Mail: 25%
Magazines: 25%
Newspapers: 40%
TV/Radio: 10%
Founded: 1975

Market rare U.S. coins & precious metals to investors & collectors.

DICK BLICK HOLDINGS INC
Subs. of Dick Blick Co
PO Box 1267
Galesburg, IL 61402-1267
Telephone: (309) 343-6181, FAX:
    (309) 343-5785, E-Mail: admin@
    dickblick.com, Web Site: www.
    dickblick.com
Pres, CEO: Bob Buchsbaum
Conducts Business: Worldwide
Employees: 550
Primary Market Served: Business &
    Consumer
Catalog available online
Direct online sales
Founded: 1911

Sells art & educational materials to schools, hospitals & individual consumers & "handy helpers" for the home, yard & garden. Branch in Emmaus, PA.

BLOOMINGDALE'S DIRECT
aka Bloomingdale's by Mail Ltd
1000 Third Ave (fl 11)
New York, NY 10022
Telephone: (212) 705-2000, (866) 593-2540, FAX: (212) 705-2805, Web
    Site: www.bloomingdales.com
Chmn Bd: Michael Gould
Pres: Franz Weiglein
Sr VP Mktg: Lisa Gavales
Employees: 381
Primary Market Served: Consumer
Founded: 2001
Gross sales or billing: $64,700,000

Catalog & mail order houses for apparel, accessories, gifts, cosmetics, housewares & more.

BLUE CORAL SLICK 50
Div. of Shell Oil Products US
    (SOPUS)
910 Louisiana St, One Shell Plaza
Houston, TX 77002-4916

Telephone: (713) 241-6161, (800) 416-1600, FAX: (713) 241-4044, E-Mail: SCD-ConsumerSolutions@Shell.com, Web Site: www.bluecoral.com
VP Shell Lubricants: Doug Boyle
PR: Deborah Breazeale
Corp Affairs: Nino Polomo
Sponsorship & Events: Victoria Moreno
Primary Market Served: Business & Consumer
Founded: 1927

Manufacturer of oil additive designed to reduce engine wear and other car care products. Slick 50 engine & fuel treatments & Blue Coral car wash.

BLUESTEM BRANDS
6509 Flying Cloud Dr
Eden Prairie, MN 55344-3307
Telephone: (952) 656-3700, Web Site: www.fingerhut.com
VP, New Customer Acq Mktg: Jennifer Kemp
Primary Market Served: Business & Consumer

BLUEWATER YACHTS
811 E Maple
Mora, MN 55051-1224
Telephone: (320) 679-3811, FAX: (320) 679-3820, E-Mail: bluewater@ncis.com, Web Site: www.bluewateryacht.com
Pres & Owner: Steve Klapmeier
Owner: Jolie Klapmeier
Mktg Dir: Kari Boster
Conducts Business: U.S., Canada, Europe, Asia, S. America
Employees: 60
Primary Market Served: Consumer
Indirect online sales
Founded: 1954

Custom luxury yachts.

BOBCAT CO
Div. of Ingersoll-Rand
250 E Beaton Dr
West Fargo, ND 58078
Telephone: (701) 241-8700, FAX: (701) 241-8704, Web Site: www.bobcat.com
Pres: Richard F. Pedtke
Pres, Bobcat: David Rowles
Pres, Europe: Scott R. Nelson
VP, Global Opers: Dennis Schneider
Conducts Business: Worldwide
Employees: 1,800
Primary Market Served: Business & Consumer
Catalog available online
Indirect online sales
Advertising/Marketing Budget Related to Direct Marketing: 0-25%
Founded: 1947

Manufacturer of BOBCAT loaders & excavators.

BODY BY JAKE GLOBAL LLC
11611 San Vicente Blvd Ste 610
Los Angeles, CA 90049-6506
Telephone: (310) 571-7101, FAX: (310) 571-7107, E-Mail: info@bodybyjake.com, Web Site: www.bodybyjake.com
Pres: Phil Scotti
CFO: Kevin Gallagher
Employees: 10
Primary Market Served: Business
Catalog available online
Direct online sales
Gross sales or billing: $1,100,000

Production, marketing & licensing.

BOEING CO
100 N Riverside
Chicago, IL 60606
Telephone: (312) 544-2000, FAX: (312) 544-2082, Web Site: www.boeing.com
Chmn, Pres & CEO: W. James McNerney Jr.
Exec VP & CFO: James A. Bell
Exec VP, Pres & CEO, Integrated Defense Sys: James F. Albaugh
Dir: John H. Biggs
Dir: John E. Bryson
Primary Market Served: Business
Catalog available online

Aerospace industry.

BOISE CASCADE HOLDINGS LLC
1111 W Jefferson St (Suite 300)
Boise, ID 83702-5389
Telephone: (208) 384-6451, FAX: (208) 384-7189, E-Mail: mediarelations@bc.com, Web Site: www.bc.com
Chmn & CEO: William Thomas Stephens
Sr VP & CFO: Thomas E. Carlile
VP, HR & Commun: John Sahlberg
Conducts Business: U.S., U.K., Australia, Canada, Mexico, New Zealand
Employees: 10,191
Primary Market Served: Business
Catalog available online
Direct online sales
Founded: 1957
Gross sales or billing: $5,780,000,000

Delivers office, building and paper solutions.

BOLIND INC
PO Box 18714
Boulder, CO 80308-1714

Telephone: (303) 443-3142, FAX: (303) 443-9889, Web Site: www.bolind.com
Pres: Katherine Lukoskie
VP: Bruce F. Lindeke
Conducts Business: U.S.
Employees: 25
Primary Market Served: Business & Consumer
Catalog available online
Direct online sales
Advertising/Marketing Budget Related to Direct Marketing: 76-100%
Founded: 1956

Stationery & return address label manufacturer selling to distributors & the consumer. Also produce a gift catalog.

BONTEX
1207 Hunakai St
Honolulu, HI 96816-4614
Telephone: (540) 261-2181, FAX: (540) 261-3784, E-Mail: bontex@bontex.com, Web Site: www.bontex.com
Pres: J.C. Kostelni
VP: Charles Kostelini
Sls Dir: Larry Morris
Conducts Business: Worldwide
Employees: 250
Primary Market Served: Business
Catalog available online
Indirect online sales
Direct Marketing ad budget: $100,000
Direct Mail: 10%
Magazines: 10%
Newspapers: 10%
TV/Radio: 70%
Gross sales or billing: $45,000,000

Producers of bontex wet web elastomeric impregnated fiberboard/nonwovens.

BOUNDLESS CORP
1916 State Route 96
Phelps, NY 14532-9705
Telephone: (631) 962-1500, (800) 231-5445, FAX: (631) 962-1505, E-Mail: sales@boundless.com, Web Site: www.boundless.com
Chmn & CEO: Xitian Wang
CFO: Xiangi Cheng
VP & Dir: Yuangie Jin
VP: Delong Song
Direct Mail Mgr: Jim Catalano
Conducts Business: U.S.
Employees: 300
Primary Market Served: Business & Consumer
Catalog available online
Advertising/Marketing Budget Related to Direct Marketing: 51-75%
Founded: 1969
Gross sales or billing: $6,000,000

Manufacturer of display terminals from text to multiconsole all the way to X, which now includes network computers.

BOWERS & MERENA AUCTIONS

18061 Fitch
Irvine, CA 92614-6018
Telephone: (949) 253-0916, (800) 458-4646, FAX: (949) 253-4091, E-Mail: auction@bowersandmerena.com, Web Site: www.bowersandmerena.com
Pres: Stephen Deeds
Dir: Jeff Ambio
Dir: Debbie McDonald
Adv Dir: Chris Karstedt
Primary Market Served: Business & Consumer
Founded: 1953

Auction house.

BOYD GAMING CORP

3883 Howard Hughes Pkwy (fl 9)
Las Vegas, NV 89169
Telephone: (702) 792-7200, FAX: (702) 792-7313, Web Site: www.boydgaming.com
Pres & CEO: Keith E. Smith
VP Mktg: Dan Stark
Media Contact: Rob Stillwell
Employees: 18,300
Primary Market Served: Business & Consumer
Gross sales or billing: $2,278,000,000

Resort & casino operator in Las Vegas, Florida, Indiana, Illinois, Louisiana, and Mississippi.

THE BRADFORD GROUP

9333 N Milwaukee Ave
Niles, IL 60714-1303
Telephone: (847) 966-2770, FAX: (847) 581-8630, Web Site: www.collectiblestoday.com
Pres & CEO: Rich Tinberg
Sr VP & Gen Mgr: Shay Gallagher
VP, Opers: Robert Del Cielo
VP, Legal: Joel Platt
Mktg Svcs Dir: Karen Cox
Mgr: Allison Fox
Conducts Business: Worldwide
Primary Market Served: Business & Consumer
Catalog available online
Direct online sales
Founded: 1973

Exchange trading, buying & selling of collector's plates. Offers of recommended plates are made periodically.

BRADFORD HEALTH SERVICES

2101 Magnolia Ave S (Suite 518)
Birmingham, AL 35205-2853
Telephone: (205) 251-7753, (800) 217-2849, Web Site: www.bradfordhealth.com
Pres & CEO: Jerry Crowder
Chief Privacy Officer: Rogen D. Cain
Conducts Business: U.S.
Employees: 350
Primary Market Served: Business & Consumer
Catalog available online
Advertising/Marketing Budget Related to Direct Marketing: 76-100%
Direct Marketing ad budget:
Direct Mail: $50,000
Magazines: $20,000
Newspapers: $20,000
TV/Radio: $400,000
Telephone: $25,000
Gross sales or billing: $20,000,000

Dedicated to making recovery from alcohol & other chemical dependencies available to the general public.

BRADY CORP

W H Brady Co
6555 W Good Hope Rd
Milwaukee, WI 53223
Telephone: (414) 358-6600, (800) 541-1686, FAX: (800) 292-2289, Web Site: www.bradycorp.com
Pres & CEO: Frank M. Jaehnert
Pres, Brady Americas: Matt O. Williamson
Pres, Direct Mktg Americas: Tom Felmer
Sr VP & CEO: David Mathieson
Sr VP, HR: Michael O. Oliver
Conducts Business: Worldwide
Employees: 8,000
Primary Market Served: Business
Catalog available online
Indirect online sales
Founded: 1914
Gross sales or billing: $1,300,000,000

Manufacturer of industrial identification products for electronic, electrical, telecommunications & automotive markets.

BRADY MARKETING CO INC

1331 N California Blvd (Suite 320)
Walnut Creek, CA 94596-4563
Telephone: (925) 676-1300, (800) 326-6080, FAX: (925) 676-3082, E-Mail: info@bradymarketing.com, Web Site: www.bradymarketing.com
Pres: Frank Brady
VP, Fin: Lorraine Brady
Conducts Business: U.S.
Employees: 25

Primary Market Served: Business & Consumer

Supply consumers with replacement coffee carafes, shaver parts, food processor parts & accessories.

BRAHMIN LEATHER WORKS

77 Alden Rd
Fairhaven, MA 02719
Telephone: (508) 994-4000, (800) 229-2428, FAX: (508) 994-4153, Web Site: www.brahminusa.com
Pres: William R. Martin
VP: Joan Martin
Acct Sls Exec: David Patton
Primary Market Served: Business & Consumer
Catalog available online
Direct online sales

Manufacture men's & women's high end hand bags & leather accessories.

BRIDGESTONE/FIRESTONE NORTH AMERICAN TIRE LLC

Div. of Bridgestone/Firestone Inc
535 Marriott Dr
Nashville, TN 37214-5092
Telephone: (615) 937-1000, (800) 543-7522, FAX: (615) 937-3721, Web Site: www.bridgestonetire.com
CEO, BFNT: Mark Emkes
Pres, BSLA & Exec VP, BSAM: Eduardo Minardi
Chmn, CEO & Pres, BSRO: Larry Magee
Chmn, CEO & Pres BATO: Asahiko Nishiyama
Pres, BBTS: Saul Solomon
Chmn, CEO & Pres, FSDP: Kenneth Weaver
Vice Chmn, BSAM & Exec VP, BATO: Narumi Zaitsu
Pres, US & Canada Consumer Tire Sls Div: Michael K. Gorey
Primary Market Served: Business & Consumer

Manufacture & distribute tires as well as other rubber products.

BRISTOL-MYERS SQUIBB CO

345 Park Ave
New York, NY 10154-0037
Telephone: (212) 546-4000, FAX: (212) 546-9544, Web Site: www.bms.com
CEO: James M. Cornelieus
Dir: James D. Robinson
Exec VP, COO Worldwide Pharmaceuticals: Lamberto Andreotti
Sr VP HR: Stephen E. Bear
Pres Healthcare Grp: John E. Celentano
Conducts Business: Worldwide

Employees: 43,000
Primary Market Served: Business
Catalog available online
Gross sales or billing: $18,000,000,000

A diversified company whose principle businesses are pharmaceuticals, consumer products, nutritional & medical devices.

BROADVISION INC
1600 Seaport Blvd (Suite 550)
Redwood City, CA 94063-5589
Telephone: (650) 542-5100, FAX:
(650) 364-3425, E-Mail: sales@
broadvision.com, Web Site: www.
broadvision.com
Pres & CEO: Dr. Pehong Chen
Chief of Staff: Shin-Yuan Tzou
VP Worldwide Opers: Dr. Albert Chen
Sr VP Engrng & Tech Support: David
Boyer
Gen Mgr: Andrea Rubei
Primary Market Served: Business &
Consumer
Catalog available online
Indirect online sales
Founded: 1993

Offer a comprehensive application system optimized for enabling global Fortune 1000 companies to establish direct consumer connection & obtain higher profit margin through dynamically marketing & selling goods & services online on a personalized one-to-one basis.

BROCADE COMMUNICATIONS SYSTEMS INC
Subs. of EMC Corp
1745 Technology Dr
San Jose, CA 95110
Telephone: (408) 333-4300, FAX:
(408) 333-8101, Web Site: www.
brocade.com
Chmn: Dave House
CEO: Michael Klayko
VP & Gen Mgr: Don Jaworski
VP & Gen Mgr: Luc Moyen
Sr VP Worldwide Sls: Ian Whiting
Primary Market Served: Business
Catalog available online
Advertising/Marketing Budget Related
to Direct Marketing: 0-25%

Design, manufacture & market network communication systems. Supplier of information switching products.

BROOKFIELD PROPERTIES
181 Bay St (Suite 330), Brookfield
Place
Toronto, ON, Canada M5J 2T3
Telephone: (416) 369-2300, FAX:
(416) 369-2301, Web Site: www.
brokfieldproperties.com
Pres & CEO: Ric Clark
Pres & COO Canadian Comml Opers:
Tom Farley
Pres & COO, US Comml Opers: Dennis Friedrich
VP Investor Rels & Communs: Melissa Coley
Employees: 2,014
Primary Market Served: Business
Gross sales or billing: $1,028,000,000

Commercial & real estate.

BROOKS SPORTS INC
Subs. of Resource Group International
19910 N Creek Pkwy (#200)
Bothell, WA 98011-8223
Telephone: (425) 402-1632, (800) 2
BROOKS, FAX: (425) 489-1975,
Web Site: www.brooksrunning.com
Pres, CEO & Dir: James M. Weber
VP Apparel Sls: Parker Karnan
VP Mktg: Dave Larson
Conducts Business: Worldwide
Employees: 150
Primary Market Served: Business
Catalog available online
Direct online sales
Advertising/Marketing Budget Related
to Direct Marketing: 0-25%
Founded: 1914
Gross sales or billing: $21,000,000

Manufacturer & marketer of technical athletic footwear, apparel & accessories.

BROWN-FORMAN BEVERAGES WORLDWIDE
Subs. of Brown-Forman Corp
850 Dixie Hwy
Louisville, KY 40210
Telephone: (502) 585-1100, FAX:
(502) 774-7185, E-Mail: Brown-
Forman@b-f.com, Web Site: www.
brown-forman.com
DM Mgr: Gail Koach
Conducts Business: U.S.
Employees: 1,100
Primary Market Served: Business &
Consumer
Advertising/Marketing Budget Related
to Direct Marketing: 0-25%

Producer & marketer of liquor & wine.

BROWN-FORMAN CORP
850 Dixie Hwy
Louisville, KY 40210
Telephone: (502) 585-1100, FAX:
(502) 774-7876, E-Mail: brown-
forman@b-f.com, Web Site: www.
brown-forman.com
Chmn & CEO: Owsley Brown II
Corp Commun Dir: Philip Lynch
Conducts Business: Worldwide
Employees: 3,750
Primary Market Served: Consumer
Indirect online sales
Founded: 1870
Gross sales or billing: $2,218,000

Produce & market consumer products.

BROWN SHOE CO
Div. of Brown Group
8300 Maryland Ave, PO Box 29
Saint Louis, MO 63105-3645
Telephone: (314) 854-4000, FAX:
(314) 854-4274, Web Site: www.
brownshoe.com
Chmn Bd & CEO: Ronald Fromm
Pres & COO: Diane M. Sullivan
Pres, NY Div: Richard M. Ausick
Sr VP & CFO: Mark E. Hood
Sr VP: Douglas Koch
Primary Market Served: Business
Catalog available online
Indirect online sales

Marketer of women's, men's & children's brand name footwear.

TONY BROWN PRODUCTIONS
2214 Frederick Douglass Blvd (Suite
124)
New York, NY 10026
Telephone: (718) 264-2226, FAX:
(718) 264-1914, E-Mail: mail@tbol.
net, Web Site: www.tonybrown.com
Pres: Tony Brown
Mktg Dir: Jim Cannaday
Primary Market Served: Consumer

Sell video cassettes to public.

BUCKS COUNTY COFFEE CO
Div. of Bucks County Nut & Coffee
Co
960 Brook Rd Ste 1
Conshohocken, PA 19428-1100
Telephone: (215) 741-1855, (800) 523-
6163, FAX: (215) 741-1799, Web
Site: www.buckscountycoffee.com
Pres: Rodger R. Owen
VP, Retail Opers: Kathy Owen
VP, Admin: Debby Prentice
Pur Mgr: Chris Vaccarella
Conducts Business: U.S., Canada, Europe
Employees: 300
Primary Market Served: Business &
Consumer
Advertising/Marketing Budget Related
to Direct Marketing: 51-75%
Direct Marketing ad budget:
Direct Mail: 85%
Magazines: 15%
Founded: 1981

Food company specializing in gourmet foods shipped throughout the U.S. & Canada. Company prepares its own fancy nutmeats, gourmet coffee, popcorn & bakery products.

BUENA VISTA WINERY

18000 Old Winery Rd
Sonoma, CA 95476
Telephone: (707) 252-7117, (800) 678-8504, FAX: (707) 252-0392, Web Site: www.buenavistawinery.com
Pres, Boisset Family Estates: Jean-Charles Boisset
Conducts Business: Worldwide
Employees: 75
Primary Market Served: Business & Consumer
Catalog available online

BUICK DIVISION GENERAL MOTORS CORP

300 Renaissance Center
Detroit, MI 48265-3000
Telephone: (313) 556-5000, (800) 521-7300, FAX: (313) 556-5108, Web Site: www.buick.com
Chmn & CEO: G. Richard Wagner Jr.
Vice-Chmn & CFO: Frederick A. Henderson
Vice-Chmn: Robert A. Lutz
VP & CIO: Ralph J. Szygenda
Advisor: Stephen J. Girsky
Employees: 280,000
Primary Market Served: Business & Consumer
Catalog available online
Indirect online sales

Automotive manufacturer.

BULL HN INFORMATION SYSTEMS

285 Billerica Rd (Suite 200)
Chelmsford, MA 01824-4174
Telephone: (978) 294-6000, FAX: (978) 294-7999, Web Site: www.bull.com/us
Dir Commun: Steve Puleo
Conducts Business: Worldwide
Employees: 7,178
Primary Market Served: Business

BUNN-O-MATIC CORP

1400 Stevenson Dr
Springfield, IL 62703-4291
Telephone: (217) 529-6601, FAX: (217) 529-6622, E-Mail: bunn@bunn.com, Web Site: www.bunn.com
CFO: Gene Wilkin
VP: Bill Taylor
Mktg Mgr: Lisa McCloud
Conducts Business: Worldwide
Primary Market Served: Business & Consumer
Catalog available online

Advertising/Marketing Budget Related to Direct Marketing: 0-25%
Direct Marketing ad budget:
Direct Mail: 100%
Founded: 1958

Manufactures coffee brewers, coffee grinders, iced tea brewers, hot water machines, coffee filters, coffee warmers, coffee decanters, water conditioning systems, espresso coffee brewers & espresso coffee grinders.

BUNZL DISTRIBUTION USA, INC

aka BUNZL
1 Cityplace Dr Ste 200
Saint Louis, MO 63141-7067
Telephone: (314) 997-5959, (888) 997-5959, FAX: (314) 997-1405, Web Site: www.bunzldistribution.com
Pres: Patrick Larmon
Sr VP Strategic Devel: Terry Frank
Dir Comp Svcs & ECommerce: John Pestka
VP Strategic Vendor Devel: Dave Fisher
Conducts Business: U.S.
Employees: 3,625
Primary Market Served: Business
Gross sales or billing: $946,100,000

Supplies a range of products including outsourced food packaging, disposable supplies, and cleaning and safety products to food processors, supermarkets, retailers, convenience stores and other users. Bunzl Distribution is the largest division of Bunzl plc, an international distribution and outsourcing group headquartered in London.

BURLINGTON COAT FACTORY

1830 Rte 130
Burlington, NJ 08016
Telephone: (609) 387-7800, FAX: (609) 387-7071, Web Site: www.coat.com
Pres: Mark Mesci
VP: Windy Siskind
Mktg Dir: Gary Graham
Primary Market Served: Consumer

Retail warehouse.

BURLINGTON INDUSTRIES INC

804 Green Valley Rd (Suite 300)
Greensboro, NC 27408-7039
Telephone: (336) 379-2000, FAX: (336) 379-2498, Web Site: www.burlington.com
Pres & COO: George Henderson
CEO: William A. Klopman
Primary Market Served: Business & Consumer

Textile manufacturing company.

BURLINGTON NORTHERN & SANTA FE RAILROAD

2650 Lou Menk Dr
Fort Worth, TX 76131-2830
Telephone: (817) 878-2000, (800) 795-2673, FAX: (817) 333-7593, Web Site: www.bnsf.com
Chmn, Pres & CEO: Matthew K. Rose
Dir: Alan L. Boeckmann
Exec VP & CFO: Thomas N. Hund
Exec VP & COO: Carl R. Ice
Exec VP, Law: Roger Nober
Conducts Business: U.S.
Primary Market Served: Business
Catalog available online

BURNS INC

350 Mariano S Bishop Blvd
Fall River, MA 02721-2365
Telephone: (508) 675-0381, (800) 341-2200, FAX: (508) 677-1300, Web Site: www.burnstools.com
Chmn Bd: John M. Burns Sr.
VP, Treas & Co-Owner: Jeffery M. Burns
Conducts Business: U.S.
Employees: 30
Primary Market Served: Business & Consumer
Catalog available online
Direct online sales
Advertising/Marketing Budget Related to Direct Marketing: 26-50%
Founded: 1934

Marketer of industrial power tools.

BUSHNELL OUTDOOR PRODUCTS

9200 Cody
Overland Park, KS 66214-1734
Telephone: (913) 752-3400, (800) 423-3537, FAX: (913) 752-3550, Web Site: www.bushnell.com
Pres: Joe Messner
CFO: Dave Broadbent
Media Rels: Jen Messelt
Conducts Business: Worldwide
Primary Market Served: Business
Catalog available online
Indirect online sales

Optical products: binoculars, telescopes, spotting scopes, rifle scopes, sunglass, laser range finders, speed guns, digital navigation, night vision, helmets and goggles.

BUSINESS AUTOMATION SYSTEMS INC

6949 Charlotte Pike Ste 106
Nashville, TN 37209-4200

Telephone: (615) 329-4585, FAX: (615) 320-0206, Web Site: www.bas-solutions.com
Pres: Raymond E. Ingram
Office Mgr: Ardith Ingram
Proj Mgr: Pamela Blackall
Conducts Business: U.S.
Employees: 13
Primary Market Served: Business & Consumer
Founded: 1985

Computer support services.

BUSINESS GRAPHICS INC

955 Dieckman
Woodstock, IL 60098-9262
Telephone: (815) 338-8222, (800) 435-4874, FAX: (815) 338-2652, E-Mail: busgraph@mc.net, Web Site: www.businessgraphics.com
Pres: Luke Johnsos
Sec & Treas: Judith Johnsos
Conducts Business: U.S.
Employees: 4
Primary Market Served: Business
Catalog available online
Direct online sales
Advertising/Marketing Budget Related to Direct Marketing: 51-75%
Direct Marketing ad budget:
Direct Mail: $50,000
Founded: 1981
Gross sales or billing: $1,000,000

Sells printed products to the business community, restaurants, hotels & hospitals.

BUSINESSONLINE

701 B St (Suite 1000)
San Diego, CA 92101-8109
Telephone: (619) 699-0767, Web Site: www.businessol.com
CEO: Thad Kahlow

BUTLER SCHEIN ANIMAL HEALTH

400 Metro Pl N Ste 100
Dublin, OH 43017-3340
Telephone: (614) 761-9095, (888) 691-2724, FAX: (888) 329-3861, Web Site: www.butlerschein.com
Chmn, Pres & CEO: Kevin Vasquez
VP Mktg & Sls Svs: Davey L. Stone
Reg Mgr: Mike Stone
Pres Comml Div: Kim Allen
VP Bus Devel: Ben Coe
Natl Dir Equine Sls Devel: Jeannie Jeffery
Reg Mgr: Bob Anderson
Reg Mgr: Dawn Burdette
Reg Mgr: Mike Powers
Conducts Business: U.S., Worldwide
Primary Market Served: Business
Catalog available online

Veterinarian supplies & drugs.

BUTLER SPECIALTY CO

8200 S Chicago Ave
Chicago, IL 60617-1804
Telephone: (773) 221-1200, (800) 799-2857, FAX: (773) 221-5892, Web Site: www.butlerspecialty.net
Chmn: Burton Bergman
Vice Chmn: Burt Fainman
Pres: David Bergman
Conducts Business: Worldwide
Employees: 25
Primary Market Served: Business
Catalog available online
Advertising/Marketing Budget Related to Direct Marketing: 0-25%
Founded: 1930

Manufacturer of accent furniture, lamps, wall curios, globes, consoles & benches.

H E BUTT GROCERY CO

646 S Main
San Antonio, TX 78204-1210
Telephone: (210) 938-8357, (800) 432-3113, FAX: (210) 938-7511, Web Site: www.heb.com
Mktg Dir: Janell Neal
Commun Coord: Miguel Carranza
Conducts Business: U.S.
Employees: 35,000
Primary Market Served: Consumer
Founded: 1905

Full-service grocery store chain throughout Texas.

CA INC

1 Ca Plz Ste 100
Islandia, NY 11749-5303
Telephone: (800) 225-5224, FAX: (631) 342-3300, E-Mail: info@ca.com, Web Site: www.ca.com
Pres & CEO: John A. Swainson
EVP, Gen Mgr Worldwide Sls: George Fischer
EVP, Chief Mktg Officer: Donald R. Friedman
Conducts Business: Worldwide
Employees: 14,500
Primary Market Served: Business
Founded: 1976
Gross sales or billing: $3,943,000,000

Develops, licenses & supports more than 500 integrated products that include enterprise computing & information management, application development, manufacturing & financial applications.

CBT DIRECT

905 E Martin Luther King Jr Dr Ste 500
Tarpon Springs, FL 34689-4830

Telephone: (727) 724-8994, (877) 872-4646, FAX: (727) 797-9143, Web Site: www.cbtdirect.com
Pres: Frank Coleman
VP, Mktg: Jamie Sene
VP, Opers: Kim Cardinale
Sr Training Advisor: Robert Roy
Conducts Business: Worldwide
Employees: 250
Primary Market Served: Business & Consumer
Advertising/Marketing Budget Related to Direct Marketing: 0-25%
Founded: 1991
Gross sales or billing: $51,000,000

Online and computer-based training for the IT industry.

CCA GLOBAL PARTNERS

670 N Commercial St
Manchester, NH 03101-1160
Telephone: (603) 626-0333, Web Site: www.ccaglobal.com
VP Mktg: Terri Daniels
Primary Market Served: Business & Consumer

CCC OF AMERICA

102 Decker Ct (Suite 204)
Irving, TX 75062
Telephone: (214) 206-3130, (800) 935-2222, FAX: (214) 206-3134, Web Site: www.cccofamerica.com
Editor: Gabe Huck
Catalog available online
Direct online sales
Founded: 1983

Manufacturer of children's animated videos.

CCI SOLUTIONS

1342 88th Ave SE, PO Box 481
Olympia, WA 98507-0481
Telephone: (360) 943-5378, (800) 426-8664, FAX: (360) 754-1566, (800) 339-TAPE, E-Mail: info@ccisolutions.com, Web Site: www.ccisolutions.com
Pres: Bob Schmidt
CEO: Denny Bradley
Sls & Adv Mgr: Jerry Lamb
Conducts Business: U.S., Canada
Employees: 47
Primary Market Served: Business & Consumer
Advertising/Marketing Budget Related to Direct Marketing: 76-100%
Direct Marketing ad budget: $100,000
Direct Mail: 80%
Magazines: 20%
Founded: 1976
Gross sales or billing: $8,000,000

Audio cassette tape supply, sound reinforcement equipment, audio/visual equipment.

CD UNIVERSE
101 N Plains Ind Rd
Wallingford, CT 06492-2165
Telephone: (203) 294-1648, Web Site:
www.cduniverse.com

CDMO INC
40 Burt Dr Ste 5, PO Box 765
Deer Park, NY 11729-5743
Telephone: (631) 242-8820, FAX:
(631) 242-5761, E-Mail: cdsales@
cdmo.com, Web Site: www.cdmo.
com
Conducts Business: U.S.
Primary Market Served: Consumer
Catalog available online
Direct online sales

Distribute DVD, CD, VHS & other
recording formats.

CDW CORP
300 N Milwaukee Ave
Vernon Hills, IL 60061
Telephone: (847) 465-6000, (800) 800-
4239
VP & Chief Mktg Officer: Diane
Primo
Primary Market Served: Business &
Consumer

CMEINFO.COM
500 Corporate Pkwy (Suite 300)
Birmingham, AL 35242
Telephone: (205) 991-9188, (800) 284-
8433, FAX: (800) 284-5964, Web
Site: www.cmeinfo.com
Mktg Dir: Rich Frankel
Primary Market Served: Business &
Consumer

Video & audio continuing medical
education program for doctors.

CPAC INC
2364 Leicester Rd
Leicester, NY 14481
Telephone: (585) 382-3223, (800) 828-
6011, FAX: (585) 382-3031, E-Mail:
cpacinfo@cpac.com, Web Site:
www.cpac.com
VP, Admin: Wendy Clay
VP, Sls & Mktg: Ernie Thompson
Corp Commun Mgr: Karen McCulley
Conducts Business: Worldwide
Employees: 44
Primary Market Served: Business &
Consumer
Advertising/Marketing Budget Related
to Direct Marketing: 0-25%
Founded: 1969

Manufacturer of processing chemicals
& silver recovery pollution control
equipment for the photo industry. Also
provide silver refining services. Manufacture and market more than 2,500
chemicals and hard goods for the
cleaning industries, commercial and
consumer.

CPI CORP
1706 Washington Ave
St Louis, MO 63103-1717
Telephone: (314) 231-1575, (877) 763-
4456, FAX: (314) 231-8150, E-Mail:
feedback@cpicorp.com, Web Site:
www.cpicorp.com
CEO: Dave Pierson
VP: Jack Krings
Dir Mktg: Sherry Kohrs
Conducts Business: U.S., Canada
Employees: 3,600
Primary Market Served: Consumer

Specialize in children's & adult/family
portrait photography taken in major
discount (K-Mart) & department stores
throughout the country.

CRM LEARNING
2218 Faraday Ave (Suite 110)
Carlsbad, CA 92008
Telephone: (760) 431-9800, (800) 421-
0833, FAX: (760) 931-5792, E-Mail:
sales@crmlearning.com, Web Site:
www.crmlearning.com
Partner & CEO: Peter Jordan
Mktg Dir: Lindy Caulder
Sls: Pan Clavert
Employees: 38
Primary Market Served: Business
Catalog available online
Direct online sales
Gross sales or billing: $6,000,000

Training videos for businesses, government, healthcare & education.

CSI
1059 Powers Rd
Conklin, NY 13748-1400
Telephone: (607) 775-7905, Web Site:
www.cleanersupply.com
Pres: Jeff Schapiro
Primary Market Served: Business &
Consumer

**CTB MACMILLAN/MCGRAW-
HILL**
20 Ryan Ranch Rd
Monterey, CA 93940
Telephone: (831) 393-0700, (800) 538-
9547, FAX: (831) 393-6528, E-Mail:
hr@ctb.com, Web Site: www.ctb.
com
VP, Sls & Mktg: Richard Dobbs
Conducts Business: U.S.

Primary Market Served: Business
Catalog available online
Direct online sales

Central testing bureau for McGraw-
Hill for grades K-12.

CTC CORP
Subs. of Starson Services Corp
254 Benmont Ave
Bennington, VT 05201
Telephone: (802) 442-6371, FAX:
(802) 442-8526
Owner: Bruce Laumeister
Treas & Sec: Wayne Massari
Sls Mgr: Philip Jordan
Conducts Business: U.S., Canada
Employees: 100
Primary Market Served: Business &
Consumer

Wholesale & retail photo-finishing lab.

CVT PRODUCTION INC
50906 Rothbury Dr
Granger, IN 46530-6291
Telephone: (574) 247-0647, Web Site:
www.destinationfitness.com
Pres: Mark Lange
Primary Market Served: Business &
Consumer
Catalog available online
Indirect online sales

Produce & distribute scenic workout
video tapes for home exercise
equipment.

CYRO INDUSTRIES
379 Interpace Pkwy Ste 1
Parsippany, NJ 07054-1131
Telephone: (973) 541-8000, (800) 631-
5384, FAX: (973) 442-6117, (973)
442-6135, Web Site: www.cyro.com
Pres: John Medina
VP: W.M. Lowman
Gen Mgr Sheet Products: D.L. Quinlan
Conducts Business: U.S., Latin
America
Employees: 750
Primary Market Served: Business
Founded: 1976

Manufacturer of acrylic sheet & molding compounds, plus polycarbonate
sheet, all sold to a variety of markets.

**CABLE SHOPPING
NETWORK**
15945 N 76th St
Scottsdale, AZ 85260-1781
Telephone: (480) 624-4446, Web Site:
www.shopcsntv.com
Dir Mktg: Steven Harris
Primary Market Served: Business &
Consumer

CABLEVISION SYSTEMS CORP

111 Stewart Ave
Bethpage, NY 11714-3533
Telephone: (516) 803-2300, FAX:
(516) 803-3134, Web Site: www.
cablevision.com
Chmn: Charles F. Dolan
CEO, Pres, Dir Madison Square Garden, Governor NY Knicks: James L.
Dolan
Dir Opers & Bus: Madeline Marcus
Exec VP, Prod Mngmt & Mktg: Patricia Gottesmann
VP, Corp Commun: Kim Kearns
Employees: 22,075
Primary Market Served: Consumer
Catalog available online
Direct online sales
Founded: 1985
Gross sales or billing: $5,927,500,000

Cable television, digital cable, movies-on-demand & VoIP telephony. Controls
Madison Square Garden, NY Knicks,
NY Rangers & Radio City Music Hall.

CADIE PRODUCTS CORP

151 E 11th St
Paterson, NJ 07524-1228
Telephone: (973) 278-8300, FAX:
(973) 278-0303, E-Mail: emeyers@
cadie.com, Web Site: www.
cadieproducts.com
Pres: Edwin W. Meyers
VP: Bob Appelbaum
VP: Dan Kellenberger
VP: Kenneth Meyers
Conducts Business: Worldwide
Employees: 70
Primary Market Served: Consumer
Catalog available online
Advertising/Marketing Budget Related
to Direct Marketing: 26-50%
Founded: 1939
Gross sales or billing: $10,000,000

Supplier of mail order specialties to
catalog houses & space advertisers.
Manufacture & distribute extensive
cleaning products to supermarkets &
mass merchandisers.

CAESARS PALACE

Harrah's Corp Office
1 Caesars Palace Dr
Las Vegas, NV 89109
Telephone: (702) 407-6000, (800) 634-
6001, FAX: (702) 407-6037, Web
Site: www.caesars.com
Chmn, CEO & Pres: Gary Loveman
CFO & Treas: Jonathon S. Halkyard
Vice Chmn Bd: Charles A. Atwood
Pres Eastern Division: Carlos Tolosa
Pres Western Division: Tom Jenkin
Conducts Business: U.S.
Employees: 58,000

Primary Market Served: Business &
Consumer
Catalog available online
Indirect online sales
Gross sales or billing: $535,000,000

Hotel, casino & convention area.

CAFE LANGO

Div. of Jeffrey Norton Publishers Inc
2351 Boston Post Rd (#101)
Guilford, CT 06437
Telephone: (203) 453-1456, (800) 243-
1234, FAX: (203) 453-5110, E-Mail:
mail@cafelango.com, Web Site:
www.audioforum.com
Pres: Jeffrey Norton
Acctg Mgr: Laura McGrady
Conducts Business: Worldwide
Employees: 10
Primary Market Served: Consumer
Catalog available online
Indirect online sales
Advertising/Marketing Budget Related
to Direct Marketing: 76-100%
Founded: 1972
Gross sales or billing: $2,000,000

Sell quality self-instructional language
courses on CDs, audio & video cassettes as well as music, literature &
personal development programs.

CALICO CORNERS

Div. of Everfast
203 Gale Ln
Kennett Square, PA 19348-1764
Telephone: (610) 444-9700, FAX:
(610) 444-1221, Web Site: www.
calicocorners.com
Mktg Dir: Dale Schier
Primary Market Served: Consumer
Founded: 1948

Retail stores across U.S. specializing in
fabrics for the home, custom labor services & custom upholstery furniture.

CALIFORNIA INSTITUTE OF TECHNOLOGY

Industrial Relations Ctr 1-90
Pasadena, CA 91125-9000
Telephone: (626) 395-3746, FAX:
(626) 795-7174, E-Mail: execedu@
caltech.edu, Web Site: www.irc.
caltech.edu
Dir, Opers & Mktg: Anne Campbell
Dir: Gaylord Nichols
Conducts Business: Worldwide
Primary Market Served: Business
Catalog available online
Direct online sales
Advertising/Marketing Budget Related
to Direct Marketing: 76-100%
Direct Marketing ad budget:
Direct Mail: 94%
Magazines: 2%

Online: 4%
Founded: 1891

Develop & provide executive educational programs that focus on effective
leadership in world class organizations.
Programs also provide a leadership
perspective that addresses critical, strategic & competitive issues.

CALIFORNIA MUSTANG PARTS & ACCESSORIES

19400 San Jose Ave
City of Industry, CA 91748
Telephone: (909) 598-3383, (800) 775-
0101, FAX: (909) 598-5611, E-Mail:
csmustang@cal-mustang.com, Web
Site: www.cal-mustang.com
Pres: Gary Lovett
Conducts Business: U.S.
Employees: 2
Primary Market Served: Business &
Consumer
Catalog available online
Direct online sales
Advertising/Marketing Budget Related
to Direct Marketing: 26-50%
Direct Marketing ad budget:
Direct Mail: 20%
Magazines: 60%
TV/Radio: 20%
Founded: 1976
Gross sales or billing: $200,000

Parts & accessories for Ford Mustang
automobiles.

CAMP HEALTHCARE INC

Div. of Trulife Group
2010 E High St
Jackson, MI 49204-3416
Telephone: (517) 787-1600, (800) 492-
1088, FAX: (800) 245-3765, E-Mail:
info@truelife.biz, Web Site: www.
camphealthcare.com
VP, Sls: Larry Knudsen
Employees: 240
Primary Market Served: Business
Catalog available online
Indirect online sales
Advertising/Marketing Budget Related
to Direct Marketing: 51-75%

Rehabilitation products for health care
professionals & facilities (breastcare-post mastectomy, orthopedics, supports
& braces, pressure care, compression
therapy & wheelchair cushions).

CAMPBELL SOUP CO

1 Campbell Pl
Camden, NJ 08103-1701
Telephone: (856) 342-4800, (800) 257-
8443, FAX: (856) 342-3878, Web
Site: www.campbellsoup.com
Pres, CEO & Dir: Douglas R. Conant
Sr Mktg Mgr: Joyce Friedberg

Sr Interactive Mktg Mgr: John Johnson
VP Sls: Walt Tullis
Employees: 24,000
Primary Market Served: Business &
    Consumer
Catalog available online
Direct online sales
Founded: 1869
Gross sales or billing: $7,343,000,000

Food manufacturers.

CANADA POST CORP
2701 Riverside Dr (Suite N1200),
    Canada Post PL
Ottawa, ON, Canada K1A 0B1
Telephone: (613) 734-8440, (866) 607-
    6301, FAX: (613) 734-3378, Web
    Site: www.canadapost.ca
Conducts Business: Canada
Employees: 57,000
Primary Market Served: Business &
    Consumer
Advertising/Marketing Budget Related
    to Direct Marketing: 51-75%
Gross sales or billing: $4,000,000,000

Canada Post, the official Postal Service
of Canada, provides trusted, integrated
solutions to support the communication, marketing and selling, distribution
and logistics needs of businesses.

CANINE COMPANIONS FOR INDEPENDENCE
PO Box 446
Santa Rosa, CA 95402-0446
Telephone: (707) 577-1700, (800) 572-
    2275, FAX: (707) 577-1711, E-Mail:
    info@cci.org, Web Site: www.
    caninecompanions.org
Pres, Bd of Dirs: Jean Schulz
Devel Dir: Jennifer Conroy
CEO: Corey Hudson
Conducts Business: U.S.
Employees: 140
Primary Market Served: Consumer
Advertising/Marketing Budget Related
    to Direct Marketing: 0-25%
Founded: 1975
Gross sales or billing: $12,665,333

Non-profit organization providing dogs
for the disabled.

CAPEZIO BALLET MAKERS INC
1 Campus Rd
Totowa, NJ 07512
Telephone: (973) 653-2093, (800) 533-
    1887, FAX: (800) 522-1222, E-Mail:
    info@balletmakers.com, Web Site:
    www.capeziodance.com
CEO: Paul Terlizzi
Pres: Michael Terlizzi
COO: Marc Terlizzi
Trustee: Donald Terlizzi

Exec Dir: Jane Remer
Employees: 400
Primary Market Served: Business &
    Consumer
Catalog available online
Direct online sales
Gross sales or billing: $23,000,000

Retail store chain & manufacturers of
dancewear products.

CAPITOL CONCIERGE INC
1400 "I" St NW (Suite 750)
Washington, DC 20005
Telephone: (202) 223-4765, FAX:
    (202) 833-2287, E-Mail:
    onlineconcierge@capitolconcierge.
    com, Web Site: www.
    capitolconcierge.com
CEO: Lynda Ellis
Employees: 100
Primary Market Served: Business &
    Consumer
Founded: 1987

Corporate concierge services for commercial & residential buildings.

CARAUSTAR
5000 Austell-Powder Springs Rd (#
    300)
Austell, GA 30106-3227
Telephone: (770) 948-3101, E-Mail:
    info@caraustar.com, Web Site: www.
    caraustar.com
Chmn: James E. Rogers
Pres, CEO & Dir: Michael J. Keough
Sr VP, CFO & Dir: Ronald J. Doma-
    nico
VP, Gen Counsel & Sec: Wilma E.
    Beaty
VP: Gregory B. Cottrell
Conducts Business: U.S.
Employees: 30
Primary Market Served: Business
Catalog available online
Gross sales or billing: $989,000,000

Manufacturer of paper, tubes, cores &
cans.

CARD TECHNOLOGY INC
Div. of NBS
10925 Bren Rd E
Hopkins, MN 55343-9613
Telephone: (201) 845-7373, FAX:
    (201) 845-3337, E-Mail: info@
    nbstech.com, Web Site: www.
    nbstech.com
Pres: Fred Muller
VP, DM: Teresa Luke
Conducts Business: U.S.
Employees: 250
Primary Market Served: Business &
    Consumer
Gross sales or billing: $16,400,000

Manufacture & distribute embossing
related equipment to the health care,
banking & retail markets.

ER CARPENTER
Div. of Carpenter Co
302 Highland Dr
Taylor, TX 76574
Telephone: (512) 365-5833, (800) 234-
    9105, FAX: (512) 352-6025, Web
    Site: www.carpenter.com
Pres & CEO: Stan Yukevich
Dir: Judie Carpenter
Dir: Dan Schecter
Dir: Ken Thompsen
Conducts Business: U.S.
Employees: 100
Primary Market Served: Business
Catalog available online
Indirect online sales
Advertising/Marketing Budget Related
    to Direct Marketing: 0-25%
Founded: 1903

Manufacturers of polyester quilt batting, pillow forms & craft fiber, mattress pads & bed pillows.

CARROT-TOP INDUSTRIES INC
328 Elizabeth Brady Rd
Hillsborough, NC 27278-9540
Telephone: (919) 732-6200, (800) 628-
    3524, FAX: (919) 732-5526, E-Mail:
    service@carrot-top.com, Web Site:
    www.carrot-top.com
Pres: Dwight A. Morris
Dir, Mktg: Eric Pennington
Conducts Business: U.S., Canada,
    Mexico
Employees: 20
Primary Market Served: Business &
    Consumer
Catalog available online
Direct online sales
Advertising/Marketing Budget Related
    to Direct Marketing: 76-100%
Direct Marketing ad budget:
Direct Mail: 75%
Telephone: 25%
Founded: 1980
Gross sales or billing: $4,800,000

Sell flags, flag poles, banners, trophies
& plaques. Also, sell supplies for
meetings & conventions.

CARSON PIRIE SCOTT & CO
Subs. of Saks Inc
331 W Wisconsin Ave
Milwaukee, WI 53203-2201
Telephone: (414) 347-1152, FAX:
    (414) 278-5748
VP, Mktg & Admin Svcs Dir: Richard
    Schwab
Mktg Dir: Cathy Jacobson
Conducts Business: U.S.

Employees: 18,000
Primary Market Served: Consumer
Advertising/Marketing Budget Related
 to Direct Marketing: 0-25%
Founded: 1854

Chain of department stores including:
Carson Pirie Scott, Boston Store,
Bergner's & Herbergers.

THE DMA CATERPILLAR INC
100 NE Adams St
Peoria, IL 61629-0002
Telephone: (309) 675-1000, Web Site:
 www.cat.com
Echannel Comml Mgr: Toni Belcher
Primary Market Served: Business

CEDAR FRESH PRODUCTS
Div. of Arbor American Corp
4207 University Dr
Coral Gables, FL 33146-1140
Telephone: (305) 870-9390, Web Site:
 www.cedarfresh.com
Pres: Jay Butera
Pres & CEO: Jonathan Mayer
Conducts Business: U.S.
Employees: 45
Primary Market Served: Business
Catalog available online
Direct online sales

Manufacturer & distributor of housewares business-to-business.

CELESTIAL SEASONINGS
Subs. of Hain
4600 Sleepytime Dr
Boulder, CO 80301-3292
Telephone: (303) 530-5300, (800) 434-
 4246, FAX: (303) 581-1249, Web
 Site: www.hain-celestial.com
Vice Chmn Hain Celestial Grp: Mo
 Siegel
Sr VP & Gen Mgr: Walt Freese
Conducts Business: U.S., Canada, Eu-
 rope, Australia
Employees: 220
Primary Market Served: Consumer
Catalog available online
Direct online sales
Founded: 1969
Gross sales or billing: $70,000,000

Manufacturer of herb and other specialty teas.

CELLULAR ONE GROUP
Div. of SBC Communications
14201 Wireless Way
Oklahoma City, OK 74134
Telephone: (509) 663-2162, (800) 545-
 5982, FAX: (425) 586-8451, Web
 Site: www.cellularone.com
Pres: Richard Lyons
CEO: Richard Watkins
Dir, Mktg: Kim Smith

PR: Camille Cadmam
Primary Market Served: Business &
 Consumer
Catalog available online
Direct online sales
Gross sales or billing: $104,000,000

Sell cellular phones.

**CENTER FOR CREATIVE
LEADERSHIP**
1 Leadership Pl
Greensboro, NC 27410-9427
Telephone: (336) 545-2810, FAX:
 (336) 282-3284, E-Mail: info@ccl.
 org, Web Site: www.ccl.org
CEO & Pres: John Ryan
Sr VP Res & Innovation: David G.
 Altman
VP HR: Paul Draeger
Exec VP Global Leadership Devel:
 Lily M. Kelly-Radford Ph.D.
VP: Portia Mount
Conducts Business: Worldwide
Employees: 350
Primary Market Served: Business
Catalog available online
Direct online sales
Advertising/Marketing Budget Related
 to Direct Marketing: 0-25%
Direct Marketing ad budget: $550,000
Direct Mail: $500,000
Magazines: $50,000
Founded: 1970
Gross sales or billing: $24,000,000

Non-profit organization. Research
based management training institution.
Produce management training seminars, assessment instruments & publications of general interest to managers,
leaders & human resource
professionals.

**CENTER FOR
PROFESSIONAL
DEVELOPMENT**
Subs. of Florida State University
555 W Pensacola St (#2027), Turnbull
 Conference Ctr
Tallahassee, FL 32306-1640
Telephone: (850) 644-8004, (850) 487-
 1691, FAX: (850) 644-2589, Web
 Site: www.Learningforlife.fsu.com
Facilities Dir: Suzanne Harrell
Assoc Dir: Susann Rudasill
Mktg Dir: Jean Martin
Dir: Bill Lindner
Conducts Business: U.S.
Employees: 50
Primary Market Served: Business &
 Consumer
Direct Marketing ad budget: $150,000
Direct Mail: 70%
Magazines: 5%
Newspapers: 20%
TV/Radio: 5%

Founded: 1980
Gross sales or billing: $2,750,000

Design & implementation of continuing education programs to audiences
primarily in southeastern United States.
Operate urban & rural meeting & conference centers for regional & national
programs. Also offer online programs.

CENTERCORE GROUP INC
aka Kobico LLC & Domore
201 Industrial Park
Marked Tree, AR 72365
Telephone: (800) 686-0821, FAX:
 (870) 358-3330, Web Site: www.
 centercoregroup.com
Pres: Ralph Berger
Conducts Business: U.S., Canada,
 Mexico
Employees: 20
Primary Market Served: Business
Founded: 1957
Gross sales or billing: $8,000,000

Contract furniture seating, open-plan
systems, wall panels, wood casegoods
& seating & custom products.

THE DMA CENTERPOINT ENERGY
800 LaSalle Ave
Minneapolis, MN 55402-2006
Telephone: (612) 372-4664, FAX:
 (612) 321-4873, E-Mail: mgc-
 businessinformation@
 centerpointenergy.com, Web Site:
 www.minnegasco.centerpointenergy.
 com
Pres & CEO: David M. McClanahan
Prod Mgr: Kelly O'Keefe
Exec VP & Gen Counsel: Scott Roz-
 zell
Grp Pres Regulated Opers: Thomas R.
 Standish
Exec VP & CFO: Gary L. Whitlock
Primary Market Served: Consumer
Founded: 1959

Gas industry, sales & marketing, business & management, household appliance merchandising, public utilities,
energy.

CENTRAL SHIPPEE INC
46 Star Lake Rd
Bloomingdale, NJ 07403-1244
Telephone: (973) 838-1100, (800) 631-
 8968, FAX: (973) 838-8273, Web
 Site: www.centralshippee.com
Chmn Bd: Donald A. Hubner
VP, Opers: Eric Hubner
Conducts Business: U.S.
Employees: 29
Primary Market Served: Business &
 Consumer
Founded: 1945

Sell flameproof felt for display &
exhibits. Also, tablecloths, banners,
Velcro compatible fabrics & banners.

CERTAINTEED CORP
Div. of St. Gobain
750 E Swedesford Rd
Valley Forge, PA 19482
Telephone: (610) 341-7000/7739, (800)
  233-8990, FAX: (610) 341-7777,
  Web Site: www.certainteed.com
VP, Mktg: Marcia Hannah
Pres & CEO: Peter Dachowski
Sr VP: Gianpaolo Caccini
VP: David Sharpe
VP & CFO: Robert Statile
Primary Market Served: Business &
  Consumer
Catalog available online
Founded: 1904

Insulation, siding, roofing & windows.

CESSNA AIRCRAFT CO
Subs. of Textron Inc
One Cessna Blvd
Wichita, KS 67215-1400
Telephone: (316) 517-6000, FAX:
  (316) 517-6640, E-Mail: pmichael@
  cessna.textron.com, Web Site: www.
  cessna.com
CEO: Gary W. Hay
VP, Mktg: Philip M. Michel
Commun Prog Dir: Thomas Zwemke
Conducts Business: Worldwide
Employees: 7,500
Primary Market Served: Business &
  Consumer
Advertising/Marketing Budget Related
  to Direct Marketing: 26-50%
Founded: 1927

Aircraft manufacturer of general aviation products for business & utility
use.

CHABIN CONCEPTS
2515 Ceanothus Ave (Suite 100)
Chico, CA 95973-7720
Telephone: (530) 345-0364, FAX:
  (530) 345-6417, E-Mail: chabininc@
  aol.com
Pres: Audrey Taylor
Employees: 5
Primary Market Served: Business
Founded: 1989

Industrial development & recruitment.

CHAMPION
A Gardner Denver Co
1800 Gardner Expressway
Quincy, IL 62305-9364
Telephone: (217) 222-5400, FAX:
  (217) 228-8260, Web Site: www.
  championpneumatic.com
Chmn: Ross J. Centanni

Pres, CEO & Dir: Barry L. Penny-
  packer
VP, Fin & CFO: Helen W. Cornell
VP, Corp Controller: David J. Anto-
  niuk
VP & Gen Mgr: Winfried Kaiser
Conducts Business: Worldwide
Employees: 150
Primary Market Served: Business
Catalog available online
Advertising/Marketing Budget Related
  to Direct Marketing: 0-25%
Founded: 1919

Air compressor manufacturer.

CHANEL INC
Nine W 57th St
New York, NY 10019
Telephone: (212) 688-5055, FAX:
  (212) 752-1851, Web Site: www.
  chanel.com
Mktg Mgr: Rebekah McCabe
Primary Market Served: Business &
  Consumer

THE DMA CHAR-BROIL
1442 Belfast Ave
Columbus, GA 31904-4432
Telephone: (706) 571-7000, Web Site:
  www.charbroil.com
VP Mktg: Rob Schwing

THE DMA CHARTER COMMUNICATIONS
12405 Powerscourt Dr (Suite 100)
Saint Louis, MO 63131-3674
Telephone: (314) 965-0555, (888) 438-
  2427, FAX: (314) 965-9745, Web
  Site: www.charter.com
Chmn: Paul G. Allen
Exec VP & COO: Michael J. Lovett
Sr Dir Digital Prod: Robert Ladd
Exec VP & CFO: Jerry T. Fisher
Exec VP & CTO: Marwan Fawaz
CMO: Robert A. Quigley
Employees: 15,500
Primary Market Served: Consumer
Catalog available online
Indirect online sales
Advertising/Marketing Budget Related
  to Direct Marketing: 76-100%
Founded: 1975
Gross sales or billing: $5,500,000,000

Advanced digital technology for home
& office via cable network systems.

CHASE INDUSTRIES, INC
dba Chase Doors
10021 Commerce Park Dr
Cincinnati, OH 45246-1333
Telephone: (513) 860-5565, (800) 543-
  4455, FAX: (800) 245-7045, Web
  Site: www.chasedoors.com
Pres: Bob Muir

VP, Sls: Mike Hegner
VP, Mktg: Rory Falato
Conducts Business: U.S.
Employees: 200
Primary Market Served: Business
Advertising/Marketing Budget Related
  to Direct Marketing: 0-25%
Founded: 1932
Gross sales or billing: $14,700,000

Manufacturer of double-acting impact
traffic doors. Chase's product line includes strip doors and sliding fire and
pharmaceutical doors.

CHATTANOOGA SHOOTING SUPPLIES INC
2600 Walker Rd
Chattanooga, TN 37421-1285
Telephone: (423) 894-3007, (800) 251-
  4808, FAX: (423) 855-5513, Web
  Site: www.chattanoogashooting.com
CFO: David Dodson
Sls Mgr: Jim Post
Pur Mgr: Chris Means
Primary Market Served: Business

Wholesaler of guns & reloading
supplies.

CHOICE COURIER SYSTEMS INC
1 Whitehall St (fl 12)
New York, NY 10004-2138
Telephone: (212) 370-1999, FAX:
  (212) 370-0440, Web Site: www.
  choicecourier.com
Chmn: Ed Katz
Pres CEO: Michael Katz
Conducts Business: U.S.
Employees: 1,200
Primary Market Served: Consumer
Direct Marketing ad budget:
  $1,000,000
Direct Mail: 50%
Magazines: 15%
Newspapers: 25%
TV/Radio: 10%
Founded: 1964

Messenger & courier service. Conduct
surveys of traffic needs.

CHOICE HOTELS INTERNATIONAL
10750 Columbia Pike
Silver Spring, MD 20901-4491
Telephone: (301) 592-6636, (888) 770-
  6800, FAX: (301) 592-6157, E-Mail:
  ihelp@choicehotels.com, Web Site:
  www.choicebuys.com
Chmn: Stewart Bainum Jr.
Vice Chmn & CEO: Charles Ledsinger
  Jr.
Sr VP Consumer Revenue Growth:
  William Carlson
CFO: David White

Sr VP, Mktg: Wayne Wielgus
Employees: 1,860
Primary Market Served: Business &
  Consumer
Gross sales or billing: $544,700,000

Publish hotel directories.

CHOICE POINT
1000 Alderman Dr
Alpharetta, GA 30005
Telephone: (770) 752-6000, (800) 342-
  5339, FAX: (770) 752-6005, Web
  Site: www.choicepoint.com
Chmn & CEO: Derek V. Smith
Pres, COO & Dir: Douglas C. Curling
CFO: David E. Trine
CTO: Stanley M. Garrison
VP, Precision Mktg: Bernadette L.
  Randall
Primary Market Served: Business &
  Consumer
Catalog available online

Public records information network.

THE DMA CHRISTIAN BRANDS
5226 S 31st Pl
Phoenix, AZ 85040-3742
Telephone: (602) 243-5200, (800) 521-
  2914, FAX: (602) 232-1855, Web
  Site: www.christian-brands.com
Pres: Paul DiGiovanni
VP: Tom DiGiovanni
Dir Mktg: Mary Ellen Wanamaker
Conducts Business: U.S.
Employees: 90
Primary Market Served: Business &
  Consumer
Catalog available online
Direct online sales
Advertising/Marketing Budget Related
  to Direct Marketing: 0-25%
Direct Marketing ad budget:
Direct Mail: 65%
Online: 35%
Founded: 1948

Church supplies & religious articles.

CINCINNATI BELL
TELEPHONE
Div. of Cincinnati Bell Inc
221 E 4th St (Suite 700)
Cincinnati, OH 45202-4137
Telephone: (513) 397-9900, FAX:
  (513) 241-8341, Web Site: www.
  cincinnatibelltelephone.com
VP, Client Tech Opers: Paul Singer
Conducts Business: U.S.
Employees: 2,500
Primary Market Served: Consumer

Telephone company using direct marketing techniques in dealings with
consumers.

CINTAS
PO Box 625737
Cincinnati, OH 45262
Telephone: (816) 474-7000, FAX:
  (816) 474-1258, Web Site: www.
  cintas.com
VP, Natl Accts: Don Richter
Conducts Business: U.S.
Employees: 2,700
Primary Market Served: Business

Manufacturer, distributor & renter of
industrial uniforms.

CIRCLE K STORES INC
935 E Tallmadge Ave
Akron, OH 44310-3566
Telephone: (330) 630-6300, Web Site:
  www.cirlcek.com
Pres: Brian Hannasch
VP: Mike Struble
CIO: Bryant Santini
Dir: Rick Hazen
Mktg Dir: Larry Brueggemier
Mktg: Kim Strode
Conducts Business: Worldwide
Employees: 14,000
Primary Market Served: Consumer
Catalog available online
Direct Marketing ad budget:
Direct Mail: 100%

Direct mail marketing of merchandise
& insurance service to credit card
holders.

CLAMPITT PAPER CO
9207 Ambassador Row
Dallas, TX 75247-4506
Telephone: (214) 638-3300, FAX:
  (214) 634-7837, E-Mail: dcrew@
  clampitt.com, Web Site: www.
  clampitt.com
Chmn: Donald Clampitt
Office Mgr: Candie Garcia
Mktg: Whitney Robinson
Sls: Tommy Liska
Conducts Business: U.S.
Employees: 74
Primary Market Served: Business &
  Consumer
Catalog available online
Indirect online sales
Founded: 1941

Wholesale distributor of fine papers.

THE CLARK GRAVE VAULT
CO
375 E Fifth Ave
Columbus, OH 43201-2819
Telephone: (614) 294-3761, FAX:
  (614) 299-2324, Web Site: www.
  clarkvault.com
Pres: David A. Beck
VP, Mfg: Mark A. Beck
VP, Mktg: Douglas Beck

Conducts Business: U.S., Canada
Employees: 100
Primary Market Served: Business
Catalog available online
Indirect online sales
Founded: 1898

Manufacturer of metal burial vaults.
Also, metal working & stamping.

CLARKS OF NORTH
AMERICA
156 Oak St
Newton, MA 02464
Telephone: (617) 964-1222, (800) 925-
  4315, FAX: (617) 243-4213, Web
  Site: www.clarks.com
Retail Mktg Coord: Janice McEwen
Primary Market Served: Business &
  Consumer

Retailer & wholesaler of men's footwear & accessories.

THE DMA CLEARSALEING INC
8415 Pulsar Pl Ste 477
Columbus, OH 43240-4093
Telephone: (614) 448-2688, (800) 592-
  0463, Web Site: www.clearsaleing.
  com
CEO: Michael Lanese
Mktg Mgr: Adam Hritzak

CLEGG INDUSTRIES INC
19032 S Vermont Ave
Gardena, CA 90248-4412
Telephone: (310) 225-3800, FAX:
  (800) 250-9851, E-Mail: sales@
  clegg.xo.com, Web Site: www.
  cleggonline.com
Pres: Kevin Clegg
VP Mktg: Frank Bennett
Primary Market Served: Business &
  Consumer
Catalog available online
Founded: 1987
Gross sales or billing: $20,000,000

Manufacturer of light, sound & voice
promotional products.

CLEMENTE NOVELTIES INC
301 Lafayette St
Utica, NY 13502-4311
Telephone: (315) 732-4145, FAX:
  (315) 732-2251, E-Mail: clemente@
  6org.com
Pres: Anthony Clemente
VP: Andrew J. Scarafile
Conducts Business: U.S.
Employees: 15
Primary Market Served: Business &
  Consumer
Founded: 1950
Gross sales or billing: $6,000,000

Direct marketing to profit organizations
& school fundraising.

THE CLOROX CO

1221 Broadway
Oakland, CA 94612-1888
Telephone: (510) 271-7000, FAX:
   (510) 832-1463, Web Site: www.
   thecloroxcompany.com
Chmn & CEO: Donald R. Kraus
VP, Corp Mktg Svcs: George Roeth
Conducts Business: Worldwide
Employees: 7,600
Primary Market Served: Consumer
Advertising/Marketing Budget Related
   to Direct Marketing: 0-25%
Direct Marketing ad budget:
Direct Mail: $500,000
TV/Radio: $500,000
Founded: 1913
Gross sales or billing: $4,847,000,000

Manufacturer of consumer products.

CLUETT PEABODY

48 W 38th St
New York, NY 10018-6248
Telephone: (212) 984-8900, FAX:
   (212) 984-8910, Web Site: www.
   arrowshirt.com
Pres: James Williams
Conducts Business: Worldwide
Employees: 4,000
Primary Market Served: Business &
   Consumer
Advertising/Marketing Budget Related
   to Direct Marketing: 0-25%
Gross sales or billing: $650,000,000

COASTAL TOOL & SUPPLY

510 New Park Ave
West Hartford, CT 06110
Telephone: (860) 233-8213, (877) 551-
   8665, FAX: (860) 233-6295, E-Mail:
   sales@coastaltool.com, Web Site:
   www.coastaltool.com
Pres: Robert S. Ludgin
Webmaster: Todd Mogren
Conducts Business: Worldwide
Employees: 10
Primary Market Served: Business &
   Consumer
Catalog available online
Direct online sales
Advertising/Marketing Budget Related
   to Direct Marketing: 0-25%
Founded: 1980
Gross sales or billing: $5,000,000

Power tools, hand tools & related
accessories.

COBALT

605 5th Ave S (Suite 800)
Seattle, WA 98104-3888
Telephone: (206) 269-6363, Web Site:
   www.cobalt.com
Corp Mktg: Tara Thomas

THE COCA-COLA CO

PO Box 1734
Atlanta, GA 30301-1734
Telephone: (404) 676-2121, FAX:
   (404) 676-6792, Web Site: www.
   cocacola.com
Chmn & CEO: E. Neville Isdell
Pres & COO: Muhtar Kent
Sr VP, Chief Mktg & Comml Officer:
   Joseph V. Tripodi
Employees: 71,000
Primary Market Served: Business &
   Consumer
Founded: 1886
Gross sales or billing: $5,080,000,000

Manufacture, distribute & market syrups & concentrates for soft drinks.
Also process citrus products & manufacture orange juice & other juices &
beverages.

THE DMA COLE-PARMER INSTRUMENT CO

625 E Bunker Ct
Vernon Hills, IL 60061-1844
Telephone: (847) 549-7600, (800) 323-
   4340, FAX: (847) 247-2929, E-Mail:
   info@coleparmer.com, Web Site:
   www.coleparmer.com
VP & CRM: Mark Graves
Dir Catalog Production & Planning:
   Bob Guttosch
Pres: Andy Greenawalt
Dir, Global Mktg: Mary Blase
Conducts Business: Worldwide
Employees: 280
Primary Market Served: Business
Catalog available online
Indirect online sales
Advertising/Marketing Budget Related
   to Direct Marketing: 76-100%
Direct Marketing ad budget:
Direct Mail: 90%
Magazines: 8%
Telephone: 2%
Founded: 1955

Distributor of laboratory & research
equipment.

COLGATE-PALMOLIVE CO

300 Park Ave
New York, NY 10022-7412
Telephone: (212) 310-2000, (800) 468-
   6502, FAX: (212) 310-2475, Web
   Site: www.colgate.com
Pres & CEO: Iam M. Cook
VP Fin, Global Sls & Adv: Leonard D.
   Smith
VP Global Bus Devel: William H.
   Lunderman
VP Global Strategy & Plng: Malcolm
   Jones
VP Global Adv: Jeff Salguero
Conducts Business: U.S.
Employees: 34,700

Primary Market Served: Consumer
Founded: 1806
Gross sales or billing: $12,237,000,000

Manufactures & sells household
products.

COLLECTIBLES TODAY NETWORK, LTD

dba Collectibles Today. Part of the
   Bradford Group.
9200 N Maryland Ave
Niles, IL 60105
Telephone: (800) 323-5577 #6, Web
   Site: www.collectiblestoday.com
Pres: Richard W. Tinberg
Conducts Business: U.S., Canada
Employees: 6
Primary Market Served: Consumer
Advertising/Marketing Budget Related
   to Direct Marketing: 76-100%

Sell direct mail collectibles to
consumers.

COLLEGIATE CAP & GOWN

Div. of Herff Jones Inc
1000 N Market St
Champaign, IL 61820-3009
Telephone: (217) 351-9500, FAX:
   (217) 351-9214, Web Site: www.
   herff-jones.com
Natl Sls Mgr: Ken Langlois
Plant Mgr: Peter Slamkowski
Adv & Promo Dir: John Moore
Gen Mgr Cap & Gown Div: Tom Tan-
   ton
Conducts Business: U.S.
Employees: 500
Primary Market Served: Business
Founded: 1926

Manufacture, rent & sell graduation
caps & gowns. Manufacture & sell
choir apparel to churches & schools.
Also, pulpit robes, academic outfits &
judicial robes.

COLUMBIA-PRESBYTERIAN MEDICAL CENTER

115 Central Park W
New York, NY 10023-4198
Telephone: (212) 305-2500, FAX:
   (212) 305-8023, Web Site: www.nyp.
   org
Chmn: John J. Mack
Pres & CEO: Herbert Pardes MD
Exec VP & COO: Steven J. Corwin
   MD
Exec VP, CFO, & Treas: Phyllis R. F.
   Lantos
Sr VP: Aurelia G. Boyer
Conducts Business: U.S.
Employees: 25
Primary Market Served: Business &
   Consumer
Founded: 1928

Gross sales or billing: $18,180,612

Provide medical care & related health services.

COLUMBIA TRISTAR HOME VIDEO

Subs. of Sony Pictures Corp
10202 W Washington Blvd (Rm 7814), SPP Bldg
Culver City, CA 90232-3119
Telephone: (310) 244-4000, FAX: (310) 244-1544, Web Site: www. cthe.com
Pres: Ben Feingold
Sr VP, Sls: Marshal Foster
Mktg: Tana Evans
Sls Promos: Betsy Caffrey
Exec VP: Marshall Forster
Conducts Business: U.S., Canada
Employees: 120
Primary Market Served: Consumer
Advertising/Marketing Budget Related to Direct Marketing: 0-25%

Film studio.

COMMEMORATIVE BRANDS INC

7211 Circle S Rd, PO Box 149079
Austin, TX 78714-9770
Telephone: (512) 444-0571, FAX: (512) 444-0065
Adv: Theresa Aradi
Conducts Business: U.S.
Primary Market Served: Business
Advertising/Marketing Budget Related to Direct Marketing: 76-100%
Founded: 1996

Sell jewelry.

THE COMPANY STORE INC

Div. of Hanover Direct Inc
455 Park Plaza Dr
La Crosse, WI 54601-4445
Telephone: (608) 785-1400, FAX: (608) 791-5790, Web Site: www. thecompanystore.com
Pres, Home Fashions: Jeffrey C. Potts
VP, Telemktg: Patrick Kelly
Mktg Mgr: Mark Freedman
Conducts Business: U.S.
Employees: 800
Primary Market Served: Consumer
Advertising/Marketing Budget Related to Direct Marketing: 76-100%
Founded: 1911

Direct marketer & manufacturer of comforters, pillows & other natural fiber & down-filled items.

COMPAQ COMPUTER CORP

Subs. of Hewlett-Packard
20555 State Hwy 249
Houston, TX 77070-2698
Telephone: (281) 370-0670, FAX: (281) 927-8835, Web Site: www. compaq.com
Chmn Bd, CEO & Pres: Mark Hurd
Exec VP & CAO: Jon Flaxman
Exec VP & CFO: Cathie Lesjak
Exec VP: Todd Bradley
Exec VP: Michael J. Holston
Primary Market Served: Business & Consumer
Catalog available online
Direct online sales

PC computer manufacturers.

COMPHEALTH

6440 Millrock Dr (Suite 175)
Salt Lake City, UT 84121-5892
Telephone: (801) 930-3000, (800) 453-3030, FAX: (801) 930-4517, E-Mail: info@comphealth.com, Web Site: www.comphealth.com
Pres: Michael Reinholtz
Conducts Business: U.S.
Employees: 150
Primary Market Served: Business
Founded: 1985

Permanent and temporary physician staffing.

CONCEPT COMMUNICATIONS CO

380-A Internationale Dr
Bolingbrook, IL 60440
Telephone: (630) 829-8450, (800) 323-3524, FAX: (630) 629-8415, E-Mail: info@cstore1.com, Web Site: www.cstore1.com
Pres: Rudolf Orisek
VP, Opers: Tim Orisek
VP, Mktg: Martin Orisek
Primary Market Served: Business
Catalog available online
Direct online sales
Founded: 1987

Marketing agent - sell merchandise to gas stations & convenience stores.

CONDOLINK

Subs. of LDM Enterprises
3012 N 93rd St
Omaha, NE 68134-4716
Telephone: (402) 592-3525, (800) 877-9600, FAX: (402) 592-4122, E-Mail: info@condolink.com, Web Site: www.condolink.com
Pres: Linda Miller
Mktg Dir: Tim Whiteman
Conducts Business: Worldwide
Employees: 10
Primary Market Served: Business & Consumer
Founded: 1978

Clearinghouse for resales & rentals of resort condominium time sharing.

THE CONFERENCE BOARD, INC

845 Third Ave
New York, NY 10022-6679
Telephone: (212) 759-0900, FAX: (212) 980-7014, Web Site: www.conference-board.org
Pres & CEO: Jonathan Spector
Sr VP, Opers: Salvatore J. Vitale
Exec VP & COO: Joan S. Dargery
Dir - Consumer Res Ctr: Lynn Franco
Conducts Business: Worldwide
Employees: 200
Primary Market Served: Business
Catalog available online
Founded: 1916
Gross sales or billing: $55,900,000

Business research institute with offices in San Ramon, CA; Washington, DC; Chicago, IL; Ottawa, ON, Canada; Brussels, Belgium; New York and Hong Kong.

CONFORM PACIFIC

PO Box 1658
Lomita, CA 90717-5658
Telephone: (800) CONFORM, FAX: (310) 496-2880, E-Mail: info@smartblock.com, Web Site: www.smartblock.com
Conducts Business: U.S.
Primary Market Served: Business
Founded: 1988

Manufacture construction materials.

CONMIO INC

570 Fashion Ave (Rm 1104)
New York, NY 10018-1629
Telephone: (917) 583-2651, Web Site: www.conmio.com
Sr VP: Floyd Weintraub

CONSUMER BENEFIT SERVICES INC

1620 Bond St
Naperville, IL 60563-0131
Telephone: (630) 420-6200, (800) 657-8309, FAX: (630) 420-2294, E-Mail: dcarlson@consumerbenefit.com, Web Site: www.consumerbenefit.com
Pres: David Carlson

CONSUMER CREDIT ADVOCATES INC

4746 S 900th E (Suite 240)
Salt Lake City, UT 84117
Telephone: (801) 265-9333, FAX: (801) 265-9595
Primary Market Served: Business & Consumer
Founded: 1989

Debt consolidators.

CONSUMER'S ENERGY
Div. of CMS Energy
212 W Michigan Ave
Jackson, MI 49201-2277
Telephone: (517) 788-0550, (800) 805-0490, FAX: (517) 788-1859, E-Mail: businesscenter@consumerenergy.com, Web Site: www.consumersenergy.com
Pres, CEO & Dir: David W. Joos
Exec VP & CFO: Thomas J. Webb
Sr VP & Gen Counsel: James E. Brunner
Sr VP & HR: John M. Butler
Sr VP: William E. Garrity
Primary Market Served: Business & Consumer

Electric & gas utility company.

CONVERSIONVOODOO.COM
10601 Tierrasanta Blvd (# G-371)
San Diego, CA 92124-2616
Telephone: (858) 625-4203, Web Site: www.conversionvoodoo.com

CONVERTIBLE SERVICE
5126 N Walnut Grove Ave
San Gabriel, CA 91776-2026
Telephone: (626) 285-2255, (800) 333-1140, FAX: (626) 285-9004, Web Site: www.convertibleparts.com
Owner: Paul Terry
Mgr: Ron Hayes
Conducts Business: Worldwide
Employees: 8
Primary Market Served: Business & Consumer
Catalog available online
Direct online sales
Advertising/Marketing Budget Related to Direct Marketing: 0-25%
Direct Marketing ad budget: $45,000
Direct Mail: 30%
Magazines: 50%
Online: 20%
Founded: 1982
Gross sales or billing: $400,000

Manufactures & sells convertible top mechanism parts.

COOPER COMMUNITIES INC
903 N 47th St
Rogers, AR 72756
Telephone: (479) 246-6500, (800) 648-6401, FAX: (479) 855-6256, E-Mail: coopernet@ccias.com, Web Site: www.cooper-communities.com
Chmn, Pres & CEO: John Cooper Jr.
Sr VP & CFO: Kent Burger
Pres, Cooper Land Dev: Randy Brucker
Pres, Cooper Homes Inc: Daniel W. Cooper
Conducts Business: U.S.
Employees: 600

Primary Market Served: Business & Consumer
Catalog available online
Advertising/Marketing Budget Related to Direct Marketing: 51-75%
Direct Marketing ad budget:
Direct Mail: $6,000,000
Telephone: $500,000
Founded: 1954
Gross sales or billing: $169,000,000

Develop entire communities & sell to middle-income consumers in about four states.

COOPER TIRE & RUBBER CO INC
dba Coopertires
701 Lima Ave
Findlay, OH 45840-2315
Telephone: (419) 423-1321, (800) 854-6288, FAX: (419) 424-4212, Web Site: www.coopertire.com
Chmn, Pres & CEO: Roy V. Armes
Sr VP, Global HR: Mark W. Krivoruchka
VP & CFO: Philip G. Weaver
Conducts Business: U.S., Europe, Middle East, China, Mexico
Employees: 13,355
Primary Market Served: Business
Founded: 1914
Gross sales or billing: $2,900,000,000

Manufacture and sale of replacement tires, including passenger, light truck, motorcycle and racing.

COPTECH INC
100 Cummings Park
Woburn, MA 01801-2128
Telephone: (781) 935-2679, (800) 934-1560, FAX: (781) 935-7673, Web Site: www.coptechinc.com
Pres: Tom Cherry
Primary Market Served: Business

COSCO INDUSTRIES INC
7220 W Wilson Ave
Chicago, IL 60706-4706
Telephone: (708) 867-5800, (800) 323-0253, FAX: (800) 323-0275
Pres & Gen Mgr: John Anthony
VP & Sec: Paul C. Becker
Sls Mgr: Liz Schmidt
Conducts Business: Worldwide
Primary Market Served: Business

Manufacturer of marking devices & machines.

COSMO INTERNATIONAL
601 Fairway Dr
Deerfield Beach, FL 33441-1867
Telephone: (954) 798-4500, FAX: (954) 798-4514
Pres: J.F. Belmont

Mktg Mgr: Felipe Martinez
Primary Market Served: Business & Consumer

Manufacture fragrances.

COTTA TRANSMISSION CO
1301 Prince Hall Dr
Beloit, WI 53511
Telephone: (608) 368-5600, FAX: (608) 368-5605, E-Mail: sales@cotta.com, Web Site: www.cotta.com
Pres: Matt Modek
VP: John Duncan Thompson
Mktg Dir: Larry Mowell
Conducts Business: U.S.
Primary Market Served: Business
Catalog available online
Advertising/Marketing Budget Related to Direct Marketing: 0-25%
Direct Marketing ad budget:
Direct Mail: 2%
Magazines: 98%
Founded: 1909

Sells industrial gearboxes to OEMs in a variety of industries.

THE COUNTRY BED SHOP
328 Richardson Rd
Ashby, MA 01431
Telephone: (978) 386-7550, FAX: (978) 386-7263, E-Mail: alan@countrybed.com, Web Site: www.countrybed.com
Pres: Alan Pease
Conducts Business: U.S.
Primary Market Served: Consumer
Catalog available online
Indirect online sales
Founded: 1975

Manufacture early American wood furniture.

THE DMA COVERDELL CANADA CORPORATION
1801 McGill College Ave (Suite 725)
Montreal, PQ, Canada H3A 2N4
Telephone: (514) 847-7800
Primary Market Served: Business

COX COMMUNICATIONS
Div. of Cox Enterprises
1400 Lake Hearn Dr
Atlanta, GA 30319-1464
Telephone: (404) 843-5000, FAX: (404) 269-2243, Web Site: www.cox.com
Pres: Patrick J. Esser
Sr VP: Dallas S. Clement
Sr VP, Opers: Jill Campbell
Sr VP & CIO: Scott Hatfield
Sr VP & CTO: Christopher J. Bowick
Conducts Business: U.S.
Employees: 825

Primary Market Served: Business &
   Consumer
Catalog available online
Indirect online sales
Advertising/Marketing Budget Related
   to Direct Marketing: 26-50%
Gross sales or billing: $133,000,000

COYNE AMERICAN INSTITUTE

330 N Green St
Chicago, IL 60607-1300
Telephone: (773) 935-2520, (800) 999-
   5220, FAX: (773) 935-2920, Web
   Site: www.coyneamerican.edu
Pres: Russell Freeman
VP: Lee Mueller
Indus Rep: Bill Austin
Conducts Business: U.S.
Employees: 200
Primary Market Served: Consumer
Catalog available online
Founded: 1899

Industrial training organization in the
areas of electronics technician, electrical maintenance, air conditioning, refrigeration, heating & computer systems skills.

THE CRACKER BOX INC

PO Box 114
Blooming Glen, PA 18911-0114
Telephone: (215) 443-7777, FAX:
   (215) 443-7777, E-Mail: walter@
   crackerboxkits.com, Web Site: www.
   crackerboxkits.com
Pres: Paul T. Caine
Conducts Business: Worldwide
Primary Market Served: Consumer
Catalog available online
Direct online sales
Founded: 1971

Catalog of 223 original beaded orna-
ment kits.

CRAFT-DISTON INDUSTRIES

Subs. of Architectural Art Mfg. Inc
PO Box 12492
Wichita, KS 67277-2492
Telephone: (316) 838-4291, (800) 835-
   0028, FAX: (316) 838-8502, Web
   Site: www.craftdiston.com
Pres & Owner: John J. Murphy
VP & Gen Mgr: Carl Fry
Conducts Business: U.S., Mexico, Car-
   ibbean, Peru, Argentina, Chile
Employees: 30
Primary Market Served: Business &
   Consumer
Catalog available online
Indirect online sales
Advertising/Marketing Budget Related
   to Direct Marketing: 26-50%
Founded: 1985
Gross sales or billing: $4,000,000

Shower & tub enclosures, mirrored
closet doors to glass houses & plumbing wholesalers.

CRANE PUMPS & SYSTEMS INC

aka CP&S
420 Third St
Piqua, OH 45356-3918
Telephone: (937) 773-2442, FAX:
   (937) 773-2238, E-Mail:
   cranepumps@cranepumps.com, Web
   Site: www.cranepumps.com
Pres: Vincent Buffa
VP Sls & Mktg: Brian O'Toole
Dir Mktg: Chuck Drake
Conducts Business: Worldwide
Employees: 811
Primary Market Served: Business
Catalog available online
Indirect online sales
Gross sales or billing: $89,800,000

Pumps, end suction, regen turbine,
self-priming, vertical multistage, sump
pumps & condensate return systems
for OEM & industrial markets.

CREATIVE HEALTH PRODUCTS

5148 Saddle Ridge Rd
Plymouth, MI 48170
Telephone: (734) 996-5900, (800) 742-
   4478, FAX: (734) 996-4650, Web
   Site: www.chponline.com
Pres: Marlene Donoghue
VP, Sec: W.C. Donoghue
Sls Mgr: Robin Mack
Mgr: Debbie Schooley
Conducts Business: Worldwide
Employees: 10
Primary Market Served: Business &
   Consumer
Catalog available online
Direct online sales
Advertising/Marketing Budget Related
   to Direct Marketing: 76-100%
Direct Marketing ad budget:
Direct Mail: 37%
Magazines: 1%
Online: 62%
Founded: 1976
Gross sales or billing: $1,500,000

Fitness testing products.

CREATIVE TEACHING ASSOCIATES

23505 Auberry Rd
Clovis, CA 93619-9648
Telephone: (559) 291-6626, (800) 767-
   4282, FAX: (559) 291-2953, Web
   Site: www.mastercta.com
Pres & CEO: Richard Wiebe
Sls & Mktg Mgr: Laurie Long
Conducts Business: Worldwide
Employees: 35

Primary Market Served: Business
Catalog available online
Advertising/Marketing Budget Related
   to Direct Marketing: 0-25%
Direct Marketing ad budget:
Direct Mail: $15,000
Magazines: $5,000
Telephone: $1,500
Founded: 1971
Gross sales or billing: $3,000,000

Manufacturer & marketer of teaching
materials such as games, teaching/
learning activities & books for math,
science, language & reading for grades
K-12.

CREATIVITY INTERNATIONAL

4930 Cascade Rd SE
Ada, MI 49546
Telephone: (616) 956-0053, FAX:
   (616) 956-6957
Pres: Sheri Lewis
Pres: Charles J. Lewis
Employees: 3
Primary Market Served: Consumer
Founded: 1978
Gross sales or billing: $120,000

Sell educational material to professional photographers via direct mail.

CREST HEALTHCARE SUPPLY

195 S Third St
Dassel, MN 55325-4511
Telephone: (800) 369-9207, (800) 328-
   8908, Web Site: www.
   cresthealthcare.com
Pres: Larry Lautt
Mktg & Sls Dir: Paul Kritzeck
IT: Adam Simons
IT: Chad Ardoff
Conducts Business: U.S., Canada, Pu-
   erto Rico
Employees: 80
Primary Market Served: Business
Catalog available online
Indirect online sales
Advertising/Marketing Budget Related
   to Direct Marketing: 76-100%
Founded: 1967
Gross sales or billing: $10,000,000

Direct marketer of hospital signal systems, nurse call equipment, pillow
speakers, bed maintenance & accessories, general maintenance, fire protection security & surveillance, blood
pressure equipment, healthcare TV,
lighting fixtures & exam lamps, cu-
bicle curtains, track & hardware, special orders, repair services, casters,
wheelchair parts & signage.

CRESTLINE SPECIALTIES, INC

Div. of Geiger Brothers
70 Mt Hope Ave
Lewiston, ME 04241
Telephone: (207) 777-7075, (866) 488-4975, FAX: (207) 784-5038, E-Mail: info@crestline.com, Web Site: www.crestline.com
VP & Gen Mgr: Judy Paradis
Conducts Business: U.S.
Employees: 62
Primary Market Served: Business
Gross sales or billing: $8,200,000

Advertising specialties & custom imprinted products for industry, education & associations.

CRONIN & CO

50 Nye Rd
Glastonbury, CT 06033-2196
Telephone: (860) 659-0514, Web Site: www.cronin-co.com
Partner & COO: Kimberly Manning
Primary Market Served: Business & Consumer

A T CROSS CO

1 Albion Rd
Lincoln, RI 02865-3700
Telephone: (401) 333-1200, (800) 282-7677, FAX: (401) 334-2861, Web Site: www.cross.com
Pres & CEO: David Whalen
VP, Fin, CFO: Kevin F. Mahoney
VP Legal & HR: Tina C. Benik
VP Strategic Devel: Robin Boss Dorman
Pres Cross Accessory Division: Charles S. Mellen
Conducts Business: U.S., Canada, Europe, Asia, Bermuda, Puerto Rico
Employees: 900
Primary Market Served: Business
Catalog available online
Direct online sales
Founded: 1846
Gross sales or billing: $139,000,000

Manufacturer & marketer of fine writing instruments & gifts.

CROSS COUNTRY AUTOMOTIVE SERVICES

1 Cabot Rd
Medford, MA 02155-5117
Telephone: (781) 393-9300, Web Site: www.cchs.com
Dir, Mktg & Communs: Katherine Bassick
Primary Market Served: Business

CROSS COUNTRY TRAVCORPS

6551 Park of Commerce Blvd
Boca Raton, FL 33487-8247
Telephone: (800) 530-6125, FAX: (561) 998-8533, Web Site: www.crosscountrytravcorps.com
Pres & CEO: Joseph A. Boshart
VP, Corp Devel & Strategy: Victor Kalafa
Conducts Business: U.S.
Employees: 1,200
Primary Market Served: Consumer
Advertising/Marketing Budget Related to Direct Marketing: 0-25%
Founded: 1978
Gross sales or billing: $655,400,000

Healthcare staffing.

CUISINART

Div. of Conair Corp
1 Cummings Point Rd
Stamford, CT 06902-7901
Telephone: (203) 975-4600, FAX: (203) 975-4660, Web Site: www.cuisinart.com
Sr VP: Barry Haber
VP, Mktg: Paul M. Ackels
VP, Sls: Jack Wilson
Sls & Mktg Opers Dir: Peter Cammarata
Grp Controller: Kevin Hudak
Conducts Business: Worldwide
Primary Market Served: Business & Consumer
Founded: 1971

Food processors & stainless steel cookware, blenders, toasters, coffee makers & cooking accessories.

CULINARY PARTS UNLIMITED

840 Folsom St
San Francisco, CA 94107
Telephone: (800) 543-7549, FAX: (415) 495-5141, Web Site: www.culinaryparts.com
Mgr: Mike Hanika
Conducts Business: U.S., Canada
Employees: 12
Primary Market Served: Business & Consumer
Advertising/Marketing Budget Related to Direct Marketing: 76-100%
Direct Marketing ad budget: $100,000
Direct Mail: 70%
Magazines: 25%
Newspapers: 5%
Gross sales or billing: $2,000,000

Replacement parts & accessories for high-end kitchenware, both European & domestic products.

ᵀᴴᴱ CUSTOM DIRECT

1802 Fashion Ct
Joppa, MD 21085-3237
Telephone: (410) 679-3300
VP, Opers: Dale Dabbs
Primary Market Served: Consumer

CYTEC INDUSTRIES INC

1405 Buffalo St
Olean, NY 14760-1139
Telephone: (716) 372-9650, FAX: (716) 372-1594, Web Site: www.conap.com
Pur Mgr: Bill Work
Admin: Marsha Topec
Conducts Business: Worldwide
Employees: 100
Primary Market Served: Business
Catalog available online
Founded: 1958

Supplies epoxy & polyurethane resin systems for potting & encapsulation, conformal coatings, adhesives, sealants, tooling resin systems & elastomers for the defense, aerospace, electronic, biomedical, computer, automotive & related markets.

DCA

889 S Matlack St
West Chester, PA 19382
Telephone: (610) 344-7488, (800) 638-6684, FAX: (610) 431-6500, E-Mail: ortho@dentalcorp.com, Web Site: www.dentalcorp.com
Pres: Don Taylor
Conducts Business: U.S., Canada, Europe, S. America, Asia, Africa
Employees: 5
Primary Market Served: Business & Consumer
Catalog available online
Direct online sales
Advertising/Marketing Budget Related to Direct Marketing: 0-25%
Founded: 1982
Gross sales or billing: $2,500,000

Sell orthodontic supplies.

DIA - NIELSEN USA INC

Subs. of DIA - Nielsen GmbH Duren Germany
41 Twosome Dr (Unit 5)
Moorestown, NJ 08057
Telephone: (856) 642-9700, (800) 893-6361, FAX: (856) 642-9709, Web Site: www.thomasregister.com
Gen Mgr: Wayne Connelly
Conducts Business: N. America, S. America
Employees: 10
Primary Market Served: Business
Catalog available online
Advertising/Marketing Budget Related to Direct Marketing: 0-25%

Founded: 1978

Manufacturer of marking systems for recording instruments.

DMB REALTY NETWORK

20789 N Pima Rd (Suite 250)
Scottsdale, AZ 85255-7206
Telephone: (480) 515-0148, Web Site:
www.dmbrealty.com
Mktg Communs: Gina Canzonetta

DMC CORP

Subs. of DMC Inc Paris France
77 S Hackensack Ave (Bldg 10F)
Kearny, NJ 07032-4688
Telephone: (973) 589-0606, FAX:
(973) 589-8931, Web Site: www.
dmc-usa.com
Mktg Mgr: Steve Mancuso
Conducts Business: Worldwide
Employees: 100
Primary Market Served: Business &
Consumer
Catalog available online
Direct online sales
Advertising/Marketing Budget Related
to Direct Marketing: 0-25%
Founded: 1934
Gross sales or billing: $21,500,000

Craft manufacturer sells to specialty & mass market outlets. Wool broadwoven fabric and wholesale nondurable goods knitting mill.

DPC COMPUTERS

42 Melnick Dr
Monsey, NY 10952
Telephone: (845) 426-3790, (866) 513-
CORP, FAX: (845) 426-6275,
E-Mail: learnmore@salestax.com,
Web Site: www.salestax.com
Pres & CEO: David Polatseck
Sls Dir & CFO: Abe Brach
VP Prof Svcs: Anthony Ward
Conducts Business: U.S., Canada
Employees: 15
Primary Market Served: Business
Catalog available online
Direct online sales
Advertising/Marketing Budget Related
to Direct Marketing: 51-75%
Direct Marketing ad budget: $200,000
Direct Mail: 25%
Magazines: 25%
Telephone: 50%
Founded: 1991
Gross sales or billing: $2,000,000

Sales tax compliance software. Provides current sales & use tax rates by zip code & covers the entire U.S., its territories & Canada. Provides stand alone systems & integration files. Provides CD-Rom of sales tax forms.

DA-LITE SCREEN CO INC

3100 N Detroit St
Warsaw, IN 46582-2288
Telephone: (574) 267-8101, (800) 622-
3737, FAX: (574) 267-7804, E-Mail:
info@da-lite.com, Web Site: www.
da-lite.com
Pres, CEO: Richard Lundin
Sr VP, Sls & Mktg: Judy Loughran
Mktg Coord: Dawn J. Stiles
Dir Mktg: Wendy Long
Conducts Business: Worldwide
Employees: 600
Primary Market Served: Business
Catalog available online
Indirect online sales
Advertising/Marketing Budget Related
to Direct Marketing: 26-50%
Founded: 1909

Projection screens, computer furniture, lecterns & audio visual equipment.

DAIRY FARMERS OF AMERICA INC

10220 N Ambassador Dr Suite 1000)
Kansas City, MO 64153-2327
Telephone: (816) 801-6455, (888) 332-
6455, FAX: (816) 801-6456, E-Mail:
webmail@dfamilk.com, Web Site:
www.dfamilk.com
Chmn: James P. Camerlo
Pres & CEO: Richard P. Smith
Sr VP, Fin: David Meyer
VP, Mktg: Mark Korsmeyer
Employees: 4,000
Primary Market Served: Business &
Consumer
Founded: 1998
Gross sales or billing: $7,800,000,000

Produce & distribute dairy products.

DAMARK INTERNATIONAL INC

PO Box 3000
La Salle, IL 61301-0300
Telephone: (877) 326-2757, Web Site:
www.damark.com
Chmn & CEO: Mark A. Cohn
Sr VP: George S. Richards
Sr VP: Michael Moroz
VP Info Sys: Rod Merry
Conducts Business: U.S.
Employees: 1,500
Primary Market Served: Consumer
Advertising/Marketing Budget Related
to Direct Marketing: 76-100%
Founded: 1986

Sell general merchandise at discounted prices to the consumer via mail order. A membership service company.

DAMILIC CORP

601 Dover Rd Ste 7
Rockville, MD 20850-1275

Telephone: (301) 251-2960, (800) 276-
7749, FAX: (301) 251-8591, E-Mail:
info@realsig.com, Web Site: www.
realsig.com
Pres: Robert Olding
Conducts Business: U.S., Canada, Europe, Central & S. America
Employees: 7
Primary Market Served: Business
Catalog available online
Founded: 1998

Manufacturer of automatic signature machines which write signatures (with notes or postscripts) or calligraphy. Operates as an attachment to an IBM/PC or compatible with automatic paper feeding.

DANKER LABORATORIES INC

6805 33rd St E, Box 1899
Sarasota, FL 34243
Telephone: (800) 237-9641, FAX:
(800) 665-5086, E-Mail: sales@
dankerlabs.com, Web Site: www.
dankerlabs.com
Owner: Frederick Danker
Office Mgr & Exec Asst: Gwen Norris
Gen Mgr: Kevin Hing
Conducts Business: U.S., Canada
Employees: 15
Primary Market Served: Business
Catalog available online
Direct online sales
Advertising/Marketing Budget Related
to Direct Marketing: 0-25%
Founded: 1958

Manufactures contact lenses, solutions & cases. Sell to ophthalmologists, optometrists, opticians, hospitals, pharmacies & drug wholesalers.

DANSK

PO Box 2006
Bristol, PA 19007-0806
Telephone: (914) 697-6400, (800) 326-
7528, FAX: (914) 697-6464, Web
Site: www.dansk.com
Pres: Dave Herman
Primary Market Served: Business &
Consumer
Founded: 1954

Manufacturer of tabletop goods.

DASSAULT FALCON JET CORP

dba Dassault Aviation
200 Riser Rd
Little Ferry, NJ 07643-1226
Telephone: (201) 440-6700, FAX:
(201) 541-4515, Web Site: www.
dassaultfalcon.com
Chmn: Charles Edelstone
Pres, CEO & Dir: John Rosanvallon

Sr VP, Fin & Admin: J. Morgan Young
Conducts Business: U.S.
Primary Market Served: Business &
Consumer
Founded: 1963

Business aircraft services.

DATA CAL CORP
1345 N Mondel Dr
Gilbert, AZ 85233
Telephone: (480) 813-3100, (800) 223-
0123, FAX: (480) 545-8090, E-Mail:
info@datacal.com, Web Site: www.
datacal.com
Pres: Jim Lunt
Mktg Mgr: Larry Karasz
Primary Market Served: Business &
Consumer
Catalog available online
Direct online sales
Founded: 1999

Computer, accessories, video & CD
computer training.

DATALEVER CORP
1515 Walnut St (Suite 200)
Boulder, CO 80302-5429
Telephone: (303) 541-1515, Web Site:
www.datalever.com
VP: Ed Sugg
Primary Market Served: Business

DATAPOINT USA INC
8122 Datapoint Dr (Suite 300)
San Antonio, TX 78229-3264
Telephone: (210) 614-9977, FAX:
(210) 614-2297, E-Mail: info@
datapointusa.com, Web Site: www.
datapointusa.com
CEO, Datapoint United Kingdom:
David Berger
Conducts Business: Worldwide
Employees: 1,500
Primary Market Served: Business
Founded: 1968
Gross sales or billing: $208,000,000

Local area networks & network serv-
ers, enterprise-wide system integration,
networked video conferencing & PCs.

DAVID DAUBER &
ASSOCIATES
50 Lexington Ave (Suite 173)
New York, NY 10010
Telephone: (212) 564-1728, FAX:
(212) 208-4524, E-Mail:
advancedbc@aol.com
Pres: David Dauber
Conducts Business: U.S.
Primary Market Served: Business
Catalog available online
Advertising/Marketing Budget Related
to Direct Marketing: 26-50%
Founded: 1991

Assists companies in establishing mail
order & internet Visa/MasterCard merchant accounts & database management and provide secure gateways,
web hosting and web creation.

THE DAVIS CENTER
19 State Route 10 (Suite 25)
Succasunna, NJ 07876-1750
Telephone: (862) 251-4637, FAX:
(862) 251-4642, E-Mail: info@
thedaviscenter.com, Web Site: www.
thedaviscenter.com
Pres & Founder: Dorinne S. Davis
Office Mgr: Nancy Puckett-Dunn
Conducts Business: U.S. Worldwide,
(Europe, Asia, other)
Employees: 4
Primary Market Served: Business &
Consumer
Catalog available online
Advertising/Marketing Budget Related
to Direct Marketing: 0-25%
Direct Marketing ad budget:
Direct Mail: $3,000
Magazines: $1,000
Newspapers: $1,000
Founded: 1998

Services for general education, therapy,
hearing & speech.

DAVOR PHOTO INC
3580 Progress Dr (Suite G)
Bensalem, PA 19020
Telephone: (215) 638-2490, (800) 334-
1531, FAX: (800) 724-6442, Web
Site: www.davor.com
Pres: Abe Orlick
Employees: 140
Primary Market Served: Business
Founded: 1966

School photography.

DAYDOTS
1801 Riverbend W Dr
Fort Worth, TX 76118
Telephone: (817) 590-4500, (800) 321-
3687, FAX: (800) 438-7002, E-Mail:
customercare@daydots.com, Web
Site: www.daydots.com
Pres: Mike Milliorn
Exec VP & CFO: Peter Currie
VP, Sls: Rob Heidemann
Mktg Mgr: Karen Combs
Primary Market Served: Business
Catalog available online
Direct online sales
Founded: 1985

Manufacture pressure sensitive labels
for food retailers. Distribution of food
safety products for restaurants.

DAYS INNS WORLDWIDE INC
Div. Wyndham Worldwide Corp
1 Sylvan Way Ste 2
Parsippany, NJ 07054-3879
Telephone: (973) 753-6000, (800) 441-
1618, Web Site: www.daysinn.com
Pres: Ken Greene
Sr VP Mktg & Communs: Betsy
O'Rourke
Conducts Business: Worldwide
Primary Market Served: Business &
Consumer
Catalog available online
Advertising/Marketing Budget Related
to Direct Marketing: 0-25%
Founded: 1970

International mid-market hotel chain.

DEERE & CO
HEADQUARTERS
1 John Deere Pl
Moline, IL 61265-8010
Telephone: (309) 765-8000, FAX:
(309) 765-5671, Web Site: www.
deere.com
Chmn, Pres & CEO: Robert W. Lane
Sr VP & CFO: Michael J. Mack Jr.
Exec VP: H.J. Markley
VP, IT: James R. Jabowski
Conducts Business: Worldwide
Primary Market Served: Business &
Consumer
Catalog available online
Direct online sales

Manufacturer of farm equipment, lawn
& ground care products & industrial
equipment.

DEL WEBB
100 Bloomfield Hills Pkwy Ste 150
Bloomfield Hills, MI 48304-2957
Telephone: (248) 644-7300, (888) 717-
9777, FAX: (248) 433-4598, Web
Site: www.delwebb.com
Chmn: William J. Pulite
Pres & CEO: Richard J. Dugas Jr.
Exec VP & CFO: Roger A. Cregg
Exec VP, HR: Leo J. Taylor
Sr VP & Gen Counsel: John R.
Stroller
Primary Market Served: Business &
Consumer
Catalog available online

Home builders--55 yrs. & over, active
adult retirement community.

DELL COMPUTER CORP
One Dell Way
Round Rock, TX 78682
Telephone: (512) 338-4400, FAX:
(512) 283-6161, Web Site: www.dell.
com
Chmn & CEO: Michael S. Dell
Dir, Mktg: Scott Helbing

Primary Market Served: Business & Consumer
Advertising/Marketing Budget Related to Direct Marketing: 76-100%

Design, manufacture, & direct market personal computers.

DELMMAR COMMUNICATIONS

920 N Ashland Dr
Cameron, MO 64429
Telephone: (816) 632-1583, (800) 872-2627, FAX: (816) 632-5107, E-Mail: sales@eradiostore.com, Web Site: www.delmmar.com
Mktg Dir: Connie Lintner
Primary Market Served: Business
Catalog available online
Direct online sales
Founded: 1987

Distributor for Motorola radius division radios & jobcom by ritroin 2 way radios

DELSTAR TECHNOLOGIES

Subs. of US Netting Inc
601 Industrial Dr
Middletown, DE 19709
Telephone: (302) 378-8888, (800) 521-6713, FAX: (302) 378-4482, Web Site: www.delstarinc.com
CEO: Mark Abrahams
VP: John Ribsam
VP, Sls & Mktg: D. Timothy Cullen
Mktg: Marjorie Wilcox
Conducts Business: U.S., Canada, Europe
Employees: 132
Primary Market Served: Business & Consumer
Catalog available online
Direct online sales
Direct Marketing ad budget:
Direct Mail: $20,000
Magazines: $100,000
Newspapers: $10,000
Founded: 1946
Gross sales or billing: $74,600,000

Manufactures extruded plastic netting used in various applications including filtration, parts protection, grocery store case liners, automotive, aquaculture & fencing. Mailing Address: PO Box 40909, Austin, TX 78704-0909.

DELTA UPSILON INTERNATIONAL FRATERNITY

8705 Founders Rd, Box 68942
Indianapolis, IN 46268
Telephone: (317) 875-8900, FAX: (317) 876-1629, E-Mail: ihq@deltau.org, Web Site: www.deltau.org
Chmn: William L. Messick

Pres: E. Bernard Franklin Dr.
Sec: Charles E. Downton
Treas: David G. Herzer
Alumni Dir: Malcom P. Branch
Conducts Business: U.S., Canada
Employees: 11
Primary Market Served: Consumer
Catalog available online
Direct online sales
Advertising/Marketing Budget Related to Direct Marketing: 0-25%
Direct Marketing ad budget:
Direct Mail: $10,000
Magazines: $100,000
Founded: 1834

Headquarters for Delta Upsilon International Fraternity chapters in the U.S. & Canada. Offers fraternity related items.

DELUXE LABORATORIES INC

Div. of Rank of London
5433 Fernwood Ave
Hollywood, CA 90027
Telephone: (323) 462-6171, FAX: (323) 960-7016, E-Mail: steven.vananda@bydeluxe.com, Web Site: www.bydeluxe.com
Pres, CEO: Peter Pacitti
Exec VP & CFO: Tom Vale
VP, Mktg: Dierdre Kurnett
VP & Gen Mgr: Michael Jackman
Conducts Business: U.S., Canada
Employees: 1,200
Primary Market Served: Business
Catalog available online
Indirect online sales
Advertising/Marketing Budget Related to Direct Marketing: 0-25%

Full-service video tape duplication, packaging & fulfillment services.

DENVER TAX SOFTWARE INC

PO Box 632285
Littleton, CO 80163-2285
Telephone: (303) 796-7780, (800) 326-6686, FAX: (888) 326-6686, Web Site: www.denvertax.com
Owner & Pres: Dave Kaufmann
Primary Market Served: Business
Catalog available online
Direct online sales

Tax software to CPAs.

DERMAC LABS INC

dba Touch of Mink
PO Box 5268
Salem, OR 97304-0268
Telephone: (503) 399-8181, (800) 547-9164, FAX: (503) 581-7439, Web Site: www.touchofmink.com
Pres & CEO: John Simpson

Conducts Business: U.S., Taiwan
Employees: 22
Primary Market Served: Business & Consumer
Advertising/Marketing Budget Related to Direct Marketing: 76-100%
Founded: 1970
Gross sales or billing: $1,800,000

Manufacturer of skin & hair care products. Supply hotel amenities. Private packaging for private labels.

DESERET BOOK

THE DMA

Div. of Deseret Book
PO Box 30178
Salt Lake City, UT 84130-0178
Telephone: (801) 534-1515, (800) 453-4532, FAX: (801) 517-3392, Web Site: www.deseretbook.com
Mgr: Rex T. Carlisle Jr.
Dir: Mark Standing
Conducts Business: Worldwide
Employees: 3
Primary Market Served: Consumer
Founded: 1871

Retail, mail & phone order sales of books & other related book store merchandise with emphasis on religion.

DETAILS INTERACTIVE LLC

30 Manchester Dr
Westfield, NJ 07090-2265
Telephone: (917) 331-0685, E-Mail: mark@detailsinteractive.com, Web Site: www.detailsinteractive.com

THE DETROIT INSTITUTE OF ARTS

5200 Woodward Ave
Detroit, MI 48202
Telephone: (313) 833-7900, FAX: (313) 833-1390, Web Site: www.dia.org
Dir: Graham W. Beal
Retail Opers Dir: Joyce Harding
Conducts Business: U.S.
Primary Market Served: Business & Consumer
Catalog available online
Direct online sales
Gross sales or billing: $55,400,000

Museum wholesale & retail merchandise.

DEVELOPMENT DIMENSIONS INTERNATIONAL

1225 Washington Pike
Bridgeville, PA 15017-2838
Telephone: (412) 257-0600, (800) 933-4463, FAX: (412) 220-2942, E-Mail: info@ddiworld.com, Web Site: www.ddiworld.com
Owner & Pres: William C. Byham

Pres: Bob Rogers
Cons DDI Direct: Jane Miller Rollman
Primary Market Served: Business

Human resources training & consulting.

DEVRY INC
1 Tower Ln Ste 2350
Oakbrook Terrace, IL 60181-4633
Telephone: (630) 571-7700, FAX: (602) 943-4108, Web Site: www.devry.com
Pres & CEO: Daniel Hamburger
VP Corp Devel & Plng: John P. Roselli
Dir Mktg: Joann Seager
Conducts Business: U.S., Canada
Employees: 4,800
Primary Market Served: Consumer
Gross sales or billing: $933,000,000

Education in electronics, computer information systems, telecommunications, business operations & accounting, either through home studies or in-house instruction.

DEXTA CORP
962 Kaiser Rd
Napa, CA 94558
Telephone: (707) 255-2454, (800) 733-3982, FAX: (707) 255-8520, Web Site: www.dexta.com
Pres: Paul Rusin
Primary Market Served: Business

Sell medical & dental equipment factory direct.

DIAGRAPH CORP
One Missouri Research Park Dr
Saint Charles, MO 63304-5685
Telephone: (636) 300-2000, (800) 722-1125, FAX: (636) 300-2004, E-Mail: info@diagraph.com, Web Site: www.diagraph.com
Mktg Dir: Bill Myers
Prod Mgr: Jackie Goodell
Conducts Business: U.S.
Primary Market Served: Business
Catalog available online
Founded: 1896

Industrial marking products including labels, ink jet printers & label printer applicators.

DIAL-A-MATTRESS
1000 S Oyster Bay Rd
Hicksville, NY 11801-3527
Telephone: (718) 472-1200, (800) 824-7777, FAX: (718) 482-6561, E-Mail: sales@mattress.com, Web Site: www.mattress.com
Pres & CEO: Napoleon Barragan
Exec VP & Gen Mgr: Joe Vicens

Exec VP & Gen Mgr: William A. Johnson
Adv Mgr: Veronica Rodas
Conducts Business: U.S.
Employees: 280
Primary Market Served: Business & Consumer
Catalog available online
Direct online sales
Advertising/Marketing Budget Related to Direct Marketing: 0-25%
Direct Marketing ad budget: $5,500,000
Direct Mail: $150,000
Magazines: $260,000
Newspapers: $340,000
TV/Radio: $4,000,000
Founded: 1976
Gross sales or billing: $170,000,000

Sell mattresses, box springs & bedding accessories via the telephone & retail in over 500 showrooms.

DIDIT
330 Old Country Rd (Suite 206)
Mineola, NY 11501-4143
Telephone: (212) 631-0157, Web Site: www.did-it.com
Exec Chmn: Kevin Lee
Primary Market Served: Consumer

THE DMA DIEBOLD INC
3792 Boettler Oaks Dr (Suite A), PO Box 3077
Uniontown, OH 44685-7769
Telephone: (330) 899-2510, (800) DIE-BOLD, FAX: (330) 490-3794, E-Mail: barronp@diebold.com, Web Site: www.diebold.com
Pres, CEO & Dir: Thomas W. Swidarski
Exec VP & CFO: Kevin J. Krakora
Chmn: John N. Lauer
DM Dir: Pamela Barron Leach
Commun Asst: Michael Jacobsen
Global Mgr, Inside Sls & Sls Support: Marta Blase
Conducts Business: Worldwide
Employees: 15,500
Primary Market Served: Business
Catalog available online
Direct online sales
Advertising/Marketing Budget Related to Direct Marketing: 26-50%
Founded: 1859
Gross sales or billing: $2,900,000,000

Sells ATM machines & supplies.

THE DMA DIGDEV DIRECT
260 SW Natura Ave (fl 2)
Deerfield Beach, FL 33441
Telephone: (954) 949-9500, Web Site: www.foundationmediagroup.com
Primary Market Served: Business & Consumer

DINN BROTHERS INC
"The Trophy People"
221 Interstate Dr
West Springfield, MA 01089
Telephone: (413) 750-3466, (800) 628-9657, FAX: (800) 876-7497, E-Mail: sales@dinntrophy.com, Web Site: www.dinntrophy.com
Pres: Bill Dinn
Sls Mgr: Michael Dinn
Conducts Business: U.S.
Primary Market Served: Business & Consumer
Catalog available online
Founded: 1956
Gross sales or billing: $8,400,000

Sell trophies & awards direct to schools, clubs & organizations.

DIRECT ENERGY
2225 Sheppard Ave E (Suite 100)
Toronto, ON, Canada M2J 5C2
Telephone: (416) 758-8700, (800) 348-2999
Exec VP: Anna Filipopoulas
Primary Market Served: Business & Consumer

DIRECT SUPPLY INC
6767 N Industrial Rd
Milwaukee, WI 53223
Telephone: (414) 358-2805, (800) 634-7328, FAX: (414) 358-2397, E-Mail: deardirect@directs.com, Web Site: www.directsupply.net
Pres & CEO: Robert J. Hillis
Conducts Business: U.S.
Employees: 600
Primary Market Served: Consumer
Catalog available online
Direct online sales
Founded: 1985
Gross sales or billing: $89,900,000

Provide long-term healthcare equipment to nursing home facilities.

THE DMA DIRECTV
Div. of Hughes Electronics Corp
2230 E Imperial Hwy
El Segundo, CA 90245
Telephone: (310) 535-5000, FAX: (310) 535-5225
Primary Market Served: Business

Sell direct broadcast satellite service to American consumers. Toll free fax# (800) DIRECTV.

DIRXION
1859 Bowles Ave (Suite 100)
Saint Louis, MO 63026-1936
Telephone: (636) 717-2300, Web Site: www.dirxion.com
Mktg Mgr: Jennifer Graham

DISCOVERY COMMUNICATIONS LLC
One Discovery Pl
Silver Spring, MD 20910
Telephone: (240) 662-2000, FAX: (240) 662-1868, Web Site: corporate. discovery.com
Founder & Chmn: John Hendricks
Pres & CEO: David Zaslav
COO: Mark Hollinger
CMO: Wonya Y. Lucas
Sr Exec VP, HR: Adria Alpert-Romm
Primary Market Served: Business & Consumer
Founded: 1982

Worldwide cable network: Travel, Discovery Channel, The Learning Channel & Animal Planet. Discovery showcase networks & multimedia on-line.

DISCOVERY TOYS
7364 Marathon Dr (Suite A)
Livermore, CA 94550-3000
Telephone: (925) 606-2600, (800) 426-4777, FAX: (925) 370-0289, Web Site: www.discoverytoysinc.net
Conducts Business: U.S., Canada, Japan
Employees: 171
Primary Market Served: Consumer
Founded: 1978

Sell developmental books, toys & games via home demonstration.

DOALL CO
1480 S Wolf Rd
Wheeling, IL 60090-6514
Telephone: (847) 824-1122, (800) 92-DOALL, FAX: (847) 699-7524, E-Mail: info@doall.com, Web Site: www.doall.com
Chmn & Pres: Michael Wilkie
COO: Clifford Gordon
Mktg Dir: Bruno Gruaz
Primary Market Served: Business
Catalog available online
Direct online sales

Provide industrial supplies & metal capital equipment for industries.

DOCTOR'S BEST INC
197 Avenida La Pata (#A)
San Clemente, CA 92673-6307
Telephone: (949) 498-3628, (800) 333-6977, FAX: (800) 754-2036, (949) 498-3952, E-Mail: info@ drbvitamins.com, Web Site: www. drbvitamins.com
Pres: Ken Halvorsrude
VP Corp Opers: Peter Dunphy
COO: Evan Falchuk
Conducts Business: U.S.
Employees: 11

Primary Market Served: Business & Consumer
Catalog available online
Indirect online sales
Advertising/Marketing Budget Related to Direct Marketing: 0-25%
Founded: 1990
Gross sales or billing: $3,000,000

Sell nutritional (food) supplements, primarily wholesale to mail order catalogers.

DOMINION RETAIL INC
120 Tredegar St
Richmond, VA 23219-4306
Telephone: (804) 819-2268, Web Site: www.dom.com
Mng Dir: R. Michael Rose
Primary Market Served: Business & Consumer

EDWARD DON & CO
2500 S Harlem Ave
North Riverside, IL 60546
Telephone: (708) 442-9400, (800) 777-4366, FAX: (708) 442-0436, Web Site: www.don.com
Chmn: Robert E. Don
Pres & CEO: Steven R. Don
COO & CFO: Jim Jones
VP: Jim Lyman
VP, HR: Mark Scheider
Conducts Business: U.S., Caribbean, U.K., Korea
Employees: 1,500
Primary Market Served: Business
Catalog available online
Direct online sales
Advertising/Marketing Budget Related to Direct Marketing: 0-25%
Founded: 1921

Distributor of food service equipment & supplies.

DOUGLAS PRESS INC
2810 Madison St
Bellwood, IL 60104-2256
Telephone: (708) 547-8400, (800) 323-0705, FAX: (708) 547-0296, Web Site: www.douglaspress.com
Pres: Frank Fienberg
VP, Mktg: Debra Fienberg
Conducts Business: U.S., Canada, Australia, U.K., Belgium
Employees: 250
Primary Market Served: Business
Catalog available online
Direct online sales
Gross sales or billing: $24,000,000

Manufacturer of games of chance used by non-profit organizations, state lotteries & sales promotion agencies.

DOW CHEMICAL USA
2030 Dow Center
Midland, MI 48674
Telephone: (989) 636-1000, (800) 447-4369, FAX: (989) 832-1465, E-Mail: jadams@dow.com, Web Site: www. dow.com
Chmn, CEO & Pres: Andrew Liveris
Exec VP, CFO & Dir: Geoffrey E. Merszei
Sr VP & CIO: David E. Kepler II
Exec VP: Michael R. Gambrell
Tax Dir: Charles J. Hahn
Conducts Business: Worldwide
Employees: 5,500
Primary Market Served: Business
Catalog available online
Gross sales or billing: $50,000,000,000

International chemical company.

DOW CORNING CORP
PO Box 994
Midland, MI 48686
Telephone: (989) 496-4000, (800) 248-2481, FAX: (989) 496-4572, Web Site: www.dowcorning.com
Chmn: Stephanie A. Burns
Pres & CEO: Robert D. Hansen
EVP & CFO: Joseph D. Sheets
Sr VP & CTO: Gregg A. Zank
Sr VP, Gen Counsel & Corp Sec: Sue K McDonnell
VP & Chief Mktg Officer: Brian J Chermside
VP & Chief HR Officer: Mike Conway
VP & CIO: Kristy Folkwein
Conducts Business: Worldwide
Employees: 9,000
Primary Market Served: Business
Catalog available online
Indirect online sales
Founded: 1943

Develop, manufacture & market silicones, related specialty chemical materials, hyperpure polycrystalline silicon, silicon-source chemicals & certain specialty healthcare products.

DRAGICH AUTO LITERATURE
PO Box 1024
Princeton, MN 55371-4024
Telephone: (763) 389-8600, FAX: (763) 389-8222, E-Mail: mail@ dragich.com, Web Site: www. dragich.com
Pres: John Dragich
Primary Market Served: Business & Consumer
Founded: 1974

Sell books on automobiles.

DRAWING BOARD INC
101 E 9th St
Waynesboro, PA 17268-2200

Telephone: (301) 739-4487, (800) 527-9530, FAX: (800) 253-1838, E-Mail: customerservice@drawingboard.com, Web Site: www.drawingboard.com
Pres: Mark Ladouceur
Conducts Business: U.S.
Primary Market Served: Business & Consumer

Sell imprinted stationery, labels, business forms, Christmas cards & continuous forms supplies to individuals & small business firms by direct mail & space advertising.

DREIS & KRUMP MANUFACTURING CO

481 Governors Hwy (Suite 2)
Peotone, IL 60468
Telephone: (708) 258-1200, FAX: (708) 258-9682, E-Mail: chicago@dreis-krump.com, Web Site: www.dreis-krump.com
Pres: R. Wolfer
VP, Fin: A. Anderson
Conducts Business: Worldwide
Employees: 50
Primary Market Served: Business
Advertising/Marketing Budget Related to Direct Marketing: 0-25%
Direct Marketing ad budget:
Magazines: 100%
Founded: 1899
Gross sales or billing: $8,000,000

Manufacturer of metal forming equipment sold worldwide.

DREXEL UNIVERSITY (GOODWIN COLLEGE OF PROFESSIONAL STUDIES)

3001 Market St (Suite 100), One Drexel Plaza
Philadelphia, PA 19104
E-Mail: goodwin@drexel.edu, Web Site: www.drexel.edu/goodwin
Dean: William F. Lynch Ph.D.
Dir Mktg & Recruitment: Elizabeth Hanson
Recruitment: Patricia Gremmel
Conducts Business: U.S.
Employees: 73
Primary Market Served: Business

Markets continuing professional education non-credit seminars, conferences & workshops for professionals. Key audiences: government employees, engineers, entrepreneurs & managers. Programs offered nationally.

THE DU-RITE GROUP INC

103 S Van Brunt St
Englewood, NJ 07631-3437

Telephone: (201) 387-7000, FAX: (201) 385-8513, E-Mail: information@duriteconstruction.com, Web Site: www.duriteconstruction.com
VP: Dennis Zysman
VP: Gary Zysman
Conducts Business: U.S.
Primary Market Served: Business

Construction company.

DUGGAN & BROWN INC

1617 Old York Rd
Abington, PA 19001
Telephone: (215) 657-3400, FAX: (215) 657-6119, E-Mail: john@dugganandbrown.com
CEO: Curtis A. Clarke
Pres: Jerry Brown
VP: John P. Duggan
Conducts Business: U.S.
Employees: 10
Primary Market Served: Business
Advertising/Marketing Budget Related to Direct Marketing: 76-100%
Founded: 1973
Gross sales or billing: $50,000,000

Manufacturer representative for direct mail.

DUNCAN AVIATION

3701 Aviation Rd, Lincoln Airport
Lincoln, NE 68524
Telephone: (402) 475-2611, (800) 228-4277, FAX: (402) 475-5541, Web Site: www.duncanaviation.com
Chmn: J. Robert Duncan
Pres: Aaron C. Hilkemann
Exec VP & COO: Mark Matthes
CFO: Jeff Lake
Gulfstream Tech Rep: John Kauppila
Conducts Business: Worldwide
Employees: 525
Primary Market Served: Business
Catalog available online
Indirect online sales
Advertising/Marketing Budget Related to Direct Marketing: 26-50%
Gross sales or billing: $123,000,000

Sell & service corporate aircraft.

DUNCRAFT INC

102 Fisherville Rd
Concord, NH 03303-9020
Telephone: (603) 224-0200, (800) 593-5656, FAX: (603) 226-3735, E-Mail: info@duncraft.com, Web Site: www.duncraft.com
CEO: Michael M. Dunn
Pres: Sharon Dunn
Conducts Business: U.S.
Employees: 55
Primary Market Served: Business & Consumer
Catalog available online

Direct online sales
Advertising/Marketing Budget Related to Direct Marketing: 76-100%
Direct Marketing ad budget: $1,000,000
Direct Mail: 90%
Online: 10%
Founded: 1952
Gross sales or billing: $6,900,000

Retail-wholesale mail order company selling wild bird supplies to the nation.

E I DUPONT DE NEMOURS & CO

1007 Market St
Wilmington, DE 19898
Telephone: (302) 774-1000, FAX: (302) 774-7321, Web Site: www.dupont.com
CEO: Charles Holliday
Chief Mktg & Sls Officer: David Bills
Primary Market Served: Business & Consumer

Operates in six principal business segments: chemical, fibers, polymers, petroleum & diversified business.

DURACELL

Div. of the Gillette Co
8 Research Dr
Bethel, CT 06801
Telephone: (203) 796-4000, FAX: (203) 207-7842, Web Site: www.duracell.com
VP, Mktg: Rick Anderson
Primary Market Served: Business & Consumer
Founded: 1916

Manufacturer of Duracell Alkaline & specialty batteries for consumer & OEM markets; manufacturer of professional products for B to B market

THE DURHAM MANUFACTURING CO

201 Main St
Durham, CT 06422-2108
Telephone: (860) 349-3427, (800) 243-3774, FAX: (800) 782-5499, (860) 349-8572, E-Mail: info@durhammfg.com, Web Site: www.durhammfg.com
Chmn: Herbert Patterson
Pres: Richard Patterson
VP, Prod Devel: John Mansfield
VP, Sls & Mktg: Joe Soja
Conducts Business: U.S., Canada, U.K., Mexico
Employees: 240
Primary Market Served: Business
Catalog available online
Indirect online sales
Advertising/Marketing Budget Related to Direct Marketing: 0-25%

Founded: 1922
Gross sales or billing: $44,000,000

Manufacturer of quality steel office products: literature racks, data processing files, security & first aid boxes, industrial storage bins, cabinets & racks.

THE DWYER GROUP
1020 N University Parks Dr
Waco, TX 76707-3863
Telephone: (254) 759-5850, Web Site:
    www.dwyergroup.com
VP Mktg: Bob Walker

DWYER INSTRUMENTS INC
102 Indiana Hwy 212
Michigan City, IN 46360-1956
Telephone: (219) 879-8868, Web Site:
    www.dwyer-inst.com
Mktg Mgr: Robert Thompson
Primary Market Served: Business

DX ENGINEERING
PO Box 1491
Akron, OH 44309-1491
Telephone: (800) 777-0703, FAX:
    (330) 572-3279, E-Mail: info@
    comteksystems.com, Web Site: www.
    comteksystems.com
Pres: Thomas J. Hayes
Pur Agent: M.C. Hayes
Conducts Business: U.S.
Employees: 7
Primary Market Served: Business
Catalog available online
Direct online sales
Advertising/Marketing Budget Related
    to Direct Marketing: 0-25%
Direct Marketing ad budget:
Direct Mail: 51%
Telephone: 49%
Founded: 1975
Gross sales or billing: $600,000

Manufacture point-of-sale systems.

DYNAMICS RESEARCH CORP
60 Frontage Rd
Andover, MA 01810
Telephone: (978) 475-9090, (800) 522-
    4321, FAX: (978) 475-8205, Web
    Site: www.drc.com
VP, Mktg: Edward Johnson
CFO: David Keleher
Employees: 1,600
Primary Market Served: Business &
    Consumer
Founded: 1955
Gross sales or billing: $259,000,000

Computer software manufacturer & content delivery services.

EMC CORP
176 South St.
Hopkinton, MA 01748
Telephone: (888) 438-3622, Web Site:
    www.emc.com
Sr VP, Corp Mktg: David A. Donatelli
Adv & Brand Strategy: Kim Chrystie
Exec VP: Jeremy Burton
Conducts Business: Worldwide
Employees: 500
Primary Market Served: Business
Advertising/Marketing Budget Related
    to Direct Marketing: 0-25%
Founded: 1979
Gross sales or billing: $11,155,090,000

Supplier of innovative, high-performance information storage products & related services for mainframe, open systems & AS400 computers.

EMED CO INC
PO Box 369
Buffalo, NY 14240-0369
Telephone: (716) 626-1616, (800) 442-
    3633, FAX: (716) 626-1630, E-Mail:
    customerservice@emedco.com, Web
    Site: www.emedco.com
Mktg Dir: Ron Doiel
Mktg Dir: Scott Wardour
Mdsg Mgr: David Ewen
Cust Svc Mgr: Bill Arnold
Mgr: Nick Colca
Conducts Business: U.S.
Primary Market Served: Business
Catalog available online
Direct online sales
Advertising/Marketing Budget Related
    to Direct Marketing: 76-100%
Direct Marketing ad budget:
Direct Mail: 95%
Telephone: 5%

Manufacturer of identification products: signs, labels, tags, markers.

EMS TECHNOLOGIES
660 Engineering Dr
Norcross, GA 30092
Telephone: (770) 263-9200, FAX:
    (770) 447-4405, Web Site: www.
    ems-t.com
Pres: Paul Domorski
Exec VP, CFO & Treas: Don T. Scartz
VP, Gen Counsel: Timothy C. Reis
VP, Bus Opers: Joanne Walker
VP: Gary Shell
Primary Market Served: Business &
    Consumer
Catalog available online

Industrial manufacturer.

ETTSI PREMIUMS & INCENTIVES
301 Indigo Dr
Daytona Beach, FL 32114-1134

Telephone: (386) 271-0204, Web Site:
    www.ettsi.com
Owner, CEO: Frank Bertalli

EXL
10 Exchange Pl
Jersey City, NJ 07302-3918
Telephone: (201) 748-4729
Methodology: Krishna Mehta

EARTHRISE
Subs. of Earthrise Trading Co
2151 Michelson Dr (Suite 258)
Irvine, CA 92648
Telephone: (949) 623-0980, FAX:
    (949) 623-0990, E-Mail: info@
    earthrise.com, Web Site: www.
    earthrise.com
Mktg Dir: Rob Kelly
Primary Market Served: Consumer
Founded: 1982

Health food manufacturer.

EASTERN MICHIGAN UNIVERSITY
1000 College Pl
Ypsilanti, MI 48197
Telephone: (734) 487-1849, FAX:
    (734) 484-1151, Web Site: www.
    emich.edu
Chair: Karen Q. Valvo
Pres: John A. Fallon III
Vice-Chair & Interim VP: Thomas W.
    Sidlik
VP, Bus & Fin Treas: John Beaghan
VP & Interim Provost: Donald M.
    Loppnow
Conducts Business: U.S.
Employees: 2,400
Primary Market Served: Business &
    Consumer
Catalog available online
Founded: 1849
Gross sales or billing: $85,000,000

Market all aspects of the university to a national market.

EASTERN MOUNTAIN SPORTS
1 Vose Farm Rd
Peterborough, NH 03458-2122
Telephone: (603) 924-9571, (800) 463-
    6367, FAX: (603) 924-4320, Web
    Site: www.ems.com
CEO: William Manzee
CFO: Steve Brooks
CMO & Mktg Mgr: Scott Barrett
Sr Mktg Mgr: Donna Edgar
Conducts Business: U.S.
Employees: 500
Primary Market Served: Consumer
Direct Marketing ad budget:
Direct Mail: 100%
Founded: 1967

Retailer of outdoor clothing & equipment.

EASTMAN CHEMICAL CO
200 S Wilcox Dr
Kingsport, TN 37660-5147
Telephone: (800) 695-4322, Web Site:
www.eatman.com
Mktg Communs: Katherine Watkins
Primary Market Served: Business

DAVID EASTON INC
5 Union Sq W (fl 3)
New York, NY 10003-3315
Telephone: (212) 334-3820, FAX:
(212) 334-3821, Web Site: www.
davideastoninc.com
Owner & Pres: David Easton
Primary Market Served: Business &
Consumer

Interior design.

EASYLINK SERVICES INTERNATIONAL CORP
33 Knightsbridge Rd
Piscataway, NJ 08854
Telephone: (800) 828-7115, FAX:
(732) 652-3810, E-Mail: sales@
easylink.com, Web Site: www.
easylink.com
CEO: Tom Stallings
VP, Sls & Mktg: Jim Walsh
Primary Market Served: Business

Designs, develops & markets variety
of business to business facsimile transmission services including fax to fax,
desktop to fax, enhanced fax & broadcast services designed to reduce the
cost of sending as international fax.

EATON CORP
8609 Six Forks Rd
Raleigh, NC 27615-2966
Telephone: (216) 523-4400, (800) 356-
5794, FAX: (216) 523-4787, Web
Site: www.eaton.com
Chmn, Pres & CEO: Alexander M.
Cutler
Exec VP & CFO: Richard H. Fearon
Sr VP: Craig Arnold
VP & CIO: William W. Blausey Jr.
VP: Richard P. Jacobs
Mktg Mgr: Kristin Somers
Conducts Business: U.S., Canada
Employees: 60,000
Primary Market Served: Business
Catalog available online
Founded: 1893
Gross sales or billing: $12,300,000,000

Manufacture & sell electrical & electronic controls to industrial & construction customers.

EBAY
2145 Hamilton Ave
San Jose, CA 95125-5905
Telephone: (408) 376-7400, Web Site:
www.ebay.com
VP, CFO Intl, Ebay Intl AG: Nicholas
Staheyeff

ECOLAB PROFESSIONAL PRODUCTS
Div. of Ecolab Inc
370 N Wabasha St, Ecolab Ctr
Saint Paul, MN 55102-2233
Telephone: (651) 293-4248, FAX:
(651) 225-3025, E-Mail: ecolabs@
ecolabs.com, Web Site: www.ecolab.
com
Dir Mktg: Mark Miller
Conducts Business: U.S., Canada
Employees: 350
Primary Market Served: Business
Advertising/Marketing Budget Related
to Direct Marketing: 26-50%
Direct Marketing ad budget:
Direct Mail: 25%
Magazines: 75%
Founded: 1923
Gross sales or billing: $3,800,000,000

Infection control & cleaning products
for healthcare & institutional/
commercial buildings.

ECONOMY HANDICRAFTS
932 46th St
Brooklyn, NY 11219
Telephone: (718) 431-9300, (800) 216-
1601, FAX: (718) 431-9309, Web
Site: www.vanguardcrafts.com
Pres: Eric Schwedock
Conducts Business: U.S.
Employees: 21
Primary Market Served: Business &
Consumer
Catalog available online
Indirect online sales
Advertising/Marketing Budget Related
to Direct Marketing: 0-25%
Direct Marketing ad budget:
Direct Mail: 75%
Magazines: 25%
Founded: 1959
Gross sales or billing: $1,700,000

Generalized & specialized arts & crafts
supplies. Sell to institutions such as
schools, hospitals & correctional facilities, as well as to individuals.

EDO INTERACTIVE
3841 Green Hills Village Dr (Suite
425)
Nashville, TN 37215-2632
Telephone: (615) 297-6080, Web Site:
www.edointeractive.com
Dir Mktg: Constance Baker

EDROY PRODUCTS CO INC
245 N Midland Ave, PO Box 998
Nyack, NY 10960-0998
Telephone: (845) 358-6600, (800) 233-
8803, FAX: (845) 358-4098, E-Mail:
sales@edroyproducts.com, Web Site:
www.edroyproducts.com
Pres: Steve Stoltze
Conducts Business: U.S., Canada
Employees: 5
Primary Market Served: Business
Catalog available online
Advertising/Marketing Budget Related
to Direct Marketing: 0-25%
Direct Marketing ad budget:
Magazines: 100%
Founded: 1937

Magnifiers & low vision aids.

EDUCATION DIRECT
Div. of A Thompson Co
925 Oak St
Scranton, PA 18515
Telephone: (570) 342-7701, FAX:
(570) 961-4851, Web Site: www.
educationdirect.com
Pres: David Beach
Conducts Business: Worldwide
Employees: 50
Primary Market Served: Consumer
Catalog available online
Advertising/Marketing Budget Related
to Direct Marketing: 76-100%

Marketer of educational training products to industry, consumers &
government.

EDUCATIONAL COIN CO
PO Box 892
Highland, NY 12528-0892
Telephone: (845) 691-6100, Web Site:
www.educationalcoin.com
Dir Mktg: Robin Danziger

EDUCATIONAL INSIGHTS, INC
Subs of Learning Resources
152 W Walnut St Ste 201
Gardena, CA 90248-3147
Telephone: (310) 884-2000, (888) 591-
9334, FAX: (310) 886-8850, E-Mail:
service@edin.com, Web Site: www.
educationalinsights.com
Pres & COO: Jim Whitney
CEO: C. Reid Calcott
VP Prod Devel: Pat Sarka
VP Mktg: Mark J. Mallardi
Conducts Business: U.S., Canada, U.K.
Employees: 100
Primary Market Served: Business
Catalog available online
Indirect online sales
Advertising/Marketing Budget Related
to Direct Marketing: 26-50%
Direct Marketing ad budget:

Direct Mail: 90%
Magazines: 5%
Telephone: 5%
Founded: 1962
Gross sales or billing: $7,500,000

Manufacturer of educational toys, games & computer software for both school & home use.

THE DMA EDUCATIONAL TESTING SERVICE
666 Rosedale Rd (M/S 40-L)
Princeton, NJ 08541-0001
Telephone: (609) 683-2292, FAX: (609) 734-5410, Web Site: www.ets.org
External Commun Dir: Tom Ewing
Grp Dir Web Svcs: Laura Miller
Conducts Business: Worldwide
Employees: 2,433
Primary Market Served: Business & Consumer
Catalog available online
Direct online sales
Founded: 1947
Gross sales or billing: $860,000,000

SAT'S, PSAT'S, High school tests, GRE, GMAT, TOEFL, NAP.

EDUTREK
155 N 400 W (Suite 150)
Salt Lake City, UT 84103-1132
Telephone: (801) 716-3924, Web Site: edutrek.com

College selection & financial aid advice services

EFFECTIVE PROMOTIONS INC
PO Box 210
Fort Johnson, NY 12070-0210
Telephone: (518) 274-0291, (888) 467-3514, FAX: (518) 274-0290, Web Site: www.efpromotions.com
Pres: Patricia M. O'Brien
Employees: 10
Primary Market Served: Business & Consumer
Catalog available online
Direct online sales

Direct mail marketing of poly bags.

EIRE DIRECT
720 N Franklin (Suite 310)
Chicago, IL 60610-3512
Telephone: (312) 640-4000, FAX: (312) 640-0324, E-Mail: info@eiredirect.com, Web Site: www.eiredirect.com
Partner: Ellen Best
Partner: Jim Kearney
Primary Market Served: Business & Consumer
Catalog available online

Advertising/Marketing Budget Related to Direct Marketing: 26-50%
Founded: 1996

U.S. office for the national telephone company of Ireland.

ELI JOURNALS
Div. of Mosaic Media Inc
2222 Sedwick Rd (Suite 101)
Durham, NC 27713-2658
Telephone: (585) 203-5248, (800) 223-8720, FAX: (585) 292-4392, Web Site: www.elijournals.com
CEO: Greg Lindberg
Conducts Business: U.S., Canada, U.K.
Primary Market Served: Business
Catalog available online
Direct online sales
Advertising/Marketing Budget Related to Direct Marketing: 76-100%
Direct Mail: 50%
Online: 50%

Publish self-study computer training materials and newsletters.

EMERGENCY ESSENTIALS INC
653 N 1500th W
Orem, UT 84057-2831
Telephone: (801) 222-9596, FAX: (801) 222-9598, E-Mail: webmaster@beprepared.com, Web Site: www.beprepared.com
CEO & Pres: David Sheets
VP: Don Pectol
VP: Matt Nettesheim
Conducts Business: U.S.
Primary Market Served: Business & Consumer
Catalog available online
Direct online sales
Founded: 1987

Specialize in home storage, first aid & camping equipment.

EMPEROR CLOCK LLC
PO Box 960
Amherst, VA 24521
Telephone: (800) 642-0011, FAX: (434) 946-1420, E-Mail: emperor@emperorclock.com, Web Site: www.emperorclock.com
VP: Eleanor Carpenter
Customer Svc Mgr: Julie George
Conducts Business: Worldwide
Employees: 25
Primary Market Served: Business & Consumer
Catalog available online
Indirect online sales
Advertising/Marketing Budget Related to Direct Marketing: 76-100%
Direct Marketing ad budget:

Direct Mail: 70%
Magazines: 20%
Newspapers: 1%
Online: 9%
Founded: 1969

Manufacturer of do-it-yourself grandfather clock kits & fully assembled grandfather clocks, wall and mantel clocks.

EMPIRE SCIENTIFIC
151 E Industry Ct
Deer Park, NY 11729-5713
Telephone: (631) 595-9206, (800) 645-7220, FAX: (631) 595-9384, (800) 343-5733, E-Mail: sales@empirescientific.com, Web Site: www.empirescientific.com
Pres: Jeffrey English
VP: Spencer Slipko
Conducts Business: U.S., Australia, Japan, England, Canada, Sweden, Italy
Employees: 30
Primary Market Served: Business
Catalog available online
Indirect online sales
Direct Marketing ad budget:
Direct Mail: $150,000
Magazines: $50,000
Telephone: $50,000
Gross sales or billing: $4,000,000

Manufacturer of video camcorder batteries, cellular phone & cordless phone batteries.

ENCORE MARKETING INTERNATIONAL
4501 Forbes Blvd
Lanham, MD 20706-4236
Telephone: (301) 459-8020, (800) 846-9398, FAX: (301) 731-0525, E-Mail: customerservice@encoremarketing.com, Web Site: www.encoremarketing.com
CEO: Stanley Plotnick
Pres: Stephen Klein
EVP Mktg: Dave Gallimore
VP Mktg: Bonnie Kasander
Conducts Business: U.S., Canada, Europe
Employees: 200
Primary Market Served: Consumer
Catalog available online
Direct online sales
Advertising/Marketing Budget Related to Direct Marketing: 76-100%
Direct Marketing ad budget: $45,000
Online: 25%
Telephone: 75%
Founded: 1978
Gross sales or billing: $75,000,000

Offer a variety of branded and unbranded Discount Clubs & Loyalty Programs.

ENERGIZER BATTERY CO INC

Subs. of Ralston Purina Corp
533 Maryville University Dr
Saint Louis, MO 63141
Telephone: (314) 985-2000, (800) 383-7323, FAX: (636) 733-4001, Web Site: www.energizer.com
CEO: J. Patrick Mulcahy
VP, Mktg: David Hatfield
Conducts Business: Worldwide
Primary Market Served: Business & Consumer

Sell batteries, lighting products & consumer packaged goods.

ENERPAC

Div. of Applied Power Inc
PO Box 9010
Menomonee Falls, WI 53052-9010
Telephone: (262) 781-6600, (800) 433-2766, FAX: (262) 781-1028, Web Site: www.enerpac.com
Chmn & Pres: Bob Arzbacher
Global Mktg Mgr: Larry Rothering
Mktg Commun Lead Mgr: Kandy Ra-ether
Conducts Business: Worldwide
Employees: 500
Primary Market Served: Business & Consumer
Advertising/Marketing Budget Related to Direct Marketing: 0-25%
Founded: 1910

Specialize in sale & design of hydraulic tools & equipment.

ENNIS INC

2441 Presidential Pkwy
Midlothian, TX 76065-3723
Telephone: (972) 775-9801, (800) 962-0944, FAX: (800) 645-8339, Web Site: www.ennis.com
Chmn, Pres & CEO: Keith S. Walters
Exec VP & Treas: Michael D. Magill
VP, Opers: Terry Pennington
VP, Fin, CFO & Sec: Richard L. Travis Jr.
VP, Admin & Dir: Ronald M. Graham
Primary Market Served: Business
Catalog available online
Direct online sales
Gross sales or billing: $584,000,000

Manufacturer of business forms & promotional & commercial products. Toll free fax: (800) 972-3100.

ENTERGY

639 Loyola Ave (Suite 300)
New Orleans, LA 70113-7106
Telephone: (504) 576-4000, (800) EN-TERGY, FAX: (504) 576-4428, Web Site: www.entergy.com
Chmn & CEO: J. Wayne Leonard

Pres & COO: Richard Smith
Exec VP & CFO: Leo Denault
Exec VP, Opers: Mark T. Savoff
Exec VP: Curt L. Hebert Jr.
Conducts Business: U.S.
Primary Market Served: Business & Consumer
Gross sales or billing: $11,000,000,000

Public utility.

ENTERPREX INTERNATIONAL CORP

12101 Clark St Ste G
Arcadia, CA 91006-6031
Telephone: (626) 256-1444, FAX: (626) 256-1404, E-Mail: premium@enterprex.com, Web Site: www.enterprex.com
Pres: Walter Yuan
VP: Dennis Chen
Conducts Business: U.S.
Employees: 7
Primary Market Served: Business & Consumer
Catalog available online
Advertising/Marketing Budget Related to Direct Marketing: 0-25%
Founded: 1973
Gross sales or billing: $4,000,000

Marketer of consumer premium merchandise.

ENTERPRISE IRELAND

345 Park Ave (17th fl)
New York, NY 10154-0037
Telephone: (212) 371-3600, FAX: (212) 371-6398, Web Site: www.enterprise-ireland.com
CEO: Frank Ryan
Dir Americas: Marina Donohoe
East Coast Mgr: Tom Cusak
Exec Dir: Gerry Murphy
Conducts Business: Australia, Central, N., S. America, Europe, Far East Realm
Employees: 16
Primary Market Served: Business & Consumer
Advertising/Marketing Budget Related to Direct Marketing: 0-25%
Founded: 1991
Gross sales or billing: $7,000,000,000

Agency of Irish government established to promote & develop exports from Ireland. Irish government trade & technology division.

ENTERTAINMENT MUSIC MARKETING CORP

dba EMMC
795 Foxhurst Rd
Baldwin, NY 11510-3530

Telephone: (631) 243-0600, FAX: (631) 243-0605, E-Mail: emmcmusic@aol.com, Web Site: www.emmcmusic.com
VP & Owner: Jeffrey Saltzman
Opers Mgr: Michael Wentz
Conducts Business: Worldwide
Employees: 9
Primary Market Served: Business
Catalog available online
Direct online sales
Advertising/Marketing Budget Related to Direct Marketing: 26-50%
Direct Marketing ad budget:
Direct Mail: $20,000
Magazines: $6,000
Telephone: $6,000
Founded: 1976
Gross sales or billing: $1,400,000

Importer & supplier of musical instruments, including string instruments, amplifiers & PA systems. Also, electronic pianos, sing-a-long machines & tapes.

ESCO CORP

2141 NW 25th Ave
Portland, OR 97210-2578
Telephone: (503) 228-2141, FAX: (503) 778-6682, Web Site: www.escocorp.com
VP & Gen Mgr Mining Div: Jim Songer
Gen Mgr Sls & Mktg, NA & SA: Tim Elbel
Gen Mgr Construction Div: Pat Fonner
Process Devel Svcs: John Hemmingson
Conducts Business: Worldwide
Employees: 2,000
Primary Market Served: Business
Advertising/Marketing Budget Related to Direct Marketing: 0-25%

Manufacture & sell earth moving equipment to the mining & construction markets. Dredging & forestry products.

ESCORT INC

5440 Westchester Rd
West Chester, OH 45069-2950
Telephone: (513) 870-8500, (800) 964-3138, FAX: (513) 870-8509, E-Mail: sales@escortradar.com, Web Site: www.escortradar.com
CEO: Greg Blair
Pres & COO: John Larson
VP Sls & Mktg: Gary Oppito
Adv & DM Mgr: Kim Schmidt
Conducts Business: U.S.
Employees: 250
Primary Market Served: Consumer
Advertising/Marketing Budget Related to Direct Marketing: 76-100%
Gross sales or billing: $20,200,000

Manufacturer & marketer of the passport line of radar & laser detectors.

ESPRIT LINE CO LTD - USA
11 Heronvue Rd
Greenwich, CT 06831-2906
Telephone: (203) 629-5124
Pres & CEO: Noboru Otani

ESSELTE AMERICAS
An Esselte Co
225 Broadhollow Rd
Melville, NY 11747-2340
Telephone: (631) 675-5700, (800) 645-6051, FAX: (631) 622-1970, Web Site: www.curtis.com
Pres & CEO: Magnus Nicolin
Conducts Business: U.S., Canada, Europe, Mexico
Primary Market Served: Business & Consumer

Manufacturer of computer accessories, furniture, printer sound enclosures & microfilm storage products.

ESTEE LAUDER INC
767 Fifth Ave
New York, NY 10153
Telephone: (212) 572-4200, (866) 467-7363, FAX: (212) 572-3942, Web Site: www.esteelauder.com
CEO: William Lauder
Exec VP Global Creative Directions: Aerin Lauder
Exec VP HR: Amy DiGeso
Exec VP: Harvey Gedeon
VP: Javier Perez
Primary Market Served: Consumer
Catalog available online
Direct online sales
Founded: 1946

Perfumes & treatment products.

ETHYL CORP
330 S Fourth St, PO Box 2189
Richmond, VA 23218
Telephone: (804) 788-5000, FAX: (804) 788-5688, Web Site: www.ethyl.com
Chmn & CEO: Bruce C. Gotwald
Pres & COO: Thomas E. Gotwald
VP, HR & External Affairs: Henry C. Page Jr
Conducts Business: Worldwide
Employees: 1,800
Primary Market Served: Business
Advertising/Marketing Budget Related to Direct Marketing: 0-25%
Founded: 1887
Gross sales or billing: $1,030,000,000

Develops, manufactures & blends performance-enhancing fuel & lubricant additives marketed worldwide to refiners & others who sell petroleum products for use in transportation & industrial equipment. Ethyl additives increase the value of gasoline, diesel & heating fuels, as well as lubricants for engines, automatic transmission, gears & hydraulic & industrial equipment.

EVEREX COMPUTER SYSTEMS INC
48319 Fremont Blvd
Fremont, CA 94538-6580
Telephone: (866) 850-8835, (800) 383-7391, FAX: (510) 683-2186, E-Mail: customerservice@everex.com, Web Site: www.everex.com
Pres: Yale Ma
Gen Mgr & VP, Sls: John Lin
Conducts Business: Worldwide
Primary Market Served: Business
Catalog available online
Direct online sales
Founded: 1983
Gross sales or billing: $500,000,000

Manufacture computer peripherals & personal computer systems.

EXECUTIVE ENTERPRISES INC
12 Skyline Dr
Hawthorne, NY 10532-2133
Telephone: (860) 701-5900, (800) 831-8333, FAX: (800) 250-3861, (860) 701-5909, E-Mail: info@ eeiconferences.com, Web Site: www. eeiconferences.com
CEO: Glenn Shapiro
COO & CFO: David Berks
Sr Mktg Mgr: Sally Sheffield
Conducts Business: U.S., Canada
Employees: 35
Primary Market Served: Business
Catalog available online
Indirect online sales
Advertising/Marketing Budget Related to Direct Marketing: $2MM%
Direct Marketing ad budget:
Direct Mail: 99.8%
Telephone: .2%
Founded: 1971
Gross sales or billing: $15,000,000

Conduct seminars & conferences for corporate executives, attorneys, engineers, accountants, bankers, insurance companies, human resource executives & government employees.

EXECUTIVE PROTECTION PRODUCTS INC
351 Second St.
Napa, CA 94559

Telephone: (707) 253-7142, FAX: (707) 253-7149, E-Mail: services@ epsecuritysolutions.com, Web Site: epsecuritysolutions.com
Pres: Gene Kelly
Primary Market Served: Business

Security consultation & systems to schools, government agencies & corporations.

EXPERIENCE IN SOFTWARE INC
2029 Durant Ave Ste 201
Berkeley, CA 94704-1564
Telephone: (510) 644-0694, (800) 678-7008, FAX: (510) 644-3823, Web Site: www.projectkickstart.com
Pres: Roy A. Nierenberg
Mktg Mgr: Carolyn Burd
Conducts Business: Worldwide
Employees: 4
Primary Market Served: Business & Consumer
Catalog available online
Indirect online sales
Advertising/Marketing Budget Related to Direct Marketing: 76-100%
Direct Marketing ad budget:
Direct Mail: 85%
Magazines: 15%
Founded: 1983

Software publisher.

EXPRESSIONS CUSTOM FURNITURE
Div. of Century Furniture Industries
401 11th St NW, PO Box 608
Hickory, NC 28603-0608
Telephone: (828) 328-1851, FAX: (828) 328-2176, Web Site: www. expressionsfurniture.com
Conducts Business: U.S.
Employees: 40
Primary Market Served: Business & Consumer

Custom furniture, case goods & accessories; manufacturer & retailer.

F P INTERNATIONAL
1090 Mills Way
Redwood City, CA 94063
Telephone: (650) 261-5300, (800) 866-9946, FAX: (650) 361-1713, Web Site: www.fpintl.com
VP Mktg: Larry Lenhart
Mktg Mgr: Jim Jensen
VP, Sls: Harry Reynolds
Sr VP Sls & Mktg: Joe Nezwek
Conducts Business: U.S.
Employees: 500
Primary Market Served: Business
Catalog available online
Indirect online sales
Advertising/Marketing Budget Related

to Direct Marketing: 0-25%
Founded: 1967
Gross sales or billing: $100,000,000

Manufacture protective packing
materials.

FAFCO INC
435 Otterson Dr
Chico, CA 95928-8207
Telephone: (530) 332-2100, (800) 994-
7652, FAX: (530) 332-2109, Web
Site: www.fafco.com
Chmn, Pres & CEO: Freeman A. Ford
Sls & Mktg Coord: Suzanne Caraveo
Employees: 62
Primary Market Served: Business &
Consumer
Catalog available online
Indirect online sales
Founded: 1969
Gross sales or billing: $7,900,000

Manufacture solar pool heating energy
panels & thermal energy & ice cool
storage systems.

FLM GRAPHICS CORP
123 Lehigh Dr
Fairfield, NJ 07004-3095
Telephone: (973) 575-9450, E-Mail:
info@flmgraphics.com, Web Site:
www.flmgraphics.com
CIO: Mark Hahn
Pres: Vince Fiorello
Founder & CEO: Frank L. Misischia
VP: Peter Burke
Conducts Business: U.S., Canada, Pu-
erto Rico, Caribbean
Employees: 75
Primary Market Served: Business &
Consumer
Catalog available online
Direct Marketing ad budget: $250,000
Direct Mail: 50%
Magazines: 50%
Gross sales or billing: $19,000,000

Process to professional photographers,
industrial photo departments, schools,
school photographers & advanced
amateurs. Includes signs, posters, murals & banners, point of purchase &
exhibitors.

FMC CORP
1735 Market St
Philadelphia, PA 19103
Telephone: (215) 299-6000, FAX:
(215) 299-5998, Web Site: www.
fmc.com
Chmn, Pres & CEO: William G.
Walter
Sr VP & CFO: William K. Foster
CIO: Michael F. Giesler
VP, Gen Mgr: Theodore H. Butz
VP, Treas: Thomas C. Deas Jr.
Conducts Business: Worldwide

Employees: 21,000
Primary Market Served: Business
Catalog available online
Founded: 1884
Gross sales or billing: $3,800,000,000

Performance & industrial chemicals,
machinery & equipment for industry &
agriculture.

FTD FLORIST TRANSWORLD DELIVERY
3113 Woodcreek Dr
Downers Grove, IL 60515
Telephone: (630) 719-7756, (800)
SEND-FTD, Web Site: www.ftd.com
Pres & CEO: Robert Norton
Conducts Business: U.S., Canada
Primary Market Served: Business &
Consumer
Catalog available online
Direct online sales
Advertising/Marketing Budget Related
to Direct Marketing: 26-50%

Flowers wire service.

FAIRFIELD INDUSTRIES INC
1111 Gillingham Ln
Sugar Land, TX 77478-2865
Telephone: (281) 275-7500, (800) 231-
9809, FAX: (281) 275-7550, E-Mail:
jblattman@fairfield.com, Web Site:
www.fairfield.com
Pres & CEO: Walt Pharris
Sls Mgr: Dennis Clark
Sls Rep: Jim Blattman
Sls Rep: Mary Rafipour
Sls Rep: Nick Shilcock
Conducts Business: U.S.
Primary Market Served: Business
Catalog available online
Gross sales or billing: $250,000

Packaging experts in meeting industrial
sub-contracting needs: shrink wrapping, labeling, skin packaging, assembly & poly bagging.

FALCON PRODUCTS INC
Subs. of CF Group
810 W Highway 25 70
Newport, TN 37821-8044
Telephone: (314) 991-9200, (800) 873-
3252, FAX: (314) 991-9227, E-Mail:
info@falconproducts.com, Web Site:
www.falconproducts.com
Chmn & CEO: Frank Jacobs
CFO & VP, Fin: Mike Dreller
Sr VP, Quality: Richard Hnatek
VP, Sls: Stephen Cohen
VP, Sys Tech & Devel: Mike Kula
Conducts Business: Worldwide
Employees: 2,000
Primary Market Served: Business
Catalog available online
Advertising/Marketing Budget Related

to Direct Marketing: 0-25%
Direct Marketing ad budget: $200,000
Magazines: 100%
Founded: 1959
Gross sales or billing: $113,000,000

Commercial furniture for healthcare,
foodservice, office & lodging
industries.

FALCON SAFETY PRODUCTS
25 Imclone Dr, Box 1229
Branchburg, NJ 08876
Telephone: (908) 707-4900, FAX:
(908) 707-8855, Web Site: www.
falconsafety.com
Pres: Phil Lapin
CFO: Greg Mas
VP, Mfg: Ron Maurer
VP, Mktg & Sls: Andy Steinman
Conducts Business: Worldwide
Employees: 60
Primary Market Served: Business &
Consumer
Catalog available online
Advertising/Marketing Budget Related
to Direct Marketing: 51-75%
Direct Marketing ad budget:
Direct Mail: 20%
Magazines: 80%
Founded: 1953
Gross sales or billing: $15,000,000

Computer/office accessories, marine
accessories; boat horns & mooring
compensators.

FAMOUS SMOKE SHOP INC
90 Mort Dr
Easton, PA 18040-9202
Telephone: (610) 559-7000, (800) 672-
5544, FAX: (610) 559-7170, E-Mail:
info@famous-smoke.com, Web Site:
www.famous-smoke.com
Pres: Arthur Zaretsky
Conducts Business: U.S.
Employees: 60
Primary Market Served: Business &
Consumer
Catalog available online
Direct online sales
Advertising/Marketing Budget Related
to Direct Marketing: 76-100%
Direct Marketing ad budget:
Direct Mail: 70%
Online: 30%
Founded: 1939
Gross sales or billing: $2,800,000

Sell brand & off-brand named cigars at
discounts. Mailing list available.

RUSSELL A FARROW LTD
Dupe of 370706
2001 Huron Church Rd
Windsor, ON, Canada N9C 2L6

Telephone: (519) 252-4415, FAX: (519) 252-0982, E-Mail: sherry.lamont@farrow.com, Web Site: www.farrow.com
Pres & CEO: Rick Farrow
Gen Mgr: Steve Cortelli
Exec VP: John Farrow
Conducts Business: U.S.
Employees: 350
Primary Market Served: Business & Consumer
Indirect online sales
Advertising/Marketing Budget Related to Direct Marketing: 0-25%
Founded: 1910
Gross sales or billing: $158,000,000

Our mission is to be the leading provider of superior customs brokerage, logistics and systems solutions which contribute to the success and profitability of North American companies engaged in international trade.

FASSON ROLL DIV
Div. of Avery Dennison Corp
5750 Heisley Rd
Mentor, OH 44060-1830
Telephone: (440) 354-7900, FAX: (440) 358-4712, (440) 358-6025, Web Site: www.fasson.com
Grp VP Fasson Roll Worldwide: Christian Simcic
Conducts Business: U.S., Canada, Europe
Employees: 160
Primary Market Served: Business

Manufactures & sells roll stock pressure sensitive materials to companies that make labels. Branches: Rancho Cucamonga, CA; Peachtree City & Atlanta, GA; Chicago, IL; Fort Wayne, IN; Kansas City, MO; Greensboro, NC; Cranbury, NJ; Quakertown, PA; Dallas, TX; Kent, WA; Neenah, WI.

FAULTLESS STARCH/BON AMI CO
1025 W Eighth St
Kansas City, MO 64101-1200
Telephone: (816) 842-1230, FAX: (816) 842-3417, E-Mail: info@faultless.com, Web Site: www.faultless.com
Chmn & Co-CEO: Gordon T. Beaham III
Pres & Co-CEO: David G. Beaham
VP, Treas & Co-CEO: Robert B. Beaham
VP: Ben Stark
Primary Market Served: Consumer
Catalog available online

Manufacture household cleaners, garden tools & products.

FEDERAL EXPRESS
3965 Airways Blvd
Memphis, TN 38116-5017
Telephone: (901) 369-3600, FAX: (901) 395-5082, Web Site: www.fedex.com
Chmn, Pres & CEO: Frederick W. Smith
Exec VP, Mkt Devel & Corp Commun: T Michael Glen
Conducts Business: Worldwide
Primary Market Served: Business & Consumer

Specialize in transportation of high priority business goods & documents.

GEORGE FENCIK ASSOCIATES
Div. of GFA Marketing Group
1006 Arnold Ave
Point Pleasant, NJ 08742
Telephone: (732) 295-8092, (800) 443-6743, FAX: (732) 295-1729, E-Mail: gfencik@aol.com
Pres: George Fencik
Conducts Business: U.S., Canada, Japan, Switzerland
Employees: 5
Primary Market Served: Business & Consumer
Advertising/Marketing Budget Related to Direct Marketing: 26-50%
Founded: 1979

Sell health and beauty aids - housewares & consumer products.

FILENE'S BASEMENT
Div. of May Co Dept Stores
1 Syms Way
Secaucus, NJ 07094-9400
Telephone: (617) 348-7000, FAX: (617) 357-2596
VP & Adv Dir: Shellie Rubin
Conducts Business: U.S.
Primary Market Served: Consumer

Department store.

FINE ARCHITECTURAL METALSMITHS
Div. of New England Tool Co Ltd
PO Box 30
Chester, NY 10918
Telephone: (845) 651-7550, FAX: (845) 651-7857, Web Site: www.iceforge.com
CEO: Ed Mack
Art Dir: Rhoda Weber Mack
Conducts Business: U.S.
Primary Market Served: Business & Consumer
Advertising/Marketing Budget Related to Direct Marketing: 51-75%
Direct Marketing ad budget:
Direct Mail: 30%

Magazines: 65%
Telephone: 5%
Founded: 1981

Ornamental iron gates with electronic openers. Ornamental iron & aluminum fencing. Ornamental iron, aluminum, stainless & brass railings. Ornamental iron furniture & sheet metal fabrications. Custom lighting. Sold to industrial parks, businesses, homeowners, architects & interior designers.

FINLEY PRODUCTS INC
1333 Beaconfield Ln
Lancaster, PA 17601-5344
Telephone: (717) 735-8200, (888) 626-5301, FAX: (717) 735-8210, E-Mail: fininfo@finleyproducts.com, Web Site: www.2X4basics.com
Pres: Howard Livingston
VP Sls Mktg: Fin Livingston Jr.
Conducts Business: Worldwide
Employees: 10
Primary Market Served: Consumer
Catalog available online
Indirect online sales
Advertising/Marketing Budget Related to Direct Marketing: 76-100%
Founded: 2001

Outdoor furniture & storage equipment, shed kits, deck bench brackets, a multifunction roofing tool, a portable desk for construction & architecture design

FIRE MOUNTAIN GEMS
1 Fire Mountain Way
Grants Pass, OR 97526-2373
Telephone: (541) 956-7890, (800) 423-2319, (800) 355-2137, FAX: (541) 470-GEMS, E-Mail: questions@firemtn.com, Web Site: www.firemtn.com
Pres: Stuart Freedman
Mgr, Direct Response: Rex T. Carlisle
VP Mktg: Christlin Freedman
Admin & Mktg: Lisa Emonds
Conducts Business: U.S., Canada
Employees: 180
Primary Market Served: Business & Consumer
Catalog available online
Direct online sales
Advertising/Marketing Budget Related to Direct Marketing: 51-75%
Direct Marketing ad budget:
Direct Mail: 90%
Magazines: 10%
Founded: 1973

Wholesale jewelry components, beads & findings.

FIRST MEDIA COMMUNICATIONS INC
9149 Jones Ct
Brentwood, TN 37027-8537

Telephone: (615) 661-0826, FAX:
(615) 661-4084, Web Site: www.
first-media.com
Pres: James L. Berk II
Employees: 2
Primary Market Served: Business &
Consumer
Catalog available online
Direct online sales
Gross sales or billing: $100,000

Music publishing, musical instruments
and supplies.

FISHER-PRICE
Div. of Mattel
636 Girard Ave
East Aurora, NY 14052-1824
Telephone: (716) 687-3300, FAX:
(716) 687-3636, Web Site: www.
fisherprice.com
CEO, Mattel: Robert A. Eckert
CFO: Kevin M. Farr
VP, Fin: Anthony DiMichel
VP, Mktg: Lisa Mancuso
Conducts Business: U.S.
Employees: 850
Primary Market Served: Business &
Consumer
Catalog available online
Direct online sales
Gross sales or billing: $76,500,000

Manufacture toys for catalog & retail
sales.

FISHER SCIENTIFIC
A Fisher Scientific Co
2000 Park Lane Dr
Pittsburgh, PA 15275-1118
Telephone: (800) 766-7000, FAX:
(800) 772-7702, Web Site: www.
fishersci.com
Safety Dir: Carl Shaw
Mktg Mgr: Tim Zeh
Mktg Mgr: Scott Daly
Conducts Business: U.S.
Employees: 450
Primary Market Served: Business
Founded: 1902

Sell safety products & controlled
environments.

FITNESS QUEST
1400 Raff Rd SW
Canton, OH 44750-2320
Telephone: (330) 478-0755, (800) 321-
9236, FAX: (330) 479-9213, E-Mail:
customersupport@fitnessquest.com,
Web Site: www.fitnessquest.com
Pres: Robert R. Schnabel Jr
VP, Bus Devel: Craig Waters
VP, Mktg: Mike Clark
Conducts Business: U.S.
Employees: 147
Primary Market Served: Consumer
Catalog available online

Direct online sales
Advertising/Marketing Budget Related
to Direct Marketing: 0-25%
Gross sales or billing: $35,300,000

Consumer direct company specializing
in health-oriented products sold
through direct marketing.

FITNESS USA SUPER CENTERS
7091 Orchard Lake Rd (Suite 300)
West Bloomfield, MI 48322
Telephone: (248) 737-7200, (800)
GET-FIT-1, FAX: (248) 932-3300,
Web Site: www.fitnessusa.com
Pres & CEO: Larry Gurney
Mgr: Michael Winger
Primary Market Served: Consumer
Catalog available online
Indirect online sales
Founded: 1958

Full service health spa for men &
women.

ᵀᴴᴱ_ᴰᴹᴬ FLEXCON
1 FLEXcon Industrial Pk
Spencer, MA 01562-2643
Telephone: (508) 885-8200, Web Site:
www.flexcon.com
Dir, Corp Communs: Joyce Laffin
Primary Market Served: Business &
Consumer

THE FLINCHBAUGH CO INC
245 Beshore School Rd
Manchester, PA 17345
Telephone: (717) 266-2202, FAX:
(717) 266-7055, E-Mail:
flinchbaugh@blazenet.net, Web Site:
www.flinchbaugh.com
Owner & Pres: Gregory Jenkings
Owner & Exec VP: Kurt Weber
Conducts Business: U.S., Canada, Aus-
tralia, U.S. Virgin Islands
Employees: 50
Primary Market Served: Business &
Consumer
Catalog available online
Indirect online sales
Advertising/Marketing Budget Related
to Direct Marketing: 0-25%
Direct Marketing ad budget:
Direct Mail: 20%
Magazines: 80%
Founded: 1936
Gross sales or billing: $3,000,000

Incline wheelchair lifts, stair climbs,
dumbwaiters & custom machine work
to dealers or direct.

FLORIDA A&M UNIVERSITY
Div. of Journalism
428 Tucker Hall
Tallahassee, FL 32307

Telephone: (850) 599-3718, FAX:
(850) 599-3086
Assoc Dean & Professor Journalism:
Jim Hawkins
Conducts Business: U.S.
Primary Market Served: Consumer

Educational institution that prepares
students for opportunities in broadcast
journalism, magazine production,
newspaper production through courses
in mass communications & public
relations.

FLORIDA POWER & LIGHT CO
PO Box 025576
Miami, FL 33102
Telephone: (305) 552-3552, (800) 468-
8243, FAX: (305) 552-2487, Web
Site: www.fpl.com
VP, Cust Svcs: Bill Hamilton
Adv & Promos Supvr: K. Robin Mon-
serrat
Conducts Business: U.S.
Primary Market Served: Business &
Consumer
Founded: 1925

Electricity utility in Florida. PO Box
14000, Juno Beach, FL 33408.

FLORIDA POWER CORP
299 First Ave N
Saint Petersburg, FL 33701
Telephone: (727) 820-5151, (800) 700-
8744, FAX: (727) 384-7865, Web
Site: www.progressenergy.com
Pres & CEO: Jeffrey J. Lyash
Exec VP & CFO: Peter M. Scott III
Sr VP: Jeffrey A. Corbet
Sr VP, Power Opers: E. Michael Will-
iams
Conducts Business: U.S.
Employees: 4,000
Primary Market Served: Business &
Consumer
Gross sales or billing: $4,600,000,000

Provider of electrical services.

FLUID METERING INC
dba Fmi
5 Aeriel Way (Suite 500)
Syosset, NY 11791-5593
Telephone: (516) 922-6050, (800) 223-
3388, FAX: (516) 624-8261, E-Mail:
pumps@fmipump.com, Web Site:
www.fmipump.com
Pres: Henry Pinkerton III
Adv Mktg: Herb Warner
Adv: George Bienenstock
Conducts Business: Worldwide
Employees: 60
Primary Market Served: Business &
Consumer
Catalog available online

Indirect online sales
Advertising/Marketing Budget Related
to Direct Marketing: 0-25%
Direct Marketing ad budget:
Direct Mail: 20%
Magazines: 80%
Founded: 1959
Gross sales or billing: $1,940,000

Manufactures valveless rotating & reciprocating piston metering pumps. Industrial business to business supplier.

FLUKE BIOMEDICAL

Div. of Fluke Corp
6920 Seaway Blvd
Everett, WA 98203-5829
Telephone: (425) 347-6100, (800) 850-4608, FAX: (425) 446-5116, Web Site: www.flukebiomedical.com
CEO: R. Kerry Clark
Exec VP, Global Communs: Shelley Bird
Exec VP Strategy & Corp Devel: Vivek Jain
Dir Mktg: Karen Higley
Conducts Business: Worldwide
Employees: 150
Primary Market Served: Business & Consumer
Catalog available online
Indirect online sales
Advertising/Marketing Budget Related
to Direct Marketing: 76-100%
Founded: 1966
Gross sales or billing: $14,600,000

Manufactures biomedical test & simulation products. Biomedical test, diagnostic imaging, radiation oncology, radiation safety, nuclear medicine, nuclear power systems, & asset management capabilities.

FOLLETT LIBRARY RESOURCES

Div. of Follett Corp
1340 Ridgeview Dr
McHenry, IL 60050
Telephone: (815) 759-1700, (800) 435-6170, FAX: (800) 852-5458, E-Mail: custserv@flr.follett.com, Web Site: www.flr.follett.com
Pres: Tom Salvetti
Conducts Business: Worldwide
Employees: 600
Primary Market Served: Business
Catalog available online
Advertising/Marketing Budget Related
to Direct Marketing: 51-75%
Founded: 1948

Wholesaler to schools of audiovisual materials & online services for grades K-12.

FOOTE-JONES/ILLINOIS GEAR

Div. of Regal Beloit
2914 Industrial Ave
Aberdeen, SD 57402-1089
Telephone: (605) 225-0360, FAX: (605) 225-0567, Web Site: www.footejones.com
VP & Gen Mgr: Louis Ertel
Natl Sls Mgr: Daniel Ward
Conducts Business: U.S., S. America
Employees: 300
Primary Market Served: Business
Advertising/Marketing Budget Related
to Direct Marketing: 0-25%
Direct Marketing ad budget:
Direct Mail: 10%
Magazines: 85%
Telephone: 5%
Founded: 1962
Gross sales or billing: $50,000,000

Custom gears & shafts, standard & special gear boxes.

FORD MOTOR CO

One American Rd
Dearborn, MI 48126-2798
Telephone: (313) 845-8540, (800) 555-5259, FAX: (313) 845-6073, Web Site: www.ford.com
Chmn: William Clay Ford
Pres & CEO: Alan Mulally
Exec VP: Michael E. Bannister
Exec VP: Lewis Booth
VP: Joe Hinrichs
Conducts Business: Worldwide
Employees: 245,000
Primary Market Served: Business & Consumer
Catalog available online
Indirect online sales
Founded: 1903
Gross sales or billing: $173,000,000,000

Automotive manufacturer.

FOREMOST INDUSTRIAL EXCHANGE

Subs. of Mared Industries
15222 Keswick St
Van Nuys, CA 91405-1068
Telephone: (818) 988-6900, FAX: (818) 787-0293
Chmn: Edward Guttenberg
Pres: Larry Phillips
Sec: Paul Cirino
Conducts Business: U.S.
Employees: 150
Primary Market Served: Business
Gross sales or billing: $25,600,000

Business-to-business supplier of cutting tools & abrasives.

THE DMA FOUR CORNERS DIRECT INC

8520 S Tamiami Trl Unit 2
Sarasota, FL 34238-3001
Telephone: (941) 364-8585
Pres: Martin Lothman
Primary Market Served: Business & Consumer

4IMPRINT INC

101 Commerce St
Oshkosh, WI 54901
Telephone: (920) 236-7272, (888) 298-8190, (877) 446-7746, FAX: (800) 355-5043, E-Mail: administrator@4imprint.com, Web Site: www.4imprint.com
Pres: Kevin Lyons-Tarr
VP Admin: Mary Curtin
VP Sls & Mktg: Greg Ebel
Conducts Business: U.S., U.K.; Germany; France; Hong Kong
Employees: 350
Primary Market Served: Business
Catalog available online
Direct online sales
Advertising/Marketing Budget Related
to Direct Marketing: 76-100%
Direct Marketing ad budget: $4,000,000
Direct Mail: $4,000,000
Founded: 1985

Imprinted promotional products.

LARRY FOX & CO LTD

PO Box 729
Valley Stream, NY 11582-0729
Telephone: (516) 791-7929, (800) 397-7923, FAX: (516) 791-1022, E-Mail: larry@larryfox.com, Web Site: www.larryfox.com
Pres: Ellen Ingber
VP: Larry Fox
Conducts Business: U.S., Australia, Canada, Japan, Germany
Employees: 7
Primary Market Served: Business & Consumer
Catalog available online
Direct online sales
Advertising/Marketing Budget Related
to Direct Marketing: 26-50%
Direct Marketing ad budget:
Direct Mail: 80%
Magazines: 15%
Newspapers: 5%
Founded: 1961

Promotional & advertising specialties. Stock Firematic items for direct sales to firefighters, emergency medical personnel & fire departments.

FRAGRANCE INTERNATIONAL INC

398 E Rayen Ave
Youngstown, OH 44505

Telephone: (330) 747-3341, (888) 547-8355, FAX: (330) 747-3343, Web Site: www.kisstell.com
Pres: Brad Levy
VP: Judy Levy
Conducts Business: U.S.
Employees: 50
Primary Market Served: Business & Consumer
Catalog available online
Direct online sales
Advertising/Marketing Budget Related to Direct Marketing: 0-25%
Direct Marketing ad budget:
Direct Mail: 25%
Online: 25%
Telephone: 50%
Founded: 1978

Perfumes, colognes, health & beauty aids.

THE DMA   THE FRANKLIN MINT

486 Thomas Jones Way Ste 240
Exton, PA 19341-2561
Telephone: (610) 497-4800, (800) THE-MINT, FAX: (610) 497-4956, E-Mail: info@franklinmint.com, Web Site: www.franklinmint.com
Chmn: Stewart Resnick
Vice Chmn: Lynda Resnick
COO: Deb Listman
VP, Mktg & Prod Devel: Gwynne Gorr
Conducts Business: Worldwide
Employees: 40
Primary Market Served: Business & Consumer
Catalog available online
Direct online sales
Advertising/Marketing Budget Related to Direct Marketing: 76-100%
Founded: 1964

Creator & marketer of fine collectibles, home decor & luxury products. Product lines offer originally designed items in a diverse range of artistic genres: sculpture, Franklin Heirloom Dolls, fashion jewelry, Franklin Mint Precision Models, home accessories, historic & artistic arms reproductions, games & collector plates.

THE DMA   FREEMAN DECORATING CO

909 Newark Tpke
Kearny, NJ 07032-4307
Telephone: (201) 998-6006

FRITO-LAY

Div. of Pepsi Co
7701 Legacy Dr
Plano, TX 75024-4099
Telephone: (972) 334-7000, (800) 352-4477, FAX: (972) 334-2019, Web Site: www.fritolay.com
Pres & CEO: Albert P. Carey
CFO: Dave Rader

Sr VP, HR: Michele Thatcher
VP, Investor Rels: Jane Nielsen
Pub Rels Dir: Lyn Markley
Conducts Business: U.S.
Primary Market Served: Business & Consumer
Catalog available online

Manufacturer of snack foods for retail sales.

FRONTIER CORP

Div. of Citizens Communications Co.
180 S Clinton Ave
Rochester, NY 14646-0002
Telephone: (716) 777-1000, Web Site: www.frontieronline.com
Chmn Bd & CEO: Mary Agnes Wilderottes
Exec VP & COO: Daniel J. McCarthy
CFO: Donald R. Shassian
Exec VP, Sls & Mktg: Peter B. Heyes
Sr VP, Gen Counsel: Hilary E. Glassman
Primary Market Served: Business & Consumer
Catalog available online
Direct online sales

Telecommunications services & products.

FUJI PHOTO FILM USA

200 Summit Lake Dr
Valhalla, NY 10595-1356
Telephone: (914) 789-8100, (800) 755-3854, FAX: (914) 789-8295, Web Site: www.fujifilmusa.com
Pres & CEO: Shingetaka Komori
Exec VP: Toshio Takahashi
Sr VP: Hisatoyo Kato
Sr VP: Tadashi Sasaki
Corp VP: Yuzo Toda
Conducts Business: U.S.
Primary Market Served: Business & Consumer
Catalog available online

Manufacture & sell cameras & film.

FUJITSU TRANSACTION SOLUTIONS INC

Subs. of Fujitsu LTD
2791 Telecom Pkwy
Richardson, TX 75082-3523
Telephone: (972) 963-2300, (800) 340-4425, Web Site: www.fujitsu.com
Pres & CEO: Masao Teramoto
COO: Ed Soladay
Sr VP: Keith McNamara
Sr VP: Bill Witte
Reg VP, Sls: Don Cramb
Conducts Business: U.S., Canada
Employees: 1,400
Primary Market Served: Business
Catalog available online
Indirect online sales

Gross sales or billing: $120,000,000

Develop, manufacture & market retail point-of-sale (POS) systems, automated teller machines (ATMs) & handheld computer systems.

THE FULLER THEOLOGICAL SEMINARY

135 N Oakland Ave
Pasadena, CA 91182
Telephone: (626) 584-5200, (800) 2-FULLER, FAX: (626) 584-5449, Web Site: www.fuller.edu/cll
Chair: Merlin W. Call
Vice Chair: Dale Wang
Pres: Richard W. Mouw
Conducts Business: U.S.
Primary Market Served: Business & Consumer
Catalog available online
Direct online sales
Founded: 1947
Gross sales or billing: $78,400,000

Hold seminars & provide supplies for pastors & lay people.

G&S PACKING CO INC

16600 S Hwy 25
Weirsdale, FL 32195
Telephone: (352) 821-2251, (800) 949-9074, FAX: (352) 821-5000, Web Site: www.gspacking.com
Pres: Earl Scales
VP: George Scales
Mktg: Doris Elkins
Conducts Business: Worldwide
Primary Market Served: Business & Consumer
Catalog available online
Founded: 1879

Fulfillment company specializing in Florida & tropical fruit.

G H BASS & CO

Div. of Phillips Van Huesen
200 Madison Ave
New York, NY 10016-3903
Telephone: (212) 381-3900, FAX: (212) 381-3950, Web Site: www.pvh.com
Pres: Scott H. Orenstein
Conducts Business: U.S.
Employees: 5,000
Primary Market Served: Business & Consumer
Catalog available online
Direct online sales
Founded: 1876
Gross sales or billing: $600,000,000

Shoes wholesaler.

G2 PROMOTIONAL MARKETING

Subs. of Grey Advertising
200 5th Ave Bsmt B
New York, NY 10010-3313
Telephone: (212) 537-3700, FAX:
(203) 352-0798, Web Site: www.
g2pm.com
Pres: Jason Press
CFO: Darren Barrett
Sr Partner: Ann Moriarty
Conducts Business: U.S.
Employees: 135
Primary Market Served: Business
Gross sales or billing: $62,300,000

Channel marketing, co-operative advertising & specializing in direct marketing.

GE CONSUMER & INDUSTRIAL LIGHTING

Div. of GE Consumer Products
1975 Noble Rd
Cleveland, OH 44112-6300
Telephone: (216) 266-2222, (216) 266-2121, FAX: (216) 266-2930, Web
Site: www.gelighting.com/na
CEO & Pres: James P. Campbell
VP, Elec Distr & Lighting Sls: Michael B. Petras
Program Mgr, Mktg Media: Leslie Redford
Primary Market Served: Business & Consumer

Light bulbs & other commercial electrical equipment.

GN NETCOM

77 Northeastern Blvd
Nashua, NH 03062-3128
Telephone: (603) 598-1100, (800) 345-8639, FAX: (603) 598-1122, Web
Site: www.jabra.com
Conducts Business: U.S., Canada
Employees: 350
Primary Market Served: Business
Catalog available online
Advertising/Marketing Budget Related to Direct Marketing: 0-25%
Founded: 1987
Gross sales or billing: $100,000

Manufactures professional, lightweight wireless and corded telephone headsets.

GACO WESTERN INC

200 W Mercer St (Suite 202)
Seattle, WA 98119-3958
Telephone: (206) 575-0450, (800) 456-4226, FAX: (206) 575-0587, E-Mail:
info@gaco.com, Web Site: www.
gaco.com
Pres: Peter Davis
Mktg Dir: Kyle Sherk

Admin Asst to Pres: Yolanda Sewell
Conducts Business: Worldwide
Employees: 51
Primary Market Served: Business & Consumer
Catalog available online
Direct online sales
Founded: 1955

Manufactures & distributes waterproofing systems, architectural coatings & sprayed-in-place polyurethane foam insulation.

GALEN WILLIAMS LANDSCAPING & GARDEN DESIGN

Seven Oyster Shores Rd
East Hampton, NY 11937-1103
Telephone: (631) 324-6220, FAX:
(631) 329-3684
Pres: Galen Williams
Primary Market Served: Business & Consumer

Landscape architects.

GALL'S INC

Subs. Aramark Uniform & Career Apparel
2680 Palumbo Dr
Lexington, KY 40509-1234
Telephone: (859) 266-7227, (800) 477-7766, FAX: (859) 268-5954, E-Mail:
help-desk@galls.com, Web Site:
www.galls.com
Pres: Thomas Vozzo
CFO: David Solomon
CIO: Robert McCormack
Conducts Business: U.S.
Employees: 450
Primary Market Served: Business & Consumer
Catalog available online
Direct online sales
Founded: 1967

Public safety equipment supplier.

GAMBRO INC

14143 Denver W Pkwy
Lakewood, CO 80401
Telephone: (303) 232-6800, (800) 525-2623, FAX: (303) 222-6810, Web
Site: www.gambro.com
Pres & CEO: David B. Perez
COO: Teresa W. Ayers
VP: Frank Corbin
VP, Opers: Gary Heath
Dir, Mktg: Anne Bonelli
Conducts Business: U.S.
Employees: 7
Primary Market Served: Business
Catalog available online
Advertising/Marketing Budget Related to Direct Marketing: 0-25%
Founded: 1984

Gross sales or billing: $6,000,000

Incentive suppliers & distributors.

GAMMA PHOTO LABS LLC

222 N Des Plains
Chicago, IL 60661-1120
Telephone: (312) 337-0022, FAX:
(312) 337-3753, Web Site: www.
photobition.com
Pres: Doug Goddard
VP, Opers: Ray Pryor
Office Mgr: Patricia Andrews
Conducts Business: U.S.
Employees: 135
Primary Market Served: Business & Consumer
Catalog available online
Advertising/Marketing Budget Related to Direct Marketing: 0-25%

Full-service custom photo lab.

GANNETT CO INC

7950 Jones Branch Dr
Mc Lean, VA 22107
Telephone: (703) 854-6000, FAX:
(703) 854-2046, E-Mail: gcishare@
gannett.com, Web Site: www.gannett.
com
Chmn, Pres & CEO: Craig A. Dubow
Exec VP & CFO: Gracia C. Martore
Sr VP HR: Roxanne V. Horning
Employees: 50,000
Primary Market Served: Business & Consumer
Gross sales or billing: $8,000,000,000

Communication media & newspapers.

GARON PRODUCTS INC

PO Box 1924
Wall, NJ 07719-1924
Telephone: (732) 449-1776, (800) 631-5380, FAX: (732) 449-6937, Web
Site: www.garonproducts.com
Pres: Arthur M. Crowley
Mktg Dir: Tara Crowley
Conducts Business: U.S.
Primary Market Served: Business
Catalog available online
Direct online sales
Direct Marketing ad budget:
Direct Mail: 85%
Telephone: 15%

Manufacturer of industrial & construction maintenance products. Sell to business & industrial markets largely through direct mail catalogs.

THE GATEWAY LEARNING CORP

Div. of Gateway
7565 Irvine Center Dr
Irvine, CA 92618
Telephone: (714) 429-2223, (800) 222-3334, FAX: (714) 338-2525

Pres & CEO: Chip Adams
Conducts Business: U.S., Canada
Primary Market Served: Consumer
Founded: 1987

Creators of Hooked-on-Phonics.

THE DMA GAYLORD BROTHERS
PO Box 4901
Syracuse, NY 13221-4901
Telephone: (315) 634-8440, Web Site:
    www.gaylord.com
VP Sls & Mktg: Coleen Gagliardo
Conducts Business: U.S.
Primary Market Served: Business

Furniture, office & library supplies.
Mailing address: PO Box 4901, Syracuse, NY 13221.

GELCO INFORMATION NETWORK
10700 Prairie Lakes Dr
Eden Prairie, MN 55344
Telephone: (952) 947-1500, (800) 444-
    6588, FAX: (952) 947-1525, Web
    Site: www.gelco.com
Pres: Neil Vill
VP, Prods & Mktg: Ralph Bernstein
Conducts Business: U.S., Canada
Employees: 300
Primary Market Served: Business
Advertising/Marketing Budget Related
    to Direct Marketing: 0-25%
Founded: 1894

A worldwide provider of complete,
outsourced trade fund & travel expense
management solutions to U.S. & multi-
national Fortune 1000 companies &
government agencies.

GEMALTO INC
dba Gem Plus Card Services
101 Park Dr
Montgomeryville, PA 18936-9613
Telephone: (215) 390-2000, E-Mail:
    us.sales@gemalto.com, Web Site:
    www.gemalto.com
VP-Pres, VP Sys: Eric Soulliard
Conducts Business: U.S., Canada, S.
    America
Employees: 400
Primary Market Served: Business
Advertising/Marketing Budget Related
    to Direct Marketing: 0-25%
Direct Marketing ad budget:
Magazines: 100%
Founded: 1953
Gross sales or billing: $29,800,000

Manufacturer of semiconductors &
related devices, magnetic stripe &
smart cards. Sell to financial, retail,
travel, entertainment & oil industries.
Firm also produces magnetic tape for
use on financial transaction cards.

GENERAL ELECTRIC CO
3135 Easton Tpke
Fairfield, CT 06828-0001
Telephone: (203) 373-2211, FAX:
    (203) 373-3131, Web Site: www.ge.
    com
Chmn & CEO: John F. Welch Jr
Sr VP, Fin: Dennis Dammerman
Primary Market Served: Business &
    Consumer

Diversified manufacturer of technology
& services.

GENERAL PENCIL CO INC
67 Fleet St
Jersey City, NJ 07306
Telephone: (201) 653-5351, FAX:
    (201) 653-2298, E-Mail: info@
    generalpencil.com, Web Site: www.
    generalpencil.com
Pres & CEO: James Weissenborn
Primary Market Served: Business &
    Consumer
Catalog available online
Direct online sales
Founded: 1864

Manufactures wood-cased pencils for
the art, craft, office, drafting & bowling industries.

GENERAL PHYSICS CORP
6095 Marshalee Dr (Suite 300)
Elkridge, MD 21075
Telephone: (410) 379-3600, (800) 727-
    6677, FAX: (410) 540-5302, E-Mail:
    info@gpworldwide.com, Web Site:
    www.gpworldwide.com
Head Engrng: Ben Parks
CEO: Jerome I. Feldman
Head Training: Jim Barnes
Primary Market Served: Business

Training & engineering services.

GENERAL VITAMIN CORP
10700 World Trade Blvd (Suite 102)
Raleigh, NC 27617-4220
Telephone: (919) 929-5785, (800) 323-
    8432, FAX: (919) 929-2458, E-Mail:
    support@generalvitamin.com, Web
    Site: www.generalvitamin.com
VP: A.C. Bushnel
Conducts Business: U.S.
Primary Market Served: Business &
    Consumer

Sell vitamins through direct response
marketing.

GENETICA DNA LABORATORIES INC
8740 Montgomery Rd (Suite 11)
Cincinnati, OH 45236-2100
Telephone: (513) 985-9777, (800) 433-
    6848, FAX: (513) 985-9983, Web
    Site: www.genetica.com

Pres & Founder: Elizabeth Panke
    M.D.; Ph.D.
Conducts Business: North & South
    America, Africa
Employees: 15
Primary Market Served: Business &
    Consumer
Catalog available online
Direct online sales
Founded: 1996

Commercial provider of DNA testing
services. Services include DNA pater-
nity tests, DNA family relationship
tests, and DNA identity tests to the
general public as well as to healthcare,
legal professionals and embassies
throughout the United States and
worldwide.

THE DMA GEORGIA POWER
241 Ralph McGill Blvd NW (Bin
    #10220)
Atlanta, GA 30308-3374
Telephone: (404) 506-3440
Mktg Commun: J. Adam Pickard
Primary Market Served: Business &
    Consumer

GERBER PRODUCTS CO
Subs. of Novartis
445 State St.
Fremont, MI 49413
Telephone: (231) 928-2000, (800) 443-
    7237, Web Site: www.gerber.com
Mktg Svcs Dir: Mack Jenks
Conducts Business: Worldwide
Employees: 3,500
Primary Market Served: Consumer
Advertising/Marketing Budget Related
    to Direct Marketing: 26-50%
Founded: 1928
Gross sales or billing: $1,300,000,000

Baby food, baby care & baby wear.

GERO VITA
1835 Newport Blvd (Suite A109,
    #439)
Costa Mesa, CA 92627-5007
Telephone: (888) 382-9175, Web Site:
    www.gvi.com
Pres: Tuong Nyugen
VP: Jim Chiang
Employees: 100
Primary Market Served: Consumer
Catalog available online
Direct online sales
Gross sales or billing: $26,000,000

Vitamins.

GET SEEN MEDIA GROUP
5115 Wilshire Blvd (Apt 235)
Los Angeles, CA 90036-4371
Telephone: (323) 424-4669, Web Site:
    www.getseenmedia.com

CEO: Frank Mustafa

GETRONICS
100 Ames Pond Dr (Suite 200)
Tewksbury, MA 01876-1240
Telephone: (978) 625-5000, Web Site:
   www.getronics.com
Vice Chmn & Exec VP: Kevin Roche
Primary Market Served: Business &
   Consumer

Manufacture & sell software &
services.

GHIRARDELLI CHOCOLATE CO
1111 139th Ave
San Leandro, CA 94578
Telephone: (510) 483-6970, (800) 877-
   9338, FAX: (510) 297-2649, Web
   Site: www.ghirardelli.com
Pres & CEO: John J. Anton
Exec VP: Randall Bruner
VP, Mktg: Tinka Gordon
VP: Jaemin Park
Conducts Business: U.S.
Primary Market Served: Business
Catalog available online
Direct online sales
Founded: 1852
Gross sales or billing: $35,800,000

Manufacturer & wholesaler of
Ghirardelli chocolates.

GLAMOUR SHOTS LICENSING
Subs. of Candid Color Systems
1300 Metropolitan Ave
Oklahoma City, OK 73108
Telephone: (405) 947-8747, (888)
   GLAMOUR-SHOTS, FAX: (405)
   951-7343, Web Site: www.
   glamourshots.com
Pres: Jack Counts
Primary Market Served: Consumer
Catalog available online

Fashion photography.

GLAS-COL
711 Hulman St, PO Box 2128
Terre Haute, IN 47808
Telephone: (812) 235-6167, FAX:
   (812) 234-6975, Web Site: www.i-2-
   r.com
Conducts Business: U.S.
Primary Market Served: Business

Manufacturer of laboratory devices.

GLAXO SMITH KLINE
Five Moore Dr
Research Triangle Park, NC 27709
Telephone: (919) 483-2100, (888) 825-
   5249, FAX: (919) 248-8383, Web
   Site: www.gsk.com
Non-Exec Chmn: Sir Christopher Gent
Non-Exec Dir: Professor Sir Roy
   Anderson
Non-Exec Dir: Dr. Stephanie Burns
CEO: Jean-Pierre Garnier
CFO: Julian Heslop
Conducts Business: Worldwide
Employees: 100,000
Primary Market Served: Consumer
Catalog available online
Indirect online sales
Founded: 1715

Pharmaceutical manufacturer selling to
wholesalers. Sell over-the-counter
products to retail industries.

GLOBAL SPECIALTIES
Div. of Interplex Electronics Inc
994 N Colony Rd (Unit 305)
Wallingford, CT 06492-5902
Telephone: (203) 272-3285, FAX:
   (203) 272-4330, Web Site: www.
   globalspecialties.com
Exec VP: John Pease
VP & Gen Mgr: Eric Blauvelt
Conducts Business: Worldwide
Employees: 56
Primary Market Served: Business

Manufacture electronic testing & pro-
totyping equipment.

GLOBE TICKET & LABEL CO
11 Eisenhower Ln S
Lombard, IL 60148-5409
Telephone: (404) 762-9711, (800) 523-
   5968, FAX: (404) 762-7019, Web
   Site: www.globeticket.com
Pres, CFO & Exec VP: Bob Puleo
Bus Devel Dir: Philip Raines
Conducts Business: U.S., U.K.
Employees: 320
Primary Market Served: Business
Indirect online sales
Direct Marketing ad budget: $100,000
Direct Mail: 20%
Magazines: 75%
Newspapers: 5%
Founded: 1868
Gross sales or billing: $30,000,000

Manufacturer of printed products (tickets, tags, labels, transfers, parking
checks, data processing cards) & commercial publications.

GO AHEAD VACATIONS
Subs. of EF Education
One Education St
Cambridge, MA 02141
Telephone: (617) 619-1000, (800) 242-
   4686, FAX: (617) 619-1001, E-Mail:
   goahead@et.com, Web Site: www.
   goaheadvacations.com
Pres: Louise Jillian
Exec VP: Chris O'Brien
Conducts Business: U.S.

Primary Market Served: Consumer
Business vacation & travel agency.

THE DMA GOLD MEDAL PRODUCTS CO
10700 Medallion Dr
Cincinnati, OH 45241-4807
Telephone: (513) 769-7676, (800) 543-
   0862, FAX: (800) 542-1496, E-Mail:
   info@gmpopcorn.com, Web Site:
   www.gmpopcorn.com
Pres: Dan Kroeger
Natl Sls Mgr: Chris Petroff
Dir Mktg: Stephanie Goodin
Conducts Business: Worldwide
Primary Market Served: Business &
   Consumer
Catalog available online
Advertising/Marketing Budget Related
   to Direct Marketing: 0-25%
Founded: 1931

Concession equipment and supplies for
fund-raising purposes. Branches: Orlando, FL; Chicago, IL; Indianapolis,
IN; New Orleans, LA; Greensboro,
NC; Pittsburgh, PA; Nashville, TN.

GOLDEN BEAR GOLF INC
11780 US Hwy 1 (Suite 500)
North Palm Beach, FL 33408-3042
Telephone: (561) 626-3900, FAX:
   (561) 626-4104, Web Site: www.
   nicklaus.com
Chmn: Jack Nicklaus
Sr VP, CFO & COO: Stephen S. Wins-
   lett
VP: Andrew O'Brien
VP: Thomas P. Hislop
Conducts Business: Worldwide
Employees: 500
Primary Market Served: Business &
   Consumer
Catalog available online
Direct online sales
Advertising/Marketing Budget Related
   to Direct Marketing: 0-25%
Founded: 1970

Design & construct golf courses, golf
centers, clothing & golf schools.

GOLDEN FLEECE DESIGNS INC
441 S Victory Blvd
Burbank, CA 91502-2353
Telephone: (818) 848-7724, FAX:
   (818) 566-7100, Web Site: www.
   mandonia.com
Chmn & CEO: Symeon D. Argyropou-
   los
VP: Maria Argyropoulos
VP: Antoinette Argyropoulos
Conducts Business: U.S., Canada, Car-
   ibbean, U.K., Japan, Greece
Employees: 20

Primary Market Served: Business &
    Consumer
Catalog available online
Direct online sales
Advertising/Marketing Budget Related
    to Direct Marketing: 0-25%
Direct Marketing ad budget: $50,000
Direct Mail: $20,000
Magazines: $15,000
Online: $15,000
Founded: 1970

Marine & industrial canvas, canvas
products & covers, flags, duffle & tote
bags, promotional goods. Nautical gifts
manufacturers, exporters & wholesale
supplier to the U.S. government.

GOLDEN GATE TRANSPORTATION DISTRICT
1011 Anderson Dr
San Rafael, CA 94901
Telephone: (415) 921-5858, FAX:
    (415) 923-2014, Web Site: www.
    goldengate.org
Pres: John J. Moylan
First VP: Albert J. Boro
Second VP: Tom Ammiano
Dir: Harold C. Brown Jr.
Dir: Gerald D. Cochran
Conducts Business: U.S.
Primary Market Served: Business
Catalog available online

Purchasing division for the transportation industry.

GOODYEAR TIRE & RUBBER CO
dba "Goodyear", "Dunlop", "Kelly
    Tires", "Sava" & "Fulda".
1144 E Market St
Akron, OH 44316
Telephone: (330) 796-3250, Web Site:
    www.goodyear.com
Chmn Bd, CEO & Pres: Robert J.
    Keegan
Pres, N American Tire: Richard J
    Kramer
Pres, Consumer Tires: Lawrence D.
    Mason
Sr VP, Global Communs: Charles L.
    Sinclair
VP Bus Devel: Laura Thompson
Gen Mgr: Barry Petrea
Conducts Business: U.S.
Employees: 77,000
Primary Market Served: Business &
    Consumer
Founded: 1894
Gross sales or billing: $20,258,000,000

Manufacturer & marketer of passenger,
truck & farm tires for replacement
markets.

GOVERNMENT TECHNOLOGY SERVICES INC
2553 Dulles View Dr (Suite 100)
Herndon, VA 20171-5228
Telephone: (703) 502-2000, (800) 234-
    GTSI, FAX: (703) 222-5218, Web
    Site: www.gtsi.com
Pres & CEO: Dendy Young
Mktg Mgr: Kim Tatarka
Conducts Business: U.S.
Employees: 380
Primary Market Served: Business
Catalog available online
Advertising/Marketing Budget Related
    to Direct Marketing: 26-50%

Provider of computer hardware & software products to federal government.

W R GRACE & CO
7500 Grace Dr
Columbia, MD 21044
Telephone: (410) 531-4000, FAX:
    (410) 531-4367, Web Site: www.
    grace.com
Pres & COO: Fred Festa
Conducts Business: Worldwide
Employees: 6,500
Primary Market Served: Business
Founded: 1899
Gross sales or billing: $2,800,000,000

Specialty chemicals & specialized
healthcare company.

GRAINGER PARTS
Div. of WW Grainger Inc
1657 Shermer Rd
North Brook, IL 60062
Telephone: (847) 498-5900, FAX:
    (847) 498-3402, Web Site: www.
    grainger.com
Grp Pres: Donald E. Brelinski
Grp Pres: Wesley Clark
Conducts Business: U.S., Canada
Employees: 350
Primary Market Served: Business
Catalog available online
Direct online sales
Advertising/Marketing Budget Related
    to Direct Marketing: 0-25%
Direct Marketing ad budget:
Direct Mail: 85%
Magazines: 5%
Telephone: 10%
Founded: 1927

Specialty distribution of replacement
parts for MRO, food & bottled water
equipment.

GRAPHIK DIMENSIONS LTD
2103 Brentwood St
High Point, NC 27263
Telephone: (336) 887-3500, (800) 221-
    0262, FAX: (336) 887-3773, E-Mail:
    customercare@pictureframes.com,
    Web Site: www.pictureframes.com
Pres: Joan Feinsod
VP: Dave Shelton
Conducts Business: Worldwide
Employees: 120
Primary Market Served: Business &
    Consumer
Catalog available online
Direct online sales
Advertising/Marketing Budget Related
    to Direct Marketing: 76-100%
Founded: 1966

Manufacture picture frames.

GREAT NORTH AMERICAN COS INC
2828 Forest Ln (Suite 2000)
Dallas, TX 75234
Telephone: (972) 481-6100, (800) 527-
    2782, FAX: (972) 243-1637, Web
    Site: www.gnamerican.com
CEO: Joseph Salatino
Mktg Dir: Lisa Copeland
Conducts Business: U.S.
Employees: 200
Primary Market Served: Business
Catalog available online
Advertising/Marketing Budget Related
    to Direct Marketing: 0-25%
Founded: 1972
Gross sales or billing: $25,000,000

Business to business telemarketing
wholesaler of office supplies and computer supplies. Advertising specialty
items for business promotions.

GROVE ENTERPRISES INC
7540 Hwy 64 W
Brasstown, NC 28902-9736
Telephone: (828) 837-9200, (800) 438-
    8155, FAX: (828) 837-2216, E-Mail:
    judy@grove-ent.com, Web Site:
    www.grove-ent.com
Pres: Robert Grove
CEO: Judy A. Grove
Conducts Business: Worldwide
Employees: 14
Primary Market Served: Business &
    Consumer
Catalog available online
Direct online sales
Advertising/Marketing Budget Related
    to Direct Marketing: 76-100%
Direct Marketing ad budget:
Direct Mail: 90%
Magazines: 10%
Founded: 1979
Gross sales or billing: $3,500,000

Shortwave, scanner radios & accessories, computer sales & service & web
page design. Publisher of monthly
magazine, Monitoring Times.

GROVER CO
PO Box 41844
Mesa, AZ 85274-1844
Telephone: (480) 827-8011, FAX:
(480) 827-8014
Pres: Rande Grover
VP: John Grover
Conducts Business: Worldwide
Employees: 10
Primary Market Served: Consumer
Advertising/Marketing Budget Related
to Direct Marketing: 0-25%
Direct Marketing ad budget:
Direct Mail: 50%
Newspapers: 40%
TV/Radio: 5%
Telephone: 5%

Sell the Marathon Mill & Kenwood
Bread Mixer plus the whole grains for
use in the mixer through mail order.
Also sell Mountain House freeze-dried
foods.

THE DMA GROWING FAMILY PORTRAITS
2003 Western Ave (Suite 460)
Seattle, WA 98121-2185
Telephone: (206) 587-0333, Web Site:
www.silversand.com

GUIDING EYES FOR THE BLIND
611 Granite Springs Rd
Yorktown Heights, NY 10598
Telephone: (914) 245-4042, (800) 942-
0149, FAX: (914) 245-1609, Web
Site: www.guidingeyes.org
Pres & CEO: Bill Badger
Dir: Carolyn Kihm
Comptroller: Jerry Attard
Conducts Business: U.S.
Primary Market Served: Business &
Consumer
Gross sales or billing: $20,434,061

Guide dog training school.

GULFSTREAM AIRCRAFT INC
500 Gulfstream Rd, PO Box 2206
Savannah, GA 31408-2206
Telephone: (912) 965-5300, FAX:
(912) 965-3775, E-Mail: info@
gulfstream.com, Web Site: www.
gulfstream.com
Pres: Bryan Moss
Conducts Business: Worldwide
Employees: 4,800
Primary Market Served: Business
Founded: 1978
Gross sales or billing: $1,500,000,000

Manufacture Gulfstream Business Jet
Aircraft; special requirement jet aircraft for government & military
purposes.

HCI DIRECT
3369 Progress Dr
Bensalem, PA 19020
Telephone: (215) 244-9600, (888) 765-
0062, FAX: (215) 244-0328, Web
Site: www.silkies.com
Pres & CEO: John F. Biagini
VP & CFO: William J. Kelly
Mktg Dir: Darrell Edwards
Conducts Business: Worldwide
Primary Market Served: Business &
Consumer
Catalog available online
Direct online sales
Advertising/Marketing Budget Related
to Direct Marketing: 76-100%
Direct Marketing ad budget:
Direct Mail: 90%
Online: 1%
Telephone: 9%
Gross sales or billing: $53,100,000

Direct marketing company for wom-
en's goods and services. Primary service is hosiery.

THE DMA HP INDIGO & INKJET PRESS SOLUTIONS
6831 E Thunderbird Rd
Scottsdale, AZ 85254-4044
Telephone: (404) 427-7418
Segment Mktg Mgr: Tonya Powers

HAGEMEYER - NORTH AMERICA
1460 Tobias Gadson Blvd
Charleston, SC 29407-4793
Telephone: (843) 745-2400, FAX:
(843) 745-6942, E-Mail: info@
hagemeyerna.com, Web Site: www.
hagemeyerna.com
Exec VP: Lisa A. Mitchell
Mgr Mktg Design Services: Anna
McGuiness
Conducts Business: U.S.
Employees: 17,600
Primary Market Served: Business
Founded: 1900
Gross sales or billing: $1,500,000,000

Industrial supplies.

HAIN CELESTIAL GROUP
58 S Service Rd
Melville, NY 11747
Telephone: (631) 730-2200, FAX:
(631) 730-2500, Web Site: www.
hain-celestial.com
Chmn, Pres & CEO: Irwin David Si-
mon
Exec VP, CFO, Sec & Treas: Ira J.
Lamel
Exec VP: John Carroll
Exec VP: Francis W. Daily
Dir: Melanie Boivin
Employees: 2,131
Primary Market Served: Business

Catalog available online
Gross sales or billing: $900,000,000

Manufacturer of 200 products-cookies,
snack bars, cereals, soups & chilies.
Primarily sold through distributors &
retailed through health stores & health
food section of supermarkets.

HALE INDIAN RIVER GROVES INC
PO Box 691237
Vero Beach, FL 32969-1237
Telephone: (800) 356-7264, FAX:
(877) 329-4253, E-Mail: marketing@
halegroves.com, Web Site: www.
hales.com
Pres: Stephen Hale III
VP: Daniel Keith Bryan
Conducts Business: U.S.
Employees: 400
Primary Market Served: Business &
Consumer
Catalog available online
Direct online sales
Advertising/Marketing Budget Related
to Direct Marketing: 76-100%
Direct Marketing ad budget:
Direct Mail: 75%
Magazines: 10%
Newspapers: 10%
TV/Radio: 5%
Founded: 1948

Sell Indian River citrus for family,
business gifts & personal use. Also
truckload shipments for fund-raisers.

HALL-ERICKSON INC
98 E Naperville Rd (Suite 200)
Westmont, IL 60559-2199
Telephone: (630) 434-7779, FAX:
(630) 434-1216
Pres: Peter H. Erickson
Primary Market Served: Business
Advertising/Marketing Budget Related
to Direct Marketing: 0-25%

Exposition management company.

THE DMA HALLMARK CARDS INC
PO Box 419580
Kansas City, MO 64141-6580
Telephone: (816) 274-5111, FAX:
(816) 274-7276, Web Site: www.
hallmark.com
Pres & CEO: Ira Hockaday
Mktg Capabilities Mgr: Zoann Merry-
field
Mktg Dir: Julie Cunnyngham
Conducts Business: U.S.
Primary Market Served: Business &
Consumer

Social expression company.

HALLS KANSAS CITY
200 E 25th St
Kansas City, MO 64108-2509
Telephone: (816) 274-8111, (800) 624-4034, FAX: (816) 545-2121, Web Site: www.hallskc.com
Chmn Bd: Donald J. Halls Sr.
CEO: Robert Leitstein
VP: Kenneth McCormack
Dir, Sls Promotion: Carnie Kline
Conducts Business: U.S.
Primary Market Served: Consumer
Catalog available online
Indirect online sales

Specialty women's retail clothing store.

HALO/LEE WAYNE
1980 Industrial Dr
Sterling, IL 61081-9064
Telephone: (815) 632-0980, (866) 840-6401, FAX: (815) 632-6900, E-Mail: moreinfo@leewayne.com, Web Site: www.leewayne.com
CEO: Marc Simon
Pres: Jack Mewhirter
VP, Sls: Dale Limes
Conducts Business: U.S., Canada, Mexico
Employees: 52
Primary Market Served: Business & Consumer
Catalog available online
Direct Marketing ad budget:
Direct Mail: $50,000
Magazines: $10,000
Telephone: $20,000
Gross sales or billing: $18,000,000

Advertising specialty distributor.

HALSOM HOME CARE INC
Subs of Tuscan Inc
7905 Clyo Rd
Centerville, OH 45459
Telephone: (937) 438-6600, (800) 345-5438, FAX: (937) 438-6620, E-Mail: main@halsom.com, Web Site: www.halsom.com
Pres: Mike Zelinskas
Conducts Business: U.S.
Employees: 11
Primary Market Served: Business & Consumer
Founded: 1936

Distributor of medical supplies to physicians & home care products to individuals.

HAMILTON BEACH/ PROCTOR-SILEX INC
4421 Waterfront Dr
Glen Allen, VA 23060-3375
Telephone: (804) 273-9777, FAX: (804) 527-7142, Web Site: www.hambeach.com
Pres & CEO: Michael J. Morecroft
Primary Market Served: Business & Consumer

Manufacturer of small appliances.

THE HAMILTON GROUP LTD INC
Subs. of The Bradford Exchange
7018 A C Skinner Pkwy (#300)
Jacksonville, FL 32256
Telephone: (904) 279-1300, FAX: (904) 279-1414, Web Site: www.collectibletoday.com
VP, Mktg: Debbie Montalao
Gen Mgr: Bernard Fazer
Employees: 330
Primary Market Served: Consumer
Advertising/Marketing Budget Related to Direct Marketing: 76-100%
Gross sales or billing: $135,000,000

Direct marketing firm.

HAMILTON WATCH
Swatch Group US
1200 Harbor Blvd
Weehawken, NJ 07086-6728
Telephone: (201) 271-1400, (800) 243-8463, Web Site: www.hamiltonwatches.com
Mgr: Dennis Phillips
Conducts Business: U.S., Canada, Europe, Asia, & S. America
Employees: 19
Primary Market Served: Business
Advertising/Marketing Budget Related to Direct Marketing: 0-25%
Founded: 1892

Manufacture & distribute complete collection of watches for retail & fine jewelry store trade & customized watches for awards as incentives.

HAMMACHER SCHLEMMER
147 E 57th St
New York, NY 10022
Telephone: (847) 581-8600, (800) 233-4800, FAX: (847) 581-8616, Web Site: www.hammacher.com
CEO: Richard W. Tinberg
VP, Mktg: Fred Barnes
Conducts Business: Worldwide
Primary Market Served: Business & Consumer
Catalog available online
Direct online sales
Founded: 1848

Publish 12 catalogs annually, with circulation exceeding 30,000,000 copies. In addition Hammacher has two retail stores located in Chicago and New York.

HAMPTON MARKETING CORP
19 Industrial Blvd
Medford, NY 11763
Telephone: (516) 924-1335, (800) 229-1019, FAX: (516) 924-1669, Web Site: www.hamptonstamp.com
CEO: R.F. Gallagher
Pres: Ronald T. Gallagher
Opers Mgr: Steven Gallagher
Conducts Business: U.S., Canada
Employees: 41
Primary Market Served: Business & Consumer
Catalog available online
Direct online sales
Advertising/Marketing Budget Related to Direct Marketing: 51-75%
Direct Marketing ad budget:
Direct Mail: 45%
Magazines: 20%
Newspapers: 30%
Telephone: 5%
Founded: 1978

Supplier of premium & mail order products both imported & domestic. Includes: manufacture of fine rubber stamps & accessories, self-inking, creative rubber stamps for the craft industry, short run custom or personalized labels, various personalized products, ink, ink pads & bar code printing. Contract rubber stamp programs.

HANLEY WOOD LLC
Owned by affiliates of JP Morgan Partners LLC
1 Thomas Cir NW (Suite 600)
Washington, DC 20005-5803
Telephone: (202) 452-0800, FAX: (202) 785-1974, Web Site: www.hanleywood.com
CEO: Frank Anton
VP Mktg: Ann Seltz
Exec Dir E-Media: Andreas Schmidt
Employees: 630
Primary Market Served: Business & Consumer
Founded: 1976
Gross sales or billing: $180,000,000

Magazine publisher & trade show producer. Four divisions: Media; Exhibitions; Marketing; Intelligence.

HANNA INSTRUMENTS INC
584 Park East Dr
Woonsocket, RI 02895
Telephone: (401) 765-7500, (800) 426-6287, FAX: (401) 765-7575, E-Mail: custsvc@hannainst.com, Web Site: www.hannainst.com
Pres: Martino Nardo
VP: Pamela Nardo
Conducts Business: Worldwide
Primary Market Served: Business

Catalog available online
Direct online sales
Founded: 1986
Gross sales or billing: $12,000,000

Manufacturer & distributor of water quality instruments.

THE HANOVER SHOE CO
Subs. of C J Clark Ltd
156 Oak St
Newton, MA 02464
Telephone: (617) 964-1222, FAX:
(617) 243-4210, Web Site: www.
clarks.com
Pres & CEO: Bob Infantino
Conducts Business: U.S.
Employees: 1,500
Primary Market Served: Consumer
Advertising/Marketing Budget Related
to Direct Marketing: 0-25%
Founded: 1899

Sell men's shoes through catalogs & other direct response methods.

CHRIS HANSEN
Subs. of Crompton & Knowles Corp
16300 W Lincoln Ave
New Berlin, WI 53151-2837
Telephone: (414) 607-5700, FAX:
(414) 607-5704, Web Site: www.chr-hansen.com
Pres, N American Div: Leif Naergaard
Mktg Commun Mgr: Cindy Stoebich
Conducts Business: Worldwide
Employees: 400
Primary Market Served: Business
Gross sales or billing: $100,000

Manufacturer of food ingredients, flavor, color, food additives, sweeteners, spices & seasonings.

HANSEN CORP
Div. of Minebea Corp
901 S First St
Princeton, IN 47670-2369
Telephone: (812) 385-3415, FAX:
(812) 385-3013, E-Mail: sales@
hansen-motor.com, Web Site: www.
hansen-motor.com
Pres & Gen Mgr: William K. Poyner
Controller: W. Michael Hollars
Dir, IT: Bonnie Reeves
Design Engrng Mgr: Lincoln Dreher
Conducts Business: U.S., Canada, Europe, Asia
Employees: 400
Primary Market Served: Business
Catalog available online
Indirect online sales
Advertising/Marketing Budget Related
to Direct Marketing: 0-25%
Direct Marketing ad budget:
Direct Mail: 5%
Magazines: 15%
Online: 80%

Founded: 1908

Design, manufacture & sale of custom timing motors, chart drives, DC Servo motors, clock movements, steppers, BLDC actuator & brake motors.

HARBOUR BAY INC
70 Orange Ave
Suffern, NY 10901
Telephone: (845) 368-2857, FAX:
(845) 368-2349
Pres: Richard Fleming
Conducts Business: U.S., Canada
Employees: 3
Primary Market Served: Business &
Consumer
Indirect online sales
Advertising/Marketing Budget Related
to Direct Marketing: 0-25%
Direct Marketing ad budget: $100,000
Direct Mail: 85%
Magazines: 10%
Newspapers: 5%
Founded: 1994
Gross sales or billing: $500,000

Seller of tobacco accessories for cigars, pipes and cigarettes.

HARLAND FINANCIAL SOLUTIONS INC
605 Crescent Executive Ct (Suite 600)
Lake Mary, FL 32746
Telephone: (407) 804-6600, (800) 815-5592, FAX: (407) 829-6702, Web
Site: www.
harlandfinancialsolutions.com
Pres: John O'Malley
Sr VP & CTO: Dan Larlee
Sr VP, Strategic Initiatives: Helen
Beckel
Exec VP: Stan Muir
VP Bus Devel & Strategic Mktg: Scott
Hansen
Employees: 120
Primary Market Served: Business &
Consumer
Catalog available online

Market software & technical support.

JOHN HARLAND CO
2939 Miller Rd
Decatur, GA 30035-4038
Telephone: (770) 981-5580, (800) 723-3690, FAX: (770) 593-5367, E-Mail:
jhhwebmaster@harland.net, Web
Site: www.harland.net
Pres & CEO: Tim Tuff
Sr VP & Gen Counsel: Phil Theodore
Sr VP: John C. Walters
Pub Rels: Dan Coleman
Conducts Business: U.S., Canada
Employees: 7,000
Primary Market Served: Business
Catalog available online

Direct online sales
Founded: 1923
Gross sales or billing: $560,000,000

Produces business forms, checks & stamps.

HARRAH'S MARKETING
219 N Center St
Reno, NV 89501-1413
Telephone: (775) 786-3232, FAX:
(775) 722-2815, Web Site: www.
harrahsreno.com
Chmn, CEO & Pres: Gary Loveman
Vice Chmn Bd: Charles L. Atwood
CFO & Treas: Jonathan S. Halkyard
Pres Eastern Division: Carlos Tolosa
Pres Western Division: Tom Jenkin
Conducts Business: U.S.
Primary Market Served: Business &
Consumer
Catalog available online
Indirect online sales

Hotel & casino.

HARRIS CORP
1025 W NASA Blvd
Melbourne, FL 32919
Telephone: (407) 727-9100, FAX:
(407) 726-5427
Chmn Bd, Pres & CEO: Howard L.
Lance
Primary Market Served: Business

Global communications company with core capabilities in wireless, office & digital television systems & microelectronics information processing defense communications.

THE HARTZ MOUNTAIN CORP
400 Plaza Dr
Secaucus, NJ 07094-3605
Telephone: (201) 271-4800, (800) 275-1414, FAX: (201) 271-0068, Web
Site: www.hartz.com
Pres & CEO: William D. Ecker
VP, Mktg: Julianne Krauss
Conducts Business: U.S.
Employees: 1,600
Primary Market Served: Business &
Consumer
Founded: 1926
Gross sales or billing: $189,300,000

Manufacture & sell pet products.

HASCO FIRST PHOTO
Div. of Hasco International Inc
3613 Mueller Rd
Saint Charles, MO 63301
Telephone: (636) 946-5115, FAX:
(636) 946-7148, Web Site: www.
growingfamily.com
Chmn & CEO: Raymond W. Harmon
Pres: Dave Van Vliet

Mktg Dir: Jim Grabowski
Conducts Business: U.S., Canada, Japan, Australia, New Zealand, France
Primary Market Served: Consumer

Infant & newborn photography.

HEALTH CARE CONCEPTS INC

3011 N IH-35
Austin, TX 78722
Telephone: (512) 479-8508, (800) 628-4201, FAX: (512) 479-8741
Pres: Charles R. Denham
Conducts Business: U.S.
Employees: 10
Primary Market Served: Business

Medical research company.

THE DMA HEALTH CARE LOGISTICS

450 Town St
Circleville, OH 43113-2244
Telephone: (800) 848-1633, Web Site:
www.healthcarelogistics.com
Mktg Mgr: Diane Taylor
Primary Market Served: Business

HEALTH O METER

11800 S Austin Ave (#B)
Alsip, IL 60803-3559
Telephone: (708) 377-0600, (800) 815-6615, FAX: (708) 377-0601, E-Mail:
HomProCS@homscales.com, Web
Site: www.homscales.com
Mktg Svcs Mgr: Barbara Vook
Mktg Mgr Medical Sls: Art Swanson
Conducts Business: U.S.
Primary Market Served: Business & Consumer

Manufacture scales.

THE HEALTHY BACK STORE

11714 Baltimore Ave
Beltsville, MD 20705-1850
Telephone: (703) 339-1700, (800) 4
MY BACK, FAX: (703) 339-0671,
E-Mail: service@healthyback.com,
Web Site: www.healthyback.com
Pres: Tony Mazlish
VP: Cliff Levin
Conducts Business: U.S.
Employees: 45
Primary Market Served: Business & Consumer
Catalog available online
Direct online sales
Advertising/Marketing Budget Related to Direct Marketing: 0-25%
Direct Marketing ad budget: $250,000
Direct Mail: 25%
Newspapers: 50%
TV/Radio: 25%
Founded: 1993
Gross sales or billing: $10,000,000

Back care products such as ergonomic office seating, car seat supports & back-friendly beds.

HECHT RUBBER CORP

6161 Phillips Hwy
Jacksonville, FL 32216-5920
Telephone: (904) 731-3401, (800) 872-3401, FAX: (904) 730-0066, Web
Site: www.hechtrubber.com
Pres: Larry M. Hecht
CFO: Stuart Hecht
Conducts Business: Worldwide
Employees: 33
Primary Market Served: Business & Consumer
Catalog available online
Advertising/Marketing Budget Related to Direct Marketing: 26-50%
Direct Marketing ad budget:
Direct Mail: 70%
Magazines: 10%
Newspapers: 1%
Telephone: 19%
Founded: 1944

Manufacturer & distributor of rubber products for business, industry, government & safety. Sell products through direct mail.

W C HELLER & CO

201 W Wabash St
Montpelier, OH 43543-1840
Telephone: (419) 485-3176, FAX:
(419) 485-8694
Pres: R.L. Heller
VP: Andrew M. Heller
Conducts Business: U.S.
Employees: 4
Primary Market Served: Business & Consumer
Catalog available online
Advertising/Marketing Budget Related to Direct Marketing: 26-50%
Direct Marketing ad budget:
Direct Mail: 60%
Magazines: 10%
Newspapers: 10%
Telephone: 20%
Founded: 1891
Gross sales or billing: $500,000

Manufacturers of wood library furniture such as book shelving, counters, tables & study carrells. Sold to schools, public & private libraries, offices & hospitals. Custom cabinets for anyone.

HELLO DIRECT

Subs. of GN Netcom
77 Northeastern Blvd
Nashua, NH 03062-3128
Telephone: (408) 972-1990, (800) 435-5634, FAX: (408) 972-8155, Web
Site: www.hello-direct.com

VP, Mktg: Ron Becht
Gen Mgr: Terry Flynn
Cntrl: Brian Ronan
Sls Dir: James Smith
Conducts Business: U.S.
Employees: 300
Primary Market Served: Business & Consumer
Direct online sales
Founded: 1987
Gross sales or billing: $26,000,000

Sell telephone systems & accessories, including headsets, handsets, fax machines & accessories, voice mail, auto attendant, teleconferencing units & small key telephone systems. Home & business offices are included.

HELLY-HANSEN

4101 C St (Suite 200)
Auburn, WA 98002
Telephone: (800) 435-5901, FAX:
(425) 649-3740, E-Mail:
webmaster@hellyhansen.com, Web
Site: www.hellyhansen.com
Mktg: John Raymer
Global Brand Mgr: Hans Gunleikscrud
Primary Market Served: Business
Catalog available online
Direct online sales
Founded: 1877
Gross sales or billing: $25,000,000

Outdoor clothing gear wholesale company sold through salesman.

HELMAN GROUP LTD

1621 Beacon Pl
Oxnard, CA 93033
Telephone: (805) 487-7772, FAX:
(805) 487-9975, E-Mail: barryh@
helmangroup.com, Web Site: www.
helmangroup.com
Pres: Andy Helman
Mgr, Sls: Lisa Latimer
CEO: Barry Helman
Conducts Business: U.S., Canada, Japan, Europe, Taiwan, Korea, Hong Kong
Employees: 50
Primary Market Served: Business
Indirect online sales
Advertising/Marketing Budget Related to Direct Marketing: 0-25%
Founded: 1969
Gross sales or billing: $30,000,000

Manufacturer of mail order products. Distribution & sales to retail accounts in the U.S. & Canada.

HELZBERG DIAMONDS

Subs. of Berkshire Hathaway
1825 Swift St
North Kansas City, MO 64116-3606

Telephone: (816) 842-7780, (800) HELZBURG, FAX: (816) 480-0294, Web Site: www.helzberg.com
Chmn & CEO: H. Marvin Beasley
Exec VP & CFO: Laura Kirsner
Exec VP HR: J. Kevin Fitzpatrick
Sr VP: John Goodman
Mktg Dir: Monica Wilkens
Conducts Business: U.S.
Employees: 3,000
Primary Market Served: Consumer
Catalog available online
Direct online sales
Advertising/Marketing Budget Related to Direct Marketing: 26-50%
Founded: 1915
Gross sales or billing: $479,700,000

Retail jewelry store.

HERMAN MILLER INC
855 E Main Ave
Zeeland, MI 49464
Telephone: (616) 654-3000, FAX: (616) 654-5234, E-Mail: investor@hermanmiller.com, Web Site: www.hermanmiller.com
Chmn: Michael A. Volkema
Pres, CEO & Dir: Brian C. Walker
CFO: Curt Pullen
VP, Investor Rels & Treas: Joe Nowicki
PR: Luke Dawson
Conducts Business: Worldwide
Employees: 3,500
Primary Market Served: Business
Catalog available online
Indirect online sales
Gross sales or billing: $1,900,000,000

Manufacturer of office furniture systems, desks & seating products.

HERR FOODS INC
20 Herr Dr
Nottingham, PA 19362
Telephone: (610) 932-9330, (800) 344-3777, FAX: (610) 932-2137, E-Mail: info@herrs.com, Web Site: www.herrfoods.com
Chmn & CEO: James Herr
Pres: Edwin Herr
VP, Sls, HR & Mktg: Richard White
Mktg Dir: Daryl Thomas
Employees: 1,200
Primary Market Served: Consumer
Catalog available online
Direct online sales
Gross sales or billing: $165,000,000

Snack foods.

HERRINGTON
Three Symmes Dr
Londonderry, NH 03053

Telephone: (603) 437-1600, (800) 903-2878, FAX: (603) 437-1340, (603) 437-3492, E-Mail: customerservice@herringtoncatalog.com, Web Site: www.herringtoncatalog.com
Pres & Owner: Lee R. Herrington
Controller: Norm Beauchesne
Conducts Business: U.S.
Employees: 64
Primary Market Served: Consumer
Catalog available online
Direct online sales
Founded: 1980

Sell upscale products: audio, video, photography, motoring, golf, boating & skiing accessories to consumers via online and mail order catalog.

HEWLETT-PACKARD CO
3000 Hanover St
Palo Alto, CA 94304-1185
Telephone: (650) 857-1501, (800) 752-0900, FAX: (650) 857-5518, Web Site: www.hp.com
Dir Marcom: Chris Sutter
Chmn, Pres & CEO: Mark V. Hurd
Exec VP & CFO: Catherine A. Lesjak
Exec VP & CIO: Randall D. Mott
Exec VP Chief Strategy & Tech Officer: Shane Robison
Exec VP Imaging & Printing Grp: Vyomesh Joshi
Employees: 156,000
Primary Market Served: Business & Consumer
Catalog available online
Direct online sales
Gross sales or billing: $91,600,000,000

Manufacturer of electronic equipment for measurement analysis & computation.

THE DMA HILTON HHONORS WORLDWIDE
7930 Jones Branch Dr
McLean, VA 22102
Telephone: (703) 883-1000, Web Site: www.hilton.com
Primary Market Served: Business

THE DMA HIPCRICKET INC
4400 Carillon Pt # 4
Kirkland, WA 98033-7353
Telephone: (425) 452-1111, Web Site: www.hipcricket.com
CMO: Jeff Hasen

THE HISTORICAL RESEARCH CENTER INTERNATIONAL INC
2107 Corporate Dr
Boynton Beach, FL 33426-6645

Telephone: (561) 732-5263, (800) 985-9956, FAX: (561) 940-7991, E-Mail: custsvc@names.com, Web Site: www.historicalresearchcenter.net
Founder: Michael Walshe
Employees: 40
Primary Market Served: Consumer
Catalog available online
Direct online sales
Advertising/Marketing Budget Related to Direct Marketing: 76-100%
Direct Marketing ad budget:
Direct Mail: 10%
Newspapers: 10%
TV/Radio: 70%
Telephone: 10%
Founded: 1988

Retail heraldic products.

HOBSONS
50 E Business Way (Suite 300)
Cincinnati, OH 45241-2398
Telephone: (513) 985-4186, Web Site: www.hobsons.com
Dir Student Mktg: Daniela Locreille

Educational professionals offering higher education CRM & other tools for student recruitment, enrollment management & student retention

THE DMA HOLLISTER INC
2000 Hollister Dr
Libertyville, IL 60048
Telephone: (847) 680-1000, (888) 740-8999, FAX: (847) 680-2123, Web Site: www.hollister.com
Pres: Alan F. Herbert
VP & CFO: Samuel P. Brilliant
Dir: Randy Klinger
Conducts Business: U.S.
Primary Market Served: Business
Catalog available online
Indirect online sales

Marketer of medical record forms to physicians.

HOLY CROSS HOSPITAL
4725 N Federal Hwy
Fort Lauderdale, FL 33308-4670
Telephone: (954) 771-8000, FAX: (954) 229-8597, Web Site: www.holy-cross.com
Pres & CEO: John Johnson
Exec VP & COO: Patrick A. Taylor MD
Sr VP: Mark R. Dissette
Sr VP Chief Nursing Officer: Nora Triola RN, Ph D
VP HR: Luisa Gutman
Conducts Business: U.S.
Employees: 1,400
Primary Market Served: Business & Consumer

Not-for-profit, privately owned, religiously affiliated facility under the direction of the Sisters of Mercy.

THE HOME DEPOT INC
2455 Paces Ferry Rd NW
Atlanta, GA 30339-1834
Telephone: (770) 433-8211, (800) 430-3376, FAX: (770) 384-2356, Web Site: www.homedepot.com
Chmn & CEO: Francis C. Blake
Exec VP & COO: Joseph J. DeAngelo
Exec VP, Corp Svcs & CFO: Carol B. Tome
Exec VP & CIO: Robert P. DeRodes
Exec VP, HR: Timothy M. Crow
Dir, CRM: Rebecca Charles
Conducts Business: U.S., Canada
Employees: 364,000
Primary Market Served: Business & Consumer
Catalog available online
Direct online sales
Founded: 1978
Gross sales or billing: $90,000,000,000

Retailer of do-it-yourself merchandise.

HOME INTERIORS & GIFTS INC
1649 Frankford Rd W
Carrollton, TX 75007-4605
Telephone: (972) 695-1000, FAX: (972) 695-1112
Pres & CEO: Mike Lohner
Primary Market Served: Consumer

HONEYWELL
101 Columbia Rd
Morristown, NJ 07962
Telephone: (973) 455-2000, FAX: (973) 455-4807, Web Site: www.honeywell.com
Chmn & CEO: Michael R. Bonsignore
Conducts Business: Worldwide
Employees: 55,000
Primary Market Served: Business
Advertising/Marketing Budget Related to Direct Marketing: 0-25%
Gross sales or billing: $6,200,000,000

Global controls company providing products, systems & services that increase comfort, environmental protection, energy conservation, productivity & safety in homes & buildings, industry, aviation & space.

HONEYWELL WINTRESS CONTROLS
100 Discovery Way
Acton, MA 01720
Telephone: (978) 264-9550, (800) 333-3282, FAX: (978) 263-0630, Web Site: www.wintress.com
Prod Line Dir: Mark Hatch

Conducts Business: Worldwide
Employees: 125
Primary Market Served: Business
Catalog available online
Indirect online sales

Safety and automation controls

THE HOPE CO INC
12777 Pennridge Dr
Bridgeton, MO 63044
Telephone: (314) 739-7254, (800) 325-4026, FAX: (314) 739-7786, E-Mail: info@hopecompany.com
Pres & CEO: John H. Finnegan, Sr
Mktg Dir: John H. Finnegan, Jr
Conducts Business: U.S.
Primary Market Served: Business
Catalog available online

Manufacture chemical home care products.

HORMEL FOODS CORP
One Hormel Pl
Austin, MN 55912-3680
Telephone: (507) 437-5611, (800) 523-4635, FAX: (507) 437-5158, Web Site: www.hormel.com
Chmn, Pres & CEO: Joel W. Johnson
VP, PR: Allan Krejci
VP: Robert Tegt
Mktg Svcs Dir: Jerry Whithaus
Primary Market Served: Business
Catalog available online
Indirect online sales

Meat packing & food processing.

F.M. HOWELL & CO
79 Pennsylvania Ave
Elmira, NY 14902-1455
Telephone: (607) 734-6291, FAX: (607) 735-0464, E-Mail: best@howellpkg.com, Web Site: www.howellpkg.com
Chmn & CEO: George Howell
Dir: Stephen D. Duff
Employees: 275
Primary Market Served: Business
Gross sales or billing: $21,000,000

Manufacture paperboard packing & thermoform plastic packaging.

THE DMA HUBERT CO
9555 Dry Fork Rd
Harrison, OH 45030-1994
Telephone: (513) 367-8767, (800) 543-7374, FAX: (513) 367-8823, Web Site: www.hubert.com
Pres: C. Bart Kohler
VP, Mktg: Andy Hallock
Dir Mktg: Mark Woodrow
Conducts Business: Worldwide
Employees: 309
Primary Market Served: Business
Catalog available online

Direct online sales
Founded: 1946

Food service store furnishings, equipment & supplies. Food service industry, merchandising displays, equipment & supplies.

HY CITE CORP
dba Royal Prestige & Ocean Blue
333 Holtzman Rd
Madison, WI 53713-2109
Telephone: (608) 273-3373, (800) 279-3373, FAX: (608) 273-0936, Web Site: www.hycite.com
Pres: Eric Johnson
Mktg Supv: Cybell Abrei
Employees: 175
Primary Market Served: Consumer
Founded: 1959
Gross sales or billing: $5,900,000

Cookware, cutlery, water filters, air purifiers & China flatware.

HY-KO PRODUCTS CO
60 Meadow Ln
Northfield, OH 44067-1415
Telephone: (330) 467-7446, Web Site: www.hy-ko.com
Project Supvr: Sarah Shebesta
Primary Market Served: Business & Consumer

HYATT HOTELS CORP
71 S Wacker Dr (Suite 1000)
Chicago, IL 60606-4716
Telephone: (312) 750-1234, FAX: (312) 780-5289, Web Site: www.hyatt.com
Pres: Doug Gioga
Pres & CEO: Mark Hoplamazian
Mktg Asst: Sarah Laughlin
Conducts Business: U.S., Canada, Caribbean
Employees: 400
Primary Market Served: Business & Consumer
Direct Marketing ad budget: $20,000,000
Direct Mail: 50%
Magazines: 20%
Newspapers: 20%
TV/Radio: 10%

Hotel management & development organization.

HYATT LEGAL PLANS INC
A Metlife Co
1111 Superior Ave E (Suite 800)
Cleveland, OH 44114-2529
Telephone: (216) 241-0022, FAX: (216) 694-4305, Web Site: www.legalplans.com
VP: Andrew Kohn
Mktg Dir: Marcia Bowers

Employees: 82
Primary Market Served: Business & Consumer
Catalog available online
Indirect online sales
Advertising/Marketing Budget Related to Direct Marketing: 0-25%
Founded: 1977
Gross sales or billing: $8,200,000

Group Legal services provider through 4,600 participating law firms in the U.S.

HYGIENIC FABRICS & FILTERS INC

1301 Erie Ave, PO Box 1005
Sheboygan, WI 53082-1005
Telephone: (920) 457-7383, (800) 876-2009, FAX: (920) 457-2558, Web Site: www.hyfab.com
Pres, Sls: John F. Wilson Jr
VP: Thomas Laiken
Employees: 6
Primary Market Served: Business & Consumer
Catalog available online
Direct online sales
Advertising/Marketing Budget Related to Direct Marketing: 0-25%
Founded: 1936

Manufacturer of filter cloths sold to the food processing industry & household soft goods sold via catalog.

THE DMA IBM CORP

1 New Orchard Rd
Armonk, NY 10504-1725
Telephone: (914) 765-1900, FAX: (914) 765-6633, Web Site: www.ibm.com
Pres & CEO: Virginia M. Rometty
Conducts Business: U.S.
Primary Market Served: Business

Financial services, leasing corporation.

IDMS INC

560 Broadhollow Rd (Suite 109)
Melville, NY 11747-3702
Telephone: (631) 249-7744, (800) 582-5831, FAX: (631) 249-4425, E-Mail: sales@idmsinc.com, Web Site: www.idmsinc.com
Pres: Jeff Goldstein
Mktg: Leslie Goldstein
Conducts Business: U.S.
Employees: 6
Primary Market Served: Business & Consumer
Catalog available online
Direct online sales
Advertising/Marketing Budget Related to Direct Marketing: 26-50%
Direct Marketing ad budget: $50,000
Online: $50,000

Founded: 1984
Gross sales or billing: $1,500,000

Custom software development & developer of integrated computer network solutions. Targeting primarily wholesalers, distributors, manufacturers & accountants. Specializing in EDI, telecommunications & bar coding.

IHOP CORP

450 N Brand Blvd Fl 7
Glendale, CA 91203-4415
Telephone: (818) 240-6055, FAX: (818) 553-3131, Web Site: www.ihop.com
Chmn & CEO: Julia A. Stewart
CFO: Thomas G. Conforti
CMO: Carolyn P. O'Keefe
VP: Jim Peros
VP, IT: Patrick J. Piccinno
Conducts Business: U.S., Canada, Japan
Primary Market Served: Consumer
Catalog available online
Advertising/Marketing Budget Related to Direct Marketing: 0-25%
Founded: 1958
Gross sales or billing: $349,000,000

Restaurant operator & franchiser of International House of Pancakes Restaurants.

INX INTERNATIONAL INK CO

150 N Martingale Rd (Suite 700)
Schaumburg, IL 60173
Telephone: (800) 631-7956, FAX: (847) 969-9758, E-Mail: info@inxink.com, Web Site: www.inxinternational.com
Pres: Rick Clendenning
VP, Fin: Bryce Kristo
Conducts Business: U.S., Canada
Employees: 1,300
Primary Market Served: Business
Advertising/Marketing Budget Related to Direct Marketing: 0-25%
Founded: 1991
Gross sales or billing: $360,000,000

Manufacturer of printing ink & coding.

ITT EDUCATIONAL SERVICES INC

13000 N Meridian St
Carmel, IN 46082
Telephone: (317) 706-9200, E-Mail: gtanner@itt-tech.edu, Web Site: www.itt-tech.edu
Chmn & CEO: Rene R. Champagne
VP, Mktg: Glen E. Tanner
Sr VP & Mktg Dir: Martin A. Grossman
CFO: Kevin M. Modany
Dir, Corp Rels: Nancy Brown

Pres, COO: Omer E. Waddles
Conducts Business: U.S.
Employees: 2,600
Primary Market Served: Consumer
Catalog available online
Direct online sales
Advertising/Marketing Budget Related to Direct Marketing: 76-100%
Founded: 1968
Gross sales or billing: $464,946,000

Provides education for 75 technical colleges in over 43 markets specializing in post secondary career-oriented degree level technical education.

ITW BEE LEITZKE

Div of Illinois Tool Works
2000 Industrial Rd
Iron Ridge, WI 53035-9535
Telephone: (920) 625-2342, FAX: (920) 625-2643, Web Site: www.itwbeeleitzke.com
COO: Barth Leatherman
Pres: Jerry DeWitz
Mktg Mgr: Mark Simmons
Conducts Business: U.S., Canada
Primary Market Served: Business
Founded: 1929

Fasteners & industrial components, industrial distribution. Manufacture fasteners.

ITW VORTEC

Div. of Illinois Tool Works
10125 Carver Rd
Cincinnati, OH 45242
Telephone: (513) 891-7474, (800) 441-7475, FAX: (513) 891-4092, E-Mail: techsupport@vortec.com, Web Site: www.vortec.com
Gen Mgr: Michael Parker
Matls Coord: Sandy Baggett
Mktg Supvr: Dave Kremp
Conducts Business: Worldwide
Primary Market Served: Business
Catalog available online
Founded: 1961

Manufacture new technology items such as specialized compressed air appliances that cool, reduce air consumption & lower plant noise level. Sell to all types of industrial customers through direct marketing promotions.

THE IAMS CO

Subs of Procter & Gamble (P&G Petcare)
7250 Poe Ave
Dayton, OH 45414-5801
Telephone: (937) 898-7387, (800) 675-3849, FAX: (937) 264-7264, Web Site: www.iams.com
CEO & Chmn Bd - P&G: A. G. Lafley
External Rels: Staci Dudley
Administrator: Nina Douglas

External Rels: Julie Franklin
Conducts Business: U.S., Canada
Employees: 1,000
Primary Market Served: Consumer
Founded: 1946
Gross sales or billing: $118,300,000

Supplier of premium pet food.

ICLIMBER INC

315 W Verdugo Ave (Suite 101)
Burbank, CA 91502-2484
Telephone: (818) 567-3030, Web Site:
    www.iclimber.com
VP Sls & Mktg: Allen Horwitz
Primary Market Served: Consumer

THE IDEA CLUB.COM(TM) &
DUMAS MARTIN
CONSULTING

101 W Mission Blvd (Suite 110-147)
Pomona, CA 91766-1245
Telephone: (909) 620-4772, FAX:
    (909) 629-4739, E-Mail:
    theideaclub@peoplepc.com, Web
    Site: www.incorpman.com
Pres & CEO: Dumas Martin Jr.
Co-Founder & VP: Eleanora O. Murph
Conducts Business: U.S.
Employees: 5
Primary Market Served: Business &
    Consumer
Catalog available online
Direct online sales
Advertising/Marketing Budget Related
    to Direct Marketing: 0-25%
Direct Marketing ad budget:
Direct Mail: $2,000
Magazines: $3,000
Newspapers: $5,000
Online: $5,000
TV/Radio: $2,000
Telephone: $5,000
Founded: 1993

Inventors Guide: ABC's of Entrepreneurial Inventing (TM). Idea development consulting service.

I/D/E/A INC

One Idea Way
Caldwell, ID 83605-6900
Telephone: (208) 459-6357, (800) 635-
    9261, FAX: (208) 459-6484, Web
    Site: www.relyonidea.com
CEO: Paul Kaye
Controller & VP: Anita Kiser
Conducts Business: U.S., Canada
Employees: 70
Primary Market Served: Business

Business-to-business printed product
marketer.

IDEAL INDUSTRIES INC

Becker Pl
Sycamore, IL 60178

Telephone: (815) 895-5181, (800) 435-
    0705, FAX: (815) 895-4800, E-Mail:
    ideal_industries@idealindustries.com,
    Web Site: www.idealindustries.com
VP Mktg: Glenn Hollister
Primary Market Served: Business

Manufacture of electrical products
through distributions.

IDEARC MEDIA CORP

2200 W Airfield Dr
Dallas, TX 75261
Telephone: (972) 453-7797
Mgr Mktg Res: David Bernstein
Primary Market Served: Consumer

ILOOP MOBILE INC

25 Metro Dr (Suite 210)
San Jose, CA 95110-1338
Telephone: (408) 907-3360, Web Site:
    www.iloopmobile.com
Exec VP Mobile Strategy: Michael
    Becker

THE DMA IMPERIAL SUPPLIES

789 Armed Forces Dr
Green Bay, WI 54304-4527
Telephone: (920) 494-5403, (800) 558-
    2808, FAX: (800) 553-8769, Web
    Site: www.imperialsupplies.com
Pres: Rob Gilson
VP, Mktg: Mitchell Mittlestadt
Dir Mktg: Pauline Schuster
Mktg Mgr: Nicole Alboushi
Conducts Business: U.S.
Employees: 120
Primary Market Served: Business &
    Consumer
Catalog available online
Indirect online sales
Advertising/Marketing Budget Related
    to Direct Marketing: 0-25%
Founded: 1958

Wholesaler & nationwide distributor of
maintenance supplies.

INDIUM CORP OF AMERICA

34 Robinson Rd
Clinton, NY 13323-1419
Telephone: (315) 853-4900, (800) 446-
    3486, FAX: (800) 221-5759, E-Mail:
    askus@indium.com, Web Site: www.
    indium.com
Chmn & CEO: William N. Macartney
    III
Pres: Gregory P. Evans
Mgr: Kevin Moore
Conducts Business: Worldwide
Employees: 240
Primary Market Served: Business
Catalog available online
Advertising/Marketing Budget Related
    to Direct Marketing: 0-25%
Direct Marketing ad budget:

Direct Mail: 5%
Magazines: 90%
Telephone: 5%
Founded: 1934
Gross sales or billing: $30,000,000

Manufacturer of indium metal & specialty solders & alloys.

INFOMART

1950 Stemmons Fwy (Suite1000)
Dallas, TX 75207
Telephone: (214) 800-8000, FAX:
    (214) 800-8100, Web Site: www.
    infomartusa.com
Pres: Tom Jones
Property Mgr: Jay Stone
Conducts Business: Worldwide
Primary Market Served: Business &
    Consumer
Advertising/Marketing Budget Related
    to Direct Marketing: 76-100%

Real estate & trade show educational
facility.

INGRAM BOOK GROUP

Div. of Ingram Industries Inc
One Ingram Blvd
La Vergne, TN 37086
Telephone: (615) 793-5000, (800) 937-
    8000, FAX: (800) 876-0186, Web
    Site: www.ipage.ingrambook.com
Pres, IBC: Jim Chandler
CEO, Ingram Book Grp: Mike Lovett
VP, Mktg, IBG: Kelley Maier
VP, Sls & Mktg: Tom Jones
Conducts Business: Worldwide
Employees: 3,500
Primary Market Served: Business
Catalog available online
Advertising/Marketing Budget Related
    to Direct Marketing: 0-25%
Founded: 1969

A leading wholesaler of trade books,
spoken audio, and magazines. Operating units include Ingram Book Company, Ingram Periodicals Inc., Ingram
International, Ingram Library Services
Inc, Spring Arbor Distributors Inc.,
Tennessee Book Company, Ingram
Fullfillment Services, and Ingram Customer Systems.

INSIGHT DIRECT INC

Div. of Insight Enterprises Inc
6820 S Harl Ave
Tempe, AZ 85283-4318
Telephone: (480) 333-3001, (800) 467-
    4448, FAX: (480) 902-1180, Web
    Site: www.insight.com
Pres: Tim A. Crown
CEO: Eric Crown
VP, Opers: Denny Chittick
VP, Sls: Rick Ridart
VP, Mktg: Dan Sager
Corp Communs: Valerie Paxton

Conducts Business: U.S., Canada, US Virgin Islands
Employees: 550
Primary Market Served: Business & Consumer
Advertising/Marketing Budget Related to Direct Marketing: 76-100%
Direct Marketing ad budget:
Direct Mail: $1,000,000
Magazines: $6,000,000
Founded: 1986
Gross sales or billing: $245,000,000

Distribution company selling computer & electronic components, peripherals & software.

INSTITUTE FOR INTERNATIONAL RESEARCH INC

708 Third Ave (4th fl)
New York, NY 10017-4103
Telephone: (212) 661-3500, (800) 345-8016, FAX: (212) 599-2192, E-Mail: register@iirusa.com, Web Site: www.iir-ny.com
Gen Mgr & Fin Dir: Debra Chipman
VP, Mktg: Roxanne John
Mktg Dir: Yemil Martinez
Conducts Business: Worldwide
Employees: 75
Primary Market Served: Business
Direct Marketing ad budget:
Direct Mail: 98%
Magazines: 2%

Business information company that organizes conferences & training programs for mid to senior level executives.

INSTITUTE FOR NATURAL RESOURCES

2352 Stanwell Dr
Concord, CA 94520
Telephone: (925) 687-0860, FAX: (925) 609-2820, E-Mail: dcheung@biocorp.com
CEO, Pres & Owner: Barry Meltzer
VP: Deborah Cheung
Primary Market Served: Consumer
Catalog available online
Direct online sales

Conducts scientific seminars for professionals.

THE INSTRUMENT WORKSHOP

PO Box 1060
Ashland, OR 97520-0050
Telephone: (541) 552-0989, (800) 442-6038, FAX: (541) 488-5846, E-Mail: shop77@fortepiano.com, Web Site: www.fortepiano.com
Partner: Lutz Bungart
Partner: Martha Bungart

Conducts Business: Worldwide
Primary Market Served: Business & Consumer
Catalog available online
Indirect online sales
Advertising/Marketing Budget Related to Direct Marketing: 51-75%
Direct Marketing ad budget:
Direct Mail: 75%
Magazines: 20%
Telephone: 5%
Founded: 1969
Gross sales or billing: $100,000

Parts & plans for early keyboard instruments: harpsichords, clavichords, virginals, forte pianos, hammer dulcimers, harps, sitars & zithers.

INTEGRETEL INC

5883 Rue Ferrari
San Jose, CA 95138-1857
Telephone: (408) 362-4000, FAX: (408) 362-2795, Web Site: www.integretel.com
CEO: Joe Lynam
Pres: Ken Dawson
Primary Market Served: Business
Direct Marketing ad budget:
Direct Mail: 15%
Magazines: 80%
Newspapers: 5%
Founded: 1988

Telephone billing company & service agency.

INTEGRITY MUSIC INC

1000 Cody Rd
Mobile, AL 36695
Telephone: (251) 633-9000, FAX: (251) 633-5202, Web Site: www.integritymusic.com
Pres: Mike Coleman
Dir: Jean C. Coleman
Conducts Business: Worldwide
Employees: 218
Primary Market Served: Consumer
Catalog available online
Direct online sales
Founded: 1987

Producer and publisher of Christian music products.

INTEL CORP

2200 Mission College Blvd
Santa Clara, CA 95052
Telephone: (408) 765-8080, (800) 548-4725, FAX: (408) 765-6187, Web Site: www.intel.com
Chmn: Craig R. Barrett
Pres & CEO: Paul S. Otellini
Exec VP & CAO: Andy D. Bryant
Exec VP & CMO: Sean M. Maloney
Exec VP: David Perlmutter
Conducts Business: Worldwide
Employees: 94,100

Primary Market Served: Business & Consumer
Founded: 1968
Gross sales or billing: $35,382,000,000

Manufacturers of electronic products.

INTERFACEFLOR LLC

1503 Orchard Hill Rd
La Grange, GA 30240-5709
Telephone: (706) 882-1891, (800) 336-0225, FAX: (706) 882-0500, Web Site: www.interfaceflor.com
Pres & CEO: David Hobbs
VP Mktg: Tracy Cook
Conducts Business: Worldwide
Employees: 1,500
Primary Market Served: Business
Advertising/Marketing Budget Related to Direct Marketing: 0-25%
Founded: 1923
Gross sales or billing: $190,000,000

Manufactures carpet tile & six foot goods. Markets tiles under the Interface & Interface Retail names in 90 different countries.

INTERGRAPH CORP

170 Graphics Dr
Madison, AL 35758
Telephone: (256) 730-2000, (800) 345-4856, FAX: (256) 730-2048, Web Site: www.intergraph.com
Pres & CEO: R. Halsey Wise
Sr VP & Treas: Larry J. Laster
Exec VP & COO: R. Reid French Jr
VP & CAO: Steven Cost
VP: David Vance Lucas
Primary Market Served: Business & Consumer
Founded: 1969

Design, manufacture, market & support turnkey computer-aided engineering, design & graphics.

INTERNATIONAL CRYSTAL MANUFACTURING CO

10 N Lee St
Oklahoma City, OK 73102
Telephone: (405) 236-3741, (800) 252-6780, FAX: (405) 235-1904, E-Mail: info@icmfg.com, Web Site: www.icmfg.com
Pres: Dana Guy
VP & Gen Sls Mgr: Steve Webb
Mktg Mgr: Mark Handley
Pur & Inventory Mgr: Barbara Thompson
Conducts Business: U.S.
Employees: 30
Primary Market Served: Business & Consumer
Catalog available online
Direct online sales
Advertising/Marketing Budget Related

to Direct Marketing: 76-100%
Direct Marketing ad budget:
Online: 25%
Telephone: 75%
Founded: 1967

Manufacture Quartz crystals & related items for two-way radios, pagers, transmitters & receivers, oscillator crystals, recrystal pagers, pager crystals & oscillators.

THE DMA INTERNATIONAL PAPER
6400 Poplar Ave
Memphis, TN 38197-0100
Telephone: (901) 419-9000, (800) 207-4003, Web Site: www.internationalpaper.com
Chmn Bd & CEO: John V. Faraci
Employees: 60,000
Primary Market Served: Business & Consumer
Gross sales or billing: $22,000,000,000

A global forest products, paper and packaging company with primary markets and manufacturing operations in the United States, Europe, Latin America and Asia, complemented by xpedx, an extensive North American merchant distribution system.

INTERNATIONAL SPECIALIZED BOOK SERVICES INC
dba Isbs
920 NE 58th Ave (Suite 300)
Portland, OR 97213
Telephone: (503) 287-3093, (800) 944-6190, FAX: (503) 280-8832, E-Mail: isbs_sales@isbs.com, Web Site: www.isbscatalog.com
Gen Mgr: Rod Walker
Mktg Mgr: Tamna Greenfield
Sec: Carl D. Dyess
Conducts Business: Worldwide
Employees: 15
Primary Market Served: Business & Consumer
Catalog available online
Indirect online sales
Advertising/Marketing Budget Related to Direct Marketing: 26-50%
Founded: 1976
Gross sales or billing: $2,000,000

Represent over 60 book publishers exclusively. 80% of business is by direct mail marketing to libraries, companies, retail outlets & special interest individuals. Self-maintained databased/computer mailing lists. Also represent English speaking foreign publishers.

INTRA BUSINESS SYSTEMS INC
PO Box 6681
South Bend, IN 46660-6681

Telephone: (574) 257-7940, FAX: (574) 257-7944, E-Mail: info@intrabusinesssystems.com, Web Site: www.intrabusinesssystems.com
Owner: John Kampars
Conducts Business: U.S.
Primary Market Served: Business & Consumer
Advertising/Marketing Budget Related to Direct Marketing: 76-100%
Direct Marketing ad budget: $72,000
Direct Mail: 5%
Magazines: 95%
Founded: 2000
Gross sales or billing: $500,000

Remanufacturer of laser printer & copier toner cartridges & office supplies.

INTROMARK INC
217 Ninth St
Pittsburgh, PA 15222-3506
Telephone: (412) 288-1300, (800) 851-6030 X1368, FAX: (412) 338-0497, E-Mail: licensing@intromark.com
Mng Dir: Richard Resnick
Licensing Mgr: John Adkins
Mktg Coord: Brian Frattaroli
Conducts Business: Worldwide
Employees: 9
Primary Market Served: Business & Consumer
Gross sales or billing: $700,000

Invention licensing and marketing service organization specializing in new products.

INVACARE CONTINUING CARE GROUP
Div. of Invacare Corp
1848 Craig Rd
Saint Louis, MO 63146-4712
Telephone: (519) 659-1395, (800) 347-5440, FAX: (636) 519-0044, Web Site: www.invacare-ccg.com
Mgr: Victoria Cote
Conducts Business: U.S., Canada, S. America, Middle East, Far East, Europe
Primary Market Served: Business
Catalog available online
Advertising/Marketing Budget Related to Direct Marketing: 0-25%

Manufacture electric & manual hospital beds & related patient room furniture sold direct to the end user through local representation.

INVACARE SUPPLY GROUP
9 Industrial Rd
Milford, MA 01757-3588

Telephone: (508) 429-1000, (800) 225-4792, FAX: (508) 429-1581, E-Mail: service.isg@invacare.com, Web Site: www.invacaresupplygroup.com
VP, Fin: Paul Patsuno
VP Cust Svc: Steve Biles
VP MIS: Paul Jandron
Conducts Business: U.S.
Employees: 100
Primary Market Served: Business
Advertising/Marketing Budget Related to Direct Marketing: 76-100%
Direct Marketing ad budget:
Direct Mail: $500,000
Founded: 1975
Gross sales or billing: $60,000,000

Wholesaler of durable medical equipment. Distribution centers in Holliston, MA; Rancho Cucamonga, CA; Grand Prairie, TX; Atlanta, GA; South Bend, IN & Edison, NJ.

INWAVE INTERNET
1131 W Enterprise Dr
Janesville, WI 53546
Telephone: (888) 469-2831, FAX: (608) 752-8981, Web Site: www.inwave.com
Pres: Mark Mitchell
Primary Market Served: Business & Consumer
Catalog available online
Advertising/Marketing Budget Related to Direct Marketing: 76-100%
Direct Marketing ad budget:
Direct Mail: 85%
Magazines: 15%
Founded: 1992

Small electronics equipment.

IOMEGA CORP
4059 S 1900 W
Roy, UT 84067
Telephone: (801) 332-1000, (888) 446-6342, FAX: (801) 332-3158, Web Site: www.iomega.com
Pres & CEO: Thomas Kampfer
CFO: Preston Romm
VP, Sls: Peter Wharton
Conducts Business: Worldwide
Primary Market Served: Business
Catalog available online
Direct online sales
Founded: 1980
Gross sales or billing: $400,000,000

Develop, manufacture & sell high-performance removable mass storage products for desktop computers. Patented Bernoulli Technology provides unlimited data storage capability by combining the removability of floppy drives with the high capacity & performance of rigid drives. Bernoulli drives are distributed through dealers/distributors domestically & internationally.

ISUZU MOTORS AMERICA INC

1400 S Douglass Rd
Anaheim, CA 92806-6904
Telephone: (562) 229-5000, (800) 255-6727, FAX: (562) 229-5463, Web Site: www.isuzu.com
Chmn: Yoshimoto Utaka
Vice Chmn: Akira Mukai
Pres: Terry Maloney
Exec VP & CFO: Matt Saito
Mktg Dir: Jeff Birdseye
Conducts Business: US
Employees: 600
Primary Market Served: Consumer
Catalog available online
Indirect online sales
Founded: 1975
Gross sales or billing: $198,000,000

Distributor of sport, utility & light trucks, commercial vehicles & diesel engines.

ITOCHU CHEMICALS AMERICA INC

360 Hamilton Ave (Suite 610)
White Plains, NY 10601-1842
Telephone: (914) 333-7800, (800) 423-6870, FAX: (914) 333-7848, Web Site: www.itochu-sc.com
Controller: Alex Tabaco
Pres: Bob Yamashita
Mktg Mgr: Shin Ishii
Conducts Business: Worldwide
Employees: 30
Primary Market Served: Business & Consumer

Pharmaceutical company that sells information storage products, including magnetic media, video related products & thermal facsimile paper to OEMs, distributors & major accounts.

JLG INDUSTRIES INC

One JLG Dr
McConnellsburg, PA 17233
Telephone: (717) 485-5161, (877) JLG-SELL, FAX: (717) 485-6417, E-Mail: comments@jlg.com, Web Site: www.jlg.com
CEO: William J. Lasky
Sr VP, Sls & Mktg Devel: Craig Paylor
VP: Dale Robertson
VP, Cust Support Svcs: John Louderback
VP, Mktg: Dan Sandonato
Mktg Commun Specialist: Mark Eckert
Conducts Business: Worldwide
Employees: 3,770
Primary Market Served: Business & Consumer
Catalog available online
Indirect online sales
Advertising/Marketing Budget Related to Direct Marketing: 0-25%
Direct Marketing ad budget:
Magazines: 100%
Founded: 1969
Gross sales or billing: $1,056,168

World's leading producer of mobile aerial work platforms and a leading manufacturer of telescopic material handlers and hydraulic excavators marketed under the JLG and Gradall Trademarks.

JT INTERNATIONAL

500 Frank W Burr Blvd (Suite 24)
Teaneck, NJ 07666-6802
Telephone: (201) 871-1210, Web Site: www.jti.com
Dir Portfolio Brand & Trade Strategy: Dirk Skogerson
Primary Market Served: Consumer

JAFF MARKETING GROUP INC

20603 Rhodes Rd
Spring, TX 77388-3714
Telephone: (281) 353-0004, FAX: (281) 288-0970
Pres: Frank J. Vross
Conducts Business: U.S.
Primary Market Served: Consumer
Advertising/Marketing Budget Related to Direct Marketing: 76-100%
Direct Marketing ad budget:
Direct Mail: 100%
Founded: 1972

Varied consumer products for the ultimate consumer, by mail order.

JARDEN CORP

14611 W Commerce Rd
Daleville, IN 47334
Telephone: (765) 557-3000, (800) 428-8150, FAX: (765) 281-5403, Web Site: www.jarden.com
Chmn & CEO: Martin E. Franklin
Vice Chmn & CFO: Ian Ashken
Pres & COO: James E. Lillie
Exec VP, Fin & Treas: Desiree D. Stefano
Sr VP: John E. Capps
Primary Market Served: Business & Consumer

The Consumer Products division handles wholesale sales of Bell canning jars & lids & 100% natural food products.

JAZ HOLDINGS LLC

dba Regent Book Co
PO Box 37, Bldg 5
Liberty Corner, NJ 07938-0037
Telephone: (973) 574-7600, (800) 999-9554, FAX: (973) 944-5073, E-Mail: webmaster@regentbook.com, Web Site: www.regentbook.com
Pres: Janice Zucker
VP: Joshua Zucker
Mgr: Charlene Iacobacci
Conducts Business: U.S.
Primary Market Served: Business
Catalog available online
Indirect online sales
Gross sales or billing: $6,500,000

Sell all types of books to libraries & schools.

JENNY PRODUCTS INC

850 N Pleasant Ave
Somerset, PA 15501-1069
Telephone: (814) 445-3400, FAX: (814) 445-2280, Web Site: www.jennyproducts.com
Pres: Peter Leiss
CFO, VP, Sec & Treas: Daniel Leiss
Svc Mgr: Donald Ryan
Prodn Mgr: Dennis Young
Office Mgr: Heather Brougher
Conducts Business: U.S., Canada, Middle East, Europe
Employees: 11
Primary Market Served: Business & Consumer
Advertising/Marketing Budget Related to Direct Marketing: 0-25%

Manufacture & sell high pressure hot water, cold water & steam cleaners to reps, distributors & jobbers.

JERDEN RECORDS/ SPEECHWORKS

Subs. of SoundWorks USA Inc
17725 NE 65th St (Suite A-160)
Redmond, WA 98052
Telephone: (425) 882-3344, (888) 401-4487, FAX: (425) 882-3494, E-Mail: jerden@aol.com, Web Site: www.soundworks.net
Pres: G.B. Dennon
VP & COO: Robert L. Wikstrom
Conducts Business: U.S.
Employees: 7
Primary Market Served: Business & Consumer
Catalog available online
Direct online sales
Advertising/Marketing Budget Related to Direct Marketing: 51-75%
Founded: 1991

Audio publisher that packages, manufactures & markets music, spoken word & video products via radio, TV & the internet to consumers.

JOBSCOPE CORP

Subs. of Gower Corp
355 Woodruff Rd (Suite 406)

Greenville, SC 29607-3481
Telephone: (864) 458-3143, (800) 443-5794, FAX: (864) 234-4852, E-Mail: marketing@jobscope.com, Web Site: www.jobscope.com
Pres: Hunter Park
VP, Sls: Bob Parrott
Mktg Dir: Dan Bryant
Sls Mgr: Jeff Maddox
Conducts Business: U.S., Canada, Europe
Employees: 65
Primary Market Served: Business
Catalog available online
Advertising/Marketing Budget Related to Direct Marketing: 51-75%
Founded: 1980

Marketer of MFG software to Make-to-Order & Engineer-to-Order manufacturers. Also aviation component repair manufacturers.

JOFCO INC
402 E 13th St, PO Box 71
Jasper, IN 47547-0071
Telephone: (812) 482-5154, (800) 23-JOFCO, FAX: (812) 634-2392, E-Mail: furniture@jofco.com, Web Site: www.jofco.com
Pres & CEO: Bill Rubino
Pur Dir: Steve Fleck
Mktg Svcs: Gene Luebbehusen
Conducts Business: U.S., Canada, Pacific Rim Area
Employees: 300
Primary Market Served: Business
Catalog available online
Indirect online sales
Advertising/Marketing Budget Related to Direct Marketing: 0-25%
Founded: 1922

Manufacturers of wood office furniture & upholstered seating.

JOHN DEERE CONSUMER PRODUCTS
One John Deere Pl
Moline, IL 61625
Telephone: (309) 765-8000, FAX: (309) 748-0114, Web Site: www.johndeere.com
VP, Mktg & Prod Plng: Rand Ruland
Chmn & CEO: Robert W. Lane
Exec VP: H.J. Markley
Sr VP: James R. Jenkins
VP: John J. Dalhoff
VP & Treas: James A. Davlin
Conducts Business: Worldwide
Employees: 1,500
Primary Market Served: Business & Consumer
Catalog available online
Indirect online sales
Advertising/Marketing Budget Related to Direct Marketing: 0-25%

Founded: 1921
Manufacturer of portable outdoor power equipment.

JOHNSON & JOHNSON
One Johnson & Johnson Plaza
New Brunswick, NJ 08933
Telephone: (732) 524-0400, FAX: (732) 214-0332, Web Site: www.jnj.com
Chmn & CEO: William C. Weldon
Worldwide Chmn Comprehensive Care Grp: Donald M. Casey Jr
VP Fin & CFO: Dominic J. Caruso
VP, Gen Counsel & Chief Compliance Officer: Russell C. Deyo
VP HR: Kaye Foster-Cheek
Worldwide Chmn Consumer Grp: Colleen Goggins
Worldwide Chmn Pharmaceuticals Grp: Sheri S. McCoy
VP Strategy & Growth: Nicolas J. Valeriani
Worldwide Chmn Surgical Care Grp: Alex Gorsky
Conducts Business: Worldwide
Employees: 93,100
Primary Market Served: Business & Consumer
Founded: 1886
Gross sales or billing: $23,657,000,000

Manufacturer of healthcare products & provider of related services for the consumer, pharmaceutical & professional markets.

JONES INTERNATIONAL LTD
9697 E Mineral Ave
Centennial, CO 80112
Telephone: (303) 792-3111, (800) 525-7002, FAX: (303) 784-8508, E-Mail: publicrelations@jones.com, Web Site: www.jones.com
Pres & CEO: Glen Jones
Grp VP & CFO: Timothy J. Burke
VP Mktg: Kim Ketchel
Conducts Business: U.S., U.K.
Employees: 2,000
Primary Market Served: Business & Consumer

Sixty systems across country provide services to subscribers. Online University (take courses online).

JOSLIN PHOTO PUZZLE CO
PO Box 914
Southampton, PA 18966-0914
Telephone: (215) 357-8346, FAX: (215) 357-0307, E-Mail: 2832@comcast.net, Web Site: www.jigsawpuzzle.com
Owner: Marcia S. Joslin
Prodn Engr: Jeffrey L. Joslin
Conducts Business: Worldwide

Primary Market Served: Business & Consumer
Catalog available online
Indirect online sales
Founded: 1972

Manufacturer of jigsaw puzzles for sales promotions, advertising campaigns & premium promotions. Also, personalized photo jigsaw puzzles & precut blank jigsaw puzzles for heat transfers.

JOSTENS, INC
THE DMA
3601 Minnesota Dr (Suite 400)
Minneapolis, MN 55435-6008
Telephone: (952) 830-3300, FAX: (952) 830-3293, Web Site: www.jostens.com
Pres & CEO: Michael Bailey
CIO: Alden Sutherland
Sr VP & Gen Mgr Printing & Emerging Mkts: Timothy M. Larson
Mktg Mgr: Chris Johnson
Dir Commun: Richard Stoebe
Employees: 6,700
Primary Market Served: Business & Consumer
Founded: 1897
Gross sales or billing: $850,000,000

Class rings, graduation announcements, caps & gowns, yearbooks, diplomas, customized awards & plaques & photography packages.

JUNIOR'S CHEESECAKE
386 Flatbush Ave Ext at Dekalb Ave
Brooklyn, NY 11238
Telephone: (718) 852-5257, (800) 458-6467, FAX: (718) 260-9849, E-Mail: info@juniorscheesecake.com, Web Site: www.juniorscheesecake.com
Pres: Walter Rosen
VP: Marvin Rosen
Mktg Mgr: Alan Rosen
Primary Market Served: Consumer
Founded: 1950

Cheesecake restaurant, bakery, cafe & bar.

JUSTTHINKINCORPORATED
85 Cranford Way
Sherwood Park, AB, Canada T8H0H9
Telephone: (780) 416-0244
Pres: Jesse Willms
Primary Market Served: Business & Consumer

K-TEL INTERNATIONAL
7500 Wayzata Blvd (Suite 28)
Golden Valley, MN 55426-1682
Telephone: (204) 889-5430, (800) 665-5021, FAX: (612) 559-6803, Web Site: www.ktel.com
Pres: Bill McMahon

VP & Gen Mgr: Mary Kuehn
Founder: Philip Kives
Primary Market Served: Consumer
Founded: 1968

Distributor of music.

KEH.COM
4900 Highlands Pkwy SE
Smyrna, GA 30082-5132
Telephone: (770) 333-4200, (800) 342-5534, FAX: (770) 333-4242, E-Mail:
sales@keh.com, Web Site: www.keh.com
Pres: W. King Grant Jr.
Gen Mgr: Pat Mulherin
Sls Mgr: Ed Warrick
Conducts Business: Worldwide
Employees: 30
Primary Market Served: Business & Consumer
Catalog available online
Direct online sales
Advertising/Marketing Budget Related to Direct Marketing: 76-100%
Founded: 1979

Buy, sell & trade new & used photographic equipment to professionals, amateurs & collectors. Catalog available.

KHL ENGINEERED PACKAGING SOLUTIONS
Div. of AMCOR Sunrise
6600 Valley View St
Buena Park, CA 90620
Telephone: (714) 690-6361
Mktg Coord: Selena Jimenez
Primary Market Served: Business & Consumer

KTM SPORTMOTORCYCLE USA INC
1119 Milan Ave
Amherst, OH 44001-1319
Telephone: (440) 985-3553, FAX: (440) 985-3060, Web Site: www.ktmusa.com
Controller: John Eric Burleson
CFO: Patrick Prugger
Dir: Stefan Pierer
Pur: Harald Plockinger
Conducts Business: U.S.
Primary Market Served: Business

Importer of Austrian-built racing motorcycles.

KADANT JOHNSON INC
805 Wood St
Three Rivers, MI 49093
Telephone: (269) 278-1715, FAX: (269) 279-5980, Web Site: www.kadantjohnson.com
Pres: Rudi Leerentueld
Pres, Kadant Canada: Mike Soucy

PR Mgr: Steve Manos
Mgr: Ivan Kroupa
Primary Market Served: Business
Catalog available online

Manufacture steam specialty items for the pulp & paper industry.

KANO LABORATORIES
1000 E Thompson Ln
Nashville, TN 37211
Telephone: (615) 833-4101, (800) 311-3374, FAX: (615) 833-5790, Web Site: www.kanolabs.com
Chmn: P.R. Zimmerman
Pres: Peter Zimmerman
Conducts Business: U.S., Canada, Europe, Japan, Middle East
Employees: 15
Primary Market Served: Business & Consumer
Catalog available online
Direct online sales
Founded: 1939

Marketer of industrial strength specialty chemicals, penetrating oil & lubricants.

KANSAS CITY CHIEFS
One Arrowhead Dr
Kansas City, MO 64129
Telephone: (816) 920-9300, (888) 99-CHIEFS, FAX: (816) 923-4719, Web Site: www.kcchiefs.com
Chmn: Clark Hunt
Pres & CEO: Carl Peterson
Exec VP & COO: Dennis Thum
CFO: Dale Young
Sr VP, Admin: Dennis Watley
Conducts Business: U.S.
Employees: 100
Primary Market Served: Business & Consumer
Direct Marketing ad budget: $150,000
Direct Mail: 25%
Newspapers: 25%
TV/Radio: 50%

Season & group Pro Football tickets.

KAPLAN INC
395 Hudson St (Rm 400)
New York, NY 10014-7455
Telephone: (212) 492-5800, (800) 527-8378, FAX: (212) 492-5933, Web Site: www.kaplan.com
Pres & COO: Andrew S. Rosen
Employees: 23,000
Primary Market Served: Business & Consumer
Founded: 1938
Gross sales or billing: $1,700,000,000

Company that prepares students for college & graduate school entrance exams.

KAYLOR'S SCHOOL SUPPLY
4152 Hwy 75 N
Albertville, AL 35951
Telephone: (256) 878-1200, (800) 239-9999, FAX: (800) 239-9998, E-Mail:
sales@kaylorsinc.com, Web Site: www.kaylorsinc.com
Pres: Jesse Kaylor
VP: Dan Kaylor
Primary Market Served: Business & Consumer

School supplies.

KEENELAND ASSOCIATION INC
4201 Versailles Rd, PO Box 1690
Lexington, KY 40588-1690
Telephone: (859) 254-3412, (800) 456-3412, FAX: (859) 255-2484, Web Site: www.keeneland.com
Pres & CEO: Nick Nicholson
VP: Harvie Wilkinson
Commun Dir: R. James Williams
Sls Dir: W.B. Rogers Beasley
Treas: Jessica A. Green
Conducts Business: U.S., E. Asia, S. America, Australia, Canada, Europe, Middle East
Employees: 125
Primary Market Served: Consumer
Catalog available online
Indirect online sales
Founded: 1936
Gross sales or billing: $700,000,000

Thoroughbred race track & auction company.

KELCO SUPPLY CO
7700 Setzler Pkwy N.
Brooklyn Park, MN 55445
Telephone: (763) 493-1260, (800) 328-7720, FAX: (763) 493-1261, E-Mail:
info@kelcosupply.com, Web Site: www.kelcosupply.com
Mktg Mgr: Lori Adamson
Owner, Pres, CEO & CFO: Alicia Carr
Conducts Business: U.S.
Employees: 25
Primary Market Served: Business & Consumer
Advertising/Marketing Budget Related to Direct Marketing: 76-100%
Direct Marketing ad budget:
Direct Mail: 100%
Gross sales or billing: $4,000,000

Sell funeral, church, school, nursing home, hospital & emergency supplies.

JJ KELLER & ASSOCIATES INC
3003 W Breezewood Ln
Neenah, WI 54957-0368

Telephone: (920) 722-2848, (800) 327-6868, FAX: (800) 727-7516, E-Mail: thines@jjkeller.com, Web Site: www.jjkeller.com/jjk
Chmn: Robert Keller
Pres: James Keller
VP, Publications & Prods: Terrence Quirk
Corp Creative Mgr: Thomas A. Hines
Conducts Business: U.S., Canada
Employees: 1,200
Primary Market Served: Business
Catalog available online
Direct online sales
Founded: 1953

Publishes training materials, videos, software, training seminars & workshops & services dealing with government regulations & management systems for the transportation, chemical process & healthcare industries, including permits & licenses.

KENDALL PRODUCTS/DRI-DEK

PO Box 8656
Naples, FL 34101-8656
Telephone: (239) 643-2244, (800) 348-2398, FAX: (800) 828-4248, E-Mail: info@dri-dek.com, Web Site: www.dri-dek.com
Pres & CEO: Lee Dees
Dir Mktg & Sls: Linda Bell
Mgr: Scott Lilly
Conducts Business: Worldwide
Primary Market Served: Business & Consumer
Catalog available online
Direct online sales

Distributor of industrial services & safety products.

KENNAMETAL INC

1600 Technology Way
Latrobe, PA 15650-0231
Telephone: (800) 222-9327, FAX: (800) 521-3319, E-Mail: mcs-na.service@kennmetal.com, Web Site: www.kennametal.com
Pres & CEO: Carlos M. Cardoso
VP: James R. Breisinger
VP: Raj Datt
VP: David W. Greenfield
VP: Dr William Y. Hsu
Employees: 14,000
Primary Market Served: Business
Catalog available online
Direct online sales
Founded: 1938

Manufacture tools & systems for metal cutting, mining & construction.

KENSINGTON TECHNOLOGY GROUP

Subs. of Acco World
333 Twin Dolphin Dr (6th fl)

Redwood Shores, CA 94065
Telephone: (650) 572-2700, FAX: (650) 267-2800, Web Site: www.kensington.com
Chm & CEO: David D. Campbell
Pres: Boris Elisman
Dir, Prod Mngmt: David Dobson
Sls & Mktg: Tom Russo
Conducts Business: U.S.
Employees: 45
Primary Market Served: Business & Consumer
Catalog available online
Direct online sales

Manufacturer of power protection, input & security devices & accessories for Apple II, Macintosh, IBM & IBM compatible computers. Provider of computer peripheral & software product accessories.

KERR-HAYS CO

PO Box 711
Ligonier, PA 15658-0711
Telephone: (724) 238-6694, FAX: (724) 238-7440
Pres: Laura Widing
Conducts Business: U.S.
Primary Market Served: Business & Consumer

Manufacturer of custom gifts & premiums.

KEY WEST ALOE HOLDINGS LLC

Div. of Key West Fragrance & Cosmetic Factory Inc
PO Box 19547
Fort Lauderdale, FL 33318-0547
Telephone: (305) 883-3166, FAX: (305) 883-3185, Web Site: www.keywestaloe.com
CEO & Pres: Nalin Patel
Conducts Business: U.S., Canada, Central America, Caribbean, Hawaii, Switzerland, Italy, Korea, Iceland, Saudi Arabia, Singapore
Employees: 50
Primary Market Served: Business & Consumer
Catalog available online
Advertising/Marketing Budget Related to Direct Marketing: 26-50%
Founded: 1971

Manufacture & sell aloe based cosmetics: skin care, bath, hair care, suntan products & fragrances for both male & female via mail order, wholesale, private label & retail.

KEYSPAN ENERGY CORP

1 Metrotech Ctr Fl 1
Brooklyn, NY 11201-3949

Telephone: (718) 403-2000, (888) 222-7359, Web Site: www.keyspanenergy.com
Chmn & CEO: Robert B. Catell
Pres & COO: Craig G. Matthews
Sr VP, Mktg: Colon Watson
CFO: Gerald Luterman
Primary Market Served: Business & Consumer

Gas & electric utility.

THE DMA KIMBERLY-CLARK CORP

2100 Winchester Rd
Neenah, WI 54956
Telephone: (920) 721-2000, (888) 525-8388, FAX: (920) 721-7722, Web Site: www.kimberly-clark.com
Chmn Bd & CEO: Thomas J. Falk
Group Pres N Atlantic Consumer Prods: Robert E. Abernathy
Pres Health Care Bus: Joanne B. Bauer
Group Pres Developing & Emerging Markets: Robert W. Black
Sr VP & Chief Strategic Officer: Christian A. Brickman
Sr VP & CFO: Mark A. Buthman
Sr VP HR: Lizanne C. Gottung
Sr VP Law, Govt Affairs & Chief Compliance Officer: Thomas J. Mielke
Sr VP & Chief Mktg Officer: Anthony J. Palmer
Pres Kimberly-Clark Prof: Jan B. Spencer
Conducts Business: Worldwide
Employees: 64,000
Primary Market Served: Consumer
Gross sales or billing: $16,700,000,000

Feminine care, infant care, adult care & household products.

KNOLL GROUP

Subs. of Westinghouse Electric Corp
76 Ninth Ave (11th fl)
New York, NY 10011
Telephone: (212) 343-4000, FAX: (212) 343-4180
VP, Mktg: Andrew Coco
Conducts Business: U.S., Canada
Employees: 100
Primary Market Served: Business & Consumer
Advertising/Marketing Budget Related to Direct Marketing: 0-25%
Gross sales or billing: $400,000,000

Manufacture & market office furniture, seating, desk accessories, textiles, executive & residential furniture & case goods.

KOEZE CO

P.O. Box 9470
Grand Rapids, MI 49509

Telephone: (800) 555-9688, E-Mail:
service@koezedirect.com, Web Site:
www.koeze.com
Pres: Jeff Koeze
Mktg Mgr: Tom Lakos
Conducts Business: U.S.
Primary Market Served: Consumer

Manufacture & sell consumer nut
products.

KOZAK AUTO DRYWASH INC

Eight S Lyon St
Batavia, NY 14020-1802
Telephone: (716) 343-8111, (800) 237-
9927, FAX: (585) 343-3732, E-Mail:
info@kozak.com, Web Site: www.
dryautowash.com
Pres, CFO & Mktg Dir: Edward R.
Harding
VP: Carol Harding
Conducts Business: Worldwide
Employees: 7
Primary Market Served: Business &
Consumer
Catalog available online
Indirect online sales
Advertising/Marketing Budget Related
to Direct Marketing: 76-100%
Direct Marketing ad budget: $75,000
Direct Mail: 80%
Magazines: 10%
Newspapers: 10%
Founded: 1926
Gross sales or billing: $700,000

Manufacturer of a Drywash(REG)
cloth that cleans & polishes cars without water. Sell to dealers, funeral directors & individual consumers. Consumer list totals about 265M names.
Also sells complete line of car care
accessories. Mailmaster (printing &
mailing) division located at same address is capable of complete lettershop
operations including printing, folding,
Cheshire(REG) labeling & mail
stuffing.

THE DMA KRAFT FOODS/GEVALIA KAFFE

Div. of Philip Morris
555 S Broadway
Tarrytown, NY 10591-6301
Telephone: (914) 335-4239, Web Site:
www.gevalia.com
CEO & VP, Philip Morris: Geoffrey
Bible
CEO & VP, Kraft Foods: Betsy
Holden
COO: William Webb
VP, Mktg & Commerce: Paula Sneed
VP, Mktg: Lance Friedman
Assoc Dir, CRM: Mark Kaczkowski
Conducts Business: U.S.

Primary Market Served: Business &
Consumer
Catalog available online
Food manufacturer. Headquarters Tele-
phone (847) 646-2000.

THE DMA KREG TOOL CO

201 Campus Dr
Huxley, IA 50124-9760
Telephone: (515) 597-6400, Web Site:
www.kregtool.com
VP Sls & Mktg: Brad Lilienthal

KROSS INC

dba Kross Kits
25682 Springbrook Ave Ste 140
Santa Clarita, CA 91350-2433
Telephone: (661) 284-3557, (800) 456-
3699, FAX: (661) 257-1914, Web
Site: www.krosskits.com
Pres: Robert M. James
Conducts Business: U.S., Canada
Employees: 12
Primary Market Served: Business &
Consumer

Supply auto emergency, first aid &
earthquake kits & other items for
credit card merchandising, premium &
advertising specialty programs.

L&L MANAGEMENT

751 N Fair Oaks Ave
Pasadena, CA 91103-3069
Telephone: (626) 568-0338, FAX:
(626) 568-9165
Owner: Joe Brown
Conducts Business: U.S., Canada
Employees: 1
Primary Market Served: Business &
Consumer
Advertising/Marketing Budget Related
to Direct Marketing: 0-25%
Direct Marketing ad budget:
Direct Mail: 65%
Magazines: 25%
Telephone: 10%
Founded: 1984

Audio/video cassette duplication company providing high volume cassette
copies for direct marketing or promotional purposes. Also provides on-site
recording of conferences.

LGP GEM LTD

10 W 46th St (Suite 4A)
New York, NY 10036-4515
Telephone: (212) 840-2510, FAX:
(212) 302-6182, E-Mail: sales@
lgpltd.com, Web Site: www.lgpltd.
com
Pres & CEO: Isaac Pollak
Exec VP: Arlene Rubin
Conducts Business: Worldwide
Employees: 16

Primary Market Served: Business
Founded: 1980

Fashion jewelry and watches design
and manufacture for direct mail
industry.

LS RECORDS

1225 Apache Ln
Madison, TN 37115
Telephone: (615) 868-7171, FAX:
(615) 860-7665, E-Mail: ls654@
home.com, Web Site: www.
cristylane.com
Pres: Lee Stoller
CFO, VP & Mktg Mgr: Kevin Stoller
Conducts Business: Worldwide
Employees: 7
Primary Market Served: Business &
Consumer
Direct Marketing ad budget:
$1,000,000
Magazines: 34%
Newspapers: 33%
TV/Radio: 33%
Gross sales or billing: $1,500,000

Television marketing & music
publishing.

LACROSSE FOOTWEAR INC

17634 NE Airport Way
Portland, OR 97230-4999
Telephone: (503) 262-0110, (800) 323-
2668, FAX: (503) 262-0115, E-Mail:
customerservice@lacrossefootwear.
com, Web Site: www.
lacrossefootwear.com
Chmn: Richard A. Rosenthal
Pres & CEO: Joseph P. Schneider
Exec VP, CFO & Secy: David P. Carl-
son
Conducts Business: U.S.
Employees: 303
Primary Market Served: Business &
Consumer
Catalog available online
Advertising/Marketing Budget Related
to Direct Marketing: 0-25%
Founded: 1897
Gross sales or billing: $107,798,000

Rainwear, specialty clothing & footwear to direct marketers.

LAITRAM MACHINERY

Subs. of The Laitram Corp
220 Laitram Ln
Harahan, LA 70123
Telephone: (504) 733-6000, FAX:
(504) 733-6111
Pres & Gen Mgr: Flemming Frederick-
son
CFO: Laurie Oerthing
Mktg Mgr: Cindy Foremaster
Conducts Business: U.S., U.K., Europe
Primary Market Served: Business

Manufacturer of food processing equipment.

LAKE SHORE INDUSTRIES
1817 Poplar St
Erie, PA 16508-0427
Telephone: (800) 458-0463, FAX:
(814) 453-4293, E-Mail: info@
lsisigns.com, Web Site: www.
lsisigns.com
Pres & CEO: Leo Bruno
Adv & Mktg: Shirley Bruno
Acct: Marie Bartlett
Conducts Business: U.S., Canada
Employees: 16
Primary Market Served: Business &
Consumer
Catalog available online
Founded: 1908
Gross sales or billing: $1,700,000

Cast aluminum signs & markers, fabricated signs, acrylic signs, vinyl graphics, ADA signs, commercial castings.

LAMINEX INC
Div. of D&K Group Inc
4211 Pleasant Rd
Fort Mill, SC 29708-9328
Telephone: (704) 679-4170, (800) 438-
8850, FAX: (704) 679-8453, Web
Site: www.laminex.com
Pres: Tim Long
Conducts Business: Worldwide
Employees: 135
Primary Market Served: Business
Founded: 1945

Manufacture hardware & software for photo I.D. & security cards. Sell by direct mail to schools, colleges, government & industry.

LAND O' LAKES INC
4001 Lexington Ave
Arden Hills, MN 55122
Telephone: (651) 481-2222, (800) 328-
9680, FAX: (651) 481-2000, Web
Site: www.landolakes.com
Chmn: Peter Kappelman
Pres & CEO: Chris Policinski
Exec VP & COO: Alan Pierson
Sr VP & CFO: Daniel E. Knutson
Conducts Business: U.S.
Employees: 8,500
Primary Market Served: Consumer
Gross sales or billing: $7,200,000,000

Food processing & marketing; farm supplies.

LANDMARK GRAPHICS CORP
Subs. of Halliburton
2101 Citywest Blvd (#200)
Houston, TX 77042-2829
Telephone: (713) 839-2000, FAX:
(713) 839-2015, E-Mail: solutions@
lgc.com, Web Site: www.lgc.com
Pres & CEO: John Gibson
CFO: Millicent Chancellor
VP Innovation & Mktg: Jonathan
Lewis
Mktg Dir: John Wilson
Employees: 1,900
Primary Market Served: Business &
Consumer
Catalog available online

Manufacture seismic interpretation software.

LANDSCAPE FORMS INC
431 Lawndale Ave
Kalamazoo, MI 49048
Telephone: (616) 381-0490, (800) 430-
6209, FAX: (616) 381-3455, E-Mail:
specify@landscapeforms.com, Web
Site: www.landscapeforms.com
Pres: Bill Main
CFO: Conrad Sutter
Mktg Svc Mgr: Janis L. Etzcorn
Conducts Business: U.S.
Primary Market Served: Business
Catalog available online

Manufacture exterior furniture for commercial spaces.

LARAN COMMUNICATIONS INC
26W482 Blair St
Winfield, IL 60190-1109
Telephone: (630) 690-2141, FAX:
(630) 690-2143, Web Site: www.
web-ads.com
Owner: Lawrence E. Spiegel
Conducts Business: U.S.
Primary Market Served: Business &
Consumer
Catalog available online
Founded: 1991

Provider of on-line advertising for direct marketers.

LATHEM TIME CORP
200 Selig Dr SW
Atlanta, GA 30336
Telephone: (404) 691-0400, (800) 241-
4990, FAX: (404) 696-6048, Web
Site: www.lathem.com
Pres: William Lathem
CFO: Ann Hooper
Mktg Mgr: Lance Whipple
Conducts Business: Worldwide
Employees: 185
Primary Market Served: Business
Advertising/Marketing Budget Related
to Direct Marketing: 51-75%
Direct Marketing ad budget:
Direct Mail: 30%
Magazines: 70%

Founded: 1919
Manufacturer of time clocks & automated time & attendance systems.

LAUGHLIN ASSOCIATES INC
2533 N Carson St
Carson City, NV 89706
Telephone: (775) 883-8484, (888) 273-
8152, FAX: (775) 883-4874
Pres & CEO: Lewis E. Laughlin
COO & Exec VP: Robert Seligman
VP Mktg & Sls: Meghan Cole
Conducts Business: U.S.
Employees: 32
Primary Market Served: Business &
Consumer
Catalog available online
Direct online sales
Advertising/Marketing Budget Related
to Direct Marketing: 0-25%
Founded: 1972
Gross sales or billing: $4,000,000

Resident agents.

LAWN DOCTOR INC
142 State Route 34 (Suite 1)
Holmdel, NJ 07733-2092
Telephone: (732) 946-0029, (800) 631-
5660, FAX: (732) 946-9089, Web
Site: www.lawndoctor.com
Pres & CEO: Russell Frith
Sr VP: Bobby Magda
VP Mktg & Franchise Devel: Scott
Frith
Conducts Business: U.S.
Employees: 72
Primary Market Served: Consumer
Advertising/Marketing Budget Related
to Direct Marketing: 51-75%
Founded: 1967
Gross sales or billing: $75,000,000

Franchised lawn care service. Has 500 franchises in 40 states.

LEA & PERRINS INC
15-01 Pollitt Dr
Fair Lawn, NJ 07410
Telephone: (201) 791-1600, FAX:
(201) 791-8945, Web Site: www.
leaperrins.com
CEO: Ralph Abrams
CFO: Brian Duffy
Mktg Dir: Michael Schwartzman
Employees: 100
Primary Market Served: Consumer

Manufacturer of condiments (steak & barbeque sauces).

LEADERSHIP SOFTWARE CORP
PO Box 725
Nyack, NY 10960

Telephone: (845) 358-0406, (800) 872-0068, FAX: (845) 358-0359, E-Mail: info@leadersoft.com, Web Site: www.leadersoft.com
Pres: Roger W. Seiler
VP: Sally Marmion
Conducts Business: Worldwide
Employees: 2
Primary Market Served: Business & Consumer
Catalog available online
Direct online sales
Advertising/Marketing Budget Related to Direct Marketing: 76-100%
Founded: 1992

Software publisher of memory training products & Human Resources software for performance assessment & planning & CBT.

LEARNCOM HR CONSULTING & TRAINING
Div. of Learning Communications Inc
5520 Trabuco Rd
Irvine, CA 92620-5705
Telephone: (515) 440-0890, (800) 698-8263, FAX: (515) 221-3149, E-Mail: nhartline@learncom.com, Web Site: www.learncomhr.com
VP, Sls: Jacqueline Hendrick
Conducts Business: Worldwide
Employees: 45
Primary Market Served: Business
Catalog available online
Direct online sales
Advertising/Marketing Budget Related to Direct Marketing: 51-75%
Direct Marketing ad budget:
Direct Mail: 50%
Magazines: 10%
Telephone: 40%
Founded: 1950

Produce & distribute video based training products in the areas of environmental & safety compliance, EEO & affirmative action compliance, labor relations issues & general management.

LEARNING CARE GROUP
21333 Haggerty Rd (Suite 300)
Novi, MI 48375-5537
Telephone: (248) 697-9115, Web Site: www.learningcaregroup.com
Chief Mktg Officer: Stacy DeWalt

LEARNING COMMUNICATIONS LLC
5520 Trabuco Rd
Irvine, CA 92620-5705
Telephone: (800) 622-3610, FAX: (949) 727-4323, E-Mail: sales@learncom.com, Web Site: www.learncom.com
Pres: Lloyd Singer

Conducts Business: Worldwide
Employees: 14
Primary Market Served: Business
Advertising/Marketing Budget Related to Direct Marketing: 0-25%
Founded: 1985

Training videos, human resources management, safety & sexual harassment.

LEVI STRAUSS & CO
1155 Battery St
San Francisco, CA 94111
Telephone: (415) 501-6000, FAX: (415) 501-7112, Web Site: www.levistrauss.com
Chmn: Robert D. Haas
Pres, CEO & Dir: R. John Anderson
Pres & COO: Phil Marinea
Pres, Levi Strauss Americas: Robert Hanson
Sr VP & CFO: Hans Ploos van Amstel
Sr VP & Gen Counsel: Hillary K. Krane
Employees: 10,600
Primary Market Served: Business & Consumer
Catalog available online
Direct online sales
Gross sales or billing: $4,100,000,000

Manufacturer of men's & women's apparel.

LEXISNEXIS
A member of the Reed Elsevier Plc Group
9443 Springboro Pike
Miamisburg, OH 45342
Telephone: (937) 865-6800, (800) 227-9597, (800) 227-4908, FAX: (800) 348-2609, E-Mail: pr@lexisnexis.com, Web Site: www.lexisnexis.com
CEO LexisNexis Grp: Andrew Prozes
Pres & CEO Corp & Federal Markets: Bill Pardue
Pres & CEO North American Legal Markets: Lou Andreozzi
Conducts Business: Worldwide
Employees: 12,000
Primary Market Served: Business
Founded: 1966

LexisNexis is a provider of data & information for the legal, corporate, government & academic markets via the web & other media.

LIBERTY ORCHARDS CO INC
117 Mission Ave, PO Box C
Cashmere, WA 98815
Telephone: (509) 782-2191, (800) 888-5696, FAX: (509) 782-1487, E-Mail: service@libertyorchards.com, Web Site: www.libertyorchards.com
Pres & CEO: Greg Taylor
CFO: Brad Thomas
VP, Sls & Mktg: J. Mike Rainey

Wholesale Admin Asst: Kathy Paine
Materials & Pur Mgr: Jim Johnson
Conducts Business: U.S.
Employees: 80
Primary Market Served: Business & Consumer
Catalog available online
Direct online sales
Founded: 1920
Gross sales or billing: $14,400,000

Manufacturer of candy.

LIEBERT CORP
Subs. of Emerison Electric Co
1050 Dearborn Dr, PO Box 29186
Columbus, OH 43085
Telephone: (614) 841-6700, (800) LIEBERT, FAX: (614) 841-6022, Web Site: www.liebert.com
Pres: Robert Bauer
Pres, Liebert North America: Scott Dysert
VP & Gen Mgr: Steve Madara
VP & Gen Mgr: Randy MacCleary
VP, Mktg: Kevin Stoll
Conducts Business: Worldwide
Employees: 5,100
Primary Market Served: Business
Catalog available online
Advertising/Marketing Budget Related to Direct Marketing: 26-50%
Gross sales or billing: $358,000,000

Manufacturer of computer support equipment.

LIFEBOAT DISTRIBUTION
Div. of Programmers Paradise Inc
1157 Shrewsbury Ave
Shrewsbury, NJ 07702
Telephone: (732) 389-8950, FAX: (732) 389-9227, Web Site: www.programmersparadise.com
Pres: Bill Willet
VP, Mktg: Jeff Largiader
Primary Market Served: Business

Distribute computer software to dealers.

LIFELOCK
60 E Rio Salado Pkwy Ste 400
Tempe, AZ 85281-9129
Telephone: (480) 457-2007, Web Site: www.lifelock.com
VP Mktg: Andrew Wyant
Primary Market Served: Business & Consumer

LIFETIPS
240 Commercial St (Suite 3B)
Boston, MA 02109-1386
Telephone: (617) 886-9001, Web Site: www.lifetips.com
Pres: Byron White
Primary Market Served: Consumer

LIGHT SOURCES INC
6220 Indian River Rd (Suite I)
Virginia Beach, VA 23464-3514
Telephone: (757) 424-8636, (800) 882-
8834, FAX: (757) 424-6186, E-Mail:
lightsources@earthlink.net, Web Site:
www.lightsourcesinc.com
Pres: Marty Pfiefer
Conducts Business: U.S., Canada
Employees: 3
Primary Market Served: Business &
Consumer
Catalog available online
Advertising/Marketing Budget Related
to Direct Marketing: 0-25%
Direct Marketing ad budget:
Direct Mail: 80%
Magazines: 20%
Founded: 1977
Gross sales or billing: $350,000

Direct sales of special lamps for studio, audiovisual, photographic, micro-
graphic, reprographic, communication
& medical equipment. Sell to schools,
churches, hospitals, libraries, museums,
theatres, television, publishers, banks,
photographers & industries using visual aids & reproduction equipment.

LIMITEDBRANDS INC
Div. of Limited Inc
5 Limited Pkwy
Reynoldsburg, OH 43068-5300
Telephone: (614) 577-5902, FAX:
(614) 415-7440, Web Site: www.
limitedbrands.com
Chmn & CEO: Leslie H. Wexner
CFO: Stuart Burgdoerfer
Exec VP, Retail Real Estate: Jamie
Bersani
VP, Mktg Opers: Gay Clay
Exec VP, Retail Opers: Mark A. Giresi
Exec VP, Corp Devel: V. Ann Hailey
Primary Market Served: Consumer

Men's retail clothing chain.

LIONS GATE TELEVISION
CORP
2700 Colorado Ave Ste 200
Santa Monica, CA 90404-5502
Telephone: (310) 449-9200, FAX:
(310) 255-3870, Web Site: www.
lionsgate.com
Pres: Kevin Beggs
COO: Sandre Stern
Sr VP, Programming & Sls: Craig
Cegielski
Sr VP, TV: Barbara Wall
Dir, Global Mktg: Douglas Friedman
Conducts Business: Worldwide
Employees: 40
Primary Market Served: Business
Catalog available online

Purchase movie rights for domestic &
international theatrical home video &
TV rights. Also produce theatrical feature films.

A LISS & CO INC
51-55 59th Pl
Woodside, NY 11377-7408
Telephone: (718) 728-0600, (800) 221-
0938, FAX: (718) 728-1227, E-Mail:
alissco@aol.com
CEO: Jerold Liss
Pres: Jeffrey Liss
Conducts Business: Worldwide
Employees: 27
Primary Market Served: Business
Founded: 1936
Gross sales or billing: $5,300,000

Distribute & sell materials handling,
industrial & safety equipment & office
furniture. Expertise in storage &
manual methods of in-plant movement.

LLADRO USA
One Lladro Dr
Moonachie, NJ 07074-1019
Telephone: (201) 807-1177, (800) 634-
9088, FAX: (201) 807-1168, E-Mail:
customer-services@us.lladro.com,
Web Site: www.lladro.com
Pres: Jose Lladro Dolz
VP Bus Devel: Glenn Conciatori
Employees: 100
Primary Market Served: Business &
Consumer
Founded: 1953
Gross sales or billing: $16,600,000

Distribute porcelain figurines.

LO-AD COMMUNICATIONS
150 E Colorado Blvd (Suite 210)
Pasadena, CA 91105
Telephone: (626) 304-7750, FAX:
(626) 304-2716, Web Site: www.lo-
ad.com
CFO: Dennis Hammilton
Mng Dir: Kris Flynn
Acct Exec: Christine David
Primary Market Served: Business

International service bureau. Communication company.

LO INK SPECIALTIES
PO Box 530B
Kennebunkport, ME 04046-1821
Telephone: (207) 967-9110, (800) 777-
6471, FAX: (800) 895-6465, E-Mail:
rwatson@loink.com, Web Site:
www.loink.com
Pres: Robert C. Watson III
Conducts Business: U.S., Canada
Employees: 1
Primary Market Served: Business
Catalog available online

Direct online sales
Advertising/Marketing Budget Related
to Direct Marketing: 76-100%
Direct Marketing ad budget:
Direct Mail: 90%
Magazines: 10%
Founded: 1985
Gross sales or billing: $500,000

Sell to architects, surveyors, engineers
& contractors.

LOCKHEED MARTIN CORP
6801 Rockledge Dr
Bethesda, MD 20817
Telephone: (301) 897-6000
Sr VP: Robert Trice
Primary Market Served: Business

Design & produce strategic missiles,
spacecraft, aircraft, electronic systems;
communications & intelligence systems; ocean & information systems;
technical information & management
services.

LOCTITE CORP
Div. of Henkel Corp-Industrial
1001 Trout Brook Crossing
Rocky Hill, CT 06067
Telephone: (860) 571-5100, (800)
LOCTITE, (800) 562-8483, FAX:
(860) 571-5465, Web Site: www.
loctite.com
Corp Commun Adv: Mike Bruno
Conducts Business: U.S., Canada,
Mexico
Employees: 400
Primary Market Served: Business &
Consumer
Catalog available online
Direct online sales
Founded: 1997

Manufacturer of adhesives, sealants,
lubricants & coatings.

LOGICAL COMPUTER
SELECTIONS
18 Winding Way
Short Hills, NJ 07078-2530
Telephone: (212) 949-2290, (800) 949-
2701, FAX: (212) 697-5786, E-Mail:
info@logicomputer.com, Web Site:
www.logicomputer.com
Pres: Satish Bhalerao
Conducts Business: U.S., Asia
Employees: 19
Primary Market Served: Business &
Consumer
Catalog available online
Direct online sales
Advertising/Marketing Budget Related
to Direct Marketing: 0-25%
Direct Marketing ad budget:
Direct Mail: 100%
Founded: 1989

Gross sales or billing: $5,000,000

Sell & service micro computers & install local area networks. Distributors of micro computer tapes & backup systems. Also, provide services for systems integration & software development.

LORILLARD TOBACCO CO
PO Box 10529
Greensboro, NC 27408-7018
Telephone: (336) 335-7000, (888) 818-3304, FAX: (336) 373-6917, E-Mail: externalaffairs@lorrilard.com, Web Site: www.lorillard.net
Chmn & CEO: A.W. Spears
Primary Market Served: Business & Consumer
Founded: 1760
Gross sales or billing: $3,500,000,000

Manufacture & sell cigarettes.

LOS ANGELES KINGS
1111 S Figeroa (Suite 3100)
Los Angeles, CA 90015
Telephone: (213) 742-7100, (888) KINGS-LA, FAX: (213) 742-7296, Web Site: kings.nhl.com
Owner: Philip F. Anschutz
CEO: Timothy J. Leiwekei
Pres & Gen Mgr: Dean Lombari
Head Coach: Marc Crawford
VP, Sls & Mktg: Chris McGowan
Conducts Business: U.S., Canada
Primary Market Served: Business & Consumer
Catalog available online
Direct online sales
Advertising/Marketing Budget Related to Direct Marketing: 26-50%
Founded: 1967

Hockey team.

LOVING PROMISES & MORE
1429 Commerce Ave
Longview, WA 98632
Telephone: (360) 425-8466, (800) 999-6909
Pres: Linda Vickers
Conducts Business: U.S.
Employees: 6
Primary Market Served: Consumer

Sell lingerie & lovers products through home parties & retail.

LUCE CORP
Div. of American Metaseal of CT
336 Putnam Ave, Box 4124
Hamden, CT 06517
Telephone: (203) 787-0281, FAX: (203) 230-2753
Pres & Mktg Mgr: Timothy F. Pagnam
VP: Mary Pagnam
Sec & VP: Julia Pagnam

Conducts Business: U.S.
Employees: 8
Primary Market Served: Business & Consumer
Gross sales or billing: $500,000

Blue magic krispy kans, mail order companies, wholesale distributors & retail stores.

LUGGAGE BASE
670 S Frontage Rd
Nipomo, CA 93444-9148
Telephone: (805) 929-8191, (888) 832-1201, FAX: (805) 929-8192, E-Mail: service@luggagebase.com, Web Site: www.luggagebase.com
Owner: Joe Williams
Owner: Susan Williams
Employees: 4
Primary Market Served: Business & Consumer
Catalog available online
Direct online sales
Advertising/Marketing Budget Related to Direct Marketing: 0-25%
Founded: 1971

Name brand luggage, travel gear, bookbags, backpacks & briefcases at discount prices.

LUNDBERG FAMILY FARMS
Div. of Wehah-Lundberg, Inc.
PO Box 369, 5370 Church St
Richvale, CA 95974-0369
Telephone: (530) 882-4551, FAX: (530) 882-4500, E-Mail: info@lundberg.com, Web Site: www.lundberg.com
Chmn: Wendell Lundberg
VP, Sls & Mktg: Tim O'Donnell
Conducts Business: Worldwide
Employees: 140
Primary Market Served: Business & Consumer
Direct Marketing ad budget:
Direct Mail: $10,000
Magazines: $70,000
Telephone: $24,000
Founded: 1937
Gross sales or billing: $8,900,000

Grow & market whole grain, brown rice & rice products.

LUSTER CARE PRODUCTS
8854 Frost Ave
Saint Louis, MO 63134-1044
Telephone: (636) 272-1885, (800) 291-5223, FAX: (636) 272-1869, Web Site: www.lusterlace.com
Pres: Robert Flores
Member: Loretta Dwyre
Conducts Business: U.S.
Employees: 6
Primary Market Served: Business
Catalog available online

Direct online sales
Advertising/Marketing Budget Related to Direct Marketing: 51-75%
Founded: 1995
Gross sales or billing: $700,000

Sell to wholesale distributors & jobbers. Products are part of a metal polishing system (patented). Luster Lace was developed specifically for polishing round & tubular objects such as brass hand & foot rails, metal furniture, auto parts & brass beds. Luster Pad is perfect for flat & uneven surfaces, brass sinks, engine parts, motorcycle & auto rims, etc. Luster Seal, newest product, is a metal sealant excellent for sealing metals against damage from oxidation.

THE DMA **MBI INC**
47 Richards Ave
Norwalk, CT 06857-0001
Telephone: (203) 853-2000, E-Mail: webmail@mbi-inc.com, Web Site: www.mbi-inc.com
Personnel Mgr: Thomas Reese
CEO: Peter Magiathlin
CFO: Michael Wilbur
Employees: 600
Primary Market Served: Consumer
Founded: 1969
Gross sales or billing: $500,000,000

Market collectibles through The Danbury Mint, The Postal Commemorative Society, The Easton Press, and The Danbury Mint, UK.

MCI INC
Subs. of MCI WorldCom Inc
22001 Loudoun Co Pkwy
Ashburn, VA 20147
Telephone: (703) 886-5600, FAX: (703) 885-0570
Exec VP of Strategy & Corp Devel: Jonathan Crane
Conducts Business: Worldwide
Primary Market Served: Consumer

Long distance telephone service.

THE DMA **MDE MARKETING**
55 Lehman St
Mahwah, NJ 07430-3050
Telephone: (201) 891-7010, Web Site: www.wdemarketing.com
Mktg Dir: Ken Ebling

MGI MANAGEMENT INSTITUTE
12 Skyline Dr
Hawthorne, NY 10532
Telephone: (914) 428-6500, (800) 932-0191, FAX: (914) 428-0773, E-Mail: mgiusa@aol.com, Web Site: www.mgi.org

VP: Gerard Cunningham
Engr: Mark Luciono
Conducts Business: Worldwide
Employees: 12
Primary Market Served: Business
Catalog available online
Indirect online sales
Advertising/Marketing Budget Related to Direct Marketing: 76-100%
Founded: 1968

Develop & administer database learning programs, both print-based and online, for many professional associates.

MGM GRAND DETROIT
1777 3rd St
Detroit, MI 48226-2561
Telephone: (877) 888-2121, Web Site: www.mgmgrand.com/det
Database Mktg Mgr: Synthia Adams

MPBS INDUSTRIES
2820 E Washington Blvd
Los Angeles, CA 90023-4217
Telephone: (323) 268-8514, (800) 421-6265, FAX: (323) 268-6305, Web Site: www.mpbs.com
Pres: Michael Dernburg
Gen Mgr: Philip Lopes
Mktg: Jim Kallenberg
Conducts Business: Worldwide
Employees: 30
Primary Market Served: Business
Advertising/Marketing Budget Related to Direct Marketing: 0-25%
Gross sales or billing: $7,000,000

Distributor of equipment & supplies for industrial meat & food processing & packaging.

MPS MULTIMEDIA INC
1222 S Amphlett Blvd
San Mateo, CA 94402-1906
Telephone: (650) 872-7100, FAX: (650) 872-7133, E-Mail: sales@gospg.com, Web Site: www.selectmedia.com
Pres & CEO: Steve Chen
VP & Mktg Dir: Edgar Chen
Primary Market Served: Business & Consumer
Catalog available online
Indirect online sales

Resale & distribution of CD-ROM titles.

MTS SYSTEMS CORP
14000 Technology Dr
Eden Prairie, MN 55344-2247
Telephone: (952) 937-4000, (800) 328-2255, FAX: (952) 937-4515, E-Mail: info@mts.com, Web Site: www.mts.com

Chmn: Sidney W. Emery Jr.
Pres, CEO & Dir: Laura B. Hamilton
VP & CFO: Susan E. Knight
Treas & Dir: Paul Runice
Primary Market Served: Business
Gross sales or billing: $421,000,000

Industrial services: make testing equipment for testing materials, structures & vehicles.

THE DMA MACY'S MARKETING
Div. of Advertex
151 W 34th St (fl 17)
New York, NY 10001-2101
Telephone: (212) 695-4400, FAX: (212) 494-1517, Web Site: www.macys.com
Chmn, Pres & CEO: Terry J. Lundgren
CIO: Larry A. Lewark
Exec VP & CFO: Karen M. Hoquet
Dir, Direct Mail/Inserts/Production: Elizabeth (Betsy) Wordsman
Conducts Business: U.S.
Employees: 188,000
Primary Market Served: Consumer
Catalog available online
Direct online sales
Founded: 1820
Gross sales or billing: $26,970,000,000

Retail department store.

MACY'S WEST
170 O'Farrell St
San Francisco, CA 94102
Telephone: (415) 954-6089, FAX: (415) 954-6103
Chmn: Robert L. Mettler
Pres: Daniel H. Edelman
Vice Chmn, Dir Stores: Rudolph J. Borneo
Conducts Business: U.S.
Employees: 38,900
Primary Market Served: Business & Consumer
Gross sales or billing: $6,002,000,000

Complete full-service department store.

MAGNAFLUX
Div. of Illinois Works Inc
3624 W Lake Ave
Glenview, IL 60026-1215
Telephone: (847) 657-5300, FAX: (847) 657-5388, Web Site: www.magnaflux.com
Gen Mgr: Steve Groeninger
Sls & Mktg Mgr: Kevin Walker
Conducts Business: Worldwide
Employees: 100
Primary Market Served: Business
Catalog available online
Advertising/Marketing Budget Related to Direct Marketing: 51-75%
Founded: 1927
Gross sales or billing: $50,000,000

Non-destructive testing equipment & materials.

MAGNATAG VISABLE SYSTEMS
Div. of WA Krapf Inc
2031 O'Neill Rd
Macedon, NY 14502-8953
Telephone: (315) 986-3033, FAX: (315) 986-4000, Web Site: www.magnatag.com
Pres: Wallace Krapf
Info Sys Mgr: Doug Weeks
Conducts Business: U.S.
Primary Market Served: Business & Consumer

Mail order house specializing in magnetic scheduling systems.

MAGNET LLC
Seven Chamber Dr, PO Box 605
Washington, MO 63090
Telephone: (636) 239-5661, (800) 458-9457, FAX: (636) 239-4490, E-Mail: contactus@themagnetgroup.com, Web Site: www.magnetllc.com
Pres & CEO: Bill Korowitz
COO: Tom Gorgonne
CFO: Paul Leone
Exec VP: David Kagel
VP, Sls: Darryl Haddox
Primary Market Served: Business
Catalog available online
Indirect online sales

Promotional magnet supplier.

THE MAGNI CO INC
Div. of The Magni Group Inc
7106 Wellington Point Rd
McKinney, TX 75070-5705
Telephone: (972) 540-2050, (800) 645-9199, FAX: (972) 540-1057, E-Mail: sales@magnico.com, Web Site: www.magnico.com; www.magnilife.com
Pres: Evan Reynolds
VP: Darlene Reynolds
Conducts Business: U.S., U.K., Australia, Canada
Employees: 7
Primary Market Served: Business & Consumer
Catalog available online
Direct online sales
Advertising/Marketing Budget Related to Direct Marketing: 26-50%
Founded: 1982
Gross sales or billing: $3,950,000

Health products in North America & Australia.

THE MAINE PHOTOGRAPHIC WORKSHOPS

2 Central St
Rockport, ME 04856-5936
Telephone: (207) 236-8581, (877) 577-7700, FAX: (207) 236-2558, E-Mail: info@theworkshops.com, Web Site: www.theworkshops.com
Dir: David H. Lyman
Conducts Business: U.S., France, Italy
Employees: 20
Primary Market Served: Business
Advertising/Marketing Budget Related to Direct Marketing: 0-25%

Create & offer workshops & training programs for working professionals in film, video & photography.

MAJESTIC PRODUCTS CO

Div. of CFM Majestic Inc
410 Admiral Blvd
Mississauga, ON, Canada L5T 2N6
Telephone: (905) 858-8010, (800) 668-5323, FAX: (905) 670-7915, Web Site: www.cfmcorp.com
Pres & COO: Mark Proudfoot
CEO: Carry R. Robinette
VP & CFO: J. David Wood
VP, Mktg: Jason Perry
Dir Mktg: Jennifer Coombe
Conducts Business: U.S., Canada, Europe
Employees: 350
Primary Market Served: Business & Consumer
Catalog available online
Direct Marketing ad budget:
Direct Mail: 25%
Magazines: 50%
Newspapers: 10%
TV/Radio: 5%
Telephone: 10%

Manufacture wood & gas stoves.

MALCO PRODUCTS INC

361 Fairview Ave
Barberton, OH 44203
Telephone: (330) 753-0361, (800) 253-2526, FAX: (330) 753-2025, Web Site: www.malcopro.com
Pres: Stuart Glauberman
VP: Jay Glauberman
Mgr: Dave Pennell
Mgr: Todd West
Conducts Business: Worldwide
Employees: 200
Primary Market Served: Business & Consumer
Catalog available online
Direct online sales

Chemical specialty manufacturer supplying automotive chemicals & specialty chemicals to direct marketing & fundraising companies under the Malco or private label.

MALM CHEMICAL CORP

Dept WEB-5, PO Box 300
Pound Ridge, NY 10576-0300
Telephone: (914) 764-5775, FAX: (914) 764-5386, E-Mail: custserv1@malms.com, Web Site: www.malms.com
Pres: Jay Kolinsky
Conducts Business: U.S., Canada
Primary Market Served: Business & Consumer
Catalog available online
Direct online sales
Advertising/Marketing Budget Related to Direct Marketing: 76-100%
Founded: 1979

Automotive wax, polishes & high speed applicators.

EF MALONEY INC

257 Mamaroneck Ave (Suite 208)
Mamaroneck, NY 10543-2686
Telephone: (718) 549-7000, FAX: (718) 549-6320, E-Mail: efmaloney@aol.com, Web Site: www.efmaloney.com
Pres: E. F. Maloney
VP: Thomas J. Carney
Conducts Business: U.S.
Employees: 16
Primary Market Served: Business & Consumer
Catalog available online
Advertising/Marketing Budget Related to Direct Marketing: 26-50%
Founded: 1953
Gross sales or billing: $1,000,000

Distributor of equipment & furniture to schools, institutions & offices.

THE MALONEY GROUP

Five E 22nd St
New York, NY 10010-5315
Telephone: (212) 777-6655, FAX: (212) 777-6600
Pres: Antoinette Maloney
Primary Market Served: Business
Founded: 1991

Marketing firm, new business consultant.

MANE SOLUTIONS

314 Fifth Ave
New York, NY 10001-3606
Telephone: (212) 736-0306, FAX: (212) 239-2039
Pres: Kenneth McBride
Conducts Business: U.S., Europe
Employees: 6
Primary Market Served: Consumer

Hair replacement.

MANNING MATERIALS

Div. of Canamould Max
680 Ben Franklin Hwy E, PO Box 250
Birdsboro, PA 19508-0250
Telephone: (610) 385-6797, (800) 445-1719, FAX: (610) 385-7524, E-Mail: mmsupport@manningmaterials.com, Web Site: www.manningmaterials.com
Pres: Drew Seibert
Gen Mgr Sls, VP Mktg: Matthew Thomas
Project Mgr: Greg Gates
Employees: 30
Primary Market Served: Business & Consumer
Catalog available online
Founded: 1980

Maintenance products for cleaning & sealing of stucco.

MARATHON NORCO AEROSPACE INC

Subs. of Transdigm Group
8301 Imperial Rd
Waco, TX 76712-6588
Telephone: (254) 776-0650, FAX: (254) 776-6558, Web Site: www.mptc.com
Pres & CEO: Nicolas Howley
Pres (Marathon): Al Rodriguez
VP & CFO: Gregory Rufus
Conducts Business: U.S.
Employees: 250
Primary Market Served: Business
Catalog available online
Direct Marketing ad budget: $500,000
Direct Mail: 50%
Magazines: 50%
Gross sales or billing: $26,000,000

Manufacturer of ni-cad batteries for airframe OEMs, government & commercial OEMs.

MARCOR REMEDIATION INC

3900 Vero Rd
Halethorpe, MD 21227-1510
Telephone: (410) 785-0001, (800) 547-0128, FAX: (410) 771-0348, E-Mail: info@marcor.com, Web Site: www.marcor.com
VP, Sls & Mktg: Steve Silicato
Dir Corp Commun: Dr. Joan Warfield Blazucki
Conducts Business: U.S.
Employees: 586
Primary Market Served: Business
Catalog available online
Indirect online sales
Founded: 1980

Full-service environmental contracting firm, with regional operations throughout the US. Services include emergency response, model remediation, IAQ, industrial cleaning & vacuuming, environmental site assessments, UST testing, clean-up & removal, soil & groundwater remediation, waste water treatment, as well as asbestos, disaster recovery, lead & other hazard abatement.

MARK JAMES & ASSOCIATES INC
PO Box 429
Oswego, IL 60543-0429
Telephone: (630) 548-8100, FAX: (630) 548-6107, E-Mail: info@markjamesassociates.com, Web Site: www.markjamesassociates.com/contact.html
Pres: Ted Fujii
Office Mgr: Sharon Geltner
Conducts Business: U.S., Australia, Canada, Europe
Employees: 2
Primary Market Served: Business
Founded: 1961
Gross sales or billing: $200,000

Manufacturer's representative of merchandise ranging from collectibles & household goods to cameras & watches. Develops & supplies merchandise offers to direct mail industry & premium incentive markets.

MARKETING AND PRODUCT STRATEGY
Globalink Inc
Nine Centennial Dr
Peabody, MA 01960
Telephone: (978) 977-2000, (800) 825-5897, FAX: (781) 238-0986, Web Site: www.lhsl.com
Sr VP, Mktg & Corp Communs: Ellen Spooren
Sr VP: Robert Weideman
Sr VP, Worldwide Sls: Gerald Calabrese
Primary Market Served: Business & Consumer

Translation software & in-house translation service.

MARKETING RESULTS INC
604 Libertyville Pl
Sicklerville, NJ 08081
Telephone: (856) 740-3334, FAX: (856) 740-3335, Web Site: www.marketingresults.net
CEO: Patrice Gianni
Pres: Gary A. Border
Dir: Kevin McElroy
Dir, Mktg: Alisa Mirabal
Sr Acct Exec: Craig Border

Sr Acct Exec: Rebecca Perger
Conducts Business: U.S., Canada
Employees: 10
Primary Market Served: Business & Consumer
Catalog available online
Advertising/Marketing Budget Related to Direct Marketing: 51-75%
Direct Marketing ad budget:
Direct Mail: $1,500,000
Magazines: $25,000
Newspapers: $100,000
TV/Radio: $500,000
Telephone: $200,000
Gross sales or billing: $3,500,000

Marketer in the casino gaming, lodging, food, beverage & cellular communications industries.

MARKWINS INTERNATIONAL CORP
22067 Ferrero Pkwy
City of Industry, CA 91789
Telephone: (909) 595-8898, FAX: (909) 595-8820, Web Site: www.markwins.com
Pres & CEO: Eric Chen
CFO: Julie Hsu
Exec VP, Gen Mgr: Mac Ritchie
Sr VP, Sls: Matt Allen
Sr VP, Mktg: Shawn Haynes
Conducts Business: U.S., Canada, Norway, Sweden, Denmark
Employees: 60
Primary Market Served: Business
Catalog available online
Advertising/Marketing Budget Related to Direct Marketing: 0-25%

Cosmetics manufacturers supplying specialty health & beauty aids to direct marketers in 20 countries.

MARMELSTEIN INC
760 S Fourth St
Philadelphia, PA 19147
Telephone: (215) 925-9862, FAX: (215) 925-3889
Pres & Owner: Judy Buchsbaum
Conducts Business: U.S.
Employees: 20
Primary Market Served: Business & Consumer
Advertising/Marketing Budget Related to Direct Marketing: 26-50%

Textile distributor to both consumer & business.

THE MARMON GROUP LLC
181 W Madison St Ste 2500
Chicago, IL 60602-4505
Telephone: (312) 372-9500, FAX: (312) 845-5305, Web Site: www.marmon.com
Pres & CEO: Frank S. Ptak

Div Pres: Kelly E. Dier
Sr VP & Gen Counsel: Robert W. Webb
VP, HR: Larry Rist
Conducts Business: Worldwide
Employees: 27,000
Primary Market Served: Business & Consumer
Advertising/Marketing Budget Related to Direct Marketing: 0-25%
Gross sales or billing: $7,000,000,000

International association of more than 60 auto manufacturing & service companies.

MARY KAY COSMETICS INC
16251 Dallas Pkwy
Addison, TX 75001-6801
Telephone: (972) 687-6300, (800) MARY KAY, FAX: (972) 687-1611, Web Site: www.marykay.com
Exec Chmn: Richard R. Rogers
Pres & CEO: David B. Holl
Exec VP & CIO: Kregg Jodie
Exec VP: Dennis Greaney
Sr VP, Fin: Terry Smith
Sr VP, Mktg: Rhonda Shasteen
Conducts Business: Worldwide
Employees: 4,500
Primary Market Served: Consumer
Catalog available online
Direct online sales
Founded: 1985
Gross sales or billing: $2,250,000,000

Manufacturer & marketer of personal care products through 200,000 independent beauty consultants.

MARY OF PUDDIN HILL INC
201 E Interstate 30 Exit 95
Greenville, TX 75402
Telephone: (903) 455-2651, (800) 545-8889, FAX: (903) 455-4522, E-Mail: customerservice@puddinhill.com, Web Site: www.puddinhill.com
Pres: Ron Massey
Conducts Business: U.S.
Employees: 118
Primary Market Served: Consumer
Catalog available online
Direct online sales
Advertising/Marketing Budget Related to Direct Marketing: 51-75%
Direct Marketing ad budget:
Direct Mail: 100%
Founded: 1839
Gross sales or billing: $3,600,000

Sell fruit cakes, candies & other food gifts by direct mail.

MASCO CORP
21001 Van Born Rd
Taylor, MI 48180

Telephone: (313) 274-7400, FAX: (313) 792-6135, E-Mail: webmaster@mascohq.com, Web Site: www.masco.com
Chmn: Richard A. Manoogian
Pres, CEO & Dir: Timothy Wadhams
Exec VP & COO: Donald J. DeMarie Jr.
VP, Corp Devel & CFO: John G. Sznewajs
VP & CIO: Timothy J. Monteith
Primary Market Served: Business & Consumer
Catalog available online
Indirect online sales

Building & home improvement products.

WB MASON CO
53 23rd St (fl 10)
New York, NY 10010-4234
Telephone: (888) 926-2766, Web Site: www.wbmason.com
Acct Exec: Mary McBride
Primary Market Served: Consumer

MASTERPIECE STUDIOS INC
PO Box 8700
Mankato, MN 56002-8700
Telephone: (507) 388-8788, (800) 447-0219, FAX: (507) 344-4606, E-Mail: masterpiecestudios@masterpiecestudios.com, Web Site: www.masterpiecestudios.com
Exec VP, Sls & Mktg: Doug Faust
Pres: John Kind
Conducts Business: U.S., Canada
Employees: 215
Primary Market Served: Business & Consumer
Gross sales or billing: $27,600,000

Manufacture & distribute stationery & copy paper for use in small presses & office copiers.

MASTERVISION INC
969 Park Ave
New York, NY 10028
Telephone: (212) 879-0448, (800) 876-0091, FAX: (212) 744-3560, E-Mail: stadin1@aol.com, Web Site: www.mastervision.com
Pres: Richard N. Stadin
Conducts Business: Worldwide
Employees: 10
Primary Market Served: Business & Consumer
Direct Marketing ad budget:
Direct Mail: 25%
Magazines: 25%
Newspapers: 25%
Online: 25%
Founded: 1980

Produce & market cultural & educational TV, video cassettes, disks, how-to's & books in the arts, humanities & sciences.

MATTEL INC
333 Continental Blvd
El Segundo, CA 90245-5012
Telephone: (310) 252-2000, FAX: (310) 252-2180, Web Site: www.mattel.com
Chmn & CEO: Robert A. Eckert
Pres - Mattel Brands: Neil Friedman
Pres, Am Girl's Brand: Ellen L. Brothers
Sr VP Mktg & Licensing: Jim Wagner
Employees: 25,000
Primary Market Served: Consumer
Founded: 1945
Gross sales or billing: $5,650,200,000

Manufacturer of family products.

MAUI JIM INC
8300 N Allen Rd
Peoria, IL 61615
Telephone: (309) 691-3700, FAX: (309) 683-2202, Web Site: www.mauijim.com
Pres: Walter Hester
VP, Mktg: Chris Abbruzzese
Primary Market Served: Business & Consumer
Catalog available online
Direct online sales

Vision care products & services, sunglasses.

MAZDA NORTH AMERICAN OPERATIONS
Div. of Mazda Corp
7755 Irvine Center Dr
Irvine, CA 92623
Telephone: (949) 727-1990, (800) 222-6500, FAX: (949) 727-6101, Web Site: www.mazdausa.com
Pres & CEO: James J. O'Sullivan
Sr VP & CFO: Matthew Foulston
Sr VP, Res & Devel: Robert Davis
VP, PR: Jay Amestoy
Dir, IT & CIO: Jim DiMarizio
Employees: 860
Primary Market Served: Business
Catalog available online
Indirect online sales
Gross sales or billing: $300,000,000

Parts & accessories & automotive distributor.

MCDONALD OBSOLETE PARTS CO
6458 W Eureka Rd
Rockport, IN 47635

Telephone: (812) 359-4965, FAX: (812) 359-5555, E-Mail: parts@mcdonaldparts.com, Web Site: www.mcdonaldparts.com
Pres & Owner: Marjorie McDonald
Parts Specialist: Robert McDonald
Parts Buyer: Will McDonald
Conducts Business: U.S.
Primary Market Served: Business & Consumer
Catalog available online
Indirect online sales
Advertising/Marketing Budget Related to Direct Marketing: 26-50%
Founded: 1974
Gross sales or billing: $150,000

Obsolete Ford, Lincoln & Mercury parts to the public & dealers.

MCFEELY'S SQUARE DRIVE SCREWS
PO Box 44976
Madison, WI 53744-4976
Telephone: (434) 846-2729, (800) 443-7937, FAX: (804) 847-7136, E-Mail: tech@mcfeelys.com, Web Site: www.mcfeelys.com
Pres: James C. Ray
Tech Dir: Daren Lawrence
Opers Mgr: Ron Pegran
Conducts Business: U.S.
Employees: 35
Primary Market Served: Business & Consumer
Catalog available online
Indirect online sales
Advertising/Marketing Budget Related to Direct Marketing: 0-25%
Direct Marketing ad budget: $1,000,000
Direct Mail: $900,000
Magazines: $100,000
Founded: 1978

Supply square drive screws for the woodworking market.

MCGRUFF SPECIALTY PRODUCTS OFFICE
Div. of National Crime Prevention Council
1 Prospect St
Amsterdam, NY 12010
Telephone: (518) 842-4388, (888) 776-7763, FAX: (800) 995-5121, E-Mail: mcgruff@spocentral.com, Web Site: www.mcgruffspo.com
Pres & CEO: Alfonso E. Lendhart
Exec Dir: Tibby Milne
Dir: Carolyn Cullen
Conducts Business: U.S.
Primary Market Served: Business
Catalog available online
Direct online sales
Advertising/Marketing Budget Related to Direct Marketing: 76-100%

Crime prevention educational products.

MCKENZIE TAXIDERMY SUPPLY
PO Box 480
Granite Quarry, NC 28072-0480
Telephone: (704) 279-7985, (800) 279-7985, Web Site: www.mckenziesp.com
CEO: Kevin McKenzie
Dir, IT: Barry McKenzie
Mgr: Eric Cantrall
Primary Market Served: Business & Consumer
Catalog available online
Direct online sales

Taxidermy supplies.

MCNICHOLS CO
PO Box 30300
Tampa, FL 33630-3300
Telephone: (813) 282-3828, FAX: (813) 288-9342, E-Mail: sales@mcnichols.com, Web Site: www.mcnichols.com
Mktg Dir: William J. Tuxhorn
Adv Dir: Sharon Robertson
Conducts Business: U.S., Mexico, Canada, Puerto Rico, Costa Rica, Chile, Colombia, Venezuela, Panama
Employees: 315
Primary Market Served: Business
Catalog available online
Indirect online sales
Advertising/Marketing Budget Related to Direct Marketing: 76-100%
Direct Marketing ad budget:
Direct Mail: 80%
Magazines: 8%
Online: 10%
Telephone: 2%
Founded: 1952
Gross sales or billing: $95,000,000

Distributor of specialty metals.

MEDTRONIC INC
710 Medtronic Pkwy NE
Minneapolis, MN 55432-5604
Telephone: (763) 514-4000, (800) 328-2518, FAX: (763) 514-4879, Web Site: www.medtronic.com
Pres & CEO: William A. Hawkins III
Sr VP & CIO: H. James Dallas
Sr VP Strategy & Bus Devel: Geoffrey Martha
Conducts Business: Worldwide
Employees: 37,000
Primary Market Served: Consumer
Advertising/Marketing Budget Related to Direct Marketing: 51-75%
Founded: 1949
Gross sales or billing: $12,300,000,000

Implantable pacing systems, heart valves, cardiopulmonary pumps, cardiac ablation systems, leads, angioplasty catheters, drug pumps, spinal stimulators & blood management products sold to doctors & hospitals. 40 U.S. locations & 120 international offices & facilities.

MEGGER
427 Bronze Way
Dallas, TX 75237-1019
Telephone: (214) 330-3539, Web Site: www.megger.com
Dir Mktg: Elsa Cantu
Primary Market Served: Business & Consumer

MEGUIAR'S INC
17991 Mitchell S, PO Box 92623
Irvine, CA 92614-6015
Telephone: (949) 752-8000, (800) 347-5700, FAX: (949) 752-6659, Web Site: www.meguiars.com
Pres & CEO: Barry Meguiar
Employees: 225
Primary Market Served: Business & Consumer
Founded: 1901
Gross sales or billing: $26,500,000

Surface cleaners, polishes & waxes for cars, boats, planes, wood, fiberglass, plastics & marble.

MELDISCO
Div. of Footstar
933 MacArthur Blvd
Mahwah, NJ 07430-2045
Telephone: (201) 934-2000, FAX: (201) 934-2570, Web Site: www.meldisco.com
Pres Footstar: John Michael Robinson
CEO Meldisco: Heffret A. Shephard
CEO Footstar: Shawn Neville
Exec VP: William Lenich
Sr VP & CFO: Mike Lynch
Primary Market Served: Consumer
Gross sales or billing: $257,000,000

Retail shoes.

MENARDI MIKROPUL LLC
1 Maxwell Dr
Trenton, SC 29847
Telephone: (803) 663-6551, (800) 321-3218, FAX: (803) 663-4029, E-Mail: info@menardifilters.com, Web Site: www.menardifilters.com
Mgr: Lisa Hayes
Conducts Business: U.S., Canada
Employees: 150
Primary Market Served: Business
Catalog available online
Advertising/Marketing Budget Related to Direct Marketing: 0-25%

Direct Marketing ad budget: $200,000
Direct Mail: 20%
Magazines: 20%
Telephone: 60%
Founded: 2000
Gross sales or billing: $9,100,000

Manufacture & service filtration products for air pollution control & product recovery in chemical, mineral, food & other industries.

MENTOR CORP
201 Mentor Dr
Santa Barbara, CA 93111-3340
Telephone: (805) 879-6000, (800) 525-0245, FAX: (805) 964-2712, Web Site: www.mentorcorp.com
Chmn: Joseph E. Whitters
Pres, CEO & Dir: Joshua H. Levine
VP, HR: Cathryn Ullery
VP & CFO: Michael O'Neil
VP & COO: Edward S. Northrop
Employees: 950
Primary Market Served: Business
Catalog available online
Founded: 1969
Gross sales or billing: $300,000,000

Manufacturer of medical devices for plastic & reconstructive surgery, clinical & consumer health care.

MERCK & CO INC
1 Merck Dr
Whitehouse Station, NJ 08889
Telephone: (908) 423-1000, Web Site: www.merck.com
Chmn, Pres & CEO: Richard T. Clark
VP Bus Devel: Richard N. Kender
Sr VP Global Process & CIO: J. Chris Scalet
Pres Mfg: Willie A. Deese
Exec VP: Kenneth C. Frazier
Conducts Business: U.S., Canada, Europe
Employees: 60,000
Primary Market Served: Business & Consumer
Gross sales or billing: $22,600,000,000

Pharmaceuticals & health products for humans.

MERISEL
127 W 30th St (5th fl)
New York, NY 10001
Telephone: (212) 594-4800, FAX: (212) 594-4488, E-Mail: corp@merisel.com, Web Site: www.merisel.com
VP, Mktg: Leslie Sinfield
Conducts Business: U.S.
Primary Market Served: Business

Distributor of computer products, and software sales.

MERSCO MEDICAL
1411 E Wells Ave
Pierre, SD 57501
Telephone: (605) 224-6687, (800) 234-1881, FAX: (605) 322-1801
Reg Admin: Steve Statz
Conducts Business: U.S.
Employees: 80
Primary Market Served: Consumer
Advertising/Marketing Budget Related to Direct Marketing: 51-75%

Home healthcare.

MERVYN'S
6200 Stoneridge Mall Rd (Suite 300)
Pleasanton, CA 94588-3705
Telephone: (510) 727-3000, (800) 480-5014, FAX: (510) 727-5851, Web Site: www.mervyns.com
Pres & CEO: Diane Neal
VP, Mktg: Lee Walker
Admin Asst: Leanne King
Primary Market Served: Consumer

Department stores. Clothing accessories, jewelry, shoes & housewares.

METSO MINERALS/WS TYLER
Div. of North American Vibrating Equipment
20965 Crossroads Cir
Waukesha, WI 53186
Telephone: (803) 699-4200, (262) 717-2500, FAX: (262) 717-2501, E-Mail: minerals.info.csr@metso.com, Web Site: www.metsominerals.com
Conducts Business: U.S., Canada, Central & South America
Employees: 550
Primary Market Served: Business & Consumer
Advertising/Marketing Budget Related to Direct Marketing: 0-25%

Manufacture & sell mining equipment.

FRED MEYER JEWELERS INC
Div. of Fred Meyer Inc
3800 SE 22nd Ave
Portland, OR 97202
Telephone: (503) 232-8844, (800) 457-5977, FAX: (503) 797-7616, Web Site: www.fredmeyerjewelers.com
Pres & CEO: Ed Dayoob
VP, Strategic Plng & Bus Devel: Mark Funasaki
Employees: 3,000
Primary Market Served: Consumer
Catalog available online
Direct online sales
Founded: 1973
Gross sales or billing: $259,000,000

Fine jewelry.

MICKWEE GROUP INC
5600 Mowry School Rd Ste 230
Newark, CA 94560-5800
Telephone: (510) 651-6522, FAX: (510) 770-9682, E-Mail: info@generatemarketing.com, Web Site: www.generatemarketing.com
Pres: Ron Mickwee
Client Grp Dir: Ann Mickwee
Conducts Business: U.S.
Employees: 35
Primary Market Served: Business
Advertising/Marketing Budget Related to Direct Marketing: 26-50%
Direct Marketing ad budget:
Direct Mail: 10%
Telephone: 90%

Provide third-party direct marketing services to the computer industry. Services include telemarketing (outbound & inbound) & direct mail.

MICRO PLASTICS INC
PO Box 149
Flippin, AR 72634
Telephone: (870) 453-2261, (800) 466-1467, FAX: (870) 453-8676, E-Mail: mpsales@microplastics.com, Web Site: www.microplastics.com
Pres: Tom Hill
Nat'l Sls Mgr: Bruce Sanders
Mktg & Adv: Tammy Killian
Creative Mktg Devel: Tony Wilson
Conducts Business: U.S., Canada, U.K., Mexico, South America, Central America, Far East
Employees: 350
Primary Market Served: Business & Consumer
Catalog available online
Direct online sales
Advertising/Marketing Budget Related to Direct Marketing: 26-50%
Founded: 1961

Manufacture & sell nylon & plastic hardware & fasteners to distributors & O.E.M. manufacturers.

MICROFLUIDICS CORP
Subs. of MFIC Corp
30 Ossipee Rd
Newton, MA 02464-1444
Telephone: (617) 969-5452, (800) 370-5452, FAX: (617) 965-1213, E-Mail: info@mfics.com, Web Site: www.microfluidicscorp.com
CEO: Michael C. Ferrara
Pres & COO: Robert Bruno
VP Sls & Mktg: Thomas Hoarty
Conducts Business: U.S., Canada, Europe, Asia
Employees: 53
Primary Market Served: Business
Advertising/Marketing Budget Related to Direct Marketing: 26-50%

Founded: 1984
Gross sales or billing: $15,600,000

MICRON CORP
89 Access Rd (Suite 5), Norwood Airport Business Park
Norwood, MA 02062-5234
Telephone: (781) 769-5771, (800) 456-0734, FAX: (781) 762-3531, E-Mail: info@microncorp.com, Web Site: www.microncorp.com
Pres: William Theos
VP, Sls: John Theos
VP Mfg: Charles W. Theos
Conducts Business: U.S.
Employees: 30
Primary Market Served: Business
Catalog available online
Direct online sales
Advertising/Marketing Budget Related to Direct Marketing: 0-25%
Founded: 1982
Gross sales or billing: $3,200,000

Assemble printed circuit boards, surface mount and through hole.

MID WEST FLOOR CO INC
2714 Breckenridge Industrial Ct
Saint Louis, MO 63144
Telephone: (314) 647-6060, FAX: (314) 647-9189, E-Mail: sales@midwestfloor.com, Web Site: www.midwestfloor.com
Pres: Virgil Hendricks
Sls: Kasie Wright
Conducts Business: U.S.
Employees: 100
Primary Market Served: Consumer
Catalog available online
Advertising/Marketing Budget Related to Direct Marketing: 0-25%
Direct Marketing ad budget: $50,000
Direct Mail: 100%
Founded: 1939
Gross sales or billing: $10,000,000

THE MIDDLEBY CORP
1400 Toastmaster Dr
Elgin, IL 60120-9272
Telephone: (847) 741-3300, FAX: (847) 741-0015, E-Mail: sales@middleby.com, Web Site: www.middleby.com
Pres & CEO: Selim A. Bassoul
VP & CFO: Timothy J. Fitzgerald
Investor Rels & PR: Darcy Bretz
Conducts Business: Worldwide
Employees: 1,282
Primary Market Served: Business
Gross sales or billing: $403,431,000

Manufacturer of commercial cooking equipment.

MIDLAND MARKETING GROUP

PO Box 8576
Saint Joseph, MO 64508-8576
Telephone: (816) 261-9007, FAX: (816) 233-0859, E-Mail: info@ midlandmarketinggroup.com, Web Site: www.midlandmarketinggroup. com
Pres: Gary Gerchen
Primary Market Served: Consumer

Greeting card distributor.

THE MILLARD GROUP

7301 N Cicero Ave
Lincolnwood, IL 60712-1613
Telephone: (847) 674-4100, (800) 339-6876, FAX: (847) 677-0790, E-Mail: sales@millardgroup.com, Web Site: www.millardgroup.com
Pres: Larry Kugler
Conducts Business: U.S.
Employees: 2,300
Primary Market Served: Business
Catalog available online
Gross sales or billing: $50,000,000

Contract custodial services to major commercial, medical & educational facilities.

MILWAUKEE ELECTRIC TOOL CORP

Div of Techtronic Industries Co Ltd, Hong Kong
13135 W Lisbon Rd
Brookfield, WI 53005-2550
Telephone: (262) 781-3600, (800) 414-6527, FAX: (262) 781-3611, (800) 638-9582, Web Site: www.mil-electric-tool.com
Pres: Steven P. Richman
Sr VP Sls, Mktg & Prod Devel: Darrell Hendrix
Conducts Business: U.S., Canada
Employees: 2,075
Primary Market Served: Business & Consumer
Catalog available online
Founded: 1924

Manufacture power tools & heavy-duty electric tools for contractors & industry.

MINITAB INC

1829 Pine Hall Rd
State College, PA 16801-3008
Telephone: (814) 238-3280, (800) 448-3555, FAX: (814) 238-4383, E-Mail: sales@minitab.com, Web Site: www.minitab.com
CEO: Barbara Ryan
Conducts Business: U.S., Canada, Europe, Asia, Australia, U.K., South America

Employees: 300
Primary Market Served: Business & Consumer
Catalog available online
Direct online sales
Founded: 1972

Provider of quality improvement software: Minitab Statistical Software, Quality Companion by Minitab & Quality Trainer by Minitab. Also provide a complete solution for Six Sigma & other projects. Companies that rely on Minitab software & services include Toshiba, DuPont & Boeing.

MIRACLE EAR

Subs. of Amplifon
5000 Cheshire Pkwy N
Minneapolis, MN 55446
Telephone: (877) 268-4264, FAX: (763) 268-4365, Web Site: www.miracle-ear.com
CEO Amplifon: Franco Moscetti
Conducts Business: U.S., Canada, Puerto Rico, Australia, Spain, Mexico
Employees: 600
Primary Market Served: Consumer
Catalog available online
Advertising/Marketing Budget Related to Direct Marketing: 26-50%
Direct Marketing ad budget:
Direct Mail: $4,000,000
TV/Radio: $6,000,000
Telephone: $2,000,000
Founded: 1948
Gross sales or billing: $96,000,000

Manufacture hearing aids.

MISSCO CORP

PO Box 321400, PO Box 5349
Flowood, MS 39232-1400
Telephone: (601) 948-8600, (800) 647-5333, FAX: (601) 987-3038
Supvr: Jim Scholtens
Proj Coord: Monique Chatman
VP, Sls: Mel Edmonds
Sls: Tracy Echols
Conducts Business: U.S.
Primary Market Served: Business & Consumer
Catalog available online

Sells office & school supplies, furniture & equipment.

MR G'S ENTERPRISES

5613 Elliott Reeder Rd
Fort Worth, TX 76117-6013
Telephone: (817) 831-3501, FAX: (817) 831-0638, E-Mail: mrgs@ mrgusa.com, Web Site: www.mrgusa.com
Owner: Glenn Garrison
Conducts Business: Worldwide
Employees: 12

Primary Market Served: Business & Consumer
Catalog available online
Indirect online sales
Advertising/Marketing Budget Related to Direct Marketing: 76-100%
Direct Marketing ad budget:
Magazines: 100%
Founded: 1974
Gross sales or billing: $500,000

Autofasteners, rechrome plastic service & screw kits for 922 models.

MR WASH CAR WASH

3817 Dupont Ave
Kensington, MD 20895
Telephone: (301) 933-4858, Web Site: www.mrwash.com
Adv & Mktg Dir: Jody Weinstein
Primary Market Served: Consumer
Catalog available online

Car wash services.

MOBILE FUSION

165 S Union Blvd Ste 405
Lakewood, CO 80228-2210
Telephone: (720) 963-8000, (800) 431-8556, Web Site: www.mobile-fusion.com
Mng Partner: Joel Morrow

MODERNAGE CUSTOM DIGITAL IMAGING LABS

555 8th Ave (Rm 2003)
New York, NY 10018-4651
Telephone: (212) 997-1800, (800) 997-2510, FAX: (212) 869-4796, E-Mail: info@modernage.com, Web Site: www.modernage.com
Pres & Co-Owner: Kenneth Troiano
VP & Co-Owner: Richard Troiano
Conducts Business: U.S.
Employees: 120
Primary Market Served: Business & Consumer
Catalog available online
Direct online sales
Advertising/Marketing Budget Related to Direct Marketing: 0-25%
Direct Marketing ad budget:
Direct Mail: 10%
Magazines: 40%
Newspapers: 50%
Founded: 1944

A full service custom photographic lab specializing in single roll development (E-6, C-41 & B&W); duratrans, duraflex or C-prints to any size; photocomposites, dupes, B&W silver gelatin prints, murals & overlaminating; full color & B&W airbrushing, retouching & restoration services. Complete digital imaging, hi-res drum scans to hi-res color negative, transparency or B&W outputs. Computer generated slides, design & layout. Direct digital C-prints & inkjet printing.

THE DMA MOEN INC

25300 Al Moen Dr
North Olmsted, OH 44070-5619
Telephone: (440) 962-2000, Web Site: www.moen.com
Dir Online & Direct Mktg: Ginny Long

MOLSON COORS BREWING CO

1225 17th St Ste 3200
Denver, CO 80202-5536
Telephone: (303) 279-6565, (800) 642-6116, FAX: (303) 277-5415, Web Site: www.molsoncoors.com
Chmn: Eric H. Molson
Vice Chmn: Peter H. Coors
CEO: Leo Kiely
VP & Global CFO: Timothy V. Wolf
Primary Market Served: Business & Consumer
Catalog available online
Founded: 1913
Gross sales or billing: $5,800,000,000

Brewery of Coors Beer.

THURSTON MOORE COUNTRY LTD

304 W Due West Ave
Madison, TN 37115-4511
Telephone: (615) 868-7448, FAX: (615) 868-3738
Pres: Thurston Moore
Treas: Tracy Guerriero
Conducts Business: Worldwide
Employees: 3
Primary Market Served: Business & Consumer
Advertising/Marketing Budget Related to Direct Marketing: 0-25%
Direct Marketing ad budget:
Direct Mail: 100%
Founded: 1975
Gross sales or billing: $200,000

Specialize in personality dollar bills, custom brochures, full color post cards, business cards & bookmarks.

JACQUES MORET INC

1411 Broadway (fl 8)
New York, NY 10018
Telephone: (212) 354-2400, FAX: (212) 354-5544, E-Mail: info@moret.com, Web Site: www.moret.com
Asst to VP Mktg: Joanne Paolucci
Conducts Business: U.S., China
Employees: 55
Primary Market Served: Business
Advertising/Marketing Budget Related to Direct Marketing: 0-25%
Founded: 1975

Sell active wear clothing & apparel to all levels of distribution.

MORITT, HOCK, HAMROFF & HOROWITZ

400 Garden City Plaza
Garden City, NY 11530-3327
Telephone: (516) 873-2000, FAX: (516) 873-2010, E-Mail: lhauser@morritthock.com, Web Site: www.morritthock.com
Pres: Neil J. Moritt
Dir Bus Devel: Laura Hauser
Partner: Alan Hock
Employees: 35
Primary Market Served: Business
Founded: 1980

Attorneys.

THOMAS MOSER CABINETMAKERS

149 Main St
Freeport, ME 04032
Telephone: (207) 865-4519, (800) 708-9041, FAX: (207) 865-6539, E-Mail: freeportshowroom@thosmoser.com, Web Site: www.thosmoser.com
Mktg Dir: Gretchen Kruysman
HR: Cindy Violet
Conducts Business: U.S.
Employees: 100
Primary Market Served: Business & Consumer
Advertising/Marketing Budget Related to Direct Marketing: 26-50%
Founded: 1973
Gross sales or billing: $7,000,000

Handcrafted solid wood furniture to direct users, architects & designers for residential, corporate & institutional use.

MOSTAD & CHRISTENSEN

PO Box 1709
Oak Harbor, WA 98277-1709
Telephone: (360) 679-4164, (800) 654-1654, FAX: (360) 679-4167, E-Mail: marketing@mostad.com, Web Site: www.mostad.com
Editor: Shirlee Christensen

Pres: Arvid Mostad
Office Mgr: Michael Coppage
Conducts Business: U.S., Canada
Employees: 9
Primary Market Served: Business

Provide marketing services such as newsletters & brochures to CPAs.

MOTIENT COMMUNICATIONS

11700 Plaza America Dr Ste 900
Reston, VA 20190-4774
Telephone: (847) 478-4330, (800) 752-2672, FAX: (703) 758-6111
VP System Engrng & Solutions: Deborah Peterson
Employees: 487
Primary Market Served: Business & Consumer
Founded: 1988

Owns & operates an integrated terrestrial/satellite network & provides a variety of mobile communications solutions for the transportation, field service, wireless email & telemetry markets.

MOTOR COACH INDUSTRIES INTERNATIONAL INC

aka MCI
1700 E Golf Rd
Schaumburg, IL 60173
Telephone: (847) 285-2000, (800) 624-2622, Web Site: www.mcicoach.com
Pres & CEO: Tom Sorrells III
Sr VP Sls & Mktg: Pete Cotter
Conducts Business: U.S., Canada, Taiwan, Australia
Employees: 2,000
Primary Market Served: Business
Founded: 1975
Gross sales or billing: $6,924,000,000

Distribution of OEM coach & bus parts to the transit & inter-city fleet companies.

MOTOROLA INC

5 Paragon Dr (#200)
Montvale, NJ 07645
Telephone: (201) 949-5500, (800) 262-8509, Web Site: www.motorola.com
Chmn: Edward J. Zander
Pres, CEO, COO & Dir: Gregory Q. Brown
Exec VP, Dir & Acting CFO: Thomas J. Meredith
Exec VP & CIO: Patricia B. Morrison
Exec VP & CMO: Kenneth C. Keller Jr.
Conducts Business: Worldwide
Employees: 66,000
Primary Market Served: Business
Catalog available online
Direct online sales

Gross sales or billing: $42,800,000,000

Analog & digital SY that provide video, audio & high speed internet/data services over cable & satellite TV networks.

MUSEUM MASTERS INC
185 E 85th St (Suite 27B)
New York, NY 10028
Telephone: (917) 273-8710, (212) 360-7100, FAX: (212) 360-7102, E-Mail: MMIMarilyn@aol.com, Web Site: www.museummasters.com
Pres: Marilyn Goldberg
Conducts Business: U.S., Canada, Europe, Japan, Korea
Employees: 5
Primary Market Served: Business
Direct Marketing ad budget: $100,000
Direct Mail: 50%
Magazines: 50%
Founded: 1980
Gross sales or billing: $1,000,000

Design & produce boutique items using images of the masters, i.e., Picasso, Van Gogh, Gaughin, Degas, Toulouse-Lautrec, Matisse, Warhol & Haring. Also, licensing of these images & merchandising for exhibitions & special events.

MUSIC CHOICE
650 Dresher Rd
Horsham, PA 19044-2204
Telephone: (215) 784-5840, Web Site: www.musicchoice.com
Pres: David Devessa
Sr VP, Sls: Christina Tancredi
Conducts Business: U.S.
Employees: 120
Primary Market Served: Business & Consumer
Founded: 1991

Provide commercial free CD music service to businesses & consumers.

MUSKEGON POWER TOOL CORP
2357 Whitehall Rd
North Muskegon, MI 49445
Telephone: (231) 766-2194, (800) 635-5465, FAX: (231) 766-3846
Pres: William A. Seyferth
Conducts Business: Worldwide
Employees: 5
Primary Market Served: Business & Consumer
Catalog available online
Advertising/Marketing Budget Related to Direct Marketing: 26-50%

Sell professional portable power tools to contractors via direct mail.

MXENERGY INC
595 Summer St (Suite 300)
Stamford, CT 06901-1407
Telephone: (203) 356-1318, Web Site: www.mxenergy.com
Mktg Mgr: Caroline Antunez

THE DMA MYRON CORP
205 Maywood Ave
Maywood, NJ 07607-1000
Telephone: (201) 843-6464, (877) 803-3358, FAX: (201) 843-8390, Web Site: www.myron.com
Pres: Marie Adler-Kravecas
CEO: Jim Adler
Conducts Business: U.S., Canada
Employees: 1,000
Primary Market Served: Business
Catalog available online
Direct online sales
Founded: 1955
Gross sales or billing: $100,000

Sell imprinted pocket & desk appointment diaries, laser engraved pens & market business to business gifts.

THE DMA MYSTIC STAMP CO INC
9700 Mill St
Camden, NY 13316
Telephone: (866) 660-7147, FAX: (800) 385-4919, E-Mail: info@mysticstamp.com, Web Site: www.mysticstamp.com
Pres: Donald J. Sundman
Mktg Mgr: Linda Stevens
Conducts Business: U.S., Canada
Employees: 100
Primary Market Served: Consumer
Catalog available online
Direct online sales
Advertising/Marketing Budget Related to Direct Marketing: 26-50%
Founded: 1923
Gross sales or billing: $19,900,000

Sell retail & wholesale postage stamps to collectors by mail.

NCR CORP
2651 Satellite Blvd
Duluth, GA 30096-5810
Telephone: (937) 445-1936, (800) CALL-NCR, FAX: (937) 445-1682, Web Site: www.ncr.com
Chmn & CEO: Bill Nuti
Sr VP: Dan Bogan
Sr VP: Macolm Collins
VP: Janet Brewer
CTO: Alan Chow
Primary Market Served: Business
Catalog available online

Computer systems; business information processing systems.

NCS
Div. of Russell and Miller Inc
60 Newtown Rd (Suite 6)
Danbury, CT 06810-6257
Telephone: (562) 946-6900, (800) 975-6804, FAX: (800) 527-2488, Web Site: www.shopncs.com; www.ncs-apparel.com
Pres: Mike Wooten
Controller: Glenn Jackmen
Acct Mgr: Minerva Deleon
Conducts Business: U.S.
Employees: 100
Primary Market Served: Business
Catalog available online
Direct online sales
Advertising/Marketing Budget Related to Direct Marketing: 76-100%
Direct Marketing ad budget:
Direct Mail: 100%
Founded: 1931

Signage & merchandising supplies for retail stores.

NCS LEARN
Div. of Pearson Education
19 Orion Way
Trabuco Canyon, CA 92679
Telephone: (949) 766-1068, Web Site: www.ncslearn.com
VP, Mktg: Steve Gardner
Conducts Business: U.S., Canada, U.K., Singapore, Japan, Australia, New Zealand
Employees: 600
Primary Market Served: Business
Advertising/Marketing Budget Related to Direct Marketing: 0-25%
Direct Marketing ad budget: $1,000,000
Direct Mail: 40%
Telephone: 60%
Founded: 1967

With greater than 60 years of research accomplished between CCC (Computer Curriculum Corp) and NCS NovaNET, NCS Learn offers the most comprehensive software (totalling more than 20,000 hours) and online learning programs. Over 5,000,000 children in schools around the world use these products.

NPI
14901 Trinity Blvd
Fort Worth, TX 76155
Telephone: (214) 634-2288, FAX: (682) 503-8214, E-Mail: sales@npisorters.com, Web Site: www.npisorters.com
Mktg Mgr: Michelle Ramirez
Primary Market Served: Business

NATIONAL AUTO WARRANTY
100 Mall Pkwy
Wentzville, MO 63385-4816

Telephone: (800) 649-1620
Chief Mktg Officer: Shawn Morris
Primary Market Served: Consumer

NATIONAL BULK EQUIPMENT INC

12838 Stainless Dr
Holland, MI 49424
Telephone: (616) 399-2220, FAX: (616) 399-7365, E-Mail: sales@nbe-inc.com, Web Site: www.nbe-inc.com
Pres: Todd Reed
CEO: Joe Reed
Exec VP, Opers: Dave Denhof
VP: Ellen Kaines
Conducts Business: U.S.
Employees: 65
Primary Market Served: Business
Catalog available online
Indirect online sales
Advertising/Marketing Budget Related to Direct Marketing: 0-25%
Founded: 1977
Gross sales or billing: $6,000,000

Manufacturer of mixing, storing & conveying equipment for use with dry bulk materials. Also handle pastes & liquids.

NATIONAL EMBLEM SALES

Div. of The American Legion National Headquarters
PO Box 36460
Indianapolis, IN 46206-0460
Telephone: (317) 630-1247, (888) 453-4466, FAX: (317) 630-1381, E-Mail: emblem@legion.org, Web Site: www.emblem.legion.org
Div Dir: Jeffrey Brown
Mktg Mgr: Kevin Carruthers
Conducts Business: U.S.
Employees: 35
Primary Market Served: Business & Consumer
Catalog available online
Direct online sales
Advertising/Marketing Budget Related to Direct Marketing: 76-100%
Founded: 1919

Sell regalia to American Legion members & posts.

NATIONAL 4-H SUPPLY SERVICE

Div. of National 4-H Council
7100 Connecticut Ave
Chevy Chase, MD 20815
Telephone: (301) 961-2959, FAX: (301) 961-2937, E-Mail: 4hsupply@fourhcouncil.edu, Web Site: www.fourhcouncil.edu
Sr VP: Edwin M. Gershon
Dir Natl 4-H Supply Svc: Kelly Carpenter

Conducts Business: U.S.
Employees: 15
Primary Market Served: Business & Consumer
Catalog available online
Direct online sales
Advertising/Marketing Budget Related to Direct Marketing: 26-50%
Direct Marketing ad budget: $300,000
Direct Mail: 60%
Online: 40%
Founded: 1924
Gross sales or billing: $4,500,000

Goods & services to the 4-H.

NATIONAL GALLERY OF ART GIFT SHOP

4th & Constitution Ave NW
Washington, DC 20565
Telephone: (202) 842-6466, (800) 697-9350, FAX: (202) 842-4043, Web Site: www.nga.gov
Chmn: John Wilmerding
Pres: Victoria P. Sant
Gallery Dir: Earl A. Powell III
Conducts Business: U.S.
Employees: 70
Primary Market Served: Consumer
Catalog available online
Indirect online sales

Sell fine art reproductions & posters to the general public.

NATIONAL RAILROAD PASSENGER CORP

dba Amtrak
60 Massachussetts Ave NE
Washington, DC 20002
Telephone: (202) 906-3000, (800) USA-RAIL, FAX: (202) 906-3306, Web Site: www.amtrak.com
Pres & CEO & Dir: Alexander K. Kummunt
Chmn Bd: Donna McLean
Sec of Transportation, US Dept of Transportation: Mary Peters
COO: William L. Crosbie
Vice Chmn Bd: R. Hunter Biden
Employees: 19,000
Primary Market Served: Business & Consumer
Catalog available online
Direct online sales
Founded: 1971
Gross sales or billing: $2,042,000,000

Railroad.

NATIONAL SEMICONDUCTOR CORP

2900 Semiconductor Dr
Santa Clara, CA 95052-8090

Telephone: (408) 721-5000, (800) 272-9959, FAX: (408) 245-0671, E-Mail: new.feedback@nsc.com, Web Site: www.national.com
Chmn & CEO: Brian Halla
Pres & COO: Donald Macleod
Sr VP & CFO: Lewis Chew
Sr VP: Edward Sweeney
Sr VP: Suneil Parulekar
Sr VP & CTO: Ahmad Bahai
Employees: 8,500
Primary Market Served: Business & Consumer
Founded: 1959
Gross sales or billing: $2,158,100,000

Semiconductors & computers.

NATIONAL SEMINARS GROUP

Div. of Rockhurst University Continuing Education Center
6901 W 63rd St (Suite 300)
Shawnee Mission, KS 66202-4005
Telephone: (913) 432-7755, (800) 258-7246, FAX: (913) 432-0824, E-Mail: cstserv@natsem.com, Web Site: www.natsem.com
Exec Dir & Founder: Mark Truitt
VP Mktg: Janette Novack
Mgr: Gary Weinberg
Facilities Mgr: Helena Conley
Conducts Business: U.S.
Employees: 200
Primary Market Served: Business
Catalog available online
Direct online sales
Advertising/Marketing Budget Related to Direct Marketing: 76-100%
Founded: 1978

One of the nation's leading business training seminar companies.

NATIONWIDE BEAUTY & BARBER SUPPLY

2600 Erie Blvd E
Syracuse, NY 13224-1287
Telephone: (315) 446-9026, FAX: (315) 446-8943, E-Mail: sales@nationwidebeauty.com, Web Site: www.nationwidebeauty.com
Pres: Norman Kassel
VP & Sec: Richard Kassel
Conducts Business: U.S., Puerto Rico
Employees: 25
Primary Market Served: Business & Consumer
Catalog available online
Indirect online sales
Direct Marketing ad budget:
Direct Mail: $120,000
Newspapers: $2,000
Telephone: $30,000
Gross sales or billing: $3,000,000

Mail order wholesale beauty & barber supplies to trade & retail consumers.

NATIONWIDE DISPLAYS INC
100 Christopher St
Ronkonkoma, NY 11779
Telephone: (631) 467-2034, FAX:
(631) 467-2079, E-Mail: info@
nationwidedisplays.com, Web Site:
www.nationwidedisplays.com
Pres: Bill Griffith
VP Sls: Steve Griffith
Conducts Business: U.S., Canada
Employees: 15
Primary Market Served: Business
Catalog available online
Indirect online sales
Direct Marketing ad budget: $75,000
Direct Mail: 100%
Founded: 1990

Portable & custom exhibits for industry installation & dismantling. Serving North America & Europe.

NAVISTAR
4201 Winfield Rd
Warrenville, IL 60555-4026
Telephone: (630) 753-5804, (800) 448-
7825, FAX: (630) 753-2303, Web
Site: www.navistar.com
Pres & CEO: Daniel Ustian
Sr VP & Treas: Terry M. Endsley
Dir, Bus Intel & Integ Mktg: Matt Aldrich
VP & CIO: Donald C. Sharp
Conducts Business: U.S.
Employees: 13,000
Primary Market Served: Business &
Consumer
Catalog available online
Indirect online sales
Direct Marketing ad budget: $500,000
Direct Mail: 90%
Telephone: 10%
Gross sales or billing: $4,000,000,000

International medium & heavy duty trucks, school buses, parts, service, engines & financing to businesses.

NAVITAR INC
200 Commerce Dr
Rochester, NY 14623-3506
Telephone: (585) 359-4000, FAX:
(585) 359-4999, E-Mail: info@
navitar.com, Web Site: www.navitar.
com
Pres: Jeremy Goldstein
Mktg Asst: Casey Lalyk
COO: Thomas McCune
Controller: Mark Smith
Conducts Business: Worldwide
Employees: 50
Primary Market Served: Business
Catalog available online
Direct Marketing ad budget:
Direct Mail: 25%
Magazines: 25%
Telephone: 50%

Manufacturer of optical lenses & audio visual equipment.

NESTLE CLINICAL NUTRITION CO
Div. of Nestle USA
12500 Whitewater Dr
Hopkins, MN 55343-9420
Telephone: (877) 463-7853, (800) 284-
9488, FAX: (877) 563-7853, Web
Site: www.nestle-nutrition.com
VP: Roy Reed
Primary Market Served: Business

Manufacture nutrition supplements.

NETWORK TELEPHONE SERVICES INC
dba Pacific Marketing
21135 Erwin St
Woodland Hills, CA 91367-3713
Telephone: (818) 992-4300, (800) 727-
6874, FAX: (818) 992-8415, Web
Site: www.nts.net
CEO: Joseph Preston
Pres: Gary Passon
VP Mktg: David Wood
Employees: 500
Primary Market Served: Business &
Consumer
Gross sales or billing: $56,200,000

Service bureau for 800, 900 & 976 telephone lines.

NEUTRON INDUSTRIES
Subs. of State Industrial Products Inc
7107 N Black Canyon Hwy
Phoenix, AZ 85021-7619
Telephone: (602) 864-0090, (888) 712-
7127, FAX: (602) 357-3996, (877)
646-7337, E-Mail: questions@
neutronindustries.com, Web Site:
www.neutronindustries.com
Pres & COO, St Indus Prods: Robert
San Julian
Mktg Mgr: T. J. McDowell
Conducts Business: U.S., Canada, U.K.
Employees: 225
Primary Market Served: Business
Catalog available online
Indirect online sales
Advertising/Marketing Budget Related
to Direct Marketing: 76-100%
Direct Marketing ad budget:
Direct Mail: 60%
Telephone: 40%
Founded: 1978

Sell maintenance, cleaning & repair products to industrial institutions & commercial accounts.

NEVCO SCOREBOARD CO
301 E Harris Ave
Greenville, IL 62246-2193

Telephone: (618) 664-0360, (800) 851-
4040, FAX: (618) 664-0398, E-Mail:
sales@nevcoscoreboards.com, Web
Site: www.nevcoscoreboards.com
Pres: MG Nevinger
Mktg Staff, Dir: Tom Harnetiaux
Admin Coord: Angie Rankers
Conducts Business: Worldwide
Employees: 92
Primary Market Served: Consumer
Catalog available online
Indirect online sales
Founded: 1934
Gross sales or billing: $5,600,000

Manufacture scoreboards for sporting events.

THE NEW PIPER AIRCRAFT INC
2926 Piper Dr
Vero Beach, FL 32960-1955
Telephone: (772) 567-4361, FAX:
(772) 978-6573, E-Mail: marketing@
piper.com, Web Site: www.newpiper.
com
Pres & CEO: James K. Bass
VP Sls: Bob Kromer
Conducts Business: Worldwide
Employees: 100
Primary Market Served: Business &
Consumer
Catalog available online
Advertising/Marketing Budget Related
to Direct Marketing: 51-75%
Founded: 1937

Manufactures the world's only complete line of piston aircraft for personal, business & utility use.

NEW YORK POWER AUTHORITY
30 S Pearl St (10th fl)
Albany, NY 12207-3425
Telephone: (518) 433-6700, Web Site:
www.nypa.gov
Chmn: Frank McCullough Jr.
Vice Chmn: Michael J. Townsend
Pres & CEO: Timothy S. Carey
Exec VP & CFO: Joseph M. Del Sindaco
Exec VP, Gen Counsel: Thomas J.
Kelley
Employees: 25
Primary Market Served: Business &
Consumer
Catalog available online

Promotes energy efficiency to customers of New York Power. Branch location.

NEWELL RUBBERMAID, INC
3 Glenlake Pkwy
Atlanta, GA 30328

Telephone: (770) 418-7000, Web Site: www.newellrubbermaid.com
Primary Market Served: Business & Consumer

NIELSEN BUSINESS MEDIA

770 Broadway
New York, NY 10003
Telephone: (646) 654-4500, FAX: (646) 654-7212, E-Mail: bmcomm@nielsen.com, Web Site: www.nielsenbusinessmedia.com
Chmn & CEO: David L Calhoun
Vice Chmn & Exec VP: Susan D Whiting
Conducts Business: Worldwide
Employees: 25
Primary Market Served: Business & Consumer
Catalog available online
Gross sales or billing: $490,000,000

Producer of major trade shows; national variety merchandise show & national merchandise show. Also produces Orlando & Atlantic City Merchandise Show.

NILODOR INC

10966 Industrial Pkwy NW
Bolivar, OH 44612-8991
Telephone: (330) 874-1017, (800) 443-4321, FAX: (330) 874-3366, E-Mail: info@nilodor.com, Web Site: www.nilodor.com
Pres: Les W. Mitson
VP, Sls: Kurt Peterson
VP Mktg: Todd Sauser
Conducts Business: U.S.
Employees: 33
Primary Market Served: Business & Consumer
Advertising/Marketing Budget Related to Direct Marketing: 0-25%
Founded: 1954
Gross sales or billing: $3,100,000

Manufacturer of deodorizing products & cleaners.

NIMLOK

7420 N Lehigh Ave
Niles, IL 60714
Telephone: (847) 647-1012, (800) 233-8870, FAX: (847) 647-2044, E-Mail: info@nimlok.com, Web Site: www.nimlok.com
Pres: Simon Perutz
Dir: Dave Fugiel
Conducts Business: U.S.
Employees: 68
Primary Market Served: Business
Catalog available online
Advertising/Marketing Budget Related to Direct Marketing: 26-50%
Gross sales or billing: $20,000,000

Display & exhibit systems: portable panel systems, pop-ups, tabletop displays & custom modular exhibit systems: exhibit shipping cases; aluminum truss system.

NISSAN NORTH AMERICA INC

4400 Regent Blvd
Irving, TX 75063-2400
Telephone: (310) 532-3111, Web Site: www.nissanusa.com
Sr VP, Sls & Mktg: Brad Bradshaw
Conducts Business: U.S.
Primary Market Served: Consumer
Catalog available online

Sales, marketing & distribution of Nissan & Infiniti automobiles in the US.

NORMAN CONTROL CO

Div. of Coffman Manufacturing Corp
305 Cary Point Dr
Cary, IL 60013-2974
Telephone: (847) 639-5721, FAX: (847) 639-5755, E-Mail: susan@coffmanmfg.com, Web Site: www.coffmanmfg.com
Pres: Richard Coffman
Co-Owner: Susan Coffman
Conducts Business: U.S.
Employees: 23
Primary Market Served: Business & Consumer
Direct Marketing ad budget:
Direct Mail: 50%
Magazines: 50%
Founded: 1948
Gross sales or billing: $1,000,000

Institutional laundry equipment - dumpers, carts, hamper dumpers, hydraulic dumpers, barrel dumpers, lighted inspection tables & towel counting units.

NORMAN ROCKWELL MUSEUM

9 Glendale Rd, Rte 183
Stockbridge, MA 01262
Telephone: (413) 298-4100, (800) 742-9450, FAX: (413) 298-4144, E-Mail: emazzer@nrm.org, Web Site: www.nrm.org
Dir: Laurie Norton Moffatt
Dir: Terry Smith
Commun Coord: Ellen S. Mazzer
Store Mgr: Mike Duffy
Conducts Business: Worldwide
Employees: 63
Primary Market Served: Business & Consumer
Direct online sales
Advertising/Marketing Budget Related to Direct Marketing: 0-25%
Founded: 1967
Gross sales or billing: $4,197,553

Sells exclusive Norman Rockwell books, prints, signed lithographs & gift items through gift shop & website.

NORTHERN CROSS

Div. of Barancorp
214 N 2100 Rd
Lecompton, KS 66050
Telephone: (785) 887-6010, (800) 625-7233, FAX: (785) 887-6263
Pres & CEO: Dennis A. Baranski
Conducts Business: U.S., Canada, Japan, Western Europe
Primary Market Served: Business & Consumer
Catalog available online
Founded: 1984

Manufacturers of safety & survival products for distribution to industry, wholesalers, retailers & individuals. Distributes its proprietary products & other safety & survival products produced by other manufacturers in the field.

ᵀᴴᴱ_ᴰᴹᴬ NORTHERN SAFETY CO INC

PO Box 4250
Utica, NY 13504-4250
Telephone: (315) 793-4900, Web Site: www.northernsafety.com
Pres: Neil Sexton
Primary Market Served: Business

NORTHERN TOOL & EQUIPMENT INC

2800 Southcross Dr W
Burnsville, MN 55306-6936
Telephone: (952) 894-9510, (800) 221-0516, FAX: (952) 894-1020, Web Site: www.northerntool.com
Chmn & CEO: Donald L. Kotula
Pres: Chuck Albrecht
CFO: Tom Erickson
VP & Mktg Dir: Jay Berlin
Mktg Dir: Kevin Huggett
Conducts Business: Worldwide
Employees: 2,000
Catalog available online
Direct online sales
Advertising/Marketing Budget Related to Direct Marketing: 51-75%
Direct Marketing ad budget:
Direct Mail: 75%
Magazines: 10%
Newspapers: 5%
TV/Radio: 10%
Founded: 1981
Gross sales or billing: $349,000,000

Mail order marketer of industrial & consumer tools.

NORWOOD PROMOTIONAL PRODUCTS
14421 Myerlake Cir
Clearwater, FL 33760-2840
Telephone: (317) 275-2500, (800) 959-9138, FAX: (317) 275-2570, Web Site: www.norwood.com
Sr VP, Chief Mktg Officer: Jim Simone
Pres: Paul Lage MAS
VP Mktg & Mdsg: Andy Roth
Employees: 3,500
Primary Market Served: Business
Founded: 1989
Gross sales or billing: $330,000,000

Supply promotional products sold through distributors.

NUANCE SPEECH SOLUTIONS
One Wayside Rd
Burlington, MA 01803
Telephone: (781) 565-5000, FAX: (781) 565-5001, E-Mail: sales@speechworks.com, Web Site: www.nuance.com
Pres Speech Solutions Div: Stuart Patterson
Exec VP, Worldwide Mktg: Steve Chambers
CEO: Paul Ricci
Sr VP Mktg & Global Strategy: Robert J. Weidman
Primary Market Served: Business

Develop advanced speech recognition software for the call-center & telephone market.

NUCOR CORP
1915 Rexford Rd Ste 400
Charlotte, NC 28211-3888
Telephone: (704) 366-7000, FAX: (704) 362-4208, E-Mail: info@nucor.com, Web Site: nucor.com
Pres: Daniel D'Micco
Primary Market Served: Business
Founded: 1966

Manufacture steel & steel products.

NUNATURALS
2220 W Second Ave (Suite 1)
Eugene, OR 97402-7112
Telephone: (541) 344-9785, (800) 753-4372, FAX: (541) 343-0915, E-Mail: info@nunaturals.com, Web Site: www.nunaturals.com
Pres: Warren Sablosky
Gen Mgr: Travis Debacker
Conducts Business: U.S.
Employees: 8
Primary Market Served: Business & Consumer
Catalog available online
Indirect online sales
Founded: 1989

Vitamins, nutrients & herbs.

NAT NUSSBAUM & ASSOCIATES INC
1440 Coral Ridge Dr
Coral Springs, FL 33071-5433
Telephone: (954) 345-9131, FAX: (954) 345-0786, E-Mail: nlnmktg@aol.com
Pres: Nathan Nussbaum
Conducts Business: U.S., Canada, U.K., Australia
Employees: 1
Primary Market Served: Business
Advertising/Marketing Budget Related to Direct Marketing: 26-50%
Direct Marketing ad budget:
Direct Mail: 70%
Magazines: 5%
Newspapers: 5%
Telephone: 20%
Founded: 1992
Gross sales or billing: $400,000

Sell jewelry, electronics & other items to the mail order industry.

NUTRITIONAL RESEARCH ASSOCIATES INC
407 E Broad St
South Whitley, IN 46787-1001
Telephone: (260) 723-4931, (800) 456-4931, FAX: (260) 723-6297, E-Mail: info@nrfeeds.com, Web Site: www.nrfeeds.com
Pres: Barbara Pook
Mgr: Kerry Flater
Conducts Business: U.S., Canada, Australia, Singapore, Mexico, Caribbean, Latin America
Employees: 11
Primary Market Served: Business & Consumer
Advertising/Marketing Budget Related to Direct Marketing: 26-50%
Direct Marketing ad budget: $25,000
Magazines: 100%
Founded: 1934
Gross sales or billing: $2,000,000

Small animal nutritional products. Small animal & bird cages & equipment. Caged bird seed mixes & nutritional supplies. Small animal complete feeds. Horse, goat, & other livestock supplements.

OSRAM SYLVANIA
100 Endicott St
Danvers, MA 01923-3782
Telephone: (978) 750-2210, Web Site: www.sylvania.com
E-Sls Direct Mail Specialist: Tara Fuller
Primary Market Served: Business

OAKWOOD HOMES CORP
7800 McCloud Rd
Greensboro, NC 27409-9634
Telephone: (336) 664-2400, (800) 822-0633, FAX: (336) 315-3249, Web Site: www.oakwoodhomes.com
Pres: Dale Holmgren
Conducts Business: U.S.
Employees: 1,200
Primary Market Served: Consumer
Catalog available online
Gross sales or billing: $150,000,000

Homes to the public.

THE OCCASIONS GROUP
1750 Tower Blvd
North Mankato, MN 56003-1706
Telephone: (507) 625-6464
VP, Sls & Mktg: Jean Andersen

OFF THE WALL MAGNETICS LLC
60 SE Main St
Portland, OR 97214-3320
Telephone: (800) 337-2637, Web Site: www.4thefridge.com
Pres: Page Mesher

OFFICE DEPOT
6600 N Military Trl
Boca Raton, FL 33496-2434
Telephone: (561) 438-4800, (800) 937-3600, FAX: (561) 438-4001, Web Site: www.officedepot.com
Chmn, Dir & CEO: Steve Oland
Exec VP & CFO: Patricia A. McKay
Exec VP: Cynthia Campbell
VP, Mdsg: Barbara Pizzella
Employees: 52,000
Primary Market Served: Business & Consumer
Founded: 1986
Gross sales or billing: $15,000,000,000

Office products distributor.

OLAN MILLS INC
6060 Shallowford Rd.
Chattanooga, TN 37421-1611
Telephone: (423) 622-5141, (800) 251-6320, FAX: (423) 629-8128, Web Site: www.olanmills.com
Chmn & CEO: Robert L. McDowell
CIO: Steve Kraus
Dir Mktg: Lynette Darr
Conducts Business: U.S., Canada, U.K.
Employees: 4,000
Primary Market Served: Consumer
Advertising/Marketing Budget Related to Direct Marketing: 76-100%
Founded: 1932
Gross sales or billing: $156,700,000

Portrait sales company.

OLEDA & CO INC
7700 Camp Bowie W
Fort Worth, TX 76116-6450
Telephone: (817) 731-1147, (800) 731-4247, FAX: (817) 731-1149, E-Mail: oleda@oleda.com, Web Site: www.oleda.com
Pres: Oleda Baker
VP, Bus Devel: James Haun
Conducts Business: Worldwide
Primary Market Served: Consumer
Catalog available online
Direct online sales
Advertising/Marketing Budget Related to Direct Marketing: 51-75%
Founded: 1969

Anti-aging, beauty, fitness & health national mail order company. Products sold through various mail order media, including TV. Sold in bulk to countries outside U.S.

OLIVER OF ADRIAN INC
PO Box 189
Adrian, MI 49221-0189
Telephone: (517) 263-2132, (877) 668-0885, FAX: (517) 265-8698, E-Mail: info@oliverinstrument.com, Web Site: www.oliverofadrian.com
Sec: Mary Smith
VP: Neal Garrison
Conducts Business: Worldwide
Employees: 6
Primary Market Served: Business & Consumer
Catalog available online
Advertising/Marketing Budget Related to Direct Marketing: 0-25%
Direct Marketing ad budget: $4,000
Online: $360
Telephone: $140
Founded: 1913
Gross sales or billing: $900,000

Manufacture a complete line of metal-working machine tools such as automatic & manual drill grinders, automatic & manual cutter & tool grinders & point thinning machines. Customers include major cutting tool manufacturers, automotive firms, construction equipment companies & farm equipment manufacturers.

OLYMPIA SALES INC
215 Moody Rd
Enfield, CT 06083-3207
Telephone: (860) 749-0751, (800) 338-9992, FAX: (860) 814-4451, E-Mail: info@olympiasales.net, Web Site: www.olympiasales.us
Chmn: Arthur O'Hara
Pres & Dir: Thomas A. O'Hara
Mktg Dir: Diane Spiro
Conducts Business: U.S.
Employees: 40

Primary Market Served: Business & Consumer
Catalog available online
Indirect online sales
Founded: 1966
Gross sales or billing: $7,200,000

Manufacturer & distributor of greeting cards, stationary, and office supplies.

OMAHA VACCINE CO
Div. of CSR
11143 Mockingbird Dr
Omaha, NE 68137-2332
Telephone: (402) 731-9600, (800) 367-4444, FAX: (800) 242-9447, E-Mail: customerservice@OmahaVaccine.com, Web Site: www.omahavaccine.com
Chmn & CEO: Scott Remington
VP: Jim Hoing
Conducts Business: Worldwide
Employees: 90
Primary Market Served: Business & Consumer
Catalog available online
Direct online sales

Market animal health & animal related products.

OMNI FARM
1369 Calloway Gap Rd
West Jefferson, NC 28694
Telephone: (336) 982-3475, (800) TREE-FARM, FAX: (336) 982-4163, E-Mail: omnifarm@omnifarm.com, Web Site: www.omnifarm.com
Pres: Hal F. Gimlin
Exec Dir: Pat Herbert
Conducts Business: U.S.
Employees: 11
Primary Market Served: Business & Consumer
Catalog available online
Direct online sales
Advertising/Marketing Budget Related to Direct Marketing: 76-100%
Direct Marketing ad budget: $30,000
Direct Mail: 50%
Online: 50%
Founded: 1972
Gross sales or billing: $1,000,000

Sell real Christmas trees, wreaths, garlands, greenery & Christmas tree stands through catalogs & direct to consumer.

ON-HAND ADHESIVES INC
940 Telser Rd
Lake Zurich, IL 60047-6714
Telephone: (847) 437-7773, (800) 323-5158, FAX: (847) 437-8006, E-Mail: help@on-hand.com, Web Site: www.on-hand.com
Chmn Bd & CEO: George L. Cooper
Pres: Michael Cooper

Sec & Treas: Margaret Cooper
Conducts Business: U.S.
Employees: 20
Primary Market Served: Business
Catalog available online
Direct online sales
Direct Marketing ad budget:
Direct Mail: $75,000
Telephone: $25,000
Gross sales or billing: $3,000,000

Industrial distributor of adhesives with branch offices in Milwaukee, Saint Louis & Los Angeles.

THE DMA 1-800-FLOWERS.COM
1 Old Country Rd (Suite 500)
Carle Place, NY 11514-1847
Telephone: (516) 237-6000, Web Site: www.1800flowers.com
Dir, Third Party Mktg: Jill Eastman Vidal
Primary Market Served: Business & Consumer

100% REAL ESTATE INC
1810 Lee Rd
Orlando, FL 32810-5702
Telephone: (800) 454-3422, E-Mail: rcs@100percentflorida.com, Web Site: www.100percentflorida.com
Pres: Robert C. Sinclair
VP: Colby Sinclair
Conducts Business: U.S., Japan, Central America, Korea
Employees: 33
Primary Market Served: Business & Consumer
Advertising/Marketing Budget Related to Direct Marketing: 51-75%
Direct Marketing ad budget: $28,000
Direct Mail: 15%
Magazines: 35%
Newspapers: 50%
Gross sales or billing: $60,000,000

Real estate broker specializing in businesses, warehouses, office buildings & land in Florida.

ONEIDA LTD
Div. of Oneida Ltd
163-181 Kenwood Ave
Oneida, NY 13421-2829
Telephone: (315) 361-3000, (888) 263-7195, FAX: (315) 361-3700, Web Site: www.oneida.com
Pres & CEO: James E. Joseph
EVP & CFO: Andrew G. Church
CIO & SVP, IT: Rob Hack
EVP: W. Tim Runyan
CMO & SVP Strat Plng: David Sank
Conducts Business: Worldwide
Employees: 905
Primary Market Served: Business & Consumer
Catalog available online

Direct online sales
Advertising/Marketing Budget Related
to Direct Marketing: 0-25%
Founded: 1880
Gross sales or billing: $350,800,000

Manufacturer and supplier of flatware,
hollow ware & giftware, crystal and
glass products.

OPEN TEXT INC

275 Frank Tompa Dr
Waterloo, ON, Canada N2L 0A1
Telephone: (519) 888-9933, (800) 499-
6544, FAX: (519) 888-0677, E-Mail:
support@opentext.com, Web Site:
www.opentext.com
Chmn: P. Thomas Jenkins
Pres, CEO & Dir: John Shackleton
CFO: Paul J. McFeeters
Exec VP, Bus Devel: M. William
Forquer
Exec VP, Worldwide Sls: John A.
Kirkham
Conducts Business: U.S.
Employees: 2,700
Primary Market Served: Business &
Consumer
Advertising/Marketing Budget Related
to Direct Marketing: 51-75%
Founded: 1971
Gross sales or billing: $595,000,000

Software developer. Publishes a
calendaring/group scheduling software
program called OnTime for the IBM
PC's & compatibles. Markets to Fortune 1000 & government agencies that
have a need for an organizational tool
to better manage their time & schedule
group meetings. Publish OnTime for
Windows Network version & On Time
Enterprise for Novell Netware, Banyan
Vines & Windows NT.

OPRYLAND

Div. of Gaylord Entertainment Co
2800 Opryland Dr
Nashville, TN 37214-1200
Telephone: (615) 889-1000, FAX:
(615) 871-7741, E-Mail: info@
gaylordhotels.com, Web Site: www.
oprylandhotels.com
Pres: Jerry Sevigny
Conducts Business: U.S.
Employees: 4,000
Primary Market Served: Business &
Consumer

Meeting, convention & entertainment
destination.

ORACLE CORP

500 Oracle Pkwy
Redwood Shores, CA 94065-1675
Telephone: (650) 506-7000, (800) 633-
0738, FAX: (650) 506-7200, Web
Site: www.oracle.com

Chmn Bd: Jeffrey O. Henley
CEO & Dir: Larry Ellison
Co-Pres, CFO & Dir: Safra A. Catz
Sr VP & Chief Mktg Officer: Judith
Sim
Conducts Business: Worldwide
Employees: 74,674
Primary Market Served: Business &
Consumer
Founded: 1977
Gross sales or billing: $17,274,000,000

Supplier of database management software & services.

ORCHARD SUPPLY HARDWARE

Subs. of Sears Holdings Corp
6450 Via Del Oro St
San Jose, CA 95119
Telephone: (408) 281-3500, FAX:
(408) 225-0388, Web Site: www.osh.
com
CEO: Jerry Post
CFO: Michael Baumann
VP, Mktg: Rick Saunders
Employees: 7,000
Primary Market Served: Consumer
Founded: 1931

Hardware.

OSMONICS INC

5951 Clearwater Dr
Minnetonka, MN 55343-8990
Telephone: (952) 264-3937, (800) 605-
6698, FAX: (952) 536-3301, Web
Site: www.osmonics.com
CEO: D. Dean Spatz
Exec VP, Bus Devel, Strategy, Sls &
Mktg: Ed Fierko
Sr VP, Sls & Mktg: Roger Miller
VP, Fin & Admin: L. Lee Runzheimer
Corp Commun Mgr: Kay A. Kettwig
Mktg Coord: Karen Schurmann
Conducts Business: Worldwide
Employees: 1,350
Primary Market Served: Business
Catalog available online
Advertising/Marketing Budget Related
to Direct Marketing: 0-25%
Founded: 1969
Gross sales or billing: $160,000,000

Manufacturer of high technology
equipment, controls & components that
purify water, separate and handle flu-
ids, remove dissolved solids, concen-
trate wastes and enable clean water to
be recycled or discharged to
environment.

OTTO ENVIRONMENTAL SYSTEMS OF NORTH AMERICA

12700 General Dr, PO Box 410251
Charlotte, NC 28273

Telephone: (704) 588-9191, (800) 227-
5885, FAX: (704) 588-5250, E-Mail:
info@otto-usa.com, Web Site: www.
otto-usa.com
CEO: Steve Stradtman
Dir Opers: Brenda Beaver

Manufacture bins & two-wheeled trash
carts for material recycling & solid
wastes.

OUR DESIGNS INC

1212 W Fourth Plain Blvd
Vancouver, WA 98660-2023
Telephone: (859) 282-5500, (800) 382-
5252, FAX: (859) 282-5508, E-Mail:
sales@ourdesigns.com, Web Site:
www.ourdesigns.com
CEO: Mike Daugherty
Pres: Carol Daugherty
Employees: 22
Primary Market Served: Business &
Consumer
Catalog available online
Direct online sales
Advertising/Marketing Budget Related
to Direct Marketing: 51-75%
Founded: 1981
Gross sales or billing: $2,600,000

Direct mail for firefighters, police officers, EMTs & paramedics.

P & H MINING EQUIPMENT

Subs. of Joy Global Inc
4400 W National Ave
Milwaukee, WI 53214-3639
Telephone: (414) 671-4400, FAX:
(414) 671-7618, Web Site: www.
phmining.com
Chmn: John Hanson
Pres & CEO: Michael W. Sutherlin
CFO & Treas: James H. Woodward Jr.
Exec VP & COO: Mark E. Readinger
Exec VP: Edward L. Doheny II
Conducts Business: Worldwide
Employees: 13,700
Primary Market Served: Business
Catalog available online
Founded: 1884
Gross sales or billing: $2,000,000,000

Manufacture & distribution of equipment for pulp and paper-making machinery, surface & underground
mining.

PC/NAMETAG INC

124 Horizon Dr
Verona, WI 53593
Telephone: (608) 845-1850, (800) 233-
9767, E-Mail: sales@pcnametag.
com, Web Site: www.pcnametag.com
Pres: Nick Topitzes
Sls Asst: Darren Walker
Employees: 45
Primary Market Served: Business
Catalog available online

Direct online sales
Advertising/Marketing Budget Related
to Direct Marketing: 76-100%
Founded: 1980

Sell meeting & conference supplies.

PI INC
213 Dennis St
Athens, TN 37303-2995
Telephone: (423) 745-6213, FAX:
(423) 745-7039, Web Site: www.pi-
inc.com
Pres: Jeff Beene
Conducts Business: Worldwide
Employees: 500
Primary Market Served: Business
Catalog available online
Indirect online sales

Supplier of injection molded plastic
components.

PVC PLASTICS CO
4406 E Morgan Ave
Evansville, IN 47715-2254
Telephone: (812) 476-3592, (800) 782-
7527, FAX: (812) 474-4531
Pres: William D. Smith
Conducts Business: U.S.
Employees: 35
Primary Market Served: Business &
Consumer
Founded: 1965

Plumbing wholesaler & distributor of
plastic pipes, valves, fittings, pumps &
drainage products.

PACCAR INC
777 106th Ave NE
Bellevue, WA 98004-5027
Telephone: (425) 468-7400, FAX:
(425) 468-8216, Web Site: www.
paccar.com
Chmn & CEO: Mark C. Piggott
Dir: Alison J. Carnwath
Dir: John M. Fluke
Pres: Thomas Plimpton
VP & CIO: Janice Skredsvig
Employees: 21,000
Primary Market Served: Business
Catalog available online
Indirect online sales
Gross sales or billing: $16,000,000,000

Manufacturer of heavy duty trucks &
industrial winches.

PACE INC
9030 Junction Dr
Annapolis Junction, MD 20701
Telephone: (910) 695-7223, FAX:
(910) 944-1724, Web Site: www.
paceworldwide.com/index.asp
CEO & Pres: Paul Dunham
Mktg: Sandra Dunham
Primary Market Served: Business

Assembly, rework & repair of highly
advanced electronics including printed
circuit assemblies. Manufactures fume
extraction systems.

PACE UNIVERSITY - DIV OF ENROLLMENT MGMT
Pace Plaza
New York, NY 10038-1598
Telephone: (212) 346-1781, (866) 722-
3338, FAX: (212) 346-1821, Web
Site: www.pace.edu/pace/
Interim VP Enrollment Mngmt: Robina
Schepp
Conducts Business: U.S.
Primary Market Served: Business &
Consumer
Founded: 1862

Sell Pace University education to both
adolescents & adults.

PACIFIC CYCLE INC
dba Mongoose, Schwinn & GT
Subs of Dorel Industries (CN)
4902 Hammersly Rd
Madison, WI 53711
Telephone: (608) 268-2468, (800) 724-
9466, FAX: (847) 236-3692, (847)
573-0602, E-Mail: info@
pacificcycle.com, Web Site: www.
pacificcycle.com
Pres & CEO: Jeff Frehner
Exec VP Mktg: Bruno Maier
Conducts Business: Worldwide
Employees: 360
Primary Market Served: Business
Gross sales or billing: $80,700,000

Manufacturer & distributor of Mongoose Pro, Mongoose, MGX, Road-
master & Flexible Flyer brand name
recreation equipment.

PACIFIC PROPELLER INC
Subs. of Precision Aerospace Corp
5802 S 228th St
Kent, WA 98032-1810
Telephone: (253) 872-7767, (800) 722-
7767, FAX: (253) 872-7221, E-Mail:
jheikke@pacprop.com, Web Site:
www.pacificpropeller.com
VP & Gen Mgr: Jeff Heikke
Prod Sls Mgr: Al Hayward
Sls & Mktg Dir: Don Lownds
Conducts Business: U.S., Canada
Primary Market Served: Business &
Consumer
Direct Marketing ad budget: $72,000
Direct Mail: 26%
Magazines: 74%
Founded: 1946

Manufacture, distribution, servicing &
maintenance of aircraft propellers.

PAL HEALTH TECHNOLOGY
1805 Riverway Dr
Pekin, IL 61554-9309
Telephone: (309) 347-8785, (800) 223-
2957, FAX: (309) 477-4456, Web
Site: www.palhealth.com
VP: Lois Barnum
Conducts Business: U.S.
Employees: 180
Primary Market Served: Business
Catalog available online
Gross sales or billing: $15,000,000

Manufacture & market national & international prescription orthotics &
insoles.

PARAGON LABORATORIES
20433 Earl St
Torrance, CA 90503-2414
Telephone: (310) 370-1563, (800) 231-
3670, FAX: (310) 370-7354, E-Mail:
sales@paragonlabsusa.com, Web
Site: www.paragonlabsusa.com
CEO: Jay Kaufman
COO: Richard Kaufman
Conducts Business: Worldwide
Employees: 50
Primary Market Served: Business &
Consumer
Gross sales or billing: $22,000,000

Manufacturer, distributor & packager
of nutritional supplements, life cycle
products & weight reduction products.

ᴛʜᴇ ᴅᴍᴀ PARKER STEEL CO
4239 Monroe St, Box 2883
Toledo, OH 43606-1943
Telephone: (419) 473-2481, (800) 333-
4140, FAX: (419) 471-2655, Web
Site: www.metricmetal.com
Pres & CEO: Paul Goldner
Pres: Jerry Hidalgo
VP: Mark Goldner
Mktg: Sharon Goldner
Sls Mgr: Jeff Meyer
Conducts Business: U.S., Canada,
Mexico
Employees: 23
Primary Market Served: Business
Catalog available online
Indirect online sales
Founded: 1955
Gross sales or billing: $6,300,000

Steel warehouse specializing in metric
sizes.

PARKER SYSTEMS INC
2880 Yadkin Rd
Chesapeake, VA 23323-0360
Telephone: (757) 485-2955, (866) 472-
7537, FAX: (757) 487-5872, E-Mail:
info@parkersystemsinc.com, Web
Site: www.parkersystemsinc.com
Pres: Ellen Parker
Opers Dir: John Parker

Sls Mgr: Pam McSwain
Conducts Business: Worldwide
Employees: 28
Primary Market Served: Business
Catalog available online
Advertising/Marketing Budget Related
  to Direct Marketing: 0-25%
Direct Marketing ad budget:
Direct Mail: 30%
Magazines: 10%
Online: 50%
Telephone: 10%
Founded: 1970

Manufacture oil spill cleaning equipment & erosion control products.

PASLODE

Div. of Illinois Tool Works
888 Forest Edge Dr
Vernon Hills, IL 60061-8117
Telephone: (847) 634-1900, (800) 222-
  6990, FAX: (847) 634-6602, E-Mail:
  tech@paslode.com, Web Site: www.
  paslode.com
Mgr: Martin Jahn
Sls Mgr: Mark Boutelle
Bus Unit Mgr: Chuck Heinlen
Conducts Business: U.S., Canada, West
  Europe, Japan, Australia
Employees: 900
Primary Market Served: Business
Catalog available online
Indirect online sales
Founded: 1935
Gross sales or billing: $150,000,000

Manufacturer & marketer of cordless & pneumatic fastening systems for construction, remodeling & industrial applications.

THE DMA PASTERNACK ENTERPRISES INC

PO Box 16759
Irvine, CA 92623-6759
Telephone: (949) 261-1920, Web Site:
  www.pasternack.com
Pres: Chuck Becker
Primary Market Served: Business

PEERLESS RATTAN

687 Miller Rd
Plainwell, MI 49080-9538
Telephone: (269) 685-1858, (877) 611-
  2263, E-Mail: sales@peerlessrattan.
  com, Web Site: www.peerlessrattan.
  com
Owner: Helen Cribbs
Conducts Business: U.S.
Primary Market Served: Business &
  Consumer
Catalog available online
Indirect online sales
Advertising/Marketing Budget Related
  to Direct Marketing: 0-25%
Gross sales or billing: $200,000

Mail order house specializing in raw materials of rattan, chair cane webbing, seagrass, basketry reeds, ash splint & fiber rush.

PENNSTREET BAKERY

Div. of Savory Foods
900 Hynes SW
Grand Rapids, MI 49507
Telephone: (616) 241-2583, (800) 84-
  CAKES, FAX: (616) 241-6332, Web
  Site: www.pennstreet.com
Pres: Dan Abraham
Conducts Business: U.S.
Employees: 30
Primary Market Served: Business &
  Consumer
Catalog available online
Direct online sales
Advertising/Marketing Budget Related
  to Direct Marketing: 0-25%
Founded: 1972

Mail order bakery goods.

PENSKE LOGISTICS

Div. of Penske Truck Leasing
Rte 10 Green Hills
Reading, PA 19603
Telephone: (610) 775-6000, (800) 529-
  6531, FAX: (610) 775-6432, Web
  Site: www.penskelogistics.com
Pres: Vincent Hartnett
Sr VP, Sls: Joe Gallick
Corp Commun Mgr: Louise Moyer
PR: Randy Ryerson
PR: Jennifer Ryan
Conducts Business: U.S.
Employees: 10,000
Primary Market Served: Business
Catalog available online
Indirect online sales
Founded: 1969
Gross sales or billing: $2,100,000,000

Provider of integrated logistics services and supply chain management.

PENTON LEARNING SYSTEMS INC

535 Fifth Ave (fl 8)
New York, NY 10017-8011
Telephone: (212) 885-2700, FAX:
  (212) 885-2703, E-Mail: info@iqpc.
  com, Web Site: www.iqpc.com
Cust Svc Dir: Patti Kahwaty
Conducts Business: U.S.
Employees: 60
Primary Market Served: Business

Marketer of business educational materials.

PERFECTION TIP CO/ CAMPING PRODUCTS CO

Subs. of Parrish Enterprises
1340 W Cowles St

Long Beach, CA 90803
Telephone: (562) 491-0076, (800) 525-
  4835, FAX: (562) 435-7599
Pres: J. Parrish
Gen Mgr: David Hill
Conducts Business: Worldwide
Employees: 12
Primary Market Served: Business
Gross sales or billing: $800,000

Manufacture guides/tips for fishing rods. Manufacture & import camping products (i.e., backpack stoves, lanterns, slingshots/ammo, butane fuel) for outdoor sports.

PERFORMANCE MEDIA SOLUTIONS INC & TRUEWORX INC

4001 S Decatur Blvd (#37-425)
Las Vegas, NV 89103-5860
Telephone: (866) 827-7077
Pres: Clive Stanley
Primary Market Served: Business &
  Consumer

PERNOD RICARD USA

Div. of Joseph E Seagram & Sons
100 Manhattanville Rd.
Purchase, NY 10577-2134
Telephone: (914) 848-4800, Web Site:
  www.pernod-ricard-usa.com
Sr VP of Mktg: Kevin Fennessey
DM Dir: Mary Ellen Griffin
Sr VP Spirits Mktg: Matt Aeppli
Conducts Business: Worldwide
Primary Market Served: Business &
  Consumer

Producer of premium liquors & wines.

PERRYGRAF

25W550 Geneva Rd (Suite 1934)
Carol Stream, IL 60188-2225
Telephone: (630) 665-3333, (800) 323-
  4433, FAX: (630) 665-3491, E-Mail:
  info2@americanperrygraf.com, Web
  Site: www.perrygraf.com
Dir Sls & Mktg: Don Hoff
Mktg Dir: Cathie Smith
Sls Mgr: Karen Vidoni
Conducts Business: Worldwide
Employees: 35
Primary Market Served: Business
Catalog available online
Advertising/Marketing Budget Related
  to Direct Marketing: 76-100%
Direct Marketing ad budget: $300,000
Direct Mail: 85%
Magazines: 5%
Telephone: 10%
Founded: 1934
Gross sales or billing: $5,000,000

Design & manufacture slide-charts, wheel-charts & pop-up calendars.

RJ PERSSON ENTERPRISES INC

1208 Kent Ave (Suite 101)
Montrose, CO 81402-5228
Telephone: (303) 249-6000, FAX:
 (303) 249-0800
Pres: Richard Persson
Conducts Business: U.S., Canada
Primary Market Served: Consumer
Founded: 1982

List owner with databases for opportunity seekers.

THE DMA PETEDGE

100 Cummings Ctr (307B)
Beverly, MA 01915-6107
Telephone: (978) 998-8100, (800) 738-
 3343, FAX: (978) 887-8499, E-Mail:
 support@petedge.com, Web Site:
 www.petedge.com
Pres: Andrew Katz
VP, Fin & Opers: Dale Robinson
Primary Market Served: Business &
 Consumer
Catalog available online
Direct online sales

Mail order pet supplies.

PFAELZER BROTHERS

Div. of Hickory Farms Inc
1505 Holland Rd
Maumee, OH 43537
Telephone: (419) 893-7611, (800) 345-
 9290, FAX: (419) 893-0164, Web
 Site: www.phaelzerbrothers.com
CEO, Pres & Chmn: John J. Langdon
Sr VP, Bus Devel: Ike Herb
VP, HR: Amy Heaton
VP, Sls & Mktg: Erik Long
VP & CFO: Mark Wagner
Conducts Business: U.S., Japan
Employees: 30
Primary Market Served: Business &
 Consumer
Catalog available online
Direct online sales
Advertising/Marketing Budget Related
 to Direct Marketing: 76-100%

Sell gourmet beef steak gift packs &
beef snack products via direct mail.
Sell beef snacks to distribution
companies.

PFIZER INC

235 E 42nd St
New York, NY 10017
Telephone: (212) 733-2323, Web Site:
 www.pfizer.com
Chmn: Henry A. McKinnell
CEO: Jeffrey B. Kindler
Conducts Business: Worldwide
Employees: 87,000
Primary Market Served: Business &
 Consumer

Catalog available online
Founded: 1849
Gross sales or billing: $48,371,000,000

Make & market agricultural, chemical,
pharmaceutical & food products.

PHARMAVITE CORP LLC (HQ)

Subs. of Otsuka
8510 Balboa
Northridge, CA 91325-3583
Telephone: (818) 221-6200, (800) 423-
 2405, FAX: (818) 221-6618, Web
 Site: www.pharmavite.com
VP Bus Devel: Tom Zimmerman
Pres & CEO: Connie Barry
Exec VP & CFO: Steve Chopp
Conducts Business: U.S., Canada, Japan
Employees: 850
Primary Market Served: Consumer
Gross sales or billing: $108,900,000

Manufacture vitamins & skin care
products. Fulfill internationally continuity for customer.

PHILIP MORRIS USA INC

Subs. Altria Holdings Group
6601 W Broad St
Richmond, VA 23230-1701
Telephone: (804) 274-2000, FAX:
 (804) 484-8231, Web Site: www.
 philipmorrisusa.com
Chmn & CEO: Michael E. Szymaczyk
Pres & CEO: William Gifford
VP, Marlboro: Francisca Rahardja
Sr VP Mfg Opers: Gary R Ruth
Primary Market Served: Business
Catalog available online
Indirect online sales
Advertising/Marketing Budget Related
 to Direct Marketing: 0-25%

Manufacture & sell tobacco & food
products.

PHILLIPS KILN SERVICE LTD

2607 Dakota Ave Ste 2
South Sioux City, NE 68776-3256
Telephone: (402) 494-6837, (800) 831-
 0876, FAX: (402) 494-6858, E-Mail:
 info@kilm.com, Web Site: www.
 kiln.com
Chmn: Eric Bertness
Pres: Daryl Austin
VP, Intl Sls: Walter M. Gebhart
Conducts Business: U.S., Canada
Employees: 60
Primary Market Served: Business
Catalog available online

Provide replacement parts, installation
& repair of industrial rotary
equipment.

PHOENIX LEARNING GROUP INC

141A Millwell Dr
Maryland Heights, MO 63043-2509
Telephone: (314) 569-0211, (800) 221-
 1274, FAX: (314) 569-2834, E-Mail:
 dealersales@phoenixlearninggroup.
 com, Web Site: www.
 phoenixlearninggroup.com
VP Market Devel: Kathy Longsworth
VP, Opers & Mngmt: Erin Bryant
Customer Svc Mgr: Rhonda Sterling
Sls Rep: Antoinette Montegrande
Sls Rep: Shane Egan
Conducts Business: Worldwide
Employees: 25
Primary Market Served: Business &
 Consumer
Catalog available online
Direct online sales
Direct Marketing ad budget:
Direct Mail: 10%
Magazines: 20%
Online: 40%
Telephone: 30%
Founded: 1973

Market video cassette & multimedia
programs in fields of health, business
& industry. Also, film & video programs in education, social services &
television.

PHOENIX POKE BOATS INC

106 Bethford Rd
McKee, KY 40447
Telephone: (606) 965-2803, E-Mail:
 pokeboat@pokeboat.com, Web Site:
 www.pokeboat.com
Pres: Tom G. Wilson
Conducts Business: Worldwide
Primary Market Served: Consumer
Catalog available online
Indirect online sales
Advertising/Marketing Budget Related
 to Direct Marketing: 0-25%
Direct Marketing ad budget:
Direct Mail: 10%
Magazines: 60%
Telephone: 30%
Founded: 1973

Manufacture & direct market small
boats & duck boats.

PHOTOWORKS

1 American Rd
Cleveland, OH 44144-2301
Telephone: (206) 281-1390, (800)
 PHOTOWORKS, FAX: (206) 284-
 5357, E-Mail: info@photoworks.
 com, Web Site: www.photoworks.
 com
Chmn: Joseph W. Waechter
Pres & CEO: Andy L. Wood
CFO: David M. Douglass
VP Bus Devel: David Kaill

VP Engrng: Dan Zimmerman
Conducts Business: U.S., Canada
Employees: 400
Primary Market Served: Consumer
Catalog available online
Direct online sales
Advertising/Marketing Budget Related
  to Direct Marketing: 0-25%
Direct Marketing ad budget:
Direct Mail: $4,000,000
Founded: 1976
Gross sales or billing: $11,000,000

Specialize in 35mm motion picture
photographic film & processing for
consumers.

PHYSICAL THERAPY INSTITUTE INC

12630 Monte Vista Rd (Suite 204)
Poway, CA 92064
Telephone: (858) 485-7103
Owner: Mary Hall
Primary Market Served: Consumer

Physical therapy.

PHYSICIANS PLANNING ASSOCIATION SERVICES

350 Fairway Dr (Suite 200), Hillsboro
  Executive Center N
Deerfield Beach, FL 33441-1834
Telephone: (954) 571-1877, (800) 221-
  2168, FAX: (954) 571-8582, E-Mail:
  insurance@assnservices.com, Web
  Site: www.physiciansplanning.com
Chmn: Patricia Arden
Sr VP: Stuart Liebowitz
Insurance Mgr: Michael Haggerty
Membership Svc Mgr: Joseph Santoli
Conducts Business: U.S.
Employees: 25
Primary Market Served: Business &
  Consumer
Catalog available online
Indirect online sales
Advertising/Marketing Budget Related
  to Direct Marketing: 76-100%
Direct Marketing ad budget:
Direct Mail: $600,000
Founded: 1963
Gross sales or billing: $11,000,000

Provide economic & financial benefits
to physicians, dentists & professionals
through American Professional Practice
Association, National Association of
Residents & Interns & National Association of the Professions.

THE PILLSBURY CO

Subs. of General Mills
PO Box 9452, General Mills Inc
Minneapolis, MN 55440-9452
Telephone: (763) 764-7600, (800) 775-
  4777, FAX: (763) 764-8330, Web
  Site: www.pillsbury.com

Chmn: Stephen W. Sanger
Pres, CEO & Dir: Kendall J. Powell
CFO: Robert Briggs
Exec VP: Y. Marc Belton
Sr VP: Rory Delaney
Conducts Business: Worldwide
Primary Market Served: Consumer
Catalog available online
Indirect online sales

International food, drink, restaurant &
retail company.

THE PIN MAN

PO Box 52817
Tulsa, OK 74152-0187
Telephone: (918) 587-2405, FAX:
  (918) 745-2162, Web Site: www.
  positivepin.com
Pres: Bern L. Gentry
VP: Michelle Gentry
Sec & Treas: Eric Cahn
Conducts Business: Canada, Germany,
  England, France
Employees: 8
Primary Market Served: Business &
  Consumer
Advertising/Marketing Budget Related
  to Direct Marketing: 51-75%
Direct Marketing ad budget: $75,000
Magazines: 100%
Founded: 1973
Gross sales or billing: $1,000,000

Custom & stock lapel pins, totes, pens,
pencils, mugs, smocks, plaques, awards
& teacher gifts.

PINE CASTLE ANIMAL HOSPITAL

5250 S Orange Ave
Orlando, FL 32809
Telephone: (407) 855-5010
Owner: Craig Lautenschlager DVM
Primary Market Served: Consumer

Animal hospital.

PINKERTON SECURITY & INVESTIGATION SERVICES

Subs Securitas Security Services USA,
  Inc
2 Campus Dr
Parsippany, NJ 07054-4499
Telephone: (973) 397-2276, (800) 724-
  1616, FAX: (973) 397-2491, Web
  Site: www.ci-pinkerton.com
Pres: Ron Long
VP Sls & Mktg: Bruce Scherer
Conducts Business: Worldwide
Primary Market Served: Business
Advertising/Marketing Budget Related
  to Direct Marketing: 26-50%
Founded: 1850

Security & investigative agency.

PIZZA HUT INC

7100 Corporate Dr
Plano, TX 75024-4100
Telephone: (972) 338-7700, (866) 298-
  6986, FAX: (972) 338-6869, Web
  Site: www.pizzahut.com
Pres: Scott Bergen
CPO: Paul Moskowitz
CFO: David Gibbs
Employees: 1,200
Primary Market Served: Business &
  Consumer
Gross sales or billing: $26,000,000

Restaurant franchiser.

POLAROID CORP

4350 Baker Rd
Minnetonka, MN 55343-8684
Telephone: (781) 386-2000, (800) 765-
  2764, FAX: (781) 386-3263, Web
  Site: www.polaroid.com
Chmn & CEO: Gary T. DiCamillo
Pres: J Michael Pocock
Dir Media Rels: Lorrie Parent
Primary Market Served: Business &
  Consumer

Design, manufacture & market worldwide a variety of products primarily in
instant imaging recording.

POLY ONE CORP

33587 Walker Rd
Avon Lake, OH 44012
Telephone: (440) 930-1000, (866)
  POLY-ONE, FAX: (440) 930-1428,
  Web Site: www.polyone.com
Pres, CEO & Chmn Bd: Steve Newlin
Sr VP & CFO: W. David Wilson
Sr VP, CIO & HR: Kenneth M. Smith
Sr VP & Gen Mgr: Bernard Baert
Sr VP: Michael E. Kahler
Conducts Business: Worldwide
Primary Market Served: Business
Catalog available online
Indirect online sales
Advertising/Marketing Budget Related
  to Direct Marketing: 0-25%
Gross sales or billing: $1,000,000,000

Business-to-business marketer of plastic raw materials.

POLYNESIAN CULTURAL CENTER

2255 Kuhio Ave (Suite 1010)
Honolulu, HI 96815-2648
Telephone: (808) 293-3333, (800) 367-
  7060, FAX: (888) 722-7339, E-Mail:
  internetrez@polynesia.com, Web
  Site: www.polynesia.com
Chmn: Ted Jacobson
Pres: Lester W.B. Moore
Sr VP, Mktg & Sls: Alfred Grace
VP, Fin: Greg Gollaher
Retail Sls & Mktg Mgr: Eric Workman

Conducts Business: U.S.
Employees: 1,000
Primary Market Served: Business & Consumer
Catalog available online
Indirect online sales
Advertising/Marketing Budget Related to Direct Marketing: 0-25%
Founded: 1963
Gross sales or billing: $1,000,000

Merchandiser of South Pacific crafts & goods. Producer & distributor of Polynesian videos, audios, books & IMAX films.

POSITION TECHNOLOGIES INC
2325 Dean St (Suite 800)
Saint Charles, IL 60175
Telephone: (630) 262-5300, FAX: (630) 232-2998, Web Site: www.positiontech.com
Pres: Ken Johnson
Primary Market Served: Business

POSTY CARDS INC
1600 Olive St
Kansas City, MO 64127-2539
Telephone: (816) 231-2323, (800) 554-5018, FAX: (888) 577-3800, E-Mail: customerservice@postycards.com, Web Site: www.postycards.com
Pres: Lance H. Jessee
Mktg Dir: Janet Coats
Conducts Business: Worldwide
Employees: 38
Primary Market Served: Business & Consumer
Catalog available online
Indirect online sales
Advertising/Marketing Budget Related to Direct Marketing: 0-25%
Founded: 1948
Gross sales or billing: $4,000,000

Manufacture & market greeting cards & calendars.

POWER & TELEPHONE SUPPLY
44 Hull St # 2
Randolph, VT 05060-1102
Telephone: (800) 451-4381, FAX: (802) 234-5006, E-Mail: cablesales@ptsupply.com, Web Site: www.ptsupply.com/enterprise
Dir Sls: Cyrus Parker
Mktg Coord: Valerie Wild
Conducts Business: U.S.
Primary Market Served: Business
Catalog available online
Advertising/Marketing Budget Related to Direct Marketing: 51-75%
Founded: 1946

Distributor of communication cables, wire, supplies & equipment, test equipment, fiber optic & security cameras.

POWER MUSIC
P.O. Box 3030
Salt Lake City, UT 84110
Telephone: (801) 292-2418, (800) 777-BEAT, FAX: (801) 292-2462, Web Site: www.powermusic.com
Owner: Richard Petty
Mktg Dir: Jodie Erickson
Primary Market Served: Business & Consumer
Direct online sales
Advertising/Marketing Budget Related to Direct Marketing: 76-100%

Exercise music tapes for health clubs & aerobics instructors & a new line of music tapes for home workouts.

PRACTICING LAW INSTITUTE
810 7th Ave (fl 21)
New York, NY 10019-5856
Telephone: (212) 824-5700, (800) 260 4PLI, FAX: (800) 321-0093, E-Mail: info@pli.edu, Web Site: www.pli.edu
Exec Dir: Victor J. Rubino
Direct Mktg Mgr: Nadine Hovan
Assoc Dir Mktg: Arlene Bein
Conducts Business: Worldwide
Employees: 160
Primary Market Served: Business
Direct online sales
Founded: 1933

Help lawyers maintain their competence by keeping up with changes in the law resulting from new statutes, decisions, regulations & developments in the social & economic climate. Offer programs, specialized law books, audio, videotapes & online services.

PRATT CORP
3035 N Shadeland Ave (Suite 100)
Indianapolis, IN 46226-6231
Telephone: (317) 924-3201, (800) 428-7728, FAX: (317) 927-0653, Web Site: www.prattcorp.com
Pres: Daniel D. Pratt Jr
VP: Thomas Pratt
Conducts Business: U.S
Employees: 100
Primary Market Served: Business

Manufacturer of promotional banners, flags, bunting, pennants, sign kits & balloons.

PREMIER FARNELL CORP
4180 Highlander Pkwy
Richfield, OH 44286-9352

Telephone: (216) 525-4300, (800) 458-3222, FAX: (216) 525-4509, E-Mail: information@premierfarnell.com, Web Site: www.premierfarnell.com
Pres Premier Holding Inc: Peter D. Costello
VP Premier Farnell Corp: Joseph Daprile
Head Corp Commun: Jenny Peters
Conducts Business: Worldwide
Employees: 4,100
Primary Market Served: Business
Founded: 1966
Gross sales or billing: $905,100,000

Manufacture fire-fighting equipment; distribute electronic components, industrial maintenance & repair products.

PREMIER PACKAGING CORP
6 Framark Dr, PO Box 352
Victor, NY 14564-1136
Telephone: (877) 924-8460, FAX: (585) 924-8753, E-Mail: info@premiercustompkg.com, Web Site: www.premiercustompkg.com
VP: Paul Dougherty
Acct Exec: Peter Ashe
Acct Exec: Glenn Marino
Sls & Mktg Mgr: David Denn
Sls Support Mgr: Bryan William
Conducts Business: U.S., Canada
Employees: 40
Primary Market Served: Business
Advertising/Marketing Budget Related to Direct Marketing: 0-25%
Founded: 1989

Manufacture custom packaging for all forms of media to be mailed/delivered to end user.

PREVIO/ALTERIS
588 W 400 St
Lindon, UT 84042
Telephone: (801) 226-8500, (888) 252-5551, FAX: (801) 226-8506, Web Site: www.previo.com
VP, Mktg: Carine Clark
Employees: 180
Primary Market Served: Business & Consumer
Catalog available online
Direct online sales
Advertising/Marketing Budget Related to Direct Marketing: 26-50%
Founded: 1983

Developer of leading disaster recovery & remote access software.

PRIME
Div. of Prime Resources
1100 Boston Ave
Bridgeport, CT 06610
Telephone: (203) 331-9100, (800) 873-7746, FAX: (203) 330-0123, Web Site: www.primeline.com

Pres: Rick Brenner
Conducts Business: Worldwide
Employees: 18
Primary Market Served: Business
Catalog available online
Direct online sales
Direct Marketing ad budget: $150,000
Direct Mail: 50%
Magazines: 35%
Newspapers: 10%
Telephone: 5%

Manufacturer of battery operated pencil sharpeners, telephone indexes, desk sets, organizers & office accessories.

PRINCESS HOUSE INC

470 Miles Standish Blvd
Taunton, MA 02780
Telephone: (508) 832-6800, (508) 823-0711, (800) 622-0039, FAX: (508) 823-5182, Web Site: www. princesshouse.com
Chmn Bd: James Northrop
Pres: Timothy J. Brown
Sr Mgr Programs: Stefani Shea
Unit Organizer: Lavena Pleva
Conducts Business: U.S., Canada, Mexico, U.K., Australia
Employees: 600
Primary Market Served: Consumer
Catalog available online
Gross sales or billing: $150,000,000

Direct sales (party plan) of crystal & porcelain tabletop products as well as other home decorative & gift items.

THE PRINCETON REVIEW

925 Oak St
Scranton, PA 18515-0999
Telephone: (212) 874-8282, FAX: (212) 874-0775, E-Mail: helpme@ review.com, Web Site: www.review. com
VP, Mktg: Linda Nessim
Primary Market Served: Consumer

Test preparation for standardized tests.

THE PROCTER & GAMBLE CO

1 Procter & Gamble Plaza
Cincinnati, OH 45202-3393
Telephone: (513) 983-4224, (800) 742-6253, FAX: (513) 983-9369, Web Site: www.pg.com
DM Promo Mgr: Scott Stewart
Global Ethics, Compliance & Privacy: Sandra Hughes
Pres & CEO: Alan G. Lafley
Conducts Business: Worldwide
Employees: 77,300
Primary Market Served: Business & Consumer
Founded: 1837

Manufacture & market laundry, cleaning & personal care products, pharmaceuticals, food & beverages.

PROFESSIONAL BINDING PRODUCTS INC

2192-A Anchor Ct
Thousand Oaks, CA 91320
Telephone: (800) 545-9413, (800) 443-7557, E-Mail: sales@probinding. com, Web Site: www.probinding.com
Pres: Michael Drew
Primary Market Served: Business & Consumer

Marketer & distributor of laminating & binding machines.

PROFILE MAILING SERVICE INC

575 Underhill Blvd (Suite 132)
Syosset, NY 11791-3416
Telephone: (516) 802-3974
Pres: Marc Goldstein
Conducts Business: U.S.
Employees: 9
Primary Market Served: Business
Advertising/Marketing Budget Related to Direct Marketing: 0-25%
Direct Marketing ad budget:
Direct Mail: 50%
Magazines: 20%
Newspapers: 20%
Telephone: 10%
Founded: 1992
Gross sales or billing: $1,300,000

Standard mailing services, data processing, laser personalization & fulfillment services.

PROGRESS SOFTWARE CORP

14 Oak Park
Bedford, MA 01730
Telephone: (781) 280-4000, (800) 477-6473, FAX: (781) 280-4095, Web Site: www.progress.com
Pres & CEO: Joseph W. Allsop
Conducts Business: Worldwide
Primary Market Served: Business
Catalog available online
Gross sales or billing: $405,376

Application development & database software.

PROJECTION VIDEO SERVICES

5803 Rolling Rd (Suite 207)
Springfield, VA 22152-1056
Telephone: (703) 912-1334, (800) 377-7650, FAX: (703) 912-1350, Web Site: www.projection.com
Pres: Dave Campbell
Corp Dir Mktg & Commun: Nancy DeBrosse
Conducts Business: U.S.

Employees: 150
Primary Market Served: Business & Consumer
Gross sales or billing: $7,000,000

Audio-visual & computer rental service firm with branches in Boston, New York, New Orleans, Philadelphia, Washington D.C., San Francisco & Anaheim.

PROSPERITY AND PROFITS UNLIMITED DISTRIBUTION SERVICES

PO Box 416
Denver, CO 80201-0416
Telephone: (303) 575-5676, FAX: (303) 575-1187, E-Mail: emailstreet@gmail.com, Web Site: www. prosperityandprofitsunlimited.com
Mktg VP & Founder: A. Doyle
Conducts Business: U.S.
Employees: 1
Primary Market Served: Business & Consumer
Catalog available online
Indirect online sales
Advertising/Marketing Budget Related to Direct Marketing: 76-100%
Direct Marketing ad budget:
Direct Mail: 5%
Online: 90%
Telephone: 5%
Founded: 1988

Distributors of cookbooks, children's books, correspondence courses, workbooks, directories, books & tapes. Content for websites, magazines, newspapers, etc. Distributors of curriculum, courses, periodicals.

PROTECTION ONE INC

1035 N Third St (Suite 101)
Lawrence, KS 66044
Telephone: (785) 856-5500, (800) GET-HELP, Web Site: www. protectionone.com
Pres, CEO & Dir: Richard Ginsburg
Exec VP & COO: Peter J. Pefanis
Dir Mktg: Robert McClarin
Exec VP & CFO: Darius G. Nevin
Sr VP: Joseph Sanchez
Mgr: Nancy Roll
Primary Market Served: Consumer
Gross sales or billing: $270,000,000

Security alarm service.

ᴛʜᴇ DMA PRUDENT PUBLISHING CO

65 Challenger Rd
Ridgefield Park, NJ 07660-2111
Telephone: (201) 641-7900, FAX: (800) 772-1144
Chmn Bd Dirs: Alan Solow
Mktg Dir: Tony Patella

Conducts Business: U.S., Canada
Employees: 80
Primary Market Served: Business &
Consumer
Gross sales or billing: $7,900,000

Sell custom imprinted Christmas cards.

FRED PRYOR SEMINARS
Div. of Park University Enterprises
5700 Broadmoor St (Suite 300)
Mission, KS 66202-2415
Telephone: (913) 967-8518, (800) 780-
8476, FAX: (913) 967-8849, E-Mail:
customerservice@pryor.com, Web
Site: www.pryor.com
CEO: Lauren Wright
Pres: John Brown
Mktg Supvr: Janet Turner
Conducts Business: U.S., U.K., Austra-
lia, New Zealand, Germany
Employees: 90
Primary Market Served: Business
Catalog available online
Direct online sales

Provide business & educational
seminars/audio & video cassettes.

PUTT PUTT FUN CENTERS
300 S Liberty St (Suite 100)
Winston-Salem, NC 27101-5279
Telephone: (336) 714-3950, (866)
PUTT-PUTT, FAX: (336) 714-3955,
Web Site: www.puttputt.com
CEO: David Callahan
Mktg Dir: Sherry Shaw
Conducts Business: U.S., Canada,
Lebanon, Japan, Indonesia
Primary Market Served: Business &
Consumer
Catalog available online
Advertising/Marketing Budget Related
to Direct Marketing: 0-25%

Sell equipment & supplies to family
amusement centers including clothing,
equipment, resale merchandise, promotional & operational supplies & construction materials. Offer supply &
design services for miniature golf,
driving ranges, batting cages, go-carts,
bumper boats & indoor soft play.

QC SUPPLY LLC
PO Box 581
Schuyler, NE 68661-0581
Telephone: (402) 352-3167, Web Site:
www.qcsupply.com
Pres: Lonnie Kitt
Primary Market Served: Business &
Consumer

QUADRANT ENGINEERING
PLASTIC PRODUCTS
PO Box 14235
Reading, PA 19612-4235

Telephone: (610) 320-6600, (800) 366-
0300, FAX: (610) 320-6868, Web
Site: www.quadrantepp.com
Pres & CEO: Glen Steady
VP, Mktg: Earl Wester
Mktg Commun Mgr: Kress Swartz
CEO: Michael Kotch
Conducts Business: U.S., Canada,
Mexico, Europe, Far East
Primary Market Served: Business
Catalog available online
Indirect online sales
Advertising/Marketing Budget Related
to Direct Marketing: 51-75%

Industrial plastics.

THE QUAKER OATS CO
Div. of PepsiCo Beverages & Foods
PO Box 049003
Chicago, IL 60604-9003
Telephone: (312) 821-1000, (800) 367-
6287, FAX: (312) 222-8323, Web
Site: www.quakeroats.com
Chmn, Pres & CEO: Robert S. Morri-
son
Sr VP, Fin & CFO: Richard M. Gunst
Sr VP, HR: Franz Hijkoop
Sr VP: Polly B. Kawalek
Sls Team Leader: Albert P. Carey
Primary Market Served: Business &
Consumer
Catalog available online
Indirect online sales

Foods & beverages.

QUILL CORP
Subs. of Staples Inc
PO Box 94080
Palatine, IL 60094-4080
Telephone: (847) 634-4800, (800) 789-
1331, FAX: (800) 789-6630, Web
Site: www.quill.com
Pres: Larry Morse
VP, Mdsg: Kyle Anderson
Printing Buyer: Vern Bush
Conducts Business: U.S., Canada
Employees: 1,000
Primary Market Served: Business

Sell office products to business & professional people.

R&S INDUSTRIES CORP
1065 Appalachian Trl
Chesterfield, MO 63017-1948
Telephone: (314) 781-5400, FAX:
(314) 781-5169, E-Mail:
sendeverything@
miraclepolishingcloth.com, Web Site:
www.miraclepolishingcloth.com
Pres & Co-Owner: Ronald B. Schwartz
VP & Co-Owner: Steven Rubin
Conducts Business: Worldwide
Employees: 10
Primary Market Served: Consumer
Catalog available online

Indirect online sales
Advertising/Marketing Budget Related
to Direct Marketing: 76-100%
Direct Marketing ad budget: $500,000
Direct Mail: 80%
Magazines: 20%
Founded: 1965
Gross sales or billing: $2,000,000

Manufacture "Miracle Polishing
Cloth," a chemically treated cotton
cloth which cleans, polishes & protects
ANY surface.

RACER'S EQUIPMENT
WAREHOUSE
111 Commerce Dr
Warwick, RI 02886-2429
Telephone: (401) 348-6010, (800) 556-
2864, FAX: (401) 348-6023, E-Mail:
scott@racers-eq.com, Web Site:
www.racers-eq.com
Pres: Ralph Accinno
HR: Nancy Accinno
VP Fin: Peter Accinno
Conducts Business: Worldwide
Employees: 25
Primary Market Served: Business
Advertising/Marketing Budget Related
to Direct Marketing: 0-25%
Direct Marketing ad budget:
Direct Mail: 60%
TV/Radio: 20%
Telephone: 20%
Founded: 1965
Gross sales or billing: $3,700,000

High performance auto parts &
accessories.

RAINBOW ART GLASS
1761 Rte 34 S
Wall, NJ 07727-3935
Telephone: (732) 681-6003, (800) 526-
2356, FAX: (732) 681-4984, E-Mail:
info@rainbowartglass.com, Web
Site: www.rainbowartglass.com
Pres: Charles M. Longo
VP: Anthony Longo
Conducts Business: U.S., Canada, Eu-
rope
Employees: 29
Primary Market Served: Business &
Consumer
Founded: 1965
Gross sales or billing: $4,500,000

Manufacture stained glass lamp kits,
supplies & other stained glass items.
Sell both wholesale & retail.

RALEY'S BEL AIR MARKETS
Div. of Raley's
500 W Capitol Ave
West Sacramento, CA 95605-2696

Telephone: (916) 373-3333, FAX:
(916) 373-6351, Web Site: www.
raleys.com
Pres & CEO: Bill Coyne
Conducts Business: U.S.
Employees: 15,000
Primary Market Served: Consumer
Founded: 1935
Gross sales or billing: $3,400,000,000

Supermarket chain in Northern
California.

RAND MATERIAL HANDLING
EQUIPMENT CO INC

Div. of Lab Safety Supply Inc
PO Box 5195
Janesville, WI 53547-5195
Telephone: (401) 751-7657, (800) 366-
2300, FAX: (800) 755-7263, E-Mail:
cs@randmh.com, Web Site: www.
randmh.com
Pres: James Fitzgerald Sr
Primary Market Served: Business
Founded: 1972

Material handling & packaging products sold to a wide range of businesses, wholesalers, manufacturers &
government agencies.

RAPIDS WHOLESALE
EQUIPMENT

6201 S Gateway Dr
Marion, IA 52302-9430
Telephone: (319) 447-1670, (800) 472-
7431, FAX: (319) 447-1680, (800)
858-0327, E-Mail: judys@
rapidswholesale.com, Web Site:
www.rapidswholesale.com
VP: Diane Dodds
Pres: Joe Schmitt
VP Mktg: Joe Dodds
VP: Geri Schmitt
Conducts Business: U.S.
Employees: 48
Primary Market Served: Business
Founded: 1936
Gross sales or billing: $14,800,000

Supplier & manufacturer of refrigeration, beer & restaurant equipment, food
service equipment & furniture.

RAYCOM SPORTS

Div. of Raycom Media
1900 W Morehead St
Charlotte, NC 28208-5228
Telephone: (704) 378-4456/4400, FAX:
(704) 378-4465, E-Mail: whicks@
raycomsports.com, Web Site:
raycomsports.com
Pres: Ken Haines
Dir ACC Properties: Lisa Shaw
Sls Dir: Jim Brannon
Dir Event Acctg: Stephanie Miller
Employees: 50

Primary Market Served: Business &
Consumer
Direct online sales
Founded: 1979

Documentary, sports & entertainment
programs produced for TV & sold to
sports fans & video distributors on a
national level.

ᵀᴴᴱ READING FOR EDUCATION
ᴰᴹᴬ

180 Freedom Ave
Murfreesboro, TN 37129-0071
Telephone: (615) 896-3800
Pres: Elijah Collard

RECOGNITION PRODUCTS
INTERNATIONAL

8706 Commerce Dr (Suite 6)
Easton, MD 21601-6903
Telephone: (410) 820-0022, (800) 292-
7354, FAX: (410) 820-5044, E-Mail:
info@recognitionproducts.com, Web
Site: www.shoprecognitionproducts.
com
Pres: Charles W. Bresloff
CEO: Donald A. Schwartz
Controller: Vickie Sharp
Sls Mgr: Mike Ridge
VP: kay Stein
Conducts Business: U.S.
Employees: 9
Primary Market Served: Business &
Consumer
Catalog available online
Direct online sales
Advertising/Marketing Budget Related
to Direct Marketing: 0-25%
Direct Marketing ad budget:
Direct Mail: 20%
Online: 80%
Founded: 2000
Gross sales or billing: $2,100,000

Manufactures wholesale awards recognition and promotional products including medals, emblematic jewelry &
plaques.

RECOGNITION SYSTEMS
(DOT WORKS)

30 Harbor Park Dr
Port Washington, NY 11050
Telephone: (516) 625-5000, FAX:
(516) 625-1507, E-Mail: wade@
dotworks.com, Web Site: www.
dotworks.com
Mktg Dir: John Bender
VP: Linda McLuster
Mktg Mgr: Liz Barrington
Conducts Business: U.S., Canada
Employees: 15
Primary Market Served: Business

Distributor of graphic arts, films &
chemicals.

RECORDING FOR THE BLIND
& DYSLEXIC INC

20 Roszel Rd
Princeton, NJ 08540-9983
Telephone: (609) 452-0606, (800) 221-
4792, FAX: (609) 520-7996, E-Mail:
info@rfbd.org, Web Site: www.rfbd.
org
Mail Mktg Dir: JoAnne Rygiel
Pres: John Kelly
Publ Editor: Paula Whitcomb
Conducts Business: U.S., Canada,
Mexico, Europe
Employees: 200
Primary Market Served: Business &
Consumer
Catalog available online
Direct online sales
Advertising/Marketing Budget Related
to Direct Marketing: 0-25%
Founded: 1948

Educational & professional audio tapes
& computer discs for visually impaired
& learning disabled nationwide.

JP REDINGTON & CO

PO Box 429
Huntington, NY 11743
Telephone: (631) 754-0111, FAX:
(631) 757-0878
Pres: Marie Ricciardi
Conducts Business: U.S., Europe, Asia
Employees: 5
Primary Market Served: Consumer
Advertising/Marketing Budget Related
to Direct Marketing: 0-25%
Founded: 1897
Gross sales or billing: $1,000,000

Manufactures public building furniture.
Church pews

ᵀᴴᴱ REED EXHIBITIONS
ᴰᴹᴬ

Div. of Reed Elsevier Inc
383 Main Ave
Norwalk, CT 06851-1500
Telephone: (203) 840-4800, (888) 745-
7644, FAX: (203) 840-5805, E-Mail:
dhalter@reedexpo.com, Web Site:
www.readerexpo.com
Group Dir, Segmentation &Targeting:
Denise Halter
VP Opers: Mike Grant
Primary Market Served: Business &
Consumer

Trade show management. Acts as relationship broker - identifying, targeting,
attracting and matching the needs of
buyers and suppliers.

REGAL WARE INC

1675 Reigle Dr
Kewaskum, WI 53040-8923

Telephone: (262) 626-2121, E-Mail:
pseitz@regalware.com, Web Site:
www.regalware.com
Pres & CEO: Jeffrey A. Reigle
COO: Douglas J. Reigle
Dir Commun: Pat Seitz
Conducts Business: U.S., Canada,
Mexico, Europe, Japan, Central
America, South America, Philip-
pines, New Zealand
Employees: 500
Primary Market Served: Business
Catalog available online
Direct online sales
Advertising/Marketing Budget Related
to Direct Marketing: 0-25%
Founded: 1945

Manufacturer of stainless steel and cast
aluminum cookware for direct marketing and retail companies.

REID SUPPLY CO
2265 Black Creek Rd
Muskegon, MI 49444-2673
Telephone: (231) 777-3951, (800) 253-
0421, FAX: (231) 767-3882, E-Mail:
mail@reidsupply.com, Web Site:
www.reidsupply.com
Mktg Dir: Greg Palmer
Conducts Business: Worldwide
Primary Market Served: Business
Catalog available online
Direct online sales
Advertising/Marketing Budget Related
to Direct Marketing: 51-75%
Founded: 1948

Global industrial supplies distributor.

RELIABLE TECHNOLOGIES
INC
55 S Commercial St
Manchester, NH 03101
Telephone: (603) 644-2528, (800) 346-
7890, FAX: (603) 627-5553, Web
Site: www.tei-imaging.com
Mktg & Sls Mgr: Sarah Scheffer
Sls Mngr: Nancy Warner
Customer Svc Mgr: Scott Spaulding
Svc Mgr: Matt Morin
Svc Supvr: Julian Reynolds
Conducts Business: Worldwide
Employees: 75
Primary Market Served: Business &
Consumer
Catalog available online
Advertising/Marketing Budget Related
to Direct Marketing: 76-100%
Gross sales or billing: $5,000,000

Direct marketing of computer supplies,
accessories, & add-ons.

THE DMA RELIANT ENERGY
1000 Main St (fl 18)
Houston, TX 77002-6336

Telephone: (713) 497-7794, Web Site:
www.reliant.com
Dir Database Mktg Devel: Tom Atkinson

RENT-A-CENTER INC
Subs. of Renter's Choice Inc
5501 Headquarters Dr
Plano, TX 75024-5837
Telephone: (972) 801-1100, (800) 275-
2996, FAX: (972) 943-0113, Web
Site: www.rentacenter.com
Pres, COO, Dir: Mitchell Fadel
Chmn & CEO: Mark E. Speese
Sr VP Fin, CFO, Treas: Robert D.
Davis
Sr VP, CIO: Tony F. Fuller
Exec VP, Opers: William S. Short
Primary Market Served: Business &
Consumer
Catalog available online
Direct online sales
Gross sales or billing: $2,400,000,000

A rent-to-own industry.

REPLOGLE GLOBES INC
2801 S 25th Ave
Broadview, IL 60155-4500
Telephone: (708) 343-0900, FAX:
(708) 343-0923, E-Mail: info@
replogleglobes.com, Web Site: www.
replogleglobes.com
Pres: Dan Dillon
Co-Pres & Treas: Ed Dieschbourg
National Acct Mgr: Rodney Wachow-
iak
New Bus Devel: Dell Torgerson
Sls Mgr: Bob Mitchell
Export Sls Mgr: Patricia Boling
Special Accts Mgr: Jane Quinn
Conducts Business: Worldwide
Employees: 150
Primary Market Served: Business
Catalog available online
Indirect online sales
Advertising/Marketing Budget Related
to Direct Marketing: 0-25%
Direct Marketing ad budget:
Direct Mail: 30%
Magazines: 65%
Telephone: 5%
Founded: 1930

Manufacturer of geographical globes.

REXCRAFT WEDDING
INVITATIONS
Div. of Artco
One Stationery Pl
Rexburg, ID 83441
Telephone: (208) 359-1000, (800) 635-
3898, FAX: (800) 826-2712, E-Mail:
cs@rexcraft.com, Web Site: www.
rexcraft.com
Pres: Garth Miller
Direct Mail Mktg Coord: Blair Taylor

Conducts Business: U.S., Canada, Aus-
tralia
Primary Market Served: Consumer
Catalog available online
Indirect online sales
Advertising/Marketing Budget Related
to Direct Marketing: 76-100%
Direct Marketing ad budget:
Magazines: 100%
Founded: 1910

Sell a varied line of wedding invitations, napkins imprinted in foil & miscellaneous reception & gift items.

THE DMA RHODE ISLAND NOVELTY
5 Industrial Rd
Cumberland, RI 02864-4714
Telephone: (401) 335-3300, (800) 528-
5599, FAX: (800) 448-1775, E-Mail:
info@rinovelty.com, Web Site: www.
rinovelty.com
Webmaster/Sys Admin: Scott Blood-
worth
Primary Market Served: Business
Catalog available online
Direct online sales
Founded: 1986

RICCI LEE HUBBART
ASSOCIATES INC
20660 Stevens Creek Blvd (Suite 177)
Cupertino, CA 95014
Telephone: (408) 725-1242, FAX:
(408) 716-2704, E-Mail: susan@
riccilee.com, Web Site: www.riccilee.
com
Pres: Susan Hubbart
Primary Market Served: Business
Founded: 1992

Search consultant agency.

RICH BRANDS
7227 N 16th St (Suite 209)
Phoenix, AZ 85020-5283
Telephone: (602) 889-4800, (877) 856-
1753, FAX: (602) 889-4830, E-Mail:
sales@esscentualbrands.com, Web
Site: esscentualbrands.com
Pres: Mark Grodsky
Direct Mktg Mgr: Susan Baler
Conducts Business: U.S., Europe
Employees: 500
Primary Market Served: Consumer
Catalog available online
Direct online sales
Gross sales or billing: $15,600,000

Manufacturer and distributor of personal care products and room
fragrances.

RICH PRODUCTS CORP
One Robert Rich Way
Buffalo, NY 14213-1701

Telephone: (716) 878-8000, (800) 828-2021, FAX: (716) 878-8765, Web Site: www.richs.com
Chmn: Robert E. Rich Jr
Vice Chmn: Melinda R. Rich
Pres, CEO & Dir: William G. Gisel Jr.
Exec VP, CFO: James Deuschle
Sr VP, CIO: Paul Klein
Conducts Business: U.S., Canada
Employees: 6,500
Primary Market Served: Business & Consumer
Catalog available online
Direct online sales
Advertising/Marketing Budget Related to Direct Marketing: 0-25%
Founded: 1983
Gross sales or billing: $2,400,000

Sell tickets & merchandise.

RICHARDSON ELECTRONICS LTD

40 W 267 Keslinger Rd
Lafox, IL 60147
Telephone: (630) 208-2200, FAX: (630) 208-2550, E-Mail: edg@rell.com, Web Site: www.rell.com
CEO & Pres: E.J. Richardson
CFO: Kathleen Dvorak
VP, Worldwide Sls: Robert Prince
VP, Mktg Opers: Brad Knechtal
Mktg Mgr: Julie Gentry
Conducts Business: Worldwide
Primary Market Served: Business & Consumer
Catalog available online
Indirect online sales
Advertising/Marketing Budget Related to Direct Marketing: 0-25%
Direct Marketing ad budget: $1,200,000
Direct Mail: 10%
Magazines: 40%
Online: 50%
Founded: 1947
Gross sales or billing: $625,000,000

Global provider of "engineered solutions," serving the RF and wireless communications, industrial power conversion, and display systems markets. Delivers engineered solutions for its customers' needs through product manufacturing, systems integration, prototype design and manufacture, testing and logistics.

RIO BRANDS

Div. of All-Luminum Products Inc
10981 Decatur Rd
Philadelphia, PA 19154-3297
Telephone: (215) 632-2800, FAX: (215) 824-1172
Chmn: Bob Cohen
Pres: Warren Cohen
Exec VP, Sls & Mktg: Mark J. Cohen

Conducts Business: U.S.
Employees: 1,650
Primary Market Served: Business
Founded: 1947
Gross sales or billing: $18,900,000

Manufacturer of folding tables, folding cots & beach chairs. Importer of office chairs. Sell to all warehouse clubs, mass merchants, drug stores & department stores.

RIO GRANDE

Div. of The Bell Group
7500 Bluewater Rd NW
Albuquerque, NM 87121-1962
Telephone: (505) 839-3000, (800) 545-6566, FAX: (800) 965-2329, E-Mail: info@riogrande.com, Web Site: www.riogrande.com
CEO: Andrea Hill
Pres: Hugh Bell
Conducts Business: Worldwide
Employees: 400
Primary Market Served: Business
Catalog available online
Direct online sales
Advertising/Marketing Budget Related to Direct Marketing: 76-100%
Direct Marketing ad budget:
Direct Mail: 100%
Founded: 1944
Gross sales or billing: $31,000,000

Wholesale distributor of supplies to the jewelry industry.

THE DMA RJ REYNOLDS TOBACCO CO

401 N Main St, Reynolds Bldg
Winston Salem, NC 27101-3804
Telephone: (336) 741-5111
Sr Dir 1 to 1 Commun Grp: Nancy Montgomery
Primary Market Served: Consumer

C H ROBINSON WORLDWIDE INC

14701 Charlson Rd
Eden Prairie, MN 55347-5076
Telephone: (952) 937-8500, FAX: (952) 937-6740, E-Mail: info@chrobinson.com, Web Site: www.chrobinson.com
Chmn, CEO & Pres: John P. Wiehoff
Sr VP: Jim Butts
VP: Molly M. DuBois
VP: Linda Feuss
VP, HR: Laura Gillund
Conducts Business: Worldwide
Employees: 3,700
Primary Market Served: Business
Advertising/Marketing Budget Related to Direct Marketing: 0-25%
Gross sales or billing: $6,600,000,000

Third party provider of all modes of transportation.

ROBINSON HOME PRODUCTS

2615 Walden Ave, PO Box 550
Buffalo, NY 14225-0550
Telephone: (716) 685-6300, FAX: (716) 685-4916
VP, Mktg: Joan Skerker
VP, Admin: Larry Skerker
VP: Robert Skerker
Conducts Business: U.S., Canada, Europe, Far East
Employees: 61
Primary Market Served: Business & Consumer
Gross sales or billing: $80,000,000

Kitchen housewares, including cutlery, kitchen tools, promotional sets, gift sets & gadgets.

ROCKWELL AUTOMATION

1201 S 2nd St
Milwaukee, WI 53204-2410
Telephone: (414) 382-2000, FAX: (414) 382-4444, Web Site: www.rockwellautomation.com
Pres, CEO & Chmn: Keith Nosbusch
Sr VP & CFO: Theodore D. Crandall
Sr VP: John D. Cohn
Sr VP: Steven A. Eisenbrown
Sr VP: Douglas M. Hagerman
Conducts Business: Worldwide
Employees: 4,000
Primary Market Served: Business
Catalog available online
Founded: 1952

Complete line of predictive maintenance tools including portable vibration meters, data collectors, analyzers, balancing machines, on-line surveillance systems, protection monitors & predictive maintenance software. Full range of technical consultation services & a comprehensive set of training courses to complement the wide family of products. These services assist its customers in establishing & successfully implementing an effective predictive maintenance program.

ROHM & HAAS CO

100 S Independence Mall W
Philadelphia, PA 19106-2320
Telephone: (215) 592-3000, (877) 288-5881, FAX: (215) 592-3377, Web Site: www.rohmhess.com
Chmn & CEO: Raj L. Gupta
Pres & COO: J. Michael Fitzpatrick
VP: Gray Wirth
VP: Phillip J. Lewis MD
VP: Richard J. Lovely
Primary Market Served: Business
Catalog available online
Direct online sales

Manufacturers of specialty chemicals.

ROLAND PRODUCTS INC
Div. of Roland Corporation
3400 W Olympic Blvd
Los Angeles, CA 90019
Telephone: (323) 731-1111, FAX:
(323) 731-9585, E-Mail: salesinfo@
rolandinc.com, Web Site: www.
rolandinc.com
Chmn: Dan Katsuyoshi
Pres, CEO & Dir: Hidezaku Tanaka
Pres & Dir, USA: Dennis Houlihan
Mgr: Joanne Kim
Conducts Business: U.S., Canada
Employees: 24
Primary Market Served: Consumer
Catalog available online
Direct online sales
Advertising/Marketing Budget Related
to Direct Marketing: 26-50%
Direct Marketing ad budget:
Magazines: 25%
Newspapers: 25%
TV/Radio: 50%
Gross sales or billing: $1,400,000

High end European houseware &
kitchenware sold to North American
consumers.

**ROLL INTERNATIONAL
CORP**
11444 W Olympic Blvd (fl 10)
Los Angeles, CA 90064-1557
Telephone: (310) 966-5700, FAX:
(310) 914-4747, Web Site: www.roll.
com
Chmn: Stewart Resnick
Co-Chmn: Lynda R. Resnick
Sr VP & Chief Tax Officer: Jordan P.
Weiss
Employees: 2,600
Primary Market Served: Consumer
Founded: 1957
Gross sales or billing: $1,400,000,000
Collectibles.

RONCO CORP
1779 Wells Branch Pkwy (#110B-337)
Austin, TX 78728
Telephone: (800) 486-1806, E-Mail:
customerservice@ronco.com, Web
Site: www.ronco.com
Pres: Terry Tigner
VP Mktg: Christian Darby
Employees: 200
Primary Market Served: Business &
Consumer
Gross sales or billing: $41,300,000,000
Direct response television advertising.

THE DMA **ROSE DISPLAYS LTD**
35 Congress St
Salem, MA 01970-5529
Telephone: (978) 219-8100, Web Site:
www.rosedisplays.com

Dir, Mktg: Melissa Santos
Primary Market Served: Business

ROSS METALS
27 W 47 St
New York, NY 10036-2806
Telephone: (212) 869-1407, (800) 654-
ROSS
Pres: Jack Angel Ross
Exec Supvr: Karin Zakarian
Sls Mgr: Sally Singh
Telemarketing Dir: Armida Moultrie
Conducts Business: Worldwide
Employees: 30
Primary Market Served: Business
Catalog available online
Direct online sales
Founded: 1974

Wholesale jewelry company.

**ROTO-ROOTER SERVICES
CO**
255 E Fifth St, 2500 Chemed Center
Cincinnati, OH 45202
Telephone: (513) 762-6690, FAX:
(513) 762-6590, Web Site: www.
rotorooter.com
Pres: Richard Arguilla
VP, Mktg: Steven Pollyea
Primary Market Served: Business &
Consumer
Advertising/Marketing Budget Related
to Direct Marketing: 0-25%

Drain cleaning & plumbing.

ROW RESOURCES INC
260 Main St (Ste 110)
Northport, NY 11768-1738
Telephone: (631) 261-0525
Pres: Kenneth Rowland
Primary Market Served: Business

ROWE POTTERY WORKS INC
404 England St
Cambridge, WI 53523
Telephone: (608) 423-3363, (800) 356-
5003, FAX: (608) 423-4273, E-Mail:
sales@rowepottery.com, Web Site:
www.rowepottery.com
Pres: James Rowe
Dir, Mktg: Greg Sanders
Primary Market Served: Business &
Consumer
Catalog available online
Direct online sales
Advertising/Marketing Budget Related
to Direct Marketing: 0-25%

Retail manufacturer of pottery &
wrought iron.

THE DMA **ROYAL CANADIAN MINT**
320 Sussex Dr
Ottawa, ON, Canada K2J 2G6
Telephone: (613) 993-1912

Primary Market Served: Business

ROYAL CANIN
500 Fountain Lakes Blvd (Suite 100)
Saint Charles, MO 63301-4354
Telephone: (636) 926-0003, Web Site:
www.royalcanin.us
Dir Mktg: Ann Hudson
Primary Market Served: Consumer

RUSH INDUSTRIES, INC
263 Horton Hwy
Mineola, NY 11501-2255
Telephone: (516) 741-0346, FAX:
(516) 741-0348, Web Site: www.
rushindustries.com
Pres: Esra Sheena
Conducts Business: U.S.
Employees: 11
Primary Market Served: Consumer
Catalog available online
Direct online sales
Direct Marketing ad budget:
Direct Mail: 50%
Magazines: 50%
Founded: 1977

General merchandise.

**RUSKIN, MOSCOU,
FALTISCHEK, PC**
190 EAB Plaza (15th fl East Tower)
Uniondale, NY 11556
Telephone: (516) 663-6600, FAX:
(516) 663-6601, E-Mail: info@
rmfpc.com, Web Site: www.rmfpc.
com
Mng Partner: Michael Faltischek
Mktg & Pub Affairs Dir: Barbara L.
Cerrone
Conducts Business: U.S.
Employees: 120
Primary Market Served: Business
Advertising/Marketing Budget Related
to Direct Marketing: 0-25%

Law firm.

RUTLAND PRODUCTS
38 Merchants Row
Rutland, VT 05701-2853
Telephone: (802) 775-5519, FAX:
(802) 775-5262, E-Mail: sales@
rutland.com, Web Site: www.rutland.
com
Pres: Thomas P. Martin
Conducts Business: U.S., Canada
Primary Market Served: Business &
Consumer
Advertising/Marketing Budget Related
to Direct Marketing: 26-50%
Founded: 1883

Manufacturer of products related to
chimney sweeping & hearth products.

SCI MANAGEMENT

1929 Allen Pkwy
Houston, TX 77019-2506
Telephone: (713) 525-7783, Web Site:
  www.sci-corp.com
Mng Dir Mktg: Russell Richmond

SLM CORP

12061 Bluemont Way
Reston, VA 20190
Telephone: (703) 810-3000, FAX:
  (703) 984-5042, Web Site: www.
  salliemae.com
CEO & Vice Chmn: Albert L. Lord
Pres: C.E. Andrews
Exec VP, Opers: Robert S. Autor
Conducts Business: U.S.
Primary Market Served: Business &
  Consumer
Catalog available online
Gross sales or billing: $9,100,000,000

Nationwide free scholarship service on
internet & provides software for financial aid packages.

SA-SO

525 N Great Southwest Pkwy
Arlington, TX 76011
Telephone: (972) 641-4911, (800) 752-
  4294, FAX: (972) 660-3684, E-Mail:
  info@sa-so.com, Web Site: www.sa-
  so.com
Co-Owner: Joe Nussbaum
Co-Owner: Becky Nussbaum
Conducts Business: U.S.
Primary Market Served: Business &
  Consumer
Catalog available online
Direct online sales
Advertising/Marketing Budget Related
  to Direct Marketing: 51-75%
Founded: 1948

Supplier of industrial & municipal
safety equipment products. Sell to industries & government by direct mail.

SAFEGUARD BUSINESS SYSTEMS INC

8585 N Stemmons Fwy (Suite 600N)
Dallas, TX 75247-3824
Telephone: (214) 905-3935, (800) 523-
  2422, FAX: (800) 439-8423, Web
  Site: www.gosafeguard.com
Pres: Tim Broadhead
VP: Elizabeth Jones
VP: David Miller
VP: Lauren Pickwoad
VP: Mark Roggenkamp
Conducts Business: U.S., Canada
Employees: 850
Primary Market Served: Business &
  Consumer
Founded: 1956
Gross sales or billing: $86,900,000

Served the small business community
for more than 47 years with business
management solutions such as continuous & laser computer checks & forms,
accounting software, one-write accounting, gift certificate & records
management solutions.

SAFTI FIRST

Div. of O'Keeffe's Architectural Build-
  ing Products Inc
325 Newhall St
San Francisco, CA 94124-1432
Telephone: (415) 824-4900, (888) 653-
  3333, FAX: (415) 824-5900, (888)
  653-4444, E-Mail: info@safti.com,
  Web Site: www.safti.com
Chmn & Pres: William O'Keeffe Jr.
Pres & CEO: William O'Keefe
Sr VP & CFO: William H. Hernandez
VP Sls & Mktg: Kathryn O'Keeffe
VP Sls: Mike Vicarra
Conducts Business: U.S., China, Saudi
  Arabia, Mexico, France
Employees: 70
Primary Market Served: Business
Catalog available online
Indirect online sales
Advertising/Marketing Budget Related
  to Direct Marketing: 26-50%
Founded: 1961
Gross sales or billing: $17,000,000

San Francisco based manufacturer of
fire rated glazing & framing systems,
standard custom skylight systems &
architectural building products for residential, commercial & industrial
buildings.

SAGE SOFTWARE INC

6561 Irvine Center Dr
Irvine, CA 92618-2118
Telephone: (949) 753-1222, (800) 854-
  3415, FAX: (949) 753-0374, Web
  Site: www.sagesoftware.com
Acting CFO: Andrew Griffith
Exec VP & CIO: John D. Bartz
Exec VP, Mktg: Dennis Frahman
Sr VP, HR: Beccie C. Dawson
Sr VP, Fin: Marshall Ford
Conducts Business: U.S., Canada
Employees: 230
Primary Market Served: Business &
  Consumer
Catalog available online
Advertising/Marketing Budget Related
  to Direct Marketing: 0-25%
Direct Marketing ad budget:
  $1,000,000
Direct Mail: 50%
Telephone: 50%
Founded: 1985
Gross sales or billing: $300,000,000

Sell accounting & business-related
software to small & medium-sized
businesses.

SAKS FIFTH AVENUE

12 E 49th St (fl 2)
New York, NY 10017-1088
Telephone: (212) 940-5195, FAX:
  (212) 940-5339, Web Site: www.
  saksfifthavenue.com
Sr VP, Mktg: Bette Chabot
DM Dir: Elizabeth Price
Conducts Business: U.S.
Primary Market Served: Business &
  Consumer
Advertising/Marketing Budget Related
  to Direct Marketing: 26-50%

Department store specializing in luxury
items.

SALES & MARKETING MANAGEMENT MAGAZINE

Div. of Bill Communications
770 Broadway
New York, NY 10003
Telephone: (800) 821-6897, FAX:
  (905) 470-8561, E-Mail: joyce.
  cooney@nielsen.com, Web Site:
  www.salesandmarketing.com
Grp Publr: Dan Corcoran
Online Editor: Stacy Straczynski
Editor In Chief: Michael McCue
Editor in Chief: Jennifer Juergens
Exec Editor: Lorrie Freifeld
Conducts Business: Worldwide
Primary Market Served: Business &
  Consumer
Catalog available online
Direct online sales
Advertising/Marketing Budget Related
  to Direct Marketing: 26-50%
Direct Marketing ad budget:
  $100,000,000
Direct Mail: 90%
Magazines: 5%
Telephone: 5%

Market books, data & directories to the
sales & marketing community.

SALES SERVICE/AMERICA INC

85 S Bragg St (Suite 600)
Alexandria, VA 22312-2793
Telephone: (703) 813-2400
VP Sls & Msdg: Greg Magnani
Primary Market Served: Consumer

Fine art print & posters, bags, banners,
buttons, printed certificates, flags, jewelry, pencils, pens, embroidered promotional gifts, thermometers, tote
boxes, signs, porcelain cups & mugs

SAMSONITE AMERICAN TOURISTER
575 West St (Suite 110)
Mansfield, MA 02048-1160
Telephone: (508) 851-1400, (800) 821-6632, FAX: (508) 851-8715, E-Mail: samsonite@casupport.ca, Web Site: www.samsonite.com
CEO: Marcello Bottoli
CFO, Treas & Dir: Richard H. Wiley
Conducts Business: U.S.
Primary Market Served: Business & Consumer
Catalog available online
Direct online sales
Gross sales or billing: $1,000,000,000

Luggage & travel accessories. Headquarters: 11200 E 45th Ave, Denver, CO 80239.

SAMSONITE CORP
575 West St (Suite 110)
Mansfield, MA 02048-1160
Telephone: (508) 851-1400, (800) 547-BAGS, FAX: (303) 373-8715, Web Site: www.samsonite.com
Chmn: John Allan
Pres & CEO: Marcello Bottoli
CFO, Treas, Sec & Dir: Richard H. Wiley
VP, HR: Lou Cimini
VP, Gen Counsel: Deborah Rasin
Conducts Business: U.S.
Employees: 1,000
Primary Market Served: Business & Consumer
Catalog available online
Direct online sales
Advertising/Marketing Budget Related to Direct Marketing: 0-25%
Founded: 1910
Gross sales or billing: $1,000,000,000

Manufacture & sell luggage.

SAN FRANCISCO BAY AREA RAPID TRANSIT DISTRICT (BART)
800 Madison St
Oakland, CA 94607-2622
Telephone: (510) 464-6000, FAX: (510) 464-7103, Web Site: www.bart.gov
Gen Mgr: Thomas E. Margro
VP: Gail Murray
Dir: Joel Keller
Dir: Bob Franklin
Dir: Carole Ward Allen
Conducts Business: U.S.
Employees: 3,400
Primary Market Served: Consumer
Catalog available online
Direct online sales
Founded: 1946

Public transportation agency serving four counties in the Bay Area with over 76 miles of track.

SANDY CORP
Div. of General Physics
300 E Big Beaver Rd (Suite 500)
Troy, MI 48083
Telephone: (800) 733-4739, FAX: (248) 729-4701, E-Mail: info@sandycorp.com, Web Site: www.sandycorp.com
Pres: Frederic Strickland
Sr VP: Dave Gugalal
Employees: 151
Primary Market Served: Business
Advertising/Marketing Budget Related to Direct Marketing: 0-25%
Founded: 1911
Gross sales or billing: $42,000,000

Full service performance improvement company. Helps clients close the gap between current performance & their full potential. Services include consulting, research, training & communication tools & media.

SANI SERV
PO Box 1089
Mooresville, IN 46158-5089
Telephone: (317) 831-7030, FAX: (317) 381-7036, Web Site: www.saniserv.com
Pres: Rob McAfee
VP, Sls & Mktg: Stephen Dowling
Conducts Business: Worldwide
Employees: 100
Primary Market Served: Business
Catalog available online
Indirect online sales
Advertising/Marketing Budget Related to Direct Marketing: 26-50%
Founded: 1929
Gross sales or billing: $20,000,000

Manufactures Soft Serv ice cream & milkshakes. Also batch freezers & cappuccino machines.

THE DMA SANTA FE NATURAL TOBACCO CO
PO Box 25140
Santa Fe, NM 87504-5140
Telephone: (505) 982-4257, Web Site: www.nascigs.com
Consumer Relationship Mktg Mgr: Johanna Stein
Primary Market Served: Business

SATORI SOFTWARE INC
1301 5th Ave (Suite 2200)
Seattle, WA 98101-2676

Telephone: (206) 357-2900, (800) 553-6477, FAX: (206) 357-2901, E-Mail: sales@satorisoftware.com, Web Site: www.satorisoftware.com
VP Sls: Joe Skop
Pres: Hugh Rogovy
Conducts Business: U.S., UK
Employees: 20
Primary Market Served: Business & Consumer
Catalog available online
Direct online sales
Advertising/Marketing Budget Related to Direct Marketing: 26-50%
Founded: 1982
Gross sales or billing: $1,800,000

Mailroom address correction & postal presorting software is sold to print shops, large companies, or list management services.

SAUNDERS MANUFACTURING CO INC
65 Nickerson Hill Rd
Readfield, ME 04355
Telephone: (207) 685-3385, (800) 341-4674, FAX: (207) 685-9918, E-Mail: jsherwood@saunders-usa.com, Web Site: www.saunders-usa.com
CEO & Owner: John Rosmarin
CFO & COO: Dann Harriman
VP Sls: Michael Stanga
Mktg Mgr: Tracy Kastning
Web Mktg Mgr: Jennifer Sherwood
Conducts Business: USA, Canada, Mexico, EU, Australia
Employees: 70
Primary Market Served: Business
Catalog available online
Indirect online sales
Advertising/Marketing Budget Related to Direct Marketing: 0-25%
Direct Marketing ad budget:
Online: 100%
Founded: 1947

Manufacturer of metal & plastic office products, especially aluminum holders for business forms, clipboards & sheetholders. Also manufacture specialty printed clipboards for sports plays as well as general office supplies. Distributor of UHU glue adhesives & Ticket Board police products.

SCAN OPTICS INC
169 Progress Dr
Manchester, CT 06040-2294
Telephone: (860) 645-7878, (800) 745-6001, FAX: (860) 645-7995, E-Mail: info@scanoptics.com, Web Site: www.scanoptics.com
Chmn: James C. Mavel
CEO: Gideon Agar
Pres: Raymond Griffin
Sr VP & COO: Richard Lieberfarb

Exec VP: Raymond Parker
Employees: 183
Primary Market Served: Business
Founded: 1968
Gross sales or billing: $28,741,000

Computer services & software sold to companies involved in large volume datacapturing for data processing.

HENRY SCHEIN INC

135 Duryea Rd
Melville, NY 11747-3834
Telephone: (631) 843-5500, (800) 472-4346, FAX: (631) 843-5658, E-Mail: custserv@henryschein.com, Web Site: www.henryschein.com
Chmn & CEO: Stanley Bergman
Pres & COO: James P. Breslawski
Exec VP, CAO & Dir: Gerald A. Benjamin
Exec VP Bus Devel: Mark E. Mlotek
Sr Advisor: Leonard A. David
Conducts Business: U.S., Canada, Europe
Employees: 1,500
Primary Market Served: Business & Consumer
Catalog available online
Direct online sales
Founded: 1932
Gross sales or billing: $5,100,000,000

Sell pharmaceutical, medical, dental & veterinary supplies to health care professionals & institutional customers.

SCHNUCK MARKETS INC

11420 Lackland Rd
Saint Louis, MO 63146-6928
Telephone: (314) 994-9900, FAX: (314) 994-4465, Web Site: www.schnucks.com
Chmn & CEO: Scott C. Schnuck
Pres: Todd Schnuck
Sr VP, Sls & Mktg: Randy Wedel
Sr Analyst: Mark Dagestad
Adv Dir: Joyce Reese
Conducts Business: U.S.
Employees: 15,000
Primary Market Served: Business & Consumer
Catalog available online
Direct online sales
Advertising/Marketing Budget Related to Direct Marketing: 0-25%
Direct Marketing ad budget:
Direct Mail: 85%
Magazines: 10%
Newspapers: 5%

Grocery items to consumers; also offer services in most of our stores - pharmacy, video rental, carry-out foods, photo finishing, bakery, check cashing services, Western Union, etc.

SCHOOL SPECIALTY INC

dba Brodhead Garrett, Frey Scientific, EPS & Childcraft
W6316 Design Dr
Greenville, WI 54942-8404
Telephone: (920) 734-5712, (888) 388-3224, FAX: (920) 734-5112, E-Mail: info@schoolspecialty.com, Web Site: www.schoolspecialty.com
Chmn Bd: Terry L. Lay
CEO: David J. Vander Zanden
Exec VP & CFO: David Vander Ploeg
Exec VP Dir Mktg: David Johnson
Commun & Investor Rels: Mark Fleming
Conducts Business: U.S.
Employees: 2,800
Primary Market Served: Business
Founded: 1959
Gross sales or billing: $1,043,200,000

Supplier of industrial, vocational & technical equipment to secondary & post secondary schools.

SCOPE 1

6490 S Sprinkle Rd
Kalamazoo, MI 49004-9706
Telephone: (269) 323-1333, Web Site: www.scope 1.com
Pres: William English
Primary Market Served: Consumer

SCORECARDS USA

200 Circuit Dr
North Kingstown, RI 02852-0298
Telephone: (401) 294-4049, (800) 553-4154, FAX: (401) 294-4076, E-Mail: sales@scorecardsusa.com, Web Site: www.scorecardsusa.com
Treas: Dennis Glass
Pres: Ed Bouclin
Mgr: Heidi Lee Strickland
Conducts Business: U.S.
Primary Market Served: Business
Advertising/Marketing Budget Related to Direct Marketing: 26-50%
Direct Marketing ad budget:
Direct Mail: 75%
Magazines: 15%
Telephone: 10%

Golf scorecards.

SCOTT SIGN SYSTEMS INC

Div. of Identity Group
7525 Pennsylvania Ave (Unit 102)
Sarasota, FL 34243-5065
Telephone: (941) 355-5171, (800) 237-9447, FAX: (941) 351-1787, E-Mail: mail@scottsigns.com, Web Site: www.scottsigns.com
Pres: Steve Evans
Art Dir: Jennifer Adkins
Conducts Business: Worldwide
Employees: 100

Primary Market Served: Business & Consumer
Catalog available online
Indirect online sales
Founded: 1957
Gross sales or billing: $8,000,000

Manufacturer of dimensional letters, logos & graphics. Also, custom fabrication of signing products.

SCOTTS-SIERRA HORTICULTURAL

14111 Scottslawn Rd
Marysville, OH 43041
Telephone: (888) 270-3714, Web Site: www.scottscompany.com
Chm & CEO: Jim Hagedorn
Conducts Business: U.S., Canada, Europe, Australia
Employees: 300
Primary Market Served: Business & Consumer
Advertising/Marketing Budget Related to Direct Marketing: 0-25%
Direct Marketing ad budget:
Direct Mail: 10%
Magazines: 10%
TV/Radio: 80%
Gross sales or billing: $100,000,000

Manufacture & sell controlled release fertilizers, soils & plant protection products to the nursery, greenhouse, turf & landscape & retail industries.

SCULPTURE HOUSE INC

405 Skillman Rd, PO Box 69
Skillman, NJ 08558
Telephone: (609) 466-2986, FAX: (888) 529-1980, E-Mail: customercare@sculpturehouse.com, Web Site: www.sculpturehouse.com
Pres: Bruner Barrie
Conducts Business: United States & Puerto Rico
Employees: 25
Primary Market Served: Business & Consumer
Catalog available online
Direct online sales
Founded: 1883

Sell sculpting supplies, tools & materials.

SEA BEAR

605 30th St
Anacortes, WA 98221
Telephone: (360) 293-4661, (800) 645-3474, FAX: (888) 487-6427, Web Site: www.seabear.com
Pres & CEO: Mike Mondello
VP, Fin: Dan Jondal
VP Direct to Consumer: Patti Fisher
Conducts Business: U.S., Canada, Japan, Hong Kong, Taiwan

Primary Market Served: Business & Consumer
Catalog available online
Direct online sales
Founded: 1957

Gift pack smoked salmon, oysters & mussels. No refrigeration required.

SEARS HOME IMPROVEMENT PRODUCTS INC

Sears Home Improvement
1024 Florida Central Pkwy
Longwood, FL 32750-7579
Telephone: (407) 767-0990, (877) 840-7126, FAX: (407) 831-1848, Web Site: www.searshomepro.com
Gen Mgr: Joseph J. Steenbeke
CEO: Arthur Martinez
Sr VP Retail Opers: Mike McCarthy
Sr VP HR: Bob Luse
Chmn Sears Holdings: Edward S. Lampert
Primary Market Served: Consumer
Catalog available online
Gross sales or billing: $748,000,000

Vinyl siding & texture coating.

SEARS, ROEBUCK & CO

3333 Beverly Rd
Hoffman Estates, IL 60179
Telephone: (847) 286-2500, FAX: (847) 286-7829, Web Site: www.sears.com
Chmn & CEO: Alan J. Lacy
Conducts Business: U.S., Canada, Mexico
Employees: 320,000
Primary Market Served: Consumer
Founded: 1886
Gross sales or billing: $34,000,000,000

General merchandising.

SECO-LARM USA INC

16842 Millikan Ave
Irvine, CA 92606
Telephone: (949) 261-2999, (800) 662-0800, FAX: (949) 261-7326, E-Mail: info@seco-larm.com, Web Site: www.seco-larm.com
VP: Michael Block
Mktg Dir: Joe Kovar
Mgr: Lawrence Hwang
Conducts Business: Worldwide
Employees: 20
Primary Market Served: Business & Consumer
Catalog available online
Advertising/Marketing Budget Related to Direct Marketing: 0-25%
Founded: 1971
Gross sales or billing: $4,400,000

Dealer direct & export of vehicle, residential & commercial security systems & access.

SEIKO CORP OF AMERICA

1111 MacArthur Blvd
Mahwah, NJ 07430
Telephone: (201) 529-5730, FAX: (201) 529-1548, Web Site: www.seiko.com
Pres & CEO: Toyoji Todaka
CFO: Tetsu Matsuda
Exec VP Sls & Mktg: Les Perry
VP Mktg: Bob Swanson
Special Markets Mgr: Brian Deis
Employees: 400
Primary Market Served: Business & Consumer
Gross sales or billing: $30,000,000,000

Sell watches & clocks.

SELECT COMFORT CORP

9800 59th Ave N
Minneapolis, MN 55442
Telephone: (763) 551-7000, (888) 411-2188, FAX: (763) 551-7826, Web Site: www.selectcomfort.com
CEO: William McLaughlin
Sr VP, CIO: Ernest Park
Sr VP, CFO: James C. Raube
Media Dir: Lynn Ferrin
Conducts Business: U.S.
Primary Market Served: Consumer
Catalog available online
Direct online sales
Advertising/Marketing Budget Related to Direct Marketing: 100%
Founded: 1987
Gross sales or billing: $806,000,000

Manufacture & sell adjustable firmness sleep systems-air beds.

SELLSTROM MANUFACTURING CO

One Sellstrom Dr
Palatine, IL 60067
Telephone: (847) 358-2000, (800) 323-7402, FAX: (847) 358-8564, E-Mail: sellstrom@sellstrom.com, Web Site: www.sellstrom.com
Pres & CEO: David Peters
VP, Sls & Mktg: Rusty Franklin
Mktg Coord: Melissa Heard
Conducts Business: Worldwide
Employees: 101
Primary Market Served: Business
Advertising/Marketing Budget Related to Direct Marketing: 0-25%
Founded: 1923
Gross sales or billing: $7,100,000

Diversified manufacturer of industrial safety products.

SENCORE INC

3200 Sencore Dr
Sioux Falls, SD 57107
Telephone: (605) 339-0100, (800) SEN-CORE, FAX: (605) 339-0317, E-Mail: sales@sencore.com, Web Site: www.sencore.com
Chmn & Pres: Al Bowden
Exec VP: Doug Bowden
Sls & Mktg Mgr: Jeffrey Murray
Conducts Business: U.S., Canada, Puerto Rico, Mexico, France
Employees: 250
Primary Market Served: Business
Catalog available online
Advertising/Marketing Budget Related to Direct Marketing: 76-100%
Founded: 1958
Gross sales or billing: $32,000,000

Manufacturer of electronic test equipment.

SENSIENT TECHNOLOGIES

2526 Baldwin St
Saint Louis, MO 63106
Telephone: (314) 889-7600, (800) 325-8110, FAX: (314) 658-7318, Web Site: www.sensient-tech.com
Chmn, Pres & CEO: Kenneth P. Manning
Sr VP & CFO: Steve Cordier
Gen Mgr: Terry Anderson
Conducts Business: Worldwide
Employees: 300
Primary Market Served: Business
Founded: 1904
Gross sales or billing: $90,000,000

Manufacturers of certified (FD&C/D&C) natural colorants supplied to food, drug, beverage, cosmetic, baking, pet food industries & pharmaceutical.

SENSORY EFFECTS POWDER SYSTEM

231 Rock Industrial Park Dr
Bridgeton, MO 63044
Telephone: (314) 291-5444, (800) 422-5444, FAX: (314) 291-3289, E-Mail: info@sensoryeffects.com
Sls & Mktg Dir: Tiffany Tyler
Conducts Business: U.S., Central America
Primary Market Served: Consumer
Advertising/Marketing Budget Related to Direct Marketing: 0-25%
Direct Marketing ad budget:
Direct Mail: 90%
Telephone: 10%
Founded: 1972

Vitamite non-dairy beverage powders for people who are lactose-intolerant.

THE DMA SETON IDENTIFICATION PRODUCTS

Div. of Tricor Direct Inc
20 Thompson Rd

Branford, CT 06405-2842
Telephone: (203) 488-8059, (800) 243-6624, FAX: (203) 488-5973, Web Site: www.seton.com
Database Mktg Assoc: Donna J. Canestin
Mktg Dir: David Giroux
Gen Mgr: Pascal Deman
Conducts Business: Worldwide
Employees: 250
Primary Market Served: Business
Catalog available online
Direct online sales
Advertising/Marketing Budget Related to Direct Marketing: 76-100%
Founded: 1956

Manufacturer of identification products: signs, tags, labels & badges. Sell by mail distributing millions of catalogs.

JA SEXAUER

Subsidiary of Wilmar Industries
570 Taxter Rd (#230)
Elmsford, NY 10523-2365
Telephone: (914) 472-7501, (800) 431-1872, FAX: (914) 472-5834, Web Site: www.jasmro.com
Pres, CEO Wilmar: Armond Waxman
Sr VP Wilmar: William Sanford
Mktg Dir: Rick Coalter
Conducts Business: U.S., Canada
Primary Market Served: Business
Catalog available online
Direct online sales
Advertising/Marketing Budget Related to Direct Marketing: 0-25%
Founded: 1921

Distributor of plumbing, heating, air conditioning & electrical maintenance products to institutional, commercial & government markets.

THE DMA SHELL OIL PRODUCTS US

PO Box 2463
Houston, TX 77252
Telephone: (713) 241-6161, Web Site: www.shell.us
Mktg Alliance Implementation Mgr: Sergio Roldan
Primary Market Served: Consumer

SHERMAN SPECIALTY TOY CO INC

300 Jericho Quadrangle (Suite 240)
Jericho, NY 11753-2719
Telephone: (516) 861-6420, (516) 546-7400, (800) 645-6513, FAX: (516) 861-1033, (800) 853-8697, E-Mail: orders@shermanspecialty.com, Web Site: www.shermanspecialty.com
Pres: Stuart Krosser
Mktg Mgr: Guy Abbate
Mktg: Shawn Hood
Conducts Business: Worldwide

Employees: 99
Primary Market Served: Business
Catalog available online
Direct online sales
Advertising/Marketing Budget Related to Direct Marketing: 0-25%
Gross sales or billing: $19,000,000

Market inexpensive toys used as premiums and a full line of party novelties.

SHILLCRAFT INC

2530 Riva Rd (Suite 308)
Annapolis, MD 21401-7414
Telephone: (410) 682-3060, (800) 638-1542, FAX: (410) 682-3130, Web Site: www.shillcraft.com
Mktg Mgr: Joyce Wehberg
Conducts Business: U.S., Canada
Employees: 24
Primary Market Served: Business & Consumer
Advertising/Marketing Budget Related to Direct Marketing: 76-100%

Sell latch hook kits for making rugs, wall hangings, pillow covers plus related needlecraft items to retail stores, chains & direct to the consumer-primarily female.

SHIPPING SOLUTIONS

PO Box 22267
Eagan, MN 55122-0267
Telephone: (651) 905-1727, (888) 890-7447, FAX: (651) 905-1827, E-Mail: info@shipsolutions.com, Web Site: www.shipsolutions.com
Pres: David M. Noah
Chief Tech Officer: Robert Hale
Employees: 5
Primary Market Served: Business
Catalog available online

Sell software to international trading companies.

SHOP.COM

21 Lower Ragsdale Dr, Bldg 1 (Suite 210
Monterey, CA 93940-5740
Telephone: (831) 647-2489, (866) 746-7005, FAX: (831) 644-9283, Web Site: www.shop.com
Pres & Co-Founder: Bruce Sellers
Sr VP Mktg: Mondy Beller
Dir Online Mktg: Robert Corelli
Mktg: Sheila Anderson
Conducts Business: U.S.
Employees: 150
Primary Market Served: Business & Consumer
Founded: 1997
Gross sales or billing: $34,500,000

Online shopping portal. Builds custom malls & stores.

SHOPSMITH INC

6530 Poe Ave
Dayton, OH 45414
Telephone: (937) 898-6070, (800) 543-7586, FAX: (937) 890-5197, Web Site: www.shopsmith.com
Chmn & CEO: John R. Folkerth
Pres: Robert Folkerth
CFO: Mark May
Dir Mktg Mgr: Karen Seabach
Conducts Business: U.S., Canada, England
Employees: 93
Primary Market Served: Business & Consumer
Founded: 1972
Gross sales or billing: $11,000,000

Manufacture & sell woodworking power tools direct to the general public through direct mail & direct sales.

SHOWTIME NETWORKS INC

Subs. of Viacom Inc
1633 Broadway
New York, NY 10019
Telephone: (212) 708-1600, FAX: (212) 708-1450, Web Site: www.sho.com
Chmn & CEO: Matthew Blank
Exec VP, Mktg & Corp Strategy Commun: Mark Greenberg
VP, DM: Rick King
Conducts Business: U.S.
Employees: 575
Primary Market Served: Consumer

Premium-cable television network.

SIEMENS IT SOLUTIONS & SERVICES INC

101 Merritt 7
Norwalk, CT 06851-1061
Telephone: (203) 642-2300, FAX: (203) 642-2399, Web Site: www.it-solutions.usa.siemens.com
CEO: John McKenna
Primary Market Served: Business & Consumer

Computer services.

SILICON GRAPHICS INC

46600 Landing Pkwy
Fremont, CA 94538-6420
Telephone: (510) 933-8300, Web Site: www.sgi.com
CEO: Robert Ewald
Primary Market Served: Business & Consumer

Manufacture 3-D computer graphic systems; some software development.

SIMON PROPERTY GROUP

115 W Washington St
Indianapolis, IN 46204

Telephone: (317) 636-1600, FAX:
(317) 263-7925, Web Site: www.
shopsimon.com
VP, Corp Mktg: Shari Simon
Conducts Business: U.S., Europe
Employees: 4,000
Primary Market Served: Business

Develop & operate enclosed shopping
malls, strip centers & mixed use
centers.

SIMPLEX GRINNELL
50 Technology Dr
Westminster, MA 01441-0001
Telephone: (978) 731-2500, (800)
SIMPLEX, FAX: (978) 731-7856,
Web Site: www.simplexgrinnel.com
Pres: Dean S. Seavers
VP & CFO: Mike Ford
VP, Mktg: Dave Baer
Dir, Mktg Commun: Chris Woodcock
Conducts Business: Worldwide
Employees: 3,000
Primary Market Served: Business
Catalog available online
Advertising/Marketing Budget Related
to Direct Marketing: 26-50%
Founded: 2001
Gross sales or billing: $1,800,000,000

Manufacture recorders & fire alarm
systems for industrial companies.

SIMPSON ELECTRIC CO
dba Lac Du Flambeau Band of Lake
Superior Chippewa Indians
520 Simpson Ave, PO Box 99
Lac Du Flambeau, WI 54538-0099
Telephone: (715) 588-3311, FAX:
(715) 588-3327, E-Mail: cservice@
simpsonelectric.com, Web Site:
www.simpsonelectric.com
CEO: William Conn
Conducts Business: U.S., Europe, Asia,
South America
Employees: 100
Primary Market Served: Business
Catalog available online
Founded: 1934
Gross sales or billing: $10,000,000

Manufacturer of analog & digital instrumentation; electrical & electronic
test equipment & accessories, panel
meters & controllers.

SIRIUS XM RADIO
1500 Eckington Pl
Washington, DC 20002
Telephone: (212) 584-5100
Primary Market Served: Business &
Consumer

SKULLDUGGERY
5433 E La Palma Ave
Anaheim, CA 92807-2022

Telephone: (714) 777-6425, (800) 3
FOSSIL, FAX: (714) 832-1215, Web
Site: www.skullduggery.com
Chmn & Pres: Peter Koehl
VP, Mktg: Emmy Koehl
Conducts Business: Worldwide
Employees: 9
Primary Market Served: Business &
Consumer

Manufacture & sell museum quality
fossil replicas to artists, executives,
physicians, dentists, scholars, geolo-
gists, anthropologists & those with
interest in the earth's past, present &
future.

SKYMALL INC
1520 E Pima St
Phoenix, AZ 85034-4600
Telephone: (602) 254-9777, (800)
SKY-MALL, FAX: (602) 254-6075,
Web Site: www.skymall.com
Pres: Christine A. Aguilera
VP Mktg: Theresa McMullan
VP Info Tech: Jay Scannell
Primary Market Served: Consumer
Catalog available online
Direct online sales
Founded: 1990
Gross sales or billing: $100,000,000

Consumer mail order products. In-
flight direct response shopping service.

SKYPOINT COMMUNICATIONS INC
7340 Mark St
Loretto, MN 55357
Telephone: (763) 548-2600, FAX:
(763) 548-2610, E-Mail: info@
skypoint.com, Web Site: www.
skypoint.com
Pres: Greg Kemmitz
Sls & Mktg Mgr: Bruce Morrows
Primary Market Served: Business
Catalog available online
Founded: 1994

Internet services provider.

SLEEPY'S INC
dba Sleepy's; Kleinsleep; 1-800-
Sleepy's
1000 S Oyster Bay Rd
Hicksville, NY 11801-3527
Telephone: (516) 844-8800, (800)
sleepys, FAX: (516) 844-8847, Web
Site: www.sleepys.com
Pres: David Acker
CFO: Joseph Graci
Exec VP, Sls: Mike Bookbinder
Conducts Business: U.S.
Employees: 2,000
Primary Market Served: Consumer
Founded: 1957
Gross sales or billing: $394,000,000

Bedding retailer.

SLIFTER
307 7th Ave (Room 2104)
New York, NY 10001-6089
Telephone: (212) 488-2222, Web Site:
www.slifter.com
Dir Corp Communs: Michelle Barna

AO SMITH CORP
11270 W Park Pl (Suite 1200)
Milwaukee, WI 53224-3643
Telephone: (414) 359-4000, FAX:
(414) 359-4064, Web Site: www.
aosmith.com
Chmn & CEO: Paul W. Jones
Exec VP & CFO: Terry M. Murphy
Sr VP IT: Randall S. Bednar
Exec VP: Christopher L. Mapes
Exec VP Corp Tech: Ronald E. Massa
Primary Market Served: Business
Catalog available online
Gross sales or billing: $2,100,000,000

Water heaters, electric motors & protective coatings.

SMITHFIELD PACKING CO INC
Div. of Smithfield Foods Inc
Hwy Ten
Smithfield, VA 23430
Telephone: (757) 357-4321, FAX:
(757) 357-1339, E-Mail:
information@smithfieldfoods.com,
Web Site: www.smithfieldfoods.com
Chmn, Pres & CEO: Joseph W. Luter
III
VP, Sls & Mktg Processed Meats: Ed
Knoblich
VP, Sls & Mktg Smoked Meats: Will-
iam Hunter
Conducts Business: U.S.
Employees: 24
Primary Market Served: Business &
Consumer
Advertising/Marketing Budget Related
to Direct Marketing: 26-50%

Pork packers.

TOM SNYDER PRODUCTIONS
Div. of Scholastic
100 Talcott Ave Ste 6
Watertown, MA 02472-5715
Telephone: (617) 926-6000, (800) 342-
0236, FAX: (800) 304-1254, E-Mail:
ask@tomsnyder.com, Web Site:
www.tomsnyder.com
Gen Mgr: Richard Abrams
Channel Mgr, Mktg: Kim Goodman
VP Mktg: John Caroll
VP & Chief Academic Officer: David
Dockerman
Dir Fin & Admin: Arlene Hawkins
Dir Prod Mngmt: Liza Debus

Dir Natl Sls: Brian McKean
Employees: 80
Primary Market Served: Business &
  Consumer
Catalog available online
Direct online sales
Founded: 1980

Sell educational software &
technology.

SOCIAL STUDIES SCHOOL SERVICE

10200 Jefferson Blvd
Culver City, CA 90232-0802
Telephone: (310) 839-2436, (800) 421-
  4246, FAX: (310) 839-2249, (800)
  944-5432, E-Mail: access@
  socialstudies.com, Web Site: www.
  socialstudies.com
Co-Pres: Irwin Levin
Co-Pres: Sanford Weiner
CEO: David Weiner
Chief Educ Officer: Aaron Willis
Conducts Business: U.S., Canada
Employees: 65
Primary Market Served: Business &
  Consumer
Catalog available online
Direct online sales
Founded: 1965

Distributor of a wide variety of supplementary curriculum materials for
educators.

SOLARCOM

One Sun Ct
Norcross, GA 30092
Telephone: (770) 449-6116, (888)
  SUN-DATA, FAX: (770) 448-7726,
  Web Site: www.solarcom.net
Chmn & CEO: Eric Prockow
Vice Chmn: John Crilly
Pres Solarcom LLC: Ted Glahn
Pres Atlantic Global Sys: Bill Woerner
VP Mktg: Randy Hicks
Gen Mgr: Jim Johnson
Mktg Coord: Barbara Ingram
Conducts Business: U.S., Europe, S.
  America, Australia, Japan, China
Employees: 356
Primary Market Served: Business
Catalog available online
Direct online sales
Advertising/Marketing Budget Related
  to Direct Marketing: 0-25%
Direct Marketing ad budget:
Direct Mail: 10%
Magazines: 50%
TV/Radio: 40%
Founded: 1976
Gross sales or billing: $250,000,000

An independent business & technology
solutions provider that delivers system
integration, data management, group-
ware solutions, Lan/Wan solutions,
product delivery & lease/financing
services.

SOLITRON DEVICES INC

3301 Electronics Way
West Palm Beach, FL 33407-4636
Telephone: (561) 848-4311, FAX:
  (561) 863-5946, E-Mail: sales@
  solitrondevices.com, Web Site: www.
  solitrondevices.com
Chmn, Pres, CFO & CEO: Shevach
  Saraf
Dir Opers: Jesse Quinn
Dir: Dr. Jacob A. Davis
Dir: Joseph Schlig
Conducts Business: U.S.
Employees: 80
Primary Market Served: Business
Catalog available online
Advertising/Marketing Budget Related
  to Direct Marketing: 0-25%
Founded: 1959
Gross sales or billing: $8,000,000

Manufactures & markets semiconductor & related products primarily to the
defense & aerospace industries.

SONY ELECTRONICS INC

Subs. of Sony Corp of America
One Sony Dr
Park Ridge, NJ 07656
Telephone: (201) 930-6173, FAX:
  (201) 930-7665, Web Site: www.
  sony.com
VP: Mary Rullo
Conducts Business: U.S.
Primary Market Served: Business

Marketer of consumer electronics.

SOUTHEAST TOYOTA DISTRIBUTORS LLC

100 Jim Moran Blvd
Deerfield Beach, FL 33442
Telephone: (954) 429-2000, Web Site:
  www.jmfamily.com
Pres: Kenneth Czubay
Mktg Mgr: Grant Wilson
Primary Market Served: Business &
  Consumer
Catalog available online

Toyota parts & services.

SOUTHERN FLAVORING CO INC

1330 Norfolk Ave
Bedford, VA 24523-2223
Telephone: (540) 586-8565, (800) 765-
  8565, FAX: (540) 586-8568, E-Mail:
  tom@southernflavoring.com, Web
  Site: www.southernflavoring.com

Pres: Earle Thomas Messier
VP, Mktg: John P. Messier
Conducts Business: U.S.
Employees: 20
Primary Market Served: Business &
  Consumer
Catalog available online
Indirect online sales
Founded: 1929

Liquid food flavorings & colors.

HUCK SPAULDING ENTERPRISES

Rte 85, New Scotland Rd
Voorheesville, NY 12186
Telephone: (518) 768-2070, (888) 982-
  8866, FAX: (518) 768-2240, E-Mail:
  orders@spaulding-rogers.com, Web
  Site: www.spaulding-rogers.com
CEO: Huck Spaulding
Pres & Sec: William Lawyer
Vice-CEO: Josephine Spaulding
VP: Jeff Lawyer
VP & Treas: Bobbi DeFranco
Pur Agent: Bob Weineski
Conducts Business: Worldwide
Employees: 56
Primary Market Served: Business &
  Consumer
Catalog available online
Indirect online sales
Founded: 1956

Huck Spaulding Ent Inc. distributor of
products by Spaulding & Rogers Mfg
Inc & Spaulding Color Corp for tattoo
equipment & supplies used by tattoo
artists, plastic surgeons, research insti-
tutes, veterinarians, ophthalmologists &
many other professionals. Also manufacture body jewelry, piercing kits &
piercing supplies.

SPEAKERS GUILD INC

78 Old Kings Hwy, PO Box 1540
Sandwich, MA 02563-1540
Telephone: (508) 888-6702, (800) 343-
  4530, FAX: (508) 888-6771, E-Mail:
  info@speakersguild.com, Web Site:
  www.speakersguild.com
Pres: Phil Frankio
Owner: Edward Larkin
Conducts Business: U.S., Canada
Employees: 6
Primary Market Served: Business
Catalog available online
Indirect online sales
Advertising/Marketing Budget Related
  to Direct Marketing: 26-50%
Direct Marketing ad budget: $150,000
Direct Mail: 95%
Telephone: 5%
Founded: 1978
Gross sales or billing: $6,500,000

Provide public speakers & seminar
leaders for meetings & conventions.

SPEAR ENGINEERING CO
3107 N Stone Ave
Colorado Springs, CO 80907
Telephone: (719) 471-9850
Pres: Spencer Katalin
VP: Joann Wall
Conducts Business: U.S.
Employees: 8
Primary Market Served: Business &
Consumer
Direct Marketing ad budget:
Direct Mail: 90%
Magazines: 10%

Manufacture & sell a line of name-
plates & signs. Solicit orders through
magazine ads & direct mail. Mailing
address: PO Box 7025, Colorado
Springs, CO 80933.

SPECIALIZED PRODUCTS CO
1100 S Kimball Ave
Southlake, TX 76092
Telephone: (817) 329-6647, (800) 866-
5353, FAX: (800) 234-8286, E-Mail:
spc@specialized.net, Web Site:
www.specialized.net
Pres: Pete Smith
Exec Asst: Lisa Oldham
Conducts Business: Worldwide
Employees: 49
Primary Market Served: Business
Catalog available online
Direct online sales
Advertising/Marketing Budget Related
to Direct Marketing: 76-100%
Founded: 1965
Gross sales or billing: $20,000,000

Sells tool kits, tools & test equipment
for installation and maintenance of
telecom, computers, fiber optics, LAN
& electronic systems. Sells extensive
line of instrument shipping cases, complete range of products for field service
& depot repair. 400+ page full color
catalog.

THE DMA SPECIALTY STORE SERVICES INC
454 Jarvis Ave
Des Plaines, IL 60018
Telephone: (847) 470-7000, (888) 441-
4440, FAX: (847) 470-5355, Web
Site: www.specialtystoreservices.com
Pres: Malcom Finke
VP, Opers: Evan Finke
VP Adv: Eric Weinstein
Employees: 85
Primary Market Served: Business
Catalog available online
Direct online sales
Advertising/Marketing Budget Related
to Direct Marketing: 76-100%
Founded: 1987
Gross sales or billing: $11,800,000

Manufacturers of displays, fixtures and
retail store supplies.

SPECTRA MERCHANDISING INTERNATIONAL INC
4230 N Normandy
Chicago, IL 60634
Telephone: (773) 202-8408, FAX:
(773) 202-8409
Pres: Patricia Schoenberg
VP: Alex Greenwood
Conducts Business: U.S., Mexico, Eu-
rope, Australia, Canada
Employees: 60
Primary Market Served: Business
Advertising/Marketing Budget Related
to Direct Marketing: 0-25%
Founded: 1981

Consumer electronics; audio, video,
calculators & telephones.

SPECTRUM CHEMICALS & LABORATORY PRODUCTS
14422 S San Pedro St
Gardena, CA 90248-2027
Telephone: (310) 516-8000, Web Site:
www.spectrumchemical.com
Dir, EBus: Larry Hilton
Primary Market Served: Business

SPEED-MAT
374 South St
Biddeford, ME 04005
Telephone: (207) 294-4358, (800) 882-
7017, FAX: (207) 882-9279, E-Mail:
info@speedmat.com, Web Site:
www.speed-mat.com
Pres: Harry F. Esterly
VP, Treas & Mktg Mgr: Diana E. Es-
terly
Conducts Business: Worldwide
Employees: 7
Primary Market Served: Business &
Consumer
Indirect online sales
Advertising/Marketing Budget Related
to Direct Marketing: 76-100%
Direct Marketing ad budget: $30,000
Direct Mail: 10%
Magazines: 80%
Telephone: 10%
Founded: 1973

SPINNEYBECK ENTERPRISES
425 Crosspoint Pkwy (Suite 100)
Getzville, NY 14068-1609
Telephone: (716) 446-2380, (800) 482-
7777, FAX: (716) 446-2396, E-Mail:
sales@spinneybeck.com, Web Site:
www.spinneybeck.com
Pres: Roger Wall
VP, Opers Mngmt: Jack Wolf
VP, Fin: Susanne Francis
Employees: 60

Primary Market Served: Business &
Consumer
Catalog available online
Indirect online sales
Founded: 1962
Gross sales or billing: $11,800,000

Wholesale Italian upholstery leather
supplier.

SPRING-GREEN LAWN CARE CORP
11909 Spaulding School Dr
Plainfield, IL 60544
Telephone: (815) 436-8777, FAX:
(815) 436-9056, Web Site: www.
spring-green.com
Pres: Thomas W. Hofer
Primary Market Served: Business

Sell lawn care franchises.

SPRINGS GLOBAL INC
Div. of Spring Industries
110 5th Ave (fl 5)
New York, NY 10011-5647
Telephone: (888) 926-7888, Web Site:
www.springs.com
Pres: Tom O'Connor
Conducts Business: Worldwide
Employees: 18,000
Primary Market Served: Business

Sell home textiles & furnishings to
department & chain stores.

SPRINT PCS
6391 Sprint Pkwy
Overland Park, KS 66251-4300
Telephone: (800) 927-2199, Web Site:
www.sprintpcs.com
Pres & CEO: Dan Hesse
CFO: Paul Saleh
Pres Sls & Distr: Mark E. Angelino
Pres Strategic Plng & Corp Initiatives:
Keith Lowan
VP Ethics & Corp Strategy: Chris A.
Hill
Primary Market Served: Business &
Consumer
Catalog available online
Direct online sales
Gross sales or billing: $41,000,000,000

Telemarketing & telecommunications
company.

SQUADRON MAIL ORDER
1115 Crowley Dr
Carrollton, TX 75011-1312
Telephone: (972) 242-8663, (877) 414-
0434, FAX: (972) 242-3775, E-Mail:
mailorder@squadron.com, Web Site:
www.squadron.com
Pres: Jerry Campbell
Mktg Dir: Charles Harransky
Conducts Business: Worldwide
Employees: 40

Primary Market Served: Consumer
Catalog available online
Indirect online sales
Direct Marketing ad budget: $300,000
Direct Mail: 80%
Magazines: 20%
Gross sales or billing: $3,000,000

Sell plastic models & military books
with an emphasis on aviation.

STANDARD COMMUNICATIONS CORP
Subs. of Marantz of Japan Inc
6260 Sequence Dr
San Diego, CA 92121-4358
Telephone: (858) 546-5300, (800) 745-
2445, FAX: (858) 546-5301, E-Mail:
satcommsales@stdcom.com, Web
Site: www.standardcomm.com
Pres & CEO: Ron Blanchard
Conducts Business: U.S.
Employees: 140
Primary Market Served: Business
Advertising/Marketing Budget Related
to Direct Marketing: 0-25%
Direct Marketing ad budget:
Direct Mail: 100%
Founded: 1969
Gross sales or billing: $60,000,000

Commercial satellite receivers.

STANLEY SUPPLY & SERVICES
335 Willow St
North Andover, MA 01845-5921
Telephone: (978) 682-9844, (800) 225-
5370, FAX: (800) 743-8141, Web
Site: www.stanleysupplyservices.com
Pres: Holly Tsourides
VP Global Sls: Bruce Westcott
Conducts Business: Worldwide
Employees: 133
Primary Market Served: Business
Catalog available online
Direct online sales
Advertising/Marketing Budget Related
to Direct Marketing: 76-100%
Founded: 1963
Gross sales or billing: $33,000,000

Direct mail distributor of hardware,
industrial equipment, mail-order house
& electronic parts.

STARCHTECH
720 Florida Ave S (#A)
Golden Valley, MN 55426-1704
Telephone: (763) 545-5400, (800) 597-
7225, FAX: (763) 545-9450, Web
Site: www.starchtech.com
CEO: Ed Boehmer
Gen Mgr, Sls: Dean Bartels
Inside Sls: Charlie Pyle
Dir, Opers: Matt Niles
Plant Mgr: Gary Barbo

Primary Market Served: Business
Catalog available online
Indirect online sales
Founded: 1997

Biodegradable packing materials.

STARCREST PRODUCTS OF CALIFORNIA INC
3660 Brennan Ave
Perris, CA 92599
Telephone: (909) 943-2011, FAX:
(909) 943-2971, E-Mail: tmc@
tstonramp.com
Pres: T.M. Calandra
VP: Michael Donnelly
Mdse Mgr: Frank Hartless
Dir Acct & HR: Betty Abramson
Conducts Business: U.S.
Employees: 1,700
Primary Market Served: Consumer
Advertising/Marketing Budget Related
to Direct Marketing: 76-100%
Direct Marketing ad budget:
$42,000,000
Direct Mail: 100%
Founded: 1976
Gross sales or billing: $300,000,000

Mail order sales of consumer products.

STARKEY LABORATORIES
6700 Washington Ave S
Eden Prairie, MN 55344-3405
Telephone: (952) 941-6401, Web Site:
www.starkey.com
Sr Dir, Mktg & Communs: Chris Mc-
Cormick
Primary Market Served: Business &
Consumer

STARZ ENTERTAINMENT GROUP
8900 Liberty Cir
Englewood, CO 80112-7057
Telephone: (720) 852-7700, Web Site:
www.starz.com
VP Brand Strategy & Mktg Comms:
Kelly Bumann
Primary Market Served: Consumer

STATE LINE TACK INC
Subs. of PetsUnited LLC
19601 N 27th Ave
Phoenix, AZ 85027-4008
Telephone: (623) 580-6100, (800) 228-
9208, FAX: (623) 580-6183, E-Mail:
customerservice@statelinetack.com,
Web Site: www.statelinetack.com
Chmn, CEO: Philip L. Francis
Pres & COO: Robert F. Moran
Sr VP & CFO: Lawrence Malloy
Sr VP & CIO: Donald E. Beaver
Sr VP: Scott A. Grozier
Employees: 38,400
Primary Market Served: Consumer

Catalog available online
Direct online sales
Founded: 1969
Gross sales or billing: $4,200,000,000

Discount equine and equestrian products & supplies, and information including an online horse forum & horse
classifieds.

STATWARE
90 Main St (Suite 213A)
Centerbrook, CT 06409
Telephone: (860) 767-9000, FAX:
(860) 767-3145, E-Mail: info@
statware.net, Web Site: www.
powerlist.com
Pres: Richard Lepoutre

Provide software to list brokers & list
managers.

STEELCASE INC
901 44th St SE
Grand Rapids, MI 49508
Telephone: (616) 247-2710, FAX:
(616) 475-2270, Web Site: www.
steelcase.com
Chmn: Robert C. Pew III
Pres, CEO & Dir: James P. Hackett
Exec VP & CFO: David C. Sylvester
Exec VP & CIO: John S. Dean
Sr VP: Mark A. Baker
Employees: 13,000
Primary Market Served: Business &
Consumer
Catalog available online
Founded: 1912

Manufacture office furniture.

STERLING FLUID SYSTEMS
2005 Dr Martin Luther King St, PO
Box 7026
Indianapolis, IN 46202-1165
Telephone: (317) 925-9661, (800) 879-
0182, FAX: (317) 924-7388, Web
Site: www.peerlesspump.com
Pres: Dean Douglas
VP, Sls & Mktg: John Kahren
CFO: David Baker
Conducts Business: Worldwide
Employees: 200
Primary Market Served: Business
Direct Marketing ad budget:
Direct Mail: 25%
Magazines: 75%
Founded: 1923

Manufacturer of chemical processing
pumps sold by authorized representatives nationally & internationally.

THE DMA STERLING JEWELERS INC
Subs. of Signet Group
375 Ghent Rd
Akron, OH 44333-4601

Telephone: (330) 668-5000, FAX: (330) 668-5052, E-Mail: webmaster@jewels.com, Web Site: www.sterlingjewelers.com
Pres & CEO: Mark Light
Chmn: Terry Burman
Exec VP & CFO: Robert Trabucco
Sr VP, Mktg: George Murray
Employees: 10,000
Primary Market Served: Consumer
Advertising/Marketing Budget Related to Direct Marketing: 26-50%
Founded: 1906
Gross sales or billing: $1,300,000,000
Retail jewelry.

STERLING NAME TAPE INC
Nine Willow St, PO Box 939
Winsted, CT 06098
Telephone: (860) 379-5142, (800) 654-5210, FAX: (860) 379-0394, E-Mail: postman@sterlingtape.com, Web Site: www.sterlingtape.com
Pres: James Barrett
Conducts Business: U.S., Canada, Europe, Mexico
Employees: 4
Primary Market Served: Business & Consumer
Catalog available online
Direct online sales
Direct Marketing ad budget: $35,000
Direct Mail: 50%
Magazines: 50%
Founded: 1901

Manufacturer of personalized garment labels.

THE DMA STEWART ENTERPRISES INC
1333 S Clearview Pkwy
Jefferson, LA 70121-1014
Telephone: (504) 729-1400, (800) 535-6017, FAX: (504) 729-1984, Web Site: www.stewartenterprises.com
Pres & CEO: Thomas J. Crawford
Chmn Bd: Frank B. Stewart Jr.
Direct Mktg Mgr: Kellie Ferrara
Integrated Mktg Commun Dir: Connie P. Ernst
Conducts Business: United States & Puerto Rico
Employees: 5,400
Primary Market Served: Consumer
Catalog available online
Advertising/Marketing Budget Related to Direct Marketing: 5-10%
Founded: 1910
Gross sales or billing: $487,000,000

Funeral home, cemetery owner & operator.

STEWART-MACDONALD
21 N Shafer, PO Box 900
Athens, OH 45701

Telephone: (740) 592-3021, (800) 848-2273, FAX: (740) 593-7922, E-Mail: hostetler@stewmac.com, Web Site: www.stewmac.com
Founder: C.E. Stewart
Co-Founder: Bill MacDonald
VP: Jay Hostetler
Builder: Dan Erlewine
Builder: Don MacRostie
Conducts Business: Worldwide
Employees: 15
Primary Market Served: Business & Consumer
Catalog available online
Direct online sales
Direct Marketing ad budget:
Direct Mail: 80%
Magazines: 20%

Manufacturer & distributor of fretted musical instruments, kits, parts & supplies.

KIRK STIEFF CO
Div. of Lenox
1414 Radcliffe St
Bristol, PA 19007
Telephone: (267) 525-7800, (800) 635-3669, Web Site: www.lenox.com
Conducts Business: U.S.
Employees: 400
Primary Market Served: Business & Consumer
Advertising/Marketing Budget Related to Direct Marketing: 0-25%

Manufacturer & designer of sterling silver, pewter & silverplate flatware, hollowware & decorative accessories.

STIMPSON CO INC
1515 SW 13th Ct
Pompano Beach, FL 33069-4789
Telephone: (954) 946-3500, (877) 765-0748, FAX: (954) 941-1921, E-Mail: customerservice@stimpson.com, Web Site: www.stimpson.com
VP Sls & Mktg: Bill Rauff
Conducts Business: U.S., Canada, U.K.
Employees: 450
Primary Market Served: Business
Catalog available online
Indirect online sales
Advertising/Marketing Budget Related to Direct Marketing: 26-50%
Direct Marketing ad budget:
Magazines: 100%
Founded: 1852
Gross sales or billing: $41,500,000

Sell industrial fasteners & attaching machinery.

STONWURKS
13218 Kerry Ln
Eden Prairie, MN 55346-3140

Telephone: (785) 526-7847, (888) 884-7881, FAX: (785) 526-7841, E-Mail: stonwurks@stonwurks.com, Web Site: www.stonwurks.com
VP: Kirk Meyer
Sls Mgr: Lloyd Frigon
Office Mgr: Joan Caskey
Conducts Business: U.S.
Employees: 5
Primary Market Served: Business & Consumer
Advertising/Marketing Budget Related to Direct Marketing: 76-100%
Founded: 1992

Fabricator of panelized light-weight stone.

STORE SMART EXPRESS/ VISUAL HORIZONS
180 Metro Park
Rochester, NY 14623-2610
Telephone: (585) 424-5300, (800) 424-1011, FAX: (585) 424-1064, E-Mail: cs@storesmart.com, Web Site: www.storesmart.com
VP & Founder: Reenie Fiengold
Mktg Mgr: Stan Fiengold
Catalog available online
Indirect online sales
Founded: 1997

Free full color catalog full of things to protect, store & organize. Clear vinyl peel & stick pockets are sized to fit business cards, 3 1/2 disks & CD-ROMs. With over 300 more sizes & the ability to have the pockets customized, the uses are endless. All products & services guaranteed. Phone/fax orders welcomed. Accepting Master Charge, VISA & American Express.

STRATEGY CORPS LLC
201 Summit View Dr (Suite 250), Summit Bldg
Brentwood, TN 37027-4645
Telephone: (615) 221-8381, (888) 577-6933, FAX: (615) 221-8479, E-Mail: info@strategycorps.com, Web Site: www.strategycorps.com
Chmn: William King
DM Mgr: Christie Skelley
Sls: David Crook
Employees: 16
Primary Market Served: Business
Advertising/Marketing Budget Related to Direct Marketing: 26-50%
Direct Marketing ad budget:
Direct Mail: 50%
Magazines: 50%
Founded: 2000
Gross sales or billing: $1,200,000

Sell accounts receivable software to banking institutions & other businesses to facilitate banks' efforts in selling small business loans & insurance products.

STRATUS TECHNOLOGIES
111 Powder Mill Rd
Maynard, MA 01754-3409
Telephone: (978) 461-7000, (800) 787-2887, FAX: (978) 461-3670, Web Site: www.stratus.com
Pres & CEO: David J. Laurello
Mktg Dir: Sue Lawrence-Longo
Primary Market Served: Business
Founded: 1980

Industrial manufacturers of computers.

STRAW HAT COOPERATIVE CORP
18 Crow Canyon Ct (Suite 150)
San Ramon, CA 94583-1669
Telephone: (925) 837-3400, FAX: (925) 820-1080, E-Mail: info@strawhatpizza.com, Web Site: www.strawhatpizza.com
Pres & CEO: Joshua Richman
Dir Mktg: Kevin Johnson
Reg Dir: Lee Dubrow
Conducts Business: U.S.
Employees: 1,000
Primary Market Served: Consumer
Founded: 1987
Gross sales or billing: $20,000,000

Franchised company of individually owned & operated pizza restaurants.

STREAM INTERNATIONAL
20 William St (Suite 310)
Wellesley, MA 02481-4145
Telephone: (781) 304-1800, (888) 264-5834, FAX: (781) 575-6999, Web Site: www.stream.com
CEO: Steven D.R. Moore
VP, Mktg: Deb Keeman

Customer relationship management & customer care services.

THE DMA STURBRIDGE YANKEE WORKSHOP INC
90 Blueberry Rd
Portland, ME 04102-1924
Telephone: (207) 774-9045, (800) 343-1144, FAX: (207) 774-2561, Web Site: www.sturbridgeyankee.com
Pres: Thomas Binnie
Sr Fin Analyst: John Alexander
Gen Mgr: Gary Boisvert
Conducts Business: U.S.
Employees: 75
Primary Market Served: Consumer
Catalog available online
Direct online sales
Advertising/Marketing Budget Related to Direct Marketing: 76-100%
Founded: 1953

Fine home furnishings & accessories.

STURGES SPORTSWEAR
7752 NC 48
Battleboro, NC 27809
Telephone: (252) 446-0096, (866) 532-6748, FAX: (252) 977-3932, E-Mail: estu73123@aol.com, Web Site: www.sturgessportswear.com
Co-Pres: Johnny Sturges
Co-Pres: Eddie Sturges
Conducts Business: U.S., Japan, Mexico, Canada
Employees: 150
Primary Market Served: Business & Consumer
Catalog available online
Indirect online sales
Advertising/Marketing Budget Related to Direct Marketing: 76-100%
Founded: 1978

Wholesale supplier of T-shirts, denim, sweatwear & ladies leisure wear to the imprintable sportswear industry.

SUEZ ENERGY NORTH AMERICA
1990 Post Oak Blvd (Suite 1900)
Houston, TX 77056-3831
Telephone: (713) 636-0000, FAX: (713) 636-1364, Web Site: www.tractebelpowerinc.com
Pres & CEO: Zin Smati
Sr VP & Gen Counsel: Bart Clark
Sr VP, HR: Mike Thompson
Exec VP, Bus Devel: Paul Gevicchi
Exec VP & CFO: Geert Peeters
Conducts Business: Worldwide
Employees: 47,000
Primary Market Served: Business
Founded: 1895
Gross sales or billing: $11,000,000,000

Independent power & industrial energy.

SUNBEAM
2381 NW Executive Center Dr
Boca Raton, FL 33431
Telephone: (561) 912-4100, FAX: (561) 912-4567, Web Site: www.sunbeam.com
CEO: Al Dunlap
Sr VP, Mktg: Jo Anne Lala
Exec VP, Fin: Russell E. Kersh
Mktg Mgr: Jerry Levin
Primary Market Served: Business & Consumer
Catalog available online
Direct online sales

Manufacture & sell small kitchen appliances, scales & therapeutic products.

SUNDANCER JEWELRY CO INC
5921 Office Blvd NE (Suite A)
Albuquerque, NM 87109
Telephone: (505) 345-7475, FAX: (505) 345-7561, E-Mail: sales@sundancer.net, Web Site: www.sundancer.net
Pres: Steven Stacy
Primary Market Served: Business
Catalog available online
Founded: 1973

Manufacture jewelry.

SUNOCO, INC
Ten Penn Ctr, 1801 Market St
Philadelphia, PA 19103-1699
Telephone: (215) 977-3000, (800) 786-6261, FAX: (215) 977-3409, E-Mail: sunoco_online@sunoil.com, Web Site: www.sunocoinc.com
Chmn, Pres & CEO: John G. Drosdick
Chmn & CEO: Robert H. Campbell
CFO: Thomas W. Hofmann
Sr VP Lubriants & Logistics: Deborah M. Fretz
Sr VP Northeast Refining & Chemicals: David E. Knoll
Sr VP & Chief Admin Officer: Sheldon L. Thompson
VP & Gen Mgr Sunoco Northeast Mktg: Robert W. Owens
Comptroller: Joseph P. Krott
Treas: Malcolm I. Ruddock
Corp Sec & Gen Attorney: Ann C. Mule
Gen Auditor: Ross S. Tippin Jr
Employees: 11,000
Primary Market Served: Business & Consumer
Advertising/Marketing Budget Related to Direct Marketing: 76-100%
Direct Marketing ad budget:
Direct Mail: 5%
Magazines: 5%
Newspapers: 10%
TV/Radio: 80%
Founded: 1886
Gross sales or billing: $8,400,000

Operates five domestic refineries & markets gasoline under the Sunoco brand through nearly 4000 service outlets & APlus convenience stores in 17 states, Maine to Virginia & west to Indiana. Sells lubricants & petrochemicals worldwide, operates domestic pipelines & our terminals produce nearly two million tons per year of metallurgical-grade coke.

SUNRISE MEDICAL INC
6899 Winchester Cir (Suite 200)
Boulder, CO 80301-3696
Telephone: (303) 218-4500, (800) 333-4000, FAX: (303) 218-4949, Web Site: www.sunrisemedical.com
Pres & CEO: Thomas Rossnagel
VP Mkeg: Bob Kaenel
Conducts Business: U.S., Canada

Employees: 2,298
Primary Market Served: Business
Catalog available online
Advertising/Marketing Budget Related
  to Direct Marketing: 0-25%
Direct Marketing ad budget:
Direct Mail: 35%
Magazines: 35%
Telephone: 30%
Founded: 1898
Gross sales or billing: $175,500,000

Electric, manual & crank-free manual
beds, dining, resident & commons area
furnishings, nationwide direct sales
force & leasing programs. Sell to
healthcare, hospital & retirement
industry.

SUNSTAR

Div. of Strategic Planning
4635 W Foster Ave
Chicago, IL 60630-1709
Telephone: (773) 777-4000, FAX:
  (773) 777-1417, E-Mail: dominico@
  sunstar.com, Web Site: www.sunstar.
  com
CEO: Hiroo Kaneda
Pres: Shigeto Yasuoka
VP: Lawrence Farrell
Gen Mgr: Noboru Masuda
Primary Market Served: Business &
  Consumer
Catalog available online
Indirect online sales
Gross sales or billing: $44,300,000

Represents pharmaceutical company
based in Japan. Oral care, health and
beauty.

SUPELCO INC

Div. of Sigma-Aldrich Co
595 N Harrison Rd
Bellefonte, PA 16823-6217
Telephone: (814) 359-3441, (800) 359-
  3041, FAX: (814) 359-3044, E-Mail:
  supelco@sial.com, Web Site: www.
  sigma-aldrich.com
Pres: Russell Gant
VP, Mktg: Shailesh Maingi
Conducts Business: Worldwide
Primary Market Served: Business
Advertising/Marketing Budget Related
  to Direct Marketing: 51-75%
Founded: 1966

Separations technology & supportive
products for analysts in the petroleum/
chemicals, life sciences, environmental
& food & beverage markets; such as
high resolution GC, capillary & HPLC
products as well as a full line of accessories & chemical standards.

SWEEPSTAKES
CLEARINGHOUSE

Subs. of Allied Marketing Group Inc
1555 Regal Row

Dallas, TX 75247
Telephone: (214) 915-7100, FAX:
  (214) 915-7458, E-Mail:
  customersupport@
  sweepstakesclearinghouse.com, Web
  Site: www.sweepstakesclearinghouse.
  com
Pres: Steven Hammond
COO: Julia Gostic
Mktg Dir: David Case
Conducts Business: U.S., Canada
Employees: 200
Primary Market Served: Consumer
Advertising/Marketing Budget Related
  to Direct Marketing: 76-100%
Direct Marketing ad budget:
Direct Mail: 100%
Founded: 1984

Discount consumer mail order
marketer.

SYLVAN LEARNING
CENTERS

Div. of Sylvan Learning Systems Inc
1001 Fleet St
Baltimore, MD 21202
Telephone: (410) 843-8000, FAX:
  (410) 843-8057, Web Site: www.
  educate.com
Pres: Mary Foster
Sr VP, Franchise Opers & Franchise
  Devel: Patty Miller
VP, Educ: Rick Bavaria
VP, Educ & Tech: Matt Myers
Internet Mktg Mgr: Mary Ingwersen
Conducts Business: U.S., Canada, Ger-
  many, Guam, Spain
Employees: 1,000
Primary Market Served: Consumer
Catalog available online
Direct Marketing ad budget:
  $15,000,000
Direct Mail: 10%
Magazines: 5%
Newspapers: 25%
TV/Radio: 55%
Telephone: 5%
Founded: 1979
Gross sales or billing: $100,000,000

Educational services & supplements
for students K-12.

SYMANTEC

350 Ellis St
Mountain View, CA 94043-2202
Telephone: (408) 517-8000, FAX:
  (408) 517-8186, Web Site: www.
  symantec.com
Pres & CEO: Enrique T. Salem
SVP Consumer Bus Unit: Rowan Trol-
  lope
VP Channel Sls: Randy Cochran
Sr VP & Chief Mktg Officer: Carine
  Clark
Employees: 17,100

Primary Market Served: Business &
  Consumer
Catalog available online
Direct online sales
Founded: 1982
Gross sales or billing: $5,199,400,000

Manufacture & market network security software for consumers and businesses and computer software systems.

SYNGENTA

410 Swing Rd
Greensboro, NC 27409-2012
Telephone: (336) 632-6000, FAX:
  (336) 632-7065
Conducts Business: U.S.
Employees: 1,500
Primary Market Served: Business &
  Consumer

Agricultural chemical manufacturer.

SYNTELLECT

Div. of Enghouse Systems, Ltd.
2095 W Pinnacle Peak Rd Ste 110
Phoenix, AZ 85027-1262
Telephone: (602) 789-2800, (800) 788-
  9733, FAX: (602) 789-2899, Web
  Site: www.syntellect.com
Chmn & CEO: Anthony Carollo
Pres: Steve Dodenhoff
VP & CFO: Timothy V. Vatuone
Dir Sls & Mktg: Andy Klune
Conducts Business: U.S., Canada
Employees: 45
Primary Market Served: Business

Design, manufacture & sell telecommunication equipment.

THE DMA SYSTEM PAVERS

3750 S Susan St (Suite 200)
Newport Beach, CA 92704-6964
Telephone: (949) 263-8300, Web Site:
  www.systempavers.com
VP Mktg: Katherine Fotch
Primary Market Served: Business &
  Consumer

SYSTEMAX INC

dba Infotel Distributors and Tiger Di-
rect
11 Harbor Park Dr
Port Washington, NY 11050
Telephone: (516) 608-7000, FAX:
  (516) 6208-7001, Web Site: www.
  systemax.com
Chmn Bd & CEO: Richard Leeds
VP Mktg: Scott Strunk
Conducts Business: U.S., Canada
Employees: 3,287
Primary Market Served: Business &
  Consumer
Gross sales or billing: $2,345,200,000

Direct marketer of computers and related products to businesses in North America and Europe. Through nearly 20 catalogs and a dozen Web sites, Systemax offers more than 100,000 brand-name and private-label items. Systemax also assembles its own computers, which are sold under the Systemax and Ultra brands.

TDS TELECOM
525 Junction Rd
Madison, WI 53717-2152
Telephone: (608) 664-4119, Web Site:
    www.tdstelecom.com
Dir, Consumer Mktg: Shane West

TNT PACKAGING INC
2390 NW 149th St
Miami, FL 33054
Telephone: (305) 769-0616, (305) 633-
    2556, (800) 327-6085, FAX: (305)
    769-0619, E-Mail: tntpackaging@
    bellsouth.net, Web Site: www.
    tntpackaging.com
Gen Mgr: Jeffrey Tokayer
Mgr Sls: Barry Tokayer
Conducts Business: Worldwide
Employees: 14
Primary Market Served: Business
Catalog available online
Indirect online sales
Founded: 1981
Gross sales or billing: $2,700,000

Direct mail marketers & manufacturers of corrugated solid fiber boxes & "lucite" products, bins, shipping cartons, office supplies & files.

TXU ENERGY
6555 Sierra Dr
Irving, TX 77002-6336
Telephone: (972) 868-8345, Web Site:
    www.txu.com
Dir Mktg: Eddie Otto

TARGET.COM
33 S 6th St
Minneapolis, MN 55402
Telephone: (612) 304-6545, Web Site:
    www.target.com

TAYLOR CORP
1725 Roe Crest Dr
North Mankato, MN 56003-1806
Telephone: (507) 625-2828, FAX:
    (507) 625-3388
Pres: Bradley J. Schreier
VP Sls & Mktg: Gary Zellmer
VP Social Div: Jean Andersen
Christmas Mgr: Patricia Savig
DM Div Mgr: Paul Schleich
Conducts Business: U.S., Canada
Employees: 100

Primary Market Served: Business & Consumer

Holding company - imprinted items, stationary pens, business cards & greeting cards.

TAYLOR-STILES DIVISION
Littleford Day Inc
7451 Empire Dr
Florence, KY 41042
Telephone: (859) 525-7600, (800) 365-
    8555, FAX: (859) 525-1446, E-Mail:
    sales@littleford.com, Web Site:
    www.littleford.com
Pres & CEO: Donald Steedman
Mktg Mgr: William R. Barker
Conducts Business: Worldwide
Employees: 150
Primary Market Served: Business
Catalog available online
Advertising/Marketing Budget Related
    to Direct Marketing: 51-75%
Founded: 1882

Manufacture & market size reduction, waste reclamation & recycling equipment to various processing industries.

TECHNI-TOOL INC
1547 N Trooper Rd
Worcester, PA 19490
Telephone: (610) 941-2400, (800) 832-
    4866, FAX: (800) 854-8665, E-Mail:
    sales@techni-tool.com, Web Site:
    www.techni-tool.com
Pres: Paul Weiss
VP, Mktg: David Weitner
Exec VP: Steven Weiss
Exec VP: Stuart Weiss
VP, Sls: Michael Ryan
Conducts Business: Worldwide
Employees: 235
Primary Market Served: Business
Catalog available online
Direct online sales
Advertising/Marketing Budget Related
    to Direct Marketing: 76-100%
Founded: 1959
Gross sales or billing: $50,000,000

Supplier of tools, tool kits, soldering, test equipment & instrumentation for electronic production, assembly & repair.

TEKTRONIX INC
14200 SW Karl Braun Dr
Beaverton, OR 97077
Telephone: (503) 627-7111, (800) 833-
    9200, FAX: (503) 627-3247, Web
    Site: www.tektronix.com
Chmn, Pres & CEO: Rick Wills
VP, Sls: Richard McBee
Mktg Mgr: Steve Dawson
Sr VP & CFO: Colin L. Slade
Sr VP Corp Devel, Gen Counsel &
    Sec: James F. Dalton

VP & Gen Mgr: Bob Agnes
Employees: 4,400
Primary Market Served: Business
Catalog available online
Gross sales or billing: $1,100,000,000

Manufacture electronic measurement, communications & display equipment.

TELCORDIA TECHNOLOGIES
One Telcordia Dr
Piscataway, NJ 08854-4151
Telephone: (732) 699-2000, FAX:
    (973) 829-2458, Web Site: www.
    telcordia.com
CEO: Richard Smith
Sr VP Mktg: Graham Palmer
Tech Licensing Dir: Andrew Dudek
Exec VP Global Sls Mktg: Patrick Jog-
    gerst
Primary Market Served: Business

Telecommunications research & software.

TELECT INC
23321 E Knox Ave
Liberty Lake, WA 99019-9461
Telephone: (509) 926-6000, FAX:
    (509) 926-8915, E-Mail: getinfo@
    telect.com, Web Site: www.telect.
    com
Pres & CEO: Wayne E. Williams
Exec VP & CFO: Stan Hilbert
Founder & Chmn Bd: Bill Williams Jr.
Dir Corp Controller: Mike Drew
Dir Global Quality: Kelly Jones
Primary Market Served: Business
Catalog available online
Direct online sales

Manufacture telecommunications hardware.

THE DMA TELEFLORA
11444 W Olympic Blvd (fl 4)
Los Angeles, CA 90064-1546
Telephone: (310) 966-3586, Web Site:
    www.teleflora.com
Dir, Partner Mktg: Pamela Ng
Primary Market Served: Business & Consumer

TELEFONIX INC
2340 Ernie Kruger Cir
Waukegan, IL 60087-3224
Telephone: (847) 244-4500, Web Site:
    www.telefonixinc.com
VP, Sls Mktg: Allison Burke
Primary Market Served: Business

TENNESSEE VALLEY AUTHORITY
400 W Summit Hill Dr
Knoxville, TN 37902-1499
Telephone: (865) 632-2101, Web Site:
    www.tva.gov

Pres & CEO: Tom Kilgore
COO: William R. McCollum Jr.
Exec VP, Power System Opers: Terry Boston
Exec VP, Customer Resources: Kenneth R. Breeden
Exec VP, Gen Counsel: Maureen H. Dunn
Primary Market Served: Business
Catalog available online
Founded: 1933
Gross sales or billing: $9,100,000,000

Electrical Utility.

THE DMA TENSAR INTERNATIONAL CORPORATION
2500 Northwinds Pkwy (Suite 500)
Alpharetta, GA 30009-2247
Telephone: (404) 250-1290, Web Site: www.tensarcorp.com
VP Mktg: Tim Oliver
Primary Market Served: Business

TERMINIX INTERNATIONAL, THE TRUGREEN COMPANIES
860 Ridge Lake Blvd
Memphis, TN 38120-9434
Telephone: (901) 766-1105, Web Site: www.trugreenchemlawn.com
Sr VP: Norman Goldenberg
Primary Market Served: Business & Consumer

TESSCO INC
11126 McCormick Rd
Hunt Valley, MD 21031
Telephone: (410) 229-1000, (800) 508-5444, FAX: (410) 527-0005, E-Mail: webhelp@tessco.com, Web Site: www.tessco.com
CEO: Robert B. Barnhill Jr.
Conducts Business: U.S., Canada
Employees: 100
Primary Market Served: Business & Consumer
Founded: 1952

Distributor of wireless communications products.

TETLEY USA INC
155 Chestnut Ridge Rd, PO Box 856
Montvale, NJ 07645-1156
Telephone: (203) 929-9200, (800) 728-0084, FAX: (203) 926-0876, Web Site: www.tetleyusa.com
VP Retail Sls: Ron Stroup
COO: Charlie Mc Carthy
Conducts Business: U.S.
Primary Market Served: Business & Consumer

Tea manufacturer.

TEXAS INDUSTRIES INC
1341 W Mockingbird Ln
Dallas, TX 75247
Telephone: (972) 647-6700, FAX: (972) 647-3878, Web Site: www.txi.com
Chmn: Robert D. Rogers
Pres: Melvin G. Brekhus
Exec VP & CFO: Richard M. Fowler
VP, Steel: Tommy A. Valenta
Primary Market Served: Business
Catalog available online
Gross sales or billing: $996,000,000

Manufacture & sell cement, concrete, steel & masonry products.

TEXWIPE CO
1210 S Park Dr
Kernersville, NC 27284-3104
Telephone: (201) 684-1800, (800) TEXWIPE, FAX: (201) 684-1801, E-Mail: info@texwipe.com, Web Site: www.texwipe.com
Pres & CEO: William Paley
Prod Mktg Mgr: Mark King
Facilities Mgr: Larry Ruvolo
Corp Acct Mgr: Tim Daly
Conducts Business: Worldwide
Employees: 200
Primary Market Served: Business
Catalog available online
Indirect online sales
Advertising/Marketing Budget Related to Direct Marketing: 26-50%
Founded: 1964

Manufacturer of contamination & control products for hospitals, laboratories & clear rooms.

THERMAL PRODUCT SOLUTIONS
Div. of Lunaire Ltd
PO Box 150
White Deer, PA 17887-0150
Telephone: (570) 538-7200, (800) 586-2473
Pres: Michael Grausam
VP: Stuart Lunick
VP: Arthur Campbell
VP Engrng: Troy Boring
Application Engrng Mgr: Glenn Cunningham
Mktg Coord: Erin Hall
Conducts Business: Worldwide
Employees: 250
Primary Market Served: Business
Catalog available online
Indirect online sales
Advertising/Marketing Budget Related to Direct Marketing: 0-25%
Direct Marketing ad budget: $90,000
Direct Mail: 20%
Magazines: 80%
Founded: 1932
Gross sales or billing: $20,000,000

Test chambers for the simulation of environmental conditions - temperature, humidity, altitude, pressure & combined environments. Burn-in, temperature cycling, thermal shock, stress screening, precision lab ovens, vacuum & clean room ovens. Sell to all industries & the government.

THERMO PRO
1600 Distribution Dr (Suite D)
Duluth, GA 30097
Telephone: (678) 475-1647, (800) 523-5542, FAX: (678) 475-1747, Web Site: www.thermopro.com
Pres: David Gould
VP: Michael L. Gould
Mktg Mgr: Nancy Prossick
Conducts Business: U.S., Canada, Great Britain, France
Employees: 30
Primary Market Served: Business & Consumer
Catalog available online
Advertising/Marketing Budget Related to Direct Marketing: 0-25%
Founded: 1970

Manufacturer & distributor of storage containers, magazine displays & literature organizers.

THETFORD CORP
7101 Jackson Rd
Ann Arbor, MI 48103
Telephone: (734) 769-6000, (800) 543-1219, FAX: (734) 769-2023, Web Site: www.thetford.com
Pres & CEO: John Arlen
VP, Opers: Don Ternes
Mktg Mgr: Armin Luzi
Conducts Business: Worldwide
Employees: 275
Primary Market Served: Business & Consumer
Catalog available online
Founded: 1963
Gross sales or billing: $75,000,000

Manufacturer of sanitation products & systems for recreational vehicle & marine industries.

THE DMA THOMAS COMPUTER CORP
203 Park Lake St
Orlando, FL 32803-3823
Telephone: (407) 855-2020, (800) 621-3906, FAX: (407) 426-2805, E-Mail: hildap@thomascompute.com, Web Site: www.thomascomputer.com
Pres: Charles Green
VP: Douglas Polkosky
VP: Hilda Polkosky
Treas & Sec: Stanley Green
Conducts Business: Worldwide
Employees: 16

Primary Market Served: Business & Consumer
Indirect online sales
Advertising/Marketing Budget Related to Direct Marketing: 76-100%
Founded: 1965

Marketer of computers, supplies & accessories.

THOMAS KLISE/CRIMSON MULTIMEDIA

PO Box 720
Mystic, CT 06355-0720
Telephone: (800) 937-0092, FAX: (860) 536-5141, E-Mail: info@crimsoninc.com, Web Site: www.crimsoninc.com
Pres: Molly Klise
Conducts Business: U.S.
Employees: 13
Primary Market Served: Business
Catalog available online
Indirect online sales
Advertising/Marketing Budget Related to Direct Marketing: 76-100%
Direct Marketing ad budget:
Direct Mail: 90%
Magazines: 5%
Newspapers: 5%
Founded: 1994
Gross sales or billing: $2,500,000

Educational & entertainment software for school & library use.

THORLO INC

2210 Newton Dr, PO Box 5399
Statesville, NC 28687
Telephone: (704) 872-6522, (888) 846-7567, FAX: (704) 838-7005, Web Site: www.thorlo.com
VP, Mktg: Robert Ravich
Employees: 350
Primary Market Served: Consumer
Founded: 1953

Sock manufacturer.

THOUGHT TECHNOLOGY LTD

2180 Belgrave Ave
Montreal, PQ, Canada H4A 2L8
Telephone: (514) 489-8251, (800) 361-3651, FAX: (514) 489-8255, E-Mail: lawrence@thoughttechnology.com, Web Site: www.thoughttechnology.com
Pres: Hal K. Myers
VP & Co-Founder: Lawrence Klein
Sales & Mktg Mgr: Shawn Tian
Conducts Business: Worldwide
Employees: 45
Primary Market Served: Business
Catalog available online
Advertising/Marketing Budget Related to Direct Marketing: 0-25%

Direct Marketing ad budget:
Direct Mail: 50%
Magazines: 25%
Telephone: 25%
Founded: 1974

Manufacturer of Bio-feedback equipment.

THOUSAND TRAILS LP

2 N Riverside Plz (Suite 800)
Chicago, IL 60606-2682
Telephone: (214) 618-7200, (800) 205-0606, FAX: (214) 618-7324, Web Site: www.1000trails.com
Pres & CEO: John Malone
CFO: Bryan D. Reed
VP, Sls & Mktg: R. Gerald Gelinas
VP, Gen Counsel: Walter B. Jaccard
VP HR: David McCrum
Conducts Business: U.S.
Employees: 2,400
Primary Market Served: Consumer
Catalog available online
Indirect online sales
Advertising/Marketing Budget Related to Direct Marketing: 51-75%
Gross sales or billing: $72,000,000

Sell memberships to a private resort network. Campsites in the US & British Columbia & recreational facilities.

THREE GEORGES AND THE NUTHOUSE

558 S Broad St
Mobile, AL 36603-1124
Telephone: (334) 433-1689, FAX: (334) 433-3364, E-Mail: sales@threegeorges.com, Web Site: www.threegeorges.com
Pres & CEO: Scott Gonzales
VP: Siobhan Gonzales
Conducts Business: U.S.
Employees: 15
Primary Market Served: Business & Consumer
Catalog available online
Direct online sales

Marketer of shelled pecans & fruit cakes sold wholesale & retail.

THE DMA 3M POST-IT DIRECT RESPONSE PRODUCTS

3M Center Bldg
Saint Paul, MN 55144-1001
Telephone: (651) 733-1110, Web Site: www.mmm.com
Mktg Supvr: Mindy Shea
Primary Market Served: Business

TIMBER CREST FARMS

4791 Dry Creek Rd
Healdsburg, CA 95448

Telephone: (707) 433-8251, FAX: (707) 433-8255, E-Mail: tcf@sonic.net, Web Site: www.sonic.net/tcf
Owner: Ronald E. Waltenspiel
Mktg Dir: Ruth Waltenspiel
Conducts Business: Worldwide
Employees: 17
Primary Market Served: Business & Consumer
Catalog available online
Direct online sales
Advertising/Marketing Budget Related to Direct Marketing: 0-25%
Direct Marketing ad budget:
Direct Mail: 10%
Magazines: 80%
Newspapers: 10%
Founded: 1957
Gross sales or billing: $4,000,000

Grow, process & package dried fruits, nuts, dried tomatoes & gift packs.

TIMBERLAND.COM

200 Domain Dr
Stratham, NH 03885
Telephone: (603) 772-9500, Web Site: www.Timberland.com
Pres: Jeffrey Swartz
Exec VP: Ken Pucker
Exec VP Fin: Brian McKeon
Conducts Business: U.S.
Employees: 600
Primary Market Served: Consumer
Direct online sales
Advertising/Marketing Budget Related to Direct Marketing: 0-25%
Direct Marketing ad budget:
Direct Mail: 100%
Founded: 1955
Gross sales or billing: $2,000,000,000

Footwear and apparel for the outdoors for our own Timberland retail and factory stores and wholesale to other retailers.

TIME PRODUCTS INTERNATIONAL

501 Pierce St
Del Rio, TX 78840-5456
Telephone: (847) 459-8885, FAX: (847) 459-8111, E-Mail: cttpi@aol.com, Web Site: www.tpi2000.com
Pres: Herbert Kwok
Sr VP, Mktg: Edward Gusfield
VP: Paul Berko
Employees: 20
Primary Market Served: Business & Consumer
Advertising/Marketing Budget Related to Direct Marketing: 0-25%
Direct Marketing ad budget:
Direct Mail: 100%
Founded: 1977
Gross sales or billing: $8,000,000

Small electronic consumer-type items - clocks, calculators & radios to direct mail & mail order. Also, promotional products.

TIME/SYSTEM
150 Front St (Fl 1 Bldg C)
Chicopee, MA 01013
Telephone: (800) 637-9942, FAX: (800) 269-3075, E-Mail: customerservice@timesystem.us, Web Site: www.timesystem.us
Pres: Sheryl Hofmann
Conducts Business: U.S., Canada
Employees: 50
Primary Market Served: Business & Consumer
Advertising/Marketing Budget Related to Direct Marketing: 0-25%
Founded: 1981

Manufacturer & distributor of productivity tools & training (i.e. paper-based management systems, software, workshops).

TIME WARNER INC
1 Time Warner Ctr
New York, NY 10019-8016
Telephone: (212) 484-8000, Web Site: www.timewarner.com
Chmn & CEO: Jeffrey L. Bewkes
Exec VP, Corp Communs: Keith Cocozza
Exec VP & Gen Counsel: Paul T. Cappuccio
Exec VP Admin: Patricia Fili-Krushel
Exec VP & CFO: John K. Martin
Exec VP Global Pub Policy: Carol A. Melton
Exec VP: Olaf Olafsson
Primary Market Served: Business & Consumer

Multimedia corporation.

TIMM MEDICAL TECHNOLOGIES, INC
9600 W 76th St Ste T
Eden Prairie, MN 55344-3922
Telephone: (952) 947-9410, (800) 438-8592, FAX: (952) 947-9411, Web Site: www.timmmedical.com
Founder & Chmn: Gerry Timm
Pres & CEO: Gerry Mattys
CFO: Bill Cook
Mgr: Camille Christianson
Employees: 120
Primary Market Served: Business & Consumer
Catalog available online
Direct online sales
Founded: 1997

Markets impotence & incontinence diagnostic & management products to doctors, pharmacists & consumers.

TOGETHER
15443 Knoll Trail (Suite 130)
Dallas, TX 75248
Telephone: (972) 407-1609, (800) 678-DATE, FAX: (972) 407-0082, Web Site: www.togetherdating.com
CEO: Paul Falzone
Primary Market Served: Consumer

Dating service.

TOLAND HOME AND GARDEN INC
273 N Otto St
Port Townsend, WA 98368-9780
Telephone: (504) 893-9503, (800) 989-6287, E-Mail: info@tolandhomeandgarden.com, Web Site: www.tolandhomeandgarden.com
Owner: Bruce Solly
Consultant: David T. Sands
Consultant: Jill Sands
Conducts Business: U.S.
Employees: 125
Primary Market Served: Business
Catalog available online
Advertising/Marketing Budget Related to Direct Marketing: 51-75%

Manufacturer of personalized door & car mats, accent rugs & pillows; including decorated flags, comfort mats & computer mouse pads.

TOMAHAWK LIVE TRAP CO
PO Box 323
Tomahawk, WI 54487-0323
Telephone: (715) 453-3550, (800) 272-8727, FAX: (715) 453-4326, E-Mail: trapem@livetrap.com, Web Site: www.livetrap.com
Pres: Greg Smith
Sls & Fin Exec: Mary S. Smith
Conducts Business: U.S., Canada, Argentina, Brazil, England, Germany, Mexico
Employees: 45
Primary Market Served: Business & Consumer
Catalog available online
Direct online sales
Founded: 1925

Traps & cages that capture animals alive & unharmed. Animal traps, cages & squeeze cages, animal control poles & protection gloves.

THE TORO CONSUMER DIV
The Toro Co
8111 Lyndale Ave S
Bloomington, MN 55420
Telephone: (952) 888-8801, (888) 384-9939, FAX: (952) 887-8258, Web Site: www.thetorocompany.com
Chmn, Pres & CEO: Mike Hoffman

VP, CFO & Treas: Stephen P. Wolfe
VP: Dennis P. Himan
Mktg Dir: Tom Swain
Sls Dir: Frank Conney
Conducts Business: Worldwide
Employees: 5,370
Primary Market Served: Consumer
Catalog available online
Indirect online sales
Gross sales or billing: $1,800,000,000

Sell electrical lawn & garden equipment & electric snow blowers.

TOTER INC
841 Meacham Rd
Statesville, NC 28677
Telephone: (704) 872-8171, (800) 424-0422, FAX: (704) 878-0734, E-Mail: info@toter.com, Web Site: www.toter.com
Pres, CEO: Larry Boppe
VP, Sls & Mktg: John Scott
CFO: Jeff Gilliam
Conducts Business: U.S., Japan
Employees: 400
Primary Market Served: Business & Consumer
Direct Marketing ad budget:
Magazines: 100%
Gross sales or billing: $65,000,000

Manufacture molded polyethylene roll-out cart systems for commercial & residential recycling & refuse collection. Special office carts are available for confidential documents, office paper & aluminum can recycling.

TOYOTA MOTOR SALES USA INC
19001 S Western Ave
Torrance, CA 90501
Telephone: (310) 468-4000, (800) 331-4331, FAX: (310) 468-7841, Web Site: www.toyota.com
Chmn & CEO: Yukitoshi Funo
Pres: James Lentz
Grp VP & CFO: Tracey C. Doi
Employees: 8,900
Primary Market Served: Business & Consumer
Catalog available online
Indirect online sales
Gross sales or billing: $2,147,500,000

Corporate headquarters office for sales division within America.

TRANCOS INC
6800 Koll Center Pkwy (Ste 170)
Pleasanton, CA 94566-7044
Telephone: (650) 364-3110, Web Site: www.trancos.com
CEO: Brian Nelson

TRANSCAT

35 Vantage Point Dr
Rochester, NY 14624-1175
Telephone: (585) 352-9460, (800) 800-5001, FAX: (585) 352-1486, Web Site: www.transcat.com
Chairman: Carl E. Sassano
Pres, CEO & COO: Charles P. Hadeed
VP Fin CFO: John J. Zimmer
VP HR: John A. DeVoldre
VP Mktg: Jay F. Woychick
Conducts Business: Worldwide
Employees: 238
Primary Market Served: Business
Catalog available online
Direct online sales
Advertising/Marketing Budget Related to Direct Marketing: 51-75%
Founded: 1964
Gross sales or billing: $66,500,000

Distributor of calibration & test instruments. Also offers calibration services.

TRANSEMANTICS INC

1337 Connecticut Ave NW (4th fl)
Washington, DC 20036
Telephone: (202) 362-2505, FAX: (202) 686-5603, E-Mail: ili@transemantics.com, Web Site: www.transemantics.com
Dir: Marie-Laurence Wax
Mgr: Allen B. Cooperman
Conducts Business: U.S., Europe
Employees: 26
Primary Market Served: Business
Advertising/Marketing Budget Related to Direct Marketing: 76-100%
Founded: 1970
Gross sales or billing: $1,500,000

All aspects of foreign language communication, including, but not limited to: translating, interpreting, cultural analysis of promotional material aimed at foreign markets, typesetting, audiovisual narration, subtitling, tape transcription, language & culture research.

TRI-CHEM INC

681 Main St Ste 24, Bldg 24
Belleville, NJ 07109-3471
Telephone: (973) 751-9200, FAX: (973) 450-1057, (973) 450-1260, E-Mail: paints@trichem.com, Web Site: www.trichem.com
CEO: Andy McKnight
VP, Sls: Linda Musgrove
Opers Mgr: Kathleen Bodrato
Conducts Business: Worldwide
Employees: 250
Primary Market Served: Consumer
Advertising/Marketing Budget Related to Direct Marketing: 76-100%
Direct Marketing ad budget:
Direct Mail: 90%

Magazines: 4%
Newspapers: 5%
Telephone: 1%
Founded: 1950
Gross sales or billing: $420,000

Direct selling company. Sell fashion painting supply items to 10,000 independent dealers (in-home demonstrators).

TRI TECH LABORATORIES INC

1000 Robins Rd
Lynchburg, VA 24504-3516
Telephone: (434) 845-7073, FAX: (434) 847-4360, Web Site: www.tritechlabs.com
Pres: Ron Rogers
Conducts Business: U.S.
Primary Market Served: Business
Direct Marketing ad budget:
Direct Mail: 65%
Magazines: 15%
Newspapers: 5%
TV/Radio: 15%

Sell cosmetics, toiletries, food, household products, jewelry & giftware to independent sales agents.

TRICOR BRAUN

2145 Internationale Pkwy Ste 800
Woodridge, IL 60517-4830
Telephone: (708) 385-9333, FAX: (708) 385-3015, Web Site: www.tricorbraun.com
Chmn: Ken Kranzberg
Pres & CEO: Keith Strope
Exec VP, Design: Craig Sawicki
Conducts Business: U.S., Canada, Mexico, Central America, South America, Europe, Asia
Employees: 300
Primary Market Served: Business
Catalog available online
Advertising/Marketing Budget Related to Direct Marketing: 0-25%

Packaging, design & supply, focus on containers for cosmetic-personal care & household chemicals & fragrance.

TRILITHIC

9710 Park Davis Dr
Indianapolis, IN 46235-2390
Telephone: (317) 423-6604, Web Site: www.trilithic.com
Dir, Mktg & Communs: Karalee Slayton
Primary Market Served: Business

TRISTAR PRODUCTS

492 US Hwy 46 E
Fairfield, NJ 07004

Telephone: (973) 575-5400, FAX: (973) 683-6708, E-Mail: infotp@tristarproductsinc.com, Web Site: www.tristarproductsinc.com
Pres & CEO: Keith Mirchandani
VP & CFO: Steve Souers
Producer: Chris Bonanno
Dir Production: John Glouatts
Dir HR: Elizabeth Sandman
Primary Market Served: Business
Catalog available online
Direct online sales

International direct response marketing company. Markets products through TV, retail & catalog advertising.

TRITON COLLEGE

2000 Fifth Ave
River Grove, IL 60171
Telephone: (708) 456-0300, FAX: (708) 583-3121, Web Site: www.triton.edu
Pres: Patricia Granados
Exec Dir Mktg: Thomas D. Olson
Conducts Business: U.S.
Primary Market Served: Business & Consumer
Catalog available online
Founded: 1964

Two year community college & business employee training facility.

THE DMA TRUE VALUE CO

8600 W Bryn Mawr Ave
Chicago, IL 60631-3579
Telephone: (773) 695-5000, Web Site: www.truevalue.com
Dir Loyalty Mktg: Chuck Sample
Primary Market Served: Consumer

TRUGREEN/CHEMLAWN

461 Enterprise Dr
Lewis Center, OH 43035-9424
Telephone: (614) 846-1800, (800) TRUE-GREEN, FAX: (614) 431-0155, Web Site: www.trugreen.com
Chmn: George W. Tamke
CEO: J. Patrick Speinhour
Sr VP & CFO: Steve J. Martin
Branch Mgr: Al Karow
Conducts Business: U.S., Canada
Employees: 700
Primary Market Served: Business & Consumer
Advertising/Marketing Budget Related to Direct Marketing: 76-100%

Offer quality lawn, tree & shrub care to residential & commercial customers.

TRUITT BROTHERS INC

1105 Front St NE
Salem, OR 97301-1034

Telephone: (503) 362-3674, (800) 547-8712, FAX: (503) 588-2868, E-Mail: truittbrothers@truittbros.com, Web Site: www.truittbros.com
Pres: Peter Truitt
VP: David Truitt
Gen Mgr Spec Prods: Jeff Geyer
Mktg Mgr: Roger Plant
Food Svc Sls Dir: Rod Friesen
Conducts Business: U.S., Pacific Rim, Mexico
Employees: 350
Primary Market Served: Business

Produce shelf stable canned, tray & pouched products for institutional, wholesale & retail markets.

TUPPERWARE
14901 S Orange Blossom Trail
Orlando, FL 32837
Telephone: (407) 826-5050, (800) 366-3800, FAX: (407) 826-8874, Web Site: www.tupperware.com
CEO: Rick Goings
Consultant: Alan Kennedy
Pres, Natl Sls: Glenn Drake
VP, Prod Devel: Robert Woodard
Dir PR: Elinor Steele
Conducts Business: Worldwide
Primary Market Served: Consumer
Catalog available online
Direct online sales

Sell Tupperware products.

20TH CENTURY FOX TELEVISION
10201 W Pico Blvd (Bldg 88, Rm 30)
Los Angeles, CA 90064-2606
Telephone: (310) 444-8100, FAX: (310) 444-8101
Chmn: Gary Newman
Exec VP & CFO: Robert Barron
Exec VP: Bob Cesa
Exec VP: Elie Dekel
Sr VP, Mktg: Steven Melnick
Conducts Business: International (except U.S., Canada)
Employees: 400
Primary Market Served: Business & Consumer
Catalog available online
Advertising/Marketing Budget Related to Direct Marketing: 51-75%
Founded: 1983

Produces &/or acquires TV products, including movies of the week, maxi & mini-series & animated features for the international marketplace for sale to foreign broadcasters.

TYCO ELECTRONICS CORP
300 Constitution Dr
Menlo Park, CA 94025-1140
Telephone: (650) 361-3333, (800) 272-9243, FAX: (800) 361-5579, Web Site: www.tycoelectronics.com
Conducts Business: U.S.
Employees: 9,000
Primary Market Served: Business
Catalog available online
Indirect online sales
Advertising/Marketing Budget Related to Direct Marketing: 0-25%
Founded: 1957
Gross sales or billing: $640,000,000

Broad based materials science company. Develop & supply high performance products (many based on radiation chemistry) for the electronics, aerospace, processed electrical power, construction, telecommunications & consumer industries.

TYCO VALVES & CONTROLS
Div. of Tyco International Ltd
10707 Clay Rd (#200)
Houston, TX 77041-5497
Telephone: (713) 986-4665, (800) 343-0990, FAX: (713) 937-5466, Web Site: www.tycovalves.com
Chmn & CEO: Edward D. Breen
VP, Mktg: Mark Fucich
VP, Sls & Dist: Gene Crouch
Mgr, Mktg Svcs: Darrel Desrochers
Conducts Business: Worldwide
Employees: 594
Primary Market Served: Business
Catalog available online

Manufacturer of Butterfly Valves: ANSI Class 150/300 2''-36,'' AWWA 3''-96,'' Resilient Seat 1''-48,'' PTFE Lined 2''-12.'' Check Valves 2''-48.'' Electric, pneumatic and hydraulic actuators & accessories for quarter turn valves.

U-HAUL INTERNATIONAL
2727 N Central Ave
Phoenix, AZ 85004
Telephone: (602) 263-6011, (800) GO-UHAUL, FAX: (602) 263-6598, Web Site: www.uhaul.com
Chmn & CEO: Joe Shoen
Pres: James Taylor
Exec VP & Chief of Staff: Renee Royer
VP: Mark Shoen
VP, Mktg & Retail Sls Mgr: Richard Herrera
Conducts Business: U.S., Canada
Employees: 15,000
Primary Market Served: Business & Consumer
Catalog available online
Indirect online sales
Advertising/Marketing Budget Related to Direct Marketing: 0-25%
Founded: 1945

Gross sales or billing: $4,000,000,000
Truck & trailer rentals.

UGL EQUIS CORP
161 N Clark St (Suite 2400)
Chicago, IL 60601-3221
Telephone: (312) 424-8000, FAX: (312) 424-8080, Web Site: www.equiscorp.com
Pres & CEO: David Montross
Exec VP & CFO: Larry O'Drobinak
Mktg Coord: Lawrence Perea
HR: Linda Gamino
Commun: Megan Brody
Conducts Business: U.S.
Primary Market Served: Business & Consumer
Catalog available online
Founded: 1984

Real estate tenant representation.

USX
600 Grant St
Pittsburgh, PA 15219
Telephone: (412) 433-1121, E-Mail: webmaster@usx.com, Web Site: www.usx.com
Chmn & CEO USX Corp: Thomas J. Usher
Vice Chmn & CFO: Robert M. Hernandez
Public Affairs Mgr: John Armstrong
Primary Market Served: Business & Consumer

Manufacture iron & steel products & oil company.

ULTIMATE OFFICE
PO Box 688
Farmingdale, NJ 07727-0688
Telephone: (732) 780-6911, (800) 631-2233, FAX: (732) 780-9833, Web Site: www.ultoffice.com
Pres: Donald McGee
Database Mgr: Michele Scott
Conducts Business: U.S.
Employees: 25
Primary Market Served: Business
Advertising/Marketing Budget Related to Direct Marketing: 76-100%
Direct Marketing ad budget:
Direct Mail: 90%
Online: 10%

Manufacture & supply magnetic visual scheduling boards. Sell through direct mail to known inquirers & buyers of direct mail items.

ULTIMATE PRODUCTS INC
1151 Bay Blvd (Suite D)
Chula Vista, CA 91911-2669

Telephone: (813) 881-1575, (800) 477-4287, FAX: (813) 881-1831, E-Mail: office@ultimatehat.com, Web Site: www.ultimatehat.com
Pres: Monica McGrath
Conducts Business: Worldwide
Employees: 8
Primary Market Served: Business & Consumer
Catalog available online
Direct online sales
Founded: 1987

Manufacturer of nautical belts & jewelry.

ULTRA DIRECT MARKETING INC

PO Box 1575
Jackson, NJ 08527
Telephone: (732) 364-8337, (800) 365-8587, FAX: (732) 364-9598, E-Mail: contact@ultradirect.com, Web Site: www.ultradirect.com
Pres: Randi Hersh
Conducts Business: U.S.
Employees: 5
Primary Market Served: Business
Catalog available online
Direct online sales

Sell computer supplies & accessories.

UNADILLA LAMINATED PRODUCTS

Div. of Unadilla Silo Co Inc
32 Clifton St
Unadilla, NY 13849
Telephone: (607) 369-9341, FAX: (607) 369-3608, E-Mail: info@unalam.com, Web Site: www.unalam.com
Pres: Craig H. Van Cott
VP, Sls: Phillip Holowacz
Conducts Business: U.S., Canada
Employees: 75
Primary Market Served: Business & Consumer
Advertising/Marketing Budget Related to Direct Marketing: 0-25%
Direct Marketing ad budget:
Direct Mail: 50%
Magazines: 50%
Founded: 1906

Manufacturer of glue laminated wood arches, beams & trusses.

UNICOM ELECTRIC INC

565 Brea Canyon Rd Ste A
Walnut, CA 91789-3004
Telephone: (626) 964-7873, (800) 346-6668, FAX: (626) 964-7880, E-Mail: info@unicomlink.com, Web Site: www.unicomlink.com
Pres: Jeffrey Lo
Sls Mgr: Sam Hen

Conducts Business: U.S., Canada
Employees: 32
Primary Market Served: Business & Consumer
Catalog available online
Advertising/Marketing Budget Related to Direct Marketing: 0-25%
Founded: 1986
Gross sales or billing: $3,100,000

Network hardware to the enterprise & Soho market.

UNILEVER BEST FOODS

Subs. of Unilever United States
800 Sylvan Ave
Englewood Cliffs, NJ 07632
Telephone: (201) 567-8000, FAX: (201) 871-8257, E-Mail: comments@unilever.com, Web Site: www.unilever.com
Pres: Michael Polk
CEO: Patrick Cescau
Market Research Dir: Donna Goldfarb
Conducts Business: Worldwide
Employees: 179,000
Primary Market Served: Consumer
Catalog available online
Gross sales or billing: $56,039,072,165

Food, beverage & gelatin products.

UNION SWITCH & SIGNAL INC

Subs. of Ansaldo Signal NV
1000 Technology Dr
Pittsburgh, PA 15219-3120
Telephone: (412) 688-2400, (800) 351-1520, FAX: (412) 688-2399, Web Site: www.switch.com
Prod Mngmt Dir: Robert Galbraith
VP Sls & Mktg: John P. Dolan
Conducts Business: Worldwide
Employees: 950
Primary Market Served: Business
Advertising/Marketing Budget Related to Direct Marketing: 0-25%
Direct Marketing ad budget: $200,000
Direct Mail: $100,000
Magazines: $100,000
Founded: 1881
Gross sales or billing: $270,900,000

Supplier of traditional & modern signal & control products & systems for Class 1, Regional & Short Line Railroads, transit & commuter applications; offer individual products, turnkey systems, maintenance & repair, engineering & service.

UNISYS

Unisys Way
Blue Bell, PA 19424-0001
Telephone: (215) 986-4011, (800) 874-8647, FAX: (215) 986-2312, Web Site: www.unisys.com

Chmn: Henry C. Duques
Pres, CEO & Dir: Joseph W. McGrath
Sr VP & CFO: Janet B. Haugen
CTO: Frederick Dillman
VP, Mktg: Timothy Lambert
Conducts Business: Worldwide
Employees: 30,000
Primary Market Served: Business
Catalog available online
Advertising/Marketing Budget Related to Direct Marketing: 0-25%
Founded: 1886
Gross sales or billing: $5,757,200,000

Marketer of office equipment, industrial mainframe, computer products & consumables.

UNITED AIR SPECIALISTS INC

Subs. of Clareor Inc
4440 Creek Rd
Cincinnati, OH 45242
Telephone: (513) 891-0400, (800) 992-4422, FAX: (513) 891-4882, E-Mail: uas@uasinc.com, Web Site: www.uasinc.com
Pres: Rich Larson
VP, Mktg: Pam Curry
Conducts Business: Worldwide
Employees: 230
Primary Market Served: Business & Consumer
Catalog available online
Indirect online sales
Advertising/Marketing Budget Related to Direct Marketing: 51-75%
Direct Marketing ad budget: $230,000
Direct Mail: $130,000
Magazines: $45,000
Newspapers: $30,000
Online: $25,000
Founded: 1966

Manufacturer & distributor of electronic air cleaners for commercial & industrial use.

UNITED SECURITY PRODUCTS INC

PO Box 785
Poway, CA 92074-0785
Telephone: (858) 413-0149, (800) 227-1592, FAX: (858) 413-0124, E-Mail: usp@unitedsecurity.com, Web Site: www.unitedsecurity.com
Pres: Ted Greene
Conducts Business: Worldwide
Employees: 32
Primary Market Served: Business & Consumer
Catalog available online
Founded: 1972
Gross sales or billing: $3,900,000

Manufacturer of burglar & fire alarm equipment.

UNITED STAFFING SYSTEMS
130 William St Fl 6
New York, NY 10038-5068
Telephone: (212) 743-0300, (800) 972-9725, FAX: (212) 576-1569, Web Site: www.unitedstaffing.com
Pres: Barry Saide
Primary Market Served: Business & Consumer
Catalog available online

Full-service personnel agency.

US BRANDING GROUP, LLC
PO Box 540957
Lake Worth, FL 33467
Telephone: (561) 966-8090
Primary Market Served: Business & Consumer

US GAS & ELECTRIC
290 NW 165th St (PH5)
Miami, FL 33169-6457
Telephone: (305) 947-7880, Web Site: www.usgande.com
Dir, Mktg: Sarah Rose

US HISTORICAL SOCIETY
8417 Glazebrook Ave
Richmond, VA 23228
Telephone: (800) 788-4478, FAX: (804) 648-0002, E-Mail: administrator@ushs.org, Web Site: www.ushs.org
Chmn: Robert H. Kline
Treas: Carole Cloudt
Conducts Business: U.S., Japan, France, Italy, Switzerland
Employees: 10
Primary Market Served: Consumer

Market artistic & historic objects in cooperation with museums & historic organizations.

US PLAYING CARD CO
Div. of Brown & Bigelow Inc
300 Gap Way
Erlanger, KY 41018-3160
Telephone: (513) 396-5700, (800) 542-7430, FAX: (513) 392-5879
Pres: Charles Zunk
VP, Sls: Gregory Huslen
Conducts Business: U.S., Canada, Europe
Primary Market Served: Business
Advertising/Marketing Budget Related to Direct Marketing: 0-25%

Manufacturer of playing cards & calendars.

UNIVERSAL CORP
1501 N Hamilton St
Richmond, VA 23230
Telephone: (804) 359-9311, FAX: (804) 254-3582, Web Site: www.universalcorp.com
Chmn & CEO: Henry H. Harrell
Pres: Allen King
Primary Market Served: Business
Founded: 1918

Importers & exporters of tobacco leaf.

UNIVERSAL ENGINEERING CORP
800 First Ave NW
Cedar Rapids, IA 52405-3999
Telephone: (319) 365-0441, (800) 366-2051, FAX: (319) 369-5440, E-Mail: info@universalcrusher.com, Web Site: www.universalcrusher.com
CEO: Daniel Ferguson
CFO: Tom J. Werning
Sls & Mktg Mgr: Gerry Mangrich
Conducts Business: Worldwide
Employees: 60
Primary Market Served: Business
Catalog available online
Direct Marketing ad budget:
Magazines: 100%
Founded: 1906
Gross sales or billing: $10,000,000

Manufacture rock crushers, shredders & apron feeders.

UNIVERSAL SECURITY INSTRUMENTS INC
11407 Cronhill Dr (Suite A)
Owings Mills, MD 21117-6218
Telephone: (410) 363-3000, FAX: (410) 363-2218, E-Mail: sales@universalsecurity.com, Web Site: www.universalsecurity.com
CEO, Sec & Treas: James B. Huff
Pres: Harvey B. Grossblatt
Office Mgr: Susie Bowles
Conducts Business: U.S.
Employees: 15
Primary Market Served: Business & Consumer
Catalog available online
Direct online sales
Founded: 1969
Gross sales or billing: $35,800,000

Designs and sells smoke alarms, carbon monoxide alarms and outdoor floodlights in retail stores. Smoke alarms for the hearing impaired are sold to distributors by USI Electric subsidiary.

UNIVERSAL TRAINING
736 N Western Ave (Suite 323)
Lake Forest, IL 60045
Telephone: (847) 235-2170, E-Mail: information@universaltraining.com, Web Site: www.universaltraining.com

Pres & Co-Owner: Carl Ruggiero
Dir Mktg & PR: Maureen Smith-McKee
Sr Cons & Co-Owner: Mary Carolan
Sr Cons & Co-Owner: John Doyle
Conducts Business: U.S., Canada & Mexico
Employees: 25
Primary Market Served: Business
Direct online sales
Advertising/Marketing Budget Related to Direct Marketing: 0-25%
Founded: 1968
Gross sales or billing: $2,000,000

Custom training.

UNIWAY MANAGEMENT CORP
dba Ucac Financial Services
5182A Old Dixie Hwy
Forest Park, GA 30297
Telephone: (404) 363-6200, (888) 386-4929, FAX: (404) 363-8848, E-Mail: uniway@bellsouth.net, Web Site: www.uniway.com
Pres: Robert C. Hardy
Chmn Bd: Robert W. Carter
Conducts Business: U.S.
Employees: 11
Primary Market Served: Consumer
Advertising/Marketing Budget Related to Direct Marketing: 51-75%
Founded: 1979
Gross sales or billing: $1,500,000

Consumer services & franchise continuing/club programs & consumer products - wholesalers/distributors.

UPSTART
Div. of Highsmith Co
PO Box 8010
Madison, WI 53708-8010
Telephone: (920) 563-9571, FAX: (800) 448-5828, Web Site: www.highsmith.com
Gen Mgr Dist: Bill Flood
Conducts Business: U.S.
Employees: 15
Primary Market Served: Business & Consumer
Direct Marketing ad budget:
Direct Mail: 95%
Magazines: 5%

Sell posters, bookmarks, T-shirts, buttons, sweatshirts, books, plastic book bags, certificates, mobiles, bulletin board decorators & balloons to libraries & schools.

URBAN MAPPING INC
690 Fifth St (Suite 200)
San Francisco, CA 94107-1517
Telephone: (415) 946-8170, Web Site: www.urbanmapping.com

CEO: Ian White

UTILITIES SUPPLY CORP
Subs. of F W Webb
50 Everberg Rd
Woburn, MA 01801-1019
Telephone: (781) 395-9023, (800) 343-7555, FAX: (781) 395-2329, (800) 232-8726, E-Mail: jge@fwwebb. com, Web Site: www.uscosupply. com
Opers Mgr: John Everett
Conducts Business: Worldwide
Employees: 35
Primary Market Served: Business & Consumer
Catalog available online
Direct online sales
Advertising/Marketing Budget Related to Direct Marketing: 76-100%
Direct Marketing ad budget: $100,000
Direct Mail: 50%
Magazines: 40%
Telephone: 10%

Distributor of thermoplastic piping products & accessories, environmental, plumbing & heating products.

VALDAWN WATCH CO
2910 Thomson Ave (6th fl)
Long Island City, NY 11101-2939
Telephone: (201) 807-1110, FAX: (201) 807-0228
Pres: Mark Schell
Mktg Dir: Amy Burdick
Conducts Business: U.S.
Employees: 15
Primary Market Served: Business
Advertising/Marketing Budget Related to Direct Marketing: 26-50%
Gross sales or billing: $3,500,000

Design & manufactures custom watches.

VALENTI CLASSICS
355 S Hwy 41
Caledonia, WI 53108
Telephone: (262) 835-2070, FAX: (262) 835-2575, Web Site: www. valenticlassics.com
CEO: Steve Valenti

THE DMA VALENTINE RESEARCH INC
10280 Alliance Rd
Cincinnati, OH 45242-4710
Telephone: (513) 984-8900, (800) 331-3030, FAX: (513) 984-8976, E-Mail: sales@valentine1.com, Web Site: www.valentine1.com
Pres: Michael D. Valentine
Dir Mktg: Pete Kaufman
Conducts Business: U.S., Canada
Primary Market Served: Consumer
Catalog available online

Direct online sales
Vertically integrated electronic products & radar locators manufacturer & direct marketer.

VANCE INDUSTRIES INC
5617 W Howard St
Niles, IL 60714-4011
Telephone: (847) 375-8900, FAX: (847) 375-6818, E-Mail: vance@ vanceind.com, Web Site: www. vanceind.com
Chmn & CEO: William Rapp
Pres: Jim Schleiter
Mktg Svcs Mgr: Lisa Walker
Retail Div: John Kensey
Conducts Business: U.S., Canada, Europe
Employees: 70
Primary Market Served: Business & Consumer
Advertising/Marketing Budget Related to Direct Marketing: 0-25%
Direct Marketing ad budget:
Direct Mail: 35%
Magazines: 55%
Telephone: 10%

Manufacturer of cutting boards, drawer organizers, kitchen sinks & bar sinks.

THE VANE BROTHERS CO
2100 Frankfurst Ave
Baltimore, MD 21226-1026
Telephone: (410) 631-5096, FAX: (410) 631-7781, E-Mail: webmaster@vanebros.com, Web Site: www.vanebros.com
Pres: Duff Hughes
Mktg Dir: Don Glenn
Primary Market Served: Business

Marine transportation of petroleum products & sale of bunker fuel to ships.

VEER
119 14th St NW (Suite 400)
Calgary, AB, Canada T2N IZ6
Telephone: (403) 234-7901, Web Site: www.veer.com
Mktg Mgr: Marla Clarke
Primary Market Served: Business

VENTYX
400 Perimeter Center Ter NE Ste 500
Atlanta, GA 30346-1231
Telephone: (770) 952-8444, (800) 868-0497, FAX: (770) 955-2977, E-Mail: support@ventyx.com, Web Site: www.ventyx.com
Pres: Gregory Dukat
VP, Mktg: Steve Roth
Event Mktg Mgr: Martha Thompson
Mktg Coord: Ronnie Norton
Conducts Business: Worldwide

Employees: 1,000
Primary Market Served: Business
Founded: 1976

Software development company, EAM.

VERIAD
Subs. of Moore Wallace
650 Columbia St
Brea, CA 92821-2912
Telephone: (714) 990-2700, (800) 962-0658, FAX: (800) 962-0658, E-Mail: info@veriad.com, Web Site: www. veriad.com
Pres: Cal Laird
Owner: David G. Smith
CEO Moore Wallace: Mark A. Angelsom
VP Customer Tech: Denise Milano
Lead Svc Mgr: Laura Richards
Info Tech Mgr: Micke Clemens
Conducts Business: U.S., Canada
Employees: 165
Primary Market Served: Business
Catalog available online
Direct online sales
Founded: 1958

Manufacturer of pressure sensitive labels supplied direct to hospitals, business & industry.

THE DMA VERIZON
1320 N Court House Rd (fl 9)
Arlington, VA 22201-2525
Telephone: (703) 351-3156, FAX: (703) 708-4297
Primary Market Served: Business & Consumer

Bell Atlantic internet service provider.

VERTEX INC
1041 Old Cassatt Rd
Berwyn, PA 19312
Telephone: (610) 640-4200, (800) 355-3500, FAX: (610) 640-5892, Web Site: www.vertexinc.com
Pres & CEO: Jeff Westphal
VP, Mktg: Gerry Hurley
VP Commun & Pub Affairs: Alex Smith
Conducts Business: U.S., Canada
Employees: 160
Primary Market Served: Business
Catalog available online
Indirect online sales
Founded: 1978

Developer & marketer of computer software for tax-related applications. Products are used for the calculation of taxes by companies doing business in several states. Sales tax software covers all taxing jurisdictions in the U.S. & Canada. Payroll software interfaces with payroll systems to calculate federal, state & local withholding taxes. Telecommunication tax software provides utility tax rate information for all taxing jurisdictions in the U.S.

THE DMA VIACOM INC
dba Viacom
1515 Broadway
New York, NY 10036-8901
Telephone: (212) 258-6000, FAX: (212) 258-6464, Web Site: www.viacom.com
Exec Chmn: Sumner E. Redstone
Pres, CEO & Dir: Philippe Dauman
Sr Exec VP, Chief Admin Officer & CFO: Thomas E. Dooley
Exec VP, Corp Commun: Carl D. Folta
Exec VP, HR & Admin: Denise White
Employees: 12,800
Primary Market Served: Business & Consumer
Gross sales or billing: $11,466,500,000

Entertainment & publishing.

VIAHEALTH
1425 Portland Ave
Rochester, NY 14621-3001
Telephone: (585) 922-4000, (585) 922-3677, FAX: (585) 922-3929, Web Site: www.viahealth.org
Pres: Mark Clement
Dir: Joseph Vasile
Sr VP: Dr. Richard Gangemi
VP, Fin Svcs: John Midolo
Dept Chief: John Schriver
Mktg: Mike Tedesco
Conducts Business: U.S.
Employees: 6,000
Primary Market Served: Business & Consumer
Catalog available online
Advertising/Marketing Budget Related to Direct Marketing: 0-25%
Direct Marketing ad budget:
Direct Mail: 50%
Newspapers: 25%
TV/Radio: 25%
Gross sales or billing: $202,000,000

Inpatient & ambulatory healthcare to community.

VIATECH PUBLISHING SOLUTIONS INC
1440 5th Ave
Bay Shore, NY 11706-4147

Telephone: (631) 968-8500, (800) 645-8558, FAX: (631) 968-0830, Web Site: www.viatechpub.com
COO: Ron Simmons
VP, Natl Sls: Thomas Bergenholtz
Conducts Business: U.S., Canada, Mexico
Employees: 500
Primary Market Served: Business
Catalog available online
Indirect online sales
Advertising/Marketing Budget Related to Direct Marketing: 0-25%
Founded: 1906

Manufacture loose leaf binders & accessories. On demand printing & fulfillment services.

VICTORY CORPS
2730 Nevada Ave N
New Hope, MN 55427
Telephone: (763) 561-5600, (800) 328-6120, FAX: (763) 561-8523, E-Mail: cs@victorycorps.com, Web Site: www.victorycorps.com
Pres: Dennis Flaherty
Sls Mgr: Brian Knoop
Mktg Coord: Stacy Handeland
Mktg Mgr: Polly Fossum
Conducts Business: U.S., Canada
Employees: 70
Primary Market Served: Business & Consumer
Catalog available online
Direct online sales
Direct Marketing ad budget: $225,000
Direct Mail: 30%
Magazines: 20%
Online: 30%
Telephone: 20%
Founded: 1904
Gross sales or billing: $10,000,000

Retail catalog sales of flags, flag poles, custom banners, parade floats & float kits, sign and banner displays, trade show displays and accessories.

VIERK NATIONAL SUPPLY
2300 Commonwealth Ave
North Chicago, IL 60064
Telephone: (847) 869-4318, (800) 428-7548, FAX: (847) 689-4412, Web Site: www.vierk.com
CFO: Amber Swift
Conducts Business: U.S.
Employees: 11
Primary Market Served: Business
Catalog available online
Indirect online sales
Advertising/Marketing Budget Related to Direct Marketing: 76-100%
Direct Marketing ad budget:
Direct Mail: $240,000
Telephone: $18,000
Founded: 1949

Gross sales or billing: $2,600,000
Wholesale distributor of plumbing/heating & industrial supplies.

VIEW VIDEO INC/ARCADIA ENTERTAINMENT CORP
PO Box 77
Saugerties, NY 12477
Telephone: (845) 246-9955, FAX: (845) 246-9966, E-Mail: sales@view.com, Web Site: www.view.com
Pres & Founder: Bob Karcy
Conducts Business: Worldwide
Employees: 15
Primary Market Served: Business & Consumer
Catalog available online
Direct online sales
Advertising/Marketing Budget Related to Direct Marketing: 26-50%
Founded: 1984

Pre-recorded home video cassettes. Broadcast quality programming in the following core areas: art, classical music, opera, dance, jazz & pop music, parenting/children's interactive, sports, modern lifestyles.

VIKING PUMP INC
Div. of IDEX Corp
406 State St, Box 8
Cedar Falls, IA 50613-0008
Telephone: (319) 266-1741, FAX: (319) 273-8157, E-Mail: info@vikingpump.com, Web Site: www.vikingpump.com
Mktg Mgr: James Mayer
VP, Mktg & Sls: Kevin Rhodes
VP, Domestic Mktg: W. Vogel
Mktg Dir: James Murphy
Conducts Business: Worldwide
Employees: 770
Primary Market Served: Business
Catalog available online
Direct online sales
Advertising/Marketing Budget Related to Direct Marketing: 0-25%
Direct Marketing ad budget:
Direct Mail: 10%
Magazines: 90%
Founded: 1911

Manufacturer of positive displacement rotary pumps. Marketed through a worldwide distribution organization to petroleum, chemical & petrochemical industries. Food, pulp and paper manufacturers & most other process industries.

VILLAGE WEAVERS
418 Villita St Ste 800
San Antonio, TX 78205-2910

Telephone: (210) 222-0776, E-Mail:
shop@villageweavers.com, Web Site:
www.villageweavers.com
Pres: Chris Van Wyk

VIRCO MANUFACTURING CORP

Hwy 65 S
Conway, AR 72033
Telephone: (501) 329-2901, (800) 448-
4726, FAX: (800) 258-7367, E-Mail:
info@virco.com, Web Site: www.
virco.com
VP, Mktg: Randal Smith
VP: Glen Parish
Facilities Mgr: Don Curran
Corp Copywriter: Bob Roskos
Primary Market Served: Business &
Consumer
Catalog available online
Direct online sales

School & office furniture manufacturer.

VIRGINIA PORT AUTHORITY

Commonwealth of Virginia
600 World Trade Ctr
Norfolk, VA 23510-1781
Telephone: (757) 683-8000, (800) 446-
8098, FAX: (757) 683-2897, Web
Site: www.portofvirginia.com
Dir Port Promo: Linda Ford
Conducts Business: U.S., Worldwide
Employees: 150

Provides port services (transportation)
to importers, exporters, S/S lines, railroads & motor carriers.

VISIBLE COMPUTER SUPPLY CORP

Subs. of Wallace Computer Services
Inc
1750 Wallace Ave
Saint Charles, IL 60174
Telephone: (630) 377-2586, (800) 323-
0628, FAX: (800) 233-2016, Web
Site: www.wallace.com
Gen Mgr: Paul Kasanders
Conducts Business: U.S.
Primary Market Served: Business
Direct Marketing ad budget:
Direct Mail: 90%
Telephone: 10%

Supplier of tax forms.

VISUAL HORIZONS

180 Metro Park
Rochester, NY 14623-2610
Telephone: (585) 424-5300, (800) 424-
1011, FAX: (800) 424-5411, E-Mail:
cs@visualhorizons.com, Web Site:
www.visualhorizons.com
Pres: Stanley Z. Feingold
VP, Co-Founder: Reenie Feingold
Conducts Business: U.S., Australia,

England, Germany, India
Employees: 10
Primary Market Served: Business
Catalog available online
Indirect online sales
Advertising/Marketing Budget Related
to Direct Marketing: 76-100%
Founded: 1971
Gross sales or billing: $2,000,000

Free 56-page full-color catalog includes "Presentation Survival Skills,"
offering advice for the beginner to the
power presenter. Offer up-to-date selection of stock slides & overheads,
LCD panels, projectors, laminating &
binding equipment, laser pointers &
thousands of hard-to-find products at
competitive prices. Some services include 35mm slide duplication, creation
of custom slides & overheads, PC/
MAC scans & imaging of slides &
overheads from PC/MAC files such as
PowerPoint, Corel Draw, Freelance etc.

THE DMA VITA-MIX CORP

8615 Usher Rd
Cleveland, OH 44138-2199
Telephone: (440) 235-4840, (800)
VITA-MIX, FAX: (440) 235-3726,
E-Mail: service@vitamix.com, Web
Site: www.vitamix.com
Pres: John Barnard
Chmn Bd Dirs: W. G. Barnard
Mktg Asst: Kristi Poltrone
Comml Mktg Mgr: DeAnne Hrabak
Conducts Business: Worldwide
Employees: 125
Primary Market Served: Consumer
Catalog available online
Direct online sales
Founded: 1921

Manufacturer of multi-purpose small
kitchen appliances.

VITASOY USA INC

1 New England Way
Ayer, MA 01432-1514
Telephone: (978) 772-6880, (800)
VITA-SOY, FAX: (978) 772-6881,
Web Site: www.vitasoy-usa.com
Gen Mgr: Walter Riglian
VP Opers: John Wareham
VP, Fin & CFO: Michael Auth
Conducts Business: U.S.
Employees: 90
Primary Market Served: Business &
Consumer
Catalog available online
Founded: 1940
Gross sales or billing: $50,000,000

Process & manufacture tofu & oriental
food products for retail consumption
under Azumaya & Nasoya labels.

VIVENDI

800 3rd Ave Bsmt B1
New York, NY 10022-7655
Telephone: (212) 572-7000, FAX:
(212) 572-1080, Web Site: www.
vivendi.com
Chmn & CEO: Jean Bernard Levy
Chmn Bd & CEO, Universal Music
Group: Doug Morris
Chmn Bd & CEO, SFR: Frank Esser
Chmn Bd, Vivendi Games: Rene Pe-
nisson
CFO: Phillipe Capron
Conducts Business: Worldwide
Employees: 381,000
Primary Market Served: Business &
Consumer
Catalog available online
Direct online sales
Founded: 1853
Gross sales or billing: $97,000,000

Consumer-focused, performance
driven, values-based global media and
communications company. Operates in
all businesses that are key to digital
communications of tomorrow: music,
TV & film, publishing, telecommunications and the Internet. Majority shareholder in Vivendi Environmental, the
world leader in environmental services.
The company is headquartered in
Paris.

VIVITAR CORP

1600 N Desert Dr (Suite 101)
Tempe, AZ 85281-1798
Telephone: (800) 592-9541, FAX:
(909) 348-6390, Web Site: www.
vivitar.com
Pres: Clifford Montgomery
Conducts Business: Worldwide
Employees: 150
Primary Market Served: Business &
Consumer
Catalog available online
Advertising/Marketing Budget Related
to Direct Marketing: 51-75%
Founded: 1938

Distributor of wide range of photographic items.

VOLKSWAGEN GROUP OF AMERICA INC

3800 Hamlin Rd
Auburn Hills, MI 48326-2829
Telephone: (248) 754-5000, FAX:
(248) 754-4930, Web Site: www.vw.
com
CEO: Stefan Jacoby
COO: Matthias Seidl
Co-Pres: Kevin V. Kelly
Exec VP: Adrian M. Hallmark
VP, Mktg: Tim Ellis
Conducts Business: U.S., Canada
Employees: 2,500

Primary Market Served: Consumer
Catalog available online
Indirect online sales
Advertising/Marketing Budget Related
to Direct Marketing: 0-25%

Distributor of German automobiles.

VOLVO CARS OF NORTH AMERICA
PO Box 914
Northvale, NJ 07647-0914
Telephone: (201) 768-7300, (800) 458-
1552, E-Mail: customercare@
volvocars.com, Web Site: www.
volvocars.com
Pres & CEO: Victor H. Doolan
Exec VP, Mktg: Thomas Anderson
Conducts Business: U.S., Canada
Employees: 4,500
Primary Market Served: Business &
Consumer
Advertising/Marketing Budget Related
to Direct Marketing: 0-25%
Gross sales or billing: $207,200,000

Import & market cars from Sweden.

ED VOYLES HYUNDAI INC
2135 Cobb Pkwy SE
Smyrna, GA 30080-7632
Telephone: (770) 952-8881, (877) 579-
0642, FAX: (770) 612-9396, Web
Site: www.edvoyleshyundai.com
Pres: Charles Edwin Voyles
Dir Internet Sls: Mike Cotter
Conducts Business: U.S.
Employees: 129
Primary Market Served: Business &
Consumer
Catalog available online
Indirect online sales
Advertising/Marketing Budget Related
to Direct Marketing: 0-25%
Direct Marketing ad budget:
Direct Mail: 20%
Magazines: 15%
Newspapers: 50%
Telephone: 15%

Auto & truck repairs; transportation
services; small business accounting &
services.

VULCAN INFORMATION PACKAGING
Div. of Ebsco Industries
PO Box 29
Vincent, AL 35178
Telephone: (205) 672-2241, (800) 633-
4526, FAX: (205) 672-1276, Web
Site: www.vulcan-online.com
CEO: J.T. Stephens
VP: Franklin Barn
Pur Mgr: Glen Jones
Conducts Business: U.S.
Employees: 300

Primary Market Served: Business &
Consumer
Catalog available online
Direct online sales
Advertising/Marketing Budget Related
to Direct Marketing: 26-50%
Founded: 1950

Manufacture loose leaf binders, magazine storage collectors, index tabs plus
custom binders.

VULCAN MATERIALS CO
1200 Urban Ctr Dr
Birmingham, AL 35242
Telephone: (205) 298-3000, FAX:
(205) 298-2960, Web Site: www.
vulcanmaterials.com
Chmn, Pres & CEO: Donald M. James
Sr VP: Guy M. Badgett III
Sr VP: Danny R. Shepherd
Sr VP: Ronald G. Mc Abee
Sr VP: Daniel F. Sansone
Primary Market Served: Business
Advertising/Marketing Budget Related
to Direct Marketing: 0-25%
Founded: 1909

Construction materials & chemicals.

WTS MEDIA
2841 Hickory Valley Rd, PO Box 8277
Chattanooga, TN 37421
Telephone: (423) 894-9427, (800) 251-
7228, FAX: (423) 894-7281, E-Mail:
customerservice@wtsmedia.com,
Web Site: www.wts-tape.com
Pres & CEO: Tom Salley Sr.
Conducts Business: U.S.
Employees: 40
Primary Market Served: Business &
Consumer
Catalog available online
Direct online sales
Advertising/Marketing Budget Related
to Direct Marketing: 76-100%
Founded: 1977

Audio, video, CD and DVD duplication service. Blank audio and video
media sales. Professional presentation
products, including projectors, micro-
phones, screens and lecterns.

WACHOVIA CENTER
AKA Comcast Spectator
3601 S Broad St Ste 1
Philadelphia, PA 19148-5250
Telephone: (215) 336-3600, FAX:
(215) 389-9518, E-Mail: info@
comcast-spectacor.com, Web Site:
www.comcast-spectacor.com
Pres & CEO: Peter Luukko
COO: John Page
Sr VP Bus Devel: Michael F. Sauers
Conducts Business: U.S.
Employees: 90

Primary Market Served: Business &
Consumer
Advertising/Marketing Budget Related
to Direct Marketing: 0-25%
Founded: 1967
Gross sales or billing: $9,500,000

All purpose arena for sports &
entertainment.

WAG/AERO GROUP
1216 North Rd
Lyons, WI 53148
Telephone: (262) 763-9586, (800) 558-
6868, FAX: (262) 763-7595, E-Mail:
wagaero-sales@wagaero.com, Web
Site: www.wagaero.com
Pres: Mary Myers
Mktg Dir: Mary Pat Henningfield
Buyer: Mary Meinen
Sls Dir: Sandy Hana
Conducts Business: Worldwide
Employees: 32
Primary Market Served: Business &
Consumer
Catalog available online
Direct online sales
Advertising/Marketing Budget Related
to Direct Marketing: 76-100%
Direct Marketing ad budget:
Direct Mail: 80%
Magazines: 5%
Online: 15%
Founded: 1961

Aircraft replacement parts, remanufac-
ture exhaust systems, engine mounts &
seatbelts.

THE DMA WAL MART STORES
702 SW 8th St, Div 1 - Legal
Bentonville, AR 72716-0001
Telephone: (479) 273-4000, (800) 925-
6278, FAX: (479) 277-1830, Web
Site: www.walmart.com
Chmn: S. Robson Walton
Vice Chmn: Eduardo Castro-Wright
Pres & CEO: Michael Terry Duke
Chmn Exec Committee Bd Dirs: H.
Lee Scott Jr.
Exec VP & CFO: Thomas M. Schoewe
Primary Market Served: Consumer
Catalog available online
Indirect online sales
Gross sales or billing:
$348,000,000,000

Retail sales.

WARNACO SWIMWEAR INC
Div. of Speedo
1201 W 5th St (Suite T1200)
Los Angeles, CA 90017-1493
Telephone: (323) 726-1262, FAX:
(323) 724-6931, Web Site: www.
speedo.com
Pres, Speedo North America: Sherry
Waterson

Pres, Designer Swimwear: Paul
Schneider
COO: Larry Burak
CFO: Michelle Pascoe
VP, Mktg Speedo: Craig Brommers
Conducts Business: U.S.
Employees: 400
Primary Market Served: Business &
Consumer
Catalog available online
Direct online sales
Gross sales or billing: $18,100,000

Sportswear & swimwear manufacturer
& retailer.

WASHINGTON GAS ENERGY
SERVICES

13865 Sunrise Valley Dr (Suite 200)
Herndon, VA 20171-6189
Telephone: (703) 793-7500, Web Site:
www.wges.com
Mgr Residential Mktg: Maria Frazzini

WASHINGTON NATIONAL
OPERA

2600 Virginia Ave (Suite 301)
Washington, DC 20037
Telephone: (202) 295-2400, (800) US-
OPERA, FAX: (202) 295-2460,
E-Mail: mail@dc-opera.org, Web
Site: www.dc-opera.org
Pres: Kenneth R. Feinberg
CFO & COO: Richard Johnson
HR Dir: Canie Odlum
Gen Dir: Placida Domingo
Music Dir: Heinz Fricke
Conducts Business: U.S., Canada, Ger-
many, U.K., France, Italy, Japan
Employees: 100
Primary Market Served: Business &
Consumer
Catalog available online
Direct online sales
Advertising/Marketing Budget Related
to Direct Marketing: 51-75%
Founded: 1956
Gross sales or billing: $6,000,000

Ticket sales to performances of the
opera, to subscribers, single ticket buyers, corporate accounts & civic
organizations.

ANDREW D WASHTON
BOOKS ON THE FINE ARTS

168 Irving Ave
Port Chester, NY 10573
Telephone: (914) 933-0479, E-Mail:
andrew@washtonbooks.com, Web
Site: www.washtonbooks.com
Pres: Andrew Washton
VP: Ruth Washton
Conducts Business: U.S., Canada, Eu-
rope, Far East
Employees: 1

Primary Market Served: Business &
Consumer
Catalog available online
Direct online sales
Advertising/Marketing Budget Related
to Direct Marketing: 0-25%
Direct Marketing ad budget: $5,000
Direct Mail: 90%
Magazines: 5%
Newspapers: 5%
Founded: 1982
Gross sales or billing: $100,000

Antiquarian book dealer in the fine
arts. Sell to dealers of art, museums,
scholars, libraries, collectors of art.
Carry mostly out-of-print books.

WATERS CORP

34 Maple St
Milford, MA 01757-3696
Telephone: (508) 482-2000, (800) 252-
4752, FAX: (508) 872-1990, Web
Site: www.waters.com
Pres & CEO: Douglas A. Berthiaume
Employees: 2,500
Primary Market Served: Business
Catalog available online
Founded: 1958
Gross sales or billing: $350,000,000

Laboratory instruments.

WAYTEK

2440 Galpin Ct
Chanhassen, MN 55317-0690
Telephone: (952) 465-0431, Web Site:
www.waytekwire.com
Mktg: Sonia Johnson
Primary Market Served: Business

WEBB DESIGNS INC

PO Box 1405
El Cajon, CA 92022-1405
Telephone: (619) 596-6400, (800) 262-
9322, FAX: (619) 596-4511, E-Mail:
awebb@webbshade.com, Web Site:
www.webbshade.com
Pres: Allison Webb Untiedt
VP, R&D: Tony Webb
Dir: Chris Latko
Conducts Business: U.S., Canada,
Mexico
Employees: 18
Primary Market Served: Business
Catalog available online
Founded: 1946
Gross sales or billing: $1,400,000

Weaving mill & manufacturer of wo-
ven wood window shades.

THE WEDDING PAGES

195 Broadway
New York, NY 10007

Telephone: (212) 219-8555, (800) 843-
4983, FAX: (212) 219-1929, Web
Site: www.theknot.com
Chmn & CEO: David Liu
Pres & CMO: Janet Scardino
COO & Dir: Sandra Stiles
CFO, Treas & Sec: Richard Szefc
CTO: Armando Cardenas-Nolazsco
Conducts Business: U.S.
Employees: 80
Primary Market Served: Business &
Consumer
Catalog available online
Direct online sales
Advertising/Marketing Budget Related
to Direct Marketing: 26-50%
Direct Marketing ad budget: $300,000
Direct Mail: $200,000
Telephone: $100,000
Founded: 1982
Gross sales or billing: $72,000,000

Database marketing to brides &
grooms. A complete bridal marketing
system for wedding professionals.

WEIGHT WATCHERS
INTERNATIONAL

11 Madison Ave (17th fl)
New York, NY 10010
Telephone: (516) 390-1400, FAX:
(516) 390-1302, Web Site: www.
weight-watchers.com
VP, Prods Publ: Wayne Perra
Primary Market Served: Consumer
Founded: 1963

Commercial weight loss company.

WEINGEROFF ENTERPRISES
INC

One Weingeroff Blvd
Cranston, RI 02910-4019
Telephone: (401) 467-2200, FAX:
(401) 785-1320, Web Site: www.
weingeroff.com
Chmn: Frederick L. Weingeroff
Pres: Gregg Weingeroff
Mktg Dir: Lisa Weingeroff
Mgr: Mona Hirson
Controller: Anthony P. Santucci
Conducts Business: Worldwide
Employees: 300
Primary Market Served: Business
Advertising/Marketing Budget Related
to Direct Marketing: 0-25%
Direct Marketing ad budget: $500,000
Direct Mail: 30%
Magazines: 10%
Newspapers: 10%
TV/Radio: 50%
Founded: 1957
Gross sales or billing: $3,000,000

Supplier of premium incentives & continuity programs to the direct mail
trade & TV markets.

WESCO

225 W Station Square Dr (Suite 700)
Pittsburgh, PA 15219
Telephone: (412) 454-2200, (800) 343-1201, E-Mail: info@wesco.com, Web Site: www.wescodist.com
Chmn & CEO: Roy W. Haley
Sr VP & COO: John J. Engel
Sr VP, CFO & CAO: Stephen A. Van Oss
VP: William E. Cenk
VP: William M. Goodwin
Corp Controller: Timothy A. Hibbard
Conducts Business: U.S.
Employees: 80
Primary Market Served: Business & Consumer
Advertising/Marketing Budget Related to Direct Marketing: 0-25%
Direct Marketing ad budget:
Direct Mail: 25%
Magazines: 25%
Telephone: 50%
Founded: 1885

Electrical & electronics distributor & contractor.

WEST BEND

Brand of Focus Electrics LLC
2845 Wingate St
West Bend, WI 53095
Telephone: (262) 334-5107, (866) 290-1851, FAX: (262) 334-6800, Web Site: www.focuselectrics.com
Pres: Mike Carpenter
VP Prod Devel: Brian Beesley
Dir Prod Devel: Howard Kaney
Conducts Business: Worldwide
Employees: 40
Primary Market Served: Business & Consumer
Catalog available online
Direct online sales
Advertising/Marketing Budget Related to Direct Marketing: 0-25%
Founded: 1911
Gross sales or billing: $11,000,000

Manufacturer of quality electrical appliances, electronics & stainless steel cookware.

WEST FARM FOODS (BRANCH)

520 Albany St
Caldwell, ID 83605
Telephone: (208) 459-3687, FAX: (208) 459-9135, Web Site: www. westfarm.com
Pres: John Miller
Conducts Business: U.S.
Employees: 90
Primary Market Served: Business

Dairy products.

WESTCON

520 Whiteplains Rd (Suite 100)
Tarrytown, NY 10591-5167
Telephone: (914) 829-7000, FAX: (914) 829-7137, Web Site: www. westcon.com
Pres & CEO: Tom Dolan
Exec VP & CFO: John P. O'Malley
Exec VP: Anthony Daley
Sr VP Opers: Brian Westfield
CMO: Duncan Potter
Conducts Business: U.S.
Employees: 25
Primary Market Served: Business
Catalog available online
Direct online sales
Advertising/Marketing Budget Related to Direct Marketing: 76-100%

Electronic trade show management company.

WESTERN PSYCHOLOGICAL SERVICES

625 Alaska Ave
Torrance, CA 90503-5124
Telephone: (310) 478-2061, (800) 648-8857, FAX: (310)) 478-7838, E-Mail: marketing@wpspublish.com, Web Site: www.wpspublish.com
Pres: Jeffrey Manson
Mktg Dir: Brian Thomas
Primary Market Served: Business & Consumer
Catalog available online
Direct online sales
Founded: 1948

Publisher of psychological and educational assessments.

WESTLAKE PLASTICS CO

PO Box 127
Lenni, PA 19052-0127
Telephone: (610) 459-1000, (800) 999-1700, FAX: (610) 459-1084, Web Site: www.westlakeplastics.com
Sls & Mktg Dir Indus Prods: Tony Caballero
Mktg Dir: Amy Gaylord
Sls Mgr: James Abbott
Pur Mgr: Elizabeth McKenna
Employees: 68
Primary Market Served: Business
Advertising/Marketing Budget Related to Direct Marketing: 76-100%
Founded: 1958
Gross sales or billing: $7,000,000

Custom bag manufacturer. All types & sizes. Plain or printed for packaging & protection.

WHIRLPOOL CORP

2000 N M-63
Benton Harbor, MI 49022-2632

Telephone: (616) 923-5000, FAX: (616) 923-2759, Web Site: www. whirlpoolcorp.com
DM Mgr Natl Sls: Tom Kibler
Conducts Business: Worldwide
Primary Market Served: Business & Consumer

Service contract sales to Whirlpool, Kitchen-Aid & Roper appliance purchasers.

WHITAKER NATIONAL

533 Fourth Ave (12th fl)
Huntington, WV 25701-1318
Telephone: (304) 525-0852, (800) 377-8721, FAX: (304) 525-0874, Web Site: www.neshold.com
Vice Chmn, Pres, & CEO: Vincent Morra
COO: G. Scott Dillon
CFP: William G. Keely
Conducts Business: U.S.
Employees: 17
Primary Market Served: Business
Gross sales or billing: $5,500,000

Emergency room management.

WHITE CAP WHOLESALE CONTRACTORS SUPPLIES

Div. of White Cap Industries Inc
PO Box 1770
Costa Mesa, CA 92628-1770
Telephone: (800) 944-8322, FAX: (866) 791-8396, E-Mail: customerservice@whitecap.com, Web Site: www.whitecapdirect.com
Pres: Greg Grosch
VP & Sls Mgr: Rik Gagnon
Sec: Diane Galbreath
Mktg Dir: Terry Anderson
Conducts Business: U.S.
Employees: 400
Primary Market Served: Business & Consumer
Advertising/Marketing Budget Related to Direct Marketing: 76-100%
Founded: 1976
Gross sales or billing: $80,000,000

Sell construction tools & accessories to the construction trade.

WHITING & DAVIS

171 Commonwealth Ave
Attleboro Falls, MA 02763-1152
Telephone: (508) 699-4412, (800) 876-MESH, FAX: (508) 695-7606, E-Mail: info@whitingdavis.com, Web Site: www.whitinganddavis.com
Pres: David Youngerman
Conducts Business: Worldwide
Employees: 50
Primary Market Served: Business & Consumer
Catalog available online

Advertising/Marketing Budget Related
   to Direct Marketing: 0-25%
Direct Marketing ad budget: $50,000
Direct Mail: 55%
Magazines: 25%
Newspapers: 20%
Founded: 1991
Gross sales or billing: $8,000,000

Safety glove manufacturer. Safety
products used in meat, pork & poultry
slaughter facilities.

WHITMAN PUBLISHING LLC

3101 Clairmont Rd
Atlanta, GA 30329
Telephone: (800) 546-2995, FAX:
   (256) 246-1116, E-Mail: info@
   whitmanbooks.com, Web Site: www.
   whitmanbooks.com
Gen Mgr: Dawn Burbank
Conducts Business: U.S., Canada
Employees: 15
Primary Market Served: Business &
   Consumer
Advertising/Marketing Budget Related
   to Direct Marketing: 51-75%
Direct Marketing ad budget:
Direct Mail: 70%
Magazines: 20%
Newspapers: 10%
Founded: 1916

Sell stamps & stamp supplies to collectors (60% by mail direct to the
consumer). Balance of business is job-
ber or dealer direct.

WIDEBAND BY KARS

PO Box 1785
New Rochelle, NY 10802-1785
Telephone: (212) 691-9000, FAX:
   (212) 691-9835, E-Mail: info@
   widebandjewelry.com, Web Site:
   www.widebandjewelry.com
Pres: Richard M. Korwin
Conducts Business: U.S.
Employees: 10
Primary Market Served: Business
Catalog available online
Founded: 1951

Jewelry manufacturer.

LT MOSES WILLARD INC

1156 US 50
Milford, OH 45150
Telephone: (513) 248-5500, (800) 621-
   8956, FAX: (513) 831-0548, E-Mail:
   info@ltmoses.com, Web Site: www.
   ltmoses.com
Owner: Christopher L. Nordloh
Conducts Business: U.S., Canada, Eu-
   rope
Employees: 19
Primary Market Served: Business
Advertising/Marketing Budget Related
   to Direct Marketing: 0-25%

Direct Marketing ad budget:
Online: 100%
Founded: 1971
Gross sales or billing: $1,500,000

Manufacturer of handmade museum
reproductions, lighting, folk art &
accessories.

WILTON ARMETALE

Plumb & Square Sts
Mount Joy, PA 17552
Telephone: (717) 653-4444, (800) 553-
   2048, FAX: (717) 653-6573, E-Mail:
   cservice@armetale.com, Web Site:
   www.armetale.com
Chmn Bd: Fred Wilton
Chief Mktg Officer: Dan Helmer
Pres: David Meckley
Conducts Business: U.S., Canada, Ja-
   pan, Germany
Employees: 180
Primary Market Served: Business &
   Consumer
Catalog available online
Direct online sales
Founded: 1892

Manufacturer of aluminum tableware,
gifts & decorative accessories.

WILTON INDUSTRIES INC

2240 W 75th St
Woodridge, IL 60517
Telephone: (630) 963-1818, (800) 794-
   5866, FAX: (630) 963-7196, E-Mail:
   info@wilton.com, Web Site: www.
   wilton.com
Pres & CEO: Vincent Naccarato
VP & Gen Mgr: Marvin Oakes
Conducts Business: Worldwide
Employees: 500
Primary Market Served: Business &
   Consumer
Catalog available online
Direct online sales

Distributor of cake decorating, candy
making & bakeware products, picture
frames & fashion kitchenware products
& gadgets.

WINDSOR VINEYARDS

205 Concourse Blvd
Santa Rosa, CA 95403-8258
Telephone: (800) 741-6070, (800) 289-
   9463, E-Mail: webmaster@
   windsorvineyards.com, Web Site:
   www.windsorvineyards.com
Principal: Patrick Roney
Principal: Leslie Rudd
Admin Asst: Gina Bertoli
Conducts Business: U.S.
Employees: 160
Primary Market Served: Business &
   Consumer
Catalog available online
Direct online sales

Founded: 1959
Gross sales or billing: $14,200,000

Sell premium California wines with
personalized labels.

HARRY WINSTON INC

718 Fifth Ave
New York, NY 10019
Telephone: (212) 245-2000, FAX:
   (212) 489-0016, E-Mail: hw@
   harrywinston.com, Web Site: www.
   harry-winston.com
Pres: Thomas O'Neill
VP, Wholesale: Steven Shonebarger
Primary Market Served: Business &
   Consumer

Retail jeweler.

WOMANSHIP

137 Conduit St
Annapolis, MD 21401
Telephone: (410) 267-6661, FAX:
   (410) 263-2036, E-Mail: sail@
   womanship.com, Web Site: www.
   womanship.com
Pres & Founder: Suzanne Pogell
Conducts Business: U.S., Canada, Brit-
   ish Virgin Islands, Europe (Greece,
   Turkey, France), New Zealand
Employees: 100
Primary Market Served: Consumer
Direct online sales
Advertising/Marketing Budget Related
   to Direct Marketing: 0-25%
Direct Marketing ad budget:
Direct Mail: 70%
Magazines: 15%
Newspapers: 10%
Telephone: 5%
Founded: 1984

Sailing school for women by women
& publisher of videos, articles &
books on collaborative learning & the
issues of women's & men's learning
styles.

WORKING ASSETS

dba CREDO
101 Market St (Suite 700)
San Francisco, CA 94105
Telephone: (800) 668-9253, FAX:
   (415) 371-1046, Web Site: www.
   workingassets.com
CEO: Laura Scher
Pres: Michael Kieschnick
Employees: 107
Primary Market Served: Consumer
Founded: 1985
Gross sales or billing: $14,200,000

Long distance phone company & credit
card.

WORLD KITCHEN INC

1 Steuben St
Corning, NY 14830-2900
Telephone: (607) 377-8000, (800) 999-3436, FAX: (607) 377-8946, Web Site: www.worldkitchen.com
Pres & CEO: Joseph T. Mallof
Sr VP: James A. Sharman
VP, Sls & Mktg: Dennis Brown
Conducts Business: Worldwide
Employees: 20,000
Primary Market Served: Consumer
Catalog available online
Direct online sales

Manufacturer of housewares.

WORLD WRESTLING ENTERTAINMENT

1241 E Main St, PO Box 3857
Stamford, CT 06902
Telephone: (203) 352-8600, FAX: (203) 359-5180, E-Mail: Gary.Davis@wwecorp.com, Web Site: www.wwe.com
Exec VP: Geoff Rochester
Conducts Business: U.S., Italy, France, Germany, Australia, Saudi Arabia, Japan, England, New Zealand
Employees: 560
Primary Market Served: Consumer
Catalog available online
Direct online sales
Gross sales or billing: $415,300,000

Exclusive distributor for all World Wrestling Entertainment products.

WORLEYPARSONS

Subs. of Parsons Corp
2675 Morgantown Rd
Reading, PA 19607
Telephone: (610) 855-2000, FAX: (610) 885-2001, Web Site: www.worleyparsons.com
Chmn & CEO: John Grill
Dir, Corp Commun: Don Lassus
Sr VP: Robert Martin
Exec VP: W. Jeffrey Osborne
Conducts Business: Worldwide
Employees: 700
Primary Market Served: Business
Founded: 1995

Global business unit of Parsons Corporation consolidating petroleum, chemical & power project services into one global entity. Full service design centers in Pasadena, CA; Reading, PA; Houston, TX & London, UK. Worldwide network of project offices. Provides full-service engineering services.

XEROX CORP

Xerox Square (12th fl)
Rochester, NY 14644
Telephone: (716) 423-5090, FAX: (716) 423-5479, Web Site: www.xerox.com
Sr VP, Corp Strategy & Mktg: Jim Firestone
Conducts Business: U.S.
Primary Market Served: Business & Consumer
Catalog available online

Sell Xerox & general office supplies through mail order.

XILINX INC

2100 Logic Dr
San Jose, CA 95124-3400
Telephone: (408) 559-7778, FAX: (408) 559-7114, Web Site: www.xilinx.com
Pres CEO & Chmn: William Roelandts
Conducts Business: U.S., Canada, Europe, Asia
Employees: 3,295
Primary Market Served: Business
Founded: 1984
Gross sales or billing: $1,842,739,000

FPGA semiconductors & related software.

YEAR ONE INC

Year One Inc
Braselton, GA 30517
Telephone: (706) 658-2140, FAX: (706) 654-5355, E-Mail: info@yearone.com, Web Site: www.yearone.com
Pres: Kevin King
VP, Opers: Mike King
Conducts Business: U.S., Canada, Europe
Employees: 175
Primary Market Served: Business & Consumer
Catalog available online
Indirect online sales
Advertising/Marketing Budget Related to Direct Marketing: 76-100%
Direct Marketing ad budget: $1,500,000
Direct Mail: 66%
Magazines: 33%
TV/Radio: 1%
Founded: 1981

Mail order antique & classic automobile parts.

YENKIN-MAJESTIC

1920 Leonard Ave
Columbus, OH 43219
Telephone: (614) 253-8511, FAX: (614) 253-6327
VP, Pur: John Gerhold
Conducts Business: U.S., Canada, Europe, Middle East
Employees: 600
Primary Market Served: Business & Consumer
Direct Marketing ad budget: $400,000
Magazines: 10%
Newspapers: 40%
TV/Radio: 50%
Founded: 1920
Gross sales or billing: $60,000,000

Manufacturers & marketers of a complete line of coatings, selling to industry, paint stores, discount store & home improvement store chains.

YOUR CHOICE OR MINE

128 N Kingston St
San Mateo, CA 94401-2063
Telephone: (650) 340-7959, FAX: (650) 340-0449
Pres: Stacy Weiss Elliott
VP: Thomas Elliott
Conducts Business: U.S., Canada
Employees: 2
Primary Market Served: Business
Indirect online sales
Direct Marketing ad budget: $20,000
Direct Mail: 50%
Magazines: 25%
Newspapers: 25%
Founded: 1985
Gross sales or billing: $1,500,000

Custom manufacture executive gifts, premiums, employee awards for advertising agencies, retailers, manufacturers, trade associations & corporate awards.

ZIG ZIGLAR CORP

5050 W Park Blvd (Suite 700)
Plano, TX 75093
Telephone: (972) 233-9191, (800) 527-0306, FAX: (469) 321-7556, E-Mail: info@ziglar.com, Web Site: www.zigziglar.com
Founder: Zig Ziglar
Pres: Tom Ziglar
COO: Richard Oates
Fin Mgr: Gail R. Arnett
Consultant: Bryan Flanagan
Consultant: Amy Jones
Conducts Business: Worldwide
Employees: 35
Primary Market Served: Business & Consumer
Catalog available online
Direct online sales
Direct Marketing ad budget:
Direct Mail: $100,000
Newspapers: $25,000
TV/Radio: $10,000
Telephone: $200,000
Gross sales or billing: $4,600,000

Promote motivational materials for training & development: books, cassettes, video tapes & seminars. Speakers bureau, customized training.

ZIM-AMERICAN ISRAELI SHIPPING CO INC

Subs. of Zim Israel Navigation Co Ltd
1110 South Ave
Staten Island, NY 10314
Telephone: (718) 313-1950, Web Site:
  www.zim.com
Mktg & Sls: Andrew Monestero
Conducts Business: Worldwide
Employees: 180
Founded: 1948

Ocean shipping.

ZIMMERMAN IRRIGATION INC

Div. of Trickl-EEZ
3550 Chambersburg Rd
Biglerville, PA 17307
Telephone: (717) 337-2727, (800) 452-
  5699, FAX: (717) 337-1785, E-Mail:
  info@trikl-eez.com, Web Site: www.
  trickl-eez.com
Pres: John Nye
VP: Sandra Nye
Mgr: Ron Mihalek
Inside Sls: Ken Ketterman
Conducts Business: U.S.
Employees: 5
Primary Market Served: Business &
  Consumer
Catalog available online
Indirect online sales
Advertising/Marketing Budget Related
  to Direct Marketing: 0-25%
Direct Marketing ad budget:
Direct Mail: 70%
Magazines: 10%
Newspapers: 20%
Founded: 1973
Gross sales or billing: $1,500,000

Sell irrigation supplies, primarily agricultural & supplies for vegetable growing needs.

ZIMMERMAN-MCDONALD MACHINERY INC

2272 Weldon Pkwy
Saint Louis, MO 63146-3206
Telephone: (314) 291-9360, FAX:
  (314) 291-2981, E-Mail: zimsales@
  zimmermanmcdonald.com, Web Site:
  www.zimmermanmcdonald.com
CEO: Stan Zimmerman
Pres: Brad Zimmerman
Employees: 15
Primary Market Served: Business &
  Consumer
Catalog available online
Advertising/Marketing Budget Related
  to Direct Marketing: 51-75%
Direct Marketing ad budget:
Direct Mail: 90%
Telephone: 10%
Founded: 1982

Sell machinery for metalworking &
fabrication.

ZOTOS INTERNATIONAL

Div. of Shiseido Cosmetics America
  Ltd
100 Tokeneke Rd
Darien, CT 06820-4894
Telephone: (203) 655-8911, (800) 242-
  WAVE, (800) 242-9283, FAX: (203)
  656-7890, E-Mail:
  HumanResources@zotosintl.com,
  Web Site: www.zotos.com
Pres, CEO & COO: Ron Krassin
VP, Sls & Sls Dir: Bruce Selan
VP, Mktg: Wolf Heim
VP, Mktg Core Brands: Richard Stella
Conducts Business: Worldwide
Employees: 450
Primary Market Served: Business &
  Consumer
Catalog available online
Indirect online sales
Gross sales or billing: $900,000,000

Manufacturer of hair care & color
products & personal care items for
salons. Products sold through professional beauty supply stores, salons &
online retailers.

Publishers (17)

ABC CLIO
130 Cremona
Santa Barbara, CA 93117
Telephone: (805) 968-1911, FAX:
(805) 685-9685, E-Mail: elott@abc/
clio.com, Web Site: www.abc-clio.
com
Dir of Sls School Div: Edward Lott
Conducts Business: U.S.
Employees: 12
Primary Market Served: Business
Advertising/Marketing Budget Related
to Direct Marketing: 26-50%
Direct Marketing ad budget:
Direct Mail: 75%
Magazines: 25%
Gross sales or billing: $1,200,000

Educational reference, software & educational videos for the K-12 & higher education market.

ACP MEDICINE
Pub by Web Md
69 John St S (Suite 310)
Hamilton, ON, Canada L8N 2B9
Telephone: (905) 522-8526, (855) 647-6511, FAX: (905) 522-9273, E-Mail:
acpmedicine@deckerpublishing.com,
Web Site: acpmedicine.com
Editor in Chief: Elizabeth Nabel MD
Conducts Business: Worldwide
Employees: 27
Primary Market Served: Business & Consumer
Catalog available online
Direct online sales
Direct Marketing ad budget:
Direct Mail: 92%
Magazines: 5%
Telephone: 3%
Founded: 1978

Publish medical information services for physicians.

ASM PRESS
Div. of American Society for Microbiology
1752 N St NW
Washington, DC 20036-2904
Telephone: (202) 737-3600, (800) 546-2416, FAX: (202) 942-9342, E-Mail:
books@asmusa.org, Web Site: www.
asmpress.org
Mktg Mgr: Jennifer Adelman
Mktg Asst: Norma Davis
Conducts Business: U.S., Canada
Employees: 9
Primary Market Served: Business & Consumer
Catalog available online
Indirect online sales
Advertising/Marketing Budget Related
to Direct Marketing: 51-75%

Direct Marketing ad budget: $300,000
Direct Mail: 80%
Magazines: 20%
Gross sales or billing: $3,000,000

Scientific publications for the microbiologist.

AARDVARK ENTERPRISES
Proprietorship of J. Alvin Speers
204 Millbank Dr SW
Calgary, AB, Canada T2Y 2H9
Telephone: (360) 779-5374
Proprietor: J. Alvin Speers
Conducts Business: U.S., Canada
Employees: 1
Primary Market Served: Business & Consumer
Advertising/Marketing Budget Related
to Direct Marketing: 26-50%
Direct Marketing ad budget: $5,000
Direct Mail: 70%
Magazines: 10%
Newspapers: 10%
Telephone: 10%
Founded: 1962

Publisher of books. Catalogue of 114 titles.

ABBOTT, LANGER ASSOCIATION SURVEYS
1725 I St NW (Suite 300)
Washington, DC 20006
Telephone: (877) 210-6563, FAX:
(877) 239-2457, E-Mail: info@
abbott-langer.com, Web Site: www.
abbott-langer.com
Pres: Steven Langer
Conducts Business: U.S.
Employees: 8
Primary Market Served: Business
Indirect online sales
Advertising/Marketing Budget Related
to Direct Marketing: 76-100%
Direct Marketing ad budget: $347,000
Direct Mail: $317,000
Online: $30,000
Founded: 1967

Sell books, salary survey reports including Compensation In Direct Marketing, to personnel departments & to specific types of executives.

HARRY N ABRAMS INC
Subs. of Le Martiniere Group
115 W 18th St (fl 5)
New York, NY 10011-4113
Telephone: (212) 206-7715, FAX:
(212) 645-8437, Web Site: www.
hnabooks.com
Pres & CEO: Michael Jacobs
VP Mktg: Maggie Kneip
Conducts Business: Worldwide

Employees: 94
Primary Market Served: Business & Consumer
Founded: 1949
Gross sales or billing: $11,400,000

Publisher of art, photographic & illustrated gift books syndicated to other mail order companies.

ACTIVE PARENTING
1220 Kennestone Cir Ste 130
Marietta, GA 30066-6022
Telephone: (770) 429-0565, (800) 825-0060, (800) 235-7755, FAX: (770) 429-0334, E-Mail: cservice@
activeparenting.com, Web Site:
www.activeparenting.com
Founder & Pres: Michael H. Popkin Ph.D.
Mktg Mgr: Virginia Murray
Employees: 17
Primary Market Served: Business & Consumer
Catalog available online
Direct online sales
Founded: 1983

Video-based programs & books for parents.

ADVANSTAR COMMUNICATIONS INC
24950 Country Club Blvd (Suite 200)
North Olmstead, OH 44070-5351
Telephone: (440) 243-8100, (800) 225-4569, FAX: (440) 891-2740, E-Mail:
info@advanstar.com, Web Site:
www.advanstarlists.com
CEO: Joe Loggia
CFO: Theodore S. Alpert
CMO: Patricia Joseph
VP Mktg Devel: Steve Morris
VP, Pub Opers: Francis Heid
VP Licensing & Mkt Devel Grp: Georgiann Decenzo
Sls Opers Dir: Casie Shipkosky
Conducts Business: U.S., Canada, U.K., Germany, France, Brazil, Hong Kong
Employees: 1,500
Primary Market Served: Business
Catalog available online
Indirect online sales
Advertising/Marketing Budget Related
to Direct Marketing: 26-50%
Founded: 1987

Business information company serving specialized markets with top business and professional publications, exhibitions and conferences, numerous web-based communities, direct marketing & database and reference products and services. Target market sectors in automotive aftermarket, fashion, healthcare, pharmaceutical, science, licensing, dental & veterinary.

AGATE PUBLISHING
1501 Madison St
Evanston, IL 60202-2033
Telephone: (847) 475-4457, (800) 326-4430, FAX: (312) 751-7334, Web Site: www.surreybooks.com
Publr, Publicity Dir & Spec Mkts Mgr: Susan Schwartz
Conducts Business: U.S.
Employees: 4
Primary Market Served: Business & Consumer
Advertising/Marketing Budget Related to Direct Marketing: 0-25%
Founded: 1982

Publishers of health, travel & career books & cookbooks distributed to catalogs, retail stores, schools & used as premiums & incentives. Direct mail sales to in-house list.

AGORA INC
14 W Mount Vernon Pl
Baltimore, MD 21201-5125
Telephone: (410) 783-8499, FAX: (410) 783-8414, E-Mail: csteam@agorapublishinggroup.com, Web Site: www.agora-inc.com
Chmn & Pres: William Bonner
CEO: Miles Norin
CFO: Bob Comppon
Publr: Kathleen Peddicord
VP: Beth Dent
Conducts Business: U.S., England, France, Germany, So Africa, Australia, Panama City
Employees: 500
Primary Market Served: Business & Consumer
Catalog available online
Indirect online sales
Advertising/Marketing Budget Related to Direct Marketing: 76-100%
Direct Marketing ad budget:
Direct Mail: 40%
Online: 60%
Founded: 1979

Publishers & marketers of health, travel & financial newsletters & books, children's books & academic titles.

AHC MEDIA
3525 Piedmont Rd NE (Suite 400)
Atlanta, GA 30305-1562
Telephone: (404) 262-7436, FAX: (404) 262-7837
Mktg Dir: Steve Ackerman
Conducts Business: Worldwide
Employees: 95
Primary Market Served: Business & Consumer
Direct Marketing ad budget:
Direct Mail: $3,800,000
Gross sales or billing: $11,000,000

Publish & sell newsletters & books, primarily health-related, to hospitals, medical & legal audiences. Continuing medical, nursing & dental education.

ALFRED PUBLISHING CO INC
16320 Roscoe Blvd (Suite 100)
Van Nuys, CA 91406-1216
Telephone: (818) 891-5999, (800) 292-6122, FAX: (818) 895-5301, E-Mail: sales@alfred.com, Web Site: www.alfred.com
CEO: Steven Manus
Pres: Morty Manus
VP, Mktg: Andrew Surmani
VP, Creative Devel: Ron Manus
Conducts Business: Worldwide
Employees: 275
Primary Market Served: Business & Consumer
Catalog available online
Direct online sales
Advertising/Marketing Budget Related to Direct Marketing: 0-25%
Direct Marketing ad budget:
Direct Mail: 40%
Magazines: 40%
Telephone: 20%
Founded: 1922
Gross sales or billing: $31,000,000

Publisher of sheet music for instrument, vocal & classroom use, music-related software, DVD, MIDI, and CD titles.

ALFREDA'S FILM WORKS
PO Box 416
Denver, CO 80201-0416
Telephone: (303) 575-5676, FAX: (303) 575-1187, E-Mail: emailstreet@gmail.com, Web Site: www.gumbomedia.com
Mktg VP & Founder: A. Doyle
Employees: 1
Primary Market Served: Business & Consumer
Catalog available online
Indirect online sales
Advertising/Marketing Budget Related to Direct Marketing: 76-100%
Direct Marketing ad budget:
Direct Mail: 5%
Online: 80%
Telephone: 15%

Founded: 1998

Programming, television & films that are educational, business related & entertaining. Scripts, plays and Reader's Theater. Content for various media outlets.

ALL STAR DIRECTORIES
2200 Alaskan Way (Suite 200)
Seattle, WA 98121
Telephone: (888) 404-8043, FAX: (707) 667-1524, Web Site: www.allstardirectories.com
Pres & CEO: Doug Brown
Corp Commun Mgr: Dana Pake
VP Mktg: Marston Gould
Primary Market Served: Business & Consumer

ALLYN & BACON
Div. of Pearson Higher Education
1 Lake St
Upper Saddle River, NJ 07458-1813
Telephone: (617) 848-7216, FAX: (781) 455-1220
Assoc Publr: Stephen Dragin
Conducts Business: Worldwide
Employees: 120
Primary Market Served: Business & Consumer
Advertising/Marketing Budget Related to Direct Marketing: 76-100%
Gross sales or billing: $3,000,000

Publisher of professional & reference books sold to educators, psychologists, audiologists & speech pathologists.

AMACOM BOOKS
Div. of American Management Association
1601 Broadway
New York, NY 10019-7434
Telephone: (212) 903-8376, FAX: (212) 903-8083, E-Mail: customerservice@amanet.org, Web Site: www.amacombooks.org
Publr: Hank Kennedy
DM Dir: Harriet Weitzner
Spec Sls Mgr: Renita Hanfling
Conducts Business: U.S.
Employees: 40
Primary Market Served: Business & Consumer
Catalog available online
Direct online sales
Advertising/Marketing Budget Related to Direct Marketing: 26-50%

Business book publisher selling a variety of titles to the professional business community.

AMERICA DIRECT BOOK SERVICE CUSTOM PUBLISHING

Div. of Gigo.com, Inc
1805 Spring Valley Rd
Ossining, NY 10562-1637
Telephone: (914) 271-3640, FAX:
(914) 271-3641, E-Mail: info@
americadirectbook.com, Web Site:
www.americadirectbook.com
CEO: Arthur G. Heydendael

Publishing-on-Demand & custom publishing.

AMERICAN BIOGRAPHICAL INSTITUTE INC

5126 Bur Oak Cir
Raleigh, NC 27612-3101
Telephone: (919) 781-8710, FAX:
(919) 781-8712, Web Site: www.
abiworldwide.com
Pres: Janet Evans
Chmn: Arlene Calhoun
Conducts Business: Worldwide
Employees: 22
Primary Market Served: Business &
Consumer
Advertising/Marketing Budget Related
to Direct Marketing: 76-100%
Direct Marketing ad budget: $150,000
Direct Mail: 100%
Founded: 1967
Gross sales or billing: $1,500,000

Publisher of biographical reference books sold primarily to individuals & libraries.

ᴛʜᴇ ᴅᴍᴀ AMERICAN COLLEGE OF PHYSICIANS

25 Massachusetts Ave NW (Suite 700)
Washington, DC 20001-7401
Telephone: (215) 351-2400, (800) 523-
1546, FAX: (215) 351-2686, Web
Site: www.acponline.org
CEO: Steven E Weinberger MD
COO: Wayne H Bylsma PhD
Sr VP: Patrick Alguire MD
Sr VP: Michael S Barr MD
Sr VP: Robert B Doherty
CFO: Ralph L Hibbs Jr
Conducts Business: Worldwide
Employees: 450
Primary Market Served: Business
Catalog available online
Direct online sales
Advertising/Marketing Budget Related
to Direct Marketing: 26-50%
Founded: 1915
Gross sales or billing: $66,000,000

Publisher of medical journals distributed to members & sold to individuals.

AMERICAN CRAFT COUNCIL

1224 Marshall St NE (Suite 200)
Minneapolis, MN 55413-1089
Telephone: (212) 274-0630, FAX:
(212) 274-0650, E-Mail: council@
craftcouncil.org, Web Site: www.
craftcouncil.org
Editor in Chief: Andrew Wagner
Publr: John Gourlay
Conducts Business: U.S.
Employees: 28
Primary Market Served: Consumer
Founded: 1943

Non-profit membership organization to stimulate interest in museum & gallery quality crafts. Publisher of bi-monthly American Craft magazine.

AMERICAN EXPRESS PUBLISHING CORP

Subs. of American Express
1120 Avenue Of The Americas Fl 9
New York, NY 10036-6700
Telephone: (212) 382-5600, (888) 461-
6180, FAX: (212) 827-6496, E-Mail:
aepc@custmersvc.com, Web Site:
www.amexpub.com
Pres & CEO: Ed Kelly
COO & Gen Mgr: Anthony Morgano
Sr VP & CMO: Mark Stanich
VP: Stacy Staaterman
Editor: Lisa Gabor
Conducts Business: U.S.
Employees: 300
Primary Market Served: Consumer
Catalog available online
Direct online sales

Publisher of magazines about travel & leisure, food & wines. Also, newsletters, one college magazine & a magazine for college student cardmembers.

AMERICAN HISTORIC INNS INC

PO Box 669
Dana Point, CA 92629-0669
Telephone: (949) 497-2232, (800) 397-
4667, FAX: (949) 497-9228, E-Mail:
comments@iloveinns.com, Web Site:
www.iloveinns.com
Pres, CEO & Publisher: Deborah Ed-
wards Sakach
Prod Devel Mgr & Editor: Stephen
Sakach
Editor: Joshua Prizer
Editor: Tim Sakach
Employees: 12
Primary Market Served: Consumer
Catalog available online
Direct online sales
Founded: 1981
Gross sales or billing: $1,000,000

Bed & Breakfast books & promotions.

AMERICAN INSTITUTE OF PHYSICS

2 Huntington Quadrangle (Suite 1NO1)
Melville, NY 11747-4502
Telephone: (516) 576-2200, (800) 892-
8259, FAX: (516) 576-2374, E-Mail:
aipinfo@aip.org, Web Site: www.aip.
org
Dir Publ Svcs Sls: Richard Kobel
Sr VP, Publ: Darlene Walters
Publ Sls & Mkt Devel: Douglas LaFre-
nier
Exec Dir & CEO: H. Frederick Dylla
Conducts Business: Worldwide
Employees: 240
Primary Market Served: Business &
Consumer
Catalog available online
Direct online sales
Advertising/Marketing Budget Related
to Direct Marketing: 0-25%
Direct Marketing ad budget:
Direct Mail: 20%
Magazines: 40%
Online: 40%
Founded: 1931

Publisher of journals, magazines & databases sold to the scientific community & libraries.

AMERICAN KENNEL CLUB

260 Madison Ave
New York, NY 10016-2401
Telephone: (212) 696-8200, FAX:
(212) 696-8217, (212) 696-8299,
Web Site: www.akc.org
VP Commun: Noreen E. Baxter
Dir Mktg: Gail Miller
Asst VP Commun: Daisy L. Okas
Conducts Business: U.S.
Employees: 450
Primary Market Served: Consumer
Catalog available online
Direct online sales
Advertising/Marketing Budget Related
to Direct Marketing: 26-50%
Direct Marketing ad budget:
Direct Mail: 90%
Telephone: 10%
Founded: 1884
Gross sales or billing: $72,700,000

AKC Kennel Gazette is the official publication of the American Kennel Club. Editorial content for breeders & exhibitors of pure-bred dogs. AKC is a registry body of pure-bred dogs & governing body of dog events.

AMERICAN MATHEMATICAL SOCIETY

201 Charles St, PO Box 6248
Providence, RI 02904-2294
Telephone: (401) 455-4000, (800) 321-
4267, FAX: (401) 331-3842, E-Mail:
ams@ams.org, Web Site: www.ams.
org
Pres: Prof. James G. Glimm
Exec Dir, Devel: Dr. John H. Ewing
Sales Admin Supvr: Lori Sprague

Conducts Business: Worldwide
Employees: 160
Primary Market Served: Business & Consumer
Catalog available online
Direct online sales
Advertising/Marketing Budget Related to Direct Marketing: 0-25%
Founded: 1888
Gross sales or billing: $24,760,000

A non-profit organization that publishes books, journals & videotapes in its effort to promote research mathematics. Sells publications & rents several mailing lists, all maintained daily.

AMERICAN TECHNICAL PUBLISHERS INC

10100 Orland Pkwy
Orland Park, IL 60467-5756
Telephone: (708) 957-1100, (800) 323-3471, FAX: (708) 957-1101, E-Mail: service@americantech.net, Web Site: www.go2atp.com
Pres: Robert Deisinger
VP, Edit: Jonathan Gosse
VP, Mktg: J. David Holloway
Conducts Business: U.S.
Employees: 32
Primary Market Served: Business & Consumer
Catalog available online
Direct online sales
Advertising/Marketing Budget Related to Direct Marketing: 76-100%
Founded: 1898

Technical training materials for education & industry.

THE AMERICAN VINTAGE LIBRARY

Div. of Vintage Newspapers
PO Box 48621
Los Angeles, CA 90048-0621
Telephone: (310) 552-3176, (800) 235-1919, Web Site: www.vintagelibrary.com
VP: Jack Wayne
Conducts Business: U.S.
Primary Market Served: Business & Consumer
Advertising/Marketing Budget Related to Direct Marketing: 76-100%
Founded: 1976

Original newspapers every day since 1880. 35 major dailies to choose from. Newspaper comes custom leather-bound & personalized, for a marriage day, birthday, retirement or any special day.

AMOS PRESS, INC

aka Amos Publishing
911 Vandemark Rd
Sidney, OH 45365
Telephone: (937) 498-2111, FAX: (937) 498-0876, Web Site: www.amospress.com
Pres: Bill Fay
Mktg Dir: Margie Bruns
Circ Dir: Terri Wise
Employees: 125
Primary Market Served: Business & Consumer
Catalog available online
Indirect online sales
Direct Marketing ad budget:
Direct Mail: 40%
Magazines: 10%
Online: 40%
Telephone: 10%
Founded: 1876
Gross sales or billing: $49,000,000

Amos Publishing is a niche publishing company producing 15 different magazines for a variety of markets including stamp and coin collectors, automotive enthusiasts and crafters.

ARCHAEOLOGY MAGAZINE

Archaeological Institute of America
3636 33rd St
Long Island City, NY 11106
Telephone: (718) 472-3050, FAX: (718) 472-3051, E-Mail: production@archaeology.org, Web Site: www.archaeology.org
Pres: Brian Rose
Exec Publr: Bonnie Clendenning
Conducts Business: Worldwide
Employees: 20
Primary Market Served: Consumer
Direct online sales
Advertising/Marketing Budget Related to Direct Marketing: 51-75%
Founded: 1948

Magazine & journal publisher.

ARIZONA HIGHWAYS MAGAZINE

Div. of Arizona Dept of Transportation
2039 W Lewis Ave
Phoenix, AZ 85009-2819
Telephone: (602) 712-2200, FAX: (602) 254-4505, E-Mail: editor@arizonahighways.com, Web Site: www.arizonahighways.com
Publr: Win Holden
Ed: Robert Stieve
Art Dir: Barbara Glynn Denney
Mktg: Debbie Klein
Conducts Business: U.S.
Employees: 58
Primary Market Served: Business & Consumer
Catalog available online
Direct online sales
Advertising/Marketing Budget Related to Direct Marketing: 76-100%

Direct Marketing ad budget:
$1,500,000
Direct Mail: 89%
Magazines: 4%
Newspapers: 1%
TV/Radio: 5%
Telephone: 1%
Founded: 1925
Gross sales or billing: $7,587,000

Publisher of Arizona Highways magazine, a travel publication exploring the state featuring full-color photography & Arizona travel-related books, videotapes, maps & gifts.

THE DMA THE ARIZONA REPUBLIC

200 E Van Buren St
Phoenix, AZ 85004-2238
Telephone: (602) 444-8000, Web Site: www.azcentral.com
Mktg Mgr Direct Response: Jennifer Botz
Primary Market Served: Consumer

ARMY TIMES PUBLISHING CO

6883 Commercial Dr
Springfield, VA 22151-4202
Telephone: (703) 750-9000, (800) 336-4590, FAX: (703) 750-8129, E-Mail: cust-svc@atpco.com, Web Site: www.armytimes.com
Pres & CEO: Elaine Howard
VP Adv: Denis Dugas
Circ Mgr: Dick Howlett
Conducts Business: U.S., Foreign, APO-FPO
Employees: 337
Primary Market Served: Business & Consumer
Catalog available online
Direct online sales
Gross sales or billing: $19,200,000

Sell both new & renewal orders by mail & telephone to Army Times, Navy Times, Air Force Times, Federal Times, Defense News & Space News.

ART NEWS MAGAZINE

Div. of Artnews LLC
48 W 38th St Fl 9
New York, NY 10018-0042
Telephone: (212) 398-1690, FAX: (212) 819-0394, E-Mail: info@artnews.com, Web Site: www.artnewsonline.com
Publr: Milton Esterow
Assoc Publr: Judith Esterow
Conducts Business: Worldwide
Employees: 40
Primary Market Served: Consumer
Direct online sales
Founded: 1902

Magazine publisher specializing in the fine arts.

THE ART OF SELF PROMOTION

1012 Park Ave, PO Box 23
Hoboken, NJ 07030-4334
Telephone: (201) 653-0783, FAX:
(201) 222-2494, E-Mail: ilise@
marketing-mentor.com, Web Site:
www.artofselfpromotion.com
Dir: Ilise Benun
Conducts Business: U.S.
Employees: 1
Primary Market Served: Business
Catalog available online
Direct online sales
Advertising/Marketing Budget Related
to Direct Marketing: 76-100%
Direct Marketing ad budget: $10,000
Direct Mail: 90%
Telephone: 10%
Founded: 1990
Gross sales or billing: $100,000

Publisher of The Art of Self Promotion, a newsletter for self-employed professionals, marketing services & talents. Inquiries regarding private consultations are welcome.

ARTECH HOUSE

Subs. of Horizon House Publications
Inc
685 Canton St
Norwood, MA 02062-2610
Telephone: (781) 769-9750, FAX:
(781) 769-6334, E-Mail: artech@
artechhouse.com, Web Site: www.
artechhouse.com
Dir Sls, Mktg & Bus Devel: John W.
Stone
Conducts Business: Worldwide
Employees: 27
Primary Market Served: Business
Catalog available online
Indirect online sales
Advertising/Marketing Budget Related
to Direct Marketing: 76-100%
Direct Marketing ad budget: $250,000
Direct Mail: 75%
Magazines: 15%
Online: 10%
Founded: 1969

Publisher of professional books for engineers & managers in nanotechnology, biomedical engineering, telecommunications, optoelectronics, microwave, radar, antennas, & other high-tech areas. Sell to corporate, university & individual technical community.

ASPEN PUBLISHERS INC

Subs. of Wolters Kluwer Group
111 Eighth Ave (fl 7)
New York, NY 10011-5201

Telephone: (800) 638-8437, FAX:
(301) 417-7655, Web Site: www.
aspenpublishers.com
VP & Mfg Dir: Deborah Bowen-Leser
Mktg Dir: Ann Marie Cocchia
Exec Dir Mktg & Sls: Kathy Flanagan
Conducts Business: Worldwide
Employees: 165
Primary Market Served: Business &
Consumer
Founded: 1958

Publisher of professional books, journals, newsletters & manuals primarily in health care, allied health, public administration, corporate administration, law & nursing markets.

ASSOCIATED CONSTRUCTION PUBLICATIONS

1200 Madison Ave (Suite LL20)
Indianapolis, IN 46225
Telephone: (317) 423-7080, FAX:
(317) 423-7094, Web Site: www.
acppubs.com
Primary Market Served: Business
Advertising/Marketing Budget Related
to Direct Marketing: 0-25%
Founded: 1901

Provide construction & business news for contractors, public officials & construction industry materials & equipment suppliers in Iowa, Kansas, Nebraska & Western & Northeastern Missouri.

ATLANTA JOURNAL & CONSTITUTION

Div. of Cox Enterprises
223 Perimeter Center Pkwy
Atlanta, GA 30303
Telephone: (404) 526-5151, FAX:
(404) 526-7122
DM Mgr: Mike Sims

Publisher of newspaper, also providing direct mail services.

THE DMA THE ATLANTIC MONTHLY

600 New Hampshire Ave NW Fl 4
Washington, DC 20037-2403
Telephone: (202) 266-6000, (800) 234-
2411, FAX: (202) 266-7280, Web
Site: www.theatlantic.com
Chmn: David Bradley
CEO & Grp Publr: John Fox Sullivan
Pres: John Galloway
Consumer Mktg Asst: Shari Boyce
Conducts Business: Worldwide
Employees: 80
Primary Market Served: Consumer
Catalog available online
Direct online sales
Founded: 1857

Publisher of The Atlantic Monthly magazine.

ATLANTIC PUBLICATION GROUP LLC

PO Box 30007
Charleston, SC 29417-0007
Telephone: (843) 747-0025, FAX:
(843) 744-0816, E-Mail: info@
atlanticpublicationgrp.com, Web Site:
www.atlanticpublicationgrp.com
Mktg Svcs Rep: Christie Michaud
Pres: Richard Barry
Pub Dir: Warren Darby
Production Coord: Melissa Berge
Sr Art Dir: Bob Durand
Art Dir & IT Dir: Ryan Wilcox
Production Svcs Rep: Elena Kozyrski
Editorial Svcs Dir: Allison Cooke
Conducts Business: U.S., U.K., Japan
Employees: 20
Primary Market Served: Business &
Consumer
Advertising/Marketing Budget Related
to Direct Marketing: 76-100%
Direct Marketing ad budget:
Direct Mail: 90%
Magazines: 10%
Gross sales or billing: $2,500,000

Specializing in developing customized organizational magazines surrounding the specific needs of various organizations. Publishing programs offered range from consultation to full scale magazine production.

AUGSBURG FORTRESS PUBLISHERS

Publishing House of the Evangelical
Lutheran Church in America
100 S Fifth St (Suite 600)
Minneapolis, MN 55402-1242
Telephone: (612) 330-3300, (800) 426-
0115, FAX: (612) 330-3455, E-Mail:
info@augsburgfortress.org, Web Site:
www.augsburgfortress.org
Pres: Rev. Beth A. Lewis
Sr VP Sls & Mktg: Tim Blevins
VP Fin: John Rahja
VP Publ: Bill Huff
VP HR: Sandra Middendorf
Dir Strategic Mktg: Tim Paulson
Conducts Business: U.S., Canada
Employees: 225
Primary Market Served: Consumer
Catalog available online
Direct online sales
Advertising/Marketing Budget Related
to Direct Marketing: 51-75%
Gross sales or billing: $36,000,000

Provide education resource materials; theological, children's & other books; music; worship resources for the congregations of the Evangelical Lutheran Church in America. Also, offers most of these materials to others, including bookstores. Publisher of the following periodicals: Christ In Our Home, Word In Season, Davey & Goliath's Devotions. Mailing address: PO Box 1209, Minneapolis, MN 55440-1209.

THE DMA AUGUST HOME PUBLISHING CO
2200 Grand Ave
Des Moines, IA 50312-5306
Telephone: (515) 875-7000, FAX: (515) 282-6741, E-Mail: ask@ workbenchmag.com, Web Site: www.augusthome.com
CEO & Owner: Donald Peschke
New Media Mgr: Gordon Gaippe
Employees: 150
Primary Market Served: Business & Consumer
Catalog available online
Indirect online sales
Founded: 1979
Gross sales or billing: $16,800,000

Woodworking & other related magazines.

AVIATION BOOK CO
7201 Perimeter Rd S (Suite C)
Seattle, WA 98108-3804
Telephone: (206) 767-5232, FAX: (206) 763-3428, E-Mail: sales@ aviationbook.com, Web Site: www. aviationbook.com
Pres: Nancy Griffith
Conducts Business: U.S., Canada
Employees: 8
Primary Market Served: Business & Consumer
Catalog available online
Direct online sales
Advertising/Marketing Budget Related to Direct Marketing: 51-75%
Founded: 1982

Publishes & sells aviation books & pilot supplies.

AVON BOOKS
Div. of Hearst Corp
10 E 53rd St
New York, NY 10022-5244
Telephone: (212) 207-7000, FAX: (212) 207-7222
Acct Exec: Patricia Santillan
Conducts Business: U.S., Canada
Primary Market Served: Business & Consumer
Catalog available online
Founded: 1817

Publisher of mass market, hardcover & trade paperback books. Sell to premium users, magazines & direct to the customer, jobbers, wholesalers & retail outlets.

BAI
Div. of Bank Administration Institute
115 S La Salle St (Suite 3300)
Chicago, IL 60603-3801
Telephone: (312) 683-2464, FAX: (312) 683-2373, E-Mail: info@bai. org, Web Site: www.bai.org
Pres, CEO: Deborah Bianucci
COO: James McNeil
Conducts Business: U.S.
Employees: 20
Primary Market Served: Business
Advertising/Marketing Budget Related to Direct Marketing: 51-75%
Direct Marketing ad budget:
Direct Mail: 80%
Telephone: 20%
Founded: 1922

Training & educational products for entry & mid-level staff at financial institutions.

BCR ENTERPRISES INC
3025 Highland Pkwy (Suite 200)
Downers Grove, IL 60515-5668
Telephone: (630) 986-1432, (800) 227-1234, FAX: (630) 323-5324, Web Site: www.bcr.com
Pres: Jerry A. Goldstone
Gen Mgr: Fred Knight
Sls Mgr: Michael Leahy
Mktg: Angela Boling
Ed: Eric Krapf
Conducts Business: U.S., Canada
Employees: 26
Primary Market Served: Business
Catalog available online
Advertising/Marketing Budget Related to Direct Marketing: 76-100%
Founded: 1971
Gross sales or billing: $14,000,000

Marketer of publications & training programs on communications network technologies.

BJU PRESS
1700 Wade Hampton Blvd
Greenville, SC 29614
Telephone: (864) 242-5100, (800) 845-5731, FAX: (800) 525-8398, (864) 271-8151, E-Mail: bjuinfo@ bjupress.com, Web Site: www. bjupress.com
Production Dir: Jim Davis
CEO: Steve Smith
Mktg & Sls Dir: John Cross
Conducts Business: U.S., Canada, Australia
Employees: 350

Primary Market Served: Business & Consumer
Catalog available online
Direct online sales
Founded: 1973

Publisher of textbooks for Christian schools & juvenile fiction.

BLS INC
501 N Lincoln St
Wilmington, DE 19805-3047
Telephone: (302) 631-1616, (800) 545-7766, FAX: (302) 631-1619, E-Mail: bls@tutorsystems.com, Web Site: www.tutorsystems.com
Pres: Bradford Siegfried
Conducts Business: U.S.
Primary Market Served: Business & Consumer
Catalog available online

Educational software publisher.

BABCOX PUBLICATIONS LLC
3550 Embassy Pkwy
Akron, OH 44333-8318
Telephone: (330) 670-1234, FAX: (330) 670-0874, E-Mail: bbabcox@ babcox.com, Web Site: www.babcox. com
Co-Publr: Becky Babcox
Co-Publr: Dave Wooldridge
Conducts Business: U.S., Canada
Employees: 65
Primary Market Served: Business
Catalog available online
Direct online sales
Advertising/Marketing Budget Related to Direct Marketing: 0-25%
Founded: 1921
Gross sales or billing: $5,000,000

Monthly updated lists of automotive aftermarket firms. Special databases available.

HH BACKER ASSOCIATES INC
18 S Michigan Ave (Suite 1100)
Chicago, IL 60604
Telephone: (312) 578-1818, FAX: (312) 578-1819, E-Mail: hhbacker@ hhbacker.com, Web Site: www. hhbacker.com
Pres: Patty Backer
VP: Mark-Christopher Mitera
Mgr: Christine Farrell Nowinski
Controller: Karen M. Pedroni
Conducts Business: U.S., Canada, Japan, Australia, Germany, Italy, England, Mexico, Spain, China, Brazil
Employees: 15
Primary Market Served: Business
Indirect online sales
Advertising/Marketing Budget Related

to Direct Marketing: 0-25%
Founded: 1966

Trade publishing & show management firm. Produce pet dealer trade shows & publish BPA audited trade book, Pet Age.

BALL PUBLISHING

Div. of Burpee Horticulture Co.
622 Town Rd
West Chicago, IL 60185-2614
Telephone: (630) 231-3675, FAX: (630) 231-5254, E-Mail: info@ ballpublishing.com, Web Site: www. ballpublishing.com
Pres & Publr: Diane Blazek
Fin & Opers: Pam Barz
Mng Editor: Catherine Evans
Conducts Business: Worldwide
Employees: 21
Primary Market Served: Consumer
Catalog available online
Founded: 1937

Books & monthly magazines for professional horticulturists. We sell direct to growers, educators & academic libraries.

BALTIMORE MAGAZINE

Div. of Rosebud Entertainment LLC
1000 Lancaster St (Suite 400)
Baltimore, MD 21202-4632
Telephone: (410) 752-4200, (800) 935-0838, FAX: (410) 625-0280, E-Mail: blori@baltimoremagazine.net, Web Site: www.baltimoremagazine.net
COO: Richard Basoco
Dir Mktg & Sls: Sally Ann Davis
Circulation Dir: Lori Birney
Conducts Business: U.S.
Employees: 30
Primary Market Served: Consumer
Catalog available online
Direct online sales
Advertising/Marketing Budget Related to Direct Marketing: 0-25%
Direct Marketing ad budget: $75,000
Direct Mail: 100%
Founded: 1907

Magazine presents lifestyle features & articles for the Baltimore metropolitan area.

BANKER & TRADESMAN

Div. of The Warren Group
280 Summer St
Boston, MA 02210-1131
Telephone: (617) 428-5100, FAX: (617) 428-5119, E-Mail: dmoore@ thewarrengroup.com, Web Site: www.thewarrengroup.com
CEO: Timothy M. Warren Jr.
Pres: David Lovins
Grp Publr: Vincent Valvo
Circ Mgr: Deborah Moore

Conducts Business: U.S.
Employees: 75
Primary Market Served: Business
Direct online sales
Advertising/Marketing Budget Related to Direct Marketing: 76-100%
Direct Marketing ad budget:
Direct Mail: 40%
Magazines: 20%
Online: 30%
TV/Radio: 10%
Founded: 1872

Publisher of weekly banking, financial & real estate newspapers in Massachusetts.

BANTAM DELL PUBLISHING GROUP INC

Div. of Random House, Inc
1745 Broadway
New York, NY 10019
Telephone: (212) 782-9000, FAX: (212) 940-7381, Web Site: www.randomhouse.com/bantamdell
VP: Carolyn Farnsworth
Conducts Business: U.S.
Primary Market Served: Consumer
Catalog available online
Direct online sales

Publisher of mass market paperbacks, trade & hardcover books. Direct marketing business is through hardcover & paperback continuity programs.

BARBOUR PUBLISHING INC

1810 Barbour Dr
Uhrichsville, OH 44683-1084
Telephone: (740) 922-6045, FAX: (740) 922-5948, (800) 220-5948, E-Mail: info@barbourbooks.com, Web Site: www.barbourbooks.com
Pres: Tim Martins
Mktg Dir: Mary Burns
Primary Market Served: Business & Consumer
Founded: 1981

Christian book publisher.

BARTERNEWS

24446 Caswell Ct
Laguna Niguel, CA 92677
Telephone: (949) 831-0607, FAX: (949) 831-9378, E-Mail: bmeyer@ barternews.com, Web Site: www.barternews.com
Publr: Robert B. Meyer
Opers Mgr: Marcia Meyer
Conducts Business: U.S., Australia, New Zealand
Employees: 8
Primary Market Served: Business
Indirect online sales
Advertising/Marketing Budget Related to Direct Marketing: 26-50%

Direct Marketing ad budget: $90,000
Direct Mail: 50%
Magazines: 25%
Newspapers: 25%
Founded: 1980
Gross sales or billing: $250,000

National magazine reporting on how barter is done for small business, corporate America & International countertrade.

BASELINE FT

3415 S Sepulveda Blvd (Suite 200)
Los Angeles, CA 90034-6032
Telephone: (310) 393-9999, (212) 254-8235, (800) 242-7546, FAX: (212) 529-3330, E-Mail: info@baseline. hollywood.com, Web Site: www. baseline.hollywood.com
Pres: Rafi Gordon
Conducts Business: Worldwide
Employees: 15
Primary Market Served: Business & Consumer
Founded: 1986

Sell reference products relating to motion picture industry to libraries & movie buffs. Online database service to entertainment industry.

BAUER PUBLISHING CO

270 Sylvan Ave
Englewood Cliffs, NJ 07632-2523
Telephone: (201) 569-6699, FAX: (201) 510-3297, Web Site: www. bauerpublishing.com
Pres & CEO: Hubert Boehle
Exec VP: Henning Lauer
Sr VP Production: Richard Buchert
Sr VP Subscriptions & Licensing: Dennis Cohen
Sr VP: Richard Parker
Conducts Business: U.S.
Employees: 200
Primary Market Served: Consumer
Catalog available online
Indirect online sales

Periodical publisher.

BAXTER BROS INC

1030 E Putnam Ave
Greenwich, CT 06830
Telephone: (203) 637-4559, (866) 280-1924, FAX: (203) 637-4550, E-Mail: info@baxterinvestment.com, Web Site: www.baxterinvestment.com
Pres: William J. Baxter Jr.
Fulfillment Mgr: S. Asher
Conducts Business: U.S., Canada
Employees: 10
Primary Market Served: Business & Consumer
Advertising/Marketing Budget Related to Direct Marketing: 0-25%
Founded: 1959

Publish a financial-economic advisory bulletin for paid subscribers once a month.

MEL BAY PUBLICATIONS INC

Four Industrial Dr
Pacific, MO 63069-0066
Telephone: (800) 8-MELBAY, FAX: (636) 257-5062, E-Mail: email@ melbay.com, Web Site: www.melbay. com
Pres: William Bay
VP: Bryndon Bay
Editor: John Zardin
Editor: Louis Hornbuster
Editor: David Barrett
Conducts Business: Worldwide
Employees: 57
Primary Market Served: Business & Consumer
Catalog available online
Indirect online sales
Advertising/Marketing Budget Related to Direct Marketing: 26-50%
Founded: 1947

Instructional music books for a wide variety of instruments & styles of play. Also, many of the books have complimenting music cassettes, CDs & videos.

BEDFORD/ST MARTIN'S

Subs. of Bedford, Freeman & Worth Publishing Group LLC
75 Arlington St
Boston, MA 02116
Telephone: (617) 426-7440, FAX: (617) 426-8582, Web Site: www. bedfordstmartins.com
Pres & Publr: Charles Christensen
Adv & Promo Mgr: Hope Tompkins
Employees: 60
Primary Market Served: Consumer
Catalog available online
Advertising/Marketing Budget Related to Direct Marketing: 51-75%
Founded: 1981

Publishers of college English, history, communications & political science books.

THE DMA BELCARO GROUP INC

7100 E Belleview Ave (Suite 208)
Greenwood Village, CO 80111-1634
Telephone: (303) 843-0302, Web Site: www.shopathome.com
Pres: Marc Braunstein
Primary Market Served: Business & Consumer

BELVOIR MEDIA GROUP LLC

800 Connecticut Ave Ste 4W02
Norwalk, CT 06854-1628
Telephone: (203) 857-3100, (800) 424-7887, FAX: (203) 857-3103, E-Mail: customer_service@belvoir.com, Web Site: www.belvoir.com
Chmn Bd & CEO: Robert Englander
Exec VP: Timothy H. Cole
COO: Phil Penny
Production Dir: Chris Burt
Conducts Business: U.S., Canada
Employees: 50
Primary Market Served: Business & Consumer
Catalog available online
Direct online sales
Direct Marketing ad budget:
Direct Mail: 100%
Founded: 1972

Publisher of reader-focused magazines, newsletters, books, web sites and electronic media.

BERKSHIRE DIRECT INC

208 Water St
Williamstown, MA 01267-2802
Telephone: (413) 458-1721, FAX: (413) 458-1727, E-Mail: info@ berkshiredirect.com, Web Site: www. berkshiredirect.com
Pres & Publr: M. John Storey
VP: Martha Storey
Adv Sls Mgr: Amy Carey
Conducts Business: Worldwide
Employees: 5
Primary Market Served: Business & Consumer
Catalog available online
Indirect online sales
Advertising/Marketing Budget Related to Direct Marketing: 26-50%
Direct Marketing ad budget: $2,000,000
Direct Mail: 100%
Founded: 2001
Gross sales or billing: $2,000,000

Publish Gardeners' Marketplace, Back-to-Basics Marketplace, Backyard Living Marketplace, and Cooperative Advertising Media.

CHANNING L BETE CO INC

One Community Pl
South Deerfield, MA 01373
Telephone: (800) 477-4776, FAX: (800) 499-6464, E-Mail: custscvs@ channing.bete.com, Web Site: www. channing-bete.com
Pres & CEO: Michael Bete
Exec VP & COO: Robert Underhill
Sr VP Adv & Publg Dir: Carol W. Wentworth-Bete

Sr VP & Dir Mktg & Sls: Daniel C. Carmody
Conducts Business: U.S., Canada, U.K., Australia, Japan
Employees: 345
Primary Market Served: Business
Catalog available online
Founded: 1954

Publish a wide range of consumer information booklets. Booklets are sold via direct mail, telemarketing & direct sale to government, business, industry, health organizations, educational institutions & religious organizations.

BETTERWAY BOOKS

Div. of FW Publications
10151 Carver Rd (Suite 200)
Blue Ash, OH 45242-4760
Telephone: (513) 531-2222, (800) 289-0963, FAX: (513) 531-4744, Web Site: www.fwpublications.com/ books.asp
Pres: Sara Domville
Mktg Dir: Karen Cooper
Conducts Business: Worldwide
Catalog available online

With nearly 3,000 titles in print and nearly a century of publishing history, F+W is one of the largest enthusiast book publishers in the world. Imprints include books on crafts, woodworking, painting, fine art, writing and more.

BLACK ENTERPRISE MAGAZINE

Div. of Earl G. Graves Ltd
130 Fifth Ave (fl 10)
New York, NY 10011-4399
Telephone: (212) 242-8000, FAX: (212) 886-9618, E-Mail: corpcomm@blackenterprise.com, Web Site: www.blackenterprise.com
Chmn Bd: Earl G. Graves Sr.
Pres & CEO: Earl "Butch" Graves
Exec VP, Corp Sls: Michael Graves
Conducts Business: U.S.
Employees: 96
Primary Market Served: Consumer
Direct Marketing ad budget:
Direct Mail: 20%
Magazines: 30%
Newspapers: 30%
TV/Radio: 20%
Founded: 1970
Gross sales or billing: $35,000,000

Publish monthly magazine Black Enterprise & Black consumer inserts.

BLETHEN MAINE NEWSPAPERS INC

390 Congress St, PO Box 1460
Portland, ME 04104-5009

Telephone: (207) 791-6650, FAX:
(207) 791-6925, Web Site: www.
mainetoday.com
Pres: Joe Michaud
CEO & Publr: Chuck Cochrane
CFO Central Maine Newspapers: Gary
Zemrak
Exec Producer: Brian Becker
Dir HR Central Maine Newspapers:
Karne O'Connor
Primary Market Served: Business &
Consumer

Newspaper publisher.

THE BLUE BOOK OF BUILDING & CONSTRUCTION
800 E Main St
Jefferson Valley, NY 10535
Telephone: (800) 431-2584, Web Site:
www.thebluebook.com
Mktg Opers Supvr: Kelly Meyering

THE DMA BOARDROOM INC
281 Tresser Blvd (fl 8)
Stamford, CT 06901-3284
Telephone: (203) 973-5900, FAX:
(203) 967-3086, E-Mail: kseaborne@
boardroom.com, Web Site: www.
boardroom.com
Publr: Marjory Abrams
VP Mktg: Brian Kurtz
Mktg Dir: Rita Shankewitz
Dir List Opers: Kristina Cassell
Conducts Business: U.S., Canada, Aus-
tralia
Employees: 89
Primary Market Served: Consumer
Catalog available online
Direct online sales
Advertising/Marketing Budget Related
to Direct Marketing: 76-100%
Direct Marketing ad budget:
Direct Mail: 55%
Magazines: 5%
Newspapers: 5%
Online: 10%
TV/Radio: 20%
Telephone: 5%
Founded: 1971

Publish newsletters & books in the
categories of health, finance, consumer
issues, psychology, retirement planning
& taxes for the executive at home.

BOOK PASSAGE CAFE
51 Tamal Vista Blvd
Corte Madera, CA 94925-1145
Telephone: (415) 927-0960, (800) 999-
7909, FAX: (415) 924-3838, Web
Site: www.BookPassage.com
Pres & Chmn Bd: Elaine Petrocelli
Retail Mgr: Janel Feierbend
Conducts Business: Worldwide
Employees: 50

Primary Market Served: Consumer
Catalog available online
Direct online sales

Retail & mail order sales of travel
books, guides, maps & language aids.
Also, complete retail line of books.

BOOK PUBLISHING INFORMATION KIT
Div. of Para Publishing
530 Ellwood Ridge
Santa Barbara, CA 93117-1047
Telephone: (805) 968-7277, (800)
PARAPUB, FAX: (805) 968-1379,
E-Mail: danpoynter@parapublishing.
com, Web Site: www.parapublishing.
com
Publr: Dan Poynter
Office Mgr: Becky Carbone
Conducts Business: Worldwide
Employees: 6
Primary Market Served: Business &
Consumer
Catalog available online
Direct online sales
Advertising/Marketing Budget Related
to Direct Marketing: 76-100%
Founded: 1969

Publish books & mailing lists.

BOOKS ON TAPE
Div. of Random House
400 Hahn Rd
Westminster, MD 21157-4627
Telephone: (800) 733-3000, Web Site:
www.booksontape.com
Publr & Pres: Madeline McIntosh
Conducts Business: U.S.
Employees: 100
Primary Market Served: Business &
Consumer
Catalog available online
Direct online sales
Advertising/Marketing Budget Related
to Direct Marketing: 0-25%
Direct Marketing ad budget:
Online: 100%
Founded: 1975

Manufacture & sell recordings of full-
length audiobooks, from classics to
current bestsellers.

BOOTH MICHIGAN
PO Box 2168
Grand Rapids, MI 49503
Telephone: (616) 222-5824, FAX:
(616) 222-5318, Web Site: www.
boothnewspapers.com
Dir, Projects: Renee Hampton
Mktg & Sls Dir: Larry Dodge
Mktg Mgr: Monique Van Epps
Sls Mgr: Kim Brown
Acct Mgr: Steve Davis

Primary Market Served: Business &
Consumer

Corporate office of eight newspapers
throughout Michigan.

THE BOSTON GLOBE
Subs. of The New York Times Co.
135 Morrissey Blvd
Boston, MA 02125
Telephone: (617) 929-2000, (888) MY-
GLOBE, FAX: (617) 929-2606, Web
Site: www.bostonglobe.com
Pres & Gen Mgr, Boston Globe: P.
Steven Ainsley
VP, Sls & Mktg: Mary Jane Patrone
Editor: Susanne Althoff
Reporter: David S. Abel
Conducts Business: U.S.
Primary Market Served: Business &
Consumer
Catalog available online
Indirect online sales

Publishes Daily & Sunday newspapers.

R R BOWKER
630 Central Ave
New Providence, NJ 07974
Telephone: (888) BOWKER-2 (269-
5372), FAX: (908) 771-8699, Web
Site: www.bowker.com
Gen Mgr: Sharon Lubrano
Sr VP Publ Svcs: Gary Aiello
VP Publ Svcs: Kelly Gallagher

Database publisher of information ref-
erences & directories available in print,
CD-ROM, internet, online & tape for
libraries & the publishing trade. Major
titles include Books in Print, Ulrich's
International Periodicals Directory,
American Library Directory, American
Book Trade Directory, Broadcasting &
Cable Yearbook & Literary Market
Place.

BOWTIE INC
3 Burroughs Ave
Irvine, CA 92618-2804
Telephone: (949) 855-8822, FAX:
(949) 855-1850, E-Mail: mevans@
bowtieinc.com, Web Site: www.
animalnetwork.com
List Mgr: Michael Evans
Conducts Business: U.S., Canada
Primary Market Served: Business &
Consumer

Magazine publisher & list manager of
25 magazines.

BOYS' LIFE & SCOUTING MAGAZINES
Subs. of Boy Scouts of America
1325 W Walnut Hill Ln, PO Box
152079
Irving, TX 75015-2079

Telephone: (972) 580-2000, (866) 584-6589, FAX: (972) 580-2079, Web Site: www.boyslife.org
Natl Commissioner: Donald D. Belcher
Pres: John C. Cushman III
Mng Ed: J.D. Owen
Sr Ed: Michael Goldman
Conducts Business: U.S.
Primary Market Served: Consumer
Founded: 1911
Gross sales or billing: $12,000,000

Publish two magazines by Boy Scouts of America totaling 2.2 million in paid circulation. Each magazine has special direct response rates for mail order advertisers.

BRANT PUBLICATIONS INC
575 Broadway
New York, NY 10012-3230
Telephone: (212) 941-2800, FAX: (212) 941-2885, Web Site: www.interviewmagazine.com
Publr: Sandra J. Brant
VP & Assoc Publr: David Hamilton
Circ Dir: Donald Liebling
Adv Dir: Cynthia Zabel
Adv Dir: Jennifer Norton
Conducts Business: Worldwide
Primary Market Served: Business & Consumer

Publisher of Art in America, The Magazine Antiques & Interview.

BRENTWOOD BENSON MUSIC PUBLISHING
2555 Meridian Blvd Ste 100
Franklin, TN 37067-6364
Telephone: (615) 261-3400, (800) 846-7664, FAX: (615) 261-3381, E-Mail: choral@brentwoodbensonmusic.com, Web Site: www.brentwoodbenson.com
Dir Mktg: Rob Collins
VP Print Prod: Jonathan Crumpton
Conducts Business: U.S.
Primary Market Served: Business & Consumer
Catalog available online
Direct online sales
Advertising/Marketing Budget Related to Direct Marketing: 76-100%
Direct Marketing ad budget:
Direct Mail: 80%
Magazines: 10%
Online: 10%
Founded: 1902

Christian music & publishing company selling direct to the public & through retail stores.

BRIEFINGS PUBLISHING GROUP
Div. of Financial Times Management
2807 N Parham Rd (Suite 200)

Richmond, VA 23294-4410
Telephone: (703) 567-1982, (800) 791-8699, FAX: (703) 684-2136, E-Mail: rmalvaso@douglaspublications.com, Web Site: www.briefings.com
Publr: Michelle Cox
Sr Mktg Mgr: Rebekah Malvaso
Editorial Dir: Barbara Clark
Conducts Business: Worldwide
Employees: 28
Primary Market Served: Business
Catalog available online
Advertising/Marketing Budget Related to Direct Marketing: 76-100%

Publisher of Communication Briefings, The Pryor Report/Managers Edge, Team Management Briefings & The Competitive Advantage monthly newsletters.

BROADWAY BOOKS
Subs. Random House
1745 Broadway
New York, NY 10019
Telephone: (212) 782-9644, FAX: (212) 782-8338, E-Mail: bwaypub@randomhouse.com, Web Site: www.randomhouse.com/broadway
Publr: Steven Rubin
Mktg Dir: Robert Allen
Conducts Business: Worldwide
Employees: 70
Primary Market Served: Consumer
Catalog available online
Direct online sales
Founded: 1996

Publisher of adult non & selective fiction. Audio division with "Books on Tape."

BROADWAY PLAY PUBLISHING INC
224 E 62nd St
New York, NY 10065-8201
Telephone: (212) 772-8334, FAX: (212) 772-8358, E-Mail: sara@broadwayplaypubl.com, Web Site: www.broadwayplaypubl.com
Pres: C.W.D. Gould
Conducts Business: U.S.
Employees: 3
Primary Market Served: Business & Consumer
Advertising/Marketing Budget Related to Direct Marketing: 76-100%
Direct Marketing ad budget:
Direct Mail: $20,000
Founded: 1982
Gross sales or billing: $500,000

Publisher of plays.

BULLETIN OF THE ATOMIC SCIENTISTS
1155 E 60th St
Chicago, IL 60637-2745

Telephone: (773) 702-6301, FAX: (773) 980-6932, E-Mail: admin@thebulletin.org, Web Site: www.thebulletin.org
Exec Dir: Kennette Benedict
Editor: Mindy Kay Bricker
Fin Dir: Lisa McCabe
Conducts Business: Worldwide
Employees: 8
Primary Market Served: Business & Consumer
Advertising/Marketing Budget Related to Direct Marketing: 0-25%
Founded: 1945

Journal dedicated to informing policy leaders & the public about risks to humanity from nuclear weapons, nuclear energy, climate change & biotechnology. By publishing expert analysis, convening scientists & policymakers & tracking trends with the Doomsday Clock, provide knowledge & solutions for a safer world.

THE BUREAU OF NATIONAL AFFAIRS, INC
1801 S Bell St
Arlington, VA 22202-4506
Telephone: (703) 341-3000, (800) 372-1033, FAX: (703) 341-1688, E-Mail: mbromley@bna.com, Web Site: www.bna.com
Pres: Paul Wojcik
Mgr Creative Svcs: Eric Roell
Library Dir: Marilyn Bromley
Conducts Business: U.S., Canada, Europe, Japan
Employees: 1,200
Primary Market Served: Business
Catalog available online
Direct online sales
Direct Marketing ad budget: $3,000,000
Direct Mail: 80%
Magazines: 20%
Founded: 1929

A publisher of print & electronic news & information services, reporting on developments in business, economics, law, taxation, labor relations, environmental protection, & other public policy issues. Products include specialized information services, books, research reports, web information services, software & printing services.

BUSINESS PUBLISHERS INC
2222 Sedwick Rd
Durham, NC 27713-2655
Telephone: (919) 281-0474, (800) 274-6737, FAX: (919) 544-3147, Web Site: www.bpinews.com
CEO: Greg Lindberg
Conducts Business: Worldwide
Employees: 60

Primary Market Served: Business
Catalog available online
Direct online sales
Advertising/Marketing Budget Related
   to Direct Marketing: 51-75%
Direct Marketing ad budget:
Direct Mail: 80%
Telephone: 20%
Founded: 1963

Washington newsletter specialists covering energy, environment, education, health, grants, transportation, law, construction & natural & human resources. Over 40 titles for high-level government & private sector executives.

CCH INC

Div. of Walters Klumer
2700 Lake Cook Rd
Riverwoods, IL 60015-3888
Telephone: (847) 267-7000, (888) 224-7377, Web Site: www.cch.com
Pres & CEO: Kevin Robert
VP & CFO: Douglas M. Winterrose
VP, Sls & Mktg: Mike Sabbatis
VP, Legal Grp: Stacey Caywood
VP: Paul Gibson
Conducts Business: Worldwide
Employees: 7,613
Primary Market Served: Business
Catalog available online
Gross sales or billing: $537,000,000

Principal products include publication of loose leaf current news reports & books, primarily on tax & business law subjects; corporate services to lawyers.

CRB

Div. of Logical Systems Inc.
330 S Wells (Suite 612)
Chicago, IL 60606-7110
Telephone: (312) 554-8456, (800) 621-5271, FAX: (312) 939-4135, E-Mail: info@crbtrader.com, Web Site: www.crbtrader.com
Pres: Davidson C. Lowdon
Conducts Business: U.S., Canada, Europe, Far East
Employees: 10
Primary Market Served: Business & Consumer
Catalog available online
Direct online sales
Advertising/Marketing Budget Related
   to Direct Marketing: 26-50%
Direct Marketing ad budget:
Direct Mail: 40%
Magazines: 60%
Founded: 1934

Financial publishing company. Publish products used by traders, money managers & brokers active in the futures & options markets. Maintains an historical database on many futures, options & cash markets as well as stock indices. Available in printed chart format, floppy diskette, CD-ROM or via the internet.

CSPI/NUTRITION ACTION HEALTH LETTER

1220 L St NW Ste 300
Washington, DC 20005-4053
Telephone: (202) 332-9110, FAX: (202) 265-4954, E-Mail: cspi@cspinet.org, Web Site: www.cspinet.org
Pres: Kathleen O'Reilly
Sec: Michael F. Jacobson Ph.D.
Treas: Mark A. Ingram
Bd Member: Tom Gegax
Bd Member: William Corr
Conducts Business: U.S., Canada
Employees: 60
Primary Market Served: Consumer
Catalog available online
Direct online sales
Advertising/Marketing Budget Related
   to Direct Marketing: 76-100%
Direct Marketing ad budget:
   $5,000,000
Direct Mail: 100%
Founded: 1971
Gross sales or billing: $16,000,000

CXO MEDIA INC

Subs. of International Data Group
492 Old Connecticut Path
Framingham, MA 01701-4584
Telephone: (508) 872-0080, (800) 859-5478, FAX: (508) 872-0618, Web Site: www.cxo.com
Pres & CEO: Michael Friedenberg
Dir, List Svcs: Kathryn Grayson-Marston
VP Mktg: Susan Yanovitch
Conducts Business: Worldwide
Employees: 144
Primary Market Served: Business
Advertising/Marketing Budget Related
   to Direct Marketing: 0-25%
Founded: 1987
Gross sales or billing: $20,900,000

Publishing firm dedicated to the information processing industry, written with a management perspective.

CALIBRE PRESS INC

200 Green St (Suite 200)
San Francisco, CA 94111-1356
Telephone: (214) 545-3060, (800) 323-0037, FAX: (866) 225-4273, Web Site: www.calibrepress.com
Consultant: Charles Remsberg

Consultant: Dave Smith
Sls Mgr: Steve Hirst
Conducts Business: Worldwide
Employees: 14
Primary Market Served: Consumer
Catalog available online
Advertising/Marketing Budget Related
   to Direct Marketing: 51-75%
Founded: 1979
Gross sales or billing: $2,700,000

Law enforcement training media & seminars.

CAMPAIGNS & ELECTIONS MAGAZINE

1901 N Moore St Ste 1105
Arlington, VA 22209-1718
Telephone: (703) 778-4028, (800) 771-8252, FAX: (703) 778-4024, Web Site: www.campaignsandelections.com
Mng Editor: James Klatell
Sr Editor: Shane D'April
Staff Writer: Jeremy Jacobs
Publr: Paul Plawin
Conducts Business: U.S., Canada, S. America, Europe
Employees: 15
Primary Market Served: Business
Catalog available online
Indirect online sales
Advertising/Marketing Budget Related
   to Direct Marketing: 51-75%
Direct Marketing ad budget:
Direct Mail: 55%
Magazines: 35%
Newspapers: 10%
Gross sales or billing: $3,000,000

Magazine for people in politics. Our 10,000 readers are elected officials, campaign managers & other political leaders.

CAMPMOR INC

400 Corporate Dr
Mahwah, NJ 07430-3606
Telephone: (201) 335-9064, (800) 525-4784, FAX: (201) 236-3601, Web Site: www.campmor.com
Chmn: Morton Jarashow
Pres: Daniel Jarashow
Conducts Business: Worldwide
Employees: 100
Primary Market Served: Consumer
Advertising/Marketing Budget Related
   to Direct Marketing: 26-50%
Direct Marketing ad budget:
   $1,500,000
Direct Mail: 90%
Magazines: 5%
Newspapers: 5%
Gross sales or billing: $19,000,000

Catalog publisher and retailer.

CANADIAN BUSINESS

Div. of CB Media Ltd
1 Mount Pleasant Rd (fl 11)
Toronto, ON, Canada M4Y 2Y5
Telephone: (416) 596-5100, FAX:
(416) 764-1200, Web Site: www.
canadianbusiness.com
Dir & Mktg: Soomi Kwak
Conducts Business: Canada
Primary Market Served: Business &
Consumer

Publisher of Canada's national business magazine. Mailing list consists of professionals & business executives.

CAPTAN ASSOCIATES INC

744 Durham Rd
Brick, NJ 08724-1064
Telephone: (732) 840-1244, FAX:
(732) 840-1211
Pres: Clara Bluestein
Conducts Business: U.S., Canada, Europe, S. America
Primary Market Served: Business
Advertising/Marketing Budget Related
to Direct Marketing: 0-25%
Direct Marketing ad budget:
Direct Mail: 30%
Magazines: 60%
Telephone: 10%
Founded: 1976

Publish & sell books & periodicals providing technology consulting to management, research & development personnel of industrial firms.

CARROLL PUBLISHING

4701 Sangamore Rd (Suite S155)
Bethesda, MD 20816-2532
Telephone: (301) 263-9800, (800) 336-
4240, FAX: (301) 263-9801, Web
Site: www.carrollpub.com
Pres: Thomas E. Carroll
Mktg Dir: Cathy Updegoss
Conducts Business: U.S.
Employees: 25
Primary Market Served: Business
Catalog available online
Direct online sales
Founded: 1973

Government directory & organization chart publisher; all levels in print & online. Also, defense organizational charts in print & online.

CATHOLIC DIGEST

Published by Bayard Magazine Group,
division of Bayard, Inc.
Sponsored by Augustinians of the
Assumption.
PO Box 6015
New London, CT 06320-1789
Telephone: (800) 321-0411, E-Mail:
catholicdigest@bayardinc.com, Web
Site: www.catholicdigest.com

Ed: Dan Connors
Mktg Dir: Kathleen Gaito
Adv Dir: Tom Rickert
Conducts Business: U.S.
Employees: 40
Primary Market Served: Consumer
Direct online sales
Advertising/Marketing Budget Related
to Direct Marketing: 76-100%
Founded: 1936

Publisher of a digest-size magazine 11 times a year.

THE CATHOLIC UNIVERSITY OF AMERICA PRESS

620 Michigan Ave NE, Leahy Hall
(Rm 240)
Washington, DC 20064
Telephone: (202) 319-5052, FAX:
(202) 319-4985, E-Mail: cua-press@
cua.edu, Web Site: www.cuapress.
cua.edu
Dir Editor in Chief: David J. McGonagle
Acq Editor: James C. Kruggel
Mng Editor: Theresa Walker
Mktg Mgr: Beth Benevides
Mktg Asst: Abigail Padou
Conducts Business: Worldwide
Primary Market Served: Business &
Consumer
Catalog available online
Direct online sales
Advertising/Marketing Budget Related
to Direct Marketing: 0-25%
Founded: 1939

Publisher of scholarly books.

MARSHALL CAVENDISH CORP

Subs. of Cavendish Times Publishing
Group
99 White Plains Rd
Tarrytown, NY 10591-5502
Telephone: (914) 332-8888, (800) 821-
9881, FAX: (914) 332-1888, Web
Site: www.marshallcavendish.com
Pres: Albert Lee
VP, Mktg: Richard Farley
Sr Editor: Liu Ling
Sr Editor of Mathematics: Varsha Primalani
Conducts Business: U.S., Canada,
U.K., Australia
Employees: 35
Primary Market Served: Business
Catalog available online
Direct online sales
Advertising/Marketing Budget Related
to Direct Marketing: 0-25%
Founded: 1970

Publisher of school & library books.
Specialize in encyclopedias.

CENGAGE LEARNING

Ult. Parent Apax Partners Inc.
10650 Toebben Dr
Independence, KY 41051-5100
Telephone: (800) 354-9706, FAX:
(800) 487-8488, Web Site: www.
delmar.com
Sr VP & CIO: Carl Urbania
CFO: Emanuel Guzman
Exec VP Sls & Mktg: Rich Foley
Employees: 275
Primary Market Served: Business &
Consumer
Catalog available online
Direct online sales
Advertising/Marketing Budget Related
to Direct Marketing: 0-25%
Founded: 1945

Education & training information provider.

CHAIN STORE GUIDE

Div. of Lebhar-Friedman Inc
3922 Coconut Palm Dr Ste 300
Tampa, FL 33619-1389
Telephone: (800) 927-9292, FAX:
(813) 627-6882, E-Mail: info@csgis.
com, Web Site: www.csgis.com
Res Dir: Mike Jarvis
Natl Acct Mgr: Kathy Marshall
Dir Sls & Mktg: Carmen Vasquez-
Perez
Publr: Art Sciarrotta
Conducts Business: U.S., Canada, Europe, Asia
Employees: 75
Primary Market Served: Business
Catalog available online
Direct online sales
Advertising/Marketing Budget Related
to Direct Marketing: 76-100%
Direct Marketing ad budget: $450,000
Direct Mail: $300,000
Magazines: $50,000
Telephone: $100,000
Founded: 1932
Gross sales or billing: $7,000,000

Maintain company data from all major retail & food service segments to provide prospect lists to manufacturers & suppliers to these industries.

CHEMICAL WEEK

140 E 45th St (Rm 4000)
New York, NY 10017-9304
Telephone: (212) 621-4900, FAX:
(212) 621-4800, E-Mail:
clientservices@chemweek.com, Web
Site: www.chemweek.com
Group VP - Publr: Lyn Tattum
Global Sls Dir: John Mennella
Conducts Business: U.S.
Primary Market Served: Business &
Consumer

Publish trade magazine.

CHICAGO MAGAZINE
Owned by K-3 Communications
435 N Michigan Ave (Suite 1100)
Chicago, IL 60611-4031
Telephone: (312) 222-8999, FAX:
(312) 222-0287, Web Site: www.
chicagomag.com
Mng Ed: Shane Tritsch
Sr Ed: David Bernstein
Sr Ed: Geoffrey Johnson
Sr Ed: Christine Newman
Ed: Richard Babcook
Conducts Business: U.S., Canada
Employees: 55
Primary Market Served: Business &
Consumer
Catalog available online
Direct online sales
Founded: 1970

Sell Chicago magazine to both advertisers & consumers who are interested
in the Chicago Area.

CHIEF EXECUTIVE MAGAZINE
Div. of Chief Executive Group
1 Sound Shore Dr (Suite 100)
Greenwich, CT 06830-7251
Telephone: (203) 930-2700, Web Site:
www.chiefexecutive.net
Editor in Chief: J.P. Donlon
VP Mktg Assoc: Robin Uhl
VP Sls: Andy Clifton
Dir Mktg: Katherin Fleming
Reprint Opers Specialist: Danielle
Marsh
Conducts Business: Worldwide
Employees: 50
Primary Market Served: Business
Catalog available online
Founded: 1977

Business publication written primarily
by & for chief executive officers in
American industry.

THE DMA CHIEF MARKETER AND MULTICHANNEL MERCHANT
249 W 17th St
New York, NY 10011-5390
Telephone: (212) 204-4228
Primary Market Served: Consumer

CHINA BOOKS & PERIODICALS INC
360 Swift Ave (#48)
South San Francisco, CA 94080
Telephone: (650) 872-7076, (800) 818-
2017, FAX: (650) 872-7808, E-Mail:
info@chinabooks.com, Web Site:
www.chinabooks.com
Pres: Greg Jones
CEO: Erik Noyes
Editor: Chris Rosyn

Conducts Business: Worldwide
Employees: 15
Primary Market Served: Business &
Consumer
Catalog available online
Direct online sales
Advertising/Marketing Budget Related
to Direct Marketing: 51-75%
Direct Marketing ad budget: $100,000
Direct Mail: $90,000
Magazines: $5,000
Telephone: $5,000
Founded: 1960
Gross sales or billing: $1,000,000

Books, periodicals & software from
China & Far East. Sold to schools,
libraries, businesses & consumers.

THE DMA CHRISTIAN BOOK DISTRIBUTORS INC
140 Summit St
Peabody, MA 01960-5156
Telephone: (978) 532-5300, FAX:
(978) 977-5010, E-Mail: javedisian@
chrbook.com, Web Site: www.
chrbook.com
Pres: Ray Hendrickson
VP, Catalog Sls: Ken Davis
Mgr: Gary Lussier
Conducts Business: Worldwide
Employees: 300
Primary Market Served: Business &
Consumer
Catalog available online
Direct online sales
Advertising/Marketing Budget Related
to Direct Marketing: 76-100%
Founded: 1978
Gross sales or billing: $76,000,000

Distributor of Christian books by mail
order.

THE CHRISTIAN SCIENCE PUBLISHING SOCIETY
210 Massachusetts Ave
Boston, MA 02115-3195
Telephone: (617) 450-2000, E-Mail:
info@christianscience.com, Web
Site: www.tfccs.com
Mng Publr, Fin & Opers: Patrick Haf-
ford
Publ Mgr: John Selover
Ed: David T. Cook
Conducts Business: Worldwide
Primary Market Served: Consumer
Indirect online sales
Advertising/Marketing Budget Related
to Direct Marketing: 76-100%
Direct Marketing ad budget:
Direct Mail: $3,000,000
Founded: 1898

Publisher of The Christian Science
Monitor & other products.

CHRISTIANITY TODAY INC
465 Gundersen Dr
Carol Stream, IL 60188-2415
Telephone: (630) 260-6200, FAX:
(630) 260-0114, Web Site: www.
christianitytoday.com
Ed-in-Chief & CEO: Harold B. Smith
Sr VP: Vicki Howard
VP, Mktg: Carol Thompson
VP: Terumi Echols
Exec Admin: Paulette De Paul
Conducts Business: Worldwide
Employees: 100
Primary Market Served: Business &
Consumer
Catalog available online
Direct online sales
Direct Marketing ad budget:
Direct Mail: 90%
Magazines: 10%

Publisher of nine evangelical Christian
magazines, continuity books &
cassettes.

CLASSIC MOTORBOOKS INC
Subs. of Motorbooks International
Publishers & Wholesalers Inc
400 1st Ave N (Suite 300)
Minneapolis, MN 55401
Telephone: (715) 294-3345, (800) 826-
6600, FAX: (715) 294-4448, Web
Site: www.motorbooks.com
VP, Global Publ: Tim Parker
Conducts Business: Worldwide
Employees: 70
Primary Market Served: Consumer
Advertising/Marketing Budget Related
to Direct Marketing: 51-75%
Gross sales or billing: $16,000,000

Publish books about motorcars. Distribute own books & books published
by others to bookstores & automotive
aviation aftermarket. Retail titles to
customers who respond to catalog featuring 6,000 titles.

CLEMENT COMMUNICATIONS
Subs. of Brady Corporation
3 Creek Pkwy
Upper Chichester, PA 19061-3148
Telephone: (610) 497-6800, (800) 253-
6368, FAX: (610) 497-6806, E-Mail:
customerservice@clement.com, Web
Site: www.clement.com; www.
bradycorp.com
Pres: George Clement
Gen Mgr: Chris Fontes
VP Mktg: Pam Scott
VP Sales: Bill Kearns
Conducts Business: U.S., Canada,
Great Britain
Employees: 38
Primary Market Served: Business
Advertising/Marketing Budget Related

to Direct Marketing: 0-25%
Founded: 1919
Gross sales or billing: $10,000,000

Full service employee communications company focused on providing awareness, education & reinforcement tools to help organizations communicate more effectively to all levels within an organization.

CLIGGOTT PUBLISHING CO

535 Connecticut Ave Ste 300
Norwalk, CT 06854-1713
Telephone: (203) 662-6400, (203) 661-0600, FAX: (203) 662-6420, Web Site: www.cmp.com
Res, Circ & Reprint Dir: Beatrix Valles
Res Mgr: Amy Erdman
Conducts Business: U.S.
Employees: 80
Primary Market·Served: Business
Advertising/Marketing Budget Related to Direct Marketing: 0-25%
Direct Marketing ad budget:
Direct Mail: 100%

Publisher of professional magazines.

COBBLESTONE PUBLISHING

30 Grove St (Suite C)
Peterborough, NH 03458-1453
Telephone: (603) 924-7209, (800) 821-0115, FAX: (603) 924-7380, E-Mail: customerservice@caruspub.com, Web Site: www.cobblestonepub.com
Mktg Mgr: Manuela Meier
Conducts Business: Worldwide
Employees: 14
Primary Market Served: Consumer
Advertising/Marketing Budget Related to Direct Marketing: 51-75%
Founded: 1979

Publisher of special interest children's magazines & related ancillary products.

COIN WORLD

Div. of Amos Press Inc
911 Vandemark Rd
Sidney, OH 45365-8974
Telephone: (937) 498-0800, (800) 253-4555, FAX: (937) 498-0812, E-Mail: cwcustomerservice@coinworld.com, Web Site: www.coinworld.com
Ed: Beth Deisher
Circ Mgr: Terri Wise
Conducts Business: U.S.
Employees: 27
Primary Market Served: Consumer
Catalog available online
Direct online sales
Advertising/Marketing Budget Related to Direct Marketing: 51-75%
Direct Marketing ad budget:
Direct Mail: 90%
Magazines: 5%

Telephone: 5%
Founded: 1960

Weekly publication containing national & international news & picture coverage plus features on U.S. & world coins, tokens, medals & paper money for beginner, intermediate & advanced collectors.

COLD SPRING HARBOR LAB PRESS

dba CSHL Press
500 Sunnyside Blvd
Woodbury, NY 11797-2924
Telephone: (516) 422-4100, (800) 843-4388, FAX: (516) 422-4097, E-Mail: cshpress@cshl.edu, Web Site: www.cshlpress.com
Exec Dir: John Inglis
Book Sls Mgr: Elizabeth Powers
Fin Dir: Stephen Nussbaum
Opers Mgr: Nancy Hodson
Book Devel Mgr, Mktg & Sls Dir: Jan Argentine
Dir Serials Mktg & Sls: Wayne Manos
Cust Svc: Geraldine Jaitlin
Conducts Business: U.S., Canada, Worldwide
Employees: 45
Primary Market Served: Business & Consumer
Catalog available online
Direct online sales
Advertising/Marketing Budget Related to Direct Marketing: 0-25%
Direct Marketing ad budget: $380,000
Direct Mail: 90%
Magazines: 10%
Founded: 1933
Gross sales or billing: $7,300,000

Publishes & sells books, journals, DVD & CD to scientists.

COLLECTOR BOOKS & AMERICAN QUILTERS SOCIETY

Div. of Schroeder Publishing Co Inc
5801 Kentucky Dam Rd, PO Box 3009
Paducah, KY 42003-9323
Telephone: (270) 898-6211, (800) 626-5420, FAX: (270) 898-8890, E-Mail: info@collectorbooks.com, Web Site: www.collectorbooks.com
CEO: Bill Shroeder Sr.
Pres: Bill Schroeder Jr.
Sec & Treas: Meredith Schroeder
Credit Mgr: Rick Loyd
Office Mgr: Paula Bunting
Conducts Business: U.S., Canada
Employees: 65
Primary Market Served: Business & Consumer
Catalog available online
Indirect online sales
Advertising/Marketing Budget Related

to Direct Marketing: 51-75%
Direct Marketing ad budget:
Direct Mail: $250,000
Magazines: $150,000
Founded: 1973

Publisher of the American Quilter Magazine. Also, sell books on quilting, antiques & collectibles through mail order.

COLLEGESOURCE INC

dba "Career Guidance Foundation"
8090 Engineer Rd
San Diego, CA 92111
Telephone: (858) 560-8051, (800) 854-2670, FAX: (858) 278-8960, Web Site: www.collegesource.org
Owner: Harry Cooper
CEO: Kerry Cooper
Mktg Mgr: Annette Crone
Conducts Business: Worldwide
Primary Market Served: Business
Founded: 1971

Non-profit publishing firm servicing the education community, libraries and government agencies.

COLUMBIA JOURNALISM REVIEW

Subs. of Columbia University Graduate School of Journalism
2950 Broadway Frnt 1, 201 Journalism Bldg
New York, NY 10027-7060
Telephone: (212) 854-2718, (888) 625-7782, FAX: (212) 854-8367, Web Site: www.cjr.org
Deputy Publr: Dennis F. Giza
Conducts Business: U.S.
Primary Market Served: Business & Consumer
Founded: 1961

Bimonthly magazine devoted to monitoring the performance of the news media.

THE COLUMBIAN

PO Box 180
Vancouver, WA 98666-0180
Telephone: (360) 694-3391, FAX: (360) 735-4503, Web Site: www.columbian.com
Pres & Publr: Scott Campbell
Circ & Production Dir: Marc Dailey
Adv Dir: Teresa Keplinger
Editor: Lou Brancaccio
Employees: 220
Primary Market Served: Business & Consumer
Advertising/Marketing Budget Related to Direct Marketing: 0-25%
Direct Marketing ad budget:
Direct Mail: 20%
Newspapers: 80%

Founded: 1890

Daily newspaper publisher.

THE COLUMBUS DISPATCH

5300 Crosswind Dr
Columbus, OH 43228-3664
Telephone: (614) 461-5000, FAX:
(614) 461-7551, E-Mail: csmith@
the.dispatch.com, Web Site: www.
dispatch.com
CEO: John F. Wolfe
Asst Circulation Dir, Mktg: Brian
Howell

COMMONWEALTH BUSINESS MEDIA INC

2 Penn Plz E Ste 2, 400 Windsor Corp
Park
Newark, NJ 07105-2251
Telephone: (609) 371-7700, (800) 221-
5488, FAX: (609) 371-7879, Web
Site: www.cbizmedia.com
Creative Svcs Dir: Robert Bertrand
Conducts Business: Worldwide
Employees: 800
Primary Market Served: Business
Direct online sales
Founded: 2000

Products include magazines and directories for the international trade and transportation market, including The Journal of Commerce, Traffic World, Air Cargo World, PIERS, The Pocket List of Railroad Officials, The Official Railway Guide, Pacific Shipper, The Florida Shipper, Shipping Digest, Gulf Shipper, Canadian Sailings, Official Export Guide, U.S. Custom House Guide, Transportation Telephone Tickler, Musical America International Directory of the Performing Arts and others.

COMMUNICATION CREATIVITY

209 Church St
Buena Vista, CO 81211
Telephone: (720) 344-4388, (800) 331-
8355, FAX: (866) 685-0307, E-Mail:
steve@steveheimberg.com, Web Site:
www.communicationcreativity.com
Pres: Marilyn Ross
VP, Production: Tom Ross
Mktg Dir: Ann Markham
Mgr: Steve Heimberg
Conducts Business: U.S.
Employees: 5
Primary Market Served: Consumer
Catalog available online
Indirect online sales

Publisher of innovative nonfiction books. Specialize in business, advertising/PR, lifestyle, career strategies & publishing "how-to" reference.

COMMUNITY NEWSPAPERS CO

150 Baker Ave Extension (Suite 201)
Concord, MA 01742-9191
Telephone: (978) 371-5200, FAX:
(978) 371-5214, Web Site: home.
wickedlocal.com
Ed in Chief: Kathy Cordeiro
Conducts Business: U.S.
Primary Market Served: Business &
Consumer
Advertising/Marketing Budget Related
to Direct Marketing: 51-75%

Newspaper publishing.

CONCORDIA PUBLISHING HOUSE

3558 S Jefferson
Saint Louis, MO 63118-3910
Telephone: (314) 268-1000, (800) 325-
3040, FAX: (314) 268-1329, E-Mail:
order@cph.org, Web Site: www.cph.
org
Pres & CEO: Bruce G. Kintz
VP, Corp Counsel: Jonathan D. Schultz
Exec Dir, Fin: Peggy Anderson
Exec Dir, IT: Steve Harris
Exec Dir, Mktg & Sls: Larry Padgett
Conducts Business: Worldwide
Employees: 350
Primary Market Served: Business &
Consumer
Catalog available online
Direct online sales
Advertising/Marketing Budget Related
to Direct Marketing: 26-50%
Direct Marketing ad budget:
Direct Mail: $1,000,000
Magazines: $100,000
Telephone: $50,000
Founded: 1869
Gross sales or billing: $35,000,000

Publisher of religious materials.

THE DMA CONDE NAST

4 Times Sq
New York, NY 10036-6561
Telephone: (212) 286-2860, FAX:
(212) 880-8289, Web Site: www.
conde.net
Chmn: S.I. Newhouse Jr.
Group Pres, Consumer Mktg: Robert
Sauerberg
Sr VP, Consumer Grp: Peter Armour
Consumer Mktg Assoc Dir & List
Mngmt: Sharron Mahoney
Printing Buyer: Naomi Farber
Conducts Business: U.S.
Primary Market Served: Consumer

Magazine publisher utilizing direct mail in subscription acquisition & renewal efforts for Vogue, Architectural Digest, Glamour, Mademoiselle, Self, GQ, Vanity Fair, Gourmet, Bon Appetit, Brides, Details & Allure. Also, handle The New Yorker, Conde Nast Traveller, House & Garden, Conde Nast Sports for Women.

CONNELL COMMUNICATIONS INC

Affiliated with International Data
Group
45 Main St Ste 102
Peterborough, NH 03458-2433
Telephone: (603) 924-7271, (800) 677-
8847, FAX: (603) 924-7013
Conducts Business: Worldwide
Employees: 55
Primary Market Served: Consumer

Consumer magazine publisher.

CONSUMERS DIGEST INC

520 Lake Cook Rd (Suite 500)
Deerfield, IL 60015-5633
Telephone: (847) 607-3000, FAX:
(847) 763-0200, E-Mail:
postmaster@consumersdigest.com,
Web Site: www.consumersdigest.com
Pres, Consumers Digest: Arthur Weber
Publr: Randy Weber
Ed-in-Chief: Dennis Fertig
Ed-in-Chief, Consumers Digest: John
Manos
VP & Gen Mgr: Chuck Mitchell
Conducts Business: U.S.
Primary Market Served: Consumer
Direct Marketing ad budget:
Direct Mail: 100%
Founded: 1960

Publisher of Consumers Digest & Your Money magazines.

CONSUMERS UNION

101 Truman Ave
Yonkers, NY 10703-1057
Telephone: (914) 378-2000, FAX:
(914) 378-2906, Web Site: www.
consumerreports.org
CFO: Conrad Harris
Direct Mail Mgr: Laurie Mellon
VP: Joel Gurin
Bus Affairs Dir: Louis J. Milani
Conducts Business: U.S.
Primary Market Served: Consumer
Advertising/Marketing Budget Related
to Direct Marketing: 76-100%

Publisher of Consumer Reports Magazine, Consumer Reports Travel Newsletter & Consumer Reports Health Newsletter.

DAVID C COOK

Subs. of Cook Communications Ministries
4050 Lee Vance View
Colorado Springs, CO 80918-7102
Telephone: (719) 536-0100, (800) 323-7543, FAX: (719) 536-3232, Web Site: www.davidccook.com
Pres & CEO: Chris Doombos
Exec VP: Alyson Bruu
Exec VP: Bob Beever
CFO & Controller: David Hatchell
Editor: C. Elvan Olmstead
Conducts Business: Worldwide
Employees: 400
Primary Market Served: Business & Consumer
Catalog available online
Direct online sales
Founded: 1875

Publish Christian books.

COOKBOOK PUBLISHERS INC

10800 Lakeview Ave
Lenexa, KS 66285-5920
Telephone: (913) 492-5900, (800) 227-7282, FAX: (913) 492-5947, E-Mail: info@cookbookpublishers.com, Web Site: www.cookbookpublishers.com
Chmn: Dennis Evans
Pres: Kevin Derry
Mktg Dir: Terri Horton
Conducts Business: U.S., Canada
Employees: 150
Primary Market Served: Consumer
Catalog available online
Indirect online sales
Advertising/Marketing Budget Related to Direct Marketing: 76-100%
Founded: 1947
Gross sales or billing: $5,000,000

Publish personalized & specialty cookbooks for individuals & organizations. Also, specialty cookbooks for retail.

CORNHUSKER PRESS

Div. of Dutton-Lainson Co
451 W Second St
Hastings, NE 68902-0729
Telephone: (402) 462-4141, FAX: (402) 460-4612, E-Mail: dlsales@dutton-lainson.com, Web Site: www.dutton-lainson.com
Pres: Charles R. Hermes
VP & CFO: David N. Brandt
VP, Sls & Mktg: Mark Bliss
VP: Jeremy L. Daniels
Conducts Business: U.S.
Employees: 60
Primary Market Served: Business & Consumer
Catalog available online
Direct online sales
Direct Marketing ad budget: $100,000

Direct Mail: 50%
Magazines: 20%
Newspapers: 5%
TV/Radio: 10%
Telephone: 15%
Founded: 1935
Gross sales or billing: $34,000,000

Sell limited edition prints, books & greeting cards on both the wholesale & retail level.

COUNCIL ON FOREIGN RELATIONS INC

dba Foreign Affairs (Magazine)
58 E 68th St
New York, NY 10021-5953
Telephone: (212) 434-9400, FAX: (212) 861-2759, E-Mail: editor@foreignaffairs.com, Web Site: www.foreignaffairs.org
Ed & Peter G Peterson Chair: James F. Huge Jr.
Publr: David Kellog
Mng Editor: Gideon Rose
Sr Mktg Mgr: Emilie Harkin
Adv Mgr: Edward Welsh
Primary Market Served: Consumer
Direct online sales
Advertising/Marketing Budget Related to Direct Marketing: 0-25%
Direct Marketing ad budget:
Direct Mail: 90%
Magazines: 1%
Telephone: 9%
Founded: 1922

Non-profit organization publishing magazine six times a year. Dedicated to improving the understanding of U.S. foreign policy & international affairs through the free & civil exchange of ideas.

COUNTRY SAMPLER GROUP

Div. of Emmis Publishing
707 Kautz Rd
Saint Charles, IL 60174
Telephone: (630) 377-8000, FAX: (630) 377-8194, Web Site: www.sampler.com
Pres & CEO: Margaret Borst
VP, Circ: Denise Boba
VP, Prodn: William Lowry
Conducts Business: Worldwide
Employees: 40
Primary Market Served: Business & Consumer
Indirect online sales
Advertising/Marketing Budget Related to Direct Marketing: 51-75%
Direct Marketing ad budget:
Direct Mail: 93%
Magazines: 5%
Telephone: 2%
Founded: 1984
Gross sales or billing: $12,000,000

Publisher of national consumer home decorating & craft magazines: Country Sampler Decorating Ideas, Country Sampler, Decorate with Paint, Country Marketplace & a trade magazine, Country Business. Also do custom publishing.

COURSESMITH

PO Box 416
Denver, CO 80201-0416
Telephone: (303) 575-5676, FAX: (303) 575-1187, E-Mail: emailstreet@gmail.com, Web Site: www.coursesmith.com
Mktg VP & Founder: A. Doyle
Employees: 1
Primary Market Served: Business & Consumer
Catalog available online
Indirect online sales
Advertising/Marketing Budget Related to Direct Marketing: 76-100%
Direct Marketing ad budget:
Direct Mail: 5%
Online: 75%
Telephone: 20%
Founded: 1999

Courses for K-12, college & non-profit organizations; content for courses and education. Prop Box Theme Box Idea Series. Courses & workshops on a variety of subjects ranging from home economics to entrepreneurship & food.

CRAIN COMMUNICATIONS INC

1155 Gratiot Ave
Detroit, MI 48207-2997
Telephone: (313) 446-6000, FAX: (313) 446-1616, Web Site: www.crain.com
Chmn: Keith Crain
Circulation Dir: Nina LaFrance
Pres: Rance Crain
Exec VP: Bill Morrow
Grp VP Mfg Circ & Tech: Robert Adams
Corp Commun Mgr: Bridget M. Kavanaugh
Conducts Business: Worldwide
Employees: 1,000
Primary Market Served: Business & Consumer
Direct online sales
Founded: 1916

Publisher of over 30 business, consumer & trade magazines including Advertising Age, Automotive News, Crain's Chicago, Detroit, New York & Cleveland Business. Extensive use of direct mail in selling advertising, subscriptions & registration to professional conferences.

CREATIVE PUBLISHING INTERNATIONAL

400 First Ave N (Suite 300)
Minneapolis, MN 55401
Telephone: (612) 344-8100, FAX:
(612) 344-8691, E-Mail: sales@
creativepub.com, Web Site: www.
creativepub.com
Pres & CEO: Ken Fund
CFO: John Harvatine
Publr: Bryan Tandem
Publr: Winnie Prentiss
VP, Sls & Mktg: Kevin Hamric
Conducts Business: Worldwide
Employees: 85
Primary Market Served: Business &
Consumer
Catalog available online
Indirect online sales
Advertising/Marketing Budget Related
to Direct Marketing: 26-50%
Founded: 1969

Sell continuity series via mail &
telephone. Also sell single titles direct
to retail & educational markets. Provide comprehensive custom publishing
& creative services for books, magazines, catalogs, brochures, ads & direct
mail packages.

CREATIVE TEACHING PRESS

15342 Graham St
Huntington Beach, CA 92549
Telephone: (714) 895-5047, (800) 287-
8879
Pres: Jim Connelly
Primary Market Served: Business &
Consumer

THE CRICKET MAGAZINE GROUP

Div. of Carus Publishing
70 E Lake St (Ste 300)
Chicago, IL 60601-5945
Telephone: (603) 924-7209, (800) 821-
0115, FAX: (815) 224-6615, E-Mail:
customerservice@caruspub.com,
Web Site: www.cricketmag.com
Chmn & CEO: Andre Carus
Publr & Ed-in-Chief: Marianne Carus
CFO: Jason Patenaude
Conducts Business: Worldwide
Employees: 50
Primary Market Served: Business &
Consumer
Catalog available online
Direct online sales
Advertising/Marketing Budget Related
to Direct Marketing: 76-100%
Founded: 1973
Gross sales or billing: $6,000,000

Children's magazine publisher. Sell
subscriptions via direct mail, space
ads, package inserts, agents, bookstores
& schools.

CROSS COUNTRY STITCHING

PO Box 180
Quakertown, PA 18951-0180
Telephone: (215) 529-6430, (800) 231-
8108, FAX: (215) 529-6434, Web
Site: www.crosscountrystitching.com
Pres: Allen Coleman
Co-Owner: Linda Coleman
Conducts Business: Worldwide
Primary Market Served: Business &
Consumer
Catalog available online
Direct online sales
Advertising/Marketing Budget Related
to Direct Marketing: 51-75%
Direct Marketing ad budget:
Direct Mail: 90%
Magazines: 10%
Founded: 1982

Publisher of Needlecraft Designs &
Projects & Counted Cross Stitch
Magazine.

CURRICULUM ASSOCIATES INC

153 Rangeway Rd
North Billerica, MA 01862-2013
Telephone: (978) 667-8000, FAX:
(978) 667-5706, E-Mail: cainfo@
curriculumassociates.com, Web Site:
www.curriculumassociates.com
Pres: Frank E. Ferguson
VP, Sls & Mktg: Katherine Harvey
Mktg Mgr: Jackie Dawson
Conducts Business: U.S.
Employees: 70
Primary Market Served: Business
Advertising/Marketing Budget Related
to Direct Marketing: 0-25%
Founded: 1969

Publisher selling educational materials
direct to schools.

CYGNUS BUSINESS MEDIA

1233 Janesville Ave
Fort Atkinson, WI 53538-2738
Telephone: (203) 227-4037, (800) 547-
7377, FAX: (203) 227-4245, Web
Site: www.cygnusb2b.com
CEO: John Franch
CFO: Paul Bonaiuto
VP, HR: Ed Wood
Conducts Business: Worldwide
Employees: 450
Primary Market Served: Business
Catalog available online
Direct online sales
Founded: 1937
Gross sales or billing: $247,000,000

Publish business-to-business trade
magazines. Also create & develop
company sponsored publications, trade
shows & online business information
sites & magazines.

DRG

306 E Parr Rd
Berne, IN 46711-1138
Telephone: (260) 589-4000, Web Site:
www.drgnetwork.com
CEO: David McKee
Primary Market Served: Business &
Consumer

DAILY COMMERCIAL NEWS & CONSTRUCTION RECORD

Div of Reed Construction Data
500 Hood Rd (4th fl)
Markham, ON, Canada L3R 9Z3
Telephone: (905) 752-5408, (800) 465-
6475, FAX: (888) 396-9413, (905)
752-5450, E-Mail: dcnonl@
reedbusiness.com, Web Site: www.
dcnonl.com
Ed: Patrick McConnell
Circ Mgr: Sonia Kalra-ali
VP & Mng Dir: Mark Casaletto
Customer Care Coord: Christine
Takashima
Mktg Mgr: Michelle Smith
Conducts Business: Canada
Primary Market Served: Business &
Consumer

Daily newspaper for the building &
construction marketplace in Ontario,
Canada.

DAILY RECORD & DISPATCH CO

99 W Broad St
Dunn, NC 28334-6031
Telephone: (910) 891-1234, FAX:
(910) 891-5253, Web Site: www.
mydailyrecord.com
Circ Dir: Tom Gilligan
Mktg Dir: Mary Kay Lashmit
Ed: Bart Adams
Mng Editor: Lisa Farmer
Conducts Business: U.S.
Employees: 50
Primary Market Served: Business &
Consumer
Catalog available online
Direct online sales
Advertising/Marketing Budget Related
to Direct Marketing: 0-25%
Direct Marketing ad budget:
Newspapers: 80%
Telephone: 20%
Founded: 1950

Newspapers.

DANTE UNIVERSITY PRESS

PO Box 812158
Wellesley, MA 02482-0014
Telephone: (781) 790-1059, FAX:
(781) 790-1056, E-Mail: dante@
danteuniversity.org, Web Site: www.
danteuniversity.com

Pres: Adolph Caso
VP: Josephine Tanner
Conducts Business: Worldwide
Primary Market Served: Business &
  Consumer
Catalog available online
Advertising/Marketing Budget Related
  to Direct Marketing: 0-25%
Direct Marketing ad budget:
Magazines: 100%
Founded: 1976

Renaissance thought & letters, Italian
language & linguistics, Italian-
American history & culture, bilingual
education; reprints, translations, pro-
grammed learning.

THE DARTNELL CORP

Div. of Eli Research
2272 Airport Rd S
Naples, FL 34112
Telephone: (585) 240-7301, (800) 447-
  4030, FAX: (585) 292-4392, E-Mail:
  customerservice@dartnellcorp.com,
  Web Site: www.dartnellcorp.com
Publr: Kenneth Kahn
Dir Editorial: Claude Werder
Editor: Paula P. Willits Ed. D.
Editor: Cynthia Gomez
Editor: Robert L. Dilenschnieder
Editor: David Dee
Employees: 350
Primary Market Served: Business
Catalog available online
Direct online sales
Advertising/Marketing Budget Related
  to Direct Marketing: 76-100%
Founded: 1917

Dedicated to supplying diverse business audiences with informational, instructional & motivational training materials, including books & manuals,
newsletters, videos, planners, audiocas-
sette programs & a speakers bureau.
Materials provide valuable training
information for salespeople, supervi-
sors, managers, secretaries, human resource professionals & customer service representatives.

DICK DAVIS DIGEST

176 North St
Salem, MA 01970-1648
Telephone: (978) 745-5532, FAX:
  (978) 745-1283, E-Mail: marketing@
  dickdavis.com, Web Site: www.
  dickdavis.com
Pres: Don Hanrahan
Gen Mgr: Roberta Norman
Conducts Business: U.S., Canada
Primary Market Served: Business &
  Consumer
Advertising/Marketing Budget Related
  to Direct Marketing: 51-75%
Direct Marketing ad budget:

Direct Mail: 85%
Newspapers: 15%
Founded: 1982

Bi-weekly financial newsletter that is
marketed to serious investors & financial professionals.

DAVIS PUBLICATIONS INC

50 Portland St
Worcester, MA 01608-2013
Telephone: (508) 754-7201, (800) 533-
  2847, FAX: (508) 753-3834, E-Mail:
  contactus@davisart.com, Web Site:
  www.davis-art.com
Pres: Wyatt Wade
Chmn: Mark Davis
Conducts Business: U.S., Canada
Employees: 35
Primary Market Served: Business &
  Consumer
Catalog available online
Indirect online sales
Advertising/Marketing Budget Related
  to Direct Marketing: 76-100%
Founded: 1901
Gross sales or billing: $8,000,000

Publish art educational work.

DEFENSE NEWS MEDIA GROUP

Subs Army Times Publishing Co
6883 Commercial Dr
Springfield, VA 22151-4202
Telephone: (703) 848-0490, FAX:
  (703) 848-0480, E-Mail: mgrant@
  atpco.com, Web Site: www.
  defensenews.com
Dir Mktg: Maurice Grant

DENTAL PRODUCTS REPORT

Div. of MEDEC Dental Communica-
  tions
641 Lexington Ave Fl 8
New York, NY 10022-4503
Telephone: (847) 441-3700, FAX:
  (847) 441-3702, Web Site: www.
  dentalproducts.net
Publr Emeritus: Dolph Sharp
Conducts Business: Worldwide
Employees: 33
Primary Market Served: Business
Founded: 1967

Publisher of dental publications with
lists of dentists & dental labs available
for rental.

DIRECT MARKETING PUBLISHERS

1304 University Dr
Yardley, PA 19067-2829
Telephone: (215) 321-3068, (800) 663-
  8387, FAX: (215) 321-9647, E-Mail:
  consulting@dmpublishers.com, Web
  Site: www.dmpublishers.com

Pres: Bernard A. Goldberg
Conducts Business: U.S., Canada
Primary Market Served: Business
Founded: 1987

Books & newsletters for business direct marketing, telephone selling &
lead generation.

DIRECT RESPONSE CONSULTING

6849 Old Dominion Dr (Suite 320)
McLean, VA 22101
Telephone: (703) 749-0010, FAX:
  (703) 749-0967, Web Site: www.
  drcs.com
Partner: Jerry Watson
Partner: Byron Hughery
Conducts Business: U.S.
Employees: 2
Primary Market Served: Business
Direct Marketing ad budget:
Direct Mail: $200,000
Gross sales or billing: $1,000,000

Publish personal biographical books
for libraries & the general public. Directories for organizations. Fund-
raising.

DISCOVER PUBLICATIONS

6797 N High St (Suite 213)
Worthington, OH 43085-2533
Telephone: (614) 785-1111, Web Site:
  www.discover.pubs.com
Pres: Leo Zupan

DOANE

77 Westport Plaza (Suite 250)
Saint Louis, MO 63146-3121
Telephone: (314) 569-2700, (866) 647-
  0918, FAX: (314) 569-1083, Web
  Site: www.doane.com
CEO: Lynn O. Henderson
VP & Mgr: Dick Stiltz
Mng Dir: Ken P. Morrison
Circ Dir: Shanon Weaver
Primary Market Served: Business &
  Consumer
Catalog available online
Direct online sales
Founded: 1920

Information & publishing.

DOVER PUBLICATIONS INC

Subs. of Courier Corp
31 E Second St
Mineola, NY 11501
Telephone: (516) 294-7000, (800) 223-
  3130, FAX: (516) 873-1401, Web
  Site: www.doverpublications.com
Pres: Paul T. Negri
Sr VP & CFO: Robert P. Story Jr.
VP Publishing: Eric Zimmerman
Natl Sls Mgr: Mary Groza Schuetz
VP Dir Sls: Jarvis Melton

Conducts Business: Worldwide
Primary Market Served: Business & Consumer
Catalog available online
Direct online sales
Founded: 1943

Publish original & out-of-print books in such fields as art, music, physical & natural sciences, crafts, needlework, linguistics, orientalia, anthropology, children's coloring books & cooking books. Books sold to individuals & institutions via direct mail, space ads, web & retail stores.

THE DMA DOW JONES & CO
PO Box 300
Princeton, NJ 08543-0300
Telephone: (609) 520-4000, FAX: (212) 416-4348, Web Site: www.dowjones.com/corp/index.html
Chmn: M. Peter McPherson
CEO: Leslie F. Hinton
Exec VP & CFO: Stephen Daintith
VP & CIO: William A. Godfrey III
VP Circulation: Lynne Brennen
Conducts Business: Worldwide
Employees: 7,400
Primary Market Served: Business & Consumer
Catalog available online
Indirect online sales
Founded: 1882
Gross sales or billing: $1,700,000,000

Publisher of the Wall Street Journal, Barron's, The Asian Wall Street Journal, The Asian Wall Street Weekly, Wall Street Journal/Europe, Dow Jones New Wires, Ottaway Newspapers, Inc. Also, Broadcast News Services, Dow Jones Interactive Publishing, WSJ Interactive Edition & Smart Money Magazine.

DOW THEORY FORECASTS
7412 Calumet Ave
Hammond, IN 46324
Telephone: (219) 931-6480, (800) 233-5922, FAX: (219) 931-6487, E-Mail: custserv@horizonpublishing.com, Web Site: www.dowtheory.com
Pres: Charles Follett
VP & Editor: Richard Moroney
Mng Editor: Bob Sweet
Editor: Charles Carlson
Anaylst: David Wright
Primary Market Served: Business & Consumer
Catalog available online
Direct online sales
Founded: 1946

Investment newsletter covering investment grade & income-oriented stocks.

EDC PUBLISHING
Div. of Educational Development Corp
10302 E 55th Pl
Tulsa, OK 74146-6515
Telephone: (918) 622-4522, (800) 475-4522, FAX: (800) 747-4509, Web Site: www.edcpub.com
Pres: Randall White
VP, USBORNE Books at Home: Kathy Plecenski
Conducts Business: U.S.
Employees: 100
Primary Market Served: Business & Consumer
Advertising/Marketing Budget Related to Direct Marketing: 0-25%
Founded: 1963
Gross sales or billing: $30,000,000

Children's educational books (USBORNE). Activity kits (kid kits).

THE DMA EAGLE PUBLISHING
One Massachusetts Ave NW
Washington, DC 20001
Telephone: (202) 216-0600, FAX: (202) 216-0612, Web Site: www.eaglepub.com
Chmn: Thomas L. Phillips
Pres: Jeffrey J. Carneal
VP Opers & CFO: Jon Heimerman
Conducts Business: U.S.
Employees: 220
Primary Market Served: Business & Consumer
Advertising/Marketing Budget Related to Direct Marketing: 0-25%
Direct Marketing ad budget:
Direct Mail: 100%
Founded: 1993
Gross sales or billing: $8,300,000

National weekly newspaper featuring political topics. Sold through direct mail subscriptions.

ECKANKAR
Eckankar Religion of the Light & Sound of God
PO Box 27300
Minneapolis, MN 55427
Telephone: (612) 544-3001, (800) 327-5113, FAX: (612) 474-1127, Web Site: www.eckankar.org
Natl Sls & Mktg Mgr: John Kulick
Conducts Business: U.S., Canada, Australia, New Zealand, Europe
Employees: 1
Primary Market Served: Business & Consumer
Founded: 1969

Distributor of books on Eckankar religion to booksellers, wholesalers & consumers.

THE ECONOMIST NEWSPAPER NA INC
Div. of The Economist Newspaper Group Inc
750 3rd Ave (fl 5)
New York, NY 10017
Telephone: (212) 554-0600, FAX: (212) 586-1191, Web Site: www.economist.com
COO: Elizabeth O'Rorke
Mktg & Res Dir: Humphry Rolleston
Adv Dir: Oliver Comyn
Circ Dir, NA: Alison Papier
Comml Dir for economist.com: Paul Rossi
Conducts Business: Worldwide
Primary Market Served: Business & Consumer
Catalog available online
Direct online sales
Founded: 1843

International weekly magazine devoted to report & commentary from a global perspective on business, politics, finance, science & technology.

EDITORIAL PROJECTS IN EDUCATION INC
6935 Arlington Rd (Suite 100)
Bethesda, MD 20814-5233
Telephone: (301) 280-3100, (800) 346-1834, FAX: (301) 280-3250, Web Site: www.edweek.org
Pres & Publr: Virginia B. Edwards
Gen Mgr: Michele Givens
Adv Dir: Michael McKenna
Primary Market Served: Business & Consumer
Founded: 1981

Publishes Education Week-weekly national newspaper for school administrators. Teacher's magazine-monthly for K-12 teachers.

EDUCATORS PROGRESS SERVICE INC
aka FreeTeachingAids.com
214 Center St
Randolph, WI 53956-1408
Telephone: (920) 326-3126, (888) 951-4469, Web Site: www.freeteachingaids.com
Pres & Publr: Kathy Nehmer
Conducts Business: Worldwide
Employees: 5
Primary Market Served: Business & Consumer
Advertising/Marketing Budget Related to Direct Marketing: 26-50%
Founded: 1934

Publisher of guides to free materials. Sell to schools, libraries, nursing homes, health & youth centers, prisons & industry.

EDWARD ELGAR PUBLISHING INC

Nine Dewey Ct, The William Pratt House
Northampton, MA 01060-3815
Telephone: (413) 584-5551, FAX: (413) 584-9933, E-Mail: sales@e-elgar.com, Web Site: www.e-elgar.com
VP: Richard Henning
Promo Mgr: Katy Wight
Publ Asst: Tara Gorvine
Conducts Business: Worldwide
Employees: 5
Primary Market Served: Business & Consumer
Catalog available online
Indirect online sales
Advertising/Marketing Budget Related to Direct Marketing: 51-75%
Direct Marketing ad budget: $300,000
Direct Mail: 100%
Founded: 1986
Gross sales or billing: $3,000,000

Academic monographs & reference books on Economics, Politics & Business to libraries, academics & professionals.

THE DMA ELKS MAGAZINE

Div. of BPO Elks of the USA
425 W Diversey Pkwy
Chicago, IL 60614-6196
Telephone: (773) 755-4700, (877) 355-7624, FAX: (773) 775-4891, E-Mail: elksmag@elks.org, Web Site: www.elks.org
Mktg Dir & Editor: Fred Oakes
Dir Circulation: Phil Claiborne
Adv Coord: Bris Hernandez
Conducts Business: U.S.
Employees: 40
Primary Market Served: Business & Consumer
Advertising/Marketing Budget Related to Direct Marketing: 0-25%
Founded: 1922

Monthly magazine (July/Aug & Dec/Jan issues combined) with heavy direct-to-consumer advertising. Reaches 1.1 million households.

ELSEVIER

360 Park Ave S
New York, NY 10010-1710
Telephone: (212) 989-5800, FAX: (212) 633-3990, Web Site: www.elsevier.com
CEO: Erik Engstrom
CEO Elsevier Health Sciences: Michael Hansen
Primary Market Served: Business

EMPLOYMENT PUBLISHING INC

175 Strafford Ave
Wayne, PA 19087-3317
Telephone: (610) 975-4539, FAX: (610) 687-7860, E-Mail: jfanning@employment911.com
Pres: Jake Fannin

THE DMA EN ESPANOL PUBLISHING GROUP LLC

250 S Beverly Dr (#301)
Beverly Hills, CA 90212-3831
Telephone: (310) 248-2680
Pres: Michaelle Fastlicht
Primary Market Served: Business & Consumer

ENCYCLOPAEDIA BRITANNICA INC

331 N LaSalle St
Chicago, IL 60654-2682
Telephone: (312) 347-7319, (800) 323-1229, FAX: (312) 347-7225
VP, Print Products Mktg: Joan Julian
Conducts Business: U.S., Canada
Primary Market Served: Business & Consumer
Direct Marketing ad budget:
Direct Mail: 60%
Magazines: 5%
TV/Radio: 35%

Obtain leads for Encyclopaedia Britannica through all direct response media. Product is sold to a demographic cross-section, primarily families with children. Marketer of children & adult products via mail order. Also performs telemarketing services for outside clients.

ENTREPRENEUR MEDIA INC

2445 McCabe Way (Suite 400)
Irvine, CA 92614
Telephone: (949) 261-2325, (800) 274-6229, FAX: (949) 261-0234, Web Site: www.entrepreneur.com
CEO: Peter Shea
Ed-in-Chief: Rieva Lesonsky
Promos Mgr: Tracy Kerley
Conducts Business: U.S., Canada
Employees: 100
Primary Market Served: Consumer
Catalog available online

Publisher of Entrepreneur magazines: Entrepreneur de Mexico, Entrepreneur Japan, Entrepreneur Philippines & Entrepreneur International.

ENVIRONMENTAL LAW INSTITUTE

2000 "L" St NW (Suite 200)
Washington, DC 20036-4919
Telephone: (202) 939-3800, FAX: (202) 939-3868, E-Mail: law@eli.org, Web Site: www.eli.org
Pres: Leslie Carothers
VP Devel: Martin Dickinson
VP Fin & Admin: Elliot D
VP Res & Policy: Elissa Parker
VP, Publications & Assoc: Scott Schang
Conducts Business: U.S.
Employees: 60
Primary Market Served: Business
Catalog available online
Gross sales or billing: $5,300,000

Publish & market books, journals, newsletters & loose-leaf services on environmental & natural resources law & policy. Publish Environmental Law Reporter (ELR).

ESQUIRE MAGAZINE

Div. of Hearst Corp
300 W 57th St (21st fl)
New York, NY 10019
Telephone: (212) 649-2000, (800) 925-0485, FAX: (212) 265-0938, E-Mail: esquire@hearst.com, Web Site: www.esquire.com
Editor in Chief: David Granger
Deputy Editor: Peter Griffin
Editorial Dir: Helene F. Runinstein
Design Dir: David Curcurito
Editorial Project Dir: Lisa Hintelmann
Exec Editor: Mark Warren
Fashion Dir: Nick Sullivan
Mng Editor: John Kenney
Art Dir: Darhil Crooks
Dir Photography: Michael Norseng
Conducts Business: U.S., Canada
Primary Market Served: Business & Consumer

Publisher of Esquire Magazine. Use various direct marketing techniques in circulation subscription efforts.

ESSENCE COMMUNICATIONS INC

135 W 50th St (4th fl)
New York, NY 10020-1201
Telephone: (212) 522-1212, FAX: (212) 921-5173, Web Site: www.essence.com
Publr & CEO: Edward Lewis
Editor-in-Chief: C.R. White
Assoc Publr Mktg: Cindy Schreibman
Gen Mgr EBM: Nancy Hegy-Martin
Pres: Michele Ebanks
Conducts Business: U.S.
Employees: 150
Primary Market Served: Consumer
Catalog available online
Direct online sales
Advertising/Marketing Budget Related to Direct Marketing: 76-100%
Direct Marketing ad budget:
Direct Mail: $10,400,000
TV/Radio: $400,000
Telephone: $45,000
Founded: 1968
Gross sales or billing: $97,000,000

Publish Essence Magazine, Latina Magazine & The Essence By Mail Catalog.

F&W PUBLICATIONS INC
10151 Carver Rd (Suite 200)
Blue Ash, OH 45242-4760
Telephone: (513) 531-2690, FAX: (513) 531-0293, Web Site: www.fwpublications.com
Pres: Steve Kent
Sr VP & Gen Mgr Book Div: W. Budge Wallis
Sr VP & Gen Mgr Magazine Div: Jeff Lapin
VP Fin & Admin: Mark Arnett
VP New Prod Devel: David Lewis
HR Dir: Kathy Schneider
Promo Dir: Colleen Cannon
Circ Dir: David Lee
Conducts Business: U.S., Canada, English-speaking countries
Employees: 300
Primary Market Served: Business & Consumer
Direct online sales
Advertising/Marketing Budget Related to Direct Marketing: 51-75%
Direct Marketing ad budget:
Direct Mail: 90%
Magazines: 10%
Founded: 1913

Publish magazines, books & courses for freelance artists, crafters, designers, woodworkers & writers. Mail several million pieces per year to solicit subscriptions, sell books & home study courses in writing, art, woodworking & design.

THE DMA FDANEWS
300 N Washington St (Suite 200)
Falls Church, VA 22046-3431
Telephone: (703) 538-7600, (888) 838-5578, FAX: (703) 538-7676, E-Mail: customerservice@fdanews.com, Web Site: www.fdanews.com
Pres: Cindy Carter
Publ: Matt Salt
Mktg Dir: Allison King
Sr Mktg Mgr: Alka Desai
Conducts Business: U.S., Canada, Worldwide
Employees: 30
Primary Market Served: Business & Consumer
Catalog available online
Direct online sales
Advertising/Marketing Budget Related to Direct Marketing: 26-50%
Founded: 1976
Gross sales or billing: $6,100,000

Premier provider of regulation, legislative and business news and information to the pharmaceutical, medical device and biotech industries.

FT PUBLICATIONS INC
Financial Times Group
1330 Ave of the Americas
New York, NY 10019
Telephone: (212) 641-6500, FAX: (212) 641-6544, E-Mail: adsales@ft.com, Web Site: www.ft.com
Pres: Steve Hoye
Comml Dir: Andrew Sollinger
Conducts Business: Worldwide
Primary Market Served: Business & Consumer
Founded: 1888

International business newspaper.

FW MEDIA
4700 E Galbraith Rd
Cincinnati, OH 45236-2726
Telephone: (513) 531-2690, Web Site: www.fwpublications.com
VP Consumer Mktg: Sara DeCarlo
Primary Market Served: Business & Consumer

FACTS ON FILE INC
Subs. of Infobase Holdings Inc
132 W 31st St (17th fl)
New York, NY 10001
Telephone: (212) 967-8800, (800) 322-8755, FAX: (212) 678-3633, Web Site: www.factsonfile.com
Pres: Mark McDonnell
CFO: James Housely
Mktg Dir: Kate Moore
Sls Dir: Paul Conklin
Edit Dir & Electronic Publ Dir: Laurie Likoff
Publicity Dir: Linda Leonard
Conducts Business: U.S., U.K.
Employees: 125
Primary Market Served: Business & Consumer
Catalog available online
Direct online sales
Advertising/Marketing Budget Related to Direct Marketing: 0-25%

Book, electronic reference & trade publisher.

FAIRCHILD BOOKS
Div. of Fairchild Publications Inc
750 Third Ave
New York, NY 10017
Telephone: (212) 630-4171, (800) 932-4724, FAX: (212) 630-3868, Web Site: www.fairchildbooks.com
CEO, Fairchild Publications, Inc: Mary Berner
Gen Mgr: Elizabeth Tighe
Exec Editor: Olga Kontzias
Editorial Devel Dir: Jennifer Crane
Prod Dir: Ginger Hillman
Conducts Business: U.S., Canada
Employees: 20

Primary Market Served: Business & Consumer
Catalog available online
Advertising/Marketing Budget Related to Direct Marketing: 76-100%
Direct Marketing ad budget: $500,000
Direct Mail: 90%
Newspapers: 5%
Telephone: 5%
Gross sales or billing: $2,000,000

Textile, apparel, design and merchandising, retail, interior design to 2 and 4 year colleges and universities, high schools and professionals.

FAIRCHILD PUBLICATIONS
750 Third Ave
New York, NY 10017-2703
Telephone: (212) 630-4000, Web Site: www.fairchildpub.com
Chmn & Editorial Dir: Patrick McCarthy
Pres & CEO: Mary Berner
Conducts Business: Worldwide
Employees: 726
Primary Market Served: Business & Consumer
Founded: 1889
Gross sales or billing: $350,000,000

Publisher of trade & consumer magazines serving the retail & industrial industries.

THE FAMILY HANDYMAN
Subs. of Reader's Digest Inc
2915 Commers Dr (Suite 700)
Eagan, MN 55121-2398
Telephone: (651) 454-9200, FAX: (651) 994-2250
Publr: Mike Rielly
Ed-in-Chief: Gary Havens
Circ Mgr: Craig Reynolds
Conducts Business: U.S., Canada
Employees: 52
Primary Market Served: Consumer
Advertising/Marketing Budget Related to Direct Marketing: 51-75%
Direct Marketing ad budget: $6,000,000
Direct Mail: 100%
Gross sales or billing: $27,000,000

Magazine for do-it-yourself homeowners.

FARM JOURNAL INC
Div. of Tribune Co
30 S 15th St Ste 900, Center Sq W
Philadelphia, PA 19102-4803
Telephone: (215) 557-8937, FAX: (215) 568-4238
Pres: Roger Randall
VP, Publ Svc: Earl Ainsworth
Conducts Business: U.S.
Employees: 230

Primary Market Served: Business &
   Consumer
Advertising/Marketing Budget Related
   to Direct Marketing: 0-25%
Direct Marketing ad budget:
Magazines: $100,000
Founded: 1877
Gross sales or billing: $35,000,000

Magazine publisher.

FARM PROGRESS CO
Subs. of Rural Press Ltd Inc
255 38th Ave (Suite P)
Saint Charles, IL 60174-5410
Telephone: (630) 690-5600, FAX:
   (630) 462-2202, E-Mail: dwilson@
   farmprogress.com, Web Site: www.
   farmprogress.com
VP Mktg Oper: Sara Hess
Conducts Business: Worldwide
Employees: 200
Primary Market Served: Business &
   Consumer
Indirect online sales
Advertising/Marketing Budget Related
   to Direct Marketing: 0-25%
Founded: 1841
Gross sales or billing: $45,000,000

Publisher of specialized agricultural
publications serving producers & agri-
businesses database management.

FARRAR STRAUS & GIROUX
INC
18 W 18th St Fl 7
New York, NY 10011-4675
Telephone: (212) 741-6900, (800) 330-
   8477, FAX: (212) 633-2427, E-Mail:
   childrens_editorial@fsgbooks.com,
   Web Site: www.fsgbooks.com
Ed-in-Chief & VP: Jonathan Galassi
CFO & Sr VP Fin: Philip Zweiger
Sls, Mktg Dir & Treas: Laurie Brown
Publr: Sarah Crichton
Conducts Business: Worldwide
Employees: 95
Primary Market Served: Business
Catalog available online
Indirect online sales
Advertising/Marketing Budget Related
   to Direct Marketing: 0-25%
Founded: 1946

Publisher of books for adults &
children.

FERGUSON PUBLISHING CO
Div. of Infobase Publishing
132 W 31st St (17 fl)
New York, NY 10001-3406
Telephone: (212) 613-2800, (800) 322-
   8755, FAX: (800) 678-3633, E-Mail:
   custserv@factsonfile.com, Web Site:
   www.fergpubco.com
Sls Dir: Paul Conklin

VP: Russ Beck
Mgr: Elizabeth Malafi
Conducts Business: U.S.
Employees: 70
Primary Market Served: Business
Advertising/Marketing Budget Related
   to Direct Marketing: 51-75%
Founded: 1939
Gross sales or billing: $8,200,000

Publisher of career education books
and reference materials. Offer the publications to direct mail companies for
their mailings.

FINANCIAL PUBLISHING CO
Div. of Carleton
1251 N Eddy St (Suite 202)
South Bend, IN 46617-1478
Telephone: (800) 247-3214, FAX:
   (574) 243-6060, Web Site: www.
   financial-publishing.com
VP, Engrng, Res & Devel & Tech:
   Deborah Grounds
Conducts Business: U.S., Canada
Employees: 25
Primary Market Served: Business
Catalog available online
Indirect online sales
Direct Marketing ad budget:
Direct Mail: 88%
Magazines: 12%

Publisher of financial books, rate
charts, schedules, micro computer software, electronic calculators & internet
products.

THE DMA FINANCIAL TIMES
1330 Avenue of the Americas
New York, NY 10019-5436
Telephone: (212) 641-6500, Web Site:
   www.ft.com
VP Consumer Mktg: Richard Varey
Primary Market Served: Business &
   Consumer

CARL FISCHER MUSIC
65 Bleecker St Fl 8
New York, NY 10012-2420
Telephone: (212) 777-0900, (800) 762-
   2328, FAX: (212) 477-6996, E-Mail:
   cf-info@carlfischer.com, Web Site:
   www.carlfischer.com
CEO: Lauren Keiser
VP Sls & Mktg: Chris Scialfa
Mktg Mgr: Alfred Fredel
Mktg Asst: Tiffany Sumner
Conducts Business: Worldwide
Employees: 40
Primary Market Served: Business &
   Consumer
Catalog available online
Advertising/Marketing Budget Related
   to Direct Marketing: 0-25%
Direct Marketing ad budget: $300,000
Direct Mail: 80%

Magazines: 20%
Founded: 1872

Sheet music & music products to dealers & consumers.

FLORIDA TODAY
AKA Cape Publications, Inc. Owned
   by Gannett Co Inc
1 Gannett Plz
Melbourne, FL 32940
Telephone: (321) 242-3500, (877) 424-
   0156, FAX: (321) 242-3729, Web
   Site: www.floridatoday.com
Exec Ed: Terry Eberle
Bus Devel Dir: Greg Watson
Sls & Mktg: Patricia Shoff
Mktg & Community Affairs: Gina Kai-
   ser
Employees: 600
Primary Market Served: Business &
   Consumer
Founded: 1966
Gross sales or billing: $34,700,000

Newspaper publishing company.

FOOD CHEMICAL NEWS
Div. of CRC Press Inc
2200 Clarendon Blvd (Suite 1401)
Arlington, VA 22201-3381
Telephone: (202) 887-6320, (888) 732-
   7070, FAX: (202) 887-6335, E-Mail:
   cs@foodregulation.com, Web Site:
   www.foodchemicalnews.com
Ed of Food Chemical News: Jay
   Fletcher
Mktg Dir: Amy Mitrani
Conducts Business: U.S.
Employees: 20
Primary Market Served: Business
Indirect online sales
Advertising/Marketing Budget Related
   to Direct Marketing: 76-100%
Direct Marketing ad budget:
Direct Mail: 90%
Telephone: 10%
Founded: 1959

Newsletters & reports on food regulations & environmental regulations.

FORBES INC
60 Fifth Ave (corner of 12th St)
New York, NY 10011-8868
Telephone: (212) 620-2200, FAX:
   (212) 620-2245, Web Site: www.
   forbesinc.com
Circ Dir: Nina LaFrance
Conducts Business: U.S., Canada
Employees: 700
Primary Market Served: Consumer
Advertising/Marketing Budget Related
   to Direct Marketing: 76-100%
Founded: 1917

Magazine for business executives &
investors.

FORUM PUBLISHING CO

383 E Main St
Centerport, NY 11721-1538
Telephone: (631) 754-5000, (800) 635-
7654, FAX: (631) 754-0630, E-Mail:
forumpublishing@aol.com, Web Site:
www.forum123.com
Pres: Martin B. Stevens
Conducts Business: U.S.
Employees: 9
Primary Market Served: Business
Catalog available online
Direct online sales
Advertising/Marketing Budget Related
to Direct Marketing: 0-25%
Direct Marketing ad budget:
Direct Mail: 25%
Magazines: 25%
Telephone: 50%
Founded: 1981
Gross sales or billing: $1,400,000

Publishers of trade magazines, con-
necting retail stores with wholesale
merchandise.

FOUR DIRECTIONS MEDIA

Div. of Oneida Nation Enterprises,
LLC
579 Main St
Oneida, NY 13421
Telephone: (315) 829-8316, Web Site:
www.fourdirectionsinc.com
Dir Mktg: Peter Wiezalis
Primary Market Served: Consumer

FRANKLIN ESTIMATING SYSTEMS

2391 S 1560 W Ste B
Woods Cross, UT 84087-2378
Telephone: (801) 303-6083, (800) 346-
7363, FAX: (801) 303-4540, E-Mail:
management@franklinestimating.
com, Web Site: www.fesys.com
Owner: Gregory Harrison
Conducts Business: U.S., Canada
Employees: 21
Primary Market Served: Business
Catalog available online
Indirect online sales
Advertising/Marketing Budget Related
to Direct Marketing: 51-75%
Direct Marketing ad budget: $120,000
Direct Mail: $50,000
Magazines: $50,000
Telephone: $20,000
Founded: 1917

Publisher of Estimating Guides to the
Graphic Arts. Catalogs include: Franklin Offset Catalog, Franklin Small
Press Catalog, Franklin Estimator for
Windows & Power Macintosh (Computer Estimating Software for Printers).
Also Data Manager, a turnkey system
for collecting time, storing, sorting &
reporting the time & production
information.

FULCRUM PUBLISHING

4690 Table Mountain Dr (Suite 100)
Golden, CO 80403
Telephone: (303) 277-1623, (800) 992-
2908, FAX: (303) 279-7111, Web
Site: www.fulcrum-books.com
Publr: Sam Scinta
Assoc Publr: Derek Lawrence
Mktg Mgr: Katie O'Neill
Conducts Business: U.S.
Employees: 25
Primary Market Served: Business &
Consumer
Catalog available online
Direct online sales
Advertising/Marketing Budget Related
to Direct Marketing: 0-25%
Founded: 1984

Books for gardeners, teachers, librarians & professors.

GALE RESEARCH INC

Subs. of The Thomson Corp
27500 Drake Rd
Farmington Hills, MI 48331-3535
Telephone: (248) 699-4253, (800) 877-
GALE, FAX: (313) 961-6083, Web
Site: www.gale.com
Pres, CEO: Dedria Bryfonski
CFO: Bill Schuetz
Exec VP, Sls & Mktg: Ben Mondloch
Exec VP, Ed & Devel: Dennis Poupard
Sr VP, Sls: Valerie MacLeod
Sr VP, Mktg & Sls: Lynda James-
Gilboe
Chief Tech Officer: Nancy Ziemski
VP, Ed & Gen Reference Publg: Ellen
Crowley
VP, Intl Sls: Lucy Schoener
Conducts Business: Worldwide
Primary Market Served: Business
Catalog available online
Founded: 1954

Information publisher providing data in
print & electronic formats.

GARLINGHOUSE CO

Sub of: Virtual Mktg Concepts
2121 Boundary St (Suite 208), Burn-
side Bldg
Beaufort, SC 29902-6812
Telephone: (703) 547-4115, (800) 235-
5700, FAX: (703) 222-9705, Web
Site: www.familyhomeplans.com
Publr & CEO: James D. McNair lll
Conducts Business: U.S., Canada
Employees: 50
Primary Market Served: Business &
Consumer
Catalog available online
Direct online sales
Direct Marketing ad budget: $250,000
Direct Mail: 15%
Magazines: 50%
Newspapers: 5%

Telephone: 30%
Founded: 1907
Gross sales or billing: $5,000,000

Publishers of Home Plan books and
magazines; blueprint sales to public
through books & magazines.

GAZETTE COMMUNICATIONS INC

dba Decisionmark; Gazette Direct
Mktg Svcs; The Gazette &
KCRG-TV 9
500 Third Ave SE, Box 511
Cedar Rapids, IA 52406
Telephone: (319) 398-8211, (800) 397-
8211, FAX: (319) 368-8834, Web
Site: www.gazettecommunications.
com
Exec VP & CFO: Ken Slaughter
Pres & COO: Charles M. Peters
CEO: Joe F. Hladky
Mgr Mktg & Promos: Stacie Bedford
Conducts Business: U.S.
Employees: 700
Primary Market Served: Business &
Consumer
Founded: 1883
Gross sales or billing: $34,700,000

Companies include a daily newspapers,
an ABC affiliate broadcast station, a
shoppers network, commercial printing,
and online services. Over 300,000
Eastern Iowans read, tune in, or log
onto their products daily.

GEBBIE PRESS INC

PO Box 1000
New Paltz, NY 12561-0017
Telephone: (845) 255-7560, FAX:
(888) 345-2790, E-Mail:
gebbiepress@pipeline.com, Web
Site: www.gebbieinc.com
Ed, Publr & Pres: Mark Gebbie
Assoc Ed: Barbara A. Edelman
Conducts Business: U.S.
Employees: 2
Primary Market Served: Business
Catalog available online
Indirect online sales
Founded: 1954
Gross sales or billing: $100,000

Publish All-in-One media directory
including all daily, weekly, Black &
Hispanic newspapers; all radio, TV,
Black & Hispanic stations; consumer
magazines, trade press, business periodicals & farm press. Also available as
text files on CD or as an online subscription service.

GEMINI PUBLISHING CO

1799 Fm 528 Rd Apt 11101
Webster, TX 77598-4721

Telephone: (281) 316-4276, E-Mail:
getgirls@getgirls.com, Web Site:
www.getgirls.com
Pres & Owner: Don Diebel
VP: Michele Diebel
Conducts Business: U.S., Canada, Europe, Asia
Employees: 3
Primary Market Served: Business &
Consumer
Catalog available online
Direct online sales
Advertising/Marketing Budget Related
to Direct Marketing: 0-25%
Direct Marketing ad budget: $10,000
Direct Mail: 10%
Newspapers: 5%
Online: 80%
Telephone: 5%
Founded: 1978
Gross sales or billing: $90,000

Books, cassettes, videos, cd's & dvd's
to help men meet, attract & succeed
with women. Free 4-page catalog
available upon request. Market products to single men & our books to mail
order businesses.

GENIUM PUBLISHING
79 The Mall
Amsterdam, NY 12010
Telephone: (518) 842-4111, FAX:
(518) 842-1843, E-Mail: sales@
genium.com, Web Site: www.
genium.com
Pres: Michael Cinquanti
Editor: Paul Hans
Tech Editor: Gary Whitmore
Conducts Business: U.S., Canada, Europe
Employees: 7
Primary Market Served: Business &
Consumer
Catalog available online
Direct online sales
Advertising/Marketing Budget Related
to Direct Marketing: 76-100%
Direct Marketing ad budget:
Direct Mail: 100%
Founded: 1984
Gross sales or billing: $1,000,000

Technical books & manuals, health &
safety booklets, manuals, videotapes &
software & vocational training
videotapes.

PETER GLENN
PUBLICATIONS
777 E Atlantic Ave (Suite C2337)
Delray Beach, FL 33483
Telephone: (561) 404-4290, (888) 332-
6700, FAX: (561) 892-5786, E-Mail:
gregjames@pgdirect.com, Web Site:
www.pgdirect.com
CEO & Publr: Gregory James

Dir: L Chip Brill
Dir: Umberto Guido III
Conducts Business: Worldwide
Employees: 9
Primary Market Served: Business &
Consumer
Catalog available online
Direct online sales
Advertising/Marketing Budget Related
to Direct Marketing: 51-75%
Founded: 1956

Publishing house for the entertainment
industry.

GLOBE SPECIALTY
PRODUCTS INC
9 Latti Farm Rd
Millbury, MA 01527-2132
Telephone: (508) 871-1900
Pres: David Dickerson
Primary Market Served: Business &
Consumer

GOLF DIGEST CO
Subs. of Advance Publications Inc
20 Westport Rd Ste 320, PO Box 850
Wilton, CT 06897-4550
Telephone: (203) 761-5100, FAX:
(203) 371-2572, Web Site: www.
golfdigest.com
Pres: Mitchell Fox
Pub Rels Mgr: Catherine Soltis
Field Sls Mgr: Mike Connelly
Conducts Business: U.S., Canada
Employees: 325
Primary Market Served: Business &
Consumer
Catalog available online
Direct online sales
Advertising/Marketing Budget Related
to Direct Marketing: 76-100%
Gross sales or billing: $7,700,000

Publish Golf Digest, Golf World, &
Golf Shop Operations. Special event
publications include programs for the
Masters & U.S. Opens. Other products
include books, videos, golf schools,
custom research & a variety of events
conducted by NYT Event Sports
Marketing.

GOODHEART-WILLCOX
PUBLISHER
18604 W Creek Dr
Tinley Park, IL 60477-6243
Telephone: (708) 687-5000, (800) 323-
0440, FAX: (708) 687-3900, E-Mail:
custserv@g-w.com, Web Site: www.
g-w.com
Pres: John F. Flanagan
VP, Sls & Mktg: Todd Scheffers
Conducts Business: Worldwide
Employees: 65
Primary Market Served: Business &
Consumer

Catalog available online
Indirect online sales
Founded: 1921
Gross sales or billing: $26,500,000

Publisher of industrial/technical, family
& consumer sciences & career textbooks for education, industry &
individuals.

GOODMAN MEDIA GROUP
INC
250 W 57th St (Suite 710)
New York, NY 10107
Telephone: (212) 262-2247, FAX:
(212) 262-2278, E-Mail: jgoodman@
gmgpub.com, Web Site: www.
goodmanmediagroup.dev.
hotresponse.com
Publr: Jason Goodman
Sls Mgr: Deena E. Brown
Primary Market Served: Consumer
Founded: 1995

Small consumer publishing firm publishing various topics, including collectibles, Victorian & women's
magazines.

GOVERNING MAGAZINE
1100 Connecticut Ave NW Ste 1300
Washington, DC 20036-4109
Telephone: (202) 862-8802, Web Site:
www.governing.com
Circulation Dir: Paula Lawrence
Primary Market Served: Business &
Consumer

GOVERNMENT DATA
PUBLICATIONS INC
2300 M St NW
Washington, DC 20037-1434
Telephone: (718) 627-0819, (800) 275-
4688, FAX: (718) 998-5960, E-Mail:
gdp@govdata.com, Web Site: www.
govdata.com
Publr: Siegfried Lobel
Mktg Dir: Gail Rand
Comptroller: Nellie Corenman
Head Computer Opers: Leonard Lobel
Prodn Mgr: Joseph Reinman
Conducts Business: U.S., Canada
Employees: 35
Primary Market Served: Business &
Consumer
Advertising/Marketing Budget Related
to Direct Marketing: 76-100%

Directories, periodicals & databases.

GRADE FINDERS INC
PO Box 944
Exton, PA 19341-0908
Telephone: (610) 524-7070, FAX:
(610) 524-8912, E-Mail: info@
gradefinders.com, Web Site: www.
gradefinders.com

CEO: W. A. Subers
Pres: Mark Subers
Conducts Business: Worldwide
Employees: 7
Primary Market Served: Business
Catalog available online
Direct online sales
Founded: 1967

Publish a directory of paper manufacturers, distributors & converters. List the brand names produced by each.

THE GREAT AMARILLO DIRECTORY

Div. of Yellow Book
2400 Lakeview Dr (Suite 113)
Amarillo, TX 79109-1532
Telephone: (806) 353-5155, FAX:
(806) 359-2974, Web Site: www.
worldpages.com
Pres & CEO: Joe Walsh
VP: John Beaver
Primary Market Served: Business
Catalog available online

Publish telephone directories.

GREENWOOD PUBLISHING GROUP INC

Div. of Houghton Mifflin Harcourt
PO Box 6926, PO Box 5007
Portsmouth, NH 03802-6926
Telephone: (203) 226-3571, FAX:
(203) 222-1502, E-Mail: sales@
greenwood.com, Web Site: www.
greenwood.com
Pres: Wayne Smith
Mktg Consultant: Roland Ochsenbein
Conducts Business: Worldwide
Employees: 264
Primary Market Served: Business &
Consumer
Founded: 1967
Gross sales or billing: $29,700,000

Publish scholarly, professional & reference books, newsletters & journals for the academic & professional markets. Approximately 700 original titles per year. Backlist contains over 12,000 titles in social sciences & humanities. Imprints: Auburn House, Praeger Publishers, Greenwood Press, Bergin & Garvey, Quorum Books.

GROLIER PUBLISHING

90 Sherman Tpke
Danbury, CT 06816-0002
Telephone: (203) 797-3500, (800) 621-
1115, FAX: (203) 797-3720, Web
Site: www.grolier.com
VP, Media: Diane Petruzzelli
VP, Adv: Nadine Rozzini
Conducts Business: Worldwide
Employees: 50
Primary Market Served: Consumer

Publisher of children's books.

GROWING CHILD, INC

Subs. of Dunn & Hargitt
PO Box 2505
West Lafayette, IN 47996-2505
Telephone: (765) 464-0920, (800) 927-
7289, FAX: (765) 423-4495, E-Mail:
service@growingchild.com, Web
Site: www.growingchild.com
Pres: Dennis Dunn
Conducts Business: U.S., Canada
Employees: 45
Primary Market Served: Business &
Consumer
Catalog available online
Direct online sales
Founded: 1971

Publisher of child-development materials & commodities investment charts.

GRUBER & ALLISON INC

7487 Falls Rd W
Boynton Beach, FL 33437
Telephone: (561) 752-9960, FAX:
(561) 752-0085
Pres: J.H. Gruber
Conducts Business: U.S., Canada, Europe
Employees: 6
Primary Market Served: Business &
Consumer
Advertising/Marketing Budget Related
to Direct Marketing: 0-25%
Founded: 1991

Newsletters.

GUILFORD PUBLICATIONS INC

72 Spring St (4th fl)
New York, NY 10012-4050
Telephone: (212) 431-9800, (800) 365-
7006, FAX: (212) 966-6708, E-Mail:
info@guilford.com, Web Site: www.
guilford.com
Pres: Robert Matloff
Mktg Dir: Marian Robinson
Asst Sls Mgr: Indre Melynis
Sls Mgr: Anne Patota
Conducts Business: Worldwide
Employees: 55
Primary Market Served: Business &
Consumer
Catalog available online
Direct online sales
Advertising/Marketing Budget Related
to Direct Marketing: 51-75%
Founded: 1973

Publish professional & trade books, DVDs, newsletters & journals in psychology & psychiatry, family therapy, learning disabilities, addictions, gender issues, education, & geography.

GULF PUBLISHING CO

2 Greenway Plz (Ste 1020)
Houston, TX 77046-0208
Telephone: (713) 529-4301, FAX:
(713) 520-4433, E-Mail:
publications@gulfpub.com, Web
Site: www.gulfpub.com
Mktg Dir: Joe Woods
Conducts Business: Worldwide
Employees: 160
Primary Market Served: Business
Catalog available online
Indirect online sales
Founded: 1916

Publish specialized books & software for engineering & scientific professionals.

HDA INC

944 Anglum Rd
Saint Louis, MO 63042
Telephone: (314) 770-2222, (800) 533-
4350, FAX: (314) 770-1454, E-Mail:
plans@hdainc.com, Web Site: www.
designamerica.com
Pres: Robert Ketterer
Sls Mgr: Michael Kirchwehm
Conducts Business: U.S., Canada
Employees: 27
Primary Market Served: Business &
Consumer
Advertising/Marketing Budget Related
to Direct Marketing: 0-25%
Direct Marketing ad budget: $60,000
Direct Mail: 12%
Magazines: 80%
TV/Radio: 8%
Founded: 1910
Gross sales or billing: $2,000,000

Blueprints, project plans, how-to books; Sunset, Ortho, BH&G & Sterling magazines.

THE HERALD & REVIEW

Div. of Lee Enterprises
601 E William St
Decatur, IL 62525-1190
Telephone: (217) 429-5151, FAX:
(217) 421-6913, E-Mail: hrdirect@
herald-review.com, Web Site: www.
herald-review.com
Editor: Tim Cain
Editor: David Dawson
Editor: Jeana Matherly
Editor: Todd Nelson
Editor: Scott Perry
Employees: 300
Primary Market Served: Business &
Consumer
Catalog available online
Direct online sales
Founded: 1873

Publisher of specialty magazines, guides & brochures; also direct mail, list rental, lettershop & postal center.

HACHETTE FILIPACCHI LIST MANAGEMENT

Div. of Hachette Filipacchi Magazines
1633 Broadway (fl 43)
New York, NY 10019-6708
Telephone: (212) 767-6677, FAX:
(212) 767-5605, Web Site: www.
hfmuslists.com
List Dir: Alan R. Zamchick
VP, Circulation/Bus Strategy: Philip
Ketonis

HAMMOCK PUBLISHING INC

3322 West End Ave Ste 100
Nashville, TN 37203-6822
Telephone: (615) 690-3400, FAX:
(615) 690-3401, E-Mail: info@
hammock.com, Web Site: www.
hammock.com
Pres: John Lavey
Mktg Dir: Barbara Logan
Admin Dir: Julia Boklage
Conducts Business: U.S.
Primary Market Served: Business &
Consumer
Catalog available online
Founded: 1991

Publishing-base relationship marketing.
Publish custom magazine, newsletter &
internet based services.

HAMMOND WORLD ATLAS CORP

Subs. of Langenscheidt Publishing
Group
245 Park Ave (Fl 24)
New York, NY 10167-2499
Telephone: (908) 206-1300, (800) 526-
4953, FAX: (908) 206-1104, E-Mail:
erika@hammondmap.com, Web Site:
www.hammondmap.com
Sr Acct Supvr: Erika F. Gold
Conducts Business: U.S.
Employees: 40
Primary Market Served: Business &
Consumer
Advertising/Marketing Budget Related
to Direct Marketing: 0-25%
Founded: 1900

Complete line of atlases, maps, gift
books and travel guides. Also premium
& advertising specialty capabilities.

HAR COURT INC

9400 Southpark Center Loop
Orlando, FL 32819-8647
Telephone: (407) 345-2000, FAX:
(407) 345-1052
Mktg: Katie Lile
Primary Market Served: Business
Publishing.

HARCOURT EDUCATIONAL MEASUREMENT

Div. of Psychological Corp
19500 Bulverde Rd
San Antonio, TX 78259-3701
Telephone: (210) 299-1061, (800) 211-
8378, FAX: (800) 232-1223, Web
Site: www.harcourtassessment.com
Pres: Eugene T. Paslov
Mktg Dir: Wayne Gressett
Exhibits Mgr: Liz Huggins
DM Mgr: Terrie Dittman
Conducts Business: U.S., Canada, Aus-
tralia, U.K.
Employees: 35
Primary Market Served: Business &
Consumer
Advertising/Marketing Budget Related
to Direct Marketing: 51-75%
Direct Marketing ad budget:
Direct Mail: 90%
Magazines: 5%
Telephone: 5%
Founded: 1968

Retail publication & distribution of
educational books, kits, video & mi-
crocomputer software to professionals
working in public & private schools,
colleges, universities, hospitals &
clinics. Wholesale distribution to college & university bookstores.

THE DMA HARLEQUIN ENTERPRISES LTD

Subs. of Torstar Corp.
225 Duncan Mill Rd
Don Mills, ON, Canada M3B 3K9
Telephone: (416) 445-5860, FAX:
(416) 445-8655, E-Mail:
customer_ecare@harlequin.ca, Web
Site: www.eharlequin.com
Pres & COO: Dana Hayes
Exec VP, New Bus Devel & Strategy:
Pamela Layock
Exec VP, Retail Mktg & Sls: Craig
Swinwood
VP, Direct Mail & Readers Svc: Chris-
tina Clifford
Conducts Business: Worldwide
Employees: 1,000
Primary Market Served: Business &
Consumer
Catalog available online
Direct online sales
Direct Marketing ad budget:
$30,000,000
Direct Mail: 100%
Gross sales or billing: $583,000,000

Publish & market paperback books in
13 languages in over 90 countries.

HARPERCOLLINS

Subs of News Corp
10 E 53rd St (fl Cellar 2)
New York, NY 10022-5299

Telephone: (212) 207-7000, (800) 242-
7737, FAX: (212) 207-7145, Web
Site: www.harpercollins.com
Pres & CEO: Jane Friedman
VP Mktg/Indep Retailing: Carl Len-
nertz
Conducts Business: U.S.
Employees: 1,425
Primary Market Served: Business &
Consumer
Gross sales or billing: $165,200,000

The company's publishing groups in-
clude HarperCollins General Books
(imprints such as Perennial, Quill),
HarperCollins Children's Book Group,
HarperCollins UK, HarperCollins
Canada, HarperCollins India, and Har-
perCollins Australia/New Zealand. Its
Zondervan unit publishes bibles and
Christian books. The company's
e-book imprint is PerfectBound.

HARPER'S MAGAZINE

Harper's Magazine Foundation
666 Broadway (11th fl)
New York, NY 10012
Telephone: (212) 420-5720, FAX:
(212) 260-1096, Web Site: www.
harpers.org
Pres & Publr: John R. MacArthur
VP & Gen Mgr: Lynn Carlson
Pub Rels: Giulia Melucci
Conducts Business: Worldwide
Primary Market Served: Consumer
Catalog available online
Direct online sales
Founded: 1850

Published since 1850, Harper's Magazine is the oldest monthly magazine in
America. Marketed to an intelligent,
literate audience of thought-leaders
through direct mail & other direct response advertising.

HARRIS INFOSOURCE INTERNATIONAL INC

Div. of Dun & Bradstreet
5005 Rockside Rd (Suite 660)
Independence, OH 44131-6827
Telephone: (330) 425-9000, (877) 359-
6308, (800) 888-5900, (800) 748-
5482, FAX: (800) 643-5997, E-Mail:
customerservice@harrisinfo.com,
Web Site: www.harrisinfo.com
VP Mktg: David Wilkof
VP Sls: Joel Braun
Sls Mgr: Christian Heller
Sls Mgr: Bill Jones
Sls Mgr: Dave Powell
Conducts Business: Worldwide
Employees: 85
Primary Market Served: Consumer
Catalog available online
Indirect online sales
Advertising/Marketing Budget Related

to Direct Marketing: 76-100%
Founded: 1972
Gross sales or billing: $3,000,000

Publisher of business information databases on CD-ROM & industrial directories for all of the U.S.& Canada, nationally or by state or region; specializes in information databases on U.S. manufacturing on CD-ROM.

HARVARD BUSINESS REVIEW

Subs. of Harvard Business School Publishing Corp
300 N Beacon St
Watertown, MA 01472
Telephone: (617) 783-7400, FAX: (617) 783-7664, Web Site: www. hbsp.harvard.edu
Conducts Business: Worldwide
Employees: 40
Primary Market Served: Business & Consumer
Advertising/Marketing Budget Related to Direct Marketing: 51-75%

In-depth articles report timely business problems affecting marketing, general management, executive training & organization mergers. Subscribers are upper level management executives.

THE DMA HARVARD BUSINESS SCHOOL PUBLISHING

60 Harvard Way
Boston, MA 02163-1001
Telephone: (617) 783-7400, Web Site: www.harvardbusiness.org
Sr Dir Consumer Mktg: Elaine Spencer
Primary Market Served: Business

HATTON-BROWN PUBLISHERS INC

225 Hanrick St
Montgomery, AL 36104-3317
Telephone: (334) 834-1170, FAX: (334) 834-4525, E-Mail: webman@ hattonbrown.com, Web Site: www. hattonbrown.com
Co-Publr: David E. Knight
COO: Dianne C. Sullivan
Conducts Business: Worldwide
Employees: 23
Primary Market Served: Business & Consumer

Publisher of trade magazine serving the forestry & wood products markets. Brochure design & database management.

HAYMARKET GROUP LTD

12 W 37th St
New York, NY 10018-7480

Telephone: (212) 239-0855, FAX: (212) 967-4184, Web Site: www. chocalatiermagazine.com
Pres: Michael Schneider
Adv Dir: Elizabeth Hall
Prodn Dir: Christina Van der Walt
Cir Dir: Charles Squires
Conducts Business: U.S., Canada
Employees: 12
Primary Market Served: Consumer
Catalog available online
Direct online sales
Advertising/Marketing Budget Related to Direct Marketing: 26-50%
Gross sales or billing: $1,100,000

Publisher of Chocolatier & Pastry Art & Design magazines.

HEALTH AFFAIRS

Div. of Project Hope
7500 Old Georgetown Rd (Suite 600)
Bethesda, MD 20814-6800
Telephone: (301) 656-7401, FAX: (301) 654-2845, Web Site: www. healthaffairs.org
Publr: John Iglehart
Circ & Mktg Dir: Georgie Goldston
Exec Dir: Don Metz
Primary Market Served: Business
Catalog available online
Direct online sales
Advertising/Marketing Budget Related to Direct Marketing: 0-25%
Founded: 1981

Bi-monthly health policy journal.

HEALTH SCIENCES CONSORTIUM

300 Silver Cedar Ct
Chapel Hill, NC 27514-1696
Telephone: (919) 942-8731, FAX: (919) 942-3689, E-Mail: tony. penta@edtsi.com, Web Site: www. healthsciencesconsortium.org
Exec Dir: Frank B. Penta Edd
Mktg Dir: Jack Adcox
Publications Dir: Tony Penta
Conducts Business: U.S., Canada
Employees: 10
Primary Market Served: Business
Catalog available online
Indirect online sales
Advertising/Marketing Budget Related to Direct Marketing: 76-100%
Direct Marketing ad budget:
Direct Mail: 95%
Magazines: 5%
Founded: 1971
Gross sales or billing: $1,000,000

Publishers of instructional video & computer-based programs in the health sciences.

HEARLIHY & CO

1002 E Adams, PO Box 1747
Pittsburg, KS 66762
Telephone: (866) 622-1003, (800) 622-1000, FAX: (800) 443-2260, Web Site: www.hearlihy.com
Pres & CEO: Harvey Dean
Treas & Sec: Sandra Hearlihy
Supvr: Beth Garrison
Conducts Business: U.S.
Primary Market Served: Business & Consumer
Catalog available online
Direct online sales
Advertising/Marketing Budget Related to Direct Marketing: 51-75%
Direct Marketing ad budget:
Direct Mail: 80%
Telephone: 20%
Founded: 1969

Publisher of Educational Curriculum for Technology Education & Life Skills.

THE HEARST CORP

300 W 57th St
New York, NY 10019-3741
Telephone: (212) 649-2000, FAX: (212) 649-2108, Web Site: www. hearst.com/magazines/
Chmn Bd: George R. Hearst
Sr VP & CFO: Ronald J. Doerfler
Vice Chmn & CEO: Frank A. Bennack Jr
Sr VP & Chief Legal & Devel Officer: James M. Asher
Pres, Hearst Magazine: Cathie Black
Pres: David Carey
Conducts Business: U.S.
Employees: 17,000
Primary Market Served: Business & Consumer
Catalog available online
Direct online sales
Founded: 1887
Gross sales or billing: $4,520,000,000

Magazine publisher.

THE DMA HEARST MAGAZINES

Subs. of The Hearst Corporation
300 W 57th St (fl 19)
New York, NY 10019-3741
Telephone: (212) 649-2824, FAX: (212) 765-3528, Web Site: www. hearst.com/magazines
Pres: Cathleen P. Black
Exec VP, Chief Mktg Officer & Publ Dir: Michael A. Clinton
Sr VP, HR: Ruth Diem
Dir, Agency & ABC Svcs: Bernadette Pace
Employees: 20,000
Primary Market Served: Business & Consumer
Catalog available online

Direct online sales

Newspapers, magazines, radio & television.

HEARTLAND BOATING MAGAZINE

319 N Fourth St (Suite 650)
Saint Louis, MO 63102
Telephone: (314) 241-4310, (800) 366-9630, FAX: (314) 241-4207, E-Mail: info@heartlandboating.com, Web Site: www.heartlandboating.com
Publr & Ed: Nelson Spencer
Sls Mgr: Kathryn Burns
Conducts Business: U.S.
Employees: 6
Primary Market Served: Consumer
Advertising/Marketing Budget Related to Direct Marketing: 76-100%
Direct Marketing ad budget: $35,000
Direct Mail: 90%
Magazines: 5%
TV/Radio: 5%
Founded: 1989
Gross sales or billing: $500,000

Boating magazine for those interested & active in boating in mid-America.

HEARTSTRINGS PRESS

Div. of Gramma's Graphics Inc
49 Starview Pl, Dept DMMP-GL
Lancaster, VA 22503
Telephone: (804) 462-0884, (800) 462-0884, FAX: (716) 462-0884, E-Mail: sue@grandloving.com, Web Site: www.grandloving.com
Co-author: Julie Carlson
Sec & Treas: F.B. Johnson
Pres: Sue Johnson
Conducts Business: Worldwide
Primary Market Served: Business & Consumer
Catalog available online
Indirect online sales
Advertising/Marketing Budget Related to Direct Marketing: 26-50%
Founded: 1980

Grandloving: Making Memories with Your Grandchildren (newly released 5th edition), Heartstrings Press features anecdotes & ideas from over 350 grandparents, parents & grandchildren worldwide. Includes over 250 innovative, inexpensive activities for grandparents to do with or mail to their grandchildren. Three hundred & eight pages include illustrated projects, index & guide to the best children's books & products. and updated to include new technology & social networking methods.

HELDREF PUBLICATIONS

Div. of Helen Dwight Reid Educational Foundation
1319 18th St NW
Washington, DC 20036-1802
Telephone: (215) 625-8900, (202) 296-6267, FAX: (202) 296-5149, Web Site: www.heldref.org
Exec Dir Gen Counsel: Douglas Kirkpatrick
Mktg Dir: Katie Pfund
Circ Dir: Fred Huber
Art Dir: Sergey Ivanov
Conducts Business: Worldwide
Employees: 80
Primary Market Served: Business & Consumer
Catalog available online
Indirect online sales
Advertising/Marketing Budget Related to Direct Marketing: 51-75%
Direct Marketing ad budget:
Direct Mail: $250,000

Publisher of scholarly journals & magazines.

HEMMINGS MOTOR NEWS

PO Box 256
Bennington, VT 05201
Telephone: (800) 227-4373, FAX: (802) 447-9631, Web Site: www.hmn.com
Publr & Ed-in-Chief: Jim Maneto
Primary Market Served: Business & Consumer

Publish a monthly magazine for collectors of antique automobiles, listing cars, parts, supplies & services.

THE DMA HIGHLIGHTS FOR CHILDREN

1800 Watermark Drive
Columbus, OH 43215-1035
Telephone: (614) 487-2601, (800) 848-8922, FAX: (614) 487-2700, Web Site: www.highlights.com
CEO: Kent S. Johnson
Exec Asst: Amy Maynard
VP Mktg: Shelly Stotzer
Conducts Business: U.S., Canada, Taiwan, Sweden, China, Singapore, Indonesia, Thailand, Korea
Employees: 600
Primary Market Served: Consumer
Catalog available online
Direct online sales
Advertising/Marketing Budget Related to Direct Marketing: 26-50%
Founded: 1946
Gross sales or billing: $120,000,000

Monthly magazine for children 2-12. Also sell books & other educational materials to parents, teachers & schools.

HIGHSCOPE EDUCATIONAL RESEARCH FOUNDATION

600 N River St
Ypsilanti, MI 48198-2898
Telephone: (734) 485-2000, (800) 40-PRESS, FAX: (734) 485-0704, E-Mail: lschweinhart@highscope.org, Web Site: www.highscope.org
Pres: Larry Schweinhart
Mktg & Commun Dir: Kathleen M. Woodard
Sr Dir, Fin & Opers: Theresa Schenk
VP: Clay Shouse
Conducts Business: U.S., U.K., Canada, Netherlands, Mexico, Singapore
Employees: 65
Primary Market Served: Business & Consumer
Catalog available online
Indirect online sales
Advertising/Marketing Budget Related to Direct Marketing: 0-25%
Founded: 1970

Educational books, videos & recordings for educators & educational researchers working primarily with early childhood education.

HOKE COMMUNICATIONS INC

54 Adams St
Garden City, NY 11530
Telephone: (516) 746-6700, FAX: (516) 294-8141
Pres: Stuart W. Boysen III
Publr: Henry Reed Hoke III
Conducts Business: Worldwide
Employees: 2
Primary Market Served: Business & Consumer
Advertising/Marketing Budget Related to Direct Marketing: 76-100%
Direct Marketing ad budget:
Direct Mail: 50%
Telephone: 50%
Founded: 1938

Publishing company.

HOLLYWOOD FILM ARCHIVE

8391 Beverly Blvd (PMB 321)
Los Angeles, CA 90048
Telephone: (323) 655-4968, Web Site: www.hfarchive.com
Pres: D. Richard Baer
Admin Dir: Howard Schiller
Conducts Business: Worldwide
Employees: 3
Primary Market Served: Business & Consumer
Catalog available online
Advertising/Marketing Budget Related to Direct Marketing: 26-50%
Direct Marketing ad budget:
Direct Mail: 60%
Magazines: 10%
Newspapers: 20%
Online: 5%

Telephone: 5%
Founded: 1972
Gross sales or billing: $200,000

Publisher of movie & TV reference material; also distributes similar works to entertainment industry, libraries & the public.

HOME PLANNERS

Wholly Owned by Hanley-Wood Inc
3275 W Ina Rd (Suite 110)
Tucson, AZ 85741-2152
Telephone: (520) 297-8200, FAX: (520) 297-6219, E-Mail: sales@ homeplanners.com, Web Site: www. homeplanners.com
Pres: Nick Foley
Mktg Dir: Julie Turetzky
Conducts Business: U.S., Canada
Employees: 80
Primary Market Served: Business & Consumer
Catalog available online
Indirect online sales
Advertising/Marketing Budget Related to Direct Marketing: 76-100%
Direct Marketing ad budget:
Direct Mail: 10%
Magazines: 90%
Founded: 1946

Publisher of home plan books & construction blueprints. Sell directly to consumers, home builders & bookstores.

HORTICULTURE MAGAZINE

Subs. of PJS Publications Inc
10151 Carver Rd (Suite 200)
Blue Ash, OH 45242-4760
Telephone: (513) 531-2690, FAX: (513) 891-7153, Web Site: www. hortmag.com
Publr: Bill Wehman
Circ Dir: Janet Lazarus
Prodn Dir: Lynda Segal
Conducts Business: U.S., Canada, Mexico, Europe
Employees: 30
Primary Market Served: Business & Consumer
Advertising/Marketing Budget Related to Direct Marketing: 76-100%
Direct Marketing ad budget:
Direct Mail: $600,000
Telephone: $50,000
Founded: 1904
Gross sales or billing: $8,000,000

Published eight times each year - gardening magazine for avid amateur gardeners.

HUMAN RESOURCE DEVELOPMENT PRESS

22 Amherst Rd
Amherst, MA 01002-9709

Telephone: (413) 253-3488, (800) 822-2801, FAX: (413) 253-3490, E-Mail: info@hrdpress.com, Web Site: www. hrdpress.com
Pres: Robert Carkhuff
CFO: Gregory Carkhuff
Employees: 21
Primary Market Served: Business
Founded: 1972
Gross sales or billing: $3,568,850

Publishing company that caters to the training & human research development market. Provide a line of customized resources to the training professional & novice that are cost & time effective.

IHS INC

321 Inverness Dr S
Englewood, CO 80112-5895
Telephone: (303) 790-0600, (800) 525-7052, FAX: (303) 754-3940, E-Mail: customer.support@ihs.com, Web Site: www.ihs.com
Chmn & CEO: Jerre L. Stead
Co Pres & Co CEO: Rohnington Mobed
Co Pres & Co CEO: Jeffrey R. Tarr
Exec VP & CFO: Michael J. Sullivan
Sr VP & CIO: H. John Oechsle
Conducts Business: Worldwide
Employees: 600
Primary Market Served: Business
Catalog available online
Founded: 1928

Supplier of oil & gas activity & earth science-related information to the oil, hazardous waste transport & disposal industries.

INC MAGAZINE

Div. of The Goldhirsh Group
Seven World Trade Center
New York, NY 10007
Telephone: (212) 389-5377, FAX: (617) 248-8090, Web Site: www.inc. com
Ed-in-Chief: George Gendron
Deputy Ed: Karen Dillon
Conducts Business: Worldwide
Primary Market Served: Business
Advertising/Marketing Budget Related to Direct Marketing: 26-50%

Publisher of monthly business magazine for growing companies. Also market management books & conferences & seminars, information services, planning guides, special reprints & newsletters. Conferences and seminars.

IDEALS PUBLICATIONS INC

2636 Elm Hill Pike (Suite 120), PO Box 305301
Nashville, TN 37214-3162

Telephone: (615) 333-0478, FAX: (615) 781-1447, Web Site: www. idealspublications.com
Pres: Simon Waterlow
Publr: Pat Pingry
Conducts Business: U.S., Canada
Employees: 30
Primary Market Served: Consumer
Direct online sales
Advertising/Marketing Budget Related to Direct Marketing: 76-100%

Publisher of Ideals Magazine, a six-issue per year publication dealing with traditional ideals & values. Also publish general interest books, specialty cookbooks & popular children's books.

IMPACT PUBLISHING INC

Potentials Unlimited
3409 47th Ave E
Bradenton, FL 34203-3974
Telephone: (941) 739-2611, (800) 4-A-NEW-ME, FAX: (941) 756-0315, E-Mail: info@impactpublishinginc. com, Web Site: www. impactpublishinginc.com
Pres: Stephanie Banfill
Bookkeeper: Alisa Begley
Dir, Mktg: Susanne Konicov
Conducts Business: Worldwide
Employees: 10
Primary Market Served: Business & Consumer
Catalog available online
Direct online sales
Advertising/Marketing Budget Related to Direct Marketing: 0-25%
Founded: 1975

Publisher of self-help, motivational & educational audio & video tapes. Ten different series with over 180 titles, including English, Spanish & French language versions; new MP3 titles available.

INDIANAPOLIS NEWSPAPERS INC

307 N Pennsylvania St
Indianapolis, IN 46204
Telephone: (317) 444-4444, FAX: (317) 633-9414, Web Site: www. indystar.com
Publr: Barbara Henry
Mktg Svc Dir: Janet Baker
Dir: Glen Perryman
Electronic News & Info Dir: Myrta Pulliam
Employees: 1,300
Primary Market Served: Business & Consumer
Gross sales or billing: $76,000,000

Publishes The Indianapolis Star & The Indianapolis News for the state of Indiana. Also provides on-line service specializing in auto racing information, Indiana basketball & local news.

INFO USA CITY DIRECTORIES

5711 S 86th Cir
Omaha, NE 68127
Telephone: (402) 593-4500, (800) 925-4654, FAX: (402) 593-4671, E-Mail: customerservice@infousacity.com, Web Site: www.infousacity.com
Chmn & CEO: Vinod Gupta
CFO: Stormy L. Dean
CTO: Dan Speicher
Exec VP & CAO: Fred Vakili
VP, Mktg: Ronald Bruggeman
Conducts Business: U.S.
Employees: 4,089
Primary Market Served: Business
Catalog available online
Indirect online sales
Direct Marketing ad budget:
Direct Mail: 90%
Telephone: 10%
Founded: 1917
Gross sales or billing: $434,000,000

Sell cross reference phone directories by mail & telephone to businesses, institutions & government agencies. Customers use directories to prepare or supplement mailing lists.

INFORMATION FOR PUBLIC AFFAIRS, INC

dba State Net
2101 K St
Sacramento, CA 95816-4920
Telephone: (916) 444-0840, (800) 726-4566, FAX: (916) 446-5369, E-Mail: info@statenet.com, Web Site: www.statenet.com
Chmn Bd: Edward Lammerding
Pres: Judson Clark
Employees: 200
Primary Market Served: Business
Founded: 1970
Gross sales or billing: $15,600,000

Provide on-line services for access to state & federal legislative & regulatory information.

INSTITUTE OF MANAGEMENT & ADMINISTRATION (IOMA)

Subs. of Bureau of National Affairs
1 Phoenix Mill Ln Fl 3
Peterborough, NH 03458-1467
Telephone: (800) 401-5937, FAX: (973) 622-0595
Pres: Joe Bremmer
Mktg Dir: James Bell
VP & Publr: Patty Patterson
Sr Mng Editor: Janice Prescott
Sr Mktg Mgr: Laraine Kelly
Conducts Business: United States
Primary Market Served: Business
Catalog available online
Direct online sales

Newsletters for professionals specializing in law office management, insurance, accounting, corporate finance, corporate compensation & benefits, manufacturing, finance, or design/construction.

INSTITUTIONAL INVESTOR INC

225 Park Ave S
New York, NY 10003
Telephone: (212) 224-3300, FAX: (212) 224-3592, Web Site: www.institutionalinvestor.com
Chmn: Padraic M. Fallon
Pres & Dir: Sir Patrick Sergeant
CCO: Collin Jones
Mng Dir: P. Richard Ensor
Editor Bus Publ: Jessica Sommar
Conducts Business: Worldwide
Primary Market Served: Business
Direct online sales
Advertising/Marketing Budget Related to Direct Marketing: 76-100%

Financial publishers.

THE DMA INSTITUTIONAL REAL ESTATE INC

2274 Camino Ramon
San Ramon, CA 94583
Telephone: (925) 244-0500, FAX: (925) 244-0520, Web Site: www.irei.com
VP Mktg: Sandy Terranova
Primary Market Served: Business

INSURANCE PUBLICATIONS INC

9404 Reeds Rd, PO Box 11310
Overland Park, KS 66207-1010
Telephone: (913) 383-9191, (800) 762-3387, FAX: (913) 383-1247, E-Mail: brokerwrld@primary.net, Web Site: www.brokerworldmag.com
Assoc Publr: Stephen P. Howard
Ed: Sharon A. Chace
Prod Mgr: Elizabeth Coleman
Circ Dir: Catherine Fritz
Circ Dir: Patty L. Godfrey
Conducts Business: U.S.
Employees: 10
Primary Market Served: Business
Catalog available online
Direct online sales
Founded: 1981

Publisher of trade magazine.

INTEREX

34 Hunt Rd
Amesbury, MA 01913
Telephone: (978) 388-8755, (800) IN-TEREX, FAX: (978) 388-8747, Web Site: www.interexexhibits.com
CEO: Ronald W. Evans

Pres: Tamara C. Olbres
Exec Dir: Darryl Armstrong
Adv Mgr: Kathy Schwartz
Conducts Business: Worldwide
Employees: 38
Primary Market Served: Business
Catalog available online
Indirect online sales
Advertising/Marketing Budget Related to Direct Marketing: 26-50%

Users group for Hewlett-Packard.

INTERNATIONAL DIRECT MEDIA CO & INFORMATION PUBLISHING CO

2801 39th Ave (Suite 100)
San Francisco, CA 94116-2744
Telephone: (415) 661-4730, E-Mail: infopubsf@aol.com, Web Site: www.bookwormproductions.com
Pres: Don D. Flaten
VP & Gen Mgr: A.R. Wrenn
Conducts Business: U.S., Canada
Employees: 6
Primary Market Served: Business & Consumer
Advertising/Marketing Budget Related to Direct Marketing: 51-75%
Direct Marketing ad budget:
Direct Mail: 80%
Magazines: 20%
Founded: 1984

General giftware merchandise, educational books, videos & tapes.

INTERNATIONAL MARINE

The McGraw-Hill Cos
90 Mechanic St
Camden, ME 04843-1844
Telephone: (207) 236-4837, FAX: (207) 236-6314, Web Site: www.internationalmarine.com
Ed Dir: Jon Eaton
Acq Ed: Thomas McCarthy
Mng Ed: Deborah Oliver
Conducts Business: Worldwide
Employees: 10
Primary Market Served: Consumer
Catalog available online
Founded: 1969

Publisher & retailer of nautical books. Send quarterly catalog to customer list.

THE DMA INTERNATIONAL MASTERS PUBLISHERS INC

948 Plaza Dr.
Montoursville, PA 17754-2400
Telephone: (800) 570-5718, E-Mail: customerservice@imp-usa.com, Web Site: www.imponline.com
CFO: Peter Saretsky
VP, New Mkts: Bennie Nordahl

Gen Counsel & Corp Sec: Rhonda
Gornitsky
Employees: 300
Primary Market Served: Consumer
Founded: 1979
Gross sales or billing: $300,000,000

Full service DM continuity publisher.

JIST PUBLISHING

875 Montreal Way
Saint Paul, MN 55102
Telephone: (800) 648-5478, FAX:
(800) 547-8329, E-Mail: info@jist.
com, Web Site: www.jist.com
Pres: Mike Farr
Publr: Janet E. Wall
VP, Sls & Mktg: Tom Abeel
Mktg Mgr: Steve Garner
Editor: Barb Terry
Conducts Business: Worldwide
Employees: 45
Primary Market Served: Business &
Consumer
Catalog available online
Direct online sales
Direct Marketing ad budget:
Direct Mail: 75%
Magazines: 15%
Telephone: 10%
Founded: 1981

Career development, job search & educational training books, videos &
software.

JANES INFORMATION GROUP

110 N Royal St (Suite 200)
Alexandria, VA 22314
Telephone: (703) 683-3700, (800) 824-
0768, FAX: (703) 836-0297, Web
Site: www.janes.com
Pres & CEO: Scott Key
Deputy CEO: Michael Dell
CFO: Michael Staton
Chief Contact Officer: Ian Kay
CIO: Jo Moon
Conducts Business: Worldwide
Employees: 300
Primary Market Served: Business &
Consumer
Catalog available online
Direct online sales
Advertising/Marketing Budget Related
to Direct Marketing: 51-75%
Founded: 1898
Gross sales or billing: $7,300,000

The leading publisher of aerospace &
defense information.

JAZZTIMES MAGAZINE INC

85 Quincy Ave (Suite 2)
Quincy, MA 02169-6764

Telephone: (617) 706-9110, FAX:
(617) 536-0102, E-Mail: info@
jazztimes.com, Web Site: www.
jazztimes.com
Publr: Glenn Sabin
Gen Mgr: Jeff Sabin
Ed: Chris Porter
Assoc Publr: Lee Mergner
Conducts Business: Worldwide
Employees: 10
Primary Market Served: Business &
Consumer
Indirect online sales
Direct Marketing ad budget:
Direct Mail: 40%
TV/Radio: 60%
Founded: 1970

Magazine which covers the spectrum
from historical styles to the sounds of
today with reviews of new releases &
reissues, profiles of artists & jazz news
here & abroad.

THE JEWISH PUBLICATION SOCIETY

2100 Arch St (2nd fl)
Philadelphia, PA 19103-1300
Telephone: (215) 832-0600, (800) 234-
3151, FAX: (215) 568-2017, E-Mail:
jewishbook@jewishpub.org, Web
Site: www.jewishpub.org
CEO & Editor in Chief: Dr. Ellen
Frankel
Sr Sls & Mktg Mgr: Laurie
Schlesinger
Conducts Business: Worldwide
Employees: 18
Primary Market Served: Business
Catalog available online
Founded: 1888

Non-profit publishing company. Publish books to promote Jewish culture &
experience.

JONES PUBLISHING INC

N7450 Aanstad Rd
Iola, WI 54945-8229
Telephone: (715) 445-5000, (800) 331-
0038, FAX: (715) 445-4053, E-Mail:
jonespub@jonespublishing.com, Web
Site: www.jonespublishing.com
Founder: Joe Jones
Pres & CEO: Joe Kools
Dir Mktg: Brandan DuChateau
Production Mgr: Jean Barth
Mktg Asst: Tammy Homan
Conducts Business: Worldwide
Employees: 34
Primary Market Served: Business &
Consumer
Catalog available online
Direct online sales
Founded: 1987

JOSSEY-BASS INC PUBLISHERS

Subs. of John Wiley & Sons, Inc
One Montgomery St (Suite 1200)
San Francisco, CA 94104-4505
Telephone: (415) 433-1740, FAX:
(415) 433-0499, E-Mail:
webperson@jbp.com, Web Site:
www.josseybass.com
Mgr: Steve Robinson
Conducts Business: U.S., Canada
Employees: 154
Primary Market Served: Business &
Consumer
Advertising/Marketing Budget Related
to Direct Marketing: 26-50%

Professional books (hardcover & paperback) & journals in the fields of
management, social & behavioral sciences, education (K-12 & higher education), non-profit sector, health administration & public administration.

THE JOURNAL NEWS

Subs. of The Gannett Co Inc
One Gannett Dr
White Plains, NY 10604
Telephone: (914) 694-9300, FAX:
(914) 696-8152, Web Site: www.
nyjournalnews.com
Pres & Publr: Gary Sherlock
VP Mktg: John Green
Coord Mktg Dept: Donna Cardillo
Conducts Business: U.S.
Primary Market Served: Business &
Consumer

Total market coverage of Westchester,
Putnam & Rockland Counties, NY
through newspaper inserts.

JOURNAL OF COMMERCE GROUP

Div. of the Economist Group Ltd
2 Penn Plz E (Suite 4)
Newark, NJ 07105-2251
Telephone: (973) 848-7000, FAX:
(973) 848-7004, Web Site: www.joc.
com
Pres: Bill Ralph
Sr VP, Mktg: Steve Brennen
Conducts Business: Worldwide
Employees: 400
Primary Market Served: Business
Advertising/Marketing Budget Related
to Direct Marketing: 76-100%
Founded: 1827

Publisher of several publications &
web sites covering logistics, trade &
transportation.

JOURNAL STAR

Subs. of Copley Press Inc
One News Plaza
Peoria, IL 61643

Telephone: (309) 686-3026, FAX:
(309) 686-3265, Web Site: www.
pjstar.com
Publr: John McConnell
Promo Pub Affairs Mgr: Joy M. Anderson
Conducts Business: US
Primary Market Served: Consumer

Daily newspaper & Copley newspaper.

KCI COMMUNICATIONS INC

Subs. of National Information Corp
7600A Leesburg Pike, West Building
(Suite 300)
Falls Church, VA 22043
Telephone: (703) 394-4931, FAX:
(703) 905-8100, Web Site: www.kci-com.com
Pres: Walter Pearce
Conducts Business: U.S., Canada, Europe
Employees: 35
Primary Market Served: Consumer
Catalog available online
Direct online sales
Direct Marketing ad budget:
Direct Mail: 100%

Publisher of financial newsletters &
books.

KET

600 Cooper Dr
Lexington, KY 40502-1669
Telephone: (859) 258-7000, (800) 432-0951, FAX: (606) 258-7396, E-Mail:
rgriffin@ket.org, Web Site: www.ket.org
Pres: Ron Griffin
Exec Dir & CEO: Virginia Gaines
Sls & Mktg Dir: Milli Fazey
Adv Mgr: Margaret Norman
Conducts Business: U.S.
Primary Market Served: Business &
Consumer
Catalog available online

KALMBACH PUBLISHING CO

21027 Crossroads Cir
Waukesha, WI 53187
Telephone: (262) 796-8776, (800) 558-1544, FAX: (262) 796-1143, Web
Site: www.kalmbach.com
Pres: Jerald Boetlcher
Sr VP & Ed: Russell Larson
Conducts Business: Worldwide
Employees: 300
Primary Market Served: Consumer
Advertising/Marketing Budget Related
to Direct Marketing: 51-75%

Publisher of hobby & leisure magazines such as Model Railroader, Astronomy, Dollhouse Miniature & 4
other magazine titles in addition to a
full line of related hobby books, calendars, posters & videos. Sold to consumers, bookstores, hobby shops,
newsstands & wholesalers.

KAPLAN PUBLISHING

205 W Randolph St (Suite 200)
Chicago, IL 60606-1814
Telephone: (312) 606-8905, (800) 245-2665, FAX: (312) 606-8985, E-Mail:
kaplanorders@kaplan.com, Web Site:
www.kaplanpublishing.com
Chmn & CEO: John Grayer
Pres & COO: Andrew S. Rosen
Sr VP & CFO: Robert L. Lane
Exec VP: Scott August
CTO: Mick Demakos
Conducts Business: Worldwide
Employees: 20
Primary Market Served: Business
Catalog available online
Direct online sales
Advertising/Marketing Budget Related
to Direct Marketing: 26-50%
Direct Marketing ad budget: $500,000
Direct Mail: 10%
Magazines: 60%
Newspapers: 20%
TV/Radio: 5%
Telephone: 5%

Trade publishing & distribution
company.

KAPPA PUBLISHING GROUP

Subs. of Games Magazine
6198 Butler Pike (Suite 200)
Blue Bell, PA 19422-2606
Telephone: (215) 643-6385, FAX:
(215) 628-3571, Web Site: www.
kappapublishing.com
Pres: Despina McNulty
Circulation Dir: Dave Tyler
Asst VP: Janis Weiner
Dir Sls: Paul Herbert
Editorial Dir: Anthony Herbert
Conducts Business: Canada
Primary Market Served: Business &
Consumer
Catalog available online
Direct online sales

Sell puzzle & game magazines.

KENSINGTON PUBLISHING CORP

119 W 40th St (fl 21)
New York, NY 10018-2522
Telephone: (212) 407-1500, (800) 221-2647, FAX: (212) 407-1590, Web
Site: www.kensingtonbooks.com
Pres: Steven Zacharius
Dir Publicity: Karen Auerbach

Conducts Business: Worldwide
Employees: 87
Primary Market Served: Consumer
Catalog available online
Founded: 1974
Gross sales or billing: $57,000,000

Sell books to consumers. Topics
include: romance, mystery, true crime,
biography, fiction, health, self-help,
suspense & horror.

KEY COMMUNICATIONS INC

385 Garrisonville Rd (Suite 116), PO
Box 569
Garrisonville, VA 22554
Telephone: (540) 720-5584, FAX:
(540) 720-5687, E-Mail: usglass@
aol.com, Web Site: www.key-com.
com
Publr: Debra A. Levy
Conducts Business: Worldwide
Employees: 17
Primary Market Served: Business
Indirect online sales
Advertising/Marketing Budget Related
to Direct Marketing: 0-25%
Direct Marketing ad budget:
Direct Mail: 99%
Telephone: 1%
Founded: 1966

Magazines, editorial & ad space.

KEYBOARD WORKSHOP

Subs. of Duane Shinn Publications
PO Box 700
Medford, OR 97501-0047
Telephone: (541) 664-7052, FAX:
(541) 664-7052, E-Mail: duane@
playpiano.com, Web Site: www.
playpiano.com
Owner: Duane Shinn
Conducts Business: U.S., Canada
Employees: 4
Primary Market Served: Consumer
Catalog available online
Direct online sales
Advertising/Marketing Budget Related
to Direct Marketing: 51-75%
Direct Marketing ad budget:
Direct Mail: $75,000
Magazines: $10,000
Online: $100,000
Founded: 1965
Gross sales or billing: $400,000

Music courses, books, cassettes to mail
order retailers such as catalog houses.
Drop-ship for most accounts. Also create non-music products to be manufactured & marketed by other marketers.

KIMBO EDUCATIONAL

Div. of United Sound Arts Inc
Ten N Third Ave
Long Branch, NJ 07740-7045

Telephone: (732) 229-4949, (800) 848-6099 (NM), (800) 631-2187 (NJ), FAX: (732) 870-3340, E-Mail: kimboed@aol.com, Web Site: www.kimboed.com
CEO: Gertrude Kimble
Pres: James Kimble
Sls & Mktg Dir: Elaine Murphy
Sr VP: Jeffrey Kimble
Prodn Mgr & Ed: Amy Laufer
Conducts Business: U.S., Canada, Australia, Japan, Singapore, New Zealand, Great Britain
Employees: 1
Primary Market Served: Business & Consumer
Catalog available online
Direct online sales
Direct Marketing ad budget:
Direct Mail: 75%
Telephone: 25%
Founded: 1962
Gross sales or billing: $2,000,000

Produce compact discs, DVD's for the educational marketplace & parent/teacher stores. Main area of concentration is on early childhood, yet products for middle grade & adult fitness programs are also released.

KING FEATURES
300 West 57th St (fl 15)
New York, NY 10019-3741
Telephone: (212) 455-4000, FAX: (212) 682-8332
Pres: T.R. Shepard III
Conducts Business: Worldwide
Primary Market Served: Business & Consumer

Syndicate comic strips for newspapers & license merchandising.

THE KIPLINGER WASHINGTON EDITORS INC
1100 13th St NW Ste 750
Washington, DC 20005-4364
Telephone: (202) 887-6400, (800) 544-0155, FAX: (202) 496-1817, Web Site: www.kiplinger.com
Pres: Knight A. Kiplinger
Sr VP & CFO: Corbin M. Wilkes
Vice Chmn & VP: Todd L. Kipplinger
Dir Mktg: Larry Fishbein
Conducts Business: U.S.
Employees: 220
Primary Market Served: Business & Consumer
Catalog available online
Direct online sales
Advertising/Marketing Budget Related to Direct Marketing: 51-75%
Founded: 1923
Gross sales or billing: $24,300,000

Publisher of Kiplinger Personal Finance Magazine & The Kiplinger Newsletters.

B KLEIN PUBLICATIONS
6037 W Atlantic Ave
Delray Beach, FL 33484-8408
Telephone: (561) 496-3316, FAX: (561) 496-5546, E-Mail: bkleinpub@aol.com
Pres: Bernard Klein
VP: Betty Klein
Conducts Business: Worldwide
Employees: 6
Primary Market Served: Business & Consumer
Advertising/Marketing Budget Related to Direct Marketing: 51-75%
Direct Marketing ad budget: $150,000
Direct Mail: 70%
Magazines: 10%
Newspapers: 10%
Telephone: 10%
Founded: 1946
Gross sales or billing: $1,000,000

Reference books, directories, mailing lists & consulting services.

KOLBE CORP
2355 E Camelback Rd Ste 610
Phoenix, AZ 85016-9040
Telephone: (602) 840-9770, (800) 642-2822, FAX: (602) 952-2706, E-Mail: info@kolbe.com, Web Site: www.kolbe.com
CEO: David Kolbe
Pres Kolbe Intl: William K. Rapp
Chmn Bd: Kathryn Kolbe
VP Mktg & Communs: Jerry Cobb
Conducts Business: Worldwide
Employees: 20
Primary Market Served: Business & Consumer
Direct online sales
Founded: 1975

Online, print, and audio/video materials for self awareness, both personal & in business; team building, change management & placement in organizational development.

WILLIAM S KONECKY ASSOCIATES INC
72 Ayers Point Rd
Old Saybrook, CT 06475
Telephone: (860) 388-0878, FAX: (860) 388-0273
Pres: William Konecky
VP: Sean Konecky
Primary Market Served: Business

Book publishers for Art & Military History.

KRAUSE PUBLICATIONS INC
Subs of F&W Publications
700 E State St
Iola, WI 54990
Telephone: (715) 445-2214, FAX: (715) 445-4087, E-Mail: info@krause.com, Web Site: www.krause.com
Chmn & CEO F&W Publications: David Steward
Conducts Business: Worldwide
Employees: 400
Primary Market Served: Business & Consumer
Catalog available online
Direct online sales
Founded: 1952

Publish books & periodicals in the following areas: collector cars, sports cards & sports memorabilia, records, coins, crafts, firearms, comic books & toy collecting, turkey hunting, deer hunting, trapping & rural building. Books & subscriptions are sold through direct marketing techniques to hobbyists & investors.

LAKESIDE PUBLISHING CO LLC
990 Grove St
Evanston, IL 60201-6510
Telephone: (847) 491-6440, FAX: (847) 491-0459, E-Mail: cs@centurysports.net, Web Site: www.centurysports.net
Pres: Norman Jacobs
Circ Mgr: Richard Kent
Conducts Business: U.S.
Employees: 15
Primary Market Served: Consumer
Catalog available online
Direct online sales
Advertising/Marketing Budget Related to Direct Marketing: 0-25%
Founded: 1969
Gross sales or billing: $20,000,000

Baseball digest & cruise travel

LANDAUER CORP
3100 NW 101st St (Suite A)
Urbandale, IA 50322-3867
Telephone: (515) 287-2144, (800) 557-2144, FAX: (515) 276-5102, E-Mail: info@landauercorp.com, Web Site: www.landauercorp.com
Pres: Jeramy Landauer
Conducts Business: U.S.
Employees: 10
Primary Market Served: Business & Consumer
Catalog available online
Indirect online sales
Advertising/Marketing Budget Related to Direct Marketing: 0-25%
Founded: 1991

Christmas cards, gifts & books.

LANDMARK COMMUNICATIONS INC

150 W Brambleton Ave, PO Box 449
Norfolk, VA 23510-2075
Telephone: (757) 446-2010, (800) 446-2004, FAX: (757) 446-2489, Web Site: www.landmark.com
Chmn & CEO: Frank Batten Jr.
Pres: Michael Alston
Pres & COO: Decker Anston
Vice Chmn: Richard F. Barry III
VP & CFO: Teresa F. Blevins
Conducts Business: U.S.
Employees: 12,000
Primary Market Served: Business & Consumer
Gross sales or billing: $1,750,000,000

Multimedia company in publishing & broadcasting.

LAS VEGAS REVIEW JOURNAL

Div. of Don Rey Media Group
1111 W Bonanza Rd, PO Box 70
Las Vegas, NV 89125
Telephone: (702) 383-0211, FAX: (702) 383-4646, Web Site: www.lvrj.com
Publ Dir: Steve Coffeen
Publr: Sherman R. Frederick
Editor: Thomas Mitchel
Gen Mgr: Alan B. Fleming
Dir Adv: Bob Brown
Conducts Business: U.S.
Employees: 817
Primary Market Served: Business & Consumer
Catalog available online
Indirect online sales
Advertising/Marketing Budget Related to Direct Marketing: 0-25%
Direct Marketing ad budget:
Direct Mail: 25%
Newspapers: 25%
Telephone: 50%

Newspaper.

LAWYER'S WEEKLY PUBLICATIONS

10 Milk St (Suite 1000)
Boston, MA 02108-4620
Telephone: (617) 451-7300, FAX: (617) 451-0132, Web Site: www.lawyersweekly.com
CEO: Jeff Baskies
Assoc Publr: Paul J. Martinek
Conducts Business: U.S.
Employees: 120
Primary Market Served: Business
Direct Marketing ad budget:
Direct Mail: 50%
Newspapers: 50%
Founded: 1972

Publish a statewide weekly legal newspaper in the states of Massachusetts, Rhode Island, Michigan, Missouri, North Carolina, Ohio & Virginia. Also publish newsletters, books & other services for attorneys in Massachusetts & New England, plus a biweekly newspaper, Lawyers Weekly USA. Sell New England attorney's kits & marketing services for those wishing to promote directly to attorneys.

LAZAR MEDIA GROUP INC

334 E Bay St (PMB 156)
Charleston, SC 29401
Telephone: (877) 579-0222, FAX: (843) 577-5542, E-Mail: email@lazarshopping.com, Web Site: www.lazarmedia.com
CEO: Elysa Lazar
Conducts Business: U.S.
Primary Market Served: Business & Consumer
Catalog available online
Direct online sales
Founded: 1986

Full service publisher of consumer books.

LEADERSHIP DIRECTORIES INC

104 Fifth Ave
New York, NY 10011
Telephone: (212) 627-4140, FAX: (212) 645-0931, E-Mail: info@leadershipdirectories.com, Web Site: www.leadershipdirectories.com
Pres & Publr: David Hurvitz
VP, Cust Svc & Sls: Nancy Scholem
List Mgr: Tony Sapp
Conducts Business: U.S.
Employees: 60
Primary Market Served: Business
Catalog available online
Advertising/Marketing Budget Related to Direct Marketing: 76-100%

Publisher of directories on corporations, federal & state government. Rent mailing lists of corporate, state & federal managers & buyers.

LEISURE ARTS INC

5701 Ranch Dr
Little Rock, AR 72223-9633
Telephone: (501) 868-8800, Web Site: www.leisurearts.com
Editorial Dir: Susan Wiles
Primary Market Served: Business & Consumer

HAL LEONARD CORP

7777 W Bluemound Rd, Box 13819
Milwaukee, WI 53213

Telephone: (414) 774-3630, FAX: (414) 774-3259, Web Site: www.halleonard.com
Chmn & CEO: Keith Mardak
Pres: Larry Morton
Sr Sls & Mktg Mgr: Brad Smith
Adv Mgr: Jim Meinhardt
Conducts Business: Worldwide
Employees: 370
Primary Market Served: Business & Consumer
Founded: 1947

Music publisher selling to distributors.

LERNER PUBLISHING GROUP

1251 Washington Ave N
Minneapolis, MN 55401
Telephone: (612) 332-3344, (800) 328-4929, FAX: (800) 332-1132, E-Mail: info@lernerbooks.com, Web Site: www.lernerbooks.com
Pres & Publr: Adam Lerner
CEO: Harry Lerner
CFO: Margaret Wunderlich
Sls & Mktg Dir: David Wexler
Mktg Mgr: Beth Heiss
Conducts Business: U.S.
Employees: 100
Primary Market Served: Business & Consumer
Catalog available online
Indirect online sales
Founded: 1959
Gross sales or billing: $8,100,000

Publisher of books for young people, grades K-12 & distributed to schools, libraries & bookstores.

LEXIS NEXIS MATTHEW BENDER

1275 Broadway
Albany, NY 12204-2628
Telephone: (518) 487-3000, (800) 424-4200, E-Mail: lexisnexis@matthewbender, Web Site: www.bender.lexisnexis.com
Sls Eastern Zone Mng Dir: Jim Mitchell
CEO: Andrew Prozes
Conducts Business: Worldwide
Employees: 1,400
Primary Market Served: Business
Advertising/Marketing Budget Related to Direct Marketing: 26-50%

Publishing company specializing in legal, tax & business publications & software for lawyers, accountants & business people.

PETER LI EDUCATION GROUP

2621 Dryden Rd (Suite 300)
Dayton, OH 45439

Telephone: (937) 293-1415, (800) 523-4625, FAX: (937) 293-1310, Web Site: www.peterli.com
Chmn: Peter Li
Pres, Publr: Bret Thomas
VP, Opers: Cathy Helmers
VP, Mktg: Terry Perkins
Corp Circulation Dir: Rosemary Walker
Mktg Mgr: Amy Baird
Conducts Business: Worldwide
Employees: 100
Primary Market Served: Consumer
Catalog available online
Direct online sales
Founded: 1971

Serves the educational & religious education markets nationwide as a publisher of magazines and teaching resources for school administrators, teachers & students.

LIFE-STUDY FELLOWSHIP FOUNDATION INC
90 Heights Rd
Darien, CT 06820
Telephone: (203) 655-1436, FAX: (203) 655-1392, Web Site: www.lifestudyfellowship.com
Pres: Theodore E. Lundberg
Exec VP: Michael Donnelly
VP, Mktg: Michael Keane
VP, Fin: John Keane Jr.
Conducts Business: Worldwide
Employees: 85
Primary Market Served: Consumer
Advertising/Marketing Budget Related to Direct Marketing: 51-75%
Direct Marketing ad budget:
Direct Mail: 80%
Newspapers: 20%
Founded: 1939

Publisher of inspirational books & pamphlets.

LIGUORI PUBLICATIONS
One Liguori Dr
Liguori, MO 63057-9999
Telephone: (636) 464-2500, (800) 325-9521, FAX: (800) 325-9526, E-Mail: liguori@liguori.org, Web Site: www.liguori.org
Pres: Rev. Mathew J. Kessler
Dir Sales & Mktg: Pamela Brown
Mktg Mgr: Angela Baumann
Bi-lingual Mktg Specialist: Rhina Portillo
Printing Buyer: Tom Houseworth
Conducts Business: Worldwide
Primary Market Served: Business & Consumer
Catalog available online
Direct online sales
Advertising/Marketing Budget Related to Direct Marketing: 76-100%

Founded: 1947
Publisher of the Liguorian magazine, parish bulletins, trade books on spirituality, prayer & Christian living & religious education materials, Spanish & English.

LINGUISYSTEMS
3100 Fourth Ave
East Moline, IL 61244-9700
Telephone: (309) 755-2300, (800) 776-4332, FAX: (800) 577-4555, E-Mail: service@linguisystems.com, Web Site: www.linguisystems.com
Co-Owner: Linda Bowers
Co-Owner: Rosemary Huisingh
Ed: Mark Barrett
Ed: Paul Johnson
Ed: Carolyn Lo Giudice
Conducts Business: U.S., Europe, Canada
Employees: 45
Primary Market Served: Business & Consumer
Catalog available online
Direct online sales
Advertising/Marketing Budget Related to Direct Marketing: 76-100%
Direct Marketing ad budget:
Direct Mail: 100%
Founded: 1984

Publisher of language & critical thinking materials for speech language pathologists, special educators & regular education teachers.

LINKS MAGAZINE
PO Box 7628
Hilton Head Island, SC 29938-7628
Telephone: (843) 842-6200, FAX: (843) 842-6233, Web Site: www.linksmagazine.com
Pres & Publr: Jack Purcell
Mktg Dir: Kevin May
Conducts Business: U.S., Canada
Employees: 25
Primary Market Served: Consumer
Direct online sales
Advertising/Marketing Budget Related to Direct Marketing: 0-25%
Direct Marketing ad budget:
Direct Mail: 50%
Magazines: 25%
Online: 20%
Telephone: 5%
Founded: 1988

Golf magazine.

LIPPINCOTT, WILLIAMS & WILKINS
Subs. of Wolters Kluwer Health
351 W Camden St
Baltimore, MD 21201-2436

Telephone: (410) 528-4000, (800) 638-0672, FAX: (410) 528-8597, E-Mail: customerservice@lww.com, Web Site: www.lww.com
Pres, Domestic Mktg: Rick Perry
Pres, Periodicals: Carole Pippen
Conducts Business: Worldwide
Employees: 350
Primary Market Served: Business & Consumer
Catalog available online
Direct online sales
Advertising/Marketing Budget Related to Direct Marketing: 26-50%
Founded: 1890
Gross sales or billing: $49,300,000

Publisher of medical, nursing (software), allied health, scientific books, journals, periodicals & newspapers.

LIVE DESIGN
249 W 17th St
New York, NY 10011
Telephone: (212) 204-4268, FAX: (212) 204-4291, Web Site: livedesignonline.com
Assoc Publr & Editorial Dir: David Johnson
Editorial Coord: Lisa Murphy
Conducts Business: U.S., Canada, Europe, Asia
Primary Market Served: Business

A creative and technical journal for live entertainment professionals in lighting, staging, and projection. Provides designers, programmers, and technicians with tips and trends, news and reviews of the latest gear, reports from the field, and industry viewpoint and commentary.

LLEWELLYN PUBLICATIONS
Div. of Llewellyn Worldwide Ltd
2143 Wooddale Dr
Woodbury, MN 55125-2989
Telephone: (651) 291-1970, (800) 843-6666, FAX: (651) 291-1908, Web Site: www.llewellyn.com
Mktg Mgr: Stephanie Clemens
Sls Dir: Rhonda Ogren
Conducts Business: U.S., Canada, U.K., Australia, New Zealand, Mexico
Employees: 75
Primary Market Served: Business & Consumer
Advertising/Marketing Budget Related to Direct Marketing: 51-75%
Founded: 1901

Oldest "new age" book & periodical publisher in North America. Books on astrology, wicca, yoga, meditation, magic, tarot & alternative health. English & Spanish language titles. Also publish New Worlds magazine & Flux - YA fiction & Midnight Inc - adult mystery fiction.

LOMBARDI PUBLISHING CORP
PO Box 428
Vaughan, ON, Canada L0J 1C0
Telephone: (905) 760-9929, Web Site: www.lombardipublishing.com
CEO: Michael Lombardi
Primary Market Served: Business & Consumer

M2MEDIA 360
1030 W Higgins Rd (Suite 230)
Park Ridge, IL 60068
Telephone: (760) 318-7000, E-Mail: cnaughton@m2media360.com, Web Site: www.m2media360.com
Pres: Marion Minor
Sr VP & Grp Publr: Charles Forman
Ed-in-Chief: Richard Brandes
Mktg Specialist: Cheryl Naughton
Conducts Business: U.S.
Employees: 10
Primary Market Served: Business & Consumer
Advertising/Marketing Budget Related to Direct Marketing: 0-25%
Gross sales or billing: $4,800,000

Trade publications for green industry.

MTS PUBLISHING
800 W 5th Ave (Suite 204A)
Naperville, IL 60563-4925
Telephone: (630) 955-9750, (800) 332-4655, FAX: (630) 955-9787, E-Mail: info@mtspbl.com, Web Site: www.mtspbl.com
Shareholder: Robert Quigley
Conducts Business: U.S., Canada, Mexico
Employees: 7
Primary Market Served: Business & Consumer
Catalog available online
Direct online sales
Advertising/Marketing Budget Related to Direct Marketing: 76-100%
Gross sales or billing: $2,000,000

Publisher of crossword puzzles sold on subscription basis.

MAGAZINE PUBLISHERS OF AMERICA
810 Seventh Ave (fl 24)
New York, NY 10019-5873
Telephone: (212) 872-3700, FAX: (212) 888-4217, Web Site: www.magazine.org
Pres, CEO: Nina Link
Exec VP, Govt Affairs: James C. Cregan
Exec VP, CMO: Ellen Oppenheim
Exec VP, Consumer Mktg: Kenneth Godshall
Exec VP: Jeremy Koch
Sr VP: Rita Cohen
Conducts Business: Worldwide
Employees: 50
Primary Market Served: Consumer
Catalog available online
Founded: 1919
Gross sales or billing: $2,425,000,000

Magazine industry association. Supports the marketing & Washington activities of over 800 U.S. magazines, representing 60% of total ABC circulation. Branch Office in Washington, DC.

MAGNA PUBLICATIONS INC
2718 Dryden Dr
Madison, WI 53704-3086
Telephone: (608) 246-3580, FAX: (608) 246-3597, Web Site: www.magnapubs.com
Pres: Bill Haight
VP & Publr: Jodi Glynn Patrick
Conducts Business: U.S., Canada
Employees: 35
Primary Market Served: Business
Catalog available online
Direct online sales
Advertising/Marketing Budget Related to Direct Marketing: 76-100%
Direct Marketing ad budget: $3,000,000
Direct Mail: 85%
Magazines: 5%
Newspapers: 5%
Telephone: 5%
Founded: 1971
Gross sales or billing: $6,000,000

Subscription newsletters to colleges, universities.

MAJORIUM
aka The American Management Development Group, Inc
2025 Main St
Stevens Point, WI 54481-3019
Telephone: (715) 342-1018, (800) 654-4935, FAX: (715) 342-1118, E-Mail: sales@majorium.com, Web Site: www.letstalkselling.com
CEO: Timothy Bednarz Ph.D.
Partner: Shirley Bednarz Ph.D.
Conducts Business: U.S.
Employees: 8
Primary Market Served: Business

Management programs for professional service businesses (Doctors, Lawyers, etc.) & small middle business management manuals. Training for sales, sales management & speaking consulting.

MARKETSHARE PUBLICATIONS INC
7171 W 95th St (Suite 600)
Overland Park, KS 66212-2300
Telephone: (913) 338-3360, (800) 488-8051, FAX: (913) 217-2895, Web Site: www.marketsharepubs.com
Pres & CEO: Howard L. Payne
Conducts Business: U.S.
Employees: 20
Primary Market Served: Business & Consumer
Founded: 1985

Direct response card pack publisher.

MARQUIS WHO'S WHO LLC
300 Connell Dr (Suite 2000)
Berkeley Heights, NJ 07922
Telephone: (908) 673-1000, (800) 473-7020, FAX: (908) 673-1179, E-Mail: info@marquiswhoswho.com, Web Site: www.marquiswhoswho.com
Chmn: James A. Finkelstein
CEO: Fred Marks
CTO: Ariel Spivakovsky
Publr: Robert Docherty
Dir Sls: Kelli MacKinnon
Conducts Business: Worldwide
Employees: 75
Primary Market Served: Business & Consumer
Catalog available online
Indirect online sales
Founded: 1898

Publisher of comprehensive biographical information available in print & online. Major Marquis Who's Who publications include Who's Who in America, Who's Who in the World, and Who's Who of American Women.

MARSHALL & SWIFT
777 S Figueroa St Fl 12
Los Angeles, CA 90017-5878
Telephone: (213) 683-9000, FAX: (213) 683-9010, Web Site: www.marshallswift.com
Mktg Dir: Leslie Lake
Mktg Res Analyst: Linda Jovanelly
Conducts Business: U.S., Canada
Primary Market Served: Business
Catalog available online
Founded: 1932

Publisher of building cost information.

MARTINDALE-HUBBELL
Div. of Reed Elsevier Inc
121 Chanlon Rd

New Providence, NJ 07974
Telephone: (908) 464-6800, (800) 526-4902, FAX: (908) 771-7740
Assoc Publr: Carol D. Cooper
Sr VP, Sls: Larry Thompson
VP, Database Prodn: Dean Hollister
VP, HR: Eileen Purelis
Sr Mktg Dir: Marilyn Canning
Conducts Business: Worldwide
Primary Market Served: Consumer
Founded: 1868

Publisher of The Martindale-Hubbell Law Directory in hardcopy, on CD-ROM, online through Lexis/Nexis & on the Internet; containing listings of over 900,000 lawyers & law firms worldwide. Other publications include Law Digest, a summary of laws from each of the 50 states and 75 countries; Martindale-Hubbell Law Directory's International Edition, designed for the international legal community and Martindale-Hubbell Bar Register of Preeminent Lawyers, listing law practices designated as outstanding by members of the legal community.

MAYO CLINIC
200 First St SW
Rochester, MN 55905
Telephone: (507) 266-2511, FAX: (507) 284-0161, Web Site: www.mayoclinic.org
CEO: Glenn S. Forbes
Chief Mktg Officer: John La Forgia
Dir Mktg: Misty Hathaway
Brand Mngmt: Amy Davis
Conducts Business: U.S., Germany, Chile, Japan, Netherlands, Saudi Arabia
Employees: 52,194
Primary Market Served: Business & Consumer
Direct online sales
Advertising/Marketing Budget Related to Direct Marketing: 0-25%
Gross sales or billing: $5,234,000,000

Produce & market reliable health information products to general consumers, including newsletters, books, CD-ROM & on-line services.

MCCLATCHY CO
2100 "Q" St
Sacramento, CA 95816-6899
Telephone: (916) 321-1855, FAX: (916) 321-1869, Web Site: www.mcclatchy.com
Chmn: Erwin Potts
Pres & CEO: Gary Pruitt
Dir Commun: Peter Tira
Employees: 16,791
Primary Market Served: Business & Consumer
Founded: 1857

Gross sales or billing: $1,675,200,000
Newspaper company.

MCDOUGAL LITTELL
Div. of Houghton Mifflin Co
1560 Sherman Ave, PO Box 1667
Evanston, IL 60201
Telephone: (847) 869-2300, FAX: (847) 869-0841, Web Site: www.mcdougallittell.com
Pres: Rita Schaefer
Ed-in-Chief: Susan Schaffrath
Conducts Business: U.S.
Employees: 300
Primary Market Served: Business
Direct online sales
Advertising/Marketing Budget Related to Direct Marketing: 0-25%
Direct Marketing ad budget: $650,000
Direct Mail: $200,000
Telephone: $450,000
Founded: 1969
Gross sales or billing: $204,000,000

Educational text books for marketing to High, Junior High & Middle Schools.

MCFARLAND & CO INC PUBLISHERS
PO Box 611
Jefferson, NC 28640-0611
Telephone: (336) 246-4460, (800) 253-2187, FAX: (336) 246-5018, E-Mail: info@mcfarlandpub.com, Web Site: www.mcfarlandpub.com
Pres: Robert Franklin
Exec Editor: Steve Wilson
Exec VP: Rhonda Herman
Dir Fin & Admin: Margie Turnmire
Sls Mgr: Karl-Heinz Roseman
Conducts Business: Worldwide
Employees: 45
Primary Market Served: Consumer
Catalog available online
Direct online sales
Advertising/Marketing Budget Related to Direct Marketing: 0-25%
Direct Marketing ad budget:
Direct Mail: 60%
Magazines: 15%
Newspapers: 5%
Online: 20%
Founded: 1979

Scholarly & reference books.

THE MCGRAW-HILL COS
1221 Ave of the Americas
New York, NY 10020-1095
Telephone: (212) 904-2000, (866) 436-8502, FAX: (212) 512-3840, Web Site: www.mcgraw-hill.com
Pres, CEO & Chmn: Harold W. McGraw III
Exec VP & CFO: Robert J. Bahash

Exec VP & CIO: Bruce D. Marcus
VP, Govt Affairs: Cynthia Braddon
Exec VP Global Strategy: Charles L. Teschner Jr.
Conducts Business: U.S.
Employees: 20,214
Primary Market Served: Business & Consumer
Gross sales or billing: $6,255,100,000

Create & produce mail & space campaigns to individuals, companies & institutions for McGraw-Hill books, software & services.

MCKNIGHT'S LONG-TERM CARE NEWS
An imprint of Haymarket Media Group, UK
One Northfield Plaza (Suite 521)
Northfield, IL 60093
Telephone: (847) 784-8706, (800) 558-1703, FAX: (847) 784-9346, E-Mail: mltcn-webmaster@mltcn.com, Web Site: www.mcknightsonline.com
VP, Assoc Publr & Editorial Dir: John O'Connor
Natl Sls Mgr: Karmen Maurer
Circ Mgr: Sherry Oommen
Conducts Business: Worldwide
Primary Market Served: Business

McKnight's long term care news publications.

MCMURRY INC
1010 E Missouri Ave
Phoenix, AZ 85014-2602
Telephone: (602) 395-5850, Web Site: www.mcmurry.com
Sr Dir Database Mktg: Joseph Abeyta

MEDCOM INC
6060 Phyllis Dr
Cypress, CA 90630
Telephone: (800) 877-1443, FAX: (714) 891-3140, E-Mail: lhammonds@medcominc.com, Web Site: www.medcominc.com
CEO: Bill Williams
VP, Sls & Mktg: Michael Zoradi
Mktg Mgr: Lisa Hammonds
Conducts Business: Worldwide
Employees: 70
Primary Market Served: Business
Catalog available online
Direct online sales
Direct Marketing ad budget: $25
Direct Mail: 80%
Telephone: 20%

Produce & market training educational materials in the health care field.

MEDIA TWO
1014 W 36th St
Baltimore, MD 21211-2415

Telephone: (410) 828-0120, FAX:
(410) 825-1002, Web Site: www.
mediatwo.com
Pres: Jonathan Witty
Mktg Coord: Bethany Vellucci

MEDICAL ECONOMICS MAGAZINE

Div. of Thomson
24950 Country Club Blvd (Suite 200)
North Olmsted, OH 44070-5351
Telephone: (440) 243-8100, FAX:
(440) 891-2735, Web Site:
medicaleconomics.modernmedicine.
com/about
Editor-in-Chief: Tara Sultz
Mng Editor: Lois A. Bowers
Sr Editor: Jeffrey Bendix
Sr Editor: Morgan Lewis Jr.
Conducts Business: U.S.
Primary Market Served: Business
Catalog available online
Indirect online sales

Lists of nurse, pharmacy, medical, lab, physician, medical equipment & supplies manufacturers, nursing home personnel & hospital personnel. $3MM+ healthcare professionals. Also offer direct response postcard decks for pharmacists, registered nurses & physicians.

MEISTER MEDIA WORLDWIDE

37733 Euclid Ave
Willoughby, OH 44094-5992
Telephone: (440) 942-2000, (800) 572-7740, FAX: (440) 975-3447, E-Mail:
info@meistermedia.com, Web Site:
www.meistermedia.com
CEO: Gary T. Fitzgerald
Pres: William Miller
Mgr Circulation: Sue Stearns
Dir Circulation: Jodie Svenson
Mktg: Christian Hendrix
Conducts Business: Worldwide
Employees: 116
Primary Market Served: Business & Consumer
Catalog available online
Direct online sales
Advertising/Marketing Budget Related to Direct Marketing: 0-25%
Direct Marketing ad budget: $700,000
Direct Mail: 80%
Magazines: 10%
Online: 10%
Gross sales or billing: $11,700,000

Publish monthly & annual farm publications sold online & via direct mail. Books, CD, DVD & video. Crop protection/pest control, fertilizer/nutrition, fruits & vegetables, ornamental horticulture, plant breeding, precision & sustainable agriculture.

MENTORING MINDS
4882 Hightech Dr
Tyler, TX 75703-2613
Telephone: (903) 509-4002
Primary Market Served: Consumer

MEREDITH CORP
1716 Locust St
Des Moines, IA 50309-3023
Telephone: (515) 284-3000, FAX:
(515) 284-2700, Web Site: www.
meredith.com
Pres & CEO: Stephen M. Lacy
CFO & VP: Suku V. Radia
Chief Devel Officer, Gen Counsel & Sec: John S. Zieser
Pres, Media Publ Grp: Jack Griffin
Pres, Media Broadcasting Grp: Paul Karpowicz
Employees: 3,300
Primary Market Served: Business & Consumer
Founded: 1902
Gross sales or billing: $1,600,000,000

Publisher of magazines & tradebooks on TV broadcasting & marketing.

THE MIAMI HERALD MEDIA CO
1 Herald Plaza
Miami, FL 33132-1609
Telephone: (305) 350-2111
Mgr, Direct Mktg Sls: Sylvia Schencker
Primary Market Served: Business

MIDWEST PUBLISHING INC
10844 N 23rd Ave
Phoenix, AZ 85029-4924
Telephone: (602) 943-1244, FAX:
(602) 331-0702
Employees: 275
Primary Market Served: Business & Consumer
Gross sales or billing: $30,500,000

MISSOURI LIFE INC
501 High St # A
Boonville, MO 65233-1211
Telephone: (660) 882-9898, (800) 492-2593, FAX: (660) 882-9899, E-Mail:
info@missourilife.com, Web Site:
www.missourilife.com
Publr: Greg Wood
Exec Office Mgr: Amy Stapleton
VP: Danita Allen Wood
Conducts Business: U.S.
Employees: 8
Primary Market Served: Business & Consumer
Catalog available online
Direct online sales
Advertising/Marketing Budget Related to Direct Marketing: 26-50%
Founded: 1973

Statewide magazine & printing & publishing company.

MITCHELL INTERNATIONAL
Thomson Publishing Corp
6220 Greenwich Dr
San Diego, CA 92122-5913
Telephone: (858) 368-7000, FAX:
(858) 238-9111, Web Site: www.
mitchell.com
Pres & CEO: James Lindner
Exec VP, Sls, Svc, Prod Mngmt & Mktg: Todd Mavis
Sr VP, Natl Sls: Bob Schachte
Mktg Dir: Chris Andrews
Conducts Business: U.S., Canada
Employees: 500
Primary Market Served: Business
Founded: 1946
Gross sales or billing: $80,000,000

Furnish technical automotive repair information to the body shop, general repair shops & insurance industries via online services & publications.

MONKEYSHINES PUBLISHERS
North Carolina Learning Institute for Fitness & Education
1608 Ilchester Ct.
Greensboro, NC 27401
FAX: (336) 292-6999, E-Mail:
mkshines@nr.infi.net, Web Site:
www.monkeyshinespublishers.com
Pres: Phyllis B. Goldman
Catalog available online
Indirect online sales
Founded: 1987

Educational resource material for K-12.

MORGAN KAUFMANN PUBLISHERS INC
30 Corporate Dr (Suite 400)
Burlington, MA 01803
Telephone: (781) 313-4700, E-Mail:
order@mkp.com, Web Site: www.
mkp.com
VP: Amy Pedersen
Mgr: Suzanne Dedell
Controller: Jill Espinola
Employees: 24
Primary Market Served: Business & Consumer
Catalog available online
Direct online sales
Advertising/Marketing Budget Related to Direct Marketing: 76-100%
Founded: 1984

Computer books, database management, science behind graphics books. Catalogs in bookstores.

MORRIS VISITORS PUBLICATIONS LLC

Div. of Morris Communications
699 Broad St (Suite 500)
Augusta, GA 30901
Telephone: (305) 892-6644, FAX:
   (305) 892-1005, E-Mail:
   mvpcustomerservice@morris.com,
   Web Site: www.
   morrisvisitorpublications.com
Conducts Business: U.S., Caribbean
Employees: 120
Primary Market Served: Business &
   Consumer
Direct online sales
Advertising/Marketing Budget Related
   to Direct Marketing: 51-75%
Direct Marketing ad budget:
Direct Mail: 60%
Magazines: 25%
Online: 5%
TV/Radio: 5%
Telephone: 5%

Publishers specializing in magazines
and travel guides.

MOTHER EARTH NEWS MAGAZINE

Subs. of Ogden Publications Inc
1503 SW 42nd St
Topeka, KS 66609-1265
Telephone: (785) 274-4300, (800) 678-
   5779, FAX: (785) 274-4305, E-Mail:
   bwelch@ogdenpubs.com, Web Site:
   www.cappers.com
Gen Mgr Pubns & Publr: Bryan Welch
Ed-in-Chief: Richard Backus
Ed-in-Chief: Kathryn C. Compton
Ed-in-Chief: Robyn Griggs Lawrence
Ed-in-Chief: David Schimke
Conducts Business: U.S., Canada
Employees: 67
Primary Market Served: Consumer
Catalog available online
Direct online sales
Advertising/Marketing Budget Related
   to Direct Marketing: 76-100%
Direct Marketing ad budget:
Direct Mail: 95%
Newspapers: 5%
Founded: 1879

Publisher of two tabloids & one bi-
monthly magazine aimed at 50+ C&D
counties nationally, biweekly. Use direct mail & space advertising to secure
salesmen & subscriptions for biweekly
magazines.

MOTHER JONES MAGAZINE

222 Sutter St (Suite 600)
San Francisco, CA 94108-4457
Telephone: (415) 321-1700, Web Site:
   www.motherjones.com
Publr: Jay Harris
CFO: Madeline Buchingham

Creative Dir: Jane Palecek
Co Chair: Jane Butcher
Editor in Chief: Russ Rymes
Conducts Business: U.S., Canada
Employees: 40
Primary Market Served: Consumer
Catalog available online
Direct online sales
Founded: 1976
Gross sales or billing: $9,500,000

Non-profit educational organization
dedicated to the dissemination of information & ideas necessary for a just
society & a healthy democracy. Publisher of Mother Jones Magazine.

MOTT MEDIA LLC

1130 Fenway Cir
Fenton, MI 48430
Telephone: (810) 714-4280, FAX:
   (810) 714-2077, E-Mail: info@
   mottmedia.com, Web Site: www.
   mottmedia.com
Pres & Member: William Hoetger
VP: Joyce Bohn
Editor: Diane Davis
Conducts Business: U.S., Canada
Employees: 14
Primary Market Served: Business &
   Consumer
Catalog available online
Indirect online sales
Advertising/Marketing Budget Related
   to Direct Marketing: 26-50%
Direct Marketing ad budget: $50,000
Direct Mail: 20%
Magazines: 70%
Telephone: 10%
Gross sales or billing: $1,200,000

Publisher of trade & textbook materials
designed for the Christian school &/or
bookstore market. Owner of the Home-
schooling Book Club.

MOUNTAIN PRESS PUBLISHING CO

PO Box 2399
Missoula, MT 59806-2399
Telephone: (406) 728-1900, (800) 234-
   5308, FAX: (406) 728-1635, E-Mail:
   info@mtnpress.com, Web Site:
   www.mountain-press.com
Publr: John A. Rimel
Bus Mgr: Rob Williams
History Ed: Gwen McKenna
Prodn Mgr: Jeannie Nuckolls
Conducts Business: U.S., Canada
Employees: 12
Primary Market Served: Business &
   Consumer
Catalog available online
Indirect online sales
Advertising/Marketing Budget Related
   to Direct Marketing: 26-50%
Direct Marketing ad budget:

Direct Mail: 80%
Magazines: 6%
Newspapers: 4%
Online: 10%
Founded: 1948
Gross sales or billing: $1,200,000

Publish books on geology, western
Americana & natural science. Titles
sold through book trade & direct mail.

MIKE MURACH & ASSOCIATES INC

4340 N Knoll Ave
Fresno, CA 93722-7825
Telephone: (559) 440-9071, (800) 221-
   5528, FAX: (559) 440-0963, E-Mail:
   murachbooks@murach.com, Web
   Site: www.murach.com
Pres: Mike Murach
Mktg Dir: Judy Taylor
Dir Mktg: Cyndi Vasquez
Employees: 12
Primary Market Served: Business &
   Consumer
Catalog available online
Direct online sales
Advertising/Marketing Budget Related
   to Direct Marketing: 76-100%
Direct Marketing ad budget:
Direct Mail: 90%
Magazines: 10%
Founded: 1972

Publishers of PC & mainframe computer books.

MUSIC SALES CORP

257 Park Ave S Fl 20
New York, NY 10010-7304
Telephone: (212) 254-2100, (800) 431-
   7187, FAX: (212) 254-2013, E-Mail:
   info@musicsales.com, Web Site:
   www.musicsales.com
Sls & Mktg Dir: Steven A. Wilson
VP: Kristin Lancino
Pub Rels Dir: Alison Wofford
COO: Chris Butler
Pres: Barrie Edwards
VP Sls & Mktg: Chris Scialfa
Conducts Business: U.S.
Employees: 100
Primary Market Served: Business &
   Consumer
Catalog available online
Direct online sales
Advertising/Marketing Budget Related
   to Direct Marketing: 0-25%
Direct Marketing ad budget:
Direct Mail: 40%
Magazines: 60%
Founded: 1935
Gross sales or billing: $7,600,000

Music books for musicians & fans.

NCP SOLUTIONS

11100 Wildlife Center Dr
Reston, VA 20190-5362
Telephone: (703) 438-6000, (800) 822-
9919, FAX: (703) 438-3570, Web
Site: www.nwf.org
Pres: Mark VanPatten
VP, Promo Activities: Diane Snyder
Conducts Business: U.S., Worldwide
Employees: 375
Primary Market Served: Business &
Consumer
Catalog available online
Advertising/Marketing Budget Related
to Direct Marketing: 0-25%
Founded: 1936

Wildlife conservation, educational materials, magazine publishing & merchandise catalog.

NADA APPRAISAL GUIDES

3186 Airway Ave (Unit K)
Costa Mesa, CA 92626
Telephone: (714) 556-8511, (800) 966-
6232, FAX: (714) 957-0302, E-Mail:
info@nadaguides.com, Web Site:
www.nadaguides.com
Pres & CEO: Donald D. Christy Jr.
VP & Gen Mgr: Lenny Sims
Conducts Business: U.S., Canada,
Mexico, Puerto Rico
Employees: 32
Primary Market Served: Business &
Consumer
Catalog available online
Indirect online sales
Advertising/Marketing Budget Related
to Direct Marketing: 26-50%
Founded: 1933

Publisher of used value guides for cars, boats, RV's, motorcycles, mobile homes, airplanes, helicopters, vans, limousines, mobile homes, & commercial trucks.

NAR PRODUCTIONS

Div. of NAR Associates
PO Box 233
Barryville, NY 12719-0233
Telephone: (845) 557-8713, FAX:
(845) 557-6770, E-Mail: info@
aodceus.com, Web Site: www.
aodceus.com
Conducts Business: U.S.
Employees: 5
Primary Market Served: Business &
Consumer
Catalog available online
Indirect online sales
Advertising/Marketing Budget Related
to Direct Marketing: 76-100%
Founded: 1977

Publishing & communications firm.

NATCOM INC

7580 E 151st St
Bixby, OK 74008
Telephone: (918) 491-6100, (800) 554-
1999, FAX: (918) 491-9410, E-Mail:
cs@natcom-publications.com, Web
Site: www.natcom-publications.com
VP, Circ Mktg: Gordon Sprouse
Primary Market Served: Business &
Consumer
Catalog available online
Direct online sales
Founded: 1988

Publishers of sporting magazines.

NATIONAL ARCHIVES & RECORDS ADMINISTRATION

8601 Adelphi Rd
College Park, MD 20740-6001
Telephone: (301) 837-0482, (86)
NARA-NARA, FAX: (301) 837-
0483, Web Site: www.archives.gov
Deputy Archivist & Chief of Staff:
Louis J. Bellardo
Archivist: John W. Carlin
Archivist: Allen Weinstein
Asst Archivist Info Svcs: Martha Morphy
Conducts Business: U.S.
Employees: 40
Primary Market Served: Business &
Consumer
Catalog available online
Advertising/Marketing Budget Related
to Direct Marketing: 51-75%
Direct Marketing ad budget: $350,000
Direct Mail: 75%
Magazines: 20%
Newspapers: 5%
Gross sales or billing: $2,000,000

Publishers of historically significant federal records. Microforms, finding aids, guides & periodicals are sold to individuals, schools, libraries, research centers & genealogists. Museum shop & catalogs.

NATIONAL AUDUBON SOCIETY

225 Varick St (7 fl)
New York, NY 10014-4396
Telephone: (212) 979-3000, FAX:
(212) 979-3188, Web Site: www.
audubon.org
Pres: John Flicker
COO: Robert Perciasepe
VP, Membership & Mktg: Alan Bayersdorfer
VP, HR: Linda H. Brooke
VP: Tamar Chotzen
VP: W. E. Scott
Conducts Business: U.S.
Employees: 600
Primary Market Served: Consumer

Advertising/Marketing Budget Related
to Direct Marketing: 51-75%
Gross sales or billing: $11,000,000

Publisher of leading environmental magazine.

NATIONAL CATHOLIC REPORTER PUBLISHING CO INC

115 E Armour Blvd
Kansas City, MO 64111-1203
Telephone: (816) 531-0538, (800) 444-
8910, FAX: (816) 968-2268, Web
Site: www.ncronline.org
Publr: Thomas Fox
Editor at Large: Tom Roberts
Adv/Prod Dir: Vicki Breashears
Mktg Dir: Sara Wiercinski
Editor: Dennis Coday
Conducts Business: Worldwide
Employees: 30
Primary Market Served: Business &
Consumer
Direct online sales
Advertising/Marketing Budget Related
to Direct Marketing: 76-100%
Direct Marketing ad budget:
$1,000,000
Direct Mail: 99%
Magazines: 1%
Newspapers: 1%
Founded: 1964
Gross sales or billing: $5,500,000

An independent newsweekly sold primarily through direct mail. Sell a homily service for churches by mail.

NATIONAL CRIME PREVENTION COUNCIL

One Prospect St
Amsterdam, NY 12010
Telephone: (518) 842-4388, (888) 776-
7763, FAX: (800) 995-5121, E-Mail:
mcgruff@spocentral.com, Web Site:
www.mcgruffspo.com
Acting Mktg Dir: Anna Podolec
Employees: 20
Primary Market Served: Business &
Consumer
Catalog available online
Direct online sales

National publication on safety.

NATIONAL ENQUIRER

Subs. of American Media Inc
1000 American Media Way
Boca Raton, FL 33464-1000
Telephone: (561) 989-1221, Web Site:
www.nationalenquirer.com
Chmn & CEO: David Pecker
Pres, Direct Response Mktg & Pub Dir
Tabloid Grp: Bette Rockmore
Conducts Business: U.S., Canada, Puerto Rico

Employees: 1,500
Primary Market Served: Consumer

Publisher of National Enquirer, Star, Globe, Country Weekly, Country Music, All to World, Mira, National Examiner, Sun, Weekly World News, Mini Mages. Our publications are proven direct response vehicles.

THE DMA **NATIONAL GEOGRAPHIC SOCIETY**
1145 17th St NW
Washington, DC 20036-4688
Telephone: (202) 857-7311, (800) NGS-LINE, FAX: (202) 457-8200, Web Site: www.nationalgeographic.com
Chmn: Gilbert Grosvenor
Pres: John Fahey
Dir, Creative Svcs: Karen Rice-Gardiner
VP, Mktg: Mary Donohoe
CEO & Exec VP: Christopher A. Liedel
Conducts Business: Worldwide
Employees: 1,400
Catalog available online
Indirect online sales
Advertising/Marketing Budget Related to Direct Marketing: 51-75%
Founded: 1888

Magazine publisher, educational products.

THE DMA **NATIONAL JOURNAL GROUP**
600 New Hampshire Ave NW Fl 4
Washington, DC 20037-2403
Telephone: (202) 266-7541
Mktg Mgr: Michael Torio
Primary Market Served: Business & Consumer

NATIONAL REVIEW
215 Lexington Ave
New York, NY 10016
Telephone: (212) 679-7330, FAX: (212) 849-2852, Web Site: www.nationalreview.com
Pres: Thomas Rhodes
Circ Dir: Theresa Maloney
Publr: Edward Capano
Ed: Richard Lowry
Conducts Business: U.S.
Employees: 50
Primary Market Served: Consumer
Catalog available online
Advertising/Marketing Budget Related to Direct Marketing: 76-100%
Direct Marketing ad budget:
Direct Mail: 100%
Founded: 1955
Gross sales or billing: $8,000,000

Magazine publisher.

NATIONAL TECHNICAL INFORMATION SERVICE
Div. of US Dept of Commerce
5301 Shawnee Rd
Alexandria, VA 22312-2379
Telephone: (703) 605-6000, FAX: (703) 605-6900, Web Site: www.ntis.gov
Dir: Ron Lawson
Conducts Business: Worldwide
Employees: 350
Primary Market Served: Business & Consumer
Advertising/Marketing Budget Related to Direct Marketing: 0-25%
Direct Marketing ad budget:
Direct Mail: $20,000
Magazines: $20,000
Newspapers: $20,000
Founded: 1945

A central clearing house & government wide resource for scientific technical engineering & other business-related information, with three million titles. Provides a wide range of products & services including online, world wide web, audiovisual materials, CD ROM & more.

THE NATIONAL UNDERWRITER CO
5081 Olympic Blvd
Erlanger, KY 41018-3164
Telephone: (800) 543-0874, FAX: (856) 692-2246, E-Mail: customerservice@nuco.com, Web Site: www.nuco.com
Pres: Garry Baumgartner
VP, Mktg: Peggy Walker
Pur Mgr: Steve Johnston
Conducts Business: U.S.
Employees: 160
Primary Market Served: Business
Catalog available online
Direct online sales
Advertising/Marketing Budget Related to Direct Marketing: 26-50%
Founded: 1897

Weekly newspapers, monthly magazines & 100 book and software publications for the insurance industry & other financial service fields.

NATURAL HISTORY MAGAZINE
American Museum of Natural History
105 W NC Highway 54 (Suite 265), PMB 204
Durham, NC 27713-6650
Telephone: (646) 356-6500, FAX: (646) 356-6511, E-Mail: nhmag@naturalhistorymag.com, Web Site: www.naturalhistorymag.com
Ed-in-Chief: Peter G. Brown
Publr: Charles Harris

Prodn Dir: Meredith Miller
Conducts Business: Worldwide
Employees: 35
Primary Market Served: Consumer
Catalog available online
Direct online sales
Advertising/Marketing Budget Related to Direct Marketing: 26-50%
Founded: 1900
Gross sales or billing: $12,500,000

Monthly magazine (ten issues annually) published by the American Museum of Natural History.

NATURE PUBLISHING GROUP
75 Varick St (fl 9)
New York, NY 10013-1917
Telephone: (212) 726-9200, FAX: (212) 696-9006, E-Mail: nature@natureny.com, Web Site: www.nature.com
Chief Tech Officer (NY): Howard Ratner
Mng Dir (London): Steven Inchcoombe
Editor in Chief (London): Phillip Campbell
Publ Dir (London): Peter Collins
CFO: Richard Hartgill
Conducts Business: Worldwide
Primary Market Served: Business
Catalog available online
Direct online sales
Advertising/Marketing Budget Related to Direct Marketing: 0-25%

Publisher of scientific journals.

NAVAL INSTITUTE PRESS
Div. of US Naval Institute
291 Wood Rd
Annapolis, MD 21402-5034
Telephone: (410) 268-6110, (800) 233-8764, FAX: (410) 571-1703, E-Mail: webmaster@usni.org, Web Site: www.usni.org/navalinstitutepress
Prod Asst: Carol Parkinson
Publr: William Miller
Dir: Rick Russell
Conducts Business: Worldwide
Employees: 60
Primary Market Served: Business & Consumer
Catalog available online
Direct online sales
Founded: 1873

The book-publishing imprint of the U.S. Naval Institute, a private professional society for members of the military services and civilians who share an interest in naval & maritime affairs. Membership includes a subscription to the monthly magazine Proceedings, substantial discounts on more than 800 books, art prints, & photographs available from the press. Direct mail is used extensively to generate new members & to promote book sales among members & non-members.

THOMAS NELSON, INC
PO Box 141000
Nashville, TN 37214
Telephone: (615) 889-9000, (800) 251-4000, FAX: (615) 889-5940, Web Site: www.thomasnelson.com
Pres & CEO: Michael S. Hyatt
EVP & CFO: Joe L. Powers
EVP: Mary Graham
EVP: Tamara L. Heim
EVP: Vance Lawson
Conducts Business: U.S.
Primary Market Served: Business & Consumer
Advertising/Marketing Budget Related to Direct Marketing: 26-50%
Direct Marketing ad budget:
Direct Mail: 40%
Magazines: 10%
TV/Radio: 10%
Telephone: 40%
Founded: 1798
Gross sales or billing: $250,000

Bibles & Christian books, audio & video tapes to churches & consumers.

⟨THE DMA⟩ NEO-TECH PUBLISHING CO
2435 W Horizon Ridge Pkwy (Suite 100)
Henderson, NV 89052-5787
Telephone: (702) 891-0303, FAX: (702) 795-8393
Gen Mgr: Steve Rapella
Primary Market Served: Consumer

Self help books.

NEVADA MAGAZINE
401 N Carson St
Carson City, NV 89701-4221
Telephone: (775) 687-5416, FAX: (775) 687-6159, E-Mail: editor@ nevadamagazine.com, Web Site: www.nevadamagazine.com
Publr: Joyce Hollister
Editor: Matt Brown
Assoc Editor: Charlie Johnston
Events Editor: Ann Henderson
Dir Sls: Carrie Roussel
Conducts Business: U.S., Canada
Employees: 10
Primary Market Served: Consumer

Catalog available online
Direct online sales
Advertising/Marketing Budget Related to Direct Marketing: 76-100%
Founded: 1936

Travel & leisure magazine of The Real West.

NEW DIRECTIONS PUBLISHING CORP
80 Eighth Ave (19th fl)
New York, NY 10011-7146
Telephone: (212) 255-0230, FAX: (212) 255-0231, E-Mail: editorial@ ndbooks.com, Web Site: www.ndpublishing.com
Pres: Peggy Fox
DM Mgr: Linda Callahan
Conducts Business: Worldwide
Employees: 10
Primary Market Served: Consumer
Catalog available online
Founded: 1936

NEW ENGLAND JOURNAL OF MEDICINE
Div. of Massachusetts Medical Society
860 Winter St
Waltham, MA 02451-1430
Telephone: (781) 893-3800, FAX: (781) 893-7729, Web Site: www.nejm.org
VP Publr: Chris Lynch
Ed: Marsha Angell
Exec Publ Svcs Dir: William H. Paige
Exec Worldwide Sls & Mktg Dir: Art Wilschek
Conducts Business: Worldwide
Employees: 270
Primary Market Served: Business

Weekly medical journal directed to physicians, residents, medical students, researchers, libraries, hospitals & other professionals in the medical field.

NEW JERSEY MONTHLY
55 Park Pl
Morristown, NJ 07960-3924
Telephone: (973) 539-8230, FAX: (973) 538-2953, E-Mail: research@ njmonthly.com, Web Site: www.njmonthly.com
Publr, EIC & Consumer Mktg: Kate S. Tomlinson
Circ Dir: Donald Seckler
Conducts Business: U.S.
Employees: 40
Primary Market Served: Consumer
Advertising/Marketing Budget Related to Direct Marketing: 26-50%
Founded: 1976

Statewide monthly consumer magazine with articles relating to New Jersey.

NEW TRACK MEDIA
90 Sherman St
Cambridge, MA 02140-3264
Telephone: (617) 758-0247

NEW WIN PUBLISHING INC
Div. of Academic Learning Co
9682 Telstar Ave (Suite 110)
El Monte, CA 91731-3009
Telephone: (626) 448-3448, FAX: (626) 602-3817, E-Mail: info@ AcademicLearningCompany.com, Web Site: www.newwinpublishing.com
Publr: Frank Gil
Conducts Business: U.S.
Employees: 3
Primary Market Served: Business & Consumer
Advertising/Marketing Budget Related to Direct Marketing: 0-25%
Founded: 1989

Publisher of non-fiction, trade titles, cookbooks, craft & how-to books. Also publish outdoor sports books under Winchester Press imprint.

THE NEW YORK TIMES CO
620 8th Ave
New York, NY 10018-1618
Telephone: (212) 556-3881, FAX: (212) 556-7389, Web Site: www.nytimes.com
Chmn NY Times Co & Publr, NY Times: Arthur O. Sulzberger Jr.
Mng Dir Acq Mktg: James Dunn
Pres & CEO, NY Times Co: Janet L. Robinson
Sr VP & CFO: James M. Follo
Sr VP, Corp Commun: Catherine J. Mathis
VP, Res & Devel Opers: Michael Zimbalist
Dir, Pub Rels: Abbe Serphos
Conducts Business: U.S., Canada
Primary Market Served: Business & Consumer
Gross sales or billing: $3,300,000,000

Agency promotes subscriptions of The New York Times newspapers.

THE NEW YORKER MAGAZINE
Subs. of Advance Publications
Four Times Sq
New York, NY 10036
Telephone: (212) 286-5400, FAX: (212) 286-5735, E-Mail: alatia_bradley@newyorker.com, Web Site: www.newyorker.com
Ed-in-Chief: Dave Remnick
Publr & VP: Louis Cona
Assoc Publr: Jannie Engel
Adv Dir: Alatia Bradley
Conducts Business: U.S.

Employees: 350
Primary Market Served: Business &
  Consumer
Founded: 1925

Weekly publication.

NEWS AMERICA
PUBLISHING INC

Subs. of The News Corporation Ltd
1211 Ave of the Americas
New York, NY 10036
Telephone: (212) 782-8000, FAX:
  (212) 852-7145
Chmn: K. Rupert Murdoch
CFO: David DeVoe
Primary Market Served: Business

Newspaper & magazine publisher, TV
stations, motion picture production.

THE NEWS TRIBUNE

1950 S State St
Tacoma, WA 98405-2817
Telephone: (253) 597-8742, E-Mail:
  reader.representative@
  thenewstribune.com, Web Site: www.
  thenewstribune.com
Publr: Elizabeth Brenner
Direct Delivery Mgr: Tanyalee Erwin
Primary Market Served: Consumer
Founded: 1880

Business newspaper publisher.

NEWSDAY

Subs. of Times Mirror
235 Pinelawn Rd
Melville, NY 11747-4250
Telephone: (631) 843-2020, FAX:
  (631) 843-5424, Web Site: www.
  newsday.com
Pres, CEO & Publr: Timothy P. Knight
Sr VP Opers & Engrng Svcs: Frank
  Toner
VP, Fin & CFO: Terry A. Jimenez
Bus Editor: Rick Green
Primary Market Served: Consumer
Catalog available online
Gross sales or billing: $50,000,000

Newspaper publisher.

™️ NEWSWEEK INC
THE DMA

Div. of Washington Post Co
555 W 18th St # 2
New York, NY 10011-2822
Telephone: (212) 445-4000, FAX:
  (212) 445-5068, Web Site: www.
  newsweek.com
Pres & CEO: Harold Shain
Sr VP, Circ: Mary Sue Rynecki
Ed-in-Chief: Richard M. Smith
Conducts Business: Worldwide
Employees: 1,000
Primary Market Served: Business &
  Consumer
Gross sales or billing: $326,000,000

Various direct marketing techniques in
Newsweek subscription promotion
efforts. Also, rent mailing lists.

NEXTSCREEN LLC

8868 Research Blvd Ste 108
Austin, TX 78758-6446
Telephone: (512) 892-8682, Web Site:
  www.avguide.com
Ed-in-Chief: Harry Pearson
Publr & VP: Mark Fisher
Editor: Roy Gregory
Editor: Chris Martens
Conducts Business: Worldwide
Employees: 18
Primary Market Served: Consumer
Catalog available online
Indirect online sales
Advertising/Marketing Budget Related
  to Direct Marketing: 0-25%
Founded: 1998
Gross sales or billing: $2,000,000

Publishes bi-monthly journal, The Absolute Sound, about high end audio
equipment & music.

THE NIELSEN CO

770 Broadway
New York, NY 10003-9595
Telephone: (646) 654-5000, E-Mail:
  contactcommunications@nielsen.
  com, Web Site: www.nielsen.com
Chm & CEO: David Calhoun
PR: Jack Coftus
PR: Gary Holmes
PR: Karen Watson
Conducts Business: U.S.
Employees: 42,000
Primary Market Served: Business
Catalog available online
Indirect online sales
Advertising/Marketing Budget Related
  to Direct Marketing: 51-75%
Founded: 1964
Gross sales or billing: $9,000,000

Information and media company in-
cluding marketing information (AC-
Nielsen), media information (Nielsen
Media Research), business publications
(Billboard, The Hollywood Reporter,
Adweek) and trade shows

NIELSEN TRADE
DIMENSIONS

40 Danbury Rd
Wilton, CT 06897-4406
Telephone: (203) 222-5750, (800) 291-
  0410, FAX: (203) 222-5701, E-Mail:
  tradedimensions.info@nielsen.com,
  Web Site: www.tradedimensions.com
Dir Mktg: Carley Staron
Dir Res Opers: Thomas Donato
VP: Mario Gutierrez
Acct Rep: Tracey Jason
Bus Devel Mgr: Joe Trovarelli

Conducts Business: U.S., Canada
Employees: 14
Primary Market Served: Business &
  Consumer
Catalog available online
Direct online sales
Advertising/Marketing Budget Related
  to Direct Marketing: 26-50%
Gross sales or billing: $3,000,000

Customized retail databases for consumer packaged goods manufacturers.
Directories on the supermarket, convenience store, mass merchandiser/chain
drug industries, plus a directory of retail tenants.

™️ NIGHTINGALE-CONANT
THE DMA
CORP

6245 W Howard St
Niles, IL 60714-3403
Telephone: (847) 647-0300, (800) 557-
  1660, FAX: (847) 647-7145, Web
  Site: www.nightingale.com
Pres: Vic Conant
Sr VP, Publ & Bus Devel: Gary
  Chapel
VP, Mktg: Sara Pond
Dir, New Prod Devel: Dan Strutzel
Dir, HR: Michael Burgess
Conducts Business: U.S., Canada,
  U.K., Australia
Employees: 250
Primary Market Served: Business &
  Consumer
Catalog available online
Direct online sales
Advertising/Marketing Budget Related
  to Direct Marketing: 51-75%
Direct Marketing ad budget:
  $20,000,000
Direct Mail: 80%
Magazines: 6%
Telephone: 14%
Gross sales or billing: $50,000,000

Publisher of audio & video cassette
programs sold to individuals & companies via direct marketing &
distributors. Syndicated radio program
to stations & sponsors via direct
marketing.

NIGHTINGALE RESOURCES

6 Chestnut St
Cold Spring, NY 10516-2517
Telephone: (718) 338-3976, (212) 753-
  5383, (800) 953-9929
Pres: L.T. Gold
Conducts Business: Worldwide
Primary Market Served: Business &
  Consumer
Indirect online sales
Founded: 1981

Publishes children's, history & cookery
books. Judaica.

NIHON KEIZAI SHIMBUN AMERICA INC

1325 Ave of the Americas (Suite 2500)
New York, NY 10019
Telephone: (212) 261-6230, FAX:
(212) 261-6239, Web Site: www.
nikkeius.com
Ed: Kenji Fukasawa
Conducts Business: U.S., Canada, S.
America
Employees: 60
Primary Market Served: Business &
Consumer
Advertising/Marketing Budget Related
to Direct Marketing: 26-50%
Direct Marketing ad budget:
Direct Mail: 50%
Magazines: 20%
Newspapers: 20%
TV/Radio: 5%
Telephone: 5%

Sells subscriptions to the Nikkei
Weekly, a Japanese business & economic newspaper written in English.

THE NONPROFIT TIMES

Publication of the Davis Information
Group
201 Littleton Rd (Suite 120)
Morris Plains, NJ 07950-2939
Telephone: (973) 401-0202, FAX:
(973) 401-0404, Web Site: www.
nptimes.com
Publr: Willy Morgan
CEO: John McIlquham
Conducts Business: U.S.
Employees: 10
Primary Market Served: Business
Advertising/Marketing Budget Related
to Direct Marketing: 0-25%
Direct Marketing ad budget: $100,000
Direct Mail: 70%
Telephone: 30%
Gross sales or billing: $1,000,000

National monthly publication for non-
profit organizations.

NORDSKOG PUBLISHING CO

Subs. of Nordskog Industries
4562 Westinghouse St (Suite E)
Ventura, CA 93003-5797
Telephone: (805) 642-2070, FAX:
(805) 642-1862, E-Mail:
pwrboatmag@aol.com, Web Site:
www.nordskogpublishing.com
Publr: Jerry Nordskog
Theology Editor: Rev. Christian Hoops
Editor: Desta Garret
Graphic Designer: Tim Belper
Proofreader: Kimberly Winters
Conducts Business: U.S., Canada
Employees: 12
Primary Market Served: Consumer
Catalog available online
Direct online sales

Advertising/Marketing Budget Related
to Direct Marketing: 26-50%
Direct Marketing ad budget: $100,000
Direct Mail: 50%
Magazines: 40%
TV/Radio: 10%
Founded: 1968
Gross sales or billing: $2,000,000

Monthly periodical. Special consumer
interest.

NUCLEAR PLANT JOURNAL

1400 Opus Pl (Suite 904)
Downers Grove, IL 60515
Telephone: (630) 858-6161, FAX:
(630) 852-8787, Web Site: www.
nuclearplantjournal.com
Sr Publr & Editor: Newal Agnihotri
Publr & Sls Mgr: Anu Agnihotri
Conducts Business: Worldwide
Employees: 4
Primary Market Served: Business
Catalog available online
Direct online sales
Advertising/Marketing Budget Related
to Direct Marketing: 0-25%
Founded: 1983

Mailing list of subscribers available for
rental. Subscribers are primarily engineers, scientists & managers in the
nuclear power industry. List is BPA
audited & updated every other month.

NYREV INC

dba New York Review of Books
435 Hudson St (Suite 300)
New York, NY 10014-3949
Telephone: (212) 757-8070, FAX:
(212) 333-5374, E-Mail: mail@
nybooks.com, Web Site: www.
nybooks.com
CEO: Rea Hederman
Ed: Barbara Epstein
Ed: Robert Silvers
Conducts Business: Worldwide
Employees: 35
Primary Market Served: Consumer
Catalog available online
Direct online sales
Advertising/Marketing Budget Related
to Direct Marketing: 0-25%
Direct Marketing ad budget:
Direct Mail: 60%
Magazines: 30%
Newspapers: 10%
Founded: 1963
Gross sales or billing: $3,200,000

Magazine - 20 times/year.

OAG WORLDWIDE

3025 Highland Pkwy (Suite 200)
Downers Grove, IL 60515
Telephone: (630) 515-5300, FAX:
(630) 515-5301, E-Mail: custsvc@
oag.com, Web Site: www.oag.com

Mgr, Customer Direct Mktg: Bonita
Glader
Conducts Business: Worldwide
Employees: 800
Primary Market Served: Business &
Consumer
Catalog available online
Direct online sales
Advertising/Marketing Budget Related
to Direct Marketing: 0-25%

Distributor & publisher of printed &
electronic travel information & other
travel related publications.

OAKSTONE PUBLISHING LLC

Div. of Haights Cross Communications
LLC
100 Corporate Pkwy (Suite 600)
Birmingham, AL 35242-8908
Telephone: (205) 991-5188, (800) 952-
0690, FAX: (205) 995-4656, Web
Site: www.oakstonepublishing.com
Chmn: Peter J. Quandt
Pres & CEO: Nancy M. McMeekin
VP Mktg: Mary Hoffman
VP, Opers: Connie Fleming
Employees: 100
Primary Market Served: Business &
Consumer
Advertising/Marketing Budget Related
to Direct Marketing: 51-75%
Founded: 1975

Publishes audiotapes and compact
discs & computer software for medical
& dental continuing education & wellness, safety & financial newsletters and
calendars sold to organizations for distribution to their employees.

OIL & GAS JOURNAL

Subs. of PennWell Publishing Co
1421 S Sheridan Rd
Tulsa, OK 74112-6600
Telephone: (918) 835-3161, (800) 331-
4463, FAX: (918) 832-9497, Web
Site: www.pennwell.com; www.ogj.
com
Presentation Ed: Robert G. Lair
Conducts Business: Worldwide
Primary Market Served: Business &
Consumer
Catalog available online
Direct online sales
Advertising/Marketing Budget Related
to Direct Marketing: 0-25%

Weekly trade magazine covering all
aspects of the petroleum industry.
Maintain & rent mailing list of subscribers & prospects.

OMNIGRAPHICS INC

PO Box 8002
Aston, PA 19014-8002

Telephone: (610) 461-3548, (800) 234-1340, FAX: (800) 875-1340, E-Mail: info@omnigraphics.com, Web Site: www.omnigraphics.com
Chmn: Frederick G. Ruffner Jr.
Pres & Publr: Peter E. Ruffner
Sr VP: Matthew Barbour
Conducts Business: Worldwide
Employees: 35
Primary Market Served: Business & Consumer
Catalog available online
Direct online sales
Advertising/Marketing Budget Related to Direct Marketing: 76-100%
Direct Marketing ad budget:
Direct Mail: 83%
Magazines: 15%
Telephone: 2%
Founded: 1985

Reference publisher serving the library, school, business & institutional markets.

THE ORANGE COUNTY REGISTER

Owned by Freedom Communications, Inc.
625 N Grand Ave
Santa Ana, CA 92701
Telephone: (877) 469-7344, E-Mail: customerservice@ocregister.com, Web Site: www.ocregister.com
Mktg Dir: Lelani Bluner
Primary Market Served: Business & Consumer
Founded: 1905

Newspaper.

ORBIS BOOKS

Subs. of Maryknoll Fathers & Brothers
PO Box 302, Price Bldg
Maryknoll, NY 10545-0302
Telephone: (914) 941-7636 X2576, (800) 258-5838, FAX: (914) 941-7005, E-Mail: orbisbooks@maryknoll.org, Web Site: www.orbisbooks.com
Mktg Mgr: Bernadette Price
Conducts Business: Worldwide
Employees: 20
Primary Market Served: Business & Consumer
Catalog available online
Indirect online sales
Advertising/Marketing Budget Related to Direct Marketing: 26-50%
Direct Marketing ad budget:
Direct Mail: 70%
Magazines: 30%
Founded: 1970
Gross sales or billing: $2,400,000

Not for profit publisher of books on religion/politics, ecology, interreligious dialogue, comparative religion, world religions, spirituality, peace studies, ethnic studies, women's issues & missiology.

THE DMA OUR SUNDAY VISITOR PUBLISHING

Div. of Our Sunday Visitor Inc
200 Noll Plaza
Huntington, IN 46750
Telephone: (260) 356-8400, (800) 348-2440, FAX: (260) 356-8472, E-Mail: athomas@osv.com, Web Site: www.osv.com
Publr: Greg Erlandson
Mktg Dir Books: Jill Kurtz
Circulation Mgr: Amy Thomas
Conducts Business: Worldwide
Employees: 53
Primary Market Served: Business & Consumer
Catalog available online
Direct online sales
Advertising/Marketing Budget Related to Direct Marketing: 0-25%
Founded: 1912

Publish & market a wide variety of books & periodicals to Catholic readers. Also market general religious & educational titles.

OXFORD UNIVERSITY PRESS INC

198 Madison Ave Fl 8
New York, NY 10016-4308
Telephone: (212) 726-6000, FAX: (212) 726-6455, Web Site: www.oup.com/us/
Pres: Laura Brown
Sr VP & Dist Dir: Brinton Strode
Dir Direct Response & Mktg Opers: Rose Pintaudi-Jones
Sr VP Fin: Richard Gehringer
Sr VP Corp Counsel Admin & Planning: John Grillos
Publr Paperbacks & Acting Publr Trade: Ellen Chodosh
Conducts Business: Worldwide
Employees: 255
Primary Market Served: Business & Consumer
Catalog available online

Sell books to retailers, distributors & through direct mail to academics, professionals & businessmen. Branch offices located worldwide.

PC WORLD

Div. of IDG Communications Inc
501 2nd St
San Francisco, CA 94107-1496

Telephone: (415) 243-0500, FAX: (415) 442-1891, Web Site: www.pcworld.com
Pres & CEO: Jeff Edman
Editorial Dir: Steve Fox
Conducts Business: Worldwide
Employees: 80
Primary Market Served: Business & Consumer

International data group company. Publisher of computer related magazines & newspapers.

PESI LLC

aka Professional Education Systems Institute
200 Spring St (Ste A)
Eau Claire, WI 54703-3663
Telephone: (800) 844-8260, FAX: (800) 554-9775, E-Mail: info@pesi.com, Web Site: www.pesi.com
Exec Dir: Rick Olson
VP Mktg: Jane Kemper
Conducts Business: U.S., Canada
Employees: 40
Primary Market Served: Business & Consumer
Founded: 1979
Gross sales or billing: $4,500,000

Provide continuing education programs for legal, nursing, construction, financial, general business & real estate professions. Also, publish & market medical & law-oriented audio tapes.

PMIC

4727 Wilshire Blvd (Suite 300)
Los Angeles, CA 90010-3873
Telephone: (323) 954-0224, (800) 633-4215, FAX: (323) 954-0253, Web Site: pmiconline.stores.yahoo.net
Pres: James Davis
Primary Market Served: Business & Consumer
Catalog available online
Direct online sales
Founded: 1989

Publish medical books.

PACE COMMUNICATIONS INC

1301 Carolina St
Greensboro, NC 27401-1032
Telephone: (336) 378-6065, FAX: (336) 275-2864, Web Site: www.pacecommunications.com
CEO: Bonnie McElveen-Hunter
Chief Mktg & Sls Officer: Craig Waller
Pres, Ecommerce: Cindy Marshall
VP Custom Publishing & Mktg Svcs: Jaci Ponzoni
Mktg Res Mgr: Emily Wright
Dir HR: Gol Casper

Conducts Business: Worldwide
Primary Market Served: Business &
Consumer

Publish In Flight magazine & trade
publication.

PALADIN PRESS

Subs. of Paladin Enterprises Inc
7077 Winchester Cir, Gunbarrel Tech
Center
Boulder, CO 80301-3505
Telephone: (303) 443-7250, (800) 392-
2400, FAX: (303) 442-8741, E-Mail:
service@paladin-press.com, Web
Site: www.paladin-press.com
Pres & Publr: Peder C. Lund
Ed Dir: Jon Ford
Sls Dir: Wendy Mannatt
Conducts Business: Worldwide
Employees: 25
Primary Market Served: Business &
Consumer
Catalog available online
Direct online sales
Direct Marketing ad budget: $100,000
Direct Mail: 20%
Magazines: 80%
Founded: 1970

Mail order publisher specializing in
books & videos on survival, self-
defense, martial arts, weaponry & military & police science. Market is primarily men, 21 to 50 years.

PANOPTIC ENTERPRISES

PO Box 11220
Burke, VA 22009-1220
Telephone: (703) 451-5953, (800) 594-
4766, FAX: (703) 451-5953, E-Mail:
panoptic@fedgovcontracts.com, Web
Site: www.fedgovcontracts.com
Pres: Vivina McVay
VP: Barry McVay
Conducts Business: U.S.
Employees: 2
Primary Market Served: Business &
Consumer
Catalog available online
Indirect online sales
Advertising/Marketing Budget Related
to Direct Marketing: 51-75%
Direct Marketing ad budget: $15,000
Direct Mail: 94%
Magazines: 2%
Newspapers: 2%
Online: 2%
Founded: 1982
Gross sales or billing: $45,000

Books, pamphlets, seminars on how to
win federal contracts. Sold nationwide
to businesses of all sizes plus individuals interested in starting a business or
working in this field.

PARA PUBLISHING

PO Box 8206
Santa Barbara, CA 93118-8206
Telephone: (805) 968-7277, (800)
PARAPUB, FAX: (805) 986-1379,
E-Mail: danpoynter@parapublishing.
com, Web Site: www.parapublishing.
com
Publr: Dan Poynter
Office Mgr: Becky Carbone
Conducts Business: Worldwide
Employees: 6
Primary Market Served: Business &
Consumer
Catalog available online
Direct online sales
Advertising/Marketing Budget Related
to Direct Marketing: 26-50%
Founded: 1969

Books & information for writers &
publishers.

PARLAY INTERNATIONAL

712 Bancroft Rd (#505)
Walnut Creek, CA 94598
Telephone: (510) 601-1000, FAX:
(510) 601-1008, E-Mail: info@
parlay.com, Web Site: www.parlay.
com
Pres & CEO: Robert Lester
Employees: 2
Primary Market Served: Business
Catalog available online
Direct online sales
Founded: 1987

PARTMINER

Div. of IHS Information Handling Ser-
vices
7807 E Peakview Ave (Suite 400)
Centennial, CO 80111-6849
Telephone: (303) 200-5500, FAX:
(303) 754-3940, Web Site: www.
partminer.com
CEO: Chris Meyer
Chmn: Jerre L. Stead
CFO: Mike Arena
Pres Partminer Direct: Dan Murphy
Sr VP & CIO: H. Hohn Oechsle
Conducts Business: Worldwide
Employees: 100
Primary Market Served: Business &
Consumer
Catalog available online
Direct online sales
Advertising/Marketing Budget Related
to Direct Marketing: 51-75%
Founded: 1956

Database publisher of electronics components & plastic materials
information.

PASTIME PUBLICATIONS INC

Div. of Pastime Company
99 Kalamath St
Denver, CO 80223-1549
Telephone: (303) 534-7867, (888) 650-
8665, FAX: (630) 214-7600, E-Mail:
post@pastimecompany.com, Web
Site: www.pastimecompany.com
Pres: Carl A. Nelson
Opers: Mike Draper
Conducts Business: Worldwide
Employees: 20
Primary Market Served: Business &
Consumer
Catalog available online
Indirect online sales
Direct Marketing ad budget:
Direct Mail: 50%
Telephone: 50%
Founded: 1990
Gross sales or billing: $250,000

PATH TO PURCHASE INSTITUTE

7400 Skokie Blvd
Skokie, IL 60077-3339
Telephone: (847) 675-7400, Web Site:
www.p2pi.org
Mktg Analyst: Meggie Smolen
Primary Market Served: Business &
Consumer

PATIENT NEWS

3909 Witmer Rd (#1080)
Niagara Falls, NY 14305-1239
Telephone: (705) 457-4030, (800) 667-
0268, FAX: (705) 457-4067, E-Mail:
jbishop@patientnews.com, Web Site:
www.patientnews.com
VP, Sls & Mktg: Joanne Bishop
Employees: 50
Primary Market Served: Business &
Consumer
Founded: 1993

PEARSON EDUCATION

Div. of Pearson plc
One Lake St
Upper Saddle River, NJ 07458-1813
Telephone: (201) 236-7000, FAX:
(201) 236-3290, E-Mail:
communications@pearsoned.com,
Web Site: www.pearsoned.com
CEO: Dame Marjorie M. Scardino
Exec VP, Pres & CEO, School
Companies: Steven A. Dowling
Exec VP, COO & CFO: George
Werner
Sr VP & CTO, Pres Pearson Educ:
Douglas G. Kubach
Sr VP Communs: Wendy Spiegel
Mktg: Jodie Bassett
Conducts Business: Worldwide
Employees: 19,186
Primary Market Served: Business
Catalog available online
Direct online sales
Advertising/Marketing Budget Related

to Direct Marketing: 0-25%
Founded: 1998
Gross sales or billing: $5,073,700,000

Publisher of textbooks, workbooks & other materials for K-12 elementary schools, higher education & professional markets. Also operates assessment & skill development divisions.

PENGUIN GROUP USA INC

Div. of Pearson Education
405 Murray Hill Pkwy
East Rutherford, NJ 07073-2136
Telephone: (201) 909-6200, FAX: (201) 236-3381, Web Site: penguingroup.com
Pres: Sally Wood
Dir, List Rental Sls: Barbara P. Semco
Bus & Fin Mktg Dir: Judy Weiss-Brown
Educ Mktg Mgr: Carol Demont
Health & Self-Improvement Mktg Mgr: John Sabine
Card Deck Sls & Adv Mgr: George Sala
Conducts Business: U.S., Canada
Employees: 200
Primary Market Served: Business & Consumer
Catalog available online
Direct online sales
Advertising/Marketing Budget Related to Direct Marketing: 76-100%
Direct Marketing ad budget: $15,000,000
Direct Mail: 95%
Magazines: 4%
Telephone: 1%

Book publisher specializing in books for business professionals, teachers & consumers. Book sales are made by direct mail.

PENGUIN PUBLISHING GROUP

Subs. of Pearson
375 Hudson St Bsmt 3
New York, NY 10014-7465
Telephone: (212) 366-2000, FAX: (212) 366-2952, Web Site: www. penguinputnam.com
CEO: Phyllis Grann
Sr VP, Sls & Mktg: Richard Heffernan
Sr VP, Spec Mkts: Barbara O'Shea
Conducts Business: U.S.
Primary Market Served: Business & Consumer

Publisher of general interest fiction & non-fiction books including adult & juvenile titles. Conduct direct mail campaigns for selected non-fiction. Health, diet, reference, cooking & children's books are successful categories.

PENGUIN PUTNAM INC

375 Hudson St
New York, NY 10014-3672
Telephone: (212) 366-2000, FAX: (212) 366-2278, Web Site: www. penguinputnam.com
Mktg Dir: John Fagan
Conducts Business: U.S.
Primary Market Served: Business & Consumer

Publisher of quality adult & children's hardcover & paperback books. Plus calendars, diaries, cassettes.

PENNSYLVANIA STATE UNIVERSITY PRESS

820 N University Dr (Suite C)
University Park, PA 16802-1012
Telephone: (814) 865-1327, (800) 326-9180, FAX: (814) 863-1408, Web Site: www.psupress.org
Editor in Chief: Patrick H. Alexander
Mng Editor: Cherene Howard
Exec Editor Art & Humanities: Eleanor Goodman
Mktg & Sls Mgr: Tony Sanfilippo
Production Coord: Patty Mitchell
Editorial Asst: Cali Buckley
Conducts Business: U.S., U.K., Canada
Employees: 26
Primary Market Served: Business & Consumer
Catalog available online
Direct online sales
Advertising/Marketing Budget Related to Direct Marketing: 26-50%
Direct Marketing ad budget: $205,980
Direct Mail: 45%
Magazines: 49%
Newspapers: 5%
TV/Radio: 1%
Founded: 1956
Gross sales or billing: $2,000,000

Scholarly books in the subject areas of history, art history, philosophy, political science, Pennsylvania history & regional interest.

PENNWELL PUBLISHING

1421 S Sheridan Rd
Tulsa, OK 74112
Telephone: (918) 835-3161, (800) 331-4463, E-Mail: headquarters@ pennwell.com, Web Site: www. pennwell.com
Pres & CEO: Brian Biochlini
Exec VP & CFO: Mark C. Wilmonth
VP: Jim Enos
VP, Digital Media: Tom Citorino
Circulation Mgr: Linda Thomas
Conducts Business: U.S., Canada, Europe, Asia
Employees: 10
Primary Market Served: Business
Catalog available online

Advertising/Marketing Budget Related to Direct Marketing: 51-75%
Direct Marketing ad budget: $500,000
Direct Mail: 75%
Magazines: 15%
TV/Radio: 5%
Telephone: 5%
Founded: 1910
Gross sales or billing: $5,000,000

Conferences, trade shows & exhibitions.

THE PENNYSAVER GROUP INC

1342 Charwood Rd
Hanover, MD 21076
Telephone: (410) 684-2600, FAX: (410) 684-2065, Web Site: www. mdpennysaver.com
Pres: Bernard Bradpiece
COO: Denny Guastaferro
Circ Dir: Wayne Johnson
Adv Dir: Dan Aquilino
Conducts Business: U.S.
Employees: 330
Primary Market Served: Business & Consumer
Catalog available online
Indirect online sales
Advertising/Marketing Budget Related to Direct Marketing: 76-100%
Direct Marketing ad budget:
Direct Mail: 100%
Founded: 1979

Saturation mailed shopper appearing weekly in over 1,284,300 households in MD & VA. Display advertising, inserts & circulars plus web press printing.

PENSIONS & INVESTMENTS

Div. of Crain Communication Inc
711 3rd Ave
New York, NY 10017-4014
Telephone: (212) 210-0100, FAX: (212) 210-0117, Web Site: www. pionline.com
Grp Publr: William T. Bisson
VP & Publr: Christopher Battaglia
Promo Dir: Michelle DeMarco
Adv Sls Dir: Richard Scanlon
Conducts Business: U.S., Canada, Europe
Employees: 50
Primary Market Served: Business
Advertising/Marketing Budget Related to Direct Marketing: 26-50%
Founded: 1973

Newspaper edited for financial executives in corporations, governments, banks, insurance companies & money management firms. Readers make investment, financing, real estate, employee benefits, leasing, brokerage & cash management decisions for their firms.

PERSONAL ACHIEVEMENT INSTITUTE

PO Box 6543, One Speaking Success Rd
Kingman, AZ 86402-6543
Telephone: (928) 753-7546, (800) 321-1225, FAX: (928) 753-7554, E-Mail: burt@burtdubin.com, Web Site: www.speakingbizsuccess.com
Pres: Burt Dubin
Conducts Business: Worldwide
Employees: 3
Primary Market Served: Business & Consumer
Catalog available online
Direct online sales
Advertising/Marketing Budget Related to Direct Marketing: 76-100%
Direct Marketing ad budget:
Online: 100%
Founded: 1978

Write & publish the Speaking Success System - a system for the mastery of the business skills & platform expertise a speaker needs.

PERSONNEL POLICY SERVICE INC

159 St Matthews Ave (Suite 5)
Louisville, KY 40207-3137
Telephone: (502) 899-5102, (800) 437-3735, FAX: (800) 755-7011, E-Mail: info@ppspublishers.com, Web Site: www.ppspublishers.com
Pres: John C. Norman Jr.
Conducts Business: U.S.
Primary Market Served: Business
Catalog available online
Direct online sales

Publisher of loose leaf services & newsletters. Mailing address: PO Box 7967, Louisville, KY 40257-0697.

PETERSON'S

Div. of Thomson Corp
2000 Lenox Dr
Lawrenceville, NJ 08648-2314
Telephone: (609) 896-1800, FAX: (609) 896-1811, E-Mail: custsvc@petersons.com, Web Site: www.petersons.com
Pres: Mary E. Gatsch
VP, Mktg: Michael H. Fleischner
Conducts Business: Worldwide
Employees: 200
Primary Market Served: Business & Consumer
Catalog available online
Direct online sales
Founded: 1966

Education publishing in the areas of college search and selection, test preparation, and financial aid online and in print.

PLAYBOY ENTERPRISES INC

9346 Civic Center Dr (#200)
Beverly Hills, CA 90210-3604
Telephone: (310) 860-1215, Web Site: www.playboyenterprises.com
Chmn & CEO: Christie Hefner
VP Corp Commun: Linda Marsicano
Sr VP Corp Commun & Investor Rels: Martha Linderman
Exec VP, Fin, Opers & CFO: Linda Havard
Exec VP: Richard S. Rosenzweig
Conducts Business: Worldwide
Employees: 643
Primary Market Served: Consumer
Gross sales or billing: $193,700,000

An international publishing & entertainment company that publishes Playboy magazine & related media, including newsstand specials & calendars; licenses 16 foreign editions of Playboy magazine; operates a direct marketing business including the Playboy & Critics' Choice Video catalogs; creates & distributes programming for domestic pay television, worldwide home video & international television; markets the Playboy trademarks on apparel, accessories & products for consumers around the world.

PNEUMA BOOKS

25 Hunter Ct
Elkton, MD 21921-1762
Telephone: (410) 441-8200, FAX: (410) 441-8201, E-Mail: gettingstarted@pneumabooks.com, Web Site: www.pneumabooks.com
Employees: 8
Primary Market Served: Business & Consumer
Advertising/Marketing Budget Related to Direct Marketing: 76-100%
Direct Marketing ad budget: $110,000
Direct Mail: $40,000
Magazines: $60,000
Telephone: $10,000
Founded: 1971
Gross sales or billing: $1,200,000

Publisher & wholesaler of financial, how-to & spare time or new career books & manuals. Interested parties should remit three dollars for complete information package, including catalogs, procedures, distributor forms, etc.

THE POHLY CO

253 Summer St Ste 303
Boston, MA 02210-1114
Telephone: (617) 451-1700, (800) 383-0888, FAX: (617) 338-7767, E-Mail: info@pohlyco.com, Web Site: www.pohlyco.com
Pres: Diana Pohly
Conducts Business: U.S.

Primary Market Served: Business & Consumer

Specializes in custom publishing, consulting, online content and creative services.

POKER PLAYER

Sub. of Gambling Times Inc
13701 Riverside Dr Ste 300
Sherman Oaks, CA 91423-2447
Telephone: (310) 674-3365, FAX: (310) 674-3205, E-Mail: ard@gamblingtimes.com, Web Site: www.gamblingtimes.com
Pres: Stanley R. Sludikoff
Mng Editor: A.R. Dyck
Editor: Lou Krieger
Conducts Business: Worldwide
Primary Market Served: Business & Consumer
Catalog available online
Indirect online sales
Founded: 1971
Gross sales or billing: $900,000

Magazines.

POWERS TELEVISION MARKETING

9731 Variel Ave
Chatsworth, CA 91311-4315
Telephone: (818) 700-1522, FAX: (818) 700-1527, E-Mail: mpowers@mpowers.com, Web Site: www.mpowers.com
Pres: Melvin Powers
Conducts Business: Worldwide
Employees: 21
Primary Market Served: Business & Consumer
Catalog available online
Direct online sales
Direct Marketing ad budget:
Direct Mail: 40%
Magazines: 25%
Newspapers: 10%
TV/Radio: 25%
Gross sales or billing: $4,000,000

Publisher of mail order books & seminars. Also act as television consultant.

PRAKKEN PUBLICATIONS INC

2851 Boardwalk St.
Ann Arbor, MI 48104
Telephone: (734) 975-2800, (800) 530-9673, FAX: (734) 975-2787, E-Mail: vanessa@techdirections.com, Web Site: www.eddigest.com; www.techdirections.com
Pres & Bus Mgr: Turalee Barlow
Mng Editor Education Digest Journal: Pamela Moore

Mng Editor Tech Directions Magazine: Suzanne Peckham
Circulation Mgr: Vanessa Revelli
Book & Adv Sls Mgr: Matt Knope
Adv Sls & Mktg Coord: Tonya White
Conducts Business: Worldwide
Employees: 6
Primary Market Served: Business & Consumer
Catalog available online
Direct online sales
Advertising/Marketing Budget Related to Direct Marketing: 51-75%
Direct Marketing ad budget: $50,000
Direct Mail: 20%
Magazines: 30%
Online: 50%
Founded: 1934
Gross sales or billing: $500,000

Publishers of The Education Digest, Tech Directions Magazine, Machinists' Ready Reference & other technology & career-technical education books, video, and CD-ROM.

PRECEPT PRESS

Div. of Bonus Books Inc
160 E Illinois St
Chicago, IL 60611-5426
Telephone: (312) 467-0580, FAX: (312) 467-9271, E-Mail: bb@bonusbooks.com, Web Site: www.bonusbooks.com
Pres: Aaron Cohodes
Conducts Business: U.S., Canada, Europe
Employees: 12
Primary Market Served: Business & Consumer
Catalog available online
Direct online sales
Advertising/Marketing Budget Related to Direct Marketing: 0-25%
Founded: 1970

Publisher of books, audio-visual materials for administrators & professionals in fundraising, education, business & clinical fields.

PRESS-ENTERPRISE CO

Div. of A H Belo Corp
3450 14th St
Riverside, CA 92501
Telephone: (951) 684-1200, FAX: (951) 368-9022, Web Site: www.pe.com
Publr & CEO: Ronald Redfern
Employees: 800
Primary Market Served: Business & Consumer
Advertising/Marketing Budget Related to Direct Marketing: 0-25%
Founded: 1878

Newspaper-Western Riverside County & South Central San Bernardino County, 162,551 daily & 170,748 circulation on Sundays.

THEODORE PRESSER CO

588 N Gulph Rd Ste B
King Of Prussia, PA 19406-2831
Telephone: (610) 592-1222, FAX: (610) 592-1229, E-Mail: webmaster@presser.com, Web Site: www.presser.com
Pres: Thomas Broido
VP: George Hotton
Controller: Don DiReso
Mktg Mgr: Dwight Munroe
Conducts Business: U.S., Canada, Mexico
Employees: 50
Primary Market Served: Business
Catalog available online
Direct online sales
Direct Marketing ad budget:
Direct Mail: 67%
Magazines: 33%
Founded: 1783

Music publishers, selling sheet music & music books to music dealers.

PRESTWICK HOUSE INC

PO Box 658
Clayton, DE 19938-0658
Telephone: (302) 659-2070, Web Site: www.prestwickhouse.com
Gen Mgr: Keith Bergstrom
Primary Market Served: Business & Consumer

PRIME MEDIA EQUINE GROUP

656 Quince Orchard Rd
Gaithersburg, MD 20878
Telephone: (301) 977-3900, FAX: (301) 990-9015, Web Site: www.equisearch.com
Pres & CEO: Dean Nelson
Exec VP & Publr: Susan Harding
Sr VP: Steve Parr
Sr VP & CFO: Kevin Neary
Conducts Business: U.S., Canada, Europe
Primary Market Served: Business & Consumer
Catalog available online
Indirect online sales

Publisher of Equus, Practical Horseman, Dressage Today, Horse & Rider & The Arabian Horse.

PRINCETON BOOK CO PUBLISHERS

dba Princeton Book Company-Dance Horizons
614 Rte 130

Hightstown, NJ 08520-2651
Telephone: (609) 426-0602, (800) 220-7149, FAX: (609) 426-1344, E-Mail: pbc@dancehorizons.com, Web Site: www.dancehorizons.com
Pres: Charles H. Woodford
Internet Coord: John McMenamin
Customer Svc: Marcia Sylvester
Conducts Business: Worldwide
Employees: 7
Primary Market Served: Business & Consumer
Catalog available online
Direct online sales
Advertising/Marketing Budget Related to Direct Marketing: 76-100%
Direct Marketing ad budget:
Direct Mail: 25%
Online: 75%
Founded: 1975
Gross sales or billing: $1,000,000

Dance books, videos, DVDs, and non-fiction books.

PRITCHETT & HULL ASSOCIATES INC

3440 Oakcliff Rd NE (Suite 110)
Atlanta, GA 30340-3079
Telephone: (770) 451-0602, (800) 241-4925, FAX: (770) 454-7130, E-Mail: sales@p-h.com, Web Site: www.p-h.com
CEO: Betty Westmoreland
COO: Cecily Shull
Conducts Business: U.S., Canada
Employees: 11
Primary Market Served: Business & Consumer
Catalog available online
Advertising/Marketing Budget Related to Direct Marketing: 51-75%
Founded: 1973

Publisher of patient education materials for hospitals & medical offices.

PRIVACY JOURNAL

PO Box 28577
Providence, RI 02908-0577
Telephone: (401) 274-7861, FAX: (401) 274-4747, E-Mail: orders@privacyjournal.net, Web Site: www.privacyjournal.net
Publr: Robert Ellis Smith
Asst to Publr: Lee Shoreham
Conducts Business: USA
Employees: 3
Primary Market Served: Business & Consumer
Catalog available online
Direct online sales
Founded: 1974
Gross sales or billing: $500,000

Monthly newsletter on credit reports, mailing lists, telemarketing, wiretaps, Internet & other privacy issues.
Subscription: $125/year.

PRO CD INC

Div. of Info USA Inc
5711 S 86th Cir
Omaha, NE 68127
Telephone: (800) 992-3766, FAX:
(402) 750-0020
VP: Bruce Lowry
Mktg Acct Exec: Melissa Powers
Primary Market Served: Business &
Consumer
Catalog available online
Direct online sales
Advertising/Marketing Budget Related
to Direct Marketing: 76-100%
Direct Marketing ad budget:
Direct Mail: 95%
Telephone: 5%

Provider of every published telephone
listing on CD-ROM for consumers,
retailers & corporate networks.

PROFESSIONAL PHOTOGRAPHER MAGAZINE

Subs. of Professional Photographers of
America
229 Peachtree St NE (Suite 2200), In-
ternational Tower
Atlanta, GA 30303-1608
Telephone: (404) 522-8600, (800) 786-
6277, FAX: (404) 614-6405, E-Mail:
csc@ppa.com, Web Site: www.ppa.
com
CEO: David Trust
Commun Mgr: Amy Walkes
Adv Mgr: Danielle Chavannes
Sr Mgr Pubns: Kris Delaney
Conducts Business: U.S., Canada
Employees: 50
Primary Market Served: Business &
Consumer
Direct online sales
Advertising/Marketing Budget Related
to Direct Marketing: 26-50%
Direct Marketing ad budget:
Direct Mail: 90%
Magazines: 10%

Monthly magazine for photographers.

PROFESSIONAL TRAINING ASSOCIATES INC

46 S Linden St (Suite C)
Duquesne, PA 15110-1091
Telephone: (412) 460-0266, FAX:
(412) 460-0269, E-Mail: info@
ptainc.com, Web Site: www.ptainc.
com
Chmn & Pres: Greg Ashman
Dir VP Trng: John Curcio
VP: William Tomlinson
Conducts Business: U.S., Canada
Employees: 4
Primary Market Served: Business
Catalog available online
Indirect online sales

Advertising/Marketing Budget Related
to Direct Marketing: 76-100%

Environmental & safety training &
customized course development for
industrial, commercial, manufacturing,
construction, consulting, government
and education sectors. Courses include
Asbestos, Lead-Based Paint,
HAZWOPER, Confined Space Entry
and Construction Safety Outreach.

PROGRESSIVE BUSINESS PUBLICATIONS

Div. of American Future Systems Inc
370 Technology Dr
Malvern, PA 19355-1315
Telephone: (610) 695-8600, (800) 220-
5000, FAX: (610) 647-8089, E-Mail:
customer_service@pbp.com, Web
Site: www.pbp.com
Pres: Ed Satell
DM Dir: Al Phillips
Conducts Business: Worldwide
Primary Market Served: Business
Advertising/Marketing Budget Related
to Direct Marketing: 76-100%
Direct Marketing ad budget:
Direct Mail: 25%
Telephone: 75%

Publisher of subscription newsletters &
posters for business.

PROMO MAGAZINE

Div. of Penton Business Media Inc
249 W 17th St (3rd fl)
New York, NY 10011
Telephone: (203) 358-9900, (800) 927-
5007, FAX: (203) 358-5816, E-Mail:
larry.jaffee@penton.com, Web Site:
www.promomagazine.com
Editor in Chief: Larry Jaffee
Group Publr: Leslie Bacon
Exec Editor: Patricia Odell
Primary Market Served: Business
Founded: 1987

Promotional marketing magazine.

THE PSYCHOLOGICAL CORP

Subs. of Harcourt Inc
Harcourt Educational Measurement
19500 Bulverde Rd
San Antonio, TX 78259
Telephone: (800) 211-8378, FAX:
(800) 232-1223, Web Site: www.
psychcorp.com
Pres & CEO: Michael Hansen
Pres, The Psychological Corp: Aurelio
Prifitera
SVP: Jean Shiunko
VP: Scott Barnes
VP: Jim Hill
Catalog available online
Indirect online sales

Publishing company.

PUBLICATIONS INTERNATIONAL LTD

7373 N Cicero Ave
Lincolnwood, IL 60712-1613
Telephone: (847) 745-9299, (800) 595-
8484, FAX: (847) 676-3671, Web
Site: www.pubint.com
VP, Special Markets: Jerry Kurtzweil
VP, Intl Division: Earl Brosnahan
Dir Acq: Jennifer Goldstein
Children's Publr: Ann Taylor
Co-editions & Special Sls Mgr: Grant
Sargent
Conducts Business: U.S.
Employees: 210
Primary Market Served: Consumer
Catalog available online
Indirect online sales
Advertising/Marketing Budget Related
to Direct Marketing: 26-50%
Founded: 1967
Gross sales or billing: $45,600,000

Consumer based publisher specializing
in the areas of cookbooks, children's,
health, automobile, sports, crafts, lifestyle & consumer information.

QUAYSIDE PUBLISHING GROUP/MBI PUBLISHING

Div. of MBI Publishing/Chronicle Pub-
lishing Co
400 1st Ave N (Suite 300)
Minneapolis, MN 55401-1721
Telephone: (715) 294-3345, (800) 826-
6600, FAX: (715) 294-4448, Web
Site: www.motorbooks.com
Pres: Tim Parker
Conducts Business: Worldwide
Employees: 70
Primary Market Served: Consumer

Publisher & distributor of automotive,
military, aviation & hobby books.

QUEUE INC

80 Hathaway Dr
Stratford, CT 06615-7304
Telephone: (203) 335-0906, (800) 232-
2224, FAX: (800) 775-2729, E-Mail:
jdk@queueinc.com, Web Site: www.
qworkbooks.com
CEO: Jonathan Kantrowitz
Controller: Peter Uhrynowski
Conducts Business: U.S., Canada, Far
& Near East, Europe, Australia
Employees: 30
Primary Market Served: Business &
Consumer
Catalog available online
Direct online sales
Advertising/Marketing Budget Related
to Direct Marketing: 76-100%
Founded: 1980
Gross sales or billing: $4,000,000

Publish educational software & CD-
ROM.

RANDOM HOUSE DIRECT MARKETING

Div. of Random House
1745 Broadway
New York, NY 10019-4305
Telephone: (212) 572-4985, (800) 678-5681, FAX: (212) 572-6018, Web Site: www.randomhousedirect.com
Dir Mktg: Tom Downing
VP & Gen Mgr: Lisa Faith Phillips
Sr Mktg Mgr: Lyn Hastings
Conducts Business: U.S.
Primary Market Served: Consumer
Catalog available online
Direct online sales
Advertising/Marketing Budget Related to Direct Marketing: 76-100%
Direct Marketing ad budget: $5,000,000
Direct Mail: 100%

Responsible for direct mailings of select Random House titles & development of Conde Nast direct mail book products.

RANDOM LENGTHS PUBLICATIONS INC

450 Country Club Rd (#240)
Eugene, OR 97401-6078
Telephone: (541) 686-9925, (888) 686-9925, FAX: (541) 686-9629, (800) 874-7979, E-Mail: rlmail@rlpi.com, Web Site: www.randomlengths.com
Publr: Jon Anderson
Mktg Dir: Nancy West
Conducts Business: Worldwide
Primary Market Served: Business
Catalog available online
Direct online sales
Advertising/Marketing Budget Related to Direct Marketing: 76-100%
Direct Marketing ad budget:
Direct Mail: 100%
Founded: 1958

Newsletters, directory to wood products & related industries.

THE READER'S DIGEST ASSOCIATION INC

750 3rd Ave
New York, NY 10017-2703
Telephone: (914) 238-3599, FAX: (914) 244-7689, Web Site: www.rd.com
Pres: Dawn Zier
Conducts Business: Worldwide
Employees: 1,800
Primary Market Served: Consumer
Gross sales or billing: $2,000,000,000

Global publisher & direct mail marketer of magazines, books & home entertainment products.

REDBOOK MAGAZINE

Div. of Hearst Corp
300 W 57th St
New York, NY 10019
Telephone: (212) 649-2000, (800) 888-0008, FAX: (212) 581-7605, Web Site: www.redbookmag.com
Exec Editor: Alison Brower
Creative Dir: Michael Picon
Mng Editor: Kim Cheney
Deputy Editor: Melanie Mannarino
Special Proj Dir: Lori Berger
Conducts Business: Worldwide
Primary Market Served: Consumer

Mail order section "Shopping with Redbook" (incorporates travel, school, camps, crafts & gardens) carries direct response advertising. "Catalogue Review" is published once a year in August for catalog advertising.

REDLEAF PRESS

Div. of Think Small
10 Yorkton Ct
Saint Paul, MN 55117-1065
Telephone: (651) 641-6621, (800) 423-8309, FAX: (800) 641-0115, E-Mail: jvoltz@redleafpress.org, Web Site: www.redleafpress.org
Publr: Linda Hein
Editor-in-Chief: David Heath
Mktg Mgr: Joanne Voltz
Sls Mgr: Inga Weberg
Opers Mgr: Paul Bloomer
Conducts Business: U.S.
Employees: 25
Primary Market Served: Business
Catalog available online
Direct online sales
Direct Marketing ad budget:
Direct Mail: 60%
Online: 35%
Telephone: 5%
Founded: 1976

Resources for early childhood education specifically books. Sell to early childhood professionals, organizations, schools, libraries, corporations, military & individuals.

REED - ELSEVIER

Lexis Nexis
125 Park Ave Fl 22
New York, NY 10017-8503
Telephone: (212) 309-5498, FAX: (212) 309-5480, Web Site: www.reed-elsevier.com
CEO: Gerard Van de Aast
Conducts Business: Worldwide
Employees: 2,000
Primary Market Served: Business & Consumer

Book publishing & packaging firm.

REGNERY PUBLISHING

Div. of Eagle Publishing
1 Massachusetts Ave NW
Washington, DC 20001-1401
Telephone: (202) 216-0600, FAX: (202) 216-0612, Web Site: www.regnery.com
Pres & Publr: Marji Ross
Mktg & Publicity: Patricia Jackson
Conducts Business: U.S.
Employees: 100
Primary Market Served: Consumer
Catalog available online
Direct online sales
Advertising/Marketing Budget Related to Direct Marketing: 76-100%
Direct Marketing ad budget:
Direct Mail: 100%
Founded: 1947
Gross sales or billing: $9,100,000

Book publishers.

REIMAN PUBLICATIONS

5400 S 60th St
Greendale, WI 53129
Telephone: (414) 423-0100, (800) 344-6913, FAX: (414) 423-3840, Web Site: www.reimanpub.com
Chmn: Roy Reiman
Pres: Russel Denson
Sr VP, Catalog & Tour Mktg: Phil Minix
Sr Circulation Bus Analyst: Kevin Nangle
VP: Heidi Reuter Loyd
Conducts Business: U.S., Canada
Employees: 525
Primary Market Served: Consumer
Catalog available online
Direct online sales
Advertising/Marketing Budget Related to Direct Marketing: 76-100%
Direct Marketing ad budget:
Direct Mail: 100%
Founded: 1965
Gross sales or billing: $56,100,000

Publisher of Country, Country EXTRA, Country Woman, Country Discoveries, Crafting Traditions, Birds & Blooms, Farm & Ranch Living, Reminisce, Reminisce EXTRA, Taste of Home & Quick Cooking & Country Store (catalog).

REMEDY MAGAZINE

Div of MediZine Healthy Living
500 Fifth Ave (Suite 1900)
New York, NY 10110
Telephone: (212) 695-2223, FAX: (212) 695-2936, E-Mail: info@rmedizine.com, Web Site: www.medizine.com
Chief Revenue Officer: Suzanne Polizzi
Pres & CEO: Traver Hutchins

Assoc Mktg Mgr: Jenna Chessari
Employees: 100
Primary Market Served: Consumer
Catalog available online
Advertising/Marketing Budget Related
   to Direct Marketing: 0-25%
Founded: 1992
Gross sales or billing: $10,000,000

REMILON LLC
100 View St Ste 202
Mountain View, CA 94041-1374
Telephone: (650) 425-7511, Web Site:
   www.remilon.com
Co-CEO: Adrian Ridner

RENO GAZETTE JOURNAL
Div. of Gannett Corp
955 Kuenzli St
Reno, NV 89520
Telephone: (775) 788-6200, FAX:
   (775) 788-6563
Publr: Sue Clark Johnson
Community Mktg Mgr: Robert Boisson
Asst to Publr: Kim Foster
Primary Market Served: Business &
   Consumer

Advertising (newspaper). Sell advertising space & newspaper distributor.

RESOURCE PUBLICATIONS INC
160 E Virginia St (Suite 290)
San Jose, CA 95112-5876
Telephone: (408) 286-8505, (888) 273-
   7782, FAX: (408) 287-8748, E-Mail:
   info@rpinet.com, Web Site: www.
   rpinet.com
Pres: William Burns
Admin Mktg: Caroline Thomas
Conducts Business: U.S.
Employees: 8
Primary Market Served: Business &
   Consumer
Catalog available online
Indirect online sales
Advertising/Marketing Budget Related
   to Direct Marketing: 51-75%
Direct Marketing ad budget:
Direct Mail: 5%
Magazines: 10%
Online: 55%
Telephone: 30%
Founded: 1973
Gross sales or billing: $800,000

Books, periodicals, software, music
services, videos & custom book
packaging.

RIZZOLI INTERNATIONAL PUBLICATIONS INC
dba Universe Publishing Div
300 Park Ave S (3rd fl)
New York, NY 10010

Telephone: (212) 387-3400, FAX:
   (212) 387-3535
Pres: Marco Ausenda
Publr & VP: Charles Miers
Conducts Business: U.S.
Employees: 50
Primary Market Served: Business
Founded: 1975
Gross sales or billing: $7,700,000

Publisher of art, architecture, photography, gardening, fashion, design, lifestyle, music & culinary books.

THE ROBLIN GROUP INC
405 Tarrytown Rd (Suite 1545)
White Plains, NY 10607
Telephone: (914) 686-7221, FAX:
   (914) 372-1028, E-Mail:
   freethingsusa@yahoo.com, Web Site:
   www.freethingsusa.com
Pres: Robert Kalian
VP: Linda Kalian
Mktg Mgr: Dennis Kalian
Conducts Business: U.S.
Employees: 7
Primary Market Served: Business &
   Consumer
Catalog available online
Direct online sales
Advertising/Marketing Budget Related
   to Direct Marketing: 76-100%
Direct Marketing ad budget:
Direct Mail: 80%
Magazines: 20%
Founded: 1980

Direct marketing of books & reports to
business & consumers. Publishes non-
fiction paperback books to general
public via direct marketing & through
dealers.

RODALE INC
33 E Minor St
Emmaus, PA 18098-0001
Telephone: (610) 967-5171, FAX:
   (610) 967-8963, Web Site: www.
   rodale.com
Chmn: Ardath Rodale
Pres, Magazine Div: Steven Murphy
Asst to Mktg Res & Books Div Mgr:
   Julie White
CMO & Pres of Integrated Mktg &
   Sls: Gregg Michaelson
Conducts Business: U.S., Canada, Eu-
   rope
Employees: 1,000
Primary Market Served: Business &
   Consumer
Gross sales or billing: $200,000,000

Publisher of Prevention, Organic Gardening, Bicycling, New Woman, Runner's World, Backpacker, Mountain
Bike, Men's Health Magazine, American Woodworker, Men's Confidential
Newsletter & other newsletters. Also
consumer books on health, nutrition,
exercise, gardening & bicycling.

ROGERS PUBLISHING LTD
333 Blour St E (6th fl)
Toronto, ON, Canada M4W 1G9
Telephone: (416) 935-7777, FAX:
   (416) 935-3597, Web Site: www.
   rogerspublishing.ca
Pres & CEO: Brian Segal
Sr VP Circulation & Devel: Michael J.
   Fox
VP, Consumer Mktg: Tracey McKinley
VP Bus Plng: Immee Chee Wah
Conducts Business: Canada
Primary Market Served: Business &
   Consumer
Founded: 1887
Gross sales or billing: $1,200,000,000

Publisher of Canadian consumer
magazines. Also, offer subscriber lists
for rental.

ROUND LAKE PUBLISHING CO
23 Chestnut Hill Rd
Trumbull, CT 06611
Telephone: (203) 459-8484, Web Site:
   www.letterworks.com
Pres: Henry J. Lefcort
Conducts Business: U.S., Far East
Primary Market Served: Business &
   Consumer
Catalog available online
Direct online sales
Founded: 1987

Publisher & marketer of business
books & business software.

SNL FINANCIAL
One SNL Plaza, PO Box 2124
Charlottesville, VA 22902
Telephone: (434) 977-1600, FAX:
   (434) 977-4466, E-Mail: support@
   sni.com, Web Site: www.snl.com
Pres: Mike Chinn
Conducts Business: U.S.
Primary Market Served: Business
Catalog available online
Indirect online sales

Researcher & publisher specializing in
financial services.

ᴛʜᴇ SRDS
ᴅᴍᴀ
Part of Kantar Media
1700 E Higgins Rd Ste 500
Des Plaines, IL 60018-5610

Telephone: (800) 851-7737, FAX:
(847) 375-5001, Web Site: www.
srds.com
VP, Publr: Joseph Hayes
VP Client Sales & Svc: Trish Delauner
Dir: Lindsay H Morrison
Dir Mktg Res: Joe Hardin
Conducts Business: Worldwide
Employees: 200
Primary Market Served: Business
Catalog available online
Indirect online sales
Direct Marketing ad budget:
Direct Mail: 25%
Founded: 1919

Publisher of SRDS Direct Marketing
List Source and SRDS Direct Net List,
research services with information on
available mailing lists for rent or
purchase. Pinpoints the sources & de-
scribes more than 68,000 mailing lists.

ST MEDIA GROUP INTERNATIONAL
dba "Signs of the Times"; "Visual
Mdsg & Str Design"; "Big Picture"
& "Signs & Screen Printing"
11262 Cornell Park Dr
Cincinnati, OH 45242-1812
Telephone: (513) 421-2050, (800) 925-
1110, FAX: (513) 421-5144, E-Mail:
customer@stmediagroup.com, Web
Site: www.signweb.com
Pres & CEO: Tedd Swormstedt
CFO: Brian Foos
Publr Signs of Times: Wade Swormst-
edt
Grp Publr: Steve Duccilli
Conducts Business: Worldwide
Employees: 45
Primary Market Served: Business
Catalog available online
Direct online sales
Advertising/Marketing Budget Related
to Direct Marketing: 0-25%
Founded: 1906
Gross sales or billing: $10,100,000

A global provider of trade information
across multiple media divisions: "ST
Publications", "ST Events", "ST Online", "ST Books".

THE SAILING CO
Subs. of Miller Sports Group Publish-
ing
PO Box 420235
Palm Coast, FL 32142-0235
Telephone: (866) 436-2460, FAX:
(401) 848-5048, Web Site: www.
sailingworld.com
Publr: Sally Helm
Mktg Dir: George Brengle
Conducts Business: Worldwide
Employees: 60

Primary Market Served: Business &
Consumer

Magazine written for those who enjoy
cruising under sail.

ST LOUIS POST-DISPATCH
Owned by St. Louis Post-Dispatch
LLC
An affiliate of Pulitzer Inc
900 N Tucker Blvd
Saint Louis, MO 63101
Telephone: (314) 340-8000, (800) 365-
0820, FAX: (314) 340-3140, Web
Site: www.postnet.com
Pres & Publr: Terry Egger
VP & Gen Mgr: Matthew G. Kraner
VP & Dir HR: Kathy Joyce
VP Fin, Treas & Asst Sec: Robin
Spears
VP, Mktg: Terrie L. Robbins
VP, Circ: Larry T. Martin
VP, Adv: Thomas L. Rees
VP, Info Tech: Dan McGuire
Conducts Business: U.S.
Employees: 1,500
Primary Market Served: Business &
Consumer
Gross sales or billing: $26,100,000

Daily & Sunday newspaper.

SALES LEADS
601 Heritage Dr (Suite 111)
Jupiter, FL 33458-2777
Telephone: (866) 725-3753, FAX:
(866) 702-5558, E-Mail: info@
salesleadsinc.com, Web Site: www.
salesleadsinc.com
Pres: John B. Beecher
Co-Founder: La Verne Beecher
VP & Ed: Michael Beecher
Conducts Business: U.S., Canada
Employees: 3
Primary Market Served: Business
Catalog available online
Direct online sales
Advertising/Marketing Budget Related
to Direct Marketing: 76-100%
Direct Marketing ad budget: $30,000
Direct Mail: 90%
Telephone: 10%
Founded: 1959

Newsletter geared towards industrial
salespeople who wish to obtain qualified leads on industrial expansions
throughout the U.S. & Canada.

SAN FRANCISCO CHRONICLE
Subs. of Hearst Corp
901 Mission St
San Francisco, CA 94103

Telephone: (415) 777-1111, FAX:
(415) 536-5178, E-Mail:
amatthews@sfchronicle.com, Web
Site: www.sfgate.com
Exec VP & Editor: Philip Bronstein
Asst Mng Editor: Allen Matthews
Conducts Business: U.S.
Primary Market Served: Business &
Consumer
Advertising/Marketing Budget Related
to Direct Marketing: 0-25%

Publish two daily newspapers (one
morning, one evening) & one combined Sunday paper.

SAN JOSE MERCURY NEWS
Subs. of Knight-Ridder Inc
750 Ridder Park Dr
San Jose, CA 95190
Telephone: (408) 920-5000, FAX:
(408) 271-3690, Web Site: www.
bayarea.com
Publr & Chmn: Jay Harris
VP, Mktg: Kathleen Slattery
Exec Ed: David Yarnold
Employees: 1,530
Primary Market Served: Business &
Consumer
Direct online sales
Advertising/Marketing Budget Related
to Direct Marketing: 0-25%
Founded: 1851

Newspaper.

THE DMA SCHOLASTIC INC
557 Broadway
New York, NY 10012-3919
Telephone: (212) 343-6100, (800)
SCHOLASTIC, FAX: (212) 343-
6484, Web Site: www.scholastic.
com/
Chmn, Pres & CEO: Richard Robinson
Exec VP, CFO & CAO: Maureen
O'Connell
Pres, Trade Publ: Ellie Berger
Exec VP & Pres Scholastic Media:
Deborah A Forte
Exec VP & Pres Scholastic Education:
Margery W Mayer
Exec VP, Gen Counsel & Sec: Andrew
S Hedden
Exec VP & Pres Book Clubs: Judith A
Newman
Exec VP: Hugh Roome
Pres, Scholastic Classroom & Library
Grp: Greg Worrell
Sr VP, HR & Employee Svcs: Cynthia
Augustine
VP, Corp Commun & Media Rels:
Kyle Good
Conducts Business: U.S., Canada,
U.K., Australia, New Zealand
Employees: 1,075
Primary Market Served: Business &
Consumer

Gross sales or billing: $206,000,000

Market educational periodicals, paperback & hard cover books, software & textbooks primarily to the educational market. Also market through wholesale, retail, public library & to selected at-home consumer markets. Publish Home Office Computing magazine.

SCHOOL ANNUAL PUBLISHING CO

2568 Park Center Blvd
State College, PA 16801-3005
Telephone: (800) 436-6030, E-Mail: yearbook@schoolannual.com, Web Site: www.schoolannual.com
COO & VP: Nancy Stone
Customer Svc Supvr: Brenda Pollock
Sls Rep: Bernard Kalt
Sls Rep: Tonya Daher
Conducts Business: Worldwide
Primary Market Served: Business & Consumer
Catalog available online
Indirect online sales
Advertising/Marketing Budget Related to Direct Marketing: 76-100%
Founded: 1953

Publisher of yearbooks, church directories, calendars, and agenda planners.

SCHOOLWISE PRESS

385 Ashton Ave (Suite 200)
San Francisco, CA 94112
Telephone: (415) 337-7971, (800) 247-8443 x 202, FAX: (415) 337-1146, E-Mail: info@schoolwisepress.com, Web Site: www.schoolwisepress.com
Pres & Editor: Steve Rees
Tech Dir: Greg Smith
Prod Mgr: Robert Ross
Mktg Dir: Alison Nakashima
Sr Project Mgr: Lee Smith Seiden
Conducts Business: U.S.
Primary Market Served: Business & Consumer

Publishers of books & information services about schools.

SCOTT PUBLICATIONS, INC

2145 W Sherman Blvd
Muskegon, MI 49441-3434
Telephone: (248) 477-6650, (800) 458-8237, FAX: (248) 477-6795, E-Mail: contactus@scottpublications.com, Web Site: www.scottpublications.com
Pres: Robert H. Keessen

SCRIPPS NETWORKS

9721 Sherrill Blvd
Knoxville, TN 37932-3330
Telephone: (865) 560-2700, Web Site: scrippsnetworks.com

SEATTLE MAGAZINE

Subs. of Tiger Oak Publications
1518 1st Ave S (Suite 500)
Seattle, WA 98134-1456
Telephone: (206) 284-1750, (800) 637-0334, FAX: (206) 284-2550, E-Mail: customerservice@seattlemag.com, Web Site: www.seattlemag.com
Publr: R. Craig Bednar
Editorial Dir: Rachel Hart
Promos, Sls Devel Dir: Jamie Peha
Promos Coord: Elizabeth Tveit
Conducts Business: U.S.
Employees: 75
Primary Market Served: Business & Consumer
Founded: 1966
Gross sales or billing: $7,000,000

Travel & lifestyle publication, published twelve times a year, for the greater northwest region. Provides service-oriented articles on travel, lodging, the outdoors, the environment, people, business & topical issues important to the region; on food & restaurants & home related subjects.

SECOND RENAISSANCE BOOKS

2121 Alton Pkwy (Suite 250)
Irvine, CA 92606-4926
Telephone: (860) 354-5448, (800) 729-6149, FAX: (860) 355-7161, Web Site: www.aynrandbookstore.com
Pres & CEO: Yaron Brook
Conducts Business: Worldwide
Employees: 6
Primary Market Served: Business & Consumer
Catalog available online
Direct online sales
Advertising/Marketing Budget Related to Direct Marketing: 76-100%
Direct Marketing ad budget: $100,000
Direct Mail: 100%
Founded: 1985
Gross sales or billing: $600,000

Books & taped lectures to individuals interested in ideas & principles of individualism, reason & freedom.

SELECT PRESS

40 Phillip Terr
Novato, CA 94945
Telephone: (415) 209-9838, E-Mail: selectpr@aol.com
Editor: Roderick Crandall
Conducts Business: Worldwide
Employees: 4
Primary Market Served: Business & Consumer
Direct Marketing ad budget:
Direct Mail: $50,000
Telephone: $10,000
Founded: 1986

Publish various publications for business. Divisions market to lawyers, academics & managers.

SERENITY

PO Box 168
Maria Stein, OH 45860-0168
Telephone: (419) 925-1215, (800) 869-1684, FAX: (419) 925-1216, E-Mail: serenity@bright.net, Web Site: www.serenitymusic.com
Pres & Owner: Jim Moeller
Conducts Business: U.S.
Employees: 9
Primary Market Served: Business & Consumer
Catalog available online
Direct online sales
Advertising/Marketing Budget Related to Direct Marketing: 26-50%
Direct Marketing ad budget: $100,000
Direct Mail: 50%
Magazines: 50%
Gross sales or billing: $500,000

Production & distribution of new age & classical music & books.

SEYBOLD PUBLICATIONS

Div. of The Joss Group, LLC
PO Box 682
Gilbertsville, PA 19525
Telephone: (610) 327-3958, (888) 544-7104, FAX: (888) 463-4814, E-Mail: molly@thejossgroup, Web Site: www.seyboldreports.com
Mktg Dir: Dorothy Engel
Conducts Business: Worldwide
Primary Market Served: Business
Catalog available online
Indirect online sales
Founded: 1971

Computer publications.

SHUTTERBUG

Div. of Primedia Enthusiast Group
1415 Chaffee Dr Ste 10
Titusville, FL 32780-7936
Telephone: (321) 269-3212, FAX: (321) 255-3146, Web Site: www.shutterbug.net
Publr: Ron Leach
Conducts Business: U.S.
Primary Market Served: Consumer
Catalog available online
Direct online sales
Advertising/Marketing Budget Related to Direct Marketing: 0-25%

Monthly photographic equipment magazine for advanced, amateur & professional photographers, featuring reviews, news & test reports.

SIMMONS-BOARDMAN PUBLISHING CORP

345 Hudson St Rm 1201
New York, NY 10014-7115
Telephone: (212) 620-7200, FAX:
   (212) 633-1165
Chmn, Pres & CEO: A.J. McGinnis Jr.
Publr & Banking: Russ Selover
Publr Rail Grp: Robert De Marco
Circ Dir: Thomas Leader
Controller: Allen Morrell
Conducts Business: Worldwide
Employees: 70
Primary Market Served: Business
Advertising/Marketing Budget Related
   to Direct Marketing: 26-50%
Direct Marketing ad budget:
Direct Mail: 47%
Telephone: 53%
Founded: 1910

Trade/business publications in the following markets: commercial banking;
railroads and rail transit; shipping
maritime; intermodal transportation;
rail track & maintenance. Railway
Educational Bureau & Book Division
in Omaha, NE. Conferences relating to
the maritime & rail industries.

SIMON & SCHUSTER INC

Subs. of Viacom Inc
1230 Ave of the Americas
New York, NY 10020
Telephone: (212) 698-7000, (800) 223-
   2348, Web Site: www.simonsays.
   com
Pres & CEO: Jonathan Newcomb
Conducts Business: U.S.
Primary Market Served: Consumer

Operate book clubs & continuity
programs. Sell direct to the consumer
through various direct response media.

SINGLE SCENE NEWS

1928 E Laguna Dr
Tempe, AZ 85282-5913
Telephone: (480) 945-6746, FAX:
   (480) 945-6746, E-Mail: publisher@
   azsinglescene.com, Web Site: www.
   azsinglescene.com
Publr: Janet Jacobsen
Publr: Jeff Jacobsen
Publr: Harlan Jacobsen
Conducts Business: U.S.
Employees: 2
Primary Market Served: Business &
   Consumer
Indirect online sales
Advertising/Marketing Budget Related
   to Direct Marketing: 0-25%
Direct Marketing ad budget:
Direct Mail: 40%
Newspapers: 60%
Founded: 1972

Monthly service newspaper of news,
advice & events for single adults.

SKYDIVING MAGAZINE

Subs. of AeroGraphics
1725 N Lexington Ave
DeLand, FL 32724
Telephone: (386) 736-4793, FAX:
   (386) 736-9786, E-Mail: admin@
   skydivingmagazine.com, Web Site:
   www.skydivingmagazine.com
Owner & Publr: Michael Truffer
Editor: Sue Clifton
Subscriptions Adv Books & Videos:
   Sandy Bobo
Conducts Business: Worldwide
Employees: 5
Primary Market Served: Business &
   Consumer
Catalog available online
Direct online sales
Advertising/Marketing Budget Related
   to Direct Marketing: 26-50%
Founded: 1979

Monthly magazine with paid circulation of over 14,000 sport parachutists
around the world.

SMART PRACTICE

Div. of Smart Health
3400 E McDowell Rd
Phoenix, AZ 85008-7899
Telephone: (800) 522-0800, FAX:
   (800) 522-8329, E-Mail: info@
   smartpractice.com, Web Site: www.
   smartpractice.com
Pres & CEO: Dr. Curt Hamann
Co-Founder: Naomi Rhode
VP: Beth Hamann
VP Mktg & Sls: Scott Maloney
Conducts Business: Worldwide
Employees: 340
Primary Market Served: Business
Catalog available online
Direct online sales
Direct Marketing ad budget:
Direct Mail: $1,500,000
Gross sales or billing: $100,000,000

Dental & medical supplies plus practice promotional products to medical
professionals, veterinarians & real estate professionals.

THE DMA SMITHSONIAN ENTERPRISES

Smithsonian Institution
420 Lexington Ave
New York, NY 10170-0002
Telephone: (212) 916-1300, (800) 766-
   2149, FAX: (212) 490-0058, E-Mail:
   email@simag.si.edu, Web Site:
   www.smithsonianmag.com
Consumer Mktg Dir: Lisa Dunham
Adv Dir: Tom Huber
Mktg Dir: Diane Lowman
List Mgr: Suzanne Eng

Conducts Business: U.S.
Employees: 100
Primary Market Served: Consumer
Catalog available online
Direct online sales
Advertising/Marketing Budget Related
   to Direct Marketing: 51-75%
Direct Marketing ad budget:
Direct Mail: 100%
Founded: 1981

Publish monthly magazine. Articles
cover science, history, fine & folk art,
& the environment. Membership in
Smithsonian National Associates includes magazine subscription. Use direct mail to promote to literate
audience.

SOURCEBOOKS INC

1935 Brookdale Rd (Suite 139)
Naperville, IL 60563-7994
Telephone: (630) 961-3900, Web Site:
   www.sourcebooks.com
Publisher & CEO: Dominique Raccah

SOUTH-WESTERN PUBLISHING

Subs. of The Thomson Corp
5191 Natorp Blvd
Madison, OH 45040
Telephone: (513) 299-1000, FAX:
   (513) 527-6992
Pres: Bob Lynch
Conducts Business: Worldwide
Employees: 700
Primary Market Served: Business
Advertising/Marketing Budget Related
   to Direct Marketing: 51-75%
Direct Marketing ad budget:
Direct Mail: $1,000,000

Publisher of business administration &
educational materials for collegiate &
secondary schools.

SOUTHERN PROGRESS CORP

Subs. of Time Inc
2100 Lake Shore Dr
Birmingham, AL 35209-6721
Telephone: (205) 877-6000, FAX:
   (205) 877-6283, Web Site: www.
   southernprogress.com
Pres & CEO: Tom K. Angelillo
Exec VP: Bruce Akin
Conducts Business: U.S.
Employees: 750
Primary Market Served: Business &
   Consumer
Founded: 1886
Gross sales or billing: $84,500,000

Publisher of Southern Living, Progressive Farmer, Southern Accents, Cooking Light, Southern Living Vacations,
Oxmoorhouse Books, Weight Watchers
& Coastal Living.

SPOKEN ARTS

195 S White Rock Rd
Holmes, NY 12531-5406
Telephone: (845) 878-9600, (800) 326-4090, FAX: (845) 878-9009, E-Mail: sales@spokenartsmedia.com, Web Site: www.spokenartsmedia.com
Pres: Daniel Welsh
COO: Susan Welsh
Conducts Business: US
Employees: 3
Primary Market Served: Business & Consumer
Catalog available online
Indirect online sales
Direct Marketing ad budget: $150,000
Direct Mail: 100%
Gross sales or billing: $300,000

Motion picture/video production. Language arts, children's tales, cassettes, videos, multimedia cassettes, audio books & read-a-longs. Sell to educational institutions, libraries, distributors & dealers.

THE SPOKESMAN-REVIEW

Div. of Cowles Publishing Co
PO Box 2160
Spokane, WA 99210-2160
Telephone: (509) 459-5060, FAX: (509) 459-5083, E-Mail: shaunh@spokesman.com, Web Site: www.spokane.net
Dir, Mktg & Sls: Shaun Higgins
Primary Market Served: Business & Consumer

Business newspaper publisher.

SPORTING CLAYS LTD

317 S Washington Ave (Suite 201)
Titusville, FL 32976-3539
Telephone: (321) 268-5010, FAX: (321) 267-7216, E-Mail: sales@sportingclays.net, Web Site: www.sportingclays.net
Publr: Dan Wade
Sales: Eileen Meister
Conducts Business: Worldwide
Primary Market Served: Consumer

Monthly magazines, sporting clays.

THE SPORTING NEWS PUBLISHING CO

Subs. of Vulcan Print Media Inc
120 W Morehead St Ste 310
Charlotte, NC 28202-1826
Telephone: (704) 973-1546, (800) 443-1886, FAX: (704) 973-1552, Web Site: www.sportingnews.com
Pres & Publr: Jeff Price
VP Digital Adv Dir: Joey Glowracki
Conducts Business: Worldwide
Employees: 120
Primary Market Served: Consumer

Catalog available online
Direct online sales
Advertising/Marketing Budget Related to Direct Marketing: 76-100%
Direct Marketing ad budget:
Direct Mail: $3,500,000
Magazines: $250,000
Newspapers: $100,000
TV/Radio: $1,700,000
Telephone: $250,000
Founded: 1886
Gross sales or billing: $60,000,000

Publisher of sports magazines & sports books.

SPRINGER SCIENCE & BUSINESS MEDIA LLC

233 Spring St
New York, NY 10013
Telephone: (212) 460-1500, FAX: (212) 473-6272, Web Site: www.springer-ny.com
Pres: Ruediger Gebauer
CEO: Derk Haank
VP Book Sls: Paul Manning
Exec VP Corp Communs: Eric Merkel-Sobotta
Conducts Business: Worldwide
Employees: 400
Primary Market Served: Business & Consumer
Catalog available online
Direct online sales
Founded: 1842
Gross sales or billing: $44,700,000

Scientific, medical & technical publisher of books & journals.

STANDARD & POOR'S CORP

Div. of McGraw-Hill Companies, Inc.
55 Water St
New York, NY 10041-0004
Telephone: (212) 438-2000, FAX: (212) 438-7375, Web Site: www.standardandpoors.com
President: Deven Sharma
Exec VP: Vickie A. Tillman
VP Global Mkt Devel: Bruce Schachne
Conducts Business: U.S., Europe, Asia
Employees: 7,500
Primary Market Served: Business
Catalog available online
Founded: 1906
Gross sales or billing: $2,400,000,000

Marketer of financial & business information to investors, financial institutions, libraries & corporations.

STANDARD PUBLISHING

Subs. of Standex International
8805 Governor's Hill Dr (Suite 400)
Cincinnati, OH 45249
Telephone: (513) 931-4050, (800) 543-1301, FAX: (877) 867-5751, Web Site: www.standardpub.com
Pres & CEO: Matthew Thibeau
VP Sls & Mktg: Steven Couture
Conducts Business: U.S., Canada, U.K., Australia, New Zealand
Primary Market Served: Business & Consumer
Catalog available online
Direct online sales
Advertising/Marketing Budget Related to Direct Marketing: 0-25%
Founded: 1866

Publish dated curriculum, summer vacation school products, Bible centered books, games & church supplies. Sell to churches direct through company owned stores (15) & religious bookstores (5000). Also a commercial printer.

STAR TRIBUNE

Acquired by Avista Capital Partners
425 Portland Ave S
Minneapolis, MN 55488
Telephone: (612) 673-4000, FAX: (612) 673-4359, E-Mail: charte@startribune.com, Web Site: www.startribunecompany.com
Publr & COB: Chris Harte
Sr VP, Mktg & Commun: Benjamin Taylor
Sr VP Sls & Strategic Devel: Michael LaBonia
Primary Market Served: Consumer
Founded: 1867

Newspaper & consumer periodical publications.

STAYWELL/KRAMES

Subs. of Vivendi Universal
1100 Grundy Ln (#2)
San Bruno, CA 94066
Telephone: (650) 742-0400, FAX: (650) 244-4568, Web Site: www.staywell.com
Pres & CEO: Patrick Cliffor
Pres & CEO Staywell Insurance: Don Davis
Sr VP, Sls: Jean Neiner
Conducts Business: U.S., Canada, Australia, Europe
Employees: 150
Primary Market Served: Business
Catalog available online
Indirect online sales
Advertising/Marketing Budget Related to Direct Marketing: 76-100%
Founded: 1974

Publish full-color booklets, brochures & posters on numerous health & safety topics for physicians, hospitals & corporations.

STECK-VAUGHN

Div. of Harcourt Education
10801 N MoPac Expy (Bldg 3)
Austin, TX 78759-5415
Telephone: (512) 343-8227, (877) 866-2586, (800) 531-5015, FAX: (512) 795-3617, (877) 265-2730, E-Mail: info@steck-vaughn.com, Web Site: www.steck-vaughn.com
Pres & CEO: Richard J. Casabonne
Pres, Educational Trade Unit: James P. Levy
Exec VP, Opers: Floyd D. Rogers
VP & CFO: Todd Wehner
Gen Mgr: Carol Wolf
Conducts Business: Worldwide
Employees: 300
Primary Market Served: Consumer
Catalog available online
Direct online sales
Advertising/Marketing Budget Related to Direct Marketing: 51-75%
Founded: 1936

Supplemental publisher of educational workbooks, books, software & manipulatives for school, library, international & direct marketing markets.

STERLING PUBLISHING CO INC

387 Park Ave S (5th fl)
New York, NY 10016-8898
Telephone: (212) 532-7160, (800) 367-9692, FAX: (212) 213-2495, Web Site: www.sterlingpublishing.com
CEO: Charles Nurn
Exec VP: Charles G. Nurnberg
VP & COO: Marcus E. Leaver
VP, Fin & Warehouse Opers: Jim Benjamin
Conducts Business: U.S., Canada, U.K., Australia, New Zealand
Employees: 250
Primary Market Served: Business
Advertising/Marketing Budget Related to Direct Marketing: 0-25%
Direct Marketing ad budget: $500,000
Direct Mail: 60%
Magazines: 20%
Newspapers: 10%
Telephone: 10%
Founded: 1949
Gross sales or billing: $28,100,000

Self help and how to books.

STEVENS PUBLISHING CO

311 W Perkins Ave
Sandusky, OH 44870-4805
Telephone: (419) 626-5592, (800) 236-5592, FAX: (419) 626-9333, Web Site: www.stephenspublishing.com
Pres: Craig S. Stevens
Conducts Business: U.S., Canada, England
Employees: 102

Primary Market Served: Business
Catalog available online
Direct online sales
Publisher of 15 professional journals.

MARTHA STEWART LIVING OMNIMEDIA

601 W 26th St (Fl 9)
New York, NY 10001-1101
Telephone: (212) 827-8000, Web Site: www.marthastewart.com
Sr VP Consumer Mktg Dir: Richard Fontaine
Primary Market Served: Business & Consumer

STORY TIME STORIES THAT RHYME

PO Box 416
Denver, CO 80201-0416
Telephone: (303) 575-5676, FAX: (303) 575-1187, E-Mail: emailstreet@gmail.com, Web Site: www.storytimestoriesthatrhyme.com
Mktg VP & Founder: A. Doyle
Conducts Business: U.S.
Employees: 1
Primary Market Served: Business & Consumer
Catalog available online
Indirect online sales
Advertising/Marketing Budget Related to Direct Marketing: 76-100%
Direct Marketing ad budget:
Direct Mail: 20%
Newspapers: 10%
Online: 60%
Telephone: 10%
Founded: 1989

Storytelling & children's stories that educate, entertain & rhyme. Workbooks & educational materials. Content for catalogs, bulletins, advertising, promotions. E- books to download online. Prop Box Theme Box Idea Series, films. Homeschool, literacy & educational articles.

STRANG COMMUNICATIONS CO

600 Rinehart Rd
Lake Mary, FL 32746-4898
Telephone: (407) 333-0600, FAX: (407) 333-7100, E-Mail: magcustsvc@strang.com, Web Site: www.strang.com
Pres & Ed: Stephen Strang
Circ Dir: Larry Bregel
Retailing Editor: Andy Butcher
Editor: J. Lee Grudy
Sr Editor: Rafael Serrano
Conducts Business: U.S.
Employees: 100
Primary Market Served: Business & Consumer

Catalog available online
Direct online sales
Direct Marketing ad budget:
Direct Mail: $500,000

Christian magazine service that publishes Charisma, Ministries Today, SpiritLed Woman, Christian Retailing, New Man & Vida Cristiana.

STRESS MARKET

PO Box 127
Port Angeles, WA 98362-0017
Telephone: (360) 457-9223, (800) 578-7377, FAX: (360) 457-9466, E-Mail: info@stressmarket.com, Web Site: www.stressmarket.com
Pres: Tim Lownstein
Conducts Business: U.S.
Employees: 3
Primary Market Served: Business & Consumer
Catalog available online
Direct online sales
Advertising/Marketing Budget Related to Direct Marketing: 76-100%
Direct Marketing ad budget:
Direct Mail: 30%
Magazines: 30%
Online: 40%
Founded: 1978
Gross sales or billing: $100,000

Educational books & cassettes, stress meters, biofeedback & holographic music. Health Master, fitness, nutrition, psychology, biodots, stress cards & relaxation.

SUCCESSFUL FARMING

Div. of Meredith Publishing Co
1716 Locust St
Des Moines, IA 50309-3023
Telephone: (515) 284-2143, (800) 678-2711, FAX: (515) 284-3127
Pres & Publr: Chris Little
Magazine Grp VP: Jerry Ward
Publr: Jim Cornick
DM Mgr: Cathy Porepp
Conducts Business: U.S.
Primary Market Served: Consumer

Publish a mail order marketplace section in each of 12 issues per year. The magazine itself provides decision making business help to large, professional farm families.

SUNBURST TECHNOLOGY

1550 Executive Dr
Elgin, IL 60123
Telephone: (914) 747-3310, FAX: (914) 747-4109, E-Mail: service@nysunburst.com, Web Site: www.sunburst.com
Pres: Conall Ryan
VP Mktg: Mike Gavelek
Ed-in-Chief: Susan Green

Mktg Dir: Tara Green
Conducts Business: Worldwide
Employees: 180
Primary Market Served: Consumer
Catalog available online
Indirect online sales
Advertising/Marketing Budget Related
    to Direct Marketing: 76-100%
Direct Marketing ad budget:
Direct Mail: 95%
Magazines: 1%
Telephone: 4%
Founded: 1973

Produce & distribute video, computer
software & print instructional materials
for use in elementary & secondary
schools, colleges, hospitals, public
agencies & homes. Products are marketed by direct mail & telemarketing
to school teachers, librarians &
administrators.

SUNRISE GREETINGS

1145 Sunrise Greetings Ct
Bloomington, IN 47404
Telephone: (812) 336-4045, (800) 457-
    4045, FAX: (812) 336-8712, E-Mail:
    info@interart.com, Web Site: www.
    interartdistribution.com
CEO: Susan Hare
Art Dir: Sara Davis
Dir, Seasonal Cards: Kandy Schwandt
Conducts Business: U.S., U.K., Canada
Employees: 475
Primary Market Served: Business
Catalog available online
Advertising/Marketing Budget Related
    to Direct Marketing: 0-25%
Founded: 1974
Gross sales or billing: $22,000,000

Greeting card publisher, stationery &
paper gifts.

SUNSET MAGAZINE

Subs. of Time Inc Magazine Co
80 Willow Rd
Menlo Park, CA 94025
Telephone: (650) 321-3600, FAX:
    (650) 328-6215
Circ Dir: Christina Olsen
Circ Mktg Mgr: Jalayne Forrester
Circ Mktg Mgr: Karen Gallion
Circ Mktg Mgr: Pamela Miller
Conducts Business: U.S.
Employees: 300
Primary Market Served: Consumer
Direct Marketing ad budget:
Direct Mail: $4,000,000
TV/Radio: $600,000
Telephone: $200,000
Founded: 1898
Gross sales or billing: $100,000,000

Publish Sunset Books & Sunset Magazine serving 13 Western States.

SURE-FIRE BUSINESS SUCCESS CATALOG

50 Follen St (#507)
Cambridge, MA 02138
Telephone: (617) 547-6372, FAX:
    (617) 547-0061, E-Mail: drjlant@
    worldprofit.com, Web Site: www.
    worldprofit.com
Pres: Jeffrey Lant
Conducts Business: Worldwide
Employees: 2
Primary Market Served: Business &
    Consumer
Catalog available online
Direct online sales
Advertising/Marketing Budget Related
    to Direct Marketing: 76-100%
Direct Marketing ad budget:
Online: 100%
Founded: 1979

Books, card decks, and software to
help businesses grow. See web site for
details.

SURPLUS RECORD

Subs. of Free Markets
20 N Wacker Dr (Suite 2400)
Chicago, IL 60606-3181
Telephone: (312) 372-9077, (800) 622-
    5449, FAX: (312) 372-6537, E-Mail:
    surplus@surplusrecord.com, Web
    Site: www.surplusrecord.com
Publr: T.C. Scanlan
CEO: Glen Meakem
Sr VP: Doug Wnorowski
Conducts Business: Worldwide
Employees: 20
Primary Market Served: Business
Catalog available online
Advertising/Marketing Budget Related
    to Direct Marketing: 76-100%
Founded: 1924

Surplus machine tools. Publisher of
Catalog/Index of Available Capital
Equipment.

SUSSEX PUBLISHERS INC

115 E 23rd St (9th fl)
New York, NY 10010
Telephone: (212) 260-7210, FAX:
    (212) 260-7445, Web Site: www.
    blues-buster.com
Editor in Chief: Kaja Perina
Exec Editor: Lysi Ma
Creative Dir: Ed Levine
Sr Editor: Jay Dixit
Assoc Editor: Carlin Flora
Primary Market Served: Business &
    Consumer
Catalog available online
Direct online sales
Publish magazines.

THOMSON REUTERS

195 Broadway Fl 4
New York, NY 10007-3124
Telephone: (212) 367-6300, (800) 950-
    1216, FAX: (212) 367-6301, Web
    Site: www.riahome.com
Mktg Dir: John Hartnett
Mktg Mgr: David O'Toole
Conducts Business: U.S.
Primary Market Served: Business
Catalog available online
Direct online sales
Advertising/Marketing Budget Related
    to Direct Marketing: 0-25%
Direct Marketing ad budget:
Direct Mail: 40%
Telephone: 60%

Publish insightful analysis & practical
guidance of laws & regulations for
CPA's, corporate tax & finance, human
resource professionals & attorneys.
Sell through mail order & national
sales force.

TL ENTERPRISES INC

Affinity Group Inc
2575 Vista Del Mar Dr
Ventura, CA 93001-3920
Telephone: (805) 667-4100, FAX:
    (805) 667-4419
Pres: Joe McAdams
Employees: 300
Primary Market Served: Business &
    Consumer
Advertising/Marketing Budget Related
    to Direct Marketing: 76-100%

Publisher & marketer of magazines,
clubs & ancillary products.

TT PUBLISHING

Div. of American Trucking Associa-
    tions
950 N Gleb Rd
Arlington, VA 22203
Telephone: (703) 838-1770, FAX:
    (703) 838-0285, Web Site: www.
    ttnews.com
Publr: Bob Rast
Publr: Howard Abramson
VP & Assoc Publr Mktg &
    Circulation: Paul Rosenthal
Conducts Business: U.S., Canada,
    Mexico
Employees: 38
Primary Market Served: Business
Catalog available online
Direct online sales
Advertising/Marketing Budget Related
    to Direct Marketing: 0-25%
Direct Marketing ad budget:
Direct Mail: $100,000
Magazines: $5,000
Newspapers: $5,000
Telephone: $10,000
Founded: 1933

Gross sales or billing: $8,200,000

Publish weekly newspaper "Transport Topics", & monthly magazines "Light & Medium Truck" & "Utility Fleet Management."

THE TAUNTON PRESS
63 S Main St, PO Box 5506
Newtown, CT 06470-2344
Telephone: (203) 426-8171, (800) 477-8727, FAX: (203) 426-3434, Web Site: www.taunton.com
Pres: Suzanne Roman
EVP: Tim Rahr
COO: Tom Luxeder
Production Mgr: Phil Van Kirk
Sr VP, CMO: Janine Scolpino
Conducts Business: U.S., Canada
Employees: 270
Primary Market Served: Business & Consumer
Gross sales or billing: $26,000,000

Publisher of magazines, books & videos.

TAX MANAGEMENT INC
Subs. of The Bureau of National Affairs Inc
3 Bethesda Metro Ctr (Suite 250), BNA Customer Contact Center
Bethesda, MD 20814-5377
Telephone: (202) 452-4200, FAX: (202) 496-6013
Pres: Dave McFarlend
Adv & Commun Mgr: Barbara Patrick
Promo Mgr: Gretchen Zekiel
Conducts Business: Worldwide
Primary Market Served: Business

Publisher of professionally oriented tax & related business services for lawyers, accountants, executives & financial planners.

THE DMA THE TEACHING CO
4151 Lafayette Center Dr
Chantilly, VA 20151-1232
Telephone: (703) 502-7300, (800) 832-2412, FAX: (703) 378-3819, Web Site: www.teach12.com
Pres: Thomas Rollins
Dir, Mktg Production: Jason Smigel
Primary Market Served: Business & Consumer
Founded: 1990

Make educational audio & video cassettes featuring teachers & professors from leading universities & high schools. Sold through mail order & retail.

THE DMA TECHNOLOGY REVIEW
Subs. of Massachusetts Institute of Technology
1 Main St (Suite 7), MIT Bldg W59

Cambridge, MA 02142-1599
Telephone: (617) 475-8000, FAX: (617) 258-5850, Web Site: www.technologyreview.com
Publr & CEO: R. Bruce Journey
VP Circulation & Consumer Mktg: Heather Holmes
Ed: John Benditt
VP & GM: Martha Connors
Mktg Dir: Marcy Dill
Conducts Business: Worldwide
Employees: 20
Primary Market Served: Business & Consumer
Catalog available online
Advertising/Marketing Budget Related to Direct Marketing: 26-50%
Direct Marketing ad budget:
Direct Mail: $2,000,000
Founded: 1899

MIT's national magazine on technological innovation across the full spectrum of technologies & industries. Coverage concentrated on areas of high technology where progress is most rapid, such as biotechnology, information technology & materials science. Coverage also provided of innovation in mature industries, such as transportation, construction & energy technology.

TELECOMMUNICATIONS REPORTS INTERNATIONAL INC
Part of Aspen Publishers
1015 15th St NW (fl 10)
Washington, DC 20005-2605
Telephone: (202) 312-6060, (800) 234-1660, FAX: (202) 312-6111, E-Mail: bhammond@tr.com, Web Site: www.tr.com
Pres: Robert Becker
Mng Ed: Brian Hammond
Conducts Business: U.S.
Primary Market Served: Business
Catalog available online
Direct online sales

Publisher of newsletters, directories & manuals to the telecommunications industry.

TELEMEDIA COMMUNICATIONS US
25 Sheppard Ave W (Suite 100)
North York, ON, Canada M2N 6S7
Telephone: (416) 733-7600, (888) 290-1466 Can., (800) 461-3773 U.S., FAX: (416) 733-3563, E-Mail: info@transcontinental.ca, Web Site: www.transcontinental.com
Chmn: Remi Marcoux
Pres & CEO: Luc Desjardins
COO: Francois Oliver
VP & CFO: Benoit Huard

Conducts Business: U.S.
Employees: 14,476
Primary Market Served: Consumer
Founded: 1976
Gross sales or billing: $2,100,000,000

Publisher of consumer magazines.

TELEPHONY
Div. of Intertec Publishing Corp
One IBM Plaza (23rd fl)
Chicago, IL 60611
Telephone: (312) 595-1080, (800) 458-0479, FAX: (312) 595-0295, Web Site: www.internettelephony.com
Pres: Cameron Bishop
Div VP: Larry Lannon
Mktg Dir: Bill McDonough
Tele Publr: Mark Hickey
Conducts Business: Worldwide
Employees: 100
Primary Market Served: Business
Founded: 1901

Publisher of the weekly journal of telecommunications - Telephony, monthly journal of telecommunications - Global Telephony. Also publisher of telecommunications books. Sponsor telecommunications seminars.

TEN SPEED PRESS
Subs. of Philip Wood, Inc.
6001 Shellmound St 4th Fl, PO Box 7123
Emeryville, CA 94608-1988
Telephone: (510) 559-1600, (800) 841-BOOK, FAX: (510) 559-1629, E-Mail: order@tenspeed.com, Web Site: www.tenspeed.com
Pres & CEO: Phillip R. Wood
Publicity Mgr: Lisa Regul
Customer Svc: Shelley Davidson
Conducts Business: U.S., U.K., Canada, Australia, New Zealand, South Africa, Singapore, India
Employees: 75
Primary Market Served: Business & Consumer
Catalog available online
Direct online sales
Advertising/Marketing Budget Related to Direct Marketing: 0-25%
Gross sales or billing: $24,000,000

Book, poster & audiotape publisher. Sell to wholesalers, distributors, bookstores, libraries & specialty accounts.

TERRITORIAL NEWSPAPERS
Div. of Wick Communications
3280 E Hemisphere Loop (Suite 180), PO Box 27087
Tucson, AZ 85726-7087
Telephone: (520) 294-1200, FAX: (520) 294-4040, Web Site: www.azbiz.com
Publr: Thomas P. Lee

List Coord: James Werner
Employees: 50

TEXAS MONTHLY
Subs. of Emmis Communications
816 Congress Ave Ste 1700
Austin, TX 78701-2643
Telephone: (512) 320-6900, (800) 759-
2000, FAX: (512) 476-9007, E-Mail:
info@texasmonthly.com, Web Site:
www.texasmonthly.com
Publr: Michael R. Levy
Sr VP Sls & Mktg: April Brumley
Hinkle
Sr VP & Gen Mgr: Lorelei Calvert
Office Mgr: Angela Clawson
Dir: Charlie Llewelin
Dir: Cynthia Winer
Conducts Business: U.S.
Employees: 125
Primary Market Served: Consumer
Catalog available online
Indirect online sales
Founded: 1973

Publish a monthly general interest consumer magazine for Texans.

THIEME MEDICAL
PUBLISHERS INC
dba Thieme New York
333 7th Ave Rm 500
New York, NY 10001-5122
Telephone: (212) 760-0888, (800) 782-
3488, FAX: (212) 947-1112, E-Mail:
info@thieme.com, Web Site: www.
thieme.com
Pres: Brian Scanlon
Dir Online Div: Sigrid Lesch
Online Mktg: Cornelia Schulze
Mktg: Verena Dieme
Employees: 50
Primary Market Served: Business
Catalog available online
Direct online sales
Advertising/Marketing Budget Related
to Direct Marketing: 51-75%
Direct Marketing ad budget:
Direct Mail: 70%
Online: 30%
Founded: 1995
Gross sales or billing: $13,800,000

Publisher of medical books & journals.

THIMBAND
PO Box 416
Denver, CO 80201-0416
Telephone: (303) 575-5676, FAX:
(303) 575-1187, E-Mail: email@
contentprovidermedia.info
Founder & Mktg VP: A. Doyle
Employees: 1
Primary Market Served: Business &
Consumer
Catalog available online
Indirect online sales

Advertising/Marketing Budget Related
to Direct Marketing: 76-100%
Direct Marketing ad budget:
Direct Mail: 10%
Online: 80%
Telephone: 10%
Founded: 1998

Patterns, crafts and notions.

THOMPSON PUBLISHING
GROUP INC
1725 "K" St
Washington, DC 20006
Telephone: (202) 872-4000, (800) 677-
3789, FAX: (800) 999-5661, E-Mail:
service@thompson.com, Web Site:
www.thompson.com
Grp Sls: Steve Ackerman
Conducts Business: U.S., Canada
Employees: 300
Primary Market Served: Business
Catalog available online
Direct online sales
Advertising/Marketing Budget Related
to Direct Marketing: 51-75%
Direct Marketing ad budget:
Direct Mail: 65%
Online: 10%
Telephone: 25%
Founded: 1972

Publish loose-leaf reference services &
newsletters. Thompson Publishing Services division in Tampa, Florida provides database systems, 800 customer
service number, distribution, cashiering
& other related fulfillment services to
publishers, associations & government
agencies. A brochure listing these services is available by calling (800) 677-
3789.

THOMSON FINANCIAL
Div. of International Thomson
195 Broadway Fl 4
New York, NY 10007-3124
Telephone: (212) 803-8200, FAX:
(212) 843-9608
Chmn: James A. Finkelstein
CEO & Pres: Phil Gabel
CFO & VP, Admin: Randy Koubek
VP, Opers: David Ludwig
Conducts Business: U.S., Canada
Employees: 400
Primary Market Served: Business
Catalog available online
Direct online sales
Direct Marketing ad budget:
Direct Mail: 75%
Telephone: 25%
Founded: 1972

Publish several publications for banking executives & professionals in the
bond business. Sell subscriptions to
senior bankers & related financial industry executives.

THOMSON-GALE
Div. of Thompson Corp
27500 Drake Rd
Farmington Hills, MI 48331
Telephone: (800) 877-4253, FAX:
(877) 363-4253, Web Site: www.
galegroup.com
CEO: Allen Paschal
Exec VP, Sls & Mktg: Rich Foley
Mktg Dir: Mary Mercatante
Conducts Business: Worldwide
Employees: 600
Primary Market Served: Business
Founded: 1954

Information publishing for libraries,
schools & businesses. The company
creates and maintains more than 600
databases that are published online, in
print & in microform.

THOMSON WEST
Subs. of Thomson Corp
610 Opperman Dr
Eagan, MN 55164
Telephone: (651) 687-7000, (800) 328-
9378, FAX: (651) 687-7849, E-Mail:
jeff.patrios@thomsonreuters.com,
Web Site: www.thomson.com
Pres & CEO: Peter Warwick
Sr VP, HR: Tom Moran
Exec VP, Chief Strategy Officer:
Charles B. Cater
Sr Dir Mktg: Jeff Patrios
Conducts Business: Worldwide
Employees: 7,000
Primary Market Served: Business
Catalog available online
Direct online sales
Advertising/Marketing Budget Related
to Direct Marketing: 51-75%
Founded: 1876
Gross sales or billing: $935,000,000

A legal publisher, headquartered in
Eagan, MN, supplying legal professionals with print & electronic source
materials including WESTLAW, a
computer-assisted legal research service; West's Legal Directory(TM);
West CD-ROM Libraries(TM); West's
Desktop Practice Systems; WESTfax;
and a full range of integrated legal
publications.

THORNDIKE PRESS
10 Water St Ste 310
Waterville, ME 04901-6566
Telephone: (207) 859-1000, (800) 223-
1244, E-Mail: gale.salesassistance@
cengage.com, Web Site: www.
galegroup.com
Publr: Karen Huyser
Conducts Business: Worldwide
Employees: 115
Primary Market Served: Business &
Consumer

Publish books in large print & books on cassettes. Also reference, library catalogs & bibliographies.

TIDBITS MEDIA

1430 I-85 Pkwy (Suite 301)
Montgomery, AL 36106-3635
Telephone: (334) 290-0225, (800) 523-3096, FAX: (334) 386-0302, E-Mail: editors@tidbitsweekly.com, Web Site: www.tidbitsweekly.com
Exec VP & Owner: Ken Woodward
Pres & Owner: Karl Dabbs
Creative Dir: Carl Adams
Conducts Business: U.S., Canada
Employees: 10
Primary Market Served: Business & Consumer
Catalog available online
Direct online sales
Advertising/Marketing Budget Related to Direct Marketing: 76-100%
Direct Marketing ad budget:
Direct Mail: 10%
Magazines: 40%
Online: 40%
Telephone: 10%
Founded: 1994

Victorian & French reproduction furniture.

ᵀᴴᴱ TIME INC
ᴰᴹᴬ

1271 6th Ave
New York, NY 10020-1300
Telephone: (212) 522-1212, Web Site: www.timeinc.com/home
Exec VP, Consumer Mktg & Sls: Steve Sachs
Primary Market Served: Business & Consumer

TOWNSEND COMMUNICATIONS LLC

20 E Gregory Blvd
Kansas City, MO 64114
Telephone: (816) 361-0616, (800) 274-8867, FAX: (816) 361-6164, Web Site: www.townsendprint.com
Chmn: H.G. Townsend Jr.
Pres & CEO: H. Guyon Townsend III
VP, Sls & Mktg: Irv Craig
Bus Devel Mgr: Beth Owens
Pre-Press Mgr: Barb Hill
Conducts Business: U.S.
Employees: 9
Primary Market Served: Business & Consumer

Publish magazines mailed direct to high school juniors & seniors.

TRANSACTION PUBLISHERS

35 Berrue Cir, Rutgers University
Piscataway, NJ 08854-8042
Telephone: (732) 445-1245, FAX: (732) 748-9801, E-Mail: trans@transactionpub.com, Web Site: www.transactionpub.com
Pres: Mary E. Curtis
Mktg Mgr: Mindy Waizer
Conducts Business: Worldwide
Employees: 30
Primary Market Served: Business & Consumer
Catalog available online
Direct online sales
Advertising/Marketing Budget Related to Direct Marketing: 26-50%
Direct Marketing ad budget:
Direct Mail: 50%
Magazines: 10%
Online: 40%
Founded: 1962

Publisher of social science books & serials since 1962. Shipping and distribution services for publishers.

TREND MAGAZINES INC

Subs. of Times Publishing Co
490 First Ave S (8th fl)
Saint Petersburg, FL 33701
Telephone: (727) 821-5800, (800) 821-5800, FAX: (727) 822-5083, E-Mail: feedback@fltrend.com, Web Site: www.floridatrend.com
Pres & Publr: Andrew P. Corty
Dir Audience Devel: Karen Tyson
Conducts Business: U.S.
Employees: 35
Primary Market Served: Business & Consumer
Catalog available online
Direct online sales
Advertising/Marketing Budget Related to Direct Marketing: 51-75%
Founded: 1958

Magazines of business & finance.

TRIBUNE CO

435 N Michigan Ave
Chicago, IL 60611-4041
Telephone: (312) 222-9100, FAX: (312) 222-1573, Web Site: www.tribune.com
Chmn & CEO: Samuel Zell
Sr VP, Fin & Admin: Donald C. Grenesko
Exec VP & CAO: Gerald A. Spector
Exec VP: Rob Gremillion
Exec VP: Randy Michaels
Employees: 21,000
Primary Market Served: Business & Consumer
Catalog available online
Indirect online sales
Gross sales or billing: $5,500,000,000

Diversified media company.

ᵀᴴᴱ TRIUMPH LEARNING
ᴰᴹᴬ

136 Madison Ave (fl 7)
New York, NY 10016-6711
Telephone: (212) 652-0200, Web Site: http://triumphlearning.com
Primary Market Served: Consumer

Publisher of state-customized, standards-aligned, K-12 instructional materials

THE TRUMPET CLUB

Subs. of Scholastic Inc
578 Broadway (Rm 807)
New York, NY 10012
Telephone: (212) 343-6100, FAX: (212) 343-7709, Web Site: www.scholastic.com
Promo Mgr: Kim Soscie
Promo Coord: Ann Klien
Conducts Business: U.S.
Employees: 100
Primary Market Served: Business & Consumer
Advertising/Marketing Budget Related to Direct Marketing: 76-100%
Direct Marketing ad budget:
Direct Mail: 100%
Founded: 1985

Books to children through schools.

TRUTV

Subs. of Time Warner
1 Time Warner Ctr (bsmt)
New York, NY 10019-6010
Telephone: (212) 973-2800, FAX: (212) 973-3210, Web Site: www.trutv.com
VP Cons PR: Vicky Kahn
SVP Mktg: Mary Corigliano
VP Adv Sls Mktg: Joanne Eckert
Conducts Business: U.S.
Primary Market Served: Business & Consumer
Founded: 1979

Television network.

TYNDALE HOUSE PUBLISHERS

351 Executive Dr
Carol Stream, IL 60188
Telephone: (630) 668-8300, FAX: (630) 668-3245
Pres: Mark Taylor
Sr VP & Grp Publr: Doug Knox
Conducts Business: U.S.
Employees: 186
Primary Market Served: Business & Consumer
Direct Marketing ad budget:
Direct Mail: 75%
Magazines: 10%
TV/Radio: 10%
Telephone: 5%

Direct marketer of religious books, bibles & children's videos.

TYSON ASSOCIATES INC
246 Federal Rd (Suite D23)
Brookfield, CT 06804
Telephone: (203) 775-9465, FAX: (203) 775-0563, E-Mail: elaine@ tysonassociates.com, Web Site: www.tysonassociates.com
Pres: Elaine Tyson

UMI PUBLICATIONS INC
1135 N Tryon St
Charlotte, NC 28206
Telephone: (800) 747-9287, FAX: (704) 374-0729, E-Mail: info@ umipub.com, Web Site: www.umipub.com
Pres: Ivan Motherhead
Controller: Lewis Patton
Mng Ed: Ward Woodbury
Conducts Business: U.S. & Canada
Employees: 15
Primary Market Served: Consumer
Catalog available online
Indirect online sales
Advertising/Marketing Budget Related to Direct Marketing: 51-75%
Direct Marketing ad budget:
Direct Mail: 75%
Magazines: 5%
Newspapers: 5%
Online: 10%
TV/Radio: 5%
Founded: 1973

Publisher of college basketball handbooks. Publisher of Official NASCAR Preview, Press Guide & NASCAR NEXTEL Cup Series Yearbook.

UNCHARTED COUNTRY PUBLISHING
dba Tai Chi Health
408 S Baldwin St
Madison, WI 53703-4805
Telephone: (575) 776-3470, E-Mail: ucp@taichihealth.com, Web Site: www.taichihealth.com
Pres: Tricia Yu
Publr: Doug Swayne
Dir: Lauri McKean
Conducts Business: U.S., Canada
Primary Market Served: Business & Consumer
Catalog available online

Sell video & audio tapes, books, seminars & classes that promote health & wellness through mind/body exercises based on T'ai Chi principles & movements.

UNICOL INC
11590 SW Ninth Ct
Pembroke Pines, FL 33025-4324
Telephone: (954) 431-7871, FAX: (954) 430-7227, E-Mail: customerservice@unicol-publishing.com, Web Site: www.unicol-publishing.com
Pres: Henry A. Rose
Conducts Business: U.S., Canada, United Kingdom
Primary Market Served: Business
Catalog available online
Direct online sales
Advertising/Marketing Budget Related to Direct Marketing: 76-100%
Founded: 1991

UNITED BUSINESS MEDIA
600 Community Dr Ste 1
Manhasset, NY 11030-3818
Telephone: (516) 562-5000, Web Site: www.ubmtechnology.com
Sr VP Mktg Strategy & Bus Devel: Kate Spellman
Grp Dir, Mktg: Felicia Hamerman
VP, Mktg: Scott Vaughan
Mktg Dir: Tara Gibb
Conducts Business: Worldwide
Primary Market Served: Business & Consumer

Publisher of 4 magazines. Sell technical & business books on telecommunications & data processing by direct mail.

UNITED COMMUNICATIONS GROUP
9737 Washingtonian Blvd (Suite 100), Two Washingtonian Center
Gaithersburg, MD 20878-7364
Telephone: (301) 287-2700, FAX: (301) 816-8945, E-Mail: webmaster@ucg.com, Web Site: www.ucg.com
Partner: Bruce Levenson
Partner: Ed Peskowitz
Partner: Bob Koran
Conducts Business: Worldwide
Employees: 85
Primary Market Served: Business
Founded: 1977
Gross sales or billing: $25,800,000

Publish business-to-business newsletters in areas of petroleum, finance, high technology, human resources & direct marketing. Also provide online data services, seminars & trade shows, computers, telecommunications & government contracting.

THE UNITED METHODIST PUBLISHING HOUSE
201 8th Ave S
Nashville, TN 37203-3919

Telephone: (615) 749-6000, (800) 672-1789, FAX: (615) 749-6417, E-Mail: productsandservices@umpublishing.com, Web Site: www.umpublishing.com
Pres & Publ: Neil Alexander
Sr VP: Ed Kowalski
VP: Tammy Gaines
VP: Larry Linville
VP: Alyce Meadors
Primary Market Served: Consumer
Founded: 1789

Consumer publishers, periodical publications; consumer non-profit organization.

US NEWS & WORLD REPORT
4 New York Plz Fl 6
New York, NY 10004-2473
Telephone: (212) 916-7360, FAX: (212) 643-7842, Web Site: www.usnews.com
Chmn & Ed in Chief: Mortimer B. Zuckerman
Pres: William D. Holiber
CFO: Thomas H. Peck
Pub Rels Dir: Cynthia Powell
Adv Sls: Barbara Bauer
Dir of Renewals, Billing, Gifts & Fulfillment: Stacie Paradis
Consumer Mktg Dir: Margaret Lorczak
Conducts Business: U.S.
Primary Market Served: Business & Consumer
Founded: 1948

Publish U.S. News & World Report magazine.

THE DMA USA TODAY
Div. of Gannett
7950 Jones Branch Dr
Mc Lean, VA 22102-3302
Telephone: (703) 854-3400, (800) 872-0001, E-Mail: accuracy@usatoday.com, Web Site: www.usatoday.com
Classified Adv Dir: Kathy Vu
Sls Mgr: Janet Lewis
Dir, Circulation Mktg: Gary Evans
Conducts Business: U.S.
Primary Market Served: Business

Direct response classified advertising space marketed to mail order & catalog advertisers.

UNITY SCHOOL OF CHRISTIANITY
1901 NW Blue Pkwy
Unity Village, MO 64065-0001
Telephone: (816) 254-3550, FAX: (816) 251-3554, E-Mail: unity@ unityonline.org, Web Site: www.unityonline.org
Sr Dir Mktg: Kim West
VP Mktg: Tim Ipema

Dir: Charles Rickert Filmore
Dir: Rev. Gregory Guice
Conducts Business: Worldwide
Employees: 600
Primary Market Served: Consumer
Catalog available online
Direct online sales

Publisher of four different religious
magazines sold to consumers by
subscription.

UNIVERSITY OF CHICAGO PRESS

1427 E 60th St
Chicago, IL 60637
Telephone: (773) 702-7700, FAX:
(773) 702-9756, Web Site: www.
press.uchicago.edu
Sr Ed: Dan Pervin
Ed: William Strunk Jr.
Mgr Dir Mktg: J. Weintraub
Conducts Business: U.S., Canada,
U.K., Europe, Japan, Australia
Employees: 200
Primary Market Served: Business &
Consumer
Catalog available online
Direct online sales
Advertising/Marketing Budget Related
to Direct Marketing: 26-50%
Direct Marketing ad budget: $400,000
Direct Mail: 100%

Publishers of scholarly books, journals
& references.

UNIVERSITY OF OKLAHOMA PRESS

4100 28th Ave NW
Norman, OK 73069-8218
Telephone: (800) 627-7377, FAX:
(405) 364-5798, Web Site: www.
oupress.com
Dir: John Drayton
Editor-in-Chief & Assoc Dir: Charles
E. Rankin
Conducts Business: Worldwide
Primary Market Served: Business &
Consumer
Catalog available online
Direct online sales
Direct Marketing ad budget:
Direct Mail: 100%
Founded: 1929

Publish books.

UNIVERSITY PRESS OF AMERICA INC

Div. of D. Rowman & Littlefield Publishing Group
4501 Forbes Blvd (Suite 200)
Lanham, MD 20706

Telephone: (301) 459-3366, (800) 462-
6420, FAX: (301) 429-5748, E-Mail:
custserv@rowman.com, Web Site:
www.univpress.com
Pres & Publr: Jed E. Lyons
Mktg Dir: Judith Rothman
Mktg Mgr: Sheila Burnett
Mktg: Dean Roxanis
Assoc Mktg Mgr: Amanda Slaybaugh
Conducts Business: Worldwide
Employees: 10
Primary Market Served: Business &
Consumer
Catalog available online
Direct online sales
Advertising/Marketing Budget Related
to Direct Marketing: 0-25%
Direct Marketing ad budget:
Direct Mail: 50%
Online: 50%
Founded: 1975
Gross sales or billing: $3,000,000

Publisher of scholarly monographs,
college texts, professional books &
reprints. Owns National Book Network, distributor of independent trade
book publishers.

URBAN RESPONSE LLC

Subs. of James Direct, Inc.
500 S Prospect Ave
Hartville, OH 44632-9403
Telephone: (330) 877-0800, (866) 550-
3501, FAX: (330) 877-0802
Pres: James DiCola
Primary Market Served: Consumer

VALUE LINE PUBLISHING INC

Div. of Value Line Inc
220 E 42nd St
New York, NY 10017
Telephone: (212) 907-1500, FAX:
(212) 818-9747, Web Site: www.
valueline.com
Mktg Dir: Lawrence Freeman
Conducts Business: Worldwide
Employees: 340
Primary Market Served: Business &
Consumer
Direct online sales
Advertising/Marketing Budget Related
to Direct Marketing: 76-100%
Founded: 1931

Investment publications, electronic
products, mutual funds, asset management & investment research.

VAN DAM INC

11 W 20th St Fl 4
New York, NY 10011-3704
Telephone: (212) 929-0416, (800) UN-
FOLDS, FAX: (212) 929-0426,
E-Mail: info@vandam.com, Web
Site: www.vandam.com

Pres: Stephan C. VanDam
Conducts Business: Worldwide
Primary Market Served: Business &
Consumer

Produce pop-up maps & guides.

THE VESTAL PRESS LTD

Div. of The Rowman & Littlefield
Publishing Group
4501 Forbes Blvd (Suite 200)
Lanham, MD 20706
Telephone: (301) 459-3366, (800) 462-
6420, FAX: (301) 429-5746, E-Mail:
sburnett@rowman.com, Web Site:
www.nbnbooks.com
Sr VP NBN Mktg: Marianne Bohr
Dir Sls Admin: Lita Orner
VP Mktg: Linda May
Conducts Business: Worldwide
Employees: 150
Primary Market Served: Consumer
Catalog available online
Indirect online sales
Advertising/Marketing Budget Related
to Direct Marketing: 0-25%
Direct Marketing ad budget: $10,000
Direct Mail: 70%
Magazines: 25%
Newspapers: 5%
Founded: 1961

Publish & sell books on technical antiquarian hobbies, early entertainment
history (including film), woodcarving.

VISUAL REFERENCE PUBLICATIONS

Subs. of Milton B Conhaim Inc
302 Fifth Ave
New York, NY 10001
Telephone: (212) 279-7000, (800) 251-
4545, FAX: (212) 279-7014
VP, Mktg: John Burr
VP & Publr: Lawrence Fuersich
Conducts Business: Worldwide
Employees: 30
Primary Market Served: Business

Publications & books for retailers, advertising agencies, designers &
architects.

WFF'N PROOF LEARNING GAMES ASSOCIATES

118 N Court St
Fairfield, IA 52556-2811
Telephone: (641) 472-0149, (800) 289-
2377, FAX: (641) 472-0693, Web
Site: www.wffnproof.com
Sr Dir Devel: Layman E. Allen
Conducts Business: Worldwide
Primary Market Served: Business &
Consumer
Catalog available online
Direct online sales
Founded: 1962

Publisher of educational games that teach logic, math, science, language, word structures & strategy. Computer software for learning math available on Apple or IBM 5.25″ DS/DD diskettes. IBM now available on 3.5″ disk. Also a teacher training video course for equations.

WALCH PUBLISHING
40 Walch Dr
Portland, ME 04103-1286
Telephone: (207) 772-2846, (800) 558-2846, FAX: (207) 772-3105, E-Mail: customerservice@walch.com, Web Site: www.walch.com
CEO: John Thoreson
Pres: Al Noyes
Controller Dir Fin: Jim Walker
Publr: Betty Merti
Conducts Business: U.S., Canada, U.K., Singapore
Employees: 35
Primary Market Served: Business & Consumer
Catalog available online
Indirect online sales
Advertising/Marketing Budget Related to Direct Marketing: 76-100%
Direct Marketing ad budget:
Direct Mail: 96%
Magazines: 4%
Founded: 1927
Gross sales or billing: $6,000,000

Educational materials for teachers & students in middle school & high school; sell directly to teachers as well as through distributors & retail stores.

WALKER PUBLISHING CO INC
Div. of Bloomsbury Publishing
175 Fifth Ave (Frnt 4)
New York, NY 10010-7728
Telephone: (212) 727-8300, (800) 289-2553, FAX: (212) 727-0984
Pres: George Gibson
CFO & Controller: Theodore Rosenfeld
Conducts Business: Worldwide
Employees: 30
Primary Market Served: Business & Consumer

Publisher of books; adult & juvenile fiction & non-fiction.

WARNER BOOKS
Subs. of Time Inc
1271 Ave of the Americas
New York, NY 10020
Telephone: (212) 364-1200, FAX: (212) 522-7989, Web Site: www.twbookmark.com
Chmn & CEO: Laurence Kirshbaum
Pres & Publr: Maureen Mahon Egen

VP, New Mkts: Jean Griffin
Direct Response Mgr: Linda Cook
Conducts Business: Worldwide
Primary Market Served: Business & Consumer
Catalog available online

Publish hard cover & paperback books of general interest; fiction, & non-fiction. Sell to consumers, retailers, wholesalers, & direct marketers.

WARNER PRESS
1201 E Fifth St
Anderson, IN 46012
Telephone: (765) 644-7721, (800) 741-7721, FAX: (765) 640-8005, E-Mail: wporders@warnerpress.org, Web Site: www.warnerpress.com
Sls Mgr: Regina Jackson
Primary Market Served: Business & Consumer
Founded: 1881

Religious publications.

WARREN COMMUNICATIONS NEWS
2115 Ward Ct NW
Washington, DC 20037-1209
Telephone: (202) 872-9200, (800) 771-9202, FAX: (202) 318-8350, E-Mail: info@warren-news.com, Web Site: www.warren-news.com
Pres & Editor: Dan Warren
Exec Publr & Chmn: Paul Warren
Publr: Albert Warren
Assoc Mng Editor: Edie Herman
Sr Editor: Mark Seavy
Sr Editor: Jeff Berman
Conducts Business: U.S.
Employees: 50
Primary Market Served: Business
Catalog available online
Direct online sales
Advertising/Marketing Budget Related to Direct Marketing: 26-50%
Founded: 1945

Publish reference books & newsletters about the telecommunications industry.

WARREN, GORHAM & LAMONT INC
Div. of Thomson Reuters
195 Broadway
New York, NY 10007-3100
Telephone: (617) 423-2020, Web Site: ria.thomsonreuters.com
Telemktg Dir: Dan Antman
Conducts Business: U.S., Canada
Primary Market Served: Business
Advertising/Marketing Budget Related to Direct Marketing: 76-100%

Publishing firm specializing in tax & legal accounting, IS & HR publications for professionals.

THE WASHINGTON MONTHLY CO
1200 18th St NW (Suite 330)
Washington, DC 20036-2556
Telephone: (202) 393-5155, FAX: (202) 393-2444, E-Mail: editors@washingtonmonthly.com, Web Site: www.washingtonmonthly.com
Ed-in-Chief: Paul Glastris
Pres: Markos Kounalakis
Bus Mgr: Claire Igeli
Mktg Svcs & Adv Sls: Linda Miller
Conducts Business: U.S.
Employees: 8
Primary Market Served: Business & Consumer
Founded: 1969

National magazine covering politics, government & public affairs.

THE WASHINGTON POST
Div. of The Washington Post Co
1150 15th St NW
Washington, DC 20071
Telephone: (202) 334-6000, (800) 627-1150, E-Mail: letters@washpost.com, Web Site: www.washingtonpost.com
Chmn & CEO: Donald E. Graham
Exec Editor: Leonard Downie Jr.
Mng Editor: Philip Bennet
Deputy Mng Editor: Milton Coleman
Pub Rels Dir: Eric Grant
Conducts Business: U.S., Europe
Employees: 3,600
Primary Market Served: Consumer
Direct online sales
Advertising/Marketing Budget Related to Direct Marketing: 0-25%
Founded: 1977

Newspaper publisher.

WASHINGTON POST DIGITAL
1150 15th St NW
Washington, DC 20071
Telephone: (202) 334-9900
VP Mktg: Denise Simpson
Primary Market Served: Business & Consumer

THE WASHINGTONIAN
1828 ″L″ St NW (Suite 200)
Washington, DC 20036
Telephone: (202) 296-3600, E-Mail: editorial@washingtonian.com, Web Site: www.washingtonian.com
Circ Dir & Controller: Michael Johnson
Adv Dir: Edward Mansfield
Conducts Business: U.S.
Employees: 50
Primary Market Served: Consumer
Catalog available online
Advertising/Marketing Budget Related to Direct Marketing: 0-25%

Founded: 1965

Monthly magazine for an educated & affluent consumer audience.

WATERING INC/HEMMINGS MOTOR NEWS

222 W Main St
Bennington, VT 05201-2103
Telephone: (802) 442-3101, (800) 227-4373, FAX: (802) 447-1561, E-Mail: hmnmail@hemmings.com, Web Site: www.hemmings.com
Chmn Bd: Ray Shaw
Conducts Business: Worldwide
Employees: 100
Primary Market Served: Consumer
Catalog available online
Direct online sales
Advertising/Marketing Budget Related to Direct Marketing: 51-75%
Founded: 1954
Gross sales or billing: $32,000,000

Publisher of periodicals & books for the antique, classic & special interest auto hobby market.

WEIDER PUBLICATIONS INC

Subs. of Weider Health & Fitness Inc
21100 Erwin St
Woodland Hills, CA 91367
Telephone: (818) 884-6800, (800) 423-5590, FAX: (818) 884-0242
Chmn: Joe Weider
Pres: Russell Denson
Sr VP, Consumer Mktg: David Foster
Conducts Business: Worldwide
Employees: 300
Primary Market Served: Business & Consumer
Founded: 1939

Publish Muscle & Fitness, SHAPE, Men's Fitness, Flex, Fit Pregnancy, Natural Health and Muscle & Fitness Here. Manufacture & distribute food supplements & exercise equipment worldwide; a "Total Fitness Company."

WEISS RESEARCH INC

15430 Endeavor Dr
Jupiter, FL 33478-6400
Telephone: (561) 627-3300, (877) 925-4833, FAX: (561) 625-6685, E-Mail: newbusiness@weissgroupinc.com, Web Site: www.weissgroupinc.com
CEO & Pres: Martin D. Weiss Ph. D.
Mktg Dir: Mary Ellen Tribley
Head Consultant: Larry Edelson
List Brokerage Mgr: Alisa Padgett
Head Consultant: Tony Sagami
Res Analyst: Amber Dakar
Res Analyst: John Burke
Dir Mktg: Jennifer Moran
Conducts Business: U.S.
Employees: 200

Primary Market Served: Business & Consumer
Catalog available online
Direct online sales
Advertising/Marketing Budget Related to Direct Marketing: 76-100%
Direct Marketing ad budget: $10,000,000
Direct Mail: 94%
Newspapers: 2%
Online: 2%
TV/Radio: 2%
Founded: 1971
Gross sales or billing: $16,800,000

Publish three financial newsletters with economic & stock market analysis. Rate insurance companies, banks & brokerage firms for financial stability.

WENNER MEDIA LLC

1290 Ave of the Americas (2nd fl)
New York, NY 10104-0298
Telephone: (212) 484-1616, FAX: (212) 484-1713
Chmn Bd & Pres: Jann S. Wenner
CFO: John Gruber
Chief Mktg Officer: Gary Armstrong
Conducts Business: U.S., Canada
Employees: 300
Primary Market Served: Business & Consumer
Founded: 1967
Gross sales or billing: $33,400,000

Publisher of Rolling Stone Magazine, US, The Entertainment Magazine & Men's Journal.

WESTGROUP

Div. of The Thomson Corp
610 Opperman Dr
Eagan, MN 55123-1340
Telephone: (800) 344-5008, Web Site: www.westgroup.com
Pres & CEO Westgroup: Brian Hall
VP Strategic Devel: Lee Bongiolatti
Conducts Business: U.S., Canada, Europe, Japan
Primary Market Served: Business
Advertising/Marketing Budget Related to Direct Marketing: 26-50%
Direct Marketing ad budget:
Direct Mail: 85%
Magazines: 5%
Telephone: 10%

Sells quality law books in areas of the law having national & international appeal. Sales are primarily to practicing attorneys.

WESTWOOD PUBLISHING CO

Div. of The Gil Boyne Group Inc
700 S Central Ave
Glendale, CA 91204
Telephone: (818) 242-1159, FAX: (818) 247-9379

Pres: Mark T. Gilboyne
Gen Mgr: Jon Younquist
Conducts Business: U.S., Canada, Malaysia, New Zealand, South Africa, Australia, U.K.
Employees: 6
Primary Market Served: Business & Consumer
Direct Marketing ad budget: $130,000
Direct Mail: 70%
Magazines: 30%
Gross sales or billing: $835,000

Mail order publisher of hypnotism, mind power & holistic studies books. Cassettes, courses & videotapes. Operate state licensed vocational school to train hypnotherapists.

WHITE MANE PUBLISHING CO INC

73 W Burd St
Shippensburg, PA 17257-1259
Telephone: (717) 532-2237, (888) 948-6263, FAX: (717) 532-6110, E-Mail: marketing@whitemane.com, Web Site: www.whitemane.com
Opers Dir: Denise Logan
Conducts Business: U.S.
Employees: 10
Primary Market Served: Business & Consumer
Catalog available online
Indirect online sales
Advertising/Marketing Budget Related to Direct Marketing: 0-25%
Direct Marketing ad budget:
Direct Mail: 50%
Magazines: 20%
Newspapers: 15%
TV/Radio: 5%
Telephone: 10%
Founded: 1987

MICHAEL WIESE PRODUCTIONS

3940 Laurel Canyon Blvd (#1111)
Studio City, CA 91604
Telephone: (818) 379-8799, (800) 833-5738, FAX: (818) 986-3408, Web Site: www.mwp.com
Pres: Michael Wiese
VP: Ken Lee
Conducts Business: Worldwide
Employees: 3
Primary Market Served: Business & Consumer
Catalog available online
Direct online sales
Advertising/Marketing Budget Related to Direct Marketing: 0-25%
Direct Marketing ad budget:
Direct Mail: 80%
Magazines: 20%

Health & educational infomercials, books, videos & audios & books for film & video professionals. Also, network television documentaries.

WILDLIFE EDUCATION LTD
1260 Audubon Rd
Park Hills, KY 41011-1904
Telephone: (858) 513-7600, FAX: (858) 513-7660, E-Mail: animals@zoobooks.com, Web Site: www.zoobooks.com
Publr: Ed Shadek
Sls Mgr: Kurt Von Hertsenberg
Online Mktg Mgr: Debi S. Ives
Circ Mgr: Jay Hillis
Conducts Business: Worldwide
Primary Market Served: Consumer
Direct online sales
Founded: 1980

Publish wildlife magazines and books for children.

JOHN WILEY & SONS CANADA LTD
Subs. of John Wiley & Sons Inc
5353 Dundaf St W
Etobicoke, ON, Canada M9B 6H8
Telephone: (416) 236-4433, FAX: (416) 236-4448, Web Site: www.wiley.com
Pres: Diane Wood
Prodn Mgr: Karen Bryan
Conducts Business: Canada
Employees: 90
Primary Market Served: Business

Professional, reference & trade books sold to educational & research institutions, industry professionals & libraries.

JOHN WILEY & SONS INC
111 River St
Hoboken, NJ 07030-5774
Telephone: (201) 748-6000, FAX: (201) 748-6088, E-Mail: info@wiley.com, Web Site: www.wiley.com
Chmn Bd: Peter Booth Riley
Pres & CEO: William J. Pesce
Sr VP, Corp Commun: Deborah E. Wiley
Dir: Bradford Wiley II
Direct Response Mktg Dir: Jack Day
Conducts Business: U.S., Canada, Europe, Australia, India, S.E. Asia
Employees: 4,900
Primary Market Served: Business & Consumer
Catalog available online
Direct online sales
Advertising/Marketing Budget Related to Direct Marketing: 51-75%
Direct Marketing ad budget:
Direct Mail: 95%
Magazines: 5%

Founded: 1807
Gross sales or billing: $1,100,000,000

Publisher of scientific, technical, business law, professional medical books & other related materials.

WILLIS MUSIC CO
7380 Industrial Rd, PO Box 548
Florence, KY 41042-0548
Telephone: (859) 283-2050, (800) 354-9799, FAX: (859) 283-1784, E-Mail: ordpt@willis-music.com, Web Site: www.willismusic.com
Owner: Edward R. Cranley
Pres: Kevin Cranley
Conducts Business: Worldwide
Employees: 150
Primary Market Served: Business & Consumer
Catalog available online
Direct Marketing ad budget:
Direct Mail: 50%
Magazines: 15%
Newspapers: 25%
TV/Radio: 10%
Founded: 1899

Music publishers. Also, musical instruments & accessories, music & stationery racks, musical gifts & collectors' items.

THE HW WILSON CO
950 University Ave
Bronx, NY 10452
Telephone: (718) 588-8400, (800) 367-6770, FAX: (800) 590-1617, E-Mail: custserv@hwwilson.com, Web Site: www.hwwilson.com
Pres & CEO: Harold Regan
VP, Sls & Mktg: Deborah V. Loeding
Conducts Business: Worldwide
Employees: 500
Primary Market Served: Business
Catalog available online
Direct online sales
Founded: 1898

Publisher of indexes, abstracts, reference books, videotapes, online database vendor & CD-ROM products.

WINN DEVON
aka CAP & Winn Devon; Div of Encore Art Group
6311 Westminster Hwy (Unit 110)
Richmond, BC, Canada V7C 4V4
Telephone: (206) 763-9544, (800) 875-4150, FAX: (206) 762-1389, Web Site: www.winndevon.com
Pres: Lisa Krieger
Creative Dir: Niki Krieger
Conducts Business: Worldwide
Employees: 60
Primary Market Served: Business
Founded: 1977
Gross sales or billing: $4,400,000

Publisher & distributor of original artworks, fine art posters and limited edition prints.

WINSLOW PUBLISHING
550 Eglinton Ave W
Toronto, ON, Canada M5N 3A8
Telephone: (416) 789-4733, E-Mail: winslow@interlog.com, Web Site: www.winslowpublishing.com
Owner & Pres: Michelle West
VP: Lawrence Merkur
Conducts Business: U.S., Canada
Employees: 2
Primary Market Served: Business & Consumer
Catalog available online
Indirect online sales
Advertising/Marketing Budget Related to Direct Marketing: 0-25%
Direct Marketing ad budget:
Direct Mail: 100%
Founded: 1981

Publish & sell books. Also, sell craft supplies & novelties.

WOLFE PUBLISHING CO INC
2180 Gulfstream (Suite A)
Prescott, AZ 86301-6182
Telephone: (928) 445-7810, (800) 899-7810, FAX: (928) 778-5124, E-Mail: wolfepub@riflemag.com, Web Site: www.riflemagazine.com
Pres & Publr: Mark Harris
Conducts Business: Worldwide
Employees: 11
Primary Market Served: Business & Consumer
Catalog available online
Founded: 1965

We publish magazines, books & art prints. Product is sold to dealers & retail consumers.

WOMAN'S MISSIONARY UNION
100 Missionary Ridge, PO Box 830010
Birmingham, AL 35283-0010
Telephone: (205) 991-8100, FAX: (205) 991-4990, E-Mail: email@wmu.org, Web Site: www.wmu.org
Mktg Svcs Dir: Dolores Jackson
Conducts Business: U.S.
Employees: 160
Primary Market Served: Consumer
Catalog available online
Direct online sales
Advertising/Marketing Budget Related to Direct Marketing: 0-25%
Founded: 1888

Publisher of Christian Missions materials, including New Hope books.

WOMAN'S DAY SPECIAL INTEREST PUBLICATIONS
Subs. of Hachette Filipacchi Magazines Publications Inc
1633 Broadway (42nd fl)
New York, NY 10019
Telephone: (212) 767-6000, FAX: (212) 767-5612, Web Site: www.womensday.com
Assoc Publr: Lynne Dominick
Conducts Business: U.S.
Primary Market Served: Consumer

Publisher of 39 special interest consumer magazines sold exclusively at supermarkets & retail outlets.

WOODALL PUBLISHING CO LP
Affinity Group
2575 Vista Del Mar Dr
Ventura, CA 93001
Telephone: (805) 667-4100, (800) 323-9076, FAX: (805) 667-4468, Web Site: www.woodalls.com
Chmn Bd, Affinity: Stephen Adams
CEO, Pres, Dir, Affinity: Michael A. Shneider
CFO & Sr VP: Thomas F. Wolfe
Pres & CEO Woodall: Linda L. Pro-Faiser
Pres & CEO Camping World: Marcus Lemonis
Conducts Business: U.S., Canada
Employees: 55
Primary Market Served: Consumer
Direct Marketing ad budget:
Direct Mail: 50%
Magazines: 10%
Newspapers: 40%
Founded: 1935

Monthly publications & annual directory for the Campground Industry.

WORDRIGHT ENTERPRISES INC
431 Dogwood Terr
Buffalo Grove, IL 60089-1820
Telephone: (847) 215-5190, Web Site: www.globalsources.com
Trade Shows Mgr: Alexis Schmookler
Conducts Business: Worldwide
Primary Market Served: Business

Business to business e-commerce.

THE WORLD BANK
1818 "H" St NW
Washington, DC 20433
Telephone: (202) 473-1000, FAX: (202) 477-6391, Web Site: www.worldbank.org
Pres: Paul Wolfowitz
Media Mgr: Amy L. Stilwell
Mgr Corp Commun: Carl Hanton
TV & Radio Mktg: Cynthia Case

Mkt Analyst: Maya Brahmam
Conducts Business: Worldwide
Employees: 10,000
Primary Market Served: Business & Consumer
Catalog available online
Indirect online sales
Advertising/Marketing Budget Related to Direct Marketing: 0-25%
Founded: 1945

Publications department disseminates economic & development research produced by World Bank.

THE DMA WORLD BOOK INC
233 N Michigan Ave (Suite 2000)
Chicago, IL 60601-5805
Telephone: (312) 729-5800, (800) 255-1750, FAX: (312) 729-5600, Web Site: www.worldbook.com
Pres: Robert Martin
Exec VP & Publr: Michael Ross
Dir, Direct Mktg: Mark Willy
Conducts Business: U.S., Canada
Employees: 178
Primary Market Served: Consumer
Catalog available online
Indirect online sales
Advertising/Marketing Budget Related to Direct Marketing: 51-75%
Direct Marketing ad budget:
$6,000,000
Direct Mail: $1,000,000
Magazines: $2,000,000
Newspapers: $1,000,000
TV/Radio: $1,000,000
Telephone: $1,000,000
Founded: 1917
Gross sales or billing: $31,000,000

Market encyclopedias (print & CD-ROM) & other reference resources to consumers, schools & libraries.

WORLD PUBLICATIONS INC
460 N Orlando Ave (Suite 200)
Winter Park, FL 32789
Telephone: (407) 628-4802, FAX: (407) 628-7061, Web Site: www.worldpub.net
Chmn: Jonas Bonnier
CEO: Terry Snow
COO: Dan Altman
VP Consumer Mktg: Bruce Miller
VP Production Opers: Lisa Earlywine
Conducts Business: U.S., Canada
Employees: 65
Primary Market Served: Business & Consumer
Catalog available online
Direct online sales
Advertising/Marketing Budget Related to Direct Marketing: 76-100%
Gross sales or billing: $350,000,000

Consumer sports-related publications & trade publications for the sports & boating industries, food & garden.

WORLDVU LLC
1906 E Pratt St
Baltimore, MD 21231-1925
Telephone: (410) 522-4223, FAX: (410) 522-4233, E-Mail: info@worldvu.com, Web Site: www.worldvu.com
Pres & Publr: Merry Law
Assoc Publr: Wayne Winkler
Conducts Business: Worldwide
Employees: 3
Primary Market Served: Business
Catalog available online
Indirect online sales
Advertising/Marketing Budget Related to Direct Marketing: 76-100%
Direct Marketing ad budget:
Direct Mail: 96%
Magazines: 2%
Telephone: 2%

Publisher of practical information for businesses worldwide, including the Guide to Worldwide Postal-Code Address Formats.

WRITER'S DIGEST BOOKS
Div. of F&W Publications
10151 Carver Rd (Suite 200)
Blue Ash, OH 45242-4760
Telephone: (513) 531-2690, (800) 666-0963, Web Site: www.fwpublications.com
Pres Book Publ & Book Clubs: William Budge Wallis
Conducts Business: Worldwide
Employees: 300
Primary Market Served: Business & Consumer
Direct online sales
Advertising/Marketing Budget Related to Direct Marketing: 0-25%
Founded: 1921

Publish instructional books for writers, artists, songwriters, woodworkers & photographers.

WYANDOTTE WEST COMMUNICATIONS INC
PO Box 12003
Kansas City, KS 66112-0003
Telephone: (913) 788-5565, FAX: (913) 788-9812, E-Mail: news@wyandottewest.com, Web Site: www.wyandottewest.com
Pres: Murrel W. Bland
Gen Mgr & Ed: Joe Keefhaver
Sls & Mktg Mgr: Jamie Ralston
Sls: Mickey Johns
Production Ed: Sarah Abend
Conducts Business: U.S.
Employees: 7

Primary Market Served: Business &
Consumer
Catalog available online
Direct online sales
Advertising/Marketing Budget Related
to Direct Marketing: 0-25%
Direct Marketing ad budget: $15,000
Direct Mail: 10%
Newspapers: 10%
Telephone: 80%
Founded: 1968
Gross sales or billing: $465,000

Community weekly newspaper. Sell
subscriptions to consumers & ads to
consumers and businesses.

WYCLIFFE BIBLE TRANSLATORS

7500 W Camp Wisdom Rd
Dallas, TX 75236-5629
Telephone: (972) 708-7522, Web Site:
www.wycliffe.org
Sustained Giving Mgr: Pixie Chris-
tensen
Primary Market Served: Consumer

YANKEE PUBLISHING INC

1121 Main St
Dublin, NH 03444
Telephone: (603) 563-8111, FAX:
(603) 563-8732, Web Site: www.
yankeemagazine.com
Chmn: C. Robertson Trowbridge
Conducts Business: U.S.
Employees: 100
Primary Market Served: Consumer

Publisher of Yankee Magazine, Old
Farmers Almanac, Travel Guide to
New England.

YELLOW BOOK USA

398 RXR Plaza
Uniondale, NY 11556-0398
Telephone: (516) 730-1900, (800) 666-
8230, FAX: (845) 278-3299, Web
Site: www.yellowbook.com
Conducts Business: U.S.
Employees: 35
Primary Market Served: Business
Founded: 1972

Publish local telephone directories &
other specialized publications.

THE DMA YOGA JOURNAL / ACTIVE INTEREST MEDIA

475 Sansome St (Suite 850)
San Francisco, CA 94111-3135
Telephone: (415) 591-0555, Web Site:
www.yogajournal.com
Grp Circulation Dir: Barbara Besser

ZIFF DAVIS MEDIA INC

28 E 28th St (11th fl)
New York, NY 10016
Telephone: (212) 503-5100, FAX:
(212) 503-5023, Web Site: www.
ziffdavis.com
Chmn: Robert F. Callahan
CEO: Jason Young
Sr VP & CFO: Mark D. Moyer
VP, Gen Counsel: Shirin Malkani
VP, HR: Beth Repeta
Primary Market Served: Business &
Consumer

Magazine publisher.

ZONDERVAN CORP

Div. of Harper Collins Publishers
5300 Patterson Ave SE
Grand Rapids, MI 49530
Telephone: (616) 698-6900, (800) 727-
3060, FAX: (616) 698-3235, Web
Site: www.zondervan.com
Pres & CEO: Bruce Ryskamp
EVP & CFO: Gary Wicker
EVP: Scott Bolinder
Conducts Business: Worldwide
Employees: 340
Primary Market Served: Business
Catalog available online
Direct online sales
Founded: 1932
Gross sales or billing: $38,600,000

Company specializing in the publication & sale of books, Bibles, curriculum & software.

Subscription Agencies (18)

This section lists agencies that distribute, sell or market magazines and newspapers to various segments of the public and industry.

AMERICAN PREFERRED READER'S SERVICE INC
1975 E Sunrise Blvd Ste 800
Fort Lauderdale, FL 33304-1455
Telephone: (954) 489-2443, FAX: (954) 492-2343, E-Mail: jfarrell@amerpref.com, Web Site: www.amerpref.com
Pres: James H. Farrell Sr.
VP Mktg: Caryn Farrell
Agency Acct Exec: Leslie S. Smith
Conducts Business: U.S.
Employees: 100
Primary Market Served: Business & Consumer
Founded: 1985
Gross sales or billing: $2,000,000

Distribute family oriented magazines, wholesale & retail.

BELLTOWER TECHNOLOGIES
7100 E Belleview Ave (Suite 208)
Greenwood Village, CO 80111
Telephone: (303) 843-0302, FAX: (303) 843-0377, Web Site: www.shopathome.com
Pres: Marc Braunstein
Sr VP, Circ: Claudia Braunstein
Primary Market Served: Consumer
Catalog available online
Direct online sales
Founded: 1986

Direct mail catalog company.

COMMUNICATION RESOURCES INC
4150 Belden Village St NW (4th fl)
Canton, OH 44718
Telephone: (800) 992-2144, FAX: (330) 493-3158, E-Mail: service@comresources.com, Web Site: www.comresources.com
Pres: Randall S. Coy
COO: Kelly Brown
Conducts Business: U.S., Canada
Employees: 25
Primary Market Served: Business & Consumer
Advertising/Marketing Budget Related to Direct Marketing: 76-100%

Periodical publications & newsletter related materials.

CUSTOMIZED NEWSPAPER ADVERTISING
aka CNA
319 E Fifth St
Des Moines, IA 50309
Telephone: (515) 244-2145, (800) 227-7636, FAX: (515) 244-4855, Web Site: www.cnaads.com
Exec Dir: Bill Monroe
Asst Dir: Chris Mudge
Employees: 15
Primary Market Served: Business

CNA facilitates multi-newspaper and on-line planning and placement locally or nationwide.

DAYTON DAILY NEWS
Div. of Cox Enterprises
1611 S Main St, Cox Ohio Publishing, Media Ctr
Dayton, OH 45409-2547
Telephone: (937) 222-5700, (888) 397-6397, FAX: (937) 225-2153, E-Mail: daytondaily@coxohio.com, Web Site: www.daytondailynews.com
Publr: Kevin Riley
Conducts Business: U.S.
Employees: 1,000
Primary Market Served: Business & Consumer
Advertising/Marketing Budget Related to Direct Marketing: 0-25%
Gross sales or billing: $58,300,000

Sells newspapers.

DETROIT NEWSPAPERS
615 W Lafayette Blvd
Detroit, MI 48226
Telephone: (313) 222-6400, FAX: (313) 222-5032, Web Site: www.freep.com
Prodn Mgr Home Delivery: Carolyn Arnold
Primary Market Served: Business & Consumer

Agent for Detroit News & Detroit Free Press.

EBSCO RECEPTION ROOM SUBSCRIPTION SERVICES
Div. of EBSCO Investment Services Inc
PO Box 830460
Birmingham, AL 35283-0460
Telephone: (205) 991-1409, (800) 527-5901, FAX: (205) 995-1621, Web Site: www.ebsco.com/errss
Pres: J.T. Stephens
VP & Gen Mgr: Jack H. Breard
Office Mgr: Susie Sims
Conducts Business: U.S., Canada
Employees: 55
Primary Market Served: Business

Direct online sales
Advertising/Marketing Budget Related to Direct Marketing: 76-100%
Direct Marketing ad budget:
Direct Mail: 100%
Founded: 1980

Provide professional offices, barber & beauty shops & business offices with one-order, one-invoice purchasing of magazines & journal subscriptions at savings up to 50%.

IN-SYNC PUBLICATIONS
800 Knob Hill Ave
Redondo Beach, CA 90277
Telephone: (310) 543-9045, FAX: (310) 543-9035, E-Mail: insyncpubs@aol.com, Web Site: www.insyncpubs.com
Owner: Robert Christy
VP: Julie Christy
Conducts Business: Worldwide
Employees: 3
Primary Market Served: Business & Consumer
Catalog available online
Indirect online sales
Advertising/Marketing Budget Related to Direct Marketing: 76-100%
Direct Marketing ad budget:
Direct Mail: 100%
Founded: 1987
Gross sales or billing: $180,000

Sales & service of motion picture & video equipment to the professional market. Our newspaper tries to put buyer & seller together.

MERRILL CORP
Subs. of Merrill Corp
4110 Clearwater Rd
Saint Cloud, MN 56301
Telephone: (320) 656-5000, FAX: (320) 656-5163
Primary Market Served: Business

Company print program.

O'CURRANCE INC
1747 Lone Peak Pkwy (Suite 100)
Draper, UT 84020-6876
Telephone: (801) 736-0500, (888) 628-7726, FAX: (801) 736-0510, E-Mail: sales@ocurrance.com, Web Site: www.ocurance.com
Pres: Carla Curran
Primary Market Served: Business & Consumer
Founded: 1994

Call center.

PERIODICAL PUBLISHER'S SERVICE BUREAU INC
One Superior St
Sandusky, OH 44870-1815
Telephone: (419) 626-0623, (800) 220-1247, FAX: (419) 626-4576, Web Site: www.ppsb.com
Sls & Mktg Dir: Steven Posti
Conducts Business: Worldwide
Primary Market Served: Business & Consumer
Catalog available online
Founded: 1910

Subscription sales & reader service processing.

THE PLAIN DEALER
1801 Superior Ave
Cleveland, OH 44114-2107
Telephone: (216) 999-5000, FAX: (216) 999-6356, Web Site: www.plaindealer.com
Pres & Publr: Terrence C.Z. Egger
Chief Mktg Ofc: Matt Kraner
VP Mktg: Bruce A. Ross
Mktg Svc Coord: Chuck Kandrach
Conducts Business: U.S.
Employees: 1,520
Primary Market Served: Consumer
Catalog available online
Direct online sales
Advertising/Marketing Budget Related to Direct Marketing: 0-25%
Direct Marketing ad budget:
Direct Mail: 10%
Magazines: 5%
Newspapers: 50%
Online: 15%
TV/Radio: 10%
Telephone: 10%
Founded: 1842
Gross sales or billing: $220,000,000

Ohio's largest newspaper. Selling ads, classifieds, subscriptions, article reprints online.

ᴛʜᴇ ᴅᴍᴀ PUBLISHERS CLEARING HOUSE
382 Channel Dr
Port Washington, NY 11050-2297
Telephone: (516) 883-5432, FAX: (516) 767-4567, E-Mail: cirving@pch.com, Web Site: www.pch.com
Chmn: Robin B. Smith
Pres & CEO: Andrew Goldberg
Conducts Business: U.S., Canada, U.K.
Employees: 500
Primary Market Served: Consumer
Catalog available online
Direct online sales
Advertising/Marketing Budget Related to Direct Marketing: 76-100%
Direct Marketing ad budget:

Direct Mail: 90%
Telephone: 10%
Founded: 1953
Gross sales or billing: $625,000,000

Publishers Clearing House is a leading multi-channel direct marketer of value-based consumer products and magazines and a respected leader in the direct marketing industry.

RAPID CITY JOURNAL
507 Main St
Rapid City, SD 57701-2733
Telephone: (605) 394-8300, FAX: (605) 394-8462, E-Mail: classifieds@rapidcityjournal.com, Web Site: www.rapidcityjournal.com
Publr: Brad Slater
Editor: Mike LeFort
Online Sls Mgr: Debbie Renner
Interactive Products Mgr: Christopher Donahue
HR Mgr: Laurel Grove
Employees: 220
Primary Market Served: Business & Consumer
Catalog available online
Gross sales or billing: $19,100,000

Sells to western South Dakota area. Printing, want ads, newspapers.

SUBSCRIPTION AGENCY.COM INC
3000 Executive Rd (Suite 12)
Winter Haven, FL 33884
Telephone: (863) 229-2557, FAX: (508) 374-8599, E-Mail: info@subscriptionagency.com, Web Site: www.subscriptionagency.com
Pres: Melanie Truesdell
Conducts Business: U.S.
Primary Market Served: Business & Consumer
Catalog available online
Direct online sales
Founded: 2003
Gross sales or billing: $2,600,000

Magazine subscriptions - clearing house for magazine agents.

SYNAPSE GROUP INC
Subs. of Time Inc.
225 High Ridge Rd, East Building
Stamford, CT 06905-3038
Telephone: (203) 595-8255, FAX: (203) 329-8237, E-Mail: webmaster@synapsemail.com, Web Site: www.synapsegroupinc.com
CEO: Jeff Blatt
Pres: Michael Loeb
HR: Dorothy Brill
Mktg Dir: Tracy Furrier
Conducts Business: U.S.
Employees: 300

Primary Market Served: Consumer
Advertising/Marketing Budget Related to Direct Marketing: 76-100%
Direct Marketing ad budget:
Direct Mail: 100%
Founded: 1991

Marketing.

TIME OUT NEW YORK
475 10th Ave (12th fl)
New York, NY 10018
Telephone: (646) 432-3000, FAX: (212) 677-9665, E-Mail: tnew@kable.com, Web Site: www.timeout.com/newyork/
Mktg Dir: Michael Rucker
Primary Market Served: Consumer

Weekly arts and entertainment guide to New York City.

TIMES PUBLISHING CO
205 W 12th St
Erie, PA 16534-0011
Telephone: (814) 870-1600, FAX: (814) 870-1808, E-Mail: terry.cascioli@timesnews.com
Pres & Publr: Rosanne Cheeseman
Dir Sls & Mktg: Terry Cascioli
Conducts Business: Newspaper
Employees: 250
Direct online sales
Founded: 1888

Newspaper for Erie County, PA.

TIMES UNION
Div. of Hearst
Box 15000, News Plaza
Albany, NY 12212
Telephone: (518) 454-5694, FAX: (518) 454-5628, Web Site: www.timesunion.com
Online Ed: Patti Hart
Online Producer: David Washburn
Primary Market Served: Business & Consumer

Local Newspaper.

UNIVERSITY SUBSCRIPTION SERVICE
1213 Butterfield Rd
Downers Grove, IL 60515
Telephone: (630) 960-3233, FAX: (630) 960-3246, Web Site: www.ussmag.com
Pres: Pethi Velu
VP: Param Velu
Conducts Business: U.S.
Employees: 30
Primary Market Served: Consumer
Catalog available online
Indirect online sales
Advertising/Marketing Budget Related to Direct Marketing: 0-25%
Founded: 1974

Gross sales or billing: $8,000,000

Sell subscriptions to consumer magazines to teachers, college students & educators by direct mail, space advertising, publication inserts & through college bookstores.

WORLD PRESS REVIEW

Div. of All Media Inc
700 Broadway
New York, NY 10003
Telephone: (212) 982-8880, Web Site:
  www.worldpressreview.com
Publr & Founder: Teri Schure
Ed-in-Chief: Alice Chasan
Prod & Design Mgr: Laura R. Custus
Adv Coord: Louisa D. Kearney
Conducts Business: Worldwide
Employees: 19
Primary Market Served: Consumer
Indirect online sales
Founded: 1997
Gross sales or billing: $400,000

Monthly magazine & website of the foreign press with translated feature articles, commentary & cartoons from leading publications throughout the world. 95% subscription sold.

Travel & Leisure (19)

AESU INC
3922 Hickory Ave
Baltimore, MD 21211-1834
Telephone: (410) 366-5494, (800) 638-7640, FAX: (410) 366-6999, E-Mail: res@aesu.com, Web Site: www.aesu.com
Pres: Fritz Satren
Conducts Business: Worldwide
Employees: 25
Primary Market Served: Business & Consumer
Catalog available online
Indirect online sales
Advertising/Marketing Budget Related to Direct Marketing: 26-50%
Founded: 1977
Gross sales or billing: $10,000,000

International tour operators. Incentive travel & specialty tours.

THE DMA AIFS
9 W Broad St
Stamford, CT 06902-3788
Telephone: (203) 399-5000, Web Site: www.aifs.com
Asst Dir Database Mktg & Direct Mktg: Richard Chow

ABSOLUTE RESERVATION CENTER INC
150 E Wildmere Ave (#108)
Longwood, FL 32750
Telephone: (407) 660-9995, Web Site: www.arcfun.com
Primary Market Served: Business & Consumer

ACADEMIC TRAVEL ABROAD INC
1920 N St NW (Suite 200)
Washington, DC 20036-1652
Telephone: (202) 785-9000, (800) 556-7896, FAX: (202) 342-0317, Web Site: www.academictravel.com
Pres: David T. Parry
Exec VP: Kate Simpson
VP: Sarah Saleh
VP: Chase Poffenberger
VP: Beverly Cutshaw
Conducts Business: U.S., Canada
Employees: 45
Primary Market Served: Business & Consumer
Founded: 1947
Gross sales or billing: $13,750,000

Tour operators for tours around the world.

AFFINITY GROUP INC
2575 Vista del Mar Dr
Ventura, CA 93001-3920
Telephone: (805) 667-4100, (800) 765-1912, FAX: (805) 667-4419, E-Mail: khurd@affinitygroup.com, Web Site: www.affinitygroup.com
Sr VP Prods & Svcs: Praibhuling Patel
Sr Dir Corp Commun: Gene Tuttle
Sr VP & CFO: Tom Wolfe
CEO: Mike Schneider
Sr VP & CMO: Murray Coker
VP New Prod Devel: Kevin Hobbs
Conducts Business: U.S., Canada
Employees: 2,000
Primary Market Served: Consumer
Catalog available online
Direct online sales
Advertising/Marketing Budget Related to Direct Marketing: 76-100%
Founded: 1993
Gross sales or billing: $450,000,000

Management of Affinity groups & clubs; member & consumer publications, insurance & financial services.

AIRTRAN AIRWAYS
1800 Phoenix Blvd (Suite 104)
Atlanta, GA 30349-5569
Telephone: (678) 254-7459, Web Site: www.airtran.com
Pres: James Fitzgerald

ALITALIA
51 Madison Ave (Suite 2000)
New York, NY 10010
Telephone: (800) 223-5730, FAX: (212) 903-3568, E-Mail: customer.relationsnyc@alitalia.it, Web Site: www.alitalia.com
Cust Rels Mgr: Barry Morrow
Conducts Business: U.S.
Employees: 550
Primary Market Served: Business & Consumer
Advertising/Marketing Budget Related to Direct Marketing: 0-25%

Air transportation to consumer & trade.

THE DMA AMBASSADOR PROGRAMS
1956 Ambassador Way
Spokane, WA 99224-4012
Telephone: (509) 568-7800, Web Site: www.ptpprograms.org
Primary Market Served: Business & Consumer

AMERICAN AIRLINES INC
Subs. of AMR Corp
PO Box 619616
Dallas, TX 75261-9616

Telephone: (817) 967-1910, FAX: (817) 967-2841
DM Mgr: Susan D. Williams
Conducts Business: Worldwide
Employees: 90,000
Primary Market Served: Business & Consumer
Gross sales or billing: $1,000,000,000

Promote air travel for American Airlines.

THE DMA AMERISTAR CASINOS
3773 Howard Hughes Pkwy 490 S
Las Vegas, NV 89169-0949
Telephone: (702) 567-7059
Primary Market Served: Consumer

ELIZABETH ARDEN SPAS LLC
300 Main St (Suite 8)
Stamford, CT 06901-3033
Telephone: (203) 905-1700, FAX: (203) 905-1716, Web Site: www.reddoorspas.com
CEO & Pres: W Todd Walter
CFO: Robert Broadhead
Chief Mktg Officer & Sr VP: Lisa Hagen
Conducts Business: U.S.
Employees: 4,200
Primary Market Served: Consumer
Direct online sales
Advertising/Marketing Budget Related to Direct Marketing: 0-25%
Direct Marketing ad budget: $500,000
Direct Mail: 100%
Gross sales or billing: $200,000,000

Spa and salon services and beauty and hair retail products to consumers.

AVIS WORLD HEADQUARTERS
6 Sylvan Way
Parsippany, NJ 07054-3826
Telephone: (973) 496-3500, Web Site: www.avis.com
VP, Adv & Mktg: Don Simon
DM Mgr: Elisa Lopez
Sr VP: Becky Alseth
Conducts Business: Worldwide
Employees: 11,000
Primary Market Served: Business & Consumer

Provide rental car services to business & leisure travelers.

THE DMA BAHAMAS MINISTRY OF TOURISM
1200 S Pine Island Rd (Suite 750)
Fort Lauderdale, FL 33324-4413

Telephone: (954) 236-9292, Web Site:
www.bahamas.com
Gen Mgr E-Commerce: Andrew
Adderley
Sr Dir Commun: Nalini Bethel
Primary Market Served: Business &
Consumer

BEAU RIVAGE RESORT & CASINO

875 Beach Blvd
Biloxi, MS 39530-4299
Telephone: (228) 386-7150, Web Site:
www.beaurivage.com
Exec Dir Adv: Brian Bork
Primary Market Served: Business &
Consumer

THE DMA BEST WESTERN INTERNATIONAL

6201 N 24th Pkwy
Phoenix, AZ 85016-2023
Telephone: (609) 957-5809, Web Site:
www.bestwestern.com
Sr Mgr Mktg Programs: Cassie Spill-
ner

BLUE STRAWBERRY RESORTS LLC

7600 Harding Ave Apt 3
Miami Beach, FL 33141-2150
Telephone: (756) 513-1456, (800) 873-
1440, Web Site: www.
bluestrawberry-resorts.com
CEO: Erika Garcia

Represents over 400 beachfront & golf
course view hotel rooms

BROADMOOR HOTEL INC

1 Lake Ave
Colorado Springs, CO 80906-4269
Telephone: (719) 634-7711, (866) 837-
9520, FAX: (719) 577-5779, Web
Site: www.broadmoor.com
Chmn & CEO: Steve Bartolin
VP, Sls & Mktg: John Washko
Dir: Karen Brandner
Resident Mgr: Ann Alba
Network Admin: Christopher Fisher
Conducts Business: U.S.
Employees: 1,500
Primary Market Served: Business &
Consumer
Catalog available online
Direct online sales
Gross sales or billing: $52,000,000

Full-service hotel & resort.

BROTHERHOOD AMERICA'S OLDEST WINERY LTD

100 Brotherhood Plaza Dr
Washingtonville, NY 10992-2262

Telephone: (845) 496-3661, FAX:
(845) 496-8720, E-Mail: contact@
brotherhoodwinery.net, Web Site:
www.brotherhoodwinery.net
VP & Winetaster: Cesar Baeza
Grp Sls Dir: Silvana Spisany
Events Dir: Randy Maduras
Pres: Hernan Donoso
Conducts Business: U.S.
Employees: 40
Primary Market Served: Consumer
Catalog available online
Direct online sales
Advertising/Marketing Budget Related
to Direct Marketing: 0-25%
Founded: 1839

Conduct tours & wine tastings. Produce a diversified line of quality wine
for local, regional & national
distribution.

CPC INC

dba International Travel Conferences
206 E Main St, PO Box 697
Babylon, NY 11702-0697
Telephone: (631) 661-6779, (800) 621-
4414, FAX: (631) 661-6914, E-Mail:
cpcus@aol.com, Web Site: www.
cpctours.com
Pres: Paul V. Elmstrom
VP: Katherine T. Monaco
Conducts Business: U.S., Canada
Employees: 5
Primary Market Served: Business &
Consumer
Catalog available online
Indirect online sales
Advertising/Marketing Budget Related
to Direct Marketing: 76-100%
Direct Marketing ad budget: $500,000
Direct Mail: 100%
Founded: 1988
Gross sales or billing: $1,000,000

Market international nursing, legal &
veterinary study tours, conferences,
seminars & business meetings.

CAESARS ATLANTIC CITY CASINO/HOTEL

Div. of Harrah's Entertainment Inc.
2100 Pacific Ave, Boardwalk at Arkan-
sas
Atlantic City, NJ 08401-6612
Telephone: (609) 348-4411, (800) 634-
6661, FAX: (609) 343-2405, Web
Site: www.harrahs.com
Dir Mktg: Christina Banks
VP Pub Rels: Alyce Parker
Conducts Business: U.S.
Employees: 3,500
Primary Market Served: Business &
Consumer
Catalog available online
Direct online sales
Gross sales or billing: $117,800,000

Promote casino, hotel & convention
facilities. Sell hotel reservations, show
tickets, and spa and other packages.

CALLAWAY GARDENS

Subs. of Ida Cason Callaway Founda-
tion
17800 US Hwy 27
Pine Mountain, GA 31822-2000
Telephone: (706) 663-2281, (800)
CALLAWAY, FAX: (706) 663-6812,
E-Mail: info@callawaygardens.com,
Web Site: www.callawaygardens.com
Chmn: Ray C. Anderson
Sr Partner: James E. Butler
VP, Sls & Mktg: Kathy Tilles
VP: Rex R. Boner
Dir: Dr. Becky Champion
Stores & Prods Dir: Kevin Bridges
PR Mgr: Rachel Crumbley
Conducts Business: U.S.
Employees: 1,100
Primary Market Served: Business &
Consumer
Catalog available online
Direct online sales
Advertising/Marketing Budget Related
to Direct Marketing: 0-25%
Founded: 1952

Full-service destination resort. Complete stores & products division headquartered at Callaway Gardens for retail & catalog sales of food items.

THE DMA CARNIVAL CRUISE LINES

3655 NW 87th Ave
Miami, FL 33178-2418
Telephone: (212) 599-2600, Web Site:
www.carnival.com
Dir Direct Mktg: Cecilia Sanguinetti
Primary Market Served: Business &
Consumer

COAST HOTELS LIMITED

dba Coast Hotels & Resorts
2003 Western Ave (Suite 500)
Seattle, WA 98121
Telephone: (206) 826-2700, FAX:
(206) 826-2701, Web Site: www.
coasthotels.com
Pres: Michael Bushaw
Exec VP: Matt Murphy
Conducts Business: Worldwide
Primary Market Served: Business &
Consumer
Catalog available online
Direct online sales
Advertising/Marketing Budget Related
to Direct Marketing: 51-75%
Direct Marketing ad budget:
Direct Mail: 40%
Magazines: 10%
Newspapers: 50%
Founded: 1972

Operator of resorts & conference centers.

COLLETTE VACATIONS
180 Middle St
Pawtucket, RI 02860-1013
Telephone: (401) 727-9000, FAX: (401) 727-1000, E-Mail: czesk@ collettetours.com, Web Site: www. collettevacations.com
Sr VP Mktg: Eric Welter

CROWNE PLAZA CHATEAU LE COMBE
Subs. of Commonwealth Hospitality
10111 Bellamy Hill
Edmonton, AB, Canada T5J 1N7
Telephone: (780) 428-6611, FAX: (780) 420-8379, E-Mail: info@ chateaulecombe.com, Web Site: www.chateaulecombe.com
Gen Mgr: Paul Stephens
Dir Sls & Mktg: Cindy Sorenson
Conducts Business: U.S., Canada
Employees: 250
Primary Market Served: Business & Consumer
Direct Marketing ad budget:
Magazines: 60%
Newspapers: 5%
Online: 35%

307 room luxury hotel in downtown Edmonton. Meeting & convention facilities to accommodate up to 800 persons. Full food & beverage facilities.

DELTA VACATIONS
Sub. of MLT Vacations
110 E Broward Blvd Fl 14
Fort Lauderdale, FL 33301-3521
Telephone: (954) 522-1440, (800) 800-1504, FAX: (954) 468-4765, Web Site: www.deltavacations.com
CFO: Celeste Allen
COO: Michael Egan
Gen Mgr Delta Vacations: John Mooney
Primary Market Served: Consumer
Catalog available online
Direct online sales
Advertising/Marketing Budget Related to Direct Marketing: 51-75%
Founded: 1981

Air-inclusive vacation packages to over 120 destinations worldwide.

DESTINATIONS IRELAND & GREAT BRITAIN
PO Box 739
Rhinebeck, NY 12572

Telephone: (800) 832-1848, FAX: (212) 265-0154, E-Mail: info@ digbtravel.com, Web Site: www. allgolftravel.com/tours
Pres: Declan O'Brien
Opers & Grp Sls: Linda Buote
Conducts Business: Worldwide
Primary Market Served: Business & Consumer
Catalog available online
Advertising/Marketing Budget Related to Direct Marketing: 0-25%
Founded: 1990

Luxury custom-designed tours.

DAN DIPERT TRAVEL SERVICE INC
7301 W Pioneer Pkwy Ste A
Arlington, TX 76013-2804
Telephone: (817) 543-3700, (800) 433-5335, FAX: (817) 543-3728, Web Site: www.dandipert.com
Pres & CEO: Dan W. Dipert
CEO & COO: Autumn Dipert
VP, Opers: Margie Brantley
Sls & Mktg Dir: Linda Dipert
Conducts Business: U.S., Canada
Employees: 25
Primary Market Served: Business & Consumer
Catalog available online
Advertising/Marketing Budget Related to Direct Marketing: 51-75%
Direct Marketing ad budget: $200,000
Direct Mail: 70%
Newspapers: 30%
Founded: 1970

Travel agency specializing in retail & wholesale escorted tours, retail travel & motorcoach charter.

DISNEY VACATION CLUB
Subs. of Walt Disney Co.
1390 Celebration Blvd
Kissimmee, FL 34747-5166
Telephone: (407) 566-3100, (800) 500-3990, FAX: (407) 566-3393
Chmn: Richard Cook
Pres: Andy Bird
Sr Exec VP, Gen Counsel & Sec: Andy Braverman
Exec VP, Dir & HR: Wes Coleman
Exec VP Corp Strategy: Kevin Mayer
Primary Market Served: Consumer
Catalog available online
Direct online sales

Vacation ownership business.

WALT DISNEY PARKS & RESORTS
PO Box 10000
Lake Buena Vista, FL 32830-1000
Telephone: (407) 824-2222, Web Site: www.disneyworld.com

Sr VP Global Customer Managed Rels: Tom Boyles

DOUBLETREE SUITES BY HILTON
400 Soldiers Field Rd
Boston, MA 02134-1893
Telephone: (617) 783-0090, (800) 222-TREE, FAX: (617) 783-0897, E-Mail: doubletree1@hilton.com
Gen Mgr: Christian Coffin
CEO: Richard Kelleher
Sr VP: David E. Worth
Exec VP: James P. Evans
Sr VP: Dave Horton
Conducts Business: U.S.
Employees: 5,200
Primary Market Served: Business & Consumer
Catalog available online
Direct online sales
Direct Marketing ad budget: $1,000,000
Direct Mail: 30%
Magazines: 35%
Newspapers: 35%
Gross sales or billing: $464,000,000

Provide travelers with first class suites, services & amenities, innovative restaurants & lounges. Flexible meeting & banquet rooms. Relaxing health & fitness facilities.

E-MILES.COM
8401 N Central Expy (#1000)
Dallas, TX 75225-4405
Telephone: (214) 757-4700, Web Site: www.e-miles.com
VP: Brad Harraman

ELMWOOD SPA
Toronto, ON, Canada M5G 1G7
Telephone: (416) 964-4515, Web Site: www.elmwoodspa.com
Sr Mgr Sls & Mktg: Gwen Hayes

EMPIRE CITY CASINO AT YONKERS RACEWAY
810 Yonkers Ave
Yonkers, NY 10704-2030
Telephone: (914) 968-4200, Web Site: www.empirecitygaming.com
Database Mgr: Darcy Murray

ENTERPRISE RENT-A-CAR
600 Corporate Park Dr
Saint Louis, MO 63105-4204
Telephone: (314) 512-5000, Web Site: www.enterprise.com
VP Mktg: Brian Curtin

EVENTFUL INC
12626 High Bluff Dr Ste 100
San Diego, CA 92130-2072

Telephone: (858) 754-3004, Web Site:
www.eventful.com
VP Opers: Paul Ramirez
Primary Market Served: Business &
Consumer

EXPEDIA INC

333 108th Ave NE (Suite 300)
Bellevue, WA 98004-5736
Telephone: (425) 679-7200, Web Site:
www.expedia.com
Mktg Mgr: Courtney Schwind
Primary Market Served: Business &
Consumer

FOUR SEASONS HOTELS & RESORTS

1165 Leslie St
Toronto, ON, Canada M3C 2K8
Telephone: (416) 449-1750, (800) 819-
5053, FAX: (416) 441-4374, Web
Site: www.fourseasons.com
Mktg Commun Dir: David Bounsall
Chmn & CEO: Isadore Sharp
Pres & COO: Kathleen Taylor
Pres Worldwide Hotel Opers: Jim
FitzGibbon
Reg VP: Stan Bromley
Reg VP: Thomas Gurtner
Conducts Business: U.S., Canada
Primary Market Served: Business &
Consumer
Catalog available online
Direct online sales
Founded: 1960

Hotel chain.

GAYLORD ENTERTAINMENT CO

One Gaylord Dr
Nashville, TN 37214
Telephone: (615) 316-6000, Web Site:
www.gaylordentertainment.com
Mgr: Peter Fisher
Primary Market Served: Consumer
Founded: 1925

Entertainment & Grand Ole Oprey.

GENERAL TOURS/TBI TOURS

53 Summer St
Keene, NH 03431
Telephone: (603) 357-5033, (800) 221-
2216, FAX: (603) 357-4548, E-Mail:
info@generaltours.com, Web Site:
www.generaltours.com
Pres: Robert Drumm
Mktg Mgr: Christine Whippie
Conducts Business: U.S.
Employees: 25
Primary Market Served: Business &
Consumer
Direct Marketing ad budget: $50,000
Direct Mail: 25%
Newspapers: 75%

Founded: 1947
Gross sales or billing: $15,000,000

Tour packages including airfare to
Russia, Eastern Europe, Israel, Egypt,
Morocco, Middle East, Japan, China,
Orient, India & Turkey.

GRAND CIRCLE TRAVEL

THE DMA

347 Congress St
Boston, MA 02210-1230
Telephone: (617) 350-7500, (800) 959-
0405, FAX: (617) 346-6030, Web
Site: www.gct.com
Chmn Bd: Allan Lewis
Vice Chmn: Harriet Lewis
VP, Pub Rels: Priscilla O'Reilly
VP Production Svcs & Creative: Diane
Rooney
Conducts Business: U.S.
Employees: 3,000
Primary Market Served: Consumer
Catalog available online
Direct online sales
Advertising/Marketing Budget Related
to Direct Marketing: 76-100%
Direct Marketing ad budget:
Direct Mail: 75%
Telephone: 25%
Founded: 1958
Gross sales or billing: $577,000,000

International travel for retired
Americans.

GRAND PACIFIC RESORTS

5900 Pasteur Ct (#200)
Carlsbad, CA 92009-7336
Telephone: (760) 827-4101, Web Site:
www.grandpacificresorts.com
VP Mktg: Randy Nakagawa

HAPPY TRAILS RESORT

17200 W Bell Rd
Surprise, AZ 85374-9740
Telephone: (623) 584-0066, FAX:
(623) 546-2968, E-Mail:
happytrails@uccinc.net, Web Site:
www.htresort.com
Assn Mgr: Beth McWilliams
Conducts Business: U.S.
Employees: 40
Primary Market Served: Business &
Consumer
Founded: 1984

Recreational vehicle & mobile home
resort. Lots are owned by occupants.

HARRAH'S ENTERTAINMENT INC

dba Harrah's, Bally's, Caesars, Grand
Casino, Horseshoe & Rio
1 Harrahs Ct
Las Vegas, NV 89119-4377

Telephone: (702) 407-6000, FAX:
(702) 407-6499, (702) 407-6500,
Web Site: www.harrahs.com
SVP Commun & Govt Rels: Janis L.
Jones
SVP Bus Devel: Richard E. Mirman
Sr VP Relationship Mktg: David W.
Norton
VP Sports & Entertainment Mktg: Jef-
frey N. Pollack
VP Channel Mktg: Katrina Lane
DM Mgr: David Kowal
Employees: 85,000
Primary Market Served: Business &
Consumer
Catalog available online
Direct online sales
Founded: 1990
Gross sales or billing: $9,673,900,000

Hospitality, gaming hotels & casinos.
Owns, operates, or manages 48 casinos
under the Harrah's, Caesar's, Bally's,
Horseshoe & Rio brand names, primarily in the US & UK.

HERSHEY PARK

Div. of HERCO
100 W Hershey Park Dr
Hershey, PA 17033
Telephone: (717) 534-3149, (800)
HERSHEY, E-Mail: info@
hersheypa.com, Web Site: www.
hersheypark.com
CEO: J. Bruce McKinney
Conducts Business: U.S.
Primary Market Served: Business &
Consumer
Founded: 1907

90-acre theme park.

HERTZ CORP

Subs. of Ford Motor Co
225 Brae Blvd
Park Ridge, NJ 07656
Telephone: (201) 307-2000, FAX:
(201) 307-2644, Web Site: www.
hertz.com
Divisional VP: Vincent J. Canale
Grp & Cmml Mktg Dir: Patricia Trot-
tere
Conducts Business: Worldwide
Primary Market Served: Business &
Consumer

Rent-A-Car service for businesses &
leisure travelers.

HILTON GRAND VACATIONS CO

THE DMA

6355 Metrowest Blvd (Suite 180)
Orlando, FL 32835-6203
Telephone: (407) 521-3100, Web Site:
www.hiltongrandvacations.com
CEO: Antoine Dagot

HILTON HOTELS CORP

7930 Jones Branch Dr Ste 100
Mc Lean, VA 22102-3389
Telephone: (310) 278-4321, (800) HIL-
TONS, FAX: (310) 205-3670, Web
Site: www.hilton.com
Pres & CEO: Christopher Nassetta
Exec VP & CEO, Americas & Global
Brands: Thomas C. Keltner
VP Multi-Brand & Loyalty Programs
Hilton Honors Worldwide: Nancy
Deck
Exec VP & CEO, Hilton Intl: Ian R.
Carter
Exec VP & CFO: Robert M. La Forgia
Exec VP & Gen Counsel: Madeline A.
Kleiner
Conducts Business: Worldwide
Primary Market Served: Business &
Consumer
Catalog available online
Indirect online sales
Advertising/Marketing Budget Related
to Direct Marketing: 0-25%
Founded: 1919
Gross sales or billing: $8,000,000,000

Hotel chain.

HOBART & WILLIAM SMITH COLLEGES

629 S Main St
Geneva, NY 14456-3165
Telephone: (315) 781-3000, (800) 852-
2256, FAX: (315) 781-3655, Web
Site: www.hws.edu
Pres: Mark D. Gearen
Dean, Faculty & Provost: Teres L.
Amott
VP, Student Affairs: Robb Flowers
VP, Finance: Peter Polinak
CIO: Fred Damiano
Conducts Business: U.S.
Employees: 4
Primary Market Served: Consumer
Catalog available online
Gross sales or billing: $69,100,000

HOLIDAY TRAVEL OF AMERICA

6405 El Camino Real
Carlsbad, CA 92009
Telephone: (760) 431-8600, (888) 732-
2479, FAX: (760) 431-3131, E-Mail:
sales@htoa.com, Web Site: www.
htoa.com
Pres: Richard J. Romanello
Exec VP: Kelly Romanello
Natl Sls Mgr: Allan Bloom
Mktg Mgr: Randy Fish
Primary Market Served: Business
Catalog available online
Founded: 1988

Wholesaler & provider of travel
certificates.

HOLIDAY VACATIONS

aka Holiday Travel Inc
2727 Henry Ave, PO Box 87
Eau Claire, WI 54701-6828
Telephone: (715) 834-5555, (800) 826-
2266, FAX: (715) 834-8554, E-Mail:
info@holidayvacations.net, Web Site:
www.holidayvacations.net
Owner: Patrick Stoffers
Employees: 100
Primary Market Served: Consumer

Tour company & travel agency.

HOMEAWAY.COM INC

1011 W Fifth St (Suite 300)
Austin, TX 78703
Telephone: (512) 782-0805, (877) 228-
3145, Web Site: www.homeaway.
com
Sr Mktg Mgr: Morgan Larkin
Primary Market Served: Business &
Consumer

INDIANAPOLIS MOTOR SPEEDWAY

4790 W 16th St
Indianapolis, IN 46222-2550
Telephone: (317) 492-6700, Web Site:
www.indianapolismotorspeedway.
com
Mgr Mktg Strategy & Res: Katie Mc-
Cauley
Primary Market Served: Business &
Consumer

INTERCONTINENTAL HOTELS GROUP

Three Ravinia Dr (Suite 100)
Atlanta, GA 30346-2149
Telephone: (770) 604-2000, (877) 424-
2449, FAX: (770) 604-8639, Web
Site: www.ichotelsgroup.com
COO: Thomas Murray
Sr VP, Sls & Mktg: Charles Brown-
field
Dir: Stephanie Yudin
Primary Market Served: Consumer
Gross sales or billing: $2,020,300,000

Hotels & resorts.

KUWAIT AIRWAYS CORP

400 Kelby St Ste 41
Fort Lee, NJ 07024-2938
Telephone: (201) 582-9222, (800)
4-KUWAIT, FAX: (212) 659-4270,
E-Mail: nyc@kuwait-airways.com,
Web Site: www.kuwait-airways.com
Mktg Mgr The Americas: Jagdish Lal
Sls Mgr Passenger NE: Kamal Jolly
Primary Market Served: Consumer

International airlines.

LEXINGTON LUGGAGE LIMITED

793 Lexington Ave Frnt 1
New York, NY 10065-8161
Telephone: (212) 223-0698, (800) 822-
0404, FAX: (212) 753-3298, E-Mail:
sales@lexingtonluggage.com, Web
Site: www.lexingtonluggage.com
Conducts Business: U.S.
Employees: 15
Primary Market Served: Business &
Consumer
Advertising/Marketing Budget Related
to Direct Marketing: 26-50%
Founded: 1949

Sell luggage, attache cases, brief cases,
garment bags & fine pens at wholesale
prices.

THE DMA LIVE NATION

9348 Civic Center Dr Lbby
Beverly Hills, CA 90210-3642
Telephone: (310) 598-4100, Web Site:
www.livenation.com
Primary Market Served: Business &
Consumer

LOEWS HOTELS

Div. of Loews Corp
667 Madison Ave (7th fl)
New York, NY 10065-8087
Telephone: (212) 521-2000, (866) 563-
9792, FAX: (212) 545-2714, Web
Site: www.loewshotels.com
Pres: Jonathan Tisch
Exec VP, Loews Hotels: Charlotte St
Martin
Individual Travel Sls & Mktg Dir: Ri-
chard Duncan
Conducts Business: Worldwide
Employees: 5,000
Primary Market Served: Business &
Consumer
Advertising/Marketing Budget Related
to Direct Marketing: 0-25%
Founded: 1956

Hotel chain.

THE DMA THE LOS ANGELES CONVENTION & VISITORS BUREAU

333 S Hope St (fl 18)
Los Angeles, CA 90071-1406
Telephone: (213) 624-7300, (800) 366-
6116, FAX: (213) 627-9746, Web
Site: discoverlosangeles.com
Dir Creative Svcs: Julia Kopischke
Conducts Business: U.S., China, Japan,
England
Employees: 75
Primary Market Served: Business
Catalog available online
Advertising/Marketing Budget Related
to Direct Marketing: 26-50%
Direct Marketing ad budget:

Direct Mail: 20%
Magazines: 20%
Newspapers: 20%
Online: 20%
TV/Radio: 20%
Founded: 1977

LUFTHANSA GERMAN AIRLINES

1640 Hempstead Tpke
East Meadow, NY 11554
Telephone: (516) 296-9416, FAX:
(516) 296-9386, Web Site: www.
lufthansa-usa.com
Gen Mgr Mktg & Eline Sls USA:
Michael Zengerle
Conducts Business: Worldwide.
Primary Market Served: Business &
Consumer
Advertising/Marketing Budget Related
to Direct Marketing: 0-25%
Founded: 1955

Global airline.

THE DMA MGM MIRAGE

3600 Las Vegas Blvd S
Las Vegas, NV 89109-4303
Telephone: (702) 693-8005, Web Site:
www.mirageresorts.com
Mktg Compliance Rep: Brittany Haid
Primary Market Served: Business &
Consumer

MARRIOTT INTERNATIONAL INC

1 Marriott Dr
Washington, DC 20058-0001
Telephone: (301) 380-3000, (301) 380-
1791, E-Mail: internet.customer.
care@marriott.com, Web Site: www.
marriott.com
Chmn & CEO: J.W. Marriott Jr.
Dir Strategic Acct Mgmt & Client
Svcs, Marriott Rewards: Phyllis
Woods
Pres: William Shaw
Conducts Business: Worldwide
Primary Market Served: Business &
Consumer

Diversified hospitality company involved in lodging & services.

MARRIOTT OWNERSHIP RESORTS SALES & MARKETING

Marriott Ownership Resorts Inc
6649 Westwood Blvd, Bldg 3 (Suite
300)
Orlando, FL 32821
Telephone: (407) 206-6000, (800) 850-
6674, FAX: (407) 851-1304
Sr VP, Mktg Sls & Svcs: Peter Watzka
VP & Gen Mgr: Robert Miller
Primary Market Served: Consumer

Marketer of time-share resorts.

MONTBLEU RESORT CASINO AND SPA

Subs. of Tropicana Casinos and Re-
sorts
55 Hwy 50
Stateline, NV 89449
Telephone: (775) 588-3515, (888) 829-
7630, FAX: (775) 586-2030, Web
Site: www.montbleuresort.com
Gen Mgr: Dave Davis
Owner & CEO: William J. Yung
Sr VP, CFO, Treas: Ted Mitchel
Employees: 1,500
Primary Market Served: Consumer
Catalog available online
Indirect online sales
Advertising/Marketing Budget Related
to Direct Marketing: 26-50%
Founded: 1979

Hotel casino resort.

NEW ZEALAND TOURISM BOARD

501 Santa Monica Blvd (Suite 300)
Santa Monica, CA 90401
Telephone: (310) 857-2213, FAX:
(310) 395-5453, E-Mail: nzinfo@
nztb.govt.nz, Web Site: www.purenz.
com
Reg Mgr USA & Canada: Gregg
Anderson
Mktg Commun Mgr: Fred Ker
Conducts Business: Globally
Employees: 10
Primary Market Served: Consumer
Advertising/Marketing Budget Related
to Direct Marketing: 0-25%
Founded: 1901

New Zealand tourism information.

1000 ISLANDS INTERNATIONAL TOURISM COUNCIL

43373 Collins Landing Rd
Alexandria Bay, NY 13607-2210
Telephone: (315) 482-2520, (800) 847-
5263, (800) 456-2267, FAX: (315)
482-5906, Web Site: www.
visit1000islands.com/visitorinfo/
Tourism Dir: Gary de Young
Mktg & Media Coord: Dawn Cole
PR Mgr: Tillie Youngs
Conducts Business: U.S., Canada
Employees: 8
Primary Market Served: Consumer
Catalog available online
Advertising/Marketing Budget Related
to Direct Marketing: 26-50%
Direct Marketing ad budget: $235,000
Direct Mail: 15%
Magazines: 5%
Newspapers: 10%

TV/Radio: 70%
Gross sales or billing: $581,000

Tourist promotion agency for the
Thousand Islands International region,
covering southeastern Ontario & Jefferson County, NY.

THE DMA ORLANDO/ ORANGE COUNTY CONVENTION & VISITOR'S BUREAU

6700 Forum Dr (Suite 100)
Orlando, FL 32821-8086
Telephone: (407) 541-4239, Web Site:
visitorlando.com
Dir Direct Mktg: Beth Leahey
Primary Market Served: Business &
Consumer

PAN PACIFIC HOTEL & RESORTS AMERICA

2125 Terry Ave
Seattle, WA 98121-2709
Telephone: (206) 264-8111, (877) 324-
4856, FAX: (206) 654-5049, Web
Site: www.panpacific.com
Conducts Business: U.S.
Employees: 479
Primary Market Served: Business &
Consumer
Advertising/Marketing Budget Related
to Direct Marketing: 26-50%
Founded: 1986
Gross sales or billing: $16,100,000

330 room hotel.

PETER PAN BUS LINES INC

1776 Main St
Springfield, MA 01102
Telephone: (413) 781-2900, (800) 343-
9999, FAX: (413) 746-8671, E-Mail:
info@peterpanbus.com, Web Site:
www.peterpanbus.com
Pres: Peter A. Picknelly
Exec VP & CFO: Brian Stefano
Exec VP: Robert Schwarz
Mktg Dir: Michele Goldberg
Conducts Business: U.S., Canada
Employees: 750
Primary Market Served: Business &
Consumer
Advertising/Marketing Budget Related
to Direct Marketing: 0-25%
Direct Marketing ad budget: $700,000
Direct Mail: 10%
Magazines: 10%
Newspapers: 50%
TV/Radio: 30%
Founded: 1933
Gross sales or billing: $53,900,000

Motorcoach transportation available for
charter & tour throughout U.S. &
Canada.

POTAWATOMI BINGO CASINO

313 N 13th St
Milwaukee, WI 53233-2244
Telephone: (800) PAYS-BIG, Web
    Site: www.paysbig.com
Process Direct Mktg Mgr: Stephenie
    Streiff
Primary Market Served: Business &
    Consumer

PRINCESS CRUISES (HQ)

24844 Avenue Rockefeller
Santa Clarita, CA 91355-3467
Telephone: (661) 753-0000, (800) Prin-
    cess, FAX: (661) 284-4765, Web
    Site: www.princesscruises.com
Sr VP Cust Svc & Sls: Jan Swartz
Pres: Alan B. Buckelew
Mktg Mgr: Jeff Andrade
Conducts Business: U.S., Canada
Employees: 22,900
Primary Market Served: Business &
    Consumer
Founded: 1965

Market cruise vacations.

RESORT CONDOMINIUMS INTERNATIONAL INC

9998 N Michigan Rd
Carmel, IN 46032
Telephone: (317) 876-1692, FAX:
    (317) 871-9699, Web Site: www.rci.
    com
CEO: Kenneth May
Exec VP, Chief Mktg Officer: Peter
    Giamalva
Conducts Business: Worldwide
Employees: 1,200
Primary Market Served: Consumer

Leisure travel company that provides
exchange service for timeshare owners.

RESORTS ATLANTIC CITY

1133 Boardwalk
Atlantic City, NJ 08401
Telephone: (609) 334-6000, (800) 336-
    6378, FAX: (609) 340-6349, Web
    Site: www.resortsac.com
Pres & CEO: Audrey Oswell
Sr VP, Opers: Steve Callendary
Conducts Business: U.S.
Employees: 3,000
Primary Market Served: Consumer
Catalog available online
Direct online sales

Hotel & casino.

RESORTS WORLDWIDE INC

Starwood Hotels
1111 Westchester Ave
White Plains, NY 10604-3525
Telephone: (914) 640-8100, (800) 325-
    3535, FAX: (914) 640-8310, Web
    Site: www.starwood.com
Chmn & CEO: Barry Sternlicht
CFO & Exec VP: Ronald C. Brown
Sr VP, Corp Devel: James H. Sabatier
Conducts Business: Worldwide
Employees: 110,000
Primary Market Served: Business &
    Consumer
Advertising/Marketing Budget Related
    to Direct Marketing: 0-25%

Provide hotel service to business &
leisure travelers.

SABRE HOLDINGS INC

3150 Sabre Dr
Southlake, TX 76092
Telephone: (682) 605-1000, Web Site:
    www.sabre.com
Dir Mktg: Renee Alexander
Primary Market Served: Business

SEASHORE VACATIONS

11 Executive Park Rd
Hilton Head Island, SC 29928-4781
Telephone: (843) 785-2191, (800) 845-
    0077, FAX: (843) 785-6450, E-Mail:
    seashorehhi@hargray.com, Web Site:
    www.seashorehhi.com
Rental Mgr: Buddy Konecny
Conducts Business: U.S.
Employees: 4
Primary Market Served: Business &
    Consumer
Advertising/Marketing Budget Related
    to Direct Marketing: 51-75%
Direct Marketing ad budget: $30,000
Direct Mail: 100%

Rental agents for condos, villas &
homes.

SOUTH SEAS ISLAND RESORT

5400 Plantation Rd
Captiva Island, FL 33924
Telephone: (866) 565-5089, FAX:
    (941) 482-2470, Web Site: www.
    southseas.com
Dir Mktg: Frank Cavella
Primary Market Served: Business &
    Consumer
Catalog available online
Indirect online sales

Own & operate nine beach front
properties.

STARWOOD HOTELS & RESORTS

1 Star Pt
Stamford, CT 06902-8911
Telephone: (914) 640-8268, FAX:
    (914) 640-8310, Web Site: www.
    starwoodhotels.com
Sr Dir Loyalty & Direct Mktg:
    Gretchen Kloke

STEPPIN' OUT & SEE AMERICA

1140 N Town Center Dr (#360)
Las Vegas, NV 89144-0501
Telephone: (702) 798-6522, E-Mail:
    sales@see-america.net, Web Site:
    steppinoutseeamerica.com
CEO: Bob Colton

Sell all catalogs for national coupon
books.

THE STRATOSPHERE LAS VEGAS

Subs. of AREP
2000 Las Vegas Blvd S
Las Vegas, NV 89104
Telephone: (702) 380-7777, (800) 998-
    6937, FAX: (702) 383-4755, Web
    Site: www.stratospherehotel.com
CEO: Richard Brown
Gen Mgr: Paul Hobson
Primary Market Served: Business &
    Consumer
Founded: 1999

Hotel & casino.

SUPER 8 HOTELS WORLDWIDE

part of Wyndham Hotel Group
22 Sylvan Way
Parsippany, NJ 07054-3879
Telephone: (973) 428-9700, (800) 800-
    8000, FAX: (973) 496-7307, Web
    Site: www.super8.com
Pres: John Valetta
VP Mktg: Heny Gabay
VP Opers: Jim Darby
Conducts Business: U.S., Canada,
    China
Primary Market Served: Business &
    Consumer
Catalog available online
Direct online sales
Advertising/Marketing Budget Related
    to Direct Marketing: 0-25%
Direct Marketing ad budget:
Direct Mail: 15%
Magazines: 2%
Online: 40%
TV/Radio: 40%
Telephone: 3%
Founded: 1973
Gross sales or billing: $1,300,000,000

Promote Super 8 Motels to users of
economy lodging throughout the
United States & Canada.

TAUCK WORLD DISCOVERY

10 Norden Pl
Norwalk, CT 06855-1454

Telephone: (203) 899-6760, Web Site:
www.tauck.com
Dir Direct & Interactive Mktg: Cheryl
DeMichael

TRAVEL PLANNERS INC
381 Park Ave S
New York, NY 10016
Telephone: (212) 532-1660, (800) 221-
3531, FAX: (212) 779-6102, Web
Site: www.tphousing.com
Pres: Ray Vastola
VP: Ira Malin
Dir Strategy & Opers: Lisa Baez
Dir IT: Becky Hansen
Dir Program Opers: Louise Alvarado
Conducts Business: U.S., Canada, W.
Europe, Orient
Primary Market Served: Business
Catalog available online
Founded: 1980

Marketer of discounted travel programs
for conventions, meetings & individual
business travel.

TRAVELCLICK
300 N Martingale Rd
Schaumburg, IL 60173-2407
Telephone: (847) 585-5016
Events Mgr: Sharon Fulton
Primary Market Served: Business &
Consumer

TREASURE CHEST
304 Park Ave S
New York, NY 10010-4301
Telephone: (212) 590-2332, Web Site:
treasurechestonline.com
Primary Market Served: Consumer

TRUMP MARINA HOTEL & CASINO
Huron Ave & Brigantine Blvd
Atlantic City, NJ 08401
Telephone: (609) 441-2000, FAX:
(609) 340-5107, Web Site: www.
trumpmarina.com
VP, Mktg: Todd Moyer
Primary Market Served: Business &
Consumer

Hotel & casino.

TRUMP PLAZA HOTEL & CASINO
Div. of Trump Entertainment Resorts
Inc.
1000 Boardwalk at Mississippi Ave
Atlantic City, NJ 08401-7415
Telephone: (609) 441-6000, FAX:
(609) 441-7727, Web Site: www.
trumpplaza.com
Pres & CEO: Fred A. Buro
VP, Mktg: Debra Cole
Dept Mgr Dir Mktg: Anthony Martone

Primary Market Served: Business &
Consumer

Hotel and casino.

USA HOSTS
657 Mission St (#202)
San Francisco, CA 94105
Telephone: (415) 695-8000, (800) 368-
4678, FAX: (415) 986-3668, Web
Site: www.usahosts.com
Gen Mgr: David Warermann
Sls Mgr: Elizabeth Bussing
VP Sls & Mktg: Molly Pengra
CEO: Terrence J. Epton
VP Admin: Marsha Reeder
Dir Natl Accts: Serena Melancon
Conducts Business: Worldwide
Employees: 6
Primary Market Served: Business
Advertising/Marketing Budget Related
to Direct Marketing: 0-25%

San Francisco Bay area travel destination services & event planning.

VAIL ASSOCIATES INC
390 Interlocken Crescent
Broomfield, CO 80021
Telephone: (303) 404-1800, (800) 842-
8062, FAX: (303) 404-6415, Web
Site: www.snow.com
Pres: Andrew P. Daily
CEO: Adam Aaron
Sr Mktg Mgr: Jennifer Maclure
Primary Market Served: Consumer

Ski resort.

VAIL RESORTS INC
PO Box 38
Keystone, CO 80435
Telephone: (970) 468-2316/845-2694,
FAX: (970) 453-3202, Web Site:
www.keystoneresort.com
CEO: John W. Rutter
Mktg Dir: Margie Bootenhoff
Primary Market Served: Consumer

Ski & golf resort & conference center.

THE DMA VIRTUOSO LTD
1001 SW Klickitat Way (Suite 105)
Seattle, WA 98134-1161
Telephone: (206) 625-0969, Web Site:
www.virtuoso.com
Dir, Direct Mktg: Laura Sport

WATER'S EDGE RESORT & SPA
1525 Boston Post Rd
Westbrook, CT 06498
Telephone: (860) 399-5901, (800) 222-
5901, FAX: (860) 399-8644, Web
Site: www.watersedgeresort.com
Pres & Treas: Michael Datillo
Gen Mgr: Tina Datillo

Conducts Business: U.S.
Employees: 300
Primary Market Served: Business &
Consumer
Catalog available online
Indirect online sales
Advertising/Marketing Budget Related
to Direct Marketing: 0-25%
Founded: 1986

Full service shoreline resort & vacation
club with restaurant.

WESTERN RIVER EXPEDITIONS
7258 Racquet Club Dr
Salt Lake City, UT 84121-4599
Telephone: (801) 942-6669, (866) 904-
1160, FAX: (801) 942-8514, Web
Site: www.westernriver.com
CEO: Brian Merrill
VP: Larry Lake
Employees: 12
Primary Market Served: Business &
Consumer
Catalog available online
Indirect online sales
Advertising/Marketing Budget Related
to Direct Marketing: 76-100%
Direct Marketing ad budget:
Direct Mail: 50%
Magazines: 25%
Newspapers: 25%
Founded: 1961
Gross sales or billing: $5,000,000

Whitewater rafting trips in Grand Can-
yon, Colorado River in Utah through
Westwater & Cataract Canyons, Green
River & Salmon River in Idaho.

WINDSTAR CRUISES
Subs. of Ambassadors International
Cruise Group Company
2101 4th Ave (Suite 210)
Seattle, WA 98121-2392
Telephone: (206) 292-9606, (800) 258-
SAIL, FAX: (206) 340-0975,
E-Mail: info@windstarcruises.com,
Web Site: www.windstarcruises.com
VP Mktg: Diane Moore
Dir Mktg: Tony Scoringe
Pub Rels Mgr: Sarah Scoltock
Pres & CEO: Joseph J. Ueberroth
Conducts Business: U.S., Canada
Employees: 12
Primary Market Served: Business &
Consumer
Catalog available online
Direct online sales
Advertising/Marketing Budget Related
to Direct Marketing: 26-50%
Direct Marketing ad budget: $100,000
Direct Mail: 50%
Magazines: 50%
Founded: 1986
Gross sales or billing: $144,000,000

Cruises: mostly Americans & Canadians; ages 20-75, mid to upper income.

THE DMA **WYNDHAM HOTEL GROUP**
1 Sylvan Way (fl 3)
Parsippany, NJ 07054-3887
Telephone: (973) 753-8925, Web Site:
  www.cendant.com
Sr Dir Loyalty & Mktg: Florence Ho
Primary Market Served: Consumer

YOUR MAN TOURS
100 N Sepulveda Blvd (Suite 1700)
El Segundo, CA 90245-5655
Telephone: (310) 649-3820, FAX:
  (310) 649-2118, E-Mail: ymt@
  earthlink.net, Web Site: www.
  ymtvacations.com
Chmn: Frank J. Dupuis
Pres: William Price
Conducts Business: U.S., Canada
Employees: 120
Primary Market Served: Consumer
Catalog available online
Indirect online sales
Advertising/Marketing Budget Related
  to Direct Marketing: 76-100%
Direct Marketing ad budget:
  $3,500,000
Direct Mail: 20%
Magazines: 12%
Newspapers: 25%
TV/Radio: 38%
Telephone: 5%
Founded: 1967
Gross sales or billing: $30,000,000

Travel tour operator selling direct to
the general public.

Direct Marketers — Geographic Index

Alabama

Alfa Insurance (15), PO Box 11000, Montgomery, 36191-0001

Award Co of America (6), 3200 Rice Mine Rd, Tuscaloosa, 35406-1510

Bradford Health Services (16), 2101 Magnolia Ave S (Suite 518), Birmingham, 35205-2853

BuyFilters.com LLC (5), PO Box 581, Silverhill, 36576

CMEinfo.com (16), 500 Corporate Pkwy (Suite 300), Birmingham, 35242

Compass Bank (14), 15 20th St S Ste 100, Birmingham, 35233-2011

Da Vinci Technologies LLC (3), PO Box 3637, Auburn, 36831

EBSCO Reception Room Subscription Services (18), PO Box 830460, Birmingham, 35283-0460

Fathers of St Edmund Southern Missions Inc (1), 1428 Broad St, Selma, 36701

GameTime Inc (11), 150 Playcore Dr, Fort Payne, 35967

Gothic Arch Greenhouses Inc (8), PO Box 1564, Mobile, 36633

Hatton-Brown Publishers Inc (17), 225 Hanrick St, Montgomery, 36104-3317

Martha M House Furniture (8), 1022 S Decatur St., Montgomery, 36104-5116

Infinity Insurance Co (15), 3700 Colonnade Pkwy (Suite 600), Birmingham, 35243-3219

Integrity Music Inc (16), 1000 Cody Rd, Mobile, 36695

Intergraph Corp (16), 170 Graphics Dr, Madison, 35758

Robert James Co Inc (10), PO Box 520, Moody, 35004

Jeffers & Co (5), 310 W Saunders Rd, Dothan, 36302-8622

Kappler Protective Apparel & Fabrics (2), 55 Grimes Dr, Guntersville, 35976

Kaylor's School Supply (16), 4152 Hwy 75 N, Albertville, 35951

Long's Electronics Inc (3), 2630 S Fifth Ave, Irondale, 35210-1209

MAX Federal Credit Union (14), PO Box 244040, Montgomery, 36124-4040

Oakstone Publishing LLC (17), 100 Corporate Pkwy (Suite 600), Birmingham, 35242-8908

Priester Pecan Co Inc (4), 208 E Old Fort Rd, Fort Deposit, 36032-4012

Protective Life Insurance Co (15), 2801 Hwy 280 S, Birmingham, 35223-2488

Redstone Federal Credit Union (1), 220 Wynn Dr NW, Huntsville, 35893-0001

Regions (14), 1900 5th Ave N Ste 300, Birmingham, 35203-2669

Regitar USA Inc (9), 2575 Container Dr, Montgomery, 36109

The Ken Roberts Co (5), 435 Village Dr, Daphne, 36526-4003

Shelby Insurance Companies (15), 300 Riverhills Business Park, Birmingham, 35242-5037

Southern Poverty Law Center (1), 400 Washington Ave, Montgomery, 36104-4344

Southern Progress Corp (17), 2100 Lake Shore Dr, Birmingham, 35209-6721

Three Georges and the Nuthouse (16), 558 S Broad St, Mobile, 36603-1124

Tidbits Media (17), 1430 I-85 Pkwy (Suite 301), Montgomery, 36106-3635

United Investors Life Insurance Co (15), 2001 3rd Ave S Bsmt, Box 10207, Birmingham, 35233-2196

University of Alabama (13), College of Continuing Studies, Box 870388, Tuscaloosa, 35487-0388

Vulcan Information Packaging (16), PO Box 29, Vincent, 35178

Vulcan Materials Co (16), 1200 Urban Ctr Dr, Birmingham, 35242

Woman's Missionary Union (17), 100 Missionary Ridge, PO Box 830010, Birmingham, 35283-0010

Alaska

Oomingmak Musk Ox Producers Cooperative (6), 604 "H" St, Anchorage, 99501

Rural Alaska Community Action Program Inc (1), 731 E 8th Ave, Anchorage, 99501-3772

St Lawrence Island Original Ivory Cooperative (6), PO Box 189, Gambell, 99742

Arizona

Alliance Defense Fund (1), 15100 N 90th St, Scottsdale, 85260-2901

American Federation of Astrologers (1), 6535 S Rural Rd, Tempe, 85283-3746

Animal Health Express, Inc (5), 3301 N Freeway Rd, Tucson, 85705-5015

Antique Electronic Supply (3), 6221 S Maple Ave, Tempe, 85283

Arizona Highways Magazine (17), 2039 W Lewis Ave, Phoenix, 85009-2819

The Arizona Republic (17), 200 E Van Buren St, Phoenix, 85004-2238

Avnet Inc (16), 2211 S 47th St, Phoenix, 85034

B Bunch Co Inc (16), 9619 N 21st Dr, Phoenix, 85021-1895

BDL Homeware (3), PO Box 11744, Glendale, 85318-1744

Best Western International (19), 6201 N 24th Pkwy, Phoenix, 85016-2023

Cable Shopping Network (16), 15945 N 76th St, Scottsdale, 85260-1781

Christian Brands (16), 5226 S 31st Pl, Phoenix, 85040-3742

Community Food Bank (1), 3003 S Country Club Rd (Ste 221), Tucson, 85713-4084

Con-Cor International (11), 8101 E Research Ct Ste 101, Tucson, 85710-6758

Crosstown Traders Inc (2), 7840 E Broadway Blvd Ste 224, Tucson, 85710-3908

Data Cal Corp (16), 1345 N Mondel Dr, Gilbert, 85233

DMB Realty Network (16), 20789 N Pima Rd (Suite 250), Scottsdale, 85255-7206

Desert Rat Truck Centers (12), 3705 S Palo Verde St, Tucson, 85713-5401

Drumbeat Indian Arts Inc (6), 4143 N 16th St (Suite 1), Phoenix, 85016-5351

Fairytale Brownies (4), 4610 E Cotton Center Blvd (Suite 100), Phoenix, 85040-8898

Food for the Hungry Inc (1), 1224 E Washington St, Phoenix, 85034-1365

Grand Canyon Association (1), 1824 S Thompson St (Suite 205), Flagstaff, 86001-2694

Grand Canyon University (13), 3300 W Camelback Rd, Phoenix, 85017-1097

Grover Co (16), PO Box 41844, Mesa, 85274-1844

Happy Trails Resort (19), 17200 W Bell Rd, Surprise, 85374-9740

HP Indigo & Inkjet Press Solutions (16), 6831 E Thunderbird Rd, Scottsdale, 85254-4044

Home Planners (17), 3275 W Ina Rd (Suite 110), Tucson, 85741-2152

ICS Audio Video Supply Inc (3), 6721 N Black Canyon Hwy, Phoenix, 85069-5489

Insight Direct Inc (16), 6820 S Harl Ave, Tempe, 85283-4318

Interfaith Community Care (1), PO Box 8450, Surprise, 85374-0124

Kolbe Corp (17), 2355 E Camelback Rd Ste 610, Phoenix, 85016-9040

LifeLock (16), 60 E Rio Salado Pkwy Ste 400, Tempe, 85281-9129

Make-A-Wish Foundation of America (1), 4742 N 24th St Ste 400, Phoenix, 85016-4862

McMurry Inc (17), 1010 E Missouri Ave, Phoenix, 85014-2602

Mechanical Breakdown Administrators Inc (14), PO Box 6545, Scottsdale, 85261-6545

Meriks Partners (10), 2509 N Campbell St (#311), Tucson, 85719-3362

Midwest Publishing Inc (17), 10844 N 23rd Ave, Phoenix, 85029-4924

Mountain West Supply Co (3), 5116 E Charter Oak, Scottsdale, 85254

Muscular Dystrophy Association (1), 3300 E Sunrise Dr, Tucson, 85718-3299

Naturmed (7), PO Box 1270, Camp Verde, 86322

Neutron Industries (16), 7107 N Black Canyon Hwy, Phoenix, 85021-7619

Nu-Parr Swimwear (2), 929 E Indian School Rd, Phoenix, 85014-4745

Nutri-Health Supplements (7), 260 Justin Dr, Cottonwood, 86326

Personal Achievement Institute (17), PO Box 6543, One Speaking Success Rd, Kingman, 86402-6543

PetSmart Inc (5), 19601 N 27th Ave, Phoenix, 85027-4010

Rich Brands (16), 7227 N 16th St (Suite 209), Phoenix, 85020-5283

Security Micro Systems Inc (3), 19135 N 94th St, Scottsdale, 85255

Sierra Scientific Inc (9), 1005 N 50th St (Suite 150), Phoenix, 85008-0117

Single Scene News (17), 1928 E Laguna Dr, Tempe, 85282-5913

SkyMall Inc (16), 1520 E Pima St, Phoenix, 85034-4600

Smart Practice (17), 3400 E McDowell Rd, Phoenix, 85008-7899

State Line Tack Inc (16), 19601 N 27th Ave, Phoenix, 85027-4008

Superior Real Estate Supply (10), 8373 W Troy St, Phoenix, 85382-8095

Syntellect (16), 2095 W Pinnacle Peak Rd Ste 110, Phoenix, 85027-1262

Territorial Newspapers (17), 3280 E Hemisphere Loop (Suite 180), PO Box 27087, Tucson, 85726-7087

U-Haul International (16), 2727 N Central Ave, Phoenix, 85004

University of Phoenix (13), 4025 S Riverpoint Pkwy, Phoenix, 85040-0723

Vemma Nutrition Co (7), 8322 E Hartford Dr, Scottsdale, 85255

Vivitar Corp (16), 1600 N Desert Dr (Suite 101), Tempe, 85281-1798

Wikco Industries Inc (5), 1467 N Grant Ave, Casa Grande, 85222

Wolfe Publishing Co Inc (17), 2180 Gulfstream (Suite A), Prescott, 86301-6182

Arkansas

Alltel (16), 1 Allied Dr, Little Rock, 72202

CenterCore Group Inc (16), 201 Industrial Park, Marked Tree, 72365

Cooper Communities Inc (16), 903 N 47th St, Rogers, 72756

Creative Irish Gifts (6), 3801 Woodland Heights Rd Ste 100, Little Rock, 72212-2410

Holland Wildflower Farm (8), PO Box 328, 290 O'Neil Lane, Elkins, 72727

Lafferty Equipment Manufacturing Inc (9), 5614 Oak Grove Rd, North Little Rock, 72118

Leisure Arts Inc (17), 5701 Ranch Dr, Little Rock, 72223-9633

Micro Plastics Inc (16), PO Box 149, Flippin, 72634

Reliance Electric (9), 5711 RS Boreham Jr St, Fort Smith, 72901-8301

AG Russell Knives Inc (11), 2900 S 26th St, Rogers, 72758-8571

Sauce Co (4), 11525 Cantrell Rd (Suite 910), Little Rock, 72212-1721

Virco Manufacturing Corp (16), Hwy 65 S, Conway, 72033

Wal Mart Stores (16), 702 SW 8th St, Div 1 - Legal, Bentonville, 72716-0001

California

ABC Clio (17), 130 Cremona, Santa Barbara, 93117

AGIA Insurance Services (15), 1155 Eugenia Pl, Carpinteria, 93013-2061

Abbeon Cal Inc (9), 123 Gray Ave, Santa Barbara, 93101-1809

Accountants' Supply House (10), PO Box 1186, Lancaster, 93584-1186

Accountemps (16), 2884 Sand Hill Rd, Menlo Park, 94025-7059

ACCUSPLIT Inc (16), 3090 Independence Dr Ste 150, Livermore, 94551-9423

Adventure Creations Inc (16), 2077 Harbor Blvd (#B), Costa Mesa, 92625-2630

Affinity Group Inc (19), 2575 Vista del Mar Dr, Ventura, 93001-3920

Air Power USA (12), 8366 Isis Ave, Los Angeles, 90045

Aircraft Spruce & Specialty Co (12), 225 Airport Cir, Corona, 92880-2527

Alfred Publishing Co Inc (17), 16320 Roscoe Blvd (Suite 100), Van Nuys, 91406-1216

Allergan Inc (16), 2525 DuPont Dr, Irvine, 92612-1531

Alliance of Area Business Publications (1), 1970 E Grand Ave (Suite 300), El Segundo, 90245-5038

Amanet (16), 7001 Eton Ave # B, Canoga Park, 91303-2112

American Association of Critical-Care Nurses (1), 101 Columbia, Aliso Viejo, 92656-4109

American Council on Exercise (1), 4851 Paramount Dr, San Diego, 92123

The American Film Institute (1), 2021 N Western Ave, Los Angeles, 90027-1657

American Historic Inns Inc (17), PO Box 669, Dana Point, 92629-0669

American Horse Products (11), 31896 Plaza Dr (Suite C4), San Juan Capistrano, 92675

American Research Corp (3), 11581 Federal Rd, El Monte, 91731

American Society on Aging (1), 71 Stevenson St (Suite 1450), San Francisco, 94105-2938

The American Vintage Library (17), PO Box 48621, Los Angeles, 90048-0621

America's Finest Pet Doors (16), 202 Tank Farm Rd (Suite F1), San Luis Obispo, 93401-7520

Amrel (16), 3445 Fletcher Ave, El Monte, 91731

Amvac Chemical Corp (8), 4100 E Washington Blvd, Los Angeles, 90023-4406

Ancient Circles (6), 190 North St, Willits, 95490-3420

Anritsu Co (16), 490 Jarvis Dr, Morgan Hill, 95037

Anthem Blue Cross (15), 1 Wellpoint Way, Westlake Village, 91362-3893

Apple Computer Inc (16), 1 Infinite Loop, Cupertino, 95014-2083

Aramark Uniform Services (2), 115 N First St, Burbank, 91502-1856

Area Electronics Systems Inc (3), 1247 N Lakeview Ave Ste C, Anaheim, 92807-1833

Art.com (8), 2100 Powell St 10th Fl, Emeryville, 94608-1893

Astronomical Society of the Pacific (1), 390 Ashton Ave, San Francisco, 94112-1722

Audio-Digest Foundation (1), 1577 E Chevy Chase Dr, Glendale, 91206-4107

Audio Editions Books-on-Cassette & CD (3), PO Box 6930, Auburn, 95604-6930

Australian Tourist Commission (16), 6100 Center Drive, Los Angeles, 90045

Autodesk Inc (16), 111 McInnis Pkwy, San Rafael, 94903

Avery Dennison Corp (10), 50 Pointe Dr, Brea, 92821-3699

The Ayn Rand Institute (1), 2121 Alton Pkwy (Suite 250), Irvine, 92606-4926

Back Designs Inc (7), PO Box 2810, Novato, 94948-2810

Bailey's Inc (9), PO Box 550, Laytonville, 95454-0550

Baker Corp (16), 3020 Old Ranch Pkwy (Suite 220), Seal Beach, 90740-8805

Balboa Life & Casualty (15), 3349 Michelson (Suite 200), Irvine, 92623-9702

Bamboo Sourcery (8), 666 Wagnon Rd, Sebastopol, 95472-9546

Bank of the West (14), 300 S Grand Ave, Los Angeles, 90071-3109

Barely Nothings Lingerie (2), 560 W Tefft St., Nipomo, 93444

BarterNews (17), 24446 Caswell Ct, Laguna Niguel, 92677

Baseline FT (17), 3415 S Sepulveda Blvd (Suite 200), Los Angeles, 90034-6032

Bathroom Machineries (8), 495 Main St, Murphys, 95247

Beauty Naturally (7), 850 Stanton Rd, Burlingame, 94010-1404

Beckman Coulter Inc (16), 250 S Kraemer Blvd., Brea, 92821-6232

Beemak Plastics Inc (16), 16711 Knott Ave, La Mirada, 90638-6013

Beeman Precision Airguns (11), 10652 Bloomfield Ave, Santa Fe Springs, 90670-3912

Bennett Marine Video (3), 2321 Abbot Kinney Blvd Ste 201, Venice, 90291-4876

Better Tools For Industry (9), 9525 Pathway St, Santee, 92071

Bick International (6), PO Box 854, Van Nuys, 91408-0854

Biomerica Inc (7), 17571 Von Karman Ave, Irvine, 92614-6207

Blue Shield Life (15), 50 Beale St, San Francisco, 94105-1813

Blue Shield of California (15), 50 Beale St, San Francisco, 94105-1808

Body by Jake Global LLC (16), 11611 San Vicente Blvd Ste 610, Los Angeles, 90049-6506

Book Passage Cafe (17), 51 Tamal Vista Blvd, Corte Madera, 94925-1145

Book Publishing Information Kit (17), 530 Ellwood Ridge, Santa Barbara, 93117-1047

Born Free USA (1), 1122 S St, Sacramento, 95811-6525

Bountiful Gardens (8), 18001 Shafer Ranch Rd, Willits, 95490-9626

Bowers & Merena Auctions (16), 18061 Fitch, Irvine, 92614-6018

BowTie Inc (17), 3 Burroughs Ave, Irvine, 92618-2804

Brady Marketing Co Inc (16), 1331 N California Blvd (Suite 320), Walnut Creek, 94596-4563

BroadVision Inc (16), 1600 Seaport Blvd (Suite 550), Redwood City, 94063-5589

Brocade Communications Systems Inc (16), 1745 Technology Dr, San Jose, 95110

Buena Vista Home Entertainment (3), 500 S Buena Vista St, Burbank, 91521

Buena Vista Winery (16), 18000 Old Winery Rd, Sonoma, 95476

BusinessOnline (16), 701 B St (Suite 1000), San Diego, 92101-8109

Butterfield Farms Inc (4), 904 Silver Spur Rd (Suite 485), Rolling Hills Estates, 90274-3800

C&T Bridge Supplies (11), 3532 Katella Ave (Suite 103), Los Alamitos, 90720-3138

Cable Car Clothiers/Robert Kirk Ltd (2), 200 Bush St, San Francisco, 94104-3500

Cable Connection (3), 1035 Mission Ct, Fremont, 94539-8203

Calbiochem-Novabiochem Corp (9), 10394 Pacific Ctr Ct, San Diego, 92121-4340

Calibre Press Inc (17), 200 Green St (Suite 200), San Francisco, 94111-1356

California Chamber of Commerce (1), 1332 N Market Blvd, Sacramento, 95834-1912

California Cosmetics Corp (7), 18757 Burbank Blvd (Suite 110), Tarzana, 91356-3345

California Institute of Technology (16), Industrial Relations Ctr 1-90, Pasadena, 91125-9000

California Mustang Parts & Accessories (16), 19400 San Jose Ave, City of Industry, 91748

California Society of CPA's (1), 1800 Gateway Dr (Suite 200), San Mateo, 94404-4072

Cane & Basket Supply Co (8), 1283 S Cochran Ave, Los Angeles, 90019-2846

Canine Companions for Independence (16), PO Box 446, Santa Rosa, 95402-0446

The Caning Shop (11), 926 Gilman St, Berkeley, 94710

Capital Insurance Group (CIG) (15), 2300 Garden Rd, Monterey, 93940-5326

Carabella Collection (2), 17662 Armstrong Ave, Irvine, 92614

Cardflex Financial Services (14), 2900 Bristol Ave Suite F-206, Costa Mesa, 92626-7911

CAIG Laboratories Inc (9), 12200 Thatcher Ct, Poway, 92064

CDMI Inc (1), 711 Pacific Coast Hwy (Unit 118), Huntington Beach, 92648-5051

CMI Direct (15), 2349 B Honolulu Ave, Montrose, 91020-2513

CRM Learning (16), 2218 Faraday Ave (Suite 110), Carlsbad, 92008

CTB MacMillan/McGraw-Hill (16), 20 Ryan Ranch Rd, Monterey, 93940

Century Photo (10), 10425 Slusher Dr, Santa Fe Springs, 90670-3750

Chabin Concepts (16), 2515 Ceanothus Ave (Suite 100), Chico, 95973-7720

Charisma Brands LLC (6), 23482 Peralta Dr Ste A, Laguna Hills, 92653-1733

Children of the Night (1), 14530 Sylvan St, Van Nuys, 91411

China Books & Periodicals Inc (17), 360 Swift Ave (#48), South San Francisco, 94080

City of Cerritos (1), PO Box 3130, Cerritos, 90703-3130

City of Hope Cancer Center (1), 1055 Wilshire Blvd, Los Angeles, 90017-2431

Civil Service Employees Insurance Group (15), 2121 N California Blvd (Suite 555), Walnut Creek, 94596-3501

Clegg Industries Inc (16), 19032 S Vermont Ave, Gardena, 90248-4412

Clients & Profits Worldwide (14), 4755 Oceanside Blvd (#200), Oceanside, 92056-3056

The Clorox Co (16), 1221 Broadway, Oakland, 94612-1888

Clothing Solutions (2), 5405 Alton Pkwy (Suite A), Irvine, 92604-3718

Collegesource Inc (17), 8090 Engineer Rd, San Diego, 92111

Columbia Tristar Home Video (16), 10202 W Washington Blvd (Rm 7814), SPP Bldg, Culver City, 90232-3119

Conform Pacific (16), PO Box 1658, Lomita, 90717-5658

CM Connolly (1), 9545 Coney Island Cir, Elk Grove, 95758-3646

Continuing Education of the Bar (CEB) (1), 2100 Franklin St Ste 500, Oakland, 94612-3098

ConversionVoodoo.com (16), 10601 Tierrasanta Blvd (# G-371), San Diego, 92124-2616

Convertible Service (16), 5126 N Walnut Grove Ave, San Gabriel, 91776-2026

Coppa Woodworking, Inc (8), 1231 Paraiso Ave, San Pedro, 90731

Corona-Lotus Inc (4), 465 Green St, San Francisco, 94133-4001

Countrywide Financial Corp (14), 4500 Park Granada, Calabasas, 91302

Creative Teaching Associates (16), 23505 Auberry Rd, Clovis, 93619-9648

Creative Teaching Press (17), 15342 Graham St, Huntington Beach, 92549

Culinary Parts Unlimited (16), 840 Folsom St, San Francisco, 94107

Cuvaison Inc (4), 4550 Silverado Trail, Calistoga, 94515

Dairy Council of California (1), 2151 Michelson Ave (Suite 235), Irvine, 92612-1339

Dalrada Financial Corp (14), 11956 Bernardo Plaza Dr (Suite 516), San Diego, 92128-2538

Data Direct Networks (HQ) (3), 9351 Deering Ave, Chatsworth, 91311

Davis Instruments Corp (8), 3465 Diablo Ave, Hayward, 94545-2746

DFS Group Limited (5), 525 Market St, First Market Tower, San Francisco, 94105-2708

D'Lights (8), 2107 Chico Ave, South El Monte, 91733

DOM Corp (5), 4305 Redwood Ave, Marina Del Rey, 90292

Delta Tech Industries (12), 1901 S Vineyard Ave # 7, Ontario, 91761-7747

DeLuxe Laboratories Inc (16), 5433 Fernwood Ave, Hollywood, 90027

Dexta Corp (16), 962 Kaiser Rd, Napa, 94558

Dharma Trading Co (2), 1805 S McDowell Boulevard Ext Ste D, Petaluma, 94954-6945

Dinyari Inc (9), 500 Phelan Ave, San Jose, 95112-2506

DIRECTV (16), 2230 E Imperial Hwy, El Segundo, 90245

Discovery Toys (16), 7364 Marathon Dr (Suite A), Livermore, 94550-3000

Diversified Photo Supply Corp (10), 333 W Alondra Blvd (Suite C), Gardena, 90248-2428

Doctor's Best Inc (16), 197 Avenida La Pata (#A), San Clemente, 92673-6307

The Doctor's Co (15), 185 Greenwood Rd, Napa, 94558

Donor Services Group (1), 6715 W Sunset Blvd, Los Angeles, 90028-7107

Draper's & Damon's (2), Nine Pasteur (Suite 200), Irvine, 92618-3804

Dream Products Inc (5), 9754 Deering Ave, Chatsworth, 91311-4301

Dynamic Development Co (12), 25512 Pampero Cir, Mission Viejo, 92691-5436

Dynamic Engineering (3), 150 Dubois St Ste C, Santa Cruz, 95060-2114

Earthrise (16), 2151 Michelson Dr (Suite 258), Irvine, 92648

Ebay (16), 2145 Hamilton Ave, San Jose, 95125-5905

Educational Insights, Inc (16), 152 W Walnut St Ste 201, Gardena, 90248-3147

ECHO - Electronic Clearing House Inc (14), 21215 Burbank Blvd (#100), Woodland Hills, 91367-6607

EOS International Inc (5), 2292 Faraday Ave Frnt, Carlsbad, 92008-7237

Electronic Arts Inc (3), 209 Redwood Shores Pkwy, Redwood City, 94065-1175

Elite Debit (14), 11450 Sheldon St, Sun Valley, 91352-1121

En ESPANOL Publishing Group LLC (17), 250 S Beverly Dr (#301), Beverly Hills, 90212-3831

Enterprex International Corp (16), 12101 Clark St Ste G, Arcadia, 91006-6031

Entrepreneur Media Inc (17), 2445 McCabe Way (Suite 400), Irvine, 92614

Epson America (10), 3840 Kilroy Airport Way, Long Beach, 90806-2469

ESignal (14), 3955 Point Eden Way, Hayward, 94545-3720

Eventful Inc (19), 12626 High Bluff Ste 100, San Diego, 92130-2072

Everex Computer Systems Inc (16), 48319 Fremont Blvd, Fremont, 94538-6580

Excelligence Learning Corp (5), 2 Lower Ragsdale Dr (Suite 125), Monterey, 93940-7810

Executive Protection Products Inc (16), 351 Second St., Napa, 94559

Experience In Software Inc (16), 2029 Durant Ave Ste 201, Berkeley, 94704-1564

F P International (16), 1090 Mills Way, Redwood City, 94063

Farmers Insurance (15), 4680 Wilshire Blvd, Los Angeles, 90010

FAFCO Inc (16), 435 Otterson Dr, Chico, 95928-8207

Fireman's Fund Insurance Co (14), 777 San Marin Dr, Novato, 94998-0002

First Advantage Membership Services (14), 12395 First American Way, Poway, 92064-6897

Fisher Investments (14), 13100 Skyline Blvd, Woodside, 94062-4542

Forecaster Publishing Co Inc (14), 19623 Ventura Blvd, Tarzana, 91356

Foremost Industrial Exchange (16), 15222 Keswick St, Van Nuys, 91405-1068

Rich Fox & Associates Inc (1), 175 Chaparral Rd, Carmel Valley, 93924-9634

Frederick's of Hollywood Group Inc (2), 6255 Sunset Blvd (fl 6), Los Angeles, 90028-7403

Freestyle Photographic Supplies (5), 5124 Sunset Blvd, Los Angeles, 90027-9897

Fresno Oxygen (9), 2825 S Elm Ave (#101), Fresno, 93706-5460

The Fuller Theological Seminary (16), 135 N Oakland Ave, Pasadena, 91182

Gallery of Cats (6), 26136 Galvez Ct, Valencia, 91355-3349

Gateway Inc (3), 7565 Irvine Center Dr, Irvine, 92618

The Gateway Learning Corp (16), 7565 Irvine Center Dr, Irvine, 92618

Geary's of Beverly Hills (6), 351 N Beverly Dr, Beverly Hills, 90210-4794

Gero Vita (16), 1835 Newport Blvd (Suite A109, #439), Costa Mesa, 92627-5007

Get Seen Media Group (16), 5115 Wilshire Blvd (Apt 235), Los Angeles, 90036-4371

GBH Communications (3), 1309 S Myrtle Ave, Monrovia, 91016-4150

Ghirardelli Chocolate Co (16), 1111 139th Ave, San Leandro, 94578

Golden Fleece Designs Inc (16), 441 S Victory Blvd, Burbank, 91502-2353

Golden Gate Transportation District (16), 1011 Anderson Dr, San Rafael, 94901

Goldline International (14), 1601 Cloverfield Blvd (Suite 100S), Santa Monica, 90404-4162

Goodwill Industries of San Francisco (1), 1500 Mission St, San Francisco, 94103-2513

Grand Pacific Resorts (19), 5900 Pasteur Ct (#200), Carlsbad, 92009-7336

Gump's By Mail Inc (6), 135 Post St, San Francisco, 94108

Gun Video Catalog/LMP (11), 4585 Murphy Canyon Rd, San Diego, 92123-4318

The Gymboree Corp (2), 500 Howard St, San Francisco, 94105-3000

Hadley Fruit Orchards Inc (4), 50130 Main St, Cabazon, 92230-3218

Harbor Freight Tools (9), 3491 Mission Oaks Blvd, Camarillo, 93012-5034

Harris Direct (1), 6800 Owensmouth Ave (Suite 200), Canoga Park, 91303-3170

Harwil Corp (9), 541 Kinetic Dr, Oxnard, 93030

Helman Group Ltd (16), 1621 Beacon Pl, Oxnard, 93033

Herbalife International of America Inc (7), PO Box 80210, Los Angeles, 90080-0210

Hewlett-Packard Co (16), 3000 Hanover St, Palo Alto, 94304-1185

Hireko Golf (11), 16185 Stephens St, City of Industry, 91745

Histacount & Expressions (10), PO Box 1186, Lancaster, 93584-4486

Holiday Travel of America (19), 6405 El Camino Real, Carlsbad, 92009

Hollywood Film Archive (17), 8391 Beverly Blvd (PMB 321), Los Angeles, 90048

Home Safeguard Industries (9), 29706 Baden Pl, Malibu, 90265

Hot Topic Inc (2), 18305 E San Jose Ave, City of Industry, 91748

Houlihan Lokey Howard & Zukin (14), 1930 Century Park W, Los Angeles, 90067

Howard Rice Nemerovski Canady Falk & Rabkin (14), 3 Embarcadero Ctr (fl 7), San Francisco, 94111-4078

Hydra Group LLC (9), 10940 Wilshire Blvd (Fl 11), Los Angeles, 90024

IClimber Inc (16), 315 W Verdugo Ave (Suite 101), Burbank, 91502-2484

The Idea Club.com(TM) & Dumas Martin Consulting (16), 101 W Mission Blvd (Suite 110-147), Pomona, 91766-1245

IHOP Corp (16), 450 N Brand Blvd Fl 7, Glendale, 91203-4415

iLoop Mobile Inc (16), 25 Metro Dr (Suite 210), San Jose, 95110-1338

In-Sync Publications (18), 800 Knob Hill Ave, Redondo Beach, 90277

Information for Public Affairs, Inc (17), 2101 K St, Sacramento, 95816-4920

Institute For Natural Resources (16), 2352 Stanwell Dr, Concord, 94520

Institute of Reading Development (1), Five Commercial Blvd, Novato, 94949

Institutional Real Estate Inc (17), 2274 Camino Ramon, San Ramon, 94583

Integretel Inc (16), 5883 Rue Ferrari, San Jose, 95138-1857

Intel Corp (16), 2200 Mission College Blvd, Santa Clara, 95052

IntelliQuote Insurance Services (15), 5170 Golden Foothill Pkwy, El Dorado Hills, 95762-9658

International Direct Media Co & Information Publishing Co (17), 2801 39th Ave (Suite 100), San Francisco, 94116-2744

Intuit (10), 2632 Marine Way, Mountain View, 94043

Involve Social (1), 44288 Fremont Blvd, Fremont, 94538-6000

Isuzu Motors America Inc (16), 1400 S Douglass Rd, Anaheim, 92806-6904

Jaffe Brothers Natural Foods (4), 28560 Lilac Rd, Valley Center, 92082

Jafra Cosmetics International Inc (7), 2451 Townsgate Rd, Westlake Village, 91361

Jameco Electronics (3), 1355 Shoreway Rd, Belmont, 94002

Jan Associates (7), 7001 Exeter Dr, Oakland, 94611

Jazzercise Inc (2), 2460 Impala Dr, Carlsbad, 92008

JDR Microdevices (3), 229 Polaris Ave Ste 17, Mountain View, 94043-4579

Jossey-Bass Inc Publishers (17), One Montgomery St (Suite 1200), San Francisco, 94104-4505

Kelsey National Corp (15), 3030 S Bundy Dr, Los Angeles, 90066

Kensington Technology Group (16), 333 Twin Dolphin Dr (6th fl), Redwood Shores, 94065

KCET (1), 4401 W Sunset Blvd, Los Angeles, 90027-6017

KHL Engineered Packaging Solutions (16), 6600 Valley View St, Buena Park, 90620

KPBS FM/TV (1), 5200 Campanile Dr San Diego State Univ, San Diego, 92182-1901

Knott's Berry Farm Foods (4), 8039 Beach Blvd, Buena Park, 90620-3200

Kross Inc (16), 25682 Springbrook Ave Ste 140, Santa Clarita, 91350-2433

Patricia Kutza Co (2), PO Box 4127, Vallejo, 94590

L&L Management (16), 751 N Fair Oaks Ave, Pasadena, 91103-3069

The LadyBug Co (8), 12857 Oroville Quincy Hwy, Berry Creek, 95916-9754

Lamkin Corp (11), 6530 Gateway Park Dr, San Diego, 92154-7510

Lark in the Morning (5), PO Box 1176, Mendocino, 95460

Larkwood Group LLC (1), 4096 Piedmont Ave (Suite 214), Oakland, 94611-5221

LearnCom HR Consulting & Training (16), 5520 Trabuco Rd, Irvine, 92620-5705

Learning Communications LLC (16), 5520 Trabuco Rd, Irvine, 92620-5705

Levi Strauss & Co (16), 1155 Battery St, San Francisco, 94111

Lexus Division of Toyota (12), 19001 S Western Ave (Suite L100), Torrance, 90501-1106

Liberty Tree Network (5), 100 Swan Way, Oakland, 94621-1428

LifeScript (7), 26001 Pala, Mission Viejo, 92691-7955

Lions Gate Television Corp (16), 2700 Colorado Ave Ste 200, Santa Monica, 90404-5502

Live Nation (19), 9348 Civic Center Dr Lbby, Beverly Hills, 90210-3642

LO-AD Communications (16), 150 E Colorado Blvd (Suite 210), Pasadena, 91105

Location Sound Corp (3), 10639 Riverside Dr, North Hollywood, 91602-2355

Longevity Pure Medicine (7), 611 S Palm Canyon Dr (Suite 7522), Palm Springs, 92264

The Los Angeles Convention & Visitors Bureau (19), 333 S Hope St (fl 18), Los Angeles, 90071-1406

Los Angeles Kings (16), 1111 S Figeroa (Suite 3100), Los Angeles, 90015

The Los Angeles Lakers Inc (11), 555 N Nash St, El Segundo, 90245

Lotions & Lace (2), 3960 Garner Rd, Riverside, 92501

Luggage Base (16), 670 S Frontage Rd, Nipomo, 93444-9148

Lundberg Family Farms (16), PO Box 369, 5370 Church St, Richvale, 95974-0369

Macy's (5), 15541 Gale Ave, City Of Industry, 91745-1512

Macy's West (16), 170 O'Farrell St, San Francisco, 94102

Magellan's Catalog (5), 110 W Sola St, Santa Barbara, 93101-3007

Making It Big (2), 525 Portal St, Cotati, 94931-3023

Markwins International Corp (16), 22067 Ferrero Pkwy, City of Industry, 91789

Marshall & Swift (17), 777 S Figueroa St Fl 12, Los Angeles, 90017-5878

Matt & Kumpany Kuzins (1), 68 Aiken Way, Sacramento, 95819-2118

Mattel Inc (16), 333 Continental Blvd, El Segundo, 90245-5012

Mazda North American Operations (16), 7755 Irvine Center Dr, Irvine, 92623

McBee (10), PO Box 1186, Lancaster, 93584-1186

McClatchy Co (17), 2100 "Q" St, Sacramento, 95816-6899

McKesson Corp (7), 1 Post St, San Francisco, 94104-5203

Medcom Inc (17), 6060 Phyllis Dr, Cypress, 90630

Medic Alert Foundation (1), 2323 Colorado Ave, Turlock, 95382

Meguiar's Inc (16), 17991 Mitchell S, PO Box 92623, Irvine, 92614-6015

Mentor Corp (16), 201 Mentor Dr, Santa Barbara, 93111-3340

Merchant E-Solutions (14), 3400 Bridge Pkwy Ste 100, Redwood City, 94065-1195

Meriks Gifts (6), 1380 Garnet Ave (Suite E-278), San Diego, 92109-3081

Mervyn's (16), 6200 Stoneridge Mall Rd (Suite 300), Pleasanton, 94588-3705

Mickwee Group Inc (16), 5600 Mowry School Rd Ste 230, Newark, 94560-5800

Microbiz Corp (3), 17075 Newhope St (Suite A), Fountain Valley, 92708-4299

Mitchell International (17), 6220 Greenwich Dr, San Diego, 92122-5913

Mitsubishi Digital Electronics America Inc (3), 9351 Geronimo Rd, Irvine, 92618

Mitsubishi Motor Sales of America Inc (1), 6400 W Katella Ave, Cypress, 90630

MCA/Universal Studios Inc (3), 111 Universal Hollywood Dr Ste 890, Universal City, 91608-1138

MPBS Industries (16), 2820 E Washington Blvd, Los Angeles, 90023-4217

MPS Multimedia Inc (16), 1222 S Amphlett Blvd, San Mateo, 94402-1906

MRV Communications (3), 20415 Nordhoff St, Chatsworth, 91311

Moby Wrap Inc (2), PO Box 1066, Chico, 95927-1066

Modern Postcard (10), 1675 Faraday Ave, Carlsbad, 92008-7314

Monex Deposit Co (14), 4910 Birch St Ste 103, Newport Beach, 92660-2188

Moon Shine Trading Co (4), 1250A Harter Ave, Woodland, 95776

Mother Jones Magazine (17), 222 Sutter St (Suite 600), San Francisco, 94108-4457

Motion Picture & Television Fund Foundation (1), 23388 Mulholland Dr, Woodland Hills, 91364-2733

Mrs Beasley's & Miss Grace Lemon Cake Co (4), PO Box 25575, Los Angeles, 90025-0575

Multi-Level Marketing International Association (MLMIA) (1), 119 Stanford Ct, Irvine, 92612-1671

Mike Murach & Associates Inc (17), 4340 N Knoll Ave, Fresno, 93722-7825

Murad Inc (7), 2121 Rosecrans Ave 5th Fl, El Segundo, 90245-4744

Musician's Friend (5), PO Box 5111, Westlake Village, 91359-5111

Mustek Inc (3), 14751 Franklin Ave Ste B, Tustin, 92780-7272

NADA Appraisal Guides (17), 3186 Airway Ave (Unit K), Costa Mesa, 92626

Narrow Way (6), 712 Moraga Rd, Lafayette, 94549-4916

National Pen Corp (6), 12121 Scripps Summit Dr (Suite 200), San Diego, 92131-4609

National Semiconductor Corp (16), 2900 Semiconductor Dr, Santa Clara, 95052-8090

National University (1), 11355 N Torrey Pines Rd, La Jolla, 92037-1013

Nestle USA (4), 800 N Brand Blvd, Glendale, 91203-1216

NetSpend (14), 901 Mariners Island Blvd Ste 300, San Mateo, 94404-5025

Network Telephone Services Inc (16), 21135 Erwin St, Woodland Hills, 91367-3713

New & Unique Videos (3), 7323 Rondel Ct, San Diego, 92119

New Win Publishing Inc (17), 9682 Telstar Ave (Suite 110), El Monte, 91731-3009

New Zealand Tourism Board (19), 501 Santa Monica Blvd (Suite 300), Santa Monica, 90401

NCS Learn (16), 19 Orion Way, Trabuco Canyon, 92679

No Load Fund*X (14), 235 Montgomery St (Suite 1049), San Francisco, 94104-2994

Nordskog Publishing Co (17), 4562 Westinghouse St (Suite E), Ventura, 93003-5797

Nor'east Miniature Roses Inc (8), PO Box 440, Arroyo Grande, 93421

Nowell's Inc (8), 615 Irwin St, San Rafael, 94901-3940

Oakley Inc (2), 1 Icon, Foothill Ranch, 92610-3000

Oracle Corp (16), 500 Oracle Pkwy, Redwood Shores, 94065-1675

The Orange County Register (17), 625 N Grand Ave, Santa Ana, 92701

Orchard Supply Hardware (16), 6450 Via Del Oro St, San Jose, 95119

Orion Telescopes & Binoculars (11), 89 Hangar Way, Watsonville, 95076

Pacific Sportswear Co Inc (5), 6160 Fairmount Ave (Suite F), San Diego, 92120-3427

PAPYRUS (5), 500 Chadbourne Rd, Fairfield, 94534-9656

Para Publishing (17), PO Box 8206, Santa Barbara, 93118-8206

Paradise Galleries (6), PO Box 57086, Irvine, 92619-7086

Paragon Laboratories (16), 20433 Earl St, Torrance, 90503-2414

Parenting Concepts Inc (2), 25060 Hancock Ave (Suite 103-124), Murrieta, 92562

Parlay International (17), 712 Bancroft Rd (#505), Walnut Creek, 94598

Parmer Books (6), 7644 Forrestal Rd, San Diego, 92120-2203

Pasternack Enterprises Inc (16), PO Box 16759, Irvine, 92623-6759

Patagonia (2), 259 W Santa Clara St, Ventura, 93001-2545

The Patio (8), 36298 Toulon Dr, PO Box 1042, Murrieta, 92564

Peet's Coffee & Tea Inc (4), PO Box 12509, Berkeley, 94712-3509

Penguin Party Products (5), PO Box 1434, Campbell, 95009-1434

Perfection Tip Co/Camping Products Co (16), 1340 W Cowles St, Long Beach, 90803

Petco Animal Supplies (5), 9125 Rehco Rd, San Diego, 92121-2270

Pharmavite Corp LLC (HQ) (16), 8510 Balboa, Northridge, 91325-3583

PhotoStamps.com (5), 12959 Coral Tree Pl, Los Angeles, 90066-7020

Physical Therapy Institute Inc (16), 12630 Monte Vista Rd (Suite 204), Poway, 92064

Planned Parenthood Mar Monte (1), 1691 The Alameda, San Jose, 95126-2203

Bud Plant Illustrated Books (6), 3809 Laguna Ave, Palo Alto, 94306-2629

Plastic View ATC (9), 4585 Runway (Suite B), Simi Valley, 93063

Playboy Enterprises Inc (17), 9346 Civic Center Dr (#200), Beverly Hills, 90210-3604

Poker Player (17), 13701 Riverside Dr Ste 300, Sherman Oaks, 91423-2447

Porta-Bote International (11), 1074 Independence Ave, Mountain View, 94043-1602

Powers Television Marketing (17), 9731 Variel Ave, Chatsworth, 91311-4315

PC Mall (3), 2555 W 190 St, Torrance, 90504

PC World (17), 501 2nd St, San Francisco, 94107-1496

PMIC (17), 4727 Wilshire Blvd (Suite 300), Los Angeles, 90010-3873

Press-Enterprise Co (17), 3450 14th St, Riverside, 92501

Princess Cruises (HQ) (19), 24844 Avenue Rockefeller, Santa Clarita, 91355-3467

Professional Binding Products Inc (16), 2192-A Anchor Ct, Thousand Oaks, 91320

Progressive Energy Corp (5), 650 Corte Raquel, San Marcos, 92069-7320

Quartermaster Uniform & Equipment Co (2), PO Box 4147, Cerritos, 90703-4147

Quick Draw Clip Systems Inc (9), 4869 McGrath St (Suite 130), Ventura, 93003-7767

Raley's Bel Air Markets (16), 500 W Capitol Ave, West Sacramento, 95605-2696

Real Goods Trading Corp (5), 27 Simms St, San Rafael, 94901

Recycled Software Inc (3), 3764 Serenity Trl, Palm Springs, 92262-9774

RedEnvelope Inc (6), 4840 Eastgate Mall, San Diego, 92121-1977

Redwood City Seed Co (8), PO Box 361, Redwood City, 94064-0361

Remilon LLC (17), 100 View St Ste 202, Mountain View, 94041-1374

Rose Resnick Lighthouse for the Blind & Visually Impaired (1), 214 Van Ness Ave, San Francisco, 94102

Resource Publications Inc (17), 160 E Virginia St (Suite 290), San Jose, 95112-5876

Ricci Lee Hubbart Associates Inc (16), 20660 Stevens Creek Blvd (Suite 177), Cupertino, 95014

Road Runner Sports Inc (11), 5549 Copley Dr, San Diego, 92111-7904

Roland Products Inc (16), 3400 W Olympic Blvd, Los Angeles, 90019

Roll International Corp (16), 11444 W Olympic Blvd (fl 10), Los Angeles, 90064-1557

Rosicrucian Order AMORC (1), 1342 Naglee Ave, San Jose, 95191

Rosland Capital LLC (14), 429 Santa Monica Blvd (Suite 450), Santa Monica, 90401-3401

Safti First (16), 325 Newhall St, San Francisco, 94124-1432

Sage Software Inc (16), 6561 Irvine Center Dr, Irvine, 92618-2118

San Francisco Bay Area Rapid Transit District (BART) (16), 800 Madison St, Oakland, 94607-2622

San Francisco Chronicle (17), 901 Mission St, San Francisco, 94103

San Francisco Herb & Natural Food Co (4), 47444 Kato Rd, Fremont, 94538-7319

San Francisco Victoriana Inc (9), 2070 Newcomb Ave, San Francisco, 94124

San Jose Mercury News (17), 750 Ridder Park Dr, San Jose, 95190

Santa Barbara Greenhouses (8), 721 Richmond Ave, Oxnard, 93030

Schoolwise Press (17), 385 Ashton Ave (Suite 200), San Francisco, 94112

Charles Schwab & Co Inc (14), 211 Main St, San Francisco, 94105-1905

SECO-LARM USA Inc (16), 16842 Millikan Ave, Irvine, 92606

Second Renaissance Books (17), 2121 Alton Pkwy (Suite 250), Irvine, 92606-4926

See's Candies Inc (4), 20600 S Alameda St, Carson, 90810-1105

Select Press (17), 40 Phillip Terr, Novato, 94945

Sequoia Nursery (8), 9133 N Stoneridge Ln, Fresno, 93720-0843

Shield Healthcare (7), 27911B Franklin Pkwy, Valencia, 91355-4110

Shop.com (16), 21 Lower Ragsdale Dr, Bldg 1 (Suite 210, Monterey, 93940-5740

Sierra Club Books (1), 85 Second St, San Francisco, 94105-3488

Silicon Graphics Inc (16), 46600 Landing Pkwy, Fremont, 94538-6420

Skullduggery (16), 5433 E La Palma Ave, Anaheim, 92807-2022

Smith & Hawken Ltd (8), 4 Hamilton Landing Ste 100, Novato, 94949-8247

Smith & Noble (8), 1181 California Ave, Corona, 92881

SOAR Inflatables (11), 20 Healdsburg Ave, Healdsburg, 95448

Social Studies School Service (16), 10200 Jefferson Blvd, Culver City, 90232-0802

Soitenly Stooges (6), 1415 Gardena Ave, Glendale, 91204-2709

Southern California Gas Co (1), 1919 S State College Blvd, Anaheim, 92806-6114

Spalding Laboratories Inc (7), 760 Printz Rd, Arroyo Grande, 93420-5022

Specialty Equipment Market Association (1), 1575 S Valley Vista Dr, Diamond Bar, 91765-3914

Spectrum Chemicals & Laboratory Products (16), 14422 S San Pedro St, Gardena, 90248-2027

Spectrum eCommerce (15), 26023 Acero (Suite 100), Mission Viejo, 92691-7942

SF Video Inc (3), 1000 Sansome St (Suite 280), San Francisco, 94111

Standard Communications Corp (16), 6260 Sequence Dr, San Diego, 92121-4358

Starcrest Products of California Inc (16), 3660 Brennan Ave, Perris, 92599

StayWell/Krames (17), 1100 Grundy Ln (#2), San Bruno, 94066

Stick-Em Up Inc (5), PO Box 5445, Pleasanton, 94566-1445

Straw Hat Cooperative Corp (16), 18 Crow Canyon Ct (Suite 150), San Ramon, 94583-1669

Student Union at SJSU (1), 211 S 9th St, San Jose, 95192-0001

Sun Hope Nutritional Health (7), 1158 26th St (#566), Santa Monica, 90403-4698

Sunset Magazine (17), 80 Willow Rd, Menlo Park, 94025

Support Systems International Corp (3), 136 S Second St, Richmond, 94804

John Sutherland & Associates (15), 6275 Lusk Blvd, San Diego, 92121-2731

Symantec (16), 350 Ellis St, Mountain View, 94043-2202

System Pavers (16), 3750 S Susan St (Suite 200), Newport Beach, 92704-6964

Tailwinds Inc (6), 775 E Blithedale (#166), Mill Valley, 94941-1554

Tamrac Inc (2), 9240 Jordan Ave, Chatsworth, 91311-5769

Teleflora (16), 11444 W Olympic Blvd (fl 4), Los Angeles, 90064-1546

Ten Speed Press (17), 6001 Shellmound St 4th Fl, PO Box 7123, Emeryville, 94608-1988

Timber Crest Farms (16), 4791 Dry Creek Rd, Healdsburg, 95448

Timberline Geodesics (8), 2015 Blake St, Berkeley, 94704

Time Motion Tools (9), 12778 Brookprinter Pl, Poway, 92064

Tools for Wellness (7), 638 Lindero Canyon Rd (Suite 128), Oak Park, 91377-5457

Toyota Motor Sales USA Inc (16), 19001 S Western Ave, Torrance, 90501

Toys To Grow On (11), 2695 E Dominguez St, Carson, 90895

Trancos Inc (16), 6800 Koll Center Pkwy (Ste 170), Pleasanton, 94566-7044

Transamerica Occidental Life Co (15), 1150 S Olive St (T-24), Los Angeles, 90015

TransAmerica Retirement Services (15), 1150 S Olive St (#T-9-10), Los Angeles, 90015-2211

TechBA - Fumec (1), 1737 1st St (Suite 110), San Jose, 95112-4522

TL Enterprises Inc (17), 2575 Vista Del Mar Dr, Ventura, 93001-3920

20th Century Fox Television (16), 10201 W Pico Blvd (Bldg 88, Rm 30), Los Angeles, 90064-2606

21st Century Insurance (15), 6301 Owensmouth Ave, Woodland Hills, 91367

Tyco Electronics Corp (16), 300 Constitution Dr, Menlo Park, 94025-1140

U-Bild (8), 821 S Tremont St Ste B, PO Box 2383, Oceanside, 92054-4158

Ultimate Products Inc (16), 1151 Bay Blvd (Suite D), Chula Vista, 91911-2669

Unicom Electric Inc (16), 565 Brea Canyon Rd Ste A, Walnut, 91789-3004

United Farm Workers of America, AFL-CIO (1), 29700 Woodford-Tehachapi Rd, Keene, 93531

United Security Products Inc (16), PO Box 785, Poway, 92074-0785

USA Hosts (19), 657 Mission St (#202), San Francisco, 94105

US Tax Shield (14), 17328 Ventura Blvd, Encino, 91316-3904

United Systems c/o Biomed (7), 2354 Stanwell Dr, Concord, 94520-4822

University of California Irvine Extension (1), PO Box 6050, Irvine, 92616-6050

Urban Mapping Inc (16), 690 Fifth St (Suite 200), San Francisco, 94107-1517

USC Viterbi School of Engineering (1), 3650 McClintock Ave, Olin Hall (Suite 5), Los Angeles, 90089-1451

Varian Medical Systems (9), 3100 Hansen Way, Palo Alto, 94304

Venture Entertainment Group (3), PO Box 55113, Sherman Oaks, 91413

Veriad (16), 650 Columbia St, Brea, 92821-2912

Visa USA (14), 800 Metro Center Blvd, Foster City, 94404-4252

Warnaco Swimwear Inc (16), 1201 W 5th St (Suite T1200), Los Angeles, 90017-1493

Warner Bros (3), 4000 Warner Blvd, Burbank, 91522-0001

Warrior Custom Golf Inc (11), 15 Mason (Suite A), Irvine, 92618-2707

Mal Warwick Associates (1), 2550 9th St (Suite 103), Berkeley, 94710-2551

Webb Designs Inc (16), PO Box 1405, El Cajon, 92022-1405

Weider Publications Inc (17), 21100 Erwin St, Woodland Hills, 91367

Wells Fargo (14), 420 Montgomery St, San Francisco, 94163

West Marine Inc (11), 500 Westridge Dr, Watsonville, 95076-4171

Western Psychological Services (16), 625 Alaska Ave, Torrance, 90503-5124

Westwood Publishing Co (17), 700 S Central Ave, Glendale, 91204

White Cap Wholesale Contractors Supplies (16), PO Box 1770, Costa Mesa, 92628-1770

Michael Wiese Productions (17), 3940 Laurel Canyon Blvd (#1111), Studio City, 91604

Simon Wiesenthal Center (1), 1399 Roxbury Dr Ste 100, Los Angeles, 90035-4709

Williams-Sonoma Inc (8), 3250 Van Ness Ave, San Francisco, 94109-1012

Windsor Vineyards (16), 205 Concourse Blvd, Santa Rosa, 95403-8258

Winetasting.com (4), 2545 Napa Valley Corporate Dr, Napa, 94558-6275

Woodall Publishing Co LP (17), 2575 Vista Del Mar Dr, Ventura, 93001

Sylvia Woods Harp Center (11), PO Box 816, Montrose, 91021

Working Assets (16), 101 Market St (Suite 700), San Francisco, 94105

Xilinx Inc (16), 2100 Logic Dr, San Jose, 95124-3400

Yoga Journal / Active Interest Media (17), 475 Sansome St (Suite 850), San Francisco, 94111-3135

Your Choice Or Mine (16), 128 N Kingston St, San Mateo, 94401-2063

Your Man Tours (19), 100 N Sepulveda Blvd (Suite 1700), El Segundo, 90245-5655

Zoological Society of San Diego (1), 2920 Zoo Dr, PO Box 120551, San Diego, 92112

Colorado

Accellos Inc (12), 90 S Cascade Ave (Suite 1200), Colorado Springs, 80903-1678

Alfreda's Film Works (17), PO Box 416, Denver, 80201-0416

American Indian College Fund (1), 8333 Greenwood Blvd Ste 120, Denver, 80221-4483

American Numismatic Association (1), 818 N Cascade Ave, Colorado Springs, 80903-3279

Belcaro Group Inc (17), 7100 E Belleview Ave (Suite 208), Greenwood Village, 80111-1634

BellTower Technologies (18), 7100 E Belleview Ave (Suite 208), Greenwood Village, 80111

Birthday Keepsakes (6), 1323 S Garfield Ave, Loveland, 80537-6334

Bolind Inc (16), PO Box 18714, Boulder, 80308-1714

Broadmoor Hotel Inc (19), 1 Lake Ave, Colorado Springs, 80906-4269

DV Burrell Seed Growers Co (8), 405 N Main St, Rocky Ford, 81067

Celestial Seasonings (16), 4600 Sleepytime Dr, Boulder, 80301-3292

Chefs Catalog (8), 5070 Centennial Blvd, Colorado Springs, 80919-2402

Coast to Coast Inc (1), PO Box 6574, Englewood, 80155-6574

Communication Creativity (17), 209 Church St, Buena Vista, 81211

Compassion International (1), 12290 Voyager Pkwy, Colorado Springs, 80921-3694

David C Cook (17), 4050 Lee Vance View, Colorado Springs, 80918-7102

Coursesmith (17), PO Box 416, Denver, 80201-0416

Creative Learning Systems Inc (9), 1140 Boston Ave (Unit A), Longmont, 80501-5890

Critter Mountain Wear (2), PO Box 975, 86 Jacqueline Lane, Crested Butte, 81224-0975

Current USA Inc (6), 1025 E Woodmen Rd, Colorado Springs, 80920-3181

DataLever Corp (16), 1515 Walnut St (Suite 200), Boulder, 80302-5429

Denver Metro Convention & Visitors Bureau (1), 1555 California St (Suite 300), Denver, 80202

Denver Tax Software Inc (16), PO Box 632285, Littleton, 80163-2285

Eagle Claw Fishing Tackle (11), 4245 E 46th Ave, Denver, 80216-3219

Estes Industries (11), 1295 "H" St, Penrose, 81240

Federal Citizen Information Center (5), Consumer Information Catalog, Pueblo, 81009

First Data Merchant Services (14), 6200 S Quebec St Ste 1, Greenwood Village, 80111-4733

Fulcrum Publishing (17), 4690 Table Mountain Dr (Suite 100), Golden, 80403

Gaiam Inc (9), PO Box 3095, Boulder, 80307-3095

Gambro Inc (16), 14143 Denver W Pkwy, Lakewood, 80401

Gates Corp (9), 1551 Wewatta St, Denver, 80202

Golden Bison LLC (4), 1395 S Platte River Dr, Denver, 80223-3467

Golf Card International (1), 64 Inverness Dr E, Englewood, 80112

Gorsuch Ltd (2), 263 E Gore Creek Dr, Vail, 81657

Great-West Life (15), 8515 E Orchard Rd, Greenwood Village, 80111

IHS Inc (17), 321 Inverness Dr S, Englewood, 80112-5895

International Bible Society (1), 1820 Jet Stream Dr, Colorado Springs, 80921-3696

Jason Natural Personal Care Products (7), 4600 Sleepytime Dr, Boulder, 80301-3284

Jones International Ltd (16), 9697 E Mineral Ave, Centennial, 80112

Leanin' Tree Inc (6), 6055 Longbow Dr, Box 9800, Boulder, 80301

Lillian Vernon Corp (6), PO Box 35980, Colorado Springs, 80935-3598

Medical Group Management Association (MGMA) (1), 104 Inverness Terr Dr E, Englewood, 80112-5306

Miller Stockman (2), 8500 Zuni St, Denver, 80260-5007

Mobile Fusion (16), 165 S Union Blvd Ste 405, Lakewood, 80228-2210

Molson Coors Brewing Co (16), 1225 17th St Ste 3200, Denver, 80202-5536

National Institute for Trial Advocacy (NITA) (1), 1685 38th St, Boulder, 80301-2735

National Jewish Health (1), 1400 Jackson St, Denver, 80206-2761

National Multiple Sclerosis Society (1), 900 S Broadway Ste 210, Denver, 80209-4269

Native American Rights Fund (1), 1506 Broadway, Boulder, 80302-6217

Paladin Press (17), 7077 Winchester Cir, Gunbarrel Tech Center, Boulder, 80301-3505

Partminer (17), 7807 E Peakview Ave (Suite 400), Centennial, 80111-6849

Pastime Publications Inc (17), 99 Kalamath St, Denver, 80223-1549

RJ Persson Enterprises Inc (16), 1208 Kent Ave (Suite 101), Montrose, 81402-5228

Play Fair Toys (11), 3043 Walnut St, Boulder, 80301-2509

ProSing Karaoke (5), PO Box 7, Nederland, 80466-0007

Prosperity And Profits Unlimited Distribution Services (16), PO Box 416, Denver, 80201-0416

Renton's Inc (10), 6551 S Revere Pkwy (Suite 205), Centennial, 80111-6411

The Right Start Inc (5), 3000 E Third Ave (#15), Denver, 80206

Rocky Mountain Chocolate Factory (4), 265 Turner Dr, Durango, 81303-7941

Society of American Magicians Inc (1), PO Box 505, Parker, 80134-0505

Spear Engineering Co (16), 3107 N Stone Ave, Colorado Springs, 80907

Starz Entertainment Group (16), 8900 Liberty Cir, Englewood, 80112-7057

Stickers 'N' Stuff Inc (6), 245 W Sycamore Ln, Louisville, 80027-2235

Story Time Stories That Rhyme (17), PO Box 416, Denver, 80201-0416

Sunrise Medical Inc (16), 6899 Winchester Cir (Suite 200), Boulder, 80301-3696

Tecra Tools Inc (9), 2925 S Umatilla St, Englewood, 80110-1217

Thimband (17), PO Box 416, Denver, 80201-0416

Trumble Greetings (6), 6055 Longbow Dr, Boulder, 80301-3203

TAB Boards International Inc (14), 11031 Sheridan Blvd, Westminster, 80020-3201

2-10 Home Buyers Warranty (15), 10375 E Harvard Ave, 1 Denver Highlands (Suite 100), Denver, 80231-3966

Vail Associates Inc (19), 390 Interlocken Crescent, Broomfield, 80021

Vail Resorts Inc (19), PO Box 38, Keystone, 80435

Weston Distance Learning (13), 2001 Lowe St, Fort Collins, 80525-3474

Connecticut

AIFS (19), 9 W Broad St, Stamford, 06902-3788

AETNA - Marketing Product & Communication (14), 151 Farmington Ave, Hartford, 06156

Affinion Group Inc (16), 6 High Ridge Park, Stamford, 06905-1327

CM Almy & Son Inc (5), 3 American Ln, Greenwich, 06831-2551

American Radio Relay League (1), 225 Main St, Newington, 06111-1494

AmeriCares (1), 88 Hamilton Ave, Stamford, 06902-3100

Anheuser-Busch Inc Promotional Products Group (6), 20 Constitution Blvd S, Shelton, 06484

Anthem Blue Cross Blue Shield (15), 370 Bassett Rd, North Haven, 06473

Elizabeth Arden Spas LLC (19), 300 Main St (Suite 8), Stamford, 06901-3033

Association of Bridal Consultants (1), 56 Danbury Rd (Suite 11), New Milford, 06776-2521

Baxter Bros Inc (17), 1030 E Putnam Ave, Greenwich, 06830

Belvoir Media Group LLC (17), 800 Connecticut Ave Ste 4W02, Norwalk, 06854-1628

BIC Corp (16), 1 BIC Way (Suite 1), Shelton, 06484-6223

RC Bigelow Inc (4), 201 Black Rock Tpke, Fairfield, 06825-5512

Boardroom Inc (17), 281 Tresser Blvd (fl 8), Stamford, 06901-3284

Cafe Lango (16), 2351 Boston Post Rd (#101), Guilford, 06437

Catholic Digest (17), PO Box 6015, New London, 06320-1789

CD Universe (16), 101 N Plains Ind Rd, Wallingford, 06492-2165

Champion America Inc (10), PO Box 3092, Branford, 06405-1692

Chief Executive Magazine (17), 1 Sound Shore Dr (Suite 100), Greenwich, 06830-7251

Clairol Inc (7), One Blachley Rd, Stamford, 06922-0003

Cliggott Publishing Co (17), 535 Connecticut Ave Ste 300, Norwalk, 06854-1713

Coastal Tool & Supply (16), 510 New Park Ave, West Hartford, 06110

Cooper Surgical Inc (7), 95 Corporate Dr, Trumbull, 06611

Crabtree & Evelyn Ltd (4), 102 Peake Brook Rd, Woodstock, 06281-3429

Cronin & Co (16), 50 Nye Rd, Glastonbury, 06033-2196

Cuisinart (16), 1 Cummings Point Rd, Stamford, 06902-7901

Down Home Comforts (8), 128 Woodland St, Windsor, 06095-3454

Duracell (16), 8 Research Dr, Bethel, 06801

The Durham Manufacturing Co (16), 201 Main St, Durham, 06422-2108

Engineering Services & Products Co (9), 1395 John Fitch Blvd, South Windsor, 06074-1029

Esprit Line Co Ltd - USA (16), 11 Heronvue Rd, Greenwich, 06831-2906

Florian Tools (8), 157 Water St, Southington, 06489-3018

Gems Sensors & Controls (9), One Cowles Rd, Plainville, 06062-1198

General Electric Co (16), 3135 Easton Tpke, Fairfield, 06828-0001

Global Specialties (16), 994 N Colony Rd (Unit 305), Wallingford, 06492-5902

Gold Line Connector Inc (3), PO Box 500, West Redding, 06896

Golf Digest Co (17), 20 Westport Rd Ste 320, PO Box 850, Wilton, 06897-4550

Good Directions Co Inc (8), 20 Commerce Dr, Danbury, 06810

Grolier Publishing (17), 90 Sherman Tpke, Danbury, 06816-0002

Guideposts (1), 39 Old Ridgebury Rd Ste 2AB, Danbury, 06810-5122

The Hartford Financial Services Inc (15), 200 Executive Blvd, Southington, 06489-1058

Hobby Surplus Sales (11), 287 Main St, New Britain, 06050-2202

Janice's LLC (8), 30 Arbor St S, Hartford, 06106

Jaypro Sports (11), 976 Hartford Tpke, Waterford, 06385-4044

William S Konecky Associates Inc (17), 72 Ayers Point Rd, Old Saybrook, 06475

Lego Direct Marketing (11), 555 Taylor Rd, Enfield, 06082-2372

Life-Study Fellowship Foundation Inc (17), 90 Heights Rd, Darien, 06820

LIMRA International (1), 300 Day Hill Rd, Windsor, 06095-1783

Loctite Corp (16), 1001 Trout Brook Crossing, Rocky Hill, 06067

Luce Corp (16), 336 Putnam Ave, Box 4124, Hamden, 06517

Matthews 1812 House Inc (4), 250 Kent Rd, Cornwall Bridge, 06754

Merrimade Stationery Co LLC (10), 200 Main St (Suite 100), Ansonia, 06401

MBI Inc (16), 47 Richards Ave, Norwalk, 06857-0001

Moore Medical LLC (7), 1690 New Britain Ave Ste A, Farmington, 06032-3361

MxEnergy Inc (16), 595 Summer St (Suite 300), Stamford, 06901-1407

Mystic Seaport Museum Stores (6), 75 Greenmanville Ave, Mystic, 06355-0990

Nielsen Trade Dimensions (17), 40 Danbury Rd, Wilton, 06897-4406

NCS (16), 60 Newtown Rd (Suite 6), Danbury, 06810-6257

Nodine's Smokehouse (4), 65 Fowler Ave, Torrington, 06790-6529

Olympia Sales Inc (16), 215 Moody Rd, Enfield, 06083-3207

Oxford Health Plans, Inc (15), 48 Monroe Turnpike, Trumbull, 06611

Pachmayr Ltd (11), 475 Smith St, Middletown, 06457-1529

People's United Bank (14), 850 Main St, Bridgeport, 06604-4917

Pitney Bowes (10), 1 Elmcroft Rd, Stamford, 06926-0700

Richard M Pordes LLC (1), 99 Dolphin Cove Quay, Stamford, 06902-7716

PPI Benefit Solutions (15), 10 Research Pkwy, Wallingford, 06492-1963

PTI Pyramid Technologies LLC (10), 45 Gracey Ave, Meriden, 06451-2284

Prime (16), 1100 Boston Ave, Bridgeport, 06610

Professional Cutlery Direct (4), 242 Branford Rd, North Branford, 06471

Queue Inc (17), 80 Hathaway Dr, Stratford, 06615-7304

Reed Exhibitions (16), 383 Main Ave, Norwalk, 06851-1500

Rinfret Ltd (8), 354 Greenwich Ave, Greenwich, 06830-6522

Round Lake Publishing Co (17), 23 Chestnut Hill Rd, Trumbull, 06611

S&S Worldwide (11), 75 Mill St, Colchester, 06415-0513

Save the Children Federation Inc (1), 54 Wilton Rd, Westport, 06880-3108

Scan Optics Inc (16), 169 Progress Dr, Manchester, 06040-2294

Seton Identification Products (16), 20 Thompson Rd, Branford, 06405-2842

Siemens IT Solutions & Services Inc (16), 101 Merritt 7, Norwalk, 06851-1061

The Silo Inc (8), 44 Upland Rd, New Milford, 06776

Soundprints (6), 353 Main Ave, Norwalk, 06851-1552

Sovereign Bank New England (14), 140 Hebron Ave, Glastonbury, 06033-4239

SSHC Inc/Radiant Heating Commercial Applications (9), Four Custom Dr, Old Saybrook, 06475-4008

Stabenfeldt Inc (13), 457 N. Main St (#3C), Danbury, 06811-4700

Starwood Hotels & Resorts (19), 1 Star Pt, Stamford, 06902-8911

Statware (16), 90 Main St (Suite 213A), Centerbrook, 06409

Sterling Name Tape Inc (16), Nine Willow St, PO Box 939, Winsted, 06098

Stew Leonard's (4), 100 Westport Ave, Norwalk, 06851

SunPorch Structures Inc (8), 495 Post Rd E, Westport, 06880-4433

Synapse Group Inc (18), 225 High Ridge Rd, East Building, Stamford, 06905-3038

Tauck World Discovery (19), 10 Norden Pl, Norwalk, 06855-1454

The Taunton Press (17), 63 S Main St, PO Box 5506, Newtown, 06470-2344

Thomas Klise/Crimson Multimedia (16), PO Box 720, Mystic, 06355-0720

Torqmaster International (9), 200 Harvard Ave, Stamford, 06902-6230

The Travelers Insurance Cos (15), 1 Tower Sq (#9PB-B), Hartford, 06183-0001

Tricor Direct Inc/Seton (9), 20 Thompson Rd, Branford, 06405-2842

Tuttle (2), 23 Village Ln, Wallingford, 06492-2426

Tyson Associates Inc (17), 246 Federal Rd (Suite D23), Brookfield, 06804

US Games Systems Inc (11), 179 Ludlow St, Stamford, 06902

Vertrue Inc (13), 20 Glover Ave, Norwalk, 06850-1219

Water's Edge Resort & Spa (19), 1525 Boston Post Rd, Westbrook, 06498

Webster Bank (14), 145 Bank St Fl 1, Waterbury, 06702-2211

White Flower Farm (8), 30 Irene St, Torrington, 06790-6657

World Wrestling Entertainment (16), 1241 E Main St, PO Box 3857, Stamford, 06902

Zotos International (16), 100 Tokeneke Rd, Darien, 06820-4894

Delaware

AAA Mid-Atlantic Insurance Groups (15), 1 River Pl, Wilmington, 19801-5125

Advanced Machinery (9), PO Box 430, New Castle, 19720

AstraZeneca (7), 1800 Concord Pike A3C-122, Wilmington, 19850

The Bank of New York/Delaware (14), PO Box 6995, Newark, 19714-6995

BLS Inc (17), 501 N Lincoln St, Wilmington, 19805-3047

Chick Harness & Supply Inc (11), 18011 S Dupont Hwy, Harrington, 19952-2135

DelStar Technologies (16), 601 Industrial Dr, Middletown, 19709

E I DuPont De Nemours & Co (16), 1007 Market St, Wilmington, 19898

WL Gore & Associates Inc (2), 555 Paper Mill Rd, Newark, 19711

Kennel Vet (11), PO Box 523, Laurel, 19956

MXT Card Services, LLC (14), 2 Penns Way (Suite 201), New Castle, 19720-2407

Prestwick House Inc (17), PO Box 658, Clayton, 19938-0658

Winterthur Museum & Country Estate (6), 5105 Kennett Pike, Wilmington, 19735

District of Columbia

AAAS/Science (1), 1200 New York Ave NW (fl 9), Washington, 20005-3928

AARP (1), 601 E St NW, Washington, 20049-0003

ADRFCO (1), 1612 K St NW (Suite 510), Washington, 20006-2849

AFL-CIO (1), 815 16th St NW (5th fl), Washington, 20006

ASM Press (17), 1752 N St NW, Washington, 20036-2904

Abbott, Langer Association Surveys (17), 1725 I St NW (Suite 300), Washington, 20006

Academic Travel Abroad Inc (19), 1920 N St NW (Suite 200), Washington, 20036-1652

Accuracy in Media Inc (1), 4455 Connecticut Ave NW (Suite 330), Washington, 20008-2372

ActionAid (1), 1420 K St NW (Suite 900), Washington, 20005-2507

African Wildlife Foundation (1), 1400 16th St NW (Suite 120), Washington, 20036-2249

Amazon.com (16), 126 C St NW Fl 2, Washington, 20001-2132

American Association for Justice (1), 777 6th St NW (Suite 200), The Leonard M Ring Law Center, Washington, 20001-3707

American Association of University Women (1), 1111 16th St NW Ste Mailrm, Washington, 20036-4809

American Bankers Association (1), 1120 Connecticut Ave NW, Washington, 20036-3959

American Chemical Society (1), 1155 16th St NW, Washington, 20036-4839

American College of Cardiology (1), 2400 N St NW, Washington, 20037-1153

American College of Physicians (17), 25 Massachusetts Ave NW (Suite 700), Washington, 20001-7401

American Forests (1), 734 15th St NW (Suite 800), Washington, 20005-1016

American Humane Association (1), 1400 16th St NW Ste 360, Washington, 20036-2215

American Institute for Cancer Research (1), 1759 R St NW, Washington, 20009-2570

American Psychological Association (1), 750 First St NE, Washington, 20002-4242

American Red Cross (1), 2025 E St NW, National HQ, Washington, 20006-5009

American Society of Interior Designers (1), 608 Massachusetts Ave NE, Washington, 20002-6006

Americans for Peace Now (1), 2100 M St NW Ste 619, Washington, 20037-1269

Arent Fox LLP (9), 1050 Connecticut Ave NW, Washington, 20036

Association of American Publishers (1), 455 Massachusetts Ave NW, Washington, 20001-2777

The Atlantic Monthly (17), 600 New Hampshire Ave NW Fl 4, Washington, 20037-2403

Black Entertainment Television Inc (16), 1900 ″W″ Pl NE, Washington, 20018-1211

B'nai B'rith International (1), 2020 K St NW (7th fl), Washington, 20006

Capitol Concierge Inc (16), 1400 ″I″ St NW (Suite 750), Washington, 20005

Care2 (1), 1100 15th S NW (Suite 600), Washington, 20005-1759

Carefirst Blue Cross Blue Shield (15), 840 First St NE, Washington, 20002-8046

The Catholic University of America Press (17), 620 Michigan Ave NE, Leahy Hall (Rm 240), Washington, 20064

CSPI/Nutrition Action Health Letter (17), 1220 L St NW Ste 300, Washington, 20005-4053

Center for Science in the Public Interest (1), 1220 L St NW Ste 300, Washington, 20005-4053

Children's Hospital Foundation (1), 111 Michigan Ave NW, Children's Hospital Foundation, Washington, 20010-2916

Citizens Against Government Waste (1), 1301 Pennsylvania Ave NW Ste 1075, Washington, 20004-1707

Civil War Preservation Trust (1), 1156 15th St NW (Suite 900), Washington, 20005-4761

Council for Advancement and Support of Education (CASE) (1), 1307 New York Ave NW (Suite 100), Washington, 20005

Defenders of Wildlife (1), 1130 17th St NW, Washington, 20036-4604

Democratic Congressional Campaign Committee (1), 430 S Capitol St SE, Washington, 20003

Eagle Publishing (17), One Massachusetts Ave NW, Washington, 20001

Edison Electric Institute (1), 701 Pennsylvania Ave NW, Washington, 20004-2696

Environmental Defense Fund (1), 1875 Connecticut Ave NW (# 600), Washington, 20009-5739

Environmental Law Institute (17), 2000 ″L″ St NW (Suite 200), Washington, 20036-4919

Fannie Mae (14), 3900 Wisconsin Ave NW, Washington, 20016-2806

Food & Water Watch (1), 1616 P St NW (Suite 300), Washington, 20036-1408

Fund for Public Interest Research (1), 218 D St SE Fl 2, Washington, 20003-1900

Georgetown University Law Center/ Continuing Legal Education Div (13), 600 New Jersey Ave NW, Georgetown CLE, Washington, 20001

Georgetown University McDonough School of Business (1), 37th & O Streets, NW, 211 Hariri Bldg, Washington, 20057

GEICO Direct (15), 1 GEICO Plaza, Washington, 20076-0005

Governing Magazine (17), 1100 Connecticut Ave NW Ste 1300, Washington, 20036-4109

Government Data Publications Inc (17), 2300 M St NW, Washington, 20037-1434

Graduate School USDA (1), 600 Maryland Ave SW, Washington, 20024

Hanley Wood LLC (16), 1 Thomas Cir NW (Suite 600), Washington, 20005-5803

Heldref Publications (17), 1319 18th St NW, Washington, 20036-1802

ICMA Retirement Corp (14), 777 N Capitol St NE (Suite 500), Washington, 20002

The Interfaith Alliance (1), 1212 New York Ave NW (#7), Washington, 20005-3905

International City/County Management Association (1), 777 N Capitol St NE (Suite 500), Washington, 20002-4201

The Kiplinger Washington Editors Inc (17), 1100 13th St NW Ste 750, Washington, 20005-4364

Lautman Maska Neill & Co (1), 1730 Rhode Island Ave NW (Suite 301), Washington, 20036-3120

Market Development Group Inc (1), 5151 Wisconsin Ave NW (Suite 400), Washington, 20016-4124

Marriott International Inc (19), 1 Marriott Dr, Washington, 20058-0001

Movie/Entertainment Book Club (13), One Massachusetts Ave, Washington, 20001

National Alliance of Business (1), 1455 Pennsylvania Ave NW (Suite 375), Washington, 20004

National Committee to Preserve Social Security & Medicare (1), 10 ″G″ St NE (Suite 600), Washington, 20002-4215

National Gallery of Art Gift Shop (16), 4th & Constitution Ave NW, Washington, 20565

National Geographic Society (17), 1145 17th St NW, Washington, 20036-4688

National Journal Group (17), 600 New Hampshire Ave NW Fl 4, Washington, 20037-2403

National Law Enforcement Officers Memorial Fund (1), 901 E St NW Ste 100, Washington, 20004-2025

National Osteoporosis Foundation (1), 1150 17th St NW (Suite 850), Washington, 20037-1216

National Railroad Passenger Corp (16), 60 Massachussetts Ave NE, Washington, 20002

National Retail Federation Inc (1), 325 Seventh St NW (Suite 1100), Washington, 20004

National Society of Collegiate Scholars (1), 2000 M St NW Ste 600, Washington, 20036-3328

National Trust for Historic Preservation (1), 1785 Massachusetts Ave NW, Washington, 20036-2189

NARAL Pro-Choice America (1), 1156 15th St NW, Washington, 20005-1704

Ocean Conservancy (1), 1300 19th St NW, Washington, 20036

OMP (1), 1133 19th St NW (Suite 300), Washington, 20036-3610

Overseas Private Investment Corp (OPIC) (14), 1100 New York Ave NW, Washington, 20527

Paralyzed Veterans of America (1), 801 18th St NW, Washington, 20006-3517

People for the American Way (1), 1101 15th St NW Ste 600, Washington, 20005-5023

Pharmaceutical Care Management Association (1), 601 Pennsylvania Ave NW Ste 740S, Washington, 20004-2699

Population Connection (1), 2120 L St NW (Suite 500), Washington, 20037-1534

Regnery Publishing (17), 1 Massachusetts Ave NW, Washington, 20001-1401

Sirius XM Radio (16), 1500 Eckington Pl, Washington, 20002

Smithsonian Institution (6), PO Box 37012, SI Bldg, Room 153 MRC 010, Washington, 20013-7012

Society for Neuroscience (1), 1121 14th St NW (Suite 1010), Washington, 20005-5642

Special Olympics International (1), 1133 19th St NW Ste 1200, Washington, 20036-3645

SOS Children's Villages - USA (1), 1001 Connecticut Ave NW Ste 1250, Washington, 20036-5520

Sustainable Forestry Initiative Inc (1), 900 17th St NW Ste 700, Washington, 20006-2515

Telecommunications Reports International Inc (17), 1015 15th St NW (fl 10), Washington, 20005-2605

Thompson Publishing Group Inc (17), 1725 "K" St, Washington, 20006

Transemantics Inc (16), 1337 Connecticut Ave NW (4th fl), Washington, 20036

Travel Industry Association (1), 1100 New York Ave NW Ste 450W, Washington, 20005-6130

Travelex America Inc (14), 1152 15th St NW (fl 7), Washington, 20005

Union Privilege, AFL-CIO (1), 1125 15th St NW (Suite 300), Washington, 20005-2707

United Nations Foundation (1), 1800 Massachusetts Ave NW (Suite 400), Washington, 20036-1218

US Chamber of Commerce (1), 1615 "H" St NW, Washington, 20062-0001

US Department of Commerce (1), Intl Trade Admin (Rm H-1124), Washington, 20230-0001

ULI-The Urban Land Institute (1), 1025 Thomas Jefferson St NW (Suite 500W), Washington, 20007-5201

Vegetarian Awareness Network/ VEGANET (1), PO Box 3545, Washington, 20027-0045

Warren Communications News (17), 2115 Ward Ct NW, Washington, 20037-1209

The Washington Monthly Co (17), 1200 18th St NW (Suite 330), Washington, 20036-2556

Washington National Opera (16), 2600 Virginia Ave (Suite 301), Washington, 20037

Washington Post Digital (17), 1150 15th St NW, Washington, 20071

The Washington Post (17), 1150 15th St NW, Washington, 20071

The Washingtonian (17), 1828 "L" St NW (Suite 200), Washington, 20036

The World Bank (17), 1818 "H" St NW, Washington, 20433

World Wildlife Fund (1), 1250 24th St NW (fl4), Washington, 20037-1145

YWCA of the USA (1), 2025 M St NW (Suite 550), Washington, 20036-3320

Florida

AAA Auto Club South (1), 1515 N Westshore Blvd, Tampa, 33607-4505

ADT Worldwide (16), 1 Town Center Rd, Boca Raton, 33486

Absolute Reservation Center Inc (19), 150 E Wildmere Ave (#108), Longwood, 32750

Achieve Global (16), 8875 Hidden River Pkwy (Suite 400), Tampa, 33637

Action Direct Inc (11), 513 NW 72nd St, Miami, 33150-3731

AeroGraphics (3), 1725 N Lexington Ave, DeLand, 32724

Air Ambulance Network Inc (16), 3607 Alt 19 Ste A, Palm Harbor, 34683-1412

Alarmingyou.com (16), One Town Center Rd., Boca Raton, 33486-1002

American Automobile Association (16), 1000 AAA Dr MS-74, Heathrow, 32746-5063

American College of Physician Executives (1), 400 N Ashley Dr (Suite 400), Tampa, 33602-4322

American Dermatological Corp (16), PO Box 565014, Miami, 33256-5014

American Nicaraguan Foundation (1), 1000 NW 57th Ct Ste 770, Miami, 33126-3288

American Preferred Reader's Service Inc (18), 1975 E Sunrise Blvd Ste 800, Fort Lauderdale, 33304-1455

Anda Inc (7), 2915 Weston Rd, Weston, 33331-3627

Arnet Pharmaceutical (7), 2525 Davie Rd, Davie, 33317

Sam Ash.Com (5), 7726 Cheri Ct, Tampa, 33634-2419

AsiaEXP (16), 1835 NE Miami Gardens Dr, Miami, 33179-5035

AvMed Health Plan Inc (1), 9400 S Dadeland Blvd, Miami, 33156-2823

Bahamas Ministry of Tourism (19), 1200 S Pine Island Rd (Suite 750), Fort Lauderdale, 33324-4413

Bankers Warranty Group (16), 11101 Roosevelt Blvd N, Saint Petersburg, 33716-2340

Battery Pros Inc (9), PO Box 54, Horseshoe Beach, 32648-0054

Bell Performance Inc (9), 1340 Bennett Dr, Longwood, 32750-7623

Bethesda Hospital Foundation (1), 2815 S Seacrest Blvd, Boynton Beach, 33435-7934

Bijoux Terner (16), 6950 NW 77th Ct, Miami, 33126-2714

Blue Cross & Blue Shield of Florida (15), 4800 Deerwood Corporate Campus Pkwy, Jacksonville, 32246

Blue Strawberry Resorts LLC (19), 7600 Harding Ave Apt 3, Miami Beach, 33141-2150

Boca Java (4), 200 S Biscayne Blvd Ste 1818, Miami, 33131-2329

Brooke Distributors Inc (3), 16250 NW 52nd Ave, Miami, 33014

Buggies Unlimited (12), 3510 Port Jacksonville Pkwy, Jacksonville, 32226

Carnival Cruise Lines (19), 3655 NW 87th Ave, Miami, 33178-2418

Casual Living USA (6), 5401 Hangar Ct, Tampa, 33634-5341

CBT Direct (16), 905 E Martin Luther King Jr Dr Ste 500, Tarpon Springs, 34689-4830

Cedar Fresh Products (16), 4207 University Dr, Coral Gables, 33146-1140

Center for Professional Development (16), 555 W Pensacola St (#2027), Turnbull Conference Ctr, Tallahassee, 32306-1640

Chain Store Guide (17), 3922 Coconut Palm Dr Ste 300, Tampa, 33619-1389

Champs Corp (11), 311 Manatee Ave W, Bradenton, 34205

Champs Software Inc (3), 1255 N Vantage Point Dr, Crystal River, 34429

Checks by Phone/Checks by Web (14), 9770 S Military Trail (Suite 380), Boynton Beach, 33436

Chico's FAS Inc (2), 11215 Metro Pkwy, Fort Myers, 33966-1206

Comp USA, Inc (3), 14951 N Dallas Pkwy, Miami, 33144

Corona Cigar Co (5), 7792 W Sand Lake Rd, Orlando, 32819

Cosmo International (16), 601 Fairway Dr, Deerfield Beach, 33441-1867

Cross Country Travcorps (16), 6551 Park of Commerce Blvd, Boca Raton, 33487-8247

Crystek Corp (9), 12730 Commonwealth Dr, Fort Myers, 33913

Cushman Fruit Co Inc (4), 3325 Forest Hill Blvd, West Palm Beach, 33406-5812

Danker Laboratories Inc (16), 6805 33rd St E, Box 1899, Sarasota, 34243

The Dartnell Corp (17), 2272 Airport Rd S, Naples, 34112

Databazaar.com (10), 12070 Miramar Pkwy, Miramar, 33025

Davidoff of Geneva Inc (6), 3001 Gateway Centre Pkwy N, Pinellas Park, 33782-6124

Decal Shop (10), 1849 Foster Dr, Jacksonville, 32216

Delta Vacations (19), 110 E Broward Blvd Fl 14, Fort Lauderdale, 33301-3521

DigDev Direct (16), 260 SW Natura Ave (fl 2), Deerfield Beach, 33441

Disney Vacation Club (19), 1390 Celebration Blvd, Kissimmee, 34747-5166

Walt Disney Parks & Resorts (19), PO Box 10000, Lake Buena Vista, 32830-1000

Dole Fresh Flowers (8), 2200 NW 70th Ave, Miami, 33122-1816

Eagle Asset Management Inc (14), PO Box 10520, Saint Petersburg, 33733-0520

Ecklers (12), 5200 S Washington Ave, Titusville, 32780-7316

Edwin Watts Golf (11), 20 Hill Ave, Fort Walton Beach, 32548

ETTSI Premiums & Incentives (16), 301 Indigo Dr, Daytona Beach, 32114-1134

Encircle (14), 1691 NW 107th Ave, Miami, 33172

FIU Online (1), 11200 SW 8th St (Marc 210), Miami, 33199

Florida A&M University (16), 428 Tucker Hall, Tallahassee, 32307

Florida Credit Union (14), PO Box 5549, Gainesville, 32627

Florida Gift Fruit Shippers Association (1), 5500 W Concord Ave, Orlando, 32808-7700

Florida Institute of CPA's (1), 325 W College Ave, Tallahassee, 32301

Florida Power & Light Co (16), PO Box 025576, Miami, 33102

Florida Power Corp (16), 299 First Ave N, Saint Petersburg, 33701

Florida Today (17), 1 Gannett Plz, Melbourne, 32940

Food for the Poor Inc (1), 6401 Lyons Rd, Coconut Creek, 33073-3602

Four Corners Direct Inc (16), 8520 S Tamiami Trl Unit 2, Sarasota, 34238-3001

G&S Packing Co Inc (16), 16600 S Hwy 25, Weirsdale, 32195

G-Neil Direct Mail (10), 720 International Pkwy, PO Box 450939, Sunrise, 33345-0939

Galloway Farms (8), 7790 SW 87th Ave, Miami, 33173

General Wig Manufacturers Inc (7), 1480 SW 3rd St (Suite 3), Pompano Beach, 33069-3225

Peter Glenn Publications (17), 777 E Atlantic Ave (Suite C2337), Delray Beach, 33483

Golden Bear Golf Inc (16), 11780 US Hwy 1 (Suite 500), North Palm Beach, 33408-3042

Golden River Fruit Co (4), 505 66th Ave SW, PO Box 2090, Vero Beach, 32961-2090

Gracewood Fruit Co (4), PO Box 370, Vero Beach, 32961-0370

Graves Lapidary Co (9), 1800 N Andrews Ave, Pompano Beach, 33069-1421

Gruber & Allison Inc (17), 7487 Falls Rd W, Boynton Beach, 33437

Gulf Coast Data Supply Inc (3), 5455 Rowe Trl, Milton, 32571-9556

Hale Indian River Groves Inc (16), PO Box 691237, Vero Beach, 32969-1237

The Hamilton Collection (6), 7018 A C Skinner Pkwy (Suite 300), Jacksonville, 32256-6975

The Hamilton Group Ltd Inc (16), 7018 A C Skinner Pkwy (#300), Jacksonville, 32256

Har Court Inc (17), 9400 Southpark Center Loop, Orlando, 32819-8647

Harland Financial Solutions Inc (16), 605 Crescent Executive Ct (Suite 600), Lake Mary, 32746

Harris Corp (16), 1025 W NASA Blvd, Melbourne, 32919

HealthPlan Services (15), 3501 E Frontage Rd, Tampa, 33607

Hecht Rubber Corp (16), 6161 Phillips Hwy, Jacksonville, 32216-5920

HR Direct (10), PO Box 452049, Sunrise, 33345-2049

HSN Inc (5), One HSN Dr, Saint Petersburg, 33729

Hilton Grand Vacations Co (19), 6355 Metrowest Blvd (Suite 180), Orlando, 32835-6203

The Historical Research Center International Inc (16), 2107 Corporate Dr, Boynton Beach, 33426-6645

Hoffman Mint (6), 1400 NW 65th Pl, Fort Lauderdale, 33309-1902

Holy Cross Hospital (16), 4725 N Federal Hwy, Fort Lauderdale, 33308-4670

Hot Sauce Harry's (4), 1077 Innovation Ave Unit 109, North Port, 34289-9345

Hyatt Fruit Co (4), PO Box 639, Vero Beach, 32961-0639

IMPACT Publishing Inc (17), 3409 47th Ave E, Bradenton, 34203-3974

InfoSource Inc (3), 1300 City View Ctr, Oviedo, 32755-5530

Investors Alliance Inc (1), PO Box 10136, Pompano Beach, 33061-6136

Johnson Smith Co (5), 4514 19th St Ct E, Bradenton, 34203-3709

Marlin P Jones & Associates Inc (3), PO Box 530400, Lake Park, 33403

Kellyco Metal Detector Distributors (11), 1085 Belle Ave, Winter Springs, 32708

Kendall Products/Dri-Dek (16), PO Box 8656, Naples, 34101-8656

Key West Aloe Holdings LLC (16), PO Box 19547, Fort Lauderdale, 33318-0547

B Klein Publications (17), 6037 W Atlantic Ave, Delray Beach, 33484-8408

Knollwood Groves at Cushman's (4), 3325 Forest Hill Blvd, West Palm Beach, 33406

Kropp Enterprises (2), 232 Longview Ave, Kissimmee, 34747-5042

Lazydays RV Center (12), 6131 Lazydays Blvd, Seffner, 33584-2968

LeadFlash (14), 6700 Broken Sound Pkwy NW, Boca Raton, 33487-5701

Levenger (5), 420 S Congress Ave Ste 101, Delray Beach, 33445-4696

Life Extension Foundation (7), 3600 W Commercial Blvd Ste 100, Fort Lauderdale, 33309-3324

Ligonier Ministries (5), 400 Technology Park, Lake Mary, 32746

LOTSolutions (14), 10151 Deerwood Park Blvd Ste 200-330, Jacksonville, 32256-0564

The Mark Group (2), 6500 Park of Commerce Blvd, Boca Raton, 33487-8293

Marriott Ownership Resorts Sales & Marketing (19), 6649 Westwood Blvd, Bldg 3 (Suite 300), Orlando, 32821

Maus & Hoffman Inc (2), 225 S Federal Hwy, Fort Lauderdale, 33301-1938

McNichols Co (16), PO Box 30300, Tampa, 33630-3300

Melitta USA (4), 13925 58th St, Clearwater, 33760-3721

The Miami Herald Media Co (17), 1 Herald Plaza, Miami, 33132-1609

MDR (7), 14101 NW Fourth St, Sunrise, 33325-6209

National Council on Compensation Insurance Inc (NCCI) (1), 901 Peninsula Corp Cir, Boca Raton, 33487

National Enquirer (17), 1000 American Media Way, Boca Raton, 33464-1000

National Golf Foundation (1), 1150 S US Hwy One (Suite 401), Jupiter, 33477

National Parkinson Foundation (1), 1501 NW 9th Ave, Miami, 33136-1407

The New Piper Aircraft Inc (16), 2926 Piper Dr, Vero Beach, 32960-1955

New York Life Insurance Co/AARP (15), 5505 W Cypress St (Suite 300), Tampa, 33607-1707

Norwood Promotional Products (16), 14421 Myerlake Cir, Clearwater, 33760-2840

Nova Southeastern University - FSEHS (1), 1750 NE 167th St, North Miami Beach, 33162-3017

Nat Nussbaum & Associates Inc (16), 1440 Coral Ridge Dr, Coral Springs, 33071-5433

Office Depot (16), 6600 N Military Trl, Boca Raton, 33496-2434

100% Real Estate Inc (16), 1810 Lee Rd, Orlando, 32810-5702

Orlando/ Orange County Convention & Visitor's Bureau (19), 6700 Forum Dr (Suite 100), Orlando, 32821-8086

Pango Pango Swimwear Corp (2), 1909 E Atlantic Blvd, Pompano Beach, 33060-6562

Physicians Planning Association Services (16), 350 Fairway Dr (Suite 200), Hillsboro Executive Center N, Deerfield Beach, 33441-1834

Pine Castle Animal Hospital (16), 5250 S Orange Ave, Orlando, 32809

The Professional Golfers' Association of America (1), 100 Avenue of the Champions, Palm Beach Gardens, 33410-9601

Racer Walsh Co (12), 1849 Foster Dr, Jacksonville, 32216-3104

Remington College (13), 500 International Pkwy (Suite 200), Heathrow, 32746-5627

The Sailing Co (17), PO Box 420235, Palm Coast, 32142-0235

St Petersburg/Clearwater Area CVB (1), 13805 58th St N (Suite 2-200), Clearwater, 33760-3716

Sales Leads (17), 601 Heritage Dr (Suite 111), Jupiter, 33458-2777

Saunders Military Insignia (6), PO Box 1831, Naples, 34106-1831

Scott Sign Systems Inc (16), 7525 Pennsylvania Ave (Unit 102), Sarasota, 34243-5065

Sears Home Improvement Products Inc (16), 1024 Florida Central Pkwy, Longwood, 32750-7579

Seta Corp of Boca Inc (5), 6400 E Rogers Cir, Boca Raton, 33499-0002

Shutterbug (17), 1415 Chaffee Dr Ste 10, Titusville, 32780-7936

Skydiving Magazine (17), 1725 N Lexington Ave, DeLand, 32724

Slocum Water Gardens (8), 921 Ave S SE, Winter Haven, 33880-4639

Solitron Devices Inc (16), 3301 Electronics Way, West Palm Beach, 33407-4636

South Seas Island Resort (19), 5400 Plantation Rd, Captiva Island, 33924

Southeast Toyota Distributors LLC (16), 100 Jim Moran Blvd, Deerfield Beach, 33442

The Sperry & Hutchinson Co Inc (6), 1625 S Congress Ave, Delray Beach, 33445

Sporting Clays Ltd (17), 317 S Washington Ave (Suite 201), Titusville, 32976-3539

Stimpson Co Inc (16), 1515 SW 13th Ct, Pompano Beach, 33069-4789

Strang Communications Co (17), 600 Rinehart Rd, Lake Mary, 32746-4898

Subscription Agency.com Inc (18), 3000 Executive Rd (Suite 12), Winter Haven, 33884

Sullivan-Victory Groves (4), PO Box 10, Cocoa, 32923-0010

Sun Harvest Citrus (6), 14810 Metro Pkwy, Fort Myers, 33912-4307

Sunbeam (16), 2381 NW Executive Center Dr, Boca Raton, 33431

Sunshine Discount Crafts (11), 12335 62nd St N, Largo, 33773

Thomas Computer Corp (16), 203 Park Lake St, Orlando, 32803-3823

Thompson Cigar Co (6), 5401 Hangar Ct, Tampa, 33634

Tiger Direct Inc (3), 7795 W Flagler St (Suite 35), Miami, 33144-2367

Trend Magazines Inc (17), 490 First Ave S (8th fl), Saint Petersburg, 33701

Trophyland USA Inc (5), 7001 W 20th Ave, Hialeah, 33014

TNT Packaging Inc (16), 2390 NW 149th St, Miami, 33054

Tupperware (16), 14901 S Orange Blossom Trail, Orlando, 32837

Unicol Inc (17), 11590 SW Ninth Ct, Pembroke Pines, 33025-4324

US BRANDING GROUP, LLC (16), PO Box 540957, Lake Worth, 33467

US Gas & Electric (16), 290 NW 165th St (PH5), Miami, 33169-6457

Venus Fashion, Inc (2), 11711 Mario Beach Dr, Jacksonville, 32224

Wasserman Uniform Co (2), 700 NW 57th Pl, Fort Lauderdale, 33309

Richard Weiner Consultant (14), 1814 NE Miami Gardens Dr (Suite 904), North Miami Beach, 33179-5043

Weiss Research Inc (17), 15430 Endeavor Dr, Jupiter, 33478-6400

Wood Carvers Supply Inc (9), PO Box 7500, Englewood, 34295-7500

World Publications Inc (17), 460 N Orlando Ave (Suite 200), Winter Park, 32789

Wrisco Industries Inc (8), 355 Hiatt Dr (Suite B), Palm Beach Gardens, 33418-7106

Georgia

ACP - Automation Control Products (16), 4080 McGinnis Ferry Rd (Suite 801), Alpharetta, 30005

AFA Service Corp (16), 3495 Piedmont Rd NE 11, Atlanta, 30305

AFLAC (15), 1932 Wynnton Rd, Columbus, 31999

AGCO Inc (9), 2782 Simpson Cir, Norcross, 30071

AMC Inc (2), 240 Peachtree St NW (Suite 2200), Atlanta, 30303-1327

ARI (16), 2523 S McDonough Rd, Orchard Hill, 30266

Active Parenting (17), 1220 Kennestone Cir Ste 130, Marietta, 30066-6022

AdvanceMe Inc (14), 2015 Vaughn Rd NW (Suite 500), Kennesaw, 30144-7831

Agco Spra-Coup (16), 4205 River Green Pkwy, Duluth, 30096

AHC Media (17), 3525 Piedmont Rd NE (Suite 400), Atlanta, 30305-1562

AirTran Airways (19), 1800 Phoenix Blvd (Suite 104), Atlanta, 30349-5569

John Alden Life Insurance Co/North Star Marketing (15), 11465 Johns Creek Pkwy (Suite 160), Duluth, 30097-1573

American Cancer Society (1), 250 Williams St NW Ste 6000, Atlanta, 30303-1034

American Family Life Assurance Co of Columbus (AFLAC) (15), 1932 Wynnton Rd, Columbus, 31999-0001

American Megatrends Inc (3), 5555 Oakbrook Pkwy (Suite 200), Norcross, 30093-2286

American 3B Scientific (16), 2189 Flintstone Dr (Suite O), Tucker, 30084-5023

Ames Taping Tool System Inc (9), 1380 Beverage Dr Ste W, Stone Mountain, 30083-2133

Arthritis Foundation (1), 1330 W Peachtree St NW (Suite 100), Atlanta, 30309-2922

Ashworth University (13), 430 Technology Pkwy, Norcross, 30092-3406

Assurant Solutions Preneed Division (15), 260 Interstate North Cir SE, Atlanta, 30339-2110

Astral Brands LLC (7), 4900 Highlands Pkwy SE, Smyrna, 30082-5132

Atlanta Cutlery Corp (11), 2147 Gees Mill Rd, Conyers, 30013-1333

Atlanta Journal & Constitution (17), 223 Perimeter Center Pkwy, Atlanta, 30303

Automod (12), 3353 W Hospital Ave, Atlanta, 30341-3419

Backyard Gardening (8), PO Box 8, Tiger, 30576-0008

Ballard Designs (8), 1670 Defoor Ave, Atlanta, 30318-7528

Benchmark Brands Inc (5), 5250 Triangle Pkwy, Norcross, 30092-2536

Bland Farms (4), 1126 Raymond Bland Rd, Glennville, 30427

Boys & Girls Clubs of America National Headquarters (1), 1275 Peachtree St NE, Atlanta, 30309-3506

Bradley Direct (8), PO Box 1240, Columbus, 31902-1240

Beverly Bremer Silver Shop (6), 3164 Peachtree Rd NE, Atlanta, 30305-1853

Byron Plantation (4), PO Box 60, Vidalia, 30475-0060

Callaway Gardens (19), 17800 US Hwy 27, Pine Mountain, 31822-2000

Caraustar (16), 5000 Austell-Powder Springs Rd (# 300), Austell, 30106-3227

CARE USA (1), 151 Ellis St NE, Atlanta, 30303-2420

Carvel Corp (4), 200 Glenridge Point Pkwy NE Ste 200, Atlanta, 30342-1450

Char-Broil (16), 1442 Belfast Ave, Columbus, 31904-4432

Choice Point (16), 1000 Alderman Dr, Alpharetta, 30005

City of LaGrange (1), 200 Ridley Ave, PO Box 430, LaGrange, 30240

The Coca-Cola Co (16), PO Box 1734, Atlanta, 30301-1734

Collector's Armoury Ltd (6), PO Box 2948, McDonough, 30253-1743

Concurrent Computer Corp (3), 4375 River Green Pkwy, Duluth, 30096-2572

Cox Communications (16), 1400 Lake Hearn Dr, Atlanta, 30319-1464

Cumberland General Store Inc (8), PO Box 4468, Alpharetta, 30023-4468

DS Waters of North America LP (4), 4170 Tanners Creek Dr, Flowery Branch, 30542

delfortgroup (10), 1530 Dunwoody Village Pkwy (Suite 130), Atlanta, 30338

EMS Technologies (16), 660 Engineering Dr, Norcross, 30092

Fiserv (14), 4411 E Jones Bridge Rd, Norcross, 30092-1615

Georgia Institute of Technology (1), 84 5th St NW Distance Learning & Profess, Atlanta, 30308-1031

Georgia Power (16), 241 Ralph McGill Blvd NW (Bin #10220), Atlanta, 30308-3374

GE Money (14), 4125 Windward Plaza Dr, Alpharetta, 30005-8738

GMAC Insurance (15), 1000 Abernathy Rd NE, 400 Northpark (Suite 275), Atlanta, 30328-5606

Golden Key International Honour Society (1), 1040 Crown Pointe Pkwy Ste 900, Atlanta, 30338-4724

Graham Field Health Products Inc (7), 2935 Northeast Pkwy, Atlanta, 30360-2808

The Green Pond Co (2), 3179 Maple Dr NE (Suite 11), Atlanta, 30305-2511

Gulfstream Aircraft Inc (16), 500 Gulfstream Rd, PO Box 2206, Savannah, 31408-2206

Habitat For Humanity International (1), 121 Habitat St, Americus, 31709-3423

John Harland Co (16), 2939 Miller Rd, Decatur, 30035-4038

Hobby Builders Supply (11), 2388 Pleasantdale Rd, Atlanta, 30340

The Home Depot Inc (16), 2455 Paces Ferry Rd NW, Atlanta, 30339-1834

IPS - Sendero Corp (14), 107 Technology Pkwy, Norcross, 30092-2909

In Touch Ministries (1), 3836 DeKalb Technology Pkwy, Atlanta, 30340-3604

InterContinental Hotels Group (19), Three Ravinia Dr (Suite 100), Atlanta, 30346-2149

InterfaceFlor LLC (16), 1503 Orchard Hill Rd, La Grange, 30240-5709

International Manufacturing Co (8), 216 Main St, Box 154, Whitesburg, 30185

Kalmed Dental Products Inc (7), 3048 Alberta Dr, Marietta, 30062-1513

KEH.com (16), 4900 Highlands Pkwy SE, Smyrna, 30082-5132

L6 Holdings Corp (14), 6555 Sugarloaf Pkwy (Suite 307), Duluth, 30097-4934

Lathem Time Corp (16), 200 Selig Dr SW, Atlanta, 30336

Magnolia Hall (8), 138 Emerald Creek Dr, Jasper, 30143

MAP International (1), 2200 Glynco Pkwy, Brunswick, 31521

Meyer Decorative Surfaces Inc (8), PO Box 43765, Atlanta, 30336-0765

Montag & Caldwell Inc (14), 3455 Peachtree Rd NE (Suite 1200), Atlanta, 30326-3248

Morris Visitors Publications LLC (17), 699 Broad St (Suite 500), Augusta, 30901

Moultrie Manufacturing Co (8), 1403 Georgia Hwy, Moultrie, 31776-2948

Newell Rubbermaid, Inc (16), 3 Glenlake Pkwy, Atlanta, 30328

NCR Corp (16), 2651 Satellite Blvd, Duluth, 30096-5810

North Point Resources (1), 4400 North Point Pkwy (Suite 152), Alpharetta, 30022-2429

Okeefe (5), 408 Woodstone W Dr., Marietta, 30068-4083

Omega Research & Development (12), 981 N Burnt Hickory Rd, Douglasville, 30134

PJT Inc (4), PO Box 1265, Savannah, 31402-1265

Pritchett & Hull Associates Inc (17), 3440 Oakcliff Rd NE (Suite 110), Atlanta, 30340-3079

Professional Photographer Magazine (17), 229 Peachtree St NE (Suite 2200), International Tower, Atlanta, 30303-1608

Ranger Joe's International Military Supply (2), 325 Farr Rd, Columbus, 31907

Raven's Nest Herbals, LLC (7), PO Box 370, Duluth, 30096

River Street Sweets (4), 13 E River St, Savannah, 31401-1295

Schermer Pecans (4), PO Box 399, Glennville, 30427

Solarcom (16), One Sun Ct, Norcross, 30092

Sportime International (11), 3155 Northwoods Pkwy, Norcross, 30071

State Mutual Insurance Co (15), PO Box 153, Rome, 30162-0153

Summit Industries Inc (5), 839 Pickens Industrial Dr, Marietta, 30062

Sunnyland Farms Inc (4), PO Box 1275, Albany, 31702-1275

Suntrust Banks Inc (14), 303 Peachtree Center Ave NE (Suite 320), Atlanta, 30303-1280

Tensar International Corporation (16), 2500 Northwinds Pkwy (Suite 500), Alpharetta, 30009-2247

Thermo Pro (16), 1600 Distribution Dr (Suite D), Duluth, 30097

TAPPI (Technical Association of the Pulp & Paper Industry) (1), 15 Technology Pkwy S, Norcross, 30092-2923

United Community Bank (14), 63 Hwy 51 S, Blairsville, 30512

Uniway Management Corp (16), 5182A Old Dixie Hwy, Forest Park, 30297

Ventyx (16), 400 Perimeter Center Ter NE Ste 500, Atlanta, 30346-1231

Ed Voyles Hyundai Inc (16), 2135 Cobb Pkwy SE, Smyrna, 30080-7632

Walk Thru The Bible Ministries Inc (1), 4201 N Peachtree Rd, Atlanta, 30341-1207

Welcomemat Services Inc (9), 3348 Peachtree Rd (Suite 1095), Atlanta, 30326-1400

Whitman Publishing LLC (16), 3101 Clairmont Rd, Atlanta, 30329

Year One Inc (16), Year One Inc, Braselton, 30517

Hawaii

Bank of Hawaii (14), PO Box 2900, Honolulu, 96846-0001

Bontex (16), 1207 Hunakai St, Honolulu, 96816-4614

Central Pacific Bank (14), 220 S King St, Honolulu, 96813-4530

First Hawaiian Bank (14), 999 Bishop St Ste 3200, Honolulu, 96813-4424

Hawaiian Host Inc (4), 500 Alakawa St (Suite 111), Honolulu, 96817-4576

Islands Tropicals (6), PO Box 1989, Keaau, 96749-1989

Polynesian Cultural Center (16), 2255 Kuhio Ave (Suite 1010), Honolulu, 96815-2648

Idaho

Angler's Catalog Co (11), 3551 W Deerfield Dr, Eagle, 83616

Boise Cascade Holdings LLC (16), 1111 W Jefferson St (Suite 300), Boise, 83702-5389

Bosom Buddy Breast Forms (7), 2417 Bank Dr (Suite 201), Boise, 83705-0731

Brookhollow Cards (10), 1 Stationary Pl, Rexburg, 83440-3567

Cascade Outfitters (11), 604 E 45th St, Boise, 83714-4848

Cattle Kate (2), 6701 W State St, Boise, 83714-7412

Coldwater Creek (2), 751 W Hanley Ave, Coeur D Alene, 83815

Cougar Mountain Software (14), 7180 Potomac Dr (Suite D), Boise, 83704

Gibson Auer LLC (7), PO Box 228, Victor, 83455-0228

I/D/E/A Inc (16), One Idea Way, Caldwell, 83605-6900

Rexcraft Wedding Invitations (16), One Stationery Pl, Rexburg, 83441

Seastrom Manufacturing Co Inc (3), 456 Seastrom St, Twin Falls, 83301

Sunshine Minting Inc (14), 7600 N Mineral Dr (Suite 700), Coeur D'Alene, 83815-9170

West Farm Foods (Branch) (16), 520 Albany St, Caldwell, 83605

Illinois

A La Carte (16), 5610 W Bloomingdale Rd, Chicago, 60639

AAA-Chicago Motor Club (1), 975 Meridian Lake Dr, Aurora, 60504-4904

ACCO North America (16), 300 Tower Pkwy, Lincolnshire, 60069

AMA Insurance Agency Inc (15), 515 N State St, Chicago, 60601

AMS Direct (13), 7020 High Grove Blvd, Burr Ridge, 60527-7637

AON Center (15), 200 E Randolph St, Chicago, 60601-6436

Aon Innovative Solutions (16), 175 W Jackson Blvd Ste 1100, Chicago, 60604-2709

Abbott (7), 100 Abbott Park Rd, North Chicago, 60064-3502

Ace Hardware Corp (16), 2200 Kensington Ct, Oak Brook, 60523-2100

Adnet USA (16), 909 N Forrest Ave, Arlington Heights, 60004-5814

Affinity Express (16), 2200 Point Blvd (Suite 130), Elgin, 60123

Agate Publishing (17), 1501 Madison St, Evanston, 60202-2033

Alexian Brothers Bonaventure House (1), 825 W Wellington Ave, Chicago, 60657

Alloyd Brands (16), 1401 Pleasant St, Dekalb, 60115-2663

Allstate Motor Club, Inc (7), 302 Wilmot Rd Ste 101, Deerfield, 60015-4618

Allstate Motor Club (13), 51 W Higgins Rd (Suite RGA), South Barrington, 60010-9300

Alzheimer's Association (1), 225 N Michigan Ave, Chicago, 60601-7757

American Association of Individual Investors (1), 625 N Michigan Ave, Chicago, 60611-3110

American Bar Association (1), 321 N Clark St (fl 16), Chicago, 60654-4740

American Health Information Management Association (1), 233 N Michigan Ave (21st fl), Chicago, 60601-5519

American Library Association-Publishing Services (1), 50 E Huron St, Chicago, 60611

American Medical Association (1), 515 N State St, Chicago, 60610

American Science & Surplus (9), 7410 N Lehigh Ave, Niles, 60714-4024

American Technical Publishers Inc (17), 10100 Orland Pkwy, Orland Park, 60467-5756

Anatomical Chart Co (7), 4025 W Peterson Ave, Chicago, 60646-6069

Andrew Wireless Solutions (16), 3 Westbrook Corporate Ctr (Suite 900), Westchester, 60154-5765

Appraisal Institute (1), 200 W Madison St Ste 1500, Chicago, 60606-3515

Arbus Capital Ltd (16), 1320 Tower Rd, Schaumburg, 60173

ArcelorMittal (16), 1 S Dearborn St, Chicago, 60603-2302

Armbrust Paper Tubes Inc (10), 6255 S Harlem Ave, Chicago, 60638-3990

Assisted Access- NFSS (3), PO Box 230, Lake Villa, 60046

HH Backer Associates Inc (17), 18 S Michigan Ave (Suite 1100), Chicago, 60604

Badge-A-Minit (16), 345 N Lewis Ave, Oglesby, 61348-9776

Ball Publishing (17), 622 Town Rd, West Chicago, 60185-2614

Bank One (14), One Bank One Plaza, Chicago, 60670

Bankers Life & Casualty Co (15), 600 W Chicago Ave, Chicago, 60654-2800

Baxter Healthcare, Renal Division (7), 1620 Waukegan Rd, Waukegan, 60085

BAI (17), 115 S La Salle St (Suite 3300), Chicago, 60603-3801

BCR Enterprises Inc (17), 3025 Highland Pkwy (Suite 200), Downers Grove, 60515-5668

BMI Home Decorating (16), 6917 Catalpa Ct, Spring Grove, 60081

BP (16), 4101 Winfield Rd (Suite 100), Warrenville, 60555-3522

Beltone (3), 2601 Patriot Blvd, Glenview, 60026-8023

Benet Academy (1), 2200 Maple Ave, Lisle, 60532-2393

William Blair & Co LLC (14), 222 W Adams St, Chicago, 60606-5312

Dick Blick Holdings Inc (16), PO Box 1267, Galesburg, 61402-1267

Blue Cross/Blue Shield of Illinois (15), 300 E Randolph, Chicago, 60601

Boeing Co (16), 100 N Riverside, Chicago, 60606

The Bradford Group (16), 9333 N Milwaukee Ave, Niles, 60714-1303

Braintree Payment Solutions LLC (14), 833 W Jackson Blvd (Suite 500), Chicago, 60607-5400

Brand New Products LLC (4), 2506 N Clark St (#280), Chicago, 60614-1848

Broadcast Electronics Inc (3), 4100 N 24th St, Quincy, 62305

Brokers/Consultants Inc (15), 1332 Dartmouth Rd, Flossmoor, 60422-1905

Brookfield Zoo (1), 3300 Golf Rd, Brookfield, 60513-1060

Bulletin of the Atomic Scientists (17), 1155 E 60th St, Chicago, 60637-2745

Bunker Hill Auctions (6), 10251 Fox River Dr, Newark, 60541-9657

Bunn-O-Matic Corp (16), 1400 Stevenson Dr, Springfield, 62703-4291

Business Graphics Inc (16), 955 Dieckman, Woodstock, 60098-9262

Butler Specialty Co (16), 8200 S Chicago Ave, Chicago, 60617-1804

C&S Sales Inc (9), 150 Carpenter Ave, Wheeling, 60090

Calendar Marketing Association (1), 214 N Hale St, Wheaton, 60187-5115

Calumet Photographic Inc (3), 890 Supreme Dr, Bensenville, 60106-1107

Career Education Corp (1), 231 N Martingale Rd Ste 100, Schaumburg, 60173-2007

CashNetUSA (14), 200 W Jackson Blvd (Suite 2400), Chicago, 60606-6941

Caterpillar Inc (16), 100 NE Adams St, Peoria, 61629-0002

Catholic Church Extension Society (1), 150 S Wacker Dr (fl 20), Chicago, 60606-4103

CCH Inc (17), 2700 Lake Cook Rd, Riverwoods, 60015-3888

CCIM Institute (1), 430 N Michigan Ave (Suite 800), Chicago, 60611-4011

CDW Computer Centers Inc (3), 200 N Milwaukee Ave, Vernon Hills, 60061

CDW Corp (16), 300 N Milwaukee Ave, Vernon Hills, 60061

CNA (15), 333 S Wabash Ave, Chicago, 60604-4107

CRB (17), 330 S Wells (Suite 612), Chicago, 60606-7110

Celtic Life Insurance Co (15), 233 S Wacker Dr (Suite 700), Chicago, 60606-6300

Champion (16), 1800 Gardner Expressway, Quincy, 62305-9364

Chiasso (6), 1440 N Dayton St (Suite 307), Chicago, 60642-2645

Chicago Convention & Tourism Bureau (1), 301 E Cermak Rd, Chicago, 60616-1578

Chicago Magazine (17), 435 N Michigan Ave (Suite 1100), Chicago, 60611-4031

Christianity Today Inc (17), 465 Gundersen Dr, Carol Stream, 60188-2415

Clubs of America (6), 426 Scotland Rd, Lakemoor, 60051

Coin Laundry Association (1), 1S660 Midwest Rd Ste 205, Oakbrook Terrace, 60181-4738

Cole-Parmer Instrument Co (16), 625 E Bunker Ct, Vernon Hills, 60061-1844

Cole's Appliance & Furniture Co (8), 4026 Lincoln Ave, Chicago, 60618-3097

Collectibles Today Network, Ltd (16), 9200 N Maryland Ave, Niles, 60105

Collegiate Cap & Gown (16), 1000 N Market St, Champaign, 61820-3009

Combined Insurance Co of America (15), 1000 Milwaukee Ave Fl 1, Glenview, 60025-2424

Concept Communications Co (16), 380-A Internationale Dr, Bolingbrook, 60440

Consumer Benefit Services Inc (16), 1620 Bond St, Naperville, 60563-0131

Consumers Digest Inc (17), 520 Lake Cook Rd (Suite 500), Deerfield, 60015-5633

Cortz Inc (5), 320 Industrial Dr, West Chicago, 60185-1817

Cosco Industries Inc (16), 7220 W Wilson Ave, Chicago, 60706-4706

Cosmetique, Inc (13), 200 Corporate Woods Pkwy, Vernon Hills, 60061-3167

Country Financial (15), PO Box 2020, Bloomington, 61702-2020

Country Sampler Group (17), 707 Kautz Rd, Saint Charles, 60174

Coverdell & Co Inc (15), 8770 W Bryn Mawr Ave (Suite 1000), Chicago, 60631-3515

Coyne American Institute (16), 330 N Green St, Chicago, 60607-1300

Crate & Barrel (8), 1250 Techny Rd, Northbrook, 60062-5419

Creative Catalogs Corp (6), 19W661 101st St, Lemont, 60439-9642

The Cricket Magazine Group (17), 70 E Lake St (Ste 300), Chicago, 60601-5945

Cunningham Group (15), 7234 W North Ave (Suite 101), Elmwood Park, 60707-4200

Custom Accessories (11), 6440 W Howard St, Niles, 60714-3391

Dairy Management Inc (1), 10255 W Higgins Rd (Suite 900), Rosemont, 60018

DAMARK International Inc (16), PO Box 3000, La Salle, 61301-0300

Deere & Co Headquarters (16), 1 John Deere Pl, Moline, 61265-8010

Design Toscano, Inc (6), 1400 Morse Ave, Elk Grove Village, 60007-5722

DeVry Inc (16), 1 Tower Ln Ste 2350, Oakbrook Terrace, 60181-4633

Discover Financial Services (14), 2500 Lake Cook Rd, Riverwoods, 60015-1838

Divine Word Missionaries (1), 1835 Waukegan Rd, Techny, 60082

DoAll Co (16), 1480 S Wolf Rd, Wheeling, 60090-6514

Edward Don & Co (16), 2500 S Harlem Ave, North Riverside, 60546

Douglas Press Inc (16), 2810 Madison St, Bellwood, 60104-2256

Douglas Shaw & Associates (1), 1717 Park St Ste 300, Naperville, 60563-4864

Dreis & Krump Manufacturing Co (16), 481 Governors Hwy (Suite 2), Peotone, 60468

Easter Seals (1), 223 S Wacker Dr (Suite 2400), Chicago, 60606-6410

Educational Resources (3), 1550 Executive Dr, Elgin, 60121-1900

Eire Direct (16), 720 N Franklin (Suite 310), Chicago, 60610-3512

Elks Magazine (17), 425 W Diversey Pkwy, Chicago, 60614-6196

Ellis Systems Corp (9), 28457 N Ballard Dr Ste F, Lake Forest, 60045-4545

Encyclopaedia Britannica Inc (17), 331 N LaSalle St, Chicago, 60654-2682

Event 360 Inc (1), 205 N Michigan Ave (Suite 2640), Chicago, 60601-5944

Farm Progress Co (17), 255 38th Ave (Suite P), Saint Charles, 60174-5410

Farrington Transportation (12), 553 S Joliet Rd (Suite B), Bolingbrook, 60440-3631

FEEDING AMERICA (1), 35 E Wacker Dr (Suite 2000), Chicago, 60601-2200

FTD Florist Transworld Delivery (16), 3113 Woodcreek Dr, Downers Grove, 60515

The Field Museum (1), 1400 S Lake Shore Dr, Chicago, 60605-2827

First to the Finish Inc (7), 1325 N Broad St, Carlinville, 62626-9770

Caimin Flannery & Associates (14), 4275 Stableford Ln, Naperville, 60564-9768

Flight Form Cases Inc (9), 6543 S Laramie Ave, Bedford Park, 60638

Follett Library Resources (16), 1340 Ridgeview Dr, McHenry, 60050

Fox Valley Systems Inc (9), 640 Industrial Dr, Cary, 60013

Frog Tool Co Ltd (11), 2169 IL Rte 26, Dixon, 61021-9217

Gamma Photo Labs LLC (16), 222 N Des Plains, Chicago, 60661-1120

General Binding Corp (10), One GBC Plaza, Northbrook, 60062

General Growth Properties (5), 110 N Wacker, Chicago, 60606-1511

GE Partnership Marketing Group (14), 200 N Martingale Rd, Schaumburg, 60173

Glenview State Bank (14), 800 Waukegan Rd, Glenview, 60025-4300

Globe Ticket & Label Co (16), 11 Eisenhower Ln S, Lombard, 60148-5409

Golden Trophy (4), 3548 N Kostner Ave, Chicago, 60641

Goodheart-Willcox Publisher (17), 18604 W Creek Dr, Tinley Park, 60477-6243

Grainger Parts (16), 1657 Shermer Rd, North Brook, 60062

WW Grainger Inc (9), 14441 W II Route 60, Lake Forest, 60045-5203

The Great Books Foundation (1), 35 E Wacker Dr (Suite 400), Chicago, 60601-2298

Guarantee Trust Life Insurance Co (15), 1275 Milwaukee Ave (Suite 100), Glenview, 60025-2489

Hall-Erickson Inc (16), 98 E Naperville Rd (Suite 200), Westmont, 60559-2199

HALO/Lee Wayne (16), 1980 Industrial Dr, Sterling, 61081-9064

Hamakor Judaica Inc (5), 7777 Merrimac, Niles, 60714

Handi-Ramp Inc (7), 510 North Ave, Libertyville, 60048-2025

Harper College (1), 1200 W Algonquin Rd, Palatine, 60067-7373

Harris Bancorp Inc (14), 111 W Monroe St (fl 21W), Chicago, 60603-4096

Health O Meter (16), 11800 S Austin Ave (#B), Alsip, 60803-3559

Heller Financial (14), 500 W Monroe St, Chicago, 60661-3671

The Herald & Review (17), 601 E William St, Decatur, 62525-1190

HIMSS (1), 33 W Monroe St Ste 1700, Chicago, 60603-5616

Hollister Inc (16), 2000 Hollister Dr, Libertyville, 60048

Home 123 Mortgage (14), 2033 Milwaukee Ave (Suite 237), Riverwoods, 60015

Hoover's Mfg Co (2), 4133 Progress Blvd, Peru, 61354-1125

Horace Mann Educators Corp (15), 1 Horace Mann Plaza, Springfield, 62715-0002

House of Wesley Inc (8), 1700 Morrissey Dr, Bloomington, 61704

Hyatt Hotels Corp (16), 71 S Wacker Dr (Suite 1000), Chicago, 60606-4716

Ideal Industries Inc (16), Becker Pl, Sycamore, 60178

INX International Ink Co (16), 150 N Martingale Rd (Suite 700), Schaumburg, 60173

Indus-Tool (12), 300 N Oakley Blvd, Chicago, 60612

Institute of Real Estate Management (1), 430 N Michigan Ave, Chicago, 60611-4090

Integrated Product Development Group (1), 30 S Wacker Dr (Suite 2200), Chicago Mercantile Exchange, Chicago, 60606-7452

Inter7 Internet Technologies Inc (3), 219 S Prospect St, Galena, 61036-2119

International Fellowship of Christians and Jews (1), 30 N La Salle St Ste 4300, Chicago, 60602-2584

Iroquois Products (10), 2220 W 56th St, Chicago, 60636-3900

J&J Commerce (5), PO Box 1517, Galesburg, 61402-1517

JC Whitney (12), 225 N Michigan Ave (Suite 9), Chicago, 60601-7757

John Deere Consumer Products (16), One John Deere Pl, Moline, 61625

Joint Commission (1), 1 Renaissance Blvd, Oakbrook Terrace, 60181-4805

Journal Star (17), One News Plaza, Peoria, 61643

K-Log (8), 1224 27th St, Zion, 60099-2673

Kaplan Publishing (17), 205 W Randolph St (Suite 200), Chicago, 60606-1814

Lakeside Publishing Co LLC (17), 990 Grove St, Evanston, 60201-6510

LaPreferida Inc (4), 3400 W 35th St, Chicago, 60632

Laran Communications Inc (16), 26W482 Blair St, Winfield, 60190-1109

Learning Seed (3), 641 W Lake St (Suite 301), Chicago, 60661-1308

Lesman Instrument Co (9), 135 Bernice Dr, Bensenville, 60106-3366

Libertyville Saddle Shop Inc (11), 306 Peterson Rd, Box M, Libertyville, 60048

Life Fitness (11), 5100 N River Rd, Schiller Park, 60176

Lincoln Park Zoo (1), 2100 N Clark St, Chicago, 60614

LinguiSystems (17), 3100 Fourth Ave, East Moline, 61244-9700

Loyola University Chicago (1), 820 N Michigan Ave, Chicago, 60611-2147

Magnaflux (16), 3624 W Lake Ave, Glenview, 60026-1215

Mark James & Associates Inc (16), PO Box 429, Oswego, 60543-0429

Marketplace of the Master Inc (5), 4790 Colt Rd, Rockford, 61109-2635

The Marmon Group LLC (16), 181 W Madison St Ste 2500, Chicago, 60602-4505

Marsh Affinity Group Services (15), 500 W Monroe St (Suite 2400), Chicago, 60661

Maui Jim Inc (16), 8300 N Allen Rd, Peoria, 61615

McDougal Littell (17), 1560 Sherman Ave, PO Box 1667, Evanston, 60201

McKnight's Long-Term Care News (17), One Northfield Plaza (Suite 521), Northfield, 60093

McMaster-Carr Supply Co (HQ) (9), 600 County Line Rd, Elmhurst, 60126-2081

Medill IMC/Northwestern University (1), 1870 Campus Dr, Evanston, 60208-0885

Melaniphy & Associates, Inc (8), 6333 N Milwaukee Ave (Suite 106), Chicago, 60646-3744

Mercy Home for Boys & Girls (1), 1140 W Jackson Blvd, Chicago, 60607-2906

Methode Electronics Inc (9), 7401 W Wilson Ave, Chicago, 60706

Meyer Partners (1), 1701 E Woodfield Rd (Suite 425), Schaumburg, 60173-5313

Mid America Designs Inc (12), 17082 N US Hwy 45, Effingham, 62401-6764

Mid America Motorworks (12), 17082 N US Hwy 45, Effingham, 62401-7107

The Middleby Corp (16), 1400 Toastmaster Dr, Elgin, 60120-9272

The Millard Group (16), 7301 N Cicero Ave, Lincolnwood, 60712-1613

The Miller Group (5), 1610 Design Way, Dupo, 62239-1820

MillerCoors LLC (4), 250 S Wacker Dr Ste 800, Chicago, 60606-5888

Miller's First Insurance Companies (15), 111 E Fourth St, PO Box 220, Alton, 62002

M2Media 360 (17), 1030 W Higgins Rd (Suite 230), Park Ridge, 60068

MTS Publishing (17), 800 W 5th Ave (Suite 204A), Naperville, 60563-4925

Morkes Chocolates (4), 1890 N Rand Rd, Palatine, 60074

Morningstar Inc (14), 22 W Washington St, Chicago, 60602

The Morton Arboretum (1), 4100 Illinois (Route 53), Lisle, 60532-1293

Motor Coach Industries International Inc (16), 1700 E Golf Rd, Schaumburg, 60173

National Association of Realtors (1), 430 N Michigan Ave, Chicago, 60611-4088

National Luggage Dealers Association (1), 1817 Elmdale Ave, Glenview, 60625-1355

The National Restaurant Association Educational Foundation (1), 175 W Jackson Blvd, Chicago, 60604

Navistar (16), 4201 Winfield Rd, Warrenville, 60555-4026

Nevco Scoreboard Co (16), 301 E Harris Ave, Greenville, 62246-2193

Newark Electronics (3), 4801 Ravenswood Ave, Chicago, 60640-4496

Nightingale-Conant Corp (17), 6245 W Howard St, Niles, 60714-3403

Nimlok (16), 7420 N Lehigh Ave, Niles, 60714

Norman Control Co (16), 305 Cary Point Dr, Cary, 60013-2974

North American Co for Life & Health Insurance (15), 525 W Van Buren St Ste 1200, Chicago, 60607-3820

The Northern Trust Co (14), 50 S La-Salle St, Chicago, 60675

Nuclear Plant Journal (17), 1400 Opus Pl (Suite 904), Downers Grove, 60515

Nuveen Investments (14), 333 W Wacker Dr, Chicago, 60606

OfficeMax Inc (10), 263 Shuman Blvd, Naperville, 60563-8147

Olesuk Financial Services (14), 5206 W Elm St (Route 120), McHenry, 60050-4000

On-Hand Adhesives Inc (16), 940 Telser Rd, Lake Zurich, 60047-6714

OAG Worldwide (17), 3025 Highland Pkwy (Suite 200), Downers Grove, 60515

OMSI Inc (1), 9480 N Demazenod Dr, Belleville, 62223-1159

Paasche Airbrush Co (10), 4311 N Normandy Ave, Chicago, 60634-1395

PAL Health Technology (16), 1805 Riverway Dr, Pekin, 61554-9309

Paris Presents Inc (7), 3800 Swanson Ct, Gurnee, 60031-1226

Paslode (16), 888 Forest Edge Dr, Vernon Hills, 60061-8117

Path to Purchase Institute (17), 7400 Skokie Blvd, Skokie, 60077-3339

Pearl Insurance Group LLC (15), 1200 E Glen Ave, Peoria Heights, 61616-5325

Perrygraf (16), 25W550 Geneva Rd (Suite 1934), Carol Stream, 60188-2225

Personal Creations (6), 1005 101st St Ste A, Lemont, 60439-9628

Polyair Packaging (9), 808 E 113th St, Chicago, 60628

Polyline LLC (3), 845 N Church St, Elmhurst, 60126

The Popcorn Factory (4), 13970 W Laurel Dr, Lake Forest, 60045-4533

Portland Cement Association (1), 5420 Old Orchard Rd, Skokie, 60077-1083

Position Technologies Inc (16), 2325 Dean St (Suite 800), Saint Charles, 60175

Precept Press (17), 160 E Illinois St, Chicago, 60611-5426

Prevent Blindness America (1), 211 W Wacker Dr (Suite 1700), Chicago, 60606-1375

Print Services Distribution Association (1), 401 N Michigan Ave Ste 2200, Chicago, 60611-4245

Protective Life Corp (15), PO Box 770, Deerfield, 60015-0770

Publications International Ltd (17), 7373 N Cicero Ave, Lincolnwood, 60712-1613

The Quaker Oats Co (16), PO Box 049003, Chicago, 60604-9003

Quill Corp (16), PO Box 94080, Palatine, 60094-4080

Reassure America Life Insurance Co (15), 1275 Sandusky Rd, Jacksonville, 62650

Reb Storage Systems International (9), 4556 W Grand Ave, Chicago, 60639-4734

Rediscover Music Catalogue (3), 705 S Washington St Ste 3, Naperville, 60540-6697

REGIT Inc (15), 1200 Roosevelt Rd (Suite 115), Glen Ellyn, 60137

Replogle Globes Inc (16), 2801 S 25th Ave, Broadview, 60155-4500

Richardson Electronics Ltd (16), 40 W 267 Keslinger Rd, Lafox, 60147

Robert Marketing Inc (5), 17 The Court of Island Point, Northbrook, 60062-3210

Rock-Tred Corp (9), 405 N Oakwood Ave, Waukegan, 60085

Sears, Roebuck & Co (16), 3333 Beverly Rd, Hoffman Estates, 60179

Sedgwick Moran Detert & Arnold LLP (9), 1 N Wacker Dr (Suite 4200), Chicago, 60606-2862

Seedburo Equipment Co (8), 2293 S Mount Prospect Rd, Des Plaines, 60018-1810

Sellstrom Manufacturing Co (16), One Sellstrom Dr, Palatine, 60067

L.H. Selman Ltd (6), 410 S Michigan Ave Ste 207, Chicago, 60605-1448

Shape LLC (3), 2105 Corporate Dr, Addison, 60101

Simply Batteries Inc (7), PO Box 948, Dekalb, 60115-0948

Smarterville Productions LLC (3), 1550 Executive Dr, Elgin, 60123-9311

Solar Cine Products Inc (5), 4247 S Kedzie Ave, Chicago, 60632

Sourcebooks Inc (17), 1935 Brookdale Rd (Suite 139), Naperville, 60563-7994

Specialty Store Services Inc (16), 454 Jarvis Ave, Des Plaines, 60018

Spectra Merchandising International Inc (16), 4230 N Normandy, Chicago, 60634

Spilsbury Puzzle Co (11), 70 W Madison St (Suite 2300), Chicago, 60602-4250

Spring-Green Lawn Care Corp (16), 11909 Spaulding School Dr, Plainfield, 60544

SRDS (17), 1700 E Higgins Rd Ste 500, Des Plaines, 60018-5610

Star Silkscreen Design Inc (2), 2281 Hubbard Ave, Decatur, 62526-2149

State Farm Insurance Cos (15), 1 State Farm Plaza, Bloomington, 61710-0001

Stock Yards Packing Co Inc (4), 340 N Oakley Blvd, Chicago, 60612

Sunburst Technology (17), 1550 Executive Dr, Elgin, 60123

Sunstar (16), 4635 W Foster Ave, Chicago, 60630-1709

Surplus Record (17), 20 N Wacker Dr (Suite 2400), Chicago, 60606-3181

Svoboda Collins LLC (5), One North Franklin (Suite 1500), Chicago, 60606

Taylor Capital Group, Inc (14), 9550 W Higgins Rd, Rosemont, 60018-4906

Telefonix Inc (16), 2340 Ernie Kruger Cir, Waukegan, 60087-3224

Telephony (17), One IBM Plaza (23rd fl), Chicago, 60611

Tempco Electric Heater Corp (9), 607 N Central Ave, Wood Dale, 60191-1452

Thoma Cressey Bravo (14), 300 N La Salle Dr (Suite 4300), Chicago, 60654-3422

Thousand Trails LP (16), 2 N Riverside Plz (Suite 800), Chicago, 60606-2682

Tower Hobbies/Hobbico (11), 2904 Research Rd, Champaign, 61822

Trans Union Corp (14), 555 W Adams St, Chicago, 60661-3614

Travelclick (19), 300 N Martingale Rd, Schaumburg, 60173-2407

Tribune Co (17), 435 N Michigan Ave, Chicago, 60611-4041

Tricor Braun (16), 2145 Internationale Pkwy Ste 800, Woodridge, 60517-4830

Triton College (16), 2000 Fifth Ave, River Grove, 60171

True Value Co (16), 8600 W Bryn Mawr Ave, Chicago, 60631-3579

Tyndale House Publishers (17), 351 Executive Dr, Carol Stream, 60188

US Foodservice (4), 9399 W Higgins Rd Ste 500, Rosemont, 60018-4992

Unitrin (15), 1 E Wacker Dr, Chicago, 60601-1883

Universal Hovercraft (11), 1204 Third St, Cordova, 61242

Universal Training (16), 736 N Western Ave (Suite 323), Lake Forest, 60045

University of Chicago GSB (1), 450 N Cityfront Plaza Dr, Chicago, 60611-5500

University of Chicago Press (17), 1427 E 60th St, Chicago, 60637

University of Illinois College of LAS, Office of Advancement (1), 2111 S Oak St (Suite 100), Champaign, 61820-0908

University of Illinois Foundation (1), 1305 W Green St (MC-386), Urbana, 61801-2962

University Subscription Service (18), 1213 Butterfield Rd, Downers Grove, 60515

UGL Equis Corp (16), 161 N Clark St (Suite 2400), Chicago, 60601-3221

ULTA Salon Cosmetics Fragrance (7), 1135 Arbor Dr, Romeoville, 60446-1174

Vance Industries Inc (16), 5617 W Howard St, Niles, 60714-4011

Vierk National Supply (16), 2300 Commonwealth Ave, North Chicago, 60064

Visible Computer Supply Corp (16), 1750 Wallace Ave, Saint Charles, 60174

Washington Mutual Home Loan, Inc (14), 3050 Highland Pkwy (Suite 100), Downers Grove, 60515-5565

Wellpoint (7), 201 N Westshore Dr (Apt 1801), Chicago, 60601-7265

Wilton Industries Inc (16), 2240 W 75th St, Woodridge, 60517

Winston Marketing Group (8), 2521 Busse Rd, Elk Grove Village, 60007-6118

Wordright Enterprises Inc (17), 431 Dogwood Terr, Buffalo Grove, 60089-1820

World Book Inc (17), 233 N Michigan Ave (Suite 2000), Chicago, 60601-5805

Zoro Tools Inc (9), 1445 Armour Blvd, Mundelein, 60060-4403

Zurich (15), 1400 American Ln, Schaumburg, 60196-5452

Indiana

Abbey Press (6), One Hill Dr, Saint Meinrad, 47577-1004

Airomat Corp (16), 2916 Engle Rd, Fort Wayne, 46809-1198

The American Legion National Headquarters (1), 5745 Lee Rd, Indianapolis, 46216-2063

American Stationery Co Inc (10), 100 N Park Ave, Box 207, Peru, 46970

Anthem Corporate Communications (15), 120 Monument Cir, Indianapolis, 46204

Aristokraft Inc (16), 1 Masterbrand Cabinets Dr, Jasper, 47547-0420

Arrow Co (16), 5457 W 79th St, Indianapolis, 46268-1675

Associated Construction Publications (17), 1200 Madison Ave (Suite LL20), Indianapolis, 46225

Bart's Watersports (11), 7581 E 800th N, North Webster, 46555-9604

Berger's Table Pad Co (8), 1501 W Market St, Indianapolis, 46222

Bits & Pieces Inc (11), PO Box 4150, Lawrenceburg, 47025

Vera Bradley (2), 2208 Production Rd, Fort Wayne, 46808-3660

Breck's Bulbs (8), 5700 Schenley Pl, Lawrenceburg, 47025-2191

Brylane (2), PO Box 8320, Indianapolis, 46283-8320

CVT Production Inc (16), 50906 Rothbury Dr, Granger, 46530-6291

Children's Better Health Institute (1), 1100 Waterway Blvd, Indianapolis, 46202

Conseco Inc (15), 11825 N Pennsylvania Ave, Carmel, 46032-4555

Da-Lite Screen Co Inc (16), 3100 N Detroit St, Warsaw, 46582-2288

DRG (17), 306 E Parr Rd, Berne, 46711-1138

Delta Upsilon International Fraternity (16), 8705 Founders Rd, Box 68942, Indianapolis, 46268

DirectBuy Inc (1), PO Box 13006, Merrillville, 46410-3006

Dow Theory Forecasts (17), 7412 Calumet Ave, Hammond, 46324

Dwyer Instruments Inc (16), 102 Indiana Hwy 212, Michigan City, 46360-1956

e-Pipeconnection (9), 4406 E Morgan Ave, Evansville, 47715-2254

ETS Inc (7), 6270 Corporate Dr, Indianapolis, 46278-2900

Elkhart Cases (2), 3605 Cooper Dr, Elkhart, 46514

Fielder's Choice Direct (8), 306 N Main St, Monticello, 47960

Financial Publishing Co (17), 1251 N Eddy St (Suite 202), South Bend, 46617-1478

Forethought Financial Services Inc (15), 1 Forethought Ctr, Batesville, 47006-1279

Gardens Alive! Inc (8), 5100 Schenley Pl, Lawrenceburg, 47025-2100

Glas-Col (16), 711 Hulman St, PO Box 2128, Terre Haute, 47808

Gohn Brothers (5), PO Box 1110, Middlebury, 46540

Golden Rule Insurance Co (15), 7440 Woodland Dr, Golden Rule Bldg, Indianapolis, 46278-1719

Growing Child, Inc (17), PO Box 2505, West Lafayette, 47996-2505

Hansen Corp (16), 901 S First St, Princeton, 47670-2369

ITT Educational Services Inc (16), 13000 N Meridian St, Carmel, 46082

Indianapolis Motor Speedway (19), 4790 W 16th St, Indianapolis, 46222-2550

Indianapolis Newspapers Inc (17), 307 N Pennsylvania St, Indianapolis, 46204

Intra Business Systems Inc (16), PO Box 6681, South Bend, 46660-6681

Ivy Tech State College (13), 50 W Fall Creek Pkwy N Dr, Indianapolis, 46208-5752

James Medical Rents & Sales Inc (7), 7821 Coldwater Rd Ste A, Fort Wayne, 46825-8412

Jarden Corp (16), 14611 W Commerce Rd, Daleville, 47334

Jofco Inc (16), 402 E 13th St, PO Box 71, Jasper, 47547-0071

Kitchen Kompact Inc (8), PO Box 868, Jeffersonville, 47131-0868

Liberty Fund Inc (1), 8335 Allison Pointe Trail (Suite 300), Indianapolis, 46250-1684

Lure-Craft (11), 513 W Central, Lagrange, 46761

McDonald Obsolete Parts Co (16), 6458 W Eureka Rd, Rockport, 47635

Mead Johnson Co (7), 2400 W Lloyd Expwy, Evansville, 47721-0001

National Emblem Sales (16), PO Box 36460, Indianapolis, 46206-0460

Nutritional Research Associates Inc (16), 407 E Broad St, South Whitley, 46787-1001

Our Sunday Visitor Publishing (17), 200 Noll Plaza, Huntington, 46750

PVC Plastics Co (16), 4406 E Morgan Ave, Evansville, 47715-2254

Pratt Corp (16), 3035 N Shadeland Ave (Suite 100), Indianapolis, 46226-6231

Professional Creations (5), 1220 Church St, New Castle, 47362

Relaxo-Bak Inc (7), PO Box 2613, Anderson, 46018-2613

Resort Condominiums International Inc (19), 9998 N Michigan Rd, Carmel, 46032

Roche Diagnostics Corp (7), 9115 Hague Rd, Indianapolis, 46256-1045

The RYTEX Co (10), 100 N Park Ave, Peru, 46970-1701

Sailrite Enterprises, Inc (11), 2390 E 100 S, Columbia City, 46725-8751

Sani Serv (16), PO Box 1089, Mooresville, 46158-5089

Scott's Dog Supply Inc (11), PO Box 34302, Indianapolis, 46234-0302

Simon Property Group (16), 115 W Washington St, Indianapolis, 46204

Sterling Fluid Systems (16), 2005 Dr Martin Luther King St, PO Box 7026, Indianapolis, 46202-1165

Stile-Tile Like Metal Roofing (9), 7800 State Rd (#60), Sellersburg, 47172

Sunrise Greetings (17), 1145 Sunrise Greetings Ct, Bloomington, 47404

Teachers Credit Union (1), 110 S Main St, South Bend, 46601-1833

Threefold (9), 5151 N Shadeland Ave, Indianapolis, 46226-2603

Touch of Class Catalog (8), 709 W 12th St, Huntingburg, 47542-8915

Trilithic (16), 9710 Park Davis Dr, Indianapolis, 46235-2390

Warner Press (17), 1201 E Fifth St, Anderson, 46012

Woodwind & Brasswind Inc (5), 6625 Network Way Ste 200, Indianapolis, 46278-1683

Iowa

ARAG (15), 400 Locust St (Suite 480), Des Moines, 50309

Agri Drain Corp (9), 1462 340th St, Adair, 50002

Amazon Drygoods (2), 411 Brady St, Davenport, 52801-1518

August Home Publishing Co (17), 2200 Grand Ave, Des Moines, 50312-5306

Aviva USA Corp (14), 611 Fifth Ave, Des Moines, 50309

Cascade Forest Nursery (8), 36460 333rd Ave, Bellevue, 52031-9691

Continental Western Group (15), 11201 Douglas Ave, Des Moines, 50322

Customized Newspaper Advertising (18), 319 E Fifth St, Des Moines, 50309

Foundation for Chiropractic Education & Research (1), PO Box 400, Norwalk, 50211-0400

Frontier Natural Products Co-op (7), 3021 78th St, PO Box 299, Norway, 52318

Gazette Communications Inc (17), 500 Third Ave SE, Box 511, Cedar Rapids, 52406

GuideOne Insurance (15), 1111 Ashworth Rd, West Des Moines, 50265-3537

Hagie Manufacturing Co (9), 721 Central Ave W, PO Box 273, Clarion, 50525

Homesteaders Life Co (15), 5700 Westown Pkwy, West Des Moines, 50266-8214

ING USA Annuity & Life Ins Co (15), 909 Locust St, Des Moines, 50309-2899

Iowa Medical Society (1), 1001 Grand Ave, West Des Moines, 50265

Iowa Student Loan Liquidity Corp (1), 6805 Vista Dr, Ashford I Bldg, West Des Moines, 50266-9362

J&P Cycles (12), 13225 Circle Dr, Anamosa, 52205-7321

John Deere Credit USA (14), 6400 NW 86th St, PO Box 6600, Johnston, 50131-6600

Kreg Tool Co (16), 201 Campus Dr, Huxley, 50124-9760

Landauer Corp (17), 3100 NW 101st St (Suite A), Urbandale, 50322-3867

Life Investors Insurance Co of America (14), 4333 Edgewood Rd NE, Cedar Rapids, 52499

Marsh US Consumer (15), 12421 Meredith Dr, Urbandale, 50398-9001

Maxon Furniture Inc (10), 505 Ford Ave, Muscatine, 52761-5662

Meredith Corp (17), 1716 Locust St, Des Moines, 50309-3023

Midwest Technology Products & Services (9), PO Box 3717, Sioux City, 51102

MI-T-M Corp (9), 8650 Enterprise Dr, Peosta, 52068-9433

Pioneer Hi-Bred International Inc (4), 7100 NW 62nd Ave, PO Box 1000, Johnston, 50131-1000

Porter's Camera Store Inc (3), 411 Viking Rd, Cedar Falls, 50613-6930

PPC (9), PO Box 246, Johnston, 50131

The Principal Financial Group (15), 711 High St, Des Moines, 50392-0330

Profit Potentials Inc (1), 1 Foreign Candy Dr, Hull, 51239-7719

Rapids Wholesale Equipment (16), 6201 S Gateway Dr, Marion, 52302-9430

Successful Farming (17), 1716 Locust St, Des Moines, 50309-3023

Transamerica Life Insurance Co (15), 4333 Edgewood Rd NE, Cedar Rapids, 52499

Universal Engineering Corp (16), 800 First Ave NW, Cedar Rapids, 52405-3999

Veridian Credit Union (1), 1827 Ansborough Ave, Waterloo, 50701-3629

Viking Pump Inc (16), 406 State St, Box 8, Cedar Falls, 50613-0008

Wellmark Blue Cross & Blue Shield of Iowa (15), PO Box 9232, 636 Grand Ave, Des Moines, 50309-2565

WFF'N PROOF Learning Games Associates (17), 118 N Court St, Fairfield, 52556-2811

Kansas

Bushnell Corporation (11), 9200 Cody, Overland Park, 66214-1734

Bushnell Outdoor Products (16), 9200 Cody, Overland Park, 66214-1734

Cable Films & Video (3), 2026 West 63rd St, Mission Hills, 66208-1975

Cessna Aircraft Co (16), One Cessna Blvd, Wichita, 67215-1400

Cookbook Publishers Inc (17), 10800 Lakeview Ave, Lenexa, 66285-5920

Craft-Diston Industries (16), PO Box 12492, Wichita, 67277-2492

Dean & Deluca Brands Inc (4), 2402 E 37th St N, Wichita, 67219-3538

Ebersole Lapidary Supply Inc (11), 5830 W Hendryx St, Wichita, 67209-1234

The Fuller Brush Co (5), One Fuller Way, Great Bend, 67530

GTM Sportswear (2), PO Box 8, Manhattan, 66505-0008

Goddard Manufacturing Co (8), 107 Mill, Logan, 67646

Hearlihy & Co (17), 1002 E Adams, PO Box 1747, Pittsburg, 66762

Industrial Uniform Co Inc (2), 902 E Indianapolis St, Wichita, 67211-2407

Insurance Publications Inc (17), 9404 Reeds Rd, PO Box 11310, Overland Park, 66207-1010

International Wine Accessories Inc (4), 4115 E Harry, Wichita, 67218

Kansas State University Division of Continuing Education (1), 13 College Ct Bldg, Manhattan, 66506-6005

Marketshare Publications Inc (17), 7171 W 95th St (Suite 600), Overland Park, 66212-2300

Mother Earth News Magazine (17), 1503 SW 42nd St, Topeka, 66609-1265

National Seminars Group (16), 6901 W 63rd St (Suite 300), Shawnee Mission, 66202-4005

Northern Cross (16), 214 N 2100 Rd, Lecompton, 66050

Payless ShoeSource Inc (2), 3231 SE 6th Ave, Topeka, 66607-2260

Peruvian Connection Ltd (2), 24535 McLouth Rd, Tonganoxie, 66086-3132

Player Piano Co Inc (11), 300 N Mead St (Suite 200), Wichita, 67202-2745

Protection One Inc (16), 1035 N Third St (Suite 101), Lawrence, 66044

Fred Pryor Seminars (16), 5700 Broadmoor St (Suite 300), Mission, 66202-2415

The Saint Francis Academy Inc (1), 509 E Elm St, Salina, 67401

Sheplers Catalog Sales Inc (2), 6501 W Kellogg, Wichita, 67209

Sprint PCS (16), 6391 Sprint Pkwy, Overland Park, 66251-4300

SW Caging Corp (14), 5342 NW 25th St, Topeka, 66618-3738

Stanley Home Products (8), 1 Fuller Way, Great Bend, 67530

Sunshine Unlimited Inc (9), Box 71, Lindsborg, 67456-0071

Uniformed Services Benefit Association (15), 10895 Grandview Dr (Suite 350), Overland Park, 66210

Vet Vax (11), 1203 E Hwy 24-40, Tonganoxie, 66086-9507

Wyandotte West Communications Inc (17), PO Box 12003, Kansas City, 66112-0003

Kentucky

Abbey of Gethsemani (1), 3642 Monks Rd, New Haven, 40051-6152

Aegon Corp (14), 400 W Market St, Louisville, 40202-4000

American Printing House for the Blind (7), 1839 Frankfort Ave, Louisville, 40206-0085

Ashland Inc (16), 50 E Rivercenter Blvd (Suite 1600), Covington, 41011-1678

Associated Photo (16), PO Box 817, Florence, 41022-0817

Baron/Barclay Bridge Supplies (11), 3600 Chamberlain Ln (Suite 206), Louisville, 40241

Brown-Forman Beverages Worldwide (16), 850 Dixie Hwy, Louisville, 40210

Brown-Forman Corp (16), 850 Dixie Hwy, Louisville, 40210

Camping World Inc (11), Box 90018, Bowling Green, 42102-9018

The Candy Factory (4), 1020 Saratoga St, Newport, 41071-2129

Cengage Learning (17), 10650 Toebben Dr, Independence, 41051-5100

Char-Broil Grill Lover's Catalog (8), PO Box 2737, Louisville, 40201-2737

Christian Appalachian Project (1), PO Box 55911, Lexington, 40555-5911

Collector Books & American Quilters Society (17), 5801 Kentucky Dam Rd, PO Box 3009, Paducah, 42003-9323

Fauntleroy Supply Co/Wing Supply (11), PO Box 368, Greenville, 42345

Gall's Inc (16), 2680 Palumbo Dr, Lexington, 40509-1234

House of Onyx, Inc (6), 120 N Main St, The Aaron Bldg, Greenville, 42345-1504

Humana Inc (7), 1951 Bishop Ln, Louisville, 40218-1930

Jefferson National (14), 9920 Corporate Campus Dr (Suite 1000), Louisville, 40223-4051

Keeneland Association Inc (16), 4201 Versailles Rd, PO Box 1690, Lexington, 40588-1690

Kentucky Bankers Association (1), 600 W Main St (Suite 400), Louisville, 40202-2998

KCEOC Community Action Partnership Inc (1), PO Box 490, Barbourville, 40906-0490

KET (17), 600 Cooper Dr, Lexington, 40502-1669

Bob Morgan Woodworking Supplies Inc (8), 6521 Jacob Dr, Westport, 40077

The National Underwriter Co (17), 5081 Olympic Blvd, Erlanger, 41018-3164

Papa John's International (4), 2002 Papa John's Blvd, Louisville, 40299-2333

Party Kits & Equestrian Gifts (6), 10920 Plantside Dr Ste C, Louisville, 40299-6113

Personnel Policy Service Inc (17), 159 St Matthews Ave (Suite 5), Louisville, 40207-3137

J Peterman Co (5), 400 Old Vine St Ste 200, Lexington, 40507-1910

Phoenix Poke Boats Inc (16), 106 Bethford Rd, McKee, 40447

Donna Salyers' Fabulous-Furs (2), 25 W Robbins St, Covington, 41011-3005

Taylor-Stiles Division (16), 7451 Empire Dr, Florence, 41042

UniFirst Corp (2), 2801 UniFirst Dr, Owensboro, 42301-7701

US Cavalry (6), 2855 Centennial Ave, Radcliff, 40160-9000

US Playing Card Co (16), 300 Gap Way, Erlanger, 41018-3160

WILD Flavors Inc (4), 1261 Pacific Ave, Erlanger, 41018-1260

Wildlife Education Ltd (17), 1260 Audubon Rd, Park Hills, 41011-1904

Willis Music Co (17), 7380 Industrial Rd, PO Box 548, Florence, 41042-0548

Xcelerated Investments Inc (14), 2940 Hebron Park Dr (Suite 307), Hebron, 41048-9573

Ztek Co (3), PO Box 967, Lexington, 40588-0967

Louisiana

AllBrands.com Sewing Machine Superstore (11), 20415 Highland Rd, Baton Rouge, 70817-7348

Amaryllis Inc (8), 1452 Glenmore Ave, Baton Rouge, 70808-1225

Arnaud's (16), 813 Bienville St, New Orleans, 70112-3121

Baton Rouge Conventions & Visitors Bureau (1), 359 3rd St Ste A, Baton Rouge, 70801-1310

Blanchard & Co Inc (16), 909 Poydras St (Suite 1900), New Orleans, 70112

Blue Cross Blue Shield of Louisiana (15), 5525 Reitz Ave, Baton Rouge, 70809-3802

Community Coffee Co (4), 3332 Partridge Ln (Bldg A), Baton Rouge, 70809-2413

DeGrado Inc (2), PO Box 1211, Mandeville, 70470

Entergy (16), 639 Loyola Ave (Suite 300), New Orleans, 70113-7106

Great Chefs Television Publishing (6), 747 Magazine St, New Orleans, 70130

Laitram Machinery (16), 220 Laitram Ln, Harahan, 70123

Louisiana Nursery (8), 5853 Hwy 182, Opelousas, 70570

Louisiana State Museum (1), 751 Chartres St, New Orleans, 70116-3205

Magic Seasonings Mail Order (4), 720 Distributors Row, New Orleans, 70183-3208

Orient Expressed Imports Inc (2), 3905 Magazine St, New Orleans, 70115

Starmount Life Insurance Co (15), 8485 Goodwood Blvd, Baton Rouge, 70806-7878

Stewart Enterprises Inc (16), 1333 S Clearview Pkwy, Jefferson, 70121-1014

Stuller, Inc (2), 302 Rue Louis XIV, PO Box 87777, Lafayette, 70508

Jimmy Swaggart Ministries (1), 8919 World Ministry Ave Ste B, Baton Rouge, 70810-9007

Maine

Akers Ski Inc (11), 51 Akers Way, Andover, 04216

Antique & Collectible Tools Inc (11), 27 Fickett Rd, Pownal, 04069

LL Bean Inc (2), Casco St, Freeport, 04033-0001

Blethen Maine Newspapers Inc (17), 390 Congress St, PO Box 1460, Portland, 04104-5009

Clarin by Hussey Seating (5), 38 Dyer St Ext, North Berwick, 03906-6763

Crestline Specialties, Inc (16), 70 Mt Hope Ave, Lewiston, 04241

Cuddledown Inc (8), 312 Canco Rd, Portland, 04103-4281

DeLorme Mapping (3), Two DeLorme Dr, Yarmouth, 04096

Ducktrap River Fish Farm (4), 57 Little River Dr, Belfast, 04915

Fieldstone Gardens Inc (8), 55 Quaker Ln, Vassalboro, 04989-3816

Gimbels of Maine Inc (6), 14 Commercial St, Boothbay Harbor, 04538-1821

Hebron Academy (1), PO Box 309 (Rte 119), Hebron, 04238-0309

International Marine (17), 90 Mechanic St, Camden, 04843-1844

The Jackson Laboratory JAX Research Systems (1), 600 Main St, Bar Harbor, 04609-1523

Lo Ink Specialties (16), PO Box 530B, Kennebunkport, 04046-1821

Mailworks Inc (1), PO Box M, Freeport, 04032-0919

The Maine Photographic Workshops (16), 2 Central St, Rockport, 04856-5936

Maine Potato Board (1), 744 Main St (Rm 1), Presque Isle, 04769

Thomas Moser Cabinetmakers (16), 149 Main St, Freeport, 04032

Nowetah's American Indian Store & Museum (6), 2 Colegrove Rd, New Portland, 04961-3821

PowerPay (14), 320 Cumberland Ave, Portland, 04101

Renaissance Greeting Cards Inc (5), PO Box 845, Springvale, 04083

Saunders Manufacturing Co Inc (16), 65 Nickerson Hill Rd, Readfield, 04355

Sheep Shop (5), 222 N High St (Rte 302), Bridgton, 04009-9400

Speed-Mat (16), 374 South St, Biddeford, 04005

Sturbridge Yankee Workshop Inc (16), 90 Blueberry Rd, Portland, 04102-1924

Thorndike Press (17), 10 Water St Ste 310, Waterville, 04901-6566

TD Bank NA (14), 70 Gray Rd, Falmouth, 04105-2019

Unum Corp (15), 2211 Congress St (Suite B118), Portland, 04122

Walch Publishing (17), 40 Walch Dr, Portland, 04103-1286

Maryland

ADRA International (1), 12501 Old Columbia Pike, Silver Spring, 20904-6601

AEGON Direct Marketing Services Inc (15), 100 Light St Fl B1, Baltimore, 21202-1098

AESU Inc (19), 3922 Hickory Ave, Baltimore, 21211-1834

AIIM International (1), 1100 Wayne Ave (Suite 1100), Silver Spring, 20910-5616

AMVETS National Service Foundation (1), 4647 Forbes Blvd, Lanham, 20706

Accounting with Debits and Credits with Coates & Hutchinson PC (14), PO Box 561, Odenton, 21113

AGORA Inc (17), 14 W Mount Vernon Pl, Baltimore, 21201-5125

Air Force Sergeants Association (1), 5211 Auth Rd, Suitland, 20746-4339

Aircraft Owners & Pilots Association (1), 421 Aviation Way, Frederick, 21701-4756

American Breast Cancer Foundation (1), 1220B E Joppa Rd (Suite 332), Baltimore, 21286-5823

American Capital (15), 2 Bethesda Metro Ctr Ste 1400, Bethesda, 20814-5390

American Health Assistance Foundation (1), 22512 Gateway Ctr Dr, Clarksburg, 20871-2005

American Kidney Fund (1), 6110 Executive Blvd (Suite 1010), Rockville, 20852-3914

American Nurses' Association (1), 8515 Georgia Ave (Suite 400), Silver Spring, 20006-4105

American Running Association (1), 4405 East-West Hwy (#405), Bethesda, 20814-4522

American Speech-Language-Hearing Association (1), 2200 Research Blvd, Rockville, 20850-3289

Association for Financial Professionals (14), 4520 East West Hwy (Suite 750), Bethesda, 20814-3574

Automotive Forms (16), 7215 Rolling Mill Rd, Baltimore, 21224-2033

Balducci Enterprises Inc (16), 12920 Cloverleaf Center Dr (Suite B), Germantown, 20874

Baltimore Magazine (17), 1000 Lancaster St (Suite 400), Baltimore, 21202-4632

Joseph A Bank Clothiers Inc (2), 500 Hanover Pike, Hampstead, 21074-2002

Barton-Cotton (16), 3030 Waterview Ave (Suite 100), Baltimore, 21230-3520

BGE Home Products & Services Inc (16), 1409 Tangiere Dr (Suite A), Baltimore, 21220-2878

BT Alex Brown Inc (14), 1 South St, Baltimore, 21202-3298

BYK-Gardner USA (16), 9104 Guilford Rd, Columbia, 21046-2677

Bill Me Later Inc (14), 9690 Deereco Rd (Suite 705), Timonium, 21093-6936

Black & Decker (US) Inc (16), 701 E Joppa Rd, Towson, 21286-5559

Blaine Window Hardware Inc (9), 17319 Blaine Dr, Hagerstown, 21740

Blissliving Home (8), 5515 Security Ln (Suite 1100), Rockville, 20852-5009

Books on Tape (17), 400 Hahn Rd, Westminster, 21157-4627

Carroll Publishing (17), 4701 Sangamore Rd (Suite S155), Bethesda, 20816-2532

Catholic Relief Services (1), 228 Lexington St, Baltimore, 21201-3443

CDR Fundraising Group (1), 16900 Science Dr (Suite 210), Bowie, 20715-4412

Chesapeake Bay Foundation (1), 6 Herndon Ave, Annapolis, 21403-4503

Choice Hotels International (16), 10750 Columbia Pike, Silver Spring, 20901-4491

CitiFinancial (14), 300 Saint Paul St Fl 3, Baltimore, 21202-2120

ClearOne Advantage (14), 7125 Thomas Edison Dr (Suite 203), Columbia, 21046-2976

The Country House Inc (6), 805 E Main St, Salisbury, 21804-5024

Custom Direct (16), 1802 Fashion Ct, Joppa, 21085-3237

Cystic Fibrosis Foundation (1), 6931 Arlington Rd, Bethesda, 20814-5231

Daedalus Books Inc (5), 9645 Gerwig Ln, Columbia, 21046-1520

Damilic Corp (16), 601 Dover Rd Ste 7, Rockville, 20850-1275

Discovery Communications LLC (16), One Discovery Pl, Silver Spring, 20910

Doorguard Systems Inc (3), 8970 D Route 108, Columbia, 21045-2145

Editorial Projects in Education Inc (17), 6935 Arlington Rd (Suite 100), Bethesda, 20814-5233

Encore Marketing International (16), 4501 Forbes Blvd, Lanham, 20706-4236

Epilepsy Foundation (1), 8301 Professional Pl, Landover, 20785-2267

Foundation Fighting Blindness (1), 7168 Columbia Gateway Dr Ste 100, Columbia, 21046-3256

Alan Furman & Co (2), 12250 Rockville Pike (Suite 270), Rockville, 20852

General Physics Corp (16), 6095 Marshalee Dr (Suite 300), Elkridge, 21075

W R Grace & Co (16), 7500 Grace Dr, Columbia, 21044

Health Affairs (17), 7500 Old Georgetown Rd (Suite 600), Bethesda, 20814-6800

The Healthy Back Store (16), 11714 Baltimore Ave, Beltsville, 20705-1850

Hopkins Medical Products (7), Five Greenwood Pl, Baltimore, 21208-2763

The Humane Society of the US (1), 700 Professional Dr, Gaithersburg, 20879-3418

The Jewish Federation of Greater Washington (1), 6101 Montrose Rd Ste 400, Rockville, 20852-4816

Jos A Bank Clothiers Inc (2), 500 Hanover Pike, Hampstead, 21074-2002

Kaiser Foundation Health Plan of the Mid-Atlantic States Inc (1), 2101 E Jefferson St, Rockville, 20852-4908

Lilypons Water Gardens (8), 6800 Lilypons Rd, PO Box 10, Adamstown, 21710

Lippincott, Williams & Wilkins (17), 351 W Camden St, Baltimore, 21201-2436

Lockheed Martin Corp (16), 6801 Rockledge Dr, Bethesda, 20817

Mailorder Gardening Association (1), 5836 Rockburn Woods Way, Elkridge, 21075-7302

MARCOR Remediation Inc (16), 3900 Vero Rd, Halethorpe, 21227-1510

The Maryland Saddlery Inc (11), 14924 Falls Rd, Butler, 21023

McCormick & Co Inc (4), 211 Schilling Cir, Hunt Valley, 21031

Media Two (17), 1014 W 36th St, Baltimore, 21211-2415

Medifast Inc (4), 11445 Cronhill Dr Ste 200, Owings Mills, 21117-2270

Meriks Inc (3), 822 Guilford Ave (#1700), Baltimore, 21202-3707

Mr Wash Car Wash (16), 3817 Dupont Ave, Kensington, 20895

National Archives & Records Administration (17), 8601 Adelphi Rd, College Park, 20740-6001

National Foundation for Cancer Research (1), 4600 E West Hwy (Suite 525), Bethesda, 20814-6900

National 4-H Supply Service (16), 7100 Connecticut Ave, Chevy Chase, 20815

Naval Institute Press (17), 291 Wood Rd, Annapolis, 21402-5034

Network for Good (1), 7920 Norfolk Ave (Suite 520), Bethesda, 20814-2571

NAACP (National Association for the Advancement of Colored People) (1), 4805 Mount Hope Dr, Baltimore, 21215-3206

NASA Federal Credit Union (1), 500 Prince Georges Blvd., Upper Marlboro, 20774-8732

NASW Assurance Services Inc (1), 50 Citizens Way (Suite 304), Frederick, 21701

NEA's Member Benefits Corp (1), 900 Clopper Rd, Gaithersburg, 20878-1360

Pace Inc (16), 9030 Junction Dr, Annapolis Junction, 20701

Pallottine Center for Apostolic Causes Inc/St Jude Shrine (1), 512 W Saratoga St, Baltimore, 21201-1896

PayPal Inc (14), 9690 Deereco Rd (Suite 705), Timonium, 21093-6936

Penny Wise Office Products (10), 6911 Laurel Bowie Rd (Suite 209), Bowie, 20715-1712

The Pennysaver Group Inc (17), 1342 Charwood Rd, Hanover, 21076

Planet Cotton (2), 8001 Cessna Ave, Gaithersburg, 20879-4116

Pneuma Books (17), 25 Hunter Ct, Elkton, 21921-1762

Prime Media Equine Group (17), 656 Quince Orchard Rd, Gaithersburg, 20878

Print Products International (9), 9030 Junction Dr, Annapolis Junction, 20701

Recognition Products International (16), 8706 Commerce Dr (Suite 6), Easton, 21601-6903

Rollyson Financial Group (14), 150 Oak Dr, Pasadena, 21122-4421

Shelburne Co (8), 3617 Old Taneytown Rd, Taneytown, 21787-2723

Shillcraft Inc (16), 2530 Riva Rd (Suite 308), Annapolis, 21401-7414

Albert S Smyth Co Inc (6), 2020 York Rd, Timonium, 21093

Sylvan Learning Centers (16), 1001 Fleet St, Baltimore, 21202

T Rowe Price Associates Inc (14), 100 E Pratt St (fl 4), Baltimore, 21202-1081

Tax Management Inc (17), 3 Bethesda Metro Ctr (Suite 250), BNA Customer Contact Center, Bethesda, 20814-5377

Tax Reduction Institute (14), 13200 Executive Park Terr, Germantown, 20874-5313

Tessco Inc (16), 11126 McCormick Rd, Hunt Valley, 21031

Texada Capital Corp (14), 62 Greenwood Shoals, Grasonville, 21638-9659

Total Care (7), PO Box 1661, Rockville, 20849-1661

Transamerica Life & Protection (15), 520 Park Ave, Baltimore, 21201-4500

The Union Labor Life Insurance Co (15), 8403 Colesville Rd, Silver Spring, 20910-6331

United Communications Group (17), 9737 Washingtonian Blvd (Suite 100), Two Washingtonian Center, Gaithersburg, 20878-7364

US Pharmacopeia (1), 5645 Fisher Ln, Rockville, 20852

Universal Security Instruments Inc (16), 11407 Cronhill Dr (Suite A), Owings Mills, 21117-6218

University Press of America Inc (17), 4501 Forbes Blvd (Suite 200), Lanham, 20706

The Vane Brothers Co (16), 2100 Frankfurst Ave, Baltimore, 21226-1026

The Vestal Press Ltd (17), 4501 Forbes Blvd (Suite 200), Lanham, 20706

Vietnam Veterans of America (1), 8719 Colesville Rd (Suite 100), Silver Spring, 20910-3710

Womanship (16), 137 Conduit St, Annapolis, 21401

World Future Society (1), 7910 Woodmont Ave (Suite 450), Bethesda, 20814

World Villages for Children (1), 180 Admiral Cochrane Dr Ste 240, Annapolis, 21401-7367

WorldVu LLC (17), 1906 E Pratt St, Baltimore, 21231-1925

Massachusetts

A-T Surgical Manufacturing Co (2), 115 Clemente St, Holyoke, 01040-5644

APW-Wright Line (16), 160 Gold Star Blvd, Worcester, 01606

ASE Technologies Inc (16), 226 Lowell St, Wilmington, 01887-3074

Abbott Products (16), 86 Finnell Dr, Weymouth, 02188-1126

Academic Management Services (14), P.O. Box 55807, Boston, 02205-8507

Aerovox Inc (16), 167 John Vertente Blvd, New Bedford, 02745-1221

Alfa Aesar-A Johnson Matthey Co (9), 26 Partridge Rd, Ward Hill, 01835-8099

Alfa CTP Systems (10), 554 Clark Rd # 2, Tewksbury, 01876-1631

AliMed Inc (7), 297 High St, Dedham, 02026-2898

Amergent (1), 9 Centennial Dr Unit 201, Peabody, 01960-7940

American Institute for Economic Research (1), 250 Division St, Great Barrington, 01230-1198

American Student Assistance (1), 100 Cambridge St (Suite 1600), Boston, 02114-2567

Americraft - The Gift Brokers Inc (16), 210 Lockes Village Rd, Wendell, 01379

Appalachian Mountain Club (1), 5 Joy St, Boston, 02108-1490

Artech House (17), 685 Canton St, Norwood, 02062-2610

Association of Marian Helpers (1), Eden Hill, Stockbridge, 01263

Atlantic Spice Co (4), PO Box 205, North Truro, 02652

Bank Boston (14), 1075 Main St, Waltham, 02451-7424

Banker & Tradesman (17), 280 Summer St, Boston, 02210-1131

The Bauman Group (14), 50 Main St, Ashland, 01721-3113

BJ's Wholesale Club Inc (13), PO Box 5230, Westborough, 01581-5230

Bedford/St Martin's (17), 75 Arlington St, Boston, 02116

Bentley College (13), 175 Forest St, Waltham, 02452-4705

Berkshire Direct Inc (17), 208 Water St, Williamstown, 01267-2802

Berkshire Record Outlet Inc (3), 461 Pleasant St, Lee, 01238-9804

Berman Group (16), 18 Tarleton Rd, Newton Center, 02459-1733

Berway Visual Products Inc (3), 668 Main St (Suite 10), Wilmington, 01887-3377

Channing L Bete Co Inc (17), One Community Pl, South Deerfield, 01373

The Black Dog Tavern Co Inc (2), PO Box 2219, 20 Beach St Extension, Vineyard Haven, 02568

Blue Raven Technology (3), 110 Fordham Rd, Wilmington, 01887-2165

Bose Corp (3), The Mountain, Framingham, 01701-9168

Boston Apparel Group (2), 42 Thomas Patten Dr, Randolph, 02368-3902

The Boston Co (14), 1 Boston Pl, Boston, 02108-4407

The Boston Globe (17), 135 Morrissey Blvd, Boston, 02125

Brahmin Leather Works (16), 77 Alden Rd, Fairhaven, 02719

Bruce Medical Supply (7), 411 Waverly Oaks Rd, Waltham, 02452-8494

Bull HN Information Systems (16), 285 Billerica Rd (Suite 200), Chelmsford, 01824-4174

Burns Inc (16), 350 Mariano S Bishop Blvd, Fall River, 02721-2365

Cape Cod Cupola Co Inc (8), 78 State Rd, North Dartmouth, 02747-2994

Casual Male Retail Group (2), 555 Turnpike St, Canton, 02021-2724

CXO Media Inc (17), 492 Old Connecticut Path, Framingham, 01701-4584

Chadwick's of Boston Inc (2), 35 United Dr, West Bridgewater, 02379-1027

Chelsea Clock Co Inc (6), 284 Everett Ave, Chelsea, 02150-1598

Christian Book Distributors Inc (17), 140 Summit St, Peabody, 01960-5156

The Christian Science Publishing Society (17), 210 Massachusetts Ave, Boston, 02115-3195

Citizens Bank (14), 770 Legacy Pl (Stop MLP250), Mail Stop MLP250, Dedham, 02026-6837

Clark's Corvair Parts, Inc (12), 400 Mohawk Trl, Shelburne Falls, 01370-8503

Clarks of North America (16), 156 Oak St, Newton, 02464

Cohasset Colonials (8), PO Box 0548, Ashburnham, 01430-0548

Community Newspapers Co (17), 150 Baker Ave Extension (Suite 201), Concord, 01742-9191

Josiah R Coppersmythe (8), 10 Mill Pond Rd, Harwich, 02645

Coptech Inc (16), 100 Cummings Park, Woburn, 01801-2128

The Country Bed Shop (16), 328 Richardson Rd, Ashby, 01431

Country Curtains Inc (8), 705 Pleasant St, Lee, 01238-9323

Country Dance and Song Society (1), 132 Main St, Haydenville, 01039-0338

Covidien International (7), 15 Hampshire St, Mansfield, 02048-1113

Cross Country Automotive Services (16), 1 Cabot Rd, Medford, 02155-5117

The Cross Country Group LLC (13), 1 Cabot Rd, Medford, 02155-5117

Curriculum Associates Inc (17), 153 Rangeway Rd, North Billerica, 01862-2013

Dana-Farber Cancer Institute (1), 44 Binney St, Boston, 02215-6013

Dante University Press (17), PO Box 812158, Wellesley, 02482-0014

Datum Timing, Test & Measurement (9), 34 Tozer Rd, Beverly, 01915

Dave's Soda & Pet City (5), 151 Springfield St, Agawam, 01001-1553

DaVinci Direct (1), 36 Cordage Park Cir (Suite 339), Plymouth, 02360-7320

Dick Davis Digest (17), 176 North St, Salem, 01970-1648

Davis Publications Inc (17), 50 Portland St, Worcester, 01608-2013

DMB Financial (14), 152 Conant St Ste 4, Beverly, 01915-1659

Deloitte & Touche (14), 200 Berkeley St, Boston, 02116

Diamond Machining Technology (9), 85 Hayes Memorial Dr, Marlborough, 01752-1831

Dinn Brothers Inc (16), 221 Interstate Dr, West Springfield, 01089

Doubletree Suites by Hilton (19), 400 Soldiers Field Rd, Boston, 02134-1893

Dover Saddlery (11), 525 Great Rd, Littleton, 01460-6221

Dynamics Research Corp (16), 60 Frontage Rd, Andover, 01810

Eastern Bank (14), 195 Market St, Lynn, 01901-1517

EMC Corp (16), 176 South St., Hopkinton, 01748

89 Degrees (9), 25 Burlington Mall Rd (Suite 610), Burlington, 01803-4100

Elderhostel Inc (1), 11 Ave de Lafayette, Boston, 02111-1736

Electric Insurance Co (15), 75 Sam Fonzo Dr, Beverly, 01915-1000

Edward Elgar Publishing Inc (17), Nine Dewey Ct, The William Pratt House, Northampton, 01060-3815

Faire Harbour Limited (5), 44 Captain Pierce Rd, Scituate, 02066-2644

Fallon Community Health Plan (1), 10 Chestnut St, Worcester, 01608-2898

Fidelity Investments (14), 82 Devonshire St, Boston, 02109-3605

FLEXcon (16), 1 FLEXcon Industrial Pk, Spencer, 01562-2643

Getronics (16), 100 Ames Pond Dr (Suite 200), Tewksbury, 01876-1240

GCC Printers (10), 209 Burlington Rd, Bedford, 01730

GRP Funding LLC (14), 1350 Main St (fl 4), Springfield, 01103-1664

Globe Specialty Products Inc (17), 9 Latti Farm Rd, Millbury, 01527-2132

Go Ahead Vacations (16), One Education St, Cambridge, 02141

Grand Circle Travel (19), 347 Congress St, Boston, 02210-1230

The Hanover Shoe Co (16), 156 Oak St, Newton, 02464

Harvard Business Review (17), 300 N Beacon St, Watertown, 01472

Harvard Business School - Executive Education (1), Soldiers Field, Teele Hall, Boston, 02163-1000

Harvard Business School Publishing (17), 60 Harvard Way, Boston, 02163-1001

Harvard Pilgrim Health Care (7), 93 Worcester St, Wellesley, 02481-3609

Hitchcock Shoes Inc (2), 225 Beal St, Hingham, 02043-1543

Honeywell Wintress Controls (16), 100 Discovery Way, Acton, 01720

Horn Packaging Corp (5), 580 Fort Pond Rd, Lancaster, 01523-3224

Human Resource Development Press (17), 22 Amherst Rd, Amherst, 01002-9709

Interex (17), 34 Hunt Rd, Amesbury, 01913

International Fund for Animal Welfare (1), 290 Summer St, Yarmouth Port, 02675-1734

Invacare Supply Group (16), 9 Industrial Rd, Milford, 01757-3588

Investors Marketing Services (14), 168 Centre St, Danvers, 01923-1321

JazzTimes Magazine Inc (17), 85 Quincy Ave (Suite 2), Quincy, 02169-6764

Jeffrey Lant Associates Inc (5), 50 Follen St (Suite 507), Cambridge, 02138

J Jill Group, Inc (2), Four Batterymarch Park, Quincy, 02169

John Hancock Financial Services Inc (15), 601 Congress St, Box 111, Boston, 02117

Johnny Appleseed's Inc (2), 30 Tozer Rd, Beverly, 01915-5510

Will Kirkpatrick Shorebird Decoys Inc (6), 124 Forest Ave, Hudson, 01749-2840

KAR Graphics (8), 31 Highland St, PO Box 2430, Mashpee, 02649

Lahey Clinic (1), 41 Mall Rd, Burlington, 01805-0002

The Law Offices of James Sokolove (14), 93 Worcester St # 101, Wellesley Hills, 02481-3609

Lawyer's Weekly Publications (17), 10 Milk St (Suite 1000), Boston, 02108-4620

Legal Sea Foods Inc (4), One Seafood Way, Boston, 02210-2702

Lemee's Inc (8), 815 Bedford St, Rtes 18 & 28, Bridgewater, 02324-3007

Liberty Mutual Group, Inc (15), 175 Berkeley St, Boston, 02116-5066

Lifetips (16), 240 Commercial St (Suite 3B), Boston, 02109-1386

Lindustries Inc (8), 21 Shady Hill Rd, Weston, 02493-1407

Litle & Co (14), 900 Chelmsford St, Lowell, 01851-8100

LDS Test & Measurement (3), 19 Bartlett St, Marlborough, 01752-3014

Mardiron Optics (11), Four Spartan Cir, Stoneham, 02180

Marian Helpers Center (1), Eden Hill, Stockbridge, 01263-0001

Marketing and Product Strategy (16), Nine Centennial Dr, Peabody, 01960

Massachusetts Horticultural Society (1), 900 Washington St (Rte 16), Wellesley, 02482

MassMutual Financial Group (15), 1295 State St, Springfield, 01111-0001

Mercury International Trading (2), 20 Alice Agnew Dr, North Attleboro, 02763-1036

Microfluidics Corp (16), 30 Ossipee Rd, Newton, 02464-1444

Micron Corp (16), 89 Access Rd (Suite 5), Norwood Airport Business Park, Norwood, 02062-5234

Miller Harness Co (11), PO Box 406, Westford, 01886-0406

Millipore Corp (9), 75 Wiggins Ave, Bedford, 01730-2337

MFS Investment Management (14), 500 Boylston St, Boston, 02116-3740

Morgan Kaufmann Publishers Inc (17), 30 Corporate Dr (Suite 400), Burlington, 01803

Motherwear (2), 110 Lyman St, Holyoke, 01040-4653

Murder by Mail (1), PO Box 789, West Tisbury, 02575

National Fire Protection Association (1), 1 Batterymarch Park Bsmt, Quincy, 02169-7484

New England Cheesemaking Supply Co (4), 54 Whately Rd Ste B, South Deerfield, 01373-9608

New England Journal of Medicine (17), 860 Winter St, Waltham, 02451-1430

New England Life Insurance Co (15), 501 Boylston St, Boston, 02110

New Track Media (17), 90 Sherman St, Cambridge, 02140-3264

Newport Creative Communications (1), 33 Railroad Ave, Duxbury, 02332-3884

NEBS (10), 500 Main St, Groton, 01471-0001

NETC (5), 50 Franklin St, Boston, 02110-1308

NNE Marketing (1), 105 Paul Revere Rd, Concord, 01742-4817

Norman Rockwell Museum (16), 9 Glendale Rd, Rte 183, Stockbridge, 01262

Nourse Farms (8), 41 River Rd, South Deerfield, 01373

Nuance Speech Solutions (16), One Wayside Rd, Burlington, 01803

OSRAM Sylvania (16), 100 Endicott St, Danvers, 01923-3782

The Original Honey Baked Ham Co of the East (4), 105 Green St, Marblehead, 01945-1439

Oxfam America (1), 226 Causeway St (5th fl), Boston, 02114-2155

Partners Village Store (11), 865 Main Rd, Westport, 02790-4315

PartyLite Gifts Inc (8), 59 Armstrong Rd, Plymouth, 02360-4840

PetEdge (16), 100 Cummings Ctr (307B), Beverly, 01915-6107

Peter Pan Bus Lines Inc (19), 1776 Main St, Springfield, 01102

Philips Lifeline (7), 111 Lawrence St, Framingham, 01702-8156

The Pohly Co (17), 253 Summer St Ste 303, Boston, 02210-1114

Potpourri Group Inc (6), 222 Mill Rd, Chelmsford, 01824-4127

PNC Global Investment Servicing (14), 66 Broadway Ste 3, Lynnfield, 01940-2369

PPN INC (7), 275 Center St (Suite 3), Holbrook, 02343-1079

Princess House Inc (16), 470 Miles Standish Blvd, Taunton, 02780

PRO Chemical & Dye Inc (10), 126 Shove St, Fall River, 02724-2039

Progress Software Corp (16), 14 Oak Park, Bedford, 01730

Putnam Investments (14), 30 Dan Rd, Canton, 02021-2809

Reebok International Ltd (2), 1895 JW Foster Blvd, Canton, 02021

The Reggio Register Co Inc (8), 31 Jytek Rd, Leominster, 01453-5934

The Renovator's Supply Inc (9), Renovator's Old Mill, Millers Falls, 01349

Rent Mother Nature (4), PO Box 380193, Cambridge, 02238-0193

LW Robbins Associates (1), 201 Summer St, Holliston, 01746-2258

Roman Research Inc/Simply Whispers Earring (2), 800 Franklin St, Hanson, 02341

Rose Displays Ltd (16), 35 Congress St, Salem, 01970-5529

Rounder Mail Order (3), One Rounder Way, Burlington, 01803

RBC Dain Rauscher (14), One Beacon St, Boston, 02108

RBS Citizens Financial Group Inc (14), 770 Legacy Pl (MLP 250), Dedham, 02026-6837

Samsonite American Tourister (16), 575 West St (Suite 110), Mansfield, 02048-1160

Samsonite Corp (16), 575 West St (Suite 110), Mansfield, 02048-1160

Savings Bank Life Insurance Co of MA (SBLI) (15), 1 Linscott Rd, Woburn, 01801-2001

Shaker Workshops (8), PO Box 8001, Ashburnham, 01430-8001

Simmons College (1), 300 Fenway, Boston, 02115-5898

Simplex Grinnell (16), 50 Technology Dr, Westminster, 01441-0001

Small Business Service Bureau Inc (1), 554 Main St, PO Box 15014, Worcester, 01615-2014

Tom Snyder Productions (16), 100 Talcott Ave Ste 6, Watertown, 02472-5715

The Soap Factory (7), 3 Burlington Rd, Bedford, 01730-1305

Speakers Guild Inc (16), 78 Old Kings Hwy, PO Box 1540, Sandwich, 02563-1540

SC Direct (2), 400 Manley St Ste 1, West Bridgewater, 02379-1085

Stanley Supply & Services (16), 335 Willow St, North Andover, 01845-5921

Staples Inc (10), 500 Staples Dr, Framingham, 01702-4474

State Street Global Advisors (14), 1 Lincoln St (fl 30), Boston, 02111-2901

Stratus Technologies (16), 111 Powder Mill Rd, Maynard, 01754-3409

Stream International (16), 20 William St (Suite 310), Wellesley, 02481-4145

Sunlife of Canada (15), 1 Sunlife Executive Park, Wellesley Hills, 02481

Sure-Fire Business Success Catalog (17), 50 Follen St (#507), Cambridge, 02138

Talbots (2), One Talbots Dr, Hingham, 02043-1583

Technology Review (17), 1 Main St (Suite 7), MIT Bldg W59, Cambridge, 02142-1599

Thermo Fisher Scientific I (9), 81 Wyman St, Waltham, 02451-1223

Thomson Research (14), 22 Thompson Pl, Boston, 02210

Time/System (16), 150 Front St (Fl 1 Bldg C), Chicopee, 01013

The Tog Shop Inc (2), 30 Tozer Rd, Beverly, 01915

THD Inc (1), 80 Hayden Ave (Suite 300), Lexington, 02421-7962

Tully & Holland Inc (14), 20 William St Ste 135, Wellesley, 02481-4133

Umass Dartmouth (1), 285 Old Westport Rd, North Dartmouth, 02747-2356

UndercoverWear Inc (2), 30 Commerce Way (Unit 2), Tewksbury, 01876

Utilities Supply Corp (16), 50 Everberg Rd, Woburn, 01801-1019

UCEA (1), 910 Commonwealth Ave, Boston, 02215-1204

The Vantage Group Inc (14), 90 Canal St, Boston, 02114

Village Software Inc (3), 76 Summer St (Suite 600), Boston, 02110-1267

Vitasoy USA Inc (16), 1 New England Way, Ayer, 01432-1514

Waters Corp (16), 34 Maple St, Milford, 01757-3696

WearGuard Corp (2), 141 Longwater Dr, Norwell, 02061-1683

Whiting & Davis (16), 171 Commonwealth Ave, Attleboro Falls, 02763-1152

Williamsburg Blacksmiths Inc (8), 26 Williams St, Williamsburg, 01096

Win-Win Giving (1), 429 Waltham St, West Newton, 02465-1939

WGBH Educational Foundation (1), 1 Guest St, Brighton, 02135-2016

Michigan

Admore Inc (10), 24707 Wood Ct, Macomb, 48042-5378

American Baseball Coaches Association (1), 108 S University (Suite 3), Mount Pleasant, 48858-2327

Amerisure Insurance Cos (15), 26777 Halsted Rd, Farmington Hills, 48331-3586

Amigo Mobility International Inc (16), 6693 Dixie Hwy, Bridgeport, 48722-9725

Amway Global (7), 7575 Fulton Rd SE, Ada, 49355-0001

Automotive Headphones (16), 44648 Mound Rd (# 161), Sterling Heights, 48314-1322

Baudville Inc (16), 5380 52nd St SE, Grand Rapids, 49512-9702

Booth Michigan (17), PO Box 2168, Grand Rapids, 49503

Bronner's Christmas Wonderland (6), 25 Christmas Ln, Frankenmuth, 48734-1807

Buick Division General Motors Corp (16), 300 Renaissance Center, Detroit, 48265-3000

Camp Healthcare Inc (16), 2010 E High St, Jackson, 49204-3416

Citizens Republic Bank (14), 328 S Saginaw St, Flint, 48502-1923

Cold Stream Farm (8), 8585 N Stephens Rd, Free Soil, 49411

Con-Way Freight (12), 2211 Old Earhart Rd Ste 100, Ann Arbor, 48105-2963

Consumer's Energy (16), 212 W Michigan Ave, Jackson, 49201-2277

Crain Communications Inc (17), 1155 Gratiot Ave, Detroit, 48207-2997

Creative Health Products (16), 5148 Saddle Ridge Rd, Plymouth, 48170

Creativity International (16), 4930 Cascade Rd SE, Ada, 49546

DaimlerChrysler Corp (12), 1000 Chrysler Dr (CIMS 485-06-73), Auburn Hills, 48326-2766

Del Webb (16), 100 Bloomfield Hills Pkwy Ste 150, Bloomfield Hills, 48304-2957

The Detroit Institute of Arts (16), 5200 Woodward Ave, Detroit, 48202

Detroit Newspapers (18), 615 W Lafayette Blvd, Detroit, 48226

Do-It Corp (9), PO Box 592, South Haven, 49090-0592

Dow Chemical USA (16), 2030 Dow Center, Midland, 48674

Dow Corning Corp (16), PO Box 994, Midland, 48686

Eastern Michigan University (16), 1000 College Pl, Ypsilanti, 48197

Elderly Instruments (5), 1100 N Washington, Box 14210, Lansing, 48901

Family Christian Stores (5), 5300 Patterson Ave SE, Grand Rapids, 49530

Farm Bureau Insurance (15), 7373 W Saginaw Hwy, Box 30400, Lansing, 48917

Fitness USA Super Centers (16), 7091 Orchard Lake Rd (Suite 300), West Bloomfield, 48322

Ford Motor Co (16), One American Rd, Dearborn, 48126-2798

Foremost Insurance Group (15), PO Box 2450, Grand Rapids, 49501-2450

Fry Inc (3), 650 Avis Dr, Ann Arbor, 48108-9649

Gale Research Inc (17), 27500 Drake Rd, Farmington Hills, 48331-3535

Gerber Products Co (16), 445 State St., Fremont, 49413

Golf Haus (11), 700 N Pennsylvania Ave, Lansing, 48906-5319

Grower's Supply Co (8), PO Box 219, Dexter, 48130-0219

Health Alliance Plan (15), 2850 W Grand Blvd, Detroit, 48202-2692

Heath Kit Co (3), 2024 Hawthorne Ave, Saint Joseph, 49085

Herman Miller Inc (16), 855 E Main Ave, Zeeland, 49464

HighScope Educational Research Foundation (17), 600 N River St, Ypsilanti, 48198-2898

Indoor Gardening Supplies (8), PO Box 527, Dexter, 48130

J&L Industrial Supply (9), 20921 Lahser Rd, Southfield, 48034-4432

Kadant Johnson Inc (16), 805 Wood St, Three Rivers, 49093

Kingsley North Inc (11), 910 Brown St, PO Box 216, Norway, 49870

Koeze Co (16), P.O. Box 9470, Grand Rapids, 49509

Landscape Forms Inc (16), 431 Lawndale Ave, Kalamazoo, 49048

Learning Care Group (16), 21333 Haggerty Rd (Suite 300), Novi, 48375-5537

Leslie Shoe Co Inc (2), 480 N Second St, Rogers City, 49779-1367

Masco Corp (16), 21001 Van Born Rd, Taylor, 48180

Mary Maxim Inc (11), 2001 Holland Ave, Port Huron, 48061-5019

Meemic Insurance Co (15), 1685 N Opdyke Rd, Auburn Hills, 48326-2656

Michigan Apple Committee (1), 13750 S Sedona Pkwy Ste 3, Lansing, 48906-8101

MGM Grand Detroit (16), 1777 3rd St, Detroit, 48226-2561

MSU Federal Credit Union (1), 3777 West Rd, East Lansing, 48823-8029

Mott Media LLC (17), 1130 Fenway Cir, Fenton, 48430

Muskegon Power Tool Corp (16), 2357 Whitehall Rd, North Muskegon, 49445

National Bulk Equipment Inc (16), 12838 Stainless Dr, Holland, 49424

The Newman Group (3), 2577 Newport Rd, Ann Arbor, 48103-2274

Okun Brothers Shoes Inc (2), 179 Portage Rd, Kalamazoo, 49007-4801

Oliver of Adrian Inc (16), PO Box 189, Adrian, 49221-0189

Parts Place Inc (12), 2300 N Opdyke Rd, Auburn Hills, 48326

Peerless Rattan (16), 687 Miller Rd, Plainwell, 49080-9538

Pennstreet Bakery (16), 900 Hynes SW, Grand Rapids, 49507

Phone Bank Systems Inc (1), 4990 Northwind Dr (Suite 235), East Lansing, 48823-5091

Praises, Prizes & Presents (5), 3822 Richmond St NW, Grand Rapids, 49534-2300

Prakken Publications Inc (17), 2851 Boardwalk St., Ann Arbor, 48104

Reid Supply Co (16), 2265 Black Creek Rd, Muskegon, 49444-2673

Resumate Inc (3), 2500 Packard (Suite 200), Ann Arbor, 48104

Sandy Corp (16), 300 E Big Beaver Rd (Suite 500), Troy, 48083

Schoolcraft College (1), 18600 Haggerty Rd, Livonia, 48152-2696

Scope 1 (16), 6490 S Sprinkle Rd, Kalamazoo, 49004-9706

Scott Publications, Inc (17), 2145 W Sherman Blvd, Muskegon, 49441-3434

B Shackman & Co Inc (6), 9964 W Miller Dr, Galesburg, 49053

Society of Manufacturing Engineers (1), One SME Dr, PO Box 930, Dearborn, 48121

Steelcase Inc (16), 901 44th St SE, Grand Rapids, 49508

Teachers' Discovery (5), 2741 Paldan Dr, Auburn Hills, 48326-1827

Terumo Cardiovascular Systems Corp (5), 6200 Jackson Rd, Ann Arbor, 48103-9586

Thetford Corp (16), 7101 Jackson Rd, Ann Arbor, 48103

Thomson-Gale (17), 27500 Drake Rd, Farmington Hills, 48331

Troy Biologicals Inc (7), 1238 Rankin, Troy, 48083

University Bank (14), 2015 Washtenaw Ave, Ann Arbor, 48104

Volkswagen Group of America Inc (16), 3800 Hamlin Rd, Auburn Hills, 48326-2829

Whirlpool Corp (16), 2000 N M-63, Benton Harbor, 49022-2632

Wholesale Tool Co (9), 12155 Stephens Dr, Warren, 48089

Wysong Corp (7), 7550 Eastman Ave, Midland, 48642-7779

Zondervan Corp (17), 5300 Patterson Ave SE, Grand Rapids, 49530

Minnesota

Activision Value (16), 7800 Equitable Dr (Suite 200), Eden Prairie, 55344

ActivStyle (16), 3100 Pacific St, Minneapolis, 55411

Agilis Co (14), 2380 Crossroads Blvd, Albert Lea, 56007-4001

Allianz Life Insurance Co of North America (15), 5701 Golden Hills Dr, PO Box 1344, Minneapolis, 55416-1297

American Academy of Neurology (1), 1080 Montreal Ave Ste 100, Saint Paul, 55116-2387

American Craft Council (17), 1224 Marshall St NE (Suite 200), Minneapolis, 55413-1089

The American Phytopathological Society (1), 3340 Pilot Knob Rd, Saint Paul, 55121-2055

Ameriprise Financial Services Inc (14), 2324 Ameriprise Financial Center, Minneapolis, 55474-0023

Apothecary Products Inc (7), 11750 12th Ave S, Burnsville, 55337-1297

Arrow Advantage (3), 7627 Anagram Dr, Eden Prairie, 55344-7310

Art Instruction Schools (13), 3400 Technology Dr, Minneapolis, 55418-6000

Asset Marketing Services Inc (16), 14101 Southcross Dr W, Burnsville, 55337-6902

Augsburg Fortress Publishers (17), 100 S Fifth St (Suite 600), Minneapolis, 55402-1242

Aveda Corp (7), 4000 Pheasant Ridge Dr, Minneapolis, 55449-7106

Bellacor (8), 2425 Enterprise Dr (Suite 900), Mendota Heights, 55120

Best Buy (3), 7601 Penn Ave S, Richfield, 55423-3683

Bluestem Brands (16), 6509 Flying Cloud Dr, Eden Prairie, 55344-3307

Bluewater Yachts (16), 811 E Maple, Mora, 55051-1224

Borbeleta Gardens (8), 15980 Canby Ave, Fairbault, 55021

Card Technology Inc (16), 10925 Bren Rd E, Hopkins, 55343-9613

Centerpoint Energy (16), 800 LaSalle Ave, Minneapolis, 55402-2006

Charmaster Products Inc (8), 2307 W US Hwy 2, Grand Rapids, 55744-2152

Classic Motorbooks Inc (17), 400 1st Ave N (Suite 300), Minneapolis, 55401

Classic Thermographers (10), 1680 Roe Crest Dr, North Mankato, 56003-2658

Courage Cards & Gifts (1), 3915 Golden Valley Rd Courage Ctr, Golden Valley, 55422-4249

Creative Banner Assemblies (9), 2730 Nevada Ave, New Hope, 55427-2807

Creative Publishing International (17), 400 First Ave N (Suite 300), Minneapolis, 55401

Crest Healthcare Supply (16), 195 S Third St, Dassel, 55325-4511

Dain Rauscher Inc (14), 60 S Sixth St, Minneapolis, 55402-4422

DEI (1), 401 N 3rd St (Suite 370), Minneapolis, 55401-1350

Digi International (3), 11001 Bren Rd E, Minnetonka, 55343-4410

Digi-Key Corp (3), 701 Brooks Ave S, Box 677, Thief River Falls, 56701

Dragich Auto Literature (16), PO Box 1024, Princeton, 55371-4024

Eckankar (17), PO Box 27300, Minneapolis, 55427

Ecolab Professional Products (16), 370 N Wabasha St, Ecolab Ctr, Saint Paul, 55102-2233

Eichten's Hidden Acres (4), 16809 310th St, PO Box 216, Center City, 55012

The Family Handyman (17), 2915 Commers Dr (Suite 700), Eagan, 55121-2398

Farm Home Offices (10), 6739 12th Ave S, Richfield, 55423

Gelco Information Network (16), 10700 Prairie Lakes Dr, Eden Prairie, 55344

General Mills Inc (8), One General Mills Blvd, Minneapolis, 55426

Gillette Children's Specialty Healthcare (1), 200 University Ave E, Saint Paul, 55101-2507

Goldsmith Agio Helms (14), 225 S 6th St Ste 4600, Minneapolis, 55402-5611

Hazelden (7), CO 3 PO Box 11, Center City, 55012-0011

Heartland America (3), 8085 Century Blvd, Chaska, 55318

HMI Marketing (7), 8000 85th Ave N, Brooklyn Park, 55445

James J Hill Reference Library (1), 80 4th St W, Saint Paul, 55102-1605

Historic Aviation (12), 640 Taft St NE, Minneapolis, 55413-2815

Hormel Foods Corp (16), One Hormel Pl, Austin, 55912-3680

ING (15), 20 Washington Ave S, Minneapolis, 55401-1908

JIST Publishing (17), 875 Montreal Way, Saint Paul, 55102

Jostens, Inc (16), 3601 Minnesota Dr (Suite 400), Minneapolis, 55435-6008

K-tel International (16), 7500 Wayzata Blvd (Suite 28), Golden Valley, 55426-1682

Kelco Supply Co (16), 7700 Setzler Pkwy N., Brooklyn Park, 55445

Land O' Lakes Inc (16), 4001 Lexington Ave, Arden Hills, 55122

Lerner Publishing Group (17), 1251 Washington Ave N, Minneapolis, 55401

Llewellyn Publications (17), 2143 Wooddale Dr, Woodbury, 55125-2989

Marshall Fields Dept Stores (5), 7235 France Ave S, Minneapolis, 55435-4337

Masterpiece Studios Inc (16), PO Box 8700, Mankato, 56002-8700

Mayo Clinic (17), 200 First St SW, Rochester, 55905

Medtronic Inc (16), 710 Medtronic Pkwy NE, Minneapolis, 55432-5604

Meriks Marketers (3), 2200 W 66th St (#190), Richfield, 55423-2196

Merrill Corp (18), 4110 Clearwater Rd, Saint Cloud, 56301

Minnesota Life (15), 400 Robert St N, Saint Paul, 55101

Minnesota Multi Housing Association (1), 1600 W 82nd St (Suite 110), Bloomington, 55431-1411

Minnesota Public Radio (1), 480 Cedar St, Saint Paul, 55101-2230

Miracle Ear (16), 5000 Cheshire Pkwy N, Minneapolis, 55446

MTS Systems Corp (16), 14000 Technology Dr, Eden Prairie, 55344-2247

Nestle Clinical Nutrition Co (16), 12500 Whitewater Dr, Hopkins, 55343-9420

North American Membership Group Inc (13), 12301 Whitewater Dr, Minnetonka, 55343-9447

Northern Tool & Equipment Inc (16), 2800 Southcross Dr W, Burnsville, 55306-6936

The Occasions Group (16), 1750 Tower Blvd, North Mankato, 56003-1706

Osmonics Inc (16), 5951 Clearwater Dr, Minnetonka, 55343-8990

Patterson Dental (10), 1031 Mendota Heights Rd, Saint Paul, 55120-1419

The Pillsbury Co (16), PO Box 9452, General Mills Inc, Minneapolis, 55440-9452

Piper Jaffray (14), 800 Nicollet Mall, Minneapolis, 55402-7000

Polaroid Corp (16), 4350 Baker Rd, Minnetonka, 55343-8684

Quayside Publishing Group/MBI Publishing (17), 400 1st Ave N (Suite 300), Minneapolis, 55401-1721

Redleaf Press (17), 10 Yorkton Ct, Saint Paul, 55117-1065

ReMark USA (15), 301 Carlson Pkwy (Suite 305), Minnetonka, 55305

C H Robinson Worldwide Inc (16), 14701 Charlson Rd, Eden Prairie, 55347-5076

Rockler Woodworking & Hardware (8), 4365 Willow Dr, Medina, 55340

Schwan's Home Service Inc (5), 115 W College Dr, Marshall, 56258-1747

Select Comfort Corp (16), 9800 59th Ave N, Minneapolis, 55442

Shady Oaks Nursery, LLC (8), PO Box 708, 1601 Fifth St SE, Waseca, 56093-0708

Shipping Solutions (16), PO Box 22267, Eagan, 55122-0267

Siegel Display Products (5), 300 Sixth Ave N (Suite 200), Minneapolis, 55401-1212

Skyline Displays (5), 3355 Discovery Rd, Saint Paul, 55121-2098

Skypoint Communications Inc (16), 7340 Mark St, Loretto, 55357

The Sportsman's Guide Inc (11), 411 Farwell Ave, South Saint Paul, 55075-2428

Star Tribune (17), 425 Portland Ave S, Minneapolis, 55488

Starchtech (16), 720 Florida Ave S (#A), Golden Valley, 55426-1704

Starkey Laboratories (16), 6700 Washington Ave S, Eden Prairie, 55344-3405

Stonwurks (16), 13218 Kerry Ln, Eden Prairie, 55346-3140

Strategic Fundraising Inc (1), 7591 9th St N, Saint Paul, 55128-6626

Stratford Hall (10), 1680 Roe Crest Dr, North Mankato, 56003-2658

Target.com (16), 33 S 6th St, Minneapolis, 55402

Taylor Corp (16), 1725 Roe Crest Dr, North Mankato, 56003-1806

Taymark Inc (1), 4875 White Bear Pkwy, White Bear Lake, 55110

Thomson West (17), 610 Opperman Dr, Eagan, 55164

3M Post-It Direct Response Products (16), 3M Center Bldg, Saint Paul, 55144-1001

Timm Medical Technologies, Inc (16), 9600 W 76th St Ste T, Eden Prairie, 55344-3922

The Toro Consumer Div (16), 8111 Lyndale Ave S, Bloomington, 55420

Turncraft Clocks Inc (6), 4310 Shoreline Dr, Spring Park, 55384-9722

US Bancorp (14), 800 Nicollet Mall, Minneapolis, 55402-7014

US Bank (14), 200 S 6th St, Minneapolis, 55402-1403

University of Minnesota Alumni Association (1), 200 Oak St SE (Suite 200), Minneapolis, 55455-2040

University of Minnesota (1), 1420 Eckles Ave 340 Coffee Hall, Saint Paul, 55108-1030

Victory Corps (16), 2730 Nevada Ave N, New Hope, 55427

Waytek (16), 2440 Galpin Ct, Chanhassen, 55317-0690

We-No-Nah Canoe Inc (11), 1252 Bundy Blvd, Box 247, Winona, 55987-4872

Westgroup (17), 610 Opperman Dr, Eagan, 55123-1340

Wilsons Leather (2), 7401 Boone Ave N, Brooklyn Park, 55428

Win Craft Inc (5), 1124 W Fifth St, PO Box 888, Winona, 55987

Xcel Energy (5), 414 Nicollet Mall (GO 6), Minneapolis, 55401-1927

Mississippi

ACBL (1), 6575 Windchase Dr, Horn Lake, 38637-1523

Beau Rivage Resort & Casino (19), 875 Beach Blvd, Biloxi, 39530-4299

FNC INC (14), 1214 Office Park Dr, Oxford, 38655-3597

Forestry Suppliers Inc (9), 205 W Rankin St, PO Box 8397, Jackson, 39284-6126

Historical Replications Inc (8), 3908 N State St, Jackson, 39206-5752

Kelly's Kids (2), 391 Liberty Rd, Natchez, 39120-4344

MISSCO Corp (16), PO Box 321400, PO Box 5349, Flowood, 39232-1400

Quality Products Inc (10), 2415 Hwy 45 N, PO Box 564, Columbus, 39703

Uncle Ben's Inc (4), 1098 N Broadway St, Greenville, 38701-2004

University of Southern Mississippi (1), 118 College Dr (Box 5016), Hattiesburg, 39406-0001

Missouri

American Century Investments (14), 4500 Main St, Box 418210, Kansas City, 64111

American Ostomy Supply (16), 13400 Lakefront Dr, Earth City, 63045-1516

American Recreation Products Inc (11), 1224 Fern Ridge Pkwy, Saint Louis, 63141-4404

Angelica Image Apparel (16), 7700 Forsyth Blvd (Suite 1010), Saint Louis, 63105-1821

Anthem Blue Cross Blue Shield (15), 1831 Chestnut St (#1), Saint Louis, 63103-2275

Association of the Miraculous Medal (1), 1811 W Saint Joseph St, Perryville, 63775-1598

Bass Pro Shops (11), 2500 E Kearney, Springfield, 65898-0001

Mel Bay Publications Inc (17), Four Industrial Dr, Pacific, 63069-0066

Beacon Shoe Co Inc (16), 11 Worthington Access Dr Stop 1, Maryland Heights, 63043-3804

Big Brothers Big Sisters of Greater Kansas City (1), 3908 Washington St, Kansas City, 64111-2925

Bissinger French Confections (4), 3983 Gratiot St, Saint Louis, 63110-1723

Brown Shoe Co (16), 8300 Maryland Ave, PO Box 29, Saint Louis, 63105-3645

Bunzl Distribution USA, Inc (16), 1 Cityplace Dr Ste 200, Saint Louis, 63141-7067

Burger's Ozark Country Cured Hams Inc (4), 32819 Hwy 87, California, 65018

Carhill Enterprises Inc (15), 1232 Washington Ave (Suite 300), Saint Louis, 63103-1983

CPI Corp (16), 1706 Washington Ave, St Louis, 63103-1717

CTA Inc (5), 1625 Larkin Williams Rd, Fenton, 63026-1205

Charter Communications (16), 12405 Powerscourt Dr (Suite 100), Saint Louis, 63131-3674

Children International (1), 2000 E Red Bridge Rd, Kansas City, 64131-3694

Clarkson Eyecare (5), 217 Clarkson Rd, Ellisville, 63011-2219

Commerce Bancshares Inc (14), 8000 Forsyth Blvd (CBIR-1), Saint Louis, 63105-1707

Con-Way Truckload (12), 4701 E 32nd St, Joplin, 64804

Concordia Publishing House (17), 3558 S Jefferson, Saint Louis, 63118-3910

Copilevitz & Canter, LLC (14), 310 W 20th St (Suite 300), Kansas City, 64108-2025

Dairy Farmers of America Inc (16), 10220 N Ambassador Dr Suite 1000), Kansas City, 64153-2327

DWS Investments Service Co (14), PO Box 219151, Attn: General Correspondence, Kansas City, 64121-9151

Deck the Walls Inc (5), 221 First Executive Ave, Saint Peters, 63376-1697

Delmmar Communications (16), 920 N Ashland Dr, Cameron, 64429

Diagraph Corp (16), One Missouri Research Park Dr, Saint Charles, 63304-5685

Dirxion (16), 1859 Bowles Ave (Suite 100), Saint Louis, 63026-1936

Doane (17), 77 Westport Plaza (Suite 250), Saint Louis, 63146-3121

Eggs by Byrd (10), HC 3 Box 3653, Wappapello, 63966-9727

Energizer Battery Co Inc (16), 533 Maryville University Dr, Saint Louis, 63141

Enterprise Rent-A-Car (19), 600 Corporate Park Dr, Saint Louis, 63105-4204

Faultless Starch/Bon Ami Co (16), 1025 W Eighth St, Kansas City, 64101-1200

Fidelity Security Life Insurance Co (15), 3130 Broadway, Kansas City, 64111-2406

First Banks Inc (14), 600 McDonnell Blvd, Hazelwood, 63042

Garden Botanika Inc (7), 8500 Valcour Ave, Saint Louis, 63123

Gilliom Manufacturing Inc (8), 500 Boonslick Rd, Saint Charles, 63301-2437

H&R Block Inc (14), 1 H&R Block Way, Kansas City, 64105-1905

Hallmark Cards Inc (16), PO Box 419580, Kansas City, 64141-6580

Halls Kansas City (16), 200 E 25th St, Kansas City, 64108-2509

Hasco First Photo (16), 3613 Mueller Rd, Saint Charles, 63301

Heartland Boating Magazine (17), 319 N Fourth St (Suite 650), Saint Louis, 63102

Helzberg Diamonds (16), 1825 Swift St, North Kansas City, 64116-3606

Herschend Family Entertainment (5), 399 Indian Point Rd, Branson, 65616

HDA Inc (17), 944 Anglum Rd, Saint Louis, 63042

Home Decorators Collection Inc (8), 8920 Pershall Rd, Hazelwood, 63042-2809

The Hope Co Inc (16), 12777 Pennridge Dr, Bridgeton, 63044

InteliSpend Prepaid Solutions (5), 1400 S Highway Dr, Fenton, 63026-2281

Invacare Continuing Care Group (16), 1848 Craig Rd, Saint Louis, 63146-4712

Edward Jones (14), 12555 Manchester Rd, Des Peres, 63131-3710

Kansas City Chiefs (16), One Arrowhead Dr, Kansas City, 64129

EC Kraus Home Wine & Beer Making Supplies (4), 733 S Northern Blvd, PO Box 7850, Independence, 64054

Liguori Publications (17), One Liguori Dr, Liguori, 63057-9999

Luster Care Products (16), 8854 Frost Ave, Saint Louis, 63134-1044

Lutheran Church Extension Fund - Missouri Synod (1), 10733 Sunset Office Dr (Suite 300), Sunset Corporate Center, Saint Louis, 63127-1020

Luzier Personalized Cosmetics (7), 7910-7912 Troost Ave, Kansas City, 64131-1920

Magna-Tel Inc (5), 775 S Kings Hwy St, Cape Girardeau, 63703

Magna Visual Inc (9), 9400 Watson Rd, Saint Louis, 63126

Magnet LLC (16), Seven Chamber Dr, PO Box 605, Washington, 63090

Maverick Ventures Product Line (5), 15698 Ferncreek Dr, Chesterfield, 63017-0702

Joyce Meyer Ministries (1), 700 Grace Pkwy, Fenton, 63026-5390

Mid West Floor Co Inc (16), 2714 Breckenridge Industrial Ct, Saint Louis, 63144

Midcontinent Financial Center Inc (14), 2614 Calvert Dr # B, Columbia, 65202-2321

Midland Marketing Group (16), PO Box 8576, Saint Joseph, 64508-8576

Missouri Landscape & Nursery Association (1), PO Box 81, Bowling Green, 63334

Missouri Life Inc (17), 501 High St # A, Boonville, 65233-1211

National Auto Warranty (16), 100 Mall Pkwy, Wentzville, 63385-4816

National Catholic Reporter Publishing Co Inc (17), 115 E Armour Blvd, Kansas City, 64111-1203

National Research Center for College & University Admissions (1), 3651 NE Ralph Powell Rd, Lees Summit, 64064-2357

Parcel Insurance Plan Inc (15), 9666 Olive Blvd (Suite 200), Saint Louis, 63132-3012

Phoenix Learning Group Inc (16), 141A Millwell Dr, Maryland Heights, 63043-2509

Posty Cards Inc (16), 1600 Olive St, Kansas City, 64127-2539

PFI Western Stores Inc (2), 2816 S Ingram Mill Rd, Springfield, 65804

R&S Industries Corp (16), 1065 Appalachian Trl, Chesterfield, 63017-1948

Royal Canin (16), 500 Fountain Lakes Blvd (Suite 100), Saint Charles, 63301-4354

St Louis Post-Dispatch (17), 900 N Tucker Blvd, Saint Louis, 63101

St Louis Slot Machine Co (6), 9617 Dielman Rock Island Industrial Dr, Saint Louis, 63132-2149

Schnuck Markets Inc (16), 11420 Lackland Rd, Saint Louis, 63146-6928

Sensient Technologies (16), 2526 Baldwin St, Saint Louis, 63106

Sensory Effects Powder System (16), 231 Rock Industrial Park Dr, Bridgeton, 63044

Soft Surroundings (2), 1100 N Lindbergh Blvd, Saint Louis, 63132-2914

Stark Brothers Fulfillment Services (8), PO Box 1800, Louisiana, 63353-7800

Stark Brothers Nurseries & Orchards (8), PO Box 1800, Louisiana, 63353

Townsend Communications LLC (17), 20 E Gregory Blvd, Kansas City, 64114

Uniforms & Scrubs.com (7), 910 Kehrs Mill Rd (Suite 106), Ballwin, 63011-2404

Unity School of Christianity (17), 1901 NW Blue Pkwy, Unity Village, 64065-0001

Upbeat Inc (9), 211 N Lindbergh Blvd (fl 2), Saint Louis, 63141-7838

Vehicle Assurance (5), 2747 W Clay, Saint Charles, 63301-2557

Veterans of Foreign Wars (VFW) of the US-National Headquarters (1), 406 W 34th St Fl 11, Kansas City, 64111-2736

Washington University (1), 1 Brookings Dr, Saint Louis, 63130-4899

Watts Radiant (9), 4500 E Progress Pl, Springfield, 65803

Westhoff Machine Co (9), 9462 Watson Industrial Park, Saint Louis, 63126

Gilbert H Wild & Son Inc (8), 2944 State Hwy 37, Reeds, 64859

Zimmerman-McDonald Machinery Inc (16), 2272 Weldon Pkwy, Saint Louis, 63146-3206

Montana

Mountain Press Publishing Co (17), PO Box 2399, Missoula, 59806-2399

Photographer's Formulary Inc (9), 7079 Hwy 83 N, Condon, 59826

St Labre Indian School (1), PO Box 77, Ashland, 59003-0077

Sims Stoves (11), PO Box 21405, Billings, 59104

Nebraska

AccuTrade Inc (14), 1005 Ameritrade Pl, PO Box 68103-2227, Bellevue, 68005

Alpha Dog Marketing Inc (1), 9060 Andermatt Dr Ste 101, Lincoln, 68526-9644

Arbor Capital 1 (14), 1414 Harney St (Suite 400), Omaha, 68102-2255

Arbor Day Foundation (1), 211 N 12th St (Suite 501), Lincoln, 68508-1411

Back to the Bible (5), 6400 Cornhusker Hwy, Lincoln, 68501-2808

Baldwin Filters (16), 4400 E Hwy 30, Kearney, 68848-6010

Behlen Manufacturing Co (16), 4025 E 23rd St, Columbus, 68601-3448

Burden Sales Co (9), 1015 W "O" St, Lincoln, 68528-1322

Cabela's Inc (11), 1 Cabela Dr, Sidney, 69160-1001

Central States Health & Life Co of Omaha (15), 1212 N 96th St, Omaha, 68114

Central States Indemnity (15), 1212 N 96th St, Omaha, 68114-2274

Commercial Federal Bank (14), 13220 California St, Omaha, 68154-5228

Condolink (16), 3012 N 93rd St, Omaha, 68134-4716

Cornhusker Press (17), 451 W Second St, Hastings, 68902-0729

Duncan Aviation (16), 3701 Aviation Rd, Lincoln Airport, Lincoln, 68524

Father Flanagan's Boy's Home (1), 234 Monsky Dr, Boys Town, 68010-7550

Garden Perennials (8), 85261 Hwy 15, Wayne, 68787

GWR Wealth Management (14), 14301 First National Bank Pkwy, Omaha, 68154-5213

Info USA City Directories (17), 5711 S 86th Cir, Omaha, 68127

KV Vet Supply Co, Inc (5), 3190 N Rd (#245), David City, 68632-5142

Manheim Steamroller (3), 9130 Mormon Bridge Rd, Omaha, 68152-1937

Medco Insurance Co (15), 1515 S 75th St, Omaha, 68124-1618

Medibadge Inc (5), PO Box 12307, Omaha, 68112-0307

Missionary Society of St Columban (1), PO Box 10, Saint Columbans, 68056-0010

Mutual of Omaha (15), Mutual of Omaha Plaza (fl 7), Omaha, 68175-0001

Omaha Creative Group Inc (4), 11030 O St, Omaha, 68137-2346

Omaha Fixture International (8), 10320 "J" St, Omaha, 68127-1092

Omaha Steaks Inc (4), 11030 "O" St, Omaha, 68137-2346

Omaha Vaccine Co (16), 11143 Mockingbird Dr, Omaha, 68137-2332

Oriental Trading Co Inc (5), 5455 S 90th St, Omaha, 68127-3501

Phillips Kiln Service LTD (16), 2607 Dakota Ave Ste 2, South Sioux City, 68776-3256

Physicians Mutual Insurance Co (15), 2600 Dodge St, Omaha, 68131

Pro CD Inc (17), 5711 S 86th Cir, Omaha, 68127

QC Supply LLC (16), PO Box 581, Schuyler, 68661-0581

Speedway (12), PO Box 81906, Lincoln, 68501-1906

Surplus Center (9), 1015 W "O" St, Lincoln, 68528-1322

Tender Heart Treasures (6), 11005 E Cir, Omaha, 68137-1228

TransFirst ePayment Services (14), 13220 Birch Dr (Suite 110), Omaha, 68164-5434

Wellness Councils of America (1), 17002 Marcy St (Suite 140), Omaha, 68118-2933

Wimmer's Meat Products Inc (4), 126 W Grant St, PO Box 286, West Point, 68788-0286

Nevada

Ameristar Casinos (19), 3773 Howard Hughes Pkwy 490 S, Las Vegas, 89169-0949

BluBlocker Corp (2), 3350 Palm Ctr Dr, Las Vegas, 89103-5668

Boyd Gaming Corp (16), 3883 Howard Hughes Pkwy (fl 9), Las Vegas, 89169

Caesars Palace (16), 1 Caesars Palace Dr, Las Vegas, 89109

California Pacific Research & New Generation (7), 300 Brinkby Ave (Suite 200), Reno, 89509-4359

EMPLOYERS Insurance (15), 10375 Professional Cir, Reno, 89521-4802

Enco Manufacturing Co (9), 400 Nevada Pacific Hwy, Fernley, 89408

Ethel M Chocolates Inc (4), One Sunset Way, Henderson, 89014

Harrah's Entertainment Inc (19), 1 Harrahs Ct, Las Vegas, 89119-4377

Harrah's Marketing (16), 219 N Center St, Reno, 89501-1413

Health Freedom Nutrition LLC (7), 255 Bell St (2nd fl), Reno, 89503-5352

IDC, Ltd (1), 2500 Paseo Verde Pkwy, Henderson, 89074

Impulse Inc (3), 8238 W Charleston Blvd, Las Vegas, 89117

Las Vegas Review Journal (17), 1111 W Bonanza Rd, PO Box 70, Las Vegas, 89125

Laughlin Associates Inc (16), 2533 N Carson St, Carson City, 89706

Longevity Network Ltd (7), 5 Longevity Dr, Henderson, 89014-2048

MGM MIRAGE (19), 3600 Las Vegas Blvd S, Las Vegas, 89109-4303

Montbleu Resort Casino and Spa (19), 55 Hwy 50, Stateline, 89449

Morcon Industrial Specialty Inc (9), 658 Hardy Way (Suite 2), Mesquite, 89027-3914

Neo-Tech Publishing Co (17), 2435 W Horizon Ridge Pkwy (Suite 100), Henderson, 89052-5787

Nevada Commission on Tourism (1), 401 N Carson St, Carson City, 89701-4221

Nevada Magazine (17), 401 N Carson St, Carson City, 89701-4221

Patagonia Mail Order Inc (2), 8550 White Fir St, Reno, 89523-2050

Performance Media Solutions Inc & TrueWorx Inc (16), 4001 S Decatur Blvd (#37-425), Las Vegas, 89103-5860

Reliapon Police Products (5), 4620 Calimesa St # 1D, Las Vegas, 89115-2364

Reno Gazette Journal (17), 955 Kuenzli St, Reno, 89520

Sportif Mail Order Inc (2), 1415 Greg St (Suite 101), Sparks, 89431

Steppin' Out & See America (19), 1140 N Town Center Dr (#360), Las Vegas, 89144-0501

The Stratosphere Las Vegas (19), 2000 Las Vegas Blvd S, Las Vegas, 89104

TVC Enterprises and the TV Collector Magazine (6), 6704 Fruit Flower Ave, Las Vegas, 89130

Vitamin Research Products (7), 4610 Arrowhead Dr, Carson City, 89706-2017

Zappos.com (2), 2280 Corporate Cir (Suite 100), Henderson, 89074-6382

New Hampshire

Brookstone Co (3), 1 Innovation Way, Merrimack, 03054-4873

CCA Global Partners (16), 670 N Commercial St, Manchester, 03101-1160

Cheap Aprons (2), 55 Crystal Ave (#265), Derry, 03038-1702

Cobblestone Publishing (17), 30 Grove St (Suite C), Peterborough, 03458-1453

Connell Communications Inc (17), 45 Main St Ste 102, Peterborough, 03458-2433

Copper Art by Morse (8), PO Box 1220, Claremont, 03743-1220

Custom Miniatures (6), 19 Winnhaven Dr, Hudson, 03051-4748

Dartmouth-Hitchcock (1), Hinman Box 7070, One Medical Center Dr, Lebanon, 03756-1000

Duncraft Inc (16), 102 Fisherville Rd, Concord, 03303-9020

Eastern Mountain Sports (16), 1 Vose Farm Rd, Peterborough, 03458-2122

Emerson Ecologics (7), 7 Commerce Dr, Bedford, 03110-6835

Gardener's Eden (8), One Innovation Way, Merrimack, 03054

Garnet Hill Inc (2), 231 Main St, Franconia, 03580

General Tours/TBI Tours (19), 53 Summer St, Keene, 03431

GN Netcom (16), 77 Northeastern Blvd, Nashua, 03062-3128

Greenwood Publishing Group Inc (17), PO Box 6926, PO Box 5007, Portsmouth, 03802-6926

Hampshire Pewter Co (6), 43 Mill St, Wolfeboro, 03894

Harman's Cheese & Country Store Inc (4), 1400 Rte 117, Sugar Hill, 03586

Hello Direct (16), 77 Northeastern Blvd, Nashua, 03062-3128

Herrington (16), Three Symmes Dr, Londonderry, 03053

Information Unlimited Inc (11), PO Box 716, Amherst, 03031-0716

Institute of Management & Administration (IOMA) (17), 1 Phoenix Mill Ln Fl 3, Peterborough, 03458-1467

Kenmore Stamp Co (6), 119 West St, PO Box 331, Milford, 03055-4855

Littleton Coin Co Inc (6), 1309 Mt Eustis Rd, Littleton, 03561

MFE Instruments (9), 32 Hampshire Rd, Salem, 03079

Northeast Hinge Distributors Inc (9), 261 Proctor Hill Rd, Hollis, 03049

Paymentech (14), Four Northeastern Blvd, Salem, 03079

Reliable Technologies Inc (16), 55 S Commercial St, Manchester, 03101

Rubber Stamps of America (6), 1110 Main St, Dublin, 03444

Solar Components Corp (9), 121 Valley St, Manchester, 03103-0237

Timberland.com (16), 200 Domain Dr, Stratham, 03885

Vermont Tubbs (8), 87 Brown St, Whitefield, 03598-3024

Village Coin Shop (6), 51C Plaistow Rd, Plaistow, 03865

Whitehorse Gear (11), 107 E Conway Rd, Center Conway, 03813-4012

Yankee Publishing Inc (17), 1121 Main St, Dublin, 03444

New Jersey

A&P (16), 2 Paragon Dr, Montvale, 07645

AAA Umbrella Co Inc (16), 230 Pegasus Ave, Northvale, 07647-1904

ADP Inc (16), 1 ADP Blvd, Roseland, 07068-1728

AT&T (16), 1 ATT Way, Bedminster, 07921-2694

Accoona Corp (16), 101 Hudson St (Suite 3606), Jersey City, 07302-3915

Ad-Lib Advertising Inc (10), 109 White Oak Ln (Suite 72A), Old Bridge, 08857

Aerosoles (2), 201 Meadow Rd, Edison, 08817-6030

Affinity Federal Credit Union (1), 73 Mountain Rd, Basking Ridge, 07920

All-State Legal (16), 1 Commerce Dr, Cranford, 07016-3508

Allyn & Bacon (17), 1 Lake St, Upper Saddle River, 07458-1813

American General Co (15), 3600 State Rte 66, Neptune, 07753

Analytical Measurements (9), 22 Mountain View Dr, Chester, 07930-3104

Anything Goes (6), 321 Main St, Allenhurst, 07711-1037

Arquest Inc (16), 14 Scotto Farm Ln., Millstone Twp, 08535-9426

The Art of Self Promotion (17), 1012 Park Ave, PO Box 23, Hoboken, 07030-4334

Audio & Video Labs Inc (16), 7905 N Route 130, Pennsauken, 08110-1402

Avis World Headquarters (19), 6 Sylvan Way, Parsippany, 07054-3826

Basic Adhesives Inc (9), 60 Webro Rd, Clifton, 07012

Bauer Publishing Co (17), 270 Sylvan Ave, Englewood Cliffs, 07632-2523

Bayer Corp Consumer Care Division (16), 36 Columbia Rd, Morristown, 07962

BOC Gases (16), 575 Mountain Ave, Murray Hill, 07974

Bearingpoint Inc (14), 50 Chestnut Ridge Rd, Montvale, 07645-1814

J&H Berge/The Lab Mart (7), 4111 S Clinton Ave, South Plainfield, 07080

Berkeley College (13), 64 E Midland Ave, Paramus, 07652-2947

Biosciences-Amersham (16), 800 Centennial Ave, PO Box 1327, Piscataway, 08855-1327

R R Bowker (17), 630 Central Ave, New Providence, 07974

Brim Electronics Inc (3), 120 Home Pl, Lodi, 07644

Burlington Coat Factory (16), 1830 Rte 130, Burlington, 08016

Butler Distributing Co (3), 730 Fairfield Ave, Kenilworth, 07033-2012

Cadie Products Corp (16), 151 E 11th St, Paterson, 07524-1228

Caesars Atlantic City Casino/Hotel (19), 2100 Pacific Ave, Boardwalk at Arkansas, Atlantic City, 08401-6612

Campbell Soup Co (16), 1 Campbell Pl, Camden, 08103-1701

Campmor Inc (17), 400 Corporate Dr, Mahwah, 07430-3606

Capezio Ballet Makers Inc (16), 1 Campus Rd, Totowa, 07512

Captan Associates Inc (17), 744 Durham Rd, Brick, 08724-1064

Caswell-Massey Co Ltd (7), 121 Fieldcrest Ave Ste A, Edison, 08837-3658

CIT (14), 1 CIT Dr, Livingston, 07039-5703

CYRO Industries (16), 379 Interpace Pkwy Ste 1, Parsippany, 07054-1131

Center for Professional Advancement (13), 25 Kennedy Blvd (Suite 400), East Brunswick, 08816-1258

Central Shippee Inc (16), 46 Star Lake Rd, Bloomingdale, 07403-1244

Chairman's Marketing Group LLC (15), 8 Lafayette Rd W, Princeton, 08540-2428

Commonwealth Business Media Inc (17), 2 Penn Plz E Ste 2, 400 Windsor Corp Park, Newark, 07105-2251

Coronis Building Systems Inc (9), 2305 Rancocas Rd., Burlington, 08016-4113

D&E Pharmaceuticals Inc (7), 700 Central Ave, Farmingdale, 07727-3787

Dassault Falcon Jet Corp (16), 200 Riser Rd, Little Ferry, 07643-1226

The Davis Center (16), 19 State Route 10 (Suite 25), Succasunna, 07876-1750

Days Inns Worldwide Inc (16), 1 Sylvan Way Ste 2, Parsippany, 07054-3879

DIA - Nielsen USA Inc (16), 41 Twosome Dr (Unit 5), Moorestown, 08057

DMC Corp (16), 77 S Hackensack Ave (Bldg 10F), Kearny, 07032-4688

Delicious Orchards (4), 36 Rte 34, Colts Neck, 07722-1987

Details Interactive LLC (16), 30 Manchester Dr, Westfield, 07090-2265

Diamond Essence (2), 3906 Cricket Cir, Edison, 08820

Diapers.com (5), PO Box 483, Jersey City, 07303

Disc Makers (3), 7905 N Route 130, Pennsauken, 08110-1402

Discovery (9), 12 Christopher Way Ste 202, Eatontown, 07724-3331

Dow Jones & Co (17), PO Box 300, Princeton, 08543-0300

Dr Leonard's Healthcare Corp (7), 100 Nixon Ln, Edison, 08837-3804

The Du-Rite Group Inc (16), 103 S Van Brunt St, Englewood, 07631-3437

Durey-Libby Edible Nuts Inc (4), 100 Industrial Rd, Carlstadt, 07072

EasyLink Services International Corp (16), 33 Knightsbridge Rd, Piscataway, 08854

Edmund Optics Inc (9), 101 E Gloucester Pike, Barrington, 08007-1331

Educational Testing Service (16), 666 Rosedale Rd (M/S 40-L), Princeton, 08541-0001

EWA & Miniature Cars USA Inc (11), 369 Springfield Ave., P.O. Box 188, Berkeley Heights, 07922-0188

EXL (16), 10 Exchange Pl, Jersey City, 07302-3918

Etchworld (11), 176-180 Fifth Ave, Hawthorne, 07506

Falcon Safety Products (16), 25 Imclone Dr, Box 1229, Branchburg, 08876

Family Foot Care (7), 530 Lakehurst Rd (Suite 205), Toms River, 08755

George Fencik Associates (16), 1006 Arnold Ave, Point Pleasant, 08742

FLM Graphics Corp (16), 123 Lehigh Dr, Fairfield, 07004-3095

Filene's Basement (16), 1 Syms Way, Secaucus, 07094-9400

Financial Executives International (1), 125 Headquarters Plaza (fl 7), Morristown, 07960

Flaghouse Inc (5), 601 Flaghouse Dr, Hasbrouck Heights, 07604

Foote, Francisco & Co (1), 19 Beverly Rd, West Caldwell, 07006-6501

Fran's Basket House, Inc (8), 295 Rte 10 E, Succasunna, 07876

Freeman Decorating Co (16), 909 Newark Tpke, Kearny, 07032-4307

Garon Products Inc (16), PO Box 1924, Wall, 07719-1924

Genada Imports (8), PO Box 204 (Dept 2), Teaneck, 07666

General Pencil Co Inc (16), 67 Fleet St, Jersey City, 07306

The Graph Co (14), PO Box 961, Vineland, 08362-0961

Haband Co Inc (2), 110 Bauer Dr, Oakland, 07436-3105

Hamilton Watch (16), 1200 Harbor Blvd, Weehawken, 07086-6728

Handy Store Fixtures Inc (8), 337 Sherman Ave, Newark, 07114-1592

Hanover Direct Inc (5), 1500 Harbor Blvd, Weehawken, 07086-6768

The Hartz Mountain Corp (16), 400 Plaza Dr, Secaucus, 07094-3605

Healthfest (5), 100 Nixon Ln, Edison, 08837-3804

Herbach & Rademan Co (9), 353 Crider Ave, Moorestown, 08057

Hertz Corp (19), 225 Brae Blvd, Park Ridge, 07656

High Point Insurance (15), PO Box 906, Lincroft, 07738-0906

Hillside Wire Cloth Co (9), PO Box 1190, Bloomfield, 07003-1190

Honeywell (16), 101 Columbia Rd, Morristown, 07962

The IEI Corp (6), 29 Emmons Dr Ste A30, Princeton, 08540-5994

Institute of Management Accountants Inc (1), Ten Paragon Dr, Montvale, 07645-1718

Herbert L Jamison & Co LLC (15), 100 Executive Dr (Suite 200), West Orange, 07052-3362

Jaz Holdings LLC (16), PO Box 37, Bldg 5, Liberty Corner, 07938-0037

JT International (16), 500 Frank W Burr Blvd (Suite 24), Teaneck, 07666-6802

Johnson & Johnson (16), One Johnson & Johnson Plaza, New Brunswick, 08933

Journal of Commerce Group (17), 2 Penn Plz E (Suite 4), Newark, 07105-2251

Kimbo Educational (17), Ten N Third Ave, Long Branch, 07740-7045

Kuwait Airways Corp (19), 400 Kelby St Ste 41, Fort Lee, 07024-2938

Lawn Doctor Inc (16), 142 State Route 34 (Suite 1), Holmdel, 07733-2092

Lea & Perrins Inc (16), 15-01 Pollitt Dr, Fair Lawn, 07410

Lifeboat Distribution (16), 1157 Shrewsbury Ave, Shrewsbury, 07702

Lin Terry (6), 185 6th Ave Ste 4, Paterson, 07524-1247

Lincoln Educational Services (13), 200 Executive Dr Ste 340, West Orange, 07052-3303

Linens n' Things (8), 80 E State Rte 4 Ste 290, Paramus, 07652-2661

Lladro USA (16), One Lladro Dr, Moonachie, 07074-1019

Logical Computer Selections (16), 18 Winding Way, Short Hills, 07078-2530

Lucent Direct Catalog (3), 600 Mountain Ave, New Providence, 07974

Maidenform Inc (2), 485-F US Hwy 1S, Iselin, 08830-3055

Maison Glass Delicacies (4), 2321 John F Kennedy Blvd., Jersey City, 07304

Marketing Results Inc (16), 604 Libertyville Pl, Sicklerville, 08081

Marquis Who's Who LLC (17), 300 Connell Dr (Suite 2000), Berkeley Heights, 07922

Martindale-Hubbell (17), 121 Chanlon Rd, New Providence, 07974

Medco Health Solutions Inc (7), 100 Parsons Pond Dr, Franklin Lakes, 07417-2604

MELDISCO (16), 933 MacArthur Blvd, Mahwah, 07430-2045

Merck & Co Inc (16), 1 Merck Dr, Whitehouse Station, 08889

Metro Speedgear (11), 70 Okner Pkwy (Suite A), Livingston, 07039

Meylan Corp (9), 543 Valley Rd (Suite 1), Montclair, 07043-1844

MDE Marketing (16), 55 Lehman St, Mahwah, 07430-3050

Modular Devices, LLC (3), 35-D Wilson Dr, Sparta, 07871

Motorola Inc (16), 5 Paragon Dr (#200), Montvale, 07645

Multiple Sclerosis Association of America (1), 706 Haddonfield Rd, Cherry Hill, 08002-2652

Myron Corp (16), 205 Maywood Ave, Maywood, 07607-1000

National Association for Printing Leadership (1), 1 Meadowlands Plz (Suite 1511), East Rutherford, 07073-2167

National Basketball Association (1), 100 Plaza Dr Fl 3, Secaucus, 07094-3677

New Jersey Institute for Continuing Legal Education (1), 1 Constitution Sq, New Brunswick, 08901-1587

New Jersey Monthly (17), 55 Park Pl, Morristown, 07960-3924

Newmark Laboratories (7), 164 Northfield Ave, Edison, 08837

Noevir Direct Marketing Inc (7), 200 W Grand Ave, Montvale, 07645-1716

The NonProfit Times (17), 201 Littleton Rd (Suite 120), Morris Plains, 07950-2939

Novartis Pharmaceuticals Corp (7), 1 Health Plaza (Bldg 701 Rm 060), East Hanover, 07936-1016

Pearson Education (17), One Lake St, Upper Saddle River, 07458-1813

Penguin Group USA Inc (17), 405 Murray Hill Pkwy, East Rutherford, 07073-2136

Peterson's (17), 2000 Lenox Dr, Lawrenceville, 08648-2314

Pilani's Live in Style (2), 284 Steelmanville Rd, Egg Harbor Township, 08234-7806

Pinkerton Security & Investigation Services (16), 2 Campus Dr, Parsippany, 07054-4499

Polo Ralph Lauren (2), 9 Polito Ave (fl 5), Lyndhurst, 07071-3406

Princeton Book Co Publishers (17), 614 Rte 130, Hightstown, 08520-2651

Prudent Publishing Co (16), 65 Challenger Rd, Ridgefield Park, 07660-2111

Prudential Financial (14), 751 Broad St, Newark, 07102-2195

Qualco, Inc (8), 225 Passaic St, Passaic, 07055-6414

Rainbow Art Glass (16), 1761 Rte 34 S, Wall, 07727-3935

Rascal (7), 591 Mantua Blvd, Sewell, 08080

Recording for the Blind & Dyslexic Inc (16), 20 Roszel Rd, Princeton, 08540-9983

Resorts Atlantic City (19), 1133 Boardwalk, Atlantic City, 08401

Roche Pharmaceuticals (7), 340 Kingsland St, Nutley, 07110-1150

Rogers & Rosenthal Inc (6), 2150 Center Ave Apt 21E, Fort Lee, 07024-5805

Saveology.com (5), 1 Cragwood Rd Ste 3, South Plainfield, 07080-2448

Jacques C Schiff Jr Inc (5), 195 Main St, Ridgefield Park, 07660-1620

The Scholar's Bookshelf (5), 21 Palmer Sq W Apt A, Princeton, 08542-3726

Schwartz & Co (6), 524 Bloomfield Ave, Verona, 07044

Sculpture House Inc (16), 405 Skillman Rd, PO Box 69, Skillman, 08558

Seiko Corp of America (16), 1111 MacArthur Blvd, Mahwah, 07430

Sensory Consumer Science (7), 300 North St, Teterboro, 07608-1204

Seton Hall University (1), 400 South Orange Ave, South Orange, 07079-2646

Skinder-Strauss Associates (14), 240 Mulberry St, Newark, 07102-3528

Software Assistance International Ltd (SAIL) (3), 85 Moraine Rd, Morris Plains, 07950

Songbird Hearing Inc (7), 1 Penbrook Ct, Princeton Junction, 08550-1805

Sony Electronics Inc (16), One Sony Dr, Park Ridge, 07656

Robert A Stanger & Co Inc (14), 1129 Broad St, Shrewsbury, 07702

The Suburban Chamber of Commerce (14), 71 Summit Ave Ste 1, Summit, 07901-3690

Super 8 Hotels Worldwide (19), 22 Sylvan Way, Parsippany, 07054-3879

The Supplies Guys (3), 268 Greenwood Ave, Midland Park, 07432-1445

Telcordia Technologies (16), One Telcordia Dr, Piscataway, 08854-4151

Tetley USA Inc (16), 155 Chestnut Ridge Rd, PO Box 856, Montvale, 07645-1156

Thomas Scientific (9), 1654 High Hill Rd, Swedesboro, 08085

Tidewater Workshop (8), 1515 Grant St, Egg Harbor City, 08215-2730

Toys "R" Us (11), 1 Geoffrey Way, Wayne, 07470-2066

Transaction Publishers (17), 35 Berrue Cir, Rutgers University, Piscataway, 08854-8042

Tri-Chem Inc (16), 681 Main St Ste 24, Bldg 24, Belleville, 07109-3471

Tristar Products (16), 492 US Hwy 46 E, Fairfield, 07004

Trump Marina Hotel & Casino (19), Huron Ave & Brigantine Blvd, Atlantic City, 08401

Trump Plaza Hotel & Casino (19), 1000 Boardwalk at Mississippi Ave, Atlantic City, 08401-7415

Ultimate Office (16), PO Box 688, Farmingdale, 07727-0688

Ultra Direct Marketing Inc (16), PO Box 1575, Jackson, 08527

Unilever Best Foods (16), 800 Sylvan Ave, Englewood Cliffs, 07632

United Retail Inc (2), 365 W Passaic St (Suite 230), Rochelle Park, 07662-3017

Universal Communication Enterprise (13), 66 Elmora Ave, Elizabeth, 07202-1630

Utretch Art Supplies (10), 6 Corporate Dr Ste 1, Cranbury, 08512-3616

UBS Wealth Management US (14), 1200 Harbor Blvd, Weehawken, 07086-6728

Vcom International Multi-Media Corp (3), 55 Ruta Ct, PO Box 3171, South Hackensack, 07606

Vitamin Specialties Co (7), 500 Halls Mill Rd, Freehold, 07728

Volvo Cars of North America (16), PO Box 914, Northvale, 07647-0914

Weichert Co (14), 1625 State Route 10, Morris Plains, 07950-2905

John Wiley & Sons Inc (17), 111 River St, Hoboken, 07030-5774

Window Coverings Exchange (8), 855 Rte 22, North Plainfield, 07060-3619

Wyndham Hotel Group (19), 1 Sylvan Way (fl 3), Parsippany, 07054-3887

Yellow Pages Association (1), 400 Connell Dr (Suite 1100), Connell Corp Park, Berkeley Heights, 07922-2818

New Mexico

American Society of Radiologic Technologists (1), 15000 Central Ave SE, Albuquerque, 87123-3909

The Bell Group Rio Grande (5), 7500 Bluewater Rd NW, Albuquerque, 87121-1962

ClingZ Inc (9), 541 Laser Dr NE, Rio Rancho, 87124-4518

Gallup Inter-tribal Indian Ceremonial (1), 202 W Coal Ave, Gallup, 87301-6306

Hooleon Corp (3), 304 W Denby Ave, Melrose, 88124

Indian Arts & Crafts Association (1), 4010 Carlisle NE (Suite C), Albuquerque, 87107

Indian House Records & Tapes (3), PO Box 472, Taos, 87571-0472

Rio Grande (16), 7500 Bluewater Rd NW, Albuquerque, 87121-1962

Santa Fe Natural Tobacco Co (16), PO Box 25140, Santa Fe, 87504-5140

Santa Fe School of Cooking (4), 116 W San Francisco St, Santa Fe, 87501

Sundancer Jewelry Co Inc (16), 5921 Office Blvd NE (Suite A), Albuquerque, 87109

New York

02Kl (4), 800 Westchester Ave (Suite S440), Rye Brook, 10573-1329

ABC Carpet & Home (8), 888 Broadway at E 19th St, New York, 10003-1280

ACN USA (1), 725 Leonard St, Brooklyn, 11222-2350

ADM Productions Inc (16), 40 Seaview Blvd, Port Washington, 11050-4618

AIG Accident & Health (15), 70 Pine St (50th fl), New York, 10270

AIG Marketing (15), 70 Pine St (40th fl), New York, 10270-0002

AIN Plastics Inc (16), 60 Fullerton Ave, Yonkers, 10704

Aon Consulting New York (15), 199 Water St (fl 12), New York, 10038-3541

APSCO (11), 7994 CR Ten, Davenport Center, 13751

ASPCA (1), 520 8th Ave (fl 7), New York, 10018-4195

AXA Equitable (15), 1290 Ave of the Americas (fl 7), New York, 10104-0101

Harry N Abrams Inc (17), 115 W 18th St (fl 5), New York, 10011-4113

Ace Communications (3), 625 Locust St Ste 300, Garden City, 11530-6557

Active Web Group (9), 30 Oser Ave (Suite 500), Hauppauge, 11788

Ad Infinitum Books (16), 7 N MacQuesten Pkwy, Mount Vernon, 10550-1811

Adirondack Direct (10), 3040 48th Ave, Long Island City, 11101

The Advertising Council Inc (1), 815 2nd Ave (Bsmt 815 2nd Ave), New York, 10017-4511

African Medical & Research Foundation Inc (AMREF USA) (1), 4 W 43rd St (fl 2), New York, 10036-7408

Air France (16), 125 W 55th St, New York, 10019

The Akadine Press Inc (16), 120 Bloomingdale Rd (Suite 100), White Plains, 10605-1522

Alitalia (19), 51 Madison Ave (Suite 2000), New York, 10010

All Star Carts & Vehicles (16), 1565-D Fifth Industrial Ct, Bay Shore, 11706-3434

Alliance Bernstein (14), 1345 Ave of the Americas, New York, 10105-0302

Alliance for the Arts (1), 330 W 42nd St (Suite 1701), New York, 10036-6902

ALSTOM Signaling Inc (16), 1025 John St, West Henrietta, 14586-9781

Amacom Books (17), 1601 Broadway, New York, 10019-7434

America Direct Book Service Custom Publishing (17), 1805 Spring Valley Rd, Ossining, 10562-1637

American Arbitration Association (1), 1633 Broadway Lowr 2C01, New York, 10019-6707

American Bible Society (1), 1865 Broadway, New York, 10023-7505

American Catalog Mailers Association (1), 188 Briarwood Dr, Somers, 10589-1810

American Civil Liberties Union Foundation (1), 125 Broad St (fl 18), New York, 10004-2454

American Express Co (14), 200 Vesey St (fl 47, New York, 10285-0002

American Express Publishing Corp (17), 1120 Avenue Of The Americas Fl 9, New York, 10036-6700

American Foundation for the Blind Inc (1), 2 Penn Plaza Rm 1102, New York, 10121-1100

American Institute of Chemical Engineers (1), 3 Park Ave, New York, 10016-5991

American Institute of CPAs (1), 1211 Avenue Of The Americas Ste 1900, New York, 10036-8702

American Institute of Physics (17), 2 Huntington Quadrangle (Suite 1NO1), Melville, 11747-4502

American International Group (15), 70 Pine St (fl 50), New York, 10270

American Kennel Club (17), 260 Madison Ave, New York, 10016-2401

American Lung Association (1), 21 W 38th St (fl 3), New York, 10018-2254

American Management Association (1), 1601 Broadway, New York, 10019-7434

American Movie Classics Holding Corp (16), 220 Jericho Quadrangle, Jericho, 11753

American National Standards Institute (1), 24 W 43rd St (fl 4), New York, 10036-7422

American Securities Capital Partners (15), 666 3rd Ave (fl 29), New York, 10017-4030

Amnesty International USA (1), Five Penn Plaza (fl 16), New York, 10001-1823

Amsterdam Printing (16), 166 Wallins Corners Rd, Amsterdam, 12010-1899

Andrea Electronics Corp (16), 65 Orville Dr (Suite 1), Bohemia, 11716-2517

Angel Records (3), 150 Fifth Ave, New York, 10011

The Angler's Den (11), 11 W Main St (Suite 4), Pawling, 12564-1341

The Animal Medical Center (16), 510 E 62nd St, New York, 10065-8314

Anne Klein (16), 1411 Broadway Rm 2002, New York, 10018-3762

Anti-Defamation League (1), 605 3rd Ave (fl 9), New York, 10158-0102

Antiquarian Booksellers Association of America Inc (1), 20 W 44th St, New York, 10036

Arbor Commercial Mortgage (14), 333 Earle Ovington Blvd, Uniondale, 11553-3610

Archaeology Magazine (17), 3636 33rd St, Long Island City, 11106

Argent Trading LLC (16), 521 5th Ave Rm 2200, New York, 10175-2900

Armento Inc (5), 1011 Military Rd, PO Box 39, Buffalo, 14217-0039

Art News Magazine (17), 48 W 38th St Fl 9, New York, 10018-0042

Arts & Entertainment Television Network (16), 235 E 45th St, New York, 10017

Aspen Publishers Inc (17), 111 Eighth Ave (fl 7), New York, 10011-5201

Associated Textile Rental Services (16), 548 Saint Paul St, Rochester, 14605-1735

Association for Computing Machinery (ACM) (1), 2 Penn Plaza (Rm 701), New York, 10121-0799

Assurant Group (15), 1 Chase Manhattan Plaza, New York, 10005-1401

Astoria Federal Savings (14), 1 Astoria Federal Plaza, Lake Success, 11042-1076

Astrologer's Fund Inc (16), 7913 Bay Pkwy (#A7), Brooklyn, 11214

At Last Naturals (7), PO Box 338, North Salem, 10560-0338

Atrinsic Inc (9), 469 7th Ave (fl 10), New York, 10018-7640

Audio Classics Ltd (3), 3501 Vestal Rd, Vestal, 13850-2244

Audiovox (16), 150 Marcus Blvd, Hauppauge, 11788-3794

Avon Books (17), 10 E 53rd St, New York, 10022-5244

Avon Products Inc (7), 1345 Ave of the Americas, New York, 10105-0302

Axis Capital (14), 430 Park Ave (fl 2), New York, 10022-3539

Bachrach Clothing Inc (2), 323 W 39th St (Fl 11), New York, 10018

Maurice Badler Fine Jewelry Ltd (2), 578 Fifth Ave, New York, 10036

Bantam Dell Publishing Group Inc (17), 1745 Broadway, New York, 10019

Barnes & Noble Direct (3), 76 9th Ave Fl 9, New York, 10011-4962

BarnesandNoble.com (16), 76 Ninth Ave (fl 9), New York, 10011

Bausch & Lomb Inc (16), 1 Bausch & Lomb Pl, Rochester, 14604-2701

BBC Worldwide Americas Inc (3), 1120 Ave of the Americas (Fl 5), New York, 10036-6700

BMG Columbia House (13), 1 Penn Plaza, New York, 10119-0002

BNY Mellon (14), 1 Wall St, New York, 10286

Beckmann Converting Inc (16), 14 Park Dr, PO Box 390, Amsterdam, 12010-5340

Bed Bath & Beyond (8), 110 Bi County Blvd (Suite 114), Farmingdale, 11735-3923

Benetton USA (2), 601 Fifth Ave, New York, 10017-1024

Bergdorf Goodman (2), 754 Fifth Ave, New York, 10019-2503

Better Health Fitness (11), 5302 New Utrecht Ave, Brooklyn, 11219-4139

The Bil-Ray Aluminum Siding Corp of Queens Inc (16), 102 Jericho Tpke, New Hyde Park, 11040-4507

Black Enterprise Magazine (17), 130 Fifth Ave (fl 10), New York, 10011-4399

Bliss World LLC (5), 75 Varick St (10th fl), New York, 10013-1917

Bloomingdale's By Mail Ltd (5), 919 Third Ave, New York, 10022

Bloomingdale's Direct (16), 1000 Third Ave (fl 11), New York, 10022

The Blue Book of Building & Construction (17), 800 E Main St, Jefferson Valley, 10535

Bobley-Harmann Corp/GiftValues.Com (5), 95 Hopper St (Unit 1), Westbury, 11590-4826

Bodyscapes Inc (2), 115 W 30th St (Rm 1202), New York, 10001-4041

Bookspan (13), 501 Franklin Ave, Garden City, 11530

Boundless Corp (16), 1916 State Route 96, Phelps, 14532-9705

The Bowery Mission (1), 132 Madison Ave, New York, 10016-7004

Brant Publications Inc (17), 575 Broadway, New York, 10012-3230

Bristol-Myers Squibb Co (16), 345 Park Ave, New York, 10154-0037

Broadway Books (17), 1745 Broadway, New York, 10019

Broadway Play Publishing Inc (17), 224 E 62nd St, New York, 10065-8201

Bronson Nutritionals LLC (7), 70 Commerce St, Hauppauge, 11788-3962

Bronx Council on the Arts (1), 1738 Hone Ave, Bronx, 10461-1486

Brooks Brothers (2), 346 Madison Ave (fl 10, New York, 10017-3788

Brotherhood America's Oldest Winery Ltd (19), 100 Brotherhood Plaza Dr, Washingtonville, 10992-2262

Arthur Brown & Bro Inc (10), 2 W 45th St Frnt 1, New York, 10036-4214

Tony Brown Productions (16), 2214 Frederick Douglass Blvd (Suite 124), New York, 10026

Burberry (2), 444 Madison Ave, New York, 10022-6903

Business Planners & Consultants Inc (15), 370 Lexington Ave (Suite 909), New York, 10017-6503

Cablevision Systems Corp (16), 111 Stewart Ave, Bethpage, 11714-3533

Cablexpress Technologies (10), 5404 S Bay Rd, Syracuse, 13212-3801

Cambridge Educational (12), 132 W 31st St Fl 17, New York, 10001-3406

Canyon Marketing (7), 43 Hunting Hollow Ct, Dix Hills, 11746-6166

Carestream Health Inc (7), 150 Verona St, Rochester, 14608

Catholic Charities - Brooklyn & Queens (1), 191 Joralemon St, Brooklyn, 11201-4306

Marshall Cavendish Corp (17), 99 White Plains Rd, Tarrytown, 10591-5502

Caviarteria New York Inc (4), 2584 Steinway St Ste A, Astoria, 11103-3706

CA Inc (16), 1 Ca Plz Ste 100, Islandia, 11749-5303

CDMO Inc (16), 40 Burt Dr Ste 5, PO Box 765, Deer Park, 11729-5743

CNY Awards & Apparel Inc (5), 33 New Hartford Shopping Center, New Hartford, 13413

CPAC Inc (16), 2364 Leicester Rd, Leicester, 14481

CPC Inc (19), 206 E Main St, PO Box 697, Babylon, 11702-0697

CSI (16), 1059 Powers Rd, Conklin, 13748-1400

Chanel Inc (16), Nine W 57th St, New York, 10019

Channel 13 WNET Catalog Division (5), 450 W 33rd St, New York, 10001-3302

Chartis (15), 70 Pine St (fl 22), New York, 10270-0001

Chem-Tainer Industries Inc (9), 361 Neptune Ave, North Babylon, 11704

Chemical Week (17), 140 E 45th St (Rm 4000), New York, 10017-9304

Chief Marketer and Multichannel Merchant (17), 249 W 17th St, New York, 10011-5390

Children's Aid Society (1), 105 E 22nd St (Rm 504), New York, 10010-5453

Choice Courier Systems Inc (16), 1 Whitehall St (fl 12), New York, 10004-2138

Christian Herald Association (1), 132 Madison Ave, New York, 10016-7004

Church Pension Fund (1), 445 5th Ave, New York, 07652-1461

Citi Cards / Citicorp Credit Services (14), 1 Court Sq, Long Island City, 11120-0001

Citibank (14), 399 Park Ave, New York, 10022-4699

Citigroup Inc (14), 399 Park Ave, New York, 10043-0001

Clemente Novelties Inc (16), 301 Lafayette St, Utica, 13502-4311

Cluett Peabody (16), 48 W 38th St, New York, 10018-6248

Coach (2), 516 W 34th St, New York, 10001-1394

Cockpit USA Inc (2), 15 W 39th St (#12), New York, 10018-0628

Cold Spring Harbor Lab Press (17), 500 Sunnyside Blvd, Woodbury, 11797-2924

Colgate-Palmolive Co (16), 300 Park Ave, New York, 10022-7412

Collector's Teapot (6), PO Box 1577, Kingston, 12402-1577

The College Board (1), 45 Columbus Ave, New York, 10023-6917

Colonial Redi-Record Corp (10), 1225 36th St, Brooklyn, 11218-2023

Columbia Journalism Review (17), 2950 Broadway Frnt 1, 201 Journalism Bldg, New York, 10027-7060

Columbia-Presbyterian Medical Center (16), 115 Central Park W, New York, 10023-4198

Columbia University, Annual Fund Programs (5), 622 W 113th St (MC4520), New York, 10025-7982

Columbian Mutual Life Insurance Co (15), Vestal Pkwy E, Binghamton, 13902-4600

Commercial Travelers Mutual Insurance Co (15), 70 Genesee St, Utica, 13502-3503

Compustar (3), 250 D Jericho Tpke, Mineola, 11501

Concern Worldwide (1), 355 Lexington Ave Fl 19, New York, 10017-6603

Conde Nast (17), 4 Times Sq, New York, 10036-6561

The Conference Board, Inc (16), 845 Third Ave, New York, 10022-6679

Conmio Inc (16), 570 Fashion Ave (Rm 1104), New York, 10018-1629

Consumers Union (17), 101 Truman Ave, Yonkers, 10703-1057

Cooper Vision (7), 370 Woodcliff Dr (Suite 200), Fairport, 14450

Cornell Lab of Ornithology (1), 159 Sapsucker Woods Rd, Ithaca, 14850-1923

Cosgrove Associates (14), 747 Third Ave (16th fl), New York, 10017-2803

Council on Foreign Relations Inc (17), 58 E 68th St, New York, 10021-5953

Covenant House International Headquarters (1), 5 Penn Plaza, New York, 10001-1810

Crohn's & Colitis Foundation of America (CCFA) (1), 386 Park Ave S (fl 17), New York, 10016-8804

Cuba Cheese Shoppe (4), 53 Genesee St, Cuba, 14727-1199

Cytec Industries Inc (16), 1405 Buffalo St, Olean, 14760-1139

David Dauber & Associates (16), 50 Lexington Ave (Suite 173), New York, 10010

Day Runner Direct (10), 101 Oneil Rd, Sidney, 13838-1055

DPC Computers (16), 42 Melnick Dr, Monsey, 10952

DealerTrack (14), 1111 Marcus Ave (Suite M04), New Hyde Park, 11042-1034

Dental Products Report (17), 641 Lexington Ave Fl 8, New York, 10022-4503

Destinations Ireland & Great Britain (19), PO Box 739, Rhinebeck, 12572

Deutsche Bank Alex Brown Inc (14), 60 Wall St, New York, 10005

Dial-A-Mattress (16), 1000 S Oyster Bay Rd, Hicksville, 11801-3527

Diamonds By Rennie Ellen (6), 15 W 47th St (Rm 503), New York, 10036

Didit (16), 330 Old Country Rd (Suite 206), Mineola, 11501-4143

The Dime Savings Bank of New York FSB (14), 209 Havemeyer St, Brooklyn, 11211

Dimmock Hill Golf Course Pro Shop (11), 638 Dimmock Hill Rd, Binghamton, 13905-9801

DineWise (4), 500 Bi-County Blvd (Suite 400), Farmingdale, 11735-3996

Christian Dior Perfumes (7), 21 E 57th St, New York, 10022-2506

Direct Brands Inc (13), W 34th St (fl 5), 1 Penn Plaza, New York, 10119-0002

Direct Marketing Association (1), 1120 Ave of the Americas, New York, 10036-6713

The Direct Marketing Club of New York Inc (1), 54 Adams St, Garden City, 11530-3918

Directory of American Business & Insurance Attorneys (15), 130 Church St (#303), New York, 10007-2906

Diversified Investment Advisors (14), PO Box 1000, Harrison, 10528-7000

Doctors Without Borders (1), 333 7th Ave (fl 2), New York, 10001-5089

DoubleVerify (9), 575 8th Ave (fl 7), New York, 10018-3186

Dover Publications Inc (17), 31 E Second St, Mineola, 11501

Dr Jays (2), 853 Broadway (Suite 1900), New York, 10003-4703

The Dreyfus Corp (14), 200 Park Ave, New York, 10166

Drug Policy Alliance (1), 131 W 33 St (fl 15), New York, 10001-2938

E-Z-EM Inc (7), 532 Broadhollow Rd Ste 126, Melville, 11747-3625

David Easton Inc (16), 5 Union Sq W (fl 3), New York, 10003-3315

The Economist Newspaper NA Inc (17), 750 3rd Ave (fl 5), New York, 10017

Economy Handicrafts (16), 932 46th St, Brooklyn, 11219

Edroy Products Co Inc (16), 245 N Midland Ave, PO Box 998, Nyack, 10960-0998

Educational Coin Co (16), PO Box 892, Highland, 12528-0892

EBA Wholesale Corp (3), 2361 Nostrand Ave, Brooklyn, 11210

EMED Co Inc (16), PO Box 369, Buffalo, 14240-0369

ESL Federal Credit Union (14), PO Box 92714, Rochester, 14692-8814

ESPN (5), 77 W 66th St (FL 4), New York, 10023-6201

Effective Promotions Inc (16), PO Box 210, Fort Johnson, 12070-0210

Elsevier (17), 360 Park Ave S, New York, 10010-1710

Emigrant Savings Bank (14), 5 E 42nd St, New York, 10017-6904

Empire Blue Cross & Blue Shield (15), 1 Liberty Plz (Suite 1300), New York, 10006-1419

Empire City Casino at Yonkers Raceway (19), 810 Yonkers Ave, Yonkers, 10704-2030

Empire Coffee & Tea Co (4), 568 9th Ave Frnt 1, New York, 10036-3726

Empire Scientific (16), 151 E Industry Ct, Deer Park, 11729-5713

Enterprise Ireland (16), 345 Park Ave (17th fl), New York, 10154-0037

Entertainment Music Marketing Corp (16), 795 Foxhurst Rd, Baldwin, 11510-3530

Episcopal Relief & Development (1), 815 2nd Ave (fl 7), New York, 10017-4503

Esquire Magazine (17), 300 W 57th St (21st fl), New York, 10019

Esselte Americas (16), 225 Broadhollow Rd, Melville, 11747-2340

Essence Communications Inc (17), 135 W 50th St (4th fl), New York, 10020-1201

Essential Products Co Inc (7), 90 Water St., New York, 10005-3511

Estee Lauder Inc (16), 767 Fifth Ave, New York, 10153

Executive Enterprises Inc (16), 12 Skyline Dr, Hawthorne, 10532-2133

Eyeglass Service Industries (2), 481 Sunrise Hwy, Lynbrook, 11563-3017

Facts On File Inc (17), 132 W 31st St (17th fl), New York, 10001

Fairchild Books (17), 750 Third Ave, New York, 10017

Fairchild Publications (17), 750 Third Ave, New York, 10017-2703

Farrar Straus & Giroux Inc (17), 18 W 18th St Fl 7, New York, 10011-4675

Fashion Institute of Technology Library (1), 227 W 27th St, Library Room (E619), New York, 10001-5902

Ferguson Publishing Co (17), 132 W 31st St (17 fl), New York, 10001-3406

Ferrara Bakery & Cafe Inc (4), 195 Grand St, New York, 10013

The FX Matt Brewing Co (4), 830 Varick St, Utica, 13502

FAO Schwarz (11), 767 Fifth Ave, New York, 10153

FCIA Management Co Inc (15), 125 Park Ave (fl 14), New York, 10017-5529

FT Publications Inc (17), 1330 Ave of the Americas, New York, 10019

Fifth Avenue Committee (1), 621 De-Graw St, Brooklyn, 11217

Films Media Group (3), 132 W 31st St Fl 17, New York, 10001-3406

Michael C Fina (6), 545 5th Ave Frnt, New York, 10017-3616

Financial Times (17), 1330 Avenue of the Americas, New York, 10019-5436

Fine Architectural Metalsmiths (16), PO Box 30, Chester, 10918

Carl Fischer Music (17), 65 Bleecker St Fl 8, New York, 10012-2420

Fisher-Price (16), 636 Girard Ave, East Aurora, 14052-1824

Fluid Metering Inc (16), 5 Aeriel Way (Suite 500), Syosset, 11791-5593

Forbes Inc (17), 60 Fifth Ave (corner of 12th St), New York, 10011-8868

Ford Foundation Office of Communications (5), 320 E 43rd St, New York, 10017-4816

Forum Publishing Co (17), 383 E Main St, Centerport, 11721-1538

Four Directions Media (17), 579 Main St, Oneida, 13421

Four Seasons Sunrooms (8), 5005 Veterans Memorial Hwy, Holbrook, 11741

Fowler's Chocolates Inc (4), 100 River Rock Dr (Suite 102), Buffalo, 14207-2163

Larry Fox & Co Ltd (16), PO Box 729, Valley Stream, 11582-0729

Franciscan Friars of the Atonement - Graymoor (1), Rte Nine, Garrison, 10524

Franciscan Mission Associates (1), 274-280 W Lincoln Ave, Mount Vernon, 10550-2509

Freeport Music Inc (11), 65 Clove Ave, Farmingville, 11738-1630

French Trade Office Embassy of France (1), 1700 Broadway Ste 3201, New York, 10019-5925

FreshDirect (5), 23-30 Borden Ave, Long Island City, 11101-4515

A I Friedman Inc (10), 44 W 18th St, New York, 10011

Frontier Corp (16), 180 S Clinton Ave, Rochester, 14646-0002

Fuji Photo Film USA (16), 200 Summit Lake Dr, Valhalla, 10595-1356

G H Bass & Co (16), 200 Madison Ave, New York, 10016-3903

G2 Promotional Marketing (16), 200 5th Ave Bsmt B, New York, 10010-3313

Galen Williams Landscaping & Garden Design (16), Seven Oyster Shores Rd, East Hampton, 11937-1103

The Gallery Shop (6), 1285 Elmwood Ave, Albright-Knox Art Gallery, Buffalo, 14222-1096

Gay Men's Health Crisis (1), 446 W 33rd St, New York, 10001-2601

Gaylord Brothers (16), PO Box 4901, Syracuse, 13221-4901

Gebbie Press Inc (17), PO Box 1000, New Paltz, 12561-0017

Genium Publishing (17), 79 The Mall, Amsterdam, 12010

Gerber Life Insurance Co (15), 1311 Mamaroneck Ave, White Plains, 10605-5221

GMG Productions Inc (3), 346 Baltustrol Cir, Roslyn, 11576-3058

Girl Scouts of the USA (1), 420 Fifth Ave, New York, 10018-2729

Glens Falls Hospital Foundation (1), 126 South St, Glens Falls, 12801-4321

Glenview Capital Management (14), 767 Fifth Ave (fl 44), New York, 10153-0023

Global Computer Corp (3), 11 Harbor Park Dr, Port Washington, 11050-4602

Global Equipment Co Inc (9), 11 Harbor Park Dr, Port Washington, 11050

Go Promos (5), PO Box 272, Gloversville, 12078

Godiva Chocolatier (4), 333 W 34th St Fl 6, New York, 10001-2566

Gold Medal Hair Products Inc (7), 104 Allen Blvd Ste H, Farmingdale, 11735-5627

Goodman Media Group Inc (17), 250 W 57th St (Suite 710), New York, 10107

Government of India Tourist Office (1), 1270 Ave of the Americas (Suite 1808), New York, 10020-1700

Grandma Brown's Beans Inc (4), 5837 Scenic Ave, Mexico, 13114

Green River Trading Co (8), 578 Boston Corners Rd, Millerton, 12546

Gridley & Co LLC (14), 10 E 53rd St (fl 24), New York, 10022-5070

Gruppo Levey & Co (14), 122 E 42nd St (fl 46), New York, 10168-0002

The Guardian Life Insurance Co (15), 7 Hanover Sq (fl 14), New York, 10004-4013

Guiding Eyes for the Blind (16), 611 Granite Springs Rd, Yorktown Heights, 10598

Guilford Publications Inc (17), 72 Spring St (4th fl), New York, 10012-4050

Hachette Filipacchi List Management (17), 1633 Broadway (fl 43), New York, 10019-6708

Hain Celestial Group (16), 58 S Service Rd, Melville, 11747

Hammacher Schlemmer (16), 147 E 57th St, New York, 10022

Hammond World Atlas Corp (17), 245 Park Ave (Fl 24), New York, 10167-2499

Hampshire Agency (14), 33 Great Neck Rd (#7), Great Neck, 11021-3335

Hampton Marketing Corp (16), 19 Industrial Blvd, Medford, 11763

Harbour Bay Inc (16), 70 Orange Ave, Suffern, 10901

HarperCollins (17), 10 E 53rd St (fl Cellar 2), New York, 10022-5299

Harper's Magazine (17), 666 Broadway (11th fl), New York, 10012

Harris Connect LLC (1), 1511 Route 22 (Suite C25), Brewster, 19047-1706

HAVE Inc (3), 350 Power Ave, Hudson, 12534-2448

Haymarket Group Ltd (17), 12 W 37th St, New York, 10018-7480

HealthRight International (1), 80 Maiden Ln, New York, 10038-4811

The Hearst Corp (17), 300 W 57th St, New York, 10019-3741

Hearst Magazines (17), 300 W 57th St (fl 19), New York, 10019-3741

Hermes of Paris (2), 55 E 59th St (front 2), New York, 10022

HSBC Bank USA, NA (14), PO Box 643, Buffalo, 14240-0643

Tommy Hilfiger (2), 601 W 26th St Rm 500, New York, 10001-1142

Hobart & William Smith Colleges (19), 629 S Main St, Geneva, 14456-3165

Hoke Communications Inc (17), 54 Adams St, Garden City, 11530

Homespun Tapes Music Instruction (3), PO Box 340, Woodstock, 12498-0340

House of Oldies (6), 35 Carmine St Frnt 1, New York, 10014-4429

F.M. Howell & Co (16), 79 Pennsylvania Ave, Elmira, 14902-1455

IBM Corp (16), 1 New Orchard Rd, Armonk, 10504-1725

IDMS Inc (16), 560 Broadhollow Rd (Suite 109), Melville, 11747-3702

INC Magazine (17), Seven World Trade Center, New York, 10007

Independent Living Aids (7), 200 Robbins Ln (Unit A), Jericho, 11753-2341

Indium Corp of America (16), 34 Robinson Rd, Clinton, 13323-1419

Institute for International Research Inc (16), 708 Third Ave (4th fl), New York, 10017-4103

Institute for Student Achievement (1), 1 Old Country Rd Ste 250, Carle Place, 11514-1818

Institute of Business Forecasting (1), 350 Northern Blvd (Suite 203), Great Neck, 11021-4809

Institutional Advancement Programs Inc (1), 35 Park View Ave (Suite 4A), Bronxville, 10708-2953

Institutional Investor Inc (17), 225 Park Ave S, New York, 10003

Instructor's Choice Dancewear (2), 5020 Sunrise Hwy, Massapequa Park, 11762-2913

International Advertising Association (1), 275 Madison Ave (Suite 2102), World Service Center, New York, 10016-1118

International Collectors Society (6), 9700 Mill St, Camden, 13316-6109

International Irrigation Systems (8), 1755 Factory Outlet Blvd, PO Box 163, Niagara Falls, 14304-0163

International Planned Parenthood Federation Western Hemisphere Region Inc (1), 125 Maiden Ln (9th Fl), New York, 10038-5063

Itochu Chemicals America Inc (16), 360 Hamilton Ave (Suite 610), White Plains, 10601-1842

J&R Music/J&R Computer World (3), 23 Park Row, New York, 10038-2302

JP Morgan Chase & Co (14), 270 Park Ave (10th fl), New York, 10017-2070

The Jordan Edmiston Group Inc (14), 150 E 52nd St (18th fl), New York, 10022-6260

The Journal News (17), One Gannett Dr, White Plains, 10604

Junior's Cheesecake (16), 386 Flatbush Ave Ext at Dekalb Ave, Brooklyn, 11238

Juvenile Diabetes Research Foundation (1), 26 Broadway (fl 14), New York, 10004-1838

Kaplan Inc (16), 395 Hudson St (Rm 400), New York, 10014-7455

Kaplan Test Prep & Admissions (1), 395 Hudson St., New York, 10014

Kensington Publishing Corp (17), 119 W 40th St (fl 21), New York, 10018-2522

Key Bank National Association (14), 19 Corporate Woods Blvd, Albany, 12211-2345

Keyspan Energy Corp (16), 1 Metrotech Ctr Fl 1, Brooklyn, 11201-3949

Kikucall (3), 14 Wall St Fl 15, New York, 10005-2139

King Features (17), 300 West 57th St (fl 15), New York, 10019-3741

Calvin Klein Cosmetics Co (7), 205 W 39th St, New York, 10018-3102

Knoll Group (16), 76 Ninth Ave (11th fl), New York, 10011

KozaK Auto Drywash Inc (16), Eight S Lyon St, Batavia, 14020-1802

Kraft Foods/Gevalia Kaffe (16), 555 S Broadway, Tarrytown, 10591-6301

Lancer Insurance Co (15), PO Box 9004, Long Beach, 11561-9004

Latest Products Corp (7), 36 Orchard Dr, Woodbury, 11797-2830

Leadership Directories Inc (17), 104 Fifth Ave, New York, 10011

Leadership Software Corp (16), PO Box 725, Nyack, 10960

League of American Orchestras (1), 33 W 60th St (5th fl), New York, 10023-7905

Leucadia National Corp (14), 315 Park Ave S (20th fl), New York, 10010

The Leukemia & Lymphoma Society (1), 1311 Mamaroneck Ave, White Plains, 10605-5228

Lexington Luggage Limited (19), 793 Lexington Ave Frnt 1, New York, 10065-8161

Lexis Nexis Matthew Bender (17), 1275 Broadway, Albany, 12204-2628

The Library of America (13), 14 E 60th St Ste 1101, New York, 10022-7115

Life Technologies (9), 3175 Staley Rd, Grand Island, 14072-2028

Lifetime Brands Inc (8), 1000 Stewart Ave, Garden City, 11530

A Liss & Co Inc (16), 51-55 59th Pl, Woodside, 11377-7408

Listening Library Inc, Random House Audio (3), 1745 Broadway, New York, 10019

Live Design (17), 249 W 17th St, New York, 10011

LGP GEM LTD (16), 10 W 46th St (Suite 4A), New York, 10036-4515

LIM College (1), 12 E 53rd St, New York, 10022-5268

Loehmann's (2), 2500 Halsey St, Bronx, 10461-3637

Loews Hotels (19), 667 Madison Ave (7th fl), New York, 10065-8087

Lufthansa German Airlines (19), 1640 Hempstead Tpke, East Meadow, 11554

M&M Health Care Apparel Co (2), 1541 60th St, Brooklyn, 11219-5023

Macy's Marketing (16), 151 W 34th St (fl 17), New York, 10001-2101

Madisonavegifts.com (6), 325 Barben Ave, Watertown, 13601-4503

Magazine Publishers of America (17), 810 Seventh Ave (fl 24), New York, 10019-5873

Magnaplan Corp (10), 1320 State Rte 9 (#3314), Champlain, 12919-5412

Magnatag Visable Systems (16), 2031 O'Neill Rd, Macedon, 14502-8953

MALM Chemical Corp (16), Dept WEB-5, PO Box 300, Pound Ridge, 10576-0300

EF Maloney Inc (16), 257 Mamaroneck Ave (Suite 208), Mamaroneck, 10543-2686

The Maloney Group (16), Five E 22nd St, New York, 10010-5315

Mane Solutions (16), 314 Fifth Ave, New York, 10001-3606

Manhattan College (1), Manhattan College Pkwy, Bronx, 10471-3915

March of Dimes Birth Defects Foundation (1), 1275 Mamaroneck Ave, White Plains, 10605

Markertek Video Supply (3), One Tower Dr, PO Box 397, Saugerties, 12477-4386

Maryknoll Fathers & Brothers (1), PO Box 304, Maryknoll, 10545-0304

WB Mason Co (16), 53 23rd St (fl 10), New York, 10010-4234

MasterCard Worldwide (14), 2000 Purchase St, Purchase, 10577

Mastervision Inc (16), 969 Park Ave, New York, 10028

The McGraw-Hill Cos (17), 1221 Ave of the Americas, New York, 10020-1095

McGruff Specialty Products Office (16), 1 Prospect St, Amsterdam, 12010

Medco Supply Co Inc (7), 500 Fillmore Ave, Tonawanda, 14150

Medical Letter Inc (1), 145 Huguenot St (Suite 312), New Rochelle, 10801-7537

Memorial Sloan Kettering Cancer Center (1), 633 3rd Ave, New York, 10017-6706

Merisel (16), 127 W 30th St (5th fl), New York, 10001

Merrill Lynch (14), 250 Vesey St (4th fl), Four World Financial Center, New York, 10080-0002

MetLife International (15), 2701 Queens Plaza N (#4E-148), Long Island City, 11101-4020

Metropolis Magazine (2), 61 W 23rd St (4th fl), New York, 10010

Metropolitan Museum of Art (8), 6 E 82nd St, New York, 10028-0304

The Metropolitan Opera (1), 3 Lincoln Center, Metropolitan Opera House, New York, 10023-7230

Microvideo Learning Systems, Inc (3), 208 E 51st St (#273), New York, 10022-6500

JE Miller Nurseries Inc (8), 5060 W Lake Rd, Canandaigua, 14424-8952

Mini City Ltd (12), 799 Holt Rd Ste 170, Webster, 14580-9188

Minnetonka By Mail (2), 229 City Island Ave., Bronx, 10464

Frank Mittermeier Inc (11), PO Box 2, Bronx, 10465-0001

MGI Management Institute (16), 12 Skyline Dr, Hawthorne, 10532

MJA International (7), 9 Roslyn Dr, Glen Head, 11545

MSC Industrial Supply Co (9), 75 Maxess Rd, Melville, 11747-3151

Modernage Custom Digital Imaging Labs (16), 555 8th Ave (Rm 2003), New York, 10018-4651

Mohawk Lifts (9), 65 Vrooman Ave, PO Box 110, Amsterdam, 12010

Jacques Moret Inc (16), 1411 Broadway (fl 8), New York, 10018

Morgan Stanley (14), 1585 Broadway, New York, 10036

Moritt, Hock, Hamroff & Horowitz (16), 400 Garden City Plaza, Garden City, 11530-3327

Motown Records (3), 1755 Broadway (fl 6), New York, 10019-3768

Murphy Bed Co Inc (8), 42 Central Ave, Farmingdale, 11735

Museum Masters Inc (16), 185 E 85th St (Suite 27B), New York, 10028

The Museum of Modern Art (5), 11 W 53rd St, New York, 10019-5497

Music Barn Inc (6), PO Box 1083, Niagara Falls, 14304-0383

Music Sales Corp (17), 257 Park Ave S Fl 20, New York, 10010-7304

Mutual of America Life Insurance Co (14), 320 Park Ave, New York, 10022-6839

Mystic Stamp Co Inc (16), 9700 Mill St, Camden, 13316

NAR Productions (17), PO Box 233, Barryville, 12719-0233

National Association for Female Executives (NAFE) (1), 2 Park Ave Fl 10, New York, 10016-5604

National Audubon Society (17), 225 Varick St (7 fl), New York, 10014-4396

National Crime Prevention Council (17), One Prospect St, Amsterdam, 12010

National League for Nursing (1), 61 Broadway (fl 33), New York, 10006-2800

National Medical Fellowships (1), 347 5th Ave (Suite 510), New York, 10016-5007

National Review (17), 215 Lexington Ave, New York, 10016

Nationwide Beauty & Barber Supply (16), 2600 Erie Blvd E, Syracuse, 13224-1287

Nationwide Displays Inc (16), 100 Christopher St, Ronkonkoma, 11779

Nature Publishing Group (17), 75 Varick St (fl 9), New York, 10013-1917

Navitar Inc (16), 200 Commerce Dr, Rochester, 14623-3506

Neighborhood Cleaners Association International (1), 252 W 29th St, New York, 10001

Neuberger & Berman Management (14), 605 3rd Ave (fl 21), New York, 10158-3698

New Directions Publishing Corp (17), 80 Eighth Ave (19th fl), New York, 10011-7146

New Wave Media Inc (5), 915 Broadway (Suite 1301), New York, 10010

New York & Co (2), 450 W 33rd St (fl 5), New York, 10001-2632

New York Blood Center Inc (1), 310 E 67th St, New York, 10021

New York Easter Seal Society (1), 40th W 37th St (Suite 503), New York, 10018-7345

New York Findings (6), 17625 Union Tpke, PMB 402, Fresh Meadows, 11366-1515

New York Foundation For The Arts (1), 20 Jay St Ste 740, Brooklyn, 11201-8352

New York Landmarks Conservancy (1), One Whitehall St, New York, 10004

New York Philharmonic (1), 10 Lincoln Ctr Plaza, Avery Fisher Hall, New York, 10023-6970

New York Power Authority (16), 30 S Pearl St (10th fl), Albany, 12207-3425

New York Road Runners Club, Inc (13), Nine E 89th St, New York, 10128-0602

The New York Times Co (17), 620 8th Ave, New York, 10018-1618

New York University Medical Center (1), 550 First Ave, New York, 10016

New York University (1), 11 W 42nd St (Rm 431), New York, 10036-8083

The New Yorker Magazine (17), Four Times Sq, New York, 10036

Newport News (2), 110 William St (11th Fl), New York, 10038-3945

News America Publishing Inc (17), 1211 Ave of the Americas, New York, 10036

Newsday (17), 235 Pinelawn Rd, Melville, 11747-4250

Newsweek Inc (17), 555 W 18th St # 2, New York, 10011-2822

Nielsen Business Media (16), 770 Broadway, New York, 10003

The Nielsen Co (17), 770 Broadway, New York, 10003-9595

Nightingale Resources (17), 6 Chestnut St, Cold Spring, 10516-2517

Nihon Keizai Shimbun America Inc (17), 1325 Ave of the Americas (Suite 2500), New York, 10019

NBTY Inc (7), 2100 Smithtown Ave, Ronkonkoma, 11779-7347

NYSARC, Inc (1), 393 Delaware Ave, Delmar, 12054

North Shore Animal League America Inc (1), 750 Port Washington Blvd, Port Washington, 11050-3720

Northern Safety Co Inc (16), PO Box 4250, Utica, 13504-4250

NutraOrigin (7), 1983 Marcus Ave (Suite 206), Lake Success, 11042-1016

Nyrev Inc (17), 435 Hudson St (Suite 300), New York, 10014-3949

Old World Mouldings Inc (9), 821 Lincoln Ave, Bohemia, 11716

Oliver Wyman (14), 1166 Avenue of the Americas, New York, 10036-2726

1-800-Flowers.com (16), 1 Old Country Rd (Suite 500), Carle Place, 11514-1847

1000 Islands International Tourism Council (19), 43373 Collins Landing Rd, Alexandria Bay, 13607-2210

One World Projects (6), 43 Ellicott Ave, Batavia, 14020-2010

Oneida Ltd (16), 163-181 Kenwood Ave, Oneida, 13421-2829

Oppenheimer Funds (14), 225 Liberty St (fl 11), 2 World Financial Ctr, New York, 10281-1005

Orbis Books (17), PO Box 302, Price Bldg, Maryknoll, 10545-0302

Our Lady of Victory Homes of Charity (1), 780 Ridge Rd, Lackawanna, 14218-1682

Oxford University Press Inc (17), 198 Madison Ave Fl 8, New York, 10016-4308

Pace University - Div of Enrollment Mgmt (16), Pace Plaza, New York, 10038-1598

Parkinson's Disease Foundation (1), 710 West 168th St., New York, 10032

Patient News (17), 3909 Witmer Rd (#1080), Niagara Falls, 14305-1239

Penguin Publishing Group (17), 375 Hudson St Bsmt 3, New York, 10014-7465

Penguin Putnam Inc (17), 375 Hudson St, New York, 10014-3672

Pensions & Investments (17), 711 3rd Ave, New York, 10017-4014

Penton Learning Systems Inc (16), 535 Fifth Ave (fl 8), New York, 10017-8011

Pernod Ricard USA (16), 100 Manhattanville Rd., Purchase, 10577-2134

Peter Pauls Nurseries (8), 4665 Chapin Rd, Canandaigua, 14424-8720

Petsky Prunier LLC (14), 60 Broad St Ste 3810, New York, 10004-2329

Pfizer Inc (16), 235 E 42nd St, New York, 10017

Phillips-Van Heusen Corp (2), 200 Madison Ave (Bsmt 1), New York, 10016-3913

Planned Parenthood Federation of America (1), 434 W 33rd St, New York, 10001-2600

Pontifical Mission Societies in the US (1), 70 W 36th St (fl 8), New York, 10018-1256

Practicing Law Institute (16), 810 7th Ave (fl 21), New York, 10019-5856

Premier Packaging Corp (16), 6 Framark Dr, PO Box 352, Victor, 14564-1136

ST Preston & Son Inc (8), 102 Main St Wharf, Greenport, 11944-1422

PricewaterhouseCoopers LLP (14), 300 Madison Ave (fl 24), New York, 10017

Profile Coverage Corp (15), PO Box 9081, Melville, 11747-9081

Profile Mailing Service Inc (16), 575 Underhill Blvd (Suite 132), Syosset, 11791-3416

Projector-Recorder Belt Corp (3), 3375 Royal Ave, Oceanside, 11572-4812

Promo Magazine (17), 249 W 17th St (3rd fl), New York, 10011

Promotion Marketing Association (PMA) Inc (1), 650 1st Ave Fl 2, New York, 10016-3207

Publishers Clearing House (18), 382 Channel Dr, Port Washington, 11050-2297

Puritan's Pride (7), 2100 Smithtown Ave, Ronkonkoma, 11779-7347

Putnam Rolling Ladder Co Inc (5), 32 Howard St, New York, 10013-3112

Quadriga Art Inc (10), 30 E 33rd St, New York, 10016-5317

Random House Children's Books (13), 1745 Broadway, New York, 10019

Random House Direct Marketing (17), 1745 Broadway, New York, 10019-4305

The Reader's Digest Association Inc (17), 750 3rd Ave, New York, 10017-2703

Recognition Systems (Dot Works) (16), 30 Harbor Park Dr, Port Washington, 11050

Redbook Magazine (17), 300 W 57th St, New York, 10019

Redcats USA (2), 463 Fashing Ave (Rm 1603), New York, 10018-7421

JP Redington & Co (16), PO Box 429, Huntington, 11743

Reed - Elsevier (17), 125 Park Ave Fl 22, New York, 10017-8503

Reliable Racing Supply (11), 643 Upper Glen St (Suite B), Queensbury, 12804-2014

REMEDY Magazine (17), 500 Fifth Ave (Suite 1900), New York, 10110

Research To Prevent Blindness Inc (1), 645 Madison Ave (fl 21), New York, 10022-1010

Resorts Worldwide Inc (19), 1111 Westchester Ave, White Plains, 10604-3525

Retawmatic Corp (9), 14911 41st Ave, Flushing, 11355-1025

Rich Products Corp (16), One Robert Rich Way, Buffalo, 14213-1701

Pete Rickard Inc (11), 115 Roy Walsh Rd, Cobleskill, 12043-4422

Right On Computer Software (3), 27 Bowdon Rd, Greenlawn, 11740-1901

Rizzoli International Publications Inc (17), 300 Park Ave S (3rd fl), New York, 10010

Robinson Home Products (16), 2615 Walden Ave, PO Box 550, Buffalo, 14225-0550

The Roblin Group Inc (17), 405 Tarrytown Rd (Suite 1545), White Plains, 10607

Rochester Institute of Technology (1), 55 Lomb Memorial Dr, Rochester, 14623-5602

RocketWear (2), 101 W 57th St (#15 D), New York, 10019

Ross Metals (16), 27 W 47 St, New York, 10036-2806

Row Resources Inc (16), 260 Main St (Ste 110), Northport, 11768-1738

Rush Industries, Inc (16), 263 Horton Hwy, Mineola, 11501-2255

Ruskin, Moscou, Faltischek, PC (16), 190 EAB Plaza (15th fl East Tower), Uniondale, 11556

St Joseph's College (1), 245 Clinton Ave, Brooklyn, 11205-3602

Saks Fifth Avenue (16), 12 E 49th St (fl 2), New York, 10017-1088

Sales & Marketing Management Magazine (16), 770 Broadway, New York, 10003

Salesian Missions (1), 2 Lefevre Ln, New Rochelle, 10801-5710

Sanky Communications Inc (1), 599 11th Ave Fl 6, New York, 10036-2110

The Sausage Maker Inc (4), 1500 Clinton St (Suite 123), Buffalo, 14206-3099

Henry Schein Inc (16), 135 Duryea Rd, Melville, 11747-3834

Scholastic Inc (17), 557 Broadway, New York, 10012-3919

Sesame Workshop (1), 1 Lincoln Plaza, New York, 10023-7163

JA Sexauer (16), 570 Taxter Rd (#230), Elmsford, 10523-2365

The Sharper Image (6), 1450 Broadway Fl 4, New York, 10018-2204

Sherman Specialty Toy Co Inc (16), 300 Jericho Quadrangle (Suite 240), Jericho, 11753-2719

Shiseido Cosmetics America (7), 900 Third Ave (15th fl), New York, 10022

Showtime Networks Inc (16), 1633 Broadway, New York, 10019

Signature Styles LLC (2), 110 Willaim St (11th Fl), New York, 10038-3945

Simmons-Boardman Publishing Corp (17), 345 Hudson St Rm 1201, New York, 10014-7115

Simon & Schuster Inc (17), 1230 Ave of the Americas, New York, 10020

Simplicity Pattern Co Inc/Style Patterns Ltd/New Look English Pattern Co Ltd (8), 261 Madison Ave (fl 4), New York, 10016-3906

Sleepy's Inc (16), 1000 S Oyster Bay Rd, Hicksville, 11801-3527

Slifter (16), 307 7th Ave (Room 2104), New York, 10001-6089

The Smile Train (1), 41 Madison Ave Rm 2801, New York, 10010-2325

Smithsonian Enterprises (17), 420 Lexington Ave, New York, 10170-0002

Peter J Solomon Co (14), 520 Madison Ave (fl 29), New York, 10022-4385

Sony DADC (3), 555 Madison Ave (#1810), New York, 10022-3301

Sotheby's (6), 1334 York Ave at 72nd St, New York, 10021-4806

Spa-Finder Inc (7), 257 Park Ave S (10th fl), New York, 10010

Huck Spaulding Enterprises (16), Rte 85, New Scotland Rd, Voorheesville, 12186

Spectronics Corp (9), 956 Brush Hollow Rd, Westbury, 11590-1731

Spiegel Brands Inc (2), 110 William St (11th Fl), New York, 10038-3945

Spinneybeck Enterprises (16), 425 Crosspoint Pkwy (Suite 100), Getzville, 14068-1609

Spoken Arts (17), 195 S White Rock Rd, Holmes, 12531-5406

Springer Science & Business Media LLC (17), 233 Spring St, New York, 10013

Springs Global Inc (16), 110 5th Ave (fl 5), New York, 10011-5647

SIFMA (1), 120 Broadway (fl 35), New York, 10271-0080

Standard & Poor's Corp (17), 55 Water St, New York, 10041-0004

Stellar Technology Inc (9), 237 Commerce Dr, Amherst, 14228-2302

Sterling Publishing Co Inc (17), 387 Park Ave S (5th fl), New York, 10016-8898

Steuben Glass (6), 667 Madison Ave Lowr Level, New York, 10065-8029

Martha Stewart Living Omnimedia (17), 601 W 26th St (Fl 9), New York, 10001-1101

Stock Drive Products (5), 2101 Jericho Tpke, New Hyde Park, 11040

Stokes Seeds Inc (8), PO Box 548, Buffalo, 14240-0548

Store Smart Express/Visual Horizons (16), 180 Metro Park, Rochester, 14623-2610

Paul Stuart (2), Madison Ave & 45th St, New York, 10017

Sunbilt Creative Sunrooms (8), 109-10 180th St, Jamaica, 11433-2622

Sunrise Business Products (10), 69 E Jericho Tpke, Mineola, 11501

Sunshine Glassworks Ltd (11), 111 Industrial Pkwy, Buffalo, 14227-2712

Sussex Publishers Inc (17), 115 E 23rd St (9th fl), New York, 10010

Syracuse University (1), 820 Comstock Ave, Syracuse, 13244-0001

Systemax Inc (16), 11 Harbor Park Dr, Port Washington, 11050

Talas (10), 330 Morgan Ave, Brooklyn, 11211

Ann Taylor Inc (2), 7 Times Square Tower (Fl 14), New York, 10036

Team Cheer (2), 131 Main St Ste 2, Geneseo, 14454-1242

Theatre Development Fund Inc (1), 520 8th Ave (Suite 801), New York, 10018-6507

Thieme Medical Publishers Inc (17), 333 7th Ave Rm 500, New York, 10001-5122

Things Deco (6), 130 E 18th St (Suite 8F), New York, 10003-2416

Thirteen/WNET (1), 450 W 33rd St, New York, 10001

Thomson Financial (17), 195 Broadway Fl 4, New York, 10007-3124

Thomson Reuters LPC (14), 3 Times Sq, New York, 10036

Tiffany & Co (6), 600 Madison Ave Fl 4, New York, 10022-1689

Time Inc (17), 1271 6th Ave, New York, 10020-1300

Time Out New York (18), 475 10th Ave (12th fl), New York, 10018

Time Warner Inc (16), 1 Time Warner Ctr, New York, 10019-8016

Times Union (18), Box 15000, News Plaza, Albany, 12212

Todaro Brothers Mail Order Co (4), 555 Second Ave, New York, 10016

Torah Umesorah Publications (5), 1090 Coney Island Ave (Suite 4), Brooklyn, 11203-2341

The Townsend Group (3), 616 W 207th St (Suite 4E), New York, 10034-2638

Transcat (16), 35 Vantage Point Dr, Rochester, 14624-1175

Transit Treasure Inc (12), 311 E 38th St (Suite 19B), New York, 10016

TransitCenter Inc (1), 1065 Avenue of the Americas, New York, 10018-1878

Travel Planners Inc (19), 381 Park Ave S, New York, 10016

Treasure Chest (19), 304 Park Ave S, New York, 10010-4301

Triumph Learning (17), 136 Madison Ave (fl 7), New York, 10016-6711

Trump University (13), 40 Wall St Ste 3200, New York, 10005-1332

The Trumpet Club (17), 578 Broadway (Rm 807), New York, 10012

truTV (17), 1 Time Warner Ctr (bsmt), New York, 10019-6010

TCJC (2), 40 W 37th St Ph A, New York, 10018-7415

Thomson Reuters (17), 195 Broadway Fl 4, New York, 10007-3124

TIAA-CREF (15), 730 Third Ave, New York, 10017

Unadilla Laminated Products (16), 32 Clifton St, Unadilla, 13849

Union Pen Co (5), PO Box 220, Hagaman, 12086-0220

United Business Media (17), 600 Community Dr Ste 1, Manhasset, 11030-3818

United Jewish Communities (1), 25 Broadway Fl 17, New York, 10004-1015

United Nations Federal Credit Union (1), 2401 44th Rd (fl 7) Ct Sq Pl, Long Island City, 11101-4605

United Spinal Association (1), 7520 Astoria Blvd, East Elmhurst, 11370-1138

United Staffing Systems (16), 130 William St Fl 6, New York, 10038-5068

United States Bronze Sign Co Inc (1), 811 Second Ave, New Hyde Park, 11040

US Digital Transactions Corporation (14), 228 Park Ave S, New York, 10003-1502

US Fund for UNICEF (6), 125 Maiden Ln, New York, 10038-4912

US News & World Report (17), 4 New York Plz Fl 6, New York, 10004-2473

United States Tennis Association (1), 70 W Red Oak Ln, White Plains, 10604-3610

Unitron Ltd (9), 73 Mall Dr, Commack, 11725-5703

University at Buffalo Center for Entrepreneurial Leadership (5), 672 Delaware Ave, Buffalo, 14209-2202

Urbani Truffles USA Corp (4), 10 West End Ave, New York, 10023

UJA/Federation of New York (1), 130 E 59th St, New York, 10022-1302

UNICEF (1), 3 United Nations Plaza, New York, 10017-4486

Valdawn Watch Co (16), 2910 Thomson Ave (6th fl), Long Island City, 11101-2939

Value Line Publishing Inc (17), 220 E 42nd St, New York, 10017

Van Dam Inc (17), 11 W 20th St Fl 4, New York, 10011-3704

Vanderbilt Advertising (14), 220 E 42nd St, New York, 10017-5806

Vector Marketing Corp (5), 1116 E State St, Olean, 14760-3814

Venator Group (2), 112 W 34th St, New York, 10020

Verizon Communications Inc (3), 140 West St LBBY 1, New York, 10007-2123

Veronis Suhler Stevenson LLC (14), 55 E 52nd St (fl 33), New York, 10055-0007

Viacom Inc (16), 1515 Broadway, New York, 10036-8901

Viahealth (16), 1425 Portland Ave, Rochester, 14621-3001

Viatech Publishing Solutions Inc (16), 1440 5th Ave, Bay Shore, 11706-4147

Victor Machinery Exchange (9), 56 Bogart St, Brooklyn, 11206-3817

Video Artists International (3), 109 Wheeler Ave, Pleasantville, 10570

VIEW Video Inc/Arcadia Entertainment Corp (16), PO Box 77, Saugerties, 12477

Visual Horizons (16), 180 Metro Park, Rochester, 14623-2610

Visual Reference Publications (17), 302 Fifth Ave, New York, 10001

Vitamin Power Inc (7), 73 Commerce Dr, Hauppauge, 11788-3902

Vivendi (16), 800 3rd Ave Bsmt B1, New York, 10022-7655

Walker Publishing Co Inc (17), 175 Fifth Ave (Frnt 4), New York, 10010-7728

Warnaco (2), 501 Fashion Ave Fl 14, New York, 10018-5942

Warner Books (17), 1271 Ave of the Americas, New York, 10020

Warren, Gorham & Lamont Inc (17), 195 Broadway, New York, 10007-3100

Andrew D Washton Books On the Fine Arts (16), 168 Irving Ave, Port Chester, 10573

Wathne Ltd (2), 156 W 56 St, New York, 10019

The Wedding Pages (16), 195 Broadway, New York, 10007

Weight Watchers International (16), 11 Madison Ave (17th fl), New York, 10010

Welch Allyn, Inc (9), 4341 State Street Rd, Skaneateles Falls, 13153-5300

Wenner Media LLC (17), 1290 Ave of the Americas (2nd fl), New York, 10104-0298

Westcon (16), 520 Whiteplains Rd (Suite 100), Tarrytown, 10591-5167

Wideband by Kars (16), PO Box 1785, New Rochelle, 10802-1785

The HW Wilson Co (17), 950 University Ave, Bronx, 10452

Wine Enthusiast Cos (4), 333 N Bedford Rd, Mount Kisco, 10523-1158

Winmill & Co (14), 11 Hanover Sq, New York, 10005-2818

Harry Winston Inc (16), 718 Fifth Ave, New York, 10019

Woman's Day Special Interest Publications (17), 1633 Broadway (42nd fl), New York, 10019

Women's Sports Foundation (1), Eisenhower Park 1899 Hemstead Turnpike, East Meadow, 11554-1099

World Kitchen Inc (16), 1 Steuben St, Corning, 14830-2900

World Press Review (18), 700 Broadway, New York, 10003

Xerox Corp (16), Xerox Square (12th fl), Rochester, 14644

Yellow Book USA (17), 398 RXR Plaza, Uniondale, 11556-0398

Your Move Chess & Games (11), 832 N Broadway, North Massapequa, 11758

David Yurman (5), 24 Vestry St, New York, 10013-1903

Ziff Davis Media Inc (17), 28 E 28th St (11th fl), New York, 10016

Zim-American Israeli Shipping Co Inc (16), 1110 South Ave, Staten Island, 10314

North Carolina

Air Chek Inc (9), PO Box 2000, Naples, 28760-5000

Ambient Shapes Inc (7), 856 21st Street Dr SE, Hickory, 28602-8376

American Biographical Institute Inc (17), 5126 Bur Oak Cir, Raleigh, 27612-3101

Asheville Compassionate Communication Center (13), 150 E Chestnut St (#1), Asheville, 28801-2337

B&G Lieberman Co Inc (16), 2420 Distribution St, Charlotte, 28203

Babyshoe.com (6), 306 Hebron St, Hendersonville, 28739-5210

Baker & Taylor Inc (16), 2550 W Tyvola Rd (#300), Charlotte, 28217-4579

Bank of America (14), 100 N Tryon St Ste 220, Bank America Corp Ctr, Charlotte, 28202-4031

Bob Barker Co Inc (5), PO Box 429, Fuquay Varina, 27526-0429

Battleground Antiques Inc (6), 3910 US Hwy 70 E, New Bern, 28560

Belk Stores Services Inc (16), 2801 W Tyvola Rd, Charlotte, 28217-4500

Bencone Uniform Connection (2), 1855 Runnymede Rd, Winston Salem, 27104-3109

Blue Cross Blue Shield of North Carolina (15), PO Box 2291, Durham, 27702-2291

The Body Shop Inc (7), 5036 One World Way, Wake Forest, 27587-7732

Boy Scouts of America/National Supply Group (1), 2109 Westinghouse Blvd, Charlotte, 28273-6310

Branch Banking & Trust Co (14), 223 W Nash St, Wilson, 27893-3801

Brooks Equipment Co (9), 10926 David Taylor Dr (Suite 300), Charlotte, 28262

Burlington Industries Inc (16), 804 Green Valley Rd (Suite 300), Greensboro, 27408-7039

Business Publishers Inc (17), 2222 Sedwick Rd, Durham, 27713-2655

Camellia Forest Nursery (8), 626 Hwy 54 W, Chapel Hill, 27516-7911

Carolina Biological Supply Co (9), 2700 York Rd, Burlington, 27215-3387

Carolina Exotic Gardens/CEG Nursery (8), 2237 Sunnyside Rd, Greenville, 27834

Carrot-Top Industries Inc (16), 328 Elizabeth Brady Rd, Hillsborough, 27278-9540

CMS Inc (14), 2650 Pilgrim Ct, Winston Salem, 27106-5238

Center for Creative Leadership (16), 1 Leadership Pl, Greensboro, 27410-9427

Chadsworth's 1-800-Columns (8), 277 N Front St, Wilmington, 28401-3907

Charlotte Chamber of Commerce (1), 330 S Tryon St (Suite 200), Charlotte, 28202-1923

The Ben Craig Center (1), 8701 Mallard Creek Rd # 106, Charlotte, 28262-6007

Daily Record & Dispatch Co (17), 99 W Broad St, Dunn, 28334-6031

Direct SAT TV LLC (3), 1930 N Poplar St (Suite 21), Southern Pines, 28387-7092

Dorothy's Ruffled Originals Inc (8), 6721 Market St, Wilmington, 28405-3703

Eaton Corp (16), 8609 Six Forks Rd, Raleigh, 27615-2966

Eli Journals (16), 2222 Sedwick Rd (Suite 101), Durham, 27713-2658

Expressions Custom Furniture (16), 401 11th St NW, PO Box 608, Hickory, 28603-0608

Foundation of FirstHealth (1), 150 Applecross Rd, Pinehurst, 28374-8520

Gardens Of The Blue Ridge Inc (8), PO Box 10, 9056 Pittman Gap Rd, Pineola, 28662

Gateway Bank and Trust (14), 2235 Gateway Access Point (Suite 200), Raleigh, 27607-3076

General Vitamin Corp (16), 10700 World Trade Blvd (Suite 102), Raleigh, 27617-4220

Glaxo Smith Kline (16), Five Moore Dr, Research Triangle Park, 27709

Gould & Goodrich (2), 709 E McNeil St, Lillington, 27546

Billy Graham Evangelistic Association (1), 1 Billy Graham Pkwy, Charlotte, 28201-0001

Graphik Dimensions Ltd (16), 2103 Brentwood St, High Point, 27263

Grove Enterprises Inc (16), 7540 Hwy 64 W, Brasstown, 28902-9736

Hallelujah Acres (5), 900 S Post Rd, Shelby, 28152-7423

Hanesbrands Inc (2), 1000 E Hanes Mill Rd, Winston Salem, 27105-1384

Happy Jack Inc (11), PO Box 475, Snow Hill, 28580

Health Sciences Consortium (17), 300 Silver Cedar Ct, Chapel Hill, 27514-1696

House of Eyes II (2), 2222 Patterson St Ste A, Greensboro, 27407-2539

ISA-The Instrumentation Systems & Automation Society (1), 67 Alexander Dr, Research Triangle Park, 27709

Inmar (14), 2650 Pilgrim Ct, Winston-Salem, 27106-5238

Jerry's Artarama (10), PO Box 58638J, Raleigh, 27658-8638

JR Tobacco/800-JR Cigar Inc (5), 2589 Eric Ln, Burlington, 27215

Kayne & Son Custom Hardware Inc (8), 100 Daniel Ridge Rd, Candler, 28715-9434

Kayser-Roth Corp Inc (2), 102 Corporate Center Blvd, Greensboro, 27408

King's Chandelier Co (6), 729 S Van Buren Rd (Hwy 14 S), Eden, 27288-5321

Klingspor's Woodworking Shop (9), 856 21st St Dr SE, Hickory, 28602

Lending Tree/Home Loan Center (14), 11115 Rushmore Dr, Charlotte, 28277-3442

Lenovo (3), 1009 Think Pl, Morrisville, 27560-9002

Local Government Federal Credit Union (14), 323 W Jones St (Suite 600), Raleigh, 27603-1369

Lorillard Tobacco Co (16), PO Box 10529, Greensboro, 27408-7018

Lowe's Companies Inc (8), 1000 Lowes Blvd, Mooresville, 28117-8520

Markson Scientific LLC (9), 336 E Montgomery St, Henderson, 27536

McFarland & Co Inc Publishers (17), PO Box 611, Jefferson, 28640-0611

McKenzie Taxidermy Supply (16), PO Box 480, Granite Quarry, 28072-0480

Monkeyshines Publishers (17), 1608 Ilchester Ct., Greensboro, 27401

National Wholesale Co Inc (2), 400 National Blvd, Lexington, 27292-2631

Natural History Magazine (17), 105 W NC Highway 54 (Suite 265), PMB 204, Durham, 27713-6650

Nucor Corp (16), 1915 Rexford Rd Ste 400, Charlotte, 28211-3888

Oakwood Homes Corp (16), 7800 McCloud Rd, Greensboro, 27409-9634

Omni Farm (16), 1369 Calloway Gap Rd, West Jefferson, 28694

One Hanes Place Catalog (2), 450 W Hanes Mill Rd, Winston Salem, 27105

Otto Environmental Systems of North America (16), 12700 General Dr, PO Box 410251, Charlotte, 28273

Overton's Inc (11), 111 Red Banks Rd, Greenville, 27858-5702

Pace Communications Inc (17), 1301 Carolina St, Greensboro, 27401-1032

PHE Inc (5), PO Box 8200, Hillsborough, 27278-8200

The Professional Putters Association (1), 300 S Liberty St (Suite 100), Winston Salem, 27101-5279

Putt Putt Fun Centers (16), 300 S Liberty St (Suite 100), Winston-Salem, 27101-5279

Raycom Sports (16), 1900 W Morehead St, Charlotte, 28208-5228

Replacements Ltd (8), 1089 Knox Rd, Greensboro, 27420-6029

RJ Reynolds Tobacco Co (16), 401 N Main St, Reynolds Bldg, Winston Salem, 27101-3804

Sandy Mush Herb Nursery (8), 316 Surrett Cove Rd, Leicester, 28748

Sara Lee Direct Home Shopping (2), 450 W Hanes Mill Rd, Winston-Salem, 27105

Sara Lee Hosiery (2), 1000 E Hanes Mill Rd, Winston Salem, 27105-1384

SIPCAMADVAN (5), 2520 Meridian Pkwy (Suite 525), Durham, 27713-4210

Southern Emblem Co (5), PO Box 8, Toast, 27049

The Sporting News Publishing Co (17), 120 W Morehead St Ste 310, Charlotte, 28202-1826

Standard Tools & Equipment Co (9), 4810 Clover Rd, Greensboro, 27405-9607

Sturges Sportswear (16), 7752 NC 48, Battleboro, 27809

Syngenta (16), 410 Swing Rd, Greensboro, 27409-2012

Texwipe Co (16), 1210 S Park Dr, Kernersville, 27284-3104

THORLO INC (16), 2210 Newton Dr, PO Box 5399, Statesville, 28687

Toter Inc (16), 841 Meacham Rd, Statesville, 28677

Turner Greenhouses (8), 1500 US Hwy 117 S, Goldsboro, 27530-8587

UMI Publications Inc (17), 1135 N Tryon St, Charlotte, 28206

Uwharrie Capital Corp (14), PO Box 338, Albemarle, 28002-0338

Village Interiors Carpet One (8), 3203 Hwy 70 SE, Newton, 28658

Wachovia Bank, National Association (14), 1 Wachovia Center, 301 S College St, Charlotte, 28228-0206

Wake Forest University Baptist Medical Center (1), Medical Center Blvd, Winston Salem, 27157-0001

North Dakota

Acme Tools (8), 1603 12th Ave N, Grand Forks, 58203-2304

Alerus Financial (14), 401 Demers Ave Ste 100, Grand Forks, 58201-4574

Bobcat Co (16), 250 E Beaton Dr, West Fargo, 58078

Northern Greenhouse Sales (8), PO Box 42, Neche, 58265-0042

Telpro Inc (9), 7251 S 42nd St, Grand Forks, 58201

Ohio

ASM International (1), 9639 Kinsman Rd, Materials Park, 44073-0002

AcuSport Corp (11), 1 Hunter Pl, Bellefontaine, 43311-3001

Adams Manufacturing Co (9), 9790 Midwest Ave, Cleveland, 44125-2497

Advanstar Communications Inc (17), 24950 Country Club Blvd (Suite 200), North Olmstead, 44070-5351

American Bronzing Co (16), 1313 Alum Creek Dr, Columbus, 43209-2706

American Greetings Corp (16), 1 American Rd, Cleveland, 44144

American Insurance Administrators Inc (15), 3070 Riverside Dr, Columbus, 43221

American Modern Insurance Group (15), 7000 Midland Blvd, Amelia, 45102-2607

American Trim (9), 1005 W Grand Ave, Lima, 45801

Amos Press, Inc (17), 911 Vandemark Rd, Sidney, 45365

Arkline Computers & Supply (3), 14524 Orchard Park Ave, Cleveland, 44111

Ashland University (1), 224 Andrews Hall, Ashland, 44805

Associated Materials (8), 3773 State Rd, Cuyahoga Falls, 44223-2603

Automation Mailing & Shipping Solutions Inc (16), 1138 W Ninth St, Cleveland, 44113-1060

Babcox Publications LLC (17), 3550 Embassy Pkwy, Akron, 44333-8318

Banana Republic (2), 5900 N Meadows Dr, Grove City, 43123-9541

Barbour Publishing Inc (17), 1810 Barbour Dr, Uhrichsville, 44683-1084

RG Barry Corp (2), 13405 Yarmouth Rd NW, Pickerington, 43147-8493

Eddie Bauer (2), PO Box 7001, Groveport, 43125-7001

Bay Manufacturing (16), PO Box 1250, Milan, 44846-1250

BBS & Associates (1), 130 Springside Dr (Suite 200), Akron, 44333-4553

BFS Credit Services Co (16), 6275 Eastland Rd, Brook Park, 44142-1301

Berean Christian Stores (5), 9415 Meridian Way, West Chester, 45069

Berkey Brendel Sheline (1), 130 Springside Dr (Suite 200), Akron, 44333-3755

Betterway Books (17), 10151 Carver Rd (Suite 200), Blue Ash, 45242-4760

Bigelow Electronics (3), 186 E Jefferson St, Bluffton, 45817-0125

Bluestone Perennials Inc (8), 7211 Middle Ridge Rd, Madison, 44057-3050

Butler Schein Animal Health (16), 400 Metro Pl N Ste 100, Dublin, 43017-3340

Cables to Go (3), 3555 Kettering Blvd, Moraine, 45439

Campbell Tools Co (9), 125 N Tecumseh Rd, Springfield, 45504-3404

Charter One Bank (14), 1215 Superior Ave, Cleveland, 44114-3299

Chase Industries, Inc (16), 10021 Commerce Park Dr, Cincinnati, 45246-1333

Cincinnati Bell Telephone (16), 221 E 4th St (Suite 700), Cincinnati, 45202-4137

Cinmar LP (8), 5566 West Chester Rd, West Chester, 45069-2914

Cintas (16), PO Box 625737, Cincinnati, 45262

Circle K Stores Inc (16), 935 E Tallmadge Ave, Akron, 44310-3566

The Clark Grave Vault Co (16), 375 E Fifth Ave, Columbus, 43201-2819

ClearSaleing Inc (16), 8415 Pulsar Pl Ste 477, Columbus, 43240-4093

Cleveland Clinic Foundation (1), 9500 Euclid Ave (AC311), Cleveland, 44195-0001

Cleveland Institute of Electronics (13), 1776 E 17th St, Cleveland, 44114-3636

The Cleveland Orchestra (1), 11001 Euclid Ave, Cleveland, 44106-1796

Coin World (17), 911 Vandemark Rd, Sidney, 45365-8974

The Columbus Dispatch (17), 5300 Crosswind Dr, Columbus, 43228-3664

Communication Resources Inc (18), 4150 Belden Village St NW (4th fl), Canton, 44718

Companion Plants (8), 7247 N Coolville Ridge Rd, Athens, 45701

Consolidated Electronics Inc (3), 705 Watervliet Ave, Dayton, 45420

Consolidated Plastics Co Inc (9), 4700 Prosper Rd, Stow, 44224-1068

Continental Supply Inc (9), PO Box 33663, Cleveland, 44133

Cooper Tire & Rubber Co Inc (16), 701 Lima Ave, Findlay, 45840-2315

Cornerstone Brands Inc (5), PO Box 1308, West Chester, 45071-1308

Council of Smaller Enterprises (COSE) (1), 100 Public Square (Suite 210), The Higbee Building, Cleveland, 44113-2227

Council of Smaller Enterprises (COSE) (9), 2535 Spring Grove Ave, Cincinnati, 45214-1729

Crane Pumps & Systems Inc (16), 420 Third St, Piqua, 45356-3918

Dalco Electronics (3), 425 S Pioneer Blvd, Springboro, 45066-1180

Dayton Daily News (18), 1611 S Main St, Cox Ohio Publishing, Media Ctr, Dayton, 45409-2547

Decko Products Inc (4), 2105 Superior St, Sandusky, 44870

Diebold Inc (16), 3792 Boettler Oaks Dr (Suite A), PO Box 3077, Uniontown, 44685-7769

Disabled American Veterans (1), PO Box 14301, Cincinnati, 45250-0301

Discover Publications (17), 6797 N High St (Suite 213), Worthington, 43085-2533

DX Engineering (16), PO Box 1491, Akron, 44309-1491

ElectroWarmth Products LLC (8), PO Box A, Danville, 43014-4601

Ellerbusch Instrument Co (9), 4505 Vine St, Cincinnati, 45217-1617

Escort Inc (16), 5440 Westchester Rd, West Chester, 45069-2950

Express LLC (2), 1 Limited Pkwy, Columbus, 43230-1498

F&W Publications Inc (17), 10151 Carver Rd (Suite 200), Blue Ash, 45242-4760

Fasson Roll Div (16), 5750 Heisley Rd, Mentor, 44060-1830

FW Media (17), 4700 E Galbraith Rd, Cincinnati, 45236-2726

Fifth Third Bank (14), 38 Fountain Square Plz, Cincinnati, 45202-3102

First Merit Bank (HQ) (14), III Cascade Plaza (7 fl), Akron, 44308-1124

FirstGroup America (12), 600 Vine St (Suite 1400), Cincinnati, 45202-2426

Fitness Quest (16), 1400 Raff Rd SW, Canton, 44750-2320

Four Wheel Drive Hardware LLC (12), 44488 State Rte 14, Columbiana, 44408-9540

Fox Lite, Inc (9), 8300 Dayton Rd, Fairborn, 45324

Fragrance International Inc (16), 398 E Rayen Ave, Youngstown, 44505

Genetica DNA Laboratories Inc (16), 8740 Montgomery Rd (Suite 11), Cincinnati, 45236-2100

Gerstner Woodworks (6), 20 Gerstner Way, Dayton, 45402-8408

GE Consumer & Industrial Lighting (16), 1975 Noble Rd, Cleveland, 44112-6300

Ghent Manufacturing Inc (10), 2999 Henkle Dr, Lebanon, 45036-9260

Gilson Co Inc (9), PO Box 200, Lewis Center, 43035-0200

Gold Medal Products Co (16), 10700 Medallion Dr, Cincinnati, 45241-4807

Goodyear Tire & Rubber Co (16), 1144 E Market St, Akron, 44316

Grimes Seeds and Plants (8), 11335 Concord Hambden Rd, Concord, 44077-0640

Halsom Home Care Inc (16), 7905 Clyo Rd, Centerville, 45459

Harris Infosource International Inc (17), 5005 Rockside Rd (Suite 660), Independence, 44131-6827

Havel's Inc (7), 3726 Lonsdale St, Cincinnati, 45227-3651

Health Care Logistics (16), 450 Town St, Circleville, 43113-2244

W C Heller & Co (16), 201 W Wabash St, Montpelier, 43543-1840

Hickory Farms (4), 1505 Holland Rd, PO Box 219, Maumee, 43537-0219

Highlights For Children (17), 1800 Watermark Drive, Columbus, 43215-1035

Hobsons (16), 50 E Business Way (Suite 300), Cincinnati, 45241-2398

The HoneyBaked Ham Co (4), 6145 Merger Dr, Holland, 43528-8430

Horticulture Magazine (17), 10151 Carver Rd (Suite 200), Blue Ash, 45242-4760

Hubert Co (16), 9555 Dry Fork Rd, Harrison, 45030-1994

Huntington Bancshares (14), 41 S High St Fl 1, Columbus, 43215-6167

HY-KO Products Co (16), 60 Meadow Ln, Northfield, 44067-1415

Hyatt Legal Plans Inc (16), 1111 Superior Ave E (Suite 800), Cleveland, 44114-2529

The Iams Co (16), 7250 Poe Ave, Dayton, 45414-5801

ITW Vortec (16), 10125 Carver Rd, Cincinnati, 45242

Improvements (8), 5566 West Chester Rd, West Chester, 45069-2914

Insurance.com (15), 29000 Aurora Rd, Solon, 44139-1843

K-D Lamp Co (12), 101 Parker Dr, Andover, 44003-9456

Kao Brands (9), 2535 Spring Grove Ave, Cincinnati, 45214

Kett Tool Co (9), 5055 Madison Rd, Cincinnati, 45227

Key Bank (14), 800 Superior Ave E Ste 1000, Cleveland, 44114-2601

KTM Sportmotorcycle USA Inc (16), 1119 Milan Ave, Amherst, 44001-1319

The Kroger Co (4), 1014 Vine St (Suite 1000), Cincinnati, 45202-1100

Laser Label Technologies Inc (10), 4560 Darrow Rd, Stow, 44224-1888

Lehman's (8), 289 N Kurzen Rd, Dalton, 44618

AM Leonard Inc (8), 241 Fox Dr, PO Box 816, Piqua, 45356-0816

LexisNexis (16), 9443 Springboro Pike, Miamisburg, 45342

Peter Li Education Group (17), 2621 Dryden Rd (Suite 300), Dayton, 45439

Liebert Corp (16), 1050 Dearborn Dr, PO Box 29186, Columbus, 43085

Life Line Screening (7), 6150 Oak Tree Blvd (Suite 200), Independence, 44131-2569

The Limited Stores Inc (2), Three Limited Pkwy, Columbus, 43230

LimitedBrands Inc (16), 5 Limited Pkwy, Reynoldsburg, 43068-5300

Lion Apparel (2), 7200 Poe Ave # 400, Dayton, 45414-2547

Luxottica Retail (2), 4000 Luxottica Pl, Mason, 45040-8114

Malco Products Inc (16), 361 Fairview Ave, Barberton, 44203

Mary's Plant Farm & Landscaping (8), 2410 Lanes Mill Rd, Hamilton, 45013-9181

T Marzetti Co Inc (4), 1105 Schrock Rd (3rd fl), Columbus, 43229-1146

Robert J Matthews Co (7), 2780 Richville Dr SE, Massillon, 44646-8396

Mead Westvaco Consumer & Office Products (10), PO Box 290001, Dayton, 45429-1290

Medical Economics Magazine (17), 24950 Country Club Blvd (Suite 200), North Olmsted, 44070-5351

Meister Media Worldwide (17), 37733 Euclid Ave, Willoughby, 44094-5992

Micro Center (3), 4119 Leap Rd, Hilliard, 43026

The Midland Co (15), 7000 Midland Blvd, Amelia, 45102-2608

Midwest Center for Stress & Anxiety Inc (7), 106 N Church St (Suite 200), PO Box 205, Oak Harbor, 43449

MCCS (14), 9111 Duke Blvd, Mason, 45040-8999

Moen Inc (16), 25300 Al Moen Dr, North Olmsted, 44070-5619

Moto Franchise Corp (3), 7086 Corporate Way, Dayton, 45459

National City Bank (14), 1900 E Ninth St, Cleveland, 44114

Nationwide Mutual Insurance Co (15), 1 Nationwide Plaza, Columbus, 43215-2220

Natural Essentials Inc (5), 1800 Miller Pkwy, Streetsboro, 44241-5067

Nilodor Inc (16), 10966 Industrial Pkwy NW, Bolivar, 44612-8991

NSA Technologies LLC (9), 3867 W Market St (Suite 256), Akron, 44333

O'Brien Manufacturing (9), 117 Industry Rd, Marietta, 45750-9355

Parker Hannifin Corp (9), 6035 Parkland Blvd, Cleveland, 44124-4186

Parker Steel Co (16), 4239 Monroe St, Box 2883, Toledo, 43606-1943

Parts Express (3), 725 Pleasant Valley Dr, Springboro, 45066-1158

Periodical Publisher's Service Bureau Inc (18), One Superior St, Sandusky, 44870-1815

Pfaelzer Brothers (16), 1505 Holland Rd, Maumee, 43537

PharmArt (6), PO Box 400, Circleville, 43113-0400

Photoworks (16), 1 American Rd, Cleveland, 44144-2301

Pinnacle Orchards (4), 1505 Holland Rd, Maumee, 43537

The Plain Dealer (18), 1801 Superior Ave, Cleveland, 44114-2107

PLAS-TANKS Industries Inc (9), 39 Standen Dr, Hamilton, 45015

Poly One Corp (16), 33587 Walker Rd, Avon Lake, 44012

Premier Farnell Corp (16), 4180 Highlander Pkwy, Richfield, 44286-9352

The Procter & Gamble Co (16), 1 Procter & Gamble Plaza, Cincinnati, 45202-3393

The Progressive Corp (15), 6300 Wilson Mills Rd, Mayfield Village, 44143-2182

Rod's Western Palace (2), 3099 Silver Dr D, Columbus, 43224-3945

Roto-Rooter Services Co (16), 255 E Fifth St, 2500 Chemed Center, Cincinnati, 45202

Rubbermaid Inc (8), 3320 W Market St, Fairlawn, 44333

Safeware, The Insurance Agency Inc (15), 6500 Busch Blvd (Suite 233), Columbus, 43229

Schneider Saddlery (11), 8255 E Washington St, Chagrin Falls, 44023

The Scotts Co Div of Lawn Service (8), 14111 Scottslawn Rd, Marysville, 43041

Scotts-Sierra Horticultural (16), 14111 Scottslawn Rd, Marysville, 43041

Selman & Co (15), 6110 Parkland Blvd, Cleveland, 44124-4187

Serenity (17), PO Box 168, Maria Stein, 45860-0168

Shopsmith Inc (16), 6530 Poe Ave, Dayton, 45414

Short Sizes Inc (2), 907 Spicers Ln, Northfield, 44067-2235

Shortage Control Inc & SC Video (5), 22643 Ascoa Ct, Strongsville, 44149-4700

The JM Smucker Co (4), 1 Strawberry Ln, Orrville, 44667-1298

South-Western Publishing (17), 5191 Natorp Blvd, Madison, 45040

Sporty's Preferred Living (5), 2001 Sportys Dr, Clermont County Airport, Batavia, 45103-9719

ST Media Group International (17), 11262 Cornell Park Dr, Cincinnati, 45242-1812

Standard Publishing (17), 8805 Governor's Hill Dr (Suite 400), Cincinnati, 45249

Standard Register (10), 600 Albany St, Dayton, 45417-3405

Sterling Jewelers Inc (16), 375 Ghent Rd, Akron, 44333-4601

Stevens Publishing Co (17), 311 W Perkins Ave, Sandusky, 44870-4805

Stewart-MacDonald (16), 21 N Shafer, PO Box 900, Athens, 45701

Suarez Corp Industries (5), 7800 Whipple Ave NW, North Canton, 44767-0001

Summit Racing Equipment (12), 1200 Southeast Ave, Tallmadge, 44278-3161

Support Plus (7), 5581 Hudson Industrial Pkwy, PO Box 500, Hudson, 44236-5019

Things Remembered (6), 5500 Avion Park Dr, Highland Heights, 44143-1992

Thompson & Morgan Inc (8), 110 W Elm St, Tipp City, 45371-1655

TruGreen/ChemLawn (16), 461 Enterprise Dr, Lewis Center, 43035-9424

United Air Specialists Inc (16), 4440 Creek Rd, Cincinnati, 45242

United Church Homes (1), 170 E Center St, Marion, 43302-3815

University of Akron (1), Business Admin Bldg 312, Akron, 44325-0001

Urban Response LLC (17), 500 S Prospect Ave, Hartville, 44632-9403

USI Affinity Collegiate Insurance Resources (15), 3070 Riverside Dr, Columbus, 43221-2547

Vagabond Creations Inc (10), 2560 Lance Dr, Dayton, 45409-1581

Valentine Research Inc (16), 10280 Alliance Rd, Cincinnati, 45242-4710

Victoria's Secret Catalogue (2), PO Box 16589, Columbus, 43216-6589

Vita-Mix Corp (16), 8615 Usher Rd, Cleveland, 44138-2199

West Shore Distributors (8), 31060 Clemens Rd, Westlake, 44145-1005

Western-Southern Life (15), 400 Broadway, Cincinnati, 45202-3312

What on Earth (5), 5581 Hudson Industrial Pkwy, Hudson, 44236-5019

Lt Moses Willard Inc (16), 1156 US 50, Milford, 45150

Writer's Digest Books (17), 10151 Carver Rd (Suite 200), Blue Ash, 45242-4760

Yenkin-Majestic (16), 1920 Leonard Ave, Columbus, 43219

Oklahoma

Alamo Rent A Car (16), 6929 N Lakewood Ave (Suite 100), Tulsa, 74117

Amcat TeleProfit Inc (16), 300 Johnny Bench Dr (# 120), Oklahoma City, 73104-2476

American Counseling Association (1), 305 N Beech Cir, Broken Arrow, 74012-2293

American Fidelity Assurance Co (15), 2000 Classen Blvd, PO Box 73125, Oklahoma City, 73106

Blue Cross & Blue Shield of Oklahoma (15), 1215 Boulder Ave, Tulsa, 74119-2827

Cellular One Group (16), 14201 Wireless Way, Oklahoma City, 74134

EDC Publishing (17), 10302 E 55th Pl, Tulsa, 74146-6515

Feed the Children (1), PO Box 36, Oklahoma City, 73101-0036

Glamour Shots Licensing (16), 1300 Metropolitan Ave, Oklahoma City, 73108

International Crystal Manufacturing Co (16), 10 N Lee St, Oklahoma City, 73102

Jantz Supply Koval Knives (9), 309 W Main, PO Box 584, Davis, 73030

Kraftbilt (10), 6504 E 44th St, Tulsa, 74145-4614

Loves Travel Stops & Country Stores (5), 10601 N Pennsylvania, Oklahoma City, 73120-4198

Lowrance Electronics (11), 12000 E Skelly Dr, Tulsa, 74128

Natcom Inc (17), 7580 E 151st St, Bixby, 74008

Oil & Gas Journal (17), 1421 S Sheridan Rd, Tulsa, 74112-6600

Oklahoma Dept of Commerce (1), 900 N Stiles Ave, Oklahoma City, 73104-3234

Optronics Inc (11), 401 S 41st St E, Muskogee, 74403

Oral Roberts University (1), Graduate Ctr (7th fl), 7777 S Lewis Ave, Tulsa, 74171

Pennwell Publishing (17), 1421 S Sheridan Rd, Tulsa, 74112

The Pin Man (16), PO Box 52817, Tulsa, 74152-0187

Reserve National Insurance Co (15), PO Box 138801, Oklahoma City, 73113-8801

Sportsmith LLC (11), 5925 S 118th Ave, Tulsa, 74146-6827

StatSoft Inc (9), 2300 E 14th St, Tulsa, 74104

Don Stewart Association (1), PO Box 21004, Tulsa, 74121-1004

University of Oklahoma Press (17), 4100 28th Ave NW, Norman, 73069-8218

Oregon

Almore International Inc (7), PO Box 25214, Portland, 97298-0214

Hanna Andersson Corp (2), 1010 NW Flanders, Portland, 97209

Bridge City Tool Works Inc (9), 2545 SW Spring Garden St (Suite 120), Portland, 97219-3942

Brownell Holly Farms (6), 17251 S Clackamas River Dr, Oregon City, 97045-9493

Catch The Wind Kite Shop (11), PO Box 973, Lincoln City, 97367-0973

Church Extension Plan (14), 4070 27th Ct SE (Suite 210), Salem, 97302-1359

Columbia Sportswear (2), 14375 NW Science Park Dr, Portland, 97229-5418

Compass Electronics (9), 397 SW Stringtown Rd, Forest Grove, 97116

Dermac Labs Inc (16), PO Box 5268, Salem, 97304-0268

Esco Corp (16), 2141 NW 25th Ave, Portland, 97210-2578

Fire Mountain Gems (16), 1 Fire Mountain Way, Grants Pass, 97526-2373

Gossler Farms Nursery (8), 1200 Weaver Rd, Springfield, 97478-9691

Greer Gardens (8), 1280 Goodpasture Island Rd, Eugene, 97401-1755

Harry & David Holdings Inc (4), 2500 S Pacific Hwy, Medford, 97501-8724

IPD Co Inc (12), 11744 NE Ainsworth Cir, Portland, 97220

Informal Education Products (11), 2517 SE Mailwell Dr, Milwaukie, 97222-7329

The Instrument Workshop (16), PO Box 1060, Ashland, 97520-0050

International Society for Technology in Education (1), 175 W Broadway (Suite 300), Eugene, 97401-2916

International Specialized Book Services Inc (16), 920 NE 58th Ave (Suite 300), Portland, 97213

Keyboard Workshop (17), PO Box 700, Medford, 97501-0047

Klahowya Native American & Nature Gift Shop (6), 4055 Royal Ave SPC 71, Bandon, 97402-6823

LaCrosse Footwear Inc (16), 17634 NE Airport Way, Portland, 97230-4999

Leslie Jordan (2), 1930 NW 24th Ave, Portland, 97210

Lithia Motors Inc (12), 360 E Jackson St, Medford, 97501-5892

Fred Meyer Jewelers Inc (16), 3800 SE 22nd Ave, Portland, 97202

Nike Inc (2), 1 SW Bowerman Dr, Beaverton, 97005-0979

Nomadics Tipi Makers (11), 17671 Snow Creek Rd, Bend, 97701-9149

NuNaturals (16), 2220 W Second Ave (Suite 1), Eugene, 97402-7112

Off the Wall Magnetics LLC (16), 60 SE Main St, Portland, 97214-3320

Oregon Freeze Dry Inc (4), 525 W 25th Ave SE, Albany, 97321-3900

Pacific Botanicals LLC (7), 4840 Fish Hatchery Rd, Grants Pass, 97527-9547

Pacific Spirit Corp (6), 1334 Pacific Ave, Forest Grove, 97116-2315

Portland Rescue Mission (1), PO Box 3713, Portland, 97208-3713

Random Lengths Publications Inc (17), 450 Country Club Rd (#240), Eugene, 97401-6078

Ronell Clock Co (5), 5001 Jerome Prairie Rd, Grants Pass, 97527

The Stash Tea Catalog (4), 7204 SW Durham Rd (Suite 200), Tigard, 97224

Tektronix Inc (16), 14200 SW Karl Braun Dr, Beaverton, 97077

Norm Thompson Outfitters Inc (2), 3188 NW Aloclek Dr, Hillsboro, 97124

Tillamook County Creamery Association (4), 4185 Hwy 101 N, Tillamook, 97141-7770

Truitt Brothers Inc (16), 1105 Front St NE, Salem, 97301-1034

Woodcrafters Lumber Sales Inc (9), 212 NE Sixth Ave, Portland, 97232-2976

Pennsylvania

A-Mark Inc (15), 715 Twining Rd (Suite 118), Dresher, 19025-1832

ASTM International (1), 100 Barr Harbor Dr, West Conshohocken, 19428-2959

Acurian (7), 2 Walnut Grove (Suite 375), Horsham, 19044-2286

Advanced Medical Nutrition Inc (7), 600 Boyce Rd, Pittsburgh, 15205-9742

Advanta Corp (14), Welsh & McKean Rd, Spring House, 19477

Ahrensdorf & Associates (16), PO Box 7494, Saint Davids, 19087-7494

Air-Scent International (16), 290 Alpha Dr, RIDC Industrial Park, Pittsburgh, 15238-2906

American Crane & Equipment Corp (16), 531 Old Swede Rd, Douglassville, 19518-1205

American Eagle Outfitters (2), 77 Hot Metal St, Pittsburgh, 15203-2382

American Marketing Solutions LLC (5), 1 Millennium Dr, Uniontown, 15401-6408

American Mint LLC (6), 5020 Louise Dr (Suite 300), Mechanicsburg, 17055-4927

American Period Lighting Inc (8), 3004 Columbia Ave, Lancaster, 17603-4001

Americansource Bergan (7), 1300 Morris Ave, Chesterbrook, 19087-5559

Ames-Tru-Temper (8), 465 Railroad Ave, Camp Hill, 17011-5611

Aon's Affinity Insurance Services Inc (15), 159 E County Line Rd, Hatboro, 19040-1218

Appalachian Nurseries, Inc (8), 1724 Clay Hill Rd, Chambersburg, 17201

Arbill Safety Products (9), 10450 Drummond Rd, Philadelphia, 19154

Arcelor Mittal (16), 139 Modena Rd, Coatesville, 19320-4036

Arrowhead Mountain Spring Water (16), PO Box 628, Wilkes Barre, 18703-0628

Artisanal LLC (8), PO Box 625, Holicong, 18928-0625

Wendell August Forge Inc (6), 390 Lincoln Ave, Grove City, 16127

Black Box Corp (3), 1000 Park Dr, Lawrence, 15055-1018

Blair Corp (2), 220 Hickory St, Warren, 16366-0001

Bucks County Coffee Co (16), 960 Brook Rd Ste 1, Conshohocken, 19428-1100

W Atlee Burpee Co (8), 300 Park Ave, Warminster, 18974-4860

Calico Corners (16), 203 Gale Ln, Kennett Square, 19348-1764

Carino Nurseries (8), PO Box 538, Indiana, 15701

Harriet Carter Gifts Inc (6), PO Box 427, Montgomeryville, 18936-0427

Catholic Health East (1), 3805 West Chester (#100), Newtown Square, 19073-2329

CJ Hummul Co (11), PO Box 522, 422 Third St, Nescapeck, 18635-0522

The Center for eBusiness & Advanced IT (1), 5340 Fryling Rd (Suite 201), Erie, 16510-4672

CertainTeed Corp (16), 750 E Swedesford Rd, Valley Forge, 19482

Charming Shoppers (2), 3750 State Rd, Bensalem, 19020-5903

Cherry Brothers LLC/ Cherrydale (1), 1900 Am Dr (Suite 203), Quakertown, 18951-6403

Children's Hospital of Pittsburgh (1), 4401 Penn Ave., Pittsburgh, 15224

CIGNA International (15), 1601 Chestnut St, 2 Liberty Pl (fl 53), Philadelphia, 19192-0003

Clement Communications (17), 3 Creek Pkwy, Upper Chichester, 19061-3148

Wm F Comly & Son Inc (9), 1825 E Boston St, Philadelphia, 19125-1201

The Cracker Box Inc (16), PO Box 114, Blooming Glen, 18911-0114

Cross Country Stitching (17), PO Box 180, Quakertown, 18951-0180

Cumberland Woodcraft Co Inc (8), PO Drawer 609, Carlisle, 17013-0609

Dansk (16), PO Box 2006, Bristol, 19007-0806

Davor Photo Inc (16), 3580 Progress Dr (Suite G), Bensalem, 19020

Day-Timers (13), 5700 Lower Macungie Rd, Macungie, 18046

DCA (16), 889 S Matlack St, West Chester, 19382

Delaware Investments (14), 2005 Market St, Philadelphia, 19103

Dentsply International (7), 570 W College Ave, York, 17401-3880

Destination Maternity Corp (2), 456 N Fifth St, Philadelphia, 19123-4007

Development Dimensions International (16), 1225 Washington Pike, Bridgeville, 15017-2838

Diakon Lutheran Social Ministries (1), 798 Hausman Rd (Suite 300), Allentown, 18104-9108

Direct Marketing Publishers (17), 1304 University Dr, Yardley, 19067-2829

Dorothy Biddle Service (8), 348 Greeley Lake Rd, Greeley, 18425-9799

Drawing Board Inc (16), 101 E 9th St, Waynesboro, 17268-2200

Drexel University (Goodwin College of Professional Studies) (16), 3001 Market St (Suite 100), One Drexel Plaza, Philadelphia, 19104

Drug Information Association (1), 800 Enterprise Rd (Suite 200), Horsham, 19044-3595

Duggan & Brown Inc (16), 1617 Old York Rd, Abington, 19001

E Hille, Angler's Supply House (11), 441 William St, Williamsport, 17701-6103

Easthill Group Inc (12), 263 Shoemaker Rd, Pottstown, 19464-6433

Education Direct (16), 925 Oak St, Scranton, 18515

Education Management Corp (1), 210 6th Ave Ste 3300, Pittsburgh, 15222-2603

Elite Sportswear LP (2), 2136 N 13th St (Ste A), Reading, 19604-1213

Employment Publishing Inc (17), 175 Strafford Ave, Wayne, 19087-3317

Entrepreneur Partners (14), 2000 Market St Ste 720, Philadelphia, 19103-3214

Everfast Inc (8), 203 Gale Ln, Kennett Square, 19348-1735

Family Album (6), 4887 Newport Rd, Kinzers, 17535-9793

Famous Smoke Shop Inc (16), 90 Mort Dr, Easton, 18040-9202

Farm Journal Inc (17), 30 S 15th St Ste 900, Center Sq W, Philadelphia, 19102-4803

Federated Investors Co (14), 1001 Liberty Ave, Federated Investors Tower, Pittsburgh, 15222-3779

FMC Corp (16), 1735 Market St, Philadelphia, 19103

Finley Products Inc (16), 1333 Beaconfield Ln, Lancaster, 17601-5344

Fisher Scientific (16), 2000 Park Lane Dr, Pittsburgh, 15275-1118

Fitness Systems Manufacturing Corp (7), 104 Evans Ave, Sinking Spring, 19608-1318

Flickinger's Nursery (8), Rte 85, Sagamore, 16250

The Flinchbaugh Co Inc (16), 245 Beshore School Rd, Manchester, 17345

Fox Chase Cancer Center (1), 333 Cottman Ave, Philadelphia, 19111-2497

The Franklin Mint (16), 486 Thomas Jones Way Ste 240, Exton, 19341-2561

Paul Fredrick Menstyle (2), 223 W Poplar St, Fleetwood, 19522

French Creek Sheep & Wool Co Inc (2), 600 Pines Swamp Rd, PO Box 110, Elverson, 19520-8917

Gary's Perennials, LLC (8), 1122 E Welsh Rd, Maple Glen, 19002-2224

Gemalto Inc (16), 101 Park Dr, Montgomeryville, 18936-9613

General Nutrition Corp (7), 300 6th Ave Fl 2, Pittsburgh, 15222-2511

Gilman's Lapidary Supply (11), 726 Durham St, Hellertown, 18055-1926

Grade Finders Inc (17), PO Box 944, Exton, 19341-0908

Herr Foods Inc (16), 20 Herr Dr, Nottingham, 19362

Hershey Foods Corp (4), 100 Crystal A Dr, Hershey, 17033

Hershey Park (19), 100 W Hershey Park Dr, Hershey, 17033

Hershey's Mail Order (4), 200 E Hersheypark Dr, PO Box 801, Hershey, 17033-0801

HCI Direct (16), 3369 Progress Dr, Bensalem, 19020

Highmark Blue Cross Blue Shield (15), 120 Fifth Ave (Suite 1044), Pittsburgh, 15222-3099

The History Book Club Inc (13), 1225 S Market St, Mechanicsburg, 17055

Home-Sew Inc (11), 1825 W Market St, PO Box 4099, Bethlehem, 18018-0099

Homecraft Veneer & Woodworker Supply (8), PO Box 776, Youngstown, 15696-0776

Hook & Hackle Co Inc (11), 607 Ann St Rear, Homestead, 15120

William B Hugg Enterprise Inc Swim Wear & Accessories (11), 44 1/2 E Butler Ave, Ambler, 19002-4517

ICIS Inc (2), 1908 Ringing Rock Rd, Upper Black Eddy, 18912

Industrial Instruments & Supplies Inc (9), 125 Countyline Indus Park, Southampton, 18966

Intelligent Direct (9), 10 1st St, Wellsboro, 16901-8167

International Masters Publishers Inc (17), 948 Plaza Dr., Montoursville, 17754-2400

Intromark Inc (16), 217 Ninth St, Pittsburgh, 15222-3506

Jenny Products Inc (16), 850 N Pleasant Ave, Somerset, 15501-1069

The Jewish Publication Society (17), 2100 Arch St (2nd fl), Philadelphia, 19103-1300

JLG Industries Inc (16), One JLG Dr, McConnellsburg, 17233

Joslin Photo Puzzle Co (16), PO Box 914, Southampton, 18966-0914

Kappa Publishing Group (17), 6198 Butler Pike (Suite 200), Blue Bell, 19422-2606

Kennametal Inc (16), 1600 Technology Way, Latrobe, 15650-0231

Kerr-Hays Co (16), PO Box 711, Ligonier, 15658-0711

Krames - Staywell (7), 780 Township Line Rd, Yardley, 19067-4200

Lake Shore Industries (16), 1817 Poplar St, Erie, 16508-0427

Lefty's Corner (6), 601 Nichols St, PO Box 615, Clarks Summit, 18411-1487

Lenox Group Inc (6), 1414 Radcliffe St, Bristol, 19007-5413

Lincoln Financial Group (15), 150 N Radnor Chester Rd (Suite A305), Radnor, 19087

Manning Materials (16), 680 Ben Franklin Hwy E, PO Box 250, Birdsboro, 19508-0250

Marastar Communications (13), 11 West Ave (Suite 220), Wayne, 19087-3224

Marmelstein Inc (16), 760 S Fourth St, Philadelphia, 19147

McPherson Associates Inc (1), 312 E King St, Malvern, 19355-2520

Minitab Inc (16), 1829 Pine Hall Rd, State College, 16801-3008

MMS Education (5), 105 Terry Dr (Suite 120), Newtown, 18940-1872

Music Choice (16), 650 Dresher Rd, Horsham, 19044-2204

New Pig Corp (9), 1 Pork Ave, Tipton, 16684

NutriSystem Inc (7), 600 Office Center Dr, Fort Washington, 19034-3232

Omnigraphics Inc (17), PO Box 8002, Aston, 19014-8002

One Point (10), 101 Poplar St Unit 2, Scranton, 18509-2745

Opus Inc (8), 69 N Locust St, Lititz, 17543

Orbit Manufacturing Co (9), 1507 W Park Ave, Perkasie, 18944

Partners Health (15), 901 Market St (Suite 500), Philadelphia, 19107

Penn Herb Co Ltd (7), 10601 Decatur Rd (Suite 2), Philadelphia, 19154-3293

Penn Mutual (15), 600 Dresher Rd, Horsham, 19044-2204

Penn State Hazleton (1), 76 University Dr, Hazleton, 18202-8025

Pennsylvania Firebacks (8), 2237 Bethel Rd, Lansdale, 19446-6003

Pennsylvania State University Press (17), 820 N University Dr (Suite C), University Park, 16802-1012

Penske Logistics (16), Rte 10 Green Hills, Reading, 19603

Peoples Benefit Life Insurance Co (15), 300 Eagleview Blvd, Exton, 19341-1155

Pets United LLC (5), One Maplewood Dr, Hazleton, 18202-9790

Pfaltzgraff Co (8), 140 E Market St, York, 17401-1219

The Philadelphia Contributorship Insurance Co (15), 212 S Fourth St, Philadelphia, 19106-3787

Philadelphia Museum of Art (1), PO Box 7646, Philadelphia, 19101-7646

Pittsburgh Parks Conservancy (1), 2000 Technology Dr (Suite 300), Pittsburgh, 15219-3137

Pocket Nurse Enterprises Inc (7), 610 Frankfort Rd, Monaca, 15061-2218

PNC Bank Corp (14), 249 5th Ave Ste 1200, One PNC Plaza, Pittsburgh, 15222-2707

Presque Isle Wine Cellars Inc (4), 9440 W Main Rd, North East, 16428

Theodore Presser Co (17), 588 N Gulph Rd Ste B, King Of Prussia, 19406-2831

The Princeton Review (16), 925 Oak St, Scranton, 18515-0999

Professional Training Associates Inc (17), 46 S Linden St (Suite C), Duquesne, 15110-1091

Progressive Business Publications (17), 370 Technology Dr, Malvern, 19355-1315

Quadrant Engineering Plastic Products (16), PO Box 14235, Reading, 19612-4235

Raybuck Autobody Parts (12), 2829 Saint John Rd, Punxsutawney, 15767-8501

Response Insurance (15), PO Box 4079, Scranton, 18505-6079

Rio Brands (16), 10981 Decatur Rd, Philadelphia, 19154-3297

Rodale Inc (17), 33 E Minor St, Emmaus, 18098-0001

Rohm & Haas Co (16), 100 S Independence Mall W, Philadelphia, 19106-2320

RMA-The Risk Management Association (1), 1801 Market St (Suite 300), Philadelphia, 19103-1628

Safe Publications Inc (11), PO Box 263, Southampton, 18966

Sage Financial Group (14), 300 Barr Harbor Dr (Suite 200), Five Tower Bridge, West Conshohocken, 19428

School Annual Publishing Co (17), 2568 Park Center Blvd, State College, 16801-3005

Schultz & Williams Inc (1), 325 Chestnut St (Suite 700), Philadelphia, 19106-2616

Sculptz (2), 1150 Northbrook Dr Ste 300, Feasterville Trevose, 19053-8443

Seybold Publications (17), PO Box 682, Gilbertsville, 19525

Sickafus Sheepskins (2), 8373 Rte 183, Strausstown, 19559

Society of Financial Service Professionals (1), 19 Campus Blvd (Suite 100), Newtown Square, 19073-3239

SAE International (6), 400 Commonwealth Dr, Warrendale, 15086-7511

SEI (14), 100 Cider Mill Rd., Oaks, 19456-9989

Stagestep Inc (5), 4701 Bath St (# 46), Philadelphia, 19137

Star Sprinkler Inc (9), 1400 Pennbrook Pkwy, Lansdale, 19446-3840

Kirk Stieff Co (16), 1414 Radcliffe St, Bristol, 19007

Sunoco, Inc (16), Ten Penn Ctr, 1801 Market St, Philadelphia, 19103-1699

Supelco Inc (16), 595 N Harrison Rd, Bellefonte, 16823-6217

Sure Fit Inc (8), 8000 Quarry Rd (Suite C), Alburtis, 18011-9599

Tafford Uniforms (2), 104 Park Dr, Montgomeryville, 18936-9612

Taylor Gifts Inc (8), 600 Cedar Hollow Rd, Paoli, 19301

Techni-Tool Inc (16), 1547 N Trooper Rd, Worcester, 19490

Teva Pharmaceuticals USA (7), 1090 Horsham Rd, Box 1090, North Wales, 19454-1090

Thermal Product Solutions (16), PO Box 150, White Deer, 17887-0150

Times Publishing Co (18), 205 W 12th St, Erie, 16534-0011

Tova Corp (7), 1200 Wilson Dr, Studio Park, West Chester, 19380

Union Switch & Signal Inc (16), 1000 Technology Dr, Pittsburgh, 15219-3120

Unisys (16), Unisys Way, Blue Bell, 19424-0001

Universal Vintage Tire Co (11), 2994 Elizabethtown Rd, Hershey, 17033

University of Pennsylvania (1), 3451 Walnut St, 601 Franklin Bldg, Philadelphia, 19104-6285

University of Pennsylvania - Veterinary Medicine (Development) (1), 3800 Spruce St (Suite 172E), Philadelphia, 19104-4192

UPMC Health Plan (1), Washington Pl (fl 9), 1 Chatham Ctr, Pittsburgh, 15219-3441

USI Affinity (15), 1 International Plz (Suite 400), Philadelphia, 19113-1535

USX (16), 600 Grant St, Pittsburgh, 15219

Vanguard (14), PO Box 2600, Valley Forge, 19482-2600

Vaxserve (7), 111 N Washington Ave Fl 1, Scranton, 18503-1841

Vertex Inc (16), 1041 Old Cassatt Rd, Berwyn, 19312

Wachovia Center (16), 3601 S Broad St Ste 1, Philadelphia, 19148-5250

WESCO (16), 225 W Station Square Dr (Suite 700), Pittsburgh, 15219

Western Pennsylvania Conservancy (1), 800 Waterfront Dr Fl 2, Pittsburgh, 15222-4718

Westlake Plastics Co (16), PO Box 127, Lenni, 19052-0127

Whirley Drink Works (5), 618 Fourth Ave, Warren, 16365

White Mane Publishing Co Inc (17), 73 W Burd St, Shippensburg, 17257-1259

The Wig Co (2), 1391 McLaughlin Run Rd, Pittsburgh, 15241

Wilton Armetale (16), Plumb & Square Sts, Mount Joy, 17552

WinterSilks LLC (2), 100 Murray Dr, Warren, 16368-0001

Wire Works (9), 200 Keystone Rd (Suite 1), Chester, 19013

Woolrich Inc (2), 2 Mill St, Woolrich, 17779

WorleyParsons (16), 2675 Morgantown Rd, Reading, 19607

XL Environmental (15), 505 Eagleview Blvd, Exton, 19341-1119

Zimmerman Irrigation Inc (16), 3550 Chambersburg Rd, Biglerville, 17307

Puerto Rico

Caribe Direct Inc (6), 107 Tres Hermanos, San Juan, 00907-2306

Joys SA Inc (2), PO Box 98, Hatillo, 00659-0098

Wireless Idea (5), 1213 Calle Luchetti (Apt 2), Condado Mansions, San Juan, 00907-1850

Rhode Island

AAA Southern New England (1), 110 Royal Little Dr, Providence, 02904-1860

Advanced Financial Services (14), 25 Enterprise Ctr, Middletown, 02842-7233

American Mathematical Society (17), 201 Charles St, PO Box 6248, Providence, 02904-2294

American Power Conversion Corp (3), 132 Fairgrounds Rd, West Kingston, 02889

Amica Insurance (15), 100 Amica Way, Lincoln, 02865-1158

Bale Co (16), 222 Public St, Providence, 02940

Bizzaro Rubber Stamps (6), PO Box 292, Greenville, 02828-0292

Brigade Quartermasters Ltd (11), 177 Georgia Ave, Providence, 02905-4422

CVS Caremark (7), 1 CVS Dr, Woonsocket, 02895-6146

Childreach US Member of Plan International (8), 155 Plan Way, Warwick, 02886

Collette Vacations (19), 180 Middle St, Pawtucket, 02860-1013

A T Cross Co (16), 1 Albion Rd, Lincoln, 02865-3700

Domestic Bank (14), 15 Park Row W, Providence, 02903-1104

Droll Yankees Inc (8), 27 Mill Rd, Foster, 02825

Emblem & Badge Inc (6), 16 Sunnyside Ave, Johnston, 02919-5318

Embrace Home Loans (14), 25 Enterprise Ctr, Middletown, 02842-7233

Hanna Instruments Inc (16), 584 Park East Dr, Woonsocket, 02895

Hasbro Inc (11), 1027 Newport Ave, Pawtucket, 02861-2500

Home Loan Investment Bank (14), One Home Loan Plaza (Suite 3), Warwick, 02886

Klitzner Industries (6), 44 Warren St, Providence, 02907

Marshall Domestics LLC (5), 12 Factory St, PO Box 107, West Warwick, 02893

Metropolitan Property & Casualty Ins (15), 700 Quaker Ln, Warwick, 02886-6681

Plan USA (1), 155 Plan Way, Warwick, 02886-1099

Posh Papers (6), 73 Terrace Ave, Riverside, 02915-4726

Privacy Journal (17), PO Box 28577, Providence, 02908-0577

Racer's Equipment Warehouse (16), 111 Commerce Dr, Warwick, 02886-2429

Rhode Island Novelty (16), 5 Industrial Rd, Cumberland, 02864-4714

Ross-Simons (6), 9 Ross Simons Dr, Cranston, 02920-4475

Scorecards USA (16), 200 Circuit Dr, North Kingstown, 02852-0298

Union Federal Savings Bank (14), 1565 Mineral Spring Ave, North Providence, 02904

Weingeroff Enterprises Inc (16), One Weingeroff Blvd, Cranston, 02910-4019

South Carolina

Atlantic Publication Group LLC (17), PO Box 30007, Charleston, 29417-0007

BJU Press (17), 1700 Wade Hampton Blvd, Greenville, 29614

Blue Cross & Blue Shield of South Carolina (15), I-20 E at Alpine Rd, Columbia, 29219

Carter & Holmes Inc (8), 629 Mendenhall Rd, Newberry, 29108

Computer Dynamics Inc (3), 7640 Pelham Rd, Greenville, 29615

Craig/Vartorella International Marketing & Advertising Inc (1), 277 Peckwood Rd, Camden, 29020

Fran's Gifts to Go (4), 3700 Clay Pond Rd, Myrtle Beach, 29577

Garlinghouse Co (17), 2121 Boundary St (Suite 208), Burnside Bldg, Beaufort, 29902-6812

Hagemeyer - North America (16), 1460 Tobias Gadson Blvd, Charleston, 29407-4793

Hyman's (2), 5809 N Rhett Ave, Hanahan, 29410-2510

Innovative Clip Art (10), 4772 Betty Davis Rd, York, 29745

The Inspiration Networks (1), 3000 World Reach Dr, Indian Land, 29707-6542

Jobscope Corp (16), 355 Woodruff Rd (Suite 406), Greenville, 29607-3481

Jones School Supply Co Inc (6), PO Box 2909, Irmo, 29063-4009

Laminex Inc (16), 4211 Pleasant Rd, Fort Mill, 29708-9328

Lazar Media Group Inc (17), 334 E Bay St (PMB 156), Charleston, 29401

Liberty Life Insurance Co (15), 2000 Wade Hampton Blvd, Greenville, 29615-1064

Links Magazine (17), PO Box 7628, Hilton Head Island, 29938-7628

Manchester Farms Inc (4), 8126 Garners Ferry Rd, Columbia, 29209-9402

Medals of America (6), 114 Southchase Blvd, Fountain Inn, 29644-9019

Menardi Mikropul LLC (16), 1 Maxwell Dr, Trenton, 29847

Mergent Inc (14), 580 Kingslet Park Dr, Fort Mill, 29715-6403

The MR Group Inc (9), 2042 Dogwood Rd, Charleston, 29414

George W Park Seed Co Inc (8), One Parkton Ave, Greenwood, 29647

Passport International Ltd (2), 4838 Jenkins Ave, North Charleston, 29405-4816

Seashore Vacations (19), 11 Executive Park Rd, Hilton Head Island, 29928-4781

Shakespeare Co (11), 7 Science Ct, Columbia, 29203-9344

Voyageur Inc (11), 111 Kayaker Way, Easley, 29642-2433

Young Pecan Co (4), 1200 Pecan St, Florence, 29501-2827

South Dakota

Dakota Digital (12), 4510 W 61st St N, Sioux Falls, 57107-0639

Foote-Jones/Illinois Gear (16), 2914 Industrial Ave, Aberdeen, 57402-1089

Great Western Bank (14), 100 N Phillips Ave, Sioux Falls, 57104-6715

Mersco Medical (16), 1411 E Wells Ave, Pierre, 57501

Rapid City Journal (18), 507 Main St, Rapid City, 57701-2733

St Joseph's Indian School (1), 1301 N Main St, Chamberlain, 57325-1656

Sencore Inc (16), 3200 Sencore Dr, Sioux Falls, 57107

Tennessee

Alco Chemical (16), 909 Mueller Dr, Chattanooga, 37406-1334

ALSAC - St. Jude (1), 501 Saint Jude Pl, Memphis, 38105-1905

Affinion Group (15), 400 Duke Dr (Suite 200), Franklin, 37067-2700

American General Life & Accident Insurance (15), American General Ctr, Nashville, 37250

American Healthways (16), 701 Cool Springs Blvd, Franklin, 37067-2697

AmMed Direct (7), 5720 Crossings Blvd, Antioch, 37013-3144

Ansar Inc (1), 6651 Bethesda Arno Rd, Thompsons Station, 37179-9216

BMI (1), 10 Music Sq E, Nashville, 37203-4321

Brentwood Benson Music Publishing (17), 2555 Meridian Blvd Ste 100, Franklin, 37067-6364

Bridgestone/Firestone North American Tire LLC (16), 535 Marriott Dr, Nashville, 37214-5092

Business Automation Systems Inc (16), 6949 Charlotte Pike Ste 106, Nashville, 37209-4200

Cancer Fund of America Inc (1), 2901 Breezewood Ln, Knoxville, 37921-1099

Catalog Music Corp (3), 4301 Hillsboro Rd (Suite 320), PO Box 159297, Nashville, 37215

Caterpillar Insurance Services Corp (15), 2120 West End Ave, Nashville, 37203

Chattanooga Shooting Supplies Inc (16), 2600 Walker Rd, Chattanooga, 37421-1285

Comdata Corp (14), 5301 Maryland Way, Brentwood, 37027

Computers for Education (1), 180 Freedom Ave, Murfreesboro, 37129-6926

Direct Auto Insurance (15), 1281 Murfreesboro Pike Ste 150, Nashville, 37217-2437

Ducks Unlimited (1), 1 Waterfowl Way, Memphis, 38120-2351

Dudley's Country Kitchen (4), 2230 Viar Rd, Dyersburg, 38024-9802

E-Z Bowz Inc (8), PO Box 1597, Gatlinburg, 37738-1597

Eastman Chemical Co (16), 200 S Wilcox Dr, Kingsport, 37660-5147

Edo Interactive (16), 3841 Green Hills Village Dr (Suite 425), Nashville, 37215-2632

Falcon Products Inc (16), 810 W Highway 25 70, Newport, 37821-8044

Federal Express (16), 3965 Airways Blvd, Memphis, 38116-5017

First Media Communications Inc (16), 9149 Jones Ct, Brentwood, 37027-8537

First Tennessee Bank (14), 165 Madison Ave Ste Mezz1, Memphis, 38103-2725

Fleet One LLC (14), 613 Bakertown Rd, Antioch, 37013-2657

Formal Approach (2), 281 W Old Andrew Johnson Hwy, Jefferson City, 37760-1805

Fostoria Industries Inc (9), PO Box 4973, Johnson City, 37502-4973

Gaylord Entertainment Co (19), One Gaylord Dr, Nashville, 37214

Genesco Inc (2), 1415 Murfeesboro Rd (Suite 190), Nashville, 37217-2895

Graceland (6), 3734 Elvis Presley Blvd, Memphis, 38116-4106

Hammock Publishing Inc (17), 3322 West End Ave Ste 100, Nashville, 37203-6822

Ideals Publications Inc (17), 2636 Elm Hill Pike (Suite 120), PO Box 305301, Nashville, 37214-3162

Ingram Book Group (16), One Ingram Blvd, La Vergne, 37086

International Paper (16), 6400 Poplar Ave, Memphis, 38197-0100

Journeys (2), 1415 Murfreesboro Pike Ste 181, Genesco Park, Nashville, 37217-2829

Kano Laboratories (16), 1000 E Thompson Ln, Nashville, 37211

King Pharmaceuticals, Inc (7), 501 Fifth St, Bristol, 37620

Lee's Nursery (8), 233 Lee's Dr, McMinnville, 37110-6939

LifeWay Christian Resources (1), 1 Lifeway Plaza, Nashville, 37234-1002

LS Records (16), 1225 Apache Ln, Madison, 37115

Lucky Heart Cosmetics Inc (7), 390 Mulberry St, Memphis, 38103-4212

Memphis Net & Twine Co Inc (11), 2481 Matthews Ave, Memphis, 38108

Merastar Insurance Co (15), 5600 Brainard Rd (Suite 1A), Chattanooga, 37411-5336

Thurston Moore Country Ltd (16), 304 W Due West Ave, Madison, 37115-4511

Thomas Nelson, Inc (17), PO Box 141000, Nashville, 37214

NFIB - National Federation of Independent Business (1), 53 Century Blvd (Suite 250), Nashville, 37214-4618

No Load Fund Investor (14), PO Box 3029, Brentwood, 37024-3029

Nylon Net Co (11), PO Box 592, Memphis, 38101-0592

Olan Mills Inc (16), 6060 Shallowford Rd., Chattanooga, 37421-1611

Opryland (16), 2800 Opryland Dr, Nashville, 37214-1200

PI Inc (16), 213 Dennis St, Athens, 37303-2995

Reading for Education (16), 180 Freedom Ave, Murfreesboro, 37129-0071

Scripps Networks (17), 9721 Sherrill Blvd, Knoxville, 37932-3330

ServiceMaster Co (8), 860 Ridge Lake Blvd, Memphis, 38120-9434

Smart Dog Products (11), 1009 S College St, Winchester, 37398

Strategy Corps LLC (16), 201 Summit View Dr (Suite 250), Summit Bldg, Brentwood, 37027-4645

Tennessee Valley Authority (16), 400 W Summit Hill Dr, Knoxville, 37902-1499

Terminix International, The Trugreen Companies (16), 860 Ridge Lake Blvd, Memphis, 38120-9434

Time Logistics Inc (12), 115 Dyer St (Suite 2), Columbia, 38401-4551

Tinsley Tool Supply Inc (9), 8038 Canter Ln, Powell, 37849-3143

Tractor Supply Co (5), 200 Powell Pl, Brentwood, 37027

The United Methodist Publishing House (17), 201 8th Ave S, Nashville, 37203-3919

VF Imagewear (2), 545 Marriott Dr (Ste 200), Nashville, 37214-5077

The Wexner Companies Inc (2), 418 S Grove Park Rd, Memphis, 38117-3518

WTS Media (16), 2841 Hickory Valley Rd, PO Box 8277, Chattanooga, 37421

Texas

A&B Equipment Co (16), 2101 Riverside Dr, Fort Worth, 76103-2120

AAFES (5), 3911 S Walton Walker Blvd, Dallas, 75236-1598

Academy of Psychic Arts & Sciences (5), PO Box 191129, Dallas, 75219-8129

Accountants Education Group (10), 8111 Lyndon B Johnson Fwy Ste 1345, Dallas, 75251-1354

American Airlines Inc (19), PO Box 619616, Dallas, 75261-9616

American Airlines (12), 4333 Amon Carter Blvd, Fort Worth, 76155-2605

American College of Emergency Physicians (1), 1125 Executive Cir, Irving, 75038-2522

American General Life Insurance Co (15), 2929 Allen Pkwy, Houston, 77019-2155

American Health & Life Insurance Co (15), 3001 Meacham Blvd (Suite 200), Fort Worth, 76137

American Heart Association (1), 7272 Greenville Ave, Dallas, 75231-5129

American Locker Security Systems Inc (16), PO Box 169, Coppell, 75019-0169

Amplify Federal Credit Union (1), PO Box 85300, Austin, 78708-5300

MD Anderson Cancer Center - Children's Art Project (1), 6900 Fannin St (Suite FHB 1.1000), Houston, 77030-3800

Anglicans United & Latimer Press (1), 904 Forest Hill Ct, Cedar Hill, 75104-5712

Annie's Attic LLC (11), 111 Corporate Dr, Big Sandy, 75755-2446

Antique Rose Emporium (8), 9300 Lueckemeyer Rd, Brenham, 77833-6453

Arch Telecom Inc (16), 210 Barton Springs (Suite 275), Austin, 78704

Astro Air, LP (9), 1653 N Fulton, Jacksonville, 75766

Balfour (16), PO Box 149107, Austin, 78714-9107

Baylor Health Care System (16), 2001 Bryan St (Suite 2300), Dallas, 75201-3063

Bear Computer Systems Inc (16), PO Box 559001, Dallas, 75355

Beauticontrol Cosmetics Inc (16), 2121 Midway Rd, Carrollton, 75006-5039

BenefitMall (15), 485 Lyndon B Johnson Fwy (Suite 1100), Dallas, 75244-6025

Blue Coral Slick 50 (16), 910 Louisiana St, One Shell Plaza, Houston, 77002-4916

Carol Bond Health Foods (7), 334 N Main St, Liberty, 77575

Boys' Life & Scouting Magazines (17), 1325 W Walnut Hill Ln, PO Box 152079, Irving, 75015-2079

Brown's Omaha Plant Farms (8), 110 McLean Ave, Omaha, 75571

Burlington Northern & Santa Fe Railroad (16), 2650 Lou Menk Dr, Fort Worth, 76131-2830

H E Butt Grocery Co (16), 646 S Main, San Antonio, 78204-1210

Careington International (7), 7400 Gaylord Pkwy (fl 3), Frisco, 75034-9463

ER Carpenter (16), 302 Highland Dr, Taylor, 76574

CAS Design Center (8), 7205 Boulevard 26, North Richland Hills, 76180

CCC of America (16), 102 Decker Ct (Suite 204), Irving, 75062

CPM Delta 1, Inc (11), 10830 Sanden Dr, Dallas, 75238

Brad Cecil & Associates (1), 2700 W Park Row, Arlington, 76013-2258

Charity Dynamics (1), 3420 Executive Center Dr Ste G100, Austin, 78731-1692

Charolette Ford Trunks (11), PO Box 495, Dumas, 79029

CheckVantage (14), 1908 Parkside Ln, Austin, 78745-3615

Clampitt Paper Co (16), 9207 Ambassador Row, Dallas, 75247-4506

Collider Media (9), 619 Congress Ave Ste B, Austin, 78701-3024

Collin Street Bakery (4), 401 W Seventh Ave, Corsicana, 75110-6362

Collis Curve Catalog Sales (7), 6110 California Rd, Brownsville, 78521

Colonial Life Insurance Co Texas (15), 2600 West Freeway, Fort Worth, 76113

Comerica Inc (14), 1717 Main St, Dallas, 75201-4612

Commemorative Brands Inc (16), 7211 Circle S Rd, PO Box 149079, Austin, 78714-9770

Compaq Computer Corp (16), 20555 State Hwy 249, Houston, 77070-2698

Computer Station Corp (3), 6611 Bissonnet (Suite 107), Houston, 77074

The Container Store (8), 500 Freeport Pkwy Ste 100, Coppell, 75019-3998

Corpus Christi Museum of Science & History (1), 1900 N Chaparral St, Corpus Christi, 78401-1114

Crazy Crow Trading Post (11), 1801 Airport Rd, PO Box 847, Pottsboro, 75076-3094

Credicorp (1), PO Box 569001, Dallas, 75356-9001

Crest Fruit Inc (4), 4000 E Goodwin Rd, Mission, 78574-9525

Datapoint USA Inc (16), 8122 Datapoint Dr (Suite 300), San Antonio, 78229-3264

Daydots (16), 1801 Riverbend W Dr, Fort Worth, 76118

D/FW Grocers Association (1), 3044 Old Denton Rd (Suite 111), Carrollton, 75007-5074

Dell Computer Corp (16), One Dell Way, Round Rock, 78682

Digital Speech Systems (3), 1241 N Glenville Dr, Richardson, 75081-2412

Dan Dipert Travel Service Inc (19), 7301 W Pioneer Pkwy Ste A, Arlington, 76013-2804

Diversified Healthcare Services (15), 800 E Campbell Rd (Suite 399), Richardson, 75081

Dunham & Co (1), 2400 Dallas Pkwy (Suite 400), Plano, 75093-4381

The Dwyer Group (16), 1020 N University Parks Dr, Waco, 76707-3863

E-Miles.com (19), 8401 N Central Expy (#1000), Dallas, 75225-4405

Educational First Steps (1), 2800 Swiss Ave, Dallas, 75204-5926

Eilenberger's Bakery Inc (4), 512 N John St, Palestine, 75801-2725

Ennis Inc (16), 2441 Presidential Pkwy, Midlothian, 76065-3723

Eye Care Centers of America (7), 175 E Houston St (6th Fl), San Antonio, 78205-2210

Fairfield Industries Inc (16), 1111 Gillingham Ln, Sugar Land, 77478-2865

Finck Cigar Co (5), 6100 West Ave, PO Box 831007, San Antonio, 78213

Fossil (2), 2323 N Central Expy, Richardson, 75080-2712

Frito-Lay (16), 7701 Legacy Dr, Plano, 75024-4099

Frost Bank (14), 100 W Houston St (Ste 100), San Antonio, 78205-1400

Fujitsu Transaction Solutions Inc (16), 2791 Telecom Pkwy, Richardson, 75082-3523

Galveston Bay Foundation (1), 17330 Hwy 3, Webster, 77598-4133

Gemini Publishing Co (17), 1799 Fm 528 Rd Apt 11101, Webster, 77598-4721

Golfsmith International Inc (11), 11000 N IH-35, Austin, 78753-3152

The Great Amarillo Directory (17), 2400 Lakeview Dr (Suite 113), Amarillo, 79109-1532

Great North American Cos Inc (16), 2828 Forest Ln (Suite 2000), Dallas, 75234

Greater Fort Worth Builders Association (1), 100 E 15th St Ste 600, Fort Worth, 76102-6569

Gulf Publishing Co (17), 2 Greenway Plz (Ste 1020), Houston, 77046-0208

Harcourt Educational Measurement (17), 19500 Bulverde Rd, San Antonio, 78259-3701

Harvard Square Records (3), PO Box 2525, Round Rock, 78680-2525

Health Care Concepts Inc (16), 3011 N IH-35, Austin, 78722

Diana Hils (5), 700 Milam, Houston, 77002-2806

Conrad N Hilton College of Hotel & Restaurant Management University of Houston (1), 229 CN Hilton Hotel College, Houston, 77204-3028

Home Interiors & Gifts Inc (16), 1649 Frankford Rd W, Carrollton, 75007-4605

HomeAway.com Inc (19), 1011 W Fifth St (Suite 300), Austin, 78703

Idearc Media Corp (16), 2200 W Airfield Dr, Dallas, 75261

Infomart (16), 1950 Stemmons Fwy (Suite1000), Dallas, 75207

International Academy - Compounding Pharmacists (1), 4638 Riverstone Blvd Ste 100, Missouri City, 77459-6157

International Currency LLC (11), 8725 Eastex Fwy, Beaumont, 77708-1307

Jaff Marketing Group Inc (16), 20603 Rhodes Rd, Spring, 77388-3714

JC Penney Inc (5), 6501 Legacy Dr, Plano, 75024-3612

Justin Discount Boots & Cowboy Outfitters (2), 101 N Hwy 156, PO Box 67, Justin, 76247

King Ranch Saddle Shop (8), PO Box 1594, Kingsville, 78364-1594

KMA Direct Communications (1), 5151 Belt Line Rd Ste 900, Dallas, 75254-6757

Susan G Komen for the Cure (1), 5005 Lyndon B Johnson Fwy (Suite 250), Dallas, 75244-6125

Landmark Graphics Corp (16), 2101 Citywest Blvd (#200), Houston, 77042-2829

Lift Outreach (1), 7370 Dogwood Pk, Richland Hills, 76118-6403

Lockhart Industries Inc (9), 9610 Skillman St, Dallas, 75243-8202

The Magni Co Inc (16), 7106 Wellington Point Rd, McKinney, 75070-5705

Marathon Norco Aerospace Inc (16), 8301 Imperial Rd, Waco, 76712-6588

Mary Kay Cosmetics Inc (16), 16251 Dallas Pkwy, Addison, 75001-6801

Mary of Puddin Hill Inc (16), 201 E Interstate 30 Exit 95, Greenville, 75402

Mastergrip Inc (11), 3410 Century Cir, Irving, 75062-4904

Megger (16), 427 Bronze Way, Dallas, 75237-1019

The Menninger Foundation (1), 2801 Gessner Dr, Menninger Clinic, Houston, 77280

Mentoring Minds (17), 4882 Hightech Dr, Tyler, 75703-2613

Michael's (11), 8000 Bent Branch, Irving, 75063-6023

Miracle of Aloe (7), PO Box 612688, Dallas, 75261-2688

Mr G's Enterprises (16), 5613 Elliott Reeder Rd, Fort Worth, 76117-6013

MoneyGram International (14), 2828 N Harwood (fl 15), Dallas, 75201

MultiView (1), 7701 Las Colinas Ridge (Suite 800), Irving, 75063-7555

National Motor Club of America Inc (1), 130 E John Carpenter Fwy, Irving, 75062-2708

Neiman-Marcus Group (8), 1618 Main St, Dallas, 75201

Neopost (9), 1335 Valwood Pkwy (Suite 111), Carrollton, 75006-6881

NestFamily.com (3), 1461 S Beltline Rd (Suite 500), Coppell, 75019-4939

NextScreen LLC (17), 8868 Research Blvd Ste 108, Austin, 78758-6446

Nissan Motor Acceptance Corp (14), 8900 Freeport Pkwy, Irving, 75063

Nissan North America Inc (16), 4400 Regent Blvd, Irving, 75063-2400

NPI (16), 14901 Trinity Blvd, Fort Worth, 76155

NRS (11), 1410 S Fm 51, Decatur, 76234-2416

No Fault Sports Products (11), 2101 Briarglen Dr, Houston, 77027-3711

North America Life Insurance Co (15), 1300 Guadalupe St Ste 200, Austin, 78701-1630

Oblate Missions (1), 323 Oblate Dr, PO Box 659432, San Antonio, 78265-9432

Oleda & Co Inc (16), 7700 Camp Bowie W, Fort Worth, 76116-6450

Orange Leap (1), 13800 Montfort Dr (Suite 220), Dallas, 75240-4347

Pecan Producers International (4), 2131 E State Hwy 31, Corsicana, 75151-1301

Pier 1 Imports Inc (8), 100 Pier 1 Pl, Fort Worth, 76102-2600

Pittman & Davis Inc (4), 801 N Expressway 77, Harlingen, 78552

Pizza Hut Inc (16), 7100 Corporate Dr, Plano, 75024-4100

Powr-Flite, a Tacony Co (9), 3101 Wichita Ct, Fort Worth, 76140-1755

The Psychological Corp (17), 19500 Bulverde Rd, San Antonio, 78259

RadioShack Corp (3), 300 Radioshack Cir (MS CF7-331), Fort Worth, 76102-1964

Ranch House Meat Co (4), PO Box 977, Menard, 76859-0977

Red Cooper (4), PO Box 3089, Mission, 78573-0052

Reliant Energy (16), 1000 Main St (fl 18), Houston, 77002-6336

Rent-A-Center Inc (16), 5501 Headquarters Dr, Plano, 75024-5837

Research Institute America (14), 2395 Midway Rd, Carrollton, 75006-2521

Rhythm Band Inc (11), 1316 E Lancaster Ave, Fort Worth, 76102-6634

Ronco Corp (16), 1779 Wells Branch Pkwy (#110B-337), Austin, 78728

Rose Electronics (3), 10707 Stancliff Rd, Houston, 77099

Sa-So (16), 525 N Great Southwest Pkwy, Arlington, 76011

Sabre Holdings Inc (19), 3150 Sabre Dr, Southlake, 76092

Safeguard Business Systems Inc (16), 8585 N Stemmons Fwy (Suite 600N), Dallas, 75247-3824

Sally Beauty Supply LLC (7), 3001 Colorado Blvd, Denton, 76210

School of Management, The University of Texas at Dallas (1), 800 W Campbell Rd (SM 32), Richardson, 75080-3021

The Scooter Store (7), PO Box 310709, New Braunfels, 78131-0709

Shell Oil Products US (16), PO Box 2463, Houston, 77252

Sheshunoff Information Services Inc (14), 4120 Friedrich Ln (Suite 100), Austin, 78744-1003

Society of Petroleum Engineers (1), 222 Palisades Creek Dr, Richardson, 75080-2040

Specialized Association Services (1), 130 E John Carpenter Fwy, Irving, 75062-2708

Specialized Products Co (16), 1100 S Kimball Ave, Southlake, 76092

Sport Supply Group (11), 1901 Diplomat Dr, Dallas, 75234

Squadron Mail Order (16), 1115 Crowley Dr, Carrollton, 75011-1312

SCA Promotions Inc (15), 3030 LBJ Fwy (Suite 300), Dallas, 75234

SCI Management (16), 1929 Allen Pkwy, Houston, 77019-2506

SWBC (14), 9311 San Pedro Ave (Suite 600), San Antonio, 78216-4459

START International (9), 4270 Airborn Dr, Addison, 75001-5182

Steck-Vaughn (17), 10801 N MoPac Expy (Bldg 3), Austin, 78759-5415

STRATMARK (1), 855 E Collins Blvd, Richardson, 75081-2251

Suez Energy North America (16), 1990 Post Oak Blvd (Suite 1900), Houston, 77056-3831

Sweepstakes Clearinghouse (16), 1555 Regal Row, Dallas, 75247

Tandy Leather Co (11), 1900 SE Loop 820, Fort Worth, 76140-1003

Texas Children's Hospital (1), 1919 S Braeswood, Houston, 77030-4412

Texas Farm Bureau Insurance Companies (1), 1200 Sycamore St, Waxahachie, 75165-2397

Texas Farm Bureau Insurance Cos (15), 7420 Fish Pond Rd, Waco, 76710-1010

Texas Industries Inc (16), 1341 W Mockingbird Ln, Dallas, 75247

Texas Monthly (17), 816 Congress Ave Ste 1700, Austin, 78701-2643

Texas Parks & Wildlife Dept (1), 4200 Smith School Rd, Austin, 78744

Texas Refinery Corp (9), 840 N Main St, Fort Worth, 76106-9419

Time Products International (16), 501 Pierce St, Del Rio, 78840-5456

Together (16), 15443 Knoll Trail (Suite 130), Dallas, 75248

TransFirst Holdings Inc (14), 5400 Lyndon B Johnson Fwy (Suite 900), Dallas, 75240-1054

TWL Knowledge Group (3), 4101 International Pkwy, Carrollton, 75007

TXU Energy (16), 6555 Sierra Dr, Irving, 77002-6336

Tucker Electronics Co (3), 1717 Reserve St, Garland, 75042

Tyco Valves & Controls (16), 10707 Clay Rd (#200), Houston, 77041-5497

Universal Fidelity Corp (14), 1445 Langham Creek Dr, Houston, 77084

University of North Texas (1), PO Box 311460, Denton, 76203-1460

University of Texas School of Law (1), 727 E Dean Keeton St, Continuing Legal Education, Austin, 78705-3224

UDL Laboratories Inc (7), 12720 Darry Ashford, Sugar Land, 77478

USAA Alliance Services Marketing (14), 9800 Fredericksburg Rd, San Antonio, 78288-0141

USAA (15), 9800 Fredericksburg Rd, USAA Building, San Antonio, 78240-4100

Village Weavers (16), 418 Villita St Ste 800, San Antonio, 78205-2910

Vintage Wood Works (8), Hwy 34 S, Quinlan, 75474

Whole Foods Market Inc (4), 550 Bowie St Ste 99, Austin, 78703-4644

Wildseed Farms (8), 100 Legacy Dr, PO Box 3000, Fredericksburg, 78624

Williamson-Dickie Manufacturing Co (2), 509 W Vickery Blvd, Fort Worth, 76104

Winning Solutions Inc (7), 4401 Diplomacy Rd, Fort Worth, 76155-2665

WRS Group Ltd (7), 5045 Franklin Ave, Waco, 76710-6919

Wycliffe Bible Translators (17), 7500 W Camp Wisdom Rd, Dallas, 75236-5629

Zale Corp (6), 901 W Walnut Hill Ln, Irving, 75038-1001

Zig Ziglar Corp (16), 5050 W Park Blvd (Suite 700), Plano, 75093

Utah

American Civil Defense Association (16), 11576 S State St (Suite 502), Draper, 84020-7111

Basic Research (7), 5742 Harold Gatty Dr, Salt Lake City, 84116-3762

Best Friends Animal Society (1), 5001 Angel Canyon Rd, Kanab, 84741-5000

CHG (7), 6440 S Millrock Dr, Salt Lake City, 84121

Children's Miracle Network (6), 205 W 700 S, Salt Lake City, 84101-2726

CollegeAmerica (1), 4021 S 700 E (Suite 300), Salt Lake City, 84107-2184

Comphealth (16), 6440 Millrock Dr (Suite 175), Salt Lake City, 84121-5892

Consumer Credit Advocates Inc (16), 4746 S 900th E (Suite 240), Salt Lake City, 84117

Deseret Book (16), PO Box 30178, Salt Lake City, 84130-0178

EduTrek (16), 155 N 400 W (Suite 150), Salt Lake City, 84103-1132

Emergency Essentials Inc (16), 653 N 1500th W, Orem, 84057-2831

Equitable Life & Casualty Insurance Co (15), Three Triad Ctr, Salt Lake City, 84180-1200

Franklin Estimating Systems (17), 2391 S 1560 W Ste B, Woods Cross, 84087-2378

Iomega Corp (16), 4059 S 1900 W, Roy, 84067

Love To Learn Inc (5), 741 N State Rd 198, Salem, 84653

Merrick Bank (14), 10705 S Jordan Gtwy (Suite 200), South Jordan, 84095-3977

O'Currance Inc (18), 1747 Lone Peak Pkwy (Suite 100), Draper, 84020-6876

1-800-Contacts (7), 51 W Center St, Orem, 84057-4605

Power Music (16), P.O. Box 3030, Salt Lake City, 84110

Previo/Alteris (16), 588 W 400 St, Lindon, 84042

Propay (14), 3400 N Ashton Blvd (Suite 200), Lehi, 84043-5310

SanSegal Sportswear (HQ) (2), 611 W 9560 S, Sandy, 84070-2587

Sundance Catalog Co (6), 3865 W 2400 S, Salt Lake City, 84120-7212

Ultradent Products Inc (7), 505 W 10200 S, South Jordan, 84095-3935

Western River Expeditions (19), 7258 Racquet Club Dr, Salt Lake City, 84121-4599

Vermont

American Meadows Inc & Vermont Wild Flowers Farm (8), 223 Ave D (#30), Williston, 05495-7139

Authentic Designs Colonial and Early American Lighting Fixtures Inc (8), The Mill Rd, West Rupert, 05776-9716

Brown & Jenkins Trading Co (4), 287 Old Route 15, Cambridge, 05444-9772

Carlson's Gardens (8), 74 Brightenback Ln, Waitsfield, 05673-6090

CTC Corp (16), 254 Benmont Ave, Bennington, 05201

Communication Industries Corp (10), 117 J L H Memorial Dr., Grafton, 05146-0116

Dakin Farm (4), 5797 Rte Seven, Ferrisburgh, 05456-9798

Dutch Gardens (8), 144 Intervale Rd, Burlington, 05401

Gardener's Supply Co (8), 128 Intervale Rd, Burlington, 05401-2804

Green Mountain Coffee Roasters, Inc (4), 33 Coffee Ln, Waterbury, 05676

Harrington's of Vermont Inc (4), 210 E Main St, Richmond, 05477-7721

Hearthside Quilts & Supplies (11), 90 Mechanicsville Rd, PO Box 610, Hinesburg, 05461

Hemmings Motor News (17), PO Box 256, Bennington, 05201

International Coins & Currency Inc (6), 62 Ridge St, Montpelier, 05602

Le Jardin Du Gourmet (8), PO Box 75 (Dept DM), Saint Johnsbury Center, 05863-0075

Maple Grove Farms of Vermont Inc (4), 1052 Portland St, Saint Johnsbury, 05819-2815

Bruce McGaw Graphics (6), PO Box 1528, Manchester Center, 05255-1528

National Pension Service Inc (14), 40 Main St (Suite 300), Burlington, 05401-8433

The Orvis Co Inc (11), Historic Rte Seven A, Manchester, 05254

Perennial Pleasures Nursery (8), 63 Brickhouse Rd, East Hardwick, 05836

Power & Telephone Supply (16), 44 Hull St # 2, Randolph, 05060-1102

Rutland Products (16), 38 Merchants Row, Rutland, 05701-2853

Spates The Florist (8), 20 Elm St, Newport, 05855

Sugarbush Farm Inc (4), 591 Sugarbush Farm Rd, Woodstock, 05091

Tuttle Printing & Engraving (10), 414 Quality Ln, Rutland, 05702

The Vermont Country Store (5), 5650 Main St, Manchester Center, 05255-9711

Vermont Ski Areas Association (1), 26 State St Ste 12, Montpelier, 05602-2943

Vermont Teddy Bear Co (6), 6655 Shelburne Rd, Shelburne, 05482

Watering Inc/Hemmings Motor News (17), 222 W Main St, Bennington, 05201-2103

Virginia

ARE Press (1), 215 67th St, Virginia Beach, 23451-2061

Affinity4 (16), 999 Waterside Dr (Suite 1910), Norfolk, 23510-3319

Airlines Reporting Corp (16), 3000 Wilson Blvd Ste 300, Arlington, 22201-3862

Airlines Reporting Corp (9), 3000 Wilson Blvd Ste 300, Arlington, 22201-3862

America (6), 21 Enterprise Ct, Fredericksburg, 22405

American Diabetes Association (1), 1701 N Beauregard St, Alexandria, 22311-1733

American Society for Training & Development (1), 1640 King St, PO Box 1443, Alexandria, 22313-2043

American Society of Civil Engineers (1), 1801 Alexander Bell Dr Ste 100, Reston, 20191-4382

American Trucking Association (1), 950 N Glebe Rd (Suite 210), Arlington, 22203-4181

Army Times Publishing Co (17), 6883 Commercial Dr, Springfield, 22151-4202

Association for Facilities Engineering (1), 12801 Worldgate Dr (Suite 500), Herndon, 20170

The Association of Fundraising Professionals (1), 4300 Wilson Blvd (Suite 300), Arlington, 22203-4179

Briefings Publishing Group (17), 2807 N Parham Rd (Suite 200), Richmond, 23294-4410

Robert Bryan Ltd (2), 909 Caroline St, Port Royal, 22535

The Bureau of National Affairs, Inc (17), 1801 S Bell St, Arlington, 22202-4506

Campaigns & Elections Magazine (17), 1901 N Moore St Ste 1105, Arlington, 22209-1718

CARFAX Inc (12), 5860 Trinity Pkwy (Suite 600), Centreville, 20120-1998

Cartouche Ltd (6), 100 S Early St, Alexandria, 22304

CMS LLC (1), 1900 Campus Commons Dr (Suite 450), Reston, 20191-1559

Chartifacts (6), 3221 Marlboro Ct, Richmond, 23225-0654

ChildFund International (1), 2821 Emerywood Pkwy, Richmond, 23294-3726

Christian Broadcasting Network Inc (1), 977 Centerville Tpke, Virginia Beach, 23463-1001

Christian Children's Fund Inc (1), 2821 Emerywood Pkwy, Richmond, 23294

Christian Relief Services Charities Inc (1), 2550 Huntington Ave (Suite 200), Alexandria, 22303-1400

Coastal Health Train (7), 500 Studio Dr, Virginia Beach, 23452-1175

The Colonial Williamsburg Foundation (1), PO Box 1776, Williamsburg, 23187-1776

Conservation International (1), 2011 Crystal Dr (Suite 500), Arlington, 22202-3787

Council of Better Business Bureaus - BBBOnline (1), 3033 Wilson Blvd Ste 600, Arlington, 22201-3863

Craver Mathews Smith & Co (1), 1900 Campus Commons Dr (Suite 450), Reston, 20191-1559

Crutchfield Corp (3), 1 Crutchfield Pk, Charlottesville, 22911-9097

Darden School Foundation Executive Foundation (1), PO Box 7186, Charlottesville, 22906-7186

Defense News Media Group (17), 6883 Commercial Dr, Springfield, 22151-4202

Direct Response Consulting (17), 6849 Old Dominion Dr (Suite 320), McLean, 22101

Direct Sports Supply (11), 1720 Curve Rd, Pearisburg, 24134

Dominion Retail Inc (16), 120 Tredegar St, Richmond, 23219-4306

Eberle & Associates Inc (1), 1420 Spring Hill Rd (Suite 490), McLean, 22102-3006

Edible Landscaping (8), 361 Spirit Ridge Ln, Afton, 22920

S Wallace Edwards & Sons Inc (4), PO Box 25, Surry, 23883-0025

Emperor Clock LLC (16), PO Box 960, Amherst, 24521

Envelope Manufacturers Association (1), 500 Montgomery St (Suite 550), Alexandria, 22314-1581

Ethyl Corp (16), 330 S Fourth St, PO Box 2189, Richmond, 23218

Evergreen Enterprises Inc (8), 5915 Midlothian Tpke, Richmond, 23225-5917

Federal Home Loan Mortgage Corp (Freddie Mac) (14), 8200 Jones Branch Dr, McLean, 22102-3110

FDAnews (17), 300 N Washington St (Suite 200), Falls Church, 22046-3431

Food Chemical News (17), 2200 Clarendon Blvd (Suite 1401), Arlington, 22201-3381

Fundamentals Co Inc (1), 411 Euclid Ave, Bristol, 24201

Gannett Co Inc (16), 7950 Jones Branch Dr, Mc Lean, 22107

Genworth Financial Inc (14), 6620 W Broad St, Richmond, 23230

The Jane Goodall Institute (1), 4245 N Fairfax Dr (Suite 600), Arlington, 22203-1698

Government Technology Services Inc (16), 2553 Dulles View Dr (Suite 100), Herndon, 20171-5228

Van Groesbeck & Co (1), 2124 Hanover Ave., Richmond, 23220

Hamilton Beach/Proctor-Silex Inc (16), 4421 Waterfront Dr, Glen Allen, 23060-3375

Heartstrings Press (17), 49 Starview Pl, Dept DMMP-GL, Lancaster, 22503

Heaven & Earth (5), 1255 Fordham Dr (Suite 120), Virginia Beach, 23464

HSP Direct (1), 13755 Sunrise Valley Dr (Suite 450), Herndon, 20171-4682

Hilton HHonors Worldwide (16), 7930 Jones Branch Dr, McLean, 22102

Hilton Hotels Corp (19), 7930 Jones Branch Dr Ste 100, Mc Lean, 22102-3389

Independent Insurance Agents & Brokers of America (1), 127 S Peyton St, Alexandria, 22314

International Auto Parts (12), PO Box 9036, Rte 29 North, Charlottesville, 22906-9036

Intersections (14), 3901 Stonecroft Blvd, Chantilly, 20151-1032

Janes Information Group (17), 110 N Royal St (Suite 200), Alexandria, 22314

Key Communications Inc (17), 385 Garrisonville Rd (Suite 116), PO Box 569, Garrisonville, 22554

KCI Communications Inc (17), 7600A Leesburg Pike, West Building (Suite 300), Falls Church, 22043

AB Lambdin Inc (2), 1134 56 St, Hampton, 23630-4000

Landmark Communications Inc (17), 150 W Brambleton Ave, PO Box 449, Norfolk, 23510-2075

Legal Defense Foundation Inc (1), 8001 Braddock Rd, Springfield, 22160-2115

Liberty Tax Service (14), 1716 Corporate Landing Pkwy, Virginia Beach, 53454-5681

Light Sources Inc (16), 6220 Indian River Rd (Suite I), Virginia Beach, 23464-3514

Long & Foster Insurance (15), 14501 George Carter Way, Chantilly, 20151-1770

George Mason University School of Management (1), 4400 University Dr (MS 1B1), Fairfax, 22030-4422

Military Officers Association of America (1), 201 N Washington St, Alexandria, 22314-2539

Military Order of the Purple Heart Svc (1), PO Box 49, Annandale, 22003-0049

MINDset Direct (1), 1700 N Jefferson St, Arlington, 22205-2817

MCI Inc (16), 22001 Loudoun Co Pkwy, Ashburn, 20147

Motient Communications (16), 11700 Plaza America Dr Ste 900, Reston, 20190-4774

The Motley Fool (14), 2000 Duke St (fl 4), Alexandria, 22314

Music Treasures Co (6), PO Box 9138, Richmond, 23227-0138

National Active & Retired Federal Employees Association (1), 606 N Washington St, Alexandria, 22314-1914

National Association of Federal Credit Unions (14), 3138 10th St N, Arlington, 22201-2160

National Association of Professional Insurance Agents (1), 400 N Washington St, Alexandria, 22314-2353

National Automated Clearing House Association (1), 13450 Sunrise Valley Dr (Suite 100), Herndon, 20171

National Community Pharmacists Association (1), 100 Daingerfield Rd, Alexandria, 22314

National Contract Management Association (1), 21740 Beaumeade Cir (Suite 125), Ashburn, 20147-6237

National Court Reporters Association (1), 8224 Old Courthouse Rd, Vienna, 22182-3808

National Defense Industrial Association (1), 2111 Wilson Blvd (Suite 400), Arlington, 22201-3061

National Relief Charities (1), 13318 Airport Dr, Elkwood, 22718-1760

National Rifle Association of America (1), 11250 Waples Mill Rd, Fairfax, 22030-7400

National Rural Electric Cooperative Association (1), 4301 Wilson Blvd, Arlington, 22203-1860

National School Boards Association Inc (1), 1680 Duke St, Alexandria, 22314

National Technical Information Service (17), 5301 Shawnee Rd, Alexandria, 22312-2379

National Wildlife Federation (1), 11100 Wildlife Center Dr, Reston, 20190-5362

Native American Heritage Associations (1), 830 John Marshall Hwy (Suite F), Front Royal, 22630-3743

The Nature Conservancy (1), 4245 N Fairfax Dr (Suite 100), Arlington, 22203-1650

Navy Federal Credit Union (14), 820 Follin Ln SE, Vienna, 22180-4907

Newspaper Association of America (1), 4401 Wilson Blvd (Suite 900), Arlington, 22203-4195

NCP Solutions (17), 11100 Wildlife Center Dr, Reston, 20190-5362

NTL Institute (1), 1901 S Bell St (Suite 300), Arlington, 22202-4503

Operation Smile Inc (1), 6435 Tidewater Dr, Norfolk, 23509-1600

Panoptic Enterprises (17), PO Box 11220, Burke, 22009-1220

Parker Systems Inc (16), 2880 Yadkin Rd, Chesapeake, 23323-0360

Philip Morris USA Inc (16), 6601 W Broad St, Richmond, 23230-1701

The Plow & Hearth Inc (8), 7021 Wolftown-Hood Rd, PO Box 5000, Madison, 22727

PBS Distribution (3), 2100 Crystal Dr, Arlington, 22202-3784

Project HOPE (1), 255 Carter Hall Ln, Millwood, 22646-0255

Projection Video Services (16), 5803 Rolling Rd (Suite 207), Springfield, 22152-1056

Rappahannock Electric Cooperative (1), 247 Industrial Ct, Fredericksburg, 22408-2443

Sales Service/America Inc (16), 85 S Bragg St (Suite 600), Alexandria, 22312-2793

The Salvation Army National Headquarters (1), 615 Slaters Ln, Alexandria, 22314-1112

Shades of Light (8), 4924 W Broad St, Richmond, 23230

Smithfield Packing Co Inc (16), Hwy Ten, Smithfield, 23430

Society for Human Resource Management (1), 1800 Duke St (Suite 100), Alexandria, 22314-3499

Software AG USA (3), 11700 Plaza America Dr (Suite 700), Reston, 20190

Southern Flavoring Co Inc (16), 1330 Norfolk Ave, Bedford, 24523-2223

Specialized Information Publishers Association (SIPA) (1), 8229 Boone Blvd (Suite 260), Vienna, 22182-2661

Sprint Nextel Corp (3), 12502 Sunrise Valley Dr, Reston, 20191-3438

SCA Direct (1), 11200 Waples Mill Rd (Suite 150), Fairfax, 22030-7418

SLM Corp (16), 12061 Bluemont Way, Reston, 20190

SNL Financial (17), One SNL Plaza, PO Box 2124, Charlottesville, 22902

Strongwell (9), 400 Commonwealth Ave, Bristol, 24201-3800

The Teaching Co (17), 4151 Lafayette Center Dr, Chantilly, 20151-1232

Tri Tech Laboratories Inc (16), 1000 Robins Rd, Lynchburg, 24504-3516

Tridium Inc (9), 3951 Westerre Pkwy, Richmond, 23233-1317

Trigon Blue Cross/Blue Shield (15), 602 S Jefferson St, PO Box 13047, Roanoke, 24011

Trout Unlimited (1), 1300 17th St N (Suite 500), Arlington, 22209-3800

TT Publishing (17), 950 N Gleb Rd, Arlington, 22203

US Historical Society (16), 8417 Glazebrook Ave, Richmond, 23228

USA TODAY (17), 7950 Jones Branch Dr, Mc Lean, 22102-3302

United Way Worldwide (1), 701 N Fairfax St, Alexandria, 22314-2058

Universal Corp (16), 1501 N Hamilton St, Richmond, 23230

USO Inc (1), 2111 Wilson Blvd Ste 1200, Arlington, 22201-3052

Van Bourgondien Bros (8), 2820 Crusader Cir, Virginia Beach, 23453-3134

Verizon (16), 1320 N Court House Rd (fl 9), Arlington, 22201-2525

The Virginia Diner Inc (4), 322 W Main St, Wakefield, 23888-2940

Virginia Home For Boys (1), 8716 W Broad St, Richmond, 23294

Virginia Port Authority (16), 600 World Trade Ctr, Norfolk, 23510-1781

Volunteers of America (1), 1660 Duke St Ste 100, Alexandria, 22314-3427

VW Credit (14), 2200 Ferdinand Porsche Dr, Herndon, 20171-5884

Wakefield Peanut Co (4), 11253 General Mahone Hwy (Rte 460), Wakefield, 23888

Washington Gas Energy Services (16), 13865 Sunrise Valley Dr (Suite 200), Herndon, 20171-6189

Washington Marketing Group (1), 5155 N 37th St, Arlington, 22207

Young America's Foundation (1), 110 Elden St, Herndon, 20170-4891

Washington

All Star Directories (17), 2200 Alaskan Way (Suite 200), Seattle, 98121

Alpha Supply Inc (16), 1225 Hollis, Bremerton, 98310-3611

Ambassador Programs (19), 1956 Ambassador Way, Spokane, 99224-4012

Ampersand Press (11), 750 Lake St, Port Townsend, 98368-2216

Aviation Book Co (17), 7201 Perimeter Rd S (Suite C), Seattle, 98108-3804

Eddie Bauer Holdings Inc (5), 10401 NE 8th St (Suite 500), Bellevue, 98004-4346

Birthday Express Inc (5), 3700 Monte Villa Pkwy (#110), Bothell, 98021-8992

Brooks Sports Inc (16), 19910 N Creek Pkwy (#200), Bothell, 98011-8223

Brown & Co (8), 8527 Semiahmoo Dr, Blaine, 98230

BUYSEASONS Inc (5), 3700 Monte Villa Pkwy (#110), Bothell, 98021-8992

CCI Solutions (16), 1342 88th Ave SE, PO Box 481, Olympia, 98507-0481

Coast Hotels Limited (19), 2003 Western Ave (Suite 500), Seattle, 98121

Coastal Hotel Group (1), 18525 36th Ave S, Seattle, 98188-4967

Cobalt (16), 605 5th Ave S (Suite 800), Seattle, 98104-3888

The Columbian (17), PO Box 180, Vancouver, 98666-0180

Crystal Records Inc (3), 28818 NE Hancock Rd, Camas, 98607

Custom Toll Free (5), 914 164th St SE (#1670), Mill Creek, 98012-6385

Ebbets Field Flannels Inc (2), 562 First Ave S (Suite 200), Seattle, 98104

Expedia Inc (19), 333 108th Ave NE (Suite 300), Bellevue, 98004-5736

Fancy Fronds (8), PO Box 1090, Gold Bar, 98251

Financial Services International Corp (14), 701 Fifth Ave (Suite 6870), Seattle, 98104

Fluke Biomedical (16), 6920 Seaway Blvd, Everett, 98203-5829

Gaco Western Inc (16), 200 W Mercer St (Suite 202), Seattle, 98119-3958

GaelSong (6), PO Box 15356, Seattle, 98115-0356

Gift Services Inc (6), 1800 W Fourth Plain Blvd (Suite 120B), Vancouver, 98660-1367

Grizzly Industrial Inc (9), PO Box 2069, Bellingham, 98227

Growing Family Portraits (16), 2003 Western Ave (Suite 460), Seattle, 98121-2185

Hear Music (3), 545 Bellevue Sq, Bellevue, 98004

Helly-Hansen (16), 4101 C St (Suite 200), Auburn, 98002

HipCricket Inc (16), 4400 Carillon Pt # 4, Kirkland, 98033-7353

Michael Jaffe Stamps Inc/Brookman Stamp Co (6), PO Box 61484, Vancouver, 98666-1484

Brian Jenner Inc (6), PO Box 2466, Pasco, 99302

Jerden Records/SpeechWorks (16), 17725 NE 65th St (Suite A-160), Redmond, 98052

Laplink Software Inc (3), 600 108th Ave NE Ste 610, Bellevue, 98004-5125

Liberty Orchards Co Inc (16), 117 Mission Ave, PO Box C, Cashmere, 98815

Loving Promises & More (16), 1429 Commerce Ave, Longview, 98632

Masterworks (1), 19462 Powder Hill Pl NE Ste 100, Poulsbo, 98370-7472

Mostad & Christensen (16), PO Box 1709, Oak Harbor, 98277-1709

Nautilus Inc (11), 16400 SE Nautilus Dr, Vancouver, 98683-5535

Nelson Crab Inc (4), 3088 Kindred Ave, Tokeland, 98590

The News Tribune (17), 1950 S State St, Tacoma, 98405-2817

Nordstrom Inc (2), 1700 7th Ave Ste 1000, Seattle, 98101-4407

Northwest Laboratories (9), 241 S Holden St, Seattle, 98108

Orion (1), 33926 9th Ave S, Federal Way, 98003-6708

Our Designs Inc (16), 1212 W Fourth Plain Blvd, Vancouver, 98660-2023

Outdoor Research (11), 2203 First Ave S (Suite 700), Seattle, 98134-1424

PACCAR Inc (16), 777 106th Ave NE, Bellevue, 98004-5027

Pacific Propeller Inc (16), 5802 S 228th St, Kent, 98032-1810

Pan Pacific Hotel & Resorts America (19), 2125 Terry Ave, Seattle, 98121-2709

PEMCO Insurance Cos (15), 325 Eastlake Ave E, Seattle, 98109-5466

Premera Blue Cross (15), 3900 E Sprague Ave (Bldg 1), Spokane, 99202-4847

Recreational Equipment Inc (11), 6750 S 228th St, Kent, 98032-4803

REI-Recreational Equipment Inc (11), 6750 S 228th St, Kent, 98032

Russell Investments (14), 1301 Second Ave (18th Fl), Seattle, 98101

Safeco Insurance Co (15), 4333 Brooklyn NE, Seattle, 98185-0001

Satori Software Inc (16), 1301 5th Ave (Suite 2200), Seattle, 98101-2676

Sea Bear (16), 605 30th St, Anacortes, 98221

Seattle Magazine (17), 1518 1st Ave S (Suite 500), Seattle, 98134-1456

Daniel Smith Inc (10), 4150 First Ave S, Seattle, 98134

The Software Labs Inc (3), 3824 140th Ave NE, Bellevue, 98005

Spokane Teachers Credit Union (14), 1620 N Signal Dr, Liberty Lake, 99019-9517

The Spokesman-Review (17), PO Box 2160, Spokane, 99210-2160

Starbucks Corp (4), 2401 Utah Ave S, PO Box 34067, Seattle, 98134

Stress Market (17), PO Box 127, Port Angeles, 98362-0017

Sur La Table (8), 5701 Sixth Ave S (Suite 486), Seattle, 98108

Symetra Financial (15), 777 108th Ave (Suite 1200), Bellevue, 98004-5135

Telect Inc (16), 23321 E Knox Ave, Liberty Lake, 99019-9461

Think Ink (10), 9709 Riverbend Dr, Bothell, 98011-4030

3D Mail Results (5), 6205 S 231st St, Kent, 98032-3208

Toland Home and Garden Inc (16), 273 N Otto St, Port Townsend, 98368-9780

University of Washington Educational Outreach (1), Box 359480, Seattle, 98195-9480

Virtuoso Ltd (19), 1001 SW Klickitat Way (Suite 105), Seattle, 98134-1161

Windstar Cruises (19), 2101 4th Ave (Suite 210), Seattle, 98121-2392

World Vision Inc (1), PO Box 9716, Federal Way, 98063-9716

Zones Inc (3), 1102 15th St SW (Suite 102), Auburn, 98001-6509

West Virginia

Almost Heaven Group (16), HC 67 Box 539 BB, Renick, 24966

Bike Nashbar (11), PO Box 1455, Crab Orchard, 25827-1455

Darco International Inc (9), 810 Memorial Blvd, Huntington, 25701-7002

The Legal Studies Forum (1), PO Box 6130 University Ave, Morgantown, 26506-6130

Mountain Craft Shop Co (11), RR1 Box 122, Proctor, 26055

National Humane Education Society (1), PO Box 340, Charles Town, 25414-0340

Sunshine Farm & Gardens (8), HC 67 Box 539B, Renick, 24966

Whitaker National (16), 533 Fourth Ave (12th fl), Huntington, 25701-1318

Woodcraft Supply Corp LLC (9), 1177 Rosemar Rd, Parkersburg, 26105-8272

Wisconsin

AW Direct Inc (12), 1125 Deming Way, Madison, 53717-1953

Air-Lec Industries Inc (16), 3300 Commercial Ave, Madison, 53714-1458

Amateur Electronic Supply LLC (16), 5710 W Good Hope Rd, Milwaukee, 53223

American Appraisal Associates (14), 411 E Wisconsin Ave (Suite 1900), Milwaukee, 53202-4466

American Family Insurance Group (15), 6000 American Pkwy, Madison, 53783-0001

American Girl Brands LLC (6), 8400 Fairway Pl, Middleton, 53562-2548

American Health & Safety Inc (16), 325 Industrial Cir, Stoughton, 53589

American Society for Quality-ASQ (1), 600 N Plankinton Ave, Milwaukee, 53203

Ameritech Services Inc (16), 722 N Broadway (fl 13), Milwaukee, 53202-4303

Amtelco (16), 4800 Curtin Dr, McFarland, 53558

As We Change (7), 250 City Center, Oshkosh, 54901

Associated Bag Co (10), 400 W Boden St, Milwaukee, 53207-7120

Assurant Health (15), 501 W Michigan St, Milwaukee, 53203-2706

Blue Cross & Blue Shield Cobalt (15), North 17 W 24340 Riverwood Dr, Waukesha, 53188

Brady Corp (16), 6555 W Good Hope Rd, Milwaukee, 53223

BrownCor International (5), 770 S 70 St, Milwaukee, 53214-3109

C&H Distributors LLC (9), 770 S 70th St, PO Box 14770, Milwaukee, 53214-0770

Camelot Enterprises (9), 8234 199th Ave, Bristol, 53104-9701

Carson Pirie Scott & Co (16), 331 W Wisconsin Ave, Milwaukee, 53203-2201

Centaur Forge LLC (9), 117 N Spring St, Burlington, 53105-1532

Cherry Tree Toys Inc (11), 12446 W State Rd 81, Beloit, 53511-8049

The Company Store Inc (16), 455 Park Plaza Dr, La Crosse, 54601-4445

Conney Safety Products LLC (7), 3202 Latham Dr, Madison, 53713-4614

Cotta Transmission Co (16), 1301 Prince Hall Dr, Beloit, 53511

Credit Union Executives Society (1), 5510 Research Park Dr, Madison, 53711-5377

CUNA Mutual Group (15), 5910 Mineral Point Rd, Madison, 53705-4498

CUNA - Trade Association (1), 5710 Mineral Point Rd, Madison, 53705-4454

Cygnus Business Media (17), 1233 Janesville Ave, Fort Atkinson, 53538-2738

Demco Inc (10), 4810 Forest Run Rd, Madison, 53704-7338

Direct Supply Inc (16), 6767 N Industrial Rd, Milwaukee, 53223

Drs Foster & Smith Inc (2), PO Box 100, Rhinelander, 54501-0100

Dozier Equipment International (9), 770 S 70th St, PO Box 88031, Milwaukee, 53288

Duluth Trading Co Inc (8), 170 Countryside Dr, PO Box 200, Belleville, 53508-0200

Eastbay Running Store Inc (2), 111 S First Ave, Wausau, 54401

Educators Progress Service Inc (17), 214 Center St, Randolph, 53956-1408

Elemental Scientific LLC (9), 1607 N Richmond St, Appleton, 54911-3553

Enerpac (16), PO Box 9010, Menomonee Falls, 53052-9010

Fair Indigo (2), 579 Donofrio Dr Ste 1, Madison, 53719-2838

FatWallet (14), 100 E Grand Ave, Beloit, 53511-6255

Figi's Inc (4), 3200 S Maple Ave, Marshfield, 54404-2000

4Imprint Inc (16), 101 Commerce St, Oshkosh, 54901

Guaranty Bank (14), 4000 W Brown Deer Rd, Brown Deer, 53209

The Guild Inc (8), 931 E Main St (Suite 9), Madison, 53703-2956

Chris Hansen (16), 16300 W Lincoln Ave, New Berlin, 53151-2837

Harley-Davidson Inc (12), 3700 W Juneau Ave, Milwaukee, 53208-2865

Herrschners Inc (11), 2800 Hoover Rd, Stevens Point, 54492-0001

Holiday Vacations (19), 2727 Henry Ave, PO Box 87, Eau Claire, 54701-6828

Hy Cite Corp (16), 333 Holtzman Rd, Madison, 53713-2109

Hygienic Fabrics & Filters Inc (16), 1301 Erie Ave, PO Box 1005, Sheboygan, 53082-1005

ITW Bee Leitzke (16), 2000 Industrial Rd, Iron Ridge, 53035-9535

Imperial Supplies (16), 789 Armed Forces Dr, Green Bay, 54304-4527

International Foundation of Employee Benefit Plans (1), 18700 W Bluemound Rd, Brookfield, 53045-2936

INWAVE Internet (16), 1131 W Enterprise Dr, Janesville, 53546

Jockey International Global Inc (2), 2300 60th St, Kenosha, 53140-3822

Jones Publishing Inc (17), N7450 Aanstad Rd, Iola, 54945-8229

JW Jung Seed Co (8), 335 S High St, Randolph, 53957-0001

Kalmbach Publishing Co (17), 21027 Crossroads Cir, Waukesha, 53187

JJ Keller & Associates Inc (16), 3003 W Breezewood Ln, Neenah, 54957-0368

Kester's Wild Game Food Nurseries Inc (8), 4582 Hwy 116 E, Omro, 54963

Miles Kimball Co (6), PO Box 3600, Oshkosh, 54903-3600

Kimberly-Clark Corp (16), 2100 Winchester Rd, Neenah, 54956

Klockit (6), PO Box 636, N3211 Country Rd H, Lake Geneva, 53147-0636

Krause Publications Inc (17), 700 E State St, Iola, 54990

Lab Safety Supply Inc (5), 401 S Wright Rd, Box 1368, Janesville, 53547-1368

Lakewood Products LLC (11), 3188 Bowling Green Ln, Suamico, 54173

Lands' End Inc (2), One Lands' End Ln, Dodgeville, 53595

Leather Unlimited Corp (2), PO Box 342, Belgium, 53004-0342

Hal Leonard Corp (17), 7777 W Bluemound Rd, Box 13819, Milwaukee, 53213

Lorman Education Services (1), 2510 Alpine Rd, Eau Claire, 54703-9560

Magna Publications Inc (17), 2718 Dryden Dr, Madison, 53704-3086

Majorium (17), 2025 Main St, Stevens Point, 54481-3019

Marshall & Ilsley Corp (14), 770 N Water St, Milwaukee, 53202

Mason Companies Inc (2), 1251 First Ave, Chippewa Falls, 54729-1408

McClure & Zimmerman (8), 335 S High St, Randolph, 53956-1425

McFeely's Square Drive Screws (16), PO Box 44976, Madison, 53744-4976

Media Management & Magnetics Inc (3), N93 W14636 Whitaker Way, Menomonee Falls, 53051

Metso Minerals/WS Tyler (16), 20965 Crossroads Cir, Waukesha, 53186

Milwaukee Electric Tool Corp (16), 13135 W Lisbon Rd, Brookfield, 53005-2550

Nancy's Notions LLC (11), 333 Beichl Ave, Beaver Dam, 53916-0683

National Business Furniture Inc (10), 735 N Water St Ste 440, Milwaukee, 53202-4103

Nelson-Jameson Inc (9), 2400 E Fifth St, PO Box 647, Marshfield, 54449-0647

NASCO (5), 901 Janesville Ave, Fort Atkinson, 53538-2497

NBI Inc (1), PO Box 3067, Eau Claire, 54702-3067

NGL Insurance Group (15), Two E Gilman St (Stop 1), Madison, 53703-1494

Norscot Group (5), 1000 W Donges Bay Rd, Mequon, 53092

Northwestern Mutual (14), 720 E Wisconsin Ave, Milwaukee, 53202-4703

officefurniture.com (8), 735 N Water (#400), Milwaukee, 53202-4103

Olsen's Mill Direct (2), 1641 S Main St, Oshkosh, 54902-6913

P & H Mining Equipment (16), 4400 W National Ave, Milwaukee, 53214-3639

Pacific Cycle Inc (16), 4902 Hammersly Rd, Madison, 53711

Pegasus Auto Racing Supplies Inc (12), 2475 S 179th St, New Berlin, 53146-2150

Pleasant Company (11), PO Box 620497, Middleton, 53562-0497

Potawatomi Bingo Casino (19), 313 N 13th St, Milwaukee, 53233-2244

PC/Nametag Inc (16), 124 Horizon Dr, Verona, 53593

PESI LLC (17), 200 Spring St (Ste A), Eau Claire, 54703-3663

Prairie Nursery (8), W5875 Dyke Ave, PO Box 306, Westfield, 53964

Priests of the Sacred Heart (1), 6889 S Lovers Ln Rd, Hales Corners, 53130-0900

Rainbow Group LLC (11), 8233 Forsythia St Ste 120, Middleton, 53562-1496

Rand Material Handling Equipment Co Inc (16), PO Box 5195, Janesville, 53547-5195

Referee Enterprises (1), PO Box 161, Franksville, 53126-0161

Regal Ware Inc (16), 1675 Reigle Dr, Kewaskum, 53040-8923

Reiman Publications (17), 5400 S 60th St, Greendale, 53129

Renaissance Learning (5), 2911 Peach St, PO Box 8036, Wisconsin Rapids, 54495-8036

Rockwell Automation (16), 1201 S 2nd St, Milwaukee, 53204-2410

Rowe Pottery Works Inc (16), 404 England St, Cambridge, 53523

RBC Funds (14), PO Box 702, Milwaukee, 53201-0701

Ruud Lighting Inc (9), 9201 Washington Ave, Racine, 53406-3772

Sax Arts & Crafts (10), PO Box 1579, Appleton, 54912-1579

School Specialty Inc (16), W6316 Design Dr, Greenville, 54942-8404

Securitec Publications (7), W175N11117 Stonewood Dr (Suite 110), Germantown, 53022-6505

Sentry Life Insurance Co (15), 1800 Northpoint Dr, Stevens Point, 54481

Sierra Inc (3), 558 State St, Racine, 53402-5132

Simpson Electric Co (16), 520 Simpson Ave, PO Box 99, Lac Du Flambeau, 54538-0099

AO Smith Corp (16), 11270 W Park Pl (Suite 1200), Milwaukee, 53224-3643

Snap-on Inc (9), 2801 80th St, Kenosha, 53141-1410

Society of the Divine Savior (1), 1303 Milwaukee Dr, New Holstein, 53061-1443

Sony Media Software (3), 8215 Greenway Blvd, Middleton, 53562-3685

Storage Battery Systems Inc (12), N 56 W 16665 Ridgewood Dr, Menomonee Falls, 53051

The Swiss Colony Inc (4), 1112 7th Ave, Monroe, 53566-1364

Tackle Craft (11), W5043 480th Ave, Ellsworth, 54011-5209

Thermo Fisher Scientific SID (9), 5225 Verona Rd, Madison, 53711-4497

Thrivent Financial for Lutherans (14), 4321 N Ballard Rd, Appleton, 54919-0001

Tomahawk Live Trap Co (16), PO Box 323, Tomahawk, 54487-0323

Total Training Solutions LLC (5), PO Box 310, Waunakee, 53597-0310

TDS Telecom (16), 525 Junction Rd, Madison, 53717-2152

Uline (5), 12575 Uline Dr, Pleasant Prairie, 53158-3686

Uncharted Country Publishing (17), 408 S Baldwin St, Madison, 53703-4805

Undergear.com (2), 455 Park Plz Dr, La Crosse, 54601

University of Wisconsin-Madison School of Business Executive Education (1), 601 University Ave Fluno Ctr for Exec Ed, Madison, 53715-1035

Upstart (16), PO Box 8010, Madison, 53708-8010

Valenti Classics (16), 355 S Hwy 41, Caledonia, 53108

Wag/Aero Group (16), 1216 North Rd, Lyons, 53148

Wm. K. Walthers Inc (11), 5601 W Florist Ave, Milwaukee, 53218

West Bend (16), 2845 Wingate St, West Bend, 53095

Wind in the Rigging (11), PO Box 249, Port Washington, 53074-0249

The Wisconsin Cheeseman (4), 301 Broadway Dr, Sun Prairie, 53590-1742

Wisconsin Historical Foundation (1), 368 Park Ave, Sun Prairie, 53590-3014

Wyoming

Queen Bee Gardens (4), 1863 Lane 11 1/2, Lovell, 82431-9751

Sierra Trading Post (2), 5025 Campstool Rd, Cheyenne, 82007-1816

Unicover Corp (6), 1 Unicover Ctr, Cheyenne, 82008-0001

Woodworker's Supply Inc (11), 1108 N Glenn Rd, Casper, 82601

CANADA
Alberta

Aardvark Enterprises (17), 204 Millbank Dr SW, Calgary, T2Y 2H9

Canada Brokerlink Insurance (15), 17520 111th Ave, Edmonton, T55 OA2

Crowne Plaza Chateau Le Combe (19), 10111 Bellamy Hill, Edmonton, T5J 1N7

ENMAX Corp (9), 141 - 50 Ave SE, Calgary, T2G 4S7

Fitter International Inc (1), 3050 - 2600 Portland St SE, Calgary, T2G 4M6

JustThinkIncorporated (16), 85 Cranford Way, Sherwood Park, T8H0H9

Veer (16), 119 14th St NW (Suite 400), Calgary, T2N IZ6

British Columbia

British Columbia Automobile Association (15), 4567 Canada Way, Burnaby, V5G 4T1

House of Orange (2), PO Box 444, Brentwood Bay, V8M 1R3

PacNet Services Ltd (14), 595 Howe St (fl 4), Vancouver, V6C 2T5

Winn Devon (17), 6311 Westminster Hwy (Unit 110), Richmond, V7C 4V4

Manitoba

Arctic Trading Co Inc (6), Kelsey & Bernier Sts Box 910, Churchill, R0B 0E0

McFayden/McConnell (8), 30 Ninth St, Brandon, R7A 6E1

Movada Media Inc (5), 3-16 Mazenod Rd, Winnipeg, R2J 4H2

Winnipeg Art Gallery (1), 300 Memorial Blvd, Winnipeg, R3C 1V1

Nova Scotia

Bear Woods Supply Co Inc (11), PO Box 275, Cornwallis, B0S 1H0

Ontario

ACP Medicine (17), 69 John St S (Suite 310), Hamilton, L8N 2B9

Alzheimer Society of Canada (1), 20 Eglinton Ave W (Suite 1200), Toronto, M4R 1K8

Bell & Howell Ltd (9), 5650 Young St (Suite 1802), North York, M2M 4G3

Berry Hill Ltd (8), 75 Burwell Rd, Saint Thomas, N5P 3R5

The Bombay Co (8), 3389 Steeles Ave E, Brampton, L6T 5W4

Brookfield Properties (16), 181 Bay St (Suite 330), Brookfield Place, Toronto, M5J 2T3

Canada Post Corp (16), 2701 Riverside Dr (Suite N1200), Canada Post PL, Ottawa, K1A 0B1

Canadian Blood Services (1), 1800 Alta Vista Dr, Ottawa, K1G 4J5

Canadian Business (17), 1 Mount Pleasant Rd (fl 11), Toronto, M4Y 2Y5

Canadian Institute of Chartered Accountants (1), 277 Wellington St W, Toronto, M5V 3H2

CAA Auto Club & Travel Agency Inc (1), 60 Commerce Valley Dr E, Thornhill, L3T 7P9

Daily Commercial News & Construction Record (17), 500 Hood Rd (4th fl), Markham, L3R 9Z3

Direct Energy (16), 2225 Sheppard Ave E (Suite 100), Toronto, M2J 5C2

Doubleday Direct (13), 5900 Finch Ave E, Scarborough, M1B 0A2

Efstonscience Inc (3), 3350 Dufferin St, Toronto, M6A 3A4

Elmwood Spa (19), ,Toronto, M5G 1G7

Russell A Farrow Ltd (16), 2001 Huron Church Rd, Windsor, N9C 2L6

Foresters (15), 789 Don Mills Rd, Toronto, M3C 1T9

Four Seasons Hotels & Resorts (19), 1165 Leslie St, Toronto, M3C 2K8

Gardenimport Inc (8), 135 W Beaver Creek Rd, PO Box 760, Richmond Hill, L4B 1C6

GE Canada (9), 2300 Meadowvale Blvd, Mississauga, L5N 5P9

Gifts Corp (6), 130 Bell Farm Rd (Unit 2), Barrie, L4M 6J4

Harlequin Enterprises Ltd (17), 225 Duncan Mill Rd, Don Mills, M3B 3K9

Ideal Industries (Canada) Corp (9), 33 Fuller Rd, Ajax, L1S 2E1

Interwood Direct (8), 50 Staples Ave - Richmond Hill, Toronto, L4B O47

John Hancock Retirement Plan Services (14), 200 Bloor St W - ET6, Toronto, M4W1E5

The Kidney Foundation of Canada/Greater Ontario Branch (1), 35 Goderich Rd (Unit 9), Hamilton, L8E 4P2

Lombardi Publishing Corp (17), PO Box 428, Vaughan, L0J 1C0

Majestic Products Co (16), 410 Admiral Blvd, Mississauga, L5T 2N6

Manulife Financial Inc (15), 2 Queen St E, Toronto, M5C 3G7

Open Text Inc (16), 275 Frank Tompa Dr, Waterloo, N2L 0A1

Peak Impact Inc (14), 2 Beaverbrook Rd (Suite 204), Ottawa, K2K 1L2

PC Ontario Fund (1), 401-19 Duncan St, Toronto, M5H 3H1

Psion Teklogix Inc (3), 2100 Meadowvale Blvd, Mississauga, L5N 719

Rogers Publishing Ltd (17), 333 Blour St E (6th fl), Toronto, M4W 1G9

Royal Bank of Canada (14), 200 Bay St, Royal Bank Plaza, Toronto, M5J 2J5

Royal Canadian Mint (16), 320 Sussex Dr, Ottawa, K2J 2G6

Sears Canada Inc (5), 222 Jarvis St, Toronto, M5B 2B8

SickKids Foundation (1), 525 University Ave (fl 14), Toronto, M5G 2L3

SDI Marketing (14), 65 International Blvd (Suite 200), Toronto, M9W 6L9

Steptoe & Wife Antiques Ltd (8), 90 Tycos Dr, Toronto, M6B 1V9

Telemedia Communications US (17), 25 Sheppard Ave W (Suite 100), North York, M2N 6S7

Stephen Thomas (1), 184 Front St E (Suite 501), Toronto, M5A 4N3

TigerDirect.ca (3), 55 E Beaver Creek Rd (Unit G), Richmond Hill, L4B 1E5

Toronto Hydro-Electric System (1), 14 Carlton St, Toronto, M5B 1K5

United Way of Greater Toronto (1), 26 Wellington St E (11th fl), Toronto, M5E 1W9

UNICEF Canada (1), 2200 Yonge St (Suite 1100), Toronto, M4S 2C6

VGH Solutions (7), 145 Anderson Ave, Markham, L6E 1A4

John Wiley & Sons Canada Ltd (17), 5353 Dundaf St W, Etobicoke, M9B 6H8

Winslow Publishing (17), 550 Eglinton Ave W, Toronto, M5N 3A8

World Vision Canada (1), One World Dr, Mississauga, L5T 2Y4

Prince Edward Island

Vesey's Seeds Ltd (8), PO Box 9000, Charlottetown, C1A 8K6

Quebec

Cancer Research Society (1), 625 President Kennedy Ave (Suite 402), Montreal, H3A 3S5

Coverdell Canada Corporation (16), 1801 McGill College Ave (Suite 725), Montreal, H3A 2N4

Desjardins Financial Securities (15), 200 Ave des Commandeurs, Levis, G6V 6R2

L'Entraide Assurance (15), 520 Charest Blvd E (fl1), Quebec-Centre Station, Quebec, G2J 0A2

Marimac Inc (8), 6395 Cote-de-Liesse, Montreal, H4T 1E5

Promotional Product Professionals of Canada (1), 6700 Cote-de-Liesse (Suite 100), Saint-Laurent, H4T 2B5

Standard Life (15), 1245 Sherbrooke St W, Montreal, H3G 1G3

Thought Technology Ltd (16), 2180 Belgrave Ave, Montreal, H4A 2L8

Yves Rocher North America Inc (7), 2199 Boul Fernaud LaFontaine, Longueuil, J4G2V7

A

A&B Equipment Co, Fort Worth, TX (16)
A La Carte, Chicago, IL (16)
A-T Surgical Manufacturing Co, Holyoke, MA (2)
AAA Auto Club South, Tampa, FL (1)
AAA-Chicago Motor Club, Aurora, IL (1)
AAA Umbrella Co Inc, Northvale, NJ (16)
ABC Carpet & Home, New York, NY (8)
ABC Clio, Santa Barbara, CA (17)
ACBL, Horn Lake, MS (1)
ACCO North America, Lincolnshire, IL (16)
ACP - Automation Control Products, Alpharetta, GA (16)
ACP Medicine, Hamilton, ON, Canada (17)
ADM Productions Inc, Port Washington, NY (16)
ADP Inc, Roseland, NJ (16)
ADRFCO, Washington, DC (1)
ADT Worldwide, Boca Raton, FL (16)
AESU Inc, Baltimore, MD (19)
AFA Service Corp, Atlanta, GA (16)
AFL-CIO, Washington, DC (1)
AGCO Inc, Norcross, GA (9)
AIG Accident & Health, New York, NY (15)
AIIM International, Silver Spring, MD (1)
AIN Plastics Inc, Yonkers, NY (16)
Alco Chemical, Chattanooga, TN (16)
AMA Insurance Agency Inc, Chicago, IL (15)
AMC Inc, Atlanta, GA (2)
AMS Direct, Burr Ridge, IL (13)
AON Center, Chicago, IL (15)
Aon Consulting New York, New York, NY (15)
Aon Innovative Solutions, Chicago, IL (16)
APSCO, Davenport Center, NY (11)
APW-Wright Line, Worcester, MA (16)
ARAG, Des Moines, IA (15)
ARE Press, Virginia Beach, VA (1)
ARI, Orchard Hill, GA (16)
ASE Technologies Inc, Wilmington, MA (16)
ASM Press, Washington, DC (17)
ASTM International, West Conshohocken, PA (1)
AT&T, Bedminster, NJ (16)
Aardvark Enterprises, Calgary, AB, Canada (17)
Abbeon Cal Inc, Santa Barbara, CA (9)
Abbey of Gethsemani, New Haven, KY (1)
Abbey Press, Saint Meinrad, IN (6)
Abbott, North Chicago, IL (7)
Abbott, Langer Association Surveys, Washington, DC (17)
Abbott Products, Weymouth, MA (16)
Harry N Abrams Inc, New York, NY (17)
Absolute Reservation Center Inc, Longwood, FL (19)
Academic Management Services, Boston, MA (14)
Academic Travel Abroad Inc, Washington, DC (19)
Academy of Psychic Arts & Sciences, Dallas, TX (5)
Accountants Education Group, Dallas, TX (10)
Accountants' Supply House, Lancaster, CA (10)
Accountemps, Menlo Park, CA (16)
Accounting with Debits and Credits with Coates & Hutchinson PC, Odenton, MD (14)
Accuracy in Media Inc, Washington, DC (1)
ACCUSPLIT Inc, Livermore, CA (16)
AccuTrade Inc, Bellevue, NE (14)
Ace Communications, Garden City, NY (3)
Ace Hardware Corp, Oak Brook, IL (16)
Achieve Global, Tampa, FL (16)
Action Direct Inc, Miami, FL (11)
Active Parenting, Marietta, GA (17)
Active Web Group, Hauppauge, NY (9)
Activision Value, Eden Prairie, MN (16)
ActivStyle, Minneapolis, MN (16)
AcuSport Corp, Bellefontaine, OH (11)
Ad-Lib Advertising Inc, Old Bridge, NJ (10)
Adams Manufacturing Co, Cleveland, OH (9)
Adirondack Direct, Long Island City, NY (10)
Admore Inc, Macomb, MI (10)
Adnet USA, Arlington Heights, IL (16)
Advanced Machinery, New Castle, DE (9)
Advanced Medical Nutrition Inc, Pittsburgh, PA (7)

Advanstar Communications Inc, North Olmstead, OH (17)
Adventure Creations Inc, Costa Mesa, CA (16)
The Advertising Council Inc, New York, NY (1)
AeroGraphics, DeLand, FL (3)
Aerovox Inc, New Bedford, MA (16)
AETNA - Marketing Product & Communication, Hartford, CT (14)
Affinity Express, Elgin, IL (16)
Affinity4, Norfolk, VA (16)
Agate Publishing, Evanston, IL (17)
Agco Spra-Coup, Duluth, GA (16)
Agilis Co, Albert Lea, MN (14)
AGORA Inc, Baltimore, MD (17)
Agri Drain Corp, Adair, IA (9)
AHC Media, Atlanta, GA (17)
Ahrensdorf & Associates, Saint Davids, PA (16)
Air Ambulance Network Inc, Palm Harbor, FL (16)
Air Chek Inc, Naples, NC (9)
Air France, New York, NY (16)
Air-Lec Industries Inc, Madison, WI (16)
Air Power USA, Los Angeles, CA (12)
Air-Scent International, Pittsburgh, PA (16)
Aircraft Spruce & Specialty Co, Corona, CA (12)
Airlines Reporting Corp, Arlington, VA (16)
The Akadine Press Inc, White Plains, NY (16)
Alamo Rent A Car, Tulsa, OK (16)
John Alden Life Insurance Co/North Star Marketing, Duluth, GA (15)
Alfa Aesar-A Johnson Matthey Co, Ward Hill, MA (9)
Alfa CTP Systems, Tewksbury, MA (10)
Alfred Publishing Co Inc, Van Nuys, CA (17)
Alfreda's Film Works, Denver, CO (17)
AliMed Inc, Dedham, MA (7)
Alitalia, New York, NY (19)
All Star Carts & Vehicles, Bay Shore, NY (16)
All Star Directories, Seattle, WA (17)
All-State Legal, Cranford, NJ (16)
AllBrands.com Sewing Machine Superstore, Baton Rouge, LA (11)
Allergan Inc, Irvine, CA (16)
Alliance Bernstein, New York, NY (14)
Alliance for the Arts, New York, NY (1)
Alliance of Area Business Publications, El Segundo, CA (1)
Allianz Life Insurance Co of North America, Minneapolis, MN (15)
Alloyd Brands, Dekalb, IL (16)
Alltel, Little Rock, AR (16)
Allyn & Bacon, Upper Saddle River, NJ (17)
Almore International Inc, Portland, OR (7)
Almost Heaven Group, Renick, WV (16)
CM Almy & Son Inc, Greenwich, CT (5)
Alpha Supply Inc, Bremerton, WA (16)
ALSTOM Signaling Inc, West Henrietta, NY (16)
Alzheimer Society of Canada, Toronto, ON, Canada (1)
Amacom Books, New York, NY (17)
Amanet, Canoga Park, CA (16)
Amaryllis Inc, Baton Rouge, LA (8)
Amateur Electronic Supply LLC, Milwaukee, WI (16)
Amazon Drygoods, Davenport, IA (2)
Ambassador Programs, Spokane, WA (19)
Ambient Shapes Inc, Hickory, NC (9)
Amcat TeleProfit Inc, Oklahoma City, OK (16)
American Airlines Inc, Dallas, TX (19)
American Appraisal Associates, Milwaukee, WI (14)
American Arbitration Association, New York, NY (1)
American Association for Justice, Washington, DC (1)
American Bankers Association, Washington, DC (1)
American Bar Association, Chicago, IL (1)
American Biographical Institute Inc, Raleigh, NC (17)
American Capital, Bethesda, MD (15)
American Century Investments, Kansas City, MO (14)
American Civil Defense Association, Draper, UT (16)
American College of Physicians, Washington, DC (17)
American Counseling Association, Broken Arrow, OK (1)
American Crane & Equipment Corp, Douglassville, PA (16)
American Express Co, New York, NY (14)

American Family Insurance Group, Madison, WI (15)
American Family Life Assurance Co of Columbus (AFLAC), Columbus, GA (15)
American Federation of Astrologers, Tempe, AZ (1)
American Fidelity Assurance Co, Oklahoma City, OK (15)
American Forests, Washington, DC (1)
American Foundation for the Blind Inc, New York, NY (1)
American General Co, Neptune, NJ (15)
American General Life Insurance Co, Houston, TX (15)
American Greetings Corp, Cleveland, OH (16)
American Health & Life Insurance Co, Fort Worth, TX (15)
American Health & Safety Inc, Stoughton, WI (16)
American Health Information Management Association, Chicago, IL (1)
American Healthways, Franklin, TN (16)
American Institute of Chemical Engineers, New York, NY (1)
American Institute of CPAs, New York, NY (1)
American Institute of Physics, Melville, NY (17)
American Insurance Administrators Inc, Columbus, OH (15)
American International Group, New York, NY (15)
American Library Association-Publishing Services, Chicago, IL (1)
American Locker Security Systems Inc, Coppell, TX (16)
American Management Association, New York, NY (1)
American Mathematical Society, Providence, RI (17)
American Meadows Inc & Vermont Wild Flowers Farm, Williston, VT (8)
American Medical Association, Chicago, IL (1)
American Megatrends Inc, Norcross, GA (3)
American Modern Insurance Group, Amelia, OH (15)
American Movie Classics Holding Corp, Jericho, NY (16)
American Ostomy Supply, Earth City, MO (16)
American Period Lighting Inc, Lancaster, PA (8)
American Power Conversion Corp, West Kingston, RI (3)
American Preferred Reader's Service Inc, Fort Lauderdale, FL (18)
American Printing House for the Blind, Louisville, KY (7)
American Psychological Association, Washington, DC (1)
American Recreation Products Inc, Saint Louis, MO (11)
American Red Cross, Washington, DC (1)
American Research Corp, El Monte, CA (3)
American Running Association, Bethesda, MD (1)
American Science & Surplus, Niles, IL (9)
American Society for Quality-ASQ, Milwaukee, WI (1)
American Society for Training & Development, Alexandria, VA (1)
American Society of Interior Designers, Washington, DC (1)
American Society on Aging, San Francisco, CA (1)
American Speech-Language-Hearing Association, Rockville, MD (1)
American Student Assistance, Boston, MA (1)
American Technical Publishers Inc, Orland Park, IL (17)
American 3B Scientific, Tucker, GA (16)
American Trim, Lima, OH (9)
American Trucking Association, Arlington, VA (1)
The American Vintage Library, Los Angeles, CA (17)
Americans for Peace Now, Washington, DC (1)
America's Finest Pet Doors, San Luis Obispo, CA (16)
Americraft - The Gift Brokers Inc, Wendell, MA (16)
Amerisure Insurance Cos, Farmington Hills, MI (15)
Ameritech Services Inc, Milwaukee, WI (16)
Ames Taping Tool System Inc, Stone Mountain, GA (9)
Amica Insurance, Lincoln, RI (15)

Amigo Mobility International Inc, Bridgeport, MI (16)
AmMed Direct, Antioch, TN (7)
Amos Press, Inc, Sidney, OH (17)
Ampersand Press, Port Townsend, WA (11)
Amrel, El Monte, CA (16)
Amsterdam Printing, Amsterdam, NY (16)
Amtelco, McFarland, WI (16)
Amvac Chemical Corp, Los Angeles, CA (8)
Analytical Measurements, Chester, NJ (9)
Anatomical Chart Co, Chicago, IL (7)
Ancient Circles, Willits, CA (6)
Anda Inc, Weston, FL (7)
Hanna Andersson Corp, Portland, OR (2)
Andrea Electronics Corp, Bohemia, NY (16)
Andrew Wireless Solutions, Westchester, IL (16)
Angelica Image Apparel, Saint Louis, MO (16)
Angler's Catalog Co, Eagle, ID (11)
Anglicans United & Latimer Press, Cedar Hill, TX (1)
Anheuser-Busch Inc Promotional Products Group, Shelton, CT (6)
Anne Klein, New York, NY (16)
Annie's Attic LLC, Big Sandy, TX (11)
Anritsu Co, Morgan Hill, CA (16)
Anthem Blue Cross, Westlake Village, CA (15)
Anthem Blue Cross Blue Shield, Saint Louis, MO (15)
Anthem Corporate Communications, Indianapolis, IN (15)
Antiquarian Booksellers Association of America Inc, New York, NY (1)
Antique & Collectible Tools Inc, Pownal, ME (11)
Antique Electronic Supply, Tempe, AZ (3)
Aon's Affinity Insurance Services Inc, Hatboro, PA (15)
Apothecary Products Inc, Burnsville, MN (7)
Appalachian Nurseries, Inc, Chambersburg, PA (8)
Apple Computer Inc, Cupertino, CA (16)
Appraisal Institute, Chicago, IL (1)
Arbill Safety Products, Philadelphia, PA (9)
Arbus Capital Ltd, Schaumburg, IL (16)
Arcelor Mittal, Coatesville, PA (16)
ArcelorMittal, Chicago, IL (16)
Arch Telecom Inc, Austin, TX (16)
Arctic Trading Co Inc, Churchill, MB, Canada (6)
Area Electronics Systems Inc, Anaheim, CA (3)
Arent Fox LLP, Washington, DC (1)
Argent Trading LLC, New York, NY (16)
Aristokraft Inc, Jasper, IN (16)
Arizona Highways Magazine, Phoenix, AZ (17)
Arkline Computers & Supply, Cleveland, OH (3)
Armbrust Paper Tubes Inc, Chicago, IL (10)
Armento Inc, Buffalo, NY (5)
Army Times Publishing Co, Springfield, VA (17)
Arnet Pharmaceutical, Davie, FL (7)
Arquest Inc, Millstone Twp, NJ (16)
Arrow Advantage, Eden Prairie, MN (3)
Arrow Co, Indianapolis, IN (16)
Arrowhead Mountain Spring Water, Wilkes Barre, PA (16)
The Art of Self Promotion, Hoboken, NJ (17)
Artech House, Norwood, MA (17)
Arthritis Foundation, Atlanta, GA (1)
Sam Ash.Com, Tampa, FL (5)
Asheville Compassionate Communication Center, Asheville, NC (13)
Ashland Inc, Covington, KY (16)
Ashworth University, Norcross, GA (13)
Aspen Publishers Inc, New York, NY (17)
Assisted Access- NFSS, Lake Villa, IL (3)
Associated Construction Publications, Indianapolis, IN (17)
Associated Photo, Florence, KY (16)
Associated Textile Rental Services, Rochester, NY (16)
Association for Computing Machinery (ACM), New York, NY (1)
Association for Facilities Engineering, Herndon, VA (1)
Association for Financial Professionals, Bethesda, MD (14)

Association of American Publishers, Washington, DC (1)
Association of Bridal Consultants, New Milford, CT (1)
Association of Marian Helpers, Stockbridge, MA (1)
Assurant Group, New York, NY (15)
Assurant Health, Milwaukee, WI (15)
Assurant Solutions Preneed Division, Atlanta, GA (15)
Astral Brands LLC, Smyrna, GA (7)
Astro Air, LP, Jacksonville, TX (9)
Astronomical Society of the Pacific, San Francisco, CA (1)
At Last Naturals, North Salem, NY (7)
Atlanta Cutlery Corp, Conyers, GA (11)
Atlantic Publication Group LLC, Charleston, SC (17)
Atlantic Spice Co, North Truro, MA (4)
Audio & Video Labs Inc, Pennsauken, NJ (16)
Audio Classics Ltd, Vestal, NY (3)
Audio-Digest Foundation, Glendale, CA (1)
Audiovox, Hauppauge, NY (16)
August Home Publishing Co, Des Moines, IA (17)
Wendell August Forge Inc, Grove City, PA (6)
Authentic Designs Colonial and Early American Lighting Fixtures Inc, West Rupert, VT (8)
Autodesk Inc, San Rafael, CA (16)
Automation Mailing & Shipping Solutions Inc, Cleveland, OH (16)
Automod, Atlanta, GA (12)
Automotive Forms, Baltimore, MD (16)
Automotive Headphones, Sterling Heights, MI (16)
Avery Dennison Corp, Brea, CA (10)
Aviation Book Co, Seattle, WA (17)
Avis World Headquarters, Parsippany, NJ (19)
Avnet Inc, Phoenix, AZ (16)
Avon Books, New York, NY (17)
Award Co of America, Tuscaloosa, AL (6)
The Ayn Rand Institute, Irvine, CA (1)

B

B Bunch Co Inc, Phoenix, AZ (16)
BAI, Chicago, IL (17)
BCR Enterprises Inc, Downers Grove, IL (17)
BGE Home Products & Services Inc, Baltimore, MD (16)
BJ's Wholesale Club Inc, Westborough, MA (13)
BJU Press, Greenville, SC (17)
BLS Inc, Wilmington, DE (17)
BMI, Nashville, TN (1)
BMI Home Decorating, Spring Grove, IL (16)
BNY Mellon, New York, NY (14)
BOC Gases, Murray Hill, NJ (16)
BP, Warrenville, IL (16)
BT Alex Brown Inc, Baltimore, MD (14)
BYK-Gardner USA, Columbia, MD (16)
Babcox Publications LLC, Akron, OH (17)
Babyshoe.com, Hendersonville, NC (6)
Back Designs Inc, Novato, CA (7)
Back to the Bible, Lincoln, NE (5)
HH Backer Associates Inc, Chicago, IL (17)
Badge-A-Minit, Oglesby, IL (16)
Bahamas Ministry of Tourism, Fort Lauderdale, FL (19)
Baker & Taylor Inc, Charlotte, NC (16)
Balboa Life & Casualty, Irvine, CA (15)
Balducci Enterprises Inc, Germantown, MD (16)
Baldwin Filters, Kearney, NE (16)
Bale Co, Providence, RI (16)
Balfour, Austin, TX (16)
Ballard Designs, Atlanta, GA (8)
Bamboo Sourcery, Sebastopol, CA (8)
Bank Boston, Waltham, MA (14)
Bank of America, Charlotte, NC (14)
Bank of Hawaii, Honolulu, HI (14)
The Bank of New York/Delaware, Newark, DE (14)
Bank One, Chicago, IL (14)
Banker & Tradesman, Boston, MA (17)
Bankers Warranty Group, Saint Petersburg, FL (16)
Barbour Publishing Inc, Uhrichsville, OH (17)
Bob Barker Co Inc, Fuquay Varina, NC (5)

BarnesandNoble.com, New York, NY (16)
Baron/Barclay Bridge Supplies, Louisville, KY (11)
RG Barry Corp, Pickerington, OH (2)
BarterNews, Laguna Niguel, CA (17)
Barton-Cotton, Baltimore, MD (16)
Bart's Watersports, North Webster, IN (11)
Baseline FT, Los Angeles, CA (17)
Basic Adhesives Inc, Clifton, NJ (9)
Bass Pro Shops, Springfield, MO (11)
Bathroom Machineries, Murphys, CA (8)
Baton Rouge Conventions & Visitors Bureau, Baton Rouge, LA (1)
Battery Pros Inc, Horseshoe Beach, FL (9)
Battleground Antiques Inc, New Bern, NC (6)
Baudville Inc, Grand Rapids, MI (16)
The Bauman Group, Ashland, MA (14)
Bausch & Lomb Inc, Rochester, NY (16)
Baxter Bros Inc, Greenwich, CT (17)
Bay Manufacturing, Milan, OH (16)
Mel Bay Publications Inc, Pacific, MO (17)
Bayer Corp Consumer Care Division, Morristown, NJ (16)
Baylor Health Care System, Dallas, TX (16)
LL Bean Inc, Freeport, ME (2)
Bear Computer Systems Inc, Dallas, TX (16)
Bear Woods Supply Co Inc, Cornwallis, NS, Canada (11)
Bearingpoint Inc, Montvale, NJ (14)
Beau Rivage Resort & Casino, Biloxi, MS (19)
Beauty Naturally, Burlingame, CA (7)
Beckman Coulter Inc, Brea, CA (16)
Beckmann Converting Inc, Amsterdam, NY (16)
Beemak Plastics Inc, La Mirada, CA (16)
Beeman Precision Airguns, Santa Fe Springs, CA (11)
Behlen Manufacturing Co, Columbus, NE (16)
Belcaro Group Inc, Greenwood Village, CO (17)
Bell & Howell Ltd, North York, ON, Canada (9)
The Bell Group Rio Grande, Albuquerque, NM (5)
Bell Performance Inc, Longwood, FL (9)
Bellacor, Mendota Heights, MN (8)
Beltone, Glenview, IL (3)
Belvoir Media Group LLC, Norwalk, CT (17)
Bencone Uniform Connection, Winston Salem, NC (2)
BenefitMall, Dallas, TX (15)
Benetton USA, New York, NY (2)
Bentley College, Waltham, MA (13)
J&H Berge/The Lab Mart, South Plainfield, NJ (7)
Berger's Table Pad Co, Indianapolis, IN (8)
Berkeley College, Paramus, NJ (13)
Berkey Brendel Sheline, Akron, OH (1)
Berkshire Direct Inc, Williamstown, MA (17)
Berkshire Record Outlet Inc, Lee, MA (3)
Berman Group, Newton Center, MA (16)
Berry Hill Ltd, Saint Thomas, ON, Canada (8)
Berway Visual Products Inc, Wilmington, MA (3)
Channing L Bete Co Inc, South Deerfield, MA (17)
Better Health Fitness, Brooklyn, NY (11)
Better Tools For Industry, Santee, CA (9)
BIC Corp, Shelton, CT (16)
Bick International, Van Nuys, CA (6)
Bigelow Electronics, Bluffton, OH (3)
Bijoux Terner, Miami, FL (16)
Biomerica Inc, Irvine, CA (7)
Biosciences-Amersham, Piscataway, NJ (16)
Bissinger French Confections, Saint Louis, MO (4)
Bizzaro Rubber Stamps, Greenville, RI (6)
Black & Decker (US) Inc, Towson, MD (16)
Black Box Corp, Lawrence, PA (3)
Black Entertainment Television Inc, Washington, DC (16)
Blaine Window Hardware Inc, Hagerstown, MD (9)
William Blair & Co LLC, Chicago, IL (14)
Bland Farms, Glennville, GA (4)
Blethen Maine Newspapers Inc, Portland, ME (17)
Dick Blick Holdings Inc, Galesburg, IL (16)
Blue Coral Slick 50, Houston, TX (16)
Blue Cross & Blue Shield Cobalt, Waukesha, WI (15)
Blue Cross & Blue Shield of Florida, Jacksonville, FL (15)
Blue Cross & Blue Shield of Oklahoma, Tulsa, OK (15)

Blue Cross & Blue Shield of South Carolina, Columbia, SC (15)
Blue Cross/Blue Shield of Illinois, Chicago, IL (15)
Blue Cross Blue Shield of Louisiana, Baton Rouge, LA (15)
Blue Raven Technology, Wilmington, MA (3)
Blue Shield Life, San Francisco, CA (15)
Blue Shield of California, San Francisco, CA (15)
Bluestem Brands, Eden Prairie, MN (16)
Bluestone Perennials Inc, Madison, OH (8)
B'nai B'rith International, Washington, DC (1)
Bobcat Co, West Fargo, ND (16)
Bobley-Harmann Corp/GiftValues.Com, Westbury, NY (5)
Body by Jake Global LLC, Los Angeles, CA (16)
Boeing Co, Chicago, IL (16)
Boise Cascade Holdings LLC, Boise, ID (16)
Bolind Inc, Boulder, CO (16)
Bontex, Honolulu, HI (16)
Book Publishing Information Kit, Santa Barbara, CA (17)
Books on Tape, Westminster, MD (17)
Booth Michigan, Grand Rapids, MI (17)
Borbeleta Gardens, Fairbault, MN (8)
Bosom Buddy Breast Forms, Boise, ID (7)
The Boston Co, Boston, MA (14)
The Boston Globe, Boston, MA (17)
Boundless Corp, Phelps, NY (16)
Bountiful Gardens, Willits, CA (8)
Bowers & Merena Auctions, Irvine, CA (16)
BowTie Inc, Irvine, CA (17)
Boyd Gaming Corp, Las Vegas, NV (16)
The Bradford Group, Niles, IL (16)
Bradford Health Services, Birmingham, AL (16)
Vera Bradley, Fort Wayne, IN (2)
Brady Corp, Milwaukee, WI (16)
Brady Marketing Co Inc, Walnut Creek, CA (16)
Brahmin Leather Works, Fairhaven, MA (16)
Branch Banking & Trust Co, Wilson, NC (14)
Brand New Products LLC, Chicago, IL (4)
Brant Publications Inc, New York, NY (17)
Brentwood Benson Music Publishing, Franklin, TN (17)
Bridgestone/Firestone North American Tire LLC, Nashville, TN (16)
Briefings Publishing Group, Richmond, VA (17)
Brigade Quartermasters Ltd, Providence, RI (11)
Brim Electronics Inc, Lodi, NJ (3)
Bristol-Myers Squibb Co, New York, NY (16)
British Columbia Automobile Association, Burnaby, BC, Canada (15)
Broadcast Electronics Inc, Quincy, IL (3)
Broadmoor Hotel Inc, Colorado Springs, CO (19)
BroadVision Inc, Redwood City, CA (16)
Broadway Play Publishing Inc, New York, NY (17)
Brocade Communications Systems Inc, San Jose, CA (16)
Brokers/Consultants Inc, Flossmoor, IL (15)
Bronson Nutritionals LLC, Hauppauge, NY (7)
Bronx Council on the Arts, Bronx, NY (1)
Brooke Distributors Inc, Miami, FL (3)
Brookfield Properties, Toronto, ON, Canada (16)
Brookhollow Cards, Rexburg, ID (10)
Brooks Equipment Co, Charlotte, NC (9)
Brooks Sports Inc, Bothell, WA (16)
Brown & Co, Blaine, WA (8)
Arthur Brown & Bro Inc, New York, NY (10)
Brown-Forman Beverages Worldwide, Louisville, KY (16)
Brown Shoe Co, Saint Louis, MO (16)
BrownCor International, Milwaukee, WI (5)
Brownell Holly Farms, Oregon City, OR (6)
Brown's Omaha Plant Farms, Omaha, TX (8)
Bruce Medical Supply, Waltham, MA (7)
Robert Bryan Ltd, Port Royal, VA (2)
Bucks County Coffee Co, Conshohocken, PA (16)
Buena Vista Home Entertainment, Burbank, CA (3)
Buena Vista Winery, Sonoma, CA (16)
Buick Division General Motors Corp, Detroit, MI (16)
Bull HN Information Systems, Chelmsford, MA (16)
Bulletin of the Atomic Scientists, Chicago, IL (17)

Bunker Hill Auctions, Newark, IL (6)
Bunn-O-Matic Corp, Springfield, IL (16)
Bunzl Distribution USA, Inc, Saint Louis, MO (16)
Burberry, New York, NY (2)
Burden Sales Co, Lincoln, NE (9)
The Bureau of National Affairs, Inc, Arlington, VA (17)
Burger's Ozark Country Cured Hams Inc, California, MO (4)
Burlington Industries Inc, Greensboro, NC (16)
Burlington Northern & Santa Fe Railroad, Fort Worth, TX (16)
Burns Inc, Fall River, MA (16)
DV Burrell Seed Growers Co, Rocky Ford, CO (8)
Bushnell Corporation, Overland Park, KS (11)
Bushnell Outdoor Products, Overland Park, KS (16)
Business Automation Systems Inc, Nashville, TN (16)
Business Graphics Inc, Woodstock, IL (16)
Business Planners & Consultants Inc, New York, NY (15)
Business Publishers Inc, Durham, NC (17)
Butler Distributing Co, Kenilworth, NJ (3)
Butler Schein Animal Health, Dublin, OH (16)
Butler Specialty Co, Chicago, IL (16)
Butterfield Farms Inc, Rolling Hills Estates, CA (4)
BUYSEASONS Inc, Bothell, WA (5)
Byron Plantation, Vidalia, GA (4)

C

C&H Distributors LLC, Milwaukee, WI (9)
C&S Sales Inc, Wheeling, IL (9)
C&T Bridge Supplies, Los Alamitos, CA (11)
CA Inc, Islandia, NY (16)
CAA Auto Club & Travel Agency Inc, Thornhill, ON, Canada (1)
CAIG Laboratories Inc, Poway, CA (9)
CAS Design Center, North Richland Hills, TX (8)
CBT Direct, Tarpon Springs, FL (16)
CCA Global Partners, Manchester, NH (16)
CCH Inc, Riverwoods, IL (17)
CCI Solutions, Olympia, WA (16)
CCIM Institute, Chicago, IL (1)
CDW Computer Centers Inc, Vernon Hills, IL (3)
CDW Corp, Vernon Hills, IL (16)
CHG, Salt Lake City, UT (7)
CIT, Livingston, NJ (14)
CMEinfo.com, Birmingham, AL (16)
CNA, Chicago, IL (15)
CNY Awards & Apparel Inc, New Hartford, NY (5)
CPAC Inc, Leicester, NY (16)
CPC Inc, Babylon, NY (16)
CPM Delta 1, Inc, Dallas, TX (11)
CRB, Chicago, IL (17)
CRM Learning, Carlsbad, CA (16)
CSI, Conklin, NY (16)
CTB MacMillan/McGraw-Hill, Monterey, CA (16)
CTC Corp, Bennington, VT (16)
CVT Production Inc, Granger, IN (16)
CXO Media Inc, Framingham, MA (17)
CYRO Industries, Parsippany, NJ (16)
Cabela's Inc, Sidney, NE (11)
Cable Connection, Fremont, CA (3)
Cable Films & Video, Mission Hills, KS (3)
Cable Shopping Network, Scottsdale, AZ (16)
Cables to Go, Moraine, OH (3)
Cablexpress Technologies, Syracuse, NY (10)
Caesars Atlantic City Casino/Hotel, Atlantic City, NJ (19)
Caesars Palace, Las Vegas, NV (16)
Calbiochem-Novabiochem Corp, San Diego, CA (9)
Calendar Marketing Association, Wheaton, IL (1)
California Chamber of Commerce, Sacramento, CA (1)
California Institute of Technology, Pasadena, CA (16)
California Mustang Parts & Accessories, City of Industry, CA (16)
California Society of CPA's, San Mateo, CA (1)
Callaway Gardens, Pine Mountain, GA (19)
Calumet Photographic Inc, Bensenville, IL (3)

Cambridge Educational, New York, NY (12)
Camelot Enterprises, Bristol, WI (9)
Camp Healthcare Inc, Jackson, MI (16)
Campaigns & Elections Magazine, Arlington, VA (17)
Campbell Soup Co, Camden, NJ (16)
Campbell Tools Co, Springfield, OH (9)
Canada Post Corp, Ottawa, ON, Canada (16)
Canadian Business, Toronto, ON, Canada (17)
Canadian Institute of Chartered Accountants, Toronto, ON, Canada (1)
Cancer Fund of America Inc, Knoxville, TN (1)
Cancer Research Society, Montreal, PQ, Canada (1)
Cane & Basket Supply Co, Los Angeles, CA (8)
The Caning Shop, Berkeley, CA (11)
Cape Cod Cupola Co Inc, North Dartmouth, MA (8)
Capezio Ballet Makers Inc, Totowa, NJ (16)
Capitol Concierge Inc, Washington, DC (16)
Captan Associates Inc, Brick, NJ (17)
Caraustar, Austell, GA (16)
Card Technology Inc, Hopkins, MN (16)
Care2, Washington, DC (1)
CARE USA, Atlanta, GA (1)
Carefirst Blue Cross Blue Shield, Washington, DC (15)
Carestream Health Inc, Rochester, NY (7)
CARFAX Inc, Centreville, VA (12)
Caribe Direct Inc, San Juan, PR (6)
Carino Nurseries, Indiana, PA (8)
Carlson's Gardens, Waitsfield, VT (8)
Carnival Cruise Lines, Miami, FL (19)
Carolina Biological Supply Co, Burlington, NC (9)
Carolina Exotic Gardens/CEG Nursery, Greenville, NC (8)
ER Carpenter, Taylor, TX (16)
Carroll Publishing, Bethesda, MD (17)
Carrot-Top Industries Inc, Hillsborough, NC (16)
Carter & Holmes Inc, Newberry, SC (8)
Cartouche Ltd, Alexandria, VA (6)
Carvel Corp, Atlanta, GA (4)
Cascade Forest Nursery, Bellevue, IA (8)
Casual Male Retail Group, Canton, MA (2)
Caterpillar Inc, Peoria, IL (16)
Caterpillar Insurance Services Corp, Nashville, TN (15)
The Catholic University of America Press, Washington, DC (17)
Cattle Kate, Boise, ID (2)
Marshall Cavendish Corp, Tarrytown, NY (17)
Caviarteria New York Inc, Astoria, NY (4)
Cedar Fresh Products, Coral Gables, FL (16)
Cellular One Group, Oklahoma City, OK (16)
Celtic Life Insurance Co, Chicago, IL (15)
Cengage Learning, Independence, KY (17)
Centaur Forge LLC, Burlington, WI (9)
Center for Creative Leadership, Greensboro, NC (16)
Center for Professional Advancement, East Brunswick, NJ (13)
Center for Professional Development, Tallahassee, FL (16)
CenterCore Group Inc, Marked Tree, AR (16)
Central Pacific Bank, Honolulu, HI (14)
Central Shippee Inc, Bloomingdale, NJ (16)
Central States Indemnity, Omaha, NE (15)
Century Photo, Santa Fe Springs, CA (10)
CertainTeed Corp, Valley Forge, PA (16)
Cessna Aircraft Co, Wichita, KS (16)
Chabin Concepts, Chico, CA (16)
Chadsworth's 1-800-Columns, Wilmington, NC (8)
Chain Store Guide, Tampa, FL (17)
Champion, Quincy, IL (16)
Champion America Inc, Branford, CT (10)
Champs Software Inc, Crystal River, FL (3)
Chanel Inc, New York, NY (16)
Channel 13 WNET Catalog Division, New York, NY (5)
Charisma Brands LLC, Laguna Hills, CA (6)
Charmaster Products Inc, Grand Rapids, MN (8)
Charolette Ford Trunks, Dumas, TX (11)
Charter One Bank, Cleveland, OH (14)
Chartifacts, Richmond, VA (6)
Chase Industries, Inc, Cincinnati, OH (16)

Chattanooga Shooting Supplies Inc, Chattanooga, TN (16)

Cheap Aprons, Derry, NH (2)

Checks by Phone/Checks by Web, Boynton Beach, FL (14)

CheckVantage, Austin, TX (14)

Chelsea Clock Co Inc, Chelsea, MA (6)

Chem-Tainer Industries Inc, North Babylon, NY (9)

Chemical Week, New York, NY (17)

Cherry Tree Toys Inc, Beloit, WI (11)

Chiasso, Chicago, IL (6)

Chicago Magazine, Chicago, IL (17)

Chick Harness & Supply Inc, Harrington, DE (11)

Chico's FAS Inc, Fort Myers, FL (2)

Chief Executive Magazine, Greenwich, CT (17)

Childreach US Member of Plan International, Warwick, RI (8)

Children of the Night, Van Nuys, CA (1)

Children's Hospital Foundation, Washington, DC (1)

China Books & Periodicals Inc, South San Francisco, CA (17)

Choice Hotels International, Silver Spring, MD (16)

Choice Point, Alpharetta, GA (16)

Christian Book Distributors Inc, Peabody, MA (17)

Christian Brands, Phoenix, AZ (16)

Christian Broadcasting Network Inc, Virginia Beach, VA (1)

Christianity Today Inc, Carol Stream, IL (17)

Church Pension Fund, New York, NY (1)

Cintas, Cincinnati, OH (16)

Citi Cards / Citicorp Credit Services, Long Island City, NY (14)

Citibank, New York, NY (14)

Citizens Against Government Waste, Washington, DC (1)

Citizens Bank, Dedham, MA (14)

City of LaGrange, LaGrange, GA (1)

Civil Service Employees Insurance Group, Walnut Creek, CA (15)

Clampitt Paper Co, Dallas, TX (16)

Clarin by Hussey Seating, North Berwick, ME (5)

The Clark Grave Vault Co, Columbus, OH (16)

Clarks of North America, Newton, MA (16)

Classic Thermographers, North Mankato, MN (10)

Clegg Industries Inc, Gardena, CA (16)

Clement Communications, Upper Chichester, PA (17)

Clemente Novelties Inc, Utica, NY (16)

Cleveland Institute of Electronics, Cleveland, OH (13)

Clients & Profits Worldwide, Oceanside, CA (14)

Cliggott Publishing Co, Norwalk, CT (17)

Clothing Solutions, Irvine, CA (2)

Clubs of America, Lakemoor, IL (6)

Cluett Peabody, New York, NY (16)

Coast Hotels Limited, Seattle, WA (19)

Coastal Hotel Group, Seattle, WA (1)

Coastal Tool & Supply, West Hartford, CT (16)

The Coca-Cola Co, Atlanta, GA (16)

Cockpit USA Inc, New York, NY (2)

Coin Laundry Association, Oakbrook Terrace, IL (1)

Cold Spring Harbor Lab Press, Woodbury, NY (17)

Cold Stream Farm, Free Soil, MI (8)

Coldwater Creek, Coeur D Alene, ID (2)

Cole-Parmer Instrument Co, Vernon Hills, IL (16)

Collector Books & American Quilters Society, Paducah, KY (17)

Collector's Armoury Ltd, McDonough, GA (6)

Collector's Teapot, Kingston, NY (6)

Collegesource Inc, San Diego, CA (17)

Collegiate Cap & Gown, Champaign, IL (16)

Collin Street Bakery, Corsicana, TX (4)

Collis Curve Catalog Sales, Brownsville, TX (7)

Colonial Redi-Record Corp, Brooklyn, NY (10)

Columbia Journalism Review, New York, NY (17)

Columbia-Presbyterian Medical Center, New York, NY (16)

The Columbian, Vancouver, WA (17)

Columbian Mutual Life Insurance Co, Binghamton, NY (15)

Comdata Corp, Brentwood, TN (14)

Comerica Inc, Dallas, TX (14)

Commemorative Brands Inc, Austin, TX (16)

Commerce Bancshares Inc, Saint Louis, MO (14)

Commercial Federal Bank, Omaha, NE (14)

Commercial Travelers Mutual Insurance Co, Utica, NY (15)

Commonwealth Business Media Inc, Newark, NJ (17)

Communication Industries Corp, Grafton, VT (10)

Communication Resources Inc, Canton, OH (18)

Community Coffee Co, Baton Rouge, LA (4)

Community Newspapers Co, Concord, MA (17)

Comp USA, Inc, Miami, FL (3)

Companion Plants, Athens, OH (8)

Compaq Computer Corp, Houston, TX (16)

Compass Bank, Birmingham, AL (14)

Compass Electronics, Forest Grove, OR (9)

Comphealth, Salt Lake City, UT (16)

Compustar, Mineola, NY (3)

Computer Station Corp, Houston, TX (3)

Computers for Education, Murfreesboro, TN (1)

Con-Way Truckload, Joplin, MO (12)

Concept Communications Co, Bolingbrook, IL (16)

Concordia Publishing House, Saint Louis, MO (17)

Concurrent Computer Corp, Duluth, GA (3)

Condolink, Omaha, NE (16)

The Conference Board, Inc, New York, NY (16)

Conform Pacific, Lomita, CA (16)

Conney Safety Products LLC, Madison, WI (7)

Consolidated Electronics Inc, Dayton, OH (3)

Consolidated Plastics Co Inc, Stow, OH (9)

Consumer Credit Advocates Inc, Salt Lake City, UT (16)

Consumer's Energy, Jackson, MI (16)

Continental Supply Inc, Cleveland, OH (9)

Continuing Education of the Bar (CEB), Oakland, CA (1)

Convertible Service, San Gabriel, CA (16)

David C Cook, Colorado Springs, CO (17)

Cooper Communities Inc, Rogers, AR (16)

Cooper Surgical Inc, Trumbull, CT (7)

Cooper Tire & Rubber Co Inc, Findlay, OH (16)

Cooper Vision, Fairport, NY (7)

Coppa Woodworking, Inc, San Pedro, CA (8)

Copper Art by Morse, Claremont, NH (8)

Josiah R Coppersmythe, Harwich, MA (8)

Coptech Inc, Woburn, MA (16)

Cornell Lab of Ornithology, Ithaca, NY (1)

Cornhusker Press, Hastings, NE (17)

Corona-Lotus Inc, San Francisco, CA (4)

Coronis Building Systems Inc, Burlington, NJ (9)

Corpus Christi Museum of Science & History, Corpus Christi, TX (1)

Cortz Inc, West Chicago, IL (5)

Cosco Industries Inc, Chicago, IL (16)

Cosgrove Associates, New York, NY (14)

Cosmo International, Deerfield Beach, FL (16)

Cotta Transmission Co, Beloit, WI (16)

Cougar Mountain Software, Boise, ID (14)

Council for Advancement and Support of Education (CASE), Washington, DC (1)

Council of Better Business Bureaus - BBBOnline, Arlington, VA (1)

Country Dance and Song Society, Haydenville, MA (1)

Country Financial, Bloomington, IL (15)

Country Sampler Group, Saint Charles, IL (17)

Countrywide Financial Corp, Calabasas, CA (14)

Courage Cards & Gifts, Golden Valley, MN (1)

Coursesmith, Denver, CO (17)

Coverdell & Co Inc, Chicago, IL (15)

Coverdell Canada Corporation, Montreal, PQ, Canada (16)

Covidien International, Mansfield, MA (7)

Cox Communications, Atlanta, GA (16)

Craft-Diston Industries, Wichita, KS (16)

The Ben Craig Center, Charlotte, NC (1)

Craig/Vartorella International Marketing & Advertising Inc, Camden, SC (1)

Crain Communications Inc, Detroit, MI (17)

Crane Pumps & Systems Inc, Piqua, OH (16)

Craver Mathews Smith & Co, Reston, VA (1)

Crazy Crow Trading Post, Pottsboro, TX (11)

Creative Health Products, Plymouth, MI (16)

Creative Learning Systems Inc, Longmont, CO (9)

Creative Publishing International, Minneapolis, MN (17)

Creative Teaching Associates, Clovis, CA (16)

Creative Teaching Press, Huntington Beach, CA (17)

Crest Healthcare Supply, Dassel, MN (16)

Crestline Specialties, Inc, Lewiston, ME (16)

The Cricket Magazine Group, Chicago, IL (17)

Critter Mountain Wear, Crested Butte, CO (2)

Cronin & Co, Glastonbury, CT (16)

A T Cross Co, Lincoln, RI (16)

Cross Country Automotive Services, Medford, MA (16)

The Cross Country Group LLC, Medford, MA (13)

Cross Country Stitching, Quakertown, PA (17)

Crowne Plaza Chateau Le Combe, Edmonton, AB, Canada (19)

Crystal Records Inc, Camas, WA (3)

Crystek Corp, Fort Myers, FL (9)

Cuba Cheese Shoppe, Cuba, NY (4)

Cuisinart, Stamford, CT (16)

Culinary Parts Unlimited, San Francisco, CA (16)

Cumberland Woodcraft Co Inc, Carlisle, PA (8)

CUNA Mutual Group, Madison, WI (15)

Cunningham Group, Elmwood Park, IL (15)

Curriculum Associates Inc, North Billerica, MA (17)

Cushman Fruit Co Inc, West Palm Beach, FL (4)

Custom Accessories, Niles, IL (11)

Custom Miniatures, Hudson, NH (6)

Customized Newspaper Advertising, Des Moines, IA (18)

Cuvaison Inc, Calistoga, CA (4)

Cygnus Business Media, Fort Atkinson, WI (17)

Cytec Industries Inc, Olean, NY (16)

D

D&E Pharmaceuticals Inc, Farmingdale, NJ (7)

DCA, West Chester, PA (16)

D/FW Grocers Association, Carrollton, TX (1)

DIA - Nielsen USA Inc, Moorestown, NJ (16)

D'Lights, South El Monte, CA (8)

DMC Corp, Kearny, NJ (16)

DPC Computers, Monsey, NY (16)

DRG, Berne, IN (17)

DS Waters of North America LP, Flowery Branch, GA (4)

DWS Investments Service Co, Kansas City, MO (14)

Da-Lite Screen Co Inc, Warsaw, IN (16)

Da Vinci Technologies LLC, Auburn, AL (3)

Daedalus Books Inc, Columbia, MD (5)

Daily Commercial News & Construction Record, Markham, ON, Canada (17)

Daily Record & Dispatch Co, Dunn, NC (17)

DaimlerChrysler Corp, Auburn Hills, MI (12)

Dain Rauscher Inc, Minneapolis, MN (14)

Dairy Council of California, Irvine, CA (1)

Dairy Farmers of America Inc, Kansas City, MO (16)

Dairy Management Inc, Rosemont, IL (1)

Dakin Farm, Ferrisburgh, VT (4)

Dakota Digital, Sioux Falls, SD (12)

Dalco Electronics, Springboro, OH (3)

Dalrada Financial Corp, San Diego, CA (14)

Damilic Corp, Rockville, MD (16)

Danker Laboratories Inc, Sarasota, FL (16)

Dansk, Bristol, PA (16)

Dante University Press, Wellesley, MA (17)

The Dartnell Corp, Naples, FL (17)

Dassault Falcon Jet Corp, Little Ferry, NJ (16)

Data Cal Corp, Gilbert, AZ (16)

Data Direct Networks (HQ), Chatsworth, CA (3)

Databazaar.com, Miramar, FL (10)

DataLever Corp, Boulder, CO (16)

Datapoint USA Inc, San Antonio, TX (16)

Datum Timing, Test & Measurement, Beverly, MA (9)

David Dauber & Associates, New York, NY (16)

Davidoff of Geneva Inc, Pinellas Park, FL (6)

The Davis Center, Succasunna, NJ (16)

Dick Davis Digest, Salem, MA (17)

Davis Instruments Corp, Hayward, CA (8)

Davis Publications Inc, Worcester, MA (17)
Davor Photo Inc, Bensalem, PA (16)
Day Runner Direct, Sidney, NY (10)
Day-Timers, Macungie, PA (13)
Daydots, Fort Worth, TX (16)
Days Inns Worldwide Inc, Parsippany, NJ (16)
Dayton Daily News, Dayton, OH (18)
DealerTrack, New Hyde Park, NY (14)
Decal Shop, Jacksonville, FL (10)
Decko Products Inc, Sandusky, OH (4)
Deere & Co Headquarters, Moline, IL (16)
Del Webb, Bloomfield Hills, MI (16)
Delaware Investments, Philadelphia, PA (14)
Dell Computer Corp, Round Rock, TX (16)
Delmmar Communications, Cameron, MO (16)
Deloitte & Touche, Boston, MA (14)
DelStar Technologies, Middletown, DE (16)
Delta Tech Industries, Ontario, CA (12)
DeLuxe Laboratories, Hollywood, CA (16)
Demco Inc, Madison, WI (10)
Democratic Congressional Campaign Committee, Washington, DC (1)
Dental Products Report, New York, NY (17)
Denver Metro Convention & Visitors Bureau, Denver, CO (1)
Denver Tax Software Inc, Littleton, CO (16)
Dermac Labs Inc, Salem, OR (16)
Desjardins Financial Securities, Levis, PQ, Canada (15)
Destinations Ireland & Great Britain, Rhinebeck, NY (19)
The Detroit Institute of Arts, Detroit, MI (16)
Detroit Newspapers, Detroit, MI (18)
Deutsche Bank Alex Brown Inc, New York, NY (14)
Development Dimensions International, Bridgeville, PA (16)
Dexta Corp, Napa, CA (16)
Dharma Trading Co, Petaluma, CA (2)
Diagraph Corp, Saint Charles, MO (16)
Dial-A-Mattress, Hicksville, NY (16)
Diamonds By Rennie Ellen, New York, NY (6)
Diebold Inc, Uniontown, OH (16)
DigDev Direct, Deerfield Beach, FL (16)
Digi International, Minnetonka, MN (3)
Digi-Key Corp, Thief River Falls, MN (3)
Digital Speech Systems, Richardson, TX (3)
The Dime Savings Bank of New York FSB, Brooklyn, NY (14)
Dimmock Hill Golf Course Pro Shop, Binghamton, NY (11)
DineWise, Farmingdale, NY (4)
Dinn Brothers Inc, West Springfield, MA (16)
Dan Dipert Travel Service Inc, Arlington, TX (19)
Direct Energy, Toronto, ON, Canada (16)
Direct Marketing Association, New York, NY (1)
The Direct Marketing Club of New York Inc, Garden City, NY (1)
Direct Marketing Publishers, Yardley, PA (17)
Direct Response Consulting, McLean, VA (17)
Direct SAT TV LLC, Southern Pines, NC (3)
Directory of American Business & Insurance Attorneys, New York, NY (15)
DIRECTV, El Segundo, CA (16)
Discover Financial Services, Riverwoods, IL (14)
Discovery Communications LLC, Silver Spring, MD (16)
Diversified Healthcare Services, Richardson, TX (15)
Diversified Investment Advisors, Harrison, NY (14)
Diversified Photo Supply Corp, Gardena, CA (10)
Divine Word Missionaries, Techny, IL (1)
Do-It Corp, South Haven, MI (9)
DoAll Co, Wheeling, IL (16)
Doane, Saint Louis, MO (17)
Doctor's Best Inc, San Clemente, CA (16)
The Doctor's Co, Napa, CA (15)
Dole Fresh Flowers, Miami, FL (8)
Domestic Bank, Providence, RI (14)
Dominion Retail Inc, Richmond, VA (16)
Edward Don & Co, North Riverside, IL (16)
Doorguard Systems Inc, Columbia, MD (3)
Dorothy Biddle Service, Greeley, PA (8)

Dorothy's Ruffled Originals Inc, Wilmington, NC (8)
Doubletree Suites by Hilton, Boston, MA (19)
Douglas Press Inc, Bellwood, IL (16)
Dover Publications Inc, Mineola, NY (17)
Dow Chemical USA, Midland, MI (16)
Dow Corning Corp, Midland, MI (16)
Dow Jones & Co, Princeton, NJ (17)
Dow Theory Forecasts, Hammond, IN (17)
Dozier Equipment International, Milwaukee, WI (9)
Dragich Auto Literature, Princeton, MN (16)
Drawing Board Inc, Waynesboro, PA (16)
Dreis & Krump Manufacturing Co, Peotone, IL (16)
Drexel University (Goodwin College of Professional Studies), Philadelphia, PA (16)
The Dreyfus Corp, New York, NY (14)
Droll Yankees Inc, Foster, RI (8)
Drug Policy Alliance, New York, NY (1)
Drumbeat Indian Arts Inc, Phoenix, AZ (6)
The Du-Rite Group Inc, Englewood, NJ (16)
Ducks Unlimited, Memphis, TN (1)
Ducktrap River Fish Farm, Belfast, ME (4)
Dudley's Country Kitchen, Dyersburg, TN (4)
Duggan & Brown Inc, Abington, PA (16)
Duncan Aviation, Lincoln, NE (16)
Duncraft Inc, Concord, NH (16)
E I DuPont De Nemours & Co, Wilmington, DE (16)
Duracell, Bethel, CT (16)
Durey-Libby Edible Nuts Inc, Carlstadt, NJ (4)
The Durham Manufacturing Co, Durham, CT (16)
Dwyer Instruments Inc, Michigan City, IN (16)
DX Engineering, Akron, OH (16)
Dynamic Development Co, Mission Viejo, CA (12)
Dynamic Engineering, Santa Cruz, CA (3)
Dynamics Research Corp, Andover, MA (16)

E

E Hille, Angler's Supply House, Williamsport, PA (11)
e-Pipeconnection, Evansville, IN (9)
E-Z Bowz Inc, Gatlinburg, TN (8)
E-Z-EM Inc, Melville, NY (7)
EBA Wholesale Corp, Brooklyn, NY (3)
EBSCO Reception Room Subscription Services, Birmingham, AL (18)
EDC Publishing, Tulsa, OK (17)
EMC Corp, Hopkinton, MA (16)
EMED Co Inc, Buffalo, NY (16)
EMS Technologies, Norcross, GA (16)
EOS International Inc, Carlsbad, CA (5)
ESL Federal Credit Union, Rochester, NY (14)
ETS Inc, Indianapolis, IN (7)
EWA & Miniature Cars USA Inc, Berkeley Heights, NJ (11)
Eagle Claw Fishing Tackle, Denver, CO (11)
Eagle Publishing, Washington, DC (17)
Eastbay Running Store Inc, Wausau, WI (2)
Eastern Bank, Lynn, MA (14)
Eastern Michigan University, Ypsilanti, MI (16)
Easthill Group Inc, Pottstown, PA (12)
Eastman Chemical Co, Kingsport, TN (16)
David Easton Inc, New York, NY (16)
EasyLink Services International Corp, Piscataway, NJ (16)
Eaton Corp, Raleigh, NC (16)
Ebbets Field Flannels Inc, Seattle, WA (2)
Ebersole Lapidary Supply Inc, Wichita, KS (11)
Eckankar, Minneapolis, MN (17)
Ecklers, Titusville, FL (12)
Ecolab Professional Products, Saint Paul, MN (16)
The Economist Newspaper NA Inc, New York, NY (17)
Economy Handicrafts, Brooklyn, NY (16)
Edible Landscaping, Afton, VA (8)
Edison Electric Institute, Washington, DC (1)
Editorial Projects in Education Inc, Bethesda, MD (17)
Edmund Optics Inc, Barrington, NJ (9)
Edroy Products Co Inc, Nyack, NY (16)
Educational Insights, Inc, Gardena, CA (16)
Educational Resources, Elgin, IL (3)

Educational Testing Service, Princeton, NJ (16)
Educators Progress Service Inc, Randolph, WI (17)
Effective Promotions Inc, Fort Johnson, NY (16)
Efstonscience Inc, Toronto, ON, Canada (9)
Eichten's Hidden Acres, Center City, MN (4)
89 Degrees, Burlington, MA (9)
Eilenberger's Bakery Inc, Palestine, TX (4)
Eire Direct, Chicago, IL (16)
Electric Insurance Co, Beverly, MA (15)
ElectroWarmth Products LLC, Danville, OH (8)
Elemental Scientific LLC, Appleton, WI (9)
Edward Elgar Publishing Inc, Northampton, MA (17)
Eli Journals, Durham, NC (16)
Elite Sportswear LP, Reading, PA (2)
Elkhart Cases, Elkhart, IN (2)
Elks Magazine, Chicago, IL (17)
Ellerbusch Instrument Co, Cincinnati, OH (9)
Ellis Systems Corp, Lake Forest, IL (9)
Elsevier, New York, NY (17)
Emblem & Badge Inc, Johnston, RI (6)
Embrace Home Loans, Middletown, RI (14)
Emergency Essentials Inc, Orem, UT (16)
Emperor Clock LLC, Amherst, VA (16)
Empire Blue Cross & Blue Shield, New York, NY (15)
Empire Coffee & Tea Co, New York, NY (4)
Empire Scientific, Deer Park, NY (16)
En ESPANOL Publishing Group LLC, Beverly Hills, CA (17)
Encircle, Miami, FL (14)
Enco Manufacturing Co, Fernley, NV (9)
Encyclopaedia Britannica Inc, Chicago, IL (17)
Energizer Battery Co Inc, Saint Louis, MO (16)
Enerpac, Menomonee Falls, WI (16)
Engineering Services & Products Co, South Windsor, CT (9)
ENMAX Corp, Calgary, AB, Canada (9)
Ennis Inc, Midlothian, TX (16)
Entergy, New Orleans, LA (16)
Enterprex International Corp, Arcadia, CA (16)
Enterprise Ireland, New York, NY (16)
Entertainment Music Marketing Corp, Baldwin, NY (16)
Entrepreneur Partners, Philadelphia, PA (14)
Envelope Manufacturers Association, Alexandria, VA (1)
Environmental Law Institute, Washington, DC (17)
Epson America, Long Beach, CA (10)
Esco Corp, Portland, OR (16)
ESignal, Hayward, CA (14)
Esquire Magazine, New York, NY (17)
Esselte Americas, Melville, NY (16)
Essential Products Co Inc, New York, NY (7)
Estes Industries, Penrose, CO (11)
Ethel M Chocolates Inc, Henderson, NV (4)
Ethyl Corp, Richmond, VA (16)
Eventful Inc, San Diego, CA (19)
Everex Computer Systems Inc, Fremont, CA (16)
Evergreen Enterprises Inc, Richmond, VA (8)
Excelligence Learning Corp, Monterey, CA (5)
Executive Enterprises Inc, Hawthorne, NY (16)
Executive Protection Products Inc, Napa, CA (16)
Expedia Inc, Bellevue, WA (19)
Experience In Software Inc, Berkeley, CA (16)
Expressions Custom Furniture, Hickory, NC (16)

F

F&W Publications Inc, Blue Ash, OH (17)
F P International, Redwood City, CA (16)
The FX Matt Brewing Co, Utica, NY (4)
FAFCO Inc, Chico, CA (16)
FCIA Management Co Inc, New York, NY (15)
FDAnews, Falls Church, VA (17)
FIU Online, Miami, FL (1)
FLM Graphics Corp, Fairfield, NJ (16)
FMC Corp, Philadelphia, PA (16)
FNC INC, Oxford, MS (14)
FT Publications Inc, New York, NY (17)

FTD Florist Transworld Delivery, Downers Grove, IL (16)
FW Media, Cincinnati, OH (17)
Facts On File Inc, New York, NY (17)
Fairchild Books, New York, NY (17)
Fairchild Publications, New York, NY (17)
Faire Harbour Limited, Scituate, MA (5)
Fairfield Industries Inc, Sugar Land, TX (16)
Fairytale Brownies, Phoenix, AZ (4)
Falcon Products Inc, Newport, TN (16)
Falcon Safety Products, Branchburg, NJ (16)
Fallon Community Health Plan, Worcester, MA (1)
Family Album, Kinzers, PA (6)
Family Christian Stores, Grand Rapids, MI (5)
Famous Smoke Shop Inc, Easton, PA (16)
Fannie Mae, Washington, DC (14)
Farm Bureau Insurance, Lansing, MI (15)
Farm Home Offices, Richfield, MN (10)
Farm Journal Inc, Philadelphia, PA (17)
Farm Progress Co, Saint Charles, IL (17)
Farrar Straus & Giroux Inc, New York, NY (17)
Farrington Transportation, Bolingbrook, IL (12)
Russell A Farrow Ltd, Windsor, ON, Canada (16)
Fasson Roll Div, Mentor, OH (16)
Father Flanagan's Boy's Home, Boys Town, NE (1)
FatWallet, Beloit, WI (7)
Federal Express, Memphis, TN (16)
Federal Home Loan Mortgage Corp (Freddie Mac), McLean, VA (14)
Federated Investors Co, Pittsburgh, PA (14)
George Fencik Associates, Point Pleasant, NJ (16)
Ferguson Publishing Co, New York, NY (17)
Ferrara Bakery & Cafe Inc, New York, NY (4)
Fidelity Investments, Boston, MA (14)
Fidelity Security Life Insurance Co, Kansas City, MO (15)
The Field Museum, Chicago, IL (1)
Fieldstone Gardens Inc, Vassalboro, ME (8)
Fifth Avenue Committee, Brooklyn, NY (1)
Fifth Third Bank, Cincinnati, OH (14)
Figi's Inc, Marshfield, WI (4)
Films Media Group, New York, NY (3)
Financial Executives International, Morristown, NJ (1)
Financial Publishing Co, South Bend, IN (17)
Financial Services International Corp, Seattle, WA (14)
Financial Times, New York, NY (17)
Fine Architectural Metalsmiths, Chester, NY (16)
Fire Mountain Gems, Grants Pass, OR (16)
Fireman's Fund Insurance Co, Novato, CA (14)
First Banks Inc, Hazelwood, MO (14)
First Data Merchant Services, Greenwood Village, CO (14)
First Hawaiian Bank, Honolulu, HI (14)
First Media Communications Inc, Brentwood, TN (16)
First Merit Bank (HQ), Akron, OH (14)
First Tennessee Bank, Memphis, TN (14)
FirstGroup America, Cincinnati, OH (12)
Carl Fischer Music, New York, NY (17)
Fiserv, Norcross, GA (14)
Fisher Investments, Woodside, CA (14)
Fisher-Price, East Aurora, NY (16)
Fisher Scientific, Pittsburgh, PA (16)
Fitness Systems Manufacturing Corp, Sinking Spring, PA (7)
Fitter International Inc, Calgary, AB, Canada (1)
Flaghouse Inc, Hasbrouck Heights, NJ (5)
Fleet One LLC, Antioch, TN (14)
FLEXcon, Spencer, MA (16)
Flickinger's Nursery, Sagamore, PA (8)
Flight Form Cases Inc, Bedford Park, IL (9)
The Flinchbaugh Co Inc, Manchester, PA (16)
Florian Tools, Southington, CT (8)
Florida Credit Union, Gainesville, FL (14)
Florida Gift Fruit Shippers Association, Orlando, FL (1)
Florida Institute of CPA's, Tallahassee, FL (1)
Florida Power & Light Co, Miami, FL (16)
Florida Power Corp, Saint Petersburg, FL (16)
Florida Today, Melbourne, FL (17)
Fluid Metering Inc, Syosset, NY (16)

Fluke Biomedical, Everett, WA (16)
Follett Library Resources, McHenry, IL (16)
Food Chemical News, Arlington, VA (17)
Foote, Francisco & Co, West Caldwell, NJ (1)
Foote-Jones/Illinois Gear, Aberdeen, SD (16)
Ford Foundation Office of Communications, New York, NY (5)
Ford Motor Co, Dearborn, MI (16)
Forecaster Publishing Co Inc, Tarzana, CA (14)
Foremost Industrial Exchange, Van Nuys, CA (16)
Foresters, Toronto, ON, Canada (15)
Forestry Suppliers Inc, Jackson, MS (9)
Forethought Financial Services Inc, Batesville, IN (15)
Forum Publishing Co, Centerport, NY (17)
Fostoria Industries Inc, Johnson City, TN (9)
Foundation for Chiropractic Education & Research, Norwalk, IA (1)
Four Corners Direct Inc, Sarasota, FL (16)
4Imprint Inc, Oshkosh, WI (16)
Four Seasons Hotels & Resorts, Toronto, ON, Canada (19)
Four Seasons Sunrooms, Holbrook, NY (8)
Four Wheel Drive Hardware LLC, Columbiana, OH (12)
Fowler's Chocolates Inc, Buffalo, NY (4)
Fox Chase Cancer Center, Philadelphia, PA (1)
Larry Fox & Co Ltd, Valley Stream, NY (16)
Fox Lite, Inc, Fairborn, OH (9)
Fox Valley Systems Inc, Cary, IL (9)
Fragrance International, Youngstown, OH (16)
Franklin Estimating Systems, Woods Cross, UT (17)
The Franklin Mint, Exton, PA (16)
Fran's Gifts to Go, Myrtle Beach, SC (4)
Paul Fredrick Menstyle, Fleetwood, PA (2)
Freeport Music Inc, Farmingville, NY (11)
Fresno Oxygen, Fresno, CA (9)
A I Friedman Inc, New York, NY (10)
Frito-Lay, Plano, TX (16)
Frog Tool Co Ltd, Dixon, IL (11)
Frontier Corp, Rochester, NY (16)
Frontier Natural Products Co-op, Norway, IA (7)
Frost Bank, San Antonio, TX (14)
Fuji Photo Film USA, Valhalla, NY (16)
Fujitsu Transaction Solutions Inc, Richardson, TX (16)
Fulcrum Publishing, Golden, CO (17)
The Fuller Brush Co, Great Bend, KS (5)
The Fuller Theological Seminary, Pasadena, CA (16)
Fundamentals Co Inc, Bristol, VA (1)

G

G&S Packing Co Inc, Weirsdale, FL (16)
G H Bass & Co, New York, NY (16)
G-Neil Direct Mail, Sunrise, FL (10)
G2 Promotional Marketing, New York, NY (16)
GBH Communications, Monrovia, CA (3)
GCC Printers, Bedford, MA (10)
GE Canada, Mississauga, ON, Canada (9)
GE Consumer & Industrial Lighting, Cleveland, OH (16)
GE Money, Alpharetta, GA (14)
GE Partnership Marketing Group, Schaumburg, IL (14)
GMG Productions Inc, Roslyn, NY (3)
GN Netcom, Nashua, NH (16)
GRP Funding LLC, Springfield, MA (14)
GWR Wealth Management, Omaha, NE (14)
Gaco Western Inc, Seattle, WA (16)
Gaiam Inc, Boulder, CO (9)
Gale Research Inc, Farmington Hills, MI (17)
Galen Williams Landscaping & Garden Design, East Hampton, NY (16)
The Gallery Shop, Buffalo, NY (6)
Gall's Inc, Lexington, KY (16)
Gallup Inter-tribal Indian Ceremonial, Gallup, NM (1)
Gambro Inc, Lakewood, CO (16)
GameTime Inc, Fort Payne, AL (11)
Gamma Photo Labs LLC, Chicago, IL (16)
Gannett Co Inc, Mc Lean, VA (16)
Gardens Of The Blue Ridge Inc, Pineola, NC (8)

Garlinghouse Co, Beaufort, SC (17)
Garon Products Inc, Wall, NJ (16)
Gary's Perennials, LLC, Maple Glen, PA (8)
Gates Corp, Denver, CO (9)
Gateway Inc, Irvine, CA (3)
Gaylord Brothers, Syracuse, NY (16)
Gazette Communications Inc, Cedar Rapids, IA (17)
Gebbie Press Inc, New Paltz, NY (17)
Gelco Information Network, Eden Prairie, MN (16)
Gemalto Inc, Montgomeryville, PA (16)
Gemini Publishing Co, Webster, TX (17)
Gems Sensors & Controls, Plainville, CT (9)
General Binding Corp, Northbrook, IL (10)
General Electric Co, Fairfield, CT (16)
General Pencil Co Inc, Jersey City, NJ (16)
General Physics Corp, Elkridge, MD (16)
General Tours/TBI Tours, Keene, NH (19)
General Vitamin Corp, Raleigh, NC (16)
Genesco Inc, Nashville, TN (2)
Genetica DNA Laboratories Inc, Cincinnati, OH (16)
Genium Publishing, Amsterdam, NY (17)
Genworth Financial Inc, Richmond, VA (14)
Georgetown University Law Center/Continuing Legal Education Div, Washington, DC (13)
Georgetown University McDonough School of Business, Washington, DC (1)
Georgia Power, Atlanta, GA (16)
Gerstner Woodworks, Dayton, OH (6)
Getronics, Tewksbury, MA (16)
Ghent Manufacturing Inc, Lebanon, OH (10)
Ghirardelli Chocolate Co, San Leandro, CA (16)
Gibson Auer LLC, Victor, ID (7)
Gift Services Inc, Vancouver, WA (6)
Gillette Children's Specialty Healthcare, Saint Paul, MN (1)
Gilman's Lapidary Supply, Hellertown, PA (11)
Gilson Co Inc, Lewis Center, OH (9)
Glas-Col, Terre Haute, IN (16)
Peter Glenn Publications, Delray Beach, FL (17)
Glenview State Bank, Glenview, IL (14)
Global Computer Corp, Port Washington, NY (3)
Global Equipment Co Inc, Port Washington, NY (9)
Global Specialties, Wallingford, CT (16)
Globe Specialty Products Inc, Millbury, MA (17)
Globe Ticket & Label Co, Lombard, IL (16)
Go Promos, Gloversville, NY (5)
Goddard Manufacturing Co, Logan, KS (8)
Gohn Brothers, Middlebury, IN (5)
Gold Line Connector Inc, West Redding, CT (3)
Gold Medal Hair Products Inc, Farmingdale, NY (7)
Gold Medal Products Co, Cincinnati, OH (16)
Golden Bear Golf Inc, North Palm Beach, FL (16)
Golden Fleece Designs Inc, Burbank, CA (16)
Golden Gate Transportation District, San Rafael, CA (16)
Golden River Fruit Co, Vero Beach, FL (4)
Golden Rule Insurance Co, Indianapolis, IN (15)
Golden Trophy, Chicago, IL (4)
Goldsmith Agio Helms, Minneapolis, MN (14)
Golf Digest Co, Wilton, CT (17)
Good Directions Co Inc, Danbury, CT (8)
Goodheart-Willcox Publisher, Tinley Park, IL (17)
Goodyear Tire & Rubber Co, Akron, OH (16)
WL Gore & Associates Inc, Newark, DE (2)
Gossler Farms Nursery, Springfield, OR (8)
Gothic Arch Greenhouses Inc, Mobile, AL (8)
Gould & Goodrich, Lillington, NC (2)
Governing Magazine, Washington, DC (17)
Government Data Publications Inc, Washington, DC (17)
Government of India Tourist Office, New York, NY (1)
Government Technology Services Inc, Herndon, VA (16)
W R Grace & Co, Columbia, MD (16)
Gracewood Fruit Co, Vero Beach, FL (4)
Grade Finders Inc, Exton, PA (17)
Graham Field Health Products Inc, Atlanta, GA (7)
Grainger Parts, North Brook, IL (16)
WW Grainger Inc, Lake Forest, IL (9)
Grand Canyon University, Phoenix, AZ (13)

Grandma Brown's Beans Inc, Mexico, NY (4)
Graphik Dimensions Ltd, High Point, NC (16)
Graves Lapidary Co, Pompano Beach, FL (9)
The Great Amarillo Directory, Amarillo, TX (17)
Great Chefs Television Publishing, New Orleans, LA (6)
Great North American Cos Inc, Dallas, TX (16)
Great-West Life, Greenwood Village, CO (15)
Greater Fort Worth Builders Association, Fort Worth, TX (1)
Green Mountain Coffee Roasters, Inc, Waterbury, VT (4)
Green River Trading Co, Millerton, NY (8)
Greenwood Publishing Group Inc, Portsmouth, NH (17)
Greer Gardens, Eugene, OR (8)
Grimes Seeds and Plants, Concord, OH (8)
Grove Enterprises Inc, Brasstown, NC (16)
Grower's Supply Co, Dexter, MI (8)
Growing Child, Inc, West Lafayette, IN (17)
Gruber & Allison Inc, Boynton Beach, FL (17)
Gruppo Levey & Co, New York, NY (14)
Guaranty Bank, Brown Deer, WI (14)
The Guardian Life Insurance Co, New York, NY (15)
GuideOne Insurance, West Des Moines, IA (15)
Guiding Eyes for the Blind, Yorktown Heights, NY (16)
Guilford Publications Inc, New York, NY (17)
Gulf Coast Data Supply Inc, Milton, FL (3)
Gulf Publishing Co, Houston, TX (17)
Gulfstream Aircraft Inc, Savannah, GA (16)
Gun Video Catalog/LMP, San Diego, CA (11)

H

H&R Block Inc, Kansas City, MO (14)
HCI Direct, Bensalem, PA (16)
HDA Inc, Saint Louis, MO (17)
The Herald & Review, Decatur, IL (17)
HMI Marketing, Brooklyn Park, MN (7)
HR Direct, Sunrise, FL (10)
HSBC Bank USA, NA, Buffalo, NY (14)
HSP Direct, Herndon, VA (1)
Habitat For Humanity International, Americus, GA (1)
Hadley Fruit Orchards Inc, Cabazon, CA (4)
Hagemeyer - North America, Charleston, SC (16)
Hagie Manufacturing Co, Clarion, IA (9)
Hain Celestial Group, Melville, NY (16)
Hale Indian River Groves Inc, Vero Beach, FL (16)
Hall-Erickson Inc, Westmont, IL (16)
Hallmark Cards Inc, Kansas City, MO (16)
HALO/Lee Wayne, Sterling, IL (16)
Halsom Home Care Inc, Centerville, OH (16)
Hamilton Beach/Proctor-Silex Inc, Glen Allen, VA (16)
Hamilton Watch, Weehawken, NJ (16)
Hammacher Schlemmer, New York, NY (16)
Hammock Publishing Inc, Nashville, TN (17)
Hammond World Atlas Corp, New York, NY (17)
Hampshire Agency, Great Neck, NY (14)
Hampshire Pewter Co, Wolfeboro, NH (6)
Hampton Marketing Corp, Medford, NY (16)
Handi-Ramp Inc, Libertyville, IL (7)
Hanley Wood LLC, Washington, DC (16)
Hanna Instruments Inc, Woonsocket, RI (16)
Chris Hansen, New Berlin, WI (16)
Hansen Corp, Princeton, IN (16)
Happy Trails Resort, Surprise, AZ (19)
Har Court Inc, Orlando, FL (17)
Harbor Freight Tools, Camarillo, CA (9)
Harbour Bay Inc, Suffern, NY (16)
Harcourt Educational Measurement, San Antonio, TX (17)
Harland Financial Solutions Inc, Lake Mary, FL (16)
John Harland Co, Decatur, GA (16)
Harlequin Enterprises Ltd, Don Mills, ON, Canada (17)
Harley-Davidson Inc, Milwaukee, WI (12)
Harman's Cheese & Country Store Inc, Sugar Hill, NH (4)

HarperCollins, New York, NY (17)
Harrah's Entertainment Inc, Las Vegas, NV (19)
Harrah's Marketing, Reno, NV (16)
Harris Bancorp Inc, Chicago, IL (14)
Harris Corp, Melbourne, FL (16)
Harry & David Holdings Inc, Medford, OR (4)
The Hartz Mountain Corp, Secaucus, NJ (16)
Harvard Business Review, Watertown, MA (17)
Harvard Business School Publishing, Boston, MA (17)
Harvard Pilgrim Health Care, Wellesley, MA (7)
Hatton-Brown Publishers Inc, Montgomery, AL (17)
HAVE Inc, Hudson, NY (3)
Hazelden, Center City, MN (7)
Health Affairs, Bethesda, MD (17)
Health Care Concepts Inc, Austin, TX (16)
Health Care Logistics, Circleville, OH (16)
Health O Meter, Alsip, IL (16)
HealthPlan Services, Tampa, FL (15)
Health Sciences Consortium, Chapel Hill, NC (17)
The Healthy Back Store, Beltsville, MD (16)
Hearlihy & Co, Pittsburg, KS (17)
The Hearst Corp, New York, NY (17)
Hearst Magazines, New York, NY (17)
Hearthside Quilts & Supplies, Hinesburg, VT (11)
Heartland America, Chaska, MN (3)
Heartstrings Press, Lancaster, VA (17)
Hecht Rubber Corp, Jacksonville, FL (16)
Heldref Publications, Washington, DC (17)
Heller Financial, Chicago, IL (14)
W C Heller & Co, Montpelier, OH (16)
Hello Direct, Nashua, NH (16)
Helly-Hansen, Auburn, WA (16)
Helman Group Ltd, Oxnard, CA (16)
Hemmings Motor News, Bennington, VT (17)
Herbach & Rademan Co, Moorestown, NJ (9)
Herbalife International of America Inc, Los Angeles, CA (7)
Herman Miller Inc, Zeeland, MI (16)
Hermes of Paris, New York, NY (2)
Herschend Family Entertainment, Branson, MO (5)
Hershey Foods Corp, Hershey, PA (4)
Hershey Park, Hershey, PA (19)
Hershey's Mail Order, Hershey, PA (4)
Hertz Corp, Park Ridge, NJ (19)
Hewlett-Packard Co, Palo Alto, CA (16)
Hickory Farms, Maumee, OH (4)
High Point Insurance, Lincroft, NJ (15)
Highmark Blue Cross Blue Shield, Pittsburgh, PA (15)
HighScope Educational Research Foundation, Ypsilanti, MI (17)
Hillside Wire Cloth Co, Bloomfield, NJ (9)
Hilton HHonors Worldwide, McLean, VA (16)
Hilton Hotels Corp, Mc Lean, VA (19)
Hireko Golf, City of Industry, CA (11)
Histacount & Expressions, Lancaster, CA (10)
Hoffman Mint, Fort Lauderdale, FL (16)
Hoke Communications Inc, Garden City, NY (17)
Holiday Travel of America, Carlsbad, CA (19)
Holland Wildflower Farm, Elkins, AR (8)
Hollister Inc, Libertyville, IL (16)
Hollywood Film Archive, Los Angeles, CA (17)
Holy Cross Hospital, Fort Lauderdale, FL (16)
The Home Depot Inc, Atlanta, GA (16)
Home Planners, Tucson, AZ (17)
Home Safeguard Industries, Malibu, CA (9)
HomeAway.com Inc, Austin, TX (19)
Homecraft Veneer & Woodworker Supply, Youngstown, PA (8)
Homespun Tapes Music Instruction, Woodstock, NY (3)
Homesteaders Life Co, West Des Moines, IA (15)
The HoneyBaked Ham Co, Holland, OH (4)
Honeywell, Morristown, NJ (16)
Honeywell Wintress Controls, Acton, MA (16)
Hook & Hackle Co Inc, Homestead, PA (11)
Hooleon Corp, Melrose, NM (3)
Hoover's Mfg Co, Peru, IL (2)
The Hope Co Inc, Bridgeton, MO (16)
Hopkins Medical Products, Baltimore, MD (7)
Hormel Foods Corp, Austin, MN (16)
Horn Packaging Corp, Lancaster, MA (5)

Horticulture Magazine, Blue Ash, OH (17)
Houlihan Lokey Howard & Zukin, Los Angeles, CA (14)
House of Eyes II, Greensboro, NC (2)
House of Oldies, New York, NY (6)
House of Onyx, Inc, Greenville, KY (6)
House of Orange, Brentwood Bay, BC, Canada (2)
Howard Rice Nemerovski Canady Falk & Rabkin, San Francisco, CA (14)
F.M. Howell & Co, Elmira, NY (16)
Hubert Co, Harrison, OH (16)
William B Hugg Enterprise Inc Swim Wear & Accessories, Ambler, PA (11)
Human Resource Development Press, Amherst, MA (17)
Humana Inc, Louisville, KY (7)
Huntington Bancshares, Columbus, OH (14)
HY-KO Products Co, Northfield, OH (16)
Hyatt Fruit Co, Vero Beach, FL (4)
Hyatt Hotels Corp, Chicago, IL (16)
Hyatt Legal Plans Inc, Cleveland, OH (16)
Hygienic Fabrics & Filters Inc, Sheboygan, WI (16)
Hyman's, Hanahan, SC (2)

I

IBM Corp, Armonk, NY (16)
ICIS Inc, Upper Black Eddy, PA (2)
ICS Audio Video Supply Inc, Phoenix, AZ (3)
IDMS Inc, Melville, NY (16)
IHS Inc, Englewood, CO (17)
INC Magazine, New York, NY (17)
ING, Minneapolis, MN (15)
ING USA Annuity & Life Ins Co, Des Moines, IA (15)
INX International Ink Co, Schaumburg, IL (16)
IPD Co Inc, Portland, OR (12)
IPS - Sendero Corp, Norcross, GA (14)
ISA-The Instrumentation Systems & Automation Society, Research Triangle Park, NC (1)
ITW Bee Leitzke, Iron Ridge, WI (16)
ITW Vortec, Cincinnati, OH (16)
The Idea Club.com(TM) & Dumas Martin Consulting, Pomona, CA (16)
I/D/E/A Inc, Caldwell, ID (16)
Ideal Industries (Canada) Corp, Ajax, ON, Canada (9)
Ideal Industries Inc, Sycamore, IL (16)
IMPACT Publishing Inc, Bradenton, FL (17)
Imperial Supplies, Green Bay, WI (16)
Improvements, West Chester, OH (8)
Impulse Inc, Las Vegas, NV (3)
In-Sync Publications, Redondo Beach, CA (18)
Independent Insurance Agents & Brokers of America, Alexandria, VA (1)
Independent Living Aids, Jericho, NY (7)
Indian Arts & Crafts Association, Albuquerque, NM (1)
Indian House Records & Tapes, Taos, NM (3)
Indianapolis Motor Speedway, Indianapolis, IN (19)
Indianapolis Newspapers Inc, Indianapolis, IN (17)
Indium Corp of America, Clinton, NY (16)
Indus-Tool, Chicago, IL (12)
Industrial Instruments & Supplies Inc, Southampton, PA (9)
Industrial Uniform Co Inc, Wichita, KS (2)
Infinity Insurance Co, Birmingham, AL (15)
Info USA City Directories, Omaha, NE (17)
Infomart, Dallas, TX (16)
Information for Public Affairs, Inc, Sacramento, CA (17)
Information Unlimited Inc, Amherst, NH (11)
InfoSource Inc, Oviedo, FL (3)
Ingram Book Group, La Vergne, TN (16)
Innovative Clip Art, York, SC (10)
Insight Direct Inc, Tempe, AZ (16)
Institute for International Research Inc, New York, NY (16)
Institute of Management Accountants Inc, Montvale, NJ (1)

Institute of Management & Administration (IOMA), Peterborough, NH (17)
Institute of Reading Development, Novato, CA (1)
Institute of Real Estate Management, Chicago, IL (1)
Institutional Advancement Programs Inc, Bronxville, NY (1)
Institutional Investor Inc, New York, NY (17)
Institutional Real Estate Inc, San Ramon, CA (17)
Instructor's Choice Dancewear, Massapequa Park, NY (2)
The Instrument Workshop, Ashland, OR (16)
Insurance.com, Solon, OH (15)
Insurance Publications Inc, Overland Park, KS (17)
Integretel Inc, San Jose, CA (16)
Intel Corp, Santa Clara, CA (16)
IntelliQuote Insurance Services, El Dorado Hills, CA (15)
Inter7 Internet Technologies Inc, Galena, IL (3)
Interex, Amesbury, MA (17)
InterfaceFlor LLC, La Grange, GA (16)
Intergraph Corp, Madison, AL (16)
International Academy - Compounding Pharmacists, Missouri City, TX (1)
International Advertising Association, New York, NY (1)
International Bible Society, Colorado Springs, CO (1)
International City/County Management Association, Washington, DC (1)
International Crystal Manufacturing Co, Oklahoma City, OK (16)
International Direct Media Co & Information Publishing Co, San Francisco, CA (17)
International Foundation of Employee Benefit Plans, Brookfield, WI (1)
International Irrigation Systems, Niagara Falls, NY (8)
International Manufacturing Co, Whitesburg, GA (8)
International Paper, Memphis, TN (16)
International Specialized Book Services Inc, Portland, OR (16)
International Wine Accessories Inc, Wichita, KS (4)
Intersections, Chantilly, VA (14)
Intra Business Systems Inc, South Bend, IN (16)
Intromark Inc, Pittsburgh, PA (16)
Intuit, Mountain View, CA (10)
Invacare Continuing Care Group, Saint Louis, MO (16)
Invacare Supply Group, Milford, MA (16)
Investors Alliance Inc, Pompano Beach, FL (1)
Investors Marketing Services, Danvers, MA (14)
INWAVE Internet, Janesville, WI (16)
Iomega Corp, Roy, UT (16)
Iowa Medical Society, West Des Moines, IA (1)
Iroquois Products, Chicago, IL (10)
Islands Tropicals, Keaau, HI (6)
Itochu Chemicals America Inc, White Plains, NY (16)

J

J&L Industrial Supply, Southfield, MI (9)
J&R Music/J&R Computer World, New York, NY (3)
J&J Commerce, Galesburg, IL (5)
JC Whitney, Chicago, IL (12)
JDR Microdevices, Mountain View, CA (3)
JIST Publishing, Saint Paul, MN (17)
JLG Industries Inc, McConnellsburg, PA (16)
JR Tobacco/800-JR Cigar Inc, Burlington, NC (5)
Jaffe Brothers Natural Foods, Valley Center, CA (4)
Jameco Electronics, Belmont, CA (3)
James Medical Rents & Sales Inc, Fort Wayne, IN (7)
Robert James Co Inc, Moody, AL (10)
Herbert L Jamison & Co LLC, West Orange, NJ (15)
Jan Associates, Oakland, CA (7)
Janes Information Group, Alexandria, VA (17)
Jantz Supply Koval Knives, Davis, OK (9)
Jarden Corp, Daleville, IN (16)
Jason Natural Personal Care Products, Boulder, CO (7)
Jaypro Sports, Waterford, CT (11)
Jaz Holdings LLC, Liberty Corner, NJ (16)
JazzTimes Magazine Inc, Quincy, MA (17)

Jeffers & Co, Dothan, AL (5)
Jefferson National, Louisville, KY (14)
Jeffrey Lant Associates Inc, Cambridge, MA (5)
Jenny Products Inc, Somerset, PA (16)
Jerden Records/SpeechWorks, Redmond, WA (16)
Jerry's Artarama, Raleigh, NC (10)
The Jewish Publication Society, Philadelphia, PA (17)
Jobscope Corp, Greenville, SC (16)
Jockey International Global Inc, Kenosha, WI (2)
Jofco Inc, Jasper, IN (16)
John Deere Consumer Products, Moline, IL (16)
John Deere Credit USA, Johnston, IA (14)
John Hancock Financial Services Inc, Boston, MA (15)
John Hancock Retirement Plan Services, Toronto, ON, Canada (14)
Johnson & Johnson, New Brunswick, NJ (16)
Edward Jones, Des Peres, MO (14)
Jones International Ltd, Centennial, CO (16)
Marlin P Jones & Associates Inc, Lake Park, FL (3)
Jones Publishing Inc, Iola, WI (17)
Jones School Supply Co Inc, Irmo, SC (6)
Joslin Photo Puzzle Co, Southampton, PA (16)
Jossey-Bass Inc Publishers, San Francisco, CA (17)
Jostens, Inc, Minneapolis, MN (16)
The Journal News, White Plains, NY (17)
Journal of Commerce Group, Newark, NJ (17)
Joys SA Inc, Hatillo, PR (2)
JustThinkIncorporated, Sherwood Park, AB, Canada (16)
Juvenile Diabetes Research Foundation, New York, NY (1)

K

K-D Lamp Co, Andover, OH (12)
KAR Graphics, Mashpee, MA (8)
KCET, Los Angeles, CA (1)
KEH.com, Smyrna, GA (16)
KET, Lexington, KY (17)
KHL Engineered Packaging Solutions, Buena Park, CA (16)
KMA Direct Communications, Dallas, TX (1)
KTM Sportmotorcycle USA Inc, Amherst, OH (16)
KV Vet Supply Co, Inc, David City, NE (5)
Kadant Johnson Inc, Three Rivers, MI (16)
Kalmed Dental Products Inc, Marietta, GA (7)
Kano Laboratories, Nashville, TN (16)
Kansas City Chiefs, Kansas City, MO (16)
Kansas State University Division of Continuing Education, Manhattan, KS (1)
Kao Brands, Cincinnati, OH (9)
Kaplan Inc, New York, NY (16)
Kaplan Publishing, Chicago, IL (17)
Kappa Publishing Group, Blue Bell, PA (17)
Kappler Protective Apparel & Fabrics, Guntersville, AL (2)
Kaylor's School Supply, Albertville, AL (16)
Kayne & Son Custom Hardware Inc, Candler, NC (8)
Kelco Supply Co, Brooklyn Park, MN (16)
JJ Keller & Associates Inc, Neenah, WI (16)
Kellyco Metal Detector Distributors, Winter Springs, FL (11)
Kelsey National Corp, Los Angeles, CA (15)
Kendall Products/Dri-Dek, Naples, FL (16)
Kennametal Inc, Latrobe, PA (16)
Kennel Vet, Laurel, DE (11)
Kensington Technology Group, Redwood Shores, CA (16)
Kentucky Bankers Association, Louisville, KY (1)
Kerr-Hays Co, Ligonier, PA (16)
Kester's Wild Game Food Nurseries Inc, Omro, WI (8)
Kett Tool Co, Cincinnati, OH (9)
Key Bank, Cleveland, OH (14)
Key Bank National Association, Albany, NY (14)
Key Communications Inc, Garrisonville, VA (17)
Key West Aloe Holdings LLC, Fort Lauderdale, FL (16)
Keyspan Energy Corp, Brooklyn, NY (16)

The Kidney Foundation of Canada/Greater Ontario Branch, Hamilton, ON, Canada (1)
Miles Kimball Co, Oshkosh, WI (6)
Kimbo Educational, Long Branch, NJ (17)
King Features, New York, NY (17)
King Ranch Saddle Shop, Kingsville, TX (8)
King's Chandelier Co, Eden, NC (6)
Kingsley North Inc, Norway, MI (11)
The Kiplinger Washington Editors Inc, Washington, DC (17)
Will Kirkpatrick Shorebird Decoys Inc, Hudson, MA (6)
Kitchen Kompact Inc, Jeffersonville, IN (8)
B Klein Publications, Delray Beach, FL (17)
Klingspor's Woodworking Shop, Hickory, NC (9)
Klockit, Lake Geneva, WI (6)
Knoll Group, New York, NY (16)
Knollwood Groves at Cushman's, West Palm Beach, FL (4)
Knott's Berry Farm Foods, Buena Park, CA (4)
Kolbe Corp, Phoenix, AZ (17)
Susan G Komen for the Cure, Dallas, TX (1)
William S Konecky Associates Inc, Old Saybrook, CT (17)
KozaK Auto Drywash Inc, Batavia, NY (16)
Kraft Foods/Gevalia Kaffe, Tarrytown, NY (16)
Kraftbilt, Tulsa, OK (10)
Krause Publications Inc, Iola, WI (17)
The Kroger Co, Cincinnati, OH (4)
Kropp Enterprises, Kissimmee, FL (2)
Kross Inc, Santa Clarita, CA (16)
Patricia Kutza Co, Vallejo, CA (2)

L

L&L Management, Pasadena, CA (16)
L6 Holdings Corp, Duluth, GA (14)
LGP GEM LTD, New York, NY (16)
LS Records, Madison, TN (16)
Lab Safety Supply Inc, Janesville, WI (5)
LaCrosse Footwear Inc, Portland, OR (16)
The LadyBug Co, Berry Creek, CA (8)
Lafferty Equipment Manufacturing Inc, North Little Rock, AR (9)
Laitram Machinery, Harahan, LA (16)
Lake Shore Industries, Erie, PA (16)
Lakewood Products LLC, Suamico, WI (11)
Laminex Inc, Fort Mill, SC (16)
Lancer Insurance Co, Long Beach, NY (15)
Landauer Corp, Urbandale, IA (17)
Landmark Communications Inc, Norfolk, VA (17)
Landmark Graphics Corp, Houston, TX (16)
Lands' End Inc, Dodgeville, WI (2)
Landscape Forms Inc, Kalamazoo, MI (16)
Laplink Software Inc, Bellevue, WA (3)
LaPreferida Inc, Chicago, IL (4)
Laran Communications Inc, Winfield, IL (16)
Lark in the Morning, Mendocino, CA (5)
Las Vegas Review Journal, Las Vegas, NV (17)
Laser Label Technologies Inc, Stow, OH (10)
Latest Products Corp, Woodbury, NY (7)
Lathem Time Corp, Atlanta, GA (16)
Laughlin Associates Inc, Carson City, NV (16)
Lautman Maska Neill & Co, Washington, DC (1)
Lawyer's Weekly Publications, Boston, MA (17)
Lazar Media Group Inc, Charleston, SC (17)
Leadership Directories Inc, New York, NY (17)
Leadership Software Corp, Nyack, NY (16)
LeadFlash, Boca Raton, FL (14)
League of American Orchestras, New York, NY (1)
Leanin' Tree Inc, Boulder, CO (6)
LearnCom HR Consulting & Training, Irvine, CA (16)
Learning Communications LLC, Irvine, CA (16)
Leather Unlimited Corp, Belgium, WI (2)
Lefty's Corner, Clarks Summit, PA (6)
Legal Defense Foundation Inc, Springfield, VA (1)
Legal Sea Foods Inc, Boston, MA (4)
The Legal Studies Forum, Morgantown, WV (1)
Lehman's, Dalton, OH (8)
Leisure Arts Inc, Little Rock, AR (17)

Lenox Group Inc, Bristol, PA (6)
L'Entraide Assurance, Quebec, PQ, Canada (15)
AM Leonard Inc, Piqua, OH (8)
Hal Leonard Corp, Milwaukee, WI (17)
Lerner Publishing Group, Minneapolis, MN (17)
Leslie Jordan, Portland, OR (2)
Lesman Instrument Co, Bensenville, IL (9)
Leucadia National Corp, New York, NY (14)
Levenger, Delray Beach, FL (5)
Levi Strauss & Co, San Francisco, CA (16)
Lexington Luggage Limited, New York, NY (19)
Lexis Nexis Matthew Bender, Albany, NY (17)
LexisNexis, Miamisburg, OH (16)
Lexus Division of Toyota, Torrance, CA (12)
Liberty Orchards Co Inc, Cashmere, WA (16)
Liberty Tree Network, Oakland, CA (5)
The Library of America, New York, NY (13)
Liebert Corp, Columbus, OH (16)
Life Extension Foundation, Fort Lauderdale, FL (7)
Life Fitness, Schiller Park, IL (11)
Life Technologies, Grand Island, NY (9)
Lifeboat Distribution, Shrewsbury, NJ (16)
LifeLock, Tempe, AZ (16)
Lifetime Brands Inc, Garden City, NY (8)
Light Sources Inc, Virginia Beach, VA (16)
Ligonier Ministries, Lake Mary, FL (5)
Liguori Publications, Liguori, MO (17)
Lilypons Water Gardens, Adamstown, MD (8)
Lin Terry, Paterson, NJ (6)
Lincoln Educational Services, West Orange, NJ (13)
Lincoln Financial Group, Radnor, PA (15)
Lindustries Inc, Weston, MA (8)
Linens n' Things, Paramus, NJ (8)
LinguiSystems, East Moline, IL (17)
Lion Apparel, Dayton, OH (2)
Lions Gate Television Corp, Santa Monica, CA (16)
Lippincott, Williams & Wilkins, Baltimore, MD (17)
A Liss & Co Inc, Woodside, NY (16)
Lithia Motors Inc, Medford, OR (12)
Live Design, New York, NY (17)
Live Nation, Beverly Hills, CA (19)
Lladro USA, Moonachie, NJ (16)
Llewellyn Publications, Woodbury, MN (17)
LO-AD Communications, Pasadena, CA (16)
Lo Ink Specialties, Kennebunkport, ME (16)
Location Sound Corp, North Hollywood, CA (3)
Lockheed Martin Corp, Bethesda, MD (16)
Loctite Corp, Rocky Hill, CT (16)
Loews Hotels, New York, NY (19)
Logical Computer Selections, Short Hills, NJ (16)
Lombardi Publishing Corp, Vaughan, ON, Canada (17)
Long & Foster Insurance, Chantilly, VA (15)
Longevity Pure Medicine, Palm Springs, CA (7)
Long's Electronics Inc, Irondale, AL (3)
The Los Angeles Convention & Visitors Bureau, Los
    Angeles, CA (19)
Los Angeles Kings, Los Angeles, CA (16)
The Los Angeles Lakers Inc, El Segundo, CA (11)
Lotions & Lace, Riverside, CA (2)
LOTSolutions, Jacksonville, FL (14)
Lowe's Companies Inc, Mooresville, NC (8)
Luce Corp, Hamden, CT (16)
Lufthansa German Airlines, East Meadow, NY (19)
Luggage Base, Nipomo, CA (16)
Lundberg Family Farms, Richvale, CA (16)
Lure-Craft, Lagrange, IN (11)
Luster Care Products, Saint Louis, MO (16)
Lutheran Church Extension Fund - Missouri Synod,
    Saint Louis, MO (1)

M

M&M Health Care Apparel Co, Brooklyn, NY (2)
M2Media 360, Park Ridge, IL (17)
MCA/Universal Studios Inc, Universal City, CA (3)
MFE Instruments, Salem, NH (9)
MGI Management Institute, Hawthorne, NY (16)
MGM MIRAGE, Las Vegas, NV (19)
MI-T-M Corp, Peosta, IA (9)

MJA International, Glen Head, NY (7)
MPBS Industries, Los Angeles, CA (16)
MPS Multimedia Inc, San Mateo, CA (16)
The MR Group Inc, Charleston, SC (9)
MRV Communications, Chatsworth, CA (3)
MSC Industrial Supply Co, Melville, NY (9)
MTS Publishing, Naperville, IL (17)
MTS Systems Corp, Eden Prairie, MN (16)
Macy's, City Of Industry, CA (5)
Macy's West, San Francisco, CA (16)
Magellan's Catalog, Santa Barbara, CA (5)
Magna Publications Inc, Madison, WI (17)
Magna-Tel Inc, Cape Girardeau, MO (5)
Magna Visual Inc, Saint Louis, MO (9)
Magnaflux, Glenview, IL (16)
Magnaplan Corp, Champlain, NY (10)
Magnatag Visable Systems, Macedon, NY (16)
Magnet LLC, Washington, MO (16)
The Magni Co Inc, McKinney, TX (16)
Mailorder Gardening Association, Elkridge, MD (1)
The Maine Photographic Workshops, Rockport, ME
    (16)
Maine Potato Board, Presque Isle, ME (1)
Maison Glass Delicacies, Jersey City, NJ (4)
Majestic Products Co, Mississauga, ON, Canada (16)
Majorium, Stevens Point, WI (17)
Malco Products Inc, Barberton, OH (16)
MALM Chemical Corp, Pound Ridge, NY (16)
EF Maloney Inc, Mamaroneck, NY (16)
The Maloney Group, New York, NY (16)
Manchester Farms Inc, Columbia, SC (4)
Manheim Steamroller, Omaha, NE (3)
Manning Materials, Birdsboro, PA (16)
Manulife Financial Inc, Toronto, ON, Canada (15)
MAP International, Brunswick, GA (1)
Maple Grove Farms of Vermont Inc, Saint Johnsbury,
    VT (4)
Marathon Norco Aerospace Inc, Waco, TX (16)
March of Dimes Birth Defects Foundation, White
    Plains, NY (1)
MARCOR Remediation Inc, Halethorpe, MD (16)
Mardiron Optics, Stoneham, MA (11)
Marimac Inc, Montreal, PQ, Canada (8)
Mark James & Associates Inc, Oswego, IL (16)
Marketing and Product Strategy, Peabody, MA (16)
Marketing Results Inc, Sicklerville, NJ (16)
Marketplace of the Master Inc, Rockford, IL (5)
Marketshare Publications Inc, Overland Park, KS (17)
Markson Scientific LLC, Henderson, NC (9)
Markwins International Corp, City of Industry, CA
    (16)
Marmelstein Inc, Philadelphia, PA (16)
The Marmon Group LLC, Chicago, IL (16)
Marquis Who's Who LLC, Berkeley Heights, NJ (17)
Marriott International Inc, Washington, DC (19)
Marsh Affinity Group Services, Chicago, IL (15)
Marsh US Consumer, Urbandale, IA (15)
Marshall & Swift, Los Angeles, CA (17)
Marshall Domestics LLC, West Warwick, RI (5)
The Maryland Saddlery Inc, Butler, MD (11)
Mary's Plant Farm & Landscaping, Hamilton, OH (8)
T Marzetti Co Inc, Columbus, OH (4)
Masco Corp, Taylor, MI (16)
Mason Companies Inc, Chippewa Falls, WI (2)
Massachusetts Horticultural Society, Wellesley, MA
    (1)
MassMutual Financial Group, Springfield, MA (15)
MasterCard Worldwide, Purchase, NY (14)
Masterpiece Studios Inc, Mankato, MN (16)
Mastervision Inc, New York, NY (16)
Robert J Matthews Co, Massillon, OH (7)
Maui Jim Inc, Peoria, IL (16)
Maverick Ventures Product Line, Chesterfield, MO (5)
Maxon Furniture Inc, Muscatine, IA (10)
Mayo Clinic, Rochester, MN (17)
Mazda North American Operations, Irvine, CA (16)
McBee, Lancaster, CA (10)
McClatchy Co, Sacramento, CA (17)
McClure & Zimmerman, Randolph, WI (8)
McCormick & Co Inc, Hunt Valley, MD (4)
McDonald Obsolete Parts Co, Rockport, IN (16)

McDougal Littell, Evanston, IL (17)
McFayden/McConnell, Brandon, MB, Canada (8)
McFeely's Square Drive Screws, Madison, WI (16)
Bruce McGaw Graphics, Manchester Center, VT (6)
The McGraw-Hill Cos, New York, NY (17)
McGruff Specialty Products Office, Amsterdam, NY
    (16)
McKenzie Taxidermy Supply, Granite Quarry, NC (16)
McKesson Corp, San Francisco, CA (7)
McKnight's Long-Term Care News, Northfield, IL
    (17)
McMaster-Carr Supply Co (HQ), Elmhurst, IL (9)
McNichols Co, Tampa, FL (16)
Mead Johnson Co, Evansville, IN (7)
Mead Westvaco Consumer & Office Products, Dayton,
    OH (10)
Mechanical Breakdown Administrators Inc, Scottsdale,
    AZ (14)
Medco Health Solutions Inc, Franklin Lakes, NJ (7)
Medco Insurance Co, Omaha, NE (15)
Medco Supply Co Inc, Tonawanda, NY (7)
Medcom Inc, Cypress, CA (17)
Media Management & Magnetics Inc, Menomonee
    Falls, WI (3)
Medibadge Inc, Omaha, NE (5)
Medical Economics Magazine, North Olmsted, OH
    (17)
Medical Group Management Association (MGMA),
    Englewood, CO (1)
Medical Letter Inc, New Rochelle, NY (17)
Megger, Dallas, TX (16)
Meguiar's Inc, Irvine, CA (16)
Meister Media Worldwide, Willoughby, OH (17)
Melaniphy & Associates, Inc, Chicago, IL (8)
Memphis Net & Twine Co Inc, Memphis, TN (11)
Menardi Mikropul LLC, Trenton, SC (16)
The Menninger Foundation, Houston, TX (1)
Mentor Corp, Santa Barbara, CA (16)
Merastar Insurance Co, Chattanooga, TN (15)
Merck & Co Inc, Whitehouse Station, NJ (16)
Mercury International Trading, North Attleboro, MA
    (2)
Meredith Corp, Des Moines, IA (17)
Mergent Inc, Fort Mill, SC (14)
Merisel, New York, NY (16)
Merrick Bank, South Jordan, UT (14)
Merrill Corp, Saint Cloud, MN (18)
Merrill Lynch, New York, NY (14)
Methode Electronics Inc, Chicago, IL (9)
Metro Speedgear, Livingston, NJ (11)
Metropolitan Museum of Art, New York, NY (8)
Metropolitan Property & Casualty Ins, Warwick, RI
    (15)
Metso Minerals/WS Tyler, Waukesha, WI (16)
Meyer Decorative Surfaces Inc, Atlanta, GA (8)
Meylan Corp, Montclair, NJ (9)
The Miami Herald Media Co, Miami, FL (17)
Michigan Apple Committee, Lansing, MI (1)
Mickwee Group Inc, Newark, CA (16)
Micro Center, Hilliard, OH (3)
Micro Plastics Inc, Flippin, AR (16)
Microbiz Corp, Fountain Valley, CA (3)
Microfluidics Corp, Newton, MA (16)
Micron Corp, Norwood, MA (16)
Microvideo Learning Systems, Inc, New York, NY (3)
Mid America Designs Inc, Effingham, IL (12)
Mid America Motorworks, Effingham, IL (12)
Midcontinent Financial Center Inc, Columbia, MO
    (14)
The Middleby Corp, Elgin, IL (16)
The Midland Co, Amelia, OH (15)
Midwest Center for Stress & Anxiety Inc, Oak Harbor,
    OH (7)
Midwest Publishing Inc, Phoenix, AZ (17)
Midwest Technology Products & Services, Sioux City,
    IA (9)
Military Officers Association of America, Alexandria,
    VA (1)
Military Order of the Purple Heart Svc, Annandale,
    VA (1)
The Millard Group, Lincolnwood, IL (16)

The Miller Group, Dupo, IL (5)
Millipore Corp, Bedford, MA (9)
Milwaukee Electric Tool Corp, Brookfield, WI (16)
Mini City Ltd, Webster, NY (12)
Minitab Inc, State College, PA (16)
Minnesota Life, Saint Paul, MN (15)
Minnesota Multi Housing Association, Bloomington, MN (1)
Minnesota Public Radio, Saint Paul, MN (1)
Minnetonka By Mail, Bronx, NY (2)
Miracle of Aloe, Dallas, TX (7)
MISSCO Corp, Flowood, MS (16)
Missouri Landscape & Nursery Association, Bowling Green, MO (1)
Missouri Life Inc, Boonville, MO (17)
Mr G's Enterprises, Fort Worth, TX (16)
Mitchell International, San Diego, CA (17)
Frank Mittermeier Inc, Bronx, NY (11)
Modern Postcard, Carlsbad, CA (10)
Modernage Custom Digital Imaging Labs, New York, NY (16)
Modular Devices, LLC, Sparta, NJ (3)
Mohawk Lifts, Amsterdam, NY (9)
Molson Coors Brewing Co, Denver, CO (16)
Montag & Caldwell Inc, Atlanta, GA (14)
Moon Shine Trading Co, Woodland, CA (4)
Moore Medical LLC, Farmington, CT (7)
Thurston Moore Country Ltd, Madison, TN (16)
Morcon Industrial Specialty Inc, Mesquite, NV (9)
Jacques Moret Inc, New York, NY (16)
Bob Morgan Woodworking Supplies Inc, Westport, KY (8)
Morgan Kaufmann Publishers Inc, Burlington, MA (17)
Morgan Stanley, New York, NY (14)
Moritt, Hock, Hamroff & Horowitz, Garden City, NY (16)
Morkes Chocolates, Palatine, IL (4)
Morris Visitors Publications LLC, Augusta, GA (17)
Thomas Moser Cabinetmakers, Freeport, ME (16)
Mostad & Christensen, Oak Harbor, WA (16)
Motient Communications, Reston, VA (16)
Motion Picture & Television Fund Foundation, Woodland Hills, CA (1)
The Motley Fool, Alexandria, VA (14)
Motor Coach Industries International Inc, Schaumburg, IL (16)
Motorola Inc, Montvale, NJ (16)
Motown Records, New York, NY (3)
Mott Media LLC, Fenton, MI (17)
Mountain Craft Shop Co, Proctor, WV (11)
Mountain Press Publishing Co, Missoula, MT (17)
Mountain West Supply Co, Scottsdale, AZ (3)
Mrs Beasley's & Miss Grace Lemon Cake Co, Los Angeles, CA (4)
Multi-Level Marketing International Association (MLMIA), Irvine, CA (1)
Mike Murach & Associates Inc, Fresno, CA (17)
Murder by Mail, West Tisbury, MA (1)
Murphy Bed Co Inc, Farmingdale, NY (8)
Muscular Dystrophy Association, Tucson, AZ (1)
Museum Masters Inc, New York, NY (16)
The Museum of Modern Art, New York, NY (5)
Music Choice, Horsham, PA (16)
Music Sales Corp, New York, NY (17)
Music Treasures Co, Richmond, VA (6)
Muskegon Power Tool Corp, North Muskegon, MI (16)
Mustek Inc, Tustin, CA (3)
Mutual of America Life Insurance Co, New York, NY (14)
Mutual of Omaha, Omaha, NE (15)
Myron Corp, Maywood, NJ (16)
Mystic Seaport Museum Stores, Mystic, CT (6)

N

NASCO, Fort Atkinson, WI (5)
NBTY Inc, Ronkonkoma, NY (7)
NCP Solutions, Reston, VA (17)

NCR Corp, Duluth, GA (16)
NCS, Danbury, CT (16)
NCS Learn, Trabuco Canyon, CA (16)
NEBS, Groton, MA (10)
NGL Insurance Group, Madison, WI (15)
NPI, Fort Worth, TX (16)
NSA Technologies LLC, Akron, OH (9)
NTL Institute, Arlington, VA (1)
NADA Appraisal Guides, Costa Mesa, CA (17)
Nancy's Notions LLC, Beaver Dam, WI (11)
NAR Productions, Barryville, NY (17)
Natcom Inc, Bixby, OK (17)
National Active & Retired Federal Employees Association, Alexandria, VA (1)
National Alliance of Business, Washington, DC (1)
National Archives & Records Administration, College Park, MD (17)
National Association for Female Executives (NAFE), New York, NY (1)
National Association for Printing Leadership, East Rutherford, NJ (1)
National Association of Realtors, Chicago, IL (1)
National Automated Clearing House Association, Herndon, VA (1)
National Bulk Equipment Inc, Holland, MI (16)
National Business Furniture Inc, Milwaukee, WI (10)
National Catholic Reporter Publishing Co Inc, Kansas City, MO (17)
National City Bank, Cleveland, OH (14)
National Community Pharmacists Association, Alexandria, VA (1)
National Contract Management Association, Ashburn, VA (1)
National Council on Compensation Insurance Inc (NCCI), Boca Raton, FL (1)
National Court Reporters Association, Vienna, VA (1)
National Crime Prevention Council, Amsterdam, NY (17)
National Emblem Sales, Indianapolis, IN (16)
National Fire Protection Association, Quincy, MA (1)
National Foundation for Cancer Research, Bethesda, MD (1)
National 4-H Supply Service, Chevy Chase, MD (16)
National Golf Foundation, Jupiter, FL (1)
National Journal Group, Washington, DC (17)
National Law Enforcement Officers Memorial Fund, Washington, DC (1)
National League for Nursing, New York, NY (1)
National Luggage Dealers Association, Glenview, IL (1)
National Medical Fellowships, New York, NY (1)
National Motor Club of America Inc, Irving, TX (1)
National Pen Corp, San Diego, CA (6)
National Pension Service Inc, Burlington, VT (14)
National Railroad Passenger Corp, Washington, DC (16)
The National Restaurant Association Educational Foundation, Chicago, IL (1)
National Retail Federation Inc, Washington, DC (1)
National Rural Electric Cooperative Association, Arlington, VA (1)
National School Boards Association Inc, Alexandria, VA (1)
National Semiconductor Corp, Santa Clara, CA (16)
National Seminars Group, Shawnee Mission, KS (16)
National Society of Collegiate Scholars, Washington, DC (1)
National Technical Information Service, Alexandria, VA (17)
The National Underwriter Co, Erlanger, KY (17)
Nationwide Beauty & Barber Supply, Syracuse, NY (16)
Nationwide Displays Inc, Ronkonkoma, NY (16)
Nationwide Mutual Insurance Co, Columbus, OH (15)
Natural Essentials Inc, Streetsboro, OH (5)
The Nature Conservancy, Arlington, VA (1)
Nature Publishing Group, New York, NY (17)
Nautilus Inc, Vancouver, WA (11)
Naval Institute Press, Annapolis, MD (17)
Navistar, Warrenville, IL (16)
Navitar Inc, Rochester, NY (16)

Navy Federal Credit Union, Vienna, VA (14)
Neighborhood Cleaners Association International, New York, NY (1)
Nelson Crab Inc, Tokeland, WA (4)
Nelson-Jameson Inc, Marshfield, WI (9)
Thomas Nelson, Inc, Nashville, TN (17)
Neopost, Carrollton, TX (9)
Nestle Clinical Nutrition Co, Hopkins, MN (16)
Nestle USA, Glendale, CA (4)
Network Telephone Services Inc, Woodland Hills, CA (16)
Neuberger & Berman Management, New York, NY (14)
Neutron Industries, Phoenix, AZ (16)
New & Unique Videos, San Diego, CA (3)
New England Cheesemaking Supply Co, South Deerfield, MA (4)
New England Journal of Medicine, Waltham, MA (17)
New England Life Insurance Co, Boston, MA (15)
New Jersey Institute for Continuing Legal Education, New Brunswick, NJ (1)
New Pig Corp, Tipton, PA (9)
The New Piper Aircraft Inc, Vero Beach, FL (16)
New Win Publishing Inc, El Monte, CA (17)
New York Blood Center Inc, New York, NY (1)
New York Easter Seal Society, New York, NY (1)
New York Findings, Fresh Meadows, NY (6)
New York Foundation For The Arts, Brooklyn, NY (1)
New York Landmarks Conservancy, New York, NY (1)
New York Power Authority, Albany, NY (16)
The New York Times Co, New York, NY (17)
New York University Medical Center, New York, NY (1)
The New Yorker Magazine, New York, NY (17)
Newark Electronics, Chicago, IL (3)
Newell Rubbermaid, Inc, Atlanta, GA (16)
The Newman Group, Ann Arbor, MI (3)
News America Publishing Inc, New York, NY (17)
Newspaper Association of America, Arlington, VA (1)
Newsweek Inc, New York, NY (17)
Nielsen Business Media, New York, NY (16)
The Nielsen Co, New York, NY (17)
Nielsen Trade Dimensions, Wilton, CT (17)
Nightingale-Conant Corp, Niles, IL (17)
Nightingale Resources, Cold Spring, NY (17)
Nihon Keizai Shimbun America Inc, New York, NY (17)
Nilodor Inc, Bolivar, OH (16)
Nimlok, Niles, IL (16)
Nissan Motor Acceptance Corp, Irving, TX (14)
No Fault Sports Products, Houston, TX (11)
No Load Fund*X, San Francisco, CA (14)
Nodine's Smokehouse, Torrington, CT (4)
Noevir Direct Marketing Inc, Montvale, NJ (7)
Nomadics Tipi Makers, Bend, OR (11)
The NonProfit Times, Morris Plains, NJ (17)
Nor'east Miniature Roses Inc, Arroyo Grande, CA (8)
Norman Control Co, Cary, IL (16)
Norman Rockwell Museum, Stockbridge, MA (16)
Norscot Group, Mequon, WI (5)
North American Co for Life & Health Insurance, Chicago, IL (15)
Northeast Hinge Distributors Inc, Hollis, NH (9)
Northern Cross, Lecompton, KS (16)
Northern Greenhouse Sales, Neche, ND (8)
Northern Safety Co Inc, Utica, NY (16)
The Northern Trust Co, Chicago, IL (14)
Northwest Laboratories, Seattle, WA (9)
Northwestern Mutual, Milwaukee, WI (14)
Norwood Promotional Products, Clearwater, FL (16)
Nourse Farms, South Deerfield, MA (8)
Novartis Pharmaceuticals Corp, East Hanover, NJ (7)
Nowell's Inc, San Rafael, CA (8)
Nu-Parr Swimwear, Phoenix, AZ (2)
Nuance Speech Solutions, Burlington, MA (16)
Nuclear Plant Journal, Downers Grove, IL (17)
Nucor Corp, Charlotte, NC (16)
NuNaturals, Eugene, OR (16)
Nat Nussbaum & Associates Inc, Coral Springs, FL (16)

The Professional Putters Association, Winston Salem, NC (1)
Professional Training Associates Inc, Duquesne, PA (17)
Profile Coverage Corp, Melville, NY (15)
Profile Mailing Service Inc, Syosset, NY (16)
Profit Potentials Inc, Hull, IA (1)
Progress Software Corp, Bedford, MA (16)
Progressive Business Publications, Malvern, PA (17)
The Progressive Corp, Mayfield Village, OH (15)
Progressive Energy Corp, San Marcos, CA (5)
Projection Video Services, Springfield, VA (16)
Projector-Recorder Belt Corp, Oceanside, NY (3)
Promo Magazine, New York, NY (17)
Promotion Marketing Association (PMA) Inc, New York, NY (1)
Promotional Product Professionals of Canada, Saint-Laurent, PQ, Canada (1)
ProSing Karaoke, Nederland, CO (5)
Prosperity And Profits Unlimited Distribution Services, Denver, CO (16)
Protective Life Corp, Deerfield, IL (15)
Protective Life Insurance Co, Birmingham, AL (15)
Prudent Publishing Co, Ridgefield Park, NJ (16)
Prudential Financial, Newark, NJ (14)
Fred Pryor Seminars, Mission, KS (16)
Psion Teklogix Inc, Mississauga, ON, Canada (3)
Putnam Investments, Canton, MA (14)
Putnam Rolling Ladder Co Inc, New York, NY (5)
Putt Putt Fun Centers, Winston-Salem, NC (16)

Q

QC Supply LLC, Schuyler, NE (16)
Quadrant Engineering Plastic Products, Reading, PA (16)
Quadriga Art Inc, New York, NY (10)
The Quaker Oats Co, Chicago, IL (16)
Qualco, Inc, Passaic, NJ (8)
Quality Products Inc, Columbus, MS (10)
Quartermaster Uniform & Equipment Co, Cerritos, CA (2)
Queen Bee Gardens, Lovell, WY (4)
Queue Inc, Stratford, CT (17)
Quick Draw Clip Systems Inc, Ventura, CA (9)
Quill Corp, Palatine, IL (16)

R

RBC Dain Rauscher, Boston, MA (14)
RBS Citizens Financial Group Inc, Dedham, MA (14)
RMA-The Risk Management Association, Philadelphia, PA (1)
Racer Walsh Co, Jacksonville, FL (12)
Racer's Equipment Warehouse, Warwick, RI (16)
Rainbow Art Glass, Wall, NJ (16)
Rainbow Group LLC, Middleton, WI (11)
Ranch House Meat Co, Menard, TX (4)
Rand Material Handling Equipment Co Inc, Janesville, WI (16)
Random Lengths Publications Inc, Eugene, OR (17)
Ranger Joe's International Military Supply, Columbus, GA (2)
Rapid City Journal, Rapid City, SD (18)
Rapids Wholesale Equipment, Marion, IA (16)
Rascal, Sewell, NJ (7)
Raybuck Autobody Parts, Punxsutawney, PA (12)
Raycom Sports, Charlotte, NC (16)
Reb Storage Systems International, Chicago, IL (9)
Recognition Products International, Easton, MD (16)
Recognition Systems (Dot Works), Port Washington, NY (16)
Recording for the Blind & Dyslexic Inc, Princeton, NJ (16)
Recycled Software Inc, Palm Springs, CA (3)
RedEnvelope Inc, San Diego, CA (6)
Redleaf Press, Saint Paul, MN (17)
Redwood City Seed Co, Redwood City, CA (8)
Reed - Elsevier, New York, NY (17)

Reed Exhibitions, Norwalk, CT (16)
Referee Enterprises, Franksville, WI (1)
Regal Ware Inc, Kewaskum, WI (5)
The Reggio Register Co Inc, Leominster, MA (8)
Regitar USA Inc, Montgomery, AL (9)
Reid Supply Co, Muskegon, MI (16)
Relaxo-Bak Inc, Anderson, IN (7)
Reliable Racing Supply, Queensbury, NY (11)
Reliable Technologies Inc, Manchester, NH (16)
Reliance Electric, Fort Smith, AR (9)
Reliapon Police Products, Las Vegas, NV (5)
Renaissance Greeting Cards Inc, Springvale, ME (5)
Renaissance Learning, Wisconsin Rapids, WI (5)
Reno Gazette Journal, Reno, NV (13)
The Renovator's Supply Inc, Millers Falls, MA (9)
Rent-A-Center Inc, Plano, TX (16)
Rent Mother Nature, Cambridge, MA (4)
Renton's Inc, Centennial, CO (10)
Replacements Ltd, Greensboro, NC (8)
Replogle Globes Inc, Broadview, IL (16)
Research Institute America, Carrollton, TX (14)
Research To Prevent Blindness Inc, New York, NY (1)
Rose Resnick Lighthouse for the Blind & Visually Impaired, San Francisco, CA (1)
Resorts Worldwide Inc, White Plains, NY (19)
Resource Publications Inc, San Jose, CA (17)
Resumate Inc, Ann Arbor, MI (3)
Retawmatic Corp, Flushing, NY (9)
Rhode Island Novelty, Cumberland, RI (16)
Rhythm Band Inc, Fort Worth, TX (11)
Ricci Lee Hubbart Associates Inc, Cupertino, CA (16)
Rich Products Corp, Buffalo, NY (16)
Richardson Electronics Ltd, Lafox, IL (16)
Pete Rickard Inc, Cobleskill, NY (11)
Right On Computer Software, Greenlawn, NY (3)
Rio Brands, Philadelphia, PA (16)
Rio Grande, Albuquerque, NM (16)
River Street Sweets, Savannah, GA (4)
Rizzoli International Publications Inc, New York, NY (17)
Robert Marketing Inc, Northbrook, IL (5)
The Ken Roberts Co, Daphne, AL (5)
C H Robinson Worldwide Inc, Eden Prairie, MN (16)
Robinson Home Products, Buffalo, NY (16)
The Roblin Group Inc, White Plains, NY (17)
Roche Pharmaceuticals, Nutley, NJ (7)
Rock-Tred Corp, Waukegan, IL (9)
RocketWear, New York, NY (2)
Rockler Woodworking & Hardware, Medina, MN (8)
Rockwell Automation, Milwaukee, WI (16)
Rocky Mountain Chocolate Factory, Durango, CO (4)
Rodale Inc, Emmaus, PA (17)
Rod's Western Palace, Columbus, OH (2)
Rogers Publishing Ltd, Toronto, ON, Canada (17)
Rohm & Haas Co, Philadelphia, PA (16)
Rollyson Financial Group, Pasadena, MD (14)
Roman Research Inc/Simply Whispers Earring, Hanson, MA (2)
Ronco Corp, Austin, TX (16)
Ronell Clock Co, Grants Pass, OR (5)
Rose Displays Ltd, Salem, MA (16)
Rose Electronics, Houston, TX (3)
Rosicrucian Order AMORC, San Jose, CA (1)
Rosland Capital LLC, Santa Monica, CA (14)
Ross Metals, New York, NY (16)
Ross-Simons, Cranston, RI (6)
Roto-Rooter Services Co, Cincinnati, OH (16)
Round Lake Publishing Co, Trumbull, CT (17)
Row Resources Inc, Northport, NY (16)
Rowe Pottery Works Inc, Cambridge, WI (16)
Royal Bank of Canada, Toronto, ON, Canada (14)
Royal Canadian Mint, Ottawa, ON, Canada (16)
Rubber Stamps of America, Dublin, NH (6)
Rubbermaid Inc, Fairlawn, OH (8)
Rural Alaska Community Action Program Inc, Anchorage, AK (1)
Ruskin, Moscou, Faltischek, PC, Uniondale, NY (16)
Rutland Products, Rutland, VT (16)
Ruud Lighting Inc, Racine, WI (9)

S

S&S Worldwide, Colchester, CT (11)
SC Direct, West Bridgewater, MA (2)
SCA Promotions Inc, Dallas, TX (15)
SDI Marketing, Toronto, ON, Canada (14)
SEI, Oaks, PA (14)
SF Video Inc, San Francisco, CA (3)
SIFMA, New York, NY (1)
SLM Corp, Reston, VA (16)
SNL Financial, Charlottesville, VA (17)
SRDS, Des Plaines, IL (17)
SSHC Inc/Radiant Heating Commercial Applications, Old Saybrook, CT (9)
ST Media Group International, Cincinnati, OH (17)
SWBC, San Antonio, TX (14)
Sa-So, Arlington, TX (16)
Sabre Holdings Inc, Southlake, TX (19)
Safe Publications Inc, Southampton, PA (11)
Safeco Insurance Co, Seattle, WA (15)
Safeguard Business Systems Inc, Dallas, TX (16)
Safeware, The Insurance Agency Inc, Columbus, OH (15)
Safti First, San Francisco, CA (16)
Sage Financial Group, West Conshohocken, PA (14)
Sage Software Inc, Irvine, CA (16)
The Sailing Co, Palm Coast, FL (17)
The Saint Francis Academy Inc, Salina, KS (1)
St Lawrence Island Original Ivory Cooperative, Gambell, AK (6)
St Louis Post-Dispatch, Saint Louis, MO (17)
St Louis Slot Machine Co, Saint Louis, MO (6)
St Petersburg/Clearwater Area CVB, Clearwater, FL (1)
Saks Fifth Avenue, New York, NY (16)
Sales & Marketing Management Magazine, New York, NY (16)
Sales Leads, Jupiter, FL (17)
Salesian Missions, New Rochelle, NY (1)
Sally Beauty Supply LLC, Denton, TX (7)
Samsonite American Tourister, Mansfield, MA (16)
Samsonite Corp, Mansfield, MA (16)
San Francisco Chronicle, San Francisco, CA (17)
San Francisco Herb & Natural Food Co, Fremont, CA (4)
San Francisco Victoriana Inc, San Francisco, CA (9)
San Jose Mercury News, San Jose, CA (17)
Sandy Corp, Troy, MI (16)
Sani Serv, Mooresville, IN (16)
SanSegal Sportswear (HQ), Sandy, UT (2)
Santa Barbara Greenhouses, Oxnard, CA (8)
Santa Fe Natural Tobacco Co, Santa Fe, NM (16)
Satori Software Inc, Seattle, WA (16)
Sauce Co, Little Rock, AR (4)
Saunders Manufacturing Co Inc, Readfield, ME (16)
Saunders Military Insignia, Naples, FL (6)
The Sausage Maker Inc, Buffalo, NY (4)
Save the Children Federation Inc, Westport, CT (1)
Sax Arts & Crafts, Appleton, WI (10)
Scan Optics Inc, Manchester, CT (16)
Henry Schein Inc, Melville, NY (16)
Schermer Pecans, Glennville, GA (4)
Jacques C Schiff Jr Inc, Ridgefield Park, NJ (5)
Schneider Saddlery, Chagrin Falls, OH (11)
Schnuck Markets Inc, Saint Louis, MO (16)
Scholastic Inc, New York, NY (17)
School Annual Publishing Co, State College, PA (17)
School Specialty Inc, Greenville, WI (16)
Schoolwise Press, San Francisco, CA (17)
Schultz & Williams Inc, Philadelphia, PA (1)
The Scooter Store, New Braunfels, TX (7)
Scorecards USA, North Kingstown, RI (16)
Scott Sign Systems Inc, Sarasota, FL (16)
The Scotts Co Div of Lawn Service, Marysville, OH (8)
Scott's Dog Supply Inc, Indianapolis, IN (11)
Scotts-Sierra Horticultural, Marysville, OH (16)
Sculpture House Inc, Skillman, NJ (16)
Sea Bear, Anacortes, WA (16)
Seashore Vacations, Hilton Head Island, SC (19)

Seattle Magazine, Seattle, WA (17)
SECO-LARM USA Inc, Irvine, CA (16)
Second Renaissance Books, Irvine, CA (17)
Security Micro Systems Inc, Scottsdale, AZ (3)
Seedburo Equipment Co, Des Plaines, IL (8)
Seiko Corp of America, Mahwah, NJ (16)
Select Press, Novato, CA (17)
Sellstrom Manufacturing Co, Palatine, IL (16)
L.H. Selman Ltd, Chicago, IL (6)
Sencore Inc, Sioux Falls, SD (16)
Sensient Technologies, Saint Louis, MO (16)
Sensory Consumer Science, Teterboro, NJ (7)
Sentry Life Insurance Co, Stevens Point, WI (15)
Sequoia Nursery, Fresno, CA (8)
Serenity, Maria Stein, OH (17)
Seton Identification Products, Branford, CT (16)
JA Sexauer, Elmsford, NY (16)
Seybold Publications, Gilbertsville, PA (17)
B Shackman & Co Inc, Galesburg, MI (6)
Shades of Light, Richmond, VA (8)
Shady Oaks Nursery, LLC, Waseca, MN (8)
Shakespeare Co, Columbia, SC (11)
Shape LLC, Addison, IL (3)
Shelby Insurance Companies, Birmingham, AL (15)
Sherman Specialty Toy Co Inc, Jericho, NY (16)
Sheshunoff Information Services Inc, Austin, TX (14)
Shield Healthcare, Valencia, CA (7)
Shillcraft Inc, Annapolis, MD (16)
Shipping Solutions, Eagan, MN (16)
Shop.com, Monterey, CA (16)
Shopsmith Inc, Dayton, OH (16)
Shortage Control Inc & SC Video, Strongsville, OH (5)
Siegel Display Products, Minneapolis, MN (5)
Siemens IT Solutions & Services Inc, Norwalk, CT (16)
Sierra Inc, Racine, WI (3)
Sierra Scientific Inc, Phoenix, AZ (9)
Silicon Graphics Inc, Fremont, CA (16)
Simmons-Boardman Publishing Corp, New York, NY (17)
Simon Property Group, Indianapolis, IN (16)
Simplex Grinnell, Westminster, MA (16)
Simplicity Pattern Co Inc/Style Patterns Ltd/New Look English Pattern Co Ltd, New York, NY (8)
Simpson Electric Co, Lac Du Flambeau, WI (16)
Sims Stoves, Billings, MT (11)
Single Scene News, Tempe, AZ (17)
Sirius XM Radio, Washington, DC (16)
Skinder-Strauss Associates, Newark, NJ (14)
Skullduggery, Anaheim, CA (16)
Skydiving Magazine, DeLand, FL (17)
Skyline Displays, Saint Paul, MN (5)
Skypoint Communications Inc, Loretto, MN (16)
Slocum Water Gardens, Winter Haven, FL (8)
Small Business Service Bureau Inc, Worcester, MA (1)
Smart Dog Products, Winchester, TN (11)
Smart Practice, Phoenix, AZ (17)
AO Smith Corp, Milwaukee, WI (16)
Smith & Hawken Ltd, Novato, CA (8)
Smithfield Packing Co Inc, Smithfield, VA (16)
The JM Smucker Co, Orrville, OH (4)
Snap-on Inc, Kenosha, WI (9)
Tom Snyder Productions, Watertown, MA (16)
The Soap Factory, Bedford, MA (7)
SOAR Inflatables, Healdsburg, CA (11)
Social Studies School Service, Culver City, CA (16)
Society for Human Resource Management, Alexandria, VA (1)
Society of Financial Service Professionals, Newtown Square, PA (1)
Society of Manufacturing Engineers, Dearborn, MI (1)
Software AG USA, Reston, VA (3)
Software Assistance International Ltd (SAIL), Morris Plains, NJ (3)
The Software Labs Inc, Bellevue, WA (3)
Solar Cine Products Inc, Chicago, IL (5)
Solar Components Corp, Manchester, NH (9)
Solarcom, Norcross, GA (16)
Solitron Devices Inc, West Palm Beach, FL (16)

Sony Electronics Inc, Park Ridge, NJ (16)
Sotheby's, New York, NY (6)
Soundprints, Norwalk, CT (6)
South Seas Island Resort, Captiva Island, FL (19)
South-Western Publishing, Madison, OH (17)
Southeast Toyota Distributors LLC, Deerfield Beach, FL (16)
Southern California Gas Co, Anaheim, CA (1)
Southern Emblem Co, Toast, NC (5)
Southern Flavoring Co Inc, Bedford, VA (16)
Southern Progress Corp, Birmingham, AL (17)
Sovereign Bank New England, Glastonbury, CT (14)
Spa-Finder Inc, New York, NY (7)
Spalding Laboratories Inc, Arroyo Grande, CA (7)
Spates The Florist, Newport, VT (8)
Huck Spaulding Enterprises, Voorheesville, NY (16)
Speakers Guild Inc, Sandwich, MA (16)
Spear Engineering Co, Colorado Springs, CO (16)
Specialized Association Services, Irving, TX (1)
Specialized Information Publishers Association (SIPA), Vienna, VA (1)
Specialized Products Co, Southlake, TX (16)
Specialty Store Services Inc, Des Plaines, IL (16)
Spectra Merchandising International Inc, Chicago, IL (16)
Spectronics Corp, Westbury, NY (9)
Spectrum Chemicals & Laboratory Products, Gardena, CA (16)
Speed-Mat, Biddeford, ME (16)
The Sperry & Hutchinson Co Inc, Delray Beach, FL (6)
Spinneybeck Enterprises, Getzville, NY (16)
Spokane Teachers Credit Union, Liberty Lake, WA (14)
Spoken Arts, Holmes, NY (17)
The Spokesman-Review, Spokane, WA (17)
Sport Supply Group, Dallas, TX (11)
Sportif Mail Order Inc, Sparks, NV (2)
Sportime International, Norcross, GA (11)
Spring-Green Lawn Care Corp, Plainfield, IL (16)
Springer Science & Business Media LLC, New York, NY (17)
Springs Global Inc, New York, NY (16)
Sprint Nextel Corp, Reston, VA (3)
Sprint PCS, Overland Park, KS (16)
Stagestep Inc, Philadelphia, PA (5)
Standard & Poor's Corp, New York, NY (17)
Standard Communications Corp, San Diego, CA (16)
Standard Life, Montreal, PQ, Canada (15)
Standard Publishing, Cincinnati, OH (17)
Standard Register, Dayton, OH (10)
Robert A Stanger & Co Inc, Shrewsbury, NJ (14)
Stanley Supply & Services, North Andover, MA (16)
Staples Inc, Framingham, MA (10)
Star Sprinkler Inc, Lansdale, PA (9)
Starbucks Corp, Seattle, WA (4)
Starchtech, Golden Valley, MN (16)
Stark Brothers Fulfillment Services, Louisiana, MO (8)
Stark Brothers Nurseries & Orchards, Louisiana, MO (8)
Starkey Laboratories, Eden Prairie, MN (16)
START International, Addison, TX (9)
State Farm Insurance Cos, Bloomington, IL (15)
State Mutual Insurance Co, Rome, GA (15)
StatSoft Inc, Tulsa, OK (9)
StayWell/Krames, San Bruno, CA (17)
Steelcase Inc, Grand Rapids, MI (16)
Stellar Technology Inc, Amherst, NY (9)
Steptoe & Wife Antiques Ltd, Toronto, ON, Canada (8)
Sterling Fluid Systems, Indianapolis, IN (16)
Sterling Name Tape Inc, Winsted, CT (16)
Sterling Publishing Co Inc, New York, NY (17)
Steuben Glass, New York, NY (6)
Stevens Publishing Co, Sandusky, OH (17)
Stew Leonard's, Norwalk, CT (4)
Stewart-MacDonald, Athens, OH (16)
Martha Stewart Living Omnimedia, New York, NY (17)
Stick-Em Up Inc, Pleasanton, CA (5)

Kirk Stieff Co, Bristol, PA (16)
Stile-Tile Like Metal Roofing, Sellersburg, IN (9)
Stimpson Co Inc, Pompano Beach, FL (16)
Stock Drive Products, New Hyde Park, NY (5)
Stock Yards Packing Co Inc, Chicago, IL (4)
Stonwurks, Eden Prairie, MN (16)
Story Time Stories That Rhyme, Denver, CO (17)
Strang Communications Co, Lake Mary, FL (17)
Strategy Corps LLC, Brentwood, TN (16)
Stratford Hall, North Mankato, MN (10)
The Stratosphere Las Vegas, Las Vegas, NV (19)
Stratus Technologies, Maynard, MA (16)
Stress Market, Port Angeles, WA (17)
Strongwell, Bristol, VA (9)
Sturges Sportswear, Battleboro, NC (16)
Subscription Agency.com Inc, Winter Haven, FL (18)
Suez Energy North America, Houston, TX (16)
Sugarbush Farm Inc, Woodstock, VT (4)
Sullivan-Victory Groves, Cocoa, FL (4)
Summit Industries Inc, Marietta, GA (5)
Summit Racing Equipment, Tallmadge, OH (12)
Sun Harvest Citrus, Fort Myers, FL (6)
Sun Hope Nutritional Health, Santa Monica, CA (7)
Sunbeam, Boca Raton, FL (16)
Sunbilt Creative Sunrooms, Jamaica, NY (8)
Sundancer Jewelry Co Inc, Albuquerque, NM (16)
Sunlife of Canada, Wellesley Hills, MA (15)
Sunnyland Farms Inc, Albany, GA (4)
Sunoco, Inc, Philadelphia, PA (16)
Sunrise Business Products, Mineola, NY (10)
Sunrise Greetings, Bloomington, IN (17)
Sunrise Medical Inc, Boulder, CO (16)
Sunshine Discount Crafts, Largo, FL (11)
Sunshine Farm & Gardens, Renick, WV (8)
Sunshine Glassworks Ltd, Buffalo, NY (11)
Sunshine Minting Inc, Coeur D'Alene, ID (14)
Sunshine Unlimited Inc, Lindsborg, KS (9)
Sunstar, Chicago, IL (16)
Suntrust Banks Inc, Atlanta, GA (14)
Supelco Inc, Bellefonte, PA (16)
Super 8 Hotels Worldwide, Parsippany, NJ (19)
Superior Real Estate Supply, Phoenix, AZ (10)
Support Systems International Corp, Richmond, CA (3)
Sur La Table, Seattle, WA (8)
Sure-Fire Business Success Catalog, Cambridge, MA (17)
Surplus Center, Lincoln, NE (9)
Surplus Record, Chicago, IL (17)
Sussex Publishers Inc, New York, NY (17)
Svoboda Collins LLC, Chicago, IL (5)
The Swiss Colony Inc, Monroe, WI (4)
Symantec, Mountain View, CA (16)
Symetra Financial, Bellevue, WA (15)
Syngenta, Greensboro, NC (16)
Syntellect, Phoenix, AZ (16)
System Pavers, Newport Beach, CA (16)
Systemax Inc, Port Washington, NY (16)

T

T Rowe Price Associates Inc, Baltimore, MD (14)
TAB Boards International Inc, Westminster, CO (14)
TAPPI (Technical Association of the Pulp & Paper Industry), Norcross, GA (1)
TCJC, New York, NY (2)
Thomson Reuters, New York, NY (17)
TIAA-CREF, New York, NY (15)
TL Enterprises Inc, Ventura, CA (17)
TNT Packaging Inc, Miami, FL (16)
TT Publishing, Arlington, VA (17)
TVC Enterprises and the TV Collector Magazine, Las Vegas, NV (6)
TWL Knowledge Group, Carrollton, TX (3)
Tackle Craft, Ellsworth, WI (11)
Tailwinds Inc, Mill Valley, CA (6)
Talas, Brooklyn, NY (10)
Tamrac Inc, Chatsworth, CA (2)
Tandy Leather Co, Fort Worth, TX (11)
The Taunton Press, Newtown, CT (17)

Tax Management Inc, Bethesda, MD (17)
Tax Reduction Institute, Germantown, MD (14)
Ann Taylor Inc, New York, NY (2)
Taylor Capital Group, Inc, Rosemont, IL (14)
Taylor Corp, North Mankato, MN (16)
Taylor-Stiles Division, Florence, KY (16)
Taymark Inc, White Bear Lake, MN (1)
Teachers' Discovery, Auburn Hills, MI (5)
The Teaching Co, Chantilly, VA (17)
Team Cheer, Geneseo, NY (2)
Techni-Tool Inc, Worcester, PA (16)
Technology Review, Cambridge, MA (17)
Tektronix Inc, Beaverton, OR (16)
Telcordia Technologies, Piscataway, NJ (16)
Telecommunications Reports International Inc, Washington, DC (17)
Telect Inc, Liberty Lake, WA (16)
Teleflora, Los Angeles, CA (16)
Telefonix Inc, Waukegan, IL (16)
Telephony, Chicago, IL (17)
Telpro Inc, Grand Forks, ND (9)
Tempco Electric Heater Corp, Wood Dale, IL (9)
Ten Speed Press, Emeryville, CA (17)
Tennessee Valley Authority, Knoxville, TN (16)
Tensar International Corporation, Alpharetta, GA (16)
Terminix International, The Trugreen Companies, Memphis, TN (16)
Tessco Inc, Hunt Valley, MD (16)
Tetley USA Inc, Montvale, NJ (16)
Teva Pharmaceuticals USA, North Wales, PA (7)
Texas Industries Inc, Dallas, TX (16)
Texas Parks & Wildlife Dept, Austin, TX (1)
Texas Refinery Corp, Fort Worth, TX (9)
Texwipe Co, Kernersville, NC (16)
Theatre Development Fund Inc, New York, NY (1)
Thermal Product Solutions, White Deer, PA (16)
Thermo Fisher Scientific I, Waltham, MA (9)
Thermo Fisher Scientific SID, Madison, WI (9)
Thermo Pro, Duluth, GA (16)
Thetford Corp, Ann Arbor, MI (16)
Thieme Medical Publishers Inc, New York, NY (17)
Thimband, Denver, CO (17)
Things Deco, New York, NY (6)
Things Remembered, Highland Heights, OH (6)
Think Ink, Bothell, WA (10)
Thirteen/WNET, New York, NY (1)
Thoma Cressey Bravo, Chicago, IL (14)
Thomas Computer Corp, Orlando, FL (16)
Thomas Klise/Crimson Multimedia, Mystic, CT (16)
Thomas Scientific, Swedesboro, NJ (9)
Stephen Thomas, Toronto, ON, Canada (1)
Thompson Publishing Group Inc, Washington, DC (17)
Thomson Financial, New York, NY (17)
Thomson-Gale, Farmington Hills, MI (17)
Thomson Research, Boston, MA (14)
Thomson Reuters LPC, New York, NY (14)
Thomson West, Eagan, MN (17)
Thorndike Press, Waterville, ME (17)
Thought Technology Ltd, Montreal, PQ, Canada (16)
3D Mail Results, Kent, WA (5)
Three Georges and the Nuthouse, Mobile, AL (16)
3M Post-It Direct Response Products, Saint Paul, MN (16)
Tidbits Media, Montgomery, AL (17)
Tiger Direct Inc, Miami, FL (3)
TigerDirect.ca, Richmond Hill, ON, Canada (3)
Tillamook County Creamery Association, Tillamook, OR (4)
Timber Crest Farms, Healdsburg, CA (16)
Timberline Geodesics, Berkeley, CA (8)
Time Inc, New York, NY (17)
Time Motion Tools, Poway, CA (9)
Time Products International, Del Rio, TX (16)
Time/System, Chicopee, MA (16)
Time Warner Inc, New York, NY (16)
Times Union, Albany, NY (18)
Timm Medical Technologies, Inc, Eden Prairie, MN (16)
Tinsley Tool Supply Inc, Powell, TN (9)
Todaro Brothers Mail Order Co, New York, NY (4)

Toland Home and Garden Inc, Port Townsend, WA (16)
Tomahawk Live Trap Co, Tomahawk, WI (16)
Torah Umesorah Publications, Brooklyn, NY (5)
Toronto Hydro-Electric System, Toronto, ON, Canada (1)
Torqmaster International, Stamford, CT (9)
Total Care, Rockville, MD (7)
Total Training Solutions LLC, Waunakee, WI (5)
Toter Inc, Statesville, NC (16)
Townsend Communications LLC, Kansas City, MO (17)
Toyota Motor Sales USA Inc, Torrance, CA (16)
Trans Union Corp, Chicago, IL (14)
Transaction Publishers, Piscataway, NJ (17)
Transamerica Occidental Life Co, Los Angeles, CA (15)
Transcat, Rochester, NY (16)
Transemantics Inc, Washington, DC (16)
TransFirst Holdings Inc, Dallas, TX (14)
Transit Treasure Inc, New York, NY (12)
Travel Industry Association, Washington, DC (1)
Travel Planners Inc, New York, NY (19)
Travelclick, Schaumburg, IL (19)
The Travelers Insurance Cos, Hartford, CT (15)
Trend Magazines Inc, Saint Petersburg, FL (17)
Tri Tech Laboratories Inc, Lynchburg, VA (16)
Tribune Co, Chicago, IL (17)
Tricor Braun, Woodridge, IL (16)
Tricor Direct Inc/Seton, Branford, CT (9)
Trigon Blue Cross/Blue Shield, Roanoke, VA (15)
Trilithic, Indianapolis, IN (16)
Tristar Products, Fairfield, NJ (16)
Triton College, River Grove, IL (16)
Trophyland USA Inc, Hialeah, FL (5)
Trout Unlimited, Arlington, VA (1)
Troy Biologicals Inc, Troy, MI (7)
TruGreen/ChemLawn, Lewis Center, OH (16)
Truitt Brothers Inc, Salem, OR (16)
Trumble Greetings, Boulder, CO (6)
Trump Marina Hotel & Casino, Atlantic City, NJ (19)
Trump Plaza Hotel & Casino, Atlantic City, NJ (19)
The Trumpet Club, New York, NY (17)
truTV, New York, NY (17)
Tucker Electronics Co, Garland, TX (3)
Tully & Holland Inc, Wellesley, MA (14)
Turncraft Clocks Inc, Spring Park, MN (6)
Tuttle, Wallingford, CT (2)
Tuttle Printing & Engraving, Rutland, VT (10)
20th Century Fox Television, Los Angeles, CA (16)
Tyco Electronics Corp, Menlo Park, CA (16)
Tyco Valves & Controls, Houston, TX (16)
Tyndale House Publishers, Carol Stream, IL (17)

U

U-Bild, Oceanside, CA (8)
U-Haul International, Phoenix, AZ (16)
UBS Wealth Management US, Weehawken, NJ (14)
UDL Laboratories Inc, Sugar Land, TX (7)
UGL Equis Corp, Chicago, IL (16)
ULI-The Urban Land Institute, Washington, DC (1)
UNICEF, New York, NY (1)
UNICEF Canada, Toronto, ON, Canada (1)
USAA, San Antonio, TX (15)
USX, Pittsburgh, PA (16)
Uline, Pleasant Prairie, WI (5)
Ultimate Office, Farmingdale, NJ (16)
Ultimate Products Inc, Chula Vista, CA (16)
Ultra Direct Marketing Inc, Jackson, NJ (16)
Umass Dartmouth, North Dartmouth, MA (1)
Unadilla Laminated Products, Unadilla, NY (16)
Uncharted Country Publishing, Madison, WI (17)
Uncle Ben's Inc, Greenville, MS (4)
Undergear.com, La Crosse, WI (2)
Unicol Inc, Pembroke Pines, FL (17)
Unicom Electric Inc, Walnut, CA (16)
Unicover Corp, Cheyenne, WY (6)
Uniforms & Scrubs.com, Ballwin, MO (7)

Union Federal Savings Bank, North Providence, RI (14)
Union Pen Co, Hagaman, NY (5)
Union Switch & Signal Inc, Pittsburgh, PA (16)
Unisys, Blue Bell, PA (16)
United Air Specialists Inc, Cincinnati, OH (16)
United Business Media, Manhasset, NY (17)
United Church Homes, Marion, OH (1)
United Communications Group, Gaithersburg, MD (17)
United Community Bank, Blairsville, GA (14)
United Investors Life Insurance Co, Birmingham, AL (15)
United Security Products Inc, Poway, CA (16)
United Spinal Association, East Elmhurst, NY (1)
United Staffing Systems, New York, NY (16)
US Bancorp, Minneapolis, MN (14)
US Bank, Minneapolis, MN (14)
US BRANDING GROUP, LLC, Lake Worth, FL (16)
United States Bronze Sign Co Inc, New Hyde Park, NY (1)
US Chamber of Commerce, Washington, DC (1)
US Department of Commerce, Washington, DC (1)
US Foodservice, Rosemont, IL (4)
US Fund for UNICEF, New York, NY (6)
US Games Systems Inc, Stamford, CT (11)
US News & World Report, New York, NY (17)
USA Hosts, San Francisco, CA (19)
USA TODAY, Mc Lean, VA (17)
US Pharmacopeia, Rockville, MD (1)
US Playing Card Co, Erlanger, KY (16)
United Systems c/o Biomed, Concord, CA (7)
United Way of Greater Toronto, Toronto, ON, Canada (1)
Unitrin, Chicago, IL (15)
Unitron Ltd, Commack, NY (9)
Universal Communication Enterprise, Elizabeth, NJ (13)
Universal Corp, Richmond, VA (16)
Universal Engineering Corp, Cedar Rapids, IA (16)
Universal Fidelity Corp, Houston, TX (14)
Universal Hovercraft, Cordova, IL (11)
Universal Security Instruments Inc, Owings Mills, MD (16)
Universal Training, Lake Forest, IL (16)
Universal Vintage Tire Co, Hershey, PA (11)
University Bank, Ann Arbor, MI (14)
University of Akron, Akron, OH (1)
University of Alabama, Tuscaloosa, AL (13)
University of Chicago Press, Chicago, IL (17)
University of Illinois Foundation, Urbana, IL (1)
University of Oklahoma Press, Norman, OK (17)
University Press of America Inc, Lanham, MD (17)
Unum Corp, Portland, ME (15)
Upbeat Inc, Saint Louis, MO (9)
Upstart, Madison, WI (16)
Urbani Truffles USA Corp, New York, NY (4)
Utilities Supply Corp, Woburn, MA (16)
Utretch Art Supplies, Cranbury, NJ (10)

V

VF Imagewear, Nashville, TN (2)
Vagabond Creations Inc, Dayton, OH (10)
Valdawn Watch Co, Long Island City, NY (16)
Value Line Publishing Inc, New York, NY (17)
Van Bourgondien Bros, Virginia Beach, VA (8)
Van Dam Inc, New York, NY (17)
Vance Industries Inc, Niles, IL (16)
Vanderbilt Advertising, New York, NY (14)
The Vane Brothers Co, Baltimore, MD (16)
Vanguard, Valley Forge, PA (14)
Varian Medical Systems, Palo Alto, CA (9)
Vaxserve, Scranton, PA (7)
Vcom International Multi-Media Corp, South Hackensack, NJ (3)
Veer, Calgary, AB, Canada (16)
Vegetarian Awareness Network/VEGANET, Washington, DC (1)
Vemma Nutrition Co, Scottsdale, AZ (7)

Venture Entertainment Group, Sherman Oaks, CA (3)
Ventyx, Atlanta, GA (16)
Venus Fashion, Inc, Jacksonville, FL (2)
Veriad, Brea, CA (16)
Veridian Credit Union, Waterloo, IA (1)
Verizon, Arlington, VA (16)
Verizon Communications Inc, New York, NY (3)
Vermont Teddy Bear Co, Shelburne, VT (6)
Vermont Tubbs, Whitefield, NH (8)
Veronis Suhler Stevenson LLC, New York, NY (14)
Vertex Inc, Berwyn, PA (16)
Vertrue Inc, Norwalk, CT (13)
Vet Vax, Tonganoxie, KS (11)
Veterans of Foreign Wars (VFW) of the US-National
    Headquarters, Kansas City, MO (1)
Viacom Inc, New York, NY (16)
Viahealth, Rochester, NY (16)
Viatech Publishing Solutions Inc, Bay Shore, NY (16)
Victor Machinery Exchange, Brooklyn, NY (9)
Victory Corps, New Hope, MN (16)
Video Artists International, Pleasantville, NY (3)
Vierk National Supply, North Chicago, IL (16)
VIEW Video Inc/Arcadia Entertainment Corp, Sauger-
    ties, NY (16)
Viking Pump Inc, Cedar Falls, IA (16)
Village Coin Shop, Plaistow, NH (6)
Village Interiors Carpet One, Newton, NC (8)
Village Software Inc, Boston, MA (3)
Vintage Wood Works, Quinlan, TX (8)
Virco Manufacturing Corp, Conway, AR (16)
The Virginia Diner Inc, Wakefield, VA (4)
Virginia Home For Boys, Richmond, VA (1)
Visa USA, Foster City, CA (14)
Visible Computer Supply Corp, Saint Charles, IL (16)
Visual Horizons, Rochester, NY (16)
Visual Reference Publications, New York, NY (17)
Vitamin Power Inc, Hauppauge, NY (7)
Vitamin Research Products, Carson City, NV (7)
Vitasoy USA Inc, Ayer, MA (16)
Vivendi, New York, NY (16)
Vivitar Corp, Tempe, AZ (16)
Volvo Cars of North America, Northvale, NJ (16)
Voyageur Inc, Easley, SC (11)
Ed Voyles Hyundai Inc, Smyrna, GA (16)
Vulcan Information Packaging, Vincent, AL (16)
Vulcan Materials Co, Birmingham, AL (16)

W

WFF'N PROOF Learning Games Associates, Fairfield,
    IA (17)
WRS Group Ltd, Waco, TX (7)
WTS Media, Chattanooga, TN (16)
Wachovia Bank, National Association, Charlotte, NC
    (14)
Wachovia Center, Philadelphia, PA (16)
Wag/Aero Group, Lyons, WI (16)
Walch Publishing, Portland, ME (17)
Walker Publishing Co Inc, New York, NY (17)
Wm. K. Walthers Inc, Milwaukee, WI (11)
Warnaco, New York, NY (2)
Warnaco Swimwear Inc, Los Angeles, CA (16)
Warner Books, New York, NY (17)
Warner Press, Anderson, IN (17)
Warren Communications News, Washington, DC (17)
Warren, Gorham & Lamont Inc, New York, NY (17)
Washington Marketing Group, Arlington, VA (1)
The Washington Monthly Co, Washington, DC (17)
Washington Mutual Home Loan, Inc, Downers Grove,
    IL (14)
Washington National Opera, Washington, DC (16)
Washington Post Digital, Washington, DC (17)
Andrew D Washton Books On the Fine Arts, Port
    Chester, NY (16)
Wasserman Uniform Co, Fort Lauderdale, FL (2)
Waters Corp, Milford, MA (16)
Water's Edge Resort & Spa, Westbrook, CT (19)
Wathne Ltd, New York, NY (2)
Watts Radiant, Springfield, MO (9)
Waytek, Chanhassen, MN (16)

We-No-Nah Canoe Inc, Winona, MN (11)
WearGuard Corp, Norwell, MA (2)
Webb Designs Inc, El Cajon, CA (16)
Webster Bank, Waterbury, CT (14)
The Wedding Pages, New York, NY (16)
Weichert Co, Morris Plains, NJ (14)
Weider Publications Inc, Woodland Hills, CA (17)
Weingeroff Enterprises Inc, Cranston, RI (16)
Weiss Research Inc, Jupiter, FL (17)
Welcomemat Services Inc, Atlanta, GA (9)
Wellmark Blue Cross & Blue Shield of Iowa, Des
    Moines, IA (15)
Wellness Councils of America, Omaha, NE (1)
Wells Fargo, San Francisco, CA (14)
Wenner Media LLC, New York, NY (17)
WESCO, Pittsburgh, PA (16)
West Bend, West Bend, WI (16)
West Farm Foods (Branch), Caldwell, ID (16)
West Marine Inc, Watsonville, CA (11)
West Shore Distributors, Westlake, OH (8)
Westcon, Tarrytown, NY (16)
Western Pennsylvania Conservancy, Pittsburgh, PA (1)
Western Psychological Services, Torrance, CA (16)
Western River Expeditions, Salt Lake City, UT (19)
Westgroup, Eagan, MN (17)
Westhoff Machine Co, Saint Louis, MO (9)
Westlake Plastics Co, Lenni, PA (16)
Weston Distance Learning, Fort Collins, CO (13)
Westwood Publishing Co, Glendale, CA (17)
Whirley Drink Works, Warren, PA (5)
Whirlpool Corp, Benton Harbor, MI (16)
Whitaker National, Huntington, WV (16)
White Cap Wholesale Contractors Supplies, Costa
    Mesa, CA (16)
White Flower Farm, Torrington, CT (8)
White Mane Publishing Co Inc, Shippensburg, PA (17)
Whitehorse Gear, Center Conway, NH (11)
Whiting & Davis, Attleboro Falls, MA (16)
Whitman Publishing LLC, Atlanta, GA (16)
Wholesale Tool Co, Warren, MI (9)
Wideband by Kars, New Rochelle, NY (16)
Michael Wiese Productions, Studio City, CA (17)
Wikco Industries Inc, Casa Grande, AZ (5)
WILD Flavors Inc, Erlanger, KY (4)
Wildseed Farms, Fredericksburg, TX (8)
John Wiley & Sons Canada Ltd, Etobicoke, ON,
    Canada (17)
John Wiley & Sons Inc, Hoboken, NJ (17)
Lt Moses Willard Inc, Milford, OH (16)
Williamsburg Blacksmiths Inc, Williamsburg, MA (8)
Williamson-Dickie Manufacturing Co, Fort Worth, TX
    (2)
Willis Music Co, Florence, KY (17)
The HW Wilson Co, Bronx, NY (17)
Wilton Armetale, Mount Joy, PA (16)
Wilton Industries Inc, Woodridge, IL (16)
Wimmer's Meat Products Inc, West Point, NE (4)
Windsor Vineyards, Santa Rosa, CA (16)
Windstar Cruises, Seattle, WA (19)
Wine Enthusiast Cos, Mount Kisco, NY (4)
Winmill & Co, New York, NY (14)
Winn Devon, Richmond, BC, Canada (17)
Winning Solutions Inc, Fort Worth, TX (7)
Winslow Publishing, Toronto, ON, Canada (17)
Harry Winston Inc, New York, NY (16)
Wire Works, Chester, PA (9)
Wolfe Publishing Co Inc, Prescott, AZ (17)
Wood Carvers Supply Inc, Englewood, FL (9)
Woodcraft Supply Corp LLC, Parkersburg, WV (9)
Woodcrafters Lumber Sales Inc, Portland, OR (9)
Woodwind & Brasswind Inc, Indianapolis, IN (5)
Woodworker's Supply Inc, Casper, WY (11)
Wordright Enterprises Inc, Buffalo Grove, IL (17)
The World Bank, Washington, DC (17)
World Future Society, Bethesda, MD (1)
World Publications Inc, Winter Park, FL (17)
World Villages for Children, Annapolis, MD (1)
WorldVu LLC, Baltimore, MD (17)
WorleyParsons, Reading, PA (16)
Wrisco Industries Inc, Palm Beach Gardens, FL (8)
Writer's Digest Books, Blue Ash, OH (17)

Wyandotte West Communications Inc, Kansas City,
    KS (17)
Wysong Corp, Midland, MI (7)

X

XL Environmental, Exton, PA (15)
Xerox Corp, Rochester, NY (16)
Xilinx Inc, San Jose, CA (16)

Y

Year One Inc, Braselton, GA (16)
Yellow Book USA, Uniondale, NY (17)
Yellow Pages Association, Berkeley Heights, NJ (1)
Yenkin-Majestic, Columbus, OH (16)
Young Pecan Co, Florence, SC (4)
Your Choice Or Mine, San Mateo, CA (16)
Your Move Chess & Games, North Massapequa, NY
    (11)
Yves Rocher North America Inc, Longueuil, PQ,
    Canada (7)

Z

Zale Corp, Irving, TX (6)
Ziff Davis Media Inc, New York, NY (17)
Zig Ziglar Corp, Plano, TX (16)
Zimmerman Irrigation Inc, Biglerville, PA (16)
Zimmerman-McDonald Machinery Inc, Saint Louis,
    MO (16)
Zondervan Corp, Grand Rapids, MI (17)
Zones Inc, Auburn, WA (3)
Zoological Society of San Diego, San Diego, CA (1)
Zotos International, Darien, CT (16)
Zurich, Schaumburg, IL (15)

0

02Kl, Rye Brook, NY (4)

A

A&P, Montvale, NJ (16)
A La Carte, Chicago, IL (16)
AAA Auto Club South, Tampa, FL (1)
AAA-Chicago Motor Club, Aurora, IL (1)
AAA Mid-Atlantic Insurance Groups, Wilmington, DE (15)
AAA Southern New England, Providence, RI (1)
AAFES, Dallas, TX (5)
ABC Carpet & Home, New York, NY (8)
ACBL, Horn Lake, MS (1)
ACCO North America, Lincolnshire, IL (16)
ACP - Automation Control Products, Alpharetta, GA (16)
ACP Medicine, Hamilton, ON, Canada (17)
ADRFCO, Washington, DC (1)
ADT Worldwide, Boca Raton, FL (16)
AEGON Direct Marketing Services Inc, Baltimore, MD (15)
AESU Inc, Baltimore, MD (19)
AFL-CIO, Washington, DC (1)
AGCO Inc, Norcross, GA (9)
AGIA Insurance Services, Carpinteria, CA (15)
AIG Accident & Health, New York, NY (15)
AIG Marketing, New York, NY (15)
AIN Plastics Inc, Yonkers, NY (16)
ALSAC - St. Jude, Memphis, TN (1)
AMA Insurance Agency Inc, Chicago, IL (15)
AMS Direct, Burr Ridge, IL (13)
AMVETS National Service Foundation, Lanham, MD (1)
AON Center, Chicago, IL (15)
Aon Consulting New York, New York, NY (15)
APSCO, Davenport Center, NY (11)
ARAG, Des Moines, IA (15)
ARE Press, Virginia Beach, VA (1)
ASM International, Materials Park, OH (1)
ASM Press, Washington, DC (17)
AT&T, Bedminster, NJ (16)
AW Direct Inc, Madison, WI (12)
Aardvark Enterprises, Calgary, AB, Canada (17)
Abbey of Gethsemani, New Haven, KY (1)
Abbey Press, Saint Meinrad, IN (6)
Abbott, North Chicago, IL (7)
Abbott Products, Weymouth, MA (16)
Harry N Abrams Inc, New York, NY (17)
Absolute Reservation Center Inc, Longwood, FL (19)
Academic Management Services, Boston, MA (14)
Academic Travel Abroad Inc, Washington, DC (19)
Academy of Psychic Arts & Sciences, Dallas, TX (5)
Accoona Corp, Jersey City, NJ (16)
Accountants Education Group, Dallas, TX (10)
Accountants' Supply House, Lancaster, CA (10)
Accuracy in Media Inc, Washington, DC (1)
ACCUSPLIT Inc, Livermore, CA (16)
AccuTrade Inc, Bellevue, NE (14)
Ace Hardware Corp, Oak Brook, IL (16)
Acme Tools, Grand Forks, ND (8)
Action Direct Inc, Miami, FL (11)
Active Parenting, Marietta, GA (17)
Activision Value, Eden Prairie, MN (16)
ActivStyle, Minneapolis, MN (16)
Acurian, Horsham, PA (7)
Adnet USA, Arlington Heights, IL (16)
Advanced Financial Services, Middletown, RI (14)
Advanced Machinery, New Castle, DE (9)
Advanced Medical Nutrition Inc, Pittsburgh, PA (7)
The Advertising Council Inc, New York, NY (1)
Aegon Corp, Louisville, KY (14)
AeroGraphics, DeLand, FL (3)
Aerovox Inc, New Bedford, MA (16)
AETNA - Marketing Product & Communication, Hartford, CT (14)
Affinity Express, Elgin, IL (16)

Affinity Federal Credit Union, Basking Ridge, NJ (1)
Affinity4, Norfolk, VA (16)
Affinity Group Inc, Ventura, CA (19)
Agate Publishing, Evanston, IL (17)
Agco Spra-Coup, Duluth, GA (16)
Agilis Co, Albert Lea, MN (14)
AGORA Inc, Baltimore, MD (17)
AHC Media, Atlanta, GA (17)
Air Ambulance Network Inc, Palm Harbor, FL (16)
Air Chek Inc, Naples, NC (9)
Air Force Sergeants Association, Suitland, MD (1)
Air France, New York, NY (16)
Air Power USA, Los Angeles, CA (12)
Aircraft Owners & Pilots Association, Frederick, MD (1)
Aircraft Spruce & Specialty Co, Corona, CA (12)
Airlines Reporting Corp, Arlington, VA (9)
The Akadine Press Inc, White Plains, NY (16)
Akers Ski Inc, Andover, ME (1)
Alamo Rent A Car, Tulsa, OK (16)
John Alden Life Insurance Co/North Star Marketing, Duluth, GA (15)
Alerus Financial, Grand Forks, ND (14)
Alexian Brothers Bonaventure House, Chicago, IL (1)
Alfa CTP Systems, Tewksbury, MA (10)
Alfa Insurance, Montgomery, AL (15)
Alfred Publishing Co Inc, Van Nuys, CA (17)
Alfreda's Film Works, Denver, CO (17)
AliMed Inc, Dedham, MA (7)
Alitalia, New York, NY (19)
All Star Directories, Seattle, WA (17)
AllBrands.com Sewing Machine Superstore, Baton Rouge, LA (11)
Allergan Inc, Irvine, CA (16)
Alliance Bernstein, New York, NY (14)
Alliance Defense Fund, Scottsdale, AZ (1)
Alliance for the Arts, New York, NY (1)
Allianz Life Insurance Co of North America, Minneapolis, MN (15)
Allstate Motor Club, South Barrington, IL (13)
Allstate Motor Club, Inc, Deerfield, IL (7)
Alltel, Little Rock, AR (16)
Allyn & Bacon, Upper Saddle River, NJ (17)
Almore International Inc, Portland, OR (7)
Almost Heaven Group, Renick, WV (1)
CM Almy & Son Inc, Greenwich, CT (5)
Alpha Supply Inc, Bremerton, WA (16)
ALSTOM Signaling Inc, West Henrietta, NY (16)
Alzheimer Society of Canada, Toronto, ON, Canada (1)
Alzheimer's Association, Chicago, IL (1)
Amacom Books, New York, NY (17)
Amaryllis Inc, Baton Rouge, LA (8)
Amateur Electronic Supply LLC, Milwaukee, WI (16)
Amazon Drygoods, Davenport, IA (2)
Ambassador Programs, Spokane, WA (19)
Ambient Shapes Inc, Hickory, NC (7)
Amcat TeleProfit Inc, Oklahoma City, OK (16)
America, Fredericksburg, VA (6)
American Airlines, Fort Worth, TX (12)
American Airlines Inc, Dallas, TX (19)
American Arbitration Association, New York, NY (1)
American Association of Critical-Care Nurses, Aliso Viejo, CA (1)
American Association of Individual Investors, Chicago, IL (1)
American Bar Association, Chicago, IL (1)
American Bible Society, New York, NY (1)
American Biographical Institute Inc, Raleigh, NC (17)
American Breast Cancer Foundation, Baltimore, MD (1)
American Bronzing Co, Columbus, OH (16)
American Capital, Bethesda, MD (15)
American Catalog Mailers Association, Somers, NY (1)
American Century Investments, Kansas City, MO (14)
American Civil Defense Association, Draper, UT (16)
American Civil Liberties Union Foundation, New York, NY (1)
American College of Cardiology, Washington, DC (1)

American College of Emergency Physicians, Irving, TX (1)
American College of Physician Executives, Tampa, FL (1)
American Council on Exercise, San Diego, CA (1)
American Counseling Association, Broken Arrow, OK (1)
American Craft Council, Minneapolis, MN (17)
American Crane & Equipment Corp, Douglassville, PA (16)
American Dermatological Corp, Miami, FL (16)
American Diabetes Association, Alexandria, VA (1)
American Express Co, New York, NY (14)
American Express Publishing Corp, New York, NY (17)
American Family Insurance Group, Madison, WI (15)
American Family Life Assurance Co of Columbus (AFLAC), Columbus, GA (15)
American Federation of Astrologers, Tempe, AZ (1)
American Fidelity Assurance Co, Oklahoma City, OK (15)
The American Film Institute, Los Angeles, CA (1)
American Forests, Washington, DC (1)
American Foundation for the Blind Inc, New York, NY (1)
American General Life & Accident Insurance, Nashville, TN (15)
American General Life Insurance Co, Houston, TX (15)
American Girl Brands LLC, Middleton, WI (6)
American Greetings Corp, Cleveland, OH (16)
American Health & Life Insurance Co, Fort Worth, TX (15)
American Health Information Management Association, Chicago, IL (1)
American Healthways, Franklin, TN (16)
American Heart Association, Dallas, TX (1)
American Historic Inns Inc, Dana Point, CA (17)
American Horse Products, San Juan Capistrano, CA (11)
American Indian College Fund, Denver, CO (1)
American Institute of Chemical Engineers, New York, NY (1)
American Institute of CPAs, New York, NY (1)
American Institute of Physics, Melville, NY (17)
American Insurance Administrators Inc, Columbus, OH (15)
American International Group, New York, NY (15)
American Kennel Club, New York, NY (17)
The American Legion National Headquarters, Indianapolis, IN (1)
American Library Association-Publishing Services, Chicago, IL (1)
American Locker Security Systems Inc, Coppell, TX (16)
American Lung Association, New York, NY (1)
American Marketing Solutions LLC, Uniontown, PA (5)
American Mathematical Society, Providence, RI (17)
American Meadows Inc & Vermont Wild Flowers Farm, Williston, VT (8)
American Megatrends Inc, Norcross, GA (3)
American Mint LLC, Mechanicsburg, PA (6)
American Movie Classics Holding Corp, Jericho, NY (16)
American Nicaraguan Foundation, Miami, FL (1)
American Nurses' Association, Silver Spring, MD (1)
American Ostomy Supply, Earth City, MO (16)
American Period Lighting Inc, Lancaster, PA (8)
American Power Conversion Corp, West Kingston, RI (3)
American Preferred Reader's Service Inc, Fort Lauderdale, FL (18)
American Printing House for the Blind, Louisville, KY (7)
American Psychological Association, Washington, DC (1)
American Radio Relay League, Newington, CT (1)
American Red Cross, Washington, DC (1)
American Research Corp, El Monte, CA (3)
American Running Association, Bethesda, MD (1)

BenefitMall, Dallas, TX (15)
Bentley College, Waltham, MA (13)
Berean Christian Stores, West Chester, OH (5)
Bergdorf Goodman, New York, NY (2)
Berger's Table Pad Co, Indianapolis, IN (8)
Berkeley College, Paramus, NJ (13)
Berkshire Direct Inc, Williamstown, MA (17)
Berkshire Record Outlet Inc, Lee, MA (3)
Berry Hill Ltd, Saint Thomas, ON, Canada (8)
Berway Visual Products Inc, Wilmington, MA (3)
Best Buy, Richfield, MN (5)
Better Health Fitness, Brooklyn, NY (11)
Better Tools For Industry, Santee, CA (9)
BIC Corp, Shelton, CT (16)
Bick International, Van Nuys, CA (6)
Bigelow Electronics, Bluffton, OH (3)
RC Bigelow Inc, Fairfield, CT (4)
Bijoux Terner, Miami, FL (16)
Bike Nashbar, Crab Orchard, WV (11)
The Bil-Ray Aluminum Siding Corp of Queens Inc, New Hyde Park, NY (16)
Biomerica Inc, Irvine, CA (7)
Birthday Express Inc, Bothell, WA (5)
Bissinger French Confections, Saint Louis, MO (4)
Bits & Pieces Inc, Lawrenceburg, IN (11)
Bizzaro Rubber Stamps, Greenville, RI (6)
Black & Decker (US) Inc, Towson, MD (16)
The Black Dog Tavern Co Inc, Vineyard Haven, MA (2)
Black Enterprise Magazine, New York, NY (17)
Black Entertainment Television Inc, Washington, DC (16)
Blaine Window Hardware Inc, Hagerstown, MD (9)
Blair Corp, Warren, PA (2)
William Blair & Co LLC, Chicago, IL (14)
Blanchard & Co Inc, New Orleans, LA (16)
Bland Farms, Glennville, GA (4)
Blethen Maine Newspapers Inc, Portland, ME (17)
Dick Blick Holdings Inc, Galesburg, IL (16)
Bliss World LLC, New York, NY (5)
Bloomingdale's By Mail Ltd, New York, NY (5)
Bloomingdale's Direct, New York, NY (16)
Blue Coral Slick 50, Houston, TX (16)
Blue Cross & Blue Shield Cobalt, Waukesha, WI (15)
Blue Cross & Blue Shield of Florida, Jacksonville, FL (15)
Blue Cross & Blue Shield of Oklahoma, Tulsa, OK (15)
Blue Cross & Blue Shield of South Carolina, Columbia, SC (15)
Blue Cross/Blue Shield of Illinois, Chicago, IL (15)
Blue Cross Blue Shield of Louisiana, Baton Rouge, LA (15)
Blue Raven Technology, Wilmington, MA (3)
Blue Shield Life, San Francisco, CA (15)
Blue Shield of California, San Francisco, CA (15)
Bluestem Brands, Eden Prairie, MN (16)
Bluestone Perennials Inc, Madison, OH (8)
Bluewater Yachts, Mora, MN (16)
Boardroom Inc, Stamford, CT (17)
Bobcat Co, West Fargo, ND (16)
Bobley-Harmann Corp/GiftValues.Com, Westbury, NY (5)
The Body Shop Inc, Wake Forest, NC (7)
Bodyscapes Inc, New York, NY (2)
Bolind Inc, Boulder, CO (16)
The Bombay Co, Brampton, ON, Canada (8)
Carol Bond Health Foods, Liberty, TX (7)
Book Passage Cafe, Corte Madera, CA (17)
Book Publishing Information Kit, Santa Barbara, CA (17)
Books on Tape, Westminster, MD (17)
Bookspan, Garden City, NY (13)
Booth Michigan, Grand Rapids, MI (17)
Borbeleta Gardens, Fairbault, MN (8)
Born Free USA, Sacramento, CA (1)
Bose Corp, Framingham, MA (3)
Bosom Buddy Breast Forms, Boise, ID (7)
The Boston Co, Boston, MA (14)
The Boston Globe, Boston, MA (17)
Boundless Corp, Phelps, NY (16)

Bountiful Gardens, Willits, CA (8)
Bowers & Merena Auctions, Irvine, CA (16)
The Bowery Mission, New York, NY (1)
BowTie Inc, Irvine, CA (17)
Boy Scouts of America/National Supply Group, Charlotte, NC (1)
Boyd Gaming Corp, Las Vegas, NV (16)
Boys & Girls Clubs of America National Headquarters, Atlanta, GA (1)
Boys' Life & Scouting Magazines, Irving, TX (17)
The Bradford Group, Niles, IL (16)
Bradford Health Services, Birmingham, AL (16)
Bradley Direct, Columbus, GA (8)
Vera Bradley, Fort Wayne, IN (2)
Brady Marketing Co Inc, Walnut Creek, CA (16)
Brahmin Leather Works, Fairhaven, MA (16)
Branch Banking & Trust Co, Wilson, NC (14)
Brand New Products LLC, Chicago, IL (4)
Brant Publications Inc, New York, NY (17)
Breck's Bulbs, Lawrenceburg, IN (8)
Beverly Bremer Silver Shop, Atlanta, GA (6)
Brentwood Benson Music Publishing, Franklin, TN (17)
Bridge City Tool Works Inc, Portland, OR (9)
Bridgestone/Firestone North American Tire LLC, Nashville, TN (16)
Brigade Quartermasters Ltd, Providence, RI (11)
British Columbia Automobile Association, Burnaby, BC, Canada (15)
Broadmoor Hotel Inc, Colorado Springs, CO (19)
BroadVision Inc, Redwood City, CA (16)
Broadway Books, New York, NY (17)
Broadway Play Publishing Inc, New York, NY (17)
Brokers/Consultants Inc, Flossmoor, IL (15)
Bronner's Christmas Wonderland, Frankenmuth, MI (6)
Bronson Nutritionals LLC, Hauppauge, NY (7)
Bronx Council on the Arts, Bronx, NY (1)
Brookfield Zoo, Brookfield, IL (1)
Brookhollow Cards, Rexburg, ID (10)
Brooks Brothers, New York, NY (2)
Brooks Equipment Co, Charlotte, NC (9)
Brookstone Co, Merrimack, NH (3)
Brotherhood America's Oldest Winery Ltd, Washingtonville, NY (19)
Brown & Co, Blaine, WA (8)
Brown & Jenkins Trading Co, Cambridge, VT (4)
Arthur Brown & Bro Inc, New York, NY (10)
Brown-Forman Beverages Worldwide, Louisville, KY (16)
Brown-Forman Corp, Louisville, KY (16)
Tony Brown Productions, New York, NY (16)
BrownCor International, Milwaukee, WI (5)
Brownell Holly Farms, Oregon City, OR (6)
Brown's Omaha Plant Farms, Omaha, TX (8)
Bruce Medical Supply, Waltham, MA (7)
Brylane, Indianapolis, IN (2)
Bucks County Coffee Co, Conshohocken, PA (16)
Buena Vista Home Entertainment, Burbank, CA (3)
Buena Vista Winery, Sonoma, CA (16)
Buggies Unlimited, Jacksonville, FL (12)
Buick Division General Motors Corp, Detroit, MI (16)
Bulletin of the Atomic Scientists, Chicago, IL (17)
Bunker Hill Auctions, Newark, IL (6)
Bunn-O-Matic Corp, Springfield, IL (16)
Burberry, New York, NY (2)
Burden Sales Co, Lincoln, NE (9)
Burger's Ozark Country Cured Hams Inc, California, MO (4)
Burlington Coat Factory, Burlington, NJ (16)
Burlington Industries Inc, Greensboro, NC (16)
Burns Inc, Fall River, MA (16)
W Atlee Burpee Co, Warminster, PA (8)
DV Burrell Seed Growers Co, Rocky Ford, CO (8)
Bushnell Corporation, Overland Park, KS (11)
Business Automation Systems Inc, Nashville, TN (16)
Business Planners & Consultants Inc, New York, NY (15)
Butler Distributing Co, Kenilworth, NJ (3)
H E Butt Grocery Co, San Antonio, TX (16)
Butterfield Farms Inc, Rolling Hills Estates, CA (4)

BUYSEASONS Inc, Bothell, WA (5)
Byron Plantation, Vidalia, GA (4)

C

C&H Distributors LLC, Milwaukee, WI (9)
C&S Sales Inc, Wheeling, IL (9)
C&T Bridge Supplies, Los Alamitos, CA (11)
CAA Auto Club & Travel Agency Inc, Thornhill, ON, Canada (1)
CAIG Laboratories Inc, Poway, CA (9)
CAS Design Center, North Richland Hills, TX (8)
CBT Direct, Tarpon Springs, FL (16)
CCA Global Partners, Manchester, NH (16)
CCI Solutions, Olympia, WA (16)
CDMI Inc, Huntington Beach, CA (1)
CDMO Inc, Deer Park, NY (16)
CDW Computer Centers Inc, Vernon Hills, IL (3)
CDW Corp, Vernon Hills, IL (16)
CHG, Salt Lake City, UT (7)
CJ Hummul Co, Nescapeck, PA (11)
CMEinfo.com, Birmingham, AL (16)
CMI Direct, Montrose, CA (15)
CMS Inc, Winston Salem, NC (14)
CNA, Chicago, IL (15)
CNY Awards & Apparel Inc, New Hartford, NY (5)
CPAC Inc, Leicester, NY (16)
CPC Inc, Babylon, NY (19)
CPI Corp, St Louis, MO (16)
CPM Delta 1, Inc, Dallas, TX (11)
CRB, Chicago, IL (17)
CSI, Conklin, NY (16)
CSPI/Nutrition Action Health Letter, Washington, DC (17)
CTA Inc, Fenton, MO (5)
CTC Corp, Bennington, VT (16)
CVS Caremark, Woonsocket, RI (7)
CVT Production Inc, Granger, IN (16)
Cabela's Inc, Sidney, NE (11)
Cable Car Clothiers/Robert Kirk Ltd, San Francisco, CA (2)
Cable Connection, Fremont, CA (3)
Cable Films & Video, Mission Hills, KS (3)
Cable Shopping Network, Scottsdale, AZ (16)
Cablexpress Technologies, Syracuse, NY (10)
Cablevision Systems Corp, Bethpage, NY (16)
Cadie Products Corp, Paterson, NJ (16)
Caesars Atlantic City Casino/Hotel, Atlantic City, NJ (19)
Caesars Palace, Las Vegas, NV (16)
Cafe Lango, Guilford, CT (16)
Calbiochem-Novabiochem Corp, San Diego, CA (9)
Calendar Marketing Association, Wheaton, IL (1)
Calibre Press Inc, San Francisco, CA (17)
Calico Corners, Kennett Square, PA (16)
California Cosmetics Corp, Tarzana, CA (7)
California Mustang Parts & Accessories, City of Industry, CA (16)
California Pacific Research & New Generation, Reno, NV (7)
California Society of CPA's, San Mateo, CA (1)
Callaway Gardens, Pine Mountain, GA (19)
Calumet Photographic Inc, Bensenville, IL (3)
Cambridge Educational, New York, NY (12)
Camellia Forest Nursery, Chapel Hill, NC (8)
Camelot Enterprises, Bristol, WI (9)
Campbell Soup Co, Camden, NJ (16)
Campbell Tools Co, Springfield, OH (9)
Camping World Inc, Bowling Green, KY (11)
Campmor Inc, Mahwah, NJ (17)
Canada Brokerlink Insurance, Edmonton, AB, Canada (15)
Canada Post Corp, Ottawa, ON, Canada (16)
Canadian Blood Services, Ottawa, ON, Canada (1)
Canadian Business, Toronto, ON, Canada (17)
Cancer Fund of America Inc, Knoxville, TN (1)
Cancer Research Society, Montreal, PQ, Canada (1)
The Candy Factory, Newport, KY (4)
Cane & Basket Supply Co, Los Angeles, CA (8)

Canine Companions for Independence, Santa Rosa, CA (16)
The Caning Shop, Berkeley, CA (11)
Canyon Marketing, Dix Hills, NY (7)
Cape Cod Cupola Co Inc, North Dartmouth, MA (8)
Capezio Ballet Makers Inc, Totowa, NJ (16)
Capitol Concierge Inc, Washington, DC (16)
Carabella Collection, Irvine, CA (2)
Card Technology Inc, Hopkins, MN (16)
Care2, Washington, DC (1)
CARE USA, Atlanta, GA (1)
Career Education Corp, Schaumburg, IL (1)
Carefirst Blue Cross Blue Shield, Washington, DC (15)
Careington International, Frisco, TX (7)
Carestream Health Inc, Rochester, NY (7)
CARFAX Inc, Centreville, VA (12)
Caribe Direct Inc, San Juan, PR (6)
Carino Nurseries, Indiana, PA (8)
Carlson's Gardens, Waitsfield, VT (8)
Carnival Cruise Lines, Miami, FL (19)
Carolina Exotic Gardens/CEG Nursery, Greenville, NC (8)
Carrot-Top Industries Inc, Hillsborough, NC (16)
Carson Pirie Scott & Co, Milwaukee, WI (16)
Carter & Holmes Inc, Newberry, SC (8)
Harriet Carter Gifts Inc, Montgomeryville, PA (6)
Cartouche Ltd, Alexandria, VA (6)
Carvel Corp, Atlanta, GA (4)
Cascade Forest Nursery, Bellevue, IA (8)
Cascade Outfitters, Boise, ID (11)
Casual Living USA, Tampa, FL (6)
Casual Male Retail Group, Canton, MA (2)
Caswell-Massey Co Ltd, Edison, NJ (7)
Catalog Music Corp, Nashville, TN (3)
Catch The Wind Kite Shop, Lincoln City, OR (11)
Caterpillar Insurance Services Corp, Nashville, TN (15)
Catholic Charities - Brooklyn & Queens, Brooklyn, NY (1)
Catholic Digest, New London, CT (17)
Catholic Relief Services, Baltimore, MD (1)
The Catholic University of America Press, Washington, DC (17)
Cattle Kate, Boise, ID (2)
Caviarteria New York Inc, Astoria, NY (4)
Celestial Seasonings, Boulder, CO (16)
Cellular One Group, Oklahoma City, OK (16)
Celtic Life Insurance Co, Chicago, IL (15)
Cengage Learning, Independence, KY (17)
Center for Professional Development, Tallahassee, FL (16)
Center for Science in the Public Interest, Washington, DC (1)
Centerpoint Energy, Minneapolis, MN (16)
Central Pacific Bank, Honolulu, HI (14)
Central Shippee Inc, Bloomingdale, NJ (16)
Central States Health & Life Co of Omaha, Omaha, NE (15)
Central States Indemnity, Omaha, NE (15)
Century Photo, Santa Fe Springs, CA (10)
CertainTeed Corp, Valley Forge, PA (16)
Cessna Aircraft Co, Wichita, KS (16)
Chadsworth's 1-800-Columns, Wilmington, NC (8)
Chadwick's of Boston Inc, West Bridgewater, MA (2)
Chairman's Marketing Group LLC, Princeton, NJ (15)
Champs Corp, Bradenton, FL (11)
Chanel Inc, New York, NY (16)
Channel 13 WNET Catalog Division, New York, NY (5)
Char-Broil Grill Lover's Catalog, Louisville, KY (8)
Charisma Brands LLC, Laguna Hills, CA (6)
Charlotte Chamber of Commerce, Charlotte, NC (1)
Charmaster Products Inc, Grand Rapids, MN (8)
Charming Shoppers, Bensalem, PA (2)
Charolette Ford Trunks, Dumas, TX (11)
Charter Communications, Saint Louis, MO (16)
Charter One Bank, Cleveland, OH (14)
Chartifacts, Richmond, VA (6)
Chartis, New York, NY (15)
Cheap Aprons, Derry, NH (2)

Chefs Catalog, Colorado Springs, CO (8)
Chem-Tainer Industries Inc, North Babylon, NY (9)
Chemical Week, New York, NY (17)
Cherry Tree Toys Inc, Beloit, WI (11)
Chiasso, Chicago, IL (6)
Chicago Convention & Tourism Bureau, Chicago, IL (1)
Chicago Magazine, Chicago, IL (17)
Chick Harness & Supply Inc, Harrington, DE (11)
Chico's FAS Inc, Fort Myers, FL (2)
Chief Marketer and Multichannel Merchant, New York, NY (17)
ChildFund International, Richmond, VA (1)
Childreach US Member of Plan International, Warwick, RI (1)
Children of the Night, Van Nuys, CA (1)
Children's Aid Society, New York, NY (1)
Children's Better Health Institute, Indianapolis, IN (1)
Children's Hospital Foundation, Washington, DC (1)
Children's Hospital of Pittsburgh, Pittsburgh, PA (1)
Children's Miracle Network, Salt Lake City, UT (6)
China Books & Periodicals Inc, South San Francisco, CA (17)
Choice Courier Systems Inc, New York, NY (16)
Choice Hotels International, Silver Spring, MD (16)
Choice Point, Alpharetta, GA (1)
Christian Appalachian Project, Lexington, KY (1)
Christian Book Distributors Inc, Peabody, MA (17)
Christian Brands, Phoenix, AZ (16)
Christian Broadcasting Network Inc, Virginia Beach, VA (1)
Christian Children's Fund Inc, Richmond, VA (1)
Christian Herald Association, New York, NY (1)
Christian Relief Services Charities Inc, Alexandria, VA (1)
The Christian Science Publishing Society, Boston, MA (17)
Christianity Today Inc, Carol Stream, IL (17)
Church Extension Plan, Salem, OR (14)
CIGNA International, Philadelphia, PA (15)
Cincinnati Bell Telephone, Cincinnati, OH (16)
Cinmar LP, West Chester, OH (8)
Circle K Stores Inc, Akron, OH (16)
Citibank, New York, NY (14)
CitiFinancial, Baltimore, MD (14)
Citigroup Inc, New York, NY (14)
Citizens Against Government Waste, Washington, DC (1)
Citizens Bank, Dedham, MA (14)
City of Cerritos, Cerritos, CA (1)
City of Hope Cancer Center, Los Angeles, CA (1)
City of LaGrange, LaGrange, GA (1)
Civil Service Employees Insurance Group, Walnut Creek, CA (15)
Clairol Inc, Stamford, CT (7)
Clampitt Paper Co, Dallas, TX (16)
Clarin by Hussey Seating, North Berwick, ME (5)
Clark's Corvair Parts, Inc, Shelburne Falls, MA (12)
Clarks of North America, Newton, MA (16)
Clarkson Eyecare, Ellisville, MO (5)
Classic Motorbooks Inc, Minneapolis, MN (17)
Classic Thermographers, North Mankato, MN (10)
Clegg Industries Inc, Gardena, CA (16)
Clemente Novelties Inc, Utica, NY (16)
Cleveland Institute of Electronics, Cleveland, OH (13)
The Cleveland Orchestra, Cleveland, OH (1)
ClingZ Inc, Rio Rancho, NM (9)
The Clorox Co, Oakland, CA (16)
Clubs of America, Lakemoor, IL (6)
Cluett Peabody, New York, NY (16)
Coach, New York, NY (2)
Coast Hotels Limited, Seattle, WA (19)
Coast to Coast Inc, Englewood, CO (1)
Coastal Tool & Supply, West Hartford, CT (16)
Cobblestone Publishing, Peterborough, NH (17)
The Coca-Cola Co, Atlanta, GA (16)
Cockpit USA Inc, New York, NY (2)
Cohasset Colonials, Ashburnham, MA (8)
Coin World, Sidney, OH (17)
Cold Spring Harbor Lab Press, Woodbury, NY (17)
Cold Stream Farm, Free Soil, MI (8)

Coldwater Creek, Coeur D Alene, ID (2)
Cole's Appliance & Furniture Co, Chicago, IL (8)
Colgate-Palmolive Co, New York, NY (16)
Collectibles Today Network, Ltd, Niles, IL (16)
Collector Books & American Quilters Society, Paducah, KY (17)
Collector's Armoury Ltd, McDonough, GA (6)
Collector's Teapot, Kingston, NY (6)
The College Board, New York, NY (1)
CollegeAmerica, Salt Lake City, UT (1)
Collider Media, Austin, TX (9)
Collin Street Bakery, Corsicana, TX (4)
Collis Curve Catalog Sales, Brownsville, TX (7)
Colonial Life Insurance Co Texas, Fort Worth, TX (15)
The Colonial Williamsburg Foundation, Williamsburg, VA (1)
Columbia Journalism Review, New York, NY (17)
Columbia-Presbyterian Medical Center, New York, NY (16)
Columbia Tristar Home Video, Culver City, CA (16)
Columbia University, Annual Fund Programs, New York, NY (5)
The Columbian, Vancouver, WA (17)
Columbian Mutual Life Insurance Co, Binghamton, NY (15)
Combined Insurance Co of America, Glenview, IL (15)
Comdata Corp, Brentwood, TN (14)
Comerica Inc, Dallas, TX (14)
Wm F Comly & Son Inc, Philadelphia, PA (9)
Commercial Federal Bank, Omaha, NE (14)
Commercial Travelers Mutual Insurance Co, Utica, NY (15)
Communication Creativity, Buena Vista, CO (17)
Communication Resources Inc, Canton, OH (18)
Community Coffee Co, Baton Rouge, LA (4)
Community Newspapers Co, Concord, MA (17)
Companion Plants, Athens, OH (8)
The Company Store Inc, La Crosse, WI (16)
Compaq Computer Corp, Houston, TX (16)
Compass Bank, Birmingham, AL (14)
Compass Electronics, Forest Grove, OR (9)
Compustar, Mineola, NY (3)
Computer Station Corp, Houston, TX (3)
Computers for Education, Murfreesboro, TN (1)
Con-Cor International, Tucson, AZ (11)
Concordia Publishing House, Saint Louis, MO (17)
Conde Nast, New York, NY (17)
Condolink, Omaha, NE (16)
Connell Communications Inc, Peterborough, NH (17)
Coney Safety Products LLC, Madison, WI (7)
Conseco Inc, Carmel, IN (15)
Conservation International, Arlington, VA (1)
Consolidated Electronics Inc, Dayton, OH (3)
Consolidated Plastics Co Inc, Stow, OH (9)
Consumer Credit Advocates Inc, Salt Lake City, UT (16)
Consumers Digest Inc, Deerfield, IL (17)
Consumer's Energy, Jackson, MI (16)
Consumers Union, Yonkers, NY (17)
Continental Supply Inc, Cleveland, OH (9)
Continental Western Group, Des Moines, IA (15)
Convertible Service, San Gabriel, CA (16)
David C Cook, Colorado Springs, CO (17)
Cookbook Publishers Inc, Lenexa, KS (17)
Cooper Communities Inc, Rogers, AR (16)
Coppa Woodworking, Inc, San Pedro, CA (8)
Copper Art by Morse, Claremont, NH (8)
Josiah R Coppersmythe, Harwich, MA (8)
Cornell Lab of Ornithology, Ithaca, NY (1)
Cornerstone Brands Inc, West Chester, OH (5)
Cornhusker Press, Hastings, NE (17)
Corona Cigar Co, Orlando, FL (5)
Corona-Lotus Inc, San Francisco, CA (4)
Coronis Building Systems Inc, Burlington, NJ (9)
Corpus Christi Museum of Science & History, Corpus Christi, TX (1)
Cortz Inc, West Chicago, IL (5)
Cosgrove Associates, New York, NY (14)
Cosmetique, Inc, Vernon Hills, IL (13)

Cosmo International, Deerfield Beach, FL (16)
Council for Advancement and Support of Education (CASE), Washington, DC (1)
Council of Better Business Bureaus - BBBOnline, Arlington, VA (1)
Council of Smaller Enterprises (COSE), Cincinnati, OH (9)
Council on Foreign Relations Inc, New York, NY (17)
The Country Bed Shop, Ashby, MA (16)
Country Curtains Inc, Lee, MA (8)
Country Dance and Song Society, Haydenville, MA (1)
Country Financial, Bloomington, IL (15)
The Country House Inc, Salisbury, MD (6)
Country Sampler Group, Saint Charles, IL (17)
Countrywide Financial Corp, Calabasas, CA (14)
Courage Cards & Gifts, Golden Valley, MN (1)
Coursesmith, Denver, CO (17)
Covenant House International Headquarters, New York, NY (1)
Coverdell & Co Inc, Chicago, IL (15)
Covidien International, Mansfield, MA (7)
Cox Communications, Atlanta, GA (16)
Coyne American Institute, Chicago, IL (16)
Crabtree & Evelyn Ltd, Woodstock, CT (4)
The Cracker Box Inc, Blooming Glen, PA (16)
Craft-Diston Industries, Wichita, KS (16)
Craig/Vartorella International Marketing & Advertising Inc, Camden, SC (1)
Crain Communications Inc, Detroit, MI (17)
Crazy Crow Trading Post, Pottsboro, TX (11)
Creative Banner Assemblies, New Hope, MN (9)
Creative Catalogs Corp, Lemont, IL (6)
Creative Health Products, Plymouth, MI (16)
Creative Irish Gifts, Little Rock, AR (6)
Creative Publishing International, Minneapolis, MN (17)
Creative Teaching Press, Huntington Beach, CA (17)
Creativity International, Ada, MI (16)
Credicorp, Dallas, TX (1)
Credit Union Executives Society, Madison, WI (1)
Crest Fruit Inc, Mission, TX (4)
The Cricket Magazine Group, Chicago, IL (17)
Critter Mountain Wear, Crested Butte, CO (2)
Crohn's & Colitis Foundation of America (CCFA), New York, NY (1)
Cronin & Co, Glastonbury, CT (16)
Cross Country Stitching, Quakertown, PA (17)
Cross Country Travcorps, Boca Raton, FL (16)
Crosstown Traders Inc, Tucson, AZ (2)
Crowne Plaza Chateau Le Combe, Edmonton, AB, Canada (19)
Crutchfield Corp, Charlottesville, VA (3)
Crystal Records Inc, Camas, WA (3)
Cuba Cheese Shoppe, Cuba, NY (4)
Cuddledown Inc, Portland, ME (8)
Cuisinart, Stamford, CT (16)
Culinary Parts Unlimited, San Francisco, CA (16)
Cumberland General Store Inc, Alpharetta, GA (8)
Cumberland Woodcraft Co Inc, Carlisle, PA (8)
CUNA Mutual Group, Madison, WI (15)
CUNA - Trade Association, Madison, WI (1)
Cunningham Group, Elmwood Park, IL (15)
Current USA Inc, Colorado Springs, CO (6)
Cushman Fruit Co Inc, West Palm Beach, FL (4)
Custom Direct, Joppa, MD (16)
Custom Miniatures, Hudson, NH (6)
Cuvaison Inc, Calistoga, CA (4)
Cystic Fibrosis Foundation, Bethesda, MD (1)

D

D&E Pharmaceuticals Inc, Farmingdale, NJ (7)
DCA, West Chester, PA (16)
DMC Corp, Kearny, NJ (16)
DOM Corp, Marina Del Rey, CA (5)
DRG, Berne, IN (17)
DS Waters of North America LP, Flowery Branch, GA (4)
DWS Investments Service Co, Kansas City, MO (14)

Da Vinci Technologies LLC, Auburn, AL (3)
Daedalus Books Inc, Columbia, MD (5)
Daily Commercial News & Construction Record, Markham, ON, Canada (17)
Daily Record & Dispatch Co, Dunn, NC (17)
DaimlerChrysler Corp, Auburn Hills, MI (12)
Dain Rauscher Inc, Minneapolis, MN (14)
Dairy Council of California, Irvine, CA (1)
Dairy Farmers of America Inc, Kansas City, MO (16)
Dairy Management Inc, Rosemont, IL (1)
Dakin Farm, Ferrisburgh, VT (4)
Dakota Digital, Sioux Falls, SD (12)
Dalco Electronics, Springboro, OH (3)
Dalrada Financial Corp, San Diego, CA (14)
DAMARK International Inc, La Salle, IL (16)
Dana-Farber Cancer Institute, Boston, MA (1)
Dansk, Bristol, PA (16)
Dante University Press, Wellesley, MA (17)
Darden School Foundation Executive Foundation, Charlottesville, VA (1)
Dartmouth-Hitchcock, Lebanon, NH (1)
Dassault Falcon Jet Corp, Little Ferry, NJ (16)
Data Cal Corp, Gilbert, AZ (16)
Databazaar.com, Miramar, FL (10)
Davidoff of Geneva Inc, Pinellas Park, FL (6)
DaVinci Direct, Plymouth, MA (1)
The Davis Center, Succasunna, NJ (16)
Dick Davis Digest, Salem, MA (17)
Davis Instruments Corp, Hayward, CA (8)
Davis Publications Inc, Worcester, MA (17)
Day Runner Direct, Sidney, NY (10)
Day-Timers, Macungie, PA (13)
Days Inns Worldwide Inc, Parsippany, NJ (16)
Dayton Daily News, Dayton, OH (18)
Dean & Deluca Brands Inc, Wichita, KS (4)
Decal Shop, Jacksonville, FL (10)
Deck the Walls Inc, Saint Peters, MO (5)
Decko Products Inc, Sandusky, OH (4)
Deere & Co Headquarters, Moline, IL (16)
DeGrado Inc, Mandeville, LA (2)
Del Webb, Bloomfield Hills, MI (16)
Delicious Orchards, Colts Neck, NJ (4)
Dell Computer Corp, Round Rock, TX (16)
DeLorme Mapping, Yarmouth, ME (3)
DelStar Technologies, Middletown, DE (16)
Delta Tech Industries, Ontario, CA (12)
Delta Upsilon International Fraternity, Indianapolis, IN (16)
Delta Vacations, Fort Lauderdale, FL (19)
Democratic Congressional Campaign Committee, Washington, DC (1)
Dentsply International, York, PA (7)
Denver Metro Convention & Visitors Bureau, Denver, CO (1)
Dermac Labs Inc, Salem, OR (16)
Deseret Book, Salt Lake City, UT (16)
Desert Rat Truck Centers, Tucson, AZ (12)
Design Toscano, Inc, Elk Grove Village, IL (6)
Desjardins Financial Securities, Levis, PQ, Canada (15)
Destinations Ireland & Great Britain, Rhinebeck, NY (19)
The Detroit Institute of Arts, Detroit, MI (16)
Detroit Newspapers, Detroit, MI (18)
DeVry Inc, Oakbrook Terrace, IL (16)
Dharma Trading Co, Petaluma, CA (2)
Diakon Lutheran Social Ministries, Allentown, PA (1)
Dial-A-Mattress, Hicksville, NY (16)
Diamond Essence, Edison, NJ (2)
Diamond Machining Technology, Marlborough, MA (9)
Diamonds By Rennie Ellen, New York, NY (6)
Didit, Mineola, NY (16)
DigDev Direct, Deerfield Beach, FL (16)
Digi International, Minnetonka, MN (3)
Digi-Key Corp, Thief River Falls, MN (3)
The Dime Savings Bank of New York FSB, Brooklyn, NY (14)
Dimmock Hill Golf Course Pro Shop, Binghamton, NY (11)
DineWise, Farmingdale, NY (4)

Dinn Brothers Inc, West Springfield, MA (16)
Christian Dior Perfumes, New York, NY (7)
Dan Dipert Travel Service Inc, Arlington, TX (19)
Direct Auto Insurance, Nashville, TN (15)
Direct Energy, Toronto, ON, Canada (16)
Direct SAT TV LLC, Southern Pines, NC (3)
Direct Sports Supply, Pearisburg, VA (11)
Direct Supply Inc, Milwaukee, WI (16)
DirectBuy Inc, Merrillville, IN (1)
Directory of American Business & Insurance Attorneys, New York, NY (15)
Disabled American Veterans, Cincinnati, OH (1)
Discovery, Eatontown, NJ (9)
Discovery Communications LLC, Silver Spring, MD (16)
Discovery Toys, Livermore, CA (16)
Disney Vacation Club, Kissimmee, FL (19)
Diversified Healthcare Services, Richardson, TX (15)
Diversified Photo Supply Corp, Gardena, CA (10)
Divine Word Missionaries, Techny, IL (1)
Do-It Corp, South Haven, MI (9)
Doane, Saint Louis, MO (17)
Doctor's Best Inc, San Clemente, CA (16)
Drs Foster & Smith Inc, Rhinelander, WI (2)
Doctors Without Borders, New York, NY (1)
Dole Fresh Flowers, Miami, FL (8)
Domestic Bank, Providence, RI (14)
Dominion Retail Inc, Richmond, VA (16)
Dorothy Biddle Service, Greeley, PA (8)
Dorothy's Ruffled Originals Inc, Wilmington, NC (8)
Doubleday Direct, Scarborough, ON, Canada (13)
Doubletree Suites by Hilton, Boston, MA (19)
DoubleVerify, New York, NY (9)
Dover Publications Inc, Mineola, NY (17)
Dow Jones & Co, Princeton, NJ (17)
Dow Theory Forecasts, Hammond, IN (17)
Down Home Comforts, Windsor, CT (8)
Dozier Equipment International, Milwaukee, WI (9)
Dr Jays, New York, NY (2)
Dr Leonard's Healthcare Corp, Edison, NJ (7)
Dragich Auto Literature, Princeton, MN (16)
Draper's & Damon's, Irvine, CA (2)
Drawing Board Inc, Waynesboro, PA (16)
Dream Products Inc, Chatsworth, CA (5)
The Dreyfus Corp, New York, NY (14)
Droll Yankees Inc, Foster, RI (8)
Drug Information Association, Horsham, PA (1)
Drug Policy Alliance, New York, NY (1)
Drumbeat Indian Arts Inc, Phoenix, AZ (6)
Ducks Unlimited, Memphis, TN (1)
Ducktrap River Fish Farm, Belfast, ME (4)
Dudley's Country Kitchen, Dyersburg, TN (4)
Duluth Trading Co Inc, Belleville, WI (8)
Duncraft Inc, Concord, NH (16)
E I DuPont De Nemours & Co, Wilmington, DE (16)
Duracell, Bethel, CT (16)
Durey-Libby Edible Nuts Inc, Carlstadt, NJ (4)
Dutch Gardens, Burlington, VT (8)
Dynamic Development Co, Mission Viejo, CA (12)
Dynamic Engineering, Santa Cruz, CA (3)
Dynamics Research Corp, Andover, MA (16)

E

E Hille, Angler's Supply House, Williamsport, PA (11)
e-Pipeconnection, Evansville, IN (9)
E-Z Bowz Inc, Gatlinburg, TN (8)
EBA Wholesale Corp, Brooklyn, NY (3)
ECHO - Electronic Clearing House Inc, Woodland Hills, CA (14)
EDC Publishing, Tulsa, OK (17)
EMS Technologies, Norcross, GA (16)
EOS International Inc, Carlsbad, CA (5)
ESL Federal Credit Union, Rochester, NY (14)
ESPN, New York, NY (5)
ETS Inc, Indianapolis, IN (7)
EWA & Miniature Cars USA Inc, Berkeley Heights, NJ (11)
Eagle Asset Management Inc, Saint Petersburg, FL (14)

G

G&S Packing Co Inc, Weirsdale, FL (16)
G H Bass & Co, New York, NY (16)
GCC Printers, Bedford, MA (10)
GE Canada, Mississauga, ON, Canada (9)
GE Consumer & Industrial Lighting, Cleveland, OH (16)
GE Partnership Marketing Group, Schaumburg, IL (14)
GEICO Direct, Washington, DC (15)
GMAC Insurance, Atlanta, GA (15)
GMG Productions Inc, Roslyn, NY (3)
GRP Funding LLC, Springfield, MA (14)
Gaco Western Inc, Seattle, WA (16)
Gaiam Inc, Boulder, CO (9)
Galen Williams Landscaping & Garden Design, East Hampton, NY (16)
Gallery of Cats, Valencia, CA (6)
The Gallery Shop, Buffalo, NY (6)
Galloway Farms, Miami, FL (8)
Gall's Inc, Lexington, KY (16)
Gallup Inter-tribal Indian Ceremonial, Gallup, NM (1)
GameTime Inc, Fort Payne, AL (11)
Gamma Photo Labs LLC, Chicago, IL (16)
Gannett Co Inc, Mc Lean, VA (16)
Garden Botanika Inc, Saint Louis, MO (7)
Garden Perennials, Wayne, NE (8)
Gardener's Eden, Merrimack, NH (8)
Gardener's Supply Co, Burlington, VT (8)
Gardenimport Inc, Richmond Hill, ON, Canada (8)
Gardens Alive! Inc, Lawrenceburg, IN (8)
Gardens Of The Blue Ridge Inc, Pineola, NC (8)
Garlinghouse Co, Beaufort, SC (17)
Garnet Hill Inc, Franconia, NH (2)
Gates Corp, Denver, CO (9)
Gateway Bank and Trust, Raleigh, NC (14)
Gateway Inc, Irvine, CA (3)
The Gateway Learning Corp, Irvine, CA (16)
Gay Men's Health Crisis, New York, NY (1)
Gaylord Entertainment Co, Nashville, TN (19)
Gazette Communications Inc, Cedar Rapids, IA (17)
Geary's of Beverly Hills, Beverly Hills, CA (6)
Gemini Publishing Co, Webster, TX (17)
Genada Imports, Teaneck, NJ (8)
General Binding Corp, Northbrook, IL (10)
General Electric Co, Fairfield, CT (16)
General Mills Inc, Minneapolis, MN (8)
General Nutrition Corp, Pittsburgh, PA (7)
General Pencil Co Inc, Jersey City, NJ (16)
General Tours/TBI Tours, Keene, NH (19)
General Vitamin Corp, Raleigh, NC (16)
General Wig Manufacturers Inc, Pompano Beach, FL (7)
Genesco Inc, Nashville, TN (2)
Genetica DNA Laboratories Inc, Cincinnati, OH (16)
Genium Publishing, Amsterdam, NY (17)
Genworth Financial Inc, Richmond, VA (14)
Georgetown University Law Center/Continuing Legal Education Div, Washington, DC (13)
Georgetown University McDonough School of Business, Washington, DC (1)
Georgia Power, Atlanta, GA (16)
Gerber Life Insurance Co, White Plains, NY (15)
Gerber Products Co, Fremont, MI (16)
Gero Vita, Costa Mesa, CA (16)
Gerstner Woodworks, Dayton, OH (6)
Getronics, Tewksbury, MA (16)
Ghent Manufacturing Inc, Lebanon, OH (10)
Gibson Auer LLC, Victor, ID (7)
Gift Services Inc, Vancouver, WA (6)
Gifts Corp, Barrie, ON, Canada (6)
Gillette Children's Specialty Healthcare, Saint Paul, MN (1)
Gilliom Manufacturing Inc, Saint Charles, MO (8)
Gilman's Lapidary Supply, Hellertown, PA (11)
Gilson Co Inc, Lewis Center, OH (9)
Gimbels of Maine Inc, Boothbay Harbor, ME (6)
Girl Scouts of the USA, New York, NY (1)
Glamour Shots Licensing, Oklahoma City, OK (16)

Glaxo Smith Kline, Research Triangle Park, NC (16)
Peter Glenn Publications, Delray Beach, FL (17)
Glens Falls Hospital Foundation, Glens Falls, NY (1)
Glenview Capital Management, New York, NY (14)
Glenview State Bank, Glenview, IL (14)
Global Equipment Co Inc, Port Washington, NY (9)
Globe Specialty Products Inc, Millbury, MA (17)
Go Ahead Vacations, Cambridge, MA (16)
Go Promos, Gloversville, NY (5)
Goddard Manufacturing Co, Logan, KS (8)
Godiva Chocolatier, New York, NY (4)
Gohn Brothers, Middlebury, IN (5)
Gold Medal Hair Products Inc, Farmingdale, NY (7)
Gold Medal Products Co, Cincinnati, OH (16)
Golden Bear Golf Inc, North Palm Beach, FL (16)
Golden Bison LLC, Denver, CO (4)
Golden Fleece Designs Inc, Burbank, CA (16)
Golden Rule Insurance Co, Indianapolis, IN (15)
Golden Trophy, Chicago, IL (4)
Goldline International, Santa Monica, CA (14)
Golf Card International, Englewood, CO (1)
Golf Digest Co, Wilton, CT (17)
Golf Haus, Lansing, MI (11)
Golfsmith International Inc, Austin, TX (11)
Good Directions Co Inc, Danbury, CT (8)
Goodheart-Willcox Publisher, Tinley Park, IL (17)
Goodman Media Group Inc, New York, NY (17)
Goodwill Industries of San Francisco, San Francisco, CA (1)
Goodyear Tire & Rubber Co, Akron, OH (16)
WL Gore & Associates Inc, Newark, DE (2)
Gorsuch Ltd, Vail, CO (2)
Gossler Farms Nursery, Springfield, OR (8)
Gothic Arch Greenhouses Inc, Mobile, AL (8)
Governing Magazine, Washington, DC (17)
Government Data Publications Inc, Washington, DC (17)
Government of India Tourist Office, New York, NY (1)
Graceland, Memphis, TN (6)
Gracewood Fruit Co, Vero Beach, FL (4)
Graduate School USDA, Washington, DC (1)
Billy Graham Evangelistic Association, Charlotte, NC (1)
Graham Field Health Products Inc, Atlanta, GA (7)
Grand Canyon University, Phoenix, AZ (13)
Grand Circle Travel, Boston, MA (19)
Grandma Brown's Beans Inc, Mexico, NY (4)
The Graph Co, Vineland, NJ (14)
Graphik Dimensions Ltd, High Point, NC (16)
Graves Lapidary Co, Pompano Beach, FL (9)
Great Chefs Television Publishing, New Orleans, LA (6)
Great Western Bank, Sioux Falls, SD (14)
Greater Fort Worth Builders Association, Fort Worth, TX (1)
Green Mountain Coffee Roasters, Inc, Waterbury, VT (4)
The Green Pond Co, Atlanta, GA (2)
Green River Trading Co, Millerton, NY (8)
Greenwood Publishing Group Inc, Portsmouth, NH (17)
Greer Gardens, Eugene, OR (8)
Gridley & Co LLC, New York, NY (14)
Grizzly Industrial Inc, Bellingham, WA (9)
Grolier Publishing, Danbury, CT (17)
Grove Enterprises Inc, Brasstown, NC (16)
Grover Co, Mesa, AZ (16)
Growing Child, Inc, West Lafayette, IN (17)
Gruber & Allison Inc, Boynton Beach, FL (17)
Guarantee Trust Life Insurance Co, Glenview, IL (15)
Guaranty Bank, Brown Deer, WI (14)
The Guardian Life Insurance Co, New York, NY (15)
Guideposts, Danbury, CT (1)
Guiding Eyes for the Blind, Yorktown Heights, NY (16)
Guilford Publications Inc, New York, NY (17)
Gulf Coast Data Supply Inc, Milton, FL (3)
Gump's By Mail Inc, San Francisco, CA (6)
Gun Video Catalog/LMP, San Diego, CA (11)

H

H&R Block Inc, Kansas City, MO (14)
HCI Direct, Bensalem, PA (16)
HDA Inc, Saint Louis, MO (17)
The Herald & Review, Decatur, IL (17)
HR Direct, Sunrise, FL (10)
HSBC Bank USA, NA, Buffalo, NY (14)
HSN Inc, Saint Petersburg, FL (5)
Haband Co Inc, Oakland, NJ (2)
Habitat For Humanity International, Americus, GA (1)
Hadley Fruit Orchards Inc, Cabazon, CA (4)
Hagie Manufacturing Co, Clarion, IA (9)
Hale Indian River Groves Inc, Vero Beach, FL (16)
Hallelujah Acres, Shelby, NC (5)
Hallmark Cards Inc, Kansas City, MO (16)
Halls Kansas City, Kansas City, MO (16)
HALO/Lee Wayne, Sterling, IL (16)
Halsom Home Care Inc, Centerville, OH (16)
Hamakor Judaica Inc, Niles, IL (5)
Hamilton Beach/Proctor-Silex Inc, Glen Allen, VA (16)
The Hamilton Collection, Jacksonville, FL (6)
The Hamilton Group Ltd Inc, Jacksonville, FL (16)
Hammacher Schlemmer, New York, NY (16)
Hammock Publishing Inc, Nashville, TN (17)
Hammond World Atlas Corp, New York, NY (17)
Hampshire Agency, Great Neck, NY (14)
Hampshire Pewter Co, Wolfeboro, NH (6)
Hampton Marketing Corp, Medford, NY (16)
Handi-Ramp Inc, Libertyville, IL (7)
Hanesbrands Inc, Winston Salem, NC (2)
Hanley Wood LLC, Washington, DC (16)
Hanover Direct Inc, Weehawken, NJ (5)
The Hanover Shoe Co, Newton, MA (16)
Happy Trails Resort, Surprise, AZ (19)
Harbor Freight Tools, Camarillo, CA (9)
Harbour Bay Inc, Suffern, NY (16)
Harcourt Educational Measurement, San Antonio, TX (17)
Harland Financial Solutions Inc, Lake Mary, FL (16)
Harlequin Enterprises Ltd, Don Mills, ON, Canada (17)
Harman's Cheese & Country Store Inc, Sugar Hill, NH (4)
HarperCollins, New York, NY (17)
Harper's Magazine, New York, NY (17)
Harrah's Entertainment Inc, Las Vegas, NV (19)
Harrah's Marketing, Reno, NV (16)
Harrington's of Vermont Inc, Richmond, VT (4)
Harris Bancorp Inc, Chicago, IL (14)
Harris Infosource International Inc, Independence, OH (17)
Harry & David Holdings Inc, Medford, OR (4)
The Hartford Financial Services Inc, Southington, CT (15)
The Hartz Mountain Corp, Secaucus, NJ (16)
Harvard Business Review, Watertown, MA (17)
Harvard Business School - Executive Education, Boston, MA (1)
Harvard Pilgrim Health Care, Wellesley, MA (7)
Harvard Square Records, Round Rock, TX (3)
Hasbro Inc, Pawtucket, RI (11)
Hasco First Photo, Saint Charles, MO (16)
Hatton-Brown Publishers Inc, Montgomery, AL (17)
Havel's Inc, Cincinnati, OH (7)
Haymarket Group Ltd, New York, NY (17)
Hazelden, Center City, MN (7)
Health Freedom Nutrition LLC, Reno, NV (7)
Health O Meter, Alsip, IL (16)
HealthPlan Services, Tampa, FL (15)
HealthRight International, New York, NY (1)
The Healthy Back Store, Beltsville, MD (16)
Hear Music, Bellevue, WA (3)
Hearlihy & Co, Pittsburg, KS (17)
The Hearst Corp, New York, NY (17)
Hearst Magazines, New York, NY (17)
Hearthside Quilts & Supplies, Hinesburg, VT (11)
Heartland America, Chaska, MN (3)
Heartland Boating Magazine, Saint Louis, MO (17)

Journal Star, Peoria, IL (17)
Journeys, Nashville, TN (2)
Joys SA Inc, Hatillo, PR (2)
JW Jung Seed Co, Randolph, WI (8)
Junior's Cheesecake, Brooklyn, NY (16)
Justin Discount Boots & Cowboy Outfitters, Justin, TX (2)
JustThinkIncorporated, Sherwood Park, AB, Canada (16)
Juvenile Diabetes Research Foundation, New York, NY (1)

K

K-tel International, Golden Valley, MN (16)
KAR Graphics, Mashpee, MA (8)
KCET, Los Angeles, CA (1)
KCI Communications Inc, Falls Church, VA (17)
KEH.com, Smyrna, GA (16)
KET, Lexington, KY (17)
KHL Engineered Packaging Solutions, Buena Park, CA (16)
KMA Direct Communications, Dallas, TX (1)
KPBS FM/TV, San Diego, CA (1)
KV Vet Supply Co, Inc, David City, NE (5)
Kalmbach Publishing Co, Waukesha, WI (17)
Kano Laboratories, Nashville, TN (16)
Kansas City Chiefs, Kansas City, MO (16)
Kansas State University Division of Continuing Education, Manhattan, KS (1)
Kaplan Inc, New York, NY (16)
Kaplan Test Prep & Admissions, New York, NY (1)
Kappa Publishing Group, Blue Bell, PA (17)
Kappler Protective Apparel & Fabrics, Guntersville, AL (2)
Kaylor's School Supply, Albertville, AL (16)
Kayne & Son Custom Hardware Inc, Candler, NC (8)
Kayser-Roth Corp Inc, Greensboro, NC (2)
Keeneland Association Inc, Lexington, KY (16)
Kelco Supply Co, Brooklyn Park, MN (16)
Kellyco Metal Detector Distributors, Winter Springs, FL (11)
Kelly's Kids, Natchez, MS (2)
Kelsey National Corp, Los Angeles, CA (15)
Kendall Products/Dri-Dek, Naples, FL (16)
Kenmore Stamp Co, Milford, NH (6)
Kennel Vet, Laurel, DE (11)
Kensington Publishing Corp, New York, NY (17)
Kensington Technology Group, Redwood Shores, CA (16)
Kerr-Hays Co, Ligonier, PA (16)
Kester's Wild Game Food Nurseries Inc, Omro, WI (8)
Kett Tool Co, Cincinnati, OH (9)
Key Bank, Cleveland, OH (14)
Key Bank National Association, Albany, NY (14)
Key West Aloe Holdings LLC, Fort Lauderdale, FL (16)
Keyboard Workshop, Medford, OR (17)
Keyspan Energy Corp, Brooklyn, NY (16)
The Kidney Foundation of Canada/Greater Ontario Branch, Hamilton, ON, Canada (1)
Miles Kimball Co, Oshkosh, WI (6)
Kimberly-Clark Corp, Neenah, WI (16)
Kimbo Educational, Long Branch, NJ (17)
King Features, New York, NY (17)
King Pharmaceuticals, Inc, Bristol, TN (7)
King Ranch Saddle Shop, Kingsville, TX (8)
King's Chandelier Co, Eden, NC (6)
Kingsley North Inc, Norway, MI (11)
The Kiplinger Washington Editors Inc, Washington, DC (17)
Will Kirkpatrick Shorebird Decoys Inc, Hudson, MA (6)
Klahowya Native American & Nature Gift Shop, Bandon, OR (6)
B Klein Publications, Delray Beach, FL (17)
Calvin Klein Cosmetics Co, New York, NY (7)
Klingspor's Woodworking Shop, Hickory, NC (9)
Klitzner Industries, Providence, RI (6)

Klockit, Lake Geneva, WI (6)
Knoll Group, New York, NY (16)
Knollwood Groves at Cushman's, West Palm Beach, FL (4)
Knott's Berry Farm Foods, Buena Park, CA (4)
Koeze Co, Grand Rapids, MI (16)
Kolbe Corp, Phoenix, AZ (17)
Susan G Komen for the Cure, Dallas, TX (1)
KozaK Auto Drywash Inc, Batavia, NY (16)
Kraft Foods/Gevalia Kaffe, Tarrytown, NY (16)
Kraftbilt, Tulsa, OK (10)
EC Kraus Home Wine & Beer Making Supplies, Independence, MO (4)
Krause Publications Inc, Iola, WI (17)
The Kroger Co, Cincinnati, OH (4)
Kropp Enterprises, Kissimmee, FL (2)
Kross Inc, Santa Clarita, CA (16)
Patricia Kutza Co, Vallejo, CA (2)
Kuwait Airways Corp, Fort Lee, NJ (19)

L

L&L Management, Pasadena, CA (16)
L6 Holdings Corp, Duluth, GA (14)
LDS Test & Measurement, Marlborough, MA (3)
LIMRA International, Windsor, CT (1)
LS Records, Madison, TN (16)
LaCrosse Footwear Inc, Portland, OR (16)
The LadyBug Co, Berry Creek, CA (8)
Lahey Clinic, Burlington, MA (1)
Lake Shore Industries, Erie, PA (16)
Lakeside Publishing Co LLC, Evanston, IL (17)
AB Lambdin Inc, Hampton, VA (2)
Land O' Lakes Inc, Arden Hills, MN (16)
Landauer Corp, Urbandale, IA (17)
Landmark Communications Inc, Norfolk, VA (17)
Landmark Graphics Corp, Houston, TX (16)
Lands' End Inc, Dodgeville, WI (2)
Laplink Software Inc, Bellevue, WA (3)
LaPreferida Inc, Chicago, IL (4)
Laran Communications Inc, Winfield, IL (16)
Lark in the Morning, Mendocino, CA (5)
Las Vegas Review Journal, Las Vegas, NV (17)
Laughlin Associates Inc, Carson City, NV (16)
Lawn Doctor Inc, Holmdel, NJ (16)
Lazar Media Group Inc, Charleston, SC (17)
Lazydays RV Center, Seffner, FL (12)
Le Jardin Du Gourmet, Saint Johnsbury Center, VT (8)
Lea & Perrins Inc, Fair Lawn, NJ (16)
Leadership Software Corp, Nyack, NY (16)
LeadFlash, Boca Raton, FL (14)
Leanin' Tree Inc, Boulder, CO (6)
Learning Seed, Chicago, IL (3)
Leather Unlimited Corp, Belgium, WI (2)
Lefty's Corner, Clarks Summit, PA (6)
Legal Defense Foundation Inc, Springfield, VA (1)
Legal Sea Foods Inc, Boston, MA (4)
Lego Direct Marketing, Enfield, CT (11)
Lehman's, Dalton, OH (8)
Leisure Arts Inc, Little Rock, AR (17)
Lemee's Inc, Bridgewater, MA (8)
Lending Tree/Home Loan Center, Charlotte, NC (14)
AM Leonard Inc, Piqua, OH (8)
Hal Leonard Corp, Milwaukee, WI (17)
Lerner Publishing Group, Minneapolis, MN (17)
Leslie Shoe Co Inc, Rogers City, MI (2)
Leucadia National Corp, New York, NY (14)
The Leukemia & Lymphoma Society, White Plains, NY (1)
Levenger, Delray Beach, FL (5)
Levi Strauss & Co, San Francisco, CA (16)
Lexington Luggage Limited, New York, NY (19)
Lexus Division of Toyota, Torrance, CA (12)
Peter Li Education Group, Dayton, OH (17)
Liberty Fund Inc, Indianapolis, IN (1)
Liberty Life Insurance Co, Greenville, SC (15)
Liberty Mutual Group, Inc, Boston, MA (15)
Liberty Orchards Co Inc, Cashmere, WA (16)
Liberty Tax Service, Virginia Beach, VA (14)

Liberty Tree Network, Oakland, CA (5)
Libertyville Saddle Shop Inc, Libertyville, IL (11)
The Library of America, New York, NY (13)
Life Extension Foundation, Fort Lauderdale, FL (7)
Life Fitness, Schiller Park, IL (11)
Life Investors Insurance Co of America, Cedar Rapids, IA (17)
Life Line Screening, Independence, OH (7)
Life-Study Fellowship Foundation Inc, Darien, CT (17)
LifeLock, Tempe, AZ (16)
Lifetips, Boston, MA (16)
Light Sources Inc, Virginia Beach, VA (16)
Ligonier Ministries, Lake Mary, FL (5)
Liguori Publications, Liguori, MO (17)
Lillian Vernon Corp, Colorado Springs, CO (6)
Lilypons Water Gardens, Adamstown, MD (8)
The Limited Stores Inc, Columbus, OH (2)
LimitedBrands Inc, Reynoldsburg, OH (16)
Lin Terry, Paterson, NJ (6)
Lincoln Educational Services, West Orange, NJ (13)
Lincoln Financial Group, Radnor, PA (15)
Lincoln Park Zoo, Chicago, IL (1)
Lindustries Inc, Weston, MA (8)
Linens n' Things, Paramus, NJ (8)
LinguiSystems, East Moline, IL (17)
Links Magazine, Hilton Head Island, SC (17)
Lion Apparel, Dayton, OH (2)
Lippincott, Williams & Wilkins, Baltimore, MD (17)
Listening Library Inc, Random House Audio, New York, NY (3)
Lithia Motors Inc, Medford, OR (12)
Litle & Co, Lowell, MA (14)
Littleton Coin Co Inc, Littleton, NH (6)
Live Nation, Beverly Hills, CA (19)
Lladro USA, Moonachie, NJ (16)
Llewellyn Publications, Woodbury, MN (17)
Local Government Federal Credit Union, Raleigh, NC (14)
Loctite Corp, Rocky Hill, CT (16)
Loehmann's, Bronx, NY (2)
Loews Hotels, New York, NY (19)
Logical Computer Selections, Short Hills, NJ (16)
Lombardi Publishing Corp, Vaughan, ON, Canada (17)
Longevity Network Ltd, Henderson, NV (7)
Longevity Pure Medicine, Palm Springs, CA (7)
Lorillard Tobacco Co, Greensboro, NC (16)
Los Angeles Kings, Los Angeles, CA (16)
The Los Angeles Lakers Inc, El Segundo, CA (11)
Lotions & Lace, Riverside, CA (2)
LOTSolutions, Jacksonville, FL (14)
Louisiana Nursery, Opelousas, LA (8)
Louisiana State Museum, New Orleans, LA (1)
Love To Learn Inc, Salem, UT (5)
Loves Travel Stops & Country Stores, Oklahoma City, OK (5)
Loving Promises & More, Longview, WA (16)
Lowe's Companies Inc, Mooresville, NC (8)
Lowrance Electronics, Tulsa, OK (11)
Luce Corp, Hamden, CT (3)
Lucky Heart Cosmetics Inc, Memphis, TN (7)
Lufthansa German Airlines, East Meadow, NY (19)
Luggage Base, Nipomo, CA (16)
Lundberg Family Farms, Richvale, CA (16)
Lure-Craft, Lagrange, IN (11)
Lutheran Church Extension Fund - Missouri Synod, Saint Louis, MO (1)
Luzier Personalized Cosmetics, Kansas City, MO (7)

M

M&M Health Care Apparel Co, Brooklyn, NY (2)
M2Media 360, Park Ridge, IL (17)
MBI Inc, Norwalk, CT (16)
MCA/Universal Studios Inc, Universal City, CA (3)
MCCS, Mason, OH (14)
MCI Inc, Ashburn, VA (16)
MDR, Sunrise, FL (7)
MFS Investment Management, Boston, MA (14)
MGM MIRAGE, Las Vegas, NV (19)

MI-T-M Corp, Peosta, IA (9)
MMS Education, Newtown, PA (5)
MPS Multimedia Inc, San Mateo, CA (16)
MRV Communications, Chatsworth, CA (3)
MTS Publishing, Naperville, IL (17)
MXT Card Services, LLC, New Castle, DE (14)
Macy's, City Of Industry, CA (5)
Macy's Marketing, New York, NY (16)
Macy's West, San Francisco, CA (16)
Madisonavegifts.com, Watertown, NY (6)
Magazine Publishers of America, New York, NY (17)
Magellan's Catalog, Santa Barbara, CA (5)
Magic Seasonings Mail Order, New Orleans, LA (4)
Magnaplan Corp, Champlain, NY (10)
Magnatag Visable Systems, Macedon, NY (16)
The Magni Co Inc, McKinney, TX (16)
Magnolia Hall, Jasper, GA (8)
Maidenform Inc, Iselin, NJ (2)
Mailorder Gardening Association, Elkridge, MD (1)
Mailworks Inc, Freeport, ME (1)
Maine Potato Board, Presque Isle, ME (1)
Maison Glass Delicacies, Jersey City, NJ (4)
Majestic Products Co, Mississauga, ON, Canada (16)
Make-A-Wish Foundation of America, Phoenix, AZ (1)
Making It Big, Cotati, CA (2)
Malco Products Inc, Barberton, OH (16)
MALM Chemical Corp, Pound Ridge, NY (16)
EF Maloney Inc, Mamaroneck, NY (16)
Manchester Farms Inc, Columbia, SC (4)
Mane Solutions, New York, NY (16)
Manhattan College, Bronx, NY (1)
Manheim Steamroller, Omaha, NE (3)
Manning Materials, Birdsboro, PA (16)
Manulife Financial Inc, Toronto, ON, Canada (15)
MAP International, Brunswick, GA (1)
Maple Grove Farms of Vermont Inc, Saint Johnsbury, VT (4)
March of Dimes Birth Defects Foundation, White Plains, NY (1)
Mardiron Optics, Stoneham, MA (11)
Marian Helpers Center, Stockbridge, MA (1)
Marimac Inc, Montreal, PQ, Canada (8)
The Mark Group, Boca Raton, FL (2)
Markertek Video Supply, Saugerties, NY (3)
Marketing and Product Strategy, Peabody, MA (16)
Marketing Results Inc, Sicklerville, NJ (16)
Marketplace of the Master Inc, Rockford, IL (5)
Marketshare Publications Inc, Overland Park, KS (17)
Marmelstein Inc, Philadelphia, PA (16)
The Marmon Group LLC, Chicago, IL (16)
Marquis Who's Who LLC, Berkeley Heights, NJ (17)
Marriott International Inc, Washington, DC (19)
Marriott Ownership Resorts Sales & Marketing, Orlando, FL (19)
Marsh Affinity Group Services, Chicago, IL (15)
Marshall & Ilsley Corp, Milwaukee, WI (14)
Marshall Fields Dept Stores, Minneapolis, MN (5)
Martindale-Hubbell, New Providence, NJ (17)
Mary Kay Cosmetics Inc, Addison, TX (16)
Mary of Puddin Hill, Greenville, TX (16)
Maryknoll Fathers & Brothers, Maryknoll, NY (1)
The Maryland Saddlery Inc, Butler, MD (11)
Mary's Plant Farm & Landscaping, Hamilton, OH (8)
T Marzetti Co Inc, Columbus, OH (4)
Masco Corp, Taylor, MI (16)
Mason Companies Inc, Chippewa Falls, WI (2)
George Mason University School of Management, Fairfax, VA (1)
WB Mason Co, New York, NY (16)
Massachusetts Horticultural Society, Wellesley, MA (1)
MassMutual Financial Group, Springfield, MA (15)
MasterCard Worldwide, Purchase, NY (14)
Mastergrip Inc, Irving, TX (11)
Masterpiece Studios Inc, Mankato, MN (16)
Mastervision Inc, New York, NY (16)
Matt & Kumpany Kuzins, Sacramento, CA (1)
Mattel Inc, El Segundo, CA (16)
Matthews 1812 House Inc, Cornwall Bridge, CT (4)
Robert J Matthews Co, Massillon, OH (7)

Maui Jim Inc, Peoria, IL (16)
MAX Federal Credit Union, Montgomery, AL (14)
Mary Maxim Inc, Port Huron, MI (11)
Maxon Furniture Inc, Muscatine, IA (10)
Mayo Clinic, Rochester, MN (17)
McClatchy Co, Sacramento, CA (17)
McClure & Zimmerman, Randolph, WI (8)
McCormick & Co Inc, Hunt Valley, MD (4)
McDonald Obsolete Parts Co, Rockport, IN (16)
McFarland & Co Inc Publishers, Jefferson, NC (17)
McFayden/McConnell, Brandon, MB, Canada (8)
McFeely's Square Drive Screws, Madison, WI (16)
The McGraw-Hill Cos, New York, NY (17)
McKenzie Taxidermy Supply, Granite Quarry, NC (16)
McKesson Corp, San Francisco, CA (7)
Mead Johnson Co, Evansville, IN (7)
Mead Westvaco Consumer & Office Products, Dayton, OH (10)
Mechanical Breakdown Administrators Inc, Scottsdale, AZ (14)
Medals of America, Fountain Inn, SC (6)
Media Management & Magnetics Inc, Menomonee Falls, WI (3)
Medibadge Inc, Omaha, NE (5)
Medic Alert Foundation, Turlock, CA (1)
Medifast Inc, Owings Mills, MD (4)
Medill IMC/Northwestern University, Evanston, IL (1)
Medtronic Inc, Minneapolis, MN (16)
Megger, Dallas, TX (16)
Meguiar's Inc, Irvine, CA (16)
Meister Media Worldwide, Willoughby, OH (17)
Melaniphy & Associates, Inc, Chicago, IL (8)
MELDISCO, Mahwah, NJ (16)
Memorial Sloan Kettering Cancer Center, New York, NY (1)
Memphis Net & Twine Co Inc, Memphis, TN (11)
The Menninger Foundation, Houston, TX (1)
Mentoring Minds, Tyler, TX (16)
Merastar Insurance Co, Chattanooga, TN (15)
Merck & Co Inc, Whitehouse Station, NJ (16)
Meredith Corp, Des Moines, IA (17)
Merrick Bank, South Jordan, UT (14)
Merrill Lynch, New York, NY (14)
Merrimade Stationery Co LLC, Ansonia, CT (10)
Mersco Medical, Pierre, SD (16)
Mervyn's, Pleasanton, CA (16)
Methode Electronics Inc, Chicago, IL (9)
Metro Speedgear, Livingston, NJ (11)
Metropolis Magazine, New York, NY (2)
Metropolitan Museum of Art, New York, NY (8)
The Metropolitan Opera, New York, NY (1)
Metso Minerals/WS Tyler, Waukesha, WI (16)
Meyer Decorative Surfaces Inc, Atlanta, GA (8)
Fred Meyer Jewelers Inc, Portland, OR (16)
Meylan Corp, Montclair, NJ (9)
Michael's, Irving, TX (11)
Michigan Apple Committee, Lansing, MI (1)
Micro Center, Hilliard, OH (3)
Micro Plastics Inc, Flippin, AR (16)
Mid America Designs Inc, Effingham, IL (12)
Mid America Motorworks, Effingham, IL (12)
Mid West Floor Co Inc, Saint Louis, MO (16)
Midcontinent Financial Center Inc, Columbia, MO (14)
The Midland Co, Amelia, OH (15)
Midland Marketing Group, Saint Joseph, MO (16)
Midwest Center for Stress & Anxiety Inc, Oak Harbor, OH (7)
Midwest Publishing Inc, Phoenix, AZ (17)
Midwest Technology Products & Services, Sioux City, IA (9)
Military Officers Association of America, Alexandria, VA (1)
Military Order of the Purple Heart Svc, Annandale, VA (1)
Miller Harness Co, Westford, MA (11)
JE Miller Nurseries Inc, Canandaigua, NY (8)
Miller Stockman, Denver, CO (2)
MillerCoors LLC, Chicago, IL (4)
Miller's First Insurance Companies, Alton, IL (15)
Milwaukee Electric Tool Corp, Brookfield, WI (16)

Mini City Ltd, Webster, NY (12)
Minitab Inc, State College, PA (16)
Minnesota Life, Saint Paul, MN (15)
Minnesota Public Radio, Saint Paul, MN (1)
Minnetonka By Mail, Bronx, NY (2)
Miracle Ear, Minneapolis, MN (16)
Miracle of Aloe, Dallas, TX (7)
MISSCO Corp, Flowood, MS (16)
Missouri Life Inc, Boonville, MO (17)
Mr G's Enterprises, Fort Worth, TX (16)
Mr Wash Car Wash, Kensington, MD (16)
Mitsubishi Digital Electronics America Inc, Irvine, CA (3)
Mitsubishi Motor Sales of America Inc, Cypress, CA (1)
Frank Mittermeier Inc, Bronx, NY (11)
Modernage Custom Digital Imaging Labs, New York, NY (16)
Modular Devices, LLC, Sparta, NJ (3)
Molson Coors Brewing Co, Denver, CO (16)
Monex Deposit Co, Newport Beach, CA (14)
MoneyGram International, Dallas, TX (14)
Montag & Caldwell Inc, Atlanta, GA (14)
Montbleu Resort Casino and Spa, Stateline, NV (19)
Moon Shine Trading Co, Woodland, CA (4)
Thurston Moore Country Ltd, Madison, TN (16)
Morcon Industrial Specialty Inc, Mesquite, NV (9)
Bob Morgan Woodworking Supplies Inc, Westport, KY (8)
Morgan Kaufmann Publishers Inc, Burlington, MA (17)
Morgan Stanley, New York, NY (14)
Morkes Chocolates, Palatine, IL (4)
Morningstar Inc, Chicago, IL (14)
Morris Visitors Publications LLC, Augusta, GA (17)
Thomas Moser Cabinetmakers, Freeport, ME (16)
Mother Earth News Magazine, Topeka, KS (17)
Mother Jones Magazine, San Francisco, CA (17)
Motherwear, Holyoke, MA (2)
Motient Communications, Reston, VA (16)
Motion Picture & Television Fund Foundation, Woodland Hills, CA (1)
The Motley Fool, Alexandria, VA (14)
Moto Franchise Corp, Dayton, OH (3)
Motown Records, New York, NY (3)
Mott Media LLC, Fenton, MI (17)
Moultrie Manufacturing Co, Moultrie, GA (8)
Mountain Craft Shop Co, Proctor, WV (11)
Mountain Press Publishing Co, Missoula, MT (17)
Mountain West Supply Co, Scottsdale, AZ (3)
Movie/Entertainment Book Club, Washington, DC (13)
Mrs Beasley's & Miss Grace Lemon Cake Co, Los Angeles, CA (4)
Multi-Level Marketing International Association (MLMIA), Irvine, CA (1)
Mike Murach & Associates Inc, Fresno, CA (17)
Murad Inc, El Segundo, CA (7)
Murder by Mail, West Tisbury, MA (1)
Murphy Bed Co Inc, Farmingdale, NY (8)
Muscular Dystrophy Association, Tucson, AZ (1)
The Museum of Modern Art, New York, NY (5)
Music Barn Inc, Niagara Falls, NY (6)
Music Choice, Horsham, PA (16)
Music Sales Corp, New York, NY (17)
Music Treasures Co, Richmond, VA (6)
Muskegon Power Tool Corp, North Muskegon, MI (16)
Mustek Inc, Tustin, CA (3)
Mutual of Omaha, Omaha, NE (15)
Mystic Seaport Museum Stores, Mystic, CT (6)
Mystic Stamp Co Inc, Camden, NY (16)

N

NAACP (National Association for the Advancement of Colored People), Baltimore, MD (1)
NASCO, Fort Atkinson, WI (5)
NASW Assurance Services Inc, Frederick, MD (1)
NBI Inc, Eau Claire, WI (1)

NBTY Inc, Ronkonkoma, NY (7)
NCP Solutions, Reston, VA (17)
NEA's Member Benefits Corp, Gaithersburg, MD (1)
NGL Insurance Group, Madison, WI (15)
NSA Technologies LLC, Akron, OH (9)
NTL Institute, Arlington, VA (1)
NYSARC, Inc, Delmar, NY (1)
NADA Appraisal Guides, Costa Mesa, CA (17)
Nancy's Notions LLC, Beaver Dam, WI (11)
NAR Productions, Barryville, NY (17)
Narrow Way, Lafayette, CA (6)
Natcom Inc, Bixby, OK (17)
National Active & Retired Federal Employees Association, Alexandria, VA (1)
National Archives & Records Administration, College Park, MD (17)
National Association for Female Executives (NAFE), New York, NY (1)
National Association of Professional Insurance Agents, Alexandria, VA (1)
National Association of Realtors, Chicago, IL (1)
National Audubon Society, New York, NY (17)
National Auto Warranty, Wentzville, MO (16)
National Automated Clearing House Association, Herndon, VA (1)
National Basketball Association, Secaucus, NJ (1)
National Business Furniture Inc, Milwaukee, WI (10)
National Catholic Reporter Publishing Co Inc, Kansas City, MO (17)
National City Bank, Cleveland, OH (14)
National Committee to Preserve Social Security & Medicare, Washington, DC (1)
National Community Pharmacists Association, Alexandria, VA (1)
National Contract Management Association, Ashburn, VA (1)
National Court Reporters Association, Vienna, VA (1)
National Crime Prevention Council, Amsterdam, NY (17)
National Defense Industrial Association, Arlington, VA (1)
National Emblem Sales, Indianapolis, IN (16)
National Enquirer, Boca Raton, FL (17)
National Foundation for Cancer Research, Bethesda, MD (1)
National 4-H Supply Service, Chevy Chase, MD (16)
National Gallery of Art Gift Shop, Washington, DC (16)
National Humane Education Society, Charles Town, WV (1)
National Jewish Health, Denver, CO (1)
National Journal Group, Washington, DC (17)
National Law Enforcement Officers Memorial Fund, Washington, DC (1)
National League for Nursing, New York, NY (1)
National Luggage Dealers Association, Glenview, IL (1)
National Medical Fellowships, New York, NY (1)
National Motor Club of America Inc, Irving, TX (1)
National Osteoporosis Foundation, Washington, DC (1)
National Pension Service Inc, Burlington, VT (14)
National Railroad Passenger Corp, Washington, DC (16)
The National Restaurant Association Educational Foundation, Chicago, IL (1)
National Retail Federation Inc, Washington, DC (1)
National Review, New York, NY (17)
National Rifle Association of America, Fairfax, VA (1)
National Semiconductor Corp, Santa Clara, CA (16)
National Society of Collegiate Scholars, Washington, DC (1)
National Technical Information Service, Alexandria, VA (17)
National University, La Jolla, CA (1)
National Wholesale Co Inc, Lexington, NC (2)
National Wildlife Federation, Reston, VA (1)
Nationwide Beauty & Barber Supply, Syracuse, NY (16)
Nationwide Mutual Insurance Co, Columbus, OH (15)
Natural Essentials Inc, Streetsboro, OH (5)

Natural History Magazine, Durham, NC (17)
The Nature Conservancy, Arlington, VA (1)
Nautilus Inc, Vancouver, WA (11)
Naval Institute Press, Annapolis, MD (17)
Navistar, Warrenville, IL (16)
Neiman-Marcus Group, Dallas, TX (8)
Nelson Crab Inc, Tokeland, WA (4)
Thomas Nelson, Inc, Nashville, TN (17)
Neo-Tech Publishing Co, Henderson, NV (17)
NestFamily.com, Coppell, TX (3)
NetSpend, San Mateo, CA (14)
Network Telephone Services Inc, Woodland Hills, CA (16)
Neuberger & Berman Management, New York, NY (14)
Nevada Commission on Tourism, Carson City, NV (1)
Nevada Magazine, Carson City, NV (17)
Nevco Scoreboard Co, Greenville, IL (16)
New & Unique Videos, San Diego, CA (3)
New Directions Publishing Corp, New York, NY (17)
New England Cheesemaking Supply Co, South Deerfield, MA (4)
New England Life Insurance Co, Boston, MA (15)
New Jersey Institute for Continuing Legal Education, New Brunswick, NJ (1)
New Jersey Monthly, Morristown, NJ (17)
New Pig Corp, Tipton, PA (9)
The New Piper Aircraft Inc, Vero Beach, FL (16)
New Wave Media Inc, New York, NY (5)
New Win Publishing Inc, El Monte, CA (17)
New York Blood Center Inc, New York, NY (1)
New York Easter Seal Society, New York, NY (1)
New York Landmarks Conservancy, New York, NY (1)
New York Life Insurance Co/AARP, Tampa, FL (15)
New York Philharmonic, New York, NY (1)
New York Power Authority, Albany, NY (16)
New York Road Runners Club, Inc, New York, NY (13)
The New York Times Co, New York, NY (17)
New York University Medical Center, New York, NY (1)
The New Yorker Magazine, New York, NY (17)
New Zealand Tourism Board, Santa Monica, CA (19)
Newark Electronics, Chicago, IL (3)
Newell Rubbermaid, Inc, Atlanta, GA (16)
The Newman Group, Ann Arbor, MI (3)
Newmark Laboratories, Edison, NJ (7)
Newport News, New York, NY (2)
The News Tribune, Tacoma, WA (17)
Newsday, Melville, NY (17)
Newspaper Association of America, Arlington, VA (1)
Newsweek Inc, New York, NY (17)
NextScreen LLC, Austin, TX (17)
Nielsen Business Media, New York, NY (16)
Nielsen Trade Dimensions, Wilton, CT (17)
Nightingale-Conant Corp, Niles, IL (17)
Nightingale Resources, Cold Spring, NY (17)
Nihon Keizai Shimbun America Inc, New York, NY (17)
Nike Inc, Beaverton, OR (2)
Nilodor Inc, Bolivar, OH (16)
Nissan North America Inc, Irving, TX (16)
No Load Fund Investor, Brentwood, TN (14)
No Load Fund*X, San Francisco, CA (14)
Nodine's Smokehouse, Torrington, CT (4)
Noevir Direct Marketing Inc, Montvale, NJ (7)
Nomadics Tipi Makers, Bend, OR (11)
Nordskog Publishing Co, Ventura, CA (17)
Nordstrom Inc, Seattle, WA (2)
Nor'east Miniature Roses Inc, Arroyo Grande, CA (8)
Norman Control Co, Cary, IL (16)
Norman Rockwell Museum, Stockbridge, MA (16)
Norscot Group, Mequon, WI (5)
North America Life Insurance Co, Austin, TX (15)
North American Co for Life & Health Insurance, Chicago, IL (15)
North American Membership Group Inc, Minnetonka, MN (13)
North Shore Animal League America Inc, Port Washington, NY (1)

Northeast Hinge Distributors Inc, Hollis, NH (9)
Northern Cross, Lecompton, KS (16)
Northern Greenhouse Sales, Neche, ND (8)
Northwestern Mutual, Milwaukee, WI (14)
Nourse Farms, South Deerfield, MA (8)
Nova Southeastern University - FSEHS, North Miami Beach, FL (1)
Novartis Pharmaceuticals Corp, East Hanover, NJ (7)
Nowell's Inc, San Rafael, CA (8)
Nowetah's American Indian Store & Museum, New Portland, ME (6)
Nu-Parr Swimwear, Phoenix, AZ (2)
NuNaturals, Eugene, OR (16)
NutriSystem Inc, Fort Washington, PA (7)
Nutritional Research Associates Inc, South Whitley, IN (16)
Nuveen Investments, Chicago, IL (14)
Nylon Net Co, Memphis, TN (11)
Nyrev Inc, New York, NY (17)

O

OAG Worldwide, Downers Grove, IL (17)
Oakley Inc, Foothill Ranch, CA (2)
Oakstone Publishing LLC, Birmingham, AL (17)
Oakwood Homes Corp, Greensboro, NC (16)
O'Brien Manufacturing, Marietta, OH (9)
Ocean Conservancy, Washington, DC (1)
O'Currance Inc, Draper, UT (18)
Office Depot, Boca Raton, FL (16)
OfficeMax Inc, Naperville, IL (10)
Oil & Gas Journal, Tulsa, OK (17)
Okun Brothers Shoes Inc, Kalamazoo, MI (2)
Olan Mills Inc, Chattanooga, TN (16)
Old World Mouldings Inc, Bohemia, NY (9)
Oleda & Co Inc, Fort Worth, TX (16)
Olesuk Financial Services, McHenry, IL (14)
Oliver of Adrian Inc, Adrian, MI (16)
Olsen's Mill Direct, Oshkosh, WI (2)
Olympia Sales Inc, Enfield, CT (16)
Omaha Creative Group Inc, Omaha, NE (4)
Omaha Steaks Inc, Omaha, NE (4)
Omaha Vaccine Co, Omaha, NE (16)
Omni Farm, West Jefferson, NC (16)
Omnigraphics Inc, Aston, PA (17)
1-800-Contacts, Orem, UT (18)
1-800-Flowers.com, Carle Place, NY (16)
One Hanes Place Catalog, Winston Salem, NC (2)
100% Real Estate Inc, Orlando, FL (16)
1000 Islands International Tourism Council, Alexandria Bay, NY (19)
Oneida Ltd, Oneida, NY (16)
Oomingmak Musk Ox Producers Cooperative, Anchorage, AK (6)
Open Text Inc, Waterloo, ON, Canada (16)
Opryland, Nashville, TN (16)
Optronics Inc, Muskogee, OK (11)
Opus Inc, Lititz, PA (8)
Oracle Corp, Redwood Shores, CA (16)
Oral Roberts University, Tulsa, OK (1)
The Orange County Register, Santa Ana, CA (17)
Orbis Books, Maryknoll, NY (17)
Orchard Supply Hardware, San Jose, CA (16)
Orient Expressed Imports Inc, New Orleans, LA (2)
Oriental Trading Co Inc, Omaha, NE (5)
The Original Honey Baked Ham Co of the East, Marblehead, MA (4)
Orion Telescopes & Binoculars, Watsonville, CA (11)
Orlando/ Orange County Convention & Visitor's Bureau, Orlando, FL (19)
The Orvis Co Inc, Manchester, VT (11)
Our Designs Inc, Vancouver, WA (16)
Our Lady of Victory Homes of Charity, Lackawanna, NY (1)
Our Sunday Visitor Publishing, Huntington, IN (17)
Overton's Inc, Greenville, NC (11)
Oxford Health Plans, Inc, Trumbull, CT (15)
Oxford University Press Inc, New York, NY (17)

P

PBS Distribution, Arlington, VA (3)
PC Mall, Torrance, CA (3)
PC Ontario Fund, Toronto, ON, Canada (1)
PC World, San Francisco, CA (17)
PESI LLC, Eau Claire, WI (17)
PFI Western Stores Inc, Springfield, MO (2)
PHE Inc, Hillsborough, NC (5)
PMIC, Los Angeles, CA (17)
PNC Bank Corp, Pittsburgh, PA (14)
PNC Global Investment Servicing, Lynnfield, MA (14)
PPC, Johnston, IA (9)
PPN INC, Holbrook, MA (7)
PVC Plastics Co, Evansville, IN (16)
Paasche Airbrush Co, Chicago, IL (10)
Pace Communications Inc, Greensboro, NC (17)
Pace University - Div of Enrollment Mgmt, New York, NY (16)
Pachmayr Ltd, Middletown, CT (11)
Pacific Botanicals LLC, Grants Pass, OR (7)
Pacific Propeller Inc, Kent, WA (16)
Pacific Spirit Corp, Forest Grove, OR (6)
Paladin Press, Boulder, CO (17)
Pallottine Center for Apostolic Causes Inc/St Jude Shrine, Baltimore, MD (1)
Pan Pacific Hotel & Resorts America, Seattle, WA (19)
Pango Pango Swimwear Corp, Pompano Beach, FL (2)
Panoptic Enterprises, Burke, VA (17)
Papa John's International, Louisville, KY (4)
PAPYRUS, Fairfield, CA (5)
Para Publishing, Santa Barbara, CA (17)
Paradise Galleries, Irvine, CA (6)
Paragon Laboratories, Torrance, CA (16)
Paralyzed Veterans of America, Washington, DC (1)
Parenting Concepts Inc, Murrieta, CA (2)
George W Park Seed Co Inc, Greenwood, SC (8)
Parker Hannifin Corp, Cleveland, OH (9)
Parmer Books, San Diego, CA (6)
Partminer, Centennial, CO (17)
Partners Health, Philadelphia, PA (15)
Partners Village Store, Westport, MA (11)
Parts Express, Springboro, OH (3)
Parts Place Inc, Auburn Hills, MI (12)
Party Kits & Equestrian Gifts, Louisville, KY (6)
Passport International Ltd, North Charleston, SC (2)
Pastime Publications Inc, Denver, CO (17)
Patagonia, Ventura, CA (2)
Patagonia Mail Order Inc, Reno, NV (2)
Path to Purchase Institute, Skokie, IL (17)
Patient News, Niagara Falls, NY (17)
The Patio, Murrieta, CA (8)
PayPal Inc, Timonium, MD (14)
Peak Impact Inc, Ottawa, ON, Canada (14)
Pecan Producers International, Corsicana, TX (4)
Peerless Rattan, Plainwell, MI (16)
Peet's Coffee & Tea Inc, Berkeley, CA (4)
Pegasus Auto Racing Supplies Inc, New Berlin, WI (12)
PEMCO Insurance Cos, Seattle, WA (15)
Penguin Group USA Inc, East Rutherford, NJ (17)
Penguin Publishing Group, New York, NY (17)
Penguin Putnam Inc, New York, NY (17)
Penn Herb Co Ltd, Philadelphia, PA (7)
Penn Mutual, Horsham, PA (15)
Penn State Hazleton, Hazleton, PA (1)
Pennstreet Bakery, Grand Rapids, MI (16)
Pennsylvania Firebacks, Lansdale, PA (8)
Pennsylvania State University Press, University Park, PA (17)
The Pennysaver Group Inc, Hanover, MD (17)
Peoples Benefit Life Insurance Co, Exton, PA (15)
People's United Bank, Bridgeport, CT (14)
Perennial Pleasures Nursery, East Hardwick, VT (8)
Performance Media Solutions Inc & TrueWorx Inc, Las Vegas, NV (16)
Periodical Publisher's Service Bureau Inc, Sandusky, OH (18)

Pernod Ricard USA, Purchase, NY (16)
Personal Achievement Institute, Kingman, AZ (17)
Personal Creations, Lemont, IL (6)
RJ Persson Enterprises Inc, Montrose, CO (16)
Petco Animal Supplies, San Diego, CA (5)
PetEdge, Beverly, MA (16)
Peter Pan Bus Lines Inc, Springfield, MA (19)
Peter Pauls Nurseries, Canandaigua, NY (8)
J Peterman Co, Lexington, KY (5)
Peterson's, Lawrenceville, NJ (17)
Pets United LLC, Hazleton, PA (5)
PetSmart Inc, Phoenix, AZ (5)
Pfaelzer Brothers, Maumee, OH (16)
Pfaltzgraff Co, York, PA (8)
Pfizer Inc, New York, NY (16)
PharmArt, Circleville, OH (6)
Pharmavite Corp LLC (HQ), Northridge, CA (16)
The Philadelphia Contributorship Insurance Co, Philadelphia, PA (15)
Philips Lifeline, Framingham, MA (7)
Phillips-Van Heusen Corp, New York, NY (2)
Phoenix Learning Group Inc, Maryland Heights, MO (16)
Phoenix Poke Boats Inc, McKee, KY (16)
Photographer's Formulary Inc, Condon, MT (9)
Photoworks, Cleveland, OH (16)
Physical Therapy Institute Inc, Poway, CA (16)
Physicians Mutual Insurance Co, Omaha, NE (15)
Physicians Planning Association Services, Deerfield Beach, FL (16)
Pilani's Live in Style, Egg Harbor Township, NJ (2)
The Pillsbury Co, Minneapolis, MN (16)
The Pin Man, Tulsa, OK (16)
Pine Castle Animal Hospital, Orlando, FL (16)
Pinnacle Orchards, Maumee, OH (4)
Pioneer Hi-Bred International Inc, Johnston, IA (4)
Pittman & Davis Inc, Harlingen, TX (4)
Pizza Hut Inc, Plano, TX (16)
The Plain Dealer, Cleveland, OH (18)
Plan USA, Warwick, RI (1)
Planet Cotton, Gaithersburg, MD (2)
Planned Parenthood Federation of America, New York, NY (1)
Planned Parenthood Mar Monte, San Jose, CA (1)
Bud Plant Illustrated Books, Palo Alto, CA (6)
Plastic View ATC, Simi Valley, CA (9)
Play Fair Toys, Boulder, CO (11)
Playboy Enterprises Inc, Beverly Hills, CA (17)
Player Piano Co Inc, Wichita, KS (11)
Pleasant Company, Middleton, WI (11)
The Plow & Hearth Inc, Madison, VA (8)
Pneuma Books, Elkton, MD (17)
Pocket Nurse Enterprises Inc, Monaca, PA (7)
The Pohly Co, Boston, MA (17)
Poker Player, Sherman Oaks, CA (17)
Polaroid Corp, Minnetonka, MN (16)
Polo Ralph Lauren, Lyndhurst, NJ (2)
Polyair Packaging, Chicago, IL (9)
Polynesian Cultural Center, Honolulu, HI (16)
The Popcorn Factory, Lake Forest, IL (4)
Population Connection, Washington, DC (1)
Porta-Bote International, Mountain View, CA (11)
Porter's Camera Store Inc, Cedar Falls, IA (3)
Portland Cement Association, Skokie, IL (1)
Posh Papers, Riverside, RI (6)
Posty Cards Inc, Kansas City, MO (16)
Potawatomi Bingo Casino, Milwaukee, WI (19)
Potpourri Group Inc, Chelmsford, MA (6)
Power Music, Salt Lake City, UT (16)
Powers Television Marketing, Chatsworth, CA (17)
Prairie Nursery, Westfield, WI (8)
Praises, Prizes & Presents, Grand Rapids, MI (5)
Prakken Publications Inc, Ann Arbor, MI (17)
Precept Press, Chicago, IL (17)
Premera Blue Cross, Spokane, WA (15)
Presque Isle Wine Cellars Inc, North East, PA (4)
Press-Enterprise Co, Riverside, CA (17)
ST Preston & Son Inc, Greenport, NY (8)
Prestwick House Inc, Clayton, DE (17)
Previo/Alteris, Lindon, UT (16)
Priester Pecan Co Inc, Fort Deposit, AL (4)

Priests of the Sacred Heart, Hales Corners, WI (1)
Prime Media Equine Group, Gaithersburg, MD (17)
Princess Cruises (HQ), Santa Clarita, CA (19)
Princess House Inc, Taunton, MA (16)
Princeton Book Co Publishers, Hightstown, NJ (17)
The Princeton Review, Scranton, PA (16)
The Principal Financial Group, Des Moines, IA (15)
Print Products International, Annapolis Junction, MD (9)
Pritchett & Hull Associates Inc, Atlanta, GA (17)
Privacy Journal, Providence, RI (17)
Pro CD Inc, Omaha, NE (17)
PRO Chemical & Dye Inc, Fall River, MA (10)
The Procter & Gamble Co, Cincinnati, OH (16)
Professional Binding Products Inc, Thousand Oaks, CA (16)
Professional Cutlery Direct, North Branford, CT (4)
The Professional Golfers' Association of America, Palm Beach Gardens, FL (1)
Professional Photographer Magazine, Atlanta, GA (17)
The Professional Putters Association, Winston Salem, NC (1)
Profit Potentials Inc, Hull, IA (1)
The Progressive Corp, Mayfield Village, OH (15)
Progressive Energy Corp, San Marcos, CA (5)
Project HOPE, Millwood, VA (1)
Projection Video Services, Springfield, VA (16)
Projector-Recorder Belt Corp, Oceanside, NY (3)
Promotion Marketing Association (PMA) Inc, New York, NY (1)
Prosperity And Profits Unlimited Distribution Services, Denver, CO (1)
Protection One Inc, Lawrence, KS (16)
Protective Life Insurance Co, Birmingham, AL (15)
Prudent Publishing Co, Ridgefield Park, NJ (16)
Publications International Ltd, Lincolnwood, IL (17)
Publishers Clearing House, Port Washington, NY (18)
Puritan's Pride, Ronkonkoma, NY (7)
Putnam Investments, Canton, MA (14)
Putnam Rolling Ladder Co Inc, New York, NY (5)
Putt Putt Fun Centers, Winston-Salem, NC (16)

Q

QC Supply LLC, Schuyler, NE (16)
Quadriga Art Inc, New York, NY (10)
The Quaker Oats Co, Chicago, IL (16)
Quartermaster Uniform & Equipment Co, Cerritos, CA (2)
Quayside Publishing Group/MBI Publishing, Minneapolis, MN (17)
Queen Bee Gardens, Lovell, WY (4)
Queue Inc, Stratford, CT (17)
Quick Draw Clip Systems Inc, Ventura, CA (9)

R

R&S Industries Corp, Chesterfield, MO (16)
RBC Dain Rauscher, Boston, MA (14)
RBC Funds, Milwaukee, WI (14)
RBS Citizens Financial Group Inc, Dedham, MA (14)
REI-Recreational Equipment Inc, Kent, WA (11)
Racer Walsh Co, Jacksonville, FL (12)
RadioShack Corp, Fort Worth, TX (3)
Rainbow Art Glass, Wall, NJ (16)
Rainbow Group LLC, Middleton, WI (11)
Raley's Bel Air Markets, West Sacramento, CA (16)
Ranch House Meat Co, Menard, TX (4)
Random House Children's Books, New York, NY (13)
Random House Direct Marketing, New York, NY (17)
Ranger Joe's International Military Supply, Columbus, GA (2)
Rapid City Journal, Rapid City, SD (18)
Rascal, Sewell, NJ (7)
Raven's Nest Herbals, LLC, Duluth, GA (7)
Raybuck Autobody Parts, Punxsutawney, PA (12)
Raycom Sports, Charlotte, NC (16)
The Reader's Digest Association Inc, New York, NY (17)

Sleepy's Inc, Hicksville, NY (16)
Slocum Water Gardens, Winter Haven, FL (8)
Smart Dog Products, Winchester, TN (11)
The Smile Train, New York, NY (1)
Smith & Hawken Ltd, Novato, CA (8)
Smith & Noble, Corona, CA (8)
Daniel Smith Inc, Seattle, WA (10)
Smithfield Packing Co Inc, Smithfield, VA (16)
Smithsonian Enterprises, New York, NY (17)
The JM Smucker Co, Orrville, OH (4)
Albert S Smyth Co Inc, Timonium, MD (6)
Snap-on Inc, Kenosha, WI (9)
Tom Snyder Productions, Watertown, MA (16)
The Soap Factory, Bedford, MA (7)
SOAR Inflatables, Healdsburg, CA (11)
Social Studies School Service, Culver City, CA (16)
Society for Human Resource Management, Alexandria, VA (1)
Society of American Magicians Inc, Parker, CO (1)
Society of Petroleum Engineers, Richardson, TX (1)
Society of the Divine Savior, New Holstein, WI (1)
Soft Surroundings, Saint Louis, MO (2)
Software Assistance International Ltd (SAIL), Morris Plains, NJ (3)
The Software Labs Inc, Bellevue, WA (3)
Soitenly Stooges, Glendale, CA (6)
Solar Cine Products Inc, Chicago, IL (5)
Solar Components Corp, Manchester, NH (9)
Songbird Hearing Inc, Princeton Junction, NJ (7)
Sotheby's, New York, NY (6)
Soundprints, Norwalk, CT (6)
South Seas Island Resort, Captiva Island, FL (19)
Southeast Toyota Distributors LLC, Deerfield Beach, FL (16)
Southern California Gas Co, Anaheim, CA (1)
Southern Emblem Co, Toast, NC (5)
Southern Flavoring Co Inc, Bedford, VA (16)
Southern Poverty Law Center, Montgomery, AL (1)
Southern Progress Corp, Birmingham, AL (17)
Sovereign Bank New England, Glastonbury, CT (14)
Spa-Finder Inc, New York, NY (7)
Spalding Laboratories Inc, Arroyo Grande, CA (7)
Spates The Florist, Newport, VT (8)
Huck Spaulding Enterprises, Voorheesville, NY (16)
Spear Engineering Co, Colorado Springs, CO (16)
Specialized Information Publishers Association (SIPA), Vienna, VA (1)
Specialty Equipment Market Association, Diamond Bar, CA (1)
Spectrum eCommerce, Mission Viejo, CA (15)
Speed-Mat, Biddeford, ME (16)
Spiegel Brands Inc, New York, NY (2)
Spilsbury Puzzle Co, Chicago, IL (11)
Spinneybeck Enterprises, Getzville, NY (16)
Spokane Teachers Credit Union, Liberty Lake, WA (14)
Spoken Arts, Holmes, NY (17)
The Spokesman-Review, Spokane, WA (17)
Sportif Mail Order Inc, Sparks, NV (2)
Sporting Clays Ltd, Titusville, FL (17)
The Sporting News Publishing Co, Charlotte, NC (17)
The Sportsman's Guide Inc, South Saint Paul, MN (11)
Sportsmith LLC, Tulsa, OK (11)
Sporty's Preferred Living, Batavia, OH (5)
Springer Science & Business Media LLC, New York, NY (17)
Sprint PCS, Overland Park, KS (16)
Squadron Mail Order, Carrollton, TX (16)
Stabenfeldt Inc, Danbury, CT (13)
Stagestep Inc, Philadelphia, PA (5)
Standard Life, Montreal, PQ, Canada (15)
Standard Publishing, Cincinnati, OH (17)
Stanley Home Products, Great Bend, KS (8)
Staples Inc, Framingham, MA (10)
Star Silkscreen Design Inc, Decatur, IL (2)
Star Sprinkler Inc, Lansdale, PA (9)
Star Tribune, Minneapolis, MN (17)
Starbucks Corp, Seattle, WA (4)
Starcrest Products of California Inc, Perris, CA (16)

Stark Brothers Fulfillment Services, Louisiana, MO (8)
Stark Brothers Nurseries & Orchards, Louisiana, MO (8)
Starkey Laboratories, Eden Prairie, MN (16)
Starmount Life Insurance Co, Baton Rouge, LA (15)
Starz Entertainment Group, Englewood, CO (16)
The Stash Tea Catalog, Tigard, OR (4)
State Farm Insurance Cos, Bloomington, IL (15)
State Line Tack Inc, Phoenix, AZ (16)
State Mutual Insurance Co, Rome, GA (15)
State Street Global Advisors, Boston, MA (14)
StatSoft Inc, Tulsa, OK (9)
Steck-Vaughn, Austin, TX (17)
Steelcase Inc, Grand Rapids, MI (16)
Steptoe & Wife Antiques Ltd, Toronto, ON, Canada (8)
Sterling Jewelers Inc, Akron, OH (16)
Sterling Name Tape Inc, Winsted, CT (16)
Steuben Glass, New York, NY (6)
Stew Leonard's, Norwalk, CT (4)
Don Stewart Association, Tulsa, OK (1)
Stewart Enterprises Inc, Jefferson, LA (16)
Stewart-MacDonald, Athens, OH (16)
Martha Stewart Living Omnimedia, New York, NY (17)
Stick-Em Up Inc, Pleasanton, CA (5)
Stickers 'N' Stuff Inc, Louisville, CO (6)
Kirk Stieff Co, Bristol, PA (16)
Stile-Tile Like Metal Roofing, Sellersburg, IN (9)
Stock Yards Packing Co Inc, Chicago, IL (4)
Stokes Seeds Inc, Buffalo, NY (8)
Stonwurks, Eden Prairie, MN (16)
Story Time Stories That Rhyme, Denver, CO (17)
Strang Communications Co, Lake Mary, FL (17)
Stratford Hall, North Mankato, MN (10)
The Stratosphere Las Vegas, Las Vegas, NV (19)
Straw Hat Cooperative Corp, San Ramon, CA (16)
Stress Market, Port Angeles, WA (17)
Strongwell, Bristol, VA (9)
Paul Stuart, New York, NY (2)
Stuller, Inc, Lafayette, LA (2)
Sturbridge Yankee Workshop Inc, Portland, ME (16)
Sturges Sportswear, Battleboro, NC (16)
Suarez Corp Industries, North Canton, OH (5)
Subscription Agency.com Inc, Winter Haven, FL (18)
The Suburban Chamber of Commerce, Summit, NJ (14)
Successful Farming, Des Moines, IA (17)
Sugarbush Farm Inc, Woodstock, VT (4)
Sullivan-Victory Groves, Cocoa, FL (4)
Summit Industries Inc, Marietta, GA (5)
Summit Racing Equipment, Tallmadge, OH (12)
Sun Harvest Citrus, Fort Myers, FL (4)
Sun Hope Nutritional Health, Santa Monica, CA (7)
Sunbeam, Boca Raton, FL (16)
Sunbilt Creative Sunrooms, Jamaica, NY (8)
Sunburst Technology, Elgin, IL (17)
Sundance Catalog Co, Salt Lake City, UT (6)
Sunlife of Canada, Wellesley Hills, MA (15)
Sunnyland Farms Inc, Albany, GA (4)
Sunoco, Inc, Philadelphia, PA (16)
SunPorch Structures Inc, Westport, CT (8)
Sunset Magazine, Menlo Park, CA (17)
Sunshine Discount Crafts, Largo, FL (11)
Sunshine Farm & Gardens, Renick, WV (8)
Sunshine Glassworks Ltd, Buffalo, NY (11)
Sunshine Minting Inc, Coeur D'Alene, ID (14)
Sunshine Unlimited Inc, Lindsborg, KS (9)
Sunstar, Chicago, IL (16)
Suntrust Banks Inc, Atlanta, GA (14)
Super 8 Hotels Worldwide, Parsippany, NJ (19)
The Supplies Guys, Midland Park, NJ (3)
Support Plus, Hudson, OH (7)
Sur La Table, Seattle, WA (8)
Sure-Fire Business Success Catalog, Cambridge, MA (17)
Surplus Center, Lincoln, NE (9)
Sussex Publishers Inc, New York, NY (17)
John Sutherland & Associates, San Diego, CA (15)
Svoboda Collins LLC, Chicago, IL (5)

Jimmy Swaggart Ministries, Baton Rouge, LA (1)
Sweepstakes Clearinghouse, Dallas, TX (16)
The Swiss Colony Inc, Monroe, WI (4)
Sylvan Learning Centers, Baltimore, MD (16)
Symantec, Mountain View, CA (16)
Symetra Financial, Bellevue, WA (15)
Synapse Group Inc, Stamford, CT (18)
Syngenta, Greensboro, NC (16)
System Pavers, Newport Beach, CA (16)
Systemax Inc, Port Washington, NY (16)

T

T Rowe Price Associates Inc, Baltimore, MD (14)
TCJC, New York, NY (2)
TD Bank NA, Falmouth, ME (14)
TIAA-CREF, New York, NY (15)
TL Enterprises Inc, Ventura, CA (17)
TVC Enterprises and the TV Collector Magazine, Las Vegas, NV (6)
Tackle Craft, Ellsworth, WI (11)
Tafford Uniforms, Montgomeryville, PA (2)
Tailwinds Inc, Mill Valley, CA (6)
Talas, Brooklyn, NY (10)
Talbots, Hingham, MA (2)
Tamrac Inc, Chatsworth, CA (2)
Tandy Leather Co, Fort Worth, TX (11)
The Taunton Press, Newtown, CT (17)
Tax Reduction Institute, Germantown, MD (14)
Ann Taylor Inc, New York, NY (2)
Taylor Capital Group, Inc, Rosemont, IL (14)
Taylor Corp, North Mankato, MN (16)
Taylor Gifts Inc, Paoli, PA (8)
Taymark Inc, White Bear Lake, MN (1)
The Teaching Co, Chantilly, VA (17)
Team Cheer, Geneseo, NY (2)
Technology Review, Cambridge, MA (17)
Teleflora, Los Angeles, CA (16)
Telemedia Communications US, North York, ON, Canada (17)
Ten Speed Press, Emeryville, CA (17)
Tender Heart Treasures, Omaha, NE (6)
Terminix International, The Trugreen Companies, Memphis, TN (16)
Tessco Inc, Hunt Valley, MD (16)
Tetley USA Inc, Montvale, NJ (16)
Texas Children's Hospital, Houston, TX (1)
Texas Farm Bureau Insurance Cos, Waco, TX (15)
Texas Monthly, Austin, TX (17)
Texas Parks & Wildlife Dept, Austin, TX (1)
Theatre Development Fund Inc, New York, NY (1)
Thermo Fisher Scientific I, Waltham, MA (9)
Thermo Pro, Duluth, GA (16)
Thetford Corp, Ann Arbor, MI (16)
Thimband, Denver, CO (17)
Things Deco, New York, NY (6)
Things Remembered, Highland Heights, OH (6)
Think Ink, Bothell, WA (10)
Thirteen/WNET, New York, NY (1)
Thomas Computer Corp, Orlando, FL (16)
Stephen Thomas, Toronto, ON, Canada (1)
Thompson & Morgan Inc, Tipp City, OH (8)
Thompson Cigar Co, Tampa, FL (6)
Norm Thompson Outfitters Inc, Hillsboro, OR (2)
THORLO INC, Statesville, NC (16)
Thorndike Press, Waterville, ME (17)
Thousand Trails LP, Chicago, IL (16)
Three Georges and the Nuthouse, Mobile, AL (16)
Threefold, Indianapolis, IN (9)
Thrivent Financial for Lutherans, Appleton, WI (14)
Tidbits Media, Montgomery, AL (17)
Tidewater Workshop, Egg Harbor City, NJ (8)
Tiffany & Co, New York, NY (6)
TigerDirect.ca, Richmond Hill, ON, Canada (3)
Tillamook County Creamery Association, Tillamook, OR (4)
Timber Crest Farms, Healdsburg, CA (16)
Timberland.com, Stratham, NH (16)
Timberline Geodesics, Berkeley, CA (8)
Time Inc, New York, NY (17)

Time Out New York, New York, NY (18)
Time Products International, Del Rio, TX (16)
Time/System, Chicopee, MA (16)
Time Warner Inc, New York, NY (16)
Times Union, Albany, NY (18)
Timm Medical Technologies, Inc, Eden Prairie, MN (16)
Todaro Brothers Mail Order Co, New York, NY (4)
The Tog Shop Inc, Beverly, MA (2)
Together, Dallas, TX (16)
Tomahawk Live Trap Co, Tomahawk, WI (16)
Tools for Wellness, Oak Park, CA (7)
Torah Umesorah Publications, Brooklyn, NY (5)
The Toro Consumer Div, Bloomington, MN (16)
Toter Inc, Statesville, NC (16)
Touch of Class Catalog, Huntingburg, IN (8)
Tova Corp, West Chester, PA (7)
Tower Hobbies/Hobbico, Champaign, IL (11)
Townsend Communications LLC, Kansas City, MO (17)
The Townsend Group, New York, NY (3)
Toyota Motor Sales USA Inc, Torrance, CA (16)
Toys "R" Us, Wayne, NJ (11)
Toys To Grow On, Carson, CA (11)
Tractor Supply Co, Brentwood, TN (5)
Transaction Publishers, Piscataway, NJ (17)
Transamerica Life Insurance Co, Cedar Rapids, IA (15)
Transamerica Occidental Life Co, Los Angeles, CA (15)
TransFirst ePayment Services, Omaha, NE (14)
Transit Treasure Inc, New York, NY (12)
TransitCenter Inc, New York, NY (1)
Travel Industry Association, Washington, DC (1)
Travelclick, Schaumburg, IL (19)
The Travelers Insurance Cos, Hartford, CT (15)
Travelex America Inc, Washington, DC (14)
Treasure Chest, New York, NY (19)
Trend Magazines Inc, Saint Petersburg, FL (17)
Tri-Chem Inc, Belleville, NJ (16)
Tribune Co, Chicago, IL (17)
Trigon Blue Cross/Blue Shield, Roanoke, VA (15)
Triton College, River Grove, IL (16)
Triumph Learning, New York, NY (17)
Trophyland USA Inc, Hialeah, FL (5)
True Value Co, Chicago, IL (16)
TruGreen/ChemLawn, Lewis Center, OH (16)
Trumble Greetings, Boulder, CO (6)
Trump Marina Hotel & Casino, Atlantic City, NJ (19)
Trump Plaza Hotel & Casino, Atlantic City, NJ (19)
The Trumpet Club, New York, NY (17)
truTV, New York, NY (17)
Tucker Electronics Co, Garland, TX (3)
Tupperware, Orlando, FL (16)
Turncraft Clocks Inc, Spring Park, MN (6)
Turner Greenhouses, Goldsboro, NC (8)
Tuttle, Wallingford, CT (2)
20th Century Fox Television, Los Angeles, CA (16)
21st Century Insurance, Woodland Hills, CA (15)
Tyndale House Publishers, Carol Stream, IL (17)

U

U-Bild, Oceanside, CA (8)
U-Haul International, Phoenix, AZ (16)
UBS Wealth Management US, Weehawken, NJ (14)
UCEA, Boston, MA (1)
UGL Equis Corp, Chicago, IL (16)
UJA/Federation of New York, New York, NY (1)
UMI Publications Inc, Charlotte, NC (17)
UNICEF, New York, NY (1)
UNICEF Canada, Toronto, ON, Canada (1)
USAA, San Antonio, TX (15)
USAA Alliance Services Marketing, San Antonio, TX (14)
USI Affinity, Philadelphia, PA (15)
USO Inc, Arlington, VA (1)
USX, Pittsburgh, PA (16)
Ultimate Products Inc, Chula Vista, CA (16)
Ultradent Products Inc, South Jordan, UT (7)

Umass Dartmouth, North Dartmouth, MA (1)
Unadilla Laminated Products, Unadilla, NY (16)
Uncharted Country Publishing, Madison, WI (17)
UndercoverWear Inc, Tewksbury, MA (2)
Undergear.com, La Crosse, WI (2)
Unicom Electric Inc, Walnut, CA (16)
Unicover Corp, Cheyenne, WY (6)
UniFirst Corp, Owensboro, KY (2)
Uniformed Services Benefit Association, Overland Park, KS (15)
Unilever Best Foods, Englewood Cliffs, NJ (16)
Union Federal Savings Bank, North Providence, RI (14)
The Union Labor Life Insurance Co, Silver Spring, MD (15)
Union Privilege, AFL-CIO, Washington, DC (1)
United Air Specialists Inc, Cincinnati, OH (16)
United Business Media, Manhasset, NY (17)
United Church Homes, Marion, OH (1)
United Community Bank, Blairsville, GA (14)
United Farm Workers of America, AFL-CIO, Keene, CA (1)
United Investors Life Insurance Co, Birmingham, AL (15)
United Jewish Communities, New York, NY (1)
The United Methodist Publishing House, Nashville, TN (17)
United Nations Federal Credit Union, Long Island City, NY (1)
United Retail Inc, Rochelle Park, NJ (2)
United Security Products Inc, Poway, CA (16)
United Spinal Association, East Elmhurst, NY (1)
United Staffing Systems, New York, NY (16)
US Bancorp, Minneapolis, MN (14)
US Bank, Minneapolis, MN (14)
US BRANDING GROUP, LLC, Lake Worth, FL (16)
United States Bronze Sign Co Inc, New Hyde Park, NY (1)
US Cavalry, Radcliff, KY (6)
US Department of Commerce, Washington, DC (1)
US Digital Transactions Corporation, New York, NY (14)
US Fund for UNICEF, New York, NY (6)
US Games Systems Inc, Stamford, CT (11)
US Historical Society, Richmond, VA (16)
US News & World Report, New York, NY (17)
US Tax Shield, Encino, CA (14)
United Systems c/o Biomed, Concord, CA (7)
United Way of Greater Toronto, Toronto, ON, Canada (1)
Unitrin, Chicago, IL (15)
Unitron Ltd, Commack, NY (9)
Unity School of Christianity, Unity Village, MO (17)
Universal Communication Enterprise, Elizabeth, NJ (13)
Universal Hovercraft, Cordova, IL (11)
Universal Security Instruments Inc, Owings Mills, MD (16)
Universal Vintage Tire Co, Hershey, PA (11)
University at Buffalo Center for Entrepreneurial Leadership, Buffalo, NY (5)
University of Akron, Akron, OH (1)
University of Alabama, Tuscaloosa, AL (13)
University of California Irvine Extension, Irvine, CA (1)
University of Chicago GSB, Chicago, IL (1)
University of Chicago Press, Chicago, IL (17)
University of Illinois Foundation, Urbana, IL (1)
University of Minnesota, Saint Paul, MN (1)
University of Minnesota Alumni Association, Minneapolis, MN (1)
University of Oklahoma Press, Norman, OK (17)
University of Pennsylvania, Philadelphia, PA (1)
University of Southern Mississippi, Hattiesburg, MS (1)
University of Texas School of Law, Austin, TX (1)
University of Wisconsin-Madison School of Business Executive Education, Madison, WI (1)
University Press of America Inc, Lanham, MD (17)
University Subscription Service, Downers Grove, IL (18)

Uniway Management Corp, Forest Park, GA (16)
Unum Corp, Portland, ME (15)
Upbeat Inc, Saint Louis, MO (9)
Upstart, Madison, WI (16)
Urban Response LLC, Hartville, OH (17)
Urbani Truffles USA Corp, New York, NY (4)
Utilities Supply Corp, Woburn, MA (16)
Utretch Art Supplies, Cranbury, NJ (10)
Uwharrie Capital Corp, Albemarle, NC (14)

V

VGH Solutions, Markham, ON, Canada (7)
VW Credit, Herndon, VA (14)
Vail Associates Inc, Broomfield, CO (19)
Vail Resorts Inc, Keystone, CO (19)
Valentine Research Inc, Cincinnati, OH (16)
Value Line Publishing Inc, New York, NY (17)
Van Bourgondien Bros, Virginia Beach, VA (8)
Van Dam Inc, New York, NY (17)
Vance Industries Inc, Niles, IL (16)
Vanderbilt Advertising, New York, NY (14)
Vanguard, Valley Forge, PA (14)
The Vantage Group Inc, Boston, MA (14)
Vcom International Multi-Media Corp, South Hackensack, NJ (3)
Vector Marketing Corp, Olean, NY (5)
Vegetarian Awareness Network/VEGANET, Washington, DC (1)
Vehicle Assurance, Saint Charles, MO (5)
Vemma Nutrition Co, Scottsdale, AZ (7)
Venator Group, New York, NY (2)
Venture Entertainment Group, Sherman Oaks, CA (3)
Venus Fashion, Inc, Jacksonville, FL (2)
Veridian Credit Union, Waterloo, IA (1)
Verizon, Arlington, VA (16)
Verizon Communications Inc, New York, NY (3)
Vermont Ski Areas Association, Montpelier, VT (1)
Vermont Teddy Bear Co, Shelburne, VT (6)
Vermont Tubbs, Whitefield, NH (8)
Vertrue Inc, Norwalk, CT (13)
Vesey's Seeds Ltd, Charlottetown, PE, Canada (8)
The Vestal Press Ltd, Lanham, MD (17)
Vet Vax, Tonganoxie, KS (11)
Veterans of Foreign Wars (VFW) of the US-National Headquarters, Kansas City, MO (1)
Viacom Inc, New York, NY (16)
Viahealth, Rochester, NY (16)
Victor Machinery Exchange, Brooklyn, NY (9)
Victoria's Secret Catalogue, Columbus, OH (2)
Victory Corps, New Hope, MN (5)
Video Artists International, Pleasantville, NY (3)
Vietnam Veterans of America, Silver Spring, MD (1)
VIEW Video Inc/Arcadia Entertainment Corp, Saugerties, NY (16)
Village Coin Shop, Plaistow, NH (6)
Village Interiors Carpet One, Newton, NC (8)
Village Software Inc, Boston, MA (3)
Vintage Wood Works, Quinlan, TX (8)
Virco Manufacturing Corp, Conway, AR (16)
The Virginia Diner Inc, Wakefield, VA (4)
Virginia Home For Boys, Richmond, VA (1)
Visa USA, Foster City, CA (14)
Vita-Mix Corp, Cleveland, OH (16)
Vitamin Power Inc, Hauppauge, NY (7)
Vitamin Research Products, Carson City, NV (7)
Vitamin Specialties Co, Freehold, NJ (7)
Vitasoy USA Inc, Ayer, MA (16)
Vivendi, New York, NY (16)
Vivitar Corp, Tempe, AZ (16)
Volkswagen Group of America Inc, Auburn Hills, MI (16)
Volunteers of America, Alexandria, VA (1)
Volvo Cars of North America, Northvale, NJ (16)
Voyageur Inc, Easley, SC (11)
Ed Voyles Hyundai Inc, Smyrna, GA (16)
Vulcan Information Packaging, Vincent, AL (16)

W

WFF'N PROOF Learning Games Associates, Fairfield, IA (17)
WGBH Educational Foundation, Brighton, MA (1)
WRS Group Ltd, Waco, TX (7)
WTS Media, Chattanooga, TN (16)
Wachovia Center, Philadelphia, PA (16)
Wag/Aero Group, Lyons, WI (16)
Wake Forest University Baptist Medical Center, Winston Salem, NC (1)
Wakefield Peanut Co, Wakefield, VA (4)
Wal Mart Stores, Bentonville, AR (16)
Walch Publishing, Portland, ME (17)
Walk Thru The Bible Ministries Inc, Atlanta, GA (1)
Walker Publishing Co Inc, New York, NY (17)
Wm. K. Walthers Inc, Milwaukee, WI (11)
Warnaco, New York, NY (2)
Warnaco Swimwear Inc, Los Angeles, CA (16)
Warner Books, New York, NY (17)
Warner Bros, Burbank, CA (3)
Warner Press, Anderson, IN (17)
Washington Marketing Group, Arlington, VA (1)
The Washington Monthly Co, Washington, DC (17)
Washington National Opera, Washington, DC (16)
The Washington Post, Washington, DC (17)
Washington Post Digital, Washington, DC (17)
Washington University, Saint Louis, MO (1)
The Washingtonian, Washington, DC (17)
Andrew D Washton Books On the Fine Arts, Port Chester, NY (16)
Wasserman Uniform Co, Fort Lauderdale, FL (2)
Watering Inc/Hemmings Motor News, Bennington, VT (17)
Water's Edge Resort & Spa, Westbrook, CT (19)
Wathne Ltd, New York, NY (2)
Watts Radiant, Springfield, MO (9)
We-No-Nah Canoe Inc, Winona, MN (11)
WearGuard Corp, Norwell, MA (2)
Webster Bank, Waterbury, CT (14)
The Wedding Pages, New York, NY (16)
Weichert Co, Morris Plains, NJ (14)
Weider Publications Inc, Woodland Hills, CA (17)
Weight Watchers International, New York, NY (16)
Richard Weiner Consultant, North Miami Beach, FL (14)
Weiss Research Inc, Jupiter, FL (17)
Welch Allyn, Inc, Skaneateles Falls, NY (9)
Welcomemat Services Inc, Atlanta, GA (9)
Wellmark Blue Cross & Blue Shield of Iowa, Des Moines, IA (15)
Wells Fargo, San Francisco, CA (14)
Wenner Media LLC, New York, NY (17)
WESCO, Pittsburgh, PA (16)
West Bend, West Bend, WI (16)
West Marine Inc, Watsonville, CA (11)
Western Pennsylvania Conservancy, Pittsburgh, PA (1)
Western Psychological Services, Torrance, CA (16)
Western River Expeditions, Salt Lake City, UT (19)
Western-Southern Life, Cincinnati, OH (15)
Westhoff Machine Co, Saint Louis, MO (9)
Weston Distance Learning, Fort Collins, CO (13)
Westwood Publishing Co, Glendale, CA (17)
The Wexner Companies Inc, Memphis, TN (2)
What on Earth, Hudson, OH (5)
Whirlpool Corp, Benton Harbor, MI (16)
White Cap Wholesale Contractors Supplies, Costa Mesa, CA (16)
White Flower Farm, Torrington, CT (8)
White Mane Publishing Co Inc, Shippensburg, PA (17)
Whitehorse Gear, Center Conway, NH (11)
Whiting & Davis, Attleboro Falls, MA (16)
Whitman Publishing LLC, Atlanta, GA (16)
Wholesale Tool Co, Warren, MI (9)
Michael Wiese Productions, Studio City, CA (17)
The Wig Co, Pittsburgh, PA (2)
Wikco Industries Inc, Casa Grande, AZ (5)
WILD Flavors Inc, Erlanger, KY (4)
Gilbert H Wild & Son Inc, Reeds, MO (8)
Wildlife Education Ltd, Park Hills, KY (17)

Wildseed Farms, Fredericksburg, TX (8)
John Wiley & Sons Inc, Hoboken, NJ (17)
Williams-Sonoma Inc, San Francisco, CA (8)
Williamsburg Blacksmiths Inc, Williamsburg, MA (8)
Willis Music Co, Florence, KY (17)
Wilsons Leather, Brooklyn Park, MN (2)
Wilton Armetale, Mount Joy, PA (16)
Wilton Industries Inc, Woodridge, IL (16)
Wimmer's Meat Products Inc, West Point, NE (4)
Win Craft Inc, Winona, MN (5)
Wind in the Rigging, Port Washington, WI (11)
Windsor Vineyards, Santa Rosa, CA (16)
Windstar Cruises, Seattle, WA (19)
Wine Enthusiast Cos, Mount Kisco, NY (4)
Winetasting.com, Napa, CA (4)
Winmill & Co, New York, NY (14)
Winning Solutions Inc, Fort Worth, TX (7)
Winnipeg Art Gallery, Winnipeg, MB, Canada (1)
Winslow Publishing, Toronto, ON, Canada (17)
Harry Winston Inc, New York, NY (16)
Winston Marketing Group, Elk Grove Village, IL (8)
WinterSilks LLC, Warren, PA (2)
Wire Works, Chester, PA (9)
Wireless Idea, San Juan, PR (5)
The Wisconsin Cheeseman, Sun Prairie, WI (4)
Wolfe Publishing Co Inc, Prescott, AZ (17)
Woman's Missionary Union, Birmingham, AL (17)
Womanship, Annapolis, MD (16)
Woman's Day Special Interest Publications, New York, NY (17)
Wood Carvers Supply Inc, Englewood, FL (9)
Woodall Publishing Co LP, Ventura, CA (17)
Woodcraft Supply Corp LLC, Parkersburg, WV (9)
Woodcrafters Lumber Sales Inc, Portland, OR (9)
Sylvia Woods Harp Center, Montrose, CA (11)
Woodwind & Brasswind Inc, Indianapolis, IN (5)
Woodworker's Supply Inc, Casper, WY (11)
Woolrich Inc, Woolrich, PA (2)
Working Assets, San Francisco, CA (16)
The World Bank, Washington, DC (17)
World Book Inc, Chicago, IL (17)
World Future Society, Bethesda, MD (1)
World Kitchen Inc, Corning, NY (16)
World Press Review, New York, NY (18)
World Publications Inc, Winter Park, FL (17)
World Villages for Children, Annapolis, MD (1)
World Vision Inc, Federal Way, WA (1)
World Wrestling Entertainment, Stamford, CT (16)
Wrisco Industries Inc, Palm Beach Gardens, FL (8)
Writer's Digest Books, Blue Ash, OH (17)
Wyandotte West Communications Inc, Kansas City, KS (17)
Wycliffe Bible Translators, Dallas, TX (17)
Wyndham Hotel Group, Parsippany, NJ (19)
Wysong Corp, Midland, MI (7)

X

Xcel Energy, Minneapolis, MN (5)
Xerox Corp, Rochester, NY (16)

Y

YWCA of the USA, Washington, DC (1)
Yankee Publishing Inc, Dublin, NH (17)
Year One Inc, Braselton, GA (16)
Yellow Pages Association, Berkeley Heights, NJ (1)
Yenkin-Majestic, Columbus, OH (17)
Young America's Foundation, Herndon, VA (1)
Young Pecan Co, Florence, SC (4)
Your Man Tours, El Segundo, CA (19)
Your Move Chess & Games, North Massapequa, NY (11)
David Yurman, New York, NY (5)
Yves Rocher North America Inc, Longueuil, PQ, Canada (7)

Z

Zale Corp, Irving, TX (6)
Ziff Davis Media Inc, New York, NY (17)
Zig Ziglar Corp, Plano, TX (16)
Zimmerman Irrigation Inc, Biglerville, PA (16)
Zimmerman-McDonald Machinery Inc, Saint Louis, MO (16)
Zoological Society of San Diego, San Diego, CA (1)
Zotos International, Darien, CT (16)
Zurich, Schaumburg, IL (15)

Consultants, Recruiters, Collection & Finance (20) — Geographic Index

Alabama

FotoBed.com, 4630 Old Looney Mill Rd., Birmingham, 35243-2607

Arizona

Billin Medina-Warren, 8655 E Via de Ventura (#G200), Scottsdale, 85258-3300

CDMC/Carefree Direct Marketing Corp, PO Box 3737, 8001 E Serene St, Carefree, 85377-3737

Robert DeLay, 4121 E Via del Cuculin, Tucson, 85718-3320

Direct Marketing Insights Inc, 15970 W Edgemont Ave, Goodyear, 85395-8112

Kennedy Inner Circle, 15433 N Tatum Blvd Ste 104, Phoenix, 85032-4231

Smith-Browning Direct Inc, 45 Camielle Ct, Sedona, 86336-5977

Andrew Yoelin & Co, 5524 E Waltann Ln, Scottsdale, 85254-1701

California

ADM Marketing, 908 N Hollywood Way, Burbank, 91505-2815

Access Business Communications Inc, 5611 Ocean Terrace Dr, Huntington Beach, 92648-7511

Allen, Matkins, Leck, Gamble & Mallory, 515 S Figueroa St (9th fl), Los Angeles, 90071-3398

Anderson/skow, 690 Texas St, San Francisco, 94107-2941

Diana Baty, 109 Sullivan Dr, Moraga, 94556-1211

Blatteis Communications, 2335 W Hedding St, San Jose, 95128-1327

Bloom, Hergott, Diemer, Rosenthal and Laviolette LLP, 150 S Rodeo Dr (fl 3), Beverly Hills, 90212-2410

Bristol Associates Inc, 5777 W Century Blvd (Suite 865), Los Angeles, 90045-5696

Brown, Van Remmen, Kanuit, Inc, 840 Apollo St Ste 300, El Segundo, 90245-4763

Browning, Jacobson & Klein LLP, 9595 Wilshire Blvd Ste 601, Beverly Hills, 90212-2506

Coleman Frost LLP, 429 Santa Monica Blvd Ste 700, Santa Monica, 90401-3435

The Copy Works, 12668 Camino Emparrado, San Diego, 92128-1404

Decker Communications Inc, 575 Market St (Suite 1925), San Francisco, 94105

Patricia Dowd Inc, 5300 San Jacinto Ave, Atascadero, 93422-2940

Employers Group, 400 Continental Blvd Ste 300, El Segundo, 90245-5080

Equity Management Inc, 4365 Executive Dr Ste 1000, San Diego, 92121-2192

Gartner Inc, 1650 Technology Dr Ste 500, San Jose, 95110-3838

Robert Half International Inc, 2884 Sand Hill Rd (Suite 200), Menlo Park, 94025

Harvest Communications, 2400 Washington Ave Ste 411, Redding, 96001-2827

HDI Group, 1 Embarcadero Ctr (Suite 500), San Francisco, 94111-3610

IJHANA, 409 W Olympic (Suite 706), Los Angeles, 90015-1635

Jasek Enterprises, 1000 Deep Wood Dr, Westlake Village, 91362-4215

JK Associates LLC, 445 Sherman Ave (Suite W), Palo Alto, 94306-1828

Joffrey Long Consultants, 17045 Chatsworth St, Granada Hills, 91344-5845

Ladd Associates Inc, 2527 Fillmore St, San Francisco, 94115

LN Marketing Associates, 25 Seki Ct, Emerald Hills, 94062-3401

Martineau & Associates, 1770 Oakdell Dr, Menlo Park, 94025

McKee Consulting LLC, 1404 W Country Club Ln, Escondido, 92026-1660

MVI Marketing Ltd, 5640 Linne Rd, Paso Robles, 93446-8443

Paul Nelson Direct Marketing, 2411 Sixth St, Santa Monica, 90405

New American Dimensions, 6955 La Tijera Blvd (Suite B), Los Angeles, 90045-1932

James Robert Parish Consulting, 4338 Gentry Ave (Suite 1), Studio City, 91604-1764

Pillsbury Winthrop Shaw Pittman LLP, 725 S Figueroa St (Suite 2800), Los Angeles, 90017-5406

Proven Prospects Inc, 1073 Monterey Blvd, Hermosa Beach, 90254-3746

Public Issues Management, 902 Rose Ave, Piedmont, 94611-4343

Publication Fulfillment Svcs, 10564 Progress Way (Suite D), Cypress, 90630-4712

Neil Ransick Marketing, 212 Teresita Blvd, San Francisco, 94127-1729

Research Boston Corp, 1160 Brown Ave, Lafayette, 94549-3102

Response ADvantage, 8635 Falmouth (#301), Playa Del Rey, 90293-8281

Responsys, 900 Cherry Ave (fl 5), San Bruno, 94066-3081

Rhino Marketing Inc, 515 S Flower St (Fl 36, Los Angeles, 90071-2221

Russ, August, & Kabat, 12424 Wilshire Blvd (Suite 1200), Los Angeles, 90025

Savitz, 5757 W Century Blvd (Suite 360), Los Angeles, 90045

Schus & Co, 1458 Royal Blvd, Glendale, 91201

Sharf Woodward & Associates Inc, 5900 Sepulveda Blvd (Suite 104), Sherman Oaks, 91411

Southwest Consultants, 17045 Chatsworth St, Granada Hills, 91344-5845

Transamerican Mailing, 355 State Pl, Escondido, 92029-1359

Unisfair, 149 Commonwealth Dr, Menlo Park, 94025-1133

Whitewing Labs, 17939 Chatsworth St (#408), Granada Hills, 91344

Zoe Marketing, 5132 Meadows del Mar, San Diego, 92130-4854

Colorado

About Books Inc, 1001 Taurus Dr, Colorado Springs, 80906-1133

The Contrino Group, 2770 Arapahoe Rd Ste 132, Lafayette, 80026-8016

Jungle Consulting, 13795 Tewkesbury Ct, Colorado Springs, 80908

Legrand Hart, 1625 Broadway (Suite 200), Denver, 80202

Qwest, 1801 California St, Denver, 80202-5555

Connecticut

The Aldrich Group, 43 Sherman Hill Rd D-104, Woodbury, 06798

Alexander & Co LLC, 178 Water St, Stonington, 06378

Blum & Co LLC, 81 Clinton St, Fairfield, 06824-6908

Bowman Circulation Marketing, 56 Ritch Ave W (fl 2), Greenwich, 06830-6918

Reggie Brady Marketing Solutions LLC, 198 Scribner Ave, Norwalk, 06854-1324

Ciarlo Consulting LLC, 39 Gary Ave, Waterbury, 06704-2034

Circulation Specialists Inc, 3 Enterprise Dr (Suite 408), Shelton, 06484-4694

Communication Managers, LLC, 604 Federal Rd, Brookfield, 06804-2070

John Condon & Associates, 38 Angus Ln, Greenwich, 06831-4402

Connecticut Marketing Associates, 12 Godfrey Pl (Suite 3), Wilton, 06897

Corry Direct Marketing LLC, 109 Limekiln Rd, Ridgefield, 06877-3418

Direct Advantage Partners, 69 Bluff Ave (Suite 100), Rowayton, 06853-1802

Direct Dynamics LLC, 85 Emanuel Church Rd, Killingworth, 06419

The Edbraham Group, PO Box 753, Westbrook, 06498-0753

JS Eliezer Associates Inc, 300 Atlantic St (fl 7), Stamford, 06901-3522

Growth Platforms Institute, 68 St Johns (Suite 200), Wilton, 06897

Imagination Works, 24 Primrose Dr, Trumbull, 06611-5043

Victoria James Executive Search Inc, 11 Stonefence Ln, South Kent, 06785-1307

Lev & Berlin, 200 Connecticut Ave Ste 10, Norwalk, 06854-1907

Madison Executive Search, 54 Danbury Rd (Suite 368), Ridgefield, 06877

Mangieri/Hull Solutions LLC, One Riverside Rd, Sandy Hook, 06482

The Marketing Alliance, 127 Field Point Dr, Fairfield, 06824-6374

Marvel Associates, 199 Sound Beach Ave, Box 504, Old Greenwich, 06870-1711

Mission: A Consulting Group, 36 Cross Hwy, Westport, 06880-2141

Platinum Press, 37 Route 80, Killingworth, 06419-1429

Polestar Group, 20 N Canton Rd, West Simsbury, 06092

The Rusin Group, LLC, 30 Hollow Tree Pl, Wilton, 06897

Smith Hanley Associates, 107 John St Ste 201, Southport, 06890-1466

Frederick Wershaw Management Co, 111 Black Rock Rd, Stamford, 06903-1430

Windsor House, Two Industrial Rd, Windsor Locks, 06096

Delaware

Epic Research LLC, 300 Centennial Cir, Greenville, 19807-2130

The Jackson Consulting Group Ltd, PO Box 246, Middletown, 19709

Mail Management Enterprises, 5616 Galestown Reliance Rd, Seaford, 19973-6044

Modern Mail, 100 Pencader Dr, Newark, 19702-3321

Morris James Hitchens & Williams, 500 Delaware Ave (Suite 1500), PO Box 2306, Wilmington, 19801-1494

District of Columbia

Baker & Hostetler LLP, 1050 Connecticut Ave NW (Suite 1100), Washington, 20036-5304

Center For Information Policy Leadership, 2200 Pennsylania Ave NW, Hunton & Williams, LLP, Washington, 20037-1701

Mary Culnan, 37th & O Sts NW, Washington, 20057

National Economic Research Associates Inc, 1255 23rd St NW (Suite 600), Washington, 20037

Venable LLP Conference Center, 575 7th St NW, Washington, 20004-1607

VMF Inc, 3313 Ross Pl NW, Washington, 20008

Florida

AVD Marketing, 4113 Trenton Ave, Hollywood, 33026-4923

Ability Commerce, 1300 NW 17th Ave Ste 200, Delray Beach, 33445-2560

Allpro Direct Marketing, 11626 Prosperous Dr, Odessa, 33556

JoAnna Brandi & Co Inc, 7491 N Federal Hwy C-5 (#304), Boca Raton, 33487

The Catalog Consultancy, 3285 West Brookfield Way, Vero Beach, 32966-3164

Thomas Dawson, 40 Casa Bella Cir, Palm Coast, 32137-1223

Direct Mail Systems, 12450 Automobile Blvd, Clearwater, 33762

Executive Connections LLC, 8466 Lockwood Ridge Rd (#330), Sarasota, 34243-2951

Jonathan Friedman, 3720 N 37th Ter, Hollywood, 33021

Ideas in SEO, 758 NE 90 St (Unit 514), Miami, 33138

IZEA, 150 N Orange Ave (Suite 412), Orlando, 32801-2317

JZ Marketing, 4532 Varsity Cir, Lehigh Acres, 33971

Kforce Inc, 1001 E Palm Ave, Tampa, 33605-3551

Leads-Plus Inc, PO Box 400, Killarney, 34740-0400

Life Works Inc, 2817 Evans St, Hollywood, 33020-1119

Mr Fantastic LLC, 55739 Holiday Cr, Astor, 32102-7991

MRI Norwalk, 2334 S Cypress Bend Dr (Suite 11), Pompano Beach, 33069-4488

Muldoon & Baer Inc, 130 Banyan Isle Rd, Palm Beach Gardens, 33416-4601

Open Systems Services, 330 SW 27 Ave (Suite 402), Miami, 33135

Postal En Espanol Inc, 8325 W Hillsborough Ave, Tampa, 33615-3805

Protocol Services Acquisitions Corp, 2805 Fruitville Rd, Sarasota, 34237-5318

The Schmidt Group International Inc, 298 Peppertree Dr S, Vero Beach, 32963

Seklemian Newell Inc (CRMC), 1521 Alton Rd (Suite 138), Miami Beach, 33139-3301

Snyder Glenn J & Assocs, 49 Quail Ln, Jacksonville Beach, 32250

UCI/Dream Giveaways, 19321-C US Hwy 19 N (Suite 605), Clearwater, 33764

West Companies Inc, 7155 Savoy Ct, Seminole, 33776-4329

Georgia

Equifax Credit Information Services Inc, 1550 Peachtree NW, Atlanta, 30309

A.S. Kleeman & Associates, 1416 Spyglass Hill Dr, Duluth, 30097-5948

Morris & Fellows, 6105 Blue Stone Rd NE (Suite A), Atlanta, 30328-3885

Plexus Marketing Group Inc, PO Box 76380, Bldg G, Atlanta, 30358-1380

Kurt Salmon Associates Inc, 1355 Peachtree St NE (Suite 900), Atlanta, 30309-3266

Hawaii

Pohaku Inc, PO Box 1121, Kailua, 96734-1121

Illinois

A Plus Marketing Ltd, 1300 Barclay Blvd, Buffalo Grove, 60089-4500

Actuarial Enterprises Ltd, 920 N Franklin (Suite 401), Chicago, 60610-3186

Applications Development Corp, 169 Buena Vista Dr, Dekalb, 60115-1069

BennettBaker Ltd, 33 W Monroe St (Suite 2110), Chicago, 60603-5414

Brothers & Thompson PC, 180 N Stetson Ave Ste 4425, Chicago, 60601-6733

Burtch Works LLC, 1603 Orrington Ave (Suite 1740), Evanston, 60201-5017

Catalog Marketing Group, 500 Davis St (Suite 812), Evanston, 60201-4668

CORS, 1 Pierce Pl (Suite 295), Itasca, 60143-1253

DM Info, 308 Royce Woods Ct, Naperville, 60565

Duggan & Brown Inc, 215 S Northwest Hwy Ste 202B, Barrington, 60010-8301

Equity Residential Properties, Two N Riverside Plaza (Suite 400), Chicago, 60606-2624

FunME Events, PO Box 463, Dekalb, 60115-0463

GasPedal, 333 W North Ave (Suite 500), Chicago, 60610-1293

Glazer-Kennedy Insider Circle, 8430 W Bryn Mawr Ave Ste 575, Chicago, 60631-3497

HealthInfo Direct, 1528 Sandburg Dr, Schaumburg, 60173-2183

High Note Media Inc, 5315 N Clark (#218), Chicago, 60640-2290

IMV, 1400 E Touhy Ave (Suite 250), Des Plaines, 60018-3339

Jacobsohn Consulting Associates, PO Box 236, Highland Park, 60035-0236

Kannon Consulting Inc, 39 S LaSalle St (Suite 1013), Chicago, 60603-1727

KesTry, 209 E Lake Shore Dr (#6E), Chicago, 60611-1307

Kobs Strategic Consulting, 222 N Columbus Dr (#2202), Chicago, 60601-7819

Herbert Krug & Associates Inc, 500 Davis St Ste 812, Evanston, 60201-4655

Learning Resources Institute, 2235 Durand Dr, Downers Grove, 60515

Steve Lytle, 425 W Randolph St, Chicago, 60606-1530

Marketing Highway, 1416 Gordon Ter, Deerfield, 60015-4739

Marnell Database Marketing, 119 W Chestnut St (Suite 3E), Chicago, 60610-3288

MCDM Strategic Direct Marketing, 12864 Bradford Ln, Plainfield, 60585-2244

Northern Illinois Consulting Inc, PO Box 7157, Libertyville, 60048-7157

O'Keefe Henry Direct Inc, 707 Lake Cook Rd (Suite 285), Deerfield, 60015-4933

James R Perdiew & Co, 1250 S Grove Ave Ste 302, Barrington, 60010-5066

S Pernick & Associates, 1616 Sheridan Rd (Unit 2H), Wilmette, 60091-1884

Peter N Carey & Associates Inc, 1010 Jorie Blvd (Suite 400), Oak Brook, 60523-2239

PCG, Inc, 1S935 Tanglewood Dr (#121), Batavia, 60510-9511

Productive Strategies Inc, 2 Northfield Plaza (Suite 365), Northfield, 60093-1272

Quigley Consulting Group, 1775 W Broadland Ln, Lake Forest, 60045-4817

Ridenour & Associates, 1555 N Sandburg Ter (Suite 602), Chicago, 60610-6324

Shapes Marketing Inc, 2086 Saint Johns Ave (Apt 207), Highland Park, 60035-2461

Silliker Inc, 111 E Wacker Dr Ste 2300, Chicago, 60601-4214

SourceLink, 500 Park Blvd (Suite 415), Itasca, 60143-1260

SpencerStuart, 353 N Clark (Suite 2400), Chicago, 60654-3479

Tesar Reynes Inc, 333 N Michigan Ave (Suite 2226), Chicago, 60601-4035

Training Consultants Inc, 1415 Sheridan Rd, Highland Park, 60035

WTB Associates Inc, 4020 Bunker Ln, Wilmette, 60091

ZS Associates, 1800 Sherman Ave, Evanston, 60201

Indiana

ACCENT Marketing Services LLC, 400 Missouri Ave (Suite 107), Jeffersonville, 47130-3086

ChaCha Mobile Answers, 14550 Clay Terrace Blvd (Suite 130), Carmel, 46032-3653

Rescott LLC Marketing & Technology, 5856 Poole Pl (Suite 263), Noblesville, 46062-7608

Brent Slinkard Consultant, 1048 W 17th St, Bloomington, 47404-3338

Iowa

Brokers International Ltd, 1200 E Main St, Panora, 50216-1100

Gazette Direct Marketing Co, 500 Third Ave SE, Cedar Rapids, 52401-1945

The Stelter Co, 10435 New York Ave, Des Moines, 50322-3774

TitanTV Media, 818 Dows Rd SE, Cedar Rapids, 52403-7000

Kansas

Rich Becker & Associates/Pump-Em-Up Publishing, In Public Relations, 9225 Woodstone Ln, Lenexa, 66219-1959

J Schmid & Associates Inc, 5800 Foxridge Dr (Suite 200), Mission, 66202-2333

StrategicOne, 6700 Antioch Rd Ste 110, Overland Park, 66204-1200

WDS Marketing & Public Relations, 8232 Hadley St, Overland Park, 66204-3542

Kentucky

DS & A Consulting, 1037 Corinthian Ct, Lexington, 40509-2508

PackStream LLC, 2400 Dundee Rd, Louisville, 40205-2047

Maryland

American Marketing & Communication Corp, 14201 Pennsylvania Ave, Hagerstown, 21742-1665

Amtower & Co Federal Direct, PO Box 314, Highland, 20777-0314

Arlen Communications Inc, 7315 Wisconsin Ave (Suite 705E), Bethesda, 20814

Creative Synergy Inc, 13660 Spinning Wheel Dr, Germantown, 20874-2819

Daly Communications, 5630 Wisconsin Ave (#903), Chevy Chase, 20815-4456

Iris Marketing, 1303 Harling Ct, Bel Air, 21015-5029

PMG, 7160 Columbia Gateway Dr Ste 300, Columbia, 21046-2134

ProjectSense, 602 Whispering Wind Ct, Gaithersburg, 20877-3418

Roland Advisors, 4 Norwood Rd, Annapolis, 21401-1227

Webb Mason, 10830 Gilroy Rd, Hunt Valley, 21031-4312

Massachusetts

Accenture, 800 Boylston St (#2300), Boston, 02199

Atlantic-ACM, One Beacon St (34th fl), Boston, 02108

Bernheimer Associates, 10 Laurel Ave, Wellesley, 02481-7534

Circinus International LLC, 283 Franklin St (Suite 400), Boston, 02110-3100

ClickSquared, 280 Summer St (Suite 600), Boston, 02210-1131

CopyDirect, 39 Forge Dr, Plymouth, 02360-2508

Cramer, 425 University Ave, Norwood, 02062-2636

MJ Curran & Associates Inc, 1 Birchwood Ln, Sandwich, 02563

DBMCatalyst, 377 Lincoln St., Lexington, 02421-7446

The Devereux Group, 47 Locust St, Little Harbour, Marblehead, 01945-2935

Directives/Targeted Marketing and Communications, 1022 Avalon Way, Plymouth, 02360-7777

Executive Search International, 1525 Centre St, Newton, 02461-1200

The Forum Corp, 265 Franklin St Ste 400, Boston, 02110-3182

Gilchrist & Partners, 542 Mass Ave, Boston, 02118-1439

iKnowtion LLC, 25 Burlington Mall Rd (Suite 409), Burlington, 01803-4156

Kochevar Research Associates, PO Box 290010, Charlestown, 02129-0201

Kowal & Associates Inc, 620 Massachusetts Ave, Cambridge, 02139-3376

Arthur D Little Inc, 1 Federal St (fl 28), Boston, 02110-2011

LoyaltyOne, 3 Bessom St (Suite 211), Marblehead, 01945-2372

Market Recognition, 112 Prescott Rd, Boxborough, 01719-1121

Monster Worldwide, 5 Clock Tower Pl (Suite 500), Maynard, 01754-2578

Percipio Media, LLC, 201 Broadway Ste 7, Cambridge, 02139-1955

Productivity Development Group Inc, PO Box 488, Westford, 01886

The Results Group, 65 E India Row (Suite 37F), Harbor Towers, Boston, 02110-3323

Bruce Rhodes, 83 Victoria Rd, Sudbury, 01776-3139

Alan Rosenspan & Associates, 34 Summit Ave, Sharon, 02067-2149

Statistical Innovations Inc, 375 Concord Ave, Belmont, 02478-3084

Systems Analytics Inc, 946 Great Plain Ave (#125), Needham, 02492-3030

Teres Consulting Inc, Nine Magnolia St, Framingham, 01701-4913

The Yankee Group, One Liberty Sq (fl 7), Boston, 02109-4868

Michigan

Advertising Network Solutions, 40 Engelwood Dr (Suite A), Lake Orion, 48359-2419

BJT Management Group, 8303 Baileau Oaks Dr NE, Ada, 49301-9764

Customer Retention Solutions, 7837 S Sprinkle Rd, Portage, 49002-9432

Directions Marketing, 505 Green Rd, Ann Arbor, 48105

Marketing Solutions, 28252 Woodworth Way, Lathrup Village, 48076-2518

Signature Inc, 4701 Midway Dr, Ann Arbor, 48103

Urban Science Applications Inc, 200 Renaissance Ctr (Suite 1800), Detroit, 48243-1306

Minnesota

Clario Analytics, 7684 Golden Triangle Dr, Eden Prairie, 55344-3732

DWS Associates, 1032 Saint Johns Bay, Saint Paul, 55129-8537

Ecoenvelopes, 17800 George Moran Dr, Eden Prairie, 55347

Engagenextgen LLC, 5463 Bartlett Blvd, Mound, 55364-1605

Group 3 Marketing, 800 Wayzata Blvd E (Suite 201), Wayzata, 55391-1765

Independent Consultant, 2307 Boxwood Ave E, Saint Paul, 55119-5670

Ovative/Group LLC, 1011 Washington Ave S Ste 350, Minneapolis, 55415-1264

Product to Market LLC, 4536 County Rd 4 SW, Cokato, 55321-4220

Reichert & Associates Inc, PO Box 268, Grand Marais, 55604

RDO Marketing LLC, 4820 W 77th St Ste 120, Minneapolis, 55435-4809

Schulte Associates, 2807 Polk St NE, Minneapolis, 55418-2954

Solutran, 3600 Holly Ln (Suite 60), Plymouth, 55447

Stockham Consulting, 7300 Butterscotch Rd, Eden Prairie, 55346-3233

Whitney Worldwide Inc, 553 Hayward Ave N Ste 250, Saint Paul, 55128-9006

Missouri

Avantus, 2463 Schuetz Rd, Maryland Heights, 63043-3314

Colarelli Meyer & Associates Inc, 7751 Carondelet Ave (Suite 302), Saint Louis, 63105-3316

Collinger & Associates, 590 Sarah Ln Apt 401, Saint Louis, 63141-6968

Hemisphere Marketing, 6437 Washington St, Kansas City, 64113-1731

LandaJob, 222 W Gregory Blvd (Suite 304), Kansas City, 64114-1127

Masten Publishing Systems, PO Box 6074, Chesterfield, 63006-6074

Outsourcing Solutions Inc, 390 S Woods Mill Rd Ste 150, Chesterfield, 63017-3667

Nebraska

First of Omaha Merchant Processing, 1620 Dodge St, Omaha, 68197

Integrated Marketing Solutions (IMS), 30108 Kimberly Dr, Ashland, 68003-3806

West Corp, 11808 Miracle Hills Dr, Omaha, 68154

Nevada

Pamela Cotrupe, 129 S Royal Ascot Dr, Las Vegas, 89144-4309

New Hampshire

ASH Recruitment Solutions, PO Box 888, Exeter, 03833-0888

Concept Communications, 400 Amherst St, Nashua, 03063-1241

DM Assistance Inc, 155 Fleet St, Portsmouth, 03801-4050

Rapid Insight Inc, 53 Technology Ln (Suite 112), Conway, 03818-5804

New Jersey

ACP American Catalog Partnerships LLC, 392 Morris Ave, Summit, 07901-4734

Allen Consulting, 89 Middletown Rd, Holmdel, 07733-2203

Alliance Direct Marketing Solutions LLC, 665 Newark Ave (Suite 408), Jersey City, 07306

Baier Stein Direct, 211 Dryden Rd, Bernardsville, 07924-1108

BBC Direct Mktg Svcs, 361 Oak Shade Rd, Shamong, 08088

Capell & Associates, 601 Central, Barnegat Light, 08006

Caugherty Hahn Communications, 233 Rock Rd (Suite 248), Glen Rock, 07452-1708

The Chubb Corp, 15 Mountainview Rd, Warren, 07059

Didactic Systems, PO Box 457, Cranford, 07016-0457

E Media Advantage, Six Hamilton Ln, Livingston, 07039-2006

Gillespie Magazine Marketing & Publishing, 3450 Princeton Pike, Lawrenceville, 08648

International Corp, 225 Division Ave, Hasbrouck Heights, 07604-1719

JRB Marketing Group, 93 Einstein Way, East Windsor, 08512-2549

Judith Kennerk, 11 Scott Ave, Princeton Junction, 08550-1005

Leaps & Bounds LLC, 100 Old Palisades Rd (Suite 2409), Fort Lee, 07024-7021

Libey-Concordia, 811 Church Rd (Suite 105), Cherry Hill, 08002

Marketing Systems Analysis, 108 N Washington Ave, Ventnor, 08406-1961

Marketsmith Inc, 14 Walsh Dr Fl 200, Parsippany, 07054-1063

Medavante, 100 American Metro Blvd (Suite 106), Hamilton, 08619-2319

Milrod Executive Search, 22 Riverside Dr, Princeton, 08540-4017

OSG Billing, 100 W Forest Ave (Suite G), Englewood, 07631-4033

Practical Computer Solutions, 154 Brentwood Dr, South Orange, 07079-1141

Privacy & Information Practices Advisory, 10 Gristmill Ln, Saddle River, 07458-1317

Response Design Corp, 5541 Simpson Ave, Ocean City, 08226-1258

Smith O'Keefe & Associates, 1566 Somers Point Rd, Egg Harbor Township, 08234-8514

Thinkalytics, 440 Millburn Ave, Millburn, 07041-1210

Tucker Capital Corp, 234 Nassau St Ste 3, Princeton, 08542-4614

USY Consulting Inc, 50 Highwood Dr, Dumont, 07628-2608

Vertical Media Group, 2200 N Central Rd, Fort Lee, 07024-7557

Williams, Caliri, Miller & Otley, 1428 Rte 23, Wayne, 07474-5826

WPI Group Inc, PO Box 65, Colts Neck, 07722-0065

New Mexico

Deborah Hoffman Copywriting, 306 Sagebrush Dr, Corrales, 87048-8552

New York

Ad Hoc Marketing Resources Inc, 15 W 72nd St, New York, 10023

Adecco Employment Services, 175 Broadhollow Rd, Melville, 11747-4902

Agency.com, 488 Madison Ave (22nd fl), New York, 10022

American Society of Mechanical Engineers, Three Park Ave, New York, 10016-5990

Analytic Recruiting Inc, 144 E 44th St Ste 301, New York, 10017-4055

Arich Corp, 150 Central Park S (Suite 3210), New York, 10019-1566

Artrinsic Inc, 469 7th Ave (fl 10), New York, 10018-7640

Auriemma Consulting Group, 120 Broadway Ste 3402, New York, 10271-3400

The Author's, Writer's & Information Book/Video Publisher's Advice-Line, 7 Putter Ln, Linick Bldg, Middle Island, 11953-0102

Black & Co, 232 Madison Ave (Suite 1400), New York, 10016

The Boston Consulting Group, 430 Park Ave Fl 14, New York, 10022-3528

Boyden Global Executive Search, 3 Manhattanville Rd (Suite 104), Building 3, Purchase, 10577-2116

Capgemini Americas Outsourcing, 623 Fifth Ave (33rd fl), New York, 10022

Career Blazers, 5 W 37th St (5th fl), New York, 10018-5384

Andrea B Cautela, 111 Worth St, New York, 10013-4008

Cohen & Co, 281 Hicks St, Brooklyn, 11201-4508

Communispond Inc, 5 Lauras Ln, East Hampton, 11937-5916

Crandall Associates Inc, 6 Litchfield Rd # 316, Port Washington, 11050-3815

John Cummings & Partners LLC, Six Blair Rd, Armonk, 10504-2522

Cynthia Fields & Co (CFC), 230 W 22nd St, New York, 10011-2701

Chet Dalzell, 145 E 29th St (Apt 6D), New York, 10016-8146

Daniel Gonzalez & Associates, 939 8th Ave (#300), New York, 10019-4205

Davis & Gilbert, 1740 Broadway, New York, 10019-4379

Bert Davis Executive Search, 425 Madison Ave (fl 14), New York, 10017-1110

DB Consulting, 550 Mamaroneck Ave., Harrison, 10528

DCJ Consulting, 6749 Exeter St, Forest Hills, 11375-4150

Denmark Francisco, 684 9th Ave (fl 4), New York, 10036-3612

Direct Marketers On Call Inc (DMOC), 45 Christopher St Apt 4A, New York, 10014-3585

Direct Ventures Inc, 18 Clover Rd, Larchmont, 10538-1749

Eastern Collection Corp, 16 Barclay Dr, Sag Harbor, 11963-4316

Edelman Direct Marketing Inc, 75 Fairview Ave, Great Neck, 11023-1350

EBM Direct Marketing Services LLC, 39 Seaview Ln, Port Washington, 11050-1737

eMarketing Strategy Group, 155 E 34th St (Suite 20-C), New York, 10016-4718

Ernan Roman Direct Marketing Corp, 3 Melrose Ln, Little Neck, 11363-1220

Ernst & Young LLP, 5 Times Sq, New York, 10036-6527

FlarePath LLC, 200 Cabrini Blvd (#119), New York, 10033-1121

Focus on the ROI, 97 Gem Ln, Massapequa Park, 11762-3222

Furgiuele & Co Inc, 276 Read Ave, Crestwood, 10707

Global Marketing Group Ltd, 119 W 57th St Ste 1405, New York, 10019-2401

Barbara Gold, 10 W 15th (Apt 1924), New York, 10011-6850

Goodman & Co, PO Box 835, New York, 10024-0540

GreenPath Sustainability Consultants, 13 Windgate Dr, New City, 10956-4434

Grey Birch Group LLC, 64 Sycamore Ln, Irvington, 10533-1931

Gordon W Grossman Inc, 254 Salem Rd, Pound Ridge, 10576-1320

Gundersen Partners LLC, 30 Irving Pl (fl 2), New York, 10003

Hal Levy & Associates, 186 Mohonk Rd, High Falls, 12440-5229

Elizabeth Hartman, 5 Azalea Dr, Syosset, 11791-2802

Hauser List Services, NMIS, 2545 Hempstead Tpke Ste 401, East Meadow, 11554-2144

Howard-Sloan-Koller Group, 300 E 42nd St Fl 15, New York, 10017-5925

EA Hughes & Co, 200 Park Ave S (Suite 1608), New York, 10003-1521

IPG, 532 W 22nd St (Apt 3C), New York, 10011-1117

Imagine 360 Marketing, 1123 Broadway (Suite 902), New York, 10010-2007

Infomorphosis/Marketing Solutions, 152 W 20th St (Suite D), New York, 10011-3635

Jack Schecterson visualmarketing Consultants, 5316 251st Pl, Little Neck, 11362-1711

JLMC, 15 Park Row (17E), New York, 10038-2301

Kenzer Group, LLC, One Penn Plaza (Suite 6300), New York, 10119

Liz Kislik Associates LLC, 100 Merrick Rd (Suite 505E), Rockville Centre, 11570-4834

LaMotta Strategic Communications Inc, 137 Old Haverstraw Rd, Congers, 10920-1607

Richard Law, 166 E 3rd St, Deer Park, 11729-5307

Nancy Liss, 233 E 32nd St, New York, 10016-6336

Lister Butler Inc, 445 Park Ave (Suite 1401), New York, 10022-8626

Loeb & Loeb Inc, 345 Park Ave, New York, 10154-0004

Mapping Analytics, 120 Allens Creek Rd, Rochester, 14618-3306

Marketrac Inc, 300 Roosevelt Way, Westbury, 11590-6700

Shannon McDonald, 205 W 88 St (#9D), New York, 10024

McKinsey & Co, 55 E 52nd St (fl 21), New York, 10055-0183

Media Recruiting Group Inc, 1 Bridge St (Suite P2), Irvington, 10533-1575

Adrian Miller Direct Marketing, 43 Park Ave, Port Washington, 11050-4010

Fred Milman Associates, 23 Selina Ct, Glen Cove, 11542-3048

MIMAARTS LLC, 535 Fifth Ave (fl 31), New York, 10017-3667

MLB Associates, 1936 Saranac Ave (Suite 2-300), Lake Placid, 12946-1114

NAK Marketing & Communications, 575 Madison Ave (Suite 700), New York, 10022-8512

Oak Knoll Limited Liability Co, 7 Hastings Ct, South Salem, 10590-2517

Glen Orenstein, 2959 Judith Dr, Merrick, 11566-5448

Paul, Hastings, Janofsky & Walker LLP, 75 E 55th St, Park Avenue Tower, New York, 10022-3205

Publishing Fulfillment Consulting LLC, 85 Settlers Hill Rd, Brewster, 10509-5210

Raab Associates, 345 Millwood Rd, Chappaqua, 10514-1002

Lynda Raihofer & Associates LLC, 48 Young Ave, Pelham, 10803-1724

Rainwater Associates Inc, 135 E 71st St, New York, 10021-4258

Redwood Partners Ltd, 60 E 42nd St (Rm 1820), New York, 10165-6210

Reed Smith Hall Dickler Advertising & Law Marketing Group, 599 Lexington Ave (29th fl), New York, 10022

Retrieval Masters Creditors Bureau Inc, 4 Westchester Plz Ste 110, Elmsford, 10523-1615

Ross Culbert & Lavery, 900 Broadway (#401), New York, 10003

Anne Ruth, 6 Alden Pl Apt 1D, Bronxville, 10708-4846

Sandler Techworks, 525 E 82nd St (Suite 2g), New York, 10028-7148

Satisfaction Software Inc, 8711 150th St, Jamaica, 11435-3107

Schupak Group Inc, 595 Madison Ave Rm 1900, New York, 10022-1958

Severini Communications LLC (Mogility), 200 W 86th St (Apt 1k), New York, 10024-3326

Shasho Jones Direct Inc, 267 W 25th St, New York, 10001-7128

David Shepard Associates Inc, 332 Altessa Blvd, Melville, 11747-5222

Kate Shifman Consulting, 179 Saint Johns Pl Apt 2, Brooklyn, 11217-3417

Ray Slyper Associates, 420 E 72nd St (Suite 2L), New York, 10021

Smart Source Direct, 1185 Ave of the Americas (fl 27), News America Marketing, New York, 10036-2603

Debbie Sorace, 70 Edwards Pl, Valley Stream, 11580-3143

SIGMA Marketing Group LLC, 1850 S Winton Rd, Rochester, 14618-3923

SKO-Brenner-American, 841 Merrick Rd CS 9320, Baldwin, 11510-9320

Stagg Direct Marketing Inc, 11 Gorham Rd, Scarsdale, 10583-1117

Stephen-Bradford Search, 261 Madison Ave Fl 11, New York, 10016-2303

Stephens Inc, 65 E 55th St Fl 22, New York, 10022-3369

Elizabeth Streitz & Associates, 255 W 108th St (Suite 9A), New York, 10025

TeleManagement Search, 6 Litchfield Rd (Suite 316), Port Washington, 11050-3815

Tolliver Inc, 303 5th Ave Rm 206, New York, 10016-6690

Towers Watson, 875 Third Ave., New York, 10022

Karen Tripi Associates, 305 Madison Ave (Suite 2319), New York, 10165-6209

The Troyanos Group Ltd, 106 N Broadway (fl 3), Irvington, 10533-1262

TSI, 12 Corporate Woods Blvd, Albany, 12211-2344

Gilbert Tweed Associates, 415 Madison Ave (20th fl), New York, 10017

Wakefield Talabisco International, 11 E 44th St (Rm 1206), New York, 10017-3608

Steve Wexler Creative Group, PO Box 219, Farmingville, 11738-0219

Winston & Winston PC, 295 Madison Ave, New York, 10017

Winterberry Group, 60 Broad St Ste 3810, New York, 10004-2329

Brian Wolfe, 418 E 59th St (Apt 26A), New York, 10022-2378

WLA Inc, 535 5th Ave (fl 31), New York, 10017-3667

RL Zapin Associates Inc, 708 Third Ave (6th fl), New York, 10017

Neil Zelenetz & Associates, 67 Transverse Rd, Garden City, 11530-1821

Zimmerman Business Consulting Inc, 44 E 92nd St (Suite 5B), New York, 10128-1319

North Carolina

AKS Marketing & Media, 200 Chimeneas Pl, Chapel Hill, 27517-8389

Altman Dedicated Direct, 853 Academy St, Rural Hall, 27045-9329

Beechtree Assoc Inc, 216 Whisperwood Dr (Suite 100), Cary, 27511

Clarity Group LLC, 600 Market St Ste 302, Chapel Hill, 27516-4057

ClementDIRECT, 72109 Moseley, Chapel Hill, 27517-8574

T A Cook Consultants Inc, 9212 Falls of Neuse Rd (Suite 201), Raleigh, 27615-2483

Direct Marketing Resources Group Inc, 4501 Newborn Ave (Suite 130-253), Raleigh, 27610-1550

Direct Marketing Resources, 517 Highland Forest Dr, Charlotte, 28270-0848

Group f/64, 1050 Arbor Rd, Winston-Salem, 27104

PrintCom Consulting Group, 1020 Farm Creek Rd, Waxhaw, 28173-7793

RSM McGladrey Inc, 4725 Piedmont Row Dr (Suite 300), Charlotte, 28210-4280

RW Consulting, 452 Sondley Woods Pl, Asheville, 28805

Ohio

The Ad Farm, 2225 Dundas Rd, Ottawa Hills, 43606-2526

American Tax Associates Inc, 31 E Whittier St, Columbus, 43206-2026

Richard L Bencin & Associates, 2616 Hidden Canyon Dr, Brecksville, 44141-3530

Dovetail Art & Design Inc, 113 Wade Dr, Dover, 44622-9460

Eadon Ventures, 11224 Reeder Ave NE, Alliance, 44601-8332

Interactive Search Group, 35104 Euclid Ave (Suite 303), Cleveland, 44094

Kramer & Associates, 8044 Montgomery Rd (Suite 200), Bank One Towers, Cincinnati, 45236-2926

L3 Virtual Solutions LLC, 450 Township Rd (#208), Marengo, 43334

Laven & Loeb Inc, 2163 Halcyon Rd, Beachwood, 44122-1301

Mac Murray Petersen & Shuster LLP, 6530 W Campus Oval (Suite 210), New Albany, 43054-7069

Mastery Marketing Group, 5650 Blazer Pkwy (Suite 141), Dublin, 43017

Richard Saunders International, 3849 Edwards Rd, Cincinnati, 45244

Sedlak, 22901 Millcreek Blvd (Suite 600), Metropolitan Plaza, Highland Hills, 44122-5724

Skystone Ryan, 635 W Seventh St (Suite 107), Cincinnati, 45203

TeleDevelopment Services Inc, PO Box 502, Richfield, 44286-0502

Transglobal Consultants Inc, 3210 Glastonbury Cir NW, Canton, 44708-1174

Wind River Group, 900 State Mill Rd, Akron, 44319-2138

Oregon

Effective Marketing Associates, Inc, 3525 Riverknoll Way, West Linn, 97068-3641

Interface Engineering, 708 SW Third Ave (Suite 400), Portland, 97204

Michel Consulting, 61903 Brokentop Dr, Bend, 97702-1085

SLR Associates, 3300 NW 185th Ave (PMB 268), Portland, 97229-3406

Pennsylvania

The Beam Group, 414 Mill Creek Rd, Gladwyne, 19035-1519

Brandywine Consulting Group Inc, 1398 Morstein Rd (Suite 4), West Chester, 19380-5848

Col Voce Consulting, 551 Newcomen Rd, Exton, 19341-1938

Corpora Consulting, 42 W Market St, Bethlehem, 18018-5703

Direct Marketing Consultant, 399 Sherman Ave, Sharon, 16146-3953

The Diversified Services Group Inc, 303 W Lancaster Ave (Suite 2E), Wayne, 19087-3938

Denny Hatch Associates Inc, 310 Gaskill St, Philadelphia, 19147-1503

David Heneberry Associates, 111 Reynolds Ln, West Grove, 19390-1371

Infomercial Monitoring Service Inc, 812 Parkway, Broomall, 19008

The Keystone Equities Group, 1003 Egypt Rd, Oaks, 19456-1155

Kistler-Tiffany Companies LLC, 1205 Westlakes Dr Ste 290, Berwyn, 19312-2405

LTD Supply Chain, 3 Black Horse Cir, Downingtown, 19335-1552

Ken Malek Associates Inc, PO Box 383, Yardley, 19067-8383

Management Science Associates Inc, 6565 Penn Ave, Pittsburgh, 15206-4490

McBee Associates Inc, 997 Old Eagle School Rd Ste 205, Wayne, 19087-1706

Media Management Services Inc, 105 Terry Dr (Suite 120), Newton, 18940-1872

Medina Associates, 12 Hilltop Rd, Rose Valley, 19086-6243

National Mail/Marketing Corp, 390 Reed Rd Fl 3, Broomall, 19008-4008

NigroNewMedia, 4004 Hermitage Hills Blvd (Apt 20), Hermitage, 16148-3420

Spectrum Retail Associates, 10 E Athens Ave (Suite 200), Ardmore, 19003

Grant Thornton LLP, Two Commerce Square (Suite 3100), Philadelphia, 19103

Wesley R. Weber & Associates, 405 Brookmeade Dr, West Chester, 19380

Rhode Island

Mac McIntosh Inc, 601 Pendar Rd, North Kingstown, 02852-6620

Spaide, Kuipers & Co, 42 Second St, Newport, 02840

South Carolina

Blexrud Direct, 215 Indian Wells Dr, Spartanburg, 29306-6625

South Dakota

Bull Dog Media Group Inc, PO Box 463, Madison, 57042-0463

Tennessee

The Buffkin Group LLC, 730 Cool Springs Blvd (Suite 120), Franklin, 37067-7290

LucidView, 80 Rolling Links Blvd, Oak Ridge, 37830-9023

Marketing Consulting Services, 2669 Suffolk St, Kingsport, 37660-5803

Texas

ABCO Inc, 1621 Wall St, Dallas, 75215-1864

Alen, (Suite 307), PMB 299, 5114 Balcones Woods Dr, Austin, 78759-5273

Audience Research & Development, 2440 Lofton Ter, Fort Worth, 76109-1123

Creating Selling Opportunities, 2902 W Lane Dr (Suite E), Houston, 77027

Creditcards.com, 8920 Business Park Dr (Suite 350), Austin, 78759-7636

Dodson & Associates, 16302 Shadybank Dr, Dallas, 75248-2957

Echotouch Corp, 5907 Carry Back Ln, Austin, 78746-1448

GC Services, 6330 Gulfton, Houston, 77081

Gibson Direct Inc, 204 Plantation Dr, Coppell, 75019-3232

Glengarry Marketing, 2303 RR 620 S Unit 135-150, Austin, 78734

Ed Golden & Associates, 7303 Shoal Creek Blvd, Austin, 78757-2028

Hatchholdings LLC, 5832 Broadwell Dr, Plano, 75093-4717

The Herman Group, 7112 Viridian Ln, Austin, 78739-2092

International Direct Marketing Consultants Inc, 3419 Westminster Ave, Dallas, 75205-1387

International Resource Management Co, 3008 Spring Valley Dr., Bedford, 76021-4245

Lion's Share Marketing Group, Inc, 5410 Schumacher Ln, Houston, 77056-6810

Moran Direct Inc, 710 N Post Oak Rd (Suite 520), Houston, 77024-3858

ProSource, 1502 Augusta Dr (Suite 100), Houston, 77057-2454

Pursuant Group, 5151 Beltline Rd (Suite 900), Dallas, 75254-6757

Sheshunoff Management Services, 2801 Via Fortuna (Suite 600), Austin, 78746

Shisler and Associates, 14917 Oaks North Dr (Suite 113), Dallas, 75254-7631

The Sound Direct Marketing Group, PO Box 162527, Austin, 78716-2527

TALX Corp, 14755 Preston Rd (Suite 525), Dallas, 75254-7898

Vermont

Continuity Shippers Association, 2351 N Bridgewater Rd, Saddlebow Farm, Woodstock, 05091-9670

de Rham & Co Inc, PO Box 889, Dorset, 05251-0889

Coleman W Hoyt Consultant, 2351 N Bridgewater Rd, Saddlebow Farm, Woodstock, 05091-9670

Printmark, 432 Johnson Rd, East Montpelier, 05651-4250

Raphel Marketing, 211 North Ave, Saint Johnsbury, 05819-1626

Timberline Interactive, 5 Park St (Suite 2), Middlebury, 05753-1169

Windward Group, 241 Spinnaker Ln, Shelburne, 05482-7779

Virginia

F Curtis Barry & Co, 2104 Willowick Ln, Henrico, 23238-3616

Blagman Creative/Direct Response, 13269 Triple Crown Loop, Gainesville, 20155-6668

Chapman Cubine Adams & Hussey, 1600 Wilson Blvd (Suite 300), Arlington, 22209-2505

Click2Mail, 3103 10th St N (Suite 201), Arlington, 22201-2191

Communications Unlimited Inc, 10129 Deepwood Cir, Richmond, 23238-4241

Dan Smolen Direct Search LLC, 44 Lightfoot Dr, Stafford, 22554-8509

DeHart & Darr Associates, 1360 Beverly Rd (Suite 201), McLean, 22101-3647

Erlandson Associates, 222 W Market St, Leesburg, 20176-2709

Foxhall Corp, 6849 Old Dominion Dr (Suite 320), McLean, 22101-3791

Foxhall Corporation, 6849 Old Dominion Dr (Suite 320), McLean, 22101-3791

Graduate Management Admission Council, 11921 Freedom Dr (Suite 300), Reston, 20190

NEW Customer Service Companies Inc, 22894 Pacific Blvd, Sterling, 20166-6722

PM Consulting Corp, 11250 Waples Mill Rd, Fairfax, 22030

Production Solutions, 1953 Gallows Rd (Suite 600), Vienna, 22182-3988

RedEngine Digital, 1485 Chain Bridge Rd (Suite 305), Mc Lean, 22101-4501

The Services Group (TSG), 2101 Wilson Blvd (Suite 700), Arlington, 22201-3060

Stateside Associates, 2300 Clarendon Blvd Ste 407, Arlington, 22201-3300

Technical Assistance Research Programs (TARP), 2425 Wilson Blvd (Suite 400), Arlington, 22201

Turtle Bay Management Co Inc, 209 86th St (Suite E), Virginia Beach, 23451

Wagner Hines & Avary Inc, 218 N Lee St, Alexandria, 22314

West Cary Group, 5 W Cary St, Richmond, 23220-5609

Washington

brandUNITY Inc, PO Box 4512, Rollingbay, 98061-0512

Emailogics Inc/Emailbrain, 8100 NE Parkway Dr (Suite 300), Vancouver, 98662-7954

Sentinel Peak LLC, 15600 Redmond Way, Redmond, 98052

Strofina, 10200 NE Garibaldi Loop, Bainbridge Island, 98110-3976

The Write Answers Copywriting & Consulting, 816 Peace Portal Dr (#82), Blaine, 98230-4010

West Virginia

Marketing/Media Dynamics Inc, 197 Shannondale Rd, Harpers Ferry, 25425-4564

Wisconsin

ABR Employment Services, 1402 Pankratz St (Suite 101), Madison, 53704-4046

Einhorn Associates Inc, 2675 N Mayfair Rd (Suite 410), Milwaukee, 53226

Hunter Business Group LLC, 4650 N Port Washington Rd Stop 8, Milwaukee, 53212-1078

The Kaiser Group Inc, 237 South St, Waukesha, 53186

Dorothy Kerr & Associates, 1509 E Standish Pl, Milwaukee, 52317-1960

Market Square Communications Inc, 1100 Centerpoint Dr (Suite 203), Stevens Point, 54481-2849

Miglautsch Marketing Inc, 555 S Industrial Dr (Suite 5), Hartland, 53029

NuEdge Systems, 4900 W Brown Deer Rd, Brown Deer, 53223

CANADA

Ontario

Cameron & Co, 83 Duggan Ave, Toronto, M4V 1Y1

Figurs*, 39a Fourth St, Toronto, M8V 2Y2

News Marketing Canada, 100 King St W (Suite 7000), One First Canadian Place, Toronto, M5X 1A4

Quebec

CakeMail Inc, 4020 St-Ambroise (Suite 145), Montreal, H4C 2C7

Ken Elo, 3863 Laval, Montreal, H2W 2H9

Komunik, 1500 St Patrick, Montreal, H3K 0A3

Publications Groupe RR International Inc, 2322 Sherbrooke E, Montreal, H2K 1E5

A PLUS MARKETING LTD
1300 Barclay Blvd
Buffalo Grove, IL 60089-4500
Telephone: (847) 537-1166, FAX:
(847) 537-5611, Web Site: www.
aplusmarketing.com
Pres: Greg Alberts

ABCO INC
1621 Wall St
Dallas, TX 75215-1864
Telephone: (214) 565-5250, Web Site:
www.abcoinc.com
Pres: Leon Kaplan

ABR EMPLOYMENT SERVICES
Div. of Forward Service Corp
1402 Pankratz St (Suite 101)
Madison, WI 53704-4046
Telephone: (608) 244-3526, FAX:
(608) 244-8279, E-Mail: info@
abrjobs.com, Web Site: www.abrjobs.
com
Mgr: Deborah Schaefer

ACP AMERICAN CATALOG PARTNERSHIPS LLC
392 Morris Ave
Summit, NJ 07901-4734
Telephone: (908) 598-1947
Chmn: Theodore Pamperin

ADM MARKETING
908 N Hollywood Way
Burbank, CA 91505-2815
Telephone: (888) 800-1001
Founder: Stephen Farr-Jones

AKS MARKETING & MEDIA
200 Chimeneas Pl
Chapel Hill, NC 27517-8389
Telephone: (919) 240-5496
CEO: Markus Wilhelm
Primary Market Served: Business &
Consumer

ASH RECRUITMENT SOLUTIONS
PO Box 888
Exeter, NH 03833-0888
Telephone: (603) 778-8888, E-Mail:
t.hall@ashrecruit.com, Web Site:
www.ashrecruit.com
Principal: Anthony Hall
Primary Market Served: Business
Advertising/Marketing Budget Related

to Direct Marketing: 76-100%
Founded: 2001

AVD MARKETING
4113 Trenton Ave
Hollywood, FL 33026-4923
Telephone: (954) 410-9000, Web Site:
www.avdmarketing.com
Principal: Andre Doren
Primary Market Served: Business &
Consumer

ABILITY COMMERCE
A Marketing Concepts Company
1300 NW 17th Ave Ste 200
Delray Beach, FL 33445-2560
Telephone: (561) 330-3151, Web Site:
www.abilitycommerce.com
Pres: Terence Jukes

ABOUT BOOKS INC
1001 Taurus Dr
Colorado Springs, CO 80906-1133
Telephone: (719) 632-8226, FAX:
(719) 471-2182, E-Mail: infoabi2@
about-books.com, Web Site: www.
about-books.com
Pres: Tom Ross

ACCENT MARKETING SERVICES LLC
400 Missouri Ave (Suite 107)
Jeffersonville, IN 47130-3086
Telephone: (812) 206-6200, Web Site:
www.accentonline.com
Pres & CEO: Kevin Foley

ACCENTURE
800 Boylston St (#2300)
Boston, MA 02199
Telephone: (617) 488-4000, FAX:
(617) 488-4001, Web Site: www.
accenture.com
Assoc Partner: Robert Mann Jr.

ACCESS BUSINESS COMMUNICATIONS INC
5611 Ocean Terrace Dr
Huntington Beach, CA 92648-7511
Telephone: (800) 675-2415, Web Site:
www.abcimarketing.com
Mng Partner: Jack Bogle

ACTUARIAL ENTERPRISES LTD
920 N Franklin (Suite 401)
Chicago, IL 60610-3186

Telephone: (312) 397-0099, E-Mail:
jay@actentltd.com
Pres: Jay M. Jaffe

THE AD FARM
2225 Dundas Rd
Ottawa Hills, OH 43606-2526
Telephone: (419) 720-5676, Web Site:
www.theadfarm.com
Pres: Jonathan Downing

AD HOC MARKETING RESOURCES INC
15 W 72nd St
New York, NY 10023
Telephone: (212) 595-1800, FAX:
(212) 656-1860, E-Mail:
adhocmrktg@aol.com, Web Site:
www.members.aol.com/adhocmrktg
Pres: Karen Hochman

ADECCO EMPLOYMENT SERVICES
175 Broadhollow Rd
Melville, NY 11747-4902
Telephone: (631) 844-7800, Web Site:
www.adecco.com
Mktg: Ed Blust

ADVERTISING NETWORK SOLUTIONS
40 Engelwood Dr (Suite A)
Lake Orion, MI 48359-2419
Telephone: (248) 475-7881, Web Site:
www.adnetworksolutions.com
Pres: Jeff Fasseel
Primary Market Served: Business &
Consumer

AGENCY.COM
488 Madison Ave (22nd fl)
New York, NY 10022
Telephone: (212) 358-2600, FAX:
(212) 358-2604, Web Site: www.
agency.com
Worldwide CEO: David Eastman

THE ALDRICH GROUP
43 Sherman Hill Rd D-104
Woodbury, CT 06798
Telephone: (860) 274-7693, (203) 263-
5505, FAX: (203) 263-5572, E-Mail:
jeff.aldrich@aldrichsearch.com, Web
Site: www.aldrichsearch.com
Principal: Jeff Aldrich

THE DMA ALEN

(Suite 307), PMB 299, 5114 Balcones
    Woods Dr
Austin, TX 78759-5273
Telephone: (512) 600-6948, (800) 630-
    2396, Web Site: www.alencorp.com/
Primary Market Served: Consumer

ALEXANDER & CO LLC

178 Water St
Stonington, CT 06378
Telephone: (860) 535-9160, FAX:
    (860) 535-9161, E-Mail: jraandco@
    aol.com
Pres: James R. Alexander

ALLEN CONSULTING

89 Middletown Rd
Holmdel, NJ 07733-2203
Telephone: (732) 946-2711, FAX:
    (732) 946-8032, E-Mail: sylvia@
    allenconsulting.com, Web Site: www.
    allenconsulting.com
Pres: Sylvia Allen

**ALLEN, MATKINS, LECK,
GAMBLE & MALLORY**

515 S Figueroa St (9th fl)
Los Angeles, CA 90071-3398
Telephone: (213) 622-5555, FAX:
    (213) 620-8816, E-Mail:
    communications@allenmatkins.com,
    Web Site: www.allenmatkins.com
Mng Partner: Brian Leck

**ALLIANCE DIRECT
MARKETING SOLUTIONS
LLC**

665 Newark Ave (Suite 408)
Jersey City, NJ 07306
Telephone: (201) 863-1360, (888) 455-
    2367, FAX: (201) 863-3910, E-Mail:
    vteran@alliancedirectleads.com, Web
    Site: www.alliancedirectleads.com
Pres: Vivian Teran
Conducts Business: US
Employees: 10
Primary Market Served: Business &
    Consumer
Direct online sales
Advertising/Marketing Budget Related
    to Direct Marketing: 0-25%
Founded: 2002
Gross sales or billing: $200,000

List broker of business, consumer,
email, data processing and printing.

**THE DMA ALLPRO DIRECT
MARKETING**

11626 Prosperous Dr
Odessa, FL 33556
Telephone: (888) 679-0255, Web Site:
    www.allprodirectmarketing.com

Primary Market Served: Business &
Consumer

**THE DMA ALTMAN DEDICATED
DIRECT**

853 Academy St
Rural Hall, NC 27045-9329
Telephone: (336) 969-9538, FAX:
    (336) 969-0187, E-Mail: saltman@
    AltmanDedicatedDirect.com, Web
    Site: www.altmandedicateddirect.com
Pres: Shari Altman

**THE DMA AMERICAN MARKETING &
COMMUNICATION CORP**

14201 Pennsylvania Ave
Hagerstown, MD 21742-1665
Telephone: (240) 625-9225, FAX:
    (240) 625-9235, E-Mail: info@
    amcc1.com, Web Site: www.
    americanmarketingcc.com
Pres & CEO: Lisa C. Boyle

**AMERICAN SOCIETY OF
MECHANICAL ENGINEERS**

Three Park Ave
New York, NY 10016-5990
Telephone: (973) 882-1167, (800) 843-
    2763, FAX: (973) 882-1717, E-Mail:
    infocentral@asme.org, Web Site:
    www.asme.org
Chair: J. R. Sims

**AMERICAN TAX ASSOCIATES
INC**

31 E Whittier St
Columbus, OH 43206-2026
Telephone: (614) 443-5343, FAX:
    (614) 443-0279
Pres: Dale H. Durley

**AMTOWER & CO FEDERAL
DIRECT**

PO Box 314
Highland, MD 20777-0314
Telephone: (240) 882-9546, E-Mail:
    markamtower@gmail.com, Web Site:
    www.federaldirect.net
Partner: Mark Amtower

THE DMA ANALYTIC RECRUITING INC

144 E 44th St Ste 301
New York, NY 10017-4055
Telephone: (212) 545-8511, FAX:
    (212) 545-8520, E-Mail: rita@
    analyticrecruiting.com, Web Site:
    www.analyticrecruiting.com
Pres: Rita Raz
Founded: 1980

Experienced in Database Marketing,
Marketing Analytics, Digital Analytics
& Strategy, Customer Insights & Marketing Management. Works with clients in matching skills, career goals &
positions.

ANDERSON/SKOW

690 Texas St
San Francisco, CA 94107-2941
Telephone: (888) 983-0880, Web Site:
    www.andersonskow.com
Pres: Kathi Skow
Primary Market Served: Business &
    Consumer

**APPLICATIONS
DEVELOPMENT CORP**

169 Buena Vista Dr
Dekalb, IL 60115-1069
Telephone: (815) 754-7432, Web Site:
    www.appdevcorp.com

ARICH CORP

150 Central Park S (Suite 3210)
New York, NY 10019-1566
Telephone: (212) 247-1800, FAX:
    (212) 247-2231, Web Site: www.
    arichinc.com
Pres: Richard F. Gray

**ARLEN COMMUNICATIONS
INC**

7315 Wisconsin Ave (Suite 705E)
Bethesda, MD 20814
Telephone: (301) 656-7940, E-Mail:
    info@arlencom.com, Web Site:
    www.arlencom.com
Pres: Gary Arlen

ARTRINSIC INC

469 7th Ave (fl 10)
New York, NY 10018-7640
Telephone: (212) 716-1977 X201, Web
    Site: www.atrinsic.com
CEO: Jeffrey Schwartz
Primary Market Served: Business

ATLANTIC-ACM

One Beacon St (34th fl)
Boston, MA 02108
Telephone: (617) 720-3700, FAX:
    (617) 720-1077, E-Mail: atlantic@
    atlantic-acm.com, Web Site: www.
    atlantic-acm.com
CEO: Judy Reed Smith

**AUDIENCE RESEARCH &
DEVELOPMENT**

2440 Lofton Ter
Fort Worth, TX 76109-1123

Telephone: (817) 924-6922, FAX:
(817) 924-7539, E-Mail: jgumbert@
ar-d.com, Web Site: www.ar-d.com
Pres & CEO: Jerry Gumbert

AURIEMMA CONSULTING GROUP
120 Broadway Ste 3402
New York, NY 10271-3400
Telephone: (516) 333-4800, FAX:
(516) 333-4815, E-Mail: info@acg.
net, Web Site: www.acg.net
Pres: Michael Auriemma

THE AUTHOR'S, WRITER'S & INFORMATION BOOK/ VIDEO PUBLISHER'S ADVICE-LINE
Div. of Linick Group International Inc
7 Putter Ln, Linick Bldg
Middle Island, NY 11953-0102
Telephone: (631) 924-3888, (631) 775-
6075, FAX: (631) 924-8555, E-Mail:
andrewlinick@gmail.com;
linickgroup@gmail.com, Web Site:
andrewlinickdirectmarketing.com;
www.asklinick.com
CEO: Dr Andrew S. Linick

AVANTUS
2463 Schuetz Rd
Maryland Heights, MO 63043-3314
Telephone: (314) 994-3449, Web Site:
www.avantus.com
Pres: Deborah Challoner
Primary Market Served: Business &
Consumer

BBC DIRECT MKTG SVCS
dba BBC Worldwide
361 Oak Shade Rd
Shamong, NJ 08088
Telephone: (877) 786-4389, FAX:
(609) 268-9939, E-Mail: csr@
bbcglobal.com, Web Site: www.
bbcglobal.com
Pres: Clarence Reichenbach Jr.
VP: C. Stephen Reichenbach
Opers Mgr: Rachel McCormick
Conducts Business: U.S., Canada
Primary Market Served: Business

3PL Transportation Logistics, Warehousing & Distribution.

BJT MANAGEMENT GROUP
8303 Baileau Oaks Dr NE
Ada, MI 49301-9764
Telephone: (616) 682-0369, Web Site:
www.bjtmgt.com
Pres & CEO: Robert Ostertag
Primary Market Served: Consumer

Provides management services to companies

BAIER STEIN DIRECT
211 Dryden Rd
Bernardsville, NJ 07924-1108
Telephone: (908) 781-7849, Web Site:
www.directcopy.com
Pres: Donna Baier Stein

BAKER & HOSTETLER LLP
1050 Connecticut Ave NW (Suite
1100)
Washington, DC 20036-5304
Telephone: (202) 861-1500, FAX:
(202) 861-1783, E-Mail:
wschweitzer@bakerlaw.com, Web
Site: www.bakerlaw.com
Partner: William H. Schweitzer

F CURTIS BARRY & CO
2104 Willowick Ln
Henrico, VA 23238-3616
Telephone: (804) 740-8743, FAX:
(804) 740-6179, E-Mail: cbarry@
fcbco.com, Web Site: www.fcbco.
com
Pres: Curt Barry

DIANA BATY
109 Sullivan Dr
Moraga, CA 94556-1211
Telephone: (202) 689-5332
Primary Market Served: Consumer

THE BEAM GROUP
414 Mill Creek Rd
Gladwyne, PA 19035-1519
Telephone: (215) 988-2100, FAX:
(215) 988-1558, Web Site: www.
beamgroup.com
Pres: Russell Glicksman
Founded: 1989

RICH BECKER & ASSOCIATES/PUMP-EM-UP PUBLISHING, IN PUBLIC RELATIONS
9225 Woodstone Ln
Lenexa, KS 66219-1959
Telephone: (913) 894-9530, FAX:
(913) 894-9530, E-Mail: rbecker@
kc.rr.com
Pres: Rich Becker

BEECHTREE ASSOC INC
216 Whisperwood Dr (Suite 100)
Cary, NC 27511
Telephone: (919) 852-1800, FAX:
(919) 852-4400, E-Mail: jfoliano@
aol.com
Pres: Jay Foliano

RICHARD L BENCIN & ASSOCIATES
2616 Hidden Canyon Dr
Brecksville, OH 44141-3530
Telephone: (440) 526-6726, FAX:
(440) 546-1623, E-Mail: rlbencin@
netzero.net, Web Site: www.rlbencin.
com
Pres: Richard L. Bencin
Conducts Business: Worldwide
Employees: 4
Primary Market Served: Business
Founded: 1981
Gross sales or billing: $1,000,000

Recruiting services for both the direct
marketing & center industries.

BENNETTBAKER LTD
33 W Monroe St (Suite 2110)
Chicago, IL 60603-5414
Telephone: (312) 252-8883, FAX:
(312) 252-8209, E-Mail: nbennett@
bennettwheelless.com, Web Site:
www.bennettbaker.com
CEO/Founder: Neysa Bennett
Recruiter: Heather Baker
Conducts Business: U.S.
Employees: 2
Primary Market Served: Business
Advertising/Marketing Budget Related
to Direct Marketing: 76-100%
Direct Marketing ad budget:
Direct Mail: 70%
Telephone: 30%
Founded: 1987

Executive search firm for the direct
marketing and internet marketing
industries.

BERNHEIMER ASSOCIATES
10 Laurel Ave
Wellesley, MA 02481-7534
Telephone: (781) 237-8910, FAX:
(781) 239-2932, E-Mail: wsbii@
hotmail.com
Pres: Walter Bernheimer II

BILLIN MEDINA-WARREN
8655 E Via de Ventura (#G200)
Scottsdale, AZ 85258-3300
Telephone: (972) 951-7291
Principal: Billin Medina-Warren

BLACK & CO
232 Madison Ave (Suite 1400)
New York, NY 10016
Telephone: (212) 867-5533, FAX:
(212) 447-0785, E-Mail:
wblack6340@aol.com
Pres: William Black

BLAGMAN CREATIVE/ DIRECT RESPONSE

13269 Triple Crown Loop
Gainesville, VA 20155-6668
Telephone: (703) 743-2493, E-Mail:
jackbee21@comcast.net
Pres: Jack Blagman

BLATTEIS COMMUNICATIONS

2335 W Hedding St
San Jose, CA 95128-1327
Telephone: (901) 356-0090, Web Site:
www.blatteis.com
Owner: Beatrice Blatteis
Primary Market Served: Business &
Consumer

BLEXRUD DIRECT

215 Indian Wells Dr
Spartanburg, SC 29306-6625
Telephone: (864) 583-7399, FAX:
(864) 583-7399, E-Mail: blexrud@
bellsouth.net
Pres: Tom Blexrud
Conducts Business: U.S.
Employees: 1
Primary Market Served: Business &
Consumer
Advertising/Marketing Budget Related
to Direct Marketing: 0-25%
Founded: 1987

Direct marketing consulting services.

BLOOM, HERGOTT, DIEMER, ROSENTHAL AND LAVIOLETTE LLP

150 S Rodeo Dr (fl 3)
Beverly Hills, CA 90212-2410
Telephone: (310) 859-6820, FAX:
(310) 860-6820, E-Mail: sfb@bhdrl.
com
Partner: Stephen F. Breimer

THE DMA BLUM & CO LLC

81 Clinton St
Fairfield, CT 06824-6908
Telephone: (203) 255-4813, FAX:
(203) 255-3936, E-Mail: e-blum@
att.net, Web Site: www.blumdirect.
com
Pres: Sandra J. Blum

THE DMA THE BOSTON CONSULTING GROUP

430 Park Ave Fl 14
New York, NY 10022-3528
Telephone: (212) 446-2800
Lead Researcher: Ginny Woodis

THE DMA BOWMAN CIRCULATION MARKETING

56 Ritch Ave W (fl 2)
Greenwich, CT 06830-6918
Telephone: (917) 913-6172, E-Mail:
nicole@nicolebowman.com, Web
Site: www.nicolebowman.com
Pres: Nicole Bowman
Conducts Business: U.S.
Primary Market Served: Business &
Consumer
Indirect online sales
Founded: 2004

Consulting consumer marketing to
publishers of magazines & newsletters.

BOYDEN GLOBAL EXECUTIVE SEARCH

3 Manhattanville Rd (Suite 104),
Building 3
Purchase, NY 10577-2116
Telephone: (914) 747-0093, E-Mail:
inquiry@boyden.com, Web Site:
www.boyden.com
Mng Dir: Tim C. McNamara

THE DMA REGGIE BRADY MARKETING SOLUTIONS LLC

198 Scribner Ave
Norwalk, CT 06854-1324
Telephone: (203) 838-8138, Web Site:
www.reggiebrady.com
Pres: Regina Brady

JOANNA BRANDI & CO INC

7491 N Federal Hwy C-5 (#304)
Boca Raton, FL 33487
Telephone: (561) 279-0027, E-Mail:
joanna@returnonhappiness.com, Web
Site: www.returnonhappiness.com
Pres: JoAnna Brandi

Training, consulting & research in customer & employee loyalty &
happiness. Twenty one years of helping
companies create customer-caring
cultures.

BRANDUNITY INC

PO Box 4512
Rollingbay, WA 98061-0512
Telephone: (206) 842-4948, E-Mail:
admin@brandunity.com, Web Site:
www.brandunity.com
Pres: Ann Jensen Warman
CTO: David Warman
Conducts Business: Worldwide
Employees: 4
Primary Market Served: Business &
Consumer
Indirect online sales
Advertising/Marketing Budget Related
to Direct Marketing: 0-25%
Direct Marketing ad budget:

Direct Mail: 25%
Magazines: 25%
Online: 50%
Founded: 2003
Gross sales or billing: $1,000,000

Integrated brand marketing, strategies
& creative services.

BRANDYWINE CONSULTING GROUP INC

1398 Morstein Rd (Suite 4)
West Chester, PA 19380-5848
Telephone: (610) 696-5872, FAX:
(610) 429-1954, Web Site: www.
brandywineconsulting.com
Pres: Benjamin J. Ventresca Jr.

BRISTOL ASSOCIATES INC

5777 W Century Blvd (Suite 865)
Los Angeles, CA 90045-5696
Telephone: (310) 670-0525, FAX:
(310) 670-4075, E-Mail: lfarber@
bristolassoc.com, Web Site: www.
bristolassoc.com
Pres: James J. Bright Jr.

THE DMA BROKERS INTERNATIONAL LTD

1200 E Main St
Panora, IA 50216-1100
Telephone: (641) 755-2775
Commun Specialist: Sara Tokheim

BROTHERS & THOMPSON PC

180 N Stetson Ave Ste 4425
Chicago, IL 60601-6733
Telephone: (312) 372-2909, FAX:
(312) 704-6693, E-Mail:
hthompson@brothersthompson.net,
Web Site: www.brothersthompson.
net
Partner: Alan W. Brothers

BROWN, VAN REMMEN, KANUIT, INC

840 Apollo St Ste 300
El Segundo, CA 90245-4763
Telephone: (310) 536-0777, FAX:
(310) 536-0606, E-Mail: info@
bvksearch.com, Web Site: www.
bvksearch.com
Pres: Roger Van Remmen
Office Mgr: Julie Smith

BROWNING, JACOBSON & KLEIN LLP

9595 Wilshire Blvd Ste 601
Beverly Hills, CA 90212-2506
Telephone: (310) 247-8777, FAX:
(310) 247-1827
Co-Owner: Kenneth L. Browning

THE DMA THE BUFFKIN GROUP LLC
730 Cool Springs Blvd (Suite 120)
Franklin, TN 37067-7290
Telephone: (615) 778-2142, E-Mail:
info@thebuffkingroup.com, Web
Site: www.thebuffkingroup.com
Mng Partner: Craig Buffkin
Primary Market Served: Business

BULL DOG MEDIA GROUP INC
PO Box 463
Madison, SD 57042-0463
Telephone: (605) 256-9103, Web Site:
www.commissionsoup.com
Pres/Co-Founder: Darin Namken

BURTCH WORKS LLC
1603 Orrington Ave (Suite 1740)
Evanston, IL 60201-5017
Telephone: (847) 328-6902, Web Site:
www.burtchworks.com
Exec Recruiter: Sandy Marmitt

CDMC/CAREFREE DIRECT MARKETING CORP
PO Box 3737, 8001 E Serene St
Carefree, AZ 85377-3737
Telephone: (480) 488-4227, FAX:
(480) 488-2841
Pres: Stephen R. Warsaw

CAKEMAIL INC
4020 St-Ambroise (Suite 145)
Montreal, PQ, Canada H4C 2C7
Telephone: (514) 316-1550, Web Site:
www.cakemail.com
Primary Market Served: Business

CAMERON & CO
83 Duggan Ave
Toronto, ON, Canada M4V 1Y1
Telephone: (416) 268-2326
Owner: Wade Cameron
Primary Market Served: Business &
Consumer

CAPELL & ASSOCIATES
601 Central
Barnegat Light, NJ 08006
Telephone: (201) 572-8774, FAX:
(609) 494-7369, E-Mail: contact@
capellandassociates.com, Web Site:
www.capell&associates.com
Pres: E Daniel Capell

CAPGEMINI AMERICAS OUTSOURCING
623 Fifth Ave (33rd fl)
New York, NY 10022
Telephone: (212) 314-8000, FAX:
(212) 314-8001
CEO: Dave Bonner

CAREER BLAZERS
5 W 37th St (5th fl)
New York, NY 10018-5384
Telephone: (212) 719-3232, FAX:
(212) 221-0452
Pres: Allen Bowers

THE CATALOG CONSULTANCY
3285 West Brookfield Way
Vero Beach, FL 32966-3164
Telephone: (772) 226-7740, FAX:
(772) 226-7740, E-Mail:
catalog321@aol.com, Web Site:
www.catalogconsultant.com
Pres: Sidney Kerber

CATALOG MARKETING GROUP
500 Davis St (Suite 812)
Evanston, IL 60201-4668
Telephone: (847) 864-8089
Pres: E. Herbert Krug
Primary Market Served: Business

CAUGHERTY HAHN COMMUNICATIONS
233 Rock Rd (Suite 248)
Glen Rock, NJ 07452-1708
Telephone: (201) 251-7778, FAX:
(201) 251-7779, Web Site: www.
chcomm.com
Pres & CEO: Lisa C. Hahn

ANDREA B CAUTELA
111 Worth St
New York, NY 10013-4008
Telephone: (212) 577-5920
Primary Market Served: Consumer

THE DMA CENTER FOR INFORMATION POLICY LEADERSHIP
at Hunton & Williams, LLP
2200 Pennsylania Ave NW, Hunton &
Williams, LLP
Washington, DC 20037-1701
Telephone: (202) 778-2264, FAX:
(202) 778-2201, Web Site: www.
policyleaders.com
Exec Dir: Martin Abrams

CHACHA MOBILE ANSWERS
14550 Clay Terrace Blvd (Suite 130)
Carmel, IN 46032-3653
Telephone: (317) 660-6680, Web Site:
partners.chacha.com
Chief Sls & Mktg Officer: Jay Highley

THE DMA CHAPMAN CUBINE ADAMS & HUSSEY
1600 Wilson Blvd (Suite 300)
Arlington, VA 22209-2505

Telephone: (703) 248-0025, Web Site:
www.ahadirect.com
Pres: James Hussey
Primary Market Served: Business &
Consumer

THE CHUBB CORP
15 Mountainview Rd
Warren, NJ 07059
Telephone: (908) 903-2000, FAX:
(908) 903-2027, Web Site: www.
chubb.com
Sr VP Customer & Mktg Intel: Jeff
Hoffman

THE DMA CIARLO CONSULTING LLC
39 Gary Ave
Waterbury, CT 06704-2034
Telephone: (203) 232-6655

CIRCINUS INTERNATIONAL LLC
283 Franklin St (Suite 400)
Boston, MA 02110-3100
Telephone: (774) 696-3517, Web Site:
www.circinusinternational.com
Pres: Brook Spaulding

CIRCULATION SPECIALISTS INC
3 Enterprise Dr (Suite 408)
Shelton, CT 06484-4694
Telephone: (888) 315-2472, FAX:
(888) 315-2507
Pres: Greg Wolfe

CLARIO ANALYTICS
7684 Golden Triangle Dr
Eden Prairie, MN 55344-3732
Telephone: (952) 653-0980, (866) 849-
3341, FAX: (952) 653-5900, E-Mail:
sales@clarioanalytics.com, Web Site:
www.clarioanalytics.com
CEO: Bill Flach
Pres: Randy Erdahl
CTO: Matt Redlon
CFO: John Miller
Employees: 22
Primary Market Served: Business
Advertising/Marketing Budget Related
to Direct Marketing: 0-25%
Direct Marketing ad budget: $20,000
Direct Mail: 50%
Online: 50%
Founded: 2002
Gross sales or billing: $1,500,000

Specializes in analyzing vast quantities
of consumer data to help companies
that have large information databases
market more efficiently.

THE DMA CLARITY GROUP LLC
600 Market St Ste 302
Chapel Hill, NC 27516-4057

Telephone: (919) 932-6036, Web Site: www.claritygroupinc.com
Founder & CEO: Craig Wood

CLEMENTDIRECT
THE DMA
72109 Moseley
Chapel Hill, NC 27517-8574
Telephone: (919) 338-2853, FAX: (206) 338-2511, Web Site: www.clementdirect.com
Pres: Coy Clement

CLICK2MAIL
THE DMA
3103 10th St N (Suite 201)
Arlington, VA 22201-2191
Telephone: (703) 521-9029, (866) 665-2787, FAX: (703) 358-8811, E-Mail: info@click2mail.com, Web Site: www.click2mail.com
Pres & CEO: Lee Garvey
Conducts Business: U.S.
Primary Market Served: Business & Consumer
Catalog available online
Direct online sales
Advertising/Marketing Budget Related to Direct Marketing: 51-75%
Direct Marketing ad budget: $25,000
Direct Mail: 50%
Online: 50%
Founded: 2003
Gross sales or billing: $18,000,000

CLICKSQUARED
THE DMA
280 Summer St (Suite 600)
Boston, MA 02210-1131
Telephone: (781) 622-1611, (866) 402-5425, FAX: (857) 246-7645, E-Mail: info@clicksquared.com, Web Site: www.clicksquared.com
Dir Mktg: Eileen Weinberg

Provider of email & cross-channel database marketing solutions, including self-service email to automated, real-time customer engagement.

COHEN & CO
281 Hicks St
Brooklyn, NY 11201-4508
Telephone: (718) 875-5065, FAX: (718) 875-5065, E-Mail: herbertjcohen@aol.com
Pres: Herbert J. Cohen

COL VOCE CONSULTING
THE DMA
551 Newcomen Rd
Exton, PA 19341-1938
Telephone: (215) 266-2992, Web Site: www.colvoce.com
Pres: Diane Rodwell
Primary Market Served: Business & Consumer

COLARELLI MEYER & ASSOCIATES INC
7751 Carondelet Ave (Suite 302)
Saint Louis, MO 63105-3316
Telephone: (314) 721-1860, (800) 459-4548, FAX: (314) 721-1992, E-Mail: cmaconsult@cmaconsult.com, Web Site: www.cmaconsult.com
Founding Member: Nick J. Colarelli

COLEMAN FROST LLP
429 Santa Monica Blvd Ste 700
Santa Monica, CA 90401-3435
Telephone: (310) 576-7312, Web Site: www.colemanfrost.com

COLLINGER & ASSOCIATES
THE DMA
590 Sarah Ln Apt 401
Saint Louis, MO 63141-6968
Telephone: (314) 991-8787, FAX: (314) 991-9797, E-Mail: bcmktr@aol.com
Pres: William Collinger

COMMUNICATION MANAGERS, LLC
THE DMA
604 Federal Rd
Brookfield, CT 06804-2070
Telephone: (203) 775-4213, FAX: (203) 775-6413, E-Mail: etalian@communicationmanagers.com, Web Site: www.communicationmanagers.com
Principal: Elizabeth Talian

COMMUNICATIONS UNLIMITED INC
10129 Deepwood Cir
Richmond, VA 23238-4241
Telephone: (804) 754-7242, E-Mail: communicationsunlimited@verizon.net
VP: Robert Carter

COMMUNISPOND INC
5 Lauras Ln
East Hampton, NY 11937-5916
Telephone: (212) 486-2300, (800) 529-5925, FAX: (212) 486-2680
Pres: Kevin Daley

CONCEPT COMMUNICATIONS
400 Amherst St
Nashua, NH 03063-1241
Telephone: (603) 577-9810, Web Site: www.conceptcommusa.com
Dir: John Fayad

JOHN CONDON & ASSOCIATES
38 Angus Ln
Greenwich, CT 06831-4402

Telephone: (203) 869-7006, FAX: (203) 622-1488
Pres & Owner: John Condon Jr.

CONNECTICUT MARKETING ASSOCIATES
12 Godfrey Pl (Suite 3)
Wilton, CT 06897
Telephone: (203) 761-9556, FAX: (203) 761-9763
VP: Steve R. Lake

CONTINUITY SHIPPERS ASSOCIATION
2351 N Bridgewater Rd, Saddlebow Farm
Woodstock, VT 05091-9670
Telephone: (802) 672-3634
Exec Dir: Coleman Hoyt

THE CONTRINO GROUP
2770 Arapahoe Rd Ste 132
Lafayette, CO 80026-8016
Telephone: (303) 664-1290, Web Site: www.thecontrinogroup.com
Pres: Kathleen Contrino

T A COOK CONSULTANTS INC
THE DMA
9212 Falls of Neuse Rd (Suite 201)
Raleigh, NC 27615-2483
Telephone: (919) 510-8142, Web Site: www.tacook.com
Primary Market Served: Consumer

THE COPY WORKS
THE DMA
12668 Camino Emparrado
San Diego, CA 92128-1404
Telephone: (858) 676-6757, Web Site: www.thecopyworks.com
Owner: Susan Fantle

COPYDIRECT
THE DMA
39 Forge Dr
Plymouth, MA 02360-2508
Telephone: (508) 732-9900, Web Site: www.belindabrewster.com
Primary Market Served: Business & Consumer

CORPORA CONSULTING
42 W Market St
Bethlehem, PA 18018-5703
Telephone: (215) 313-9229
Pres: Placido Corpora

CORRY DIRECT MARKETING LLC
THE DMA
109 Limekiln Rd
Ridgefield, CT 06877-3418

Telephone: (203) 438-1478, FAX:
(203) 431-0217, E-Mail: tom@
corrydirect.com, Web Site: www.
corrydirect.com
Pres: Thomas P. Corry

CORS
1 Pierce Pl (Suite 295)
Itasca, IL 60143-1253
Telephone: (630) 250-8677, (800) 323-
1352, FAX: (630) 250-7362, Web
Site: www.cors.com
Mktg Commun Supvr: Therese De-
Francesco

THE DMA PAMELA COTRUPE
129 S Royal Ascot Dr
Las Vegas, NV 89144-4309
Telephone: (818) 624-0087

CRAMER
425 University Ave
Norwood, MA 02062-2636
Telephone: (781) 278-2387, Web Site:
www.crameronline.com
Dir Mktg: Rebecca Hodgkins

THE DMA CRANDALL ASSOCIATES INC
6 Litchfield Rd # 316
Port Washington, NY 11050-3815
Telephone: (516) 767-6800, E-Mail:
joyce@crandallassociates.com, Web
Site: www.crandallassociates.com
Pres: Wendy Weber

CREATING SELLING
OPPORTUNITIES
2902 W Lane Dr (Suite E)
Houston, TX 77027
Telephone: (713) 622-6936, FAX:
(713) 622-2924, E-Mail: annci@
sbcglobal.net
Owner: Ann C. Iverson

THE DMA CREATIVE SYNERGY INC
13660 Spinning Wheel Dr
Germantown, MD 20874-2819
Telephone: (301) 515-9397, Web Site:
kimschwalm.com

CREDITCARDS.COM
8920 Business Park Dr (Suite 350)
Austin, TX 78759-7636
Telephone: (512) 996-8663, Web Site:
www.creditcards.com
VP Strategic Mktg: Jody Farmer

MARY CULNAN
Georgetown University
37th & O Sts NW
Washington, DC 20057

Telephone: (202) 687-4031, (202) 687-
0100, Web Site: www.georgetown.
edu
Prof: Betsy Sigman

JOHN CUMMINGS &
PARTNERS LLC
Six Blair Rd
Armonk, NY 10504-2522
Telephone: (914) 273-4691, FAX:
(914) 206-3007, E-Mail: john@
dbmscan.com, Web Site: www.
dbmscan.com
Pres: John J. Cummings
Partner: Robert Cummings

MJ CURRAN & ASSOCIATES
INC
1 Birchwood Ln
Sandwich, MA 02563
Telephone: (617) 247-7700, FAX:
(617) 267-6429
Pres: Martin J. Curran

CUSTOMER RETENTION
SOLUTIONS
7837 S Sprinkle Rd
Portage, MI 49002-9432
Telephone: (269) 324-7385
Pres: David Disser

CYNTHIA FIELDS & CO
(CFC)
230 W 22nd St
New York, NY 10011-2701
Telephone: (212) 242-6063
Owner: Cindy Fields

DB CONSULTING
550 Mamaroneck Ave.
Harrison, NY 10528
Telephone: (914) 698-2008, E-Mail:
darcybev@yahoo.com
CEO: Darcy Bevelacqua
CEO & Partner: Kandal Antik
Partner: Mark Wilcox

DBMCATALYST
377 Lincoln St.
Lexington, MA 02421-7446
Telephone: (339) 227-7591

DCJ CONSULTING
6749 Exeter St
Forest Hills, NY 11375-4150
Telephone: (718) 575-8357
Primary Market Served: Consumer

DM ASSISTANCE INC
155 Fleet St
Portsmouth, NH 03801-4050
Telephone: (603) 964-6156
Pres: Wes DeVries

Sec: Sharon Brown

DM INFO
308 Royce Woods Ct
Naperville, IL 60565
Telephone: (630) 357-0732, FAX:
(630) 527-8136, E-Mail: dminfo@
dmcsweeney.com
Owner: David McSweeney
Conducts Business: U.S.
Primary Market Served: Business &
Consumer
Advertising/Marketing Budget Related
to Direct Marketing: 76-100%
Founded: 2003

Database and program analysis, list
brokerage utilities, non-profit and direct marketers services.

DS & A CONSULTING
1037 Corinthian Ct
Lexington, KY 40509-2508
Telephone: (973) 530-4198
Principal: Dany Sfeir

THE DMA DWS ASSOCIATES
1032 Saint Johns Bay
Saint Paul, MN 55129-8537
Telephone: (602) 321-6512, Web Site:
www.dwstevenson.com
CEO: Dudley Stevenson

DALY COMMUNICATIONS
5630 Wisconsin Ave (#903)
Chevy Chase, MD 20815-4456
Telephone: (301) 951-9110, E-Mail:
speaker@johnjaydaly.com, Web Site:
www.johnjaydaly.com
Pres: John Jay Daly APR, PREA

THE DMA CHET DALZELL
145 E 29th St (Apt 6D)
New York, NY 10016-8146
Telephone: (917) 608-2251
Primary Market Served: Consumer

DAN SMOLEN DIRECT
SEARCH LLC
44 Lightfoot Dr
Stafford, VA 22554-8509
Telephone: (703) 835-9900, FAX:
(703) 835-9966, E-Mail: dsmolen@
dansmolen.com, Web Site: www.
dansmolen.com
Pres: Daniel T. Smolen
Conducts Business: U.S.
Employees: 2
Primary Market Served: Business &
Consumer
Advertising/Marketing Budget Related
to Direct Marketing: 76-100%
Direct Marketing ad budget:
Direct Mail: 15%
Newspapers: 85%

Founded: 2005
Gross sales or billing: $600,000
Executive search services for direct marketing, interactive marketing & consumer insights.

ᴛʜᴇ ᴅᴍᴀ DANIEL GONZALEZ & ASSOCIATES

939 8th Ave (#300)
New York, NY 10019-4205
Telephone: (212) 682-0333
Pres: Daniel Gonzalez

ᴛʜᴇ ᴅᴍᴀ DAVIS & GILBERT

1740 Broadway
New York, NY 10019-4379
Telephone: (212) 468-4800, FAX: (212) 468-4888, Web Site: www. dglaw.com
Partner: Ronald R. Urbach

BERT DAVIS EXECUTIVE SEARCH

Bert Davis Publishing Placement Consultants
425 Madison Ave (fl 14)
New York, NY 10017-1110
Telephone: (212) 838-4000, FAX: (212) 935-3291, E-Mail: info@ bertdavis.com, Web Site: www. bertdavis.com
Pres: Bert Davis
Sr VP: Wendy Baker
Sr VP: Kathy Berlowe
Mktg & Research Dir: Kristi Johnston
Exec VP: Sally Dougan
Primary Market Served: Business & Consumer
Founded: 1977

THOMAS DAWSON

40 Casa Bella Cir
Palm Coast, FL 32137-1223
Telephone: (303) 250-9000

DE RHAM & CO INC

PO Box 889
Dorset, VT 05251-0889
Telephone: (802) 867-0155, (888) 867-0155, FAX: (802) 867-0361, Web Site: www.derham.com
Pres: Abbott de Rham
Conducts Business: U.S.
Primary Market Served: Business & Consumer
Founded: 1993

Automated speech solutions for direct marketers. End-to-end services for customer service and marketing call center, direct marketing consulting.

DECKER COMMUNICATIONS INC

575 Market St (Suite 1925)
San Francisco, CA 94105
Telephone: (877) 485-0700, FAX: (415) 543-8103, E-Mail: info@ deckercommunications.com, Web Site: www.deckercommunications. com
Pres & CEO: Bert Decker

ᴛʜᴇ ᴅᴍᴀ DEHART & DARR ASSOCIATES

1360 Beverly Rd (Suite 201)
McLean, VA 22101-3647
Telephone: (703) 448-1000, FAX: (703) 790-3460
VP: Daniel Smith
Consultant: Anne Darr

ᴛʜᴇ ᴅᴍᴀ ROBERT DELAY

4121 E Via del Cuculin
Tucson, AZ 85718-3320
Telephone: (520) 615-8235

DENMARK FRANCISCO

684 9th Ave (fl 4)
New York, NY 10036-3612
Telephone: (212) 444-8157, Web Site: www.dsfnyc.com
Primary Market Served: Consumer

THE DEVEREUX GROUP

47 Locust St, Little Harbour
Marblehead, MA 01945-2935
Telephone: (781) 631-9213, FAX: (781) 639-3044, E-Mail: roeser@ devereuxgroup.com, Web Site: www. devereuxgroup.com
Pres: Prugh Roeser

DIDACTIC SYSTEMS

PO Box 457
Cranford, NJ 07016-0457
Telephone: (908) 276-5413, FAX: (908) 276-7174, E-Mail: didacticra@ aol.com
Pres: Erwin Rausch

ᴛʜᴇ ᴅᴍᴀ DIRECT ADVANTAGE PARTNERS

69 Bluff Ave (Suite 100)
Rowayton, CT 06853-1802
Telephone: (203) 286-7100

DIRECT DYNAMICS LLC

85 Emanuel Church Rd
Killingworth, CT 06419
Telephone: (860) 614-4816, E-Mail: info@direct-dynamics.com, Web Site: direct-dynamics.com
Mng Partner: Francis Barkyoumb

DIRECT MAIL SYSTEMS

12450 Automobile Blvd
Clearwater, FL 33762
Telephone: (727) 573-1985, (800) 683-6245, FAX: (727) 573-1747, E-Mail: info@direct-mail-systems.com, Web Site: www.direct-mail-systems.com
Pres: Roger Pennington

DIRECT MARKETERS ON CALL INC (DMOC)

45 Christopher St Apt 4A
New York, NY 10014-3585
Telephone: (212) 691-1942, FAX: (212) 924-1331, E-Mail: info@ dmoc-inc.com, Web Site: www. dmoc-inc.com
Pres: Heather Frayne
Opers Mgr: Nicole Allen
Comptroller: Amy Gotbetter
Employees: 6
Primary Market Served: Business & Consumer
Indirect online sales
Advertising/Marketing Budget Related to Direct Marketing: 76-100%
Direct Marketing ad budget:
Direct Mail: 50%
Magazines: 50%
Founded: 1989

Freelance and consulting service for the direct marketing industry, servicing ad agencies, and corporations in the New York Metro Region.

DIRECT MARKETING CONSULTANT

399 Sherman Ave
Sharon, PA 16146-3953
Telephone: (724) 699-0230
Direct Mktg Consultant: Lynne Nigro

DIRECT MARKETING INSIGHTS INC

15970 W Edgemont Ave
Goodyear, AZ 85395-8112
Telephone: (843) 817-7488, E-Mail: jimp@dminsights.com, Web Site: www.dminsights.com
Pres: James L. Padgitt

Expert direct response consulting help for entrepreneurial owners of catalog & ecommerce businesses.

DIRECT MARKETING RESOURCES

517 Highland Forest Dr
Charlotte, NC 28270-0848
Telephone: (704) 845-5890, (888) 644-4DMR, E-Mail: dan@dmresources. com, Web Site: www.dmresources. com
Pres: Daniel J. Sullivan
Conducts Business: U.S.

Employees: 4
Primary Market Served: Business &
 Consumer
Advertising/Marketing Budget Related
 to Direct Marketing: 26-50%
Direct Marketing ad budget:
Direct Mail: 20%
Telephone: 80%
Founded: 1988
Gross sales or billing: $1,000,000

Executive search firm specializing in
the direct marketing industry, both corporate and agency and all functional
areas.

DIRECT MARKETING
RESOURCES GROUP INC

4501 Newborn Ave (Suite 130-253)
Raleigh, NC 27610-1550
Telephone: (919) 231-2728, (800) 517-
 5253, Web Site: www.
 improvedmarketingresults.com
Mktg Dir: George Wehmann

DIRECT VENTURES INC

18 Clover Rd
Larchmont, NY 10538-1749
Telephone: (914) 833-9842, FAX:
 (914) 834-3883, E-Mail: bsideroff@
 directventuresmcinc.wm
Pres: Barry Sideroff

DIRECTIONS MARKETING

505 Green Rd
Ann Arbor, MI 48105
Telephone: (734) 930-2820, FAX:
 (734) 930-9189, E-Mail: directions@
 directions.com.eg, Web Site: www.
 directions.com.eg
Pres: Bruce S. Moyer

DIRECTIVES/TARGETED
MARKETING AND
COMMUNICATIONS

1022 Avalon Way
Plymouth, MA 02360-7777
Telephone: (215) 546-7817, Web Site:
 www.directivesmarketing.com
Pres: Carolyn Gould
Founded: 1988

Specializes in multi-channel, integrated
marketing and communications. Over
the years, its clients have included
consumer and business-to-business
marketers, ranging from small retailers
to Fortune 200 companies. Experienced in all types of industry segments
- from fashion to finance, technology
to travel, health to hard goods - and a
wide variety of communications channels - bricks and mortar, catalog, internet, solo direct mail, telemarketing,
publishing, advertising, and television.

THE DIVERSIFIED SERVICES
GROUP INC

303 W Lancaster Ave (Suite 2E)
Wayne, PA 19087-3938
Telephone: (610) 989-1710, FAX:
 (610) 989-1730, E-Mail: rfgrieb@
 dsg-network.com, Web Site: www.
 dsg-network.com
Principal & Founder: Robert F. Grieb

DODSON & ASSOCIATES

16302 Shadybank Dr
Dallas, TX 75248-2957
Telephone: (972) 931-1020
Principal: Gordon O. Dodson

DOVETAIL ART & DESIGN
INC

113 Wade Dr
Dover, OH 44622-9460
Telephone: (303) 987-9300, Web Site:
 www.dovetailart.com
Primary Market Served: Consumer

PATRICIA DOWD INC

5300 San Jacinto Ave
Atascadero, CA 93422-2940
Telephone: (805) 985-8243, E-Mail:
 pdowd@pdisearch.com, Web Site:
 www.pdisearch.com
Pres: Patricia Dowd

The first recruiter to specialize in database marketing placing all levels of
database marketing professionals since
1988.

DUGGAN & BROWN INC

215 S Northwest Hwy Ste 202B
Barrington, IL 60010-8301
Telephone: (847) 381-8484, FAX:
 (847) 381-8499
Pres: Jerry J. Brown

E MEDIA ADVANTAGE

Six Hamilton Ln
Livingston, NJ 07039-2006
Telephone: (917) 994-3685, FAX:
 (973) 455-1312, E-Mail: tnevitt@
 emediaadvantage.com, Web Site:
 emediaadvantage.com
Pres: Toni Nevitt

THE DMA EBM DIRECT MARKETING
SERVICES LLC

39 Seaview Ln
Port Washington, NY 11050-1737
Telephone: (516) 874-7839, Web Site:
 www.ebmdirectmarketing.com
Member: Eric Mohr

EADON VENTURES

11224 Reeder Ave NE
Alliance, OH 44601-8332

Telephone: (330) 418-4298
Pres: David Conway

EASTERN COLLECTION
CORP

16 Barclay Dr
Sag Harbor, NY 11963-4316
Telephone: (631) 563-2112, (800) 243-
 1204, FAX: (631) 563-2471, E-Mail:
 ecc1626@aol.com
Pres: Arleen Rossi

ECHOTOUCH CORP

5907 Carry Back Ln
Austin, TX 78746-1448
Telephone: (512) 327-5638, Web Site:
 www.echotouch.com
CEO: Brian McClure

ECOENVELOPES

17800 George Moran Dr
Eden Prairie, MN 55347
Telephone: (612) 605-4885, (888) 428-
 4364, FAX: (651) 392-8924, E-Mail:
 info@ecoenvelopes.com, Web Site:
 www.ecoenvelopes.com
Founder & CEO: Ann DeLaVergne

THE DMA THE EDBRAHAM GROUP

PO Box 753
Westbrook, CT 06498-0753
Telephone: (860) 664-4120, Web Site:
 www.theedbrahamgroup.com
Principal: Shirley Edbrooke
Primary Market Served: Business

EDELMAN DIRECT
MARKETING INC

75 Fairview Ave
Great Neck, NY 11023-1350
Telephone: (516) 829-9398
Pres: Robert Edelman
Pres Consumer Mktg & Global Cre-
ative Dir: Mitch Markson

EFFECTIVE MARKETING
ASSOCIATES, INC

aka EMA
3525 Riverknoll Way
West Linn, OR 97068-3641
Telephone: (503) 657-5859, FAX:
 (503) 657-5886, Web Site: www.e-
 m-a.com
Pres: Stephen B. Garner

EINHORN ASSOCIATES INC

2675 N Mayfair Rd (Suite 410)
Milwaukee, WI 53226
Telephone: (414) 453-4488, FAX:
 (414) 453-4831, Web Site: www.
 einhornassociates.com
Pres: Stephen Einhorn

JS ELIEZER ASSOCIATES INC
300 Atlantic St (fl 7)
Stamford, CT 06901-3522
Telephone: (203) 658-1300
Assoc: Andrew Gruber

EMAILOGICS INC/ EMAILBRAIN
8100 NE Parkway Dr (Suite 300)
Vancouver, WA 98662-7954
Telephone: (866) 873-3019, Web Site:
www.emailbrain.com
Bus Devel: Stephanie Lazardi

THE DMA EMARKETING STRATEGY GROUP
155 E 34th St (Suite 20-C)
New York, NY 10016-4718
Telephone: (212) 679-6486, Web Site:
www.ruthstevens.com
Pres: Ruth Stevens

EMPLOYERS GROUP
400 Continental Blvd Ste 300
El Segundo, CA 90245-5080
Telephone: (800) 748-8484, Web Site:
www.employesgroup.com
Mktg Mgr: Nicole Vierzba
Primary Market Served: Consumer

Human Resources consulting firm offering custom consulting services, training, seminars, publications & products

ENGAGENEXTGEN LLC
5463 Bartlett Blvd
Mound, MN 55364-1605
Telephone: (952) 905-4474
Primary Market Served: Consumer

EPIC RESEARCH LLC
300 Centennial Cir
Greenville, DE 19807-2130
Telephone: (302) 467-5445, Web Site:
www.epicresearch.net
Chief Mktg Officer: Ben Brake

EQUIFAX CREDIT INFORMATION SERVICES INC
1550 Peachtree NW
Atlanta, GA 30309
Telephone: (404) 885-8000, (800) 685-5000, FAX: (404) 885-8988, Web
Site: www.equifax.com
Chmn & CEO: Richard F. Smith
VP & Chief Mktg Officer: Paul J. Springman

EQUITY MANAGEMENT INC
4365 Executive Dr Ste 1000
San Diego, CA 92121-2192

Telephone: (858) 558-2500, FAX:
(858) 558-2547, Web Site: www.
equitymanagementinc.com
Chmn & CEO: Glen Konkle

EQUITY RESIDENTIAL PROPERTIES
Two N Riverside Plaza (Suite 400)
Chicago, IL 60606-2624
Telephone: (312) 474-1300, FAX:
(312) 474-8703, E-Mail:
mgraycraddock@eqr.com, Web Site:
www.eqr.com
Corp Mktg Dir: Mary Gray Craddock

ERLANDSON ASSOCIATES
222 W Market St
Leesburg, VA 20176-2709
Telephone: (703) 669-0889, E-Mail:
bgerlandso@aol.com
Pres: Barbara Erlandson

THE DMA ERNAN ROMAN DIRECT MARKETING CORP
3 Melrose Ln
Little Neck, NY 11363-1220
Telephone: (718) 225-4151, FAX:
(718) 225-4889, E-Mail: ernan@
erdm.com, Web Site: www.erdm.com
Pres: Ernan Roman
Sr Partner: Scott Hornstein
Conducts Business: U.S.
Primary Market Served: Business & Consumer
Advertising/Marketing Budget Related to Direct Marketing: 76-100%
Founded: 1983

Integrated direct marketing and consensual opt-in marketing consulting services.

THE DMA ERNST & YOUNG LLP
5 Times Sq
New York, NY 10036-6527
Telephone: (212) 773-6146, FAX:
(312) 879-4000, Web Site: www.ey.
com
Dir, Direct Mktg Distr: Ingrid McGuire

THE DMA EXECUTIVE CONNECTIONS LLC
8466 Lockwood Ridge Rd (#330)
Sarasota, FL 34243-2951
Telephone: (941) 323-8300, Web Site:
www.executiveconnectionsllc.com
CEO: Jeff Gundersen
Chief Coaching Officer: Lorraine White
Mktg Dir: Jackie Bivins
Search Consultant: Paula Fontana
Conducts Business: U.S.
Employees: 8
Primary Market Served: Business & Consumer

Catalog available online
Direct online sales
Advertising/Marketing Budget Related to Direct Marketing: 51-75%
Founded: 2003
Gross sales or billing: $5,000,000

Specializes in executive search consulting and executive coaching.

EXECUTIVE SEARCH INTERNATIONAL
1525 Centre St
Newton, MA 02461-1200
Telephone: (617) 527-8787, E-Mail:
info@execsearchintl.com, Web Site:
www.execsearchintl.com
Mng Partner: Les Gore

FIGURS*
39a Fourth St
Toronto, ON, Canada M8V 2Y2
Telephone: (416) 826-9083
Primary Market Served: Business

FIRST OF OMAHA MERCHANT PROCESSING
Subs. of First National Bank of Omaha
1620 Dodge St
Omaha, NE 68197
Telephone: (402) 341-0500, (800) 228-2443
Chmn: Bruce Lawitzen

THE DMA FLAREPATH LLC
200 Cabrini Blvd (#119)
New York, NY 10033-1121
Telephone: (212) 927-1296
Co-Pres: Mark Oberski

FOCUS ON THE ROI
97 Gem Ln
Massapequa Park, NY 11762-3222
Telephone: (917) 620-1838
Primary Market Served: Consumer

THE FORUM CORP
265 Franklin St Ste 400
Boston, MA 02110-3182
Telephone: (617) 523-7300, (800) 367-8611, FAX: (617) 371-3300, E-Mail:
forum@forum.com, Web Site: www.
forum.com
Pres & CEO: Ed Boswell

FOTOBED.COM
4630 Old Looney Mill Rd.
Birmingham, AL 35243-2607
Telephone: (888) 368-6233, E-Mail:
service@fotobed.com, Web Site:
www.fotobed.com
Pres: John Castleberry

FOXHALL CORP
6849 Old Dominion Dr (Suite 320)
McLean, VA 22101-3791
Telephone: (703) 749-3126
Pres: Byron Hughey

THE
DMA **FOXHALL CORPORATION**
6849 Old Dominion Dr (Suite 320)
McLean, VA 22101-3791
Telephone: (703) 749-3126
Pres: Bryon Hughey
Primary Market Served: Business &
Consumer

THE
DMA **JONATHAN FRIEDMAN**
3720 N 37th Ter
Hollywood, FL 33021
Telephone: (954) 416-3419
Primary Market Served: Business &
Consumer

FUNME EVENTS
Div. of Creative Marketing Enterprises
Inc
PO Box 463
Dekalb, IL 60115-0463
Telephone: (800) 386-6321, FAX:
(815) 787-3100, E-Mail:
funMEevents@aol.com, Web Site:
www.funMEevents.com
Pres: Michael T. Embrey

FURGIUELE & CO INC
276 Read Ave
Crestwood, NY 10707
Telephone: (914) 793-0045, FAX:
(914) 779-6447, E-Mail: fci@fcidms.
com, Web Site: www.fcidms.com
Pres: Joseph Furgiuele

GC SERVICES
6330 Gulfton
Houston, TX 77081
Telephone: (713) 777-4441, FAX:
(713) 776-6535, E-Mail: marketing.
communications@gcserv.com, Web
Site: www.gcserv.com
Pres: Frank Taylor

THE
DMA **GARTNER INC**
1650 Technology Dr Ste 500
San Jose, CA 95110-3838
Telephone: (408) 468-8000, (800) 419-
3282, FAX: (408) 954-1780, E-Mail:
tom.mccall@gartner.com, Web Site:
www.gartner.com
Sr Dir, Pub Rels: Tom McCall

THE
DMA **GASPEDAL**
333 W North Ave (Suite 500)
Chicago, IL 60610-1293
Telephone: (312) 932-9000, Web Site:
www.gaspedal.net
CEO: Andy Sernovitz

Primary Market Served: Business &
Consumer

**GAZETTE DIRECT
MARKETING CO**
Subs. of Gazette Co
500 Third Ave SE
Cedar Rapids, IA 52401-1945
Telephone: (319) 399-5997, FAX:
(319) 399-5998, Web Site: www.
gazette.com
CEO & Pub: Joe Haldy

THE
DMA **GIBSON DIRECT INC**
204 Plantation Dr
Coppell, TX 75019-3232
Telephone: (972) 462-7580, FAX:
(972) 304-9202
Pres: Steve E. Gibson

GILCHRIST & PARTNERS
542 Mass Ave
Boston, MA 02118-1439
Telephone: (617) 314-4096, (866) 617-
5070

**GILLESPIE MAGAZINE
MARKETING &
PUBLISHING**
Div. of Gillespie
3450 Princeton Pike
Lawrenceville, NJ 08648
Telephone: (609) 895-0200, FAX:
(609) 895-0222, Web Site: www.
gillespie.com
Exec VP Mng Dir: Jamie Pack

THE
DMA **GLAZER-KENNEDY INSIDER
CIRCLE**
8430 W Bryn Mawr Ave Ste 575
Chicago, IL 60631-3497
Telephone: (410) 825-8600, Web Site:
www.dankennedy.com
Pres: William Glazer

GLENGARRY MARKETING
2303 RR 620 S Unit 135-150
Austin, TX 78734
Telephone: (800) 883-1924
CEO: Robert Stutz
Founded: 2004

**GLOBAL MARKETING
GROUP LTD**
119 W 57th St Ste 1405
New York, NY 10019-2401
Telephone: (212) 247-6060, FAX:
(212) 586-5446, E-Mail: kimglobal@
aol.com, Web Site: www.
gmgsolution.com
Pres: Kenneth Miller

BARBARA GOLD
10 W 15th (Apt 1924)
New York, NY 10011-6850
Telephone: (917) 750-4038
Primary Market Served: Consumer

ED GOLDEN & ASSOCIATES
7303 Shoal Creek Blvd
Austin, TX 78757-2028
Telephone: (512) 458-8222, FAX:
(512) 454-3536
Pres: Ed Golden

GOODMAN & CO
PO Box 835
New York, NY 10024-0540
Telephone: (212) 579-0020, Web Site:
www.goodmancompany.com
Chmn & CEO: Susan Goodman
Primary Market Served: Business &
Consumer

**GRADUATE MANAGEMENT
ADMISSION COUNCIL**
11921 Freedom Dr (Suite 300)
Reston, VA 20190
Telephone: (703) 668-9813, Web Site:
www.mba.com
Primary Market Served: Business

THE
DMA **GREENPATH
SUSTAINABILITY
CONSULTANTS**
13 Windgate Dr
New City, NY 10956-4434
Telephone: (914) 980-8346
Pres: David Refkin

GREY BIRCH GROUP LLC
64 Sycamore Ln
Irvington, NY 10533-1931
Telephone: (914) 479-5088, Web Site:
www.greybirch.com
Principal: Anne Schaeffer

GORDON W GROSSMAN INC
254 Salem Rd
Pound Ridge, NY 10576-1320
Telephone: (914) 238-9387, FAX:
(914) 238-1635
Pres: Gordon W. Grossman

GROUP F/64
1050 Arbor Rd
Winston-Salem, NC 27104
Telephone: (336) 748-8272, FAX:
(336) 748-8780
Pres: Cynthia Skaar

GROUP 3 MARKETING
800 Wayzata Blvd E (Suite 201)
Wayzata, MN 55391-1765

Telephone: (952) 475-3269, (888) 571-
6554, FAX: (952) 449-0403, E-Mail:
info@group3marketing.com, Web
Site: www.group3marketing.com
Pres: Bart Foreman

**GROWTH PLATFORMS
INSTITUTE**
68 St Johns (Suite 200)
Wilton, CT 06897
Telephone: (203) 529-0500, E-Mail:
info@growthplatforms.org, Web Site:
www.growthplatforms.org
Pres, Consulting: Neil Kleinfeld

GUNDERSEN PARTNERS LLC
30 Irving Pl (fl 2)
New York, NY 10003
Telephone: (212) 677-7660, FAX:
(212) 358-0275, Web Site: www.
gundersenpartners.com
Principal: Steven Gundersen
Mgr Opers: Ed Steffen
Founded: 1984

THE DMA HDI GROUP
1 Embarcadero Ctr (Suite 500)
San Francisco, CA 94111-3610
Telephone: (415) 794-3320, Web Site:
www.hobbsdirect.com
Pres: Michele Hobbs
Primary Market Served: Business &
Consumer

HAL LEVY & ASSOCIATES
186 Mohonk Rd
High Falls, NY 12440-5229
Telephone: (845) 687-4400
Pres: Hal Levy

**ROBERT HALF
INTERNATIONAL INC**
2884 Sand Hill Rd (Suite 200)
Menlo Park, CA 94025
Telephone: (650) 234-6000, FAX:
(650) 234-6930, E-Mail:
webmaster@rhi.com, Web Site:
www.rhii.com
CEO: Harold M. Messmer Jr

THE DMA ELIZABETH HARTMAN
5 Azalea Dr
Syosset, NY 11791-2802
Telephone: (516) 650-8862
VP: Elizabeth Hartman

**THE DMA HARVEST
COMMUNICATIONS**
2400 Washington Ave Ste 411
Redding, CA 96001-2827
Telephone: (800) 303-6405, FAX:
(800) 926-8038, Web Site: www.
harvest-communications.com

Admin: Jeanelle Couch

**DENNY HATCH ASSOCIATES
INC**
310 Gaskill St
Philadelphia, PA 19147-1503
Telephone: (215) 627-9103, FAX:
(215) 627-6610, E-Mail:
dennyhatch@yahoo.com, Web Site:
www.dennyhatch.com
Pres: Denny Hatch

HATCHHOLDINGS LLC
5832 Broadwell Dr
Plano, TX 75093-4717
Telephone: (214) 505-4697
Principal: William Randall

**THE DMA HAUSER LIST SERVICES,
NMIS**
2545 Hempstead Tpke Ste 401
East Meadow, NY 11554-2144
Telephone: (516) 935-8603, FAX:
(516) 935-8626, E-Mail: david@
hausernet.com, Web Site: www.
hausertrack.com
Chmn: Barry Hauser
EVP: David Hauser

HEALTHINFO DIRECT
1528 Sandburg Dr
Schaumburg, IL 60173-2183
Telephone: (630) 936-9465
Principal: Matthew Stone

THE DMA HEMISPHERE MARKETING
6437 Washington St
Kansas City, MO 64113-1731
Telephone: (816) 444-5439, Web Site:
www.hemispheremarketing.com
Owner: Gina Valentino

**DAVID HENEBERRY
ASSOCIATES**
111 Reynolds Ln
West Grove, PA 19390-1371
Telephone: (203) 778-0692, FAX:
(203) 778-0699
Pres: David Heneberry

THE HERMAN GROUP
7112 Viridian Ln
Austin, TX 78739-2092
Telephone: (336) 210-3547, E-Mail:
info@hermangroup.com, Web Site:
www.hermangroup.com
CEO: Joyce L. Gioia

THE DMA HIGH NOTE MEDIA INC
5315 N Clark (#218)
Chicago, IL 60640-2290
Telephone: (773) 980-6873, Web Site:
www.highnotemedia.com

**THE DMA DEBORAH HOFFMAN
COPYWRITING**
306 Sagebrush Dr
Corrales, NM 87048-8552
Telephone: (505) 440-8725
Primary Market Served: Consumer

**HOWARD-SLOAN-KOLLER
GROUP**
300 E 42nd St Fl 15
New York, NY 10017-5925
Telephone: (212) 661-5250, FAX:
(212) 557-9178, E-Mail: ekoller@
hsksearch.com, Web Site: www.
hsksearch.com
Pres: Edward R. Koller Jr.
Dir, Res: Steven Unger

**COLEMAN W HOYT
CONSULTANT**
2351 N Bridgewater Rd, Saddlebow
Farm
Woodstock, VT 05091-9670
Telephone: (802) 672-3634, FAX:
(802) 672-5116, E-Mail: cwhoyt@
vermontel.net
Principal: Coleman W. Hoyt

EA HUGHES & CO
200 Park Ave S (Suite 1608)
New York, NY 10003-1521
Telephone: (212) 689-4600, FAX:
(212) 689-4975, E-Mail: hr@
eahughes.com, Web Site: www.
eahughes.com
Pres: Elaine A. Hughes

**THE DMA HUNTER BUSINESS GROUP
LLC**
4650 N Port Washington Rd Stop 8
Milwaukee, WI 53212-1078
Telephone: (414) 203-8060, (800) 423-
4010, FAX: (414) 203-8225, E-Mail:
hunter@hunterbusiness.com, Web
Site: www.hunterbusiness.com
Pres: Victor Hunter
COO: Nedra Sadorf

IJHANA
409 W Olympic (Suite 706)
Los Angeles, CA 90015-1635
Telephone: (213) 268-4283, (888) 421-
9222, E-Mail: info@ijhana.com,
Web Site: www.ijhana.com
Managing Partner & CTO: Kevin Cal-
loway
Mng Partner: Thomas Dillmann

Global technology consulting firm

IMV
1400 E Touhy Ave (Suite 250)
Des Plaines, IL 60018-3339

Telephone: (847) 297-1404, FAX: (847) 297-5010, E-Mail: sales@imvinfo.com, Web Site: www.imvlimited.com
VP: Gail Prochaska

THE DMA IPG
532 W 22nd St (Apt 3C)
New York, NY 10011-1117
Telephone: (646) 229-2255
Primary Market Served: Consumer

IZEA
150 N Orange Ave (Suite 412)
Orlando, FL 32801-2317
Telephone: (321) 332-6830, Web Site: www.izea.com
Internet Mktg Specialist: Ashley Edwards

IDEAS IN SEO
758 NE 90 St (Unit 514)
Miami, FL 33138
Telephone: (786) 280-6051
Primary Market Served: Business & Consumer

THE DMA IKNOWTION LLC
25 Burlington Mall Rd (Suite 409)
Burlington, MA 01803-4156
Telephone: (781) 494-9989, Web Site: www.iknowtion.com
Mng Partner: William Duffy

IMAGINATION WORKS
24 Primrose Dr
Trumbull, CT 06611-5043
Telephone: (203) 377-1747, FAX: (203) 377-7401, E-Mail: jim@imaginationworks.net, Web Site: www.imaginationworks.net
Principal: Jim Lang

IMAGINE 360 MARKETING
1123 Broadway (Suite 902)
New York, NY 10010-2007
Telephone: (212) 313-9616, Web Site: www.i360m.com
Pres & CEO: Yael Penn

INDEPENDENT CONSULTANT
2307 Boxwood Ave E
Saint Paul, MN 55119-5670
Telephone: (612) 239-6572
Consultant: Mary Scundi

INFOMERCIAL MONITORING SERVICE INC
812 Parkway
Broomall, PA 19008

Telephone: (610) 328-6902, FAX: (610) 328-6791, E-Mail: catanese@imstv.com, Web Site: www.imstv.com
Pres & CEO: Samuel R. Catanese

INFOMORPHOSIS/ MARKETING SOLUTIONS
152 W 20th St (Suite D)
New York, NY 10011-3635
Telephone: (212) 366-6216, FAX: (212) 255-4784, E-Mail: dfain@nyc.rr.com
Principal: Deborah Fain

INTEGRATED MARKETING SOLUTIONS (IMS)
30108 Kimberly Dr
Ashland, NE 68003-3806
Telephone: (402) 486-3151, FAX: (402) 486-3161
Pres: Chris Peterson

INTERACTIVE SEARCH GROUP
35104 Euclid Ave (Suite 303)
Cleveland, OH 44094
Telephone: (216) 255-3388, Web Site: www.isgstaffingnow.com
Pres: Jason Peterson

INTERFACE ENGINEERING
708 SW Third Ave (Suite 400)
Portland, OR 97204
Telephone: (503) 382-2266, FAX: (503) 382-2262, E-Mail: solutions@interfaceengineering.com, Web Site: www.ieice.com
Pres & Treas: Omid Nabipoor
Sr VP: David Pickett
Principal: Joel Cruz
Assoc Principal: Andrew Briones
Assoc Principal: David Chesley
Founded: 1969

Consulting engineering firm designing mechanical, electrical lighting, telecommunications fire safety and life safety systems.

INTERNATIONAL CORP
225 Division Ave
Hasbrouck Heights, NJ 07604-1719
Telephone: (201) 203-3083, Web Site: www.datadirectsolutions.com
Primary Market Served: Consumer

INTERNATIONAL DIRECT MARKETING CONSULTANTS INC
3419 Westminster Ave
Dallas, TX 75205-1387

Telephone: (214) 443-9494, FAX: (214) 443-9512, E-Mail: billmcnutt@charter.net, Web Site: www.dmtrademissions.com
Pres: William McNutt III

INTERNATIONAL RESOURCE MANAGEMENT CO
3008 Spring Valley Dr.
Bedford, TX 76021-4245
Telephone: (817) 861-9191, FAX: (817) 277-0868, E-Mail: james@irmco.net, Web Site: www.irmco.net
Dir: James E. Johnson

IRIS MARKETING
1303 Harling Ct
Bel Air, MD 21015-5029
Telephone: (443) 742-1232
Pres: Vayia Skinner

JK ASSOCIATES LLC
445 Sherman Ave (Suite W)
Palo Alto, CA 94306-1828
Telephone: (650) 838-9816, FAX: (650) 838-9867, Web Site: www.jk-associates.com
Pres: Judith W. Kincaid

JLMC
15 Park Row (17E)
New York, NY 10038-2301
Telephone: (917) 476-3072
Primary Market Served: Consumer

JRB MARKETING GROUP
93 Einstein Way
East Windsor, NJ 08512-2549
Telephone: (301) 758-2334, FAX: (302) 348-2490, E-Mail: jrblitman@gmail.com
Principal & CEO: Joan Blitman

THE DMA JZ MARKETING
4532 Varsity Cir
Lehigh Acres, FL 33971
Telephone: (239) 693-7567, Web Site: www.jzmktg.com
Primary Market Served: Business & Consumer

JACK SCHECTERSON VISUALMARKETING CONSULTANTS
5316 251st Pl
Little Neck, NY 11362-1711
Telephone: (718) 225-3536
Pres: Jack Schecterson

THE JACKSON CONSULTING GROUP LTD
PO Box 246
Middletown, DE 19709

Telephone: (302) 378-0218, (866) 450-7005, FAX: (302) 378-0219, E-Mail: djack98489@aol.com, Web Site: www.jcg-ltd.com
Chmn: Donald R. Jackson

JACOBSOHN CONSULTING ASSOCIATES
Div. of American Slicing Machine Co
PO Box 236
Highland Park, IL 60035-0236
Telephone: (312) 543-3330, E-Mail: jacobsohnr@aol.com
Pres: Richard H. Jacobsohn
Conducts Business: U.S., Canada, Europe, Japan
Employees: 10
Primary Market Served: Business & Consumer
Advertising/Marketing Budget Related to Direct Marketing: 51-75%
Direct Marketing ad budget:
Direct Mail: 50%
Online: 50%
Founded: 1904
Gross sales or billing: $5,000,000

Consulting for direct sales of consumer products through direct mail, magazines & credit cards, syndicated to oil & credit card companies, catalogs, internet.

THE DMA VICTORIA JAMES EXECUTIVE SEARCH INC
11 Stonefence Ln
South Kent, CT 06785-1307
Telephone: (203) 750-8838 X101, FAX: (203) 547-6284, E-Mail: vjames@victoriajames.com, Web Site: www.victoriajames.com
Pres: Victoria James

JASEK ENTERPRISES
1000 Deep Wood Dr
Westlake Village, CA 91362-4215
Telephone: (805) 379-2871, FAX: (805) 379-9839
Pres: Alexander M. Kushner

JOFFREY LONG CONSULTANTS
17045 Chatsworth St
Granada Hills, CA 91344-5845
Telephone: (818) 635-1777, Web Site: www.southwestbancorp.com
Pres: Joffrey Long

JUNGLE CONSULTING
13795 Tewkesbury Ct
Colorado Springs, CO 80908
Telephone: (702) 596-4366
Owner & CEO: Gary Moore
Primary Market Served: Business

Dental practice consultants

THE KAISER GROUP INC
237 South St
Waukesha, WI 53186
Telephone: (262) 544-4971, FAX: (262) 544-6271, Web Site: www.kaisergrp.com
Pres: Peter Kaiser

KANNON CONSULTING INC
39 S LaSalle St (Suite 1013)
Chicago, IL 60603-1727
Telephone: (312) 346-2244, FAX: (312) 346-3665, Web Site: www.kannon.com
Pres: Barbara Cohen

KEN ELO
3863 Laval
Montreal, PQ, Canada H2W 2H9
Telephone: (514) 926-6945
Mktg Consultant: Kenza Elouazzani
Primary Market Served: Business & Consumer

KENNEDY INNER CIRCLE
15433 N Tatum Blvd Ste 104
Phoenix, AZ 85032-4231
Telephone: (602) 269-3111, FAX: (602) 269-3113
Pres: Dan S. Kennedy

THE DMA JUDITH KENNERK
11 Scott Ave
Princeton Junction, NJ 08550-1005
Telephone: (609) 240-2876
Primary Market Served: Consumer

KENZER GROUP, LLC
One Penn Plaza (Suite 6300)
New York, NY 10119
Telephone: (212) 308-4300, FAX: (917) 534-6280, E-Mail: info@kenzergroup.com, Web Site: kenzergroup.com
Chmn: Robert Kenzer

DOROTHY KERR & ASSOCIATES
1509 E Standish Pl
Milwaukee, WI 52317-1960
Telephone: (414) 228-0335, FAX: (414) 228-0337
Pres: Dorothy Kerr

Strategic planning, copywriting, marketing evaluation, mentoring.

THE DMA KESTRY
209 E Lake Shore Dr (#6E)
Chicago, IL 60611-1307
Telephone: (312) 664-6060, FAX: (312) 664-6059, E-Mail: kkestnbaum@earthlink.net
Pres: Kate Kestnbaum

Conducts Business: U.S.
Primary Market Served: Business & Consumer
Advertising/Marketing Budget Related to Direct Marketing: 76-100%
Founded: 1967

Marketing consulting services.

THE KEYSTONE EQUITIES GROUP
1003 Egypt Rd
Oaks, PA 19456-1155
Telephone: (610) 415-6300, (800) 715-9905, FAX: (610) 415-6328, Web Site: www.keystoneequities.com
Pres: William B. Fretz Jr.
Chmn: Richard A. Hansen
Mng Dir: Kevin M. Leigh
Mng Dir: Mark A. Zimmer
Exec Dir: Jack Freeman
Exec Dir: L. Keith Fretz
Exec Dir: John J. Harrison
Sr VP: Noel J. Atkinson
Employees: 15
Primary Market Served: Business
Indirect online sales
Advertising/Marketing Budget Related to Direct Marketing: 26-50%
Direct Marketing ad budget: $25,000
Direct Mail: 25%
Newspapers: 75%
Founded: 2003
Gross sales or billing: $5,000,000

Investment banking services (capital & M&A advisory) for direct marketing companies.

KFORCE INC
1001 E Palm Ave
Tampa, FL 33605-3551
Telephone: (813) 552-2394, Web Site: www.kforce.com

THE DMA LIZ KISLIK ASSOCIATES LLC
100 Merrick Rd (Suite 505E)
Rockville Centre, NY 11570-4834
Telephone: (516) 568-2932, FAX: (516) 568-2936, Web Site: www.lizkislik.com
Pres: Liz Kislik
Exec Asst: Lauren Norris

Specialize in assessment, training, coaching and mentoring for all aspects of management, organizational design and customer care.

KISTLER-TIFFANY COMPANIES LLC
1205 Westlakes Dr Ste 290
Berwyn, PA 19312-2405
Telephone: (610) 722-3300, (866) 250-5413, Web Site: www.ktadv.com
Partner: David Kovach

A.S. KLEEMAN & ASSOCIATES
1416 Spyglass Hill Dr
Duluth, GA 30097-5948
Telephone: (770) 752-0500, FAX:
(770) 752-0066
Pres: Alan Kleeman

ᴛʜᴇ/ᴅᴍᴀ KOBS STRATEGIC CONSULTING
222 N Columbus Dr (#2202)
Chicago, IL 60601-7819
Telephone: (312) 938-4430, FAX:
(847) 934-1194, E-Mail: kobs4ksc@
aol.com
Pres: Jim Kobs
Advertising/Marketing Budget Related
to Direct Marketing: 76-100%
Founded: 1989

KOCHEVAR RESEARCH ASSOCIATES
PO Box 290010
Charlestown, MA 02129-0201
Telephone: (617) 242-4332, FAX:
(617) 242-8009, E-Mail: kra@
bigfoot.com, Web Site: www.
kochevarresearch.com
Pres: John J. Kochevar

KOMUNIK
1500 St Patrick
Montreal, PQ, Canada H3K 0A3
Telephone: (514) 904-0710, Web Site:
www.komunik.com
VP Sls: Patrick Gagne
Primary Market Served: Business

KOWAL & ASSOCIATES INC
620 Massachusetts Ave
Cambridge, MA 02139-3376
Telephone: (617) 577-0700, FAX:
(617) 577-0500, E-Mail: pkowal@
kowalassociates.com, Web Site:
www.kowalassociates.com
Pres: G. Paul Kowal
Employees: 5
Founded: 1988

Assists companies improve the connection with their customers & prospects
by helping them create a customer-
centric corporate culture.

KRAMER & ASSOCIATES
8044 Montgomery Rd (Suite 200),
Bank One Towers
Cincinnati, OH 45236-2926
Telephone: (513) 792-5700, (800) 281-
1400, FAX: (513) 792-5709, E-Mail:
eservice@kramerandassociates.com,
Web Site: www.kramerandassociates.
com
Mngmt Dir: Lyn Kramer

HERBERT KRUG & ASSOCIATES INC
500 Davis St Ste 812
Evanston, IL 60201-4655
Telephone: (847) 864-0550, FAX:
(847) 864-0575
Pres: E Herbert Krug

L3 VIRTUAL SOLUTIONS LLC
450 Township Rd (#208)
Marengo, OH 43334
Telephone: (740) 625-6535, Web Site:
www.l3vs.com
Mktg Commun Consultant: Lark Lamontagne

ᴛʜᴇ/ᴅᴍᴀ LN MARKETING ASSOCIATES
25 Seki Ct
Emerald Hills, CA 94062-3401
Telephone: (650) 368-7181
Pres: Lisa Nash
Primary Market Served: Business &
Consumer

LTD SUPPLY CHAIN
3 Black Horse Cir
Downingtown, PA 19335-1552
Telephone: (610) 458-3636, FAX:
(610) 458-8039, E-Mail: tomc@
ltdsupplychain.com, Web Site: www.
ltdsupplychain.com
Pres: Thomas W. Craig

LADD ASSOCIATES INC
2527 Fillmore St
San Francisco, CA 94115
Telephone: (415) 921-1001, FAX:
(415) 921-2311, E-Mail: info@
laddassociates.com, Web Site:
laddassociates.com
Pres: Jack W. Ladd

LAMOTTA STRATEGIC COMMUNICATIONS INC
137 Old Haverstraw Rd
Congers, NY 10920-1607
Telephone: (845) 358-6301, Web Site:
www.lamottastrategic.com
Pres: Connie LaMotta
Primary Market Served: Business &
Consumer

LANDAJOB
222 W Gregory Blvd (Suite 304)
Kansas City, MO 64114-1127
Telephone: (816) 523-1881, (800) 931-
8806, FAX: (816) 523-1876, E-Mail:
adstaff@landajobnow.com, Web Site:
www.landajobnow.com
Pres: Landa Williams

LAVEN & LOEB INC
2163 Halcyon Rd
Beachwood, OH 44122-1301
Telephone: (623) 217-2101, (216) 291-
3483, E-Mail: alaven@lavenandloeb.
com; vtaylor@lavenandloeb.com,
Web Site: www.lavenandloeb.com
Pres: Ava Laven
VP: Richard Loeb
Admin Mgr: Victor Taylor
Conducts Business: U.S.
Employees: 4
Primary Market Served: Business
Catalog available online
Advertising/Marketing Budget Related
to Direct Marketing: 0-25%
Founded: 2004

RICHARD LAW
166 E 3rd St
Deer Park, NY 11729-5307
Telephone: (917) 267-8293
Primary Market Served: Consumer

LEADS-PLUS INC
PO Box 400
Killarney, FL 34740-0400
Telephone: (800) 548-4571, E-Mail:
eurekaman43@hotmail.com, Web
Site: www.salesprospectingexpert.
com
Pres: Gordie Allen

ᴛʜᴇ/ᴅᴍᴀ LEAPS & BOUNDS LLC
100 Old Palisades Rd (Suite 2409)
Fort Lee, NJ 07024-7021
Telephone: (201) 947-5459
Mng Dir: Jerry Reisberg

LEARNING RESOURCES INSTITUTE
Lilly Associates Inc
2235 Durand Dr
Downers Grove, IL 60515
Telephone: (630) 963-0398
Mng Dir: Sam Lilly

LEGRAND HART
1625 Broadway (Suite 200)
Denver, CO 80202
Telephone: (303) 298-8470, FAX:
(303) 298-8570, Web Site: www.
legrandhart.com
CEO: DeeDee Legrand-Hart

LEV & BERLIN
200 Connecticut Ave Ste 10
Norwalk, CT 06854-1907
Telephone: (203) 838-8500, (800) 377-
4508, FAX: (203) 854-1652, E-Mail:
info@levberlin.com, Web Site: www.
levberlin.com
Counsel: Bruce Lev

LIBEY-CONCORDIA
811 Church Rd (Suite 105)
Cherry Hill, NJ 08002
Telephone: (877) 903-9448, FAX:
(856) 885-5068, E-Mail: libey@
libey.com, Web Site: www.libey.com
Pres: Donald R. Libey

LIFE WORKS INC
2817 Evans St
Hollywood, FL 33020-1119
Telephone: (954) 929-8428, (888) 780-
9400, FAX: (954) 925-3365, Web
Site: www.healthwagon.com
Pres: Doug Brown

Sells Health & Wellness Products

LION'S SHARE MARKETING GROUP, INC
5410 Schumacher Ln
Houston, TX 77056-6810
Telephone: (713) 686-4252, Web Site:
www.lionsshare.com
Owner: Sharon Lyon
Primary Market Served: Consumer

NANCY LISS
233 E 32nd St
New York, NY 10016-6336
Telephone: (646) 418-5000
Primary Market Served: Consumer

LISTER BUTLER INC
445 Park Ave (Suite 1401)
New York, NY 10022-8626
Telephone: (212) 951-6100, FAX:
(212) 481-0230, Web Site: www.
listerbutler.com
Pres & CEO: Anita K. Hersh

ARTHUR D LITTLE INC
1 Federal St (fl 28)
Boston, MA 02110-2011
Telephone: (617) 532-9550, FAX:
(617) 261-6630, Web Site: www.
adlittle-us.com
CEO: Michael Tram

LOEB & LOEB INC
345 Park Ave
New York, NY 10154-0004
Telephone: (212) 407-4000, Web Site:
www.loeb.com
Partner: James Taylor

LOYALTYONE
3 Bessom St (Suite 211)
Marblehead, MA 01945-2372
Telephone: (781) 990-8844, Web Site:
www.speechrep.com
Primary Market Served: Business &
Consumer

THE DMA LUCIDVIEW
80 Rolling Links Blvd
Oak Ridge, TN 37830-9023
Telephone: (888) 582-4384, Web Site:
www.lucidview.com
Pres: Gordon Bell

STEVE LYTLE
425 W Randolph St
Chicago, IL 60606-1530
Telephone: (312) 894-7000

MCDM STRATEGIC DIRECT MARKETING
12864 Bradford Ln
Plainfield, IL 60585-2244
Telephone: (815) 436-5194, FAX:
(815) 439-5941
Pres: Mike Capetanakis

Produces leads via all online & office
media. Expertise in customer retention
& copywriting.

THE DMA MLB ASSOCIATES
1936 Saranac Ave (Suite 2-300)
Lake Placid, NY 12946-1114
Telephone: (518) 523-2371, FAX:
(518) 523-9011, E-Mail: mlbassoc@
aol.com, Web Site: www.
mlbassociates.com
Exec Search-Database Mktg: Mary
Lou Brown

MRI NORWALK
Div. of MRI Management Recruiters
International
2334 S Cypress Bend Dr (Suite 11)
Pompano Beach, FL 33069-4488
Telephone: (203) 926-1200, FAX:
(203) 926-1211, E-Mail: jbgurn@
mricoastalgroup.com, Web Site:
www.mricoastalgroup.com
Pres: Jim Gurn

MVI MARKETING LTD
5640 Linne Rd
Paso Robles, CA 93446-8443
Telephone: (805) 459-4455, (805) 239-
2994, FAX: (805) 239-2947, E-Mail:
info@mvimarketing.com, Web Site:
www.mvimarketing.com
Pres: Elizabeth Chatelain
CEO: Marty Hurwitz

MAC MCINTOSH INC
601 Pendar Rd
North Kingstown, RI 02852-6620
Telephone: (401) 294-7730, (800) 944-
5553, FAX: (401) 679-0176, E-Mail:
info@sales-lead-experts.com, Web
Site: www.sales-lead-experts.com
Pres: M.H. McIntosh

THE DMA MAC MURRAY PETERSEN & SHUSTER LLP
6530 W Campus Oval (Suite 210)
New Albany, OH 43054-7069
Telephone: (614) 939-9955, FAX:
(614) 939-9955, E-Mail: dbryson@
mpslawyers.com, Web Site: www.
mpslawyers.com
Attorney & Partner: Helen Mac Murray
Office Mgr: Destiny Bryson

MADISON EXECUTIVE SEARCH
54 Danbury Rd (Suite 368)
Ridgefield, CT 06877
Telephone: (203) 431-6565, FAX:
(203) 431-6060, E-Mail: mimi@
directexec.com, Web Site: www.
directexec.com
Partner: M. Ward Perrott
Partner: Mimi D'Amelio

MAIL MANAGEMENT ENTERPRISES
5616 Galestown Reliance Rd
Seaford, DE 19973-6044
Telephone: (410) 883-3224, FAX:
(410) 883-3392, E-Mail: mailmgt@
aol.com, Web Site: www.
mailmanagemententerprises.com
Pres: Jacquelyn McPeak

KEN MALEK ASSOCIATES INC
PO Box 383
Yardley, PA 19067-8383
Telephone: (215) 579-2070, FAX:
(215) 860-3498, Web Site: www.
kenmalek.com
Pres: Kenneth Malek

MANAGEMENT SCIENCE ASSOCIATES INC
6565 Penn Ave
Pittsburgh, PA 15206-4490
Telephone: (412) 362-2000, (800)
MSA-INFO, FAX: (412) 363-5598,
E-Mail: info@msa.com, Web Site:
www.msa.com
Pres: Dr Alfred A. Kuehn
Mgr, Mktg Communs: Sharon Motta

MANGIERI/HULL SOLUTIONS LLC
One Riverside Rd
Sandy Hook, CT 06482
Telephone: (203) 270-4800, FAX:
(203) 270-4815, E-Mail: chris@
mhrecruiters.com, Web Site: www.
mhrecruiters.com
Pres & Owner: Christopher J. Mangieri

MAPPING ANALYTICS
120 Allens Creek Rd
Rochester, NY 14618-3306
Telephone: (585) 271-6490, (877) 893-6490, FAX: (585) 271-1132, E-Mail: sales@mappinganalytics.com, Web Site: www.mappinganalytics.com
Pres: Ralph Rothfelder
Office Mgr: Kate Ralston
Sr Sls Consultant: George Bauman
Conducts Business: U.S.
Employees: 10
Primary Market Served: Business
Advertising/Marketing Budget Related to Direct Marketing: 0-25%
Founded: 1989
Gross sales or billing: $2,000,000

Decision support for sales & marketing professionals who are interested in customer profiling, site selection, sale & service territory management & design.

MARKET RECOGNITION
112 Prescott Rd
Boxborough, MA 01719-1121
Telephone: (978) 314-0127, Web Site: www.marketrecognition.com
VP: Jane Shurtleff

MARKET SQUARE COMMUNICATIONS INC
1100 Centerpoint Dr (Suite 203)
Stevens Point, WI 54481-2849
Telephone: (715) 344-4609, FAX: (715) 344-6885
Pres: Ann Garber

THE MARKETING ALLIANCE
127 Field Point Dr
Fairfield, CT 06824-6374
Telephone: (203) 254-0474
Principal: James McAlister

MARKETING CONSULTING SERVICES
2669 Suffolk St
Kingsport, TN 37660-5803
Telephone: (423) 288-5866, FAX: (423) 288-5576
Pres: John Buckles

THE DMA MARKETING HIGHWAY
1416 Gordon Ter
Deerfield, IL 60015-4739
Telephone: (312) 502-3732, E-Mail: info@marketinghighway.com, Web Site: www.marketinghighway.com
Mng Partner: Sid Liebenson

MARKETING/MEDIA DYNAMICS INC
197 Shannondale Rd
Harpers Ferry, WV 25425-4564

Telephone: (304) 725-1119
Pres: Mary Sue Jedele

MARKETING SOLUTIONS
28252 Woodworth Way
Lathrup Village, MI 48076-2518
Telephone: (248) 443-5252, FAX: (248) 443-5252
Pres: Allen Weaks

MARKETING SYSTEMS ANALYSIS
Div. of SCI, LLC
108 N Washington Ave
Ventnor, NJ 08406-1961
Telephone: (609) 487-9340, FAX: (866) 214-3208, E-Mail: ernie@schell.com, Web Site: www.schell.com
Pres: Ernest H. Schell
Conducts Business: U.S., U.K.
Employees: 2
Primary Market Served: Business & Consumer
Advertising/Marketing Budget Related to Direct Marketing: 76-100%
Direct Marketing ad budget:
Direct Mail: 10%
Online: 90%
Founded: 1987

Publishes online guide for direct commerce systems & services

MARKETRAC INC
300 Roosevelt Way
Westbury, NY 11590-6700
Telephone: (516) 365-4330, FAX: (516) 365-5789
Pres: Louise Donnelly

MARKETSMITH INC
14 Walsh Dr Fl 200
Parsippany, NJ 07054-1063
Telephone: (973) 889-0006, Web Site: www.marketsmithinc.com
VP Mktg: Davey Rosenbaum

MARNELL DATABASE MARKETING
119 W Chestnut St (Suite 3E)
Chicago, IL 60610-3288
Telephone: (312) 944-3511
Pres: Thomas J. Marnell

MARTINEAU & ASSOCIATES
1770 Oakdell Dr
Menlo Park, CA 94025
Telephone: (650) 326-5030, FAX: (650) 329-0883
Partner: Catherine Martineau

MARVEL ASSOCIATES
199 Sound Beach Ave, Box 504
Old Greenwich, CT 06870-1711
Telephone: (203) 637-4777
Pres: Hunter M. Marvel

MASTEN PUBLISHING SYSTEMS
PO Box 6074
Chesterfield, MO 63006-6074
Telephone: (636) 527-1810, (800) 616-9476, E-Mail: steve@mastensystems.com, Web Site: www.mastensystems.com
CEO: Steve Masten

MASTERY MARKETING GROUP
5650 Blazer Pkwy (Suite 141)
Dublin, OH 43017
Telephone: (703) 938-0101, (203) 544-8997, (800) MKT-0121, FAX: (203) 544-8397, (703) 938-0144, E-Mail: info@masterymg.com, Web Site: www.masterymktgrp.com
Pres: Paul Hall

MCBEE ASSOCIATES INC
997 Old Eagle School Rd Ste 205
Wayne, PA 19087-1706
Telephone: (610) 964-9680, Web Site: www.mcbeeassociates.com
Dir, Mktg: Tanya McTaggart

SHANNON MCDONALD
205 W 88 St (#9D)
New York, NY 10024
Telephone: (917) 838-2057
Primary Market Served: Consumer

MCKEE CONSULTING LLC
1404 W Country Club Ln
Escondido, CA 92026-1660
Telephone: (760) 738-8200, Web Site: www.trainyourcallcenter.com
Partner: Sally Cordova

THE DMA MCKINSEY & CO
55 E 52nd St (fl 21)
New York, NY 10055-0183
Telephone: (212) 446-7000, FAX: (212) 446-8575, Web Site: www.mckinsey.com
Knowledge Opers Coord: Kelly Brennan
Employees: 14,190
Gross sales or billing: $4,370,000,000

MEDAVANTE
100 American Metro Blvd (Suite 106)
Hamilton, NJ 08619-2319
Telephone: (609) 528-9413, Web Site: www.metavante.com

Primary Market Served: Consumer

MEDIA MANAGEMENT SERVICES INC

105 Terry Dr (Suite 120)
Newton, PA 18940-1872
Telephone: (215) 579-8590, (800) 523-5948, FAX: (215) 579-8589, Web Site: www.mmseducation.com
VP: Connie Schofer

MEDIA RECRUITING GROUP INC

1 Bridge St (Suite P2)
Irvington, NY 10533-1575
Telephone: (914) 591-5511, FAX: (914) 591-8911, E-Mail: resume@mediarecruiting.com, Web Site: www.mediarecruiting.com
Exec VP: Steve Goldberg

MRG are leaders in executive search for digital media sales and marketing placements including: sales, marketing/SEO/SEM, social media marketing. We also place within other mediums (like print). Launched in 2009, MRG also has a Digital Sales & Marketing Course Division designed to empower media professionals in today's rapidly changing times.

THE DMA MEDINA ASSOCIATES

12 Hilltop Rd
Rose Valley, PA 19086-6243
Telephone: (610) 565-8836, FAX: (610) 565-8184, E-Mail: kurtmedina@aol.com, Web Site: www.medinaassociates.com
Pres: Kurt Medina
Conducts Business: U.S.
Employees: 2
Primary Market Served: Consumer
Advertising/Marketing Budget Related to Direct Marketing: 76-100%
Direct Marketing ad budget: $20,000,000
Direct Mail: 20%
Magazines: 10%
TV/Radio: 60%
Telephone: 10%
Founded: 1991

Direct response marketing consulting specializing in the 50 plus mature market.

MICHEL CONSULTING

61903 Brokentop Dr
Bend, OR 97702-1085
Telephone: (541) 633-7838
Pres: Bill Michel

MIGLAUTSCH MARKETING INC

555 S Industrial Dr (Suite 5)
Hartland, WI 53029
Telephone: (262) 369-3900, FAX: (262) 369-3915, E-Mail: info@migmar.com, Web Site: www.migmar.com
Owner: John Miglautsch

ADRIAN MILLER DIRECT MARKETING

43 Park Ave
Port Washington, NY 11050-4010
Telephone: (516) 767-9288, E-Mail: amiller@adrianmiller.com, Web Site: www.adrianmiller.com
Pres: Adrian Miller

FRED MILMAN ASSOCIATES

23 Selina Ct
Glen Cove, NY 11542-3048
Telephone: (516) 625-8075, FAX: (516) 625-5927, E-Mail: fmilman@compuserve.com
Pres: Fred Milman

MILROD EXECUTIVE SEARCH

22 Riverside Dr
Princeton, NJ 08540-4017
Telephone: (609) 683-8787, FAX: (609) 683-8221
Pres: Jane Milrod

MIMAARTS LLC

535 Fifth Ave (fl 31)
New York, NY 10017-3667
Telephone: (212) 584-1810
Primary Market Served: Consumer

MISSION: A CONSULTING GROUP

Div. of Mission Inc
36 Cross Hwy
Westport, CT 06880-2141
Telephone: (203) 227-9475, FAX: (203) 227-6512, E-Mail: info@mission-consulting.com, Web Site: www.mission-consulting.com
Mng Partner: Dorothy E. Curran

MR FANTASTIC LLC

55739 Holiday Cr
Astor, FL 32102-7991
Telephone: (407) 719-2020, E-Mail: sbillue@usa2net.net, Web Site: www.stanbillue.com
Pres & Owner: Stan Billue
Conducts Business: Worldwide
Employees: 5
Primary Market Served: Business
Catalog available online
Indirect online sales

Direct Marketing ad budget: $120,000
Direct Mail: 10%
Magazines: 10%
Newspapers: 10%
Online: 20%
Telephone: 50%
Founded: 1983
Gross sales or billing: $1,000,000

Audio & video tapes and live seminars for telemarketing sales training, motivation, and consulting.

MODERN MAIL

100 Pencader Dr
Newark, DE 19702-3321
Telephone: (302) 391-1200, Web Site: www.triggermarketing.com
Pres: Doug Ainsworth

THE DMA MONSTER WORLDWIDE

5 Clock Tower Pl (Suite 500)
Maynard, MA 01754-2578
Telephone: (888) MONSTER, Web Site: www.monster.com
VP CRM: Matthew Resteghini

THE DMA MORAN DIRECT INC

710 N Post Oak Rd (Suite 520)
Houston, TX 77024-3858
Telephone: (713) 880-3725, FAX: (713) 263-7647, E-Mail: rmoran@morandirect.com, Web Site: www.morandirect.com
Pres: Ron Moran

MORRIS & FELLOWS

6105 Blue Stone Rd NE (Suite A)
Atlanta, GA 30328-3885
Telephone: (404) 250-0225
Pres Fin: Cheri Morris
Office Mgr: Ginger Pepper

MORRIS JAMES HITCHENS & WILLIAMS

500 Delaware Ave (Suite 1500), PO Box 2306
Wilmington, DE 19801-1494
Telephone: (302) 888-6800, FAX: (302) 571-1750, Web Site: www.morrisjames.com
Partner: Edward M. McNally

MULDOON & BAER INC

130 Banyan Isle Rd
Palm Beach Gardens, FL 33416-4601
Telephone: (561) 630-0999, FAX: (561) 630-9466, Web Site: www.muldoonandbaer.com
Pres: Katie Muldoon
VP: J. Baer

THE DMA **NAK MARKETING & COMMUNICATIONS**
575 Madison Ave (Suite 700)
New York, NY 10022-8512
Telephone: (212) 505-9290, Web Site:
www.nakcomm.com
Pres: Thaddeus Kubis

NATIONAL ECONOMIC RESEARCH ASSOCIATES INC
1255 23rd St NW (Suite 600)
Washington, DC 20037
Telephone: (202) 466-3510, FAX:
(202) 466-3605, E-Mail: andrew.
carron@nera.com, Web Site: www.
nera.com
Pres: Dr Andrew Carron

NATIONAL MAIL/ MARKETING CORP
390 Reed Rd Fl 3
Broomall, PA 19008-4008
Telephone: (610) 544-8200, FAX:
(610) 544-1819, Web Site: www.
natlmail.com
Pres: Vince Jennings

PAUL NELSON DIRECT MARKETING
2411 Sixth St
Santa Monica, CA 90405
Telephone: (310) 392-9533
Creative Dir: Paul Nelson

NEW AMERICAN DIMENSIONS
6955 La Tijera Blvd (Suite B)
Los Angeles, CA 90045-1932
Telephone: (310) 670-6800
Pres: David Morse

NEW CUSTOMER SERVICE COMPANIES INC
22894 Pacific Blvd
Sterling, VA 20166-6722
Telephone: (703) 707-1582, Web Site:
www.newcorp.com
Primary Market Served: Consumer

NEWS MARKETING CANADA
100 King St W (Suite 7000), One First
Canadian Place
Toronto, ON, Canada M5X 1A4
Telephone: (416) 775-3000, FAX:
(416) 775-3055, E-Mail:
spetkovich@newsmarketing.ca, Web
Site: www.newsmarketing.ca
Sr VP: Adam North

NIGRONEWMEDIA
4004 Hermitage Hills Blvd (Apt 20)
Hermitage, PA 16148-3420

Telephone: (724) 699-0230
Primary Market Served: Consumer

NORTHERN ILLINOIS CONSULTING INC
PO Box 7157
Libertyville, IL 60048-7157
Telephone: (847) 828-1999, Web Site:
www.cmsbusiness.com
Pres: John Coxon
Primary Market Served: Business &
Consumer

NUEDGE SYSTEMS
Div. of Metavante Corp
4900 W Brown Deer Rd
Brown Deer, WI 53223
Telephone: (800) 236-3282, Web Site:
www.nuedgesystems.com
Pres & CEO: Frank R. Martire

OSG BILLING
100 W Forest Ave (Suite G)
Englewood, NJ 07631-4033
Telephone: (201) 871-1100, Web Site:
www.osgbilling.com
Sr Mktg Coord: Alexandria Pasckvale

THE DMA **OAK KNOLL LIMITED LIABILITY CO**
7 Hastings Ct
South Salem, NY 10590-2517
Telephone: (914) 533-0208
Principal: Charles Prescott
Primary Market Served: Business &
Consumer

O'KEEFE HENRY DIRECT INC
707 Lake Cook Rd (Suite 285)
Deerfield, IL 60015-4933
Telephone: (847) 681-9200, FAX:
(847) 681-9299, Web Site: www.
okeefehenrydirect.com
Pres: Peter Henry

OPEN SYSTEMS SERVICES
330 SW 27 Ave (Suite 402)
Miami, FL 33135
Telephone: (305) 541-1970
Pres: Alexander Lopez

GLEN ORENSTEIN
2959 Judith Dr
Merrick, NY 11566-5448
Telephone: (516) 359-8785
Primary Market Served: Consumer

OUTSOURCING SOLUTIONS INC
390 S Woods Mill Rd Ste 150
Chesterfield, MO 63017-3667

Telephone: (847) 419-1790, FAX:
(847) 419-1818
EVP & Chief Mktg Officer: Steven K.
Richards

THE DMA **OVATIVE/GROUP LLC**
1011 Washington Ave S Ste 350
Minneapolis, MN 55415-1264
Telephone: (612) 886-1010, Web Site:
www.ovative.com

PCG, INC
1S935 Tanglewood Dr (#121)
Batavia, IL 60510-9511
Telephone: (630) 482-9300, FAX:
(630) 454-3750, E-Mail: sasmith@
pcgnow.com, Web Site: www.
pcgnow.com
Partner: Meg Goodman

PM CONSULTING CORP
11250 Waples Mill Rd
Fairfax, VA 22030
FAX: (703) 272-1500, Web Site: www.
ecnext.com
VP: Michael McAllister

THE DMA **PMG**
7160 Columbia Gateway Dr Ste 300
Columbia, MD 21046-2134
Telephone: (410) 290-0667, Web Site:
www.pmgdirect.net
Pres: Rick Powell

PACKSTREAM LLC
2400 Dundee Rd
Louisville, KY 40205-2047
Telephone: (502) 552-9624, Web Site:
www.packstream.com
CEO: Erik Nelson

JAMES ROBERT PARISH CONSULTING
4338 Gentry Ave (Suite 1)
Studio City, CA 91604-1764
Telephone: (818) 753-9455, FAX:
(818) 505-6509, E-Mail: jrparish@
sbcglobal.net, Web Site: www.
jamesrobertparish.com
Pres & Owner: James Robert Parish

PAUL, HASTINGS, JANOFSKY & WALKER LLP
75 E 55th St, Park Avenue Tower
New York, NY 10022-3205
Telephone: (212) 318-6037, FAX:
(212) 319-4090, E-Mail:
robertsherman@paulhastings.com,
Web Site: www.paulhastings.com
DMA Gen Counsel: Robert Sherman
Esq.

THE DMA PERCIPIO MEDIA, LLC
201 Broadway Ste 7
Cambridge, MA 02139-1955
Telephone: (617) 995-7855

JAMES R PERDIEW & CO
1250 S Grove Ave Ste 302
Barrington, IL 60010-5066
Telephone: (847) 842-8525, FAX:
(847) 842-8518, E-Mail: jrpco@
perdiew.com, Web Site: www.
perdiew.com
Pres: James R. Perdiew

S PERNICK & ASSOCIATES
1616 Sheridan Rd (Unit 2H)
Wilmette, IL 60091-1884
Telephone: (847) 256-0115
Conducts Business: U.S., Canada
Primary Market Served: Business &
Consumer
Founded: 1989

Telemanagement of outsourced
programs.

**PETER N CAREY &
ASSOCIATES INC**
1010 Jorie Blvd (Suite 400)
Oak Brook, IL 60523-2239
Telephone: (630) 573-4260, (877) PN-
CAREY, FAX: (630) 573-0529,
E-Mail: pncarey1@sbcglobal.net
Pres: Peter N. Carey
Conducts Business: U.S.
Employees: 2
Primary Market Served: Business &
Consumer
Advertising/Marketing Budget Related
to Direct Marketing: 0-25%
Direct Marketing ad budget:
Direct Mail: 100%
Founded: 1996

Executive recruiting for direct marketing and graphic arts industries.

**PILLSBURY WINTHROP
SHAW PITTMAN LLP**
725 S Figueroa St (Suite 2800)
Los Angeles, CA 90017-5406
Telephone: (213) 488-7100, Web Site:
www.pillsburywinthrop.com
Partner: Deborah Thoren-Peden

PLATINUM PRESS
37 Route 80
Killingworth, CT 06419-1429
Telephone: (860) 663-3882, FAX:
(718) 825-5065, E-Mail:
herbertjcohen@aol.com
Pres: Herbert Cohen

**PLEXUS MARKETING GROUP
INC**
PO Box 76380, Bldg G
Atlanta, GA 30358-1380
Telephone: (770) 390-9692, (800)
9-PLEXUS, FAX: (770) 390-9693,
Web Site: www.plexusmarketing.com
Pres: Michael McClellan

POHAKU INC
PO Box 1121
Kailua, HI 96734-1121
Telephone: (319) 653-2569, Web Site:
www.gopohaku.com
Pres & CEO: Wendy Gady
Primary Market Served: Business &
Consumer

POLESTAR GROUP
20 N Canton Rd
West Simsbury, CT 06092
Telephone: (860) 658-4992
Pres: Peter Brinkerhoff

POSTAL EN ESPANOL INC
8325 W Hillsborough Ave
Tampa, FL 33615-3805
Telephone: (813) 885-8888, Web Site:
www.postalenespanol.com
Gen Mgr & Mktg Consultant: Jeff
Devin

**PRACTICAL COMPUTER
SOLUTIONS**
154 Brentwood Dr
South Orange, NJ 07079-1141
Telephone: (973) 761-6099, FAX:
(215) 243-8283, E-Mail: dbsteig@
alum.mit.edu, Web Site: www.
donsteig.com
Pres: Donald B. Steig

**PRINTCOM CONSULTING
GROUP**
1020 Farm Creek Rd
Waxhaw, NC 28173-7793
Telephone: (704) 843-5350, FAX:
(704) 843-5352, E-Mail: printcom@
aol.com
Pres: William Lamparter

PRINTMARK
432 Johnson Rd
East Montpelier, VT 05651-4250
Telephone: (802) 229-9743, FAX:
(802) 229-9746, E-Mail: alex@
printmark.net, Web Site: www.
printmark.net
Pres: Alex Brown

**PRIVACY & INFORMATION
PRACTICES ADVISORY**
10 Gristmill Ln
Saddle River, NJ 07458-1317
Telephone: (201) 887-2157

THE DMA PRODUCT TO MARKET LLC
4536 County Rd 4 SW
Cokato, MN 55321-4220
Telephone: (320) 286-9997
Owner: Mark Koivisto
Primary Market Served: Business

THE DMA PRODUCTION SOLUTIONS
1953 Gallows Rd (Suite 600)
Vienna, VA 22182-3988
Telephone: (703) 734-5700
Pres & CEO: George Lizama

**PRODUCTIVE STRATEGIES
INC**
2 Northfield Plaza (Suite 365)
Northfield, IL 60093-1272
Telephone: (847) 446-0008, FAX:
(847) 446-0211, E-Mail: pkrone@
productivestrategies.com, Web Site:
www.productivestrategies.com
Pres: Philip Krone

**PRODUCTIVITY
DEVELOPMENT GROUP
INC**
PO Box 488
Westford, MA 01886
Telephone: (978) 692-1818, FAX:
(978) 692-5080, E-Mail: info@
martinstankard.com
Pres: Martin F. Stankard

THE DMA PROJECTSENSE
602 Whispering Wind Ct
Gaithersburg, MD 20877-3418
Telephone: (240) 476-1677, Web Site:
www.projectsense.net

PROSOURCE
1502 Augusta Dr (Suite 100)
Houston, TX 77057-2454
Telephone: (713) 667-3690, FAX:
(713) 660-9629, Web Site: www.
prosourcedev.com
VP Mktg: April Merrill
Primary Market Served: Business &
Consumer

**PROTOCOL SERVICES
ACQUISITIONS CORP**
2805 Fruitville Rd
Sarasota, FL 34237-5318
Telephone: (941) 906-9000, Web Site:
www.protocolusa.com
SVP Mktg Svcs: Jill Compton

THE DMA PROVEN PROSPECTS INC
1073 Monterey Blvd
Hermosa Beach, CA 90254-3746
Telephone: (805) 448-6253, Web Site:
www.provemprospects.com
CEO: Ben Kennedy

**PUBLIC ISSUES
MANAGEMENT**
902 Rose Ave
Piedmont, CA 94611-4343
Telephone: (510) 654-9114, FAX:
(510) 654-0196
Principal: Karen Joffe

**PUBLICATION
FULFILLMENT SVCS**
aka Edwards-Pullin Consulting
10564 Progress Way (Suite D)
Cypress, CA 90630-4712
Telephone: (714) 226-9785, FAX:
(714) 226-9733, E-Mail: janpullin@
pfsmag.com, Web Site: www.pfsmag.
com
Pres: Jan Edwards-Pullin

**PUBLICATIONS GROUPE RR
INTERNATIONAL INC**
2322 Sherbrooke E
Montreal, PQ, Canada H2K 1E5
Telephone: (514) 521-8148
VP Opers: Diane Tanguay
Primary Market Served: Business &
Consumer

**PUBLISHING FULFILLMENT
CONSULTING LLC**
85 Settlers Hill Rd
Brewster, NY 10509-5210
Telephone: (845) 278-2800, Web Site:
www.fulfillmentconsulting.com
Pres: William Dugan

THE DMA PURSUANT GROUP
5151 Beltline Rd (Suite 900)
Dallas, TX 75254-6757
Telephone: (214) 866-7700, Web Site:
pursuant.net
Primary Market Served: Consumer

**QUIGLEY CONSULTING
GROUP**
1775 W Broadland Ln
Lake Forest, IL 60045-4817
Telephone: (847) 604-6773
Pres: Robert Quigley

QWEST
1801 California St
Denver, CO 80202-5555
Telephone: (303) 992-1400, (800) 603-
6000, FAX: (303) 896-8515, Web
Site: www.qwest.com

Chmn & CEO: Eduard R. Mueller

THE DMA RDO MARKETING LLC
4820 W 77th St Ste 120
Minneapolis, MN 55435-4809
Telephone: (952) 746-7585

THE DMA RSM MCGLADREY INC
4725 Piedmont Row Dr (Suite 300)
Charlotte, NC 28210-4280
Telephone: (980) 233-4700, Web Site:
www.rsmmcgladrey.com
Sr Dir Mktg Svcs & Brand: Eric Webb
Primary Market Served: Business &
Consumer

RW CONSULTING
452 Sondley Woods Pl
Asheville, NC 28805
Telephone: (828) 299-3645, Web Site:
www.rwconsulting.net
Pres: Bob Weinberg
Conducts Business: U.S.
Employees: 2
Primary Market Served: Business &
Consumer
Advertising/Marketing Budget Related
to Direct Marketing: 51-75%
Founded: 1996

Provide strategic and database analytic
services to direct and database
marketers. Expertise includes business
evaluations, program and product improvement and database conceptual
design.

RAAB ASSOCIATES
345 Millwood Rd
Chappaqua, NY 10514-1002
Telephone: (914) 241-2117, FAX:
(914) 241-0080, E-Mail: info@
raabassociates.com, Web Site: www.
raabassociates.com
Partner: David M. Raab

**LYNDA RAIHOFER &
ASSOCIATES LLC**
48 Young Ave
Pelham, NY 10803-1724
Telephone: (914) 738-8282
Owner: Lynda Raihofer

**RAINWATER ASSOCIATES
INC**
135 E 71st St
New York, NY 10021-4258
Telephone: (212) 861-2856, FAX:
(212) 861-1729, E-Mail: rainwine@
aol.com
Pres: Michael Michaelson

NEIL RANSICK MARKETING
212 Teresita Blvd
San Francisco, CA 94127-1729
Telephone: (415) 664-6728
Principal Owner: Neil Ransick

RAPHEL MARKETING
211 North Ave
Saint Johnsbury, VT 05819-1626
Telephone: (802) 751-8802, FAX:
(802) 751-8804, E-Mail: neil@
raphel.com, Web Site: www.raphel.
com
Pres: Neil Raphel

RAPID INSIGHT INC
53 Technology Ln (Suite 112)
Conway, NH 03818-5804
Telephone: (603) 447-0240, Web Site:
www.rapidinsightinc.com

THE DMA REDENGINE DIGITAL
1485 Chain Bridge Rd (Suite 305)
Mc Lean, VA 22101-4501
Telephone: (703) 556-6951, Web Site:
www.redenginedigital.com
Pres: Liz Murphy

REDWOOD PARTNERS LTD
60 E 42nd St (Rm 1820)
New York, NY 10165-6210
Telephone: (212) 843-8585, FAX:
(212) 843-9093, E-Mail: info@
redwoodpartners.com, Web Site:
www.redwoodpartners.com
Mng Dir: Michael D. Flannery

**REED SMITH HALL
DICKLER ADVERTISING &
LAW MARKETING GROUP**
599 Lexington Ave (29th fl)
New York, NY 10022
Telephone: (212) 549-0377, FAX:
(212) 521-5450, Web Site: www.
reedsmith.com
Exec Partner: Douglas Wood
Asst Mktg VP: Andrea Mouzakis

**REICHERT & ASSOCIATES
INC**
PO Box 268
Grand Marais, MN 55604
Telephone: (218) 387-1095, E-Mail:
reichertln@aol.com
Pres: Leo N. Reichert

**RESCOTT LLC MARKETING
& TECHNOLOGY**
5856 Poole Pl (Suite 263)
Noblesville, IN 46062-7608
Telephone: (317) 816-0700, Web Site:
www.rescott.com
Pres: Toby Reeves

RESEARCH BOSTON CORP
1160 Brown Ave
Lafayette, CA 94549-3102
Telephone: (978) 225-8030, FAX:
(267) 295-8704, Web Site: www.
researchboston.com
Pres: Paul Teplitz

THE DMA RESPONSE ADVANTAGE
8635 Falmouth (#301)
Playa Del Rey, CA 90293-8281
Telephone: (310) 577-0389, Web Site:
www.responseadvantage.com
Pres: Stephanie Beckman

RESPONSE DESIGN CORP
5541 Simpson Ave
Ocean City, NJ 08226-1258
Telephone: (609) 601-5866, (800) 366-
4732, FAX: (609) 788-3619, E-Mail:
rdc@responsedesign.com, Web Site:
www.responsedesign.com
Pres: Kathryn E. Jackson

THE DMA RESPONSYS
900 Cherry Ave (fl 5)
San Bruno, CA 94066-3081
Telephone: (650) 745-1700, Web Site:
www.responsys.com
Chief Mktg Officer: Scott Olrich

THE RESULTS GROUP
aka Verdant Results Group
65 E India Row (Suite 37F), Harbor
Towers
Boston, MA 02110-3323
Telephone: (617) 227-0229, Web Site:
www.verdant-results-group.com
Pres: Vincent Vassallo

**RETRIEVAL MASTERS
CREDITORS BUREAU INC**
4 Westchester Plz Ste 110
Elmsford, NY 10523-1615
Telephone: (914) 592-0055, (800) 666-
8097, FAX: (914) 345-5023, E-Mail:
info@retrievalmasters.com, Web
Site: www.retrievalmasters.com
Pres: Michael Ghort

RHINO MARKETING INC
515 S Flower St (Fl 36
Los Angeles, CA 90071-2221
Telephone: (604) 472-3240, (877) 605-
7022, FAX: (604) 637-5619, Web
Site: www.rhino.ca
Chief Rhino: Doug Morneau
Primary Market Served: Business &
Consumer

BRUCE RHODES
83 Victoria Rd
Sudbury, MA 01776-3139
Telephone: (978) 443-8389

Pres: Bruce Rhodes

RIDENOUR & ASSOCIATES
1555 N Sandburg Ter (Suite 602)
Chicago, IL 60610-6324
Telephone: (312) 787-8228, FAX:
(312) 787-8528, E-Mail:
ssridenour@aol.com, Web Site:
www.ridenourassociates.com
Pres: Suzanne S. Ridenour

THE DMA ROLAND ADVISORS
4 Norwood Rd
Annapolis, MD 21401-1227
Telephone: (410) 268-3648
Principal: Donald Roland
Primary Market Served: Business &
Consumer

**THE DMA ALAN ROSENSPAN &
ASSOCIATES**
34 Summit Ave
Sharon, MA 02067-2149
Telephone: (781) 784-2228, Web Site:
www.alanrosenspan.com
Pres: Alan Rosenspan

ROSS CULBERT & LAVERY
900 Broadway (#401)
New York, NY 10003
Telephone: (212) 206-0044, Web Site:
www.rclnyc.com
Pres: Peter Ross

THE RUSIN GROUP, LLC
30 Hollow Tree Pl
Wilton, CT 06897
Telephone: (203) 529-3257

RUSS, AUGUST, & KABAT
12424 Wilshire Blvd (Suite 1200)
Los Angeles, CA 90025
Telephone: (310) 826-7474, FAX:
(310) 826-6991, E-Mail: info@
raklaw.com, Web Site: www.raklaw.
com
Pres, Mng Partner: Larry C. Russ

ANNE RUTH
6 Alden Pl Apt 1D
Bronxville, NY 10708-4846
Telephone: (914) 337-7931
Marketing: Anne Ruth

**SIGMA MARKETING GROUP
LLC**
1850 S Winton Rd
Rochester, NY 14618-3923
Telephone: (585) 473-7300, (888) 277-
9837, FAX: (585) 473-0332, E-Mail:
mbush@sigmamarketing.com, Web
Site: www.sigmamarketing.com;
www.jthgearanalytics.com (Blog)

CEO: Kenyon Blunt
CFO: Jaime Sanchez
Exec VP Client Svcs: Jim Dellavilla
SVP Strategy & Mktg: Martha Bush
Chief Technology Officer: Mike Fuqua
Employees: 85
Founded: 1985
Gross sales or billing: $15,300,000

Analytics+Strategy+Technology=Making
it Work. SIGMA Marketing turns data
into customer intelligence & innovative
marketing solutions: online & offline.
Our direct & digital solutions focus on
multichannel marketing strategies, data
& technology integration, web analytics & sales enablement. We build long
term customer relationships and drive
Marketing ROI.

SKO-BRENNER-AMERICAN
841 Merrick Rd CS 9320
Baldwin, NY 11510-9320
Telephone: (516) 771-4400, (800) 645-
3390, FAX: (516) 771-7810, E-Mail:
collect@skobrenner.com, Web Site:
www.skobrenner.com
Chmn & CEO: Stuart Brenner

SLR ASSOCIATES
3300 NW 185th Ave (PMB 268)
Portland, OR 97229-3406
Telephone: (503) 645-0675
Pres: Stacy Rollins

**KURT SALMON ASSOCIATES
INC**
Subs. of Management Consulting
Group PLC
1355 Peachtree St NE (Suite 900)
Atlanta, GA 30309-3266
Telephone: (404) 892-0321, FAX:
(404) 898-9590, E-Mail:
infoksaweb@kurtsalmon.com, Web
Site: www.kurtsalmon.com
Chmn: Mark Wietecha
CEO: Jerry T. Black
CFO: William Beckemeyer
CIO: Bruce Seeber
VP & Pres Health Care Div: James
Berarducci
Editorial Mgr: Katherine Lombardo
Conducts Business: Worldwide
Employees: 60
Catalog available online
Indirect online sales
Founded: 1935

Global management consultant that
specializes in health care providers.
Strategy, facility planning & information technology for multi-hospital systems, community hospitals, academic
medical centers, children's hospitals, &
physician group practices in the US.
Also serves retail & consumer products
industries.

SANDLER TECHWORKS
525 E 82nd St (Suite 2g)
New York, NY 10028-7148
Telephone: (917) 697-9678, Web Site:
www.sandlertechworks.com
Primary Market Served: Consumer

SATISFACTION SOFTWARE INC
8711 150th St
Jamaica, NY 11435-3107
Telephone: (732) 382-8736, FAX:
(732) 382-8736, E-Mail: db@biink.
com
Pres: David Beardsley

RICHARD SAUNDERS INTERNATIONAL
3849 Edwards Rd
Cincinnati, OH 45244
Telephone: (513) 271-9911, FAX:
(513) 271-9966, E-Mail: doug@
eurekaranch.com, Web Site: www.
eurekaranch.com
Pres: Douglas B. Hall

SAVITZ
5757 W Century Blvd (Suite 360)
Los Angeles, CA 90045
Telephone: (310) 642-4799, FAX:
(310) 642-7795, E-Mail: lmoran@
savitzfieldandfocus.com, Web Site:
www.savitzfieldandfocus.com
Mgr: Lynn Moran

THE DMA J SCHMID & ASSOCIATES INC
5800 Foxridge Dr (Suite 200)
Mission, KS 66202-2333
Telephone: (913) 236-8988, FAX:
(913) 236-8987, E-Mail: info@
jschmid.com, Web Site: www.
jschmid.com
Pres & Chief Creative Officer: Lois
Boyle

THE SCHMIDT GROUP INTERNATIONAL INC
298 Peppertree Dr S
Vero Beach, FL 32963
Telephone: (772) 492-0073, FAX:
(772) 492-0293, E-Mail:
catalogprofit@att.net, Web Site:
www.the-schmidt-group.com
Pres: Alfred M. Schmidt Jr.

SCHULTE ASSOCIATES
2807 Polk St NE
Minneapolis, MN 55418-2954
Telephone: (612) 788-1673, FAX:
(612) 788-1147, E-Mail: schulte@
nmoa.org, Web Site: www.nmoa.org/
schulte
Pres: John D. Schulte

SCHUPAK GROUP INC
595 Madison Ave Rm 1900
New York, NY 10022-1958
Telephone: (212) 582-4210
CEO: Donald Schupak

SCHUS & CO
1458 Royal Blvd
Glendale, CA 91201
Telephone: (818) 550-8100, E-Mail:
sschus@aol.com
Pres: Stephanie Schus

SEDLAK
22901 Millcreek Blvd (Suite 600),
Metropolitan Plaza
Highland Hills, OH 44122-5724
Telephone: (216) 206-4700, FAX:
(216) 206-4840, E-Mail: info@
jasedlak.com, Web Site: www.
jasedlak.com
Pres: Jeffrey B. Graves
Mktg Commun: N. Evans

SEKLEMIAN NEWELL INC (CRMC)
1521 Alton Rd (Suite 138)
Miami Beach, FL 33139-3301
Telephone: (310) 622-5405, FAX:
(520) 842-7344, Web Site: www.
thecrmc.com
Pres: Devon Wylie

Customer Relationship Management
Conference (CRMC).

SENTINEL PEAK LLC
15600 Redmond Way
Redmond, WA 98052
Telephone: (360) 293-7271, Web Site:
www.sentinel-peak.com
Principal: Bart Pestarino

THE SERVICES GROUP (TSG)
2101 Wilson Blvd (Suite 700)
Arlington, VA 22201-3060
Telephone: (703) 528-7444, FAX:
(703) 522-2329, E-Mail: tsq@tsginc.
com, Web Site: www.tsginc.com
CEO: Hugh Doyle

THE DMA SEVERINI COMMUNICATIONS LLC (MOGILITY)
200 W 86th St (Apt 1k)
New York, NY 10024-3326
Telephone: (917) 734-3991, Web Site:
mogilityny.com
Primary Market Served: Consumer

SHAPES MARKETING INC
2086 Saint Johns Ave (Apt 207)
Highland Park, IL 60035-2461
Telephone: (847) 291-1110, FAX:
(847) 291-1308, Web Site: www.
shapesmarket.com
Chmn: John L. Shapin
Pres: Margaret Shapin

SHARF WOODWARD & ASSOCIATES INC
5900 Sepulveda Blvd (Suite 104)
Sherman Oaks, CA 91411
Telephone: (818) 988-2200, (877) 482-
6687, Web Site: www.swjobs.com
Owner: Bernie Sharf

SHASHO JONES DIRECT INC
267 W 25th St
New York, NY 10001-7128
Telephone: (212) 929-2300, E-Mail:
glenda@sjdirect.com, Web Site:
www.sjdirect.com
Pres: Glenda Shasho Jones
Pres: Rey Cruz
Founded: 1991

Catalog consulting, branding & creative development.

DAVID SHEPARD ASSOCIATES INC
332 Altessa Blvd
Melville, NY 11747-5222
Telephone: (516) 271-5567, FAX:
(516) 271-5589, E-Mail:
davidshepard@dsadirect.com, Web
Site: www.dsadirect.com
Pres: David B. Shepard

SHESHUNOFF MANAGEMENT SERVICES
2801 Via Fortuna (Suite 600)
Austin, TX 78746
Telephone: (512) 472-4000, (800) 477-
1772, FAX: (512) 479-8189, E-Mail:
info@smslp.com, Web Site: www.
ashesh.com
Partner: Alex Sheshunoff

THE DMA KATE SHIFMAN CONSULTING
179 Saint Johns Pl Apt 2
Brooklyn, NY 11217-3417
Telephone: (917) 710-0219
Primary Market Served: Consumer

SHISLER AND ASSOCIATES
14917 Oaks North Dr (Suite 113)
Dallas, TX 75254-7631
Telephone: (972) 387-8656
Partner: Jack Shisler

SIGNATURE INC
4701 Midway Dr
Ann Arbor, MI 48103

Telephone: (734) 426-2000, FAX: (734) 426-2109, E-Mail: johnagno@ signatureseries.com, Web Site: www. mentoringandcoaching.com
Pres: John Agno

SILLIKER INC
111 E Wacker Dr Ste 2300
Chicago, IL 60601-4214
Telephone: (708) 957-7878, FAX: (708) 957-3798, E-Mail: cjx@ netcom.com, Web Site: www.silliker. com
Dir, Mktg Commun: Jessica Sawyer-Lueck

SKYSTONE RYAN
635 W Seventh St (Suite 107)
Cincinnati, OH 45203
Telephone: (513) 241-6778, FAX: (513) 241-0551, E-Mail: cincinnati@ skystoneryan.com, Web Site: www. skystoneryan.com
Pres: J. Patrick Ryan

BRENT SLINKARD CONSULTANT
1048 W 17th St
Bloomington, IN 47404-3338
Telephone: (812) 336-1111
Pres: Brent Slinkard

RAY SLYPER ASSOCIATES
420 E 72nd St (Suite 2L)
New York, NY 10021
Telephone: (212) 439-0710
Pres: Ray Slyper

SMART SOURCE DIRECT
Div. of News America Marketing
1185 Ave of the Americas (fl 27), News America Marketing
New York, NY 10036-2603
Telephone: (617) 375-0404, FAX: (617) 425-0115, Web Site: www. newsamerica.com

**THE
DMA SMITH-BROWNING DIRECT INC**
45 Camielle Ct
Sedona, AZ 86336-5977
Telephone: (928) 203-9420
VP: Timothy C. Smith
Co Owner: Elizabeth Smith

**THE
DMA SMITH HANLEY ASSOCIATES**
107 John St Ste 201
Southport, CT 06890-1466
Telephone: (203) 319-4300, (888) 221-2900, FAX: (203) 319-4320, Web Site: www.smithhanley.com
Pres: Tom Hanley
Mng Dir: Jacqueline Paige

Recruiter: Eda Zullo
Recruiter: Peg Hoerres
Recruiter: Kim McStocker
Recruiter: Nikki Quist
Employees: 100
Founded: 1980

Highly specialized recruiting firm with long term dedicated professionals focusing on the needs of our clients.

SMITH O'KEEFE & ASSOCIATES
1566 Somers Point Rd
Egg Harbor Township, NJ 08234-8514
Telephone: (609) 653-0400, (800) 222-0461, FAX: (609) 653-6483, E-Mail: info@smithokeefe.com, Web Site: www.smithokeefe.com
CEO: Kenneth P. Smith

SNYDER GLENN J & ASSOCS
49 Quail Ln
Jacksonville Beach, FL 32250
Telephone: (904) 246-6223, FAX: (904) 246-6229
Owner: Glenn J. Snyder

SOLUTRAN
3600 Holly Ln (Suite 60)
Plymouth, MN 55447
Telephone: (763) 559-2225, (888) 765-8872, FAX: (763) 559-8872, E-Mail: solutions@solutran.com, Web Site: www.solutran.com
Pres & CEO: Barry J. Nordstrand

DEBBIE SORACE
70 Edwards Pl
Valley Stream, NY 11580-3143
Telephone: (516) 659-5614
Primary Market Served: Consumer

THE SOUND DIRECT MARKETING GROUP
PO Box 162527
Austin, TX 78716-2527
Telephone: (512) 306-0879
Pres: Robert Rogin

**THE
DMA SOURCELINK**
500 Park Blvd (Suite 415)
Itasca, IL 60143-1260
Telephone: (866) 947-6872, Web Site: www.sourcelink.com
Pres & CEO: Don McKenzie

SOUTHWEST CONSULTANTS
17045 Chatsworth St
Granada Hills, CA 91344-5845
Telephone: (818) 635-1777, Web Site: www.southwestbancorp.com
Pres: Joffrey Long

SPAIDE, KUIPERS & CO
42 Second St
Newport, RI 02840
Telephone: (610) 668-8296, FAX: (610) 579-3844, E-Mail: spaide@ spaidekuipers.com, Web Site: www. spaidekuipers.com
Principal: William J. Spaide

SPECTRUM RETAIL ASSOCIATES
10 E Athens Ave (Suite 200)
Ardmore, PA 19003
Telephone: (610) 645-9520, (800) 570-6565, FAX: (610) 645-9524
Chmn: Scott C. Borowsky
Dir: Eileen Vogel

Specializes in direct sales, catalog and graphic arts.

SPENCERSTUART
353 N Clark (Suite 2400)
Chicago, IL 60654-3479
Telephone: (312) 822-0088, FAX: (312) 822-0116, Web Site: www. spencerstuart.com
Chmn: Kevin M Connelly
CEO: David S Daniel
Mng Dir N America: Michael J Anderson
CFO & Chief Admin Officer: Richard M Kurkow
Conducts Business: U.S., Canada, Worldwide
Employees: 1,400
Primary Market Served: Business
Gross sales or billing: $435,000,000

Senior level executive search for CEOs/general managers and key functional leaders. Clients include leading direct and interactive marketing companies and suppliers/agencies to the industry.

STAGG DIRECT MARKETING INC
11 Gorham Rd
Scarsdale, NY 10583-1117
Telephone: (914) 725-3990, FAX: (914) 472-7298
Pres: Phyllis C. Stagg

STATESIDE ASSOCIATES
2300 Clarendon Blvd Ste 407
Arlington, VA 22201-3300
Telephone: (703) 525-7466 X228
Pres & CEO: Constance Campanella
Primary Market Served: Business

STATISTICAL INNOVATIONS INC
375 Concord Ave
Belmont, MA 02478-3084

Telephone: (617) 489-4490, FAX:
(617) 489-4499, E-Mail:
statisticalinnovations@gmail.com,
Web Site: www.
statisticalinnovations.com
Pres: Jay Magidson

THE STELTER CO
10435 New York Ave
Des Moines, IA 50322-3774
Telephone: (800) 331-6881
Creative Dir: Beverly Hutney

**STEPHEN-BRADFORD
SEARCH**
261 Madison Ave Fl 11
New York, NY 10016-2303
Telephone: (212) 221-6333, X346,
(800) 720-0922, FAX: (212) 391-
7826, E-Mail: info@stephenbradford.
com, Web Site: www.
stephenbradford.com
Pres: Erika Weinstein

STEPHENS INC
65 E 55th St Fl 22
New York, NY 10022-3369
Telephone: (212) 891-1777, Web Site:
www.stephens.com
Mng Dir: Ken Wasik

STOCKHAM CONSULTING
7300 Butterscotch Rd
Eden Prairie, MN 55346-3233
Telephone: (952) 250-2206
Mktg Consultant: Maria Stockham

STRATEGICONE
6700 Antioch Rd Ste 110
Overland Park, KS 66204-1200
Telephone: (913) 342-9100 x102, Web
Site: www.strategic-one.com
Pres: Mike Rogers
Primary Market Served: Business &
Consumer

**ELIZABETH STREITZ &
ASSOCIATES**
255 W 108th St (Suite 9A)
New York, NY 10025
Telephone: (212) 749-3152
Pres: Elizabeth Streitz

THE DMA STROFINA
10200 NE Garibaldi Loop
Bainbridge Island, WA 98110-3976
Telephone: (206) 855-9681

SYSTEMS ANALYTICS INC
946 Great Plain Ave (#125)
Needham, MA 02492-3030

Telephone: (781) 444-4837, E-Mail:
info@systemsanalytics.com, Web
Site: www.systemsanalytics.com
Pres: John Zhang

TALX CORP
Div. of Equifax
14755 Preston Rd (Suite 525)
Dallas, TX 75254-7898
Telephone: (972) 755-2100, FAX:
(972) 755-2080, E-Mail:
consulting@managementinsights.
com, Web Site: www.
managementinsights.com
Dir TCI Services: Gayle Malone
Client Svcs Relations: Kelly Connel

TSI
12 Corporate Woods Blvd
Albany, NY 12211-2344
Telephone: (518) 463-5555, FAX:
(518) 463-4504, E-Mail: tsi@capital.
net, Web Site: www.tsidrivers.com
Pres: Peter Mirabille

**TECHNICAL ASSISTANCE
RESEARCH PROGRAMS
(TARP)**
2425 Wilson Blvd (Suite 400)
Arlington, VA 22201
Telephone: (703) 524-1456, FAX:
(703) 524-6374, Web Site: www.
tarp.com
Pres: John Goodman

**TELEDEVELOPMENT
SERVICES INC**
PO Box 502
Richfield, OH 44286-0502
Telephone: (330) 659-4441, FAX:
(330) 659-4442, E-Mail: jkaplan@
teledevelopment.com, Web Site:
www.teledevelopment.com
Founder & Pres: Jon E. Kaplan

**TELEMANAGEMENT
SEARCH**
6 Litchfield Rd (Suite 316)
Port Washington, NY 11050-3815
Telephone: (516) 767-6990, FAX:
(516) 767-6980, E-Mail: connie@
tmrecruiters.com, Web Site: www.
tmrecruiters.com
Pres: Connie Caroli

TERES CONSULTING INC
Nine Magnolia St
Framingham, MA 01701-4913
Telephone: (508) 872-4922, FAX:
(253) 595-6748, E-Mail: info@
teresconsulting.com, Web Site: www.
teresconsulting.com
Principal: Wayne Teres

TESAR REYNES INC
333 N Michigan Ave (Suite 2226)
Chicago, IL 60601-4035
Telephone: (312) 726-1900, E-Mail:
tony@tesar-reynes.com, Web Site:
www.tesar-reynes.com
Partner: Anthony Reynes

THINKALYTICS
440 Millburn Ave
Millburn, NJ 07041-1210
Telephone: (973) 671-1590, Web Site:
www.thinkalytics.com
Primary Market Served: Consumer

GRANT THORNTON LLP
Two Commerce Square (Suite 3100)
Philadelphia, PA 19103
Telephone: (215) 561-4200, FAX:
(215) 561-1066, Web Site: www.
grantthornton.com
Mng Partner: Richard Gebert

TIMBERLINE INTERACTIVE
5 Park St (Suite 2)
Middlebury, VT 05753-1169
Telephone: (802) 388-8377, Web Site:
www.timberlineinteractive.com
Pres & CEO: Bud Reed

TITANTV MEDIA
Owned by Turnstone & Capital CBC
New Media
818 Dows Rd SE
Cedar Rapids, IA 52403-7000
Telephone: (319) 365-5597, (800) 365-
7629, FAX: (319) 365-5694, E-Mail:
mktg@titantv.com, Web Site: www.
titantv.com
Pres & COO: Mark Effron

TOLLIVER INC
303 5th Ave Rm 206
New York, NY 10016-6690
Telephone: (212) 758-7344, FAX:
(212) 750-8617, E-Mail: tolliver12@
aol.com
Pres: Susan Taliaferro

TOWERS WATSON
Subs. of The Wyatt Co
875 Third Ave.
New York, NY 10022
Telephone: (212) 725-7550, FAX:
(212) 644-7432, Web Site: www.
towerswatson.com
Mktg Dir: Bob Crane

**TRAINING CONSULTANTS
INC**
1415 Sheridan Rd
Highland Park, IL 60035

Telephone: (847) 432-9428, FAX:
(847) 432-9318, E-Mail: wetrain2@
home.com
Pres: Andrea Crane

TRANSAMERICAN MAILING
355 State Pl
Escondido, CA 92029-1359
Telephone: (760) 745-5343, Web Site:
www.transdirect.com
VP: Heather Benjamin

**TRANSGLOBAL
CONSULTANTS INC**
Div. of International Services Group
3210 Glastonbury Cir NW
Canton, OH 44708-1174
Telephone: (330) 477-6450, E-Mail:
transglobal@earthlink.net
Dir: Lawrence J Chaido

THE DMA KAREN TRIPI ASSOCIATES
305 Madison Ave (Suite 2319)
New York, NY 10165-6209
Telephone: (212) 972-5258, FAX:
(212) 599-3809, E-Mail: karen@
karentripi.com, Web Site: www.
karentripi.com
Pres: Karen Tripi

THE DMA THE TROYANOS GROUP LTD
106 N Broadway (fl 3)
Irvington, NY 10533-1262
Telephone: (914) 479-1801, FAX:
(914) 993-9554, E-Mail: dennis@
troyanosgroup.com, Web Site: www.
troyanosgroup.com
Pres: Dennis Troyanos
Employees: 4
Primary Market Served: Business
Founded: 1991

Executive search in the direct marketing industry.

TUCKER CAPITAL CORP
234 Nassau St Ste 3
Princeton, NJ 08542-4614
Telephone: (609) 924-5710, FAX:
(609) 924-5027, E-Mail: info@
tuckercapital.com, Web Site: www.
tuckercapital.com
Mng Dir: Craig L. Battle

**TURTLE BAY MANAGEMENT
CO INC**
209 86th St (Suite E)
Virginia Beach, VA 23451
Telephone: (757) 422-2760, FAX:
(757) 422-1434, E-Mail: jimlant@
turtlebaymanagement.com, Web Site:
www.turtlebaymanagement.com
Principal: Jim Lant

**GILBERT TWEED
ASSOCIATES**
415 Madison Ave (20th fl)
New York, NY 10017
Telephone: (212) 758-3000, FAX:
(212) 832-1040, E-Mail: hrdptgt@
gmail.com, Web Site: www.
gilberttweed.com
Owner & CEO: Janet Tweed

THE DMA UCI/DREAM GIVEAWAYS
19321-C US Hwy 19 N (Suite 605)
Clearwater, FL 33764
Telephone: (727) 536-2777, Web Site:
www.dreamgiveaways.com
Primary Market Served: Business &
Consumer

USY CONSULTING INC
50 Highwood Dr
Dumont, NJ 07628-2608
Telephone: (201) 585-7402, FAX:
(201) 585-2754, E-Mail:
usyconsulting@hotmail.com
Pres: Reizo Yoshida

UNISFAIR
149 Commonwealth Dr
Menlo Park, CA 94025-1133
Telephone: (866) 354-4030, Web Site:
www.unisfair.com
Mktg Mgr: Nhien Le
Primary Market Served: Business

**THE DMA URBAN SCIENCE
APPLICATIONS INC**
200 Renaissance Ctr (Suite 1800)
Detroit, MI 48243-1306
Telephone: (313) 259-9900, Web Site:
www.urbanscience.com
Global Practice Dir: Mark Yuhn

VMF INC
3313 Ross Pl NW
Washington, DC 20008
Telephone: (202) 966-3361, FAX:
(202) 362-8409, E-Mail: veflei@
aol.com
Pres: Virginia Fleischman

**THE DMA VENABLE LLP CONFERENCE
CENTER**
575 7th St NW
Washington, DC 20004-1607
Telephone: (202) 344-4860, (202) 344-
4000, (888) VENABLE, FAX: (202)
344-8300, E-Mail: info@venable.
com, Web Site: www.venable.com
Partner: Ian Volner

VERTICAL MEDIA GROUP
2200 N Central Rd
Fort Lee, NJ 07024-7557

Telephone: (201) 245-7935
Pres: Jeff Holland

**WDS MARKETING & PUBLIC
RELATIONS**
8232 Hadley St
Overland Park, KS 66204-3542
Telephone: (913) 362-4541, FAX:
(913) 362-7342, E-Mail: bwilson@
wdspr.com, Web Site: www.wdspr.
com
Owner: Becky S. Wilson

THE DMA WLA INC
535 5th Ave (fl 31)
New York, NY 10017-3667
Telephone: (212) 584-1810
CEO: Worth Linen
Primary Market Served: Business &
Consumer

WPI GROUP INC
PO Box 65
Colts Neck, NJ 07722-0065
FAX: (212) 202-3742, E-Mail: info@
wpinj.com, Web Site: www.wpinj.
com
Pres: Aditya Aluhawalia

WTB ASSOCIATES INC
4020 Bunker Ln
Wilmette, IL 60091
Telephone: (847) 251-4188
Chmn: William T. Bringham Sr.
Pres: William T. Bringham Jr.

**WAGNER HINES & AVARY
INC**
218 N Lee St
Alexandria, VA 22314
Telephone: (703) 684-7740, FAX:
(703) 548-3721
Chmn: Robert Avary

**WAKEFIELD TALABISCO
INTERNATIONAL**
11 E 44th St (Rm 1206)
New York, NY 10017-3608
Telephone: (212) 661-8600, FAX:
(212) 661-8832, Web Site: www.
wtali.com
Pres: Barbara Talabisco

WEBB MASON
10830 Gilroy Rd
Hunt Valley, MD 21031-4312
Telephone: (410) 785-1111, Web Site:
www.webbmason.com
HR Dir: Marty Levine
Primary Market Served: Business

WESLEY R. WEBER & ASSOCIATES
405 Brookmeade Dr
West Chester, PA 19380
Telephone: (610) 909-8040, E-Mail:
wesweber@aol.com
Pres: Wesley R. Weber

FREDERICK WERSHAW MANAGEMENT CO
111 Black Rock Rd
Stamford, CT 06903-1430
Telephone: (203) 329-3000, FAX:
(203) 329-3044
Pres: Frederick I. Wershaw

THE DMA **WEST CARY GROUP**
5 W Cary St
Richmond, VA 23220-5609
Telephone: (804) 343-2029
Primary Market Served: Consumer

WEST COMPANIES INC
7155 Savoy Ct
Seminole, FL 33776-4329
Telephone: (212) 319-7069
Pres: Larry J. West
Founded: 1984

Mergers & acquisitions for direct marketing & e commerce cos.

WEST CORP
11808 Miracle Hills Dr
Omaha, NE 68154
Telephone: (800) 841-9000, FAX:
(402) 963-1602, E-Mail: sales@west.
com, Web Site: www.west.com
VP, Mktg: Mark Meudt

THE DMA **STEVE WEXLER CREATIVE GROUP**
PO Box 219
Farmingville, NY 11738-0219
Telephone: (631) 736-6565, Web Site:
www.wexdirect.com
CEO: Steve Wexler

WHITEWING LABS
17939 Chatsworth St (#408)
Granada Hills, CA 91344
Telephone: (800) 950-3030, FAX:
(818) 240-2785, E-Mail: service@
whitewing.com, Web Site: www.
whitewing.com
Pres: Cynthia A. Kolke

WHITNEY WORLDWIDE INC
553 Hayward Ave N Ste 250
Saint Paul, MN 55128-9006
Telephone: (651) 748-5000, (800) 597-
0227, FAX: (651) 748-4000, Web
Site: www.whitneyworld.com
Pres & CEO: Les Layton

WILLIAMS, CALIRI, MILLER & OTLEY
1428 Rte 23
Wayne, NJ 07474-5826
Telephone: (973) 694-0800, FAX:
(973) 694-0302, Web Site: www.
wcmolaw.com
Administrator: Barbara Jerchower

WIND RIVER GROUP
900 State Mill Rd
Akron, OH 44319-2138
Telephone: (330) 644-7774, FAX:
(330) 645-2045
Pres: Ed Jacobs

WINDSOR HOUSE
Div. of Windsor Marketing
Two Industrial Rd
Windsor Locks, CT 06096
Telephone: (860) 627-5927, FAX:
(860) 627-0252, E-Mail: ahalley@
windsormarketing.com, Web Site:
windsormarketing.com
Pres & Treas: Kevin Armata

WINDWARD GROUP
241 Spinnaker Ln
Shelburne, VT 05482-7779
Telephone: (802) 985-3631, Web Site:
www.windwardgroup.us
Mng Partner: Rebecca Jewett

THE DMA **WINSTON & WINSTON PC**
295 Madison Ave
New York, NY 10017
Telephone: (212) 922-9483, FAX:
(212) 532-2722, Web Site: www.
winstonandwinston.com
Sr Partner: Arthur Winston

THE DMA **WINTERBERRY GROUP**
Subs. of Petsky Prunier LLC
60 Broad St Ste 3810
New York, NY 10004-2329
Telephone: (212) 842-6000, FAX:
(212) 842-6010, E-Mail: info@
winterberrygroup.com, Web Site:
www.winterberrygroup.com
Sr Mng Dir: Bruce Biegel

THE DMA **BRIAN WOLFE**
418 E 59th St (Apt 26A)
New York, NY 10022-2378
Telephone: (516) 840-3748
Primary Market Served: Consumer

THE WRITE ANSWERS COPYWRITING & CONSULTING
816 Peace Portal Dr (#82)
Blaine, WA 98230-4010

Telephone: (888) 331-0322, Web Site:
www.thewriteanswers.com
Resultant: Peter Britton

THE YANKEE GROUP
One Liberty Sq (fl 7)
Boston, MA 02109-4868
Telephone: (617) 598-7200, E-Mail:
info@yankeegroup.com, Web Site:
www.yankeegroup.com
Chief Strategy Officer: Berge Ayvazian

ANDREW YOELIN & CO
5524 E Waltann Ln
Scottsdale, AZ 85254-1701
Telephone: (602) 482-6214, E-Mail:
corpdating@aol.com
Pres: Andrew Yoelin

ZS ASSOCIATES
1800 Sherman Ave
Evanston, IL 60201
Telephone: (847) 492-3600, FAX:
(847) 864-6280, E-Mail: inquiry@
zsassociates.com, Web Site: www.
zsassociates.com
Founder & Co Chmn Bd: Andris Zoltners

RL ZAPIN ASSOCIATES INC
708 Third Ave (6th fl)
New York, NY 10017
Telephone: (212) 297-6248, E-Mail:
roni@rlzapinassociates.com, Web
Site: www.rlzapinassociates.com
Pres: Roni L. Zapin
Primary Market Served: Business &
Consumer

NEIL ZELENETZ & ASSOCIATES
67 Transverse Rd
Garden City, NY 11530-1821
Telephone: (516) 746-2981, E-Mail:
nzelenetz@aol.com
Pres: Neil Zelenetz

ZIMMERMAN BUSINESS CONSULTING INC
44 E 92nd St (Suite 5B)
New York, NY 10128-1319
Telephone: (212) 860-3107, FAX:
(212) 860-7730, E-Mail: ljzzbci@
aol.com, Web Site: www.zbcinc.com
Pres: Leonard J. Zimmerman

ZOE MARKETING
5132 Meadows del Mar
San Diego, CA 92130-4854
Telephone: (858) 408-1700
Pres: Russell Levine

Full Service Direct Mail Companies (21) — Geographic Index

Alabama

Action In Mailing, 4521 Troy Hwy, Montgomery, 36116-5121

Mail Enterprises LLC, 3810 5th Ct N, Birmingham, 35222-1308

NCP Solutions, 5200 E Lake Blvd, Birmingham, 35217

Arizona

Cactus Mailing Company, 16121 N 78th St (Suite 103), Scottsdale, 85260

FMP Direct Inc, 15560 N Frank Lloyd Wright Blvd Ste B4, Scottsdale, 85260-2020

LPL, PO Box 15610, Scottsdale, 85267-5610

Market Builder Inc, 5135 E Ingram St Ste 2, Mesa, 85205-3465

Arkansas

The Marketing Advantage Inc, 1525 Merrill Dr (Suite 1500), Little Rock, 72211-1662

McKee & Associates Inc, PO Box 2838, Hot Springs National Park, 71914-2838

Sumotext, Inc, 10825 Financial Centre Pkwy Ste 123, Little Rock, 72211-3557

California

AMC MMI, 1050 Valencia Dr, Fullerton, 92831

Active Voice, 600 Townsend St (#140 W), San Francisco, 94103

CDMG, 21171 S Western (Suite 260), Torrance, 90501

Chewning Direct Marketing, 4 Candlebush, Irvine, 92603-3727

Direct Mail Center, 1099 Mariposa St, San Francisco, 94107

Dufford Marketing, 2233 Brigden Rd, Pasadena, 91104-3304

ERS Direct Marketing, 1336 Morrpark Rd (#302), Thousand Oaks, 91360

GenerH, Inc, 1605 Date Ave, Torrance, 90503-6109

GSI Commerce, 10303 Norris Ave, Pacoima, 91331

New Income Sources, 141 Linden St, Hermosa Beach, 90254

Buck Owens' Crystal Palace, 2800 Buck Owens Blvd, Bakersfield, 93308-6314

Professional Print & Mail Inc, 2818 E Hamilton Ave, Fresno, 93721-3209

Service Mailers Inc, 3101 Exposition Pl, Los Angeles, 90018-4030

Technicolor, 3233 E Mission Oaks Blvd, Camarillo, 93012

Towne Allpoints Communications, 3441 W MacArthur Blvd, Santa Ana, 92704

Western Graphics, 7614 Lemon Ave, Lemon Grove, 91945-1619

World Marketing, Inc (HQ), 14407 Alondra Blvd, La Mirada, 90638

XDM Corp, 235 Montgomery St Ste 834, San Francisco, 94104-3002

Zumbox, 31364 Via Colinas (Suite 103), Westlake Village, 91362-6844

Colorado

Advanced Direct Marketing Inc, 712 E Eisenhower Blvd, Loveland, 80537-3920

DMX-Direct, Inc, 8955 E Nichols Ave (Suite 200), Centennial, 80112-3498

Eagle:xm, 5105 E 41st Ave, Denver, 80216-4420

First Class Direct Inc, 5610 Boeing Dr, Loveland, 80538

McCaffrey Enterprises, 1331 Red Cedar Cir, Fort Collins, 80524

Bob Stone Inc, 2317 Interstate Ave (Unit B), Grand Junction, 81505-8674

G.A. Wright Direct Marketing, 10325 E 47th Ave, Denver, 80238

Connecticut

ADVO Inc, One Targeting Centre, Windsor, 06095

The Harty Press Inc, 25 James St, New Haven, 06513-4218

Marketing Solutions Unlimited LLC, 109 Talcott Rd, West Hartford, 06110-1228

Media Horizons Inc, 40 Richards Ave, Norwalk, 06854-2320

Phoenix Marketing Group Ltd, PO Box 599, Georgetown, 06829-0599

WordCom Inc, 56 Main St, PO Box 308, Ellington, 06029-3360

Florida

Cox Target Media/DBA Valpak, 8605 Largo Lakes Dr, Largo, 33773

Globe Marketing Systems, 11950 NW 39th St (Suite B), Coral Springs, 33065

Hill Mailing & Printing of Florida Inc, PO Box 3331, Brandon, 33509-3331

Hyphos360 Inc, 19337 US Hwy 19 N (Suite 500), Clearwater, 33764-3151

Innovative Marketing Direct Inc, 3200 Henderson Blvd Ste 100, Tampa, 33609-3054

Marketing Visions Inc, 3338 Deer Creek Alba Way, Deerfield Beach, 33442

MediaWorks Advertising & Marketing Inc, 725 W Granada Blvd, Ormond Beach, 32174-9406

Nature Trade Center, 1915 Trade Center Way, Naples, 34109-6220

Nordis Direct, 4401 NW 124th Ave, Coral Springs, 33065-7636

Precision Response Corp, 8151 Peters Rd (Suite 4000), Plantation, 33324-4012

Progressive Communications, 1001 Sand Pond Rd, Lake Mary, 32746-3354

Pronto Post, 7885 W 20th Ave, Hialeah, 33014-3228

Protocol Integrated Direct Marketing, 2805 Fruitville Rd, Sarasota, 34237-5318

Sentinel Direct, 633 N Orange Ave (MP122), Orlando, 32801

Georgia

ACE Marketing Service, 1961 S Cobb Industrial Blvd, Smyrna, 30082-4915

Gardella & Co, PO Box 20121, Atlanta, 30325-0121

Imagemakers Marketing Inc, 1843 Blackwater Dr, Marietta, 30066-6713

Loyaltyworks Inc, 2337 Perimeter Park Dr Ste 220, Atlanta, 30341-1313

Stezzi Direct Inc, 2775 Bankers Industrial Dr, Atlanta, 30360

Hawaii

FireFly, 999 Bishop St (21 fl), Honolulu, 96813

Illinois

Active Graphics Inc, 5500 W 31st St, Cicero, 60804-3957

Liberty Creative Solutions, 18625 W Creek Dr, Tinley Park, 60477-6247

Northern Printing Network Inc, 1400 S Wolf Rd (Suite 102), Wheeling, 60090-6524

Premier Print and Service Group Inc, 120 S Riverside Plz (Suite 1650), Chicago, 60606-3938

Prima-Nelson Printing Inc, 911 Elmdale Rd, Glenview, 60025-3905

Print Arts, 2001 W 21st St, Broadview, 60155

Priority Systems Inc, PO Box 289, Grayslake, 60030-0289

Programmers Investment Corp, 125 E Algonquin Rd, Arlington Heights, 60005

United Marketing Group LLC, 929 N Plum Grove Rd, Schaumburg, 60173-4704

Indiana

Bacompt Systems Inc, 12742 Hamilton Crossing Blvd, Carmel, 46032-5422

Sigma Micro LLC, 9100 Purdue Rd Ste 400, Indianapolis, 46268-1180

Iowa

Typed Letters Corp, PO Box 799, Mount Pleasant, 52641-0799

Kansas

MarketAide Services Inc, PO Box 500, Salina, 67402-0500

Midwest Direct Marketing Inc, 501 N Webster, Spring Hill, 66083

Kentucky

Gannett Direct Marketing Services Inc, 3400 Robards Ct, Louisville, 40218-4544

Icon Marketing Communications, 7000 Houston Rd Ste 10, Florence, 41042-4874

Louisiana

Direct Mail Marketing Inc, 509 Market St (Suite 100), Shreveport, 71101-3259

Maine

GG Direct, 351 Riverside Industrial Pkwy, Portland, 04103-1415

Maryland

Creative Marketing Management, 2703 Colston Dr, Chevy Chase, 20815-3033

DataLab USA, 202561 Goldenrod Ln, Germantown, 20876-4063

Doner Direct, 400 E Pratt St (10th fl), Baltimore, 21202-3116

EU Services, 649 N Horners Ln, Rockville, 20850-1233

KCMS, 201 Commerce Dr, Upper Marlboro, 20774-8762

Suman Inc, 10805 Whiterim Dr, Potomac, 20854-1786

Massachusetts

B&W Press Inc, 401 E Main St, Georgetown, 01833-2513

Community Newspaper Co, 254 2nd Ave Ste 1, Needham, 02494-2829

DS Graphics Inc, 120 Stedman St, Lowell, 01851

Direct Results, 2005 Riverdale St, West Springfield, 01089-1067

The Field Companies Inc, 385 Pleasant St, PO Box 78, Watertown, 02471-0078

Mail Computer Service, 321 Manley St, West Bridgewater, 02379

Masscot Internet Inc, 20 Grove St, West Yarmouth, 02673

Signature Communications, 45 West Side Rd, Milton, 02186-3018

Tiziani Whitmyre, 2 Commercial St, Sharon Commerce Ctr, Sharon, 02067

W.A. Wilde Co, 201 Summer St, Holliston, 01746-2258

Michigan

ICS Marketing Support Services, 4225 Legacy Pkwy, Lansing, 48911-4246

Minnesota

Development Resources, 790 Cleveland Ave S (Suite 200), Saint Paul, 55116-3858

Direct Response Insurance Administrative Services Inc (DRIASI), 7930 Century Blvd, Chanhassen, 55317-8001

Diversified Graphics Inc, 3301 Como Ave SE, Minneapolis, 55414-2809

IC System Inc, 444 Hwy 96 E, Saint Paul, 55164-2557

IQ Marketing, 19990 Sweetwater Curve, Excelsior, 55331-8134

IWCO Direct, 7951 Powers Blvd, Chanhassen, 55317-9502

James M Laing & Associates, 7086 Pontiac Cir, Chanhassen, 55317

MRC Marketing Inc, 2 Red Pine Rd, Saint Paul, 55127-2028

Pro/Phase Marketing Inc, 6554 Edenvale Blvd, Eden Prairie, 55346-2502

Mississippi

First American Printing & Direct Mail, 1 Choctaw Trail, Ocean Springs, 39564-4107

Missouri

Ad Sell Co, 5001 Southwest Ave, Saint Louis, 63110-3427

American Direct Marketing Resources Inc, 400 Chesterfield Ctr (Suite 500), Chesterfield, 63017-7703

Creative Marketing Programs, 412 Oak St, Kansas City, 64106-1133

Emfluence, 106 W 11th St (Suite 2220), Kansas City, 64105-1823

Fiorella's Jack Stack Barbecue, 8250 NE Underground Dr, Pillar 140 (Bldg 32A), Kansas City, 64161-9734

Gabriel Group, 3190 Rider Trail S, Earth City, 63045

Sales Development Associates Inc, 7850 Manchester Rd, Saint Louis, 63143-2710

STAR Direct, 215 E 18th St, Kansas City, 64108

Vestcom Saint Louis, 4288 Rider Trail N, Earth City, 63045-1105

Wilkes Direct Mail Co, 3401 Chouteau Ave, Saint Louis, 63103

Nebraska

Omaha Print, 4700 "F" St, Omaha, 68117

New Hampshire

Direct Print, Five Brown Rd, Windham, 03087-1231

Fred B Estabrook Co Inc, 39 Ridge Rd, New Hampton, 03256

PEP Direct, 19 Stoney Brook Dr, Wilton, 03086-5151

New Jersey

Asbury Park Press Addresses Unlimited, 3601 Hwy 66, Neptune, 07753-2604

The Corporate Communications Group, 14 Henderson Dr, West Caldwell, 07006-6608

Hummel Integrated Marketing Solutions, 850 Springfield Rd, Union, 07083-8614

Interactive Marketing Group Inc, 50 Commerce Dr., Allendale, 07401

Promark Direct Marketing Concepts Inc, One University Plaza Dr (Suite 8), Hackensack, 07601-6207

Red Clay Media, 33 W 8th St, Bayonne, 07002

Telebrands Corp, 81 Two Bridges Rd, Bldg One, Fairfield, 07004

Trimensions Inc, 1 Engle St (Suite 202), Englewood, 07631-2941

New York

Adrea Rubin Marketing Inc, 19 W 44th St (Suite 1415), New York, 10036-6101

Advertising Distributors of America Inc, 230 Adams Ave., Hauppauge, 11788

Austin & Williams, 125 Kennedy Dr (Suite 100), Hauppauge, 11788-4017

Cathedral Corp, 632 Ellsworth Rd, Griffiss Technology Park, Rome, 13441

CGT Marketing, 275-B Dixon Ave, Amityville, 11701-2874

Design Distributors, Inc, 300 Marcus Blvd, Deer Park, 11729-4500

Ground Truth, 116 W 23rd St (fl 5), New York, 10011-2599

The Horah Group, 351 Manville Rd (Suite 105), Pleasantville, 10570-2166

Lazarus Marketing, 3530 Oceanside Rd, Oceanside, 11572

Manhattan Media Services Inc, 535 5h Ave (#1012), New York, 10017-8004

North American Communications, 20 Maple Ave, Armonk, 10504-0430

Prime Access Inc, 345 Seventh Ave (10th fl), New York, 10001

Quality Letter Service Inc, 22 W 32nd St (fl 10), New York, 10001-3807

Relationship1, 2 2nd St, Rye, 10580-2927

The St John Associates Inc, 3450 Baychester Ave, Bronx, 10475-1407

Tyme Direct Mail Service, 3030 47th Ave Ste 300, c/o Century Direct, LLC, Long Island City, 11101-3445

UniWorld Group, 1 Metro Tech Center N (fl 11), Brooklyn, 11201

Xpandomedia, 340 Nagel Dr, Buffalo, 14225

North Carolina

Advanced Direct, 4221 Tudor Ln, Greensboro, 27410-8105

Dex One, 1001 Winstead Dr, Cary, 27513-2117

RCS Response Technologies Inc, 6420 Rea Rd (Suite 210), Charlotte, 28217

Ohio

Americalist, 8050 Freedom Ave NW, North Canton, 44720

AmeriMark Holdings LLC, 6864 Engle Rd, Cleveland, 44130-7910

Optimum Group, 310 Culvert St (fl 5), c/o Mktg Inc, Cincinnati, 45202-2229

Resource Marketing Inc, 343 N Front St Ste 300, Columbus, 43215-2266

Workflow One, 220 E Monument Ave, Dayton, 45402-1223

Oregon

McIntyre Direct, 700 N Hayden Island Dr (Suite 390), Portland, 97217-8185

Reed/Harris, PO Box 3100, Portland, 97208-3100

Pennsylvania

Alternative Marketing Solutions Inc, 342 Nutt Rd, Phoenixville, 19460

Antares Information Tech, 110 Commons Ct, Chadds Ford, 19317-9716

The Ted Barkus Co Inc, 8017 Anderson St, Philadelphia, 19118-2936

Communication Concepts Inc, 1044 Pulinski Rd, Ivyland, 18974-1534

Direct Mail Service Inc, 939 W North Ave, Pittsburgh, 15233-1605

Forecast Direct Marketing Group, 37 Terminal Way, Pittsburgh, 15219

ICS Corp, 2225 Richmond St, Philadelphia, 19125

Mailing Services of Pittsburgh Inc, 155 Commerce Dr, Freedom, 15042-9202

Nice Lines Direct Mail, 1210 Stanbridge St Ste 4, Norristown, 19401-5318

PlusNetMarketing Inc, 415 Eagleview Blvd (#116), Exton, 19341-1143

USA Direct Inc, 2901 Blackbridge Rd, York, 17402

Rhode Island

Catalog Design Studios, 8 Barnes St, Providence, 02906-1517

Tennessee

Baber Inc, 3135 Millbranch Rd, Memphis, 38116-1917

ClientLogic, 3102 W End Ave (Suite 1000), Two American Center, Nashville, 37203

DataMarketing Network Inc, 701 Murfreesboro Pike, Nashville, 37210-4521

Strategic Direct Marketing Inc, 208 Centre St, Pleasant View, 37146-7053

Thompson & Co Marketing Communications, 85 Union Ave (fl 3), Memphis, 38103-5127

Texas

Allied Marketing Group Inc, 1555 Regal Row, Dallas, 75247-3619

Altman Direct Marketing, 4102 Balcones Dr, Austin, 78731-5704

The EZ-Forms Co, 317 Sidney Baker S (#317), Kerrville, 78028

GS Marketing, 1345 Enclave Pkwy, Houston, 77077-2026

Inter Direct USA, 1001 S Dairy Ashford St Ste 450, Houston, 77077-2386

Premier IMS, 815 Live Oak St, Houston, 77003-3220

Print Mailers Inc, 707 West Rd, Houston, 77038-2505

TABS Direct, 2800 Story Rd W, Irving, 75038-5267

Topp Direct Marketing, 1117 N Stuart Place Rd Ste 103, Harlingen, 78552-4344

Vermont

Direct Communications Corp, 23 Court St, Rutland, 05702

Virginia

Commonwealth Lists, 11208 Maples Mill Rd, Fairfax, 22030

Communications Corp of America, 13195 Freedom Way, Boston, 22713-4114

Huntsinger & Jeffer Inc, 809 Brook Hill Cir, Richmond, 23227-2503

L & E Meridian, 7400 Fullerton Rd (Suite 110), Springfield, 22153-2286

O'Connell Meier LLC, PO Box 10252, Alexandria, 22310

Washington

Kaye-Smith, 4101 Oakesdale Ave SW, Renton, 98057-4817

Mailing Lists Plus Inc, 12819 SE 38th St, PMB 203, Bellevue, 98006-1326

Wisconsin

AB Data Ltd, 600 A B Data Dr, Milwaukee, 53217-4931

IMS Group II Communications, 11311 W Forest Home Ave, Franklin, 53132

Novo 1 Inc, 20935 Swenson Dr Ste 360, Waukesha, 53186-2076

Pragalz Metro Graphx Inc, 2500 E Lakeshore Dr, Twin Lakes, 53181-9371

Prospect Direct Inc, 2266 N Prospect Ave (Suite 336), Milwaukee, 53202-6306

Publishers Diversified Mail Service Inc, 10545 W Donges Ct, Milwaukee, 53224-1182

CANADA
British Columbia

Benwell Atkins, 901 Great Northern Way, Vancouver, V5T 1E1

Leader Direct Marketing Ltd, 1688 152nd St (Suite 207), Surrey, V4A 4N2

PDQ Post Group, 19134 95A Ave (Unit 7), Surrey, V4N 4P2

Ontario

ActionPak, 125 Nashdene Rd (Unit 1), Scarborough, M1V 2W3

The Interprovincial Group, 1315 Morningside Ave, Scarborough, M1B 3C5

Prism Data Services Ltd, 200-1599 Hurontario St, Mississauga, L5G 4S1

Saatchi & Saatchi Canada, Two Bloor St E (Suite 600), Toronto, M4W 1A8

Smart DM, 342 Horner Ave (Unit A), Toronto, M8W 1Z3

Spring, 6655 Airport Rd, Mississauga, L4V 1V8

Tann Selective Communications Inc, 100 Granton Dr, Richmond Hill, L4B 1H7

TDC Direct, 75 Superior Blvd, Mississauga, L5T 2X9

Westminster International, 174 W Beaver Creek, Richmond Hill, L4B 1B4

Quebec

Harling Marketing Inc, 18103 Rte Transcanadienne, Kirkland, H9J 3Z4

Full Service Direct Mail Companies (21)

AB DATA LTD
Div. of AB Data Ltd
600 A B Data Dr
Milwaukee, WI 53217-4931
Telephone: (414) 961-6400, FAX:
(414) 961-6410, E-Mail: info@
abdata.com, Web Site: www.abdata.
com
Co-Mng Dir: Bruce Arbit

ADVO INC
One Targeting Centre
Windsor, CT 06095
Telephone: (860) 285-6100, FAX:
(860) 285-1567, Web Site: www.
advo.com
Chmn & CEO: Gary Mulloy

AMC MMI
1050 Valencia Dr
Fullerton, CA 92831
Telephone: (888) 304-4664, FAX:
(714) 888-8855
Pres: William Rivera

ACE MARKETING SERVICE
Div. of World Marketing Co
1961 S Cobb Industrial Blvd
Smyrna, GA 30082-4915
Telephone: (770) 431-2500, (800) 962-
4514, FAX: (770) 431-2517, E-Mail:
mail@ace-marketing.com, Web Site:
www.ace-marketing.com
Pres: Charles Thompson

ACTION IN MAILING
4521 Troy Hwy
Montgomery, AL 36116-5121
Telephone: (334) 286-4667, (800) 277-
6245, FAX: (334) 286-6008, E-Mail:
info@actioninmailing.com, Web Site:
www.actioninmailing.com
CEO: Pat Parvin

ACTIONPAK
aka Q-Ponz Inc
dba Open and Save
125 Nashdene Rd (Unit 1)
Scarborough, ON, Canada M1V 2W3
Telephone: (416) 321-2222, FAX:
(416) 321-5286, Web Site: www.
openandsave.com
Pres: Terry Shaw
VP Fin: Eric Blom

ACTIVE GRAPHICS INC
5500 W 31st St
Cicero, IL 60804-3957
Telephone: (312) 733-4343, FAX:
(312) 733-4614, E-Mail: info@
activegraphics.net, Web Site: www.
activegraphics.net
Pres: George Hayes Jr.

ACTIVE VOICE
600 Townsend St (#140 W)
San Francisco, CA 94103
Telephone: (415) 487-2000, FAX:
(415) 487-2260, E-Mail: info@
activevoice.net, Web Site: www.
activevoice.net
Exec Dir: Ellen Schneider

AD SELL CO
5001 Southwest Ave
Saint Louis, MO 63110-3427
Telephone: (314) 773-0500, FAX:
(314) 773-0555, Web Site: www.
adsell.com
Pres: Mark W. Shocker

ADREA RUBIN MARKETING INC
19 W 44th St (Suite 1415)
New York, NY 10036-6101
Telephone: (212) 983-0020, FAX:
(212) 983-0107, E-Mail: sales@
adrearubin.com, Web Site: www.
adrearubin.com
CEO: Adrea Rubin
Employees: 20

Integrated direct marketing agency.

ADVANCED DIRECT
4221 Tudor Ln
Greensboro, NC 27410-8105
Telephone: (336) 299-0800, (800) 786-
2812, FAX: (336) 299-2619, E-Mail:
info@advdirectinc.com, Web Site:
www.advdirectinc.com
Pres: Jeff Burkett

ADVANCED DIRECT MARKETING INC
712 E Eisenhower Blvd
Loveland, CO 80537-3920
Telephone: (970) 669-9800, (888) 553-
1230, FAX: (970) 669-1920, E-Mail:
sales@admimail.com
Pres: Darrell Burbeck

ADVERTISING DISTRIBUTORS OF AMERICA INC
230 Adams Ave.
Hauppauge, NY 11788
Telephone: (631) 231-5700, FAX:
(631) 434-1063
Pres & CEO: Dominick Iannaccone

ALLIED MARKETING GROUP INC
1555 Regal Row
Dallas, TX 75247-3619
Telephone: (214) 915-7000, FAX:
(214) 905-5133, E-Mail: support@
alliedmarketinggroup.com, Web Site:
www.alliedmarketinggroup.com
Pres: Stevan Hammond

ALTERNATIVE MARKETING SOLUTIONS INC
342 Nutt Rd
Phoenixville, PA 19460
Telephone: (610) 783-1320, FAX:
(610) 783-1324, E-Mail: guntick@
amsolutions.com, Web Site: www.
amsolutions.com
Pres: Michael Guntick

ALTMAN DIRECT MARKETING
Div. of Altman Business Services Inc
4102 Balcones Dr
Austin, TX 78731-5704
Telephone: (210) 590-2062, (800) 324-
2062, FAX: (210) 590-2945, E-Mail:
altman@altmandirect.com, Web Site:
www.altmandirect.com
Pres: William M. Altman

AMERICALIST
Div. of Haines & Co Inc
8050 Freedom Ave NW
North Canton, OH 44720
Telephone: (330) 494-9111, (888) 219-
LIST, FAX: (330) 494-0226, Web
Site: www.americalist.com
VP: Richard Toriello

AMERICAN DIRECT MARKETING RESOURCES INC
400 Chesterfield Ctr (Suite 500)
Chesterfield, MO 63017-7703
Telephone: (636) 532-7703, FAX:
(636) 532-2427, Web Site: www.
admr.com

Pres: Ed Smith

AMERIMARK HOLDINGS LLC

6864 Engle Rd
Cleveland, OH 44130-7910
Telephone: (440) 325-2000, FAX:
(440) 234-8925, Web Site: www.
amerimark.com
Pres: Gary Giesler

Holding company for AmeriMark Direct which is a direct marketer of women's apparel, shoes, cosmetics, fragrance & jewelry

ANTARES INFORMATION TECH

110 Commons Ct
Chadds Ford, PA 19317-9716
Telephone: (631) 234-5700, (800) 330-2579, FAX: (631) 234-5472, E-Mail:
steve@antares-iti.com, Web Site:
www.antares-iti.com
Pres: Jeff Safran
CEO: Arthur Epstein
VP: Steve Hertz
Conducts Business: U.S.
Employees: 400
Primary Market Served: Business
Founded: 1983

ASBURY PARK PRESS ADDRESSES UNLIMITED

Address Unlimited
3601 Hwy 66
Neptune, NJ 07753-2604
Telephone: (732) 922-6000, FAX:
(732) 462-3282
Pres: Robert T. Collins

AUSTIN & WILLIAMS

125 Kennedy Dr (Suite 100)
Hauppauge, NY 11788-4017
Telephone: (631) 231-6600, (888) 281-9200, FAX: (212) 434-7022, E-Mail:
info@austin-williams.com, Web Site:
www.austin-williams.com
Pres CEO: William Pesce

B&W PRESS INC

401 E Main St
Georgetown, MA 01833-2513
Telephone: (978) 352-6100, (877) 246-3467, FAX: (978) 352-5955, E-Mail:
csr@bwpress.com, Web Site: www.
bwpress.com
Pres & Treas: Paul J. Beegan
CFO: Russell Beegan
Plant Mgr: Dan Kimball
Press Room Mgr: Dave Dillon
Mfg Mgr: Mark Gaudet
Mktg: Karen Talbott
Conducts Business: U.S., Canada
Employees: 47

Primary Market Served: Business & Consumer
Direct Marketing ad budget: $300,000
Direct Mail: 40%
Magazines: 50%
Telephone: 10%
Founded: 1965
Gross sales or billing: $12,550,000

Direct response products with/without a built-in BRE. Order forms, package inserts, 2-way mailers, etc. 10-page Mini "Slim" catalog mailers--mail less pages, target markers all year, prospect more, increase web traffic---standard letter rates---a multi-channel solution provider. Inside/outside personalization.

BABER INC

3135 Millbranch Rd
Memphis, TN 38116-1917
Telephone: (901) 332-6300, (800) 847-7040, FAX: (901) 332-6441, E-Mail:
info@baberweb.com, Web Site:
www.baberweb.com
Pres: Michael Baber

BACOMPT SYSTEMS INC

12742 Hamilton Crossing Blvd
Carmel, IN 46032-5422
Telephone: (317) 574-7474, (800) 533-7109, FAX: (317) 574-7475, E-Mail:
customer.service@bacompt.com,
Web Site: www.bacompt.com
VP: Tracy Cunningham

THE TED BARKUS CO INC

8017 Anderson St
Philadelphia, PA 19118-2936
Telephone: (215) 545-0616, FAX:
(215) 545-7976
Pres: Alan Barkus
Sr VP: Harriet Barkus
Founded: 1958

BENWELL ATKINS

A RR Donnelley Company
901 Great Northern Way
Vancouver, BC, Canada V5T 1E1
Telephone: (604) 872-2326, FAX:
(604) 872-4235, E-Mail: vancouver.
reception@rrd.com, Web Site:
rrdonnelley.com/wwwbenwell/
Gen Mgr: Eddis Nowworthy

CDMG

21171 S Western (Suite 260)
Torrance, CA 90501
Telephone: (310) 212-5727, FAX:
(310) 212-5773, E-Mail: infomat@
biz.com, Web Site: www.cdmginc.
com
Pres: Craig A. Huey
Acctg: Lynn Falconer

CGT MARKETING

275-B Dixon Ave
Amityville, NY 11701-2874
Telephone: (631) 842-4600, FAX:
(631) 842-6301, Web Site: www.
cgtmarketing.com
Principal: Vincent Grucci
Partner: Fred Candiotti

Direct mail advertising

CACTUS MAILING COMPANY

16121 N 78th St (Suite 103)
Scottsdale, AZ 85260
Telephone: (480) 443-1442, (866) 443-1442, FAX: (480) 443-2518, E-Mail:
info@cactusmailing.com, Web Site:
www.cactusmailing.com
Pres: Michael Ryan
Founded: 2001

Direct mail marketing

CATALOG DESIGN STUDIOS

8 Barnes St
Providence, RI 02906-1517
Telephone: (888) 409-9992, Web Site:
www.catalogdesignstudios.com
Creative Dir: Sarah Fletcher

Catalog design services

CATHEDRAL CORP

632 Ellsworth Rd, Griffiss Technology Park
Rome, NY 13441
Telephone: (315) 338-0021, (800) 698-0299, FAX: (315) 338-5874, E-Mail:
sales@cathedralstewardship.com,
Web Site: www.cathedralcorporation.
com
Pres & COO: Marianne W. Gaige
VP Mktg: Larry J. Beasley

CHEWNING DIRECT MARKETING

4 Candlebush
Irvine, CA 92603-3727
Telephone: (949) 854-5401, E-Mail:
hchewning@cdmdirect.com, Web
Site: www.cdmdirect.com
Pres: Hugh Chewning

Provides direct mail solutions for consumer, nonprofit & business-to-business groups. Direct mail, copywriting, consulting & strategy.

CLIENTLOGIC

3102 W End Ave (Suite 1000), Two American Center
Nashville, TN 37203
Telephone: (615) 301-7100, E-Mail:
bobfet@clientlogic.com
CEO: Tom Harbison

COMMONWEALTH LISTS
Steve Cram & Associates
11208 Maples Mill Rd
Fairfax, VA 22030
Telephone: (703) 273-3231, FAX:
(703) 279-5970, E-Mail: info@
commonwealthlists.com, Web Site:
www.commonwealthlists.com
Pres: Steve Cram

COMMUNICATION CONCEPTS INC
1044 Pulinski Rd
Ivyland, PA 18974-1534
Telephone: (215) 672-6900, FAX:
(215) 957-4362, E-Mail: info@
ccgroupnet.com, Web Site: www.
ccgroupnet.com
Pres & CEO: E. McKenzie

COMMUNICATIONS CORP OF AMERICA
13195 Freedom Way
Boston, VA 22713-4114
Telephone: (540) 547-1700, FAX:
(540) 547-4600, E-Mail: contact@
cca.net, Web Site: www.cca.net
Pres: Steven R. Fisher

COMMUNITY NEWSPAPER CO
Subs. of GateHouse Media
254 2nd Ave Ste 1
Needham, MA 02494-2829
Telephone: (781) 433-6700, FAX:
(781) 433-6701, E-Mail:
customerservice@cnc.com, Web Site:
www.nvo.com/communitynews
Adv Dir: Michael Mosses
Employees: 1,800

THE CORPORATE COMMUNICATIONS GROUP
14 Henderson Dr
West Caldwell, NJ 07006-6608
Telephone: (973) 386-1444, FAX:
(973) 808-9740, E-Mail: useccg@
corpcomm.com, Web Site: www.
corpcomm.com
Pres: James E. Pinkin

COX TARGET MEDIA/DBA VALPAK
8605 Largo Lakes Dr
Largo, FL 33773
Telephone: (727) 399-3000, (800) 678-
2743, FAX: (727) 399-3061, E-Mail:
contact_sales@coxtarget.com, Web
Site: www.coxdirect.com
CEO: Bill Disbrow

CREATIVE MARKETING MANAGEMENT
2703 Colston Dr
Chevy Chase, MD 20815-3033
Telephone: (301) 650-4160, FAX:
(301) 650-4161
Pres: Marti Campbell

CREATIVE MARKETING PROGRAMS
412 Oak St
Kansas City, MO 64106-1133
Telephone: (816) 472-6843, (800) 373-
6843, FAX: (816) 472-8184, E-Mail:
getresults@cmpkc.com, Web Site:
www.cmpkc.com
Pres: Dwight W. Orr
Acct Supvr: Tamara Cauton

DMX-DIRECT, INC
8955 E Nichols Ave (Suite 200)
Centennial, CO 80112-3498
Telephone: (303) 339-9300, FAX:
(303) 388-6363, Web Site: www.
dmx-direct.com
Pres: James Kennel

THE DMA DS GRAPHICS INC
120 Stedman St
Lowell, MA 01851
Telephone: (617) 389-5350, (800) 536-
8253, FAX: (617) 387-7752, E-Mail:
sales@dsgraphics.com, Web Site:
www.dsgraphics.com
VP Mailing Svcs: Bob Cipriani

THE DMA DATALAB USA
202561 Goldenrod Ln
Germantown, MD 20876-4063
Telephone: (301) 972-1430, Web Site:
www.datalabusa.com
Exec VP Bus Devel: Alex Aigner
Primary Market Served: Business &
Consumer

DATAMARKETING NETWORK INC
701 Murfreesboro Pike
Nashville, TN 37210-4521
Telephone: (615) 313-7000, Web Site:
www.datamarketingnetwork.com
CEO: Jono Huddleston

DESIGN DISTRIBUTORS, INC
300 Marcus Blvd
Deer Park, NY 11729-4500
Telephone: (631) 242-2000, FAX:
(631) 242-7367, E-Mail: info@
designdistributors.com, Web Site:
www.designdistributors.com
Pres: Adam Avrick
Admin Asst: Michael Conley

DEVELOPMENT RESOURCES
790 Cleveland Ave S (Suite 200)
Saint Paul, MN 55116-3858
Telephone: (651) 695-5558, FAX:
(888) 805-1070, E-Mail: info@
developmentresources.com, Web
Site: www.developmentresources.
com
Pres: Timothy Puffer

DEX ONE
1001 Winstead Dr
Cary, NC 27513-2117
Telephone: (919) 297-1600

DIRECT COMMUNICATIONS CORP
23 Court St
Rutland, VT 05702
Telephone: (802) 747-3322, FAX:
(802) 747-3376, E-Mail:
information@direct-com.com, Web
Site: www.direct-com.com
Pres: Jerry Henkel

DIRECT MAIL CENTER
1099 Mariposa St
San Francisco, CA 94107
Telephone: (415) 252-1600, FAX:
(415) 252-9100, E-Mail: dmc@
directmailctr.com, Web Site: www.
directmailctr.com
Gen Mgr: Pierre Smit

DIRECT MAIL MARKETING INC
509 Market St (Suite 100)
Shreveport, LA 71101-3259
Telephone: (318) 631-4081, FAX:
(318) 621-9150, E-Mail:
james_dmm@bizsport.rr.com
Pres: James Breedlove

DIRECT MAIL SERVICE INC
939 W North Ave
Pittsburgh, PA 15233-1605
Telephone: (412) 471-6300
Owner: Ray Fragal

DIRECT PRINT
Five Brown Rd
Windham, NH 03087-1231
Telephone: (603) 437-6831
Owner: William Crucius

DIRECT RESPONSE INSURANCE ADMINISTRATIVE SERVICES INC (DRIASI)
7930 Century Blvd
Chanhassen, MN 55317-8001

Telephone: (952) 556-5600, (800) 688-0760, FAX: (952) 556-8200, E-Mail: tpa@driasi.com, Web Site: www.driasi.com
Pres & CEO: Richard H. Votel
Exec VP: Dodi Iverson
Mktg Coord: Heidi Orcholski
Conducts Business: U.S., Canada
Employees: 130
Primary Market Served: Business & Consumer
Founded: 1982

Insurance administrators.

DIRECT RESULTS
2005 Riverdale St
West Springfield, MA 01089-1067
Telephone: (413) 732-8310, FAX: (413) 732-8361
Pres: John Epstein

DIVERSIFIED GRAPHICS INC
3301 Como Ave SE
Minneapolis, MN 55414-2809
Telephone: (800) 233-7454, FAX: (612) 331-4079, Web Site: www.dgi.net
Digital Mktg Mgr: Kris Morrow
Conducts Business: U.S.
Employees: 500
Primary Market Served: Business
Founded: 1949
Gross sales or billing: $60,000,000

DGI is a business communications provider via commercial printing, digital printing, direct mail marketing services, fulfillment, technology services including web-to-print.

DONER DIRECT
Div. of W B Doner & Co
400 E Pratt St (10th fl)
Baltimore, MD 21202-3116
Telephone: (248) 354-9700, FAX: (248) 827-0880
Pres: Tony Everett
Exec VP & Gen Mgr: Ted Thompson

DUFFORD MARKETING
2233 Brigden Rd
Pasadena, CA 91104-3304
Telephone: (626) 665-2268, E-Mail: donnduff@aol.com
Pres: Donn Dufford

ERS DIRECT MARKETING
Div. of ERS Media Services Inc
1336 Morrpark Rd (#302)
Thousand Oaks, CA 91360
Telephone: (805) 499-1129, FAX: (805) 499-3189, E-Mail: eileen@ersdirect.com, Web Site: www.ersdirect.com
Pres: Eileen Sonheim

ᴛʜᴇ ᴅᴍᴀ EU SERVICES
649 N Horners Ln
Rockville, MD 20850-1233
Telephone: (301) 424-3300, (800) 230-3362, FAX: (301) 424-3696, Web Site: www.euservices.com
Pres: Karen Allen
Mktg Mgr: Crystal Uppercue

THE EZ-FORMS CO
317 Sidney Baker S (#317)
Kerrville, TX 78028
Telephone: (281) 667-4414, FAX: (281) 667-4415, E-Mail: ezformscontactus@gmail.com, Web Site: www.ez-forms.com
Gen Mgr: Ed Marion

EAGLE:XM
5105 E 41st Ave
Denver, CO 80216-4420
Telephone: (303) 320-5411, (800) 426-5376, FAX: (303) 393-6884, E-Mail: bettersolutions@eaglexm.com, Web Site: www.eaglexm.com
Pres: Howard Harris

ᴛʜᴇ ᴅᴍᴀ EMFLUENCE
106 W 11th St (Suite 2220)
Kansas City, MO 64105-1823
Telephone: (816) 472-4455, Web Site: www.emfluence.com
Mktg Mgr: Jessica Best

FRED B ESTABROOK CO INC
39 Ridge Rd
New Hampton, NH 03256
Telephone: (603) 744-6316
Pres: A.G. Estabrook

ᴛʜᴇ ᴅᴍᴀ FMP DIRECT INC
15560 N Frank Lloyd Wright Blvd Ste B4
Scottsdale, AZ 85260-2020
Telephone: (847) 816-1919, (800) 995-3343, FAX: (847) 816-1969, E-Mail: info@fmpdirect.com, Web Site: www.fmpdirect.com
CEO: Michael J. Wilmet
Pres: Rachel A. Wilmet
Conducts Business: U.S.
Employees: 9
Primary Market Served: Business
Catalog available online
Indirect online sales
Advertising/Marketing Budget Related to Direct Marketing: 0-25%
Direct Marketing ad budget:
Direct Mail: $50,000
Magazines: $30,000
Telephone: $20,000
Founded: 1987
Gross sales or billing: $4,000,000

Exclusively offer the National Credit Register (145 million credit qualified individuals), the New Movers Register (1.8 million monthly new movers), the New Credit Additions File (1.5 million monthly) & the Access America Databank (166 million American shoppers). All lists are complete with demographics, mail order buyer, donor information & financial lifestyle data. Also provide creative, production & fulfillment services.

THE FIELD COMPANIES INC
Div. of The Field Companies
385 Pleasant St, PO Box 78
Watertown, MA 02471-0078
Telephone: (617) 926-5550, (800) 346-6552, FAX: (617) 924-9011, E-Mail: info@fieldcompanies.com, Web Site: www.fieldcompanies.com
Pres & Treas: Joseph McDonald

FIORELLA'S JACK STACK BARBECUE
8250 NE Underground Dr, Pillar 140 (Bldg 32A)
Kansas City, MO 64161-9734
Telephone: (816) 452-1185, Web Site: www.jackstackbbq.com
Gen Mgr: Wiley Fisher
Primary Market Served: Consumer

FIREFLY
Div. of Milici Valenti Ng Pack
999 Bishop St (21 fl)
Honolulu, HI 96813
Telephone: (808) 545-2122, FAX: (808) 535-1655, Web Site: www.fireflyhawaii.com
Mng Dir: Susan Moss

FIRST AMERICAN PRINTING & DIRECT MAIL
An Enterprise of the Mississippi Band of Choctaw Indians
1 Choctaw Trail
Ocean Springs, MS 39564-4107
Telephone: (228) 875-8199, (800) 967-2637, FAX: (228) 875-8198, E-Mail: sales@fapdm.com, Web Site: www.fapdm.com
Pres: Jon Murphy

FIRST CLASS DIRECT INC
Div. of Vision Graphics Inc
5610 Boeing Dr
Loveland, CO 80538
Telephone: (970) 613-0608, Web Site: www.firstclassdirect.com
Sls & Bus Devel Mgr: Bill Jones

FORECAST DIRECT MARKETING GROUP

37 Terminal Way
Pittsburgh, PA 15219
Telephone: (412) 481-5699, FAX:
(412) 481-0872, E-Mail: forecast@
sgi.net
Pres: William Ferari

GG DIRECT

351 Riverside Industrial Pkwy
Portland, ME 04103-1415
Telephone: (207) 772-0414, FAX:
(207) 871-1444, E-Mail: info@
ggdirect.com, Web Site: www.
ggdirect.com
Pres: William Sweeney

THE DMA GS MARKETING

1345 Enclave Pkwy
Houston, TX 77077-2026
Telephone: (713) 580-3900, FAX:
(713) 580-5950, E-Mail: angie.
sherrell@gsmarketing.com, Web
Site: www.gsmarketing.com
VP & Gen Mgr: Angie Sherrell

GSI COMMERCE

10303 Norris Ave
Pacoima, CA 91331
Telephone: (818) 834-8800, (800) 244-
7371, FAX: (818) 834-8840, Web
Site: www.gsicommerce.com

GABRIEL GROUP

3190 Rider Trail S
Earth City, MO 63045
Telephone: (314) 743-5700, FAX:
(314) 576-5573, E-Mail: sales@
gabrielgr.com, Web Site: www.
gabrielgr.com
Pres: Arthur F. Kerckhoff III

GANNETT DIRECT MARKETING SERVICES INC

3400 Robards Ct
Louisville, KY 40218-4544
Telephone: (502) 454-6660, (800) 345-
5654, FAX: (502) 459-7479, Web
Site: www.gdms.com
Pres: David Worland

GARDELLA & CO

PO Box 20121
Atlanta, GA 30325-0121
Telephone: (404) 355-1005, FAX:
(404) 355-4888, E-Mail:
gardellastudio@comcast.com
Owner: Patricia Gardella

GENERH, INC

1605 Date Ave
Torrance, CA 90503-6109
Telephone: (888) 312-3443, E-Mail:
info@generh.com, Web Site: www.
generh.com
Principal: Alex Sobol
Principal Acct Plng Dir: Marcelino
Miyares Jr
Acct Exec, Japanese Market: Mitsue
Burak
Acct Exec, Hispanic Market: Yolanda
Lopez
Conducts Business: U.S., Latin
America
Employees: 15
Primary Market Served: Business &
Consumer
Catalog available online
Advertising/Marketing Budget Related
to Direct Marketing: 26-50%
Founded: 2004
Gross sales or billing: $5,000,000

We are a multicultural ad agency, offering advertising, marketing and creative services for the U.S. and Latin
American markets.

GLOBE MARKETING SYSTEMS

11950 NW 39th St (Suite B)
Coral Springs, FL 33065
Telephone: (954) 753-7173, (800) 382-
9013, FAX: (954) 741-1369, Web
Site: www.globemarketingsystems.
com
Pres: Dwight Jewett

THE DMA GROUND TRUTH

116 W 23rd St (fl 5)
New York, NY 10011-2599
Telephone: (212) 851-4000
Primary Market Served: Consumer

HARLING MARKETING INC

dba Harling Direct
18103 Rte Transcanadienne
Kirkland, PQ, Canada H9J 3Z4
Telephone: (514) 695-1430, FAX:
(514) 695-0530, E-Mail: info@
harlingdirect.com, Web Site: www.
harlingdirect.com
Pres: Randy Yates

THE HARTY PRESS INC

25 James St
New Haven, CT 06513-4218
Telephone: (203) 562-5112, (800) 654-
0562, FAX: (203) 782-9168, E-Mail:
gplatt@hartynet.com, Web Site:
www.hartynet.com
Pres: George R. Platt

HILL MAILING & PRINTING OF FLORIDA INC

PO Box 3331
Brandon, FL 33509-3331
Telephone: (813) 258-5220
Pres: Robert S. Lee

THE HORAH GROUP

Horah Graphics Inc
351 Manville Rd (Suite 105)
Pleasantville, NY 10570-2166
Telephone: (914) 495-3200, FAX:
(914) 769-8802, E-Mail:
dgoldsmith@horah.com, Web Site:
www.horah.com
Pres: Richard Goldsmith

HUMMEL INTEGRATED MARKETING SOLUTIONS

850 Springfield Rd
Union, NJ 07083-8614
Telephone: (908) 688-5300, FAX:
(908) 688-6020, E-Mail:
hummelmlg@aol.com
Pres: John Hummel

THE DMA HUNTSINGER & JEFFER INC

809 Brook Hill Cir
Richmond, VA 23227-2503
Telephone: (804) 266-2499, FAX:
(804) 266-8563, E-Mail: vickil@
huntsinger-jeffer.com, Web Site:
www.huntsinger-jeffer.com
Pres: Victoria Lester
Sr Writer: Willis Turner

HYPHOS360 INC

19337 US Hwy 19 N (Suite 500)
Clearwater, FL 33764-3151
Telephone: (727) 532-0700, (800) 733-
1817, FAX: (727) 524-3424, Web
Site: www.hyphos360.com
Pres: Michael Dykstra
Conducts Business: U.S.
Employees: 40
Primary Market Served: Business
Advertising/Marketing Budget Related
to Direct Marketing: 76-100%
Direct Mail: 90%
Magazines: 10%
Founded: 1992
Gross sales or billing: $10,000,000

Campaign processing, analytical services & database marketing services.

IC SYSTEM INC

444 Hwy 96 E
Saint Paul, MN 55164-2557
Telephone: (651) 483-0585, (800) 245-
8875, FAX: (651) 481-6363, E-Mail:
promo@icsystem.com, Web Site:
www.icsystem.com
Pres & CEO: Ken Rapp

ICS CORP
2225 Richmond St
Philadelphia, PA 19125
Telephone: (888) 223-2840, FAX:
(215) 634-1522, E-Mail: info@ics-
corporation.com, Web Site: www.ics-
corporation.com
Pres: Matthew J. Bastian

**ICS MARKETING SUPPORT
SERVICES**
4225 Legacy Pkwy
Lansing, MI 48911-4246
Telephone: (517) 394-1890, (888) 394-
1890, FAX: (517) 394-7408, E-Mail:
sales@icshq.com, Web Site: www.
icshq.com
Pres: Ken Orr
Sr VP & Chmn: Marty Jerick
Sr VP Sls & Mktg: Kevin Harlow
Conducts Business: U.S.
Employees: 50
Primary Market Served: Business &
Consumer
Advertising/Marketing Budget Related
to Direct Marketing: 26-50%
Direct Marketing ad budget: $10,000
Direct Mail: 50%
Online: 50%
Founded: 1990
Gross sales or billing: $6,000,000

Advanced marketing and technological
solutions for business growth.

**IMS GROUP II
COMMUNICATIONS**
11311 W Forest Home Ave
Franklin, WI 53132
Telephone: (414) 425-2080, FAX:
(414) 425-6029, Web Site: www.
groupii.com
New Bus Contact: Todd Cromheecke

IQ MARKETING
19990 Sweetwater Curve
Excelsior, MN 55331-8134
Telephone: (952) 897-7300, FAX:
(952) 820-8041, Web Site: www.
iqmarketing.com
Pres & CEO: Jan Finken

IWCO DIRECT
7951 Powers Blvd
Chanhassen, MN 55317-9502
Telephone: (952) 474-0961, FAX:
(952) 474-6467
CEO: Jeffrey S. Jurick
Pres: Stephen Paladino
Exec VP: Raymond D. Amedeo
Exec VP & Chief Mktg Officer: Tom
Wicka
Employees: 600
Founded: 1916

Offers a full array of direct mail production services including sheet-fed
and continuous form printing, variable
data printing solutions, personalization,
lettershop, response management, fulfillment, presorting, commingling and
international mailing. No matter where
you mail, Fala delivers.

**ICON MARKETING
COMMUNICATIONS**
7000 Houston Rd Ste 10
Florence, KY 41042-4874
Telephone: (859) 647-7271, FAX:
(859) 647-0615, E-Mail: shawn@
iconmc.com, Web Site: www.iconmc.
com
VP: Ron Daniel

**IMAGEMAKERS
MARKETING INC**
1843 Blackwater Dr
Marietta, GA 30066-6713
Telephone: (770) 926-9552, FAX:
(770) 926-9558, Web Site: www.
imagemakersmarketing.com
Pres: Elaine Gossett

**INNOVATIVE MARKETING
DIRECT INC**
3200 Henderson Blvd Ste 100
Tampa, FL 33609-3054
Telephone: (813) 873-7909, FAX:
(813) 873-7918, Web Site: www.
innovativedirectmail.com
Primary Market Served: Business

INTER DIRECT USA
1001 S Dairy Ashford St Ste 450
Houston, TX 77077-2386
Telephone: (281) 497-7606, FAX:
(281) 497-7616, E-Mail:
scotthaney@interdirectusa.com, Web
Site: www.interdirectusa.com

**INTERACTIVE MARKETING
GROUP INC**
50 Commerce Dr.
Allendale, NJ 07401
Telephone: (201) 327-0974, FAX:
(201) 327-3596, E-Mail: info@
imgusa.com, Web Site: www.imgusa.
com/index.aspx
Chm: K.A. George
Founder, Vice Chm & CEO: Chris
George
Pres: Matthew W. Staudt

**THE INTERPROVINCIAL
GROUP**
dba Interprovincial Printing Ltd & In-
terpro Mailings Ltd
1315 Morningside Ave
Scarborough, ON, Canada M1B 3C5

Telephone: (416) 283-5555, FAX:
(416) 283-6643, E-Mail: info@
interprovincialgroup.com, Web Site:
www.interprovincialgroup.com
Mgr: Lee Barker

KCMS
201 Commerce Dr
Upper Marlboro, MD 20774-8762
Telephone: (301) 853-1300, FAX:
(301) 853-1390, Web Site: www.
kcms.com
Pres: Ken Rubin

KAYE-SMITH
4101 Oakesdale Ave SW
Renton, WA 98057-4817
Telephone: (425) 228-8600, (800) 822-
9987, FAX: (425) 226-4312, E-Mail:
info@kayesmith.com, Web Site:
www.kayesmith.com
Sls Mgr: Dick Erehig

L & E MERIDIAN
7400 Fullerton Rd (Suite 110)
Springfield, VA 22153-2286
Telephone: (703) 913-0300, (800) 555-
1556, FAX: (703) 913-7052, E-Mail:
pmaaseide@l-e.com, Web Site:
www.l-e.com
VP Acct Svcs: Peter Maaseide

LPL
PO Box 15610
Scottsdale, AZ 85267-5610
Telephone: (480) 457-2007, Web Site:
www.lifelock.com

**JAMES M LAING &
ASSOCIATES**
7086 Pontiac Cir
Chanhassen, MN 55317
Telephone: (952) 474-1138
Pres: James M. Laing

LAZARUS MARKETING
3530 Oceanside Rd
Oceanside, NY 11572
Telephone: (516) 678-5107, FAX:
(516) 766-3160, E-Mail: warrenl@
lazmkt.com, Web Site: www.
lazarusmarketing.com
Pres: Warren S. Lazarus

**LEADER DIRECT
MARKETING LTD**
Div. of The Leader Group
1688 152nd St (Suite 207)
Surrey, BC, Canada V4A 4N2
Telephone: (604) 542-2026, FAX:
(604) 542-2090, E-Mail: listinfo@
leaderdirect.ca, Web Site: www.
theleadergroup.ca

Dir: Karl Folia
Conducts Business: U.S., Canada, Germany, France, Austria, Switz., Australia, U.K.
Employees: 100
Primary Market Served: Business
Advertising/Marketing Budget Related to Direct Marketing: 76-100%
Gross sales or billing: $12,000,000

Direct marketing services.

THE DMA LIBERTY CREATIVE SOLUTIONS

18625 W Creek Dr
Tinley Park, IL 60477-6247
Telephone: (708) 633-7450, Web Site:
www.libertycreativesolutions.com
Mktg Coord: Julie Calzaretta

LOYALTYWORKS INC

2337 Perimeter Park Dr Ste 220
Atlanta, GA 30341-1313
Telephone: (678) 539-5000, (800) 844-5000, FAX: (678) 539-5173, Web Site: www.loyaltyworks.com
Exec VP, Client Svcs: David Thomas
Sr VP Mktg: Loren Weaver
Conducts Business: U.S., Canada
Employees: 80
Primary Market Served: Business & Consumer
Advertising/Marketing Budget Related to Direct Marketing: 76-100%

Designs, builds & manages loyalty & incentive marketing programs, from recognition & performance improvement programs to complete consumer relationship marketing solutions. Also support clients with a full range of capabilities and services, all toward helping clients to meet their objectives.

MRC MARKETING INC

2 Red Pine Rd
Saint Paul, MN 55127-2028
Telephone: (612) 759-2069, E-Mail:
info@mrcmarketing.com, Web Site:
www.mrcmarketing.com
Pres: James A. Parker

MAIL COMPUTER SERVICE

321 Manley St
West Bridgewater, MA 02379
Telephone: (508) 584-6490, (800) 640-8530, FAX: (508) 584-2890
Pres: Ron Menconi

MAIL ENTERPRISES LLC

3810 5th Ct N
Birmingham, AL 35222-1308
Telephone: (205) 595-4945, (800) 595-4945, FAX: (205) 595-4943, Web Site: www.mailent.com
CEO: R. Scott Swedenburg

Conducts Business: U.S.
Primary Market Served: Business & Consumer
Advertising/Marketing Budget Related to Direct Marketing: 76-100%
Direct Marketing ad budget:
Direct Mail: 95%
Telephone: 5%
Founded: 1964

Direct Mail services.

MAILING LISTS PLUS INC

12819 SE 38th St, PMB 203
Bellevue, WA 98006-1326
Telephone: (425) 451-3335, (877) 339-4584, FAX: (425) 646-4485, E-Mail: info@mailinglistsplus.com, Web Site: www.mailinglistsplus.com
Pres: Carol Kollmann

Direct mail & email marketing services, national & international.

MAILING SERVICES OF PITTSBURGH INC

155 Commerce Dr
Freedom, PA 15042-9202
Telephone: (724) 774-3244, (800) 876-3211, FAX: (724) 774-6996, Web Site: www.msp-pgh.com
Pres: Richard E. Bushee III
Mktg: Kirstan Tervo

MANHATTAN MEDIA SERVICES INC

535 5h Ave (#1012)
New York, NY 10017-8004
Telephone: (212) 808-4077, FAX: (212) 808-4080, E-Mail: mmorello@manhmedia.com, Web Site: www.manhmedia.com
Pres & CEO: Marianna Morello
Sr Acct Exec: Viraya Myint
Controller: J Redger
Dir Mktg & Sales: Celia Mollica
Sr Account Exec: Marc Sibal
Conducts Business: U.S.
Employees: 10
Primary Market Served: Consumer
Advertising/Marketing Budget Related to Direct Marketing: 76-100%
Direct Marketing ad budget:
Magazines: 70%
Newspapers: 30%
Founded: 1995
Gross sales or billing: $30,000,000

Full service direct response/branding advertising agency specializing in place print media at substantially discounted rates.

MARKET BUILDER INC

5135 E Ingram St Ste 2
Mesa, AZ 85205-3465

Telephone: (480) 641-6200, FAX: (480) 641-6239, E-Mail: info@themarketbuilder.com, Web Site: www.themarketbuilder.com
Pres: Keith Lawson

MARKETAIDE SERVICES INC

Subs. of Harris Enterprises
PO Box 500
Salina, KS 67402-0500
Telephone: (785) 825-7161, (800) 204-2433, FAX: (785) 825-4697, E-Mail: kcarlgren@marketaide.com, Web Site: www.marketaide.com
Pres: Dee Warren
Media Dir: Kendi Carlgren

THE MARKETING ADVANTAGE INC

dba freevacations.com
1525 Merrill Dr (Suite 1500)
Little Rock, AR 72211-1662
Telephone: (501) 954-7771, FAX: (501) 954-7879, E-Mail: central_reservations@tmae.net, Web Site: www.freevacations.com
Owner: William J. Hoag
List Mgr: Terri L. Gjestvang
Conducts Business: U.S.
Employees: 30
Primary Market Served: Consumer
Direct online sales
Advertising/Marketing Budget Related to Direct Marketing: 76-100%
Direct Marketing ad budget:
Direct Mail: 90%
Online: 10%
Founded: 1991
Gross sales or billing: $10,000,000

Direct Marketing Agency - direct mail, telemarketing (IB & DB), market research, lead generation.

MARKETING SOLUTIONS UNLIMITED LLC

109 Talcott Rd
West Hartford, CT 06110-1228
Telephone: (860) 523-0670, FAX: (860) 523-0675, E-Mail: info@msudirectmail.com, Web Site: www.msudirectmail.com
Pres: Heidi Buckley

MARKETING VISIONS INC

3338 Deer Creek Alba Way
Deerfield Beach, FL 33442
Telephone: (954) 421-2002, E-Mail: marvisions@aol.com
Pres: E. Burke

MASSCOT INTERNET INC

20 Grove St
West Yarmouth, MA 02673

Telephone: (508) 778-6320, (877) 627-7268, FAX: (888) 884-9960, E-Mail: admin@masscot.net, Web Site: www.masscothosting.com
Pres: John McDonald

MCCAFFREY ENTERPRISES
1331 Red Cedar Cir
Fort Collins, CO 80524
Telephone: (970) 493-4840, FAX: (970) 493-8781
Pres: Neil T. McCaffrey III

THE DMA MCINTYRE DIRECT
700 N Hayden Island Dr (Suite 390)
Portland, OR 97217-8185
Telephone: (503) 286-1400, FAX: (503) 286-7622, Web Site: www.mcintyredirect.com
Pres: Susan McIntyre
Founded: 1991

Full service agency & consulting firm for catalogers

MCKEE & ASSOCIATES INC
PO Box 2838
Hot Springs National Park, AR 71914-2838
Telephone: (501) 623-8833, (888) 883-4988, FAX: (501) 620-6856, E-Mail: newmoverexperts@mckeeandassociates.net, Web Site: www.newmoverexperts.com
Partner Bus Devel: Brandi Davis
Conducts Business: U.S.
Advertising/Marketing Budget Related to Direct Marketing: 76-100%
Founded: 1997

Direct Marketing/Tele programs to consumers. Businesses wanting to reach consumer market.

MEDIA HORIZONS INC
40 Richards Ave
Norwalk, CT 06854-2320
Telephone: (203) 857-0770, FAX: (203) 857-0296, E-Mail: mhict@mediahorizons.com, Web Site: www.mediahorizons.com
Pres & CEO: James Kabakow
Sr VP, New Bus: Peter Burgess
Sr VP, Mktg: Tom Reynolds
Pres, Catalog Mktg: Joyce Beggs
Employees: 53
Founded: 1988

Full service direct marketing & media company. Services include strategic planning, media buying (alternative media, print & broadcast), direct mail, website development, e-mail and alternative media program management.

MEDIAWORKS ADVERTISING & MARKETING INC
725 W Granada Blvd
Ormond Beach, FL 32174-9406
Telephone: (407) 909-1903, E-Mail: mmalys@cfl.rr.com, Web Site: www.mediaworksusa.com
Pres: Scott Reid
Sr Partner Client Svcs: Marcia Malys

THE DMA MIDWEST DIRECT MARKETING INC
501 N Webster
Spring Hill, KS 66083
Telephone: (913) 686-2220, E-Mail: info@midwestdm.com, Web Site: www.midwestdm.com
Pres: Scott Robbins

NCP SOLUTIONS
5200 E Lake Blvd
Birmingham, AL 35217
Telephone: (250) 849-5200, Web Site: www.ncprint.com
CEO: Steve Greenwalt
VP, Direct Mktg: LeighAnn Duaybes

THE DMA NATURE TRADE CENTER
1915 Trade Center Way
Naples, FL 34109-6220
Telephone: (239) 592-7611, Web Site: www.naturerx.com
VP Direct Mail: Al Laufer

Direct response agency

NEW INCOME SOURCES
141 Linden St
Hermosa Beach, CA 90254
Telephone: (310) 376-9238, (800) 288-7058, FAX: (310) 376-9258, E-Mail: pk@nisdm.com
CEO: Paula Kaye

NICE LINES DIRECT MAIL
1210 Stanbridge St Ste 4
Norristown, PA 19401-5318
Telephone: (610) 279-1100, (888) 815-NICE, FAX: (610) 279-7800, Web Site: www.nicelines.com
Mng Dir: John Rafner
Dir Mktg: Andrew Katz

THE DMA NORDIS DIRECT
4401 NW 124th Ave
Coral Springs, FL 33065-7636
Telephone: (954) 323-5500, (800) 208-1169, FAX: (954) 323-0100, E-Mail: sdolan@nordisdirect.com, Web Site: www.nordisdirect.com
Pres & CEO: Ronnie Selinger
Sr VP & Gen Mgr: Dennis Darnio
Mktg Mgr: Shelley Dolan
Dir Client Svcs: Deborah Riseh
Conducts Business: U.S.

Employees: 100
Primary Market Served: Business
Advertising/Marketing Budget Related to Direct Marketing: 76-100%
Direct Marketing ad budget:
Direct Mail: 90%
Magazines: 10%
Founded: 1989

THE DMA NORTH AMERICAN COMMUNICATIONS
20 Maple Ave
Armonk, NY 10504-0430
Telephone: (914) 273-8620, FAX: (914) 273-3135, E-Mail: info@nacmail.com, Web Site: www.nacmail.com
CEO: Nicholas Robinson
Employees: 2,000
Founded: 1979

NORTHERN PRINTING NETWORK INC
1400 S Wolf Rd (Suite 102)
Wheeling, IL 60090-6524
Telephone: (847) 215-7300, FAX: (847) 215-7314, E-Mail: sales@northernprint.com, Web Site: www.northernprint.com
Pres: John Fox
Exec VP: Artie Collins
VP, Direct Mktg & Sls: Rick Drucker
Employees: 30
Founded: 1985
Gross sales or billing: $25,000,000

Full service direct mail production company specializing in print (forms, letters, brochures, envelopes), personalization, bindery and lettershop.

NOVO 1 INC
20935 Swenson Dr Ste 360
Waukesha, WI 53186-2076
Telephone: (262) 827-6400, (877) 810-7171, FAX: (262) 827-6440, Web Site: www.novo1.com
Chmn, Pres & CEO: George D. Dalton
Conducts Business: U.S.
Employees: 2,500
Primary Market Served: Business & Consumer
Advertising/Marketing Budget Related to Direct Marketing: 26-50%
Direct Marketing ad budget:
Direct Mail: 100%
Founded: 2000
Gross sales or billing: $78,500,000

Specializes in market research, I/B and D/B teleservices, and personalized print.

O'CONNELL MEIER LLC
PO Box 10252
Alexandria, VA 22310

Telephone: (703) 635-2893, (866) 391-1415, FAX: (703) 739-0478, E-Mail: info@omdirect.com, Web Site: www.omdirect.com
Pres: Rich Meier
CEO & Creative Dir: Lynn O'Connell

OMAHA PRINT
4700 "F" St
Omaha, NE 68117
Telephone: (402) 734-4400, (800) 369-0033, FAX: (402) 734-7492, E-Mail: shayes@omahaprint.com, Web Site: www.omahaprint.com
CEO: Steve Hayes

OPTIMUM GROUP
310 Culvert St (fl 5), c/o Mktg Inc
Cincinnati, OH 45202-2229
Telephone: (513) 577-7000, FAX: (513) 577-7099, E-Mail: info@coactivemarketing.com, Web Site: www.getcoactive.com
Admin Asst: Patricia Williams

BUCK OWENS' CRYSTAL PALACE
2800 Buck Owens Blvd
Bakersfield, CA 93308-6314
Telephone: (661) 328-7560, FAX: (805) 328-7565, Web Site: www.buckowens.com
Gen Mgr: Terry Christoffersen

PDQ POST GROUP
19134 95A Ave (Unit 7)
Surrey, BC, Canada V4N 4P2
Telephone: (604) 888-0676, (888) 998-9878, FAX: (604) 888-4467, E-Mail: lorraine@pdqpostgroup.com, Web Site: www.pdqpostgroup.com
Pres: Lorraine Duclos
Founded: 1991

PEP DIRECT
19 Stoney Brook Dr
Wilton, NH 03086-5151
Telephone: (603) 654-6141, Web Site: www.pep-direct.com
Sls & Mktg Specialist: Andrea Manseau

PHOENIX MARKETING GROUP LTD
PO Box 599
Georgetown, CT 06829-0599
Telephone: (203) 762-8665, FAX: (203) 762-8285
Pres: Bruce Side

PLUSNETMARKETING INC
415 Eagleview Blvd (#116)
Exton, PA 19341-1143

Telephone: (610) 458-0707, Web Site: www.pnmarketing.com
Primary Market Served: Consumer

PRAGALZ METRO GRAPHX INC
2500 E Lakeshore Dr
Twin Lakes, WI 53181-9371
Telephone: (708) 449-2700, FAX: (708) 449-2711
Pres: Robert J. Van Hyfte

PRECISION RESPONSE CORP
8151 Peters Rd (Suite 4000)
Plantation, FL 33324-4012
Telephone: (954) 693-3700, FAX: (954) 693-3767, Web Site: www.prcnet.com
CEO: Thomas L. Cardella

PREMIER IMS
815 Live Oak St
Houston, TX 77003-3220
Telephone: (713) 222-8871, FAX: (713) 222-0334, E-Mail: norm2@mailplex.com, Web Site: www.premiercompany.com
Pres: Martha Justice

PREMIER PRINT AND SERVICE GROUP INC
120 S Riverside Plz (Suite 1650)
Chicago, IL 60606-3938
Telephone: (312) 648-2266, (800) 648-3677, FAX: (312) 648-1361, E-Mail: blabin@premierprint.com, Web Site: www.premierprint.com
Pres: Ronald C. La Bine

PRIMA-NELSON PRINTING INC
911 Elmdale Rd
Glenview, IL 60025-3905
Telephone: (847) 729-8410, FAX: (847) 244-1421
Pres: Roger Pettenger

PRIME ACCESS INC
345 Seventh Ave (10th fl)
New York, NY 10001
Telephone: (212) 868-6800, FAX: (212) 868-9495, E-Mail: contact@primeaccess.net, Web Site: www.primeaccess.net
Pres & CEO: C.H. Buford

PRINT ARTS
2001 W 21st St
Broadview, IL 60155
Telephone: (708) 938-1600, Web Site: www.printarts.com

PRINT MAILERS INC
707 West Rd
Houston, TX 77038-2505
Telephone: (832) 201-2000, (800) 656-8883, FAX: (832) 201-2001, E-Mail: steve@pminet.com, Web Site: www.pminet.com
Pres & Founder: Steve Johns

PRIORITY SYSTEMS INC
PO Box 289
Grayslake, IL 60030-0289
Telephone: (773) 539-1884, (800) 330-3448, FAX: (773) 539-1755, E-Mail: sbender@priority.com, Web Site: www.priority.com
Pres: William Mehren

PRISM DATA SERVICES LTD
200-1599 Hurontario St
Mississauga, ON, Canada L5G 4S1
Telephone: (905) 278-5556, FAX: (905) 278-6603, E-Mail: bill.cram@prism-data.com; sales@prism-data.com, Web Site: www.prism-data.com
Pres: William Cram
VP: Dave Quinn

PRO/PHASE MARKETING INC
6554 Edenvale Blvd
Eden Prairie, MN 55346-2502
Telephone: (952) 974-1100, (866) 876-2737, FAX: (952) 974-7874, E-Mail: inquiry@repeatrewards.com, Web Site: www.ppmi.com
Pres & CEO: Elliot B. Eskin

PROFESSIONAL PRINT & MAIL INC
2818 E Hamilton Ave
Fresno, CA 93721-3209
Telephone: (559) 237-7468, (800) 654-7468, FAX: (559) 237-4929, E-Mail: dcarlile@printfresno.com, Web Site: www.printfresno.com
Pres & CEO: D.B. Carlile

PROGRAMMERS INVESTMENT CORP
125 E Algonquin Rd
Arlington Heights, IL 60005
Telephone: (847) 227-4500, FAX: (847) 299-8286, E-Mail: pic@pic-online.com, Web Site: www.pic-online.com
CEO: Gary W. Scherer

PROGRESSIVE COMMUNICATIONS
1001 Sand Pond Rd
Lake Mary, FL 32746-3354

Telephone: (407) 333-9500, FAX: (407) 333-7979, E-Mail: info@ progressivecommunications.com, Web Site: www. progressivecommunications.com
Pres: Mark Mills

PROMARK DIRECT MARKETING CONCEPTS INC

One University Plaza Dr (Suite 8)
Hackensack, NJ 07601-6207
Telephone: (201) 489-0532, (800) 776-6275, FAX: (201) 489-2680, E-Mail: jdunetz@promarkdirectmarketing. com
Pres: Janet Dunetz

PRONTO POST

7885 W 20th Ave
Hialeah, FL 33014-3228
Telephone: (305) 621-7900
Pres: Joshua Blank
Conducts Business: U.S., Canada
Employees: 51
Primary Market Served: Business
Founded: 1982
Gross sales or billing: $5,000,000

Direct mail & marketing services to the trade.

PROSPECT DIRECT INC

2266 N Prospect Ave (Suite 336)
Milwaukee, WI 53202-6306
Telephone: (414) 271-3313, (800) 624-9050, FAX: (414) 271-4244, E-Mail: info@prospect-direct.com, Web Site: www.prospect-direct.com
Pres: Jill Cohen

PROTOCOL INTEGRATED DIRECT MARKETING

2805 Fruitville Rd
Sarasota, FL 34237-5318
Telephone: (800) 677-2001, (800) 351-3774, FAX: (941) 906-9099, Web Site: www.protocolmarketing.com
Pres & CEO: Charles Dall'Acqua
Exec VP, Mktg & Sls: Gregg Sullivan
Sr VP & CIO: Jim Ferrato
Employees: 3,400

PUBLISHERS DIVERSIFIED MAIL SERVICE INC

10545 W Donges Ct
Milwaukee, WI 53224-1182
Telephone: (414) 354-1423, FAX: (414) 354-9338, E-Mail: webmaster@publishersmail.com, Web Site: www.publishersmail.com
Pres: Ronald Friedle

QUALITY LETTER SERVICE INC

"the lettersmiths"(R) "the datas-marts"(R)
22 W 32nd St (fl 10)
New York, NY 10001-3807
Telephone: (212) 268-3400, FAX: (212) 268-3401, E-Mail: info@ qletter.com, Web Site: www.qletter. com
Pres: Gary Weinberg

RCS RESPONSE TECHNOLOGIES INC

6420 Rea Rd (Suite 210)
Charlotte, NC 28217
Telephone: (704) 522-1919, FAX: (704) 522-9092, E-Mail: data@ rcsdirect.com, Web Site: www. rcsdirect.com
Pres & COO: Joseph A. Rowell

RED CLAY MEDIA

33 W 8th St
Bayonne, NJ 07002
Telephone: (866) Red-List, Web Site: www.redclaymedia.com
Founded: 1998

Direct mail, mailing list acquisition, data analytics, creative design, production & measurability

REED/HARRIS

aka Reed/Harris Direct Marketing, Inc
PO Box 3100
Portland, OR 97208-3100
Telephone: (503) 224-1812, (800) 238-1812, FAX: (503) 223-8283, E-Mail: info@reedharris.com, Web Site: www.reedharris.com
Pres: Michael Oberg

THE DMA RELATIONSHIP1

2 2nd St
Rye, NY 10580-2927
Telephone: (914) 921-4400, E-Mail: marketing@relationship1.com, Web Site: www.relationship1.com
CEO & Pres: David L. Ganz
COO: Howard W. Mertz
Conducts Business: U.S., Canada, Europe
Employees: 24
Primary Market Served: Business & Consumer
Founded: 1993
Gross sales or billing: $8,000,000

Build and maintain customized marketing databases from which we offer analysis, modeling, and reporting; direct mail and catalog lettershop; list brokerage; strategic consulting.

RESOURCE MARKETING INC

343 N Front St Ste 300
Columbus, OH 43215-2266
Telephone: (614) 621-2888, (800) 550-5815, FAX: (614) 621-2873, E-Mail: inquiry@resource.com, Web Site: www.resource.com
Exec Dir: Dr. Nita Rollins

SAATCHI & SAATCHI CANADA

Subs. of Saatchi & Saatchi Advertising Inc
Two Bloor St E (Suite 600)
Toronto, ON, Canada M4W 1A8
Telephone: (416) 359-9595, FAX: (416) 866-8485, Web Site: www. saatchi.ca
Exec VP & Mng Dir: John McCarter

THE ST JOHN ASSOCIATES INC

3450 Baychester Ave
Bronx, NY 10475-1407
Telephone: (718) 655-2500, FAX: (718) 655-0295, E-Mail: stjmail@ aol.com, Web Site: www.stjohn1.com
Pres & CEO: Mark G. Lewis

SALES DEVELOPMENT ASSOCIATES INC

7850 Manchester Rd
Saint Louis, MO 63143-2710
Telephone: (314) 862-8828, FAX: (314) 862-8829, E-Mail: patb@ sdasti.com
Pres: Patricia Biggerstaff

SENTINEL DIRECT

633 N Orange Ave (MP122)
Orlando, FL 32801
Telephone: (407) 420-5270, FAX: (407) 420-5282, Web Site: www. orlandosentinel.com
VP: Lou Stancampiano

SERVICE MAILERS INC

3101 Exposition Pl
Los Angeles, CA 90018-4030
Telephone: (323) 292-0133, FAX: (323) 292-1038, E-Mail: dgsteinhart@gmail.com, Web Site: www.servicemailersinc.com
Pres: David Steinhart

SIGMA MICRO LLC

9100 Purdue Rd Ste 400
Indianapolis, IN 46268-1180
Telephone: (317) 631-0907, (800) 383-4421, FAX: (317) 631-6585, Web Site: www.sigma-micro.com
Sls Mgr: Jeffrey T. Long
Mktg Commun: Jesse Kurth

SIGNATURE COMMUNICATIONS

Also dba "Signature Publications Inc."
45 West Side Rd
Milton, MA 02186-3018
Telephone: (617) 642-1300, FAX: (617) 696-2144, E-Mail: info@signaturecom.com, Web Site: www.signaturecom.com
Principal: Betsey Hartford
Controller: Owen Hartford
Conducts Business: U.S.
Primary Market Served: Business & Consumer
Founded: 1981

Direct mail creative & campaign strategy, full production services, list acquisition, merge/purge & back-end analysis for non-profit organizations of all sizes.

SMART DM

342 Horner Ave (Unit A)
Toronto, ON, Canada M8W 1Z3
Telephone: (416) 461-9271, FAX: (416) 461-9201, E-Mail: info@smartdm.ca, Web Site: www.smartdm.ca
Pres: Robert Tier

SPRING

aka Spring Global Mail
6655 Airport Rd
Mississauga, ON, Canada L4V 1V8
Telephone: (905) 678-2770, (888) 624-5327, FAX: (905) 678-9788, E-Mail: lou.laforet@springglobalmail.com, Web Site: www.springglobalmail.com
Gen Mgr: Lou LaForet

A global joint venture among TNT, Royal Mail Group and Singapore Post.

STAR DIRECT

Div. of The Kansas City Star
215 E 18th St
Kansas City, MO 64108
Telephone: (816) 234-4203, (800) 829-0151, FAX: (816) 234-4189, E-Mail: mtully@kcstar.com, Web Site: www.kcstardirect.com

STEZZI DIRECT INC

2775 Bankers Industrial Dr
Atlanta, GA 30360
Telephone: (770) 448-9900, (800) 954-5100, FAX: (770) 448-9480, E-Mail: info@stezzi.com, Web Site: www.stezzi.com
Pres: Joseph Stezzi

BOB STONE INC

2317 Interstate Ave (Unit B)
Grand Junction, CO 81505-8674

Telephone: (970) 256-9297, E-Mail: rfstone@mymailstation.com
CEO: Bob Stone
Conducts Business: U.S.
Employees: 1
Primary Market Served: Business & Consumer
Advertising/Marketing Budget Related to Direct Marketing: 76-100%
Direct Marketing ad budget: $100,000
Direct Mail: 100%
Gross sales or billing: $250,000

Consultant services to marketing firms.

STRATEGIC DIRECT MARKETING INC

208 Centre St
Pleasant View, TN 37146-7053
Telephone: (615) 834-9555, (800) 843-8861, FAX: (615) 834-6698, E-Mail: sales@sdmi3.com, Web Site: www.sdmi3.com
Pres: Randall Putala

SUMAN INC

10805 Whiterim Dr
Potomac, MD 20854-1786
Telephone: (301) 461-7625, E-Mail: sales@sumaninc.com, Web Site: www.sumaninc.com
CEO & Pres: Dr Anil Chaturvedi
VP: Abha Chaturvedi
Employees: 2
Primary Market Served: Business
Direct online sales
Advertising/Marketing Budget Related to Direct Marketing: 26-50%
Founded: 1999
Gross sales or billing: $200,000

Sell state-of-the-art marketing analytic solutions to marketing companies. Products include EZ Predict & EZ Map for direct marketing.

SUMOTEXT, INC

10825 Financial Centre Pkwy Ste 123
Little Rock, AR 72211-3557
Telephone: (800) 480-1248, Web Site: www.sumotext.com

TDC DIRECT

75 Superior Blvd
Mississauga, ON, Canada L5T 2X9
Telephone: (905) 564-6616, FAX: (905) 564-6621, E-Mail: nam@tdcdirect.com, Web Site: www.tdcdirect.com
Owner & Pres: Nam Nguyen

TABS DIRECT

Div. of Grizzard Advertising Inc
2800 Story Rd W
Irving, TX 75038-5267

Telephone: (281) 499-0417, (800) 231-0697, FAX: (281) 208-6081, E-Mail: tabsdirect@tabsdirect.com, Web Site: www.tabsdirect.com
SVP: Larry Cook

TANN SELECTIVE COMMUNICATIONS INC

aka Tann Selective
100 Granton Dr
Richmond Hill, ON, Canada L4B 1H7
Telephone: (905) 881-1030, FAX: (416) 881-1035
Pres: Jack Flynn

TECHNICOLOR

Div. of Thomson
3233 E Mission Oaks Blvd
Camarillo, CA 93012
Telephone: (805) 445-1122, (800) 732-4555, FAX: (805) 445-4280, E-Mail: info@technicolor.com, Web Site: www.technicolor.com
Mktg Dir: Michelle Menzel

TELEBRANDS CORP

81 Two Bridges Rd, Bldg One
Fairfield, NJ 07004
Telephone: (973) 244-0300, FAX: (973) 244-0233, Web Site: www.telebrands.com
Pres: A.J. Khubani

THOMPSON & CO MARKETING COMMUNICATIONS

85 Union Ave (fl 3)
Memphis, TN 38103-5127
Telephone: (901) 527-8000, FAX: (901) 527-3697, E-Mail: info@thompson-co.com, Web Site: www.thompson-co.com
Pres: Dave Diersen

TIZIANI WHITMYRE

2 Commercial St, Sharon Commerce Ctr
Sharon, MA 02067
Telephone: (781) 793-9380, FAX: (781) 793-9395, E-Mail: info@tizinc.com, Web Site: www.tizinc.com
CEO: Robert Tiziani
Pres: Rick Whitmyre

Advertising, public relations, internet marketing communications

TOPP DIRECT MARKETING

1117 N Stuart Place Rd Ste 103
Harlingen, TX 78552-4344
Telephone: (956) 421-5750, FAX: (956) 421-5721, E-Mail: info@toppmarketing.com

CEO: John W. Topp
Founded: 1983

TOWNE ALLPOINTS COMMUNICATIONS
3441 W MacArthur Blvd
Santa Ana, CA 92704
Telephone: (714) 540-3095, (800) 243-8099, FAX: (714) 540-4192, E-Mail: info@towne.com, Web Site: www.towne.com
Chmn & Owner: Jerry Monroe

TRIMENSIONS INC
1 Engle St (Suite 202)
Englewood, NJ 07631-2941
Telephone: (212) 254-5554, FAX: (212) 473-6524
Pres: Cliff Wood

TYME DIRECT MAIL SERVICE
3030 47th Ave Ste 300, c/o Century Direct, LLC
Long Island City, NY 11101-3445
Telephone: (212) 691-4444, FAX: (212) 691-6747, E-Mail: info@tymedirect.com, Web Site: www.tymedirect.com
Pres: Bill Abrams

TYPED LETTERS CORP
PO Box 799
Mount Pleasant, IA 52641-0799
Telephone: (316) 729-9093, FAX: (316) 729-9933, E-Mail: janet@typeletters.com, Web Site: www.typedletters.com
Owner: Randal A. Johnson

THE DMA UNITED MARKETING GROUP LLC
929 N Plum Grove Rd
Schaumburg, IL 60173-4704
Telephone: (847) 240-2005, FAX: (847) 240-2177, E-Mail: info@unitedmarket.com, Web Site: www.unitedmarket.com
Pres & CEO: Alan Portelli

USA DIRECT INC
2901 Blackbridge Rd
York, PA 17402
Telephone: (717) 852-1000, (800) 441-1850, FAX: (717) 852-1030, Web Site: www.usamailnow.com
CEO: Richard M. Osborne
Exec VP, Corp Devel, Sls, Mktg: Bruce Jackson

UNIWORLD GROUP
1 Metro Tech Center N (fl 11)
Brooklyn, NY 11201

Telephone: (212) 219-1600, FAX: (212) 219-6395, E-Mail: fhicks@uniworldgroup.com, Web Site: www.uniworldgroup.com
Dir: Mark Robertson
Founded: 1969

VESTCOM SAINT LOUIS
4288 Rider Trail N
Earth City, MO 63045-1105
Telephone: (314) 209-8443, (800) 264-0965, FAX: (314) 291-2195, E-Mail: sreinis@vestcom.com, Web Site: www.vestcom.com
Pres: Steve Ardwell
COO: Deno Colombo

WESTERN GRAPHICS
7614 Lemon Ave
Lemon Grove, CA 91945-1619
Telephone: (619) 668-4736, FAX: (619) 668-4742, E-Mail: jim@westerngraphics.org, Web Site: www.westerngraphics.org
Pres: James W. Elliott

WESTMINSTER INTERNATIONAL
174 W Beaver Creek
Richmond Hill, ON, Canada L4B 1B4
Telephone: (416) 494-6245, FAX: (905) 771-9349
Pres: Steve Falk

THE DMA W.A. WILDE CO
201 Summer St
Holliston, MA 01746-2258
Telephone: (508) 429-5515, FAX: (508) 893-0399, E-Mail: info@wilde.com, Web Site: www.wilde.com
Pres: Thomas A. Wilde

WILKES DIRECT MAIL CO
3401 Chouteau Ave
Saint Louis, MO 63103
Telephone: (314) 776-5555, (800) 331-6441, FAX: (314) 776-0913, E-Mail: sales@wilkesdirect.com, Web Site: www.wilkesdirect.com
Pres: Jim Poneta

WORDCOM INC
56 Main St, PO Box 308
Ellington, CT 06029-3360
Telephone: (860) 875-7373, (800) 875-7373, (800) 822-0622, FAX: (860) 872-2713, E-Mail: sales@wordcom-inc.com, Web Site: www.wordcom-inc.com
Chmn Bd & CEO: George Wachtel
Pres: Christopher Wachtel

WORKFLOW ONE
Sub. of Workflow Mgmt Inc
220 E Monument Ave
Dayton, OH 45402-1223
Telephone: (877) 735-4966, E-Mail: clientservices@workflowone.com, Web Site: www.sfinet.com
CEO: Dean Truitt

WORLD MARKETING, INC (HQ)
14407 Alondra Blvd
La Mirada, CA 90638
Telephone: (714) 994-6245, (800) 244-3003, FAX: (714) 776-2590, E-Mail: results@worldmarkinc.com, Web Site: www.worldmarkinc.com
Exec VP Mktg: Jeff Thies

G.A. WRIGHT DIRECT MARKETING
GA Wright Inc
10325 E 47th Ave
Denver, CO 80238
Telephone: (303) 333-4453, FAX: (303) 333-4660, E-Mail: gaming@gawright.com, Web Site: www.gawrightcasinomarketing.com
CEO: Gary A Wright
Pres: Tony Aveni
Sr VP: Jack Breslin

XDM CORP
235 Montgomery St Ste 834
San Francisco, CA 94104-3002
Telephone: (415) 989-3000, FAX: (925) 934-0599, E-Mail: info@xdm.com, Web Site: www.xdm.com
Pres: Ann Fairclough

XPANDOMEDIA
340 Nagel Dr
Buffalo, NY 14225
Telephone: (716) 836-9668
Pres: James Sabio

ZUMBOX
31364 Via Colinas (Suite 103)
Westlake Village, CA 91362-6844
Telephone: (818) 707-7400, Web Site: www.zumbox.com
VP Prod Devel: Dave Elkins
Primary Market Served: Business & Consumer

Computer Services, Data Processing, List & Subscription Fulfillment Companies (22) — Geographic Index

Arizona

Infolure, 1705 W Parkside Ln, Phoenix, 85027-1333

JDA Software Group Inc, 14400 N 87th St, Scottsdale, 85260-3649

Professional Marketing Associates, 405 W Fairmont Dr, Tempe, 85282-2007

Arkansas

Acxiom Corp, 601 E 3rd St, Little Rock, 72201-1709

CognitiveDATA Inc, 500 President Clinton Ave (Suite 301), Little Rock, 72201

California

AccountMate Software Corp, 1445 Technology Ln (Suite A5), Petaluma, 94954-7613

AcquireWEB Inc, 1065 E Hillsdale Blvd (Suite 310), Foster City, 94404-1689

Adobe Systems Inc, 345 Park Ave (#W17-506), San Jose, 95110-2704

Aptimus, 199 Fremont St (Suite 1800), San Francisco, 94105

Business Objects, 3410 Hillview Ave, Palo Alto, 94304-1395

CAM Commerce Solutions, 17075 Newhope St Ste A, Fountain Valley, 92708-4299

Christian Resource Management, 2322 N Batavia (Suite 108), Orange, 92865-2000

Cisco Systems Inc, 170 W Tasman Dr, San Jose, 95134-1700

COMPITSS INC, 1000 Business Center Dr (Suite 107), Newbury Park, 91320-1237

Contact Center Compliance, 350 E St (Suite 100), Santa Rosa, 95404-4438

CrownPeak, 5880 W Jefferson Blvd (Suite G), Los Angeles, 90016-3160

The Customer Connection Inc, 621 S Andreasen Dr (Suite B), Escondido, 92029-1904

CyberDefender, 617 W 7th St (Suite 401), Los Angeles, 90017-3800

DMRA, 201 San Antonio Cir (Suite 280), Mountain View, 94040-1256

ESRI, 380 New York St, Redlands, 92373-8118

FileMaker Inc, 5201 Patrick Henry, Santa Clara, 95054-1164

Fujitsu Computer Systems, 1250 E Arques Ave MS 122, Sunnyvale, 94085-3470

Global Ware Solutions, 1089 Mills Way, Redwood City, 94063-3119

Hitachi Data Systems, 2020 Main St (Suite 1120), Irvine, 92614-8234

Information Sources Inc, 2175 Cactus Ct Apt 1, Walnut Creek, 94595-2531

Input Systems Inc, 16308 Orange Ave, Paramount, 90723

Integrated Marketing Technology Inc, 2269 Chestnut St (#992), San Francisco, 94123-2600

Island Pacific Inc, 17310 Red Hill Ave Ste 320, Irvine, 92614-5600

KXEN, 201 Mission St (Suite 1950), San Francisco, 94105-1880

Magento, 10441 Jefferson Blvd (Suite 200), Culver City, 90232-3512

Mailer's Software, 22382 Avenida Empresa, Rancho Santa Margarita, 92688-2112

Melissa Data Corp, 22382 Avenida Empresa, Rancho Santa Margarita, 92688-2112

MindFireInc, 30 Corporate Park (Suite 301), Irvine, 92606-5133

MSC, 6200 Canoga Ave (Suite 102), Woodland Hills, 91367-2429

Old Vine Marketing, 147 Old Vine Way, Napa, 94558-7028

Phoenix Technologies Ltd, 915 Murphy Ranch Rd, Milpitas, 95035-7912

QMSI, 5700 Ager Beswick Rd, Montague, 96064-9495

Response Management Technologies Inc, 2550 9th St (Suite 103), Berkeley, 94710-2516

Salford Systems, 9685 Via Excelencia Ste 208, San Diego, 92126-7500

Savicom, 44 Montgomery St (Suite 1600), San Francisco, 94104

Sybase Inc, 1 Sybase Dr, Dublin, 94568-7976

TheLaw.net Corp, 6640 Lusk Blvd (Suite A205), San Diego, 92121-2777

TRUSTe, 835 Market St (Suite 800), San Francisco, 94103-1905

Vision Solutions, 15300 Barranca Pkwy, Irvine, 92618

Western Digital Corp, 3355 Michelson Dr (Suite 100), Irvine, 92612-5694

Yousendit Inc, 1919 S Bascom Ave (fl 3), Campbell, 95008-2220

Colorado

Complete Mailing Solutions, 217 12th St SW, Loveland, 80537

Core Technologies, 1320 Pearl St Ste 240, Boulder, 80302-5279

Corporate Express, One Environmental Way, Broomfield, 80021

Covalent Marketing, 2021 S Ogden St, Denver, 80210-4134

Demographic Research Co, 1552 Pennsylvania St, Denver, 80203

Dovetail, 1221 W Mineral Ave (Suite 102), Littleton, 80120-4544

Global IntelliSystems, 1153 Bergen Pkwy (#45), Evergreen, 80439-9501

Jeppesen, 55 Inverness Dr E, Englewood, 80112-5412

RealData Services Inc, 322 Van Dorn Dr, Glenwood Springs, 81601-9524

Rigden Inc, PO Box 17187, Boulder, 80308-0187

TeleTech, 9197 S Peoria St, Englewood, 80112-5833

Wiland Direct, 6309 Monarch Park Pl Ste 201, Niwot, 80503-7198

Connecticut

As Seen On PC Network, 25 Walls Dr (Suite 1-C), Fairfield, 06824

Connex International, 50 Federal Rd, Danbury, 06810

Data Square LLC, 396 Danbury Rd, Wilton, 06897

Fairfield Marketing Group Inc, 830 Sport Hill Rd, Easton, 06612-1241

Interactive Marketing Solutions, 777 Summer St (Suite 502), Stamford, 06901-1042

Lissan Computing Co Inc, 25 Beaver Brook Rd, Ridgefield, 06877-1001

MDF Systems, 780 James P Casey Rd, Bristol, 06010-8537

Pitney Bowes Software Systems, One Elmcroft Rd, Stamford, 06926-0700

Shepard's Inc, 32 Henry St, Bethel, 06801

Software Marketing Associates Inc, 1086 Elm St (Suite 200), Rocky Hill, 06067-2341

Suntel Inc, 1890 Dixwell Ave (Suite 205), Hamden, 06514-3171

Wired Assets Data Corp, 284 Riversville Rd, Greenwich, 06831-3253

District of Columbia

Triplex, 900 17th St NW (Suite 850), Washington, 20006-2523

Florida

Alvion LLC, 2503 Del Prado Blvd (Suite 502), Cape Coral, 33904

August Marketing, 18522 SE Sea Oaks Ln, Tequesta, 33469-1409

Bamboo Cricket Service, 1415 Chaffee Dr (Unit 10), Titusville, 32780

Citrix Systems, Inc, 851 W Cypress Creek Rd, Fort Lauderdale, 33309-2040

Computer Solutions Inc, 13701 SW 88th St Ste 306, Bldg H33, Miami, 33186-1309

Data Partners Inc, 12857 Banyan Creek Dr, Fort Myers, 33908-3083

DataMentors LLC, 2319-104 Oak Myrtle Ln, Wesley Chapel, 33544

Geoscape, 2100 W Flagler St (fl 2), Miami, 33135-1619

The Information Engine, 9105 Hammock Edge Pl, Bradenton, 34212-3254

Latin Force Group LLC, 2100 W Flagler St, Miami, 33145

Logicnology Inc, 720 International Pkwy, Sunrise, 33325-6219

MarketLeverage, 1515 International Pkwy Ste 2013, Lake Mary, 32746-7635

Parker Software, 4767 New Broad St, Orlando, 32814

Precision Play Media / MarketLeverage, 701 International Pkwy Ste 200, Lake Mary, 32746-5624

PrimeNet, 2100 Palmetto St Ste A, Clearwater, 33765-2101

Rapid Progress Marketing & Modeling LLC, 1760 Delaware Ave NE, Saint Petersburg, 33703-5439

REWAY Inc, 3132 SW 165th Ave, Miramar, 33027

Support Services Corp, 2401 First St, Fort Myers, 33901

Time Customer Service Inc, One N Dale Mabry Hwy, Tampa, 33609-2700

Georgia

Airs Inc, 4080 Hwy 92, Douglasville, 30135-4404

Colinear Systems, 2650 Holcomb Bridge Rd (Suite 610), Alpharetta, 30022-5343

Computer Business Services Inc, 205 W Forsyth St, PO Box A, Americus, 31709-3533

First Wave Technologies, 7000 Central Pkwy NE (Suite 330), Atlanta, 30328-4589

Gates Marketing, 3909 Oakcliff Industrial Ct, Atlanta, 30340-3408

Infor, 13560 Morris Rd (Suite 4100), Alpharetta, 30004

Nexxlinx (HQ), 3565 Piedmont Rd NE (Bldg 2-310), Atlanta, 30305-8204

North American Mailing Technologies Inc, 141 B Buford Dr, Lawrenceville, 30045-4926

O2 Consulting Inc, 7760 Landowne Dr, Atlanta, 30350-1064

Peachtree Data Inc, 2905 Premiere Pkwy (Suite 200), Duluth, 30097-5275

Performance Direct Inc, 3525 Piedmont Rd, Atlanta, 30305-1530

PossibleNOW Inc, 4400 River Green Pkwy, Duluth, 30096-8316

Premiere Global Services Inc, 3280 Peachtree Rd NE (Suite 1000), Atlanta, 30305-2451

Scott Computing Systems, 2780 Bert Adams Rd (Suite 400), Atlanta, 30339-3926

Stibo Systems, 33550 George Busbee Pkwy NW (Suite 350), Kennesaw, 30144-2122

Touch-Base Computing, PO Box 213, Silver Creek, 30173

Hawaii

DataCraft Inc, 28 Kainehe St Ste A1, Kailua, 96734-6130

Illinois

ACG/Computech Direct, 2155 Stonington Ave (Suite 215), Hoffman Estates, 60195-2058

The Allant Group, 2056 Westings Ave (Suite 500), Naperville, 60563-2485

Alterian, 35 Wacker Dr (Suite 200), Chicago, 60601-2104

Anthem Marketing, 549 W Randolph St Ste 702, Chicago, 60661-1478

Audience Identification Inc, PO Box 3305, Lisle, 60532-8305

Creative Automation, 220 Fencl Ln, Hillside, 60162-2002

Customer Asset Consulting Group Inc, 1870 N Roselle Rd (Suite 101), Schaumburg, 60195-3100

Daystar Data Group Inc, 155 W Central Rd, Schaumburg, 60195-1945

DKP & Associates, Inc, 7847 Lowell Ave (Suite 200), Skokie, 60076-3535

Direct Logic Solutions, 4507 N Sterling Ave (Suite 402), Peoria, 61615-3860

Hartley Data Service Inc, 1807 Glenview Rd (Suite 100), Glenview, 60025-2944

Information Command Inc, 5700 N Sheridan Rd (#904), Chicago, 60660-4740

Integrated Business Services Inc, 736 N Western Ave (# 125), Lake Forest, 60045-1820

Kable Fulfillment Services, 16 S Wesley Ave, Mount Morris, 61054-1473

MarketerNet LLC, 233 S Wacker Dr (Suite 1800), Sears Tower, Chicago, 60606-6462

Omeda, 555 Huehl Rd, Northbrook, 60062-2336

Partners Marketing Inc, 1750 E Main St (Suite 10), Saint Charles, 60174-2363

Peak Computer Systems, 6400 W Main St (Suite 1A), Belleville, 62223

Phoenix Data Processing, One Oak Hill Center (Suite 301), Westmont, 60559

Scientific Computing Associates, 525 N Lincoln Ave, Villa Park, 60181-1306

Spectrum Data, 131 N 3rd St, Oregon, 61061-1410

SPSS Inc, 233 S Wacker Dr (Suite 1100), Chicago, 60606-6307

Strategic Data Intelligence LLC, 555 Skokie Blvd, Northbrook, 60062-2812

SubscriberMail LLC, 3333 Warrenville Rd (Suite 350), Lisle, 60532-4551

Indiana

Fifth Gear, 9100 Purdue Rd (Suite 400), Indianapolis, 46268-1180

Service Net, 650 Missouri Ave, Jeffersonville, 47130-3081

Iowa

B2E Direct Marketing Inc, 209 S Main St, Grimes, 50111-2192

BWB Marketing Services, PO Box 802, Ankeny, 50021-0802

CDS Global, 1901 Bell Ave, Des Moines, 50315-1099

Kansas

Datasystem Solutions Inc, 6310 Lamar Ave (Suite 200), Overland Park, 66202-4284

Lexinet Corp, 701 N Union St, Council Grove, 66846-9358

Ruf Strategic Solutions, 1533 E Spruce St, Olathe, 66061-3698

Kentucky

DirecTech, 33 W Second St (Suite 504), Maysville, 41056

Maryland

Barcoding Inc, 2220 Boston St Fl 2, Baltimore, 21231-3058

Data Services Inc, 31516 Winterplace Pkwy, Salisbury, 21804-1882

Decision Software Inc, 6911 Old Landover Rd, Hyattsville, 20785-1503

Group 1 Software Inc, 4200 Parliament Pl (Suite 600), Lanham, 20706-1844

Lewis Direct, 325 E Oliver St, Baltimore, 21202-2948

Lotame Solutions, 8850 Stanford Blvd (Suite 2000), Columbia, 21045-4726

Merkle Inc, 7001 Columbia Gateway Dr, Columbia, 21046-2289

MMI Direct, 7160 Columbia Gateway Dr (Suite 300), Columbia, 21046-2134

Saturn Corp, 4701 Lydell Rd, Hyattsville, 20781-1117

Sisk Fulfillment Service Inc, 1900 Industrial Park Dr, Box 463, Federalsburg, 21632

Stockton Inc, 8341 Beechcraft Ave, Gaithersburg, 20879-1509

Vocus, 12051 Indian Creek Ct, Beltsville, 20705-1246

Massachusetts

Access International, 1035 Cambridge St (Suite 2), Cambridge, 02141-1154

Bitstream Inc, 500 Nickerson Rd, Marlborough, 01752-4695

CommercialWare Inc, 1800 W Park Dr (Suite 250), Westboro, 01581-3960

Computerworld DataBase Div, 1 Speen St, Framingham, 01701-4644

Customer Portfolios LLC, 306 Northern Ave, Boston, 02210-2324

D&B Sales and Marketing Solutions, 460 Totten Pond Rd, Waltham, 02451-1908

Datamatics Technologies, 56 Middlesex Tpke (Suite 250), Burlington, 01803-4973

Direxxis Inc, 250 1st Ave (Suite 102), Needham, 02494-2847

Elcom International Inc, Ten Oceana Way, Norwood, 02062

Equifax Database Marketing, 500 Edgewater Dr (Suite 525), Wakefield, 01880

FreshAddress Inc, 36 Crafts St, Newton, 02458-1249

Galvin Associates Inc, PO Box 700, Marstons Mills, 02648-0700

GMC Software Technology Inc, 529 Main St (Suite 205), Charlestown, 02129-1121

Inforonics LLC, 25 Porter Rd Ste 4, Littleton, 01460-1434

Intellidyn Corp, 175 Derby St (Suite 40), Hingham, 02043-4053

Ipswitch Inc, 10 Maguire Rd (Suite 220), Lexington, 02421-3120

L-Com Inc, 45 Beechwood Dr, Andover, 01845-1092

Neolane, 300-334 Washington St, 1 Gateway Ctr (Suite 709), Newton, 02458-2804

NetProspex Inc, 300 3rd Ave # 2, Waltham, 02451-7525

Novell Inc, 404 Wyman St Ste 500A, Waltham, 02451-1264

Pluris, 550 Cochituate Rd Ste 7, Framingham, 01701-4600

Portrait International Inc, 125 Summer St Ste 1600, Boston, 02110-1636

PTC, 140 Kendrick St Ste C120, Needham, 02494-2743

3Com Corp, 153 Taylor St, Littleton, 01460-1407

Unica Corp, 170 Tracer Ln, Waltham, 02451-1379

Window Book Inc, 300 Franklin St, Cambridge, 02139-3781

Zircon Co Inc, 67 Aurora Ln., Salem, 01970-6803

Zoominfo Inc, 307 Waverley Oaks Rd Ste 405, Waltham, 02452-8413

Michigan

ANCOR, 1911 Woodslee Dr, Troy, 48083-2236

CRK Computer Services, 16250 Northland Dr (Suite 12), Southfield, 48075-5226

Dundee Internet Services Inc, 15000 Ostrander Rd, Azalia, 48110-9704

MarketNet Services LLC, 14998 Cleveland St (Suite E), Spring Lake, 49456-8993

Renkim Corp, 13333 Allen Rd, Southgate, 48195

Sage Direct Inc, 3400 Raleigh Ave SE, Grand Rapids, 49512-2042

Super Disk, PO Box 2797, Ann Arbor, 48106-2797

TechniServe Inc, 2065 Livernois Rd, Troy, 48083-1737

Thomson Tax & Accounting, 7322 Newman Blvd, Dexter, 48130

Minnesota

Artful Dragon Press Inc, 14108 Lake St Ext, Minnetonka, 55345-3019

Corporate Graphics Direct Marketing Solutions, 1170 Grey Fox Rd, Arden Hills, 55112-6908

Credit Index, 25 6th Ave N, Saint Cloud, 56303-4729

eBureau LLC, 25 6th Ave N, Saint Cloud, 56303-4729

ENTIERA, 3515 Plymouth Blvd (Suite 205), Minneapolis, 55447-1382

Fair Isaac Corp, 901 Marquette Ave (Suite 3200), Minneapolis, 55402

FG Companies, 901 Twelve Oaks Center Dr Ste 934, Wayzata, 55391-4721

FICO, 901 Marquette Ave (Suite 3200), Minneapolis, 55402-3232

Lorton Data Inc, 2 Pine Tree Dr (Suite 302), Arden Hills, 55112-3715

OPIN Systems Inc, 7900 International Dr (Suite 770), Bloomington, 55425-2556

Sara Isaac, 4295 Lexington Ave N, Saint Paul, 55126

SCICOM Data Services Ltd, 10101 Bren Rd E, Minnetonka, 55343-9065

Missouri

Data Dash Inc, 3928 Delor St, Saint Louis, 63116

Direct Marketing Audit Systems, 3159 Fee Fee Rd (Suite 221), Bridgeton, 63044-3299

Inquiry Intelligence Systems, 18 N Central Dr, O'Fallon, 63366

Marco Data Service, 12537 Petermoore Ln, De Soto, 63020-4760

Wooden Information Services, 13358 Windbrooke Ln, Saint Louis, 63146-2224

Nebraska

Data University, 6550 S 34th St, Lincoln, 68516-5454

PRIORITY Data Systems Inc, 5035 S 110th St, Omaha, 68137-2376

UAA Clearinghouse, 6912 N 97th Cir, Omaha, 68122-1010

New Hampshire

NextMark Inc, 2 Buck Rd Ste 8, Hanover, 03755-2715

PC Connection, Route 101A, 730 Milford Rd, Merrimack, 03054-4631

TomTom North American, 11 Lafayette St., Lebanon, 03766-1445

New Jersey

ARGI - Automated Resources Group Inc, 135 Chestnut Ridge Rd, Montvale, 07645-1152

Accurate Marketing Systems, 122 Voorhis Ave, River Edge, 07661-1522

Applied Info Group, 100 Market St, Kenilworth, 07033-1722

Business Development Solutions Inc, 1022 Red Oak Dr, Cherry Hill, 08003-2631

(C) Systems LLC, 510 Thornall St (Suite 310), Edison, 08837-2207

Commerce Register Inc, 190 Godwin Ave, Midland Park, 07432-1841

Commercial Data Processing Inc, 30 Northover Pl, Red Bank, 07701-6311

COREMedia Systems Inc, 695 US Hwy 46 (Suite 403), Fairfield, 07004-1561

Cornwell Data Services Inc, 352 Evelyn St, Paramus, 07652-2908

Createch Marketing, 180 Summit Ave (Suite 203), Montvale, 07645-1722

D&B, 3 Sylvan Way, Parsippany, 07054-3821

The Data Base Inc, 1710 Hwy 35, Oakhurst, 07755

DataBridge Marketing Systems Corp, 1 Hollow Wood Ln, Montvale, 07645-1350

DirectSmile LLC, 300 Broadacres Dr (fl 4), Bloomfield, 07003-3153

Dydacomp Development Corp, 9 Campus Dr Ste 1, Parsippany, 07054-4412

The Fidelis Group Inc, 223 Gates Rd (Unit A), Little Ferry, 07643-1900

Global Turnkey Systems Inc, 2001 US Highway 46 Ste 203, Parsippany, 07054-1315

GrayHair Software, 124 Gaither Dr (Suite 160), Mount Laurel, 08054-1719

Heritage Direct, 1710 Hwy 35, Oakhurst, 07755-2910

IPacesetters, 135 Chestnut Ridge Rd, Montvale, 07645-1152

Millions By Marketing Inc, 88 E Main St (Suite 411), Mendham, 07945-1832

Publishers Computer Corp, 209 Main St, New Milford, 07646-1733

Raritan Inc, 400 Cottontail Ln, Somerset, 08873-1238

The Total Mailing System, 551 Mid-Atlantic Pkwy, West Deptford, 08066

Veratad Technologies LLC, 500 Frank W Burr Blvd Ste 14, Teaneck, 07666-6802

New Mexico

King Computer Services Inc, PO Box 1590, Las Cruces, 88004-1590

New York

Alliant, 301 Fields Ln Ste 8, Brewster, 10509-2654

Anchor Computer Inc, 1900 New Hwy, Farmingdale, 11735-1537

BCC Software Inc, 75 Josons Dr, Rochester, 14623-3494

BT Americas, 620 8th Ave (fl 45), New York, 10018-1741

Blue Hill Marketing Solutions Inc, 1 Blue Hill Plz (Ste 1674), Pearl River, 10965-6159

Bureau Van Dijk, 40 Wall St (fl 27), New York, 10005-1364

Cambey & West Inc, 120 N Rte 9W, Congers, 10920-1729

CRC Data Systems, 47-10 32nd Pl, Long Island City, 11101

Center for International Earth Science Information Network, 61 Rte 9 W, Palisades, 10964-1707

Collective - The Audience Engine, 99 Park Ave (fl 5), New York, 10016-1601

Cross Country Computer Corp, 570 S Research Pl, Central Islip, 11722-4415

CyberData, 20 Max Ave, Hicksville, 11801

D&D Associates Inc, PO Box 9150, Garden City, 11530-9150

Datran Media, 345 Hudson St Ste 500, New York, 10014-7402

Db Marketing, 550 Mamaroneck Ave., Harrison, 10528

DMRS Group Inc, 304 Park Ave S (fl 11), New York, 10010-4305

Direct Access Marketing Services Inc, 6851 Jericho Tpke (Suite 245), Syosset, 11791-4421

Direct Data Capture Ltd, PO Box 589, Huntington Station, 11746-0458

Drake Direct, 225 E 46th St (Penthouse D), New York, 10017-2928

Easy Analytic Software Inc, 7359 196th St, Fresh Meadows, 11366-1810

Emailvision, 545 5th Ave Rm 1000, New York, 10017-3633

Enertex Marketing, 99 Madison Ave (10th fl), New York, 10016-7419

Fulcrum, 70 W 40th St (fl 10), New York, 10018-2621

The Hyiad Group, 400 Garden City Plz (Suite 403), Garden City, 11530-3336

Insight Out of Chaos, 220 E 23rd St (Suite 600), New York, 10010-4658

Walter Karl Inc, 2 Blue Hill Plz Ste 1662, Pearl River, 10965-3115

Mercury Commerce Inc, 1100 Shames Dr (Suite 200), Westbury, 11590

MBS, 265 Broadhollow Rd Ste 400, Melville, 11747-4833

MESA, 39 N Bayles Ave, Port Washington, 11050-2930

Pegg Nadler Associates Inc, 400 E 77th St (Suite 16b), New York, 10075-2337

PNT Marketing Services, Inc, 2420 Jackson Ave (Suite 203), Long Island City, 11101-4332

Professional Advertising Systems Inc, 200 Business Park Dr (Suite 304), Armonk, 10504-1751

Profit Center Software Inc, 11 Harbor Park Dr, Port Washington, 11050-4656

QED Marketing Inc, 570 S Research Pl, Central Islip, 11722-4415

Return Path Inc, 304 Park Ave S (fl 7), New York, 10010-4311

SofTrek Corp, 30 Bryant Woods N, Amherst, 14228-3601

Type-A-Scan Inc, 115 W 29th St, New York, 10001-5106

LG Wilson & Associates, 6 Butler Hill Rd, Somers, 10589-2404

XMPIE Inc, 767 3rd Ave (fl 3), New York, 10017-2023

North Carolina

Conclusive Marketing, 6900 Northpark Blvd Ste G, Charlotte, 28216-1393

Global Demand Publishing Inc, 101 B Middle St (Suite 101 B), Jacksonville, 28546-6798

Quaero Corp, 1930 Camden Rd (Suite 2060), Charlotte, 28203-5900

SAS Institute, PO Box 610, Cary, 27512-0610

Technekes LLC, 1927 S Tryon St (Suite 310), Charlotte, 28203

Web Decisions, 303 Pisgah Church Rd (Suite 2A), Greensboro, 27455-2756

Wheaton Group, 201 Bolinas Ct, Chapel Hill, 27517-8344

Yankelovich Inc, 400 Meadowmont Village Cir (Suite 431), Chapel Hill, 27517-7505

Ohio

Alltel Publishing Corp, 100 Executive Pkwy, Hudson, 44236-1630

Automation Research Inc, 1651 NW Professional Plaza, Columbus, 43220-3866

CTRAC Information Solutions, 16855 Foltz Pkwy, Strongsville, 44149-5517

International Data Management - a Dmh Marketing Partners Co, 490 White Pond Dr, Akron, 44320-1122

NFocus Consulting Inc, 1594 Hubbard Dr, Lancaster, 43130-8124

SBDP Corp, 4208 Airport Rd, Cincinnati, 45226-1646

Teradata Corp, 10000 Innovation Dr, Miamisburg, 45342-4927

Oklahoma

A La Mode Inc, 3705 W Memorial Rd (Suite 402), Oklahoma City, 73134-1507

Data Management & Marketing Services LLC, 508 N Aster Ave, Broken Arrow, 74012-9446

Marketing Information Network, 120 N Bryant Ave (Suite A1), Edmond, 73034

Myriad Systems Inc, 2627 E-I-44 Service Rd, Oklahoma City, 73111-8302

Oregon

AccuDirect Response, PO Box 10246, Portland, 97296-0246

Pennsylvania

Advanced Software Applications, 3117 Washington Pike, Bridgeville, 15017-1434

Echo Data, 735 Fox Chase Ste 101, Highlands Corp Ctr, Coatesville, 19320-1897

Elliott Marketing Group Inc, 2281 Sidgefield Ln, Pittsburgh, 15241-2713

The IDT Group, 1650 Market St Fl 36, Philadelphia, 19103-7334

Innovative Systems Inc, 790 Holiday Dr, Pittsburgh, 15220-8127

LSSiData, 1 Sentry Pkwy (Suite 1000), Blue Bell, 19422-2310

Mac Direct, 185 Discovery Drive, Colmar, 18915

Mail Movers & Mailing Services, 325 S 69th St, Upper Darby, 19082

Neat Co, 1601 Market St (Suite 3500), Philadelphia, 19103

Alan Senegeto, 808 Waverly Rd, Kennett Square, 19348-1451

Sungard Computer Services, 680 E Swedesford Rd, Wayne, 19087

Telephone Look-Up Service Co, PO Box 316, Jamison, 18929-0316

Volt Delta, 1 Sentry Pkwy E Ste 6000, Blue Bell, 19422-2310

Puerto Rico

Database Marketing Services, PO Box 2995, Guaynabo, 00970-2995

South Carolina

Blackbaud Inc, 2000 Daniel Island Dr, Charleston, 29492-7541

Tennessee

Data Intelligence Group, PO Box 682063, Franklin, 37068-2063

Texas

Affiliated Computer Services Inc (ACS), 2828 N Haskell Ave, Dallas, 75204-2909

Artemis International Solutions Corp, 401 Congress Ave Ste 2650, Austin, 78701-3708

Bowman & Partners, 1914 Spring Dr (Suite 101), Roanoke, 76262-7416

Convio Inc, 11501 Domain Dr (Suite 200), Austin, 78758-3406

Data Dallas Corp, 1111 W Mockingbird Ln (Suite 300), Dallas, 75247-5017

Epsilon, 4401 Regent Blvd, Irving, 75063-2404

Harte-Hanks, 2800 Wells Branch Pkwy, Austin, 78728-6762

Hoover's, 5800 Airport Blvd, Austin, 78752-4204

KBM Group, 2050 N Greenville Ave, Richardson, 75082-4322

MLS Data Management Solutions, 6115 Camp Bowie Blvd (Suite 200), Fort Worth, 76116-5500

Reynolds & Reynolds Co, 6700 Hollister St (fl 2), Houston, 77040-5331

Trinity Technical Group, Inc, 1360 Post N Paddock (Suite 500), Grand Prairie, 75050-1255

Vermont

AIDC (American International Distribution Corp), 50 Winter Sport Ln, Williston, 05495-0080

Datamann Inc, PO Box 1930, Wilder, 05088-1930

Global-Z International Inc, 395 Shields Dr, Bennington, 05201-9810

Virginia

CACI International Inc, 1100 N Glebe Rd, Arlington, 22201-4714

Data Management Inc, 8300 Greensboro Dr (Suite 800), Mc Lean, 22102-3661

The Database Centre, 11210 Waples Mill Rd (Suite 100), Fairfax, 22030

DM Data Solutions LLC, 7508 Manigold Ct, Alexandria, 22315-3838

Eloqua Corp, 1921 Gallows Rd (Suite 250), Vienna, 22182-3994

Marketing1by1 LLC, 3877 Fairfax Ridge Rd Ste 200N, Fairfax, 22030-0977

Relevate, 6883 Commercial Dr, Springfield, 22159-0310

Strategic Software Systems LLC, 1508 Willow Lawn Dr (Suite 111), Richmond, 23230-3421

TARGUSinfo, 1861 International Dr Fl 6, Mc Lean, 22102-4420

Washington

Compact Information Systems Inc, 7120 185th Ave NE, Redmond, 98052-0575

Concur, 18400 NE Union Hill Rd, Redmond, 98052-3332

Intelius Inc, 500 108th Ave (fl 22), Bellevue, 98004-5500

Microsoft Corp, 1 Microsoft Way, Redmond, 98052-8300

PacificEast, PO Box 439, Sumas, 98295-0439

Tableau Software, 837 N 34th St (Suite 400), Seattle, 98103-8882

Wisconsin

Advanced Concepts Inc, 8875 N 55th St (Suite 200), Milwaukee, 53223-2311

Arrow Companies, LLC, 310 O'Connor Dr, PO Box 410, Elkhorn, 53121

Communication Logistics, Inc, 2040 Jay Mar Rd, Plover, 54467-3257

TEC Mailing Solutions, LLC, 804 Liberty Blvd (Suite 201), Sun Prairie, 53590-9269

WennSoft, 1970 S Calhoun Rd, New Berlin, 53151-2214

CANADA
Nova Scotia

Epic Marketing Solutions, 6054 Quinpool Rd, Halifax, B3L 1A1

The Oyster Group, 59 Prince Albert Rd, Dartmouth, B2Y 1M1

Ontario

Andsor Research Inc, 40 Richview Rd (Suite 1501), Etobicoke, M9A 5C1

Complete Mailing Service, 8 Dohme Ave, Toronto, M4B 1Y8

Cornerstone Group of Companies, 20 Eglinton Ave W (4th fl), Toronto, M4R 1K8

LoyaltyOne, 438 University Ave (Suite 600), Toronto, M5G 2L1

Northern Response (International) Ltd, 50 Staples Ave, Toronto, L4B 0A7

Promotional Products Fulfillment & Distribution Ltd, 80 William Smith Dr, Whitby, L1N 9W1

Research in Motion Corp, 185 Columbia St W, Waterloo, N2L 5Z5

Wilson, Hugh & Associate Consultants Ltd, Four Long Bridge Rd, Thornhill, L4J 1L5

Quebec

Coveo, 2800 St-Jean-Baptiste Ave (Suite 212), Quebec, G2E 6J5

NSB Group, 2800 Trans-Canada Hwy, Pointe-Claire, H9R 1B1

Computer Services, Data Processing, List & Subscription Fulfillment Companies (22)

THE DMA A LA MODE INC
3705 W Memorial Rd (Suite 402)
Oklahoma City, OK 73134-1507
Telephone: (405) 359-6587, Web Site:
    www.alamode.com
Chief Mktg Officer: Ellana Walker
Primary Market Served: Consumer

ACG/COMPUTECH DIRECT
2155 Stonington Ave (Suite 215)
Hoffman Estates, IL 60195-2058
Telephone: (847) 843-3200, FAX:
    (847) 843-8060, E-Mail: info@acg-
    computech-direct.com, Web Site:
    www.acg-computech-direct.com
Pres: Rick Botthof

**AIDC (AMERICAN
    INTERNATIONAL
    DISTRIBUTION CORP)**
50 Winter Sport Ln
Williston, VT 05495-0080
Telephone: (800) 678-2432, FAX:
    (802) 864-7626, E-Mail: jmacon@
    aidcvt.com, Web Site: www.aidcvt.
    com
Pres: Peter A. Miller
Opers Mgr: Michael Pelland
Chief Opers: Marilyn McConnell

**ARGI - AUTOMATED
    RESOURCES GROUP INC**
135 Chestnut Ridge Rd
Montvale, NJ 07645-1152
Telephone: (201) 391-1500, FAX:
    (201) 391-8357, Web Site: www.
    callargi.com
Pres & CEO: Raymond Butkus
Employees: 65
Founded: 1971

An Application Service Provider (ASP)
offering web enabled CRM solutions,
such as business intelligence, campaign
management, one-to-one marketing,
data-mining, subscription and product
fulfillment, and data select. Our database management solutions include
database design, data warehousing,
data cleansing, merge-purge, data enhancement and consumer namebank.

ACCESS INTERNATIONAL
1035 Cambridge St (Suite 2)
Cambridge, MA 02141-1154

Telephone: (617) 218+5000, (877)
    433-9097, FAX: (617) 494-8404,
    E-Mail: info@accessint.com, Web
    Site: www.accessint.com
Pres: Bill Wood
Employees: 70
Founded: 1978

**ACCOUNTMATE SOFTWARE
    CORP**
1445 Technology Ln (Suite A5)
Petaluma, CA 94954-7613
Telephone: (415) 883-8873, FAX:
    (415) 883-5863, E-Mail:
    information@accountmate.com, Web
    Site: www.accountmate.com
Pres: David Dierke
Dir, Prod Devel: Donna DeRose
Founded: 1984

THE DMA ACCUDIRECT RESPONSE
PO Box 10246
Portland, OR 97296-0246
Telephone: (503) 223-2076, Web Site:
    accdirectnw.com
Primary Market Served: Consumer

**ACCURATE MARKETING
    SYSTEMS**
122 Voorhis Ave
River Edge, NJ 07661-1522
Telephone: (201) 265-5198
VP: Barry Holmes

ACQUIREWEB INC
1065 E Hillsdale Blvd (Suite 310)
Foster City, CA 94404-1689
Telephone: (650) 212-2233, Web Site:
    www.acquireWEB.com
Pres: Albert Gadbut
Primary Market Served: Business

ACXIOM CORP
601 E 3rd St
Little Rock, AR 72201-1709
Telephone: (501) 342-1000, Web Site:
    www.acxiom.com
Co-Leader: Charles Morgan

ADOBE SYSTEMS INC
345 Park Ave (#W17-506)
San Jose, CA 95110-2704
Telephone: (408) 536-6000, (800) 833-
    6687, FAX: (408) 537-6000, Web
    Site: www.adobe.com

Pres & CEO: Shantanu Narayen
EVP & CFO: Mark Garrett
Dir Mktg Enterprise: Carl Steffens
Sr VP: Karen Cottle
Sr VP: Donna Morris
Conducts Business: Worldwide
Employees: 6,677
Primary Market Served: Consumer
Founded: 1982
Gross sales or billing: $2,575,000,000

Sell software through OEM's, retail &
via direct mail business-to-business.

ADVANCED CONCEPTS INC
8875 N 55th St (Suite 200)
Milwaukee, WI 53223-2311
Telephone: (414) 362-9640, FAX:
    (414) 362-9646, E-Mail: info@
    advanced-concepts.com, Web Site:
    www.advanced-concepts.com
Pres: Jeff Wohlfahrt
VP Opers: Mary A. Kunze

**ADVANCED SOFTWARE
    APPLICATIONS**
3117 Washington Pike
Bridgeville, PA 15017-1434
Telephone: (412) 220-9300, E-Mail:
    asa@asacorp.com, Web Site: www.
    asacorp.com
Pres: Bill Gossman
CMO: Ken Ramoutar

**AFFILIATED COMPUTER
    SERVICES INC (ACS)**
2828 N Haskell Ave
Dallas, TX 75204-2909
Telephone: (214) 841-6111, Web Site:
    www.acs-inc.com
Pres & CEO: Lynn Blodgett

AIRS INC
4080 Hwy 92
Douglasville, GA 30135-4404
Telephone: (770) 949-0133, FAX:
    (770) 949-2773, E-Mail: estacks@
    aol.com
Pres: Ed Stacks

THE DMA THE ALLANT GROUP
2056 Westings Ave (Suite 500)
Naperville, IL 60563-2485

Telephone: (800) 367-7311, FAX: (630) 355-3090, E-Mail: dirwin@ allantgroup.com, Web Site: www. allantgroup.com
EVP Sales & Mktg: Dave Irwin

THE DMA ALLIANT
301 Fields Ln Ste 8
Brewster, NY 10509-2654
Telephone: (845) 276-2600, Web Site: www.alliantdata.com
Pres & CEO: JoAnne Monfradi Dunn
Primary Market Served: Business

ALLTEL PUBLISHING CORP
Subs. of Alltel Corp
100 Executive Pkwy
Hudson, OH 44236-1630
Telephone: (330) 650-7100, FAX: (330) 650-7883, Web Site: www. alltel.com
Pres: Jerry Weaver

ALTERIAN
35 Wacker Dr (Suite 200)
Chicago, IL 60601-2104
Telephone: (312) 704-1700, Web Site: www.alterian.com
Brand & Field Mktg Mgr: Linda Vetter
Primary Market Served: Business & Consumer

ALVION LLC
2503 Del Prado Blvd (Suite 502)
Cape Coral, FL 33904
Telephone: (239) 574-8600, (877) 528-7800, FAX: (239) 574-8551, Web Site: www.alvion.com
CEO: Robert Sher

ANCHOR COMPUTER INC
1900 New Hwy
Farmingdale, NY 11735-1537
Telephone: (631) 293-6100, Web Site: www.anchorcomputer.com
Pres: Mark Schenker
Primary Market Served: Business & Consumer

ANCOR
aka Anchor Information Management
1911 Woodslee Dr
Troy, MI 48083-2236
Telephone: (248) 740-8866, (800) 229-3860, FAX: (248) 740-9025, Web Site: www.anchorinfo.com
Exec Dir Opers: Dave Bartkowiak

ANDSOR RESEARCH INC
40 Richview Rd (Suite 1501)
Etobicoke, ON, Canada M9A 5C1
Telephone: (416) 245-8073, FAX: (416) 240-8473
Pres: Andrei Sorin

THE DMA ANTHEM MARKETING
549 W Randolph St Ste 702
Chicago, IL 60661-1478
Telephone: (312) 441-0382
Pres: John Keenan
Primary Market Served: Business & Consumer

THE DMA APPLIED INFO GROUP
100 Market St
Kenilworth, NJ 07033-1722
Telephone: (908) 241-7007, Web Site: www.appliedinfogroup.com
Pres: Mitchell Rubin
Mgr HR: Frank A. Nasta

APTIMUS
199 Fremont St (Suite 1800)
San Francisco, CA 94105
Telephone: (415) 896-2123
Mktg: Tim Choate

ARROW COMPANIES, LLC
310 O'Connor Dr, PO Box 410
Elkhorn, WI 53121
Telephone: (262) 741-1660, FAX: (262) 723-6750, Web Site: www. arrowcompanies.com
Pres: Jerry Voors

ARTEMIS INTERNATIONAL SOLUTIONS CORP
401 Congress Ave Ste 2650
Austin, TX 78701-3708
Telephone: (512) 874-3030, (800) 477-6648, FAX: (512) 874-8900, Web Site: www.aisc.com
Pres & CEO: Randall Jacops

ARTFUL DRAGON PRESS INC
14108 Lake St Ext
Minnetonka, MN 55345-3019
Telephone: (612) 221-8908, Web Site: www.artfuldragon.com
Primary Market Served: Business & Consumer

AS SEEN ON PC NETWORK
25 Walls Dr (Suite 1-C)
Fairfield, CT 06824
Telephone: (203) 256-9897, FAX: (203) 256-9507, E-Mail: info@ asseenonpc.com, Web Site: www. asseenonpc.com
Pres: Jess F. Clarke Jr.

AUDIENCE IDENTIFICATION INC
PO Box 3305
Lisle, IL 60532-8305
Telephone: (630) 435-0460, FAX: (630) 435-0470, E-Mail: rmarsh@ audienceid.com

Pres: Ronald K. Marsh

AUGUST MARKETING
18522 SE Sea Oaks Ln
Tequesta, FL 33469-1409
Telephone: (561) 747-1325, Web Site: www.augustmktg.com
VP: Lorna Berry
Primary Market Served: Business & Consumer

AUTOMATION RESEARCH INC
1651 NW Professional Plaza
Columbus, OH 43220-3866
Telephone: (614) 538-1507
VP: Steven Kraft

BCC SOFTWARE INC
Subs. of Bowe Bell & Howell
75 Josons Dr
Rochester, NY 14623-3494
Telephone: (585) 272-9130, (800) 453-3130, FAX: (585) 340-8850, Web Site: www.bccsoftware.com
Pres & CEO: K. Jon Runstrom
VP Mktg: Mark Higgins
Conducts Business: U.S.
Employees: 65
Primary Market Served: Business
Advertising/Marketing Budget Related to Direct Marketing: 0-25%
Founded: 1978

BT AMERICAS
Subs. of BT Group
620 8th Ave (fl 45)
New York, NY 10018-1741
Telephone: (646) 487-7400, (800) 331-4568, FAX: (646) 487-3370, Web Site: www.btglobalservices.com
Pub Rels Mgr: Diane Noe

BWB MARKETING SERVICES
PO Box 802
Ankeny, IA 50021-0802
Telephone: (515) 986-1992, Web Site: www.bwbmarketing.com
Pres: Keith Snow
Primary Market Served: Business & Consumer

B2E DIRECT MARKETING INC
209 S Main St
Grimes, IA 50111-2192
Telephone: (515) 986-1992, Web Site: www.bwbmarketing.com
Pres: Keith Snow

BAMBOO CRICKET SERVICE
1415 Chaffee Dr (Unit 10)
Titusville, FL 32780

Telephone: (888) 634-7097, FAX: (646) 390-6313, E-Mail: info@bamboocricket.com, Web Site: www.bamboocricket.com
Pres: Barbara Westhorpe
VP Mktg: Chuck Mora
VP Sls: Jeff LeCates
VP Product Mngmt: Helen Ching
Conducts Business: Worldwide
Employees: 10
Primary Market Served: Business
Direct online sales
Direct Marketing ad budget:
Online: 100%
Founded: 2006
Gross sales or billing: $1,500,000

Online customer service.

BARCODING INC
2220 Boston St Fl 2
Baltimore, MD 21231-3058
Telephone: (410) 385-8532, (888) 860-SCAN, (888) 860-7226, FAX: (410) 385-8559, E-Mail: info@barcoding.com, Web Site: www.barcoding.com
Pres: Jay Steinmetz
Employees: 50
Founded: 1998
Gross sales or billing: $20,000,000

Designs, develops, implements and supports barcode and wireless technology for warehouse management, package tracking, lead and order automation. Our complete solutions include hardware, software and professional services. Contact us for a free solutions guide and consultation.

BITSTREAM INC
500 Nickerson Rd
Marlborough, MA 01752-4695
Telephone: (617) 497-6222, Web Site: www.bitstream.com
Dir Mktg: Katherine Reisz-Hanson

BLACKBAUD INC
2000 Daniel Island Dr
Charleston, SC 29492-7541
Telephone: (800) 443-9441
Dir Corp Rels: Rachel Hutchisson
Primary Market Served: Business & Consumer

BLUE HILL MARKETING SOLUTIONS INC
dba LiftEngine
1 Blue Hill Plz (Ste 1674)
Pearl River, NY 10965-6159
Telephone: (845) 627-6600, FAX: (845) 735-3985, Web Site: www.liftengine.com
Pres: Keith Huntoon
Gen Mgr: Joanne Petrone

Primary Market Served: Business & Consumer

BOWMAN & PARTNERS
1914 Spring Dr (Suite 101)
Roanoke, TX 76262-7416
Telephone: (817) 431-3441, Web Site: www.bowman-partners.com
Principal: Paul Bowman
Primary Market Served: Business & Consumer

BUREAU VAN DIJK
40 Wall St (fl 27)
New York, NY 10005-1364
Telephone: (212) 797-3550, Web Site: www.bvdinfo.com
Mktg Dir Americas: Leela Hauser
Primary Market Served: Business & Consumer

BUSINESS DEVELOPMENT SOLUTIONS INC
1022 Red Oak Dr
Cherry Hill, NJ 08003-2631
Telephone: (856) 787-1500, Web Site: www.bdsdatabase.com
Pres: Robert Bloom
Primary Market Served: Business & Consumer

BUSINESS OBJECTS
3410 Hillview Ave
Palo Alto, CA 94304-1395
Telephone: (408) 933-6000, (888) 788-9004, Web Site: www.businessobjects.com
CEO: John Schwartz

(C) SYSTEMS LLC
510 Thornall St (Suite 310)
Edison, NJ 08837-2207
Telephone: (732) 548-6100, Web Site: www.csystemsllc.net
Mng Dir: Lee Hornstein

CACI INTERNATIONAL INC
1100 N Glebe Rd
Arlington, VA 22201-4714
Telephone: (703) 841-7800, FAX: (703) 841-7882, Web Site: www.caci.com
Pres & CEO CACI: Paul M. Cofoni
Exec VP, PR & Bus Communs: Jody A. Brown
Publications Specialist: Michael M. Pino

CAM COMMERCE SOLUTIONS
17075 Newhope St Ste A
Fountain Valley, CA 92708-4299

Telephone: (714) 241-9241, Web Site: www.camcommerce.com
VP Sls & Mktg: Chester Ritchie

CDS GLOBAL
Subs. of The Hearst Corp
1901 Bell Ave
Des Moines, IA 50315-1099
Telephone: (515) 247-7500, FAX: (515) 246-6882, E-Mail: dluther@cdsfulfillment.com, Web Site: www.cdsfulfillment.com
VP Mktg: Dennis Luther

CRC DATA SYSTEMS
Affiliate of Opinion Access Corp
47-10 32nd Pl
Long Island City, NY 11101
Telephone: (718) 729-2622, E-Mail: jrafael@opinionaccess.com, Web Site: www.opinionaccess.com
VP Bus Devel: Lance Hoffman

THE DMA CRK COMPUTER SERVICES
16250 Northland Dr (Suite 12)
Southfield, MI 48075-5226
Telephone: (248) 569-3050, FAX: (248) 569-5259, E-Mail: information@crkusa.com, Web Site: www.crkusa.com
Pres: Dan Neagoe
Founded: 1974

Provider of Direct Marketing Computer Services, specializing in complete database design with CRM functionality and list rental maintenance with on-line counts, business and consumer merge/purge and magazine fulfillment. In house FASTforward, zip modeling and decease suppression, match back analysis, data enhancement, data append, postal presorts, inkjet tape creation and email marketing.

CTRAC INFORMATION SOLUTIONS
16855 Foltz Pkwy
Strongsville, OH 44149-5517
Telephone: (440) 572-1000, FAX: (440) 572-3330, E-Mail: ctrac@ctrac.com, Web Site: www.ctrac.com
Pres: Susan Williamson

CAMBEY & WEST INC
120 N Rte 9W
Congers, NY 10920-1729
Telephone: (845) 267-3006, FAX: (845) 267-3503, E-Mail: info@cambeywest.com, Web Site: www.cambeywest.com
Dir Bus Devel: Jane Giles

CENTER FOR INTERNATIONAL EARTH SCIENCE INFORMATION NETWORK
61 Rte 9 W
Palisades, NY 10964-1707
Telephone: (845) 365-8988, FAX: (845) 365-8922, E-Mail: ciesin. info@ciesin.columbia.edu, Web Site: www.ciesin.org
Dir: Robert S. Chen

CHRISTIAN RESOURCE MANAGEMENT
2322 N Batavia (Suite 108)
Orange, CA 92865-2000
Telephone: (714) 974-0754, FAX: (714) 974-7845, E-Mail: CRMOrange@aol.com, Web Site: www.crmorange.com
Pres: Craig Bryson

CISCO SYSTEMS INC
170 W Tasman Dr
San Jose, CA 95134-1700
Telephone: (408) 526-4000, (800) 553-NETS, FAX: (408) 526-4100, Web Site: www.cisco.com
Mktg Opers Mgr, Corp Mktg: Karin Poe

CITRIX SYSTEMS, INC
851 W Cypress Creek Rd
Fort Lauderdale, FL 33309-2040
Telephone: (954) 267-8427, Web Site: www.citrix.com
Primary Market Served: Business & Consumer

COGNITIVEDATA INC
Sub. of Merkle
500 President Clinton Ave (Suite 301)
Little Rock, AR 72201
Telephone: (501) 975-7580, (866) 243-7883, E-Mail: info@cognitivedata. com, Web Site: www.cognitivedata. com
Founder & CEO: Rod Ford
Primary Market Served: Business & Consumer

COLINEAR SYSTEMS
2650 Holcomb Bridge Rd (Suite 610)
Alpharetta, GA 30022-5343
Telephone: (770) 643-0000, (800) COLINEAR, FAX: (770) 643-0265, E-Mail: sales@colinear.com, Web Site: www.colinear.com
Pres: Lloyd Merriam

COLLECTIVE - THE AUDIENCE ENGINE
99 Park Ave (fl 5)
New York, NY 10016-1601

Telephone: (646) 380-2744
Primary Market Served: Consumer

COMMERCE REGISTER INC
190 Godwin Ave
Midland Park, NJ 07432-1841
Telephone: (201) 445-3000, FAX: (201) 445-5806, E-Mail: cri@ comreginc.com, Web Site: www. comreginc.com
VP: Frank J. Castellvi
Office Mgr: Debra Rader

COMMERCIAL DATA PROCESSING INC
30 Northover Pl
Red Bank, NJ 07701-6311
Telephone: (800) 242-3731, FAX: (973) 882-0387, E-Mail: vivieng@ dataprocess.com, Web Site: www. dataprocess.com
Owner: Tom Fahmie

COMMERCIALWARE INC
1800 W Park Dr (Suite 250)
Westboro, MA 01581-3960
Telephone: (508) 655-7500, FAX: (508) 647-9495, E-Mail: info@ micros-retail.com, Web Site: www. commercialware.com
Pres: Donald Askin

COMMUNICATION LOGISTICS, INC
2040 Jay Mar Rd
Plover, WI 54467-3257
Telephone: (715) 341-6180, FAX: (715) 341-7971, Web Site: www. comloginc.com
Pres Creative/Mktg Svcs: Sarah Straub
Primary Market Served: Business

COMPACT INFORMATION SYSTEMS INC
7120 185th Ave NE
Redmond, WA 98052-0575
Telephone: (425) 869-1379, Web Site: www.cisdirect.com
Owner: Pat Wiley

COMPITSS INC
1000 Business Center Dr (Suite 107)
Newbury Park, CA 91320-1237
Telephone: (805) 823-2286, Web Site: www.compitss.com
Pres: Al Lakshmanan

COMPLETE MAILING SERVICE
8 Dohme Ave
Toronto, ON, Canada M4B 1Y8

Telephone: (416) 755-7761, (888) 683-2501, FAX: (416) 755-8231, E-Mail: sales@completemailing.com, Web Site: www.completemailing.com

COMPLETE MAILING SOLUTIONS
217 12th St SW
Loveland, CO 80537
Telephone: (303) 761-0681, (888) 843-9937, FAX: (303) 761-7837, Web Site: www.comp-mail.com

COMPUTER BUSINESS SERVICES INC
205 W Forsyth St, PO Box A
Americus, GA 31709-3533
Telephone: (229) 924-4408, (866) 924-4408, FAX: (229) 924-3644, E-Mail: cdill@combusser.com, Web Site: www.combusser.com
VP & CEO: Bill Bennett
CIO: Chris Dill
Project Mgr: Crystal Mays
Conducts Business: U.S.
Employees: 30
Primary Market Served: Business
Advertising/Marketing Budget Related to Direct Marketing: 0-25%
Direct Marketing ad budget: $100,000
Telephone: 100%
Founded: 1974
Gross sales or billing: $5,000,000

COMPUTER SOLUTIONS INC
13701 SW 88th St Ste 306, Bldg H33
Miami, FL 33186-1309
Telephone: (305) 558-7000, FAX: (305) 557-0003, E-Mail: mail@ csiflorida.com, Web Site: www. csiflorida.com
VP: Ernie Smith

COMPUTERWORLD DATABASE DIV
Div. of Computer World Inc
1 Speen St
Framingham, MA 01701-4644
Telephone: (508) 879-0700, (800) 343-6474, FAX: (508) 875-4394, Web Site: www.computerworld.com
Pres: Matthew Sweeney

CONCLUSIVE MARKETING
6900 Northpark Blvd Ste G
Charlotte, NC 28216-1393
Telephone: (615) 261-7600, (800) 346-0073, FAX: (615) 843-7244, E-Mail: info@conclusivemarketing.com, Web Site: www.conclusivemarketing.com
Pres & CEO: D. Leyrer
Dir Sls LCU Div: Jim Drummond

CONCUR
18400 NE Union Hill Rd
Redmond, WA 98052-3332
Telephone: (425) 702-8808, Web Site:
www.concur.com
Sr Mgr Direct & Channel Mktg: Kathleen Connor

CONNEX INTERNATIONAL
50 Federal Rd
Danbury, CT 06810
Telephone: (800) 426-6639, FAX:
(203) 731-5425, E-Mail: marketing@
connexintl.com, Web Site: www.
connexintl.com
Mktg Mgr: Gail Teixeira

**CONTACT CENTER
COMPLIANCE**
350 E St (Suite 100)
Santa Rosa, CA 95404-4438
Telephone: (800) 308-0258, Web Site:
www.dnc.com
CEO: Michael Kovatch
Primary Market Served: Business &
Consumer

CONVIO INC
11501 Domain Dr (Suite 200)
Austin, TX 78758-3406
Telephone: (888) 528-9501, Web Site:
www.convio.com
Dir Mktg Commun: Jennifer Judkins

CORE TECHNOLOGIES
1320 Pearl St Ste 240
Boulder, CO 80302-5279
Telephone: (614) 231-3031, (866) 624-
5927, FAX: (303) 395-1474, E-Mail:
support@core-tech.com, Web Site:
www.mailware.com
CEO: Bruce Kowkabany
Primary Market Served: Consumer

COREMEDIA SYSTEMS INC
695 US Hwy 46 (Suite 403)
Fairfield, NJ 07004-1561
Telephone: (973) 276-0882, Web Site:
www.coremedia-systems.com
CEO: Glenn DeKraker
Primary Market Served: Business &
Consumer

**CORNERSTONE GROUP OF
COMPANIES**
20 Eglinton Ave W (4th fl)
Toronto, ON, Canada M4R 1K8
Telephone: (416) 932-9555, FAX:
(416) 932-9566, E-Mail: info@
cstonecanada.com, Web Site: www.
cstonecanada.com
Pres & CEO: Ossie Hinds
VP, Mktg: Susan Oliver
Conducts Business: U.S., Canada

Employees: 275
Primary Market Served: Business &
Consumer
Founded: 1987
Gross sales or billing: $25,000,000

Canadian supplier of information-based products & services: List brokerage, list management, list processing, data products, fundraising services, publishing services & marketing database services.

**CORNWELL DATA SERVICES
INC**
352 Evelyn St
Paramus, NJ 07652-2908
Telephone: (201) 261-1050, FAX:
(201) 261-7569, E-Mail: jpiretra@
cornwelldata.com, Web Site: www.
cornwelldata.com
Pres: Peter Cornwell
Gen Acct Mgr: Judy Piretra
Conducts Business: U.S.
Employees: 30
Catalog available online
Founded: 1967
Gross sales or billing: $2,000,000

CORPORATE EXPRESS
One Environmental Way
Broomfield, CO 80021
Telephone: (303) 664-2000, (888) 238-
6329, Web Site: www.cexp.com
Pres & CEO: Mark Hoffman

THE
DMA **CORPORATE GRAPHICS
DIRECT MARKETING
SOLUTIONS**
1170 Grey Fox Rd
Arden Hills, MN 55112-6908
Telephone: (651) 494-1740, Web Site:
www.cgids.com
Mktg Dir: Mark Wilkes
Primary Market Served: Business &
Consumer

COVALENT MARKETING
2021 S Ogden St
Denver, CO 80210-4134
Telephone: (303) 588-7754, Web Site:
www.covalentmarketing.com
Principal: Stanton Willins
Primary Market Served: Business

THE
DMA **COVEO**
2800 St-Jean-Baptiste Ave (Suite 212)
Quebec, PQ, Canada G2E 6J5
Telephone: (418) 263-1111, Web Site:
www.coveo.com
VP Mktg & Commun: Diane Berry

CREATECH MARKETING
180 Summit Ave (Suite 203)
Montvale, NJ 07645-1722
Telephone: (201) 326-3000, Web Site:
www.createchmarketing.com
Primary Market Served: Consumer

CREATIVE AUTOMATION
Division of VMark (parent company)
220 Fencl Ln
Hillside, IL 60162-2002
Telephone: (708) 449-2800, (800) 773-
1588, FAX: (708) 449-3282, E-Mail:
busmgr@cauto.com, Web Site: www.
cauto.com
Pres: Martin Kurpiel
Dir New Bus Devel & Corp Mktg:
Bob Rajan

CREDIT INDEX
25 6th Ave N
Saint Cloud, MN 56303-4729
Telephone: (973) 770-4007, FAX:
(973) 770-4006, Web Site: www.
ebureau.com
Exec VP: Mark Doman
Pres: Linda McKenna

**CROSS COUNTRY
COMPUTER CORP**
570 S Research Pl
Central Islip, NY 11722-4415
Telephone: (631) 231-4200, Web Site:
www.crosscountrycomputer.com
Pres: Thomas Berger
Primary Market Served: Business &
Consumer

CROWNPEAK
5880 W Jefferson Blvd (Suite G)
Los Angeles, CA 90016-3160
Telephone: (310) 841-5920, Web Site:
www.crownpeak.com
Dir Mktg: Christopher Bartik

**CUSTOMER ASSET
CONSULTING GROUP INC**
1870 N Roselle Rd (Suite 101)
Schaumburg, IL 60195-3100
Telephone: (847) 805-9800, Web Site:
www.cac-group.com
Pres: Bradley Rukstales

**THE CUSTOMER
CONNECTION INC**
621 S Andreasen Dr (Suite B)
Escondido, CA 92029-1904
Telephone: (760) 489-8339, (800) 477-
7166, FAX: (760) 489-1075, E-Mail:
judd@custcon.com, Web Site: www.
custcon.com
Pres: Judd Goldfedder

THE DMA **CUSTOMER PORTFOLIOS LLC**
306 Northern Ave
Boston, MA 02210-2324
Telephone: (617) 224-9501, Web Site:
www.customerportfolios.com
Mng Partner: Augie MacCurrach

CYBERDATA
20 Max Ave
Hicksville, NY 11801
Telephone: (516) 942-8000, FAX:
(516) 942-0800, E-Mail: info@
cyberdata.com, Web Site: www.
cyberdata.com
Pres: Ralph Potente

CYBERDEFENDER
617 W 7th St (Suite 401)
Los Angeles, CA 90017-3800
Telephone: (213) 689-8631x114, Web
Site: www.cyberdefender.com
CEO: Gary Guseinov

THE DMA **D&B**
3 Sylvan Way
Parsippany, NJ 07054-3821
Telephone: (973) 921-5500, Web Site:
www.dnb.com
Sr Dir Mktg: Tariq Sharif

D&B SALES AND MARKETING SOLUTIONS
460 Totten Pond Rd
Waltham, MA 02451-1908
Telephone: (781) 672-9200, (800) 590-
0065, FAX: (781) 672-9290, Web
Site: www.b2bsalesandmarketing.
com
Pres & CEO: Steven W. Alesio

D&D ASSOCIATES INC
PO Box 9150
Garden City, NY 11530-9150
Telephone: (516) 326-8800, (800) 554-
0347
Pres: Marvin Nagourney

DB MARKETING
550 Mamaroneck Ave.
Harrison, NY 10528
Telephone: (914) 698-2008
CEO: Darcy Bevelacqua
Primary Market Served: Business

DKP & ASSOCIATES, INC
7847 Lowell Ave (Suite 200)
Skokie, IL 60076-3535
Telephone: (847) 933-9808, E-Mail:
dpearlman@dkpassociates.com, Web
Site: www.dkpassociates.com
Pres: Deborah E. Pearlman
COO: Katherine J. Katner

DM DATA SOLUTIONS LLC
7508 Manigold Ct
Alexandria, VA 22315-3838
Telephone: (703) 415-6222, Web Site:
www.dmdatasolutions.com
Pres: Mike Thornsbury
Primary Market Served: Business

THE DMA **DMRA**
201 San Antonio Cir (Suite 280)
Mountain View, CA 94040-1256
Telephone: (650) 650-9988, Web Site:
www.dmrainc.com
CMO: Allen Dyon
Primary Market Served: Business

DMRS GROUP INC
304 Park Ave S (fl 11)
New York, NY 10010-4305
Telephone: (212) 590-2340, FAX:
(212) 590-2341, E-Mail:
bgrossman@dmrsgroup.com, Web
Site: www.dmrsgroup.com
Pres: Bernice Grossman

THE DATA BASE INC
1710 Hwy 35
Oakhurst, NJ 07755
Telephone: (732) 531-4600, FAX:
(732) 531-4798, E-Mail: don.
nissim@heritagedirectdm.com, Web
Site: www.heritagedirectdm.com
Owner/Proprietor: Donald Nissim

THE DMA **DATA DALLAS CORP**
1111 W Mockingbird Ln (Suite 300)
Dallas, TX 75247-5017
Telephone: (214) 638-2007, Web Site:
www.ddci.net
Mgr Direct Mktg Svcs: Ron Rocek

DATA DASH INC
3928 Delor St
Saint Louis, MO 63116
Telephone: (314) 832-5788, (800) 211-
5988, FAX: (314) 832-5775, E-Mail:
info@datadash.com, Web Site: www.
datadash.com
Pres: Sue Morton

THE DMA **DATA INTELLIGENCE GROUP**
PO Box 682063
Franklin, TN 37068-2063
Telephone: (615) 595-9591, Web Site:
www.wedigdata.com
Regulator/COO: Robert Cucullu

DATA MANAGEMENT & MARKETING SERVICES LLC
508 N Aster Ave
Broken Arrow, OK 74012-9446

Telephone: (918) 392-0500, Web Site:
www.dm-ms.net

THE DMA **DATA MANAGEMENT INC**
8300 Greensboro Dr (Suite 800)
Mc Lean, VA 22102-3661
Telephone: (703) 893-5627, (800) 334-
8331, FAX: (703) 356-1698, E-Mail:
info@data-management.com, Web
Site: www.data-management.com
CEO & Pres: Jim Strasbourger
Conducts Business: U.S.
Employees: 45
Primary Market Served: Business &
Consumer
Advertising/Marketing Budget Related
to Direct Marketing: 0-25%
Founded: 1961

Database management, merge/purge,
and compiled lists.

DATA PARTNERS INC
12857 Banyan Creek Dr
Fort Myers, FL 33908-3083
Telephone: (239) 267-8762, (866) 423-
1818, FAX: (239) 267-9043, E-Mail:
info@data-partners.com, Web Site:
www.datapartners.com
Pres: Brigid Berry
Sls & Mktg Dir, Co-Founder: Jody
Pelfrey
COO, House Counsel: Scott Martin
Conducts Business: U.S.
Employees: 21
Primary Market Served: Business
Indirect online sales
Founded: 2002
Gross sales or billing: $3,800,000

Customized data and data solutions in
direct marketing and collections
industries.

THE DMA **DATA SERVICES INC**
31516 Winterplace Pkwy
Salisbury, MD 21804-1882
Telephone: (410) 546-2206, (800) 432-
4066, FAX: (410) 546-2274, Web
Site: www.dataservicesinc.com
Dir Fin & Admin: Bernadette M.
Dowling
Pres & CEO: Jerry Messer
VP & Dir Mktg: Bridget Amabili

THE DMA **DATA SQUARE LLC**
396 Danbury Rd
Wilton, CT 06897
Telephone: (203) 964-9733, E-Mail:
info@datasquare.com, Web Site:
www.datasquare.com
CEO & Founder: Devyani Sadh
Exec VP: C Olivia Parr Rud
Chief Fin & Enterprise Svcs Officer:
Raj Kumar
Head Opers: Judith Walters

Primary Market Served: Business

DATA UNIVERSITY
6550 S 34th St
Lincoln, NE 68516-5454
Telephone: (402) 742-2179, (866) 328-2848, E-Mail: info@datauniversity.com, Web Site: www.datauniversity.org
Pres: Mark Graham

Database marketing.

THE DMA THE DATABASE CENTRE
11210 Waples Mill Rd (Suite 100)
Fairfax, VA 22030
Telephone: (703) 359-2400, Web Site: www.databasecentre.co.uk
Mng Dir: Kim Way
Primary Market Served: Business & Consumer

THE DMA DATABASE MARKETING SERVICES
PO Box 2995
Guaynabo, PR 00970-2995
Telephone: (787) 792-7005
Pres: Kenneth Sewell
Primary Market Served: Business & Consumer

THE DMA DATABRIDGE MARKETING SYSTEMS CORP
1 Hollow Wood Ln
Montvale, NJ 07645-1350
Telephone: (201) 664-3883, Web Site: www.Data-Bridge.org
Pres: Jim Frustieri
Primary Market Served: Business & Consumer

DATACRAFT INC
28 Kainehe St Ste A1
Kailua, HI 96734-6130
Telephone: (808) 263-5583, Web Site: www.dcraftinc.com
Pres: Steven Hinaga
Primary Market Served: Business & Consumer

THE DMA DATAMANN INC
PO Box 1930
Wilder, VT 05088-1930
Telephone: (802) 295-6600, (800) 451-4263, FAX: (802) 296-3623, Web Site: www.datamann.com
Pres: John Mann
CFO: Kathy Reagan

DATAMATICS TECHNOLOGIES
56 Middlesex Tpke (Suite 250)
Burlington, MA 01803-4973

Telephone: (781) 425-5240, FAX: (781) 425-5232, Web Site: www.datamaticstech.com
Vice Chmn & CEO: Rahul L. Kanodia

DATAMENTORS LLC
2319-104 Oak Myrtle Ln
Wesley Chapel, FL 33544
Telephone: (813) 960-7800, FAX: (813) 960-7811, E-Mail: 1bedgood@datamentors.com, Web Site: www.datamentors.com
Pres & CEO: Robert S. Orf
Admin Asst: Ambrosia Pounders
Sls & Mktg Coord: Larisa Bedgood

Offers a variety of software solutions designed to address the data quality and business intelligence issues of the marketplace.

DATASYSTEM SOLUTIONS INC
6310 Lamar Ave (Suite 200)
Overland Park, KS 66202-4284
Telephone: (913) 362-6969, FAX: (913) 362-6383, E-Mail: sales@mutipub.com, Web Site: www.datasystem.com
Pres: Gay Manning

DATRAN MEDIA
345 Hudson St Ste 500
New York, NY 10014-7402
Telephone: (212) 706-9781, Web Site: www.datranmedia.com
VP: Lana McGilvray
Primary Market Served: Business

DAYSTAR DATA GROUP INC
155 W Central Rd
Schaumburg, IL 60195-1945
Telephone: (847) 202-0100, FAX: (847) 202-0107, E-Mail: sales@daystardg.com, Web Site: www.daystardg.com
Pres: Jim Calhoun
VP: Phil Jewison
VP, Mktg: Mary Staples
Conducts Business: U.S.
Employees: 24
Primary Market Served: Consumer
Advertising/Marketing Budget Related to Direct Marketing: 0-25%
Founded: 1990

Daystar creates and delivers client-focused database marketing solutions. From marketing databases to metrics and analysis, from campaign management and execution to data processing and list services, Daystar combines technology-based solutions with practical direct marketing expertise to help you leverage data to make better marketing decisions faster.

DECISION SOFTWARE INC
6911 Old Landover Rd
Hyattsville, MD 20785-1503
Telephone: (301) 459-9000, FAX: (301) 459-3072, E-Mail: clientservices@dsoftware.biz, Web Site: www.dsoftware.biz
Pres: Jeff Fowler
Dir Client Svcs: Eli Black
Conducts Business: U.S.
Employees: 14
Primary Market Served: Business
Indirect online sales
Advertising/Marketing Budget Related to Direct Marketing: 0-25%
Founded: 1989

DSI provides database design & hosting services as well as campaign management software. Clients include BB & BC catalogers, insurance, manufacturing, fundraisers, retailers, energy & utility and publishers.

DEMOGRAPHIC RESEARCH CO
1552 Pennsylvania St
Denver, CO 80203
Telephone: (310) 766-5590, FAX: (303) 831-9181, Web Site: www.drcmodel.com
Pres & CEO: Richard P. Li

DIRECT ACCESS MARKETING SERVICES INC
6851 Jericho Tpke (Suite 245)
Syosset, NY 11791-4421
Telephone: (516) 364-2777, FAX: (516) 364-0644, E-Mail: info@daxcess.com, Web Site: www.daxcess.com
Pres: Thomas Saracco
VP, Sls & Mktg: Neil Mason

DIRECT DATA CAPTURE LTD
PO Box 589
Huntington Station, NY 11746-0458
Telephone: (631) 547-5500, FAX: (631) 547-6800, E-Mail: jan@datacapture.com, Web Site: www.datacapture.com
Pres: Jan A. Trevalyan

DIRECT LOGIC SOLUTIONS
4507 N Sterling Ave (Suite 402)
Peoria, IL 61615-3860
Telephone: (309) 688-5500, FAX: (309) 688-5502, E-Mail: nedbarrett@direct-logic.com, Web Site: www.direct-logic.com
Pres: Edward V. Barrett
CEO: Chris Cusack
VP, Client Analytics: Jeff Muckler

Conducts Business: U.S., Canada, Europe

Primary Market Served: Business & Consumer

Indirect online sales

Founded: 1999

Direct response consulting services.

DIRECT MARKETING AUDIT SYSTEMS

3159 Fee Fee Rd (Suite 221)
Bridgeton, MO 63044-3299
Telephone: (314) 739-7480, FAX: (314) 739-7284, Web Site: www. dmasinc.com
Pres: Dennis Hupp

DIRECTECH

aka DirecTECH Holding Co, Inc
33 W Second St (Suite 504)
Maysville, KY 41056
Telephone: (866) 550-5030, E-Mail: ceo@directech.com, Web Site: www. directech.com
Pres & CEO: Thomas Beaudreau

DIRECTSMILE LLC

300 Broadacres Dr (fl 4)
Bloomfield, NJ 07003-3153
Telephone: (973) 780-0018, Web Site: www.directsmile.com
VP: Mike Beard

DIREXXIS INC

250 1st Ave (Suite 102)
Needham, MA 02494-2847
Telephone: (781) 444-7900, Web Site: www.direxxismarketing.com
Pres: Steve Scruton
Primary Market Served: Business

THE DMA DOVETAIL

1221 W Mineral Ave (Suite 102)
Littleton, CO 80120-4544
Telephone: (303) 904-4771, FAX: (303) 904-4776, E-Mail: welcome@ dovetailnet.com, Web Site: www. dovetailnet.com
VP Bus Devel: Jeff Barela
Pres & CEO: Paul Vannett
Conducts Business: U.S., Canada
Employees: 12
Primary Market Served: Business
Advertising/Marketing Budget Related to Direct Marketing: 0-25%
Founded: 1995

Builds and manages marketing databases for business-to-consumer companies.

THE DMA DRAKE DIRECT

225 E 46th St (Penthouse D)
New York, NY 10017-2928
Telephone: (212) 759-1225, FAX: (212) 759-9756, E-Mail: Rhonda@ DrakeDirect.com, Web Site: www. drakedirect.com
Pres: Rhonda Knehans Drake
VP: Perry Drake

THE DMA DUNDEE INTERNET SERVICES INC

15000 Ostrander Rd
Azalia, MI 48110-9704
Telephone: (734) 529-5331, Web Site: mailing-list-services.com/dundee.net

DYDACOMP DEVELOPMENT CORP

9 Campus Dr Ste 1
Parsippany, NJ 07054-4412
Telephone: (973) 237-9415, (800) 858-3666, FAX: (973) 237-9043, E-Mail: sales@dydacomp.com, Web Site: www.dydacomp.com
Pres & Founder: David Kopp
CEO: John Healy

EASY ANALYTIC SOFTWARE INC

7359 196th St
Fresh Meadows, NY 11366-1810
Telephone: (718) 740-7930, Web Site: www.easidemographics.com
Pres: Robert Katz

EBUREAU LLC

25 6th Ave N
Saint Cloud, MN 56303-4729
Telephone: (320) 534-5000, Web Site: www.ebureau.com
Pres: Gordon Meyer

ECHO DATA

735 Fox Chase Ste 101, Highlands Corp Ctr
Coatesville, PA 19320-1897
Telephone: (610) 466-2100, (800) 511-3870, FAX: (610) 466-2110, E-Mail: sroberts@echodata.com, Web Site: www.echodata.com
Vice Chmn: Stephen H. Roberts

ELCOM INTERNATIONAL INC

Ten Oceana Way
Norwood, MA 02062
Telephone: (781) 440-3333, FAX: (781) 762-1540, Web Site: www. elcom.com
Chmn: Sean P. Lewis

ELLIOTT MARKETING GROUP INC

2281 Sidgefield Ln
Pittsburgh, PA 15241-2713

Telephone: (412) 831-1183
Pres: John Elliott

ELOQUA CORP

1921 Gallows Rd (Suite 250)
Vienna, VA 22182-3994
Telephone: (416) 864-0440, Web Site: www.eloqua.com
Primary Market Served: Consumer

EMAILVISION

545 5th Ave Rm 1000
New York, NY 10017-3633
Telephone: (212) 257-6018, Web Site: www.emailvision.com
Mktg Mgr: James Jankay

ENERTEX MARKETING

99 Madison Ave (10th fl)
New York, NY 10016-7419
Telephone: (212) 532-3115, FAX: (212) 532-1878, E-Mail: info@ enertexmarketing.com, Web Site: www.enertexmarketing.com
Mailing List Mgr: Jaime Sommella

ENTIERA

3515 Plymouth Blvd (Suite 205)
Minneapolis, MN 55447-1382
Telephone: (866) 387-4271, Web Site: www.entiera.com
CEO: Patrick O'Halloran
Primary Market Served: Consumer

EPIC MARKETING SOLUTIONS

6054 Quinpool Rd
Halifax, NS, Canada B3L 1A1
Telephone: (902) 455-5100, Web Site: www.epicmarketing.ca
Pres: Ash Chugh
Primary Market Served: Business

THE DMA EPSILON

4401 Regent Blvd
Irving, TX 75063-2404
Telephone: (972) 582-9600, (800) 309-0505, FAX: (972) 582-9700, E-Mail: info@epsilon.com, Web Site: www. epsilon.com
CEO: Bryan Kennedy
Employees: 700
Gross sales or billing: $50,000,000

EQUIFAX DATABASE MARKETING

Subs. of Equifax
500 Edgewater Dr (Suite 525)
Wakefield, MA 01880
Telephone: (781) 246-0040, (800) 660-5125, FAX: (781) 246-3720, E-Mail: monica.baker@equifax.com
Senior VP: Thomas McGinley

THE DMA ESRI
380 New York St
Redlands, CA 92373-8118
Telephone: (909) 793-2853, Web Site:
www.esri.com
Bus Solutions Mgr: Simon Thompson

FG COMPANIES
901 Twelve Oaks Center Dr Ste 934
Wayzata, MN 55391-4721
Telephone: (952) 540-4901, Web Site:
www.fgcompanies.com
Mng Dir: Mark Van Ert
Primary Market Served: Business

THE DMA FICO
901 Marquette Ave (Suite 3200)
Minneapolis, MN 55402-3232
Telephone: (651) 486-1870
Sr Dir: Scott Blommer

FAIR ISAAC CORP
901 Marquette Ave (Suite 3200)
Minneapolis, MN 55402
Telephone: (612) 758-5200, E-Mail:
info@fairisaac.com, Web Site: www.
fairisaac.com
VP & Chief Mktg Officer: Eric J. Educate

**FAIRFIELD MARKETING
GROUP INC**
Div. of FMG Inc
830 Sport Hill Rd
Easton, CT 06612-1241
Telephone: (203) 261-5585 X205,
(203) 261-5568, FAX: (203) 261-
0884, E-Mail: ed@
fairfieldmarketing.com, Web Site:
www.fairfieldmarketing.com
Pres: Edward Washchilla Jr.

THE FIDELIS GROUP INC
223 Gates Rd (Unit A)
Little Ferry, NJ 07643-1900
Telephone: (410) 721-3450, Web Site:
www.thefidelisgroup.net
Pres/ CEO: Livleen Singh
Primary Market Served: Business &
Consumer

THE DMA FIFTH GEAR
9100 Purdue Rd (Suite 400)
Indianapolis, IN 46268-1180
Telephone: (317) 631-0907, Web Site:
www.sigma-micro.com
Primary Market Served: Business &
Consumer

THE DMA FILEMAKER INC
5201 Patrick Henry
Santa Clara, CA 95054-1164
Telephone: (408) 987-7347, Web Site:
www.filemaker.com

VP Legal & HR: John Pinheiro

**FIRST WAVE
TECHNOLOGIES**
7000 Central Pkwy NE (Suite 330)
Atlanta, GA 30328-4589
Telephone: (770) 431-1200, FAX:
(770) 431-1201

FRESHADDRESS INC
36 Crafts St
Newton, MA 02458-1249
Telephone: (617) 965-4500, (800) 321-
3009, FAX: (617) 965-4551, Web
Site: www.freshaddress.com
CEO: Bill Kaplan
Conducts Business: U.S.
Employees: 25
Primary Market Served: Business
Advertising/Marketing Budget Related
to Direct Marketing: 0-25%
Founded: 1999

Provides services to help companies
build and update their e-mail address
databases and manage, monitor, and
improve their e-mail deliverability.

**FUJITSU COMPUTER
SYSTEMS**
1250 E Arques Ave MS 122
Sunnyvale, CA 94085-3470
Telephone: (408) 746-6000, (800) 538-
8460, FAX: (408) 992-2674, E-Mail:
solutions@us.fujitsu.com, Web Site:
www.fujitsu.com
Sr VP Sls & Mktg: Dennis Mull

FULCRUM
70 W 40th St (fl 10)
New York, NY 10018-2621
Telephone: (888) 245-9450
CEO: David King

**GMC SOFTWARE
TECHNOLOGY INC**
529 Main St (Suite 205)
Charlestown, MA 02129-1121
Telephone: (617) 712-1200, Web Site:
www.gmc.net
Primary Market Served: Business

GALVIN ASSOCIATES INC
PO Box 700
Marstons Mills, MA 02648-0700
Telephone: (508) 420-8100, FAX:
(508) 420-1973, E-Mail: info-1@
galvinassociates.com, Web Site:
www.galvinassociates.com
Pres: Kevin Galvin

GATES MARKETING
3909 Oakcliff Industrial Ct
Atlanta, GA 30340-3408

Telephone: (770) 455-9662, FAX:
(770) 455-8785
Pres: Robert Gates

GEOSCAPE
2100 W Flagler St (fl 2)
Miami, FL 33135-1619
Telephone: (305) 860-1460, Web Site:
www.geoscape.com
CEO: Cesar Melgoza

**GLOBAL DEMAND
PUBLISHING INC**
101 B Middle St (Suite 101 B)
Jacksonville, NC 28546-6798
Telephone: (910) 937-0562, FAX:
(910) 455-1937, E-Mail:
globaldemandpublishing@yahoo.com
Mktg: Louann Driver

THE DMA GLOBAL INTELLISYSTEMS
1153 Bergen Pkwy (#45)
Evergreen, CO 80439-9501
Telephone: (800) 707-7074, Web Site:
www.gliq.com
CEO/Founder: John Brogan
Primary Market Served: Business &
Consumer

**GLOBAL TURNKEY SYSTEMS
INC**
2001 US Highway 46 Ste 203
Parsippany, NJ 07054-1315
Telephone: (973) 331-1010, FAX:
(973) 331-0042, E-Mail: sales@
gtsystems.com, Web Site: www.
gtsystems.com
Pres: Al Alteslane

GLOBAL WARE SOLUTIONS
1089 Mills Way
Redwood City, CA 94063-3119
Telephone: (650) 363-2200, (800) 469-
7500, FAX: (650) 599-3280, E-Mail:
sales@gwsmail.com, Web Site:
www.globalwaresolutions.com
CEO: David Beatson

**THE DMA GLOBAL-Z INTERNATIONAL
INC**
395 Shields Dr
Bennington, VT 05201-9810
Telephone: (802) 445-1011, FAX:
(802) 445-1016, E-Mail: info@
globalz.com, Web Site: www.globalz.
com
VP Opers: Dimitri Garder

THE DMA GRAYHAIR SOFTWARE
124 Gaither Dr (Suite 160)
Mount Laurel, NJ 08054-1719
Web Site: www.grayhairsoftware.com
Primary Market Served: Consumer

GROUP 1 SOFTWARE INC
Subs. of Pitney Bowes
4200 Parliament Pl (Suite 600)
Lanham, MD 20706-1844
Telephone: (301) 731-2300, (888) 413-6763, FAX: (301) 731-0360, E-Mail: info@g1.com, Web Site: www.g1.com
Pres: Christopher Baker

HARTE-HANKS
THE DMA
2800 Wells Branch Pkwy
Austin, TX 78728-6762
Telephone: (512) 434-1100, (800) 456-9748, FAX: (512) 244-9222, Web Site: www.harte-hanks.com
VP, Bus Devel: Kevin Kerner
Pres & Corp Officer: Gary Skidmore

HARTLEY DATA SERVICE INC
1807 Glenview Rd (Suite 100)
Glenview, IL 60025-2944
Telephone: (847) 724-9280, (800) 433-2796, FAX: (847) 729-2199, Web Site: www.hartleydata.com
Pres: Dan Koolish

HERITAGE DIRECT
1710 Hwy 35
Oakhurst, NJ 07755-2910
Telephone: (732) 531-2212, FAX: (732) 531-4798, Web Site: www.actionmarkets.com
Pres: Donald Nissim

HITACHI DATA SYSTEMS
2020 Main St (Suite 1120)
Irvine, CA 92614-8234
Telephone: (408) 970-1000, Web Site: www.hds.com
Mktg Dir Americas: Clemencia Fonseca

HOOVER'S
5800 Airport Blvd
Austin, TX 78752-4204
Telephone: (512) 374-4500
Mktg Mgr: Allen Shukers

THE HYIAD GROUP
400 Garden City Plz (Suite 403)
Garden City, NY 11530-3336
Telephone: (516) 433-3800, FAX: (516) 822-6670, Web Site: www.thehyiadgroup.com
Pres: Richard Levinson
VP & Comptroller: Barbara Cheny
VP, Client Svcs: Janine Levinson
VP, HR: Tom Monks
VP, Sls: Tom Clarken
Conducts Business: U.S.
Employees: 300
Primary Market Served: Business

Founded: 1969

THE IDT GROUP
1650 Market St Fl 36
Philadelphia, PA 19103-7334
Telephone: (215) 487-4420, FAX: (215) 487-3110, Web Site: www.idthospitality.com
Pres: Harry W. Rivkin

INFOLURE
1705 W Parkside Ln
Phoenix, AZ 85027-1333
Telephone: (602) 308-6700, FAX: (602) 308-6801, E-Mail: glenn.gottfried@infolure.com, Web Site: www.infolure.com
CEO: Glenn Gottfried
Exec VP & CFO: Cynthia Hanson
Employees: 25
Primary Market Served: Business
Advertising/Marketing Budget Related to Direct Marketing: 76-100%
Direct Marketing ad budget: $100,000
Direct Mail: 10%
Magazines: 90%
Founded: 1992
Gross sales or billing: $10,000,000

INFOR
13560 Morris Rd (Suite 4100)
Alpharetta, GA 30004
Telephone: (864) 422-5310, Web Site: www.infor.com
Primary Market Served: Business & Consumer

INFORMATION COMMAND INC
5700 N Sheridan Rd (#904)
Chicago, IL 60660-4740
Telephone: (312) 245-1111, (800) 376-6654, FAX: (312) 245-1128, E-Mail: gon@phonebiz2000.com, Web Site: www.info2u.com
VP, Mktg: Donald Young

THE INFORMATION ENGINE
THE DMA
9105 Hammock Edge Pl
Bradenton, FL 34212-3254
Telephone: (904) 645-6000, Web Site: www.informationeng.com
Primary Market Served: Business & Consumer

INFORMATION SOURCES INC
Also dba "TecTrends"
2175 Cactus Ct Apt 1
Walnut Creek, CA 94595-2531
Telephone: (510) 525-6220, FAX: (510) 525-1568, Web Site: www.tectrends.com
Pres: Ruth Koolish

INFORONICS LLC
25 Porter Rd Ste 4
Littleton, MA 01460-1434
Telephone: (978) 698-7400, FAX: (978) 698-7500, E-Mail: info@inforonics.com, Web Site: www.inforonics.com
Pres & CEO: Bruce Buckland

INNOVATIVE SYSTEMS INC
790 Holiday Dr
Pittsburgh, PA 15220-8127
Telephone: (412) 937-9300, (800) 622-6390, FAX: (412) 937-9309, E-Mail: info@innovativesystems.com, Web Site: www.innovativesystems.com
Pres & CEO: Robert J. Colonna
VP Mktg: Karin O'Sullivan

INPUT SYSTEMS INC
16308 Orange Ave
Paramount, CA 90723
Telephone: (562) 634-1170, (800) 327-9337, FAX: (562) 634-0993, E-Mail: info@sweepssoftware.com, Web Site: www.sweepssoftware.com
Pres: Harley D. Hancock

INQUIRY INTELLIGENCE SYSTEMS
18 N Central Dr
O'Fallon, MO 63366
Telephone: (636) 281-2129, (800) 467-2329, FAX: (636) 281-1517, E-Mail: sales@iqsalespro.com, Web Site: www.inquiry-tracking.com
Mgr: Janice Crawford

INSIGHT OUT OF CHAOS
THE DMA
220 E 23rd St (Suite 600)
New York, NY 10010-4658
Telephone: (212) 935-0044, Web Site: www.iooc.com
Pres: Spencer Hapoienu

INTEGRATED BUSINESS SERVICES INC
736 N Western Ave (# 125)
Lake Forest, IL 60045-1820
Telephone: (847) 735-1690, Web Site: www.medbase200.com
Pres & CEO: Samuel Tartamella

INTEGRATED MARKETING TECHNOLOGY INC
2269 Chestnut St (#992)
San Francisco, CA 94123-2600
Telephone: (415) 699-2280, FAX: (917) 591-5333, E-Mail: information@imtnetwork.com, Web Site: www.imtnetwork.com
Pres & CEO: James Tucker
COO: Sandy Dotson
VP Acct Mngmt: Therese Lodewick

Conducts Business: Worldwide
Employees: 15
Primary Market Served: Business
Indirect online sales
Advertising/Marketing Budget Related
 to Direct Marketing: 0-25%
Direct Marketing ad budget:
Direct Mail: 20%
Online: 80%
Founded: 1993
Gross sales or billing: $10,000,000

An outsourced marketing database
provider. Specializes in building, housing and maintaining marketing data
and performing critical marketing
analysis.

THE DMA INTELIUS INC
500 108th Ave (fl 22)
Bellevue, WA 98004-5500
Telephone: (425) 974-6100, Web Site:
 www.intelius.com

INTELLIDYN CORP
175 Derby St (Suite 40)
Hingham, MA 02043-4053
Telephone: (781) 741-5503, (866) 773-
 5756, FAX: (631) 390-0458, E-Mail:
 kmf@intellidyn.com, Web Site:
 www.intellidyn.com
Pres & CEO: Peter E. Harvey
Acct List Mgr: Veronica Egan
Admin: Kathie Fleischer
Employees: 24
Primary Market Served: Business
Catalog available online
Direct online sales
Advertising/Marketing Budget Related
 to Direct Marketing: 0-25%
Founded: 1998

Data Integration/warehousing, analytic,
strategic planning, database marketing
& targeted list sales sold to Fortune
100 companies such as Chase, AOL,
and Household Finance.

THE DMA INTERACTIVE MARKETING SOLUTIONS
777 Summer St (Suite 502)
Stamford, CT 06901-1042
Telephone: (203) 653-2746
Pres: Frank Rigano
Primary Market Served: Business &
 Consumer

THE DMA INTERNATIONAL DATA MANAGEMENT - A DMH MARKETING PARTNERS CO
490 White Pond Dr
Akron, OH 44320-1122
Telephone: (330) 869-8500, Web Site:
 www.idmi.com
Exec VP: Christopher Moore

Primary Market Served: Business &
 Consumer

THE DMA IPACESETTERS
135 Chestnut Ridge Rd
Montvale, NJ 07645-1152
Telephone: (201) 391-1500, Web Site:
 www.ipacesetters.com
Primary Market Served: Consumer

IPSWITCH INC
10 Maguire Rd (Suite 220)
Lexington, MA 02421-3120
Telephone: (781) 676-5700, Web Site:
 www.whatsupgold.com

ISLAND PACIFIC INC
Div. of Synaro
17310 Red Hill Ave Ste 320
Irvine, CA 92614-5600
Telephone: (303) 754-4700, (800) 569-
 1122, Web Site: www.
 islandpacific.com
VP Mktg: Jeffrey Busch

JDA SOFTWARE GROUP INC
14400 N 87th St
Scottsdale, AZ 85260-3649
Telephone: (480) 308-3000, (800) 479-
 7382, FAX: (480) 308-3001, Web
 Site: www.jda.com
Dir, Pres & CEO: Hamish Brewer
Primary Market Served: Business

JEPPESEN
55 Inverness Dr E
Englewood, CO 80112-5412
Telephone: (303) 799-9090, Web Site:
 www.jeppesen.com
Mgr Aviation Mktg: Rhonda Larance
Primary Market Served: Consumer

THE DMA KBM GROUP
2050 N Greenville Ave
Richardson, TX 75082-4322
Telephone: (972) 664-3600, FAX:
 (972) 664-3656, E-Mail: info@
 knowledgebasemarketing.com, Web
 Site: www.kbm1.com
CEO: Gary Laben
VP Mktg Commun: Mary Wall

KXEN
201 Mission St (Suite 1950)
San Francisco, CA 94105-1880
Telephone: (415) 904-4160, Web Site:
 www.kxen.com
Mktg Mgr: Michele Moussavi

KABLE FULFILLMENT SERVICES
Kable News Co Inc
16 S Wesley Ave

Mount Morris, IL 61054-1473
Telephone: (815) 734-4151, FAX:
 (815) 734-5228
VP Sls & Mktg: Karly Becker

WALTER KARL INC
Div. of Donnelley Marketing Company
2 Blue Hill Plz Ste 1662
Pearl River, NY 10965-3115
Telephone: (845) 620-0700, FAX:
 (845) 620-1885, E-Mail: info@
 walterkarl.infousa.com, Web Site:
 www.walterkarl.com
Pres: Joann Kropp
VP: Rob Fitzgerald
Creative Dir: Eric Francais
VP: Rosalie Garcia
VP: Kathy Elter
Employees: 100
Founded: 1955
Gross sales or billing: $22,000,000

Walter Karl, the industry's leading direct and interactive marketing firm, is
the "marketing partner" of over 500
management and brokerage clients in
all B2B and consumer areas. Our marketing power is derived from our talented and experienced professionals
who provide large company services
with individual attention and
commitment.

KING COMPUTER SERVICES INC
PO Box 1590
Las Cruces, NM 88004-1590
Telephone: (818) 951-5240, FAX:
 (818) 353-1278, E-Mail:
 kingsoftware@aol.com, Web Site:
 www.kingcomputerservices.com
Pres: Morrison J. Budlong

L-COM INC
45 Beechwood Dr
Andover, MA 01845-1092
Telephone: (978) 682-6936, Web Site:
 www.L-com.com
Dir Mktg: Mary Ann Kleinfelter

THE DMA LSSIDATA
Subs. of VoltDelta
1 Sentry Pkwy (Suite 1000)
Blue Bell, PA 19422-2310
Telephone: (610) 825-7720, (800) 210-
 9021, E-Mail: info@lssi.net, Web
 Site: www.dataserve.info
VP, Sls: Kevin O'Connell
Exec Dir Mktg: Steve Chirokas
Conducts Business: Worldwide
Primary Market Served: Business &
 Consumer
Founded: 1995

Directory assistance.

LATIN FORCE GROUP LLC
2100 W Flagler St
Miami, FL 33145
Telephone: (305) 860-1460, FAX:
(305) 860-6161, Web Site: www.
latinforce.com
Pres: Cesar M. Melgoza

LEWIS DIRECT
325 E Oliver St
Baltimore, MD 21202-2948
Telephone: (410) 539-5100, FAX:
(410) 539-4700
Exec VP: James G. Dickman

THE DMA LEXINET CORP
701 N Union St
Council Grove, KS 66846-9358
Telephone: (620) 767-7000
Pres: Lisa Boyer
Primary Market Served: Business &
Consumer

LISSAN COMPUTING CO INC
25 Beaver Brook Rd
Ridgefield, CT 06877-1001
Telephone: (203) 431-8755, FAX:
(203) 431-3302, E-Mail: info@
lissan.com, Web Site: www.lissan.
com
Pres: Richard Josephs

LOGICNOLOGY INC
720 International Pkwy
Sunrise, FL 33325-6219
Telephone: (954) 851-1200, FAX:
(954) 846-8552
Pres: Terry Jukes

LORTON DATA INC
2 Pine Tree Dr (Suite 302)
Arden Hills, MN 55112-3715
Telephone: (651) 203-8200, FAX:
(612) 362-0299, Web Site: www.
lortondata.com
CEO: Tony Evans
Pres: Lori Evans
Dir Sls & Mktg: Pamela Corbeille-
Lepel
Mktg Comm Mgr: Trudy Weiss
Conducts Business: U.S.
Employees: 20
Primary Market Served: Business
Direct online sales
Direct Marketing ad budget:
Direct Mail: 100%
Founded: 1989
Gross sales or billing: $2,500,000

Database services to the direct marketing industry to help businesses improve their ROI of their direct marketing dollars.

THE DMA LOTAME SOLUTIONS
8850 Stanford Blvd (Suite 2000)
Columbia, MD 21045-4726
Telephone: (410) 379-2195, Web Site:
www.lotame.com

THE DMA LOYALTYONE
438 University Ave (Suite 600)
Toronto, ON, Canada M5G 2L1
Telephone: (416) 228-6500, Web Site:
www.loyalty.com; www.airmiles.ca
Assoc Dir: Susan Park
Assoc Mgr Brand & Comm: Tara Win-
ter

A global provider of loyalty strategy,
loyalty programs, customer analytics
and relationship marketing with 1400
associates across North America.

THE DMA MBS
265 Broadhollow Rd Ste 400
Melville, NY 11747-4833
Telephone: (631) 851-5000, Web Site:
www.mbsinsight.com
Chief Client Officer: Andrea Misk-
ovsky
Primary Market Served: Business &
Consumer

MDF SYSTEMS
780 James P Casey Rd
Bristol, CT 06010-8537
Telephone: (860) 584-4750, FAX:
(860) 584-4759, Web Site: www.
mdfsystems.com
VP Opers: Joseph Cardello
VP Sls & Tech: Edward Burke

MESA
39 N Bayles Ave
Port Washington, NY 11050-2930
Telephone: (516) 767-6720, Web Site:
www.mesalliance.org/
Dir Devel: Guy Finley
Primary Market Served: Business &
Consumer

Provides information resources to entertainment technology professionals

**THE DMA MLS DATA MANAGEMENT
SOLUTIONS**
6115 Camp Bowie Blvd (Suite 200)
Fort Worth, TX 76116-5500
Telephone: (817) 804-6900, FAX:
(817) 804-6999, Web Site: www.
mlsc.com
Pres & COO: John Kirkland
Mktg Mgr: Manda Bilby
Founded: 1986

A member company as mailing list
systems. At MLS, we help you collect,
integrate, organize, store and interpret
the data your business generates. We
specialize in acquisition marketing,
data quality, data warehouseing and
business intelligence solutions.

THE DMA MMI DIRECT
7160 Columbia Gateway Dr (Suite
300)
Columbia, MD 21046-2134
Telephone: (410) 561-1500, FAX:
(410) 561-0805, Web Site: www.
mmidirect.com
Pres: Charles Dashner
VP Sls & Mktg: John Bell

THE DMA MSC
6200 Canoga Ave (Suite 102)
Woodland Hills, CA 91367-2429
Telephone: (818) 346-1600, FAX:
(818) 712-0122, Web Site: www.
mscnet.com
Pres & Chief Mktg Officer: Kevin
Blayne

MAC DIRECT
185 Discovery Drive
Colmar, PA 18915
Telephone: (215) 822-5775, (800) 278-
1154, FAX: (215) 822-7977, E-Mail:
info@macdirect.com, Web Site:
www.macdirect.com
Dir Sls: Brad Currie

MAGENTO
10441 Jefferson Blvd (Suite 200)
Culver City, CA 90232-3512
Telephone: (310) 367-5334, Web Site:
www.magento.com

**MAIL MOVERS & MAILING
SERVICES**
325 S 69th St
Upper Darby, PA 19082
Telephone: (610) 888-6969, (610) 734-
1220, FAX: (610) 734-1200, E-Mail:
mailmovers@rcn.com, Web Site:
www.mailmoversandmore.com
Pres: Gaile La Bar

MAILER'S SOFTWARE
Div. of Melissa Data Co
22382 Avenida Empresa
Rancho Santa Margarita, CA 92688-
2112
Telephone: (949) 858-3000, (800) 635-
4772, FAX: (949) 589-5211, Web
Site: www.mailerssoftware.com
Principal: Ray Melissa

MARCO DATA SERVICE
12537 Petermoore Ln
De Soto, MO 63020-4760
Telephone: (636) 337-3109, FAX:
(636) 586-1938
Owner: Barbara Marco

MARKETERNET LLC
233 S Wacker Dr (Suite 1800), Sears
Tower
Chicago, IL 60606-6462
Telephone: (312) 775-9320, (888) 443-
3684, FAX: (312) 775-9328, E-Mail:
info@marketernet.com, Web Site:
www.marketernet.com
Pres: Richard Scolio
COO: Tim Hunnewell
CFO: Jim Mackey

MARKETING INFORMATION NETWORK
120 N Bryant Ave (Suite A1)
Edmond, OK 73034
Telephone: (405) 516-1215, FAX:
(405) 516-1230, Web Site: www.
minokc.com
Pres: Scott R. Chilcutt

MARKETING1BY1 LLC
3877 Fairfax Ridge Rd Ste 200N
Fairfax, VA 22030-0977
Telephone: (703) 934-6020, Web Site:
marketing1by1.com
CEO: Keith Wardell

MARKETLEVERAGE
1515 International Pkwy Ste 2013
Lake Mary, FL 32746-7635
Telephone: (407) 805-8800, Web Site:
www.precisionplaymedia.com
CEO: Michael Jenkins

THE DMA MARKETNET SERVICES LLC
14998 Cleveland St (Suite E)
Spring Lake, MI 49456-8993
Telephone: (616) 847-7992, Web Site:
www.marketnet1.com
Gen Partner: J. T. McDonald

THE DMA MELISSA DATA CORP
22382 Avenida Empresa
Rancho Santa Margarita, CA 92688-
2112
Telephone: (949) 589-5200, (800) 800-
6245, FAX: (949) 589-5211, E-Mail:
sales@melissadata.com, Web Site:
www.melissadata.com
Pres: Raymond Melissa
VP Sls & Mktg: Gary Van Rockel
Conducts Business: U.S., Canada
Employees: 75
Primary Market Served: Business
Catalog available online
Direct online sales

Founded: 1985
Provides mailing software, databases,
programming tools, business and consumer lists, data enhancement and hygiene services.

MERCURY COMMERCE INC
1100 Shames Dr (Suite 200)
Westbury, NY 11590
Telephone: (212) 307-7001, FAX:
(646) 219-3982, E-Mail: contact@
mercury-commerce.com, Web Site:
www.mercury-commerce.com
Pres: Jeff Eisenberg
Conducts Business: U.S.
Primary Market Served: Business
Catalog available online
Indirect online sales
Advertising/Marketing Budget Related
to Direct Marketing: 0-25%
Direct Marketing ad budget:
Direct Mail: 97%
Newspapers: 3%
Founded: 1999

THE DMA MERKLE INC
7001 Columbia Gateway Dr
Columbia, MD 21046-2289
Telephone: (443) 542-4000, (877)
9MERKLE, Web Site: www.
merkleinc.com
Pres & CEO: David Williams
VP Mktg: Mike Savage
Sr Creative Dir: Bob Ball
Pres Response Svcs: Bill Sayre
Employees: 785
Gross sales or billing: $27,000,000

A database marketing agency.

THE DMA MICROSOFT CORP
1 Microsoft Way
Redmond, WA 98052-8300
Telephone: (425) 882-8080, FAX:
(425) 936-7329, Web Site: www.
microsoft.com
VP, Corp Mktg: Mich Mathews
Sr Privacy Strategist: Jennifer Garone

MILLIONS BY MARKETING INC
88 E Main St (Suite 411)
Mendham, NJ 07945-1832
Telephone: (973) 222-0011, Web Site:
www.millionsbymarketing.com
CEO: Greg Morris

THE DMA MINDFIREINC
30 Corporate Park (Suite 301)
Irvine, CA 92606-5133
Telephone: (949) 474-4418w, Web
Site: www.mindfireinc.com
Web Mktg Specialist: Mikkle Bringard
Primary Market Served: Consumer

MYRIAD SYSTEMS INC
2627 E-I-44 Service Rd
Oklahoma City, OK 73111-8302
Telephone: (405) 478-9000, (866) 505-
1730, FAX: (405) 478-8315, Web
Site: www.myriadsystems.com
Pres: Charles Riney

NSB GROUP
2800 Trans-Canada Hwy
Pointe-Claire, PQ, Canada H9R 1B1
Telephone: (514) 426-0822, E-Mail:
infona@nsbgroup.com, Web Site:
www.nsbgroup.com
CEO: David Henning

THE DMA NEAT CO
1601 Market St (Suite 3500)
Philadelphia, PA 19103
Telephone: (866) 632-8732, Web Site:
neatco.com
Primary Market Served: Consumer

THE DMA NEOLANE
300-334 Washington St, 1 Gateway Ctr
(Suite 709)
Newton, MA 02458-2804
Telephone: (617) 467-6760, Web Site:
www.neolane.com
Sr Dir Mktg: Kristin Hambleton

THE DMA NETPROSPEX INC
300 3rd Ave # 2
Waltham, MA 02451-7525
Telephone: (888) 826-4877, E-Mail:
sales@netprospex.com, Web Site:
www.netprospex.com
CEO: Gary Halliwell
Primary Market Served: Business &
Consumer
Founded: 2006

THE DMA NEXTMARK INC
2 Buck Rd Ste 8
Hanover, NH 03755-2715
Telephone: (603) 643-1307, Web Site:
www.nextmark.com
Pres: Joseph Pych

NEXXLINX (HQ)
3565 Piedmont Rd NE (Bldg 2-310)
Atlanta, GA 30305-8204
Telephone: (770) 250-0349, Web Site:
www.nexxlinx.com
VP Sls: William I. Coffeen III

A business communication solution
provider.

THE DMA NFOCUS CONSULTING INC
1594 Hubbard Dr
Lancaster, OH 43130-8124
Telephone: (740) 654-5809, Web Site:
www.nfocusconsulting.com

Pres: Douglas Cronin

NORTH AMERICAN MAILING TECHNOLOGIES INC
141 B Buford Dr
Lawrenceville, GA 30045-4926
Telephone: (770) 962-5833
Owner/Operator: Cassandra Lee
Primary Market Served: Business & Consumer

NORTHERN RESPONSE (INTERNATIONAL) LTD
50 Staples Ave
Toronto, ON, Canada L4B 0A7
Telephone: (905) 737-6698, (866) 584-1694, FAX: (905) 737-0099, E-Mail: general@nresponse.com, Web Site: www.shopnorthern.com
Owner: Richard Stacey

NOVELL INC
404 Wyman St Ste 500A
Waltham, MA 02451-1264
Telephone: (801) 861-4272, (800) 529-3400, FAX: (781) 464-8100, E-Mail: crc@novell.com, Web Site: www.novell.com
Chmn: Thomas G. Plaskett
Pres, CEO & Dir: Ronald W. Hovespain
Sr VP & CMO: John Dragoon
Sr VP & CFO: Dana C. Russell
Exec VP: Tom Francese
Conducts Business: Worldwide
Employees: 2,300
Primary Market Served: Business & Consumer
Catalog available online
Indirect online sales
Gross sales or billing: $932,000,000

Provider of networking connectivity products & systems. Computer software company.

O2 CONSULTING INC
7760 Landowne Dr
Atlanta, GA 30350-1064
Telephone: (404) 384-3990
Pres: Timothy Olzer

OLD VINE MARKETING
147 Old Vine Way
Napa, CA 94558-7028
Telephone: (707) 694-9647, E-Mail: info@oldvinemarketing.com, Web Site: www.oldvinemarketing.com
Owner: Steven Bowden

OMEDA
555 Huehl Rd
Northbrook, IL 60062-2336
Telephone: (847) 564-8900, Web Site: www.omeda.com

Pres: Aaron Oberman

OPIN SYSTEMS INC
7900 International Dr (Suite 770)
Bloomington, MN 55425-2556
Telephone: (651) 994-6555, (800) 888-1804, FAX: (651) 994-7828, E-Mail: judywy@opin.com, Web Site: www.opin.com
CEO: Ray Pinson
Assoc Dir Mktg: Judy Wise

THE OYSTER GROUP
59 Prince Albert Rd
Dartmouth, NS, Canada B2Y 1M1
Telephone: (877) 405-4858, E-Mail: fdrinnan@theoystergroup.ca, Web Site: www.theoystergroup.ca
Pres: Faith Drinnan

PC CONNECTION
Route 101A, 730 Milford Rd
Merrimack, NH 03054-4631
Telephone: (603) 683-2167, (800) 800-0014, FAX: (603) 683-5773, E-Mail: pr@pcconnection.com, Web Site: www.pcconnection.com, macconnection.com
Pres & CEO: Timothy McGrath
Sr VP Corp Mktg & Creative Svcs: David Beffa-Negrini
Sr VP Treas & CFO: Jack Ferguson
Sr VP HR: Bradley Mousseau
Corp Communs: Lynn McKensie
Conducts Business: U.S., Canada, Europe
Employees: 1,000
Primary Market Served: Business & Consumer
Catalog available online
Direct online sales
Founded: 1982

Provider of a full range of information technology solutions to business, government & education markets.

PNT MARKETING SERVICES, INC
2420 Jackson Ave (Suite 203)
Long Island City, NY 11101-4332
Telephone: (703) 761-0291, (888) 768-2210, FAX: (914) 428-0504, E-Mail: tony@pntmarketingservices.com, Web Site: www.pntmarketingservices.com
Co-CEO: Tony Coretto
Co-CEO: Phil Jarymiszyn
Dir Client Svcs: Adam Isler
Conducts Business: U.S.
Employees: 20
Primary Market Served: Business
Indirect online sales
Advertising/Marketing Budget Related to Direct Marketing: 0-25%
Direct Marketing ad budget: $20,000

Direct Mail: 25%
Online: 75%
Founded: 1988
Gross sales or billing: $3,900,000

PNT provides marketing support services (database marketing, data mining & analytics, list management, technology support & strategy consulting) to the financial services & other industries.

PTC
140 Kendrick St Ste C120
Needham, MA 02494-2743
Telephone: (781) 370-5000, Web Site: www.ptc.com
Dir, Direct Response Mktg: Michael Baldani

PACIFICEAST
PO Box 439
Sumas, WA 98295-0439
Telephone: (800) 665-8400, Web Site: www.pacificeast.com
CEO: Garth Froese
Primary Market Served: Business & Consumer

PARKER SOFTWARE
4767 New Broad St
Orlando, FL 32814
Telephone: (800) 680-7712, Web Site: www.parker-software.com
Primary Market Served: Business & Consumer

PARTNERS MARKETING INC
1750 E Main St (Suite 10)
Saint Charles, IL 60174-2363
Telephone: (630) 524-9901, FAX: (630) 524-9909, E-Mail: georgeb@partnersmarketing.com, Web Site: www.partnersmarketing.com
VP, Opers: Jerry Jones
EVP & Gen Mgr: George Bardenheier Jr.
Conducts Business: U.S., Canada
Primary Market Served: Consumer
Founded: 1992

Marketing consulting with expertise for marketing projects and services to expecting, new and experienced parents.

PEACHTREE DATA INC
2905 Premiere Pkwy (Suite 200)
Duluth, GA 30097-5275
Telephone: (678) 987-4600, Web Site: www.peachtreedata.com
Pres: Richard West
Primary Market Served: Business & Consumer

PEAK COMPUTER SYSTEMS

Div of Peak Communications Inc
6400 W Main St (Suite 1A)
Belleville, IL 62223
Telephone: (618) 398-5612, E-Mail:
    info@peaknet.net, Web Site: www.
    peaknet.net
Pres: Grant Wuller

THE DMA PEGG NADLER ASSOCIATES INC

400 E 77th St (Suite 16b)
New York, NY 10075-2337
Telephone: (212) 861-0846
Pres: Pegg Nadler
Primary Market Served: Business

PERFORMANCE DIRECT INC

3525 Piedmont Rd
Atlanta, GA 30305-1530
Telephone: (678) 608-2820, (800) 869-
    2300, FAX: (404) 869-2547, E-Mail:
    info@performancede.com
Pres & CEO: Carter S.D. Taylor

PHOENIX DATA PROCESSING

One Oak Hill Center (Suite 301)
Westmont, IL 60559
Telephone: (630) 654-4400, FAX:
    (630) 654-4470, E-Mail: sales@
    phoenixdataprocessing.com, Web
    Site: www.phoenixdataprocessing.
    com
Pres: John L. Montandon
Sls Mgr: Bryan Rich

PHOENIX TECHNOLOGIES LTD

915 Murphy Ranch Rd
Milpitas, CA 95035-7912
Telephone: (408) 570-1000, (800) 677-
    7305, FAX: (408) 570-1001, Web
    Site: www.phoenix.com
Pres & CEO: Woodson Hobbs

THE DMA PITNEY BOWES SOFTWARE SYSTEMS

One Elmcroft Rd
Stamford, CT 06926-0700
Telephone: (800) 624-5377, Web Site:
    www.pitneybowes.com
Pres & CEO: Murray D. Martin

THE DMA PLURIS

550 Cochituate Rd Ste 7
Framingham, MA 01701-4600
Telephone: (508) 663-1100, Web Site:
    www.plurisinc.com
CEO: Michael Caccavale
Primary Market Served: Consumer

PORTRAIT INTERNATIONAL INC

125 Summer St Ste 1600
Boston, MA 02110-1636
Telephone: (617) 457-5223, Web Site:
    www.portraitsoftware.com
Exec VP: Mark Smith

THE DMA POSSIBLENOW INC

4400 River Green Pkwy
Duluth, GA 30096-8316
Telephone: (770) 255-1020, Web Site:
    www.dncsolution.com
Pres & CEO: Scott Frey

PRECISION PLAY MEDIA / MARKETLEVERAGE

701 International Pkwy Ste 200
Lake Mary, FL 32746-5624
Telephone: (407) 805-8800, Web Site:
    www.precisionplaymedia.com
CEO: Michael Jenkins

PREMIERE GLOBAL SERVICES INC

3280 Peachtree Rd NE (Suite 1000)
Atlanta, GA 30305-2451
Telephone: (404) 262-8400, (800) 546-
    1541, FAX: (913) 661-9042, Web
    Site: www.PGiConnect.com
Chmn & CEO: Peter Olson
CFO & CAO: Edward Volini
Solutions Dir EMktg: Andrew Oster-
    day
Sr VP, Opers & Tech: Andrew Weber
VP, Controller: Tom Allen
Dir, Mktg: Kim Hovey
Primary Market Served: Business &
    Consumer
Catalog available online
Indirect online sales

Provide audio teleconferencing services, blast faxing & fax-on-demand,
automated recording replay programs,
as well as training & educational
consultants.

PRIMENET

Subs. of Journal Communications
2100 Palmetto St Ste A
Clearwater, FL 33765-2101
Telephone: (651) 405-4000, FAX:
    (651) 405-4100, Web Site: www.
    pnms.com
Pres: Mark Keefe

PRIORITY DATA SYSTEMS INC

5035 S 110th St
Omaha, NE 68137-2376
Telephone: (402) 592-2550, (877) 273-
    7774, FAX: (402) 592-5052, E-Mail:
    sales@pdomaha.com, Web Site:
    www.priority-data.com

Pres & Treas: Marcella E. Flynn

THE DMA PROFESSIONAL ADVERTISING SYSTEMS INC

200 Business Park Dr (Suite 304)
Armonk, NY 10504-1751
Telephone: (914) 765-0500, FAX:
    (914) 765-0503, E-Mail: info@
    paslists.com, Web Site: www.paslists.
    com
Pres: Eric Raskin

PROFESSIONAL MARKETING ASSOCIATES

405 W Fairmont Dr
Tempe, AZ 85282-2007
Telephone: (480) 829-0131, FAX:
    (480) 829-9202, Web Site: www.
    pmafulfillment.com
Pres: Chris Roth

PROFIT CENTER SOFTWARE INC

11 Harbor Park Dr
Port Washington, NY 11050-4656
Telephone: (516) 414-6300, (888) 446-
    6240, FAX: (516) 414-6304, E-Mail:
    jmarrah@profitcenter.com, Web Site:
    www.profitcenter.com
Exec VP: George Winter
Exec VP: Solomon Niyazov
Pres & CEO: John Marrah
Conducts Business: U.S. & Canada
Advertising/Marketing Budget Related
    to Direct Marketing: 76-100%
Founded: 2002

Multichannel sales, order, fulfillment &
accounting solution.

PROMOTIONAL PRODUCTS FULFILLMENT & DISTRIBUTION LTD

80 William Smith Dr
Whitby, ON, Canada L1N 9W1
Telephone: (905) 668-5060, (800) 263-
    4678, FAX: (800) 993-0543, E-Mail:
    sales@ppfd.com, Web Site: www.
    ppfd.com
CEO: Gilbert Kee

PUBLISHERS COMPUTER CORP

209 Main St
New Milford, NJ 07646-1733
Telephone: (201) 261-3700, FAX:
    (201) 261-9110, E-Mail: mail@
    publisherscomputer.com, Web Site:
    www.publisherscomputer.com
Pres: Andrew Johnston

QED MARKETING INC
570 S Research Pl
Central Islip, NY 11722-4415
Telephone: (631) 851-4254
Pres: Peter Muzzy
Primary Market Served: Business &
Consumer

QMSI
5700 Ager Beswick Rd
Montague, CA 96064-9495
Telephone: (530) 459-0910, Web Site:
www.quintmail.com

THE DMA QUAERO CORP
1930 Camden Rd (Suite 2060)
Charlotte, NC 28203-5900
Telephone: (877) 570-2199, Web Site:
www.quaero.com
SVP & Gen Mgr: Naras Eechambadi

**THE DMA RAPID PROGRESS
MARKETING & MODELING
LLC**
1760 Delaware Ave NE
Saint Petersburg, FL 33703-5439
Telephone: (727) 528-8578, Web Site:
www.rpmsquared.com
Pres: Scott Terry

THE DMA RARITAN INC
400 Cottontail Ln
Somerset, NJ 08873-1238
Telephone: (732) 764-8886, Web Site:
www.raritan.com
Dir Online Mktg: Scott Helias

REALDATA SERVICES INC
322 Van Dorn Dr
Glenwood Springs, CO 81601-9524
Telephone: (970) 945-2456, FAX:
(970) 945-5356, E-Mail: rick@
realdataservices.com, Web Site:
www.realdataservices.com
VP: Rick Hilleary

THE DMA RELEVATE
6883 Commercial Dr
Springfield, VA 22159-0310
Telephone: (703) 658-8300, (800) 523-
7346, FAX: (703) 658-8301, E-Mail:
sales@relevategroup.com, Web Site:
www.relevategroup.com
VP Reg Sls: Kelly Idol
VP Mktg: Gay Bitter
CEO: Peg Kuman
CEO: Steven Rao
VP Data Solutions: Scott Johnson
VP Database Mktg & Analytics: Andy
Pappas
Founded: 1979

Relevate builds, manages & analyzes
data in order to provide behavioral
targeting & data driven solutions. Solutions include Telematch phone append, database marketing & campaign
management, data enhancement, proprietary new mover & auto owner
data, merge/purge, modeling & analytics & email append & solutions.

RENKIM CORP
13333 Allen Rd
Southgate, MI 48195
Telephone: (734) 374-8300, FAX:
(734) 374-8323, E-Mail: info@
renkim.com, Web Site: www.renkim.
com
Pres & CEO: Gary Perlick

**RESEARCH IN MOTION
CORP**
185 Columbia St W
Waterloo, ON, Canada N2L 5Z5
Telephone: (519) 888-7465, Web Site:
www.rim.com
Mktg Mgr Direct Mktg: Donal Byrne

**RESPONSE MANAGEMENT
TECHNOLOGIES INC**
aka RMT
2550 9th St (Suite 103)
Berkeley, CA 94710-2516
Telephone: (510) 843-8180, FAX:
(510) 843-8020, E-Mail: info@
respmgt.com, Web Site: www.
respmgt.com
Pres: Julie Weidenbach

THE DMA RETURN PATH INC
304 Park Ave S (fl 7)
New York, NY 10010-4311
Telephone: (212) 905-5500, FAX:
(212) 905-5501, Web Site: www.
returnpath.biz
CEO & Co-Founder: Matt Blumberg
Pres & Co-Founder: George Bilbrey
COO, CFO & Co-Founder: Jack Sin-
clair

REWAY INC
3132 SW 165th Ave
Miramar, FL 33027
Telephone: (954) 205-1996, Web Site:
www.rewayconsulting.com
Pres: Lavanya Manchikatla
Primary Market Served: Business

THE DMA REYNOLDS & REYNOLDS CO
6700 Hollister St (fl 2)
Houston, TX 77040-5331
Telephone: (713) 718-1800, (800) 231-
6347, FAX: (713) 718-1471, Web
Site: www.reyrey.com
Pres: Robert Brockman

Sr Prod Mgr: Les Hall

RIGDEN INC
PO Box 17187
Boulder, CO 80308-0187
Telephone: (303) 442-8190, FAX:
(303) 442-8686, E-Mail: rigden@
rigden.com, Web Site: www.rigden.
com
Pres: James Jobson

THE DMA RUF STRATEGIC SOLUTIONS
1533 E Spruce St
Olathe, KS 66061-3698
Telephone: (800) 829-8544, Web Site:
www.ruf.com
VP: Jake Ruf

THE DMA SAS INSTITUTE
PO Box 610
Cary, NC 27512-0610
Telephone: (919) 677-8000, Web Site:
www.sas.com
Primary Market Served: Business &
Consumer

THE DMA SBDP CORP
4208 Airport Rd
Cincinnati, OH 45226-1646
Telephone: (513) 871-7019, FAX:
(513) 871-0134, E-Mail: info@sbdp.
com, Web Site: www.sbdp.com
Pres: William R. Fryer

SPSS INC
233 S Wacker Dr (Suite 1100)
Chicago, IL 60606-6307
Telephone: (312) 651-3000, (800) 543-
2185, FAX: (312) 651-3690, E-Mail:
sales@spss.com, Web Site: www.
spss.com
Pres, CEO: Jack Noonan
Mktg Dir: Jennifer London

SAGE DIRECT INC
3400 Raleigh Ave SE
Grand Rapids, MI 49512-2042
Telephone: (616) 940-8311, (800) 729-
8310, FAX: (616) 940-3383, E-Mail:
sageinc@sagedirect.com, Web Site:
www.sagedirect.com
Pres: Gary Sage
VP: Pamela Sage

THE DMA SALFORD SYSTEMS
9685 Via Excelencia Ste 208
San Diego, CA 92126-7500
Telephone: (619) 543-8880, Web Site:
www.salford-systems.com
Bus Devel Mgr: Lisa Solomon
Primary Market Served: Business &
Consumer

SARA ISAAC
Subs. of Fair Isaac & Company
4295 Lexington Ave N
Saint Paul, MN 55126
Telephone: (651) 482-8593, FAX:
(651) 481-8077, Web Site: www.
saraisaac.com
CEO: Tom Grudnowski

THE DMA SATURN CORP
4701 Lydell Rd
Hyattsville, MD 20781-1117
Telephone: (301) 772-7000, (800)
USA-0090, FAX: (301) 386-4538,
E-Mail: sales@saturncorp.com, Web
Site: www.saturncorp.com
CEO: Fielding Yost

SAVICOM
44 Montgomery St (Suite 1600)
San Francisco, CA 94104
Telephone: (415) 983-0990, FAX:
(415) 445-9999, E-Mail: sales@
savicom.net, Web Site: www.
savicom.net
CEO: Ted Bernard
VP Worlwide Sls: Patrick B. Scoggin
VP Mktg: Bill McGee
Employees: 28
Primary Market Served: Business
Founded: 1996
Gross sales or billing: $6,500,000

Hosts web based list management and
e-mail delivery services to marketers,
agencies, and publishers.

SCICOM DATA SERVICES LTD
10101 Bren Rd E
Minnetonka, MN 55343-9065
Telephone: (952) 933-4200, (800) 488-
9087, FAX: (952) 936-4132, Web
Site: www.scicom.com
VP: Greg Oman
Sr VP: Martin Kiener

SCIENTIFIC COMPUTING ASSOCIATES
525 N Lincoln Ave
Villa Park, IL 60181-1306
Telephone: (630) 834-8512, Web Site:
www.scausa.com
Dir Database Mktg: John Sfondouris

SCOTT COMPUTING SYSTEMS
2780 Bert Adams Rd (Suite 400)
Atlanta, GA 30339-3926
Telephone: (770) 432-7000, (800) 241-
7576, FAX: (770) 432-7500, Web
Site: www.rylandscott.com
Pres: C. Ryland Scott

ALAN SENEGETO
808 Waverly Rd
Kennett Square, PA 19348-1451
Telephone: (610) 444-8955
Primary Market Served: Business &
Consumer

THE DMA SERVICE NET
650 Missouri Ave
Jeffersonville, IN 47130-3081
Telephone: (812) 258-4722, Web Site:
www.servicenet.com
Primary Market Served: Consumer

SHEPARD'S INC
32 Henry St
Bethel, CT 06801
Telephone: (203) 830-8300, (800) 243-
0993, FAX: (203) 830-8389, Web
Site: www.shepardsinc.com
Pres: Michael Goodman

SISK FULFILLMENT SERVICE INC
1900 Industrial Park Dr, Box 463
Federalsburg, MD 21632
Telephone: (410) 754-8141, FAX:
(410) 754-8223, Web Site: www.
siskfulfillment.com
Pres: John Phillips

SOFTREK CORP
30 Bryant Woods N
Amherst, NY 14228-3601
Telephone: (800) 442-9211, Web Site:
www.softrek.com
VP Sls & Mktg: Robert Girardi

SOFTWARE MARKETING ASSOCIATES INC
1086 Elm St (Suite 200)
Rocky Hill, CT 06067-2341
Telephone: (860) 721-8929, FAX:
(860) 257-9679, E-Mail: sma@sma-
promail.com, Web Site: www.sma-
promail.com
Exec VP: Denise S. Lunden

THE DMA SPECTRUM DATA
131 N 3rd St
Oregon, IL 61061-1410
Telephone: (815) 732-6567
Pres: David Murray
Primary Market Served: Business &
Consumer

STIBO SYSTEMS
33550 George Busbee Pkwy NW
(Suite 350)
Kennesaw, GA 30144-2122
Telephone: (770) 425-3282, Web Site:
www.stibocatalog.com
Pres: Andreas Lorenzen

STOCKTON INC
8341 Beechcraft Ave
Gaithersburg, MD 20879-1509
Telephone: (301) 527-1550, FAX:
(301) 527-1503, E-Mail: info@
stocktoninc.com, Web Site: www.
stocktoninc.com
Pres: Stephen Strack

THE DMA STRATEGIC DATA INTELLIGENCE LLC
555 Skokie Blvd
Northbrook, IL 60062-2812
Telephone: (847) 897-5706, FAX:
(847) 897-5715, E-Mail: inquiry@
sdintelligence.com, Web Site: www.
sdintelligence.com
CEO & Principal: Michael Brostoff
Bus Mgr: Irene Diehl
Conducts Business: U.S.
Primary Market Served: Business
Founded: 2007

Data hygiene for direct and email
companies. Develop, maintain and host
marketing databases, call center
solutions.

STRATEGIC SOFTWARE SYSTEMS LLC
1508 Willow Lawn Dr (Suite 111)
Richmond, VA 23230-3421
Telephone: (804) 288-8827x110, Web
Site: www.sss1.com
Mng Partner: William Hungerford
Primary Market Served: Business &
Consumer

SUBSCRIBERMAIL LLC
3333 Warrenville Rd (Suite 350)
Lisle, IL 60532-4551
Telephone: (630) 303-5000, Web Site:
www.subscribermail.com
CEO & Chmn: Jordan Ayan

SUNGARD COMPUTER SERVICES
Div. of Sungard Data Systems
680 E Swedesford Rd
Wayne, PA 19087
Telephone: (484) 582-5673, E-Mail:
GetInfo@SunGard.com, Web Site:
www.sungard.com
Mktg: Jenn Rebain

SUNTEL INC
1890 Dixwell Ave (Suite 205)
Hamden, CT 06514-3171
Telephone: (203) 287-9114, FAX:
(203) 248-3883, E-Mail: info@
suntelinc.com, Web Site: www.
suntelinc.com
Mgr: Sachin Parikh

SUPER DISK
PO Box 2797
Ann Arbor, MI 48106-2797
Telephone: (734) 996-8888
CEO: Ken Ascher

SUPPORT SERVICES CORP
2401 First St
Fort Myers, FL 33901
Telephone: (239) 332-5300, FAX:
(239) 332-4555, E-Mail: steve@ss-
corp.com, Web Site: www.ss-corp.
com
Pres: Stephen Ward

SYBASE INC
1 Sybase Dr
Dublin, CA 94568-7976
Telephone: (925) 236-5000, Web Site:
www.sybase.com/product/
datawarehousing
Dir Product Mktg: Lisa Hopkins
Primary Market Served: Consumer

THE DMA TEC MAILING SOLUTIONS, LLC
804 Liberty Blvd (Suite 201)
Sun Prairie, WI 53590-9269
Telephone: (608) 825-8525

THE DMA TABLEAU SOFTWARE
837 N 34th St (Suite 400)
Seattle, WA 98103-8882
Telephone: (206) 633-3400, Web Site:
www.tableausoftware.com
Mktg Programs Mgr: Amy Schneider
Primary Market Served: Consumer

THE DMA TARGUSINFO
1861 International Dr Fl 6
Mc Lean, VA 22102-4420
Telephone: (703) 272-6200, Web Site:
www.TARGUSinfo.com
Sr Mktg Commun Mgr: Kara Cartin
Primary Market Served: Business

THE DMA TECHNEKES LLC
1927 S Tryon St (Suite 310)
Charlotte, NC 28203
Telephone: (704) 342-2900, FAX:
(704) 342-2975, Web Site: www.
technekes.com
Principal & Founder: Preston Fay

TECHNISERVE INC
2065 Livernois Rd
Troy, MI 48083-1737
Telephone: (248) 989-0100, FAX:
(248) 989-0111, E-Mail: info@
techni-serve.com, Web Site: www.
techni-serve.com
Pres: Nancy Gardner
Mgr Software Devel: Sam Phomsopha

Primary Market Served: Business &
Consumer

Provides software and services that
support customers' core business
functions.

TELEPHONE LOOK-UP SERVICE CO
PO Box 316
Jamison, PA 18929-0316
Telephone: (215) 321-0706, (800) 366-
0706, FAX: (215) 321-3229, E-Mail:
computer@telephonelookup.com,
Web Site: www.telephonelookup.com
Pres: Michael W. Schoedler

TELETECH
9197 S Peoria St
Englewood, CO 80112-5833
Telephone: (303) 397-8100, (800)
TELETECH, FAX: (303) 397-8199,
E-Mail: solutions@TeleTech.com,
Web Site: www.teletech.com
Chmn Bd & CEO: Kenneth Tuchman
Dir Demand Generation & Direct
Resp: Andrew Scantland

TERADATA CORP
10000 Innovation Dr
Miamisburg, OH 45342-4927
Telephone: (937) 242-4800, Web Site:
www.teradata.com
Solutions Mktg VP: Sam Gragg
Primary Market Served: Business &
Consumer

THELAW.NET CORP
6640 Lusk Blvd (Suite A205)
San Diego, CA 92121-2777
Telephone: (858) 554-0583, Web Site:
www.thelaw.net
Pres: Mark Whitney

THOMSON TAX & ACCOUNTING
7322 Newman Blvd
Dexter, MI 48130
Telephone: (800) 968-8900, FAX:
(734) 426-3750, E-Mail: jack.larue@
thomson.com, Web Site: www.cs.
thomson.com
Sr VP, Mktg: Jack LaRue

3COM CORP
153 Taylor St
Littleton, MA 01460-1407
Telephone: (508) 323-5000, FAX:
(508) 323-1111

TIME CUSTOMER SERVICE INC
A Time Warner Co
One N Dale Mabry Hwy

Tampa, FL 33609-2700
Telephone: (813) 878-6100, (800) 723-
NCOA, FAX: (813) 878-6452, Web
Site: www.timecustomerservice.com
VP, Postal & Dist Policy: Robert
O'Brien

TOMTOM NORTH AMERICAN
Subs. of Sony Corp of America
11 Lafayette St.
Lebanon, NH 03766-1445
Telephone: (603) 643-0330, (800) 331-
7881, FAX: (603) 653-0249, Web
Site: www.tomtom.com
CEO: Alain De Taeye
CEO: Bill Henry

THE TOTAL MAILING SYSTEM
551 Mid-Atlantic Pkwy
West Deptford, NJ 08066
Telephone: (856) 628-8800, FAX:
(856) 628-8810, Web Site: www.
ttms.com
Dir Bus Devel: Jim Capanna

TOUCH-BASE COMPUTING
PO Box 213
Silver Creek, GA 30173
Telephone: (706) 378-0964, E-Mail:
sales@touchbase.com, Web Site:
www.touchbase.com
Pres: Philip Boylan
VP Special Mktg: Keith Camille

TRINITY TECHNICAL GROUP, INC
1360 Post N Paddock (Suite 500)
Grand Prairie, TX 75050-1255
Telephone: (817) 879-7907, E-Mail:
info@trinitytechnicalgroup.com, Web
Site: www.trinitytechnicalgroup.com
Primary Market Served: Business &
Consumer

TRIPLEX
an infoUSA company
900 17th St NW (Suite 850)
Washington, DC 20006-2523
Telephone: (202) 887-8001, (866) 872-
8099, FAX: (202) 887-8008, E-Mail:
info@tdmc.com, Web Site: www.
tdmc.com
Pres: Daniel Gust

THE DMA TRUSTE
835 Market St (Suite 800)
San Francisco, CA 94103-1905
Telephone: (415) 520-3490, Web Site:
www.truste.org
Mktg/Sls Assoc: Mary Anne Timothy
Founded: 1997

Online privacy solutions provider

TYPE-A-SCAN INC
115 W 29th St
New York, NY 10001-5106
Telephone: (212) 367-8406, FAX:
(212) 691-8134, E-Mail: info@
typeascan.com, Web Site: www.
typeascan.com
Pres: Jeff Steinfeld

UAA CLEARINGHOUSE
6912 N 97th Cir
Omaha, NE 68122-1010
Telephone: (402) 991-2810, Web Site:
www.uaaclearinghouse.com
Pres: Matt Newman
Pres: Mark Shada

UNICA CORP
170 Tracer Ln
Waltham, MA 02451-1379
Telephone: (781) 839-8000, Web Site:
www.unicacorp.com

VERATAD TECHNOLOGIES LLC
500 Frank W Burr Blvd Ste 14
Teaneck, NJ 07666-6802
Telephone: (201) 510-6000, FAX:
(201) 510-6036
Pres: Pattie Dillion
CIO: Kenneth Galle
Conducts Business: U.S.
Employees: 8
Primary Market Served: Business
Direct online sales
Advertising/Marketing Budget Related
to Direct Marketing: 0-25%
Direct Marketing ad budget:
Direct Mail: 60%
Magazines: 5%
Telephone: 35%

Specializing in age and identity authentication, online tools, resourcing billions of public and government records with results in seconds. Volume pricing available.

VISION SOLUTIONS
15300 Barranca Pkwy
Irvine, CA 92618
Telephone: (949) 253-6500, (800) 683-4667, FAX: (949) 253-6501, E-Mail:
info@visionsolutions.com, Web Site:
www.visionsolutions.com
Pres & CEO: Nicholaas Vlok

VOCUS
12051 Indian Creek Ct
Beltsville, MD 20705-1246
Telephone: (301) 459-2590, Web Site:
www.vocus.com
Primary Market Served: Consumer

VOLT DELTA
Subs. of Volt Information Svcs
1 Sentry Pkwy E Ste 6000
Blue Bell, PA 19422-2310
Telephone: (610) 825-7720, FAX:
(610) 567-5698, Web Site: www.
voltdelta.com
CEO: Robert Pines

WEB DECISIONS
303 Pisgah Church Rd (Suite 2A)
Greensboro, NC 27455-2756
Telephone: (336) 545-7817 x100
CEO: Kim Addington
Primary Market Served: Business

WENNSOFT
1970 S Calhoun Rd
New Berlin, WI 53151-2214
Telephone: (262) 317-3717, Web Site:
www.wennsoft.com
Dir Mktg: Thomas Cunningham

WESTERN DIGITAL CORP
3355 Michelson Dr (Suite 100)
Irvine, CA 92612-5694
Telephone: (949) 672-7000, FAX:
(949) 672-7837, Web Site: www.
westerndigital.com
Chmn, Pres & CEO: Mathew Massengill

WHEATON GROUP
201 Bolinas Ct
Chapel Hill, NC 27517-8344
Telephone: (919) 969-8859, FAX:
(425) 675-6014, E-Mail: jim.
wheaton@wheatongroup.com, Web
Site: www.wheatongroup.com
Principal: Cynthia Wheaton
Principal: Jim Wheaton
Principal: Boris Gendelev
Principal: Leo Sterk
Conducts Business: U.S.
Employees: 6
Primary Market Served: Business &
Consumer
Founded: 2000

Builds and maintains marketing databases. Specializes in data mining and direct and database marketing consulting.

WILAND DIRECT
6309 Monarch Park Pl Ste 201
Niwot, CO 80503-7198
Telephone: (303) 485-8686, Web Site:
www.wilanddirect.com
Founder & CEO: Phillip Wiland

WILSON, HUGH & ASSOCIATE CONSULTANTS LTD
Four Long Bridge Rd
Thornhill, ON, Canada L4J 1L5
Telephone: (905) 764-5312
Pres: Hugh Wilson

LG WILSON & ASSOCIATES
6 Butler Hill Rd
Somers, NY 10589-2404
Telephone: (914) 649-5928, Web Site:
www.lgwilson.com
Pres: Lisa Wilson

WINDOW BOOK INC
300 Franklin St
Cambridge, MA 02139-3781
Telephone: (617) 441-3500, Web Site:
www.windowbook.com
CEO & Founder: Jeffrey Peoples

WIRED ASSETS DATA CORP
284 Riversville Rd
Greenwich, CT 06831-3253
Telephone: (203) 340-2316, Web Site:
www.wiredassets.com
Pres & CFO: Dean Eaker

WOODEN INFORMATION SERVICES
13358 Windbrooke Ln
Saint Louis, MO 63146-2224
Telephone: (314) 576-1124
Pres: Roger Wooden

XMPIE INC
767 3rd Ave (fl 3)
New York, NY 10017-2023
Telephone: (212) 479-5166, Web Site:
www.xmpie.com
Worldwide Mktg Mgr: Lawrence Zusman

YANKELOVICH INC
400 Meadowmont Village Cir (Suite
431)
Chapel Hill, NC 27517-7505
Telephone: (919) 932-8600, Web Site:
www.yankelovich.com
CFO: Jim Cain

YOUSENDIT INC
1919 S Bascom Ave (fl 3)
Campbell, CA 95008-2220
Telephone: (408) 879-9118, Web Site:
www.yousendit.com

ZIRCON CO INC
67 Aurora Ln.
Salem, MA 01970-6803
Telephone: (978) 741-7000, FAX:
(978) 532-0012

Pres: Curtis B. Flory III

THE DMA ZOOMINFO INC
307 Waverley Oaks Rd Ste 405
Waltham, MA 02452-8413
Telephone: (781) 693-7500, Web Site:
www.zoominfo.com
Gen Mgr: Leah Daniels

List Brokers & Compilers (23) — Geographic Index

Alabama

Info Direct, 2619 Trailway Rd SE, Huntsville, 35801-1473

Precision Mailing Solutions, 101 Colt Cir, Huntsville, 35811

Arizona

AAA BEST Mailing Lists Inc, 7507 E Tanque Verde Rd, Best Mailing Lists Inc, Tucson, 85715-3667

Direct Approach, 4131 N 24th St Ste C202, Phoenix, 85016-6256

Direct Mail Source Inc, 7729 E Pinchot, Scottsdale, 85251

Dunnings Diversified LLC, 4307 E Desert Sky Ct, Cave Creek, 85331

Jordan Direct, 40704 N Bell Meadow Tr, Phoenix, 85086-2949

Lawyers & Judges Publishing Co Inc, PO Box 30040, Tucson, 85751-0040

LeadPile, 2355 E Camelback Rd Ste 825, Phoenix, 85016-9069

Medicx Media Solutions, 9364 E Raintree Dr (Suite 101), Scottsdale, 85260-2200

California

AccuList Inc, 2140 Eastman Ave Ste 105, Ventura, 93003-7786

Active Network Media & Marketing, 10182 Telesis Ct (Suite 300), San Diego, 92121-4777

AD-Vantage Marketing, 455 Tesconi Cir, Santa Rosa, 95401-4619

Advisor Media Inc, PO Box 503350, San Diego, 92150-3350

American Leads Co, PO Box 1425, Benicia, 94510-4425

ArtNetwork-Artworld Mailing Lists, 10655 Park Ave Ext, Nevada City, 95959-8890

Autobytel Inc, 18872 Macarthur Blvd, Irvine, 92612-1448

Avrick Direct Inc, 979 Saint Mary's Ln, Santa Barbara, 93111-1034

Business Mailing Center, 200 N Elevar St, Oxnard, 93030

Byrum & Fleming, 321 San Anselmo Ave, San Anselmo, 94960-2647

Carnegie Marketing Associates, 3878 Carson St (Suite 220), Torrance, 90503-6707

Carney Direct Marketing, 15520 Rockfield Blvd (Suite C), Irvine, 92618-2792

Computerized Research & Development Inc, 6110 Auburn Folsom Rd, Granite Bay, 95746-5868

DataQuick, 9620 Towne Centre Dr, San Diego, 92121-1963

Demandbase Inc, 301 Howard St Ste 1800, San Francisco, 94105-6614

Direct List Technology Inc, 1582 N Batavia St (Suite 3), Orange, 92867-3544

DS Direct Communications, 1840 S Elena Ave (Suite 210), Redondo Beach, 90277-5717

Fasano & Associates, 333 S Beverly Dr Ste 214, Beverly Hills, 90212-4306

Frontline Direct Inc, 2658 del Mar Heights Rd (#203), Del Mar, 92014-3100

Healthcare Data Solutions, 26741 Portola Pkwy, Foothill Ranch, 92610-1743

Homeowners Marketing Services Inc, 12444 Victory Blvd (2nd fl), North Hollywood, 91606-3156

IBux, PO Box 4675, Chico, 95927-4675

IC DIRECT List Brokers, 4047 Meadow Wood Dr, El Dorado Hills, 95762-7513

Infocore Inc, 2375 Camino Vida Roble (Suite A), Carlsbad, 92011-1556

Jefferson Mailing Lists, 12350 Oak Knoll Rd, Poway, 92064-5320

List Alliance Inc, 3000 Danville Blvd (Suite F), PMB 519, Alamo, 94507-1572

List Pro of America, 3089-C Clairemont Dr (#267), San Diego, 92117-6802

List Team, 14458 Ventura Blvd, Sherman Oaks, 91423-2607

The Marketing Place, 12708 Branford St, Sun Valley, 91352

Martin Worldwide Inc, 638 Lindero Canyon Rd (#200), Oak Park, 91377

Mega Media Associates Inc, Box 4259, Newport Beach, 92661

Name-Finders Lists Inc, 8080 Capwell Dr Ste 100, Oakland, 94621-2120

Names in the News, 1300 Clay St (fl 11), Oakland, 94612-1429

NetHawk Interactive, 1255 Park Ave Ste D, Emeryville, 94608-3679

Pacific Lists Inc, 180 Grand Ave Ste 1545, Oakland, 94612-3799

Peppermill Marketing Inc, 8335 W Sunset Blvd Ste 246, Los Angeles, 90069-1529

Premier Data Group, 616 Corte Regalo, Camarillo, 93010-9107

Premier Data Solution, 2510-G Las Posas (#234), Camarillo, 93010-9107

SK&A Information Services Inc, 2601 Main St (Suite 650), Irvine, 92614-4228

George Sterne Agency Inc, 1588 S Mission Rd Ste 220, Fallbrook, 92028-4112

T O Printing & Mailing Services, 5334 Sterling Ctr Dr, Westlake Village, 91361-4612

US Data Corp, 30501 Agoura Rd Ste 102, Agoura Hills, 91301-4399

Wilson Marketing Group, 11924 W Washington Blvd, Los Angeles, 90066

Colorado

Data-Dynamix Inc, 781 Canyon Dr, Castle Rock, 80104-1844

DataLogix, 10075 Westmoor Dr (Suite 200), Westminster, 80021-2570

I-Behavior Inc, 2051 Dogwood St (Suite 220), Louisville, 80027-3042

Lewis Direct Inc, 400 Andrew Way, Superior, 80027-8300

Mailgraphics, 1668 Valtec Ln (Suite F), Boulder, 80301-4635

Connecticut

Andrew Associates Inc, Six Pearson Way, Enfield, 06082

The Catamount Group, 200 Pequot Ave Ste 1, Southport, 06890-1371

D-J Associates, 42 Old Ridgebury Rd, Danbury, 06810-5129

Gelderman Group Inc, 19 Junction Rd, Brookfield, 06804

Key Marketing Advantage LLC, 24 Stony Hill Rd (Suite 101), Bethel, 06801-1166

List Services Fundraising, PO Box 516, Bethel, 06801-0516

Market Data Retrieval, 6 Armstrong Rd (Suite 301), Shelton, 06484

Pont Media Direct, 10 E Meadow Ln, Norwalk, 06851-2902

Quality Education Data (QED), 6 Armstrong Rd (Suite 301), Shelton, 06484-4722

RMI Direct Marketing Inc, 42 Old Ridgebury Rd, Danbury, 06810-5129

Senior Citizens Unlimited Inc, PO Box 3036, Westport, 06880-8036

Sound Beach Marketing Partners LLC, Two Rocky Point Rd, Old Greenwich, 06870

Statlistics, 69 Kenosia Ave, Danbury, 06810-7303

District of Columbia

JC Lists Co, 3100 Connecticut Ave NW (Suite 4340), Washington, 20008-5148

List America, 5151 Wisconsin Ave NW (4th fl), Washington, 20016

Packer List Inc, 902 Pennsylvania Ave SE, Washington, 20003-2140

Florida

AccuData Integrated Marketing, 5220 Summerlin Commons Blvd (Suite 200), Fort Myers, 33907-2150

The Alesco Data Group, 5276 Summerlin Commons Way Ste 703, Fort Myers, 33907-2159

Alliance Strategies Group, Inc, 7700 Congress Ave, Suite 3208, Boca Raton, 33487

American Database Marketing Inc, 12627 San Jose Blvd (#603), Jacksonville, 32223-8642

Best ROI Lists, 21218 Saint Andrews Blvd (Suite 202), Boca Raton, 33433-2449

Blackstone Lists, 4280 Galt Ocean Dr (Suite 25D), Fort Lauderdale, 33308-6153

Computermail South, 200 Second Ave S (Suite 160), Saint Petersburg, 33701-4313

Contempo Marketing Co, 2101 NW 33rd St (Suite 100A), Pompano Beach, 33069-1046

Custom List Services Inc, 1810 Harbour Cir, c/o Pittman, Cape Coral, 33914-2510

The Data Group, 425 S Avalon Park Blvd., Orlando, 32828-6703

Direct Mail Advertising Corp, 5301 NW 37th Ave, Miami, 33142-3207

Dresden Direct Inc, 109 Saint Edward Pl, Palm Beach Gardens, 33418-4606

Dunhill International List Co Inc, 6400 Congress Ave Ste 1750, Boca Raton, 33487-2898

Gulf Coast List Service, PO Box 47645, Tampa, 33646-0114

LatinLists, 8424 NW 56th St (CCS 00511), Miami, 33166-3327

LeadCreations.Com LLC, 201 Alhambra Cir (Suite 501), Coral Gables, 33134-5105

ListAbility Inc, 11841 Granite Woods Loop, Venice, 34292-4113

LISTS Inc, 2950 Halcyon Ln Ste 401, Jacksonville, 32223-6691

MARKET SHARE, 5726 Cortez Rd W (#303), Bradenton, 34210-2701

Mastermailer Inc, 3700 N 29th Ave (Suite 203), Hollywood, 33020-1019

Media Source Solutions, 950 S Pine Island Rd (Suite A-150), Plantation, 33324-3918

MetaResponse Group Inc, 700 W Hillsboro Blvd (Suite 4-107), Deerfield Beach, 33441-1619

MDI Lists, 4581 Weston Rd (PMB 192), Weston, 33331-3141

Nexx Group Inc, 12734 Kenwood Ln Ste 87, Fort Myers, 33907-5638

Political Resources, PO Box 1403, Lake Worth, 33460-1403

Professional Direct Marketing & Mailing List Inc, 6400 Congress Ave Ste 2150, Boca Raton, 33487-2850

SalesLeadsTv (Federal Union Inc), 2701 NW Second Ave (Suite 213), Boca Raton, 33431

Sunvest Resorts, 425 N Federal Hwy, Hallandale, 33009

Vayan Marketing Group LLC, 6615 Boynton Beach Blvd, Boynton Beach, 33437-3526

Weiss Publishing & Marketing Inc, 15430 Endeavour Dr, Jupiter, 33478

Worldata, 3000 N Military Trl, Boca Raton, 33431-6321

Georgia

Alpha List Marketing Inc, 837 Thackston Dr, Marietta, 30068-4365

A Caldwell List Co Inc, 3295 River Exchange Dr Ste 380, Norcross, 30092-4238

Capitol Hill Lists, 1252 Rambling Rill Cir, Statham, 30666-3602

Direct Partner Solutions Inc, 6386 Nichols Rd, Flowery Branch, 30542-2619

Dirmark Group Inc, 90 W Moreno St, Buford, 30518-3037

Equifax Marketing Services, 1550 Peachtree St NE, Atlanta, 30309-2402

Equifax, 1550 Peachtree NE, Atlanta, 30309-8000

Goldleaf Data Corp, 3325 Paddock Pkwy (Suite 300), Suwanee, 30024-6060

Home Owner Data Services Inc, 1424 N Brown Rd Ste 400, Lawrenceville, 30043-8107

Marketing Solutions Now Inc, 11285 Elkins Rd (Suite H6B), Roswell, 30076-5840

My Mailing Service, Inc, 2100 Faulkner Rd NE, Atlanta, 30324-4259

Touchpoint Data Solutions, 6910 Bucks Rd, Cumming, 30040-0232

Illinois

Amacai Information Corp, 2 Mid America Plz Ste 606, Oakbrook Terrace, 60181-4716

American Hotel Register Co, 100 S Milwaukee Ave Ste 100, Vernon Hills, 60061-4321

American Student Marketing LLC, 473 Central Ave (Suite 7)), Highland Park, 60035-2691

ATP List Services, 1300 S Grove Ave (Suite 105), Barrington, 60010-5246

Burnett Marketing Inc, 800 W Central Rd (Suite 108), Mount Prospect, 60056-2383

Catalog Media Network Inc, 500 Davis Ctr (Suite 812), Evanston, 60201-4655

Cross Marketing USA, 1310 N Ritchie Ct (Suite 16-C), Chicago, 60610-8401

Direct Response Services, 111 Northlane Dr, Glen Carbon, 62034

Farm Market iD, 1 E Oakhill Dr (Ste 301), Westmont, 60559-5540

First National List Service Inc, 2257 W Irving Park Rd., Chicago, 60618-3840

GlaserDirect Inc, 800 Rossevelt Rd (Bldg B, Ste 414), Glen Ellyn, 50137

Global Business Information Services Inc (GLOBIS), 1820 N Lincoln Ave, Chicago, 60614-5812

Infutor Data Solutions, 111 Zapata Ln, Minooka, 60447-9355

Manufacturers-News Inc, 1633 Central St, Evanston, 60201-1505

Marketing Economics Inc, 1636 N Wells (#3112), Chicago, 60614-6023

PJ McCarthy & Associates Inc, 5413 Maplewood Pl, Downers Grove, 60515-4814

Midwest Lists & Media, 9333 N Milwaukee Ave, Niles, 60714

MSI List Marketing, 738 E Dundee Rd (Suite 321), Palatine, 60074-2858

Tri-Media Marketing Services Inc, 3330 Old Glenview Rd (#2), Wilmette, 60091-2963

Indiana

Harris Marketing Inc, PO Box 20428, Indianapolis, 46220-0428

S&G Business Associates Inc, 58135 Benham Ave, Elkhart, 46517

Iowa

Cornerstone Business Services Inc, PO Box 1636, Council Bluffs, 51502-1636

Datahouse Inc, 1141 Prarie View Dr, West Des Moines, 50266-7515

HR Direct Inc, 508 N 2nd St Ste 202, Fairfield, 52556-2474

Mancoma Inc, 315 W Fourth St, Davenport, 52801-1204

MidAmerica Lists Inc, 5001 1st Ave SE (Suite 105), Cedar Rapids, 52402-3251

Kansas

List Locators & Managers, 7171 W 95th (Suite 600), Overland Park, 66210

Williams Direct Inc, PO Box 205, Burlington, 66839-0205

Kentucky

American Clearinghouse Inc, 2201 Plantside Dr, Louisville, 40299-1940

Maryland

All American List Corp, 201 Skipjack Rd, Prince Frederick, 20678-3411

Mary Elizabeth Granger & Associates Inc, 110 West Rd (Suite 235), Baltimore, 21204-2343

NameBank International LLC, 100 W Monument St, Baltimore, 21201-4701

National Fundraising Lists, 16900 Science Dr (Suite 210), Bowie, 20715-4412

The Right Lists Ltd, 6417 Erin Dr, Clarksville, 21029-1290

Massachusetts

ACT ONE LISTS, 100 Cummings Ctr (Suite 434J), Beverly, 01915-6122

Advantage List Marketing Inc, 780 Marshall St, Holliston, 01746-1438

Commercial Mailing Lists, 26 Carver Rd, Framingham, 01701-4493

Direct Channel Inc, 234 W Center St Ste 2, West Bridgewater, 02379-1633

Healy List Marketing, 153 Andover St (Suite 108A), Danvers, 01923-5307

Intelitec, 154 Taylor St, Granby, 01033-9526

MGM Mailing Lists, Ten Leslin Ln, South Sandwich, 02563

PCS List & Information Technologies, PO Box 1507, Manchester, 01944-0860

Total Data Solutions, 48 Fox Hill Rd, North Andover, 01845-2936

Michigan

Advertising That Works, 6375 Westmoor Rd, Bloomfield Hills, 48301-1360

Burnett Direct Inc, 8585 P G A Dr (Suite 203), Commerce Township, 48390-1605

LED Signs, 104 Herbert St, Stockbridge, 49285-9808

RL Polk & Co, 26533 Evergreen Rd Ste 900, Southfield, 48076-4249

Minnesota

Aldata, 2 Pine Tree Dr # 302, Saint Paul, 55112-3715

BDirect Marketing, 4506 Margaret St, Saint Paul, 55110-3774

Missouri

CROSSLISTS CROSS & CO INC, 678 NW Hwy Z, Bates City, 64011-9120

The List Emporium, 171 English Landing Dr (Suite 200), Parkville, 64152

MCH Strategic Data, 601 E Marshall St, Sweet Springs, 65351-9613

Sorkins Inc, 319 South New Ballas Rd, Saint Louis, 63146

Nebraska

ACTON Group Ltd, 5760 Cornhusker Hwy (Suite 1), Lincoln, 68507-3121

CAS Inc, 10303 Crown Point Ave, Omaha, 68134-1061

Certified Lists Inc, 2823 N 81 St., Omaha, 68134

Cole Information Services, 17041 Lakeside Hills Plz Ste 2, Omaha, 68130-4677

Compass Marketing Solutions, 808 P St (Suite 300), Lincoln, 68508-1383

First Direct Marketing LLC, 1508 J F Kennedy Dr (Suite 103), Bellevue, 68005-6611

Info USA, 5711 S 86th Cir, Omaha, 68127

infoGROUP, 5711 S 86th Cir, Omaha, 68127-4146

infoUSA Inc, 5711 S 86th Cir, Omaha, 68127

New Business USA, 5711 S 86th Cir, PO Box 27086, Omaha, 68127-0086

Nevada

Collins List Exchange Inc, 2312 N Green Valley Pkwy (#2922), Henderson, 89014-3118

Exhibitrac Direct Marketing, 8290 W Sahara Ave (Suite 280), Las Vegas, 89117-8933

Firebrand Group, 7251 W Lake Mead Blvd (Suite 300), Las Vegas, 89128-8380

New Hampshire

Direct Media Millard, Ten Vose Farm Rd, Peterborough, 03458

F1rstmark Inc, 25 Vintinner Rd, Campton, 03223

Market Street Lists Inc, 7 Pleasant St, Exeter, 03833-1821

New Jersey

ALC Inc, 4300 US Hwy 1, Princeton, 08540-5706

Acxiom Co, 9004 Lincoln Dr W (Suite C), Marlton, 08053-3206

Borelli Direct Marketing Inc, 3530 State Route 27 Ste 207, Kendall Park, 08824-1055

Catalyst Direct Marketing/DNA, 109 Wanaque Ave, Pompton Lakes, 07422-2101

Central Letter Shop Inc, 14 Henderson Dr, West Caldwell, 07006-6608

Conrad Direct Inc, 300 Knickerbocker Rd, Cresskill, 07626-1350

Dataline, 5 Vaughn Dr (Suite 307), Princeton, 08540-6313

Direct Network Inc, PO Box 546, Allentown, 08501-0546

Ethnic Technologies LLC, 600 Huyler St Ste 5, South Hackensack, 07606-1734

Focus USA Inc, 1 University Plz (Suite 300), Hackensack, 07601-6205

Global DM Solutions, 416 Main St, Boonton, 07005-1714

Jamax Direct LLC, 375 Sylvan Ave (Suite 2), Englewood Cliffs, 07632-2714

Kroll Direct Marketing Inc, 101 Morgan Ln (Suite 120), Plainsboro, 08536-3345

List Service Direct Inc, 2 Christie Heights St, Leonia, 07605-2233

The List Source Inc, Four Hickory Ln, Cherry Hill, 08003-1408

Media Directions Inc, 50 Tice Blvd Ste A12, Woodcliff Lake, 07677-7681

NCRI List Management, 455 Sylvan Ave, Englewood Cliffs, 07632-2703

The Other List Co Inc, PO Box 286, Matawan, 07747

Redi-Data, 5 Audrey Pl, Fairfield, 07004-3401

SECO Financial Services Inc, 1288 Route 73 South, Mount Laurel, 08054

Specialists Marketing Services Inc, 777 Terrace Ave (fl 4), Hasbrouck Heights, 07604-3113

Trinity Direct, 10 Park Pl Ste 12, Butler, 07405-1370

V12 Group, 141 W Front St (Suite 410), Red Bank, 07701-6422

Vision Marketing Inc, 455 Sylvan Ave, Englewood Cliffs, 07632-2703

New York

Adpress Inc, 135 E 54th St (Penthouse F), New York, 10022-4539

American Student List LLC, 2 Dubon Ct, Farmingdale, 11735-1008

AmeriList Inc, 978 Route 45 Ste L2, Pomona, 10970-3565

The Center for Thanatology Research & Education Inc, 391 Atlantic Ave, Brooklyn, 11217-1701

Complete Mailing Lists LLC, 66 Palmer Ave Ste 149, Bronxville, 10708-3420

Contact Marketing LLC, 228 Park Ave S, New York, 10003-1502

Country Marketing Ltd, 26 Pine St, Ilion, 13357-1114

CoverClicks LLC, 817 Broadway (Floor 5), New York, 10003-4709

Directory of Major Malls, PO Box 837, Nyack, 10960-0837

Donnelley Marketing, 2 Blue Hill Plz (Suite 1662), Pearl River, 10965-3115

Hugo Dunhill Mailing Lists Inc, 542 Main St Ste 400, New Rochelle, 10801-7270

DUNN DATA Co Inc, 2022 Rte 22 S, Patterson Business Park E, Brewster, 10509-5946

Eclipse Direct Marketing, 173 Mineola Blvd (Suite 402), Mineola, 11501-2555

Leon Henry Inc, 200 N Central Ave (Suite 220), Hartsdale, 10530-9915

Horizon Lists, 126 W 227th St (Suite A), Bronx, 10463-6703

Hotline List Corp, 1071 Ave of the Americas, New York, 10018

Infinite Media, 190 E Post Rd, White Plains, 10601-4912

Info USA Services Group, 2 Blue Hill Plz (Suite 1662), Pearl River, 10965-3115

JF Direct Marketing Inc, 73 Croton Ave (Suite 106), Ossining, 10562-4973

Lake Group Media Inc, 1 Byram Brook Pl, Armonk, 10504

Lead Gen Media Group, 1000 South Ave (Suite 103), Staten Island, 10314-3431

List Advisor Inc, 500 Bi County Blvd (Suite 125), Farmingdale, 11735-3996

The List Connection Inc, 1015 Constable Dr, Mamaroneck, 10543

List Process Co Inc, 404 E 79th St (#23G), New York, 10075-1483

List Strategies Inc, 244 Madison Ave, New York, 10016-2817

LDS Group Inc, 555 8th Ave (Suite 1110), New York, 10018-4308

LS Direct Marketing, 4 Suffern Pl., Suffern, 10901

Macromark Inc, 185 Rte 312 (Suite 303), Brewster, 10509-2338

Mazzone Marketing Group LLC, 164 20th St (Suite 2B), Brooklyn, 11232-1151

Media Distribution Services (MDS), 307 W 36th St (fl 8), New York, 10018-6403

The MEDIA Organization Inc, 53 Holiday Dr (Suite 100), Woodbury, 11797-2319

The Merging Technologies Group LLC, 175 Commerce Dr (Suite K), Hauppauge, 11788-3920

MeritDirect, 333 Westchester Ave, White Plains, 10604-2910

Net 60 LLC, 228 Park Ave S (Suite 83872), New York, 10003-1502

Paradysz, 5 Hanover Sq, New York, 10004-2614

Research & Response International, 250 W 57th St (Suite 1326), New York, 10107-1309

Rickard List Marketing, 190 Motor Pkwy Ste 103, Hauppauge, 11788-5159

Riffkin Direct Inc, 64 Appletree Ln, Roslyn Heights, 11577-2432

Edith Roman Associates Inc, 1 Blue Hill Plz (Suite 16), Pearl River, 10965-3100

Select List Corp, 31 Glen Head Rd, Glen Head, 11545-1446

The Senior Source, 70 Sierra Vista Ln, Valley Cottage, 10989-2701

Singer Direct, 195 Broadway Fl 12, New York, 10007-3126

Fred Singer Direct Marketing Inc, 800 Westchester Ave (Suite 400), Rye Brook, 10573-1340

Sobelsohn School, 275 W 96th St, New York, 10025

SIE (Select Information Exchange), 175 W 79th St, New York, 10024

Student Marketing Group Inc, 777 Sunrise Hwy (Suite 300), Lynbrook, 11563-2950

Thor Information Services Inc, 3032 State Rte 28, Old Forge, 13420-1167

3 Gen Co, 544 Empire Blvd, Brooklyn, 11225

Triangle Marketing Services Inc, 245 W 17th St (Suite 1250), New York, 10011

USADATA Inc, 292 Madison Ave (fl 3), New York, 10017-6322

Weekly Reader Corp, 44 S Broadway, White Plains, 10601-4425

Fred Woolf List Co Inc, PO Box 346, Somers, 10589-0346

Zeppo Marketing Inc, 358 5th Ave Rm 1103, New York, 10001-2221

North Carolina

BIZ Journal Business Leads, 120 W Morehead St (Suite 100), Charlotte, 28202-1854

FJ Associates LLC, PO Box 12771, Wilmington, 28405-0138

IHFRA, 209 S Main (#M1405), High Point, 27260

The List Place Inc, 8508 Park Rd, PMB #173, Charlotte, 28210-5803

Roseberry Direct List Management & Brokerage, 265 Timberline Trl, Elon, 27244-8088

Ohio

Matt Brown & Associates Inc, 2769 Orchard Run Rd, Dayton, 45449-2831

Hippo Direct, 34472 Summerset Dr, Solon, 44139

List Marketing Group Inc, 19885 Detroit Rd (Suite 207), Cleveland, 44116-1815

Prime Target Direct LLC, 7788 W Bay Dr, Mason, 45040-8440

Speedeon Data Corp, 6655 Parkland Blvd, Cleveland, 44139-4345

Pennsylvania

Amichetti, Lewis & Associates Inc, 814 Wetherill Ln, Wayne, 19087

Great Lakes Fulfillment Inc, 3126 Peach St, Erie, 16508-2734

The Guild Co, 1500 Spring Garden St (fl 12), Philadelphia, 19130-4094

International Direct Response Inc, 1125 Lancaster Ave Ste 2, Berwyn, 19312-2601

Listmasters Direct Mail Services, 1296 Adams Rd, Bensalem, 19020

Market Force Corp, 3605 Chapel Rd (Suite C), Newtown Square, 19073-3602

Neighborhood Greetings, 328 W Charlotte St, Millersville, 17551-9516

North American Publishing Co, 1500 Spring Garden St (Suite 1200), Philadelphia, 19130-4069

Paramount Lists Inc, 3126 Peach St, Erie, 16508-2734

Pennrich, 8890 Hamot Rd, Waterford, 16441-9240

WS Ponton Inc, 5149 Butler St, The Ponton Bldg, Pittsburgh, 15201-2606

SWAT Marketing Team, 433 S Broad St, Grove City, 16127-2201

South Carolina

Evergreen Marketing, 116 Ram Cat Aly (Suite 201), Seneca, 29678-3263

List Connection Inc, PO Box 1712, Simpsonville, 29681-1712

Rein Associates Inc, PO Box 50878, Myrtle Beach, 29579-0015

Specialized Fundraising Services, 300 E Henry St Ste 102, Spartanburg, 29302-2630

South Dakota

CommissionSoup, 114 N Egan Ave, PO Box 463, Madison, 57042

Tennessee

Altair Data Resources, 730 Cool Springs Blvd Ste 130, Franklin, 37067-7290

Beach List Direct Inc, 4605 Villa Green Dr, Nashville, 37215-4331

Sitel, 3102 West End Ave (Suite 1000), Two American Center, Nashville, 37203-1324

Triax Data, 8911 Linksvue Dr, Knoxville, 37922-5254

Texas

Fred E Allen Inc, 2726 W Ferguson, Mount Pleasant, 75455-6516

AllMedia Inc, 5601 Democracy Dr Ste 255, Plano, 75024-3699

American Direct Marketing Services, 14900 Landmark Blvd (Suite 350), Dallas, 75254

Bush Co Inc, 4309 Hartwood Cir, Fort Worth, 76109-1508

Business Extension Bureau of Texas Inc, 4802 Travis St, Houston, 77002-9740

Gnames Media Group, 1452 Hughes Rd Ste 320, Grapevine, 76051-7369

Manning Media International, 2128 Surrey Ln, Mc Kinney, 75070-7132

Market Approach Consulting, 111 E Center St, Lorena, 76655-9651

Marketing Signals Group, 6801 Gaylord Pkwy Ste 200, Frisco, 75034-5979

Names in the Mail Inc, 10710 Shiloh Rd, Dallas, 75228-2640

Paragon Printing & Mailing, 10423 McKalla Pl, Bldg A (Suite 100), Austin, 78758-4448

ReachForce, 9020-1 Capital of TX Hwy N (Suite 270), Austin, 78750

Spirit Direct Marketing Services, 11777 Katy Fwy (#120), Houston, 77079-1705

TKL Interactive, 3700 Standridge Dr (Suite 210), The Colony, 75056-4149

Utah

American Name Services Inc, 774 S 400 E, Orem, 84097-6322

Vermont

Meling & Associates, 962 West Rd., West Rutland, 05777-9235

New England List Services Inc, 171 Mountain View Dr, Danville, 05828-9641

Virginia

All-n-One List Marketing Inc, PO Box 862, Fishersville, 22939-0862

American Mailing Lists Corp, 9625 Surveyer Ct (Suite 400), Manassas, 20110

Atlantic List Company Inc, 2425 Wilson Blvd (Suite 500), Arlington, 22201-3326

Carol Enters List Co Inc, 9663-C Main St (Suite C), Fairfax, 22031-3758

Frontline Data Group, 1953 Gallows Rd (Suite 600), Vienna, 22182-3988

GreatLists.com, 21351 Gentry Dr (Suite 135), Dulles, 20166

Infocus Marketing Inc, 4245 Sigler Rd, Warrenton, 20187-3940

Innovative List Marketing Inc, 9663 Main St (Suite C), Fairfax, 22031-3758

Integrated Direct Marketing, 12120 Sunset Hills Rd (Suite 450), Reston, 20190-5858

Lawrence Direct Marketing Inc, 26 Ashby St, Warrenton, 20186-3201

Tony Murray & Associates, 9663-C Main St, Fairfax, 22031

Omega List Co, 1420 Spring Hill Rd (Suite 490), McLean, 22102-3028

O'Neill Marketing Co, 10805 Main St (#400), Fairfax, 22030-4747

Pinnacle List Co, 2800 Shirlington Rd (Suite 970), Arlington, 22206-3613

Response Unlimited, 284 Shalom Rd, c/o The Old Plantation, Waynesboro, 22980-7349

Robertson Mailing List Co, 44084 Riverside Pkwy (Suite 350), Leesburg, 20176-6823

TMA Direct, 12120 Sunset Hills Rd (Suite 450), Reston, 20190-5858

Washington Lists Inc, 6849 Old Dominion Dr (Suite 320), McLean, 22101

Washington

DATA SOLUTIONS OF AMERICA INC, 7120 185th Ave NE Ste 150, Redmond, 98052-0576

LexisNexis Risk & Information Analytics, 13427 NE 16th St, Bellevue, 98005-2307

Marketfish Inc, 524 2nd Ave Ste 200, Seattle, 98104-2323

Marketry Inc, 11400 SE 8th St (Suite 370), Bellevue, 98004-6468

Wisconsin

McCarthy Media Group Inc, 1620 Eighth St, Monroe, 53566-1628

Omar's Touch Therapy, 905 Lorraine Dr, Madison, 53705-1133

CANADA
British Columbia

JR Direct Response International Inc, 4917 Delta St, Delta, V4K 2V1

JS Direct Address Limited, 1429 Dominion St (#203), North Vancouver, V7J 1B4

Ontario

Fixed Address Marketing Inc, 136 Pinnacle Tr, Aurora, L4G 7G7

ICOM Information & Communications Inc, 41 Metropolitan Rd, Toronto, M1R 2T5

InfoCANADA, 1290 Central Pkwy W (Suite 104), Mississauga, L5C 4R3

LMC Direct, 1475 Star Top Rd (Unit Eight), Ottawa, K1B 3W5

Quebec

Communications Real Laforte Inc, 1955 Rue Robertine Brry, Montreal, H4N 3G2

JonCas PostExperts Inc, 7875 Trans-Canada Hwy, Ville Saint Laurent, H4S 1L3

List Brokers & Compilers (23)

AAA BEST MAILING LISTS INC
7507 E Tanque Verde Rd, Best Mailing Lists Inc
Tucson, AZ 85715-3667
Telephone: (520) 885-0400, (800) 692-2378, FAX: (520) 885-3100, E-Mail: best@bestmailing.com, Web Site: www.bestmailing.com
Pres: Karen J. Kirsch
VP: Herbert Kirsch
Conducts Business: Worldwide
Employees: 15
Founded: 1984

ALC INC
4300 US Hwy 1
Princeton, NJ 08540-5706
Telephone: (609) 580-2800, (800) ALC-LIST, FAX: (609) 580-2888, E-Mail: info@alc.com, Web Site: www.alc.com
CEO: Donn Rappaport
Mktg Mgr: Tracie Larino

THE DMA ACCUDATA INTEGRATED MARKETING
5220 Summerlin Commons Blvd (Suite 200)
Fort Myers, FL 33907-2150
Telephone: (239) 425-4400, (800) 732-3440, FAX: (239) 425-4401, E-Mail: info@accudata.com, Web Site: www.accudata.com
Media Rels: Heather Krasnow
Pres: Rich Lancaster
Sr Dir Product Mktg: Crystal Fischer
Dir Mktg: Tara Beauchesne

ACCULIST INC
2140 Eastman Ave Ste 105
Ventura, CA 93003-7786
Telephone: (805) 644-1966, Web Site: www.acculist.com
Pres & Founder: David Kanter

THE DMA ACT ONE LISTS
100 Cummings Ctr (Suite 434J)
Beverly, MA 01915-6122
Telephone: (781) 639-1919, (800) 228-5478, FAX: (781) 639-2733, E-Mail: info@act1lists.com, Web Site: www.act1lists.com
Pres & CEO: Steven M. Cushinsky

ACTIVE NETWORK MEDIA & MARKETING
10182 Telesis Ct (Suite 300)
San Diego, CA 92121-4777
Telephone: (858) 964-6064, (877) 228-4808, Web Site: www.activemarketinggroup.com
Sr VP: Eric Magnuson
Sr Acct Mgr: Barbara Heisser

ACTON GROUP LTD
5760 Cornhusker Hwy (Suite 1)
Lincoln, NE 68507-3121
Telephone: (402) 742-2820, FAX: (402) 470-2673, E-Mail: info@acton.com, Web Site: www.acton.com
Chmn Bd: Jon Lambert
Pres: Kraig Prange
Dir Pur: Frank Lambert
Sr Database Specialist: Debb Bovett
Asia Bus Devel: Hiro Koga

Full service international direct marketing agency who develops marketing programs that yield the highest number of customers at the lowest acquisition cost possible. Specializes in full mail package creative, print, lettershop & postal logistics or a multimedia immersion campaign & full coverage country specific consumer & business database license agreements.

ACXIOM CO
Div. of Acxiom Corp
9004 Lincoln Dr W (Suite C)
Marlton, NJ 08053-3206
Telephone: (800) 635-5833, FAX: (856) 988-6662
Team Leader ARI: Pam Holden

AD-VANTAGE MARKETING
455 Tesconi Cir
Santa Rosa, CA 95401-4619
Telephone: (707) 578-8700, FAX: (707) 578-0258, Web Site: www.ad-vantagemarketing.com
Dir: Glen Rankin
Sls: Aaron Rankin

ADPRESS INC
135 E 54th St (Penthouse F)
New York, NY 10022-4539
Telephone: (212) 679-1710, FAX: (212) 532-9508, E-Mail: adpressinc@aol.com, Web Site: www.adpressinc.com
Pres: Bill Meyer

ADVANTAGE LIST MARKETING INC
780 Marshall St
Holliston, MA 01746-1438
Telephone: (508) 429-4400, FAX: (508) 429-7117
Pres: Mark J. Murphy

ADVERTISING THAT WORKS
6375 Westmoor Rd
Bloomfield Hills, MI 48301-1360
Telephone: (248) 626-2264, FAX: (248) 626-2264, Web Site: www.advertisingthatworks.us
Pres & Owner: Steven Bartley

ADVISOR MEDIA INC
PO Box 503350
San Diego, CA 92150-3350
Telephone: (858) 278-5600, FAX: (858) 278-5600, Web Site: www.advisor.com
Pres: Jeanne Hawkins

ALDATA
2 Pine Tree Dr # 302
Saint Paul, MN 55112-3715
Telephone: (952) 432-6900, FAX: (952) 432-7064, E-Mail: mharris@aldata.com, Web Site: www.aldata.com
Pres: H. Michael Harris

THE DMA THE ALESCO DATA GROUP
5276 Summerlin Commons Way Ste 703
Fort Myers, FL 33907-2159
Telephone: (239) 275-5006, (800) 701-6531, FAX: (239) 275-7737, E-Mail: marketing@alescodata.com, Web Site: www.alescodata.com
CEO: Michael Sklorenko
Primary Market Served: Business

ALL AMERICAN LIST CORP
201 Skipjack Rd
Prince Frederick, MD 20678-3411
Telephone: (301) 420-5760, (800) 690-2252, FAX: (301) 420-5765, E-Mail: info@allamericanlist.com, Web Site: www.allamericanlist.com
Pres: Hawley Van Wyck

ALL-N-ONE LIST MARKETING INC
PO Box 862
Fishersville, VA 22939-0862

Telephone: (703) 717-5621, Web Site:
www.alln1lists.com
Pres: Greg Sholes
Primary Market Served: Business

FRED E ALLEN INC
2726 W Ferguson
Mount Pleasant, TX 75455-6516
Telephone: (903) 572-1701, FAX:
(903) 572-1703
Pres: Fred E. Allen

ALLIANCE STRATEGIES GROUP, INC
7700 Congress Ave, Suite 3208
Boca Raton, FL 33487
Telephone: (561) 499-3201, Web Site:
www.bestroilists.com
Primary Market Served: Business &
Consumer

ALLMEDIA INC
5601 Democracy Dr Ste 255
Plano, TX 75024-3699
Telephone: (469) 467-9100, FAX:
(214) 291-5431, E-Mail:
lmcclendon@allmediainc.com, Web
Site: www.allmediainc.com
Pres: Laura McClendon
VP Sales: Richard Becker
VP: Mary Loeffler
Acct Exec, Intl Div: Scott Caufield
Acct Exec, Interactive Div: Jon Mens-
ing
Conducts Business: Worldwide
Employees: 25
Primary Market Served: Business &
Consumer
Founded: 1981

Provides targeted media for measurable
results. Account teams provide expert
advice to marketers regarding the purchase and use of email, postal &
telemarketing prospect lists & related
data management services. Help clients
implement lead generation programs,
insert media & online media to meet
marketing goals.

ALPHA LIST MARKETING INC
837 Thackston Dr
Marietta, GA 30068-4365
Telephone: (404) 995-7049, (800) 822-
2902, FAX: (404) 601-0826, E-Mail:
info@alphalistmarketing.com
Pres: Judith B. Kelly

ALTAIR DATA RESOURCES
730 Cool Springs Blvd Ste 130
Franklin, TN 37067-7290

Telephone: (615) 468-6800, (866) 261-
4695, FAX: (615) 468-6878, E-Mail:
info@altairdata.com, Web Site:
www.altairdata.com
Pres: David Hadaway
Employees: 30
Primary Market Served: Business
Direct online sales
Advertising/Marketing Budget Related
to Direct Marketing: 51-75%
Direct Marketing ad budget:
Direct Mail: 10%
Telephone: 90%
Founded: 2001

Compiled direct mail & telemarketing
lists.

AMACAI INFORMATION CORP
Subs. of TARGUSinfo
2 Mid America Plz Ste 606
Oakbrook Terrace, IL 60181-4716
Telephone: (800) 434-1555, FAX:
(312) 924-3001, E-Mail: info@
amacai.com, Web Site: www.amacai.
com
VP Corp Devel: Jeff Beard
Employees: 100
Indirect online sales
Advertising/Marketing Budget Related
to Direct Marketing: 0-25%
Founded: 2001

Consumer and business data to companies, whose core business is built upon
complete and accurate name, address
and phone information.

AMERICAN CLEARINGHOUSE INC
2201 Plantside Dr
Louisville, KY 40299-1940
Telephone: (800) 944-6361, Web Site:
www.americanclearinghouse.com
Owner: Renee Jones
Primary Market Served: Business

AMERICAN DATABASE MARKETING INC
12627 San Jose Blvd (#603)
Jacksonville, FL 32223-8642
Telephone: (904) 886-0744, (888) 565-
7724, FAX: (888) 270-4338, E-Mail:
admdun@cs.com, Web Site: www.
admdun.com
Sls Dir: Brant Turner

AMERICAN DIRECT MARKETING SERVICES
14900 Landmark Blvd (Suite 350)
Dallas, TX 75254
Telephone: (214) 634-2361, (800) 527-
5080, FAX: (214) 905-3829, Web
Site: www.dmlist.com
Pres: Scott Casson

Office Mgr: Connie Hill

AMERICAN HOTEL REGISTER CO
100 S Milwaukee Ave Ste 100
Vernon Hills, IL 60061-4321
Telephone: (708) 743-4163, FAX:
(708) 564-5797, Web Site: www.
americanhotel.com
Pres: James Leahy
Mktg Analyst: Lisa Falk

AMERICAN LEADS CO
PO Box 1425
Benicia, CA 94510-4425
Telephone: (707) 747-6334, FAX:
(707) 747-5323, Web Site: www.
american-leads.com
VP: Richard E. Bottom

AMERICAN MAILING LISTS CORP
9625 Surveyer Ct (Suite 400)
Manassas, VA 20110
Telephone: (571) 292-5806, FAX:
(571) 292-5807, E-Mail: dorothy@
amlc.info, Web Site: www.amlc.info

AMERICAN NAME SERVICES INC
774 S 400 E
Orem, UT 84097-6322
Telephone: (801) 235-8061, (800) 434-
1851, FAX: (801) 764-0613, E-Mail:
sales@americannameservices.com,
Web Site: www.
americannameservices.com
Pres: Jill Grammer

AMERICAN STUDENT LIST LLC
2 Dubon Ct
Farmingdale, NY 11735-1008
Telephone: (516) 248-6100, (888) 462-
5600, FAX: (516) 248-6364, E-Mail:
sales@studentlist.com, Web Site:
www.studentlist.com
Fin Dir: Frank Mangano
Pres: Donald Damore

AMERICAN STUDENT MARKETING LLC
473 Central Ave (Suite 7))
Highland Park, IL 60035-2691
Telephone: (847) 432-4329, Web Site:
www.asmdm.com
VP: Rich Johnson

AMERILIST INC
978 Route 45 Ste L2
Pomona, NY 10970-3565
Telephone: (800) 457-2899, Web Site:
www.amerilist.com

Pres: Ravi Buckredan

AMICHETTI, LEWIS & ASSOCIATES INC
814 Wetherill Ln
Wayne, PA 19087
Telephone: (610) 341-9545, E-Mail:
ala300@aol.com
Pres: Dennis Amichetti

ANDREW ASSOCIATES INC
Six Pearson Way
Enfield, CT 06082
Telephone: (860) 253-0000, FAX:
(860) 741-0850, Web Site: www.
andrewmail.com
Pres & Treas: Judith A. Knapp

ARTNETWORK-ARTWORLD MAILING LISTS
10655 Park Ave Ext
Nevada City, CA 95959-8890
Telephone: (530) 478-0920, (800) 383-
0677, FAX: (530) 470-0256, E-Mail:
info@artmarketing.com, Web Site:
www.artmarketing.com
Contact: Sarah Meyers

ATLANTIC LIST COMPANY INC
2425 Wilson Blvd (Suite 500)
Arlington, VA 22201-3326
Telephone: (703) 528-7482, Web Site:
www.atlanticlist.com
Primary Market Served: Business

ATP LIST SERVICES
Div. of Applied Tech Pub
1300 S Grove Ave (Suite 105)
Barrington, IL 60010-5246
Telephone: (800) 223-3423, Web Site:
www.atplists.com
List Mgr: Ellen Sandkam

AUTOBYTEL INC
18872 Macarthur Blvd
Irvine, CA 92612-1448
Telephone: (949) 225-4500, Web Site:
www.autobytel.com
Direct Mktg Analyst: Troy Vo

AVRICK DIRECT INC
979 Saint Mary's Ln
Santa Barbara, CA 93111-1034
Telephone: (805) 683-6551, FAX:
(805) 965-6181, E-Mail: david@
avrick.com, Web Site: www.
avrickdirect.com
Pres: David Avrick
COO: Doreen Ellen Burk
Conducts Business: Worldwide
Primary Market Served: Business &
Consumer

Direct online sales
Advertising/Marketing Budget Related
to Direct Marketing: 76-100%
Founded: 1996

Mailing list owner.

BDIRECT MARKETING
4506 Margaret St
Saint Paul, MN 55110-3774
Telephone: (651) 483-3260, FAX:
(651) 483-3267, E-Mail:
bdirectlists@comcast.net, Web Site:
www.bdirectlists.com
Owner & List Sls Mgr: Robert Shoen

BEACH LIST DIRECT INC
4605 Villa Green Dr
Nashville, TN 37215-4331
Telephone: (615) 356-1100, Web Site:
www.beachlistdirect.com
Mng Dir: T. Clay Beach
Primary Market Served: Business &
Consumer

BEST ROI LISTS
21218 Saint Andrews Blvd (Suite 202)
Boca Raton, FL 33433-2449
Telephone: (561) 499-3201, Web Site:
www.bestroilists.com
Pres: Bryan Rudnick
Primary Market Served: Business &
Consumer

BIZ JOURNAL BUSINESS LEADS
Div of American City Business Jour-
nals
120 W Morehead St (Suite 100)
Charlotte, NC 28202-1854
Telephone: (704) 973-1273
Gen Mgr: James Penegar

BLACKSTONE LISTS
Project Management Inc
4280 Galt Ocean Dr (Suite 25D)
Fort Lauderdale, FL 33308-6153
Telephone: (954) 568-6411
Pres: J. Schwartz

BORELLI DIRECT MARKETING INC
3530 State Route 27 Ste 207
Kendall Park, NJ 08824-1055
Telephone: (732) 940-1500, Web Site:
www.borellidirect.com
Owner: Joe Borelli
Primary Market Served: Business &
Consumer

THE DMA MATT BROWN & ASSOCIATES INC
2769 Orchard Run Rd
Dayton, OH 45449-2831

Telephone: (937) 434-3949, (800) 233-
3949, FAX: (937) 434-6272, E-Mail:
mba@mbalists.com, Web Site: www.
mbalists.com
Pres: Bernice Willis

BURNETT DIRECT INC
8585 P G A Dr (Suite 203)
Commerce Township, MI 48390-1605
Telephone: (248) 313-9120, E-Mail:
bdisales@burnett.com, Web Site:
www.burnett.com
Pres: Mark Burnett

BURNETT MARKETING INC
800 W Central Rd (Suite 108)
Mount Prospect, IL 60056-2383
Telephone: (800) 837-6906, FAX:
(800) 837-6978, E-Mail:
burnettmkt@aol.com, Web Site:
www.burnettmarketing.com
Pres: Robert Anderson

BUSH CO INC
4309 Hartwood Cir
Fort Worth, TX 76109-1508
Telephone: (949) 752-4210, FAX:
(949) 752-4220, E-Mail: barb@
bushlists.com, Web Site: www.
bushlists.com
Pres: Barbara Spaulding

THE DMA BUSINESS EXTENSION BUREAU OF TEXAS INC
4802 Travis St
Houston, TX 77002-9740
Telephone: (713) 528-5568, (800) 969-
5568, FAX: (713) 528-1648, E-Mail:
ronr@bebtexas.com, Web Site: www.
bebtexas.com
Pres & CEO: Ron Royall
Chmn: Robert L. Royall
VP Sales: Ro Royall

BUSINESS MAILING CENTER
Div. of Ventura Printing
200 N Elevar St
Oxnard, CA 93030
Telephone: (805) 981-2600, (800) 882-
1844, FAX: (805) 981-1180, E-Mail:
answers@venturaprint.com, Web
Site: www.venturaprint.com
Gen Mgr, BMC: Sean Russell
Gen Mgr, Ventura: David Wilson

THE DMA BYRUM & FLEMING
321 San Anselmo Ave
San Anselmo, CA 94960-2647
Telephone: (415) 457-1700, Web Site:
www.byrumfleming.com
Partner: Robert Fleming
Primary Market Served: Business &
Consumer

CAS INC
10303 Crown Point Ave
Omaha, NE 68134-1061
Telephone: (402) 964-9998, (800) 524-
0908 X2071, FAX: (402) 963-2103,
E-Mail: sales@cas-online.com, Web
Site: www.cas-online.com
Pres: Drew Lundgren

A CALDWELL LIST CO INC
3295 River Exchange Dr Ste 380
Norcross, GA 30092-4238
Telephone: (770) 662-0255, (800) 241-
7425, FAX: (770) 662-0351, Web
Site: www.caldwell-list.com
Pres: Cheslie Lachnicht

CAPITOL HILL LISTS
1252 Rambling Rill Cir
Statham, GA 30666-3602
Telephone: (706) 546-0282
Pres: Paul Kilgore

CARNEGIE MARKETING ASSOCIATES
3878 Carson St (Suite 220)
Torrance, CA 90503-6707
Telephone: (310) 540-4757, FAX:
(310) 540-7407
Pres: Janie Thompson

THE DMA CARNEY DIRECT MARKETING
15520 Rockfield Blvd (Suite C)
Irvine, CA 92618-2792
Telephone: (949) 581-51000, (800)
240-3349, Web Site: www.
carneydirect.com
Pres: Pete Carney

CATALOG MEDIA NETWORK INC
500 Davis Ctr (Suite 812)
Evanston, IL 60201-4655
Telephone: (847) 864-0550, FAX:
(847) 864-0575, Web Site: www.
thelistbank.com
Pres: E. Herbert Krug

CATALYST DIRECT MARKETING/DNA
109 Wanaque Ave
Pompton Lakes, NJ 07422-2101
Telephone: (973) 831-4222, FAX:
(973) 831-1933, E-Mail: info@
catalystdm.com, Web Site: www.
catalystdm.com
Pres: Fred Litzky
VP: Becky Santaniello
Dir, Sls & Mktg: Gene Carbine
Conducts Business: U.S.
Founded: 1984

THE CATAMOUNT GROUP
200 Pequot Ave Ste 1
Southport, CT 06890-1371
Telephone: (203) 778-4110, FAX:
(203) 778-4130, E-Mail: tina@
catamountgroup.net, Web Site: www.
catamountgroup.net
Pres: Tina MacNicholl
VP: Amy Bericewicz
Sr Acct Exec: Becky Hagadasn
Acct Exec: Bridget Hartigan
Conducts Business: U.S.
Employees: 8
Primary Market Served: Business &
Consumer
Catalog available online
Direct online sales
Advertising/Marketing Budget Related
to Direct Marketing: 76-100%
Founded: 1997

Direct marketing agency.

THE CENTER FOR THANATOLOGY RESEARCH & EDUCATION INC
391 Atlantic Ave
Brooklyn, NY 11217-1701
Telephone: (718) 858-3026, FAX:
(718) 852-1846, E-Mail:
thanatology@pipeline.com, Web
Site: www.thanatology.org
Dir: Roberta Halporn

CENTRAL LETTER SHOP INC
14 Henderson Dr
West Caldwell, NJ 07006-6608
Telephone: (973) 808-9595, FAX:
(973) 808-8339, E-Mail: lena@
centrallettershop.com, Web Site:
www.centrallettershop.com
Pres: Jim Pinkin

CERTIFIED LISTS INC
2823 N 81 St.
Omaha, NE 68134
Telephone: (402) 201-2087, (866) 537-
7569, FAX: (877) 655-8733, E-Mail:
contact@certified-lists.com, Web
Site: www.certified-lists.com
Owner: Bryce Coes

THE DMA COLE INFORMATION SERVICES
Div. of Experian
17041 Lakeside Hills Plz Ste 2
Omaha, NE 68130-4677
Telephone: (800) 403-5894, Web Site:
www.coleinformation.com
Chmn: D. Van Skilling
CFO: Paul Brooks
CEO: Jim Eggleston
Conducts Business: U.S., Canada
Primary Market Served: Business

Catalog available online
Indirect online sales
Advertising/Marketing Budget Related
to Direct Marketing: 76-100%
Direct Marketing ad budget:
Direct Mail: 50%
Newspapers: 10%
Online: 5%
Telephone: 35%
Founded: 1947

Publish a directory listing telephone
subscribers by house number and
street. Used by direct mailers, telephone marketers & door-to-door
vendors.

COLLINS LIST EXCHANGE INC
2312 N Green Valley Pkwy (#2922)
Henderson, NV 89014-3118
Telephone: (702) 369-6015, Web Site:
www.collinslist.com
Owner & Pres: Melody Collins

COMMERCIAL MAILING LISTS
Subs. of The Forman Group Ltd
26 Carver Rd
Framingham, MA 01701-4493
Telephone: (508) 879-2647, (800) 875-
8345, FAX: (508) 879-2911, E-Mail:
bruce@commercialmailinglists.com,
Web Site: www.
commercialmailinglists.com
Pres: William E. Forman

COMMISSIONSOUP
Div. of CreditSoup Inc
114 N Egan Ave, PO Box 463
Madison, SD 57042
Telephone: (605) 256-9103, (866) 309-
7687, FAX: (605) 256-1522, E-Mail:
info@creditsoup.com, Web Site:
www.commissionsoup.com
Founder & Pres: Darin Namken
Founder & CEO: Todd Knodel
Founder & Dir: Chad Ekroth
Conducts Business: U.S., Canada
Employees: 16
Primary Market Served: Business &
Consumer
Catalog available online
Direct online sales
Advertising/Marketing Budget Related
to Direct Marketing: 76-100%
Founded: 2000
Gross sales or billing: $3,500,000

E-business marketing solutions through
a performance based affiliate marketing
network.

COMMUNICATIONS REAL LAFORTE INC
1955 Rue Robertine Brry
Montreal, PQ, Canada H4N 3G2
Telephone: (514) 335-1523, (800) 836-7766, FAX: (514) 335-5981
Pres: Real Laforte

THE DMA COMPASS MARKETING SOLUTIONS
808 P St (Suite 300)
Lincoln, NE 68508-1383
Telephone: (402) 438-3222, Web Site: www.cmsdm.com
Partner: Michelle Brown

THE DMA COMPLETE MAILING LISTS LLC
66 Palmer Ave Ste 149
Bronxville, NY 10708-3420
Telephone: (914) 771-6640, (866) 314-5478, FAX: (914) 771-6645, E-Mail: ewoolf@cml-llc.com, Web Site: www.cml-llc.com
Mng Partner: Mike Jorgovan

Mailing list compiler and broker. We sell targeted lists to customers who represent all industries.

THE DMA COMPUTERIZED RESEARCH & DEVELOPMENT INC
6110 Auburn Folsom Rd
Granite Bay, CA 95746-5868
Telephone: (916) 652-0497, Web Site: www.computerizedresearch.com
Pres: Judy Groom

COMPUTERMAIL SOUTH
200 Second Ave S (Suite 160)
Saint Petersburg, FL 33701-4313
Telephone: (727) 579-1000, (800) 551-5478, FAX: (727) 823-5474, E-Mail: sales@computermailsouth.com, Web Site: computermailsouth.com
Pres: John L. Cissna
Partner: Lynn M. Cissna

CONRAD DIRECT INC
300 Knickerbocker Rd
Cresskill, NJ 07626-1350
Telephone: (201) 567-3200, FAX: (201) 567-1530, Web Site: www.conraddirect.com
Pres & CEO: Jerry Gould
Exec VP: Barbara Schonwald
VP: Sharon Traina

CONTACT MARKETING LLC
228 Park Ave S
New York, NY 10003-1502
Telephone: (201) 530-0200, (800) 848-7501, FAX: (201) 530-2205, E-Mail: info@cmlists.com, Web Site: www.contactmarketingllc.com
Pres: Ari Ginsberg

CONTEMPO MARKETING CO
2101 NW 33rd St (Suite 100A)
Pompano Beach, FL 33069-1046
Telephone: (954) 978-8215, (800) 322-5089, FAX: (954) 978-8217
Pres: Charles Lifton
Founded: 1977

CORNERSTONE BUSINESS SERVICES INC
PO Box 1636
Council Bluffs, IA 51502-1636
Telephone: (712) 256-4987, Web Site: www.conerstonelist.com
Pres & CEO: Peggy Shields

THE DMA COUNTRY MARKETING LTD
26 Pine St
Ilion, NY 13357-1114
Telephone: (315) 895-7737, FAX: (315) 895-7392, E-Mail: al@countrymarketing.com, Web Site: www.countrymarketing.com
Pres: Susan Nabinger

COVERCLICKS LLC
817 Broadway (Floor 5)
New York, NY 10003-4709
Telephone: (888) 624-1340, FAX: (212) 239-2850, E-Mail: info@coverclicksmail.com, Web Site: www.coverclicks.com
CEO: Joshua Blumenfeld
VP Direct Mktg: Gene Zacharewicz

THE DMA CROSS MARKETING USA
1310 N Ritchie Ct (Suite 16-C)
Chicago, IL 60610-8401
Telephone: (312) 440-3700, (866) 440-3700, FAX: (312) 943-5813, E-Mail: ronbernstein@crossmarketing.us, Web Site: www.crossmarketing.us
VP: Ronald A. Bernstein
Primary Market Served: Consumer

CROSSLISTS CROSS & CO INC
678 NW Hwy Z
Bates City, MO 64011-9120
Telephone: (816) 697-3306, FAX: (816) 697-3317, E-Mail: jmbrown@crosscompany.com, Web Site: www.crosscompany.com
CEO: Joy Brown

CUSTOM LIST SERVICES INC
1810 Harbour Cir, c/o Pittman
Cape Coral, FL 33914-2510
Telephone: (301) 497-1858, FAX: (301) 497-1858
List Svcs Mgr: Cori Reider

D-J ASSOCIATES
42 Old Ridgebury Rd
Danbury, CT 06810-5129
Telephone: (203) 431-8777, FAX: (203) 431-3302, E-Mail: info@djassoc.com, Web Site: www.djassoc.com
Pres: Kathy Duggan-Josephs

DATA-DYNAMIX INC
781 Canyon Dr
Castle Rock, CO 80104-1844
Telephone: (720) 855-9282, (888) 314-0078, FAX: (720) 855-9099, Web Site: www.data-dynamix.com
Pres: Brent Fankhauser
Dir Opers: Marie Fontenot
Admin Asst: Grace Casias
Dir Sls: Lisa Wise
Conducts Business: U.S., Canada, U.K.
Employees: 6
Indirect online sales
Advertising/Marketing Budget Related to Direct Marketing: 0-25%
Direct Marketing ad budget:
Direct Mail: 100%
Founded: 1999
Gross sales or billing: $1,200,000

List brokerage/list management.

THE DATA GROUP
425 S Avalon Park Blvd.
Orlando, FL 32828-6703
Telephone: (800) 262-5609, E-Mail: questions@thedatagrouponline.com, Web Site: www.thedatagrouponline.com

DATA SOLUTIONS OF AMERICA INC
7120 185th Ave NE Ste 150
Redmond, WA 98052-0576
Telephone: (239) 540-2992, Web Site: www.dsoai.com
Pres: Elizabeth Blank

DATAHOUSE INC
1141 Prarie View Dr
West Des Moines, IA 50266-7515
Telephone: (508) 480-0012, (866) 640-3282, E-Mail: data@datahouseinc.com, Web Site: www.datahouseinc.com
Pres: Richard Mestas
Conducts Business: U.S.
Employees: 1

Primary Market Served: Business & Consumer
Catalog available online
Indirect online sales
Advertising/Marketing Budget Related to Direct Marketing: 0-25%
Direct Marketing ad budget:
Direct Mail: 10%
Online: 90%
Founded: 2003
Gross sales or billing: $200,000

Prospect or mailing lists and data services.

THE DMA DATALINE
5 Vaughn Dr (Suite 307)
Princeton, NJ 08540-6313
Telephone: (609) 452-6014, Web Site: www.datalinedata.com
Pres & CEO: Paul Sobel
Primary Market Served: Business & Consumer

THE DMA DATALOGIX
10075 Westmoor Dr (Suite 200)
Westminster, CO 80021-2570
Telephone: (303) 327-1600, FAX: (303) 327-1650, Web Site: www.datalogix.com
CEO & Pres: Eric Roza
Mktg Coord: Sarah Kinnel

THE DMA DATAQUICK
Subs of MacDonald, Dettwiler & Assocs LTD
9620 Towne Centre Dr
San Diego, CA 92121-1963
Telephone: (856) 597-3100, (800) 950-9171, Web Site: www.primerasource.com
Pres: John Walsh
Mktg Specialist: Sara Stephenson
Founded: 1978

DEMANDBASE INC
301 Howard St Ste 1800
San Francisco, CA 94105-6614
Telephone: (415) 683-2660, Web Site: www.demandbase.com
Sr Mgr Demand Gen: Jason Stewart

DIRECT APPROACH
4131 N 24th St Ste C202
Phoenix, AZ 85016-6256
Telephone: (602) 955-0649, FAX: (602) 955-0654, E-Mail: tbarker@directapproachlists.com, Web Site: www.directapproachlists.com
VP: Tina Barker
Office Mgr: Debra Wells
Conducts Business: U.S.
Employees: 3
Primary Market Served: Business & Consumer

Advertising/Marketing Budget Related to Direct Marketing: 0-25%
Gross sales or billing: $1,000,000

Mailing lists and list brokerage.

DIRECT CHANNEL INC
234 W Center St Ste 2
West Bridgewater, MA 02379-1633
Telephone: (508) 588-4448, FAX: (508) 588-4644, E-Mail: directch@mindspring.com, Web Site: www.directchannel.com
Pres: Paul O'Neill

DIRECT LIST TECHNOLOGY INC
1582 N Batavia St (Suite 3)
Orange, CA 92867-3544
Telephone: (714) 772-3282, (888) 772-6947, FAX: (714) 772-6947, E-Mail: apieter@directlist.com, Web Site: www.directlist.com
Pres: Andy Pieter

DIRECT MAIL ADVERTISING CORP
5301 NW 37th Ave
Miami, FL 33142-3207
Telephone: (305) 557-4153, (800) 683-3622, FAX: (305) 634-1896, Web Site: www.directmac.com
Pres & Owner: Jack Hurley

DIRECT MAIL SOURCE INC
7729 E Pinchot
Scottsdale, AZ 85251
Telephone: (602) 947-1552
Pres: Pat McCauley

DIRECT MEDIA MILLARD
Ten Vose Farm Rd
Peterborough, NH 03458
Telephone: (603) 924-9262, FAX: (603) 924-9420, Web Site: www.millard.com
Pres: Larry May
Pres, Consumer Mngmt Grp: Jeff Kelley

DIRECT NETWORK INC
PO Box 546
Allentown, NJ 08501-0546
Telephone: (732) 821-7090, FAX: (732) 821-7202, E-Mail: dirnet@verizon.net, Web Site: www.dirnetnetworklists.com
Pres: David Nussbaum

DIRECT PARTNER SOLUTIONS INC
6386 Nichols Rd
Flowery Branch, GA 30542-2619

Telephone: (678) 762-9869, Web Site: www.directpartnersolutions.com
CEO: Deborah Simone-Holmes

DIRECT RESPONSE SERVICES
aka R Co Inc
111 Northlane Dr
Glen Carbon, IL 62034
Telephone: (618) 288-8811, (800) 795-5478, FAX: (618) 288-3005, E-Mail: drs@drslist.com, Web Site: www.drslist.com
Pres: Kenneth Petersen

DIRECTORY OF MAJOR MALLS
PO Box 837
Nyack, NY 10960-0837
Telephone: (845) 348-7000, (800) 898-6255, Web Site: www.shoppingcenters.com
Pres: Tama J. Shor

Detailed information & primary contacts for the major shopping centers & malls in the U.S. & Canada. Titles include: owner, leasing, manager & marketing director.

DIRMARK GROUP INC
Div. of Oberstein Enterprises Inc
90 W Moreno St
Buford, GA 30518-3037
Telephone: (678) 727-9677, (888) 395-6727, FAX: (800) 881-2303, E-Mail: mnewton@dirmark.com, Web Site: www.accurateleads.com
Pres: Michael Newton

DONNELLEY MARKETING
Div. of info USA
2 Blue Hill Plz (Suite 1662)
Pearl River, NY 10965-3115
Telephone: (201) 476-2300, FAX: (201) 476-2151, Web Site: www.infousa.com
Pres, Donnelley Group: Ed Mallin
HR Dir: Barbara Klumack

DRESDEN DIRECT INC
109 Saint Edward Pl
Palm Beach Gardens, FL 33418-4606
Telephone: (561) 622-3400, Web Site: www.dresdendirect.com
Pres: Phillip Dresden

THE DMA DS DIRECT COMMUNICATIONS
1840 S Elena Ave (Suite 210)
Redondo Beach, CA 90277-5717
Telephone: (310) 540-4313
Pres & Owner: Debra Stanley

HUGO DUNHILL MAILING LISTS INC

542 Main St Ste 400
New Rochelle, NY 10801-7270
Telephone: (212) 213-9300, (800) 611-0557, FAX: (212) 213-9245, E-Mail: info@hdml.com, Web Site: www.hdml.com
Mktg Mgr: Ingrid Jacques
VP Retail Sls: Maurice Herrera
Dir New Bus Devel-Wholesale: Nancy Scheutele
Dir Healthcare Sls & Mktg: Al Terrazas
Conducts Business: U.S.
Employees: 50
Primary Market Served: Business
Direct online sales
Advertising/Marketing Budget Related to Direct Marketing: 0-25%
Founded: 1936

Mailing lists, email lists, medical leads & sales leads.

THE DMA DUNHILL INTERNATIONAL LIST CO INC

6400 Congress Ave Ste 1750
Boca Raton, FL 33487-2898
Telephone: (561) 998-7800, (800) 386-4455, FAX: (561) 998-7880, E-Mail: sales@dunhills.com, Web Site: www.dunhills.com
Pres: Robert Dunhill
VP Opers: Cindy Dunhill
VP: Andy Dunhill
VP Sales: Candy Hachenburg
Employees: 25
Founded: 1938
Gross sales or billing: $5,000,000

Specializing in business and consumer categories such as executives by job function, professionals, vacationers, investors, business owners and more. Maintains 30,000 list categories. Inquire about e-mail appending and list management.

DUNN DATA CO INC

2022 Rte 22 S, Patterson Business Park E
Brewster, NY 10509-5946
Telephone: (845) 278-1200, Web Site: www.dunndataco.com
Pres & CEO: Stephen Dunn

DUNNINGS DIVERSIFIED LLC

4307 E Desert Sky Ct
Cave Creek, AZ 85331
Telephone: (480) 585-5230, FAX: (480) 585-4565, E-Mail: jack.dundiv@cox.net
Pres: Jack E. Dunning

ECLIPSE DIRECT MARKETING

173 Mineola Blvd (Suite 402)
Mineola, NY 11501-2555
Telephone: (212) 931-8344, FAX: (212) 931-8377, E-Mail: jkaiser@eclipsedm.com, Web Site: www.eclipsedm.com
Pres: Jane Kaiser
Mng Partner: John Hammersley
Mng Partner: Kris Thelen
Mng Partner: David Waldman

Provide list broker and list management services.

CAROL ENTERS LIST CO INC

9663-C Main St (Suite C)
Fairfax, VA 22031-3758
Telephone: (703) 425-0052, FAX: (703) 425-0056, E-Mail: listmanagement@carolenters.com, Web Site: www.carolenterslists.com
Pres: Barbara Sims

EQUIFAX

1550 Peachtree NE
Atlanta, GA 30309-8000
Telephone: (248) 603-3000, (888) 202-4025, FAX: (248) 603-3085, Web Site: www.equifax.com

EQUIFAX MARKETING SERVICES

1550 Peachtree St NE
Atlanta, GA 30309-2402
Telephone: (800) 466-5897, Web Site: www.equifax.com/consumer/marketing
VP Mktg: Rosemary Griesmer

THE DMA ETHNIC TECHNOLOGIES LLC

600 Huyler St Ste 5
South Hackensack, NJ 07606-1734
Telephone: (201) 440-8923, (866) 333-8324, FAX: (201) 440-2168, E-Mail: candace@ethnictechnologies.com, Web Site: www.ethnictechnologies.com
CEO: Zachary Wilhoit
Sls Dir: Candace Kennedy

EVERGREEN MARKETING

116 Ram Cat Aly (Suite 201)
Seneca, SC 29678-3263
Telephone: (864) 882-1170, FAX: (864) 882-1112, E-Mail: evawn@evergreenmarketing.com, Web Site: www.evergreenmarketing.com
VP, Brokerage & Mngmt: Evawn R. Lewis

EXHIBITRAC DIRECT MARKETING

8290 W Sahara Ave (Suite 280)
Las Vegas, NV 89117-8933
Telephone: (303) 988-6601, FAX: (303) 988-6602, E-Mail: sales@exhibitrac.com, Web Site: www.exhibitrac.com
Pres: Kyle Landrum

FJ ASSOCIATES LLC

PO Box 12771
Wilmington, NC 28405-0138
Telephone: (910) 452-2643, FAX: (630) 982-1056
Pres: Fran Milberg
VP: Jeffrey Milberg
Conducts Business: U.S.
Employees: 2
Primary Market Served: Business & Consumer
Founded: 1999

List broker & teleservices outsourcing.

FARM MARKET ID

1 E Oakhill Dr (Ste 301)
Westmont, IL 60559-5540
Telephone: (630) 654-5700, (800) 313-4778, FAX: (630) 654-4470, Web Site: www.farmmarketid.com
VP Mktg: Dick Olmsted

FASANO & ASSOCIATES

333 S Beverly Dr Ste 214
Beverly Hills, CA 90212-4306
Telephone: (818) 728-9030, FAX: (818) 728-9070, E-Mail: pfasano@fasano-accoc.com, Web Site: www.fasano-assoc.com
Pres: Patricia A. Fasano

THE DMA FIREBRAND GROUP

7251 W Lake Mead Blvd (Suite 300)
Las Vegas, NV 89128-8380
Telephone: (877) 776-4771, Web Site: www.firebrandgroup.biz
Primary Market Served: Consumer

THE DMA FIRST DIRECT MARKETING LLC

1508 J F Kennedy Dr (Suite 103)
Bellevue, NE 68005-6611
Telephone: (402) 403-0000, (866) 363-9575, FAX: (402) 403-0001, E-Mail: sales@firstdirectmarketing.com, Web Site: www.firstdirectmarketing.com
Partner: Joel Buhr
Partner: Scott Peterson
Conducts Business: U.S.
Employees: 5
Primary Market Served: Business
Direct online sales
Direct Marketing ad budget: Direct Mail: 25%

Online: 50%
Telephone: 25%
Founded: 2005

Mailing lists, data processing, printing, mail services, campaign management, direct marketing consulting services.

FIRST NATIONAL LIST SERVICE INC

2257 W Irving Park Rd.
Chicago, IL 60618-3840
Telephone: (773) 509-1266, (888) 621-5548, FAX: (773) 509-1277, E-Mail: firstnl@sbcglobal.net
Pres: Lyle Sammons

Over 35 years in the list business. We have every list in the USA! Call us with your list needs. Format Selects: 4-up chesire labels, galley w/phone numbers, pressure sensitive labels, 3x5 cards w/phone numbers, free bulk mail sorting. Demographic Selects: age, presence of children, length of residence, nationality, gender, credit card holders. Geographic Selects: state, country, zip code, telephone area code, carrier rolls, metropolitan area. Any Type of Lists: including, magazine subscribers, business airplane owners, pilots, professionals by profession, mail order buyers by product & more. Remember, research is our specialty!

F1RSTMARK INC

25 Vintinner Rd
Campton, NH 03223
Telephone: (603) 726-4800, (800) 729-2600, FAX: (603) 726-4840, E-Mail: info@firstmark.com, Web Site: www.firstmark.com
Pres: Michael H. Pomerantz

FIXED ADDRESS MARKETING INC

136 Pinnacle Tr
Aurora, ON, Canada L4G 7G7
Telephone: (905) 750-0029, Web Site: www.fixedaddressmarketing.com
Pres: Tara Dockeray

THE DMA FOCUS USA INC

1 University Plz (Suite 300)
Hackensack, NJ 07601-6205
Telephone: (201) 489-2525, FAX: (201) 489-4499, E-Mail: suzanne@focus-usa-l.com, Web Site: www.focus-usa-l.com
Pres: Chicca D'Agostino
Dir Adv: Suzanne Schmid

THE DMA FRONTLINE DATA GROUP

1953 Gallows Rd (Suite 600)
Vienna, VA 22182-3988
Telephone: (703) 734-5700)

Primary Market Served: Consumer

FRONTLINE DIRECT INC

2658 del Mar Heights Rd (#203)
Del Mar, CA 92014-3100
Telephone: (858) 638-1515, Web Site: www.frontlinedirect.com
VP: Amanda Currie
Primary Market Served: Business & Consumer

GELDERMAN GROUP INC

19 Junction Rd
Brookfield, CT 06804
Telephone: (203) 740-9000, FAX: (203) 702-7096, E-Mail: geldermangroup@earthlink.net
Pres: Harriet Schopfer

THE DMA GLASERDIRECT INC

800 Rossevelt Rd (Bldg B, Ste 414)
Glen Ellyn, IL 50137
Telephone: (630) 469-2075, FAX: (630) 790-5244, E-Mail: jglaser@glaserdirect.com, Web Site: www.glaserdirect.com
CEO: Joseph Glaser
Sr VP: Barb Toschak
Sr VP: Bert Des Rosiers
Conducts Business: U.S.
Employees: 12
Primary Market Served: Business & Consumer
Founded: 1974

Full service list brokerage & list management.

THE DMA GLOBAL BUSINESS INFORMATION SERVICES INC (GLOBIS)

1820 N Lincoln Ave
Chicago, IL 60614-5812
Telephone: (773) 220-4000, Web Site: www.glo-bis.com
Mng Dir: Louise Kern

THE DMA GLOBAL DM SOLUTIONS

416 Main St
Boonton, NJ 07005-1714
Telephone: (973) 402-2205, (866) 402-2205, FAX: (973) 402-2305, E-Mail: contact@globaldmsolutions.com, Web Site: www.globaldmsolutions.com
Pres: Sheila Donovan

GNAMES MEDIA GROUP

1452 Hughes Rd Ste 320
Grapevine, TX 76051-7369
Telephone: (972) 871-2828, FAX: (972) 871-2929, E-Mail: info@gnames.com, Web Site: www.gnames.com
Principal: Holly Hammond

Offers a full range of marketing services including data acquisition for direct mail campaigns, email marketing programs & digital media placement. Also provide exceptional data management services for consumer & business lists & alternate media programs.

THE DMA GOLDLEAF DATA CORP

3325 Paddock Pkwy (Suite 300)
Suwanee, GA 30024-6060
Telephone: (888) 936-3282, Web Site: www.goldleafdata.com
Pres: Jason Butler

MARY ELIZABETH GRANGER & ASSOCIATES INC

110 West Rd (Suite 235)
Baltimore, MD 21204-2343
Telephone: (410) 842-1170, (800) 296-5157, FAX: (410) 842-1185, E-Mail: bonnie@maryegranger.com, Web Site: www.maryegranger.com
Pres & Owner: Mary E. Granger
VP: Linda Martin
Sr Acct Mgr: Kris Evans
Conducts Business: U.S.
Employees: 10
Primary Market Served: Consumer
Catalog available online
Indirect online sales
Advertising/Marketing Budget Related to Direct Marketing: 76-100%
Direct Marketing ad budget:
Direct Mail: 100%
Founded: 1983

Mailing list brokerage and management services.

THE DMA GREAT LAKES FULFILLMENT INC

3126 Peach St
Erie, PA 16508-2734
Telephone: (814) 456-2175, (800) 964-5478, FAX: (814) 455-1942, E-Mail: info@greatlakeslists.com, Web Site: www.greatlakeslists.com
Pres: Brian Kowalawski

GREATLISTS.COM

21351 Gentry Dr (Suite 135)
Dulles, VA 20166
Telephone: (703) 821-8130, (800) 296-0888, FAX: (703) 821-8243, E-Mail: info@greatlists.com, Web Site: www.greatlists.com
Pres: Paul Taybi
Brokerage Mgr: Eileen Giaramita

THE GUILD CO

Subs. of Mail Marketing Inc
1500 Spring Garden St (fl 12)
Philadelphia, PA 19130-4094

Telephone: (201) 750-3222, FAX: (201) 750-4961, E-Mail: mmi-guild@mailmkt.com, Web Site: www.mailmkt.com
Pres: Hal Roberson

GULF COAST LIST SERVICE
Div. of Gulf Coast Enterprises
PO Box 47645
Tampa, FL 33646-0114
Telephone: (813) 962-3594, FAX: (813) 907-8463, E-Mail: tg@gulfcoastlist.com
Owner: Tina Genovese

Providing Sales Leads to Businesses Nationwide.

HR DIRECT INC
Sub. of AstroView, Inc
508 N 2nd St Ste 202
Fairfield, IA 52556-2474
Telephone: (641) 472-7188, FAX: (641) 472-5729, E-Mail: info@hrdirect.net, Web Site: www.hrdirect.net
Pres: David Hawthorne

HARRIS MARKETING INC
PO Box 20428
Indianapolis, IN 46220-0428
Telephone: (317) 251-9729, E-Mail: hmdataindy@msn.com, Web Site: www.listsandmail.com
Pres: Janet I. Harris

THE DMA HEALTHCARE DATA SOLUTIONS
26741 Portola Pkwy
Foothill Ranch, CA 92610-1743
Telephone: (949) 421-5971, Web Site: www.healthcaredatasolutions.com
Pres & CEO: Tim Slevin
Primary Market Served: Business

THE DMA HEALY LIST MARKETING
153 Andover St (Suite 108A)
Danvers, MA 01923-5307
Telephone: (978) 578-1868

LEON HENRY INC
200 N Central Ave (Suite 220)
Hartsdale, NY 10530-9915
Telephone: (914) 285-3456, FAX: (914) 285-3450, E-Mail: lh@leonhenryinc.com, Web Site: www.leonhenryinc.com
Chmn & CEO: Leon Henry
Exec VP: Gail Henry
Exec VP: Lynn Henry
VP, Mngmt Div: Jody Smith
Conducts Business: U.S., Canada, England/UK
Employees: 28

Primary Market Served: Business & Consumer
Indirect online sales
Advertising/Marketing Budget Related to Direct Marketing: 76-100%
Founded: 1956

Insert Media/Mailing List Brokers/Managers.

HIPPO DIRECT
34472 Summerset Dr
Solon, OH 44139
Telephone: (440) 519-0730, FAX: (440) 519-0727, E-Mail: rapidresponse@hippodirect.com, Web Site: www.hippodirect.com
Pres: Greg Branstetter

HOME OWNER DATA SERVICES INC
1424 N Brown Rd Ste 400
Lawrenceville, GA 30043-8107
Telephone: (770) 925-9000, FAX: (770) 925-8977, E-Mail: hdsi@newhomedata.net, Web Site: www.newhomedata.net
Pres: George F. O'Neil

HOMEOWNERS MARKETING SERVICES INC
12444 Victory Blvd (2nd fl)
North Hollywood, CA 91606-3156
Telephone: (818) 506-1507, (800) 232-2134, FAX: (818) 505-9729, (818) 506-4110, E-Mail: lists@homeown.org, Web Site: www.homeown.org
Pres: Barry Weiner
HR: Marco Salgado

HORIZON LISTS
126 W 227th St (Suite A)
Bronx, NY 10463-6703
Telephone: (845) 300-4932, Web Site: www.horizonlists.com
Primary Market Served: Consumer

HOTLINE LIST CORP
1071 Ave of the Americas
New York, NY 10018
Telephone: (212) 840-8135, FAX: (212) 840-8139
Pres: Bonnie Dursi

THE DMA I-BEHAVIOR INC
2051 Dogwood St (Suite 220)
Louisville, CO 80027-3042
Telephone: (303) 228-5000, FAX: (303) 926-1367, E-Mail: contactus@i-behavior.com, Web Site: www.i-behavior.com
Pres & CEO: Chris Dice

IBUX
PO Box 4675
Chico, CA 95927-4675
Telephone: (530) 895-0431
CEO: R. Jon Scott

IC DIRECT LIST BROKERS
4047 Meadow Wood Dr
El Dorado Hills, CA 95762-7513
Telephone: (916) 941-7605, (877) ICD-UST, FAX: (916) 941-7615, E-Mail: info@icdlist.com, Web Site: www.icdlist.com
Pres: Ira Cohen

ICOM INFORMATION & COMMUNICATIONS INC
41 Metropolitan Rd
Toronto, ON, Canada M1R 2T5
Telephone: (416) 297-4058, (800) 603-4555, FAX: (416) 297-7084, E-Mail: info@i-com.com, Web Site: www.i-com.com
VP Mktg: Peter Meyers

IHFRA
209 S Main (#M1405)
High Point, NC 27260
Telephone: (336) 889-3920, FAX: (336) 464-2125, E-Mail: ihfra@ihfra.org, Web Site: www.ihfra.org
Exec Dir: Kathy Parks

THE DMA INFINITE MEDIA
190 E Post Rd
White Plains, NY 10601-4912
Telephone: (914) 949-1547, FAX: (914) 949-1605, E-Mail: mail@infinite-media.com, Web Site: www.infinite-media.com
Pres: Steven Sheck

INFO DIRECT
2619 Trailway Rd SE
Huntsville, AL 35801-1473
Telephone: (256) 534-5478, (800) 239-5478, FAX: (256) 536-0705, E-Mail: dklib@hiway.net, Web Site: www.infodirectlists.com
Pres: Daniel Klibanoff

INFO USA
5711 S 86th Cir
Omaha, NE 68127
Telephone: (800) 321-0869, E-Mail: help@infousa.com, Web Site: www.infousa.com
Pres Infogroup: Clare Hart

INFO USA SERVICES GROUP
2 Blue Hill Plz (Suite 1662)
Pearl River, NY 10965-3115

Telephone: (201) 476-2000, (888) 322-5323, FAX: (201) 476-2301, Web Site: www.infousa.com
Pres: Edward C. Mallin

INFOCANADA
Div. of InfoUSA
1290 Central Pkwy W (Suite 104)
Mississauga, ON, Canada L5C 4R3
Telephone: (866) 373-2066, FAX: (905) 306-7272, E-Mail: customerservice@infocanada.ca, Web Site: www.infocanada.ca
Pres: Dan Cadieux

THE DMA INFOCORE INC
2375 Camino Vida Roble (Suite A)
Carlsbad, CA 92011-1556
Telephone: (760) 607-2500, FAX: (760) 607-2505, E-Mail: bstewart@infocoreinc.com, Web Site: www.infocoreinc.com
Pres & CEO: Peter Joop
Pres: Scott Neuberger
Sr VP: Douglas Sacks
VP List Brokerage: Amy MacNabb
List Mgr: Carrie James
Conducts Business: Worldwide
Primary Market Served: Business & Consumer
Direct online sales
Advertising/Marketing Budget Related to Direct Marketing: 26-50%
Founded: 1992

THE DMA INFOCUS MARKETING INC
4245 Sigler Rd
Warrenton, VA 20187-3940
Telephone: (540) 428-3240, Web Site: www.infocuslists.com
Dir Mktg: Jeannine Gibson

THE DMA INFOGROUP
5711 S 86th Cir
Omaha, NE 68127-4146
Telephone: (800) 555-5335 X4541, Web Site: www.infoUSA.com
CEO: Bill Fairfield

INFOUSA INC
5711 S 86th Cir
Omaha, NE 68127
Telephone: (402) 593-4500, (800) 321-0869, FAX: (402) 596-8902, Web Site: www.infousa.com
VP Mktg & Adv: Ronald Bruggeman

THE DMA INFUTOR DATA SOLUTIONS
111 Zapata Ln
Minooka, IL 60447-9355
Telephone: (815) 467-0601, Web Site: www.infutor.com
CEO: Gary Walter

INNOVATIVE LIST MARKETING INC
9663 Main St (Suite C)
Fairfax, VA 22031-3758
Telephone: (703) 425-5356, Web Site: www.ilmlists.com
Pres: Jerry Hopkins

THE DMA INTEGRATED DIRECT MARKETING
12120 Sunset Hills Rd (Suite 450)
Reston, VA 20190-5858
Telephone: (703) 547-4961, E-Mail: info@integrated-dm.com, Web Site: www.integrated-dm.com
Pres: Chad Slater
Conducts Business: U.S., Canada
Employees: 15
Primary Market Served: Business & Consumer
Founded: 2003
Gross sales or billing: $10,000,000

A list brokerage & database consulting company serving the unique needs of large multi-channel direct marketers.

INTELITEC
154 Taylor St
Granby, MA 01033-9526
Telephone: (413) 467-7420, FAX: (413) 467-9476, E-Mail: info@intelitec.com, Web Site: www.intelitec.com
Pres: Joseph Furnia
Conducts Business: U.S., Germany, Europe
Primary Market Served: Business & Consumer
Direct Marketing ad budget: $100,000,000
Direct Mail: 40%
Online: 60%
Founded: 1991

Specialty multi-channel marketing solutions using web crawling and traditional data channels to create customer targeting.

THE DMA INTERNATIONAL DIRECT RESPONSE INC
1125 Lancaster Ave Ste 2
Berwyn, PA 19312-2601
Telephone: (610) 993-0500, FAX: (610) 993-9938, E-Mail: idr@idronline.com, Web Site: www.idronline.com
Pres: Douglas Guyer

JC LISTS CO
3100 Connecticut Ave NW (Suite 4340)
Washington, DC 20008-5148

Telephone: (202) 364-2705, FAX: (202) 364-2450, E-Mail: jcoogan@JClists.com
Pres: Jennie Coogan

JF DIRECT MARKETING INC
73 Croton Ave (Suite 106)
Ossining, NY 10562-4973
Telephone: (914) 762-8633, FAX: (914) 762-9247, E-Mail: jfdirect@bestweb.net, Web Site: www.jfdirectmarketing.com
Pres: John Ferrini

A full service direct marketing company consisting of list brokerage, list management, e-mail marketing, list compliatiion, data appending, M/P, lettershop & fulfillment.

THE DMA JR DIRECT RESPONSE INTERNATIONAL INC
4917 Delta St
Delta, BC, Canada V4K 2V1
Telephone: (604) 940-0277, FAX: (604) 946-1419, E-Mail: tammythackray@jrdirect.com, Web Site: www.jrdirect.com
Pres: Tammy Thackray
Sales Mgr: Malcolm Smillie

JS DIRECT ADDRESS LIMITED
1429 Dominion St (#203)
North Vancouver, BC, Canada V7J 1B4
Telephone: (604) 987-1282, FAX: (604) 987-1283
Pres: Jim Slight

THE DMA JAMAX DIRECT LLC
375 Sylvan Ave (Suite 2)
Englewood Cliffs, NJ 07632-2714
Telephone: (201) 569-4540
Pres & Owner: David Malamed

JEFFERSON MAILING LISTS
Div. of The Jefferson Corp
12350 Oak Knoll Rd
Poway, CA 92064-5320
Telephone: (858) 679-1233, FAX: (858) 679-1279
Owner: Jeff Figler
List Mgr: Sandra Sauceda

JONCAS POSTEXPERTS INC
Div. of Quebecor
7875 Trans-Canada Hwy
Ville Saint Laurent, PQ, Canada H4S 1L3
Telephone: (514) 333-7480, FAX: (514) 332-6915, E-Mail: sherif.zaky@quebecorworld.com, Web Site: www.postexperts.com
Gen Dir: Sherif Zaky

JORDAN DIRECT
40704 N Bell Meadow Tr
Phoenix, AZ 85086-2949
Telephone: (623) 551-2728, FAX:
(623) 551-2730, E-Mail: dori@
jordandirect.net
Co-Owner: Dori Thomas
VP Opers: Chuck Cowley
Direct online sales

**THE DMA KEY MARKETING
ADVANTAGE LLC**
24 Stony Hill Rd (Suite 101)
Bethel, CT 06801-1166
Telephone: (203) 744-9011, Web Site:
www.keymarketingadvantage.com
Pres: Linda Bridson
Primary Market Served: Business &
Consumer

**THE DMA KROLL DIRECT MARKETING
INC**
101 Morgan Ln (Suite 120)
Plainsboro, NJ 08536-3345
Telephone: (609) 275-2900, FAX:
(609) 275-6606, E-Mail: lee@
krolldirect.com, Web Site: www.
krolldirect.com
Pres: Leland Kroll
Catalog available online

THE DMA LDS GROUP INC
555 8th Ave (Suite 1110)
New York, NY 10018-4308
Telephone: (646) 390-5702, FAX:
(646) 390-5715, E-Mail: rvergara@
ldsgroupinc.com, Web Site: www.
ldsgroupinc.com
CO & CEO: Richard Vergara
Co-CEO: Jeff Kobil
Exec VP: Nick Sarnitakos
Conducts Business: U.S., Canada
Employees: 8
Primary Market Served: Business
Founded: 2002

Provides list & data strategies to direct
marketers in the publishing, entertainment, continuity, financial & travel
markets.

LED SIGNS
Div. of Finest Services Inc
104 Herbert St
Stockbridge, MI 49285-9808
Telephone: (954) 771-5488, FAX:
(954) 267-0551, Web Site: www.
finest.com
PR Mgr: Sharon Dreyfuss

LMC DIRECT
1475 Star Top Rd (Unit Eight)
Ottawa, ON, Canada K1B 3W5
Telephone: (613) 521-8181, FAX:
(613) 521-3015

Pres: Leonard Mandel

LS DIRECT MARKETING
4 Suffern Pl.
Suffern, NY 10901
Telephone: (845) 357-1238, E-Mail:
info@ls-direct.com, Web Site: www.
ls-direct.com

LAKE GROUP MEDIA INC
1 Byram Brook Pl
Armonk, NY 10504
Telephone: (914) 925-2400, FAX:
(914) 925-2499, E-Mail:
joerobinson@lakegroupmedia.com,
Web Site: www.lakegroupmedia.com
Sr VP: Joe Robinson
CEO: Ryan Lake

THE DMA LATINLISTS
8424 NW 56th St (CCS 00511)
Miami, FL 33166-3327
Telephone: (954) 302-1795, Web Site:
www.latinlists.net
CEO: Noel Poler
Primary Market Served: Business &
Consumer

**LAWRENCE DIRECT
MARKETING INC**
26 Ashby St
Warrenton, VA 20186-3201
Telephone: (540) 349-9278, FAX:
(540) 347-7885
Pres: E. Michael Lawrence

**LAWYERS & JUDGES
PUBLISHING CO INC**
PO Box 30040
Tucson, AZ 85751-0040
Telephone: (520) 323-1500, FAX:
(520) 323-0055, E-Mail: sales@
lawyersandjudges.com, Web Site:
www.lawyersandjudges.com
Pres: Steve Weintraub

LEAD GEN MEDIA GROUP
1000 South Ave (Suite 103)
Staten Island, NY 10314-3431
Telephone: (718) 215-2233, Web Site:
leadgenmediagroup.com
Primary Market Served: Consumer

LEADCREATIONS.COM LLC
201 Alhambra Cir (Suite 501)
Coral Gables, FL 33134-5105
Telephone: (305) 851-8110, Web Site:
www.leadcreations.com
Fin Mgr: Umut Vadar
Primary Market Served: Business &
Consumer

LEADPILE
2355 E Camelback Rd Ste 825
Phoenix, AZ 85016-9069
Telephone: (602) 909-9890, Web Site:
www.leadpile.com

LEWIS DIRECT INC
400 Andrew Way
Superior, CO 80027-8300
Telephone: (303) 494-0730, FAX:
(303) 494-0729, E-Mail:
lewismails@aol.com, Web Site:
www.lewis-direct.com
Pres: Mark Lewis

**LEXISNEXIS RISK &
INFORMATION ANALYTICS**
13427 NE 16th St
Bellevue, WA 98005-2307
Telephone: (908) 673-2648, Web Site:
http://risk.lexisnexis.com

LIST ADVISOR INC
500 Bi County Blvd (Suite 125)
Farmingdale, NY 11735-3996
Telephone: (631) 777-2900, FAX:
(631) 777-3050
Pres: Thomas R. Frenz

LIST ALLIANCE INC
3000 Danville Blvd (Suite F), PMB
519
Alamo, CA 94507-1572
Telephone: (925) 820-3151, E-Mail:
info@listalliance.com, Web Site:
www.listalliance.com
Pres: Randy Robertson
Primary Market Served: Business &
Consumer

LIST AMERICA
Div. of Market Development Group
Inc
5151 Wisconsin Ave NW (4th fl)
Washington, DC 20016
Telephone: (202) 298-9206, (202) 298-
8030, FAX: (202) 244-4999, (202)
244-7294, Web Site: www.mdg.nc.
org
Grp VP: Gerry Gretschel

LIST CONNECTION INC
PO Box 1712
Simpsonville, SC 29681-1712
Telephone: (864) 962-0761, Web Site:
www.listconnection.net
VP List Mngmt & Sls: Ken Wood

THE DMA THE LIST CONNECTION INC
1015 Constable Dr
Mamaroneck, NY 10543
Telephone: (914) 381-2010, FAX:
(914) 381-2163
Pres: Elaine Canter

THE LIST EMPORIUM
171 English Landing Dr (Suite 200)
Parkville, MO 64152
Telephone: (816) 505-2111, FAX:
(816) 505-2112, E-Mail: listinfo@
listmart.com, Web Site: www.
listmart.com
Pres: Mark Coulter

**LIST LOCATORS &
MANAGERS**
Div. of Marketshare Group
7171 W 95th (Suite 600)
Overland Park, KS 66210
Telephone: (913) 338-5055, (800) 487-
8720, FAX: (913) 338-5055
Pres: Ellen Payne

**LIST MARKETING GROUP
INC**
19885 Detroit Rd (Suite 207)
Cleveland, OH 44116-1815
Telephone: (216) 990-2000, Web Site:
www.listmarketinggroup.com
CEO: Frances Anderson

THE LIST PLACE INC
8508 Park Rd, PMB #173
Charlotte, NC 28210-5803
Telephone: (704) 672-3174, FAX:
(704) 676-4755, E-Mail: bryan@
thelistplace.net, Web Site: www.
thelistplace.net
VP List Svcs: Bryan Borower
Conducts Business: U.S., Canada
Primary Market Served: Business &
Consumer
Direct online sales
Advertising/Marketing Budget Related
to Direct Marketing: 0-25%
Founded: 1997

LIST PRO OF AMERICA
3089-C Clairemont Dr (#267)
San Diego, CA 92117-6802
Telephone: (858) 483-1410, FAX:
(858) 270-6669, Web Site: www.
swmall.com
Founder: Diane O'Brien

LIST PROCESS CO INC
404 E 79th St (#23G)
New York, NY 10075-1483
Telephone: (212) 517-8550, FAX:
(212) 517-9728, Web Site: www.
listprocesscompany.com
Pres & CEO: Paulette Kranjac
Acct Execs: Lydia Imbrilc

LIST SERVICE DIRECT INC
2 Christie Heights St
Leonia, NJ 07605-2233

Telephone: (201) 585-1447, (800) 371-
5487, FAX: (201) 585-1732, E-Mail:
info@listservicedirect.com, Web
Site: www.listservicedirect.com
Pres & Owner: Micah Raskin

**LIST SERVICES
FUNDRAISING**
PO Box 516
Bethel, CT 06801-0516
Telephone: (203) 743-2600, Web Site:
www.listservices.com
CEO: Malcolm McCluskey
Primary Market Served: Business &
Consumer

THE LIST SOURCE INC
Four Hickory Ln
Cherry Hill, NJ 08003-1408
Telephone: (856) 795-3344, FAX:
(856) 795-9498
Pres: Allan D. Bilofsky

LIST STRATEGIES INC
244 Madison Ave
New York, NY 10016-2817
Telephone: (212) 767-1000, FAX:
(212) 541-4408, E-Mail: joel@
liststrategies.com, Web Site: www.
liststrategies.com
Pres: Joel Cooper

LIST TEAM
14458 Ventura Blvd
Sherman Oaks, CA 91423-2607
Telephone: (818) 986-1166, Web Site:
www.listteam.com
Pres: Glenn Levine

LISTABILITY INC
11841 Granite Woods Loop
Venice, FL 34292-4113
Telephone: (866) 446-2055, (800) 626-
6500, Web Site: www.listability.com
Pres: Christopher Dyer

**LISTMASTERS DIRECT MAIL
SERVICES**
1296 Adams Rd
Bensalem, PA 19020
Telephone: (215) 633-8200, (800) 234-
5478, FAX: (215) 633-8209, E-Mail:
sales@listmastersdirect.com, Web
Site: www.listmastersdirect.com
Pres: David Geer

LISTS INC
2950 Halcyon Ln Ste 401
Jacksonville, FL 32223-6691
Telephone: (904) 733-6106, (800) 805-
5478, FAX: (904) 730-7540, Web
Site: www.lists-inc.com
Mgr: Pauline Aldridge

THE
DMA **MCH STRATEGIC DATA**
601 E Marshall St
Sweet Springs, MO 65351-9613
Telephone: (660) 335-6373, (800) 776-
6373, FAX: (660) 335-4157, E-Mail:
tonyab@mchdata.com, Web Site:
www.mchdata.com
CEO: Peter E. Long
Pub Rels Coord: Jackie Finnegan
HR Dir: Brenda Viets
Mktg Commun Mgr: Tonya Bennett

THE
DMA **MDI LISTS**
4581 Weston Rd (PMB 192)
Weston, FL 33331-3141
Telephone: (954) 384-1557, FAX:
(954) 389-0939, Web Site: www.
mdilists.com
Mng Dir: David Raff
Conducts Business: U.S., Canada
Employees: 5
Primary Market Served: Business &
Consumer
Founded: 1998
Gross sales or billing: $3,000,000

List brokerage and management.

MGM MAILING LISTS
Ten Leslin Ln
South Sandwich, MA 02563
Telephone: (508) 539-1300, (800) 660-
5322, FAX: (508) 539-0700
Pres: Mark Linse

MSI LIST MARKETING
738 E Dundee Rd (Suite 321)
Palatine, IL 60074-2858
Telephone: (847) 934-1111, FAX:
(847) 890-6700, E-Mail: jeff@
msilist.com, Web Site: www.msilist.
com
Pres: Jeff Sutton

THE
DMA **MACROMARK INC**
185 Rte 312 (Suite 303)
Brewster, NY 10509-2338
Telephone: (845) 230-6300, FAX:
(845) 278-0650, E-Mail: david@
macromark.com, Web Site: www.
macromark.com
CEO & Pres: David Klein
Chmn: Howard Linzer
Exec VP Sls: Steven Keats
Exec VP Sls: Adam Moran
Sr VP Sls: Norman Newman
Employees: 46
Founded: 1985

MAILGRAPHICS
1668 Valtec Ln (Suite F)
Boulder, CO 80301-4635
Telephone: (303) 449-4053, FAX:
(303) 938-1544, E-Mail: questions@
mailgraphics.com

Pres: Bruce Chiddister

MANCOMA INC
315 W Fourth St
Davenport, IA 52801-1204
Telephone: (563) 323-6245, FAX:
(563) 323-0804, E-Mail: b.mangan@
mancoma.com
Pres: Benjamin W. Mangan

**THE DMA MANNING MEDIA
INTERNATIONAL**
2128 Surrey Ln
Mc Kinney, TX 75070-7132
Telephone: (972) 562-6960, Web Site:
www.manningmedia.com
Pres: Mike Manning

**MANUFACTURERS-NEWS
INC**
1633 Central St
Evanston, IL 60201-1505
Telephone: (847) 864-7000, (888) 752-
5200, FAX: (847) 332-1100, E-Mail:
hdubin@manufacturersnews.com,
Web Site: www.manufacturersnews.
com
Chmn & Treas: Howard S. Dubin
Pres & CEO: Thomas G. Dubin
VP: Scott Kartsounes
COO: George Kartsounes
Conducts Business: U.S., Europe,
China
Employees: 100
Primary Market Served: Business
Catalog available online
Direct online sales
Advertising/Marketing Budget Related
to Direct Marketing: 76-100%
Direct Marketing ad budget:
$4,000,000
Direct Mail: $1,600,000
Online: $600,000
Telephone: $1,800,000
Founded: 1912
Gross sales or billing: $11,500,000

Publish detailed information on manufacturing establishments and industrial
distributors from original research.
This information is sold to businesses
in the form of industrial directories,
electronic databases, custom lists, &
search & download from the internet.

**THE DMA MARKET APPROACH
CONSULTING**
111 E Center St
Lorena, TX 76655-9651
Telephone: (254) 857-7017, Web Site:
www.marketapproach.net
Pres: Mark McLean

MARKET DATA RETRIEVAL
A Dun & Bradstreet Co
6 Armstrong Rd (Suite 301)
Shelton, CT 06484
Telephone: (203) 926-4800, (800) 333-
8802, FAX: (203) 929-5253, E-Mail:
mdrinfo@dnb.com, Web Site: www.
schooldata.com
Pres: Mike Baldwin

MARKET FORCE CORP
3605 Chapel Rd (Suite C)
Newtown Square, PA 19073-3602
Telephone: (610) 356-5220, FAX:
(610) 356-5110, E-Mail:
davethomas@marketforcecorp.com,
Web Site: www.
marketforcecorporation.com
CMO: Dave Thomas
Pres: David Biddulph

MARKET SHARE
5726 Cortez Rd W (#303)
Bradenton, FL 34210-2701
Telephone: (941) 794-6059, FAX:
(941) 794-6059, E-Mail:
rsouthwick@tampabay.rr.com
Pres: Ruth Southwick

MARKET STREET LISTS INC
7 Pleasant St
Exeter, NH 03833-1821
Telephone: (603) 772-6666, (888) 675-
LIST, FAX: (603) 772-0184, E-Mail:
info@market-street.com, Web Site:
www.market-street.com
Pres: Christopher L. Velletri

THE DMA MARKETFISH INC
524 2nd Ave Ste 200
Seattle, WA 98104-2323
Telephone: (206) 905-1090, FAX:
(206) 694-2564, Web Site: www.
marketfish.com
CEO: David Scott
Chief Tech Officer: Andy Thomas
Chief Privacy Officer: David Fowler
CFO: Michael Goffin
Primary Market Served: Business

**MARKETING ECONOMICS
INC**
1636 N Wells (#3112)
Chicago, IL 60614-6023
Telephone: (312) 642-2188, FAX:
(312) 642-3091, E-Mail: codyh@
meimedia.com, Web Site: www.
meimedia.com
Pres: F. Cody Heiderer

THE MARKETING PLACE
Div. of Oberstein Enterprises Inc
12708 Branford St
Sun Valley, CA 91352

Telephone: (818) 834-8500, FAX:
(818) 834-8511, E-Mail:
mktgplace@aol.com, Web Site:
wwwthemarketingplace.com
Response Mktg Svcs Dir: Howard
Oberstein

**MARKETING SIGNALS
GROUP**
6801 Gaylord Pkwy Ste 200
Frisco, TX 75034-5979
Telephone: (386) 761-4840, Web Site:
www.movesignals.com
Primary Market Served: Consumer

**MARKETING SOLUTIONS
NOW INC**
11285 Elkins Rd (Suite H6B)
Roswell, GA 30076-5840
Telephone: (770) 777-4121, Web Site:
www.marketingsolutionsnow.com
Pres: Dan McDonald
Primary Market Served: Business &
Consumer

MARKETRY INC
11400 SE 8th St (Suite 370)
Bellevue, WA 98004-6468
Telephone: (425) 451-1262, (800) 346-
2013, FAX: (425) 451-1941, E-Mail:
greg@marketry.com, Web Site:
www.marketry.com
Pres: Greg Swent

MARTIN WORLDWIDE INC
638 Lindero Canyon Rd (#200)
Oak Park, CA 91377
Telephone: (888) 694-5478, Web Site:
www.martinworldwide.net
Pres: Giovanni Garile
Sr Mktg Consultant: Eddie Hren
Primary Market Served: Business &
Consumer

MASTERMAILER INC
3700 N 29th Ave (Suite 203)
Hollywood, FL 33020-1019
Telephone: (954) 921-0000, (800) 771-
LIST, FAX: (954) 925-7900, Web
Site: www.mastermailer.com
Pres: Theresa Bograkos

**THE DMA MAZZONE MARKETING
GROUP LLC**
164 20th St (Suite 2B)
Brooklyn, NY 11232-1151
Telephone: (718) 369-0001, (866) 928-
5478, FAX: (718) 369-0099, E-Mail:
info@mazzonemarketinggroup.com,
Web Site: www.
mazzonemarketinggroup.com
Pres: Michael R. Mazzone Jr
Conducts Business: U.S.

Primary Market Served: Business &
    Consumer
Catalog available online
Direct online sales
Advertising/Marketing Budget Related
    to Direct Marketing: 0-25%
Direct Marketing ad budget:
Direct Mail: 80%
Online: 20%
Founded: 2007

Mailing list compiler, broker &
manager. Specializing in niche markets, political donors, non-profit organizations, medical lists and many
more.

MCCARTHY MEDIA GROUP INC

1620 Eighth St
Monroe, WI 53566-1628
Telephone: (608) 837-4343, (800) 410-
    5352, FAX: (608) 837-5006, E-Mail:
    lists@mccarthymediagroup.com,
    Web Site: www.
    mccarthymediagroup.com
Pres: Michael McCarthy

PJ MCCARTHY & ASSOCIATES INC

5413 Maplewood Pl
Downers Grove, IL 60515-4814
Telephone: (630) 969-3532, FAX:
    (630) 969-3565, E-Mail: KDicola@
    aol.com
Chmn: P.J. McCarthy
Pres: Kathleen McCarthy DiCola
List Mgr: Megan McCarthy Schroeder

THE DMA MEDIA DIRECTIONS INC

50 Tice Blvd Ste A12
Woodcliff Lake, NJ 07677-7681
Telephone: (201) 930-4949, FAX:
    (201) 930-9229, E-Mail: mail@
    media-directions.com, Web Site:
    www.media-directions.com
Pres: Jeffrey Feldman
VP: Scott Miller
Conducts Business: U.S., Canada,
    Worldwide
Employees: 6
Primary Market Served: Business &
    Consumer
Advertising/Marketing Budget Related
    to Direct Marketing: 0-25%
Founded: 2001
Gross sales or billing: $5,000,000

Mailing list management and mailing
list brokerage.

MEDIA DISTRIBUTION SERVICES (MDS)

Div. of Allied Lettercraft Inc
307 W 36th St (fl 8)
New York, NY 10018-6403

Telephone: (212) 279-4800, (800)
    MDS-DATA, FAX: (212) 643-0576,
    E-Mail: services@mdsconnect.com,
    Web Site: www.mdsconnect.com
Pres: Daniel Cantelmo

THE MEDIA ORGANIZATION INC

53 Holiday Dr (Suite 100)
Woodbury, NY 11797-2319
Telephone: (516) 496-2577, FAX:
    (516) 496-3331
Pres: William J. Levine

THE DMA MEDIA SOURCE SOLUTIONS

950 S Pine Island Rd (Suite A-150)
Plantation, FL 33324-3918
Telephone: (954) 788-0213, Web Site:
    www.mediasourcesolutions.com
Pres List Bargains Div: Any Ben-
    icewicz
Primary Market Served: Business &
    Consumer

THE DMA MEDICX MEDIA SOLUTIONS

9364 E Raintree Dr (Suite 101)
Scottsdale, AZ 85260-2200
Telephone: (480) 614-0060, Web Site:
    www.medicxmedia.com

MEGA MEDIA ASSOCIATES INC

Box 4259
Newport Beach, CA 92661
Telephone: (949) 673-2290, E-Mail:
    info@megamediaassociaes.com, Web
    Site: www.megamediaassociates.com
Pres: Stuart A. Cogan

MELING & ASSOCIATES

962 West Rd.
West Rutland, VT 05777-9235
Telephone: (802) 774-1030
Pres & Owner: Sara Meling

THE MERGING TECHNOLOGIES GROUP LLC

Div. of Two Star Films Inc
175 Commerce Dr (Suite K)
Hauppauge, NY 11788-3920
Telephone: (631) 435-2955, FAX:
    (631) 952-0664, E-Mail: info@mt-
    group.com, Web Site: www.mt-
    group.com
Member: Russell Paterson

THE DMA MERITDIRECT

333 Westchester Ave
White Plains, NY 10604-2910
Telephone: (914) 368-1000, Web Site:
    www.meritdirect.com
CEO: Ralph Drybrough

Primary Market Served: Business &
    Consumer

THE DMA METARESPONSE GROUP INC

700 W Hillsboro Blvd (Suite 4-107)
Deerfield Beach, FL 33441-1619
Telephone: (954) 360-0644, FAX:
    (954) 360-7712, Web Site: www.
    metaresponse.com
VP: Alfred DiBlasi
Pres: Jerry Whiteway
Employees: 12
Primary Market Served: Business &
    Consumer
Direct Marketing ad budget:
Direct Mail: 70%
Magazines: 20%
Telephone: 10%
Founded: 1999

Full service list brokerage/list management organization servicing the direct
mail and e-mail needs of mailers
within the financial newsletter,
business-to-business and consumer
markets. Integrated direct response
marketing services include direct mail
and e-mail list brokerage and list management, media plan development,
copy consultation, response analysis,
merge/purge and more. Utilizing 40+
years of knowledge and experience in
direct response marketing, our corporate mission is to help marketers effectively harness the power of direct mail
and e-mail to obtain new subscribers,
generate targeted leads, secure direct
sales while also maximizing list-rental
income.

MIDAMERICA LISTS INC

5001 1st Ave SE (Suite 105)
Cedar Rapids, IA 52402-3251
Telephone: (800) 747-5900, FAX:
    (888) 312-5478, E-Mail: sales@
    malists.com, Web Site: www.malists.
    com
VP Sls: Blair Gretter

MIDWEST LISTS & MEDIA

Part of The Bradford Group, Marketing
    Services
9333 N Milwaukee Ave
Niles, IL 60714
Telephone: (847) 966-2770, FAX:
    (847) 966-8630, Web Site: www.
    thebradfordgroup.com
Mktg: Mike Briggs

TONY MURRAY & ASSOCIATES

9663-C Main St
Fairfax, VA 22031
Telephone: (703) 425-5356, (800) 783-
    6400, FAX: (703) 425-4537
VP: Mike Murray

MY MAILING SERVICE, INC
2100 Faulkner Rd NE
Atlanta, GA 30324-4259
Telephone: (404) 321-6222, E-Mail:
info@mymailingservice.com, Web
Site: www.mymailingservice.com
Pres: Marc Sherman

THE DMA NCRI LIST MANAGEMENT
455 Sylvan Ave
Englewood Cliffs, NJ 07632-2703
Telephone: (201) 541-9500, FAX:
(201) 541-1944, E-Mail: info@
ncrilists.com, Web Site: www.
ncrilists.com
VP: Melissa Trotta

THE DMA NAME-FINDERS LISTS INC
8080 Capwell Dr Ste 100
Oakland, CA 94621-2120
Telephone: (415) 955-8585, (800) 221-
5009, FAX: (415) 955-8581, E-Mail:
dm@namefinderslists.com, Web Site:
www.namefinderslists.com
CEO: Rosalie A. Bulach
Pres: Norman Garcia

**THE DMA NAMEBANK
INTERNATIONAL LLC**
100 W Monument St
Baltimore, MD 21201-4701
Telephone: (410) 783-8460, FAX:
(410) 783-8464, E-Mail: beth@
namebank.com, Web Site: www.
namebank.com
Pres: Beth Ketzner

NAMES IN THE MAIL INC
10710 Shiloh Rd
Dallas, TX 75228-2640
Telephone: (972) 681-5701, (800) 688-
5701, FAX: (972) 681-5786, E-Mail:
nimnames@att.net
Pres: Judy Ashley
VP: Melba Frozies

THE DMA NAMES IN THE NEWS
1300 Clay St (fl 11)
Oakland, CA 94612-1429
Telephone: (415) 989-3350, FAX:
(415) 433-7796, E-Mail: name@
nincal.com, Web Site: www.nincal.
com
CEO: Susan Anstrand

**NATIONAL FUNDRAISING
LISTS**
16900 Science Dr (Suite 210)
Bowie, MD 20715-4412
Telephone: (410) 721-5700, FAX:
(410) 721-5795, E-Mail: info@
nflists.com, Web Site: www.
nflists.com
Sr VP: Pat Rainey

**NEIGHBORHOOD
GREETINGS**
328 W Charlotte St
Millersville, PA 17551-9516
Telephone: (717) 871-9053, (800) 332-
9200, FAX: (717) 871-9053, E-Mail:
info@neighborhoodgreetings.net,
Web Site: www.
neighborhoodgreetings.net
Pres: Will Stone

THE DMA NET 60 LLC
228 Park Ave S (Suite 83872)
New York, NY 10003-1502
Telephone: (201) 833-9003, FAX:
(201) 336-9088, E-Mail: chaim@
net60.com, Web Site: www.net60.
com
Pres: Chaim Lazar
Primary Market Served: Business

NETHAWK INTERACTIVE
1255 Park Ave Ste D
Emeryville, CA 94608-3679
Telephone: (510) 595-2220, Web Site:
www.nethawk.net
VP: James McManis
Primary Market Served: Business &
Consumer

NEW BUSINESS USA
Div. of Info USA
5711 S 86th Cir, PO Box 27086
Omaha, NE 68127-0086
Telephone: (800) 321-0869, FAX:
(402) 331-0176, E-Mail: help@
infousa.com, Web Site: www.infousa.
com
Founder, CEO, & Chmn: Vinod Gupta

**THE DMA NEW ENGLAND LIST
SERVICES INC**
171 Mountain View Dr
Danville, VT 05828-9641
Telephone: (802) 684-1179, (877) 252-
2100, FAX: (802) 684-2113, E-Mail:
dave@nelists.com, Web Site: www.
nelists.com
Pres: David Hare

NEXX GROUP INC
12734 Kenwood Ln Ste 87
Fort Myers, FL 33907-5638
Telephone: (239) 225-1516, (800) 566-
1183, FAX: (239) 288-4968, Web
Site: www.nexxagroup.com
Pres: Holly Paulus

**NORTH AMERICAN
PUBLISHING CO**
1500 Spring Garden St (Suite 1200)
Philadelphia, PA 19130-4069

Telephone: (215) 238-5300, FAX:
(215) 238-5412, Web Site: www.
napco.com
Pres: Ned S. Borowsky

OMAR'S TOUCH THERAPY
905 Lorraine Dr
Madison, WI 53705-1133
Telephone: (608) 658-6718, E-Mail:
omar@omarstouch.com, Web Site:
www.omarstouch.com
Pres: Howard C. Nelson

OMEGA LIST CO
Subs. of Eberle Communications
Group
1420 Spring Hill Rd (Suite 490)
McLean, VA 22102-3028
Telephone: (703) 821-1890, FAX:
(703) 821-8794, E-Mail: mhiban@
omegalist.com, Web Site: www.
omegalist.com
Pres: Michael Hiban
Founded: 1975

THE DMA O'NEILL MARKETING CO
10805 Main St (#400)
Fairfax, VA 22030-4747
Telephone: (703) 934-0272, Web Site:
www.oneillmarketing.com
Pres: Rita O'Neill

THE OTHER LIST CO INC
PO Box 286
Matawan, NJ 07747
Telephone: (732) 591-1180, FAX:
(732) 591-8472
Pres: Ernie Tacinelli

**PCS LIST & INFORMATION
TECHNOLOGIES**
PO Box 1507
Manchester, MA 01944-0860
Telephone: (978) 532-7100, (800) 532-
LIST, FAX: (978) 532-9181, E-Mail:
info@pcslist.com, Web Site: www.
pcslist.com
Pres & CEO: Ann Guyer
Dir Bus Devel: Charles Crowley
Asst to Pres: Milena Azevedo

PACIFIC LISTS INC
Subs. of "Names in the News"
180 Grand Ave Ste 1545
Oakland, CA 94612-3799
Telephone: (415) 945-9450, FAX:
(415) 945-9451, E-Mail: listinfo@
pacificlists.com, Web Site: www.
pacificlists.com
Pres: Deborah Hayden

PACKER LIST INC
902 Pennsylvania Ave SE
Washington, DC 20003-2140

Telephone: (202) 546-1889, FAX:
(202) 546-1897, E-Mail: listpacker@
aol.com
Pres: Donna Packer

THE DMA PARADYSZ
5 Hanover Sq
New York, NY 10004-2614
Telephone: (952) 544-5121, (212) 387-
0300, (800) 254-0300, FAX: (212)
387-7647, (952) 544-6320, Web Site:
www.paradysz.com
Co-CEO: Chris Paradysz
Mktg Mgr: Brenda Booth

**PARAGON PRINTING &
MAILING**
10423 McKalla Pl, Bldg A (Suite 100)
Austin, TX 78758-4448
Telephone: (512) 821-0222, FAX:
(512) 821-0200, E-Mail: paragon@
paragonprinting.com, Web Site:
paragonprinting.com
Pres: Katherine Harp

PARAMOUNT LISTS INC
3126 Peach St
Erie, PA 16508-2734
Telephone: (814) 459-8787, (800) 723-
5478, FAX: (814) 459-1398, Web
Site: www.paramountlists.com
Pres: Kristin Genovese

PENNRICH
8890 Hamot Rd
Waterford, PA 16441-9240
Telephone: (814) 866-2412, FAX:
(814) 864-3908
Pres: Richard E. Hess

**THE DMA PEPPERMILL MARKETING
INC**
8335 W Sunset Blvd Ste 246
Los Angeles, CA 90069-1529
Telephone: (310) 659-8900, (877) 600-
7775, FAX: (310) 659-8901, E-Mail:
inquiry@peppermillmarketing.com,
Web Site: www.peppermillmarketing.
com
Pres: Michael Franchino
AE List Mngmt & Brokerage: Pia P.
Feng
Dir, Interactive Mktg: Gus Ozgen
Conducts Business: U.S.
Primary Market Served: Business &
Consumer
Direct online sales
Advertising/Marketing Budget Related
to Direct Marketing: 51-75%
Founded: 1995

List managers and list brokers for both
consumer and business to business in
direct mail and e-mail marketing.

PINNACLE LIST CO
2800 Shirlington Rd (Suite 970)
Arlington, VA 22206-3613
Telephone: (703) 379-4394, FAX:
(703) 379-5312, E-Mail: holly@
pinnlistco.com, Web Site: www.
pinnlistco.com
Pres: Holly Ruble

POLITICAL RESOURCES
PO Box 1403
Lake Worth, FL 33460-1403
Telephone: (800) 423-2677, FAX:
(561) 533-0104, E-Mail: info@
politicalresources.com, Web Site:
www.politicalresources.com
Pres: Carol Hess

THE DMA PONT MEDIA DIRECT
10 E Meadow Ln
Norwalk, CT 06851-2902
Telephone: (203) 354-8074, FAX:
(203) 956-9227, E-Mail: stefanie@
listgoddess.com, Web Site: www.
pontmediadirect.com
Mng Partner: Stefanie Pont
Conducts Business: U.S., Canada, Eu-
rope & Asia
Primary Market Served: Business &
Consumer
Founded: 2004

List brokerage & consulting services.

THE DMA WS PONTON INC
5149 Butler St, The Ponton Bldg
Pittsburgh, PA 15201-2606
Telephone: (412) 782-2360, (800) 628-
7806, FAX: (412) 782-1109, E-Mail:
joseph@wsponton.com, Web Site:
www.wsponton.com
VP, Sls: Joseph Marchese

**PRECISION MAILING
SOLUTIONS**
101 Colt Cir
Huntsville, AL 35811
Telephone: (256) 852-1963, FAX:
(256) 852-1963, E-Mail:
precisionmailing@mchsi.com
Pres: Michele Fleming
Conducts Business: U.S.
Employees: 1
Primary Market Served: Business &
Consumer
Advertising/Marketing Budget Related
to Direct Marketing: 0-25%
Founded: 2002
Gross sales or billing: $20,000

List broker.

PREMIER DATA GROUP
616 Corte Regalo
Camarillo, CA 93010-9107

Telephone: (805) 445-7522, FAX:
(805) 445-8876, Web Site: www.
premierdatagroup.com
CEO: Mary Ann Parshall
Conducts Business: U.S.
Primary Market Served: Business &
Consumer
Catalog available online
Indirect online sales
Advertising/Marketing Budget Related
to Direct Marketing: 0-25%
Founded: 2000

THE DMA PREMIER DATA SOLUTION
2510-G Las Posas (#234)
Camarillo, CA 93010-9107
Telephone: (805) 987-2789, (800) 537-
3282, (800) 333-DATA, FAX: (800)
333-6974, E-Mail: info@
premierdatasolution.com, Web Site:
www.premierdatasolution.com
Pres: Mary Ann Parshall

PRIME TARGET DIRECT LLC
7788 W Bay Dr
Mason, OH 45040-8440
Telephone: (513) 234-8977, E-Mail:
tom@primetargetdirect.com
Mng Member: Thomas P. Smith
Conducts Business: U.S.
Primary Market Served: Business

List brokerage and analytical services.

**PROFESSIONAL DIRECT
MARKETING & MAILING
LIST INC**
6400 Congress Ave Ste 2150
Boca Raton, FL 33487-2850
Telephone: (561) 241-4414, (800) 777-
5478, FAX: (561) 241-5878, E-Mail:
pdm@pdmm.info, Web Site: www.
pdmm.us
CEO: Rick Krna
Pres: Joseph Vergolino
Sr VP: Kevin Muth

**QUALITY EDUCATION DATA
(QED)**
A Scholastic Company
6 Armstrong Rd (Suite 301)
Shelton, CT 06484-4722
Telephone: (203) 926-4800, (800) 333-
8802, E-Mail: mdrinfor@dnb.com,
Web Site: www.schooldata.com
Pres: Andy Lacy
Mktg Mgr: Emily Garner

THE DMA REDI-DATA
Subs. of Redi-Direct Co
5 Audrey Pl
Fairfield, NJ 07004-3401

Telephone: (973) 808-4500, FAX:
(973) 808-5511, E-Mail: sales@
redimail.com, Web Site: www.
redidata.com
Founder & CEO: Tom Buckley
Dir Mktg: Michael Hayden

RL POLK & CO
26533 Evergreen Rd Ste 900
Southfield, MI 48076-4249
Telephone: (248) 728-7100, (800) GO-
4-POLK, FAX: (248) 728-4444, Web
Site: www.polk.com
Pres: Joe Walker
Chmn & CEO: Stephen Polk

THE DMA RMI DIRECT MARKETING INC
42 Old Ridgebury Rd
Danbury, CT 06810-5129
Telephone: (203) 798-0448, FAX:
(203) 778-6130, E-Mail: info@
rmidirect.com, Web Site: www.
rmidirect.com
CEO: Martin Stein
VP Bus Devel: Cyndi Lee

REACHFORCE
9020-1 Capital of TX Hwy N (Suite
270)
Austin, TX 78750
Telephone: (512) 327-9000, FAX:
(512) 327-9090, E-Mail: info@
reachforce.com, Web Site: www.
reachforce.com
CEO: Suaad Sait
COO: Bob Riazzi
VP Prods: Jason Morio
Mktg Dir: Amy Hawthorne
Conducts Business: U.S.
Employees: 35
Primary Market Served: Business
Advertising/Marketing Budget Related
to Direct Marketing: 51-75%
Founded: 2005

Delivers data and software solutions
that enable B2B companies to laser
target their lead generation initiatives.

REIN ASSOCIATES INC
PO Box 50878
Myrtle Beach, SC 29579-0015
Telephone: (732) 741-8111, FAX:
(732) 741-6666, E-Mail: info@
reinassociates.com, Web Site: www.
reinassociates.com
Pres: J.M. Rein

THE DMA RESEARCH & RESPONSE INTERNATIONAL
250 W 57th St (Suite 1326)
New York, NY 10107-1309

Telephone: (212) 489-8610, FAX:
(212) 262-3474, E-Mail: rrespe@
bway.net, Web Site: www.rrespe.com
Pres: George C. Collins

RESPONSE UNLIMITED
284 Shalom Rd, c/o The Old Plantation
Waynesboro, VA 22980-7349
Telephone: (540) 943-6721, FAX:
(540) 943-0841, E-Mail: info@ru-
lists.com, Web Site: www.
responseunlimited.com
Pres: Philip Zodhiates
Sls Mgr: Matt Laporta

THE DMA RICKARD LIST MARKETING
Div. of R&R Direct Mail Inc
190 Motor Pkwy Ste 103
Hauppauge, NY 11788-5159
Telephone: (631) 249-8710, FAX:
(631) 249-9655, E-Mail: mrickard@
rickardlist.com, Web Site: www.
rickardlist.com
Pres: Mark Rickard

RIFFKIN DIRECT INC
64 Appletree Ln
Roslyn Heights, NY 11577-2432
Telephone: (516) 621-1076, FAX:
(516) 621-7127
Pres: Ronald Riffkin

THE DMA THE RIGHT LISTS LTD
6417 Erin Dr
Clarksville, MD 21029-1290
Telephone: (410) 531-0467, Web Site:
www.rightlists.com
Pres: Bill Fletcher

ROBERTSON MAILING LIST CO
44084 Riverside Pkwy (Suite 350)
Leesburg, VA 20176-6823
Telephone: (703) 726-2822, (800) 788-
4564, FAX: (703) 726-9882, E-Mail:
vnorman@rmlc.net, Web Site: www.
rmlc.net
VP: Vickie L. Norman
Dir Mktg: Molly Rinaldi

EDITH ROMAN ASSOCIATES INC
1 Blue Hill Plz (Suite 16)
Pearl River, NY 10965-3100
Telephone: (845) 620-9000, (800) 223-
2194, FAX: (845) 620-9035
List Mgr: Michael Murphy

ROSEBERRY DIRECT LIST MANAGEMENT & BROKERAGE
265 Timberline Trl
Elon, NC 27244-8088
Telephone: (336) 532-1000, Web Site:
www.roseberrydirect.com
Pres: Claudia Hurteau

S&G BUSINESS ASSOCIATES INC
58135 Benham Ave
Elkhart, IN 46517
Telephone: (574) 295-0163
Pres: Judy Miller

SIE (SELECT INFORMATION EXCHANGE)
175 W 79th St
New York, NY 10024
Telephone: (212) 496-6435, FAX:
(212) 787-4269, Web Site: www.
siecom.com
List Mgr: Alex Wein
Pres: George Wein

SK&A INFORMATION SERVICES INC
2601 Main St (Suite 650)
Irvine, CA 92614-4228
Telephone: (949) 476-2051, (800) 752-
5478, FAX: (949) 476-2168, E-Mail:
skasales@skainfo.com, Web Site:
www.skainfo.com
Pres: Al Cosentino
VP Fin: Ramiro Tavares

SWAT MARKETING TEAM
433 S Broad St
Grove City, PA 16127-2201
Telephone: (412) 851-9700, FAX:
(412) 291-1155, Web Site: www.
swatmarketingteam.com
Pres: Christopher Bloch
Conducts Business: Worldwide
Employees: 5
Primary Market Served: Business
Founded: 1999
Gross sales or billing: $500,000

Provides prospecting lists and databases to companies in the computer
industry.

SALESLEADSTV (FEDERAL UNION INC)
2701 NW Second Ave (Suite 213)
Boca Raton, FL 33431
Telephone: (561) 981-8777, (800) 590-
5323, FAX: (561) 981-8786, E-Mail:
contact_us@salesleads.tv, Web Site:
www.salesleads.tv
Pres: John Fischer

SECO FINANCIAL SERVICES INC
1288 Route 73 South
Mount Laurel, NJ 08054
Telephone: (856) 273-0050, (800) 898-SECO, FAX: (856) 273-9228, Web Site: www.secofinancial.com
Pres: Stephen I. Einhorn

SELECT LIST CORP
31 Glen Head Rd
Glen Head, NY 11545-1446
Telephone: (516) 676-7831, FAX: (516) 676-9746
Pres: Edwin Smith

SENIOR CITIZENS UNLIMITED INC
PO Box 3036
Westport, CT 06880-8036
Telephone: (914) 273-6672, (800) 431-1712, FAX: (914) 273-6617, E-Mail: listsales@sculists.com, Web Site: www.sculists.com

THE SENIOR SOURCE
70 Sierra Vista Ln
Valley Cottage, NY 10989-2701
Telephone: (800) 882-9930, FAX: (845) 358-8772, Web Site: www.theseniorsource.com
Pres: Susan Juskiw

SINGER DIRECT
195 Broadway Fl 12
New York, NY 10007-3126
Telephone: (212) 209-1900, Web Site: www.singerdirect.com
SVP: David Levy

FRED SINGER DIRECT MARKETING INC
800 Westchester Ave (Suite 400)
Rye Brook, NY 10573-1340
Telephone: (914) 472-7100, FAX: (914) 472-9022, E-Mail: info@singerdirect.com, Web Site: www.singerdirect.com
Pres: Fred Singer

SITEL
Subs. of LCS Industries
3102 West End Ave (Suite 1000), Two American Center
Nashville, TN 37203-1324
Telephone: (615) 301-7100, (866) 95-SITEL, E-Mail: pr-na@sitet.com, Web Site: www.sitel.com
Pres & CEO: David Garner

SOBELSOHN SCHOOL
275 W 96th St
New York, NY 10025

Telephone: (917) 441-9740, FAX: (917) 441-9740, E-Mail: sobelsohnschool@yahoo.com, Web Site: www.sobelsohnschool.com
Dir: Richard Sobelsohn
Dir Mktg: John Pliny Jr

SORKINS INC
319 South New Ballas Rd
Saint Louis, MO 63146
Telephone: (800) 758-3228, FAX: (800) 721-5478, E-Mail: customerservice@sorkins.com, Web Site: www.sorkins.com
Chmn & CEO: Murray L. Sorkin

SOUND BEACH MARKETING PARTNERS LLC
Two Rocky Point Rd
Old Greenwich, CT 06870
Telephone: (203) 698-0708, FAX: (203) 698-0712, E-Mail: thudock@soundbeachmarketing.com, Web Site: www.soundbeachmarketing.com
Mng Owner: Terry Hudock
Mktg Asst: Deb Tether
Conducts Business: U.S.
Employees: 2
Primary Market Served: Business & Consumer
Advertising/Marketing Budget Related to Direct Marketing: 76-100%
Founded: 2001
Gross sales or billing: $1,000,000

Lists to Brokers, mailers.

SPECIALISTS MARKETING SERVICES INC
aka SMS
777 Terrace Ave (fl 4)
Hasbrouck Heights, NJ 07604-3113
Telephone: (201) 865-5800, FAX: (201) 288-4295, E-Mail: listinfo@specialistsms.com, Web Site: www.specialistsms.com
VP Sls & Mktg: Amy L. Lyons

THE DMA **SPECIALIZED FUNDRAISING SERVICES**
300 E Henry St Ste 102
Spartanburg, SC 29302-2630
Telephone: (864) 579-7755, Web Site: www.specializedfundraising.net
Pres: Lisa Greene
Primary Market Served: Business & Consumer

THE DMA **SPEEDEON DATA CORP**
6655 Parkland Blvd
Cleveland, OH 44139-4345
Telephone: (440) 287-7306, Web Site: www.speedeondata.com
Pres: Gerard Daher

THE DMA **SPIRIT DIRECT MARKETING SERVICES**
11777 Katy Fwy (#120)
Houston, TX 77079-1705
Telephone: (281) 496-5614
Pres & Broker: Steve Mayes

THE DMA **STATLISTICS**
69 Kenosia Ave
Danbury, CT 06810-7303
Telephone: (203) 778-8700, Web Site: www.statlistics.com
CEO: John Papalia
Mktg Dir: Barbara Salles

GEORGE STERNE AGENCY INC
1588 S Mission Rd Ste 220
Fallbrook, CA 92028-4112
Telephone: (760) 432-6913, (800) 772-8174, FAX: (760) 432-9570, E-Mail: mim@georgesterneagency.com, Web Site: www.georgesterneagency.com
Pres: Don Dominick

STUDENT MARKETING GROUP INC
777 Sunrise Hwy (Suite 300)
Lynbrook, NY 11563-2950
Telephone: (516) 593-8877, Web Site: www.studentmarketing.net
Pres: Peggy Klang

SUNVEST RESORTS
425 N Federal Hwy
Hallandale, FL 33009
Telephone: (954) 239-4200

T O PRINTING & MAILING SERVICES
5334 Sterling Ctr Dr
Westlake Village, CA 91361-4612
Telephone: (818) 991-0068
Pres: Robert J. Peters

THE DMA **TKL INTERACTIVE**
3700 Standridge Dr (Suite 210)
The Colony, TX 75056-4149
Telephone: (972) 370-7878, (800) 789-3893, FAX: (972) 370-7879, Web Site: www.tklinteractive.com
Pres: Ken Walker
VP Sls & Mktg: Sherri Jones
Conducts Business: Worldwide
Primary Market Served: Business & Consumer
Catalog available online
Direct online sales
Founded: 1998

Full service interactive agency-e-mail, direct mail, creative services, marketing strategy, execution and buys.

TMA DIRECT
12120 Sunset Hills Rd (Suite 450)
Reston, VA 20190-5858
Telephone: (703) 547-4940, Web Site:
www.tmalist.com
Pres & CEO: Mike Murray

**THOR INFORMATION
SERVICES INC**
3032 State Rte 28
Old Forge, NY 13420-1167
Telephone: (315) 369-3872, FAX:
(315) 369-2330, E-Mail: sales@
thorinfo.com
Pres: Sheila Brady

3 GEN CO
544 Empire Blvd
Brooklyn, NY 11225
Telephone: (718) 773-3388, FAX:
(718) 467-0843
Pres: Moshe Kugel

TOTAL DATA SOLUTIONS
48 Fox Hill Rd
North Andover, MA 01845-2936
Telephone: (978) 686-2311, Web Site:
www.ttldatasolutions.com
Pres: Mark Hammar

**TOUCHPOINT DATA
SOLUTIONS**
6910 Bucks Rd
Cumming, GA 30040-0232
Telephone: (770) 886-8611, Web Site:
www.touchpointdata.com
CEO: Max Korgman

**TRI-MEDIA MARKETING
SERVICES INC**
3330 Old Glenview Rd (#2)
Wilmette, IL 60091-2963
Telephone: (800) 874-4062, Web Site:
www.trimediaonline.com
Pres & Sls Mng: Neal Siegel
VP Mktg: Fran Pintozzi
VP Opers & Data Svcs Mng: Wayne
Luttrell
Conducts Business: U.S., Canada
Employees: 27
Primary Market Served: Business
Catalog available online
Founded: 1989

Provides direct-marketing options targeting churches, home schoolers, and consumers. Also provides card decks, mailing/e-mail lists, and ad booklets.

**TRIANGLE MARKETING
SERVICES INC**
245 W 17th St (Suite 1250)
New York, NY 10011

Telephone: (212) 242-4040, FAX:
(212) 242-1344, Web Site: www.tms-ny.com
List Mgr: Stephanie Cipriani
Sls Mgr: Neil Serendensky
Conducts Business: U.S.
Employees: 5
Primary Market Served: Consumer
Founded: 1995
Gross sales or billing: $1,000,000

Full service mailing list firm specializing in the gay and lesbian market. Nation's leading manager of gay and lesbian mailing lists.

THE
DMA **TRIAX DATA**
8911 Linksvue Dr
Knoxville, TN 37922-5254
Telephone: (865) 971-4333, Web Site:
www.triaxdata.com
Dir: Jonathan Brooks

THE
DMA **TRINITY DIRECT**
10 Park Pl Ste 12
Butler, NJ 07405-1370
Telephone: (973) 283-3600, Web Site:
www.trinitydirect.net
Pres: John Kehoe

THE
DMA **US DATA CORP**
30501 Agoura Rd Ste 102
Agoura Hills, CA 91301-4399
Telephone: (818) 444-4590, Web Site:
www.usdatacorp.net
Mktg Dir: Mollie Benton

USADATA INC
292 Madison Ave (fl 3)
New York, NY 10017-6322
Telephone: (212) 679-1411, Web Site:
www.usadata.com
Data & Leads Group: Dominic Le-Claire

THE
DMA **V12 GROUP**
141 W Front St (Suite 410)
Red Bank, NJ 07701-6422
Telephone: (732) 842-1001, Web Site:
www.v12group.com
Dir Mktg: Christina Galbornetti
Primary Market Served: Business &
Consumer

**VAYAN MARKETING GROUP
LLC**
6615 Boynton Beach Blvd
Boynton Beach, FL 33437-3526
Telephone: (561) 955-9660, Web Site:
www.vayan.com
VP Bus Devel: Warren Corpus

THE
DMA **VISION MARKETING INC**
455 Sylvan Ave
Englewood Cliffs, NJ 07632-2703
Telephone: (201) 816-1560, FAX:
(201) 816-1610, Web Site: www.
visionmarketing.com
Pres: Michael Young

WASHINGTON LISTS INC
6849 Old Dominion Dr (Suite 320)
McLean, VA 22101
Telephone: (703) 749-3110, FAX:
(703) 749-0960, E-Mail:
emahoney@washingtonlists.com,
Web Site: www.washingtonlists.com
Gen Mgr: Erin Mahoney

WEEKLY READER CORP
44 S Broadway
White Plains, NY 10601-4425
Telephone: (914) 242-4019, (914) 242-4000, (800) 446-3355, Web Site:
www.weeklyreader.com
Pres: Peter Bergen

**WEISS PUBLISHING &
MARKETING INC**
15430 Endeavour Dr
Jupiter, FL 33478
Telephone: (561) 627-3300, (800) 844-1773, Web Site: www.martinweiss.com
Pres: Martin D. Weiss

WILLIAMS DIRECT INC
PO Box 205
Burlington, KS 66839-0205
Telephone: (620) 364-8431, FAX:
(620) 364-8432
Pres: Caroline Williams

**WILSON MARKETING
GROUP**
11924 W Washington Blvd
Los Angeles, CA 90066
Telephone: (800) 445-2089, FAX:
(310) 397-4980, E-Mail: wilsonmg@
earthlink.net
Pres: Mike Wilson

FRED WOOLF LIST CO INC
PO Box 346
Somers, NY 10589-0346
Telephone: (914) 694-4466, (800) 431-1557, FAX: (914) 694-1710, E-Mail:
info@woolflist.com, Web Site: www.
woolflist.com
Pres: Fred Woolf
Sr VP: Sheila Woolf
Founded: 1972

THE DMA WORLDATA
3000 N Military Trl
Boca Raton, FL 33431-6321
Telephone: (561) 393-8200, (800) 331-8102, FAX: (561) 368-8345, E-Mail: mail@worldata.com, Web Site: www.worldata.com
Corp VP: Jay Schwedelson

ZEPPO MARKETING INC
358 5th Ave Rm 1103
New York, NY 10001-2221
Telephone: (212) 308-5734, Web Site: www.zeppomarketing.com
Pres: Harley Weber
Primary Market Served: Business & Consumer

List Managers & Owners (24) — Geographic Index

California

DAJ Direct Inc, 427 E 17th St (Suite 253), Costa Mesa, 92627

ETR Associates, 251 Rhode Island St Ste 204, San Francisco, 94103-5168

HomeData, 1021 Tremonto Rd, Santa Barbara, 93103-1740

Jigsaw, 777 Mariners Island Blvd (Suite 400), San Mateo, 94404

MSC Lists, 450 Los Verdes Dr, Santa Barbara, 93111-1506

Prestige Mailing Lists Inc, 7746 Gloria Ave, Van Nuys, 91406-1610

Word Dynamics of St Helena, 1998 Spring St, Saint Helena, 94574-2323

Colorado

Accutrend Data Corp, 7860 E Berry Place (Suite 200), Greenwood Village, 80111-2303

Connecticut

Direct Media List Management, 200 Pemberwick Rd, Greenwich, 06831-4273

Ginsburg Global, 1200 Summer St (Suite 105), Stamford, 06905-5541

LIST Inc, 69 Kenosia Ave (Suite 1), Danbury, 06810-7318

World Innovators Inc, 22 Bacon Rd, Roxbury, 06783-1817

District of Columbia

National Association of Home Builders, 1201 15th St NW, Washington, 20005-2800

Florida

Acxiom Xpress, 2503 Del Prado Blvd S (Suite 300), Cape Coral, 33904-5709

Bisk/Totaltape Lists, 9417 Princess Palm Ave, Tampa, 33619

Getko Direct Response, 5830 Coral Ridge Dr (Suite 240), Coral Springs, 33076

Lighthouse List Co, 27 SE 24th Ave (Suite 6), Pompano Beach, 33062-5346

Newsmax Media Inc, PO Box 20989, West Palm Beach, 33416-0989

Outsource America Inc, 715 60th St Court E, Bradenton, 34208-6262

Georgia

Lifestyle Change Communications, 1000 Cobb Place Blvd (Suite 500B), Kennesaw, 30144

Illinois

Educational Lists Services Inc, 5300 Katrine Ave, Downers Grove, 60515-4049

The List Bank, 500 Davis Ctr (Suite 812), Evanston, 60201-4655

Mardev-DM2, 333 E Butterfield Rd (Suite 700), Lombard, 60148-5619

Medical Marketing Service Inc, 185 Hansen Ct (Suite 110), Wood Dale, 60191-1168

Maryland

Bethesda List Center Inc, 4300 Montgomery Ave (Suite 204B), Bethesda, 20814-4463

Columbia Books, Inc, 8120 Woodmont Ave (Suite 110), Bethesda, 20814

InvestorPlace Media LLC, 9201 Corporate Blvd, Rockville, 20850-3202

Name Exchange, 712 N East St, Frederick, 21701

Massachusetts

Affinity Marketing Group, 30 Washington St, Wellesley Hills, 02481-1905

IDG List Services, 492 Old Connecticut Path (Suite 311), Framingham, 01701

Nebraska

American Church Lists Inc, 5711 S 86th Cir, Omaha, 68127-4146

American Medical Information Inc, 5711 S 86th Cir, Omaha, 68127-4146

William-Neil Associates, One Cabela Dr (Suite 2114), Sidney, 69160

Nevada

TCI Direct, PO Box 3936, Stateline, 89449-3936

New Hampshire

Institute Lists/IOMA, 1 Phoenix Mill Ln Fl 3, Peterborough, 03458-1467

New Jersey

The Information Refinery Inc, 200 Rte 17 (Suite 5), Mahwah, 07430-1267

Lawyers Diary and Manual, 240 Mulberry St, Newark, 07101-3528

The List Authority Inc, 192 Third Ave (#7), Westwood, 07675

List Management Center, 148 Princeton-Hightstown Rd, Hightstown, 08520-1450

Profile America List Co Inc, 455 Sylvan Ave, Englewood Cliffs, 07632-2703

New Mexico

NAM Mailing Lists, PO Box 970, Santa Cruz, 87567

New York

Blue Book Direct Mail & Database Service, 360 Park Ave S, New York, 10010-1710

Columbia House, 250 W 34th St, One Penn Plaza, New York, 10119-0002

DMG-Lists, 60 E Industry Ct Ste 5, DMG Corporate Plaza, Deer Park, 11729-4726

Estee Marketing Group Inc, 270 North Ave (Suite 805), New Rochelle, 10801-5105

Graphic Arts Blue Book/AF Lewis Marketing, 360 Park Ave S (15th fl), New York, 10010-1731

Hearst Business Communications, 50 Charles Lindbergh Blvd (Suite 100), Uniondale, 11553-3600

IEEE/Spectrum Magazine, 3 Park Ave (fl 17), New York, 10016-5902

LH Management, 200 N Central Ave, Hartsdale, 10530-1931

Mardev, 360 Park Ave S (fl 12), New York, 10010-1710

Metamorphics Media, 332 Bleecker St (Suite 212), New York, 10014-2980

RAD Marketing & Cable Towns, 167 Crary On-The-Park, Mount Vernon, 10550

The Rich List Co, PO Box 294, Wainscott, 11975-0294

Eleanor L Stark, 954 Lexington Ave (Suite 200), New York, 10021-5055

Teikoku Databank America Inc, 780 3rd Ave (Rm 2200), New York, 10017-2179

Thomas Business Lists, Five Penn Plz, New York, 10001

21st Century Marketing, 1200 Veterans Hwy (Suite 100), Hauppauge, 11788-3052

North Carolina

Preferred Communications, 410 Central Ave, Butner, 27509-1916

Oklahoma

Chilcutt Direct Marketing, 9301 Cedar Lake Ave, Oklahoma City, 73114-7899

Dental Economics, 1421 S Sheridan Rd, Tulsa, 74112-6619

PennWell Lists, 1421 S Sheridan Rd, Tulsa, 74112-6600

Pennsylvania

Charles Moore Associates Inc, PO Box 6, Southampton, 18966-0006

Promissor, Three Bala Plaza W (Suite 300), Bala Cynwyd, 19004

Virginia

Media Mart, 7600A Leesburg Pike, Falls Church, 22043-2000

Salem Web Network, 111 Virginia St (Suite 500), Richmond, 23219

Washington

Twin Peaks Press, PO Box 8, Vancouver, 98666-0008

CANADA
Ontario

CLB Media Inc, 240 Edward St, Aurora, L4G 3S9

MapInfo, Canada, 26 Wellington St E (Suite 500), Toronto, M5E 1S2

List Managers & Owners (24)

ACCUTREND DATA CORP

7860 E Berry Place (Suite 200)
Greenwood Village, CO 80111-2303
Telephone: (303) 488-0011, FAX:
    (303) 488-0133, E-Mail: info@
    accutrend.com, Web Site: www.
    accutrend.com
CEO: Vicki Reavis
Exec Asst: Janie Bowen

We directly acquire raw business
records from government jurisdictions,
standardizes, processes, links & up-
dates daily. ADC data is collected directly at the SOS, county & city levels
on a daily, daily-random, bi-weekly &
monthly ongoing basis. Our customized in-house proprietary technology
gives us the ability to track the history
of new business records from the original filing date to the dissolution &
merge date of corporations.

ACXIOM XPRESS

2503 Del Prado Blvd S (Suite 300)
Cape Coral, FL 33904-5709
Telephone: (800) 732-9250, E-Mail:
    iblexpress@acxiom.com

AFFINITY MARKETING GROUP

30 Washington St
Wellesley Hills, MA 02481-1905
Telephone: (781) 239-9310, FAX:
    (781) 239-9645, E-Mail: info@
    affinitymg.com, Web Site: www.
    affinitymg.com
CEO: Douglas D. Furbush III

AMERICAN CHURCH LISTS INC

Div. of Info USA
5711 S 86th Cir
Omaha, NE 68127-4146
Telephone: (402) 596-8905, (888) 733-
    1812, FAX: (402) 596-8907, E-Mail:
    americanchurchlists@infousa.com,
    Web Site: www.americanchurchlists.
    com
Gen Mgr: Corey Grause

AMERICAN MEDICAL INFORMATION INC

Div. of InfoUSA Inc
5711 S 86th Cir
Omaha, NE 68127-4146
Telephone: (402) 593-4500, (866) 241-
    9044, FAX: (402) 331-1505, E-Mail:
    support@drlists.com, Web Site:
    americanmedicalinfo.com
CEO: Vinod Gupta

BETHESDA LIST CENTER INC

4300 Montgomery Ave (Suite 204B)
Bethesda, MD 20814-4463
Telephone: (301) 986-1455, FAX:
    (301) 907-4870, E-Mail: info@
    bethesda-list.com, Web Site: www.
    bethesda-list.com
Mktg Mgr: John P. Rucker
Broker: Mary Mowrey-Reise
List Prodn: Barbara-Jean Hogan
List Prodn Mgr: Dan Zebroski
Conducts Business: U.S., Canada,
    Worldwide
Primary Market Served: Business
Catalog available online
Indirect online sales
Advertising/Marketing Budget Related
    to Direct Marketing: 76-100%
Founded: 1993

Business-to-business list manager and
broker. Specialties: medical/health care,
associations, IT and training

BISK/TOTALTAPE LISTS

Div. of Totaltape Publishing
9417 Princess Palm Ave
Tampa, FL 33619
Telephone: (813) 621-6200, (800) 874-
    7877, FAX: (813) 627-9442, E-Mail:
    lists@bisk.com, Web Site: www.
    listpro.com
Acct Exec: Rudd Johnson

BLUE BOOK DIRECT MAIL & DATABASE SERVICE

Subs. of AF Lewis Market Info Svc
360 Park Ave S
New York, NY 10010-1710
Telephone: (646) 746-7398, FAX:
    (646) 746-7434, Web Site: www.
    gabb.com
Mktg Mgr: Greg Bastug

CLB MEDIA INC

240 Edward St
Aurora, ON, Canada L4G 3S9
Telephone: (905) 727-0077, FAX:
    (905) 727-0017, E-Mail: km@
    industrialsourcebook.com, Web Site:
    www.clbmedia.ca
Gen Mgr: Kent Milford

THE DMA CHILCUTT DIRECT MARKETING

9301 Cedar Lake Ave
Oklahoma City, OK 73114-7899
Telephone: (405) 478-7245, FAX:
    (405) 478-2984, Web Site: www.
    cdmlist.com
Pres: Matt Chilcutt
VP: Jane McCoy

COLUMBIA BOOKS, INC

8120 Woodmont Ave (Suite 110)
Bethesda, MD 20814
Telephone: (202) 464-1662, (888) 265-
    0600, FAX: (202) 464-1775, E-Mail:
    info@columbiabooks.com, Web Site:
    www.columbiabooks.com
Dir Mktg: Brittany English

COLUMBIA HOUSE

250 W 34th St, One Penn Plaza
New York, NY 10119-0002
Telephone: (212) 596-2000, Web Site:
    www.columbiahouse.com
Pres & CEO: Stuart Goldfarb

DAJ DIRECT INC

427 E 17th St (Suite 253)
Costa Mesa, CA 92627
Telephone: (949) 722-0506, FAX:
    (949) 722-8026, Web Site: www.
    dajdirect.com
CEO & Pres: Daniel Jacobs
Conducts Business: U.S.
Primary Market Served: Business &
    Consumer
Catalog available online
Advertising/Marketing Budget Related
    to Direct Marketing: 76-100%
Direct Marketing ad budget:
Direct Mail: 90%
Telephone: 10%
Founded: 1993

List managers & brokers specializing
in business & financial opportunities,
health & credit lists.

DMG-LISTS

60 E Industry Ct Ste 5, DMG Corpo-
    rate Plaza
Deer Park, NY 11729-4726
Telephone: (631) 586-5800, FAX:
    (631) 586-6080, E-Mail: kathyb@
    dmgltd.org, Web Site: www.dmgltd.
    org
Exec VP: Maureen Rose
Pres & Owner: Keitha Rocco

DENTAL ECONOMICS
Div. of PennWell Publishing Co
1421 S Sheridan Rd
Tulsa, OK 74112-6619
Telephone: (918) 835-3161, FAX:
(918) 831-9804, E-Mail: kellib@
pennwell.com, Web Site: www.
dentaleconomics.com
Mng Editor: Kevin Henry

**DIRECT MEDIA LIST
MANAGEMENT**
200 Pemberwick Rd
Greenwich, CT 06831-4273
Telephone: (203) 532-1000, FAX:
(203) 532-3766, Web Site: www.
directmedia.com
Chmn: David W. Florence

ETR ASSOCIATES
251 Rhode Island St Ste 204
San Francisco, CA 94103-5168
Telephone: (831) 438-4060, (800) 321-
4407, FAX: (800) 435-8433, E-Mail:
webmaster@etr.org, Web Site: www.
etr.org
Dir: Michael E. Bird

**EDUCATIONAL LISTS
SERVICES INC**
5300 Katrine Ave
Downers Grove, IL 60515-4049
Telephone: (630) 968-1290, FAX:
(630) 968-6010, E-Mail: jquinn@
educationallist.com, Web Site: www.
educationallist.com
VP & Gen Mgr: Jeffery C. Quinn

**ESTEE MARKETING GROUP
INC**
270 North Ave (Suite 805)
New Rochelle, NY 10801-5105
Telephone: (914) 235-7080, FAX:
(914) 235-6518, E-Mail: info@
esteemarketing.com, Web Site: www.
esteemarketing.com
Pres: Chris Ragusa
Dir Client Svcs: Felecia Pucci

GETKO DIRECT RESPONSE
5830 Coral Ridge Dr (Suite 240)
Coral Springs, FL 33076
Telephone: (800) 642-8732, FAX:
(954) 320-7565, E-Mail:
gdrservices@getkodirect.com, Web
Site: www.getkodirect.com
Dir: Julie A. Greenbaum

GINSBURG GLOBAL
1200 Summer St (Suite 105)
Stamford, CT 06905-5541

Telephone: (203) 359-2420, FAX:
(203) 325-4443, E-Mail: gerry@
ginsburgglobal.com, Web Site: www.
ginsburgglobal.com
Pres: Gerry L. Ginsburg

**GRAPHIC ARTS BLUE BOOK/
AF LEWIS MARKETING**
360 Park Ave S (15th fl)
New York, NY 10010-1731
Telephone: (646) 746-7429, FAX:
(212) 519-7434, Web Site: www.
gabb.com
Dir of Sls & Mktg Svcs: Carl Sartori

**HEARST BUSINESS
COMMUNICATIONS**
50 Charles Lindbergh Blvd (Suite 100)
Uniondale, NY 11553-3600
Telephone: (516) 227-1300, FAX:
(516) 227-1901
Circ Dir: Barry Greene

HOMEDATA
Div. of Dominion Enterprises
1021 Tremonto Rd
Santa Barbara, CA 93103-1740
Telephone: (516) 605-0451, (800) 628-
9456, FAX: (516) 605-0455, E-Mail:
info@homedata.com, Web Site:
www.homedata.com
VP Sls: Julie Greenbaum
Conducts Business: U.S.
Employees: 6
Primary Market Served: Business &
Consumer
Direct online sales
Advertising/Marketing Budget Related
to Direct Marketing: 76-100%
Founded: 1982
Gross sales or billing: $5,000,000

The leading provider of new homeowner and new mover data to the direct marketing industry.

THE DMA IDG LIST SERVICES
Subs. of International Data Group
492 Old Connecticut Path (Suite 311)
Framingham, MA 01701
Telephone: (888) 434-5478, FAX:
(508) 370-0020, Web Site: www.
idglist.com
Gen Mgr: Andrew Sambrook
Mktg Dir: Patricia Sims

THE DMA IEEE/SPECTRUM MAGAZINE
3 Park Ave (fl 17)
New York, NY 10016-5902
Telephone: (212) 419-7768, FAX:
(212) 419-7589, E-Mail:
i.rodriguez@ieee.org, Web Site:
www.spectrum.ieee.org
Direct Mail Mktg Mgr: Ilia Rodriguez

Primary Market Served: Business &
Consumer
Member mailing list.

**THE DMA THE INFORMATION
REFINERY INC**
200 Rte 17 (Suite 5)
Mahwah, NJ 07430-1267
Telephone: (201) 529-2600, (800) 529-
9020, FAX: (201) 529-4030, E-Mail:
info@inforefinery.com, Web Site:
www.inforefinery.com
Pres: Gordon M. Clotworthy
EVP: Brian Clotworthy

THE DMA INSTITUTE LISTS/IOMA
1 Phoenix Mill Ln Fl 3
Peterborough, NH 03458-1467
Telephone: (973) 718-4766, FAX:
(973) 622-0595, E-Mail: lists@
institutelists.com, Web Site: www.
institutelists.com
Pres, Institute Lists: Debra Goldfarb
Primary Market Served: Business

**INVESTORPLACE MEDIA
LLC**
9201 Corporate Blvd
Rockville, MD 20850-3202
Telephone: (800) 219-8592, Web Site:
www.investorplace.com
Chmn: Thomas J. Phillips

JIGSAW
777 Mariners Island Blvd (Suite 400)
San Mateo, CA 94404
Telephone: (650) 235-8400, Web Site:
www.jigsaw.com
CEO & Co-Founder: Jim Fowler
VP Community & Co-Founder: Garth
Moulton
VP Mktg: Susan Chenoweth
VP Sls: Kevin Akeroyd
Dir Mktg: Shannon Duffy
Conducts Business: Worldwide
Employees: 100
Primary Market Served: Business
Founded: 2004

Jigsaw is an online directory of over 8
million complete business contacts,
designed for multi-channel (mail, email
& phone) B2B campaigns.

LH MANAGEMENT
Div. of Leon Henry Inc
200 N Central Ave
Hartsdale, NY 10530-1931
Telephone: (914) 285-3456, FAX:
(914) 285-3450, E-Mail: lh@
leonhenryinc.com, Web Site: www.
leonhenryinc.com
Pres: Thelma Henry
Exec VP: Lynn Henry
VP: Debra Goldstein

LAWYERS DIARY AND MANUAL

240 Mulberry St
Newark, NJ 07101-3528
Telephone: (208) 762-5403, (800) 444-4041, FAX: (973) 242-1905, E-Mail: mail@lawdiary.com, Web Site: www.lawdiary.com
List Mgr: Jill Rueckel
Conducts Business: U.S.
Primary Market Served: Business & Consumer
Advertising/Marketing Budget Related to Direct Marketing: 76-100%

Attorney mailing lists.

LIFESTYLE CHANGE COMMUNICATIONS

1000 Cobb Place Blvd (Suite 500B)
Kennesaw, GA 30144
Telephone: (770) 218-8200, (800) 411-5771, FAX: (770) 218-8211, E-Mail: experts@lifestylechange.com, Web Site: www.lifestylechange.com
List Mgr: Michelle Gatehouse

LIGHTHOUSE LIST CO

27 SE 24th Ave (Suite 6)
Pompano Beach, FL 33062-5346
Telephone: (954) 489-3008, (800) 684-2180, FAX: (954) 489-0850, E-Mail: mtlistdude@aol.com, Web Site: www.lighthouselist.com
VP: Mark Traverso

THE LIST AUTHORITY INC

192 Third Ave (#7)
Westwood, NJ 07675
Telephone: (201) 666-0100
Pres: Stephen Kallet

THE LIST BANK

Div. of Catalog Media Network Inc
500 Davis Ctr (Suite 812)
Evanston, IL 60201-4655
Telephone: (847) 864-0550, FAX: (847) 864-0575, E-Mail: catalogmed@aol.com, Web Site: www.thelistbank.com
Pres: E. Herbert Krug

LIST INC

69 Kenosia Ave (Suite 1)
Danbury, CT 06810-7318
Telephone: (914) 765-0700, FAX: (914) 765-0046, E-Mail: info@l-i-s-t.com, Web Site: www.l-i-s-t.com
Pres: Glenn Freedman
VP Client Svcs: Lisa Horder
VP Bus Devel: David Waldman
VP Sls: Steve Brinley
Conducts Business: U.S., Canada, Europe
Employees: 35

Founded: 1987
Mailing list consultations & list management firm specializing in high technology industries including computers, communications, publishing, seminars, software, hardware & all information technology & industrial related business-to-business markets. Company offers free directory, consultation & research on over 500 technology & business lists. Westchester Office: 84 Business Park Dr., Suite 202, Armonk, NY 10504 Telephone: (914) 765-0700, Fax: (914) 765-0046 Contact: Steve Brinley, VP.

LIST MANAGEMENT CENTER

The McGraw-Hill Companies
148 Princeton-Hightstown Rd
Hightstown, NJ 08520-1450
Telephone: (609) 426-5695, FAX: (609) 426-5096, E-Mail: renee_krug@mcgraw-hill.com, Web Site: www.mcgraw-hill.com
Dir: Maurice Persiani

MSC LISTS

450 Los Verdes Dr
Santa Barbara, CA 93111-1506
Telephone: (805) 967-4955, FAX: (805) 964-1702, E-Mail: kingstock@juno.com
Pres: Maureen Lance

MAPINFO, CANADA

26 Wellington St E (Suite 500)
Toronto, ON, Canada M5E 1S2
Telephone: (416) 594-5200, (800) 268-3282, FAX: (416) 594-5201, E-Mail: canada.sales@mapinfo.com, Web Site: www.mapinfo.com
VP Global Mktg: Reid Hislop

MARDEV

Div. of Reed Elsevier
360 Park Ave S (fl 12)
New York, NY 10010-1710
Telephone: (212) 584-9370, (800) 545-8517, FAX: (212) 584-9371, E-Mail: sales@mardev.com, Web Site: www.mardev.com
Sr VP Intl: Karie Burt

MARDEV-DM2

Div. of Reed Business Information
333 E Butterfield Rd (Suite 700)
Lombard, IL 60148-5619
Telephone: (800) 323-4958, FAX: (303) 265-5457, E-Mail: info@mardevdm2.com, Web Site: www.mardevdm2.com
VP & Gen Mgr: Steve Rourke

Mktg Program Specialist: Greg Talarico
Sls Dir: Jeff Adee
Dir Fin: Glen Svenningsen
Sls Dir: John Yedinak
Campaign Planner: Michelle McMillan
Conducts Business: U.S., Canada
Employees: 35
Catalog available online
Indirect online sales
Advertising/Marketing Budget Related to Direct Marketing: 0-25%
Direct Marketing ad budget:
Direct Mail: 17%
Magazines: 33%
Online: 33%
Telephone: 17%
Founded: 1946

DM2-DecisionMaker is direct marketing to decision makers, more than 35 million of them. Established as a list manager, DM2 now delivers industry-specific, targeted, highly responsive B-to-B direct marketing services, including database marketing, lead qualification, event marketing and market research that quickly and dramatically improve companies' sales and marketing effectiveness.

MEDIA MART

7600A Leesburg Pike
Falls Church, VA 22043-2000
Telephone: (703) 905-4532, FAX: (703) 905-8097, E-Mail: mgallogly@media-mart.com, Web Site: www.media-mart.com
List Sls Mgr: Meg Gallogly

THE DMA MEDICAL MARKETING SERVICE INC

185 Hansen Ct (Suite 110)
Wood Dale, IL 60191-1168
Telephone: (630) 477-1559, (800) 633-5478, FAX: (630) 350-1896, E-Mail: t-nugent@mmslists.com, Web Site: www.mmslists.com
Pres: Richard M. Elliott
VP Mktg: Terence J. Nugent

METAMORPHICS MEDIA

332 Bleecker St (Suite 212)
New York, NY 10014-2980
Telephone: (212) 924-1845, FAX: (212) 253-4053, E-Mail: info@metamorphics.com, Web Site: www.metamorphics.com
Sr Consult: Mark de Solla Price

CHARLES MOORE ASSOCIATES INC

PO Box 6
Southampton, PA 18966-0006

Telephone: (215) 355-6084, FAX: (215) 364-2212, E-Mail: cmadirectmail@yahoo.com, Web Site: www.cmadirectmail.com
CEO & Programmer: Charles Moore

NAM MAILING LISTS
PO Box 970
Santa Cruz, NM 87567
Telephone: (505) 753-5086, FAX: (505) 753-9249, E-Mail: nam@newmexico.com
Pres & Sls Mgr: P.S. Khalsa

NAME EXCHANGE
712 N East St
Frederick, MD 21701
Telephone: (301) 695-6140, FAX: (301) 695-5572, E-Mail: chris@nameexchange.us, Web Site: www.nameexchange.us
List Broker: Shawn Burns

NATIONAL ASSOCIATION OF HOME BUILDERS
1201 15th St NW
Washington, DC 20005-2800
Telephone: (202) 266-8200, (800) 368-5242, FAX: (202) 266-8400, Web Site: www.nahb.org
VP & CEO: Jerry Howard

THE DMA NEWSMAX MEDIA INC
PO Box 20989
West Palm Beach, FL 33416-0989
Telephone: (888) 766-7542, E-Mail: sales@newsmax.com, Web Site: www.newsmax.com/advertise
Pres: Christopher Ruddy
VP Mktg: Nancy Harrington
Primary Market Served: Consumer

OUTSOURCE AMERICA INC
715 60th St Court E
Bradenton, FL 34208-6262
Telephone: (800) 729-5694, FAX: (441) 746-3595, E-Mail: sales@oaiworld.com, Web Site: www.oaiworld.com
VP: Scott Stewart

PENNWELL LISTS
1421 S Sheridan Rd
Tulsa, OK 74112-6600
Telephone: (918) 835-3161, (800) 331-4463, FAX: (918) 831-9497, Web Site: www.pennwell.com
Exec VP: Jim Pfister

THE DMA PREFERRED COMMUNICATIONS
410 Central Ave
Butner, NC 27509-1916

Telephone: (919) 575-4600, (877) 589-9800, Web Site: www.satstar.com
Pres & CEO: Bob Meeker

THE DMA PRESTIGE MAILING LISTS INC
7746 Gloria Ave
Van Nuys, CA 91406-1610
Telephone: (818) 374-1320, FAX: (818) 374-1344, E-Mail: Debbie@prestigemaillists.com, Web Site: www.prestigemailinglists.com
Pres, Mngmt & Brokerage: Deborah Hile
Acct Mgr: Ron Stock

THE DMA PROFILE AMERICA LIST CO INC
455 Sylvan Ave
Englewood Cliffs, NJ 07632-2703
Telephone: (201) 569-7272, FAX: (201) 569-5552, E-Mail: annt@profileamerica.com, Web Site: www.profileamerica.com
Sr VP: Ann Tepper

PROMISSOR
Three Bala Plaza W (Suite 300)
Bala Cynwyd, PA 19004
Telephone: (610) 617-9300, FAX: (610) 617-9301, Web Site: www.promissor.com
President: Robert Whelan

THE DMA RAD MARKETING & CABLE TOWNS
167 Crary On-The-Park
Mount Vernon, NY 10550
Telephone: (914) 668-3563, FAX: (914) 668-4247, E-Mail: cabletowns@verizon.net
Pres: Robert Dadarria

THE RICH LIST CO
Div. of Leslie Mandel Enterprises Inc
PO Box 294
Wainscott, NY 11975-0294
Telephone: (212) 737-8917, FAX: (212) 861-5384, E-Mail: richlistco@aol.com, Web Site: www.richlist.com
Pres & CEO: Leslie Mandel

SALEM WEB NETWORK
111 Virginia St (Suite 500)
Richmond, VA 23219
Telephone: (804) 205-9700, FAX: (804) 205-9648, E-Mail: info@salemwebnetwork.com, Web Site: www.salemwebnetwork.com
Dir Adv: Jonathan Yang

ELEANOR L STARK
954 Lexington Ave (Suite 200)
New York, NY 10021-5055
Telephone: (212) 879-9510, FAX: (212) 879-6252, E-Mail: elstarkco@aol.com
Pres: Eleanor L. Stark

TCI DIRECT
PO Box 3936
Stateline, NV 89449-3936
Telephone: (818) 752-1800, FAX: (818) 752-1808
Pres: James E. Thulin

THE DMA TEIKOKU DATABANK AMERICA INC
780 3rd Ave (Rm 2200)
New York, NY 10017-2179
Telephone: (212) 421-9805, FAX: (212) 421-9806, E-Mail: info@teikoku.com, Web Site: www.teikoku.com
Pres & CEO: Tamotsu Inami
Exec VP: Hirofumi Hatanaka
Mktg: Keiko Oyamatsu

THOMAS BUSINESS LISTS
Div. of Thomas Publishing Co
Five Penn Plz
New York, NY 10001
Telephone: (212) 695-0500, FAX: (212) 290-7362, E-Mail: contact@thomaspublishing.com, Web Site: www.thomaspublishing.com
Dir: Laura Kuras

21ST CENTURY MARKETING
1200 Veterans Hwy (Suite 100)
Hauppauge, NY 11788-3052
Telephone: (631) 293-8550, FAX: (631) 293-8974, E-Mail: info@21stcm.com, Web Site: www.21stcm.com
Pres: David O. Schwartz
Exec VP: Janine Vosseler
Exec Asst: Rita Schultz
VP: Rick Blume
Sr VP: Theresa Horn

TWIN PEAKS PRESS
PO Box 8
Vancouver, WA 98666-0008
Telephone: (360) 694-2462, (800) 637-2256, FAX: (360) 696-3210, E-Mail: info@twinpeakspress.com, Web Site: www.twinpeakspress.com
Pres: Helen Hecker

WILLIAM-NEIL ASSOCIATES
One Cabela Dr (Suite 2114)
Sidney, NE 69160

Telephone: (800) 216-2214, FAX:
   (308) 254-6102, Web Site: www.
   william-neil.com
List Mgr: Beanie Obermier

**WORD DYNAMICS OF ST
   HELENA**
1998 Spring St
Saint Helena, CA 94574-2323
Telephone: (707) 963-8000, FAX:
   (707) 963-8000
Owner: Valerie S. Presten

THE DMA **WORLD INNOVATORS INC**
22 Bacon Rd
Roxbury, CT 06783-1817
Telephone: (860) 210-8088, FAX:
   (860) 210-7829, E-Mail: apeterson@
   worldinnovators.com, Web Site:
   www.worldinnovators.com
Pres: Anne M. Peterson

Paper Suppliers (25) — Geographic Index

Colorado

Bloomin Promotions, 3080 Valmont Rd, Boulder, 80301-2152

Idea Art Inc, PO Box 35750, Colorado Springs, 80935-3750

Connecticut

AT Clayton & Co Inc, 300 Atlantic St (fl 7), Stamford, 06901-3513

Horizon Paper Co Inc, 1010 Washington Blvd, Stamford, 06901-2202

Myllykoski North America, 101 Merritt 7, Norwalk, 06851-1059

Georgia

Georgia-Pacific Corp LLC, 133 Peachtree St NE, Atlanta, 30303

Unisource Worldwide, Inc, 6600 Governors Lake Pkwy, Norcross, 30071-1114

Websource & Paper Corp, 6600 Governors Lake Pkwy, Norcross, 30071-1114

Illinois

Amerikal Products, 2115 Northwestern Ave, Waukegan, 60087-4144

Midland Paper, 101 E Palatine Rd, Wheeling, 60090-9032

Saint Mary's Paper Corp, 312 S Hale St, Wheaton, 60187

United Stationers, 1 Pkwy N Blvd, Deerfield, 60015-2559

UPM North America, 999 Oakmont Plaza Dr (Suite 200), Westmont, 60559-5517

Wade Paper Corp, 1101 Lake Cook Rd Ste B, Deerfield, 60015-5233

xpedx Stores Division, 3351 W Addison St, Chicago, 60618-4303

Maine

Fraser Papers Inc, 82 Bridge Ave, Madawaska, 04756-1229

Massachusetts

Ecological Fibers Inc, 40 Pioneer Dr, Lunenburg, 01462-1699

Hampden Papers Inc, 100 Water St, Holyoke, 01040

Sappi Fine Paper North America, 225 Franklin St, Boston, 02110-2884

Michigan

Manistique Papers Inc, 453 S Mackinac Ave, Manistique, 49854

Millcraft of Michigan, 35255 Glendale St, Livonia, 48150-1254

Minnesota

American Solutions for Business, PO Box 218, Glenwood, 56334

New Hampshire

Monadnock Paper Mills Inc, 117 Antrim Rd, Bennington, 03442

New Jersey

Richard Bauer & Co Inc, 310 Cedar Ln Fl 2-1, Teaneck, 07666-3441

Central Lewmar, 261 River Rd, Clifton, 07014-1551

Roosevelt Paper Co, One Roosevelt Dr, Mount Laurel, 08054-6312

New York

AdPack/ITOCHU International Inc, 335 Madison Ave, New York, 10017-4611

Bulkley Dunton Publishing Group, 250 W 34th St (Suite 2814), New York, 10119-2814

Central National-Gottesman Inc, Three Manhattanville Rd (Suite 301B), Purchase, 10577-2123

Finch Paper, One Glen St, Glens Falls, 12801

Gould Paper Corp, 11 Madison Ave, New York, 10010

Mead Fine Paper Division, PO Box 400, Sidney, 13838-0400

Mohawk, 465 Saratoga St, Cohoes, 12047

Prestone Printing Co Inc, 47-50 30th St, Long Island City, 11101-3404

Ohio

Elmers Products Inc, 460 Polaris Pkwy Ste 500, Westerville, 43082-6091

Graphic Communications Holdings Inc, 5700 Darrow Rd (Suite 110), Hudson, 44236-5026

NewPage Corp, 8540 Gander Creek Dr, Miamisburg, 45342-5439

xpedx, 6285 Tri-Ridge Blvd, Loveland, 45140-8318

Pennsylvania

Glatfelter, 96 S George St (Suite 500), York, 17401

South Carolina

Bowater Inc, PO Box 1028, Greenville, 29602-1028

Domtar Inc, 100 Kingsley Park Dr, PO Box 5003, Fort Mill, 29715-6476

Tennessee

Verso Paper, 6775 Lenox Center Ct (Suite 400), Memphis, 38115-4436

Texas

Olmsted-Kirk Paper Co, 2420 Butler, Dallas, 75235-7816

Washington

Longview Fibre Co, PO Box 639, 300 Fibre Way, Longview, 98632-7411

Weyerhaeuser Co, 33663 Weyerhaeuser Co, PO Box 9777, Federal Way, 98063

Wisconsin

American Fine Paper Co, 5793 Grande Market Dr, Appleton, 54913-8470

Appleton Coated LLC, 540 Prospect St, Combined Locks, 54113-1120

Appleton Papers Inc, 825 E Wisconsin Ave, Appleton, 54911-3873

Mail Advertising Supply Co Inc, W222N5710 Miller Way, Box 363, Sussex, 53089-3988

Wausau Paper Mills Co, PO Box 305,
Brokaw, 54417-0305

ADPACK/ITOCHU INTERNATIONAL INC
335 Madison Ave
New York, NY 10017-4611
Telephone: (212) 818-8000, Web Site:
www.adpackusa.com
Pres: Steve Jacobs
Sr Accts Mgr: Corin Lines

AMERICAN FINE PAPER CO
5793 Grande Market Dr
Appleton, WI 54913-8470
Telephone: (920) 733-6100, (800) 458-5446, FAX: (920) 380-8711, E-Mail:
found@americanfinepaper.com, Web
Site: www.americanfinepaper.com
Pres: David Grayson

AMERICAN SOLUTIONS FOR BUSINESS
PO Box 218
Glenwood, MN 56334
Telephone: (320) 634-5471, FAX:
(320) 634-5265, Web Site: www.
americanbus.com
COO: Craig McLain

AMERIKAL PRODUCTS
2115 Northwestern Ave
Waukegan, IL 60087-4144
Telephone: (847) 244-3600, FAX:
(847) 244-2860, E-Mail: info@
amerikal.com, Web Site: www.
amerikal.com
Pres: R. Danielson

APPLETON COATED LLC
540 Prospect St
Combined Locks, WI 54113-1120
Telephone: (920) 968-3999, Web Site:
www.appletoncoated.com
VP Mktg: Phil Cavalier

APPLETON PAPERS INC
825 E Wisconsin Ave
Appleton, WI 54911-3873
Telephone: (920) 734-9841, FAX:
(920) 991-8796, Web Site: www.
appletonideas.com
Pres & CEO: Mark R. Richards

RICHARD BAUER & CO INC
310 Cedar Ln Fl 2-1
Teaneck, NJ 07666-3441
Telephone: (201) 692-1005, (800) 995-7881, FAX: (201) 692-8626, E-Mail:
info@richardbauer.com, Web Site:
www.richardbauer.com
CEO: Robert Cipolaro

BLOOMIN PROMOTIONS
3080 Valmont Rd
Boulder, CO 80301-2152
Telephone: (303) 443-3591, Web Site:
www.bloominpromotions.com
Pres: Don Martin

BOWATER INC
Subs. of Abitibi Bowater
PO Box 1028
Greenville, SC 29602-1028
Telephone: (864) 271-7733, (800) 921-3244, FAX: (864) 282-9563, E-Mail:
hrsc@abitibibowater.com, Web Site:
www.bowater.com
Pres & CEO: David J. Paterson

BULKLEY DUNTON PUBLISHING GROUP
Div. of International Paper
250 W 34th St (Suite 2814)
New York, NY 10119-2814
Telephone: (212) 863-1800, FAX:
(212) 863-1979, Web Site: www.
internationalpaper.com
Pres: George J. Doehner

CENTRAL LEWMAR
261 River Rd
Clifton, NJ 07014-1551
Telephone: (973) 622-6377, (800) 772-7301, FAX: (973) 623-4323, E-Mail:
dan.watkoske@expedx.com, Web
Site: www.centrallewmar.com
Pres & CEO: Leslie F. Stern

CENTRAL NATIONAL-GOTTESMAN INC
Three Manhattanville Rd (Suite 301B)
Purchase, NY 10577-2123
Telephone: (914) 696-9000, FAX:
(914) 696-1066, E-Mail: purchase@
cng-inc.com, Web Site: www.cng-inc.com
Pres & CEO: Kenneth L. Wallach

AT CLAYTON & CO INC
300 Atlantic St (fl 7)
Stamford, CT 06901-3513
Telephone: (203) 658-1200, E-Mail:
webmaster@atclayton.com, Web
Site: www.atclayton.com
Chmn Bd: W.F. Vallely Jr

DOMTAR INC
100 Kingsley Park Dr, PO Box 5003
Fort Mill, SC 29715-6476
Telephone: (803) 802-8283, FAX:
(810) 982-7124, Web Site: www.
domtar.com
Resident Mgr: A. Richard Wagner
Dir Publ Papers: Ann Reiser

ECOLOGICAL FIBERS INC
40 Pioneer Dr
Lunenburg, MA 01462-1699
Telephone: (978) 537-0003, FAX:
(978) 537-2238, E-Mail: jquill@
ecofibers.com
Pres: John Quill

ELMERS PRODUCTS INC
Subs. of Berwind Group
460 Polaris Pkwy Ste 500
Westerville, OH 43082-6091
Telephone: (614) 985-2600, (800) 848-9400, FAX: (614) 985-2605, E-Mail:
comments@elmers.com, Web Site:
www.elmers.com
Primary Market Served: Consumer

FINCH PAPER
dba Finch Paper Holdings, LLC
One Glen St
Glens Falls, NY 12801
Telephone: (518) 793-2541, (800) 833-9983, FAX: (518) 743-9656, E-Mail:
amcdowell@finchpaper.com, Web
Site: www.finchpaper.com
VP Sls & Mktg: Anthony T. McDowell

FRASER PAPERS INC
82 Bridge Ave
Madawaska, ME 04756-1229
Telephone: (203) 705-2800, FAX:
(203) 705-2801
VP, New Bus Devel & Intl Sls: Paul
Beaudoin

GEORGIA-PACIFIC CORP LLC
133 Peachtree St NE
Atlanta, GA 30303
Telephone: (404) 652-4000, Web Site:
www.gp.com
Media Dir: Gregory Guest

THE DMA GLATFELTER
96 S George St (Suite 500)
York, PA 17401
Telephone: (717) 225-4711, (866) 744-
7380, FAX: (717) 225-6834, E-Mail:
info@glatfelter.com, Web Site: www.
glatfelter.com
Chmn & CEO: George H. Glatfelter II

GOULD PAPER CORP
11 Madison Ave
New York, NY 10010
Telephone: (212) 301-0000, (800) 221-
3043, FAX: (212) 481-0067, Web
Site: www.gouldpaper.com
VP & CIO: Robert Bunsick
Employees: 464
Gross sales or billing: $1,150,000,000

**GRAPHIC
COMMUNICATIONS
HOLDINGS INC**
5700 Darrow Rd (Suite 110)
Hudson, OH 44236-5026
Telephone: (330) 650-5522, E-Mail:
info@graphiccommunications.com,
Web Site: www.
graphiccommunications.com
COO: Ken Russell
Sr VP: John Patneau

HAMPDEN PAPERS INC
100 Water St
Holyoke, MA 01040
Telephone: (413) 536-1000, FAX:
(413) 532-9161
VP, Sls & Mktg: Robert J. Fitzgerald
Employees: 150
Gross sales or billing: $30,000,000

HORIZON PAPER CO INC
1010 Washington Blvd
Stamford, CT 06901-2202
Telephone: (203) 358-0855, (866) 358-
0855, FAX: (203) 358-0828, Web
Site: www.horizonpaper.com
Chmn & CEO: Robert B. Obernier

IDEA ART INC
PO Box 35750
Colorado Springs, CO 80935-3750
Telephone: (615) 889-4989, (800) 433-
2278, FAX: (615) 889-6731, E-Mail:
customerservice@ideaart.com, Web
Site: www.ideaart.com
Chmn: Chris Chamberlain

LONGVIEW FIBRE CO
PO Box 639, 300 Fibre Way
Longview, WA 98632-7411
Telephone: (360) 425-1550, FAX:
(360) 230-5135, E-Mail: info@
longviewfibre.com, Web Site: www.
longfibre.com

Pres: Randy Nebel
CFO: Heidi Pozzo
VP Sls & Mktg: Lou Loosbrock

**MAIL ADVERTISING SUPPLY
CO INC**
Sub. of Lauterbach Group
W222N5710 Miller Way, Box 363
Sussex, WI 53089-3988
Telephone: (262) 549-1730, (800) 558-
2126, FAX: (800) 784-2591
Pres: Shane Lauterbach

MANISTIQUE PAPERS INC
Div. of Kruger Inc
453 S Mackinac Ave
Manistique, MI 49854
Telephone: (906) 341-2175, FAX:
(906) 341-5635
Pres: Leif Christensen

MEAD FINE PAPER DIVISION
Div. of The Mead Corp
PO Box 400
Sidney, NY 13838-0400
Telephone: (800) 936-9811, Web Site:
www.mead.com

MIDLAND PAPER
101 E Palatine Rd
Wheeling, IL 60090-9032
Telephone: (847) 777-2700, (800) 323-
8522, FAX: (847) 777-2552, E-Mail:
whl@midlandpaper.com, Web Site:
www.midlandpaper.com
Pres & CEO: Stan Hooker

MILLCRAFT OF MICHIGAN
35255 Glendale St
Livonia, MI 48150-1254
Telephone: (734) 266-3710, (800) 482-
0556, FAX: (734) 266-3705, Web
Site: www.millcraft.com
COO & VP: John Orlando

MOHAWK
aka Mohawk Fine Papers Inc
465 Saratoga St
Cohoes, NY 12047
Telephone: (518) 237-1740, (800) 843-
6455, FAX: (518) 237-7394, E-Mail:
info@mohawkpaper.com, Web Site:
www.mohawkconnects.com
Sr VP Mktg Communs: Laura Shore
CEO: Jr. Thomas D. O'Connor
Pres: Jack Haren
Dir Communs: Jane Monast

**MONADNOCK PAPER MILLS
INC**
117 Antrim Rd
Bennington, NH 03442

Telephone: (603) 588-3311, (800) 221-
2159, FAX: (603) 588-3158, Web
Site: www.monadnockpaper.com
Chm & CEO: Richard G. Verney

**MYLLYKOSKI NORTH
AMERICA**
101 Merritt 7
Norwalk, CT 06851-1059
Telephone: (203) 229-7400, Web Site:
www.myllykoski.com
Dir Mktg: William Crane

THE DMA NEWPAGE CORP
8540 Gander Creek Dr
Miamisburg, OH 45342-5439
Telephone: (937) 242-9068, (877) 855-
7243, FAX: (937) 242-9327, Web
Site: www.newpagecorp.com
VP Commun & Govt Affairs: Amber
Garwood
VP: Mark Lukacs

OLMSTED-KIRK PAPER CO
2420 Butler
Dallas, TX 75235-7816
Telephone: (214) 637-2220, (800) 367-
6526, FAX: (214) 637-7630, E-Mail:
sales@okpaper.com, Web Site: www.
okpaper.com
Pres: Charles Clark

**PRESTONE PRINTING CO
INC**
47-50 30th St
Long Island City, NY 11101-3404
Telephone: (347) 468-7900, FAX:
(347) 468-7885, Web Site: www.
prestoneprinting.com
Pres: Rob Alder

ROOSEVELT PAPER CO
One Roosevelt Dr
Mount Laurel, NJ 08054-6312
Telephone: (856) 303-4200, (856) 303-
4100, (800) 523-3470, FAX: (856)
642-1949, (856) 642-1950, Web Site:
www.rooseveltpaper.com
Chmn Bd: Ted Kosloff
Pres: David Kosloff
VP Sls Mktg: Eric Conine
Sls Mgr: Dean Egan

SAINT MARY'S PAPER CORP
312 S Hale St
Wheaton, IL 60187
Telephone: (630) 668-6279, FAX:
(630) 668-6292, Web Site: www.
stmarys-paper.com
Pres: Walter Vail
Sr VP: Rick Howe III

SAPPI FINE PAPER NORTH AMERICA
Subs. of Sappi Fine Paper
225 Franklin St
Boston, MA 02110-2884
Telephone: (617) 423-7300, FAX:
(617) 423-5494, Web Site: www.
sappi.com
Pres & CEO: Mark Gardner
Dir Creative Svcs: Molly Foshay

UPM NORTH AMERICA
Div. of UPM-Kymmene Inc.
999 Oakmont Plaza Dr (Suite 200)
Westmont, IL 60559-5517
Telephone: (630) 850-3310, (866) 300-
4175, FAX: (630) 850-3510, Web
Site: www.upm-kymmene.com
Pres: Kevin Lyden
Mgr Mktg & Bus Devel: Scott Hall

UNISOURCE WORLDWIDE, INC
Subs. of Georgia Pacific
6600 Governors Lake Pkwy
Norcross, GA 30071-1114
Telephone: (770) 447-9000, (800) 864-
7687, FAX: (770) 729-0385, Web
Site: www.unisourcelink.com
Sr VP Mktg: Ed Farley
Dir, Corp Commun: Kevin Feeney

UNITED STATIONERS
1 Pkwy N Blvd
Deerfield, IL 60015-2559
Telephone: (847) 627-7000, Web Site:
www.unitedstationers.com
VP Content Mngmt & Publ: Laura
Gale

VERSO PAPER
6775 Lenox Center Ct (Suite 400)
Memphis, TN 38115-4436
Telephone: (901) 369-4241, Web Site:
www.versopaper.com
Dir Mktg: Steve Gentner

WADE PAPER CORP
1101 Lake Cook Rd Ste B
Deerfield, IL 60015-5233
Telephone: (847) 940-9777, (800) 828-
8318, FAX: (847) 940-1077, E-Mail:
info@wadepaper.com, Web Site:
www.wadepaper.com
Pres: Kevin P. Wade

WAUSAU PAPER MILLS CO
PO Box 305
Brokaw, WI 54417-0305
Telephone: (715) 675-3361, FAX:
(715) 675-5181, Web Site: www.
wausaupaper.com
Pres & CEO: Tom Howatt

WEBSOURCE & PAPER CORP
Subs. of Unisource Worldwide Inc a
Georgia Pacific Co
6600 Governors Lake Pkwy
Norcross, GA 30071-1114
Telephone: (212) 255-1600, FAX:
(212) 463-7095, Web Site: www.
websource-paper.com
Pres: James O'Toole
Pres Asst: Julie Wintz

WEYERHAEUSER CO
33663 Weyerhaeuser Co, PO Box 9777
Federal Way, WA 98063
Telephone: (253) 924-2345, (800) 525-
5440, FAX: (253) 924-2685, Web
Site: www.wy.com
VP iLevel Mktg & Tech: Brian Greber

XPEDX
Div. of Mead Paper Co
6285 Tri-Ridge Blvd
Loveland, OH 45140-8318
Telephone: (513) 965-2900, FAX:
(513) 965-2849, Web Site: www.
xpedx.com
Pres: Mary Laschinger

XPEDX STORES DIVISION
3351 W Addison St
Chicago, IL 60618-4303
Telephone: (773) 442-6200, (800) 600-
0064, FAX: (630) 628-6310, Web
Site: www.epedxstores.com
VP Mktg & Mdsg: Mike Cape

California

Golden State Envelopes, PO Box 3367, Thousand Oaks, 91359-0367

Connecticut

GBE Plus, PO Box 750, 10 Midland St, Hartford, 06142-0750

Florida

Double Envelope, 2500 NE 39th Ave, Gainesville, 32609-2098

Illinois

Colfax Envelope Corp, 20 Carlyle Ln, Buffalo Grove, 60089-6696

Continental Envelope Corp, 1700 Averill Rd, Geneva, 60134-1668

Diamond Envelope Corp, 2270 White Oak Cir, Aurora, 60504

Federal Envelope Co, 608 Country Club Dr, Bensenville, 60106-1303

Forest Envelope Co, 1958 University Ln, Lisle, 60532

Gaw-O'Hara Envelope Co, PO Box 325, Western Springs, 60558-0325

Office Express Inc, 1320 Sherman Ave (Suite 104), Evanston, 60201

Pactiv Corp, 1900 West Field Ct, Lake Forest, 60045

Royal Envelope Corp, 4114 S Peoria St, Chicago, 60609

Victor Envelope Co, 301 Arthur Ct, Bensenville, 60106-3381

Indiana

Bowers Envelope Co, 5331 N Tacoma Ave, Indianapolis, 46220-3613

Kansas

National Envelope-Midwest, 11068 Strang Line Rd, PO Box 15064, Lenexa, 66215-2113

Maryland

Oles Envelope Corp, 532 E 25th St, Baltimore, 21218-5403

Massachusetts

Ames Specialty Packaging & Digital Print, 12 Tyler St, Somerville, 02143-3241

Envelope Products Group, 2001 Roosevelt Ave, PO Box 3300, Springfield, 01102-3300

Mac Pac Inc, 90 Corporate Park Dr (Unit 1440), Pembroke, 02359-4935

MeadWestvaco, 2001 Roosevelt Ave, Springfield, 01104-1657

Sheppard Envelope Co, 133 Southbridge St, PO Box 358, Auburn, 01501

Super Coups, 350 Revolutionary Dr, East Taunton, 02718

Worcester Envelope, 22 Millburn St, Auburn, 01501

Michigan

Husky Envelope Products, 1225 E W Maple Rd, PO Box 868, Walled Lake, 48390-0868

Wolf Envelope Co, 1280 Redding Rd, Birmingham, 48009-1024

Minnesota

MackayMitchell Envelope Co, 2100 Elm St SE, Minneapolis, 55414-2533

Quality Park Products, 1200 Washington Ave S (Suite 217), Minneapolis, 55415-1111

Missouri

American Mail-Well Envelope Co/St Louis Div, 101 Workman Ct, Eureka, 63025

The Envelope Man Plus, 5235 Cherry St, Kansas City, 64110-2427

Tension Envelope Corp, 819 E 19th St, Kansas City, 64108-1781

Nebraska

Burkley Envelope Co, 1600 N Chestnut, Wahoo, 68066

New Jersey

Liberty Envelope Inc, 45 E Fifth St, Paterson, 07524-1101

Mail-Well Envelope, 25 Linden Ave E, Jersey City, 07305-4726

Sealed Air Corp, 200 Riverfront Blvd Ste 301, Elmwood Park, 07407-1038

New York

Commercial Envelope Manufacturing Co Inc, 350 Wireless Blvd Ste 102, Hauppauge, 11788-3947

Conformer Expansion Products Inc, 60 Cuttermill Rd (Suite 407), Great Neck, 11021-3104

Craig Envelope Corp, 1201 44th Ave, Long Island City, 11101-6917

Dupli Envelope & Graphics Corp, One Dupli Park Dr, Syracuse, 13218-1436

Innovative Packaging of Westchester, Two Barrie Dr, Spring Valley, 10977-1617

Mercury Envelope Co Inc, 100 Merrick Rd (Suite 204E), Rockville Centre, 11570-4801

Poly-Flex Corp, 250 Executive Dr Ste S, Edgewood, 11717-8354

United Envelope, 4511 33rd St, Long Island City, 11101-2405

Ohio

American Church Inc, PO Box 3120, Youngstown, 44513-3120

Ohio Envelope Manufacturing Co, 5161 W 164th St, Cleveland, 44142

Specialty Envelope Inc, 4890 Spring Grove Ave, Cincinnati, 45232

Pennsylvania

National Envelope Advertising Co Inc, 982 Dale Rd, Meadowbrook, 19046

North American Communications Inc (East), 141 NAC Dr, Duncansville, 16635-9428

Tri-State Envelope Corp, 20th & Market St, Ashland, 17921-1622

Rhode Island

Admiral Packaging Inc, Ten Admiral St, Providence, 02908

Texas

International Filing Corp, 2505 Ridge Rd # 201, Rockwall, 75087-5510

Love Envelopes Inc, 1130 Quaker St, Dallas, 75205

National Envelope Corp, 601 National Dr, Ennis, 75119-7823

Virginia

ColorTree of Virginia Inc, 8000 Villa Park Dr, Richmond, 23228-6500

Washington

Cenveo Commercial Envelope Group, 6520 S 190th St (Suite 100), Kent, 98032

PAC Worldwide, 15435 NE 92nd St, Redmond, 98052-3516

Wisconsin

Wisconsin Converting Inc, 1689 Morrow St, Green Bay, 54302

CANADA
Ontario

Supremex Inc, 400 Humberline Dr, Etobicoke, M9W 5T3

Quebec

Montreal Envelope Inc, 7355 Notre-Dame est, Montreal, H1N 3S7

Supremex Inc, 7213 Cordner, La Salle, H8N 2J7

Envelope Manufacturers & Suppliers (26)

ADMIRAL PACKAGING INC
Ten Admiral St
Providence, RI 02908
Telephone: (800) 262-0027, FAX:
(401) 331-1910, Web Site: www.
admiralpkg.com
Pres: Harley Frank

AMERICAN CHURCH INC
PO Box 3120
Youngstown, OH 44513-3120
Telephone: (330) 758-4545, (800) 250-
7112, FAX: (800) 763-8772, E-Mail:
sales@americanchurch.com, Web
Site: www.americanchurch.com
Pres: Kyle Hamilton

**AMERICAN MAIL-WELL
ENVELOPE CO/ST LOUIS
DIV**
Div. of Cenveo
101 Workman Ct
Eureka, MO 63025
Telephone: (314) 966-2000, (800) 800-
8845, FAX: (314) 966-4725, E-Mail:
info@cenveo.com, Web Site: www.
mail-well.com
Mgr: Frank Bow

**AMES SPECIALTY
PACKAGING & DIGITAL
PRINT**
12 Tyler St
Somerville, MA 02143-3241
Telephone: (617) 776-3360, (800) 521-
2637, FAX: (617) 623-8895, E-Mail:
info@amespage.com, Web Site:
www.amespage.com
VP Sales & Mktg: Richard Erwin
Employees: 450
Founded: 1929
Gross sales or billing: $53,480,000

BOWERS ENVELOPE CO
5331 N Tacoma Ave
Indianapolis, IN 46220-3613
Telephone: (317) 253-4321, FAX:
(317) 254-2231, Web Site: www.
bowersenvelope.com
Pres: Tom Marshall

BURKLEY ENVELOPE CO
1600 N Chestnut
Wahoo, NE 68066
Telephone: (402) 443-3010, FAX:
(402) 443-4029, E-Mail: info@
burkley.com, Web Site: www.
burkley.com

Pres: Robert W. Burkley

**CENVEO COMMERCIAL
ENVELOPE GROUP**
6520 S 190th St (Suite 100)
Kent, WA 98032
Telephone: (206) 576-4300, (800) 347-
6989, FAX: (206) 574-8013, E-Mail:
info@cenveo.com, Web Site: www.
cenveo.com
VP Sls: Joe Ritchie

COLFAX ENVELOPE CORP
20 Carlyle Ln
Buffalo Grove, IL 60089-6696
Telephone: (847) 215-1122, FAX:
(847) 215-1145, Web Site: www.
colfaxenv.com
Pres: Charles R. Patten

**COLORTREE OF VIRGINIA
INC**
8000 Villa Park Dr
Richmond, VA 23228-6500
Web Site: www.colortree.com
Dir Mktg: Ed Glaser

**COMMERCIAL ENVELOPE
MANUFACTURING CO INC**
350 Wireless Blvd Ste 102
Hauppauge, NY 11788-3947
Telephone: (631) 242-2500, FAX:
(631) 242-6122, Web Site: www.
commercial-envelope.com
Sls Mgr: John N. Knoesel

**CONFORMER EXPANSION
PRODUCTS INC**
60 Cuttermill Rd (Suite 407)
Great Neck, NY 11021-3104
Telephone: (516) 504-6300, E-Mail:
support@conformerinc.com, Web
Site: www.conformerinc.com
Pres: Marvin Makofsky
VP Bus Devel: Sari McConnell
VP & Gen Mgr: Bob Makofsky
Conducts Business: U.S., Canada
Primary Market Served: Business
Advertising/Marketing Budget Related
to Direct Marketing: 0-25%
Founded: 1972

Created a full line of packaging designed specifically to save money on
postage.

**CONTINENTAL ENVELOPE
CORP**
1700 Averill Rd
Geneva, IL 60134-1668
Telephone: (630) 262-8080, (800) 621-
8155, FAX: (630) 262-1450, Web
Site: www.continentalenvelope.com
Pres: Jacob Margulies

CRAIG ENVELOPE CORP
1201 44th Ave
Long Island City, NY 11101-6917
Telephone: (718) 392-9304, (888) 272-
4436, FAX: (718) 937-8178, E-Mail:
info@craigenvelope.com, Web Site:
www.craigenvelope.com
Pres: Lawrence Aaronson

DIAMOND ENVELOPE CORP
2270 White Oak Cir
Aurora, IL 60504
Telephone: (630) 499-2800, FAX:
(630) 499-2801
Pres: Alan Jania

DOUBLE ENVELOPE
Div. of BSC Ventures
2500 NE 39th Ave
Gainesville, FL 32609-2098
Telephone: (800) 543-5275, Web Site:
www.double-envelope.com
CEO: Brian Sass

**DUPLI ENVELOPE &
GRAPHICS CORP**
One Dupli Park Dr
Syracuse, NY 13218-1436
Telephone: (315) 472-1316, (800) 724-
2477, FAX: (315) 422-3637, Web
Site: www.duplionline.com
Pres: J. Kemper Matt Sr.

THE ENVELOPE MAN PLUS
5235 Cherry St
Kansas City, MO 64110-2427
Telephone: (816) 474-5555, (800) 597-
1099, FAX: (816) 221-3700, E-Mail:
sales@envelopeman.com, Web Site:
www.envelopeman.com
Pres: Paul C. Guignon III

**ENVELOPE PRODUCTS
GROUP**
Div. of Meadwestvaco Corp
2001 Roosevelt Ave, PO Box 3300
Springfield, MA 01102-3300

Telephone: (413) 736-7211, (888) 715-6641, (800) 628-9265, FAX: (413) 787-9749, E-Mail: envelopes@meadwestvaco.com, Web Site: www.meadwestvaco.com/envelopeprod.nsf
Div Mgr: John C. Taylor

THE DMA FEDERAL ENVELOPE CO
608 Country Club Dr
Bensenville, IL 60106-1303
Telephone: (630) 595-2000, FAX: (630) 595-1212, E-Mail: postmaster@federalenvelope.com, Web Site: www.federalenvelope.com
Pres: Michael Shaw
VP: Lee Shaw

FOREST ENVELOPE CO
1958 University Ln
Lisle, IL 60532
Telephone: (630) 515-1200
VP: Jack Wagner

GBE PLUS
Div. of Massachusetts Envelope Co
PO Box 750, 10 Midland St
Hartford, CT 06142-0750
Telephone: (860) 727-9100, (800) 842-0139, FAX: (860) 527-6041, Web Site: www.gbeplus.com
Pres: Linda Martyn

GAW-O'HARA ENVELOPE CO
PO Box 325
Western Springs, IL 60558-0325
Telephone: (773) 638-1200, (888) 385-8439, FAX: (773) 638-1208, E-Mail: info@gawohara.com, Web Site: www.gawohara.com
Pres: Brian Dietrich

GOLDEN STATE ENVELOPES
PO Box 3367
Thousand Oaks, CA 91359-0367
Telephone: (818) 865-7940, (800) 252-7600, FAX: (818) 865-0012, E-Mail: answers@golden-state-env.com, Web Site: www.golden-state-env.com
Gen Mgr: Mark W. Goggin

HUSKY ENVELOPE PRODUCTS
1225 E W Maple Rd, PO Box 868
Walled Lake, MI 48390-0868
Telephone: (248) 624-7070, FAX: (248) 624-5990, E-Mail: bmuehl@huskyenvelope.com, Web Site: www.huskyenvelope.com
Mktg Mgr: Bob Muehl

INNOVATIVE PACKAGING OF WESTCHESTER
Two Barrie Dr
Spring Valley, NY 10977-1617
Telephone: (845) 364-9500
Pres: Bruce Hollander

INTERNATIONAL FILING CORP
Subs. of Cenveo Inc
2505 Ridge Rd # 201
Rockwall, TX 75087-5510
Telephone: (800) 647-3070, FAX: (800) 633-7053, E-Mail: pcoerper@intfiling.com, Web Site: www.intfiling.com
Pres & CEO: Phil Coerper

LIBERTY ENVELOPE INC
45 E Fifth St
Paterson, NJ 07524-1101
Telephone: (973) 546-5600, FAX: (973) 546-4721
Pres: Ligia Guarderas

LOVE ENVELOPES INC
1130 Quaker St
Dallas, TX 75205
Telephone: (214) 637-5900, (800) 569-5683, FAX: (214) 951-0469, E-Mail: sales.dallas@loveenvelopes.com, Web Site: www.loveenvelopes.com
Pres: Mike Love

MAC PAC INC
90 Corporate Park Dr (Unit 1440)
Pembroke, MA 02359-4935
Telephone: (781) 826-6900, FAX: (781) 826-6880, E-Mail: jsargeant@macpacinc.com, Web Site: www.macpacinc.com
Pres: Richard MacDowell
Mktg Dir: Julie Sargeant
Conducts Business: U.S., Canada
Catalog available online
Indirect online sales
Advertising/Marketing Budget Related to Direct Marketing: 0-25%
Founded: 1999

Decorative mailers envelopes ("Deco Bags") and Decorative Bobble mailers ("Mac Pac Deco Bubble Bags").

THE DMA MACKAYMITCHELL ENVELOPE CO
2100 Elm St SE
Minneapolis, MN 55414-2533
Telephone: (800) 622-5299, Web Site: www.mackayenvelope.com
Exec VP: Daryl Walsh

MAIL-WELL ENVELOPE
25 Linden Ave E
Jersey City, NJ 07305-4726
Telephone: (201) 434-2100, (800) 526-3020, E-Mail: info@cenveo.com, Web Site: www.mail-well.com
Branch Mgr: George Napiorkowski

MEADWESTVACO
2001 Roosevelt Ave
Springfield, MA 01104-1657
Telephone: (888) 715-6641, Web Site: www.mwvenvelopes.com
Dir Sls: Bryan Jamgochian

MERCURY ENVELOPE CO INC
100 Merrick Rd (Suite 204E)
Rockville Centre, NY 11570-4801
Telephone: (516) 678-6744, FAX: (516) 678-6764, E-Mail: mercuryenvelope@aol.com
Pres: Stanley Deutsch

MONTREAL ENVELOPE INC
aka Enveloppe Montreal Inc
7355 Notre-Dame est
Montreal, PQ, Canada H1N 3S7
Telephone: (514) 331-7110, (800) 655-2709, FAX: (514) 748-7322, E-Mail: ybrochu@enveloppe-montreal.com, Web Site: www.enveloppe-montreal.com
Sls Mgr: Yvan Brochu

NATIONAL ENVELOPE ADVERTISING CO INC
982 Dale Rd
Meadowbrook, PA 19046
Telephone: (215) 887-8496, FAX: (215) 887-2652
Pres: Steven H. Beck

THE DMA NATIONAL ENVELOPE CORP
601 National Dr
Ennis, TX 75119-7823
Telephone: (800) 696-0409, Web Site: www.nationalenvelope.com
Exec VP & Mktg: Bernard Mathieu
VP: Dave Erwin

NATIONAL ENVELOPE-MIDWEST
11068 Strang Line Rd, PO Box 15064
Lenexa, KS 66215-2113
Telephone: (913) 888-3282, FAX: (913) 888-8743, E-Mail: sales@natenv.com, Web Site: www.nationalenvelope.com
VP: Jim Brown

**NORTH AMERICAN
COMMUNICATIONS INC
(EAST)**
141 NAC Dr
Duncansville, PA 16635-9428
Telephone: (814) 696-3553, (800) 624-
1533, FAX: (814) 696-1180, E-Mail:
info@nacmail.com, Web Site: www.
nacmail.com
Pres: Robert Herman

OFFICE EXPRESS INC
aka envelopesexpress.com
1320 Sherman Ave (Suite 104)
Evanston, IL 60201
Telephone: (888) 526-8438, FAX:
(773) 341-7322, E-Mail: sales@
envelopesexpress.com, Web Site:
www.envelopesexpress.com
Pres: Bill Raspe

**OHIO ENVELOPE
MANUFACTURING CO**
5161 W 164th St
Cleveland, OH 44142
Telephone: (216) 267-2920, (800) 989-
0336, FAX: (216) 267-1765, E-Mail:
mgmt@ohioenvelope.com, Web Site:
www.ohioenvelope.com
Pres: Rick Gould
Founded: 1936

OLES ENVELOPE CORP
532 E 25th St
Baltimore, MD 21218-5403
Telephone: (410) 243-1520, (800) 822-
6537, FAX: (410) 366-7022, Web
Site: www.olesenvelope.com
Chmn Bd: John R. Young

PAC WORLDWIDE
Subs. of PAC Worldwide
15435 NE 92nd St
Redmond, WA 98052-3516
Telephone: (425) 885-9330, (800) 535-
0039, FAX: (425) 885-2934, Web
Site: www.pac.com
Sr VP, Sls & Mktg: Tim B. Magee

PACTIV CORP
1900 West Field Ct
Lake Forest, IL 60045
Telephone: (847) 482-2000, (800) 828-
2850, FAX: (847) 482-4738, Web
Site: www.pactiv.com
Chmn Bd & CEO: Richard L.
Wambold

POLY-FLEX CORP
250 Executive Dr Ste S
Edgewood, NY 11717-8354

Telephone: (631) 586-9500, FAX:
(631) 586-6631, E-Mail: info@poly-
flexcorp.com, Web Site: www.poly-
flexcorp.com
Pres: Barry Neustein

QUALITY PARK PRODUCTS
1200 Washington Ave S (Suite 217)
Minneapolis, MN 55415-1111
Telephone: (651) 645-0251, (800) 547-
4252, (800) 328-2990, FAX: (800)
637-5770, (800) 701-3291, E-Mail:
mktg@qualitypark.com, Web Site:
www.qualitypark.com
Pres: Allen Conway

ROYAL ENVELOPE CORP
4114 S Peoria St
Chicago, IL 60609
Telephone: (773) 376-1212, (800) 279-
0142, FAX: (773) 376-0011, E-Mail:
mattp@royalenv.com, Web Site:
www.royalenv.com
Pres: Anthony Pusatera
Gen Mgr: Matt Pusatera

SEALED AIR CORP
200 Riverfront Blvd Ste 301
Elmwood Park, NJ 07407-1038
Telephone: (201) 791-7600, FAX:
(201) 712-7070, Web Site: www.
sealedair.com
VP Mktg: Hugh L. Sargant

SHEPPARD ENVELOPE CO
133 Southbridge St, PO Box 358
Auburn, MA 01501
Telephone: (508) 791-5588, (800) 325-
6622, FAX: (508) 754-3108, E-Mail:
sales@sheppardenvelope.com, Web
Site: www.sheppardenvelope.com
CEO: J. Lincoln Spaulding

SPECIALTY ENVELOPE INC
4890 Spring Grove Ave
Cincinnati, OH 45232
Telephone: (513) 542-4700, (800) 288-
8884, FAX: (513) 542-5260, E-Mail:
info@specialtyenvelope.com, Web
Site: www.specialtyenevelope.com
Pres: Sam Peters

SUPER COUPS
Subs. of ADVO Inc
350 Revolutionary Dr
East Taunton, MA 02718
Telephone: (508) 977-2000, (800) 626-
2620, FAX: (508) 977-0644, Web
Site: www.supercoups.com
VP, Mktg: Bill Matthews

SUPREMEX INC
7213 Cordner
La Salle, PQ, Canada H8N 2J7

Telephone: (514) 595-0555, Web Site:
www.supremex.com
Gen Mgr US Bus Devel: Lorne Hill

SUPREMEX INC
400 Humberline Dr
Etobicoke, ON, Canada M9W 5T3
Telephone: (416) 675-9370, (800) 465-
7603, FAX: (416) 675-1952, (416)
848-8388, E-Mail: sales.central@
supremex.com, Web Site: www.
supremex.com
Sales Mgr: Murray J. Rundle

TENSION ENVELOPE CORP
819 E 19th St
Kansas City, MO 64108-1781
Telephone: (816) 471-3800, FAX:
(816) 283-1498, Web Site: www.
tension.com
Pres & CEO: William Berkley
Dir Adv: Dan Imler

THE
DMA **TRI-STATE ENVELOPE CORP**
20th & Market St
Ashland, PA 17921-1622
Telephone: (570) 875-0433, (800) 233-
3102, FAX: (570) 875-0125, E-Mail:
tsecny@attglobal.net, Web Site:
www.tristateenvelope.com
CEO: Joel Orgler
Pres: John C Swenson
VP: Frank DeCarlo
Conducts Business: U.S.
Employees: 500
Primary Market Served: Business &
Consumer
Advertising/Marketing Budget Related
to Direct Marketing: 76-100%
Founded: 1966

Envelope manufacturer producing
25,000,000 envelopes daily.

UNITED ENVELOPE
4511 33rd St
Long Island City, NY 11101-2405
Telephone: (718) 707-0700, FAX:
(718) 729-8671, E-Mail: marketing@
unitedenvelope.com, Web Site: www.
unitedenvelope.com
Pres: Steven Bunker
Dir Sls & Mktg: John Sorrentino

THE
DMA **VICTOR ENVELOPE CO**
301 Arthur Ct
Bensenville, IL 60106-3381
Telephone: (630) 616-2750, Web Site:
www.victorenvelope.com
Pres: Kent Dahlgren

**WISCONSIN CONVERTING
INC**
1689 Morrow St
Green Bay, WI 54302

Telephone: (920) 437-6400, (800) 544-
1935, FAX: (920) 436-4964, E-Mail:
wci@wisconsinconverting.com, Web
Site: www.wisconsinconverting.com
Pres: Rich Bierman
Employees: 50
Founded: 1987

Converters of ECO-SHIPPER(R) liner-
board utility mailers, DURA-BAG(R)
laminated, reinforced mailers; both
available in flat or gusseted, with or
without Peel & Seal Closure(TM).
Multi-color graphics. Sales to direct
marketers, catalog & fulfillment operations through national distribution.

WOLF ENVELOPE CO

1280 Redding Rd
Birmingham, MI 48009-1024
Telephone: (248) 687-2745, (800) 466-
WOLF, FAX: (248) 687-2751, Web
Site: www.wolfenvelope.com
Pres: Hugh F. Mahler

THE DMA WORCESTER ENVELOPE

22 Millburn St
Auburn, MA 01501
Telephone: (800) 343-1398, FAX:
(508) 832-3796, Web Site: www.
worcester-envelope.com
Sls & Mktg Mgr: Jim Dufresne

Printing & Related Services (27) — Geographic Index

Alabama

RayPress Corp, 380 Riverchase Pkwy E, Birmingham, 35244-1813

Arizona

White Electronic Designs, 3601 E University Dr, Phoenix, 85034-7217

Arkansas

Mays Mission for the Handicapped Inc, 604 Colonial Dr, Heber Springs, 72543-3425

California

Apperson Print Management Services, 13910 Cerritos Corporate Dr, Cerritos, 90703-2457

California Offset Printers, 620 W Elk Ave, Glendale, 91204

Creel Printing of California, 151 Kalmus Dr Ste H11, Costa Mesa, 92626-5971

Crush Creative, 1919 Empire Ave, Burbank, 91504-3404

The Dico Group Inc, PO Box 2067, Toluca Lake, 91610-0067

Dome Printing, 340 Commerce Cir, Sacramento, 95815-4213

Foremost Packaging, 9120 Center Ave, Rancho Cucamonga, 91730-5130

Franchise Services Inc, 26772 Plaza, Mission Viejo, 92691

MailBlazer, 2020 S Eastwood Ave, Santa Ana, 92705-5208

The Monaco Group, 1011 S Linwood Ave, Santa Ana, 92705-4323

Multi-Media Publishing & Packaging Inc, 14621 Titus St Ste A, Panorama City, 91402-4904

O'Neil Data Systems Inc, 12655 Beatrice St, Los Angeles, 90066-7300

Penn Industries Inc, PO Box 3067, Cerritos, 90703-3067

Precise Media Services Inc, 5678 E Concours Ave, Ontario, 91764

Rapidforms Inc, PO Box 1186, Lancaster, 93584-1186

Shutterfly, 2800 Bridge Pkwy, Redwood City, 94065-1192

Sumi Printing, 1139 E Janis St, Carson, 90746-1306

TFC Inc, 690 Airpark Rd, Napa, 94558-7516

USDiscs, 2387 Buena Vista St, Duarte, 91010-3301

V3, 200 N Elevar St, Oxnard, 93030-7969

Colorado

CPI Card Group, 10368 W Centennial Rd Ste A, Littleton, 80127-4296

Connecticut

Allied Printing Services Inc, 1 Allied Way, PO Box 850, Manchester, 06040-2728

Cenveo Inc, 1 Canterbury Green, Stamford, 06901-2032

Danbury Printing & Litho Inc, 1 Prindle Ln, Danbury, 06811-5115

National Graphics Inc, 248 Branford Rd (Suite One), North Branford, 06471-1303

Quebecor-World Infiniti, 96 Phoenix Ave, Enfield, 06082

Quebecor World North America, 291 State St, North Haven, 06473

Structural Graphics, 38 Plains Rd, Essex, 06426-1520

Delaware

Dupont Color Proofing, PO Box 80030, Wilmington, 19880-0030

Foxfire Printing & Packaging Inc, 750 Dawson Dr, Newark, 19713-3414

District of Columbia

Meriks Mayan Chocolaterie, 142 36 St NE, Washington, 20019-2601

Florida

Action Communications Inc, 500 NE Spanish River Blvd Ste 26, Boca Raton, 33431-4517

Angstrom Graphics, 2025 McKinley St, Hollywood, 33020

BBF Integrated Solutions, 10950 Belcher Rd S, Largo, 33777-1438

Continental Plastic Card Co, 1801 Green Rd Ste B, Pompano Beach, 33064-1052

Dynacolor Graphics Inc, 950 SE 8th St, Hialeah, 33010

Foilmania, 9730 NW 25th St, Miami, 33172-2201

Hi-Tech Marketing Solutions, 3410 NE 6th Ter, Pompano Beach, 33064

The Inkpen, 811 SW 113th Ave, Pembroke Pines, 33025-3419

Interprint Web & Sheetfed, 12350 US Hwy 19 N, Clearwater, 33764

Media Printing Corp, 4300 N Powerline Rd, Pompano Beach, 33073-3071

Modern Graphic Arts, 1527 102nd Ave N, Saint Petersburg, 33716-5049

Naylor Inc, 5950 NW 1st Pl, Gainesville, 32607-6018

Peninsular Printing of Daytona Beach Inc, 3 Timberline Trl (#A), Ormond Beach, 32174-4923

Printing Corp of the Americas Inc (PCA), 620 SW 12th Ave, Pompano Beach, 33069-4526

Rex Three Inc, 15431 SW 14th St, Sunrise, 33326

Rose Printing Co Inc, 2503 Jackson Bluff Rd, Tallahassee, 32304-4405

Solo Printing, 7860 NW 66th St, Miami, 33166-2708

Think Shapes Mail, 5463 W Waters Ave (Suite 820), Tampa, 33634

Web Graphics, 7731 Cottesmore Dr, Naples, 34113-3180

Georgia

Atlanta Offset, 120 James Aldredge Blvd SW, Atlanta, 30336-2102

Beacon Printing & Graphics Inc, 1628A James P Rodgers Dr, Valdosta, 31601

Curtis 1000 Inc, 1725 Breckinridge Pkwy (Suite 500), Duluth, 30096-8994

IPD Printing & Distributing Inc, 5800 Peachtree Rd, Atlanta, 30341-2302

Printed Communications Inc, 1929 Mountain Industrial Blvd, Tucker, 30084

Sauers Group, Inc, 1585 Roadhaven Dr, Stone Mountain, 30083-1315

Williams Printing Co/an RR Donnelley Co, 1240 Spring St NW, Atlanta, 30309-2808

Wise, 555 McFarland 400 Dr, Alpharetta, 30004-3375

Worldcolor, 3101 McCall Dr, Atlanta, 30340-2807

Hawaii

Hagadone Printing Co, 274 Pu'uhale Rd, Honolulu, 96819-2234

Idaho

Selkirk Press, 1714 Industrial Dr, PO Box 875, Sandpoint, 83864

Illinois

A&H Lithoprint Inc, 2540 S 27th Ave, Broadview, 60155-3851

ABS Graphics, 901 S Rohlwing Rd (Suite M), Addison, 60101-4229

American Graphics Network Inc, 1701 E Lake Ave Ste 475, Glenview, 60025-2036

American Slide-Chart Corp, 25W550 Geneva Rd, Carol Stream, 60188-2225

Art, Tape & Label Co, 444 Interstate Rd, Addison, 60101-4518

Aspen Packaging Corp, 5253 W Roosevelt Rd, Cicero, 60804-1222

Badger Press Inc, 32941 N Stone Manor Dr, Grayslake, 60030-3051

Benchmark Imaging & Display, 221 Lively Blvd, Elk Grove Village, 60007-1622

Berlin Industries Inc, 175 Mercedes Dr, Carol Stream, 60188-9409

Carqueville Graphics Inc, 1536 Bourbon Pkwy, Streamwood, 60107-1808

CDI Network Inc, 4311 Ariel Ct, Naperville, 60564-3188

CPE, 329 W 18th St (fl 18), Chicago, 60616-1121

Chicago Decal Co, 101 Tower Dr, Burr Ridge, 60527-5779

Classic Color, 2424 S 25th Ave, Broadview, 60155-3874

JJ Collins' Sons Inc, 7125 Janes Ave (Suite 200), Woodridge, 60517-2341

Continental Web Press Inc, 1430 Industrial Dr, Itasca, 60143-1848

Creative Printing Services Inc, 1701 Birchwood Ave, Des Plaines, 60018-3005

Darwill, 11900 W Roosevelt Rd, Hillside, 60162-2069

Datamart Direct Inc, 279 Madsen Dr (Suite 101), Bloomingdale, 60108-2692

Dependable Business Forms, 843 South Myrtle Ave, Villa Park, 60181-3353

Des Plaines Printing Co, 999 Commerce Ct, Buffalo Grove, 60089-2375

Domino Amjet Inc, 1290 Lakeside Dr, Gurnee, 60031-2499

E&D Web Printing Inc, 1100A S Main St, Rochelle, 61068-3509

FCL Graphics Inc, 4600 N Olcott Ave, Harwood Heights, 60656

Stephen Fossler Co Inc, 1600 E Touhy Ave, Des Plaines, 60018-3607

The Garvey Group, 7400 N Lehigh Ave, Niles, 60714

Impressions Unlimited Inc, PO Box 1349, Deerfield, 60015-6005

Innovative Plastic Printing Corp, 534 Congress Cir N, Roselle, 60172

Integrated Print & Graphics, 645 Stevenson Rd, South Elgin, 60177-1134

Jet LithoColor Inc, 1500 Centre Cir, Downers Grove, 60515

JD Graphic Co, 1101 Arthur Ave, Elk Grove Village, 60707

Kingery Printing Co, 3012 S Banker, Box 727, Effingham, 62401-0727

Lake County Press Inc, PO Box 9209, Waukegan, 60079-9209

Lehigh Direct, 1900 S 25th Ave, Broadview, 60155-2800

Marking Specialists Group, 1000 Asbury Dr (Suite 2), Buffalo Grove, 60089-4551

Marvin Envelope & Paper Co, 288 W Palatine Rd, Wheeling, 60090-5815

Metropolitan Graphic Arts, 930 Turret Ct, Mundelein, 60060-3821

MAR Graphics, 523 S Meyer Ave, Valmeyer, 62295-3120

O'Brien Document Solutions, 1273 Humbracht Cir, Bartlett, 60103-1606

Perfect Plastic Printing Corp, 311 Kautz Rd Ste 4, Saint Charles, 60174-5304

Plastic Graphic, 255 Industrial Dr, Wauconda, 60084

PPS - Packaging Printing Specialists, 3915 Stern Ave, Saint Charles, 60174-5441

PSA, 485 E Half Day Rd Ste 500, Buffalo Grove, 60089-8808

Prime Graphics Inc, 501 N Central Ave, Wood Dale, 60191-1473

Print Management Partners, 701 Lee St (Suite 1050), Des Plaines, 60016-4572

Quantum Color, 6511 Oakton St, Morton Grove, 60053-2728

Rainbow Graphics Inc, 933 Tower Rd, Mundelein, 60060-3811

Schawk DesPlaines, 1600 Sherwin Ave, Des Plaines, 60018-3013

Schawk Inc, 1695 River Rd, Des Plaines, 60018

The Segerdahl Corp, 1351 S Wheeling Rd, Wheeling, 60090-5997

Segerdahl Graphics, 385 Gilman Ave, Wheeling, 60090-5807

Service Web Offset Corp, 2500 S Dearborn St, Chicago, 60616-2299

Specialty Print Communications, 6019 W Howard St, Niles, 60714-4801

SAF Financial Services Inc, 635 Remington Rd (Unit F), Schaumburg, 60173

TempoGraphics Inc, 455 E North Ave, Carol Stream, 60188

Triangle Printers Inc, 3737 Chase Ave, Skokie, 60076-4008

Unique Embossing Services Inc & Global Cards, 1213 Butterfield Rd, Downers Grove, 60515

Versatile Card Technology Inc, 5200 Thatcher Rd, Downers Grove, 60515

Wallace Targeted Communications, 1750 Wallace Ave, Saint Charles, 60174-3401

Indiana

Dynamic Graphics, 7210 Zionsville Rd, Indianapolis, 46268-2165

Newcomb Marketing Solutions, 605 E 9th St, Michigan City, 46360-3651

PIP Printing and Marketing Services, 6330 E 75th St (Suite 138), Indianapolis, 46250-2717

Shindigz, One Party Pl, South Whitley, 46787

Iowa

Fisher Group Inc, 1250 N Center Point Rd, Hiawatha, 52233-1226

The Printer Inc, 1220 Thomas Beck Rd, Des Moines, 50315-1068

Kansas

Digital Vision Resources Group - DVRG, 8238 Nieman Rd, Overland Park, 66214-1507

Heart Thoughts Inc, 1480 N Stratford Ln, Wichita, 67206-1165

McCormick-Armstrong Co Inc, 1501 E Douglas, Wichita, 67211-1608

Kentucky

Allegra Print & Imaging - East, 2680 Technology Dr, Louisville, 40299-6424

CCL Label, 1187 Industrial Rd, Cold Spring, 41076

Champion Printing Inc, 4205 Dixie Hwy, Elsmere, 41018-1817

Fetter Label, 700 Locust Ln, Louisville, 40217-2997

Publishers Press Inc, 100 Frank E Simon Ave, Shepherdsville, 40165-6013

VG Reed & Sons, 1002 S 12th St, Louisville, 40210-1302

Louisiana

National Mail-It Inc, 9151 Youree Dr, Shreveport, 71115-3303

Maine

The Dingley Press, 119 Lisbon St, Lisbon, 04250-6005

Formsource, 170 Summer St, Lewiston, 04240-7532

The Maine Connection, 246 Deering Ave, Univ of Maine School of Law, Portland, 04102-2837

Maryland

Editors Press Inc, 1701 Cabin Branch Dr, Hyattsville, 20785-3820

Image Checks, PO Box 2, Bel Air, 21014

McArdle Printing Co Inc, 800 Commerce Dr, Upper Marlboro, 20774-8792

Omni Print Inc, 9700 Philadelphia Ct, Lanham, 20706-4405

Reese Press Inc, 7085 Milford Industrial Rd, Pikesville, 21208-6013

Tidewater Direct LLC, 300 Tidewater Dr, Centreville, 21617

Massachusetts

Arthur Blank & Co Inc, 225 Rivermoor St, Boston, 02132

Boston Color Graphics, 755 Middlesex Tpke, Billerica, 01821-3927

CM Consulting Services, 7 Maple Ln, Marshfield, 02050-3466

Connecticut Color, 8 Emerald St, Hingham, 02043-2402

48HourPrint.com, 33 Farnsworth St (Suite 2), Boston, 02210-1210

HubCast Inc, 500 Edgewater Dr (Suite 568), Wakefield, 01880-6222

Lasermax Roll Systems, 4 Suburban Park Dr., Billerica, 01821-3904

Linguistic Systems Inc, 201 Broadway, Cambridge, 02139

Pilgrim Printed Promotional Plastics, 1200 W Chestnut St, Brockton, 02301-5574

The Pond-Ekberg Co, 660 Broadway St, Chicopee, 01020-2400

Presskits, 8 Rose Ct Way, East Walpole, 02032-1185

UniGraphic Inc, 110 Commerce Way Ste 6, Woburn, 01801-1098

VistaPrint USA Inc, 95 Hayden Ave, Lexington, 02421-7942

Michigan

Allegra Network, LLC, 47585 Galleon Dr, Plymouth, 48170-2466

Data-Matic Systems Co, 5545 Enterprise Dr, Lansing, 48911-4131

Inland Press, 2001 W Lafayette Blvd, Detroit, 48216

John Henry Packaging, 5800 W Grand River Ave, Lansing, 48906-9111

Mitchell Graphics Inc, 2363 Mitchell Park Dr, Petoskey, 49770

Quebecor World Midland, 1700 James Savage Rd, Midland, 48642

Sheridan Books Inc, 613 E Industrial Dr, Chelsea, 48118-1536

Sir Speedy Grand Rapids, 4513 Broadmoor Ave SE (Suite A), Grand Rapids, 49512-5369

Minnesota

Ambassador Press, 1400 Washington Ave N, Minneapolis, 55411-3422

American Spirit Graphics Corp, 801 SE 9th St, Minneapolis, 55414-1306

Anderberg-Lund Printing, 6999 Oxford St, Saint Louis Park, 55426

Deluxe Corp, 3680 Victoria St N, Shoreview, 55126-2906

Japs-Olson Co, 7500 Excelsior Blvd, Saint Louis Park, 55426-4519

Medical Arts Press, 8500 Wyoming Ave N, Minneapolis, 55445-1825

Nahan Printing Inc, 7000 Saukview Dr, Saint Cloud, 56303-0814

OlymPak, 6010 Earle Brown Dr (Suite 100), Minneapolis, 55430-4516

PGI Companies Inc, 220 S 6th St Ste 2125, Minneapolis, 55402-4517

Schmidt, 1101 Frontage Rd NW, Byron, 55920

Missouri

Bernadette Business Forms Inc, 601 Cannonball Ln, O Fallon, 63366-4411

Cenveo Color Art Inc, 101 Workman Ct, Eureka, 63025-1079

Felco Printing & Mailing, 1910 Walnut St, Kansas City, 64108-1810

Greystone Graphics, 4010 Washington St Ste 100, Kansas City, 64111-2614

Midland Lithographing Co, 1841 Vernon St, North Kansas City, 64116-4430

MWM Dexter Inc, 107 Washington Ave, Aurora, 65605

US Tape & Label Corp, 2092 Westport Ctr Dr, Saint Louis, 63146

Universal Printing, 1234 S Kingshighway Blvd, Saint Louis, 63110

Henry Wurst Inc, 1331 Saline St, North Kansas City, 64116-4410

Nebraska

Interstate Printing Co, 2002N 16th St, Omaha, 68110

Lancer Label, 301 S 74th St, Omaha, 68114

Redfield & Co Inc, 1901 Howard St, Omaha, 68102-2594

Surdell & Partners, 3738 S 149th St Ste 109, Omaha, 68144-5564

York Label, 13321 California St (Suite 400), Omaha, 68154-6047

Nevada

Rapid Color Printing, 6445 Karms Park Ct, Las Vegas, 89118-1414

New Hampshire

Concord Litho, 92 Old Turnpike Rd, Concord, 03301-7305

Goss International, 121 Technology Dr, Durham, 03824-4716

Relyco, 121 Broadway, Dover, 03820-3299

Sterling Print & Mail System, 206 Concord St, Peterborough, 03458

New Jersey

A&E Promotions LLC, 153 1st Ave, Atlantic Highlands, 07716-1265

AC Pedreiro, 15 Diane Dr, Morganville, 07751-1370

American Bank Note Holographics Inc, 2 Applegate Dr, Robbinsville, 08691-2342

Applied Printing Technologies, 77 Moonachie Ave, Moonachie, 07074

The Ballantine Corp, 1700 Rte 23 N, Wayne, 07470-7536

C.R.W. Graphics, 9100 Pennsauken Hwy, Pennsauken, 08110-1206

Clients First, 84 Elm St Ste 1, Westfield, 07090-2181

Driscoll Label Co Inc, 19 West St, East Hanover, 07936-2822

Federal Direct, 95 Main Ave Ste 2, Clifton, 07014-1749

Stephen Gould Paper Co Inc, 35 S Jefferson Rd, Whippany, 07981

Hannecke Display Systems Inc, 91 Fulton St (#3), Boonton, 07005

Hatteras, 56 Park Rd, Tinton Falls, 07724-9715

Imtek, 2075 High Hill Rd, Bridgeport, 08014

Invitation Hotline, 68 Hawkins Rd, Manalapan, 07726

Jersey Printing Associates Inc, 153 First Ave, PO Box 355, Atlantic Highlands, 07716-0355

Keystone Promotions Inc, 63 Vacari Way, Little Egg Harbor, 08087-4029

L.P. THEBAULT CO., 249 Pomeroy Rd, PO Box 169, Parsippany, 07054-3727

MediaTree, 77 E Haley Rd, Parsippany, 07054

Quadra Graphics Inc, PO Box 555, Cherry Hill, 08003-0555

Real Media Solutions, 77 Green Knolls Dr, Wayne, 07470-6123

RONED Printing & Reproduction Inc, Six DeForest Ave, East Hanover, 07936

Sherwood Design & Development Center, One Kero Rd, Carlstadt, 07072

Unz & Co, 333 Cedar Ave Ste 2, Middlesex, 08846-2400

New York

Andell Packaging Corp, 19 Nightingale Ct (Suite 2), Manhasset, 11030-4039

Benton Announcements Inc, 3006 Bailey Ave, Buffalo, 14215-2898

Brown Printing Co, 1500 Broadway (Suite 505), New York, 10036-4055

Center for Book Arts, 28 W 27th St (fl 3), New York, 10001-6906

Chase Media Group, 1520 Front St, Yorktown Heights, 10598

Clean Lists Associates Inc, 122 E 42nd St (Suite 1700), New York, 10168-0002

DNP America Inc, 335 Madison Ave (3rd fl), New York, 10017

Disc Graphics Inc, Ten Gilpin Ave, Hauppauge, 11788

Eastman Kodak Co, 343 State St, Rochester, 14650-0001

Essex Printing Co Inc, 14 Westminster Dr, Croton On Hudson, 10520-1008

The Flexi Group Inc, 2675 Henry Hudson Pkwy, PO Box 316, Bronx, 10463

Grafek Direct, PO Box 11500, Dupli Park Dr, Syracuse, 13218-1500

Hi-C Production, Nine Tottenham Pl, New Hyde Park, 11040-3516

Kodak Graphic Communications, 343 State St, Rochester, 14650-0002

Magjak Printing Corp, 114 Pearl St, Port Chester, 10573-4663

Media Link Communications, 321 E 22nd St (Suite 3K), New York, 10010

Minuteman Press (Westchester), 120 E Main St, Elmsford, 10523

Official Offset Corp, 8600 New Horizons Blvd, Amityville, 11701-1183

Pollack Graphics Inc, 536 Merrick Rd, Lynbrook, 11563

PCI Paper Conversions Inc, 6761 Thompson Rd N, Syracuse, 13211-2119

Printing Spectrum, 12 Research Way Ste 1, East Setauket, 11733-3531

Sir Speedy Westbury, 75 State St, Westbury, 11590-5004

Spire Creative Group, 110 W 40th St (Rm 1702), New York, 10018-8508

SPIRE Printing & Packaging LLC, 501 5th Ave (Suite 811), New York, 10017-7849

Stickertape, PO Box 483, Nesconset, 11767-0483

Tucker Printers, 270 Middle Rd, Henrietta, 14467-9312

Web Graphics, PO Box 308, Glens Falls, 12801

Wilen Group, 5 Wellwood Ave, Farmingdale, 11735-1213

William Charles Printing, 7 Fairchild Ct Ste 100, Plainview, 11803-1734

North Carolina

The Hickory Printing Group, 725 Reese Dr SW, Conover, 28613

Modern Information Services Inc, 313-B S Center St, Statesville, 28677-5879

Source 4 Inc, 16740 Birkdale Commons Pkwy (Suite 208), Huntersville, 28078-4462

Ohio

Ampac, 12025 Tricon Rd, Cincinnati, 45246-1719

Caraustar Ashland Carton Plant, 600 Union St, Ashland, 44805

Color Q Inc, 540 Richard St, Miamisburg, 45342

Cyril-Scott Co, 3950 State Route 37 E, PO Box 310, Lancaster, 43130

The Gray Printing Co, 401 E North St, Fostoria, 44830-2828

Great Lakes Integrated, 4005 Clark Ave, Cleveland, 44109-1186

Hess Print Solutions, 3765 Sunnybrook Rd, Kent, 44240

Industrial Printing Co Inc, 1635 Coining Dr, Toledo, 43612

Kreber Graphics Inc, 2580 Westbelt Dr, Columbus, 43228

Miller Printing, 581 W Leffel Ln, Springfield, 45501

Top USA Corp, 771 Dearborn Park Ln (Ste N), Worthington, 43085-5720

Univenture Inc, 13311 Industrial Pkwy, Marysville, 43040-9589

Oklahoma

Zed Marketing Group, 1210 Roosevelt St (Suite 220), Edmond, 73034-5176

Oregon

AKA Direct, PO Box 5217, Portland, 97208-5217

Pennsylvania

Action Mailers Inc, 90 Commerce Dr, Aston, 19014-3286

American Thermoplastic Co, 106 Gamma Dr, Pittsburgh, 15238-2985

Bartash Media Group, 5400 Grays Ave, Philadelphia, 19143-5897

Communifx, 1253 Freedom Rd (Suite 500), Cranberry, 16066-4952

Consolidated Printing Inc, 5050 Parkside Ave, Philadelphia, 19131-4714

Fry Communciations Inc, 800 W Church Rd, Mechanicsburg, 17055-3198

Graphic Arts Information Network (GAIN), 200 Deer Run Rd, Sewickley, 15143-2324

IBSDirect, 431 Yerkes Rd, King of Prussia, 19406-3556

Innovation Printing, 11601 Caroline Rd, Philadelphia, 19154

Intelligencer Printing Co, 330 Eden Rd, Lancaster, 17601-4218

International Fulfillment Inc, 2800 Black Lake Pl (Suite D), Philadelphia, 19154-1024

MACORP Print Group, 261 Schoolhouse Rd (Suite 8), Souderton, 18964

McCourt Label Co, 20 Egbert Ln, Lewis Run, 16738-3802

National Mail Graphics Corp, 300 Old Mill Ln, Exton, 19341-2582

Neibauer Press, 20 Industrial Dr, Warminster, 18974-1433

Printing + Quick Copy, 8799 Frankford Ave, Philadelphia, 19136

Sir Speedy of Newtown, 760 Newtown-Yardley Rd, Newtown, 18940-4500

Spring Hill Laser Services, PO Box 79, Sterling, 18463-0079

Valley Forge Tape & Label Co Inc, 119 Summit Dr, Exton, 19341

York Label, 405 Willow Springs Ln, York, 17405-6047

Rhode Island

Colorlith Corp, 321 S Main St Ste 301, Providence, 02903-7109

The Foxon Co, 235 W Park St, Providence, 02908-4881

South Dakota

Western Web Printing, 4005 S Western Ave, Sioux Falls, 57105

Tennessee

Arcade Marketing, Inc, 3800 Amnicola Hwy, Chattanooga, 37406-1003

Donihe Graphics Inc, 766 Brookside Dr, Kingsport, 37660

King Printing Solutions, 531 Straight Creek Rd., New Tazewell, 37825

Morrison Printing Co, 1039 Walters Dr, Morristown, 37814-6133

M Lee Smith Publishers LLC, 100 Winners Cir N Ste 300, Brentwood, 37027-1003

Texas

ADS Direct Media, 12758 Cimarron Path (Suite B-128), San Antonio, 78249-3426

American Color, 2010 Westridge Dr, Irving, 75038-2900

Clear Visions Inc, 121 Interpark Blvd (Suite 801), San Antonio, 78216

Dockery House Publishing Inc, 906 Main St (Suite B), Lindale, 75771

Graphic Arts Center, 2514 National Dr, Garland, 75041-2329

Graphics International Inc, 3883 Turtle Creek Blvd (Apt 1406), Dallas, 75219-4430

Lone Star Web Inc, 1412 Main St Ste 2400, Dallas, 75202-4011

Nationwide Graphic/Premier Print Organizations, 2500 W Loop S (Suite 500), Houston, 77027-4521

Performance Printing/ Optigraphics, 2929 N Stemmons Fwy, Dallas, 75247-6102

Printing for Systems Inc, 1617 W Crosby Rd Ste 100, Carrollton, 75006-6486

Shopguide.com, 3223 Commerce St, Amarillo, 79109-3275

Teraco Inc, 2080 Commerce Dr, Midland, 79703-7502

Texas Graphic Resource, 1234 Round Table Dr, Dallas, 75247-3504

Venture Encoding Service Inc, 4401 Cambridge, Fort Worth, 76155-2629

Williamson Printing, 6700 Denton Dr, Dallas, 75235-9827

Xpressdocs, 1000 Forest Park Blvd Ste 200, Fort Worth, 76110-1169

Utah

AlphaGraphics World Headquarters, 268 S State St (Suite 300), Salt Lake City, 84111-5314

Westpro Inc, 2294 Mountain Vista Ln, Provo, 84606-6206

Vermont

The Offset House Inc, 89 Sand Hill Rd, Essex Junction, 05452-3909

Virginia

Aptara, Inc, 3110 Fairview Park Dr (Suite 900), Falls Church, 22042

Balmar Inc, 2818 Fallfax Dr, Falls Church, 22042-2804

Catalogs America, 1 American Pl, Gordonsville, 22942

Datamatx Inc, 10430 Lakeridge Pkwy, Ashland, 23005

Folder Factory Inc, 5421 Main St (Suite 300), Mount Jackson, 22843-9537

Industrial Arts & Graphics, 22714 Melrose Farm Ln, Middleburg, 20117

Membership Cards Only LLC, 8000 Towers Crescent Dr (Suite 1350), Vienna, 22182-6219

Progress Printing Co, 2677 Waterlick Rd, Lynchburg, 24502

Stephenson Printing Inc, 5731 General Washington Dr, Alexandria, 22312

Washington

Labels West Inc, 17629 130th Ave NE, Woodinville, 98072

Sir Speedy Printing and Marketing Services, 7450 S Tacoma Way (Suite B1), Tacoma, 98409-3906

Wisconsin

Arandell Corp, N82 W13118 Leon Rd, Menomonee Falls, 53051

Badger Press/Photographics Inc, 7325 30th Ave, Kenosha, 53142-4401

Fox River Paper Co, 600 S Vulcan St, Appleton, 54915

Graphic Communications Center, 3001 E Venture Dr, Box 357, Appleton, 54911-8309

Heavy Rotation, 3720 N Fratney St (Studios 3F), Milwaukee, 53212

Kwik-File, 619 N Commerce St, Sheboygan, 53081-3901

Mandel Co, PO Box 12124, Milwaukee, 53212-0124

Outlook Group Corp, 1180 American Dr, Neenah, 54956-1306

Ripon Printers, 656 S Douglas St, Ripon, 54971-9044

Sells Printing Co, 16000 W Rogers Dr, New Berlin, 53151

Service Litho Print Inc, 50 W Fernau, Oshkosh, 54902-0875

Sir Speedy - Green Bay, 333 Packerland Dr, Green Bay, 54303-4815

CANADA
Ontario

Crook & Grant Lithographers Ltd, 279 Yorkland Blvd, North York, M2J 1S5

Embassy Digital, 2880 Brighton Rd (Unit 1), Oakville, L6H 5S3

General Printers, 1001 Ritson Rd S, Oshawa, L1H 4G5

Grant's Mailing Services Inc, 940 Matheson Blvd E, Mississauga, L4W 2R8

Litho-Web Inc, 24 Huddersfield Rd, Etobicoke, M9W 5Z6

PointOne Graphics Inc, 14 Vansco Rd, Toronto, M8Z 5J4

St Joseph Communications, 50 MacIntosh Blvd, Concord, L4K 4P3

St Joseph Print Thorn, 50 MacIntosh Blvd, Concord, L4K 4P3

TransContinental Yorkville - O'Keefe, Eight Tidemore Ave, Etobicoke, M9W 5H4

Quebec

Scientific Games Canada, 3000 boul de l' Assomption, Montreal, H1N 3V5

Saskatchewan

PrintWest Communications Ltd, 1150
Eighth Ave, Regina, S4R 1C9

Printing & Related Services (27)

THE DMA A&E PROMOTIONS LLC
153 1st Ave
Atlantic Highlands, NJ 07716-1265
Telephone: (732) 275-1520, Web Site:
www.aepromo.com
VP: Eugene Veltri

A&H LITHOPRINT INC
2540 S 27th Ave
Broadview, IL 60155-3851
Telephone: (708) 345-1196, FAX:
(708) 345-1225, Web Site: www.
ahlithoprint.com
Pres: David Ashley

ABS GRAPHICS
901 S Rohlwing Rd (Suite M)
Addison, IL 60101-4229
Telephone: (630) 495-2400, FAX:
(630) 495-0728, E-Mail: info@
absinet.com, Web Site: www.absinet.
com
Pres: Ken VanderVeen

THE DMA AC PEDREIRO
15 Diane Dr
Morganville, NJ 07751-1370
Telephone: (732) 598-6766
Pres: Anna Pedreiro

ADS DIRECT MEDIA
12758 Cimarron Path (Suite B-128)
San Antonio, TX 78249-3426
Telephone: (210) 655-6613, Web Site:
www.adsmediagroup.com
VP Sls: Jim Stewart
Primary Market Served: Consumer

AKA DIRECT
PO Box 5217
Portland, OR 97208-5217
Telephone: (503) 454-2233, Web Site:
www.akadirect.com
Primary Market Served: Consumer

AMPAC
12025 Tricon Rd
Cincinnati, OH 45246-1719
Telephone: (513) 671-1777, (800) 543-
7030, FAX: (513) 671-2920, Web
Site: www.ampaconline.com
Pres: John Baumann

**ACTION COMMUNICATIONS
INC**
500 NE Spanish River Blvd Ste 26
Boca Raton, FL 33431-4517

Telephone: (561) 995-1995, (800) 558-
5085, FAX: (561) 995-1990
Pres: Don Golden

THE DMA ACTION MAILERS INC
Div. of The Action Group
90 Commerce Dr
Aston, PA 19014-3286
Telephone: (610) 859-0500, (800) 258-
5992, FAX: (610) 859-0505, Web
Site: www.actionmailer.com
Pres: Daniel Dobbin
VP Sls & Mktg: Larry Mills

THE DMA ALLEGRA NETWORK, LLC
47585 Galleon Dr
Plymouth, MI 48170-2466
Telephone: (248) 596-8600, FAX:
(248) 596-8601, Web Site: www2.
allegranetwork.com
Chmn & Mng: Bill McIntyre
Majority Investor & Chief Strategy
Officer: Mike Marcantonio
Pres & CEO: Carl Gerhardt

**THE DMA ALLEGRA PRINT &
IMAGING - EAST**
2680 Technology Dr
Louisville, KY 40299-6424
Telephone: (502) 895-1530, Web Site:
www.allegra-east.com
Dir Sls: Karen Olson

**ALLIED PRINTING SERVICES
INC**
1 Allied Way, PO Box 850
Manchester, CT 06040-2728
Telephone: (860) 643-1101, (800) 225-
8777, (800) 224-8894, FAX: (860)
643-9723, E-Mail: allied@
alliedprinting.com, Web Site: www.
alliedprinting.com
Pres: John G. Sommers
Mktg: Gunner Hicks

**THE DMA ALPHAGRAPHICS WORLD
HEADQUARTERS**
268 S State St (Suite 300)
Salt Lake City, UT 84111-5314
Telephone: (801) 595-7270, (800) 955-
6246, FAX: (801) 595-7271, E-Mail:
contactus@alphagraphics.com, Web
Site: www.alphagraphics.com
Pres & CEO: Kevin Cushing
Exec Asst to CEO: Maggie Cooper

AMBASSADOR PRESS
1400 Washington Ave N
Minneapolis, MN 55411-3422
Telephone: (612) 521-0123, (800) 544-
9112, FAX: (612) 521-4587, E-Mail:
info@ambpress.com, Web Site:
www.ambpress.com
VP, Opers: Jackie Burgoon

**AMERICAN BANK NOTE
HOLOGRAPHICS INC**
2 Applegate Dr
Robbinsville, NJ 08691-2342
Telephone: (609) 632-0800, FAX:
(609) 632-0850, Web Site: www.
abnh.com
VP Corp Devel & Mktg: Adam L.A.
Scheer

AMERICAN COLOR
2010 Westridge Dr
Irving, TX 75038-2900
Telephone: (602) 333-1000, FAX:
(602) 333-1099, Web Site: www.
amcolor.com
Head Tech Svcs: Dave Norinski

**AMERICAN GRAPHICS
NETWORK INC**
1701 E Lake Ave Ste 475
Glenview, IL 60025-2036
Telephone: (847) 729-7220, FAX:
(847) 724-5080, E-Mail: info@
agninc.com, Web Site: www.agninc.
com
Pres: Wanda M. Sclaventis

**AMERICAN SLIDE-CHART
CORP**
25W550 Geneva Rd
Carol Stream, IL 60188-2225
Telephone: (630) 665-3333, (800) 323-
4433, FAX: (630) 665-3491, E-Mail:
info2@americanslidechart.com, Web
Site: www.americanslidechart.com
Dir, Sls & Mktg: Don Hoff

**THE DMA AMERICAN SPIRIT
GRAPHICS CORP**
801 SE 9th St
Minneapolis, MN 55414-1306
Telephone: (612) 623-3333, FAX:
(612) 623-9314, E-Mail: asgc@asgc.
com, Web Site: www.asgc.com
Chmn: A. Oscar Carlson
Pres & COO: Myron Angel
CEO: Darren Carlson
Exec VP: Lauren Drevlow

VP, Opers: Tim Franzen
Conducts Business: U.S.
Employees: 200
Quality 4 & 5 color heatset web offset commercial printer specializing in direct response formats, coupon books, publication inserts, brochures & small format catalogs. Featuring innovative in-line, press-finished formats for direct marketers. 2- 6-color sheetfed lithography. Inserting/mailing, personalization available through American Spirit Mailing.

AMERICAN THERMOPLASTIC CO
106 Gamma Dr
Pittsburgh, PA 15238-2985
Telephone: (412) 967-0900, (800) 245-6600, FAX: (412) 967-9990, E-Mail: atc@binders.com, Web Site: www.binders.com
Pres: S. Silberman
Adv Mgr: Joseph Sprumont

ANDELL PACKAGING CORP
19 Nightingale Ct (Suite 2)
Manhasset, NY 11030-4039
Telephone: (718) 937-6500, FAX: (718) 482-9416
Pres: Sandor Schaeffer

ANDERBERG-LUND PRINTING
6999 Oxford St
Saint Louis Park, MN 55426
Telephone: (952) 920-9720, (800) 231-9777, FAX: (952) 920-1103, E-Mail: sales@anderberglund.com, Web Site: www.anderberglund.com
Pres & CEO: Jack Anderberg

ANGSTROM GRAPHICS
2025 McKinley St
Hollywood, FL 33020
Telephone: (954) 920-7300, E-Mail: wayne.angstrom@st-ives-usa.com, Web Site: www.angstromgraphics.com
Pres & CEO: Wayne Angstrom

APPERSON PRINT MANAGEMENT SERVICES
13910 Cerritos Corporate Dr
Cerritos, CA 90703-2457
Telephone: (562) 356-3333, (800) 877-2341, FAX: (562) 356-3310, E-Mail: sales@appersonprint.com, Web Site: www.appersonprint.com
Chmn & Pres: R.P. Apperson

APPLIED PRINTING TECHNOLOGIES
77 Moonachie Ave
Moonachie, NJ 07074
Telephone: (201) 635-9447, (888) 282-4141, FAX: (201) 896-6839, E-Mail: vpsales@appliedprinting.com, Web Site: www.appliedprinting.com
Exec VP: Frank Brusco Jr.

APTARA, INC
3110 Fairview Park Dr (Suite 900)
Falls Church, VA 22042
Telephone: (703) 352-0001, E-Mail: info@aptaracorp.com, Web Site: www.aptaracorp.com
Pres & CEO: Ranjit Singh

ARANDELL CORP
N82 W13118 Leon Rd
Menomonee Falls, WI 53051
Telephone: (262) 255-4400, (800) 558-8724, FAX: (262) 253-3162, E-Mail: jft@arandell.com, Web Site: www.arandell.com
Exec VP Sls & Mktg: James Treis

ARCADE MARKETING, INC
3800 Amnicola Hwy
Chattanooga, TN 37406-1003
Telephone: (423) 624-3301, FAX: (423) 622-4635
Chmn: Bill Fox

ART, TAPE & LABEL CO
444 Interstate Rd
Addison, IL 60101-4518
Telephone: (630) 543-8100, FAX: (630) 543-8153, Web Site: arttapeandlabel.com
Pres: Allan Cameron Jr

ASPEN PACKAGING CORP
5253 W Roosevelt Rd
Cicero, IL 60804-1222
FAX: (708) 652-6444, Web Site: www.aspenpkg.com
Pres: Gary Stearns

ATLANTA OFFSET
Subs. of Gannett Co Inc
120 James Aldredge Blvd SW
Atlanta, GA 30336-2102
Telephone: (404) 699-6200, FAX: (404) 699-1393, Web Site: www.gannett.com/about/map/offset.htm
Gen Mgr: Charlie Arthur

BBF INTEGRATED SOLUTIONS
10950 Belcher Rd S
Largo, FL 33777-1438
Telephone: (800) 666-8082, Web Site: www.bbfprinting.com
Pres & CEO: Donald Huttlin

BADGER PRESS INC
32941 N Stone Manor Dr
Grayslake, IL 60030-3051
Telephone: (847) 996-1190, E-Mail: info@badgerpressinc.com, Web Site: www.badgerpressinc.com
Pres: Katherine Dederich

BADGER PRESS/ PHOTOGRAPHICS INC
7325 30th Ave
Kenosha, WI 53142-4401
Telephone: (262) 658-1628, (800) 635-9773, FAX: (262) 658-0307
Pres: Todd Bundies

THE BALLANTINE CORP
1700 Rte 23 N
Wayne, NJ 07470-7536
Telephone: (973) 305-1500, Web Site: www.ballantine.com
Dir Mktg: Ryan Cote

BALMAR INC
2818 Fallfax Dr
Falls Church, VA 22042-2804
Telephone: (703) 289-9000, FAX: (703) 289-9143, E-Mail: marketing@balmar.com, Web Site: www.balmar.com
Mktg Mgr: Kathleen Harding

BARTASH MEDIA GROUP
5400 Grays Ave
Philadelphia, PA 19143-5897
Telephone: (215) 724-1700, Web Site: www.bartash.com
Primary Market Served: Consumer

BEACON PRINTING & GRAPHICS INC
1628A James P Rodgers Dr
Valdosta, GA 31601
Telephone: (912) 244-5634, (800) 227-7377, FAX: (912) 247-4405, Web Site: www.uspress.com
Pres: Kent A. Buescher

BENCHMARK IMAGING & DISPLAY
Subs. of William McKinley Studios
221 Lively Blvd
Elk Grove Village, IL 60007-1622
Telephone: (847) 292-5150, FAX: (847) 292-5159, Web Site: www.benchmarkimaging.com
Pres: Bill McKinley

BENTON ANNOUNCEMENTS INC
3006 Bailey Ave
Buffalo, NY 14215-2898
Telephone: (716) 836-4100, FAX: (716) 836-4161
Chmn: Michael J. Guerra Sr.
Pres: Philip J. Guerra
VP: Michael J. Guerra Jr.
Conducts Business: U.S., Canada
Employees: 10
Primary Market Served: Business & Consumer
Advertising/Marketing Budget Related to Direct Marketing: 0-25%
Direct Marketing ad budget: $5,000
Telephone: 100%
Founded: 1935
Gross sales or billing: $600,000

Sell invitations with services that include embossing, leaf stamping, thermography, printing, die cutting, gluing, taping, numbering and scoring.

BERLIN INDUSTRIES INC
175 Mercedes Dr
Carol Stream, IL 60188-9409
Telephone: (630) 682-0600, FAX: (630) 682-3093, E-Mail: info@berlinindustries.com, Web Site: www.berlinindustries.com
Pres: Tina Tromiczak

BERNADETTE BUSINESS FORMS INC
601 Cannonball Ln
O Fallon, MO 63366-4411
Telephone: (314) 522-1700, (800) 862-7288, FAX: (314) 524-6161, Web Site: www.bbf.com
Pres & COO: George Mitschele

ARTHUR BLANK & CO INC
225 Rivermoor St
Boston, MA 02132
Telephone: (617) 325-9600, (800) 776-7333, FAX: (617) 327-1235, E-Mail: abco@abco.com, Web Site: www.arthurblank.com
Pres: Stuart Blank
Programming Mgr: Paul Blanchard

BOSTON COLOR GRAPHICS
755 Middlesex Tpke
Billerica, MA 01821-3927
Telephone: (978) 528-7999, (800) 767-0067, FAX: (978) 528-7609, E-Mail: sales@bostoncolorgraphics.com, Web Site: www.bostoncolorgraphics.com
Pres: Charles Noonan
Founded: 2003

BCG provides on-demand print, premedia and targeted, personalized communications.

BROWN PRINTING CO
1500 Broadway (Suite 505)
New York, NY 10036-4055
Telephone: (212) 782-7800, FAX: (212) 782-7878, E-Mail: contact.us@bpc.com, Web Site: www.bpc.com
Sr VP, Sls & Mktg: Bill Guthrie
Dir Mktg: Bill Gesele
Mktg Coord: Brittany Thomez

CCL LABEL
1187 Industrial Rd
Cold Spring, KY 41076
Telephone: (859) 781-6161, (800) 422-6633, FAX: (859) 781-6339
HR: Cheryl Romano

CDI NETWORK INC
4311 Ariel Ct
Naperville, IL 60564-3188
Telephone: (708) 409-8585, FAX: (708) 409-8589, Web Site: www.cdinet.biz
Pres & CEO: Walter D. Schenk

CM CONSULTING SERVICES
7 Maple Ln
Marshfield, MA 02050-3466
Telephone: (781) 749-5000, FAX: (801) 749-5009, E-Mail: cmalpine3@gmail.com
Acct Exec: Charles M. McAlpine

CPE
329 W 18th St (fl 18)
Chicago, IL 60616-1121
Telephone: (312) 427-5370, FAX: (312) 427-7836, E-Mail: wgavin@cpe1.com, Web Site: www.cpe1.com
Pres: William Gavin

CPI CARD GROUP
10368 W Centennial Rd Ste A
Littleton, CO 80127-4296
Telephone: (303) 973-9311, FAX: (303) 973-8420, E-Mail: mbarber@cpicardgroup.com, Web Site: www.cpicardgroup.com
VP Mktg: Bob Clark
Natl Accts Mgr: Jay Schwisow
Conducts Business: U.S.
Primary Market Served: Business
Advertising/Marketing Budget Related to Direct Marketing: 0-25%
Founded: 1982
Gross sales or billing: $10,200,000

Manufactures plastic cards for retail, grocery, financial, direct mail, and many others. Visa/MasterCard certified.

C.R.W. GRAPHICS
9100 Pennsauken Hwy
Pennsauken, NJ 08110-1206
Telephone: (856) 662-9111, (800) 820-3000, FAX: (856) 665-1789, E-Mail: service@crwgraphics.com, Web Site: www.crwgraphics.com
Pres: Mark Weiss

CALIFORNIA OFFSET PRINTERS
620 W Elk Ave
Glendale, CA 91204
Telephone: (818) 291-1100, (800) 280-6446, FAX: (818) 291-1190, E-Mail: info@copprints.com, Web Site: www.copprints.com
Pres: William Rittwage

CARAUSTAR ASHLAND CARTON PLANT
600 Union St
Ashland, OH 44805
Telephone: (419) 289-2666, FAX: (419) 281-5415, Web Site: www.caraustar.com
Chmn Bd: Daniel P. Casey

CARQUEVILLE GRAPHICS INC
Subs. of Consolidated Graphics
1536 Bourbon Pkwy
Streamwood, IL 60107-1808
Telephone: (630) 837-4500, FAX: (630) 837-4510, Web Site: www.carqueville.com
Pres & CEO: Robert Swindal

CATALOGS AMERICA
Div. of American Press LLC
1 American Pl
Gordonsville, VA 22942
Telephone: (540) 832-2253, (800) 283-4666, FAX: (540) 832-7253, E-Mail: dsayin@catalogsamerica.com, Web Site: www.catalogsamerica.com
VP, Sls: Dan Sayin

CENTER FOR BOOK ARTS
28 W 27th St (fl 3)
New York, NY 10001-6906
Telephone: (212) 481-0295, FAX: (866) 708-8994, E-Mail: info@centerforbookarts.org, Web Site: www.centerforbookarts.org
Exec Dir: Alexander Campos
External Affairs Mgr: James Copeland

CENVEO COLOR ART INC
101 Workman Ct
Eureka, MO 63025-1079
Telephone: (314) 966-2000, FAX: (314) 966-4725, E-Mail: scott.turner@cenveo.com, Web Site: www.colorart.com
Midwest Reg Mgr: Gary Lorenz

CENVEO INC
1 Canterbury Green
Stamford, CT 06901-2032
Telephone: (410) 633-4200, (800) 638-2850, FAX: (410) 633-1202, Web Site: www.cenveo.com
Pres: Robert G. Burton Sr.

CHAMPION PRINTING INC
4205 Dixie Hwy
Elsmere, KY 41018-1817
Telephone: (513) 541-1100, (800) 543-1957, FAX: (513) 541-9398, E-Mail: cpi@championprintinginc.com, Web Site: www.championprintinginc.com
Pres: Brian Sass

CHASE MEDIA GROUP
1520 Front St
Yorktown Heights, NY 10598
Telephone: (914) 962-3871, FAX: (914) 962-2040, Web Site: www.chasemultimedia.com
Pres & Publr: Carla Chase
Classified Adv Mgr: Lisa Thomas
Chase Press Acct Exec: Glen Seaman
Mktg Mgr: Leslie Mancuso
Direct Mail Acct Exec: Amy Bambace
Conducts Business: U.S.
Primary Market Served: Consumer
Catalog available online
Direct online sales
Founded: 1958

Advertising shoppers, serving 355,949 homes weekly with 28 editions throughout upper Westchester, Putnam, Dutchess & Fairfield counties.

CHICAGO DECAL CO
101 Tower Dr
Burr Ridge, IL 60527-5779
Telephone: (630) 850-2122, (888) DE-CALS R US, (888) 332-2577, FAX: (630) 850-7177, E-Mail: sales@chicagodecal.com, Web Site: www.chicagodecal.com
CEO: Fred Sasser
Pres: Frank Riggio

CLASSIC COLOR
2424 S 25th Ave
Broadview, IL 60155-3874
Telephone: (708) 484-0000, FAX: (708) 344-2233, Web Site: www.classic-color.com
Pres: Raymond E. Bell

CLEAN LISTS ASSOCIATES INC
122 E 42nd St (Suite 1700)
New York, NY 10168-0002
Telephone: (212) 551-1013, FAX: (212) 551-1107, E-Mail: cleanlists@mindspring.com

Pres: Tamara Beck

CLEAR VISIONS INC
Div. of Consolidated Graphics
121 Interpark Blvd (Suite 801)
San Antonio, TX 78216
Telephone: (210) 496-6006, FAX: (210) 496-9225, E-Mail: bidrequest@clearvisionsinc.com, Web Site: www.clearvisionsinc.com
Pres: Jim Potts

CLIENTS FIRST
84 Elm St Ste 1
Westfield, NJ 07090-2181
Telephone: (908) 232-1200, (800) 634-0040, FAX: (908) 233-8833, E-Mail: info@clientsfirst.com, Web Site: www.clientsfirst.com
Pres: Jeffrey Becker

JJ COLLINS' SONS INC
7125 Janes Ave (Suite 200)
Woodridge, IL 60517-2341
Telephone: (630) 960-2525, (800) 972-2296, FAX: (630) 960-7487, E-Mail: sales@jjcollins.com, Web Site: www.jjcollins.com
Exec VP: Thomas M. Collins Jr

COLOR Q INC
540 Richard St
Miamisburg, OH 45342
Telephone: (937) 866-4001, (800) 999-9818, FAX: (937) 866-4101, E-Mail: info@colorq.com, Web Site: www.colorqinc.com
Chmn Bd: Irwin Roth
Pres: Frank G. Klan
VP Sls: Rick Hunter
Conducts Business: U.S.
Employees: 30
Primary Market Served: Business & Consumer
Founded: 1963

Fine arts reproduction company.

COLORLITH CORP
321 S Main St Ste 301
Providence, RI 02903-7109
Telephone: (508) 837-6100, (800) 556-7171, FAX: (508) 677-4466, E-Mail: lep@colorlith.net, Web Site: www.colorlith.net
Pres: Larry Pierce

COMMUNIFX
1253 Freedom Rd (Suite 500)
Cranberry, PA 16066-4952
Telephone: (724) 935-8655, Web Site: www.communifax.com
CEO: Gene Ferruzza

THE DMA CONCORD LITHO
92 Old Turnpike Rd
Concord, NH 03301-7305
Telephone: (603) 225-3328, FAX: (603) 225-6120, E-Mail: print@concordlitho.com, Web Site: www.concordlitho.com
CEO: Peter Cook
Dir Mktg: Ali Westcott

THE DMA CONNECTICUT COLOR
8 Emerald St
Hingham, MA 02043-2402
Telephone: (781) 749-1005

CONSOLIDATED PRINTING INC
5050 Parkside Ave
Philadelphia, PA 19131-4714
Telephone: (215) 879-1400, (800) 347-0119, FAX: (215) 879-9130, Web Site: www.condrake.com
CEO: Michael George

CONTINENTAL PLASTIC CARD CO
1801 Green Rd Ste B
Pompano Beach, FL 33064-1052
Telephone: (954) 794-0040, (800) 543-0670, FAX: (954) 755-4493, E-Mail: info@continentalplasticcard.com, Web Site: www.continentalplasticcard.com
Pres & CEO: Gordon M Kramer

CONTINENTAL WEB PRESS INC
1430 Industrial Dr
Itasca, IL 60143-1848
Telephone: (630) 773-1903, FAX: (630) 773-1909, Web Site: www.continentalweb.com
Chmn & Pres: Kenneth W. Field

CREATIVE PRINTING SERVICES INC
1701 Birchwood Ave
Des Plaines, IL 60018-3005
Telephone: (847) 803-2800, (800) 932-2750, FAX: (847) 803-3299, E-Mail: info@creativepsi.com, Web Site: www.creativepsi.com
Pres: John Chesney
Mktg Dir: Jeff Kincaid

CREEL PRINTING OF CALIFORNIA
151 Kalmus Dr Ste H11
Costa Mesa, CA 92626-5971
Telephone: (714) 540-7005, FAX: (714) 979-1496
Gen Mgr: Jim Crowfoot

CROOK & GRANT LITHOGRAPHERS LTD
279 Yorkland Blvd
North York, ON, Canada M2J 1S5
Telephone: (416) 499-1011, FAX:
(416) 499-1821
Pres: Steve Crook

CRUSH CREATIVE
1919 Empire Ave
Burbank, CA 91504-3404
Telephone: (818) 842-1121, (800) 300-3686, FAX: (818) 840-0185, E-Mail:
john.davies@crushcreative.com, Web
Site: www.crushcreative.com
Sls Mgr: Charles Wherry

CURTIS 1000 INC
Subs. of American Business Products
Inc
1725 Breckinridge Pkwy (Suite 500)
Duluth, GA 30096-8994
Telephone: (678) 380-9095, (800) 766-1007, FAX: (770) 717-1890, E-Mail:
info@curtis1000.com, Web Site:
www.curtis1000.com
Bus Segment Mgr: Chad Davis
Pres: Steve Geiger

CYRIL-SCOTT CO
3950 State Route 37 E, PO Box 310
Lancaster, OH 43130
Telephone: (740) 654-2112, FAX:
(740) 654-7712, E-Mail: postoffice@
cyrilscott.com, Web Site: www.
cyrilscott.com
Pres: E.L. McClelland

DNP AMERICA INC
Div. of Dai Nippon Printing Co Ltd
335 Madison Ave (3rd fl)
New York, NY 10017
Telephone: (212) 503-1060, FAX:
(212) 679-0613
Pres: Yoshitoshi Kitajima

DANBURY PRINTING & LITHO INC
Subs. of Banta Corp
1 Prindle Ln
Danbury, CT 06811-5115
Telephone: (203) 792-5500, FAX:
(203) 744-5633
Pres: Jim Cize

THE DMA **DARWILL**
11900 W Roosevelt Rd
Hillside, IL 60162-2069
Telephone: (708) 236-4900, Web Site:
www.darwill.com

DATA-MATIC SYSTEMS CO
5545 Enterprise Dr
Lansing, MI 48911-4131
Telephone: (517) 882-4401, FAX:
(517) 882-1188, Web Site: www.
datamatic.net
Pres: Frank S. Kotulka

DATAMART DIRECT INC
279 Madsen Dr (Suite 101)
Bloomingdale, IL 60108-2692
Telephone: (630) 307-7100, FAX:
(630) 307-8059, E-Mail: info@
datamartdirect.com, Web Site: www.
datamartdirect.com
Pres: Rosemary Bussert
Mktg Mgr: Julie Leder

Marketing, variable digital printing,
pod, mailing & fullment.

DATAMATX INC
10430 Lakeridge Pkwy
Ashland, VA 23005
Telephone: (804) 550-2513, (800) 943-5240, FAX: (804) 550-2527, Web
Site: www.datamatx.com
Pres: Harry Stevens

DELUXE CORP
3680 Victoria St N
Shoreview, MN 55126-2906
Telephone: (651) 490-8000, FAX:
(651) 481-4163, Web Site: www.
deluxe.com
Chmn: Stephen P. Nachtsheim

DEPENDABLE BUSINESS FORMS
843 South Myrtle Ave
Villa Park, IL 60181-3353
Telephone: (630) 530-1734, FAX:
(630) 530-1789, E-Mail: j.zawaski@
comcast.net, Web Site: www.
dependablebusinessforms.com
Owner: John K. Zawaski

DES PLAINES PRINTING CO
Div. of Des Plaines Publishing Co
999 Commerce Ct
Buffalo Grove, IL 60089-2375
Telephone: (847) 824-1111, (800) 283-1776, FAX: (847) 824-1112, E-Mail:
custserv@dppc.com, Web Site:
www.dppc.com
CEO: Michael H. Ford

THE DICO GROUP INC
PO Box 2067
Toluca Lake, CA 91610-0067
Telephone: (323) 264-2000, FAX:
(323) 264-2600
Pres: Fern Haberman

Manufacturing of printing products.

DIGITAL VISION RESOURCES GROUP - DVRG
8238 Nieman Rd
Overland Park, KS 66214-1507
Telephone: (913) 754-8121, Web Site:
www.dvrg.com
Pres & CEO: Diane St Louis

THE DINGLEY PRESS
119 Lisbon St
Lisbon, ME 04250-6005
Telephone: (207) 353-4151, (800) 317-4574, FAX: (207) 353-9886, E-Mail:
webrequest@dingley.com, Web Site:
www.dingley.com
Chmn Bd: Christopher A. Pierce
CEO & Pres: Robert Moore

DISC GRAPHICS INC
Ten Gilpin Ave
Hauppauge, NY 11788
Telephone: (631) 234-1400, FAX:
(631) 234-1460, E-Mail: info@
discgraphics.com, Web Site: www.
discgraphics.com
Sr VP Mktg & New Bus: John Rebecchi

DOCKERY HOUSE PUBLISHING INC
906 Main St (Suite B)
Lindale, TX 75771
Telephone: (903) 882-6900, FAX:
(903) 882-6902, E-Mail: questions@
dockerypublishing.com, Web Site:
www.dockerypublishing.com
Pres: Rod Dockery

DOME PRINTING
340 Commerce Cir
Sacramento, CA 95815-4213
Telephone: (800) 343-3139
Partner: Robert Poole

DOMINO AMJET INC
1290 Lakeside Dr
Gurnee, IL 60031-2499
Telephone: (847) 244-2501, FAX:
(847) 244-2645, Web Site: www.
dominoamjet.com
Chmn: Peter Byrom

DONIHE GRAPHICS INC
Div. of Champion Industries Inc
766 Brookside Dr
Kingsport, TN 37660
Telephone: (423) 246-2800, (800) 251-0337, FAX: (423) 246-7025, Web
Site: www.champion-industries.com
Chmn & CEO: Marshall T. Reynolds

DRISCOLL LABEL CO INC
19 West St
East Hanover, NJ 07936-2822
Telephone: (973) 575-8492, FAX:
(800) 342-1195, (973) 575-8345,
E-Mail: info@driscolllabel.com, Web
Site: www.driscolllabel.com
Pres: John Raguso

DUPONT COLOR PROOFING
Dupont Photopolymers & Electronic
Materials
PO Box 80030
Wilmington, DE 19880-0030
Telephone: (800) 345-9999, FAX:
(302) 892-8030, Web Site: www.
dupont.com/proofing
CEO: Chad Holliday

DYNACOLOR GRAPHICS INC
Div. of Franklin Dodd Communications
950 SE 8th St
Hialeah, FL 33010
Telephone: (305) 625-5388, (800) 624-
8840, FAX: (305) 888-9903, E-Mail:
dmail@dynacolor.com, Web Site:
www.dynacolor.com
Pres: Donald M. Duncanson

DYNAMIC GRAPHICS
dba PIP Printing
7210 Zionsville Rd
Indianapolis, IN 46268-2165
Telephone: (317) 328-2555, Web Site:
www.dgiink.com
Primary Market Served: Consumer

E&D WEB PRINTING INC
1100A S Main St
Rochelle, IL 61068-3509
Telephone: (708) 656-6600, (800) 323-
5733, FAX: (708) 656-8390, E-Mail:
info@eanddweb.com, Web Site:
www.eanddweb.com
CEO: Christopher Love

EASTMAN KODAK CO
343 State St
Rochester, NY 14650-0001
Telephone: (585) 724-0251, (800) 698-
3324, FAX: (585) 724-1089, Web
Site: www.kodak.com
Chmn & CEO: Antonio M. Perez
Pres & COO: Philip J. Faraci
EDP: Pat McGrew
Exec VP & CFO: Frank S. Sklarsky
VP & CIO: Kim E. Van Gelder
Conducts Business: Worldwide
Employees: 40,000
Primary Market Served: Business &
Consumer
Catalog available online
Direct online sales
Advertising/Marketing Budget Related

to Direct Marketing: 51-75%
Founded: 1880
Gross sales or billing: $13,274,000
Manufacturer & marketer of imaging
products.

EDITORS PRESS INC
Subs. of Kelly Press Inc
1701 Cabin Branch Dr
Hyattsville, MD 20785-3820
Telephone: (301) 853-4900, (888) 853-
4900, FAX: (301) 853-4961, Web
Site: www.edpress.com
Pres: Michael Kelly

EMBASSY DIGITAL
Div. of Embassy Graphics Ltd
2880 Brighton Rd (Unit 1)
Oakville, ON, Canada L6H 5S3
Telephone: (905) 829-9969, (888) 477-
8629, FAX: (905) 829-9429, E-Mail:
info@embassydigital.com, Web Site:
www.embassydigital.com
Opers Dir: Chris Whalen
Conducts Business: U.S., Canada
Employees: 17
Primary Market Served: Business
Advertising/Marketing Budget Related
to Direct Marketing: 51-75%
Direct Marketing ad budget: $40,000
Direct Mail: 60%
Telephone: 40%
Founded: 1990
Gross sales or billing: $2,500,000

ESSEX PRINTING CO INC
14 Westminster Dr
Croton On Hudson, NY 10520-1008
Telephone: (212) 688-4720, (800) 443-
9113, FAX: (212) 308-2764, E-Mail:
essexptg@aol.com, Web Site: www.
essex-printing.com
Pres: Alvin B. Glaser

FCL GRAPHICS INC
4600 N Olcott Ave
Harwood Heights, IL 60656
Telephone: (708) 867-5500, (800) 274-
3380, FAX: (708) 867-7768
Pres: Frank Calabrese Sr

FEDERAL DIRECT
95 Main Ave Ste 2
Clifton, NJ 07014-1749
Telephone: (973) 667-9800, Web Site:
www.feddirect.com
Sr VP: Angela Stubbs

**FELCO PRINTING &
MAILING**
1910 Walnut St
Kansas City, MO 64108-1810

Telephone: (816) 421-5164, (800) 467-
0805, FAX: (816) 421-1607, E-Mail:
felco@felco.net, Web Site: www.
felco.net
Pres: Jill Long

FETTER LABEL
700 Locust Ln
Louisville, KY 40217-2997
Telephone: (502) 634-4771, (800) 234-
4771, FAX: (502) 634-3587, E-Mail:
info@fettergroup.com
Pres: James W. Hyder Jr.

FISHER GROUP INC
1250 N Center Point Rd
Hiawatha, IA 52233-1226
Telephone: (319) 393-5405, FAX:
(319) 393-2738, E-Mail: info@
fishergroup.com, Web Site: www.
fishergroup.com
Sr VP Sls & Mktg: Rick Sartorius

THE FLEXI GROUP INC
2675 Henry Hudson Pkwy, PO Box
316
Bronx, NY 10463
Telephone: (718) 543-8699, (800) 665-
8053, FAX: (718) 543-8609, E-Mail:
info@flexigroup.com, Web Site:
www.flexigroup.com
Gen Mgr: Howard Bromberg

FOILMANIA
9730 NW 25th St
Miami, FL 33172-2201
Telephone: (305) 854-8525, Web Site:
www.foilmania.com
Pres: Luis Soublette

FOLDER FACTORY INC
Div. of Gentile Brothers Screen Printing
5421 Main St (Suite 300)
Mount Jackson, VA 22843-9537
Telephone: (540) 984-8852, (800) 296-
4321, FAX: (540) 477-9677, E-Mail:
webmaster@folders.com, Web Site:
www.folders.com
VP: Dave Gentile

FOREMOST PACKAGING
9120 Center Ave
Rancho Cucamonga, CA 91730-5130
Telephone: (909) 941-1713, FAX:
(909) 941-4092, E-Mail: foremost.
mail@verizon.net, Web Site: www.
foremostpackaging.com
Pres: John Painter

FORMSOURCE
170 Summer St
Lewiston, ME 04240-7532

Telephone: (207) 782-3311, (877) 782-3311, FAX: (207) 783-0157, E-Mail: service@formsource1.com, Web Site: www.formsource1.com
Pres: Mark Hartnett
Design & Mktg: Jim Davis

THE DMA 48HOURPRINT.COM
33 Farnsworth St (Suite 2)
Boston, MA 02210-1210
Telephone: (800) 844-0599, Web Site: www.48hourprint.com
VP Mktg & Bus Devel: Peter Dammann

STEPHEN FOSSLER CO INC
1600 E Touhy Ave
Des Plaines, IL 60018-3607
Telephone: (800) 762-0030, FAX: (800) 424-9292, E-Mail: customerservice@fossler.com, Web Site: sfc.stephen-fossler.com
Pres: John Trimberger

FOX RIVER PAPER CO
Div. of Neenah Paper
600 S Vulcan St
Appleton, WI 54915
Telephone: (920) 733-7341, (800) 558-8327, FAX: (920) 733-2975, E-Mail: info@foxriverpaper.com, Web Site: www.foxriverpaper.com
Pres & CEO: Jeff Miller
Mktg Project Coord: Mindy Wipesyenski

FOXFIRE PRINTING & PACKAGING INC
750 Dawson Dr
Newark, DE 19713-3414
Telephone: (302) 368-9466, (800) 497-0516, FAX: (302) 368-9219, E-Mail: info@foxfiresigns.com, Web Site: www.foxfiresigns.com
Mgr: Anthony Cosmi

THE FOXON CO
235 W Park St
Providence, RI 02908-4881
Telephone: (401) 421-2386, (800) 556-6943, FAX: (401) 421-8996
Pres & Owner: William D. Ewing

FRANCHISE SERVICES INC
26772 Plaza
Mission Viejo, CA 92691
Telephone: (949) 282-3800, Web Site: www.pip.com
VP Strategic Devel: Kelly Kimberlin

FRY COMMUNCIATIONS INC
800 W Church Rd
Mechanicsburg, PA 17055-3198
Telephone: (717) 766-0211

Dir Postal Affairs/Distr: Glenn Solbenberger

THE GARVEY GROUP
aka Ed Garvey & Co
7400 N Lehigh Ave
Niles, IL 60714
Telephone: (847) 647-1900, FAX: (847) 647-6550, E-Mail: info@thegarveygroup.com, Web Site: www.thegarveygroup.com
Pres: Ed J. Garvey Jr.

GENERAL PRINTERS
Div. of Consolidated Graphics Canada Ltd
1001 Ritson Rd S
Oshawa, ON, Canada L1H 4G5
Telephone: (416) 490-6000, (888) 718-6600, FAX: (905) 436-0813, E-Mail: thornley@generalprinters.com, Web Site: www.generalprinters.com
VP Sls: Fred Thornley

GOSS INTERNATIONAL
121 Technology Dr
Durham, NH 03824-4716
Telephone: (603) 749-6600, FAX: (603) 750-6860, Web Site: www.gossinternational.com
Mktg Dir: Greg Norris

STEPHEN GOULD PAPER CO INC
35 S Jefferson Rd
Whippany, NJ 07981
Telephone: (973) 428-1500, FAX: (973) 428-5274, Web Site: www.stephengould.com
Pres: Michael Golden

GRAFEK DIRECT
Div. of Matt Industries
PO Box 11500, Dupli Park Dr
Syracuse, NY 13218-1500
Telephone: (315) 422-4732, (800) 724-2477, FAX: (315) 425-9624, E-Mail: grafek@duplionline.com, Web Site: www.duplionline.com
Pres: Kemper J. Matt

GRANT'S MAILING SERVICES INC
940 Matheson Blvd E
Mississauga, ON, Canada L4W 2R8
Telephone: (905) 624-9082, FAX: (905) 624-0007, E-Mail: info@grants-mailing.ca, Web Site: www.grants-mailing.ca
Pres: Norman Keyes

GRAPHIC ARTS CENTER
2514 National Dr
Garland, TX 75041-2329
Telephone: (972) 271-0591, (800) 865-7086, FAX: (972) 271-8392
Admin Asst: Kimberly Radcliff

GRAPHIC ARTS INFORMATION NETWORK (GAIN)
200 Deer Run Rd
Sewickley, PA 15143-2324
Telephone: (412) 741-6860, (800) 910-4283, FAX: (412) 741-2311, E-Mail: printing@printing.org, Web Site: www.gain.net
Mktg Mgr: Rebecca Blunt

GRAPHIC COMMUNICATIONS CENTER
3001 E Venture Dr, Box 357
Appleton, WI 54911-8309
Telephone: (920) 733-4483, (800) 422-3696, FAX: (920) 733-1700
Pres: Harry Kachain

GRAPHICS INTERNATIONAL INC
3883 Turtle Creek Blvd (Apt 1406)
Dallas, TX 75219-4430
Telephone: (214) 352-7565, FAX: (214) 528-0114
Pres: L. Marcus Dean

THE GRAY PRINTING CO
401 E North St
Fostoria, OH 44830-2828
Telephone: (419) 435-6638
Pres & Treas: Robert A. Gray

GREAT LAKES INTEGRATED
4005 Clark Ave
Cleveland, OH 44109-1186
Telephone: (216) 651-1500, (800) 745-4846, FAX: (216) 651-8311, E-Mail: bbemer@glintegrated.com, Web Site: www.gll.com
Chmn Bd, Pres & CEO: James R. Schultz

GREYSTONE GRAPHICS
4010 Washington St Ste 100
Kansas City, MO 64111-2614
Telephone: (913) 342-1393, (800) 458-7407, FAX: (913) 621-4856, E-Mail: info@greystonegraphics.com, Web Site: www.greystonegraphics.com
Chmn Bd: Joel D. Vile

HAGADONE PRINTING CO
274 Pu'uhale Rd
Honolulu, HI 96819-2234

Telephone: (808) 847-5310, (800) 491-4888, FAX: (808) 841-0094, E-Mail: sales@hagadoneprinting.com, Web Site: www.hagadoneprinting.com
Pres: Erwin Hudelist

HANNECKE DISPLAY SYSTEMS INC
91 Fulton St (#3)
Boonton, NJ 07005
Telephone: (973) 335-0434, FAX: (973) 335-1274, E-Mail: info.usa@hannecke.com, Web Site: www.hannecke.com
Sls Mgr: Hans Klein

HATTERAS ᵀᴴᴱ ᴰᴹᴬ
56 Park Rd
Tinton Falls, NJ 07724-9715
Telephone: (732) 223-9888, Web Site: www.hatterascpc.com
VP Mailing & Data Svcs: Jim Figuccio

HEART THOUGHTS INC
1480 N Stratford Ln
Wichita, KS 67206-1165
Telephone: (316) 688-5781, (800) 524-2229, FAX: (316) 687-2846, Web Site: www.heart-thoughts.com
Pres: Grant Goodvin

HEAVY ROTATION
3720 N Fratney St (Studios 3F)
Milwaukee, WI 53212
Telephone: (414) 384-5200, (800) 886-4759, FAX: (414) 434-9318, E-Mail: info@holoubekstudios.com, Web Site: heavytees.com
Pres: Brian Holoubek

HESS PRINT SOLUTIONS
3765 Sunnybrook Rd
Kent, OH 44240
Telephone: (330) 677-3353, FAX: (330) 677-8256, E-Mail: sshowerman@hessprintsolutions.com, Web Site: www.thepressofohio.com
VP Sls: Jim Fetherston
Pres: Jim Kersten
Mktg Mgr: Sandy Showerman

HI-C PRODUCTION
Nine Tottenham Pl
New Hyde Park, NY 11040-3516
Telephone: (516) 746-2142, FAX: (516) 294-1964, E-Mail: haponte435@aol.com
Pres: Hiram Aponte Jr

HI-TECH MARKETING SOLUTIONS ᵀᴴᴱ ᴰᴹᴬ
3410 NE 6th Ter
Pompano Beach, FL 33064
Telephone: (954) 784-3830, Web Site: www.coastmailers.com
Primary Market Served: Business & Consumer

THE HICKORY PRINTING GROUP
725 Reese Dr SW
Conover, NC 28613
Telephone: (828) 465-3431, (800) 442-5679, FAX: (828) 465-2517, E-Mail: gglisan@hickoryprinting.com, Web Site: www.hickoryprinting.com
Pres: George Glisan

HUBCAST INC ᵀᴴᴱ ᴰᴹᴬ
500 Edgewater Dr (Suite 568)
Wakefield, MA 01880-6222
Telephone: (781) 221-7200, Web Site: www.hubeast.com
Mktg Mgr: Melissa Albert

IPD PRINTING & DISTRIBUTING INC
Graphic Industries Inc
5800 Peachtree Rd
Atlanta, GA 30341-2302
Telephone: (770) 458-6351, FAX: (770) 454-6236
Pres: George Gribble

IBSDIRECT ᵀᴴᴱ ᴰᴹᴬ
431 Yerkes Rd
King of Prussia, PA 19406-3556
Telephone: (610) 265-8210, Web Site: www.ibsdm.com
VP Client Svcs: Donna Mastrangelo

IMAGE CHECKS
PO Box 2
Bel Air, MD 21014
Telephone: (800) 562-8768, FAX: (410) 676-8269, Web Site: www.imagechecks.com
Pres: Jim Browning

IMPRESSIONS UNLIMITED INC
PO Box 1349
Deerfield, IL 60015-6005
Telephone: (630) 705-6464, FAX: (630) 705-1598, E-Mail: info@impressionsunltd.com, Web Site: www.impressionsunltd.com
Pres: Ron Gion

IMTEK
2075 High Hill Rd
Bridgeport, NJ 08014

Telephone: (800) 346-8354, FAX: (856) 467-8967, Web Site: www.imtek.com
Pres: David Lesniak

INDUSTRIAL ARTS & GRAPHICS
22714 Melrose Farm Ln
Middleburg, VA 20117
Telephone: (540) 687-6770, (866) 324-7746, FAX: (215) 765-6625
Pres: George Drexel

INDUSTRIAL PRINTING CO INC
1635 Coining Dr
Toledo, OH 43612
Telephone: (419) 476-9101, (800) 472-9101, FAX: (800) 293-5225, E-Mail: steve.gross@cenveo.com, Web Site: www.ipcohio.com
Pres: Chuck Delaney

THE INKPEN
811 SW 113th Ave
Pembroke Pines, FL 33025-3419
Telephone: (954) 450-9220, FAX: (305) 624-5126, Web Site: www.theinkpen.com
Pres: Jerry Mayer

INLAND PRESS
Subs. of Detroit Legal News
2001 W Lafayette Blvd
Detroit, MI 48216
Telephone: (313) 961-6000, FAX: (313) 961-7817, Web Site: www.inlandpress.com
Pres: Bradley L. Thompson

INNOVATION PRINTING
11601 Caroline Rd
Philadelphia, PA 19154
Telephone: (215) 969-4600, FAX: (215) 464-7664
CEO: Dave Carpenter

INNOVATIVE PLASTIC PRINTING CORP
534 Congress Cir N
Roselle, IL 60172
Telephone: (630) 665-0003, (800) 238-7686, FAX: (630) 665-7752, Web Site: www.innov8cards.com
VP Sls & Mktg: Lou Darby

INTEGRATED PRINT & GRAPHICS
645 Stevenson Rd
South Elgin, IL 60177-1134
Telephone: (847) 695-6777, Web Site: www.ipandginc.com
Sls Mgr: Douglas Marecek

THE DMA INTELLIGENCER PRINTING CO
330 Eden Rd
Lancaster, PA 17601-4218
Telephone: (717) 291-3100, (800) 233-0107, FAX: (717) 569-2643, Web Site: www.intellprinting.com
VP: Kevin Franz
Mktg & Bus Devel Mgr: Todd Foster

INTERNATIONAL FULFILLMENT INC
2800 Black Lake Pl (Suite D)
Philadelphia, PA 19154-1024
Telephone: (215) 638-8060, (800) 962-8080, FAX: (215) 638-8091, Web Site: www.ifionline.net
Pres: James Bowman

INTERPRINT WEB & SHEETFED
Subs. of Morten Enterprises
12350 US Hwy 19 N
Clearwater, FL 33764
Telephone: (727) 531-8957, (800) 749-5152, FAX: (727) 536-0647, E-Mail: customerservice@printerusa.com, Web Site: www.printerusa.com
Pres: James E. Morten

INTERSTATE PRINTING CO
2002N 16th St
Omaha, NE 68110
Telephone: (402) 341-8028, (800) 788-4177, FAX: (402) 341-6168, E-Mail: printer@interstateprinting.com, Web Site: www.interstateprinting.com
Pres: Eugene W. Peter
Admin Asst: Karen Sasinski

INVITATION HOTLINE
68 Hawkins Rd
Manalapan, NJ 07726
Telephone: (732) 536-9115, (800) 800-4355, FAX: (732) 972-4875, E-Mail: info@invitationhotline.com, Web Site: www.invitationhotline.com

JD GRAPHIC CO
1101 Arthur Ave
Elk Grove Village, IL 60707
Telephone: (847) 364-4000, (888) 364-6216, FAX: (847) 364-4024, E-Mail: jim@jdgraphic.com, Web Site: www.jdgraphic.com
Pres: James DeBlasio Jr

THE DMA JAPS-OLSON CO
7500 Excelsior Blvd
Saint Louis Park, MN 55426-4519
Telephone: (952) 932-9393, (800) 548-2897, FAX: (612) 912-1900, Web Site: www.japsolson.com
CEO: Michael Beddor

VP Sls & Mktg: Debbie Roth

JERSEY PRINTING ASSOCIATES INC
153 First Ave, PO Box 355
Atlantic Highlands, NJ 07716-0355
Telephone: (732) 872-9654, FAX: (732) 872-9309, E-Mail: sales@jerseyprinting.com, Web Site: www.jerseyprinting.com

JET LITHOCOLOR INC
1500 Centre Cir
Downers Grove, IL 60515
Telephone: (630) 932-9000, (800) 932-1JET, (800) 932-1538, FAX: (630) 932-9101, E-Mail: sales@jetlitho.com, Web Site: www.jetlitho.com
Owner: Philip S. Dominick
Pres: George Bogdanovic

JOHN HENRY PACKAGING
5800 W Grand River Ave
Lansing, MI 48906-9111
Telephone: (707) 778-1250, (800) 327-5997, FAX: (707) 762-1253, Web Site: www.jhpackaging.com
Mktg Mgr: Dan Welty

KEYSTONE PROMOTIONS INC
63 Vacari Way
Little Egg Harbor, NJ 08087-4029
Telephone: (908) 688-6713, FAX: (908) 688-6645, E-Mail: mgunther_kpi@msn.com, Web Site: www.keystonepromotionsinc.com

KING PRINTING SOLUTIONS
531 Straight Creek Rd.
New Tazewell, TN 37825
Telephone: (423) 626-7700, (800) 251-9236, FAX: (423) 526-5225, E-Mail: sales@kbfcorp.com, Web Site: www.kbfcorp.com
Pres: Jim King
Founded: 1972

KINGERY PRINTING CO
3012 S Banker, Box 727
Effingham, IL 62401-0727
Telephone: (217) 347-5151, FAX: (217) 540-5400, Web Site: www.kingeryprinting.com
Pres: John F. Kingery

KODAK GRAPHIC COMMUNICATIONS
343 State St
Rochester, NY 14650-0002
Telephone: (800) 944-6171, Web Site: www.kpgraphics.com
CMO: Jeff Hayzlett

KREBER GRAPHICS INC
2580 Westbelt Dr
Columbus, OH 43228
Telephone: (614) 529-5701, (800) 777-3501, FAX: (614) 777-4890, E-Mail: info@kreber.com, Web Site: www.kreber.com
Pres & CEO: Frank Kreber

KWIK-FILE
619 N Commerce St
Sheboygan, WI 53081-3901
Telephone: (763) 572-1980, (800) 822-8037, FAX: (763) 572-0168, Web Site: www.mayline.com
VP Sls: Todd Nelson

L.P. THEBAULT CO.
Div. of EarthColor Inc.
249 Pomeroy Rd, PO Box 169
Parsippany, NJ 07054-3727
Telephone: (973) 884-1300, FAX: (973) 952-8296, Web Site: www.earthcolor.com
Chmn: Brian Thebault
CEO EarthColor: Robert Kashan

LABELS WEST INC
17629 130th Ave NE
Woodinville, WA 98072
Telephone: (425) 486-8484, (800) 540-3009, FAX: (425) 486-8488, Web Site: www.labelswest.com
Dir Sls & Mktg: Lance Wilson

LAKE COUNTY PRESS INC
PO Box 9209
Waukegan, IL 60079-9209
Telephone: (847) 336-4333
CEO & Pres: Ralph Johnson
Primary Market Served: Business & Consumer

LANCER LABEL
Div. of Mail-Well
301 S 74th St
Omaha, NE 68114
Telephone: (402) 390-9119, (800) 228-7074, FAX: (800) 344-9456, E-Mail: info@lancerlabel.com, Web Site: www.lancerlabel.com
Chmn Bd: Nancy Riley Bush

LASERMAX ROLL SYSTEMS
4 Suburban Park Dr.
Billerica, MA 01821-3904
Telephone: (978) 608-0500, FAX: (978) 608-0558, Web Site: www.lasermaxroll.com
Xerox Alliance Progs Dir: Pete Miller

THE DMA LEHIGH DIRECT
1900 S 25th Ave
Broadview, IL 60155-2800

Telephone: (708) 681-3612, FAX:
(708) 681-4694, Web Site: www.
lehighdirect.com
Pres: Paul Palmer

LINGUISTIC SYSTEMS INC
201 Broadway
Cambridge, MA 02139
Telephone: (877) 654-5006, FAX:
(617) 528-7491, E-Mail: info@
linguist.com, Web Site: www.
linguist.com
Pres: Martin Roberts
Mktg Dir: Bill Lawson
Founded: 1967

LITHO-WEB INC
24 Huddersfield Rd
Etobicoke, ON, Canada M9W 5Z6
Telephone: (416) 674-8899, (800) 490-
6688, FAX: (416) 674-8537, E-Mail:
inquiry@lithoweb.ca, Web Site:
www.lithoweb.ca
Pres: Barry Moyer

LONE STAR WEB INC
1412 Main St Ste 2400
Dallas, TX 75202-4011
Telephone: (214) 443-2200, FAX:
(214) 630-4364, E-Mail: jerry@
lonestarweb.com, Web Site: www.
lonestarweb.com
Pres & CEO: Michael R. Hansen
VP, Client Svcs: Rena Mainprice

MAR GRAPHICS
523 S Meyer Ave
Valmeyer, IL 62295-3120
Telephone: (800) 851-4460, Web Site:
www.margraphics.com
Sls & Mktg: Brian Coats

MACORP PRINT GROUP
261 Schoolhouse Rd (Suite 8)
Souderton, PA 18964
Telephone: (215) 703-0500, (877)
4MACORP, FAX: (215) 703-0501,
E-Mail: info@4macorp.com, Web
Site: www.4macorp.com
Pres: John P. Magagna

MAGJAK PRINTING CORP
114 Pearl St
Port Chester, NY 10573-4663
Telephone: (914) 939-8800, Web Site:
www.magjak.com
CEO: Bruce Browning

MAILBLAZER
2020 S Eastwood Ave
Santa Ana, CA 92705-5208
Telephone: (714) 662-5396, Web Site:
www.mailblazer.com
Sls & Mktg Mgr: Ted Robison

THE MAINE CONNECTION
246 Deering Ave, Univ of Maine
School of Law
Portland, ME 04102-2837
Telephone: (207) 780-4355, FAX:
(207) 780-4239, E-Mail: ghopkins@
midcoast.com
Pres: George E. Hopkins Jr.

MANDEL CO
PO Box 12124
Milwaukee, WI 53212-0124
Telephone: (414) 271-6970, (800) 888-
6970, FAX: (414) 271-1254, E-Mail:
rick.mandel@mandelcompany.com,
Web Site: www.mandelcompany.com
Pres: Rick Mandel

MARKING SPECIALISTS GROUP
1000 Asbury Dr (Suite 2)
Buffalo Grove, IL 60089-4551
Telephone: (847) 793-8100, (800) 678-
8073, FAX: (847) 793-8109, E-Mail:
info@marking-specialists.com, Web
Site: www.marking-specialists.com
Pres: Cliff Modlin

MARVIN ENVELOPE & PAPER CO
288 W Palatine Rd
Wheeling, IL 60090-5815
Telephone: (773) 489-3300, (800) 227-
0011, FAX: (773) 489-4783, E-Mail:
marvinenvelope@aol.com
Pres: Jose Garza

THE DMA MAYS MISSION FOR THE HANDICAPPED INC
604 Colonial Dr
Heber Springs, AR 72543-3425
Telephone: (501) 362-7526, (888) 503-
7955, FAX: (501) 362-7529, E-Mail:
sniehaus@maysmission.org, Web
Site: www.maysmission.org
Pres & Exec Dir: Sherry Niehaus
Prodn Mgr: Roland Stroud
DP Supvr: Brenda Johnson
Conducts Business: U.S.
Employees: 30
Primary Market Served: Business &
Consumer
Advertising/Marketing Budget Related
to Direct Marketing: 0-25%
Founded: 1972

Web printing, direct mail services, data
processing services.

MCARDLE PRINTING CO INC
Subs. of Bureau of National Affairs Inc
800 Commerce Dr
Upper Marlboro, MD 20774-8792

Telephone: (301) 390-8500, FAX:
(301) 390-8052, Web Site: www.
mcardleprinting.com
Pres: Jack Jenc

MCCORMICK-ARMSTRONG CO INC
1501 E Douglas
Wichita, KS 67211-1608
Telephone: (316) 264-1363, (800) 733-
1363, FAX: (316) 263-4511, E-Mail:
sales@mccormickarmstrong.com,
Web Site: www.
mccormickarmstrong.com
Pres: Jacob W. Shaffer

THE DMA MCCOURT LABEL CO
20 Egbert Ln
Lewis Run, PA 16738-3802
Telephone: (800) 458-2390, Web Site:
www..mccourtlabel.com
Primary Market Served: Consumer

MEDIA LINK COMMUNICATIONS
Div. of Robert Rose Enterprises
321 E 22nd St (Suite 3K)
New York, NY 10010
Telephone: (212) 674-8843, FAX:
(212) 260-8489, E-Mail: mlinkcom@
aol.com, Web Site: www.getprinted.
com
Pres: Robert Rose

MEDIA PRINTING CORP
4300 N Powerline Rd
Pompano Beach, FL 33073-3071
Telephone: (954) 984-7300, FAX:
(954) 888-8542
Pres: James Grubman

MEDIATREE
Div. of Telenations Inc
77 E Haley Rd
Parsippany, NJ 07054
Telephone: (800) 475-8703, FAX:
(973) 781-1071, E-Mail: sales@
mediatreegroup.com, Web Site:
www.mediatreegroup.com
Dir & Sr VP Mktg: Rob Watson
Pres: Bill Grassmyer
Conducts Business: U.S.
Employees: 15
Primary Market Served: Business
Catalog available online
Advertising/Marketing Budget Related
to Direct Marketing: 0-25%
Founded: 1996
Gross sales or billing: $10,000,000

Promotional stored value content such
as music downloads, ringtones &
phone time. Plastic printing facility
printing on premises.

MEDICAL ARTS PRESS
8500 Wyoming Ave N
Minneapolis, MN 55445-1825
Telephone: (763) 493-7300, (800) 328-
2179, FAX: (800) 328-0023, Web
Site: www.medicalartspress.com

THE DMA **MEMBERSHIP CARDS ONLY
LLC**
8000 Towers Crescent Dr (Suite 1350)
Vienna, VA 22182-6219
Telephone: (800) 772-2737, Web Site:
wwww.membershipcards.com
Pres: Richard Faust

**MERIKS MAYAN
CHOCOLATERIE**
142 36 St NE
Washington, DC 20019-2601
Telephone: (787) 721-0000
Pres: Paul Patino
Pres: Paul Pampano

THE DMA **METROPOLITAN GRAPHIC
ARTS**
930 Turret Ct
Mundelein, IL 60060-3821
Telephone: (847) 566-9502, FAX:
(847) 566-9519, Web Site: www.
mgaprinting.com
CEO: Joseph Szymanski
VP: Greg Szymanski

**MIDLAND LITHOGRAPHING
CO**
1841 Vernon St
North Kansas City, MO 64116-4430
Telephone: (816) 842-2224, FAX:
(816) 842-4530
Pres: James Rosenberg
Reg Mgr: Tammy Budd

MILLER PRINTING
Div. of Graphic Paper Products Corp
581 W Leffel Ln
Springfield, OH 45501
Telephone: (937) 325-5503, (877) 325-
5503, FAX: (937) 324-5697, Web
Site: www.miller-printing.com
CEO: Jeanne Lampe

**MINUTEMAN PRESS
(WESTCHESTER)**
Div. of Cronin Enterprises, Inc
120 E Main St
Elmsford, NY 10523
Telephone: (914) 347-5050, FAX:
(914) 347-2563, E-Mail: gcronin@
minutemanpress.com, Web Site:
www.westchester.minutemanpress.
com
Owner: Gary Cronin

MITCHELL GRAPHICS INC
2363 Mitchell Park Dr
Petoskey, MI 49770
Telephone: (231) 347-4635, (800) 583-
9401, FAX: (231) 347-9255, E-Mail:
info@mitchellgraphics.com, Web
Site: www.mitchellgraphics.com
Pres: Gary Fedus

MODERN GRAPHIC ARTS
Subs. of Sandy Alexander Inc
1527 102nd Ave N
Saint Petersburg, FL 33716-5049
Telephone: (727) 579-1527, FAX:
(727) 579-1528
Opers Mgr: Sal Campanaro

THE DMA **MODERN INFORMATION
SERVICES INC**
dba Sir Speedy
313-B S Center St
Statesville, NC 28677-5879
Telephone: (704) 872-1020
Primary Market Served: Consumer

THE MONACO GROUP
1011 S Linwood Ave
Santa Ana, CA 92705-4323
Telephone: (714) 505-5180, FAX:
(714) 505-5187, E-Mail: service@
monaco.com, Web Site: www.
monacogroup.com
Pres: Vince Monaco

MORRISON PRINTING CO
1039 Walters Dr
Morristown, TN 37814-6133
Telephone: (423) 586-4812, (800) 251-
0975, FAX: (423) 586-0322, E-Mail:
info@morrcom.com, Web Site:
www.morrcom.com
Pres & CEO: Maudie Briggs

**MULTI-MEDIA PUBLISHING
& PACKAGING INC**
14621 Titus St Ste A
Panorama City, CA 91402-4904
Telephone: (818) 341-7484, (800) 982-
8138, FAX: (818) 341-2807, E-Mail:
sales@mmppinc.com, Web Site:
www.mmppinc.com
Pres: Luke Stefanki

MWM DEXTER INC
107 Washington Ave
Aurora, MO 65605
Telephone: (888) 833-1242, FAX:
(417) 841-1040, Web Site: www.
mwmdexter.com
Chmn & Pres: John W. Burkhart
Dir Mktg: Kim Lehere
Mktg Dir: Gary Bennett

THE DMA **NAHAN PRINTING INC**
7000 Saukview Dr
Saint Cloud, MN 56303-0814
Telephone: (320) 251-7611, Web Site:
www.nahan.com
Mktg Specialist: Laura Cedeno
Corp Svcs: Tracy Hansen

NATIONAL GRAPHICS INC
248 Branford Rd (Suite One)
North Branford, CT 06471-1303
Telephone: (203) 481-2351, FAX:
(203) 483-0256

**NATIONAL MAIL GRAPHICS
CORP**
300 Old Mill Ln
Exton, PA 19341-2582
Telephone: (610) 524-1600, FAX:
(610) 524-7638, E-Mail: jsikorski@
nmgcorp.com, Web Site: www.
nmgcorp.com
Pres: John Sikorski

NATIONAL MAIL-IT INC
9151 Youree Dr
Shreveport, LA 71115-3303
Telephone: (318) 683-0093, Web Site:
www.nationalmailit.com
Pres: Michael Riordan

**NATIONWIDE GRAPHIC/
PREMIER PRINT
ORGANIZATIONS**
2500 W Loop S (Suite 500)
Houston, TX 77027-4521
Telephone: (713) 961-4700, Web Site:
www.nationwidegraphics.com
Corp Mktg Mgr: Bill Cline

THE DMA **NAYLOR INC**
5950 NW 1st Pl
Gainesville, FL 32607-6018
Telephone: (404) 739-7280, Web Site:
www.naylorinc.com

NEIBAUER PRESS
20 Industrial Dr
Warminster, PA 18974-1433
Telephone: (215) 322-6200, (800) 322-
6203, FAX: (215) 322-2495, E-Mail:
sales@neibauer.com, Web Site:
www.neibauer.com
Pres: Nathan Neibauer
VP: Ruth Neibauer

**NEWCOMB MARKETING
SOLUTIONS**
605 E 9th St
Michigan City, IN 46360-3651
Telephone: (219) 874-3201, (800) 921-
1221, FAX: (219) 874-8156, Web
Site: www.newcombsolutions.com

Pres: Kelly Newcomb

O'BRIEN DOCUMENT SOLUTIONS
1273 Humbracht Cir
Bartlett, IL 60103-1606
Telephone: (630) 830-0990, FAX:
(630) 830-0062, E-Mail:
obrien_info@obinc.com, Web Site:
www.obinc.com
Owner: Kevin O'Brien

OFFICIAL OFFSET CORP
8600 New Horizons Blvd
Amityville, NY 11701-1183
Telephone: (631) 957-8500
VP: Frank Paulino

THE OFFSET HOUSE INC
89 Sand Hill Rd
Essex Junction, VT 05452-3909
Telephone: (802) 878-4440, FAX:
(802) 879-4865, Web Site: www.
offsethouse.com
Pres: John McGrath
VP: Kevin McGrath

OLYMPAK
6010 Earle Brown Dr (Suite 100)
Minneapolis, MN 55430-4516
Telephone: (763) 504-5400, (800) 967-
1705, FAX: (763) 504-5401, E-Mail:
jgibas@olympak.com, Web Site:
www.olympak.com
Sls Mgr: Jeff Gibas

OMNI PRINT INC
9700 Philadelphia Ct
Lanham, MD 20706-4405
Telephone: (301) 731-7000, FAX:
(301) 731-7001, E-Mail: info@
omniprint.net, Web Site: www.
omniprint.net
Chmn & CEO: Kenneth A. Kaufman

O'NEIL DATA SYSTEMS INC
12655 Beatrice St
Los Angeles, CA 90066-7300
Telephone: (310) 448-6400, Web Site:
www.oneildata.com
Gen Mgr: James Lucanish

OUTLOOK GROUP CORP
1180 American Dr
Neenah, WI 54956-1306
Telephone: (920) 722-2333, FAX:
(920) 727-8529, E-Mail: path@
outlookgroup.com, Web Site: www.
outlookgroup.com
Mktg Dir: David Schanke

PCI PAPER CONVERSIONS INC
6761 Thompson Rd N
Syracuse, NY 13211-2119
Telephone: (315) 437-1641, FAX:
(315) 437-3634, E-Mail: sales@
padmaker.com, Web Site: www.
padmaker.com
Mktg Dir: Charles Michaud

PGI COMPANIES INC
220 S 6th St Ste 2125
Minneapolis, MN 55402-4517
Telephone: (952) 933-5745, FAX:
(952) 933-5864, E-Mail: ddallum@
pgicompanies.com, Web Site: www.
pgicompanies.com
VP: Jim Ripka
Pres: Dan Dallum

THE DMA PPS - PACKAGING PRINTING SPECIALISTS
3915 Stern Ave
Saint Charles, IL 60174-5441
Telephone: (630) 513-8060, (877) 573-
8060, FAX: (630) 513-8062, E-Mail:
pps@ppsofil.com, Web Site: www.
PPSofIL.com
Gen Mgr: Ken Russo
Sls: Debbie Ingram
Sls: Mark Johnson
Sls: Maureen Hernandez
Conducts Business: U.S., Canada
Employees: 21
Primary Market Served: Business
Advertising/Marketing Budget Related
to Direct Marketing: 51-75%
Direct Marketing ad budget: $100,000
Direct Mail: 75%
Telephone: 25%
Founded: 1983
Gross sales or billing: $7,000,000

Producers of membership cards, coupons, inserts, scratch off games, peel n
reveal games, 3D specialty graphics

PRECISE MEDIA SERVICES INC
5678 E Concours Ave
Ontario, CA 91764
Telephone: (908) 481-3305, (800) 444-
4217, FAX: (908) 481-3405, Web
Site: www.precisemedia.com
Pres: Robert Miller

PSA
485 E Half Day Rd Ste 500
Buffalo Grove, IL 60089-8808
Telephone: (847) 478-6000, Web Site:
www.psa.com

PENINSULAR PRINTING OF DAYTONA BEACH INC
3 Timberline Trl (#A)
Ormond Beach, FL 32174-4923
Telephone: (386) 274-4837, FAX:
(386) 274-5023, E-Mail: penprint@
bellsouth.net, Web Site: www.
peninsularprinting.com
Pres: William Maguire

PENN INDUSTRIES INC
PO Box 3067
Cerritos, CA 90703-3067
Telephone: (562) 926-0455, FAX:
(562) 926-8955, Web Site: www.
pennlitho.com
Pres: Charles Stay
CEO: Jeffrey Alkazian

PERFECT PLASTIC PRINTING CORP
311 Kautz Rd Ste 4
Saint Charles, IL 60174-5304
Telephone: (630) 584-1600, FAX:
(630) 584-0648, E-Mail: ppp@
perfectplastic.com, Web Site: www.
perfectplastic.com
VP Sls: Dave Moser
VP Mktg: Matt Smoczynski

PERFORMANCE PRINTING/ OPTIGRAPHICS
Div. of Pinnacle Brands Inc
2929 N Stemmons Fwy
Dallas, TX 75247-6102
Telephone: (214) 665-1038, (800) 662-
2813, FAX: (214) 665-1090, Web
Site: www.performancecompanies.
com
Pres: Brad Bartlett

PILGRIM PRINTED PROMOTIONAL PLASTICS
Div. of Star Printing
1200 W Chestnut St
Brockton, MA 02301-5574
Telephone: (508) 436-6300, (800) 343-
7810, FAX: (508) 580-3542, E-Mail:
pilgrimsales@pilgrimplastics.com,
Web Site: www.pilgrimplastics.com
VP & Owner: Neal Abrams

THE DMA PIP PRINTING AND MARKETING SERVICES
6330 E 75th St (Suite 138)
Indianapolis, IN 46250-2717
Telephone: (317) 849-6244, Web Site:
www.pip.com/pipindy
Primary Market Served: Consumer

PLASTIC GRAPHIC
255 Industrial Dr
Wauconda, IL 60084

Telephone: (847) 487-2030, FAX:
(847) 487-2050, E-Mail:
bgrimespgc@sbcglobal.net, Web
Site: www.plasticgraphic.com
VP, Sls: Brian Grimes

POINTONE GRAPHICS INC
14 Vansco Rd
Toronto, ON, Canada M8Z 5J4
Telephone: (416) 255-8202, Web Site:
www.point-one.com
Mktg Mgr: Tanya Low

POLLACK GRAPHICS INC
Div of IDC Printing & Stationery
536 Merrick Rd
Lynbrook, NY 11563
Telephone: (800) 884-9140, FAX:
(516) 599-8422, E-Mail: sales@
pollack.com, Web Site: www.pollack.
com
Founded: 1975

THE POND-EKBERG CO
660 Broadway St
Chicopee, MA 01020-2400
Telephone: (413) 594-7511, (800) 225-
7511, FAX: (413) 594-2179, E-Mail:
sales@pond-ekberg.com, Web Site:
www.pondekberg.com
Pres: Jonathan Kratovil
Pres: Kevin Morris

PRESSKITS
Subs. of Ardmore Graphic Services Inc
8 Rose Ct Way
East Walpole, MA 02032-1185
Telephone: (781) 762-3003, (800) 472-
3497, FAX: (781) 255-7791, Web
Site: www.presskits.com
Pres: Tom Spiegel

PRIME GRAPHICS INC
501 N Central Ave
Wood Dale, IL 60191-1473
Telephone: (630) 227-1300, FAX:
(630) 227-1823, E-Mail: moreinfo@
primegraphicsinc.com, Web Site:
www.primegraphicsinc.com
Pres & CEO: Willard M. Hunter
VP Sales & Mktg: Cy Harris

THE DMA **PRINT MANAGEMENT
PARTNERS**
701 Lee St (Suite 1050)
Des Plaines, IL 60016-4572
Telephone: (847) 699-2999, Web Site:
www.ourpartners.com
Pres: James O'Brien
Primary Market Served: Business

**PRINTED
COMMUNICATIONS INC**
1929 Mountain Industrial Blvd
Tucker, GA 30084
Telephone: (770) 934-4732, Web Site:
www.printpci.com

THE PRINTER INC
dba TPI
1220 Thomas Beck Rd
Des Moines, IA 50315-1068
Telephone: (515) 288-7241, FAX:
(515) 288-9234, E-Mail: info@the-
printer.com, Web Site: www.the-
printer.com
Mktg Dir: Dave Rittman

PRINTING + QUICK COPY
8799 Frankford Ave
Philadelphia, PA 19136
Telephone: (215) 331-5999
Owner: Bonnie Kaiser

**PRINTING CORP OF THE
AMERICAS INC (PCA)**
620 SW 12th Ave
Pompano Beach, FL 33069-4526
Telephone: (954) 781-8100, (866) 721-
1PCA, FAX: (954) 781-8421, Web
Site: www.pcaprinting.com
CEO: Murray Tuchman

PRINTING FOR SYSTEMS INC
1617 W Crosby Rd Ste 100
Carrollton, TX 75006-6486
Telephone: (203) 245-4200, FAX:
(203) 245-0349, Web Site: www.
printingforsystems.com
Pres: Ralph W. Rotermund

PRINTING SPECTRUM
12 Research Way Ste 1
East Setauket, NY 11733-3531
Telephone: (631) 689-1010, Web Site:
www.printingspectrum.com
VP Customer Rels: John Visconti

**PRINTWEST
COMMUNICATIONS LTD**
Div. of PW Group
1150 Eighth Ave
Regina, SK, Canada S4R 1C9
Telephone: (306) 525-2304, (800) 236-
6438, FAX: (306) 757-2439, E-Mail:
info@printwest.com, Web Site:
www.printwest.com
VP, Sls & Mktg: Ken Benson

PROGRESS PRINTING CO
2677 Waterlick Rd
Lynchburg, VA 24502

Telephone: (434) 239-9213, (800) 527-
7804, FAX: (434) 237-1618, Web
Site: www.progressprinting.net
Pres: Mike Thornton

PUBLISHERS PRESS INC
100 Frank E Simon Ave
Shepherdsville, KY 40165-6013
Telephone: (502) 955-6526, Web Site:
www.pubpress.com
Mktg Dir: Cathy Phillips

QUADRA GRAPHICS INC
PO Box 555
Cherry Hill, NJ 08003-0555
Telephone: (856) 665-4060, FAX:
(856) 665-7324, E-Mail: richard.
nixon@qgi.com
Pres: Robert J. Camm
VP: Richard R. Nixon
Conducts Business: U.S.
Employees: 65
Primary Market Served: Business &
Consumer
Gross sales or billing: $8,000,000

Electronic publishing & prepress printing & finishing services for direct marketing & publishing.

QUANTUM COLOR
6511 Oakton St
Morton Grove, IL 60053-2728
Telephone: (847) 967-3600, FAX:
(847) 967-3610, Web Site: www.
cpipress.com
VP: James J. Campise

QUEBECOR-WORLD INFINITI
Quebecor-World (USA) Inc
96 Phoenix Ave
Enfield, CT 06082
Telephone: (860) 741-0150, (800) 221-
6052, FAX: (860) 741-2553, E-Mail:
clint.humphrey@quebecorworld.com,
Web Site: www.infinitigraphics.com
Pres: Clint Humphrey
Advertising/Marketing Budget Related
to Direct Marketing: 76-100%

**QUEBECOR WORLD
MIDLAND**
1700 James Savage Rd
Midland, MI 48642
Telephone: (989) 496-3333, (800) 448-
4288, FAX: (989) 496-1921, Web
Site: www.quebecorworldinc.com
Gen Mgr: Jim Houvener

**QUEBECOR WORLD NORTH
AMERICA**
291 State St
North Haven, CT 06473

Telephone: (203) 288-2468, FAX: (203) 248-6478, Web Site: www. quebecorworldinc.com
Sr VP, Premedia Opers: Jerry Cacciatore

RAINBOW GRAPHICS INC
933 Tower Rd
Mundelein, IL 60060-3811
Telephone: (847) 824-9600, Web Site: www.rainbowgraphics.com
Pres: Jeff Koszuta

RAPID COLOR PRINTING
6445 Karms Park Ct
Las Vegas, NV 89118-1414
Telephone: (702) 792-6055, FAX: (702) 792-1437, Web Site: www. rapidocolor.com
Owner: David Huckabay

RAPIDFORMS INC
Subs. of New England Business Service Inc
PO Box 1186
Lancaster, CA 93584-1186
Telephone: (856) 384-1144, (800) 257-8354, FAX: (856) 384-1697, Web Site: www.rapidforms.com
VP, Mktg: Thomas Jule

THE DMA RAYPRESS CORP
380 Riverchase Pkwy E
Birmingham, AL 35244-1813
Telephone: (205) 989-3731, Web Site: www.raypress.com
VP Sls & Mktg: Robert Alden

REAL MEDIA SOLUTIONS
77 Green Knolls Dr
Wayne, NJ 07470-6123
Telephone: (973) 835-7060, Web Site: www.get-realmedia.com
Pres: Michael Aslett
Graphic Design: Robert M Bovasso

THE DMA REDFIELD & CO INC
1901 Howard St
Omaha, NE 68102-2594
Telephone: (402) 341-0364, Web Site: www.redfieldandcompany.com
Owner: Tom Beachler

VG REED & SONS
1002 S 12th St
Louisville, KY 40210-1302
Telephone: (502) 589-3770, (800) 635-9788, FAX: (502) 560-0197, E-Mail: info@vgreed.com, Web Site: www. vgreed.com
Pres: Howard Reed

REESE PRESS INC
7085 Milford Industrial Rd
Pikesville, MD 21208-6013
Telephone: (410) 467-9200, FAX: (410) 467-9520
Chmn: David B. Baker Jr

RELYCO
121 Broadway
Dover, NH 03820-3299
Telephone: (603) 516-3610, Web Site: www.relyco.com
VP Mktg: Ronald Wimbley

REX THREE INC
15431 SW 14th St
Sunrise, FL 33326
Telephone: (954) 452-8301, (800) 782-6509, FAX: (954) 452-0569, E-Mail: info@rex3.com, Web Site: www. rexthree.com
Exec VP: Howard Shusterman

THE DMA RIPON PRINTERS
656 S Douglas St
Ripon, WI 54971-9044
Telephone: (920) 748-3136, (800) 321-3136, FAX: (920) 748-3741, E-Mail: info@riponprinters.com, Web Site: www.riponprinters.com
Pres: Andy Lyke
Sls & Mktg Mgr: Jeff Hopp

RONED PRINTING & REPRODUCTION INC
Six DeForest Ave
East Hanover, NJ 07936
Telephone: (973) 386-1848, FAX: (973) 386-0969, E-Mail: info@ roned.com, Web Site: www.roned. com
Pres: Ronald N. Russo

ROSE PRINTING CO INC
2503 Jackson Bluff Rd
Tallahassee, FL 32304-4405
Telephone: (850) 576-4151, (800) 227-3725, FAX: (850) 576-4153, E-Mail: roseprt@roseprinting.com, Web Site: www.roseprinting.com
Pres: Charles Rosenberg
Direct online sales

SAF FINANCIAL SERVICES INC
Subs. of American Community Bankers
635 Remington Rd (Unit F)
Schaumburg, IL 60173
Telephone: (800) 323-3000, FAX: (847) 310-8969
Pres: David Koltonuk

SAUERS GROUP, INC
1585 Roadhaven Dr
Stone Mountain, GA 30083-1315
Telephone: (770) 621-8888, (866) 458-5212, FAX: (770) 621-8866, E-Mail: info@sauersgroup.com, Web Site: www.sauersgroup.com
Pres: Richard S. Sauers

SCHAWK DESPLAINES
1600 Sherwin Ave
Des Plaines, IL 60018-3013
Telephone: (847) 296-6000, (800) 629-1909, FAX: (847) 296-4694, Web Site: www.schawk.com
Mng Dir: David Hamm

SCHAWK INC
1695 River Rd
Des Plaines, IL 60018
Telephone: (847) 827-9494, (800) 621-1909, FAX: (847) 827-1264, E-Mail: information@schawk.com, Web Site: www.schawk.com
Pres, CEO & Dir: David A. Schawk

SCHMIDT
Div. of Taylor Corp
1101 Frontage Rd NW
Byron, MN 55920
Telephone: (507) 775-6400, FAX: (507) 775-6655, Web Site: www. schmidt.com
VP, Sls: Todd Alexander

SCIENTIFIC GAMES CANADA
3000 boul de l' Assomption
Montreal, PQ, Canada H1N 3V5
Telephone: (514) 254-3000, FAX: (514) 254-1411, Web Site: www. scientificgames.com
Sr VP Sls & Global Mktg: James Kennedy

THE DMA THE SEGERDAHL CORP
1351 S Wheeling Rd
Wheeling, IL 60090-5997
Telephone: (847) 541-1080, FAX: (847) 541-5237, Web Site: www. segerdahl.com/frameset.html
Chmn: Earl E. Segerdahl
Exec VP: John Annell

SEGERDAHL GRAPHICS
385 Gilman Ave
Wheeling, IL 60090-5807
Telephone: (847) 850-8800, FAX: (773) 477-2051
VP, Corp Mktg: Susan Herman

SELKIRK PRESS
1714 Industrial Dr, PO Box 875
Sandpoint, ID 83864

Telephone: (208) 263-7523, FAX:
(208) 263-2229, E-Mail:
selkirkpress@nidlink.com
Pres: Gary L. Pietsch

SELLS PRINTING CO
16000 W Rogers Dr
New Berlin, WI 53151
Telephone: (262) 784-9500, (800) 728-
9501, FAX: (262) 784-7876, Web
Site: www.sells.com
Sr VP & Sls Mgr: David Wilson

SERVICE LITHO PRINT INC
50 W Fernau
Oshkosh, WI 54902-0875
Telephone: (920) 231-3060, (800) 544-
1493, FAX: (920) 231-1272, E-Mail:
slp@service-litho.com
CEO: Steve Elbing

Specialty printing and packaging and
related services including up to 48 pt
substrates, lenticular, polypropylene
tubs, removable pressure sensitive, UV
printing, foil stamping, embossing,
folding and gluing, and specialty point
of sale.

SERVICE WEB OFFSET CORP
aka Service Communications & Solutions, LLC
2500 S Dearborn St
Chicago, IL 60616-2299
Telephone: (312) 567-7000, (800) 621-
1567, FAX: (312) 567-9121, E-Mail:
jhamilton@swoc.com, Web Site:
www.swoc.com
Pres: John Hamilton

SHERIDAN BOOKS INC
613 E Industrial Dr
Chelsea, MI 48118-1536
Telephone: (734) 662-3291, (734) 475-
9145, (800) 999-BOOK, FAX: (734)
475-7337, E-Mail: info@
sheridanbooks.com, Web Site: www.
sheridanbooks.com
VP, Sls: Joe Thomson
Mktg Mgr: Pam Eddington
Mktg Asst: Laura Baker

**SHERWOOD DESIGN &
DEVELOPMENT CENTER**
One Kero Rd
Carlstadt, NJ 07072
Telephone: (201) 372-3900, FAX:
(201) 372-0917
Pres: Duncan Watson

SHINDIGZ
One Party Pl
South Whitley, IN 46787

Telephone: (219) 723-5171, (800) 314-
8736, FAX: (219) 723-6976, E-Mail:
csr@shindigz.com, Web Site: www.
shindigz.com
Exec VP, Mktg: Wendy Moyle
Pres & CEO: Shep Moyle
Founded: 1926

SHOPGUIDE.COM
3223 Commerce St
Amarillo, TX 79109-3275
Telephone: (806) 351-0005, FAX:
(806) 351-0059, E-Mail: info@
shopguide.com, Web Site: www.
shopguide.com
Pres: Donald J. Melancon
VP: Lloyd Kruckeberg

SHUTTERFLY
2800 Bridge Pkwy
Redwood City, CA 94065-1192
Telephone: (650) 610-5200, Web Site:
www.shutterfly.com
Sr Mktg Mgr: Steven Marjon
Chief Mktg Officer: John Boris

THE DMA **SIR SPEEDY GRAND RAPIDS**
4513 Broadmoor Ave SE (Suite A)
Grand Rapids, MI 49512-5369
Telephone: (616) 554-7777, Web Site:
www.sirspeedy.com

THE DMA **SIR SPEEDY - GREEN BAY**
333 Packerland Dr
Green Bay, WI 54303-4815
Web Site: www.sirspeedygb.com

THE DMA **SIR SPEEDY OF NEWTOWN**
760 Newtown-Yardley Rd
Newtown, PA 18940-4500
Telephone: (215) 968-2080, Web Site:
www.sirspeedynewtown.com
Primary Market Served: Consumer

THE DMA **SIR SPEEDY PRINTING AND
MARKETING SERVICES**
7450 S Tacoma Way (Suite B1)
Tacoma, WA 98409-3906
Telephone: (253) 473-0765), Web Site:
www..sirspeedy0905.com

THE DMA **SIR SPEEDY WESTBURY**
75 State St
Westbury, NY 11590-5004
Telephone: (516) 334-7400, Web Site:
www.sirspeedyny.net
Primary Market Served: Consumer

**M LEE SMITH PUBLISHERS
LLC**
100 Winners Cir N Ste 300
Brentwood, TN 37027-1003

Telephone: (615) 373-7517, (800) 274-
6774, FAX: (615) 373-5183, E-Mail:
custserv@mleesmith.com, Web Site:
www.mleesmith.com
Publr & Chmn: M. Lee Smith
VP Content: Brad Forrister

SOLO PRINTING
7860 NW 66th St
Miami, FL 33166-2708
Telephone: (305) 594-8699, Web Site:
www.soloprinting.com
Dir Sls & Mktg: John Carr

SOURCE 4 INC
16740 Birkdale Commons Pkwy (Suite
208)
Huntersville, NC 28078-4462
Telephone: (704) 602-0110, (800) 541-
5400, FAX: (704) 602-0119, E-Mail:
source4newyork@source4.com, Web
Site: www.source4.com
Pres: Charles Calman

THE DMA **SPECIALTY PRINT
COMMUNICATIONS**
6019 W Howard St
Niles, IL 60714-4801
Telephone: (847) 588-2580, Web Site:
www.specialtyprintcomm.com
Exec VP: Dustin LeFebvre

SPIRE CREATIVE GROUP
110 W 40th St (Rm 1702)
New York, NY 10018-8508
Telephone: (212) 391-0200, Web Site:
www.spirecreativegroup.com
VP Bus: Bruce Weiser

THE DMA **SPIRE PRINTING &
PACKAGING LLC**
501 5th Ave (Suite 811)
New York, NY 10017-7849
Telephone: (212) 661-1157, Web Site:
www.spireprintingandpackaging.com
Primary Market Served: Consumer

**SPRING HILL LASER
SERVICES**
PO Box 79
Sterling, PA 18463-0079
Telephone: (570) 689-0970, FAX:
(570) 689-7915, E-Mail: kkshls@
icontech.com, Web Site: www.
springhilllaser.com

**ST JOSEPH
COMMUNICATIONS**
50 MacIntosh Blvd
Concord, ON, Canada L4K 4P3
Telephone: (905) 660-3111, FAX:
(905) 669-1972, Web Site: www.
stjoseph.com

VP Mktg: Michael O'Connor

ST JOSEPH PRINT THORN
Div of St Joseph Communications
50 MacIntosh Blvd
Concord, ON, Canada L4K 4P3
Telephone: (416) 441-1411, FAX:
(416) 441-3158, Web Site: www.
stjoseph.com
Dir Sls: John Carley

STEPHENSON PRINTING INC
5731 General Washington Dr
Alexandria, VA 22312
Telephone: (703) 642-9000, (800) 336-
4637, FAX: (703) 354-0384, E-Mail:
gstephenson@stephensonprinting.
com, Web Site: www.
stephensonprinting.com
Pres & CEO: George W. Stephenson

STERLING PRINT & MAIL SYSTEM
Subs. of Sterling Business Corp
206 Concord St
Peterborough, NH 03458
Telephone: (603) 924-9401, (800) 439-
9401, FAX: (603) 924-7925, E-Mail:
sbc@sbc.mv.com, Web Site: www.
mv.com/ipusers/sbc
Pres: George A. Sterling

STICKERTAPE
PO Box 483
Nesconset, NY 11767-0483
Telephone: (800) 811-2891, FAX:
(800) 727-5577, E-Mail:
CustomerService@stickertape.com,
Web Site: www.stickertape.com
VP, Sls: Stacy Moller

THE DMA STRUCTURAL GRAPHICS
38 Plains Rd
Essex, CT 06426-1520
Telephone: (860) 767-2661, Web Site:
www.structuralgraphics.com
CEO: Michael Maguire

SUMI PRINTING
1139 E Janis St
Carson, CA 90746-1306
Telephone: (310) 769-1600, Web Site:
www.getsumi.com
Exec VP: Michael Sumi

SURDELL & PARTNERS
3738 S 149th St Ste 109
Omaha, NE 68144-5564
Telephone: (402) 501-7488, (800) 733-
7765, FAX: (402) 733-2083, E-Mail:
dsurdell@surdellpartners.com, Web
Site: www.surdellpartners.com
Pres: Daniel L. Surdell
Partner & COO: Pat Jung

TFC INC
690 Airpark Rd
Napa, CA 94558-7516
Telephone: (707) 224-6161, Web Site:
www.tfcinc.com
Pres & Founder: Constance Hill

TEMPOGRAPHICS INC
455 E North Ave
Carol Stream, IL 60188
Telephone: (630) 462-8200, FAX:
(630) 462-0350
Pres: Mike Polucci

TERACO INC
2080 Commerce Dr
Midland, TX 79703-7502
Telephone: (888) 837-2261, Web Site:
www.teraco.com
Natl Mktg Mgr: Steve Pruitt

TEXAS GRAPHIC RESOURCE
1234 Round Table Dr
Dallas, TX 75247-3504
Telephone: (214) 630-2800, FAX:
(214) 630-0713
Pres & CEO: Joe Cangelose

THINK SHAPES MAIL
5463 W Waters Ave (Suite 820)
Tampa, FL 33634
Telephone: (813) 885-2225, (800) 889-
4406, Web Site: www.jigsawprinting.
com
Founder: Glenn Nagle

TIDEWATER DIRECT LLC
300 Tidewater Dr
Centreville, MD 21617
Telephone: (410) 758-1500, FAX:
(410) 758-2478, Web Site: www.
tidewaterdirect.com
VP, Sls: Larry McCormick

TOP USA CORP
771 Dearborn Park Ln (Ste N)
Worthington, OH 43085-5720
Telephone: (614) 431-1601, (800) 843-
3381, FAX: (614) 431-1239, E-Mail:
info@topusa.com, Web Site: www.
topusa.com
Pres, Mktg: Pia Wendel

TRANSCONTINENTAL YORKVILLE - O'KEEFE
Eight Tidemore Ave
Etobicoke, ON, Canada M9W 5H4
Telephone: (416) 741-1900, (800) 361-
9690, FAX: (416) 401-2220, Web
Site: www.transcontinentalprinting.
com
Gen Mgr: Marcel Courville

TRIANGLE PRINTERS INC
3737 Chase Ave
Skokie, IL 60076-4008
Telephone: (847) 675-3700, FAX:
(847) 674-1230, E-Mail: blevin@
triangleprinters.com, Web Site: www.
triangleprinters.com
Mktg Specialist: Barb Levin
Pres: David Saltzman
Production Mgr: Michael Mueller
Creative Svcs Mgr: Monica Grier
VP Technology: Steve Farber
Employees: 45
Founded: 1955

Provides sheetfed and digital printing,
photography, design, bindery, mailing
and fulfillment for all marketing
material. Also provides banners, signs,
fleet graphics, trade show graphics and
countertop displays. Manages entire
project in-house.

TUCKER PRINTERS
270 Middle Rd
Henrietta, NY 14467-9312
Telephone: (585) 359-3030, Web Site:
www.tuckerprinters.com
VP Packaging Solutions: Glenn Marino

UNIGRAPHIC INC
110 Commerce Way Ste 6
Woburn, MA 01801-1098
Telephone: (781) 231-7200, FAX:
(781) 938-7727, E-Mail: info@uni-
graphic.com, Web Site: www.uni-
graphic.com

UNIQUE EMBOSSING SERVICES INC & GLOBAL CARDS
1213 Butterfield Rd
Downers Grove, IL 60515
Telephone: (630) 960-3337 X23, FAX:
(630) 960-3618, Web Site: www.
globalcrd.com
Pres: Pethi Velu

US TAPE & LABEL CORP
2092 Westport Ctr Dr
Saint Louis, MO 63146
Telephone: (314) 824-4444, (800) 569-
1906, FAX: (314) 824-4400, E-Mail:
harrisonc@ustl.com, Web Site: www.
ustl.com
Chmn: William Eiseman Jr

UNIVENTURE INC
13311 Industrial Pkwy
Marysville, OH 43040-9589
Telephone: (937) 645-4600, Web Site:
www.univenture.com
VP Sls & Mktg: David Coho

UNIVERSAL PRINTING
1234 S Kingshighway Blvd
Saint Louis, MO 63110
Telephone: (314) 771-6900, FAX:
(314) 771-7987, E-Mail: info@
universalprintingco.com, Web Site:
www.universalprintingco.com
VP Sls & Mktg: Janis A. Thouvenot

UNZ & CO
Div. of Scott Printing Co
333 Cedar Ave Ste 2
Middlesex, NJ 08846-2400
Telephone: (732) 868-0706, (800) 631-
3098, FAX: (732) 868-0260, E-Mail:
unzco@unzco.com, Web Site: www.
unzco.com
Pres, Scott Printing Co: Daniel T. Scott

USDISCS
2387 Buena Vista St
Duarte, CA 91010-3301
Telephone: (626) 359-9955, Web Site:
www.usdiscs.com

THE DMA V3
200 N Elevar St
Oxnard, CA 93030-7969
Telephone: (800) 882-1844, Web Site:
www.v3corporation.com
VP Sls & Client Svcs: Michael Szanger

**VALLEY FORGE TAPE &
LABEL CO INC**
119 Summit Dr
Exton, PA 19341
Telephone: (610) 524-8900, (800) 345-
1323, FAX: (610) 524-8906, E-Mail:
vfsales@vftl.com, Web Site: www.
vftl.com
Pres: Paul Myers

**VENTURE ENCODING
SERVICE INC**
4401 Cambridge
Fort Worth, TX 76155-2629
Telephone: (817) 283-9500, FAX:
(817) 868-1705, E-Mail: sales@
venture-encoding.com, Web Site:
www.venture-encoding.com
Pres: Kenny Hargis

**VERSATILE CARD
TECHNOLOGY INC**
5200 Thatcher Rd
Downers Grove, IL 60515
Telephone: (630) 852-5600, FAX:
(630) 852-5817, Web Site: www.
versacard.com
Chmn Bd & CEO: Pethinaidu Veluchamy

THE DMA VISTAPRINT USA INC
95 Hayden Ave
Lexington, MA 02421-7942
Telephone: (800) 961-2075, Web Site:
www.vistaprint.com
Pres & CEO: Robert Keane
CMO: Janet Holian
Pub Rels Mgr: Jason Keith
COO: Alex Schwotka
CPO: Anne Drapeau
Pub Rels Coord: Nick Gosselin
VP: Manya Chait
Conducts Business: Worldwide
Employees: 2,200
Primary Market Served: Business &
Consumer
Catalog available online
Direct online sales
Advertising/Marketing Budget Related
to Direct Marketing: 76-100%
Founded: 2000
Gross sales or billing: $515,800,000

The leading online supplier of high-
quality, low-cost graphic design services & customized printed products to
small business & consumers.

**WALLACE TARGETED
COMMUNICATIONS**
Subs. of Wallace Computer Services
Inc
1750 Wallace Ave
Saint Charles, IL 60174-3401
Telephone: (630) 313-7000, FAX:
(630) 377-4622, Web Site: www.
wallace.com
VP: Doug Lazverini

WEB GRAPHICS
PO Box 308
Glens Falls, NY 12801
Telephone: (518) 792-6501, (800) 833-
8863, FAX: (518) 792-9353, (800)
833-8861, E-Mail: marketing@
printatweb.com, Web Site: www.
printatweb.com
Pres: Mark Maher
Dir Sls & Mktg: Brooks Warner

WEB GRAPHICS
7731 Cottesmore Dr
Naples, FL 34113-3180
Telephone: (239) 775-2295
Pres: Vern Froelich

WESTERN WEB PRINTING
4005 S Western Ave
Sioux Falls, SD 57105
Telephone: (605) 339-2383, (888) 855-
4563, FAX: (605) 339-1523, E-Mail:
info@westernwebprinting.com, Web
Site: www.westernwebprinting.com
Pres: K.A. Lesnar
Employees: 65
Founded: 1973

Gross sales or billing: $8,000,000
Fast turnaround design, print & mail
all under one roof.

WESTPRO INC
2294 Mountain Vista Ln
Provo, UT 84606-6206
Telephone: (801) 373-2525, (800) 533-
3885, FAX: (801) 373-8778, E-Mail:
sales@westpro.net, Web Site:
westpro.net
Pres: Stephen H. Clement

**WHITE ELECTRONIC
DESIGNS**
3601 E University Dr
Phoenix, AZ 85034-7217
Telephone: (614) 279-6326, Web Site:
www.whiteedc.com
Sls Mgr: Andrew Davis

WILEN GROUP
5 Wellwood Ave
Farmingdale, NY 11735-1213
Telephone: (631) 439-5000, Web Site:
www.wilengroup.com
Pres: Darrin Wilen

**WILLIAM CHARLES
PRINTING**
7 Fairchild Ct Ste 100
Plainview, NY 11803-1734
Telephone: (516) 349-0900, Web Site:
www.williamcharlesprinting.com
Sls Rep: Donald Seaman

**WILLIAMS PRINTING CO/AN
RR DONNELLEY CO**
1240 Spring St NW
Atlanta, GA 30309-2808
Telephone: (404) 875-6611, (800) 950-
7588, FAX: (404) 872-4025, Web
Site: www.rrdonnelley.com
Pres: Bill Tucker

WILLIAMSON PRINTING
6700 Denton Dr
Dallas, TX 75235-9827
Telephone: (214) 904-2100, (800) 843-
5423, FAX: (214) 352-1842, E-Mail:
jandagu@twpc.com, Web Site: www.
wpcnet.com
CEO: Jerry Williamson

WISE
555 McFarland 400 Dr
Alpharetta, GA 30004-3375
Telephone: (770) 442-1060
Primary Market Served: Business &
Consumer

WORLDCOLOR
3101 McCall Dr
Atlanta, GA 30340-2807
Telephone: (770) 936-7100, Web Site:
   www.worldcolor.com
VP Mktg: Maura Packham

HENRY WURST INC
1331 Saline St
North Kansas City, MO 64116-4410
Telephone: (816) 842-3113, FAX:
   (816) 472-6221, E-Mail: info@
   henrywurst.com, Web Site: www.
   henrywurst.com
Pres: Michael S. Wurst
Mktg Mgr: Stephanie Fite
Founded: 1937

THE DMA XPRESSDOCS
1000 Forest Park Blvd Ste 200
Fort Worth, TX 76110-1169
Telephone: (817) 547-9705, Web Site:
   www.xpressdocs.com
CMO: Darrin Rayner

YORK LABEL
13321 California St (Suite 400)
Omaha, NE 68154-6047
Telephone: (402) 829-4594, FAX:
   (402) 445-4282, Web Site: www.
   yorklabel.com
Pres & CEO: Richard Egan

YORK LABEL
405 Willow Springs Ln
York, PA 17405-6047
Telephone: (717) 266-9675, FAX:
   (717) 266-9834, Web Site: www.
   yorklabel.com
VP Sls: John Attayek

ZED MARKETING GROUP
1210 Roosevelt St (Suite 220)
Edmond, OK 73034-5176
Telephone: (405) 348-8145, FAX:
   (405) 348-5541, E-Mail: zed@
   zedmktg.com, Web Site: www.
   zedmktg.com
Pres: Jim Zuckermandel

Lettershops, Mailing Services & Product Fulfillment Companies (28) — Geographic Index

Alabama

High Cotton, PO Box 101568, Birmingham, 35210-6568

Arizona

Artichoke Ink, 1265 S La Arboleta St, Gilbert, 85296-4134

OnTrac, 3401 E Harbour Dr, Phoenix, 85034-7229

Arkansas

LSC Marketing, 2207 Cantrell Rd, Little Rock, 72203

Mailmaster Corp, 3401 One Pl, Jonesboro, 72404

California

A&M Direct Mail Service Inc, 949 N Cataract Ave (Suite 1), San Dimas, 91773-1464

Advanced Image Direct, 1415 S Acacia Ave., Fullerton, 92831-5317

Advantage Mailing Inc, PO Box 66013, Anaheim, 92816-6013

Adwest Mailers Inc, 19320 Londelius St, Northridge, 91324-3509

Arrow Mailing Service II Inc, 13040 Cerise Ave, Hawthorne, 90250-5523

Bullseye Marketing Inc, 9025 Owensmouth Ave, Canoga Park, 91304-1417

Business Services Network, 1275 Fairfax Ave Ste 103, San Francisco, 94124-1759

Comac Inc, 565 Sinclair Frontage Rd, Milpitas, 95035

Complete Mailing Service Inc, 108 Dubois St, Santa Cruz, 95060-2109

Creative Mailing & Marketing, 879 W 190th St Ste 400, Gardena, 90248-4223

Fulfillment Express Inc, 7271 Paramount Blvd, Pico Rivera, 90660

Goodkind & Goodkind Direct Inc, 1433 11 St (Suite I), Arcata, 95521-5712

Imagine Fulfillment Services, 20100 S Vermont Ave, Torrance, 90502-1361

Jenco Productions Inc, 401 S J St, San Bernardino, 92410-2605

Mail Boxes Etc, 6060 Cornerstone Ct W, San Diego, 92121-3795

Mail Communications, 533 Rowland Blvd, Novato, 94947-4618

The Mailing House Inc, 5600 Bandini Blvd, Bell, 90201

Mailing Source, 1760 Monrovia Ave (#C1), Costa Mesa, 92627

Matrix Manager, 1430 Blue Oaks Blvd (Suite 280), Roseville, 95747-5156

MCRB Fulfillment Corp, 4039 Mariner Cir, Westlake Village, 91361

Specialized Mailing Services Inc, 17451 Nichols Ln (Unit J), Huntington Beach, 92647

Taubenpost Inc, 20702 Linear Ln, Lake Forest, 92630

XPO, 3541 Lomita Blvd, Torrance, 90505-5016

Colorado

First Data Corp, 6200 S Quebec St, Greenwood Village, 80111-4729

The Mail Room Inc, 2110 Busch Ave, Colorado Springs, 80904

Connecticut

BMI Fulfillment Services, PO Box 3285, Danbury, 06813-3285

Better Lists Inc, 64 Sunnyside, Stamford, 06902-4792

Com-Pak, PO Box 7312, Berlin, 06037-7312

Data-Mail Inc, 240 Hartford Ave, Newington, 06111-2054

DST Output, 125 Ellington Rd, South Windsor, 06074-4112

Fosdick Fulfillment Corp, 26 Barnes Industrial Park Rd N, Wallingford, 06492

Meyer Fulfillment, 255 Long Beach Blvd, Stratford, 06615-7117

3PL Worldwide Inc, 500 Bic Dr, Milford, 06461-1734

Delaware

Sheeran Direct Marketing, 71 Southgate Blvd, New Castle, 19720-2000

District of Columbia

UNICOR- Services Business Group, 400 1st St NW, Washington, 20534-0004

US Postal Service-Library, 475 L'Enfant Plz SW, Washington, 20260-1540

Florida

A-1 Direct Mail Marketing Inc, 11950 SW 128th St, Miami, 33186-5207

The Bureau Inc, 2809 SE Monroe St, Stuart, 34997-5904

Crane Duplicating Service Inc, 4915 Rattlesnake Hammock Rd, Naples, 34113-6959

DHL Express, 1200 S Pine Island Rd (Suite 600), Plantation, 33324

DHL Global Mail, 2700 S Commerce Pkwy (Suite 400), Weston, 33331-3631

Direct One Inc, 7224 Sandscove Ct (Suite 7), Winter Park, 32792-6903

Direct Response Marketing, 12450 Automobile Blvd, Clearwater, 33762

MBI Direct Mail, 710 W New Hampshire Ave, Deland, 32720-7231

New Valley, 100 SE 2nd St (fl 32), Miami, 33131-2108

Palm Coast Data LLC, 11 Commerce Blvd, Palm Coast, 32164-7961

Southern Fulfillment Services, 1650 90th Ave, Vero Beach, 32966

ThinkDirect Marketing Group, 8285 Bryan Dairy Rd (Suite 150), Largo, 33777-1306

Georgia

Innotrac Corp, 6465 E Johns Xing Ste 400, Duluth, 30097-1581

PBD Worldwide Fulfillment Services, 1650 Bluegrass Lakes Pkwy, Alpharetta, 30004-7714

United Parcel Service, 55 Glenlake Pkwy NE, Atlanta, 30328

Hawaii

Cardinal Mailing Services Ltd, 197 Sand Island Access Rd Ste 211, Honolulu, 96819-4901

Idaho

ESP Printing & Mailing Inc, 317 E 37th St (Suite 5), Boise, 83714-6475

Illinois

A-KD Mailing & Fulfillment Service, 6850 N Central Park, Lincolnwood, 60712-2704

Advance Mailing Services Inc, 1130 Carolina Dr (Unit A), West Chicago, 60185-5163

Advantage Marketing Group, 1550 Howard St, Elk Grove Village, 60007

Alert Marketing, 2 S 180 Kent Rd, Glen Ellyn, 60137

aNETorder/American Mailers, 820 Frontenac Rd, Naperville, 60563-1743

BFC, 1051 N Kirk Rd, Batavia, 60510-1438

Calmark Inc, 1400 W 44th St, Chicago, 60609-3332

Compuletter Inc, 7460 N Lehigh Ave, Niles, 60714-4024

Data Direct, 8120 River Dr, Morton Grove, 60053

Direct Mail Solutions LLC, 775 Kimberly Dr, Carol Stream, 60188-9407

Direct Mail Source, PO Box 8033, Wilmette, 60091-8033

The Envelope Connection Inc, 4424 N Ravenswood, Chicago, 60640

Finishing Plus, Inc, 4546 W 47th St, Chicago, 60632

Form House Inc, 5750 Old Orchard Rd (Suite 520), Skokie, 60077-1081

Fulfillment Xcellence Inc (FXI), 5235 Thatcher Rd, Downers Grove, 60515-4027

Hogard Business Services Inc, 450 S Schuyler Ave, Bradley, 60915-2344

Johnson & Quin Inc, 7460 N Lehigh Ave, Niles, 60714-4099

Mailways Enterprises Inc, 6105 Factory Rd (Suite 1), Crystal Lake, 60014-7965

Mid-Central Printing & Mailing Inc, 1225 Central Ave, Wilmette, 60091

Northwest Mailing Service Inc, 5501 W Grand Ave, Chicago, 60639-2909

Prodigy Mailing Services, 389 E South Frontage Rd, Bolingbrook, 60440-3029

Promotion Support Services Inc, 2832 5th St Ste 1, Rock Island, 61201-4027

Reliant Data Processing, 197 Alder Dr, North Aurora, 60542-1471

Strategic Marketing & Mailing, PO Box 6013, Champaign, 61826-6013

ThreeSource Fulfillment, 655 Mulberry, Manteno, 60950-9219

Tribune Direct Marketing, 505 Northwest Ave (Suite A), Northlake, 60164-1662

Tripar International Inc, 20 Presidential Dr, Roselle, 60172

Unique Data Services Inc, 5300 Katrine Ave, Downers Grove, 60515

Unique Mailing Services Inc, 325 Marmon Dr, Bolingbrook, 60440

United Wire Service, 8512 N Allen Rd, Peoria, 61615-1527

Wit Postal Logistics LLC, 350 N La Salle Dr (Suite 1100), Chicago, 60654-5131

Indiana

Faris Mailing Inc, 701 N Holt Rd Ste 3, Indianapolis, 46222-3455

The Order Fulfillment Group, 7313 Mayflower Park Dr, Zionsville, 46077-7903

Pentera Inc, 8650-G Commerce Park Pl, Indianapolis, 46268-3126

Iowa

Alaniz - a Dmh Marketing Partners Co, 425 N Iris Rd, Box 799, Mount Pleasant, 52641-3109

The Pioneer Group, 316 W 5th St, Waterloo, 50701-5508

Promotion Fulfillment Ctr, 311 21st St, Camanche, 52730-9699

Rees Associates Inc, 1800 SW 2nd St, Des Moines, 50315-7147

Kansas

Consolidated Mailing Corp, 5735 Kessler Ln, Shawnee Mission, 66203-2591

Midpoint National Inc, 1263 Southwest Blvd, Kansas City, 66103-1901

Southwest Publishing & Mailing Corp, 2600 NW Topeka Blvd, Topeka, 66617-1160

Kentucky

American Mailing Service Inc, 336 13th St, Ashland, 41101-7536

Blue Grass Mailing, Data & Fulfillment Services, 833 Nandino Blvd, Lexington, 40511-1202

dmh Marketing Partners - Louisville, 12101 Westport Rd, Louisville, 40245-1759

Premier Direct Marketing Inc, 7725 National Tpke (Unit 100), Louisville, 40214-4803

Maine

Cloutier Direct Inc, 3 Washington Ave, Scarborough, 04074-9782

Maryland

DirectMail.com, 201 Skipjack Rd, Prince Frederick, 20678-3411

Distribution Postal Co Inc, 6200 Frankford Ave, Baltimore, 21206-4902

Mail Advertising Services Inc, 15711 Pagano Ln, Darnestown, 20874-3115

PMDS Inc, 9050 Junction Dr Ste 2, Annapolis Junction, 20701-1134

A Rapid Mailing Inc, 8221 Preston Ct, Jessup, 20794-9368

Sisk Mailing Service, 203 Log Canoe Cir, Stevensville, 21666-9270

USA Fulfillment, 313 Talbot Blvd, Chestertown, 21620-1016

Vertis Media & Marketing Services, 250 W Pratt St (Suite 1800), Baltimore, 21201-6813

ZIP Mailing Services Inc, 6304 Sheriff Rd (Suite Z), Landover, 20785-4361

Massachusetts

International Mailing Solutions LLC, 25 Corporate Dr (Suite 175), Burlington, 01803-4243

JLS Mailing Services Inc, 672 Crescent St, Brockton, 02302-3360

ONTIME COMPANIES, 201 Crescent Ave, Chelsea, 02150-3072

Arleen Smith Marketing Inc, 60 Mayflower Ln, Stoughton, 02072-3024

Staples Industrial, 500 Staples Dr, Framingham, 01702-4478

Michigan

Alternate Marketing Networks Inc, 4675 32nd Ave Ste B, Hudsonville, 49426-8012

On-Demand Mail Services, 2083 Pontiac Rd Ste B, Auburn Hills, 48326-2485

Progressive Distribution Services Inc, 5505 36th St SE, Grand Rapids, 49512

Wolverine Mailing & Packaging Warehouse, 1601 Clay St, Detroit, 48211-1902

Minnesota

American Spirit Mailing, 401 13th Ave N, PO Box 707, Howard Lake, 55349-0707

Archway Marketing Services, 19850 S Diamond Lake Rd, Rogers, 55374

Charnstrom, 5391 12th Ave E, Shakopee, 55379-1896

Ideagroup Mail Service, 4455 White Bear Pkwy, Saint Paul, 55110

Impact Mailing, 4600 Lyndale Ave N, Minneapolis, 55412-1408

Irresistible Ink Inc, 4444 Haines Rd, Duluth, 55811

Mail Handling Services, 7550 Corporate Way, Eden Prairie, 55344-2045

The John Roberts Co, 9687 E River Rd, Minneapolis, 55433

Young America Corp, 717 Faxon Rd, Young America, 55397-9481

Mississippi

Sacred Heart League, 6050 Hwy 161 N, Walls, 38686-0001

Missouri

Directory Distributing Associates Inc, 1602 Park 370 Ct, Hazelwood, 63042-4418

Impressions Direct, 2116 59th St, Saint Louis, 63110-2808

Innovative Industries Inc, 421 W Centennial Ave, Carthage, 64836-3528

Nebraska

Aim Marketing, 525 North D, PO Box 522, Fremont, 68025-5051

World Marketing Inc, 10918 Emiline St, La Vista, 68128-5725

Nevada

The Bender Group, 345 Parr Cir, Reno, 89512

SilverState Marketing Solutions, 3585 E Patrick Ln (#200), Las Vegas, 89120-6211

Universal Distribution Services, 4910 Longley Ln (Suite 101), Reno, 89502

New Hampshire

Polaris Direct, 300 Technology Dr, Hooksett, 03106-2520

New Jersey

A+ Letter Service, 200 Syracuse Ct, Lakewood, 08701

Advertising Mailers Inc, PO Box 6378, Edison, 08818-6378

Barton & Cooney, 300 Richards Run, Burlington, 08016-2120

Com-Pak Services Inc, 365 New Albany Rd Ste A, Moorestown, 08057-1105

Direct Link Worldwide, 700 Dowd Ave, Elizabeth, 07201-2108

Direct Mail Depot Inc, 200 Circle Dr N, Piscataway, 08854-3705

Direct Market Designs Inc, 45 E 5th St, Paterson, 07524-1101

The First Occupational Center of New Jersey, 391 Lakeside Ave, Orange, 07050-2809

GMI Distribution, 305 Churchill Ave, Somerset, 08873

Gordon Management Inc, 305 Churchill Ave, Somerset, 08873-3486

Hays International Mailing Services, 26 Hilliard Ave (Apt 1), Edgewater, 07020-1200

The Hibbert Group, 400 Pennington Ave, Trenton, 08618-3105

Just Packaging Inc, 450 Oak Tree Ave, South Plainfield, 07080

Mailco Inc, 1430 State Route 23, Wayne, 07470-5826

Mercury International, 365 Blair Rd (Suite C), Avenel, 07001-2231

Pitney Bowes International Mail Services, 158 Mount Olivet Ave, Newark, 07114-2114

Professional Mailing Services Inc, 12 Commerce St, Springfield, 07081-2996

Reliable Mail Service Inc, 121 Fieldcrest Ave Ste C, Edison, 08837-3658

Swan Packaging Fulfillment, 415 Hamburg Tpke (Suite G), Wayne, 07470-2164

New York

Access Direct Systems Inc, 91 Executive Blvd, Farmingdale, 11735-4710

The Added Touch, 2221 Niagara Falls Blvd Ste 4, Box 4, Niagara Falls, 14304-1696

Advanced Marketing Direct, 99 Thielman Dr, Buffalo, 14206-2365

Automatic Mail Services Inc, 4700 34th St, Long Island City, 11101-2412

Brigar Xpress Solutions, Inc, 5 Sand Creek Rd Ste 100, Albany, 12205-1400

The CPW Group, 60 Trade Zone Ct, Ronkonkoma, 11779-7395

Century Direct, 30-30 47th Ave, Long Island City, 11101

Challenge Industries Inc, 950 Danby Rd (Suite 179), Ithaca, 14850-5793

Direct Mail of NY-Posthaste, 199 Albany Post Rd (Suite 158), Buchanan, 10511-1624

Direct Mail Trackers, 3002 Chestnut Ave, Medford, 11763

Dispatch Letter Service, 344 W 38th St (4th fl), New York, 10018

Fulfillment Plus Inc, 889 Waverly Ave, Holtsville, 11742

G-Plex Direct Mail, 194 Morris Ave (Unit 9), Holtsville, 11742-1452

Graphnet Inc, 40 Fulton St Fl 28, New York, 10038-5074

Hand Assembly & Packaging Inc (HAPI), PO Box 617, Plainview, 11803-0019

Howell Marketing Services, 100 E Miller St., Elmira, 14904

Interstate EDP & Direct Mail Center Inc, 754 4th Ave, Brooklyn, 11232-1414

Key Computer Service of Chelsea, 227 E 56th St Rm 403, New York, 10022-3775

Key Mail Group of Companies, 266 Elmwood Ave # 514, Buffalo, 14222-2202

Lazarus Fulfillment House, 3530 Oceanside Rd, Oceanside, 11572-5829

Lettergraphics Inc, 433 W Onondaga St, Syracuse, 13201-1295

The Mailbox of Ithaca Inc, 1650 Hanshaw Rd, Ithaca, 14850-6348

Mailmen Inc, 15 Enter Ln, Hauppauge, 11749-4897

MVS Mailers Inc, 31 Crossways E Rd, Bohemia, 11716-1204

PDS International Mail Service, 85 Corporate Dr, Hauppauge, 11788

Prompt Mailers Inc, 66 Willow Ave (Suite 1), Staten Island, 10305-1848

Shakespeare Mailing Service, PO Box 8357, New York, 10116-8357

TNT International Express, 68 S Service Rd (Suite 340, Melville, 11747-2358

Unimail Corp, 655 Pullman Ave, Rochester, 14615-3313

US Monitor, 86 Maple Ave, New City, 10956-5019

Wolff/SMG, 1641 Commons Pkwy, Macedon, 14502-9190

WMG USA Inc, 1560 Broadway (fl 10), New York, 10036-1518

North Carolina

Excalibur Enterprises Inc, 4820 Bethania Station Rd, Winston Salem, 27105-1201

PBM Graphics, 415 Westcliff Rd, Greensboro, 27409

Sterling Business Services, 202 Dunhagan Pl, Cary, 27511-5049

Trinity Road LLC, PO Box 7445, Charlotte, 28241-7445

Ohio

Amity Unlimited Inc, 1221 Harrison Ave., Cincinnati, 45214-1719

Beuke Printing & Mailing, 3249 Fredonia Ave, Cincinnati, 45229-3309

JC Direct Mail Inc, 4241 Williams Rd, Groveport, 43125

Macke Bindery Inc, 10355 Spartan Dr, Cincinnati, 45215

Marketing Communication Resource Inc, 4800 E 345th St, Willoughby, 44094-4607

PJ McNerney & Associates Inc, 440 N Land Blvd, Cincinnati, 45240

Source Link, 3303 West Tech Rd, Miamisburg, 45342-0817

Vincent Graphics, LLC, PO Box 39, Box 386, Hilliard, 43026-0039

Oklahoma

DeLong Mailing Service, 3908 NW 3rd St, Oklahoma City, 73107-6606

Oregon

Co-operations, 20049 SW 112th Ave, Tualatin, 97062

Pennsylvania

ABDI, Inc Global Order Fulfillment, Ave A- Bldg 16, Buncher Commerce Park, Leetsdale, 15056-1304

Brokers Worldwide LLC, 701 Ashland Ave, Ashland Ctr III, Folcroft, 19032-2022

FedEx Ground, 1000 FedEx Dr, Coraopolis, 15108-9373

Walter Garson Jr & Associates Inc, 1370 Adams Rd, Bensalem, 19020

Karol Media, 375 Stewart Rd, PO Box 7600, Wilkes-Barre, 18773-7600

The Letter Shop Inc, 511 Towne Square Way, Brentwood Towne Center, Pittsburgh, 15227-3256

Mailing Specialists Inc, PO Box 230, Greensburg, 15601-0230

National Fulfillment Services, 100 Pine Ave, Holmes, 19043-1444

Pittsburgh Mailing, 4777 Streets Run Rd, Pittsburgh, 15236-1200

David J Thompson Mailing Corp, 21 Naus Way, Bloomsburg, 17815

Rhode Island

The Allied Group, 25 Amflex Dr, Cranston, 02921

Mercury Print & Mail Co Inc, 1110 Central Ave, Pawtucket, 02861-2262

Tennessee

MT&L Card Products & Fulfillment Services, 2911 Kraft Dr, Nashville, 37204-3618

Newroads Inc, 5751 Uptain Rd Ste 526, Chattanooga, 37411-5675

TechniPak, 149 Old Gray Station Rd, Gray, 37615-3470

Texas

Alliance Data, 7500 Dallas Pkwy Ste 700, Plano, 75024-4006

Focus Direct - a Dmh Marketing Partners Co, 9707 Broadway, San Antonio, 78217-0568

The JM Group Inc, 12716 O'Connor Rd, San Antonio, 78233

Mail Advertising Corp, 400 W 7th St, Fort Worth, 76102-4701

National Mail Advertising Inc, 2299 White St, Houston, 77007

QuantumDigital, PO Box 140825, Austin, 78714-0825

The Service Center LTD, 6450 Clara St (Suite 100), Houston, 77041

Summit Direct Mail Inc, 1655 Terre Colony Ct, Dallas, 75212-6222

Zachry Associates Inc, 500 Chestnut (Suite 2000), Abilene, 79602

Virginia

AmeriComm, 804 Greenbrier Cir, Chesapeake, 23320-2680

Direct Mail Solutions, 4500 Sarellen Rd, Henrico, 23231-4435

Mail America Communications - a Dmh Marketing Partners Co, 1174 Elkton Farm Rd, Forest, 24551-2128

Oberthur Card Systems, 4250 Pleasant Valley Rd, Chantilly, 20151

Washington

EDMS LLC, 17317 E Lake Goodwin Rd, Stanwood, 98292

Wisconsin

Advanced Mail Inc, 2908 Melby St, Eau Claire, 54703-0564

Freedom Graphic Systems Inc, 1101 S Janesville St, Milton, 53563-1838

Integrated Mail Industries Ltd, 3450 W Hopkins St, Milwaukee, 53216-1700

JHL Mail Marketing Inc, 3100 Borham Ave, Stevens Point, 54481-5097

Quad/Graphics, N63 W23075 Hwy 74, Sussex, 53089-2827

CANADA
Alberta

Globel Direct, 1324 36th Ave NE, Calgary, T2E 8S1

British Columbia

International Direct Response Services Ltd, 10159 Nordel Ct, Delta, V4G1J8

Ontario

ArrowMail Canada, 1415 Janette Ave, Windsor, N8X 1Z1

canadaplus.com, 2001 Huron Church Rd, Windsor, N9C 2L6

The Helicopter Group, 200 W Beaver Creek Rd (Unit 1), Richmond Hill, L4B 1B4

Interact Direct Marketing Inc, 787 Industrial Rd, London, N5V 4J4

Marco Sales & Incentives Ltd, 470 Hardy Rd, Brantford, N3V 6T1

Market Focus Direct, 550 Alden Rd (Suite 207), Markham, L3R 6A8

Post Linx Corp, 1170 Birchmount Rd, Scarborough, M1P 5E3

Wood & Associates Direct Marketing Services Ltd, 2-237 Finchdene Sq, Scarborough, M1X 2E1

World Wide Mailers, 2744 Edna St, Windsor, N8Y 1V2

Lettershops, Mailing Services & Product Fulfillment Companies (28)

A&M DIRECT MAIL SERVICE INC
949 N Cataract Ave (Suite 1)
San Dimas, CA 91773-1464
Telephone: (909) 599-3905, (909) 579-0111, (800) 735-3905, FAX: (909) 599-3516, E-Mail: mail@amdirectmail.com
Pres: A.F. Feldbush

A-1 DIRECT MAIL MARKETING INC
11950 SW 128th St
Miami, FL 33186-5207
Telephone: (305) 251-3187
Pres: William Bowne

A+ LETTER SERVICE
200 Syracuse Ct
Lakewood, NJ 08701
Telephone: (732) 905-2010, FAX: (732) 905-4662, E-Mail: aplus@apluletter.com, Web Site: www.aplusletters.com
Pres: Ray Finnegan

THE DMA A-KD MAILING & FULFILLMENT SERVICE
6850 N Central Park
Lincolnwood, IL 60712-2704
Telephone: (847) 673-0186, (866) 330-6245, FAX: (874) 673-0188, E-Mail: dan@kdmailing.com, Web Site: www.kdmailing.com
Pres: Hal Cohen
VP: Dan Goldberg
VP, Fulfillment: Jim Schwartz
Sls Assoc: Bill Heynes
Primary Market Served: Business & Consumer
Founded: 1951
Mailing & fulfillment services.

ABDI, INC GLOBAL ORDER FULFILLMENT
Ave A- Bldg 16, Buncher Commerce Park
Leetsdale, PA 15056-1304
Telephone: (412) 741-1142, (800) 796-6471, FAX: (412) 741-4161, E-Mail: info@abdintl.com, Web Site: www.abdintl.com
Pres: Judy G. Cheteyan
Dir Fin & IT: Brian A. Cox
CEO: Michael D. Cheteyan II

THE DMA ACCESS DIRECT SYSTEMS INC
91 Executive Blvd
Farmingdale, NY 11735-4710
Telephone: (631) 420-0700, Web Site: www.accessdirect.com
Exec VP: Lori Messina

THE ADDED TOUCH
2221 Niagara Falls Blvd Ste 4, Box 4
Niagara Falls, NY 14304-1696
Telephone: (905) 828-4041, (888) AD-TOUCH, FAX: (905) 338-1486, E-Mail: addedtouch@gmail.com, Web Site: www.addedtouch.com
Pres: Garrett Hall
Conducts Business: U.S., Canada
Employees: 20
Primary Market Served: Business & Consumer
Catalog available online
Indirect online sales
Advertising/Marketing Budget Related to Direct Marketing: 76-100%
Direct Marketing ad budget:
Direct Mail: 85%
Magazines: 10%
Newspapers: 5%
Founded: 1961
Gross sales or billing: $4,000,000

Sell unique, practical household items and call center/fulfillment services.

ADVANCE MAILING SERVICES INC
1130 Carolina Dr (Unit A)
West Chicago, IL 60185-5163
Telephone: (630) 293-0707, FAX: (630) 293-9268
Pres: Dave Devendran

ADVANCED IMAGE DIRECT
1415 S Acacia Ave.
Fullerton, CA 92831-5317
Telephone: (714) 502-3900, (800) 540-3848, FAX: (714) 502-3901, Web Site: www.advancedimagedirect.com
Pres: Frank Verrill
VP Sales: Perry Wilson

ADVANCED MAIL INC
2908 Melby St
Eau Claire, WI 54703-0564
Telephone: (715) 839-8801, FAX: (715) 839-8906, Web Site: www.amailinc.com

Pres: Gary Dreher

ADVANCED MARKETING DIRECT
99 Thielman Dr
Buffalo, NY 14206-2365
Telephone: (800) 696-7567, Web Site: www.amdirect.com
Mktg & New Bus: John Loury

THE DMA ADVANTAGE MAILING INC
PO Box 66013
Anaheim, CA 92816-6013
Telephone: (714) 538-3881, (888) 909-6245, FAX: (714) 282-3903, Web Site: www.advantagemailinginc.com
Sls Mgr: Diane Denish

ADVANTAGE MARKETING GROUP
1550 Howard St
Elk Grove Village, IL 60007
Telephone: (847) 952-2100, FAX: (847) 952-3348, Web Site: www.goamg.com
Pres: Patricia Hermann

ADVERTISING MAILERS INC
PO Box 6378
Edison, NJ 08818-6378
Telephone: (732) 225-3404, (800) 427-8513, FAX: (732) 225-7429, E-Mail: admailers@aol.com
Chmn: Sidney A. Jarvis
Pres: A.L. Garcia

ADWEST MAILERS INC
19320 Londelius St
Northridge, CA 91324-3509
Telephone: (818) 982-3720, FAX: (818) 982-3786, E-Mail: sales@adwest.com, Web Site: www.adwest.com
Pres: Frank Grijalva
Sls: Arthur Grijalva

AIM MARKETING
525 North D, PO Box 522
Fremont, NE 68025-5051
Telephone: (402) 721-2077, FAX: (402) 721-9171, E-Mail: aim@solution-group.com
Pres: C.J. Tighe

THE DMA **ALANIZ - A DMH MARKETING PARTNERS CO**
425 N Iris Rd, Box 799
Mount Pleasant, IA 52641-3109
Telephone: (319) 385-7259, FAX: (319) 385-2825, E-Mail: info@ alanizdirect.com, Web Site: www. alanizdirect.com
Pres: Randy Seberg
Dir Procurement: Ethan Burd

THE DMA **ALERT MARKETING**
2 S 180 Kent Rd
Glen Ellyn, IL 60137
Telephone: (630) 790-0386, Web Site: www.alertmarketing.com
Pres: David Leyden

ALLIANCE DATA
7500 Dallas Pkwy Ste 700
Plano, TX 75024-4006
Telephone: (972) 348-5100, Web Site: www.alliancedata.com
Chmn & CEO: Ken Murphy
Pres Retail Svcs: Ivan Szeftel

THE ALLIED GROUP
25 Amflex Dr
Cranston, RI 02921
Telephone: (401) 946-6100, Web Site: www.thealliedgrp.com
Pres & CEO: Bob Clement
Founded: 1946

Marketing communications & Fulfillment Services

ALTERNATE MARKETING NETWORKS INC
4675 32nd Ave Ste B
Hudsonville, MI 49426-8012
Telephone: (616) 662-6420, FAX: (616) 662-6422, Web Site: www. altmarknet.com
Chmn & CEO: Philip D. Miller

AMERICAN MAILING SERVICE INC
Div. of The Gallaher Group
336 13th St
Ashland, KY 41101-7536
Telephone: (606) 329-2741, (800) 678-8384, FAX: (606) 325-8558, Web Site: www.thegallahergroup.com
Pres: John Gallaher

AMERICAN SPIRIT MAILING
Div. of A.H.L. Services Inc
401 13th Ave N, PO Box 707
Howard Lake, MN 55349-0707
Telephone: (320) 543-3737, FAX: (320) 543-3228, E-Mail: asgc@asgc-mail.com, Web Site: www.asgc.com

Gen Mgr: Dennis Duval

AMERICOMM
804 Greenbrier Cir
Chesapeake, VA 23320-2680
Telephone: (303) 371-4400, FAX: (303) 371-2527, Web Site: www. americomm.net
Gen Mgr: David Stoll

AMITY UNLIMITED INC
1221 Harrison Ave.
Cincinnati, OH 45214-1719
Telephone: (513) 554-4500, FAX: (513) 554-0450, Web Site: www. amityunlimited.com
Chmn: Robert Janszen

ANETORDER/AMERICAN MAILERS
820 Frontenac Rd
Naperville, IL 60563-1743
Telephone: (630) 579-8800, Web Site: www.anetorder.com
Pres: Shane Randall

ARCHWAY MARKETING SERVICES
19850 S Diamond Lake Rd
Rogers, MN 55374
Telephone: (763) 428-3300, (866) 779-9855 X1933, FAX: (763) 488-6803, E-Mail: sales@archway.com, Web Site: www.archway.com
CEO: Clay Perfall
Conducts Business: U.S., Canada
Employees: 2,400
Primary Market Served: Business Advertising/Marketing Budget Related to Direct Marketing: 0-25%
Founded: 1953
Gross sales or billing: $33,000,000

ARROW MAILING SERVICE II INC
13040 Cerise Ave
Hawthorne, CA 90250-5523
Telephone: (310) 219-7740, FAX: (310) 219-3335
Pres: Robert A. Tappan

THE DMA **ARROWMAIL CANADA**
1415 Janette Ave
Windsor, ON, Canada N8X 1Z1
Telephone: (313) 961-8334, FAX: (313) 961-7849, E-Mail: info@ mailingcanada.com, Web Site: www. mailingcanada.com
VP: Jeff Williams

ARTICHOKE INK
1265 S La Arboleta St
Gilbert, AZ 85296-4134

Telephone: (480) 792-9597, Web Site: www.artichokeink.com

AUTOMATIC MAIL SERVICES INC
4700 34th St
Long Island City, NY 11101-2412
Telephone: (718) 361-3091, FAX: (718) 937-8568, E-Mail: data@ automatic-mail.com, Web Site: www. automatic-mail.com
Pres: Michael Waskover

THE DMA **BFC**
1051 N Kirk Rd
Batavia, IL 60510-1438
Telephone: (630) 879-9240, Web Site: www.bfcprint.com
Pres: Joseph Novak

THE DMA **BMI FULFILLMENT SERVICES**
Subs. of Blumenfield Marketing Inc
PO Box 3285
Danbury, CT 06813-3285
Telephone: (203) 546-5580, FAX: (203) 546-5575, E-Mail: barry@ bmigroup.com, Web Site: www. bmigroup.com
CEO: Barry Blumenfield
Dir: Arthur Blumenfield

BARTON & COONEY
300 Richards Run
Burlington, NJ 08016-2120
Telephone: (609) 747-9300, FAX: (609) 747-9700, E-Mail: pmdoyle@ bartoncooney.com, Web Site: www. bartoncooney.com
Pres: Patrick Doyle
Controller: Linda Malin
Founded: 1920

Printing & Mailing

THE BENDER GROUP
345 Parr Cir
Reno, NV 89512
Telephone: (775) 788-8800, (800) 621-9402, FAX: (775) 788-8811, E-Mail: salesinfo@benderwhs.com, Web Site: www.bendergroup.com
Mgr Bus Devel: Jared Lindwall
Mgr, Bender Intl: William Dalton

BETTER LISTS INC
64 Sunnyside
Stamford, CT 06902-4792
Telephone: (203) 324-4171, FAX: (203) 358-0384, E-Mail: tim@ betterlists.com, Web Site: www. betterlists.com
Pres: George S. Rath
VP: Colin D Rath

BEUKE PRINTING & MAILING
3249 Fredonia Ave
Cincinnati, OH 45229-3309
Telephone: (513) 221-0008, FAX:
(513) 221-0038, E-Mail: info@
beuke.com, Web Site: www.beuke.
com
Pres: Chuck Beuke
Mktg Dir: Bobbie Beuke

BLUE GRASS MAILING, DATA & FULFILLMENT SERVICES
833 Nandino Blvd
Lexington, KY 40511-1202
Telephone: (859) 231-7272, (800) 928-
6245, FAX: (859) 259-1214, E-Mail:
info@bgmailing.com, Web Site:
www.bgmailing.com
Pres: Thomas B. Nichols

BRIGAR XPRESS SOLUTIONS, INC
5 Sand Creek Rd Ste 100
Albany, NY 12205-1400
Telephone: (518) 438-7817, (877) 437-
7817, FAX: (518) 438-0224, E-Mail:
general@brigarxpress.com, Web Site:
www.brigarxpress.com
Pres & CEO: Jack McGrath

THE DMA **BROKERS WORLDWIDE LLC**
701 Ashland Ave, Ashland Ctr III
Folcroft, PA 19032-2022
Telephone: (610) 461-3661, (800)
MAIL-287, FAX: (610) 461-4239,
E-Mail: csmith@brokersworldwide.
com, Web Site: www.
brokersworldwide.com
Sr VP Sls & Mktg: Gary Shunk
Mktg Coord: Colleen M. Smith

BULLSEYE MARKETING INC
9025 Owensmouth Ave
Canoga Park, CA 91304-1417
Telephone: (818) 888-8700, Web Site:
www.bullseyeb2b.com
Pres: Scott Barker

THE BUREAU INC
2809 SE Monroe St
Stuart, FL 34997-5904
Telephone: (561) 845-8400, FAX:
(561) 845-7979, Web Site: www.
bureauinc.com
Pres: Resa Arnold

BUSINESS SERVICES NETWORK
1275 Fairfax Ave Ste 103
San Francisco, CA 94124-1759

Telephone: (415) 282-8161, FAX:
(415) 282-8176, E-Mail: sales@bsnc.
com, Web Site: www.bsnc.com
CEO: Frank P. Sargent

THE DMA **THE CPW GROUP**
60 Trade Zone Ct
Ronkonkoma, NY 11779-7395
Telephone: (888) 641-7901
CEO: Lorraine Chaudhry-Ekinci
Pres: John P. Plate

CALMARK INC
1400 W 44th St
Chicago, IL 60609-3332
Telephone: (773) 247-7200, FAX:
(773) 247-3199, E-Mail: ljakobi@
calmark-inc.com, Web Site: www.
clamark-inc.com
Pres & CEO: Jim Fitzgerald

THE DMA **CANADAPLUS.COM**
Business unit of Russell A Farrow Ltd
2001 Huron Church Rd
Windsor, ON, Canada N9C 2L6
Telephone: (519) 966-3003, (877) 966-
3003, FAX: (519) 966-1749, E-Mail:
canadaplusinfo@canadaplus.com,
Web Site: www.canadaplus.com
Dir Intl Logistics: Michael Meixner
Conducts Business: U.S., Canada
Employees: 500
Primary Market Served: Business
Indirect online sales
Advertising/Marketing Budget Related
to Direct Marketing: 0-25%
Founded: 1911
Gross sales or billing: $30,000,000

3rd party logistics, reduce cost, improve customer service, help build
your Canadian Market, time definite,
returns logistics, pick a pack & more.

CARDINAL MAILING SERVICES LTD
197 Sand Island Access Rd Ste 211
Honolulu, HI 96819-4901
Telephone: (808) 538-3884, FAX:
(808) 521-1419, E-Mail: mail@
cardinalservicesltd.com, Web Site:
www.cardinalservicesltd.com
Pres: Malia Lageman

CENTURY DIRECT
30-30 47th Ave
Long Island City, NY 11101
Telephone: (212) 349-0600, FAX:
(718) 349-9528, E-Mail: info@
centurydirect.net, Web Site: www.
centurydirect.net

CHALLENGE INDUSTRIES INC
950 Danby Rd (Suite 179)
Ithaca, NY 14850-5793
Telephone: (607) 272-8990, FAX:
(607) 277-7865, E-Mail: info@
aboutchallenge.org, Web Site: www.
aboutchallenge.org
Pres: Patrick McKee

CHARNSTROM
5391 12th Ave E
Shakopee, MN 55379-1896
Telephone: (952) 403-0303, (800) 328-
2962, FAX: (800) 916-3215, E-Mail:
mail@charnstrom.com, Web Site:
www.charnstrom.com
Pres: Greg Hedlund
VP: John Herntier
Sls Mgr: Kathy Lundy

CLOUTIER DIRECT INC
3 Washington Ave
Scarborough, ME 04074-9782
Telephone: (207) 883-9599, Web Site:
www.cloutierdirect.com
Pres: Scott Provencher

CO-OPERATIONS
20049 SW 112th Ave
Tualatin, OR 97062
Telephone: (503) 620-7977, (866) 228-
6362, FAX: (503) 620-7917, E-Mail:
info@fsipdx.com, Web Site: www.
fsipdx.com
CEO: Patricia Granum

COM-PAK
PO Box 7312
Berlin, CT 06037-7312
Telephone: (856) 802-1900, (856) 802-
3097, E-Mail: info@com-pak.com,
Web Site: www.marketpointdirect.
com
Pres/CEO: Ken McGovern
Pres: Steve Walk

COM-PAK SERVICES INC
365 New Albany Rd Ste A
Moorestown, NJ 08057-1105
Telephone: (856) 802-1900, Web Site:
www.com-pak.com
VP Sales & Client Svc: Pamela Spain

COMAC INC
565 Sinclair Frontage Rd
Milpitas, CA 95035
Telephone: (408) 945-1600, (866)
COMAC4U, FAX: (408) 946-1135,
E-Mail: info@comac.com, Web Site:
www.comac.com
CEO: Kevin Westerhouse

COMPLETE MAILING SERVICE INC
108 Dubois St
Santa Cruz, CA 95060-2109
Telephone: (831) 425-5556, FAX: (831) 425-0306, Web Site: www.completemail.com
Pres: Lawrence Selman

COMPULETTER INC
7460 N Lehigh Ave
Niles, IL 60714-4024
Telephone: (847) 647-6200, FAX: (847) 647-2309, E-Mail: directmail@compuletter.com, Web Site: www.compuletter.com
Pres: Gary M. Ross
Exec VP: Steven B. Ross

CONSOLIDATED MAILING CORP
5735 Kessler Ln
Shawnee Mission, KS 66203-2591
Telephone: (913) 262-4400, (800) 706-6245, FAX: (913) 262-7801, E-Mail: cmcmail@swbell.net, Web Site: www.consolidatedmailing.com
Pres: Buz Prosser

CRANE DUPLICATING SERVICE INC
4915 Rattlesnake Hammock Rd
Naples, FL 34113-6959
Telephone: (305) 280-6742, FAX: (239) 732-8415, Web Site: www.craneduplicating.com
Pres: Richard W. Price

CREATIVE MAILING & MARKETING
Subs. of FYI Inc
879 W 190th St Ste 400
Gardena, CA 90248-4223
Telephone: (310) 637-7100, FAX: (714) 998-9001, Web Site: www.creativemandm.com
Pres: Barrie Robertson
Mng Dir: Jack Jordan

DHL EXPRESS
1200 S Pine Island Rd (Suite 600)
Plantation, FL 33324
Telephone: (954) 888-7000, (800) 225-5345, FAX: (954) 888-7310, Web Site: www.dhl.com
Pres: Vick Guinasso

THE DMA DHL GLOBAL MAIL
Sub. of DPWN
2700 S Commerce Pkwy (Suite 400)
Weston, FL 33331-3631

Telephone: (954) 903-6300, (866) 616-MAIL, FAX: (954) 903-6310, E-Mail: contact@dhlglobalmail.com, Web Site: www.dhlglobalmail.com
Sr VP Mktg: David Marinkovich
Dir Commun: Edith Wollin
Dir Mktg: Jane Bergos

THE DMA DMH MARKETING PARTNERS - LOUISVILLE
12101 Westport Rd
Louisville, KY 40245-1759
Telephone: (502) 339-6442, Web Site: www.thednrgroup.com

DST OUTPUT
125 Ellington Rd
South Windsor, CT 06074-4112
Telephone: (860) 290-7337, (800) 441-7587, Web Site: www.dstoutput.com
Pres & CEO: Steve Towle
VP Sls & Corp Commun: Cheryl Kananowicz

DATA DIRECT
8120 River Dr
Morton Grove, IL 60053
Telephone: (847) 966-8327, FAX: (847) 966-8382
Pres: Hector Rodriguez

THE DMA DATA-MAIL INC
240 Hartford Ave
Newington, CT 06111-2054
Telephone: (860) 666-0399, FAX: (860) 665-1226, E-Mail: brucem@data-mail.com, Web Site: www.data-mail.com
Pres: Andrew J. Mandell
Dir Corp Devel: Mark Mandell

DELONG MAILING SERVICE
3908 NW 3rd St
Oklahoma City, OK 73107-6606
Telephone: (405) 272-9401
Pres: Christi Everest

THE DMA DIRECT LINK WORLDWIDE
700 Dowd Ave
Elizabeth, NJ 07201-2108
Telephone: (908) 289-0703, (800) 223-7967, FAX: (908) 289-0705, E-Mail: infousa@directlink.com, Web Site: www.directlink.com
Pres: John Cucciniello

THE DMA DIRECT MAIL DEPOT INC
200 Circle Dr N
Piscataway, NJ 08854-3705
Telephone: (732) 469-5900, FAX: (732) 469-8414, E-Mail: sales@directmaildepot.com, Web Site: www.directmaildepot.com

Exec VP Sls & Mktg: Mitchell Goldklank
COO: Carmen Ocello
CFO: Chris Trainor
Conducts Business: U.S.
Employees: 250
Primary Market Served: Business
Advertising/Marketing Budget Related to Direct Marketing: 0-25%
Direct Marketing ad budget: $50,000
Direct Mail: 100%
Founded: 1990

Specializing in laser personalization and complete lettershop services. Serving the direct mail industry.

DIRECT MAIL OF NY-POSTHASTE
Div. of MCS Marketing Group Inc
199 Albany Post Rd (Suite 158)
Buchanan, NY 10511-1624
Telephone: (914) 736-2239
Sr Acct Rep: Christine Saluto

THE DMA DIRECT MAIL SOLUTIONS
4500 Sarellen Rd
Henrico, VA 23231-4435
Telephone: (804) 254-8300, Web Site: www.directmailsolutions.com
Dir Bus Devel: Stephanie Hoy

DIRECT MAIL SOLUTIONS LLC
775 Kimberly Dr
Carol Stream, IL 60188-9407
Telephone: (630) 653-6863, FAX: (630) 653-7144, E-Mail: support@dmspostal.com, Web Site: www.dmspostal.com
Partner: Robert Hopkins
Partner: Bob Zunker
Partner: Jerry Gately
Employees: 10

Chicago area direct mail company.

DIRECT MAIL SOURCE
Div. of Women Entrepreneurs Inc
PO Box 8033
Wilmette, IL 60091-8033
Telephone: (847) 676-3744, E-Mail: dms@directmailsource.net
Pres: Debra Izenstark

DIRECT MAIL TRACKERS
Div. of List Technology Systems Group Inc
3002 Chestnut Ave
Medford, NY 11763
Telephone: (631) 758-0984, E-Mail: info@dmtrackers.com, Web Site: www.dmtrackers.com
Pres: Kevin Haining

DIRECT MARKET DESIGNS INC
45 E 5th St
Paterson, NJ 07524-1101
Telephone: (973) 925-9600, Web Site:
www.dmd-liberty.com
VP: Darwin Guarderas

DIRECT ONE INC
7224 Sandscove Ct (Suite 7)
Winter Park, FL 32792-6903
Telephone: (407) 673-4500, FAX:
(407) 673-4501, E-Mail: wariagno@
directoneinc.com, Web Site: www.
directoneinc.com
CEO: Jeff Lauridsen
Exec VP: William G. Ariagno
Exec Mgr: Vicki Fosdyck
Conducts Business: U.S., Canada
Employees: 25
Primary Market Served: Business
Advertising/Marketing Budget Related
to Direct Marketing: 0-25%
Founded: 1999
Gross sales or billing: $4,000,000

Full service direct mail service.

DIRECT RESPONSE MARKETING
12450 Automobile Blvd
Clearwater, FL 33762
Telephone: (727) 573-1985, (800) 683-
6245, FAX: (727) 573-1747, E-Mail:
drmclwr@tampabay.rr.com, Web
Site: www.dmsmails.com
Pres: Roger Pennington

THE DMA DIRECTMAIL.COM
Div. of DM Group
201 Skipjack Rd
Prince Frederick, MD 20678-3411
Telephone: (888) 690-2252, FAX:
(301) 855-9810, Web Site: www.
directmail.com
Pres: Joseph Salta
VP: E. Hawley Van Wyck
VP: Robert Salta
VP: Kirk L. Swain
VP, Prod: Cindy Vance
VP, Devel: Price Anderson
Conducts Business: U.S.
Employees: 20
Primary Market Served: Business
Direct online sales
Advertising/Marketing Budget Related
to Direct Marketing: 0-25%
Direct Marketing ad budget:
Direct Mail: $200,000
Founded: 1972
Gross sales or billing: $3,000,000

Direct mail fund-raising counsel.

DIRECTORY DISTRIBUTING ASSOCIATES INC
1602 Park 370 Ct
Hazelwood, MO 63042-4418
Telephone: (314) 592-8600, (800) 325-
1964, FAX: (314) 592-8790, E-Mail:
corporate@directrac.com, Web Site:
www.ddai.com
Chmn: John Runk

DISPATCH LETTER SERVICE
Subs. of Dispatch Graphics Inc
344 W 38th St (4th fl)
New York, NY 10018
Telephone: (212) 307-5943, FAX:
(212) 307-6103, Web Site: www.
dispatchletterservice.com
Pres & CEO: Paul A. Grech
Pres: Stephen Grech

DISTRIBUTION POSTAL CO INC
6200 Frankford Ave
Baltimore, MD 21206-4902
Telephone: (410) 488-1002, (800) 992-
4525, FAX: (410) 488-2344, E-Mail:
louishaber@distpost.com, Web Site:
www.distpost.com
VP: Louis Haber

EDMS LLC
17317 E Lake Goodwin Rd
Stanwood, WA 98292
Telephone: (360) 654-0448, (866) 222-
3367, FAX: (360) 652-6199, E-Mail:
info@edmsllc.com, Web Site: www.
edmsllc.com
Owner: Elaine Delack

ESP PRINTING & MAILING INC
317 E 37th St (Suite 5)
Boise, ID 83714-6475
Telephone: (800) 338-6789, FAX:
(208) 345-4765, E-Mail: data@
espmap.com
Pres: Ernest S. Puopolo

THE ENVELOPE CONNECTION INC
4424 N Ravenswood
Chicago, IL 60640
Telephone: (773) 275-3500, Web Site:
www.artofbarter.com/
EnvelopeConnectionProfile.html
VP Sls: Andrew Calvimontes

THE DMA EXCALIBUR ENTERPRISES INC
4820 Bethania Station Rd
Winston Salem, NC 27105-1201

Telephone: (336) 744-5000, (800) 441-
4193, FAX: (336) 767-8257, E-Mail:
info@excaliburmail.com, Web Site:
www.excaliburmail.com
Pres: Jackson D. Wilson Jr

FARIS MAILING INC
701 N Holt Rd Ste 3
Indianapolis, IN 46222-3455
Telephone: (317) 246-3315, FAX:
(317) 246-3330, E-Mail:
farismailing@iquest.net, Web Site:
farismailing.com
Pres: Robert L. Faris Jr

FEDEX GROUND
dba FedEx Ground Package System,
Inc
1000 FedEx Dr
Coraopolis, PA 15108-9373
Telephone: (412) 269-1000, (800) 762-
3725, FAX: (412) 747-4295, Web
Site: www.fedex.com/us/ground/main
Pres & CEO: David F. Rebholz

FINISHING PLUS, INC
4546 W 47th St
Chicago, IL 60632
Telephone: (773) 523-5510, FAX:
(773) 523-9155, E-Mail: info@
finishingplus.com, Web Site: www.
finishingplus.com
VP: Frank Puisis

THE DMA FIRST DATA CORP
6200 S Quebec St
Greenwood Village, CO 80111-4729
Telephone: (303) 488-8000, (800) 735-
3362, Web Site: www.firstdata.com
CEO & Chmn: Henry C. Duques
Mktg Dir: Lisa Fugate

THE FIRST OCCUPATIONAL CENTER OF NEW JERSEY
391 Lakeside Ave
Orange, NJ 07050-2809
Telephone: (973) 672-5800, FAX:
(973) 672-0065, E-Mail: ocnj@ocnj.
org, Web Site: www.ocnj.org
Pres & CEO: Rocco J. Meola
Admin Asst: Francine Faragi

THE DMA FOCUS DIRECT - A DMH MARKETING PARTNERS CO
9707 Broadway
San Antonio, TX 78217-0568
Telephone: (210) 247-1634, (800) 299-
9185, FAX: (210) 247-1691, Web
Site: www.focusdirect.com
Pres & CEO: Fred B. Lederman

FORM HOUSE INC
Div. of Diam International
5750 Old Orchard Rd (Suite 520)
Skokie, IL 60077-1081
Telephone: (708) 594-7300, FAX:
   (708) 594-7390, E-Mail: ktalbot@
   theformhouse.com, Web Site: www.
   theformhouse.com
Sr VP: Keith Talbot

FOSDICK FULFILLMENT CORP
26 Barnes Industrial Park Rd N
Wallingford, CT 06492
Telephone: (203) 269-0211, (800) 759-
   5588, FAX: (203) 679-3290, E-Mail:
   sales@fosdickcorp.com, Web Site:
   www.fosdickfulfillment.com
VP New Bus Dev: George C. Fanolis
Mng Dir: Steven J. Edelstein

ᴅᴹᴬ FREEDOM GRAPHIC SYSTEMS INC
1101 S Janesville St
Milton, WI 53563-1838
Telephone: (608) 868-7007, (800) 334-
   3540, FAX: (608) 868-7006, E-Mail:
   information@fgs.com, Web Site:
   www.freedomgraphicsystems.com
Mgr: Tony Allighen

FULFILLMENT EXPRESS INC
7271 Paramount Blvd
Pico Rivera, CA 90660
Telephone: (562) 948-4400, (800) 700-
   9295, FAX: (562) 948-4459, E-Mail:
   information@fex.com, Web Site:
   www.fex.com
Pres: Dieter Ammann

FULFILLMENT PLUS INC
889 Waverly Ave
Holtsville, NY 11742
Telephone: (631) 758-8300, FAX:
   (631) 758-8360, E-Mail: jeff.
   ehrlich@fulfillmentplusny.com, Web
   Site: www.fulfillmentplusny.com
Pres: Jeffrey Ehrlich

FULFILLMENT XCELLENCE INC (FXI)
5235 Thatcher Rd
Downers Grove, IL 60515-4027
Telephone: (630) 852-7600, FAX:
   (630) 852-5817, Web Site: www.fx-
   inc.com
VP & Gen Mgr: Doug Bensing

G-PLEX DIRECT MAIL
194 Morris Ave (Unit 9)
Holtsville, NY 11742-1452
Telephone: (631) 447-9500, Web Site:
   www.g-plex.net
Sls Mgr: Glen Faulhaber

GMI DISTRIBUTION
Div. of Gordon Management Inc
305 Churchill Ave
Somerset, NJ 08873
Telephone: (732) 846-4800, FAX:
   (732) 846-4709, E-Mail: keith@
   gmidistribution.com, Web Site:
   www.gmidistribution.com
Pres: Keith Gordon

WALTER GARSON JR & ASSOCIATES INC
1370 Adams Rd
Bensalem, PA 19020
Telephone: (215) 245-6610, FAX:
   (215) 245-0281, E-Mail: walt@
   garsonmail.com
Pres: Walter Garson Jr.

GLOBEL DIRECT
1324 36th Ave NE
Calgary, AB, Canada T2E 8S1
Telephone: (403) 531-6500, (800) 551-
   5721, FAX: (403) 531-6560, E-Mail:
   jr.richardson@globel.com, Web Site:
   www.globel.com
Pres & CEO: J.R. Richardson

GOODKIND & GOODKIND DIRECT INC
1433 11 St (Suite I)
Arcata, CA 95521-5712
Telephone: (712) 347-6114, (800) 690-
   9342, FAX: (712) 347-5754, E-Mail:
   mail@goodkind.com, Web Site:
   www.goodkind.com
COO & CFO: Dan Goodkind
Pres: Kathi Goodkind

GORDON MANAGEMENT INC
aka GMI Distribution
305 Churchill Ave
Somerset, NJ 08873-3486
Telephone: (732) 846-4800, FAX:
   (732) 846-4709, E-Mail: keith@
   gmidistribution.com, Web Site:
   www.gmidistribution.com
Pres: Keith Gordon
VP: Kenneth Gordon

GRAPHNET INC
40 Fulton St Fl 28
New York, NY 10038-5074
Telephone: (212) 994-1100, (800) 327-
   1800, FAX: (212) 994-1188, E-Mail:
   custsvc@graphnet.com, Web Site:
   www.graphnet.com
Pres & CEO: Yaakov Elkon
COO: Idan Elkon

HAND ASSEMBLY & PACKAGING INC (HAPI)
Div. of Your Mail Sack Inc
PO Box 617

Plainview, NY 11803-0019
Telephone: (718) 699-3400, FAX:
   (718) 699-3409
Pres: Leonard Berse

HAYS INTERNATIONAL MAILING SERVICES
26 Hilliard Ave (Apt 1)
Edgewater, NJ 07020-1200
Telephone: (201) 307-8888, E-Mail:
   ltucker@haysmailing.com, Web Site:
   www.haysmailing.com
Pres: Larry Tucker

ᴅᴹᴬ THE HELICOPTER GROUP
200 W Beaver Creek Rd (Unit 1)
Richmond Hill, ON, Canada L4B 1B4
Telephone: (905) 731-2440, Web Site:
   www.thehelicoptergroup.com
Pres: Kishan Gunasekaram

ᴅᴹᴬ THE HIBBERT GROUP
400 Pennington Ave
Trenton, NJ 08618-3105
Telephone: (609) 394-7500, (800) 545-
   4747, FAX: (609) 695-6553, Web
   Site: www.hibbertco.com
Owner: Joan Moonan
VP Account Mgmt: Paul Zukowski

HIGH COTTON
PO Box 101568
Birmingham, AL 35210-6568
Telephone: (877) 838-2345, FAX:
   (205) 836-5587, E-Mail: sales@
   highscottonusa.com, Web Site: www.
   highcottonusa.com
Pres: Thomas S. McGahey
Sls Mgr Direct Mail: John H. Meich
Prod Mgr Fulfillment: Chris Clark
Conducts Business: U.S.
Employees: 100
Primary Market Served: Business &
   Consumer
Advertising/Marketing Budget Related
   to Direct Marketing: 76-100%
Founded: 1963

Full service direct marketing and fulfillment company - our suite of services include: database marketing, lists,
data processing, printing, lettershop
and fulfillment.

HOGARD BUSINESS SERVICES INC
450 S Schuyler Ave
Bradley, IL 60915-2344
Telephone: (815) 932-1835, FAX:
   (815) 932-4793, E-Mail: hogards@
   att.net, Web Site: www.
   hogardbusinessservices.com
Pres: Myrna Sullivan

HOWELL MARKETING SERVICES

Div. of F.M. Howell & Co
100 E Miller St.
Elmira, NY 14904
Telephone: (607) 734-6291, FAX:
(607) 734-6759, E-Mail: gl@
howellmarketingservices.com, Web
Site: www.howellmarketingservices.
com
Pres: Katherine H. Roehlke
Admin Asst: Barbara James

IDEAGROUP MAIL SERVICE

4455 White Bear Pkwy
Saint Paul, MN 55110
Telephone: (651) 490-2903, FAX:
(651) 490-0728, E-Mail: ideagroup@
visi.com
Owner: Steven Butler

IMAGINE FULFILLMENT SERVICES

20100 S Vermont Ave
Torrance, CA 90502-1361
Telephone: (310) 217-4610, FAX:
(310) 217-9632, E-Mail: andya@
imaginefulfillment.com, Web Site:
www.imaginefulfillment.com
Sls & Mktg: Marcel Tsai
Conducts Business: U.S.
Employees: 300
Primary Market Served: Business
Catalog available online
Advertising/Marketing Budget Related
to Direct Marketing: 0-25%
Direct Marketing ad budget: $250,000
Direct Mail: 25%
Magazines: 25%
Newspapers: 25%
Telephone: 25%
Founded: 1998
Gross sales or billing: $20,000,000

Services include - pick, pack & ship.
For direct mailers, e-commerce promotional items, sweepstakes, DRTV, POP.

IMPACT MAILING

4600 Lyndale Ave N
Minneapolis, MN 55412-1408
Telephone: (612) 521-6245, FAX:
(612) 521-1349, E-Mail: sales@
impactmailing.com, Web Site: www.
impactmailing.com
Pres: Mark Anderson

ᴛʜᴇ IMPRESSIONS DIRECT
ᴅᴍᴀ

2116 59th St
Saint Louis, MO 63110-2808
Telephone: (314) 951-2100, Web Site:
www.impressions-direct.com
VP: John Moresi

INNOTRAC CORP

6465 E Johns Xing Ste 400
Duluth, GA 30097-1581
Telephone: (678) 584-4000, FAX:
(678) 475-5840, Web Site: www.
innotrac.com
VP Sls: Sandy Probst

INNOVATIVE INDUSTRIES INC

421 W Centennial Ave
Carthage, MO 64836-3528
Telephone: (417) 358-6891, (800) 344-
7467, FAX: (417) 358-1849, E-Mail:
info@innovativeindustries.com, Web
Site: www.innovativeindustries.com
Gen Mgr: Larry Lloyd

INTEGRATED MAIL INDUSTRIES LTD

3450 W Hopkins St
Milwaukee, WI 53216-1700
Telephone: (414) 908-3500, FAX:
(414) 449-2906, E-Mail: sales@
integratedmail.com, Web Site: www.
integratedmail.com
VP: Jerry Benjamin

ᴛʜᴇ INTERACT DIRECT
ᴅᴍᴀ MARKETING INC

787 Industrial Rd
London, ON, Canada N5V 4J4
Telephone: (519) 439-6245, Web Site:
www.interactdirect.com
Pres: Jeffrey Bisset

INTERNATIONAL DIRECT RESPONSE SERVICES LTD

10159 Nordel Ct
Delta, BC, Canada V4G1J8
Telephone: (604) 951-6855, Web Site:
www.idrs.ca
Pres & CEO: Mark Weeks

INTERNATIONAL MAILING SOLUTIONS LLC

25 Corporate Dr (Suite 175)
Burlington, MA 01803-4243
Telephone: (718) 376-5000, Web Site:
www.mailims.com
Mng Partner: Gary Harnum

INTERSTATE EDP & DIRECT MAIL CENTER INC

754 4th Ave
Brooklyn, NY 11232-1414
Telephone: (718) 965-2500, FAX:
(718) 965-2504, E-Mail: info@
interstateedp.com, Web Site: www.
interstateedp.com
Pres: Max Houss
VP: Joseph Houss

IRRESISTIBLE INK INC

Subs. of Hallmark Cards Inc
4444 Haines Rd
Duluth, MN 55811
Telephone: (218) 336-4200, (800) 543-
8396, Web Site: www.irresistibleink.
com
Gen Mgr: Joe Torago

JC DIRECT MAIL INC

4241 Williams Rd
Groveport, OH 43125
Telephone: (614) 836-4848, FAX:
(614) 836-4847, E-Mail: pwhite@
wcnjcd.com
Pres: Wayne Caltrider
Mgr Customer Svc: Patricia White

JHL MAIL MARKETING INC

3100 Borham Ave
Stevens Point, WI 54481-5097
Telephone: (715) 341-0581, (800) 236-
0581, FAX: (715) 341-9645, E-Mail:
ren@jhl.com, Web Site: www.jhl.
com
Supvr: Lorena Berry

JLS MAILING SERVICES INC

672 Crescent St
Brockton, MA 02302-3360
Telephone: (508) 313-1050, (866) JLS-
MAIL, FAX: (508) 313-1093,
E-Mail: rparkinson@jlsms.com, Web
Site: www.jlsms.com
Pres: James Clark
VP Sls: Ron Parkinson

THE JM GROUP INC

12716 O'Connor Rd
San Antonio, TX 78233
Telephone: (210) 637-0404, FAX:
(210) 637-0081
Owner: Chad Elseth

JENCO PRODUCTIONS INC

401 S J St
San Bernardino, CA 92410-2605
Telephone: (909) 381-9453, Web Site:
www.jencoproductions.com
Owner & Pres: Jennifer Imbriani

ᴛʜᴇ JOHNSON & QUIN INC
ᴅᴍᴀ

7460 N Lehigh Ave
Niles, IL 60714-4099
Telephone: (847) 588-4800, FAX:
(847) 647-6949, E-Mail: jqinfo@j-
quin.com, Web Site: www.j-quin.com
Pres & CEO: Dave Henkel
VP: Robert Arkema
Dir Sls: Brad Anliker
Mgr Corp Accts: Andrew Henkel
Employees: 110
Founded: 1876
Gross sales or billing: $22,000,000

Full service direct mail production company. Services include: pre-press, printing, data processing, personalization, card imaging, affixing, lettershop, and hand assembly.

JUST PACKAGING INC
450 Oak Tree Ave
South Plainfield, NJ 07080
Telephone: (908) 753-6700, FAX:
(908) 753-6709, E-Mail: sfischbein@
justpackaging.com, Web Site: www.
justpackaging.com
Pres: Stephen Fischbein

KAROL MEDIA
375 Stewart Rd, PO Box 7600
Wilkes-Barre, PA 18773-7600
Telephone: (570) 822-8899, (800) 526-
4773, FAX: (570) 822-8226, Web
Site: www.karolmedia.com
VP: Michael Kincheloe

KEY COMPUTER SERVICE OF CHELSEA
227 E 56th St Rm 403
New York, NY 10022-3775
Telephone: (212) 206-8060, FAX:
(212) 206-8398
Pres: Timothy Hunter

KEY MAIL GROUP OF COMPANIES
266 Elmwood Ave # 514
Buffalo, NY 14222-2202
Telephone: (800) 863-3128, Web Site:
www.key-mail.com
Mng Dir: Richard Thornton

LSC MARKETING
2207 Cantrell Rd
Little Rock, AR 72203
Telephone: (501) 374-2332, (866)
LSC-MKGT, FAX: (501) 372-6570,
Web Site: www.lscmarketing.com
Pres: C. Scott Schuh

LAZARUS FULFILLMENT HOUSE
Div. of Lazarus Marketing Inc
3530 Oceanside Rd
Oceanside, NY 11572-5829
Telephone: (516) 678-5107, (212) 431-
3337, FAX: (516) 766-3160, Web
Site: www.lazarusmarketing.com
Pres: Warren Lazarus

THE LETTER SHOP INC
511 Towne Square Way, Brentwood
Towne Center
Pittsburgh, PA 15227-3256

Telephone: (412) 882-6200, FAX:
(412) 882-7200, E-Mail: info@
lettershopcanton.com
Mgr: Carol Bailey

LETTERGRAPHICS INC
433 W Onondaga St
Syracuse, NY 13201-1295
Telephone: (315) 476-8328, FAX:
(315) 476-1818, E-Mail: nancyo@
broadviewnet.net, Web Site:
lettergraphics.net
Pres: Nancy Osborn

MBI DIRECT MAIL
710 W New Hampshire Ave
Deland, FL 32720-7231
Telephone: (386) 736-9998, Web Site:
www.directmail-mbi.com
Bus Devel Mgr: John Grogan

MCRB FULFILLMENT CORP
MCRB Service Bureau Inc
4039 Mariner Cir
Westlake Village, CA 91361
Telephone: (818) 407-4300, (800) 942-
MCRB, FAX: (818) 407-0248,
E-Mail: sallen@mcrb.com, Web Site:
www.mcrb.com
Asst: Kristin Latzer
CEO: Steve Allen

THE DMA MT&L CARD PRODUCTS & FULFILLMENT SERVICES
2911 Kraft Dr
Nashville, TN 37204-3618
Telephone: (615) 254-9471, Web Site:
www.mtlcard.com
VP Bus Devel: Michael Hale

MVS MAILERS INC
31 Crossways E Rd
Bohemia, NY 11716-1204
Telephone: (800) 641-7917, FAX:
(631) 699-0101, E-Mail: muraco@
mvsmailers.com, Web Site: www.
mvsmailers.com
CEO & Pres: Steven Muraco
Gen Mgr: Marcos Quinones
VP Sls: Steve Winkoff
VP Sls: Joseph Amalfitano
Conducts Business: U.S.
Employees: 35
Primary Market Served: Business
Advertising/Marketing Budget Related
to Direct Marketing: 0-25%
Direct Marketing ad budget:
Direct Mail: 95%
Magazines: 5%
Founded: 1986
Gross sales or billing: $15,000,000

Advertising, design and printing, international mailing and courier services, shareholder communication and website services.

MACKE BINDERY INC
10355 Spartan Dr
Cincinnati, OH 45215
Telephone: (513) 771-7500, FAX:
(531) 771-3830, Web Site: www.
mackebrothers.com
Pres: Joseph D. Macke Sr.

MAIL ADVERTISING CORP
dba MAC Direct
Subs. of Fort Worth Star Telegram
400 W 7th St
Fort Worth, TX 76102-4701
Telephone: (817) 390-7726, FAX:
(817) 390-7223, E-Mail:
wjjohnson@star-telegram.com, Web
Site: www.macus.com
Production Mgr: Dwight Anderson

MAIL ADVERTISING SERVICES INC
15711 Pagano Ln
Darnestown, MD 20874-3115
Telephone: (301) 762-9015
Owner: R. Jurgena

THE DMA MAIL AMERICA COMMUNICATIONS - A DMH MARKETING PARTNERS CO
1174 Elkton Farm Rd
Forest, VA 24551-2128
Telephone: (434) 534-8000, Web Site:
www.mail-america.com
VP: Daryl Collins

MAIL BOXES ETC
6060 Cornerstone Ct W
San Diego, CA 92121-3795
Telephone: (858) 455-8800, FAX:
(858) 546-7488, Web Site: www.
mbe.com
Pres: Stuart Mathis

MAIL COMMUNICATIONS
533 Rowland Blvd
Novato, CA 94947-4618
Telephone: (415) 883-2383, FAX:
(415) 883-3238, E-Mail: george@
mailcomusa.com, Web Site: www.
mailcomusa.com
Pres: Ron George

MAIL HANDLING SERVICES
7550 Corporate Way
Eden Prairie, MN 55344-2045

Telephone: (952) 975-5000, FAX: (952) 975-5030, Web Site: www. mailhandling.com
Pres: Wayne Cummings

THE MAIL ROOM INC
2110 Busch Ave
Colorado Springs, CO 80904
Telephone: (719) 636-1303, (888) 686-1303, FAX: (719) 636-1814, E-Mail: wpowell@themailroominc.com, Web Site: www.themailroominc.com
Pres: Wes Powell

THE MAILBOX OF ITHACA INC
1650 Hanshaw Rd
Ithaca, NY 14850-6348
Telephone: (607) 257-3865, (800) 382-6348, FAX: (607) 266-0508, E-Mail: mailbox@lightlink.com, Web Site: www.mailboxofithaca.com
Pres: David C. Updyke

MAILCO INC
1430 State Route 23
Wayne, NJ 07470-5826
Telephone: (973) 777-9500, FAX: (973) 777-5469, E-Mail: marvin@mailcoinc.com, Web Site: www.mailcoinc.com
Pres: Donald L. Hecht

THE MAILING HOUSE INC
5600 Bandini Blvd
Bell, CA 90201
Telephone: (323) 262-6000, FAX: (323) 262-6622, E-Mail: tmh4mail@themailinghouse.com, Web Site: www.themailinghouse.com
Pres: David Willock

MAILING SOURCE
1760 Monrovia Ave (#C1)
Costa Mesa, CA 92627
Telephone: (949) 722-9391
Owner: Cheryl Keating

MAILING SPECIALISTS INC
PO Box 230
Greensburg, PA 15601-0230
Telephone: (724) 832-3840, (888) 216-1056, FAX: (724) 832-8419, E-Mail: sales@mailmsi.com, Web Site: www.mailmsi.com
Owner: David Gallatin

MAILMASTER CORP
3401 One Pl
Jonesboro, AR 72404
Telephone: (870) 972-8845, (800) 551-7018, FAX: (870) 972-0877, E-Mail: info@mail-master.com, Web Site: www.mail-master.com

Pres: Steve Smith
VP: Kathy Smith
Mgr Mail Svcs Grp: Laramie McMurtry

THE DMA MAILMEN INC
15 Enter Ln
Hauppauge, NY 11749-4897
Telephone: (631) 582-6900, FAX: (631) 582-6948, E-Mail: getresults@mailmeninc.com, Web Site: www.mailmeninc.com
Dir Sls: Michael Vignola

MAILWAYS ENTERPRISES INC
6105 Factory Rd (Suite 1)
Crystal Lake, IL 60014-7965
Telephone: (815) 455-4850, FAX: (815) 455-7327, E-Mail: dave@mailways.com, Web Site: www.mailways.com
Pres: David Carson

Inkjet addressing, hand assembly & polybagging.

MARCO SALES & INCENTIVES LTD
470 Hardy Rd
Brantford, ON, Canada N3V 6T1
Telephone: (519) 751-2227, (888) 636-6161, FAX: (519) 751-0561, E-Mail: sales@themarcocorporation.com, Web Site: www.themarcocorporation.com
Pres: Robert Martin

MARKET FOCUS DIRECT
aka Market Focus Distribution Services Inc
550 Alden Rd (Suite 207)
Markham, ON, Canada L3R 6A8
Telephone: (905) 477-0801, FAX: (905) 477-4473, E-Mail: info@market-focus.com, Web Site: www.market-focus.com
Pres: Paul Gaynor

MARKETING COMMUNICATION RESOURCE INC
4800 E 345th St
Willoughby, OH 44094-4607
Telephone: (440) 484-3010, FAX: (440) 484-3020
Pres: Frank Piunno

MATRIX MANAGER
1430 Blue Oaks Blvd (Suite 280)
Roseville, CA 95747-5156

Telephone: (916) 783-1536, (877)-258-9037, E-Mail: info@mymatrixmanager.com, Web Site: www.mymatrixmanager.com
Pres: Ann Bouchard

PJ MCNERNEY & ASSOCIATES INC
440 N Land Blvd
Cincinnati, OH 45240
Telephone: (513) 825-5547, FAX: (513) 825-5601, E-Mail: tim@pjmcnerney.com, Web Site: www.pjmcnerney.com
Pres: Patrick McNerney

MERCURY INTERNATIONAL
365 Blair Rd (Suite C)
Avenel, NJ 07001-2231
Telephone: (732) 396-9555, FAX: (732) 396-1492, Web Site: www.mercuryinternational.com
Pres: Andy Curshen
Postal Liaison: Arlene Buyotski

MERCURY PRINT & MAIL CO INC
1110 Central Ave
Pawtucket, RI 02861-2262
Telephone: (401) 724-7600, FAX: (401) 724-9920, Web Site: www.mpmri.com
CEO: Steve Cronin
Gross sales or billing: $10,800,000

MEYER FULFILLMENT
Div. of William B Meyer Inc
255 Long Beach Blvd
Stratford, CT 06615-7117
Telephone: (203) 375-5801, (800) 873-6393, E-Mail: vdarish@meyerfulfillment.com, Web Site: www.meyerfulfillment.com
Mktg: Penny Shawah

MID-CENTRAL PRINTING & MAILING INC
1225 Central Ave
Wilmette, IL 60091
Telephone: (847) 251-4040, FAX: (847) 251-8615, E-Mail: mcpm@mcpm.com, Web Site: www.mcpm.com
Pres: J.T. Korzak

MIDPOINT NATIONAL INC
1263 Southwest Blvd
Kansas City, KS 66103-1901
Telephone: (913) 362-7400, (800) 228-4321, FAX: (913) 362-7401, E-Mail: info@midpt.com, Web Site: www.midpointorderfulfillment.com
Pres: Ronald Freund

**NATIONAL FULFILLMENT
SERVICES**
100 Pine Ave
Holmes, PA 19043-1444
Telephone: (610) 532-4700, (800)
NFS-1306, FAX: (610) 586-3232,
E-Mail: tkrueger@nfsrv.com, Web
Site: www.nfsrv.com
Pres: Eugene C. Krueger
VP Mktg: Thomas Krueger

**NATIONAL MAIL
ADVERTISING INC**
2299 White St
Houston, TX 77007
Telephone: (713) 869-8551, FAX:
(713) 868-5743, E-Mail: sales@
nationalmail.com, Web Site: www.
nationalmail.com
Pres: Ron Garrow

NEW VALLEY
100 SE 2nd St (fl 32)
Miami, FL 33131-2108
Telephone: (305) 579-8000, FAX:
(305) 579-8001, Web Site: www.
newvalley.com
Vice Chmn, Pres & CEO: Bennett
LeBow

NEWROADS INC
5751 Uptain Rd Ste 526
Chattanooga, TN 37411-5675
Telephone: (423) 867-9081, FAX:
(423) 867-8508
Pres: Larry Price
Pres: Dean Arnold

**NORTHWEST MAILING
SERVICE INC**
5501 W Grand Ave
Chicago, IL 60639-2909
Telephone: (773) 237-2264, Web Site:
www.nwmail.com
VP Opers: Thomas Orgler

OBERTHUR CARD SYSTEMS
Div. of De La Rue Plc
4250 Pleasant Valley Rd
Chantilly, VA 20151
Telephone: (703) 263-0100, FAX:
(703) 263-0503, E-Mail: info@
oberthurcs.com, Web Site: www.
oberthurcs.com
CEO: Philippe Geyres

**ON-DEMAND MAIL
SERVICES**
2083 Pontiac Rd Ste B
Auburn Hills, MI 48326-2485
Telephone: (888) 954-6245, Web Site:
www.odmailservices.com
Pres: Timothy Laura

Primary Market Served: Business &
Consumer

ONTIME COMPANIES
201 Crescent Ave
Chelsea, MA 02150-3072
Telephone: (617) 884-8488, Web Site:
www.ontimecompanies.com
Pres: Richard Connolly
Primary Market Served: Business

ONTRAC
3401 E Harbour Dr
Phoenix, AZ 85034-7229
Telephone: (602) 333-4417, (800) 334-
5000

**THE ORDER FULFILLMENT
GROUP**
7313 Mayflower Park Dr
Zionsville, IN 46077-7903
Telephone: (317) 733-7755, FAX:
(317) 733-8799, E-Mail: thughes@
tofg.com, Web Site: www.tofg.com
Pres: Tony Hughes

**PBD WORLDWIDE
FULFILLMENT SERVICES**
1650 Bluegrass Lakes Pkwy
Alpharetta, GA 30004-7714
Telephone: (770) 442-8633, FAX:
(770) 442-9742, E-Mail: sales.
marketing@pbd.com, Web Site:
www.pbd.com
Chmn & CEO: James E. Dockter

PBM GRAPHICS
415 Westcliff Rd
Greensboro, NC 27409
Telephone: (336) 664-5800, (800) 849-
8200, FAX: (336) 931-0965, Web
Site: www.pbmgraphics.com
Plant Mgr: Steve Welch

**PDS INTERNATIONAL MAIL
SERVICE**
Div Flexible International Mail Sys-
tems
85 Corporate Dr
Hauppauge, NY 11788
Telephone: (631) 815-1750, Web Site:
www.pdsmail.com; www.
internationalmail.com
Pres: Joseph Saggio

PMDS INC
9050 Junction Dr Ste 2
Annapolis Junction, MD 20701-1134
Telephone: (301) 604-3305
Project Mgr: Nancy Thomas

PALM COAST DATA LLC
Div. of Kable Media Services
11 Commerce Blvd
Palm Coast, FL 32164-7961
Telephone: (386) 445-4662, FAX:
(386) 445-2728, Web Site: www.
palmcoastd.com
Sr VP, Mktg: Peter Beaudet
Sr VP: Robert Elkin

PENTERA INC
8650-G Commerce Park Pl
Indianapolis, IN 46268-3126
Telephone: (617) 277-5033, Web Site:
www.pentera.com
Dir Consulting Svcs: Claudine Donikian

THE PIONEER GROUP
Subs. of Pioneer Group
316 W 5th St
Waterloo, IA 50701-5508
Telephone: (319) 234-8969, FAX:
(319) 234-8518, E-Mail: jslife@
thepioneergroup.com, Web Site:
www.pioneergroup.com
CEO: James H. Slife

**PITNEY BOWES
INTERNATIONAL MAIL
SERVICES**
158 Mount Olivet Ave
Newark, NJ 07114-2114
Telephone: (800) 521-0080, FAX:
(973) 368-6301, E-Mail: marketing@
pb.com, Web Site: www.intmail.com
VP Sls: Michael Vassalatti
VP Mktg: Cindy Katri

PITTSBURGH MAILING
dba Pittsburgh Mailing Systems, Inc
4777 Streets Run Rd
Pittsburgh, PA 15236-1200
Telephone: (412) 922-8181, FAX:
(412) 937-1730, E-Mail:
ksmallhoover@pittsburghmailing.
com, Web Site: www.
pitsburghmailing.com
Pres: Kurt Smallhoover

POLARIS DIRECT
300 Technology Dr
Hooksett, NH 03106-2520
Telephone: (603) 626-5800, E-Mail:
info@polarisdirect.net, Web Site:
www.polarisdirect.net
Dir: Judith Maloy
Exec Asst: Ashley Colburn

POST LINX CORP
Div. of Pitney Bowes
1170 Birchmount Rd
Scarborough, ON, Canada M1P 5E3

Telephone: (416) 752-8100, FAX:
(416) 752-8239, Web Site: www.
postlinx.com
Pres: Frank Mangialardi
VP Bus Devel: Michael Price

**PREMIER DIRECT
MARKETING INC**
7725 National Tpke (Unit 100)
Louisville, KY 40214-4803
Telephone: (502) 367-6441, (800) 737-
0205, FAX: (502) 361-2961, E-Mail:
rmeredith@premierdm.net, Web Site:
www.premierdm.net
Gen Mgr: Rick Meredith

**PRODIGY MAILING
SERVICES**
389 E South Frontage Rd
Bolingbrook, IL 60440-3029
Telephone: (630) 783-9070, Web Site:
www.prodigymailing.com
Primary Market Served: Business

**PROFESSIONAL MAILING
SERVICES INC**
12 Commerce St
Springfield, NJ 07081-2996
Telephone: (973) 376-0607, (800) 238-
1316, FAX: (973) 376-0949, E-Mail:
jschobel@profmail.com, Web Site:
www.profmail.com
Pres: Jeffrey Schobel

**PROGRESSIVE
DISTRIBUTION SERVICES
INC**
5505 36th St SE
Grand Rapids, MI 49512
Telephone: (616) 957-5900, (800) 304-
3699, FAX: (616) 957-2990, E-Mail:
sales@progressive-commerce.com,
Web Site: www.prodist.com
Pres: John C. McGovern
Bus Devel: Cassie Nieto
Bus Devel Coord: Tracey Jobse

**PROMOTION FULFILLMENT
CTR**
311 21st St
Camanche, IA 52730-9699
Telephone: (563) 259-0105, (800) 493-
7063, FAX: (563) 259-0110, E-Mail:
info@pfcfulfills.com, Web Site:
www.pfcfulfills.com
Mktg Mgr: Mike Fraiser

**PROMOTION SUPPORT
SERVICES INC**
2832 5th St Ste 1
Rock Island, IL 61201-4027

Telephone: (309) 788-4400, FAX:
(309) 788-4465, E-Mail: dbender@
pss-inc.net, Web Site: www.pss-inc.
net
Pres & CEO: David A. Bender

PROMPT MAILERS INC
66 Willow Ave (Suite 1)
Staten Island, NY 10305-1848
Telephone: (718) 447-6206, FAX:
(718) 981-7333, E-Mail: info@
promptmailers.com, Web Site: www.
promptmailers.com
Pres: Richard Masucci

**THE
DMA QUAD/GRAPHICS**
N63 W23075 Hwy 74
Sussex, WI 53089-2827
Telephone: (414) 566-6000, E-Mail:
qgraphics@qg.com, Web Site: www.
QG.com
Pres & CEO: Joel Quadracci

**THE
DMA QUANTUMDIGITAL**
PO Box 140825
Austin, TX 78714-0825
Telephone: (800) 637-7373, Web Site:
www.quantumdigital.com
Pres & CEO: Steve Damman

A RAPID MAILING INC
8221 Preston Ct
Jessup, MD 20794-9368
Telephone: (410) 792-4000, (800) US-
RAPID, FAX: (301) 776-3690,
E-Mail: info@rairapid.com, Web
Site: www.rairapid.com
Pres: Neal H. Ruchman

**THE
DMA REES ASSOCIATES INC**
1800 SW 2nd St
Des Moines, IA 50315-7147
Telephone: (515) 243-2127, FAX:
(515) 243-1026, Web Site: www.
reesassociates.com
Pres: Stephen D. Lundstrom
Admin Asst: Marcia Moore

**RELIABLE MAIL SERVICE
INC**
121 Fieldcrest Ave Ste C
Edison, NJ 08837-3658
Telephone: (732) 346-9779, (800) 773-
6338, FAX: (732) 346-9799, E-Mail:
bdobin@reliablemailservice.com,
Web Site: www.reliablemailservice.
com
Pres: Bruce Dobin

RELIANT DATA PROCESSING
197 Alder Dr
North Aurora, IL 60542-1471

Telephone: (630) 844-4210, FAX:
(630) 844-9530, E-Mail: rdpmail@
aol.com
Pres: Joyce Bousquet

THE JOHN ROBERTS CO
9687 E River Rd
Minneapolis, MN 55433
Telephone: (763) 755-5500, (800) 551-
1534, FAX: (763) 755-0394, E-Mail:
jfoster@johnroberts.com, Web Site:
www.johnroberts.com
Pres & CEO: Michael Keene

SACRED HEART LEAGUE
6050 Hwy 161 N
Walls, MS 38686-0001
Telephone: (662) 781-1360, (800) 232-
9079, FAX: (662) 781-3340, E-Mail:
comments@shl.org, Web Site: www.
shl.org
Pres: Ed Savage

THE SERVICE CENTER LTD
6450 Clara St (Suite 100)
Houston, TX 77041
Telephone: (713) 690-8175, FAX:
(713) 690-6844, Web Site: www.
calltsc.com
Sr Sls Exec: Gale Pashia

**SHAKESPEARE MAILING
SERVICE**
PO Box 8357
New York, NY 10116-8357
Telephone: (212) 560-8958, E-Mail:
support@shakespearemailing.com,
Web Site: www.shakespearemailing.
com
Pres: Hal Hochhauser

**SHEERAN DIRECT
MARKETING**
71 Southgate Blvd
New Castle, DE 19720-2000
Telephone: (302) 324-0200, (888) 325-
2101, FAX: (302) 324-0213, E-Mail:
jjs@jjsheeran.com, Web Site: www.
jjsheeran.com
Chmn & CEO: Joseph J. Sheeran

**SILVERSTATE MARKETING
SOLUTIONS**
3585 E Patrick Ln (#200)
Las Vegas, NV 89120-6211
Telephone: (702) 489-2124, Web Site:
www.silverstateprintmail.com
Pres & Owner: John Evans

SISK MAILING SERVICE
203 Log Canoe Cir
Stevensville, MD 21666-9270

Telephone: (410) 643-7900, FAX:
(410) 643-7933, E-Mail:
clyde_sisk@siskmail.com, Web Site:
www.siskmail.com
Pres: Clyde Sisk

ARLEEN SMITH MARKETING INC

60 Mayflower Ln
Stoughton, MA 02072-3024
Telephone: (781) 341-0882, FAX:
(781) 344-0710, Web Site: www.
arleensmithmarketing.com
Pres: Arleen Smith

SOURCE LINK

3303 West Tech Rd
Miamisburg, OH 45342-0817
Telephone: (937) 885-8000, (800) 305-
9414, FAX: (937) 885-8010, E-Mail:
nesbit@commdata.com, Web Site:
www.sourcelink.com
Pres & CEO: Christopher Behrens

SOUTHERN FULFILLMENT SERVICES

1650 90th Ave
Vero Beach, FL 32966
Telephone: (772) 226-3321
Primary Market Served: Business &
Consumer

THE DMA SOUTHWEST PUBLISHING & MAILING CORP

2600 NW Topeka Blvd
Topeka, KS 66617-1160
Telephone: (785) 233-5662, Web Site:
www.swpks.com
VP: Angie McAtee

SPECIALIZED MAILING SERVICES INC

17451 Nichols Ln (Unit J)
Huntington Beach, CA 92647
Telephone: (714) 274-2284, E-Mail:
info@specializedmailing.com, Web
Site: www.specializedmailing.com
Pres: Alicia Mishica

STAPLES INDUSTRIAL

500 Staples Dr
Framingham, MA 01702-4478
Telephone: (978) 443-9592, (800) 638-
9899, FAX: (978) 443-2678
Customer Svc Mgr: Jeff Provost

STERLING BUSINESS SERVICES

202 Dunhagan Pl
Cary, NC 27511-5049
Telephone: (919) 467-5062
Pres: Edward B. Rickless

THE DMA STRATEGIC MARKETING & MAILING

PO Box 6013
Champaign, IL 61826-6013
Telephone: (217) 355-2600, Web Site:
www.strategicmail.com
COO: Gary Shae
Primary Market Served: Business

THE DMA SUMMIT DIRECT MAIL INC

1655 Terre Colony Ct
Dallas, TX 75212-6222
Telephone: (469) 916-5170, Web Site:
www.summitdm.com
Pres: John Barber

SWAN PACKAGING FULFILLMENT

415 Hamburg Tpke (Suite G)
Wayne, NJ 07470-2164
Telephone: (973) 790-8417, FAX:
(973) 790-0216, E-Mail: info@
swanpkg.com, Web Site: www.
swanpackaging.com
Pres: Timothy S. Werkley
Employees: 40
Founded: 1986

SPF provides 3rd party pick-pack fulfillment services for B2C & B2B product marketers in the e-commerce &
catalog markets, specializing in books,
CDs, clothing, gifts & other products.
We offer electronic reports & shipping
via USPS, UPS, & FedEx. Our 85,000
sq. ft. facility is located 20 miles from
NYC & maintains secured client storage in flow rack, shelving & pallet
storage environments. SPF also provides value-added packaging services
such as kit assembly & automated
packaging. We are a USPS plant-load-
approved vendor, offering bulk mailing
services through our in-house post
office.

TNT INTERNATIONAL EXPRESS

Div. of TNT USA Inc
68 S Service Rd (Suite 340
Melville, NY 11747-2358
Telephone: (800) 558-5555
Pres: Matthew J. McDonough

TAUBENPOST INC

20702 Linear Ln
Lake Forest, CA 92630
Telephone: (949) 770-3233, FAX:
(949) 380-3940, E-Mail: info@
taubenpost.com, Web Site: www.
taubenpost.com
Pres: Carroll Goldsworth

TECHNIPAK

149 Old Gray Station Rd
Gray, TN 37615-3470
Telephone: (800) 385-1964, Web Site:
www.technipak.com
Pres: Mark Scheidt

THE DMA THINKDIRECT MARKETING GROUP

8285 Bryan Dairy Rd (Suite 150)
Largo, FL 33777-1306
Telephone: (727) 369-2700, E-Mail:
info@tdmg.com, Web Site: www.
tdmg.com
Chmn & CEO: Dennis A Cahill
Pres: Thomas H Ripley
CFO: Doug Lombardo

DAVID J THOMPSON MAILING CORP

21 Naus Way
Bloomsburg, PA 17815
Telephone: (570) 759-6690, FAX:
(570) 759-7160, E-Mail: sales@
thompsonmailing.com, Web Site:
www.thompsonmailing.com
Exec VP: Joan E. Thompson

3PL WORLDWIDE INC

500 Bic Dr
Milford, CT 06461-1734
Telephone: (203) 567-1099, Web Site:
www.3plworldwide.com
Pres: Clyde Mount

THREESOURCE FULFILLMENT

655 Mulberry
Manteno, IL 60950-9219
Telephone: (815) 936-1094 x4179,
(888) 673-4650, FAX: (815) 936-
9743, E-Mail: sandyp@threesource.
tv, Web Site: www.threesource.tv
Pres & Co-Owner: Marty Bothwell
Dir Sls: Sandy Poppie
Sls Mgr: Toby Cahilll

THE DMA TRIBUNE DIRECT MARKETING

505 Northwest Ave (Suite A)
Northlake, IL 60164-1662
Telephone: (708) 836-2712, Web Site:
www.tribunedirect.com
Dir Mktg Svcs: Erik Haugen

THE DMA TRINITY ROAD LLC

PO Box 7445
Charlotte, NC 28241-7445
Telephone: (704) 940-2240
Dir Mktg: Nicolas Cole

TRIPAR INTERNATIONAL INC
20 Presidential Dr
Roselle, IL 60172
Telephone: (630) 980-5100, (800) 222-1142, FAX: (800) 648-9015, E-Mail: sales@tripar.com, Web Site: www.tripar.com
VP Sls & Mktg: Gretchen Kroll

UNICOR- SERVICES BUSINESS GROUP
400 1st St NW
Washington, DC 20534-0004
Telephone: (202) 305-3500, Web Site: www.unicor.gov/services
Prog Mgr: Vaughn Gardineer

UNIMAIL CORP
655 Pullman Ave
Rochester, NY 14615-3313
Telephone: (585) 254-7510, (800) 688-6878, FAX: (585) 254-2367
VP Fin: Michael Bader

UNIQUE DATA SERVICES INC
5300 Katrine Ave
Downers Grove, IL 60515
Telephone: (630) 968-6000, Web Site: www.uniquedata.com
Pres: Ronald Farrey
VP Sls: Charles A. Kerber

UNIQUE MAILING SERVICES INC
325 Marmon Dr
Bolingbrook, IL 60440
Telephone: (630) 739-4848, FAX: (630) 783-1838, E-Mail: info@uniqmail.com, Web Site: www.uniqmail.com
Pres: Dan Khouri

UNITED PARCEL SERVICE
dba UPS
55 Glenlake Pkwy NE
Atlanta, GA 30328
Telephone: (404) 828-6000, (800) 874-5877, FAX: (404) 828-6562, Web Site: www.ups.com
Chmn & CEO: D. Scott Davis

THE DMA US MONITOR
86 Maple Ave
New City, NY 10956-5019
Telephone: (845) 634-1331, (800) 767-7967, FAX: (845) 634-9618, E-Mail: info@usmonitor.com, Web Site: www.usmonitor.com
Pres: Anita Sass

USA FULFILLMENT
313 Talbot Blvd
Chestertown, MD 21620-1016
Telephone: (410) 810-0800, (800) 777-8872, FAX: (410) 810-0910, E-Mail: sroy@usafill.com, Web Site: www.usafill.com
Dir Sls & Mktg: Sheila Roy

US POSTAL SERVICE- LIBRARY
Corporate Information Services, Information Systems
475 L'Enfant Plz SW
Washington, DC 20260-1540
Telephone: (202) 268-2904, FAX: (202) 268-6436, Web Site: www.usps.com
Librarian: Robert Gardner

UNITED WIRE SERVICE
Div. of ChoicePoint
8512 N Allen Rd
Peoria, IL 61615-1527
Telephone: (309) 689-6160, FAX: (309) 689-6488, E-Mail: julie.finney@choicepoint.com, Web Site: www.unitedwire.net
Acct Exec: Julie Finney

UNIVERSAL DISTRIBUTION SERVICES
Div. of InnoTrac Inc
4910 Longley Ln (Suite 101)
Reno, NV 89502
Telephone: (775) 332-5700, FAX: (775) 332-5715, E-Mail: sales@udsi.com, Web Site: www.udsi.com
Pres: Patrick West

VERTIS MEDIA & MARKETING SERVICES
Div. of Vertis Inc
250 W Pratt St (Suite 1800)
Baltimore, MD 21201-6813
Telephone: (410) 528-9800, (800) 577-8371, E-Mail: Info@VertisInc.com, Web Site: www.vertisinc.com
Chmn & CEO: Michael DuBose

VINCENT GRAPHICS, LLC
PO Box 39, Box 386
Hilliard, OH 43026-0039
Telephone: (614) 771-5440, (800) 331-0517, FAX: (614) 771-5449
Pres & CEO: Ty Vincent

WMG USA INC
1560 Broadway (fl 10)
New York, NY 10036-1518
Telephone: (212) 278-0066, E-Mail: business@wmg-group.com, Web Site: www.wmg-group.com
CEO: S. K. Ng

WIT POSTAL LOGISTICS LLC
350 N La Salle Dr (Suite 1100)
Chicago, IL 60654-5131
Telephone: (815) 215-5100, Web Site: www.witpostal.com
Pres: David Rush

WOLFF/SMG
Div. of SMG Direct, Inc
1641 Commons Pkwy
Macedon, NY 14502-9190
Telephone: (315) 986-1155, FAX: (315) 986-1161, E-Mail: rdelmonte@wolff-smg.com, Web Site: www.wolff-smg.com
CEO: Ray Del Monte

WOLVERINE MAILING & PACKAGING WAREHOUSE
1601 Clay St
Detroit, MI 48211-1902
Telephone: (313) 873-6800, FAX: (313) 873-8730, Web Site: www.wolverinemail.com
CEO: Bob Tokar

WOOD & ASSOCIATES DIRECT MARKETING SERVICES LTD
2-237 Finchdene Sq
Scarborough, ON, Canada M1X 2E1
Telephone: (416) 293-2511, FAX: (416) 293-2594, E-Mail: clientservices@wood-and-associates.com, Web Site: www.wood-and-associates.com
Pres: Annabelle Wood

WORLD MARKETING INC
10918 Emiline St
La Vista, NE 68128-5725
Telephone: (402) 384-0800, (800) 438-8797, FAX: (402) 384-0801, E-Mail: results@worldmarkinc.com, Web Site: www.worldmarkinc.com
Pres & CEO: Mac Rodgers

WORLD WIDE MAILERS
2744 Edna St
Windsor, ON, Canada N8Y 1V2
Telephone: (519) 254-6245, FAX: (519) 254-2608, E-Mail: tab@worldwidemailers.com, Web Site: www.worldwidemailers.com
Pres: Sandra Meredith

THE DMA XPO
3541 Lomita Blvd
Torrance, CA 90505-5016
Telephone: (310) 784-8485, Web Site: www.xpomail.com
CEO: Kelly Herold-Martinez
Primary Market Served: Business & Consumer

YOUNG AMERICA CORP
717 Faxon Rd
Young America, MN 55397-9481
Telephone: (952) 467-1100, FAX:
    (952) 467-3895, Web Site: www.
    young-america.com
Pres & CEO: Roger Anderson

ZACHRY ASSOCIATES INC
500 Chestnut (Suite 2000)
Abilene, TX 79602
Telephone: (325) 677-1342, E-Mail:
    pfulham@zachryinc.com, Web Site:
    www.zachryinc.com
Pres: Paul Fulham

ᴛʜᴇ ᴅᴍᴀ ZIP MAILING SERVICES INC
6304 Sheriff Rd (Suite Z)
Landover, MD 20785-4361
Telephone: (301) 386-3633, FAX:
    (301) 386-3637, E-Mail: zipmail@
    zipmailing.com, Web Site: www.
    zipmailing.com
Pres: Charlain L Bland

Alabama

ASK Telemarketing, 5815 Carmichael Rd, Montgomery, 36117

Arizona

Direct Response Enhancements LLC, 12772 E Sunnyside Dr, Scottsdale, 85259-3438

TeleDirect International Inc, 17255 N 82nd St, Scottsdale, 85255

Virido LLC, 6626 E Oberlin Way, Scottsdale, 85266-6786

Arkansas

The Heritage Co, 2402 Wildwood Ave (Suite 500), North Little Rock, 72120-5094

California

ACP Interactive, PO Box 192952, San Francisco, 94119-2952

AT&T Language Line Services, 1 Lower Ragsdale Dr (Bldg 2), Monterey, 93940-5747

Alorica Inc, 14726 Ramona Ave (fl 3), Chino, 91710-5730

Ansafone Communications, 145 E Columbine Ave, Santa Ana, 92707-4401

Concorde Communications, 3699 Wilshire Blvd (#850), Los Angeles, 90010-2718

Direct Marketing Partners, 2045 Hallmark Dr (Suite 5), Sacramento, 95825-2224

Infinian Corp, 4856 El Camino Real (Suite 200), Los Altos, 94022

LiveOps Inc, 5425 Stevens Creek Blvd, Santa Clara, 95051-7203

Lucas & Associates, 617 N Seventh St, Montebello, 90640-3536

Marketeers, PO Box 3571, Mission Viejo, 92690-1571

Omega Mobile, 350 Townsend St Ste 220, San Francisco, 94107-1671

SmartReply Inc, 6410 Oak Canyon Rd (Suite 100), Irvine, 92618-5225

Telecom Inc, 2201 Broadway (Suite 103), Oakland, 94612-3028

TollFreeForwarding.com, 5959 W Century Blvd (Suite 1108), Los Angeles, 90045-6512

Colorado

Mountain West Communications Inc, 110 E Hotchkiss Ave, PO Box 216, Hotchkiss, 81419

Connecticut

American Customer Care Inc, 225 N Main St, Bristol, 06010-4997

Frontier Communications, 3 High Ridge Dr, Stamford, 06905-3806

Lester Inc, 19 Business Park Dr (Suite A), Branford, 06405-2936

Scholastic Direct Mktg, 90 Sherman Tpke, Danbury, 06816-0001

Technology Marketing Corp/TMC, 800 Connecticut Ave, Norwalk, 06854-1631

District of Columbia

TRG World, 1700 Pennsylvania Ave NW (Suite 560), Washington, 20006

Florida

America's Call Center, 7901 Baymeadows Way (Suite 14), Jacksonville, 32256-8535

ChoiceConnex, 13555 Automobile Blvd (Suite 530), Clearwater, 33762-3838

Global Response Corp, 777 S State Rd 7, Margate, 33068-2803

ICT Group Inc, 400 N Ashley Dr (Suite 2500), Tampa, 33602-4348

Interactive Response Technologies Inc, 4500 N State Rd Seven (Suite 301), Fort Lauderdale, 33319

Alan Morgan & Associates Inc, 2854 Lake Vista Rd, Jacksonville, 32223-7934

The Office Gurus, 10055 Seminole Blvd, Seminole, 33772-2539

One World Telecom, 2620 SW 27th Ave, Miami, 33133

Prosodie Interactive, 855 SW 78th Ave (Suite 100), Plantation, 33324-3223

Protocol, 2805 Fruitville Rd, Sarasota, 34237-5318

Teleperformance Interactive, 1601 Washington Ave (Suite 400), Miami Beach, 33139-3166

White Point Leads Group LLC, 362 Gulf Breeze Pkwy (Suite 350), Gulf Breeze, 32561-4492

Winn Technology Group Inc, 523 Palm Harbor Blvd, Palm Harbor, 34682-0927

Georgia

JAK Productions, 4501 Circle 75 Pkwy SE (Suite E5280), Atlanta, 30339-3025

Teletrack Inc, 5550-A Peachtree Pkwy (Suite 600), Norcross, 30092

Idaho

Intelesure LLC, 104 E Fairview Ave (#262), PMB 262, Meridian, 83642-1733

Illinois

APAC Customer Services Inc, 2333 Waukegan Rd Ste W100, Bannockburn, 60015-1545

Afni Inc, 404 Brock Dr, Bloomington, 61701-2654

AmeriCall Group Inc, 1230 E Diehl Rd (Suite 300), Naperville, 60563-7813

Carlyle Marketing Corp, 723 Interlochen Ct, Riverwoods, 60015-3869

CTC Teleservices, 304 N 6th St, De Kalb, 60115-3484

Consolidated Market Response, 700 W Lincoln (Suite 200), Charleston, 61920

Conversational Voice Technologies Corp, 28 N US Highway 12 Apt E, Fox Lake, 60020-1257

Creative Compliance, 900 N Franklin (Suite 706), Chicago, 60610

Edge Teleservices, Inc, 4020 W 111th St (Suite 1102), Oak Lawn, 60453-5783

FTD Group Inc, 3113 Woodcreek Dr, Downers Grove, 60515

Greene an RMG Direct Co, 300 Tri-State Intl (Suite 272), Lincolnshire, 60069-4415

Lieber & Associates, 3740 N Lake Shore Dr (Ste 15B-2), Chicago, 60613-4237

National Systems Corp, 414 N Orleans St (Suite 501), Chicago, 60610-4498

ORC ProTel LLC, 17233 Continental Dr, Lansing, 60438-6005

PSI Marketing Consultants Inc, 2340 S River Rd (Suite 208), Des Plaines, 60018-3223

Tele Business USA, 1945 Techny Rd (Suite 3), Northbrook, 60062

TTC Marketing Solutions, 3945 N Neenah Ave, Chicago, 60634-2419

Indiana

American Inbound, 1111 N Walnut, Bloomington, 47404

TeleServices Direct, 5305 Lakeshore Pkwy South Dr, Indianapolis, 46268-4113

Iowa

Prism Marketing Group, 111 W Second St, Schaller, 51053

TMone, 1925 Boyrum, Iowa City, 52240

WS Live LLC, 131 W 10th St, Dubuque, 52001

Kansas

Blue Valley Tele-Marketing Inc, 1555 Pony Express Hwy, Home, 66438

Sprint Corp, 6130 Sprint Pkwy (Mailstop KSOPHJO102), Overland Park, 66251

Louisiana

Century Telephone Enterprises Inc, 100 Century Tel Dr, Monroe, 71203

Maine

Innovative Marketing Solutions LLC, 121 Target Cir, Bangor, 04401-5717

Maryland

TeleRep, 14 Wellham Ave, Glen Burnie, 21061

Massachusetts

Aspect Softwear, 300 Apollo Dr, Chelmsford, 01824

Carroll Enterprises Inc, 554 Main St, Worcester, 01608-2014

OnBrand24, 100 Cummings Ctr (Suite 306L), Beverly, 01915-6107

Power Seminars, 53 New Ocean St (Suite 3), Swampscott, 01907-1840

Share Group Inc, 79 Chapel St, Newton, 02458-1010

Michigan

Amrigon, 1815 Long Lake Shore Dr, Bloomfield Hills, 48302-1234

Demand Telemarketing Inc, 377 Fisher Rd (Suite D), Grosse Pointe, 48230-1600

Dialogue Marketing, 3252 University Dr (Suite 165), Auburn Hills, 48326-2786

Minacs Worldwide, 34115 W Twelve Mile Rd, Farmington Hills, 48331-3368

Minnesota

A Marketing Resource, 1185 Concord St N (Suite 228), South St Paul, 55075-1157

Answer America, 1600 University Ave (Suite 208), Saint Paul, 55104-3825

Arrowhead Promotion & Fulfillment, 1105 Eighth St SE, Grand Rapids, 55744-4099

CareCall Inc, 200 14th Ave E, Sartell, 56377-4500

The Connection Contact Center Services, 11351 Rupp Dr, Burnsville, 55337-1200

The Connection Outsourced Call Ctr, 11351 Rupp Dr, Burnsville, 55337-1200

CustomerLink, 11 E Superior St Ste 430, Duluth, 55802-3013

Link Telemarketing Inc, 5935 Hillendale St, Excelsior, 55331

Meyer Associates Teleservices, 14 7th Ave N, Saint Cloud, 56303-4753

Tele Resources Inc, 222 W Superior St Ste 100, Duluth, 55802-1940

Time Communications, 4444 Centerville Rd (Suite 245), Saint Paul, 55127-3712

Missouri

Communication Solutions LLC, 310 S Ingram Mill Rd, Springfield, 65802-6104

800 Call KC, 1616 N Corrington Ave, Kansas City, 64120

USA 800 Inc, 9808 E 66 Ter, Raytown, 64133

Nebraska

Affinitas Corp, 1015 N 98th St (Suite 100), Omaha, 68114-2357

Call Interactive, 10910 Mill Valley Rd, Omaha, 68154-3930

CSG Interactive Messaging, 2525 N 117th Ave, Omaha, 68164-3679

CSS Direct, 3707 N 200th St, Elkhorn, 68022-2922

Hamilton Contact Center Services, 1006 12th St, Aurora, 68818-2003

Quality Contact Solutions Inc, 808 4th St, Aurora, 68818-2201

Telenational Marketing, 2918 N 72nd St, Omaha, 68134-5107

Timberline Total Solutions LLC, 8429 Blood St, Omaha, 68134-1051

US Data Corp, 17310 Wright St (Suite 100), Omaha, 68130-2405

New Hampshire

Abacus Communications, 540 Commercial St (2nd fl), Manchester, 03101

Marketing Connections Corp, 10 Corporate Dr (Suite 206), Bedford, 03110

New Jersey

Centrac Inc, 759 Bloomfield Ave (#359), West Caldwell, 07006-6701

Colwell & Salmon Communications Inc, 100 Hillside Ave, Cresskill, 07626-1612

Cyber City Teleservices Marketing Inc, 401 Hackensack Ave (fl 3), Hackensack, 07601-6405

Cyber Marketing Services, 70 Chestnut Ridge Rd (Suite K), Montvale, 07645

Data Services Direct, 959 Rte 46 (Suite 302), Parsippany, 07054

DialAmerica Marketing Inc, 960 Macarthur Blvd, Mahwah, 07430-2040

Global Crossing Telecom Inc, 200 Park Ave (Suite 300), Florham Park, 07932

Person to Person Marketing LLC, 8 N Corporate Dr, Riverdale, 07457

Selltel Inc, 393 Mantoloking Rd, Brick, 08723

TMP Direct, PO Box 308, Budd Lake, 07828-0308

New York

Atlantic Business Products, 134 W 26th St, New York, 10001-6803

Call Compliance Inc, 90 Pratt Oval, Glen Cove, 11542-1413

Circulation by Phone Inc, 60 E 42nd St (Rm 1630), New York, 10165-0656

ETI Sales Support, 465 Columbus Ave Ste 280, Valhalla, 10595-2301

Bernard C Harris Publishing Co Inc, 1511 Route 22 (Suite C-25), Brewster, 10509-4085

King Teleservices, 48 Wall St Fl 23, New York, 10005-2922

Kurant Direct Inc, 372 Central Park W (Suite 7B), New York, 10025-8205

Joel Linchitz Consulting Services/Phone for Success, 2578 Broadway (Suite 135), New York, 10025

Milberg Penn *International, 116 Radio Cir (Suite 206), Mount Kisco, 10549-2632

PTM Communications, 330 W 38th St (Suite 801), New York, 10018-8465

SpeechSoft Inc, 49 The Crossing, Armonk, 10504

Stratmar Systems Inc, 109 Willet Ave, Port Chester, 10573

North Carolina

1-800-DialWord.com, 1095 E King St Box 10, Boone, 28607-4325

Walker & Associates, 7129 Old Hwy 52 N, PO Box 1029, Welcome, 27374-1029

Ohio

Incept Corp, 4150 Belden Village St NW (Suite 205), Canton, 44718-3643

Influent Inc, 565 Metro Pl S (Suite 250), Dublin, 43017-7312

InfoCision Management Corp, 325 Springside Dr, Akron, 44333-4504

National Administrative Service Co LLC, 400 Metro Pl N (Suite 360), Dublin, 43017-3318

PCCW Teleservices, 565 Metro Pl S (Suite 250), Dublin, 43017-7312

Synergy Direct Marketing Solutions LLC, 480 W Tuscarawas Ave Ste 307, Barberton, 44203-2597

Unicall International Inc, 3250 W Market St, Fairlawn, 44333

Oklahoma

United America Advertising Inc, 1018 West Cherry Ave, Enid, 73703

Oregon

Advanced Business Teleservices, Inc, 304 E Main St, Talent, 97540-9752

Group2Marketing, 1214 Stowe Ave, Medford, 97501-6611

Pennsylvania

Advanced Telecom Services Inc, 996 Old Eagle School Rd (Suite 1105), Wayne, 19087-1806

AnswerNet Network, 2325 Maryland Rd (Suite 210), Willow Grove, 19090

Thomas L Cardella & Associates, 2100 Kimberton Rd, Kimberton, 19442-0816

Direct Advantage Marketing, 2100 Wharton St Ste 510, Pittsburgh, 15203-1691

Falzone & Associates LLC, 5 Narothyn Rd, Sellersville, 18960-2958

Inter-Media Marketing Solutions, 204 Carter Dr, West Chester, 19382

MarketMakers Group Inc, 687 W Lancaster Ave, Wayne, 19087-2545

NCO Financial Systems, 507 Prudential Rd, Horsham, 19044

One Call Systems Inc, 155 McCartney Ln, Baden, 15005-2827

OKS-Ameridial Inc, 303 Parsons Ave, Bala Cynwyd, 19004

Sykes Acquisition, 100 Brandywine Blvd, Newtown, 18940-4000

Telerx, 723 Dresher Rd, Horsham, 19044-2299

Visions Marketing Services, 425 Dolly Dr, Lancaster, 17601-3619

Yellowbook, 2201 Renaissance Blvd, King of Prussia, 19406-2766

Rhode Island

Barterbing.com, 18 Chestnut Ave, Cranston, 02910-4625

Providence Journal Telemarketing, 75 Fountain St, Providence, 02902-0050

South Dakota

Midco Call Center Services, 4901 E 26th St, Sioux Falls, 57110-6950

Tennessee

Eperformax Inc, 100 Saddle Springs Blvd (Suite 100), Thompsons Station, 37179-5328

Texas

Aegis Communications, 8201 Ridgepoint Dr., Irving, 75063-3160

Calling Solutions, 2200 McCullough Ave, San Antonio, 78212-3751

Etech Inc, 106 N John Redditt Dr, Lufkin, 75904-2640

Integrated Alliance Limited Partnership, 5800 N Interstate 35 (Suite 200B), Denton, 76207-1438

MKS Marketing Inc, 3404 San Mateo Dr, Austin, 78733

NOVO1, 4301 Cambridge Rd, Fort Worth, 76155-2627

Our Data Works Inc, 1504 Fairway Dr, Lewisville, 75057-2329

Premier Messaging LP, 9850 Sagepike Dr, Houston, 77089-3514

Skytel Communications Inc, 1720 Lakepoint Dr, Lewisville, 75057-6408

Sturner & Klein, 4301 Cambridge Rd, Fort Worth, 76155-2627

Telesystems Marketing Inc, 3600 S Gessner Rd (Suite 250), Houston, 77063

Warrantech Direct Inc, 2200 Hwy 121 (Suite 105), Bedford, 76021-5983

Utah

Convergys Corp, 1400 W 4400 S, Ogden, 84405-3300

Virginia

Access Worldwide Communications Inc, 6402 Arlington Blvd Ste 400, Falls Church, 22042-2343

Bridgewell Associates, 405 S Union St, Alexandria, 22314-3825

InteliTarget, 212 Fort Collier Rd, Winchester, 22603-5738

Neustar Inc, 46000 Center Oak Plz Ste 1, Sterling, 20166-6579

Public Interest Communications Inc, 7700 Leesburg Pike (Suite 301), Falls Church, 22043

Washington

T-Mobile, 12920 SE 38th St, Bellevue, 98006-1350

Wisconsin

Alta Resources (West Coast Office), 120 N Commercial St, Neenah, 54956-3006

An-Ser Services, 2761 Allied St, Green Bay, 54304

Charlton, 222 W Washington Ave (Suite 200), Madison, 53703-2719

iMarketing Solutions Group Inc, 700 W Virginia St (Suite 700), Timbers Building, Milwaukee, 53204-1555

JC Penney Telemarketing Inc, 11800 W Burleigh St, Milwaukee, 53222-3110

Spectrum Communication Services Inc, 125 N Executive Dr Ste 300, Brookfield, 53005-6035

Torcom Inbound Telemarketing, 25 Kessel Ct (Suite 107), Madison, 53711-6227

CANADA
British Columbia

MarCom Technologies, 337 Rio Dr S, Kelowna, V1V 2V1

Manitoba

The Faneuil Group, 363 Broadway (Suite 906), Winnipeg, R3C 3N9

FineLine, 290 Garry St, Winnipeg, R3C 1H3

Integrated Messaging Inc, 550 Berry St, Winnipeg, R3H 0R9

Ontario

Omega Direct Response Inc, 30 Wertheim Ct (Unit 12), Richmond Hill, L4B 1B9

Ventriloquist Voice Solutions International Inc, 5025 Orbitor Dr (Suite 300), Bldg 1, Mississauga, L4W 4Y5

Voicelogic, 662 King St W, Toronto, M5V 1M7

Quebec

Voxdata Telecom, 1155 Metcalfe St (Suite 1860), Montreal, H3B 2V6

Saskatchewan

Marketlinc, 105 21 St E (Suite 100), Saskatoon, S7K 0B3

THE DMA A MARKETING RESOURCE
1185 Concord St N (Suite 228)
South St Paul, MN 55075-1157
Telephone: (651) 451-1765, Web Site:
www.amr-advantage.com
Pres: Ed Spagnola

ACP INTERACTIVE
PO Box 192952
San Francisco, CA 94119-2952
Telephone: (415) 357-5100, (800) 357-
5177, FAX: (415) 357-5110, E-Mail:
info@acpinteractive.com, Web Site:
www.callgistics.com
Pres: Camille Wehner

APAC CUSTOMER SERVICES INC
2333 Waukegan Rd Ste W100
Bannockburn, IL 60015-1545
Telephone: (847) 374-4980, (800) 688-
7687, FAX: (847) 236-5453, Web
Site: www.apaccustomerservices.com
Pres, CEO & Dir: Michael P. Marrow

AT&T LANGUAGE LINE SERVICES
1 Lower Ragsdale Dr (Bldg 2)
Monterey, CA 93940-5747
Telephone: (831) 648-5861, (877) 886-
3885, FAX: (800) 821-9040, E-Mail:
wecare@languageline.com, Web
Site: www.languageline.com
Gen Mgr: Chris Ensign

ABACUS COMMUNICATIONS
540 Commercial St (2nd fl)
Manchester, NH 03101
Telephone: (800) 888-3188, FAX:
(603) 645-5093, E-Mail: michael@
call-centers.com, Web Site: www.
callabacus.com
VP Mktg: Michael Holzberg

ACCESS WORLDWIDE COMMUNICATIONS INC
6402 Arlington Blvd Ste 400
Falls Church, VA 22042-2343
Telephone: (571) 384-7400, (800) 522-
3447, FAX: (703) 531-0711, Web
Site: www.accessww.com
Dir New Bus Development: Mike
Bowling

ADVANCED BUSINESS TELESERVICES, INC
304 E Main St
Talent, OR 97540-9752
Telephone: (800) 866-9220, FAX:
(541) 535-6942, E-Mail: randy@
abtc.com, Web Site: www.abtc.com
VP & Gen Mgr: Randy Eek

ADVANCED TELECOM SERVICES INC
996 Old Eagle School Rd (Suite 1105)
Wayne, PA 19087-1806
Telephone: (610) 688-6000, (800) 247-
1287, FAX: (610) 964-9117, E-Mail:
bobb@advancedtele.com, Web Site:
www.advancedtele.com
Mktg & Sls Dir: Bob Bentz

The leader in automated telepromotion
services for over a decade. Extensive
industry experience in sweepstakes,
contests and games; product information and public affairs; surveys and
market research; couponing, sampling
and lead generating; web integrated
programs. Detailed call reporting, fulfillment, live operator redirect. Turnkey
marketing support and unsurpassed
customer service.

AEGIS COMMUNICATIONS
8201 Ridgepoint Dr.
Irving, TX 75063-3160
Telephone: (972) 830-1800, (800) 332-
0266, FAX: (972) 830-1801, E-Mail:
info@aegisglobal.com, Web Site:
www.aegiscomgroup.com
Pres & CEO: Kannan Ramasamy
Sr Dir of Mktg: Kevin Nolan

THE DMA AFFINITAS CORP
1015 N 98th St (Suite 100)
Omaha, NE 68114-2357
Telephone: (402) 397-7077, (800) 369-
6495, FAX: (402) 397-7576, Web
Site: www.affinitas.net
Pres: Jim Schinco
VP: Steven Gilbert

THE DMA AFNI INC
404 Brock Dr
Bloomington, IL 61701-2654
Telephone: (800) 767-2364, Web Site:
www.afni.com

ALORICA INC
14726 Ramona Ave (fl 3)
Chino, CA 91710-5730

Telephone: (909) 606-3600, (866) 256-
7422, FAX: (909) 606-7708, E-Mail:
info@alorica.com, Web Site: www.
alorica.com
CEO & Founder: Andy Lee

ALTA RESOURCES (WEST COAST OFFICE)
120 N Commercial St
Neenah, WI 54956-3006
Telephone: (920) 751-5800, (877) 934-
6377, Web Site: www.altaresources.
com
Bus Devel: Tim Reiball
Employees: 800
Founded: 1995

AMERICALL GROUP INC
1230 E Diehl Rd (Suite 300)
Naperville, IL 60563-7813
Telephone: (630) 955-9100, (800) 688-
0078, FAX: (630) 955-9955, E-Mail:
sales@americallgroup.com, Web
Site: www.americallgroup.com
Chmn & CEO: George Kestler
Sr VP, Sls & Mktg: Shireen Wedlock
COO: Ben Martorano
CFO: Stephen Oscarson
CTO: Mike Novak
Conducts Business: U.S.
Primary Market Served: Business &
Consumer
Catalog available online
Advertising/Marketing Budget Related
to Direct Marketing: 0-25%
Gross sales or billing: $317,000,000

Full-service, all line insurance agency
specializing in mass marketing of insurance products to the customers of
financial institutions & mortgage
companies. Provide outbound telemarketing by licensed agents, database
management & customer service.

AMERICAN CUSTOMER CARE INC
225 N Main St
Bristol, CT 06010-4997
Telephone: (866) 400-6886, Web Site:
www.americancustomercare.com
VP Strategic Sales: Staci Kress

AMERICAN INBOUND
1111 N Walnut
Bloomington, IN 47404
Telephone: (800) 322-6445, FAX:
(800) 224-3583, Web Site: www.
americanbound.com

Pres: Don Adams

AMERICA'S CALL CENTER
7901 Baymeadows Way (Suite 14)
Jacksonville, FL 32256-8535
Telephone: (904) 224-2000, (800) 598-
2580, FAX: (904) 737-1107, E-Mail:
info@webcallusa.com, Web Site:
www.webcallusa.com
Pres: Dick Emberson
VP: Barry Krawchuk

AMRIGON
1815 Long Lake Shore Dr
Bloomfield Hills, MI 48302-1234
Telephone: (248) 332-2300, FAX:
(248) 333-9710
Partner: Richard Smith

AN-SER SERVICES
2761 Allied St
Green Bay, WI 54304
Telephone: (920) 490-7000, (800) 723-
0000, E-Mail: allanf@anser.com,
Web Site: www.anser.com
Owner: Allan Fromm

ANSAFONE
COMMUNICATIONS
145 E Columbine Ave
Santa Ana, CA 92707-4401
Telephone: (714) 560-1000, Web Site:
www.ansafone.com
Dir Contact Ctr Sls: Stewart Wolfen-
son

ANSWER AMERICA
1600 University Ave (Suite 208)
Saint Paul, MN 55104-3825
Telephone: (800) 258-2669, FAX:
(651) 644-8295, E-Mail: sales@
answeramerica.com, Web Site: www.
answeramerica.com

ANSWERNET NETWORK
2325 Maryland Rd (Suite 210)
Willow Grove, PA 19090
Telephone: (800) 411-5777, FAX:
(215) 659-6486, Web Site: www.
answernetnetwork.com
CEO: Gary Pudles

ARROWHEAD PROMOTION
& FULFILLMENT
1105 Eighth St SE
Grand Rapids, MN 55744-4099
Telephone: (218) 327-1165, FAX:
(218) 327-2576, Web Site: www.
apfco.com
CEO: Keith Arnold

ASK TELEMARKETING
5815 Carmichael Rd
Montgomery, AL 36117
Telephone: (334) 387-ASKT, FAX:
(334) 387-2759, E-Mail: rburley@
asktelemarketing.com, Web Site:
www.asktelemarketing.com
CEO: Rick Burley

ASPECT SOFTWEAR
300 Apollo Dr
Chelmsford, MA 01824
Telephone: (978) 250-7900, FAX:
(978) 244-7410, E-Mail: info@
aspect.com, Web Site: www.aspect.
com
CEO: Jim Foy

ATLANTIC BUSINESS
PRODUCTS
Ascom
134 W 26th St
New York, NY 10001-6803
Telephone: (212) 741-6400, FAX:
(212) 645-1518, E-Mail: info@
tomorrowsoffice.com, Web Site:
www.tomorrowsoffice.com
Pres: Larry Weiss

BARTERBING.COM
18 Chestnut Ave
Cranston, RI 02910-4625
Telephone: (800) 345-6733, FAX:
(401) 679-0326, Web Site: www.
barterbing.com
Pres: Bill Rosenberg

BLUE VALLEY TELE-
MARKETING INC
Subs. of Blue Valley Telephone Co
1555 Pony Express Hwy
Home, KS 66438
Telephone: (785) 799-3500, (800) 882-
0803, FAX: (785) 799-3504
Gen Mgr: Judy Zimmerling

BRIDGEWELL ASSOCIATES
405 S Union St
Alexandria, VA 22314-3825
Telephone: (703) 360-6500

CSG INTERACTIVE
MESSAGING
2525 N 117th Ave
Omaha, NE 68164-3679
Telephone: (402) 398-4100, (800) 888-
3151, FAX: (402) 398-4000, Web
Site: www.prairiesys.com
Pres & CEO: Thomas Nichting

CSS DIRECT
3707 N 200th St
Elkhorn, NE 68022-2922

Telephone: (402) 359-1515, FAX:
(402) 359-1516, E-Mail: custserv@
cssdirect.com, Web Site: www.
cssdirect.com
Sls Exec: Matt Haynes

CTC TELESERVICES
304 N 6th St
De Kalb, IL 60115-3484
Telephone: (815) 748-4200, FAX:
(630) 773-4765, Web Site: www.
ctcteleservices.com
Pres: Guy J. Scarpelli

CALL COMPLIANCE INC
90 Pratt Oval
Glen Cove, NY 11542-1413
Telephone: (516) 674-4545, FAX:
(516) 676-2420, E-Mail: sales@
callcompliance.com, Web Site: www.
callcompliance.com
Pres: Alison Garfinkel Andrews
Chmn: Dean Garfinkel
CFO: Barry Brookstein
VP Admin: Phyllis Gorham
VP Sales & Mktg: Keith Altman
Conducts Business: U.S.
Employees: 25
Primary Market Served: Business
Direct online sales
Advertising/Marketing Budget Related
to Direct Marketing: 76-100%
Direct Marketing ad budget:
Direct Mail: 45%
Magazines: 35%
Newspapers: 10%
Telephone: 10%
Founded: 2001

CALL INTERACTIVE
Subs. of First Data Corp
10910 Mill Valley Rd
Omaha, NE 68154-3930
Telephone: (402) 498-7000, FAX:
(402) 498-7900, Web Site: www.
callit.com
Pres: Tom Nichting

CALLING SOLUTIONS
2200 McCullough Ave
San Antonio, TX 78212-3751
Telephone: (210) 822-7400, (800) 683-
5500, FAX: (210) 491-1777, E-Mail:
pepe@callingsolutions.com, Web
Site: www.callingsolutions.com
Pres: Louis Cooper

THOMAS L CARDELLA &
ASSOCIATES
2100 Kimberton Rd
Kimberton, PA 19442-0816
Telephone: (610) 933-3822, Web Site:
www.tlcassociates.com
Sr VP Sls & Mktg: Jeff Bauernschmidt

CARECALL INC
200 14th Ave E
Sartell, MN 56377-4500
Telephone: (320) 253-0800, Web Site:
www.arraysg.com
VP Bus Devel: Ed Beber

**CARLYLE MARKETING
CORP**
723 Interlochen Ct
Riverwoods, IL 60015-3869
Telephone: (847) 948-9295, FAX:
(847) 948-0465, E-Mail: carlylemi@
gmail.com
Pres: Eugene D. Sollo

CARROLL ENTERPRISES INC
554 Main St
Worcester, MA 01608-2014
Telephone: (508) 770-0206, Web Site:
www.sbsb.com
Pres & COO: Brian Carroll

CENTRAC INC
759 Bloomfield Ave (#359)
West Caldwell, NJ 07006-6701
Telephone: (973) 402-0999, FAX:
(973) 402-0993, E-Mail: rleeds@
centrac.com, Web Site: www.centrac.
com
Pres: Ronald Leeds

**CENTURY TELEPHONE
ENTERPRISES INC**
100 Century Tel Dr
Monroe, LA 71203
Telephone: (318) 388-9000, (800) 201-
4102, Web Site: centurytel.com
VP Corp Commun: Patricia Cameron

CHARLTON
222 W Washington Ave (Suite 200)
Madison, WI 53703-2719
Telephone: (608) 259-8004, FAX:
(608) 259-8061, E-Mail: jdragisic@
tcgcorp.net, Web Site: www.tcgcorp.
net
Chmn Bd: John Dragisic
Administrative Asst: Kristi Larson

**THE
DMA CHOICECONNEX**
13555 Automobile Blvd (Suite 530)
Clearwater, FL 33762-3838
Telephone: (727) 571-3302, Web Site:
www.choiceconnex.com
Country Head: Sriram Iyengar

**CIRCULATION BY PHONE
INC**
60 E 42nd St (Rm 1630)
New York, NY 10165-0656
Telephone: (212) 557-2777
Pres: Nancy Bauman

**COLWELL & SALMON
COMMUNICATIONS INC**
100 Hillside Ave
Cresskill, NJ 07626-1612
Telephone: (518) 482-1596, (800) 724-
5318, FAX: (518) 482-1998, E-Mail:
sales@colwell-salmon.com, Web
Site: www.colwell-salmon.com
Pres Global Cust Rels: Wayne Colwell

**COMMUNICATION
SOLUTIONS LLC**
310 S Ingram Mill Rd
Springfield, MO 65802-6104
Telephone: (417) 862-4567, Web Site:
www.comsolllc.com
VP: Tony Ridenour
Primary Market Served: Business

**CONCORDE
COMMUNICATIONS**
3699 Wilshire Blvd (#850)
Los Angeles, CA 90010-2718
Telephone: (310) 854-4411, (800) 800-
4411, FAX: (310) 854-0551, Web
Site: www.concordecommunications.
com
Pres: Sylviane Herzog

**THE CONNECTION
CONTACT CENTER
SERVICES**
11351 Rupp Dr
Burnsville, MN 55337-1200
Telephone: (952) 948-5335, (800) 883-
5777, FAX: (952) 948-5498, E-Mail:
sales@the-connection.com, Web Site:
www.the-connection.com
Sls & Mktg Specialist: Erin Brooks
VP New Bus Devel: Corey Kotlarz
VP Sls & Mktg: Tim Austrums
Dir Sls: Michael McMillan

**THE
DMA THE CONNECTION
OUTSOURCED CALL CTR**
11351 Rupp Dr
Burnsville, MN 55337-1200
Telephone: (800) 883-5777, Web Site:
www.the-connection.com
VP Sls & Mktg: Tim Austrums

**CONSOLIDATED MARKET
RESPONSE**
A McLeod USA Company
700 W Lincoln (Suite 200)
Charleston, IL 61920
Telephone: (217) 348-7050, FAX:
(217) 348-7060
Chmn Bd: Richard A. Lumpkin

CONVERGYS CORP
1400 W 4400 S
Ogden, UT 84405-3300

Telephone: (630) 668-6174, Web Site:
www.convergys.com
Pres, CEO & Dir: David F. Dougherty
Sr Dir Bus Devel: Jim Mitchell

**CONVERSATIONAL VOICE
TECHNOLOGIES CORP**
28 N US Highway 12 Apt E
Fox Lake, IL 60020-1257
Telephone: (847) 265-4901, (800) 994-
4400, FAX: (847) 265-4915, E-Mail:
sales@conservit.com, Web Site:
www.conservit.com
Pres: Peter F. Theis

CREATIVE COMPLIANCE
900 N Franklin (Suite 706)
Chicago, IL 60610
Telephone: (916) 216-3379, E-Mail:
info@creativecompliance.com, Web
Site: www.creativecompliance.com
Principal: Joan Mullen
Principal: Sandy Pernick
Principal: Randi Wine
Conducts Business: U.S.
Primary Market Served: Business
Advertising/Marketing Budget Related
to Direct Marketing: 0-25%
Direct Marketing ad budget:
Direct Mail: 50%
Telephone: 50%
Founded: 2003

Help businesses keep current with the
continually changing legislative and
regulatory climate of the teleservices
industry.

**THE
DMA CUSTOMERLINK**
11 E Superior St Ste 430
Duluth, MN 55802-3013
Telephone: (218) 722-2800, (866) 245-
5569, FAX: (218) 722-3287, E-Mail:
info@customerlinkone.com, Web
Site: www.customerlinkone.com
Dir: Jason Broska
Conducts Business: U.S., Canada
Employees: 150
Primary Market Served: Business &
Consumer
Advertising/Marketing Budget Related
to Direct Marketing: 76-100%
Direct Marketing ad budget:
Direct Mail: 20%
Telephone: 80%
Founded: 1988

Call center services, outbound sales,
inbound sales and service to the energy
industries and medical industries.

**CYBER CITY TELESERVICES
MARKETING INC**
401 Hackensack Ave (fl 3)
Hackensack, NJ 07601-6405

Telephone: (201) 487-1616, (800) 213-4144, E-Mail: info@cctll.com, Web Site: www.cctll.com
Sr VP Bus Devel: Fred Shadding
Conducts Business: U.S.
Employees: 3,000
Primary Market Served: Business & Consumer
Advertising/Marketing Budget Related to Direct Marketing: 0-25%
Founded: 1999

Call center & back office processing services.

CYBER MARKETING SERVICES
70 Chestnut Ridge Rd (Suite K)
Montvale, NJ 07645
Telephone: (201) 505-1743, FAX: (201) 391-4907, E-Mail: info@crmxchange.com, Web Site: www.crmxchange.com
Principal: Larry Matte

DATA SERVICES DIRECT
959 Rte 46 (Suite 302)
Parsippany, NJ 07054
Telephone: (973) 331-8101, FAX: (973) 331-8108, Web Site: www.dataservicesdirect.com
Exec VP Bus Devel: Russell Thomas

THE DMA DEMAND TELEMARKETING INC
377 Fisher Rd (Suite D)
Grosse Pointe, MI 48230-1600
Telephone: (313) 823-8598, (888) 977-2256, FAX: (313) 823-8598, E-Mail: wpatterson@create-demand.com, Web Site: www.create-demand.com
Pres: William Patterson
Dir Opers: Ronne Newton
Dir Mktg Analytics: Nede Salane
Conducts Business: U.S.
Employees: 3
Primary Market Served: Business
Advertising/Marketing Budget Related to Direct Marketing: 76-100%
Direct Marketing ad budget: $1,500,000
Direct Mail: 35%
Magazines: 35%
Telephone: 30%
Founded: 2003
Gross sales or billing: $1,500,000

Full service direct & database marketing agency focusing on business to business lead generation customer acquisition & retention.

THE DMA DIALAMERICA MARKETING INC
960 Macarthur Blvd
Mahwah, NJ 07430-2040
Telephone: (201) 327-0200, (800) 531-3131, FAX: (201) 327-4875, Web Site: www.dialamerica.com
Pres & CEO: Arthur Conway

DIALOGUE MARKETING
3252 University Dr (Suite 165)
Auburn Hills, MI 48326-2786
Telephone: (734) 374-8400, (800) 523-5867, FAX: (248) 836-2601, Web Site: www.dialogue-marketing.com
CEO: Alejandro Vargas

DIRECT ADVANTAGE MARKETING
2100 Wharton St Ste 510
Pittsburgh, PA 15203-1691
Telephone: (412) 381-2300, E-Mail: information@dam.com, Web Site: www.dam.com
Pres: Jay P. Fairbrother
Principal: Sheila Hollums

THE DMA DIRECT MARKETING PARTNERS
2045 Hallmark Dr (Suite 5)
Sacramento, CA 95825-2224
Telephone: (916) 974-6969, (800) 909-2626, FAX: (916) 920-5156, E-Mail: info@dirmkt.com, Web Site: www.directmarketingpartners.com
Pres: Debra Da Costa
VP Bus Devel & Strategy: Tom Judge
Conducts Business: U.S., Canada, Western Europe
Primary Market Served: Business
Founded: 1991

A B2B direct marketing and teleservices provider. This U.S. based call center specializes in the complex sale and provides metrics-driven refinements to achieve client goals.

DIRECT RESPONSE ENHANCEMENTS LLC
12772 E Sunnyside Dr
Scottsdale, AZ 85259-3438
Telephone: (480) 451-7384, FAX: (480) 661-8460, E-Mail: drellc@aol.com, Web Site: www.dreteleconsultants.com
Pres: Gail K. Eberlein

ETI SALES SUPPORT
465 Columbus Ave Ste 280
Valhalla, NY 10595-2301
Telephone: (914) 747-3030, (800) 466-4384, FAX: (914) 747-3466, E-Mail: info@etisales.com, Web Site: www.etisales.com
Pres: Michael Falkson

EDGE TELESERVICES, INC
4020 W 111th St (Suite 1102)
Oak Lawn, IL 60453-5783
Telephone: (708) 857-5000, (800) 394-2323, FAX: (708) 857-5029, E-Mail: contactme@edgeteleservices.com, Web Site: www.edgeteleservices.com
Pres: Thomas Wogan

800 CALL KC
1616 N Corrington Ave
Kansas City, MO 64120
Telephone: (816) 231-4321, (800) 722-5554, FAX: (816) 241-2743, E-Mail: sales@call-kc.com, Web Site: www.call-kc.com
Pres: Roy Nafzinger

EPERFORMAX INC
100 Saddle Springs Blvd (Suite 100)
Thompsons Station, TN 37179-5328
Telephone: (901) 751-4800, (888) 384-7004, FAX: (901) 751-4805, E-Mail: info0609@eperformax.com, Web Site: www.eperformax.com
Pres: Teresa Hartsaw

ETECH INC
106 N John Redditt Dr
Lufkin, TX 75904-2640
Telephone: (936) 633-9333, Web Site: www.effectiveteleservices.com
COO: Matt Rocco

FTD GROUP INC
3113 Woodcreek Dr
Downers Grove, IL 60515
Telephone: (630) 719-7800, (800) 788-9000, FAX: (630) 719-6170, E-Mail: ftdmemberservices@ftdi.com, Web Site: www.ftdi.com
Chmn Bd, CEO & Pres: Michael J. Soenen
EVP Sls FTD Inc: George T. Kanganis
VP Mktg FTD.com: Michael Dorian

FALZONE & ASSOCIATES LLC
5 Narothyn Rd
Sellersville, PA 18960-2958
Telephone: (215) 822-8941
Pres: Mary Ann Falzone

THE FANEUIL GROUP
363 Broadway (Suite 906)
Winnipeg, MB, Canada R3C 3N9
Telephone: (204) 934-1900, (866) FA-NEUIL, FAX: (617) 742-3666, Web Site: www.faneuil.com
VP: Mark Leonard

THE DMA FINELINE
290 Garry St
Winnipeg, MB, Canada R3C 1H3

Telephone: (204) 942-4242, Web Site: www.finelinesolutions.com
CEO: Polly Craik

FRONTIER COMMUNICATIONS
3 High Ridge Dr
Stamford, CT 06905-3806
Telephone: (203) 614-5600, Web Site: www.czn.com
VP Residential Mktg & Customer Experience: Diane Quennoz

GLOBAL CROSSING TELECOM INC
200 Park Ave (Suite 300)
Florham Park, NJ 07932
Telephone: (800) 466-4600, FAX: (973) 937-0100, E-Mail: iccc@ globalcrossing.com, Web Site: www. globalcrossing.com
CEO: John Legere

GLOBAL RESPONSE CORP
777 S State Rd 7
Margate, FL 33068-2803
Telephone: (954) 973-7300, (800) 537-8000, FAX: (954) 968-9862, E-Mail: wendys@globalresponse.com, Web Site: www.globalresponse.com
Chmn & Owner: Herman Shooster
Co-CEO: Frank Shooster

GREENE AN RMG DIRECT CO
300 Tri-State Intl (Suite 272)
Lincolnshire, IL 60069-4415
Telephone: (847) 948-7400, (800) 356-1300 x1809, FAX: (847) 948-0400, Web Site: www.rmgdirectinc.com
Pres: Randy Greenberg
Bus Devel Mgr: Thomas Kijewski

GROUP2MARKETING
1214 Stowe Ave
Medford, OR 97501-6611
Telephone: (541) 734-2565, Web Site: www.group2marketing.net
VP & Gen Mgr: Bob Mylenek

HAMILTON CONTACT CENTER SERVICES
1006 12th St
Aurora, NE 68818-2003
Telephone: (402) 694-4343, (800) 972-3237, FAX: (402) 694-4433, Web Site: www.hamiltontm.com
VP, Contact Center Svcs: Angela M. Morris
Mktg Mgr: Gary Lewien

BERNARD C HARRIS PUBLISHING CO INC
Div. of Bernard C. Harris Publishing Company Inc
1511 Route 22 (Suite C-25)
Brewster, NY 10509-4085
Telephone: (800) 326-6600, FAX: (845) 940-0801, E-Mail: moreinfo@ harrisconnect.com, Web Site: www. bcharrispub.com
Chmn & CEO: William K. Harris

THE DMA THE HERITAGE CO
2402 Wildwood Ave (Suite 500)
North Little Rock, AR 72120-5094
Telephone: (501) 835-5000 x1142, FAX: (501) 835-5834, Web Site: www.theheritagecompany.com
Pres & CEO: John Braune

ICT GROUP INC
400 N Ashley Dr (Suite 2500)
Tampa, FL 33602-4348
Telephone: (215) 757-0200, (800) 799-6880, Web Site: www.ictgroup.com
CEO: Charles Sykes

THE DMA IMARKETING SOLUTIONS GROUP INC
700 W Virginia St (Suite 700), Timbers Building
Milwaukee, WI 53204-1555
Telephone: (414) 224-0701, (800) 879-0076, FAX: (414) 224-0943, Web Site: imarketingsolutionsgroup.com
Dir Opers: Wendy Wenaas
COO: Andrew Langhorne

INCEPT CORP
4150 Belden Village St NW (Suite 205)
Canton, OH 44718-3643
Telephone: (330) 649-8000, Web Site: www.inceptcorp.com
Pres: Jeff White
Primary Market Served: Business & Consumer

INFINIAN CORP
4856 El Camino Real (Suite 200)
Los Altos, CA 94022
Telephone: (415) 260-8142, Web Site: www.infinian.com
Sr VP Sls & Bus Devel: Dave Bakke
Primary Market Served: Business & Consumer

INFLUENT INC
565 Metro Pl S (Suite 250)
Dublin, OH 43017-7312
Telephone: (614) 280-1600, (800) 856-6768, FAX: (614) 280-1610, E-Mail: info@influentinc.com, Web Site: www.influentinc.com

Pres & CEO: Andrew Jacobs
Conducts Business: U.S., Panama, Philippines
Employees: 1,600
Primary Market Served: Business & Consumer
Advertising/Marketing Budget Related to Direct Marketing: 0-25%
Direct Marketing ad budget:
Direct Mail: 75%
Telephone: 25%
Founded: 1992
Gross sales or billing: $30,000,000

Provides multi-lingual outsourced sales and customer service and a full service resource for inbound and outbound customer contact solutions. Industry specialization includes financial services, insurance, telecommunications, business services, and Hispanic marketing.

THE DMA INFOCISION MANAGEMENT CORP
325 Springside Dr
Akron, OH 44333-4504
Telephone: (330) 668-1400, FAX: (330) 668-1401, E-Mail: infocision@ infocision.com, Web Site: www. infocision.com
Pres: Gary Taylor
Chief Mktg Officer: Ken Dawson

INNOVATIVE MARKETING SOLUTIONS LLC
121 Target Cir
Bangor, ME 04401-5717
Telephone: (207) 262-6233, Web Site: www.imsmaine.net
Pres: Vincent Wank

INTEGRATED ALLIANCE LIMITED PARTNERSHIP
5800 N Interstate 35 (Suite 200B)
Denton, TX 76207-1438
Telephone: (940) 565-9415, FAX: (940) 383-1876, E-Mail: ryoung@ integratedalliance.com, Web Site: www.integratedalliance.com
CEO: Randy Keylor
Mktg Mgr: Lucy Quintanilla
HR/Opers: Liz Foster

INTEGRATED MESSAGING INC
550 Berry St
Winnipeg, MB, Canada R3H 0R9
Telephone: (204) 786-7630, (800) 561-3734, FAX: (204) 786-7718, E-Mail: sales@imi.mb.ca, Web Site: www. imi.mb.ca
Pres: Wendy Bailey
Conducts Business: U.S., Canada
Employees: 200

Primary Market Served: Business & Consumer
Advertising/Marketing Budget Related to Direct Marketing: 76-100%
Direct Marketing ad budget:
Direct Mail: 5%
Magazines: 80%
Newspapers: 5%
Telephone: 10%
Founded: 1989
Gross sales or billing: $6,000,000

Twenty four seven inbound order entry & customer service including fulfillment.

INTELESURE LLC
104 E Fairview Ave (#262), PMB 262
Meridian, ID 83642-1733
Telephone: (866) 808-7366, Web Site:
   www.intelesure.com
CEO: Tobe Brockner

INTELITARGET
212 Fort Collier Rd
Winchester, VA 22603-5738
Telephone: (540) 409-4801, Web Site:
   www.intelitarget.com
Pres & CEO: Joseph Smith

INTER-MEDIA MARKETING SOLUTIONS
204 Carter Dr
West Chester, PA 19382
Telephone: (800) 835-3466, FAX:
   (610) 429-5137, Web Site: www.
   intermediamarketing.com
Partner: Edmund A. Thompson

INTERACTIVE RESPONSE TECHNOLOGIES INC
4500 N State Rd Seven (Suite 301)
Fort Lauderdale, FL 33319
Telephone: (954) 484-4973, (800) 700-
   3033, FAX: (954) 484-0818, E-Mail:
   hglass@callcenter.com, Web Site:
   www.callcenter.com
Pres: Howard Glass

JC PENNEY TELEMARKETING INC
Subs. of JC Penney Co Inc
11800 W Burleigh St
Milwaukee, WI 53222-3110
Telephone: (262) 792-5504, (800) 323-
   4343, FAX: (262) 792-5598, Web
   Site: www.jcpenney.com
Sr VP: Len Leininger

JAK PRODUCTIONS
4501 Circle 75 Pkwy SE (Suite E5280)
Atlanta, GA 30339-3025

Telephone: (770) 612-1386, FAX:
   (770) 612-9163, E-Mail: jkeller2@
   ix.netcom.com
Pres: Jack Keller

KING TELESERVICES
Div. of DF King
48 Wall St Fl 23
New York, NY 10005-2922
Telephone: (718) 361-4100, (800) 817-
   5468, E-Mail: info@king-
   teleservices.com, Web Site: www.
   king-teleservices.com
Pres: Mark Intregila

KURANT DIRECT INC
372 Central Park W (Suite 7B)
New York, NY 10025-8205
Telephone: (212) 866-0770, FAX:
   (212) 866-0806, E-Mail: gkurant@
   aol.com, Web Site: www.
   kurantdirect.com
Pres: Gloria L. Kurant

Strategic & tactical contact center consulting; global inbound and outbound.

LESTER INC
19 Business Park Dr (Suite A)
Branford, CT 06405-2936
Telephone: (203) 488-5265, (800) 999-
   5265, FAX: (203) 483-0408, Web
   Site: www.lesterusa.com
Pres: Rajiv Samant
SVP: Joan Marcus

THE DMA LIEBER & ASSOCIATES
3740 N Lake Shore Dr (Ste 15B-2)
Chicago, IL 60613-4237
Telephone: (773) 325-9400, FAX:
   (773) 325-0621, E-Mail: info@
   lieberandassociates.com, Web Site:
   www.lieberandassociates.com
Pres: Mitchell A. Lieber

Consultants Enhancing Contact Renters.

JOEL LINCHITZ CONSULTING SERVICES/ PHONE FOR SUCCESS
Joel Linchitz Associates
2578 Broadway (Suite 135)
New York, NY 10025
Telephone: (212) 431-6700, FAX:
   (212) 865-2008, E-Mail:
   phoneforsuccess@compuserve.com,
   Web Site: www.callcenter-
   salestraining.com/index.php
Pres: Joel Linchitz

LINK TELEMARKETING INC
Subs. of Link to Success Inc
5935 Hillendale St
Excelsior, MN 55331

Telephone: (952) 404-1609, FAX:
   (952) 474-0529, Web Site: www.
   roimark.com/link
Pres: James Daughton

LIVEOPS INC
5425 Stevens Creek Blvd
Santa Clara, CA 95051-7203
Telephone: (408) 844-2400, Web Site:
   www.liveops.com
Pur Mgr: Sandy Mar

LUCAS & ASSOCIATES
617 N Seventh St
Montebello, CA 90640-3536
Telephone: (323) 728-7899
Pres: Ned Lucas

MKS MARKETING INC
3404 San Mateo Dr
Austin, TX 78733
Telephone: (512) 263-8017, (800) 544-
   8989, FAX: (402) 333-9610, E-Mail:
   info@telemarketingoutsource.com,
   Web Site: www.
   telemarketingoutsource.com
Pres: Jerry Schoemann

MARCOM TECHNOLOGIES
337 Rio Dr S
Kelowna, BC, Canada V1V 2V1
Telephone: (250) 868-9352, FAX:
   (250) 868-9362
Pres: Henry Schuyler

MARKETEERS
PO Box 3571
Mission Viejo, CA 92690-1571
Telephone: (949) 364-1669, FAX:
   (949) 582-0829, E-Mail: wbower@
   apc.net
Co-Owner: W. Bower

MARKETING CONNECTIONS CORP
10 Corporate Dr (Suite 206)
Bedford, NH 03110
Telephone: (603) 472-8989, (800) 472-
   1818, FAX: (603) 472-9881, E-Mail:
   lcasey@mccnh.com, Web Site: www.
   mcciq.com
Pres: Larry Casey

MARKETLINC
105 21 St E (Suite 100)
Saskatoon, SK, Canada S7K 0B3
Telephone: (306) 956-7000, FAX:
   (306) 668-5812, E-Mail: info@
   marketlinc.com, Web Site: www.
   marketlinc.com
Gen Mgr: Donna Ghuman
Primary Market Served: Business & Consumer

MARKETMAKERS GROUP INC
687 W Lancaster Ave
Wayne, PA 19087-2545
Telephone: (610) 254-8924, FAX: (610) 254-9190, E-Mail: rlail@ marketmakers.com, Web Site: www. marketmakersgroup.com
Pres: Robert Lail
HR Assoc: Karen Boyle
Conducts Business: U.S.
Employees: 70
Primary Market Served: Business
Catalog available online
Direct online sales
Advertising/Marketing Budget Related to Direct Marketing: 76-100%
Founded: 1996
Gross sales or billing: $21,000,000

Business to business telemarketing.

MEYER ASSOCIATES TELESERVICES
aka Meyer Teleservices
14 7th Ave N
Saint Cloud, MN 56303-4753
Telephone: (320) 259-4000, (800) 676-9233, FAX: (320) 259-4044, E-Mail: info@callmeyer.com, Web Site: www.callmeyer.com
Pres: Lawrence R Meyer
CEO: Nick Gerten

THE DMA MIDCO CALL CENTER SERVICES
Subs. of Midcontinent Media
4901 E 26th St
Sioux Falls, SD 57110-6950
Telephone: (605) 330-4125, (800) 843-8800, FAX: (605) 357-5414, Web Site: www.midcocall.com
Gen Mgr: Doreen West

MILBERG PENN *INTERNATIONAL
116 Radio Cir (Suite 206)
Mount Kisco, NY 10549-2632
Telephone: (914) 241-0858, (914) 239-4300, E-Mail: contact@ mpioutsourcing.com, Web Site: www.mpioutsourcing.com
Pres: Jeffrey A. Milberg
CEO: Richard E. Penn
Conducts Business: U.S., Worldwide
Employees: 25
Primary Market Served: Business & Consumer
Advertising/Marketing Budget Related to Direct Marketing: 76-100%
Direct Marketing ad budget: $10,000
Direct Mail: 65%
Telephone: 35%
Founded: 2005

Program management company for direct marketing, call centers services.

MINACS WORLDWIDE
34115 W Twelve Mile Rd
Farmington Hills, MI 48331-3368
Telephone: (416) 380-3800, FAX: (416) 380-3830, E-Mail: info@ minacs.com, Web Site: www.minacs. com
Chmn & CEO: Elaine Minac

ALAN MORGAN & ASSOCIATES INC
2854 Lake Vista Rd
Jacksonville, FL 32223-7934
Telephone: (904) 262-1316, FAX: (904) 880-6182, E-Mail: amorgan@ alanmorgan.com, Web Site: www.alanmorgan.com
Pres: Alan Morgan

MOUNTAIN WEST COMMUNICATIONS INC
110 E Hotchkiss Ave, PO Box 216
Hotchkiss, CO 81419
Telephone: (970) 872-2500, (800) 642-9378, FAX: (970) 872-3862, E-Mail: sales@mountainwest.com, Web Site: www.mountainwest.com
CEO: Kirby Clock

NCO FINANCIAL SYSTEMS
Subs of NCO Group Inc
507 Prudential Rd
Horsham, PA 19044
Telephone: (215) 441-3000, (800) 220-2274, FAX: (215) 441-3923, E-Mail: marketing@ncogroup.com, Web Site: www.ncogroup.com
Sr VP Mktg: Lisa Hagee

NATIONAL ADMINISTRATIVE SERVICE CO LLC
400 Metro Pl N (Suite 360)
Dublin, OH 43017-3318
Telephone: (614) 358-1500
Member: Haytehm ElZayn
Primary Market Served: Business

NATIONAL SYSTEMS CORP
414 N Orleans St (Suite 501)
Chicago, IL 60610-4498
Telephone: (312) 855-1000, FAX: (312) 222-1605, E-Mail: support@ nationalsystems.com, Web Site: www.nationalsystems.com
Sls Mgr: Eric Beamont

THE DMA NEUSTAR INC
46000 Center Oak Plz Ste 1
Sterling, VA 20166-6579

Telephone: (571) 434-5400, Web Site: www.tcpacompliance.us
VP Mobile Svcs: Diane Strahan

NOVO1
4301 Cambridge Rd
Fort Worth, TX 76155-2627
Telephone: (817) 355-6899, FAX: (817) 355-8505, Web Site: www. novo1.com
Sr VP Devel: Jack Wilkie
CEO: Mary Marcott
CFO: John Sykstus
COO: Eric Rothert
CTO: Mitch Swindell
Employees: 1,800
Founded: 1984
Gross sales or billing: $50,000,000

NOVO1 contact centers reduce complexity for clients and enhance the customer experience through a proprietary customer obsession program and smart desktop solution.

OKS-AMERIDIAL INC
303 Parsons Ave
Bala Cynwyd, PA 19004
Telephone: (610) 667-3000, FAX: (610) 667-3002, E-Mail: info@ oksgroup.com, Web Site: www. oksameridial.com
Pres & CEO: Vinit Khanna

THE DMA ORC PROTEL LLC
17233 Continental Dr
Lansing, IL 60438-6005
Telephone: (708) 418-7413, FAX: (708) 418-7457, Web Site: www. orcprotel.com
CEO: Ruth R. Wolf
Exec VP Mktg: Allen E. Wolf

THE OFFICE GURUS
10055 Seminole Blvd
Seminole, FL 33772-2539
Telephone: (727) 803-7114, Web Site: www.theofficegurus.com
Mng Dir: Dominic Leide

OMEGA DIRECT RESPONSE INC
30 Wertheim Ct (Unit 12)
Richmond Hill, ON, Canada L4B 1B9
Telephone: (905) 482-2340, FAX: (905) 482-9721, E-Mail: odrsales@ omegadirect.com, Web Site: www. omegadirect.com
Pres & CEO: Bharat Hansraj
VP & COO: Everton Thompson
CFO: Paul Pullano
Sr VP, Bus Devel: ick Jiwa
Conducts Business: U.S., Canada, Worldwide

Primary Market Served: Business &
  Consumer
Founded: 1997
Gross sales or billing: $22,000,000
Telemarket for various clients.

OMEGA MOBILE
350 Townsend St Ste 220
San Francisco, CA 94107-1671
Telephone: (415) 596-6342, Web Site:
  www.omegamobile.com

ONBRAND24
100 Cummings Ctr (Suite 306L)
Beverly, MA 01915-6107
Telephone: (855) 662-7263

ONE CALL SYSTEMS INC
155 McCartney Ln
Baden, PA 15005-2827
Telephone: (412) 415-5000, (800) 845-
  9945, FAX: (412) 415-5023, E-Mail:
  jmcnamara@1-call.com, Web Site:
  www.1-call.com
VP Mktg: John McNamara

THE DMA 1-800-DIALWORD.COM
1095 E King St Box 10
Boone, NC 28607-4325
Telephone: (800) DIALWORD, FAX:
  (877) 329-3627, Web Site: www.
  1800dialword.com
Pres: Andy Owens

THE DMA ONE WORLD TELECOM
2620 SW 27th Ave
Miami, FL 33133
Telephone: (786) 664-6100 x6672,
  Web Site: www.nopin.us
Primary Market Served: Business &
  Consumer

OUR DATA WORKS INC
1504 Fairway Dr
Lewisville, TX 75057-2329
Telephone: (469) 546-3000, (800) 268-
  2505, FAX: (469) 546-3013, E-Mail:
  info@ourdataworks.com, Web Site:
  www.ourdataworks.com
Pres: Bruce Klotzman
VP: Michelle Harris

PCCW TELESERVICES
565 Metro Pl S (Suite 250)
Dublin, OH 43017-7312
Telephone: (614) 280-1600, Web Site:
  www.influentinc.com
Primary Market Served: Consumer

THE DMA PSI MARKETING
  CONSULTANTS INC
2340 S River Rd (Suite 208)
Des Plaines, IL 60018-3223

Telephone: (773) 878-0800, (800) 933-
  4774, FAX: (773) 878-4219
Pres: Phillip S. Immergluck
VP Mktg: Mike Baker

PERSON TO PERSON
  MARKETING LLC
8 N Corporate Dr
Riverdale, NJ 07457
Telephone: (973) 835-8112, FAX:
  (973) 835-8525, E-Mail: sales@
  persontopersondirect.com, Web Site:
  www.persontopersondirect.com
Pres: Steve Alario

POWER SEMINARS
The Learning Center
53 New Ocean St (Suite 3)
Swampscott, MA 01907-1840
Telephone: (781) 595-9990, FAX:
  (781) 595-0770, Web Site: www.
  gailcohen.com
Pres: Gail Cohen

PREMIER MESSAGING LP
9850 Sagepike Dr
Houston, TX 77089-3514
Telephone: (888) 405-7000, E-Mail:
  sales@premiermessaging.com, Web
  Site: www.premiermessaging.com
Primary Market Served: Business &
  Consumer

PRISM MARKETING GROUP
111 W Second St
Schaller, IA 51053
Telephone: (800) 862-4827, FAX:
  (712) 275-4855, E-Mail: cjgrothe@
  schallertel.net, Web Site: www.
  prismktg.com
Gen Mgr: Chris Grothe
Conducts Business: U.S.
Primary Market Served: Business &
  Consumer
Founded: 1994

PROSODIE INTERACTIVE
855 SW 78th Ave (Suite 100)
Plantation, FL 33324-3223
Telephone: (954) 671-6500, (866) 776-
  7634, FAX: (954) 915-0567, E-Mail:
  info@prosodiemail.com, Web Site:
  www.ivrinc.com
Dir Mktg: Ross Krisel
Conducts Business: U.S., Canada
Employees: 986
Primary Market Served: Business
Advertising/Marketing Budget Related
  to Direct Marketing: 0-25%
Founded: 1986
Gross sales or billing: $264,000,000

Interactive voice response, inbound
call routing, automated call distribution, automated surveys, customer experience enhancements.

PROTOCOL
2805 Fruitville Rd
Sarasota, FL 34237-5318
Telephone: (800) 800-8627, FAX:
  (203) 271-4970, Web Site: www.
  protocolmarketing.com
Pres: John Heltzer
Dir Mktg: Cheryl Walsh

PROVIDENCE JOURNAL
  TELEMARKETING
75 Fountain St
Providence, RI 02902-0050
Telephone: (401) 277-7000, FAX:
  (401) 277-8046, E-Mail: bnauman@
  projo.com, Web Site: www.projo.
  com
Sr Dir Consumer Mktg: Barbara Nauman

PTM COMMUNICATIONS
330 W 38th St (Suite 801)
New York, NY 10018-8465
Telephone: (212) 643-5458, FAX:
  (212) 643-5486, E-Mail: info@
  ptmcomm.com, Web Site: www.
  ptmcomm.com
Pres: Gail Stone

PUBLIC INTEREST
  COMMUNICATIONS INC
7700 Leesburg Pike (Suite 301)
Falls Church, VA 22043
Telephone: (703) 847-8300, FAX:
  (703) 734-9620, Web Site: www.
  pubintcom.com
Pres: Kenneth Whitaker

QUALITY CONTACT
  SOLUTIONS INC
808 4th St
Aurora, NE 68818-2201
Telephone: (402) 210-2692, (866) 963-
  2889, FAX: (402) 210-2692, E-Mail:
  info@qualitycontactsolutions.com,
  Web Site: www.
  qualitycontactsolutions.com
Pres: Angela Morris
Dir Opers: Nathan Teahon
COO: Dean Garfinkel
Dir Client Svcs: Melissa Hinrichs
Dir Back Office Opers: Kelsey Olsen
Conducts Business: U.S., Canada
Employees: 45
Primary Market Served: Business &
  Consumer
Advertising/Marketing Budget Related
  to Direct Marketing: 76-100%
Direct Marketing ad budget:

Telephone: 100%
Founded: 2007
Gross sales or billing: $4,600,000

Provides business to business telemarketing & call center solutions. Helps clients with inbound, outbound and e-contact strategies.

SCHOLASTIC DIRECT MKTG
Subs. of Scholastic Inc
90 Sherman Tpke
Danbury, CT 06816-0001
Telephone: (203) 797-3500, FAX: (203) 797-3667
Pres: George Saul

SELLTEL INC
393 Mantoloking Rd
Brick, NJ 08723
Telephone: (732) 920-8700, (888) 840-9481, FAX: (732) 903-0836, E-Mail: info@nationalprotection.com
Pres: David Gartenberg
Controller: Lucy M. Hull

SHARE GROUP INC
79 Chapel St
Newton, MA 02458-1010
Telephone: (617) 629-4500, FAX: (617) 629-4510, E-Mail: info@sharegroup.com, Web Site: www.sharegroup.com
CEO: Susan Paine

SKYTEL COMMUNICATIONS INC
A Worldcom Company
1720 Lakepoint Dr
Lewisville, TX 75057-6408
Telephone: (800) 759-8737, Web Site: www.skytel.com
Dir Sls: Kevin Calvey

SMARTREPLY INC
6410 Oak Canyon Rd (Suite 100)
Irvine, CA 92618-5225
Telephone: (949) 340-0700, Web Site: www.smartreply.com
Dir Mktg: Tania Eckweiler
Primary Market Served: Business & Consumer

SPECTRUM COMMUNICATION SERVICES INC
125 N Executive Dr Ste 300
Brookfield, WI 53005-6035
Telephone: (262) 821-8400, (800) 701-3559, FAX: (262) 821-1492, E-Mail: sales@spectrumcomm.com, Web Site: www.spectrumcomm.com
Pres: Roy Osmon

SPEECHSOFT INC
49 The Crossing
Armonk, NY 10504
Telephone: (914) 273-5560, (800) 878-8117, E-Mail: sales@speechsoft.com, Web Site: www.speechsoft.com
Pres: Morris Neuman

SPRINT CORP
6130 Sprint Pkwy (Mailstop KSOPHJO102)
Overland Park, KS 66251
Telephone: (913) 624-3313, FAX: (913) 624-5386
Corp Communs: Sandy Wickhander

STRATMAR SYSTEMS INC
dba "Intercept" & "Stratmar Retail Svcs"
109 Willet Ave
Port Chester, NY 10573
Telephone: (914) 937-7171, (800) 866-2399, FAX: (914) 937-6045, E-Mail: info@stratmar.com, Web Site: www.stratmar.com
Sr VP Sls & Mktg: Clayton Zimmerman

STURNER & KLEIN
Div. of NOVI
4301 Cambridge Rd
Fort Worth, TX 76155-2627
Telephone: (800) 678-4960, FAX: (301) 881-3745
Pres: Jerry Sturner

SYKES ACQUISITION
100 Brandywine Blvd
Newtown, PA 18940-4000
Telephone: (800) 799-6880, Web Site: www.ictgroup.com
Chmn & CEO: John Brennan

THE DMA SYNERGY DIRECT MARKETING SOLUTIONS LLC
480 W Tuscarawas Ave Ste 307
Barberton, OH 44203-2597
Telephone: (330) 869-5886, Web Site: www.synmar.biz
Pres: Alexander Stavarz
Primary Market Served: Business & Consumer

THE DMA T-MOBILE
12920 SE 38th St
Bellevue, WA 98006-1350
Telephone: (425) 999-2084, Web Site: www.t-mobile.com

TMP DIRECT
PO Box 308
Budd Lake, NJ 07828-0308

Telephone: (973) 347-9400, (800) 328-2439, FAX: (973) 347-8773, E-Mail: ron.pearl@tmpwdirect.com, Web Site: www.tmpwdirect.com
VP: Ron Pearl
VP: Mary Ann Kerr
Pres: Daniel Collins

THE DMA TRG WORLD
1700 Pennsylvania Ave NW (Suite 560)
Washington, DC 20006
Telephone: (202) 289-9898
Primary Market Served: Business & Consumer

THE DMA TTC MARKETING SOLUTIONS
3945 N Neenah Ave
Chicago, IL 60634-2419
Telephone: (773) 545-0407, (800) 777-6348, FAX: (773) 545-4034, E-Mail: sales@ttcmarketingsolutions.com, Web Site: www.ttcmarketingsolutions.com
Pres: Mary Shanley
VP: Bob Aloisio

TECHNOLOGY MARKETING CORP/TMC
800 Connecticut Ave
Norwalk, CT 06854-1631
Telephone: (203) 852-6800, (800) 243-6002, FAX: (203) 953-2845, E-Mail: tmc@tmcnet.com, Web Site: www.tmcnet.com
CEO: Nadji Tehrani
Mktg Mgr: Jan Perret

TELE BUSINESS USA
1945 Techny Rd (Suite 3)
Northbrook, IL 60062
Telephone: (847) 480-1560, FAX: (847) 897-4120, Web Site: www.tbiz.com
CEO: Larry Kaplan
Pres: Jeff Levine
Exec VP: Robert Levy

Tele Business USA is the nation's premier business-to-business teleservices resource. More than just a telemarketing service bureau, we are the leading professional teleservices agency for inbound and outbound outsourced sales, lead generation and qualification, account management, appointment setting, market research, customer service, and database management.

TELE RESOURCES INC
222 W Superior St Ste 100
Duluth, MN 55802-1940

Telephone: (888) 698-8787 X114, FAX: (218) 724-2466, E-Mail: mark.swanson@teleresources.net, Web Site: www.teleresources.net
Dir Bus Devel: Mark Swanson
Pres & CEO: Jack L. Keenan
Conducts Business: U.S.
Employees: 120
Primary Market Served: Business & Consumer
Advertising/Marketing Budget Related to Direct Marketing: 0-25%
Direct Marketing ad budget:
Direct Mail: 60%
Magazines: 40%
Founded: 1996
Gross sales or billing: $5,000,000

Tele Resources Inc., is an outbound only call center with both B to B and B to C capabilities, providing custom program management and analysis, with a hands on operating team devoted to our clients and their programs. Tele Resources Inc., places years of quality telemarketing experience into every program.

THE DMA TELECOM INC
2201 Broadway (Suite 103)
Oakland, CA 94612-3028
Telephone: (510) 873-8283, (800) 243-3101, FAX: (510) 873-8293, Web Site: www.telecominc.com
Pres CEO & Owner: Jonathan Martin
Exec VP & Owner: William M Smith
Chief Tech Officer: Greg Haggerty
VP Mktg & Bus Devel: Hywel ap Rees

TELEDIRECT INTERNATIONAL INC
17255 N 82nd St
Scottsdale, AZ 85255
Telephone: (480) 585-6464, (800) 531-6440, FAX: (480) 585-3373, Web Site: www.tdirect.com
Prod Mngmt Dir: Mark Moore

TELENATIONAL MARKETING
2918 N 72nd St
Omaha, NE 68134-5107
Telephone: (800) 333-6106 X132, FAX: (402) 391-2044, Web Site: www.telenational.com
VP Mktg: Bonnie P. Powell

TELEPERFORMANCE INTERACTIVE
1601 Washington Ave (Suite 400)
Miami Beach, FL 33139-3166
Telephone: (786) 437-3300, FAX: (786) 276-8452, Web Site: www.teleperformance.com

Pres: Jeff Cohen

TELEREP
14 Wellham Ave
Glen Burnie, MD 21061
Telephone: (800) 638-2000, FAX: (410) 761-3357, Web Site: www.telerep.com
Pres: Sandra S. Olson

TELERX
723 Dresher Rd
Horsham, PA 19044-2299
Telephone: (800) 2TELERX, Web Site: www.telerx.com
Sr Dir Sls & Mktg: Loralee Hare
Conducts Business: Worldwide
Primary Market Served: Business
Founded: 1980

Contact center and BPO services.

THE DMA TELESERVICES DIRECT
5305 Lakeshore Pkwy South Dr
Indianapolis, IN 46268-4113
Telephone: (888) 646-6626, Web Site: www.teleservicesdirect.com
CEO & Pres: Patricia Totton

TELESYSTEMS MARKETING INC
3600 S Gessner Rd (Suite 250)
Houston, TX 77063
Telephone: (713) 784-3439, (800) 622-0190, FAX: (713) 780-5974, E-Mail: kimberly@nwpros.com, Web Site: www.telesystemsmarketing.com
Pres: Robin Fisher

TELETRACK INC
5550-A Peachtree Pkwy (Suite 600)
Norcross, GA 30092
Telephone: (770) 449-8809
Mktg Mgr: Katie Bryson
Primary Market Served: Business

TIMBERLINE TOTAL SOLUTIONS LLC
8429 Blood St
Omaha, NE 68134-1051
Telephone: (402) 397-6945, (877) 575-2255, FAX: (402) 255-5045, E-Mail: rleavitt@timberlinesolutions.com
CEO: Russell Leavitt

Provides inbound customer service supplemented with outbound sales and service to the existing business relationship market. Has over 200 customer service professionals and 15 years experience.

TIME COMMUNICATIONS
Div. of Bell Telephone Inc
4444 Centerville Rd (Suite 245)

Saint Paul, MN 55127-3712
Telephone: (800) 486-8581, FAX: (612) 298-1945, E-Mail: info@timecommunications.biz, Web Site: www.timecommunications.biz
Pres: Michael Eastwood

TMONE
1925 Boyrum
Iowa City, IA 52240
Telephone: (868) 577-2461, E-Mail: srteam@tmone.com, Web Site: www.tmone.com
CEO: Jason Hall
Pres: Anthony Marlowe
COO: John Burchert
Primary Market Served: Business

TOLLFREEFORWARDING.COM
5959 W Century Blvd (Suite 1108)
Los Angeles, CA 90045-6512
Telephone: (213) 452-1505, Web Site: www.tollfreeforwarding.com

TORCOM INBOUND TELEMARKETING
25 Kessel Ct (Suite 107)
Madison, WI 53711-6227
Telephone: (800) 832-4939, FAX: (608) 275-6557, E-Mail: torcom@torcom.com, Web Site: www.torcom.com
Natl Sls Mgr: Elin Torvik
Dir Opers: John Poehling
Client Svcs Mgr: John Ross

UNICALL INTERNATIONAL INC
3250 W Market St
Fairlawn, OH 44333
Telephone: (330) 864-9364, FAX: (330) 864-9367, E-Mail: harrisb@unicallinc.com, Web Site: www.unicallinc.com
Pres: Benjamin C. Harris
Conducts Business: U.S.
Employees: 150
Primary Market Served: Business & Consumer
Catalog available online
Direct online sales
Advertising/Marketing Budget Related to Direct Marketing: 76-100%
Direct Marketing ad budget:
Telephone: 100%
Founded: 1999
Gross sales or billing: $5,000,000

UNITED AMERICA ADVERTISING INC
1018 West Cherry Ave
Enid, OK 73703
Telephone: (580) 233-7200, FAX: (580) 548-8432

Pres: Tim H. Morgan

US DATA CORP
17310 Wright St (Suite 100)
Omaha, NE 68130-2405
Telephone: (402) 502-5623, (888) 578-
3282, FAX: (402) 502-5623, Web
Site: www.usdatacorporation.com
Pres: Dan Siburg
Pres: John DotJe

USA 800 INC
9808 E 66 Ter
Raytown, MO 64133
Telephone: (816) 358-1303, (800) 821-
7539, FAX: (816) 358-8845, E-Mail:
dlabatt@usa-800.com, Web Site:
www.usa-800.com
Pres: Tom Davis

THE DMA VENTRILOQUIST VOICE SOLUTIONS INTERNATIONAL INC
5025 Orbitor Dr (Suite 300), Bldg 1
Mississauga, ON, Canada L4W 4Y5
Telephone: (866) 446-0860, E-Mail:
info@vvsii.com, Web Site: www.
vvsii.com
Pres & CEO: J. Hunt
Exec VP Sales & Mktg: L Dykun
VP Opers & Customer Svc: C Hunt
VP Sales & Bus Devel: M Strauss
VP Mktg: Joe Palombo
Sr VP Sales & Mktg: R Savein
Employees: 9
Founded: 1999

Interactive voice-messaging platform
offers customer-centric organizations a
complementary low-cost tool to increase contact penetration and improve
response rates of customer care
communications. Improve call centre
effectiveness by using voice for rou-
tine, yet important, customer service
calls. Implement voice for retention,
collections, notifications, surveys, marketing initiatives and more.

VIRIDO LLC
6626 E Oberlin Way
Scottsdale, AZ 85266-6786
Telephone: (480) 419-9063, Web Site:
www.virido.com
Pres & Owner: Gary Finney

VISIONS MARKETING SERVICES
425 Dolly Dr
Lancaster, PA 17601-3619
Telephone: (717) 381-2100, (800) 222-
1577, FAX: (717) 295-8020, Web
Site: www.wecloseloans.com
Pres: Allan Geller

VOICELOGIC
662 King St W
Toronto, ON, Canada M5V 1M7
Telephone: (888) 552-8858, Web Site:
www.voicelogic.com
Bus Devel Mgr: Laura Leduc

THE DMA VOXDATA TELECOM
Subs. of Voxdata Telecom Inc
1155 Metcalfe St (Suite 1860)
Montreal, PQ, Canada H3B 2V6
Telephone: (514) 871-1920, (800) 861-
9599, FAX: (514) 871-0445, E-Mail:
fcouture@voxdata.com, Web Site:
www.voxdata.com
Pres: France Couture
Exec VP: Jason Drum

WS LIVE LLC
Sub. of Working Solutions
131 W 10th St
Dubuque, IA 52001
Telephone: (563) 582-9501, (800) 582-
9501, FAX: (563) 582-2003, Web
Site: www.wslive.com
CEO: Tim Houhlne
Compliance Mgr: Jeff L. Schmitt
Founded: 1988

WALKER & ASSOCIATES
7129 Old Hwy 52 N, PO Box 1029
Welcome, NC 27374-1029
Telephone: (336) 731-6391, (800)
WALKER-1, FAX: (336) 731-7253/
6973, E-Mail: info@walkerfirst.com,
Web Site: www.walkerfirst.com
CEO: Virginia Walker

WARRANTECH DIRECT INC
Subs. of Warrantech Corp
2200 Hwy 121 (Suite 105)
Bedford, TX 76021-5983
Telephone: (817) 786-1000, (800) 833-
8801, FAX: (817) 786-1020, Web
Site: www.warrantech.com
Pres & Gen Mgr: Randall San Antonio
VP: Mary Aldrich
Conducts Business: U.S.
Employees: 120
Primary Market Served: Business &
Consumer
Advertising/Marketing Budget Related
to Direct Marketing: 76-100%
Founded: 1990

Direct marketing of extended service
contracts to consumers, businesses &
wholesalers.

THE DMA WHITE POINT LEADS GROUP LLC
362 Gulf Breeze Pkwy (Suite 350)
Gulf Breeze, FL 32561-4492
Telephone: (850) 934-5577, Web Site:
www.whitepointleads.com

Pres: J. Glenn Goodroe
Primary Market Served: Business &
Consumer

WINN TECHNOLOGY GROUP INC
523 Palm Harbor Blvd
Palm Harbor, FL 34682-0927
Telephone: (727) 789-0006, (800) 444-
5622, FAX: (727) 789-0638, E-Mail:
winn@winntech.net, Web Site: www.
winntech.net
Pres: G. Swallow
Mktg Mgr: Judith Woodward

THE DMA YELLOWBOOK
2201 Renaissance Blvd
King of Prussia, PA 19406-2766
Telephone: (610) 731-2335, Web Site:
www.yellowbook.com
Primary Market Served: Consumer

Alabama

Compass Media, 175 Northshore Pl, Gulf Shores, 36542

Arizona

Higher Power Marketing, PO Box 71250, Phoenix, 85050-1005

Arkansas

ChoicePoint Precision Marketing, 601 E 3rd St, Little Rock, 72201-1709

California

Advanced Research Services, 31510 Anacap View Dr, Malibu, 90265-5123

Advantage Plus Marketing Group, 13 Crestview, Aliso Viejo, 92656-1818

AutoPacific Inc, 2991 Dow Ave, Tustin, 92780

Broadcast Media Associates, PO Box 1233, Santa Maria, 93456-1233

Cheskin, 255 Shoreline Dr (Suite 350), Redwood Shores, 94065

Colligent, 20975 Valley Green Dr (#262), Cupertino, 95014-1852

Continuum Global, 431 Bryant St, San Francisco, 94107-1303

DMRA & Matchkey Corp, 201 San Antonio Cir (Suite 200), Mountain View, 94040-1271

The Dohring Co, 450 N Brand Blvd, Glendale, 91203

Experian, 475 Anton Blvd, Costa Mesa, 92626

Facts 'n Figures, 15301 Ventura Blvd (Bldg B, Suite 500), Garden Bldg B, Sherman Oaks, 91403

First American CoreLogic, 4- 1st American Way, Santa Ana, 92707-5913

First National Information Network, 3727 W Magnolia Blvd (Suite 711), Burbank, 91505-2818

Frost & Sullivan Inc, 331 E Evelyn Ave (# 100), Mountain View, 94041-1530

Kenneth Hollander Associates Inc, 45431 Greenling Cir, Mendocino, 95460-9729

House of Marketing Research, 2555 E Colorado Blvd (Suite 205), Pasadena, 91107

Nielsen Claritas, 9276 Scranton Rd Ste 200, San Diego, 92121-7703

Nimblefish Technologies, 100 Spear St (Suite 740), San Francisco, 94105-1525

JD Power Associates, 2625 Townsgate Rd, Westlake Village, 91361-5751

Sales Portal, 13101 Diericx Dr, Mountain View, 94040-3915

The Sausalito Group, PO Box 1559, Sausalito, 94966-1559

Triggerfish Marketing, 200 Townsend St (#45), San Francisco, 94107-5703

Where 2 Get It Inc, 5101 E La Palma Ave Ste 107, Anaheim, 92807-2056

Wpromote Inc, 1700 E Walnut Ave Fl 5, El Segundo, 90245-2610

Colorado

Paragon Media Strategies, 7550 W Yale Ave Ste B204, Denver, 80227-3460

Connecticut

Ipsos-ASI Inc, 301 Merritt Seven (Suite 15), Norwalk, 06851-6200

SHR Capital Partners, 165 Mason St, Greenwich, 06830

Delaware

Trellist Marketing and Technology, 117 N Market St (Suite 300), Wilmington, 19801-2538

Bill Ward Inc, 1010 Philadelphia Pike, Wilmington, 19809-2029

District of Columbia

Guideline Washington DC, 900 17th St NW (Suite 850), Washington, 20006-2523

Hamilton Campaigns, 4201 Connecticut Ave (Suite 610), Washington, 20008

National Research LLC, 4201 Connecticut Ave NW (Suite 212), Washington, 20008-1162

Florida

AMD Research & Marketing LLC, 881 Harbor Hill Dr, Safety Harbor, 34695-4130

Behavioral Science Research, 2121 Ponce De Leon Blvd (Suite 250), Coral Gables, 33134-5221

Bolton Research Corp, 2709 SW 22nd Ave, Miami, 33133-3101

Catalogs.com, 2800 Glades Cir, Fort Lauderdale, 33327

Cherry Communications Co, 227 N Bronough St (#4100), Tallahassee, 32301

Franklin & Welker Direct Marketing Services, 12555 Biscayne Blvd (PMB 440), Miami, 33181-2522

Interdata, PO Box 129, Sanibel, 33957-0129

Lead Me Media, 8927 Hypoluxo Rd (Suite A-4), Lake Worth, 33467-5249

Mars Research, 6365 NW 6th Way (Suite 150), Fort Lauderdale, 33309

Matrix, 5244 N Bay Rd, Miami Beach, 33140

Take 5 Solutions LLC, 2385 NW Executive Center Dr (Suite 320), Boca Raton, 33431-8530

Georgia

AnalyticsIQ Inc, 115 Perimeter Center Pl NE (Suite 312), Atlanta, 30346-1244

CSM Inc, 1339 Canton Rd (Suite C), Marietta, 30066

Fry Consultants Inc, 2100 Powers Ferry Rd (Suite 125), Atlanta, 30339-5014

Integrative Logic LLC, 3370 Sugarloaf Pkwy (Suite G2-305), Lawrenceville, 30044-5478

Message Technologies Inc, 1995 N Park Pl, Meridian (5th fl), Atlanta, 30339

Tangent Media LLC, 570 Westover Dr NW (Suite 200), Atlanta, 30305-3538

Illinois

ACNielsen, 150 N Martingale Rd, Schaumburg, 60173-2076

Affina, 2001 Ruppman Plaza, Peoria, 61614-7917

CompetiScan, 200 S Michigan Ave Ste 1060, Chicago, 60604-2421

Exhibitgroup/Giltspur, 6800 Santa Fe Dr # B, Hodgkins, 60525-7638

Group O Inc, PO Box 170, Milan, 61264-0170

BW Hill & Associates LLC, 7115 W North Ave (Suite 375), Oak Park, 60302-1002

Ifbyphone, 8800 Bronx, Skokie, 60077-1804

Information Resources Inc, 150 N Clinton St, Chicago, 60661-1416

Market Focus Inc, 333 Barton Ave # 1, Evanston, 60202-3363

Marketing Synergy Inc, 1700 Park St (Suite 103), Naperville, 60563

The McIlvaine Co, 191 Waukegan Rd (Suite 208), Northbrook, 60093

Mintel International, 351 W Hubbard St (fl 8), Chicago, 60654-4941

PartnerData LLC, 2119 Dewey Ave (Suite B), Evanston, 60201-3035

Strata Marketing Inc, 30 W Monroe (Suite 1900), Chicago, 60603

Indiana

JEM Research, 802 Evans Ave Ste 2, Valparaiso, 46383-3667

RSC The Quality Measurement Co, 110 Walnut St, Evansville, 47708

Iowa

Frank N Magid Associates Inc, One Research Ctr, Marion, 52302-5868

Kansas

Ruf Corp, 1533 E Spruce St, Olathe, 66061

Maryland

GXS Corp, 100 Edison Park Dr, Gaithersburg, 20878-3204

Massachusetts

Atlantic Research & Consulting Inc, 90 Canal St (Suite 600), Boston, 02114

Boston Research Group, 1 Ash St (Suite 3), Hopkinton, 01748-1886

Market Response International, PO Box 26, South Orleans, 02662-0026

OTOlabs LLC, 465 Medford St (Suite 300), Charlestown, 02129-1454

Research Communications Ltd, 95 Washington St (401-357), Canton, 02021-4006

RJ Olsen Inc, 41 Indian Ridge Rd, Natick, 01760-5635

Michigan

Editorial Code & Data Inc, 814 Wolverine Dr (Suite 2), Walled Lake, 48390-2377

ForeSee Results Inc, 2500 Green Rd (Suite 400), Ann Arbor, 48105-1573

Morpace Inc, 31700 Middlebelt Rd Ste 200, Farmington Hills, 48334-2375

W J Schroer Co, Two W Michigan Ave, Battle Creek, 49017-3609

Minnesota

Anderson Niebuhr & Associates Inc, 6 Pine Tree Dr (Suite 200), Northpark Corp Ctr, Arden Hills, 55112-3790

Ideas To Go Inc, One Main St SE (Suite 504), Minneapolis, 55414-1036

Sight Marketing, 400 1st Ave N (Suite 100), Minneapolis, 55401-1764

Missouri

Magnets 4 Media, 7 Chamber Dr, Washington, 63090-5258

Marketing Horizons Inc, 1001 Craig Rd (Suite 100), Saint Louis, 63146

Outrider North America, 111 Westport Plaza (Suite 350), Saint Louis, 36146-3099

Montana

A & A Research, 690 Sunset Blvd, Kalispell, 59901-3641

Nebraska

The MSR Group, 1121 N 102nd Ct (Suite 100), Omaha, 68114-1947

Vente Inc, 4509 S 143rd St (Suite 9), Omaha, 68137-4521

Nevada

Cobbey & Associates Marketing Research, PO Box 12, Carson City, 89702-0012

New Jersey

Aurora Marketing Inc, 66 Witherspoon St (Suite 600), Princeton, 08542-3239

Bruno & Ridgway Research Associates Inc, 3131 Princeton Pike, Lawrenceville, 08648-2201

CMMC Market Research, PO Box 306, Mount Freedom, 07970-0306

Data Analytics Corp, 44 Hamilton Ln, Plainsboro, 08536-1126

Education Dynamics LLC, 5 Marine View Plz Ste 212, Hoboken, 07030-5722

Elephant Group Inc, 1 Cragwood Rd Ste 3, South Plainfield, 07080-2448

Environmental Research Associates, 279 Wall St, Princeton, 08540-1519

Glickman Research Associates/GRA Focus Center, 160 Paris Ave., Northvale, 07647-0006

Industrial Marketing Associates, PO Box 481, Cranford, 07016

Knowledge Networks/SRI, 103 Eisenhower Pkwy (Suite 303), Roseland, 07068

James M. Sears Associates, 375 S Washington Ave, Bergenfield, 07621-4323

Spectrum Research, 5000 Boardwalk (Suite 602), Ventnor City, 08406-2918

New York

ACNielsen, 770 Broadway, New York, 10003

The Arbitron Co, 575 5th Ave (fl 22), New York, 10017-2420

Beta Research Corp, 6400 Jericho Tpke, Syosset, 11791-4497

CBSI, 550 Mamaroneck Ave Ste 309, Harrison, 10528-1615

Claritas Express, 53 Brown Rd, Ithaca, 14850

Mark Clements Research Inc, 25 Barker St (#309), Mount Kisco, 10549-1630

Electric Media, 169 S Main St (PMB 311), New York, 10956-3353

Epic Media Group, 512 Fashion Ave (fl 12), New York, 10018-0816

Erdos & Morgan Inc, 6400 Jericho Turnpike (Suite 102), Syosset, 11791

Experian Simmons, 1271 Avenue Of The Americas Ste C2, New York, 10020-1309

Focus Plus Inc, 100 5th Ave Fl 2, New York, 10011-6903

Friedman Marketing Svcs, 500 Mamaroneck Ave Ste 103, Harrison, 10528-1600

GFK Custom Research North America, 75 Ninth Ave (fl 5), New York, 10011-7076

Guideline Research Corp, 625 Ave of the Americas (2nd fl), New York, 10011-2020

Guideline, 625 Ave of the Americas, New York, 10011-2020

Harris Interactive, 161 Sixth Ave, New York, 10013

Norman Hecht Research Inc, 33 Queens St Ste 301, Syosset, 11791-3063

House Party Inc, One Bridge St (Suite 3), Irvington, 10533

Informed Sources Inc, 88 Sunnyside Blvd Ste 201, Plainview, 11803-1507

Innovative Concepts, 266 Duffy Ave # A, Hicksville, 11801-3605

JP Management Consulting (North America) Inc, 52 Vanderbilt Ave (Suite 1005), New York, 10017-3842

JRH Marketing Services Inc, 2440 Broadway (Suite 232), New York, 10024-1158

Market Discovery Group, 302 Baltustrol Cir, Roslyn, 11576

Market Probe International Inc, 805 3rd Ave Rm 1103, New York, 10022-7567

Media Monitors Inc, 445 Hamilton Ave Ste 700, White Plains, 10601-1828

Mediamark Research Inc, 75 Ninth Ave (5th fl), New York, 10011

MSW Research, 1111 Marcus Ave (Suite MZ 200), Lake Success, 11042-1034

Nielsen Media Research, Inc, 770 Broadway, New York, 10003-9595

The NPD Group Inc, 900 W Shore Rd, Port Washington, 11050

ORC Macro International, 40 Wall St (Suite 3400), New York, 10005-1325

Oxbridge Communications Inc, 186 5th Ave, New York, 10010-5202

Ruder Finn Inc, 301 E 57th St (fl 3), New York, 10022-5997

SRB Marketing Inc, 10 Caroline Way, New Paltz, 12561-1157

Synovate, 360 Park Ave S (fl 5), New York, 10010-1712

Tabline Data Services Inc, 625 Ave of the Americas (2nd fl), New York, 10001-2020

The Teleconference Network, 137 E Townline Rd, Nanuet, 10954

Thomas Marketing Information Center, Five Penn Plaza, New York, 10001

TNS Intersearch, 3 Barker Ave (#3), White Plains, 10601-1509

North Carolina

Ad Facts Inc, 1251 NW Maynard Rd (Suite 358), Cary, 27513

Bellomy Research Inc, 175 Sunnynoll Ct, Winston Salem, 27106-5076

Coleman Research Inc, 4020 Aerial Center Pkwy (Suite 102), Morrisville, 27560-8563

The Dialog Corp, 2250 Perimeter Park Dr (Suite 300), Morrisville, 27560

Leibowitz Market Research Associates Inc, 3120 Whitehall Park Dr, Charlotte, 28273

North Carolina Electric Membership Corp, 3400 Summer Blvd, Raleigh, 27616-7306

TSE Services, 3400 Summer Blvd, Raleigh, 27611-7306

Ohio

Hanson Inc, 1695 Indian Wood Cir Ste 200, Maumee, 43537-4082

MarketVision Research Inc, 10300 Alliance Rd, Cincinnati, 45242

Q Fact Marketing Research Inc & Videoconferencing Center, 9908 Carver Rd, Cincinnati, 45242-5502

SummitQwest, 446 Windsor Park Dr, Dayton, 45459-4111

Oregon

Eastlan Ratings, PO Box 3500, Sisters, 97759-3500

Pennsylvania

Delta Market Research Inc, 333 N York Rd, Hatboro, 19040

GENESYS Sampling Systems, 755 Business Center Dr (Suite 200), Horsham, 19044

Impact Ratings Inc, 3402 Horton Rd, Newtown, 19073

Marshall Marketing & Communications Inc, 2600 Boyce Plaza Rd (Suite 210), Pittsburgh, 15241

MTI Information Technologies LLC, 1 Oxford Vly (Suite 500), Langhorne, 19047-3314

Phoenix Marketing International, 132 Welsh Rd Ste 100, Horsham, 19044-2217

Sindlinger & Co Inc, 405 Osborne Ln, Wallingford, 19086

Taylor Nelson Sofres Intersearch, 410 Horsham Rd Frnt, Horsham, 19044-2041

Rhode Island

Horton Interpreting Inc, 225 Chapman St Ste 303, Providence, 02905-4533

MacIntosh Survey Center, 450 Veterans Memorial Pkwy (Suite 201), East Providence, 02914-5300

Marketing & Media Services LLC, 931 Jefferson Blvd (Suite 1001), Warwick, 02886-2247

Texas

The Benchmark Co, 907 S Congress Ave Ste C, Austin, 78704-1741

Buxton, 2651 S Polaris Dr, Fort Worth, 76137-4804

Consumer Focus, 6505 W Park Blvd (Suite 306-368), Plano, 75093-6212

DMS Insights, 19111 N Dallas Pkwy (Suite 350), Dallas, 75287

Decision Analyst Inc, 604 Ave "H" E, Arlington, 76011-3100

Galloway Research Service, 4751 Hamilton Wolfe Rd Ste 100, San Antonio, 78229-3458

Innovative Marketing Services Inc, 16360 Park Ten Pl (Suite 102), Houston, 77084

Javelin, 7850 N Belt Line Rd, Irving, 75063-6062

NuStats Inc, 206 Wild Basin Rd Ste A300, Building A, West Lake Hills, 78746-3437

Relevant Insights LLC, 2508 Salmon Run Ln, Euless, 76039-6096

Who's Calling, 200 Quality Cir, College Station, 77845

Virginia

Berry Best Services Ltd, 12210 Fairfax Town Center #924, Fairfax, 22033

Comsearch, 19700 Janelia Farm Blvd, Janelia Technology Park, Ashburn, 20147-2405

Decision Demographics, 4312 39th St N, Arlington, 22207-4606

Issues & Answers Network Inc, 5151 Bonney Rd (Suite 100), Virginia Beach, 23462-4384

JetSpring, 4022 Monument Ave, Richmond, 23230-3908

Magnets USA, 817 Connecticut Ave NE, Roanoke, 24012-5317

Nathan Associates Inc, 2101 Wilson Blvd Ste 1200, Arlington, 22201-3049

2ergo, 2020 N 14th St (Suite 500), Arlington, 22201-2515

Veritas Analytics Inc, 21351 Gentry Dr, Sterling, 20166-8510

Washington

Consumer Opinion Services Inc, 12825 First Ave S, Seattle, 98168-2618

Wisconsin

TMP Directional Marketing, PO Box 1448, Waukesha, 53187-1448

CANADA
Manitoba

Faneuil ISG, 363 Broadway (Suite 1600), Winnipeg, R3C 3N9

Ontario

BBM Canada Inc, 1500 Don Mills Rd (Suite 305), Don Mills, M3B 3L7

Custometrics Inc, 30 E Beaver Creek (Unit 210), Richmond Hill, L4B 1J2

D&B Canada, 5770 Hurontario St, Mississauga, L5R 3G5

TNF, 900-2 Bloor St E, Toronto, M4W 3H8

Quebec

IRPP, 1470 Peel St (Suite 200), Montreal, H3A 1T1

Market Research (30)

A & A RESEARCH
690 Sunset Blvd
Kalispell, MT 59901-3641
Telephone: (406) 752-7857
Pres: Judith Doonan

ACNIELSEN
150 N Martingale Rd
Schaumburg, IL 60173-2076
Telephone: (847) 605-5000, FAX:
　(847) 605-2000, E-Mail: mkarr@
　datamartdirect.com, Web Site: www.
　datamartdirect.com
VP, Communs: Art Massa

ACNIELSEN
770 Broadway
New York, NY 10003
Telephone: (646) 654-5000, FAX:
　(646) 654-5002, E-Mail: globalc@
　nielsen.com, Web Site: www.
　acnielsen.com
Pres & CEO: John Lewis

AD FACTS INC
1251 NW Maynard Rd (Suite 358)
Cary, NC 27513
Telephone: (919) 388-3015, (800) 923-
　3228, E-Mail: adfacts@adfacts.com,
　Web Site: www.adfacts.com
Pres: Michelle S. Dawson

**ADVANCED RESEARCH
SERVICES**
31510 Anacap View Dr
Malibu, CA 90265-5123
Telephone: (310) 589-0223, Web Site:
　www.tvsurveys.com
Pres: Scott V. Tallal

**ADVANTAGE PLUS
MARKETING GROUP**
13 Crestview
Aliso Viejo, CA 92656-1818
Telephone: (714) 573-7300, (800) 432-
　9466, FAX: (714) 573-7301, E-Mail:
　info@apmg.com, Web Site: www.
　apmg.com
Pres: Barry Lieberman
Conducts Business: U.S.
Employees: 15
Primary Market Served: Business &
　Consumer
Direct online sales
Advertising/Marketing Budget Related
　to Direct Marketing: 76-100%
Founded: 1992
Gross sales or billing: $2,000,000

We revitalize a company's marketing
to create a truly measurable ROI. We
bridge the gap between marketing and
sales. We offer web, email, postal mail
and telephone marketing services.

AFFINA
2001 Ruppman Plaza
Peoria, IL 61614-7917
Telephone: (309) 685-5901, (877) 4
　AFFINA, Web Site: www.affina.com
Exec VP Sls & Mktg: Steven Gonzales

**AMD RESEARCH &
MARKETING LLC**
881 Harbor Hill Dr
Safety Harbor, FL 34695-4130
Telephone: (727) 409-1087, Web Site:
　www.amdresearch-marketing.com
Owner: Anna Marie Dunn
Primary Market Served: Business &
　Consumer

ANALYTICSIQ INC
115 Perimeter Center Pl NE (Suite
　312)
Atlanta, GA 30346-1244
Telephone: (770) 407-8855, Web Site:
　www.analytics-iq.com
Pres: David Kelly
Primary Market Served: Business &
　Consumer

**ANDERSON NIEBUHR &
ASSOCIATES INC**
6 Pine Tree Dr (Suite 200), Northpark
　Corp Ctr
Arden Hills, MN 55112-3790
Telephone: (651) 486-8712, (800) 678-
　5577, FAX: (651) 486-0536, E-Mail:
　info@ana-inc.com, Web Site: www.
　ana-inc.com
Pres: John F. Anderson
Admin Asst: Jennifer Koper

THE ARBITRON CO
Div. of Ceridian Corp
575 5th Ave (fl 22)
New York, NY 10017-2420
Telephone: (212) 887-1314, FAX:
　(212) 887-1558, Web Site: www.
　arbitron.com
CEO: Steve Morris

**ATLANTIC RESEARCH &
CONSULTING INC**
90 Canal St (Suite 600)
Boston, MA 02114
Telephone: (617) 720-0174, FAX:
　(617) 589-3731, E-Mail:
　generalmailbox@guideline.com, Web
　Site: www.guideline.com
VP of Admin: Elaine Becker

AURORA MARKETING INC
66 Witherspoon St (Suite 600)
Princeton, NJ 08542-3239
Telephone: (908) 904-1125, FAX:
　(908) 359-1108, E-Mail: aurora2@
　voicenet.com, Web Site: www.
　auroramarketing.net
Pres: Doreen V. Blanc

AUTOPACIFIC INC
2991 Dow Ave
Tustin, CA 92780
Telephone: (714) 838-4234, FAX:
　(714) 838-4260, Web Site: www.
　autopacific.com
Pres: George C. Peterson

BBM CANADA INC
1500 Don Mills Rd (Suite 305)
Don Mills, ON, Canada M3B 3L7
Telephone: (416) 445-9800, FAX:
　(416) 445-8644, E-Mail: info@bbm.
　ca, Web Site: www.bbm.ca
Pres & CEO: Jim MacLeod
Dir Communs: Tom Jenks

**BEHAVIORAL SCIENCE
RESEARCH**
2121 Ponce De Leon Blvd (Suite 250)
Coral Gables, FL 33134-5221
Telephone: (305) 443-2000, (800) 282-
　2771, FAX: (305) 448-6825
Pres & Res Dir: Robert Ladner

BELLOMY RESEARCH INC
175 Sunnynoll Ct
Winston Salem, NC 27106-5076
Telephone: (336) 721-1140, FAX:
　(336) 721-1597, E-Mail: bellomy@
　interpath.com, Web Site: www.
　bellomyresearch.com
Pres: John Sessions

THE BENCHMARK CO
907 S Congress Ave Ste C
Austin, TX 78704-1741

Telephone: (512) 707-7500, FAX: (512) 707-7757, E-Mail: thebenc@earthlink.net, Web Site: www.thebenchmarkcompany.net
Pres & CEO: Dr Robert E. Balon

BERRY BEST SERVICES LTD
12210 Fairfax Town Center #924
Fairfax, VA 22033
Telephone: (202) 293-4964, FAX: (202) 293-4964, E-Mail: samf@berrybest.com, Web Site: www.berrybest.com
Pres: Thomas L. Berry

BETA RESEARCH CORP
6400 Jericho Tpke
Syosset, NY 11791-4497
Telephone: (516) 935-3800, FAX: (516) 935-4092, E-Mail: beta@nybeta.com, Web Site: www.nybeta.com
Exec VP Sls & Mktg: Gail C. Disimile

BOLTON RESEARCH CORP
2709 SW 22nd Ave
Miami, FL 33133-3101
Telephone: (305) 854-3887, FAX: (305) 854-3807, E-Mail: brcted@aol.com, Web Site: www.boltonresearch.com
Pres: Ted Bolton

BOSTON RESEARCH GROUP
1 Ash St (Suite 3)
Hopkinton, MA 01748-1886
Telephone: (508) 497-2555, FAX: (508) 497-2592, E-Mail: BRGrep@BostonResearchGroup.com, Web Site: www.bostonresearchgroup.com
Partner: James Fazzio

BROADCAST MEDIA ASSOCIATES
PO Box 1233
Santa Maria, CA 93456-1233
Telephone: (805) 937-1553, E-Mail: cliffhunter@cliffhunter.com, Web Site: www.broadcastmediabroker.com
Pres: Clifford M. Hunter

BRUNO & RIDGWAY RESEARCH ASSOCIATES INC
3131 Princeton Pike
Lawrenceville, NJ 08648-2201
Telephone: (609) 895-9889, FAX: (609) 895-6665, E-Mail: info@brunoandridway.com, Web Site: www.brra.com
Pres: Joseph Ridgway

THE DMA BUXTON
2651 S Polaris Dr
Fort Worth, TX 76137-4804
Telephone: (817) 332-3681, Web Site: www.buxtonco.com
Dir Database & Analytics: Eric Rossi
Primary Market Served: Business & Consumer

CBSI
550 Mamaroneck Ave Ste 309
Harrison, NY 10528-1615
Telephone: (914) 381-5353, Web Site: www.cbsiservices.com
VP: Kenneth Kraetzer
Primary Market Served: Business

CMMC MARKET RESEARCH
PO Box 306
Mount Freedom, NJ 07970-0306
Telephone: (973) 989-0229, FAX: (973) 366-1185, E-Mail: dmmp@cmmcinc.com, Web Site: www.cmmcinc.com
Pres & CEO: Richard W. Pavely

CSM INC
1339 Canton Rd (Suite C)
Marietta, GA 30066
Telephone: (800) 849-6788, FAX: (770) 514-6799, E-Mail: info@csmresearch.com, Web Site: www.csmresearch.com
Pres: Frank Sanders

CATALOGS.COM
2800 Glades Cir
Fort Lauderdale, FL 33327
Telephone: (954) 659-9005, FAX: (954) 659-9007, Web Site: www.catalogs.com
VP Bus Devel: Trish Baron

CHERRY COMMUNICATIONS CO
227 N Bronough St (#4100)
Tallahassee, FL 32301
Telephone: (850) 561-3600, FAX: (850) 561-1155, E-Mail: phones@cherrycomm.com, Web Site: www.cherrycomm.com
Pres: Linda Z. Cherry

CHESKIN
255 Shoreline Dr (Suite 350)
Redwood Shores, CA 94065
Telephone: (650) 802-2100, FAX: (650) 593-1125, E-Mail: info@cheskin.com, Web Site: www.cheskin.com
Principal & CEO: Darrel Rhea

CHOICEPOINT PRECISION MARKETING
601 E 3rd St
Little Rock, AR 72201-1709
Telephone: (978) 738-0544, (800) 937-4232, FAX: (978) 738-0582, Web Site: www.cp-pm.com
Pres: James N. Alvarez

CLARITAS EXPRESS
53 Brown Rd
Ithaca, NY 14850
Telephone: (607) 257-5757, (866) 737-7429, FAX: (607) 266-0425, E-Mail: info@claritas.com, Web Site: www.claritas.com/express
VP: Barbara Policay

MARK CLEMENTS RESEARCH INC
25 Barker St (#309)
Mount Kisco, NY 10549-1630
Telephone: (914) 241-1803, FAX: (914) 241-7763, E-Mail: mjfharvey@aol.com, Web Site: www.markclementsresearch.com
Pres: Mark Clements
VP, Dir Research Sales: Martin J Feldman

COBBEY & ASSOCIATES MARKETING RESEARCH
PO Box 12
Carson City, NV 89702-0012
Telephone: (775) 847-0321, (877) 433-3242, E-Mail: cobbey@cobbey.com, Web Site: www.cobbey.com
Pres: Robin Cobbey

COLEMAN RESEARCH INC
4020 Aerial Center Pkwy (Suite 102)
Morrisville, NC 27560-8563
Telephone: (919) 571-0000, FAX: (919) 571-9999, E-Mail: callcoleman@colemaninsights.com, Web Site: www.colemaninsights.com
Pres: Jon Coleman

COLLIGENT
20975 Valley Green Dr (#262)
Cupertino, CA 95014-1852
Telephone: (425) 641-1130
Owner: Sree Nagarajan
Primary Market Served: Business & Consumer

THE DMA COMPASS MEDIA
175 Northshore Pl
Gulf Shores, AL 36542
Telephone: (251) 968-4600, Web Site: www.compassmedia.com

COMPETISCAN
200 S Michigan Ave Ste 1060
Chicago, IL 60604-2421
Telephone: (312) 488-1814, Web Site:
www.competiscan.com
CEO: Richard Goldman
Primary Market Served: Business &
Consumer

COMSEARCH
19700 Janelia Farm Blvd, Janelia
Technology Park
Ashburn, VA 20147-2405
Telephone: (703) 726-5500, FAX:
(703) 726-5600, Web Site: www.
comsearch.com
Sr Mktg Mgr: Jeanette Carlisle

CONSUMER FOCUS
6505 W Park Blvd (Suite 306-368)
Plano, TX 75093-6212
Telephone: (972) 378-9697, E-Mail:
sstewart@consumerfocusco.com,
Web Site: www.consumerfocusco.
com
Pres: Sue Stewart
Primary Market Served: Business &
Consumer

CONSUMER OPINION SERVICES INC
12825 First Ave S
Seattle, WA 98168-2618
Telephone: (206) 241-6050, FAX:
(206) 241-5213, E-Mail: info@
cosvc.com, Web Site: www.cosvc.
com
Pres: Jerry Carter

THE DMA CONTINUUM GLOBAL
431 Bryant St
San Francisco, CA 94107-1303
Telephone: (415) 685-3301, Web Site:
www.continuumglobal.com
CEO: Suresh Mathai

CUSTOMETRICS INC
30 E Beaver Creek (Unit 210)
Richmond Hill, ON, Canada L4B 1J2
Telephone: (905) 886-4161, E-Mail:
info@custometrics.ca, Web Site:
www.custometrics.com
CEO: David Beaton
Primary Market Served: Business &
Consumer

D&B CANADA
Subs. of Dun & Bradstreet International
5770 Hurontario St
Mississauga, ON, Canada L5R 3G5
Telephone: (905) 568-6000, FAX:
(905) 568-6197, Web Site: www.
dnb.ca

Applications Specialist & Sls: Adrian
Tucci
Pres: Lawrence Franco
VP Mktg: Geoff Vincent
Commun Coord: Emelie Sater

DMRA & MATCHKEY CORP
201 San Antonio Cir (Suite 200)
Mountain View, CA 94040-1271
Telephone: (650) 856-9988, FAX:
(650) 856-9986
Pres: Michael E. Green

DMS INSIGHTS
Div. of United Sample, Inc.
19111 N Dallas Pkwy (Suite 350)
Dallas, TX 75287
Telephone: (972) 874-5080, (800) 409-
6262, FAX: (972) 353-2450, E-Mail:
info@dmsinsights.com, Web Site:
www.dmsdallas.com
Pres & CEO: Dennis E. Gonier
Founded: 1995

DATA ANALYTICS CORP
44 Hamilton Ln
Plainsboro, NJ 08536-1126
Telephone: (609) 936-899, Web Site:
www.dataanalyticscorp.com
Pres: Walter Paczkowski
Primary Market Served: Business &
Consumer

DECISION ANALYST INC
604 Ave "H" E
Arlington, TX 76011-3100
Telephone: (817) 640-6166, (800) 262-
5974, FAX: (817) 640-6567, E-Mail:
jthomas@decisionanalyst.com, Web
Site: www.decisionanalyst.com
Pres & CEO: Jerry W. Thomas
Mktg Dir: Cristi Allen

DECISION DEMOGRAPHICS
4312 39th St N
Arlington, VA 22207-4606
Telephone: (703) 931-9200, FAX:
(703) 527-1448, E-Mail: tordella@
decision-demographics.com, Web
Site: www.decision-demographics.
com
Pres: Stephen J. Tordella

DELTA MARKET RESEARCH INC
333 N York Rd
Hatboro, PA 19040
Telephone: (215) 674-1180, FAX:
(215) 674-1271, E-Mail:
information@deltamarketresearch.
com, Web Site: www.
deltamarketresearch.com
Mktg Dir: Chris Bonner

THE DIALOG CORP
2250 Perimeter Park Dr (Suite 300)
Morrisville, NC 27560
Telephone: (919) 804-6400, (800) 3
DIALOG, FAX: (919) 804-6410,
E-Mail: customer@dialog.com, Web
Site: www.dialog.com
Gen Mgr: Suzanne BeDell

THE DOHRING CO
450 N Brand Blvd
Glendale, CA 91203
Telephone: (818) 242-1600, FAX:
(818) 649-8291, E-Mail: info@
dohring.com, Web Site: www.
dohring.com
Chmn & CEO: Doug C. Dohring

EASTLAN RATINGS
PO Box 3500
Sisters, OR 97759-3500
Telephone: (877) 886-3320, FAX:
(541) 318-4646, E-Mail: info@
eastlanratings.com, Web Site: www.
eastlanratings.com
Pres & CEO: A. Michael Gould
Founded: 1999

EDITORIAL CODE & DATA INC
814 Wolverine Dr (Suite 2)
Walled Lake, MI 48390-2377
Telephone: (248) 926-5187, FAX:
(248) 926-6047, E-Mail: Monique@
marketsize.com, Web Site: www.
marketsize.com
VP: Monique Darnay Magee
Founded: 1990

THE DMA EDUCATION DYNAMICS LLC
5 Marine View Plz Ste 212
Hoboken, NJ 07030-5722
Telephone: (201) 377-3001
Chmn & CEO: Steven Isaac

ELECTRIC MEDIA
169 S Main St (PMB 311)
New York, NY 10956-3353
Telephone: (201) 461-5252
Pres: Arthur Cohen

ELEPHANT GROUP INC
1 Cragwood Rd Ste 3
South Plainfield, NJ 07080-2448
Telephone: (866) 755-9008, Web Site:
www.elephantgroup.com
Dir Pub Rels: Tamar Burton
Primary Market Served: Business &
Consumer

ENVIRONMENTAL RESEARCH ASSOCIATES

Div. of Integrated Marketing Services
279 Wall St
Princeton, NJ 08540-1519
Telephone: (609) 683-4860, FAX:
(609) 683-8398
Pres: Lois Kaufman

EPIC MEDIA GROUP

512 Fashion Ave (fl 12)
New York, NY 10018-0816
Telephone: (212) 308-8509, Web Site:
www.epicadvertising.com
CMO: Michael Sprouse
Primary Market Served: Business &
Consumer

ERDOS & MORGAN INC

6400 Jericho Turnpike (Suite 102)
Syosset, NY 11791
Telephone: (516) 935-6959, FAX:
(516) 935-4040, E-Mail: info@
erdosmorgan.com, Web Site: www.
erdosmorgan.com
CEO, NY Office: Nick Ferrari

EXHIBITGROUP/GILTSPUR

6800 Santa Fe Dr # B
Hodgkins, IL 60525-7638
Telephone: (972) 538-3031, (800) 843-
3944, Web Site: www.e-g.com
CEO: John Jastrem

EXPERIAN

THE DMA

475 Anton Blvd
Costa Mesa, CA 92626
Telephone: (714) 830-7000, (888) EX-
PERIAN, Web Site: www.experian.
com
VP Pub Affairs: Donald Girard

EXPERIAN SIMMONS

1271 Avenue Of The Americas Ste C2
New York, NY 10020-1309
Telephone: (212) 471-2850, FAX:
(212) 471-2940, E-Mail: ellenr@
smrb.com, Web Site: www.smrb.com
Pres & COO: Chris Wilson

FACTS 'N FIGURES

15301 Ventura Blvd (Bldg B, Suite
500), Garden Bldg B
Sherman Oaks, CA 91403
Telephone: (661) 222-2278, (818) 986-
6600, FAX: (661) 222-2287, Web
Site: www.factsnfiguresinc.com
Mktg Dept: Steven Escoe

FANEUIL ISG

363 Broadway (Suite 1600)
Winnipeg, MB, Canada R3C 3N9
Telephone: (866) Faneuil, Web Site:
www.faneuil.com

CEO: Brian Cornick
VP: Chris Stanvick

FIRST AMERICAN CORELOGIC

4- 1st American Way
Santa Ana, CA 92707-5913
Telephone: (866) 774-3282, Web Site:
www.facorelogic.com
Senior Mktg Mgr: Colleen Harrison
Primary Market Served: Consumer

FIRST NATIONAL INFORMATION NETWORK

3727 W Magnolia Blvd (Suite 711)
Burbank, CA 91505-2818
Telephone: (855) 909-6800, FAX:
(818) 558-6663, E-Mail: info@fnin.
com, Web Site: www.fnin.com
CEO: Mark Savoy
VP Sls & Mktg: David Kieran
Conducts Business: U.S.
Advertising/Marketing Budget Related
to Direct Marketing: 26-50%
Direct Marketing ad budget:
Direct Mail: 10%
Magazines: 10%
Telephone: 80%
Founded: 1992

Provider of investor profiling, custom
lead generation, internet marketing,
direct response and list management
services.

FOCUS PLUS INC

100 5th Ave Fl 2
New York, NY 10011-6903
Telephone: (212) 675-0142, (800) 340-
8846, FAX: (212) 645-3171, E-Mail:
info@focusplusny.com, Web Site:
www.focusplusny.com
Pres: Elizabeth Markham

FORESEE RESULTS INC

2500 Green Rd (Suite 400)
Ann Arbor, MI 48105-1573
Telephone: (734) 205-2600, Web Site:
www.foreseeresults.com
Pres & CEO: Larry Freed
Primary Market Served: Business &
Consumer

FRANKLIN & WELKER DIRECT MARKETING SERVICES

12555 Biscayne Blvd (PMB 440)
Miami, FL 33181-2522
Telephone: (305) 758-6690, FAX:
(305) 758-9399
Pres: Leonard G. Franklin

FRIEDMAN MARKETING SVCS

aka gfk
500 Mamaroneck Ave Ste 103
Harrison, NY 10528-1600
Telephone: (914) 698-9591, FAX:
(914) 698-0485, E-Mail: paula.
wynne@gfk.com, Web Site: www.
friedmanmktg.com
Sr VP: David Smith

FROST & SULLIVAN INC

331 E Evelyn Ave (# 100)
Mountain View, CA 94041-1530
Telephone: (877) 690-3329, (877) 463-
7678, FAX: (877) 690-3329, E-Mail:
myfrost@frost.com, Web Site: www.
frost.com
Chmn: David Frigstad

FRY CONSULTANTS INC

2100 Powers Ferry Rd (Suite 125)
Atlanta, GA 30339-5014
Telephone: (770) 226-8888, FAX:
(770) 226-8899, E-Mail: mail@
fryconsultants.com, Web Site: www.
fryconsultants.com
Pres & CEO: L. Lyne Smith III

GFK CUSTOM RESEARCH NORTH AMERICA

75 Ninth Ave (fl 5)
New York, NY 10011-7076
Telephone: (212) 240-5300, (800) 274-
3577, FAX: (212) 240-5353, E-Mail:
info@gfkamerica.com, Web Site:
www.gfkamerica.com
Chmn: Elaine Riddell

GXS CORP

100 Edison Park Dr
Gaithersburg, MD 20878-3204
Telephone: (301) 340-4000, (800) 560-
4347, FAX: (301) 340-5299, Web
Site: www.gxs.com
CEO: Gary Greenfield

GALLOWAY RESEARCH SERVICE

4751 Hamilton Wolfe Rd Ste 100
San Antonio, TX 78229-3458
Telephone: (210) 734-4346, FAX:
(210) 732-4500, E-Mail: lbrazel@
gallowayresearch.com, Web Site:
www.gallowayresearch.com
Pres: Elisa Galloway

GENESYS SAMPLING SYSTEMS

755 Business Center Dr (Suite 200)
Horsham, PA 19044

Telephone: (215) 653-7100, (800) 336-7674, FAX: (215) 653-7115, E-Mail: info@m-s-g.com, Web Site: www.m-s-g.com
Pres: Dale Kulp

GLICKMAN RESEARCH ASSOCIATES/GRA FOCUS CENTER
160 Paris Ave.
Northvale, NJ 07647-0006
Telephone: (201) 767-8888, (800) 334-3978, FAX: (201) 767-6933, E-Mail: j.glickman@glickmanresearch.com, Web Site: www.glickmanresearch.com
Pres: James Glickman

THE DMA GROUP O INC
PO Box 170
Milan, IL 61264-0170
Telephone: (309) 736-8300, Web Site: www.groupo.com
Corp Mktg Mgr: Tiffany Williams

THE DMA GUIDELINE
625 Ave of the Americas
New York, NY 10011-2020
Telephone: (212) 645-4500, (866) GUIDELINE, FAX: (212) 645-7681, Web Site: www.findsvp.com
Chmn & CEO: David M. Walke
Pres & COO: Marc C. Litvinoff
CFO: Peter M. Stone
Sr Analyst: Jay Crane
Conducts Business: U.S.
Employees: 239
Primary Market Served: Business
Advertising/Marketing Budget Related to Direct Marketing: 0-25%
Direct Marketing ad budget:
Direct Mail: 100%
Founded: 1969
Gross sales or billing: $46,300,000

Consulting by telephone service that provides executives with access to 150 research consultants.

GUIDELINE RESEARCH CORP
625 Ave of the Americas (2nd fl)
New York, NY 10011-2020
Telephone: (212) 947-5140, FAX: (212) 629-0061, Web Site: www.guidelineresearch.com
Chmn: Jay Friedland

GUIDELINE WASHINGTON DC
900 17th St NW (Suite 850)
Washington, DC 20006-2523

Telephone: (703) 312-6004, (866) GUIDELINE, E-Mail: fdudley@guideline.com, Web Site: www.guideline.com
VP Mktg: Frank Dudley

HAMILTON CAMPAIGNS
4201 Connecticut Ave (Suite 610)
Washington, DC 20008
Telephone: (202) 686-5900, FAX: (202) 686-7080, E-Mail: info@hamiltoncampaigns.com, Web Site: www.hamiltoncampaigns.com
Pres: David Beattie

HANSON INC
1695 Indian Wood Cir Ste 200
Maumee, OH 43537-4082
Telephone: (419) 327-6100, Web Site: www.hansoninc.com
Acct Dir: Anne Dalton

HARRIS INTERACTIVE
161 Sixth Ave
New York, NY 10013
Telephone: (585) 272-8400, (800) 866-7655, FAX: (585) 272-8680, E-Mail: info@harrisinteractive.com, Web Site: www.harrisinteractive.com
Pres & CEO: Kimberly Till

NORMAN HECHT RESEARCH INC
33 Queens St Ste 301
Syosset, NY 11791-3063
Telephone: (516) 496-8866, FAX: (516) 496-8165, E-Mail: nhr@normanhechtresearch.com, Web Site: www.normanhechtresearch.com
Co-Pres & COO: Laura Greenberg

THE DMA HIGHER POWER MARKETING
PO Box 71250
Phoenix, AZ 85050-1005
Telephone: (480) 837-3580, (888) 922-3580, FAX: (480) 837-3589, E-Mail: info@hpowermarketing.com, Web Site: www.hpowermarketing.com
Pres & CEO: Peter Feinstein
DP Mgr: Rod Mel
Traffic: Stephanie Klein
Affiliate Rels: Regina McDuel
Quality Control: Rian Wing
Founded: 1999

We're Higher Power Marketing, the per inquiry advertising specialists! We create and place per inquiry advertising in radio, on TV, over the Internet and on Movie Screens. Our clients receive measurable, trackable results, or they get their money back... GUARANTEED!

BW HILL & ASSOCIATES LLC
7115 W North Ave (Suite 375)
Oak Park, IL 60302-1002
Telephone: (800) 431-3183, Web Site: www.bwhillassociates.com
Pres: Benjamin Hill

KENNETH HOLLANDER ASSOCIATES INC
45431 Greenling Cir
Mendocino, CA 95460-9729
Telephone: (707) 962-1648, FAX: (707) 962-1635
Pres: Ken Hollander

HORTON INTERPRETING INC
225 Chapman St Ste 303
Providence, RI 02905-4533
Telephone: (401) 331-4798, (800) 345-2135, FAX: (401) 331-2822, Web Site: www.language-link.com
Pres & CEO: Juana I Horton

HOUSE OF MARKETING RESEARCH
2555 E Colorado Blvd (Suite 205)
Pasadena, CA 91107
Telephone: (626) 486-1400, FAX: (626) 486-1404, Web Site: www.hmr-research.com
Pres: Amy Siadak

HOUSE PARTY INC
One Bridge St (Suite 3)
Irvington, NY 10533
Telephone: (720) 496-2500, (888) 591-1678, E-Mail: help@houseparty.com, Web Site: www.houseparty.com
Mktg Dir: Robin Jacobs

IFBYPHONE
8800 Bronx
Skokie, IL 60077-1804
Telephone: (877) 295-5100, Web Site: www.ifbyphone.com
VP: Todd Curry
Primary Market Served: Consumer

IRPP
aka Institute for Research on Public Policy
1470 Peel St (Suite 200)
Montreal, PQ, Canada H3A 1T1
Telephone: (514) 985-2461, FAX: (514) 985-2559, E-Mail: irpp@irpp.org, Web Site: www.irpp.org
Pres: Mel Cappe

IDEAS TO GO INC
One Main St SE (Suite 504)
Minneapolis, MN 55414-1036

Telephone: (612) 331-1570, FAX: (612) 331-1602, E-Mail: cebert@ideastogo.com, Web Site: www.ideastogo.com
Consultant: Nancy Francis

IMPACT RATINGS INC
3402 Horton Rd
Newtown, PA 19073
Telephone: (610) 353-8311, FAX: (610) 353-8344
Chmn Bd: Mike Gerhardt

INDUSTRIAL MARKETING ASSOCIATES
PO Box 481
Cranford, NJ 07016
Telephone: (908) 276-4256, E-Mail: ken@industrialmarketingassociates.com, Web Site: www.industrialmarketingassociates.com
Pres: Ken S. Eisenberg

INFORMATION RESOURCES INC
150 N Clinton St
Chicago, IL 60661-1416
Telephone: (312) 726-1221, Web Site: www.infores.com
Chmn Bd: Romesh Wadhwani

INFORMED SOURCES INC
88 Sunnyside Blvd Ste 201
Plainview, NY 11803-1507
Telephone: (800) 201-6060, FAX: (516) 576-0249, E-Mail: info@informed-sources.com, Web Site: www.informed-sources.com
Pres: Stuart Goldberg
VP, Mktg & Sls: Robert Kasper

INNOVATIVE CONCEPTS
266 Duffy Ave # A
Hicksville, NY 11801-3605
Telephone: (516) 479-2200, (800) 631-0209, FAX: (516) 479-2215, E-Mail: info@ic-mr.com, Web Site: www.ic-mr.com
Pres: Jerry Sycoff

INNOVATIVE MARKETING SERVICES INC
16360 Park Ten Pl (Suite 102)
Houston, TX 77084
Telephone: (281) 398-0321, (800) 231-4678, FAX: (281) 398-0679, E-Mail: mfisher@imstcorp.com, Web Site: www.imstcorp.com
Pres & CEO: James B. Fisher

INTEGRATIVE LOGIC LLC
3370 Sugarloaf Pkwy (Suite G2-305)
Lawrenceville, GA 30044-5478

Telephone: (678) 638-2600, Web Site: www.integrativelogic.com
Pres & CEO: John Gardner
Primary Market Served: Business

INTERDATA
PO Box 129
Sanibel, FL 33957-0129
Telephone: (941) 472-1119, FAX: (941) 472-4272, E-Mail: jfisher435@aol.com, Web Site: www.interdata.org
Pres: Joseph C. Fisher

IPSOS-ASI INC
301 Merritt Seven (Suite 15)
Norwalk, CT 06851-6200
Telephone: (203) 840-3400, FAX: (203) 840-3450, E-Mail: info@ipsos-asi.com, Web Site: www.ipsos-asi.com
Pres & CEO: Jim Thompson

ISSUES & ANSWERS NETWORK INC
5151 Bonney Rd (Suite 100)
Virginia Beach, VA 23462-4384
Telephone: (757) 456-1100, FAX: (757) 456-0377, E-Mail: info@issans.com, Web Site: www.issans.com
Pres: Peter J. McGuinness

JEM RESEARCH
802 Evans Ave Ste 2
Valparaiso, IN 46383-3667
Telephone: (219) 464-4668, FAX: (219) 464-7011
Pres: Kathleen DeWitt

JP MANAGEMENT CONSULTING (NORTH AMERICA) INC
Div. of Jaakko Poyry Consulting Inc
52 Vanderbilt Ave (Suite 1005)
New York, NY 10017-3842
Telephone: (914) 332-4000, FAX: (914) 332-4411
Chmn: Henrik Ehrnrooth

JRH MARKETING SERVICES INC
2440 Broadway (Suite 232)
New York, NY 10024-1158
Telephone: (718) 786-9640, FAX: (718) 786-9642, E-Mail: office@jrhmarketingservices.com, Web Site: www.jrhmarketingservices.com
Pres & Owner: J. Robert Harris II

THE DMA **JAVELIN**
7850 N Belt Line Rd
Irving, TX 75063-6062

Telephone: (972) 443-7000, E-Mail: info@javelin.mg, Web Site: javelin.mg
Mgr Bus Devel: Stacie Bon

JETSPRING
4022 Monument Ave
Richmond, VA 23230-3908
Telephone: (877) 695-3834, Web Site: www.jetspring.com
VP Program Devel: Paul Glancy
Primary Market Served: Consumer

KNOWLEDGE NETWORKS/ SRI
103 Eisenhower Pkwy (Suite 303)
Roseland, NJ 07068
Telephone: (908) 497-8000, FAX: (908) 497-8001, E-Mail: mclancey@knowledgenetworks.com, Web Site: www.knowledgenetworks.com
Sr VP Custom Res: Maura Clancey
CMO: Patricia Graham

THE DMA **LEAD ME MEDIA**
8927 Hypoluxo Rd (Suite A-4)
Lake Worth, FL 33467-5249
Telephone: (888) 445-3282, Web Site: www.leadmedia.com
CEO: Robert Clouse
Primary Market Served: Business

LEIBOWITZ MARKET RESEARCH ASSOCIATES INC
3120 Whitehall Park Dr
Charlotte, NC 28273
Telephone: (704) 357-1961, FAX: (704) 357-1965, E-Mail: info@leibowitz-research.com, Web Site: www.leibowitz-research.com
Pres & CEO: Teri Leibowitz
Founded: 1959

THE MSR GROUP
1121 N 102nd Ct (Suite 100)
Omaha, NE 68114-1947
Telephone: (402) 392-0755, (800) 737-0755, FAX: (402) 392-1068, E-Mail: info@theMSRgroup.com, Web Site: www.theMSRgroup.com
Pres & CEO: Dick Worick

MTI INFORMATION TECHNOLOGIES LLC
1 Oxford Vly (Suite 500)
Langhorne, PA 19047-3314
Telephone: (267) 569-2400, Web Site: www.mtiadvantage.com
CTO: Robert McCracken

MACINTOSH SURVEY CENTER

450 Veterans Memorial Pkwy (Suite 201)
East Providence, RI 02914-5300
Telephone: (401) 438-8330, FAX: (401) 434-9219, E-Mail: macsurvey@aol.com
Pres: Ann MacIntosh

FRANK N MAGID ASSOCIATES INC

One Research Ctr
Marion, IA 52302-5868
Telephone: (319) 377-7345, FAX: (319) 377-5861, E-Mail: mailIA@magid.com, Web Site: www.magid.com
Sr VP, Mng Dir: Mike Vorhaus

THE DMA MAGNETS 4 MEDIA

Div. of The Magnet Group
7 Chamber Dr
Washington, MO 63090-5258
Telephone: (843) 216-6665, (800) 642-6384, FAX: (636) 390-5147, E-Mail: sales@magnets4media.com, Web Site: www.magnets4media.com
VP Sls: Alissa Baker
Natl Sls Mgr: Kurt Kalish
Sls & Mktg Coord: Lucy Hendrix
Conducts Business: U.S.
Primary Market Served: Business
Catalog available online
Advertising/Marketing Budget Related to Direct Marketing: 26-50%
Founded: 1983

Sells promotional magnets to the direct mail & printing industry.

THE DMA MAGNETS USA

817 Connecticut Ave NE
Roanoke, VA 24012-5317
Telephone: (540) 857-3045, Web Site: www.magnetsusa.com
CEO: Alan Turner

MARKET DISCOVERY GROUP

302 Baltustrol Cir
Roslyn, NY 11576
Telephone: (516) 365-8555, E-Mail: schiffmanl@aol.com
Pres: Leon Schiffman

MARKET FOCUS INC

333 Barton Ave # 1
Evanston, IL 60202-3363
Telephone: (847) 328-2900, FAX: (847) 328-8121
Pres: Richard C. Fowler

MARKET PROBE INTERNATIONAL INC

805 3rd Ave Rm 1103
New York, NY 10022-7567
Telephone: (212) 725-7676, FAX: (212) 725-7529, E-Mail: info@marketprobeint.com, Web Site: www.marketprobeint.com
Pres & CEO: Alan Appelbaum

MARKET RESPONSE INTERNATIONAL

PO Box 26
South Orleans, MA 02662-0026
Telephone: (508) 240-1877, FAX: (508) 945-4010, E-Mail: rmiller@capecod.net, Web Site: www.millerinternational.com
Mng Partner: Richard N. Miller

THE DMA MARKETING & MEDIA SERVICES LLC

931 Jefferson Blvd (Suite 1001)
Warwick, RI 02886-2247
Telephone: (401) 737-7730, Web Site: www.mmsipitv.com
Pres: Sally Dickson
Primary Market Served: Business

MARKETING HORIZONS INC

1001 Craig Rd (Suite 100)
Saint Louis, MO 63146
Telephone: (314) 432-1957, (800) 669-0839, FAX: (314) 432-7014, E-Mail: jkramer@mhorizons.com
Pres & CEO: Robert G. Jasper

MARKETING SYNERGY INC

1700 Park St (Suite 103)
Naperville, IL 60563
Telephone: (630) 328-9550, FAX: (630) 328-9553, E-Mail: RHlavac@MSINetwork.com, Web Site: www.msinetwork.com
Pres: Randy Hlavac

MARKETVISION RESEARCH INC

10300 Alliance Rd
Cincinnati, OH 45242
Telephone: (513) 791-3100, FAX: (513) 794-3500, E-Mail: jpinnell@mv-research.com, Web Site: www.marketvisionresearch.com
Pres: Jon Pinnell

MARS RESEARCH

6365 NW 6th Way (Suite 150)
Fort Lauderdale, FL 33309
Telephone: (954) 771-7725, (877) 755-2805, FAX: (954) 771-8824, E-Mail: ron@marsresearch.com, Web Site: www.marsresearch.com
Dir Mktg Bus Devel: Ron Teblum

MARSHALL MARKETING & COMMUNICATIONS INC

2600 Boyce Plaza Rd (Suite 210)
Pittsburgh, PA 15241
Telephone: (412) 914-0970, FAX: (412) 914-0971, Web Site: www.mm-c.com
Pres: Craig A. Marshall

MATRIX

5244 N Bay Rd
Miami Beach, FL 33140
Telephone: (305) 865-7000, FAX: (305) 864-3114
Pres: Richard Postrel

THE MCILVAINE CO

191 Waukegan Rd (Suite 208)
Northbrook, IL 60093
Telephone: (847) 784-0012, FAX: (847) 784-0061, E-Mail: editor@mcilvainecompany.com, Web Site: www.mcilvainecompany.com
Pres: Robert McIlvaine

MEDIA MONITORS INC

445 Hamilton Ave Ste 700
White Plains, NY 10601-1828
Telephone: (914) 428-5971, FAX: (914) 428-4541, E-Mail: jselig@mediamonitors.com, Web Site: www.mediamonitors.com
Pres & CEO: John L. Selig

MEDIAMARK RESEARCH INC

Subs. of GFK
75 Ninth Ave (5th fl)
New York, NY 10011
Telephone: (212) 884-9200, (800) 310-3305, FAX: (212) 884-9339, Web Site: www.mediamark.com
Pres & CEO: Kathi Love
Dir, Third Party Data Mngmt: Jeanine Taylor
Conducts Business: U.S.
Employees: 90

Syndicated media research data that includes demos, lifestyle and product data. We sell to advertising agencies, direct marketing agencies and advertisers.

MESSAGE TECHNOLOGIES INC

1995 N Park Pl, Meridian (5th fl)
Atlanta, GA 30339
Telephone: (770) 240-8000, (800) 868-3684, FAX: (770) 240-7474, E-Mail: info@messagetech.com, Web Site: www.messagetech.com
CEO: Mark Abramson
Pres: Darrell Knight

THE DMA MINTEL INTERNATIONAL
351 W Hubbard St (fl 8)
Chicago, IL 60654-4941
Telephone: (312) 932-0500, Web Site:
www.comperemedia.com
Pres: Pam McHugh
Primary Market Served: Business &
Consumer

MORPACE INC
31700 Middlebelt Rd Ste 200
Farmington Hills, MI 48334-2375
Telephone: (248) 737-5300, FAX:
(248) 737-5326, E-Mail:
information@morpace.com, Web
Site: www.morpace.com
Pres: Valerie Utley

MSW RESEARCH
Div. of MSW-McCollum Spielman
Worldwide
1111 Marcus Ave (Suite MZ 200)
Lake Success, NY 11042-1034
Telephone: (516) 394-6000, FAX:
(516) 394-6001, E-Mail: mail@
mswresearch.com, Web Site: www.
mswresearch.com
CEO: Harold Spielman

THE NPD GROUP INC
900 W Shore Rd
Port Washington, NY 11050
Telephone: (516) 625-0700, FAX:
(516) 625-2444, Web Site: www.npd.
com
VP, Corp Commun: Leslie Singer

NATHAN ASSOCIATES INC
2101 Wilson Blvd Ste 1200
Arlington, VA 22201-3049
Telephone: (703) 516-7700, FAX:
(703) 351-6162, Web Site: www.
nathaninc.com
CEO & Bd Chmn: John Beyer

NATIONAL RESEARCH LLC
4201 Connecticut Ave NW (Suite 212)
Washington, DC 20008-1162
Telephone: (202) 686-9350, FAX:
(202) 686-7163, E-Mail: survey@
nationalres.com, Web Site: www.
nationalres.com
Pres: Becky Craig

THE DMA NIELSEN CLARITAS
9276 Scranton Rd Ste 200
San Diego, CA 92121-7703
Telephone: (800) 866-6520, Web Site:
www.claritas.com
Pres: Matt O'Grady
Primary Market Served: Business &
Consumer

NIELSEN MEDIA RESEARCH, INC
770 Broadway
New York, NY 10003-9595
Telephone: (646) 654-8300, Web Site:
en-us.nielsen.com
Sr VP & Chief HR Officer: Betsy Williams

NIMBLEFISH TECHNOLOGIES
100 Spear St (Suite 740)
San Francisco, CA 94105-1525
Telephone: (415) 247-7000, Web Site:
www.nimblefish.com
Mktg Mgr: Catalina Garreton

NORTH CAROLINA ELECTRIC MEMBERSHIP CORP
3400 Summer Blvd
Raleigh, NC 27616-7306
Telephone: (919) 872-0800, (800) 662-
8835, FAX: (919) 645-3410, E-Mail:
info@ncemcs.com, Web Site: www.
ncemcs.com
Pres: J. Ronald McElheney

NUSTATS INC
206 Wild Basin Rd Ste A300, Building
A
West Lake Hills, TX 78746-3437
Telephone: (512) 306-9065, (800) 44-
STATS, FAX: (512) 306-9065, Web
Site: www.nustats.com
Pres: Carlos Arce

ORC MACRO INTERNATIONAL
Div. of Macro International
40 Wall St (Suite 3400)
New York, NY 10005-1325
Telephone: (212) 941-5555, FAX:
(212) 941-7031, E-Mail: info@icfi.
com, Web Site: www.icfi.com
Chmn: Tibor Weiss Sr

OTOLABS LLC
465 Medford St (Suite 300)
Charlestown, MA 02129-1454
Telephone: (617) 236-8400, Web Site:
www.otolabs.com
Dir Prod Mngmt: Mitchel Ahern

OUTRIDER NORTH AMERICA
111 Westport Plaza (Suite 350)
Saint Louis, MO 36146-3099
Telephone: (314) 209-1005, FAX:
(314) 209-1126, Web Site: www.
outrider.com
Sr Partner: Chris Copeland
Dir Corp Commun: Cindy Kerber
Spellman

OXBRIDGE COMMUNICATIONS INC
186 5th Ave
New York, NY 10010-5202
Telephone: (212) 741-0231, (800) 955-
0231, FAX: (212) 633-2938, E-Mail:
custserv@oxbridge.com, Web Site:
www.mediafinder.com; www.
oxbridge.com
CEO: Louis Hagood
Treas: Patricia Hagood
Editorial Dir: Deborah Striplin
Customer Svc & Mktg: Johanna Barwick
Primary Market Served: Business &
Consumer
Catalog available online
Direct online sales
Founded: 1961

Most comprehensive database of U.S.
and Canadian periodicals and catalogs,
in print and interactive online service.
Used by direct marketers, research,
reference and marketing to printers,
publishers, editors, etc.

PARAGON MEDIA STRATEGIES
7550 W Yale Ave Ste B204
Denver, CO 80227-3460
Telephone: (303) 922-5600, FAX:
(303) 922-1589, E-Mail: info@
paragonmediastrategies.com, Web
Site: www.paragonmediastrategies.
com
Pres: John Stevens
VP Mktg: Michele Tharp

PARTNERDATA LLC
2119 Dewey Ave (Suite B)
Evanston, IL 60201-3035
Telephone: (847) 733-0819
Dir Mktg: Lisa Henthorn

PHOENIX MARKETING INTERNATIONAL
132 Welsh Rd Ste 100
Horsham, PA 19044-2217
Telephone: (215) 392-0264, Web Site:
www.phoenixmi.com
Pres Response Mktg: John Schiela
Primary Market Served: Business &
Consumer

JD POWER ASSOCIATES
2625 Townsgate Rd
Westlake Village, CA 91361-5751
Telephone: (805) 418-8000, (888) 537-
6937, FAX: (805) 418-8900, E-Mail:
information@jdpa.com, Web Site:
www.jdpower.com
Sr Dir Bus Devel: Tom Petro
Primary Market Served: Consumer

Q FACT MARKETING RESEARCH INC & VIDEOCONFERENCING CENTER
9908 Carver Rd
Cincinnati, OH 45242-5502
Telephone: (513) 891-2271, FAX:
(513) 984-7464, E-Mail: info@qfact.
com, Web Site: www.qfact.com
VP, Res & Opers: Mary Swart

RJ OLSEN INC
41 Indian Ridge Rd
Natick, MA 01760-5635
Telephone: (508) 647-3777, FAX:
(508) 647-6777, E-Mail: dickolsen@
aol.com
Pres: Richard J. Olsen

RSC THE QUALITY MEASUREMENT CO
110 Walnut St
Evansville, IN 47708
Telephone: (812) 425-4562, FAX:
(812) 425-2844
Exec VP: Allan Kuse

RELEVANT INSIGHTS LLC
2508 Salmon Run Ln
Euless, TX 76039-6096
Telephone: (817) 545-8017
Pres: Michaela Mora
Primary Market Served: Business & Consumer

RESEARCH COMMUNICATIONS LTD
95 Washington St (401-357)
Canton, MA 02021-4006
Telephone: (781) 341-1190, FAX:
(781) 341-1191, E-Mail: info@
researchcommunications.com
Pres: Valerie Crane

RUDER FINN INC
301 E 57th St (fl 3)
New York, NY 10022-5997
Telephone: (212) 593-6400, FAX:
(212) 715-1556, E-Mail:
rfnewyork@ruderfinn.com, Web Site:
www.ruderfinn.com
VP: Dan Carlson

RUF CORP
1533 E Spruce St
Olathe, KS 66061
Telephone: (913) 782-8544, (800) 829-8544, FAX: (913) 782-0150, E-Mail:
solutions@ruf.com, Web Site: www.
ruf.com
VP, Sls & Mktg: Kurtis M. Ruf
Office Mgr: Sharon Crozier

SHR CAPITAL PARTNERS
165 Mason St
Greenwich, CT 06830
Telephone: (203) 618-1110
Primary Market Served: Business

SRB MARKETING INC
10 Caroline Way
New Paltz, NY 12561-1157
Telephone: (866) 210-1183, Web Site:
www.srbmarketing.com
Mng Dir: Perry Goldschein

SALES PORTAL
13101 Diericx Dr
Mountain View, CA 94040-3915
Telephone: (800) 634-3474, Web Site:
www.salesportal.com
Pres: Kevin Sandhu

THE SAUSALITO GROUP
PO Box 1559
Sausalito, CA 94966-1559
Telephone: (415) 332-3333, FAX:
(415) 332-6571, Web Site: www.
sausolitogroup.com
Founder & CEO: Peter Sealey Ph.D.

W J SCHROER CO
Two W Michigan Ave
Battle Creek, MI 49017-3609
Telephone: (269) 963-4874, FAX:
(269) 963-5930, E-Mail: info@
socialmarketing.org, Web Site: www.
socialmarketing.org
Pres: William J. Schroer

JAMES M. SEARS ASSOCIATES
375 S Washington Ave
Bergenfield, NJ 07621-4323
Telephone: (201) 501-9977, FAX:
(201) 453-0833
Principal: James M. Sears

THE DMA SIGHT MARKETING
400 1st Ave N (Suite 100)
Minneapolis, MN 55401-1764
Telephone: (651) 379-4059, Web Site:
www.sightmarketing.com
Dir Mktg: Ted Loken

SINDLINGER & CO INC
405 Osborne Ln
Wallingford, PA 19086
Telephone: (610) 565-0247, E-Mail:
nelSind@aol.com
Chmn: Nellie H. Sindlinger

SPECTRUM RESEARCH
5000 Boardwalk (Suite 602)
Ventnor City, NJ 08406-2918

Telephone: (609) 822-0056, E-Mail:
peter@spectrumresearch.com
Pres: Peter Mokover

STRATA MARKETING INC
30 W Monroe (Suite 1900)
Chicago, IL 60603
Telephone: (312) 222-1555, FAX:
(312) 222-2510, Web Site: www.
stratag.com
Pres, Sls & Mktg: Bruce W. Johnson

SUMMITQWEST
446 Windsor Park Dr
Dayton, OH 45459-4111
Telephone: (937) 291-4333, Web Site:
www.sqinteractive.com
Interactive Mktg Svcs: Patrick Sepate

SYNOVATE
360 Park Ave S (fl 5)
New York, NY 10010-1712
Telephone: (212) 293-6100, FAX:
(212) 293-6666
CEO North America: Robert Skolnick

TMP DIRECTIONAL MARKETING
PO Box 1448
Waukesha, WI 53187-1448
Telephone: (212) 351-7595, Web Site:
www.tmpdm.com
VP Mktg & Strategy: Monica Ho

TNF
Div. of NFO World Group
900-2 Bloor St E
Toronto, ON, Canada M4W 3H8
Telephone: (416) 924-5751, FAX:
(416) 923-7085, Web Site: www.tnf-
cf.com
Pres: Michael LoPresti

TNS INTERSEARCH
3 Barker Ave (#3)
White Plains, NY 10601-1509
Telephone: (914) 684-6100, FAX:
(914) 684-6078, Web Site: www.tns-
global.com
VP Mktg: Brenda Edwards

TSE SERVICES
3400 Summer Blvd
Raleigh, NC 27611-7306
Telephone: (919) 875-3037, Web Site:
www.ncemcs.com
Sr Analyst: Scott Staff
Primary Market Served: Consumer
Founded: 1998

Cooperative market research organization

TABLINE DATA SERVICES INC
625 Ave of the Americas (2nd fl)
New York, NY 10001-2020
Telephone: (212) 695-4873, FAX:
(212) 629-4423
VP & Mng Dir: Arye Lubovitz

THE DMA TAKE 5 SOLUTIONS LLC
2385 NW Executive Center Dr (Suite 320)
Boca Raton, FL 33431-8530
Telephone: (561) 819-5555, (866) 861-8862, FAX: (561) 819-0245, E-Mail:
sales@take5s.com, Web Site: www.take5solutions.com
COO of Data: Alex Radetich
Dir Mktg & Commun: John J Lofquist

TANGENT MEDIA LLC
570 Westover Dr NW (Suite 200)
Atlanta, GA 30305-3538
Telephone: (404) 444-2357, Web Site:
www.tangentmedia.us
CEO: Dr. Kevin McCarthy
Primary Market Served: Business

TAYLOR NELSON SOFRES INTERSEARCH
410 Horsham Rd Frnt
Horsham, PA 19044-2041
Telephone: (419) 725-8560, E-Mail:
info@intersearch.tnsofres.com, Web
Site: www.intersearch.tnsofres.com
VP, Mktg: Melanie Mumper

THE TELECONFERENCE NETWORK
Div. of Market Navigation Inc
137 E Townline Rd
Nanuet, NY 10954
Telephone: (845) 624-0633, FAX:
(845) 623-9394, E-Mail: nospam@
mnav.com, Web Site: www.market-navigation.com
Pres, CEO, & Founder: George Silverman

THOMAS MARKETING INFORMATION CENTER
Div. of Thomas Publishing Co
Five Penn Plaza
New York, NY 10001
Telephone: (212) 695-0500, FAX:
(212) 290-7362, E-Mail: contact@
thomaspublishing.com, Web Site:
www.thomaspublishing.com
Pres: John L. Lindsey

TRELLIST MARKETING AND TECHNOLOGY
117 N Market St (Suite 300)
Wilmington, DE 19801-2538

Telephone: (302) 778-1300, Web Site:
www.trellist.com
Mng Partner: David Atadan

TRIGGERFISH MARKETING
200 Townsend St (#45)
San Francisco, CA 94107-5703
Telephone: (415) 671-4699, Web Site:
www.triggerfish.com
Pres & CEO: Scott Gregory

2ERGO
2020 N 14th St (Suite 500)
Arlington, VA 22201-2515
Telephone: (703) 879-3400, Web Site:
www.2ergo.com
Dir Mktg: Lindsay Woodworth

VENTE INC
4509 S 143rd St (Suite 9)
Omaha, NE 68137-4521
Telephone: (402) 898-6800, (877) 899-9691, FAX: (402) 334-4829, Web
Site: www.venteinc.com
Mgr, Prod Mngmt: Katie Geilenkrichen

VERITAS ANALYTICS INC
21351 Gentry Dr
Sterling, VA 20166-8510
Telephone: (703) 707-5620, Web Site:
www.veritas-analytics.com
Principal Staff Analyst: Eric Qualkenbush
Program Mgr: Roger Andrews
Primary Market Served: Business & Consumer

BILL WARD INC
1010 Philadelphia Pike
Wilmington, DE 19809-2029
Telephone: (302) 762-6600, FAX:
(302) 397-2153, E-Mail: billward@
billwardinc.com
Pres: William F. Ward Jr

WHERE 2 GET IT INC
5101 E La Palma Ave Ste 107
Anaheim, CA 92807-2056
Telephone: (888) 377-2767, Web Site:
www.where2getit.com
VP Mktg & Bus: Vickie McGee

THE DMA WHO'S CALLING
200 Quality Cir
College Station, TX 77845
Telephone: (866) 688-9300, FAX:
(888) 821-4260, E-Mail: contact@
whoscalling.com, Web Site: www.
whoscalling.com
Mktg Mgr: Susan DeSantis
Primary Market Served: Business

WPROMOTE INC
1700 E Walnut Ave Fl 5
El Segundo, CA 90245-2610
Telephone: (310) 421-4844, Web Site:
www.wpromote.com
Dir Mktg: Jamie Lane
Primary Market Served: Business & Consumer

Arkansas

Vestcom International Inc, 7304 Kanis Rd, Little Rock, 72204

California

Los Angeles Times, 202 W First St, Los Angeles, 90012-4105

Money Mailer LLC, 12131 Western Ave, Garden Grove, 92841

Publisher's Media, 1145 N Second St, El Cajon, 92021-5024

Senior Publishers Media Group, 4141 Jutland Dr (Suite 300, San Diego, 92117-7316

Vegetarian Times, 300 N Continental Blvd (Suite 650), El Segundo, 90245

Zinio Systems Inc, 114 Sansome St (fl 4), San Francisco, 94104

Colorado

Dex Direct Marketing, 9380 Station St, Lone Tree, 80124-6807

Connecticut

Bayard Inc, 1 Montauk Ave (Suite 3), New London, 06320-4967

Choice Magazine, 100 Riverview Ctr, Middletown, 06457-3401

The Hartford Courant, 285 Broad St, Hartford, 06115-2510

Madison Direct Marketing Ltd, 60 Long Ridge Rd (Suite 306), Stamford, 06902-1841

Media Dynamics LLC, 12 Choctaw Ln, Greenwich, 06831-3203

Media Horizons Management LLC, 40 Richards Ave, Norwalk, 06854

Media Space Solutions, 101 Merritt 7 Corporate Park (3rd fl), Norwalk, 06851

Multichannel Merchant Magazine, 11 River Bend Dr S, Stamford, 06907-0242

Newspapers First, 501 Westport Ave (Suite 73), Norwalk, 06851-4411

Valassis, 1 Targeting Ctr, Windsor, 06095-2639

District of Columbia

Capitol Advantage/Roll Call Group, 77 K St NE (fl 8), Washington, 20002-4681

Florida

Alternative Media Group, 999 Vanderbilt Beach Rd Ste 200, Naples, 34108-3512

The Doyle Group Inc, 5150 Palm Valley Rd (Suite 103), Ponte Vedra Beach, 32082

First Marketing Co, 3300 Gateway Dr, Pompano Beach, 33069

Fortent, 80 SW 8th St (Suite 2300), Miami, 33130-3031

RSVP Publications, 6730 W Linebaugh Ave (Suite 201), Tampa, 33625-4914

Valpak Direct Marketing Systems Inc, 8605 Largo Lakes Dr, Largo, 33773-4912

Georgia

AAVIM, 220 Smithsonia Rd, Winterville, 30683-1418

Ashrae Learning Institute, 1791 Tullie Cir NE, Atlanta, 30329-2305

Harland Clarke Marketing Services, 2939 Miller Rd, Decatur, 30035-4038

Morris Communications Corp, 725 Broad St, PO Box 936, Augusta, 30903-0936

Primedia Inc, 3585 Engineering Dr (Suite 100), Norcross, 30092

Illinois

Angel Sales Inc, 4147 N Ravenswood, Chicago, 60613

BBS Chicago, 111 S Wacker Dr, Chicago, 60606-4301

Chicago Sun-Times, 350 N Orleans St (fl 10), Chicago, 60654-1700

Chicago Tribune, 777 W Chicago Ave, Chicago, 60654-2823

RR Donnelley & Sons Co, 111 S Wacker Dr, Chicago, 60606-4304

Fox Associates Inc, 116 W Kinzie St, Chicago, 60654-4655

Reilly Communications Group, 3030 W Salt Creek Ln Ste 201, Arlington Heights, 60005-5002

RR Donnelley Response Marketing Services, 3075 Highland Pkwy Ste 400, Downers Grove, 60515-5560

Solar Communications, 400 S County Farm Rd (Suite 330), Wheaton, 60187-4547

Today's Christian Woman, 465 Gundersen Dr, Carol Stream, 60188

Winfield Marketing Corp, 5724 N Palaski Rd, Chicago, 60646

Kansas

YP Talk, 1101 Cedar Crest Dr, Pittsburg, 66762-6631

Kentucky

AMC Publishing/Agent Media Corp, 5081 Olympic Blvd, Erlanger, 41018-3164

Maine

On-Line Technologies Inc, 605 US Route 1 (Suite 3), Scarborough, 04074-9617

Maryland

Automated Graphic Systems Inc, 4590 Graphics Dr, White Plains, 20695

Massachusetts

AMI Instore, 945 Concord St, Framingham, 01701

The Christian Science Monitor, 210 Massachusetts Ave, Boston, 02115-3012

Course Technology, 20 Channel Ctr St, Boston, 02210-3402

The MarketPlace Group Inc, 9 Jaybarry Ln, Norwood, 02062-1925

The NH Broadcaster, 491 Dutton St (Suite 1), Lowell, 01854-4292

Michigan

Entertainment Publications Inc, 1414 E Maple Rd, Troy, 48083-4019

Minnesota

CardSource, 1286 Trapp Rd, Eagan, 55121-1217

Duplication Factory Inc, 4275 Norex Dr, Chaska, 55318-3046

Machalek Communications, 12550 W Frontage Rd (Suite 220), Burnsville, 55337

Novus Media Inc, 2 Carlson Pkwy (Suite 400), Plymouth, 55447-4470

Vocational Biographies Inc, 414 S Sixth St, PO Box 31, Sauk Centre, 56378-0031

Missouri

AT&T Advertising & Publishing, 13075 Manchester Rd, Saint Louis, 63131

Commercial Lithographing Co Inc, 1226 Chestnut Ave, Kansas City, 64127-2022

Roberts & Buchanan Inc, 513 S Travis St, Concordia, 64020-7329

Montana

The Missoulian, PO Box 8029, Missoula, 59807

Nebraska

First Cyber Services, 13624 Montclair Dr, Omaha, 68144-2438

International Gamco Inc, 9335 N 48th St, Omaha, 68152

Papillion Times Group, 604 Fort Crook Rd N, Bellevue, 68005-4557

New Hampshire

Choice Media, 15 Danbury Cir, Amherst, 03031-2016

New Jersey

Cable Direct Marketing Inc, One Gabriel Dr, Montville, 07045

Direct Mail Strategy Group (DMSG), 300 Knickerbocker Rd, Cresskill, 07626

Michele Jaworski, 65 Forest Ave, Ramsey, 07446-2706

New York Daily News, 125 Theodore Conrad Dr, Jersey City, 07305-4615

Sancoa International, 92 Ark Rd, Lumberton, 08048-4103

We Deliver America Inc, 68 Irving Ave., Englewood Cliffs, 07632

New York

ARA Media Solutions Inc, 347 W 57th St (fl 18), New York, 10019-3173

Adriana Associates Ltd, 2 W 45th St Ste 1403, New York, 10036-4240

Better Homes & Gardens, 125 Park Ave Fl 20, New York, 10017-8501

Bon Appetit Magazine, 4 Times Sq, New York, 10036-6518

Butler Till Media Services, 1565 Jefferson Rd Ste 200, Rochester, 14623-3178

Computer Shopper, 28 E 28th (#10), New York, 10016

Editorial Freelance Association, 71 W 23rd St (4th fl), New York, 10010-4181

Everyday Media, 230 Old Albany Post Rd, Garrison, 10524-3711

Family Circle Magazine Inc, 125 Park Ave, New York, 10017

David Geller Associates, 1071 Ave of the Americas, New York, 10018-3704

GLM Communications, 242 W 27th St (Suite 1B), New York, 10001-5926

Google, 76 Ninth Ave, New York, 10011

Guidance Associates, 31 Pine View Rd, Mount Kisco, 10549

Halogen Response Media, 1675 Broadway, New York, 10019-5820

Hearst Direct Response Advertising Sales, 300 W 57th St, New York, 10019-5239

InterMedia Outdoors Inc, 512 Fashion Ave Rm 1100, New York, 10018-4618

Karaban Labiner Associates, 225 W 36th St (Suite 1202), New York, 10018

Main Street Direct, 575 Lexington Ave Fl 4, New York, 10022-6146

Marvel Entertainment Inc, 135 W 50th St Fl 4, New York, 10020-1201

Media People Inc, 122 E 42nd St (Suite 725), New York, 10168-0601

Media Resource Group Inc, 100 S Bedford Rd (Suite 320), Mount Kisco, 10549-3444

Metropolitan Newspaper Advertising Services Inc, 8 W 38th St (fl 4), New York, 10018-0154

Military Direct Marketing Inc, 1 Bushwick Rd, Poughkeepsie, 12603-3839

News America Marketing, 1185 Ave of the Americas (fl 27), New York, 10036-2603

Parade Publications, 711 Third Ave, New York, 10017-4014

The Allen Schluger Co Inc, 21 W 68th St, New York, 10023

Iris Shokoff Associates, 845 3rd Ave Fl 6, New York, 10022-6630

Specialized Marketing Inc, 162 Prospect Hill Rd Ste 203, Brewster, 10509-2374

Spectra Products LLC, 1364 Reynolds Rd, Johnson City, 13790-4837

Stanton Direct Marketing Inc, 315 W Water St, Elmira, 14901-2914

TV Guide Magazine, 11 W 42nd St (fl 17), New York, 10036-8002

USA Weekend, 535 Madison Ave, New York, 10022

Working Mother, 2 Park Ave (fl 10), New York, 10016

ZCard North America, 39 Broadway (fl 32), New York, 10006-3047

North Carolina

News & Record, 200 E Market St, Greensboro, 27401

Ohio

JB Dollar Stretcher Magazine, 3105 Farnham Rd, Richfield, 44286

Sales Building Systems, 9325 Progress Pkwy, Mentor, 44060

Town Money Saver, 6 E Main St, Lucas, 44843-9701

Oregon

New Customer Acquisition, 620 Franquette St, Medford, 97501-7832

Pennsylvania

Campus Dimensions Inc, 1880 John F Kennedy Blvd (Suite 1710), Philadelphia, 19103-7424

Clipper Magazine, 3708 Hempland Rd, Mountville, 17554-1542

H & H Graphics, 854 N Prince St, Lancaster, 17603-2752

IMC - Multi Media Marketing, 930 Fox Pavilion, Jenkintown, 19046

The Philadelphia Inquirer & Daily News, 400 N Broad St, Box 8263, Philadelphia, 19101

Target Marketing Group, 1500 Spring Garden St (Suite 1200), Philadelphia, 19130-4069

TelAmerica Media Inc, 1701 John F Kennedy Blvd (Suite 2510), Philadelphia, 19103-2876

South Carolina

Miller Direct Inc, 1741 Gold Hill Rd (Suite 102), Fort Mill, 29708-8240

The Press & Standard, 1025 Bells Hwy, Walterboro, 29488

Tennessee

Alternative Concepts Inc, 10420 Jackson Oaks Way Ste 103, Knoxville, 37922-0708

Texas

The Houston Chronicle, 801 Texas Ave
(Suite 300), Houston, 77002-2996

SuperMedia LLC, 2200 W Airfield Dr,
Dallas, 75261

Virginia

Taradel LLC, 4325 Cox Rd, Glen Allen,
23060-3359

CANADA
Ontario

Scott's Directories, 1450 Don Mills Rd,
Don Mills, M3B 2X7

Quebec

Trans Continental Inc, One Place Ville
Marie (Suite 3315), Montreal, H3B 3N2

AAVIM
220 Smithsonia Rd
Winterville, GA 30683-1418
Telephone: (706) 742-5355, (800) 228-4689, FAX: (706) 742-7005, E-Mail: gary@aavim.com, Web Site: www.aavim.com
Dir: Gary Farmer
Bus Mgr: Kim Butler
Conducts Business: U.S.
Employees: 4
Primary Market Served: Business & Consumer
Catalog available online
Direct online sales
Advertising/Marketing Budget Related to Direct Marketing: 76-100%
Direct Marketing ad budget:
Magazines: 5%
Newspapers: 85%
Online: 10%
Founded: 1949
Gross sales or billing: $300,000

Develop, produce & distribute instructional materials for vocational education, including publications, videos & computer software.

AMC PUBLISHING/AGENT MEDIA CORP
5081 Olympic Blvd
Erlanger, KY 41018-3164
Telephone: (727) 446-1100, (800) 933-9449, FAX: (727) 446-1166, E-Mail: sales@agentmediacorp.com, Web Site: www.agentmediacorp.com
CEO: Roscoe Smith

AMI INSTORE
945 Concord St
Framingham, MA 01701
Telephone: (508) 652-0200, (877) 652-0200, FAX: (508) 652-0101, E-Mail: info@advancemarketing.com, Web Site: www.advancemarketing.com
CEO: Joel Goodfader
Office Mgr: Marlene Evernden

ARA MEDIA SOLUTIONS INC
347 W 57th St (fl 18)
New York, NY 10019-3173
Telephone: (212) 245-6691, Web Site: www.aramediasolutions.com
Pres: Arlene Rosen

AT&T ADVERTISING & PUBLISHING
aka AT&T Yellow Pages
13075 Manchester Rd
Saint Louis, MO 63131
Telephone: (314) 957-5100, FAX: (314) 957-5050, Web Site: www.att.com
Mktg Mgr: Ravi Batheja

THE DMA ADRIANA ASSOCIATES LTD
2 W 45th St Ste 1403
New York, NY 10036-4240
Telephone: (212) 719-5952, FAX: (212) 398-6414
Pres: Adriana Delogu

ALTERNATIVE CONCEPTS INC
10420 Jackson Oaks Way Ste 103
Knoxville, TN 37922-0708
Telephone: (865) 690-1990, FAX: (865) 692-0072, E-Mail: info@acmarketing.biz, Web Site: www.acmarketing.biz
Primary Market Served: Business

ALTERNATIVE MEDIA GROUP
999 Vanderbilt Beach Rd Ste 200
Naples, FL 34108-3512
Telephone: (732) 741-0585, FAX: (732) 741-0489, Web Site: www.amg-global.com
Pres: James Cunningham
VP Sls & Bus Devel: Judd Bergenfeld

ANGEL SALES INC
4147 N Ravenswood
Chicago, IL 60613
Telephone: (773) 883-8858, FAX: (773) 883-8889, E-Mail: info@angelsales.com, Web Site: www.angelsales.com
Pres: Robert Engel
VP: Laura Engel

ASHRAE LEARNING INSTITUTE
1791 Tullie Cir NE
Atlanta, GA 30329-2305
Telephone: (404) 636-8400, (800) 527-4723, FAX: (404) 321-5478, E-Mail: ashrae@ashrae.org, Web Site: www.ashrae.org
Exec VP: Jeff Littleton
Outside Sls: Ed Farley

AUTOMATED GRAPHIC SYSTEMS INC
4590 Graphics Dr
White Plains, MD 20695
Telephone: (301) 843-1800, (800) 678-8760, FAX: (301) 843-6339, E-Mail: info@ags.com, Web Site: www.ags.com
Pres: John Green

BBS CHICAGO
Div of RR Donnelley
111 S Wacker Dr
Chicago, IL 60606-4301
Telephone: (312) 326-8000, Web Site: www.rrdonnelley.com
Pres & COO: Joe McSpadden

BAYARD INC
1 Montauk Ave (Suite 3)
New London, CT 06320-4967
Telephone: (860) 437-3012, Web Site: www.bayard-inc.com
Pub Rels Assoc: Danielle Drolet

BETTER HOMES & GARDENS
Subs. of Meredith Corp
125 Park Ave Fl 20
New York, NY 10017-8501
Telephone: (212) 551-7097, FAX: (212) 551-6917, E-Mail: support@bhg.com, Web Site: www.bhg.com
Editor in Chief: Dan Hickey

BON APPETIT MAGAZINE
Div. of Conde Nast Publications
4 Times Sq
New York, NY 10036-6518
Telephone: (212) 286-2860, FAX: (212) 286-2536, E-Mail: paul_jowdy@bonappetit.com, Web Site: www.bonappetit.com
VP & Publr: Paul Jowdy

BUTLER TILL MEDIA SERVICES
1565 Jefferson Rd Ste 200
Rochester, NY 14623-3178
Telephone: (585) 473-3740, Web Site: www.butlertill.com
Email Mktg Dir: Jennifer Favata
Primary Market Served: Consumer

CABLE DIRECT MARKETING INC
One Gabriel Dr
Montville, NJ 07045

Telephone: (973) 244-0010, FAX: (973) 244-0302, E-Mail: cabledm@aol.com
Pres: Michael Klein

CAMPUS DIMENSIONS INC
1880 John F Kennedy Blvd (Suite 1710)
Philadelphia, PA 19103-7424
Telephone: (215) 568-1700, (800) 592-2121, FAX: (215) 568-1701, E-Mail: recruitment@cdicccc.com, Web Site: www.cdicccc.com
Pres & Founder: Edward Solomon
Founded: 1976

CAPITOL ADVANTAGE/ROLL CALL GROUP
77 K St NE (fl 8)
Washington, DC 20002-4681
Telephone: (202) 6550-6500, (800) 432-2250, E-Mail: sales@cq.com
Sr Mktg Mgr: Lara Perkins
Primary Market Served: Business

CARDSOURCE
1286 Trapp Rd
Eagan, MN 55121-1217
Telephone: (651) 686-0660, Web Site: www.cardsource.com

CHICAGO SUN-TIMES
Subs. of The Sun-Times Co
350 N Orleans St (fl 10)
Chicago, IL 60654-1700
Telephone: (312) 321-3000, FAX: (312) 321-9655, E-Mail: jmorawez@suntimes.com, Web Site: www.suntimes.com
Adv Svcs Coord: Joy Morawez

CHICAGO TRIBUNE
Subs. of Tribune Co
777 W Chicago Ave
Chicago, IL 60654-2823
Telephone: (312) 222-3232, (800) 874-2863, FAX: (312) 222-2353, E-Mail: consumerservices@tribune.com, Web Site: www.chicagotribune.com
Direct Response Mgr: Peggy Kirkeng

CHOICE MAGAZINE
Div. of American Library Association
100 Riverview Ctr
Middletown, CT 06457-3401
Telephone: (860) 347-6933, (860) 347-1387, FAX: (860) 346-8586, E-Mail: adsales@ala-choice.org, Web Site: www.ala.org/ala/acrl/acrlpubs/choice/home.cfm
Editorial Dir: Francine Graf
Adv Sls Mgr: Pamela Marino

THE DMA CHOICE MEDIA
15 Danbury Cir
Amherst, NH 03031-2016
Telephone: (603) 672-3338, FAX: (603) 249-9732, E-Mail: choicemedia@comcast.net
Pres: Diane Caruso
Primary Market Served: Business

THE DMA THE CHRISTIAN SCIENCE MONITOR
The Christian Science Publishing Society
210 Massachusetts Ave
Boston, MA 02115-3012
Telephone: (617) 450-2000, FAX: (617) 450-2031, Web Site: www.csmonitor.com
Mng Publr: Stephen Gray

THE DMA CLIPPER MAGAZINE
3708 Hempland Rd
Mountville, PA 17554-1542
Telephone: (717) 569-5100, Web Site: www.clippermagazine.com
Founder, Pres: Steven Zuckerman

COMMERCIAL LITHOGRAPHING CO INC
1226 Chestnut Ave
Kansas City, MO 64127-2022
Telephone: (816) 241-2218, FAX: (816) 241-6091, E-Mail: sjohnson@commercial-lithographing.com, Web Site: www.clitho.com
Pres & CEO: William E. Pfeiffer
VP HR: John E. Sloss

Sheetfed commercial printing.

COMPUTER SHOPPER
Div. of Ziff Davis Publishing
28 E 28th (#10)
New York, NY 10016
Telephone: (646) 472-4000, FAX: (646) 472-3912, E-Mail: feedback@computershopper.com, Web Site: www.computershopper.com
Editor in Chief: John Burek

COURSE TECHNOLOGY
Div. of Cengage Learning
20 Channel Ctr St
Boston, MA 02210-3402
Telephone: (617) 757-7900, (800) 648-7450, (800) 354-9706, FAX: (617) 487-8488, E-Mail: ed.moura@cengage.com, Web Site: www.course.com
Pres: Ed Moura

DEX DIRECT MARKETING
Div of R.H. Donnelley
9380 Station St
Lone Tree, CO 80124-6807

Telephone: (800) 999-4630, Web Site: www.dexlist.com
Sls/Mktg Mgr: Linda Langhoff
Primary Market Served: Business & Consumer

DIRECT MAIL STRATEGY GROUP (DMSG)
Div. of Conrad Direct
300 Knickerbocker Rd
Cresskill, NJ 07626
Telephone: (201) 567-3200, FAX: (201) 567-1530, E-Mail: bschonwald@conraddirect.com, Web Site: www.conraddirect.com
CEO: Barbara Schonwald
COO: Steven Maier

Direct Response Marketing Agency specializing in print media planning and buying (on-the-page and insert space), merge/purge management, on-the-page advertising sales, strategic consulting, creative (copy/design) and production (printing/mailing) management, and analytical data services.

RR DONNELLEY & SONS CO
111 S Wacker Dr
Chicago, IL 60606-4304
Telephone: (312) 326-8000, FAX: (312) 326-7156, Web Site: www.rrdonnelly.com
Pres, CEO & Dir: Thomas J. Quinlan III
Sr VP & CIO: Kenneth E. O'Brien
Sr VP Pub Affairs: Gian-Carlo Peressutti
Conducts Business: North America, Latin America, Asia & Europe
Employees: 60,000
Primary Market Served: Business
Founded: 1864
Gross sales or billing: $9,316,600,000

Book, catalog, magazine, direct marketing, commercial printing, fulfillment and distribution services company.

THE DOYLE GROUP INC
5150 Palm Valley Rd (Suite 103)
Ponte Vedra Beach, FL 32082
Telephone: (904) 285-6020, FAX: (904) 285-9944
Pres: Joseph D. Doyle Jr

DUPLICATION FACTORY INC
4275 Norex Dr
Chaska, MN 55318-3046
Telephone: (952) 448-9912, (800) 279-2009, FAX: (952) 448-3983, E-Mail: info@duplicationfactory.com, Web Site: www.duplicationfactory.com
Pres: Peter McCarthy

EDITORIAL FREELANCE ASSOCIATION
71 W 23rd St (4th fl)
New York, NY 10010-4181
Telephone: (212) 929-5400, (866) 929-5400, FAX: (212) 929-5439, E-Mail: office@the-efa.org, Web Site: www.the-efa.org
Pres: Eileen Kramer
Office Mgr: Judith Greenstein
Founded: 1970

ENTERTAINMENT PUBLICATIONS INC
Subs. of IAC/Inter Active Corporation
1414 E Maple Rd
Troy, MI 48083-4019
Telephone: (248) 404-1000, (888) 231-SAVE, FAX: (248) 404-1915, Web Site: www.entertainment.com
Pres: MaryAnn D. Rivers
Mktg Mgr: Kimberly Kwant

EVERYDAY MEDIA
230 Old Albany Post Rd
Garrison, NY 10524-3711
Telephone: (845) 788-3900, FAX: (212) 481-7800, Web Site: www.everydaymedia.com
Pres: Lisa Martens

FAMILY CIRCLE MAGAZINE INC
Div. of Meredith Corp.
125 Park Ave
New York, NY 10017
Telephone: (212) 557-6600, Web Site: www.familycircle.com
Publr: James Carr
Assoc Publr: Noreen Rafferty

FIRST CYBER SERVICES
13624 Montclair Dr
Omaha, NE 68144-2438
Telephone: (402) 330-3222, (888) 977-3222, FAX: (402) 330-3444, E-Mail: cat@1csinc.com, Web Site: www.firstcyberserv.com
Pres: Andy Fitzmorris

FIRST MARKETING CO
3300 Gateway Dr
Pompano Beach, FL 33069
Telephone: (954) 979-0700, FAX: (954) 971-4707, Web Site: www.first-marketing.com
Pres & CEO: Ronald Drenning

FORTENT
80 SW 8th St (Suite 2300)
Miami, FL 33130-3031
Telephone: (305) 530-0500, (800) 232-3652, FAX: (305) 530-9434, Web Site: www.fortent.com

Gen Mgr: Kathleen Richardson
Primary Market Served: Business & Consumer

FOX ASSOCIATES INC
116 W Kinzie St
Chicago, IL 60654-4655
Telephone: (312) 644-3888, FAX: (312) 644-8718, Web Site: www.foxrep.com
Pres: Marlys Fox

GLM COMMUNICATIONS
242 W 27th St (Suite 1B)
New York, NY 10001-5926
Telephone: (212) 929-1300, FAX: (212) 929-9574, Web Site: www.glmcommunications.com
Pres: Gerald L. Massa

DAVID GELLER ASSOCIATES
1071 Ave of the Americas
New York, NY 10018-3704
Telephone: (212) 455-0100, FAX: (212) 455-0164
Pres: Milton Shapiro

THE DMA GOOGLE
76 Ninth Ave
New York, NY 10011
Telephone: (212) 565-0000, FAX: (212) 565-0001, Web Site: www.google.com
Dir Global Acquisition Mktg: Arjan Dijk
Primary Market Served: Business

GUIDANCE ASSOCIATES
Subs. of Guidance Associates
31 Pine View Rd
Mount Kisco, NY 10549
Telephone: (914) 666-4100, (800) 431-1242, FAX: (914) 666-5319, E-Mail: willg1961@gmail.com, Web Site: www.guidanceassociates.com
Pres: Will Goodman
Conducts Business: U.S., Canada, Singapore, Hong Kong, Europe
Employees: 100
Primary Market Served: Business
Catalog available online
Direct online sales
Founded: 1971

Publisher of audio-visual material & internet software for the educational marketplace.

THE DMA H & H GRAPHICS
854 N Prince St
Lancaster, PA 17603-2752
Telephone: (717) 393-3941, Web Site: www.hhgraphicsgroup.com
Primary Market Served: Consumer

THE DMA HALOGEN RESPONSE MEDIA
1675 Broadway
New York, NY 10019-5820
Telephone: (212) 468-4000, Web Site: www.halogenresponse.com
SVP: Jason Lim

THE DMA HARLAND CLARKE MARKETING SERVICES
2939 Miller Rd
Decatur, GA 30035-4038
Telephone: (866) 609-8609, Web Site: www.harlandclarke.com
Admin Asst Mktg: Gloriane Littlefield
Primary Market Served: Consumer

THE HARTFORD COURANT
285 Broad St
Hartford, CT 06115-2510
Telephone: (860) 241-6200, FAX: (860) 241-3865, Web Site: www.courant.com
Publr: Steve Carver
Mktg Specialist: Pashea Wojcik

HEARST DIRECT RESPONSE ADVERTISING SALES
Div. of Hearst Corp
300 W 57th St
New York, NY 10019-5239
Telephone: (212) 649-2920, Web Site: www.hearst.com
VP & Dir: Mary S. Hayes

THE DMA THE HOUSTON CHRONICLE
801 Texas Ave (Suite 300)
Houston, TX 77002-2996
Telephone: (713) 362-7171, Web Site: www.houstonchronicle.com
Exec Dir: Katherine English
Primary Market Served: Business & Consumer

IMC - MULTI MEDIA MARKETING
Div. of IMC Inc
930 Fox Pavilion
Jenkintown, PA 19046
Telephone: (215) 887-5700 X107, FAX: (215) 887-7076, E-Mail: berylwolk@aol.com, Web Site: berylsworld.com
Chmn Bd: Beryl Wolk

THE DMA INTERMEDIA OUTDOORS INC
512 Fashion Ave Rm 1100
New York, NY 10018-4618
Telephone: (212) 852-6600
VP Consumer Mktg: Peter Watt
Primary Market Served: Business & Consumer

INTERNATIONAL GAMCO INC
9335 N 48th St
Omaha, NE 68152
Telephone: (402) 571-2449, (800) 524-2626, FAX: (402) 571-7941, E-Mail: mark.stevens@intlgamco.com, Web Site: www.intlgamco.com
VP, Mktg: Mark Stevens

JB DOLLAR STRETCHER MAGAZINE
3105 Farnham Rd
Richfield, OH 44286
Telephone: (330) 659-3590, (800) 673-2531, FAX: (330) 659-6741, Web Site: www.jbdollar.com
Pres: Robert J. Minchak Jr
Asst to Pres: Pat Berganti

MICHELE JAWORSKI
65 Forest Ave
Ramsey, NJ 07446-2706
Telephone: (201) 825-6932
Principal: Michele Jaworski
Primary Market Served: Business & Consumer

KARABAN LABINER ASSOCIATES
225 W 36th St (Suite 1202)
New York, NY 10018
Telephone: (212) 840-0660, FAX: (212) 944-1884, E-Mail: gkaraban@klapublishing.com, Web Site: www.klapublishing.com
Pres: Glenn Karaban

LOS ANGELES TIMES
202 W First St
Los Angeles, CA 90012-4105
Telephone: (213) 237-5000, (800) 528-4637, FAX: (213) 237-7679, E-Mail: rob.barrett@latimes.com, Web Site: www.latimes.com
VP: Rob Barrett

MACHALEK COMMUNICATIONS
12550 W Frontage Rd (Suite 220)
Burnsville, MN 55337
Telephone: (952) 736-8000, (800) 846-5520, FAX: (886) 490-8834, E-Mail: publisher@machalek.com, Web Site: www.machalek.com
CEO: Jon Machalek

MADISON DIRECT MARKETING LTD
60 Long Ridge Rd (Suite 306)
Stamford, CT 06902-1841
Telephone: (203) 653-3200, FAX: (203) 316-0518, Web Site: www.madisondm.com

Pres: Chris Hulse

THE DMA MAIN STREET DIRECT
575 Lexington Ave Fl 4
New York, NY 10022-6146
Telephone: (212) 779-3000, FAX: (212) 779-3061, E-Mail: jkern@mainstreetdirect.com, Web Site: www.mainstreetdirect.com
Mng Dir: Dan Kern

THE MARKETPLACE GROUP INC
9 Jaybarry Ln
Norwood, MA 02062-1925
Telephone: (781) 762-6600, FAX: (781) 762-1300
Pres: Andrew C. Nimmo

MARVEL ENTERTAINMENT INC
135 W 50th St Fl 4
New York, NY 10020-1201
Telephone: (212) 576-4000, FAX: (847) 579-1277, Web Site: www.marvel.com
CEO: Alan Fine

MEDIA DYNAMICS LLC
12 Choctaw Ln
Greenwich, CT 06831-3203
Telephone: (203) 531-6600, FAX: (203) 531-6661, E-Mail: bjann@mediadynamx.com, Web Site: www.Media-Dynamics.com
CEO: Bill Jann

MEDIA HORIZONS MANAGEMENT LLC
40 Richards Ave
Norwalk, CT 06854
Telephone: (203) 857-0770, FAX: (203) 857-0296, E-Mail: info@mediahorizons.com, Web Site: www.mediahorizons.com
VP: Walter Chistoni
VP, Acct Mngmt: Liz Russell

Alternative media program management.

MEDIA PEOPLE INC
122 E 42nd St (Suite 725)
New York, NY 10168-0601
Telephone: (212) 779-7172, FAX: (212) 779-7248, Web Site: www.mediapeople.com
Pres: Greg Pepe
Chmn: Ed Kabakow

THE DMA MEDIA RESOURCE GROUP INC
100 S Bedford Rd (Suite 320)
Mount Kisco, NY 10549-3444

Telephone: (914) 471-4448, FAX: (914) 244-4458, Web Site: www.mrginc.com
Pres: Thomas Marianacci

MEDIA SPACE SOLUTIONS
101 Merritt 7 Corporate Park (3rd fl)
Norwalk, CT 06851
Telephone: (203) 849-8855, (888) 672-2100, FAX: (203) 849-5946, E-Mail: nsb@mindspring.com, Web Site: www.mediaspacesolutions.com
Chmn: Peter M. Anderson

METROPOLITAN NEWSPAPER ADVERTISING SERVICES INC
8 W 38th St (fl 4)
New York, NY 10018-0154
Telephone: (212) 689-8200, FAX: (212) 532-1710, E-Mail: getinfo@metrosn.com, Web Site: www.metrosn.com
Pres & COO: Michael Baratoff

THE DMA MILITARY DIRECT MARKETING INC
1 Bushwick Rd
Poughkeepsie, NY 12603-3839
Telephone: (845) 454-7900, FAX: (845) 454-7987
CEO: John Bradbury
Mgr, Sls Research: Lori J. Nutting

MILLER DIRECT INC
1741 Gold Hill Rd (Suite 102)
Fort Mill, SC 29708-8240
Telephone: (803) 548-6900, FAX: (803) 548-8701
Pres: Steve Miller

THE MISSOULIAN
Div. of Lee Enterprises
PO Box 8029
Missoula, MT 59807
Telephone: (406) 523-5334, FAX: (406) 523-5221, Web Site: www.missoulian.com
Publr: Stacy Mueller
Editor: Sherry Devlin
Sls Mgr: Jim McGowan
List Mgr: Jackie Maunder
Mktg Mgr: Stephanie Bull
Employees: 160
Primary Market Served: Business & Consumer
Catalog available online
Direct online sales
Advertising/Marketing Budget Related to Direct Marketing: 0-25%
Founded: 1873

Newspaper covering five counties.

MONEY MAILER LLC
12131 Western Ave
Garden Grove, CA 92841
Telephone: (714) 889-1590, Web Site:
www.moneymailer.net
VP Natl Acct: Don Hubert

**MORRIS COMMUNICATIONS
CORP**
725 Broad St, PO Box 936
Augusta, GA 30903-0936
Telephone: (706) 724-0851, FAX:
(706) 722-0011, Web Site: www.
morris.com
Pres: William S. Morris IV

**THE
DMA MULTICHANNEL
MERCHANT MAGAZINE**
a subs. of Penton Media
11 River Bend Dr S
Stamford, CT 06907-0242
Telephone: (203) 358-4386, FAX:
(203) 358-5823, E-Mail: melissa.
dowling@penton.com, Web Site:
www.multichannelmerchant.com
Mng Editor: Melissa Dowling

THE NH BROADCASTER
Div of The Sun
491 Dutton St (Suite 1)
Lowell, MA 01854-4292
Telephone: (978) 458-7100, Web Site:
www.nhbroadcaster.com
Pres & Publr: Mark O'Neil
Chmn Bd: Kendall Wallace
CFO: John Habbee

**NEW CUSTOMER
ACQUISITION**
Div. of Jon Jay Corp
620 Franquette St
Medford, OR 97501-7832
Telephone: (541) 779-9999, FAX:
(541) 779-1935, E-Mail: bobk@
postage-exempt.com
Pres: Bob Karl

**THE
DMA NEW YORK DAILY NEWS**
125 Theodore Conrad Dr
Jersey City, NJ 07305-4615
Telephone: (212) 210-1844, Web Site:
www.nydailynews.com
Mktg Database Administrator: Irina
Ratner

**NEWS AMERICA
MARKETING**
1185 Ave of the Americas (fl 27)
New York, NY 10036-2603
Telephone: (212) 852-8000, (800) 462-
0852, FAX: (212) 575-5845, Web
Site: www.newsamerica.com
Chmn & CEO: K. Rupert Murdoch

NEWS & RECORD
Div. of Landmark Communications
200 E Market St
Greensboro, NC 27401
Telephone: (336) 373-7000, (800) 553-
6880
Mgr: Jeff Newman

NEWSPAPERS FIRST
501 Westport Ave (Suite 73)
Norwalk, CT 06851-4411
Telephone: (212) 692-7100, FAX:
(212) 286-9004, E-Mail: adunstan@
newspapersfirst.com, Web Site:
www.newspapersfirst.com
Pres & CEO: Jay T. Zitz

NOVUS MEDIA INC
2 Carlson Pkwy (Suite 400)
Plymouth, MN 55447-4470
Telephone: (612) 758-8600, Web Site:
www.npmnetwork.com
VP Bus Devel: Patrick Soli

**ON-LINE TECHNOLOGIES
INC**
605 US Route 1 (Suite 3)
Scarborough, ME 04074-9617
Telephone: (207) 396-5172, (207) 396-
5101, Web Site: www.on-
linetechnologies.com
Primary Market Served: Business

PAPILLION TIMES GROUP
Subs. of Omaha World Herald
604 Fort Crook Rd N
Bellevue, NE 68005-4557
Telephone: (402) 339-3331, (877) 476-
4237, FAX: (402) 537-2997, E-Mail:
advertising@papilliontimes.com,
Web Site: www.papilliontimes.com
Publr: Shon Barenklau

**THE
DMA PARADE PUBLICATIONS**
711 Third Ave
New York, NY 10017-4014
Telephone: (212) 450-7000, FAX:
(212) 450-7284, Web Site: www.
parade.com
VP, Direct Response Adv: Marie
Tassini

**THE PHILADELPHIA
INQUIRER & DAILY NEWS**
Div. of Knight-Ridder Inc
400 N Broad St, Box 8263
Philadelphia, PA 19101
Telephone: (215) 854-2000, FAX:
(215) 854-4788, Web Site: www.
phil.com/inquirer
Sr VP, Adv: Todd Brownrout

THE PRESS & STANDARD
Div. of Walterboro Newspaper
1025 Bells Hwy
Walterboro, SC 29488
Telephone: (843) 549-2586, Web Site:
colletontoday.com
Gen Mgr: Anne Padgett

PRIMEDIA INC
3585 Engineering Dr (Suite 100)
Norcross, GA 30092
Telephone: (678) 421-3000, (800) 216-
1423, Web Site: www.primedia.com
Chmn: Dean Nelson
Pres & CEO: Charles Stubbs
Sr VP & CFO: Kim Payne
Sr VP, Gen Counsel & Sec: Keith
Belknap
Dir of Commun: Nichole Bigley
Conducts Business: U.S., Brazil
Employees: 1,000
Primary Market Served: Business &
Consumer
Catalog available online
Founded: 1975
Gross sales or billing: $73,400,000

Publisher of free print and online consumer guides such as, apartment guide,
new home guide and rentals.com.

PUBLISHER'S MEDIA
Div. of Hoelscher Marketing Group
1145 N Second St
El Cajon, CA 92021-5024
Telephone: (619) 588-2155, FAX:
(619) 588-9103, E-Mail: rvhmedia@
aol.com
Pres: Russ von Hoelscher

**RR DONNELLEY RESPONSE
MARKETING SERVICES**
3075 Highland Pkwy Ste 400
Downers Grove, IL 60515-5560
Telephone: (800) 722-9001, FAX:
(630) 322-6270, Web Site: www.rms.
rrd.com
Sr VP, Sls: Mark Gaier

RR Donnelley Response Marketing
Services offers the most comprehensive
single-source direct mail and marketing
solutions. Services include: Direct
Marketing Strategy, CRM and Database Marketing, Literature Management, List Processing, Creative Design,
Direct Mail Print and Production,
Postal Logistics and Project
Management. We combine quality
commercial and web printing with
powerful imaging, for highly personalized, feature rich direct mail that delivers Outstanding Financial Results.

RSVP PUBLICATIONS
6730 W Linebaugh Ave (Suite 201)
Tampa, FL 33625-4914
Telephone: (813) 960-7787, Web Site:
  www.MailToTheAffluent.com
Co-CEO: Lawrence Golden
Primary Market Served: Business

REILLY COMMUNICATIONS GROUP
3030 W Salt Creek Ln Ste 201
Arlington Heights, IL 60005-5002
Telephone: (847) 882-6336, FAX:
  (847) 519-0166, E-Mail: info@
  rcgpubs.com, Web Site: new.
  reillycomm.com
Pres: John Reilly

ROBERTS & BUCHANAN INC
513 S Travis St
Concordia, MO 64020-7329
Telephone: (660) 463-2192, E-Mail:
  kmroberts@centurytel.net
Pres: Margaret Rose Roberts

SALES BUILDING SYSTEMS
Div. of Contract Marketing Inc
9325 Progress Pkwy
Mentor, OH 44060
Telephone: (800) 435-7576, FAX:
  (440) 639-9190, E-Mail: sales@
  sbsteam.com, Web Site: www.
  sbsteam.com
Pres & CEO: Patricia White
Mktg Coord: MaryAnn Shetler

SANCOA INTERNATIONAL
92 Ark Rd
Lumberton, NJ 08048-4103
Telephone: (856) 273-0700, FAX:
  (856) 273-2710, E-Mail: sancoa@
  sancoa.com
Pres & CEO: Joseph Saski
Pur Mgr: Kevin Austin

THE ALLEN SCHLUGER CO INC
Strategic Direct Response Three Dimensional Packaging
21 W 68th St
New York, NY 10023
Telephone: (212) 873-8577, FAX:
  (212) 873-0452
Pres: Allen Schluger

SCOTT'S DIRECTORIES
Div. of Business Information Group
1450 Don Mills Rd
Don Mills, ON, Canada M3B 2X7
Telephone: (416) 442-2010, (800) 408-
  9431, FAX: (416) 442-2078, E-Mail:
  sales@scottsinfo.com, Web Site:
  www.scottsinfo.com
Grp Mgr Mktg: Jennifer Hunter

SENIOR PUBLISHERS MEDIA GROUP
Div. of Motivate Inc
4141 Jutland Dr (Suite 300
San Diego, CA 92117-7316
Telephone: (858) 272-9023, (800) 727-
  3646, FAX: (858) 272-7275, E-Mail:
  marcia@spmg.com, Web Site: www.
  spmg.com
Pres & Natl Sls Mgr: Marcia A.
  Hansen

IRIS SHOKOFF ASSOCIATES
845 3rd Ave Fl 6
New York, NY 10022-6630
Telephone: (212) 295-9191, FAX:
  (212) 293-3779
Pres: Iris Shokoff
Media Planner: Nadia Kaneva

SOLAR COMMUNICATIONS
400 S County Farm Rd (Suite 330)
Wheaton, IL 60187-4547
Telephone: (630) 983-1400, (800) 890-
  6906, FAX: (630) 983-6125, Web
  Site: www.solarcommunications.com
CEO & Pres: Frank Hudetz

SPECIALIZED MARKETING INC
162 Prospect Hill Rd Ste 203
Brewster, NY 10509-2374
Telephone: (845) 278-6100, FAX:
  (845) 278-6150, Web Site: www.
  specialized-mktg.com
Pres: Bob Wood

THE DMA SPECTRA PRODUCTS LLC
1364 Reynolds Rd
Johnson City, NY 13790-4837
Telephone: (607) 770-1985, FAX:
  (607) 798-7771, E-Mail: info@
  spectraproducts.com, Web Site:
  www.spectraproducts.com
Pres: Anthony Aquino

THE DMA STANTON DIRECT MARKETING INC
315 W Water St
Elmira, NY 14901-2914
Telephone: (607) 734-1665, (877) 734-
  1665, FAX: (607) 734-3708, Web
  Site: www.stantondirect.com
Pres: Aloysius F. Stanton

SUPERMEDIA LLC
2200 W Airfield Dr
Dallas, TX 75261
Telephone: (972) 453-7797
Mgr Mktg Res: David Bernstein

TV GUIDE MAGAZINE
Div. of News America Publications Inc
11 W 42nd St (fl 17)
New York, NY 10036-8002
Telephone: (212) 852-7500, (800) 866-
  1400, Web Site: www.tvguide.com
Gen Mgr: Christy Tanner
VP Natl Digital Sls: Ian Wallin
VP East Coast Digital Sls: Keith
  Bockus
Dir Mktg: Carrie Hoffman

TARADEL LLC
4325 Cox Rd
Glen Allen, VA 23060-3359
Telephone: (804) 364-8444, Web Site:
  www.taradel.com
Pres: James Fitzgerald

THE DMA TARGET MARKETING GROUP
1500 Spring Garden St (Suite 1200)
Philadelphia, PA 19130-4069
Telephone: (215) 238-5300, Web Site:
  www.targetonline.com
Group Pres & Publishing Dir: Peggy
  Hatch
Primary Market Served: Consumer

TELAMERICA MEDIA INC
1701 John F Kennedy Blvd (Suite
  2510)
Philadelphia, PA 19103-2876
Telephone: (215) 568-7066, FAX:
  (215) 564-5388, Web Site: www.
  telamericamedia.com
VP, Direct Response Media Sls: Ivan
  Silverman

TODAY'S CHRISTIAN WOMAN
Div. of Christianity Today International
465 Gundersen Dr
Carol Stream, IL 60188
Telephone: (630) 260-6200, FAX:
  (630) 260-0114, E-Mail: tcwedit@
  christianitytoday.com, Web Site:
  www.todayschristianwoman.net
Editor in Chief & CEO: Harold B.
  Smith

THE DMA TOWN MONEY SAVER
6 E Main St
Lucas, OH 44843-9701
Telephone: (419) 892-1913, Web Site:
  www.townmoneysaver.com
Pres: William Zirzow
Primary Market Served: Business

TRANS CONTINENTAL INC
One Place Ville Marie (Suite 3315)
Montreal, PQ, Canada H3B 3N2

Telephone: (514) 954-4000, FAX: (514) 954-4016, Web Site: www. transcontinental-gtc.com
Pres: Remi Marcoux

USA WEEKEND
Div. of Gannett Co
535 Madison Ave
New York, NY 10022
Telephone: (800) 487-4956, FAX: (703) 854-2122, Web Site: www. usaweekend.com
Pres & Publr: Charles Gabrielson
Mktg Asst: Christa Hylton

THE DMA VALASSIS
1 Targeting Ctr
Windsor, CT 06095-2639
Telephone: (860) 285-6100, FAX: (203) 845-5338, Web Site: www. valassis.com
VP: Mike Kowalczyk
Sr VP Govt Rels: Vincent Guiliano

VALPAK DIRECT MARKETING SYSTEMS INC
8605 Largo Lakes Dr
Largo, FL 33773-4912
Telephone: (727) 399-3000, Web Site: www.valpak.com
Channel Mktg Mgr: Keith Brickell

VEGETARIAN TIMES
Div. of Active Interest Media
300 N Continental Blvd (Suite 650)
El Segundo, CA 90245
Telephone: (310) 356-4100, FAX: (310) 356-4110, Web Site: www. vegetariantimes.com
Group Publr Healthy Living Group: Bill Harper

VESTCOM INTERNATIONAL INC
7304 Kanis Rd
Little Rock, AR 72204
Telephone: (501) 663-0100, (800) 264-0965, FAX: (501) 663-2451, Web Site: www.vestcom.com
VP, Sls: Darrel Risberg

VOCATIONAL BIOGRAPHIES INC
dba Project Special Education; vocbiosonline.com
414 S Sixth St, PO Box 31
Sauk Centre, MN 56378-0031
Telephone: (320) 352-6516, (800) 255-0752, FAX: (320) 352-5546, E-Mail: careers@vocbios.com, Web Site: www.vocbio.com
Pres: Toby P. Behnen
*Gen Mgr: Roxann Kleinschmidt
Conducts Business: U.S., Canada

Employees: 4
Primary Market Served: Business & Consumer
Direct online sales
Advertising/Marketing Budget Related to Direct Marketing: 76-100%

Career success stories of real people in easy-to-read four page career profiles showing how real people deal with career upheavals in real life inspiring you to discover your dream career. As well as content rich special education programs using minimum prep time, no adapting non-threatening, easy to teach.

WE DELIVER AMERICA INC
68 Irving Ave.
Englewood Cliffs, NJ 07632
Telephone: (201) 307-8888, FAX: (201) 307-1200, E-Mail: info@we-deliver-america.com, Web Site: www.we-deliver-america.com
CEO: Larry Tucker
Opers Mgr: Barb Keller
Customer Svc Mgr: Kim D'Aurizio
CFO: Herb Lefkowitz
CMO: Neil Boggart
Employees: 20
Primary Market Served: Business
Founded: 1994
Gross sales or billing: $10,000,000

Insert Media: Consumer Co-ops, Packages, Statements, ride-a-longs, hand-outs, take-ones. Take-Ones: College, post office, malls, retail, bowling alleys, fast food, hotels, motels, RV parks, tourist centers. New Mover Media: Co-op & lists 400,000 to 525,000 weekly pre movers. Sampling: Families, teens, fifty plus. Shopping malls: Sampling, take-ones, handouts. National, regional, local.

WINFIELD MARKETING CORP
5724 N Palaski Rd
Chicago, IL 60646
Telephone: (773) 743-8784, FAX: (440) 764-4871
Pres: Audrey Garrett

WORKING MOTHER
Part of The Parenting.com, Div. of Bonnier Corp
2 Park Ave (fl 10)
New York, NY 10016
Telephone: (212) 221-9595, FAX: (212) 219-7448, Web Site: www. workingmother.com
Pres: Carol Evans
Group Publr: Joan Sheridan Labarge
Editor in Chief: Suzanne Riss

YP TALK
1101 Cedar Crest Dr
Pittsburg, KS 66762-6631
Telephone: (620) 308-6434, E-Mail: info@yptalk.com, Web Site: www. yptalk.com
Publr: Kenneth Clark
Conducts Business: U.S.
Primary Market Served: Business
Direct online sales
Advertising/Marketing Budget Related to Direct Marketing: 76-100%
Founded: 2004

Industry enewsletter, recruiting & consulting.

THE DMA ZCARD NORTH AMERICA
39 Broadway (fl 32)
New York, NY 10006-3047
Telephone: (212) 797-3450, Web Site: www.zcard.com
Fin Mgr: Denise Eagle

ZINIO SYSTEMS INC
114 Sansome St (fl 4)
San Francisco, CA 94104
Telephone: (415) 494-2700, FAX: (415) 494-2701, Web Site: www. zinio.com
Global Exec VP & CMO: Jeanniey Mullen Founder

Arizona

iCrossing, 15169 N Scottsdale Rd, Scottsdale, 85254-2429

Whitehat Inc, 4665 S Ash Ave Ste G-10, Tempe, 85282-6765

Arkansas

Windstream Communications Inc, 4001 N Rodney Parham Rd Ste 202, Little Rock, 72212-2497

California

Actividentity Corp, 6623 Dumbarton Cir, Fremont, 94555-3614

Bunchball, 2200 Bridge Pkwy (Suite 201), Redwood City, 94065-1187

Catalyst Computer Services Inc, 2271 Prosser Ave, Los Angeles, 90064-2321

Caudill & Associates Inc, 1334 E Chapman Ave, Orange, 92866-2219

CCI Digital, 2921 W Alameda Ave, Burbank, 91505

ClickMail Marketing Inc, 155 Bovet Rd (Suite 310), San Mateo, 94401-3135

ClickSpark LLC, 116 New Montgomery St (Suite 233), San Francisco, 94105-3640

Coremetrics, 1840 Gateway Sr (Suite 320), San Mateo, 94404-4303

Creative Campaigns Inc, 22287 Mulholland Hwy (Suite 410), Calabasas, 91302

Dial 800 LLC, 911 Pico Blvd (Suite 1200), Los Angeles, 90035

Direct Response Marketing Inc, 39205 Leopard St (#E), Palm Desert, 92211-1149

The Disney ABC Cable Network Group, 3800 W Alameda Ave (Suite B), Burbank, 91505-4303

E! Entertainment Television, 5750 Wilshire Blvd, Los Angeles, 90036

Empire Burbank Studios, 1845 Empire Ave, Burbank, 91504

Erlich Communications, 8339 Via Panacea, San Diego, 92129

Far West Media Services, 4140 Norse Way, Long Beach, 90808-1531

Future Thunder Productions, 6506 Colbath Ave, Van Nuys, 91401-1503

Golden Millennium Productions Inc, 622 E Villa St (Suite B), Pasadena, 91101-1120

Goodmail Systems Inc, 100 Pine St (Suite 475), San Francisco, 94111-5120

Goolara LLC, 2150 Mariner Square Dr (Suite 100), Alameda, 94501-1085

Alan Gordon Enterprises, 5625 Melrose Ave, Hollywood, 90038

The Gourley Group, 1621 W 25th St (Suite 204), San Pedro, 90732

Guthy-Renker Corp, 41550 Eclectic St, Palm Desert, 92260-1967

Healthcare Communications Group, 909 N Sepulveda Blvd (Suite 550), El Segundo, 90245

Image Direct, 12021 Wilshire Blvd (#449), Los Angeles, 90025-1206

Infomercial Marketing Report, 9528 Dalegrove Dr, Beverly Hills, 90210-1711

Infomercial Solutions Inc, PO Box 1803, Agoura Hills, 91376

Intagio Trading Network, PO Box 190515, San Francisco, 94119-0515

Intium Services LLC, PO Box 4626, Diamond Bar, 91765-0626

Tylie Jones & Associates, 58 E Santa Anita Ave, Burbank, 91502

Kappa Studios, 3619 W Magnolia Blvd, Burbank, 91505

King World CBS, 2401 Colorado Ave (Suite 110), Santa Monica, 90404

KICU-TV, 2102 Commerce Dr, San Jose, 95131

KTVU Retail Services, Two Jack London Sq, Oakland, 94607-3727

KWHY-TV Channel 22, 3400 W Olive Ave (Suite 600), Burbank, 91505

Kragen & Co, 14039 Aubrey Rd, Beverly Hills, 90210

Lieberman Productions, 455 Ninth St, San Francisco, 94103-4410

Local.com, 7555 Irvine Center Dr, Irvine, 92618-2930

Lyris Inc, 6401 Hollis St Ste 125, Emeryville, 94608-1462

Marketing Resources Network Inc, 578 Washington Blvd (Suite 803), Marina Del Rey, 90292

Marketing Solutions Group Inc, 480 St John St (Suite 150), Pleasanton, 94566-6682

Marketing Works Inc, PO Box 93293, Los Angeles, 90093-0293

Media Funding Corp, 29201 Heather Cliff Rd, Malibu, 90265

Mercury Media, 520 Broadway (Suite 400), Santa Monica, 90401

Muscle Dynamics Fitness Network Inc, 14133 Freeway Dr, Santa Fe Springs, 90670-5813

NEC Group Inc, 2504 N Ontario St, Burbank, 91504

NTN Communications Inc, 5966 La Place Ct (Suite 100), Carlsbad, 92008-8895

Nor1, 440 N Wolfe Rd, Sunnyvale, 94085-3869

Online Print Solutions, 268 Bush St (#4045), San Francisco, 94104-3503

Onyx Productions Inc, 2355 Westwood Blvd (#401), Los Angeles, 90064-2109

PM Productions, 5882 W Bowcroft St (#2), Los Angeles, 90016-4907

ReputationDefender, 2688 Middlefield Rd Ste C, Redwood City, 94063-3483

Results Producers, 130 S Beaudry Ave (Suite D), Los Angeles, 90012

Script to Screen Inc, 200 N Tustin Ave (Suite 200), Santa Ana, 92705

Smart Inventions Inc, 6421 E Alondra Blvd, Paramount, 90723

Smarthome, 16542 Millikan Ave, Irvine, 92606

Strongmail Systems Inc, 1300 Island Dr (Suite 200), Redwood City, 94065-5171

Studio M Productions Unlimited, 4032 Wilshire Blvd (#403), Los Angeles, 90010-3405

Submit Express, 315 W Verdugo Ave (Suite 101), Burbank, 91502-2484

Tactara, 50 S Hope St (Suite 2825), Los Angeles, 90071-2683

Unified Precious Metals Inc, 9010 Eton Ave, Canoga Park, 91304-1616

Vidi Emi Inc, 2450 Washington Ave (Suite 220), San Leandro, 94577-5996

Voice Message Broadcasting Corp, 8105 Irvine Center Dr (Suite 900), Irvine, 92618

Walker/Fitzgibbon TV & Film Productions, 2399 Mount Olympus Dr, Los Angeles, 90046-1660

Jordan Whitney Inc, 360 E First St (#593), Tustin, 92780

YELLOWPAGES.COM/ Ingenio, 201 Mission St (Suite 200), San Francisco, 94105-1832

Colorado

Intermap Technologies, 8310 S Valley Hwy (Suite 400), Englewood, 80112-5809

Location3 Media, 1515 Arapahoe St Ste 2-400, Denver, 80202-2128

Net-Results, 691 Corporate Cir, Golden, 80401-5622

Product Information Network, 9697 Mineral Ave, PO Box 3309, Englewood, 80112

Connecticut

CRN International Inc, One Circular Ave, Hamden, 06514-4002

Color Film Media Group, 45 Keeler Ave, Norwalk, 06854-2307

eWay Direct, 200 Pewuot Ave (fl 1), Southport, 06890-1371

Liquid Focus Direct LLC, 1335 Wood Ave Ste 1, Bridgeport, 06604-1442

National Broadcast Finance Corp, 27 Harrison St, Box 3167, New Haven, 06515

Robert Rosenheim Associates, Five Gay St, PO Box 308, Sharon, 06069-2000

Webloyalty.com, 101 Merritt 7 (Suite 7), Norwalk, 06851-1060

Delaware

Direct Response Media, PO Box 1680, Wilmington, 19899-1680

District of Columbia

American Life TV Network, 1133 19th St NW (Suite 800), Washington, 20036-3655

BET Services, 1900 "W" Pl NE, Washington, 20018

Florida

Bamboo Cricket, 224 Datura St (Suite 508), West Palm Beach, 33401

Cendyn, 1515 N Federal Hwy Ste 419, Boca Raton, 33432-1954

CityTwist, 111 SE 1st St, Boca Raton, 33432-4812

eTargetMedia.com Inc, 6810 Lyons Technology Pkwy, Coconut Creek, 33073-4322

Health International Corp, 11880 28th St N Ste 100, Saint Petersburg, 33716-1824

Home Shopping Network, One HSN Dr, Saint Petersburg, 33729

Ion Media Networks Inc, 601 Clearwater Park Rd, West Palm Beach, 33401

Marcus Productions Inc, 3107 Stirling Rd Ste 204, Fort Lauderdale, 33312-8500

MoreVisibility, 925 S Federal Hwy (Suite 750), Boca Raton, 33432-6147

Publishers Circulation Fulfillment Inc, 3351-B McLemore Dr, Pensacola, 32514-7074

Sales Magic Inc, 2107 Corporate Dr, Boynton Beach, 33426-6645

ValCom Inc, 2113 A Gulf Blvd, Indian Rocks Beach, 33785-3806

Georgia

allconnect, 4 Concourse Pkwy (Suite 410), Atlanta, 30328-6199

ListK, 1200 Abernathy Rd (Suite 1700), NorthPark Ctr, Atlanta, 30328-5671

Response Media, 3155 Medlock Bridge Rd, Norcross, 30071-1423

SilverPop, 200 Galleria Pkwy (Suite 750), Atlanta, 30339-5945

ThePort Network, 5500 N Interstate Pkwy (#550), Atlanta, 30328

TNT (Turner Network Television LP), 1050 Techwood Dr NW, Atlanta, 30318

Turner Broadcasting System Inc, 190 Marietta St NW Bsmt, Atlanta, 30303-2714

Illinois

ClickStream, 14628 John Humphrey Dr, Orland Park, 60462-2642

Dotomi Inc, 168 N Clinton (Suite 400), Chicago, 60661-1419

International Newspaper Network, 1510 47th Ave, Moline, 61265

Kelly, Scott & Madison Inc, 35 E Wacker Dr (Suite 1400), Chicago, 60601

Northern Lights Direct, 150 N Michigan Ave (Suite 800), Chicago, 60601-7585

SMY Media Inc, 211 E Ontario (Suite 900), Chicago, 60611

US Cellular, 8410 W Bryn Mawr Ave (Suite 700), Chicago, 60631-3463

Indiana

DEFENDER Direct Inc, 3750 Priority Way S Dr (Suite 200), Indianapolis, 46240-3815

Delivra, 9365 Counselors Row Ste 210, Indianapolis, 46240-6418

ExactTarget Inc, 20 N Meridian St (Suite 200), Indianapolis, 46204-3023

Iowa

David Chaladoff Media, PO Box 498, Fairfield, 52556-0009

Kansas

Visible Results USA Inc, 12603 Hemlock St, Overland Park, 66213

Kentucky

Impact Communications Inc, 414 Baxter Ave (Suite 215), Louisville, 40204-1195

Louisiana

Dukky, 1200 W Causeway Approach (Suite 24), Mandeville, 70471

Maine

Groff DRTV, PO Box 8673, Portland, 04104

Maryland

Americatel Corp, 7361 Calhoun Pl Ste 520, Derwood, 20855-2774

Blue Sky Factory, 40 E Cross St Ste 2, Baltimore, 21230-4558

E-Centives Inc, 4350 East West Hwy Ste 1050, Bethesda, 20814-4481

JDSU, 1 Milestone Center Ct, Germantown, 20876-7106

The Learning Channel, 1 Discovery Pl, Silver Spring, 20910

Message Systems, 7070 Samuel Morse Dr (Suite 150), Columbia, 21046-3427

STARTEC, 7361 Calhoun Pl (Suite 520), Rockville, 20855-2774

Massachusetts

@utoRevenue, 1 Fenn St Ste 3, Pittsfield, 01201-6279

Constant Contact, 1601 Trapelo Rd (Suite 329), Waltham, 02451-7357

E-Dialog Inc, 65 Network Dr (fl 4), Burlington, 01830-2756

Fox Media Services, 5 Rockland Terrace, Natick, 01760-5858

IMN, 200 5th Ave, Waltham, 02451-8779

September Productions, 15 Madaket Rd, Nantucket, 02554-2618

SmartSource Corp, 3 New England Executive Park Ste 115, Burlington, 01803-5006

SoundBite Communications, 22 Crosby Dr Ste 200, Bedford, 01730-1429

Minnesota

Electrosonic, 10320 Bren Rd E, Minnetonka, 55343-9048

Jump Technologies Inc, 2640 Eagan Woods Dr (Suite 240), Eagan, 55121-1466

TopRank Online Marketing, PO Box 397, Mound, 55364-0397

ValueVision Media Inc, 6740 Shady Oak Rd, Eden Prairie, 55344-3433

Missouri

Adknowledge, 4600 Madison Ave (Suite 1000), Kansas City, 64112-3042

Avatar Studios, 2675 Scott Ave, Saint Louis, 63103

Schwartz & Associates Creative, 212 S Bemiston (Suite 3), Clayton, 63105-1904

SEOinhouse, 5214 Cedarfield Dr, Saint Charles, 63304-8014

Nevada

Infomercial Sales Inc, 5921 Palmyra Ave, Las Vegas, 89146

Ben Kalb Productions, 5905 S Decatur Blvd Ste 1, Las Vegas, 89118-3087

Price Target Media, 108 Kentuck Ln, Carson City, 89706-0712

Rapid Response Marketing, 7500 W Lake Mead Blvd (#9-463), Las Vegas, 89128-0297

New Hampshire

Level 5 Communications Inc, 1283 Main St, Dublin, 03444

New Hampshire Public Television, 268 Mast Rd, Durham, 03824-4601

New Jersey

CNBC-Consumer & Business Channel, 900 Sylvan Ave, Englewood Cliffs, 07632

Concepts TV Productions Inc, 328 W Main St, Boonton, 07005-1148

ESA - A Sandy Alexander Co, 200 Entin Rd, Clifton, 07014-1423

Nassau Broadcasting Co, 619 Alexander Rd (fl 3), Princeton, 08540

Virgin Mobile USA LLC, 10 Independence Blvd Ste 200, Warren, 07059-2730

Vonage, PO Box 310, Holmdel, 07733-0310

New York

ACTV Inc, 233 Park Ave S (fl 10), New York, 10003

The Artists Co, 79 Mercer St (#5), New York, 10012-4430

Canoe Ventures LLC, 1251 Avenue of the Americas (39th Floor), New York, 10020

Cinema World Studios, 220 Dupont St, Greenpoint, 11222

The Collegebound Network, 1200 South Ave (Suite 202), Staten Island, 10314-3424

Comedy Central, 513 W 54th St, New York, 10019-5014

Conversa Marketing LLC, 17 Huntington Rd, Garden City, 11530-3014

Crescent Beach Enterprises LLC, 3900 Veterans Memorial Hwy (Suite 141), Bohemia, 11717

Crossroads Films, 166 5th Ave Fl 4, New York, 10010-5958

Discovery Communications, 850 Third Ave, New York, 10022

Fujisankei Communications International Inc, 150 E 52nd St (34th fl), New York, 10022-6017

In Demand, 345 Hudson St (fl 17), New York, 10014-4520

Initiative Media Worldwide, 1 Dag Hammarskjold Plz Fl 3, New York, 10017-2209

Katz Television Direct Response, 125 W 55th St, New York, 10019-5366

KickApps Corp, 26 W 17th St Fl 2, New York, 10011-5719

King World Productions Inc, 1700 Broadway Fl 33, New York, 10019-5905

LinkShare Corp, 215 Park Ave S Fl 9, New York, 10003-1622

Lions Gate Entertainment, 75 Rockefeller Plaza (#1600), New York, 10019-6904

Media Consultants Inc, 29-15 Bell Blvd, Bayside, 1360-2543

Mediacom Communications Corp, 100 Crystal Run Rd, Middletown, 10914

MTV Networks, 1515 Broadway, New York, 10036

National Cable Communications, 405 Lexington Ave (fl 6), New York, 10174

Petry Television Inc, One Penn Plaza (55th fl), New York, 10119

Rocket Direct Marketing Inc, 156 E 37th St (Suite 5A), New York, 10016

Saatchi & Saatchi, 375 Hudson St, New York, 10014-3660

Sci-Fi Channel, 30 Rockefeller Plaza, New York, 10112

SAS Group, 220 White Plains Rd Ste 100, Tarrytown, 10591-5823

TowerData, 379 Park Ave S (fl 5), New York, 10016-8811

TNS Media Intelligence, 11 Madison Ave (fl 12), New York, 10010

USA Network, 30 Rockefeller Plz Ste 270E, New York, 10112-0299

Video Ordnance Inc, 611 Broadway (Suite 307), New York, 10012-2654

Visible World, 460 W 34th St (fl 14), New York, 10001-2350

The Weather Channel, 205 E 42nd St (Fl 19), New York, 10017

WLNY-TV, 270 S Service Rd (Suite 55), Melville, 11747-2399

Yahoo Inc, 1065 Ave of the Americas (fl 9), New York, 10018-0786

Zeta Interactive, 99 Park Ave Fl 23, New York, 10016-1601

North Carolina

Emisare, 620 Elm St (Suite 332), Greensboro, 27406-1467

iContact, 5221 Paramount Pkwy (Suite 200), Morrisville, 27560-5423

INSP - The Inspirational Network, 9700 Southern Pine Blvd, Charlotte, 28273

Mass Transmit, 8701 Mallard Creed Rd (fl 3), Charlotte, 28262-6007

Sunbelt Media Service, PO Box 3116, Chapel Hill, 27515-3116

WCPE-FM, PO Box 828, Wake Forest, 27588-0828

Ohio

AG Interactive, 1 American Rd, Cleveland, 44144-2301

admail.net/List Media, 251 W Garfield Rd (Suite 284), Aurora, 44202-8856

Consolidated Technologies Group LLC, 1614 E 40th St, Cleveland, 44103-2319

Rootblast International, PO Box 20109, 2207 Kimball Rd SE, Canton, 44701

Oklahoma

TV Guide, 7140 S Lewis Ave, Tulsa, 74136-5401

Oregon

Group Mojo, 800 NW Sixth Ave (Suite 313), Portland, 97209-3700

SuccessWorks Search Marketing Inc, 2509 Snowberry Ridge Ct, West Linn, 97068-5190

Pennsylvania

Comcast Cable Communications, 1500 Market St, Philadelphia, 19102-2100

Harmelin Direct, 525 Righters Ferry Rd, Bala Cynwyd, 19004

Listrak, 529 Main St, Lititz, 17543-2121

Patriot Communications LLC, 1275 Drummers Ln (Suite 104), Wayne, 19087-1571

QDirect, 1200 Wilson Dr, Studio Park, West Chester, 19380-4262

QVC Inc, 1200 Wilson Dr, West Chester, 19380

Rajant Corp, 400 E King St (Suite 1), Malvern, 19355

Voice Systems Engineering Inc, 900 Wheeler Way (Suite A), Langhorne, 19047-1706

Tennessee

Shop At Home LLC, 10001 Kingston Pike (Suite 57), Knoxville, 37922-6909

Texas

AT&T Inc, 175 E Houston St, San Antonio, 78205-2233

501 Post, 501 N IH-35, Austin, 78702

Koeppel Direct, 16200 Dallas Pkwy (Suite 270), Dallas, 75248-6875

LinkWorth, 417 Oakbend (Suite C1), Lewisville, 75067-2361

Skylist, 701 Brazos St (Suite 800), Austin, 78701

Video Plus Inc, 200 Swisher Rd, Lake Dallas, 75065-2324

Utah

Bloosky Interactive, PO Box 1941, Orem, 84059-1941

Prosper Inc, 5252 N Edgewood Dr (Suite 150), Provo, 84604-5853

Steve Scott Group LLC, 7090 Union Park Ctr (Suite 500), Midvale, 84047-6059

Vermont

800 Response, PO Box 1049, Burlington, 05402-1049

Resolution Inc, 327 Holly Ct Ste 20, Williston, 05495-4440

Virginia

America Online Inc, 22270 Pacific Blvd, Dulles, 20166-6924

Ingenix, 12081 Sunrise Valley Dr (Suite 400), Reston, 20191

Network Solutions LLC, 13681 Sunrise Valley Dr, Herndon, 20171

Proxicom, 1902 Campus Commons (Suite 600), Reston, 20191-1586

Washington

Innovyx Inc, 1000 2nd Ave Ste 900, Seattle, 98104-1076

Wisconsin

Cannella Response Television Inc, 848 Liberty Dr, Burlington, 53105-9384

Nesco American Harvest, 1700 Monroe St, PO Box 237, Two Rivers, 54241

CANADA
Ontario

Movie Central, 25 Dockside Dr, Corus Quay, Toronto, M5A 0B5

The Production Partners, 2 Duncan Mill Rd (Suite 202), Toronto, M3B 1Z4

Protus, 2379 Holly Ln (Suite 210), Ottawa, K1V 7P2

ACTV INC
233 Park Ave S (fl 10)
New York, NY 10003
Telephone: (415) 962-5000

AG INTERACTIVE
1 American Rd
Cleveland, OH 44144-2301
Telephone: (216) 889-5000, Web Site:
www.aginteractive.com
Dir Online Mktg: Tarik Dekkar
Primary Market Served: Business &
Consumer

ACTIVIDENTITY CORP
6623 Dumbarton Cir
Fremont, CA 94555-3614
Telephone: (510) 574-0100, (800) 529-
9499, FAX: (510) 574-0101, Web
Site: www.actividentity.com
CEO: Thomas John

THE DMA ADKNOWLEDGE
4600 Madison Ave (Suite 1000)
Kansas City, MO 64112-3042
Telephone: (816) 931-1771, Web Site:
www.adknowledge.com
VP Mktg: Tim Kidder

THE DMA ADMAIL.NET/LIST MEDIA
Div. of List Media Inc
251 W Garfield Rd (Suite 284)
Aurora, OH 44202-8856
Telephone: (330) 995-0864, FAX:
(330) 995-0873, E-Mail: sales@
admail.net, Web Site: www.admail.
net
Pres: Robert Hicks
Conducts Business: U.S., Canada
Employees: 5
Primary Market Served: Business &
Consumer
Advertising/Marketing Budget Related
to Direct Marketing: 76-100%
Founded: 1991
Gross sales or billing: $1,000,000

ALLCONNECT
4 Concourse Pkwy (Suite 410)
Atlanta, GA 30328-6199
Telephone: (404) 260-2449, Web Site:
www.allconnect.com
Exec VP Mktg & eCommerce: Scott
Klinger

AMERICA ONLINE INC
22270 Pacific Blvd
Dulles, VA 20166-6924

Telephone: (703) 265-1000
Chmn Bd & CEO: Jonathon Miller
Exec VP Access Mktg: Kimberly Par-
toll

AMERICAN LIFE TV NETWORK
1133 19th St NW (Suite 800)
Washington, DC 20036-3655
Telephone: (202) 289-6633, FAX:
(202) 289-6632, Web Site: www.
goodtv.com
Pres: Squire Rushnell

THE DMA AMERICATEL CORP
7361 Calhoun Pl Ste 520
Derwood, MD 20855-2774
Telephone: (301) 610-4354, Web Site:
www.startec.com
Mktg Dir: Anna Porteus

THE ARTISTS CO
79 Mercer St (#5)
New York, NY 10012-4430
Telephone: (212) 679-7199, FAX:
(212) 741-1519, E-Mail: nyc@
artists-ar.com
Pres: Roberto Cecchini

AT&T INC
175 E Houston St
San Antonio, TX 78205-2233
Telephone: (210) 821-4105, FAX:
(210) 351-2071, Web Site: www.
bellsouth.com
VP Consumer Mktg: Joey Schultz
Primary Market Served: Business &
Consumer

@UTOREVENUE
1 Fenn St Ste 3
Pittsfield, MA 01201-6279
Telephone: (413) 243-4800, Web Site:
www.autorevenue.com
Dir Opers: Gaye Weinberger

AVATAR STUDIOS
2675 Scott Ave
Saint Louis, MO 63103
Telephone: (314) 533-2242, FAX:
(314) 533-3349, Web Site: www.
avatar-studios.com
Pres: Bill Faris

BET SERVICES
1900 "W" Pl NE
Washington, DC 20018

Telephone: (202) 608-2000, (800) 626-
9911, FAX: (202) 635-3761, Web
Site: www.bet.com
Exec VP: Kelli Lawson

BAMBOO CRICKET
224 Datura St (Suite 508)
West Palm Beach, FL 33401
Telephone: (561) 768-7968, (800) 260-
8050, FAX: (561) 653-3990, Web
Site: www.bamboocricket.com
CEO: Paul Westhorpe
Pres: Barbara Westhorpe
VP Client Svcs: Susan O'Neil
Founded: 2006

BLOOSKY INTERACTIVE
PO Box 1941
Orem, UT 84059-1941
Telephone: (888) 203-2433, FAX:
(888) 465-7166, Web Site: www.
bloosky.com
Mktg Dir: Blair Jackson
Primary Market Served: Business &
Consumer
Founded: 2007

BLUE SKY FACTORY
40 E Cross St Ste 2
Baltimore, MD 21230-4558
Telephone: (410) 230-0061, Web Site:
www.blueskyfactory.com
Mktg Mgr: Amy Garland

BUNCHBALL
2200 Bridge Pkwy (Suite 201)
Redwood City, CA 94065-1187
Telephone: (408) 985-2034, Web Site:
www.bunchball.com
CEO: Peter Daboll
VP Mktg: Mike Earhart

CCI DIGITAL
2921 W Alameda Ave
Burbank, CA 91505
Telephone: (818) 562-6300, FAX:
(818) 562-8222, Web Site: www.
ccidigital.com
Pres: Rick Morris

CNBC-CONSUMER & BUSINESS CHANNEL
CNBC Viewer Services
900 Sylvan Ave
Englewood Cliffs, NJ 07632

Telephone: (201) 735-2622, FAX: (201) 735-3200, Web Site: www. cnbc.com
Pres: Mark Hoffman

CRN INTERNATIONAL INC
One Circular Ave
Hamden, CT 06514-4002
Telephone: (203) 288-2002, FAX: (203) 281-3291, E-Mail: info@ crnradio.com, Web Site: www. crnradio.com
Pres: Barry Berman
Mktg Coord: Barbara Johnson

CANNELLA RESPONSE TELEVISION INC
848 Liberty Dr
Burlington, WI 53105-9384
Telephone: (262) 763-4810, FAX: (262) 763-2875, E-Mail: frank@ tvinfomercial.com, Web Site: www. tvinfomercial.com
Founder & CEO: Frank Cannella

THE DMA CANOE VENTURES LLC
1251 Avenue of the Americas (39th Floor)
New York, NY 10020
Telephone: (212) 364-3600, FAX: (212) 364 3601, Web Site: www. canoe-ventures.com
Chief Privacy Officer: Louis Mastria

CATALYST COMPUTER SERVICES INC
2271 Prosser Ave
Los Angeles, CA 90064-2321
Telephone: (310) 441-4300, (800) 659-2267, FAX: (310) 441-4332, E-Mail: sales@catalystsoftware.com, Web Site: www.catalystsoftware.com
Pres: Richard Shaw

CAUDILL & ASSOCIATES INC
1334 E Chapman Ave
Orange, CA 92866-2219
Telephone: (714) 210-2585, FAX: (714) 210-2595, E-Mail: bobc@ caudill4production.com, Web Site: www.caudill4production.com
Pres: Robert S. Caudill

CENDYN
1515 N Federal Hwy Ste 419
Boca Raton, FL 33432-1954
Telephone: (561) 750-3173, Web Site: www.cendyn.com
CEO: Charles Deyo
Primary Market Served: Business

DAVID CHALADOFF MEDIA
PO Box 498
Fairfield, IA 52556-0009
Telephone: (641) 472-6700, FAX: (641) 472-7736, E-Mail: david@ dcimediainc.com
Pres: David Chaladoff

CINEMA WORLD STUDIOS
220 Dupont St
Greenpoint, NY 11222
Telephone: (718) 389-9800, FAX: (718) 389-9897, E-Mail: cinemaworldfd@verizon.net, Web Site: www.cinemaworldstudios.com
Pres & CEO: Maurice Keshner

THE DMA CITYTWIST
111 SE 1st St
Boca Raton, FL 33432-4812
Telephone: (561) 989-8480, Web Site: www.citytwist.com
Founder: Lou Nobile

CLICKMAIL MARKETING INC
155 Bovet Rd (Suite 310)
San Mateo, CA 94401-3135
Telephone: (650) 653-8055, Web Site: www.clickmarketing.com
Mktg Mgr: Rebecca Dao

CLICKSPARK LLC
116 New Montgomery St (Suite 233)
San Francisco, CA 94105-3640
Telephone: (800) 878-5709, E-Mail: amy@clickspark.com, Web Site: www.clickspark.com
CEO: Brian Einhaus
Opers Mgr: Amy Penrose

CLICKSTREAM
14628 John Humphrey Dr
Orland Park, IL 60462-2642
Telephone: (949) 439-2888, Web Site: www.clickstreamtv.com
Dir Sales: Keith Kubik

THE DMA THE COLLEGEBOUND NETWORK
1200 South Ave (Suite 202)
Staten Island, NY 10314-3424
Telephone: (718) 761-4800, Web Site: www.collegebound.net
VP: Carole Gervasi
Primary Market Served: Consumer

COLOR FILM MEDIA GROUP
45 Keeler Ave
Norwalk, CT 06854-2307

Telephone: (203) 202-2929, (800) 882-1120, FAX: (203) 702-5800, E-Mail: info@colorfilm.com, Web Site: www.colorfilm.com
Cust Svc Mgr: Dawn Palmer

THE DMA COMCAST CABLE COMMUNICATIONS
1500 Market St
Philadelphia, PA 19102-2100
Telephone: (215) 665-1700, Web Site: www.comcast.com
Sr Sales Coord: Melissa Kraft
Primary Market Served: Consumer

COMEDY CENTRAL
513 W 54th St
New York, NY 10019-5014
Telephone: (212) 767-8600, FAX: (212) 767-4284, Web Site: www. comedycentral.com
VP: Aileen Budow

CONCEPTS TV PRODUCTIONS INC
328 W Main St
Boonton, NJ 07005-1148
Telephone: (973) 331-1500, FAX: (973) 331-1550, E-Mail: collette@ conceptstv.com, Web Site: www. conceptstv.com
Pres: Collette Liantonio

THE DMA CONSOLIDATED TECHNOLOGIES GROUP LLC
1614 E 40th St
Cleveland, OH 44103-2319
Telephone: (216) 426-5328, Web Site: www.ctgadvisor.com
Primary Market Served: Consumer

CONSTANT CONTACT
1601 Trapelo Rd (Suite 329)
Waltham, MA 02451-7357
Telephone: (781) 472-8101, Web Site: www.constantcontact.com

CONVERSA MARKETING LLC
17 Huntington Rd
Garden City, NY 11530-3014
Telephone: (516) 209-3822
Founder & CEO: Michael Della Penna

COREMETRICS
1840 Gateway Sr (Suite 320)
San Mateo, CA 94404-4303
Telephone: (877) 721-2673, Web Site: www.coremetrics.com
Dir Mktg: Caroline Waterson

CREATIVE CAMPAIGNS INC
22287 Mulholland Hwy (Suite 410)
Calabasas, CA 91302
Telephone: (818) 340-2713, FAX:
(818) 337-2446, E-Mail: info@
creativecampaigns.com, Web Site:
www.creativecampaigns.com
Pres: Marcia Pellitteri

CRESCENT BEACH ENTERPRISES LLC
3900 Veterans Memorial Hwy (Suite 141)
Bohemia, NY 11717
Telephone: (631) 588-6600, FAX:
(631) 588-7077, E-Mail: rjd@cbnet.
com, Web Site: www.cbprod.com
Pres: Roy Dahl

CROSSROADS FILMS
166 5th Ave Fl 4
New York, NY 10010-5958
Telephone: (212) 647-1300, FAX:
(212) 647-9090, Web Site: www.
crossroadfilms.com
Pres: Daniel Lingau

THE DMA DEFENDER DIRECT INC
3750 Priority Way S Dr (Suite 200)
Indianapolis, IN 46240-3815
Telephone: (800) 860-0303, Web Site:
www.defenderdirect.com
Pres: David Lindsey

THE DMA DELIVRA
9365 Counselors Row Ste 210
Indianapolis, IN 46240-6418
Telephone: (317) 915-9400, Web Site:
www.delivra.com
Dir Deliverability: Kris Dougherty
Mktg Coord: Lavon Temple

THE DMA DIAL 800 LLC
911 Pico Blvd (Suite 1200)
Los Angeles, CA 90035
Telephone: (310) 273-9023, (800) 564-
8685, Web Site: www.dial800.com
CEO: Scott Richards
COO: James Diorio
Fulfillment: Chris Lowe
Opers: Eddie Treizman

DIRECT RESPONSE MARKETING INC
39205 Leopard St (#E)
Palm Desert, CA 92211-1149
Telephone: (760) 360-5900, FAX:
(760) 360-7266
Pres: Elaine Roth

DIRECT RESPONSE MEDIA
PO Box 1680
Wilmington, DE 19899-1680

Telephone: (610) 995-0200, (800) 898-
3761, FAX: (610) 995-0300, E-Mail:
info@directresponsemedia.com, Web
Site: www.directresponsemedia.com
CEO: Maria B. Eden

DISCOVERY COMMUNICATIONS
850 Third Ave
New York, NY 10022
Telephone: (212) 548-5555, Web Site:
www.discovery.com

THE DISNEY ABC CABLE NETWORK GROUP
3800 W Alameda Ave (Suite B)
Burbank, CA 91505-4303
Telephone: (818) 569-7500, FAX:
(818) 848-6925, Web Site: www.
disneyabctv.com
Co-Chair Disney Media Networks &
Pres Disney ABC Media: Anne
Sweeney

DOTOMI INC
168 N Clinton (Suite 400)
Chicago, IL 60661-1419
Telephone: (312) 588-3600, Web Site:
www.dotomi.com
Prod Mgr: David Scrim
Primary Market Served: Business

THE DMA DUKKY
1200 W Causeway Approach (Suite 24)
Mandeville, LA 70471
Telephone: (985) 626-5155, E-Mail:
info@dukky.com, Web Site: www.
dukky.com
Primary Market Served: Business &
Consumer

E-CENTIVES INC
4350 East West Hwy Ste 1050
Bethesda, MD 20814-4481
Telephone: (240) 333-6100, (877) 323-
6848, FAX: (240) 333-6250, E-Mail:
sales@e-centives.com, Web Site:
www.e-centives.com
Chm, CEO & Co-founder: Kamran
Amjadi
Pres, Chief Mktg Officer: Dadi Akhavan

E-DIALOG INC
65 Network Dr (fl 4)
Burlington, MA 01830-2756
Telephone: (888) 256-7687, Web Site:
www.e-dialog.com
Dir Mktg: Nancy Darish

E! ENTERTAINMENT TELEVISION
5750 Wilshire Blvd
Los Angeles, CA 90036
Telephone: (323) 937-3408, FAX:
(323) 954-2660, Web Site: www.
eonline.com
Editor in Chief: Linda Friendman

THE DMA ESA - A SANDY ALEXANDER CO
200 Entin Rd
Clifton, NJ 07014-1423
Telephone: (973) 470-8100, Web Site:
www.tbccolor.com
VP Bus Devel: Jack Emery
Primary Market Served: Business

800 RESPONSE
PO Box 1049
Burlington, VT 05402-1049
Telephone: (802) 860-0378, (800)
NEW-SALES, FAX: (800) NEW-
ORDER, E-Mail: sales@
800response.com, Web Site: www.
800response.com
VP Mktg & Corp Commun: Laura
Noonan
VP Sls: Kathy Rossner
PR Mgr: Jeanne Landau
VP Direct Sls & Customer Svc: Rick
Royer
Conducts Business: U.S.
Primary Market Served: Business
Catalog available online
Founded: 1989

Provides top quality vanity 800 numbers which boost ad response for regional advertisers.

ELECTROSONIC
10320 Bren Rd E
Minnetonka, MN 55343-9048
Telephone: (952) 931-7500, FAX:
(952) 938-9311, E-Mail:
information@electrosonic.com, Web
Site: www.electrosonic.com
Pres & CEO: Kyle Carpenter

EMISARE
620 Elm St (Suite 332)
Greensboro, NC 27406-1467
Telephone: (336) 378-0510, Web Site:
www.emisare.com
Pres: Scott Williams

EMPIRE BURBANK STUDIOS
1845 Empire Ave
Burbank, CA 91504
Telephone: (818) 840-1400, FAX:
(818) 567-1062
Mktg Dir: Todd Cintron

ERLICH COMMUNICATIONS
8339 Via Panacea
San Diego, CA 92129
Telephone: (858) 780-9595, FAX:
(858) 780-2922, E-Mail: gde@
erlcomm.com
Pres: Gary Erlich

ETARGETMEDIA.COM INC
6810 Lyons Technology Pkwy
Coconut Creek, FL 33073-4322
Telephone: (954) 480-8470, (888) 805-
3282, FAX: (954) 480-8489, E-Mail:
info@etargetmedia.com, Web Site:
www.etargetmedia.com
Sr VP: Harris Kreichman

EWAY DIRECT
200 Pewuot Ave (fl 1)
Southport, CT 06890-1371
Telephone: (888) 655-0464, Web Site:
www.ewaydirect.com
CEO: Neil Rosen

THE DMA EXACTTARGET INC
20 N Meridian St (Suite 200)
Indianapolis, IN 46204-3023
Telephone: (317) 423-3928, Web Site:
www.exacttarget.com
Dir E-Mktg & Education: Joel Book

FAR WEST MEDIA SERVICES
4140 Norse Way
Long Beach, CA 90808-1531
Telephone: (562) 496-3342, FAX:
(562) 496-4329, Web Site: www.
farwestmedia.com
Pres: Robert A. Ranaldi

501 POST
501 N IH-35
Austin, TX 78702
Telephone: (512) 476-3876, FAX:
(512) 477-3912, E-Mail: godwyer@
501studios.com, Web Site: www.
501post.com
Exec Producer: George O'Dwyer

FOX MEDIA SERVICES
Subs. of Fox Advertising & Marketing
5 Rockland Terrace
Natick, MA 01760-5858
Telephone: (508) 655-5665, (800) 369-
2327, FAX: (419) 715-5628, E-Mail:
joe@foxmediaservices.com, Web
Site: www.foxmediaservices.com
Pres: Joseph M. Fox

**FUJISANKEI
COMMUNICATIONS
INTERNATIONAL INC**
150 E 52nd St (34th fl)
New York, NY 10022-6017

Telephone: (212) 753-8100, FAX:
(212) 702-0420, Web Site: www.
fujisankei.com
Pres: Takashi Hoga

**FUTURE THUNDER
PRODUCTIONS**
6506 Colbath Ave
Van Nuys, CA 91401-1503
Telephone: (818) 986-9494, FAX:
(818) 986-6644, E-Mail: jim@
futurethunder.com, Web Site: www.
futurethunder.com
Pres: Jim Caldwell

**GOLDEN MILLENNIUM
PRODUCTIONS INC**
622 E Villa St (Suite B)
Pasadena, CA 91101-1120
Telephone: (818) 500-1099, E-Mail:
info@goldenproductions.com, Web
Site: www.goldenproductions.com
Sr Exec: Robert Hernandez

GOODMAIL SYSTEMS INC
100 Pine St (Suite 475)
San Francisco, CA 94111-5120
Telephone: (877) 650-6505, Web Site:
www.goodmailsystems.com
CEO: Daniel Dreymann

GOOLARA LLC
2150 Mariner Square Dr (Suite 100)
Alameda, CA 94501-1085
Telephone: (510) 522-800, Web Site:
www.goolara.com
Pres: Philip Thorne

**ALAN GORDON
ENTERPRISES**
5625 Melrose Ave
Hollywood, CA 90038
Telephone: (323) 466-3561, FAX:
(323) 871-2193, E-Mail: info@
alangordon.com, Web Site: www.
alangordon.com
Pres: Grant Loucks
VP: Don Sahlein

THE GOURLEY GROUP
1621 W 25th St (Suite 204)
San Pedro, CA 90732
Telephone: (310) 519-1324, (888) 656-
1324, FAX: (310) 519-9323, E-Mail:
issuestoday@yahoo.com, Web Site:
www.issuestodayradio.com
Pres: Bob Gourley

GROFF DRTV
PO Box 8673
Portland, ME 04104

Telephone: (207) 415-1374, FAX:
(207) 771-5320, E-Mail: regfilm@
gmail.com, Web Site: www.
groffvideo.com
Pres: Reginald Groff
Exec Producer: Robert Barnes
Mktg Dir: Richard Boghosian
Primary Market Served: Business
Founded: 1982

Direct response television and radio
production.

THE DMA GROUP MOJO
800 NW Sixth Ave (Suite 313)
Portland, OR 97209-3700
Telephone: (503) 493-2242, FAX:
(503) 493-2246, E-Mail: sam@
mojops.com, Web Site: www.
groupmojo.com
Pres: Sam Rath
Principal: Roger Thompson
Conducts Business: U.S., Canada
Primary Market Served: Consumer
Advertising/Marketing Budget Related
to Direct Marketing: 51-75%
Founded: 2003

Long form direct response, short form
DR, long form content for distribution.
Web and tradeshow distribution pre-
sentation sales.

THE DMA GUTHY-RENKER CORP
41550 Eclectic St
Palm Desert, CA 92260-1967
Telephone: (760) 773-9022, (800) 274-
4910, FAX: (760) 773-9016, Web
Site: www.guthy-renker.com
CEO: Greg Renker
VP, Mktg Matls Procurement: Lisa
Riofrio

HARMELIN DIRECT
Div. of Harmelin Media
525 Righters Ferry Rd
Bala Cynwyd, PA 19004
Telephone: (610) 668-7900, FAX:
(610) 668-9257, E-Mail: president@
harmelin.com, Web Site: www.
harmelin.com
CEO: Joanne Harmelin

**HEALTH INTERNATIONAL
CORP**
11880 28th St N Ste 100
Saint Petersburg, FL 33716-1824
Telephone: (800) 780-6744, FAX:
(727) 595-6456, Web Site: www.
tonylittle.com
Owner & Pres: Tony Little

**HEALTHCARE
COMMUNICATIONS GROUP**
909 N Sepulveda Blvd (Suite 550)
El Segundo, CA 90245

Telephone: (310) 606-5703, (800) 504-0933, FAX: (310) 606-5705, E-Mail: fkilpatrick@hcg.com, Web Site: www.hcg.com
Pres: Frank S. Kilpatrick

HOME SHOPPING NETWORK
One HSN Dr
Saint Petersburg, FL 33729
Telephone: (727) 872-1000, FAX: (727) 571-1803, Web Site: www.hsn.com
PR: Brad Bohnert

THE DMA IMN
200 5th Ave
Waltham, MA 02451-8779
Telephone: (781) 890-4700, Web Site: www.imninc.com

THE DMA ICONTACT
5221 Paramount Pkwy (Suite 200)
Morrisville, NC 27560-5423
Telephone: (866) 803-9462, Web Site: www.icontact.com
Trade Show Mgr: Christina Jaromin

THE DMA ICROSSING
15169 N Scottsdale Rd
Scottsdale, AZ 85254-2429
Telephone: (480) 505-5800, FAX: (480) 505-5801
Assoc Pub Rels Mgr: Kristen Deye

IMAGE DIRECT
12021 Wilshire Blvd (#449)
Los Angeles, CA 90025-1206
Telephone: (310) 312-4884
EVP: Shirley Gross
Primary Market Served: Business

IMPACT COMMUNICATIONS INC
414 Baxter Ave (Suite 215)
Louisville, KY 40204-1195
Telephone: (502) 587-9084, (800) 556-9084, FAX: (502) 589-6538, E-Mail: info@impactvideo.com, Web Site: www.321impact.net
Pres: Watson Courtenay

IN DEMAND
345 Hudson St (fl 17)
New York, NY 10014-4520
Telephone: (646) 486-1010, FAX: (646) 486-0855, Web Site: www.indemand.com
VP, Sls & Mktg: Gavin Harvey

INFOMERCIAL MARKETING REPORT
9528 Dalegrove Dr
Beverly Hills, CA 90210-1711

Telephone: (310) 826-8810, FAX: (310) 826-0097, E-Mail: clarkkent@aol.com
Pres: Steven Dworman

INFOMERCIAL SALES INC
5921 Palmyra Ave
Las Vegas, NV 89146
Telephone: (702) 253-0433, FAX: (702) 871-0759, Web Site: www.infomercialsalesinc.com
Pres & Owner: Jill L. Smith

INFOMERCIAL SOLUTIONS INC
PO Box 1803
Agoura Hills, CA 91376
Telephone: (818) 879-1140, FAX: (818) 879-1148, E-Mail: david@infomercialsolutions.com, Web Site: www.infomercialsolutions.com
Pres: David Schwartz

INGENIX
Div. of Applied Healthcare Informatics
12081 Sunrise Valley Dr (Suite 400)
Reston, VA 20191
Telephone: (571) 521-7661, (800) 765-6713, FAX: (571) 521-7237, E-Mail: inform@ingenix.com, Web Site: www.ingenix.com
Sr Dir Mkt Intelligence: Angela Bailey
CEO: Andy Slavitt
COO: Lee Valenta
CFO: Paul Emerson
Chief Admin Officer: Michael Michaux
Exec VP: Theodore Chien
Conducts Business: U.S.
Employees: 150
Primary Market Served: Business
Catalog available online
Direct online sales
Advertising/Marketing Budget Related to Direct Marketing: 76-100%

Publish coding, billing & managed care information resources for hospitals, managed care organizations, physician's offices & other health care providers.

INITIATIVE MEDIA WORLDWIDE
1 Dag Hammarskjold Plz Fl 3
New York, NY 10017-2209
Telephone: (212) 605-7000, FAX: (212) 605-7200, Web Site: www.initiativemedia.com
Sr VP, Client Svcs: Ed Lehmen

THE DMA INNOVYX INC
1000 2nd Ave Ste 900
Seattle, WA 98104-1076
Telephone: (212) 817-6900, Web Site: www.innovyx.com

VP Bus Devel: Lisa Klieman

INSP - THE INSPIRATIONAL NETWORK
9700 Southern Pine Blvd
Charlotte, NC 28273
Telephone: (704) 525-9800, FAX: (704) 525-9899, E-Mail: info@insp.com, Web Site: www.insp.com
Pres: David Cerullo

INTAGIO TRADING NETWORK
PO Box 190515
San Francisco, CA 94119-0515
Telephone: (415) 247-9500, FAX: (415) 543-0375, Web Site: www.intagio.com
CEO: Phillip Letts
Dir, Mktg: Stacy O'Connell

INTERMAP TECHNOLOGIES
8310 S Valley Hwy (Suite 400)
Englewood, CO 80112-5809
Telephone: (303) 708-0955, FAX: (303) 708-0952, Web Site: www.intermap.com
Pres & CEO: Todd Oseth
Sr VP Global Sls: David Cunningham
Sr VP & CFO: Richard Mohr
VP Worldwide Mktg: Kevin Burns
VP Engrng: J. Keith Tennant
Pres Dir PT ExsaMap Asia: Nigel D. Jackson
Primary Market Served: Business

INTERNATIONAL NEWSPAPER NETWORK
1510 47th Ave
Moline, IL 61265
Telephone: (309) 743-0800, (800) 293-9576, FAX: (309) 743-0830, E-Mail: info@TownNews.com, Web Site: www.townnews.com
CEO & Gen Mgr: Marc Wilson

INTIUM SERVICES LLC
PO Box 4626
Diamond Bar, CA 91765-0626
Telephone: (909) 743-6182, Web Site: www.intiumservices.com
Pres: Ryan Champion

ION MEDIA NETWORKS INC
601 Clearwater Park Rd
West Palm Beach, FL 33401
Telephone: (561) 659-4122, (800) 646-7296, FAX: (561) 659-4252, Web Site: www.ionmedia.tv
Mktg: Robert LeRoach
Employees: 520
Gross sales or billing: $228,000,000

THE DMA JDSU
1 Milestone Center Ct
Germantown, MD 20876-7106
Telephone: (301) 353-1550, Web Site:
www.jdsu.com
Direct Mktg Mgr: Angela Davis

TYLIE JONES & ASSOCIATES
58 E Santa Anita Ave
Burbank, CA 91502
Telephone: (800) 922-0662, E-Mail:
tylie@tylie.com, Web Site: www.
tylie.com
CEO: Tylie Jones

JUMP TECHNOLOGIES INC
2640 Eagan Woods Dr (Suite 240)
Eagan, MN 55121-1466
Telephone: (651) 287-6000, Web Site:
www.jumptech.com
Primary Market Served: Consumer

KICU-TV
Div. of KICU Inc
2102 Commerce Dr
San Jose, CA 95131
Telephone: (408) 953-3636, FAX:
(408) 953-3610, Web Site: www.
ktvu.com
Pres & Gen Mgr: Thomas Raponi

KTVU RETAIL SERVICES
Div. of KTVU/Cox Communications
Two Jack London Sq
Oakland, CA 94607-3727
Telephone: (510) 874-0228, FAX:
(510) 874-0229, Web Site: www.
ktvu.com
VP & Gen Mgr: Tim McVay

KWHY-TV CHANNEL 22
3400 W Olive Ave (Suite 600)
Burbank, CA 91505
Telephone: (213) 344-3700, E-Mail:
info@canal22.tv, Web Site: www.
kwhy.com
VP & Gen Mgr: Raul Rodriguez
Dir Mktg & Commun: Jesse Nunez

BEN KALB PRODUCTIONS
5905 S Decatur Blvd Ste 1
Las Vegas, NV 89118-3087
Telephone: (702) 871-8787, FAX:
(702) 597-0741, E-Mail: benkalb@
benkalbproductions.com, Web Site:
www.benkalbproductions.com
Exec Producer: Ben Kalb

Infomercial production company

KAPPA STUDIOS
3619 W Magnolia Blvd
Burbank, CA 91505
Telephone: (818) 843-3400, FAX:
(818) 559-2418, E-Mail: info@
kappastudios.com, Web Site: www.
kappastudios.com
Pres: Paul Long

KATZ TELEVISION DIRECT RESPONSE
Div. of Katz Media Corp
125 W 55th St
New York, NY 10019-5366
Telephone: (212) 424-6124, FAX:
(212) 424-6130, E-Mail: chickie.
bucco@katz-media.com, Web Site:
www.katzdirect.com
VP & Direct Response Sls Dir:
Chickie Bucco

KELLY, SCOTT & MADISON INC
35 E Wacker Dr (Suite 1400)
Chicago, IL 60601
Telephone: (312) 977-0772, FAX:
(312) 977-0874, Web Site: www.
ksmmedia.com
Pres & Owner: Leonard Cohen

KICKAPPS CORP
26 W 17th St Fl 2
New York, NY 10011-5719
Telephone: (212) 730-4558, Web Site:
www.kickapps.com
Sr VP, Prod Mktg: Michael Sommers

KING WORLD CBS
Div. of Viacom
2401 Colorado Ave (Suite 110)
Santa Monica, CA 90404
Telephone: (310) 264-3300, Web Site:
www.kingworld.com

KING WORLD PRODUCTIONS INC
1700 Broadway Fl 33
New York, NY 10019-5905
Telephone: (212) 315-4000, Web Site:
www.kingworld.com
Chmn & CEO: Roger King

KOEPPEL DIRECT
16200 Dallas Pkwy (Suite 270)
Dallas, TX 75248-6875
Telephone: (972) 732-6110, FAX:
(972) 248-2759, E-Mail: pkoeppel@
koeppelinc.com, Web Site: www.
koeppeldirect.com
Pres: Peter Koeppel
Dir Acct Svcs: Christena Gardune
Sr Media Buyer: David Jacobs
Conducts Business: U.S.
Employees: 15
Primary Market Served: Business &
Consumer
Advertising/Marketing Budget Related

to Direct Marketing: 76-100%
Direct Marketing ad budget:
Magazines: 10%
TV/Radio: 90%
Founded: 1995
Gross sales or billing: $25,000,000

Direct response media-buying agency,
specializing in integrated direct response TV and online advertising campaigns, designed to maximize clients'
ROI from their marketing initiatives.

KRAGEN & CO
14039 Aubrey Rd
Beverly Hills, CA 90210
Telephone: (310) 854-4400, (877) 808-
0698, FAX: (310) 854-0238, E-Mail:
kenkragen@aol.com, Web Site:
www.partsamerica.com
Pres: Ken Kragen

THE LEARNING CHANNEL
Div. of Discovery Communications
1 Discovery Pl
Silver Spring, MD 20910
Telephone: (240) 662-2000, Web Site:
tlc.discovery.com
Pres, Discovery Communs: John Hen-
dricks

LEVEL 5 COMMUNICATIONS INC
dba Desktop Engineering Online
1283 Main St
Dublin, NH 03444
Telephone: (603) 563-1631, FAX:
(603) 563-8912, Web Site: www.
deskeng.com
Publr: Brian Vaillancourt
Exec Editor: Amy Rowell
Adv Coord: Carol Laughner
Primary Market Served: Business &
Consumer
Catalog available online
Direct online sales

LIEBERMAN PRODUCTIONS
455 Ninth St
San Francisco, CA 94103-4410
Telephone: (415) 955-0855, FAX:
(415) 955-0822
Pres: Lenny Lieberman

THE DMA LINKSHARE CORP
215 Park Ave S Fl 9
New York, NY 10003-1622
Telephone: (646) 654-6000, Web Site:
www.linkshare.com
CMO: Mark Kirschner

LINKWORTH
417 Oakbend (Suite C1)
Lewisville, TX 75067-2361

Telephone: (214) 440-3901, Web Site:
www.linkworth.com
Pres: Ron Wicker

LIONS GATE ENTERTAINMENT
75 Rockefeller Plaza (#1600)
New York, NY 10019-6904
Telephone: (212) 577-2400, FAX:
(212) 962-2872, Web Site: www.
liensgatefilms.com
CEO: John Feltheimer
Vice Chm: Michael Burns
Pres: Steve Beeks
Primary Market Served: Business
Founded: 2003

LIQUID FOCUS DIRECT LLC
1335 Wood Ave Ste 1
Bridgeport, CT 06604-1442
Telephone: (203) 635-4382, Web Site:
www.liquidfocus.com
CEO: Kenneth Osborn

LISTK
1200 Abernathy Rd (Suite 1700),
NorthPark Ctr
Atlanta, GA 30328-5671
Telephone: (800) 600-3389, FAX:
(800) 878-2489, Web Site: www.
listk.com
Pres: John Sabol
Conducts Business: U.S., Canada
Primary Market Served: Business
Founded: 2002

Online & email append services

LISTRAK
529 Main St
Lititz, PA 17543-2121
Telephone: (717) 627-4528, Web Site:
www.listrak.com
Pres & CEO: Ross Kramer

LOCAL.COM
7555 Irvine Center Dr
Irvine, CA 92618-2930
Telephone: (949) 784-0800, Web Site:
www.local.com
VP Mktg: Jennifer Black

THE DMA LOCATION3 MEDIA
1515 Arapahoe St Ste 2-400
Denver, CO 80202-2128
Telephone: (877) 462-9764, Web Site:
www.Location3.com
Pres: Andrew Beckman

LYRIS INC
6401 Hollis St Ste 125
Emeryville, CA 94608-1462

Telephone: (510) 844-1551, (800) 768-
2929, FAX: (510) 844-1598, E-Mail:
sales@lyris.com, Web Site: www.
lyris.com
Dir Commun: Eric Mott
Conducts Business: Worldwide
Employees: 40
Primary Market Served: Business
Catalog available online
Direct online sales
Advertising/Marketing Budget Related
to Direct Marketing: 0-25%
Founded: 1994
Gross sales or billing: $12,000,000

Develops e-mail marketing software
and hosts services for medium and
large sized businesses

MARCUS PRODUCTIONS INC
3107 Stirling Rd Ste 204
Fort Lauderdale, FL 33312-8500
Telephone: (954) 922-9166, E-Mail:
steve@marcusproductions.com, Web
Site: www.marcusproductions.com
Pres: Steven Marcus

MARKETING RESOURCES NETWORK INC
578 Washington Blvd (Suite 803)
Marina Del Rey, CA 90292
Telephone: (310) 459-2271, FAX:
(310) 459-2287
Pres: Richard Sutter

MARKETING SOLUTIONS GROUP INC
480 St John St (Suite 150)
Pleasanton, CA 94566-6682
Telephone: (510) 331-7625, E-Mail:
info@marketingsolutionsgroup.biz,
Web Site: www.
marketingsolutionsgroup.biz
Pres: Gary O. Bosley

MARKETING WORKS INC
PO Box 93293
Los Angeles, CA 90093-0293
Telephone: (323) 436-2000, FAX:
(213) 382-7538, E-Mail:
marketingwork@mediaone.net, Web
Site: www.mworks-inc.com
CEO: Charles Salmore

MASS TRANSMIT
8701 Mallard Creed Rd (fl 3)
Charlotte, NC 28262-6007
Telephone: (704) 248-8817, Web Site:
www.masstransmit.com
CEO: Adam Holden-Bache

MEDIA CONSULTANTS INC
29-15 Bell Blvd
Bayside, NY 1360-2543

Telephone: (718) 423-6300, FAX:
(718) 428-7482, E-Mail:
mediaconsults@aol.com
Pres: Jill Albert

MEDIA FUNDING CORP
29201 Heather Cliff Rd
Malibu, CA 90265
Telephone: (310) 457-4140, FAX:
(310) 774-1234, E-Mail: info@
mediafunding.com, Web Site:
mediafunding.com
Pres: Peter Bieler

MEDIACOM COMMUNICATIONS CORP
100 Crystal Run Rd
Middletown, NY 10914
Telephone: (845) 695-2600, FAX:
(845) 695-2699, Web Site: www.
mediacomcc.com
Chmn & CEO: Rocco B. Commisso

MERCURY MEDIA
520 Broadway (Suite 400)
Santa Monica, CA 90401
Telephone: (310) 451-2900, FAX:
(310) 451-0180, Web Site: www.
mercurymedia.com
CEO: John Cabrinha
Mgr: Edar Lee

THE DMA MESSAGE SYSTEMS
7070 Samuel Morse Dr (Suite 150)
Columbia, MD 21046-3427
Telephone: (410) 872-4910, (877) 887-
3031, FAX: (410) 872-4912, E-Mail:
information@messagesystems.com,
Web Site: www.messagesystems.com
VP Field Opers: Barry Abel
Dir Mktg: Erin Ickes
Conducts Business: U.S., Canada, Eu-
rope & Asia
Primary Market Served: Business
Advertising/Marketing Budget Related
to Direct Marketing: 26-50%
Founded: 1997

Ecelerity & the high performance
email software solution.

THE DMA MOREVISIBILITY
925 S Federal Hwy (Suite 750)
Boca Raton, FL 33432-6147
Telephone: (561) 620-9682, Web Site:
www.morevisibility.com
Pres: Andrew Wetzler

MOVIE CENTRAL
25 Dockside Dr, Corus Quay
Toronto, ON, Canada M5A 0B5
Telephone: (416) 479-6784, E-Mail:
info@moviecentral.ca, Web Site:
www.moviecentral.ca
Pres: Paul Robertson

VP Mktg: Jim Johnson

MTV NETWORKS
Subs. of Viacom Inc
1515 Broadway
New York, NY 10036
Telephone: (212) 258-8000, FAX:
(212) 258-8100, Web Site: www.mtv.
com
VP, Mktg: Pete Danielsen

**MUSCLE DYNAMICS
FITNESS NETWORK INC**
14133 Freeway Dr
Santa Fe Springs, CA 90670-5813
Telephone: (310) 323-9055, (800) 544-
2944, FAX: (310) 323-7608, E-Mail:
info@muscledynamics.com, Web
Site: www.maxicam.com
Pres: Brian Lewallen

NEC GROUP INC
2504 N Ontario St
Burbank, CA 91504
Telephone: (818) 909-9963, Web Site:
www.thehomeshow.com
Pres: Dan Greene

NTN COMMUNICATIONS INC
5966 La Place Ct (Suite 100)
Carlsbad, CA 92008-8895
Telephone: (760) 438-7400, (888)
PLAY-NTN, (888) 752-9686, FAX:
(760) 438-3505, Web Site: www.ntn.
com
Chmn: Barry Bergsman
CEO & Dir: Dario L. Santana

NASSAU BROADCASTING CO
Div. of Nassau Broadcasting Partners
LP
619 Alexander Rd (fl 3)
Princeton, NJ 08540
Telephone: (609) 419-0300, (800) 248-
WPST, FAX: (609) 915-9778,
E-Mail: lrios@wpst.com, Web Site:
www.wpst.com
VP & Gen Mgr: Gregg Stiansen

**NATIONAL BROADCAST
FINANCE CORP**
27 Harrison St, Box 3167
New Haven, CT 06515
Telephone: (203) 389-6000, FAX:
(203) 389-6020
Pres: David C. Cherhoniak

**NATIONAL CABLE
COMMUNICATIONS**
405 Lexington Ave (fl 6)
New York, NY 10174

Telephone: (212) 548-3300, FAX:
(212) 519-0099, Web Site: www.
spotcable.com
VP: Paul Widman

NESCO AMERICAN HARVEST
Div. of American Harvest
1700 Monroe St, PO Box 237
Two Rivers, WI 54241
Telephone: (920) 793-1368, (800) 288-
4545, FAX: (920) 794-3161, Web
Site: www.nesco.com
Pres: Wesley Drumm

NET-RESULTS
691 Corporate Cir
Golden, CO 80401-5622
Telephone: (303) 771-2552, Web Site:
www.net-results.com
Mktg Dir: Emily Long

THE
DMA **NETWORK SOLUTIONS LLC**
13681 Sunrise Valley Dr
Herndon, VA 20171
Telephone: (703) 668-4600, Web Site:
www.networksolutions.com
Sr Dir Legal & Bus Affairs: Statton
Hammock

**NEW HAMPSHIRE PUBLIC
TELEVISION**
268 Mast Rd
Durham, NH 03824-4601
Telephone: (603) 868-1100, E-Mail:
themailbox@nhptv.org, Web Site:
www.nhptv.org
Pres & CEO: Peter A. Frid
Chief Content Officer: Dawn DeAnge-
lis
Dir Corp Rels: Jeff Morris
Chief Devel Officer: Dennis Malloy
Founded: 1959

NHPTV is New Hampshire's PBS
station. In addition to serving the state,
our signal and services reach metro
Boston, southern Maine and eastern
Vermont.

THE
DMA **NOR1**
440 N Wolfe Rd
Sunnyvale, CA 94085-3869
Telephone: (408) 852-9248, Web Site:
www.nor1.com
CFO: Mark Holtzman

NORTHERN LIGHTS DIRECT
150 N Michigan Ave (Suite 800)
Chicago, IL 60601-7585
Telephone: (312) 263-8686, FAX:
(312) 624-7701, E-Mail: contact@
northernlightsdirect.com, Web Site:
www.northernlightsdirect.com
CEO: Sandy French
Pres & Exec Creative Dir: Ian French

Sls Mktg Mgr: Helen Suk
VP: Luc Bourgon
Conducts Business: U.S., Canada
Employees: 15
Primary Market Served: Business
Founded: 1985

Direct response television agency -
provides services to brand advertisers.
Strategy, media, creative and production services for DRTV campaigns.

ONLINE PRINT SOLUTIONS
268 Bush St (#4045)
San Francisco, CA 94104-3503
Telephone: (415) 651-4157, Web Site:
www.onlineprintsolutions.com
CEO: Mark Mcgowan

ONYX PRODUCTIONS INC
2355 Westwood Blvd (#401)
Los Angeles, CA 90064-2109
Telephone: (323) 692-9830, FAX:
(323) 692-9832, E-Mail: info@
onyxprod.com, Web Site: www.
onyxprod.com
Pres: Joan Renfrow

PM PRODUCTIONS
5882 W Bowcroft St (#2)
Los Angeles, CA 90016-4907
Telephone: (310) 559-3127, FAX:
(310) 559-3168, E-Mail:
odellmack@hotmail.com, Web Site:
wwwmyvideozationnetwork.com
Producer: Odell Mack

**PATRIOT
COMMUNICATIONS LLC**
1275 Drummers Ln (Suite 104)
Wayne, PA 19087-1571
Telephone: (610) 225-0100, FAX:
(610) 687-3835
Mng Dir Sls: David Gregitis

PETRY TELEVISION INC
Sub. of Petry Media Corp
One Penn Plaza (55th fl)
New York, NY 10119
Telephone: (212) 230-5600, FAX:
(323) 655-2862, E-Mail: info@
petrymedia.com, Web Site: www.
petrymedia.com
Pres & CEO: Val Napalitno

PRICE TARGET MEDIA
108 Kentuck Ln
Carson City, NV 89706-0712
Telephone: (775) 434-4451, FAX:
(206) 888-2403, E-Mail: info@
pricetargetmedia.com, Web Site:
pricetargetmedia.com
Pres: Eric Stevenson
Primary Market Served: Consumer

PRODUCT INFORMATION NETWORK

Div. of Jones International Ltd
9697 Mineral Ave, PO Box 3309
Englewood, CO 80112
Telephone: (303) 792-3111, (800) 525-7002, FAX: (303) 784-8549, Web Site: www.pinnet.com
CEO: Glen Jones

THE PRODUCTION PARTNERS

Div. of CFA
2 Duncan Mill Rd (Suite 202)
Toronto, ON, Canada M3B 1Z4
Telephone: (416) 504-5071, FAX: (416) 504-7390, Web Site: www.cfacommunications.com
Dir, Mktg: Maria Kelenc

PROSPER INC

5252 N Edgewood Dr (Suite 150)
Provo, UT 84604-5853
Telephone: (801) 371-0755, (800) 748-5799, FAX: (801) 374-2358, Web Site: www.prospering.com
Dir Mktg: Dan Vanorman
Primary Market Served: Consumer

PROTUS

2379 Holly Ln (Suite 210)
Ottawa, ON, Canada K1V 7P2
Telephone: (888) 733-0000, Web Site: www.protus.com
VP Mktg: Steve Adams

PROXICOM

1902 Campus Commons (Suite 600)
Reston, VA 20191-1586
Telephone: (703) 262-3200, FAX: (703) 262-3201, Web Site: www.proxicom.com
CEO: Raul Fernandez

PUBLISHERS CIRCULATION FULFILLMENT INC

3351-B McLemore Dr
Pensacola, FL 32514-7074
Telephone: (850) 475-2000
Govt Affairs: Matt Laubacker

QDIRECT

Div. of QVC
1200 Wilson Dr, Studio Park
West Chester, PA 19380-4262
Telephone: (484) 701-1000, FAX: (484) 701-1599, Web Site: www.qdirect.com
Pres & CEO: Michael George

QVC INC

1200 Wilson Dr
West Chester, PA 19380
Telephone: (484) 701-1000, FAX: (484) 701-8500, Web Site: www.qvc.com
Pres: Douglas Briggs

RAJANT CORP

400 E King St (Suite 1)
Malvern, PA 19355
Telephone: (484) 595-0233, FAX: (484) 595-0244, E-Mail: moreinfo@rajant.com, Web Site: www.rajant.com
CEO: Robert Schena

RAPID RESPONSE MARKETING

7500 W Lake Mead Blvd (#9-463)
Las Vegas, NV 89128-0297
Telephone: (702) 631-9714, (866) 997-7297, FAX: (702) 216-4038, Web Site: www.xy7.com
CEO: Kevin Devincenzi
Dir Opers: Rhianna Ross
Conducts Business: U.S., Canada
Employees: 8
Primary Market Served: Business & Consumer
Catalog available online
Advertising/Marketing Budget Related to Direct Marketing: 51-75%
Founded: 1998

Internet marketing.

REPUTATIONDEFENDER

2688 Middlefield Rd Ste C
Redwood City, CA 94063-3483
Telephone: (650) 241-7491, (888) 720-3332, E-Mail: helpdesk@reputation.com, Web Site: www.reputationdefender.com
Sr Mgr Bus Devel: Noah Lang
Sr Mgr Bus Devel: David Rust
Mktg Mgr: Adam Faughnan

RESOLUTION INC

327 Holly Ct Ste 20
Williston, VT 05495-4440
Telephone: (802) 862-8881, (800) 862-8900, FAX: (802) 865-2308, E-Mail: schubart@resodirect.com, Web Site: www.resodirect.com
Pres: Bill Schubart

RESPONSE MEDIA

3155 Medlock Bridge Rd
Norcross, GA 30071-1423
Telephone: (770) 451-5478, FAX: (770) 451-4929, E-Mail: babion@responsemedia.com, Web Site: www.responsemedia.com
Pres: Joshua Perlstein
CEO: Betty Abion
COO: Doug Brauer
Chief Innovations Officer: Pat Rogge

Chief Technical Officer: Keith Perlstein
Conducts Business: Worldwide
Employees: 40
Primary Market Served: Business & Consumer
Advertising/Marketing Budget Related to Direct Marketing: 76-100%
Founded: 1978
Gross sales or billing: $18,000,000

Customer acquisition and database management.

RESULTS PRODUCERS

130 S Beaudry Ave (Suite D)
Los Angeles, CA 90012
Telephone: (213) 481-7400, FAX: (213) 481-7474, E-Mail: info@resultsproducers.com, Web Site: www.resultsproducers.com
CEO: Patrick Finn

ROCKET DIRECT MARKETING INC

156 E 37th St (Suite 5A)
New York, NY 10016
Telephone: (212) 689-5800, FAX: (212) 689-0635, E-Mail: info@rocketdirect.com, Web Site: www.rocketdirect.com
Pres: Jonathan Salkin

ROOTBLAST INTERNATIONAL

PO Box 20109, 2207 Kimball Rd SE
Canton, OH 44701
Telephone: (330) 453-5828, FAX: (330) 453-5170, Web Site: www.rootblast.cc
Gen Mgr: Brent Kackley

ROBERT ROSENHEIM ASSOCIATES

Five Gay St, PO Box 308
Sharon, CT 06069-2000
Telephone: (860) 364-0050, FAX: (860) 364-5577, Web Site: rrallc.com
Pres: Robert Rosenheim

SAS GROUP

220 White Plains Rd Ste 100
Tarrytown, NY 10591-5823
Telephone: (914) 332-7878, FAX: (914) 332-7859, E-Mail: ssobo@sasgroup.com, Web Site: www.sasgroup.com
Pres: Michael Sobo

SEOINHOUSE

5214 Cedarfield Dr
Saint Charles, MO 63304-8014
Telephone: (650) 589-8720, Web Site: www.seoinhouse.com
Pres & Founder: Jessica Bowman

SMY MEDIA INC
211 E Ontario (Suite 900)
Chicago, IL 60611
Telephone: (312) 621-9600, FAX:
(312) 621-0924, E-Mail: info@
smymedia.com, Web Site: www.
smymedia.com
VP Sls: Gerald Grant

SAATCHI & SAATCHI
375 Hudson St
New York, NY 10014-3660
Telephone: (212) 463-2000, FAX:
(212) 463-9855, Web Site: www.
saatchiny.com
CEO, Worldwide: Kevin Roberts

SALES MAGIC INC
Div. of Historical Research Center
2107 Corporate Dr
Boynton Beach, FL 33426-6645
Telephone: (561) 732-5263, (800) 940-
7991, FAX: (561) 375-9413, Web
Site: www.names.com
VP: Nancy Marquis

SCHWARTZ & ASSOCIATES CREATIVE
212 S Bemiston (Suite 3)
Clayton, MO 63105-1904
Telephone: (314) 531-6810, FAX:
(314) 531-1448, E-Mail: info@
sacreative.com, Web Site: www.
sacreative.com
Pres: William J. Schwartz
Dir Bus Devel: Tyler Schwartz
Schwartz

SCI-FI CHANNEL
Div. of USA Networks
30 Rockefeller Plaza
New York, NY 10112
Telephone: (212) 413-5000, FAX:
(212) 413-6509, Web Site: www.
scifi.com
Pres: Bonnie Hammer

SCRIPT TO SCREEN INC
200 N Tustin Ave (Suite 200)
Santa Ana, CA 92705
Telephone: (714) 558-3971, (800) 453-
0003, FAX: (714) 558-1759, E-Mail:
newbusiness@scripttoscreen.com,
Web Site: www.scripttoscreen.com
Sr VP: Tony Kerry

SEPTEMBER PRODUCTIONS
15 Madaket Rd
Nantucket, MA 02554-2618
Telephone: (508) 332-3577, FAX:
(508) 228-3853, E-Mail: info@
september.com, Web Site: www.
september.com
CEO: Dan Driscoll

SHOP AT HOME LLC
10001 Kingston Pike (Suite 57)
Knoxville, TN 37922-6909
Telephone: (615) 263-8000, (866) 366-
4010, E-Mail: public.relations@jtv.
com, Web Site: www.shopathometv.
com
Pub Rels Contact: Kelly Fletcher

THE DMA SILVERPOP
200 Galleria Pkwy (Suite 750)
Atlanta, GA 30339-5945
Telephone: (866) 745-8767, FAX:
(678) 247-0501, E-Mail: info@
silverpop.com, Web Site: www.
silverpop.com
Corporate Comun Mgr: Kay Cavender
Mktg Dir: Mitch Diamond
Conducts Business: U.S., Canada
Primary Market Served: Business
Indirect online sales
Advertising/Marketing Budget Related
to Direct Marketing: 76-100%
Direct Marketing ad budget:
Online: 100%
Founded: 1999

Highly ranked email service provider.

SKYLIST
701 Brazos St (Suite 800)
Austin, TX 78701
Telephone: (877) 250-2922, FAX:
(512) 857-0368, E-Mail: sales@
skylist.com, Web Site: www.skylist.
net
VP Mktg: Lana McGilvray
Conducts Business: U.S.
Employees: 50
Primary Market Served: Business
Advertising/Marketing Budget Related
to Direct Marketing: 26-50%
Direct Marketing ad budget: $600,000
Telephone: 100%
Founded: 1996
Gross sales or billing: $6,000,000

Email marketing automation software
(ASP) hosted & license options.

SMART INVENTIONS INC
6421 E Alondra Blvd
Paramount, CA 90723
Telephone: (562) 272-1416, (800) 275-
7494, FAX: (562) 272-1423, E-Mail:
customerservice@smartinventions.
com, Web Site: www.
smartinventions.com
CEO & Founder: Jon Nokes

SMARTHOME
Div of Smart Labs
16542 Millikan Ave
Irvine, CA 92606

Telephone: (949) 221-9200, (800) 762-
7846, FAX: (949) 221-9240, E-Mail:
feedback@smarthome.com, Web
Site: www.smarthome.com
Pres: Rajeev Kapur
Mktg: Ricki Darbee

SMARTSOURCE CORP
3 New England Executive Park Ste
115
Burlington, MA 01803-5006
Telephone: (781) 785-3375, Web Site:
www.smartsourceonline.com
CEO: David Tarrant

SOUNDBITE COMMUNICATIONS
22 Crosby Dr Ste 200
Bedford, MA 01730-1429
Telephone: (781) 359-2200, Web Site:
www.soundbite.com
Dir Mktg Communs: Debbie Braunert

STARTEC
7361 Calhoun Pl (Suite 520)
Rockville, MD 20855-2774
Telephone: (310) 610-4300, Web Site:
www.startec.com
Mktg Dir: Anna Porteus

STEVE SCOTT GROUP LLC
7090 Union Park Ctr (Suite 500)
Midvale, UT 84047-6059
Telephone: (801) 277-8900, (800) 220-
6481, FAX: (801) 277-8986, Web
Site: www.totalgymdirect.com
Mgr: Steven Scott

THE DMA STRONGMAIL SYSTEMS INC
1300 Island Dr (Suite 200)
Redwood City, CA 94065-5171
Telephone: (800) 971-0380, Web Site:
www.strongmail.com
Dir Corporate Mktg: Kristin Hersant

STUDIO M PRODUCTIONS UNLIMITED
4032 Wilshire Blvd (#403)
Los Angeles, CA 90010-3405
Telephone: (213) 389-7372, (888) 389-
7372
Senator: Mike Michaels

SUBMIT EXPRESS
315 W Verdugo Ave (Suite 101)
Burbank, CA 91502-2484
Telephone: (818) 567-3030, Web Site:
www.iclimber.com
VP Sales & Mktg: Allen Horwitz

SUCCESSWORKS SEARCH MARKETING INC
2509 Snowberry Ridge Ct
West Linn, OR 97068-5190
Telephone: (503) 922-3627, Web Site:
www.seocopywriting.com
CEO: Heather Lloyd-Martin

SUNBELT MEDIA SERVICE
PO Box 3116
Chapel Hill, NC 27515-3116
Telephone: (919) 967-7174, FAX:
(919) 967-6050
Pres & Media Dir: Joel Kluger

TNS MEDIA INTELLIGENCE
11 Madison Ave (fl 12)
New York, NY 10010
Telephone: (212) 991-6000, FAX:
(212) 991-6010, Web Site: www.tns-mi.com
Pres: Mark Nesbitt

TNT (TURNER NETWORK TELEVISION LP)
Div. of Turner Broadcasting
1050 Techwood Dr NW
Atlanta, GA 30318
Telephone: (404) 827-1700, E-Mail:
tnt@turner.com, Web Site: www.tnt.tv
Chief Mktg Officer: Jeff Gregor
Employees: 100
Gross sales or billing: $1,571,000,000

TV GUIDE
7140 S Lewis Ave
Tulsa, OK 74136-5401
Telephone: (918) 488-4000, FAX:
(918) 488-4200, Web Site: www.tvguideinc.com
CEO: Rich Battista

TACTARA
50 S Hope St (Suite 2825)
Los Angeles, CA 90071-2683
Telephone: (213) 221-3200, Web Site:
www.tactara.com

THEPORT NETWORK
5500 N Interstate Pkwy (#550)
Atlanta, GA 30328
Telephone: (703) 431-2208
VP Mktg & Strategy: Suzanne Carawan

TOPRANK ONLINE MARKETING
PO Box 397
Mound, MN 55364-0397
Telephone: (952) 400-0194, Web Site:
www.toprankresults.com
CEO: Lee Odden

THE DMA TOWERDATA
379 Park Ave S (fl 5)
New York, NY 10016-8811
Telephone: (646) 742-1771, Web Site:
www.towerdata.com
Pres: Tom Burke

TURNER BROADCASTING SYSTEM INC
190 Marietta St NW Bsmt
Atlanta, GA 30303-2714
Telephone: (404) 827-1700, FAX:
(404) 827-1575, Web Site: www.turner.com
Exec VP Opers & Strategy: Jim Mc-Caffrey

UNIFIED PRECIOUS METALS INC
9010 Eton Ave
Canoga Park, CA 91304-1616
Telephone: (818) 889-7797, FAX:
(818) 735-8878
Pres: Alan Van Vliet

THE DMA US CELLULAR
8410 W Bryn Mawr Ave (Suite 700)
Chicago, IL 60631-3463
Telephone: (773) 339-8900, Web Site:
www.uscellular.com
Mgr Direct Mktg: Jennifer Dakin

USA NETWORK
30 Rockefeller Plz Ste 270E
New York, NY 10112-0299
Telephone: (212) 664-4444, FAX:
(212) 664-6365, Web Site: www.usanetwork.com
Pres: Steven Chao

VALCOM INC
2113 A Gulf Blvd
Indian Rocks Beach, FL 33785-3806
Telephone: (702) 385-9000, FAX:
(702) 382-2802, Web Site: www.valcom.tv
Chmn: Vince Vellardita
COO: Thomas Martin
CFO: Steven Cantrock

VALUEVISION MEDIA INC
6740 Shady Oak Rd
Eden Prairie, MN 55344-3433
Telephone: (952) 943-6000, FAX:
(952) 943-6711, Web Site: www.valuevisionmedia.com
Chmn & Interim CEO: John D. Buck

VIDEO ORDNANCE INC
611 Broadway (Suite 307)
New York, NY 10012-2654

Telephone: (212) 334-3939, (800) 377-7773, FAX: (212) 219-1969, E-Mail:
info@videoordnance.com, Web Site:
www.videoordnance.com
Pres: Marlene Cardin

VIDEO PLUS INC
200 Swisher Rd
Lake Dallas, TX 75065-2324
Telephone: (940) 497-9700, (800) 752-2030, FAX: (940) 497-9987, E-Mail:
support@videoplus.com, Web Site:
www.videoplus.com
VP, Sls & Mktg: Paul Adams

THE DMA VIDI EMI INC
2450 Washington Ave (Suite 220)
San Leandro, CA 94577-5996
Telephone: (510) 667-9999, FAX:
(510) 352-9999, E-Mail: info@vidiemi.com, Web Site: www.vidiemi.com
Mktg Coord: Robin Simmons
CMO: Kevin Reneau
CTO: Rick George
Bus Devel: Fred F. Tabsharani
Conducts Business: U.S.
Employees: 15
Primary Market Served: Business
Advertising/Marketing Budget Related
to Direct Marketing: 0-25%
Direct Marketing ad budget: $20,000
Magazines: 50%
Telephone: 50%
Founded: 2001
Gross sales or billing: $1,000,000

VIRGIN MOBILE USA LLC
10 Independence Blvd Ste 200
Warren, NJ 07059-2730
Telephone: (908) 607-4000, Web Site:
www.virginmobileusa.com
Dir Customer Base Mngmt: Charles
Seelig

VISIBLE RESULTS USA INC
12603 Hemlock St
Overland Park, KS 66213
Telephone: (913) 851-9400, FAX:
(913) 851-0628, E-Mail: info@visibleresults.com, Web Site: www.visibleresults.com
Gen Mgr: George Stevens
Dir Bus Devel: Steve Marquis

VISIBLE WORLD
460 W 34th St (fl 14)
New York, NY 10001-2350
Telephone: (212) 739-1914
Primary Market Served: Consumer

THE DMA **VOICE MESSAGE BROADCASTING CORP**
8105 Irvine Center Dr (Suite 900)
Irvine, CA 92618
Telephone: (714) 437-0600, FAX: (714) 242-1989, Web Site: www.vmbc.com
CEO: Jesse Crowe
Conducts Business: U.S.
Primary Market Served: Business & Consumer
Founded: 1997

Voice & mobile broadcasting services.

THE DMA **VOICE SYSTEMS ENGINEERING INC**
900 Wheeler Way (Suite A)
Langhorne, PA 19047-1706
Telephone: (215) 953-8568, Web Site: www.vseinc.com
Mktg Dir: Maryanne Fiedler

VONAGE
PO Box 310
Holmdel, NJ 07733-0310
Telephone: (732) 528-2600, Web Site: www.vonage.com
Production Mgr: Meeta Wood

WCPE-FM
PO Box 828
Wake Forest, NC 27588-0828
Telephone: (919) 556-5178, Web Site: www.theclassicalstation.org
Bus Mgr: David Sackett
Primary Market Served: Consumer

Classical music broadcasting

WLNY-TV
270 S Service Rd (Suite 55)
Melville, NY 11747-2399
Telephone: (631) 622-9420, FAX: (631) 420-4846, Web Site: www.wlnytv.com
VP & Dir of Sls: Elliot Simmons
Founded: 1985

Long Island based commercial broadcast TV station serving New York, New Jersey & Connecticut. Syndicated programming, live news, blockbuster movies.

WALKER/FITZGIBBON TV & FILM PRODUCTIONS
2399 Mount Olympus Dr
Los Angeles, CA 90046-1660
Telephone: (323) 469-6800, FAX: (323) 878-0600, E-Mail: mo@walkerfitzgibbon.com, Web Site: www.walkerfitzgibbon.com

THE WEATHER CHANNEL
205 E 42nd St (Fl 19)
New York, NY 10017
Telephone: (212) 856-5200, FAX: (212) 856-5215, Web Site: www.weather.com
EVP Corp Commun: Shirley Powell
VP: R J Maloney
VP: Terrence Sekel
VP Ad Sls Southern Region: Liz Wilson Thorington

WEBLOYALTY.COM
101 Merritt 7 (Suite 7)
Norwalk, CT 06851-1060
Telephone: (203) 846-3300, Web Site: www.webloyalty.com
Sr VP Mktg: Marty Isaac
VP Corp Commun: Beth Kitchener
Employees: 300
Founded: 1999

THE DMA **WHITEHAT INC**
4665 S Ash Ave Ste G-10
Tempe, AZ 85282-6765
Telephone: (480) 858-9000, FAX: (480) 858-9001, Web Site: www.whitehat.com
Pres/CEO: Rodney Joffe

JORDAN WHITNEY INC
360 E First St (#593)
Tustin, CA 92780
Telephone: (714) 832-3353, FAX: (714) 832-4422, E-Mail: info@jwgreensheet.com, Web Site: www.jwgreensheet.com
Publr: John Kogler
Pres: Clare Kogler

WINDSTREAM COMMUNICATIONS INC
4001 N Rodney Parham Rd Ste 202
Little Rock, AR 72212-2497
Telephone: (501) 748-7000
VP Mktg Communs: Ron Proleika

THE DMA **YAHOO INC**
1065 Ave of the Americas (fl 9)
New York, NY 10018-0786
Telephone: (212) 381-6829
Sr Dir Customer Contact Strategy: Barbara O'Connor
Primary Market Served: Business

YELLOWPAGES.COM/ INGENIO
201 Mission St (Suite 200)
San Francisco, CA 94105-1832
Telephone: (415) 248-4000, Web Site: www.ingenio.com
Mktg Coord: Wes Womack

THE DMA **ZETA INTERACTIVE**
99 Park Ave Fl 23
New York, NY 10016-1601
Telephone: (646) 834-9400, Web Site: www.zustek.com
Pres: Al DiGuido

Alabama

The Source, 2495 Washington St, PO Box 3888, Huntsville, 35810

Arizona

LT Associates, 18419 E Stirrup Ln, Rio Verde, 85263-7114

California

Aloft Group, 4607 Lakeview Canyon Rd (#434), Westlake Village, 91361

Casablanca Express, 6300 Canoga Ave (Suite 500), Woodland Hills, 91367

Cascade Promotions Corp, 1201 Radio Rd (#100), Redwood City, 94065-1217

CX&B United Corp, 1301 W 253rd St, Harbor City, 90710-2805

de Emley & Associates Inc, 33702 Calle Miramar, San Juan Capistrano, 92675-4926

Premium Incentives, 2240 E Cedar St, Ontario, 91761-8033

Promotional Media Inc, 727 N Main St, Orange, 92868-1105

Top Year International Inc, 22425 E La Palma, Yorba Linda, 92887-3803

Colorado

Blakar Inc, PO Box 5156, Englewood, 80155-5156

Incentives America, 285 S 39th St, Boulder, 80305-5409

Connecticut

Barker Specialty Co, 27 Realty Dr, Cheshire, 06410-1656

Gulbenkian Swim Inc, 16 Beaver Brook Rd, Danbury, 06810-6201

H&M Associates, 3 Dogwood Dr, Danbury, 06813

Lewtan Industries Corp, 30 High St (3rd fl), Hartford, 06103-1906

McWeeney Marketing Group, 53 Robinson Blvd, Orange, 06477-3623

John Michaels Associates Inc, 94 Holmes Rd, Newington, 06110-1708

Product Marketplace, 1128 Stratford Ave., Stratford, 06615

Putnam Group Ltd, 35 Corporate Dr Ste 1065, Trumbull, 06611-6320

Robustelli Merchandise, PO Box 17295, Stamford, 06907-7295

JM Wechter & Associates Inc, 569 Main St, Monroe, 06468-2806

Florida

BIC Graphic USA, 14421 Myerlake Cir, PO Box 23088, Clearwater, 33760-2840

Destination Rewards, 1225 Broken Sound Pkwy NW Ste A, Boca Raton, 33487-3533

King Direct Marketing Inc, 1184 Pelican Bay Dr, Daytona Beach, 32119

Nat Com Marketing, 80 SW 8th St (Suite 2230), Brickell Bayview Ctr, Miami, 33130-3004

Wilcox & Associates, 258 Short Ave, Longwood, 32750

Georgia

J&L Concepts Inc, PO Box 3716, Valdosta, 31604-3716

Ted's Promotions Inc, 144 Lake Ridge Trail, Baldwin, 30511

Illinois

AD-Sells Inc, 1440 Maple Ave (#1A), Lisle, 60532-4135

Creative Awards by Lane, 1713 Elmhurst Rd, Elk Grove Village, 60007-5924

EMAK Worldwide, 350 N Orleans St Ste 5, Chicago, 60654-1605

Elite Promotions, 2105 Painters Lake Rd, Highland Park, 60035-2121

Executive Buying Corp, 1620 Bond St, Naperville, 60563

Four Star Marketing Inc, 3732 W Morse Ave, Lincolnwood, 60645

Gorham's Inc, 1615 S Fifth St, Springfield, 62703

Grace Nathan & Associates, 100 E Bellevue Pl Apt 4A, Chicago, 60611-5198

Great Ideas Inc/CSP, 1633 Ravine Ln, Highland Park, 60035

Halo Branded Solutions, 1980 Industrial Dr, Sterling, 61081-9064

Hinda Incentives, 2440 W 34th St, Chicago, 60608

Ideas Companies Inc, 2337 Riverwoods Drive, Naperville, 60565

Irving Kannett & Associates Inc, 6212 W Oakton, Morton Grove, 60053-2721

Konik & Co Inc, 7535 N Lincoln Ave, Skokie, 60076-3851

Madison Sales Group, 3029 Commercial Ave, Northbrook, 60062-1912

Mar-San, 6045 N Keystone Ave, Chicago, 60646-5209

Marketing Incentives International Inc, 1310 N Ritchie Ct (Suite 16C), Chicago, 60610-8401

Preferred Premium & Fulfillment Corp, 361 Kelburn Rd (Apt 211), Deerfield, 60015-4354

RB Toy Design Inc, 3838 Chester Dr, Glenview, 60026-1013

Indiana

Kipp Brothers Inc, 351 W Muskegon Dr, Greenfield, 46140-3071

Special Markets Sales Co, 7435 E 86th St, Indianapolis, 46256-1207

Iowa

ITAGroup, 4800 Westown Pkwy (Suite 300), West Des Moines, 50266-6700

Impact Sales Inc, 818 Dows Rd Ste 100, Cedar Rapids, 52403-7000

Kansas

American Identity, 7500 W 110th St, Overland Park, 66210

Cannon Marketing Corp, 8275 Monrovia St, Lenexa, 66215-2752

Alvin M Clayman Enterprises Inc, 3200 Merriam Ln, Kansas City, 66106-4618

Incentive Associates Inc, PO Box 12065, Overland Park, 66282-2065

Kid Stuff Marketing, Inc, 929 SW University Blvd (Suite B-1), Topeka, 66619

Midwest Premiums & Promotions, PO Box 6006, Leawood, 66206-0006

The Promotional Resources Group of Companies, Inc, PO Box 19235, Topeka, 66619-0235

Swag Inc, 69 Via Verde, Wichita, 67230

Zouire, PO Box 7287, Overland Park, 66207-0287

Kentucky

MPC Louisville Promotions, 4300 Produce Rd, Louisville, 40218-3062

Stonebridge Press Ltd, 7620 WH Negley Rd, Henderson, 42420-9182

Louisiana

Augie Leopold Advertising Specialties, 3214 Roman St, Metairie, 70001-5224

Maine

Andersen Design, 1 Andersen Rd, East Boothbay, 04544-0246

Geiger Brothers, 70 Mount Hope Ave, Lewiston, 04240-1021

Maryland

Merjo Advertising & Sales Promotions Co, 90 Painters Mill Rd (#134), Owings Mills, 21117-3610

Massachusetts

All Star Premium Products Inc, 660 Main St, PO Box 980, Sturbridge Office Park, Fiskdale, 01518

Corporate Incentive Solutions, 101 Federal St Ste 1701, Boston, 02110-1807

Michigan

General Motivation Co, 3085 Walkent Dr NW, Grand Rapids, 49544

Morley Companies, 1 Morley Plaza, Saginaw, 48603-1305

Rohlik Specialties Co, 42505 Woodward Ave, Bloomfield Hills, 48304

Twin City Engraving/Premier Promotions, 1232 Broad St, Box 85, Saint Joseph, 49085

A. Dean Watkins, 2395 Jolly Rd (Suite 170), Okemos, 48864

Minnesota

Cassidy & Co, 2005 Pin Oak Dr (Suite 3), Eagan, 55122-2480

M R Group Inc, 4280 Rosewood Ln N, Plymouth, 55442

Strategic Marketing Services, PO Box 21686, Eagan, 55121-0686

Missouri

Accent Advertising Inc, 1227 Clay St, North Kansas City, 64116-4026

Bowers & Associates Inc, 2025 S Brentwood Blvd (Suite 207), Saint Louis, 63144-1851

CWC Inventories Inc, 2644 Metro Blvd, Maryland Heights, 63403

Clark & Clark Inc, 13221 W Watson Rd, Saint Louis, 63127-1920

Lipic's Recognition, 10030 Big Bend Rd, Saint Louis, 63122

Preferred Advertising Inc, 202 Country Creek Ct, Ballwin, 63011-3814

Nevada

The Premium Connection, 6165 S Pecos, Las Vegas, 89120

Marty Wolf Game Co, 3601 E Wyoming Ave (SPC 107), Las Vegas, 89104-4937

New Jersey

All-Ways Advertising Co, 1442 Broad St, Bloomfield, 07003

Award Marketing Services LLC, Eight Salem Park, PO Box 175, Whitehouse, 08888

BI, 535 Springfield Ave, Summit, 07901-2631

Business Promotion Ideas Inc, 20 Chestnut St (Suite 6A), Tenafly, 07670-1700

Ben Loeb Inc, 25 Pier Ln W, Fairfield, 07004

Porter Wallace Corp, 1304 Indian Hill Rd, Toms River, 08753-2879

Supreme Specialty Advertising, 34 Mulberry Ln, Mount Arlington, 07856-1383

UniServ Advertising Inc, 37 Hwy 35, Neptune City, 07753

New York

Advertising Gifts Inc, 79 Main St (Suite 302), Port Washington, 11050-2938

Allied Premium Co, 53 N Park Ave Ste 204, Rockville Centre, 11570-4118

Carina Associates, 425 Blinn Rd, Croton on Hudson, 10520-3604

Fire Light Group, PO Box 267, White Plains, 10602

Sheri Gregory Inc, Four Cricket Ln, Dobbs Ferry, 10522-1202

David Hargreaves Ltd, 67 Pine Ridge Dr, Hopewell Junction, 12533-5665

MJM Incentives Inc, PO Box 23678, Rochester, 14692

Mortimer Spiller Co Inc, 163 High Park Blvd, Buffalo, 14226

The Print Box Inc, 8802 Flatlands Ave, Brooklyn, 11236-3612

RPM Industries Inc, 26 Aurelius Ave, Auburn, 13021-0400

Standard Buying Service Ltd, 424 W 33rd St (Rm 230), New York, 10001-2656

Stromberg Brand, 200 N Water St, Peekskill, 10566-2024

Ohio

Associated Premium Corp, 1870 Summit Rd, Cincinnati, 45237-2804

GIE Import Export Corp, 6663 Huntley Rd (Suite H), Columbus, 43085-1038

Lester B Martin & Associates Inc, 2105 Pump Station Rd, Sugar Grove, 43155

Jim Mersfelder & Associates Inc, 2202 Superior Ave E Ste 1, Cleveland, 44114-4259

Partners for Incentives, 6545 Carnegie Ave, Cleveland, 44103-4619

S Group Inc, 661 W Market St, Akron, 44303

Pennsylvania

Chase Advertising Co, 2549 Mosside Blvd, Monroeville, 15146-3510

J Edward Connelly Associates, Inc, 4 Parkway Ctr W Ste 101, Pittsburgh, 15220-3516

Market Incentives Corp, 11 N Bacton Hill Rd, Frazer, 19355

Rhode Island

Capital Design, 1 Richmond Sq Ste 210E, Providence, 02906-5166

Peck Rock Associates, Seven Peck Rock, Box 49, Bristol, 02809

South Carolina

Professional Marketing Associates, PO Box 1772, Mount Pleasant, 29465-1772

Tennessee

American Accessories International, 550 W Main St (Suite 825), Knoxville, 37902-2542

Safe Specialties, 223 Green Acres Rd, Kingston, 37763

Texas

Alfax Wholesale Furniture Inc, 13901 Midway Rd (Suite 102-428), Farmers Branch, 75244-4388

The B&F System Inc, 3920 S Walton Walker Blvd, Dallas, 75236-1510

BC & Associates Representatives Inc, 106 Industrial Dr, Fate, 75132

Merit Industries Inc, 119 Serenada Dr, Georgetown, 78628

SA-SO/Time Wise, 525 N Great Southwest Pkwy, Arlington, 76011-5422

Virginia

Fiddler's Rock Communications Inc, 6841 Elm St., Box 6510, McLean, 22106

Washington

Costco Wholesale, 999 Lake Dr, Issaquah, 98027-8990

Wisconsin

CSE Inc, 5400 S Westridge Dr, New Berlin, 53151-7905

Del Enterprises, 816 Walnut St, Verona, 53593-1609

William W Schwartz Associates Inc, 1907 Erie Ave, Sheboygan, 53081-3708

CANADA
Ontario

Intrepid Distributors Inc, 2213 Dunwin Dr, Mississauga, L5L IXI

Quebec

Americ Disc, 2525 Canadien, Drummondville, J2C 7W2

Premium Wholesalers & Agents (33)

ACCENT ADVERTISING INC
1227 Clay St
North Kansas City, MO 64116-4026
Telephone: (816) 842-1860, FAX: (816) 471-4836, E-Mail: ideasaccentadv@sbcglobal.net, Web Site: www.accentadv.com
Pres: Paul J. Weishar Jr.

AD-SELLS INC
1440 Maple Ave (#1A)
Lisle, IL 60532-4135
Telephone: (630) 241-0090
Pres: Allen D. Kovarik

ADVERTISING GIFTS INC
79 Main St (Suite 302)
Port Washington, NY 11050-2938
Telephone: (516) 767-3577, (877) 496-8762, E-Mail: sales@adgiftsinc.com, Web Site: www.adgiftsinc.com
Pres: Eric Weintraub

ALFAX WHOLESALE FURNITURE INC
13901 Midway Rd (Suite 102-428)
Farmers Branch, TX 75244-4388
Telephone: (212) 947-9560, (800) 221-5710, FAX: (212) 947-4734, Web Site: www.alfaxfurniture.com
Pres: George Mosher
Gen Mgr: Gary Heller
Conducts Business: U.S.
Employees: 2
Primary Market Served: Business & Consumer
Catalog available online
Direct online sales
Advertising/Marketing Budget Related to Direct Marketing: 76-100%
Direct Marketing ad budget: $1,000,000
Direct Mail: 100%
Founded: 1946
Gross sales or billing: $15,000,000

Direct marketing of furniture & equipment to churches, schools & other institutions & businesses. Branch offices in Atlanta, Los Angeles & Milwaukee.

ALL STAR PREMIUM PRODUCTS INC
Subs. of All Star Incentive Marketing
660 Main St, PO Box 980, Sturbridge Office Park
Fiskdale, MA 01518

Telephone: (508) 347-7672, (800) 526-8629, FAX: (508) 347-5404, E-Mail: sales@incentiveusa.com, Web Site: www.incentiveusa.com
Pres: Brian A. Galonek

ALL-WAYS ADVERTISING CO
1442 Broad St
Bloomfield, NJ 07003
Telephone: (973) 338-0700, (800) 255-9291, FAX: (973) 338-1410, Web Site: www.all-waysadvertising.com
Pres: Robert Jay Lieberman

ALLIED PREMIUM CO
53 N Park Ave Ste 204
Rockville Centre, NY 11570-4118
Telephone: (516) 766-5300
Pres: Bernard Rosten

ALOFT GROUP
4607 Lakeview Canyon Rd (#434)
Westlake Village, CA 91361
Telephone: (805) 494-3700, Web Site: www.aloftgroup.com
Partner & Chief Strategy Partner: Mark Winningham
Pres & CEO: Matt Bowen

AMERIC DISC
2525 Canadien
Drummondville, PQ, Canada J2C 7W2
Telephone: (800) 263-0419, FAX: (819) 478-4575, Web Site: www.americdisc.com
Exec VP, Sls & Mktg: Claude Fragman

AMERICAN ACCESSORIES INTERNATIONAL
550 W Main St (Suite 825)
Knoxville, TN 37902-2542
Telephone: (865) 525-9100, FAX: (865) 525-0889
Pres: Eric Zeanah

AMERICAN IDENTITY
7500 W 110th St
Overland Park, KS 66210
Telephone: (913) 319-3100, (800) 848-8028
Mktg Svcs: Amy Turley

ANDERSEN DESIGN
1 Andersen Rd
East Boothbay, ME 04544-0246

Telephone: (207) 350-4057, (866) 711-8421, E-Mail: studio@andersenstudio.com, Web Site: www.andersenstudio.com
Pres: Weston Andersen
Admin, Dir: Nancy Andersen
Other: Susan Mackenzie Andersen
Other: Elise Anderson

ASSOCIATED PREMIUM CORP
1870 Summit Rd
Cincinnati, OH 45237-2804
Telephone: (513) 679-4444, FAX: (513) 679-4447, Web Site: www.associatedpremium.com
Pres: Randy Ficke

AWARD MARKETING SERVICES LLC
Eight Salem Park, PO Box 175
Whitehouse, NJ 08888
Telephone: (908) 534-5700, FAX: (908) 534-0903, E-Mail: grcanose@aol.com, Web Site: www.awardmarketingservices.com
Pres: Gregory Canose

THE B&F SYSTEM INC
3920 S Walton Walker Blvd
Dallas, TX 75236-1510
Telephone: (214) 333-2111, FAX: (214) 333-2137, E-Mail: service@bnfusa.com, Web Site: www.bnfusa.com
Pres: John Meyer

BC & ASSOCIATES REPRESENTATIVES INC
106 Industrial Dr
Fate, TX 75132
Telephone: (972) 722-7365, (800) 275-1298, FAX: (972) 722-7714, E-Mail: terri@bcincentives.com, Web Site: www.bcincentives.com
CEO: Murray Jones
Pres: Terri L. Jones
Exec VP Mktg: Barclay Walker

BI
535 Springfield Ave
Summit, NJ 07901-2631
Telephone: (908) 722-4222, FAX: (908) 722-9199, Web Site: www.Biworldwide.com
VP: Gary Bernstein

BARKER SPECIALTY CO
27 Realty Dr
Cheshire, CT 06410-1656
Telephone: (203) 272-2222, (800)
    BARKERS, (800) 227-5377, FAX:
    (203) 272-2727, Web Site: www.
    barkerspecialty.com
Pres: Gerald Barker
Dir Mktg: Bridget Ann Kingsbury
Employees: 98
Founded: 1951
Gross sales or billing: $29,545,000

Celebrating over 60 years in business.
Service oriented, innovative promotional marketing agency, specializing
in branded apparel, premium merchandise & promotional advertising.

BIC GRAPHIC USA
Div. of BIC Corporation
14421 Myerlake Cir, PO Box 23088
Clearwater, FL 33760-2840
Telephone: (727) 536-7895, FAX:
    (800) 753-5890, Web Site: www.
    bicgraphic.com
Trade Prod Mgr: Christina Szott
Gen Mgr: Nicolas Paillot

BLAKAR INC
PO Box 5156
Englewood, CO 80155-5156
Telephone: (201) 672-0705, FAX:
    (201) 673-0725, Web Site: www.
    blakar.com
Chmn: Norman Somer

BOWERS & ASSOCIATES INC
2025 S Brentwood Blvd (Suite 207)
Saint Louis, MO 63144-1851
Telephone: (314) 963-4477, FAX:
    (314) 963-4483
Pres & Treas: Thomas M. Bowers

**BUSINESS PROMOTION
IDEAS INC**
20 Chestnut St (Suite 6A)
Tenafly, NJ 07670-1700
Telephone: (201) 569-9777, FAX:
    (201) 569-2642, Web Site: www.
    buspromoideas.com
Promo Coord: Bonnie Burgess

CSE INC
5400 S Westridge Dr
New Berlin, WI 53151-7905
Telephone: (262) 786-8400, (800) 999-
    0001, FAX: (262) 796-2089, E-Mail:
    ask@csecatalog.com, Web Site:
    www.csepromo.com
CEO: Charlie Caliendo

CWC INVENTORIES INC
2644 Metro Blvd
Maryland Heights, MO 63403

Telephone: (314) 739-1311, FAX:
    (314) 739-7398, E-Mail: frankg@
    cwcinventories.com, Web Site: www.
    cwcinventories.com
Chmn: Frank Ginsberg

CX&B UNITED CORP
1301 W 253rd St
Harbor City, CA 90710-2805
Telephone: (310) 530-2102, (800) 292-
    8258, FAX: (310) 530-2513, E-Mail:
    sales@cxbunited.com, Web Site:
    www.cxbunited.com
Pres: Fenton Mitchell
VP: Rod Mitchell
Founded: 1970

CANNON MARKETING CORP
8275 Monrovia St
Lenexa, KS 66215-2752
Telephone: (913) 338-3340, (800) 444-
    0972, FAX: (913) 273-0808, E-Mail:
    jack@cannonmktg.com, Web Site:
    www.cannonmktg.com
Pres: Jack Cannon

CAPITAL DESIGN
1 Richmond Sq Ste 210E
Providence, RI 02906-5166
Telephone: (401) 270-6777, FAX:
    (401) 438-9360, E-Mail: info@
    freemiums.com, Web Site: www.
    freemiums.com
Pres: Judith S. Mann
VP Sls, Mktg: Jill Querceto
Founded: 1987

CARINA ASSOCIATES
425 Blinn Rd
Croton on Hudson, NY 10520-3604
Telephone: (914) 271-8600, FAX:
    (914) 271-8354
Pres: Alan Hochman

CASABLANCA EXPRESS
6300 Canoga Ave (Suite 500)
Woodland Hills, CA 91367
Telephone: (818) 992-5100, Web Site:
    www.casablancaexpress.com
Pres: Charles McClendon

**CASCADE PROMOTIONS
CORP**
1201 Radio Rd (#100)
Redwood City, CA 94065-1217
Telephone: (650) 594-1757
Pres: Stu Birger

CASSIDY & CO
2005 Pin Oak Dr (Suite 3)
Eagan, MN 55122-2480

Telephone: (651) 452-4485, FAX:
    (651) 452-0561, E-Mail: sarah@
    cassidycompany.com, Web Site:
    www.cassidycompany.com
Owner: Bill Cassidy

CHASE ADVERTISING CO
2549 Mosside Blvd
Monroeville, PA 15146-3510
Telephone: (412) 372-5980, FAX:
    (412) 372-6097, E-Mail: chaseadv@
    nb.net, Web Site: www.logomall.
    com/chaseadv
Owner: Florinda Chase

CLARK & CLARK INC
13221 W Watson Rd
Saint Louis, MO 63127-1920
Telephone: (314) 994-9155, FAX:
    (314) 994-0573, E-Mail: jim.clark@
    clark-clark.net
Pres & Owner: Jim Clark

**ALVIN M CLAYMAN
ENTERPRISES INC**
3200 Merriam Ln
Kansas City, KS 66106-4618
Telephone: (913) 384-3600, FAX:
    (913) 384-1227, E-Mail: bclayman@
    alvinclayman.com, Web Site: www.
    alvinmclayman.com
Pres: Alvin Clayman

**J EDWARD CONNELLY
ASSOCIATES, INC**
4 Parkway Ctr W Ste 101
Pittsburgh, PA 15220-3516
Telephone: (412) 920-4100, (800) 245-
    6532, FAX: (412) 920-4070, Web
    Site: www.jeca.com
Chmn: John Connelly

**CORPORATE INCENTIVE
SOLUTIONS**
101 Federal St Ste 1701
Boston, MA 02110-1807
Telephone: (301) 340-1600, (877) 244-
    4505, FAX: (301) 251-5887
VP, Strategic Devel: Richard Spector

THE DMA COSTCO WHOLESALE
999 Lake Dr
Issaquah, WA 98027-8990
Telephone: (425) 313-8647, Web Site:
    www.costco.com
Dir Strategic Mktg: Robert Csonaki
Primary Market Served: Business &
    Consumer

**CREATIVE AWARDS BY
LANE**
1713 Elmhurst Rd
Elk Grove Village, IL 60007-5924

Telephone: (847) 593-7700, FAX: (847) 593-1155, E-Mail: info@creativeawardsbylane.com, Web Site: www.creativeawardsbylane.com
Pres: John Erskine

DE EMLEY & ASSOCIATES INC

33702 Calle Miramar
San Juan Capistrano, CA 92675-4926
Telephone: (949) 493-5117, FAX: (949) 493-6382
Pres: Fredi Thorndike Emley

DEL ENTERPRISES

Div. of Delenterprises.com
816 Walnut St
Verona, WI 53593-1609
Telephone: (608) 845-6322, (800) 611-8045, FAX: (608) 845-3530, E-Mail: delips@tds.net, Web Site: www.delenterprises.com
Pres: Donald E. Lipske
Catalog available online
Direct online sales
Founded: 1982

Specials for 501(C) groups & fundraisers.

DESTINATION REWARDS

1225 Broken Sound Pkwy NW Ste A
Boca Raton, FL 33487-3533
Telephone: (561) 997-9940, (800) 242-6260, FAX: (561) 997-9945, Web Site: www.drloyalty.com
CEO: Jack Finn
Pres: John Lavin
VP Bus Devel: David Shaw
Natl Sls: Mickey Finn
Conducts Business: U.S.
Employees: 20
Primary Market Served: Business
Catalog available online
Direct online sales
Advertising/Marketing Budget Related to Direct Marketing: 26-50%
Direct Marketing ad budget:
Direct Mail: 10%
Telephone: 90%
Founded: 2001

Provider loyalty retention & incentive programs.

EMAK WORLDWIDE

350 N Orleans St Ste 5
Chicago, IL 60654-1605
Telephone: (323) 932-4300, E-Mail: jim.holbrook@emak.com, Web Site: www.emak.com
CEO & Dir: Jim Holbrook

ELITE PROMOTIONS

2105 Painters Lake Rd
Highland Park, IL 60035-2121
Telephone: (773) 282-0338, FAX: (773) 282-9081, E-Mail: mike@elitepromotions.com, Web Site: www.elitepromotions.com
Pres: Mike Silver

EXECUTIVE BUYING CORP

Div. of CBSi
1620 Bond St
Naperville, IL 60563
Telephone: (630) 420-6200, FAX: (630) 420-2294, Web Site: www.consumerbenefit.com
Chmn: William Sefton

FIDDLER'S ROCK COMMUNICATIONS INC

6841 Elm St., Box 6510
McLean, VA 22106
Telephone: (703) 406-1500, FAX: (703) 406-1595, Web Site: www.frmktg.com
Pres: Christopher S. Paul

FIRE LIGHT GROUP

PO Box 267
White Plains, NY 10602
Telephone: (608) 441-3473, E-Mail: mincentive@aol.com, Web Site: www.incentivesmotivate.com
Pres & CEO: Sandra Daniel
Exec Consultant: Arnold H. Light
Dir Opers: Anjee M. Sorge
Mng Dir: Krintin Briggs

FOUR STAR MARKETING INC

aka conventionbags.com
3732 W Morse Ave
Lincolnwood, IL 60645
Telephone: (800) 888-2991, FAX: (847) 679-6449, E-Mail: sales@conventionbags.com, Web Site: www.conventionbags.com
Pres: Will Moss

GIE IMPORT EXPORT CORP

6663 Huntley Rd (Suite H)
Columbus, OH 43085-1038
Telephone: (614) 888-5850, FAX: (614) 436-0723
Pres: Leonard S. Glick

GEIGER BROTHERS

70 Mount Hope Ave
Lewiston, ME 04240-1021
Telephone: (207) 755-2000, FAX: (207) 755-2422, E-Mail: ggeiger@geiger.com, Web Site: www.geiger.com
Pres: Eugene Geiger
VP Sls & Mktg: Jim Habzda

GENERAL MOTIVATION CO

3085 Walkent Dr NW
Grand Rapids, MI 49544
Telephone: (616) 647-3085, FAX: (616) 647-5909, E-Mail: motivate@i2k.com, Web Site: www.generalmotivation.com
VP: Richard Bennett

GORHAM'S INC

1615 S Fifth St
Springfield, IL 62703
Telephone: (217) 544-1727, (800) 500-3949, FAX: (217) 544-1623, E-Mail: gorhams@gorhams.com, Web Site: www.gorhams.com
Pres: Stephen J. Zink

GRACE NATHAN & ASSOCIATES

100 E Bellevue Pl Apt 4A
Chicago, IL 60611-5198
Telephone: (847) 763-1174
Pres: Grace Nathan

GREAT IDEAS INC/CSP

1633 Ravine Ln
Highland Park, IL 60035
Telephone: (847) 432-9060, (800) 611-5515, FAX: (800) 956-4443, E-Mail: sales@greatideasinc.com, Web Site: www.greatideasinc.com
Pres: Scott Rubin

SHERI GREGORY INC

Four Cricket Ln
Dobbs Ferry, NY 10522-1202
Telephone: (914) 693-2499, FAX: (914) 693-2393, E-Mail: sgi.inc@verizon.net, Web Site: www.puffaliciouspoufs.com
Pres: Sheri Gregory

GULBENKIAN SWIM INC

16 Beaver Brook Rd
Danbury, CT 06810-6201
Telephone: (203) 790-0800, (800) 431-2586, FAX: (203) 791-1449, Web Site: www.gulbenkianswim.com
Pres & CEO: Ed Gulbenkian Jr.
VP: Lauren Druckman
Conducts Business: Worldwide
Employees: 12
Primary Market Served: Business & Consumer
Catalog available online
Direct online sales
Advertising/Marketing Budget Related to Direct Marketing: 0-25%
Direct Marketing ad budget: $25,000
Direct Mail: 83%
Magazines: 10%
Newspapers: 2%
Online: 1%

TV/Radio: 1%
Telephone: 3%
Founded: 1961
Gross sales or billing: $1,500,000
Lifeguard uniforms, swimsuits & equipment. Sell to department stores, high schools, colleges, Y's, & swim clubs.

H&M ASSOCIATES
3 Dogwood Dr
Danbury, CT 06813
Telephone: (203) 748-8248, FAX: (203) 792-9555
Pres: Heidi A. Reed

HALO BRANDED SOLUTIONS
1980 Industrial Dr
Sterling, IL 61081-9064
Telephone: (877) 592-4256, (866) 840-6401, FAX: (815) 632-6900, E-Mail: moreinfo@haloleewayne.com, Web Site: www.haloleewayne.com
CEO & Dir: Marc S. Simon

DAVID HARGREAVES LTD
67 Pine Ridge Dr
Hopewell Junction, NY 12533-5665
Telephone: (516) 944-9443, FAX: (516) 944-5825, E-Mail: dhltd@optonline.net
Pres: David Hargreaves

HINDA INCENTIVES
2440 W 34th St
Chicago, IL 60608
Telephone: (773) 890-5900, (800) 621-4412, FAX: (773) 890-4606, E-Mail: contact@hinda.com, Web Site: www.hinda.com
VP Domestic & Global Sls: Bill Termini

ITAGROUP
4800 Westown Pkwy (Suite 300)
West Des Moines, IA 50266-6700
Telephone: (515) 224-3400, (800) 257-1985, FAX: (515) 224-3589, Web Site: www.itagroup.com
Pres & COO: Tom Mahoney

IDEAS COMPANIES INC
2337 Riverwoods Drive
Naperville, IL 60565
Telephone: (630) 357-7522, (800) 323-5656, FAX: (630) 357-7538
Owner Attention! Inc: Joanne Dutcher Maxwell

IMPACT SALES INC
818 Dows Rd Ste 100
Cedar Rapids, IA 52403-7000
Telephone: (319) 363-2641, FAX: (319) 362-5481
Pres: Jeanne Kewley

INCENTIVE ASSOCIATES INC
PO Box 12065
Overland Park, KS 66282-2065
Telephone: (913) 722-2848, FAX: (913) 722-6854, E-Mail: incentiveassociate@sbcglobal.net
Pres: Jack Buckley

INCENTIVES AMERICA
285 S 39th St
Boulder, CO 80305-5409
Telephone: (303) 494-8845, FAX: (303) 494-8404
Pres: Roy Boyer

INTREPID DISTRIBUTORS INC
2213 Dunwin Dr
Mississauga, ON, Canada L5L IXI
Telephone: (905) 607-5170, (800) 263-6011, FAX: (800) 361-6307, E-Mail: sales@intrepid.on.ca, Web Site: www.intrepid.on.ca
Pres: T. Mehendale

J&L CONCEPTS INC
PO Box 3716
Valdosta, GA 31604-3716
Telephone: (800) 346-5083, FAX: (912) 247-2468, E-Mail: promo@jlconcepts.com, Web Site: www.jlconcepts.com
Pres: Joyce Aigen

IRVING KANNETT & ASSOCIATES INC
6212 W Oakton
Morton Grove, IL 60053-2721
Telephone: (847) 965-8810, FAX: (847) 965-8826, Web Site: www.kannett.com
Pres: Jeff Kannett

KID STUFF MARKETING, INC
929 SW University Blvd (Suite B-1)
Topeka, KS 66619
Telephone: (785) 862-3707, (800) 677-4712, FAX: (785) 862-0070, E-Mail: info@kidstuff.com, Web Site: www.kidsstuff.com
Pres: William L. Miller
CEO: Joe Tindall
Sls Acct: Dina Stewart
Conducts Business: U.S., Canada, Europe
Employees: 40
Primary Market Served: Consumer
Catalog available online
Direct online sales
Advertising/Marketing Budget Related to Direct Marketing: 76-100%
Founded: 1982
Gross sales or billing: $4,000,000
Perfectly Safe Catalog sells infant & children's safety products, toys & education products via mail order catalogs and internet. Kids Club Catalog sells products for infants, children & parents; including toys, educational items, hard goods & clothing. Natural Baby Catalog sells natural & organic clothing, diapers, nursing products & wooden toys.

KING DIRECT MARKETING INC
1184 Pelican Bay Dr
Daytona Beach, FL 32119
Telephone: (386) 788-8925, FAX: (386) 761-0234
Owner: Cathy King

KIPP BROTHERS INC
Div. of Indiana Novelty International Inc
351 W Muskegon Dr
Greenfield, IN 46140-3071
Telephone: (317) 634-5507, (800) 428-1153, FAX: (800) 832-5477, E-Mail: toys@kippbro.com
VP, Premium Div: Irving Freeman

THE DMA KONIK & CO INC
7535 N Lincoln Ave
Skokie, IL 60076-3851
Telephone: (847) 933-1800, FAX: (847) 933-1818, E-Mail: stan@konik.com, Web Site: www.konik.com
Pres, Owner: Stan Konik

LT ASSOCIATES
18419 E Stirrup Ln
Rio Verde, AZ 85263-7114
Telephone: (952) 943-9790, FAX: (952) 943-9794, E-Mail: thouse2az@aol.com, Web Site: www.ltapromotions.net
Pres: Tom House

AUGIE LEOPOLD ADVERTISING SPECIALTIES
3214 Roman St
Metairie, LA 70001-5224
Telephone: (504) 836-0525, FAX: (504) 836-2396, E-Mail: aleopold@bellsouth.net
CEO: Augie Leopold Jr.

LEWTAN INDUSTRIES CORP
30 High St (3rd fl)
Hartford, CT 06103-1906

Telephone: (860) 278-9800, FAX: (860) 278-9019, E-Mail: lewtan@snet.net, Web Site: www.lewtan8.com
Pres: Douglas Lewtan

LIPIC'S RECOGNITION
10030 Big Bend Rd
Saint Louis, MO 63122
Telephone: (314) 775-2500, (800) 771-4640, FAX: (314) 775-2501, E-Mail: lipic@lipic.com, Web Site: www.lipics.com
Pres: Steve Lipic

BEN LOEB INC
25 Pier Ln W
Fairfield, NJ 07004
Telephone: (973) 882-9022, (800) 854-8275, FAX: (973) 882-8647, Web Site: www.bsloeb.com
Pres: Ben Goldstein

M R GROUP INC
4280 Rosewood Ln N
Plymouth, MN 55442
Telephone: (763) 550-0760, FAX: (763) 550-0760, E-Mail: webmaster@mrgrp.com, Web Site: www.mrgrp.com
Pres: Mark Rue

MJM INCENTIVES INC
PO Box 23678
Rochester, NY 14692
Telephone: (585) 424-6720, FAX: (585) 424-4387, E-Mail: cmeier@mjmincentives.com, Web Site: www.mjmincentives.com
Pres: Michael J. Murphy

MPC LOUISVILLE PROMOTIONS
4300 Produce Rd
Louisville, KY 40218-3062
Telephone: (502) 451-4900, (800) 331-0989, FAX: (502) 451-5075, E-Mail: service@mpcpromotions.com, Web Site: www.mpcpromotions.com
Mgr: Don Dobina

MADISON SALES GROUP
3029 Commercial Ave
Northbrook, IL 60062-1912
Telephone: (847) 480-2370, FAX: (847) 480-7437
Pres: George Denenberg

MAR-SAN
aka Products Fulfillment Inc
6045 N Keystone Ave
Chicago, IL 60646-5209

Telephone: (773) 583-5700, (800) 621-5582, FAX: (773) 583-1740, E-Mail: sales@mar-san.com, Web Site: www.mar-san.com
Sls Mgr: Mark Boncher

MARKET INCENTIVES CORP
11 N Bacton Hill Rd
Frazer, PA 19355
Telephone: (610) 644-5700, (800) 486-8881, FAX: (610) 889-9636, E-Mail: micpa@marketincentives.com, Web Site: www.marketincentives.com
Pres: Harold Sheinbach

MARKETING INCENTIVES INTERNATIONAL INC
1310 N Ritchie Ct (Suite 16C)
Chicago, IL 60610-8401
Telephone: (312) 440-3700, (866) 440-3700, FAX: (312) 943-5813, E-Mail: miibenefits@rcn.com, Web Site: www.mktgincentiveintl.com
Pres: Ronald A. Bernstein
Employees: 2
Founded: 1995

Value added benefit broker. See website for benefits, clubs, and premiums.

LESTER B MARTIN & ASSOCIATES INC
2105 Pump Station Rd
Sugar Grove, OH 43155
Telephone: (740) 746-8842, (614) 261-1722, (800) 262-1692, FAX: (614) 447-8417, (740) 746-8849, E-Mail: service@lesterbmartin.com, Web Site: www.lesterbmartin.com
Pres: Denise Detman

ᵀᴴᴱ_ᴰᴹᴬ MCWEENEY MARKETING GROUP
53 Robinson Blvd
Orange, CT 06477-3623
Telephone: (203) 891-8100, (800) 272-3440, FAX: (203) 891-0775, E-Mail: george@mcweeneymarketing.com, Web Site: www.mcweeneymarketing.com
Pres: George McWeeney
VP: Kali Dewey
VP: John Kelly
Corp Program Mgr: Deb Hayducky
Employees: 8
Founded: 1989
Gross sales or billing: $2,500,000

Offers a complete range of promotional products & apparel. Also offers warehouse & fulfillment programs for their many corporate & company store programs.

MERIT INDUSTRIES INC
119 Serenada Dr
Georgetown, TX 78628
Telephone: (512) 863-8541, (800) 637-4823, FAX: (512) 863-9861
Pres: Herbert Piller
Employees: 109
Founded: 1956

Imports thousands of different low cost novelty and electronic products from the Orient and offers them to direct marketing companies worldwide. In addition, there are dozens of horticultural products such as good luck bamboo plants available.

MERJO ADVERTISING & SALES PROMOTIONS CO
90 Painters Mill Rd (#134)
Owings Mills, MD 21117-3610
Telephone: (410) 345-9000, FAX: (410) 345-9002, E-Mail: merjoadv@qis.net, Web Site: www.promoplace.com/merjo
Owner: Mervyn Margolies

JIM MERSFELDER & ASSOCIATES INC
2202 Superior Ave E Ste 1
Cleveland, OH 44114-4259
Telephone: (216) 574-9009, FAX: (216) 574-9721, Web Site: www.jma-usa.com
Pres: Ron Hajek

JOHN MICHAELS ASSOCIATES INC
94 Holmes Rd
Newington, CT 06110-1708
Telephone: (860) 666-1414, FAX: (860) 666-1515, E-Mail: john@jmalogos.com, Web Site: www.johnmichaelinc.com
Pres: John J. Papa

MIDWEST PREMIUMS & PROMOTIONS
PO Box 6006
Leawood, KS 66206-0006
Telephone: (913) 383-9333, FAX: (913) 383-9555, E-Mail: dudleymidwestpremiums@yahoo.com
Owner: Steve Dudley

MORLEY COMPANIES
1 Morley Plaza
Saginaw, MI 48603-1305
Telephone: (989) 791-2550, (800) 336-5554, FAX: (989) 792-1002, E-Mail: info@morleynet.com, Web Site: www.morleynet.com
Chmn: L. Furlo
Founded: 1863

MORTIMER SPILLER CO INC
163 High Park Blvd
Buffalo, NY 14226
Telephone: (716) 834-0860
Pres & CEO: Mortimer Spiller

NAT COM MARKETING
80 SW 8th St (Suite 2230), Brickell
Bayview Ctr
Miami, FL 33130-3004
Telephone: (786) 425-0028, FAX:
(786) 425-0067, E-Mail: info@
natcom-marketing.com, Web Site:
www.natcom-marketing.com
Sr VP: Robert Bauer
Pres: Robert Rodriguez

PARTNERS FOR INCENTIVES
6545 Carnegie Ave
Cleveland, OH 44103-4619
Telephone: (216) 881-3000, (800) 292-
7371, FAX: (216) 881-7413, Web
Site: www.pfi-awards.com
Sls & Mktg Mgr: Joy Smith

PECK ROCK ASSOCIATES
Seven Peck Rock, Box 49
Bristol, RI 02809
Telephone: (401) 253-9307, FAX:
(401) 254-0424, E-Mail: pra@aol.
com, Web Site: www.peckrock.com
Pres: Katherine Waite

PORTER WALLACE CORP
1304 Indian Hill Rd
Toms River, NJ 08753-2879
Telephone: (732) 505-1675, FAX:
(201) 505-1632, E-Mail: inquiries@
porterwallace.com, Web Site: www.
porterwallace.com
Pres: Herbert Bixon

PREFERRED ADVERTISING INC
202 Country Creek Ct
Ballwin, MO 63011-3814
Telephone: (314) 298-8555, (800) 289-
7858, FAX: (314) 298-8557, E-Mail:
websales@preferredadvertising.com,
Web Site: www.preferredadvertising.
com
Pres: Dick Pecher

PREFERRED PREMIUM & FULFILLMENT CORP
361 Kelburn Rd (Apt 211)
Deerfield, IL 60015-4354
Telephone: (847) 677-3080, FAX:
(847) 564-5738
Pres: Benjamin Michaels

THE PREMIUM CONNECTION
6165 S Pecos
Las Vegas, NV 89120
Telephone: (702) 434-6900, (800) 683-
0933, FAX: (702) 434-9715, Web
Site: www.premiumconnection.net
Pres: Ron Worth

PREMIUM INCENTIVES
2240 E Cedar St
Ontario, CA 91761-8033
Telephone: (951) 599-8220, (800) 950-
5131, FAX: (949) 599-8244, E-Mail:
mhidalgo@promotebusiness.com,
Web Site: http://premiumincentives.
awardselection.com/index.icrt

THE PRINT BOX INC
Sub. of Promobrands
8802 Flatlands Ave
Brooklyn, NY 11236-3612
Telephone: (212) 741-1381, (800) 546-
4011, FAX: (212) 463-9071, E-Mail:
info@promobrands.com, Web Site:
www.promobrands.com
Sls Mgr: Jeff Huvar

PRODUCT MARKETPLACE
1128 Stratford Ave.
Stratford, CT 06615
Telephone: (203) 375-8371, (800) 286-
4768, FAX: (203) 386-1203, E-Mail:
rita@sabinc.com
Pres: Bruce T. Silverstone

PROFESSIONAL MARKETING ASSOCIATES
PO Box 1772
Mount Pleasant, SC 29465-1772
Telephone: (843) 971-8150, FAX:
(843) 971-8159
Pres: David Mann

PROMOTIONAL MEDIA INC
727 N Main St
Orange, CA 92868-1105
Telephone: (714) 639-6590, (800) 346-
5348, FAX: (714) 639-6270, E-Mail:
contactus@promotionalmedia.com,
Web Site: www.promotionalmedia.
com
Pres: Peter Bodourian

THE PROMOTIONAL RESOURCES GROUP OF COMPANIES, INC
PO Box 19235
Topeka, KS 66619-0235
Telephone: (785) 862-3707, (800) 467-
4712, FAX: (785) 862-1424, E-Mail:
info@kidstuff.com, Web Site: www.
kidstuffnet.com

PUTNAM GROUP LTD
35 Corporate Dr Ste 1065
Trumbull, CT 06611-6320
Telephone: (203) 452-7270, FAX:
(203) 268-8071, E-Mail: info@
putnamgroup.net, Web Site:
putnamgroup.net
Pres: Terrance M. Bussen

RB TOY DESIGN INC
3838 Chester Dr
Glenview, IL 60026-1013
Telephone: (847) 577-5683, FAX:
(847) 272-4034, E-Mail: info@
rbtoydesign.com, Web Site: www.
rbtoy.com
Pres: Dennis Kupperman

RPM INDUSTRIES INC
26 Aurelius Ave
Auburn, NY 13021-0400
Telephone: (315) 255-1105, (800) 669-
3676, FAX: (315) 252-1167, Web
Site: www.rpmdisplays.com
VP, Sls: Roger P. Mueller

ROBUSTELLI MERCHANDISE
PO Box 17295
Stamford, CT 06907-7295
Telephone: (203) 965-0200, FAX:
(203) 965-0387, Web Site: www.
robustelli.com
Pres: Richard Robustelli

ROHLIK SPECIALTIES CO
42505 Woodward Ave
Bloomfield Hills, MI 48304
Telephone: (248) 858-8880, FAX:
(248) 858-7323
Pres: Thomas Griesen

S GROUP INC
661 W Market St
Akron, OH 44303
Telephone: (330) 535-2103, (800) 686-
7435, FAX: (330) 535-1723, E-Mail:
info@s-groupinc.com, Web Site:
www.s-groupinc.com
VP: Jeff Sheeks

SAFE SPECIALTIES
223 Green Acres Rd
Kingston, TN 37763
Telephone: (865) 675-2815, (800) 695-
2815, FAX: (865) 717-8249, E-Mail:
black223@aol.com, Web Site: www.
safespec.com
CEO: Betty Blackburn
Primary Market Served: Business &
Consumer
Catalog available online
Direct online sales
Advertising/Marketing Budget Related
to Direct Marketing: 0-25%

Direct Marketing ad budget:
Online: 50%
Telephone: 50%
Founded: 1989

Office equipment merchant wholesalers

WILLIAM W SCHWARTZ ASSOCIATES INC
1907 Erie Ave
Sheboygan, WI 53081-3708
Telephone: (920) 458-4661, FAX:
(920) 458-6297, E-Mail: wws1503@
excel.net, Web Site: www.wschwartz.
com
Pres: Jeff Schwartz

SA-SO/TIME WISE
525 N Great Southwest Pkwy
Arlington, TX 76011-5422
Telephone: (972) 641-4911, (800) 523-
8060, FAX: (972) 660-5684, E-Mail:
info@sa-so.com, Web Site: www.sa-
so.com
Customer Service: Debbie Galling
Pres: Becky Nussbaum

THE SOURCE
Div. of Wholesale Trophies
2495 Washington St, PO Box 3888
Huntsville, AL 35810
Telephone: (256) 536-7305, (800) 433-
2375, FAX: (256) 539-8547, Web
Site: www.thesource-wti.com
Pres: Barry Tittsworth

SPECIAL MARKETS SALES CO
7435 E 86th St
Indianapolis, IN 46256-1207
Telephone: (317) 595-6587, FAX:
(317) 595-9853, E-Mail: info@
specialmkts.com, Web Site: www.
specialmkts.com
Pres: Robert J. Estka

STANDARD BUYING SERVICE LTD
424 W 33rd St (Rm 230)
New York, NY 10001-2656
Telephone: (212) 686-6800, FAX:
(212) 532-4102, E-Mail: info@
sbspromo.com, Web Site: www.
standardbuying.com
Pres: Kevin Geiger

STONEBRIDGE PRESS LTD
7620 WH Negley Rd
Henderson, KY 42420-9182
Telephone: (270) 826-0341, FAX:
(270) 826-8325
Prodn Coord: Susan Pinkston

STRATEGIC MARKETING SERVICES
PO Box 21686
Eagan, MN 55121-0686
Telephone: (651) 456-0100, E-Mail:
sms@fishnet.com
Pres: Scott Larson

STROMBERG BRAND
200 N Water St
Peekskill, NY 10566-2024
Telephone: (914) 739-7410, (800) 724-
0996, FAX: (914) 739-8642, E-Mail:
info@stromberggroup.com, Web
Site: www.strombergbrand.com
Pres: Helen Stromberg

SUPREME SPECIALTY ADVERTISING
34 Mulberry Ln
Mount Arlington, NJ 07856-1383
Telephone: (973) 770-8700, FAX:
(973) 770-0808
Owner: Donald Chopoorian

SWAG INC
69 Via Verde
Wichita, KS 67230
Telephone: (316) 685-3811, FAX:
(316) 685-4422, E-Mail: swag@cox.
net, Web Site: www.swagpromos.
com
Owner: Walter Burdick

TED'S PROMOTIONS INC
144 Lake Ridge Trail
Baldwin, GA 30511
Telephone: (770) 972-8081, FAX:
(770) 573-3141, E-Mail: ted@
tedspromotions.com, Web Site:
www.tedspromotions.com
Pres: Ted Lehmen

TOP YEAR INTERNATIONAL INC
dba Akira
22425 E La Palma
Yorba Linda, CA 92887-3803
Telephone: (714) 692-6688, (800) 942-
8722, FAX: (714) 692-8691, E-Mail:
sales@akirausa.com, Web Site:
www.akirausa.com
Pres: Susan Tsai

TWIN CITY ENGRAVING/ PREMIER PROMOTIONS
1232 Broad St, Box 85
Saint Joseph, MI 49085
Telephone: (616) 983-0601, (800) 222-
7752, FAX: (616) 983-3571, Web
Site: www.premierpromos.com
Pres & Travel Buyer: Jerry Jones

UNISERV ADVERTISING INC
37 Hwy 35
Neptune City, NJ 07753
Telephone: (732) 774-1010, FAX:
(732) 774-3311, Web Site: www.
uniservinc.com
Pres & CEO: Glen Suchecki

A. DEAN WATKINS
2395 Jolly Rd (Suite 170)
Okemos, MI 48864
Telephone: (517) 349-7700, FAX:
(517) 349-7748, E-Mail:
adeanwatkins@aol.com, Web Site:
www.adeanwatkins.com
Pres: Robert Watkins

JM WECHTER & ASSOCIATES INC
569 Main St
Monroe, CT 06468-2806
Telephone: (203) 452-0063, FAX:
(203) 452-0414, Web Site: www.
wechter.com
Pres: Janet Wechter

WILCOX & ASSOCIATES
258 Short Ave
Longwood, FL 32750
Telephone: (407) 830-4808, FAX:
(407) 830-5265
Pres: Jack Wilcox

MARTY WOLF GAME CO
3601 E Wyoming Ave (SPC 107)
Las Vegas, NV 89104-4937
Telephone: (702) 385-2963, FAX:
(702) 385-6963, E-Mail: info@
gamblersjunkyard.com, Web Site:
www.gamblersjunkyard.com
Owner: Marty Wolf

ZOUIRE
PO Box 7287
Overland Park, KS 66207-0287
Telephone: (913) 384-6888, (800) 346-
8991, FAX: (913) 384-5757, E-Mail:
info@zouire.com, Web Site: www.
zouire.com
CEO: Houston Hale

Equipment & Supplies (34) — Geographic Index

Arizona

Salt River Project, 1521 N Project Dr, Tempe, 85281

California

Advent Software Inc, 600 Townsend (fl 5), San Francisco, 94103-4945

Auto Anything, 6602 Convoy Ct # 200, San Diego, 92111-1009

Avaya Communication, 41460 Bellerive Ct, Temecula, 92591-7942

CIDCO, 2181 W Sam Brano Ave, Fresno, 93711-2834

Dataprint Corp, 1650 Borel Pl Ste 206, San Mateo, 94402-3508

HB Distributors, 21612 Marilla St, Chatsworth, 91311-4123

HD Supply, 10641 Scripps Summit Ct, San Diego, 92131-3961

IMSI/Design LLC, 25 Leveroni Ct Ste B, Novato, 94949-5726

Johnson Wilshire Distributors Service Corp, 11650 Burke St, Santa Fe Springs, 90670-2544

Parker Boiler Co, 5930 Bandini Blvd, Los Angeles, 90040-2999

PFE Inc, 475 Goddard (Suite 150), Irvine, 92626

Toyota Racing Development USA Inc, 335 E Baker St, Costa Mesa, 92626-4518

Vertical Communications Inc, 3940 Freedom Cr, Santa Clara, 95054-1204

Colorado

Quark Inc, 1225 17th St Ste 1200, Denver, 80202-5503

Stolle Machinery LLC, 6949 S Potomac St, Centennial, 80112

Connecticut

A&R Mailing Machine Inc, 757 Goodwin St, East Hartford, 06108-1202

Cooper-Atkins Corp, 33 Reeds Gap Rd, Middlefield, 06455-0450

Gerber Garment Technology Inc, 24 Industrial Park Rd W, Tolland, 06084

Hasler Mailing Systems and Solutions, 478 Wheelers Farms Rd, Milford, 06461

HB Communications, 60 Dodge Ave, North Haven, 06473

Tamarkin & Co, 270 Amity Rd (Suite 125), Woodbridge, 06525

Florida

BH Bunn Co, 2730 Drane Field Rd, Lakeland, 33811-1325

East Coast Industrial Equipment & Tire, 1330 W Beaver St, Jacksonville, 32209

Modular Mailing Systems, 4913 W Laurel St, Tampa, 33607

OCE North America Inc, 5600 Broken Sound Blvd, Boca Raton, 33487

Strong Enterprises, 11236 Satellite Blvd, Orlando, 32837

Georgia

Apollo Industries Inc, 1850 S Cobb Industrial Blvd, Smyrna, 30082

The Linton Co, 400 Baker Ln, Darien, 31305

New Hermes Inc, 2200 Northmont Pkwy, Duluth, 30096

Staples Business Advantage, 2077 Convention Center Concourse Ste 125, Atlanta, 30337-4205

Idaho

KNG Inc, 2102 E Karcher Rd, Nampa, 83687-3000

Illinois

Colorworks Graphics Inc, 451 N Racine, Chicago, 60622-5841

FP Mailing Solutions, 140 N Mitchell Ct, Addison, 60101-5629

Global Infomercial Services Inc, 745 McClintock Dr (Suite 220), Burr Ridge, 60527-0863

Gummed Papers of America, 8740 W 50th St, Mc Cook, 60525-3149

Heyer Corp, 642 Glacier Trl, Roselle, 60172-1035

Hurletron Inc, 1820 Tempel Dr, Libertyville, 60048

Jacobsen Lenticular Tool & Cylinder Engraving Technologies Co (Jacotech), PO Box 4289, Itasca, 60143-4289

Jon-Don, 400 Medinah Rd, Roselle, 60172-2329

Old World Ind, 4065 Commercial Ave, Northbrook, 60062-1828

Royal Performance Group, 2100 Western Ct (Suite 80), Lisle, 60532-1971

USG Corp, 550 W Adams St, Chicago, 60661-3665

UV Process Supply, 1229 W Cortland St, Chicago, 60614-4805

Video Jet Technologies Inc, 1500 Mittel Blvd, Wood Dale, 60191-1073

Wells Lamont Industry Group, 6640 W Touhy Ave, Niles, 60714

Western Printing Machinery (WPM), 9229 Ivanhoe St, Schiller Park, 60176

Indiana

Bemis Co Inc, 1350 N Fruitfidge Ave, Terre Haute, 47804

Merchandising Equipment Group (MEG), 502 S Green St, Cambridge City, 47327

Iowa

Business Technologies, 3350 Center Grove Dr Ste 4, Dubuque, 52003-5200

Maine

Shape Global Technology, 90 Community Dr, Sanford, 04073

Maryland

Healthy Directions LLC, 7811 Montrose Rd, Potomac, 20854-3363

925 Business Furniture, 10400 Connecticut Ave (Suite 402), Kensington, 20895-3943

Massachusetts

Ahern Communications Corp, 30 Chestnut St Ste 1, Quincy, 02169-5344

Cognitronics Corp, 124 Washington St (Suite 101), Foxboro, 02035-1368

Data Translation Inc, 100 Locke Dr, Marlborough, 01752-7235

Durasol Corp, One Oakland St, PO Box 35, Amesbury, 01913

Empire Imports Inc, PO Box 2728, Amherst, 01004-2728

Titan Manufacturing, 27 Maple Ave Ste 5, Holbrook, 02343-1077

Michigan

Haworth Inc, One Haworth Ctr, Holland, 49423

Interior Concepts Corp, 18525 Trimble Ct, Spring Lake, 49456-9570

Jesco Industries Inc, 950 Anderson Rd, Litchfield, 49252

Minnesota

Buhrs Americas Inc, 5255 E River Rd (Suite 210), Minneapolis, 55421-1005

Datacard Ga-Vehren Corp, 11111 Bren Rd W, Hopkins, 55343-9015

GS Direct Inc, 6490 Carlson Dr, Eden Prairie, 55346-1729

Postmatic Inc, 9405 Holly St (Suite D), Minneapolis, 55433

Streamfeeder, 315 27th Ave NE, Minneapolis, 55418-2715

TENNANT Co, 701 N Lilac Dr, Minneapolis, 55422-4687

Missouri

Dispensa-Matic Label Dispensers, 725 N 23rd St, Saint Louis, 63103-1533

VisiPak, 13515 Barrett Pkwy Dr, Saint Louis, 63021

Nebraska

Direct Tech Inc, 13259 Millard Ave Ste 306, Omaha, 68137-1782

New Hampshire

Perimeter Technology Inc, 540 N Commercial St, Manchester, 03101-1122

Presstek Inc, 55 Executive Dr, Hudson, 03051

New Jersey

Check Point Systems, 101 Wolf Dr, Thorofare, 08086

Flex Products, 640 Dell Rd Ste 1, Carlstadt, 07072-2202

LogEtronics Corp, 520 Lafayette Rd, Sparta, 07871

Opex Corp, 305 Commerce Dr, Moorestown, 08057-4234

New York

Automated Equipment Service Inc, 60 Noxon Rd, Poughkeepsie, 12603

The Colonial Co, 1225 36th St, Brooklyn, 11204

DeSantis Holster & Leather Goods Co, 431 Bayview Ave, Amityville, 11701

Global Computer Supplies, 11 Harbor Park Dr, Port Washington, 11050

Laerdal Medical, 167 Myers Corners Rd, Wappingers Falls, 12590-3869

Mailing and Fulfillment Service Association of New York, 411 E 53 St (Suite 20B), New York, 10022

MSC Metalworking, 75 Maxess Rd, Melville, 11747-3151

OccuNomix, 585 Bicycle Path (Suite 52), Port Jefferson Station, 11776-3431

The Staplex Co, 777 Fifth Ave, Brooklyn, 11232-1626

Surchin Advanced Mailing Technologies, 80 E Jefryn Blvd (Suite C), Deer Park, 11729-5755

Ty Pac, 7858 River Rd, Baldwinsville, 13027

Ulano Corp, 110 Third Ave, Brooklyn, 11217

Ward's Natural Science, PO Box 92912, Rochester, 14692-9012

North Carolina

Bowe Bell & Howell, 3791 S Alston Ave, Durham, 27713-1803

Rochling Engineered Plastics, 903 Gstonia Technology Pkwy, Dallas, 28034-7791

Ohio

Aspen Imaging International Inc, 3830 Kelley Ave, Cleveland, 44114-4534

Hamilton Sorter Co, 3158 Production Dr, Fairfield, 45014-4228

SGD Golf Co, 350 Tacoma Ave, Tallmadge, 44278-2717

Washington Products Inc, PO Box 644, Massillon, 44648-0644

Oklahoma

Hilti North America, 5400 S 122nd East Ave, Tulsa, 74146-6007

Petra Industries, 2101 S Kelly Ave, Edmond, 73013-3665

Oregon

Datalogic Scanning, 959 Terry St, Eugene, 97402-9150

NTP Distribution, 27150 SW Kinsman Rd, Wilsonville, 97070-9241

Pennsylvania

ATD American Co, 135 Greenwood Ave, Wyncote, 19095-1396

Calloway House Inc, 451 Richardson Dr, Lancaster, 17603-4098

Case Design Corp, 333 School Ln, Telford, 18969-2047

Crane Environmental, 2650 Eisenhower Ave (Suite 100A), PO Box 60191, Norristown, 19403-2337

Decision One, 426 W Lancaster Ave, Devon, 19333

Foster Manufacturing Co, 204B Progress Dr, Montgomeryville, 18936-9616

Frank Mobility Systems Inc, 1003 International Dr, Oakdale, 15071-9226

S Morantz Inc, 9984 Gantry Rd, Philadelphia, 19115-1002

Playworld Systems, 1000 Buffalo Rd, Lewisburg, 17837-9795

Red Hill Corp, PO Box 4234, 1540 Biglerville Rd, Gettysburg, 17325

Roovers Inc, 125 Butler Dr, Hazleton, 18201

FL Smithe Machine Co Inc, 899 Old Rte 220 N, Duncansville, 16635-9432

Styled Packaging LLC, PO Box 30299, Philadelphia, 19103-8299

VWR International, 100 Matsonford Rd (Suite 200), Radnor Corporate Ctr Bldg 1, Radnor, 19087-4560

Rhode Island

APC By Schneider Electric, 132 Fairgrounds Rd, West Kingston, 02892-1511

South Dakota

Fenske Media Corp, 3635 Homestead St, Rapid City, 57703-8101

Texas

Automated Mailing Systems Corp, 10730 Spangler Rd, Dallas, 75220-7102

Carlton Industries CP, PO Box 280, La Grange, 78945-0280

Echnologist Scrub Tech, 2701 Cameron Way, Mesquite, 75181-4405

Infinity Trading Co Inc, PO Box 9685, Spring, 77387-6685

NCH Corp, 2801 Turtle Creek Blvd (Apt 9W), Dallas, 75219

Stevens International Inc, 5700 E Belknap St, Fort Worth, 76117

Swords Music Co Inc, 4300 E Lancaster Ave, Fort Worth, 76103-3225

Thomson, 2395 Midway Rd, Carrollton, 75006-2521

Virginia

National Electrical Manufacturers Association (NEMA), 1300 N 17th St (Suite 1752), Rosslyn, 22209-3806

Spectrum Systems Inc, 11325 Random Hills Rd (Suite 600), Fairfax, 22030-0987

SER Solutions Inc, 1001 Campus Comons Dr (Suite 500), Reston, 20191-1572

United Way Store, 85 S Bragg St Ste 600, Alexandria, 22312-2793

Wisconsin

HK Systems Inc, 2855 S James Dr, New Berlin, 53151

Lewis Cleaning Systems, 502 Hwy 67, Kiel, 53042

SIG Pack Inc Doboy Div, 869 S Knowles Ave, New Richmond, 54017

Windway Capital Corp, 630 Riverfront Dr (Suite 200), Sheboygan, 53082-0897

CANADA
Ontario

Nortel Networks Corp, 5945 Airport Rd (Suite 360), Mississauga, L4V 1R9

Pitney Bowes of Canada Limited, 5500 Explorer Dr, Mississauga, L4W 5C7

Equipment & Supplies (34)

A&R MAILING MACHINE INC
757 Goodwin St
East Hartford, CT 06108-1202
Telephone: (860) 290-6640
Pres: Arthur Ringuette

ATD AMERICAN CO
135 Greenwood Ave
Wyncote, PA 19095-1396
Telephone: (215) 576-1380, (866) 283-9327, FAX: (215) 576-1827, E-Mail: janet@atd.com, Web Site: www.atdamerican.com
Pres: Janet Wischnia

THE DMA ADVENT SOFTWARE INC
600 Townsend (fl 5)
San Francisco, CA 94103-4945
Telephone: (415) 645-1200, Web Site: www.advent.com
Primary Market Served: Business

AHERN COMMUNICATIONS CORP
30 Chestnut St Ste 1
Quincy, MA 02169-5344
Telephone: (617) 471-1100, (800) 451-3280, FAX: (617) 328-9070, E-Mail: info@aherncorp.com, Web Site: www.aherncorp.com
VP: Alison B. Smith
Employees: 10
Founded: 1987
Gross sales or billing: $1,800,000

THE DMA APC BY SCHNEIDER ELECTRIC
132 Fairgrounds Rd
West Kingston, RI 02892-1511
Telephone: (401) 789-5735, Web Site: www.apc.com
Global Dir Customer Retention: Evan Kent

APOLLO INDUSTRIES INC
1850 S Cobb Industrial Blvd
Smyrna, GA 30082
Telephone: (770) 433-0210, (800) 533-3548, FAX: (770) 433-0132, Web Site: www.apolloind.com

ASPEN IMAGING INTERNATIONAL INC
3830 Kelley Ave
Cleveland, OH 44114-4534

Telephone: (216) 881-5300, (800) 955-5555, FAX: (216) 881-8380, (800) 756-0990
Pres: William Dillingham

AUTO ANYTHING
Div. of Motorlamb Accessories International
6602 Convoy Ct # 200
San Diego, CA 92111-1009
Telephone: (858) 569-8111, (800) 874-8888, FAX: (858) 569-8503, E-Mail: customerservice@autoanything.com, Web Site: www.autoanything.com
Sls & Mktg: David Klein

AUTOMATED EQUIPMENT SERVICE INC
60 Noxon Rd
Poughkeepsie, NY 12603
Telephone: (845) 452-2100, (800) 468-4068, FAX: (845) 485-8221, E-Mail: info@aesmailpro.com, Web Site: www.aesmailpro.com
Pres: James T. Maine

AUTOMATED MAILING SYSTEMS CORP
10730 Spangler Rd
Dallas, TX 75220-7102
Telephone: (972) 869-2844, (800) 527-1668, FAX: (972) 869-2735, E-Mail: amsco@amscodallas.com
Pres: Tom Helsley

AVAYA COMMUNICATION
41460 Bellerive Ct
Temecula, CA 92591-7942
Web Site: www.avaya.com
Opers Mgr, North America Mktg: Cynthia Syroka

BEMIS CO INC
1350 N Fruitfidge Ave
Terre Haute, IN 47804
Telephone: (812) 466-2213, FAX: (812) 460-6370, E-Mail: contact@beemis.com, Web Site: www.bemis.com
CEO: Jerry S. Curler

BOWE BELL & HOWELL
Subs. of Bell & Howell Co
3791 S Alston Ave
Durham, NC 27713-1803

Telephone: (919) 767-6400, (800) 220-3030, E-Mail: marketing@bowebellhowell.com, Web Site: www.bowebellhowell.com
Dir Mktg Communs: Ted Seward
CEO: John Lombard

BUHRS AMERICAS INC
Subs. of Buhrs Holdings BB
5255 E River Rd (Suite 210)
Minneapolis, MN 55421-1005
Telephone: (763) 557-9100, FAX: (763) 557-9700, Web Site: www.buhrs.com
Pres: Kevin Thompson

BH BUNN CO
2730 Drane Field Rd
Lakeland, FL 33811-1325
Telephone: (863) 647-1555, (800) 222-2866, FAX: (863) 686-2866, E-Mail: info@bunntyco.com, Web Site: www.bunntyco.com
Pres & CEO: John R. Bunn

BUSINESS TECHNOLOGIES
3350 Center Grove Dr Ste 4
Dubuque, IA 52003-5200
Telephone: (563) 556-7994, (800) 451-0399, FAX: (563) 556-2512
Pres: Robert J. Bell

CALLOWAY HOUSE INC
451 Richardson Dr
Lancaster, PA 17603-4098
Telephone: (717) 299-5703, (800) 233-0290, FAX: (717) 299-6754, Web Site: www.callowayhouse.com
CEO: Barbara Ternoban

THE DMA CARLTON INDUSTRIES CP
PO Box 280
La Grange, TX 78945-0280
Telephone: (979) 242-5055, (800) 231-5988, FAX: (800) 231-5934, E-Mail: sales@carltonusa.com, Web Site: www.carltonusa.com
Pres: Kay Carlton

CASE DESIGN CORP
333 School Ln
Telford, PA 18969-2047
Telephone: (215) 703-0130, (800) 847-4176, FAX: (215) 703-0139, E-Mail: sales@casedesigncorp.com, Web Site: www.casedesigncorp.com
Pres: Roger Ernst
VP, Sls: Paul Lowman

Conducts Business: U.S.
Employees: 150
Primary Market Served: Business
Catalog available online
Indirect online sales
Advertising/Marketing Budget Related
   to Direct Marketing: 0-25%
Founded: 1921
Gross sales or billing: $5,000,000

Design & manufacture sample, display
& video equipment cases.

CHECK POINT SYSTEMS
101 Wolf Dr
Thorofare, NJ 08086
Telephone: (856) 848-1800, (800) 257-
   5540, FAX: (856) 848-0937, Web
   Site: www.checkpointsystems.com
Pres: Nicholas Khalil

CIDCO
Div. of RKR International Marketing
   & Associates
2181 W Sam Brano Ave
Fresno, CA 93711-2834
Telephone: (559) 497-9414, FAX:
   (559) 497-9435
Mng Dir: John Knapp

COGNITRONICS CORP
124 Washington St (Suite 101)
Foxboro, MA 02035-1368
Telephone: (508) 624-7600, (888) 228-
   5061, FAX: (508) 624-0289, E-Mail:
   info@thinkengine.com, Web Site:
   www.cognitronics.com
Pres & CEO: Michael G. Mitchell

THE COLONIAL CO
1225 36th St
Brooklyn, NY 11204
Telephone: (718) 972-7433, FAX:
   (718) 972-7438

COLORWORKS GRAPHICS INC
451 N Racine
Chicago, IL 60622-5841
Telephone: (312) 666-7642, FAX:
   (312) 666-0473, E-Mail:
   colorworks@ameritech.net, Web
   Site: www.colorworksgraphics.com
Mgr: Gene Young

COOPER-ATKINS CORP
33 Reeds Gap Rd
Middlefield, CT 06455-0450
Telephone: (860) 347-2256, (800) 835-
   5011, FAX: (860) 347-5135, Web
   Site: www.cooper-atkins.com
Mktg Mgr: Sharon LeGault
Mktg Asst: Jillian Camarata
Conducts Business: Worldwide
Employees: 105

Primary Market Served: Business
Catalog available online
Advertising/Marketing Budget Related
   to Direct Marketing: 0-25%
Direct Marketing ad budget:
Direct Mail: 20%
Magazines: 80%
Founded: 1885

Sells temperature, time & humidity
instruments for HVAC/R, foodservice,
industrial, consumer, OEM & export
markets, measuring success for 125
years!

CRANE ENVIRONMENTAL
2650 Eisenhower Ave (Suite 100A),
   PO Box 60191
Norristown, PA 19403-2337
Telephone: (610) 631-7700, (800) 828-
   2447, FAX: (610) 630-6656, E-Mail:
   purwater@cranenv.com, Web Site:
   www.cranenv.com
Pres & CEO: Don Borden

DATA TRANSLATION INC
100 Locke Dr
Marlborough, MA 01752-7235
Telephone: (508) 481-3700, (800) 525-
   8528, FAX: (508) 481-8620, Web
   Site: www.datatranslation.com
Pres: Alfred Molinari

DATACARD GA-VEHREN CORP
Subs. of Datacard Group
11111 Bren Rd W
Hopkins, MN 55343-9015
Telephone: (952) 933-1223, (800) 621-
   6972 x6930, FAX: (952) 931-0418,
   E-Mail: info@datacard.com, Web
   Site: www.gavehren.com
Pres & CEO: Jeffrey J. Hattara

DATALOGIC SCANNING
959 Terry St
Eugene, OR 97402-9150
Telephone: (800) 695-5700, FAX:
   (541) 345-7140, Web Site: www.
   scanning.datalogic.com
Pres & CEO: Bill Parnell

DATAPRINT CORP
1650 Borel Pl Ste 206
San Mateo, CA 94402-3508
Telephone: (650) 340-0550, (800) 227-
   6191, FAX: (650) 340-7028, Web
   Site: www.dataprint.com
Exec VP: Donna Misa

DECISION ONE
426 W Lancaster Ave
Devon, PA 19333

Telephone: (800) 767-2876, FAX:
   (610) 296-2910, Web Site: www.
   decisionone.com
Pres & CEO: Neal Bibeau

DESANTIS HOLSTER & LEATHER GOODS CO
431 Bayview Ave
Amityville, NY 11701
Telephone: (631) 841-6300, (800)
   GUNHIDE, FAX: (631) 841-6320,
   E-Mail: contact@desantisholster.
   com, Web Site: www.desantisholster.
   com
Sec & Treas: Helen DeSantis

DIRECT TECH INC
13259 Millard Ave Ste 306
Omaha, NE 68137-1782
Telephone: (402) 895-2100, Web Site:
   www.direct-tech.com
Pres: Craig Harding

DISPENSA-MATIC LABEL DISPENSERS
725 N 23rd St
Saint Louis, MO 63103-1533
Telephone: (314) 231-6006, (800) 325-
   7303, FAX: (314) 621-1602, E-Mail:
   info@dispensamatic.com, Web Site:
   www.dispensa-matic.com
Pres: Allen H. Oglander

DURASOL CORP
One Oakland St, PO Box 35
Amesbury, MA 01913
Telephone: (978) 388-2020, (800) 370-
   0683, FAX: (978) 388-9762, Web
   Site: www.durasolcorp.com
Pres: Walter Israel

EAST COAST INDUSTRIAL EQUIPMENT & TIRE
1330 W Beaver St
Jacksonville, FL 32209
Telephone: (904) 358-1229, (800) 874-
   1942, FAX: (904) 354-0888
CEO: Jim Burch

ECHNOLOGIST SCRUB TECH
2701 Cameron Way
Mesquite, TX 75181-4405
Telephone: (520) 208-6314
Mgr: Keith Howe
Primary Market Served: Business &
   Consumer

EMPIRE IMPORTS INC
PO Box 2728
Amherst, MA 01004-2728

Telephone: (413) 256-4917, (800) 544-4744, FAX: (413) 256-4645, E-Mail: info@empireimports.com, Web Site: www.empireimports.com
Pres: Andy Beall

FP MAILING SOLUTIONS
140 N Mitchell Ct
Addison, IL 60101-5629
Telephone: (800) 341-6052, FAX: (630) 693-0626, Web Site: www.fp-usa.com
CEO: Mike Doumas
Commun Mgr: Diane Odom

FENSKE MEDIA CORP
aka Fenskemedia.com
3635 Homestead St
Rapid City, SD 57703-8101
Telephone: (605) 343-6070, (800) 821-6343, FAX: (605) 348-2108, E-Mail: tomf@fenskemedia.com, Web Site: www.fenskemedia.com
Partner: Tom Fenske

FLEX PRODUCTS
640 Dell Rd Ste 1
Carlstadt, NJ 07072-2202
Telephone: (201) 933-3030, (800) 526-6273, FAX: (201) 933-2396, E-Mail: info@flex-products.com, Web Site: www.flex-products.com
Pres: Ed Friedhoff

FOSTER MANUFACTURING CO
204B Progress Dr
Montgomeryville, PA 18936-9616
Telephone: (215) 442-1700, (800) 523-4855, FAX: (215) 442-1313, E-Mail: information@fostermfg.com, Web Site: www.fostermfg.com
Pres: Ted Borowsky

FRANK MOBILITY SYSTEMS INC
1003 International Dr
Oakdale, PA 15071-9226
Telephone: (888) 426-8581, FAX: (724) 695-3710, E-Mail: info@lfrankmobility.com, Web Site: www.lifestandusa.com

GS DIRECT INC
6490 Carlson Dr
Eden Prairie, MN 55346-1729
Telephone: (952) 942-6115, (800) 234-3729, FAX: (952) 942-0216, Web Site: www.gsdirect.net
Conducts Business: U.S.
Primary Market Served: Business & Consumer
Catalog available online
Indirect online sales

Advertising/Marketing Budget Related to Direct Marketing: 51-75%
Direct Marketing ad budget:
Direct Mail: 70%
Online: 20%
Telephone: 10%
Founded: 1988

National distributor of graphic supplies & equipment. Products include: wide format printers, paper, media & supplies.

GERBER GARMENT TECHNOLOGY INC
24 Industrial Park Rd W
Tolland, CT 06084
Telephone: (860) 871-8082, FAX: (860) 871-6007, E-Mail: info@gerbertechnology.com, Web Site: www.gerbertechnology.com
Pres: John Hancock

GLOBAL COMPUTER SUPPLIES
11 Harbor Park Dr
Port Washington, NY 11050
Telephone: (732) 264-8200, (800) 446-9662, FAX: (732) 888-8316, Web Site: www.globalcomputer.com
Gen Mgr: John White

THE DMA GLOBAL INFOMERCIAL SERVICES INC
745 McClintock Dr (Suite 220)
Burr Ridge, IL 60527-0863
Telephone: (708) 229-2424, FAX: (708) 229-2407, E-Mail: info@giservices.tv, Web Site: www.giservices.tv

GUMMED PAPERS OF AMERICA
8740 W 50th St
Mc Cook, IL 60525-3149
Telephone: (773) 650-2020, (800) 395-9000, FAX: (708) 485-8603, (800) 395-3581, E-Mail: info@labelexperts.com, Web Site: www.labelexperts.com
Pres: Michael Ratcliff
Mktg Communs: Lori DeFrenza

HB COMMUNICATIONS
60 Dodge Ave
North Haven, CT 06473
Telephone: (203) 234-9246, (800) 243-4414, FAX: (203) 234-2013, E-Mail: info@hbcommunications.com, Web Site: www.hbcommunications.com
Pres: Mackey Barron
Mktg Dir: Nathan Berger

HB DISTRIBUTORS
21612 Marilla St
Chatsworth, CA 91311-4123
Telephone: (818) 882-0000, (800) 266-3478, FAX: (818) 700-1808, Web Site: www.hddistributors.com
Mktg Mgr: Sharon McAdams

HD SUPPLY
10641 Scripps Summit Ct
San Diego, CA 92131-3961
Telephone: (858) 831-2000
Mktg Mgr: Kevin Jacobson

HK SYSTEMS INC
2855 S James Dr
New Berlin, WI 53151
Telephone: (262) 860-7000, (800) HK SYSTEMS, FAX: (262) 860-7010, E-Mail: hkinfo@hksystems.com, Web Site: www.hksystems.com
Exec VP: David Bartley

HAMILTON SORTER CO
Div. of Workstream
3158 Production Dr
Fairfield, OH 45014-4228
Telephone: (513) 870-4400, (800) 503-9966, FAX: (800) 503-9963, E-Mail: sstreight@hamiltonsorter.com, Web Site: www.hamiltonsorter.com
VP: Steve Streight

HASLER MAILING SYSTEMS AND SOLUTIONS
478 Wheelers Farms Rd
Milford, CT 06461
Telephone: (203) 301-3400, (800) 995-2035, FAX: (203) 301-2600, E-Mail: info@haslerinc.com, Web Site: www.haslerinc.com
Pres: John Vavra

HAWORTH INC
One Haworth Ctr
Holland, MI 49423
Telephone: (616) 393-3000, (800) 344-2600, FAX: (616) 393-1570, Web Site: www.haworth.com
VP Sls: Todd James

THE DMA HEALTHY DIRECTIONS LLC
7811 Montrose Rd
Potomac, MD 20854-3363
Telephone: (301) 340-7788, Web Site: www.healthydirections.com

HEYER CORP
642 Glacier Trl
Roselle, IL 60172-1035
Telephone: (708) 398-7646, FAX: (866) 542-9858, E-Mail: info@heyerco.com, Web Site: www.heyerco.com

Pres: Bill Heyer

HILTI NORTH AMERICA
5400 S 122nd East Ave
Tulsa, OK 74146-6007
Telephone: (918) 252-6000, Web Site:
　www.hilti.com
Sr Mgr Customer Fidelity: Vanessa
　Komara

HURLETRON INC
1820 Tempel Dr
Libertyville, IL 60048
Telephone: (847) 680-7022, FAX:
　(847) 680-7338, Web Site: www.
　hurletron.com
Gen Mgr: Dave Klein

IMSI/DESIGN LLC
25 Leveroni Ct Ste B
Novato, CA 94949-5726
Telephone: (415) 483-8000, (800) 833-
　4674, FAX: (415) 884-9023, Web
　Site: www.imsisoft.com
COO: Bob Mayer

INFINITY TRADING CO INC
PO Box 9685
Spring, TX 77387-6685
Telephone: (281) 931-8000, FAX:
　(281) 931-8139, E-Mail: sales@
　infinitytradingcompany.com, Web
　Site: www.
　infinitytradingcompany.com
Pres & Owner: Ben Baker

INTERIOR CONCEPTS CORP
18525 Trimble Ct
Spring Lake, MI 49456-9570
Telephone: (616) 842-5550, (800) 678-
　5550, FAX: (616) 842-7122, Web
　Site: www.interiorconcepts.com
Pres: David Kendrick

JACOBSEN LENTICULAR TOOL & CYLINDER ENGRAVING TECHNOLOGIES CO (JACOTECH)
Div. of Web Communications Group,
　Inc.
PO Box 4289
Itasca, IL 60143-4289
Telephone: (630) 467-0900, FAX:
　(630) 467-0900, E-Mail: gj@
　jacotech.com, Web Site: www.
　jacotech.com; www.lenticlearlens.
　com
CEO & Pres: Gary A. Jacobsen Ph.D.

Full Service Cylinder Engraving &
Optical Engineering.

JESCO INDUSTRIES INC
950 Anderson Rd
Litchfield, MI 49252
Telephone: (517) 542-2903, (888) 463-
　1246, FAX: (517) 542-2501, E-Mail:
　jesco@jescoonline.com, Web Site:
　www.jescoonline.com
Pres: Bonny DesJardin

JOHNSON WILSHIRE DISTRIBUTORS SERVICE CORP
11650 Burke St
Santa Fe Springs, CA 90670-2544
Telephone: (562) 777-0088, (800) 922-
　2456, FAX: (562) 777-0099, (800)
　993-9699, E-Mail: jwigloves@aol.
　com, Web Site: www.
　johnsonwilshire.com
Pres: David Pang

THE DMA JON-DON
400 Medinah Rd
Roselle, IL 60172-2329
Telephone: (800) 556-6366, Web Site:
　www.jondon.com
Mktg Mgr: Jacki Fry
Primary Market Served: Business

THE DMA KNG INC
2102 E Karcher Rd
Nampa, ID 83687-3000
Telephone: (208) 318-0188, Web Site:
　www.kng.com

LAERDAL MEDICAL
167 Myers Corners Rd
Wappingers Falls, NY 12590-3869
Telephone: (877) 523-7325, Web Site:
　www.laerdal.com
Prod Mktg Mgr: Marion Young
Primary Market Served: Business &
　Consumer

LEWIS CLEANING SYSTEMS
Subs. of Polar Wave Co
502 Hwy 67
Kiel, WI 53042
Telephone: (920) 894-2293, FAX:
　(920) 894-7029, Web Site: www.
　lewissonics.com
Pres: Robert Hunter

THE LINTON CO
400 Baker Ln
Darien, GA 31305
Telephone: (912) 638-3538, (800) 841-
　0200, FAX: (912) 437-3195, E-Mail:
　cinfo@davientel.net, Web Site: www.
　lintonlabels.com
Pres: D.B. Linton

LOGETRONICS CORP
Div. of Amergraph Corp
520 Lafayette Rd
Sparta, NJ 07871
Telephone: (703) 912-7745, FAX:
　(703) 912-7610, Web Site: www.
　logetronics.com
Pres: Ray Luca
Svc Mgr: Charlie Biern

MAILING AND FULFILLMENT SERVICE ASSOCIATION OF NEW YORK
411 E 53 St (Suite 20B)
New York, NY 10022
Telephone: (212) 217-6824, (800) 394-
　5106, FAX: (212) 217-6824, E-Mail:
　info@mfsany.com, Web Site: www.
　mfsany.com
Co-Dir: Jim Prendergast
Co-Dir: Risa Sudnow Cohen

Trade organization for professional
mailing organizations to provide an
active network for participation &
growth.

MERCHANDISING EQUIPMENT GROUP (MEG)
Div. of Hirsch
502 S Green St
Cambridge City, IN 47327
Telephone: (765) 478-3141, (800) 645-
　3315, FAX: (765) 478-4439, E-Mail:
　meginfo@megfixtures.com, Web
　Site: www.megfixtures.com
Pres: Tom Hilkert

MODULAR MAILING SYSTEMS
4913 W Laurel St
Tampa, FL 33607
Telephone: (305) 826-9077, (800) 881-
　MAIL, E-Mail: sales@
　modularmailing.com, Web Site:
　www.modularmailing.com
Gen Mgr: Art Wagaheim

S MORANTZ INC
9984 Gantry Rd
Philadelphia, PA 19115-1002
Telephone: (215) 969-0266, (800) 695-
　4522, FAX: (215) 969-0566, E-Mail:
　info@morantz.com, Web Site: www.
　morantz.com
Pres: Stan Morantz

MSC METALWORKING
75 Maxess Rd
Melville, NY 11747-3151
Telephone: (516) 812-2000, (800) 521-
　9520, E-Mail: inquiry@rutlandtool.
　com, Web Site: www.rutlandtool.com
Pres: Andrew Verey

VP Sls: Paul Martin
VP, Pur: Rich Lawce
Employees: 207
Primary Market Served: Business &
 Consumer
Founded: 1955
Gross sales or billing: $17,000,000

NCH CORP
2801 Turtle Creek Blvd (Apt 9W)
Dallas, TX 75219
Telephone: (972) 438-0211, FAX:
 (972) 438-0186, Web Site: www.nch.
 com
Chmn: Lester A. Levy

NTP DISTRIBUTION
27150 SW Kinsman Rd
Wilsonville, OR 97070-9241
Telephone: (503) 570-0171, Web Site:
 www.ntpdistribution.com
Mktg Mgr: Jeff Johnson
Primary Market Served: Business

**NATIONAL ELECTRICAL
MANUFACTURERS
ASSOCIATION (NEMA)**
1300 N 17th St (Suite 1752)
Rosslyn, VA 22209-3806
Telephone: (703) 841-3200, FAX:
 (703) 841-5900, E-Mail:
 communications@nema.org, Web
 Site: www.nema.org
Pres & CEO: Evan R. Gaddis
Sr VP Opers: Stephen Gold
VP Bus Info Svcs: Donald Leavens
VP Govt Affairs: Kyle Pitsor
VP Tech Svcs: Alvin Scolnik
Conducts Business: Worldwide
Employees: 100
Primary Market Served: Business &
 Consumer
Advertising/Marketing Budget Related
 to Direct Marketing: 0-25%
Direct Marketing ad budget: $17,000
Direct Mail: 100%
Founded: 1926
Gross sales or billing: $400,000

Standard development organization for
the electrical manufacturing industry.

NEW HERMES INC
2200 Northmont Pkwy
Duluth, GA 30096
Telephone: (770) 623-0331, (800) 843-
 7637, FAX: (800) 533-7637, E-Mail:
 sales@gravograph-newhermes.com,
 Web Site: www.gravograph.com/usa/
 government/index.php
Pres: John Norris

925 BUSINESS FURNITURE
10400 Connecticut Ave (Suite 402)
Kensington, MD 20895-3943

Telephone: (800) 525-0302, FAX:
 (302) 349-4587, E-Mail: bjfreed@
 erols.com, Web Site: www.
 natcofurniture.com
Mktg Dir: Bernie Freed

NORTEL NETWORKS CORP
5945 Airport Rd (Suite 360)
Mississauga, ON, Canada L4V 1R9
Telephone: (905) 863-7000, (888) 901-
 7286, Web Site: www.nortel.com
Sr VP Fin: John M Doolittle

OCCUNOMIX
585 Bicycle Path (Suite 52)
Port Jefferson Station, NY 11776-3431
Telephone: (631) 791-1912, Web Site:
 www.occunomix.com
Dir Mktg: Jennifer McCoy
Primary Market Served: Business &
 Consumer

OCE NORTH AMERICA INC
Sub. Canon Inc
5600 Broken Sound Blvd
Boca Raton, FL 33487
Telephone: (561) 997-3100, (800) 523-
 5444, FAX: (561) 998-9160, Web
 Site: www.oceproductionprinting.
 com
Dir Mktg: Stacy West
Transactional & Direct Mail Segment
 Mgr: Chad Skelton
Graphic Arts Segment Mgr: Tonya
 Powers

THE DMA OLD WORLD IND
4065 Commercial Ave
Northbrook, IL 60062-1828
Telephone: (847) 559-2137, Web Site:
 www.oldworldind.com

OPEX CORP
305 Commerce Dr
Moorestown, NJ 08057-4234
Telephone: (856) 727-1100, FAX:
 (856) 727-1955, Web Site: www.
 opex.com
CEO & Pres: Mark Stevens

PFE INC
475 Goddard (Suite 150)
Irvine, CA 92626
Telephone: (949) 417-0330, FAX:
 (949) 417-0331, Web Site: www.
 pfeinc.com
Gen Mgr: Jonathan Garcia

PARKER BOILER CO
5930 Bandini Blvd
Los Angeles, CA 90040-2999

Telephone: (323) 727-9800, FAX:
 (323) 722-2848, E-Mail: mleeming@
 parkerboiler.com, Web Site: www.
 parkerboiler.com
Pres: Sid D. Danenhauer
VP Engrng: Greg Danenhauer
Natl Sls Mgr,: Michael J. Leeming
Sls Mgr Los Angeles: Bob Jones
Sls Mgr San Diego: Bob Johnson
Conducts Business: U.S.
Employees: 65
Primary Market Served: Business
Catalog available online
Advertising/Marketing Budget Related
 to Direct Marketing: 0-25%
Founded: 1919
Gross sales or billing: $20,000,000

Manufacturer & distributor of steam &
hot water boilers, thermal fluid, water
heaters, tanks & accessories.

**PERIMETER TECHNOLOGY
INC**
540 N Commercial St
Manchester, NH 03101-1122
Telephone: (603) 645-1616, (800) 645-
 1650, FAX: (603) 645-1424, Web
 Site: www.perimetertechnology.com
Pres: Mike Dobbins

PETRA INDUSTRIES
2101 S Kelly Ave
Edmond, OK 73013-3665
Telephone: (405) 216-2100, Web Site:
 www.patra.com
Dir Mktg: Gregg Viall
Primary Market Served: Business

**PITNEY BOWES OF CANADA
LIMITED**
Subs. of Pitney Bowes Inc (Stamford
 CT)
5500 Explorer Dr
Mississauga, ON, Canada L4W 5C7
Telephone: (905) 219-3000, (866) 669-
 6627, FAX: (905) 219-3826, Web
 Site: www.pitneybowes.ca
VP & Gen Mgr SBS & Strategic
 Mktg: William Mackrell

THE DMA PLAYWORLD SYSTEMS
1000 Buffalo Rd
Lewisburg, PA 17837-9795
Telephone: (570) 522-9800, Web Site:
 www.playworldsystems.com
Brand Mgr: Victoria Cook
Primary Market Served: Business &
 Consumer

POSTMATIC INC
9405 Holly St (Suite D)
Minneapolis, MN 55433

Telephone: (763) 784-6046, (888) 784-6046, FAX: (763) 784-9433, E-Mail: info@postmatic.net, Web Site: www.postmatic.com
Pres: John Talbot

PRESSTEK INC
55 Executive Dr
Hudson, NH 03051
Telephone: (800) 422-3616
Pres & CEO: Edward J. Marino

QUARK INC
1225 17th St Ste 1200
Denver, CO 80202-5503
Telephone: (303) 894-3832, Web Site: www.quark.com
Pres & CEO: Raymond Schiavone
CIO: Jim Haggerty
CFO: Kevin Mammel
Gen Counsel: Peter Jensen
Sr VP Sls, Americas, Pacific & Japan: Mark Benfer
Sr VP Sls, EMEA & Asia: Matthew Wallis
Sr VP Prod Mngmt: PG Bartlett
VP HR: Claire Hancock
VP Alliances & Emerging Tech: Dave White
VP Mktg: Gavin Drake
Founded: 1981

RED HILL CORP
PO Box 4234, 1540 Biglerville Rd
Gettysburg, PA 17325
Telephone: (717) 337-3038, (800) 822-4003, FAX: (717) 337-0732, E-Mail: custserv@supergrit.com, Web Site: www.supergrit.com
Pres: Arturo M. Ottolenghi
Mgr: Ginny Mowen
It Mgr: Laura Ripple
Conducts Business: Worldwide
Employees: 5
Primary Market Served: Business & Consumer
Catalog available online
Indirect online sales
Advertising/Marketing Budget Related to Direct Marketing: 76-100%
Direct Marketing ad budget: $100,000
Direct Mail: 50%
Magazines: 45%
Online: 5%
Founded: 1978
Gross sales or billing: $1,300,000

Sanding & polishing supplies for auto body, wood & metal working.

ROCHLING ENGINEERED PLASTICS
Subs. of Rochling Haren KG
903 Gstonia Technology Pkwy
Dallas, NC 28034-7791

Telephone: (704) 922-7814, (800) 541-4419, FAX: (704) 922-7651, E-Mail: rep@roechling-plastics.us, Web Site: www.roechling-plastics.us
Partner: Lewis Carter

ROOVERS INC
125 Butler Dr
Hazleton, PA 18201
Telephone: (570) 455-7548, FAX: (570) 454-1477
Pres: Nancy M. Andrasko

THE DMA ROYAL PERFORMANCE GROUP
2100 Western Ct (Suite 80)
Lisle, IL 60532-1971
Telephone: (630) 353-7900, Web Site: www.rpggiftcards.com

SER SOLUTIONS INC
1001 Campus Comons Dr (Suite 500)
Reston, VA 20191-1572
Telephone: (703) 948-5500, (800) 274-5676, FAX: (703) 430-7738, E-Mail: info@ser.com, Web Site: www.ser.com
VP, Prod Mngmt & Mktg: Sandra Wade

SGD GOLF CO
350 Tacoma Ave
Tallmadge, OH 44278-2717
Telephone: (330) 745-4400, (800) 321-3411, FAX: (330) 745-4420, (888) 299-4240, Web Site: www.sgdgolf.com
Chmn & CEO: Donald C. Nelson

SIG PACK INC DOBOY DIV
Div. of SIG Pack Inc
869 S Knowles Ave
New Richmond, WI 54017
Telephone: (715) 246-6511, FAX: (715) 246-6539, Web Site: www.doboy.com
Pres: Bill Heilhecker

THE DMA SALT RIVER PROJECT
1521 N Project Dr
Tempe, AZ 85281
Telephone: (602) 236-5929, Web Site: www.srpnet.com
Sr Program Mgr: Jeff Cree

SHAPE GLOBAL TECHNOLOGY
90 Community Dr
Sanford, ME 04073
Telephone: (207) 324-5200, (800) 627-5836, FAX: (207) 324-0875, E-Mail: info@shapeglobal.com, Web Site: www.shapenet.com

CEO: Vincent Boragine

FL SMITHE MACHINE CO INC
899 Old Rte 220 N
Duncansville, PA 16635-9432
Telephone: (814) 695-5521, FAX: (814) 695-0860, E-Mail: info@flsmithe.com, Web Site: www.flsmithe.com
Pres: Edgar Smithe Jr

SPECTRUM SYSTEMS INC
11325 Random Hills Rd (Suite 600)
Fairfax, VA 22030-0987
Telephone: (703) 591-7400 X217, (800) 929-3781, FAX: (703) 591-9780, E-Mail: spectrum@spectrum-systems.com, Web Site: www.spectrum-systems.com
Chmn & Pres: Ronald Segal
Mktg Devel Mgr: Nancy Fallon
Dir, Mktg: Lynda Stewart

STAPLES BUSINESS ADVANTAGE
2077 Convention Center Concourse Ste 125
Atlanta, GA 30337-4205
Telephone: (770) 997-2512, (877) 826-7754, FAX: (888) 387-9592, Web Site: www.staples.com
Chmn & CEO: Ronald L. Sargent

THE STAPLEX CO
777 Fifth Ave
Brooklyn, NY 11232-1626
Telephone: (718) 768-3333, (800) 221-0822, FAX: (718) 965-0750, E-Mail: info@staplex.com, Web Site: www.staplex.com
Sls Mgr: Doug Butler
Commun Mgr: Phil Reed

STEVENS INTERNATIONAL INC
5700 E Belknap St
Fort Worth, TX 76117
Telephone: (817) 831-3911, FAX: (817) 222-0162, E-Mail: main@stevensintl.com
Pres: Richard I. Stevens

STOLLE MACHINERY LLC
6949 S Potomac St
Centennial, CO 80112
Telephone: (303) 708-9044, (800) 228-4593, FAX: (303) 708-9045, E-Mail: cmd.info@stollemachinery.com, Web Site: www.stollemachinery.com
Member: Dave Groetsch

STREAMFEEDER
315 27th Ave NE
Minneapolis, MN 55418-2715
Telephone: (763) 502-0000, FAX:
(763) 502-0100, Web Site: www.
streamfeeder.com
Pres: Mitch Speicher

STRONG ENTERPRISES
Div. of SE Inc
11236 Satellite Blvd
Orlando, FL 32837
Telephone: (407) 859-9317, (800) 344-
6319, FAX: (407) 850-6978, E-Mail:
sales@strongparachutes.com, Web
Site: www.strongparachutes.com
Pres: Ted Strong

STYLED PACKAGING LLC
PO Box 30299
Philadelphia, PA 19103-8299
Telephone: (610) 529-4122, FAX:
(610) 520-9662, E-Mail: bill@
styledpackaging.com, Web Site:
www.styledpackaging.com
Pres: William R. Fenkel

**SURCHIN ADVANCED
MAILING TECHNOLOGIES**
80 E Jefryn Blvd (Suite C)
Deer Park, NY 11729-5755
Telephone: (631) 667-0200, (800) 645-
5240, FAX: (631) 667-0242, E-Mail:
info@surchin.com, Web Site: www.
surchin.com
Pres: Hyman M. Surchin

SWORDS MUSIC CO INC
4300 E Lancaster Ave
Fort Worth, TX 76103-3225
Telephone: (817) 53-MUSIC, (800)
522-3028, FAX: (817) 536-4293,
E-Mail: daveshep4300@sbcglobal.
net, Web Site: www.swordsmusicinc.
com
Pres: Logan Swords
Sls Mgr: David Sheppard
Conducts Business: U.S.
Employees: 3
Primary Market Served: Business &
Consumer
Catalog available online
Direct online sales
Advertising/Marketing Budget Related
to Direct Marketing: 0-25%
Direct Marketing ad budget: $5,000
Direct Mail: 30%
Newspapers: 20%
Online: 40%
TV/Radio: 10%
Founded: 1969
Gross sales or billing: $400,000

Retail sales of musical instruments to
individuals, schools, churches &
businesses.

TAMARKIN & CO
270 Amity Rd (Suite 125)
Woodbridge, CT 06525
Telephone: (203) 397-9191, (800) 289-
5342, FAX: (203) 397-9393, E-Mail:
info@tamarkin.com, Web Site: www.
tamarkin.com
Pres: Stan Tamarkin

TENNANT CO
701 N Lilac Dr
Minneapolis, MN 55422-4687
Telephone: (763) 540-1200, (800) 553-
8033, FAX: (763) 513-2142, E-Mail:
info@tennantco.com, Web Site:
www.tennantco.com
Pres & CEO: Chris Killingstad

THOMSON
2395 Midway Rd
Carrollton, TX 75006-2521
Telephone: (972) 250-7000, Web Site:
www.thomson.com
Mktg Commun Mgr: John Mims

TITAN MANUFACTURING
27 Maple Ave Ste 5
Holbrook, MA 02343-1077
Telephone: (781) 767-1963, Web Site:
www.americantitan.com
Pres: Gregory Hill

**TOYOTA RACING
DEVELOPMENT USA INC**
Subs. of Toyota Technocraft Co Ltd &
Toyota Motor Sales USA Inc
335 E Baker St
Costa Mesa, CA 92626-4518
Telephone: (714) 444-1188, FAX:
(714) 444-0339, Web Site: www.
trdusa.com
CFO: David Inglis

TY PAC
7858 River Rd
Baldwinsville, NY 13027
Telephone: (315) 638-9431, (800) 356-
8964, FAX: (315) 638-9433, E-Mail:
ty-pac@hotmail.com
Pres: Glenn Jaeck

USG CORP
550 W Adams St
Chicago, IL 60661-3665
Telephone: (312) 436-4000, (800) 621-
9622, FAX: (312) 672-4093, Web
Site: www.usg.com
Chmn & CEO: William Foote
Interactive Mktg Mgr: Richard Long

UV PROCESS SUPPLY
1229 W Cortland St
Chicago, IL 60614-4805

Telephone: (773) 248-0099, (800) 621-
1296, FAX: (773) 880-6647, E-Mail:
info@uvps.com, Web Site: www.
uvprocess.com
Pres: Stephen Siegel

ULANO CORP
Div. of Kissel & Wolf GmbH Group of
Cos
110 Third Ave
Brooklyn, NY 11217
Telephone: (718) 237-4700, (800) 221-
0616, FAX: (718) 802-1119, E-Mail:
ulano@ulano.com, Web Site: www.
ulano.com
Pres: Alfred Guercio

UNITED WAY STORE
85 S Bragg St Ste 600
Alexandria, VA 22312-2793
Telephone: (703) 212-6300, (800) 772-
0008, FAX: (703) 212-6319, E-Mail:
customerservice@unitedwaystore.
com, Web Site: www.unitedwaystore.
com
Pres: Edmund Cochran

VWR INTERNATIONAL
100 Matsonford Rd (Suite 200), Rad-
nor Corporate Ctr Bldg 1
Radnor, PA 19087-4560
Telephone: (610) 386-1700, (800) 932-
5000, FAX: (866) 329-2897, Web
Site: www.vwrsp.com
Pres & CEO: John Ballbach

**VERTICAL
COMMUNICATIONS INC**
3940 Freedom Cr
Santa Clara, CA 95054-1204
Telephone: (617) 354-0600, (800)
COMDIAL, FAX: (617) 452-9159,
Web Site: www.comdial.com
Chmn & CEO: William Y. Tauscher

**VIDEO JET TECHNOLOGIES
INC**
Subs. of Danaher Corp
1500 Mittel Blvd
Wood Dale, IL 60191-1073
Telephone: (630) 860-7300, (800) 654-
4663, FAX: (630) 616-3657, E-Mail:
info@videojet.com, Web Site: www.
videojet.com
Pres & CEO: Craig Purse

VISIPAK
Div. of Sinclair & Rush Inc
13515 Barrett Pkwy Dr
Saint Louis, MO 63021
Telephone: (636) 282-6800, (800) 922-
9391, FAX: (636) 282-6888, E-Mail:
visipak@sinclair-rush.com, Web Site:
www.visipak.com

Mktg Coord: Mary Lou Pudlowski

WARD'S NATURAL SCIENCE

PO Box 92912
Rochester, NY 14692-9012
Telephone: (585) 359-2502, (800) 962-
   2660, FAX: (585) 334-6174, E-Mail:
   customer_service@wardsci.com,
   Web Site: www.wardsci.com
CEO: Mike Colyer
Commun Dir: Noel Vache
Conducts Business: Worldwide
Employees: 400
Primary Market Served: Business &
   Consumer
Catalog available online
Direct online sales
Advertising/Marketing Budget Related
   to Direct Marketing: 76-100%
Direct Marketing ad budget:
Direct Mail: 80%
Magazines: 5%
Online: 15%
Founded: 1862
Gross sales or billing: $25,000,000

Full line of science education supplies
for grades five through college. Micro-
scope slides, lab equipment, living &
preserved specimens, microscopes,
models, AV, etc.

WASHINGTON PRODUCTS
INC

PO Box 644
Massillon, OH 44648-0644
Telephone: (330) 837-5101, FAX:
   (330) 837-5401
Pres: Robert Russell

WELLS LAMONT INDUSTRY
GROUP

6640 W Touhy Ave
Niles, IL 60714
Telephone: (847) 647-8200, (800) 247-
   3295, FAX: (847) 470-1026, Web
   Site: www.wellslamontindustry.com
Pres: Steve Duffy

WESTERN PRINTING
MACHINERY (WPM)

9229 Ivanhoe St
Schiller Park, IL 60176
Telephone: (847) 678-1740, FAX:
   (847) 678-6176, E-Mail: info@wpm.
   com, Web Site: www.wpm.com
CEO: Michael K. Musgrave

THE DMA WINDWAY CAPITAL CORP

630 Riverfront Dr (Suite 200)
Sheboygan, WI 53082-0897
Telephone: (920) 457-8600
Mktg & Projects Dir: Gerald Baumann

Creative Services (35-39)

Agencies: Advertising, Direct Response & Sales Promotion (35) — Geographic Index

Alabama

Dees Communications/Fuller Fund Raising, 2540 E 5th St (Ste A), Montgomery, 36107-3152

Hatchett & Fagan Direct, 950 22nd St N (Suite 700), Birmingham, 35203-1128

Arizona

AmazingMail Inc, 8300 E Raintree Dr (Suite 201), Scottsdale, 85260-2598

Michael Bolchalk Marketing, 310 S Williams Blvd (Suite 260), Tucson, 85711-7703

CustomerFunding.com Inc, PO Box 24255, Tempe, 85285-4255

Direct Alliance, 8123 S Hardy Dr, Tempe, 85284-1106

IMPACT International Marketing, 151 Riviera Dr (Bldg B Suite 201), Lake Havasu City, 86403-5696

Intrasight, 8300 E Raintree Dr (Suite 200), Scottsdale, 85260-2598

LemmonTree Marketing Group, 3010 S Priest Dr (Suite 103), Tempe, 85282

Nova Power Marketing, 4225 E Avalon Dr, Phoenix, 85018-7207

Phillips Direct Marketing Group, 11445 E Via Linda (Suite 2), Scottsdale, 85259-2554

The Sales and Marketing Institute, 8255 E Raintree Dr (Suite 200), Scottsdale, 85260-2684

Shaver Direct Inc, 912 E Annette Dr, Phoenix, 85022-1100

SHR Perceptual Management, 2575 E Camelback Rd Ste 450, Phoenix, 85016-9288

California

The Adcentive Group Inc, 4801 Viewridge Ave, San Diego, 92123-1643

Anderson Direct Marketing, 12650 Danielson Ct, Poway, 92064-6822

Ariago Designs, 51 E Campbell Ave (Suite 126), Campbell, 95008-2055

Beasley Direct Marketing Inc, 15227 Perry Ln, Morgan Hill, 95037-9659

Berson/Dean/Stevens Inc, PO Box 3997, Westlake Village, 91359-3997

Bizo, 225 Bush St (#1150), San Francisco, 94104-4215

Bleu Marketing Solutions Inc, 3025 Fillmore St, San Francisco, 94123-4009

Carson & Co, 1740 E Garry Ave (Suite 231), Santa Ana, 92705-5844

Celebrity Endorsement Network (CEN), 23679 Calabasas Rd (#728), Calabasas, 91302-1502

Cimarron Group, 6855 Santa Monica Blvd, Hollywood, 90038

Creative Lift, 115 Sansome St Ste 600, San Francisco, 94104-3618

CustomerMining, 2901 Park Ave (Suite C4), Soquel, 95073-2831

Database Marketing Group Inc, 5 Peters Canyon Rd (Suite 150), Irvine, 92606-1793

DDB Direct Los Angeles, 10960 Wilshire Blvd (fl 16), Los Angeles, 90024-3802

Digispace Solutions LLC, 2323 Broadway (Suite 202), San Diego, 92102

Direct Cinema Ltd, PO Box 10003, Santa Monica, 90410-1003

Direct Partners, 4755 Alla Rd, Marina Del Rey, 90292-6311

DMS Marketing Inc, 26035 Acero Ste 100, Mission Viejo, 92691-7951

Eagle Marketing Services Inc, PO Box 60666, San Diego, 92166-8666

Easy Color Printing, 2725 Miller St, San Leandro, 94577-5619

Eleven Inc, 445 Bush St (fl 8), San Francisco, 94108-3729

Euro RSCG 4D Worldwide, 1355 Sansome St (#4), San Francisco, 94111-6213

FMS Direct, 18344 Oxnard St (Suite 101), Tarzana, 91356-6724

Front Porch Inc, 14520 Mono Way (Suite 200), Sonora, 95370-7829

Galanty & Co Inc, 1640 Fifth St (Suite 202), Santa Monica, 90401

Game Show Placements Ltd, 7011 Willoughby Ave, Hollywood, 90038-2332

Gennera Knab & Co, 1953 N Ontario St, Burbank, 91505-1231

Goodman Marketing Partners Inc, 4340 Redwood Hwy (Suite 52), San Rafael, 94903-2107

Grizzard Advertising, 110 N Maryland Ave, Glendale, 91206

Gumas Advertising, 99 Shotwell St, San Francisco, 94103-3625

Hahn, Crane & Associates Advertising Inc, 2404 Loring St, San Diego, 92109-2347

Hemmings IV Direct, 505 E Colorado Blvd (Suite 201D), Pasadena, 91101-2002

HHC Direct, 5287 Linda Vista Rd, San Diego, 92110-2604

High Octane Communications, 20 N San Pedro Rd (Suite 2014), San Rafael, 94903-4158

The Hitchins Corp, 22756 Hartland St, Canoga Park, 91307-2604

Icon Media Direct Inc, 5910 Lemona Ave, Van Nuys, 91411-3006

Imahara Associates Inc, 3528 Willow Wren, Fremont, 94555

InterMedia Advertising, 15760 Ventura Blvd Ste 110, Encino, 91436-3007

International Marketing Partners Ltd, 6371 W 79th St, Los Angeles, 90045-1442

InterTrend Communications Inc, 555 E Ocean Blvd Ste 900, Long Beach, 90802-5056

IVisionMobile Inc, 9566 Topanga Cyn Blvd, Chatsworth, 91311

JWT Inside, 2425 Olympic Blvd, Santa Monica, 90404

Jones & O'Malley Advertising, 10123 Camarillo St, Toluca Lake, 91602-1601

Karlen Design, 863 Pacific St, San Luis Obispo, 93401

Kern Direct Marketing, 20955 Warner Center Ln, Woodland Hills, 91367

The Kern Organization, 20955 Warner Center Ln, Woodland Hills, 91367-6511

LENSER, 899 Northgate Dr (Suite 530), San Rafael, 94903-3667

Linkin Communications, 11362 Charnock Rd, Los Angeles, 90066-2918

Majestic Marketing Inc, 1160 California Ave, Corona, 92881-3324

Marchese Communications Inc, 4652 Via Marina (#104), Marina Del Rey, 90292

Market-Ability Inc, 1520 Rancho View Dr, Lafayette, 94549-2232

MARKOTS, 405 El Camino Real (#248), Menlo Park, 94025-5240

The Marx Group, 2175 E Francisco Blvd (Suite F), San Rafael, 94901

Mayo Marketing Ideas, 2785 Pacific Coast Hwy (#E288), Torrance, 90505

Media Stream Direct, 14724 Ventura Blvd Ste 1200, Sherman Oaks, 91403-3512

Mighty Net Inc, 26010 Mureau Rd Ste 130, PO Box 9153, Calabasas, 91302-3176

The Miller Group Advertising, 1516 S Bundy (Suite 200), Los Angeles, 90025

Money Mailer Direct Marketing, 12131 Western Ave, Garden Grove, 92841-2914

MyPoints.Com Inc, 50 California St (3rd fl.), San Francisco, 94111-4632

New Day Marketing Ltd, 923 Olive St Ste 2, Santa Barbara, 93101-1447

Nostrum Inc, 401 E Ocean Blvd Ste M101, Long Beach, 90802-8900

Pacific Media Exchange, 1629-A 6th St, Berkeley, 94710-1803

Paradigm Promotions LLC, 561 34th Ave, San Francisco, 94121-2705

Pasadena Advertising, 51 W Dayton St Ste 100, Pasadena, 91105-2025

PowerDirect, 4700 Von Karman Ave (Suite 100), Newport Beach, 92660-2194

Practice Builders, 1 Technology Dr Ste I829, Irvine, 92618-5320

Quigley Simpson, 11601 Wilshire Blvd, Los Angeles, 90025-0509

Rauxa Direct, 275A McCormick Ave, Costa Mesa, 92626

Red Edge Labs LLC, 26985 Aliso Creek Rd (Suite B330), Aliso Viejo, 92656

The Response Shop Inc, 7486 La Jolla Blvd (#164), La Jolla, 92037

BP Rice & Co, 1205 E Grand Ave, El Segundo, 90245-4220

Ron Perrella DRS (DR Specialists), 29632 Seriana, Laguna Niguel, 92677-7967

Russ Reid Co, 2 N Lake Ave (Suite 600), Pasadena, 91101-1868

David Sams Industries Inc/TV First, 28720 Roadside Dr (Suite 198), Agoura Hills, 91301

Brody Smythe Direct Inc, 8665 Wilshire Blvd (#301), Beverly Hills, 90211

Social Reality, 102 La Patera Dr, Camarillo, 93010-7457

Specific Media Inc, Four Park Plaza (Suite 1900), Irvine, 92614

The Spector Agency, 4600 Dietz Way (Suite 100), Fair Oaks, 95628

Spizel Marketing/Advertising/Public Relations, 2610 Torrey Pines Rd (#C31), La Jolla, 92037

Starbird Creative, PO Box 1722, Sebastopol, 95473-1722

Strategic Marketing and Advertising Inc, 1792 Blackbird Cir, Carlsbad, 92011

Team One Advertising, 1960 E Grand Ave, El Segundo, 90245

The Testimonial Wrangler, 7486 La Jolla Blvd (#164), La Jolla, 92037-5029

Thane International Inc, 78140 Calle Tampico Ste 3, La Quinta, 92253-2985

TBWA, 5353 Grosvenor Rd, Los Angeles, 90066-6913

TVA Productions Inc (The Video Agency), 3950 Vantage Ave, Studio City, 91604-3613

Vision Media, 5437 Parker Rd, Modesto, 95357-0640

WebMetro, 160 Via Verde # 100, San Dimas, 91773-3901

Wikreate, 145 Vallejo St (#6), San Francisco, 94111-1415

Williams Worldwide Television, 3130 Wilshire Blvd (Suite 300), Santa Monica, 90403-2300

WNR Direct Response Consultants, 30423 Canwood St (Suite 234), Agoura Hills, 91301

Xpectrum Marketing Group, 1953 Ainsley Rd, San Diego, 92123

Yates Advertising, 305 Bridgeway, Sausalito, 94965-2451

Colorado

Be Somebody Be Yourself, PO Box 416, Denver, 80201-0416

Booyah Networks, 11030 Circle Point Rd (Suite 350), Westminster, 80020

Cohorts, 1624 Market St (Suite 311), Denver, 80202

The Communique Group, 10559 E Democrat Rd, Parker, 80134-5004

Concepts Unlimited, 16535 Grays Way, Broomfield, 80023-8333

The Creative Alliance Inc, 2675 Northpark Dr (Suite 200), Lafayette, 80026-3483

Customer Communications Group, 165 S Union Blvd Ste 260, Lakewood, 80228-2241

Direct Marketing Designs Inc, 6565 S Dayton (Suite 2200), Greenwood Village, 80111-5386

Heinrich Marketing, 2228 Blake St, Denver, 80205-2120

Ariss Kahan Database Marketing Group Inc, 7270 S Ivy Ct, Englewood, 80112-1506

Walt Klein & Associates Inc, 2000 S Colorado Blvd (Suite 10200), Denver, 80222-7918

Klondike Marketing Inc, PO Box 11127, Boulder, 80301-0006

Point To Point Marketing Inc, 11562 N County Rd 17, Fort Collins, 80524-8786

John Romero Direct Marketing, 10625 Woodhaven Ridge Rd, Parker, 80134-5017

Connecticut

ADV Marketing Group Inc, 33 Glenn Terr, Stamford, 06906-1402

Agency RAV, 71 Rangely Dr, Trumbull, 06611-2840

Charles F Beardsley Advertising, 31 E Main St, Avon, 06001-3805

Catalyst Marketing Communications Inc, 2777 Summer St (Suite 301), Stamford, 06905-4310

CGSM Inc, 11 Grumman Hill Rd, Wilton, 06897-4500

Customer Growth, Blau Moritz Klang Inc, 6 Willow Walk, Westport, 06880-2737

Customer Marketing Group LLC, 7 Hill Farm Rd, Weston, 06883-2007

Direct Channel LLC, 574 Heritage Rd (Suite 201A), Southbury, 06488-1868

The Directors Network, 36 Lostbrook Rd, West Hartford, 06117-1928

FPS Marketing Communications, 91 Shelter Cove Rd, Milford, 06460-6548

Fosina Marketing Group Inc, 51-53 Kenosia Ave, Danbury, 06810-2301

The GRI Marketing Group Inc, 115 Technology Dr (Suite B307), Trumbull, 06611-6339

Gray & Graham Inc, 136 Main St (Suite 6), Westport, 06880-3304

Keiler & Co, 304 Main St, Farmington, 06032-2985

Leverage Marketing Group, 117-119 S Main St, Newtown, 06470-2380

Marquardt, Roche & Partners, 5 High Ridge Park Ste 2C, Stamford, 06905-1326

Martino & Binzer, 270 Farmington Ave Ste 128, Farmington, 06032-1920

MD&C Advertising, PO Box 8446, New Haven, 06530-0446

Modem Media, 107 Elm St Ste 907, Stamford, 06902-3808

Morris Group Inc, 910 Day Hill Rd, Windsor, 06095

Mystic Logistics, 2187 New London Tpke, South Glastonbury, 06073

One On One Advertising Inc, 584 Middletown Ave, New Haven, 06513-1011

1to1 Media, 1111 Summer St Fl 5, Stamford, 06905-5511

Pappas MacDonnell Inc, 135 Rennell Dr, Southport, 06890-1450

PlusMedia LLC, 100 Mill Plain Rd (Fl 4), Danbury, 06811-5189

PromoWriting, 13 Frenchtown Rd, Trumbull, 06611-4729

Ryan IDirect, 50 Danbury Rd, Wilton, 06897-4406

School Market Research Institute Inc, 1721 Saybrook Rd, Haddam, 06438-1324

Silverstone, Adkins & Breit Inc, 35 Corporate Dr Ste 1090, Trumbull, 06611-1355

Sinish Marketing Communications, 650 Hilltop Dr (Suite B), Stratford, 06614-2414

Source Marketing, 761 Main Ave, Norwalk, 06851-1080

Tamayo Miyares & Sherman, 325 Lafayette St (Suite 5203), Bridgeport, 06604

Tanen Directed Advertising, 12 S Main St Ste 401, Norwalk, 06854-2980

District of Columbia

Concepts & Strategies Inc, 256 Eighth St SE, Washington, 20003-2107

Gitlitz Consulting, 3916 Highwood Ct NW, Washington, 20007-2132

JAM Communications, 1108 K St NW (3rd fl), Washington, 20005-6819

Meadows Design Office, 3800 Yuma St NW, Washington, 20016

RTC Relationship Marketing, 1055 Thomas Jefferson St NW (Suite 500), Washington, 20007-5256

Schramm & Associates Inc, 1250 24th St NW (Suite 300), Washington, 20037

Florida

Americana Sales Ventures Inc, 1000 Sunshine Ln, Altamonte Springs, 32714-3805

Andersen Advertising, 1752 Clemson Rd, Jacksonville, 32217

AnswerThink Inc, 1001 Brickell Bay Dr (Suite 3000), Miami, 33131

Aspen Interactive, 150 Second Ave N (# 470), Saint Petersburg, 33701

Axia, 200 E Forsyth St, Jacksonville, 32202-3320

Beber Silverstein Group, 89 N E 27th St (Suite 102), Miami, 33137-4409

George Blake & Associates, 6015 Courtside Dr, Bradenton, 34210-4018

Sandi Brown Associates, 4342 14th Way NE, Saint Petersburg, 33703-5349

Cade & Associates Advertising, 1645 Metropolitan Blvd, Tallahassee, 32308-3730

Clarke Advertising & Public Relations, 401 N Cattlemen Rd (Suite 200), Sarasota, 34232-6439

Jess Clarke & Sons Inc, 5808 42nd St E, Bradenton, 34203-5579

Clickbooth.com LLC, 5901 N Honore Ave, Sarasota, 34243-2632

CO-OP PROMOTIONS, 2301 S Ocean Dr (Suite 2504), Hollywood, 33019

Colorama LLC, 4872 Waterbridge Down, Sarasota, 34235-7215

Gene Cowell & Associates Inc, 17820 NW 149th Pl, Alachua, 32615-5259

Crispin, Porter & Bogusky, 3390 Mary St (Suite 300), Miami, 33133

Foundation Media Group, 260 SW Natura Ave, Deerfield Beach, 33441-3026

Lois Geller Marketing Group, 2028 Hamson St (Suite 202), Hollywood, 33020

GHW Associates, 13063 SW Pembroke Cir N, Lake Suzy, 34269-6914

Infotrends Inc, 2019 Corporate Dr, Boynton Beach, 33426

Integrated Advertising Inc, 8677 Southern Glen Dr, Jacksonville, 32256-9542

Interval International, 6262 Sunset Dr Ste 400, South Miami, 33143-4843

Kelley Swofford Roy Inc, 50 NE 29th St, Miami, 33137-4413

Kobie Marketing Inc, 100 Second Ave S (Suite 1000), Saint Petersburg, 33701

List Management Services Inc, 5728 Major Blvd (Suite 650), Orlando, 32819-7963

The Marketing Agency LLC, 2881 E Oakland Park Blvd (Suite 425), Fort Lauderdale, 33306-1813

Marketing III Direct Response, PO Box 121278, Clermont, 34712-8712

The Media Crew, 1803 Park Center Dr Ste 102, Orlando, 32835-6216

Media Response Inc, 2450 Hollywood Blvd (Suite 200), Hollywood, 33020-6620

The Mesa Group, 1281 Blue Heron Blvd E (# 125), West Palm Beach, 33404-4739

MoreMedia Direct Inc, 329 W 28 St., Miami Beach, 33140-4306

Myers, Myers & Adams Advertising Inc, 934 N Victoria Park Rd, Fort Lauderdale, 33304-4478

Omnidirect, 1680 Michigan Ave (Suite 1016), Miami Beach, 33139

Premier World Marketing, 3191 Coral Way (PH 202), Miami, 33145

QUAXAR, 25 SE 2nd Ave (Suite 305), The Ingraham Bldg, Miami, 33131-1509

S&H Solutions, 1625 S Congress Ave Ste 200, Delray Beach, 33445-6304

Safian Communications Services Inc, 112 Kaiser Ln, Longwood, 32750-4100

SendTec Inc, 877 Executive Center Dr W (Suite 300), Saint Petersburg, 33702

Spirit Incentives, 2455 E Sunrise Blvd Ste 150, Fort Lauderdale, 33304-3129

Spot Behavior LLC, 1121 S Military Trail (#220), Deerfield Beach, 33442-7604

Turkel, 2871 Oak Ave, Coconut Grove, 33133

Zimmerman & Partners, 2200 W Commercial Blvd (Suite 300), Fort Lauderdale, 33309-3064

Georgia

ATM Advertising, PO Box 88824, Atlanta, 30356-8824

Advantage Direct Inc, 805 Jamerson Rd (Bldg 2), Marietta, 30066-1057

BAM! Direct Inc, 3651 Peachtree Pkwy (Suite E-211), Suwanee, 30024-6034

BKV Inc, 3390 Peachtree Rd NE Ste 1000, Atlanta, 30326-1108

Broadus Advertising/Public Relations, 1008 Sea Palms West Dr, Saint Simons Island, 31522-5243

Business Direct Marketing Associates Inc, 6825 Polo Fields Pkwy, Cumming, 30040-5731

Frank W Cawood & Associates Inc, 103 Clover Green, Peachtree City, 30269-1672

Crawford & Co, 1001 Summit Blvd Ste 500, Atlanta, 30319-6410

Cypress Media Group, 630 Leather Hinge Tr, Roswell, 30075-4187

Engauge Direct, 1230 Peachtree St NE (Suite 2200), Atlanta, 30309

Fitzgerald + Co, 3333 Piedmont Rd NE Ste 1100, One Buckhead Plz, Atlanta, 30305-1740

Franklin Advertising Inc, 87 N Main St, Blakely, 39823

Marc G Gault Advertising & Marketing Consulting, 5380 Smoke Rise Dr (Suite B), Stone Mountain, 30087-1529

Grizzard Communications Group Inc, 229 Peachtree St NE (Suite 1400), Atlanta, 30303-1620

Haynes Marketing Network, 721 Walnut St (Suite B), Macon, 31201-2630

Kilgannon, 1360 Peachtree St NE (Suite 700), Atlanta, 30309-3262

MarketPower Direct Marketing, 1449 Druid Valley Dr NE (Suite C), Atlanta, 30329-2967

Response Mine Interactive, 3390 Peachtree Rd NE (Suite 800), Atlanta, 30326-2840

Seaside Publications, 201 Marina Dr, Saint Simons Island, 31522

Selling Solutions Inc, 3525 Piedmont Rd NE Bldg 5-515, Atlanta, 30305-1586

Target MarkeTeam, 1050 Crown Pointe Pkwy (Suite 1850), Atlanta, 30338-7709

22squared Inc, 1170 Peachtree St NE, Atlanta, 30309-7649

Vesdia Corp, 3348 Peachtree Rd NE (Suite 300), Atlanta, 30326-1456

Visual Response Marketing Group, 2125 Ellis Farm Dr, Marietta, 30064-2879

Hawaii

Dik & Associates Direct Marketing, 2626 Peter St, Honolulu, 96816

IMC Direct, 81 S Hotel St (Suite 315), Honolulu, 96813

Milici Valenti Ng Pack, 999 Bishop St (24th fl), Honolulu, 96813

Idaho

Oliver Russell & Associates, 217 S 11th St, Boise, 83702-6902

Illinois

Abelson-Taylor Inc, 33 W Monroe St, Chicago, 60603-5300

Adtron Inc, 1700 Morrissey Dr, Bloomington, 61704-7107

American Marketing Systems Inc, 7020 High Grove Blvd, Burr Ridge, 60527-7595

Arends, 515 N River St Ste 101, Batavia, 60510-2390

Aspen Marketing Services, 1240 W North Ave, West Chicago, 60185-1087

August Bishop & Meier Inc, 155 N Harbor Dr (Suite 4903), Chicago, 60601-7326

Keith Bates & Associates Inc, 4319 N Lowell Ave, Chicago, 60641-2015

Benoit & Associates, 279 S Schuyler Ave, Kankakee, 60901-3809

Beyond Quota LLC, 537 King Muir Rd, Lake Forest, 60045-1640

Black Dot Group, 329 W 18th St Ste 800, Chicago, 60616-1103

Black Olive Co, 125 S Wacker Dr (Suite 300), Chicago, 60606-4421

Breath Appeal, 2000 S 25th Ave (Suite N), Broadview, 60155

Leo Burnett USA, 35 W Wacker Dr (21st fl), Chicago, 60601-1723

CI Productions Inc, 3N506 Linda Ln, Addison, 60101-3037

CMC & Design, 3510 15th St Ct, Rock Island, 61201-6119

CPO Direct Inc, 736 N Western Ave (#147), Lake Forest, 60045-1820

Cooper & Cooper Direct Marketing, 540 Frontage Rd (Suite 3035), Northfield, 60093-1223

Cramer-Krasselt, 225 N Michigan Ave, Chicago, 60601-7684

DDB Chicago, 200 E Randolph St (Suite 3800), Chicago, 60601

Diamond Marketing Solutions, 280 Madsen Dr Ste 100, Bloomingdale, 60108-2693

The Direct Marketing Specialists Inc, 900 N Franklin (Suite 706), Chicago, 60610-3124

Donahoe Purohit Miller Advertising, 111 S Wacker Dr Fl 1, Chicago, 60606-4309

Edward G Dorn & Associates Inc, 121 W State St, Geneva, 60134-2254

Draftfcb Chicago (HQ), 633 N Saint Clair St, Chicago, 60611-3234

A Eicoff & Co, 401 N Michigan Ave (Suite 400), Chicago, 60611-4232

Ronald D Erkes & Associates, Box 117, Glencoe, 60022-0117

Esrock Partners, 14550 S 94th Ave, Orland Park, 60462-2652

Feldman & Associates Inc, 191 Waukegan Rd (Suite 103), Northfield, 60093-2743

Finerty & Wolfe Advertising Inc, 2418 N Burling St, Chicago, 60614

Flair Communications Agency Inc, 214 W Erie, Chicago, 60610

Fujii Communications Inc, 7369 E Prairie Rd, Lincolnwood, 60712-1039

GSP Marketing Services, 320 W Ohio, Chicago, 60610

Glidden & Boyles Inc, 2N School St, Mount Prospect, 60056-2539

Grove Communications, 3918 Valley View Rd, Crystal Lake, 60012

Hult Fritz Matuszak Associates, 401 SW Water St (Suite 601), Peoria, 61602-1586

The Ignition Network, 125 S Wacker Dr (Suite 1750), Chicago, 60606-4401

Industrial Marketing Services, 2375 Touhy Ave, Elk Grove Village, 60007-5330

Interline Creative Group Inc, 553 N North Ct (Suite 160), Palatine, 60067-8124

Jacobs & Clevenger Inc, 515 N State St (Suite 1700), Chicago, 60654-4776

Jones & Thomas Inc, 788 N Sunnyside Rd, Decatur, 62522

Killian & Co, 322 S Green St (Suite 510), Chicago, 60607-3579

Kokopelli Communications Group Inc, 449 N Clark St Ste 301, Chicago, 60654-4500

Kollias & Associates, 210 N Wells St Apt 4108, Chicago, 60606-1352

Kryl & Co Inc, 39 S Lasalle St (Suite 200), Chicago, 60603-1702

Laughlin/Constable, 200 S Michigan Ave (Suite 1700), Chicago, 60604-2460

Leapfrog Online, 807 Greenwood St, Evanston, 60201-4311

Leo Burnett USA, 35 W Wacker Dr, Chicago, 60601-1723

LEC Ltd, 12 E Ohio St (#400), Chicago, 60611-3098

LKH&S Inc, 54 W Hubbard (Suite 100), Chicago, 60610

Manley & Associates Inc, 6414 Marshall Dr, Woodridge, 60517-1223

Marketing Innovators, 9701 W Higgins Rd Ste 400, Rosemont, 60018-4717

Marketing Out-of-the-Box Inc, 600 W Chicago Ave Ste 850, Chicago, 60654-2529

The Marketing Store, 701 E 22nd St Ste 200, Lombard, 60148-5024

MarketSense, 7020 High Grove Blvd, Burr Ridge, 60527-7595

The Jack Morton Co, 875 N Michigan Ave Ste 2400, Chicago, 60611-1877

NAVTEQ, 425 W Randolph St Fl 7, Chicago, 60606-1515

Noble, 33 W Monroe St, Chicago, 60603-5300

Nova Communications Inc, 27 S 1st St, Geneva, 60134-2243

The Pampered Pet Mart, 6486 Haover Ct, Lisle, 60532-3218

Progressive Impressions International, 1 Hardman Dr, Bloomington, 61701-6934

Propco Promotional Marketing, 7360 N Lincoln Ave (Suite 100), Lincolnwood, 60712-1705

Quantum Group, 6511 Oakton St, Morton Grove, 60053-2728

Robinson & Maites Inc, 35 E Wacker Dr (Suite 3500), Chicago, 60601

Schawk, 1695 S River Rd, Des Plaines, 60018

Gloria Shurn Creative Services, 1422 N Mohawk St, Chicago, 60610

SMG Direct Market, 3000 Lakeside Dr (Suite 305S), Bannockburn, 60015-1230

Sturm, Rosenburg, King & Co, 737 N Michigan Ave (Suite 1400), Chicago, 60611-7021

Sutter Marketing Inc, 800 E Northwest Hwy (Suite 430), Palatine, 60067

Target & Response Inc, 420 N Wabash Ave (Suite 201), Chicago, 60611-3569

TargetCom Inc, 444 N Michigan Ave (33rd fl), Chicago, 60611

Tech Image, 1130 W Lake Cook Rd (Suite 250), Buffalo Grove, 60089-1994

Temkin & Temkin, 156 Barberry, Highland Park, 60035-4420

Three Sixty Inc, 200 E Delaware Pl (Suite 5B), Chicago, 60611

Tower Media Advertising Inc, 233 N Michigan Ave (Suite 2350), Chicago, 60601-5701

Unicom Marketing Group Inc, 2875 S 25th Ave, Broadview, 60155-4531

Web Direct Marketing Inc, 1900 Chestnut Ave Apt 201, Glenview, 60025-1658

Zephyr Media Group Inc, 990 Grove St (Suite 300), Evanston, 60201-6513

Indiana

CompuTrack, 10100 Lantern Rd (Suite 225), Fishers, 46037-9692

5Metacom, 630 W Carmel Dr (Suite 180), Carmel, 46032

Haynes & Partners Communications Inc, 5745 Lee Rd, Indianapolis, 46216

Interact Multimedia Corp, 115 N William St (#3000), South Bend, 46601-1509

The Jackson Group, 5804 Churchman By-Pass, Indianapolis, 46203

Tri-State Advertising Co Inc, 307 S Buffalo St, Warsaw, 46580-4304

Iowa

Action-AD, 1035 Lincoln Dr (Suite 109), PO Box 810, Bettendorf, 52722-4149

Hawthorne Direct Inc, 300 N 16th St, PO Box 1366, Fairfield, 52556-2604

Integer Group, 2633 Fleur Dr, Des Moines, 50321-1753

the meyocks group, 6800 Lake Dr (Suite 150), West Des Moines, 50266

Strategic America, 6600 Westown Pkwy Ste 100, West Des Moines, 50266-7708

ZLR Ignition, 303 Watson Powell Jr Way (Suite 100), Des Moines, 50309-1799

Kansas

Affiliate Strategies Inc, 112 S Pearl St (Suite 104), Paola, 66071-1755

Associated Integrated Marketing, 330 N Mead (Suite 200), Wichita, 67202-2828

BKV, 10561 Barkley (Suite 200), Overland Park, 66212

ClickSpeed, 6709 W 119th St (Suite 396), Overland Park, 66209-2013

Consolidated Printing & Sty Co, 319 S 5th St, Salina, 67401-3907

NAPR - National Association of Publishers Representatives, 10965 Cleveland Ave, Kansas City, 66109

Plattform Advertising, 15500 W 113th St (Suite 200), Lenexa, 66219-5106

Steinhardt Direct Inc, 12700 Antioch Rd Ste 65, Overland Park, 66213-2826

TradeNet Publishing Inc, 1200 Energy Center Dr, Gardner, 66030-1599

Zillner Marketing Communications Inc, 8725 Rosehill Rd (Suite 200), Lenexa, 66215-4611

Kentucky

Creative Media Inc, 59 Summertree Ct, Nicholasville, 40356-9780

Finelight Inc, 600 E Main St Ste 102, Louisville, 40202-1077

Monster Magnet, 7725 National Tpke (Unit 100), Louisville, 40214-4813

Price Weber Marketing Communications Inc, 10701 Shelbyville Rd, Louisville, 40243-1241

Tabler Communications, PO Box 3964, Louisville, 40201

Tobe Direct, 9700 Park Plaza (Unit 210), Louisville, 40241-2287

Louisiana

Brydels Marketing LLC, 4315 Bluebonnet Blvd (Suite A), Baton Rouge, 70809-9643

Foster Direct, 3909 Ambassador Caffery Pkwy (Suite F), Lafayette, 70503-5280

Keating Magee Advertising, 600 Decatur St, New Orleans, 70130

Peter A Mayer Advertising Inc, 324 Camp St, New Orleans, 70130-2804

Response Resources, 68 Belle Helene Dr, Destrehan, 70047

Maine

McCabe & Duval Advertising, Ten Moulton St (4th fl), Portland, 04101-5039

Maryland

BeaconFey LLC, 1107 Kenilworth Dr (Suite 307), Towson, 21204

Boscobel Marketing Communications Inc, 8606 Second Ave, Silver Spring, 20910-3326

Columbia Direct Marketing Corp, 1 S Acton Pl, Annapolis, 21401-2713

Creative Strategy Inc, 5425 Wisconsin Ave (Suite 1655), Chevy Chase, 20815-6906

Customer Retention Management Group Inc, PO Box 539, Severna Park, 21146-0539

Diamondback Direct - a Dmh Marketing Partners Co, 844 Ritchie Hwy (Suite 202), Severna Park, 21146-4137

Direct Marketing Dynamics Inc, 18633 Village Fountain Dr, Germantown, 20874-2122

GKV, 1500 Whetstone Way Ste 400, The Cascade Bldg, Baltimore, 21230-4768

Keary Advertising Co Inc, 7215 Rolling Mill Rd, Baltimore, 21224-2033

MGP Direct Inc, PO Box 694, Fulton, 20759-0694

New Village Media Inc, 9194 Red Branch Rd (Suite G), Columbia, 21045-2005

Silver Marketing Inc, 7910 Woodmont Ave (Suite 914), Bethesda, 20814-7028

Siquis Ltd, 1340 Smith Ave (Suite 300), Baltimore, 21209-3731

TBC Direct Inc, 900 S Wolfe St, Baltimore, 21231-3514

Massachusetts

AAI, 63 South St (Suite 295), Hopkinton, 01748-2241

Arnold Worldwide, 101 Huntington Ave, Boston, 02199

Arrco Medical Advertising, 1600 Providence Hwy Ste 63, Walpole, 02081-2542

BBK Worldwide, 320 Needham St (Suite 150), Newton, 02464-1515

Conversen, 2 Burlington Woods (Suite 200), Burlington, 01803-4515

Data Marketing Solutions Inc, 70 Atlantic Ave (Suite 8), Marblehead, 01945-3042

Digitas, 33 Arch St, Boston, 02110-1437

Direct Advertising, 83 Dalton Rd, Holliston, 01746-2416

Direct Impact Group, 200 Highland Ave (Suite 403), Needham, 02494-3019

EMI Strategic Marketing Inc, 15 Broad St Ste 10, Boston, 02109-3812

Geiger Donnelly Marketing LLC, 71 Elm St (Unit 8), Foxboro, 02035-2519

Greystone Services Inc, PO Box 482, Beverly, 01915-0482

Hill Holliday, 53 State St (fl 33), Boston, 02109-2802

Robert Hohler Associates, 545 Columbus Ave, Boston, 02118-1115

Ikon Communications Consultants Inc, 554 Washington St, Wellesley, 02482-6449

LCH Direct Inc, 74 Boyton St, Waltham, 02453-2866

Irma S Mann Strategic Marketing Inc, 420 Boylston St Ste 600, Boston, 02116-4017

McCarthy & King Marketing Inc, Eight Esther Dr, Milford, 01757-1057

MediaConcepts Corp, 25 N Main St, Assonet, 02702-1136

MKE Enterprises, 193 Haverhill St, North Reading, 01864

MRW Communications, 2 Fairfield St, Hingham, 02043

Mullen, 40 Broad St, Boston, 02109-4316

O'Rourke Hospitality Marketing LLC, 7 Prince Pl (#3), Newburyport, 01950-2644

Pike Communications Inc, 100 Cummings Ctr (Suite 250E), Beverly, 01915-6133

Precision Arts Advertising Inc, 57 Fitchburg Rd, Ashburnham, 01430-1409

Publicity Inc, 39 S Main St, Mansfield, 02048-2527

Rockett Communications Inc, 11 Juniper Ridge Rd (Suite 1100), Danvers, 01923-1741

Sage Communications, 428 Main St, Hudson, 01749-1851

Strategic Planning Marketing Scouting & Sales, 5 Independence Dr, Foxboro, 02035-2215

Target Direct Marketing Inc, 185 Main St (Suite 7), Gloucester, 01930-5745

THARLER DIRECTs, 4 Cabot Rd, Wayland, 01778-3716

Trinity Communications Inc, 180 Canal St Ste 300, Boston, 02114-1804

Webb & Co, 222 Mill Rd, Chelmsford, 01824-4127

WebReply.com Inc, 1085 Worcester St, Natick, 01760-1531

George Zahka, 865 Central Ave Apt L501, Needham, 02492-1389

Michigan

Perry Ballard Inc, 526 Upton Dr E, Saint Joseph, 49085-1091

Biggs/Gilmore Communications, 261 E Kalamazoo Ave (Suite 300), Kalamazoo, 49007-3990

Budco, 13700 Oakland St, Highland Park, 48203-3174

Campbell Ewald Co, 30400 Van Dyke Ave, Warren, 48093-2368

Chemistri, 3310 W Big Beaver Rd (Suite 107), Troy, 48084-2807

Duffey, Petrosky & Co, 39303 Country Club Dr (Suite A18), Farmington Hills, 48331-3482

Dziurman Dzign Inc, 620 S Main St, Clawson, 48017

GM Customer Relationship Management, 100 Renaissance Ctr, Detroit, 48265-0001

Harris Marketing Group, 102 Pierce St, Birmingham, 48009-6030

Johnson Rauhoff Inc, 2525 Lake Pine Dr, Saint Joseph, 49085-0003

Leo Burnett Detroit, 3310 W Big Beaver Rd Ste 107, Troy, 48084-2807

Maxwell & Miller Marketing Communications, 141 E Michigan Ave (Suite 500), Kalamazoo, 49007

Oneupweb, 13561 S West Bay Shore Dr (Suite 3000), Traverse City, 49684-6292

Pontis Group, 18530 Mack Ave (#369), Grosse Pointe, 48236-3254

PMH/Caramanning, 34705 W Twelve Mile Rd (Suite 200), Farmington Hills, 48331-3273

Simons-Michelson-Zieve Inc (SMZ), 900 Wilshire Dr (Suite 102), Troy, 48084

Strategy Network, PO Box 702545, Plymouth, 48170-0983

Minnesota

Aimia, 1405 Xenium Ln N (Suite 150), Minneapolis, 55441-4449

Campbell Mithun, 222 S 9th St Ste 2100, Minneapolis, 55402-3327

Carmichael Lynch Inc, 110 N Fifth St, Minneapolis, 55403

Colle+McVoy, 400 First Ave N, Minneapolis, 55401

Compass Communications Inc, 22035 Stratford Pl, Excelsior, 55331

Corporate Media Services Inc, 9801 Dupont Ave S (#408), Bloomington, 55431

Cuneo Advertising, 1401 American Blvd East (Suite 6), Bloomington, 55425-1105

Direct Marketing Group, 7550 Corporate Way, Eden Prairie, 55344-2045

d.trio marketing group, 401 N 3rd St (Suite 480), Minneapolis, 55401-1351

Fallon, 900 Marquette Ave (Suite 2400), Minneapolis, 55402

R Falls Agency, 900 6th Ave SE Ste 105, Minneapolis, 55414-1379

Gage, 10000 Hwy 55, Minneapolis, 55441-6300

Infinity Direct Inc, 13220 County Rd 6 (Suite 200), Plymouth, 55441-8791

The Lacek Group, 900 Second Ave S (Suite 1800), Minneapolis, 55402-1099

Lorex Inc, 19131 Industrial Blvd NW (Suite 1), Elk River, 55330-2438

Markgraf & Wells Marketing, 2939 Toledo Ave S, Minneapolis, 55416-1926

Martin Williams Advertising, 60 S 6th St (Suite 2800), Minneapolis, 55402-4444

Olson & Co, 420 N 5th St, Loring Corners, Minneapolis, 55401-1348

Penn Garritano Direct Response Marketing, 701 N Third St (Suite 201), Minneapolis, 55401-1157

Periscope Inc, 921 Washington Ave S, Minneapolis, 55415-1257

Popular Front Interactive Communications, 555 First Ave NE, Minneapolis, 55413-2209

Presentation Packaging, 870 Louisiana Ave S, Minneapolis, 55426

Response Marketing Inc, 6900 Shady Oak Rd, Eden Prairie, 55344-3403

Risdall Linnihan Advertising, 550 Main St, New Brighton, 55112-3271

TN Marketing, 1903 Wayzata Blvd, Wayzata, 55391-2047

Wolters Kluwer Financial Services, 100 S 5th St (Suite 700), Minneapolis, 55402-1219

Mississippi

Maris West & Baker, 18 Northtown Dr, Jackson, 39211

Missouri

Barkley, 1740 Main St, Kansas City, 64108-1311

Bernstein-Rein Advertising, 4600 Madison Ave, Kansas City, 64112-1283

Direct Impact Inc, 12747 Olive Blvd (Suite 300), Saint Louis, 63141-6269

Gragg Advertising, 450 E 4th St (Suite 100), Kansas City, 64106-1171

The Hughes Group Inc, 1141 S 7th St, Saint Louis, 63104-3623

iMarlin LLC, 1200 E Woodhurst Dr Ste V, Bldg V, Springfield, 65804-4240

InteliSpend, 1400 S Highway Dr, Fenton, 63099-0001

Kuhn & Wittenborn Inc, 2405 Grand Blvd (Suite 600), Kansas City, 64108

Latin-Pak, 141 Chesterfield Business Pkwy, Chesterfield, 63005-1233

Lundmark Advertising & Design Inc, 104 W Ninth St (Suite 104), Kansas City, 64105

Maritz, 1375 N Highway Dr, Fenton, 63026

Marketing Direct Inc, 530 Maryville Centre Dr (Suite 300), Saint Louis, 63141-5825

Nestle Purina/Checkmark Communications, 1111 Chouteau Ave, Saint Louis, 63102-1025

Nicholson Kovac Inc, 1513 NE 52nd St, Kansas City, 64118-5705

Summit Marketing, 3 Cityplace Dr Ste 500, Saint Louis, 63141-7091

West End Diving Centers Inc, 12464 Natural Bridge Rd, Bridgeton, 63044-2321

Montana

DB Duff & Associates, 26205 Show Horse Ln, Arlee, 59821-9145

Nebraska

Lortz Direct Marketing Inc, 13936 Gold Cir, Omaha, 68144-9803

Skar Advertising, 111 S 108th Ave, Omaha, 68154

TD Ameritrade Holding Corp, 4211 S 102nd St, Omaha, 68127

Nevada

Applied Marketing Sciences LLC, 1500 Tropicana Ave, Las Vegas, 89119-6516

Red Rock Marketing Group LLC, 1930 Village center Cr (Suite 3-516), Las Vegas, 89134-6299

VastCast Media, 6280 S Valley View Blvd Ste 318, Las Vegas, 89118-3890

New Hampshire

Cooper Wight Associates Inc, 133 Hay Hill, Francestown, 03043

New Jersey

Beacon Marketing Group, 311 S New York Rd Ste 25, Galloway, 08205-6025

David H Block Advertising Inc, 3 Claridge Dr, Verona, 07044-3000

Brush Fire, 2 Wing Dr, Cedar Knolls, 07927

Community Direct, 1402 Chapel Hill Rd, Mountainside, 07092-1405

Creative Marketing Alliance Inc, 191 Clarksville Rd, Princeton Junction, 08550

D2: Direct, 54 Cedar Lake W, Bldg # 2, Denville, 07834-1704

DKI Direct, 160 Summit Ave, Montvale, 07645-1750

Dentino Marketing, 515 Executive Dr, Princeton, 08540-1527

Echomax, 883 Columbus Dr, Teaneck, 07666-6612

Eclipse Marketing Services, 490 Headquarters Plz (N Towers fl 10), Morristown, 07960-4642

FocalPoint Marketing LLC, 323 Main St, Metuchen, 08840-2476

Fort Group, 100 Challenger Rd (Suite 800), Ridgefield Park, 07660-2119

Fractal Analytics, 2500 Plaza Ave, Jersey City, 07311

Gillespie, 3450 Princeton Pike, Lawrenceville, 08543-3333

The Goldmark Group Inc, 1155 Bloomfield Ave, Clifton, 07012

Grafica Group, 67 E Park Pl (Suite 425), Morristown, 07960-7103

Harvey Associates-Direct Marketing Solutions, 63 Hoover Dr, Cresskill, 07626

Hercky-Pasqua-Herman, 324 Chestnut St, Roselle Park, 07204-1904

iMarketing LTD Inc, 100 Canal Pointe Blvd Ste 216, Princeton, 08540-7063

Intermedia Consultants Inc, 100 Overlook Center (fl 2), Princeton, 08540-7814

Lanmark Group Inc, 804 Broadway Ste 4, West Long Branch, 07764-2203

Largie LLC, 903 Cedar St, Riverton, 08077-1718

Leverte Associates Inc, 1000 Wyckoff Ave, Mahwah, 07430-3164

The Lifestyle Marketing Corp, 310 Gramercy Pl, Glen Rock, 07452-2226

Linett & Harrison, 2500 Morris Ave, Union, 07083-5675

The Magna Group, 208 Harristown Rd., Glen Rock, 07452

Marketing & Promotions Group, 55-A E Ridgewood Ave, Ridgewood, 07450

Media Consultants, 205B Chubb Ave (2nd fl), Lyndhurst, 07071

Nationwide Yellow Pages Service, 104 Mountain Ct, Hackettstown, 07840-2300

Nixle LLC, PO Box 2881, Westfield, 07091-2881

The Nulman Group, 100 Davidson Ave (Suite 202), Somerset, 08873-1312

PCI, 5 W First St, Keyport, 07735-1010

Princeton Marketech, 2 Alice Rd, Princeton Junction, 08550-3027

Princeton Partners Inc, 205 Rockingham Row, Princeton, 08540-5759

Results Advertising Inc, 777 Terrace Ave Ste 506, Hasbrouck Heights, 07604-3114

RPM Direct LLC, 24 Arnett Ave (Suite 100), Lambertville, 08530-1500

Sawtooth Group, 100 Woodbridge Ctr Dr (Suite 102), Woodbridge, 07095-1162

Scientific Marketing Services Inc, 145 E Weymouth Rd, Landisville, 08326

Source Communications, 433 Hackensack Ave, Hackensack, 07601

Techcom Inc, Box 8257, Princeton, 08543-8257

Technical Marketing Group, 175 Fairfield Ave (Suite 3C), West Caldwell, 07006-6415

TRANZACT, 2200 Fletcher Ave (fl 4), Fort Lee, 07024-5016

New Mexico

Western Data Services Inc, 3010 National Parks Hwy, Carlsbad, 88220

New York

ACTIMAIL INC, 12 W 27th St Fl 13, New York, 10001-6903

Ad Pro Services Inc, 479 N Greenbush Rd, Blauvelt, 10913

Alloy Media Marketing, 151 W 26th St (fl 9), New York, 10001-6810

ANDREWS WHARTON INC, 2171 Jericho Tpke Ste 240, Commack, 11725-2900

Atmosphere BBDO, 1285 Avenue Of The Americas (Fl 5), New York, 10019-6008

Avalanche Creative Services Inc, 135 W 29th St (Suite 302), New York, 10001-5187

Banner & Greif Ltd, 119 W 72nd St (#252), New York, 10023-3201

DL Blair Inc, 400 Post Ave Ste 400, Westbury, 11590-2226

Blass Communications LLC, 17 Drowne Rd, Old Chatham, 12136-3006

Carl Bloom Associates Inc, 81 Main St (Unit 126), White Plains, 10601-1745

Bodden Partners, 102 Madison Ave Fl 7, New York, 10016-7417

Brashe Advertising Inc, 11 Jan Ln, Woodbury, 11797-2107

Broadford & Maloney Inc, 445 Park Ave (fl 10), New York, 10022-2606

Byowner.com, PO Box 667, Shoreham, 11786

C L & B Capital Management, 7583 Hunt Ln, Fayetteville, 13066-2554

The Carnegie Hall Corp, 881 Seventh Ave (fl 7), New York, 10019-8077

Catalyst, 110 Marina Dr, Rochester, 14626-5104

CCMR Advertising/Marketing Communications, 260 Fair St, Kingston, 12401-3808

Channel Neutral Marketing, 60 Peerless Dr, Oyster Bay, 11771-3615

Charter Direct Marketing, 132 E 43rd St (#727), New York, 10017

Chase Online Marketing Strategies, 79 Pine St (#102), New York, 10005

Chief Media, 875 6th Ave, New York, 10001-3507

George P Clarke Advertising Inc, 27 E 21st St (2nd fl), New York, 10010

Command Financial Press, 75 Varick St, New York, 10013

Communications Plus, 102 Madison Ave Fl 7, New York, 10016-7417

Company C, 160 Varick (fl 4), New York, 10013-1273

Compu-Mail, 1342 Military Rd, Niagara Falls, 14304-1730

The Computer Studio, 1280 Saw Mill River Rd Frnt 1, Yonkers, 10710-2738

Concept Media Partners, 1992 Commerce St (#307), Yorktown Heights, 10598-4412

ConvergeDirect, 33 E 33rd St (fl 3), New York, 10016-5335

TheCooperGroup, 381 Park Ave S (fl 8), New York, 10016-8806

CoreBrand, 122 W 27th St (Fl9), New York, 10001

Corinthian Direct, 500 8th Ave, New York, 10018-6504

CorporateRewards.com LLC, 307 5th Ave (fl 4), New York, 10016-6517

Crawford Advertising Associates LTD, 216 Congers Rd Ste 2C, New City, 10956-6280

Cross Commerce Media, 130 Madison Ave (fl 3), New York, 10016-7026

DeBow Communications Ltd, 235 W 56th St Apt 29H, New York, 10019-4334

Design Matters Inc!, 448 W 37th St Apt 9F, New York, 10018-4023

Dexposito & Partners, 875 Avenue of the Americas, New York, 10001-3507

Doremus & Co, 200 Varick St, New York, 10014-4810

E&M Advertising Inc, 462 Seventh Ave (8th fl), New York, 10018-7437

E & M Media Group Inc, 1410 Broadway (Suite 1002), New York, 10018-9359

EGC Group Inc, 1175 Walt Whitman Rd (Suite 200), Melville, 11747-3030

Eidel Marketing Communication Corp, Seven Lodge Rd, Briarcliff Manor, 10510

Euro RSCG Worldwide, 350 Hudson St, New York, 10014

Exposed Brick, 1 Astor Pl (# 7T), New York, 10003-6937

FCB HealthCare & ProHealth, 100 W 33rd St, New York, 10001

First Direct Corp, 2345 Route 52 (Suite 1B), Hopewell Junction, 12533-3220

Flamm Advertising Inc, 25 Highland Pl, Great Neck, 11020

Furman Roth Advertising, 801 Second Ave (Suite 1400), New York, 10017-8639

Garvan Communications Inc, PO Box 302, Locust Valley, 11560-0302

Garver Advertising Service Inc, 440 E 57th St (Suite 5C), New York, 10022-3047

Karen Gedney Communications, 272 87th St, Brooklyn, 11209

G2 Worldwide, 200 5th Ave Bsmt B, New York, 10010-3313

Grey Healthcare Group, 114 Fifth Ave (5th fl), New York, 10011

Group M Inc, 15 N Mill St (Suite 210), Nyack, 10960-3015

GroupM Direct, 825 7th Ave, New York, 10019-6014

Harris Publishing, 1511 Route 22 (Suite C-25), Brewster, 10509-4085

Holsted Marketing Inc, 135 Madison Ave (fl 8), New York, 10016-6727

Huntington Associates, 850 Seventh Ave (Suite 1200), New York, 10019-5230

Indros Group, 1 Meadow St (Suite 202), Brooklyn, 11206-1741

AB Isacson Associates Inc, 29 Broadway (Suite 1300), New York, 10006

Don Jagoda Associates Inc, 100 Marcus Dr, Melville, 11747

JSR Advertising Corp, 21 Astor Pl (Suite 2D), New York, 10003-6931

Kang & Lee Advertising Inc/K&L Direct, 285 Madison Ave (23rd fl), New York, 10017

Karasea Inc, 1337 Saw Mill River Rd (#102), Hastings On Hudson, 10706-3630

Katz Dochtermann & Epstein, 102 Madison Ave (fl 10), New York, 10016

The Keehn Co, 43 Cradle Rock Rd, Pound Ridge, 10576

Ketchum, 1285 Avenue of the Americas (Rm 401), New York, 10019-6029

Kirshenbaum, Bond & Partners, 160 Varick St (4th fl), New York, 10013

KPR, 711 3rd Ave Rm 1200, New York, 10017-9204

KZS Advertising, 811 W Jericho Tpke (Suite 109-E), Smithtown, 11787-3220

Klemtner Advertising Inc, 375 Hudson St Bsmt 1, New York, 10014-7464

Kyp Systems Inc, 380 Lexington Ave (fl 17), New York, 10168-1799

The Linick Group Inc, Seven Putter Ln, Linick Bldg, Middle Island, 11953-0102

Little & King Co LLC, 98 Cuttermill Rd Ste 479N, Great Neck, 11021-3037

LHH & F Inc, 2638 Route 23, Hillsdale, 12529

Lockard & Wechsler, 2 Bridge St, Irvington, 10533-1593

Lowe Worldwide, 111 8th Ave, New York, 10011

Loyalty E-Marketing, 81 Main St (Suite 101), White Plains, 10601

The Lustigman Firm P C, 65 E 55th St Fl 3, New York, 10022-3372

Marden-Kane Inc, 1055 Franklin Ave (Suite 300), Garden City, 11530-2903

Marke Communications Inc, 45 W 45th St Ste 16L, New York, 10036-4602

Marketing Visions Inc, 520 White Plains Rd (Suite 500), Tarrytown, 10591-5118

McCann Relationship Mktg, 622 Third Ave, New York, 10017

Meltzer Media Productions, 70 W 36th St (Suite 1000), New York, 10018

MM Batch, PO Box 1548, Westhampton Beach, 11978-7548

MRM Worldwide, 622 3rd Ave, New York, 10017-6707

MVBMS EURO RSCG, 350 Hudson St Fl 8, New York, 10014-4505

Morton Advertising Inc, 875 Ave of the Americas (Suite 1111), New York, 10001-3577

Eric Mower & Associates, 28 E Main St Ste 1960, Rochester, 14614-1988

Mullen & McCaffrey Direct Response, 197 Hog Creek Rd, East Hampton, 11937-4307

NextWeb Media, 350 7th Ave (fl 2), New York, 10001-5013

Ogilvy & Mather Direct, 1100 Avenue of the Americas (Frnt 3), New York, 10036-6712

OgilvyOne Worldwide, 636 11th Ave, New York, 10036-2005

Omnicom Media Group Direct, 195 Broadway, New York, 10007-3100

O2K1, 3 W 18th St (fl 4), New York, 10011-4662

Parise Marketing Group, Five Schuman Rd, Millwood, 10546

Pedone, 49 W 27th St Fl 6, New York, 10001-6936

Pluzynski & Associates Inc, 6123 190th St, PMB 515, Fresh Meadows, 11365-2720

Progressive Direct Marketing, 5800 Transit Rd, Depew, 14043-2820

Rapp Collins Worldwide, 437 Madison Ave (4th fl), New York, 10022-7043

Howard Rapp Enterprises Inc, 88 Pine St (Suite 2610), New York, 10005-1831

Richartz Fliss Clark & Pope Inc, 1 Minetta Ln, New York, 10012-1206

Roberts Communications Inc, 64 Commercial St, Rochester, 14614

Rola-Kimmerling Associates, 501 Fifth Ave (3rd fl), New York, 10017-7805

Roth Advertising Inc, PO Box 96, Sea Cliff, 11579-0096

RFM Broadcasting, 70 Devonshire Rd, New Rochelle, 10804

Sandy Goldshein Associates Inc, 38 W 21st St (#8th), New York, 10010-6906

Sanna Mattson MacLeod, 811 W Jericho Tpke, Smithtown, 11787

Smart Marketing, 23 Highland Blvd, Dix Hills, 11746

Sperber Direct Inc, 201 W 72nd St Apt 9A, New York, 10023-2766

Spring O'Brien & Co, 30 W 26th St Fl 4L, New York, 10010-2090

SCP Rapp Collins Media, 437 Madison Ave (3rd fl), New York, 10022

SKM Group, 6350 Transit Rd Ste 3, Depew, 14043-1039

The Stanford Group, 70 W 40th St Fl 8, New York, 10018-2623

STEEL MEDIA, 350 5th Ave (fl 59), New York, 10118-5999

Stein Rogan & Partners, 432 Park Ave S Fl 16, New York, 10016-8013

Stephan Partners Inc, 233 Spring St (Suite 801), New York, 10013-1522

Stromberg Consulting, 1285 Ave of the Americas (3rd fl), New York, 10019

Sutherland Global Services, 1160 Pittsford/Victor Rd, Pittsford, 14534

Joseph Tardi Associates, 2690 Troy Schenectady Rd, Niskayuna, 12309

Team Nash Inc, 4 Jonathan Dr, East Hampton, 11937-2110

Tobol Group Inc, 275 Dixon Ave (Unit B), Amityville, 11701-2874

True North Inc, 630 3rd Ave Rm 1200, New York, 10017-6749

TBWA/Chiat/Day Inc, 488 Madison Ave (fl 7), New York, 10022-5727

Two Roths, 7020 108th St (#10E), Forest Hills, 11375-4442

UMarketing LLC, 1350 Broadway (Rm 800), New York, 10018-0950

Underline Communications LLC, 12 W 27th St (fl 14), New York, 10001-6903

Unit 7, 30 Irving Pl (11th fl), New York, 10003-2303

Valmark Associates LLC, 4242 Ridge Lea Rd Ste 5, Buffalo, 14226-5122

Vane & Friends, 734 King St, Chappaqua, 10514-3811

Vanguard Direct, 519 8th Ave (23rd fl), New York, 10018-4570

Ventura Associates International LLC, 1040 Ave of the Americas (fl 20), New York, 10018-3714

The Verdi Group Inc, 135 Sully's Trail (Suite 4), Pittsford, 14534

The Vidal Partnership, 228 E 45th St Fl 14, New York, 10017-3303

Videoware Corp, 53 Doral Greens Dr W, Rye Brook, 10573

Wilson Relationship Marketing Services, 333 7th Ave (fl 5), New York, 10001-5004

Wunderman, 285 Madison Ave (Lbby 2), New York, 10017-6401

Zenith Direct, 299 W Houston St, New York, 10014-4806

North Carolina

Barringer & Associates Ltd, 224 Third Ave NW, Hickory, 28603-2525

The Burris Agency Inc, 1175 Revolution Mill Dr (Suite 11), Greensboro, 27405-5053

Cakuun, 1 W Pack Sq (Suite 510), BB&T Bldg, Asheville, 28801

Concinnity Marketing & Technology Consulting Inc, 201 N Broad St (Suite 105), Winston Salem, 27101-2744

Definitely Duffy, 3 Chestnut Mountain Rd, Asheville, 28803

FGI Research, 431 Meadowmont Village Cir, Chapel Hill, 27517-7506

Fletcher Direct, 126 Castlewood Dr, Cary, 27511-5510

Ned Herrmann Group, 794 Buffalo Creed Rd, Lake Lure, 28746-9903

Keller Crescent Co, 1072 Boulder Rd, Greensboro, 27409-9106

Mail Order Media & Marketing Inc, 5500 Linkside Ct (2A), Fuquay Varina, 27526-8499

Marketing Efficiency Corp, 20306 N Main St, Cornelius, 28031-8520

Maxim Direct, PO Box 35565, Greensboro, 27425-5565

Mower & Associates, 1001 Moorehead Sq (5th fl), Charlotte, 28203

PeterAlex Media Corp, 10130 Mallard Creek Rd (Suite 300), Charlotte, 28262

The Signature Agency, 4601 Six Forks Rd (Suite 103), Raleigh, 27609-2572

Wendover Associates Inc, 309-A Edwardia Dr, Greensboro, 27409

North Dakota

Flint Communications, 101 N 10th St (Suite 300), Fargo, 58107-4600

SUNDOG, 2000 44th St SW (fl 6), Fargo, 58103-7411

Swanson Health Products, 4075 40th Ave SW, Fargo, 58104-3912

Ohio

Acerra & Associates Inc, 3800 Boardman-Canfield Rd (Suite One), Canfield, 44406

Adcom Communications, 1370 W 6th St (3rd Fl.), Cleveland, 44113-1315

The Berry Co, 3170 Kettering Blvd, Dayton, 45439-1975

Burkholder Flint Associates, 300 Spruce St (Suite 275), Columbus, 43215-1174

Clay Creative Direct, 1550 Lewis Center Rd (Suite C), Lewis Center, 43035-8232

Cognis Corp, 5051 Este Creek Dr, Cincinnati, 45232-1446

Direct Options, 9565 Cincinnati Columbus Rd, West Chester, 45069

DirectConnect Group Ltd, 5501 Cass Ave, Cleveland, 44102-2121

Emerging Marketing, 29 W Third Ave, Columbus, 43201-3208

Fahlgren, 414 Walnut St (Suite 1006), Cincinnati, 45202-3935

G&A Marketing, 1001 Ford Cir Ste B, Milford, 45150-2740

Gianfagna Strategic Marketing Inc, 1991 Crocker Rd Ste 225, Westlake, 44145-6970

Hammond Paradigm Communications Group, 10549 Reading Rd, Cincinnati, 45241-2524

IR/ARO, 209 N Main St, Bryan, 43506-1319

Influence Inc, 3189 Princeton Rd, Hamilton, 45011-5338

Innis Maggiore Group Inc, 4715 Whipple Ave NW, Canton, 44718-2651

Liggett-Stashower Direct, 1240 Huron Rd., Cleveland, 44115-1831

Lunarcow Design, 137 S Main St (Suite 202), Akron, 44308-1416

Metrics Marketing, 905 Corporate Way, Westlake, 44145-1519

Miami Valley Marketing Group Inc, 1500 Devereux Dr, Dayton, 45419

Northlich, 720 E Pete Rose Way, Cincinnati, 45202-3579

The Ohlmann Group Direct, 1605 N Main St, Dayton, 45405-4141

Richards Communications, 3201 Enterprise Pkwy (Suite 400), Beachwood, 44122

Saint Gregory Group, 4000 Executive Park Dr (#200), Cincinnati, 45241-4007

Sherman & Associates Inc, 333 Harmon NW, Warren, 44483

Robert Silverman Direct Marketing, 1614 E 40th St, Cleveland, 44103

SBC Advertising, 333 W Nationwide Blvd, Columbus, 43215-2311

ST&P Marketing Communications Inc, 320 Springside Dr, Fairlawn, 44333

Stephens Direct Inc, 417 E Stroop Rd, Kettering, 45429-2829

Telestar Media, 4601 Malsbary Rd, Cincinnati, 45242-5659

Universal Media Syndicate Inc, 3939 Everhard Rd NW, Canton, 44709-4004

Wolf Blumberg Krody Inc, 537 E Pete Rose Way (Suite 100), Cincinnati, 45202-3578

Wyse Direct, 25 W Prospect Ave, Cleveland, 44115

Yeck Brothers Co, 2222 Arbor Blvd, Dayton, 45439-1594

Oklahoma

Bullseye Database Marketing LLC, 5546 S 104th East Ave, Tulsa, 74146-6505

Oregon

APS Technologies, 22985 NW Evergreen Pkwy, Hillsboro, 97124-7165

Atomic Direct LLC, 1219 SE Lafayette St, Portland, 97202-3802

Babcock & Jenkins, 711 SW Alder St Ste 200, Portland, 97205-3415

Citrus Inc, 919 NW Bond St Ste 209, Bend, 97701-2767

Direct Marketing Solutions Inc, 8534 NE Alderwood Rd, Portland, 97220-1347

Gard Communications, 711 SW Alder St (Suite 400), Portland, 97205-3417

R2C Group, 207 NW Park Ave, Portland, 97209-3316

Rosen Inc, 1631 NE Broadway (Suite 615), Portland, 97232-1425

Pennsylvania

Danielle Adams Publishing Co, PO Box 100, Merion Station, 19066

Advertising Idea Stores, 37 E Lancaster Ave, Ardmore, 19003-2319

Backe Digital Brand Marketing, 100 Matsonford Rd (Bldg 3, Suite 101), Radnor Corporate Center, Radnor, 19087

Boyd Tamney Cross Inc, 994 Old Eagle School Rd (Suite 1015), Wayne, 19087-1802

Brabender Cox, 1218 Grandview Ave, Pittsburgh, 15211-1239

Brunner, 11 Stanwix St (5th fl), Pittsburgh, 15222-1312

BullsEye Marketing Systems LLC, 1157 Phoenixville Pike (Suite 107), West Chester, 19380-4254

Catalogs By Lorel, 590 N Gulph Rd, Graphic Arts Bldg, King of Prussia, 19406-2800

Creative Commerce LLC, 1230 American Blvd, West Chester, 19380-4264

DMW Worldwide LLC, 701 Lee Rd (Suite 103), Chesterbrook, 19087-5612

Direct Choice Inc, 480 E Swedesford Rd (Suite 210), Wayne, 19087-1860

Direct Success Communications Inc, 308 Lynne Pl, Chester Springs, 19425

Donovan Advertising, 180 W Airport Rd, Lititz, 17543

Doran & Forgacs Inc, 1306 Barkway Dr, West Chester, 19380-5820

Dudnyk Advertising & Public Relations, 5 Walnut Grove Dr (Suite 280), Horsham, 19044-2282

Excelsior Direct, 8 N Queen St (#800), Lancaster, 17603-3855

Fried-Cassorla Communications Inc, 7408 Woodlawn Ave, Melrose Park, 19027

Goodway Group, 261 Old York Rd (Suite 930), Jenkintown, 19046-3711

GroupLevinson, 128 Chestnut St (Suite 403), Philadelphia, 19106

Hanobik Communications, 140 Convair Dr, Coraopolis, 15108-2404

Hoff Communications Inc, 23 S Lansdowne Ave, Lansdowne, 19050

IdeaOverTen LLC, 3140 W Tilghman St (Suite 128), Allentown, 18104-4268

JVW Direct, 309 W Hutchinson Ave, Pittsburgh, 15218-1325

Kenney Marketing & Advertising Inc, 150 S Warner Rd (Suite 250), King of Prussia, 19406

Al Paul Lefton Co Inc, 125 S 9th St Ste 801, Rohm & Haas Bldg, Philadelphia, 19107-5123

LevLane Advertising, 100 Penn Square E (4th fl), The Wonamaker Bldg, Philadelphia, 19107

Marc USA, 225 W Station Square Dr Ste 500, Pittsburgh, 15219-1174

Mitchell & Resnikoff/Weightman, 8003 Old York Rd, Elkins Park, 19027-1410

National A-1 Advertising Inc, 101 S Eighth St, Philadelphia, 19106-3204

Nova DM, 633 E Drinker St, Dunmore, 18512-2505

Our Community Phone Book, One Sentry Pkwy (Suite 1000), Blue Bell, 19422

Quattro Direct LLC, 1175 Lancaster Ave Ste 200, Berwyn, 19312-1297

Radio Direct Response, 1400 N Providence Rd (Suite 4000), Media, 19063-2061

Robinson Direct, 6945 Wards Ln, Center Valley, 18034

Roska Direct Advertising, 211B Progress Dr, Montgomeryville, 18936-9618

The Scholl Group, 316 Highland Ln, Bryn Mawr, 19010-3742

Tom Sheehan Advertising, 645 Penn St (Suite 301), Reading, 19601-3527

Spencer Zahn & Associates, 2015 Sansom St, Philadelphia, 19103-4416

SWB & R, 3865 Adler Pl, Bethlehem, 18017

Tierney Communications, 200 S Broad St Fl 10, Philadelphia, 19102-3845

Topak Marketing Inc, Seven N Columbus Blvd, Philadelphia, 19106

TrueSense Marketing, 155 Commerce Dr, Freedom, 15042-9202

TPG Direct Inc, 7 N Columbus Blvd, Philadelphia, 19106-1422

WOL Direct Inc, 925 Oak St, Scranton, 18515-0999

Puerto Rico

MFP&W Promotions Direct, PO Box 2125, San Juan, 00922-2125

Rhode Island

Chaffee & Communications, 310 Maple Ave #2, Barrington, 02806-3430

Creating Results/New England, PO Box 305, Barrington, 02806-0305

JJI International Inc, 200 1st Ave, Cranston, 02910-5029

Martin Thomas International, 42 Riverside Dr, Barrington, 02806-3612

South Carolina

Chernoff Newman, 1411 Gervais St (Ste 500), Columbia, 29201-3379

Ferillo & Associates, 1938 College St, Columbia, 29201-3922

Henderson Advertising Inc, PO Box 27044, Greenville, 29616-2044

Kenworthy Marketing & Promotional Products, 41 Polo Ridge Cir, Columbia, 29223-2800

Marketing Strategies, 4603 Oleander Dr (Suite 4), North Myrtle Beach, 29577-5738

Rawle-Murdy Associates Inc, Two Beaufain St, Charleston, 29401-1932

Richard Ricelli Inc, 23 Charlotte St, Charleston, 29403

TargetMail Marketing, PO Box 239, Clover, 29710-0239

Tennessee

The Affinion Group, 400 Dukee Dr, Franklin, 37067

Allegiant Direct Inc, 278 Franklin Rd (Suite 290), Brentwood, 37027-3222

Archer/Malmo, 65 Union Ave Ste 500, Memphis, 38103-5137

Atlas Pen & Pencil Corp, 408 Madison St (# 126), Shelbyville, 37160-3339

Corporate Promotions, 1437 Donelson Pike, Nashville, 37217-2957

Gish, Sherwood & Friends Inc, 4235 Hillsboro Rd, Nashville, 37215-3347

Good Advertising, 5100 Poplar Ave (Suite 1700), Memphis, 38137

JP Hogan & Co, 107 W Fifth Ave, Knoxville, 37917

Ibis Communications Inc, 1024 17th Ave S, Nashville, 37212

National Mailroom Service Inc, 6924 Karnes Crossing Ln, Knoxville, 37931-2571

Nationwide Card Services Inc, 7535 Bartlett Corporate Dr (Suite A), Memphis, 38133

Oden, 119 S Main St (Suite 300), Memphis, 38103-3677

tangerine direct - a service of archer malmo, 65 Union Ave (Suite 500), Memphis, 38103-5137

Tigert Communications, 2815 Dogwood Pl, Nashville, 37204

White Post Media Group Inc, PO Box 50180, Nashville, 37205-0180

Texas

AdPlex, 650 Century Plaza Dr (Suite 120), Houston, 77073-6014

Bigham Direct & Digital, 2301 Ohio (Suite 150), One Preston Park, Plano, 75093-4079

Brierley & Partners, 5800 Tennyson Pkwy, Plano, 75024-3993

Bromley Communications, 401 E Houston St, San Antonio, 78205-2615

Cartel Creativo, PO Box 29389, San Antonio, 78229-0389

DMN3, 2010 North Loop W (Suite 240), Houston, 77018

Dieste Harmel & Partners, 1999 Bryan St (Suite 2700), Dallas, 75201-6817

Dieste, 1999 Bryan St (Suite 2700), Dallas, 75201-6817

Farstar, 7110 Main St, Frisco, 75034-4225

FKM, 1800 West Loop S (Suite 2100), Houston, 77027-3281

GSD&M Idea City, 828 W 6th St, Austin, 78703-5420

hawkeye, 2828 Routh St (Suite 300), Dallas, 75201-7605

Hennerberg Group Inc, 5501 Willow Ln, Colleyville, 76034-5149

Internet Direct Response, Inc, 5332 Rush Creek Ct, Fort Worth, 76244

Ivie, 601 Silveron Blvd (Suite 200), Flower Mound, 75028-4030

Kruse Asset Management, 11202 Disco Dr (Suite 100), San Antonio, 78216-2860

Levenson & Brinker Public Relations, 717 N Harwood (20th fl), Dallas, 75201-6501

Lopez Negrete Communications, 3336 Richmond Ave (Suite 200), Houston, 77098-3022

n Fusion Group, 5000 Plaza on the Lake (Suite 200), Austin, 78746

Pop Labs Inc, 7850 Parkwood Circle Dr (Suite B-3), Houston, 77036-6761

Publicis, 7300 Lonestar Dr (Suite C 200), Plano, 75024

RAZOR Transaction Building Experts, 15851 Dallas Pkwy (Suite 725), Addison, 75001-3360

Richards Partners, 8750 N Central Expwy (Suite 1100), Dallas, 75231-4104

San Antonio Express-News, PO Box 2171, San Antonio, 78297-2171

The Snyder Agency, 2918 Plantation Wood Ln, Missouri City, 77459

Tacito Direct Marketing, 14165 Proton Rd, Dallas, 75244-3604

Targetbase, 7850 N Beltline Rd, Irving, 75063-6062

Tocquigny, 401 Congress Ave (fl 17), Austin, 78701-4071

Tracy Locke Partnership, 1999 Bryan St (Suite 2800), Dallas, 75201

Utah

Access Development, 1012 W Beardsley Pl, Salt Lake City, 84119-1522

Bonneville Communications, 5 Triad Ctr (Suite 700), Salt Lake City, 84180-1121

Datamark Inc, 2305 Presidents Dr, Salt Lake City, 84120-7230

HealthCare Insight, 10897 River Front Pkwy (Suite 200), South Jordan, 84095-5730

Merrell Remington & Associates, 1847 W 2300th S, Salt Lake City, 84119

Rastar, 2305 S 1070 W, Salt Lake City, 84119-1564

Redirect Relationship Marketing, 2825 E Cottonwood Pkwy (Suite 310), Salt Lake City, 84121-7282

Response Agency Inc, 936 Granite Peak Dr (Suite 1100), Sandy, 84094

Studeo Interactive Direct, 6405 S 3000th E (3rd fl), Salt Lake City, 84121

ThomasArts, PO Box 70, Farmington, 84025-0070

Vermont

802 Creative Partners Inc, PO Box 54, Bethel, 05032-0054

Gaylord Communications Unlimited, PO Box 28, Bridgewater, 05034-0028

Kelliher Samets Volk, 212 Battery St, Burlington, 05401

Russo & Kelly, 69 Oak Cir, Colchester, 05446

Vermont Media, PO Box 310, West Dover, 05356-0310

Virginia

Affinity Marketing Services, 6666 Avignon Blvd, Falls Church, 22043-1723

American Target Advertising Inc, 9625 Surveyor Ct (Suite 400), Manassas, 20110-4408

Barker Campbell & Farley, 4500 Main St Ste 600, Virginia Beach, 23462-3362

BMD, 901 N Washington St Ste 300, Alexandria, 22314-5506

Cadmus Communications Corp, 2901 Byrdhill Rd, Richmond, 23228

Catalyst Marketing Group, 207 E Main St, Richmond, 23219-3714

CRC Public Relations, 2760 Eisenhower Ave (fl 4), Alexandria, 22314-4569

DeBellis & Ferrara, 2136 Gallows Rd (Suite E), Vienna, 22027-1036

Eberle Communications Group Inc, 1420 Springhill Rd (Suite 490), McLean, 22102-3028

Edelmann Scott Inc, 3751 Westerre Pkwy (Suite A), Richmond, 23233-1472

EdgeMark Partners Inc, 4510 Cox Rd (Suite 305), Glen Allen, 23060-6759

Edmonds Associates Inc, 8221 Old Courthouse Rd (Suite 204), Vienna, 22182-3839

Globalization Partners, 1600 Tysons Blvd (fl 8), Mc Lean, 22102-4872

Marketing General Inc, 209 Madison St Ste 300, Alexandria, 22314-1764

The Martin Agency, 1 Shockoe Plaza, Richmond, 23219-4132

McDonald Enterprises Ltd, 2111 Polo Pointe Dr, Vienna, 22181-2804

Nexus Direct, 2101 Parks Ave (Suite 600), Virginia Beach, 23451-4135

Odell, Simms & Associates Inc, 7704 Leesburg Pike Ste 2, Falls Church, 22043-2625

OTM Partners, 901 N Glebe Rd (Suite 340), Arlington, 22203-1854

Parmelee Associates, PO Box 5557, Arlington, 22205-0057

Pilot Direct, 150 W Brambleton Ave, Norfolk, 23510-2018

Response Dynamics Inc, 2070 Chain Bridge Rd (Suite 520), Vienna, 22182-2569

Rightminds, 1802 Bayberry Ct Ste 400, Richmond, 23226-3773

The Stone Group Inc, 205 S Whiting St (Suite 250), Alexandria, 22304

TMP Worldwide, 1600 Tysons Blvd, Mc Lean, 22102-4865

Wexler Marketing Group Inc, 3403 Holly St, Alexandria, 22305

White & Partners, 13665 Dulles Technology Dr (Suite 150), Herndon, 20171

Washington

Cole & Weber United, 221 Yale Ave N (Suite 600), Seattle, 98109-5490

Direct Resources Group, 1221 2nd Ave Ste 300, Seattle, 98101-2986

Eenigenburg & Co, 14504 SE 47th Pl, Bellevue, 98006-3142

Firepower Marketing Inc, 1124 Fir Ave (#161), Blaine, 98230-9702

GC Direct, 911 Western Ave (Suite 509), Seattle, 98104-1047

Hacker Group Inc, 1215 4th Ave (Suite 2100), Seattle, 98161-1018

Hunt Marketing Group, 1809 7th Ave Ste 411, Seattle, 98101-4403

Northwest Direct Inc, 13240 NE 20th St (Suite 18), Bellevue, 98005-2022

Sweetgrass, 1101 Alaskan Way (Suite 200), Pier 55, Seattle, 98101

West Virginia

Mail America, 89 Bridge St Plaza, Wheeling, 26003-5209

Wisconsin

Bader Rutter & Associates, 13845 Bishops Dr Ste 300, Brookfield, 53005-6617

Boelter + Lincoln Marketing Communications, 222 E Erie St (Suite 400), Milwaukee, 53202-6062

DCI Marketing Inc, 2727 W Good Hope Rd, Milwaukee, 53209-2091

DMC Advertising, One Creative Way, Pewaukee, 53072-5797

Henke & Associates Inc, PO Box 147, PO Box 147, Cedarburg, 53012-0147

The Hiebing Group, 315 Wisconsin Ave, Madison, 53703

Johnson Direct LLC, 250 N Sunnyslope Rd (Suite 203), Brookfield, 53005-4824

Frank Mayer & Associates Inc, 1975 Wisconsin Ave, Grafton, 53024

MediaGraphics, PO Box 162, Eau Claire, 54702-0162

Milwaukee Direct Marketing Inc, 675 N Barker Rd (Suite 130), Brookfield, 53045

News Notes LLC, 2348 Pinehurst Dr Ste 1, Middleton, 53562-2587

Ovation Marketing, 201 Main St Ste 902, La Crosse, 54601-3392

Pro Media-Streff Marketing Group, W127N8690 Westbrook Crossing, Menomonee Falls, 53051-3342

The Scan Group, W222 N625 Cheaney Dr, Waukesha, 53186

Seroka & Associates Inc, N17 W24 222 Riverwood Dr, Waukesha, 53188-1133

Staples Marketing Communications, N28W23050 Roundy Dr Ste 101, Pewaukee, 53072-4095

Stephan & Brady Inc, 1850 Hoffman St, Madison, 53704-2594

STIR, 135 W Wells St (Suite 800), Milwaukee, 53203-1807

Waldbillig & Besteman, 8001 Excelsior Dr (Suite 110), Madison, 53717-1956

Wyoming

Marquis Awards & Specialties Inc, 108 N Bent, Powell, 82435-2712

CANADA
British Columbia

C-W Agencies Inc, 2020 Yukon St, Vancouver, V5Y 3N8

Grow Communications, 894 Saddle St, Coquitlam, V3C 3N2

Ordenza Marketing Group Inc, 4370 Dominion St (fl 6), Burnaby, V5G 4L7

Ontario

Arnold Brand Response, 473 Adelaide St W (3rd Fl), Toronto, M5V 1T1

Array Marketing Group Inc, 45 Progress Ave, Toronto, M1P 2Y6

Blitz Direct Data & Promotion, 502 King St W, Toronto, M5V 1L7

Blue Vidalia, 1-5595 Finch Ave E, Toronto, M1B 2T9

brandedmerchandise.ca, 647 Neal Dr, Peterborough, K9J 6Z7

MacLaren McCann, Ten Bay St, Toronto, M5J 2S3

MacPhee Marketing Communications, 1 rue Yonge St (Suite 2000), Toronto, M5E IE5

MC Group, 350 Talbot St, London, N6A 2R6

Padulo Integrated, One St Clair Ave W (10th fl), Padulo Bldg, Toronto, M4V 1K7

The PENTE Corp, 250 The Esplanade, Toronto, M5A 1J2

Pinnacle Direct Response, 1200 Sheppard Ave E (Suite 105), North York, M2K 2S5

Research and Management Corporation/WSI, 5580 Explorer Dr (Suite 600), Mississauga, L4W 4Y1

Response Innovations Inc, 256 Adelaide St E, Toronto, M5A 1N1

Teleperformance Canada, 365 Bloor St E, Toronto, M4W 3L4

Valassis Canada, 47 Jutland Rd, Toronto, M8Z 2G6

Quebec

Baker-Blais Marketing Inc, 295 Hymus Blvd, Pointe-Claire, H9R 6A5

Cossette Communications Group Inc, 801 Grande Allee Quest (Suite 200), Quebec, G1S 1C1

Transcontinental Interactive, 1 Place Ville Marie (Suite 3315), Montreal, H3B 3N2

AAI
Div. of Marketing Assistance Inc
63 South St (Suite 295)
Hopkinton, MA 01748-2241
Telephone: (508) 544-1250, (877) 866-8500, FAX: (508) 544-1253, E-Mail: info@aai-agency.com, Web Site: www.aai-agency.com
Chmn & CEO: A.R. Hersum
Exec VP: Mark Hersum
Media Coord: Nicole Smith

ADV MARKETING GROUP INC
33 Glenn Terr
Stamford, CT 06906-1402
Telephone: (203) 356-9621, FAX: (203) 324-4680
Pres: Alexander Virvo

THE AFFINION GROUP
Subs. of CUC International Inc
400 Dukee Dr
Franklin, TN 37067
Telephone: (610) 933-3645, (800) 251-2148, FAX: (610) 933-7744, Web Site: www.affiniongroup.com
Pres & CEO: Nathaniel J. Lipman

APS TECHNOLOGIES
Div. of LaCie Ltd
22985 NW Evergreen Pkwy
Hillsboro, OR 97124-7165
Telephone: (503) 844-4500, (800) 233-7550, FAX: (503) 844-4508, E-Mail: sales@lacie.com, Web Site: www.lacie.com
Pres: Scott Phillips

ATM ADVERTISING
PO Box 88824
Atlanta, GA 30356-8824
Telephone: (770) 671-0404, Web Site: www.sagpromo.com
Pres: Pete Severens

ABELSON-TAYLOR INC
33 W Monroe St
Chicago, IL 60603-5300
Telephone: (312) 894-5500, FAX: (312) 894-5526, E-Mail: info@abelsontaylor.com, Web Site: www.abelson-taylor.com
Chmn & CEO: Dale Taylor

THE DMA ACCESS DEVELOPMENT
1012 W Beardsley Pl
Salt Lake City, UT 84119-1522
Telephone: (801) 656-1529
Oper Mgr: Rebecca Compton

ACERRA & ASSOCIATES INC
3800 Boardman-Canfield Rd (Suite One)
Canfield, OH 44406
Telephone: (330) 533-5599, FAX: (330) 533-6005
Pres: John J. Acerra

ACTIMAIL INC
Subs. of Actimail Group
12 W 27th St Fl 13
New York, NY 10001-6903
Telephone: (212) 245-2272, FAX: (212) 245-2523, E-Mail: actimail.usa@actimail.com, Web Site: www.actimail.com
Mgr: Xavier Morel
Branch Mgr: Audrey Conor
Office Mgr: David Joseph
Production Mgr: Arnold Seller
Conducts Business: U.S., Canada, Europe
Employees: 4
Primary Market Served: Business & Consumer
Advertising/Marketing Budget Related to Direct Marketing: 76-100%
Founded: 2000

ACTION-AD
1035 Lincoln Dr (Suite 109), PO Box 810
Bettendorf, IA 52722-4149
Telephone: (563) 355-9581, FAX: (563) 355-9586
Pres: Roger Enke

AD PRO SERVICES INC
479 N Greenbush Rd
Blauvelt, NY 10913
Telephone: (845) 359-8332, FAX: (914) 359-3843
Pres: Peter C. Wade

DANIELLE ADAMS PUBLISHING CO
PO Box 100
Merion Station, PA 19066
Telephone: (610) 642-1000, Web Site: www.danielleadams.com

Pres: Jeffrey Dobkin

THE ADCENTIVE GROUP INC
4801 Viewridge Ave
San Diego, CA 92123-1643
Telephone: (858) 278-9200, FAX: (858) 278-9079, E-Mail: info@adcentive.com, Web Site: www.adcentive.com
Pres: Robert Jorgensen

ADCOM COMMUNICATIONS
1370 W 6th St (3rd Fl.)
Cleveland, OH 44113-1315
Telephone: (216) 574-9100, FAX: (216) 574-6131, E-Mail: adcom@adcom1.com, Web Site: www.adcom1.com
Pres: Joe Kubic

ADPLEX
650 Century Plaza Dr (Suite 120)
Houston, TX 77073-6014
Telephone: (281) 821-5522, Web Site: www.adplex.com
Corp Mktg Specialist: Jennifer Schulte

ADTRON INC
1700 Morrissey Dr
Bloomington, IL 61704-7107
Telephone: (309) 662-1221, FAX: (309) 663-6691
Pres: Richard B. Owen

ADVANTAGE DIRECT INC
805 Jamerson Rd (Bldg 2)
Marietta, GA 30066-1057
Telephone: (678) 921-2134, FAX: (770) 592-4746, E-Mail: ed@advantage-direct.com, Web Site: www.advantage-direct.com
Pres: Edwin C. Reams

ADVERTISING IDEA STORES
37 E Lancaster Ave
Ardmore, PA 19003-2319
Telephone: (610) 642-1990, FAX: (610) 649-5593, E-Mail: uniongoods@msn.com, Web Site: www.uniongoods.com
VP Sls: Marc S. Goldberg

AFFILIATE STRATEGIES INC
112 S Pearl St (Suite 104)
Paola, KS 66071-1755

Telephone: (913) 294-9093
Pres: Kris Rogers

AFFINITY MARKETING SERVICES
6666 Avignon Blvd
Falls Church, VA 22043-1723
Telephone: (703) 917-9822, FAX:
(703) 917-9804, E-Mail: serota@
affinitymarketingservicescorp.com
Pres: Gary Serota

THE DMA AGENCY RAV
71 Rangely Dr
Trumbull, CT 06611-2840
Telephone: (203) 895-7993

THE DMA AIMIA
1405 Xenium Ln N (Suite 150)
Minneapolis, MN 55441-4449
Telephone: (763) 445-3453, FAX:
(763) 496-3453, Web Site: www.
carlsonmarketing.com
Chief Marketing Officer: Mike Kust
Commun Specialist/Mktg & Commun:
Lori Ziebarth

ALLEGIANT DIRECT INC
278 Franklin Rd (Suite 290)
Brentwood, TN 37027-3222
Telephone: (615) 373-2042, FAX:
(615) 373-2099, E-Mail: welcome@
allegiantdirect.com, Web Site: www.
allegiantdirect.com
Pres & Creative Dir: Wayne Gurley
Founded: 1984

THE DMA ALLOY MEDIA MARKETING
151 W 26th St (fl 9)
New York, NY 10001-6810
Telephone: (212) 244-4307, (877) 360-
9688, FAX: (212) 244-4311, E-Mail:
contactus@alloymerch.com, Web
Site: www.alloymarketing.com
Chmn & CEO: Matthew C Diamond
COO & Pres: James K. Johnson
SVP Direct Mktg: Andrew Belth

AMAZINGMAIL INC
8300 E Raintree Dr (Suite 201)
Scottsdale, AZ 85260-2598
Telephone: (480) 281-4800, Web Site:
www.amazingmail.com
Dir Mktg: Dean Batson

AMERICAN MARKETING SYSTEMS INC
dba Professional Education Institute
7020 High Grove Blvd
Burr Ridge, IL 60527-7595

Telephone: (630) 382-1000, FAX:
(630) 325-0825, E-Mail:
studentservices@thepei.com, Web
Site: www.amsdirect.com
Pres PEI: Mark Holecek

AMERICAN TARGET ADVERTISING INC
Sub. of The Viguerie Company
9625 Surveyor Ct (Suite 400)
Manassas, VA 20110-4408
Telephone: (703) 392-7676, FAX:
(703) 392-7654
Chm: Richard A. Viguerie
VP Admin: Viola Shields

AMERICANA SALES VENTURES INC
1000 Sunshine Ln
Altamonte Springs, FL 32714-3805
Telephone: (407) 862-8388, (800) 445-
4302, FAX: (407) 862-6535, Web
Site: www.americanashopper.com
Pres: Timothy Randolph

ANDERSEN ADVERTISING
1752 Clemson Rd
Jacksonville, FL 32217
Telephone: (904) 733-7240, (877) 653-
9621, E-Mail: bob@
andersenadvertising.com, Web Site:
www.andersenadvertising.com
Pres: Bob Andersen

THE DMA ANDERSON DIRECT MARKETING
12650 Danielson Ct
Poway, CA 92064-6822
Telephone: (888) 694-5094, Web Site:
www.andersondirectmarketing.com
VP Bus Devel: Michael Campbell

ANDREWS WHARTON INC
2171 Jericho Tpke Ste 240
Commack, NY 11725-2900
Telephone: (631) 470-4546
Pres & CEO: Jack Lee

ANSWERTHINK INC
1001 Brickell Bay Dr (Suite 3000)
Miami, FL 33131
Telephone: (305) 375-8005, FAX:
(305) 379-8810, Web Site: www.
answerthink.com
COO & Dir: David N. Dungan

THE DMA APPLIED MARKETING SCIENCES LLC
1500 Tropicana Ave
Las Vegas, NV 89119-6516
Telephone: (702) 220-3383, Web Site:
www.appliedmktg.com
Conducts Business: U.S.

Primary Market Served: Business &
Consumer
Advertising/Marketing Budget Related
to Direct Marketing: 0-25%

ARCHER/MALMO
Archer/Malmo
65 Union Ave Ste 500
Memphis, TN 38103-5137
Telephone: (901) 523-2000, FAX:
(901) 524-5578, Web Site: www.
archermalmo.com
Exec VP & Principal: Mary Caywood
Bus Devel: Jennifer Anton

ARENDS
515 N River St Ste 101
Batavia, IL 60510-2390
Telephone: (630) 990-0220, FAX:
(630) 990-2556, Web Site: www.
arends-inc.com
CEO & Pres: John Arends

ARIAGO DESIGNS
51 E Campbell Ave (Suite 126)
Campbell, CA 95008-2055
Telephone: (408) 668-0400, FAX:
(408) 688-0401, Web Site: www.
ariago.com
Founder & Pres: Denise Dahart

ARNOLD BRAND RESPONSE
Div of Arnold Worldwide Canada
473 Adelaide St W (3rd Fl)
Toronto, ON, Canada M5V 1T1
Telephone: (416) 355-5009, Web Site:
www.arnoldworldwide.com
Mng Dir: Deni Baschiera
Pres: Pam Hamlin
Chmn: Bill Sharpe

ARNOLD WORLDWIDE
101 Huntington Ave
Boston, MA 02199
Telephone: (617) 587-8000, FAX:
(617) 587-8070, Web Site: www.
arnoldworldwide.com
CEO: Fran Kelly

ARRAY MARKETING GROUP INC
45 Progress Ave
Toronto, ON, Canada M1P 2Y6
Telephone: (800) 295-4120, FAX:
(416) 292-9759, E-Mail: info@
arraymarketing.com, Web Site: www.
arraymarketing.com
Pres & CEO: Rick DeHerder

ARRCO MEDICAL ADVERTISING
1600 Providence Hwy Ste 63
Walpole, MA 02081-2542

Telephone: (781) 769-7190, FAX: (781) 769-9480, E-Mail: info@arrco. com, Web Site: www.arrco.com
Pres: Jerome Reicher

ASPEN INTERACTIVE
150 Second Ave N (# 470)
Saint Petersburg, FL 33701
Telephone: (727) 823-7144, (800) 777-2255, FAX: (727) 823-6523
Pres & CEO: Brad Wendkos
Mktg Svcs Dir: Colin Shaw

ASPEN MARKETING SERVICES
1240 W North Ave
West Chicago, IL 60185-1087
Telephone: (847) 318-9010, FAX: (847) 318-9036, E-Mail: info@ etownsend.com, Web Site: www. aspenms.com

ASSOCIATED INTEGRATED MARKETING
330 N Mead (Suite 200)
Wichita, KS 67202-2828
Telephone: (316) 683-4691, Web Site: www.meetassociated.com
Sr Dir Strategy, Planning, Media: Lisa Haus

ATLAS PEN & PENCIL CORP
408 Madison St (# 126)
Shelbyville, TN 37160-3339
Telephone: (954) 920-4444, (800) 327-3232, FAX: (954) 920-8899, E-Mail: sales@atlaspen.com, Web Site: www. atlaspen.com
Exec VP: Eric Schneider

ATMOSPHERE BBDO
1285 Avenue Of The Americas (Fl 5)
New York, NY 10019-6008
Telephone: (212) 827-2500, FAX: (212) 827-2525, Web Site: www. atmospherebbdo.com
Dir Commun: Michelle Parks McCourt

THE DMA ATOMIC DIRECT LLC
1219 SE Lafayette St
Portland, OR 97202-3802
Telephone: (503) 296-6131, Web Site: www.atomicdirect.com
Founder & CEO: Doug Garnett

AUGUST BISHOP & MEIER INC
155 N Harbor Dr (Suite 4903)
Chicago, IL 60601-7326
Telephone: (312) 988-9200, FAX: (312) 988-9861
Pres: Norman August

AVALANCHE CREATIVE SERVICES INC
135 W 29th St (Suite 302)
New York, NY 10001-5187
Telephone: (212) 206-9335, FAX: (212) 206-1538, E-Mail: info@ avalanchecreative.tv, Web Site: www.avalanchecreative.tv
Pres: Ava Seavey
Assoc Producer: Josh Weber

AXIA
200 E Forsyth St
Jacksonville, FL 32202-3320
Telephone: (904) 425-6652, (866) 999-AXIA, FAX: (904) 425-6653, E-Mail: tellmemore@axia.net, Web Site: www.axia.net
PR Mgr: Craig TerBlanche

BBK WORLDWIDE
320 Needham St (Suite 150)
Newton, MA 02464-1515
Telephone: (617) 630-4477, Web Site: www.bbkworldwide.com
Creative Direction & Opers: Matthew Stumm

BKV
10561 Barkley (Suite 200)
Overland Park, KS 66212
Telephone: (913) 648-8333, FAX: (913) 648-5024, Web Site: www.bkv. com
CEO: Barbara Murphy
Founded: 1981

BKV INC
3390 Peachtree Rd NE Ste 1000
Atlanta, GA 30326-1108
Telephone: (404) 233-0332, FAX: (404) 233-0302, E-Mail: sylviam@ bkv.com, Web Site: www.bkv.com
Pres: Maribett Varner
Vice Chmn: Brent Kuhn

BMD
901 N Washington St Ste 300
Alexandria, VA 22314-5506
Telephone: (703) 549-3500, Web Site: www.b-m-d.com
Pres: Gregory Munford

BABCOCK & JENKINS
711 SW Alder St Ste 200
Portland, OR 97205-3415
Telephone: (503) 629-6090, FAX: (503) 629-8570, E-Mail: billb@bnj. com, Web Site: www.bnj.com
CEO: Bill Babcock
Pres: Denise Barnes

BACKE DIGITAL BRAND MARKETING
100 Matsonford Rd (Bldg 3, Suite 101), Radnor Corporate Center
Radnor, PA 19087
Telephone: (610) 947-6901, E-Mail: jbacke@backemarketing.com, Web Site: www.backemarketing.com
CEO: John Backe
Sr VP & Dir Client Svcs: Malcolm Brown

THE DMA BADER RUTTER & ASSOCIATES
13845 Bishops Dr Ste 300
Brookfield, WI 53005-6617
Telephone: (262) 784-7200, FAX: (262) 938-5595, Web Site: www. baderrutter.com
Pres: Greg Nickerson

THE DMA BAKER-BLAIS MARKETING INC
295 Hymus Blvd
Pointe-Claire, PQ, Canada H9R 6A5
Telephone: (514) 693-9900, Web Site: www.bakerblais.com
Pres: Don Baker

PERRY BALLARD INC
526 Upton Dr E
Saint Joseph, MI 49085-1091
Telephone: (616) 983-0611, (800) 800-9547, FAX: (616) 983-0747, Web Site: www.perryballard.com
Pres & Chmn: Perry Ballard

BAM! DIRECT INC
3651 Peachtree Pkwy (Suite E-211)
Suwanee, GA 30024-6034
Telephone: (678) 947-1943, Web Site: www.bamdirect.com
VP Acct Dir: Pamela Evans
Primary Market Served: Business & Consumer

BANNER & GREIF LTD
119 W 72nd St (#252)
New York, NY 10023-3201
Telephone: (212) 847-0010, FAX: (212) 949-9806
Pres: Jim Greif

BARKER CAMPBELL & FARLEY
4500 Main St Ste 600
Virginia Beach, VA 23462-3362
Telephone: (757) 497-4811, FAX: (757) 497-3684, Web Site: www.bc-f.com
Pres: Art Webb

BARKLEY
1740 Main St
Kansas City, MO 64108-1311
Telephone: (816) 842-1500, Web Site:
　www.barkleyUS.com
CEO: Brian Brooker
VP, Dir Insight/Impact: Chris Dickey

**BARRINGER & ASSOCIATES
LTD**
224 Third Ave NW
Hickory, NC 28603-2525
Telephone: (828) 322-5550, FAX:
　(828) 327-8440, E-Mail: barringer@
　barringeragency.com, Web Site:
　www.barringeragency.com
Pres: Phil Barringer

**KEITH BATES &
ASSOCIATES INC**
4319 N Lowell Ave
Chicago, IL 60641-2015
Telephone: (773) 205-7992, FAX:
　(773) 205-7988, E-Mail: keithbates@
　kbates.com, Web Site: www.kbates.
　com
Pres: Keith Bates

**BE SOMEBODY BE
YOURSELF**
PO Box 416
Denver, CO 80201-0416
Telephone: (303) 575-5676, FAX:
　(303) 575-1187, E-Mail:
　emailstreet@gmail.com, Web Site:
　www.besomebodybeyourself.com
Founder & Mktg VP: A. Doyle
Employees: 1
Primary Market Served: Business &
　Consumer
Catalog available online
Indirect online sales
Advertising/Marketing Budget Related
　to Direct Marketing: 76-100%
Direct Marketing ad budget:
Direct Mail: 100%
Founded: 1990

Trophies, games, posters, t-shirts, cups,
tennis shoes, shopping bags & other
items.

ᴛʜᴇ
**ᴅᴍᴀ BEACON MARKETING
GROUP**
311 S New York Rd Ste 25
Galloway, NJ 08205-6025
Telephone: (609) 677-4776, Web Site:
　www.beaconmktg.com
Principal: Phillip Kening

BEACONFEY LLC
1107 Kenilworth Dr (Suite 307)
Towson, MD 21204

Telephone: (410) 583-1203, FAX:
　(410) 583-1506, E-Mail: info@
　beaconfey.com, Web Site: www.
　beaconfey.com
Pres: Paul J. Wingate

**CHARLES F BEARDSLEY
ADVERTISING**
31 E Main St
Avon, CT 06001-3805
Telephone: (860) 676-0256, FAX:
　(860) 674-1917, E-Mail: charles.
　beardsley@snet.net
Owner: David Ketchiff

**BEASLEY DIRECT
MARKETING INC**
15227 Perry Ln
Morgan Hill, CA 95037-9659
Telephone: (408) 782-0046, FAX:
　(408) 782-9604, E-Mail: lbeasley@
　beasleydirect.com, Web Site: www.
　beasleydirect.com
Pres: Laurie Beasley

BEBER SILVERSTEIN GROUP
89 N E 27th St (Suite 102)
Miami, FL 33137-4409
Telephone: (305) 856-9800, (800)
　ASKBEBR, FAX: (305) 854-7686,
　E-Mail: jennifer@thinkbsq.com, Web
　Site: www.thinkbsq.com
Pres: Jennifer Beber
Exec VP: Ann Marie Drozd

BENOIT & ASSOCIATES
279 S Schuyler Ave
Kankakee, IL 60901-3809
Telephone: (815) 932-2582, FAX:
　(815) 932-2594, E-Mail: mbenoit@
　benoit-associates.com, Web Site:
　www.benoit-associates.com
Pres: Michael J. Benoit

**BERNSTEIN-REIN
ADVERTISING**
4600 Madison Ave
Kansas City, MO 64112-1283
Telephone: (816) 756-0640, Web Site:
　www.brbrg.com
SVP Dir Mktg & Strategic Planning:
　Joseph Greene

THE BERRY CO
Subs of AT&T
3170 Kettering Blvd
Dayton, OH 45439-1975
Telephone: (937) 296-2121, FAX:
　(937) 296-2011, Web Site: www.
　lmberry.com
Pres & CEO: Dan Graham

BERSON/DEAN/STEVENS INC
PO Box 3997
Westlake Village, CA 91359-3997
Telephone: (818) 713-0134, (877) 447-
　0134, E-Mail: info@
　bersondeanstevens.com, Web Site:
　www.bersondeanstevens.com
Pres: Lori Berson

BEYOND QUOTA LLC
537 King Muir Rd
Lake Forest, IL 60045-1640
Telephone: (847) 234-9475, FAX:
　(847) 234-5260, E-Mail:
　megrinnell@beyondquota.com, Web
　Site: www.beyondquota.com
Principal: Maureen Eddy Grinnell

**BIGGS/GILMORE
COMMUNICATIONS**
261 E Kalamazoo Ave (Suite 300)
Kalamazoo, MI 49007-3990
Telephone: (269) 349-7711, FAX:
　(269) 349-9657, E-Mail: info@
　biggs-gilmore.com, Web Site: www.
　biggs-gilmore.com
Pres: Mike Gerfen
Employees: 80
Founded: 1973

BIGHAM DIRECT & DIGITAL
2301 Ohio (Suite 150), One Preston
　Park
Plano, TX 75093-4079
Telephone: (972) 801-2600, FAX:
　(972) 801-2649, E-Mail: pbigham@
　bighamagency.com, Web Site: www.
　bighamagency.com
Pres: Paul Bigham
Conducts Business: Worldwide
Employees: 10
Primary Market Served: Business &
　Consumer
Catalog available online
Indirect online sales
Advertising/Marketing Budget Related
　to Direct Marketing: 51-75%
Direct Marketing ad budget:
Direct Mail: 80%
Magazines: 15%
TV/Radio: 5%
Founded: 1983
Gross sales or billing: $10,000,000

Direct response, online/off-line creative
and strategy, business/corporate
consultant.

ᴛʜᴇ
ᴅᴍᴀ BIZO
225 Bush St (#1150)
San Francisco, CA 94104-4215
Telephone: (866) 497-5505, Web Site:
　www.bizo.com
CEO: Russell Glass

BLACK DOT GROUP
329 W 18th St Ste 800
Chicago, IL 60616-1103
Telephone: (815) 459-8520, FAX:
(815) 459-7259, E-Mail: sales@
blackdot.com, Web Site: www.
blackdot.com
VP Sls & Mktg: Craig Robinson
Conducts Business: U.S.
Employees: 1,700
Primary Market Served: Business &
Consumer
Advertising/Marketing Budget Related
to Direct Marketing: 0-25%
Founded: 1963

Provides turnkey catalog services, marketing consultation, creative, page layout, production, photography, color
correction and prepress services.

THE DMA BLACK OLIVE CO
125 S Wacker Dr (Suite 300)
Chicago, IL 60606-4421
Telephone: (312) 893-5454, FAX:
(312) 276-8636, E-Mail: pittenger@
blackoliveco.com, Web Site: www.
blackoliveco.com
Pres: Karen Pittenger
Brandologist & Strategic Devel: Nila
Nealy
Creative Specialist: Steve Nealy
Online Specialist: John Brooks
Conducts Business: U.S.
Employees: 10
Primary Market Served: Business &
Consumer
Indirect online sales
Advertising/Marketing Budget Related
to Direct Marketing: 26-50%
Direct Marketing ad budget:
Direct Mail: 50%
Online: 40%
TV/Radio: 5%
Telephone: 5%
Founded: 2003
Gross sales or billing: $2,000,000

Strategic & creative development for
B2B & multichannel advertisers focused on brand, ROI & direct
marketing.

DL BLAIR INC
400 Post Ave Ste 400
Westbury, NY 11590-2226
Telephone: (516) 746-3700, FAX:
(516) 746-3889, Web Site: www.
dlblair.com
Chmn: T.J. Conlon

**GEORGE BLAKE &
ASSOCIATES**
6015 Courtside Dr
Bradenton, FL 34210-4018
Telephone: (941) 755-8637, E-Mail:
single14all@verizon.net

Pres: George Blake

**BLASS COMMUNICATIONS
LLC**
17 Drowne Rd
Old Chatham, NY 12136-3006
Telephone: (518) 766-2222, FAX:
(518) 766-2445, E-Mail: kenb@
blasscommunications.com, Web Site:
www.blasscommunications.com
Pres: Kenneth L. Blass

**BLEU MARKETING
SOLUTIONS INC**
3025 Fillmore St
San Francisco, CA 94123-4009
Telephone: (415) 345-3300, FAX:
(415) 353-0299, E-Mail: helpdesk@
bleumarketing.com, Web Site: www.
bleumarketing.com
Pres & CEO: Laura van Galen
Conducts Business: U.S., Canada,
Worldwide
Employees: 20
Primary Market Served: Business
Founded: 2001
Gross sales or billing: $3,000,000

Direct marketing, consulting and
services.

**BLITZ DIRECT DATA &
PROMOTION**
502 King St W
Toronto, ON, Canada M5V 1L7
Telephone: (416) 922-6434, Web Site:
www.cossette.com
SVP & Mng Dir: Anna Percy-Dove

**DAVID H BLOCK
ADVERTISING INC**
3 Claridge Dr
Verona, NJ 07044-3000
Telephone: (973) 857-3900, FAX:
(973) 857-4041, Web Site: www.
blockadvertising.com
Pres: Bill Decorso

**CARL BLOOM ASSOCIATES
INC**
81 Main St (Unit 126)
White Plains, NY 10601-1745
Telephone: (914) 761-2800, FAX:
(914) 761-2744, E-Mail: info@
carlbloom.com, Web Site: www.
carlbloom.com
Pres: Carl Bloom
VP Creative: Rob Bloom
VP Gen Mgr: Brooke Coneys
VP Mktg & Bus Devel: George
Whelan
Conducts Business: U.S.
Employees: 14
Primary Market Served: Business
Catalog available online

Indirect online sales
Advertising/Marketing Budget Related
to Direct Marketing: 76-100%
Direct Marketing ad budget:
Online: 100%
Founded: 1976
Gross sales or billing: $7,604,457

Direct marketing full service direct
response fundraising agency.

THE DMA BLUE VIDALIA
1-5595 Finch Ave E
Toronto, ON, Canada M1B 2T9
Telephone: (416) 572-5222, E-Mail:
info@bluevidalia.ca, Web Site: www.
bluevidalia.ca
Primary Market Served: Business

BODDEN PARTNERS
102 Madison Ave Fl 7
New York, NY 10016-7417
Telephone: (212) 328-1111, Web Site:
www.boddenpartners.com
Pres & Exec Creative Dir: Chris Bodden

**BOELTER + LINCOLN
MARKETING
COMMUNICATIONS**
222 E Erie St (Suite 400)
Milwaukee, WI 53202-6062
Telephone: (414) 271-0101, FAX:
(414) 271-1436, Web Site: www.
boelterlincoln.com
Chmn: Robert Boelter
VP & CFO: Terrie Treland

**MICHAEL BOLCHALK
MARKETING**
310 S Williams Blvd (Suite 260)
Tucson, AZ 85711-7703
Telephone: (520) 745-8221, FAX:
(520) 745-5540, E-Mail: michael@
adwiz.com, Web Site: www.adwiz.
com
Pres: Michael Bolchalk

**BONNEVILLE
COMMUNICATIONS**
Div. of Bonneville International Corp
5 Triad Ctr (Suite 700)
Salt Lake City, UT 84180-1121
Telephone: (801) 237-2600, (888)
BONCOM, FAX: (801) 237-2614,
E-Mail: bonneville@bonneville.com,
Web Site: www.bonneville.com
VP & Gen Mgr: Gregg D. Garber

BOOYAH NETWORKS
11030 Circle Point Rd (Suite 350)
Westminster, CO 80020

Telephone: (303) 426-7776, FAX: (303) 345-6700, E-Mail: support@ booyahnetworks.com, Web Site: www.booyahnetworks.com
Pres & CFO: Mike Shehan
Dir, Search Engine Mktg: Troy Lemer
Dir: Dan Craig
Mktg & Commun Mgr: Valerie Quintanilla
Conducts Business: U.S.
Employees: 27
Primary Market Served: Business
Founded: 2001

Online marketing: Company featuring search engine marketing capabilities and broadband video.

BOSCOBEL MARKETING COMMUNICATIONS INC
8606 Second Ave
Silver Spring, MD 20910-3326
Telephone: (301) 588-2900, E-Mail: info@boscobel.com, Web Site: www.boscobel.com
Pres: Joyce L. Bosc

BOYD TAMNEY CROSS INC
994 Old Eagle School Rd (Suite 1015)
Wayne, PA 19087-1802
Telephone: (610) 293-0500, FAX: (610) 687-8199, E-Mail: info@ btcmarketing.com, Web Site: www.boydtamneycross.com
Pres: Joseph Tamney

BRABENDER COX
1218 Grandview Ave
Pittsburgh, PA 15211-1239
Telephone: (412) 434-6320, FAX: (412) 424-6391, E-Mail: tiffany@ brabendercox.com, Web Site: www.brabendercox.com
Pres: John A. Brabender
VP, Client Svcs: Tiffany D'Alessandro

BRANDEDMERCHANDISE.CA
647 Neal Dr
Peterborough, ON, Canada K9J 6Z7
Telephone: (705) 944-5632, (800) 461-1788, FAX: (705) 944-7500, E-Mail: info@brandedmerchandise.ca, Web Site: www.brandedmerchandise.ca
Pres: Ted Cooney

Integrated promotional marketing company.

BRASHE ADVERTISING INC
11 Jan Ln
Woodbury, NY 11797-2107
Telephone: (516) 935-5544, FAX: (516) 931-1722
CEO: Harvey Cherkis

BREATH APPEAL
2000 S 25th Ave (Suite N)
Broadview, IL 60155
Telephone: (800) 300-3910, E-Mail: info@breathappeal.com, Web Site: www.breathappeal.com
Pres: Mark Goroff

BRIERLEY & PARTNERS
5800 Tennyson Pkwy
Plano, TX 75024-3993
Telephone: (214) 760-8700, FAX: (214) 743-5511, E-Mail: bpayton@ brierley.com, Web Site: www.brierley.com
Chmn & CEO: Harold M. Brierley
Pres, Retail Practice: Billy Payton

BROADFORD & MALONEY INC
445 Park Ave (fl 10)
New York, NY 10022-2606
Telephone: (212) 836-4710, FAX: (917) 322-2105, E-Mail: m.maloney@bmcorp.com, Web Site: bmcorp.com
Owner: Julie Maloney

BROADUS ADVERTISING/ PUBLIC RELATIONS
1008 Sea Palms West Dr
Saint Simons Island, GA 31522-5243
Telephone: (912) 638-0897, FAX: (912) 638-0958, E-Mail: jenniferbroadus@broadus.com, Web Site: www.broadus.com
CEO: Robert Broadus

BROMLEY COMMUNICATIONS
Subs. of The BCom3 Group
401 E Houston St
San Antonio, TX 78205-2615
Telephone: (210) 244-2000, Web Site: www.bromleyville.com
CEO: Ernest Bromley

SANDI BROWN ASSOCIATES
4342 14th Way NE
Saint Petersburg, FL 33703-5349
Telephone: (727) 528-6980, FAX: (703) 960-4492
Pres: Sandi Brown

BRUNNER
11 Stanwix St (5th fl)
Pittsburgh, PA 15222-1312
Telephone: (412) 995-9500, FAX: (412) 995-9501, Web Site: www.brunnerworks.com
Dir Mktg: Amy Mastrippolito
SVP Digital Strategy: Ken Johns

BRUSH FIRE
2 Wing Dr
Cedar Knolls, NJ 07927
Telephone: (973) 871-1700, FAX: (973) 871-1717, Web Site: www.brushfireinc.com
CEO: John Leonardi
Exec VP & Mngmt Dir: Joan Mueller
Sr VP & Creative Dir: Ken Musto
Sr VP & Media Dir: John Thompsen
Sr VP & Pub Rels Grp Dir: Valerie Warner
VP & HR Dir: Kathy Laudadio
VP Brdcst: Kathy Partis

BRYDELS MARKETING LLC
4315 Bluebonnet Blvd (Suite A)
Baton Rouge, LA 70809-9643
Telephone: (225) 773-1011
Pres: John Brydels

THE DMA BUDCO
13700 Oakland St
Highland Park, MI 48203-3174
Telephone: (313) 957-5100, Web Site: www.budco.com
VP Mktg & Prod Devel: Jeff Sierra

THE DMA BULLSEYE DATABASE MARKETING LLC
5546 S 104th East Ave
Tulsa, OK 74146-6505
Telephone: (918) 587-1731, FAX: (918) 587-0450, E-Mail: inquiries@ bullseyedm.com, Web Site: www.bullseyedm.com
Pres: Mark Jennemann

BULLSEYE MARKETING SYSTEMS LLC
1157 Phoenixville Pike (Suite 107)
West Chester, PA 19380-4254
Telephone: (484) 356-2240, Web Site: bullseyemarketingsystems.com
Primary Market Served: Consumer

BURKHOLDER FLINT ASSOCIATES
300 Spruce St (Suite 275)
Columbus, OH 43215-1174
Telephone: (614) 228-2425, FAX: (614) 228-0631, E-Mail: bfa1@ burkholderflint.com, Web Site: www.burkholderflint.com
VP: Vickie Easterday

LEO BURNETT USA
35 W Wacker Dr (21st fl)
Chicago, IL 60601-1723
Telephone: (312) 220-5959, FAX: (312) 220-3299, Web Site: www.leoburnett.com
Pres: Rich Stoddart

THE BURRIS AGENCY INC
1175 Revolution Mill Dr (Suite 11)
Greensboro, NC 27405-5053
Telephone: (336) 378-1221, FAX:
(336) 378-1221, E-Mail: mburris@
burris.com, Web Site: www.burris.
com
CEO: J. Mark Burris

BUSINESS DIRECT MARKETING ASSOCIATES INC
6825 Polo Fields Pkwy
Cumming, GA 30040-5731
Telephone: (770) 888-8300, FAX:
(770) 888-6482, E-Mail: bdmainc@
aol.com, Web Site: www.bdmainc.
com
Pres: Joe A. Staffieri Jr

BYOWNER.COM
PO Box 667
Shoreham, NY 11786
Telephone: (800) BY-OWNER, FAX:
(866) BY-OWNER, Web Site: www.
byowner.com
Pres: Kevin Wood
Founded: 1995

C L & B CAPITAL MANAGEMENT
7583 Hunt Ln
Fayetteville, NY 13066-2554
Telephone: (315) 637-0915, FAX:
(413) 403-7145, Web Site: www.
clbcm.com
Owner: Rick Labs

ᴛʜᴇ/ᴅᴍᴀ C-W AGENCIES INC
2020 Yukon St
Vancouver, BC, Canada V5Y 3N8
Telephone: (604) 871-3400, FAX:
(604) 871-3482, E-Mail:
c-wreception@c-wgroup.com, Web
Site: www.c-wgroup.com
VP, Media Commun: Al DeJoseph

CCMR ADVERTISING/ MARKETING COMMUNICATIONS
260 Fair St
Kingston, NY 12401-3808
Telephone: (845) 331-4620, FAX:
(845) 331-3026, Web Site: www.
gotoccmr.com
Mng Dir: Frank Rocco

CGSM INC
11 Grumman Hill Rd
Wilton, CT 06897-4500
Telephone: (203) 563-9233, FAX:
(203) 563-9239, Web Site: www.
cgsm.com
Pres: Mark Kolier

VP & Dir Production Svcs: Kristie
McGonigle
Conducts Business: U.S., Canada
Employees: 7
Primary Market Served: Business
Founded: 1996
Gross sales or billing: $5,000,000

Print management company offering
production of direct mail pieces, packages, and inserts to business and consumer marketers.

CI PRODUCTIONS INC
3N506 Linda Ln
Addison, IL 60101-3037
Telephone: (708) 431-2800, FAX:
(630) 458-1080
Pres: James R. Behrenfeld
Founded: 1989

Specializes in restaurant marketing and
has developed a results proven customer traffic building strategic program
that can generate an increase in sales
by 8-13% within a pre-determiined
time schedule, on target, on time & on
budget.

CMC & DESIGN
3510 15th St Ct
Rock Island, IL 61201-6119
Telephone: (309) 786-2888, FAX:
(309) 786-9887, E-Mail:
cmcanddesign@aol.com
Pres: Jodie Kavensky

CPO DIRECT INC
736 N Western Ave (#147)
Lake Forest, IL 60045-1820
Telephone: (847) 735-7365, FAX:
(847) 735-9825, E-Mail: ngoldring@
cpodirect.com, Web Site: www.
cpodirect.com
Conducts Business: U.S., Canada
Primary Market Served: Consumer
Founded: 1980

Direct response agency services to
consumer marketers.

CRC PUBLIC RELATIONS
2760 Eisenhower Ave (fl 4)
Alexandria, VA 22314-4569
Telephone: (703) 683-5004, FAX:
(703) 683-1703, E-Mail: crc@
crcpublicrelations.com, Web Site:
www.crc4pr.com
Chmn: Leif E. Noren

CADE & ASSOCIATES ADVERTISING
1645 Metropolitan Blvd
Tallahassee, FL 32308-3730

Telephone: (850) 385-0300, (800) 715-
CADE, FAX: (850) 385-1165,
E-Mail: webmaster@cade1.com,
Web Site: www.cade1.com
Pres: Rick Shapley

CADMUS COMMUNICATIONS CORP
Subs. of Cadmus Communications Inc
2901 Byrdhill Rd
Richmond, VA 23228
Telephone: (804) 264-2711, FAX:
(804) 262-6419, Web Site: www.
cenveo.com
CEO: Harry Vinson

CAKUUN
1 W Pack Sq (Suite 510), BB&T Bldg
Asheville, NC 28801
Telephone: (828) 225-5505, E-Mail:
transformyourbrand@cakuun.com,
Web Site: cakuun.com
CEO: David Anderson

ᴛʜᴇ/ᴅᴍᴀ CAMPBELL EWALD CO
The Interpublic Group of Cos
30400 Van Dyke Ave
Warren, MI 48093-2368
Telephone: (586) 574-3400, FAX:
(810) 575-9925, Web Site: www.
campbell-ewald.com
Exec VP: Tracie Reihm

CAMPBELL MITHUN
222 S 9th St Ste 2100
Minneapolis, MN 55402-3327
Telephone: (612) 347-1000, FAX:
(612) 347-1515, Web Site: www.
campbellmithun.com
CEO: Jack Rooney
SVP, Dir Direct Mktg: Michelle Arn-
tzen
Employees: 700
Founded: 1933

Campbell Mithun is a full-service na-
tional advertising & marketing commu-
nications agency with billings of $1.1
Billion. Key clients include: Ace Hard-
ware, ADC, Andersen Windows Corpo-
ration, Bumble Bee Seafoods, Burger
King (Big Kids), The Coca-Cola Com-
pany, General Mills, Inc., H&R Block,
Heinz North America, Hunt-Wesson
Foods, Interstate Bakeries Corporation,
Kimberly-Clark Corporation, Land
O'Lakes, Inc., The Medicine Shoppe,
Mutual of Omaha, National Pork Pro-
ducer's Council, Omni Hotels, San
Diego Zoo & Wild Animal Park, Sara
Lee Coffee & Tea, Schwan's, Shop-
NBC, St. Paul Companies, Time
Warner Cable, The Toro Company,
Verizon Wireless.

CARMICHAEL LYNCH INC
110 N Fifth St
Minneapolis, MN 55403
Telephone: (612) 334-6000, FAX:
  (612) 334-6101, E-Mail: roman.
  paluta@clynch.com, Web Site: www.
  carmichaellynch.com
Chief Mktg Officer: Roman Paluta

THE CARNEGIE HALL CORP
881 Seventh Ave (fl 7)
New York, NY 10019-8077
Telephone: (212) 247-7800, FAX:
  (212) 373-0500, E-Mail: feedback@
  carnegiehall.org, Web Site: www.
  carnegiehall.org
Mktg Dir: Richard Haney Jardine

CARSON & CO
1740 E Garry Ave (Suite 231)
Santa Ana, CA 92705-5844
Telephone: (949) 477-9400, E-Mail:
  gcarson@carsonandcompany.com,
  Web Site: www.carsonpr.com
Pres: George Carson

CARTEL CREATIVO
PO Box 29389
San Antonio, TX 78229-0389
Telephone: (210) 892-0700, FAX:
  (210) 696-4299, Web Site: www.
  thecartel.com
Partner: Victoria Varela
Conducts Business: U.S.
Employees: 10
Primary Market Served: Business &
  Consumer
Advertising/Marketing Budget Related
  to Direct Marketing: 26-50%
Founded: 1995

Direct, relationship & database marketing agency.

CATALOGS BY LOREL
590 N Gulph Rd, Graphic Arts Bldg
King of Prussia, PA 19406-2800
Telephone: (800) 967-2682, Web Site:
  www.catalogdesignstudios.com
Pres: Christine Carrington

THE DMA CATALYST
110 Marina Dr
Rochester, NY 14626-5104
Telephone: (585) 453-8300, (800) 836-
  7720, FAX: (585) 453-8360, E-Mail:
  info@catalystinc.com, Web Site:
  www.catalystinc.com
Mng Dir: Michael Osborn
Mng Dir: Jeff Cleary
Exec Creative Dir: John Brogan
Dir Production Svcs: Cindy West
Dir Communs: Robyn Federman
Conducts Business: U.S. Canada
Employees: 45

Primary Market Served: Business &
  Consumer
Advertising/Marketing Budget Related
  to Direct Marketing: 76-100%
Founded: 1990
Gross sales or billing: $40,000,000

A direct & digital marketing agency
that helps clients acquire, retain & develop long term relationships with their
customers. The agency takes the guess-
work out of marketing decisions by
combining intellectual curiosity with
hard-core analytics, deep customer insight & a measurement mindset.

CATALYST MARKETING COMMUNICATIONS INC
2777 Summer St (Suite 301)
Stamford, CT 06905-4310
Telephone: (203) 348-7541, FAX:
  (203) 348-5688, E-Mail: b2b@
  catalystmc.com, Web Site: www.
  catalystmc.com
Owner & Pres: Charles Wintrub
VP & Pub Rels: Melissa A. LoParco

CATALYST MARKETING GROUP
207 E Main St
Richmond, VA 23219-3714
Telephone: (804) 288-9440, FAX:
  (804) 288-9824, E-Mail: info@
  catalyst121.com, Web Site: www.
  catalyst121.com
Dir Bus Devel: Jason Angus

FRANK W CAWOOD & ASSOCIATES INC
103 Clover Green
Peachtree City, GA 30269-1672
Telephone: (770) 487-6307, Web Site:
  www.fca.com
Creative Dir: Jo Bauer

CELEBRITY ENDORSEMENT NETWORK (CEN)
23679 Calabasas Rd (#728)
Calabasas, CA 91302-1502
Telephone: (818) 225-7090, FAX:
  (818) 880-0898, E-Mail: info@
  celebrityendorsement.com, Web Site:
  www.celebrityendorsement.com
Pres: Noreen S. Jenney

CHAFFEE & COMMUNICATIONS
310 Maple Ave #2
Barrington, RI 02806-3430
Telephone: (401) 247-2300, FAX:
  (401) 247-2002, E-Mail: nchaffee@
  fullchannel.net, Web Site: www.
  chaffeecommunications.com
CEO: David S. Chaffee
Pres: Nancy Chaffee

CHANNEL NEUTRAL MARKETING
60 Peerless Dr
Oyster Bay, NY 11771-3615
Telephone: (516) 992-7887, FAX:
  (516) 983-1617, Web Site: www.
  channelneutralmarketing.com
Pres: Deborah Kennedy

CHARTER DIRECT MARKETING
Div. of The Charter Group
132 E 43rd St (#727)
New York, NY 10017
Telephone: (212) 717-2770, FAX:
  (561) 245-7559, E-Mail:
  terrykollman@
  charterdirectmarketing.com, Web
  Site: www.charterdirectmarketing.
  com
Pres: Terry Kollman
Creative Dir: John Golden
Media Dir: Tony Durante
Founded: 1986

CHASE ONLINE MARKETING STRATEGIES
79 Pine St (#102)
New York, NY 10005
Telephone: (212) 619-4780
Pres: Larry Chase

CHEMISTRI
Subs. of Publicis Groupe SA
3310 W Big Beaver Rd (Suite 107)
Troy, MI 48084-2807
Telephone: (248) 458-8300, FAX:
  (248) 458-8729
Commun Dir: R. Patrick McCarthy

CHERNOFF NEWMAN
1411 Gervais St (Ste 500)
Columbia, SC 29201-3379
Telephone: (803) 254-8158, FAX:
  (803) 252-2016, E-Mail: david.
  campbell@cnsg.com, Web Site:
  www.chernoffnewman.com
Pres: David Campbell

CHIEF MEDIA
875 6th Ave
New York, NY 10001-3507
Telephone: (212) 300-8491
Research Analyst: Joe Agostino

CIMARRON GROUP
6855 Santa Monica Blvd
Hollywood, CA 90038
Telephone: (323) 337-0300, FAX:
  (323) 337-0333, Web Site: www.
  cimarrongroup.com
Exec VP, Admin: Jeanne Carelli

CITRUS INC
919 NW Bond St Ste 209
Bend, OR 97701-2767
Telephone: (541) 388-2003, FAX:
(541) 388-4381, Web Site: www.
citrusbegin.com
CEO & Pres: Peter Levitan
Conducts Business: U.S.
Employees: 15
Primary Market Served: Business
Founded: 1986
Gross sales or billing: $3,000,000

Specializes in marketing communications through advertising, direct response campaigns, collateral materials to financial institutions, resorts, casinos, and healthcare industries.

CLARKE ADVERTISING &
PUBLIC RELATIONS
401 N Cattlemen Rd (Suite 200)
Sarasota, FL 34232-6439
Telephone: (941) 365-2710, FAX:
(941) 366-4940, E-Mail: tclarke@
clarkeadvertising.com, Web Site:
www.clarkeadvertising.com
Pres: Tim Clarke

GEORGE P CLARKE
ADVERTISING INC
27 E 21st St (2nd fl)
New York, NY 10010
Telephone: (212) 545-7400, FAX:
(212) 545-7433, E-Mail: info@
gpclarke.com, Web Site: gpclarke.
com
Pres: Richard A. Clarke

JESS CLARKE & SONS INC
5808 42nd St E
Bradenton, FL 34203-5579
Telephone: (941) 727-0042, FAX:
(941) 753-5394, E-Mail: catalogjfc@
aol.com, Web Site: www.
miracleofaloe.com
Pres: Jess F. Clarke Jr
VP: Jess F. Clarke III

CLAY CREATIVE DIRECT
1550 Lewis Center Rd (Suite C)
Lewis Center, OH 43035-8232
Telephone: (740) 548-0307, FAX:
(740) 548-0898, E-Mail: frank@
claycreativegroup.com, marketing@
claycreativegroup.com, Web Site:
www.claydm.com
Creative Dir: Franklin Clay
New Bus Mgr: Alicia Politti
Art Dir: Jessica Clay
Conducts Business: U.S.
Employees: 10
Primary Market Served: Business &
Consumer
Advertising/Marketing Budget Related
to Direct Marketing: 26-50%

Direct Marketing ad budget:
Direct Mail: 65%
Magazines: 20%
Newspapers: 10%
TV/Radio: 5%
Founded: 1977
Gross sales or billing: $900,000

Marketing communications. Clients -
top Fortune 400 clients.

CLICKBOOTH.COM LLC
5901 N Honore Ave
Sarasota, FL 34243-2632
Telephone: (941) 483-4188, Web Site:
www.integraclick.com
CEO: John Lemp

CLICKSPEED
6709 W 119th St (Suite 396)
Overland Park, KS 66209-2013
Telephone: (913) 383-1500, Web Site:
www.clickspeed.com
Pres: Matt Kirk
Primary Market Served: Business

CO-OP PROMOTIONS
2301 S Ocean Dr (Suite 2504)
Hollywood, FL 33019
Telephone: (954) 922-2323, FAX:
(954) 922-2071, E-Mail: art@co-
oppromotions.com, Web Site: www.
co-oppromotions.com
Pres: Art Averbook

COGNIS CORP
5051 Este Creek Dr
Cincinnati, OH 45232-1446
Telephone: (513) 482-3000, FAX:
(513) 482-5501, E-Mail: kathy.
bollmer@cognis.com, Web Site:
www.cognis-us.com
Pres: Bob Betz

COHORTS
Div. of IXI Corp
1624 Market St (Suite 311)
Denver, CO 80202
Telephone: (303) 893-8600, FAX:
(303) 893-8611, E-Mail: info@
cohorts.com, Web Site: www.cohorts.
com
Grp VP: Jim Walkley

COLE & WEBER UNITED
221 Yale Ave N (Suite 600)
Seattle, WA 98109-5490
Telephone: (206) 447-9595, Web Site:
www.cwunited.com
Partner: Britt Peterson
Primary Market Served: Business

COLLE+MCVOY
400 First Ave N
Minneapolis, MN 55401
Telephone: (612) 305-6000, FAX:
(612) 305-6500, E-Mail: info@
collemcvoy.com, Web Site: www.
collemcvoy.com
Pres: Christine Fruechte

COLORAMA LLC
4872 Waterbridge Down
Sarasota, FL 34235-7215
Telephone: (941) 378-5700, FAX:
(941) 371-1844
Owner: James L. Dean

COLUMBIA DIRECT
MARKETING CORP
1 S Acton Pl
Annapolis, MD 21401-2713
Telephone: (410) 268-8881, FAX:
(410) 268-8999
Pres: William J. Kardash

COMMAND FINANCIAL
PRESS
75 Varick St
New York, NY 10013
Telephone: (212) 274-6070, FAX:
(212) 274-8262, E-Mail: csd@
commandfinancial.com, Web Site:
www.commandfinancial.com
Pres: Jim Penders

COMMUNICATIONS PLUS
102 Madison Ave Fl 7
New York, NY 10016-7417
Telephone: (212) 686-9570, FAX:
(212) 686-9687, E-Mail: jrandolph@
getcp.com, Web Site: www.
boddenpartners.com
Pres: Chris Bodden

THE COMMUNIQUE GROUP
10559 E Democrat Rd
Parker, CO 80134-5004
Telephone: (617) 527-2230, FAX:
(617) 965-6763
Pres: James Kurland
Employees: 9
Founded: 1984

COMMUNITY DIRECT
1402 Chapel Hill Rd
Mountainside, NJ 07092-1405
Telephone: (212) 996-8222, FAX:
(908) 789-2995, E-Mail: slipton@
gocommunitydirect.com
Pres: Shelly Lipton
Conducts Business: U.S.
Primary Market Served: Business &
Consumer
Founded: 2003

Hispanic direct marketing and consulting services.

COMPANY C
160 Varick (fl 4)
New York, NY 10013-1273
Telephone: (212) 561-6009, FAX:
(212) 260-3710, E-Mail: nnocca@
companycmarketing.com, Web Site:
www.companycmarketing.com
Pres: Nick Nocca

COMPASS COMMUNICATIONS INC
22035 Stratford Pl
Excelsior, MN 55331
Telephone: (952) 470-2017, Web Site:
www.compasscommunications.com
Pres: William J. Tomlinson

COMPU-MAIL
1342 Military Rd
Niagara Falls, NY 14304-1730
Telephone: (716) 297-0553, (800) 255-
0670, FAX: (716) 297-0822, Web
Site: www.compu-mail.com
Pres & CEO: Michael L. Vitch

THE COMPUTER STUDIO
1280 Saw Mill River Rd Frnt 1
Yonkers, NY 10710-2738
Telephone: (914) 968-1212, FAX:
(914) 968-1228, E-Mail: sales@
webbusconnect.com, Web Site:
www.webbusconnect.com
Pres: Alan J. Goldstein

COMPUTRACK
Div. of DGS Marketing Engineers
10100 Lantern Rd (Suite 225)
Fishers, IN 46037-9692
Telephone: (317) 813-2222, FAX:
(317) 813-2233, E-Mail: info@
dgsmarketingengineers.com, Web
Site: www.dgsmarketingengineers.
com
Pres & CEO: Marc Diabold

THE DMA CONCEPT MEDIA PARTNERS
1992 Commerce St (#307)
Yorktown Heights, NY 10598-4412
Telephone: (914) 767-0032, FAX:
(914) 514-1711, E-Mail: karen@
conceptmediapartners.com, Web Site:
www.conceptmediapartners.com
Pres: Karen Capalbo

CONCEPTS & STRATEGIES INC
Div. of RxCheck
256 Eighth St SE
Washington, DC 20003-2107

Telephone: (202) 251-9951, FAX:
(202) 478-1750, E-Mail: info@
constrat.net
CEO: Mary Clare Gumbleton
Pres: Jason Hinton

CONCEPTS UNLIMITED
16535 Grays Way
Broomfield, CO 80023-8333
Telephone: (303) 449-2907, FAX:
(303) 449-2967, E-Mail:
conceptsunlimited@estreet.com, Web
Site: www.conceptsunlimitedinc.com
Owner: Pam McKinnie

THE DMA CONCINNITY MARKETING & TECHNOLOGY CONSULTING INC
201 N Broad St (Suite 105)
Winston Salem, NC 27101-2744
Telephone: (336) 245-4561, Web Site:
www.concinnitymarketing.com
Primary Market Served: Consumer

CONSOLIDATED PRINTING & STY CO
319 S 5th St
Salina, KS 67401-3907
Telephone: (785) 823-6356, FAX:
(785) 823-9187
Gen Mgr: Don Commerford

THE DMA CONVERGEDIRECT
33 E 33rd St (fl 3)
New York, NY 10016-5335
Telephone: (212) 213-0111, Web Site:
www.convergedirect.com
Primary Market Served: Consumer

THE DMA CONVERSEN
2 Burlington Woods (Suite 200)
Burlington, MA 01803-4515
Telephone: (781) 425-1110, Web Site:
www.conversen.com

COOPER & COOPER DIRECT MARKETING
540 Frontage Rd (Suite 3035)
Northfield, IL 60093-1223
Telephone: (847) 446-1123, FAX:
(847) 446-1564, E-Mail: coopsdm@
earthlink.net
Pres: Tom Cooper

COOPER WIGHT ASSOCIATES INC
133 Hay Hill
Francestown, NH 03043
Telephone: (603) 547-2144
Pres: Nelson Wight

THE DMA THECOOPERGROUP
381 Park Ave S (fl 8)
New York, NY 10016-8806
Telephone: (212) 696-2512, Web Site:
www.thecoopergroup.com
CEO & Principal: Harold Cooper

COREBRAND
122 W 27th St (Fl9)
New York, NY 10001
Telephone: (212) 329-3030, FAX:
(212) 329-3031, E-Mail: jgregory@
corebrand.com, Web Site: www.
corebrand.com
Chmn & Founder: James Gregory
Mgr Sls & Mktg: Stefanie Kubanka

CORINTHIAN DIRECT
Div. of Corinthian Media Inc
500 8th Ave
New York, NY 10018-6504
Telephone: (212) 279-5700, FAX:
(212) 239-1772, E-Mail: jonz@
mediabuying.com, Web Site: www.
mediabuying.com
Owner & Pres: Larry Miller
Exec VP Acct Svcs: Ellen Carry
Exec VP Brdcst Buying: Tina Snitzer
Exec VP: Bob Klein
Exec VP Corinthian Direct: Larry
Schneiderman

CORPORATE MEDIA SERVICES INC
9801 Dupont Ave S (#408)
Bloomington, MN 55431
Telephone: (952) 881-8081, E-Mail:
info@corporatemediaservices.com,
Web Site: corporatemediaservices.
com
Pres: John Foltz

CORPORATE PROMOTIONS
Div. of FL Companies
1437 Donelson Pike
Nashville, TN 37217-2957
Telephone: (615) 242-0501, FAX:
(615) 256-0862, Web Site: www.
promoville.com
Pres: Bobby Rosenblum

CORPORATEREWARDS.COM LLC
307 5th Ave (fl 4)
New York, NY 10016-6517
Telephone: (212) 689-1200, Web Site:
www.corporaterewards.com
Pres, COO: Edward Brookshire

COSSETTE COMMUNICATIONS GROUP INC
801 Grande Allee Quest (Suite 200)
Quebec, PQ, Canada G1S 1C1

Telephone: (418) 647-2727, FAX:
(418) 647-2564, E-Mail:
infomaster@cossette.com, Web Site:
www.cossette.com
Sr VP Corp Devel: Georges Morin

**GENE COWELL &
ASSOCIATES INC**
17820 NW 149th Pl
Alachua, FL 32615-5259
Telephone: (352) 495-5757, FAX:
(352) 495-0804, E-Mail: gcdirect@
acceleration.net
Pres: Eugene I. Cowell

CRAMER-KRASSELT
Div. of Cramer-Krasselt Co
225 N Michigan Ave
Chicago, IL 60601-7684
Telephone: (312) 616-9600, FAX:
(312) 938-3157, E-Mail: pkrivkov@
c-k.com, Web Site: www.c-k.com
Pres & CEO: Peter Krivkovich

**CRAWFORD ADVERTISING
ASSOCIATES LTD**
216 Congers Rd Ste 2C
New City, NY 10956-6280
Telephone: (914) 946-2444, FAX:
(914) 946-9236, E-Mail: crawads@
aol.com, Web Site: www.
crawfordadv.com
Pres: Howard A. Wolfe

CRAWFORD & CO
1001 Summit Blvd Ste 500
Atlanta, GA 30319-6410
Telephone: (404) 300-1000, (800) 241-
2541, FAX: (404) 300-1905, Web
Site: www.crawfordandcompany.com
Chmn: Thomas W. Crawford
Pres & CEO: Jeffrey T. Bowman
Dir Mktg: Kara Pardini

**CREATING RESULTS/NEW
ENGLAND**
Div. of Creating Results LLC
PO Box 305
Barrington, RI 02806-0305
Telephone: (401) 289-2500, (888) 205-
8899, FAX: (401) 427-6963, E-Mail:
erin@creatingresults.com, Web Site:
www.creatingresults.com
New England Mktg Programs Dir: Erin
Read Ruddick
Pres: Todd Harff
Conducts Business: U.S.
Primary Market Served: Consumer

Strategic marketing, communications
& advertising that drives demand for
life style products & services; Special
expertise in reaching the fifty plus
consumer.

**THE CREATIVE ALLIANCE
INC**
2675 Northpark Dr (Suite 200)
Lafayette, CO 80026-3483
Telephone: (303) 665-8101, (888) 293-
8101, FAX: (303) 665-3136, E-Mail:
t@thecreativealliance.com, Web Site:
www.creativealliance.com
Pres: T. Robert Taylor

CREATIVE COMMERCE LLC
1230 American Blvd
West Chester, PA 19380-4264
Telephone: (212) 625-1700
CEO: Edwin Garrubbo

THE
DMA **CREATIVE LIFT**
115 Sansome St Ste 600
San Francisco, CA 94104-3618
Telephone: (415) 248-3174, Web Site:
www.creativelift.net
Owner: Tim Carr

**CREATIVE MARKETING
ALLIANCE INC**
191 Clarksville Rd
Princeton Junction, NJ 08550
Telephone: (609) 799-6000, FAX:
(609) 799-7032, Web Site: www.
cmasolutions.com
Pres & CEO: Jeffrey E. Barnhart

CREATIVE MEDIA INC
59 Summertree Ct
Nicholasville, KY 40356-9780
Telephone: (859) 219-9667
Pres: Gene Doyle

CREATIVE STRATEGY INC
5425 Wisconsin Ave (Suite 1655)
Chevy Chase, MD 20815-6906
Telephone: (301) 718-4550, FAX:
(301) 718-8828, E-Mail: info@
creativestrategy.com, Web Site:
www.creativestrategy.com
Pres: Sally Roffman

**CRISPIN, PORTER &
BOGUSKY**
3390 Mary St (Suite 300)
Miami, FL 33133
Telephone: (305) 859-2070, FAX:
(305) 854-3419, Web Site: www.
cpbgroup.com
Pres: Jeff Hicks

CROSS COMMERCE MEDIA
130 Madison Ave (fl 3)
New York, NY 10016-7026
Telephone: (646) 400-5095, Web Site:
www.crosscommercemedia.com
CEO: Tad Martin

CUNEO ADVERTISING
1401 American Blvd East (Suite 6)
Bloomington, MN 55425-1105
Telephone: (952) 707-1212, FAX:
(952) 707-1295, E-Mail: agency@
cuneocom.com, Web Site: www.
cuneocom.com
Pres & CEO: Laurence A. Cuneo

THE
DMA **CUSTOMER
COMMUNICATIONS GROUP**
165 S Union Blvd Ste 260
Lakewood, CO 80228-2241
Telephone: (303) 986-3000, (800) 525-
0313, FAX: (303) 989-4805, E-Mail:
info@customer.com, Web Site:
www.customer.com
Pres & CEO: Sandra Gudat

**CUSTOMER GROWTH, BLAU
MORITZ KLANG INC**
6 Willow Walk
Westport, CT 06880-2737
Telephone: (203) 226-8795, FAX:
(203) 227-8601, E-Mail: josh.
moritz@customer-growth.com, Web
Site: www.customer-growth.com
Mng Partner: Joshua Moritz
Conducts Business: U.S.
Employees: 20
Primary Market Served: Business &
Consumer
Direct online sales
Advertising/Marketing Budget Related
to Direct Marketing: 76-100%
Direct Marketing ad budget:
Direct Mail: 50%
Magazines: 25%
Online: 15%
TV/Radio: 10%
Founded: 2001
Gross sales or billing: $20,000,000

Direct and Interactive Advertising.

**CUSTOMER MARKETING
GROUP LLC**
7 Hill Farm Rd
Weston, CT 06883-2007
Telephone: (203) 226-9845, FAX:
(203) 226-9837, E-Mail: bill@4cmg.
com, Web Site: www.4cmg.com
Pres: William E. McKinney

**CUSTOMER RETENTION
MANAGEMENT GROUP INC**
PO Box 539
Severna Park, MD 21146-0539
Telephone: (410) 280-1720, (888) 822-
8574, FAX: (410) 280-1723
COO: Jim Green

CUSTOMERFUNDING.COM INC
PO Box 24255
Tempe, AZ 85285-4255
Telephone: (480) 784-1030, Web Site:
  www.customerfunding.com
EVP & Dir Bus Devel: Eduardo Flores

CUSTOMERMINING
2901 Park Ave (Suite C4)
Soquel, CA 95073-2831
Telephone: (831) 465-0890, Web Site:
  www.customermining.com
Pres: Beverly Capwell

CYPRESS MEDIA GROUP
630 Leather Hinge Tr
Roswell, GA 30075-4187
Telephone: (770) 640-9918, E-Mail:
  info@cypressmedia.net, Web Site:
  www.cypressmedia.net
Pres: Randall P. Whatley

D2: DIRECT
54 Cedar Lake W, Bldg # 2
Denville, NJ 07834-1704
Telephone: (973) 627-4410, FAX:
  (973) 627-3703, E-Mail: info@
  d2direct.com, Web Site: www.
  d2direct.com
Pres: Peter Marshall
Dir, Media Svcs: Maxeen Schanfeld
Dir, Creative Svcs: Neil Callari
Conducts Business: U.S.
Employees: 8
Primary Market Served: Business &
  Consumer
Founded: 1995
Gross sales or billing: $10,000,000

Direct response advertising agency.

DCI MARKETING INC
Subs. of Cannon Solutions
2727 W Good Hope Rd
Milwaukee, WI 53209-2091
Telephone: (414) 228-7000, (800) 284-
  6318, FAX: (414) 228-3411, Web
  Site: www.dcimarketing.com
Dir Mktg Svcs: Jane Horner

DDB CHICAGO
Subs. of DDB Needham Worldwide
200 E Randolph St (Suite 3800)
Chicago, IL 60601
Telephone: (312) 552-6000, FAX:
  (312) 552-2370, Web Site: www.
  ddbchi.com
Chief Creative Officer: Ewan Patterson

DDB DIRECT LOS ANGELES
10960 Wilshire Blvd (fl 16)
Los Angeles, CA 90024-3802

Telephone: (310) 907-1500, FAX:
  (310) 907-1990, Web Site: www.
  ddbla.com
Pres & CEO: Nick Bishop
Mng Partner & Dir Client Svcs:
  Chelsea Roe
Dir Online & Digital: Jefferson Burress
Integrated Commun Dir: Marianne El-
  lis
Conducts Business: U.S.
Employees: 51
Primary Market Served: Business &
  Consumer
Advertising/Marketing Budget Related
  to Direct Marketing: 76-100%
Direct Marketing ad budget:
  $200,000,000
Direct Mail: 50%
Magazines: 5%
Newspapers: 5%
TV/Radio: 40%
Founded: 1995
Gross sales or billing: $200,000,000

Integrated marketing communications
agency services. Full service direct
response marketing.

DKI DIRECT
160 Summit Ave
Montvale, NJ 07645-1750
Telephone: (201) 391-6000, Web Site:
  www.dkidirect.com
Pres: Daniella Koren

DMC ADVERTISING
One Creative Way
Pewaukee, WI 53072-5797
Telephone: (262) 523-2000, (800) 952-
  9165, FAX: (262) 523-2012, E-Mail:
  info@dmcadvertising.com, Web Site:
  www.dmcadvertising.com
Pres & CEO: Jeffrey G. Nowak

DMN3
2010 North Loop W (Suite 240)
Houston, TX 77018
Telephone: (713) 868-3000, (800) 625-
  8320, FAX: (713) 868-1388, E-Mail:
  contact@dmn3.com, Web Site: www.
  dmn3.com
Pres: Pam Lockard
COO: John LaCour
Employees: 25
Primary Market Served: Business &
  Consumer
Indirect online sales
Advertising/Marketing Budget Related
  to Direct Marketing: 0-25%
Direct Marketing ad budget: $150,000
Direct Mail: 90%
Magazines: 10%
Founded: 1992
Gross sales or billing: $9,000,000

DMN is a full-service direct response
marketing agency that delivers results
to businesses and consumers through
offline and online solutions.

DMW WORLDWIDE LLC
701 Lee Rd (Suite 103)
Chesterbrook, PA 19087-5612
Telephone: (610) 407-0407, (877) 744-
  3699, FAX: (610) 407-9201, E-Mail:
  whunter@dmwdirect.com, Web Site:
  www.dmwdirect.com
Chmn & CEO: Warren Hunter
Exec VP & Chief Creative Officer: Bill
  Spink
Pres & COO: Mark Mandia
SVP Agency Opers: Gina Kneib
Exec VP & CMO: Linda Reed
EVP & Pres Non-Profit Div: Tom Hur-
  ley
Exec VP Acct Svcs: Linda Armstrong
Conducts Business: U.S. & Canada
Employees: 75
Primary Market Served: Business &
  Consumer
Advertising/Marketing Budget Related
  to Direct Marketing: 76-100%
Founded: 1984
Gross sales or billing: $31,000,000

Full service direct response advertising
agency providing direct marketing services, insurance, healthcare, financial
services, fund raising, consumer &
B-to-B, and non-profit industries building market-driven programs grounded
in consumer intelligence & delivered
through multimedia, multichannel
integration.

THE DMA DATA MARKETING SOLUTIONS INC
70 Atlantic Ave (Suite 8)
Marblehead, MA 01945-3042
Telephone: (781) 639-3270, Web Site:
  www.businesswatchnetwork.com
Pres: Mark Ulian

DATABASE MARKETING GROUP INC
5 Peters Canyon Rd (Suite 150)
Irvine, CA 92606-1793
Telephone: (714) 727-0800, Web Site:
  www.dbmgroup.com
CEO: John Engstrom
Primary Market Served: Business &
  Consumer

DATAMARK INC
2305 Presidents Dr
Salt Lake City, UT 84120-7230
Telephone: (801) 886-2002, (800) 279-
  9335, FAX: (801) 886-0102, E-Mail:
  info@datamark-inc.com, Web Site:
  www.datamark-inc.com
Pres: Tom Dearden

THE DMA DEBELLIS & FERRARA
2136 Gallows Rd (Suite E)
Vienna, VA 22027-1036
Telephone: (301) 986-4499, (888) 748-2133, E-Mail: info@debellis-ferrara.com, Web Site: www.debellis-ferrara.com
Pres: GE Donohue
Acctg Mgr: Jean Duffy

DEBOW COMMUNICATIONS LTD
235 W 56th St Apt 29H
New York, NY 10019-4334
Telephone: (212) 977-8815, FAX: (212) 977-8376, E-Mail: info@debow.com, Web Site: www.debow.com
Creative Dir: Thomas J. DeBow Jr.

DEES COMMUNICATIONS/ FULLER FUND RAISING
2540 E 5th St (Ste A)
Montgomery, AL 36107-3152
Telephone: (334) 263-4436, FAX: (334) 263-4437, Web Site: www.athleticpubco.com
Pres: Allen Dees

DEFINITELY DUFFY
3 Chestnut Mountain Rd
Asheville, NC 28803
Telephone: (828) 333-5860, FAX: (866) 852-4686, E-Mail: dennis@definitelyduffy.com, Web Site: www.definitelyduffy.com
Pres: Dennis Duffy
Conducts Business: U.S., Brazil
Employees: 50
Primary Market Served: Business
Advertising/Marketing Budget Related to Direct Marketing: 76-100%
Founded: 2001
Gross sales or billing: $6,000,000

Loyalty and Direct Marketing services to consumer marketing companies.

THE DMA DENTINO MARKETING
515 Executive Dr
Princeton, NJ 08540-1527
Telephone: (201) 332-1219, (800) 477-8372, FAX: (201) 332-4262, E-Mail: karl@dentinomarketing.com, Web Site: www.dentinomarketing.com
Pres: Karl Dentino
VP, Creative: Joel Rubinstein
VP, Production: John Craig
VP, Acct Mngmt: Carole Molnar
Employees: 31
Direct Marketing ad budget:
Direct Mail: 85%
Gross sales or billing: $10,000,000

Full service direct marketing agency: Strategy, planning, database management, creative, production, fulfillment, interactive media and web, testing, results analysis internal & investor communications.

DESIGN MATTERS INC!
448 W 37th St Apt 9F
New York, NY 10018-4023
Telephone: (212) 560-0681, Web Site: www.designmattersinc.com
Creative Dir & CEO: Stephen McAllister

THE DMA DEXPOSITO & PARTNERS
875 Avenue of the Americas
New York, NY 10001-3507
Telephone: (646) 747-8800, Web Site: www.dexpositoandpartners.com
Primary Market Served: Consumer

THE DMA DIAMOND MARKETING SOLUTIONS
280 Madsen Dr Ste 100
Bloomingdale, IL 60108-2693
Telephone: (630) 523-5250, FAX: (630) 523-0403, Web Site: www.dmsolutions.com
CEO: Bruce D'Angelo
Pres, Production Svcs: Greg Waite
VP, Corp Sls: John Brahn
Pres: Cyndi Greenglass
Employees: 360
Primary Market Served: Business & Consumer
Advertising/Marketing Budget Related to Direct Marketing: 76-100%
Founded: 1975
Gross sales or billing: $50,000,000

A full service direct marketing firm providing targeted & strategic services from database through creative to fulfillment & direct mail production.

THE DMA DIAMONDBACK DIRECT - A DMH MARKETING PARTNERS CO
844 Ritchie Hwy (Suite 202)
Severna Park, MD 21146-4137
Telephone: (410) 975-0001, Web Site: www.diamondbackdirect.com
Acct Exec: Elizabeth Morrow

DIESTE
1999 Bryan St (Suite 2700)
Dallas, TX 75201-6817
Telephone: (214) 259-8000, FAX: (214) 259-8040, E-Mail: bbutler@dieste.com, Web Site: www.diesteharmel.com
Gen Mgr: Brenda Butler
Conducts Business: U.S., Latin America

Employees: 180
Primary Market Served: Consumer
Advertising/Marketing Budget Related to Direct Marketing: 0-25%
Founded: 1996

Hispanic advertising & direct marketing agency.

THE DMA DIESTE HARMEL & PARTNERS
1999 Bryan St (Suite 2700)
Dallas, TX 75201-6817
Telephone: (214) 259-8000, Web Site: www.dieste.com
Gen Mgr: Brenda Butler

DIGISPACE SOLUTIONS LLC
2323 Broadway (Suite 202)
San Diego, CA 92102
Telephone: (619) 684-6737, Web Site: www.digispace.com
Lead Opers Officer: Stacia Fiore

THE DMA DIGITAS
33 Arch St
Boston, MA 02110-1437
Telephone: (617) 867-1000, FAX: (617) 867-1111, E-Mail: contact@digitas.com, Web Site: www.digitas.com
CEO: Laura Lang

DIK & ASSOCIATES DIRECT MARKETING
2626 Peter St
Honolulu, HI 96816
Telephone: (808) 734-8868, FAX: (808) 734-8868, E-Mail: susandik@gmail.com
Owner & Pres: Susan Dik

DIRECT ADVERTISING
83 Dalton Rd
Holliston, MA 01746-2416
Telephone: (508) 429-7488, E-Mail: priority@dir-adv.com, Web Site: www.dir-adv.com
Pres & CEO: Angelo A. Stamoulis

THE DMA DIRECT ALLIANCE
8123 S Hardy Dr
Tempe, AZ 85284-1106
Telephone: (800) 546-0582, Web Site: www.directalliance.com
VP Mktg: Jonathon Gray
Primary Market Served: Business

THE DMA DIRECT CHANNEL LLC
574 Heritage Rd (Suite 201A)
Southbury, CT 06488-1868
Telephone: (203) 262-0588, Web Site: www.directchannel.net
Pres: Bill Dreska

DIRECT CHOICE INC
480 E Swedesford Rd (Suite 210)
Wayne, PA 19087-1860
Telephone: (610) 995-2111, Web Site:
    www.directchoiceinc.com
Pres: Nickolas Lanzi

DIRECT CINEMA LTD
PO Box 10003
Santa Monica, CA 90410-1003
Telephone: (310) 636-8200, FAX:
    (310) 636-8228, E-Mail: orders@
    directcinemalimited.com, Web Site:
    www.directcinema.com
Pres: Mitchell W. Block

ᵀʰᵉ DMA DIRECT IMPACT GROUP
200 Highland Ave (Suite 403)
Needham, MA 02494-3019
Telephone: (781) 453-2200, FAX:
    (781) 453-1200, E-Mail: info@
    directimpactgroup.com, Web Site:
    www.directimpactgroup.com
Pres: Andrew Gordon
Primary Market Served: Business &
    Consumer

Full-service direct marketing frim specializing in results-oriented television,
radio, direct mail, print & electronic
marketing. Has 29 yrs lead generation
experience in the arena of Direct Response Lead Generation.

DIRECT IMPACT INC
12747 Olive Blvd (Suite 300)
Saint Louis, MO 63141-6269
Telephone: (314) 567-0024, FAX:
    (314) 567-1497, E-Mail: info@
    directimpactinc.com, Web Site:
    www.directimpactinc.com
Mng Partner: Susan M. Chistensen
Partner & VP Mktg: Jan Devine

DIRECT MARKETING DESIGNS INC
6565 S Dayton (Suite 2200)
Greenwood Village, CO 80111-5386
Telephone: (303) 649-9888, FAX:
    (303) 649-1917, E-Mail: info@
    directmarketingdesigns.com, Web
    Site: www.directmarketingdesigns.
    com
Pres: James Morris

DIRECT MARKETING DYNAMICS INC
18633 Village Fountain Dr
Germantown, MD 20874-2122
Telephone: (301) 916-3900, FAX:
    (301) 515-0404, E-Mail: jim@
    directmarketingdynamics.com, Web
    Site: www.directmarketingdynamics.
    com
Pres: James Gribble

DIRECT MARKETING GROUP
7550 Corporate Way
Eden Prairie, MN 55344-2045
Telephone: (952) 975-5060, Web Site:
    www.directamsc.com
VP Sales & Mktg: Jay Carroll

DIRECT MARKETING SOLUTIONS INC
8534 NE Alderwood Rd
Portland, OR 97220-1347
Telephone: (503) 281-1400, Web Site:
    www.teamdms.com
Data Center Dir: Emilio Ramirez

ᵀʰᵉ DMA THE DIRECT MARKETING SPECIALISTS INC
900 N Franklin (Suite 706)
Chicago, IL 60610-3124
Telephone: (312) 266-7906, FAX:
    (312) 266-9230, E-Mail: rwinedms@
    winestarmail.com
Pres: Randi Wine

DIRECT OPTIONS
9565 Cincinnati Columbus Rd
West Chester, OH 45069
Telephone: (513) 779-4416, FAX:
    (513) 779-4426, E-Mail: inform@
    directoptions.com, Web Site: www.
    directoptions.com
Pres: Jan S. Moore

DIRECT PARTNERS
4755 Alla Rd
Marina Del Rey, CA 90292-6311
Telephone: (310) 482-4200, FAX:
    (310) 482-4201, Web Site: www.
    directpartners.com
Founder & Mng Partner: Skip Reed
Founder & Mng Partner: Jerry McRuer

ᵀʰᵉ DMA DIRECT RESOURCES GROUP
1221 2nd Ave Ste 300
Seattle, WA 98101-2986
Telephone: (206) 749-0001, E-Mail:
    results@drg.com, Web Site: www.
    drg.com
Pres: Stephan Jensen
Mng Partner: Scott Zorn
VP Acct Svcs: Brad Douglas
Conducts Business: U.S., Canada
Employees: 18
Primary Market Served: Business &
    Consumer
Advertising/Marketing Budget Related
    to Direct Marketing: 76-100%
Direct Marketing ad budget:
Direct Mail: 99%
Online: 1%
Founded: 1993

Direct marketing - outsourcing of strategy, program development, production,
mail printing & personalization & response analysis - usually on a project
basis.

DIRECT SUCCESS COMMUNICATIONS INC
308 Lynne Pl
Chester Springs, PA 19425
Telephone: (610) 321-0321, FAX:
    (610) 321-0322
Pres: Stephanie G. Schmidt

DIRECTCONNECT GROUP LTD
5501 Cass Ave
Cleveland, OH 44102-2121
Telephone: (216) 634-8481, Web Site:
    www.directgroup.com
Dir EMarketing: Catherine Wojtus

THE DIRECTORS NETWORK
aka TDN
36 Lostbrook Rd
West Hartford, CT 06117-1928
Telephone: (818) 906-0006, FAX:
    (818) 506-4662, Web Site: www.
    tdnartists.com
Pres: Steve Lewis

DMS MARKETING INC
26035 Acero Ste 100
Mission Viejo, CA 92691-7951
Telephone: (949) 460-7300, Web Site:
    http://www.dms-marketing.com
SVP: Lucy Belcher

DONAHOE PUROHIT MILLER ADVERTISING
111 S Wacker Dr Fl 1
Chicago, IL 60606-4309
Telephone: (312) 341-8100, FAX:
    (312) 341-8119, Web Site: www.
    dpmadvert.com
Chmn: Ed Donahoe

DONOVAN ADVERTISING
180 W Airport Rd
Lititz, PA 17543
Telephone: (717) 560-1333, FAX:
    (717) 560-2034, Web Site: www.
    donovanadv.com
Pres & CEO: William Donovan Jr.

DORAN & FORGACS INC
1306 Barkway Dr
West Chester, PA 19380-5820
Telephone: (610) 344-0570, FAX:
    (610) 344-7203
Pres: Barbara H. Doran

DOREMUS & CO
Subs. of Diversified Agency Services
& Div. of Omnicom Group
200 Varick St
New York, NY 10014-4810
Telephone: (212) 366-3000, FAX:
(212) 366-3060, E-Mail: anderson@
doremus.com, Web Site: www.
doremus.com
Chief Mktg Officer: Lou Robin

**EDWARD G DORN &
ASSOCIATES INC**
121 W State St
Geneva, IL 60134-2254
Telephone: (630) 232-2010, FAX:
(630) 232-2033, Web Site: www.
egdinc.com
Pres: Brian Dorn

THE DMA DRAFTFCB CHICAGO (HQ)
Div. of IPG
633 N Saint Clair St
Chicago, IL 60611-3234
Telephone: (312) 425-5000, FAX:
(312) 425-5010, E-Mail: linda.
liming@draftfcb.com, Web Site:
www.draftfcb.com
Chmn & CEO: Howard Draft

THE DMA D.TRIO MARKETING GROUP
401 N 3rd St (Suite 480)
Minneapolis, MN 55401-1351
Telephone: (612) 436-0323, Web Site:
www.dtrio.com
Partner: Megan Devine

**DUDNYK ADVERTISING &
PUBLIC RELATIONS**
5 Walnut Grove Dr (Suite 280)
Horsham, PA 19044-2282
Telephone: (215) 443-9406, (800) 438-
3695, E-Mail: fpowers@dudnyk.
com, Web Site: www.dudnyk.com
CEO: Christopher Tobias

DB DUFF & ASSOCIATES
26205 Show Horse Ln
Arlee, MT 59821-9145
Telephone: (724) 224-5513, FAX:
(724) 224-5186
Pres: Dale B. Duff

DUFFEY, PETROSKY & CO
39303 Country Club Dr (Suite A18)
Farmington Hills, MI 48331-3482
Telephone: (248) 489-8300, FAX:
(248) 994-1600, E-Mail: info@dp-
company.com, Web Site: www.dp-
company.com
Dir Opers & Admin Svcs: Mark
Petrosky

DZIURMAN DZIGN INC
620 S Main St
Clawson, MI 48017
Telephone: (248) 288-8800 X1, FAX:
(248) 288-8804, E-Mail: dziurman@
dzdzign.com, Web Site: www.
dzdzign.com
Pres: Mark Dziurman

E&M ADVERTISING INC
aka Impart Media Advertising or E&M
Impart
462 Seventh Ave (8th fl)
New York, NY 10018-7437
Telephone: (212) 981-5901, FAX:
(212) 981-2121, E-Mail: mmedico@
emadv.com, Web Site: www.emadv.
com
CEO: Michael L. Medico
Employees: 35
Gross sales or billing: $9,600,000

E & M MEDIA GROUP INC
1410 Broadway (Suite 1002)
New York, NY 10018-9359
Telephone: (212) 455-0177, Web Site:
www.emtvsales.com
Pres: Bonnie Schalle

EGC GROUP INC
1175 Walt Whitman Rd (Suite 200)
Melville, NY 11747-3030
Telephone: (516) 935-4944, FAX:
(516) 935-7030, E-Mail: contact@
egcgroup.com
Pres: Ernest Canadeo

**EMI STRATEGIC
MARKETING INC**
15 Broad St Ste 10
Boston, MA 02109-3812
Telephone: (617) 451-9451, FAX:
(617) 451-1193, E-Mail: cedlund@
emiboston.com, Web Site: www.
emiboston.com
Pres: Campbell Edlund
Devel Dir: F. Macy Jones

**EAGLE MARKETING
SERVICES INC**
PO Box 60666
San Diego, CA 92166-8666
Telephone: (619) 223-1273, (800) 548-
5858, FAX: (727) 803-0512, E-Mail:
gettunedin@eaglemarketing.com,
Web Site: www.eaglemarketing.com
CEO: Carl Evans

EASY COLOR PRINTING
2725 Miller St
San Leandro, CA 94577-5619
Telephone: (510) 580-6500, FAX:
(510) 580-6570, Web Site: www.
easycolorprinting.com

Pres: Alan Hui

**THE DMA EBERLE COMMUNICATIONS
GROUP INC**
Div. of Eberle Communications Group
1420 Springhill Rd (Suite 490)
McLean, VA 22102-3028
Telephone: (703) 893-1095, FAX:
(703) 821-0920, Web Site: www.
eberleassociates.com
Pres: Bruce Eberle

ECHOMAX
883 Columbus Dr
Teaneck, NJ 07666-6612
Telephone: (201) 837-1371, FAX:
(201) 837-6142
Sr Partner: Robert DeStefano

**THE DMA ECLIPSE MARKETING
SERVICES**
490 Headquarters Plz (N Towers fl 10)
Morristown, NJ 07960-4642
Telephone: (800) 837-4648
SVP Mktg & Client Svcs: Joan Coyne

EDELMANN SCOTT INC
3751 Westerre Pkwy (Suite A)
Richmond, VA 23233-1472
Telephone: (804) 643-1931, FAX:
(804) 643-1934, E-Mail: dickscott@
edelmannscott.com, Web Site: www.
edelmannscott.com
Pres & CEO: Richard Scott
CFO: Bob Judge

EDGEMARK PARTNERS INC
4510 Cox Rd (Suite 305)
Glen Allen, VA 23060-6759
Telephone: (804) 967-2000, Web Site:
www.edgemarkpartners.com
EVP: Doug Glasco

EDMONDS ASSOCIATES INC
8221 Old Courthouse Rd (Suite 204)
Vienna, VA 22182-3839
Telephone: (703) 448-8221, (703) 448-
8000, Web Site: www.
edmondsassociates.com
Pres: Thomas Edmonds

EENIGENBURG & CO
14504 SE 47th Pl
Bellevue, WA 98006-3142
Telephone: (425) 649-0777, FAX:
(425) 649-0719
Pres: Jill Eenigenburg

A EICOFF & CO
Div. of Ogilvy & Mather
401 N Michigan Ave (Suite 400)
Chicago, IL 60611-4232

Telephone: (312) 527-7100, FAX:
(312) 527-7192, E-Mail: bill.
mccabe@eicoff.com, Web Site:
www.eicoff.com
Pres & CEO: Ronald Bliwas
Dir HR: Bonnie Brunsell

**EIDEL MARKETING
COMMUNICATION CORP**
Seven Lodge Rd
Briarcliff Manor, NY 10510
Telephone: (914) 762-4985, FAX:
(914) 762-4986
Pres: Zeneth Eidel

**802 CREATIVE PARTNERS
INC**
PO Box 54
Bethel, VT 05032-0054
Telephone: (802) 234-9755, FAX:
(802) 234-6719, E-Mail: info@
802creative.com, Web Site: www.
802creative.com
Pres & Mktg Dir: Mike Hickey

ELEVEN INC
445 Bush St (fl 8)
San Francisco, CA 94108-3729
Telephone: (415) 707-1111, Web Site:
www.eleveninc.com
Dir Commun Strategy: Karen Halstead

EMERGING MARKETING
29 W Third Ave
Columbus, OH 43201-3208
Telephone: (614) 923-6000 X229,
FAX: (614) 424-6200, E-Mail:
chris@360em.com, Web Site: www.
emergingmarketing.com
Pres: Chris McGovern
Dir: Meg Mannion
Dir: Brian Sullivan

ᴛʜᴇ ENGAUGE DIRECT
ᴅᴍᴀ
1230 Peachtree St NE (Suite 2200)
Atlanta, GA 30309
Telephone: (404) 601-4332, (804) 363-
5715, Web Site: www.engauge.com
Mng Partner: Scott Hildebrand
Pres: Jeff Hillimire
Employees: 300
Founded: 2007

**RONALD D ERKES &
ASSOCIATES**
Box 117
Glencoe, IL 60022-0117
Telephone: (847) 835-1867, FAX:
(847) 835-9233
Pres: Ronald D. Erkes

ESROCK PARTNERS
14550 S 94th Ave
Orland Park, IL 60462-2652
Telephone: (708) 349-8400, (888) ES-
ROCKS, FAX: (708) 349-8471,
E-Mail: clay@esrock.com, Web Site:
www.esrock.com
Pres & CEO: Jack Coughlin

EURO RSCG WORLDWIDE
350 Hudson St
New York, NY 10014
Telephone: (212) 886-2000, FAX:
(212) 886-2016, Web Site: www.
eurorscg.com
Global CEO: David Jones

EXCELSIOR DIRECT
8 N Queen St (#800)
Lancaster, PA 17603-3855
Telephone: (717) 399-3550, FAX:
(717) 399-3200
Pres: Carol Aubitz

EXPOSED BRICK
1 Astor Pl (# 7T)
New York, NY 10003-6937
Telephone: (212) 226-0060, FAX:
(212) 941-8566, E-Mail: andrewc@
exposedbrick.com, Web Site: www.
exposedbrick.com
Pres: Andrew Cohen

EURO RSCG 4D WORLDWIDE
1355 Sansome St (#4)
San Francisco, CA 94111-6213
Telephone: (415) 345-7700, FAX:
(415) 345-7701
Other: Kim Kline

**FCB HEALTHCARE &
PROHEALTH**
100 W 33rd St
New York, NY 10001
Telephone: (212) 672-2300, FAX:
(212) 672-2301
Chm, CEO & Worldwide Creative Dir:
Tom Domanico

FGI RESEARCH
431 Meadowmont Village Cir
Chapel Hill, NC 27517-7506
Telephone: (919) 929-7759, FAX:
(919) 932-8829, E-Mail: info@
fgiresearch.com, Web Site: www.
fgiresearch.com

FKM
1800 West Loop S (Suite 2100)
Houston, TX 77027-3281
Telephone: (713) 862-5100, FAX:
(713) 869-6560, E-Mail: rklein@
fkmagency.com, Web Site: www.
fkmagency.com

Principal: Rich Klein

FMS DIRECT
18344 Oxnard St (Suite 101)
Tarzana, CA 91356-6724
Telephone: (818) 708-7814, FAX:
(818) 708-7906, Web Site: www.
fmsdirect.com
Pres: Rodney H. Buchser

**ᴛʜᴇ FPS MARKETING
ᴅᴍᴀ COMMUNICATIONS**
91 Shelter Cove Rd
Milford, CT 06460-6548
Telephone: (203) 783-1940, FAX:
(203) 783-1950, E-Mail: info@
fpsmarketing.com, Web Site: www.
fpsmarketing.com
Pres: Thomas Cabeen

FAHLGREN
414 Walnut St (Suite 1006)
Cincinnati, OH 45202-3935
Telephone: (513) 241-9200, FAX:
(513) 241-5982, Web Site: www.
fahlgren.com
Sr VP & Gen Mgr: Peter Craig

FALLON
900 Marquette Ave (Suite 2400)
Minneapolis, MN 55402
Telephone: (612) 758-2345, FAX:
(612) 758-2346, Web Site: www.
fallon.com
DM Mgr: Kelly Harmon-Schmitt

R FALLS AGENCY
900 6th Ave SE Ste 105
Minneapolis, MN 55414-1379
Telephone: (612) 872-6372, (800) 339-
1119, FAX: (612) 872-1018, E-Mail:
info@fallsagency.com, Web Site:
www.fallsagency.com
VP & CFO: Toni Baraga
Partner: Sharon Lund

ᴛʜᴇ FARSTAR
ᴅᴍᴀ
7110 Main St
Frisco, TX 75034-4225
Telephone: (214) 649-0422, Web Site:
http://www.wedontplayfair.com
Primary Market Served: Consumer

**FELDMAN & ASSOCIATES
INC**
191 Waukegan Rd (Suite 103)
Northfield, IL 60093-2743
Telephone: (847) 784-0404, FAX:
(847) 784-0664, E-Mail: rfeldman@
feldmans.net
Pres: Roger S. Feldman

FERILLO & ASSOCIATES
1938 College St
Columbia, SC 29201-3922
Telephone: (803) 771-6106, FAX:
(803) 799-8019
Pres: Charles Ferillo

FINELIGHT INC
600 E Main St Ste 102
Louisville, KY 40202-1077
Telephone: (502) 589-5896, E-Mail:
info@finelight.com, Web Site: www.
finelight.com
Owner & CEO: Sherman Rogers
CFO: Kevin Todd
Exec VP: Alan Pope
Creative Dir: Mike Haukins
IT Dir: Penny McQueen
SVP Direct Response: Jeannene Manning
Employees: 200
Primary Market Served: Business &
Consumer
Advertising/Marketing Budget Related
to Direct Marketing: 51-75%
Direct Marketing ad budget:
Direct Mail: 20%
Newspapers: 5%
TV/Radio: 70%
Telephone: 5%
Gross sales or billing: $12,000,000

Multi channel direct marketing services
to health insurances, hospital systems
and related industries.

FINERTY & WOLFE ADVERTISING INC
2418 N Burling St
Chicago, IL 60614
Telephone: (773) 348-3918, FAX:
(773) 348-5873, Web Site: www.
finertyandwolfe.com
Pres: Judith E. Finerty

THE DMA FIREPOWER MARKETING INC
1124 Fir Ave (#161)
Blaine, WA 98230-9702
Telephone: (604) 940-6900, Web Site:
www.roryfatt.com
Pres: Rory Fatt

FIRST DIRECT CORP
2345 Route 52 (Suite 1B)
Hopewell Junction, NY 12533-3220
Telephone: (845) 221-3800, (800) 935-
4386, E-Mail: info@1stdirect.com,
Web Site: www.1stdirect.com
Pres: Robert Ritter

FITZGERALD + CO
Div. of Interpublic Group
3333 Piedmont Rd NE Ste 1100, One
Buckhead Plz
Atlanta, GA 30305-1740
Telephone: (404) 504-6900, FAX:
(404) 239-0548, E-Mail: dave.
fitzgerald@fitzco.com, Web Site:
www.fitzco.com
Pres & CEO: David Fitzgerald
Chief Mktg Officer: Jay Shields

5METACOM
630 W Carmel Dr (Suite 180)
Carmel, IN 46032
Telephone: (317) 580-7540, FAX:
(317) 580-7550, E-Mail: mail@
5metacom.com, Web Site: www.
5metacom.com
CEO: Chris Wirthwein

FLAIR COMMUNICATIONS AGENCY INC
214 W Erie
Chicago, IL 60610
Telephone: (312) 943-5959, (800) 621-
8317, FAX: (312) 943-0881, E-Mail:
lflaherty@flairagency.com, Web Site:
www.flairpromo.com
Chmn & CEO: Lee F. Flaherty
Pres: Allyn Miller

FLAMM ADVERTISING INC
25 Highland Pl
Great Neck, NY 11020
Telephone: (516) 466-2090
Pres: Joseph D. Flamm

FLETCHER DIRECT
126 Castlewood Dr
Cary, NC 27511-5510
Telephone: (919) 460-9513, FAX:
(240) 757-1110, E-Mail: billf@
fletcherdirect.com
Pres: William U. Fletcher

THE DMA FLINT COMMUNICATIONS
101 N 10th St (Suite 300)
Fargo, ND 58107-4600
Telephone: (701) 237-4850, FAX:
(701) 234-9680, Web Site: www.
flintcom.com
Mgr/Dir: Alexander Heiser

FOCALPOINT MARKETING LLC
323 Main St
Metuchen, NJ 08840-2476
Telephone: (877) 252-4305, Web Site:
www.nipgroup.com
Pres: Fred Ey

FORT GROUP
100 Challenger Rd (Suite 800)
Ridgefield Park, NJ 07660-2119
Telephone: (201) 445-0202, FAX:
(201) 445-0626, Web Site: www.
fortgroup.com

FOSINA MARKETING GROUP INC
51-53 Kenosia Ave
Danbury, CT 06810-2301
Telephone: (203) 790-0013
Pres & CEO: Jim Fosina

FOSTER DIRECT
Div. of Foster Marketing Communications
3909 Ambassador Caffery Pkwy (Suite F)
Lafayette, LA 70503-5280
Telephone: (337) 235-1848, FAX:
(337) 237-7246, E-Mail: gfoster@
fostermarketing.com, Web Site:
www.fostermarketing.com
Pres & CEO: George Foster

FOUNDATION MEDIA GROUP
260 SW Natura Ave
Deerfield Beach, FL 33441-3026
Telephone: (954) 949-9500, (800) 873-
5137, FAX: (954) 337-0251, Web
Site: www.foundationmediagroup.
com
CEO: Michael Richmond
Primary Market Served: Business &
Consumer

FRACTAL ANALYTICS
2500 Plaza Ave
Jersey City, NJ 07311
Telephone: (201) 633-8728, Web Site:
www.fractalanalytics.com
Primary Market Served: Consumer

FRANKLIN ADVERTISING INC
87 N Main St
Blakely, GA 39823
Telephone: (229) 723-3665, FAX:
(407) 386-6666, E-Mail:
franklinad@aol.com, Web Site:
www.franklinadv.com
Pres: Roger Franklin

FRIED-CASSORLA COMMUNICATIONS INC
7408 Woodlawn Ave
Melrose Park, PA 19027
Telephone: (215) 635-5189, FAX:
(215) 635-0461, E-Mail: albert@
fried-cas.com, Web Site: www.fried-
cas.com
Pres: Albert Fried-Cassorla

FRONT PORCH INC
14520 Mono Way (Suite 200)
Sonora, CA 95370-7829
Telephone: (209) 288-5500, Web Site:
www.frontporch.com

FUJII COMMUNICATIONS INC
7369 E Prairie Rd
Lincolnwood, IL 60712-1039
Telephone: (847) 677-0542, FAX:
(847) 677-0523, E-Mail: fujiicom@
flash.net
Partner: Laurie Fujii Falcone

FURMAN ROTH ADVERTISING
801 Second Ave (Suite 1400)
New York, NY 10017-8639
Telephone: (212) 687-2300, FAX:
(212) 687-0858, Web Site: www.
furmanroth.com
Pres: Ernie M. Roth

G&A MARKETING
1001 Ford Cir Ste B
Milford, OH 45150-2740
Telephone: (513) 965-6301, (800) 688-
1370, E-Mail: info@gamarketing.
com, Web Site: www.gamarketing.
com
Pres: Pat Gunning
Corp Mktg Mgr: Kristen Skunza

G2 WORLDWIDE
200 5th Ave Bsmt B
New York, NY 10010-3313
Telephone: (212) 537-3700, Web Site:
www.g2dd.com
Pres: Wendy Lurrie
Primary Market Served: Business &
Consumer

THE DMA GC DIRECT
911 Western Ave (Suite 509)
Seattle, WA 98104-1047
Telephone: (206) 262-1999, Web Site:
www.gcdirect.com
Pres: Mike Gilbert

GHW ASSOCIATES
13063 SW Pembroke Cir N
Lake Suzy, FL 34269-6914
Telephone: (941) 625-4293, E-Mail:
ghw@ghw-associates.com, Web Site:
www.ghw-associates.com
Principal: George H. Wojtkiewicz

GKV
1500 Whetstone Way Ste 400, The
Cascade Bldg
Baltimore, MD 21230-4768
Telephone: (410) 539-5400, FAX:
(410) 234-2441, E-Mail:
newbusiness@gkv.com, Web Site:
www.gvk.com
Chmn & CEO: Roger Gray

THE DMA GM CUSTOMER RELATIONSHIP MANAGEMENT
100 Renaissance Ctr
Detroit, MI 48265-0001
Telephone: (313) 667-2621
Dir Devel & Opers: Ed Vogt
Primary Market Served: Business &
Consumer

THE DMA THE GRI MARKETING GROUP INC
115 Technology Dr (Suite B307)
Trumbull, CT 06611-6339
Telephone: (203) 261-3337, (800) 356-
4890, FAX: (203) 261-1113, E-Mail:
bsnider@gridirect.com, Web Site:
www.gridirect.com
Pres: Brian S. Snider

THE DMA GSD&M IDEA CITY
828 W 6th St
Austin, TX 78703-5420
Telephone: (512) 242-4736, Web Site:
www.gsdm.com
SVP Direct Svcs: David Hennagin

GSP MARKETING SERVICES
320 W Ohio
Chicago, IL 60610
Telephone: (312) 944-3000, FAX:
(312) 944-8587, E-Mail: mikes@
gspmarketing.com, Web Site: www.
gspmarketing.com
Pres: Richard Grunsten

GAGE
10000 Hwy 55
Minneapolis, MN 55441-6300
Telephone: (763) 595-5800, Web Site:
www.heinrich.com
SVP: Jane Blanco

GALANTY & CO INC
1640 Fifth St (Suite 202)
Santa Monica, CA 90401
Telephone: (310) 451-2525, FAX:
(310) 451-5020, E-Mail: galanty@ix.
netcom
VP: Mark Galanty

GAME SHOW PLACEMENTS LTD
7011 Willoughby Ave
Hollywood, CA 90038-2332
Telephone: (323) 874-7818, E-Mail:
gsp@ix.netcom.com, Web Site:
www.gspltd.com
Pres: Ben Robertson

GARD COMMUNICATIONS
711 SW Alder St (Suite 400)
Portland, OR 97205-3417
Telephone: (503) 221-0100, FAX:
(503) 226-4854, Web Site: www.
gardcommunications.com
VP, Gen Mgr: V Edwards

GARVAN COMMUNICATIONS INC
PO Box 302
Locust Valley, NY 11560-0302
Telephone: (516) 827-4000, FAX:
(516) 827-4001, Web Site: www.
garvan.com
Pres & CEO: Gary Andersen

GARVER ADVERTISING SERVICE INC
440 E 57th St (Suite 5C)
New York, NY 10022-3047
Telephone: (212) 371-3325, E-Mail:
garverads@aol.com
Pres: Arthur Ball

THE DMA MARC G GAULT ADVERTISING & MARKETING CONSULTING
5380 Smoke Rise Dr (Suite B)
Stone Mountain, GA 30087-1529
Telephone: (770) 938-0781
Adv & Mktg Consultant: Marc G.
Gault

GAYLORD COMMUNICATIONS UNLIMITED
PO Box 28
Bridgewater, VT 05034-0028
Telephone: (802) 672-6200, FAX:
(802) 672-6226
Partner: Jeremy P. Gaylord

KAREN GEDNEY COMMUNICATIONS
272 87th St
Brooklyn, NY 11209
Telephone: (718) 680-1627, FAX:
(917) 591-5547, E-Mail: kg@
karengedney.com, Web Site: www.
karengedney.com
Owner: Karen Gedney

GEIGER DONNELLY MARKETING LLC
Subs. of Geiger Inc
71 Elm St (Unit 8)
Foxboro, MA 02035-2519

Telephone: (508) 549-0909, FAX:
(508) 549-0916
Pres: Christopher Donnelly

**LOIS GELLER MARKETING
GROUP**
2028 Hamson St (Suite 202)
Hollywood, FL 33020
Telephone: (646) 723-3231, FAX:
(954) 921-2005, E-Mail: loisgeller@
loisgellermarketinggroup.com, Web
Site: www.loisgellermarketinggroup.
com
Pres & Owner: Lois Geller
Gen Mgr: Dwain Jeworski
Conducts Business: U.S., Can., S.
America, Europe
Employees: 10
Primary Market Served: Business
Advertising/Marketing Budget Related
to Direct Marketing: 76-100%
Direct Marketing ad budget:
Direct Mail: 70%
Magazines: 20%
TV/Radio: 5%
Telephone: 5%
Founded: 1997
Gross sales or billing: $2,500,000

Strategic direct marketing agency providing complete planning through
implementation. Expertise with publishing, banking, insurance, catalogs,
business to business, collectibles and
travel clients.

GENNERA KNAB & CO
dba Priva
1953 N Ontario St
Burbank, CA 91505-1231
Telephone: (312) 337-2010, FAX:
(312) 337-2433, E-Mail: cleveland-
office@priva.com, Web Site: www.
priva.com
Pres & Creative Dir: Michael Knab

**ᴛʜᴇ
ᴅᴍᴀ GIANFAGNA STRATEGIC
MARKETING INC**
1991 Crocker Rd Ste 225
Westlake, OH 44145-6970
Telephone: (440) 808-4700, FAX:
(440) 808-4707, E-Mail:
tellmemore@gianfagnamarketing.
com, Web Site: www.
gianfagnamarketing.com
Pres: Jean M. Gianfagna

GILLESPIE
Div. of MRM Partners Worldwide
3450 Princeton Pike
Lawrenceville, NJ 08543-3333
Telephone: (609) 895-0200, FAX:
(609) 895-0222, Web Site: www.
gillespie.com
Pres: Richard J. Gillespie

**GISH, SHERWOOD &
FRIENDS INC**
4235 Hillsboro Rd
Nashville, TN 37215-3347
Telephone: (615) 385-1100, (800) 241-
3325, FAX: (615) 783-0500, Web
Site: www.gish.com
Owner: Dale Gish

**ᴛʜᴇ
ᴅᴍᴀ GITLITZ CONSULTING**
3916 Highwood Ct NW
Washington, DC 20007-2132
Telephone: (202) 965-6185

GLIDDEN & BOYLES INC
2N School St
Mount Prospect, IL 60056-2539
Telephone: (847) 398-5746, FAX:
(847) 756-7619, E-Mail: e:marcom@
gbmarcom.com, Web Site: www.
glidden-boyles.com
Pres: William R. Boyles

GLOBALIZATION PARTNERS
1600 Tysons Blvd (fl 8)
Mc Lean, VA 22102-4872
Telephone: (703) 268-2193
Primary Market Served: Consumer

**THE GOLDMARK GROUP
INC**
1155 Bloomfield Ave
Clifton, NJ 07012
Telephone: (973) 777-5720, (800) 632-
9632, FAX: (973) 777-2390, E-Mail:
info@goldmarkgroup.com, Web Site:
www.goldmarkgroup.com
Principal: Joseph Goldbrenner

GOOD ADVERTISING
5100 Poplar Ave (Suite 1700)
Memphis, TN 38137
Telephone: (901) 761-0741, (800) 325-
9857, FAX: (901) 682-2568, Web
Site: www.goodadvertising.com
Pres: Dale Cox

**GOODMAN MARKETING
PARTNERS INC**
4340 Redwood Hwy (Suite 52)
San Rafael, CA 94903-2107
Telephone: (415) 507-9060, FAX:
(415) 507-9067, E-Mail: info@
goodmanmarketing.com, Web Site:
www.goodmanmarketing.com
Pres & Creative Dir: Carolyn Good-
man
Sr Art Dir: Leah Prahm
Production Mgr: Hollis Brush
Controller: Deborah Ryken
Conducts Business: U.S., Canada,
Worldwide
Employees: 15

Primary Market Served: Business &
Consumer
Advertising/Marketing Budget Related
to Direct Marketing: 76-100%
Founded: 2002
Gross sales or billing: $4,500,000

Full-service direct marketing agency.

GOODWAY GROUP
Subs. of IGI Printing Co Inc
261 Old York Rd (Suite 930)
Jenkintown, PA 19046-3711
Telephone: (215) 887-5700, FAX:
(215) 881-2239, E-Mail: david@
goodwaygroup.com, Web Site: www.
goodwaygroup.com
Pres: David Wolk

GRAFICA GROUP
67 E Park Pl (Suite 425)
Morristown, NJ 07960-7103
Telephone: (973) 309-7500, FAX:
(973) 309-7501, E-Mail: info@
grafica.com, Web Site: www.
grafica.com
VP, Mktg: Jason Bacharach
VP, Mktg Dept: Jim Hathaway
Conducts Business: U.S.
Employees: 52
Primary Market Served: Business &
Consumer
Advertising/Marketing Budget Related
to Direct Marketing: 26-50%
Direct Marketing ad budget:
Direct Mail: 75%
Magazines: 5%
Newspapers: 10%
TV/Radio: 5%
Telephone: 5%
Founded: 1986

Multi-channel, integrated direct marketing, advertising, web site design and
public relations.

**ᴛʜᴇ
ᴅᴍᴀ GRAGG ADVERTISING**
450 E 4th St (Suite 100)
Kansas City, MO 64106-1171
Telephone: (816) 931-0050, Web Site:
www.graggadv.com
Primary Market Served: Consumer

GRAY & GRAHAM INC
136 Main St (Suite 6)
Westport, CT 06880-3304
Telephone: (203) 227-3900, FAX:
(203) 227-3593, Web Site: www.
graygraham.com
Pres: Jeff R. Gray

GREY HEALTHCARE GROUP
114 Fifth Ave (5th fl)
New York, NY 10011

Telephone: (212) 886-3000, FAX:
(212) 886-3297, E-Mail: info@
ghgroup.com, Web Site: www.
ghgroup.com
CEO: Lynn O'Connor-Vos

GREYSTONE SERVICES INC
PO Box 482
Beverly, MA 01915-0482
Telephone: (978) 535-9185, FAX:
(978) 535-7826, E-Mail: greystone@
gstone.biz
Pres: Lee Yaffa

GRIZZARD ADVERTISING
Subs. of Grizzard Advertising Atlanta
110 N Maryland Ave
Glendale, CA 91206
Telephone: (818) 325-4892, (800) 241-
9351, FAX: (818) 543-1308, Web
Site: www.grizzard.com
Pres: Michael Dzvonik
Sr VP: Phil Stolberg

**GRIZZARD
COMMUNICATIONS GROUP
INC**
229 Peachtree St NE (Suite 1400)
Atlanta, GA 30303-1620
Telephone: (404) 522-8330, Web Site:
www.grizzard.com
CEO: Chip Grizzard

GROUP M INC
15 N Mill St (Suite 210)
Nyack, NY 10960-3015
Telephone: (201) 227-0747, E-Mail:
gmi.prm@gmail.com, Web Site:
www.groupm.org
Pres: Rosemarie Monaco
Conducts Business: Worldwide
Employees: 6
Primary Market Served: Business
Founded: 1990

Integrated public relations and direct
marketing company to boost effectiveness of direct marketing efforts.

GROUPLEVINSON
128 Chestnut St (Suite 403)
Philadelphia, PA 19106
Telephone: (215) 627-3030, Web Site:
grouplevinson.com
CEO: Leo Levinson

THE
DMA **GROUPM DIRECT**
825 7th Ave
New York, NY 10019-6014
Telephone: (212) 474-0830, Web Site:
www.groupm.com
Pres: Marion Murphy

GROVE COMMUNICATIONS
3918 Valley View Rd
Crystal Lake, IL 60012
Telephone: (312) 884-0270, FAX:
(312) 884-0275, Web Site: www.
grovecommunications.com
Pres: Robert Grzelewski

GROW COMMUNICATIONS
894 Saddle St
Coquitlam, BC, Canada V3C 3N2
Telephone: (778) 822-0431, Web Site:
www.growcommunications.com
Pres: Kelsey Breakey

GUMAS ADVERTISING
99 Shotwell St
San Francisco, CA 94103-3625
Telephone: (415) 621-7575, FAX:
(415) 255-8804, E-Mail: jgumas@
gumas.com, Web Site: www.gumas.
com
Pres: John Gumas

HHC DIRECT
NSB Technologies Inc
5287 Linda Vista Rd
San Diego, CA 92110-2604
Telephone: (800) 358-8765, FAX:
(619) 220-0988, Web Site: www.
hhcdirect.com
Client & Acct Svcs: Eli Katkin

THE
DMA **HACKER GROUP INC**
Div. of FCB Seattle
1215 4th Ave (Suite 2100)
Seattle, WA 98161-1018
Telephone: (206) 805-1500, E-Mail:
info@hackergroup.com, Web Site:
www.hackergroup.com
Pres & CEO: Spyro Kourtis
VP Bus Devel: Brad Douglas

**HAHN, CRANE &
ASSOCIATES ADVERTISING
INC**
2404 Loring St
San Diego, CA 92109-2347
Telephone: (858) 581-8561
Principal: Fred E. Hahn

**HAMMOND PARADIGM
COMMUNICATIONS GROUP**
10549 Reading Rd
Cincinnati, OH 45241-2524
Telephone: (513) 381-7100, (800) 898-
4121, FAX: (513) 381-8756, Web
Site: www.hammondcg.com
Sls & Mktg Dir: Dean Reverman

**HANOBIK
COMMUNICATIONS**
140 Convair Dr
Coraopolis, PA 15108-2404
Telephone: (412) 264-3077, FAX:
(412) 264-0321
Pres & Owner: Raymond G. Hanobik

HARRIS MARKETING GROUP
102 Pierce St
Birmingham, MI 48009-6030
Telephone: (248) 723-6300, FAX:
(248) 723-6301, E-Mail: info@
harris-hmg.com, Web Site: www.
harris-hmg.com
Pres: Janice Shukle

HARRIS PUBLISHING
1511 Route 22 (Suite C-25)
Brewster, NY 10509-4085
Telephone: (800) 326-6600, FAX:
(914) 287-2144, E-Mail: moreinfo@
harrisconnect.com, Web Site: www.
bcharrispub.com
Chief Sls & Mktg Officer: Paul A.
Gangi

**HARVEY ASSOCIATES-
DIRECT MARKETING
SOLUTIONS**
63 Hoover Dr
Cresskill, NJ 07626
Telephone: (201) 962-8463, E-Mail:
harveyfnj@optonline.net
Pres: Harvey A. Feldman

**HATCHETT & FAGAN
DIRECT**
950 22nd St N (Suite 700)
Birmingham, AL 35203-1128
Telephone: (205) 458-8200, Web Site:
www.hfdirect.com
CEO: Ray Fagan
Primary Market Served: Business &
Consumer

THE
DMA **HAWKEYE**
2828 Routh St (Suite 300)
Dallas, TX 75201-7605
Telephone: (214) 749-0080, Web Site:
www.hawkeyeww.com
Chmn & Founder: G Steven Dapper

THE
DMA **HAWTHORNE DIRECT INC**
300 N 16th St, PO Box 1366
Fairfield, IA 52556-2604
Telephone: (641) 472-3800, FAX:
(641) 472-6043, E-Mail: drtv@
hawthornedirect.com, Web Site:
www.hawthornedirect.com
Founder, Chmn & Creative Dir: Timothy R. Hawthorne
CEO/Pres: Thomas Kelly

HAYNES & PARTNERS COMMUNICATIONS INC
5745 Lee Rd
Indianapolis, IN 46216
Telephone: (317) 860-3000, FAX:
(317) 860-3001, E-Mail: levans@hp-inc.com, Web Site: www.hp-inc.com
Pres: Charles Krupa
Acct Supvr & Exec: Lynn Evans

HAYNES MARKETING NETWORK
721 Walnut St (Suite B)
Macon, GA 31201-2630
Telephone: (912) 742-5266, Web Site:
www.haynesmarketing.com
Pres: Phil Haynes

HEALTHCARE INSIGHT
10897 River Front Pkwy (Suite 200)
South Jordan, UT 84095-5730
Telephone: (801) 285-5800, Web Site:
www.hcinsight.com
VP Mktg: Darin Johnson

THE DMA HEINRICH MARKETING
2228 Blake St
Denver, CO 80205-2120
Telephone: (303) 233-8660, (800) 356-5036, FAX: (303) 239-5352, E-Mail:
georgeeddy@heinrich.com, Web
Site: www.heinrich.com
Pres: George Eddy

THE DMA HEMMINGS IV DIRECT
505 E Colorado Blvd (Suite 201D)
Pasadena, CA 91101-2002
Telephone: (626) 796-7188
Pres: Robert Hemmings

HENDERSON ADVERTISING INC
PO Box 27044
Greenville, SC 29616-2044
Telephone: (864) 232-5733, FAX:
(864) 298-1280, Web Site: www.
hendersonadv.com
CEO: Ralph W. Callahan

HENKE & ASSOCIATES INC
PO Box 147, PO Box 147
Cedarburg, WI 53012-0147
Telephone: (262) 375-9090, FAX:
(262) 375-2262, E-Mail: jhenke@
henkeinc.com, Web Site: www.
henkeinc.com
Pres & Creative Dir: Jack Henke

THE DMA HENNERBERG GROUP INC
5501 Willow Ln
Colleyville, TX 76034-5149

Telephone: (817) 318-8100, E-Mail:
gary@hennerberg.com, Web Site:
www.hennerberg.com
Analytic Consultant & Copywriter:
Gary Hennerberg

HERCKY-PASQUA-HERMAN
324 Chestnut St
Roselle Park, NJ 07204-1904
Telephone: (908) 241-9474, FAX:
(908) 241-8961, E-Mail: hercky@
hph-comm.com
Pres: Peter Hercky

THE DMA NED HERRMANN GROUP
dba Herrmann International
794 Buffalo Creed Rd
Lake Lure, NC 28746-9903
Telephone: (828) 625-9153, Web Site:
www.hbdi.com
CEO: Ann Herrmann-Nehdi

THE HIEBING GROUP
315 Wisconsin Ave
Madison, WI 53703
Telephone: (608) 256-6357, FAX:
(608) 256-0693, E-Mail: ideas@
hiebing.com, Web Site: www.
hiebing.com
Exec Recruiter: Dave Florin

HIGH OCTANE COMMUNICATIONS
20 N San Pedro Rd (Suite 2014)
San Rafael, CA 94903-4158
Telephone: (415) 256-9369, FAX:
(415) 256-8988, E-Mail: chris@
hocadvertising.com, Web Site: www.
hocadvertising.com
CEO: Christopher E. Orlie

HILL HOLLIDAY
53 State St (fl 33)
Boston, MA 02109-2802
Telephone: (617) 366-4000, Web Site:
www.hhcc.com
SVP Mng Dir: Mark Mylan

THE HITCHINS CORP
22756 Hartland St
Canoga Park, CA 91307-2604
Telephone: (818) 715-0510, FAX:
(818) 715-0510
Pres: William E. Hitchins

HOFF COMMUNICATIONS INC
23 S Lansdowne Ave
Lansdowne, PA 19050
Telephone: (610) 623-2091, E-Mail:
service@hoffcomm.com, Web Site:
www.hoffcommunications.com
Pres: Jennifer Hoff

JP HOGAN & CO
107 W Fifth Ave
Knoxville, TN 37917
Telephone: (865) 546-7661, FAX:
(865) 523-7300, E-Mail: dhogan@
thehogancompany.net, Web Site:
www.thehogancompany.net
Pres & CEO: Douglas W. Hogan

ROBERT HOHLER ASSOCIATES
545 Columbus Ave
Boston, MA 02118-1115
Telephone: (617) 531-0010, FAX:
(617) 531-0015, E-Mail: hohassoc@
aol.com
Pres: Robert Hohler

THE DMA HOLSTED MARKETING INC
135 Madison Ave (fl 8)
New York, NY 10016-6727
Telephone: (212) 686-8537, FAX:
(212) 481-0415
CEO & Chmn: Victor N. Benson

THE HUGHES GROUP INC
1141 S 7th St
Saint Louis, MO 63104-3623
Telephone: (314) 571-6300, FAX:
(314) 862-1616, E-Mail:
jschnurbusch@hughes-stl.com, Web
Site: www.hughesgroup.com
Pres: Jim Schnurbusch

HULT FRITZ MATUSZAK ASSOCIATES
401 SW Water St (Suite 601)
Peoria, IL 61602-1586
Telephone: (309) 673-8191, FAX:
(309) 674-5530, E-Mail: jflynn@
hfma.com, Web Site: www.hfma.com
Pres: Jim Flynn

THE DMA HUNT MARKETING GROUP
1809 7th Ave Ste 411
Seattle, WA 98101-4403
Telephone: (206) 447-5665, Web Site:
www.hmgseattle.com
Pres: Brian Hunt

HUNTINGTON ASSOCIATES
850 Seventh Ave (Suite 1200)
New York, NY 10019-5230
Telephone: (212) 582-1870, FAX:
(212) 586-3291, E-Mail: huntassoc@
aol.com
Pres: Patricia S. Huntington
Exec Asst: Diane Corick

IMC DIRECT
81 S Hotel St (Suite 315)
Honolulu, HI 96813

Telephone: (808) 545-1680, FAX:
(808) 528-4293
Owner: Victor Fujita

IR/ARO
Div. of Ingersoll-Rand Co
209 N Main St
Bryan, OH 43506-1319
Telephone: (419) 636-4242, (800) 495-
0276, FAX: (419) 633-1674, E-Mail:
russ_w_davies@irco.com, Web Site:
www.arozone.com
Mktg Commun: Russ Davies

IBIS COMMUNICATIONS INC
1024 17th Ave S
Nashville, TN 37212
Telephone: (615) 777-1900, FAX:
(615) 777-1906, E-Mail:
mhowland@ibiscommunications.
com, Web Site: www.
ibiscommunications.com
Pres: MaryAnne Howland

ᴛʜᴇ ᴅᴍᴀ ICON MEDIA DIRECT INC
5910 Lemona Ave
Van Nuys, CA 91411-3006
Telephone: (818) 995-6400, FAX:
(818) 995-6405, E-Mail: info@
iconmediadirect.com, Web Site:
www.iconmediadirect.com
Pres & CEO: Nancy Lazkani
Dir Print Svcs: Rebecca Rodriguez

IDEAOVERTEN LLC
3140 W Tilghman St (Suite 128)
Allentown, PA 18104-4268
Telephone: (610) 437-4340, (866) 864-
2836, FAX: (866) 414-6165, E-Mail:
marketing@ideaover10.com, Web
Site: www.ideaover10.com
Pres: Dr. Edward Kundahl
Employees: 15
Primary Market Served: Business &
Consumer
Founded: 1994

THE IGNITION NETWORK
125 S Wacker Dr (Suite 1750)
Chicago, IL 60606-4401
Telephone: (312) 420-4398, Web Site:
www.theignitionnetwork.com

IKON COMMUNICATIONS CONSULTANTS INC
554 Washington St
Wellesley, MA 02482-6449
Telephone: (781) 237-6060, FAX:
(781) 235-3504
Pres: Daniel F. Sweeney

IMAHARA ASSOCIATES INC
3528 Willow Wren
Fremont, CA 94555

Telephone: (510) 742-3289, FAX:
(510) 742-3289, E-Mail: imahara@
aol.com, Web Site: www.imahara.
com
Pres: Alan Imahara

IMARKETING LTD INC
100 Canal Pointe Blvd Ste 216
Princeton, NJ 08540-7063
Telephone: (609) 921-0400, FAX:
(609) 921-0491, E-Mail: info@
imarketingltd.com, Web Site: www.
imarketingltd.com
CEO: Keith Kochberg
Founded: 1999

iMarketing LTD (www.imarketingltd.
com) is a leading full-service online
marketing agency delivering measurable results for clients across a broad
range of industries. With a focus on
ROI and proven experience across
multiple verticals, iMarketing's innovative programs help acquire new customers and increase revenues through a
wide range of online channels.

IMARLIN LLC
Sub. of The Marlin Company
1200 E Woodhurst Dr Ste V, Bldg V
Springfield, MO 65804-4240
Telephone: (417) 887-7446, FAX:
(417) 887-3643, E-Mail: info@
imarlin.com, Web Site: www.imarlin.
com
Gen Mgr: Linda J. Bortis
Conducts Business: U.S., Canada
Employees: 7
Primary Market Served: Business
Founded: 2000

Provides custom web solutions, online
training, e-mail and e-mmercials, online media, application service products, Extend customizable print system,
and the My Menu Recipe System to
manufacturers.

ᴛʜᴇ ᴅᴍᴀ IMPACT INTERNATIONAL MARKETING
151 Riviera Dr (Bldg B Suite 201)
Lake Havasu City, AZ 86403-5696
Telephone: (866) 389-0798, E-Mail:
salesinfo@imgroup.com, Web Site:
www.imgroup.com
Pres: Kathryn Felke

ᴛʜᴇ ᴅᴍᴀ INDROS GROUP
1 Meadow St (Suite 202)
Brooklyn, NY 11206-1741
Telephone: (866) 463-7671, Web Site:
www.easypurl.com
Primary Market Served: Consumer

INDUSTRIAL MARKETING SERVICES
2375 Touhy Ave
Elk Grove Village, IL 60007-5330
Telephone: (847) 258-8850, FAX:
(847) 593-0462, E-Mail:
whindman@imscomm.com
Pres: W.J. Hindman

INFINITY DIRECT INC
13220 County Rd 6 (Suite 200)
Plymouth, MN 55441-8791
Telephone: (763) 559-1111, Web Site:
www.infinitydirect.com
Exec VP: Shawn Harding

INFLUENCE INC
3189 Princeton Rd
Hamilton, OH 45011-5338
Telephone: (513) 825-8600, FAX:
(513) 825-9213, E-Mail: info@
influenceinc.com, Web Site: www.
influenceinc.com
Pres: Greg Stagg

INFOTRENDS INC
Div. of Historical Research Center
2019 Corporate Dr
Boynton Beach, FL 33426
Telephone: (561) 732-5263, (800) 940-
7991, FAX: (800) 400-7534, E-Mail:
info@names.com, Web Site: www.
names.com
Media Dir: Mike Dell

INNIS MAGGIORE GROUP INC
4715 Whipple Ave NW
Canton, OH 44718-2651
Telephone: (330) 492-5500, FAX:
(330) 492-5568, E-Mail: dick@
innismaggiore.com, Web Site: www.
innismaggiore.com
Pres & CEO: Dick Maggiore

ᴛʜᴇ ᴅᴍᴀ INTEGER GROUP
Part of Omnicom Group Inc (NYSE:
OMC)
2633 Fleur Dr
Des Moines, IA 50321-1753
Telephone: (515) 288-7910, FAX:
(515) 288-8439, E-Mail: fmaher@
integermidwest.com, Web Site:
www.integer.com
Group Pres & COO: Frank Maher
CRM Dir: David Ausley

INTEGRATED ADVERTISING INC
8677 Southern Glen Dr
Jacksonville, FL 32256-9542
Telephone: (904) 296-1700, E-Mail:
mary@integratedadvertising.com
Pres: Mary T. Lopez

INTELISPEND
1400 S Highway Dr
Fenton, MO 63099-0001
Telephone: (636) 226-2000, Web Site:
 intelispend.com
CEO: Darryl A Hutson
Pres: Jim Menadier

**INTERACT MULTIMEDIA
CORP**
115 N William St (#3000)
South Bend, IN 46601-1509
Telephone: (574) 232-3400, FAX:
 (219) 255-6091, E-Mail: johnd@
 interactmultimedia.com
Pres: Steve Colucci

**INTERLINE CREATIVE
GROUP INC**
553 N North Ct (Suite 160)
Palatine, IL 60067-8124
Telephone: (847) 358-4848, FAX:
 (847) 358-8089, E-Mail: info@
 interlinegroup.com, Web Site: www.
 interlinegroup.com
Pres: James A. Nowakowski

THE
DMA **INTERMEDIA ADVERTISING**
15760 Ventura Blvd Ste 110
Encino, CA 91436-3007
Telephone: (818) 995-1455, FAX:
 (818) 995-7115, Web Site: www.
 intermedia-advertising.com
VP: Betty Globus
Pres: Robert Yallen

**INTERMEDIA CONSULTANTS
INC**
100 Overlook Center (fl 2)
Princeton, NJ 08540-7814
Telephone: (609) 430-8460, Web Site:
 http://iprintmedia.com
Pres: Darr Kartychak
Employees: 4
Founded: 1980

Provide end-to-end print media production, using new & emerging
technologies. We can expertly design,
print, finish, kit, store, direct mail &
distribute nationwide almost any product . Over 50+ printed & promotional
product categories, as well as apparel,
across many industries.

**INTERNATIONAL
MARKETING PARTNERS
LTD**
6371 W 79th St
Los Angeles, CA 90045-1442
Telephone: (310) 665-1155, FAX:
 (310) 665-1155, E-Mail: info@
 intermarketingonline.com
Pres: Donald Marrs
Dir: Allyson Stewart-Allen

**INTERNET DIRECT
RESPONSE, INC**
5332 Rush Creek Ct
Fort Worth, TX 76244
Telephone: (817) 562-1506, E-Mail:
 operations@4idr.com, Web Site:
 www.4dr.com
Pres: Tom Broderick

THE
DMA **INTERTREND
COMMUNICATIONS INC**
555 E Ocean Blvd Ste 900
Long Beach, CA 90802-5056
Telephone: (562) 733-1852, Web Site:
 www.intertrend.com
Acct Supvr: Liza Legaspi

THE
DMA **INTERVAL INTERNATIONAL**
6262 Sunset Dr Ste 400
South Miami, FL 33143-4843
Telephone: (305) 925-7019, Web Site:
 www.intervalworld.com
AVP: Patricia Rasekhi

INTRASIGHT
8300 E Raintree Dr (Suite 200)
Scottsdale, AZ 85260-2598
Telephone: (480) 603-9400, FAX:
 (480) 603-9460, Web Site: www.
 intrasightmarketing.com
Exec VP: Bob Gilbert

**AB ISACSON ASSOCIATES
INC**
29 Broadway (Suite 1300)
New York, NY 10006
Telephone: (212) 529-4500, FAX:
 (212) 529-4442, Web Site: www.
 abipr.com
Pres: Alan Isacson

THE
DMA **IVIE**
601 Silveron Blvd (Suite 200)
Flower Mound, TX 75028-4030
Telephone: (972) 899-5000
Primary Market Served: Consumer

IVISIONMOBILE INC
9566 Topanga Cyn Blvd
Chatsworth, CA 91311
Telephone: (866) 655-5302, Web Site:
 www.ivisionmobile.com
CEO & Co-Founder: Omer Samiri
CTO & Co-Founder: Derek Simms

JJI INTERNATIONAL INC
200 1st Ave
Cranston, RI 02910-5029
Telephone: (401) 732-8668, (866) 732-
 8668, FAX: (401) 732-8778, E-Mail:
 info@jjiinternational.com, Web Site:
 www.jjiinternational.com
Pres: Lisa Weingeroff

Employees: 14
Premiums, confined goods & logo
merchandise.

JSR ADVERTISING CORP
The Quant Method
21 Astor Pl (Suite 2D)
New York, NY 10003-6931
Telephone: (212) 995-1661, E-Mail:
 jsr@nyc.rr.com, Web Site: www.
 quantmethod.com
Pres: Jay Rosenberg

JVW DIRECT
309 W Hutchinson Ave
Pittsburgh, PA 15218-1325
Telephone: (412) 241-5920, FAX:
 (412) 241-5850, E-Mail: john@
 jvwdirect.com
Pres: Jay van Wagenen
Partner: John C. O'Connor

JWT INSIDE
Subs. of J Walter Thompson
2425 Olympic Blvd
Santa Monica, CA 90404
Telephone: (310) 309-8282, (877) 665-
 8768, FAX: (310) 309-8283, E-Mail:
 conversations@jwtinside.com, Web
 Site: www.jwtworks.com
CEO: Rob Quish
Pres US: John Windolph
CFO: Jeff Press

THE JACKSON GROUP
5804 Churchman By-Pass
Indianapolis, IN 46203
Telephone: (888) 522-5766, Web Site:
 www.jacksongroup.com
CEO: Norm Cosand

THE
DMA **JACOBS & CLEVENGER INC**
515 N State St (Suite 1700)
Chicago, IL 60654-4776
Telephone: (312) 894-3000, FAX:
 (312) 645-9825, E-Mail: mail@
 jacobsclevenger.com, Web Site:
 www.jacobsclevenger.com
Pres: Ron Jacobs

**DON JAGODA ASSOCIATES
INC**
100 Marcus Dr
Melville, NY 11747
Telephone: (631) 454-1800, FAX:
 (631) 454-1834, E-Mail:
 information@dja.com, Web Site:
 www.dja.com
Pres: Don Jagoda
Exec VP: Bruce Hollander

JAM COMMUNICATIONS
1108 K St NW (3rd fl)
Washington, DC 20005-6819
Telephone: (202) 986-4750, FAX:
   (202) 232-9146, E-Mail: neil@
   jamagency.com, Web Site: www.
   jamagency.com
Pres: Neil Griffen

JOHNSON DIRECT LLC
250 N Sunnyslope Rd (Suite 203)
Brookfield, WI 53005-4824
Telephone: (262) 782-2750, (800) 710-
   2750, FAX: (262) 782-2751, E-Mail:
   info@johnsondirect.com, Web Site:
   www.johnsondirect.com
Pres: Grant A. Johnson

JOHNSON RAUHOFF INC
2525 Lake Pine Dr
Saint Joseph, MI 49085-0003
Telephone: (269) 428-3377, (800) 572-
   3996, FAX: (269) 428-3312, Web
   Site: www.johnsonrauhoff.com
Pres: Jackie Hui

JONES & O'MALLEY ADVERTISING
10123 Camarillo St
Toluca Lake, CA 91602-1601
Telephone: (818) 762-8353, FAX:
   (818) 762-6736
Pres & Owner: Jana O. Collins

JONES & THOMAS INC
788 N Sunnyside Rd
Decatur, IL 62522
Telephone: (217) 423-1889, FAX:
   (217) 425-0680, E-Mail: bill@
   jonesthomas.com, Web Site: www.
   jonesthomas.com
Pres: Bill Lehmann

KPR
711 3rd Ave Rm 1200
New York, NY 10017-9204
Telephone: (212) 856-8400, FAX:
   (212) 856-8660, Web Site: www.
   kprny.com
Pres & CEO: Robert Muratore

KZS ADVERTISING
811 W Jericho Tpke (Suite 109-E)
Smithtown, NY 11787-3220
Telephone: (651) 348-1440, FAX:
   (631) 348-1449, Web Site: www.
   kzsadvertising.com
Mng Partner: Ken Kopf
Pres: Jack Schultheis
Sec: Linda Rexon

ARISS KAHAN DATABASE MARKETING GROUP INC
7270 S Ivy Ct
Englewood, CO 80112-1506
Telephone: (303) 368-9800, FAX:
   (720) 274-5000, E-Mail: info@
   dbmktg.com, Web Site: www.
   arisskahan.com
Pres: Ronald Kahan

KANG & LEE ADVERTISING INC/K&L DIRECT
285 Madison Ave (23rd fl)
New York, NY 10017
Telephone: (212) 375-8111, FAX:
   (212) 375-8255, E-Mail: info@
   kanglee.com, Web Site: www.
   kanglee.com
Pres: Cynthia Park
Exec VP, Strategic Svcs & New Bus:
   Saul Gitlin

KARASEA INC
1337 Saw Mill River Rd (#102)
Hastings On Hudson, NY 10706-3630
Telephone: (914) 646-4481
Principal: Angel Alicea

KARLEN DESIGN
863 Pacific St
San Luis Obispo, CA 93401
Telephone: (805) 541-6561, E-Mail:
   info@karlendesign.com, Web Site:
   www.karlendesign.com
Partner: Cindi Karlen

KATZ DOCHTERMANN & EPSTEIN
102 Madison Ave (fl 10)
New York, NY 10016
Telephone: (212) 686-0006, FAX:
   (212) 686-6991, E-Mail: info@
   kdande.com, Web Site: www.kdande.
   com
Pres: Erik Dochtermann

KEARY ADVERTISING CO INC
7215 Rolling Mill Rd
Baltimore, MD 21224-2033
Telephone: (410) 285-3700, (800) 428-
   5429, FAX: (410) 284-8418, E-Mail:
   wayne@keary.com, Web Site: www.
   keary.com
Pres & Owner: Wayne Keary

KEATING MAGEE ADVERTISING
600 Decatur St
New Orleans, LA 70130
Telephone: (504) 299-8000, FAX:
   (504) 525-6647, E-Mail: jmagee@
   keatingmagee.com, Web Site: www.
   keatingmagee.com

CEO: Jennifer Keating Magee

THE KEEHN CO
43 Cradle Rock Rd
Pound Ridge, NY 10576
Telephone: (914) 764-8591, FAX:
   (914) 764-5388, E-Mail: dkeehnco@
   optonline.net
Pres: Dennis Keehn

KEILER & CO
304 Main St
Farmington, CT 06032-2985
Telephone: (860) 677-8821, FAX:
   (860) 676-8164, E-Mail: newbiz@
   keiler.com, Web Site: www.keiler.
   com
Mng Partner: Lynn Taylor

KELLER CRESCENT CO
1072 Boulder Rd
Greensboro, NC 27409-9106
Telephone: (508) 478-7641, FAX:
   (508) 634-3709, Web Site: www.
   kellercrescent.com
HR Mgr: Pat Perkins

KELLEY SWOFFORD ROY INC
Div. of Middlebrook International
50 NE 29th St
Miami, FL 33137-4413
Telephone: (305) 444-0004, (800) 537-
   5565, FAX: (305) 444-9057, E-Mail:
   skelley@ksrteam.com, Web Site:
   www.kelleyswoffordroy.com
Pres: Susan Kelley

KELLIHER SAMETS VOLK
212 Battery St
Burlington, VT 05401
Telephone: (802) 862-8261, FAX:
   (802) 863-4724, E-Mail: info@ksvc.
   com, Web Site: www.ksvc.com
Mng Dir: Yoram Samets
Chief Mktg Officer: Dawn DEC

KENNEY MARKETING & ADVERTISING INC
150 S Warner Rd (Suite 250)
King of Prussia, PA 19406
Telephone: (610) 341-0430, FAX:
   (610) 341-0480, E-Mail: info@
   kmaphl.com, Web Site: www.
   kmaphl.com
Pres & CEO: Robert Kenney

KENWORTHY MARKETING & PROMOTIONAL PRODUCTS
John Kenworthy Enterprises
41 Polo Ridge Cir
Columbia, SC 29223-2800

Telephone: (803) 765-2222, (800) JKE-IDEA, FAX: (803) 765-2121, Web Site: www.discountpromotions. com
Pres: John Kenworthy

KERN DIRECT MARKETING
20955 Warner Center Ln
Woodland Hills, CA 91367
Telephone: (818) 703-8775, FAX: (818) 703-8458, Web Site: www. kerndirect.com
Pres: Russell Kern

THE KERN ORGANIZATION
20955 Warner Center Ln
Woodland Hills, CA 91367-6511
Telephone: (818) 703-8775, Web Site: www.kerndirect.com
Pres & CEO: Russell Kern

KETCHUM
1285 Avenue of the Americas (Rm 401)
New York, NY 10019-6029
Telephone: (646) 935-3900, FAX: (646) 935-4482, E-Mail: editor@ketchum.com, Web Site: www. ketchum.com
CEO & Sr Partner: Ray Kotcher

KILGANNON
1360 Peachtree St NE (Suite 700)
Atlanta, GA 30309-3262
Telephone: (404) 876-2800, FAX: (404) 876-2830, E-Mail: contact@kilgannon.com, Web Site: www. kilgannon.com
Principal: Rena Kilgannon
Office Mgr: Lauren P. Scott

KILLIAN & CO
322 S Green St (Suite 510)
Chicago, IL 60607-3579
Telephone: (312) 836-0050, E-Mail: bob@killianadvertising.com, Web Site: www.killianadvertising.com
Pres: Bob Killian

KIRSHENBAUM, BOND & PARTNERS
160 Varick St (4th fl)
New York, NY 10013
Telephone: (212) 633-0080, FAX: (212) 463-8643, E-Mail: press@kb. com, Web Site: www.kb.com
COO: Stephen Fick

WALT KLEIN & ASSOCIATES INC
2000 S Colorado Blvd (Suite 10200)
Denver, CO 80222-7918

Telephone: (303) 298-8015, FAX: (303) 298-8194, Web Site: www. wka.com
Owner: Walt Klein
Owner: Susan Klein

KLEMTNER ADVERTISING INC
Div. of Saatchi & Saatchi Advertising
375 Hudson St Bsmt 1
New York, NY 10014-7464
Telephone: (212) 463-3400, FAX: (212) 463-3541
Pres & CEO: Gavin A. Scotti

KLONDIKE MARKETING INC
PO Box 11127
Boulder, CO 80301-0006
Telephone: (720) 406-1177, (888) 395-5438, FAX: (888) 395-5438, Web Site: www.klondikemarketing.com
Pres & Mktg Dir: Caswell Forrest

KOBIE MARKETING INC
100 Second Ave S (Suite 1000)
Saint Petersburg, FL 33701
Telephone: (727) 822-5353, (800) 821-7892, FAX: (727) 822-5265, Web Site: www.kobie.com
VP Mktg: Sharon Avery

KOKOPELLI COMMUNICATIONS GROUP INC
449 N Clark St Ste 301
Chicago, IL 60654-4500
Telephone: (312) 726-5656, Web Site: www.kcgi.net
Principal: Michael Fogarty

KOLLIAS & ASSOCIATES
210 N Wells St Apt 4108
Chicago, IL 60606-1352
Telephone: (312) 857-7707
Pres & CEO: George Kollias

KRUSE ASSET MANAGEMENT
11202 Disco Dr (Suite 100)
San Antonio, TX 78216-2860
Telephone: (210) 499-0777, (800) 952-1973, FAX: (210) 499-4217, E-Mail: sales@kruseasset.com, Web Site: www.kruseasset.com
Pres & CEO: Daniel J. Kruse

KRYL & CO INC
39 S Lasalle St (Suite 200)
Chicago, IL 60603-1702
Telephone: (312) 641-0338, FAX: (312) 641-0314, E-Mail: info@krylandco.com, Web Site: www. krylandco.com

Pres: Susan Kryl

KUHN & WITTENBORN INC
2405 Grand Blvd (Suite 600)
Kansas City, MO 64108
Telephone: (816) 471-7888, FAX: (816) 471-7530, E-Mail: humanresources@kuhnwitt.com, Web Site: www.kuhnwitt.com
Pres: Whitey Kuhn

KYP SYSTEMS INC
380 Lexington Ave (fl 17)
New York, NY 10168-1799
Telephone: (212) 551-7878, FAX: (917) 591-1514, E-Mail: steves@kyp.com, Web Site: www.ikyp.com
CEO: Nicholas Miller
Mktg Dir: Steve Shapiro

Creating engagement marketing solutions that allow brands to connect with target audiences through intuitive experiences that begin in the physical world.

LCH DIRECT INC
74 Boynton St
Waltham, MA 02453-2866
Telephone: (978) 664-2900, FAX: (978) 664-4812, E-Mail: info@lchdirect.com, Web Site: www. lchdirect.com
Pres: Bill Licata
Conducts Business: U.S.
Primary Market Served: Business
Founded: 1988

LEC LTD
12 E Ohio St (#400)
Chicago, IL 60611-3098
Telephone: (312) 670-0077, Web Site: www.lecltd.com
Controller: Mary Hayes

LHH & F INC
2638 Route 23
Hillsdale, NY 12529
Telephone: (518) 325-4000, (800) 955-1129
Pres: Robert E. Launey

LKH&S INC
54 W Hubbard (Suite 100)
Chicago, IL 60610
Telephone: (312) 595-0200, FAX: (312) 595-0300, E-Mail: lkhs@lkhs. com, Web Site: www.lkhs.com
Mng Dir: Stanton Lewin

THE LACEK GROUP
The Loyalty Practice of OgilvyOne Worldwide
900 Second Ave S (Suite 1800)

Minneapolis, MN 55402-1099
Telephone: (612) 359-3700, FAX:
(612) 359-9395, E-Mail: info@lacek.
com, Web Site: www.lacek.com
Pres: William Baker
Mng Partner & Chief Creative Officer:
Mark Weninger

LANMARK GROUP INC
804 Broadway Ste 4
West Long Branch, NJ 07764-2203
Telephone: (732) 389-4500, FAX:
(732) 389-4998, E-Mail: info@
lanmarkgroup.com, Web Site: www.
lanmarkgroup.com
CEO: Howard Klein

LARGIE LLC
903 Cedar St
Riverton, NJ 08077-1718
Telephone: (609) 870-8187
Primary Market Served: Consumer

LATIN-PAK
141 Chesterfield Business Pkwy
Chesterfield, MO 63005-1233
Telephone: (636) 536-5344, (800) 625-
4283, FAX: (636) 536-9456, E-Mail:
latinpak@latinpak.com, Web Site:
www.latinpak.com
Pres & CEO: Vincent Andaloro
Founded: 1996

LAUGHLIN/CONSTABLE
200 S Michigan Ave (Suite 1700)
Chicago, IL 60604-2460
Telephone: (312) 422-5900, FAX:
(312) 422-5901, Web Site: www.
laughlin.com
Exec VP: Renee Haber
Primary Market Served: Business &
Consumer

THE DMA LEAPFROG ONLINE
807 Greenwood St
Evanston, IL 60201-4311
Telephone: (847) 492-1968, Web Site:
www.leapfrogonline.com
Chief Strategy Officer: Jason Wadler

AL PAUL LEFTON CO INC
125 S 9th St Ste 801, Rohm & Haas
Bldg
Philadelphia, PA 19107-5123
Telephone: (215) 923-9600, FAX:
(215) 351-4298, Web Site: www.
lefton.com
Pres & CEO: Al Paul Lefton Jr.
Acct Supv: Betty Amoroso

LEMMONTREE MARKETING GROUP
Div. of LemmonTree Enterprises Inc
3010 S Priest Dr (Suite 103)

Tempe, AZ 85282
Telephone: (480) 967-1405, (888) 536-
6243, FAX: (480) 967-1407, E-Mail:
7solutions@lemmontree.com, Web
Site: www.lemmontree.com
Pres: Nicolette Lemmon
Client Svc Coord: Amanda Dillard
Exec Asst: Kris Johnson

LENSER
899 Northgate Dr (Suite 530)
San Rafael, CA 94903-3667
Telephone: (415) 446-2500, E-Mail:
carol@lenser.com, Web Site: www.
lenser.com
Pres: John Lenser
VP Circulation: Michelle Houston
Partner, Creative Svcs: Carol
Worthington-Levy
Conducts Business: U.S., Canada
Employees: 22
Primary Market Served: Business &
Consumer
Founded: 1994
Gross sales or billing: $2,000,000

Specialist in multi-channel mktg. Clients range from small & startup to
large companies who have presence in
one or more channels such as catalog,
retail, e-commerce or direct mail.

LEO BURNETT DETROIT
3310 W Big Beaver Rd Ste 107
Troy, MI 48084-2807
Telephone: (248) 458-8331, FAX:
(248) 458-8736, Web Site: www.
leoburnett.com
Pres: James Moore

THE DMA LEO BURNETT USA
35 W Wacker Dr
Chicago, IL 60601-1723
Telephone: (312) 220-3200, Web Site:
www.leoburnett.com
VP Information Svcs: Douglas Buffo

LEVENSON & BRINKER PUBLIC RELATIONS
Div. of Levenson Group
717 N Harwood (20th fl)
Dallas, TX 75201-6501
Telephone: (214) 932-6076, (214) 880-
0200, FAX: (214) 880-0628, E-Mail:
s.levenson@levensonbrinkerpr.com,
Web Site: www.levensonbrinkerpr.
com
Co-Founder & CEO: Stanley R. Levenson

LEVERAGE MARKETING GROUP
Div. of Goodwick/Liazon Company
117-119 S Main St
Newtown, CT 06470-2380

Telephone: (203) 426-1267, FAX:
(203) 426-5934, E-Mail: info@
leverage-marketing.com, Web Site:
www.leverage-marketing.com
Pres: David Goodwick

LEVERTE ASSOCIATES INC
1000 Wyckoff Ave
Mahwah, NJ 07430-3164
Telephone: (203) 221-4900, FAX:
(203) 221-4901, E-Mail: rleverte@
leverte.com, Web Site: www.leverte.
com
Chmn & CEO: Robert J. Leverte

LEVLANE ADVERTISING
100 Penn Square E (4th fl), The Wonamaker Bldg
Philadelphia, PA 19107
Telephone: (215) 825-9600, FAX:
(215) 825-9601
Media Mgr: Lynn Eckenard

THE LIFESTYLE MARKETING CORP
310 Gramercy Pl
Glen Rock, NJ 07452-2226
Telephone: (201) 670-7985, FAX:
(201) 251-2443
Pres: Jim Kapotes

LIGGETT-STASHOWER DIRECT
Div. of Liggett-Stashower Inc
1240 Huron Rd.
Cleveland, OH 44115-1831
Telephone: (216) 348-8500, (800) 877-
4573, FAX: (216) 736-8118, E-Mail:
mnylander@liggett.com, Web Site:
www.liggett.com
Data Analyst: Kenneth Barhoover
Sr Database Mgr: Karen Abdallah
CEO: Mark Nylander
Employees: 100

Full-service direct marketing agency
with expertise in database marketing,
creative execution that sells, and winning direct response strategy. We work
with consumer marketers, business to
business, insurance and retail.

LINETT & HARRISON
2500 Morris Ave
Union, NJ 07083-5675
Telephone: (908) 686-0606, FAX:
(908) 686-0623, E-Mail: sharrison@
linettandharrison.com, Web Site:
www.linettandharrison.com
Controller: Valerie Marks
Pres & COO: Sam Harrison

Advertising, Branding, Media Planning
& Direct Marketing, Sales Promotion,
Internet Advertising, Websites, Bro-
chures, Annual Reports.

THE LINICK GROUP INC
Seven Putter Ln, Linick Bldg
Middle Island, NY 11953-0102
Telephone: (631) 924-3888, E-Mail:
linickgroup@gmail.com, Web Site:
www.andrewlinickdirectmarketing.
com
CEO: Dr. Andrew Linick
VP: Roger Dextor

LINKIN COMMUNICATIONS
11362 Charnock Rd
Los Angeles, CA 90066-2918
Telephone: (310) 391-1288
Owner & Mktg Dir: Gerald Linkin

**LIST MANAGEMENT
SERVICES INC**
5728 Major Blvd (Suite 650)
Orlando, FL 32819-7963
Telephone: (407) 876-5544, Web Site:
www.lmsonline.com
Pres: Steve Cohen

LITTLE & KING CO LLC
98 Cuttermill Rd Ste 479N
Great Neck, NY 11021-3037
Telephone: (516) 377-1377 X12, FAX:
(212) 575-0739, E-Mail: lkinfo@
littleandking.com, Web Site: www.
littleandking.com
Pres: Karen McCarthy

THE
DMA **LOCKARD & WECHSLER**
2 Bridge St
Irvington, NY 10533-1593
Telephone: (914) 591-6600
Pres: Richard Wechsler

**LOPEZ NEGRETE
COMMUNICATIONS**
3336 Richmond Ave (Suite 200)
Houston, TX 77098-3022
Telephone: (713) 877-8777, FAX:
(713) 877-8796, E-Mail:
LNCmailbox@lopeznegrete.com,
Web Site: www.lopeznegrete.com
Pres & CEO: Alex Lopez Negrete
Direct Mktg/CRM Initiatives: Kathleen
Jones
Primary Market Served: Consumer
Founded: 1985

Full service advertising agency.

LOREX INC
19131 Industrial Blvd NW (Suite 1)
Elk River, MN 55330-2438
Telephone: (763) 441-0055, Web Site:
www.lorexinc.com
Pres: Ken Janc

**LORTZ DIRECT MARKETING
INC**
13936 Gold Cir
Omaha, NE 68144-9803
Telephone: (800) 366-7686, Web Site:
www.lortzdirect.com
VP List: Richard Stanley

LOWE WORLDWIDE
Deutsch Inc
111 8th Ave
New York, NY 10011
Telephone: (212) 981-7600, E-Mail:
info@loweworldwide.com, Web Site:
www.loweworldwide.com
Chmn: Donny Deutsch
CEO: Val DiFebo
CEO & Chief Creative Office: Eric
Hirshberg
CEO, North America: Linda Sawyer
CEO, Deutsch LA: Mike Sheldon

LOYALTY E-MARKETING
Subs. of Carl Bloom Associates Inc
81 Main St (Suite 101)
White Plains, NY 10601
Telephone: (914) 761-2800, Web Site:
www.carlbloom.com
Pres: Carl P. Bloom

LUNARCOW DESIGN
137 S Main St (Suite 202)
Akron, OH 44308-1416
Telephone: (330) 253-9000, (800) 594-
9620, FAX: (330) 253-9001, E-Mail:
info@lunarcow.com, Web Site:
www.lunarcow.com
Pres: Benjamin Harris
Conducts Business: U.S., Canada
Employees: 10
Primary Market Served: Business
Catalog available online
Direct online sales
Advertising/Marketing Budget Related
to Direct Marketing: 26-50%
Direct Marketing ad budget:
Direct Mail: 10%
Online: 30%
Telephone: 60%
Founded: 1999
Gross sales or billing: $2,000,000

Sells branding, marketing communication services, live web sites, creative
design services, print services, email
marketing, search.

**LUNDMARK ADVERTISING &
DESIGN INC**
104 W Ninth St (Suite 104)
Kansas City, MO 64105
Telephone: (816) 842-5236, FAX:
(816) 221-7175, Web Site: www.
lundonline.net
Pres: Fred Trent

THE LUSTIGMAN FIRM P C
65 E 55th St Fl 3
New York, NY 10022-3372
Telephone: (212) 683-9180, FAX:
(212) 683-9181, E-Mail: andy@
lfirm.com, Web Site: www.
lustigmanfirm.com
Partner: Andrew Lustigman
Founding Partner: Sheldon Lustigman
Conducts Business: U.S.
Employees: 4
Primary Market Served: Business &
Consumer
Founded: 1989

Attorneys to the direct marketing
industry- Advertising review, sweepstakes regulatory defense.

MC GROUP
Part of Ogilvy, owned by WPP
350 Talbot St
London, ON, Canada N6A 2R6
Telephone: (519) 660-8460, FAX:
(519) 660-8476, Web Site: www.
themcgroup.com
Pres & CEO: John Besterd

MD&C ADVERTISING
PO Box 8446
New Haven, CT 06530-0446
Telephone: (203) 624-4151, FAX:
(203) 401-6134, Web Site: www.
mdcads.com
Mng Principal & Exec Art Dir: Pas-
quale Del Vecchio

**MFP&W PROMOTIONS
DIRECT**
Div. of Promotion Direct J Walter Th-
ompson
PO Box 2125
San Juan, PR 00922-2125
Telephone: (787) 781-1616, FAX:
(787) 793-5355, Web Site: www.
jwtworld.com
Gen Mgr: Carlos Gonzalez

MGP DIRECT INC
PO Box 694
Fulton, MD 20759-0694
Telephone: (410) 531-0383, FAX:
(410) 531-8142, E-Mail: roberta@
mgpdirect.com, Web Site: www.
mgpdirect.com
Pres & CEO: Roberta Rosenberg

MKE ENTERPRISES
193 Haverhill St
North Reading, MA 01864
Telephone: (978) 664-3877, FAX:
(978) 664-2835, E-Mail: mke@
theworld.com, Web Site: www.mke-
enterprises.com
Pres: Marilyn Ewer

MM BATCH
dba Banner Direct
PO Box 1548
Westhampton Beach, NY 11978-7548
Telephone: (212) 737-0700, FAX:
　(212) 454-1124, E-Mail: christine@
　bannerdirect.com, Web Site: www.
　bannerdirect.com
Pres: Christine Fontana
Strategic Devel Mgr: Rosalyn Piecka
VP, Acct Mngmt & Strategic Planning:
　Patricia Kelly
Founded: 1990

MRM WORLDWIDE
622 3rd Ave
New York, NY 10017-6707
Telephone: (646) 865-6230, Web Site:
　www.mrmworldwide.com
CEO: Reuben Hendell

MRW COMMUNICATIONS
2 Fairfield St
Hingham, MA 02043
Telephone: (781) 740-4525, FAX:
　(718) 926-0371, E-Mail: jim@
　mrwinc.com, Web Site: www.
　mrwinc.com
Creative Dir: Tom Matzell

MVBMS EURO RSCG
Subs. of EURO RSCG
350 Hudson St Fl 8
New York, NY 10014-4505
Telephone: (212) 886-2000, FAX:
　(212) 886-2016, E-Mail:
　northamerica@eurorscg.com, Web
　Site: www.eurorscg.com
CEO & Chm: Jim Neekin
Exec VP & Gen Mgr: Lisa Fabiano

MACLAREN MCCANN
Div. of McCann-Erickson
Ten Bay St
Toronto, ON, Canada M5J 2S3
Telephone: (416) 594-6000, FAX:
　(416) 643-7026, Web Site: www.
　maclaren.com
Pres & COO: Doug Turney

MACPHEE MARKETING COMMUNICATIONS
1 rue Yonge St (Suite 2000)
Toronto, ON, Canada M5E IE5
Telephone: (416) 868-1370
VP: Dave Orthocofski

THE MAGNA GROUP
208 Harristown Rd.
Glen Rock, NJ 07452
Telephone: (201) 652-8600, Web Site:
　www.themagnagroup.com
Primary Market Served: Consumer

THE DMA MAIL AMERICA
89 Bridge St Plaza
Wheeling, WV 26003-5209
Telephone: (304) 242-8081, Web Site:
　www.mailamerica.com
VP: Leo Bartsch

MAIL ORDER MEDIA & MARKETING INC
5500 Linkside Ct (2A)
Fuquay Varina, NC 27526-8499
Telephone: (203) 254-9390, FAX:
　(203) 254-3253, E-Mail:
　mailordermedia2000@yahoo.com
Pres: Toni Menoudakos

MAJESTIC MARKETING INC
1160 California Ave
Corona, CA 92881-3324
Telephone: (951) 280-2400, Web Site:
　www.bagmasters.com
Pres: Richard Whittier
Catalog available online

MANLEY & ASSOCIATES INC
6414 Marshall Dr
Woodridge, IL 60517-1223
Telephone: (630) 963-1123, FAX:
　(630) 963-1124
Pres: Eugene Manley

IRMA S MANN STRATEGIC MARKETING INC
420 Boylston St Ste 600
Boston, MA 02116-4017
Telephone: (617) 353-1822, FAX:
　(617) 266-1890, Web Site: www.
　irmamann.com
Pres & CEO: Gary Leopold

MARC USA
225 W Station Square Dr Ste 500
Pittsburgh, PA 15219-1174
Telephone: (412) 562-2015, FAX:
　(412) 562-2022, Web Site: www.
　marcusa.com
Mng Supv & PR Dir: Marilyn Kail

MARCHESE COMMUNICATIONS INC
4652 Via Marina (#104)
Marina Del Rey, CA 90292
Telephone: (213) 533-6444, (213) 399-
　5999, (866) 441-8086, E-Mail:
　david@marchesecommunications.
　com, Web Site: www.
　marchesecommunications.com
Pres: David Marchese
Employees: 5
Founded: 1986

Specializing in generating superior response-acquisition, retention, and conversion through the integration of DR TV, online marketing, and sales promotion.

MARDEN-KANE INC
1055 Franklin Ave (Suite 300)
Garden City, NY 11530-2903
Telephone: (516) 365-3999, FAX:
　(516) 365-5250, E-Mail: expert@
　mardenkane.com, Web Site: www.
　mardenkane.com
CFO: Alan Richter
EVP: Marc Wortsman

MARIS WEST & BAKER
18 Northtown Dr
Jackson, MS 39211
Telephone: (601) 977-9200, FAX:
　(601) 977-9257, Web Site: www.
　mwb.com
Pres: Peter Marks

MARITZ
1375 N Highway Dr
Fenton, MO 63026
Telephone: (636) 827-4246, FAX:
　(636) 827-8929, Web Site: www.
　maritz.com
VP: Michael J. Donnelly

THE DMA MARKE COMMUNICATIONS INC
45 W 45th St Ste 16L
New York, NY 10036-4602
Telephone: (212) 201-0600, (800) 716-
　2753, FAX: (212) 213-0785, Web
　Site: www.marke.com
EVP: Allen G. Rosenberg
Pres: Larry Krampf

MARKET-ABILITY INC
1520 Rancho View Dr
Lafayette, CA 94549-2232
Telephone: (925) 299-7900, (800) 434-
　6275, FAX: (925) 284-2331, Web
　Site: www.market-ability.net
Pres: Mike Hughes

THE MARKETING AGENCY LLC
2881 E Oakland Park Blvd (Suite 425)
Fort Lauderdale, FL 33306-1813
Telephone: (954) 771-1177, FAX:
　(866) 379-5788, E-Mail: marketing@
　themarketingagency.com, Web Site:
　www.themarketingagency.com
Pres: David A. Kramer

Specializing in sweepstakes & contests for over twenty five years.

MARKETING & PROMOTIONS GROUP
55-A E Ridgewood Ave
Ridgewood, NJ 07450
Telephone: (201) 251-8339, FAX:
(201) 251-8340, Web Site: www.
promowave.com
Pres: Michael W. Gray

MARKETING DIRECT INC
530 Maryville Centre Dr (Suite 300)
Saint Louis, MO 63141-5825
Telephone: (314) 590-8300, FAX:
(314) 966-5632, E-Mail: dbarnes@
marketingdirect.com, Web Site:
www.marketingdirect.com
Pres: Dennis Barnes

MARKETING EFFICIENCY CORP
20306 N Main St
Cornelius, NC 28031-8520
Telephone: (704) 896-5995, FAX:
(704) 896-3426
Pres: Chris Burton

MARKETING GENERAL INC
209 Madison St Ste 300
Alexandria, VA 22314-1764
Telephone: (703) 739-1000, (800) 644-
6646, FAX: (703) 549-6057, E-Mail:
info@marketinggeneral.com, Web
Site: www.marketinggeneral.com
Sr VP: Tony Rossell

MARKETING INNOVATORS
9701 W Higgins Rd Ste 400
Rosemont, IL 60018-4717
Telephone: (847) 696-1111, (800) 543-
7373, FAX: (847) 696-3194, E-Mail:
info@marketinginnovators.com, Web
Site: www.marketinginnovators.com
Pres: Richard A. Blabolil

MARKETING OUT-OF-THE-BOX INC
600 W Chicago Ave Ste 850
Chicago, IL 60654-2529
Telephone: (847) 588-8100, (888) 588-
8100, FAX: (847) 294-0706, E-Mail:
possibilities@motb.com, Web Site:
motb.com
Pres: David E. Newberger

THE MARKETING STORE
701 E 22nd St Ste 200
Lombard, IL 60148-5024
Telephone: (630) 693-1400, Web Site:
www.themarketingstore.com
Sr VP & Client Svc Dir: Mark Watson

MARKETING STRATEGIES
4603 Oleander Dr (Suite 4)
North Myrtle Beach, SC 29577-5738
Telephone: (843) 692-9662, FAX:
(843) 272-4913, E-Mail: pr@
marketingstrategiesinc.com, Web
Site: www.marketingstrategiesinc.
com
Pres & Owner: Denise Blackburn

MARKETING III DIRECT RESPONSE
PO Box 121278
Clermont, FL 34712-8712
Telephone: (352) 241-8040, FAX:
(352) 241-4533, E-Mail:
marketing35th@aol.com
Pres: Patrice O'Callahan
VP: Dan O. Callahan

MARKETING VISIONS INC
520 White Plains Rd (Suite 500)
Tarrytown, NY 10591-5118
Telephone: (914) 631-3900, FAX:
(914) 631-3003, E-Mail:
marvisions@aol.com
Pres: Jay Sloofman

MARKETPOWER DIRECT MARKETING
1449 Druid Valley Dr NE (Suite C)
Atlanta, GA 30329-2967
Telephone: (404) 433-5555, E-Mail:
joel@marketpoweronline.com, Web
Site: www.marketpoweronline.com
Pres: Joel Alpert

THE DMA MARKETSENSE
7020 High Grove Blvd
Burr Ridge, IL 60527-7595
Telephone: (630) 654-0170, Web Site:
www.market-sense.com
EVP: Peter Wroblewski

MARKGRAF & WELLS MARKETING
2939 Toledo Ave S
Minneapolis, MN 55416-1926
Telephone: (612) 870-8550
Pres: Richard J. Markgraf
Direct Mktg Specialist: Paul Haker

Specializing in segment isolation &
description of metrics & demographics.
Commercial, industrial, consumer, non-
profit & government.

MARKOTS
405 El Camino Real (#248)
Menlo Park, CA 94025-5240
Telephone: (925) 240-0093, Web Site:
www.markots.com
CEO: Ray Gulam

MARQUARDT, ROCHE & PARTNERS
5 High Ridge Park Ste 2C
Stamford, CT 06905-1326
Telephone: (203) 327-0890, FAX:
(203) 353-8487, E-Mail: ideas@mrp-
website.com, Web Site: www.mrp-
website.com
Pres: Howard Meditz
Chief Creative Officer: Gerry O'Hara

MARQUIS AWARDS & SPECIALTIES INC
108 N Bent
Powell, WY 82435-2712
Telephone: (307) 754-2272, (800) 327-
2446, FAX: (307) 754-9577, Web
Site: www.rushawards.com
Pres: John Collins

THE DMA THE MARTIN AGENCY
1 Shockoe Plaza
Richmond, VA 23219-4132
Telephone: (804) 698-8000, FAX:
(804) 698-8001, Web Site: www.
martinagency.com
Partner Integrated Svcs: Barbara
Thornhill Joynes
Employees: 380
Founded: 1965
Gross sales or billing: $402,000,000

Full-service integrated direct response
advertising from a nationally renowned
creative shop. Winner of the Direct
Marketing Association's highest global
honor - the Diamond Echo. Focus on
measurable programs using interactive,
mail, broadcast and print to drive sales
while building strong brands. End-to-
end program development and management for acquisition and CRM including data warehouse, mining and
fulfillment.

MARTIN THOMAS INTERNATIONAL
42 Riverside Dr
Barrington, RI 02806-3612
Telephone: (401) 245-8500, FAX:
(401) 245-0694, E-Mail: contact@
martinthomas.com, Web Site: www.
martinthomas.com
Pres: Martin K. Pottle

Business to business marketing firm.
Helps businesses grow & prosper using
cost effective modeling tools.

MARTIN WILLIAMS ADVERTISING
60 S 6th St (Suite 2800)
Minneapolis, MN 55402-4444
Telephone: (612) 342-9739, FAX:
(612) 342-9700, Web Site: www.
martinwilliams.com

Chmn & CFO: Tim Frojd
Mgr: Jennifer Hahs

THE DMA MARTINO & BINZER
270 Farmington Ave Ste 128
Farmington, CT 06032-1920
Telephone: (860) 678-4300, Web Site:
 www.goodbait.com
Pres: David Martino

THE MARX GROUP
Subs. of Marx Advertising Inc
2175 E Francisco Blvd (Suite F)
San Rafael, CA 94901
Telephone: (415) 453-0844, FAX:
 (415) 451-0166, E-Mail: info@
 themarxgrp.com, Web Site: www.
 themarxgrp.com
Pres: Tom Marx
Pub Rels Dir: Gary McCoy

MAXIM DIRECT
PO Box 35565
Greensboro, NC 27425-5565
Telephone: (336) 841-6892, FAX:
 (336) 886-1655, Web Site: www.
 maximdirect.com
Pres: Will Spivey

**MAXWELL & MILLER
MARKETING
COMMUNICATIONS**
141 E Michigan Ave (Suite 500)
Kalamazoo, MI 49007
Telephone: (269) 382-4060 x26, FAX:
 (269) 382-0504, E-Mail: info@
 maxwellandmiller.com, Web Site:
 www.maxwellandmiller.com
Pres: Greg Miller

**FRANK MAYER &
ASSOCIATES INC**
1975 Wisconsin Ave
Grafton, WI 53024
Telephone: (262) 377-4700, (800) 837-
 1232, FAX: (262) 377-3449, E-Mail:
 dave.zoerb@frankmayer.com, Web
 Site: www.frankmayer.com
Pres & COO: Mike Mayer

**THE DMA PETER A MAYER
ADVERTISING INC**
324 Camp St
New Orleans, LA 70130-2804
Telephone: (504) 581-7191, Web Site:
 www.peteramayer.com
Pres: Mark Mayer

MAYO MARKETING IDEAS
2785 Pacific Coast Hwy (#E288)
Torrance, CA 90505
Telephone: (310) 517-9272, FAX:
 (310) 517-9279

Owner: Forrest Mayo

**MCCABE & DUVAL
ADVERTISING**
Ten Moulton St (4th fl)
Portland, ME 04101-5039
Telephone: (207) 773-4538, (800) 603-
 6069, FAX: (207) 773-7245, Web
 Site: www.mccabe-duval.com
Pres: Christopher Duval

**MCCANN RELATIONSHIP
MKTG**
Div. of McCann-Erickson Worldwide
622 Third Ave
New York, NY 10017
Telephone: (646) 865-6000, FAX:
 (646) 487-9610, Web Site: www.
 mrmworldwide.com
Pres & CEO: Nick Brien

**MCCARTHY & KING
MARKETING INC**
Eight Esther Dr
Milford, MA 01757-1057
Telephone: (508) 473-8643, FAX:
 (508) 473-7294, Web Site: www.
 mccarthyandking.com
Pres: Robert McCarthy

**MCDONALD ENTERPRISES
LTD**
2111 Polo Pointe Dr
Vienna, VA 22181-2804
Telephone: (703) 813-6040, FAX:
 (703) 847-9662
Principal: B. McDonald

MEADOWS DESIGN OFFICE
3800 Yuma St NW
Washington, DC 20016
Telephone: (202) 966-6007, FAX:
 (202) 966-6733, E-Mail: mdo@
 mdomedia.com, Web Site: www.
 mdomedia.com
Creative Dir: Marc Meadows

MEDIA CONSULTANTS
205B Chubb Ave (2nd fl)
Lyndhurst, NJ 07071
Telephone: (201) 933-2015, FAX:
 (201) 933-6314, E-Mail: hlhirsch@
 earthlink.net, Web Site: www.
 mediaconsultants.net
Pres: Harvey Hirsch

THE MEDIA CREW
1803 Park Center Dr Ste 102
Orlando, FL 32835-6216
Telephone: (407) 839-0390, Web Site:
 www.themediacrew.com
Gen Mgr: Nick Foley

MEDIA RESPONSE INC
2450 Hollywood Blvd (Suite 200)
Hollywood, FL 33020-6620
Telephone: (954) 967-9899, (888) 801-
 9899, FAX: (954) 967-9321, E-Mail:
 info@media-response.com, Web Site:
 www.media-response.com
Pres: Ellis Kahn

THE DMA MEDIA STREAM DIRECT
14724 Ventura Blvd Ste 1200
Sherman Oaks, CA 91403-3512
Telephone: (800) 817-8000, E-Mail:
 ecohen@mediastreamdirect.com,
 Web Site: www.mediastreamdirect.
 com
Pres: Eitan Cohen

MEDIACONCEPTS CORP
25 N Main St
Assonet, MA 02702-1136
Telephone: (508) 644-3131, FAX:
 (508) 644-5201, E-Mail: at3@
 mediaconceptscorp.com, Web Site:
 www.mediaconceptscorp.com
Owner & Pres: Paul Beaulieu
Exec VP & Creative Dir: Greg Dobos
Acct Mgr Bus Devel: Emily Boyd

MEDIAGRAPHICS
Subs. of Dev. Kinney/MediaGraphics
PO Box 162
Eau Claire, WI 54702-0162
Telephone: (751) 590-4488, (866) 324-
 1658, E-Mail: mediagraphics@
 devkinney.com, Web Site: www.
 devkinney.com
Owner & CEO: J.D. Kinney

**MELTZER MEDIA
PRODUCTIONS**
70 W 36th St (Suite 1000)
New York, NY 10018
Telephone: (212) 868-4600, FAX:
 (212) 302-6175, E-Mail:
 jeffmeltzer@earthlink.net
Pres: Jeff Meltzer

**MERRELL REMINGTON &
ASSOCIATES**
1847 W 2300th S
Salt Lake City, UT 84119
Telephone: (801) 975-0109, (800) 347-
 7468, FAX: (801) 975-0107, Web
 Site: www.merrellremington.com
CEO: A. Kent Merrell

THE MESA GROUP
1281 Blue Heron Blvd E (# 125)
West Palm Beach, FL 33404-4739
Telephone: (212) 645-9666, (888) 637-
 2477, FAX: (212) 243-0564, E-Mail:
 info@mesagrp.com, Web Site: www.
 mesagrp.com

METRICS MARKETING
905 Corporate Way
Westlake, OH 44145-1519
Telephone: (440) 331-1688, Web Site:
www.precisiondialogue.com
Partner: Daniel Rose

THE MEYOCKS GROUP
6800 Lake Dr (Suite 150)
West Des Moines, IA 50266
Telephone: (515) 225-1200, FAX:
(515) 225-6400, E-Mail: dougjeske@
areyoubrave.com, Web Site: www.
areyoubrave.com
COO: Doug Jeske

**MIAMI VALLEY MARKETING
GROUP INC**
1500 Devereux Dr
Dayton, OH 45419
Telephone: (937) 299-1825, FAX:
(937) 299-9967, E-Mail:
tomnorwalk@aol.com
Pres: Thomas S. Norwalk

MIGHTY NET INC
dba "CreditReport.com" and
"CreditWatch".
26010 Mureau Rd Ste 130, PO Box
9153
Calabasas, CA 91302-3176
Telephone: (818) 407-4620, FAX:
(818) 407-4630, E-Mail: info@
mightynet.com, Web Site: www.
mightynet.com
CEO: Adam Kasower

MILICI VALENTI NG PACK
999 Bishop St (24th fl)
Honolulu, HI 96813
Telephone: (808) 536-0881, FAX:
(808) 529-6208, E-Mail: info@
mvnp.com, Web Site: www.mvnp.
com
Mktg Dir: Lori Kimura

**THE MILLER GROUP
ADVERTISING**
1516 S Bundy (Suite 200)
Los Angeles, CA 90025
Telephone: (310) 442-0101, FAX:
(310) 442-0107, E-Mail:
TMGConnect@millergroup.net, Web
Site: www.millergroup.net
Pres & Creative Dir: Renee Miller

**MILWAUKEE DIRECT
MARKETING INC**
675 N Barker Rd (Suite 130)
Brookfield, WI 53045
Telephone: (262) 789-2240, FAX:
(262) 789-2250, E-Mail: info@
milwaukeedirect.com, Web Site:
www.milwaukeedirect.com

Pres: Ron Davis

**MITCHELL & RESNIKOFF/
WEIGHTMAN**
8003 Old York Rd
Elkins Park, PA 19027-1410
Telephone: (215) 635-1000, FAX:
(215) 635-6542, E-Mail: info@
mitch-res.com, Web Site: www.
Mitch-Res.com
Pres & CEO: Ronald B. Resnikoff
Controller: Lucille Thomas

MODEM MEDIA
107 Elm St Ste 907
Stamford, CT 06902-3808
Telephone: (203) 299-7000, FAX:
(203) 299-7060, Web Site: www.
modemmedia.com
Pres & CEO: Martin Reidy

**MONEY MAILER DIRECT
MARKETING**
12131 Western Ave
Garden Grove, CA 92841-2914
Telephone: (800) 416-1713, Web Site:
www.moneymailerdirect.com
Pres & CEO: Godfred Otuteye

MONSTER MAGNET
7725 National Tpke (Unit 100)
Louisville, KY 40214-4813
Telephone: (800) 255-0234, Web Site:
www.monstermagnet.com
Pres & CEO: Joe Martin
Acct Exec: Shannon Clark

MOREMEDIA DIRECT INC
329 W 28 St.
Miami Beach, FL 33140-4306
Telephone: (305) 672-9793, E-Mail:
info@moremediadirect.com, Web
Site: www.moremediadirect.com
Pres & CEO: Mickey Silverman

MORRIS GROUP INC
910 Day Hill Rd
Windsor, CT 06095
Telephone: (860) 687-3475, FAX:
(860) 687-3476, E-Mail:
jmorris_lee@morris-lee.com, Web
Site: www.morrisgroupinc.com
Pres: Brad Morris

MORTON ADVERTISING INC
875 Ave of the Americas (Suite 1111)
New York, NY 10001-3577
Telephone: (212) 465-2250, FAX:
(212) 465-1575, E-Mail: don@
mortonad.com, Web Site: www.
mortonad.com
Pres: Donald Reisfeld

THE JACK MORTON CO
875 N Michigan Ave Ste 2400
Chicago, IL 60611-1877
Telephone: (312) 274-6060, FAX:
(312) 274-6061, E-Mail:
experience@jackmorton.com, Web
Site: www.jackmorton.com
CEO: Josh McCall

MOWER & ASSOCIATES
1001 Moorehead Sq (5th fl)
Charlotte, NC 28203
Telephone: (704) 375-0123, FAX:
(704) 375-0222, Web Site: www.
mower.com
Media Dir: Gene Hallacy

**ERIC MOWER &
ASSOCIATES**
28 E Main St Ste 1960
Rochester, NY 14614-1988
Telephone: (585) 385-2000, Web Site:
www.mower.com
Chmn & CEO: Eric Mower
Acct Execs: Tony Astran
Direct Mktg: Keith Schofield Broad-
bent

MULLEN
40 Broad St
Boston, MA 02109-4316
Telephone: (978) 468-1155, Web Site:
www.mullen.com
SVP Grp Acct Dir: Bill Doyle

**MULLEN & MCCAFFREY
DIRECT RESPONSE**
197 Hog Creek Rd
East Hampton, NY 11937-4307
Telephone: (631) 324-4265, FAX:
(631) 324-2135, E-Mail:
mullenmccaffrey@aol.com, Web
Site: www.mullenandmccaffrey.com
Partner: Mary Ann McCaffrey

**MYERS, MYERS & ADAMS
ADVERTISING INC**
934 N Victoria Park Rd
Fort Lauderdale, FL 33304-4478
Telephone: (954) 523-6262, FAX:
(954) 523-3517, E-Mail: pete@
mmanda.com, Web Site: www.
mmanda.com
Pres & Natl Sls Mgr: Peter Myers

MYPOINTS.COM INC
Subs. UAL
50 California St (3rd fl.)
San Francisco, CA 94111-4632
Telephone: (415) 856-0877, FAX:
(415) 615-1122, E-Mail:
memberservices@mypoints.com,
Web Site: www.mypoints.com
Co-Pres: John H. Fullmer

MYSTIC LOGISTICS

2187 New London Tpke
South Glastonbury, CT 06073
Telephone: (860) 659-1566, (800) 969-
1566, FAX: (860) 659-1420, Web
Site: www.mysticlogistics.com
Chmn: Samuel J. Campbell
Customer Svc Mgr: Danielle Hobart
Dir Postal Affairs: Richard Domagala

N FUSION GROUP

5000 Plaza on the Lake (Suite 200)
Austin, TX 78746
Telephone: (512) 716-7000, FAX:
(512) 716-7001, Web Site: www.
nfusion.com
CEO: John Ellett
Sr VP & Exec Creative Dir: Matt
Monroe
CTO & Sr VP: Bill Parkes
Conducts Business: U.S., Canada,
Worldwide
Employees: 50
Primary Market Served: Business &
Consumer
Advertising/Marketing Budget Related
to Direct Marketing: 26-50%
Direct Marketing ad budget:
$4,734,000
Direct Mail: 36%
Magazines: 64%
Founded: 2001
Gross sales or billing: $12,000,000

A results-oriented integrated marketing
agency that applies a unique methodology to developing strategy-driven programs, executed with insightful creative & supported by the most
effective marketing technologies.

NAPR - NATIONAL ASSOCIATION OF PUBLISHERS REPRESENTATIVES

10965 Cleveland Ave
Kansas City, KS 66109
Telephone: (913) 708-8344, FAX:
(913) 708-8618, E-Mail: napr@
naprassoc.com, Web Site: www.
naprassoc.com
Pres: Janice L. Mason
Primary Market Served: Business
Catalog available online
Founded: 1952

Over 300 independent ad space representatives handling consumer, trade,
business, international print & electronic media. Regional meetings.

THE DMA NAVTEQ

425 W Randolph St Fl 7
Chicago, IL 60606-1515
Telephone: (312) 780-1989
Channel Mktg Mgr: Reshelle Scheffler

NATIONAL A-1 ADVERTISING INC

101 S Eighth St
Philadelphia, PA 19106-3204
Telephone: (215) 418-2700, (800) 245-
4647, FAX: (215) 627-4026, Web
Site: www.nationala-1.com

NATIONAL MAILROOM SERVICE INC

6924 Karnes Crossing Ln
Knoxville, TN 37931-2571
Telephone: (866) 862-4141, FAX:
(800) 231-4141, E-Mail: info@
nationalmailroom.com, Web Site:
www.nationalmailroom.com
Pres: Ken Mayfield

NATIONWIDE CARD SERVICES INC

7535 Bartlett Corporate Dr (Suite A)
Memphis, TN 38133
Telephone: (901) 383-4405, Web Site:
www.nationwidecardservices.com
VP Mktg: Scott Langdon

NATIONWIDE YELLOW PAGES SERVICE

104 Mountain Ct
Hackettstown, NJ 07840-2300
Telephone: (973) 765-9600, (800) 526-
2718, FAX: (973) 765-0004, E-Mail:
info@nationwideyp.com, Web Site:
www.nationwideyp.com
Pres: Paul Morgan

THE DMA NESTLE PURINA/ CHECKMARK COMMUNICATIONS

Div. of Nestle Purina
1111 Chouteau Ave
Saint Louis, MO 63102-1025
Telephone: (314) 982-1000, FAX:
(314) 982-3580, Web Site: www.
purina.com
Database & Target Mktg Dir: Margaret
Forster
Dir: Margaret Gurgol

NEW DAY MARKETING LTD

923 Olive St Ste 2
Santa Barbara, CA 93101-1447
Telephone: (805) 965-7833, FAX:
(805) 965-1284, Web Site: www.
newdaymarketing.com
Pres: Robert Hunt

NEW VILLAGE MEDIA INC

9194 Red Branch Rd (Suite G)
Columbia, MD 21045-2005
Telephone: (443) 832-4007, E-Mail:
jskillington@newvillagemedia.com
CEO: James Skillington

NEWS NOTES LLC

2348 Pinehurst Dr Ste 1
Middleton, WI 53562-2587
Telephone: (608) 831-9600, Web Site:
www.news-notes.com
Mktg Dir: John Short

THE DMA NEXTWEB MEDIA

350 7th Ave (fl 2)
New York, NY 10001-5013
Telephone: (212) 588-1180, Web Site:
www.nextwebmedia.com
CEO: Eyal Yechezkell

THE DMA NEXUS DIRECT

2101 Parks Ave (Suite 600)
Virginia Beach, VA 23451-4135
Telephone: (757) 340-5960, (800) 965-
0577, FAX: (757) 340-5980, E-Mail:
info@nexusdirect.com, Web Site:
www.nexusdirect.com
CEO: Suzanne Cole Nowers
Pres: Robert Wilke
Primary Market Served: Business &
Consumer

NICHOLSON KOVAC INC

1513 NE 52nd St
Kansas City, MO 64118-5705
Telephone: (816) 842-8881, FAX:
(816) 842-6340, E-Mail: nk@
nicholsonkovac.com, Web Site:
www.nkhw.com
Pres: Pete Kovac
SVP Media Svcs: Sheree Johnson

NIXLE LLC

PO Box 2881
Westfield, NJ 07091-2881
Telephone: (856) 427-9000, Web Site:
www.nixle.com
Primary Market Served: Consumer

NOBLE

33 W Monroe St
Chicago, IL 60603-5300
Telephone: (312) 670-2900, FAX:
(312) 670-7420, Web Site: www.
noble.net
Pres: Andy Hopson

NORTHLICH

720 E Pete Rose Way
Cincinnati, OH 45202-3579
Telephone: (513) 421-8840, FAX:
(513) 287-1858, E-Mail: northlich@
northlich.com, Web Site: www.
northlich.com
Pres & CEO: Mark Serrianne

NORTHWEST DIRECT INC

13240 NE 20th St (Suite 18)
Bellevue, WA 98005-2022

Telephone: (425) 643-7917, Web Site:
www.nwdirectmarketing.com
CEO: Michael J. Knorre

NOSTRUM INC

401 E Ocean Blvd Ste M101
Long Beach, CA 90802-8900
Telephone: (562) 437-2200, Web Site:
www.nostruminc.com
Pres: Susan Collida
Acct Exec: Abby Schwerin
Acct Supvr: Kerry Wurzelbacher
Conducts Business: U.S.
Employees: 20
Primary Market Served: Business &
Consumer
Direct online sales
Gross sales or billing: $10,000,000

Full service advertising agency specializing in customizable web to print direct mail products.

NOVA COMMUNICATIONS INC

27 S 1st St
Geneva, IL 60134-2243
Telephone: (630) 377-1889, (800) 816-6682, FAX: (630) 377-1899, E-Mail:
sales@novacominc.com, Web Site:
www.novacominc.com
Pres: James P. Emma

NOVA DM

633 E Drinker St
Dunmore, PA 18512-2505
Telephone: (570) 342-8668
VP: John McNeff
Primary Market Served: Business &
Consumer

NOVA POWER MARKETING

4225 E Avalon Dr
Phoenix, AZ 85018-7207
Telephone: (602) 558-7540, FAX:
(602) 926-8351, E-Mail:
novamarkdm@cox.net, Web Site:
www.novamarkdm.com
Principal & Creative Dir: John Seeliger

THE NULMAN GROUP

100 Davidson Ave (Suite 202)
Somerset, NJ 08873-1312
Telephone: (908) 534-4041, (888) 440-3367, FAX: (908) 534-5023, E-Mail:
pnulman@nulmangroup.com, Web
Site: www.nulmangroup.com
CEO: Philip R. Nulman
Dir Client Svcs: Claire L. Curry

O2K1

3 W 18th St (fl 4)
New York, NY 10011-4662
Telephone: (646) 839-6254, Web Site:
www.02kl.com

Pres: Tracey Owens

OTM PARTNERS

901 N Glebe Rd (Suite 340)
Arlington, VA 22203-1854
Telephone: (800) 759-2244, Web Site:
www.otmpartners.biz
VP Opers Dir Rels Mktg: Lisa Wynn

ODELL, SIMMS & ASSOCIATES INC

7704 Leesburg Pike Ste 2
Falls Church, VA 22043-2625
Telephone: (703) 903-9797, FAX:
(703) 903-8850, E-Mail:
webmaster@odellsimms.com, Web
Site: www.odellsimms.com
Pres: John Simms
DM Mgr: Patrick Pyles

ODEN

119 S Main St (Suite 300)
Memphis, TN 38103-3677
Telephone: (901) 578-8055, FAX:
(901) 578-1911, Web Site: www.
oden.com
Principal/CEO: Bill Carkeet

OGILVY & MATHER DIRECT

Subs. of Ogilvy & Mather Inc
1100 Avenue of the Americas (Frnt 3)
New York, NY 10036-6712
Telephone: (212) 237-6000, FAX:
(212) 237-5123, Web Site: www.
ogilvy.com
Exec VP & US Media Dir: Larry Cole

THE OGILVYONE WORLDWIDE
DMA

Sub of WPP Group plc
636 11th Ave
New York, NY 10036-2005
Telephone: (212) 237-6000, Web Site:
www.ogilvy-canada.com
Chmn & CEO: Brian Fetherstonhaugh

THE OHLMANN GROUP DIRECT

Div. of Ohlmann Group
1605 N Main St
Dayton, OH 45405-4141
Telephone: (937) 278-0681, FAX:
(937) 277-1723, E-Mail: info@
ohlmanngroup.com, Web Site: www.
ohlmanngroup.com
Pres & CEO: Walter Ohlmann

OLIVER RUSSELL & ASSOCIATES

217 S 11th St
Boise, ID 83702-6902
Telephone: (208) 344-1734, FAX:
(208) 344-1211, Web Site: www.
oliverrussell.com

Founder: Russ Stoddard
Mng Dir: David Jenson
Studio Dir: Jane Nallon
Commun Mgr: Julie Robinson
Bus Devel Dir: Boyd Karren
Conducts Business: U.S.
Employees: 30
Primary Market Served: Business &
Consumer
Direct Marketing ad budget:
Direct Mail: 80%
Magazines: 5%
Online: 15%

Direct & engagement marketing.

OLSON & CO

420 N 5th St, Loring Corners
Minneapolis, MN 55401-1348
Telephone: (612) 215-9800, FAX:
(612) 215-9801, E-Mail: info@oco.
com, Web Site: www.oco.com
Pres & CEO: John Olson
Mktg Dir: Ryan Linder

THE OMNICOM MEDIA GROUP
DMA **DIRECT**

195 Broadway
New York, NY 10007-3100
Telephone: (212) 590-7012
Mng Dir: Wendy Arnon

OMNIDIRECT

1680 Michigan Ave (Suite 1016)
Miami Beach, FL 33139
Telephone: (800) 459-4034, Web Site:
www.omnidirect.tv
Founder & Pres: Alex Agurcia
VP Opers: Denira Borrero

ONE ON ONE ADVERTISING INC

584 Middletown Ave
New Haven, CT 06513-1011
Telephone: (203) 562-6259, FAX:
(203) 789-1253
Pres: Stephen Nevard

1TO1 MEDIA

Div. of Peppers & Rogers Group
1111 Summer St Fl 5
Stamford, CT 06905-5511
Telephone: (203) 642-5121, FAX:
(203) 316-5121, (203) 642-5126,
Web Site: www.1to1media.com
Co-Founder: Don Peppers
Dir Mktg: Thomas Schmazl

ONEUPWEB

13561 S West Bay Shore Dr (Suite
3000)
Traverse City, MI 49684-6292

Telephone: (231) 922-9977, (877) 568-7477, FAX: (231) 922-9966, E-Mail: info@oneupweb.com, Web Site: www.oneupweb.com
Founder/CEO: Lisa Wehr
Media Planner: Rebecca Martin

ORDENZA MARKETING GROUP INC

4370 Dominion St (fl 6)
Burnaby, BC, Canada V5G 4L7
Telephone: (604) 451-1414, Web Site: www.odenza.com
Dir Mktg: Pav Sangha
Primary Market Served: Business & Consumer

O'ROURKE HOSPITALITY MARKETING LLC

7 Prince Pl (#3)
Newburyport, MA 01950-2644
Telephone: (978) 465-5955, Web Site: www.orourkehospitality.com
CEO: Tom O'Rourke

OUR COMMUNITY PHONE BOOK

Div. of Volt
One Sentry Pkwy (Suite 1000)
Blue Bell, PA 19422
Telephone: (610) 825-7720, (877) THE-RED-1, (877) 843-7731, FAX: (610) 825-5758, E-Mail: robynfine@community-phonebook.com, Web Site: www.communitybook.com
Pres: Jerry DiPippo

OVATION MARKETING

201 Main St Ste 902
La Crosse, WI 54601-3392
Telephone: (608) 785-2460, FAX: (608) 785-2496
Pres: Ralph Heath

PCI

Subs. of Creative Packaging Solutions
5 W First St
Keyport, NJ 07735-1010
Telephone: (732) 335-3700, (888) 826-1646, FAX: (732) 264-9313, E-Mail: conil@packaging-usa.com, Web Site: www.packaging-usa.com
Pres & Mktg Dir: Coni Lefferts

PMH/CARAMANNING

34705 W Twelve Mile Rd (Suite 200)
Farmington Hills, MI 48331-3273
Telephone: (248) 488-5300, FAX: (248) 488-5363, E-Mail: marketing@pmh.com, Web Site: www.pmh.com
Pres: John Schufelt
Employees: 50
Founded: 1982
Gross sales or billing: $7,800,000

PACIFIC MEDIA EXCHANGE

1629-A 6th St
Berkeley, CA 94710-1803
Telephone: (510) 528-9181, FAX: (510) 528-3449, E-Mail: pacificmedia@comcast.net, Web Site: www.pacificmediaexchange.com
Pres: K.C. Jones

PADULO INTEGRATED

One St Clair Ave W (10th fl), Padulo Bldg
Toronto, ON, Canada M4V 1K7
Telephone: (416) 966-4000, (800) 454-5321, FAX: (416) 966-4012, E-Mail: rpadulo@padulo.ca, Web Site: www.padulo.ca
CFO & COO: Kamel Mikhael
Chmn & CEO: Richard Padulo

THE PAMPERED PET MART

6486 Haover Ct
Lisle, IL 60532-3218
Telephone: (630) 660-0056, FAX: (630) 810-1934, E-Mail: dickdixon@aol.com, Web Site: www.dixondirect.com
Pres: Dick Dixon

PAPPAS MACDONNELL INC

135 Rennell Dr
Southport, CT 06890-1450
Telephone: (203) 254-1944, FAX: (203) 256-8232, E-Mail: info@pappasmacdonnell.com, Web Site: www.pappasmacdonnell.com
Principal: Susan F. Pappas

PARADIGM PROMOTIONS LLC

561 34th Ave
San Francisco, CA 94121-2705
Telephone: (415) 387-2158, FAX: (415) 387-2185, E-Mail: brian@brianharris.com, Web Site: www.paradigmpromotions.com
Mng Dir: Brian Harris

PARISE MARKETING GROUP

Five Schuman Rd
Millwood, NY 10546
Telephone: (914) 941-7467, FAX: (914) 941-7931, Web Site: www.parise.com
VP, Client Mktg: Chip Williams

PARMELEE ASSOCIATES

PO Box 5557
Arlington, VA 22205-0057
Telephone: (703) 502-0161
Pres: James Parmelee

PASADENA ADVERTISING

51 W Dayton St Ste 100
Pasadena, CA 91105-2025
Telephone: (626) 584-0011, Web Site: www.pasadenaadvertising.com
Pres & CEO: Suzanne Marks

PEDONE

49 W 27th St Fl 6
New York, NY 10001-6936
Telephone: (212) 627-3300, FAX: (212) 627-3388, E-Mail: info@pedone.com, Web Site: www.pedonepartners.com
Pres & CEO: Michael F. Pedone

PENN GARRITANO DIRECT RESPONSE MARKETING

701 N Third St (Suite 201)
Minneapolis, MN 55401-1157
Telephone: (612) 333-3775, FAX: (612) 333-3775, Web Site: www.penngarritano.com
CEO: Steve Penn
Pres: Joe Garritano
Conducts Business: U.S., Canada
Employees: 12
Primary Market Served: Business & Consumer

Full spectrum of traditional & digital marketing.

THE PENTE CORP

250 The Esplanade
Toronto, ON, Canada M5A 1J2
Telephone: (416) 214-2014, FAX: (416) 214-1202, Web Site: www.wiredpente.com
Pres: Bob Pente

THE DMA PERISCOPE INC

921 Washington Ave S
Minneapolis, MN 55415-1257
Telephone: (612) 339-0663, (800) 339-2103, FAX: (612) 339-0600, E-Mail: bill@ps-mpls.com, Web Site: www.periscope.com
CEO: Bill Simpson
Sr Acct Exec: Sarah Husnik

PETERALEX MEDIA CORP

10130 Mallard Creek Rd (Suite 300)
Charlotte, NC 28262
Telephone: (704) 947-9082, (888) 818-3849, FAX: (704) 947-9083, E-Mail: info@peteralex.com, Web Site: www.peteralex.com
Pres & CEO: Patricia Fletcher
Conducts Business: U.S.
Primary Market Served: Business
Catalog available online
Indirect online sales
Advertising/Marketing Budget Related to Direct Marketing: 26-50%

PHILLIPS DIRECT MARKETING GROUP
11445 E Via Linda (Suite 2)
Scottsdale, AZ 85259-2554
Telephone: (480) 368-7200 X224,
FAX: (480) 368-7222, E-Mail: tina@
pdmg.tv, Web Site: www.pdldrtv.com
Pres: Tina Phillips

PIKE COMMUNICATIONS INC
100 Cummings Ctr (Suite 250E)
Beverly, MA 01915-6133
Telephone: (978) 524-8777, (800) 331-7453, FAX: (978) 524-8585, E-Mail:
info@pikecommunications.com, Web
Site: www.pikecommunications.com
Pres: Dorothy A. Pike

PILOT DIRECT
150 W Brambleton Ave
Norfolk, VA 23510-2018
Telephone: (757) 446-2874, Web Site:
www.pilotdirect.com
Sales Mgr: Sara Lovell

PINNACLE DIRECT RESPONSE
1200 Sheppard Ave E (Suite 105)
North York, ON, Canada M2K 2S5
Telephone: (416) 756-9536
Pres: Husayn Remtulla

THE DMA **PLATTFORM ADVERTISING**
15500 W 113th St (Suite 200)
Lenexa, KS 66219-5106
Telephone: (913) 254-6000, (800) 279-9988, FAX: (913) 538-5078, E-Mail:
info@plattformad.com, Web Site:
www.plattformad.com
Pres: Lyle Kraft
CEO: Michael Platt
VP, Sls: Sean Pittman
Chief Growth Officer: Brad Gibbs
Employees: 67
Primary Market Served: Business
Catalog available online
Founded: 1985

Full service agency providing design,
printing, direct mail, telemarketing &
fulfillment services.

THE DMA **PLUSMEDIA LLC**
100 Mill Plain Rd (Fl 4)
Danbury, CT 06811-5189
Telephone: (203) 748-6500, FAX:
(203) 748-6600, E-Mail: contact@
plusme.com, Web Site: www.plusme.
com
Pres: Sherry Scapperotti
Mktg Commun Specialist: Jessica
Carnrick
Conducts Business: U.S., Canada
Employees: 25

Primary Market Served: Business
Indirect online sales
Advertising/Marketing Budget Related
to Direct Marketing: 76-100%
Founded: 1998
Gross sales or billing: $50,000,000

Media brokerage firm specializing in
direct response ad campaigns in print
& insert media.

PLUZYNSKI & ASSOCIATES INC
6123 190th St, PMB 515
Fresh Meadows, NY 11365-2720
Telephone: (212) 645-1414, FAX:
(212) 645-2013, E-Mail: ed@
pluzynski.com, Web Site: www.
pluzynski.com
CEO: Ed Pluzynski

THE DMA **POINT TO POINT MARKETING INC**
11562 N County Rd 17
Fort Collins, CO 80524-8786
Telephone: (970) 472-0131, Web Site:
www.ptpmarketing.com
COO: Mark Heiden

PONTIS GROUP
18530 Mack Ave (#369)
Grosse Pointe, MI 48236-3254
Telephone: (614) 764-1274, FAX:
(614) 210-0598, E-Mail:
cbirchfield@pontisgroup.com, Web
Site: www.pontisgroup.com
Chmn & CEO: H Doug Jones
VP Mktg & Client Svcs: Cyndy Birch-field

THE DMA **POP LABS INC**
7850 Parkwood Circle Dr (Suite B-3)
Houston, TX 77036-6761
Telephone: (713) 243-4500, Web Site:
www.poplabs.com
Pres: Gene McCubbin
Primary Market Served: Business &
Consumer

POPULAR FRONT INTERACTIVE COMMUNICATIONS
555 First Ave NE
Minneapolis, MN 55413-2209
Telephone: (612) 362-0900, FAX:
(612) 362-0999, E-Mail: guestlist@
popularfront.com, Web Site: www.
popularfront.com
Pres, Mng Dir, Media Dir & New Bus
Contact: Laurence Bricker
VP Mktg: Sarah Bratnober

THE DMA **POWERDIRECT**
4700 Von Karman Ave (Suite 100)
Newport Beach, CA 92660-2194
Telephone: (949) 253-3440, Web Site:
www.powerdirect.net
CEO: William Borneman

PRACTICE BUILDERS
Subs. of Ascend Media Agency, LLC
1 Technology Dr Ste I829
Irvine, CA 92618-5320
Telephone: (714) 751-7960, (800) 679-1262, FAX: (714) 751-7801, E-Mail:
info@practicebuilders.com, Web
Site: www.practicebuilders.com
Member: Curtis Pickelle

PRECISION ARTS ADVERTISING INC
57 Fitchburg Rd
Ashburnham, MA 01430-1409
Telephone: (978) 855-7648, E-Mail:
sales@precisionarts.com, Web Site:
www.precisionarts.com
Pres & Owner: Terri Adams
Founded: 1985

Provides professional advertising ser-vices to small businesses, industrial
manufacturers & distributors.

THE DMA **PREMIER WORLD MARKETING**
3191 Coral Way (PH 202)
Miami, FL 33145
Telephone: (305) 445-1077, Web Site:
www.karismahotels.com
Primary Market Served: Business &
Consumer

PRESENTATION PACKAGING
870 Louisiana Ave S
Minneapolis, MN 55426
Telephone: (763) 540-9544, (800) 818-2698, FAX: (763) 540-9522, Web
Site: www.presentationpackaging.
com
CFO: David Lenzen

PRICE WEBER MARKETING COMMUNICATIONS INC
10701 Shelbyville Rd
Louisville, KY 40243-1241
Telephone: (502) 499-9220, FAX:
(502) 491-5593, Web Site: www.
priceweber.com
Pres & CEO: Shanna Columbus

PRINCETON MARKETECH
2 Alice Rd
Princeton Junction, NJ 08550-3027

Telephone: (609) 936-0021, FAX:
(609) 936-0015, E-Mail: bzyontz@
princetonmarketech.com, Web Site:
www.princetonmarketech.com
Pres: Robert Zyontz

PRINCETON PARTNERS INC
205 Rockingham Row
Princeton, NJ 08540-5759
Telephone: (609) 452-8500, FAX:
(609) 452-7212, E-Mail: mlandis@
princetonpartners.com, Web Site:
www.princetonpartners.com
Pres & CEO: Thomas Sullivan

PRO MEDIA-STREFF MARKETING GROUP
W127N8690 Westbrook Crossing
Menomonee Falls, WI 53051-3342
Telephone: (262) 532-2600, (800) 328-
0439, FAX: (800) 951-5955, E-Mail:
info@promediaus.com, Web Site:
www.promediaus.com
Principal: Mark Roethle
Employees: 30

THE DMA PROGRESSIVE DIRECT MARKETING
Div. of HSIRI Co
5800 Transit Rd
Depew, NY 14043-2820
Telephone: (716) 681-6848, (800) 344-
7593, FAX: (716) 681-9173, Web
Site: www.pdmny.com
Exec VP: Thomas Occhiat

THE DMA PROGRESSIVE IMPRESSIONS INTERNATIONAL
1 Hardman Dr
Bloomington, IL 61701-6934
Telephone: (309) 664-0444, Web Site:
www.whateverittakes.com
Pres: Jamie Huff

PROMOWRITING
13 Frenchtown Rd
Trumbull, CT 06611-4729
Telephone: (203) 371-0654, E-Mail:
shira@promowriting.com, Web Site:
www.promowriting.com
Copywriter/Creative Consultant: Shira
Linden

PROPCO PROMOTIONAL MARKETING
7360 N Lincoln Ave (Suite 100)
Lincolnwood, IL 60712-1705
Telephone: (773) 463-9193, FAX:
(773) 463-6673, E-Mail: propco@
propco.com, Web Site: www.propco.
com
Owner, Pres: Dennis Propp

PUBLICIS
7300 Lonestar Dr (Suite C 200)
Plano, TX 75024
Telephone: (972) 628-7500, FAX:
(972) 628-7671, Web Site: www.
publicis-usa.com
Mktg Dir: Diane Colburn

PUBLICITY INC
39 S Main St
Mansfield, MA 02048-2527
Telephone: (617) 367-3555, FAX:
(617) 367-3557
Chmn & CEO: Al Longo

QUAXAR
25 SE 2nd Ave (Suite 305), The Ingraham Bldg
Miami, FL 33131-1509
Telephone: (305) 350-1919, Web Site:
www.quaxar.com

QUANTUM GROUP
6511 Oakton St
Morton Grove, IL 60053-2728
Telephone: (847) 967-3600, Web Site:
www.quantumgroup.com
VP Sales: Jay Garstecki

THE DMA QUATTRO DIRECT LLC
1175 Lancaster Ave Ste 200
Berwyn, PA 19312-1297
Telephone: (610) 993-0070, Web Site:
www.quattrodirect.com
Mng Dir: Thomas McNamara

QUIGLEY SIMPSON
11601 Wilshire Blvd
Los Angeles, CA 90025-0509
Telephone: (310) 996-5820, Web Site:
www.quigleysimpson.com
CEO: Gerald Bagg

THE DMA R2C GROUP
207 NW Park Ave
Portland, OR 97209-3316
Telephone: (503) 222-0025, Web Site:
www.r2cgroup.com
Dir Corp Mktg: Jake Mora

RFM BROADCASTING
70 Devonshire Rd
New Rochelle, NY 10804
Telephone: (914) 633-0725, FAX:
(914) 206-4144, E-Mail: andrew@
rfmitv.com
Pres: Andrew Morrison

THE DMA RPM DIRECT LLC
24 Arnett Ave (Suite 100)
Lambertville, NJ 08530-1500
Telephone: (609) 566-7150, Web Site:
www.r4pm.com

VP: Rita Huff

RTC RELATIONSHIP MARKETING
1055 Thomas Jefferson St NW (Suite
500)
Washington, DC 20007-5256
Telephone: (202) 625-2111, FAX:
(202) 424-7900, Web Site: www.
rtcrm.com
CEO: Barry Kessel

THE DMA RADIO DIRECT RESPONSE
1400 N Providence Rd (Suite 4000)
Media, PA 19063-2061
Telephone: (610) 892-7300, FAX:
(610) 892-1899, E-Mail: info@
radiodirect.com, Web Site: www.
radiodirect.com
Pres & CEO: Mark Lipsky

THE DMA RAPP COLLINS WORLDWIDE
Subs. of Omnicom
437 Madison Ave (4th fl)
New York, NY 10022-7043
Telephone: (212) 817-6800, FAX:
(212) 686-7047, Web Site: www.
rappcollins.com
Pres: Jim Lyons
Chief Client Opers: Anne Marie
Schiller

HOWARD RAPP ENTERPRISES INC
88 Pine St (Suite 2610)
New York, NY 10005-1831
Telephone: (212) 247-6646, FAX:
(212) 247-6645, E-Mail:
hrapp3678@aol.com
Pres: Howard Rapp

RASTAR
2305 S 1070 W
Salt Lake City, UT 84119-1564
Telephone: (801) 973-6720, Web Site:
www.rastek.com
Pres: Grant Fletcher

THE DMA RAUXA DIRECT
275A McCormick Ave
Costa Mesa, CA 92626
Telephone: (714) 427-1271, Web Site:
www.rauxa.com
Pres: Johanna Bracken
COO: Robin Fish

RAWLE-MURDY ASSOCIATES INC
Two Beaufain St
Charleston, SC 29401-1932

Telephone: (843) 577-7327, FAX: (843) 722-3960, E-Mail: contact@ rawlemurdy.com, Web Site: www. rawle-murdy.com
Chmn: David L. Rawle

RAZOR TRANSACTION BUILDING EXPERTS
15851 Dallas Pkwy (Suite 725)
Addison, TX 75001-3360
Telephone: (972) 663-1100, Web Site: www.razordriven.com
Co-Pres & Mng Principal: Tom Cole

RED EDGE LABS LLC
26985 Aliso Creek Rd (Suite B330)
Aliso Viejo, CA 92656
Telephone: (800) 931-1055, Web Site: www.rededgelabs.com
Pres & CEO: Craig Kurtz

THE DMA RED ROCK MARKETING GROUP LLC
1930 Village center Cr (Suite 3-516)
Las Vegas, NV 89134-6299
Telephone: (702) 944-9604, FAX: (702) 838-9673, E-Mail: info@ redrockmarketing.net, Web Site: www.redrockmarketing.net
Pres: Ted Foth

REDIRECT RELATIONSHIP MARKETING
2825 E Cottonwood Pkwy (Suite 310)
Salt Lake City, UT 84121-7282
Telephone: (801) 453-0100, Web Site: www.redirectnow.com
Pres: Wendy Jackson

RESEARCH AND MANAGEMENT CORPORATION/WSI
5580 Explorer Dr (Suite 600)
Mississauga, ON, Canada L4W 4Y1
Telephone: (888) 678-7588
Primary Market Served: Business

THE DMA RESPONSE AGENCY INC
936 Granite Peak Dr (Suite 1100)
Sandy, UT 84094
Telephone: (801) 352-9100, Web Site: www.responseagency.com
Chmn: Steve Cuno

THE DMA RESPONSE DYNAMICS INC
2070 Chain Bridge Rd (Suite 520)
Vienna, VA 22182-2569
Telephone: (703) 442-7595, FAX: (703) 790-8564
Pres: Ronald Kanfer

THE DMA RESPONSE INNOVATIONS INC
256 Adelaide St E
Toronto, ON, Canada M5A 1N1
Telephone: (416) 368-6217
Pres: Stephen Forchon

RESPONSE MARKETING INC
6900 Shady Oak Rd
Eden Prairie, MN 55344-3403
Telephone: (952) 949-4913
CEO: Judith J. Swenson

THE DMA RESPONSE MINE INTERACTIVE
3390 Peachtree Rd NE (Suite 800)
Atlanta, GA 30326-2840
Telephone: (404) 233-0370, Web Site: www.responsemine.com
*Mktg Coord: Lianne Lopez-Cepero

RESPONSE RESOURCES
Subs. of Sunbelt Marketing Group
68 Belle Helene Dr
Destrehan, LA 70047
Telephone: (985) 725-0162, FAX: (504) 764-2839
Pres: Ray Lewis

THE RESPONSE SHOP INC
7486 La Jolla Blvd (#164)
La Jolla, CA 92037
Telephone: (858) 456-6180, FAX: (858) 456-5090, E-Mail: marla@ responseshop.com, Web Site: www. responseshop.com
Pres: Marla Hoskins
Conducts Business: U.S.
Employees: 8
Primary Market Served: Business & Consumer
Advertising/Marketing Budget Related to Direct Marketing: 76-100%
Founded: 1997
Gross sales or billing: $2,600,000

Full-service agency specializing in direct response TV and radio.

RESULTS ADVERTISING INC
777 Terrace Ave Ste 506
Hasbrouck Heights, NJ 07604-3114
Telephone: (201) 288-7888, FAX: (201) 288-5112, E-Mail: info@ resultsinc.com, Web Site: www. resultsinc.com
Pres: David I. Green

BP RICE & CO
1205 E Grand Ave
El Segundo, CA 90245-4220
Telephone: (562) 926-5861, FAX: (562) 404-7130, E-Mail: info@ bprco.com, Web Site: www.bprco. com

Pres: B.P. Rice
Admin: Lorraine Hastings

RICHARD RICELLI INC
23 Charlotte St
Charleston, SC 29403
Telephone: (843) 727-0183, FAX: (843) 727-0184, E-Mail: richard@ ricelli.com, Web Site: www.ricelli. com
Pres: Richard Riccelli

RICHARDS COMMUNICATIONS
3201 Enterprise Pkwy (Suite 400)
Beachwood, OH 44122
Telephone: (216) 514-7800, FAX: (216) 514-7801, E-Mail: jrichards@ richardsgo.com, Web Site: www. richardsgo.com
Pres & CEO: John Richards
Founded: 1981

Full service marketing communications agency.

RICHARDS PARTNERS
Div. of Richards Group
8750 N Central Expwy (Suite 1100)
Dallas, TX 75231-4104
Telephone: (214) 891-5700, FAX: (214) 891-3515, E-Mail: ruth_fitzgibbons@richards.com, Web Site: www.richardspartners.com
Principal: Ruth Fitzgibbons
Gross sales or billing: $5,650,000

RICHARTZ FLISS CLARK & POPE INC
1 Minetta Ln
New York, NY 10012-1206
Telephone: (212) 286-9339, FAX: (212) 682-4748, E-Mail: pope@rfcp. com
Partner: Wendell Pope

RIGHTMINDS
1802 Bayberry Ct Ste 400
Richmond, VA 23226-3773
Telephone: (804) 755-7000, FAX: (804) 755-7200, Web Site: www. rightminds.com
Pres: Chris Thurston

RISDALL LINNIHAN ADVERTISING
550 Main St
New Brighton, MN 55112-3271
Telephone: (651) 286-6700, (888) RIS-DALL, (888) 747-3255, FAX: (651) 631-2561, E-Mail: info@risdall.com, Web Site: www.risdall.com
Chmn: John Risdall

ROBERTS COMMUNICATIONS INC
64 Commercial St
Rochester, NY 14614
Telephone: (716) 325-6000, FAX:
(716) 325-6001, Web Site: www.
robertscomm.com
CEO: Paul H. Hudson

ROBINSON & MAITES INC
35 E Wacker Dr (Suite 3500)
Chicago, IL 60601
Telephone: (312) 372-9333, FAX:
(312) 372-0682, E-Mail: amaites@
robinsonmaites.com, Web Site: www.
robinsonmaites.com
Pres: Alan Maites

ROBINSON DIRECT
6945 Wards Ln
Center Valley, PA 18034
Telephone: (610) 838-5426, FAX:
(610) 838-5589
Pres: Carole Robinson

ROCKETT COMMUNICATIONS INC
11 Juniper Ridge Rd (Suite 1100)
Danvers, MA 01923-1741
Telephone: (978) 774-1780, E-Mail:
rockett.comm@verizon.net
Pres: Brian Rockett

ROLA-KIMMERLING ASSOCIATES
501 Fifth Ave (3rd fl)
New York, NY 10017-7805
Telephone: (646) 367-4815, FAX:
(646) 367-4901, E-Mail: p_kimhov@
rkadv.com, Web Site: www.rkadv.
com
Pres: Fernando E. Rola
Dir: Pamela Kimmerling Hoveling

JOHN ROMERO DIRECT MARKETING
10625 Woodhaven Ridge Rd
Parker, CO 80134-5017
Telephone: (303) 805-2507, FAX:
(303) 805-2509, E-Mail:
romeromkt@aol.com, Web Site:
www.romeromarketing.com
Pres: John Romero
Founded: 1985

Casino direct mail & direct response
advertising.

THE DMA **RON PERRELLA DRS (DR SPECIALISTS)**
29632 Seriana
Laguna Niguel, CA 92677-7967

Telephone: (949) 495-7661, FAX:
(949) 495-7660, E-Mail: rperrdrs@
aol.com, Web Site: www.
ronperrelladrs.com
Pres: Ronald Perrella
Conducts Business: U.S.
Employees: 3
Primary Market Served: Business &
Consumer
Advertising/Marketing Budget Related
to Direct Marketing: 76-100%
Direct Marketing ad budget:
Direct Mail: 55%
Magazines: 10%
Newspapers: 10%
TV/Radio: 20%
Telephone: 5%
Founded: 1994

Direct response advertising & marketing consultancy.

THE DMA **ROSEN INC**
1631 NE Broadway (Suite 615)
Portland, OR 97232-1425
Telephone: (503) 224-9811, E-Mail:
info@rgrosen.com, Web Site: www.
rgrosen.com
Pres & CEO: Richard Rosen
Conducts Business: U.S.
Employees: 15
Primary Market Served: Business &
Consumer
Advertising/Marketing Budget Related
to Direct Marketing: 26-50%
Founded: 1990

ROSKA DIRECT ADVERTISING
211B Progress Dr
Montgomeryville, PA 18936-9618
Telephone: (215) 699-9200, FAX:
(215) 699-9240, E-Mail: jr@
roskadirect.com, Web Site: www.
RoskaDirect.com
CEO: Jon Roska
Pres: Jay Bolling

ROTH ADVERTISING INC
PO Box 96
Sea Cliff, NY 11579-0096
Telephone: (516) 674-8603, FAX:
(516) 674-8606, E-Mail: charles@
rothadvertising.com, Web Site: www.
rothadvertising.com
Pres: Daniel J. Roth
Founder & Pres: Charles A. Roth

RUSS REID CO
Subs. of Omnicom
2 N Lake Ave (Suite 600)
Pasadena, CA 91101-1868
Telephone: (626) 449-6100, FAX:
(626) 449-6190, E-Mail: info@
russreid.com, Web Site: www.
russreid.com

CFO & SVP: Don Haggstrom

RUSSO & KELLY
69 Oak Cir
Colchester, VT 05446
Telephone: (802) 655-7007, FAX:
(802) 655-4994, E-Mail: info@
russandkelly.com
Co-Founder: Tim Russo

RYAN IDIRECT
50 Danbury Rd
Wilton, CT 06897-4406
Telephone: (203) 210-3000, FAX:
(203) 210-7926, Web Site: www.
ryanpartnership.com
CEO: Dave Ryan
Pres: John Kuendig

S&H SOLUTIONS
1625 S Congress Ave Ste 200
Delray Beach, FL 33445-6304
Telephone: (561) 454-7600, FAX:
(561) 265-2493, E-Mail:
customerservice@shsolutions.com,
Web Site: www.shsolutions.com
Pres & CEO: Ron Pedersen

SBC ADVERTISING
333 W Nationwide Blvd
Columbus, OH 43215-2311
Telephone: (614) 891-7070, FAX:
(614) 891-3664, E-Mail: info@
sbcadv.com, Web Site: www.sbcadv.
com
Pres: David M. Dennis

SCP RAPP COLLINS MEDIA
437 Madison Ave (3rd fl)
New York, NY 10022
Telephone: (212) 817-6800, Web Site:
www.rappcollins.com
Pres: Thomas Benelli

SHR PERCEPTUAL MANAGEMENT
2575 E Camelback Rd Ste 450
Phoenix, AZ 85016-9288
Telephone: (480) 483-3700, FAX:
(480) 483-9675, E-Mail: info@
shrbranding.com, Web Site: www.
shrbranding.com
Principal: Will Rodgers

THE DMA **SKM GROUP**
6350 Transit Rd Ste 3
Depew, NY 14043-1039
Telephone: (716) 989-3200, FAX:
(716) 989-3220, E-Mail: info@
skmgroup.com, Web Site: www.
skmgroup.com
Pres & CEO: Susan Meany
Sr VP & Exec Creative Dir: Mike
Mathis

SMG DIRECT MARKET
Subs. of Saatchi & Saatchi Advertising
3000 Lakeside Dr (Suite 305S)
Bannockburn, IL 60015-1230
Telephone: (585) 249-6100, FAX:
   (585) 249-6309
Info Coord: Kate Savoca

**ST&P MARKETING
COMMUNICATIONS INC**
320 Springside Dr
Fairlawn, OH 44333
Telephone: (330) 668-1932, FAX:
   (330) 668-2078, Web Site: www.
   stpinc.com
Pres & CEO: Rick Kenney

SWB & R
3865 Adler Pl
Bethlehem, PA 18017
Telephone: (610) 866-0611, FAX:
   (610) 866-8650, Web Site: www.
   swb.com
Partner & CEO: Ernie Steigler

**SAFIAN COMMUNICATIONS
SERVICES INC**
112 Kaiser Ln
Longwood, FL 32750-4100
Telephone: (407) 644-6996, E-Mail:
   ssafian@earthlink.net
Pres & Creative Dir: Shelley Safian

THE DMA SAGE COMMUNICATIONS
428 Main St
Hudson, MA 01749-1851
Telephone: (978) 567-8888, Web Site:
   www.sagecommunications.com
Partner: Josef Kottler
Partner: Anne Kottler
Creative Dir: Peter Einstein
Designer: Jen Winston
Conducts Business: U.S.
Employees: 5
Primary Market Served: Business &
   Consumer
Founded: 1998

Ad agency specializing in direct mail
and circulation promotions.

SAINT GREGORY GROUP
4000 Executive Park Dr (#200)
Cincinnati, OH 45241-4007
Telephone: (513) 769-8440, FAX:
   (513) 769-1640, E-Mail: pmartin@
   stgregory.com, Web Site: www.
   stgregory.com
Pres: Patrick C. Martin

**THE SALES AND
MARKETING INSTITUTE**
8255 E Raintree Dr (Suite 200)
Scottsdale, AZ 85260-2684

Telephone: (480) 473-5777, (888) 714-
   5544, FAX: (623) 979-8843, Web
   Site: www.b2bmarketing.com
Pres: John M. Coe

**DAVID SAMS INDUSTRIES
INC/TV FIRST**
Sams Communications
28720 Roadside Dr (Suite 198)
Agoura Hills, CA 91301
Telephone: (818) 707-7022, FAX:
   (818) 707-8130, E-Mail:
   customerservice@samsdirect.com,
   Web Site: www.tvfirst.com
COO: Renee Kenneth

**THE DMA SAN ANTONIO EXPRESS-
NEWS**
PO Box 2171
San Antonio, TX 78297-2171
Telephone: (210) 250-2601, Web Site:
   www.express-news.net
Precision Mktg Mgr: Johnny Flores

**THE DMA SANDY GOLDSHEIN
ASSOCIATES INC**
38 W 21st St (#8th)
New York, NY 10010-6906
Telephone: (212) 366-5105, Web Site:
   www.sgany.com
Pres: Sandy Goldshein

SANNA MATTSON MACLEOD
aka SMM
811 W Jericho Tpke
Smithtown, NY 11787
Telephone: (631) 265-5160, FAX:
   (631) 265-5185, E-Mail: info@
   smmadagency.com, Web Site: www.
   smmadagency.com
Pres: Charles MacLeod

SAWTOOTH GROUP
100 Woodbridge Ctr Dr (Suite 102)
Woodbridge, NJ 07095-1162
Telephone: (732) 636-6600, FAX:
   (732) 602-4212, Web Site: www.
   sawtoothgroup.com
Chmn: Bill Schmermund

THE DMA THE SCAN GROUP
W222 N625 Cheaney Dr
Waukesha, WI 53186
Telephone: (262) 521-1365, Web Site:
   www.scangroup.net
Mktg Creative Dir: Kathy Reading

SCHAWK
1695 S River Rd
Des Plaines, IL 60018
Telephone: (847) 827-9494, FAX:
   (847) 827-1264, Web Site: www.
   schawk.com

Bus Devel & Mktg Dir: Paula J. Jeske

THE SCHOLL GROUP
316 Highland Ln
Bryn Mawr, PA 19010-3742
Telephone: (610) 527-7310, FAX:
   (610) 527-7323, E-Mail:
   schman1034@aol.com
Pres: Richard J. Scholl

**SCHOOL MARKET
RESEARCH INSTITUTE INC**
1721 Saybrook Rd
Haddam, CT 06438-1324
Telephone: (860) 345-8183, (800) 838-
   3444, FAX: (860) 345-3985, E-Mail:
   info@smriinc.com, Web Site: www.
   smriinc.com
Pres: Bob Stimolo

**SCHRAMM & ASSOCIATES
INC**
1250 24th St NW (Suite 300)
Washington, DC 20037
Telephone: (202) 466-0555, FAX:
   (202) 466-0541, E-Mail: schramm@
   schrammadvertising.com, Web Site:
   www.schrammadvertising.com
Pres: Joseph F. Schramm

**SCIENTIFIC MARKETING
SERVICES INC**
145 E Weymouth Rd
Landisville, NJ 08326
Telephone: (856) 697-1257, FAX:
   (856) 697-9639, E-Mail: info@
   smsmktg.com, Web Site: www.
   smsmktg.com
Pres: Robert W. Norton
Mktg Consultant: David Zappariello

In-house capabilities include web design and hosting, advertising, mailing
fulfillment, copywriting, photography,
branding. publicity, video production,
and graphic design. Popular services
include e-mail blasting, trade show
design/graphics, brochures and catalog
production, public relations, and search
engine optimization.

SEASIDE PUBLICATIONS
dba Homes & Land Magazine
201 Marina Dr
Saint Simons Island, GA 31522
Telephone: (912) 634-9596, Web Site:
   www.southeastcoastalgeorgia.com

SELLING SOLUTIONS INC
3525 Piedmont Rd NE Bldg 5-515
Atlanta, GA 30305-1586

Telephone: (404) 261-4966, FAX: (404) 264-1767, E-Mail: information@selsol.com, Web Site: www.selsol.com
Pres & CEO: William Paullin
Pres Creative: James Paullin

SENDTEC INC
877 Executive Center Dr W (Suite 300)
Saint Petersburg, FL 33702
Telephone: (727) 576-6630, FAX: (727) 576-4864, Web Site: www.sendtec.com
CEO: Paul Soltoff
Conducts Business: U.S.
Employees: 40
Primary Market Served: Business
Advertising/Marketing Budget Related to Direct Marketing: 76-100%
Founded: 1996

DRTV and digital creative production, media planning/buying and tracking technology.

SEROKA & ASSOCIATES INC
N17 W24 222 Riverwood Dr
Waukesha, WI 53188-1133
Telephone: (262) 523-3740, FAX: (262) 523-3760, E-Mail: information@seroka.com, Web Site: www.seroka.com
Pres & CEO: Patrick H. Seroka

SHAVER DIRECT INC
912 E Annette Dr
Phoenix, AZ 85022-1100
Web Site: www.dickshaver.com

TOM SHEEHAN ADVERTISING
645 Penn St (Suite 301)
Reading, PA 19601-3527
Telephone: (610) 478-8448, FAX: (610) 478-8449, E-Mail: info@tomsheehan.com, Web Site: www.tomsheehan.com
Pres: Thomas F. Sheehan Jr.

SHERMAN & ASSOCIATES INC
333 Harmon NW
Warren, OH 44483
Telephone: (330) 399-4500, FAX: (330) 399-6747, E-Mail: info@shermanexperience.com, Web Site: www.shermanexperience.com
Pres: Jonathan Sherman

GLORIA SHURN CREATIVE SERVICES
1422 N Mohawk St
Chicago, IL 60610

Telephone: (312) 337-0032, FAX: (312) 337-3958
Mng Dir: Gloria J. Shurn

THE SIGNATURE AGENCY
4601 Six Forks Rd (Suite 103)
Raleigh, NC 27609-2572
Telephone: (919) 878-8989, (800) 870-8700, FAX: (919) 878-3939, E-Mail: info@signatureagency.com, Web Site: www.signatureagency.com
Pres: Sidney Reynolds
VP: Anne Shelton
Intl Commun Mgr: Elizabeth Willison
Employees: 16
Advertising/Marketing Budget Related to Direct Marketing: 0-25%
Direct Marketing ad budget: $100,000
Direct Mail: 25%
Magazines: 25%
Newspapers: 25%
TV/Radio: 25%
Founded: 1987
Gross sales or billing: $3,000,000

Direct response advertising, public relations & digital marketing agency specializing in health & beauty & life sciences.

THE DMA SILVER MARKETING INC
7910 Woodmont Ave (Suite 914)
Bethesda, MD 20814-7028
Telephone: (301) 951-3505, FAX: (301) 652-3691, E-Mail: psilver@silvermktg.com, Web Site: www.silvermarketing.com
Pres: Patricia Silver

ROBERT SILVERMAN DIRECT MARKETING
Div. of Consolidated Graphics Group Inc
1614 E 40th St
Cleveland, OH 44103
Telephone: (216) 881-9191, (888) 884-9191, FAX: (216) 881-3442, Web Site: www.cgginc.com
Oper Mgr: Matt Revel

SILVERSTONE, ADKINS & BREIT INC
35 Corporate Dr Ste 1090
Trumbull, CT 06611-1355
Telephone: (203) 375-2887, FAX: (203) 386-1203, E-Mail: info@sabinc.com, Web Site: www.sabinc.com
Pres & Creative Dir: Bruce T. Silverstone

SIMONS-MICHELSON-ZIEVE INC (SMZ)
900 Wilshire Dr (Suite 102)
Troy, MI 48084

Telephone: (248) 362-4242, FAX: (248) 362-2014, Web Site: www.smz.com
Chmn: James A. Michelson

SINISH MARKETING COMMUNICATIONS
650 Hilltop Dr (Suite B)
Stratford, CT 06614-2414
Telephone: (203) 375-1919, E-Mail: jon@sinishmarketing.com, Web Site: www.sinishmarketing.com
Pres: Jon Sinish

SIQUIS LTD
1340 Smith Ave (Suite 300)
Baltimore, MD 21209-3731
Telephone: (410) 323-4800, FAX: (410) 323-4113, Web Site: www.siquis.com
Dir: David Melnick

SKAR ADVERTISING
111 S 108th Ave
Omaha, NE 68154
Telephone: (402) 330-0110, FAX: (402) 330-8791, E-Mail: skar@skar.com, Web Site: www.skar.com
Pres: Greg Ahrens

SMART MARKETING
aka Levine-Martin Inc
23 Highland Blvd
Dix Hills, NY 11746
Telephone: (631) 254-5259, FAX: (631) 254-4814, E-Mail: info@smartmarket.com, Web Site: www.smartmarket.com
Pres: Bruce Levine

BRODY SMYTHE DIRECT INC
8665 Wilshire Blvd (#301)
Beverly Hills, CA 90211
Telephone: (310) 360-0887, FAX: (310) 360-1078, E-Mail: rsollish@brodysmythe.com, Web Site: www.brodysmythe.com
Pres & CEO: Rochelle Sollish
Conducts Business: U.S.
Employees: 12
Founded: 1996

Direct response mail & advertising strategies and tactics.

THE SNYDER AGENCY
2918 Plantation Wood Ln
Missouri City, TX 77459
Telephone: (281) 437-9200, FAX: (832) 460-3022, E-Mail: info@snyderagency.com, Web Site: www.snyderagency.com
CEO: Philip R. Snyder

SOCIAL REALITY
102 La Patera Dr
Camarillo, CA 93010-7457
Telephone: (415) 744-1509, Web Site:
  www.socialreality.com

SOURCE COMMUNICATIONS
433 Hackensack Ave
Hackensack, NJ 07601
Telephone: (201) 343-5222
Pres & Partner: Larry Ronstein
Exec VP & Partner: Barry Bluestein
Exec VP & Creative Dir: Dennis Koye
CMO: Marcia Wasser
Conducts Business: U.S., Canada
Employees: 50
Primary Market Served: Business &
  Consumer
Advertising/Marketing Budget Related
  to Direct Marketing: 0-25%
Founded: 1983

Full service ad agency.

**THE
DMA SOURCE MARKETING**
Subs. of Maxxcom
761 Main Ave
Norwalk, CT 06851-1080
Telephone: (203) 222-2741, FAX:
  (203) 291-4010, E-Mail: bardes@
  source-marketing.com, Web Site:
  www.source-marketing.com
Pres: Howard Steinberg
Mng Partner: Rich Feldman

SPECIFIC MEDIA INC
Four Park Plaza (Suite 1900)
Irvine, CA 92614
E-Mail: info@specificmedia.com, Web
  Site: www.specificmedia.com
VP & Bus Devel: Tom Hernandez
Employees: 50
Primary Market Served: Business
Direct online sales
Direct Marketing ad budget:
Online: 100%
Founded: 1999

Online marketing services company
reaching audiences across premium site
advertising network through IAB standard ad units. Multiple targeting selects available.

THE SPECTOR AGENCY
4600 Dietz Way (Suite 100)
Fair Oaks, CA 95628
Telephone: (916) 966-1605, E-Mail:
  spector@cwnet.com
Pres: Paul Spector

**SPENCER ZAHN &
  ASSOCIATES**
2015 Sansom St
Philadelphia, PA 19103-4416

Telephone: (215) 564-5979, FAX:
  (215) 564-6205
Pres: Spencer Zahn
Employees: 5
Founded: 1970

SPERBER DIRECT INC
201 W 72nd St Apt 9A
New York, NY 10023-2766
Telephone: (212) 459-0403, FAX:
  (212) 459-0249, E-Mail: miless@
  bway.net
Pres: Miles Sperber

SPIRIT INCENTIVES
2455 E Sunrise Blvd Ste 150
Fort Lauderdale, FL 33304-3129
Telephone: (800) 860-5880, Web Site:
  www.spirit-incentives.com
Mktg Dir: Debbie Conroy

**SPIZEL MARKETING/
  ADVERTISING/PUBLIC
  RELATIONS**
2610 Torrey Pines Rd (#C31)
La Jolla, CA 92037
Telephone: (858) 455-1932, E-Mail:
  hootspa@aol.com
Pres: Edgar S. Spizel

SPOT BEHAVIOR LLC
1121 S Military Trail (#220)
Deerfield Beach, FL 33442-7604
Telephone: (888) 767-7542, Web Site:
  www.spotbehavior.com

SPRING O'BRIEN & CO
30 W 26th St Fl 4L
New York, NY 10010-2090
Telephone: (212) 620-7100, FAX:
  (212) 620-7166, Web Site: www.
  spring-obrien.com
Pres: Christopher Spring

THE STANFORD GROUP
70 W 40th St Fl 8
New York, NY 10018-2623
Telephone: (212) 333-5514, FAX:
  (212) 581-4202, E-Mail: info@
  stanfordgroupinc.com, Web Site:
  www.standfordgroupinc.com
Pres: Sheila Stanford

**STAPLES MARKETING
  COMMUNICATIONS**
N28W23050 Roundy Dr Ste 101
Pewaukee, WI 53072-4095
Telephone: (262) 650-9900, (800) 867-
  1890, FAX: (262) 650-3160, Web
  Site: www.staplesmarketing.com
Principal: Jim Staples

STARBIRD CREATIVE
PO Box 1722
Sebastopol, CA 95473-1722
Telephone: (707) 778-7277, E-Mail:
  info@starbirdcreative.com, Web Site:
  www.starbirdcreative.com
Owner: Susan Starbird

**THE
DMA STEEL MEDIA**
350 5th Ave (fl 59)
New York, NY 10118-5999
Telephone: (212) 920-9599, Web Site:
  www.steelmediainc.com
Pres: Richard Steel

STEIN ROGAN & PARTNERS
Div. of True North Communications
432 Park Ave S Fl 16
New York, NY 10016-8013
Telephone: (212) 213-1112, FAX:
  (212) 779-7305, E-Mail: tstein@
  steinrogan.com, Web Site: www.
  steinrogan.com
Pres & CEO: Thomas Stein

STEINHARDT DIRECT INC
12700 Antioch Rd Ste 65
Overland Park, KS 66213-2826
Telephone: (913) 764-6400, FAX:
  (913) 780-6401, E-Mail: sdirect2@
  home.com
Pres: William Steinhardt

STEPHAN & BRADY INC
1850 Hoffman St
Madison, WI 53704-2594
Telephone: (608) 241-4141, FAX:
  (608) 241-4246, E-Mail: gwhitely@
  stephanbrady.com, Web Site: www.
  stephanbrady.com
Pres: George Whitely

STEPHAN PARTNERS INC
233 Spring St (Suite 801)
New York, NY 10013-1522
Telephone: (212) 524-8583, E-Mail:
  george@stephenpartners.com, Web
  Site: www.stephanpartners.com
Pres: George N. Stephan
Mgr: Brian Hack
Creative Dir: Bob Feinberg
Creative Dir: Jeff Bretl
Creative Dir: Carol Bokuniewicz
Creative Dir: Jim Parry
Creative Dir: Steve Meltzer

STEPHENS DIRECT INC
417 E Stroop Rd
Kettering, OH 45429-2829
Telephone: (937) 299-4993, FAX:
  (937) 299-9355, E-Mail: phil.
  stephens@stephensdirect.com
Pres: Phillip Stephens II

STIR
135 W Wells St (Suite 800)
Milwaukee, WI 53203-1807
Telephone: (414) 278-0040, FAX:
    (414) 278-0390, E-Mail: brianb@
    stirstuff.com, Web Site: www.
    stirstuff.com
Principal: Brian Bennett

THE STONE GROUP INC
205 S Whiting St (Suite 250)
Alexandria, VA 22304
Telephone: (703) 370-8282, FAX:
    (703) 370-8287, E-Mail: tsgrp@aol.
    com, Web Site: www.
    tsgdirectresponse.com
CEO: Ann E.W. Stone

THE DMA STRATEGIC AMERICA
6600 Westown Pkwy Ste 100
West Des Moines, IA 50266-7708
Telephone: (515) 453-2000, (888) 898-
    6400, FAX: (515) 224-4181, Web
    Site: www.strategicamerica.com
CEO: Mike Schreurs
Sr Production Mgr: Jill Stilwell

STRATEGIC MARKETING AND ADVERTISING INC
Div. Response FX
1792 Blackbird Cir
Carlsbad, CA 92011
Telephone: (760) 930-6123, E-Mail:
    dmservices@smaresource.com, Web
    Site: www.responsefx.com
Sr VP: Karen J Marchetti

STRATEGIC PLANNING MARKETING SCOUTING & SALES
5 Independence Dr
Foxboro, MA 02035-2215
Telephone: (781) 215-5117, (866) 638-
    5323, FAX: (774) 215-5117, E-Mail:
    cmay@dmcommunications.com, Web
    Site: www.dmcommunications.com
Pres: Christy May

STRATEGY NETWORK
PO Box 702545
Plymouth, MI 48170-0983
Telephone: (734) 464-8100, FAX:
    (734) 464-4133, E-Mail: info@
    strategynetwork.com, Web Site:
    www.strategy-network.com
Pres: Kathy Nagy
Employees: 20
Primary Market Served: Consumer
Founded: 1999

Marketing company that conceives &
implements strategic programs. Strategic planning; market research; custom
publishing; web based relationship,
college & diversity marketing.

STROMBERG CONSULTING
1285 Ave of the Americas (3rd fl)
New York, NY 10019
Telephone: (646) 935-4177, (212) 812-
    6400, FAX: (212) 812-6300, E-Mail:
    info@strombergconsulting.com, Web
    Site: www.strombergconsulting.com
CEO: Michael M. Chayes
Other: Cynthia Roy

STUDEO INTERACTIVE DIRECT
6405 S 3000th E (3rd fl)
Salt Lake City, UT 84121
Telephone: (801) 993-2300, FAX:
    (801) 993-2301, E-Mail: info@
    studeo.com, Web Site: www.studeo.
    com
Pres: David Allen

STURM, ROSENBURG, KING & CO
737 N Michigan Ave (Suite 1400)
Chicago, IL 60611-7021
Telephone: (312) 943-1881, FAX:
    (312) 943-2346, Web Site: www.
    sturmads.com
Chmn & CEO: Arthur M. Sturm
Pres: Robert Rosenberg
Corp Opers: Donna King

SUMMIT MARKETING
Div. of Summit Marketing Group
3 Cityplace Dr Ste 500
Saint Louis, MO 63141-7091
Telephone: (314) 569-3737, FAX:
    (314) 569-0037, E-Mail: info@
    summitmarketing.com, Web Site:
    www.summitmarketing.com
VP: Susan Cheney
CEO: Daniel Renz

SUNDOG
2000 44th St SW (fl 6)
Fargo, ND 58103-7411
Telephone: (701) 235-5525, (888)
    9-SUNDOG, FAX: (701) 235-8941,
    Web Site: www.sundog.net
Pres: Greg Ness

THE DMA SUTHERLAND GLOBAL SERVICES
1160 Pittsford/Victor Rd
Pittsford, NY 14534
Telephone: (585) 586-5757, (800) 388-
    4557, FAX: (585) 419-2418, E-Mail:
    katie-laird@suth.com, Web Site:
    www.suth.com
Mktg Commun: Katie Laird

SUTTER MARKETING INC
800 E Northwest Hwy (Suite 430)
Palatine, IL 60067
Telephone: (847) 358-3100, FAX:
    (847) 705-7900, Web Site: www.
    suttermarketing.com
Pres: Lynn R. Sutter

THE DMA SWANSON HEALTH PRODUCTS
4075 40th Ave SW
Fargo, ND 58104-3912
Telephone: (701) 356-2800, (800) 824-
    4491, FAX: (800) 726-7691, E-Mail:
    customercare@swansonvitamins.
    com, Web Site: www.
    swansonvitamins.com
Pres: Doug Anderson
Market Research: Maggie McCalip

SWEETGRASS
aka Sweetgrass Advertising
1101 Alaskan Way (Suite 200), Pier 55
Seattle, WA 98101
Telephone: (206) 343-9000, FAX:
    (206) 447-2663, E-Mail: bill.
    toliver@sweetgrassadvertising.com,
    Web Site: www.
    sweetgrassadvertising.com
Exec Dir: Bill Toliver

THE DMA TBC DIRECT INC
900 S Wolfe St
Baltimore, MD 21231-3514
Telephone: (410) 347-7500, FAX:
    (410) 986-1299, E-Mail: direct@tbc.
    us, Web Site: www.tbcadv.us
VP Acct Dir: Tracey Morgan
Pres: Thomas Burden

THE DMA TBWA
5353 Grosvenor Rd
Los Angeles, CA 90066-6913
Telephone: (310) 305-5000
Dir Intelligence: Velda Ruddock

TBWA/CHIAT/DAY INC
488 Madison Ave (fl 7)
New York, NY 10022-5727
Telephone: (212) 804-1000, FAX:
    (212) 804-1200, E-Mail: jamie.
    gallo@tbwachiat.com, Web Site:
    www.tbwachiat.com
Chmn & Chief Creative Officer: Mark
    Figliulo
Mng Dir New York: Jamie Gallo
Worldwide Strategy Dir: Suzanne Pow-
    ers
Exec Dir Audience Plng: Shane An-
    keney
CFO & COO: Jeffrey Wu
US Pub Rels Dir: Marianne Stefanow-
    icz

TD AMERITRADE HOLDING CORP
4211 S 102nd St
Omaha, NE 68127
Telephone: (402) 331-7856, (800) 237-8692, FAX: (402) 597-7789, Web Site: www.amtd.com
Exec VP & CFO: William J. Gerber

TMP WORLDWIDE
1600 Tysons Blvd
Mc Lean, VA 22102-4865
Telephone: (703) 269-0144, FAX: (703) 269-0115, E-Mail: john.refo@ tmp.com, Web Site: www.tmp.com
Dir Strategic Mktg: John Refo

THE DMA TN MARKETING
1903 Wayzata Blvd
Wayzata, MN 55391-2047
Telephone: (763) 577-1216, Web Site: www.tnmarketing.com
Pres: Cal Franklin

THE DMA TPG DIRECT INC
7 N Columbus Blvd
Philadelphia, PA 19106-1422
Telephone: (215) 592-8303, Web Site: www.tpgadvertising.com
CEO: Steve Longley

TVA PRODUCTIONS INC (THE VIDEO AGENCY)
3950 Vantage Ave
Studio City, CA 91604-3613
Telephone: (818) 505-8300, (888) 322-4296, FAX: (818) 505-8370, E-Mail: info@tvaproductions.com, Web Site: www.tvaproductions.com
Pres & Exec Producer: Jeffrey Goddard
Sr VP, Pub Rels: Anne Klenman
Mktg Strategist: David Mangone
Conducts Business: Worldwide
Employees: 15
Primary Market Served: Business & Consumer
Advertising/Marketing Budget Related to Direct Marketing: 51-75%
Founded: 1987
Gross sales or billing: $12,000,000

Film/video production, duplication & packaging.

TABLER COMMUNICATIONS
PO Box 3964
Louisville, KY 40201
Telephone: (502) 585-2299, FAX: (502) 585-3574, E-Mail: biggs@ tablercommunications.com, Web Site: www.tablercommunications. com
Pres: William Biggs Tabler

TACITO DIRECT MARKETING
14165 Proton Rd
Dallas, TX 75244-3604
Telephone: (972) 458-2026, (800) 621-2225, FAX: (972) 490-6520, Web Site: www.tacito.com
CEO: Anthony J. Tacito

TAMAYO MIYARES & SHERMAN
325 Lafayette St (Suite 5203)
Bridgeport, CT 06604
Telephone: (203) 416-5718, FAX: (203) 416-5721, E-Mail: lsherman@ tmsdr.com, Web Site: www.tmsdr. com
Partner: Len Sherman

TANEN DIRECTED ADVERTISING
12 S Main St Ste 401
Norwalk, CT 06854-2980
Telephone: (203) 855-5855, FAX: (203) 855-5865, Web Site: www. tanendirected.com
Pres: Ilene Cohn Tanen

TANGERINE DIRECT - A SERVICE OF ARCHER MALMO
65 Union Ave (Suite 500)
Memphis, TN 38103-5137
Telephone: (901) 523-2000, Web Site: www.archermalmo.com
VP Grp Svcs: Patricia Emory-Walker

JOSEPH TARDI ASSOCIATES
2690 Troy Schenectady Rd
Niskayuna, NY 12309
Telephone: (518) 782-1211, FAX: (518) 782-9488, Web Site: www. tardiassociates.com
Pres & Mktg Dir: Joseph Tardi

THE DMA TARGET & RESPONSE INC
420 N Wabash Ave (Suite 201)
Chicago, IL 60611-3569
Telephone: (312) 321-0500, FAX: (312) 321-0051, Web Site: www. target-response.com
Pres: Gary Kretchmer

TARGET DIRECT MARKETING INC
185 Main St (Suite 7)
Gloucester, MA 01930-5745
Telephone: (978) 281-5967, Web Site: www.targetdirectmarketing.com
Pres: John Pirroni

TARGET MARKETEAM
1050 Crown Pointe Pkwy (Suite 1850)
Atlanta, GA 30338-7709
Telephone: (770) 274-3700, FAX: (770) 274-3730, Web Site: www. tmtinc.com
Pres: Ron Bell
Primary Market Served: Consumer

TARGETBASE
An Omnicom Group Inc Company
7850 N Beltline Rd
Irving, TX 75063-6062
Telephone: (972) 506-3400, (800) 446-6603, FAX: (972) 506-3505, E-Mail: info@targetbase.com, Web Site: www.targetbase.com
Pres & CEO: David Scholes
Dir, Corp Commun: Cynthia Edwards
Founded: 1979

TARGETCOM INC
444 N Michigan Ave (33rd fl)
Chicago, IL 60611
Telephone: (312) 822-1100, FAX: (312) 822-9628, E-Mail: tcomcontact@targetcom.com, Web Site: www.targetcom.com
Pres: Nora Ligurotis
Founded: 1978

Full Service Direct Response Agency.

TARGETMAIL MARKETING
PO Box 239
Clover, SC 29710-0239
Telephone: (540) 837-9337
Owner: Jennifer Spitzer

THE DMA TEAM NASH INC
4 Jonathan Dr
East Hampton, NY 11937-2110
Telephone: (646) 497-0297, (631) 267-3385, E-Mail: results@teamnash. com, Web Site: www.teamnash.com
CEO: Edward Nash
VP: Ayse Gurzap
CD: Lisa Sardinas
Media: Lisa Hays
Employees: 14
Founded: 1995
Gross sales or billing: $2,346,000

Specialty DM agency serving packaged goods companies and direct marketers with advanced applications using unique proprietary prospect targeting and research methods. Headed by "master strategist" Edward Nash, international lecturer and author of seven books including "Direct Marketing: Strategy, Planning & Execution."

TEAM ONE ADVERTISING
1960 E Grand Ave
El Segundo, CA 90245

Telephone: (310) 615-2000, FAX:
(310) 322-7565, E-Mail: b.sheehan@
teamoneadv.com, Web Site: www.
teamone-usa.com
Pres: Brian Sheehan

TECH IMAGE
1130 W Lake Cook Rd (Suite 250)
Buffalo Grove, IL 60089-1994
Telephone: (847) 279-0022, (888)
4-TECH-PR, FAX: (847) 279-8922,
E-Mail: info@techimage.com, Web
Site: www.techimage.com
Pres & CEO: Mike Nicholich

TECHCOM INC
Box 8257
Princeton, NJ 08543-8257
Telephone: (609) 734-0004, FAX:
(609) 520-0263, E-Mail: techcom1@
juno.com
Pres: Frank Sardi

**TECHNICAL MARKETING
GROUP**
175 Fairfield Ave (Suite 3C)
West Caldwell, NJ 07006-6415
Telephone: (856) 751-9585, FAX:
(856) 751-9729, E-Mail: tldirenzo@
aol.com, Web Site: www2.
techmktgrp.com
Owner: Thomas G. DiRenzo

**TELEPERFORMANCE
CANADA**
Subs. Sr Teleperformance Group
365 Bloor St E
Toronto, ON, Canada M4W 3L4
Telephone: (416) 922-3519, Web Site:
www.teleperformance.ca
Pres & CEO: Erifili Morfidis
COO: Charlotte Gummesson

TELESTAR MEDIA
4601 Malsbary Rd
Cincinnati, OH 45242-5659
Telephone: (513) 699-3300, Web Site:
www.telestarmedia.com
Primary Market Served: Consumer

TEMKIN & TEMKIN
156 Barberry
Highland Park, IL 60035-4420
Telephone: (847) 831-0237, FAX:
(847) 851-0409, Web Site: www.
temkin.com
Pres: Steve Temkin

**THE TESTIMONIAL
WRANGLER**
7486 La Jolla Blvd (#164)
La Jolla, CA 92037-5029
Telephone: (858) 735-7646

Chief Wrangler: Marla Hoslins

**THANE INTERNATIONAL
INC**
78140 Calle Tampico Ste 3
La Quinta, CA 92253-2985
Telephone: (760) 777-0217, FAX:
(760) 777-0214, Web Site: www.
thane.com
CEO: Amir Tukulj
Employees: 600
Founded: 1990
Gross sales or billing: $350,000,000

Global leader in the multi-channel direct marketing of consumer products in
the fitness, health, beauty and housewares categories. Thane's distribution
channels in the United States, and in
80 countries around the world, include
direct response TV, home shopping,
catalogs, retail, print, and the Internet.

THARLER DIRECTS
4 Cabot Rd
Wayland, MA 01778-3716
Telephone: (508) 358-3554, Web Site:
www.tharlerdirects.com
Chief Guide: Steven R. Tharler

THE
DMA **THOMASARTS**
PO Box 70
Farmington, UT 84025-0070
Telephone: (801) 451-5365, Web Site:
www.thomasarts.com
Media Dir: Lisa Roberts

THREE SIXTY INC
200 E Delaware Pl (Suite 5B)
Chicago, IL 60611
Telephone: (312) 255-0360, FAX:
(312) 255-1932, E-Mail: 360@360-
communications.com, Web Site:
www.360-communications.com
Creative Dir: Sharon Johnson

**TIERNEY
COMMUNICATIONS**
Div. of Interpublic Groups
200 S Broad St Fl 10
Philadelphia, PA 19102-3845
Telephone: (215) 790-4100, FAX:
(215) 545-0188, Web Site: www.
tierneyagency.com
Pres & CEO: Mary Stengel Austen

TIGERT COMMUNICATIONS
2815 Dogwood Pl
Nashville, TN 37204
Telephone: (615) 298-9957, Web Site:
www.tigertcommunications.com
Owner, Pres & Mktg Dir: Bob Tigert

THE
DMA **TOBE DIRECT**
9700 Park Plaza (Unit 210)
Louisville, KY 40241-2287
Telephone: (502) 423-9898, Web Site:
www.tobedirect.com
Pres: John Tobe

TOBOL GROUP INC
275 Dixon Ave (Unit B)
Amityville, NY 11701-2874
Telephone: (516) 767-8182, FAX:
(516) 767-8185, E-Mail: mt@
tobolgroup.com, Web Site: www.
tobolgroup.com
Pres: Mitch Tobol

TOCQUIGNY
401 Congress Ave (fl 17)
Austin, TX 78701-4071
Telephone: (512) 532-2800, Web Site:
www.tocquigny.com
Primary Market Served: Consumer

TOPAK MARKETING INC
Seven N Columbus Blvd
Philadelphia, PA 19106
Telephone: (215) 574-8307, FAX:
(215) 574-8316
Pres: Nan Williams

**TOWER MEDIA
ADVERTISING INC**
233 N Michigan Ave (Suite 2350)
Chicago, IL 60601-5701
Telephone: (312) 856-9200, FAX:
(312) 856-1300, E-Mail: info@
towermedia.com, Web Site: www.
towermedia.com
Pres: Phil Rozansky
Media Asst: Cherie Weyers

**TRACY LOCKE
PARTNERSHIP**
1999 Bryan St (Suite 2800)
Dallas, TX 75201
Telephone: (214) 969-9000, FAX:
(214) 259-3550, E-Mail: tlpinfo@tlp.
com, Web Site: www.tlp.com
Pres & CEO: Gary Von Kennel

TRADENET PUBLISHING INC
1200 Energy Center Dr
Gardner, KS 66030-1599
Telephone: (800) 884-7301, Web Site:
www.tradenetonline.com
Pres: Tom Mertz
Primary Market Served: Business

**TRANSCONTINENTAL
INTERACTIVE**
1 Place Ville Marie (Suite 3315)
Montreal, PQ, Canada H3B 3N2

Telephone: (514) 954-4000, FAX:
(514) 954-4016
Primary Market Served: Business

TRANZACT
2200 Fletcher Ave (fl 4)
Fort Lee, NJ 07024-5016
Telephone: (201) 461-5665, Web Site:
www.tranzact.net
EVP: Mitchell Ginzburg

TRI-STATE ADVERTISING CO INC
307 S Buffalo St
Warsaw, IN 46580-4304
Telephone: (574) 267-5178, FAX:
(574) 267-2965, E-Mail: info@tri-
stateadv.com, Web Site: www.tri-
stateadv.com
Pres: Clayton R. Kreicker
Controller: Barbara Bolles

TRINITY COMMUNICATIONS INC
180 Canal St Ste 300
Boston, MA 02114-1804
Telephone: (617) 292-7300, FAX:
(617) 292-7400, E-Mail: info@
trinitynet.com, Web Site: www.
trinitynet.com
Mktg Client Svcs: Kerry Weiss-Pena

THE DMA TRUE NORTH INC
630 3rd Ave Rm 1200
New York, NY 10017-6749
Telephone: (212) 557-4202, Web Site:
www.truenorthinc.com
CEO: Steve Fuchs

THE DMA TRUESENSE MARKETING
155 Commerce Dr
Freedom, PA 15042-9202
Telephone: (877) 878-6584, Web Site:
www.truesense.com
SVP Strategic Plng & Mktg: Jeff
Nickel

TURKEL
2871 Oak Ave
Coconut Grove, FL 33133
Telephone: (305) 445-9111, FAX:
(305) 448-6691, Web Site: www.
braindarts.com
Exec Creative Dir: Bruce Turkel

TWO ROTHS
7020 108th St (#10E)
Forest Hills, NY 11375-4442
Telephone: (718) 268-1998, FAX:
(718) 793-3972, E-Mail: tworoths@
rcn.com
Partner: Leah Roth

22SQUARED INC
1170 Peachtree St NE
Atlanta, GA 30309-7649
Telephone: (404) 347-8700, FAX:
(404) 347-8800, Web Site: www.
22squared.com
CEO, Pres & Dir: Richard Ward
Dir Mktg: Randy Bentley

UMARKETING LLC
1350 Broadway (Rm 800)
New York, NY 10018-0950
Telephone: (630) 916-1717, Web Site:
www.umarketing.com
CEO: George Wiedemann
Conducts Business: New York, Chi-
cago, Columbus & Omaha
Employees: 57
Founded: 2007
Gross sales or billing: $53,800,000

Provides accountable communications.
Communicates in all channels - offline
& online - & captures results on an
analaytics platform, so that performance is continuously measured &
optimized.

UNDERLINE COMMUNICATIONS LLC
12 W 27th St (fl 14)
New York, NY 10001-6903
Telephone: (212) 994-4340, Web Site:
www.underlinecom.com
Primary Market Served: Consumer

UNICOM MARKETING GROUP INC
2875 S 25th Ave
Broadview, IL 60155-4531
Telephone: (312) 738-1404, FAX:
(312) 738-1405, E-Mail: info@
unicommarketing.com, Web Site:
www.unicommarketing.com
Pres: Joe Iazzetto

UNIT 7
30 Irving Pl (11th fl)
New York, NY 10003-2303
Telephone: (212) 209-1600, FAX:
(212) 209-1800, E-Mail: lbabcock@
unit7.com, Web Site: www.unit7.com
Chm & CEO: Loreen Babcock

UNIVERSAL MEDIA SYNDICATE INC
3939 Everhard Rd NW
Canton, OH 44709-4004
Telephone: (330) 966-9000, Web Site:
www.uni-syn.com
VP: Laura Fish-Rogers

VALASSIS CANADA
47 Jutland Rd
Toronto, ON, Canada M8Z 2G6
Telephone: (416) 259-3600, Web Site:
www.valassis.com
Pres: Mark McHugh
Sr VP Sls: Frank Turner

THE DMA VALMARK ASSOCIATES LLC
4242 Ridge Lea Rd Ste 5
Buffalo, NY 14226-5122
Telephone: (716) 893-1494, Web Site:
www.valmarkassociates.com
Pres: Joseph Lojacono

VANE & FRIENDS
734 King St
Chappaqua, NY 10514-3811
Telephone: (914) 238-8890, E-Mail:
info@vaneandfriends.com, Web Site:
www.vaneandfriends.com
Pres: Penny Vane
VP, Strategic Plng & Bus Devel: Kelly
Anderson
VP, Interactive: Cara Bowler
VP & Creative Dir: Wil Rushford
Employees: 8
Primary Market Served: Business &
Consumer
Founded: 1997

A marketing communications agency
providing strategic planning, creative
and vendor management services for
direct-to-consumer and business-to-
business clients. Experience includes
new customer acquisition, lead generation, customer retention, sales support
and employee program.

THE DMA VANGUARD DIRECT
519 8th Ave (23rd fl)
New York, NY 10018-4570
Telephone: (212) 736-0770, FAX:
(212) 736-8305, Web Site: www.
vanguarddirect.com
Pres: Bob O'Connell
Dir Creative Svcs: Paul Wry

THE DMA VASTCAST MEDIA
6280 S Valley View Blvd Ste 318
Las Vegas, NV 89118-3890
Telephone: (702) 221-8261, Web Site:
www.vastcastmedia.com
CEO: Jared Dingwerth

THE DMA VENTURA ASSOCIATES INTERNATIONAL LLC
Subs. of Mickelberry Corporation
1040 Ave of the Americas (fl 20)
New York, NY 10018-3714
Telephone: (212) 302-8277, FAX:
(212) 302-2587, E-Mail: info@
sweepspros.com, Web Site: www.
sweepspros.com

Pres: Al B. Wester III
CEO: Marla Altberg

THE VERDI GROUP INC
135 Sully's Trail (Suite 4)
Pittsford, NY 14534
Telephone: (585) 381-4275, FAX:
(585) 381-4293, E-Mail: info@
theverdigroup.com, Web Site: www.
theverdigroup.com
Pres: Robert A. Green Jr.

VERMONT MEDIA
PO Box 310
West Dover, VT 05356-0310
Telephone: (802) 464-3388, FAX:
(802) 464-7255, E-Mail: vickic@
vermontmedia.com, Web Site: www.
dvalnews.com
Publr: Randy Capitani
Gen Mgr: Victoria Capitani

VESDIA CORP
3348 Peachtree Rd NE (Suite 300)
Atlanta, GA 30326-1456
Telephone: (678) 405-9208, Web Site:
www.vesdia.com
VP: Sarah Arvin

THE DMA THE VIDAL PARTNERSHIP
228 E 45th St Fl 14
New York, NY 10017-3303
Telephone: (646) 356-6600, FAX:
(212) 661-7650, Web Site: www.
vidalpartnership.com
Pres & CEO: Manny Vidal
Mng Partner: Alberto Ferrer

VIDEOWARE CORP
53 Doral Greens Dr W
Rye Brook, NY 10573
Telephone: (914) 937-6007, FAX:
(914) 937-6414, E-Mail: info@
videoware.com, Web Site: www.
videoware.com
Chmn & CEO: Dick Hubert

VISION MEDIA
5437 Parker Rd
Modesto, CA 95357-0640
Telephone: (209) 526-6500, FAX:
(209) 522-2100, E-Mail: info@
visionmediatv.com, Web Site: www.
visionmediatv.com
Pres: Kim L. Murray

**VISUAL RESPONSE
MARKETING GROUP**
2125 Ellis Farm Dr
Marietta, GA 30064-2879
Telephone: (678) 881-9400

**WNR DIRECT RESPONSE
CONSULTANTS**
30423 Canwood St (Suite 234)
Agoura Hills, CA 91301
Telephone: (818) 865-6300, FAX:
(818) 865-8559, E-Mail: gwetter@
wnrtv.com, Web Site: www.wnrtv.
com
Pres: Gary L. Wetter

WOL DIRECT INC
925 Oak St
Scranton, PA 18515-0999
Telephone: (570) 961-4043, Web Site:
www.pennfoster.edu

WALDBILLIG & BESTEMAN
8001 Excelsior Dr (Suite 110)
Madison, WI 53717-1956
Telephone: (608) 829-0900, (800) 395-
4767, FAX: (608) 829-0901, E-Mail:
info@waldbest.com, Web Site: www.
waldbest.com
Pres: Michael Knapstein
COO: Thomas Senatori
Gen Mgr: Irving Chung

**WEB DIRECT MARKETING
INC**
1900 Chestnut Ave Apt 201
Glenview, IL 60025-1658
Telephone: (847) 459-0800, (877) 841-
2841, FAX: (847) 459-7378, E-Mail:
info@webdirectmktg.com, Web Site:
www.webdirectmktg.com
Pres: Vernon L. Carson
Sr VP: Sy Dordick
Admin Asst: Linda O'Donnell

WEBB & CO
Subs. of Catalog Ventures
222 Mill Rd
Chelmsford, MA 01824-4127
Telephone: (978) 250-9262, FAX:
(978) 250-9262
VP, Mktg: Robert L. Webb

THE DMA WEBMETRO
160 Via Verde # 100
San Dimas, CA 91773-3901
Telephone: (909) 599-8885, Web Site:
www.webmetro.com
CEO & Pres: Carlos Ugalde

WEBREPLY.COM INC
1085 Worcester St
Natick, MA 01760-1531
Telephone: (508) 318-4600, Web Site:
www.webreply.com
CEO: Henry Haugland

**WENDOVER ASSOCIATES
INC**
309-A Edwardia Dr
Greensboro, NC 27409
Telephone: (336) 299-6611, FAX:
(336) 292-4261
Pres & Mktg Dir: Betty Hooker

**WEST END DIVING CENTERS
INC**
12464 Natural Bridge Rd
Bridgeton, MO 63044-2321
Telephone: (314) 209-7200, E-Mail:
info@westenddiving.com, Web Site:
www.2dive.com
Pres: D.C. Goergens

**WESTERN DATA SERVICES
INC**
3010 National Parks Hwy
Carlsbad, NM 88220
Telephone: (505) 234-2927, FAX:
(505) 234-9637, E-Mail: directmail@
wdsi.net, Web Site: www.wdsi.net
Dir Mktg: Aaron Jones

**WEXLER MARKETING
GROUP INC**
3403 Holly St
Alexandria, VA 22305
Telephone: (703) 548-4336, FAX:
(703) 548-4393, E-Mail: wexler@
compuserve.com
Pres: Sheila Wexler

WHITE & PARTNERS
13665 Dulles Technology Dr (Suite
150)
Herndon, VA 20171
Telephone: (703) 793-3000, FAX:
(703) 793-1495, E-Mail: tawnyas@
whiteandpartners.com, Web Site:
www.whiteandpartners.com
Pres & CEO: Matthew C. White
Sr Graphics Specialist: Tawnya Setterlund

**WHITE POST MEDIA GROUP
INC**
PO Box 50180
Nashville, TN 37205-0180
Telephone: (615) 730-7566
Primary Market Served: Consumer

WIKREATE
145 Vallejo St (#6)
San Francisco, CA 94111-1415
Telephone: (415) 362-0440, Web Site:
www.wikreate.com
Principal: Ezequiel Trivino

WILLIAMS WORLDWIDE TELEVISION
3130 Wilshire Blvd (Suite 300)
Santa Monica, CA 90403-2300
Telephone: (310) 449-4506, FAX:
(310) 449-4556, E-Mail: curious@
williamsworldwidetv.com, Web Site:
www.williamsworldwidetv.com
Pres & CEO: Alain Bransford
Mktg Coord: Caitlin Cooper

WILSON RELATIONSHIP MARKETING SERVICES
333 7th Ave (fl 5)
New York, NY 10001-5004
Telephone: (212) 473-6900, Web Site:
www.wilsonrms.com
Pres: David Wilson

WOLF BLUMBERG KRODY INC
537 E Pete Rose Way (Suite 100)
Cincinnati, OH 45202-3578
Telephone: (513) 784-0066, FAX:
(513) 784-0986, E-Mail: sklein@
wbk.com, Web Site: www.wbk.com
Pres: Steve Klein

WOLTERS KLUWER FINANCIAL SERVICES
100 S 5th St (Suite 700)
Minneapolis, MN 55402-1219
Telephone: (612) 656-7724, Web Site:
www.wolterskluwerfs.com
Mktg Dir: Tom Teynor

WUNDERMAN
Div. of Young & Rubicam Inc
285 Madison Ave (Lbby 2)
New York, NY 10017-6401
Telephone: (212) 941-3000, FAX:
(212) 888-7520, Web Site: www.
wunderman.com
Chmn & Global CEO: Daniel Morel
Chmn Emeritus: Lester Wunderman
Vice Chmn Pres Wunderman World
Wide: David Sable
Pres & CEO Knowledge Base Mktg:
Gary Laben
CIO Y&R/Wunderman: Mark Taylor
Exec VP Global HR: Bill Manfredi
Sr VP Global Mktg & Communs:
Nancy Maffucci
Exec VP & CFO North America: Seth
Rothstein
VP Dir Learning & Education: Cindy
Zimmerer
Conducts Business: Worldwide
Primary Market Served: Business &
Consumer
Founded: 1958

WYSE DIRECT
Div. of WYSE Advertising
25 W Prospect Ave
Cleveland, OH 44115
Telephone: (216) 696-2427, FAX:
(216) 736-4440, Web Site: www.
wysedirect.com
Pres: Dan Karp

XPECTRUM MARKETING GROUP
1953 Ainsley Rd
San Diego, CA 92123
Telephone: (858) 277-0079, FAX:
(858) 277-0076, E-Mail: info@
xpectrummg.com, Web Site: www.
xpectrummg.com
CEO: William Lopez

YATES ADVERTISING
305 Bridgeway
Sausalito, CA 94965-2451
Telephone: (415) 887-9545, FAX:
(415) 887-9549
Pres: Susan Yates

THE DMA YECK BROTHERS CO
2222 Arbor Blvd
Dayton, OH 45439-1594
Telephone: (937) 294-4000, (800) 417-
2767, FAX: (937) 294-6985, E-Mail:
byeck@yeck.com, Web Site: www.
yeck.com
Pres: Robert Yeck
Mgr Mktg & Creative: Sherry Hang

ZLR IGNITION
303 Watson Powell Jr Way (Suite 100)
Des Moines, IA 50309-1799
Telephone: (515) 244-4456, FAX:
(515) 244-5749, Web Site: www.zlr.
com
Pres: Louie Laurent

THE DMA GEORGE ZAHKA
865 Central Ave Apt L501
Needham, MA 02492-1389
Telephone: (617) 332-6797
Pres: George Zahka

ZENITH DIRECT
299 W Houston St
New York, NY 10014-4806
Telephone: (212) 859-5100, Web Site:
www.zodirect.com
COO: Joel Feldman

THE DMA ZEPHYR MEDIA GROUP INC
990 Grove St (Suite 300)
Evanston, IL 60201-6513
Telephone: (847) 328-1519, Web Site:
www.zephyr-media.com
Pres: Daniel Zefkin

THE DMA ZILLNER MARKETING COMMUNICATIONS INC
8725 Rosehill Rd (Suite 200)
Lenexa, KS 66215-4611
Telephone: (913) 599-3230, Web Site:
www.zillner.com
Direct Mktg Supvr: Chris Gray

ZIMMERMAN & PARTNERS
Div. of Omnicom
2200 W Commercial Blvd (Suite 300)
Fort Lauderdale, FL 33309-3064
Telephone: (954) 731-2900, FAX:
(954) 731-2977, Web Site: www.
zadv.com
Pres: Jordan Zimmerman

Art Services (36) — Geographic Index

Arizona

Asciutto Art Representatives Inc, 1712 E Butler Cir, Chandler, 85225-5786

California

Crawshaw Design, 120 Bayview Dr, San Rafael, 94901-2502

Jack Lucey Art & Illustration, 84 Crestwood Dr, San Rafael, 94901

Jim M'Guinness Design, 1122 Golden Way, Los Altos, 94024-5059

Stuart Karten Design, 4204 Glencoe Ave, Marina Del Rey, 90292

Edward Weston Fine Art & Photography, PO Box 3098, Chatsworth, 91311

Greg Zerovnik, 1805 N First Ave, Upland, 91784-1623

Florida

American Writers & Artists Inc, 245 NE 4th Ave (Suite 102), Delray Beach, 33483-4568

Illinois

AMD Industries Inc, 4620 W 19th St, Cicero, 60804-2502

BN Creative Advertising, 9201 King St, Franklin Park, 60131-2111

Graphic Converting Inc, 877 N Larch Ave, Elmhurst, 60126

Ion Exhibits, 700 District Dr, Itasca, 60143-1320

Jupiterimages Corp, 6000 N Forest Park Dr, Peoria, 61614

Swimmer Design Associates, 4 Piper Ln (Suite F), Prospect Heights, 60070-1741

Kansas

Pat Friesen & Co LLC, 9636 Meadow Ln, Leawood, 66206-2259

Kentucky

Beau Graphics Ltd Inc, 1910 Harrodsburg Rd, Lexington, 40503-1247

Maryland

EPI Colorspace, 8435 Helgerman Ct, Gaithersburg, 20877

Massachusetts

Rodelinde Graphic Design, PO Box 444, Lenox Dale, 01242-0444

Michigan

Pangborn Design Ltd, 275 Iron St, Detroit, 48207-4305

Presence II Productions, 3810 Mystic Valley Dr, Bloomfield Hills, 48302-1437

Minnesota

Sense of Design Inc, 5800 Baker Rd, Minnetonka, 55345-5965

New Jersey

Miller Advertising Inc, 24 Nottingham Rd, Edison, 08820

Robert Burger Illustration, 145 Kingwood Stockton Rd, Stockton, 08559

New York

Blakeney Design, 61 Horatio St, New York, 10014-1505

Cecile Brunswick, 127 W 96th St (Suite 15D), New York, 10025-6482

Karen Levy Calligraphy, 370 E 76th St, New York, 10021

Nostradamus Advertising, 884 W End Ave (Suite 2), New York, 10025

Paul Chevannes, 445A 5th St, Brooklyn, 11215-3401

Carl Waltzer Digital Service Bureau, 873 Broadway (Rm 412), New York, 10003

Westbeth Gallery, 55 Bethane St (#219), New York, 10014

North Carolina

Synergy Arts Interactive, PO Box 15085, Asheville, 28813-0085

Oregon

Skies America International Publishing & Communications, 9655 SW Sunshine Ct (Suite 500), Beaverton, 97005

Pennsylvania

Inkwell Inc, 2256 High Rd, Cresco, 18326

Interdisciplinary Design Team, 75 Toll Dr, Southhampton, 18966-3074

Texas

Olivette Hubler Graphics Inc, 1568 Bar Harbor Dr, Dallas, 75232-3016

Virginia

Gramma's Graphics Inc, 49 Starview Pl, Lancaster, 22503

Wisconsin

Communicor, 629 E Keefe Ave, Milwaukee, 53212-1612

Art Services (36)

AMD INDUSTRIES INC
4620 W 19th St
Cicero, IL 60804-2502
Telephone: (708) 863-8900, (800) 367-9999, FAX: (708) 863-2065, Web Site: www.amdpop.com
Pres & CEO: David E. Allen

AMERICAN WRITERS & ARTISTS INC
245 NE 4th Ave (Suite 102)
Delray Beach, FL 33483-4568
Telephone: (561) 278-5557, Web Site: www.awaionline.com
Exec Dir: Kate Yeakle

ASCIUTTO ART REPRESENTATIVES INC
1712 E Butler Cir
Chandler, AZ 85225-5786
Telephone: (480) 814-8010, E-Mail: aartreps@cox.net, Web Site: wwwaartreps.com
Art Rep: Mary Anne Asciutto
Founded: 1980

Represents professional artists for quality children's book illustrations.

BN CREATIVE ADVERTISING
9201 King St
Franklin Park, IL 60131-2111
Telephone: (847) 577-1300, FAX: (847) 577-2101
Pres: James M. Bataille

BEAU GRAPHICS LTD INC
1910 Harrodsburg Rd
Lexington, KY 40503-1247
Telephone: (859) 277-2328, (877) 279-2328, FAX: (859) 278-6193, Web Site: www.beaugraphics.com
Pres: Margaret Veach

BLAKENEY DESIGN
61 Horatio St
New York, NY 10014-1505
Telephone: (212) 243-0109, FAX: (212) 243-0109
Pres: Leslie Blakeney

CECILE BRUNSWICK
127 W 96th St (Suite 15D)
New York, NY 10025-6482
Telephone: (212) 222-2088, E-Mail: cbrunswick@nyc.rr.com, Web Site: www.cecilebrunswicknyc.com
Owner: Cecile Brunswick

Original colorful oil abstract paintings are available.

COMMUNICOR
629 E Keefe Ave
Milwaukee, WI 53212-1612
Telephone: (414) 961-5999, FAX: (414) 961-5990, Web Site: www.communicor.com
Pres: Robert Jarr

CRAWSHAW DESIGN
120 Bayview Dr
San Rafael, CA 94901-2502
Telephone: (415) 456-5544, FAX: (415) 456-4319, E-Mail: crawshawdesign@earthlink.net, Web Site: www.crawshawdesign.com
Owner & Pres: Todd Crawshaw

EPI COLORSPACE
8435 Helgerman Ct
Gaithersburg, MD 20877
Telephone: (301) 230-2023, FAX: (301) 990-7890, E-Mail: jcriscuoli@epicolorspace.com, Web Site: www.epicolorspace.com
VP, Corp Communs: Joseph Criscuoli

THE DMA PAT FRIESEN & CO LLC
9636 Meadow Ln
Leawood, KS 66206-2259
Telephone: (913) 341-1211, FAX: (913) 341-4343, Web Site: www.patfriesen.com
Pres: Patricia Friesen

GRAMMA'S GRAPHICS INC
49 Starview Pl
Lancaster, VA 22503
Telephone: (804) 462-0884, FAX: (804) 462-0884, E-Mail: sunprints@grandloving.com, Web Site: www.bubblink.com/donnelly
Pres: Susan Johnson
Sec & Treas: F.B. Johnson
Conducts Business: U.S., Canada
Primary Market Served: Business & Consumer
Catalog available online
Indirect online sales
Advertising/Marketing Budget Related to Direct Marketing: 0-25%
Founded: 1980

Sun print kits for blueprinting photos or opaque objects onto fabric. Also sun print kits for sun printing note cards in three colors. Sell unconditionally guaranteed kits to quilters, crafters, craft clubs, schools, retailers & wholesalers. For information send $1 & legal self addressed stamped envelope.

GRAPHIC CONVERTING INC
877 N Larch Ave
Elmhurst, IL 60126
Telephone: (630) 758-4100, (800) 447-1935, FAX: (630) 833-1058, E-Mail: sales@graphicconverting.com, Web Site: www.graphicconverting.com
Pres & Owner: John Tinnon

OLIVETTE HUBLER GRAPHICS INC
1568 Bar Harbor Dr
Dallas, TX 75232-3016
Telephone: (214) 941-9444
Pres: Olivette Hubler

INKWELL INC
2256 High Rd
Cresco, PA 18326
Telephone: (570) 595-3344, E-Mail: philip@inkwellinc.com
Pres: Philip Gruber

INTERDISCIPLINARY DESIGN TEAM
75 Toll Dr
Southhampton, PA 18966-3074
Telephone: (215) 364-5608, FAX: (215) 364-6509, E-Mail: rich.bomze@gmail.com
Graphic Designer, Creative Dir & Consultant IDT: Rich Bomze

ION EXHIBITS
700 District Dr
Itasca, IL 60143-1320
Telephone: (630) 285-9500, FAX: (630) 235-9501, E-Mail: info@ionexhibits.com, Web Site: www.ionexhibits.com
Pres: Michael Levi

JUPITERIMAGES CORP
6000 N Forest Park Dr
Peoria, IL 61614
Telephone: (312) 980-6111, (800) 764-7427, Web Site: www.jupiterimages.com

Owner: Allan Meckler

KAREN LEVY CALLIGRAPHY
370 E 76th St
New York, NY 10021
Telephone: (212) 472-1669
Owner: Karen Levy

**JACK LUCEY ART &
ILLUSTRATION**
84 Crestwood Dr
San Rafael, CA 94901
Telephone: (415) 453-3172, E-Mail:
clucey1@sbcglobal.net
Artist: Jack Lucey

JIM M'GUINNESS DESIGN
1122 Golden Way
Los Altos, CA 94024-5059
Telephone: (650) 967-3811
Pres: Jim M'Guinness

MILLER ADVERTISING INC
24 Nottingham Rd
Edison, NJ 08820
Telephone: (732) 494-5611, FAX:
(732) 494-6075
Pres: Joseph Miller

**NOSTRADAMUS
ADVERTISING**
Div. of Advocate Enterprises Inc
884 W End Ave (Suite 2)
New York, NY 10025
Telephone: (212) 581-1362, E-Mail:
nos@nostradamus.net, Web Site:
www.nostradamus.net
Pres: Barry Sher

PANGBORN DESIGN LTD
275 Iron St
Detroit, MI 48207-4305
Telephone: (313) 259-3400, FAX:
(313) 259-5690, E-Mail: info@
pangborndesign.com, Web Site:
www.pangborndesign.com
Pres: Dominic Pangborn
Press Contact: Sarah Perkins

PAUL CHEVANNES
445A 5th St
Brooklyn, NY 11215-3401
Telephone: (718) 788-3550
Pres: Paul Chevannes

PRESENCE II PRODUCTIONS
3810 Mystic Valley Dr
Bloomfield Hills, MI 48302-1437
Telephone: (248) 763-8581, Web Site:
www.presenceiiproductions.com

**ROBERT BURGER
ILLUSTRATION**
145 Kingwood Stockton Rd
Stockton, NJ 08559
Telephone: (609) 397-3737, E-Mail:
burgerbobz@aol.com
Pres: Robert Burger

**RODELINDE GRAPHIC
DESIGN**
PO Box 444
Lenox Dale, MA 01242-0444
Telephone: (413) 243-4350, FAX:
(413) 243-3066, E-Mail: rodelinde@
earthlink.net
Pres & Owner: Rodelinde Albrecht

SENSE OF DESIGN INC
5800 Baker Rd
Minnetonka, MN 55345-5965
Telephone: (952) 935-8827
Pres: Lynda Dahlheimer
Owner: Kelly Marshik

**SKIES AMERICA
INTERNATIONAL
PUBLISHING &
COMMUNICATIONS**
9655 SW Sunshine Ct (Suite 500)
Beaverton, OR 97005
Telephone: (503) 520-1955, FAX:
(503) 520-1275, E-Mail: skies@
skies.com, Web Site: www.skies.com
Owner: Jim Rullo

STUART KARTEN DESIGN
4204 Glencoe Ave
Marina Del Rey, CA 90292
Telephone: (310) 827-8722, FAX:
(310) 821-4492, Web Site: www.
kartendesign.com
Pres: Stuart Karten

**SWIMMER DESIGN
ASSOCIATES**
4 Piper Ln (Suite F)
Prospect Heights, IL 60070-1741
Telephone: (847) 215-0900, FAX:
(847) 215-9821, E-Mail: mail@
swimmerdesign.com, Web Site:
www.swimmerdesign.com
Owner: Mark Swimmer

**SYNERGY ARTS
INTERACTIVE**
PO Box 15085
Asheville, NC 28813-0085
Telephone: (914) 997-7222, FAX:
(914) 997-8893, E-Mail: bgeorge@
synergyarts.com, Web Site: www.
synergyarts.com
Pres: Bill George

**CARL WALTZER DIGITAL
SERVICE BUREAU**
Affiliate of Waltzer Photography Studio
873 Broadway (Rm 412)
New York, NY 10003
Telephone: (212) 475-8748, FAX:
(212) 475-9359, E-Mail: cwdigital@
aol.com, Web Site: www.waltzer.com
Pres: Carl Waltzer

WESTBETH GALLERY
55 Bethane St (#219)
New York, NY 10014
Telephone: (212) 989-4650
Dir: Jack Dowling

**EDWARD WESTON FINE ART
& PHOTOGRAPHY**
Subs. of Edward Weston Graphics Inc
PO Box 3098
Chatsworth, CA 91311
Telephone: (818) 885-1044, FAX:
(818) 885-1021, E-Mail:
edwardweston@westoncollection.
com, Web Site: edward-weston.com
Pres: Ann Weston

GREG ZEROVNIK
1805 N First Ave
Upland, CA 91784-1623
Telephone: (909) 982-3787, FAX:
(909) 931-2402
Pres: Greg Zerovnik

Photographers (37) — Geographic Index

California

The Icon, 5450 Wilshire Blvd, Los Angeles, 90036

Lynn McAfee, 11324 1/2 Hatteras St, North Hollywood, 91601-1276

Connecticut

Peter Glass Photography, 15 Oakwood St, East Hartford, 06108

The Lakeville Journal LLC, PO Box 1688, 33 Bissell St, Lakeville, 06039-1688

Florida

Phil Brodatz, 100 Edgewater Dr (Suite 226), Coral Gables, 33133-6979

Christopher Morrow Photography, 522 NW Blue Lake Dr, Port Saint Lucie, 34986-2650

Illinois

Dennis Jourdan Photography Inc, 1417 Rose Blvd, Buffalo Grove, 60089-3263

Hodes Photography, 503 Crown Point Dr, Buffalo Grove, 60089

William Koechling Photography, 1307 E Harrison Ave, Wheaton, 60187

Omega Studios, 168 E Highland Ave, Elgin, 60120-5564

Massachusetts

Frank Siteman Photography, 136 Pond St, Winchester, 01890

Sarah Putnam, 320 Brookline St, Cambridge, 02139

Michigan

Photographix, PO Box 8213, Ann Arbor, 48107-8213

Missouri

Our365, 3613 Neller Rd, Saint Charles, 63301

Montana

Laurance Aiuppy, Box 26, Livingston, 59047-0026

New Mexico

Eduardo Fuss, 2462 Camino Capitan, Santa Fe, 87505-6464

New York

Ann Chwatsky Photography, PO Box 271, Sag Harbor, 11963-0005

Henry Grossman, 100 W 76th St (Apt 6N), New York, 10023-8444

Imagestate, 29 E 19th St (4th fl), New York, 10003-1307

E Trina Lipton, 60 E Eighth St (#15F), New York, 10003

Shelly Rusten, PO Box 120, Hankins, 12741-0120

Walter Weissman Photo Studio, 463 West St (Suite B-332), New York, 10014-2031

North Carolina

Alderman Co, 325 Model Farm Rd, High Point, 27263

Photo Shuttle Japan, 1501 Ford Rd Lot 37, Chapel Hill, 27516-5749

Ohio

Michael Wilson Photographer, 1604 Manss Ave, Cincinnati, 45205

Pennsylvania

David K Horowitz Studio Inc, 915 N 28th St, Philadelphia, 19130

Tennessee

Borum Photographics Inc, 625 Fogg St, Nashville, 37203-4605

Virginia

Michael Carpenter Photography, 7704 Carrleigh Pkwy, Springfield, 22152-1304

Washington

Hollenbeck Productions, 19241 Normandy Park Dr SW, Seattle, 98166

Photographers (37)

LAURANCE AIUPPY
Box 26
Livingston, MT 59047-0026
Telephone: (406) 222-7308, FAX:
(406) 222-7308, E-Mail: aiuppix@
wispwest.net, Web Site: www.agpix.
com/aiuppy
Bus Mgr: Janis M. Aiuppy

ALDERMAN CO
325 Model Farm Rd
High Point, NC 27263
Telephone: (336) 889-6121, FAX:
(336) 889-7717, E-Mail: sales@
aldermancompany.com, Web Site:
www.aldermancompany.com
Chmn: Pete Williams

**BORUM PHOTOGRAPHICS
INC**
625 Fogg St
Nashville, TN 37203-4605
Telephone: (615) 254-0063, (888) 254-
0063, FAX: (615) 242-2334, Web
Site: www.chromatics.com
Pres: Michael Borum

PHIL BRODATZ
100 Edgewater Dr (Suite 226)
Coral Gables, FL 33133-6979
Telephone: (305) 661-5771

**MICHAEL CARPENTER
PHOTOGRAPHY**
7704 Carrleigh Pkwy
Springfield, VA 22152-1304
Telephone: (703) 644-9666
Owner: Michael Carpenter

**ANN CHWATSKY
PHOTOGRAPHY**
PO Box 271
Sag Harbor, NY 11963-0005
Telephone: (212) 673-5689, FAX:
(212) 673-5689, E-Mail:
annphotog@aol.com, Web Site:
www.annchwatskyphoto.com
Owner: Ann Chwatsky

**DENNIS JOURDAN
PHOTOGRAPHY INC**
1417 Rose Blvd
Buffalo Grove, IL 60089-3263
Telephone: (847) 564-2570, FAX:
(847) 255-5976, E-Mail: info@
djphoto.com, Web Site: www.
djphoto.com

Pres: Dennis Jourdan

**FRANK SITEMAN
PHOTOGRAPHY**
136 Pond St
Winchester, MA 01890
Telephone: (781) 729-3747, E-Mail:
frank@franksiteman.com, Web Site:
www.franksiteman.com
Owner: Frank Siteman
Employees: 1
Founded: 1985
Gross sales or billing: $200,000

EDUARDO FUSS
2462 Camino Capitan
Santa Fe, NM 87505-6464
Telephone: (505) 424-0304, FAX:
(505) 424-0602
Owner: Eduardo Fuss

**PETER GLASS
PHOTOGRAPHY**
15 Oakwood St
East Hartford, CT 06108
Telephone: (860) 528-8559, E-Mail:
peter@peterglass.com, Web Site:
www.peterglass.com
Owner: Peter Glass

HENRY GROSSMAN
100 W 76th St (Apt 6N)
New York, NY 10023-8444
Telephone: (212) 580-7751
Owner: Henry Grossman

HODES PHOTOGRAPHY
Subs. of Close Encounter Productions
503 Crown Point Dr
Buffalo Grove, IL 60089
Telephone: (847) 215-3939, E-Mail:
hodesphotography@comcast.net,
Web Site: www.hodesphotography.
com
Dir: Chuck Hodes

**HOLLENBECK
PRODUCTIONS**
19241 Normandy Park Dr SW
Seattle, WA 98166
Telephone: (206) 592-1800, FAX:
(206) 592-9199, E-Mail: pixhot@aol.
com, Web Site: www.
hollenbeckproductions.com
Creative Dir: Nancy Hollenbeck

**DAVID K HOROWITZ
STUDIO INC**
915 N 28th St
Philadelphia, PA 19130
Telephone: (215) 765-3600, FAX:
(215) 763-1056
VP: Robert Horowitz

THE ICON
5450 Wilshire Blvd
Los Angeles, CA 90036
Telephone: (323) 933-1666, E-Mail:
icon@iconia.com, Web Site: www.
iconia.com

IMAGESTATE
29 E 19th St (4th fl)
New York, NY 10003-1307
Telephone: (212) 982-1915, FAX:
(212) 725-1241, E-Mail: photo@
internationalstock.com

**WILLIAM KOECHLING
PHOTOGRAPHY**
1307 E Harrison Ave
Wheaton, IL 60187
Telephone: (630) 665-4379, Web Site:
www.koechlingphoto.com
Owner: William Koechling

**THE LAKEVILLE JOURNAL
LLC**
PO Box 1688, 33 Bissell St
Lakeville, CT 06039-1688
Telephone: (860) 435-9873, FAX:
(860) 435-4802
Publr & Ed-in-Chief: Janet Manko

E TRINA LIPTON
60 E Eighth St (#15F)
New York, NY 10003
Telephone: (917) 327-6886, (212) 674-
5558, FAX: (212) 674-3523, E-Mail:
trinalipton@hotmail.com
Dir: E. Trina Lipton
Founded: 1970

LYNN MCAFEE
11324 1/2 Hatteras St
North Hollywood, CA 91601-1276
Telephone: (818) 763-0227
Photographer: Lynn D. McAfee
Founded: 1974

Services - product shots, studio photography, production stills for movies, tv, music videos & commercials, photo journalism, home layouts, photo sessions on location.

CHRISTOPHER MORROW PHOTOGRAPHY

522 NW Blue Lake Dr
Port Saint Lucie, FL 34986-2650
Telephone: (845) 325-1233, E-Mail:
    chris@chrismorrow.com, Web Site:
    www.chrismorrow.com
Owner: Christopher Morrow

OMEGA STUDIOS

168 E Highland Ave
Elgin, IL 60120-5564
Telephone: (972) 444-8556, FAX:
    (972) 444-8559, E-Mail:
    omegastudios@rrd.com, Web Site:
    www.omega-studios.com
VP, Sls: Larry Quinn

THE DMA OUR365

3613 Neller Rd
Saint Charles, MO 63301
Telephone: (636) 946-5136, Web Site:
    www.growingfamily.com
VP, New Bus Devel: Gay Bredemeier

PHOTO SHUTTLE JAPAN

1501 Ford Rd Lot 37
Chapel Hill, NC 27516-5749
Telephone: (919) 967-1585, E-Mail:
    sonia@photoshuttle.com, Web Site:
    www.photoshuttle.com
Dir: Sonia Katchian

PHOTOGRAPHIX

PO Box 8213
Ann Arbor, MI 48107-8213
FAX: (734) 476-2068, E-Mail:
    lkburghardt@comcast.net
Owner: Lance Burghardt

SHELLY RUSTEN

PO Box 120
Hankins, NY 12741-0120
Telephone: (917) 421-0980, (845) 887-
    5662, E-Mail: srusten@msn.com,
    Web Site: www.shellyrusten.com
Pres: Shelly Rusten

SARAH PUTNAM

320 Brookline St
Cambridge, MA 02139
Telephone: (617) 547-3758, E-Mail:
    sarah@sarahputnam.com, Web Site:
    www.sarahputnam.com
Pres: Sarah Putnam

WALTER WEISSMAN PHOTO STUDIO

463 West St (Suite B-332)
New York, NY 10014-2031
Telephone: (212) 989-9694, FAX:
    (212) 989-9694, E-Mail:
    wweissmanphoto@nyc.rr.com, Web
    Site: www.weissmanphoto.com
Pres: Walter Weissman

MICHAEL WILSON PHOTOGRAPHER

1604 Manss Ave
Cincinnati, OH 45205
Telephone: (513) 289-3855, E-Mail:
    michaelwilson@fuse.net, Web Site:
    www.michaelwilsonphotographer.
    com
Owner: Mike Wilson

Stock Photo Agencies (38) — Geographic Index

Arizona

Jupiter Images, 5232 E Pima St (Suite 200-C), Tucson, 85712

The Source Stock Footage Library Inc, 140 S Camino Seco (Suite 308), Tucson, 85710-4473

California

Animal Fund, Fort Mason (Quarters 35 N), San Francisco, 94123-1313

Biological Photo Service & Terraphotographics, 80 Eureka Sq (Suite 146), Pacifica, 94044-2676

eFootage, 87 N Raymond Ave (Suite 850), Pasadena, 91103-3968

Foster Travel Publishing, Box 5715, Berkeley, 94705

Jeroboam, 120 27th St, San Francisco, 94110-4313

Minden Pictures, 558 Main St, Watsonville, 95076-4318

PhotoEdit Inc, 3505 Cadillac Ave (Suite P101), Costa Mesa, 92626-1434

Shooting Star International, 1441 N McCadden, Hollywood, 90028

Underwood Photo Archives Inc, 143 Alta Vista Rd, Woodside, 94062

University of Southern California, University Library, Dept of Special Collections, Los Angeles, 90089-0189

Colorado

Viesti Associates Inc, 361 S Camino Del Rio (Suite 111), Durango, 81303

Connecticut

Ideal Images, 324 Cavan Ln, Glastonbury, 06033-2485

New England Stock Photo, 2389 Main St (Suite 303), Glastonbury, 06033-6399

Florida

Tom Stack & Associates Inc, 154 Tequesta St, Tavernier, 33070

Superstock Inc, 6622 Southpoint Dr S Ste 230, Jacksonville, 32216-6171

Idaho

David R Frazier Photolibrary Inc, 1921 Cataldo Dr, PO Box 5242, Boise, 83705

Illinois

Stock Montage Inc, 1817 N Mulligan Ave, Chicago, 60639

Tony Stone Images, 122 S Michigan Ave (Suite 900), Chicago, 60603

Indiana

Trends International LLC, 5188 W 74th St, Indianapolis, 46268

Louisiana

DDB Stock Photography LLC, 4845 Newcomb Dr, Baton Rouge, 70808-4747

Maine

North Wind Picture Archives, 12 Waterboro Rd, Alfred, 04002-3243

Maryland

History (Reference & Preservation) Division, 291 Wood Rd, Annapolis, 21402-5035

Massachusetts

Anthro Photo File, 33 Hurlbut St, Cambridge, 02138-1603

Davis Art Images, 50 Portland St, Worcester, 01608-2013

Image Photos/Clemens Kalischer, 34 Main St, Stockbridge, 01262

LLR/Research, 21 Wingate St, Haverhill, 01832

Stock Boston LLC, 258 Harvard St (#355), Brookline, 02446

Michigan

ChinaStock/WorldViews, 2506 Country Village, Ann Arbor, 48103-6500

Minnesota

Chip Peterson Photos, 1711 Lincoln Ave, Saint Paul, 55105-1952

Scenic Photo!, 9208 32nd Ave N, Minneapolis, 55427-2325

New Jersey

Bergman Medical/Scientific/Technical Collection, PO Box AG, Princeton, 08542-0872

New York

AP Images, 450 W 33rd St, New York, 10001

American Heritage Picture Library, 90 Fifth Ave, New York, 10011-7629

Animals Animals/Earth Scenes, 17 Railroad Ave, Chatham, 12037-1117

Art Resource Inc, 536 Broadway (fl 5), New York, 10012-3915

Black Star Publishing Co, 1 Water St, White Plains, 10601-1009

Corbis Images, 250 Hudson St (fl 5), New York, 10013

Culver Pictures Inc, 5102 21st St, Long Island City, 11101-5838

Desion Conceptions, 112 Fourth Ave (4th fl), New York, 10003-5421

Esto Photographics Inc, 222 Valley Pl, Mamaroneck, 10543

eStock Photo, 27-28 Thomson Ave (Suite 628), Long Island City, 11101

Ewing Galloway Inc, PO Box 343, Oceanside, 11572-0343

Fundamental Photographs, 210 Forsyth St, New York, 10002

Globe Photos Inc, 24 Edmore Ln S, West Islip, 11795-4016

Joel Gordon Photography, 112 Fourth Ave (4th fl), New York, 10003-5421

The Granger Collection, 381 Park Ave S (Suite 901), New York, 10016-8827

Al Grotell, Underwater Photography, 170 Park Row (#15D), New York, 10038-1154

The Image Bank, 75 Varick St (5th fl), New York, 10013

The Image Works Inc, PO Box 443, Woodstock, 12498

Magnum Photos Inc, 151 W 25th St, New York, 10001-7204

The New York Times Agency - Photo, 620 8th Ave., New York, 10018

Photo Researchers Inc, 307 5th Ave Fl 3, New York, 10016-6517

Photofest, 32 E 31st St (5th fl), New York, 10016-6881

Phototake/The Creative Link, 260 W 35th St, New York, 10001

Sipa Press, 307 Seventh Ave (Suite 807), New York, 10001-6066

Sports Illustrated Picture Sales, 135 W 50th St, New York, 10020

VAGA (Visual Artists & Galleries Associations Inc), 350 Fifth Ave (Suite 2820), New York, 10118

North Carolina

Billy E Barnes, 313 Severin St, Chapel Hill, 27516-1512

Novastock Photo Agency, 1306 Matthews Plantation Dr, Matthews, 28105

Ohio

Lincoln Picture Studio, 225 Lookout Dr, Dayton, 45419-3813

Pennsylvania

Brown Brothers, 100 Bortree Rd, Sterling, 18463-0050

Grant Heilman Photography Inc, 506 W Lincoln Ave, PO Box 317, Lititz, 17543-8707

H Armstrong Roberts Inc, 4203 Locust St, Philadelphia, 19104

Roberts Stock/Classic Stock, 4203 Locust St, Philadelphia, 19104-5228

Rhode Island

Envision, 27 Hoppin Rd, Newport, 02840

Utah

The Stock Solution Inc, 6640 S 2200 W, West Jordan, 84084-2203

Virginia

Photri Images LLC, 9653 Sherman Oaks Ct, Fairfax, 22032-2816

Washington

Getty Images, 605 Fifth Ave S (Suite 400), Seattle, 98104-3887

West Virginia

AppaLight, 230 Griffith Run Rd, Spencer, 25276-6809

Wisconsin

PhotoSource International, 1910 35th Rd, Pine Lake Farm, Osceola, 54020-5602

CANADA
Quebec

Keystone Press Agency Inc, 664 Grosvenor Ave, Montreal, H3Y 2S8

Stock Photo Agencies (38)

AP IMAGES
Subs. of The Associated Press
450 W 33rd St
New York, NY 10001
Telephone: (212) 621-1930, FAX:
(212) 621-1955, E-Mail:
apimages_us@ap.org, Web Site:
www.apimages.com

**AMERICAN HERITAGE
PICTURE LIBRARY**
Forbes Inc
90 Fifth Ave
New York, NY 10011-7629
Telephone: (212) 206-5107, (800) 777-
1222, FAX: (212) 367-3151, Web
Site: www.americanheritage.com
Editor: Joshua Zeitz

ANIMAL FUND
Fort Mason (Quarters 35 N)
San Francisco, CA 94123-1313
Telephone: (415) 775-4636, E-Mail:
delphinus@aol.com, Web Site: www.
animalfund.org
Exec Dir: Stan Minasian

**ANIMALS ANIMALS/EARTH
SCENES**
17 Railroad Ave
Chatham, NY 12037-1117
Telephone: (518) 392-5500, (800) 392-
5503, FAX: (518) 392-5550, E-Mail:
info@animalsanimals.com, Web Site:
www.animalsanimals.com
Exec VP: Nancy Carrizales

ANTHRO PHOTO FILE
33 Hurlbut St
Cambridge, MA 02138-1603
Telephone: (617) 868-4784, FAX:
(617) 484-6428, Web Site: www.
anthrophoto.com
Pres: Nancy S. DeVore

APPALIGHT
230 Griffith Run Rd
Spencer, WV 25276-6809
Telephone: (304) 927-2978, E-Mail:
wyro@appalight.com, Web Site:
www.appalight.com
Owner: Chuck Wyrostok
Founded: 1988

Provides photo assignment coverage in
the Charleston WV region & a wide
array of stock images from Appalachia.

ART RESOURCE INC
536 Broadway (fl 5)
New York, NY 10012-3915
Telephone: (212) 505-8700, FAX:
(212) 505-2053, E-Mail: requests@
artres.com, Web Site: www.artres.
com
Pres: Ted Feder

**BERGMAN MEDICAL/
SCIENTIFIC/TECHNICAL
COLLECTION**
Div. of Project Masters Inc
PO Box AG
Princeton, NJ 08542-0872
Telephone: (609) 921-0749, E-Mail:
information@pmiprinceton.com, Web
Site: www.pmiprinceton.com
Pres: Richard L. Bergman
VP: Victoria Bergman

BILLY E BARNES
313 Severin St
Chapel Hill, NC 27516-1512
Telephone: (919) 942-6350, FAX:
(919) 942-6350, E-Mail:
bbarnes218@aol.com, Web Site:
www.billybarnes.com
Pres: Billy E. Barnes

**BIOLOGICAL PHOTO
SERVICE &
TERRAPHOTOGRAPHICS**
80 Eureka Sq (Suite 146)
Pacifica, CA 94044-2676
Telephone: (650) 359-6219, FAX:
(650) 359-6219, E-Mail: bpsterra@
pacbell.net, Web Site: www.agpix.
com/biologicalphoto
Owner: Carl W. May

**BLACK STAR PUBLISHING
CO**
1 Water St
White Plains, NY 10601-1009
Telephone: (212) 679-3288, FAX:
(212) 889-2052, Web Site: www.
blackstar.com
Pres & Mktg Dir: Benjamin J. Chadnick

BROWN BROTHERS
100 Bortree Rd
Sterling, PA 18463-0050
Telephone: (570) 689-9688, FAX:
(570) 689-7873, E-Mail: info@
brownbrotherusa.com, Web Site:
www.brownbrothersusa.com

Pres: Raymond A. Collins

CHINASTOCK/WORLDVIEWS
Subs. of Dennis Cox LLC
2506 Country Village
Ann Arbor, MI 48103-6500
Telephone: (734) 996-1440, (800) 315-
4462, FAX: (734) 996-1481, E-Mail:
decoxphoto@aol.com, Web Site:
www.denniscox.com
Pres: Dennis Cox

CHIP PETERSON PHOTOS
1711 Lincoln Ave
Saint Paul, MN 55105-1952
Telephone: (651) 699-4286, FAX:
(651) 698-7667
Mktg Dir: Rosa Maria de la Cueva-
Peterson

CORBIS IMAGES
Div. of Corbis
250 Hudson St (fl 5)
New York, NY 10013
Telephone: (212) 777-6200, FAX:
(212) 375-7700, Web Site: www.
corbis.com
Sr VP, Div of Corbis: Leslie Hughes

CULVER PICTURES INC
5102 21st St
Long Island City, NY 11101-5838
Telephone: (718) 752-9393, FAX:
(718) 752-9394, Web Site: www.
culverpictures.com
Pres & Mktg Dir: Harriet Culver

**DDB STOCK PHOTOGRAPHY
LLC**
4845 Newcomb Dr
Baton Rouge, LA 70808-4747
Telephone: (225) 763-6235, FAX:
(225) 763-6894, E-Mail: info@
ddbstock.com, Web Site: www.
ddbstock.com
Pres: Douglas Donne Bryant

DAVIS ART IMAGES
Div. of Davis Publications Inc
50 Portland St
Worcester, MA 01608-2013
Telephone: (508) 754-7201, (800) 533-
2847, FAX: (508) 753-3834, (508)
831-9260, E-Mail: lkeenekendrick@
davisart.com, Web Site: www.
davisartimages.com
Mktg Coord: Lydia Keene-Kendrick

Dir: Wyatt Wade

DESION CONCEPTIONS
Subs. of Joel Gordon Photography
112 Fourth Ave (4th fl)
New York, NY 10003-5421
Telephone: (212) 254-1688, FAX:
(212) 533-0760, E-Mail: joel.
gordon@verizon.net, Web Site:
joelgordonphotography.com
Dir: Joel Gordon

EFOOTAGE
87 N Raymond Ave (Suite 850)
Pasadena, CA 91103-3968
Telephone: (626) 395-9593, FAX:
(626) 395-5394, E-Mail: info@
efootage.com, Web Site: www.
efootage.com
VP: Lawrence Faso

ENVISION
27 Hoppin Rd
Newport, RI 02840
Telephone: (401) 619-1500, (800) 524-
8238, FAX: (401) 619-0130, E-Mail:
envision@att.net, Web Site: www.
envision-stock.com
Pres: Sue Pashko

ESTO PHOTOGRAPHICS INC
222 Valley Pl
Mamaroneck, NY 10543
Telephone: (914) 698-4060, FAX:
(914) 698-1033, E-Mail: esto@esto.
com, Web Site: www.esto.com
Pres: Erica Stoller
Photo Researcher: Christine Cordazzo

ESTOCK PHOTO
27-28 Thomson Ave (Suite 628)
Long Island City, NY 11101
Telephone: (212) 689-5580, (800) 284-
3399, FAX: (212) 545-1185, E-Mail:
sales@estockphoto.com, Web Site:
www.estockphoto.com

EWING GALLOWAY INC
PO Box 343
Oceanside, NY 11572-0343
Telephone: (516) 764-8620, E-Mail:
ewinggalloway@aol.com, Web Site:
www.indexstock.com
Mgr: Janet McDermott

FOSTER TRAVEL
PUBLISHING
Box 5715
Berkeley, CA 94705
Telephone: (510) 549-2202, FAX:
(510) 549-1131, E-Mail: lee@
fostertravel.com, Web Site: www.
fostertravel.com
Pres: Lee Foster

DAVID R FRAZIER
PHOTOLIBRARY INC
1921 Cataldo Dr, PO Box 5242
Boise, ID 83705
Telephone: (208) 342-9250, (800) 342-
3283, FAX: (208) 342-2307, E-Mail:
dave@drfphoto.com, Web Site:
www.drfphoto.com
Pres & Mktg Mgr: David R. Frazier

FUNDAMENTAL
PHOTOGRAPHS
210 Forsyth St
New York, NY 10002
Telephone: (212) 473-5770, FAX:
(212) 228-5059, E-Mail: mail@
fphoto.com, Web Site: www.fphoto.
com
Dir: Richard Megna

THE DMA GETTY IMAGES
605 Fifth Ave S (Suite 400)
Seattle, WA 98104-3887
Telephone: (206) 925-5018, (800) 462-
4379, Web Site: www.gettyimages.
com
Co-Founder, Chmn: Mark Getty
Co-Founder & CEO: Jonathan Klein
Sr VP & Bus Devel: Richard Ellis
Dir Global Direct Mktg: Kimberly
Stewart
Sr VP Imagery & Svcs: Nick Evans-
Lombe

GLOBE PHOTOS INC
24 Edmore Ln S
West Islip, NY 11795-4016
Telephone: (212) 645-9292, FAX:
(212) 627-8932
COO & Mktg Dir: Raymond F.
Whelan

JOEL GORDON
PHOTOGRAPHY
112 Fourth Ave (4th fl)
New York, NY 10003-5421
Telephone: (212) 254-1688, E-Mail:
joel.gordon@verizon.net, Web Site:
www.joelgordonphotography.com
Pres: Joel Gordon

THE GRANGER
COLLECTION
381 Park Ave S (Suite 901)
New York, NY 10016-8827
Telephone: (212) 447-1789, FAX:
(212) 447-1492, Web Site: www.
granger.com
Mng Dir: Lila Dlaboha
VP Sls: Richard Becker
VP: Mary Loeffler
Founded: 1981

The Granger collection is an historical
picture library encompassing people,
places, things and events of the world
from prehistoric times through the
mid-20th century.

AL GROTELL, UNDERWATER
PHOTOGRAPHY
170 Park Row (#15D)
New York, NY 10038-1154
Telephone: (212) 349-3165, FAX:
(212) 349-4363
Owner: Al Grotell

GRANT HEILMAN
PHOTOGRAPHY INC
506 W Lincoln Ave, PO Box 317
Lititz, PA 17543-8707
Telephone: (717) 626-0296, (800) 622-
2046, FAX: (717) 626-0971, E-Mail:
info@heilmanphoto.com, Web Site:
www.heilmanphoto.com
Pres: Sonia Shaner Wasco

HISTORY (REFERENCE &
PRESERVATION) DIVISION
US Naval Institute
291 Wood Rd
Annapolis, MD 21402-5035
Telephone: (410) 268-6110, (800) 233-
8764, FAX: (410) 571-7940, E-Mail:
dsheehan@usni.org, Web Site: www.
usni.org
HRP Dir: Paul Stillwell
Adv Mgr: Dave Sheehan

IDEAL IMAGES
324 Cavan Ln
Glastonbury, CT 06033-2485
Telephone: (860) 633-8600, FAX:
(860) 659-3235
Pres: Rich James

THE IMAGE BANK
75 Varick St (5th fl)
New York, NY 10013
Telephone: (646) 613-4000, FAX:
(646) 613-4601, Web Site: www.
gettyimages.com
Pres: Mark Getty

IMAGE PHOTOS/CLEMENS
KALISCHER
34 Main St
Stockbridge, MA 01262
Telephone: (413) 298-5500, FAX:
(413) 298-5500, E-Mail: inform@
bcn.net
Dir & Owner: Clemens Kalischer

THE IMAGE WORKS INC
PO Box 443
Woodstock, NY 12498

Telephone: (845) 679-8500, (800) 475-
8801, FAX: (845) 679-0606, E-Mail:
info@theimageworks.com, Web Site:
www.theimageworks.com
Pres: Mark Antman

JEROBOAM
120 27th St
San Francisco, CA 94110-4313
Telephone: (415) 312-0198 cell,
E-Mail: jeroboamster@gmail.com
Owner & Pres: Ellen Bunning

JUPITER IMAGES
5232 E Pima St (Suite 200-C)
Tucson, AZ 85712
Telephone: (520) 881-8101, (800) 764-
7427, FAX: (520) 881-1841, Web
Site: www.jupiterimages.com
Pres: Judy Curiale

KEYSTONE PRESS AGENCY INC
664 Grosvenor Ave
Montreal, PQ, Canada H3Y 2S8
Telephone: (514) 482-5312, (877) 482-
5312, FAX: (514) 483-9005, E-Mail:
pictures@keystonepressagency.com,
Web Site: www.ketstonepressagency.
com
Founder: Bob Moynier

LLR/RESEARCH
21 Wingate St
Haverhill, MA 01832
Telephone: (978) 374-0931, FAX:
(978) 374-1008
Owner: Linda L. Rill

LINCOLN PICTURE STUDIO
225 Lookout Dr
Dayton, OH 45419-3813
Telephone: (937) 439-9633
Owner: Dan Ostendorf

Lincoln & civil war photographs,
original art.

MAGNUM PHOTOS INC
151 W 25th St
New York, NY 10001-7204
Telephone: (212) 929-6000, FAX:
(212) 929-9325, E-Mail:
photography@magnumphotos.com,
Web Site: www.magnumphotos.com
Mng Dir: Mark Lubell

MINDEN PICTURES
558 Main St
Watsonville, CA 95076-4318
Telephone: (831) 761-3600, (888) 825-
0641, FAX: (831) 761-3233, E-Mail:
info@mindenpictures.com, Web Site:
www.mindenpictures.com

Pres: Larry Minden

NEW ENGLAND STOCK PHOTO
2389 Main St (Suite 303)
Glastonbury, CT 06033-6399
FAX: (860) 659-3235
Owner: Rich James

THE NEW YORK TIMES AGENCY - PHOTO
Div. of The New York Times
620 8th Ave.
New York, NY 10018
Telephone: (212) 556-4939, (888)
NYT-PHOTO, FAX: (212) 556-5257,
E-Mail: photosales@nytimes.com,
Web Site: www.nytimesagency.com

NORTH WIND PICTURE ARCHIVES
12 Waterboro Rd
Alfred, ME 04002-3243
Telephone: (207) 490-1940, (800) 952-
0703, FAX: (207) 490-3627, E-Mail:
mail@northwindpictures.com, Web
Site: www.northwindpictures.com
Dir: Nancy L. Carter

NOVASTOCK PHOTO AGENCY
1306 Matthews Plantation Dr
Matthews, NC 28105
Telephone: (704) 847-6185, (888) 894-
8622, FAX: (704) 841-8181, E-Mail:
novastock@aol.com, Web Site:
www.creativeshake.com/novastock
Pres: Gerard Fritz

PHOTO RESEARCHERS INC
307 5th Ave Fl 3
New York, NY 10016-6517
Telephone: (212) 758-3420, (800) 833-
9033, FAX: (212) 355-0731, E-Mail:
info@photoresearchers.com, Web
Site: www.photoresearchers.com
Pres: Robert L. Zentmaier

PHOTOEDIT INC
3505 Cadillac Ave (Suite P101)
Costa Mesa, CA 92626-1434
Telephone: (800) 860-2098, FAX:
(800) 804-3707, E-Mail: sales@
photoeditinc.com, Web Site: www.
photoeditinc.com
Pres: Leslye Borden

PHOTOFEST
32 E 31st St (5th fl)
New York, NY 10016-6881
Telephone: (212) 633-6330, FAX:
(212) 366-9062, E-Mail: requests@
photofestnyc.com

Pres: Howard Mandelbaum

PHOTOSOURCE INTERNATIONAL
1910 35th Rd, Pine Lake Farm
Osceola, WI 54020-5602
Telephone: (715) 248-3800, X27, (800)
223-3860, FAX: (715) 248-3800,
E-Mail: info@photosource.com, Web
Site: www.photosource.com
Editor: Lela LaBree
Dir: Rohn Engh

PHOTOTAKE/THE CREATIVE LINK
260 W 35th St
New York, NY 10001
Telephone: (212) 736-2525, (800) 542-
3686, FAX: (212) 736-1919, E-Mail:
photoinfo@phototakeusa.com, Web
Site: www.phototakeusa.com
Pres & CEO: Yoav Levy

PHOTRI IMAGES LLC
9653 Sherman Oaks Ct
Fairfax, VA 22032-2816
Telephone: (703) 978-0129, E-Mail:
info@photriimages.com, Web Site:
www.photriimages.com
Owner: Gail Schooefield
Owner: Sharon Dupuis

H ARMSTRONG ROBERTS INC
4203 Locust St
Philadelphia, PA 19104
Telephone: (212) 685-3870, (800) 786-
6300, FAX: (800) 786-1920, E-Mail:
info@robertstock.com, Web Site:
www.robertstock.com

ROBERTS STOCK/CLASSIC STOCK
4203 Locust St
Philadelphia, PA 19104-5228
Telephone: (213) 386-4600, (800) 786-
6300, FAX: (213) 365-7171, E-Mail:
aspstockpix@earthlink.net, Web Site:
www.americanstockphotos.com
Pres: Christopher C. Johnson

SCENIC PHOTO!
9208 32nd Ave N
Minneapolis, MN 55427-2325
Telephone: (612) 810-0797, E-Mail:
manager@scenicphoto.com, Web
Site: www.scenicphoto.com
Owner: Conrad Bloomquist

SHOOTING STAR INTERNATIONAL

Div. of Shooting Star International
  Photo Agency
1441 N McCadden
Hollywood, CA 90028
Telephone: (323) 469-2020, FAX:
  (323) 464-0880, Web Site: www.
  shootingstaragency.com
Pres: Yoram Kahana

SIPA PRESS

307 Seventh Ave (Suite 807)
New York, NY 10001-6066
Telephone: (212) 463-0150, FAX:
  (212) 463-0160, E-Mail: sipa@usa.
  com, Web Site: www.sipa.com
Dir: Blake Sell

THE SOURCE STOCK FOOTAGE LIBRARY INC

140 S Camino Seco (Suite 308)
Tucson, AZ 85710-4473
Telephone: (520) 298-4810, FAX:
  (520) 290-8831, E-Mail: requests@
  sourcefootage.com, Web Site: www.
  sourcefootage.com
Pres: Bill Briggs
Library Mgr: Don French
Founded: 1982

SPORTS ILLUSTRATED PICTURE SALES

Div. of AOL Time Warner
135 W 50th St
New York, NY 10020
FAX: (212) 522-0102, E-Mail:
  andrew_judelson@timeinc.com
CMO: Andrew Judelson

TOM STACK & ASSOCIATES INC

154 Tequesta St
Tavernier, FL 33070
Telephone: (305) 852-5520, E-Mail:
  tomstack@earthlink.net, Web Site:
  www.tomstackassociatesphotoshelter.
  com
VP: Tom Stack

STOCK BOSTON LLC

258 Harvard St (#355)
Brookline, MA 02446
Telephone: (617) 266-2300, FAX:
  (617) 277-0502, E-Mail: requests@
  stockboston.com, Web Site: www.
  stockboston.com
Pres: Michael Mazzaschi

STOCK MONTAGE INC

1817 N Mulligan Ave
Chicago, IL 60639
Telephone: (773) 637-9790, (800) 404-
  0425, FAX: (773) 637-9794, E-Mail:
  mail@stockmontage.com, Web Site:
  www.stockmontage.com
Gen Mgr: Tom Neiman

THE STOCK SOLUTION INC

6640 S 2200 W
West Jordan, UT 84084-2203
Telephone: (801) 566-8684, (888) 366-
  0430, FAX: (801) 961-8030, E-Mail:
  info@tssphoto.com, Web Site: www.
  tssphoto.com
Pres: Royce Bair

SUPERSTOCK INC

6622 Southpoint Dr S Ste 230
Jacksonville, FL 32216-6171
Telephone: (904) 565-0066, (800) 828-
  4545, FAX: (904) 641-4480, E-Mail:
  yourfriends@superstock.com, Web
  Site: www.superstockimages.com
CEO: Thomas V. Butta

TONY STONE IMAGES

Subs. of Getty Images (London)
122 S Michigan Ave (Suite 900)
Chicago, IL 60603
Telephone: (800) 234-7880, FAX:
  (312) 922-9075, Web Site: www.
  getty-images.com
Pres: Andrew Duncomb

TRENDS INTERNATIONAL LLC

5188 W 74th St
Indianapolis, IN 46268
Telephone: (317) 388-1212, (800) 354-
  4639, FAX: (317) 388-1414, E-Mail:
  info@trendsinternational.com, Web
  Site: www.trendsinternational.com
Dir: Steve Patterson

UNDERWOOD PHOTO ARCHIVES INC

143 Alta Vista Rd
Woodside, CA 94062
Telephone: (650) 851-5190, FAX:
  (650) 851-5193, E-Mail: ray@
  underwoodarchives.com, Web Site:
  www.underwoodarchives.com
Pres: Raymond Chipault

UNIVERSITY OF SOUTHERN CALIFORNIA

University Library, Dept of Special
  Collections
Los Angeles, CA 90089-0189
Telephone: (213) 821-2366, FAX:
  (213) 740-2343, E-Mail: taube@usc.
  edu, Web Site: www.usc.edu
Reg History Collection Librarian: Dace
  Taube

VAGA (VISUAL ARTISTS & GALLERIES ASSOCIATIONS INC)

350 Fifth Ave (Suite 2820)
New York, NY 10118
Telephone: (212) 736-6666, FAX:
  (212) 736-6767, E-Mail: rpanzer@
  vaga.erols.com
Pres: Richard Anuszkiewicz

VIESTI ASSOCIATES INC

361 S Camino Del Rio (Suite 111)
Durango, CO 81303
Telephone: (970) 382-2600, FAX:
  (970) 382-2700, E-Mail: photos@
  viestiphoto.com, Web Site: www.
  viestiassociates.com
Pres: Joe Viesti

Copywriters (39) — Geographic Index

California

Carnival Creations, 126 Agostino, Irvine, 92614-8420

Catalyst Creative Services, 619 Marion Pl, Palo Alto, 94301-4251

Steven P d'Adolf, 2008 Harbor Dr N, Oceanside Marinia Inn, Oceanside, 92054-1034

The Marketing Machine, 4790 Irvine Blvd (Suite 105), Irvine, 92620-1998

Mayne Associates, PO Box 48, Lafayette, 94549

McNamara & Associates, 6647 Peach Ave, Van Nuys, 91406

Lea Pierce Direct Response Strategy & Execution, 1007B W College Ave (#190), Santa Rosa, 95401-5029

Colorado

The Write Direction, 948 North St (#12), Boulder, 80304-3386

Connecticut

Al Bredenberg Creative Services, 211 Greenwood Ave 2-2 (Suite 234), Bethel, 06801

Jane Corcillo, 17 Karen Dr, Norwalk, 06851-6012

O'Halloran Advertising, 270 Saugatuck Ave, Westport, 06880-6431

Florida

Creative Freelancers Inc, 7133 W Country Club Dr N Apt 150, Sarasota, 34243-3519

Jim Kerwin Freelance Copywriter, 12013 Covent Garden Ct (#2902), Naples, 34120-4689

Lewis Enterprises, 451 Heritage Dr (Suite 215), Pompano Beach, 33060-7778

Richard K Neukranz Associates, 4569 Glen Kernan Pkwy E, Jacksonville, 32224-5628

Galen Stilson Copywriter, 1338 Kinsmore Dr, Trinity, 34655

Illinois

Across The Board Marketing Inc, 1636 N Wells St (#2515), Chicago, 60614-6037

Bauer Associates, 301 N Water St, Batavia, 60510

Paul Connors Creative, 213 Surrey Ln, Lake Forest, 60045-3488

Creative Copywriting, 4300 Glenlow Dr, Plainfield, 60586-7813

Bill Gershon Marketing Communications, 9828 Crawford Ave, Skokie, 60076-1107

Steve A Glaser Communications Services, 1903 Southwood Dr, Champaign, 61821-5428

Holden Copywriting, PO Box 5, Deerfield, 60015-0005

JSA Creative Services LLC, 2525 N Talman Ave, Chicago, 60647

Kevin J. Shea & Associates, 311 N Hickory Ave, Arlington Heights, 60004-6210

Maine

John Lovell Communication Services, 59 Richardson St, Portland, 04103-2518

Maryland

Daly Direct Marketing, 8911 Bradley Blvd, Potomac, 20854-4602

Frank Joseph, 5617 Warwick Pl, Chevy Chase, 20815-5503

J Stack & Associates, 4402 Wickford Rd, Baltimore, 21210

Massachusetts

Joan Greenfield Creative, 111 Perkins St (Suite 043), Jamaica Plain, 02130

Brian Turley & Co, 61 Sheffield Rd, Melrose, 02176

Michigan

Barbara S Anderson, 706 W Davis, Ann Arbor, 48103-4855

Susan K Jones & Associates, 251 Plymouth Ave SE, Grand Rapids, 49506-1755

Minnesota

S Connelly & Co Inc, 9687 Jeske Ave NW, Annandale, 55302-2936

Colleen Szot - Wonderful Writer Inc, 13615 61st Ave N, Minneapolis, 55446-3503

New Hampshire

Duncan Direct Associates, 16 Elm St, Peterborough, 03458

New Jersey

Bob Bly, 590 Delcina Dr, River Vale, 07675-6111

The Copy Pro, 684 Park Ave, Oradell, 07649-2008

The Copy Shoppe, 186 Mendham Rd E, Mendham, 07945-3012

The Wordstation, 526 Main St Ste 2, Avon By The Sea, 07717-1061

New Mexico

John Nicksic, 707 E Palace Ave (#2), Santa Fe, 87501

Open Horizons, PO Box 2887, Taos, 87571-2887

New York

B-T-B Internet Marketing Solutions, 7 Putter Ln, Linick Bldg, Middle Island, 11953-1920

Backman Writing & Communications, 32 Hillview Ave, Rensselaer, 12144-3513

Monte Brick, Wordsmith, Six Inwood Pl, Melville, 11747

Copywriter's Council of America - (Freelancers), 7 Putter Ln, Middle Island, 11953-1920

Samuel Feldman, 165 West End Ave (Suite 10H), New York, 10023

Diane Gallo Associates, PO Box 106, Gilbertsville, 13776-0106

Jack Galub, 1339 York Ave, New York, 10021-4707

Greenberg Consulting, 390A Heritage Hills, Somers, 10589-1989

Max Lent Communications, 812 Conventry Dr, Webster, 14580

Lerose Copywriting, 628 Meadowbrook Rd, Uniondale, 11553-2620

Robert Lerose, 628 Meadowbrook Rd, Uniondale, 11553-2620

Andrew S Linick PhD-The Copyologist (R), PO Box 102, Linick Bldg, Middle Island, 11953-0102

Martin Gross & Friends, 145 E 27th St (Penthouse C), New York, 10016-9039

Geraldine Newman Communications, 315 E 72nd St (Suite 5K), New York, 10021

Tom Pelletier, 204 Bay Ave, Patchogue, 11772-4006

Richard Silverman, 83-33 Austin St, Kew Gardens, 11415-1814

GJ Whalen & Co Inc, 451 High Cliffe Ln, Tarrytown, 10591

North Carolina

Charlie Browne Communications, 3002 Atando Ct, Apex, 27502-4150

Clausen Enterprises, 128A Main St, Hendersonville, 28792-5065

Creative Direct Marketing, 402 Whitehead Cir, Chapel Hill, 27514-4833

JL Green & Associates, 7727 Goshen Rd, Oxford, 27565-5502

Ohio

Direct Creative, 701 Lookout Ridge Dr, Westerville, 43082-8601

Don Pendell & Associates, 2622 Wayland Ave, Dayton, 45420

Profit Boosters Copywriting, 525 Club Dr, Aurora, 44202

Pennsylvania

Barcia Direct Marketing, 19 Oxford Dr, Langhorne, 19047-2056

CoreMessagink, 334 Valleybrook Dr, Lancaster, 17601-4633

Hebden Direct, 634 Spruce St, Philadelphia, 19106

Mark Everett Johnson Inc, 1201 Sadler Dr, Carlisle, 17013-4262

Texas

Luther Brock PhD, The Letter Doctor, 2911 Nottingham Dr, Denton, 76209-1352

Utah

Stephen Kimball DM Copywriting, 9489 N Canyon Heights Dr, Cedar Hills, 84062-8812

Copywriters (39)

**ACROSS THE BOARD
MARKETING INC**
1636 N Wells St (#2515)
Chicago, IL 60614-6037
Telephone: (312) 787-1642, FAX:
 (312) 787-1645, E-Mail: info@
 acrosstheboardmarketing.com, Web
 Site: www.acrosstheboardmarketing.
 com
Pres: Anne Aldrich

BARBARA S ANDERSON
706 W Davis
Ann Arbor, MI 48103-4855
Telephone: (734) 995-0125, FAX:
 (734) 994-5207
Copywriter & Graphic Artist: Barbara
 Anderson

**B-T-B INTERNET
MARKETING SOLUTIONS**
Div. of The Linick Group Inc
7 Putter Ln, Linick Bldg
Middle Island, NY 11953-1920
Telephone: (631) 924-3888, E-Mail:
 linickgroup@gmail.com, Web Site:
 www.linick.net; 222.asklinick.com
Pres: Gaylen Andrews
Exec VP: Shane Clarke
VP: Roger Dexter

**BACKMAN WRITING &
COMMUNICATIONS**
32 Hillview Ave
Rensselaer, NY 12144-3513
Telephone: (518) 449-4985, FAX:
 (518) 449-7273, E-Mail: johnb@
 backwrite.com, Web Site: www.
 backwrite.com
Principal: John Backman

**BARCIA DIRECT
MARKETING**
19 Oxford Dr
Langhorne, PA 19047-2056
Telephone: (215) 757-5785, FAX:
 (215) 757-5785, E-Mail:
 j.barciadirect@comcast.net
Pres: Joseph A. Barcia

BAUER ASSOCIATES
301 N Water St
Batavia, IL 60510
Telephone: (630) 406-8595, FAX:
 (630) 406-8596, E-Mail: lbauer@
 bauerassoc.net, Web Site: www.
 bauerassoc.net
Owner: Larry Bauer

BOB BLY
590 Delcina Dr
River Vale, NJ 07675-6111
Telephone: (201) 505-9451, FAX:
 (201) 573-4094, E-Mail: rwbly@bly.
 com, Web Site: www.bly.com
Copywriter: Bob Bly

**AL BREDENBERG CREATIVE
SERVICES**
Div. of Bredenberg Associates Inc
211 Greenwood Ave 2-2 (Suite 234)
Bethel, CT 06801
Telephone: (203) 743-1946, E-Mail:
 ab@copywriter.com, Web Site:
 www.copywriter.com
Pres: Al Bredenberg

MONTE BRICK, WORDSMITH
Six Inwood Pl
Melville, NY 11747
Telephone: (631) 549-9640, FAX:
 (631) 549-9640
Pres: Monte Brick

**LUTHER BROCK PHD, THE
LETTER DOCTOR**
2911 Nottingham Dr
Denton, TX 76209-1352
Telephone: (940) 387-8058
Pres: Luther A. Brock Jr

**CHARLIE BROWNE
COMMUNICATIONS**
3002 Atando Ct
Apex, NC 27502-4150
Telephone: (919) 267-9271, FAX:
 (919) 267-9271, E-Mail:
 cbrownecom@sbcglobal.net
Pres: Charlie Browne

CARNIVAL CREATIONS
126 Agostino
Irvine, CA 92614-8420
Telephone: (949) 833-9370, FAX:
 (949) 955-2078
VP & Creative Dir: Steven Finkelstein

**CATALYST CREATIVE
SERVICES**
619 Marion Pl
Palo Alto, CA 94301-4251
Telephone: (650) 325-1500, E-Mail:
 chief@catalystcreative.us, Web Site:
 www.catalystcreative.us
Owner: Dennis Briskin

CLAUSEN ENTERPRISES
dba copy-design.com
128A Main St
Hendersonville, NC 28792-5065
Telephone: (828) 777-7339, E-Mail:
 jhclausen@mchsi.com, Web Site:
 www.copy-design.com
Owner: John Clausen

S CONNELLY & CO INC
9687 Jeske Ave NW
Annandale, MN 55302-2936
Telephone: (320) 274-7054, E-Mail:
 sconco@aol.com
Pres: Stephen P. Connelly

PAUL CONNORS CREATIVE
213 Surrey Ln
Lake Forest, IL 60045-3488
Telephone: (847) 295-8746
Pres: Paul F. Connors

THE COPY PRO
684 Park Ave
Oradell, NJ 07649-2008
Telephone: (201) 986-1080, FAX:
 (201) 986-1170, E-Mail:
 thecopypro@aol.com, Web Site:
 www.thecopypronj.com
Response Dir & Sls Promo
 Copywriter: Kristina Elliot

THE COPY SHOPPE
Div. of CataLogistics Inc
186 Mendham Rd E
Mendham, NJ 07945-3012
Telephone: (973) 543-2679, FAX:
 (973) 543-2679, E-Mail:
 catalogistics@juno.com, Web Site:
 www.catalogistics.com
Pres: Jack Schrier

**COPYWRITER'S COUNCIL
OF AMERICA -
(FREELANCERS)**
Div. of The Linick Group Inc. aka
 CCA
7 Putter Ln
Middle Island, NY 11953-1920
Telephone: (631) 924-3888, FAX:
 (631) 924-8555, E-Mail:
 cca4dmcopy@gmail.com, Web Site:
 www.linick.net; www.
 andrewlinickdirectmarketing.com
Exec VP: Roger Dextor
Pres: Gaylen Andrews

COREMESSAGINK
334 Valleybrook Dr
Lancaster, PA 17601-4633
Telephone: (717) 207-0212, Web Site:
www.cormessagink.com
Pres & Co-Founder: Lindy Litrides
Conducts Business: U.S.
Primary Market Served: Business &
Consumer
Founded: 2001

Inspired creative messaging to attract,
maintain and advance your donor
relationships.

CREATIVE COPYWRITING
4300 Glenlow Dr
Plainfield, IL 60586-7813
Telephone: (815) 439-9160, FAX:
(815) 439-9158
Pres: John M. Mora

CREATIVE DIRECT MARKETING
402 Whitehead Cir
Chapel Hill, NC 27514-4833
Telephone: (919) 929-5757, E-Mail:
jeffb.cdm@mindspring.com
Principal: Jeff D. Bryant

CREATIVE FREELANCERS INC
7133 W Country Club Dr N Apt 150
Sarasota, FL 34243-3519
Telephone: (203) 532-2924, (800) 398-
9544, E-Mail: cfonline@freelancers.
com, Web Site: www.freelancers.com
Pres: Marilyn Howard

STEVEN P D'ADOLF
2008 Harbor Dr N, Oceanside Marinia
Inn
Oceanside, CA 92054-1034
Telephone: (858) 451-2130, FAX:
(858) 451-2130
Pres: Steve Adolf

DALY DIRECT MARKETING
8911 Bradley Blvd
Potomac, MD 20854-4602
Telephone: (301) 365-3201, FAX:
(301) 365-7514
Pres: M. Virginia Daly

DIRECT CREATIVE
701 Lookout Ridge Dr
Westerville, OH 43082-8601
Telephone: (614) 882-8823, E-Mail:
dean@directcreative.com, Web Site:
www.directcreative.com
Pres: Dean Rieck

DUNCAN DIRECT ASSOCIATES
16 Elm St
Peterborough, NH 03458
Telephone: (603) 924-3121, FAX:
(603) 924-8511, E-Mail:
duncandirect@pobox.com, Web Site:
www.duncandirect.com
Pres: George Duncan

SAMUEL FELDMAN
165 West End Ave (Suite 10H)
New York, NY 10023
Telephone: (212) 362-9517, E-Mail:
samuelfeldman@verizon.net
Pres: Samuel Feldman

FRANK JOSEPH
5617 Warwick Pl
Chevy Chase, MD 20815-5503
Telephone: (301) 656-8753, E-Mail:
mr.dm@verizon.net
Pres: Frank Joseph

DIANE GALLO ASSOCIATES
PO Box 106
Gilbertsville, NY 13776-0106
Telephone: (607) 783-2386, E-Mail:
dgallo@stny.rr.com, Web Site: www.
dianegallo.com
Owner: Diane Gallo

JACK GALUB
1339 York Ave
New York, NY 10021-4707
Telephone: (212) 737-9013
Pres: Jack Galub

BILL GERSHON MARKETING COMMUNICATIONS
9828 Crawford Ave
Skokie, IL 60076-1107
Telephone: (847) 676-9452, FAX:
(847) 674-7205, E-Mail: gershcom@
yahoo.com
Owner & Creative Dir: Bill Gershon

STEVE A GLASER COMMUNICATIONS SERVICES
1903 Southwood Dr
Champaign, IL 61821-5428
Telephone: (217) 351-0981, FAX:
(217) 351-0981, E-Mail: steve@
sagcs.net, Web Site: www.sags.net
Pres: Steve A. Glaser

JL GREEN & ASSOCIATES
7727 Goshen Rd
Oxford, NC 27565-5502
Telephone: (919) 693-3713
Pres: Jim Green

GREENBERG CONSULTING
390A Heritage Hills
Somers, NY 10589-1989
Telephone: (914) 669-8588, FAX:
(914) 669-8888, E-Mail: mgreenb@
sover.net
Pres: Martin Greenberg

JOAN GREENFIELD CREATIVE
111 Perkins St (Suite 043)
Jamaica Plain, MA 02130
Telephone: (617) 983-2055, FAX:
(617) 983-2056, E-Mail: jgcreative@
aol.com
Pres: Joan Greenfield

HEBDEN DIRECT
634 Spruce St
Philadelphia, PA 19106
Telephone: (215) 923-3891, E-Mail:
hebdendirect@comcast.net
Pres & Partner: William Hebden

HOLDEN COPYWRITING
PO Box 5
Deerfield, IL 60015-0005
Telephone: (847) 236-0669, E-Mail:
holdendm@aol.com
Pres: Stan Holden

JSA CREATIVE SERVICES LLC
2525 N Talman Ave
Chicago, IL 60647
Telephone: (773) 772-3445, FAX:
(773) 772-3446, E-Mail:
jsacreative@comcast.net, Web Site:
www.jsacreative.com
Pres: Jill Shtulman

JANE CORCILLO
17 Karen Dr
Norwalk, CT 06851-6012
Telephone: (203) 866-2008, FAX:
(203) 299-0844, E-Mail: queries@
corcillodirect.com, Web Site: www.
corcillodirect.com
Pres: Jane Corcillo

MARK EVERETT JOHNSON INC
1201 Sadler Dr
Carlisle, PA 17013-4262
Telephone: (603) 465-3888, FAX:
(603) 465-3889, E-Mail: mark@
copy.pro
Pres: Mark E. Johnson

SUSAN K JONES & ASSOCIATES
251 Plymouth Ave SE
Grand Rapids, MI 49506-1755

Telephone: (616) 458-0305, E-Mail:
sjones9200@aol.com
Owner: Susan K. Jones

JIM KERWIN FREELANCE COPYWRITER
12013 Covent Garden Ct (#2902)
Naples, FL 34120-4689
Telephone: (239) 597-4445, E-Mail:
jwkerwin@mac.com
Owner: Jim Kerwin

THE DMA STEPHEN KIMBALL DM COPYWRITING
9489 N Canyon Heights Dr
Cedar Hills, UT 84062-8812
Telephone: (801) 796-7234, FAX:
(801) 796-5799, E-Mail: stephen@
skcopywriting.com, Web Site: www.
skcopywriting.com
Owner: Stephen Kimball
Conducts Business: U.S. & Canada
Employees: 1
Primary Market Served: Business
Founded: 2005
Gross sales or billing: $500,000

Direct response copywriting.

MAX LENT COMMUNICATIONS
812 Conventry Dr
Webster, NY 14580
Telephone: (585) 670-9707, E-Mail:
max@maxlent.com, Web Site: www.
maxlent.com
Dir: Max Lent

THE DMA LEROSE COPYWRITING
628 Meadowbrook Rd
Uniondale, NY 11553-2620
Telephone: (516) 486-0472, FAX:
(516) 486-0386, E-Mail: robertler@
optonline.net, Web Site: www.
robertlerose.com
Pres: Robert Lerose

ROBERT LEROSE
628 Meadowbrook Rd
Uniondale, NY 11553-2620
Telephone: (516) 486-0472, FAX:
(516) 486-0386, E-Mail: robertler@
optonline.net, Web Site: www.
robertlerose.com
Pres: Robert Lerose
Conducts Business: U.S.
Employees: 1
Primary Market Served: Business
Advertising/Marketing Budget Related
to Direct Marketing: 26-50%
Founded: 1994

Provides marketing and corporate communications copywriting to business-to-business and consumer marketers.

LEWIS ENTERPRISES
451 Heritage Dr (Suite 215)
Pompano Beach, FL 33060-7778
Telephone: (954) 782-1750, FAX:
(954) 785-3391, E-Mail: hglewis1@
aol.com; hgl@herschellgordonlewis.
com, Web Site: www.
herschellgordonlewis.com
Author: Herschell Gordon Lewis
Primary Market Served: Business &
Consumer
Catalog available online
Founded: 1984

3rd edition, On the Art of Writing
Copy, ISBN: 0-9704515-4-7. 4th edition 2011: Internet marketing tips,
tricks & tactics. Marketing mayhem.

ANDREW S LINICK PHD-THE COPYOLOGIST (R)
Div. of The Linick Group Inc
PO Box 102, Linick Bldg
Middle Island, NY 11953-0102
Telephone: (631) 924-3888, (631) 775-
6075, FAX: (631) 924-8555, E-Mail:
andrewlinick@gmail.com; andrew@
asklinick.com, Web Site: www.
andrewlinickdirectmarketing.com;
www.asklinick.com
Pres: Dr. Andrew S. Linick

JOHN LOVELL COMMUNICATION SERVICES
59 Richardson St
Portland, ME 04103-2518
Telephone: (207) 774-0232, FAX:
(207) 774-0232
Dir: John Lovell

THE MARKETING MACHINE
4790 Irvine Blvd (Suite 105)
Irvine, CA 92620-1998
Telephone: (949) 733-3778, (949) 733-
1778, FAX: (949) 559-6993, E-Mail:
request@the-marketing-machine.
com, Web Site: www.mktgmach.com
Pres: Virginia Nicols

MARTIN GROSS & FRIENDS
145 E 27th St (Penthouse C)
New York, NY 10016-9039
Telephone: (212) 689-0772, FAX:
(212) 481-0552, E-Mail:
grossdirect@aol.com
Pres: Martin Gross

MAYNE ASSOCIATES
PO Box 48
Lafayette, CA 94549
Telephone: (925) 284-8500, FAX:
(925) 284-8502
Owner: Clifton P. Mayne

MCNAMARA & ASSOCIATES
6647 Peach Ave
Van Nuys, CA 91406
Telephone: (818) 907-6212, E-Mail:
jim@mcdrtv.com, Web Site: www.
mcdrtv.com
Owner & Pres: Jim McNamara

RICHARD K NEUKRANZ ASSOCIATES
4569 Glen Kernan Pkwy E
Jacksonville, FL 32224-5628
Telephone: (904) 998-1201, FAX:
(904) 998-1579, E-Mail: rneukranz@
bellsouth.net
Pres: Richard K. Neukranz

GERALDINE NEWMAN COMMUNICATIONS
315 E 72nd St (Suite 5K)
New York, NY 10021
Telephone: (212) 988-3395, FAX:
(212) 988-3407, E-Mail: ger@
newthynk.com, Web Site: www.
newthynk.com
Owner: Geraldine Newman

JOHN NICKSIC
707 E Palace Ave (#2)
Santa Fe, NM 87501
Telephone: (505) 983-7656, FAX:
(505) 983-7159, E-Mail: nicksic@
mindspring.com
Pres: John Nicksic

O'HALLORAN ADVERTISING
270 Saugatuck Ave
Westport, CT 06880-6431
Telephone: (203) 571-6203
Dir Sls: Mark O'Halloran
Primary Market Served: Consumer

A full service agency specializing in
D/R, Directory (YP) advertising &
local searchs as well as general advertising for regional & national clients.

OPEN HORIZONS
Div. of Open Horizons
PO Box 2887
Taos, NM 87571-2887
Telephone: (575) 751-3398, FAX:
(575) 751-3100, E-Mail: info@
bookmarket.com, Web Site: www.
bookmarket.com
Pres: John Kremer

TOM PELLETIER
204 Bay Ave
Patchogue, NY 11772-4006
Telephone: (631) 569-5552, FAX:
(413) 825-7968, E-Mail: tom@
tompelletier.com, Web Site: www.
tompelletier.com
Owner & Writer: Tom Pelletier

DON PENDELL & ASSOCIATES
2622 Wayland Ave
Dayton, OH 45420
Telephone: (937) 254-4210
Pres: Don Pendell

LEA PIERCE DIRECT RESPONSE STRATEGY & EXECUTION
1007B W College Ave (#190)
Santa Rosa, CA 95401-5029
Telephone: (707) 571-1586, (800) 932-4748, E-Mail: info@leapierce.com,
Web Site: www.leapierce.com
Owner: Lea Pierce

PROFIT BOOSTERS COPYWRITING
525 Club Dr
Aurora, OH 44202
Telephone: (330) 963-0330, FAX: (330) 562-2446, E-Mail:
mikepavlish@profitboosterscopy.com, Web Site: www.profitboosterscopy.com
Pres: Mike Pavlish

KEVIN J. SHEA & ASSOCIATES
311 N Hickory Ave
Arlington Heights, IL 60004-6210
Telephone: (847) 392-2713
Owner & Pres: Kevin J. Shea

RICHARD SILVERMAN
83-33 Austin St
Kew Gardens, NY 11415-1814
Telephone: (718) 441-5358, FAX: (718) 441-5358, E-Mail: vze268ci@verizon.net
Owner: Richard Silverman

J STACK & ASSOCIATES
4402 Wickford Rd
Baltimore, MD 21210
Telephone: (410) 889-3327, FAX: (410) 889-9039
Owner: J. Stack

GALEN STILSON COPYWRITER
1338 Kinsmore Dr
Trinity, FL 34655
Telephone: (727) 372-2032, E-Mail: galen@galenstilson.com, Web Site: www.galenstilson.com
Pres: Galen Stilson

COLLEEN SZOT - WONDERFUL WRITER INC
13615 61st Ave N
Minneapolis, MN 55446-3503
Telephone: (763) 557-7116, (888) 557-7116, FAX: (763) 551-4831, E-Mail: colleen@wonderfulwriter.com, Web Site: www.wonderfulwriter.com
Owner & Pres: Colleen Szot

BRIAN TURLEY & CO
61 Sheffield Rd
Melrose, MA 02176
Telephone: (781) 662-8538, FAX: (781) 662-5590, E-Mail: turley@shore.net
Pres: Brian C. Turley
Employees: 1
Founded: 1981

GJ WHALEN & CO INC
451 High Cliffe Ln
Tarrytown, NY 10591
Telephone: (914) 333-0085, E-Mail: george@gjwhalen.com, Web Site: www.whalen.cc
Pres: George J. Whalen

THE WORDSTATION
526 Main St Ste 2
Avon By The Sea, NJ 07717-1061
Telephone: (732) 774-4831, FAX: (732) 869-1822, E-Mail: pattyshannone@optonline.net
Owner: Patty Shannon

THE WRITE DIRECTION
948 North St (#12)
Boulder, CO 80304-3386
Telephone: (808) 635-8031, E-Mail: debra@writedirection.com, Web Site: www.writedirection.com
Owner & Copywriter: Debra Jason

Direct Marketing Associations, Clubs & Organizations (40)

Listed in this section are associations, clubs and membership organizations related to all areas of the direct marketing industry.

THE DMA ADVERTISING RESEARCH FOUNDATION

432 Park Ave S (fl 6)
New York, NY 10016-8013
Telephone: (212) 751-5656, FAX:
(212) 319-5265, E-Mail: info@
thearf.org, Web Site: www.thearf.org
Pres: Bob Barocci
Membership Svcs: Jacqueline
McLoughlin
Sr VP, Opers: Carole White
Conducts Business: Worldwide
Employees: 18
Primary Market Served: Business &
Consumer

Non-profit professional association devoted to advertising research.

ALLIANCE OF NONPROFIT MAILERS

1211 Connecticut Ave NW (Suite 610)
Washington, DC 20036-2705
Telephone: (202) 462-5132, FAX:
(202) 462-0423, E-Mail: alliance@
nonprofitmailers.org, Web Site:
www.nonprofitmailers.org
Exec Dir: Neal Denton
Exec Dir: Anthony W. Conway
Asst Dir: Heidi Kustz
Policy & Program Asst: Melissa Simonich
Conducts Business: U.S.
Employees: 3
Primary Market Served: Business
Catalog available online
Advertising/Marketing Budget Related
to Direct Marketing: 0-25%
Founded: 1980

Represent non-profit mailers before the U.S. Congress, U.S. Postal Service & Postal Rate Commission.

THE DMA AMERICAN ASSOCIATION OF ADVERTISING AGENCIES

1065 Avenue Of The Americas Fl 16
New York, NY 10018-0174
Telephone: (212) 682-2500, FAX:
(212) 682-8391, Web Site: www.
aaaa.org
Pres: O. Burtch Drake

Exec VP & CFO: James Martucci
Exec VP: Michael D. Donahue
Sr VP: Marsha Appel
Bd Sec: Michele Adams
Conducts Business: U.S.
Employees: 95
Primary Market Served: Business
Catalog available online
Founded: 1917

Advertising trade association of full service advertising agency members.

AMERICAN INSTITUTE OF GRAPHIC ARTS (AIGA)

164 Fifth Ave
New York, NY 10010-5901
Telephone: (212) 807-1990, FAX:
(212) 807-1799, E-Mail: grefe@aiga.
org, Web Site: www.aiga.org
Exec Dir: Richard Grefe
Founded: 1914
Gross sales or billing: $5,400,000

National non-profit organization for the graphic design profession.

THE DMA AMERICAN ISRAEL PUBLIC AFFAIRS COMMITTEE

251 H St NW
Washington, DC 20001-2604
Telephone: (202) 639-5226, Web Site:
www.aipac.org
Primary Market Served: Business &
Consumer

AMERICAN MARKETING ASSOCIATION

311 S Wacker Dr (Suite 5800)
Chicago, IL 60606-6629
Telephone: (312) 542-9000, FAX:
(312) 542-9001, Web Site: www.
ama.org
CEO: Dennis Dunlap
Sr Mktg Dir: Nancy Costopulos
Employees: 63
Primary Market Served: Business
Catalog available online
Advertising/Marketing Budget Related
to Direct Marketing: 0-25%
Founded: 1937

Professional society of marketing & marketing research executives, sales & promotion managers, advertising specialists, academics & others interested in marketing. Foster research, sponsors & seminars & provide educational placement.

AMERICAN MARKETING ASSOCIATION/NEW YORK CHAPTER

116 E 27th St
New York, NY 10016-8942
Telephone: (212) 687-3280, FAX:
(212) 557-9242, E-Mail: mlkeane@
nyama.org, Web Site: www.nyama.
org
Exec Dir: Marylee Keane
Mktg Dir: Bart Lewin
Conducts Business: U.S.
Primary Market Served: Business
Catalog available online
Direct online sales

Association of marketing & market research professionals with international headquarters in Chicago, IL. Branch offices nationwide.

AMERICAN SOCIETY OF MEDIA PHOTOGRAPHERS (ASMP)

150 N Second St
Philadelphia, PA 19106-1912
Telephone: (215) 451-ASMP, FAX:
(215) 451-0880, Web Site: www.
asmp.org
Exec Dir: Eugene Mopsik
Gen Counsel: Victor Perlman
Gen Mgr: Elene Goertz
Bookkeeper: Chris Chandler
Dir Commun: Peter Dyson
Employees: 7
Primary Market Served: Business
Catalog available online
Indirect online sales
Founded: 1944

Maintain & promote high ethics in photography; cultivate mutual understanding among photographers; protect & promote photographer's interests.

AMERICAN TELESERVICES ASSOCIATION

8500 Keystone Xing Ste 480
Indianapolis, IN 46240-2460
Telephone: (317) 816-9336, (877) 779-3974, FAX: (317) 218-0323, Web
Site: www.ataconnect.org
Intirim Pres: Bob Kobek
Exec VP Bus Devel: Tom Chandler
Dir, Fin: Bill Morris
Mgr, Admin Svcs: Ken Hennenfent
Conducts Business: U.S., Canada, Australia, Japan, Europe, Mexico, South
America
Employees: 12
Primary Market Served: Business
Catalog available online
Indirect online sales
Advertising/Marketing Budget Related
to Direct Marketing: 0-25%
Direct Marketing ad budget:
Direct Mail: 20%
Telephone: 80%
Founded: 1983

Provide education & leadership in the
ethical use of the telephone in commerce & advocacy in relevant legislative affairs.

THE ARIZONA DIRECT MARKETING ASSOCIATION

2107 N 69th Pl
Scottsdale, AZ 85257-2630
Telephone: (480) 970-8643, FAX:
(480) 893-1157, E-Mail: julie@
brownies.com, Web Site: www.
azdma.org
Administrator: Julie Gaffney
Conducts Business: U.S.
Employees: 280
Primary Market Served: Business &
Consumer
Advertising/Marketing Budget Related
to Direct Marketing: 76-100%
Founded: 1979

Statewide direct marketing association.

THE DMA ASSOCIATION FOR POSTAL COMMERCE

1421 Prince St (Suite 410)
Alexandria, VA 22314-2806
Telephone: (703) 524-0096, FAX:
(703) 524-1871, Web Site: www.
postcom.org
Pres: Gene A. Del Polito
VP: Anthony Gallo
Admin Dir: Donna Hoffman
Conducts Business: U.S.
Employees: 4
Catalog available online
Advertising/Marketing Budget Related
to Direct Marketing: 76-100%
Direct Marketing ad budget: $20,000
Direct Mail: 100%
Founded: 1947

Gross sales or billing: $1,200,000
Interested in all legislation pertaining
to postal laws & regulations. Keep
members informed about happenings in
Congress, the U.S. Postal Service &
the Postal Rate Commission.

ASSOCIATION OF COUPON PROFESSIONALS

1051 Pontiac Rd
Drexel Hill, PA 19026-4816
Telephone: (610) 789-1478, FAX:
(610) 789-5309, E-Mail: john.
morgan@acp-hq.org, Web Site:
www.couponpros.org
Exec Dir: John Morgan
Primary Market Served: Business
Catalog available online
Direct online sales

Represent companies in the coupon
industry, including manufacturers, retailers, processors & suppliers. Membership is limited to corporations paying annual membership dues.

ASSOCIATION OF DESK-TOP PUBLISHERS (AD-TP)

3401 Adams Ave (#800)
San Diego, CA 92116-2490
Telephone: (619) 563-9714, FAX:
(619) 280-3778
Exec Dir: N.E. Paddock
Primary Market Served: Business

International trade association for desktop publishers.

ASSOCIATION OF ENERGY ENGINEERS

4025 Pleasantdale Rd (Suite 420)
Atlanta, GA 30340-4264
Telephone: (770) 447-5083 x210, FAX:
(770) 446-3969, E-Mail: info@
aeecenter.org, Web Site: www.
aeecenter.org
Dir: Brian Douglas
Dir Info Sys: Ruth Marie
Conducts Business: Worldwide
Employees: 12
Primary Market Served: Business
Catalog available online
Direct online sales
Founded: 1977

Technical conferences, seminars, exhibitions, certification & book programs
for energy engineers.

ASSOCIATION OF NATIONAL ADVERTISERS INC

708 3rd Ave
New York, NY 10017-4201
Telephone: (212) 697-5950, FAX:
(212) 687-7310, Web Site: www.ana.
net

COO: Christina Manna
Pres & CEO: Robert Liodice
Exec VP: Michael Palmer
Sr VP: William Zengel
Sr Dir: Tracy Owens
Sr Dir: Brian Davidson
Conducts Business: U.S.
Employees: 25
Primary Market Served: Business
Catalog available online
Direct online sales
Founded: 1910
Gross sales or billing: $16,000,000

Organization exclusively dedicated to
serving the interests of corporations
that advertise either regionally or
nationally. Membership is a cross section of American industry, consisting
of manufacturers, retailers, service providers, & financial institutions. Markets
to consumers & other companies.

BUSINESS MARKETING ASSOCIATION

1833 Center Point Cir (Suite 123)
Naperville, IL 60563-4848
Telephone: (630) 544-5054, FAX:
(630) 544-5055, E-Mail: info@
marketing.org, Web Site: www.
marketing.org
Chmn: Michael Lotti
Chmn: Debra Ringold
Pres: Colin Hageny
CEO: Dennis L. Dunlap
Sr Dir: Jack Hollfelder
Conducts Business: U.S., Canada, Europe, Asia, S. America
Employees: 4
Primary Market Served: Business
Catalog available online
Direct online sales
Advertising/Marketing Budget Related
to Direct Marketing: 0-25%
Founded: 1922

Association with over 4000 members
involved in business marketing & marketing communications.

THE DMA CANADIAN MARKETING ASSOCIATION

1 Concorde Gate (Suite 607)
Don Mills, ON, Canada M3C 3N6
Telephone: (416) 391-2362, FAX:
(416) 441-4062, E-Mail: info@the-cma.org, Web Site: www.the-cma.org
Sr Dir Commun: Ed Cartwright
Conducts Business: Canada
Employees: 28
Primary Market Served: Business &
Consumer
Catalog available online
Founded: 1967

Organization of Canadian individuals, companies, corporations, businesses, firms or undertakings that are users, creators, suppliers, servicers or producers of any form of information-based marketing. National convention & trade show held annually.

CHICAGO ASSOCIATION OF DIRECT MARKETING

PO Box 578
Westmont, IL 60559-0578
Telephone: (312) 849-2236, FAX: (312) 849-2239, E-Mail: info@cadm. org, Web Site: www.cadm.org
Pres: Joe DeCosmo
VP: Michelle Blechman
Conducts Business: U.S.
Primary Market Served: Business
Catalog available online

Hold monthly meetings, workshops, seminars & an annual two day conference in February to advance new ideas, current trends & future prospects in the direct response industry.

CROSSBOW GROUP

136 Main St Ste 5
Westport, CT 06880-3304
Telephone: (203) 222-2244, FAX: (203) 226-7838, E-Mail: info@ crossbowgroup.com, Web Site: www. crossbowgroup.com
Founder: H.W. Mirbach
Pres & CEO: Jay Bower
COO: Mary Plamieniak
Primary Market Served: Business & Consumer
Founded: 1984
Gross sales or billing: $1,250,000

Help companies quickly & efficiently acquire & retain new customers using traditional & digital media.

DMA (DIRECT MARKETING ASSOCIATION)

1120 Ave of the Americas
New York, NY 10036-6700
Telephone: (212) 768-7277, FAX: (212) 302-6714, E-Mail: customerservice@the-dma.org, Web Site: www.the-dma.org
Chmn: Donn Rappaport
Pres & CEO: John A. Greco Jr.
Exec VP & COO: Ramesh A. Lakshmi-Ratan Ph D.
Treas: David Kelly
Conducts Business: U.S.
Employees: 75
Primary Market Served: Business
Catalog available online
Direct online sales

A national association of direct marketing advertising agencies dedicated to education & service to direct marketing agencies. Membership roster is available.

DMG DIRECT INC

13335 SW Chimney Ridge Ct
Tigard, OR 97223-1849
Telephone: (503) 579-5609, (888) 282-2122, FAX: (503) 579-4919, E-Mail: dmg@dirmarketing.com, Web Site: www.dirmarketing.com/dmginc
Pres: Greg Bassine
Employees: 3
Primary Market Served: Business & Consumer
Founded: 1984
Gross sales or billing: $71,000

Provides the direct marketing community with an ongoing source of awareness, education, information & networking through the interaction of direct marketing professionals while maintaining the highest levels of ethics & standards within the direct marketing industry.

DMSA INC

One Enterprise Dr (Bldg H)
Newfoundland, PA 18445-0080
Telephone: (570) 676-6000
Mng Dir: Gerry Pike

DATADIRECT

American Marketing Association
2707 Peach Tree Sq
Atlanta, GA 30360-2634
Telephone: (678) 530-0034, FAX: (678) 530-9563, E-Mail: info@ ddirect.com, Web Site: www.ddirect. com
Pres: Tom Coggin
Conducts Business: U.S.
Employees: 20
Primary Market Served: Business & Consumer

Regional direct marketing association.

DIRECT MARKETING ASSOCIATION OF DETROIT

PO Box 70
Royal Oak, MI 48068-0070
Telephone: (248) 478-4888, FAX: (248) 478-6437, E-Mail: dmad@ ameritech.net, Web Site: www.dmad. org
Pres: Dan Chester
Treas: Bruce Moyer
Sec: Alex Della Torre
Dir: Terry Burnett
Dir: Dan Dembicki
Conducts Business: U.S.
Employees: 500

Primary Market Served: Business & Consumer
Founded: 1958

Hold monthly meetings & a "Direct Marketing Day" in the fall of each year. Also, monthly meetings first Thursday of each month, September through June.

DIRECT MARKETING ASSOCIATION OF NORTHERN CALIFORNIA

Sub. of www.the-dma.org
Div. of www.the-dma.org
15227 Perry Ln
Morgan Hill, CA 95037-9659
Telephone: (800) 613-9266, FAX: (800) 613-8819, E-Mail: lbeasley@ beasleydirect.com, Web Site: www. dmanc.org
Pres: Laurie Beasley
Primary Market Served: Business & Consumer

DIRECT MARKETING ASSOCIATION OF SAINT LOUIS

PO Box 1005
Washington, MO 63090-8005
Telephone: (866) 516-0121, FAX: (636) 239-2324, E-Mail: mparisien@ mac.com, Web Site: www.dmastl.org
Exec Dir: Sue Cullinane
VP: George Snyder
Pres: Maurice R. Parisien
Sec & Treas: Glenna Phillips
Conducts Business: U.S.
Primary Market Served: Business
Founded: 1975

A not-for-profit professional business association of users & suppliers of direct marketing media.

DIRECT MARKETING ASSOCIATION OF SOUTHERN CALIFORNIA

1800 Hillcrest Dr (#297)
Newbury Park, CA 91320
Telephone: (818) 541-1152, FAX: (818) 541-1959, Web Site: www. ladma.org
Pres: Steve Stullman
Exec Dir: Bob Hughes
Conducts Business: U.S.
Primary Market Served: Business & Consumer
Catalog available online
Direct online sales
Founded: 1980

Non-profit trade association of diners.

DIRECT MARKETING ASSOCIATION OF TORONTO

75 Superior Blvd
Toronto, ON, Canada M8V 4A1
Telephone: (905) 564-6616, FAX:
(905) 564-6621, E-Mail: pete@
themose.ca, Web Site: www.
dmatoronto.org
Pres: Alan Brodeur
Conducts Business: Canada
Primary Market Served: Business &
Consumer
Founded: 1962

Direct marketing association. Networking & ideas exchange form for Direct Marketing professionals.

DIRECT MARKETING ASSOCIATION OF WASHINGTON

11709 Bowman Green Dr
Reston, VA 20190
Telephone: (703) 689-DMAW, FAX:
(703) 481-DMAW, E-Mail: info@
dmaw.org, Web Site: www.dmaw.org
Exec Dir: Donna Tschiffely
Conducts Business: U.S.
Primary Market Served: Business
Founded: 1955

Professional association for 1500 DM professionals in the Washington metro area, with chapters in Central Virginia & Baltimore. Comprehensive schedule of seminars, monthly meetings & in-house training. Annual Conference & Expo is The Bridge Conference, co-hosted with Assn. of Fundraising Professionals, DC Metro Chapter and attended by more than 1500. Monthly newsletter & annual directory of members.

DIRECT SELLING ASSOCIATION

1667 K St NW (Suite 1100)
Washington, DC 20006-1660
Telephone: (202) 452-8866, FAX:
(202) 452-9010, E-Mail: info@dsa.
org, Web Site: www.dsa.org
Pres: Joseph Mariano
Exec VP: Adolfo Franco
VP & CMO: Amy Robinson
VP, Education & Meeting: Melissa
Brunton
Dir Opers: Jennifer Dunleavey
Conducts Business: US
Employees: 20
Primary Market Served: Business
Advertising/Marketing Budget Related
to Direct Marketing: 0-25%
Founded: 1910
Gross sales or billing: $6,000,000

Represents manufacturers & distributors selling consumer products door-to-door, by appointment & through home-party plans.

DIRECT SELLING EDUCATION FOUNDATION

1667 K St (Suite 1100)
Washington, DC 20006-1660
Telephone: (202) 452-8866, FAX:
(202) 452-9015, Web Site: www.
dsef.org
Sr Program Dir: Bettie Smith
Exec Dir: Judith A. Cranford
Employees: 6
Primary Market Served: Consumer
Catalog available online
Advertising/Marketing Budget Related
to Direct Marketing: 0-25%
Founded: 1973

Advocates of marketplace ethics, consumer knowledge & consumer satisfaction.

DISCMAIL DIRECT COALITION

39 North Bayles Ave
Port Washington, NY 11050-2930
Telephone: (516) 757-6720, Web Site:
http://mesalliance.org/
Primary Market Served: Consumer

FLORIDA DIRECT MARKETING ASSOCIATION

7154 University Dr (# 244)
Tamarac, FL 33321
Telephone: (786) 357-3275, E-Mail:
president@fdma.org, Web Site:
www.fdma.org
Pres: Keith Fletcher
Employees: 1
Primary Market Served: Business &
Consumer
Founded: 1977

A 500 member direct marketing association dedicated to the networking & education of direct marketers. In addition to monthly meetings, the association's annual convention DM Summit is held annually. Call for more information. Governer of the state of Florida proclaims that week as "Direct Market Industry Week."

FOOD MARKETING INSTITUTE (FMI)

2345 Crystal Dr (Suite 800)
Arlington, VA 22202
Telephone: (202) 452-8444, FAX:
(202) 429-4519, E-Mail: fmi@fmi.
org, Web Site: www.fmi.org
Pres & CEO: Tim Hammonds
Employees: 70
Primary Market Served: Business

Founded: 1971

A non-profit trade association representing the supermarket industry, both retail & wholesale.

THE DMA GREENPEACE USA

702 H St NW (Suite 300)
Washington, DC 20001
Telephone: (202) 462-1177, Web Site:
www.greenpeace.org
Primary Market Served: Business &
Consumer

HOUSTON DIRECT MARKETING ASSOCIATION

Box 2382
Houston, TX 77252-2382
Telephone: (281) 931-8883, FAX:
(281) 820-4023, Web Site: www.
houstondma.org
Pres: Dan Singer
VP Programs Chair: Deborah Hayden
Sec: Kent Guida
Treas: Art Fallon
Arrangements: Barbara Kilawee
Past Pres Membership: Steve Fowler
Newsletter: Harry Romberg
Direct Mktg Day Programs Chair:
Gem Smith
Sponsorships: James Helsley
July Social Mixer: Jim Richards
Direct Mktg Day Facilities: Tom Filla
Member at Large: Barbara Hicks
Member at Large: Elroy Forbes
Member at Large: Jennifer Hoff
Primary Market Served: Business &
Consumer
Founded: 1953

Purpose is: to eliminate trade abuse, upgrade the image of the direct marketing industry, improve operations & self-promotion methods, establish better industry communications, maintain a code of ethics among all direct marketers, foster friendship among those in the industry, conduct a conference for all direct marketers & promote Houston's direct marketing community.

THE DMA HUMAN RIGHTS CAMPAIGN

1640 Rhode Island Ave NW
Washington, DC 20036-3200
Telephone: (202) 216-1500, Web Site:
www.hrc.org
Primary Market Served: Business &
Consumer

IDEALLIANCE

SIG of Printing Industries of America
1421 Prince St (Suite 230)
Alexandria, VA 22314-2805
Telephone: (703) 837-1070, FAX:
(703) 837-1072
Pres & CEO: David J. Steinhardt

Conducts Business: Worldwide
Employees: 21
Primary Market Served: Business
Catalog available online
Founded: 1966

Volunteer, non-profit membership association for the printing & publishing industry. The purpose is to bring about the coordination among industry segments necessary to apply technologies & in other ways increase productivity & market responsiveness in the addressing & distribution of print & information products.

INCENTIVE MANUFACTURERS REPRESENTATIVES ASSOCIATION (IMRA)

Subs. of Incentive Marketing Assoc
1601 Bond St (Suite 303)
Naperville, IL 60563-3801
Telephone: (630) 369-7786, FAX:
(630) 369-3773, E-Mail: tom@
imraorg.net, Web Site: www.imraorg.net
Exec Dir: Thomas F. Renk
Pres: Gary Slavonic
Primary Market Served: Business & Consumer
Founded: 1963

An independent representative & supplier of products to the premium & incentive industry.

INTERNATIONAL PREPAID COMMUNICATIONS ASSOCIATION

904 Massachusetts Ave NE
Washington, DC 20002
Telephone: (202) 544-4448, FAX:
(202) 547-7417
Exec Dir: Howard Segermark
Employees: 6
Primary Market Served: Business
Founded: 1995
Gross sales or billing: $400,000

The trade association for the pre-paid phone card industry.

THE INTERNET ALLIANCE

1615 L St NW (Suite 1100)
Washington, DC 20036
Telephone: (202) 861-2476, FAX:
(202) 955-8081, E-Mail: info@
internetalliance.org, Web Site: www.internetalliance.org
Exec Dir: Emily T. Hackett
Conducts Business: U.S., Canada
Employees: 1
Primary Market Served: Business
Advertising/Marketing Budget Related to Direct Marketing: 0-25%
Founded: 1981

Trade association for interactive telecommunications services.

KANSAS CITY DIRECT MARKETING ASSOCIATION

638 W 39th St, PO Box 419264
Kansas City, MO 64141
Telephone: (816) 561-5323, FAX:
(816) 561-1991, E-Mail: info@
kcdma.org, Web Site: www.kcdma.org
Pres: Jill Intravartolo
Exec Dir: Jane Male
Conducts Business: U.S.
Employees: 450
Primary Market Served: Business
Founded: 1948

Association of direct marketers in Greater Kansas City. Hold monthly meetings (2nd Tuesday of every month), an annual direct marketing day in March & an annual awards program. Provide scholarships through the KCDMA educational foundation.

THE DMA LANGEVIN LEARNING SERVICES

38 Antares Dr (Suite 1200)
Ottawa, ON, Canada K2E 7V2
Telephone: (613) 288-3064, Web Site: www.langevin.com
Pres: Erin Langevin
Primary Market Served: Business

LICENSING INDUSTRY MERCHANDISERS' ASSOCIATION (LIMA)

350 Fifth Ave (Suite 1408)
New York, NY 10118-0110
Telephone: (212) 244-1944, FAX:
(212) 563-6552, E-Mail: info@
licensing.org, Web Site: www.licensing.org
Pres: Charles M. Riotto
Admin Dir: Janet Lawlor
Conducts Business: U.S., U.K., Germany, Japan
Employees: 5
Primary Market Served: Business
Catalog available online
Indirect online sales
Advertising/Marketing Budget Related to Direct Marketing: 0-25%
Founded: 1985
Gross sales or billing: $1,500,000

The International Trade Association for the advancement of professionalism in licensing.

LOUISVILLE DIRECT MARKETING ASSOCIATION

PO Box 36034
Louisville, KY 40233-6034

Telephone: (888) 392-1941, E-Mail:
ldmacontact@ldma.org, Web Site:
www.ldma.org
Pres: Al Klein
Treas: Jo Holt
Primary Market Served: Business
Advertising/Marketing Budget Related to Direct Marketing: 51-75%
Founded: 1983

Educational & social association dedicated to educating members in direct marketing.

THE DMA MAILING & FULFILLMENT SERVICE ASSOCIATION (MFSA)

1421 Prince St (Suite 410)
Alexandria, VA 22314-2805
Telephone: (703) 836-9200, (800) 333-6272, FAX: (703) 548-8204, E-Mail:
mfsa-mail@mfsanet.org, Web Site:
www.mfsanet.org
Dir Commun: William Stevenson
Pres & CEO: J. Kenneth Garner
Conducts Business: U.S., U.K., Canada, Japan, Australia, Germany
Employees: 10
Primary Market Served: Business
Catalog available online
Indirect online sales
Advertising/Marketing Budget Related to Direct Marketing: 76-100%
Direct Marketing ad budget: $100,000
Direct Mail: 75%
Magazines: 5%
Online: 20%
Founded: 1920
Gross sales or billing: $2,000,000

Trade association to mailing and fulfillment industry. Approximately 700 member companies-consisting primarily of mailing service companies.

MARKETING AGENCIES ASSOCIATION WORLDWIDE

89 Woodland Cr
Minneapolis, MN 55424
Telephone: (952) 922-0130, FAX:
(203) 969-1499, E-Mail: keith.
mccracker@maaw.org, Web Site:
www.maaw.org
VP, Global Opers: Brad Byen
Pres: Kieran Kileen
Sec: Rico Di Giovanni
Treas: Rich Butwinick
Conducts Business: Worldwide
Primary Market Served: Business
Founded: 1961

Provide support to agencies in the promotion & marketing field, concentrating on the development & growth of agencies.

MARKETING RESEARCH ASSOCIATION

1156 15th St NW Ste 302
Washington, DC 20005-1745
Telephone: (860) 682-1000, FAX:
(860) 682-1010, E-Mail: email@
mra-net.org, Web Site: www.mra-net.
org
CEO: Larry Brownell
COO: Kristen Darby
CFO: Tasha Jackson
Dir: Bruce Mendelsohn
Dir: Lucy Haydu
Membership Mgr: Lisa Lockwood
Conducts Business: Latin America,
Europe, Asia, Middle East, South
America
Employees: 12
Primary Market Served: Business &
Consumer
Catalog available online
Indirect online sales
Founded: 1954

Not-for-profit association dedicated to
promoting excellence in marketing &
opinion research members, includes
more than 3,000 full service research
companies, data collectors, end users
& more.

MID AMERICA DIRECT MARKETING ASSOCIATION

Subs. of NATIL DMA
1620 Dodge St
Omaha, NE 68197
Telephone: (402) 964-8444, FAX:
(402) 964-8484, Web Site: www.
madma.org
Pres: Matt Smolsky
VP: Jim Svoboda
VP: Mary Vorthmann
Primary Market Served: Business
Catalog available online
Indirect online sales

Professional organization of individual
members who share a common interest
in direct marketing.

MIDWEST DIRECT MARKETING ASSOCIATION INC

1821 University Ave W (Suite S-256)
Saint Paul, MN 55104
Telephone: (651) 999-5351, FAX:
(651) 917-1835, E-Mail: mdma@
mdma.org, Web Site: www.mdma.
org
Pres Elect: Joan Forde
Pres: Kevin Sheehy
Exec Dir: Lisa Larson
Conducts Business: U.S.
Employees: 1
Primary Market Served: Business
Advertising/Marketing Budget Related
to Direct Marketing: 76-100%

Founded: 1960

Members meet regularly to exchange
ideas & information about the direct
marketing field. Monthly newsletters,
monthly meetings, a direct marketing
conference in the spring, & an annual
awards competition recognizing excellence in Midwest direct marketing.

MODERNAD MEDIA LLC

2200 SW 10th St
Deerfield Beach, FL 33442-7622
Telephone: (561) 750-5131 X206, Web
Site: www.modernad.com
COO: Greg Vanhorn

NATIONAL CABLE & TELECOMMUNICATIONS ASSOCIATION

25 Massachusetts Ave NW (Suite 400)
Washington, DC 20001
Telephone: (202) 222-2300, FAX:
(202) 775-3675, Web Site: www.
ncta.com
Pres & CEO: Kyle McSlasrow
Sr VP: Eleanor Winites
Catalog available online
Advertising/Marketing Budget Related
to Direct Marketing: 0-25%
Founded: 1952
Gross sales or billing: $6,600,000

Represent the cable television industry.

NATIONAL MAIL ORDER ASSOCIATION (NMOA)

2807 Polk St NE
Minneapolis, MN 55418-2954
Telephone: (612) 788-1673, E-Mail:
info@nmoa.org, Web Site: www.
nmoa.org
Pres: John D. Schulte
Editor: Brad Lee
Conducts Business: Worldwide
Primary Market Served: Business
Catalog available online
Direct online sales
Advertising/Marketing Budget Related
to Direct Marketing: 76-100%
Direct Marketing ad budget:
Direct Mail: 75%
Magazines: 25%
Founded: 1972

Helps small & medium firms
(50,000,000 & under) in the area of
mail order & direct mail marketing.
Publishers of Mail Order Digest &
Washington Newsletter. Operates "The
Mail Order Connection" website. Also
operates the mail order trade show on
www.nmoadirect.com &
marketingdemographics.com; a con-
necting spot for manufacturers & merchandise buyers.

NETWEB/OMNI LLC

PO Box 1298
Ellicott City, MD 21041-1298
Telephone: (410) 591-1900, E-Mail:
barry@netwebomni.com, Web Site:
www.netwebomni.com
Pres: Barry Dennis
Webmaster: Daniel Dennis
Conducts Business: Worldwide
Employees: 15
Primary Market Served: Business &
Consumer
Catalog available online
Indirect online sales
Advertising/Marketing Budget Related
to Direct Marketing: 76-100%
Direct Marketing ad budget: $100,000
Direct Mail: 25%
Magazines: 20%
Newspapers: 25%
Online: 20%
Telephone: 10%
Founded: 1997

Online internet marketing consulting.
Review, design & monitor online &
offline marketing programs. Design &
recommend marketing programs that
maximize response to client websites
& offline marketing.

NETWORKING ALTERNATIVES FOR PUBLISHERS, RETAILERS & ARTISTS, INC

PO Box 9
Eastsound, WA 98245-0009
Telephone: (360) 376-2702, (800) 367-
1907, FAX: (360) 376-2704, E-Mail:
futureweb@rockisland.com
Exec Dir Membership & Trade Shows:
Suzanne Homes
Dir: Marilyn McGuire
Mng Ed Napra Review: Michael
Weaver
Employees: 12
Primary Market Served: Business
Catalog available online
Advertising/Marketing Budget Related
to Direct Marketing: 26-50%
Founded: 1986
Gross sales or billing: $1,000,000

Education, networking, bimonthly journal, trade show representation, membership gatherings.

NEW ENGLAND DIRECT MARKETING ASSOCIATION

354 Washington St (Suite 223)
Wellesley Hills, MA 02481-6221
Telephone: (781) 237-1366, FAX:
(781) 431-8118, E-Mail: info@
nedma.com, Web Site: www.nedma.
com
Pres: Craig Blake
VP Conference: Gary Lubarsky

VP Awards & Fin: Bruce McMeekin
VP Membership: Sherry Taylor Gil-
christ
VP Education: Christine J. Erna
Conducts Business: U.S.
Employees: 725
Primary Market Served: Business &
Consumer

Regional association of more than 900
firms & individuals using & supplying
direct marketing services - mail order,
direct mail or direct response. Meets
monthly; features direct marketing day
annually in the spring, plus awards
competition & special events.

THE DMA NEW ENGLAND MAIL ORDER ASSOCIATION

PO Box 658
Scarborough, ME 04070-0658
Telephone: (207) 885-0090, (860) 691-
1260, FAX: (207) 885-0097, Web
Site: www.nemoa.org
Pres: Jean Giesmann
VP: Margot Murphy Moore
Exec Dir: Janie Downey
Treas: Marlies Duke
Conducts Business: U.S.
Employees: 1
Primary Market Served: Business &
Consumer
Founded: 1947

Organization of over 250 members in
the catalog industry. Dedicated to information exchange. Holds conferences
in March & September.

NEWS & OBSERVER DIRECT MARKETING

215 S McDowell St
Raleigh, NC 27601-1331
Telephone: (919) 836-5658
Direct Mktg Mgr: Doug Rogers
Primary Market Served: Consumer

POPAI-THE GLOBAL ASSOCIATION FOR MARKETING AT-RETAIL

440 N Wells St (Suite 740)
Chicago, IL 60654
Telephone: (312)-863-2900, FAX:
(312) 229-1152, Web Site: www.
popai.com
Pres: Richard Winter
Primary Market Served: Business
Founded: 1936

Provides its members with a variety of
benefits designed to promote, protect
& advance the broader issues of point-
of-purchase advertising.

PHILADELPHIA DIRECT MARKETING ASSOCIATION INC

PO Box 1155
Havertown, PA 19083-0155
Telephone: (215) 473-1668, FAX:
(215) 477-1109, E-Mail: contact@
the-pdma.org, Web Site: www.the-
pdma.org
Pres: Lisa Formica
Conducts Business: U.S.
Primary Market Served: Business &
Consumer
Founded: 1943

Professional association for those involved in all aspects of direct marketing, primarily serving Pennsylvania,
New Jersey & Delaware. Holds
monthly meetings, publish monthly
newsletter & annual directory of
members. Also holds a two-day conference & exhibition.

PHOTOGRAPHIC SOCIETY OF AMERICA INC (PSA)

3000 United Founders Blvd (Suite
103)
Oklahoma City, OK 73112-4294
Telephone: (405) 843-1437, FAX:
(405) 843-1438, E-Mail: HQ@psa-
photo.org, Web Site: www.psa-photo.
org
Pres: Albert Sieg
Opers Mgr: Linda Lowery
Conducts Business: Worldwide
Employees: 3
Primary Market Served: Consumer
Catalog available online
Founded: 1934

Sponsor workshops & awards for
members.

THE DMA PROMOTIONAL PRODUCTS ASSOCIATION INTERNATIONAL

3125 Skyway Cir N
Irving, TX 75038-3526
Telephone: (972) 252-0404, FAX:
(800) I-AM-PPAI, (972) 258-3004,
E-Mail: membership@ppa.org, Web
Site: www.ppa.org
Pres: Steve Slagle
Dir: Rick Merrill
Exec VP: Paul Bellatone
Exec Office Mgr: Lisa Beck
Conducts Business: Worldwide
Employees: 56
Primary Market Served: Business
Catalog available online
Indirect online sales
Advertising/Marketing Budget Related
to Direct Marketing: 26-50%
Direct Marketing ad budget:
Direct Mail: $100,000
Magazines: $20,000

Founded: 1904
Gross sales or billing: $10,000,000

Membership trade association representing the manufacturers & distributors of promotional products, incentives, gifts, awards & premiums.

PUBLISHERS MARKETING ASSOCIATION (PMA)

627 Aviation Way
Manhattan Beach, CA 90266-7107
Telephone: (310) 372-2732, FAX:
(310) 374-3342, E-Mail: info@pma-
online.org, Web Site: www.pma-
online.org
Exec Dir: Jan Nathan
Mktg Dir: Amanda Ballard
Conducts Business: U.S., Germany,
Japan, Mexico, U.K., New Zealand,
Canada
Employees: 6
Primary Market Served: Business
Catalog available online
Direct online sales
Advertising/Marketing Budget Related
to Direct Marketing: 26-50%
Direct Marketing ad budget:
Direct Mail: 60%
Magazines: 40%
Founded: 1983

A national non-profit publishers' cooperative which coordinates discounted
participation in major book & library
exhibits & trade shows throughout the
country, as well as ad placement in
major publications & direct mail
programs.

Q INTERACTIVE

1 N Dearborn St (12th fl)
Chicago, IL 60602-4337
Telephone: (312) 977-0390, (888) 729-
6465, FAX: (312) 224-5001, E-Mail:
solutions@qinteractive.com, Web
Site: www.qinteractive.com
Pres & CEO: Matthew Moog
Sr VP, Sls: Christine McNicholas
VP Mktg: Melissa Lederer
Sr VP Mktg Prod Mngmt: Matt Wise
Employees: 135
Primary Market Served: Business &
Consumer
Indirect online sales
Advertising/Marketing Budget Related
to Direct Marketing: 76-100%
Direct Marketing ad budget:
$8,000,000
Direct Mail: 2%
Online: 98%
Founded: 1995
Gross sales or billing: $40,000,000

Interactive marketing services co for
advertisers, their agencies &
publishers. Provide lead generation,
email coupons & loyalty across a
broad distribution network.

SAN DIEGO DIRECT MARKETING ASSOCIATION

PO Box 91055
San Diego, CA 92191-0854
Telephone: (858) 503-1471, E-Mail:
webmaster@sddma.org, Web Site:
www.sddma.org
Exec Dir: Michele Nowicki
VP Communs: Carey Gansert
Conducts Business: U.S.
Primary Market Served: Business &
Consumer
Direct online sales
Advertising/Marketing Budget Related
to Direct Marketing: 76-100%
Founded: 1977

Hold monthly meetings & an annual
direct marketing day.

SPECIAL LIBRARIES ASSOCIATION (SLA)

331 S Patrick St
Alexandria, VA 22314-3501
Telephone: (703) 647-4900, FAX:
(703) 647-4901, E-Mail: sla@sla.org,
Web Site: www.sla.org
Mng Dir Conferences: Alicia Dimaio

ᵀᴴᴱ US CHAMBER INSTITUTE ᴰᴹᴬ FOR LEGAL REFORM

1615 H St NW (fl 2)
Washington, DC 20062-0001
Telephone: (202) 778-6063, Web Site:
www.uschamber.com
Primary Market Served: Business &
Consumer

VERMONT/NEW HAMPSHIRE DIRECT MARKETING GROUP

3016 Barberry Hill
Woodstock, VT 05091-1336
Telephone: (802) 457-2807, FAX:
(802) 457-2807, E-Mail: vtnhmg@
vtnhmg, Web Site: www.vtnhmg.org
Pres: Peter Cameron
VP Mktg: Sundeep Kapur
Exec Admin: Sari White
Employees: 1
Primary Market Served: Business &
Consumer
Advertising/Marketing Budget Related
to Direct Marketing: 76-100%
Founded: 1988

Trade association of direct marketers
and allied professionals in Vermont
and New Hampshire.

WESTERN FULFILLMENT MANAGEMENT ASSOCIATION INC

PO Box 15281
North Hollywood, CA 91615-5281

Telephone: (310) 323-7220, FAX:
(310) 323-7231, E-Mail: mjordan@
espcomp.com, Web Site: www.wfma.
org
Pres: Mike Popalardo
VP, Programs: John Brooks
VP, Membership: Michael Jordan
VP Publicity: Laura Simkins
Treas: Peter Klehm
Primary Market Served: Business
Catalog available online

THE WILDERNESS SOCIETY

1615 M St NW
Washington, DC 20036-3209
Telephone: (202) 429-2609, Web Site:
www.wilderness.org
Primary Market Served: Business &
Consumer

WISCONSIN DIRECT MARKETING ASSOCIATION

PO Box 13036
Milwaukee, WI 53213-0036
Telephone: (414) 760-9362, FAX:
(414) 431-4195, E-Mail: info@
wdma.org, Web Site: www.wdma.org
Exec Dir: Jane Svinicki
Conducts Business: U.S.
Employees: 2
Primary Market Served: Business

Statewide association of direct marketing professionals whose primary purpose is to provide educational & networking opportunities & to promote
excellence in direct marketing. Meet
monthly & host annual convention &
trade show in May. Membership roster
is available to members only.

ᵀᴴᴱ WOMEN FOR WOMEN ᴰᴹᴬ INTERNATIONAL

4455 Connecticut Ave NW (Suite 200)
Washington, DC 20008-2300
Telephone: (202) 737-7705, Web Site:
www.womenforwomen.org
Primary Market Served: Business &
Consumer

WOMEN IN DIRECT MARKETING INTERNATIONAL

285 Madison Ave (14th fl), c/o Wun-
derman
New York, NY 10017
Telephone: (516) 746-6700, FAX:
(516) 294-8141, Web Site: www.
wdmi.org
Pres: Bernice Ladden
Reg Pres: Dorothy Liquori
VP: Victoria James
VP: Michele Napoli
Events Dir: Barbara Lewis
Conducts Business: U.S.

Primary Market Served: Business
Catalog available online
Indirect online sales
Advertising/Marketing Budget Related
to Direct Marketing: 76-100%
Founded: 1970

Provide a mutual support network to
encourage career & educational development for professionals in the direct
response industry. Sponsor industry
wide luncheons, educational workshops
in direct marketing, the annual Direct
Marketing Woman of the Year Award,
job placement services & publish a
quarterly newsletter. Luncheons &
seminars are held monthly. Not for
women only.

ALABAMA STATE UNIVERSITY/COLLEGE OF BUSINESS ADMINISTRATION

915 S Jackson
Montgomery, AL 36101-0271
Telephone: (334) 229-4124, FAX: (334) 229-4870, E-Mail: pvaughn@ alasu.edu, Web Site: www. cobanetworks.com
Chmn & Bus Admin: Janet Bell Haynes
Dean & Mktg Professor: Percy Vaughn Jr.
Conducts Business: U.S.
Primary Market Served: Business & Consumer
Founded: 1874

Courses titled: Elements of Direct Marketing & Creating Direct Market Response, Advertising & Promotion.

AMERICAN MANAGEMENT ASSOCIATION INTERNATIONAL

1601 Broadway
New York, NY 10019
Telephone: (212) 586-8100, (800) 262-9699, FAX: (212) 903-8168
Mng Dir Padgett-Thompson Div: Railen Dietz
Exec Dir, Mktg & Print Prodn: Susan Powell
Conducts Business: U.S., Canada, England
Advertising/Marketing Budget Related to Direct Marketing: 76-100%
Founded: 1978

A two-day hands-on training workshop in direct mail that includes choosing mailing lists, planning copy, building a database & designing packages. Call for more information.

AUBURN UNIVERSITY AT MONTGOMERY

Dept of Marketing
7300 University Dr
Montgomery, AL 36117-3596
Telephone: (334) 244-3621, (800) 227-2649, FAX: (334) 244-3826, Web Site: www.aum.edu
Pres: Jay Gogue
Prof: Don Self
Prof & Head of Mktg Dept: Vaughn C. Judd Ph.D.
Prof: Dr. William S. Richardson
Asst Professor, Mktg: Jeffrey A. Periatt
Assoc Professor/Head Mktg Dept: Venessa Funches
Conducts Business: U.S.
Founded: 1971

Course titled: Direct Marketing.

BARUCH COLLEGE - DEPT OF MKTG & INTERNATIONAL BUS

Div. of City University of New York
1 Bernard Baruch Way
New York, NY 10010-5585
Telephone: (646) 312-3270, FAX: (646) 312-3271, E-Mail: mktIB@ baruch.cuny.edu, Web Site: www. baruch.cuny.edu
Chmn, Dept of Mktg & Intl Bus: Kapil Bawa
Conducts Business: U.S.
Primary Market Served: Business & Consumer
Founded: 1953

Offer courses in direct marketing & direct response advertising, sales promotion, publicity & a broad spectrum of marketing - including retailing. Has one-of-a-kind "Direct & Interactive Marketing Lab".

BELMONT UNIVERSITY

School of Business
1900 Belmont Blvd
Nashville, TN 37212-3757
Telephone: (615) 460-6000, FAX: (615) 460-6455, Web Site: www. belmont.edu
Dean: Jim Clapper
Professor, Mktg: Robert Lambert
Conducts Business: U.S.
Employees: 350
Primary Market Served: Business & Consumer
Founded: 1990

Course entitled "Marketing by Mail" #399; three semester hours of credit. Spring semester only.

CALIFORNIA STATE POLYTECHNIC UNIVERSITY BUSINESS ADMINISTRATION DEPT

Business Administration/Mktg Dept
San Luis Obispo, CA 93407-0001
Telephone: (805) 756-1413, FAX: (805) 756-5057, Web Site: www. calpoly.edu
Sec, Treas & Dean: David Wehner
Chmn & VP Admin & Fin: Lawrence Kelley
Vice Chmn & Chief of Staff: Dan Howard-Greene
Provost: Robert Koob
Employees: 18
Primary Market Served: Business & Consumer
Catalog available online

Founded: 1901
Course title: Direct Marketing, elements for marketing, selling international marketing, marketing management, research & management.

CALIFORNIA STATE UNIVERSITY AT FRESNO

School of Business in Administrative Science
Dept of Mktg & Logistics, 5245 N Backer St
Fresno, CA 93740-8001
Telephone: (559) 278-7830, FAX: (559) 278-8577, Web Site: www. csufresno.edu
Chmn: Charles Sherwood
Pres: John Welty
Assoc VP: Janette Redd Williams
Dept Chair: Dr. Reza Motameni
Professor: Al McLeod
Conducts Business: U.S.
Employees: 1,000
Primary Market Served: Business & Consumer
Advertising/Marketing Budget Related to Direct Marketing: 51-75%
Direct Marketing ad budget:
Direct Mail: 100%

COLLEGE OF BUSINESS

University of Cincinnati
Carl H Lindner Hall, PO Box 210020
Cincinnati, OH 45221-0020
Telephone: (513) 556-7002, FAX: (513) 556-4891, E-Mail: business@ uc.edu, Web Site: www.business.uc. edu
Mkgt Dept Head: Karen A. Machleit Ph.D.
Dir - MS Mktg Program: Ric Sweeney
Conducts Business: U.S.
Employees: 16
Primary Market Served: Business & Consumer

Courses titled: Direct Marketing; E-marketing for managers.

COLLEGE OF BUSINESS ADMINISTRATION

Drexel University Marketing Dept
3141 Chestnut St
Philadelphia, PA 19104
Telephone: (215) 895-2145, Web Site: www.drexel.edu
Dean Bus & Admin: William Harrel
Head Mktg Dept: Trina Larsen Andras
Conducts Business: U.S.
Employees: 23
Primary Market Served: Business & Consumer
Catalog available online

Course titled: Direct Marketing.

COLUMBIA COLLEGE CHICAGO

600 S Michigan Ave
Chicago, IL 60605-1996
Telephone: (312) 663-1600, FAX: (312) 344-0869, Web Site: www.colum.edu
Chmn: Allen M. Turner
Pres: Warrick L. Carter
VP, Fin & CFO: Michael DeSalle
VP & Provost: Steve Kapelke
Catalog available online

Course offered: Database Marketing. Teach techniques of direct marketing, providing direct marketing workshops, cases & practice & advertising workshops.

DMA - EVENTS-CONFERENCE PROGRAMMING/EXHIBITORS/SPEAKERS

1120 Ave of the Americas
New York, NY 10036-6700
Telephone: (212) 768-7277 X1419, FAX: (212) 302-6714, E-Mail: consumer@the-dma.org, Web Site: www.the-dma.org
VP: Julie Hogan
Employees: 135
Primary Market Served: Business & Consumer
Founded: 1917
Gross sales or billing: $35,800,000

Public & in-house programs to help direct marketing professionals sharpen their own skills, or train their support staffs. Broad range of direct marketing topics covered, with industry leaders as instructors.

DEPAUL UNIVERSITY

One E Jackson Blvd
Chicago, IL 60604-2201
Telephone: (312) 362-8000, (800) 4-DEPAUL, FAX: (312) 362-6639, E-Mail: skelly@wppost.depaul.edu, Web Site: www.depaul.edu
Chancellor: Rev. John T. Richardson
Pres: Rev. Dennis H. Holtscheider
VP, Fin: Robert L. Kozoman
Provost: Helmut P. Epp
Primary Market Served: Business & Consumer
Catalog available online
Advertising/Marketing Budget Related to Direct Marketing: 51-75%
Founded: 1989
Gross sales or billing: $378,000,000

We offer the following programs: The Vachel Pennebaker Certificate Program in Direct Marketing, authorized by the Chicago Association of Direct Marketing Educational Foundation. This is a 26 week program, offered one night per week from September to early May. Power Forums, one-day short courses on selected areas of direct marketing such as Database Marketing, Integrated Marketing, Marketing Research for Direct Marketers, & Buisiness-to-Business Direct Marketing. Courses offered throughout the year.

DIRECT MARKETING BOOT CAMP

2028 Harrison St. (Suite 202)
Hollywood, FL 33020
Telephone: (646) 723-3230, (800) 331-7114, FAX: (954) 921-2005, E-Mail: loisgeller@loisgellermarketinggroup.com, Web Site: www.masongeller.com
Pres & Chief Instructor: Lois Geller
VP & Creative Dir: Mike McCormick
Conducts Business: U.S., Canada, Europe
Employees: 4
Primary Market Served: Business
Advertising/Marketing Budget Related to Direct Marketing: 76-100%
Direct Marketing ad budget: $50,000
Direct Mail: 50%
Magazines: 20%
Telephone: 30%
Founded: 1999

Direct Marketing training for corporations and associations. 1-2 day educational seminar on your premises for groups of 10-100 by leading practitioners.

DIRECT MARKETING INTERNATIONAL LTD

7777 Center Ave (Suite 350)
Huntington Beach, CA 92647-9133
Telephone: (877) 596-1919
VP Sls, Direct Mktg: Brian Tennyson
Primary Market Served: Business & Consumer

DIRECT RESPONSE ACADEMY

140 Lotus Cir
Austin, TX 78737-8728
Telephone: (512) 301-5900, FAX: (512) 301-7900, E-Mail: info@dracademy.org, Web Site: www.dracademy.org
CEO: Greg Sarnow
Conducts Business: US, Canada, Europe
Employees: 3

Catalog available online
Advertising/Marketing Budget Related to Direct Marketing: 26-50%
Founded: 2000
Gross sales or billing: $1,000,000

Courses & seminars on direct response marketing.

FLAGG MANAGEMENT INC

353 Lexington Ave Rm 1002
New York, NY 10016-0031
Telephone: (212) 286-0333, FAX: (212) 286-0086, E-Mail: flaggmgmt@msn.com, Web Site: www.flaggmgmt.com
Pres: Russell E. Flagg
Conducts Business: U.S.
Employees: 6
Primary Market Served: Business
Catalog available online
Advertising/Marketing Budget Related to Direct Marketing: 26-50%
Founded: 1983
Gross sales or billing: $4,000,000

Business-to-business market expositions & conferences.

FORDHAM UNIVERSITY GRADUATE SCHOOL OF BUSINESS ADMINISTRATION

33 W 60th St
New York, NY 10023
Telephone: (212) 636-6200, (800) 825-4422, FAX: (212) 636-7076, Web Site: www.fordham.edu
Chmn: Alfred C. Holden
Dean: Howard Tuckman
Conducts Business: U.S.
Primary Market Served: Business & Consumer
Founded: 1841

Courses titled: Direct Marketing & Interactive Electronic Marketing.

FORT HAYS STATE UNIVERSITY

Dept of Business Administration
600 Park St
Hays, KS 67601-4099
Telephone: (785) 628-FHSU, FAX: (785) 628-4046, Web Site: www.fhsu.edu
Pres & CEO: Virgil A. Scott Jr.
Dir: Ruth Heffel
Dir: Cathy Van Doren
Controller: Francine Hestermann
Acctg: Kathy Neiman
Catalog available online

Course titled: Services Marketing.

GLOBAL VILLAGE MARKETING & DATA SERVICES INC

2710 Thomes Ave (Suite 547)
Cheyenne, WY 82001-3029
Telephone: (425) 829-9060, Web Site:
www.globalvillagemktg.com

HAROLD WALTER SIEBENS SCHOOL OF BUSINESS

Buena Vista College.
610 W Fourth St
Storm Lake, IA 50588-1713
Telephone: (712) 749-2410, (800) 383-2821, FAX: (712) 749-2037, Web
Site: www2.bvu.edu/academics/
business
Dept Sec: Cindy L. McDonough
Prof Mktg: Dr Steven J. Remington
Asst Prof Mktg: Scott Anderson
Conducts Business: U.S.
Primary Market Served: Business &
Consumer
Founded: 1891

Harold Walter Siebens Sch of Bus -
Educational institution offering a major
in marketing.

HAWORTH COLLEGE OF BUSINESS

Western Michigan University
3120 Schneider Hall
Kalamazoo, MI 49008-3812
Telephone: (616) 387-6062, FAX:
(616) 387-5710, E-Mail: jay.
lindquist@wmich.edu, Web Site:
www.hcob.wmich.edu/mktg
Chmn & Professor Mktg: Andrew A.
Brugowicz
Professor Mktg: Jay D. Lindquist
Conducts Business: U.S.
Primary Market Served: Business &
Consumer
Founded: 1903

Interactive Marketing Strategy/473 -
Basic Advertising/374 - Marketing
Research/371 - Media Planning/472 -
Distribution Strategy/672.

WALTER E HELLER COLLEGE OF BUSINESS ADMINISTRATION

Subs. of Roosevelt University
18 S Michigan Ave (Room 400)
Chicago, IL 60605
Telephone: (312) 281-3293, FAX:
(312) 281-3290, Web Site: www.
roosevelt.edu
Professor Mktg: Paul Wellen
Professor Mktg: Sumaria Mohan-Neill
Professor Mktg: Allen Marber
Conducts Business: U.S.
Primary Market Served: Business &
Consumer

Catalog available online
Founded: 1945
Offer an M.S. in Marketing Communications oriented to direct mail.

HOFSTRA UNIVERSITY

Div. of Professional Development:
Business Studies
Univ College for Continuing Educ,
250 Hofstra Univ
Hempstead, NY 11549-2500
Telephone: (516) 463-7200, FAX:
(516) 463-4833, E-Mail: ccepa@
hofstra.edu, Web Site: ccepa.hofstra.
edu
Sr Program Dir, Hofstra Solutions:
Colleen Slattery
Asst Dir, Hofstra Solutions: June Mullan
Dir, Mktg: Debbie Hanorof
Conducts Business: U.S.
Employees: 2,000
Primary Market Served: Business &
Consumer
Catalog available online
Advertising/Marketing Budget Related
to Direct Marketing: 0-25%
Direct Marketing ad budget:
Direct Mail: 90%
Newspapers: 5%
Telephone: 5%
Founded: 1935
Gross sales or billing: $317,000,000

Marketing courses.

INTERACTIVE MARKETING INSTITUTE

Div. of Virginia Commonwealth University School of Business
901 W Main St, PO Box 84-2034
Richmond, VA 23284
Telephone: (800) 925-5308, Web Site:
www.imi.vcu.edu
Exec Dir: Pamela Kiecker
Mng Dir: Steve Isaac
Conducts Business: U.S.
Primary Market Served: Business &
Consumer
Catalog available online
Direct online sales
Advertising/Marketing Budget Related
to Direct Marketing: 76-100%
Founded: 1996

Specializes in education-professional
certificate program (certified direct
marketer) direct and interactive marketing, consulting, and research.

JOHNSON & WALES UNIVERSITY

8 Abbott Park Pl
Providence, RI 02903-3703

Telephone: (401) 598-1000, (800)
DIAL-JWU, FAX: (401) 598-1833,
E-Mail: admissions.pvd@jwu.edu,
Web Site: www.jwu.edu
Chmn: John A. Yena
Chancellor & Chmn Emeritus: Morris
J.W. Gaebe
Pres & Trustee: John J. Bowen
Assoc Professor: Mark Neckes
Conducts Business: U.S.
Employees: 1,027
Primary Market Served: Business &
Consumer
Catalog available online
Gross sales or billing: $341,000,000

Marketing, retailing & fashion merchandising courses. Direct response
retailing major.

KENNESAW STATE UNIVERSITY

Michael J. Coles College of Business
1000 Chastain Rd (Mail Stop 0406)
Kennesaw, GA 30144-5588
Telephone: (770) 423-6060, FAX:
(770) 499-3261, Web Site: www.
kennesaw.edu
Dept Chair: Dr. Keith Tudor
Dir Mktg: Mandy T. Brooks
Conducts Business: U.S.
Employees: 500
Catalog available online
Founded: 1963

Course titled: Direct Response
Marketing.

LCA VISION

7840 Montgomery Rd (3rd fl)
Cincinnati, OH 45236
Telephone: (513) 792-9292, FAX:
(513) 792-5620, Web Site: www.
lasikplus.com
VP: David Rose

MERRIMACK COLLEGE

Office of Admission
315 Turnpike Dr (Mailstop 07)
North Andover, MA 01845
Telephone: (978) 837-5154, E-Mail:
denise.tuccelli@merrimack.edu, Web
Site: www.merrimack.edu
Pub Rels: Heather Notaro
Employees: 6
Primary Market Served: Business &
Consumer
Direct online sales
Advertising/Marketing Budget Related
to Direct Marketing: 76-100%
Direct Marketing ad budget:
Direct Mail: 90%
Telephone: 10%
Founded: 1993

Courses offered at Merrimack College.

NASSAU COMMUNITY COLLEGE

1 Education Dr
Garden City, NY 11530-6793
Telephone: (516) 572-7501, E-Mail:
  marketing-communications@ncc.edu,
  Web Site: www.ncc.edu
Pres: Dr. Sean A. Fanelli
VP Academic Affairs: Jack Ostling
VP Legal & External Affairs: Anna
  Marie Mascolo
VP Fin: Alan Gurien
VP Admin & Planning: Ezra Delaney
Conducts Business: U.S.
Catalog available online

Professional instruction in product selection, advertising creativity, media
alternatives, list use & catalog
preparation. Guest speakers from
LIDMC. Course offered through college's Marketing-Retailing Department.

NEW MEXICO STATE UNIVERSITY

Marketing Department
PO Box 30001, MSC 5280
Las Cruces, NM 88003-8001
Telephone: (575) 646-0111, (505) 646-
  3341, FAX: (505) 646-1498, Web
  Site: www.nmsu.edu
Asst Dir: Nathan Bauds
Dept Head: Gerald Hampton
Professor: David Carlson
Professor: Eric Pratt
Professor: Mike Hyman
Professor: Robin Peterson
Professor: Elise Sautter
Professor Golf Mngmt: Pat Gavinson
Asst Professor: Shaun McQuitty
Conducts Business: U.S.
Employees: 12
Primary Market Served: Business &
  Consumer
Advertising/Marketing Budget Related
  to Direct Marketing: 0-25%

Course: MKTG 456 Direct Marketing.

NEW YORK UNIVERSITY/ CENTER FOR MARKETING

44 W 4th St (Suite 9-170), Henry
  Kaufman Management Ctr
New York, NY 10012-1106
Telephone: (212) 998-0500, FAX:
  (212) 995-4006, E-Mail: mkt@stern.
  nyu.edu, Web Site: w4.stern.nyu.edu/
  marketing
Academic Dir: Renee Harris
Exec Dir: Dawn Lesh
Conducts Business: U.S., Asia, Europe,
  South America
Employees: 25
Primary Market Served: Business &
  Consumer
Catalog available online
Direct online sales

Advertising/Marketing Budget Related
  to Direct Marketing: 26-50%
Founded: 1934

The Center for Direct and Interactive
Marketing offers a 42-credit Master's
Degree in direct and interactive marketing, plus non-credit direct marketing
courses in specialized areas such as:
direct mail, DM math & finance, DM
& the Internet, copywriting & catalog.

NEWHOUSE SCHOOL OF PUBLIC COMMUNICATIONS

Div. of Syracuse University
215 University Pl
Syracuse, NY 13244-2100
Telephone: (315) 443-3611, FAX:
  (315) 443-4426, Web Site:
  newhouse.syr.edu
Chmn Bd: John A. Couri
Vice Chmn: Wendy H. Cohen
Vice Chmn: Gerald B. Cramer
Vice Chmn: Michael A. Dritz
Vice Chmn: Daniel N. Mezzalingua
VP, Pub Affairs: Kevin C. Quinn
Conducts Business: U.S.
Employees: 50
Catalog available online

Advanced advertising instruction.

NON-PROFIT MANAGEMENT PROGRAM/MILANO - THE NEW SCHOOL OF MANAGEMENT & URBAN POLICY

Div. of New School for Social Re-
  search
72 Fifth Ave
New York, NY 10011
Telephone: (212) 229-5400, FAX:
  (212) 229-5354, E-Mail:
  milanoadmissions@newschool.edu,
  Web Site: www.newschool.edu/
  milano
Dean: Fred P. Hochberg
Professor Prof Practice: Dennis Der-
  ryck
Professor Prof Practice: Aida Rod-
  riguez
Conducts Business: U.S.
Primary Market Served: Consumer

NORTHERN KENTUCKY UNIVERSITY

Nunn Dr
Highland Heights, KY 41099
Telephone: (859) 572-5220, (800) 637-
  9948, FAX: (859) 572-6177, Web
  Site: www.nku.edu
Pres: Dr. James C. Votruha
VP & Provost: Dr. Gail W. Wells
Mgr: Mary P. Schuh
Conducts Business: U.S.

Employees: 15
Primary Market Served: Business &
  Consumer
Catalog available online
Founded: 1968
Gross sales or billing: $104,000,000

Course titled: 390 selected topics in
marketing: Direct Marketing. Spring
Session course: International
Marketing.

THE DMA NORTHWESTERN UNIVERSITY

Integrated Mktg Communications Dept
  Medill School of Journalism
633 Clark St
Evanston, IL 60208-2980
Telephone: (847) 491-3741, FAX:
  (847) 491-8406, E-Mail:
  webmaster@northwestern.edu, Web
  Site: www.northwestern.edu
Pres: Henry S. Bienen
Sr VP, Bus & Fin: Eugene S. Sunshine
Provost: Daniel H. Linzer
Asst Provost: John D. Margolis
Asst Provost: Michael E. Millis
Conducts Business: U.S., Europe, Asia,
  South America
Catalog available online
Founded: 1950
Gross sales or billing: $1,300,000,000

Master's degree program in integrated
marketing & communications.

OAKTON COMMUNITY COLLEGE

1600 E Golf Rd
Des Plaines, IL 60016-1234
Telephone: (847) 635-1600, FAX:
  (847) 635-1706, Web Site: www.
  oakton.edu
Pres: Margaret B. Lee
Dir: Paul Grassman
Mgr: Daniel Foster
Conducts Business: U.S.
Catalog available online
Founded: 1969

Courses in direct marketing leading to
certificate & degree.

PARSONS SCHOOL OF DESIGN HUMAN RESOURCE DEPT

Div. of The New School for Social
  Research
79 Fifth Ave (5th fl)
New York, NY 10003
Telephone: (212) 229-5671, FAX:
  (212) 229-8975, E-Mail:
  communications@newschool.edu,
  Web Site: www.parsons.edu
Sr VP HR & Labor Rels: Carol S.
  Cantrell
Asst VP HR: Warren Petty

Dir Labor Rels: Stephanie Basta
HR Project Mgr: Sheila Slaughter
Conducts Business: U.S.
Primary Market Served: Business &
  Consumer
Catalog available online
Indirect online sales
Founded: 1896

Continuing education offering day,
evening & Saturday classes for New
York metropolitan students.

POST UNIVERSITY

School of Business
800 Country Club Rd
Waterbury, CT 06708-3240
Telephone: (203) 596-4520, (800) 345-
  2562, E-Mail: admissions@post.edu,
  Web Site: www.post.edu
Professor: Rosemary Werner
Conducts Business: U.S.
Primary Market Served: Business &
  Consumer
Catalog available online
Founded: 1890

Courses titled: Direct Marketing, Marketing on the Internet.

QUEENS COLLEGE/CUNY PROFESSIONAL AND CONTINUING STUDIES (PCS)

City University of New York
65-30 Kissena Blvd (Kiely Hall 111)
Flushing, NY 11367-1575
Telephone: (718) 997-5700, FAX:
  (718) 997-5723, E-Mail: pcs@qc.
  cuny.edu, Web Site: www.qc.cuny.
  edu/pcs
Pres: James L. Muyskens
Exec Dir Professional & Continuing
  Studies: Douglas A Boethner
English Language Institute Dir: Donna
  Gruber
Dir Fin & Budget (PCS): Selena Chu
Conducts Business: U.S., China
Primary Market Served: Business &
  Consumer
Catalog available online
Direct online sales
Advertising/Marketing Budget Related
  to Direct Marketing: 0-25%
Direct Marketing ad budget:
Direct Mail: 10%
Newspapers: 80%
TV/Radio: 10%

Offer non-credit certificate & certificate
courses & seminars to general public,
business & industry.

QUINNIPIAC COLLEGE

Dept. of Marketing & International
  Business
275 Mount Carmel Ave

Hamden, CT 06518-1908
Telephone: (203) 582-8600, (203) 582-
  8200, (800) 462-1944, FAX: (203)
  281-8664, Web Site: www.
  quinnipiac.edu
Chmn Bd: William Spears
Pres: John L. Lahey
VP, Academic Affairs: John Bennett
Dept Chair: Nancy Worthington
Dept Chair: Xiaohong He
Conducts Business: U.S.
Employees: 750
Primary Market Served: Consumer
Catalog available online
Founded: 1929
Gross sales or billing: $155,000,000

Course titled: Direct marketing.

ROCKY MOUNTAIN DIRECT MARKETING ASSOCIATION

PO Box 462612
Aurora, CO 80046-2612
Telephone: (720) 922-9413, FAX:
  (720) 922-9414, E-Mail: rmdma-
  ed@rmdma.org, Web Site: www.
  rmdma.org
Exec Dir: Ed Swartley
Employees: 1
Primary Market Served: Business
Advertising/Marketing Budget Related
  to Direct Marketing: 51-75%
Founded: 1980

A professional trade organization with
250 direct marketing professionals in
the Rocky Mountain region.

SAMFORD UNIVERSITY

800 Lakeshore Dr
Birmingham, AL 35229
Telephone: (205) 726-2011, Web Site:
  www.samford.edu
Professor: David Shipley
Conducts Business: U.S.
Primary Market Served: Business &
  Consumer

Course offered: Direct Advertising
Methods.

SAN FRANCISCO STATE UNIVERSITY

1600 Holloway Ave
San Francisco, CA 94132
Telephone: (415) 338-1111, FAX:
  (415) 338-0501, Web Site: www.
  sfsu.edu
Professor: Dan Wardlow
Pres: Robert A. Corrigan
VP Academic Affairs & Provost: John
  M. Gemello
VP Admin & Fin: Leroy M. Morishita
Dept Chair: Nikos Kazantzakis
Conducts Business: U.S.
Primary Market Served: Business &
  Consumer

Catalog available online
Course titled: Sales Promotion (Course
443).

SCHOOL OF BUSINESS & ECONOMICS

California State University Los Ange-
  les Small Business Institute
5151 State University Dr
Los Angeles, CA 90032-4226
Telephone: (323) 343-2800, FAX:
  (323) 343-2813, Web Site: cbe.
  calstatela.edu
Mktg Prof: Jens D. Biermeier
Mktg Prof: Tyrone W. Jackson
Mktg Prof: Richard H. Kao
Mktg Prof: Freddy S. Lee
Mktg Prof: Shirley M. Stretch
Conducts Business: U.S.
Primary Market Served: Business &
  Consumer
Catalog available online

Marketing, mail order, direct mail &
research.

SCHOOL OF BUSINESS ADMINISTRATION

Portland State University
631 SW Harrison St
Portland, OR 97201-3548
Telephone: (503) 725-3712, FAX:
  (503) 725-5850, E-Mail: info@sba.
  pdx.edu, Web Site: www.sba.pdx.edu
Dean: Scott Dawson
Dir, External Affairs: Kristin Mihalko
Primary Market Served: Business &
  Consumer
Founded: 1946

Course titled: Direct Marketing.

SCHOOL OF MANAGEMENT

New York Institute of Technology,
  Wisser Library, Northern Blvd
Old Westbury, NY 11568-8000
Telephone: (516) 686-1000, (800) 345-
  NYIT, (800) 345-6948, Web Site:
  www.nyit.edu
Pres & CEO: Edward Guiliano
Mktg Dir: Paul Kutasovic
Mktg & Mngmt Professor: Donald Na-
  gourney
Mktg & Mngmt Professor: Abram
  Proctzer
Conducts Business: U.S.
Employees: 303
Primary Market Served: Business &
  Consumer
Catalog available online
Direct online sales
Founded: 1961
Gross sales or billing: $171,100,000

Course titled: Direct Response
Marketing.

STATE UNIVERSITY OF NEW YORK-COLLEGE OF PLATTSBURGH

School of Business & Economics
101 Broad St
Plattsburgh, NY 12901-2637
Telephone: (518) 564-2000, FAX: (518) 564-3183, E-Mail: nancy. church@plattsburgh.edu, Web Site: www.plattsburgh.edu
Professor & Chm, Dept Mktg & Entrepreneurship: Dr. Nancy J. Church
Professor: Dr. Lise Heroux
Professor: Dr. James Csipak
Conducts Business: U.S.
Primary Market Served: Consumer
Catalog available online
Founded: 1889

Courses MKE401-Interactive Marketing and ECommerce.

STETSON UNIVERSITY

School of Business Administration
421 N Woodland Blvd, Campus Box 8398
Deland, FL 32723
Telephone: (904) 822-7405/7406, FAX: (904) 822-7430, Web Site: www. stetson.edu
Chmn Mktg Dept: Michelle DeMoss
Conducts Business: U.S.
Primary Market Served: Business & Consumer
Founded: 1883

Two courses titled Channels & Global Internet Marketing.

TEMPLE UNIVERSITY

Small Business Development Center
1510 Cecil B Moore Ave
Philadelphia, PA 19121
Telephone: (215) 204-7282, FAX: (215) 204-4554, Web Site: www. sbm.temple.edu
Pres: Ann Weaver Hart
Dir: Eustace Kangaju
Conducts Business: U.S.
Employees: 15
Catalog available online
Gross sales or billing: $1,800,000,000

Courses in marketing, management, entrepreneurial development & free consulting for small businesses.

THE PETER A TOBIN COLLEGE OF BUSINESS

Div. of St John's University
8000 Utopia Pkwy
Jamaica, NY 11439
Telephone: (718) 990-2600, FAX: (718) 990-1868, Web Site: www. stjohns.edu
Dean: Steven D. Papamarcos Ph.D.

Asst Dean Staten Island Campus: Susan V. Bradley
Asst Dean Queens Campus: Nicole Bryan
Dir Mktg: Maureen Furlong-Weber
Asst Dean Queens Campus: Susan McCall
Conducts Business: U.S.
Primary Market Served: Business & Consumer
Catalog available online
Advertising/Marketing Budget Related to Direct Marketing: 0-25%
Founded: 1872

Course titled: Direct Marketing.

UF COLLEGE OF ADVERTISING, JOURNALISM, & COMMUNICATIONS

University of Florida
2086 Weimer Hall
Gainesville, FL 32611
Telephone: (352) 392-4046, FAX: (352) 392-3919, Web Site: www.jou. ufl.edu
Sec: Christina Barnes
Adv Dept Chmn: John Sutherland PhD
Conducts Business: Florida
Primary Market Served: Business & Consumer
Catalog available online
Indirect online sales
Founded: 1925

Course title: Direct Response Advertising & Promotional Writing. Special Study in Advertising.

UNIVERSITY OF MISSOURI

School of Journalism
321 University Hall
Columbia, MO 65211-3020
Telephone: (573) 882-6333, (800) 856-2181, FAX: (573) 882-2721, E-Mail: visitus@missouri.edu, Web Site: www.missouri.edu
Pres: Elson S. Floyd
VP, Fin & Admin: Natalie R. Krawitz
VP, IT: Gary K. Allen
VP, HR: R. Kenneth Hutchinson
Conducts Business: U.S.
Primary Market Served: Business & Consumer
Catalog available online
Founded: 1908

Offers Direct & Mail Order Advertising Class (Journalism/327).

UNIVERSITY OF MISSOURI/ KANSAS CITY

Henry W Bloch School of Business & Public Administration
5110 Cherry St (Rm 115)
Kansas City, MO 64110

Telephone: (816) 235-2215, FAX: (816) 235-2312, Web Site: www. umkc.edu
Chmn: Richard Hamilton
Professor: Gene Brown
Conducts Business: U.S.
Primary Market Served: Business
Catalog available online
Advertising/Marketing Budget Related to Direct Marketing: 76-100%
Founded: 1985

Offer M.B.A. degree programs in direct marketing. Also, continuing education courses in direct marketing, including professional certification and in-house training & seminars.

UNIVERSITY OF PITTSBURGH AT BRADFORD

300 Campus Dr
Bradford, PA 16701-2812
Telephone: (814) 362-7500, FAX: (814) 362-5150, E-Mail: admissions@www.upb.pitt.edu, Web Site: www.upd.pitt.edu
Pres: Dr. Livingston Alexander
Dept Chair: Alberto Cardello
Dept Chair: Lisa Fiorentino
Asst Dean: James L. Baldwin
Assoc Professor: David Blackmore
Conducts Business: U.S.
Catalog available online
Direct Marketing ad budget:
Direct Mail: $30,000
Telephone: $5,000

Course title: Direct Marketing.

USC MARSHALL SCHOOL OF BUSINESS DEPT OF MARKETING

Marshall School of Business
3660 Trousdale Pkwy, ACC 306E
Los Angeles, CA 90089-0443
Telephone: (213) 740-5033, FAX: (213) 740-7828, E-Mail: dennis. rook@marshall.usc.edu
Professor: Gary Frazier
Chmn Mktg Dept: Valerie Folks
Conducts Business: Worldwide

Course titled: Direct Response Mktg.

ᴛʜᴇ ᴅᴍᴀ VALPAK OF NEW YORK

875 Avenue of the Americas (Suite 910)
New York, NY 10001-3578
Telephone: (212) 560-9400, Web Site: www.valpaknewyork.com
Primary Market Served: Consumer

ᴛʜᴇ ᴅᴍᴀ WEST VIRGINIA UNIVERSITY

School of Journalism
Martin Hall
Morgantown, WV 26506

Telephone: (304) 293-3505, FAX:
(304) 293-3072, E-Mail:
wvuwebmaster@mail.wvu.edu, Web
Site: www.wvu.edu
Dean & Professor: Kristina M. Martin
IMC Coord & Asst Professor: Robyn
Blakeman
Asst Professor: Kurt Schimmel
Conducts Business: U.S.
Employees: 5
Founded: 1939

School of Journalism offering courses
in advertising, public relations, broadcast news & print journalism. Direct
marketing courses offered through the
advertising department.

WESTERN CONNECTICUT STATE UNIVERSITY
Ancell School of Business
181 White St
Danbury, CT 06810
Telephone: (203) 837-8200, FAX:
(203) 837-8527, E-Mail: hills@wcsu.
edu, Web Site: www.wcsu.edu
Co-Chmn, Mktg Dept: John Kakalik
Co-Chmn, Mktg Dept: Ronald
Drozdenko
Conducts Business: U.S.
Primary Market Served: Consumer
Founded: 1903

Course titled: Direct Response Marketing (327).

WRIGHT STATE UNIVERSITY
Dept of Marketing, Raj Soin College
of Business
3640 Colonel Glen Hwy, 266 Rike
Hall
Dayton, OH 45435
Telephone: (937) 775-3047, FAX:
(513) 775-3952, E-Mail: teresa.
stelmat@wright.edu, Web Site:
www.wright.edu/business/acad/
marketing
Chair: Dr. James Munch
Conducts Business: U.S.
Employees: 14
Primary Market Served: Business &
Consumer
Catalog available online
Indirect online sales
Founded: 1964

Courses titled: Integrated Mktg Communs; Technologies in Mktg; Database
Mktg; Internet Mktg.

YOUNGSTOWN STATE UNIVERSITY
Williamson College of Business Ad-
ministration
One University Plaza
Youngstown, OH 44555

Telephone: (330) 742-3064, Web Site:
www.ysu.edu
Chmn, Mktg Dept: Dr James Kohut
Conducts Business: U.S.
Employees: 10
Primary Market Served: Business &
Consumer
Founded: 1906

Advertising & public relations/direct
mail advertising. Direct Marketing
(#811).

ABA/BMA TRUST WEALTH MANAGEMENT AND MARKETING CONFERENCE

Bank Marketing Association
1120 Connecticut Ave NW (3rd fl)
Washington, DC 20036
Telephone: (202) 663-5000, (800)
   BANKERS, FAX: (202) 828-4540,
   E-Mail: custserv@aba.com, Web
   Site: www.aba.com
Chmn: Bradley E. Rock
Vice Chmn: Arthur C. Johnson
Co-Chmn: Mark E. Macomber
Co-Chmn: Earl D. McVicker
Treas: Warren K. Luke
Employees: 354
Primary Market Served: Business
Founded: 1875
Gross sales or billing: $83,693,841

ARF ANNUAL CONVENTION & RESEARCH INFOPLEX

Advertising Research Foundation
432 Park Ave S (fl 6)
New York, NY 10016-8013
Telephone: (212) 751-5656, FAX:
   (212) 319-5265, E-Mail: info@
   theARF.org, Web Site: www.theARF.
   org
Chmn: Artie Bulgrin
Pres & CEO: Robert L. Baroco
PR Dir: Heather Feeley
Sec: James Nyce
Treas: Bernard Bradpiece

AMERICASMART ATLANTA

AMC Inc
240 Peachtree St NW (Suite 2200)
Atlanta, GA 30303-1327
Telephone: (404) 220-3000, FAX:
   (404) 220-3030, Web Site: www.
   americasmart.com
VP Mktg & Sls Svcs: Brett Austin
Adv Sls: Katie Beneal
Conducts Business: Worldwide
Employees: 7
Primary Market Served: Business &
   Consumer
Advertising/Marketing Budget Related
   to Direct Marketing: 51-75%
Founded: 1961

Provides an opportunity for manufacturers & retailers of gifts & related products to meet together, on an international level, for order-writing purposes.

BOSTON GIFT SHOW

Urban Exposition
1090 Roberts Blvd NW (Suite 111)
Kennesaw, GA 30144
Telephone: (678) 285-3976, (800) 272-
   SHOW, FAX: (678) 285-7469, Web
   Site: www.bostongiftshow.com
Pub Rels Rep: Suzanne Pruitt
Pres: Doug Miller
Show Dir: Erica Guess
Employees: 150
Primary Market Served: Business
Catalog available online

Regional gift show for New England, Northeastern & Canadian markets. Semi-annual show is attended by gift & department stores, jewelers, mail order & catalog houses, antique & craft shops, boutiques & resort shops. Markets represented are gifts, stationery, souvenirs, traditional & New England crafts, novelties, toys, decorative & personal accessories & other items.

CMA AWARDS

One Concorde Gate (Suite 607)
Don Mills, ON, Canada M3C 3N6
Telephone: (416) 391-2362, FAX:
   (416) 441-4062, E-Mail: info@the-
   cma.org, Web Site: www.the-cma.
   org/awards
Pres & CEO: John Gustavson
VP, Pub Affairs: Wally Hill
Sr Mgr, Events Mktg & Sls: Andra
   Thurton
Sr Mgr, Corp Svcs: Sandra Stock
Primary Market Served: Business &
   Consumer
Founded: 1967

Marketers will gather to pay tribute to the best marketing campaigns of the year. The awards recognize outstanding achievements in all facets of marketing, from concept & execution to final results.

CUES EXPERIENCE CONFERENCE

Credit Union Executives Society, Inc
PO Box 14167
Madison, WI 53714-0167
Telephone: (608) 271-2664, (800) 252-
   2664, FAX: (608) 271-2303, Web
   Site: www.cues.org
Dir Mktg: Jessica Hrubes
Pres & CEO: Fred Johnson
Employees: 47
Primary Market Served: Business
Catalog available online
Direct online sales
Founded: 1962
Gross sales or billing: $13,500,000

Immersion Learning for Mktg, Tech & Opers Leaders. CUES Nexus & Executive Technology Forum combined.

THE CABLE SHOW NATIONAL CABLE TELEVISION ASSOCIATION

Dobson & Associates Ltd
25 Massachusetts Ave (Suite 100)
Washington, DC 20001
Telephone: (202) 222-2300, E-Mail:
   webmaster@ncta.com, Web Site:
   www.ncta.com
Pres & CEO: Kyle McSlarrow
Employees: 10
Primary Market Served: Business
Founded: 1979

CANADIAN MARKETING ASSOCIATION NATIONAL CONVENTION & TRADE SHOW

One Concorde Gate (Suite 607)
Don Mills, ON, Canada M3C 3N6
Telephone: (416) 391-2362, FAX:
   (416) 441-4062, E-Mail:
   pmckenzie@the-cma.org, Web Site:
   www.the-cma.org
Primary Market Served: Business

Marketplace for financial institutions, publishers, cataloguers & charities to contact suppliers to the industry.

COMMUNICATIONS SOLUTIONS EXPO

Div. of Technology Marketing Corp
One Technology Plaza
Norwalk, CT 06854
Telephone: (203) 852-6800, (877) 243-
   6002, FAX: (203) 853-2845, E-Mail:
   info@tmcnet.com, Web Site: www.
   tmcnet.com
Chmn & CEO: Nadji Tehrani
Pres & Grp Publr: Rich Tehrani
VP, Pubns & Trade Shows & Assoc
   Grp Publr: Marc Fubins
VP, Expositions & Conferences: Hilary
   Inman
VP: Linda Driscoll
Exposition Opers Dir: Stephanie Bauer
Conducts Business: U.S., Canada
Employees: 60
Primary Market Served: Business &
   Consumer
Catalog available online
Direct online sales
Advertising/Marketing Budget Related
   to Direct Marketing: 51-75%
Direct Marketing ad budget:
Direct Mail: $1,000,000
Magazines: $50,000
Newspapers: $100,000
TV/Radio: $200,000
Telephone: $100,000
Founded: 1972

Emerging products, deployment issues and benefits of wireless IP telephony solutions. Internet Telephony Conference & Expo,

COMNET WASHINGTON
IDG World Expo
3 Speen St (Suite 320)
Framingham, MA 01701
Telephone: (508) 879-6700, FAX: (508) 370-4325, Web Site: www. comnetexpo.com
Event Opers: Stephanie Merrill
VP Event Svcs: Darrell Baker
Mgr: Robert Ricchie
Event Opers: Nora Risti
Event Opers: Amy Scott

Event showcases multi-vender connectivity, public networking, internetworking & network computing.

THE COMPTEL ANNUAL CONVENTION & TRADE EXPOSITION
Competitive Telecommunications Association
900 17th St NW (Suite 400)
Washington, DC 20006
Telephone: (202) 296-6650, FAX: (202) 296-7585, Web Site: www. comptel.org
Chmn: J. Sherman Henderson III
Vice Chmn: Paget Alves
CEO: Jerry James
Exec VP Fin & Admin: Stephan D. Trotman
Gen Counsel: Jonathan Lee
Show Coord: Amy McCormick
Employees: 18
Primary Market Served: Business
Catalog available online
Founded: 1981

Exhibits products & services regarding network management systems, voice & data communications, electronic mail & teleconferencing services.

ELECTRONIC RETAILING ASSOCIATION
607 14th St NW Ste 530
Washington, DC 20005-2018
Telephone: (703) 841-1751, FAX: (703) 841-1860, E-Mail: askera@ retailing.org, Web Site: www. retailing.org
Pres & CEO: Barbara Tulipane
VP, Meetings & Conventions: Karla Kelly
Conducts Business: Worldwide
Employees: 15
Primary Market Served: Business & Consumer
Catalog available online
Direct online sales
Founded: 1990

IAEE ANNUAL MEETING AND EXHIBITION
International Association of Exhibitions and Events
12700 Park Central Dr (Suite 308)
Dallas, TX 75251-1526
Telephone: (972) 458-8002, FAX: (972) 458-8119, E-Mail: info@iaee. com, Web Site: www.iaee.com
Pres: Steven Hacker
Dir, Convention & Events: Karen Pipkin
Employees: 21
Primary Market Served: Business
Catalog available online
Founded: 1928

INPEX
Div. of Technosystems Service Corp
217 Ninth St
Pittsburgh, PA 15222-3506
Telephone: (412) 288-1343, (412) 288-1300, (888) 544-6739, (888) 54-INPEX, FAX: (412) 288-4546, E-Mail: info@inpex.com, Web Site: www.inpex.com
Trade Show Dir: Jennifer Lawlor
Pub Rels Specialist: Jennifer Mullen
Conducts Business: Worldwide
Employees: 7
Primary Market Served: Business & Consumer
Catalog available online
Indirect online sales
Advertising/Marketing Budget Related to Direct Marketing: 51-75%
Founded: 1984

Invention, new product & innovation trade show for business & industry.

INTERNATIONAL SIGN ASSOCIATION
1001 N Fairfax St (Suite 301)
Alexandria, VA 22314-1587
Telephone: (703) 836-4012, FAX: (703) 836-8353, Web Site: www. signs.org
Sr VP, Tradeshows: Brian McNamara
Pres & CEO: Lori Anderson
Employees: 22
Primary Market Served: Business
Founded: 1944

Exhibits lighting products & other products & services used in sign manufacturing.

INTERNATIONAL SIGN ASSOCIATION INTERNATIONAL CONVENTION
International Sign Association
1001 N Fairfax St (Suite 301)
Alexandria, VA 22314-1587

Telephone: (703) 836-4012, (866) WHY-SIGN, FAX: (703) 836-8353, Web Site: www.signs.org
Pres & CEO: Lori Anderson
Exec Admin: Jonathan Kaupanger
Office Mgr: Allison Hacker
VP Fin & Admin: Bill Winslow
Mgr: Kenny Peskin
Employees: 22
Primary Market Served: Business
Catalog available online
Indirect online sales
Founded: 1944

Exhibit lighting products & other products & services used in sign manufacturing.

MERCHANDISE GROUP
Div. of Nielsen Business Media
11835 W Olympic Blvd (Suite 550 E)
Los Angeles, CA 90064-5810
Telephone: (310) 481-7300, (800) 421-4511, FAX: (310) 481-1900, E-Mail: adsales@merchandisegroup.com, Web Site: www.merchandisegroup. com
Conducts Business: Worldwide
Employees: 15
Primary Market Served: Business
Advertising/Marketing Budget Related to Direct Marketing: 76-100%
Founded: 1985

THE MERCHANDISE MART
222 Merchandise Mart (Suite 470)
Chicago, IL 60654
Telephone: (312) 527-4141, (800) 677-6278, Web Site: www. merchandisemart.com
Pres: Chris Kennedy
Sr VP & Gen Mgr: Myron Maurer
Sr VP: Joan Ulrich
VP, Mktg: Craig Dooley
Dir, Mktg: Ann Fruland
Employees: 11

Domestic handcrafted gift show.

THE MOTIVATION SHOW
Hall-Erickson
98 E Naperville Rd (Suite 201)
Westmont, IL 60559
Telephone: (630) 434-7779, (800) 752-6312, FAX: (630) 434-1216, E-Mail: moti@heiexpo.com, Web Site: www. motivationshow.com
Sr VP: Carl Fojtik
Dir: Vince Adamo
Primary Market Served: Business
Catalog available online
Founded: 1933

Features more than 100,000 ideas to motivate consumers to buy, salespeople & dealers to sell & employees to work more productively.

**NATIONAL AGRI
MARKETING CONFERENCE
& EXPOSITION**

National Agri Marketing Association
11020 King St (Suite 205)
Overland Park, KS 66210
Telephone: (913) 491-6500, FAX:
(913) 491-6502, E-Mail: agrimktg@
nama.org, Web Site: www.nama.org
Exec Dir: Eldon White
COO & Dir, Commun & Admin:
Jenny Picket
Mgr: Kathi Conrad
Mgr, Acctg Svcs: Sherry Pfaf

**NATIONAL ASSOCIATION
BROADCASTERS ANNUAL
CONFERENCE & EXPO**

National Association Broadcasters
1771 "N" St NW
Washington, DC 20036
Telephone: (202) 429-5300, (800) 622-
3976, FAX: (202) 429-4199, E-Mail:
nab@nab.org, Web Site: www.nab.
org
Chmn: Philip J. Lombardo
Pres & CEO: David K. Rehr
CFO: Michael J. Williams
Exec VP Media Rels: Dennis Wharton
Sr VP: Chris Brown
Employees: 200
Primary Market Served: Business
Founded: 1923
Gross sales or billing: $13,000,000

Exhibits of radio & television broadcasting equipment, computer software,
post/television production equipment,
radio & audio services & internet
streaming.

**NATIONAL HARDWARE
SHOW**

Reed Exhibition Companies
Reed Exhibitions, 383 Main Ave
Norwalk, CT 06851
Telephone: (203) 840-5622, (888) 425-
9377, FAX: (203) 840-9622, E-Mail:
inquiry@hardware.reedexpo.com,
Web Site: www.
nationalhardwareshow.com
Client Svcs: Jonathan Snowdon

THE DMA NATIONAL POSTAL FORUM

3998 Fair Ridge Dr (Suite 300)
Fairfax, VA 22033-2907
Telephone: (703) 218-5015, FAX:
(703) 218-5020, E-Mail: info@npf.
org, Web Site: www.npf.org
Dir, Mktg & Exhibits: Mary Guthrie
Exec Dir & COO: Michael Genick
Employees: 12
Primary Market Served: Business
Catalog available online
Direct online sales
Advertising/Marketing Budget Related

to Direct Marketing: 51-75%
Founded: 1968

Brings together business mailers,
postal equipment, service providers &
the U.S. Postal Service. It features
more than 100 informative sessions on
postal developments & an exhibition of
mailing, sorting, addressing, printing &
more.

**NATIONAL STATIONERY
SHOW**

George Little Management LLC
1133 Westchester Ave (Suite N136)
White Plains, NY 10604-3547
Telephone: (914) 421-3200, (800) 272-
SHOW, FAX: (914) 948-6180,
E-Mail: cate_doyle@glmshows.com,
Web Site: www.glmshows.com
Chmn & Co Pres: Mike Cooke
Co Pres: George F. Little II
EVP: Alan E. Steel
EVP: Jack Withiam Jr
Sr VP: Philip D. Robinson
Primary Market Served: Business
Founded: 1924

Provides an annual domestic & international marketplace for greeting
cards, postcards, note paper, social stationery, gift wrappings & related products such as rubber stamps, picture
frames, games, toys, calendars, party
goods, desk accessories, writing instruments, small leather goods, prints &
posters, balloons, baby & wedding
gifts, back-to-school & holiday
merchandise.

**NEW YORK INTERNATIONAL
GIFT FAIR**

George Little Management LLC
1133 Westchester Ave (Suite N136)
White Plains, NY 10604-3547
Telephone: (914) 421-3200, (800) 272-
SHOW, FAX: (914) 948-6180, Web
Site: www.nyigf.com
Chmn & Co Pres: Mike Cooke
Co Pres: George F. Little II
EVP: Alan E. Steel
Show Mgr: Deborah Hilfman
Employees: 150
Primary Market Served: Business
Catalog available online

Provides a gift & decorative accessories market in the U.S. Held twice a
year, it houses ten major merchandise
sections at the Jacob K. Javits Convention Center & the Passenger Ship
Terminal. Handmade in the U.S., a
wholesale craft market juried section is
held biannually in conjunction with the
January Gift Fair.

NIELSEN

770 Broadway
New York, NY 10003-9595
Telephone: (703) 488-2700, (800) 765-
7615, FAX: (703) 488-2800, E-Mail:
bmcomm@nielsen.com, Web Site:
www.nielsenbusinessmedia.com
Mktg Dir: Dawn Wasson
Primary Market Served: Business

**SOCIETY FOR HEALTHCARE
STRATEGY & MARKET
DEVELOPMENT**

Div. of American Hospital Asssociation
One N Franklin (31st fl)
Chicago, IL 60606
Telephone: (312) 422-3888, FAX:
(312) 422-4579, E-Mail: stratsoc@
aha.org, Web Site: www.stratsociety.
org
Exec Dir: Lauren Barnett
Assoc Dir: Gayle Irvin
Assoc Dir: Karen Porter
Mgr: Michele Cohen
Mktg Mgr: Alyse Kittner
Conducts Business: U.S.
Employees: 7
Primary Market Served: Business
Catalog available online
Direct online sales
Advertising/Marketing Budget Related
to Direct Marketing: 0-25%
Founded: 1996

Exhibits of audiovisual, communications, printing & computer equipment.
Services for health care profession include strategic planning, public relations & fund-raising consulting.

**TRADE SHOW EXHIBITORS
ASSOCIATION**

2301 S Lake Shore Dr (Suite 1005)
Chicago, IL 60616
Telephone: (312) 842-8732, FAX:
(312) 842-8744, Web Site: www.
tsea.org
Pres & CEO: Margit B. Weisgal
VP Mktg & Membership: David R.
Brulll
Dir Mktg & Membership: Krislynne
Markey
Employees: 7
Primary Market Served: Business
Catalog available online
Direct online sales
Founded: 1966

Offers an array of products & services
for the corporate exhibit manager, sales
& marketing executive. Features 101
sessions on improving tradeshow results, reducing costs & future planning.

**WINTER MARKETING
EDUCATORS'
CONFERENCE**

American Marketing Association
311 S Wacker Dr (Suite 5800)

Chicago, IL 60606
Telephone: (312) 542-9000, (800) 262-
  1150, FAX: (312) 542-9001, E-Mail:
  info@ama.org, Web Site: www.ama.
  org
CEO: Dennis L. Dunlap
Conducts Business: Worldwide
Employees: 80
Primary Market Served: Business
Catalog available online
Indirect online sales
Direct Marketing ad budget:
Direct Mail: 90%
Magazines: 10%
Founded: 1932

Provides a forum where marketing
educators can share ideas, explore
findings, discuss issues and trends, and
network with colleagues.

Bibliography (43)

Direct Marketing Books & Periodicals (43)

ACADEMY OF MARKETING SCIENCE JOURNAL
Sage Publications Inc
2455 Teller Rd
Thousand Oaks, CA 91320-9924
Telephone: (805) 499-0721, FAX:
  (800) 583-2665, (805) 499-0871,
  Web Site: www.sagepub.com
Pres & CEO: Blaise R. Simqu
Exec VP, Higher Ed: Alison Mudditt
Sr VP & CIO: Tracy A. Ozmina
Mktg Dir: Helen Samon
Conducts Business: US, London, India
Primary Market Served: Business
Catalog available online
Advertising/Marketing Budget Related
  to Direct Marketing: 51-75%

Scholarly research academic journal
(Quarterly).

ADVERTISING AGE
Div. of Crain Communications
711 Third Ave
New York, NY 10017-4014
Telephone: (212) 210-0100, FAX:
  (212) 210-0111, Web Site: www.
  crain.com
Sr VP: Gloria Scoby
VP: David Klein
Conducts Business: Worldwide
Employees: 100
Primary Market Served: Business
Advertising/Marketing Budget Related
  to Direct Marketing: 51-75%
Direct Marketing ad budget:
  $3,000,000
Direct Mail: 70%
Magazines: 30%
Founded: 1930
Gross sales or billing: $40,000,000

Weekly magazine serving advertising
& marketing executives with news &
feature material, $3.

ALL-IN-ONE DIRECTORY
Gebbie Press
Box 1000
New Paltz, NY 12561-0017
Telephone: (845) 255-7560, FAX:
  (888) 345-2790, E-Mail:
  gebbiepress@pipeline.com, Web
  Site: www.gebbieinc.com
Publr & Ed: Mark Gebbie
Assoc Ed: Barbara Edelman
Conducts Business: Worldwide

Employees: 2
Primary Market Served: Business
Catalog available online
Direct online sales
Advertising/Marketing Budget Related
  to Direct Marketing: 51-75%
Founded: 1955

Listings for 24,000+ public relations
outlets in all media. Also available on
excel spreadsheet, PR Pro online app.

AMERICAN BUSINESS DIRECTORIES
Div. of info USA Inc
5711 S 86th Cir
Omaha, NE 68127
Telephone: (402) 593-4600, (800) 555-
  6124, FAX: (402) 596-0475, Web
  Site: www.infousa.com
Pres: Vin Gupta
VP: Bill Mattern
Mktg Mgr: Jan Wilson
Conducts Business: U.S., Canada
Employees: 1,000
Primary Market Served: Business &
  Consumer
Catalog available online
Direct online sales
Advertising/Marketing Budget Related
  to Direct Marketing: 76-100%
Direct Marketing ad budget:
Direct Mail: 95%
Telephone: 5%
Founded: 1972

Print business directories that are used
as a source of suppliers & a sales prospecting tool.

AMERICAN SOCIETY OF JOURNALISTS & AUTHORS DIRECTORY
American Society of Journalists & Au-
thors
1501 Broadway (Suite 302)
New York, NY 10036-5505
Telephone: (212) 997-0947, FAX:
  (212) 768-7414, E-Mail: asjany@
  ibm.net
Exec Dir: Alexandra Owens
Admin Asst: Heather Van Arsdel
Employees: 2
Primary Market Served: Business &
  Consumer
Founded: 1948

Lists more than 1000 freelance writers,
cross-indexed by geographic location,
pseudonym, media expertise & over
100 subject specialties. Annual. ISBN#
188083202X; $75.

AUDIENCE DEVELOPMENT
10 Norden Pl, Red 7 Media
Norwalk, CT 06855-1452
Telephone: (203) 854-6730, FAX:
  (203) 854-6735, E-Mail: inolan@
  red7media.com, Web Site: www.
  audiencedevelopment.com
Editor & Publr: Tony Silber
Mng Editor: Bill Mickey
Mktg Mgr: Irene Nolan
Audience Devel Mgr: Jeff Hartford
Conducts Business: U.S.
Primary Market Served: Business
Advertising/Marketing Budget Related
  to Direct Marketing: 51-75%

Comprehensive source on strategic
trends and ongoing developments affecting circulation management, as
well as in-depth, practical advice on
every aspect of circulation management and marketing.

BOOK NEWS INC
5739 NE Sumner St
Portland, OR 97218-2642
Telephone: (503) 281-9230, FAX:
  (503) 287-4485, E-Mail: booknews@
  booknews.com
Pres: Fred Gullette
Employees: 6
Primary Market Served: Business &
  Consumer
Founded: 1971

Paid advertising, news & information
pertinent to mail order book sales. $3
an issue, three publications per year.

BTOB MAGAZINE
Crain Communications Inc
711 Third Ave
New York, NY 10017-4014
Telephone: (212) 210-0206, FAX:
  (212) 210-0422, E-Mail:
  aholtzman@crain.com, Web Site:
  www.btobonline.com
Mktg Mgr: Tara Curran
VP Publr: Bob Felsenthal
Adv Dir: David Bernstein

Circulation Mgr: Hamilton Maher
Editor: Ellis Booker
Conducts Business: US
Employees: 1,000
Primary Market Served: Business
Catalog available online
Direct online sales
Founded: 1930

News monthly concerning the how-to strategic & tactical marketing, sales & advertising for business-to-business products & services; $59 year.

CISION US INC
332 S Michigan Ave (Suite 900)
Chicago, IL 60604-4393
Telephone: (312) 922-2400, (866) 639-5087, FAX: (312) 922-3126, E-Mail: info.us@cision.com, Web Site: us.cision.com
Chmn: Stephen Newman
Publr: Ruth McFarland
CEO: Joe Bernardo
Sr VP & CFO: Michael F. Czlonka
Sr VP, IT: Scott Thompson
Exec VP: Peter Granet
Employees: 550
Primary Market Served: Business
Catalog available online
Advertising/Marketing Budget Related to Direct Marketing: 26-50%

COASTAL LIVING
Imprint of Southern Progress Corp; Subs of Time, Inc.
2100 Lakeshore Dr
Birmingham, AL 35209
Telephone: (205) 877-6007, FAX: (205) 445-8655, E-Mail: coastalliving@customersvc.com, Web Site: www.coastalliving.com
Office Mgr: Mamie Walling
Pres & CEO Southern Progress: Thomas Angelillo
Sr Trvl Ed: Larry Bleiberg
On-line Editor: Gayle K. Christopher
Editor-in-Chief: Kay Fuston
Conducts Business: U.S.
Founded: 1997

Magazine emphasizing home design, architecture, coastal lifestyles & topics.

COMMERCIAL ATLAS & MARKETING GUIDE
Published by Rand McNally & Co
8255 Central Park Ave
Skokie, IL 60076-2970
Telephone: (800) 678-7263, FAX: (800) 934-3479, Web Site: www.randmcnally.com
Chmn: Peter Nolan
VP, Mktg: Betsy Owens
Employees: 636
Primary Market Served: Business & Consumer

Catalog available online
Direct online sales
Founded: 1857

DM NEWS
Div. of Courtenay Communications
114 W 26th St (Fl 4)
New York, NY 10001-6812
Telephone: (212) 925-7300, FAX: (212) 925-8752, Web Site: www.dmnews.com
Pres: Adrian Courtenay
Promo Dir: Robert DiGioia
Publr: Ron Sichler
Ed-in-Chief: Tad Clarke
Prodn Dir: Joe Oakes
Conducts Business: U.S., Canada, Europe, Asia
Employees: 50
Primary Market Served: Business
Catalog available online
Direct online sales
Advertising/Marketing Budget Related to Direct Marketing: 51-75%
Direct Marketing ad budget: $200,000
Direct Mail: 50%
Newspapers: 50%
Founded: 1979

As a weekly newspaper serving a BPA audited circulation of 40,000 direct marketers, DM News provides news coverage of new direct marketing campaigns, postal rate changes & delivery problems, sales tax disputes, new lists & databases & many other topics of interest to the people & firms involved in direct marketing. Staff reported news coverage is supplemented with columns & articles by industry experts, special reports, regular departments & op/ed pieces. ISSN# 0914-3588; 48 issues, $49. (Canada $99 & Mexico $149). (Europe) by written request only.

DMA STATISTICAL FACT BOOK
1120 Ave of the Americas
New York, NY 10036-6700
Telephone: (212) 790-1500, FAX: (212) 302-6714, E-Mail: customerservice@the-dma.org, Web Site: www.the-dma.org
Employees: 135
Primary Market Served: Business & Consumer
Catalog available online
Direct online sales
Founded: 1917
Gross sales or billing: $35,800,000

Covers many aspects of direct marketing including: media & market growth & usage trends, consumer & business attitudes, buying habits, expectations & outlooks, production & operating cost figures & environmental issues concerns.

DIANE PUBLISHING CO
PO Box 617
Darby, PA 19023-0617
Telephone: (610) 461-6200, E-Mail: hbaron@dianepublishing.net, Web Site: www.dianepublishing.net
Pres & Publr: Herman Baron
Conducts Business: Worldwide
Employees: 6
Primary Market Served: Business
Catalog available online
Direct online sales
Advertising/Marketing Budget Related to Direct Marketing: 0-25%
Founded: 1987

Books, reports & documents primarily from government sources, sold to businesses, libraries & governments & distributes hard to find remainder books.

DICTIONARY OF MARKETING TERMS
Barron's Education Series Inc
250 Wireless Blvd
Hauppauge, NY 11788-3924
Telephone: (631) 434-3311, (800) 645-3476, FAX: (631) 434-3723, E-Mail: barrons@barronseduc.com, Web Site: www.barronseduc.com
Dir Mktg: Lonny Stein
Author: Jane Imber
Author: Betsy-Ann Toffler
Conducts Business: Worldwide
Primary Market Served: Business & Consumer
Catalog available online
Direct online sales
Advertising/Marketing Budget Related to Direct Marketing: 0-25%
Direct Marketing ad budget:
Online: 100%
Founded: 1941

ISBN# 978-0-7641-3935-2; $14.99, 4th Edition, 2008. Publishes test preparation manuals including SAT, ACT & Regent's exam, Profiles of American Colleges, business & financial books & audio & video learning materials.

DIRECT MAGAZINE
Intertec Publishing
249 W 17th St
New York, NY 10011-5390
Telephone: (212) 204-4228, FAX: (212) 683-3986
Editor-in-Chief: Ray Schultz
Mng Edit: Charles Vietri

Publr: Jeff Reinhardt
Primary Market Served: Business

Magazine that provides editorial coverage for all users of direct marketing & all methods of direct response by reporting on the news, the people, the companies, the technologies & the trends.

DIRECT MARKETING DIGEST

Div. of National Mail Order Association LLC
2807 Polk St NE
Minneapolis, MN 55418
Telephone: (612) 788-1673, E-Mail: info@nmoa.org, Web Site: www. nmoa.org
Pres: John Schulte
Conducts Business: Worldwide
Primary Market Served: Business
Catalog available online
Direct online sales
Advertising/Marketing Budget Related to Direct Marketing: 76-100%
Founded: 1972

Publication for direct marketers & mail order sellers

DIRECT MARKETING MARKET PLACE

National Register Publishing
300 Connell Dr (Suite 2000)
Berkeley Heights, NJ 07922
Telephone: (908) 673-1000, (800) 473-7020, FAX: (908) 673-1179
Chmn: James A. Finkelstein
CEO: Fred Marks
CTO: Ariel Spivakovsky
Publr: Robert Docherty

Reference & mailing list source designed to enable direct marketing professionals to find new business, locate service & supply sources (printers, lettershop, list brokers, managers & computer services), find advertising agencies, consultants, design studios, freelance artists, writers & locate key executives & companies. Includes 43 categories of information & almost 28,000 key organizations & executives.

DIRECT MARKETING NEWS

Div. of Lloydmedia Inc
302-137 Main St N
Markham, ON, Canada L3P 1Y2
Telephone: (905) 201-6600, (800) 668-1838, FAX: (905) 201-6601, E-Mail: home@dmn.ca, Web Site: www. dmn.ca
Sls Mgr & Publr: Mark Henry
Pres & CEO: Steve Lloyd
Editor: Ron Glen
Conducts Business: U.S., Canada

Primary Market Served: Business
Catalog available online
Direct Marketing ad budget:
Direct Mail: 70%
Magazines: 20%
Telephone: 10%
Founded: 1988

Canadian publication for direct marketers. Also provide conferences & seminars for advertising & marketing executives. 12 issues: $60-U.S., $48-Canada.

DIRECT MARKETING STRATEGY, PLANNING & EXECUTION (FOURTH EDITION)

McGraw-Hill Publishers
PO Box 545
Blacklick, OH 43004-0545
Telephone: (614) 755-4152, (800) 722-4726, Web Site: www.mcgraw-hill. com
Author: Edward Nash
Primary Market Served: Business & Consumer

ISBN# 0-07-1352872: Comprehensive "how to" publication used worldwide in schools & for company training.

DIRECT MARKETING TOOL KIT FOR SMALL BUSINESS

Div. of Marketing Logistics Inc
2807 Polk St NE
Minneapolis, MN 55418-2954
Telephone: (612) 788-1673, E-Mail: info@nmoa.org, Web Site: www. nmoa.org/directmarketingtoolkit
Pres & Chmn: John Schulte
Contributor: Dan Argenas
Contributor: Ken Boone
Contributor: Peter Candito
Contributor: Jeffrey Dobkin
Primary Market Served: Business & Consumer

THE DIRECTORY OF BUSINESS INFORMATION RESOURCES

Grey House Publishing
185 Millerton Rd, PO Box 860
Millerton, NY 12546
Telephone: (518) 789-8700, (800) 562-2139, FAX: (518) 789-0556, E-Mail: cstupak@greyhouse.com, Web Site: www.greyhouse.com
Publr: Leslie MacKenzie
Pres: Richard Gottlieb
VP Mktg: Jessica Moody
Mktg Asst: Caitlin Stupak
Primary Market Served: Business
Catalog available online
Direct online sales
Founded: 1979

DIRECTORY OF MAIL ORDER CATALOGS

Grey House Publishing
185 Millerton Rd, PO Box 860
Millerton, NY 12546
Telephone: (518) 789-8700, (800) 562-2139, FAX: (518) 789-0556, E-Mail: cstupak@greyhouse.com, Web Site: www.greyhouse.com
Pres: Richard Gottlieb
Publr: Leslie MacKenzie
VP Mktg: Jessica Moody
Mkgt Asst: Caitlin Stupak
Primary Market Served: Business
Catalog available online
Direct online sales
Founded: 1979

Complete coverage of the consumer mail order industry for sales & marketing managers. Published annually in December. Available in print and online.

DIRECTORY OF MAIL ORDER CATALOGS

National Mail Order Association
2807 Polk St NE
Minneapolis, MN 55418
Telephone: (612) 788-1673, E-Mail: info@nmoa.org, Web Site: www. nmoa.org
Pres: John Schulte
Primary Market Served: Business & Consumer
Catalog available online
Direct online sales

Annual information base directory of all mail order businesses with sales of $5MM or more & all mail order subsidiaries. 2000 directory listings, including sales data.

DIRECTORY OF MAJOR MAILERS & WHAT THEY MAIL

Div. of North American Publishing Co
1500 Spring Garden St (Suite 1200),
North American Publishing Co
Philadelphia, PA 19130-4094
Telephone: (800) 777-8074, FAX: (215) 238-5412, E-Mail: customerservice@napco.com, Web Site: www.majormailers.com
Publr: Patty Perkins
Ed: Tiffini Weddle
Conducts Business: Worldwide
Primary Market Served: Business
Catalog available online
Indirect online sales
Advertising/Marketing Budget Related to Direct Marketing: 51-75%

A single volume, listing over 6000 top direct mail users, including the names, addresses, phone & fax numbers of key personnel. Also shows if mailers are using color, carrier sorting, the dimensions & number of pages of their latest mailings, size of their house files & more. Subscribers also gain access to the Who's Mailing What! Archive, a library of over 150,000 samples of direct mail packages. Published annually. $395 printed; $645 CD ROM.

DIRECTORY OF PREMIUM, INCENTIVE & TRAVEL BUYERS

Div. of The Salesman's Guide A Unit of Douglas Publications Inc
2807 N Parham Rd (Suite 200)
Richmond, VA 23294
Telephone: (804) 762-4455, (800) 223-1797, FAX: (804) 935-0271, E-Mail: amdouglas4@aol.com, Web Site: www.douglaspublications.com
Edit Dir: Keith Cavedo
Mktg Dir: Rusty Hopkins
Sls Dir: Jim Desborough
Employees: 50
Primary Market Served: Business & Consumer
Catalog available online
Indirect online sales
Founded: 1985

Provides information on premium & incentive & travel usage & dollar amounts spent during the past year. Indicates names of premium incentive & travel buyers.

DO IT YOURSELF DIRECT MARKETING

John Wiley & Sons Inc
111 River St
Hoboken, NJ 07030-5774
Telephone: (201) 748-6000, FAX: (201) 748-6088, E-Mail: info@wiley.com, Web Site: www.wiley.com
Chmn Bd: Peter Booth Wiley
Pres & CEO: William J. Pesce
Sr VP Corp Commun: Deborah E. Wiley
Dir: Bradford Wiley II
Dir Response Mktg Dir: Jack Day
Employees: 4,900
Primary Market Served: Business & Consumer
Catalog available online
Direct online sales
Founded: 1807
Gross sales or billing: $1,100,000,000

Subtitled Secrets for a Small Business. This book provides information for anyone initiating or enhancing a direct marketing program. 304 pages. ISBN: 0471163848; $19.95 paperback.

FRAUD & THEFT INFORMATION BUREAU

9770 S Military Trail (Suite 380)
Boynton Beach, FL 33436-3207
Telephone: (561) 737-8700, FAX: (561) 737-5800, E-Mail: sales@fraudandtheft.com, Web Site: www.fraudandtheftinfo.com
Pres & Publr: Larry Schwartz
VP: Pearl Sax
Employees: 8
Primary Market Served: Business
Catalog available online
Direct online sales
Advertising/Marketing Budget Related to Direct Marketing: 51-75%
Direct Marketing ad budget:
Direct Mail: 20%
Magazines: 20%
Online: 20%
Telephone: 40%
Founded: 1982
Gross sales or billing: $4,000,000

Publishers of credit card, check fraud control, loss prevention manuals and databases.

FRIDAY REPORT

Div. of Hoke Communications
54 Adams St
Garden City, NY 11530-3918
Telephone: (516) 746-6700, FAX: (516) 294-8141
Ed: George Reis
Employees: 40
Primary Market Served: Business
Founded: 1938

Newsletter covering the direct marketing industry. $165 (52 issues).

FUND RAISING MANAGEMENT

Div. of Hoke Communications
54 Adams St
Garden City, NY 11530-3918
Telephone: (516) 746-6700, FAX: (516) 294-8141
Ed: George Reis
Pres & Publ: Henry Hoke
Conducts Business: U.S., Canada
Employees: 40
Primary Market Served: Business
Advertising/Marketing Budget Related to Direct Marketing: 76-100%
Direct Marketing ad budget:
Direct Mail: 40%
Magazines: 40%
Telephone: 20%
Founded: 1938

Monthly magazine serving the informational needs of decision makers in nonprofit organizations. Paid circulation. $58 annually.

GRAPHIC ARTS BLUE BOOK ONLINE

Div. of Reed Business Information
2000 Clearwater Dr
Oak Brook, IL 60523
Telephone: (630) 288-8333, (800) 323-4958, Web Site: www.gammag.com
Primary Market Served: Business
Founded: 1929

GREENBOOK WORLDWIDE DIRECTORY OF MARKETING RESEARCH COMPANIES & SERVICES

American Marketing Association (New York)
4301 32nd St W (Suite E-11)
Bradenton, FL 34208
Telephone: (212) 849-2752, (800) 792-9202, FAX: (212) 202-7920, E-Mail: info@greenbrook.org, Web Site: www.greenbook.org
Publr: Camille Crifasi
Coord: Penny Guerrero
Employees: 9
Primary Market Served: Business
Catalog available online
Indirect online sales
Advertising/Marketing Budget Related to Direct Marketing: 0-25%
Direct Marketing ad budget:
Direct Mail: 90%
Magazines: 10%
Founded: 1962

Lists over 2,000 marketing research companies & research services from 50 countries.

GREY HOUSE PUBLISHING

4919 Rte 22
Amenia, NY 12501
Telephone: (518) 789-8700, (800) 562-2139, FAX: (518) 789-0556, E-Mail: books@greyhouse.com, Web Site: www.greyhouse.com
Publr, VP: Leslie MacKenzie
Pres: Richard Gottlieb
VP, Mktg: Jessica Moody
Mktg Asst: Caitlin Stupak
Editorial Dir: Laura Mars-Povietti
Conducts Business: Worldwide
Employees: 84
Primary Market Served: Business
Catalog available online
Direct online sales
Founded: 1979
Gross sales or billing: $7,300,000

GUIDE TO AMERICAN & INTERNATIONAL DIRECTORIES

B Klein Publications
6037 W Atlantic Ave
Delray Beach, FL 33484-8408

Telephone: (561) 367-3799, FAX: (561) 451-0803, E-Mail: bkleinpub@aol.com
Pres & Ed: Bernard Klein
Employees: 10
Primary Market Served: Business & Consumer
Catalog available online
Advertising/Marketing Budget Related to Direct Marketing: 51-75%
Direct Marketing ad budget:
Direct Mail: 70%
Magazines: 10%
Newspapers: 10%
Telephone: 10%
Founded: 1946
Gross sales or billing: $1,000,000

ISBN:0-317-55573; $65.

HOW I GROSSED MORE THAN $1 MILLION IN DIRECT MAIL ORDER STARTING WITH LITTLE CASH & LESS KNOW HOW

International Wealth Success Inc
24 Canterbury Rd
Rockville Centre, NY 11570-1310
Telephone: (516) 766-5850, (800) 323-0548, FAX: (516) 766-5919, Web Site: www.iwsmoney.com
Pres: Tyler G. Hicks
Employees: 1
Primary Market Served: Business & Consumer
Catalog available online
Indirect online sales
Founded: 1967

INSIDE DIRECT MAIL

Div. of North American Publishing Co
1500 Spring Green St (Suite 1200)
Philadelphia, PA 19130-4069
Telephone: (215) 238-5300, (800) 777-8074, FAX: (215) 238-5412, E-Mail: customservice@napco.com, Web Site: www.insidedirectmail.com
Mktg Mgr & Circ Dir: Patty Perkins
Editor-in-Chief: Hallie Mummert
Editor: Ethan Boldt
Copy Editor: Mavis Linnemann
Conducts Business: Worldwide
Primary Market Served: Business
Catalog available online
Direct online sales
Advertising/Marketing Budget Related to Direct Marketing: 51-75%
Founded: 1974

Monthly newsletter: Analysis & Record of Direct Mail in America. In-depth features and articles on all facets of direct marketing: consumer, business, fund-raising & catalogs. Detailed log of more than 1500 mailings received the prior month, plus subscribers can receive photocopies of mailings from the Who's Mailing What! Archive, a library of more than 150,000 mailings in over 200 categories. Also publisher of: The Directory of Major Mailers & What They Mail. $165 annual, 12 monthly issues.

JOURNAL OF MARKETING RESEARCH

American Marketing Association
311 S Wacker Dr (Suite 5800)
Chicago, IL 60606
Telephone: (312) 542-9000, (800) AMA-1150, FAX: (312) 542-9001, E-Mail: info@ama.org, Web Site: www.marketingpower.org
Dir HR: Rebecca Youngberg
Primary Market Served: Business & Consumer
Catalog available online
Direct online sales
Advertising/Marketing Budget Related to Direct Marketing: 0-25%
Founded: 1936

Marketing research. ISSN# 0022437; $200 library. Published quarterly.

LITERARY MARKET PLACE

Information Today Inc
630 Central Ave
New Providence, NJ 07974-1506
Telephone: (800) 409-4929, FAX: (908) 219-0192, E-Mail: khallard@infotoday.com, Web Site: www.literarymarketplace.com
Mng Ed: Karen Hallard
Primary Market Served: Business & Consumer
Catalog available online

Directory of over 28,000 companies & individuals in U.S. & Canadian publishing. Areas covered include book publishers, associations, book trade events, courses, conferences & contests; agents & agencies, services & suppliers, book manufacturers, direct mail promotion, sales & distribution, magazines & reference books for the trade. 2 vol set. Indexes. Annual 2012 (72 nd) Edition; ISBN: 978-1-57387-420-5; $339.00 (2 vol set).

MAIL ORDER BUSINESS

Subs. of Kendall Hunt Publishing Co
4050 Westmark Dr
Dubuque, IA 52002

Telephone: (319) 589-1000 X1076, (800) 772-9165, FAX: (319) 589-1046, Web Site: www.kendallhunt.com
Primary Market Served: Consumer
Advertising/Marketing Budget Related to Direct Marketing: 0-25%

ISBN# 0-8403-71748; $22.95.

MAIL ORDER BUSINESS DIRECTORY

B Klein Publications
PO Box 970392
Boca Raton, FL 33497-0392
Telephone: (561) 367-3799, FAX: (561) 451-0803, E-Mail: bkleinpub@aol.com
Pres: Bernard Klein
Conducts Business: Worldwide
Employees: 10
Primary Market Served: Business & Consumer
Advertising/Marketing Budget Related to Direct Marketing: 51-75%
Direct Marketing ad budget: $150,000
Direct Mail: 70%
Magazines: 10%
Newspapers: 10%
Telephone: 10%
Gross sales or billing: $1,000,000

Contains the names of the 5,000 most active mail order houses, listed geographically with indexes. Annual. 19th edition, 2002. ISBN: 0-915344-92-0; $95.

MARKETING ADVENTS

Direct Marketing Association of Washington
209 Madison St (Suite 300)
Alexandria, VA 22314
Telephone: (703) 706-0387, FAX: (703) 836-2181, E-Mail: info@dmaw.org, Web Site: www.dmaw.org
Ed: Nancy Scott
Exec Dir DMAW: Barbara Armentrout
Conducts Business: U.S.
Employees: 4
Primary Market Served: Business
Direct online sales
Founded: 1955

Covers news of the DMAW's events & information of professional interest to members, including postal related news. Free with $175 membership.

MARKETING NEWS

American Marketing Association
311 S Wacker Dr (Suite 5800)
Chicago, IL 60606
Telephone: (312) 542-9000, (800) 262-1150, FAX: (312) 542-9001, E-Mail: news@ama.org, Web Site: www.ama.org

Chmn-Elect: Michael Lotti
Chmn: Debra Ringold
Pres, Prof Chapters: Colin Hageny
Sr Dir: Jack Hollfelder
Primary Market Served: Business
Catalog available online
Direct online sales
Advertising/Marketing Budget Related
 to Direct Marketing: 0-25%
Founded: 1936

Reports on marketing & its
association. ISSN# 00253790;
membership-no additional fee: $100
non-member; $130 library, $130
institution. Published bi-weekly.

MARKETING SCIENCE INSTITUTE REVIEW

Marketing Science Institute
1000 Massachusetts Ave
Cambridge, MA 02138-5396
Telephone: (617) 491-2060, FAX:
 (617) 491-2065, E-Mail: msi@msi.
 org, Web Site: www.msi.org
COO: Marni Z. Clippinger
Chief Mktg Officer: Earl Taylor
Exec Dir: Russell Winer
Employees: 10
Primary Market Served: Business &
 Consumer
Founded: 1961

Covers events, research findings, conferences & membership of the institute, a research center whose purpose
is to advance marketing practice &
knowledge. Free; published semi-
annually.

O'DWYERS DIRECTORY OF PUBLIC RELATIONS FIRMS

JR O'Dwyer Co
271 Madison Ave (Suite 600)
New York, NY 10016-1013
Telephone: (212) 679-2471, (866) 395-
 7710, FAX: (212) 683-2750, E-Mail:
 john@odwyerpr.com, Web Site:
 www.odwyerpr.com
Publr: Jack O'Dwyer
Conducts Business: Worldwide
Employees: 10
Primary Market Served: Business &
 Consumer
Catalog available online
Founded: 1968

1001 WAYS TO MARKET YOUR BOOKS

Open Horizons Publishing Co
PO Box 2887
Taos, NM 87571
Telephone: (575) 751-3398, FAX:
 (575) 751-3100, E-Mail: info@
 bookmarket.com, Web Site: www.
 bookmarket.com
Pres: John Kremer

Conducts Business: Worldwide
Primary Market Served: Business &
 Consumer
Catalog available online
Indirect online sales
Advertising/Marketing Budget Related
 to Direct Marketing: 0-25%
Founded: 1986

A comprehensive introduction to marketing your books. Contains practical,
easy-to-use information designed to
help anyone develop a successful marketing program. $27.95.

PHOTOGRAPHER'S MARKET

Div. of Writer's Digest Books / F & W
 Publications
10151 Carver Rd (Suite 200)
Blue Ash, OH 45242-4760
Telephone: (513) 531-2690, FAX:
 (513) 531-2686, E-Mail:
 photomarket@fwpubs.com, Web
 Site: www.photographersmarket.com
Mktg Mgr: Scott Francis
Market Books Dept: Alice Pope
Employees: 1
Primary Market Served: Business
Catalog available online
Indirect online sales
Founded: 1977

More than 2000 listings of photo buyers with complete contact information;
for freelance & stock photographers.
Annual publication; $24.99.

THE DMA RESPONSE MAGAZINE

Div. of Questex Media Group Inc
201 Sandpointe Ave (Suite 500)
Santa Ana, CA 92707-8716
Telephone: (714) 513-8624, (800) 371-
 6897, FAX: (714) 338-6710, Web
 Site: www.responsemagazine.com
Publr: John Yarrington
Conducts Business: U.S., Canada
Primary Market Served: Business
Advertising/Marketing Budget Related
 to Direct Marketing: 26-50%
Founded: 1992

Published monthly. Covers all aspects
of the direct response marketing
industry. From the 30-second spot, to
the infomercial, to online & internet
programming for the marketing, advertising & television executive. ISSN#
1077-5439.

STANDARD DIRECTORY OF ADVERTISING AGENCIES

Advertising Red Books A Member of
 the LexisNexis Group
121 Chanlon Rd
New Providence, NJ 07974
Telephone: (800) 521-8110, FAX:
 (908) 790-5405

Gen Mgr: Tom W. Derry

SUCCESS MAGAZINE

200 Swisher Rd
Lake Dallas, TX 75065
Telephone: (800) 570-6414, Web Site:
 www.successmagazine.com
Publ & Editorial Dir: Darren Hardy
Editor-in-Chief: Deborah Heisz
Conducts Business: Worldwide
Employees: 3
Primary Market Served: Business &
 Consumer
Founded: 2006

Entrepreneurial Magazine.

TARGET MARKETING MAGAZINE

North American Publishing Co
1500 Spring Garden St (12th fl)
Philadelphia, PA 19130-4094
Telephone: (215) 238-5300, (800) 777-
 8074, FAX: (215) 238-5270, Web
 Site: www.targetmarketingmag.com
Pres & Grp Publr: Peggy Hatch
Editor-in-Chief: Hallie Mummert
Primary Market Served: Business

The monthly magazine of how-to,
hands-on, information for direct
marketers. $65 annually; Free to quali-
fied subscribers.

TELEPHONE SELLING REPORT

Div. of Business By Phone Inc
14005 E Cholla Dr
Scottsdale, AZ 85259-4619
Telephone: (402) 895-9399, FAX:
 (402) 896-3353, E-Mail: arts@
 businessbyphone.com, Web Site:
 www.businessbyphone.com
Pres & Publr: Art Sobczak
Conducts Business: Worldwide
Employees: 3
Primary Market Served: Business
Catalog available online
Direct online sales
Advertising/Marketing Budget Related
 to Direct Marketing: 76-100%
Founded: 1983

Monthly "how-to" newsletter providing
proven ideas & techniques for sales
reps who use the phone to prospect,
qualify, set appointments & sell by
telephone. Also have catalog of tele-
sales training audio tapes, videos,
books & other how-to resources. Provide training seminars.

THE DMA WEIDER HISTORY GROUP

350 Bennetts Farm Rd
Ridgefield, CT 06877
Telephone: (203) 273-1092

WHO'S WHO - THE MFSA BUYERS' GUIDE TO BLUE RIBBON MAILING SERVICES

Mailing & Fulfillment Service Association
1421 Prince St (Suite 410)
Alexandria, VA 22314-2805
Telephone: (703) 836-9200, FAX: (703) 548-8204, E-Mail: masamail@masa.org, Web Site: www.mfsanet.org
Pres: J Kenneth Garner
Dir Mktg & Programs: Bill Stevenson
Dir Membership: Tyler Keeney
Employees: 11
Catalog available online
Founded: 1920

Lists over 750 mailhouses, fulfillment lettershops & direct mail agencies. Latest edition, 2002. No charge to buyers of mailing services.

WILSHIRE BOOK CO

9731 Variel Ave
Chatsworth, CA 91311-4315
Telephone: (818) 700-1522, FAX: (818) 700-1527, E-Mail: mpowers@mpowers.com, Web Site: www.mpowers.com
Publr & Pres: Melvin Powers
Conducts Business: U.S., Worldwide
Employees: 21
Primary Market Served: Business & Consumer
Catalog available online
Direct online sales
Founded: 1947
Gross sales or billing: $5,000,000

ISBN # 0-87980-397-5; $20. How To Write A Good Advertisement.

Alphabetical Index to Companies & Individuals

This alphabetical index interfiles the companies and individuals found within all sections of DMMP.

A

A & A Research, Kalispell, MT. Tel: (406) 752-7857 (30)

A&B Equipment Co, Fort Worth, TX. Tel: (817) 332-8361, (800) 426-0683, FAX: (817) 332-8430, Web Site: www.abequipmentcompany.com (16)

A&E Promotions LLC, Atlantic Highlands, NJ. Tel: (732) 275-1520, Web Site: www.aepromo.com (27)

A&H Lithoprint Inc, Broadview, IL. Tel: (708) 345-1196, FAX: (708) 345-1225, Web Site: www.ahlithoprint.com (27)

A&M Direct Mail Service Inc, San Dimas, CA. Tel: (909) 599-3905, (909) 579-0111, (800) 735-3905, FAX: (909) 599-3516, E-Mail: mail@amdirectmail.com (28)

A&P, Montvale, NJ. Tel: (201) 573-9700, (866) 44 FRESH, FAX: (201) 505-3054, E-Mail: apcustomerrel@aptea.com, Web Site: www.aptea.com (16)

A&R Mailing Machine Inc, East Hartford, CT. Tel: (860) 290-6640 (34)

A La Carte, Chicago, IL. Tel: (773) 745-5900, (800) 723-2370, FAX: (773) 237-3075, E-Mail: info@alacarteline.com, Web Site: www.alacarteline.com (16)

A La Mode Inc, Oklahoma City, OK. Tel: (405) 359-6587, Web Site: www.alamode.com (22)

A-Mark Inc, Dresher, PA. Tel: (215) 886-4740, FAX: (215) 886-4749 (15)

A Marketing Resource, South St Paul, MN. Tel: (651) 451-1765, Web Site: www.amr-advantage.com (29)

A-1 Direct Mail Marketing Inc, Miami, FL. Tel: (305) 251-3187 (28)

A+ Letter Service, Lakewood, NJ. Tel: (732) 905-2010, FAX: (732) 905-4662, E-Mail: aplus@aplusletter.com, Web Site: www.aplusletters.com (28)

A Plus Marketing Ltd, Buffalo Grove, IL. Tel: (847) 537-1166, FAX: (847) 537-5611, Web Site: www.aplusmarketing.com (20)

A-T Surgical Manufacturing Co, Holyoke, MA. Tel: (413) 532-4551, (800) 225-2023, FAX: (413) 532-0826, E-Mail: atsmci@a-surgical.com, Web Site: www.atsurgical.com (2)

A-KD Mailing & Fulfillment Service, Lincolnwood, IL. Tel: (847) 673-0186, (866) 330-6245, FAX: (874) 673-0188, E-Mail: dan@kdmailing.com, Web Site: www.kdmailing.com (28)

AAA Auto Club South, Tampa, FL. Tel: (813) 289-1344, FAX: (813) 289-1340, Web Site: www.aaa.com (1)

AAA BEST Mailing Lists Inc, Tucson, AZ. Tel: (520) 885-0400, (800) 692-2378, FAX: (520) 885-3100, E-Mail: best@bestmailing.com, Web Site: www.bestmailing.com (23)

AAA-Chicago Motor Club, Aurora, IL. Tel: (847) 390-9000, (866) 968-7222, FAX: (847) 390-7738, Web Site: www.aaa.com (1)

AAA Mid-Atlantic Insurance Groups, Wilmington, DE. Tel: (302) 299-4700, (800) 451-5921, FAX: (215) 864-5486, Web Site: www.aaamidatlantic.com (15)

AAA Southern New England, Providence, RI. Tel: (401) 868-2005, FAX: (401) 868-2085, Web Site: www.aaa.com (1)

AAA Umbrella Co Inc, Northvale, NJ. Tel: (201) 784-3242, (800) 426-7446, FAX: (201) 226-0041, Web Site: www.aaaumbrella.com (16)

AAAS/Science, Washington, DC. Tel: (202) 326-6400, FAX: (202) 371-9526, E-Mail: webmaster@aaas.org, Web Site: www.aaas.org (1)

AAFES, Dallas, TX. Tel: (214) 312-6700, (800) 527-6790, FAX: (214) 312-3000, Web Site: www.aafes.com (5)

AAI, Hopkinton, MA. Tel: (508) 544-1250, (877) 866-8500, FAX: (508) 544-1253, E-Mail: info@aai-agency.com, Web Site: www.aai-agency.com (35)

AARP, Washington, DC. Tel: (202) 434-2277, Web Site: www.aarp.org (1)

AAVIM, Winterville, GA. Tel: (706) 742-5355, (800) 228-4689, FAX: (706) 742-7005, E-Mail: gary@aavim.com, Web Site: www.aavim.com (31)

AB Data Ltd, Milwaukee, WI. Tel: (414) 961-6400, FAX: (414) 961-6410, E-Mail: info@abdata.com, Web Site: www.abdata.com (21)

ABA/BMA Trust Wealth Management and Marketing Conference, Washington, DC. Tel: (202) 663-5000, (800) BANKERS, FAX: (202) 828-4540, E-Mail: custserv@aba.com, Web Site: www.aba.com (42)

ABC Carpet & Home, New York, NY. Tel: (212) 473-3000, (800) 888-RUGS, FAX: (212) 777-3713, Web Site: www.abccarpet.com (8)

ABC Clio, Santa Barbara, CA. Tel: (805) 968-1911, FAX: (805) 685-9685, E-Mail: elott@abc/clio.com, Web Site: www.abc-clio.com (17)

ABCO Inc, Dallas, TX. Tel: (214) 565-5250, Web Site: www.abcoinc.com (20)

ABDI, Inc Global Order Fulfillment, Leetsdale, PA. Tel: (412) 741-1142, (800) 796-6471, FAX: (412) 741-4161, E-Mail: info@abdintl.com, Web Site: www.abdintl.com (28)

ABR Employment Services, Madison, WI. Tel: (608) 244-3526, FAX: (608) 244-8279, E-Mail: info@abrjobs.com, Web Site: www.abrjobs.com (20)

ABS Graphics, Addison, IL. Tel: (630) 495-2400, FAX: (630) 495-0728, E-Mail: info@absinet.com, Web Site: www.absinet.com (27)

AC Pedreiro, Morganville, NJ. Tel: (732) 598-6766 (27)

ACBL, Horn Lake, MS. Tel: (901) 332-5586, FAX: (901) 398-7754, E-Mail: service@acbl.org, Web Site: www.acbl.org (1)

ACCO North America, Lincolnshire, IL. Tel: (847) 541-9500, (800) 222-6462, FAX: (847) 478-0073, Web Site: www.acco.com (16)

ACG/Computech Direct, Hoffman Estates, IL. Tel: (847) 843-3200, FAX: (847) 843-8060, E-Mail: info@acg-computech-direct.com, Web Site: www.acg-computech-direct.com (22)

ACN USA, Brooklyn, NY. Tel: (212) 334-5340, Web Site: www.churchinneed.org (1)

ACNielsen, Schaumburg, IL. Tel: (847) 605-5000, FAX: (847) 605-2000, E-Mail: mkarr@datamartdirect.com, Web Site: www.datamartdirect.com (34)

ACP American Catalog Partnerships LLC, Summit, NJ. Tel: (908) 598-1947 (20)

ACP - Automation Control Products, Alpharetta, GA. Tel: (678) 990-0945, FAX: (678) 990-0951, E-Mail: info@thinmanager.com, Web Site: www.thinmanager.com (16)

ACP Interactive, San Francisco, CA. Tel: (415) 357-5100, (800) 357-5177, FAX: (415) 357-5110, E-Mail: info@acpinteractive.com, Web Site: www.callgistics.com (29)

ACP Medicine, Hamilton, ON Canada. Tel: (905) 522-8526, (855) 647-6511, FAX: (905) 522-9273, E-Mail: acpmedicine@deckerpublishing.com, Web Site: acpmedicine.com (17)

ACTV Inc, New York, NY. Tel: (415) 962-5000 (32)

ADM Marketing, Burbank, CA. Tel: (888) 800-1001 (20)

ADM Productions Inc, Port Washington, NY. Tel: (516) 484-6900, (800) ADM-DIAL, FAX: (516) 621-2531, Web Site: www.admpro.com (16)

ADP Inc, Roseland, NJ. Tel: (973) 974-5000, (800) 225-5237, FAX: (973) 974-3334, Web Site: www.adp.com (16)

ADRA International, Silver Spring, MD. Tel: (301) 680-6373, Web Site: www.adra.org (1)

ADRFCO, Washington, DC. Tel: (202) 293-9640, Web Site: www.adrfco.org (1)

ADS Direct Media, San Antonio, TX. Tel: (210) 655-6613, Web Site: www.adsmediagroup.com (27)

ADT Worldwide, Boca Raton, FL. Tel: (561) 988-3600, FAX: (561) 988-3673, Web Site: www.tycofireandsecurity.com (16)

ADV Marketing Group Inc, Stamford, CT. Tel: (203) 356-9621, FAX: (203) 324-4680 (35)

ADVO Inc, Windsor, CT. Tel: (860) 285-6100, FAX: (860) 285-1567, Web Site: www.advo.com (21)

AEGON Direct Marketing Services Inc, Baltimore, MD. Tel: (410) 209-5617, FAX: (410) 209-5932, Web Site: www.aegondms.com (15)

AESU Inc, Baltimore, MD. Tel: (410) 366-5494, (800) 638-7640, FAX: (410) 366-6999, E-Mail: res@aesu.com, Web Site: www.aesu.com (19)

AFA Service Corp, Atlanta, GA. Tel: (404) 262-2729, (404) 237-2964, Web Site: www.arbys.com (16)

The Affinion Group, Franklin, TN. Tel: (610) 933-3645, (800) 251-2148, FAX: (610) 933-7744, Web Site: www.affiniongroup.com (35)

AFL-CIO, Washington, DC. Tel: (202) 637-5000, FAX: (202) 637-5058, (202) 637-5323, Web Site: www.aflcio.org (1)

AFLAC, Columbus, GA. Tel: (706) 243-5428, Web Site: www.aflac.com (15)

AG Interactive, Cleveland, OH. Tel: (216) 889-5000, Web Site: www.aginteractive.com (32)

AGCO Inc, Norcross, GA. Tel: (770) 447-6990, FAX: (770) 446-2102, Web Site: www.agcomarble.com (9)

AGIA Insurance Services, Carpinteria, CA. Tel: (805) 566-9191, FAX: (805) 566-1887, Web Site: www.agia.com (15)

AIDC (American International Distribution Corp), Williston, VT. Tel: (800) 678-2432, FAX: (802) 864-7626, E-Mail: jmacon@aidcvt.com, Web Site: www.aidcvt.com (22)

AIFS, Stamford, CT. Tel: (203) 399-5000, Web Site: www.aifs.com (19)

AIG Accident & Health, New York, NY. Tel: (212) 770-7000, (877) 638-4244, FAX: (212) 509-9705, Web Site: www.aig.com (15)

AIG Marketing, New York, NY. Tel: (212) 770-7000, (212) 770-2237, Web Site: www.agac.com (15)

AIIM International, Silver Spring, MD. Tel: (301) 587-8202, (800) 477-2446, FAX: (301) 587-2711, E-Mail: aiim@aiim.org, Web Site: www.aiim.org (1)

AIN Plastics Inc, Yonkers, NY. Tel: (914) 668-6800, (800) 431-2451, FAX: (914) 668-8820, Web Site: www.ainplastics.com (16)

AKA Direct, Portland, OR. Tel: (503) 454-2233, Web Site: www.akadirect.com (27)

AKS Marketing & Media, Chapel Hill, NC. Tel: (919) 240-5496 (20)

ALC Inc, Princeton, NJ. Tel: (609) 580-2800, (800) ALC-LIST, FAX: (609) 580-2888, E-Mail: info@alc.com, Web Site: www.alc.com (23)

Alco Chemical, Chattanooga, TN. Tel: (423) 629-1405, FAX: (423) 698-8723, Web Site: www.alcochemical.com (16)

ALSAC - St. Jude, Memphis, TN. Tel: (901) 495-3300, FAX: (901) 495-3103, Web Site: www.stjude.org (1)

AMA Insurance Agency Inc, Chicago, IL. Tel: (312) 464-2425, (800) 458-5736, FAX: (312) 419-5096, Web Site: www.amainsure.com (15)

AMC Inc, Atlanta, GA. Tel: (404) 220-2000, FAX: (404) 220-3030 (2)

AMC MMI, Fullerton, CA. Tel: (888) 304-4664, FAX: (714) 888-8855 (21)

AMC Publishing/Agent Media Corp, Erlanger, KY. Tel: (727) 446-1100, (800) 933-9449, FAX: (727) 446-1166, E-Mail: sales@agentmediacorp.com, Web Site: www.agentmediacorp.com (31)

AMD Industries Inc, Cicero, IL. Tel: (708) 863-8900, (800) 367-9999, FAX: (708) 863-2065, Web Site: www.amdpop.com (36)

AMI Instore, Framingham, MA. Tel: (508) 652-0200, (877) 652-0200, FAX: (508) 652-0101, E-Mail: info@advancemarketing.com, Web Site: www.advancemarketing.com (31)

Ampac, Cincinnati, OH. Tel: (513) 671-1777, (800) 543-7030, FAX: (513) 671-2920, Web Site: www.ampaconline.com (27)

AMS Direct, Burr Ridge, IL. Tel: (630) 382-1000, FAX: (630) 325-0825, Web Site: www.amsdirect.com (13)

AMVETS National Service Foundation, Lanham, MD. Tel: (301) 459-6181, (877) 726-8387, FAX: (301) 459-5578, Web Site: www.amvets.org (1)

AON Center, Chicago, IL. Tel: (312) 381-1000, FAX: (312) 381-6032, Web Site: www.aon.com (15)

Aon Consulting New York, New York, NY. Tel: (212) 792-9759, (212) 792-9700, (212) 441-2000, FAX: (212) 792-9720, E-Mail: garry_sullivan@aoncons.com (15)

Aon Innovative Solutions, Chicago, IL. Tel: (303) 279-2900, FAX: (303) 216-1732, Web Site: www.aon.com (16)

AP Images, New York, NY. Tel: (212) 621-1930, FAX: (212) 621-1955, E-Mail: apimages_us@ap.org, Web Site: www.apimages.com (38)

APAC Customer Services Inc, Bannockburn, IL. Tel: (847) 374-4980, (800) 688-7687, FAX: (847) 236-5453, Web Site: www.apaccustomerservices.com (29)

APS Technologies, Hillsboro, OR. Tel: (503) 844-4500, (800) 233-7550, FAX: (503) 844-4508, E-Mail: sales@lacie.com, Web Site: www.lacie.com (35)

APSCO, Davenport Center, NY. Tel: (607) 278-6218, FAX: (607) 278-6218, E-Mail: webmaster@antiquephono.com, Web Site: www.antiquephono.com (11)

APW-Wright Line, Worcester, MA. Tel: (508) 852-4300, (800) 225-7348, FAX: (508) 852-3060, Web Site: www.wrightline.com (16)

ARA Media Solutions Inc, New York, NY. Tel: (212) 245-6691, Web Site: www.aramediasolutions.com (31)

ARAG, Des Moines, IA. Tel: (800) 247-4184, FAX: (515) 246-8710, E-Mail: service@ARAGgroup.com, Web Site: www.araggroup.com (15)

ARE Press, Virginia Beach, VA. Tel: (757) 491-0689, (888) 273-3400, FAX: (757) 491-0689, Web Site: www.arepress.com (1)

ARF Annual Convention & Research Infoplex, New York, NY. Tel: (212) 751-5656, FAX: (212) 319-5265, E-Mail: info@theARF.org, Web Site: www.theARF.org (42)

ARGI - Automated Resources Group Inc, Montvale, NJ. Tel: (201) 391-1500, FAX: (201) 391-8357, Web Site: www.callargi.com (22)

ARI, Orchard Hill, GA. Tel: (770) 227-8222, (800) 241-5064, FAX: (770) 227-9190, Web Site: www.halt.com (16)

ASE Technologies Inc, Wilmington, MA. Tel: (978) 658-0009, FAX: (978) 658-9990, E-Mail: info@ase-tech.com, Web Site: www.ase-tech.com (16)

ASH Recruitment Solutions, Exeter, NH. Tel: (603) 778-8888, E-Mail: t.hall@ashrecruit.com, Web Site: www.ashrecruit.com (20)

ASM International, Materials Park, OH. Tel: (440) 338-5151, (800) 336-5152, FAX: (440) 338-4634, E-Mail: customerservice@asminternational.org, Web Site: www.asminternational.org (1)

ASM Press, Washington, DC. Tel: (202) 737-3600, (800) 546-2416, FAX: (202) 942-9342, E-Mail: books@asmusa.org, Web Site: www.asmpress.org (17)

ASPCA, New York, NY. Tel: (212) 876-7700, Web Site: www.aspca.org (1)

ASTM International, West Conshohocken, PA. Tel: (610) 832-9500, FAX: (610) 832-9555, E-Mail: service@astm.org, Web Site: www.astm.org (1)

AT&T, Bedminster, NJ. Tel: (800) 222-0300, FAX: (908) 532-1675, Web Site: www.att.com (16)

AT&T Advertising & Publishing, Saint Louis, MO. Tel: (314) 957-5100, FAX: (314) 957-5050, Web Site: www.att.com (31)

AT&T Language Line Services, Monterey, CA. Tel: (831) 648-5861, (877) 886-3885, FAX: (800) 821-9040, E-Mail: wecare@languageline.com, Web Site: www.languageline.com (29)

ATD American Co, Wyncote, PA. Tel: (215) 576-1380, (866) 283-9327, FAX: (215) 576-1827, E-Mail: janet@atd.com, Web Site: www.atdamerican.com (34)

ATM Advertising, Atlanta, GA. Tel: (770) 671-0404, Web Site: www.sagpromo.com (35)

AVD Marketing, Hollywood, FL. Tel: (954) 410-9000, Web Site: www.avdmarketing.com (20)

AW Direct Inc, Madison, WI. Tel: (860) 828-7800, (800) 243-3194, FAX: (800) 828-9678, E-Mail: contactus@awdirect.com, Web Site: www.awdirect.com (12)

AXA Equitable, New York, NY. Tel: (212) 554-1234, (212) 314-2956, Web Site: www.axaonline.com (15)

Aagaard, Peter, J., Steuben Glass, New York, NY. Tel: (607) 974-8659, (800) STEUBEN, FAX: (607) 974-8441, E-Mail: info@steuben.com, Web Site: www.steuben.com (6)

Aardvark Enterprises, Calgary, AB Canada. Tel: (360) 779-5374 (17)

Aaron, Adam, Vail Associates Inc, Broomfield, CO. Tel: (303) 404-1800, (800) 842-8062, FAX: (303) 404-6415, Web Site: www.snow.com (19)

Aaron, M., Brim Electronics Inc, Lodi, NJ. Tel: (201) 796-2886, FAX: (973) 778-2792, E-Mail: info@brimelectronics.com, Web Site: www.brimelectronics.com (3)

Aaronson, Lawrence, Craig Envelope Corp, Long Island City, NY. Tel: (718) 392-9304, (888) 272-4436, FAX: (718) 937-8178, E-Mail: info@craigenvelope.com, Web Site: www.craigenvelope.com (26)

Abacus Communications, Manchester, NH. Tel: (800) 888-3188, FAX: (603) 645-5093, E-Mail: michael@call-centers.com, Web Site: www.callabacus.com (29)

Abbate, Guy, Sherman Specialty Toy Co Inc, Jericho, NY. Tel: (516) 861-6420, (516) 546-7400, (800) 645-6513, FAX: (516) 861-1033, (800) 853-8697, E-Mail: orders@shermanspecialty.com, Web Site: www.shermanspecialty.com (16)

Abbeon Cal Inc, Santa Barbara, CA. Tel: (805) 966-0810, (800) 922-0977, FAX: (805) 966-7659, E-Mail: abbeoncal@abbeon.com, Web Site: www.abbeon.com (9)

Abbey of Gethsemani, New Haven, KY. Tel: (502) 549-3117, FAX: (502) 549-4124, Web Site: www.monks.org (1)

Abbey Press, Saint Meinrad, IN. Tel: (812) 357-8011, FAX: (812) 357-8388, Web Site: www.abbeypress.com (4)

Abbot, Jonathan, C., WGBH Educational Foundation, Brighton, MA. Tel: (617) 300-5400, FAX: (617) 300-1026, Web Site: www.wgbh.org (1)

Abbott, Allen, Paul Fredrick Menstyle, Fleetwood, PA. Tel: (610) 944-0909, (800) 247-1417, FAX: (610) 944-6452, E-Mail: custserv@menstyle.com, Web Site: www.paulfredricks.com (2)

Abbott, Bruce, Continental Supply Inc, Cleveland, OH. Tel: (440) 864-6231, (800) 672-0321, FAX: (888) 672-9808 (9)

Abbott, James, Westlake Plastics Co, Lenni, PA. Tel: (610) 459-1000, (800) 999-1700, FAX: (610) 459-1084, Web Site: www.westlakeplastics.com (16)

Abbott, Steve, International Society for Technology in Education, Eugene, OR. Tel: (541) 349-7575, Web Site: www.iste.org (1)

Abbott, North Chicago, IL. Tel: (847) 937-8641, FAX: (847) 937-9555, Web Site: www.abbott.com (7)

Abbott, Langer Association Surveys, Washington, DC. Tel: (877) 210-6563, FAX: (877) 239-2457, E-Mail: info@abbott-langer.com, Web Site: www.abbott-langer.com (17)

Abbott Products, Weymouth, MA. Tel: (781) 331-2030, (800) 392-7700, FAX: (781) 331-2030, Web Site: www.abbottproducts.com (16)

Abbruzzese, Chris, Maui Jim Inc, Peoria, IL. Tel: (309) 691-3700, FAX: (309) 683-2202, Web Site: www.mauijim.com (16)

Abdallah, Karen, Liggett-Stashower Direct, Cleveland, OH. Tel: (216) 348-8500, (800) 877-4573, FAX: (216) 736-8118, E-Mail: mnylander@liggett.com, Web Site: www.liggett.com (35)

Abeel, Tom, JIST Publishing, Saint Paul, MN. Tel: (800) 648-5478, FAX: (800) 547-8329, E-Mail: info@jist.com, Web Site: www.jist.com (17)

Abel, Barry, Message Systems, Columbia, MD. Tel: (410) 872-4910, (877) 887-3031, FAX: (410) 872-4912, E-Mail: information@messagesystems.com, Web Site: www.messagesystems.com (32)

Abel, David, S., The Boston Globe, Boston, MA. Tel: (617) 929-2000, (888) MY-GLOBE, FAX: (617) 929-2606, Web Site: www.bostonglobe.com (17)

Abele Jr., James, A., Robert James Co Inc, Moody, AL. Tel: (205) 640-7081, (800) 633-8296, FAX: (205) 640-7087 (10)

Abeloe, Dave, Patagonia Mail Order Inc, Reno, NV. Tel: (775) 747-1992, (800) 638-6464, FAX: (775) 747-6159, Web Site: www.patagonia.com (2)

Abelove, David, Associated Textile Rental Services, Rochester, NY. Tel: (585) 454-5988, (800) 639-4624, Web Site: www.associatedtextile.com (16)

Abelow, Justin, New York Landmarks Conservancy, New York, NY. Tel: (212) 995-5260, FAX: (212) 995-5268, Web Site: www.nylandmarks.org (1)

Abels, Stephen, Mutual of Omaha, Omaha, NE. Tel: (402) 342-7600, (800) 775-6000, FAX: (402) 351-2775, Web Site: www.mutualofomaha.com (15)

Abelson-Taylor Inc, Chicago, IL. Tel: (312) 894-5500, FAX: (312) 894-5526, E-Mail: info@abelsontaylor.com, Web Site: www.abelson-taylor.com (35)

Abend, Sarah, Wyandotte West Communications Inc, Kansas City, KS. Tel: (913) 788-5565, FAX: (913) 788-9812, E-Mail: news@wyandottewest.com, Web Site: www.wyandottewest.com (17)

Abercrombie, George, Roche Pharmaceuticals, Nutley, NJ. Tel: (973) 235-5000, FAX: (973) 235-7605, Web Site: www.rocheusa.com (7)

Abernathy, Robert, E., Kimberly-Clark Corp, Neenah, WI. Tel: (920) 721-2000, (888) 525-8388, FAX: (920) 721-7722, Web Site: www.kimberly-clark.com (16)

Abeyta, Joseph, McMurry Inc, Phoenix, AZ. Tel: (602) 395-5850, Web Site: www.mcmurry.com (17)

Abi-Karam, Leslie, Pitney Bowes, Stamford, CT. Tel: (203) 356-5000, (800) MR-BOWES, Web Site: www.pitneybowes.com (10)

Ability Commerce, Delray Beach, FL. Tel: (561) 330-3151, Web Site: www.abilitycommerce.com (20)

Abion, Betty, Response Media, Norcross, GA. Tel: (770) 451-5478, FAX: (770) 451-4929, E-Mail: babion@responsemedia.com, Web Site: www.responsemedia.com (32)

Abney, Wendy, Brigade Quartermasters Ltd, Providence, RI. Tel: (770) 428-1248, (800) 338-4327, FAX: (800) 892-2992, Web Site: www.actiongear.com (11)

About Books Inc, Colorado Springs, CO. Tel: (719) 632-8226, FAX: (719) 471-2182, E-Mail: infoabi2@about-books.com, Web Site: www.about-books.com (20)

Abraham, Dan, Pennstreet Bakery, Grand Rapids, MI. Tel: (616) 241-2583, (800) 84-CAKES, FAX: (616) 241-6332, Web Site: www.pennstreet.com (16)

Abraham, Terri, HMI Marketing, Brooklyn Park, MN. Tel: (800) 468-4144, FAX: (800) 468-8814, Web Site: www.hmimarketing.com (7)

Abrahams, Mark, DelStar Technologies, Middletown, DE. Tel: (302) 378-8888, (800) 521-6713, FAX: (302) 378-4482, Web Site: www.delstarinc.com (16)

Abrahamson, Kathy, Rose Resnick Lighthouse for the Blind & Visually Impaired, San Francisco, CA. Tel: (415) 431-1481, FAX: (415) 863-7568, E-Mail: executive@lighthouse-sf.org, Web Site: www.lighthouse-sf.org (1)

Abrams, Bill, Tyme Direct Mail Service, Long Island City, NY. Tel: (212) 691-4444, FAX: (212) 691-6747, E-Mail: info@tymedirect.com, Web Site: www.tymedirect.com (21)

Abrams, Marjory, Boardroom Inc, Stamford, CT. Tel: (203) 973-5900, FAX: (203) 967-3086, E-Mail: kseaborne@boardroom.com, Web Site: www.boardroom.com (17)

Abrams, Martin, Center For Information Policy Leadership, Washington, DC. Tel: (202) 778-2264, FAX: (202) 778-2201, Web Site: www.policyleaders.com (20)

Abrams, Mike, Iowa Medical Society, West Des Moines, IA. Tel: (515) 223-1401, FAX: (515) 223-0590, Web Site: www.iowamedical.org (1)

Abrams, Neal, Pilgrim Printed Promotional Plastics, Brockton, MA. Tel: (508) 436-6300, (800) 343-7810, FAX: (508) 580-3542, E-Mail: pilgrimsales@pilgrimplastics.com, Web Site: www.pilgrimplastics.com (27)

Abrams, Ralph, Lea & Perrins Inc, Fair Lawn, NJ. Tel: (201) 791-1600, FAX: (201) 791-8945, Web Site: www.leaperrins.com (16)

Abrams, Richard, Tom Snyder Productions, Watertown, MA. Tel: (617) 926-6000, (800) 342-0236, FAX: (800) 304-1254, E-Mail: ask@tomsnyder.com, Web Site: www.tomsnyder.com (16)

Harry N Abrams Inc, New York, NY. Tel: (212) 206-7715, FAX: (212) 645-8437, Web Site: www.hnabooks.com (17)

Abramson, Betty, Starcrest Products of California Inc, Perris, CA. Tel: (909) 943-2011, FAX: (909) 943-2971, E-Mail: tmc@tstonramp.com (16)

Abramson, Howard, TT Publishing, Arlington, VA. Tel: (703) 838-1770, FAX: (703) 838-0285, Web Site: www.ttnews.com (17)

Abramson, Mark, Message Technologies Inc, Atlanta, GA. Tel: (770) 240-8000, (800) 868-3684, FAX: (770) 240-7474, E-Mail: info@messagetech.com, Web Site: www.messagetech.com (30)

Abramson, Robert, House of Oldies, New York, NY. Tel: (212) 243-0500, FAX: (212) 989-1697, E-Mail: rabramson@houseofoldies.com, Web Site: www.houseofoldies.com (6)

Abrei, Cybell, Hy Cite Corp, Madison, WI. Tel: (608) 273-3373, (800) 279-3373, FAX: (608) 273-0936, Web Site: www.hycite.com (16)

Absolute Reservation Center Inc, Longwood, FL. Tel: (407) 660-9995, Web Site: www.arcfun.com (19)

Academic Management Services, Boston, MA. Tel: (508) 235-2900, (800) 891-4203, FAX: (508) 235-2991, E-Mail: info@amsweb.com, Web Site: www.amsweb.com (14)

Academic Travel Abroad Inc, Washington, DC. Tel: (202) 785-9000, (800) 556-7896, FAX: (202) 342-0317, Web Site: www.academictravel.com (19)

Academy of Marketing Science Journal, Thousand Oaks, CA. Tel: (805) 499-0721, FAX: (800) 583-2665, (805) 499-0871, Web Site: www.sagepub.com (43)

Academy of Psychic Arts & Sciences, Dallas, TX. Tel: (214) 219-2020, FAX: (214) 599-0040, E-Mail: academy@psychic2020.com (5)

Acampora, Carmela, ULI-The Urban Land Institute, Washington, DC. Tel: (202) 624-7000, FAX: (202) 624-7140, Web Site: www.uli.org (1)

Accellos Inc, Colorado Springs, CO. Tel: (719) 433-7000, Web Site: www.accellos.com (12)

Accent Advertising Inc, North Kansas City, MO. Tel: (816) 842-1860, FAX: (816) 471-4836, E-Mail: ideasaccentadv@sbcglobal.net, Web Site: www.accentadv.com (33)

ACCENT Marketing Services LLC, Jeffersonville, IN. Tel: (812) 206-6200, Web Site: www.accentonline.com (20)

Accenture, Boston, MA. Tel: (617) 488-4000, FAX: (617) 488-4001, Web Site: www.accenture.com (20)

Access Business Communications Inc, Huntington Beach, CA. Tel: (800) 675-2415, Web Site: www.abcimarketing.com (20)

Access Development, Salt Lake City, UT. Tel: (801) 656-1529 (35)

Access Direct Systems Inc, Farmingdale, NY. Tel: (631) 420-0700, Web Site: www.accessdirect.com (28)

Access International, Cambridge, MA. Tel: (617) 218+5000, (877) 433-9097, FAX: (617) 494-8404, E-Mail: info@accessint.com, Web Site: www.accessint.com (22)

Access Worldwide Communications Inc, Falls Church, VA. Tel: (571) 384-7400, (800) 522-3447, FAX: (703) 531-0711, Web Site: www.accessww.com (29)

Accinno, Nancy, Racer's Equipment Warehouse, Warwick, RI. Tel: (401) 348-6010, (800) 556-2864, FAX: (401) 348-6023, E-Mail: scott@racers-eq.com, Web Site: www.racers-eq.com (16)

Accinno, Peter, Racer's Equipment Warehouse, Warwick, RI. Tel: (401) 348-6010, (800) 556-2864, FAX: (401) 348-6023, E-Mail: scott@racers-eq.com, Web Site: www.racers-eq.com (16)

Accinno, Ralph, Racer's Equipment Warehouse, Warwick, RI. Tel: (401) 348-6010, (800) 556-2864, FAX: (401) 348-6023, E-Mail: scott@racers-eq.com, Web Site: www.racers-eq.com (16)

Accoona Corp, Jersey City, NJ. Tel: (201) 557-9388, Web Site: www.accoona.com (16)

Accountants Education Group, Dallas, TX. Tel: (214) 373-3486, (800) 627-7310, FAX: (800) 627-7310, E-Mail: customerservice@accountantsed.com, Web Site: www.accountantsed.com (10)

Accountants' Supply House, Lancaster, CA. Tel: (856) 384-1144, (800) 342-5274, FAX: (800) 468-4446, Web Site: www.rapidforms.com (10)

Accountemps, Menlo Park, CA. Tel: (650) 234-6000, (800) 803-8367, FAX: (650) 234-6998, Web Site: www.accountemps.com (16)

Accounting with Debits and Credits with Coates & Hutchinson PC, Odenton, MD. Tel: (800) 833-5933, FAX: (301) 912-3364, E-Mail: info@awdc.org (14)

AccountMate Software Corp, Petaluma, CA. Tel: (415) 883-8873, FAX: (415) 883-5863, E-Mail: information@accountmate.com, Web Site: www.accountmate.com (22)

AccuData Integrated Marketing, Fort Myers, FL. Tel: (239) 425-4400, (800) 732-3440, FAX: (239) 425-4401, E-Mail: info@accudata.com, Web Site: www.accudata.com (23)

AccuDirect Response, Portland, OR. Tel: (503) 223-2076, Web Site: acddirectnw.com (22)

AccuList Inc, Ventura, CA. Tel: (805) 644-1966, Web Site: www.acculist.com (23)

Accuracy in Media Inc, Washington, DC. Tel: (202) 364-4401, FAX: (202) 364-4098, E-Mail: info@aim.org, Web Site: www.aim.org (1)

Accurate Marketing Systems, River Edge, NJ. Tel: (201) 265-5198 (22)

ACCUSPLIT Inc, Livermore, CA. Tel: (925) 226-0888, (800) 935-1996, FAX: (925) 463-0147, E-Mail: sales@accusplit.com, Web Site: www.accusplit.com (16)

AccuTrade Inc, Bellevue, NE. Tel: (800) 882-4887, FAX: (816) 243-3762, E-Mail: info@accutrade.com (14)

Accutrend Data Corp, Greenwood Village, CO. Tel: (303) 488-0011, FAX: (303) 488-0133, E-Mail: info@accutrend.com, Web Site: www.accutrend.com (24)

Ace Communications, Garden City, NY. Tel: (718) 458-3800, (800) 468-7667, FAX: (516) 872-8156, Web Site: www.aceav.com (3)

Ace Hardware Corp, Oak Brook, IL. Tel: (630) 990-6600, FAX: (630) 990-6838, Web Site: www.acehardware.com (16)

ACE Marketing Service, Smyrna, GA. Tel: (770) 431-2500, (800) 962-4514, FAX: (770) 431-2517, E-Mail: mail@ace-marketing.com, Web Site: www.ace-marketing.com (21)

Acerra, John, J., Acerra & Associates Inc, Canfield, OH. Tel: (330) 533-5599, FAX: (330) 533-6005 (35)

Acerra & Associates Inc, Canfield, OH. Tel: (330) 533-5599, FAX: (330) 533-6005 (35)

Achieve Global, Tampa, FL. Tel: (813) 631-5500, (800) 566-0630, FAX: (813) 631-5796, Web Site: www.achieveglobal.com (16)

Achilles, Charles, A., Institute of Real Estate Management, Chicago, IL. Tel: (312) 329-6000, (800) 837-0706, FAX: (800) 338-4736, E-Mail: custserv@irem.org, Web Site: www.irem.org (1)

Achtman, Larry, Dole Fresh Flowers, Miami, FL. Tel: (305) 925-7900, Web Site: www.dole.com (8)

Ackels, Paul, M., Cuisinart, Stamford, CT. Tel: (203) 975-4600, FAX: (203) 975-4660, Web Site: www.cuisinart.com (16)

Acker, David, Sleepy's Inc, Hicksville, NY. Tel: (516) 844-8800, (800) sleepys, FAX: (516) 844-8847, Web Site: www.sleepys.com (16)

Acker, Jan, The Stash Tea Catalog, Tigard, OR. Tel: (800) 547-1514, FAX: (503) 684-4424, E-Mail: stash@stashtea.com, Web Site: www.stashtea.com (14)

Ackerman, Steve, AHC Media, Atlanta, GA. Tel: (404) 262-7436, FAX: (404) 262-7837 (17)

Ackerman, Steve, Thompson Publishing Group Inc, Washington, DC. Tel: (202) 872-4000, (800) 677-3789, FAX: (800) 999-5661, E-Mail: service@thompson.com, Web Site: www.thompson.com (17)

Ackford, Rob, Ideal Industries (Canada) Corp, Ajax, ON. Tel: (905) 683-3400, (800) 824-3325, FAX: (905) 683-0209, E-Mail: nick.shkordoff@idealindustries.com, Web Site: www.idealindustries.com (9)

Acme Tools, Grand Forks, ND. Tel: (701) 746-2881, Web Site: www.acmetoolcrib.com (8)

ACNielsen, New York, NY. Tel: (646) 654-5000, FAX: (646) 654-5002, E-Mail: globalc@nielsen.com, Web Site: www.acnielsen.com (30)

Acosta, De Ann, American Humane Association, Washington, DC. Tel: (303) 925-9497, Web Site: www.americanhumane.org (1)

AcquireWEB Inc, Foster City, CA. Tel: (650) 212-2233, Web Site: www.acquireWEB.com (22)

Acquistapace, James S., Davis Instruments Corp, Hayward, CA. Tel: (510) 732-9229, (510) 670-0589, E-Mail: info@davisnet.com, Web Site: www. davisnet.com (8)

Acree, Anthony, American Society of Radiologic Technologists, Albuquerque, NM. Tel: (505) 298-4500, Web Site: www.asrt.org (1)

Across The Board Marketing Inc, Chicago, IL. Tel: (312) 787-1642, FAX: (312) 787-1645, E-Mail: info@acrosstheboardmarketing.com, Web Site: www.acrosstheboardmarketing.com (39)

ACT ONE LISTS, Beverly, MA. Tel: (781) 639-1919, (800) 228-5478, FAX: (781) 639-2733, E-Mail: info@act1lists.com, Web Site: www.act1lists.com (23)

ACTIMAIL INC, New York, NY. Tel: (212) 245-2272, FAX: (212) 245-2523, E-Mail: actimail.usa@ actimail.com, Web Site: www.actimail.com (35)

Action-AD, Bettendorf, IA. Tel: (563) 355-9581, FAX: (563) 355-9586 (35)

Action Communications Inc, Boca Raton, FL. Tel: (561) 995-1995, (800) 558-5085, FAX: (561) 995-1990 (27)

Action Direct Inc, Miami, FL. Tel: (305) 969-0056, E-Mail: info@action-direct.com, Web Site: www. action-direct.com (11)

Action In Mailing, Montgomery, AL. Tel: (334) 286-4667, (800) 277-6245, FAX: (334) 286-6008, E-Mail: info@actioninmailing.com, Web Site: www.actioninmailing.com (21)

Action Mailers Inc, Aston, PA. Tel: (610) 859-0500, (800) 258-5992, FAX: (610) 859-0505, Web Site: www.actionmailer.com (27)

ActionAid, Washington, DC. Tel: (202) 835-1240, Web Site: www.actionaidusa.org (1)

ActionPak, Scarborough, ON Canada. Tel: (416) 321-2222, FAX: (416) 321-5286, Web Site: www. openandsave.com (21)

Active Graphics Inc, Cicero, IL. Tel: (312) 733-4343, FAX: (312) 733-4614, E-Mail: info@ activegraphics.net, Web Site: www.activegraphics. net (21)

Active Network Media & Marketing, San Diego, CA. Tel: (858) 964-6064, (877) 228-4808, Web Site: www.activemarketinggroup.com (23)

Active Parenting, Marietta, GA. Tel: (770) 429-0565, (800) 825-0060, (800) 235-7755, FAX: (770) 429-0334, E-Mail: cservice@activeparenting.com, Web Site: www.activeparenting.com (17)

Active Voice, San Francisco, CA. Tel: (415) 487-2000, FAX: (415) 487-2260, E-Mail: info@activevoice. net, Web Site: www.activevoice.net (21)

Active Web Group, Hauppauge, NY. Tel: (800) 978-3417, FAX: (800) 719-4402, E-Mail: info@ activewebgroup.com, Web Site: www. activewebgroup.com (9)

Actividentity Corp, Fremont, CA. Tel: (510) 574-0100, (800) 529-9499, FAX: (510) 574-0101, Web Site: www.actividentity.com (32)

Activision Value, Eden Prairie, MN. Tel: (952) 918-9400, FAX: (952) 918-9560 (16)

ActivStyle, Minneapolis, MN. Tel: (612) 520-9333, (800) 651-6223, FAX: (612) 520-9300, Web Site: www.activstyle.com (16)

Acton, Elizabeth, S., Comerica Inc, Dallas, TX. Tel: (800) 521-1190, FAX: (925) 941-1999, Web Site: www.comerica.com (14)

Acton, Randy, US Cavalry, Radcliff, KY. Tel: (270) 351-1164, FAX: (270) 352-0266, E-Mail: hq@ uscavalry.com, Web Site: www.uscavalry.com (6)

ACTON Group Ltd, Lincoln, NE. Tel: (402) 742-2820, FAX: (402) 470-2673, E-Mail: info@acton. com, Web Site: www.acton.com (23)

Actuarial Enterprises Ltd, Chicago, IL. Tel: (312) 397-0099, E-Mail: jay@actentltd.com (20)

Acurian, Horsham, PA. Tel: (215) 323-9000, Web Site: www.acurian.com (7)

AcuSport Corp, Bellefontaine, OH. Tel: (937) 593-7010, FAX: (937) 592-5625, E-Mail: mwsales@ acusport.com, Web Site: www.acusport.com (11)

Acxiom Co, Marlton, NJ. Tel: (800) 635-5833, FAX: (856) 988-6662 (23)

Acxiom Corp, Little Rock, AR. Tel: (501) 342-1000, Web Site: www.acxiom.com (22)

Acxiom Xpress, Cape Coral, FL. Tel: (800) 732-9250, E-Mail: iblexpress@acxiom.com (24)

Ad Facts Inc, Cary, NC. Tel: (919) 388-3015, (800) 923-3228, E-Mail: adfacts@adfacts.com, Web Site: www.adfacts.com (30)

The Ad Farm, Ottawa Hills, OH. Tel: (419) 720-5676, Web Site: www.theadfarm.com (20)

Ad Hoc Marketing Resources Inc, New York, NY. Tel: (212) 595-1800, FAX: (212) 656-1860, E-Mail: adhocmrktg@aol.com, Web Site: www.members. aol.com/adhocmrktg (20)

Ad Infinitum Books, Mount Vernon, NY. Tel: (914) 664-5930, (800) 697-0402, FAX: (914) 664-2642, E-Mail: aibservice@adinfinitumbooks.com, Web Site: www.adinfinitumbooks.com (16)

Ad-Lib Advertising Inc, Old Bridge, NJ. Tel: (732) 679-9226, (800) 622-3542, FAX: (732) 679-9511, E-Mail: info@adlibadvertising.com, Web Site: www.adlibadvertising.com (10)

Ad Pro Services Inc, Blauvelt, NY. Tel: (845) 359-8332, FAX: (914) 359-3843 (35)

Ad Sell Co, Saint Louis, MO. Tel: (314) 773-0500, FAX: (314) 773-0555, Web Site: www.adsell.com (21)

AD-Sells Inc, Lisle, IL. Tel: (630) 241-0090 (33)

AD-Vantage Marketing, Santa Rosa, CA. Tel: (707) 578-8700, FAX: (707) 578-0258, Web Site: www. ad-vantagemarketing.com (23)

Adam, Joan, Stokes Seeds Inc, Buffalo, NY. Tel: (716) 695-6980, (800) 396-9238, FAX: (888) 834-3334, Web Site: www.stokeseeds.com (8)

Adames, Fermin, Tempco Electric Heater Corp, Wood Dale, IL. Tel: (630) 350-2252, (800) 323-6859, FAX: (630) 350-0232, E-Mail: dpadlo@tempco. com, Web Site: www.tempco.com (9)

Adamo, Vince, The Motivation Show, Westmont, IL. Tel: (630) 434-7779, (800) 752-6312, FAX: (630) 434-1216, E-Mail: moti@heiexpo.com, Web Site: www.motivationshow.com (42)

Adams, Andrea, The Menninger Foundation, Houston, TX. Tel: (713) 275-5000, (800) 351-9058, FAX: (713) 275-5107, Web Site: www.menningerclinic. com (1)

Adams, Bart, Daily Record & Dispatch Co, Dunn, NC. Tel: (910) 891-1234, FAX: (910) 891-5253, Web Site: www.mydailyrecord.com (17)

Adams, Carl, Tidbits Media, Montgomery, AL. Tel: (334) 290-0225, (800) 523-3096, FAX: (334) 386-0302, E-Mail: editors@tidbitsweekly.com, Web Site: www.tidbitsweekly.com (17)

Adams, Chip, The Gateway Learning Corp, Irvine, CA. Tel: (714) 429-2223, (800) 222-3334, FAX: (714) 338-2525 (16)

Adams, Dan, The Scotts Co Div of Lawn Service, Marysville, OH. Tel: (937) 644-0011, FAX: (937) 644-7261, Web Site: www.scotts.com (8)

Adams, Don, American Inbound, Bloomington, IN. Tel: (800) 322-6445, FAX: (800) 224-3583, Web Site: www.americanbound.com (29)

Adams, Leslie, Checks by Phone/Checks by Web, Boynton Beach, FL. Tel: (561) 737-8700, FAX: (561) 737-5800, E-Mail: LarrySchwartz@ checksbyphone.com, Web Site: www. checksbyphone.com (14)

Adams, Marvin, Fidelity Investments, Boston, MA. Tel: (617) 563-7000, (800) 343-3548, FAX: (617) 476-6150, Web Site: www.fidelity.com (14)

Adams, Michele, American Association of Advertising Agencies, New York, NY. Tel: (212) 682-2500, FAX: (212) 682-8391, Web Site: www.aaaa.org (40)

Adams, Paul, Video Plus Inc, Lake Dallas, TX. Tel: (940) 497-9700, (800) 752-2030, FAX: (940) 497-9987, E-Mail: support@videoplus.com, Web Site: www.videoplus.com (32)

Adams, Robert, Crain Communications Inc, Detroit, MI. Tel: (313) 446-6000, FAX: (313) 446-1616, Web Site: www.crain.com (17)

Adams, Stephen, Golf Card International, Englewood, CO. Tel: (800) 321-8269, FAX: (303) 792-7332, Web Site: www.golfcard.com (1)

Adams, Stephen, Woodall Publishing Co LP, Ventura, CA. Tel: (805) 667-4100, (800) 323-9076, FAX: (805) 667-4468, Web Site: www.woodalls.com (17)

Adams, Steve, Protus, Ottawa, ON Canada. Tel: (888) 733-0000, Web Site: www.protus.com (32)

Adams, Synthia, MGM Grand Detroit, Detroit, MI. Tel: (877) 888-2121, Web Site: www.mgmgrand. com/det (16)

Adams, Terri, Precision Arts Advertising Inc, Ashburnham, MA. Tel: (978) 855-7648, E-Mail: sales@ precisionarts.com, Web Site: www.precisionarts. com (35)

Danielle Adams Publishing Co, Merion Station, PA. Tel: (610) 642-1000, Web Site: www. danielleadams.com (35)

Adams Manufacturing Co, Cleveland, OH. Tel: (216) 587-6801, FAX: (216) 587-6807, E-Mail: adamsx@att.net, Web Site: www. adamsmanufacturing.com (9)

Adamson, Lori, Kelco Supply Co, Brooklyn Park, MN. Tel: (763) 493-1260, (800) 328-7720, FAX: (763) 493-1261, E-Mail: info@kelcosupply.com, Web Site: www.kelcosupply.com (16)

The Adcentive Group Inc, San Diego, CA. Tel: (858) 278-9200, FAX: (858) 278-9079, E-Mail: info@ adcentive.com, Web Site: www.adcentive.com (35)

Adcom Communications, Cleveland, OH. Tel: (216) 574-9100, FAX: (216) 574-6131, E-Mail: adcom@ adcom1.com, Web Site: www.adcom1.com (35)

Adcox, Jack, Health Sciences Consortium, Chapel Hill, NC. Tel: (919) 942-8731, FAX: (919) 942-3689, E-Mail: tony.penta@edtsi.com, Web Site: www.healthsciencesconsortium.org (17)

The Added Touch, Niagara Falls, NY. Tel: (905) 828-4041, (888) AD-TOUCH, FAX: (905) 338-1486, E-Mail: addedtouch@gmail.com, Web Site: www. addedtouch.com (28)

Adderley, Andrew, Bahamas Ministry of Tourism, Fort Lauderdale, FL. Tel: (954) 236-9292, Web Site: www.bahamas.com (19)

Addington, Kim, Web Decisions, Greensboro, NC. Tel: (336) 545-7817 x100 (22)

Adecco Employment Services, Melville, NY. Tel: (631) 844-7800, Web Site: www.adecco.com (20)

Adee, Jeff, Mardev-DM2, Lombard, IL. Tel: (800) 323-4958, FAX: (303) 265-5457, E-Mail: info@ mardevdm2.com, Web Site: www.mardevdm2.com (24)

Adelman, Jennifer, ASM Press, Washington, DC. Tel: (202) 737-3600, (800) 546-2416, FAX: (202) 942-9342, E-Mail: books@asmusa.org, Web Site: www. asmpress.org (17)

Ades, Abraham, Anything Goes, Allenhurst, NJ. Tel: (732) 531-8040, Web Site: www.heavenlytreasures. com (6)

Adey, W., Richard, Analytical Measurements, Chester, NJ. Tel: (800) 635-5580, FAX: (973) 399-1446, E-Mail: phmeter@bellatlantic.net, Web Site: www. analyticalmeasurements.com (9)

Adiletti, John, Civil Service Employees Insurance Group, Walnut Creek, CA. Tel: (925) 817-6300, (415) 274-7803, (800) 282-6848, Web Site: www. cseinsurance.com (15)

Adirondack Direct, Long Island City, NY. Tel: (718) 932-4003, (800) 221-2444, FAX: (800) 477-1330, E-Mail: info@adirondackdirect.com, Web Site: www.adirondackdirect.com (10)

Adkins, Jennifer, Scott Sign Systems Inc, Sarasota, FL. Tel: (941) 355-5171, (800) 237-9447, FAX: (941) 351-1787, E-Mail: mail@scottsigns.com, Web Site: www.scottsigns.com (16)

Adkins, John, Intromark Inc, Pittsburgh, PA. Tel: (412) 288-1300, (800) 851-6030 X1368, FAX: (412) 338-0497, E-Mail: licensing@intromark.com (16)

Adknowledge, Kansas City, MO. Tel: (816) 931-1771, Web Site: www.adknowledge.com (32)

Adler, Allan, Association of American Publishers, Washington, DC. Tel: (202) 347-3375, FAX: (202) 347-3690, Web Site: www.publishers.org (1)

Adler, Jim, Myron Corp, Maywood, NJ. Tel: (201) 843-6464, (877) 803-3358, FAX: (201) 843-8390, Web Site: www.myron.com (16)

Adler-Kravecas, Marie, Myron Corp, Maywood, NJ. Tel: (201) 843-6464, (877) 803-3358, FAX: (201) 843-8390, Web Site: www.myron.com (16)

admail.net/List Media, Aurora, OH. Tel: (330) 995-0864, FAX: (330) 995-0873, E-Mail: sales@admail.net, Web Site: www.admail.net (32)

Admiral Packaging Inc, Providence, RI. Tel: (800) 262-0027, FAX: (401) 331-1910, Web Site: www.admiralpkg.com (26)

Admore, Inc, Macomb, MI. Tel: (810) 949-8200, (800) 523-6673, FAX: (800) 215-2664, Web Site: www.admoreonline.com (10)

Adnet USA, Arlington Heights, IL. Tel: (847) 483-5300, FAX: (773) 304-2700, Web Site: www.adnet.us (16)

Adobe Systems Inc, San Jose, CA. Tel: (408) 536-6000, (800) 833-6687, FAX: (408) 537-6000, Web Site: www.adobe.com (22)

Adolf, Steve, Steven P d'Adolf, Oceanside, CA. Tel: (858) 451-2130, FAX: (858) 451-2130 (39)

AdPack/ITOCHU International Inc, New York, NY. Tel: (212) 818-8000, Web Site: www.adpackusa.com (25)

AdPlex, Houston, TX. Tel: (281) 821-5522, Web Site: www.adplex.com (35)

Adpress Inc, New York, NY. Tel: (212) 679-1710, FAX: (212) 532-9508, E-Mail: adpressinc@aol.com, Web Site: www.adpressinc.com (23)

Adrea Rubin Marketing Inc, New York, NY. Tel: (212) 983-0020, FAX: (212) 983-0107, E-Mail: sales@adrearubin.com, Web Site: www.adrearubin.com (21)

Adriana Associates Ltd, New York, NY. Tel: (212) 719-5952, FAX: (212) 398-6414 (31)

Adtron Inc, Bloomington, IL. Tel: (309) 662-1221, FAX: (309) 663-6691 (35)

Advance Mailing Services Inc, West Chicago, IL. Tel: (630) 293-0707, FAX: (630) 293-9268 (28)

Advanced Business Teleservices, Inc, Talent, OR. Tel: (800) 866-9220, FAX: (541) 535-6942, E-Mail: randy@abtc.com, Web Site: www.abtc.com (29)

Advanced Concepts Inc, Milwaukee, WI. Tel: (414) 362-9640, FAX: (414) 362-9646, E-Mail: info@advanced-concepts.com, Web Site: www.advanced-concepts.com (22)

Advanced Direct, Greensboro, NC. Tel: (336) 299-0800, (800) 786-2812, FAX: (336) 299-2619, E-Mail: info@advdirectinc.com, Web Site: www.advdirectinc.com (21)

Advanced Direct Marketing Inc, Loveland, CO. Tel: (970) 669-9800, (888) 553-1230, FAX: (970) 669-1920, E-Mail: sales@admimail.com (21)

Advanced Financial Services, Middletown, RI. Tel: (401) 846-3100, Web Site: www.afsfitfinance.com (14)

Advanced Image Direct, Fullerton, CA. Tel: (714) 502-3900, (800) 540-3848, FAX: (714) 502-3901, Web Site: www.advancedimagedirect.com (28)

Advanced Machinery, New Castle, DE. Tel: (302) 322-2226, (800) 727-6553, FAX: (866) 686-1615, E-Mail: jean@advmachinery.com, Web Site: www.advmachinery.com (9)

Advanced Mail Inc, Eau Claire, WI. Tel: (715) 839-8801, FAX: (715) 839-8906, Web Site: www.amailinc.com (28)

Advanced Marketing Direct, Buffalo, NY. Tel: (800) 696-7567, Web Site: www.amdirect.com (28)

Advanced Medical Nutrition Inc, Pittsburgh, PA. Tel: (412) 494-0100, (800) 879-2664, (800) 437-8888, FAX: (888) 245-4440, Web Site: www.douglaslabs.com (7)

Advanced Research Services, Malibu, CA. Tel: (310) 589-0223, Web Site: www.tvsurveys.com (30)

Advanced Software Applications, Bridgeville, PA. Tel: (412) 220-9300, E-Mail: asa@asacorp.com, Web Site: www.asacorp.com (22)

Advanced Telecom Services Inc, Wayne, PA. Tel: (610) 688-6000, (800) 247-1287, FAX: (610) 964-9117, E-Mail: bobb@advancedtele.com, Web Site: www.advancedtele.com (29)

AdvanceMe Inc, Kennesaw, GA. Tel: (888) 700-8181, Web Site: www.advanceme.com (14)

Advanstar Communications Inc, North Olmstead, OH. Tel: (440) 243-8100, (800) 225-4569, FAX: (440) 891-2740, E-Mail: info@advanstar.com, Web Site: www.advanstarlists.com (17)

Advanta Corp, Spring House, PA. Tel: (215) 657-4000, (800) 255-0022, Web Site: www.advanta.com (14)

Advantage Direct Inc, Marietta, GA. Tel: (678) 921-2134, FAX: (770) 592-4746, E-Mail: ed@advantage-direct.com, Web Site: www.advantage-direct.com (35)

Advantage List Marketing Inc, Holliston, MA. Tel: (508) 429-4400, FAX: (508) 429-7117 (23)

Advantage Mailing Inc, Anaheim, CA. Tel: (714) 538-3881, (888) 909-6245, FAX: (714) 282-3903, Web Site: www.advantagemailinginc.com (28)

Advantage Marketing Group, Elk Grove Village, IL. Tel: (847) 952-2100, FAX: (847) 952-3348, Web Site: www.goamg.com (28)

Advantage Plus Marketing Group, Aliso Viejo, CA. Tel: (714) 573-7300, (800) 432-9466, FAX: (714) 573-7301, E-Mail: info@apmg.com, Web Site: www.apmg.com (30)

Advent Software Inc, San Francisco, CA. Tel: (415) 645-1200, Web Site: www.advent.com (34)

Adventure Creations Inc, Costa Mesa, CA. Tel: (949) 515-3600, FAX: (949) 515-3933, E-Mail: sales@adv-creations.com, Web Site: www.adv-creations.com (16)

Advertising Age, New York, NY. Tel: (212) 210-0100, FAX: (212) 210-0111, Web Site: www.crain.com (43)

The Advertising Council Inc, New York, NY. Tel: (212) 922-1500, FAX: (212) 922-1676, E-Mail: info@adcouncil.org, Web Site: www.adcouncil.org (1)

Advertising Distributors of America Inc, Hauppauge, NY. Tel: (631) 231-5700, FAX: (631) 434-1063 (21)

Advertising Gifts Inc, Port Washington, NY. Tel: (516) 767-3577, (877) 496-8762, E-Mail: sales@adgiftsinc.com, Web Site: www.adgiftsinc.com (33)

Advertising Idea Stores, Ardmore, PA. Tel: (610) 642-1990, FAX: (610) 649-5593, E-Mail: uniongoods@msn.com, Web Site: www.uniongoods.com (35)

Advertising Mailers Inc, Edison, NJ. Tel: (732) 225-3404, (800) 427-8513, FAX: (732) 225-7429, E-Mail: admailers@aol.com (28)

Advertising Network Solutions, Lake Orion, MI. Tel: (248) 475-7881, Web Site: www.adnetworksolutions.com (20)

Advertising Research Foundation, New York, NY. Tel: (212) 751-5656, FAX: (212) 319-5265, E-Mail: info@thearf.org, Web Site: www.thearf.org (40)

Advertising That Works, Bloomfield Hills, MI. Tel: (248) 626-2264, FAX: (248) 626-2264, Web Site: www.advertisingthatworks.us (23)

Advisor Media Inc, San Diego, CA. Tel: (858) 278-5600, FAX: (858) 278-5600, Web Site: www.advisor.com (23)

Adwest Mailers Inc, Northridge, CA. Tel: (818) 982-3720, FAX: (818) 982-3786, E-Mail: sales@adwest.com, Web Site: www.adwest.com (28)

Aegis Communications, Irving, TX. Tel: (972) 830-1800, (800) 332-0266, FAX: (972) 830-1801, E-Mail: info@aegisglobal.com, Web Site: www.aegiscomgroup.com (29)

Aegon Corp, Louisville, KY. Tel: (502) 560-2000, FAX: (502) 560-2611, Web Site: www.aegonins.com (14)

Aeling, Jim, CMI Direct, Montrose, CA. Tel: (951) 300-1700, FAX: (866) 723-5433, Web Site: www.cmidirect.net (15)

Aeppli, Matt, Pernod Ricard USA, Purchase, NY. Tel: (914) 848-4800, Web Site: www.pernod-ricard-usa.com (16)

AeroGraphics, DeLand, FL. Tel: (386) 736-4793, FAX: (386) 736-9786, Web Site: www.skydivingmagazine.com (3)

Aerosoles, Edison, NJ. Tel: (732) 985-6900, FAX: (732) 985-3697, E-Mail: bgarris@aerosoles.com, Web Site: www.aerosoles.com (2)

Aerovox Inc, New Bedford, MA. Tel: (508) 994-9661, (888) AEROVOX, FAX: (508) 995-3000, E-Mail: sales1@aerovox.com, Web Site: www.aerovox.com (16)

AETNA - Marketing Product & Communication, Hartford, CT. Tel: (860) 273-0123, (800) 872-3862, FAX: (860) 273-3971, Web Site: www.aetna.com (14)

Affiliate Strategies Inc, Paola, KS. Tel: (913) 294-9093 (35)

Affiliated Computer Services Inc (ACS), Dallas, TX. Tel: (214) 841-6111, Web Site: www.acs-inc.com (22)

Affina, Peoria, IL. Tel: (309) 685-5901, (877) 4 AF-FINA, Web Site: www.affina.com (30)

Affinion Group, Franklin, TN. Tel: (800) 251-2148, Web Site: www.progenymarketing.com (15)

Affinion Group Inc, Stamford, CT. Tel: (203) 956-1176, Web Site: www.affiniongroup.com (16)

Affinitas Corp, Omaha, NE. Tel: (402) 397-7077, (800) 369-6495, FAX: (402) 397-7576, Web Site: www.affinitas.net (29)

Affinity Express, Elgin, IL. Tel: (847) 930-3200, FAX: (847) 930-3299, E-Mail: kellyg@affinityexpress.com, Web Site: www.affinityexpress.com (16)

Affinity Federal Credit Union, Basking Ridge, NJ. Tel: (908) 860-7306, Web Site: www.affinityfcu.org (1)

Affinity4, Norfolk, VA. Tel: (757) 465-4602, Web Site: www.affinity4.com (16)

Affinity Group Inc, Ventura, CA. Tel: (805) 667-4100, (800) 765-1912, FAX: (805) 667-4419, E-Mail: khurd@affinitygroup.com, Web Site: www.affinitygroup.com (19)

Affinity Marketing Group, Wellesley Hills, MA. Tel: (781) 239-9310, FAX: (781) 239-9645, E-Mail: info@affinitymg.com, Web Site: www.affinitymg.com (24)

Affinity Marketing Services, Falls Church, VA. Tel: (703) 917-9822, FAX: (703) 917-9804, E-Mail: serota@affinitymarketingservicescorp.com (35)

Afni Inc, Bloomington, IL. Tel: (800) 767-2364, Web Site: www.afni.com (29)

African Medical & Research Foundation Inc (AMREF USA), New York, NY. Tel: (212) 768-2440, Web Site: www.amref.org (1)

African Wildlife Foundation, Washington, DC. Tel: (202) 939-3333, Web Site: www.awf.org (1)

Agar, Gideon, Scan Optics Inc, Manchester, CT. Tel: (860) 645-7878, (800) 745-6001, FAX: (860) 645-7995, E-Mail: info@scanoptics.com, Web Site: www.scanoptics.com (24)

Agate Publishing, Evanston, IL. Tel: (847) 475-4457, (800) 326-4430, FAX: (312) 751-7334, Web Site: www.surreybooks.com (17)

Agco Spra-Coup, Duluth, GA. Tel: (320) 231-9400, FAX: (320) 231-9413, Web Site: www.agcocorp.com (16)

Agency.com, New York, NY. Tel: (212) 358-2600, FAX: (212) 358-2604, Web Site: www.agency.com (20)

Agency RAV, Trumbull, CT. Tel: (203) 895-7993 (35)

Aggarwal, Bharat, Pilani's Live in Style, Egg Harbor Township, NJ. Tel: (609) 927-4686, (800) 537-1832, FAX: (609) 927-5686, E-Mail: sihart@aol.com (2)

Aggarwal, Sanjay, Pilani's Live in Style, Egg Harbor Township, NJ. Tel: (609) 927-4686, (800) 537-1832, FAX: (609) 927-5686, E-Mail: sihart@aol.com (2)

Agilis Co, Albert Lea, MN. Tel: (507) 377-5028 (14)

Agiropolous, Kathleen, O., Airlines Reporting Corp, Arlington, VA. Tel: (703) 816-8135, FAX: (703) 816-8104, E-Mail: corpcom@arccorp.com, Web Site: www.arccorp.com (16)

Agnes, Bob, Tektronix Inc, Beaverton, OR. Tel: (503) 627-7111, (800) 833-9200, FAX: (503) 627-3247, Web Site: www.tektronix.com (16)

Agnihotri, Anu, Nuclear Plant Journal, Downers Grove, IL. Tel: (630) 858-6161, FAX: (630) 852-8787, Web Site: www.nuclearplantjournal.com (17)

Agnihotri, Newal, Nuclear Plant Journal, Downers Grove, IL. Tel: (630) 858-6161, FAX: (630) 852-8787, Web Site: www.nuclearplantjournal.com (17)

Agno, John, Signature Inc, Ann Arbor, MI. Tel: (734) 426-2000, FAX: (734) 426-2109, E-Mail: johnagno@signatureseries.com, Web Site: www.mentoringandcoaching.com (20)

AGORA Inc, Baltimore, MD. Tel: (410) 783-8499, FAX: (410) 783-8414, E-Mail: csteam@agorapublishinggroup.com, Web Site: www.agora-inc.com (17)

Agostino, Joe, Chief Media, New York, NY. Tel: (212) 300-8491 (35)

Agri Drain Corp, Adair, IA. Tel: (641) 742-5211, (800) 232-4742, FAX: (641) 742-5222, (800) 282-3353, E-Mail: info@agridrain.com, Web Site: www.agridrain.com (9)

Aguilera, Christine, A., SkyMall Inc, Phoenix, AZ. Tel: (602) 254-9777, (800) SKY-MALL, FAX: (602) 254-6075, Web Site: www.skymall.com (16)

Agurcia, Alex, Omnidirect, Miami Beach, FL. Tel: (800) 459-4034, Web Site: www.omnidirect.tv (35)

Ahad, Edward, Promotional Product Professionals of Canada, Saint-Laurent, PQ. Tel: (514) 489-5359, FAX: (514) 489-7760, (800) 489-8741, E-Mail: gladys@pppc.ca, Web Site: www.pppc.ca (1)

AHC Media, Atlanta, GA. Tel: (404) 262-7436, FAX: (404) 262-7837 (17)

Ahern, Mitchel, OTOlabs LLC, Charlestown, MA. Tel: (617) 236-8400, Web Site: www.otolabs.com (30)

Ahern Communications Corp, Quincy, MA. Tel: (617) 471-1100, (800) 451-3280, FAX: (617) 328-9070, E-Mail: info@aherncorp.com, Web Site: www.aherncorp.com (34)

Ahmad, Mush, Involve Social, Fremont, CA. Tel: (510) 396-3941, Web Site: www.involvesocial.com (1)

Ahmed, Haleema, Fifth Avenue Committee, Brooklyn, NY. FAX: (718) 237-5366, Web Site: www.fifthave.org (1)

Ahrens, Greg, Skar Advertising, Omaha, NE. Tel: (402) 330-0110, FAX: (402) 330-8791, E-Mail: skar@skar.com, Web Site: www.skar.com (35)

Ahrensdorf, Lee, Ahrensdorf & Associates, Saint Davids, PA. Tel: (610) 971-0500, FAX: (610) 971-9530, E-Mail: leeahrensdorf@att.net (16)

Ahrensdorf & Associates, Saint Davids, PA. Tel: (610) 971-0500, FAX: (610) 971-9530, E-Mail: leeahrensdorf@att.net (16)

Aiello, Gary, R R Bowker, New Providence, NJ. Tel: (888) BOWKER-2 (269-5372), FAX: (908) 771-8699, Web Site: www.bowker.com (17)

Aigen, Joyce, J&L Concepts Inc, Valdosta, GA. Tel: (800) 346-5083, FAX: (912) 247-2468, E-Mail: promo@jlconcepts.com, Web Site: www.jlconcepts.com (33)

Aigner, Alex, DataLab USA, Germantown, MD. Tel: (301) 972-1430, Web Site: www.datalabusa.com (21)

Aiken, Karen, The Animal Medical Center, New York, NY. Tel: (212) 838-8100, FAX: (212) 832-9630, Web Site: www.amcny.org (16)

Aiken, Robert, US Foodservice, Rosemont, IL. Tel: (410) 312-7100, FAX: (410) 312-7167, Web Site: www.usfoodservice.com (4)

Aim Marketing, Fremont, NE. Tel: (402) 721-2077, FAX: (402) 721-9171, E-Mail: aim@solution-group.com (28)

Aimia, Minneapolis, MN. Tel: (763) 445-3453, FAX: (763) 496-3453, Web Site: www.carlsonmarketing.com (35)

Ainsley, P., Steven, The Boston Globe, Boston, MA. Tel: (617) 929-2000, (888) MY-GLOBE, FAX: (617) 929-2606, Web Site: www.bostonglobe.com (17)

Ainsworth, Doug, Modern Mail, Newark, DE. Tel: (302) 391-1200, Web Site: www.triggermarketing.com (20)

Ainsworth, Earl, Farm Journal Inc, Philadelphia, PA. Tel: (215) 557-8937, FAX: (215) 568-4238 (17)

Air Ambulance Network Inc, Palm Harbor, FL. Tel: (727) 934-3999, (800) 327-1966, FAX: (727) 937-0276, Web Site: www.airambulancenetwork.com (16)

Air Chek Inc, Naples, NC. Tel: (828) 684-0893, (800) AIR-CHEK, FAX: (828) 684-8498, Web Site: www.radon.com (9)

Air Force Sergeants Association, Suitland, MD. Tel: (301) 899-3500, (800) 638-0594, FAX: (301) 899-8136, E-Mail: staff@hqafsa.org, Web Site: www.hqafsa.org (1)

Air France, New York, NY. Tel: (212) 830-4000, FAX: (212) 830-4244, Web Site: www.airfrance.fr.com (16)

Air-Lec Industries Inc, Madison, WI. Tel: (608) 244-4754, FAX: (608) 246-7676, E-Mail: info@air-lec.com, Web Site: www.air-lec.com (16)

Air Power USA, Los Angeles, CA. Tel: (310) 641-0830, (888) 888-8231, FAX: (310) 641-8515, Web Site: www.airpowerusa.com (12)

Air-Scent International, Pittsburgh, PA. Tel: (800) 247-0770, FAX: (412) 252-2000, E-Mail: laura@aromaresource.com, Web Site: www.airscent.com (16)

Aircraft Owners & Pilots Association, Frederick, MD. Tel: (301) 695-2000, (800) 872-2672, FAX: (301) 695-2375, E-Mail: aopahq@aopa.org, Web Site: www.aopa.org (1)

Aircraft Spruce & Specialty Co, Corona, CA. Tel: (909) 372-9555, (877) 4-Spruce, FAX: (909) 372-0555, E-Mail: info@aircraft-spruce.com, Web Site: www.aircraft-spruce.com (12)

Airlines Reporting Corp, Arlington, VA. Tel: (703) 816-8135, FAX: (703) 816-8104, E-Mail: corpcom@arccorp.com, Web Site: www.arccorp.com (16)

Airlines Reporting Corp, Arlington, VA. Tel: (703) 816-8135, Web Site: www.arccorp.com (9)

Airomat Corp, Fort Wayne, IN. Tel: (260) 747-7408, (800) 348-4905, FAX: (260) 747-7409, E-Mail: airomat@airomat.com, Web Site: www.mymatting.com (16)

Airs Inc, Douglasville, GA. Tel: (770) 949-0133, FAX: (770) 949-2773, E-Mail: estacks@aol.com (22)

AirTran Airways, Atlanta, GA. Tel: (678) 254-7459, Web Site: www.airtran.com (19)

Aitken, Ian, The Menninger Foundation, Houston, TX. Tel: (713) 275-5000, (800) 351-9058, FAX: (713) 275-5107, Web Site: www.menningerclinic.com (1)

Aitken, Stuart, Michael's, Irving, TX. Tel: (972) 409-1300, FAX: (972) 409-1551, Web Site: www.michaels.com (11)

Aiuppy, Janis, M., Laurance Aiuppy, Livingston, MT. Tel: (406) 222-7308, FAX: (406) 222-7308, E-Mail: aiuppix@wispwest.net, Web Site: www.agpix.com/aiuppy (37)

Laurance Aiuppy, Livingston, MT. Tel: (406) 222-7308, FAX: (406) 222-7308, E-Mail: aiuppix@wispwest.net, Web Site: www.agpix.com/aiuppy (37)

Ajeska, Craig, West Marine Inc, Watsonville, CA. Tel: (831) 761-4825, (800) BOATING, (800) 262-8464, FAX: (831) 768-5000, E-Mail: customercare@westmarine.com, Web Site: www.westmarine.com (11)

The Akadine Press Inc, White Plains, NY. Tel: (914) 747-0777, FAX: (914) 747-0778, Web Site: www.commonreader.com (16)

Akeroyd, Kevin, Jigsaw, San Mateo, CA. Tel: (650) 235-8400, Web Site: www.jigsaw.com (24)

Akers, Jennifer, Sara Lee Direct Home Shopping, Winston-Salem, NC. Tel: (336) 519-4400, (800) 671-5056, E-Mail: ohp.managor@onehanesplace.com, Web Site: www.onehanesplace.com (2)

Akers, Leon, Akers Ski Inc, Andover, ME. Tel: (207) 392-4582, FAX: (207) 392-1225, E-Mail: sales@akers-ski.com, Web Site: www.akers-ski.com (11)

Akers Ski Inc, Andover, ME. Tel: (207) 392-4582, FAX: (207) 392-1225, E-Mail: sales@akers-ski.com, Web Site: www.akers-ski.com (11)

Akhavan, Dadi, E-Centives Inc, Bethesda, MD. Tel: (240) 333-6100, (877) 323-6848, FAX: (240) 333-6250, E-Mail: sales@e-centives.com, Web Site: www.e-centives.com (32)

Akin, Bruce, Southern Progress Corp, Birmingham, AL. Tel: (205) 877-6000, FAX: (205) 877-6283, Web Site: www.southernprogress.com (17)

Alabama State University/College of Business Administration, Montgomery, AL. Tel: (334) 229-4124, FAX: (334) 229-4870, E-Mail: pvaughn@alasu.edu, Web Site: www.cobanetworks.com (41)

Alaimo, Ross, Paul Fredrick Menstyle, Fleetwood, PA. Tel: (610) 944-0909, (800) 247-1417, FAX: (610) 944-6452, E-Mail: custserv@menstyle.com, Web Site: www.paulfredricks.com (2)

Alamo Rent A Car, Tulsa, OK. Tel: (918) 401-6000, Web Site: www.alamo.com (16)

Alaniz - a Dmh Marketing Partners Co, Mount Pleasant, IA. Tel: (319) 385-7259, FAX: (319) 385-2825, E-Mail: info@alanizdirect.com, Web Site: www.alanizdirect.com (16)

Alarie, Dave, PLAS-TANKS Industries Inc, Hamilton, OH. Tel: (513) 942-3800, FAX: (513) 942-3993, E-Mail: info@plastanks.com, Web Site: www.plastanks.com (9)

Alario, Steve, Person to Person Marketing LLC, Riverdale, NJ. Tel: (973) 835-8112, FAX: (973) 835-8525, E-Mail: sales@persontopersondirect.com, Web Site: www.persontopersondirect.com (29)

Alarmingyou.com, Boca Raton, FL. Tel: (714) 981-2900, Web Site: www.alarmingyou.com (16)

Alba, Ann, Broadmoor Hotel Inc, Colorado Springs, CO. Tel: (719) 634-7711, (866) 837-9520, FAX: (719) 577-5779, Web Site: www.broadmoor.com (19)

Albaugh, James, F., Boeing Co, Chicago, IL. Tel: (312) 544-2000, FAX: (312) 544-2082, Web Site: www.boeing.com (16)

Albe, Chriss, Hershey's Mail Order, Hershey, PA. Tel: (717) 534-7381, (800) 544-1347, FAX: (717) 534-7947, E-Mail: hersheygiftsinfo@hersheys.com, Web Site: www.hersheygifts.com (4)

Alber, Laura J., Williams-Sonoma Inc, San Francisco, CA. Tel: (415) 421-7900, FAX: (415) 983-9887, Web Site: www.williams-sonomainc.com (8)

Albergetis, Charlotte, KPBS FM/TV, San Diego, CA. Tel: (619) 594-1515, Web Site: www.kpbs.org (1)

Albert, Andrew, B., Svoboda Collins LLC, Chicago, IL. Tel: (312) 267-8750, FAX: (312) 267-6025, E-Mail: info@svoco.com, Web Site: www.svoco.com (5)

Albert, Diane, TVC Enterprises and the TV Collector Magazine, Las Vegas, NV. Tel: (760) 495-7956, E-Mail: tvcinquiries@happyretrogirl.com, Web Site: www.angelfire.com/ma/tvcollector/home.html (6)

Albert, Jill, Media Consultants Inc, Bayside, NY. Tel: (718) 423-6300, FAX: (718) 428-7482, E-Mail: mediaconsults@aol.com (32)

Albert, Melissa, HubCast Inc, Wakefield, MA. Tel: (781) 221-7200, Web Site: www.hubeast.com (27)

Alberts, Greg, A Plus Marketing Ltd, Buffalo Grove, IL. Tel: (847) 537-1166, FAX: (847) 537-5611, Web Site: www.aplusmarketing.com (20)

Alboushi, Nicole, Imperial Supplies, Green Bay, WI. Tel: (920) 494-5403, (800) 558-2808, FAX: (800) 553-8769, Web Site: www.imperialsupplies.com (16)

Albrecht, Chuck, Northern Tool & Equipment Inc, Burnsville, MN. Tel: (952) 894-9510, (800) 221-0516, FAX: (952) 894-1020, Web Site: www.northerntool.com (16)

Albrecht, Rodelinde, Rodelinde Graphic Design, Lenox Dale, MA. Tel: (413) 243-4350, FAX: (413) 243-3066, E-Mail: rodelinde@earthlink.net (36)

Aldata, Saint Paul, MN. Tel: (952) 432-6900, FAX: (952) 432-7064, E-Mail: mharris@aldata.com, Web Site: www.aldata.com (23)

Alden, Jim, Garnet Hill Inc, Franconia, NH. Tel: (603) 823-5545, FAX: (603) 823-7034, Web Site: www.garnethill.com (2)

Alden, Robert, RayPress Corp, Birmingham, AL. Tel: (205) 989-3731, Web Site: www.raypress.com (27)

John Alden Life Insurance Co/North Star Marketing, Duluth, GA. Tel: (678) 473-1211, (800) 768-6288, FAX: (678) 473-9573, Web Site: www.nstarmarketing.com (15)

Alder, Rob, Prestone Printing Co Inc, Long Island City, NY. Tel: (347) 468-7900, FAX: (347) 468-7885, Web Site: www.prestoneprinting.com (25)

Alderman Co, High Point, NC. Tel: (336) 889-6121, FAX: (336) 889-7717, E-Mail: sales@aldermancompany.com, Web Site: www.aldermancompany.com (37)

Aldred, Donald, ESL Federal Credit Union, Rochester, NY. Tel: (585) 336-1000, (800) 848-2265, FAX: (585) 336-1138, Web Site: www.esl.org (14)

Aldrich, Anne, Across The Board Marketing Inc, Chicago, IL. Tel: (312) 787-1642, FAX: (312) 787-1645, E-Mail: info@acrosstheboardmarketing.com, Web Site: www.acrosstheboardmarketing.com (39)

Aldrich, Brenda, Harman's Cheese & Country Store Inc, Sugar Hill, NH. Tel: (603) 823-8000, E-Mail: cheese@harmanscheese.com, Web Site: www.HarmansCheese.com (4)

Aldrich, Jeff, The Aldrich Group, Woodbury, CT. Tel: (860) 274-7693, (203) 263-5505, FAX: (203) 263-5572, E-Mail: jeff.aldrich@aldrichsearch.com, Web Site: www.aldrichsearch.com (20)

Aldrich, Mary, Warrantech Direct Inc, Bedford, TX. Tel: (817) 786-1000, (800) 833-8801, FAX: (817) 786-1020, Web Site: www.warrantech.com (29)

Aldrich, Matt, Navistar, Warrenville, IL. Tel: (630) 753-5804, (800) 448-7825, FAX: (630) 753-2303, Web Site: www.navistar.com (16)

Aldrich, Maxine, Harman's Cheese & Country Store Inc, Sugar Hill, NH. Tel: (603) 823-8000, E-Mail: cheese@harmanscheese.com, Web Site: www.HarmansCheese.com (4)

The Aldrich Group, Woodbury, CT. Tel: (860) 274-7693, (203) 263-5505, FAX: (203) 263-5572, E-Mail: jeff.aldrich@aldrichsearch.com, Web Site: www.aldrichsearch.com (20)

Aldridge, Pauline, LISTS Inc, Jacksonville, FL. Tel: (904) 733-6106, (800) 805-5478, FAX: (904) 730-7540, Web Site: www.lists-inc.com (23)

Aleksov, Marin, Rosland Capital LLC, Santa Monica, CA. Tel: (800) 891-2341, Web Site: www.roslandcapital.com (14)

Alen, Austin, TX. Tel: (512) 600-6948, (800) 630-2396, Web Site: www.alencorp.com/ (20)

Alert Marketing, Glen Ellyn, IL. Tel: (630) 790-0386, Web Site: www.alertmarketing.com (28)

Alerus Financial, Grand Forks, ND. Tel: (701) 795-3200, (800) 279-3200, Web Site: www2.alerusfinancial.com (14)

The Alesco Data Group, Fort Myers, FL. Tel: (239) 275-5006, (800) 701-6531, FAX: (239) 275-7737, E-Mail: marketing@alescodata.com, Web Site: www.alescodata.com (23)

Alesio, Steven, W., D&B Sales and Marketing Solutions, Waltham, MA. Tel: (781) 672-9200, (800) 590-0065, FAX: (781) 672-9290, Web Site: www.b2bsalesandmarketing.com (22)

Alexander, Dr. Livingston, University of Pittsburgh at Bradford, Bradford, PA. Tel: (814) 362-7500, FAX: (814) 362-5150, E-Mail: admissions@www.upb.pitt.edu, Web Site: www.upd.pitt.edu (41)

Alexander, Frank, C., Zoological Society of San Diego, San Diego, CA. Tel: (619) 231-1515, FAX: (619) 557-3937, Web Site: www.sandiegozoo.org (1)

Alexander, Ginny, USAA Alliance Services Marketing, San Antonio, TX. Tel: (210) 456-9857, FAX: (210) 498-4542, Web Site: www.usaa.com (14)

Alexander, Jack, Stark Brothers Fulfillment Services, Louisiana, MO. Tel: (573) 754-5511, (800) 325-4180, FAX: (573) 754-5290, E-Mail: info@starkbros.com, Web Site: www.starkbros.com (8)

Alexander, James, R., Alexander & Co LLC, Stonington, CT. Tel: (860) 535-9160, FAX: (860) 535-9161, E-Mail: jraandco@aol.com (20)

Alexander, John, Sturbridge Yankee Workshop Inc, Portland, ME. Tel: (207) 774-9045, (800) 343-1144, FAX: (207) 774-2561, Web Site: www.sturbridgeyankee.com (16)

Alexander, Lloyd, International Planned Parenthood Federation Western Hemisphere Region Inc, New York, NY. Tel: (212) 248-6400, (866) IPPFWHR, FAX: (212) 248-2441, E-Mail: info@ippfwhr.org, Web Site: www.ippfwhr.org (1)

Alexander, Neil, The United Methodist Publishing House, Nashville, TN. Tel: (615) 749-6000, (800) 672-1789, FAX: (615) 749-6417, E-Mail: productsandservices@umpublishing.com, Web Site: www.umpublishing.com (17)

Alexander, Patrick, H., Pennsylvania State University Press, University Park, PA. Tel: (814) 865-1327, (800) 326-9180, FAX: (814) 863-1408, Web Site: www.psupress.org (17)

Alexander, Renee, Sabre Holdings Inc, Southlake, TX. Tel: (682) 605-1000, Web Site: www.sabre.com (19)

Alexander, S., Tyrone, Highmark Blue Cross Blue Shield, Pittsburgh, PA. Tel: (412) 544-7000, FAX: (412) 544-5350, Web Site: www.highmark.com (15)

Alexander, Todd, Schmidt, Byron, MN. Tel: (507) 775-6400, FAX: (507) 775-6655, Web Site: www.schmidt.com (27)

Alexander & Co LLC, Stonington, CT. Tel: (860) 535-9160, FAX: (860) 535-9161, E-Mail: jraandco@aol.com (20)

Alexian Brothers Bonaventure House, Chicago, IL. Tel: (773) 327-9921, FAX: (773) 327-9113, E-Mail: info@abam.org, Web Site: www.bonaventurehouse.org (1)

Alfa Aesar-A Johnson Matthey Co, Ward Hill, MA. Tel: (800) 343-0660, FAX: (800) 322-4757, E-Mail: info@alfa.com, Web Site: www.alfa.com (9)

Alfa CTP Systems, Tewksbury, MA. Tel: (603) 689-1101, FAX: (603) 689-1197, Web Site: www.alfactp.com (10)

Alfa Insurance, Montgomery, AL. Tel: (334) 288-3900, Web Site: www.alfains.com (15)

Alfax Wholesale Furniture Inc, Farmers Branch, TX. Tel: (212) 947-9560, (800) 221-5710, FAX: (212) 947-4734, Web Site: www.alfaxfurniture.com (33)

Alford, Brad, Nestle USA, Glendale, CA. Tel: (818) 549-6000, (800) 225-2270, FAX: (818) 549-6952, Web Site: www.nestleusa.com (4)

Alfred Publishing Co Inc, Van Nuys, CA. Tel: (818) 891-5999, (800) 292-6122, FAX: (818) 895-5301, E-Mail: sales@alfred.com, Web Site: www.alfred.com (17)

Alfreda's Film Works, Denver, CO. Tel: (303) 575-5676, FAX: (303) 575-1187, E-Mail: emailstreet@gmail.com, Web Site: www.gumbomedia.com (17)

Alguire MD, Patrick, American College of Physicians, Washington, DC. Tel: (215) 351-2400, (800) 523-1546, FAX: (215) 351-2686, Web Site: www.acponline.org (17)

Alicea, Angel, Karasea Inc, Hastings On Hudson, NY. Tel: (914) 646-4481 (35)

Alicea, Noel, Gay Men's Health Crisis, New York, NY. Tel: (212) 367-1000, FAX: (212) 367-1220, E-Mail: webmaster@gmhc.org, Web Site: www.gmhc.org (1)

AliMed Inc, Dedham, MA. Tel: (781) 329-2900, (800) 225-2610, FAX: (781) 329-8392, (800) 437-2966, E-Mail: info@alimed.com, Web Site: www.alimed.info (7)

Alin, Michael, American Society of Interior Designers, Washington, DC. Tel: (202) 546-3480, FAX: (202) 546-3240, E-Mail: asid@asid.org, Web Site: www.asid.org (1)

Alitalia, New York, NY. Tel: (800) 223-5730, FAX: (212) 903-3568, E-Mail: customer.relationsnyc@alitalia.it, Web Site: www.alitalia.com (19)

Alkazian, Jeffrey, Penn Industries Inc, Cerritos, CA. Tel: (562) 926-0455, FAX: (562) 926-8955, Web Site: www.pennlitho.com (27)

Alkinburgh, Scott, Pete Rickard Inc, Cobleskill, NY. Tel: (518) 234-2731, (800) 282-5663, FAX: (518) 234-2454, E-Mail: info@peterickard.com, Web Site: www.peterickard.com (11)

All American List Corp, Prince Frederick, MD. Tel: (301) 420-5760, (800) 690-2252, FAX: (301) 420-5765, E-Mail: info@allamericanlist.com, Web Site: www.allamericanlist.com (23)

All-In-One Directory, New Paltz, NY. Tel: (845) 255-7560, FAX: (888) 345-2790, E-Mail: gebbiepress@pipeline.com, Web Site: www.gebbieinc.com (43)

All-n-One List Marketing Inc, Fishersville, VA. Tel: (703) 717-5621, Web Site: www.alln1lists.com (23)

All Star Carts & Vehicles, Bay Shore, NY. Tel: (631) 666-5252, (800) 831-3166, FAX: (631) 666-1319, Web Site: www.allstarcarts.com (16)

All Star Directories, Seattle, WA. Tel: (888) 404-8043, FAX: (707) 667-1524, Web Site: www.allstardirectories.com (17)

All Star Premium Products Inc, Fiskdale, MA. Tel: (508) 347-7672, (800) 526-8629, FAX: (508) 347-5404, E-Mail: sales@incentiveusa.com, Web Site: www.incentiveusa.com (33)

All-State Legal, Cranford, NJ. Tel: (908) 272-0800, (800) 222-0510, FAX: (800) 634-5184, E-Mail: sjacobs@aslegal.com, Web Site: www.aslegal.com (16)

All-Ways Advertising Co, Bloomfield, NJ. Tel: (973) 338-0700, (800) 255-9291, FAX: (973) 338-1410, Web Site: www.all-waysadvertising.com (33)

Allan, Elyse, GE Canada, Mississauga, ON Canada. Tel: (905) 858-5100, Web Site: www.ge.com/canada (9)

Allan, John, Samsonite Corp, Mansfield, MA. Tel: (508) 851-1400, (800) 547-BAGS, FAX: (303) 373-8715, Web Site: www.samsonite.com (16)

Allanson, Tom, H&R Block Inc, Kansas City, MO. Tel: (816) 572-6446, (800) 472-5625, FAX: (816) 854-8500, Web Site: www.hrblock.com (14)

The Allant Group, Naperville, IL. Tel: (800) 367-7311, FAX: (630) 355-3090, E-Mail: dirwin@allantgroup.com, Web Site: www.allantgroup.com (22)

AllBrands.com Sewing Machine Superstore, Baton Rouge, LA. Tel: (225) 923-1285, (866) 255-2726, FAX: (225) 923-1261, E-Mail: info@allbrands. com, Web Site: www.allbrands.com (11)

allconnect, Atlanta, GA. Tel: (404) 260-2449, Web Site: www.allconnect.com (32)

Allegiant Direct Inc, Brentwood, TN. Tel: (615) 373-2042, FAX: (615) 373-2099, E-Mail: welcome@ allegiantdirect.com, Web Site: www.allegiantdirect. com (35)

Allegra Network, LLC, Plymouth, MI. Tel: (248) 596-8600, FAX: (248) 596-8601, Web Site: www2. allegranetwork.com (27)

Allegra Print & Imaging - East, Louisville, KY. Tel: (502) 895-1530, Web Site: www.allegra-east.com (27)

Allen, Brian, United Church Homes, Marion, OH. Tel: (740) 382-4885, (800) 750-0750, FAX: (740) 382-4884, Web Site: www.unitedchurchhomes.org (1)

Allen, Carole, Ward, San Francisco Bay Area Rapid Transit District (BART), Oakland, CA. Tel: (510) 464-6000, FAX: (510) 464-7103, Web Site: www. bart.gov (16)

Allen, Celeste, Delta Vacations, Fort Lauderdale, FL. Tel: (954) 522-1440, (800) 800-1504, FAX: (954) 468-4765, Web Site: www.deltavacations.com (19)

Allen, Charlotte, American Meadows Inc & Vermont Wild Flowers Farm, Williston, VT. Tel: (802) 985-9455, (877) 309-7333, FAX: (802) 985-9268, E-Mail: erin@americanmeadows.com, Web Site: www.americanmeadows.com (8)

Allen, Christopher, Financial Executives International, Morristown, NJ. Tel: (973) 765-1000, FAX: (973) 765-1018, Web Site: www.financialexecutives.org (1)

Allen, Chy, American Meadows Inc & Vermont Wild Flowers Farm, Williston, VT. Tel: (802) 985-9455, (877) 309-7333, FAX: (802) 985-9268, E-Mail: erin@americanmeadows.com, Web Site: www. americanmeadows.com (8)

Allen, Cristi, Decision Analyst Inc, Arlington, TX. Tel: (817) 640-6166, (800) 262-5974, FAX: (817) 640-6567, E-Mail: jthomas@decisionanalyst.com, Web Site: www.decisionanalyst.com (30)

Allen, David, E., AMD Industries Inc, Cicero, IL. Tel: (708) 863-8900, (800) 367-9999, FAX: (708) 863-2065, Web Site: www.amdpop.com (36)

Allen, David, Studeo Interactive Direct, Salt Lake City, UT. Tel: (801) 993-2300, FAX: (801) 993-2301, E-Mail: info@studeo.com, Web Site: www. studeo.com (35)

Allen, Fred, E., Fred E Allen Inc, Mount Pleasant, TX. Tel: (903) 572-1701, FAX: (903) 572-1703 (23)

Allen, Gary, K., University of Missouri, Columbia, MO. Tel: (573) 882-6333, (800) 856-2181, FAX: (573) 882-2721, E-Mail: visitus@missouri.edu, Web Site: www.missouri.edu (41)

Allen, George, Tillamook County Creamery Association, Tillamook, OR. Tel: (503) 842-4481, (800) 542-7290, FAX: (503) 842-6039, Web Site: www. tillamookcheese.com (4)

Allen, Gordie, Leads-Plus Inc, Killarney, FL. Tel: (800) 548-4571, E-Mail: eurekaman43@hotmail. com, Web Site: www.salesprospectingexpert.com (20)

Allen, Karen, EU Services, Rockville, MD. Tel: (301) 424-3300, (800) 230-3362, FAX: (301) 424-3696, Web Site: www.euservices.com (21)

Allen, Kathleen, Millipore Corp, Bedford, MA. Tel: (781) 533-6000, FAX: (781) 533-3110, Web Site: www.millipore.com (9)

Allen, Kim, Butler Schein Animal Health, Dublin, OH. Tel: (614) 761-9095, (888) 691-2724, FAX: (888) 329-3861, Web Site: www.butlerschein.com (16)

Allen, Kim, Eggs by Byrd, Wappapello, MO. Tel: (573) 222-7999, (800) 235-EGGS, FAX: (573) 222-8009, E-Mail: eggsbybyrd@dishmail.net (10)

Allen, Layman E., WFF'N PROOF Learning Games Associates, Fairfield, IA. Tel: (641) 472-0149, (800) 289-2377, FAX: (641) 472-0693, Web Site: www.wffnproof.com (17)

Allen, Mark, ServiceMaster Co, Memphis, TN. Tel: (901) 766-1400, (901) 597-8502, (888) 937-3783, (866) 782-6787, FAX: (901) 766-1491, Web Site: www.servicemaster.com (8)

Allen, Matt, Markwins International Corp, City of Industry, CA. Tel: (909) 595-8898, FAX: (909) 595-8820, Web Site: www.markwins.com (16)

Allen, Michael, Dutch Gardens, Burlington, VT. Tel: (802) 660-3500, (800) 950-4470, FAX: (800) 551-6712, E-Mail: info@dutchgardens.com, Web Site: www.dutchgardens.com (8)

Allen, Nicole, Direct Marketers On Call Inc (DMOC), New York, NY. Tel: (212) 691-1942, FAX: (212) 924-1331, E-Mail: info@dmoc-inc.com, Web Site: www.dmoc-inc.com (20)

Allen, Patty, Theatre Development Fund Inc, New York, NY. Tel: (212) 912-9770, E-Mail: info@tdf. org, Web Site: www.tdf.org (1)

Allen, Paul, G., Charter Communications, Saint Louis, MO. Tel: (314) 965-0555, (888) 438-2427, FAX: (314) 965-9745, Web Site: www.charteroom.com (16)

Allen, Ray, American Meadows Inc & Vermont Wild Flowers Farm, Williston, VT. Tel: (802) 985-9455, (877) 309-7333, FAX: (802) 985-9268, E-Mail: erin@americanmeadows.com, Web Site: www. americanmeadows.com (8)

Allen, Robert, Broadway Books, New York, NY. Tel: (212) 782-9644, FAX: (212) 782-8338, E-Mail: bwaypub@randomhouse.com, Web Site: www. randomhouse.com/broadway (17)

Allen, Robert, Direct Marketing Association, New York, NY. Tel: (212) 768-7277, Web Site: www. the-dma.org (1)

Allen, Steve, MCRB Fulfillment Corp, Westlake Village, CA. Tel: (818) 407-4300, (800) 942-MCRB, FAX: (818) 407-0248, E-Mail: sallen@mcrb.com, Web Site: www.mcrb.com (28)

Allen, Sylvia, Allen Consulting, Holmdel, NJ. Tel: (732) 946-2711, FAX: (732) 946-8032, E-Mail: sylvia@allenconsulting.com, Web Site: www. allenconsulting.com (20)

Allen, Terry, Orbit Manufacturing Co, Perkasie, PA. Tel: (215) 453-9228, (888) 895-0958, FAX: (215) 257-7399, Web Site: www.orbitmfg.com (9)

Allen, Tom, Premiere Global Services Inc, Atlanta, GA. Tel: (404) 262-8400, (800) 546-1541, FAX: (913) 661-9042, Web Site: www.PGiConnect.com (22)

Allen Consulting, Holmdel, NJ. Tel: (732) 946-2711, FAX: (732) 946-8032, E-Mail: sylvia@ allenconsulting.com, Web Site: www. allenconsulting.com (20)

Fred E Allen Inc, Mount Pleasant, TX. Tel: (903) 572-1701, FAX: (903) 572-1703 (23)

Allen, Matkins, Leck, Gamble & Mallory, Los Angeles, CA. Tel: (213) 622-5555, FAX: (213) 620-8816, E-Mail: communications@allenmatkins.com, Web Site: www.allenmatkins.com (20)

Allen Wood, Danita, Missouri Life Inc, Boonville, MO. Tel: (660) 882-9898, (800) 492-2593, FAX: (660) 882-9899, E-Mail: info@missourilife.com, Web Site: www.missourilife.com (17)

Allergan Inc, Irvine, CA. Tel: (714) 246-4500, (800) 433-8871, FAX: (714) 246-4971, Web Site: www. allergan.com (16)

Alliance Bernstein, New York, NY. Tel: (212) 969-1000, (800) 962-2134, FAX: (212) 969-2229, Web Site: www.alliancebernstein.com (14)

Alliance Data, Plano, TX. Tel: (972) 348-5100, Web Site: www.alliancedata.com (28)

Alliance Defense Fund, Scottsdale, AZ. Tel: (480) 444-0020, Web Site: www.telladf.org (1)

Alliance Direct Marketing Solutions LLC, Jersey City, NJ. Tel: (201) 863-1360, (888) 455-2367, FAX: (201) 863-3910, E-Mail: vteran@

alliancedirectleads.com, Web Site: www. alliancedirectleads.com (20)

Alliance for the Arts, New York, NY. Tel: (212) 947-6340, FAX: (212) 947-6416, E-Mail: info@ allianceforarts.org, Web Site: www.nyc-arts.org (1)

Alliance of Area Business Publications, El Segundo, CA. Tel: (323) 937-5514, FAX: (323) 937-0959, E-Mail: info@bizpubs.org, Web Site: www. bizpubs.org (1)

Alliance of Nonprofit Mailers, Washington, DC. Tel: (202) 462-5132, FAX: (202) 462-0423, E-Mail: alliance@nonprofitmailers.org, Web Site: www. nonprofitmailers.org (40)

Alliance Strategies Group, Inc, Boca Raton, FL. Tel: (561) 499-3201, Web Site: www.bestroilists.com (23)

Alliant, Brewster, NY. Tel: (845) 276-2600, Web Site: www.alliantdata.com (22)

Allianz Life Insurance Co of North America, Minneapolis, MN. Tel: (763) 765-6500, (800) 950-5872, Web Site: www.allianzlife.com (15)

The Allied Group, Cranston, RI. Tel: (401) 946-6100, Web Site: www.thealliedgrp.com (28)

Allied Marketing Group Inc, Dallas, TX. Tel: (214) 915-7000, FAX: (214) 905-5133, E-Mail: support@alliedmarketinggroup.com, Web Site: www.alliedmarketinggroup.com (21)

Allied Premium Co, Rockville Centre, NY. Tel: (516) 766-5300 (33)

Allied Printing Services Inc, Manchester, CT. Tel: (860) 643-1101, (800) 225-8777, (800) 224-8894, FAX: (860) 643-9723, E-Mail: allied@ alliedprinting.com, Web Site: www.alliedprinting. com (27)

Allighen, Tony, Freedom Graphic Systems Inc, Milton, WI. Tel: (608) 868-7007, (800) 334-3540, FAX: (608) 868-7006, E-Mail: information@fgs.com, Web Site: www.freedomgraphicsystems.com (28)

Allison, Steve, Lion Apparel, Dayton, OH. Tel: (937) 898-1949, (800) 548-6614, FAX: (937) 913-5667, Web Site: www.lionapparel.com (2)

AllMedia Inc, Plano, TX. Tel: (469) 467-9100, FAX: (214) 291-5431, E-Mail: lmcclendon@allmediainc. com, Web Site: www.allmediainc.com (23)

Alloy Media Marketing, New York, NY. Tel: (212) 244-4307, (877) 360-9688, FAX: (212) 244-4311, E-Mail: contactus@alloymerch.com, Web Site: www.alloymarketing.com (35)

Alloyd Brands, Dekalb, IL. Tel: (815) 756-8451, (800) 756-7639, FAX: (815) 756-5187/9192, Web Site: www.alloyd.com (16)

Allpro Direct Marketing, Odessa, FL. Tel: (888) 679-0255, Web Site: www.allprodirectmarketing.com (20)

Allred, Betty, National Wholesale Co Inc, Lexington, NC. Tel: (336) 248-5904, (800) 480-4673, FAX: (336) 248-2880, E-Mail: customerservice@ shopnational.com, Web Site: www.shopnational. com (2)

Allsop, Joseph W., Progress Software Corp, Bedford, MA. Tel: (781) 280-4000, (800) 477-6473, FAX: (781) 280-4095, Web Site: www.progress.com (16)

Allstate Motor Club, South Barrington, IL. Tel: (847) 551-2300, (800) 998-8697 (13)

Allstate Motor Club, Inc, Deerfield, IL. Tel: (847) 914-2972, FAX: (847) 914-2804, Web Site: www. walgreens.com (7)

Alltel, Little Rock, AR. Tel: (501) 905-2590, (877) 446-3628, FAX: (501) 905-5444, Web Site: www. alltel.com (16)

Alltel Publishing Corp, Hudson, OH. Tel: (330) 650-7100, FAX: (330) 650-7883, Web Site: www.alltel. com (22)

Allyn, William F, Welch Allyn, Inc, Skaneateles Falls, NY. Tel: (315) 685-4100, Web Site: www. welchallyn.com (9)

Allyn & Bacon, Upper Saddle River, NJ. Tel: (617) 848-7216, FAX: (781) 455-1220 (17)

Almore International Inc, Portland, OR. Tel: (503) 643-6633, (800) 547-1511, FAX: (503) 643-9748, E-Mail: info@almore.com, Web Site: www.almore.com (7)

Almost Heaven Group, Renick, WV. Tel: (304) 645-2310, FAX: (304) 497-2698, E-Mail: art@almostheaven.net, Web Site: www.almostheaven.net (16)

Almquist, Hank, AMC Inc, Atlanta, GA. Tel: (404) 220-2000, FAX: (404) 220-3030 (2)

CM Almy & Son Inc, Greenwich, CT. Tel: (203) 552-7600, FAX: (203) 552-7605, E-Mail: almyaccess@almy.com, Web Site: www.almy.com (5)

Aloft Group, Westlake Village, CA. Tel: (805) 494-3700, Web Site: www.aloftgroup.com (33)

Aloisio, Bob, TTC Marketing Solutions, Chicago, IL. Tel: (773) 545-0407, (800) 777-6348, FAX: (773) 545-4034, E-Mail: sales@ttcmarketingsolutions.com, Web Site: www.ttcmarketingsolutions.com (29)

Alorica Inc, Chino, CA. Tel: (909) 606-3600, (866) 256-7422, FAX: (909) 606-7708, E-Mail: info@alorica.com, Web Site: www.alorica.com (29)

Alperson, Joel, Omaha Fixture International, Omaha, NE. Tel: (402) 592-3720, (800) 531-6627, FAX: (402) 593-5716, (800) 531-6627, Web Site: www.omahafixture.com (8)

Alperstein, Betsy, General Growth Properties, Chicago, IL. Tel: (312) 960-5413, Web Site: www.generalgrowth.com (5)

Alpert, Jacob, Professional Cutlery Direct, North Branford, CT. Tel: (203) 871-1000, FAX: (203) 871-1010, E-Mail: terri@cutlery.com, Web Site: www.cutlery.com (4)

Alpert, Joel, MarketPower Direct Marketing, Atlanta, GA. Tel: (404) 433-5555, E-Mail: joel@marketpoweronline.com, Web Site: www.marketpoweronline.com (35)

Alpert, Terri, S., Professional Cutlery Direct, North Branford, CT. Tel: (203) 871-1000, FAX: (203) 871-1010, E-Mail: terri@cutlery.com, Web Site: www.cutlery.com (4)

Alpert, Theodore, S., Advanstar Communications Inc, North Olmsted, OH. Tel: (440) 243-8100, (800) 225-4569, FAX: (440) 891-2740, E-Mail: info@advanstar.com, Web Site: www.advanstarlists.com (17)

Alpert-Romm, Adria, Discovery Communications LLC, Silver Spring, MD. Tel: (240) 662-2000, FAX: (240) 662-1868, Web Site: corporate.discovery.com (16)

Alpha Dog Marketing Inc, Lincoln, NE. Tel: (402) 486-0668, Web Site: www.alphadogmktg.com (1)

Alpha List Marketing Inc, Marietta, GA. Tel: (404) 995-7049, (800) 822-2902, FAX: (404) 601-0826, E-Mail: info@alphalistmarketing.com (23)

Alpha Supply Inc, Bremerton, WA. Tel: (360) 373-3302, (800) 257-4211, FAX: (360) 377-9235 (16)

AlphaGraphics World Headquarters, Salt Lake City, UT. Tel: (801) 595-7270, (800) 955-6246, FAX: (801) 595-7271, E-Mail: contactus@alphagraphics.com, Web Site: www.alphagraphics.com (27)

Alphin, J., Steele, Bank of America, Charlotte, NC. Tel: (704) 386-5681, (800) 841-4000, FAX: (704) 386-6699, Web Site: www.bankofamerica.com (14)

Alseth, Becky, Avis World Headquarters, Parsippany, NJ. Tel: (973) 496-3500, Web Site: www.avis.com (19)

ALSTOM Signaling Inc, West Henrietta, NY. Tel: (585) 279-2228, Web Site: www.alstomsignalingsolutions.com (16)

Alston, Michael, Landmark Communications Inc, Norfolk, VA. Tel: (757) 446-2010, (800) 446-2004, FAX: (757) 446-2489, Web Site: www.landmark.com (17)

Alta Resources (West Coast Office), Neenah, WI. Tel: (920) 751-5800, (877) 934-6377, Web Site: www.altaresources.com (29)

Altair Data Resources, Franklin, TN. Tel: (615) 468-6800, (866) 261-4695, FAX: (615) 468-6878, E-Mail: info@altairdata.com, Web Site: www.altairdata.com (23)

Altberg, Marla, Ventura Associates International LLC, New York, NY. Tel: (212) 302-8277, FAX: (212) 302-2587, E-Mail: info@sweepspros.com, Web Site: www.sweepspros.com (35)

Altenpohl, Kathy, Laser Label Technologies Inc, Stow, OH. Tel: (800) 882-4050, FAX: (800) 395-4721, E-Mail: sales@lltproducts.com, Web Site: www.lltproducts.com (16)

Alter, Dennis, Advanta Corp, Spring House, PA. Tel: (215) 657-4000, (800) 255-0022, Web Site: www.advanta.com (14)

Alter, Sy, Spectrum eCommerce, Mission Viejo, CA. Tel: (949) 600-7900, Web Site: elifemarketers.com (15)

Alterian, Chicago, IL. Tel: (312) 704-1700, Web Site: www.alterian.com (22)

Alternate Marketing Networks Inc, Hudsonville, MI. Tel: (616) 662-6420, FAX: (616) 662-6422, Web Site: www.altmarknet.com (28)

Alternative Concepts Inc, Knoxville, TN. Tel: (865) 690-1990, FAX: (865) 692-0072, E-Mail: info@acmarketing.biz, Web Site: www.acmarketing.biz (31)

Alternative Marketing Solutions Inc, Phoenixville, PA. Tel: (610) 783-1320, FAX: (610) 783-1324, E-Mail: guntick@amsolutions.com, Web Site: www.amsolutions.com (21)

Alternative Media Group, Naples, FL. Tel: (732) 741-0585, FAX: (732) 741-0489, Web Site: www.amg-global.com (31)

Alteslane, Al, Global Turnkey Systems Inc, Parsippany, NJ. Tel: (973) 331-1010, FAX: (973) 331-0042, E-Mail: sales@gtsystems.com, Web Site: www.gtsystems.com (22)

Althof, Timothy D., NEBS, Groton, MA. Tel: (978) 448-6111, (888) 823-6327, (800) 225-6380, FAX: (800) 234-4324, (978) 448-3653, E-Mail: customerservice@nebs.com, Web Site: www.nebs.com (10)

Althoff, Susanne, The Boston Globe, Boston, MA. Tel: (617) 929-2000, (888) MY-GLOBE, FAX: (617) 929-2606, Web Site: www.bostonglobe.com (17)

Altman, Alan, The Menninger Foundation, Houston, TX. Tel: (713) 275-5000, (800) 351-9058, FAX: (713) 275-5107, Web Site: www.menningerclinic.com (1)

Altman, Allan, Video Artists International, Pleasantville, NY. Tel: (914) 769-3691, (800) 477-7146, FAX: (914) 769-5407, E-Mail: orders@vaimusic.com, Web Site: www.vaimusic.com (3)

Altman, Dan, World Publications Inc, Winter Park, FL. Tel: (407) 628-4802, FAX: (407) 628-7061, Web Site: www.worldpub.net (17)

Altman, David, G., Center for Creative Leadership, Greensboro, NC. Tel: (336) 545-2810, FAX: (336) 282-3284, E-Mail: info@ccl.org, Web Site: www.ccl.org (16)

Altman, Keith, Call Compliance Inc, Glen Cove, NY. Tel: (516) 674-4545, FAX: (516) 676-2420, E-Mail: sales@callcompliance.com, Web Site: www.callcompliance.com (29)

Altman, Linda, Abbey Press, Saint Meinrad, IN. Tel: (812) 357-8011, FAX: (812) 357-8388, Web Site: www.abbeypress.com (6)

Altman, Shari, Altman Dedicated Direct, Rural Hall, NC. Tel: (336) 969-9538, FAX: (336) 969-0187, E-Mail: saltman@AltmanDedicatedDirect.com, Web Site: www.altmandedicateddirect.com (20)

Altman, William M., Altman Direct Marketing, Austin, TX. Tel: (210) 590-2062, (800) 324-2062, FAX: (210) 590-2945, E-Mail: altman@altmandirect.com, Web Site: www.altmandirect.com (21)

Altman Dedicated Direct, Rural Hall, NC. Tel: (336) 969-9538, FAX: (336) 969-0187, E-Mail: saltman@AltmanDedicatedDirect.com, Web Site: www.altmandedicateddirect.com (20)

Altman Direct Marketing, Austin, TX. Tel: (210) 590-2062, (800) 324-2062, FAX: (210) 590-2945, E-Mail: altman@altmandirect.com, Web Site: www.altmandirect.com (21)

Altschul, Alfred, Airlines Reporting Corp, Arlington, VA. Tel: (703) 816-8135, FAX: (703) 816-8104, E-Mail: corpcom@arccorp.com, Web Site: www.arccorp.com (11)

Altstadt, Manfred, Mutual of America Life Insurance Co, New York, NY. Tel: (212) 224-1600, (800) 468-3785, FAX: (212) 224-2539, Web Site: www.mutualofamerica.com (11)

Alty, Julia, Beemak Plastics Inc, La Mirada, CA. Tel: (310) 886-5880, (800) 421-4393, FAX: (310) 764-0330, E-Mail: info@beemak.com, Web Site: www.beemak.com (16)

Aluhawalia, Aditya, WPI Group Inc, Colts Neck, NJ. FAX: (212) 202-3742, E-Mail: info@wpinj.com, Web Site: www.wpinj.com (20)

Alvarado, Louise, Travel Planners Inc, New York, NY. Tel: (212) 532-1660, (800) 221-3531, FAX: (212) 779-6102, Web Site: www.tphousing.com (19)

Alvarez, James, N., ChoicePoint Precision Marketing, Little Rock, AR. Tel: (978) 738-0544, (800) 937-4232, FAX: (978) 738-0582, Web Site: www.cp-pm.com (30)

Alves, Carlos M., HSBC Bank USA, NA, Buffalo, NY. Tel: (716) 841-2424, FAX: (716) 841-5391, Web Site: www.banking.us.hsbc.com (14)

Alves, Paget, The CompTEL Annual Convention & Trade Exposition, Washington, DC. Tel: (202) 296-6650, FAX: (202) 296-7585, Web Site: www.comptel.org (42)

Alvion LLC, Cape Coral, FL. Tel: (239) 574-8600, (877) 528-7800, FAX: (239) 574-8551, Web Site: www.alvion.com (22)

Alzheimer Society of Canada, Toronto, ON Canada. Tel: (416) 488-8772, (800) 616-8816, FAX: (416) 488-3778, E-Mail: gpage@alzheimer.ca, Web Site: www.alzheimer.ca (1)

Alzheimer's Association, Chicago, IL. Tel: (312) 335-8700, Web Site: www.alz.org (1)

Amabili, Bridget, Data Services Inc, Salisbury, MD. Tel: (410) 546-2206, (800) 432-4066, FAX: (410) 546-2274, Web Site: www.dataservicesinc.com (22)

Amacai Information Corp, Oakbrook Terrace, IL. Tel: (800) 434-1555, FAX: (312) 924-3001, E-Mail: info@amacai.com, Web Site: www.amacai.com (23)

Amacker, Carl, Neopost, Carrollton, TX. Tel: (510) 489-6800, (800) 636-7678, FAX: (510) 475-6317, (510) 487-6704, Web Site: www.neopostinc.com (9)

Amacom Books, New York, NY. Tel: (212) 903-8376, FAX: (212) 903-8083, E-Mail: customerservice@amanet.org, Web Site: www.amacombooks.org (17)

Amalfitano, Joseph, MVS Mailers Inc, Bohemia, NY. Tel: (800) 641-7917, FAX: (631) 699-0101, E-Mail: muraco@mvsmailers.com, Web Site: www.mvsmailers.com (28)

Amanet, Canoga Park, CA. Tel: (818) 786-1113, FAX: (818) 786-5736, E-Mail: info@amanet-usa.com, Web Site: www.amanet.com (16)

Amaral, Terri, Berway Visual Products Inc, Wilmington, MA. Tel: (978) 694-9195, (800) 452-0410, FAX: (978) 694-9212, E-Mail: sales@berway.com, Web Site: www.berway.com (3)

Amaryllis Inc, Baton Rouge, LA. Tel: (225) 924-5560 (8)

Amatetti, Rosemary, Craver Mathews Smith & Co, Reston, VA. Tel: (703) 258-0000, FAX: (703) 258-0001, Web Site: www.craveronline.com (1)

Amateur Electronic Supply LLC, Milwaukee, WI. Tel: (414) 558-0333, (800) 558-0411, FAX: (414) 358-3337, Web Site: www.aesham.com (16)

Amato, Sheri, L., Hobby Surplus Sales, New Britain, CT. Tel: (860) 223-0600, (800) 233-0872, FAX: (860) 225-5316, E-Mail: amatohobby@sbcglobal. net, Web Site: www.hobbysurplus.com (11)

Amato, Steven, Hobby Surplus Sales, New Britain, CT. Tel: (860) 223-0600, (800) 233-0872, FAX: (860) 225-5316, E-Mail: amatohobby@sbcglobal. net, Web Site: www.hobbysurplus.com (11)

Amato, Vincent, Hobby Surplus Sales, New Britain, CT. Tel: (860) 223-0600, (800) 233-0872, FAX: (860) 225-5316, E-Mail: amatohobby@sbcglobal. net, Web Site: www.hobbysurplus.com (11)

AmazingMail Inc, Scottsdale, AZ. Tel: (480) 281-4800, Web Site: www.amazingmail.com (35)

Amazon.com, Washington, DC. Tel: (202) 347-7390 (16)

Amazon Drygoods, Davenport, IA. Tel: (800) 798-7979, FAX: (563) 322-4003, E-Mail: info@ amazondrygoods.com, Web Site: www. amazondrygoods.com (2)

Ambassador Press, Minneapolis, MN. Tel: (612) 521-0123, (800) 544-9112, FAX: (612) 521-4587, E-Mail: info@ambpress.com, Web Site: www. ambpress.com (27)

Ambassador Programs, Spokane, WA. Tel: (509) 568-7800, Web Site: www.ptpprograms.org (19)

Ambient Shapes Inc, Hickory, NC. Tel: (800) 438-2244, FAX: (800) 872-2005, E-Mail: sales@ ambientshapes.com, Web Site: www. ambientshapes.com (7)

Ambio, Jeff, Bowers & Merena Auctions, Irvine, CA. Tel: (949) 253-0916, (800) 458-4646, FAX: (949) 253-4091, E-Mail: auction@bowersandmerena. com, Web Site: www.bowersandmerena.com (16)

Amble, Rey, Meriks Gifts, San Diego, CA. Tel: (787) 721-0000 (6)

Amboian, John, P., Nuveen Investments, Chicago, IL. Tel: (312) 917-7700, (800) 257-8787, FAX: (312) 917-8049, Web Site: www.nuveen.com (14)

Amcat TeleProfit Inc, Oklahoma City, OK. Tel: (405) 216-8080, (800) 364-5518, FAX: (405) 216-8063, E-Mail: smart@amcat.com, Web Site: www.amcat. com (16)

AMD Research & Marketing LLC, Safety Harbor, FL. Tel: (727) 409-1087, Web Site: www.amdresearch-marketing.com (30)

Amedeo, Raymond, D., IWCO Direct, Chanhassen, MN. Tel: (952) 474-0961, FAX: (952) 474-6467 (21)

Amergent, Peabody, MA. Tel: (800) 370-7500, Web Site: www.amergent.com (1)

Americ Disc, Drummondville, PQ Canada. Tel: (800) 263-0419, FAX: (819) 478-4575, Web Site: www. americdisc.com (33)

America, Fredericksburg, VA. Tel: (540) 658-3388, (800) 927-8277, FAX: (540) 658-3389, Web Site: www.americastore.com (6)

America Direct Book Service Custom Publishing, Ossining, NY. Tel: (914) 271-3640, FAX: (914) 271-3641, E-Mail: info@americadirectbook.com, Web Site: www.americadirectbook.com (17)

America Online Inc, Dulles, VA. Tel: (703) 265-1000 (32)

Americalist, North Canton, OH. Tel: (330) 494-9111, (888) 219-LIST, FAX: (330) 494-0226, Web Site: www.americalist.com (21)

AmeriCall Group Inc, Naperville, IL. Tel: (630) 955-9100, (800) 688-0078, FAX: (630) 955-9955, E-Mail: sales@americallgroup.com, Web Site: www.americallgroup.com (29)

American Academy of Neurology, Saint Paul, MN. Tel: (651) 695-2793, Web Site: www.aan.com (1)

American Accessories International, Knoxville, TN. Tel: (865) 525-9100, FAX: (865) 525-0889 (33)

American Airlines, Fort Worth, TX. Tel: (817) 963-1234 (12)

American Airlines Inc, Dallas, TX. Tel: (817) 967-1910, FAX: (817) 967-2841 (19)

American Appraisal Associates, Milwaukee, WI. Tel: (414) 271-7240, (800) 558-8650, FAX: (414) 225-1271, Web Site: www.american-appraisal.com (14)

American Arbitration Association, New York, NY. Tel: (212) 716-5800, (800) 778-7879, FAX: (212) 716-5905, E-Mail: kesslerw@adr.org, Web Site: www. adr.org (1)

American Association for Justice, Washington, DC. Tel: (202) 965-3500, (800) 424-2725, FAX: (202) 625-7313, Web Site: www.justice.org (1)

American Association of Advertising Agencies, New York, NY. Tel: (212) 682-2500, FAX: (212) 682-8391, Web Site: www.aaaa.org (40)

American Association of Critical-Care Nurses, Aliso Viejo, CA. Tel: (949) 362-2000, (800) 809-CARE, FAX: (949) 362-2020, E-Mail: info@aacn.com, Web Site: www.aacn.org (1)

American Association of Individual Investors, Chicago, IL. Tel: (312) 280-0170, FAX: (312) 280-9883, E-Mail: adam@aaii.com, Web Site: www. aaii.com (1)

American Association of University Women, Washington, DC. Tel: (202) 725-7611, Web Site: www. aauw.org (1)

American Automobile Association, Heathrow, FL. Tel: (407) 444-7282, Web Site: www.aaa.com (16)

American Bank Note Holographics Inc, Robbinsville, NJ. Tel: (609) 632-0800, FAX: (609) 632-0850, Web Site: www.abnh.com (27)

American Bankers Association, Washington, DC. Tel: (202) 789-0300, (800) BANKERS, FAX: (202) 296-9258, Web Site: www.aba.com (1)

American Bar Association, Chicago, IL. Tel: (312) 988-5435, FAX: (312) 988-5455, Web Site: www. abanet.org (1)

American Baseball Coaches Association, Mount Pleasant, MI. Tel: (989) 775-3300, FAX: (989) 775-3600, E-Mail: abca@abca.org, Web Site: www. abca.org (1)

American Bible Society, New York, NY. Tel: (212) 408-1200, FAX: (212) 408-1264, Web Site: www. americanbible.org (1)

American Biographical Institute Inc, Raleigh, NC. Tel: (919) 781-8710, FAX: (919) 781-8712, Web Site: www.abiworldwide.com (17)

American Breast Cancer Foundation, Baltimore, MD. Tel: (410) 825-9388, Web Site: www.abcf.org (1)

American Bronzing Co, Columbus, OH. Tel: (614) 252-7388, (800) 423-5678, FAX: (614) 252-4602, E-Mail: bronzeinfo@bronshoe.com, Web Site: www.abcbronze.com (16)

American Business Directories, Omaha, NE. Tel: (402) 593-4600, (800) 555-6124, FAX: (402) 596-0475, Web Site: www.infousa.com (43)

American Cancer Society, Atlanta, GA. Tel: (404) 471-5852, (800) ACS-2345, FAX: (404) 982-3677, Web Site: www.cancer.org (1)

American Capital, Bethesda, MD. Tel: (301) 951-6122, FAX: (301) 654-6714, E-Mail: info@ americancapital.com, Web Site: www. americancapital.com (15)

American Catalog Mailers Association, Somers, NY. Tel: (914) 669-8391, Web Site: www. catalogmailers.org (1)

American Century Investments, Kansas City, MO. Tel: (816) 531-5575, (800) 345-2021, FAX: (816) 340-7962, Web Site: www.americancentury.com (14)

American Chemical Society, Washington, DC. Tel: (202) 872-4600, (800) 227-5558, FAX: (202) 833-7716, E-Mail: service@acs.org, Web Site: www. acs.org (1)

American Church Inc, Youngstown, OH. Tel: (330) 758-4545, (800) 250-7112, FAX: (800) 763-8772, E-Mail: sales@americanchurch.com, Web Site: www.americanchurch.com (26)

American Church Lists Inc, Omaha, NE. Tel: (402) 596-8905, (888) 733-1812, FAX: (402) 596-8907, E-Mail: americanchurchlists@infousa.com, Web Site: www.americanchurchlists.com (24)

American Civil Defense Association, Draper, UT. Tel: (800) 501-0077, FAX: (800) 403-1369, E-Mail: info@tacda.org, Web Site: www.tacda.org (16)

American Civil Liberties Union Foundation, New York, NY. Tel: (212) 549-2600, Web Site: www. aclu.org (1)

American Clearinghouse Inc, Louisville, KY. Tel: (800) 944-6361, Web Site: www. americanclearinghouse.com (23)

American College of Cardiology, Washington, DC. Tel: (202) 375-6426, Web Site: www.acc.org (1)

American College of Emergency Physicians, Irving, TX. Tel: (972) 550-0911, Web Site: www..acep.org (1)

American College of Physician Executives, Tampa, FL. Tel: (813) 287-2000, (800) 562-8088, FAX: (813) 287-8993, E-Mail: acpe@acpe.org, Web Site: www.acpe.org (1)

American College of Physicians, Washington, DC. Tel: (215) 351-2400, (800) 523-1546, FAX: (215) 351-2686, Web Site: www.acponline.org (17)

American Color, Irving, TX. Tel: (602) 333-1000, FAX: (602) 333-1099, Web Site: www.amcolor. com (27)

American Council on Exercise, San Diego, CA. Tel: (858) 279-8227, (888) 825-3636, FAX: (858) 279-8064, E-Mail: kristie.spalding@acefitness.org, Web Site: www.acefitness.org (1)

American Counseling Association, Broken Arrow, OK. Tel: (703) 823-6862, FAX: (703) 823-0252, E-Mail: webmaster@counseling.org, Web Site: www.counseling.org (1)

American Craft Council, Minneapolis, MN. Tel: (212) 274-0630, FAX: (212) 274-0650, E-Mail: council@craftcouncil.org, Web Site: www. craftcouncil.org (17)

American Crane & Equipment Corp, Douglassville, PA. Tel: (610) 385-6061, (877) 877-6778, FAX: (610) 385-3191/4876, E-Mail: info@ americancrane.com, Web Site: www.americancrane. com (16)

American Customer Care Inc, Bristol, CT. Tel: (866) 400-6886, Web Site: www.americancustomercare. com (29)

American Database Marketing Inc, Jacksonville, FL. Tel: (904) 886-0744, (888) 565-7724, FAX: (888) 270-4338, E-Mail: admdun@cs.com, Web Site: www.admdun.com (23)

American Dermatological Corp, Miami, FL. Tel: (305) 573-0763, (888) 573-0763, FAX: (305) 573-1704, E-Mail: info@dermatique.com, Web Site: www. dermatique.com (16)

American Diabetes Association, Alexandria, VA. Tel: (703) 549-1500, Web Site: www.diabetes.org (1)

American Direct Marketing Resources Inc, Chesterfield, MO. Tel: (636) 532-7703, FAX: (636) 532-2427, Web Site: www.admr.org (21)

American Direct Marketing Services, Dallas, TX. Tel: (214) 634-2361, (800) 527-5080, FAX: (214) 905-3829, Web Site: www.dmlist.com (23)

American Eagle Outfitters, Pittsburgh, PA. Tel: (412) 432-3382, Web Site: www.ae.com (2)

American Express Co, New York, NY. Tel: (212) 640-2000, FAX: (212) 619-9802, Web Site: www. americanexpress.com (14)

American Express Publishing Corp, New York, NY. Tel: (212) 382-5600, (888) 461-6180, FAX: (212) 827-6496, E-Mail: aepc@custmersvc.com, Web Site: www.amexpub.com (17)

American Family Insurance Group, Madison, WI. Tel: (608) 249-2111, FAX: (608) 243-6525, E-Mail: akin1@amfam.com, Web Site: www.amfam.com (15)

American Family Life Assurance Co of Columbus (AFLAC), Columbus, GA. Tel: (706) 323-3431, (800) 992-3522, FAX: (706) 660-7446, Web Site: www.aflac.com (15)

American Federation of Astrologers, Tempe, AZ. Tel: (480) 838-1751, (888) 301-7630, FAX: (480) 838-8293, E-Mail: afa@msn.com, Web Site: www.astrologers.com (1)

American Fidelity Assurance Co, Oklahoma City, OK. Tel: (405) 525-6900, FAX: (405) 523-5215, Web Site: www.afadvantage.com (15)

The American Film Institute, Los Angeles, CA. Tel: (323) 856-7600, FAX: (323) 467-4578, Web Site: www.afi.com (1)

American Fine Paper Co, Appleton, WI. Tel: (920) 733-6100, (800) 458-5446, FAX: (920) 380-8711, E-Mail: found@americanfinepaper.com, Web Site: www.americanfinepaper.com (25)

American Forests, Washington, DC. Tel: (202) 737-1944, FAX: (202) 737-2457, E-Mail: info@amfor.org, Web Site: www.americanforests.org (1)

American Foundation for the Blind Inc, New York, NY. Tel: (212) 502-7600, FAX: (212) 502-7777, E-Mail: afbinfo@afb.org, Web Site: www.afb.org/afb (1)

American General Co, Neptune, NJ. Tel: (732) 922-7000, FAX: (732) 922-7595 (15)

American General Life & Accident Insurance, Nashville, TN. Tel: (615) 749-1000, (800) 888-2452, Web Site: www.agla.com (15)

American General Life Insurance Co, Houston, TX. Tel: (713) 522-1111, FAX: (713) 522-8531, Web Site: www.aglife.com (15)

American Girl Brands LLC, Middleton, WI. Tel: (608) 836-4848, Web Site: www.americangirl.com (6)

American Graphics Network Inc, Glenview, IL. Tel: (847) 729-7220, FAX: (847) 724-5080, E-Mail: info@agninc.com, Web Site: www.agninc.com (27)

American Greetings Corp, Cleveland, OH. Tel: (216) 252-7300, FAX: (216) 252-6777 (16)

American Health & Life Insurance Co, Fort Worth, TX. Tel: (817) 348-7500, (800) 995-2274, FAX: (817) 348-7553, Web Site: www.citifinancial.com (15)

American Health & Safety Inc, Stoughton, WI. Tel: (630) 413-5662, (800) 522-7554, FAX: (800) 326-3245, Web Site: www.ahsafety.com (16)

American Health Assistance Foundation, Clarksburg, MD. Tel: (301) 948-3224 (1)

American Health Information Management Association, Chicago, IL. Tel: (312) 233-1100, FAX: (312) 233-1090, E-Mail: info@ahima.org, Web Site: www.ahima.org (1)

American Healthways, Franklin, TN. Tel: (615) 665-7716, FAX: (615) 665-7697, Web Site: www.americanhealthways.com (16)

American Heart Association, Dallas, TX. Tel: (214) 373-6300, (800) AHA-USA-1, FAX: (214) 373-3406, Web Site: www.americanheart.org (1)

American Heritage Picture Library, New York, NY. Tel: (212) 206-5107, (800) 777-1222, FAX: (212) 367-3151, Web Site: www.americanheritage.com (38)

American Historic Inns Inc, Dana Point, CA. Tel: (949) 497-2232, (800) 397-4667, FAX: (949) 497-9228, E-Mail: comments@iloveinns.com, Web Site: www.iloveinns.com (17)

American Horse Products, San Juan Capistrano, CA. Tel: (949) 248-5300, (800) 500-0799, FAX: (949) 248-5305, E-Mail: zjim@sbcglobal.net, Web Site: www.americanhorseproducts.com (11)

American Hotel Register Co, Vernon Hills, IL. Tel: (708) 743-4163, FAX: (708) 564-5797, Web Site: www.americanhotel.com (23)

American Humane Association, Washington, DC. Tel: (303) 925-9497, Web Site: www.americanhumane.org (1)

American Identity, Overland Park, KS. Tel: (913) 319-3100, (800) 848-8028 (33)

American Inbound, Bloomington, IN. Tel: (800) 322-6445, FAX: (800) 224-3583, Web Site: www.americanbound.com (29)

American Indian College Fund, Denver, CO. Tel: (303) 426-8900, Web Site: www.collegefund.org (1)

American Institute for Cancer Research, Washington, DC. Tel: (202) 328-7744, (800) 843-8114, FAX: (202) 328-7226, E-Mail: aicrweb@aicr.org, Web Site: www.aicr.org (1)

American Institute for Economic Research, Great Barrington, MA. Tel: (413) 528-1216, (888) 528-1216, E-Mail: info@aier.org, Web Site: www.aier.org (1)

American Institute of Chemical Engineers, New York, NY. Tel: (203) 702-7660, (800) 242-4363, FAX: (203) 775-5177, E-Mail: xpress@aiche.org, Web Site: www.aiche.org (1)

American Institute of CPAs, New York, NY. Tel: (212) 596-6200, (888) 777-7077, FAX: (212) 596-6213, Web Site: www.aicpa.org (1)

American Institute of Graphic Arts (AIGA), New York, NY. Tel: (212) 807-1990, FAX: (212) 807-1799, E-Mail: grefe@aiga.org, Web Site: www.aiga.org (40)

American Institute of Physics, Melville, NY. Tel: (516) 576-2200, (800) 892-8259, FAX: (516) 576-2374, E-Mail: aipinfo@aip.org, Web Site: www.aip.org (17)

American Insurance Administrators Inc, Columbus, OH. Tel: (614) 486-5388, FAX: (614) 486-2728 (15)

American International Group, New York, NY. Tel: (212) 770-7000, (877) 638-4244, FAX: (212) 742-8692, Web Site: www.aig.com (15)

American Israel Public Affairs Committee, Washington, DC. Tel: (202) 639-5226, Web Site: www.aipac.org (40)

American Kennel Club, New York, NY. Tel: (212) 696-8200, FAX: (212) 696-8217, (212) 696-8299, Web Site: www.akc.org (17)

American Kidney Fund, Rockville, MD. Tel: (301) 881-3052, Web Site: www.kidneyfund.org (1)

American Leads Co, Benicia, CA. Tel: (707) 747-6334, FAX: (707) 747-5323, Web Site: www.american-leads.com (23)

The American Legion National Headquarters, Indianapolis, IN. Tel: (317) 630-1247, FAX: (317) 630-1369, E-Mail: acy@legion.org, Web Site: www.legion.org (1)

American Library Association-Publishing Services, Chicago, IL. Tel: (312) 944-6780, (800) 545-2433, FAX: (312) 280-4380, Web Site: www.ala.org (1)

American Life TV Network, Washington, DC. Tel: (202) 289-6633, FAX: (202) 289-6632, Web Site: www.goodtv.com (32)

American Locker Security Systems Inc, Coppell, TX. Tel: (817) 329-1600, (800) 828-9118, E-Mail: info@americanlocker.com, Web Site: www.americanlocker.com (16)

American Lung Association, New York, NY. Tel: (212) 889-3370, (800) LUNGUSA, FAX: (212) 889-3375, E-Mail: info@alany.org, Web Site: www.lungusa.org (1)

American Mail-Well Envelope Co/St Louis Div, Eureka, MO. Tel: (314) 966-2000, (800) 800-8845, FAX: (314) 966-4725, E-Mail: info@cenveo.com, Web Site: www.mail-well.com (1)

American Mailing Lists Corp, Manassas, VA. Tel: (571) 292-5806, FAX: (571) 292-5807, E-Mail: dorothy@amlc.info, Web Site: www.amlc.info (23)

American Mailing Service Inc, Ashland, KY. Tel: (606) 329-2741, (800) 678-8384, FAX: (606) 325-8558, Web Site: www.thegallahergroup.com (28)

American Management Association, New York, NY. Tel: (212) 586-8100, FAX: (212) 903-8186, Web Site: www.amanet.org (1)

American Management Association International, New York, NY. Tel: (212) 586-8100, (800) 262-9699, FAX: (212) 903-8168 (41)

American Marketing & Communication Corp, Hagerstown, MD. Tel: (240) 625-9225, FAX: (240) 625-9235, E-Mail: info@amcc1.com, Web Site: www.americanmarketingcc.com (20)

American Marketing Association, Chicago, IL. Tel: (312) 542-9000, FAX: (312) 542-9001, Web Site: www.ama.org (40)

American Marketing Association/New York Chapter, New York, NY. Tel: (212) 687-3280, FAX: (212) 557-9242, E-Mail: mlkeane@nyama.org, Web Site: www.nyama.org (40)

American Marketing Solutions LLC, Uniontown, PA. Tel: (724) 437-3707 (5)

American Marketing Systems Inc, Burr Ridge, IL. Tel: (630) 382-1000, FAX: (630) 325-0825, E-Mail: studentservices@thepei.com, Web Site: www.amsdirect.com (35)

American Mathematical Society, Providence, RI. Tel: (401) 455-4000, (800) 321-4267, FAX: (401) 331-3842, E-Mail: ams@ams.org, Web Site: www.ams.org (17)

American Meadows Inc & Vermont Wild Flowers Farm, Williston, VT. Tel: (802) 985-9455, (877) 309-7333, FAX: (802) 985-9268, E-Mail: erin@americanmeadows.com, Web Site: www.americanmeadows.com (8)

American Medical Association, Chicago, IL. Tel: (312) 464-5000, (800) 621-8335, FAX: (312) 464-4184, Web Site: www.ama-assn.org (1)

American Medical Information Inc, Omaha, NE. Tel: (402) 593-4500, (866) 241-9044, FAX: (402) 331-1505, E-Mail: support@drlists.com, Web Site: americanmedicalinfo.com (24)

American Megatrends Inc, Norcross, GA. Tel: (770) 246-8600, (800) 828-9264, FAX: (770) 246-8790, Web Site: www.ami.com (3)

American Mint LLC, Mechanicsburg, PA. Tel: (717) 458-9200, (877) 807-MINT, FAX: (717) 458-9211, E-Mail: contact@americanmint.com, Web Site: www.americanmint.com (6)

American Modern Insurance Group, Amelia, OH. Tel: (513) 943-7200, (800) 759-9008, FAX: (513) 947-4779, (800) 217-5150, E-Mail: customer_care@amig.com, Web Site: www.amig.com (15)

American Movie Classics Holding Corp, Jericho, NY. Tel: (516) 803-3000, FAX: (516) 803-3003, Web Site: www.amctv.com (16)

American Name Services Inc, Orem, UT. Tel: (801) 235-8061, (800) 434-1851, FAX: (801) 764-0613, E-Mail: sales@americannameservices.com, Web Site: www.americannameservices.com (23)

American National Standards Institute, New York, NY. Tel: (212) 642-4900, Web Site: www.ansi.org (1)

American Nicaraguan Foundation, Miami, FL. Tel: (305) 374-3391, Web Site: www.aidnicaragua.org (1)

American Numismatic Association, Colorado Springs, CO. Tel: (719) 632-2646, Web Site: www.money.org (1)

American Nurses' Association, Silver Spring, MD. Tel: (301) 628-5000, (800) 284-2378, (800) 274-4262, FAX: (301) 628-5001, Web Site: www.nursingworld.org (1)

American Ostomy Supply, Earth City, MO. Tel: (314) 291-2900, (800) 858-5858, FAX: (800) 545-0065 (16)

American Period Lighting Inc, Lancaster, PA. Tel: (717) 392-5649, FAX: (717) 509-3127, E-Mail: conygham@yahoo.com, Web Site: www.americanperiod.com (8)

The American Phytopathological Society, Saint Paul, MN. Tel: (651) 454-7250, Web Site: www.apsnet.org (1)

American Power Conversion Corp, West Kingston, RI. Tel: (401) 789-5735, (800) 788-2208, FAX: (401) 789-3710, E-Mail: public.relations@apcc.com, Web Site: www.apcc.com (3)

American Preferred Reader's Service Inc, Fort Lauderdale, FL. Tel: (954) 489-2443, FAX: (954) 492-2343, E-Mail: jfarrell@amerpref.com, Web Site: www.amerpref.com (18)

American Printing House for the Blind, Louisville, KY. Tel: (502) 895-2405, (800) 223-1839, FAX: (502) 899-2274, E-Mail: info@aph.org, Web Site: www.aph.org (7)

American Psychological Association, Washington, DC. Tel: (202) 336-5500, (800) 374-2721, FAX: (202) 336-5568, E-Mail: order@apa.org, Web Site: www.apa.org (1)

American Radio Relay League, Newington, CT. Tel: (860) 594-0200, Web Site: www.arrl.org (1)

American Recreation Products Inc, Saint Louis, MO. Tel: (314) 576-8000, FAX: (314) 576-8072 (11)

American Red Cross, Washington, DC. Tel: (703) 303-5000 X5, (800) RED-CROSS, Web Site: www.redcross.org (1)

American Research Corp, El Monte, CA. Tel: (626) 284-1904, (800) FIND-ARC, (800) 346-3272, FAX: (626) 284-4213, E-Mail: arcinfo@800findarc.com, Web Site: www.800findarc.com (3)

American Running Association, Bethesda, MD. Tel: (301) 913-9517, (800) 776-2732, FAX: (301) 913-9520, E-Mail: run@americanrunning.org, Web Site: www.americanrunning.org (1)

American Science & Surplus, Niles, IL. Tel: (847) 647-0020, (800) SCI-PLUS, FAX: (847) 647-5010, E-Mail: info@sciplus.com, Web Site: www.sciplus.com (9)

American Securities Capital Partners, New York, NY. Tel: (212) 476-8000, Web Site: www.american-securities.com (15)

American Slide-Chart Corp, Carol Stream, IL. Tel: (630) 665-3333, (800) 323-4433, FAX: (630) 665-3491, E-Mail: info2@americanslidechart.com, Web Site: www.americanslidechart.com (27)

American Society for Quality-ASQ, Milwaukee, WI. Tel: (414) 272-8575, (800) 248-1946, FAX: (414) 272-1734, E-Mail: help@asq.org, Web Site: www.asq.org (1)

American Society for Training & Development, Alexandria, VA. Tel: (703) 683-8100, (800) NAT-ASTD, FAX: (703) 683-8103, Web Site: www.astd.org (1)

American Society of Civil Engineers, Reston, VA. Tel: (703) 295-6000, (800) 548-2723, FAX: (703) 295-6343, Web Site: www.asce.org (1)

American Society of Interior Designers, Washington, DC. Tel: (202) 546-3480, FAX: (202) 546-3240, E-Mail: asid@asid.org, Web Site: www.asid.org (1)

American Society of Journalists & Authors Directory, New York, NY. Tel: (212) 997-0947, FAX: (212) 768-7414, E-Mail: asjany@ibm.net (43)

American Society of Mechanical Engineers, New York, NY. Tel: (973) 882-1167, (800) 843-2763, FAX: (973) 882-1717, E-Mail: infocentral@asme.org, Web Site: www.asme.org (1)

American Society of Media Photographers (ASMP), Philadelphia, PA. Tel: (215) 451-ASMP, FAX: (215) 451-0880, Web Site: www.asmp.org (40)

American Society of Radiologic Technologists, Albuquerque, NM. Tel: (505) 298-4500, Web Site: www.asrt.org (1)

American Society on Aging, San Francisco, CA. Tel: (415) 974-9600, (800) 537-9728, FAX: (415) 974-0300, E-Mail: info@asaging.org, Web Site: www.asaging.org (1)

American Solutions for Business, Glenwood, MN. Tel: (320) 634-5471, FAX: (320) 634-5265, Web Site: www.americanbus.com (25)

American Speech-Language-Hearing Association, Rockville, MD. Tel: (301) 897-5700, (800) 638-8255, E-Mail: productsales@asha.org, Web Site: www.asha.org (1)

American Spirit Graphics Corp, Minneapolis, MN. Tel: (612) 623-3333, FAX: (612) 623-9314, E-Mail: asgc@asgc.com, Web Site: www.asgc.com (27)

American Spirit Mailing, Howard Lake, MN. Tel: (320) 543-3737, FAX: (320) 543-3228, E-Mail: asgc@asgc-mail.com, Web Site: www.asgc.com (28)

American Stationery Co Inc, Peru, IN. Tel: (765) 473-4438, (800) 822-2577, FAX: (800) 253-9054, Web Site: www.americanstationery.com (10)

American Student Assistance, Boston, MA. Tel: (800) 999-9000, Web Site: www.amsa.com (1)

American Student List LLC, Farmingdale, NY. Tel: (516) 248-6100, (888) 462-5600, FAX: (516) 248-6364, E-Mail: sales@studentlist.com, Web Site: www.studentlist.com (23)

American Student Marketing LLC, Highland Park, IL. Tel: (847) 432-4329, Web Site: www.asmdm.com (23)

American Target Advertising Inc, Manassas, VA. Tel: (703) 392-7676, FAX: (703) 392-7654 (35)

American Tax Associates Inc, Columbus, OH. Tel: (614) 443-5343, FAX: (614) 443-0279 (20)

American Technical Publishers Inc, Orland Park, IL. Tel: (708) 957-1100, (800) 323-3471, FAX: (708) 957-1101, E-Mail: service@americantech.net, Web Site: www.go2atp.com (17)

American Teleservices Association, Indianapolis, IN. Tel: (317) 816-9336, (877) 779-3974, FAX: (317) 218-0323, Web Site: www.ataconnect.org (40)

American Thermoplastic Co, Pittsburgh, PA. Tel: (412) 967-0900, (800) 245-6600, FAX: (412) 967-9990, E-Mail: atc@binders.com, Web Site: www.binders.com (27)

American 3B Scientific, Tucker, GA. Tel: (770) 492-9111, Web Site: www.a3bs.com (16)

American Trim, Lima, OH. Tel: (419) 228-1145, FAX: (419) 996-4850, E-Mail: sales@amtrim.com, Web Site: www.amtrim.com (9)

American Trucking Association, Arlington, VA. Tel: (703) 838-1700, FAX: (800) 254-2571, E-Mail: atamembership@trucking.org, Web Site: www.truckline.com (1)

The American Vintage Library, Los Angeles, CA. Tel: (310) 552-3176, (800) 235-1919, Web Site: www.vintagelibrary.com (17)

American Writers & Artists Inc, Delray Beach, FL. Tel: (561) 278-5557, Web Site: www.awaionline.com (36)

Americana Sales Ventures Inc, Altamonte Springs, FL. Tel: (407) 862-8388, (800) 445-4302, FAX: (407) 862-6535, Web Site: www.americanashopper.com (35)

Americans for Peace Now, Washington, DC. Tel: (202) 408-9898, FAX: (202) 728-1895, E-Mail: apndc@peacenow.org (1)

Americansource Bergan, Chesterbrook, PA. Tel: (610) 727-7000, (800) 829-3132, E-Mail: info@amerisourcebergan.com, Web Site: www.amerisourcebergan.com (7)

AmeriCares, Stamford, CT. Tel: (203) 658-9500, Web Site: www.americares.org (1)

America's Call Center, Jacksonville, FL. Tel: (904) 224-2000, (800) 598-2580, FAX: (904) 737-1107, E-Mail: info@webcallusa.com, Web Site: www.webcallusa.com (29)

America's Finest Pet Doors, San Luis Obispo, CA. Tel: (805) 781-7700 X201, (800) 826-2871, FAX: (805) 781-9734, E-Mail: alan@petdoors.com, Web Site: www.petdoors.com (18)

AmericasMart Atlanta, Atlanta, GA. Tel: (404) 220-3000, FAX: (404) 220-3030, Web Site: www.americasmart.com (42)

Americatel Corp, Derwood, MD. Tel: (301) 610-4354, Web Site: www.startec.com (32)

AmeriComm, Chesapeake, VA. Tel: (303) 371-4400, FAX: (303) 371-2527, Web Site: www.americomm.net (23)

Americraft - The Gift Brokers Inc, Wendell, MA. Tel: (978) 544-7330, (800) 866-2723, FAX: (978) 544-2771, E-Mail: info@americraft.us, Web Site: www.americraft.us (16)

Amerikal Products, Waukegan, IL. Tel: (847) 244-3600, FAX: (847) 244-2860, E-Mail: info@amerikal.com, Web Site: www.amerikal.com (25)

AmeriList Inc, Pomona, NY. Tel: (800) 457-2899, Web Site: www.amerilist.com (23)

AmeriMark Holdings LLC, Cleveland, OH. Tel: (440) 325-2000, FAX: (440) 234-8925, Web Site: www.amerimark.com (21)

Ameriprise Financial Services Inc, Minneapolis, MN. Tel: (651) 671-3434, (612) 671-3131, (800) 386-2042, Web Site: www.ameriprise.com (14)

Ameristar Casinos, Las Vegas, NV. Tel: (702) 567-7059 (19)

Amerisure Insurance Cos, Farmington Hills, MI. Tel: (248) 615-9000, (800) 257-1900, FAX: (248) 615-8224, Web Site: www.amerisure.com (15)

Ameritech Services Inc, Milwaukee, WI. Tel: (800) 924-1000, Web Site: www.ameritech.com (16)

Amerson, Ken, Oblate Missions, San Antonio, TX. Tel: (210) 736-1685, FAX: (210) 736-1314 (1)

Ames Specialty Packaging & Digital Print, Somerville, MA. Tel: (617) 776-3360, (800) 521-2637, FAX: (617) 623-8895, E-Mail: info@amespage.com, Web Site: www.amespage.com (26)

Ames Taping Tool System Inc, Stone Mountain, GA. Tel: (770) 243-2647, FAX: (770) 243-2658, Web Site: www.amestools.com (9)

Ames-Tru-Temper, Camp Hill, PA. Tel: (304) 424-3000, FAX: (304) 424-3330 (8)

Amestoy, Jay, Mazda North American Operations, Irvine, CA. Tel: (949) 727-1990, (800) 222-6500, FAX: (949) 727-6101, Web Site: www.mazdausa.com (16)

Amica Insurance, Lincoln, RI. Tel: (401) 334-6000, (800) 652-6422, FAX: (401) 334-4241, Web Site: www.amica.com (15)

Amichetti, Dennis, Amichetti, Lewis & Associates Inc, Wayne, PA. Tel: (610) 341-9545, E-Mail: ala300@aol.com (23)

Amichetti, Lewis & Associates Inc, Wayne, PA. Tel: (610) 341-9545, E-Mail: ala300@aol.com (23)

Amigo Mobility International Inc, Bridgeport, MI. Tel: (989) 777-0910, (800) 692-6446, FAX: (989) 777-8184, E-Mail: info@myamigo.com, Web Site: www.myamigo.com (16)

Amiral, Tracy, Making It Big, Cotati, CA. Tel: (707) 795-1995, (877) 644-1995, FAX: (707) 795-4874, E-Mail: mib@makingitbig.com, Web Site: www.makingitbig.com (2)

Amity Unlimited Inc, Cincinnati, OH. Tel: (513) 554-4500, FAX: (513) 554-0450, Web Site: www.amityunlimited.com (28)

Amjadi, Kamran, E-Centives Inc, Bethesda, MD. Tel: (240) 333-6100, (877) 323-6848, FAX: (240) 333-6250, E-Mail: sales@e-centives.com, Web Site: www.e-centives.com (32)

Ammann, Dieter, Fulfillment Express Inc, Pico Rivera, CA. Tel: (562) 948-4400, (800) 700-9295, FAX: (562) 948-4459, E-Mail: information@fex.com, Web Site: www.fex.com (28)

AmMed Direct, Antioch, TN. Tel: (615) 941-3900, Web Site: www.ammeddirect.com (7)

Ammendola, John, Response Insurance, Scranton, PA. Tel: (203) 634-7255, (800) 518-2984, FAX: (203) 634-7319, E-Mail: webcs@response.com, Web Site: www.response.com (15)

Ammiano, Tom, Golden Gate Transportation District, San Rafael, CA. Tel: (415) 921-5858, FAX: (415) 923-2014, Web Site: www.goldengate.org (16)

Amnesty International USA, New York, NY. Tel: (212) 807-8400, FAX: (212) 989-5478, E-Mail: vpotter@aiusa.org, Web Site: www.amnestyusa.org (1)

Amoroso, Betty, Al Paul Lefton Co Inc, Philadelphia, PA. Tel: (215) 923-9600, FAX: (215) 351-4298, Web Site: www.lefton.com (35)

Amos, Daniel, P., American Family Life Assurance Co of Columbus (AFLAC), Columbus, GA. Tel: (706) 323-3431, (800) 992-3522, FAX: (706) 660-7446, Web Site: www.aflac.com (15)

Amos Press, Inc, Sidney, OH. Tel: (937) 498-2111, FAX: (937) 498-0876, Web Site: www.amospress. com (17)

Amott, Teres L., Hobart & William Smith Colleges, Geneva, NY. Tel: (315) 781-3000, (800) 852-2256, FAX: (315) 781-3655, Web Site: www.hws.edu (19)

Ampersand Press, Port Townsend, WA. Tel: (360) 379-5187, (800) 624-4263, FAX: (360) 379-0324, E-Mail: info@ampersandpress.com, Web Site: www.ampersandpress.com (11)

Amplify Federal Credit Union, Austin, TX. Tel: (512) 834-6519, Web Site: www.goamplify.com (1)

Amrel, El Monte, CA. Tel: (626) 443-6818, (800) 654-9838, FAX: (626) 443-8600, E-Mail: amrel@ amrel.com, Web Site: www.amrel.com (16)

Amrigon, Bloomfield Hills, MI. Tel: (248) 332-2300, FAX: (248) 333-9710 (29)

Amsterdam Printing, Amsterdam, NY. Tel: (518) 842-6000, (800) 203-9917, FAX: (518) 843-5204, E-Mail: customerservice@amsterdamprinting.com, Web Site: www.amsterdamprinting.com (16)

Amtelco, McFarland, WI. Tel: (608) 838-4194, (800) 356-9148, FAX: (608) 838-8367, E-Mail: info@ amtelco.com, Web Site: www.amtelco.com (16)

Amtower, Mark, Amtower & Co Federal Direct, Highland, MD. Tel: (240) 882-9546, E-Mail: markamtower@gmail.com, Web Site: www. federaldirect.net (20)

Amtower & Co Federal Direct, Highland, MD. Tel: (240) 882-9546, E-Mail: markamtower@gmail. com, Web Site: www.federaldirect.net (20)

Amvac Chemical Corp, Los Angeles, CA. Tel: (323) 264-3910, FAX: (323) 268-1028, Web Site: www. amvac-chemical.com (8)

Amway Global, Ada, MI. Tel: (616) 787-6000, Web Site: www.amwayglobal.com (7)

An-Ser Services, Green Bay, WI. Tel: (920) 490-7000, (800) 723-0000, E-Mail: allanf@anser.com, Web Site: www.anser.com (29)

Analytic Recruiting Inc, New York, NY. Tel: (212) 545-8511, FAX: (212) 545-8520, E-Mail: rita@ analyticrecruiting.com, Web Site: www. analyticrecruiting.com (20)

Analytical Measurements, Chester, NJ. Tel: (800) 635-5580, FAX: (973) 399-1446, E-Mail: phmeter@ bellatlantic.net, Web Site: www. analyticalmeasurements.com (9)

AnalyticsIQ Inc, Atlanta, GA. Tel: (770) 407-8855, Web Site: www.analytics-iq.com (30)

Anatomical Chart Co, Chicago, IL. Tel: (847) 679-4700, (800) 621-7500, FAX: (847) 674-0211, E-Mail: service@anatomical.com, Web Site: www. anatomical.com (7)

Anchor Computer Inc, Farmingdale, NY. Tel: (631) 293-6100, Web Site: www.anchorcomputer.com (22)

Ancient Circles, Willits, CA. Tel: (800) 726-8032, FAX: (707) 459-0261, E-Mail: ancient@pacific.net, Web Site: www.ancientcircles.com (8)

ANCOR, Troy, MI. Tel: (248) 740-8866, (800) 229-3860, FAX: (248) 740-9025, Web Site: www. anchorinfo.com (22)

Anda Inc, Weston, FL. Tel: (954) 217-4144, Web Site: www.andanet.com (7)

Andaloro, Vincent, Latin-Pak, Chesterfield, MO. Tel: (636) 536-5344, (800) 625-4283, FAX: (636) 536-9456, E-Mail: latinpak@latinpak.com, Web Site: www.latinpak.com (35)

Andell Packaging Corp, Manhasset, NY. Tel: (718) 937-6500, FAX: (718) 482-9416 (27)

Anderberg, Jack, Anderberg-Lund Printing, Saint Louis Park, MN. Tel: (952) 920-9720, (800) 231-9777, FAX: (952) 920-1103, E-Mail: sales@ anderberglund.com, Web Site: www.anderberglund. com (27)

Anderberg-Lund Printing, Saint Louis Park, MN. Tel: (952) 920-9720, (800) 231-9777, FAX: (952) 920-1103, E-Mail: sales@anderberglund.com, Web Site: www.anderberglund.com (27)

Andersen, Bob, Andersen Advertising, Jacksonville, FL. Tel: (904) 733-7240, (877) 653-9621, E-Mail: bob@andersenadvertising.com, Web Site: www. andersenadvertising.com (35)

Andersen, Gary, Garvan Communications Inc, Locust Valley, NY. Tel: (516) 827-4000, FAX: (516) 827-4001, Web Site: www.garvan.com (35)

Andersen, Jan, Bellacor, Mendota Heights, MN. Tel: (651) 294-2500, (877) 723-5522, FAX: (651) 294-2595, E-Mail: customerservice@bellacor.com, Web Site: www.bellacor.com (8)

Andersen, Jean, Taylor Corp, North Mankato, MN. Tel: (507) 625-2828, FAX: (507) 625-3388 (16)

Andersen, Jean, The Occasions Group, North Mankato, MN. Tel: (507) 625-6464 (16)

Andersen, John, Admore Inc, Macomb, MI. Tel: (810) 949-8200, (800) 523-6673, FAX: (800) 215-2664, Web Site: www.admoreonline.com (10)

Andersen, Nancy, Andersen Design, East Boothbay, ME. Tel: (207) 350-4057, (866) 711-8421, E-Mail: studio@andersenstudio.com, Web Site: www. andersenstudio.com (33)

Andersen, Paul, Current USA Inc, Colorado Springs, CO. Tel: (719) 594-4100, (877) 665-4458, FAX: (719) 531-2283, Web Site: www.currentinc.com (6)

Andersen, Weston, Andersen Design, East Boothbay, ME. Tel: (207) 350-4057, (866) 711-8421, E-Mail: studio@andersenstudio.com, Web Site: www. andersenstudio.com (33)

Andersen Advertising, Jacksonville, FL. Tel: (904) 733-7240, (877) 653-9621, E-Mail: bob@ andersenadvertising.com, Web Site: www. andersenadvertising.com (35)

Andersen Design, East Boothbay, ME. Tel: (207) 350-4057, (866) 711-8421, E-Mail: studio@ andersenstudio.com, Web Site: www. andersenstudio.com (33)

Anderson, A. Richard, T Marzetti Co Inc, Columbus, OH. Tel: (614) 846-2232, FAX: (614) 848-8330, Web Site: www.marzetti.com (4)

Anderson, A., Dreis & Krump Manufacturing Co, Peotone, IL. Tel: (708) 258-1200, FAX: (708) 258-9682, E-Mail: chicago@dreis-krump.com, Web Site: www.dreis-krump.com (16)

Anderson, Al, Minnesota Public Radio, Saint Paul, MN. Tel: (651) 290-1500, (800) 228-7123, FAX: (651) 290-1260, E-Mail: mail@mpr.org, Web Site: www.mpr.org (1)

Anderson, Anna, Marie, Blue Cross & Blue Shield Cobalt, Waukesha, WI. Tel: (262) 523-4020, Web Site: www.bcbsuw.org (15)

Anderson, Barbara, Barbara S Anderson, Ann Arbor, MI. Tel: (734) 995-0125, FAX: (734) 994-5207 (39)

Anderson, Bob, Butler Schein Animal Health, Dublin, OH. Tel: (614) 761-9095, (888) 691-2724, FAX: (888) 329-3861, Web Site: www.butlerschein.com (16)

Anderson, Carole, A, American Society on Aging, San Francisco, CA. Tel: (415) 974-9600, (800) 537-9728, FAX: (415) 974-0300, E-Mail: info@ asaging.org, Web Site: www.asaging.org (1)

Anderson, David, Cakuun, Asheville, NC. Tel: (828) 225-5505, E-Mail: transformyourbrand@cakuun. com, Web Site: cakuun.com (13)

Anderson, Doug, Swanson Health Products, Fargo, ND. Tel: (701) 356-2800, (800) 824-4491, FAX: (800) 726-7691, E-Mail: customercare@ swansonvitamins.com, Web Site: www. swansonvitamins.com (35)

Anderson, Dwight, Mail Advertising Corp, Fort Worth, TX. Tel: (817) 390-7726, FAX: (817) 390-7223, E-Mail: wjjohnson@star-telegram.com, Web Site: www.macus.com (28)

Anderson, Elise, Andersen Design, East Boothbay, ME. Tel: (207) 350-4057, (866) 711-8421, E-Mail: studio@andersenstudio.com, Web Site: www. andersenstudio.com (33)

Anderson, Frances, List Marketing Group Inc, Cleveland, OH. Tel: (216) 990-2000, Web Site: www. listmarketinggroup.com (23)

Anderson, Gregg, New Zealand Tourism Board, Santa Monica, CA. Tel: (310) 857-2213, FAX: (310) 395-5453, E-Mail: nzinfo@nztb.govt.nz, Web Site: www.purenz.com (19)

Anderson, Harold, Vermont Tubbs, Whitefield, NH. Tel: (603) 837-2547, E-Mail: dogurkis@ vermonttubbs.com, Web Site: www.vermonttubbs. com (8)

Anderson, Jan, AIIM International, Silver Spring, MD. Tel: (301) 587-8202, (800) 477-2446, FAX: (301) 587-2711, E-Mail: aiim@aiim.org, Web Site: www. aiim.org (1)

Anderson, Janet, Edible Landscaping, Afton, VA. Tel: (434) 361-9134, (800) 524-4156, FAX: (434) 361-1916, E-Mail: info@ediblelandscaping.com, Web Site: www.eat-it.com (8)

Anderson, John, F., Anderson Niebuhr & Associates Inc, Arden Hills, MN. Tel: (651) 486-8712, (800) 678-5577, FAX: (651) 486-0536, E-Mail: info@ ana-inc.com, Web Site: www.ana-inc.com (30)

Anderson, Jon, Random Lengths Publications Inc, Eugene, OR. Tel: (541) 686-9925, (888) 686-9925, FAX: (541) 686-9629, (800) 874-7979, E-Mail: rlmail@rlpi.com, Web Site: www.randomlengths. com (17)

Anderson, Joy, M., Journal Star, Peoria, IL. Tel: (309) 686-3026, FAX: (309) 686-3265, Web Site: www. pjstar.com (17)

Anderson, Karen, MI-T-M Corp, Peosta, IA. Tel: (863) 556-7484, Web Site: www.mitm.com (9)

Anderson, Kathy, Florida Institute of CPA's, Tallahassee, FL. Tel: (850) 224-2727, (800) 342-3197 (FL), FAX: (850) 222-8190, E-Mail: msc@ficpa.org, Web Site: www.ficpa.org (1)

Anderson, Kelly, Vane & Friends, Chappaqua, NY. Tel: (914) 238-8890, E-Mail: info@vaneandfriends. com, Web Site: www.vaneandfriends.com (35)

Anderson, Kent, National Business Furniture Inc, Milwaukee, WI. Tel: (414) 276-8511, (800) 558-1010, FAX: (414) 276-8371, Web Site: www. nationalbusinessfurniture.com (10)

Anderson, Kent, officefurniture.com, Milwaukee, WI. Tel: (414) 272-6080, (800) 933-0053, FAX: (414) 272-0248, (800) 468-1526, Web Site: www. officefurniture.com (8)

Anderson, Kyle, Quill Corp, Palatine, IL. Tel: (847) 634-4800, (800) 789-1331, FAX: (800) 789-6630, Web Site: www.quill.com (16)

Anderson, Lori, International Sign Association International Convention, Alexandria, VA. Tel: (703) 836-4012, (866) WHY-SIGN, FAX: (703) 836-8353, Web Site: www.signs.org (42)

Anderson, Lori, International Sign Association, Alexandria, VA. Tel: (703) 836-4012, FAX: (703) 836-8353, Web Site: www.signs.org (42)

Anderson, Mark, Demco Inc, Madison, WI. Tel: (608) 241-1201, FAX: (608) 241-1799, E-Mail: custserv@demco.com, Web Site: www.demco.com (10)

Anderson, Mark, Impact Mailing, Minneapolis, MN. Tel: (612) 521-6245, FAX: (612) 521-1349, E-Mail: sales@impactmailing.com, Web Site: www.impactmailing.com (28)

Anderson, Mary, CheckVantage, Austin, TX. Tel: (512) 442-2332, (877) 243-2501, FAX: (512) 442-5515, E-Mail: marya@checkvantage.com, Web Site: www.checkvantage.com (14)

Anderson, Michael, J, SpencerStuart, Chicago, IL. Tel: (312) 822-0088, FAX: (312) 822-0116, Web Site: www.spencerstuart.com (20)

Anderson, Norma, B., American Psychological Association, Washington, DC. Tel: (202) 336-5500, (800) 374-2721, FAX: (202) 336-5568, E-Mail: order@apa.org, Web Site: www.apa.org (1)

Anderson, Peggy, Concordia Publishing House, Saint Louis, MO. Tel: (314) 268-1000, (800) 325-3040, FAX: (314) 268-1329, E-Mail: order@cph.org, Web Site: www.cph.org (17)

Anderson, Peter M., Media Space Solutions, Norwalk, CT. Tel: (203) 849-8855, (888) 672-2100, FAX: (203) 849-5946, E-Mail: nsb@mindspring.com, Web Site: www.mediaspacesolutions.com (31)

Anderson, Price, DirectMail.com, Prince Frederick, MD. Tel: (888) 690-2252, FAX: (301) 855-9810, Web Site: www.directmail.com (28)

Anderson, Professor Sir Roy, Glaxo Smith Kline, Research Triangle Park, NC. Tel: (919) 483-2100, (888) 825-5249, FAX: (919) 248-8383, Web Site: www.gsk.com (16)

Anderson, R., John, Levi Strauss & Co, San Francisco, CA. Tel: (415) 501-6000, FAX: (415) 501-7112, Web Site: www.levistrauss.com (16)

Anderson, R., The Doctor's Co, Napa, CA. Tel: (707) 226-0176, E-Mail: info@thedoctors.com, Web Site: www.thedoctors.com (15)

Anderson, Ray, C., Callaway Gardens, Pine Mountain, GA. Tel: (706) 663-2281, (800) CALLAWAY, FAX: (706) 663-6812, E-Mail: info@callawaygardens.com, Web Site: www.callawaygardens.com (19)

Anderson, Rick, Duracell, Bethel, CT. Tel: (203) 796-4000, FAX: (203) 207-7842, Web Site: www.duracell.com (16)

Anderson, Robert, Burnett Marketing Inc, Mount Prospect, IL. Tel: (800) 837-6906, FAX: (800) 837-6978, E-Mail: burnettmkt@aol.com, Web Site: www.burnettmarketing.com (23)

Anderson, Robert, D., Winmill & Co, New York, NY. Tel: (212) 785-0900, (800) 400-MIDAS, FAX: (212) 363-1100, E-Mail: info@midasfunds.com, Web Site: www.midasfunds.com (14)

Anderson, Roger, Young America Corp, Young America, MN. Tel: (952) 467-1100, FAX: (952) 467-3895, Web Site: www.young-america.com (28)

Anderson, Scott, Harold Walter Siebens School of Business, Storm Lake, IA. Tel: (712) 749-2410, (800) 383-2821, FAX: (712) 749-2037, Web Site: www2.bvu.edu/academics/business (41)

Anderson, Sean, Vegetarian Awareness Network/VEGANET, Washington, DC. Tel: (800) USA-VEGE, (800) 872-8343, FAX: (877) 329-8343 (1)

Anderson, Sheila, Shop.com, Monterey, CA. Tel: (831) 647-2489, (866) 746-7005, FAX: (831) 644-9283, Web Site: www.shop.com (16)

Anderson, Terry, Sensient Technologies, Saint Louis, MO. Tel: (314) 889-7600, (800) 325-8110, FAX: (314) 658-7318, Web Site: www.sensient-tech.com (16)

Anderson, Terry, White Cap Wholesale Contractors Supplies, Costa Mesa, CA. Tel: (800) 944-8322, FAX: (866) 791-8396, E-Mail: customerservice@whitecap.com, Web Site: www.whitecapdirect.com (16)

Anderson, Thelma, Stokes Seeds Inc, Buffalo, NY. Tel: (716) 695-6980, (800) 396-9238, FAX: (888) 834-3334, Web Site: www.stokeseeds.com (8)

Anderson, Thomas, Volvo Cars of North America, Northvale, NJ. Tel: (201) 768-7300, (800) 458-1552, E-Mail: customercare@volvocars.com, Web Site: www.volvocars.com (16)

Barbara S Anderson, Ann Arbor, MI. Tel: (734) 995-0125, FAX: (734) 994-5207 (39)

Anderson Direct Marketing, Poway, CA. Tel: (888) 694-5094, Web Site: www.andersondirectmarketing.com (35)

MD Anderson Cancer Center - Children's Art Project, Houston, TX. Tel: (713) 745-2575, (800) 231-1580, FAX: (713) 794-1950, E-Mail: krenner@mdanderson.org, Web Site: www.childrensart.org (1)

Anderson Niebuhr & Associates Inc, Arden Hills, MN. Tel: (651) 486-8712, (800) 678-5577, FAX: (651) 486-0536, E-Mail: info@ana-inc.com, Web Site: www.ana-inc.com (30)

Anderson/skow, San Francisco, CA. Tel: (888) 983-0880, Web Site: www.andersonskow.com (20)

Hanna Andersson Corp, Portland, OR. Tel: (503) 242-0920, (800) 222-0544, FAX: (503) 321-5289, Web Site: www.hannaandersson.com (2)

Andrade, Jeff, Princess Cruises (HQ), Santa Clarita, CA. Tel: (661) 753-0000, (800) Princess, FAX: (661) 284-4765, Web Site: www.princesscruises.com (19)

Andrade, Luis, Union Pen Co, Hagaman, NY. Tel: (800) 846-6600, FAX: (518) 770-7018, Web Site: www.unionpen.com (5)

Andrasko, Nancy M., Roovers Inc, Hazleton, PA. Tel: (570) 455-7548, FAX: (570) 454-1477 (34)

Andre, Julie, Starmount Life Insurance Co, Baton Rouge, LA. Tel: (225) 926-2888, (888) 729-7827, (888) 729-5433, E-Mail: info@starmountlife.com, Web Site: www.starmountlife.com (15)

Andrea, Douglas, Andrea Electronics Corp, Bohemia, NY. Tel: (631) 719-1800, (800) 442-7787, FAX: (631) 719-1950, Web Site: www.andreaelectronics.com (16)

Andrea, John, Andrea Electronics Corp, Bohemia, NY. Tel: (631) 719-1800, (800) 442-7787, FAX: (631) 719-1950, Web Site: www.andreaelectronics.com (16)

Andrea Electronics Corp, Bohemia, NY. Tel: (631) 719-1800, (800) 442-7787, FAX: (631) 719-1950, Web Site: www.andreaelectronics.com (16)

Andrea Jr, Frank A.D., Andrea Electronics Corp, Bohemia, NY. Tel: (631) 719-1800, (800) 442-7787, FAX: (631) 719-1950, Web Site: www.andreaelectronics.com (16)

Andreotti, Lamberto, Bristol-Myers Squibb Co, New York, NY. Tel: (212) 546-4000, FAX: (212) 546-9544, Web Site: www.bms.com (16)

Andreozzi, Lou, LexisNexis, Miamisburg, OH. Tel: (937) 865-6800, (800) 227-9597, (800) 227-4908, FAX: (800) 348-2609, E-Mail: pr@lexisnexis.com, Web Site: www.lexisnexis.com (16)

Andrew Associates Inc, Enfield, CT. Tel: (860) 253-0000, FAX: (860) 741-0850, Web Site: www.andrewmail.com (23)

Andrew Wireless Solutions, Westchester, IL. Tel: (800) 349-5444, Web Site: www.andrew.com (16)

Andrews, C.E., SLM Corp, Reston, VA. Tel: (703) 810-3000, FAX: (703) 984-5042, Web Site: www.salliemae.com (16)

Andrews, Chris, Mitchell International, San Diego, CA. Tel: (858) 368-7000, FAX: (858) 238-9111, Web Site: www.mitchell.com (17)

Andrews, Gaylen, B-T-B Internet Marketing Solutions, Middle Island, NY. Tel: (631) 924-3888, E-Mail: linickgroup@gmail.com, Web Site: www.linick.net; 222.asklinick.com (39)

Andrews, Gaylen, Copywriter's Council of America - (Freelancers), Middle Island, NY. Tel: (631) 924-3888, FAX: (631) 924-8555, E-Mail: cca4dmcopy@gmail.com, Web Site: www.linick.net; www.andrewlinickdirectmarketing.com (39)

Andrews, Jim, Sierra Inc, Racine, WI. Tel: (262) 638-1851, FAX: (414) 638-1852, E-Mail: support@sierrainc.com, Web Site: www.sierra.com (3)

Andrews, Patricia, Gamma Photo Labs LLC, Chicago, IL. Tel: (312) 337-0022, FAX: (312) 337-3753, Web Site: www.photobition.com (16)

Andrews, Roger, Veritas Analytics Inc, Sterling, VA. Tel: (703) 707-5620, Web Site: www.veritas-analytics.com (30)

ANDREWS WHARTON INC, Commack, NY. Tel: (631) 470-4546 (35)

Andriessen, Roel, G.M., Golden Trophy, Chicago, IL. Tel: (800) 835-6607, FAX: (800) 835-6601, E-Mail: goldentrophy@bruss.com, Web Site: www.giftsteaksonline.com (4)

Andrzejewski, Steve, King Pharmaceuticals, Inc, Bristol, TN. Tel: (423) 989-8000, (888) 840-5370, FAX: (423) 274-8677, Web Site: www.kingpharm.com (7)

Andsor Research Inc, Etobicoke, ON Canada. Tel: (416) 245-8073, FAX: (416) 240-8473 (22)

aNETorder/American Mailers, Naperville, IL. Tel: (630) 579-8800, Web Site: www.anetorder.com (28)

Angel, Myron, American Spirit Graphics Corp, Minneapolis, MN. Tel: (612) 623-3333, FAX: (612) 623-9314, E-Mail: asgc@asgc.com, Web Site: www.asgc.com (27)

Angel Records, New York, NY. Tel: (212) 786-8600, FAX: (212) 253-3119, Web Site: www.angelrecords.com (3)

Angel Sales Inc, Chicago, IL. Tel: (773) 883-8858, FAX: (773) 883-8889, E-Mail: info@angelsales.com, Web Site: www.angelsales.com (31)

Angelica Image Apparel, Saint Louis, MO. Tel: (314) 854-3800, (800) 235-8410, Web Site: www.angelica.com (16)

Angelillo, Thomas, Coastal Living, Birmingham, AL. Tel: (205) 877-6007, FAX: (205) 445-8655, E-Mail: coastalliving@customersvc.com, Web Site: www.coastalliving.com (43)

Angelillo, Tom, K., Southern Progress Corp, Birmingham, AL. Tel: (205) 877-6000, FAX: (205) 877-6283, Web Site: www.southernprogress.com (17)

Angelino, Mark, E., Sprint PCS, Overland Park, KS. Tel: (800) 927-2199, Web Site: www.sprintpcs.com (16)

Angell, Marsha, New England Journal of Medicine, Waltham, MA. Tel: (781) 893-3800, FAX: (781) 893-7729, Web Site: www.nejm.org (17)

Angelsom, Mark, A., Veriad, Brea, CA. Tel: (714) 990-2700, (800) 962-0658, FAX: (800) 962-0658, E-Mail: info@veriad.com, Web Site: www.veriad.com (16)

Angevine, Sandy, ADP Inc, Roseland, NJ. Tel: (973) 974-5000, (800) 225-5237, FAX: (973) 974-3334, Web Site: www.adp.com (16)

Angler's Catalog Co, Eagle, ID. Tel: (208) 378-9536, (800) 657-8040, FAX: (208) 735-8758, E-Mail: sales@anglers-catalog.com, Web Site: www.anglers-catalog.com (11)

The Angler's Den, Pawling, NY. Tel: (845) 855-5182, E-Mail: flyfish@anglersden.net, Web Site: www.anglersden.net (11)

Anglicans United & Latimer Press, Cedar Hill, TX. Tel: (972) 293-7443, (800) 553-3645, FAX: (972) 293-7559, E-Mail: anglicansunited@sbcglobal.net, Web Site: www.anglicansunited.com, www.latimerpress.com (1)

Angstrom, Wayne, Angstrom Graphics, Hollywood, FL. Tel: (954) 920-7300, E-Mail: wayne.angstrom@st-ives-usa.com, Web Site: www.angstromgraphics.com (27)

Angstrom Graphics, Hollywood, FL. Tel: (954) 920-7300, E-Mail: wayne.angstrom@st-ives-usa.com, Web Site: www.angstromgraphics.com (27)

Angus, Jason, Catalyst Marketing Group, Richmond, VA. Tel: (804) 288-9440, FAX: (804) 288-9824, E-Mail: info@catalyst121.com, Web Site: www.catalyst121.com (35)

Anheuser-Busch Inc Promotional Products Group, Shelton, CT. Tel: (800) 742-5283, Web Site: www.budshop.com (6)

Animal Fund, San Francisco, CA. Tel: (415) 775-4636, E-Mail: delphinus@aol.com, Web Site: www.animalfund.org (38)

Animal Health Express, Inc, Tucson, AZ. Tel: (520) 888-0294, (800) 533-8115, FAX: (520) 888-0297, (800) 437-9898, E-Mail: info@animalhealthexpress.com, Web Site: www.animalhealthexpress.com (5)

The Animal Medical Center, New York, NY. Tel: (212) 838-8100, FAX: (212) 832-9630, Web Site: www.amcny.org (16)

Animals Animals/Earth Scenes, Chatham, NY. Tel: (518) 392-5500, (800) 392-5503, FAX: (518) 392-5550, E-Mail: info@animalsanimals.com, Web Site: www.animalsanimals.com (38)

Ankeney, Shane, TBWA/Chiat/Day Inc, New York, NY. Tel: (212) 804-1000, FAX: (212) 804-1200, E-Mail: jamie.gallo@tbwachiat.com, Web Site: www.tbwachiat.com (35)

Anliker, Brad, Johnson & Quin Inc, Niles, IL. Tel: (847) 588-4800, FAX: (847) 647-6949, E-Mail: jqinfo@j-quin.com, Web Site: www.j-quin.com (28)

Annastas, Tom, BMI, Nashville, TN. Tel: (615) 401-2000, (800) 925-8451, FAX: (615) 401-2812, E-Mail: genlic@bmi.com, Web Site: www.bmi.com (1)

Anne Klein, New York, NY. Tel: (212) 536-9000, FAX: (212) 536-9000 (16)

Annell, John, The Segerdahl Corp, Wheeling, IL. Tel: (847) 541-1080, FAX: (847) 541-5237, Web Site: www.segerdahl.com/frameset.html (27)

Annie's Attic LLC, Big Sandy, TX. Tel: (903) 636-4303, FAX: (903) 636-4088, Web Site: www.anniesattic.com (11)

Annis, Mike, Rounder Mail Order, Burlington, MA. Tel: (617) 354-0700, (800) 768-6337, FAX: (617) 868-8769, E-Mail: info@rounder.com, Web Site: www.rounder.com (3)

Anop, Mike, Sheplers Catalog Sales Inc, Wichita, KS. Tel: (316) 946-3838, (800) 835-4004, FAX: (316) 946-3729, Web Site: www.sheplers.com (2)

Anritsu Co, Morgan Hill, CA. Tel: (408) 778-2000, (800) 267-4878, FAX: (408) 776-1744, Web Site: www.us.anritsu.com (16)

Ansafone Communications, Santa Ana, CA. Tel: (714) 560-1000, Web Site: www.ansafone.com (29)

Ansar Inc, Thompsons Station, TN. Tel: (615) 368-2025, Web Site: www.ansarinc.com (1)

Anschutz, Philip, F., Los Angeles Kings, Los Angeles, CA. Tel: (213) 742-7100, (888) KINGS-LA, FAX: (213) 742-7296, Web Site: kings.nhl.com (16)

Anson, Mark, J.P., Nuveen Investments, Chicago, IL. Tel: (312) 917-7700, (800) 257-8787, FAX: (312) 917-8049, Web Site: www.nuveen.com (14)

Anston, Decker, Landmark Communications Inc, Norfolk, VA. Tel: (757) 446-2010, (800) 446-2004, FAX: (757) 446-2489, Web Site: www.landmark.com (17)

Anstrand, Susan, Names in the News, Oakland, CA. Tel: (415) 989-3350, FAX: (415) 433-7796, E-Mail: name@nincal.com, Web Site: www.nincal.com (23)

Answer America, Saint Paul, MN. Tel: (800) 258-2669, FAX: (651) 644-8295, E-Mail: sales@answeramerica.com, Web Site: www.answeramerica.com (29)

AnswerNet Network, Willow Grove, PA. Tel: (800) 411-5777, FAX: (215) 659-6486, Web Site: www.answernetnetwork.com (29)

AnswerThink Inc, Miami, FL. Tel: (305) 375-8005, FAX: (305) 379-8810, Web Site: www.answerthink.com (35)

Antares Information Tech, Chadds Ford, PA. Tel: (631) 234-5700, (800) 330-2579, FAX: (631) 234-5472, E-Mail: steve@antares-iti.com, Web Site: www.antares-iti.com (21)

Anthem Blue Cross, Westlake Village, CA. Tel: (805) 557-6655, (800) 333-0912, FAX: (800) 557-6872, Web Site: www.bluecrossca.com (15)

Anthem Blue Cross Blue Shield, North Haven, CT. Tel: (203) 239-8381, (800) 545-0948, FAX: (203) 985-7918, Web Site: www.anthem.com (15)

Anthem Blue Cross Blue Shield, Saint Louis, MO. Tel: (314) 923-4444, (888) 877-9125, FAX: (314) 923-5151, E-Mail: moreinfo@bcbsmo.com, Web Site: www.bcbsmo.com (15)

Anthem Corporate Communications, Indianapolis, IN. Tel: (207) 822-7000, FAX: (207) 822-7741, Web Site: www.anthem.com (15)

Anthem Marketing, Chicago, IL. Tel: (312) 441-0382 (22)

Anthony, John, Cosco Industries Inc, Chicago, IL. Tel: (708) 867-5800, (800) 323-0253, FAX: (800) 323-0275 (16)

Anthony, Mark, Gardener's Eden, Merrimack, NH. Tel: (603) 888-9500, (800) 822-9600, FAX: (603) 577-8005, E-Mail: gsweeney@brookstone.com (8)

Anthony, Michael, F., Things Remembered, Highland Heights, OH. Tel: (440) 473-2000, (866) 902-4438, FAX: (440) 473-2018, E-Mail: customerservice@thingsremembered.com, Web Site: www.thingsremembered.com (6)

Anthro Photo File, Cambridge, MA. Tel: (617) 868-4784, FAX: (617) 484-6428, Web Site: www.anthrophoto.com (38)

Anti-Defamation League, New York, NY. Tel: (212) 885-5870, Web Site: www.adl.org (1)

Antik, Kandal, DB Consulting, Harrison, NY. Tel: (914) 698-2008, E-Mail: darcybev@yahoo.com (20)

Antiquarian Booksellers Association of America Inc, New York, NY. Tel: (212) 944-8291, FAX: (212) 944-8293, E-Mail: sbenne@abaa.org, Web Site: www.abaa.org (1)

Antique & Collectible Tools Inc, Pownal, ME. Tel: (207) 688-4962, FAX: (207) 688-4831, E-Mail: ceb@finetoolj.com, Web Site: www.finetoolj.com (11)

Antique Electronic Supply, Tempe, AZ. Tel: (480) 820-5411, (800) 706-6789, FAX: (480) 820-4643, E-Mail: info@tubesandmore.com, Web Site: www.tubesandmore.com (3)

Antique Rose Emporium, Brenham, TX. Tel: (800) 441-0002, FAX: (979) 836-0928, E-Mail: roses@industyinet.com, Web Site: www.weareroses.com (8)

Antman, Dan, Warren, Gorham & Lamont Inc, New York, NY. Tel: (617) 423-2020, Web Site: ria.thomsonreuters.com (17)

Antman, Mark, The Image Works Inc, Woodstock, NY. Tel: (845) 679-8500, (800) 475-8801, FAX: (845) 679-0606, E-Mail: info@theimageworks.com, Web Site: www.theimageworks.com (38)

Anton, Frank, Hanley Wood LLC, Washington, DC. Tel: (202) 452-0800, FAX: (202) 785-1974, Web Site: www.hanleywood.com (16)

Anton, Jennifer, Archer/Malmo, Memphis, TN. Tel: (901) 523-2000, FAX: (901) 524-5578, Web Site: www.archermalmo.com (35)

Anton, John, J., Ghirardelli Chocolate Co, San Leandro, CA. Tel: (510) 483-6970, (800) 877-9338, FAX: (510) 297-2649, Web Site: www.ghirardelli.com (16)

Antoniuk, David, J., Champion, Quincy, IL. Tel: (217) 222-5400, FAX: (217) 228-8260, Web Site: www.championpneumatic.com (16)

Antunez, Caroline, MxEnergy Inc, Stamford, CT. Tel: (203) 356-1318, Web Site: www.mxenergy.com (16)

Anuszkiewicz, Richard, VAGA (Visual Artists & Galleries Associations Inc), New York, NY. Tel: (212) 736-6666, FAX: (212) 736-6767, E-Mail: rpanzer@vaga.erols.com (38)

Anything Goes, Allenhurst, NJ. Tel: (732) 531-8040, Web Site: www.heavenlytreasures.com (6)

Aon's Affinity Insurance Services Inc, Hatboro, PA. Tel: (215) 773-4600, Web Site: www.aon.com (15)

APC By Schneider Electric, West Kingston, RI. Tel: (401) 789-5735, Web Site: www.apc.com (34)

Apollo Industries Inc, Smyrna, GA. Tel: (770) 433-0210, (800) 533-3548, FAX: (770) 433-0132, Web Site: www.apolloind.com (34)

Aponte Jr, Hiram, Hi-C Production, New Hyde Park, NY. Tel: (516) 746-2142, FAX: (516) 294-1964, E-Mail: haponte435@aol.com (27)

Apostolou, Theana, American Movie Classics Holding Corp, Jericho, NY. Tel: (516) 803-3000, FAX: (516) 803-3003, Web Site: www.amctv.com (16)

Apothecary Products Inc, Burnsville, MN. Tel: (952) 890-1940, (800) 328-2742, FAX: (800) 328-1584, Web Site: www.apothecaryproducts.com (7)

Appalachian Mountain Club, Boston, MA. Tel: (617) 523-0655, Web Site: www.outdoors.com (1)

Appalachian Nurseries, Inc, Chambersburg, PA. Tel: (717) 597-0066, (877) 743-4733, E-Mail: info@appnursery.com, Web Site: www.appnursery.com (8)

AppaLight, Spencer, WV. Tel: (304) 927-2978, E-Mail: wyro@appalight.com, Web Site: www.appalight.com (38)

Appel, Marsha, American Association of Advertising Agencies, New York, NY. Tel: (212) 682-2500, FAX: (212) 682-8391, Web Site: www.aaaa.org (40)

Appelbaum, Alan, Market Probe International Inc, New York, NY. Tel: (212) 725-7676, FAX: (212) 725-7529, E-Mail: info@marketprobeint.com, Web Site: www.marketprobeint.com (30)

Appelbaum, Bob, Cadie Products Corp, Paterson, NJ. Tel: (973) 278-8300, FAX: (973) 278-0303, E-Mail: emeyers@cadie.com, Web Site: www.cadieproducts.com (16)

Apperson, R.P., Apperson Print Management Services, Cerritos, CA. Tel: (562) 356-3333, (800) 877-2341, FAX: (562) 356-3310, E-Mail: sales@appersonprint.com, Web Site: www.appersonprint.com (27)

Apperson Print Management Services, Cerritos, CA. Tel: (562) 356-3333, (800) 877-2341, FAX: (562) 356-3310, E-Mail: sales@appersonprint.com, Web Site: www.appersonprint.com (27)

Apple Computer Inc, Cupertino, CA. Tel: (408) 996-1010, FAX: (408) 996-0275, Web Site: www.apple.com (16)

Appleton Coated LLC, Combined Locks, WI. Tel: (920) 968-3999, Web Site: www.appletoncoated.com (27)

Appleton Papers Inc, Appleton, WI. Tel: (920) 734-9841, FAX: (920) 991-8796, Web Site: www.appletonideas.com (25)

Applewhaite, Eleanor, Thirteen/WNET, New York, NY. FAX: (212) 560-1314, Web Site: www.thirteen.org (1)

Applications Development Corp, Dekalb, IL. Tel: (815) 754-7432, Web Site: www.appdevcorp.com (20)

Applied Info Group, Kenilworth, NJ. Tel: (908) 241-7007, Web Site: www.appliedinfogroup.com (22)

Applied Marketing Sciences LLC, Las Vegas, NV. Tel: (702) 220-3383, Web Site: www.appliedmktg.com (35)

Applied Printing Technologies, Moonachie, NJ. Tel: (201) 635-9447, (888) 282-4141, FAX: (201) 896-6839, E-Mail: vpsales@appliedprinting.com, Web Site: www.appliedprinting.com (27)

Appraisal Institute, Chicago, IL. Tel: (312) 335-4100, FAX: (312) 335-4400, E-Mail: info@appraisalinstitute.org, Web Site: www.appraisalinstitute.org (1)

Aptara, Inc, Falls Church, VA. Tel: (703) 352-0001, E-Mail: info@aptaracorp.com, Web Site: www.aptaracorp.com (16)

Aptimus, San Francisco, CA. Tel: (415) 896-2123 (22)

Aquilino, Dan, The Pennysaver Group Inc, Hanover, MD. Tel: (410) 684-2600, FAX: (410) 684-2065, Web Site: www.mdpennysaver.com (17)

Aquino, Anthony, Spectra Products LLC, Johnson City, NY. Tel: (607) 770-1985, FAX: (607) 798-7771, E-Mail: info@spectraproducts.com, Web Site: www.spectraproducts.com (31)

Arabea, George, Alco Chemical, Chattanooga, TN. Tel: (423) 629-1405, FAX: (423) 698-8723, Web Site: www.alcochemical.com (16)

Aradi, Theresa, Commemorative Brands Inc, Austin, TX. Tel: (512) 444-0571, FAX: (512) 444-0065 (16)

Aramark Uniform Services, Burbank, CA. Tel: (818) 953-2022, Web Site: www.aramark-uniform.com (2)

Arandell Corp, Menomonee Falls, WI. Tel: (262) 255-4400, (800) 558-8724, FAX: (262) 253-3162, E-Mail: jft@arandell.com, Web Site: www.arandell.com (27)

Arang, Renee, Baton Rouge Conventions & Visitors Bureau, Baton Rouge, LA. Tel: (225) 383-1825, (800) LA-ROUGE, FAX: (225) 346-1253, E-Mail: br@bracvb.com, Web Site: www.bracvb.com (1)

Arbill Safety Products, Philadelphia, PA. Tel: (215) 632-2000, (800) 523-5367, FAX: (800) 426-5808, E-Mail: orders@arbill.com, Web Site: www.arbill.com (9)

Arbit, Bruce, AB Data Ltd, Milwaukee, WI. Tel: (414) 961-6400, FAX: (414) 961-6410, E-Mail: info@abdata.com, Web Site: www.abdata.com (21)

The Arbitron Co, New York, NY. Tel: (212) 887-1314, FAX: (212) 887-1558, Web Site: www.arbitron.com (30)

Arbor Capital 1, Omaha, NE. Tel: (402) 991-4962 (14)

Arbor Commercial Mortgage, Uniondale, NY. Tel: (516) 229-6615, Web Site: www.thearbornet.com (14)

Arbor Day Foundation, Lincoln, NE. Tel: (402) 474-5655, Web Site: www.arborday.org (1)

Arbus Capital Ltd, Schaumburg, IL. Tel: (847) 290-9600, FAX: (847) 290-9601 (16)

Arcade Marketing, Inc, Chattanooga, TN. Tel: (423) 624-3301, FAX: (423) 622-4635 (27)

Arcamone, Gail, Save the Children Federation Inc, Westport, CT. Tel: (203) 221-4000, (800) 728-3843, FAX: (203) 222-1067, E-Mail: twebster@savethechildren.org, Web Site: www.savethechildren.org (1)

Arce, Carlos, NuStats Inc, West Lake Hills, TX. Tel: (512) 306-9065, (800) 44-STATS, FAX: (512) 306-9065, Web Site: www.nustats.com (30)

Arce, Maria, Battery Pros Inc, Horseshoe Beach, FL. Tel: (352) 498-2477, (800) 451-7171, FAX: (352) 498-2482, E-Mail: sales@probattery.com, Web Site: www.probattery.com (9)

Arcelor Mittal, Coatesville, PA. Tel: (610) 383-2000, FAX: (610) 383-5036, Web Site: www.arcelormittal.com (16)

ArcelorMittal, Chicago, IL. Tel: (312) 899-3440, FAX: (312) 899-3504, Web Site: www.mittalsteel.com (16)

Arch Telecom Inc, Austin, TX. Tel: (512) 492-0735, (800) 890-7575, FAX: (512) 495-7101, Web Site: www.archtelecom.com (16)

Archaeology Magazine, Long Island City, NY. Tel: (718) 472-3050, FAX: (718) 472-3051, E-Mail: production@archaeology.org, Web Site: www.archaeology.org (17)

Archer/Malmo, Memphis, TN. Tel: (901) 523-2000, FAX: (901) 524-5578, Web Site: www.archermalmo.com (35)

Archibald, Nolan, Black & Decker (US) Inc, Towson, MD. Tel: (410) 239-5000, (800) 544-6986, FAX: (410) 239-5227, Web Site: www.blackanddecker.com (16)

Archway Marketing Services, Rogers, MN. Tel: (763) 428-3300, (866) 779-9855 X1933, FAX: (763) 488-6803, E-Mail: sales@archway.com, Web Site: www.archway.com (28)

Arctic Trading Co Inc, Churchill, MB Canada. Tel: (204) 675-8804, (800) 665-0431, FAX: (204) 675-2164, E-Mail: atcpenny@mts.net, Web Site: www.arctictradingco.com (6)

Arden, Patricia, Physicians Planning Association Services, Deerfield Beach, FL. Tel: (954) 571-1877, (800) 221-2168, FAX: (954) 571-8582, E-Mail: insurance@assnservices.com, Web Site: www.physiciansplanning.com (16)

Elizabeth Arden Spas LLC, Stamford, CT. Tel: (203) 905-1700, FAX: (203) 905-1716, Web Site: www.reddoorspas.com (19)

Ardoff, Chad, Crest Healthcare Supply, Dassel, MN. Tel: (800) 369-9207, (800) 328-8908, Web Site: www.cresthealthcare.com (16)

Ardwell, Steve, Vestcom Saint Louis, Earth City, MO. Tel: (314) 209-8443, (800) 264-0965, FAX: (314) 291-2195, E-Mail: sreinis@vestcom.com, Web Site: www.vestcom.com (21)

Area Electronics Systems Inc, Anaheim, CA. Tel: (714) 993-0300, (800) 796-1580, FAX: (714) 993-0987, E-Mail: areasales@areasys.com, Web Site: www.areasys.com (3)

Aredia, Phil, BrownCor International, Milwaukee, WI. Tel: (414) 443-9700, (800) 327-2278, FAX: (800) 343-9228, Web Site: www.bcadvantage.com (5)

Arena, Mike, Partminer, Centennial, CO. Tel: (303) 200-5500, FAX: (303) 754-3940, Web Site: www.partminer.com (17)

Arends, John, Arends, Batavia, IL. Tel: (630) 990-0220, FAX: (630) 990-2556, Web Site: www.arends-inc.com (35)

Arends, Batavia, IL. Tel: (630) 990-0220, FAX: (630) 990-2556, Web Site: www.arends-inc.com (35)

Arent Fox LLP, Washington, DC. Tel: (202) 715-8582, Web Site: www.arentfox.com (9)

Arett, Kent, The Popcorn Factory, Lake Forest, IL. Tel: (847) 362-0028, (888) 216-0235, FAX: (888) 333-4595, E-Mail: service@thepopcornfactory.com, Web Site: www.thepopcornfactory.com (4)

Argenas, Dan, Direct Marketing Tool Kit for Small Business, Minneapolis, MN. Tel: (612) 788-1673, E-Mail: info@nmoa.org, Web Site: www.nmoa.org/directmarketingtoolkit (43)

Argent Trading LLC, New York, NY. Tel: (212) 697-8800, FAX: (212) 697-8606, Web Site: www.Argenttrading.com (16)

Argentine, Jan, Cold Spring Harbor Lab Press, Woodbury, NY. Tel: (516) 422-4100, (800) 843-4388, FAX: (516) 422-4097, E-Mail: cshpress@cshl.edu, Web Site: www.cshlpress.com (17)

Arguilla, Richard, Roto-Rooter Services Co, Cincinnati, OH. Tel: (513) 762-6690, FAX: (513) 762-6590, Web Site: www.rotorooter.com (16)

Argyropoulos, Antoinette, Golden Fleece Designs Inc, Burbank, CA. Tel: (818) 848-7724, FAX: (818) 566-7100, Web Site: www.mandonia.com (16)

Argyropoulos, Maria, Golden Fleece Designs Inc, Burbank, CA. Tel: (818) 848-7724, FAX: (818) 566-7100, Web Site: www.mandonia.com (16)

Argyropoulos, Symeon, D., Golden Fleece Designs Inc, Burbank, CA. Tel: (818) 848-7724, FAX: (818) 566-7100, Web Site: www.mandonia.com (16)

Ariagno, William G., Direct One Inc, Winter Park, FL. Tel: (407) 673-4500, FAX: (407) 673-4501, E-Mail: wariagno@directoneinc.com, Web Site: www.directoneinc.com (28)

Ariago Designs, Campbell, CA. Tel: (408) 668-0400, FAX: (408) 688-0401, Web Site: www.ariago.com (35)

Arich Corp, New York, NY. Tel: (212) 247-1800, FAX: (212) 247-2231, Web Site: www.arichinc.com (20)

Aristokraft Inc, Jasper, IN. Tel: (812) 482-2527, FAX: (812) 482-9872, Web Site: www.aristokraft.com (16)

The Arizona Direct Marketing Association, Scottsdale, AZ. Tel: (480) 970-8643, FAX: (480) 893-1157, E-Mail: julie@brownies.com, Web Site: www.azdma.org (40)

Arizona Highways Magazine, Phoenix, AZ. Tel: (602) 712-2000, FAX: (602) 254-4505, E-Mail: editor@arizonahighways.com, Web Site: www.arizonahighways.com (17)

The Arizona Republic, Phoenix, AZ. Tel: (602) 444-8000, Web Site: www.azcentral.com (17)

Arkema, Robert, Johnson & Quin Inc, Niles, IL. Tel: (847) 588-4800, FAX: (847) 647-6949, E-Mail: jqinfo@j-quin.com, Web Site: www.j-quin.com (28)

Arkline Computers & Supply, Cleveland, OH. Tel: (216) 252-6560, (800) 695-1441, FAX: (216) 671-2037, Web Site: www.geocities.com (3)

Arlen, Gary, Arlen Communications Inc, Bethesda, MD. Tel: (301) 656-7940, E-Mail: info@arlencom.com, Web Site: www.arlencom.com (20)

Arlen, John, Thetford Corp, Ann Arbor, MI. Tel: (734) 769-6000, (800) 543-1219, FAX: (734) 769-2023, Web Site: www.thetford.com (16)

Arlen Communications Inc, Bethesda, MD. Tel: (301) 656-7940, E-Mail: info@arlencom.com, Web Site: www.arlencom.com (20)

Armata, Kevin, Windsor House, Windsor Locks, CT. Tel: (860) 627-5927, FAX: (860) 627-0252, E-Mail: ahalley@windsormarketing.com, Web Site: windsormarketing.com (20)

Armault, Bernard, Christian Dior Perfumes, New York, NY. Tel: (212) 931-2200, FAX: (212) 931-2954, Web Site: www.dior.com (7)

Armbrust, Bernerd, Armbrust Paper Tubes Inc, Chicago, IL. Tel: (773) 586-3232, FAX: (773) 586-8997, E-Mail: tubesrus@corecomm.net, Web Site: www.tubesrus.com (10)

Armbrust, Marc, Armbrust Paper Tubes Inc, Chicago, IL. Tel: (773) 586-3232, FAX: (773) 586-8997, E-Mail: tubesrus@corecomm.net, Web Site: www.tubesrus.com (10)

Armbrust Paper Tubes Inc, Chicago, IL. Tel: (773) 586-3232, FAX: (773) 586-8997, E-Mail: tubesrus@corecomm.net, Web Site: www.tubesrus.com (10)

Armbuster, Michael, ESL Federal Credit Union, Rochester, NY. Tel: (585) 336-1000, (800) 848-2265, FAX: (585) 336-1138, Web Site: www.esl.org (14)

Armento Inc, Buffalo, NY. Tel: (716) 875-2423, (866) 276-3686, FAX: (716) 875-8011, E-Mail: armento@aol.com, Web Site: www.armento-columbarium.com (5)

Armentrout, Barbara, Marketing Advents, Alexandria, VA. Tel: (703) 706-0387, FAX: (703) 836-2181, E-Mail: info@dmaw.org, Web Site: www.dmaw.org (43)

Armes, Roy, V., Cooper Tire & Rubber Co Inc, Findlay, OH. Tel: (419) 423-1321, (800) 854-6288, FAX: (419) 424-4212, Web Site: www.coopertire.com (16)

Armour, Peter, Conde Nast, New York, NY. Tel: (212) 286-2860, FAX: (212) 880-8289, Web Site: www.conde.net (17)

Armstrong, Ashley, The American Phytopathological Society, Saint Paul, MN. Tel: (651) 454-7250, Web Site: www.apsnet.org (1)

Armstrong, Darryl, Interex, Amesbury, MA. Tel: (978) 388-8755, (800) INTEREX, FAX: (978) 388-8747, Web Site: www.interexexhibits.com (17)

Armstrong, David, American General Co, Neptune, NJ. Tel: (732) 922-7000, FAX: (732) 922-7595 (15)

Armstrong, Durrell, Player Piano Co Inc, Wichita, KS. Tel: (316) 263-3241, FAX: (316) 263-5480, Web Site: www.playerpianocompany.com (11)

Armstrong, Gary, Wenner Media LLC, New York, NY. Tel: (212) 484-1616, FAX: (212) 484-1713 (17)

Armstrong, John, USX, Pittsburgh, PA. Tel: (412) 433-1121, E-Mail: webmaster@usx.com, Web Site: www.usx.com (16)

Armstrong, Linda, DMW Worldwide LLC, Chesterbrook, PA. Tel: (610) 407-0407, (877) 744-3699, FAX: (610) 407-9201, E-Mail: whunter@dmwdirect.com, Web Site: www.dmwdirect.com (35)

Armstrong, R., Stephen, Patterson Dental, Saint Paul, MN. Tel: (651) 686-1600, (800) 328-5536, FAX: (651) 686-9331, Web Site: www.pattersondental.com (10)

Armstrong, Steve, Improvements, West Chester, OH. Tel: (216) 591-9148, (800) 634-9484, FAX: (216) 831-4026, Web Site: www.improvementscatalog.com (8)

Armstrong, Steve, MSC Industrial Supply Co, Melville, NY. Tel: (516) 812-2000, (800) 645-7270, FAX: (800) 255-5067, E-Mail: executive@mscdirect.com, Web Site: www.mscdirect.com (9)

Army Times Publishing Co, Springfield, VA. Tel: (703) 750-9000, (800) 336-4590, FAX: (703) 750-8129, E-Mail: cust-svc@atpco.com, Web Site: www.armytimes.com (17)

Arnaud's, New Orleans, LA. Tel: (504) 523-0611, (866) 230-8895, FAX: (504) 581-7908, Web Site: www.arnauds.com (16)

Arnet Pharmaceutical, Davie, FL. Tel: (954) 236-9053, (800) 968-6673, FAX: (954) 370-2508, E-Mail: arnet@arnetusa.com, Web Site: www.arnetusa.com (7)

Arnett, Gail R., Zig Ziglar Corp, Plano, TX. Tel: (972) 233-9191, (800) 527-0306, FAX: (469) 321-7556, E-Mail: info@ziglar.com, Web Site: www.zigziglar.com (16)

Arnett, Mark, F&W Publications Inc, Blue Ash, OH. Tel: (513) 531-2690, FAX: (513) 531-0293, Web Site: www.fwpublications.com (17)

Arney, Mark, Michigan Apple Committee, Lansing, MI. Tel: (517) 669-8353, (800) 456-2753, FAX: (517) 669-9506, E-Mail: staff@michiganapples.com, Web Site: www.michiganapples.com (1)

Arnold, Bill, EMED Co Inc, Buffalo, NY. Tel: (716) 626-1616, (800) 442-3633, FAX: (716) 626-1630, E-Mail: customerservice@emedco.com, Web Site: www.emedco.com (16)

Arnold, Carolyn, Detroit Newspapers, Detroit, MI. Tel: (313) 222-6400, FAX: (313) 222-5032, Web Site: www.freep.com (18)

Arnold, Craig, Eaton Corp, Raleigh, NC. Tel: (216) 523-4400, (800) 356-5794, FAX: (216) 523-4787, Web Site: www.eaton.com (16)

Arnold, Dean, Newroads Inc, Chattanooga, TN. Tel: (423) 867-9081, FAX: (423) 867-8508 (28)

Arnold, Dorothy, The Stash Tea Catalog, Tigard, OR. Tel: (800) 547-1514, FAX: (503) 684-4424, E-Mail: stash@stashtea.com, Web Site: www.stashtea.com (4)

Arnold, Judy, SEI, Oaks, PA. Tel: (610) 676-1000, E-Mail: webmaster@seic.com, Web Site: www.seic.com (14)

Arnold, Keith, Arrowhead Promotion & Fulfillment, Grand Rapids, MN. Tel: (218) 327-1165, FAX: (218) 327-2576, Web Site: www.apfco.com (29)

Arnold, Lauren, Denver Metro Convention & Visitors Bureau, Denver, CO. Tel: (303) 892-1112, FAX: (303) 892-1636, Web Site: www.denver.org (1)

Arnold, Martha, G., International Manufacturing Co, Whitesburg, GA. Tel: (770) 834-2094, FAX: (770) 834-2096, E-Mail: textilenterprise@aol.net (8)

Arnold, Mary, ChildFund International, Richmond, VA. Tel: (804) 756-2700, Web Site: www.ChildFund.org (1)

Arnold, Mary, Christian Children's Fund Inc, Richmond, VA. Tel: (804) 756-2700, (800) 776-6767, FAX: (804) 756-2718, Web Site: www.christianchildrensfund.org (1)

Arnold, Resa, The Bureau Inc, Stuart, FL. Tel: (561) 845-8400, FAX: (561) 845-7979, Web Site: www.bureauinc.com (28)

Arnold Brand Response, Toronto, ON Canada. Tel: (416) 355-5009, Web Site: www.arnoldworldwide.com (35)

Arnold Worldwide, Boston, MA. Tel: (617) 587-8000, FAX: (617) 587-8070, Web Site: www.arnoldworldwide.com (35)

Arnon, Wendy, Omnicom Media Group Direct, New York, NY. Tel: (212) 590-7012 (35)

Arntzen, Michelle, Campbell Mithun, Minneapolis, MN. Tel: (612) 347-1000, FAX: (612) 347-1515, Web Site: www.campbellmithun.com (35)

Aronoff, Roger, Accuracy in Media Inc, Washington, DC. Tel: (202) 364-4401, FAX: (202) 364-4098, E-Mail: info@aim.org, Web Site: www.aim.org (1)

Arquest Inc, Millstone Twp, NJ. Tel: (609) 395-9500, (888) ARQUEST, (888) 270-8378, FAX: (609) 395-9778, Web Site: www.arquest.com (16)

Array Marketing Group Inc, Toronto, ON Canada. Tel: (800) 295-4120, FAX: (416) 292-9759, E-Mail: info@arraymarketing.com, Web Site: www.arraymarketing.com (35)

Arrco Medical Advertising, Walpole, MA. Tel: (781) 769-7190, FAX: (781) 769-9480, E-Mail: info@arrco.com, Web Site: www.arrco.com (35)

Arrigo, Paul, J., Baton Rouge Conventions & Visitors Bureau, Baton Rouge, LA. Tel: (225) 383-1825, (800) LA-ROUGE, FAX: (225) 346-1253, E-Mail: br@bracvb.com, Web Site: www.bracvb.com (1)

Arriola, Dennis, Southern California Gas Co, Anaheim, CA. Tel: (714) 634-3054, (800) 427-2200, FAX: (714) 937-7712, E-Mail: Tjavid@socalgas.com, Web Site: www.socalgas.com (1)

Arrow Advantage, Eden Prairie, MN. Tel: (952) 906-7100, (800) 833-3557, FAX: (952) 906-7135, Web Site: www.arrow.com (3)

Arrow Co, Indianapolis, IN. Tel: (317) 692-6666, FAX: (317) 692-6769, Web Site: www.aearo.com (16)

Arrow Companies, LLC, Elkhorn, WI. Tel: (262) 741-1660, FAX: (262) 723-6750, Web Site: www.arrowcompanies.com (22)

Arrow Mailing Service II Inc, Hawthorne, CA. Tel: (310) 219-7740, FAX: (310) 219-3335 (28)

Arrowhead Mountain Spring Water, Wilkes Barre, PA. Tel: (800) 873-7775, Web Site: www.arrowheadwater.com (16)

Arrowhead Promotion & Fulfillment, Grand Rapids, MN. Tel: (218) 327-1165, FAX: (218) 327-2576, Web Site: www.apfco.com (29)

ArrowMail Canada, Windsor, ON Canada. Tel: (313) 961-8334, FAX: (313) 961-7849, E-Mail: info@mailingcanada.com, Web Site: www.mailingcanada.com (28)

Arroyo, Gladys, Ranger Joe's International Military Supply, Columbus, GA. Tel: (706) 689-0082, (800) 247-4541, FAX: (706) 682-8840, E-Mail: customerservice@rangerjoes.com, Web Site: www.rangerjoes.com (2)

Art.com, Emeryville, CA. Tel: (510) 879-4700, Web Site: www.art.com (8)

Art Instruction Schools, Minneapolis, MN. Tel: (612) 362-5075, FAX: (612) 362-5260, Web Site: www.artinstructionschools.edu (13)

Art News Magazine, New York, NY. Tel: (212) 398-1690, FAX: (212) 819-0394, E-Mail: info@artnews.com, Web Site: www.artnewsonline.com (17)

The Art of Self Promotion, Hoboken, NJ. Tel: (201) 653-0783, FAX: (201) 222-2494, E-Mail: ilise@marketing-mentor.com, Web Site: www.artofselfpromotion.com (17)

Art Resource Inc, New York, NY. Tel: (212) 505-8700, FAX: (212) 505-2053, E-Mail: requests@artres.com, Web Site: www.artres.com (38)

Art, Tape & Label Co, Addison, IL. Tel: (630) 543-8100, FAX: (630) 543-8153, Web Site: arttapeandlabel.com (27)

Artandi, George, The History Book Club Inc, Mechanicsburg, PA. Tel: (718) 918-2665, E-Mail: paula.batson@dgna.com, Web Site: www.historybookclub.com (13)

Artech House, Norwood, MA. Tel: (781) 769-9750, FAX: (781) 769-6334, E-Mail: artech@artechhouse.com, Web Site: www.artechhouse.com (17)

Artemis International Solutions Corp, Austin, TX. Tel: (512) 874-3030, (800) 477-6648, FAX: (512) 874-8900, Web Site: www.aisc.com (22)

Artful Dragon Press Inc, Minnetonka, MN. Tel: (612) 221-8908, Web Site: www.artfuldragon.com (22)

Arthritis Foundation, Atlanta, GA. Tel: (404) 872-7100, FAX: (404) 872-0457, Web Site: www.arthritis.org (1)

Arthur, Bradley, J., National Community Pharmacists Association, Alexandria, VA. Tel: (703) 683-8200, (800) 544-7447, FAX: (703) 683-3619, E-Mail: info@ncpanet.org, Web Site: www.ncpanet.org (1)

Arthur, Charlie, Atlanta Offset, Atlanta, GA. Tel: (404) 699-6200, FAX: (404) 699-1393, Web Site: www.gannett.com/about/map/offset.htm (27)

Artichoke Ink, Gilbert, AZ. Tel: (480) 792-9597, Web Site: www.artichokeink.com (28)

Artisanal LLC, Holicong, PA. Tel: (215) 862-8000, FAX: (215) 862-8008, E-Mail: info@artisanaldesign.com, Web Site: www.artisanaldesign.com (8)

The Artists Co, New York, NY. Tel: (212) 679-7199, FAX: (212) 741-1519, E-Mail: nyc@artists-ar.com (32)

ArtNetwork-Artworld Mailing Lists, Nevada City, CA. Tel: (530) 478-0920, (800) 383-0677, FAX: (530) 470-0256, E-Mail: info@artmarketing.com, Web Site: www.artmarketing.com (23)

Artrinsic Inc, New York, NY. Tel: (212) 716-1977 X201, Web Site: www.atrinsic.com (20)

Arts & Entertainment Television Network, New York, NY. Tel: (212) 210-1400, FAX: (212) 210-1326, Web Site: www.aetv.com (13)

Artz, Jim, Nowell's Inc, San Rafael, CA. Tel: (415) 332-4933, FAX: (415) 332-4936, E-Mail: contact@nowellslighting.com, Web Site: www.nowellslighting.com (8)

Arum, Herbert R., Stock Drive Products, New Hyde Park, NY. Tel: (516) 328-3300, FAX: (516) 326-8827, E-Mail: sdp-sisupport@sdp-si.com, Web Site: www.sdp.si.com (5)

Arvin, Sarah, Vesdia Corp, Atlanta, GA. Tel: (678) 405-9208, Web Site: www.vesdia.com (35)

Aryai, Sean, Global Equipment Co Inc, Port Washington, NY. Tel: (516) 484-3100, (888) 978-7759, FAX: (516) 608-7111, Web Site: www.globalindustrial.com (9)

Arzbacher, Bob, Enerpac, Menomonee Falls, WI. Tel: (262) 781-6600, (800) 433-2766, FAX: (262) 781-1028, Web Site: www.enerpac.com (16)

As Seen On PC Network, Fairfield, CT. Tel: (203) 256-9897, FAX: (203) 256-9507, E-Mail: info@asseenonpc.com, Web Site: www.asseenonpc.com (22)

As We Change, Oshkosh, WI. Tel: (619) 213-2200, (800) 993-0192, FAX: (619) 213-2253, E-Mail: help@aswechange.com, Web Site: www.aswechange.com (7)

Asburn, Margie, American Cancer Society, Atlanta, GA. Tel: (404) 471-5852, (800) ACS-2345, FAX: (404) 982-3677, Web Site: www.cancer.org (1)

Asbury Park Press Addresses Unlimited, Neptune, NJ. Tel: (732) 922-6000, FAX: (732) 462-3282 (21)

Ascher, Ken, Super Disk, Ann Arbor, MI. Tel: (734) 996-8888 (22)

Aschkenasy, Herbert, Oregon Freeze Dry Inc, Albany, OR. Tel: (541) 926-6001, FAX: (541) 967-6527, Web Site: www.ofd.com (4)

Asciutto, Mary Anne, Asciutto Art Representatives Inc, Chandler, AZ. Tel: (480) 814-8010, E-Mail: aartreps@cox.net, Web Site: wwwaartreps.com (36)

Asciutto Art Representatives Inc, Chandler, AZ. Tel: (480) 814-8010, E-Mail: aartreps@cox.net, Web Site: wwwaartreps.com (36)

Ash, Paul, J., Sam Ash.Com, Tampa, FL. Tel: (800) 472-6274, E-Mail: sales@samash.com, Web Site: www.samash.com (5)

Sam Ash.Com, Tampa, FL. Tel: (800) 472-6274, E-Mail: sales@samash.com, Web Site: www.samash.com (5)

Ashby, Carol, Children's Hospital of Pittsburgh, Pittsburgh, PA. Tel: (412) 692-5325, FAX: (412) 692-7140, Web Site: www.chp.edu (1)

Ashby, Joan, Pango Pango Swimwear Corp, Pompano Beach, FL. Tel: (954) 786-0255, (800) 858-9431, FAX: (954) 786-7745, E-Mail: pango_swimwear@bellsouth.net, Web Site: www.pango-pangoswimwear.com (2)

Ashe, Peter, Premier Packaging Corp, Victor, NY. Tel: (877) 924-8460, FAX: (585) 924-8753, E-Mail: info@premiercustompkg.com, Web Site: www. premiercustompkg.com (16)

Asher, James, M., The Hearst Corp, New York, NY. Tel: (212) 649-2000, FAX: (212) 649-2108, Web Site: www.hearst.com/magazines/ (17)

Asher, Paula, C&S Sales Inc, Wheeling, IL. Tel: (847) 541-0710, (800) 292-7711, FAX: (847) 541-9904, E-Mail: sales@cs-sales.com, Web Site: www. cs_sales.com (9)

Asher, S., Baxter Bros Inc, Greenwich, CT. Tel: (203) 637-4559, (866) 280-1924, FAX: (203) 637-4550, E-Mail: info@baxterinvestment.com, Web Site: www.baxterinvestment.com (17)

Asheville Compassionate Communication Center, Asheville, NC. Tel: (828) 252-0538, E-Mail: jerry@ashevilleccc.com, Web Site: ashevilleccc. com (13)

Ashken, Ian, Jarden Corp, Daleville, IN. Tel: (765) 557-3000, (800) 428-8150, FAX: (765) 281-5403, Web Site: www.jarden.com (16)

Ashland Inc, Covington, KY. Tel: (859) 815-3333, Web Site: www.ashland.com (16)

Ashland University, Ashland, OH. Tel: (419) 289-5063, Web Site: www.ashland.edu (1)

Ashley, David, A&H Lithoprint Inc, Broadview, IL. Tel: (708) 345-1196, FAX: (708) 345-1225, Web Site: www.ahlithoprint.com (27)

Ashley, Judy, Names in the Mail Inc, Dallas, TX. Tel: (972) 681-5701, (800) 688-5701, FAX: (972) 681-5786, E-Mail: nimnames@att.net (23)

Ashley, Richard W., Abbott, North Chicago, IL. Tel: (847) 937-8641, FAX: (847) 937-9555, Web Site: www.abbott.com (7)

Ashley, Timothy, P., Comerica Inc, Dallas, TX. Tel: (800) 521-1190, FAX: (925) 941-1999, Web Site: www.comerica.com (14)

Ashman, Greg, Professional Training Associates Inc, Duquesne, PA. Tel: (412) 460-0266, FAX: (412) 460-0269, E-Mail: info@ptainc.com, Web Site: www.ptainc.com (17)

Ashmore, Doug, Amvac Chemical Corp, Los Angeles, CA. Tel: (323) 264-3910, FAX: (323) 268-1028, Web Site: www.amvac-chemical.com (8)

Ashrae Learning Institute, Atlanta, GA. Tel: (404) 636-8400, (800) 527-4723, FAX: (404) 321-5478, E-Mail: ashrae@ashrae.org, Web Site: www.ashrae. org (31)

Ashtin, Voleen, Meriks Inc, Baltimore, MD. Tel: (787) 721-0000 (3)

Ashworth University, Norcross, GA. Tel: (770) 729-8400, (800) 957-5412, FAX: (770) 729-9294, E-Mail: info@ashworthuniversity.edu, Web Site: www.ashworthuniversity.edu (13)

AsiaEXP, Miami, FL. Tel: (305) 675-5969, Web Site: www.asiaexp.com (16)

ASK Telemarketing, Montgomery, AL. Tel: (334) 387-ASKT, FAX: (334) 387-2759, E-Mail: rburley@ asktelemarketing.com, Web Site: www. asktelemarketing.com (29)

Askew, Lynn, E., Patterson Dental, Saint Paul, MN. Tel: (651) 686-1600, (800) 328-5536, FAX: (651) 686-9331, Web Site: www.pattersondental.com (10)

Askin, Donald, CommercialWare Inc, Westboro, MA. Tel: (508) 655-7500, FAX: (508) 647-9495, E-Mail: info@micros-retail.com, Web Site: www. commercialware.com (22)

Aslett, Michael, Real Media Solutions, Wayne, NJ. Tel: (973) 835-7060, Web Site: www.get-realmedia.com (27)

Aspect Softwear, Chelmsford, MA. Tel: (978) 250-7900, FAX: (978) 244-7410, E-Mail: info@aspect. com, Web Site: www.aspect.com (29)

Aspen Imaging International Inc, Cleveland, OH. Tel: (216) 881-5300, (800) 955-5555, FAX: (216) 881-8380, (800) 756-0990 (34)

Aspen Interactive, Saint Petersburg, FL. Tel: (727) 823-7144, (800) 777-2255, FAX: (727) 823-6523 (35)

Aspen Marketing Services, West Chicago, IL. Tel: (847) 318-9010, FAX: (847) 318-9036, E-Mail: info@etownsend.com, Web Site: www.aspenms. com (35)

Aspen Packaging Corp, Cicero, IL. FAX: (708) 652-6444, Web Site: www.aspenpkg.com (27)

Aspen Publishers Inc, New York, NY. Tel: (800) 638-8437, FAX: (301) 417-7655, Web Site: www. aspenpublishers.com (17)

Asset Marketing Services Inc, Burnsville, MN. Tel: (952) 707-7000, Web Site: www.amsi-corp.com (16)

Assinin, Ferdinando L., The Bil-Ray Aluminum Siding Corp of Queens Inc, New Hyde Park, NY. Tel: (516) 616-4200, (800) 474-4415, FAX: (516) 616-4030, Web Site: www.homeclub.com (16)

Assisted Access- NFSS, Lake Villa, IL. Tel: (847) 265-8022, (800) 950-9655, FAX: (888) 552-1708, E-Mail: sales@nfss.com, Web Site: www.nfss.com (3)

Associated Bag Co, Milwaukee, WI. Tel: (414) 769-1000, (800) 926-6100, FAX: (800) 926-4610, E-Mail: customerservice@associatedbag.com, Web Site: www.associatedbag.com (10)

Associated Construction Publications, Indianapolis, IN. Tel: (317) 423-7080, FAX: (317) 423-7094, Web Site: www.acppubs.com (17)

Associated Integrated Marketing, Wichita, KS. Tel: (316) 683-4691, Web Site: www.meetassociated. com (35)

Associated Materials, Cuyahoga Falls, OH. Tel: (330) 922-2182, Web Site: www.alside.com (8)

Associated Photo, Florence, KY. Tel: (859) 344-1460, (800) 727-2580, FAX: (859) 282-0032 (16)

Associated Premium Corp, Cincinnati, OH. Tel: (513) 679-4444, FAX: (513) 679-4447, Web Site: www. associatedpremium.com (33)

Associated Textile Rental Services, Rochester, NY. Tel: (585) 454-5988, (800) 639-4624, Web Site: www.associatedtextile.com (16)

Association for Computing Machinery (ACM), New York, NY. Tel: (212) 869-7440, FAX: (212) 944-1318, Web Site: www.acm.org (1)

Association for Facilities Engineering, Herndon, VA. Tel: (571) 203-7171, FAX: (571) 766-2142, E-Mail: info@afe.org, Web Site: www.afe.org (1)

Association for Financial Professionals, Bethesda, MD. Tel: (301) 907-2862, FAX: (301) 907-2864, Web Site: www.afponline.org (14)

Association for Postal Commerce, Alexandria, VA. Tel: (703) 524-0096, FAX: (703) 524-1871, Web Site: www.postcom.org (40)

Association of American Publishers, Washington, DC. Tel: (202) 347-3375, FAX: (202) 347-3690, Web Site: www.publishers.org (1)

Association of Bridal Consultants, New Milford, CT. Tel: (860) 355-0464, FAX: (860) 354-1404, E-Mail: office@bridalassn.com, Web Site: www. bridalassn.com (1)

Association of Coupon Professionals, Drexel Hill, PA. Tel: (610) 789-1478, FAX: (610) 789-5309, E-Mail: john.morgan@acp-hq.org, Web Site: www. couponpros.org (40)

Association of Desk-Top Publishers (AD-TP), San Diego, CA. Tel: (619) 563-9714, FAX: (619) 280-3778 (40)

Association of Energy Engineers, Atlanta, GA. Tel: (770) 447-5083 x210, FAX: (770) 446-3969, E-Mail: info@aeecenter.org, Web Site: www. aeecenter.org (40)

The Association of Fundraising Professionals, Arlington, VA. Tel: (800) 666-3863, Web Site: www. afpnet.org (1)

Association of Marian Helpers, Stockbridge, MA. Tel: (413) 298-3691, Web Site: www.marian.org (1)

Association of National Advertisers Inc, New York, NY. Tel: (212) 697-5950, FAX: (212) 687-7310, Web Site: www.ana.net (40)

Association of the Miraculous Medal, Perryville, MO. Tel: (573) 547-8343, (800) 264-6279, FAX: (573) 547-1389, E-Mail: amm1@amm.org, Web Site: www.amm.org (1)

Assurant Group, New York, NY. Tel: (305) 253-2244, FAX: (305) 252-6987, Web Site: www.assurant. com (15)

Assurant Health, Milwaukee, WI. Tel: (414) 244-0658, (800) 800-1212, FAX: (414) 224-0472, Web Site: www.assuranthealth.com (15)

Assurant Solutions Preneed Division, Atlanta, GA. Tel: (770) 763-1000, (800) PRE NEED, FAX: (770) 859-4325, Web Site: www.assurantpreneed. com (15)

Astoria Federal Savings, Lake Success, NY. Tel: (516) 327-7000, Web Site: www.astoriafederal.com (14)

Astral Brands LLC, Smyrna, GA. Tel: (678) 303-3088, Web Site: www.astralbrands.com (7)

Astran, Tony, Eric Mower & Associates, Rochester, NY. Tel: (585) 385-2000, Web Site: www.mower. com (35)

AstraZeneca, Wilmington, DE. Tel: (302) 866-1482, Web Site: www.astrazeneca-us.com (7)

Astro Air, LP, Jacksonville, TX. Tel: (903) 586-3691, FAX: (903) 589-8094, E-Mail: sales@astroair.com, Web Site: www.astroair.com (9)

Astrologer's Fund Inc, Brooklyn, NY. Tel: (212) 949-7275, FAX: (212) 608-6964, E-Mail: books@ afund.com, Web Site: www.afund.com (16)

Astronomical Society of the Pacific, San Francisco, CA. Tel: (415) 337-1100, (800) 335-2624, FAX: (415) 337-5205, E-Mail: service@astrosociety.org, Web Site: www.astrosociety.org (1)

AT&T Inc, San Antonio, TX. Tel: (210) 821-4105, FAX: (210) 351-2071, Web Site: www.bellsouth. com (32)

At Last Naturals, North Salem, NY. Tel: (800) 527-8123, FAX: (914) 747-3791, E-Mail: info@ atlastnaturals.com, Web Site: www.atlastnaturals. com (7)

@utoRevenue, Pittsfield, MA. Tel: (413) 243-4800, Web Site: www.autorevenue.com (32)

Atadan, David, Trellist Marketing and Technology, Wilmington, DE. Tel: (302) 778-1300, Web Site: www.trellist.com (30)

Atkins, Clint, Tower Hobbies/Hobbico, Champaign, IL. Tel: (217) 398-3636, (800) 637-6050, FAX: (217) 398-1104, Web Site: www.towerhobbies.com (11)

Atkins, Howard, I., Wells Fargo, San Francisco, CA. Tel: (866) 878-5865, (800) 869-3557, FAX: (626) 312-3015, Web Site: www.wellsfargo.com (14)

Atkins, Tony, Neopost, Carrollton, TX. Tel: (510) 489-6800, (800) 636-7678, FAX: (510) 475-6317, (510) 487-6704, Web Site: www.neopostinc.com (9)

Atkinson, Jeff, Burden Sales Co, Lincoln, NE. Tel: (402) 474-4055, (800) 488-3407, FAX: (402) 474-5198, E-Mail: ccole@surpluscenter.com (9)

Atkinson, Jeff, Surplus Center, Lincoln, NE. Tel: (402) 474-4055, (800) 488-3407, FAX: (402) 474-5198, E-Mail: customerservice1@surpluscenter.com, Web Site: www.surpluscenter.com (9)

Atkinson, Mesonga, Oomingmak Musk Ox Producers Cooperative, Anchorage, AK. Tel: (907) 272-9225, (888) 360-9665, FAX: (907) 258-4225, E-Mail: oomingmak@qiviut.com, Web Site: www.qiviut. com (6)

Atkinson, Noel, J., The Keystone Equities Group, Oaks, PA. Tel: (610) 415-6300, (800) 715-9905, FAX: (610) 415-6328, Web Site: www. keystoneequities.com (20)

Atkinson, Ron, American Society for Quality-ASQ, Milwaukee, WI. Tel: (414) 272-8575, (800) 248-1946, FAX: (414) 272-1734, E-Mail: help@asq. org, Web Site: www.asq.org (1)

Atkinson, Tom, Reliant Energy, Houston, TX. Tel: (713) 497-7794, Web Site: www.reliant.com (16)

Atlanta Cutlery Corp, Conyers, GA. Tel: (770) 922-3700, (800) 833-8838, FAX: (770) 760-8993, E-Mail: webmaster@atlantacutlery.com, Web Site: www.atlantacutlery.com (11)

Atlanta Journal & Constitution, Atlanta, GA. Tel: (404) 526-5151, FAX: (404) 526-7122 (17)

Atlanta Offset, Atlanta, GA. Tel: (404) 699-6200, FAX: (404) 699-1393, Web Site: www.gannett.com/about/map/offset.htm (27)

Atlantic-ACM, Boston, MA. Tel: (617) 720-3700, FAX: (617) 720-1077, E-Mail: atlantic@atlantic-acm.com, Web Site: www.atlantic-acm.com (20)

Atlantic Business Products, New York, NY. Tel: (212) 741-6400, FAX: (212) 645-1518, E-Mail: info@tomorrowsoffice.com, Web Site: www.tomorrowsoffice.com (29)

Atlantic List Company Inc, Arlington, VA. Tel: (703) 528-7482, Web Site: www.atlanticlist.com (23)

The Atlantic Monthly, Washington, DC. Tel: (202) 266-6000, (800) 234-2411, FAX: (202) 266-7280, Web Site: www.theatlantic.com (17)

Atlantic Publication Group LLC, Charleston, SC. Tel: (843) 747-0025, FAX: (843) 744-0816, E-Mail: info@atlanticpublicationgrp.com, Web Site: www.atlanticpublicationgrp.com (17)

Atlantic Research & Consulting Inc, Boston, MA. Tel: (617) 720-0174, FAX: (617) 589-3731, E-Mail: generalmailbox@guideline.com, Web Site: www.guideline.com (30)

Atlantic Spice Co, North Truro, MA. Tel: (508) 487-6100, (800) 316-7965, FAX: (508) 487-2550, E-Mail: mark@atlanticspice.com, Web Site: www.atlanticspice.com (4)

Atlas Pen & Pencil Corp, Shelbyville, TN. Tel: (954) 920-4444, (800) 327-3232, FAX: (954) 920-8899, E-Mail: sales@atlaspen.com, Web Site: www.atlaspen.com (35)

Atmosphere BBDO, New York, NY. Tel: (212) 827-2500, FAX: (212) 827-2525, Web Site: www.atmospherebbdo.com (35)

Atomic Direct LLC, Portland, OR. Tel: (503) 296-6131, Web Site: www.atomicdirect.com (35)

ATP List Services, Barrington, IL. Tel: (800) 223-3423, Web Site: www.atplists.com (23)

Atrinsic Inc, New York, NY. Tel: (212) 716-1977, Web Site: www.atrinsic.com (9)

Attard, Jerry, Guiding Eyes for the Blind, Yorktown Heights, NY. Tel: (914) 245-4042, (800) 942-0149, FAX: (914) 245-1609, Web Site: www.guidingeyes.org (16)

Attayek, John, York Label, York, PA. Tel: (717) 266-9675, FAX: (717) 266-9834, Web Site: www.yorklabel.com (27)

Attenborough, Neale, Johnny Appleseed's Inc, Beverly, MA. Tel: (978) 922-2040, (800) 767-6666, FAX: (978) 922-7001, Web Site: www.appleseeds.com (2)

Attenborough, Neale, Norm Thompson Outfitters Inc, Hillsboro, OR. Tel: (503) 614-4600, (800) 547-1160, FAX: (503) 614-4599, Web Site: www.normthompson.com (2)

Attfield, Mary, Stephen Thomas, Toronto, ON. Tel: (416) 690-8801, FAX: (416) 690-7256, E-Mail: mail@stephenthomas.ca, Web Site: www.stephenthomas.ca (1)

Atvel, Hope, Appraisal Institute, Chicago, IL. Tel: (312) 335-4100, FAX: (312) 335-4400, E-Mail: info@appraisalinstitute.org, Web Site: www.appraisalinstitute.org (1)

Atwater, Frank, G., National Active & Retired Federal Employees Association, Alexandria, VA. Tel: (703) 838-7760, (800) 456-8410, FAX: (703) 838-7785, Web Site: www.narfe.org (1)

Atwood, Charles, A., Caesars Palace, Las Vegas, NV. Tel: (702) 407-6000, (800) 634-6001, FAX: (702) 407-6037, Web Site: www.caesars.com (16)

Atwood, Charles, L., Harrah's Marketing, Reno, NV. Tel: (775) 786-3232, FAX: (775) 722-2815, Web Site: www.harrahsreno.com (16)

Aubitz, Carol, Excelsior Direct, Lancaster, PA. Tel: (717) 399-3550, FAX: (717) 399-3200 (35)

Auburn, Susan, Chartifacts, Richmond, VA. Tel: (804) 272-7120 (6)

Auburn University at Montgomery, Montgomery, AL. Tel: (334) 244-3621, (800) 227-2649, FAX: (334) 244-3826, Web Site: www.aum.edu (41)

Audience Development, Norwalk, CT. Tel: (203) 854-6730, FAX: (203) 854-6735, E-Mail: inolan@red7media.com, Web Site: www.audiencedevelopment.com (43)

Audience Identification Inc, Lisle, IL. Tel: (630) 435-0460, FAX: (630) 435-0470, E-Mail: rmarsh@audienceid.com (22)

Audience Research & Development, Fort Worth, TX. Tel: (817) 924-6922, FAX: (817) 924-7539, E-Mail: jgumbert@ar-d.com, Web Site: www.ar-d.com (20)

Audio & Video Labs Inc, Pennsauken, NJ. Tel: (856) 663-9030, (800) 468-9353, FAX: (856) 661-3450, E-Mail: info@discmakers.com, Web Site: www.discmakers.com (16)

Audio Classics Ltd, Vestal, NY. Tel: (607) 766-3501, FAX: (607) 766-3502, E-Mail: steve@audioclassics.com, Web Site: www.audioclassics.com (3)

Audio-Digest Foundation, Glendale, CA. Tel: (818) 240-7500, (800) 423-2308, FAX: (818) 240-7379, Web Site: www.audio-digest.org (1)

Audio Editions Books-on-Cassette & CD, Auburn, CA. Tel: (800) 231-4261, FAX: (800) 882-1840, E-Mail: info@audioeditions.com, Web Site: www.audioeditions.com (3)

Audiovox, Hauppauge, NY. Tel: (631) 231-7750, (800) 645-4994, FAX: (631) 434-3995, Web Site: www.audiovox.com (16)

Auerbach, Carolyn, Kellyco Metal Detector Distributors, Winter Springs, FL. Tel: (407) 699-8700, (800) 327-9697, FAX: (407) 695-6671, E-Mail: customerservice@kellycodetectors.com, Web Site: www.kellycodetectors.com (11)

Auerbach, Karen, Kensington Publishing Corp, New York, NY. Tel: (212) 407-1500, (800) 221-2647, FAX: (212) 407-1590, Web Site: www.kensingtonbooks.com (17)

Auerbach, Stuart, Kellyco Metal Detector Distributors, Winter Springs, FL. Tel: (407) 699-8700, (800) 327-9697, FAX: (407) 695-6671, E-Mail: customerservice@kellycodetectors.com, Web Site: www.kellycodetectors.com (11)

Augsburg Fortress Publishers, Minneapolis, MN. Tel: (612) 330-3300, (800) 426-0115, FAX: (612) 330-3455, E-Mail: info@augsburgfortress.org, Web Site: www.augsburgfortress.org (17)

August, Norman, August Bishop & Meier Inc, Chicago, IL. Tel: (312) 988-9200, FAX: (312) 988-9861 (35)

August, Scott, Kaplan Publishing, Chicago, IL. Tel: (312) 606-8905, (800) 245-2665, FAX: (312) 606-8985, E-Mail: kaplanorders@kaplan.com, Web Site: www.kaplanpublishing.com (17)

August Bishop & Meier Inc, Chicago, IL. Tel: (312) 988-9200, FAX: (312) 988-9861 (35)

August Home Publishing Co, Des Moines, IA. Tel: (515) 875-7000, FAX: (515) 282-6741, E-Mail: ask@workbenchmag.com, Web Site: www.augusthome.com (17)

August Marketing, Tequesta, FL. Tel: (561) 747-1325, Web Site: www.augustmktg.com (22)

Wendell August Forge Inc, Grove City, PA. Tel: (724) 458-8360, (800) 923-1390, FAX: (724) 458-0906, E-Mail: info@wendell.com, Web Site: www.wendellaugust.com (6)

Augustine, Cynthia, Scholastic Inc, New York, NY. Tel: (212) 343-6100, (800) SCHOLASTIC, FAX: (212) 343-6484, Web Site: www.scholastic.com/ (17)

Augusto, Carl, American Foundation for the Blind Inc, New York, NY. Tel: (212) 502-7600, FAX: (212) 502-7777, E-Mail: afbinfo@afb.org, Web Site: www.afb.org/afb (1)

Aurand, Layne, No Load Fund Investor, Brentwood, TN. Tel: (800) 706-6364, FAX: (800) 785-9212, E-Mail: NoLoad@mleesmith.com, Web Site: www.noloadfundinvestor.com (14)

Auriemma, Michael, Auriemma Consulting Group, New York, NY. Tel: (516) 333-4800, FAX: (516) 333-4815, E-Mail: info@acg.net, Web Site: www.acg.net (20)

Auriemma Consulting Group, New York, NY. Tel: (516) 333-4800, FAX: (516) 333-4815, E-Mail: info@acg.net, Web Site: www.acg.net (20)

Aurora Marketing Inc, Princeton, NJ. Tel: (908) 904-1125, FAX: (908) 359-1108, E-Mail: aurora2@voicenet.com, Web Site: www.auroramarketing.net (30)

Ausenda, Marco, Rizzoli International Publications Inc, New York, NY. Tel: (212) 387-3400, FAX: (212) 387-3535 (17)

Ausick, Richard, M., Brown Shoe Co, Saint Louis, MO. Tel: (314) 854-4000, FAX: (314) 854-4274, Web Site: www.brownshoe.com (16)

Ausley, David, Integer Group, Des Moines, IA. Tel: (515) 288-7910, FAX: (515) 288-8439, E-Mail: fmaher@integermidwest.com, Web Site: www.integer.com (35)

Austen, Mary, Stengel, Tierney Communications, Philadelphia, PA. Tel: (215) 790-4100, FAX: (215) 545-0188, Web Site: www.tierneyagency.com (35)

Austin, Bill, Coyne American Institute, Chicago, IL. Tel: (773) 935-2520, (800) 999-5220, FAX: (773) 935-2920, Web Site: www.coyneamerican.edu (16)

Austin, Brett, AmericasMart Atlanta, Atlanta, GA. Tel: (404) 220-3000, FAX: (404) 220-3030, Web Site: www.americasmart.com (42)

Austin, Daryl, Phillips Kiln Service LTD, South Sioux City, NE. Tel: (402) 494-6837, (800) 831-0876, FAX: (402) 494-6858, E-Mail: info@kilm.com, Web Site: www.kiln.com (16)

Austin, David, Family Christian Stores, Grand Rapids, MI. Tel: (616) 554-8700, (888) 319-0319, FAX: (616) 554-8694, E-Mail: info@fcsdirect.familychristian.com, Web Site: www.familychristian.com (5)

Austin, Jeff, Pioneer Hi-Bred International Inc, Johnston, IA. Tel: (515) 270-3200, FAX: (515) 270-3581, E-Mail: web.editor@pioneer.com, Web Site: www.pioneer.com (4)

Austin, Kevin, Sancoa International, Lumberton, NJ. Tel: (856) 273-0700, FAX: (856) 273-2710, E-Mail: sancoa@sancoa.com (31)

Austin, Sarah, Veridian Credit Union, Waterloo, IA. Tel: (319) 236-5692, (800) 235-3228, FAX: (319) 833-1185, E-Mail: sarahma@veridiancu.org, Web Site: www.veridiancu.org (1)

Austin & Williams, Hauppauge, NY. Tel: (631) 231-6600, (888) 281-9200, FAX: (212) 434-7022, E-Mail: info@austin-williams.com, Web Site: www.austin-williams.com (21)

Australian Tourist Commission, Los Angeles, CA. Tel: (310) 695-3200, Web Site: www.australia.com (16)

Austrums, Tim, The Connection Contact Center Services, Burnsville, MN. Tel: (952) 948-5335, (800) 883-5777, FAX: (952) 948-5498, E-Mail: sales@the-connection.com, Web Site: www.the-connection.com (29)

Austrums, Tim, The Connection Outsourced Call Ctr, Burnsville, MN. Tel: (800) 883-5777, Web Site: www.the-connection.com (29)

Auth, Michael, Vitasoy USA Inc, Ayer, MA. Tel: (978) 772-6880, (800) VITA-SOY, FAX: (978) 772-6881, Web Site: www.vitasoy-usa.com (16)

Auth, Mike, NASW Assurance Services Inc, Frederick, MD. Tel: (800) 668-4274, E-Mail: zxi@naswasi.org, Web Site: www.naswinsurancetrust.org (1)

Authentic Designs Colonial and Early American Lighting Fixtures Inc, West Rupert, VT. Tel: (802) 394-7713, (800) 844-9416, FAX: (802) 394-2422, E-Mail: mail@authenticdesigns.com, Web Site: www.authenticdesigns.com (8)

The Author's, Writer's & Information Book/Video Publisher's Advice-Line, Middle Island, NY. Tel: (631) 924-3888, (631) 775-6075, FAX: (631) 924-8555, E-Mail: andrewlinick@gmail.com; linickgroup@gmail.com, Web Site: andrewlinickdirectmarketing.com; www.asklinick.com (20)

Auto Anything, San Diego, CA. Tel: (858) 569-8111, (800) 874-8888, FAX: (858) 569-8503, E-Mail: customerservice@autoanything.com, Web Site: www.autoanything.com (34)

Autobytel Inc, Irvine, CA. Tel: (949) 225-4500, Web Site: www.autobytel.com (23)

Autodesk Inc, San Rafael, CA. Tel: (415) 507-5000, FAX: (415) 507-5100, Web Site: www.autodesk.com (16)

Automated Equipment Service Inc, Poughkeepsie, NY. Tel: (845) 452-2100, (800) 468-4068, FAX: (845) 485-8221, E-Mail: info@aesmailpro.com, Web Site: www.aesmailpro.com (34)

Automated Graphic Systems Inc, White Plains, MD. Tel: (301) 843-1800, (800) 678-8760, FAX: (301) 843-6339, E-Mail: info@ags.com, Web Site: www.ags.com (31)

Automated Mailing Systems Corp, Dallas, TX. Tel: (972) 869-2844, (800) 527-1668, FAX: (972) 869-2735, E-Mail: amsco@amscodallas.com (34)

Automatic Mail Services Inc, Long Island City, NY. Tel: (718) 361-3091, FAX: (718) 937-8568, E-Mail: data@automatic-mail.com, Web Site: www.automatic-mail.com (28)

Automation Mailing & Shipping Solutions Inc, Cleveland, OH. Tel: (216) 241-4487, (800) 883-7935, FAX: (216) 241-5918, E-Mail: service@mailshipsolutions.com, Web Site: www.mailshipsolutions.com (16)

Automation Research Inc, Columbus, OH. Tel: (614) 538-1507 (22)

Automod, Atlanta, GA. Tel: (770) 457-9663, (800) 241-1832, FAX: (770) 457-6089, Web Site: www.automod.net (12)

Automotive Forms, Baltimore, MD. Tel: (410) 285-3700, FAX: (410) 284-8418, E-Mail: sales@autoforms.com, Web Site: www.autoforms.com (16)

Automotive Headphones, Sterling Heights, MI. Tel: (586) 292-6166 (16)

AutoPacific Inc, Tustin, CA. Tel: (714) 838-4234, FAX: (714) 838-4260, Web Site: www.autopacific.com (30)

Autor, Robert, S., SLM Corp, Reston, VA. Tel: (703) 810-3000, FAX: (703) 984-5042, Web Site: www.salliemae.com (16)

Avalanche Creative Services Inc, New York, NY. Tel: (212) 206-9335, FAX: (212) 206-1538, E-Mail: info@avalanchecreative.tv, Web Site: www.avalanchecreative.tv (35)

Avantus, Maryland Heights, MO. Tel: (314) 994-3449, Web Site: www.avantus.com (20)

Avary, Robert, Wagner Hines & Avary Inc, Alexandria, VA. Tel: (703) 684-7740, FAX: (703) 548-3721 (20)

Avatar Studios, Saint Louis, MO. Tel: (314) 533-2242, FAX: (314) 533-3349, Web Site: www.avatar-studios.com (32)

Avaya Communication, Temecula, CA. Web Site: www.avaya.com (34)

Aveda Corp, Minneapolis, MN. Tel: (763) 951-4201, Web Site: www.aveda.com (7)

Aveni, Ted, Neighborhood Cleaners Association International, New York, NY. Tel: (212) 967-3002, (800) 888-1622, FAX: (212) 967-2240, E-Mail: info@nca-i.com, Web Site: www.nca-i.com (1)

Aveni, Tony, G.A. Wright Direct Marketing, Denver, CO. Tel: (303) 333-4453, FAX: (303) 333-4660, E-Mail: gaming@gawright.com, Web Site: www.gawrightcasinomarketing.com (21)

Averbook, Art, CO-OP PROMOTIONS, Hollywood, FL. Tel: (954) 922-2323, FAX: (954) 922-2071, E-Mail: art@co-oppromotions.com, Web Site: www.co-oppromotions.com (35)

Avery, Sharon, Kobie Marketing Inc, Saint Petersburg, FL. Tel: (727) 822-5353, (800) 821-7892, FAX: (727) 822-5265, Web Site: www.kobie.com (35)

Avery, William, J., Lincoln Financial Group, Radnor, PA. Tel: (215) 448-1400, (877) 275-5462, FAX: (215) 448-3962, Web Site: www.lfg.com (15)

Avery Dennison Corp, Brea, CA. Tel: (714) 674-8500, (800) 462-8379, FAX: (714) 674-6929, Web Site: www.avery.com (10)

Avet, Jon, The American Film Institute, Los Angeles, CA. Tel: (323) 856-7600, FAX: (323) 467-4578, Web Site: www.afi.com (1)

Aviation Book Co, Seattle, WA. Tel: (206) 767-5232, FAX: (206) 763-3428, E-Mail: sales@aviationbook.com, Web Site: www.aviationbook.com (17)

Avis World Headquarters, Parsippany, NJ. Tel: (973) 496-3500, Web Site: www.avis.com (19)

Avitan, Guy, MRV Communications, Chatsworth, CA. Tel: (818) 773-0900, FAX: (818) 773-0906, Web Site: www.mrv.com (3)

Aviva USA Corp, Des Moines, IA. Tel: (515) 362-3600, FAX: (800) 531-0038, Web Site: www.avivausa.com (14)

Avletta, Karen, REI-Recreational Equipment Inc, Kent, WA. Tel: (253) 891-2500, (800) 426-4840, FAX: (253) 891-2523, Web Site: www.rei.com (11)

AvMed Health Plan Inc, Miami, FL. Tel: (305) 671-5437, Web Site: www.avmed.org (1)

Avnet Inc, Phoenix, AZ. Tel: (480) 643-2000, FAX: (480) 643-7240, Web Site: www.avnet.com (16)

Avon Books, New York, NY. Tel: (212) 207-7000, FAX: (212) 207-7222 (17)

Avon Products Inc, New York, NY. Tel: (212) 282-7000, (800) 367-2866, FAX: (212) 282-6225, Web Site: www.avon.com (7)

Avrick, Adam, Design Distributors, Inc, Deer Park, NY. Tel: (631) 242-2000, FAX: (631) 242-7367, E-Mail: info@designdistributors.com, Web Site: www.designdistributors.com (21)

Avrick, David, Avrick Direct Inc, Santa Barbara, CA. Tel: (805) 683-6551, FAX: (805) 965-6181, E-Mail: david@avrick.com, Web Site: www.avrickdirect.com (23)

Avrick Direct Inc, Santa Barbara, CA. Tel: (805) 683-6551, FAX: (805) 965-6181, E-Mail: david@avrick.com, Web Site: www.avrickdirect.com (23)

Award Co of America, Tuscaloosa, AL. Tel: (205) 349-2990, FAX: (205) 752-0930, Web Site: www.randallpub.com (6)

Award Marketing Services LLC, Whitehouse, NJ. Tel: (908) 534-5700, FAX: (908) 534-0903, E-Mail: grcanose@aol.com, Web Site: www.awardmarketingservices.com (33)

Axia, Jacksonville, FL. Tel: (904) 425-6652, (866) 999-AXIA, FAX: (904) 425-6653, E-Mail: tellmemore@axia.net, Web Site: www.axia.net (35)

Axis Capital, New York, NY. Tel: (212) 500-7743 (14)

Axmacher, Thomas, Global Equipment Co Inc, Port Washington, NY. Tel: (516) 484-3100, (888) 978-7759, FAX: (516) 608-7111, Web Site: www.globalindustrial.com (9)

Ayan, Jordan, SubscriberMail LLC, Lisle, IL. Tel: (630) 303-5000, Web Site: www.subscribermail.com (22)

Aycock, Thomas, United Investors Life Insurance Co, Birmingham, AL. Tel: (205) 325-4300, (800) 288-2722, FAX: (205) 325-4157, Web Site: www.uilic.com (15)

Ayer, Ramani, The Hartford Financial Services Inc, Southington, CT. Tel: (860) 843-8070, (860) 547-5000, FAX: (860) 547-2680, Web Site: www.thehartford.com (15)

Ayers, Scott, Beckmann Converting Inc, Amsterdam, NY. Tel: (518) 842-0073, FAX: (518) 842-0282, E-Mail: ppiusz@beckmannconverting.com, Web Site: www.beckmannconverting.com (16)

Ayers, Teresa, W., Gambro Inc, Lakewood, CO. Tel: (303) 232-6800, (800) 525-2623, FAX: (303) 222-6810, Web Site: www.gambro.com (16)

The Ayn Rand Institute, Irvine, CA. Tel: (949) 222-6550, FAX: (949) 222-6558, E-Mail: mail@aynrand.org, Web Site: www.aynrand.org (1)

Ayvazian, Berge, The Yankee Group, Boston, MA. Tel: (617) 598-7200, E-Mail: info@yankeegroup.com, Web Site: www.yankeegroup.com (20)

Azevedo, Milena, PCS List & Information Technologies, Manchester, MA. Tel: (978) 532-7100, (800) 532-LIST, FAX: (978) 532-9181, E-Mail: info@pcslist.com, Web Site: www.pcslist.com (23)

B

The B&F System Inc, Dallas, TX. Tel: (214) 333-2111, FAX: (214) 333-2137, E-Mail: service@bnfusa.com, Web Site: www.bnfusa.com (33)

B&G Lieberman Co Inc, Charlotte, NC. Tel: (704) 376-0717, (800) 438-0346, FAX: (800) 248-2696, E-Mail: bgl@bglieberman.com, Web Site: www.bglieberman.com (16)

B&W Press Inc, Georgetown, MA. Tel: (978) 352-6100, (877) 246-3467, FAX: (978) 352-5955, E-Mail: csr@bwpress.com, Web Site: www.bwpress.com (21)

B Bunch Co Inc, Phoenix, AZ. Tel: (602) 997-6452, FAX: (602) 997-7266, E-Mail: sales@bbunch.com, Web Site: www.bbunch.com (16)

B-T-B Internet Marketing Solutions, Middle Island, NY. Tel: (631) 924-3888, E-Mail: linickgroup@gmail.com, Web Site: www.linick.net; 222.asklinick.com (39)

BAI, Chicago, IL. Tel: (312) 683-2464, FAX: (312) 683-2373, E-Mail: info@bai.org, Web Site: www.bai.org (1)

BBC Direct Mktg Svcs, Shamong, NJ. Tel: (877) 786-4389, FAX: (609) 268-9939, E-Mail: csr@bbcglobal.com, Web Site: www.bbcglobal.com (20)

BBC Worldwide Americas Inc, New York, NY. Tel: (212) 705-9300, (800) 898-4921, FAX: (212) 888-0576, Web Site: www.bbcamerica.com (3)

BBF Integrated Solutions, Largo, FL. Tel: (800) 666-8082, Web Site: www.bbfprinting.com (27)

BBK Worldwide, Newton, MA. Tel: (617) 630-4477, Web Site: www.bbkworldwide.com (35)

BBM Canada Inc, Don Mills, ON Canada. Tel: (416) 445-9800, FAX: (416) 445-8644, E-Mail: info@bbm.ca, Web Site: www.bbm.ca (30)

BBS & Associates, Akron, OH. Tel: (330) 665-5227, Web Site: www.servantheart.com (1)

BBS Chicago, Chicago, IL. Tel: (312) 326-8000, Web Site: www.rrdonnelley.com (31)

BC & Associates Representatives Inc, Fate, TX. Tel: (972) 722-7365, (800) 275-1298, FAX: (972) 722-7714, E-Mail: terri@bcincentives.com, Web Site: www.bcincentives.com (33)

BCC Software Inc, Rochester, NY. Tel: (585) 272-9130, (800) 453-3130, FAX: (585) 340-8850, Web Site: www.bccsoftware.com (22)

BCR Enterprises Inc, Downers Grove, IL. Tel: (630) 986-1432, (800) 227-1234, FAX: (630) 323-5324, Web Site: www.bcr.com (17)

BDL Homeware, Glendale, AZ. Tel: (623) 572-5038, (800) BDL-4BDL, FAX: (623) 572-5082 (3)

BET Services, Washington, DC. Tel: (202) 608-2000, (800) 626-9911, FAX: (202) 635-3761, Web Site: www.bet.com (32)

BFC, Batavia, IL. Tel: (630) 879-9240, Web Site: www.bfcprint.com (28)

BFS Credit Services Co, Brook Park, OH. Tel: (216) 362-5094, FAX: (216) 362-5236, E-Mail: lupinettijim@bfsusa.com (16)

BGE Home Products & Services Inc, Baltimore, MD. Tel: (888) 243-4663, Web Site: www.bgehome.com (16)

BI, Summit, NJ. Tel: (908) 722-4222, FAX: (908) 722-9199, Web Site: www.Biworldwide.com (33)

BJ's Wholesale Club Inc, Westborough, MA. Tel: (508) 651-7400, FAX: (508) 651-6167, Web Site: www.bjs.com (13)

BJT Management Group, Ada, MI. Tel: (616) 682-0369, Web Site: www.bjtmgt.com (20)

BJU Press, Greenville, SC. Tel: (864) 242-5100, (800) 845-5731, FAX: (800) 525-8398, (864) 271-8151, E-Mail: bjupinfo@bjupress.com, Web Site: www.bjupress.com (17)

BKV, Overland Park, KS. Tel: (913) 648-8333, FAX: (913) 648-5024, Web Site: www.bkv.com (35)

BKV Inc, Atlanta, GA. Tel: (404) 233-0332, FAX: (404) 233-0302, E-Mail: sylviam@bkv.com, Web Site: www.bkv.com (35)

BLS Inc, Wilmington, DE. Tel: (302) 631-1616, (800) 545-7766, FAX: (302) 631-1619, E-Mail: bls@tutorsystems.com, Web Site: www.tutorsystems.com (17)

BMD, Alexandria, VA. Tel: (703) 549-3500, Web Site: www.b-m-d.com (35)

BMG Columbia House, New York, NY. Tel: (212) 287-0081, E-Mail: cs1@bmgmusicservice.com (13)

BMI, Nashville, TN. Tel: (615) 401-2000, (800) 925-8451, FAX: (615) 401-2812, E-Mail: genlic@bmi.com, Web Site: www.bmi.com (1)

BMI Fulfillment Services, Danbury, CT. Tel: (203) 546-5580, FAX: (203) 546-5575, E-Mail: barry@bmigroup.com, Web Site: www.bmigroup.com (28)

BMI Home Decorating, Spring Grove, IL. Tel: (815) 675-3703, FAX: (815) 675-3703, E-Mail: bmigroup@aol.com (16)

BN Creative Advertising, Franklin Park, IL. Tel: (847) 577-1300, FAX: (847) 577-2101 (36)

BNY Mellon, New York, NY. Tel: (412) 234-5000, (212) 495-1784, FAX: (412) 234-1928, Web Site: www.bnymellon.com (14)

BOC Gases, Murray Hill, NJ. Tel: (908) 464-8100, (800) 262-4273, FAX: (410) 749-4073, E-Mail: info@linde.com, Web Site: www.boc-gases.com (16)

BP, Warrenville, IL. Tel: (630) 821-3000, (800) 638-5672, Web Site: www.bp.com (16)

BT Alex Brown Inc, Baltimore, MD. Tel: (410) 727-1700, (800) 638-2956, Web Site: www.dbalexbrown.com (14)

BT Americas, New York, NY. Tel: (646) 487-7400, (800) 331-4568, FAX: (646) 487-3370, Web Site: www.btglobalservices.com (22)

BWB Marketing Services, Ankeny, IA. Tel: (515) 986-1992, Web Site: www.bwbmarketing.com (22)

BYK-Gardner USA, Columbia, MD. Tel: (310) 483-6500, Web Site: www.byk.com (16)

B2E Direct Marketing Inc, Grimes, IA. Tel: (515) 986-1992, Web Site: www.bwbmarketing.com (22)

Ba, Sujuan, National Foundation for Cancer Research, Bethesda, MD. Tel: (301) 654-1250, (800) 321-CURE, FAX: (301) 654-5824, E-Mail: info@nfcr.org, Web Site: www.nfcr.org (1)

Babb Jr., Ralph, W., Comerica Inc, Dallas, TX. Tel: (800) 521-1190, FAX: (925) 941-1999, Web Site: www.comerica.com (14)

Babcock, Bill, Babcock & Jenkins, Portland, OR. Tel: (503) 629-6090, FAX: (503) 629-8570, E-Mail: billb@bnj.com, Web Site: www.bnj.com (35)

Babcock, Loreen, Unit 7, New York, NY. Tel: (212) 209-1600, FAX: (212) 209-1800, E-Mail: lbabcock@unit7.com, Web Site: www.unit7.com (35)

Babcock & Jenkins, Portland, OR. Tel: (503) 629-6090, FAX: (503) 629-8570, E-Mail: billb@bnj.com, Web Site: www.bnj.com (35)

Babcook, Richard, Chicago Magazine, Chicago, IL. Tel: (312) 222-8999, FAX: (312) 222-0287, Web Site: www.chicagomag.com (17)

Babcox, Becky, Babcox Publications LLC, Akron, OH. Tel: (330) 670-1234, FAX: (330) 670-0874, E-Mail: bbabcox@babcox.com, Web Site: www.babcox.com (17)

Babcox Publications LLC, Akron, OH. Tel: (330) 670-1234, FAX: (330) 670-0874, E-Mail: bbabcox@babcox.com, Web Site: www.babcox.com (17)

Baber, Michael, Baber Inc, Memphis, TN. Tel: (901) 332-6300, (800) 847-7040, FAX: (901) 332-6441, E-Mail: info@baberweb.com, Web Site: www.baberweb.com (21)

Baber Inc, Memphis, TN. Tel: (901) 332-6300, (800) 847-7040, FAX: (901) 332-6441, E-Mail: info@baberweb.com, Web Site: www.baberweb.com (21)

Babiak, Jennifer, Miracle of Aloe, Dallas, TX. Tel: (800) 966-2563, FAX: (800) 859-9881, E-Mail: LJohnson@miracleofaloe.com, Web Site: www.miracleofaloe.com (7)

Babyshoe.com, Hendersonville, NC. Tel: (828) 697-5811, (800) 543-8566, FAX: (828) 697-5815, E-Mail: info@babyshoe.com, Web Site: www.babyshoe.com (6)

Bacharach, Jason, Grafica Group, Morristown, NJ. Tel: (973) 309-7500, FAX: (973) 309-7501, E-Mail: info@grafica.com, Web Site: www.grafica.com (35)

Bachrach Clothing Inc, New York, NY. Tel: (630) 523-5035, Web Site: www.bachrach.com (2)

Back Designs Inc, Novato, CA. Tel: (415) 883-4683, FAX: (510) 549-0837, E-Mail: info@backdesigns.com, Web Site: www.backdesigns.com (7)

Back to the Bible, Lincoln, NE. Tel: (402) 464-7200, (800) 811-2397, FAX: (402) 464-7474, E-Mail: info@backtothebible.org, Web Site: www.backtothebible.org (5)

Backe, John, Backe Digital Brand Marketing, Radnor, PA. Tel: (610) 947-6901, E-Mail: jbacke@backemarketing.com, Web Site: www.backemarketing.com (35)

Backe Digital Brand Marketing, Radnor, PA. Tel: (610) 947-6901, E-Mail: jbacke@backemarketing.com, Web Site: www.backemarketing.com (35)

Backer, Patty, HH Backer Associates Inc, Chicago, IL. Tel: (312) 578-1818, FAX: (312) 578-1819, E-Mail: hhbacker@hhbacker.com, Web Site: www.hhbacker.com (17)

HH Backer Associates Inc, Chicago, IL. Tel: (312) 578-1818, FAX: (312) 578-1819, E-Mail: hhbacker@hhbacker.com, Web Site: www.hhbacker.com (17)

Backman, John, Backman Writing & Communications, Rensselaer, NY. Tel: (518) 449-4985, FAX: (518) 449-7273, E-Mail: johnb@backwrite.com, Web Site: www.backwrite.com (39)

Backman Writing & Communications, Rensselaer, NY. Tel: (518) 449-4985, FAX: (518) 449-7273, E-Mail: johnb@backwrite.com, Web Site: www.backwrite.com (39)

Backus, Richard, Mother Earth News Magazine, Topeka, KS. Tel: (785) 274-4300, (800) 678-5779, FAX: (785) 274-4305, E-Mail: bwelch@ogdenpubs.com, Web Site: www.cappers.com (17)

Backyard Gardening, Tiger, GA. Tel: (706) 782-4224, (800) 681-3962, FAX: (800) 311-9539, E-Mail: info@yardzone.com, Web Site: www.yardzone.com (8)

Bacompt Systems Inc, Carmel, IN. Tel: (317) 574-7474, (800) 533-7109, FAX: (317) 574-7475, E-Mail: customer.service@bacompt.com, Web Site: www.bacompt.com (21)

Bacon, Leslie, Promo Magazine, New York, NY. Tel: (203) 358-9900, (800) 927-5007, FAX: (203) 358-5816, E-Mail: larry.jaffee@penton.com, Web Site: www.promomagazine.com (17)

Baden, Erik, American General Life Insurance Co, Houston, TX. Tel: (713) 522-1111, FAX: (713) 522-8531, Web Site: www.aglife.com (15)

Bader, Michael, Unimail Corp, Rochester, NY. Tel: (585) 254-7510, (800) 688-6878, FAX: (585) 254-2367 (28)

Bader Rutter & Associates, Brookfield, WI. Tel: (262) 784-7200, FAX: (262) 938-5595, Web Site: www.baderrutter.com (35)

Badge-A-Minit, Oglesby, IL. Tel: (815) 883-8822, (800) 223-4103, FAX: (815) 883-9696, Web Site: www.badgeaminit.com (16)

Badger, Bill, Guiding Eyes for the Blind, Yorktown Heights, NY. Tel: (914) 245-4042, (800) 942-0149, FAX: (914) 245-1609, Web Site: www.guidingeyes.org (16)

Badger Press Inc, Grayslake, IL. Tel: (847) 996-1190, E-Mail: info@badgerpressinc.com, Web Site: www.badgerpressinc.com (27)

Badger Press/Photographics Inc, Kenosha, WI. Tel: (262) 658-1628, (800) 635-9773, FAX: (262) 658-0307 (27)

Badgett III, Guy, M., Vulcan Materials Co, Birmingham, AL. Tel: (205) 298-3000, FAX: (205) 298-2960, Web Site: www.vulcanmaterials.com (16)

Badin, Chris, CVS Caremark, Woonsocket, RI. Tel: (401) 765-1500, FAX: (401) 769-4488, Web Site: www.cvs.com (7)

Badler, Jeffrey, P., Maurice Badler Fine Jewelry Ltd, New York, NY. Tel: (212) 575-9632, (800) M-BADLER, FAX: (212) 575-9205, E-Mail: info@badler.com, Web Site: www.badler.com (2)

Maurice Badler Fine Jewelry Ltd, New York, NY. Tel: (212) 575-9632, (800) M-BADLER, FAX: (212) 575-9205, E-Mail: info@badler.com, Web Site: www.badler.com (2)

Bado, Ken, Autodesk Inc, San Rafael, CA. Tel: (415) 507-5000, FAX: (415) 507-5100, Web Site: www.autodesk.com (16)

Baer, D. Richard, Hollywood Film Archive, Los Angeles, CA. Tel: (323) 655-4968, Web Site: www.hfarchive.com (17)

Baer, Dave, Simplex Grinnell, Westminster, MA. Tel: (978) 731-2500, (800) SIMPLEX, FAX: (978) 731-7856, Web Site: www.simplexgrinnel.com (16)

Baer, J., Muldoon & Baer Inc, Palm Beach Gardens, FL. Tel: (561) 630-0999, FAX: (561) 630-9466, Web Site: www.muldoonandbaer.com (20)

Baert, Bernard, Poly One Corp, Avon Lake, OH. Tel: (440) 930-1000, (866) POLY-ONE, FAX: (440) 930-1428, Web Site: www.polyone.com (16)

Baez, Lisa, Travel Planners Inc, New York, NY. Tel: (212) 532-1660, (800) 221-3531, FAX: (212) 779-6102, Web Site: www.tphousing.com (19)

Baeza, Cesar, Brotherhood America's Oldest Winery Ltd, Washingtonville, NY. Tel: (845) 496-3661, FAX: (845) 496-8720, E-Mail: contact@brotherhoodwinery.net, Web Site: www.brotherhoodwinery.net (19)

Bafaro, Tami, Anheuser-Busch Inc Promotional Products Group, Shelton, CT. Tel: (800) 742-5283, Web Site: www.budshop.com (6)

Bagg, Gerald, Quigley Simpson, Los Angeles, CA. Tel: (310) 996-5820, Web Site: www.quigleysimpson.com (35)

Baggett, Sandy, ITW Vortec, Cincinnati, OH. Tel: (513) 891-7474, (800) 441-7475, FAX: (513) 891-4092, E-Mail: techsupport@vortec.com, Web Site: www.vortec.com (16)

Bahai, Ahmad, National Semiconductor Corp, Santa Clara, CA. Tel: (408) 721-5000, (800) 272-9959, FAX: (408) 245-0671, E-Mail: new.feedback@nsc.com, Web Site: www.national.com (16)

Bahamas Ministry of Tourism, Fort Lauderdale, FL. Tel: (954) 236-9292, Web Site: www.bahamas.com (19)

Bahash, Robert, J., The McGraw-Hill Cos, New York, NY. Tel: (212) 904-2000, (866) 436-8502, FAX: (212) 512-3840, Web Site: www.mcgraw-hill.com (17)

Bahler, Gary, M., Champs Corp, Bradenton, FL. Tel: (941) 748-0577, (800) 991-6813, E-Mail: customer_service@champssports.com, Web Site: www.champssports.com (11)

Bai, Henry, Compustar, Mineola, NY. Tel: (516) 747-2510, FAX: (516) 747-4349, E-Mail: compustar@hotmail.com, Web Site: www.compustar-usa.com (3)

Baia, Paul, E., Datum Timing, Test & Measurement, Beverly, MA. Tel: (978) 927-8220, FAX: (978) 927-4099, E-Mail: wriley@datum.com, Web Site: www.datum.com (9)

Baier Stein, Donna, Baier Stein Direct, Bernardsville, NJ. Tel: (908) 781-7849, Web Site: www.directcopy.com (20)

Baier Stein Direct, Bernardsville, NJ. Tel: (908) 781-7849, Web Site: www.directcopy.com (20)

Baik-Kromalic, Sue, S., ASM International, Materials Park, OH. Tel: (440) 338-5151, (800) 336-5152, FAX: (440) 338-4634, E-Mail: customerservice@asminternational.org, Web Site: www.asminternational.org (1)

Bailey, Angela, Ingenix, Reston, VA. Tel: (571) 521-7661, (800) 765-6713, FAX: (571) 521-7237, E-Mail: inform@ingenix.com, Web Site: www.ingenix.com (32)

Bailey, Anne, Collector's Teapot, Kingston, NY. Tel: (845) 339-1109, (800) 724-3306, FAX: (845) 339-5530, Web Site: www.collectorsteapot.com (6)

Bailey, Bonnie, CUNA - Trade Association, Madison, WI. Tel: (608) 231-4215, Web Site: www.cuna.org (1)

Bailey, Carol, The Letter Shop Inc, Pittsburgh, PA. Tel: (412) 882-6200, FAX: (412) 882-7200, E-Mail: info@lettershopcanton.com (28)

Bailey, Hal, Family Christian Stores, Grand Rapids, MI. Tel: (616) 554-8700, (888) 319-0319, FAX: (616) 554-8694, E-Mail: info@fcsdirect.familychristian.com, Web Site: www.familychristian.com (5)

Bailey, Jim, Collector's Teapot, Kingston, NY. Tel: (845) 339-1109, (800) 724-3306, FAX: (845) 339-5530, Web Site: www.collectorsteapot.com (6)

Bailey, Michael, Jostens, Inc, Minneapolis, MN. Tel: (952) 830-3300, FAX: (952) 830-3293, Web Site: www.jostens.com (16)

Bailey, Mike, Reb Storage Systems International, Chicago, IL. Tel: (773) 252-0400, (800) 252-5955, FAX: (773) 252-0303, E-Mail: sales@rebsteel.com, Web Site: www.industrialebuy.com (9)

Bailey, Nik, Bailey's Inc, Laytonville, CA. Tel: (707) 984-6133, (800) 322-4539, FAX: (707) 984-8115, E-Mail: baileys@bbaileys.com, Web Site: www.baileys-online.com (9)

Bailey, Victoria, Theatre Development Fund Inc, New York, NY. Tel: (212) 912-9770, E-Mail: info@tdf.org, Web Site: www.tdf.org (1)

Bailey, Wendy, Integrated Messaging Inc, Winnipeg, MB Canada. Tel: (204) 786-7630, (800) 561-3734, FAX: (204) 786-7718, E-Mail: sales@imi.mb.ca, Web Site: www.imi.mb.ca (29)

Bailey's Inc, Laytonville, CA. Tel: (707) 984-6133, (800) 322-4539, FAX: (707) 984-8115, E-Mail: baileys@bbaileys.com, Web Site: www.baileys-online.com (9)

Bailis, David, P., First Data Merchant Services, Greenwood Village, CO. Tel: (303) 488-8000, (800) 735-3362, Web Site: www.firstdata.com (14)

Bain, Judith, S., Epson America, Long Beach, CA. Tel: (562) 981-3840, (800) 873-7766, FAX: (562) 290-5220, Web Site: www.epson.com (10)

Bainum Jr., Stewart, Choice Hotels International, Silver Spring, MD. Tel: (301) 592-6636, (888) 770-6800, FAX: (301) 592-6157, E-Mail: ihelp@choicehotels.com, Web Site: www.choicebuys.com (16)

Bair, Royce, The Stock Solution Inc, West Jordan, UT. Tel: (801) 566-8684, (888) 366-0430, FAX: (801) 961-8030, E-Mail: info@tssphoto.com, Web Site: www.tssphoto.com (38)

Baird, Amy, Peter Li Education Group, Dayton, OH. Tel: (937) 293-1415, (800) 523-4625, FAX: (937) 293-1310, Web Site: www.peterli.com (17)

Baird, Richard, L., PricewaterhouseCoopers LLP, New York, NY. Tel: (646) 471-4000, FAX: (646) 471-4444, Web Site: www.pwc.com (14)

Bakehorn, Michael, American Stationery Co Inc, Peru, IN. Tel: (765) 473-4438, (800) 822-2577, FAX: (800) 253-9054, Web Site: www.americanstationery.com (10)

Bakehorn, Mike, The RYTEX Co, Peru, IN. Tel: (317) 872-8553, (800) 277-5458, FAX: (317) 872-8535, (800) 329-1669, Web Site: www.rytex.com (10)

Baker Jr, David, B., Reese Press Inc, Pikesville, MD. Tel: (410) 467-9200, FAX: (410) 467-9520 (27)

Baker, Alissa, Magnets 4 Media, Washington, MO. Tel: (843) 216-6665, (800) 642-6384, FAX: (636) 390-5147, E-Mail: sales@magnets4media.com, Web Site: www.magnets4media.com (30)

Baker, Ben, Infinity Trading Co Inc, Spring, TX. Tel: (281) 931-8000, FAX: (281) 931-8139, E-Mail: sales@infinitytradingcompany.com, Web Site: www.infinitytradingcompany.com (34)

Baker, Charles, D., Harvard Pilgrim Health Care, Wellesley, MA. Tel: (617) 509-1000, FAX: (617) 509-7590, Web Site: www.harvardpilgrim.org (7)

Baker, Christopher, Group 1 Software Inc, Lanham, MD. Tel: (301) 731-2300, (888) 413-6763, FAX: (301) 731-0360, E-Mail: info@g1.com, Web Site: www.g1.com (22)

Baker, Constance, Edo Interactive, Nashville, TN. Tel: (615) 297-6080, Web Site: www.edointeractive.com (14)

Baker, Craig, A., Domestic Bank, Providence, RI. Tel: (401) 943-1600, (800) 566-6600, FAX: (401) 943-6708, Web Site: www.domesticbank.com (14)

Baker, Darrell, COMNET Washington, Framingham, MA. Tel: (508) 879-6700, FAX: (508) 370-4325, Web Site: www.comnetexpo.com (42)

Baker, David, Sterling Fluid Systems, Indianapolis, IN. Tel: (317) 925-9661, (800) 879-0182, FAX: (317) 924-7388, Web Site: www.peerlesspump.com (16)

Baker, Don, Baker-Blais Marketing Inc, Pointe-Claire, PQ Canada. Tel: (514) 693-9900, Web Site: www.bakerblais.com (35)

Baker, Heather, BennettBaker Ltd, Chicago, IL. Tel: (312) 252-8883, FAX: (312) 252-8209, E-Mail: nbennett@bennettwheelless.com, Web Site: www.bennettbaker.com (20)

Baker, Janet, Indianapolis Newspapers Inc, Indianapolis, IN. Tel: (317) 444-4444, FAX: (317) 633-9414, Web Site: www.indystar.com (17)

Baker, Jeff, Domestic Bank, Providence, RI. Tel: (401) 943-1600, (800) 566-6600, FAX: (401) 943-6708, Web Site: www.domesticbank.com (14)

Baker, Laura, Sheridan Books Inc, Chelsea, MI. Tel: (734) 662-3291, (734) 475-9145, (800) 999-BOOK, FAX: (734) 475-7337, E-Mail: info@sheridanbooks.com, Web Site: www.sheridanbooks.com (27)

Baker, Mark, A., Steelcase Inc, Grand Rapids, MI. Tel: (616) 247-2710, FAX: (616) 475-2270, Web Site: www.steelcase.com (16)

Baker, Mike, PSI Marketing Consultants Inc, Des Plaines, IL. Tel: (773) 878-0800, (800) 933-4774, FAX: (773) 878-4219 (29)

Baker, Nathaniel, Domestic Bank, Providence, RI. Tel: (401) 943-1600, (800) 566-6600, FAX: (401) 943-6708, Web Site: www.domesticbank.com (14)

Baker, Oleda, Oleda & Co Inc, Fort Worth, TX. Tel: (817) 731-1147, (800) 731-4247, FAX: (817) 731-1149, E-Mail: oleda@oleda.com, Web Site: www.oleda.com (16)

Baker, Rick, Herschend Family Entertainment, Branson, MO. Tel: (417) 338-3810, FAX: (417) 338-8144, Web Site: www.silverdollarcity.com (5)

Baker, Tim, Shield Healthcare, Valencia, CA. Tel: (661) 294-4200, (800) 228-7150, FAX: (661) 294-1043, Web Site: www.shieldhealthcare.com (7)

Baker, Wendy, Bert Davis Executive Search, New York, NY. Tel: (212) 838-4000, FAX: (212) 935-3291, E-Mail: info@bertdavis.com, Web Site: www.bertdavis.com (20)

Baker, William, F., Channel 13 WNET Catalog Division, New York, NY. Tel: (212) 560-2000, FAX: (212) 582-3297, Web Site: www.thirteen.org (5)

Baker, William, The Lacek Group, Minneapolis, MN. Tel: (612) 359-3700, FAX: (612) 359-9395, E-Mail: info@lacek.com, Web Site: www.lacek.com (35)

Baker & Hostetler LLP, Washington, DC. Tel: (202) 861-1500, FAX: (202) 861-1783, E-Mail: wschweitzer@bakerlaw.com, Web Site: www.bakerlaw.com (20)

Baker & Taylor Inc, Charlotte, NC. Tel: (704) 998-3100, (800) 775-1800, FAX: (704) 998-3316, E-Mail: btinfo@btol.com, Web Site: www.btol.com (16)

Baker-Blais Marketing Inc, Pointe-Claire, PQ Canada. Tel: (514) 693-9900, Web Site: www.bakerblais.com (35)

Baker Corp, Seal Beach, CA. Tel: (562) 430-6262 (16)

Baker Schwenk, Donna, PartyLite Gifts Inc, Plymouth, MA. Tel: (508) 830-3100, FAX: (508) 830-0026, Web Site: www.partylite.com (8)

Bakke, Dave, Infinian Corp, Los Altos, CA. Tel: (415) 260-8142, Web Site: www.infinian.com (29)

Balakrishan, T., Government of India Tourist Office, New York, NY. Tel: (212) 586-4901, (800) 953-9399, FAX: (212) 582-3274, Web Site: www.incredibleindia.org (1)

Balboa Life & Casualty, Irvine, CA. Tel: (949) 222-8000, (800) 854-6115, FAX: (949) 222-8777, Web Site: www.balboainsurance.com (15)

Baldani, Michael, PTC, Needham, MA. Tel: (781) 370-5000, Web Site: www.ptc.com (22)

Baldelli, Steven, Direct SAT TV LLC, Southern Pines, NC. Tel: (910) 693-3042, (800) 595-4101, FAX: (866) 935-4097, Web Site: www.directsattv.com (3)

Baldridge, Sally, Jazzercise Inc, Carlsbad, CA. Tel: (760) 476-1750, (800) FIT IS IT, FAX: (760) 602-7180, E-Mail: info@jazzercise.com, Web Site: www.jazzercise.com (2)

Balducci Enterprises Inc, Germantown, MD. Tel: (240) 403-2440, FAX: (240) 403-2520 (16)

Baldwin, Anita, S., Rose Resnick Lighthouse for the Blind & Visually Impaired, San Francisco, CA. Tel: (415) 431-1481, FAX: (415) 863-7568, E-Mail: executive@lighthouse-sf.org, Web Site: www.lighthouse-sf.org (1)

Baldwin, Barbara, American Running Association, Bethesda, MD. Tel: (301) 913-9517, (800) 776-2732, FAX: (301) 913-9520, E-Mail: run@americanrunning.org, Web Site: www.americanrunning.org (1)

Baldwin, James, L., University of Pittsburgh at Bradford, Bradford, PA. Tel: (814) 362-7500, FAX: (814) 362-5150, E-Mail: admissions@www.upb.pitt.edu, Web Site: www.upd.pitt.edu (41)

Baldwin, Mike, Market Data Retrieval, Shelton, CT. Tel: (203) 926-4800, (800) 333-8802, FAX: (203) 929-5253, E-Mail: mdrinfo@dnb.com, Web Site: www.schooldata.com (23)

Baldwin Filters, Kearney, NE. Tel: (308) 234-1951, (800) 822-5394, FAX: (800) 828-4453, E-Mail: info@baldwinfilter.com, Web Site: www.baldwinfilter.com (16)

Bale Co, Providence, RI. Tel: (800) 822-5350, FAX: (401) 831-5500, Web Site: www.bale.com (16)

Baler, Susan, Rich Brands, Phoenix, AZ. Tel: (602) 889-4800, (877) 856-1753, FAX: (602) 889-4830, E-Mail: sales@esscentualbrands.com, Web Site: esscentualbrands.com (16)

Bales, Gary, Carvel Corp, Atlanta, GA. Tel: (404) 255-3250, (800) 227-8353, FAX: (404) 255-4978, Web Site: www.carvel.com (16)

Balfour, Austin, TX. Tel: (512) 444-0571, FAX: (512) 440-1138, Web Site: www.artcarved.com (16)

Balkema, Gary, Bayer Corp Consumer Care Division, Morristown, NJ. Tel: (973) 254-5000, FAX: (973) 408-8215, Web Site: www.bayercare.com (16)

Ball, Arthur, Garver Advertising Service Inc, New York, NY. Tel: (212) 371-3325, E-Mail: garverads@aol.com (35)

Ball, Bob, Merkle Inc, Columbia, MD. Tel: (443) 542-4000, (877) 9MERKLE, Web Site: www. merkleinc.com (22)

Ball, F., Michael, Allergan Inc, Irvine, CA. Tel: (714) 246-4500, (800) 433-8871, FAX: (714) 246-4971, Web Site: www.allergan.com (16)

Ball, George, W Atlee Burpee Co, Warminster, PA. Tel: (215) 674-4900, (800) 333-5808, FAX: (215) 674-4170, Web Site: www.burpee.com (8)

Ball, Les, Miller Stockman, Denver, CO. Tel: (303) 428-5696, FAX: (303) 430-1130 (2)

Ball Publishing, West Chicago, IL. Tel: (630) 231-3675, FAX: (630) 231-5254, E-Mail: info@ ballpublishing.com, Web Site: www.ballpublishing. com (17)

The Ballantine Corp, Wayne, NJ. Tel: (973) 305-1500, Web Site: www.ballantine.com (27)

Ballard, Amanda, Publishers Marketing Association (PMA), Manhattan Beach, CA. Tel: (310) 372-2732, FAX: (310) 374-3342, E-Mail: info@pma-online.org, Web Site: www.pma-online.org (40)

Ballard, Monica, V., RBC Funds, Milwaukee, WI. Tel: (800) 422-2766, Web Site: us.rbcgam.com (14)

Ballard, Perry, Perry Ballard Inc, Saint Joseph, MI. Tel: (616) 983-0611, (800) 800-9547, FAX: (616) 983-0747, Web Site: www.perryballard.com (35)

Ballard Designs, Atlanta, GA. Tel: (404) 352-8486, (800) 367-2775, FAX: (404) 352-1660, Web Site: www.ballarddesigns.com (8)

Perry Ballard Inc, Saint Joseph, MI. Tel: (616) 983-0611, (800) 800-9547, FAX: (616) 983-0747, Web Site: www.perryballard.com (35)

Ballbach, John, VWR International, Radnor, PA. Tel: (610) 386-1700, (800) 932-5000, FAX: (866) 329-2897, Web Site: www.vwrsp.com (34)

Ballek, Garry, Allstate Motor Club, South Barrington, IL. Tel: (847) 551-2300, (800) 998-8697 (13)

Ballen, Morris, Audio & Video Labs Inc, Pennsauken, NJ. Tel: (856) 663-9030, (800) 468-9353, FAX: (856) 661-3450, E-Mail: info@discmakers.com, Web Site: www.discmakers.com (16)

Ballenger, Judy, The Limited Stores Inc, Columbus, OH. Tel: (614) 415-2000, FAX: (614) 415-2057, Web Site: www.limited.com (2)

Balmar Inc, Falls Church, VA. Tel: (703) 289-9000, FAX: (703) 289-9143, E-Mail: marketing@balmar. com, Web Site: www.balmar.com (27)

Balon, Dr Robert, E., The Benchmark Co, Austin, TX. Tel: (512) 707-7500, FAX: (512) 707-7757, E-Mail: thebenc@earthlink.net, Web Site: www. thebenchmarkcompany.net (30)

Balsbaugh, Tod, Virginia Home For Boys, Richmond, VA. Tel: (804) 270-6566, FAX: (804) 270-6574, Web Site: www.boyshome.org (1)

Baltimore Dr., David, AAAS/Science, Washington, DC. Tel: (202) 326-6400, FAX: (202) 371-9526, E-Mail: webmaster@aaas.org, Web Site: www. aaas.org (1)

Baltimore Magazine, Baltimore, MD. Tel: (410) 752-4200, (800) 935-0838, FAX: (410) 625-0280, E-Mail: blori@baltimoremagazine.net, Web Site: www.baltimoremagazine.net (17)

BAM! Direct Inc, Suwanee, GA. Tel: (678) 947-1943, Web Site: www.bamdirect.com (35)

Bambace, Amy, Chase Media Group, Yorktown Heights, NY. Tel: (914) 962-3871, FAX: (914) 962-2040, Web Site: www.chasemultimedia.com (27)

Bamber, Dennis, Woodwind & Brasswind Inc, Indianapolis, IN. Tel: (574) 251-3500, (800) 348-5003, FAX: (574) 251-3501, Web Site: www.wwbw.com (5)

Bamboo Cricket, West Palm Beach, FL. Tel: (561) 768-7968, (800) 260-8050, FAX: (561) 653-3990, Web Site: www.bamboocricket.com (32)

Bamboo Cricket Service, Titusville, FL. Tel: (888) 634-7097, FAX: (646) 390-6313, E-Mail: info@ bamboocricket.com, Web Site: www. bamboocricket.com (22)

Bamboo Sourcery, Sebastopol, CA. Tel: (707) 823-5866, FAX: (707) 829-8106, E-Mail: bamboosource@earthlink.net, Web Site: www. bamboosourcery.com (8)

Banana Republic, Grove City, OH. Tel: (888) 277-8953, FAX: (888) 906-2465, Web Site: www. bananarepublic.com (2)

Banfill, Stephanie, IMPACT Publishing Inc, Bradenton, FL. Tel: (941) 739-2611, (800) 4-A-NEW-ME, FAX: (941) 756-0315, E-Mail: info@ impactpublishinginc.com, Web Site: www. impactpublishinginc.com (17)

Bank Boston, Waltham, MA. Tel: (781) 788-7795, FAX: (781) 788-2513, Web Site: www.bankboston. com (14)

Joseph A Bank Clothiers Inc, Hampstead, MD. Tel: (410) 239-2700, (800) 285-2265, FAX: (410) 239-5911, E-Mail: service@jos-a-bank.com, Web Site: www.josbank.com (2)

Bank of America, Charlotte, NC. Tel: (704) 386-5681, (800) 841-4000, FAX: (704) 386-6699, Web Site: www.bankofamerica.com (14)

Bank of Hawaii, Honolulu, HI. Tel: (808) 537-8398, FAX: (808) 536-9433, Web Site: www.boh.com (14)

The Bank of New York/Delaware, Newark, DE. Tel: (302) 451-2500, (800) 942-1977, FAX: (302) 451-2537, Web Site: www.bankofny.com (14)

Bank of the West, Los Angeles, CA. Tel: (509) 736-0131, Web Site: www.bankofthewest.com (14)

Bank One, Chicago, IL. Tel: (888) 963-4000, (866) 265-1727, (800) 452-3141, Web Site: www. bankone.com (14)

Banker & Tradesman, Boston, MA. Tel: (617) 428-5100, FAX: (617) 428-5119, E-Mail: dmoore@ thewarrengroup.com, Web Site: www. thewarrengroup.com (17)

Bankers Life & Casualty Co, Chicago, IL. Tel: (312) 396-6000, (800) 231-9150, Web Site: www. bankerslife.com (15)

Bankers Warranty Group, Saint Petersburg, FL. Tel: (800) 431-5843, E-Mail: info@ bankerswarrantygroup.com, Web Site: www. bankerswarrantygroup.com (16)

Banks, Christina, Caesars Atlantic City Casino/Hotel, Atlantic City, NJ. Tel: (609) 348-4411, (800) 634-6661, FAX: (609) 343-2405, Web Site: www. harrahs.com (19)

Banner, Robert, Children's Miracle Network, Salt Lake City, UT. Tel: (801) 214-7400, Web Site: www.cmn.org (6)

Banner & Greif Ltd, New York, NY. Tel: (212) 847-0010, FAX: (212) 949-9806 (35)

Banninger, Peter, Davidoff of Geneva Inc, Pinellas Park, FL. Tel: (203) 323-5811, (800) 328-4365, FAX: (203) 975-0090 (6)

Bannister, Michael, E., Ford Motor Co, Dearborn, MI. Tel: (313) 845-8540, (800) 555-5259, FAX: (313) 845-6073, Web Site: www.ford.com (16)

Bantam Dell Publishing Group Inc, New York, NY. Tel: (212) 782-9000, FAX: (212) 940-7381, Web Site: www.randomhouse.com/bantamdell (17)

Bantivoglio, Barbara, Channel 13 WNET Catalog Division, New York, NY. Tel: (212) 560-2000, FAX: (212) 582-3297, Web Site: www.thirteen.org (5)

Baptiste, Margaret, National Active & Retired Federal Employees Association, Alexandria, VA. Tel: (703) 838-7760, (800) 456-8410, FAX: (703) 838-7785, Web Site: www.narfe.org (1)

Baraga, Anthony, R., University of Minnesota Alumni Association, Minneapolis, MN. Tel: (612) 624-2323, (800) UM-ALUMS, FAX: (612) 626-8167, E-Mail: umalumni@umn.edu, Web Site: www. umaa.umn.edu (1)

Baraga, Toni, R Falls Agency, Minneapolis, MN. Tel: (612) 872-6372, (800) 339-1119, FAX: (612) 872-1018, E-Mail: info@fallsagency.com, Web Site: www.fallsagency.com (35)

Baranski, Dennis, A., Northern Cross, Lecompton, KS. Tel: (785) 887-6010, (800) 625-7233, FAX: (785) 887-6263 (16)

Baratoff, Michael, Metropolitan Newspaper Advertising Services Inc, New York, NY. Tel: (212) 689-8200, FAX: (212) 532-1710, E-Mail: getinfo@ metrosn.com, Web Site: www.metrosn.com (31)

Barbato, Anthony, Associated Textile Rental Services, Rochester, NY. Tel: (585) 454-5988, (800) 639-4624, Web Site: www.associatedtextile.com (16)

Barbeosch, George T., United States Bronze Sign Co Inc, New Hyde Park, NY. Tel: (516) 352-5155, FAX: (516) 352-1761, Web Site: www.usbronze. com (1)

Barber, Dar, Biomerica Inc, Irvine, CA. Tel: (949) 645-2111, FAX: (949) 722-6674, E-Mail: bmra@ biomerica.com, Web Site: www.biomerica.com (7)

Barber, Howard, Shelby Insurance Companies, Birmingham, AL. Tel: (800) 443-1573, FAX: (877) 837-8203, Web Site: www.vesta.com (15)

Barber, John, Summit Direct Mail Inc, Dallas, TX. Tel: (469) 916-5170, Web Site: www.summitdm. com (28)

Barber, Michael, J., Biosciences-Amersham, Piscataway, NJ. Tel: (732) 457-8000, FAX: (732) 457-0557, Web Site: www.amersham.com (16)

Barbo, Gary, Starchtech, Golden Valley, MN. Tel: (763) 545-5400, (800) 597-7225, FAX: (763) 545-9450, Web Site: www.starchtech.com (16)

Barbour, Matthew, Omnigraphics Inc, Aston, PA. Tel: (610) 461-3548, (800) 234-1340, FAX: (800) 875-1340, E-Mail: info@omnigraphics.com, Web Site: www.omnigraphics.com (17)

Barbour Publishing Inc, Uhrichsville, OH. Tel: (740) 922-6045, FAX: (740) 922-5948, (800) 220-5948, E-Mail: info@barbourbooks.com, Web Site: www. barbourbooks.com (17)

Barcia, Joseph, A., Barcia Direct Marketing, Langhorne, PA. Tel: (215) 757-5785, FAX: (215) 757-5785, E-Mail: j.barciadirect@comcast.net (39)

Barcia Direct Marketing, Langhorne, PA. Tel: (215) 757-5785, FAX: (215) 757-5785, E-Mail: j.barciadirect@comcast.net (39)

Barcoding Inc, Baltimore, MD. Tel: (410) 385-8532, (888) 860-SCAN, (888) 860-7226, FAX: (410) 385-8559, E-Mail: info@barcoding.com, Web Site: www.barcoding.com (2)

Bardenheier Jr., George, Partners Marketing Inc, Saint Charles, IL. Tel: (630) 524-9901, FAX: (630) 524-9909, E-Mail: georgeb@partnersmarketing.com, Web Site: www.partnersmarketing.com (22)

Bardin, Dan R., Conseco Inc, Carmel, IN. Tel: (317) 817-6100, FAX: (317) 817-2847, Web Site: www. conseco.com (15)

Barefoot, Glenn, P., Strongwell, Bristol, VA. Tel: (276) 645-8000, FAX: (276) 645-8132, E-Mail: gbarefoot@strongwell.com, Web Site: www. strongwell.com (9)

Barela, Jeff, Dovetail, Littleton, CO. Tel: (303) 904-4771, FAX: (303) 904-4776, E-Mail: welcome@ dovetailnet.com, Web Site: www.dovetailnet.com (22)

Barely Nothings Lingerie, Nipomo, CA. Tel: (805) 489-5591, (800) 422-7359, FAX: (888) 489-5987, E-Mail: lingerie@barelynothings.com, Web Site: www.getpassionhere.com (2)

Barenklau, Shon, Papillion Times Group, Bellevue, NE. Tel: (402) 339-3331, (877) 476-4237, FAX: (402) 537-2997, E-Mail: advertising@ papilliontimes.com, Web Site: www.papilliontimes. com (31)

Barg, Ron, Apothecary Products Inc, Burnsville, MN. Tel: (952) 890-1940, (800) 328-2742, FAX: (800) 328-1584, Web Site: www.apothecaryproducts.com (7)

Bargas, Michael, Things Remembered, Highland Heights, OH. Tel: (440) 473-2000, (866) 902-4438, FAX: (440) 473-2018, E-Mail: customerservice@ thingsremembered.com, Web Site: www. thingsremembered.com (6)

Barham, Blaine, The Union Labor Life Insurance Co, Silver Spring, MD. Tel: (202) 962-2945, FAX: (202) 962-8429, E-Mail: info@ullico.com, Web Site: www.unioncare.com (15)

Barhoover, Kenneth, Liggett-Stashower Direct, Cleveland, OH. Tel: (216) 348-8500, (800) 877-4573, FAX: (216) 736-8118, E-Mail: mnylander@liggett. com, Web Site: www.liggett.com (35)

Baritz, Leonard, Eyeglass Service Industries, Lynbrook, NY. Tel: (516) 599-1135, FAX: (516) 599-4825 (2)

Barker, Gerald, Barker Specialty Co, Cheshire, CT. Tel: (203) 272-2222, (800) BARKERS, (800) 227-5377, FAX: (203) 272-2727, Web Site: www. barkerspecialty.com (33)

Barker, Lee, The Interprovincial Group, Scarborough, ON Canada. Tel: (416) 283-5555, FAX: (416) 283-6643, E-Mail: info@interprovincialgroup.com, Web Site: www.interprovincialgroup.com (21)

Barker, Scott, Bullseye Marketing Inc, Canoga Park, CA. Tel: (818) 888-8700, Web Site: www. bullseyeb2b.com (28)

Barker, Tina, Direct Approach, Phoenix, AZ. Tel: (602) 955-0649, FAX: (602) 955-0654, E-Mail: tbarker@directapproachlists.com, Web Site: www. directapproachlists.com (23)

Barker, William, R., Taylor-Stiles Division, Florence, KY. Tel: (859) 525-7600, (800) 365-8555, FAX: (859) 525-1446, E-Mail: sales@littleford.com, Web Site: www.littleford.com (16)

Bob Barker Co Inc, Fuquay Varina, NC. Tel: (919) 552-3431, Web Site: www.bobbarker.com (5)

Barker Campbell & Farley, Virginia Beach, VA. Tel: (757) 497-4811, FAX: (757) 497-3684, Web Site: www.bc-f.com (35)

Barker Specialty Co, Cheshire, CT. Tel: (203) 272-2222, (800) BARKERS, (800) 227-5377, FAX: (203) 272-2727, Web Site: www.barkerspecialty. com (33)

Barkley, Jackson, Manheim Steamroller, Omaha, NE. Tel: (402) 457-4341, FAX: (402) 457-4332, E-Mail: mailbox@amgram.com, Web Site: www. manheimsteamroller.com (3)

Barkley, Kansas City, MO. Tel: (816) 842-1500, Web Site: www.barkleyUS.com (35)

Barkus, Alan, The Ted Barkus Co Inc, Philadelphia, PA. Tel: (215) 545-0616, FAX: (215) 545-7976 (21)

Barkus, Harriet, The Ted Barkus Co Inc, Philadelphia, PA. Tel: (215) 545-0616, FAX: (215) 545-7976 (21)

The Ted Barkus Co Inc, Philadelphia, PA. Tel: (215) 545-0616, FAX: (215) 545-7976 (21)

Barkyoumb, Francis, Direct Dynamics LLC, Killingworth, CT. Tel: (860) 614-4816, E-Mail: info@ direct-dynamics.com, Web Site: direct-dynamics. com (20)

Barlow, Deborah, Forestry Suppliers Inc, Jackson, MS. Tel: (601) 354-3565, (800) 543-4203, FAX: (601) 292-0165, E-Mail: fsi@forestry-suppliers.com, Web Site: www.forestry-suppliers.com (9)

Barlow, Turalee, Prakken Publications Inc, Ann Arbor, MI. Tel: (734) 975-2800, (800) 530-9673, FAX: (734) 975-2787, E-Mail: vanessa@techdirections. com, Web Site: www.eddigest.com; www. techdirections.com (17)

Barn, Franklin, Vulcan Information Packaging, Vincent, AL. Tel: (205) 672-2241, (800) 633-4526, FAX: (205) 672-1276, Web Site: www.vulcan-online.com (16)

Barna, Michelle, Slifter, New York, NY. Tel: (212) 488-2222, Web Site: www.slifter.com (16)

Barnaby, Paul, Delta Tech Industries, Ontario, CA. Tel: (714) 577-8028, FAX: (714) 577-0140, E-Mail: sales@deltatechindustries.com, Web Site: www.deltatechindustries.com (12)

Barnard, John, Vita-Mix Corp, Cleveland, OH. Tel: (440) 235-4840, (800) VITA-MIX, FAX: (440) 235-3726, E-Mail: service@vitamix.com, Web Site: www.vitamix.com (16)

Barnard, W., G., Vita-Mix Corp, Cleveland, OH. Tel: (440) 235-4840, (800) VITA-MIX, FAX: (440) 235-3726, E-Mail: service@vitamix.com, Web Site: www.vitamix.com (16)

Barnes, Billy, E., Billy E Barnes, Chapel Hill, NC. Tel: (919) 942-6350, FAX: (919) 942-6350, E-Mail: bbarnes218@aol.com, Web Site: www. billybarnes.com (38)

Barnes, Christina, UF College of Advertising, Journalism, & Communications, Gainesville, FL. Tel: (352) 392-4046, FAX: (352) 392-3919, Web Site: www.jou.ufl.edu (41)

Barnes, David, Fresno Oxygen, Fresno, CA. Tel: (559) 233-6684, (800) 404-9353, FAX: (559) 233-4206, E-Mail: info@fresnooxygen.com, Web Site: www. fresnooxygen.com (9)

Barnes, Denise, Babcock & Jenkins, Portland, OR. Tel: (503) 629-6090, FAX: (503) 629-8570, E-Mail: billb@bnj.com, Web Site: www.bnj.com (35)

Barnes, Dennis, Marketing Direct Inc, Saint Louis, MO. Tel: (314) 590-8300, FAX: (314) 966-5632, E-Mail: dbarnes@marketingdirect.com, Web Site: www.marketingdirect.com (35)

Barnes, Doug, Ducks Unlimited, Memphis, TN. Tel: (901) 758-3825, (800) 45DUCKS, FAX: (901) 758-3850, Web Site: www.ducks.org (1)

Barnes, Fred, Hammacher Schlemmer, New York, NY. Tel: (847) 581-8600, (800) 233-4800, FAX: (847) 581-8616, Web Site: www.hammacher.com (16)

Barnes, Gerald, A, Neiman-Marcus Group, Dallas, TX. Tel: (214) 743-7600, (888) 888-4757, FAX: (214) 573-5320, Web Site: www.neimanmarcus. com (8)

Barnes, Heidi, Accuracy in Media Inc, Washington, DC. Tel: (202) 364-4401, FAX: (202) 364-4098, E-Mail: info@aim.org, Web Site: www.aim.org (1)

Barnes, Jim, General Physics Corp, Elkridge, MD. Tel: (410) 379-3600, (800) 727-6677, FAX: (410) 540-5302, E-Mail: info@gpworldwide.com, Web Site: www.gpworldwide.com (16)

Barnes, Karen, Beauty Naturally, Burlingame, CA. Tel: (650) 697-1845, (800) 432-4323, FAX: (650) 697-1970, E-Mail: sales@beautynaturally.com, Web Site: www.beautynaturally.com (7)

Barnes, Mike, Fresno Oxygen, Fresno, CA. Tel: (559) 233-6684, (800) 404-9353, FAX: (559) 233-4206, E-Mail: info@fresnooxygen.com, Web Site: www. fresnooxygen.com (9)

Barnes, Nancy, First Banks Inc, Hazelwood, MO. Tel: (314) 592-5000, (800) 760-2265, Web Site: www. firstbanks.com (14)

Barnes, Red, Fresno Oxygen, Fresno, CA. Tel: (559) 233-6684, (800) 404-9353, FAX: (559) 233-4206, E-Mail: info@fresnooxygen.com, Web Site: www. fresnooxygen.com (9)

Barnes, Robert, Groff DRTV, Portland, ME. Tel: (207) 415-1374, FAX: (207) 771-5320, E-Mail: regfilm@gmail.com, Web Site: www. groffvideo.com (32)

Barnes, Scott, The Psychological Corp, San Antonio, TX. Tel: (800) 211-8378, FAX: (800) 232-1223, Web Site: www.psychcorp.com (17)

Barnes, Simon, American Bible Society, New York, NY. Tel: (212) 408-1200, FAX: (212) 408-1264, Web Site: www.americanbible.org (1)

Barnes, Trevor, Markson Scientific LLC, Henderson, NC. Tel: (808) 791-0490, (800) 528-5114, FAX: (800) 858-2243, E-Mail: sales@markson.com, Web Site: www.markson.com (9)

Barnes & Noble Direct, New York, NY. Tel: (212) 414-6000, FAX: (212) 414-6171, Web Site: www. barnesandnoble.com (3)

BarnesandNoble.com, New York, NY. Tel: (212) 414-6000, (800) THE-BOOK, FAX: (212) 414-6140, E-Mail: service@barnesandnoble.com, Web Site: www.barnesandnoble.com (16)

Barnett, George, Teva Pharmaceuticals USA, North Wales, PA. Tel: (215) 591-3000, (888) TEVAUSA, FAX: (215) 591-8600, Web Site: www.tevausa.com (7)

Barnett, Lauren, Society for Healthcare Strategy & Market Development, Chicago, IL. Tel: (312) 422-3888, FAX: (312) 422-4579, E-Mail: stratsoc@aha. org, Web Site: www.stratsociety.org (42)

Barney, George, B., Portland Cement Association, Skokie, IL. Tel: (847) 966-6200, FAX: (847) 966-9781, Web Site: www.cement.org (1)

Barnhart, Jeffrey E., Creative Marketing Alliance Inc, Princeton Junction, NJ. Tel: (609) 799-6000, FAX: (609) 799-7032, Web Site: www.cmasolutions.com (35)

Barnhill Jr., Robert, B., Tessco Inc, Hunt Valley, MD. Tel: (410) 229-1000, (800) 508-5444, FAX: (410) 527-0005, E-Mail: webhelp@tessco.com, Web Site: www.tessco.com (16)

Barnhill, Chris, Better Tools For Industry, Santee, CA. Tel: (619) 562-3071, FAX: (619) 562-0592, Web Site: www.bti-tool.com (9)

Barnhill, Jim, Better Tools For Industry, Santee, CA. Tel: (619) 562-3071, FAX: (619) 562-0592, Web Site: www.bti-tool.com (9)

Barnum, Lois, PAL Health Technology, Pekin, IL. Tel: (309) 347-8785, (800) 223-2957, FAX: (309) 477-4456, Web Site: www.palhealth.com (16)

Barnum, Michael, P., Key Bank, Cleveland, OH. Tel: (216) 689-3000, (888) 539-2968, FAX: (207) 874-7044, Web Site: www.key.com (14)

Barocci, Bob, Advertising Research Foundation, New York, NY. Tel: (212) 751-5656, FAX: (212) 319-5265, E-Mail: info@thearf.org, Web Site: www. thearf.org (40)

Baroco, Robert, L., ARF Annual Convention & Research Infoplex, New York, NY. Tel: (212) 751-5656, FAX: (212) 319-5265, E-Mail: info@ theARF.org, Web Site: www.theARF.org (42)

Baron, Herman, Diane Publishing Co, Darby, PA. Tel: (610) 461-6200, E-Mail: hbaron@dianepublishing. net, Web Site: www.dianepublishing.net (43)

Baron, Mary, Baron/Barclay Bridge Supplies, Louisville, KY. Tel: (502) 426-0410, (800) 274-2221, FAX: (502) 426-2044, E-Mail: baronbarclay@ baronbarclay.com, Web Site: www.baronbarclay. com (11)

Baron, Randall, Baron/Barclay Bridge Supplies, Louisville, KY. Tel: (502) 426-0410, (800) 274-2221, FAX: (502) 426-2044, E-Mail: baronbarclay@ baronbarclay.com, Web Site: www.baronbarclay. com (11)

Baron, Trish, Catalogs.com, Fort Lauderdale, FL. Tel: (954) 659-9005, FAX: (954) 659-9007, Web Site: www.catalogs.com (30)

Baron/Barclay Bridge Supplies, Louisville, KY. Tel: (502) 426-0410, (800) 274-2221, FAX: (502) 426-2044, E-Mail: baronbarclay@baronbarclay.com, Web Site: www.baronbarclay.com (11)

Barozzini, Brenda, Admore Inc, Macomb, MI. Tel: (810) 949-8200, (800) 523-6673, FAX: (800) 215-2664, Web Site: www.admoreonline.com (10)

Barr MD, Michael, S, American College of Physicians, Washington, DC. Tel: (215) 351-2400, (800) 523-1546, FAX: (215) 351-2686, Web Site: www. acponline.org (17)

Barr, Jim, Christian Broadcasting Network Inc, Virginia Beach, VA. Tel: (757) 226-3542, FAX: (757) 226-2017, Web Site: www.cbn.org (1)

Barragan, Napoleon, Dial-A-Mattress, Hicksville, NY. Tel: (718) 472-1200, (800) 824-7777, FAX: (718) 482-6561, E-Mail: sales@mattress.com, Web Site: www.mattress.com (16)

Barrett, Craig, R., Intel Corp, Santa Clara, CA. Tel: (408) 765-8080, (800) 548-4725, FAX: (408) 765-6187, Web Site: www.intel.com (16)

Barrett, Darren, G2 Promotional Marketing, New York, NY. Tel: (212) 537-3700, FAX: (203) 352-0798, Web Site: www.g2pm.com (16)

Barrett, David, Mel Bay Publications Inc, Pacific, MO. Tel: (800) 8-MELBAY, FAX: (636) 257-5062, E-Mail: email@melbay.com, Web Site: www.melbay.com (17)

Barrett, Edward V., Direct Logic Solutions, Peoria, IL. Tel: (309) 688-5500, FAX: (309) 688-5502, E-Mail: nedbarrett@direct-logic.com, Web Site: www.direct-logic.com (22)

Barrett, James, Sterling Name Tape Inc, Winsted, CT. Tel: (860) 379-5142, (800) 654-5210, FAX: (860) 379-0394, E-Mail: postman@sterlingtape.com, Web Site: www.sterlingtape.com (16)

Barrett, John, Vesey's Seeds Ltd, Charlottetown, PE. Tel: (902) 368-7333, (800) 363-7333, FAX: (800) 686-0329, E-Mail: customerservice@veseys.com, Web Site: www.veseys.com (8)

Barrett, Mark, LinguiSystems, East Moline, IL. Tel: (309) 755-2300, (800) 776-4332, FAX: (800) 577-4555, E-Mail: service@linguisystems.com, Web Site: www.linguisystems.com (17)

Barrett, Rob, Los Angeles Times, Los Angeles, CA. Tel: (213) 237-5000, (800) 528-4637, FAX: (213) 237-7679, E-Mail: rob.barrett@latimes.com, Web Site: www.latimes.com (31)

Barrett, Scott, Eastern Mountain Sports, Peterborough, NH. Tel: (603) 924-9571, (800) 463-6367, FAX: (603) 924-4320, Web Site: www.ems.com (16)

Barrie, Bruner, Sculpture House Inc, Skillman, NJ. Tel: (609) 466-2986, FAX: (888) 529-1980, E-Mail: customercare@sculpturehouse.com, Web Site: www.sculpturehouse.com (16)

Barrie, Jason, DealerTrack, New Hyde Park, NY. Tel: (866) 339-5723, Web Site: www.dealertract.com (14)

Barringer, Phil, Barringer & Associates Ltd, Hickory, NC. Tel: (828) 322-5550, FAX: (828) 327-8440, E-Mail: barringer@barringeragency.com, Web Site: www.barringeragency.com (35)

Barringer & Associates Ltd, Hickory, NC. Tel: (828) 322-5550, FAX: (828) 327-8440, E-Mail: barringer@barringeragency.com, Web Site: www.barringeragency.com (35)

Barrington, Allyson, Suntrust Banks Inc, Atlanta, GA. Tel: (404) 588-7914, (800) 786-8787, FAX: (404) 532-0550, E-Mail: emmett.harmon@suntrust.com, Web Site: www.suntrust.com (14)

Barrington, Liz, Recognition Systems (Dot Works), Port Washington, NY. Tel: (516) 625-5000, FAX: (516) 625-1507, E-Mail: wade@dotworks.com, Web Site: www.dotworks.com (16)

Barron, Daniel, American Health Information Management Association, Chicago, IL. Tel: (312) 233-1100, FAX: (312) 233-1090, E-Mail: info@ahima.org, Web Site: www.ahima.org (1)

Barron, Mackey, HB Communications, North Haven, CT. Tel: (203) 234-9246, (800) 243-4414, FAX: (203) 234-2013, E-Mail: info@hbcommunications.com, Web Site: www.hbcommunications.com (34)

Barron, Robert, 20th Century Fox Television, Los Angeles, CA. Tel: (310) 444-8100, FAX: (310) 444-8101 (16)

Barron Leach, Pamela, Diebold Inc, Uniontown, OH. Tel: (330) 899-2510, (800) DIEBOLD, FAX: (330) 490-3794, E-Mail: barronp@diebold.com, Web Site: www.diebold.com (16)

Barrows, Cliff, Billy Graham Evangelistic Association, Charlotte, NC. Tel: (704) 401-2491, (877) 2-GRAHAM, Web Site: www.billygraham.org (1)

Barry III, Richard, F., Landmark Communications Inc, Norfolk, VA. Tel: (757) 446-2010, (800) 446-2004, FAX: (757) 446-2489, Web Site: www.landmark.com (17)

Barry, Connie, Pharmavite Corp LLC (HQ), Northridge, CA. Tel: (818) 221-6200, (800) 423-2405, FAX: (818) 221-6618, Web Site: www.pharmavite.com (16)

Barry, Curt, F Curtis Barry & Co, Henrico, VA. Tel: (804) 740-8743, FAX: (804) 740-6179, E-Mail: cbarry@fcbco.com, Web Site: www.fcbco.com (20)

Barry, Richard, Atlantic Publication Group LLC, Charleston, SC. Tel: (843) 747-0025, FAX: (843) 744-0816, E-Mail: info@atlanticpublicationgrp.com, Web Site: www.atlanticpublicationgrp.com (17)

F Curtis Barry & Co, Henrico, VA. Tel: (804) 740-8743, FAX: (804) 740-6179, E-Mail: cbarry@fcbco.com, Web Site: www.fcbco.com (20)

RG Barry Corp, Pickerington, OH. FAX: (614) 866-9787, E-Mail: sales@rgbarry.com, Web Site: www.rgbarry.com (16)

Bartash Media Group, Philadelphia, PA. Tel: (215) 724-1700, Web Site: www.bartash.com (27)

Bartel, Warren, Astro Air, LP, Jacksonville, TX. Tel: (903) 586-3691, FAX: (903) 589-8094, E-Mail: sales@astroair.com, Web Site: www.astroair.com (9)

Bartels, Dean, Starchtech, Golden Valley, MN. Tel: (763) 545-5400, (800) 597-7225, FAX: (763) 545-9450, Web Site: www.starchtech.com (16)

Barterbing.com, Cranston, RI. Tel: (800) 345-6733, FAX: (401) 679-0326, Web Site: www.barterbing.com (29)

BarterNews, Laguna Niguel, CA. Tel: (949) 831-0607, FAX: (949) 831-9378, E-Mail: bmeyer@barternews.com, Web Site: www.barternews.com (17)

Barth, Jean, Jones Publishing Inc, Iola, WI. Tel: (715) 445-5000, (800) 331-0038, FAX: (715) 445-4053, E-Mail: jonespub@jonespublishing.com, Web Site: www.jonespublishing.com (17)

Bartik, Christopher, CrownPeak, Los Angeles, CA. Tel: (310) 841-5920, Web Site: www.crownpeak.com (22)

Bartkowiak, Dave, ANCOR, Troy, MI. Tel: (248) 740-8866, (800) 229-3860, FAX: (248) 740-9025, Web Site: www.anchorinfo.com (22)

Bartlett, Bob, John Alden Life Insurance Co/North Star Marketing, Duluth, GA. Tel: (678) 473-1211, (800) 768-6288, FAX: (678) 473-9573, Web Site: www.nstarmarketing.com (15)

Bartlett, Brad, Performance Printing/ Optigraphics, Dallas, TX. Tel: (214) 665-1038, (800) 662-2813, FAX: (214) 665-1090, Web Site: www.performancecompanies.com (27)

Bartlett, Marie, Lake Shore Industries, Erie, PA. Tel: (800) 458-0463, FAX: (814) 453-4293, E-Mail: info@lsisigns.com, Web Site: www.lsisigns.com (16)

Bartlett, PG, Quark Inc, Denver, CO. Tel: (303) 894-3832, Web Site: www.quark.com (34)

Bartley, David, HK Systems Inc, New Berlin, WI. Tel: (262) 860-7000, (800) HK SYSTEMS, FAX: (262) 860-7010, E-Mail: hkinfo@hksystems.com, Web Site: www.hksystems.com (34)

Bartley, Steven, Advertising That Works, Bloomfield Hills, MI. Tel: (248) 626-2264, FAX: (248) 626-2264, Web Site: www.advertisingthatworks.us (23)

Bartolin, Steve, Broadmoor Hotel Inc, Colorado Springs, CO. Tel: (719) 634-7711, (866) 837-9520, FAX: (719) 577-5779, Web Site: www.broadmoor.com (19)

Barton, J. Gary, State Mutual Insurance Co, Rome, GA. Tel: (706) 291-1054, FAX: (706) 291-9459 (15)

Barton, Jeb, Nomadics Tipi Makers, Bend, OR. Tel: (541) 389-3980, FAX: (541) 389-3980, Web Site: www.tipi.com (11)

Barton & Cooney, Burlington, NJ. Tel: (609) 747-9300, FAX: (609) 747-9700, E-Mail: pmdoyle@bartoncooney.com, Web Site: www.bartoncooney.com (28)

Barton-Cotton, Baltimore, MD. Tel: (410) 247-4800, (800) 348-1102, FAX: (410) 536-0491, E-Mail: info@bartoncotton.com, Web Site: www.bartoncotton.com (16)

Bartruff, Lori, Nancy's Notions LLC, Beaver Dam, WI. Tel: (920) 887-0391, (800) 833-0690, FAX: (800) 255-8119, E-Mail: comments@nancysnotions.com, Web Site: www.nancysnotions.com (11)

Bart's Watersports, North Webster, IN. Tel: (574) 834-7666, (800) 348-5016, FAX: (574) 834-4246, E-Mail: info@barts.com, Web Site: www.bartswatersports.com (11)

Bartsch, Leo, Mail America, Wheeling, WV. Tel: (304) 242-8081, Web Site: www.mailamerica.com (35)

Bartz, Carol, Autodesk Inc, San Rafael, CA. Tel: (415) 507-5000, FAX: (415) 507-5100, Web Site: www.autodesk.com (16)

Bartz, John, D., Sage Software Inc, Irvine, CA. Tel: (949) 753-1222, (800) 854-3415, FAX: (949) 753-0374, Web Site: www.sagesoftware.com (16)

Baruch College - Dept of Mktg & International Bus, New York, NY. Tel: (646) 312-3270, FAX: (646) 312-3271, E-Mail: mktIB@baruch.cuny.edu, Web Site: www.baruch.cuny.edu (41)

Barwick, Johanna, Oxbridge Communications Inc, New York, NY. Tel: (212) 741-0231, (800) 955-0231, FAX: (212) 633-2938, E-Mail: custserv@oxbridge.com, Web Site: www.mediafinder.com; www.oxbridge.com (30)

Barz, Pam, Ball Publishing, West Chicago, IL. Tel: (630) 231-3675, FAX: (630) 231-5254, E-Mail: info@ballpublishing.com, Web Site: www.ballpublishing.com (17)

Barzacchini, Mike, Harper College, Palatine, IL. Tel: (847) 925-6000, Web Site: www.harpercollege.com (1)

Basan, Edward, J., Carefirst Blue Cross Blue Shield, Washington, DC. Tel: (202) 479-8000, FAX: (301) 470-8049, Web Site: www.carefirst.com (15)

Basch, Jeffrey, W., The Progressive Corp, Mayfield Village, OH. Tel: (440) 461-5000, (800) PROGRESSIVE, (800) 776-4737, FAX: (800) 456-6590, Web Site: www.progressive.com (15)

Baschiera, Deni, Arnold Brand Response, Toronto, ON Canada. Tel: (416) 355-5009, Web Site: www.arnoldworldwide.com (35)

Baseline FT, Los Angeles, CA. Tel: (310) 393-9999, (212) 254-8235, (800) 242-7546, FAX: (212) 529-3330, E-Mail: info@baseline.hollywood.com, Web Site: www.baseline.hollywood.com (17)

Basham, Barbara, Celtic Life Insurance Co, Chicago, IL. Tel: (312) 332-5401, FAX: (312) 441-0341, E-Mail: info@celtic-net.com, Web Site: www.celtic-net.com (15)

Basic Adhesives Inc, Clifton, NJ. Tel: (718) 497-5200, (800) 394-9310, FAX: (718) 366-1425, E-Mail: info@basicadhesives.com, Web Site: www.basicadhesives.com (9)

Basic Research, Salt Lake City, UT. Tel: (801) 234-7000, Web Site: www.silversage.com (7)

Baskies, Jeff, Lawyer's Weekly Publications, Boston, MA. Tel: (617) 451-7300, FAX: (617) 451-0132, Web Site: www.lawyersweekly.com (17)

Basoco, Richard, Baltimore Magazine, Baltimore, MD. Tel: (410) 752-4200, (800) 935-0838, FAX: (410) 625-0280, E-Mail: blori@baltimoremagazine.net, Web Site: www.baltimoremagazine.net (17)

Bass, Barbara, Hear Music, Bellevue, WA. Tel: (425) 452-5534, E-Mail: gail@hearmusic.com, Web Site: www.hearmusic.com (3)

Bass, Barbara, Starbucks Corp, Seattle, WA. Tel: (206) 447-1575, (800) 344-1575, FAX: (206) 447-0828, Web Site: www.starbucks.com (4)

Bass, Bill, Charming Shoppers, Bensalem, PA. Tel: (215) 245-9100, Web Site: www.charmingshoppers.com (2)

Bass, Bill, Fair Indigo, Madison, WI. Tel: (608) 824-8974, Web Site: www.fairindigo.com (2)

Bass, Carl, Autodesk Inc, San Rafael, CA. Tel: (415) 507-5000, FAX: (415) 507-5100, Web Site: www. autodesk.com (16)

Bass, Dennis, Center for Science in the Public Interest, Washington, DC. Tel: (202) 332-9110, FAX: (202) 265-4954, E-Mail: circ@cspinet.org, Web Site: www.cspinet.org (1)

Bass, James K., The New Piper Aircraft Inc, Vero Beach, FL. Tel: (772) 567-4361, FAX: (772) 978-6573, E-Mail: marketing@piper.com, Web Site: www.newpiper.com (16)

Bass, Mercedes, T., The Metropolitan Opera, New York, NY. Tel: (212) 799-3100, (212) 362-6000, FAX: (212) 870-7695, Web Site: www.metopera. org (1)

Bass Pro Shops, Springfield, MO. Tel: (417) 873-5000, FAX: (417) 873-5882, Web Site: www. basspro.com (11)

Bassett, David, Midwest Center for Stress & Anxiety Inc, Oak Harbor, OH. Tel: (419) 898-4357, (800) 611-0857, FAX: (419) 898-0669, Web Site: www. stresscenter.com (7)

Bassett, Jodie, Pearson Education, Upper Saddle River, NJ. Tel: (201) 236-7000, FAX: (201) 236-3290, E-Mail: communications@pearsoned.com, Web Site: www.pearsoned.com (17)

Bassett, Lucinda, Midwest Center for Stress & Anxiety Inc, Oak Harbor, OH. Tel: (419) 898-4357, (800) 611-0857, FAX: (419) 898-0669, Web Site: www.stresscenter.com (7)

Bassett-Baran, Maureen, Bissinger French Confections, Saint Louis, MO. Tel: (314) 534-2401, (800) 325-8881, FAX: (314) 534-2419, Web Site: www. bissingers.com (4)

Bassick, Katherine, Cross Country Automotive Services, Medford, MA. Tel: (781) 393-9300, Web Site: www.cchs.com (16)

Bassine, Greg, DMG Direct Inc, Tigard, OR. Tel: (503) 579-5609, (888) 282-2122, FAX: (503) 579-4919, E-Mail: dmg@dirmarketing.com, Web Site: www.dirmarketing.com/dmginc (40)

Bassiri, David, Cougar Mountain Software, Boise, ID. Tel: (208) 375-4455, (800) 388-3038, FAX: (208) 375-4460, E-Mail: sales@cougarmtn.com, Web Site: www.cougarmtn.com (14)

Bassoul, Selim A., The Middleby Corp, Elgin, IL. Tel: (847) 741-3300, FAX: (847) 741-0015, E-Mail: sales@middleby.com, Web Site: www.middleby. com (16)

Basta, Stephanie, Parsons School of Design Human Resource Dept, New York, NY. Tel: (212) 229-5671, FAX: (212) 229-8975, E-Mail: communications@newschool.edu, Web Site: www. parsons.edu (41)

Bastian, Matthew, J., ICS Corp, Philadelphia, PA. Tel: (888) 223-2840, FAX: (215) 634-1522, E-Mail: info@ics-corporation.com, Web Site: www.ics-corporation.com (21)

Bastug, Greg, Blue Book Direct Mail & Database Service, New York, NY. Tel: (646) 746-7398, FAX: (646) 746-7434, Web Site: www.gabb.com (24)

Bataille, James M., BN Creative Advertising, Franklin Park, IL. Tel: (847) 577-1300, FAX: (847) 577-2101 (36)

Bateman, Paul, T., JP Morgan Chase & Co, New York, NY. Tel: (212) 270-6000, E-Mail: jpmcinvestorrelations@jpmchase.com, Web Site: www.jpmorgan.com (14)

Bates, Keith, Keith Bates & Associates Inc, Chicago, IL. Tel: (773) 205-7992, FAX: (773) 205-7988, E-Mail: keithbates@kbates.com, Web Site: www. kbates.com (35)

Keith Bates & Associates Inc, Chicago, IL. Tel: (773) 205-7992, FAX: (773) 205-7988, E-Mail: keithbates@kbates.com, Web Site: www.kbates. com (35)

Batheja, Ravi, AT&T Advertising & Publishing, Saint Louis, MO. Tel: (314) 957-5100, FAX: (314) 957-5050, Web Site: www.att.com (31)

Bathroom Machineries, Murphys, CA. Tel: (209) 728-3860, FAX: (209) 728-2320, E-Mail: info@deabath.com, Web Site: www.deabath.com (8)

Baton Rouge Conventions & Visitors Bureau, Baton Rouge, LA. Tel: (225) 383-1825, (800) LA-ROUGE, FAX: (225) 346-1253, E-Mail: br@bracvb.com, Web Site: www.bracvb.com (1)

Batson, Dean, AmazingMail Inc, Scottsdale, AZ. Tel: (480) 281-4800, Web Site: www.amazingmail.com (35)

Batson, Paula, BMG Columbia House, New York, NY. Tel: (212) 287-0081, E-Mail: cs1@bmgmusicservice.com (13)

Batson, Paula, The History Book Club Inc, Mechanicsburg, PA. Tel: (718) 918-2665, E-Mail: paula. batson@dgna.com, Web Site: www. historybookclub.com (13)

Battaglia, Christopher, Pensions & Investments, New York, NY. Tel: (212) 210-0100, FAX: (212) 210-0117, Web Site: www.pionline.com (17)

Batten Jr., Frank, Landmark Communications Inc, Norfolk, VA. Tel: (757) 446-2010, (800) 446-2004, FAX: (757) 446-2489, Web Site: www.landmark. com (17)

Battery Pros Inc, Horseshoe Beach, FL. Tel: (352) 498-2477, (800) 451-7171, FAX: (352) 498-2482, E-Mail: sales@probattery.com, Web Site: www. probattery.com (13)

Battista, Rich, TV Guide, Tulsa, OK. Tel: (918) 488-4000, FAX: (918) 488-4200, Web Site: www. tvguideinc.com (32)

Battle, Craig, L., Tucker Capital Corp, Princeton, NJ. Tel: (609) 924-5710, FAX: (609) 924-5027, E-Mail: info@tuckercapital.com, Web Site: www. tuckercapital.com (20)

Battleground Antiques Inc, New Bern, NC. Tel: (252) 636-3039, FAX: (252) 637-1862, E-Mail: tarheelrebel2000@aol.com, Web Site: www. civilwarantiques.com (6)

Batts, Ron, Things Remembered, Highland Heights, OH. Tel: (440) 473-2000, (866) 902-4438, FAX: (440) 473-2018, E-Mail: customerservice@thingsremembered.com, Web Site: www. thingsremembered.com (6)

Diana Baty, Moraga, CA. Tel: (202) 689-5332 (20)

Baudot, L., Craig, Blanchard & Co Inc, New Orleans, LA. Tel: (504) 837-3010, (800) 880-4653, FAX: (504) 837-4884, Web Site: www.blanchardonline. com (16)

Bauds, Nathan, New Mexico State University, Las Cruces, NM. Tel: (575) 646-0111, (505) 646-3341, FAX: (505) 646-1498, Web Site: www.nmsu.edu (41)

Baudville Inc, Grand Rapids, MI. Tel: (616) 698-0889, (800) 728-0888, FAX: (616) 698-0554, E-Mail: service@baudville.com, Web Site: www.baudville. com (16)

Bauer, Barbara, US News & World Report, New York, NY. Tel: (212) 916-7360, FAX: (212) 643-7842, Web Site: www.usnews.com (17)

Bauer, Gerhard, Bausch & Lomb Inc, Rochester, NY. Tel: (585) 338-6000, (800) 344-8815, FAX: (585) 338-6007, Web Site: www.bausch.com (16)

Bauer, Jo, Frank W Cawood & Associates Inc, Peachtree City, GA. Tel: (770) 487-6307, Web Site: www.fca.com (35)

Bauer, Joanne, B., Kimberly-Clark Corp, Neenah, WI. Tel: (920) 721-2000, (888) 525-8388, FAX: (920) 721-7722, Web Site: www.kimberly-clark.com (16)

Bauer, Larry, Bauer Associates, Batavia, IL. Tel: (630) 406-8595, FAX: (630) 406-8596, E-Mail: lbauer@bauerassoc.net, Web Site: www.bauerassoc.net (39)

Bauer, Richard, Asset Marketing Services Inc, Burnsville, MN. Tel: (952) 707-7000, Web Site: www. amsi-corp.com (16)

Bauer, Robert, Liebert Corp, Columbus, OH. Tel: (614) 841-6700, (800) LIEBERT, FAX: (614) 841-6022, Web Site: www.liebert.com (16)

Bauer, Robert, Nat Com Marketing, Miami, FL. Tel: (786) 425-0028, FAX: (786) 425-0067, E-Mail: info@natcom-marketing.com, Web Site: www. natcom-marketing.com (33)

Bauer, Stephanie, Communications Solutions Expo, Norwalk, CT. Tel: (203) 852-6800, (877) 243-6002, FAX: (203) 853-2845, E-Mail: info@tmcnet. com, Web Site: www.tmcnet.com (42)

Bauer Associates, Batavia, IL. Tel: (630) 406-8595, FAX: (630) 406-8596, E-Mail: lbauer@bauerassoc. net, Web Site: www.bauerassoc.net (39)

Eddie Bauer, Groveport, OH. Tel: (425) 882-6100, (800) 426-8020, FAX: (425) 556-7696, Web Site: www.eddiebauer.com (2)

Eddie Bauer Holdings Inc, Bellevue, WA. Tel: (425) 755-6100, Web Site: www.ediebauer.com (5)

Bauer Publishing Co, Englewood Cliffs, NJ. Tel: (201) 569-6699, FAX: (201) 510-3297, Web Site: www. bauerpublishing.com (17)

Richard Bauer & Co Inc, Teaneck, NJ. Tel: (201) 692-1005, (800) 995-7881, FAX: (201) 692-8626, E-Mail: info@richardbauer.com, Web Site: www. richardbauer.com (25)

Bauernschmidt, Jeff, Thomas L Cardella & Associates, Kimberton, PA. Tel: (610) 933-3822, Web Site: www.tlcassociates.com (29)

Bauhof, Bernie, Siegel Display Products, Minneapolis, MN. Tel: (612) 340-1493, (800) 626-0322, FAX: (800) 230-5598, E-Mail: mwendel@siegeldisplay. com, Web Site: www.siegeldisplay.com (5)

Baum, J., Robert, Highmark Blue Cross Blue Shield, Pittsburgh, PA. Tel: (412) 544-7000, FAX: (412) 544-5350, Web Site: www.highmark.com (15)

Baum, Jay, ACBL, Horn Lake, MS. Tel: (901) 332-5586, FAX: (901) 398-7754, E-Mail: service@acbl.org, Web Site: www.acbl.org (1)

Baum, Michael, The Guild Inc, Madison, WI. Tel: (608) 257-2590, Web Site: www.guild.com (8)

Bauman, George, Mapping Analytics, Rochester, NY. Tel: (585) 271-6490, (877) 893-6490, FAX: (585) 271-1132, E-Mail: sales@mappinganalytics.com, Web Site: www.mappinganalytics.com (20)

Bauman, Marcia, The Bauman Group, Ashland, MA. Tel: (508) 879-3009, (800) 876-3009, FAX: (508) 875-3751, E-Mail: info@bauman.com, Web Site: www.bauman.com (14)

Bauman, Nancy, Circulation by Phone Inc, New York, NY. Tel: (212) 557-2777 (29)

The Bauman Group, Ashland, MA. Tel: (508) 879-3009, (800) 876-3009, FAX: (508) 875-3751, E-Mail: info@bauman.com, Web Site: www. bauman.com (14)

Baumann, Angela, Liguori Publications, Liguori, MO. Tel: (636) 464-2500, (800) 325-9521, FAX: (800) 325-9526, E-Mail: liguori@liguori.org, Web Site: www.liguori.org (17)

Baumann, Brian, Brooks Brothers, New York, NY. Tel: (212) 682-8800, (800) 274-1815, FAX: (212) 309-7273, Web Site: www.brooksbrothers.com (2)

Baumann, Gerald, Windway Capital Corp, Sheboygan, WI. Tel: (920) 457-8600 (34)

Baumann, John, Ampac, Cincinnati, OH. Tel: (513) 671-1777, (800) 543-7030, FAX: (513) 671-2920, Web Site: www.ampaconline.com (27)

Baumann, John, The Swiss Colony Inc, Monroe, WI. Tel: (608) 328-8400, FAX: (608) 328-8457, Web Site: www.swisscolony.com (4)

Baumann, Michael, Orchard Supply Hardware, San Jose, CA. Tel: (408) 281-3500, FAX: (408) 225-0388, Web Site: www.osh.com (16)

Baumgarten, Ed, Mid America Designs Inc, Effingham, IL. Tel: (217) 540-4200, (800) 350-4543, FAX: (217) 540-4800, E-Mail: mail@mamotorworks.com, Web Site: www. mamotorworks.com (12)

Baumgarten, Jay, ASE Technologies Inc, Wilmington, MA. Tel: (978) 658-0009, FAX: (978) 658-9990, E-Mail: info@ase-tech.com, Web Site: www.ase-tech.com (16)

Baumgartner, Garry, The National Underwriter Co, Erlanger, KY. Tel: (800) 543-0874, FAX: (856) 692-2246, E-Mail: customerservice@nuco.com, Web Site: www.nuco.com (17)

Baurenfeind, Eva, Davidoff of Geneva Inc, Pinellas Park, FL. Tel: (203) 323-5811, (800) 328-4365, FAX: (203) 975-0090 (6)

Bausch & Lomb Inc, Rochester, NY. Tel: (585) 338-6000, (800) 344-8815, FAX: (585) 338-6007, Web Site: www.bausch.com (16)

Bavaria, Rick, Sylvan Learning Centers, Baltimore, MD. Tel: (410) 843-8000, FAX: (410) 843-8057, Web Site: www.educate.com (16)

Bavaro, Anthony F., Herbert L Jamison & Co LLC, West Orange, NJ. Tel: (973) 731-0806, (800) JAMISON, (800) 526-4766, FAX: (973) 731-3035, Web Site: www.jamisongroup.com (15)

Bawa, Kapil, Baruch College - Dept of Mktg & International Bus, New York, NY. Tel: (646) 312-3270, FAX: (646) 312-3271, E-Mail: mktIB@baruch.cuny.edu, Web Site: www.baruch.cuny.edu (41)

Baxter Jr., William, J., Baxter Bros Inc, Greenwich, CT. Tel: (203) 637-4559, (866) 280-1924, FAX: (203) 637-4550, E-Mail: info@baxterinvestment.com, Web Site: www.baxterinvestment.com (17)

Baxter, Noreen E., American Kennel Club, New York, NY. Tel: (212) 696-8200, FAX: (212) 696-8217, (212) 696-8299, Web Site: www.akc.org (17)

Baxter Bros Inc, Greenwich, CT. Tel: (203) 637-4559, (866) 280-1924, FAX: (203) 637-4550, E-Mail: info@baxterinvestment.com, Web Site: www.baxterinvestment.com (17)

Baxter Healthcare, Renal Division, Waukegan, IL. Tel: (847) 473-6586 (7)

Bay, Bryndon, Mel Bay Publications Inc, Pacific, MO. Tel: (800) 8-MELBAY, FAX: (636) 257-5062, E-Mail: email@melbay.com, Web Site: www.melbay.com (17)

Bay, William, Mel Bay Publications Inc, Pacific, MO. Tel: (800) 8-MELBAY, FAX: (636) 257-5062, E-Mail: email@melbay.com, Web Site: www.melbay.com (17)

Bay Manufacturing, Milan, OH. Tel: (419) 499-4602, FAX: (419) 499-4603, Web Site: www.baymfg.com (16)

Mel Bay Publications Inc, Pacific, MO. Tel: (800) 8-MELBAY, FAX: (636) 257-5062, E-Mail: email@melbay.com, Web Site: www.melbay.com (17)

Bayard Inc, New London, CT. Tel: (860) 437-3012, Web Site: www.bayard-inc.com (31)

Bayer, Greg, Sportime International, Norcross, GA. Tel: (770) 449-5700, (800) 283-5700, FAX: (770) 510-7290, E-Mail: orders@sportime.com, Web Site: www.sportime.com (11)

Bayer Corp Consumer Care Division, Morristown, NJ. Tel: (973) 254-5000, FAX: (973) 408-8215, Web Site: www.bayercare.com (16)

Bayersdorfer, Alan, National Audubon Society, New York, NY. Tel: (212) 979-3000, FAX: (212) 979-3188, Web Site: www.audubon.org (17)

Baylor Health Care System, Dallas, TX. Tel: (214) 820-4901, (800) 4Baylor, FAX: (214) 820-7499, Web Site: www.baylorhealth.com (16)

Bayol, Yzes, Tiger Direct Inc, Miami, FL. Tel: (305) 415-2200, (800) 800-8300, FAX: (305) 415-2202, Web Site: biz.tigerdirect.com (3)

BDirect Marketing, Saint Paul, MN. Tel: (651) 483-3260, FAX: (651) 483-3267, E-Mail: bdirectlists@comcast.net, Web Site: www.bdirectlists.com (23)

Be Somebody Be Yourself, Denver, CO. Tel: (303) 575-5676, FAX: (303) 575-1187, E-Mail: emailstreet@gmail.com, Web Site: www.besomebodybeyourself.com (35)

Beach, David, Education Direct, Scranton, PA. Tel: (570) 342-7701, FAX: (570) 961-4851, Web Site: www.educationdirect.com (16)

Beach, T., Clay, Beach List Direct Inc, Nashville, TN. Tel: (615) 356-1100, Web Site: www.beachlistdirect.com (23)

Beach List Direct Inc, Nashville, TN. Tel: (615) 356-1100, Web Site: www.beachlistdirect.com (23)

Beachler, Tom, Redfield & Co Inc, Omaha, NE. Tel: (402) 341-0364, Web Site: www.redfieldandcompany.com (27)

Beacon Marketing Group, Galloway, NJ. Tel: (609) 677-4776, Web Site: www.beaconmktg.com (35)

Beacon Printing & Graphics Inc, Valdosta, GA. Tel: (912) 244-5634, (800) 227-7377, FAX: (912) 247-4405, Web Site: www.uspress.com (27)

Beacon Shoe Co Inc, Maryland Heights, MO. Tel: (636) 488-5444, FAX: (636) 488-3103 (16)

BeaconFey LLC, Towson, MD. Tel: (410) 583-1203, FAX: (410) 583-1506, E-Mail: info@beaconfey.com, Web Site: www.beaconfey.com (35)

Beaghan, John, Eastern Michigan University, Ypsilanti, MI. Tel: (734) 487-1849, FAX: (734) 484-1151, Web Site: www.emich.edu (16)

Beaham III, Gordon, T., Faultless Starch/Bon Ami Co, Kansas City, MO. Tel: (816) 842-1230, FAX: (816) 842-3417, E-Mail: info@faultless.com, Web Site: www.faultless.com (16)

Beaham, David, G., Faultless Starch/Bon Ami Co, Kansas City, MO. Tel: (816) 842-1230, FAX: (816) 842-3417, E-Mail: info@faultless.com, Web Site: www.faultless.com (16)

Beaham, Robert, B., Faultless Starch/Bon Ami Co, Kansas City, MO. Tel: (816) 842-1230, FAX: (816) 842-3417, E-Mail: info@faultless.com, Web Site: www.faultless.com (16)

Beal, Graham, W., The Detroit Institute of Arts, Detroit, MI. Tel: (313) 833-7900, FAX: (313) 833-1390, Web Site: www.dia.org (16)

Beale, Greg, Amtelco, McFarland, WI. Tel: (608) 838-4194, (800) 356-9148, FAX: (608) 838-8367, E-Mail: info@amtelco.com, Web Site: www.amtelco.com (16)

Beall, Andy, Empire Imports Inc, Amherst, MA. Tel: (413) 256-4917, (800) 544-4744, FAX: (413) 256-4645, E-Mail: info@empireimports.com, Web Site: www.empireimports.com (34)

Bealor, Tim, Broadcast Electronics Inc, Quincy, IL. Tel: (217) 224-9600, FAX: (217) 224-9607, E-Mail: bdcast@bdcast.com, Web Site: www.bdcast.com (3)

The Beam Group, Gladwyne, PA. Tel: (215) 988-2100, FAX: (215) 988-1558, Web Site: www.beamgroup.com (20)

Beamont, Eric, National Systems Corp, Chicago, IL. Tel: (312) 855-1000, FAX: (312) 222-1605, E-Mail: support@nationalsystems.com, Web Site: www.nationalsystems.com (29)

LL Bean Inc, Freeport, ME. Tel: (207) 865-4761, (800) 441-5713, FAX: (207) 552-3080, Web Site: www.llbean.com (2)

Beane, Chris, E Hille, Angler's Supply House, Williamsport, PA. Tel: (570) 323-7564, (800) 326-6612, FAX: (570) 323-9995, Web Site: www.anglersupplyhouse.com (11)

Beane, Cindi, E Hille, Angler's Supply House, Williamsport, PA. Tel: (570) 323-7564, (800) 326-6612, FAX: (570) 323-9995, Web Site: www.anglersupplyhouse.com (11)

Beane, Ken, E Hille, Angler's Supply House, Williamsport, PA. Tel: (570) 323-7564, (800) 326-6612, FAX: (570) 323-9995, Web Site: www.anglersupplyhouse.com (11)

Bear, Stephen, E., Bristol-Myers Squibb Co, New York, NY. Tel: (212) 546-4000, FAX: (212) 546-9544, Web Site: www.bms.com (16)

Bear Computer Systems Inc, Dallas, TX. Tel: (818) 509-0459, (800) 252-1691, FAX: (818) 769-3055, E-Mail: info@bearcom.com, Web Site: www.bearcom.com (16)

Bear Woods Supply Co Inc, Cornwallis, NS Canada. Tel: (902) 638-8622, (800) 565-5066, FAX: (902) 638-8637, Web Site: www.bearwood.com, www.woodparts.ca (11)

Beard, Cathy, Camping World Inc, Bowling Green, KY. Tel: (270) 781-2718, (800) 626-6189, FAX: (270) 796-8991, Web Site: www.campingworld.com (11)

Beard, James, S., Caterpillar Insurance Services Corp, Nashville, TN. Tel: (615) 386-5800, Web Site: www.cat.com (15)

Beard, Jeff, Amacai Information Corp, Oakbrook Terrace, IL. Tel: (800) 434-1555, FAX: (312) 924-3001, E-Mail: info@amacai.com, Web Site: www.amacai.com (23)

Beard, Mike, DirectSmile LLC, Bloomfield, NJ. Tel: (973) 780-0018, Web Site: www.directsmile.com (22)

Beardon, Blanche, Long's Electronics Inc, Irondale, AL. Tel: (205) 956-6767, (800) 633-3410, FAX: (800) 633-2530, E-Mail: info@longselectronics.com, Web Site: www.longselectronics.com (3)

Beardsley, David, Satisfaction Software Inc, Jamaica, NY. Tel: (732) 382-8736, FAX: (732) 382-8736, E-Mail: db@biink.com (20)

Beardsley, Nichelle, Liberty Tree Network, Oakland, CA. Tel: (510) 568-6047, (800) 927-8733, FAX: (510) 568-6040, E-Mail: info@liberty-tree.com, Web Site: www.liberty-tree.org (5)

Charles F Beardsley Advertising, Avon, CT. Tel: (860) 676-0256, FAX: (860) 674-1917, E-Mail: charles.beardsley@snet.net (35)

Bearingpoint Inc, Montvale, NJ. Tel: (201) 307-7000, FAX: (201) 505-3765, Web Site: www.bearingpoint.com (14)

Beasley, Glen, A, Arbor Day Foundation, Lincoln, NE. Tel: (402) 474-5655, Web Site: www.arborday.org (1)

Beasley, H., Marvin, Helzberg Diamonds, North Kansas City, MO. Tel: (816) 842-7780, (800) HELZBURG, FAX: (816) 480-0294, Web Site: www.helzberg.com (16)

Beasley, Larry, J., Cathedral Corp, Rome, NY. Tel: (315) 338-0021, (800) 698-0299, FAX: (315) 338-5874, E-Mail: sales@cathedralstewardship.com, Web Site: www.cathedralcorporation.com (21)

Beasley, Laurie, Beasley Direct Marketing Inc, Morgan Hill, CA. Tel: (408) 782-0046, FAX: (408) 782-9604, E-Mail: lbeasley@beasleydirect.com, Web Site: www.beasleydirect.com (35)

Beasley, Laurie, Direct Marketing Association of Northern California, Morgan Hill, CA. Tel: (800) 613-9266, FAX: (800) 613-8819, E-Mail: lbeasley@beasleydirect.com, Web Site: www.dmanc.org (40)

Beasley, W.B. Rogers, Keeneland Association Inc, Lexington, KY. Tel: (859) 254-3412, (800) 456-3412, FAX: (859) 255-2484, Web Site: www.keeneland.com (16)

Beasley Direct Marketing Inc, Morgan Hill, CA. Tel: (408) 782-0046, FAX: (408) 782-9604, E-Mail: lbeasley@beasleydirect.com, Web Site: www.beasleydirect.com (35)

Beaton, David, Custometrics Inc, Richmond Hill, ON Canada. Tel: (905) 886-4161, E-Mail: info@custometrics.ca, Web Site: www.custometrics.com (30)

Beatson, David, Global Ware Solutions, Redwood City, CA. Tel: (650) 363-2200, (800) 469-7500, FAX: (650) 599-3280, E-Mail: sales@gwsmail.com, Web Site: www.globalwaresolutions.com (22)

Beattie, David, Hamilton Campaigns, Washington, DC. Tel: (202) 686-5900, FAX: (202) 686-7080, E-Mail: info@hamiltoncampaigns.com, Web Site: www.hamiltoncampaigns.com (30)

Beattie, John, C., GMAC Insurance, Atlanta, GA. Tel: (314) 493-8000, (800) GMAC-123, FAX: (314) 493-8114, Web Site: www.gmacinsurance.com (15)

Beatty, Robert, Alzheimer's Association, Chicago, IL. Tel: (312) 335-8700, Web Site: www.alz.org (1)

Beaty, Wilma, E., Caraustar, Austell, GA. Tel: (770) 948-3101, E-Mail: info@caraustar.com, Web Site: www.caraustar.com (16)

Beau Graphics Ltd Inc, Lexington, KY. Tel: (859) 277-2328, (877) 279-2328, FAX: (859) 278-6193, Web Site: www.beaugraphics.com (36)

Beau Rivage Resort & Casino, Biloxi, MS. Tel: (228) 386-7150, Web Site: www.beaurivage.com (19)

Beauchamp, Thomas, Hot Topic Inc, City of Industry, CA. Tel: (626) 839-4681, (800) 275-9169, FAX: (626) 839-4686, Web Site: www.hottopic.com (2)

Beauchemin, Ken, Voyageur Inc, Easley, SC. Tel: (802) 496-3127, (800) 311-7245, FAX: (802) 496-6247 (11)

Beauchesne, Norm, Herrington, Londonderry, NH. Tel: (603) 437-1600, (800) 903-2878, FAX: (603) 437-1340, (603) 437-3492, E-Mail: customerservice@herringtoncatalog.com, Web Site: www.herringtoncatalog.com (16)

Beauchesne, Tara, AccuData Integrated Marketing, Fort Myers, FL. Tel: (239) 425-4400, (800) 732-3440, FAX: (239) 425-4401, E-Mail: info@accudata.com, Web Site: www.accudata.com (23)

Beaudet, Peter, Palm Coast Data LLC, Palm Coast, FL. Tel: (386) 445-4662, FAX: (386) 445-2728, Web Site: www.palmcoastd.com (28)

Beaudoin, Paul, Fraser Papers Inc, Madawaska, ME. Tel: (203) 705-2800, FAX: (203) 705-2801 (25)

Beaudreau, Thomas, DirecTech, Maysville, KY. Tel: (866) 550-5030, E-Mail: ceo@directech.com, Web Site: www.directech.com (22)

Beaufort, Allen, New York Easter Seal Society, New York, NY. Tel: (312) 726-6200, (212) 943-4364, (800) 221-6827, FAX: (212) 695-4807, (312) 726-4258, Web Site: ny.easterseals.com (1)

Beaulieu, Paul, MediaConcepts Corp, Assonet, MA. Tel: (508) 644-3131, FAX: (508) 644-5201, E-Mail: at3@mediaconceptscorp.com, Web Site: www.mediaconceptscorp.com (35)

Beaumont, Sarah, StatSoft Inc, Tulsa, OK. Tel: (918) 749-1119, FAX: (918) 749-2217, E-Mail: info@statsoft.com, Web Site: www.statsoft.com (9)

Beaupre, Sue, American Automobile Association, Heathrow, FL. Tel: (407) 444-7282, Web Site: www.aaa.com (16)

Beauregard, Alain, MFE Instruments, Salem, NH. Tel: (603) 893-8778, (800) 843-8011, FAX: (603) 893-8851, Web Site: www.stockeryale.com (9)

Beauticontrol Cosmetics Inc, Carrollton, TX. Tel: (972) 458-0601, (800) BEAUTI-1, FAX: (972) 458-6904, E-Mail: clientservices@beauticontrol.com, Web Site: www.beauticontrol.com (16)

Beauty Naturally, Burlingame, CA. Tel: (650) 697-1845, (800) 432-4323, FAX: (650) 697-1970, E-Mail: sales@beautynaturally.com, Web Site: www.beautynaturally.com (7)

Beaver, Brenda, Otto Environmental Systems of North America, Charlotte, NC. Tel: (704) 588-9191, (800) 227-5885, FAX: (704) 588-5250, E-Mail: info@otto-usa.com, Web Site: www.otto-usa.com (16)

Beaver, Donald E., PetSmart Inc, Phoenix, AZ. Tel: (623) 587-2009, (800) 738-1385, FAX: (623) 580-6183, Web Site: www.petsmart.com (5)

Beaver, Donald E., State Line Tack Inc, Phoenix, AZ. Tel: (623) 580-6100, (800) 228-9208, FAX: (623) 580-6183, E-Mail: customerservice@statelinetack.com, Web Site: www.statelinetack.com (16)

Beaver, John, The Great Amarillo Directory, Amarillo, TX. Tel: (806) 353-5155, FAX: (806) 359-2974, Web Site: www.worldpages.com (17)

Beavers, Kay, Associated Bag Co, Milwaukee, WI. Tel: (414) 769-1000, (800) 926-6100, FAX: (800) 926-4610, E-Mail: customerservice@associatedbag.com, Web Site: www.associatedbag.com (10)

Beavin, William, American Printing House for the Blind, Louisville, KY. Tel: (502) 895-2405, (800) 223-1839, FAX: (502) 899-2274, E-Mail: info@aph.org, Web Site: www.aph.org (7)

Bebell, Garrett, Torqmaster International, Stamford, CT. Tel: (203) 326-5945, (888) 414-4643, FAX: (203) 326-5944, E-Mail: info@torqmaster.com, Web Site: www.torqmaster.com (9)

Beber, Ed, CareCall Inc, Sartell, MN. Tel: (320) 253-0800, Web Site: www.arraysg.com (29)

Beber, Jennifer, Beber Silverstein Group, Miami, FL. Tel: (305) 856-9800, (800) ASKBEBR, FAX: (305) 854-7686, E-Mail: jennifer@thinkbsq.com, Web Site: www.thinkbsq.com (35)

Beber Silverstein Group, Miami, FL. Tel: (305) 856-9800, (800) ASKBEBR, FAX: (305) 854-7686, E-Mail: jennifer@thinkbsq.com, Web Site: www.thinkbsq.com (35)

Becht, Ron, Hello Direct, Nashua, NH. Tel: (408) 972-1990, (800) 435-5634, FAX: (408) 972-8155, Web Site: www.hello-direct.com (16)

Beck, David, A., The Clark Grave Vault Co, Columbus, OH. Tel: (614) 294-3761, FAX: (614) 299-2324, Web Site: www.clarkvault.com (16)

Beck, DeAnna, Foundation for Chiropractic Education & Research, Norwalk, IA. Tel: (515) 282-7118 (1)

Beck, Douglas, The Clark Grave Vault Co, Columbus, OH. Tel: (614) 294-3761, FAX: (614) 299-2324, Web Site: www.clarkvault.com (16)

Beck, Lisa, Promotional Products Association International, Irving, TX. Tel: (972) 252-0404, FAX: (800) I-AM-PPAI, (972) 258-3004, E-Mail: membership@ppa.org, Web Site: www.ppa.org (40)

Beck, Mark, A., The Clark Grave Vault Co, Columbus, OH. Tel: (614) 294-3761, FAX: (614) 299-2324, Web Site: www.clarkvault.com (16)

Beck, Russ, Ferguson Publishing Co, New York, NY. Tel: (212) 613-2800, (800) 322-8755, FAX: (800) 678-3633, E-Mail: custserv@factsonfile.com, Web Site: www.fergpubco.com (17)

Beck, Scott, CHG, Salt Lake City, UT. Tel: (801) 930-3000, (800) 453-3030, Web Site: www.comphealth.com (7)

Beck, Steven, H., National Envelope Advertising Co Inc, Meadowbrook, PA. Tel: (215) 887-8496, FAX: (215) 887-2652 (26)

Beck, Tamara, Clean Lists Associates Inc, New York, NY. Tel: (212) 551-1013, FAX: (212) 551-1107, E-Mail: cleanlists@mindspring.com (27)

Beckel, Helen, Harland Financial Solutions Inc, Lake Mary, FL. Tel: (407) 804-6600, (800) 815-5592, FAX: (407) 829-6702, Web Site: www.harlandfinancialsolutions.com (16)

Beckemeyer, William, Kurt Salmon Associates Inc, Atlanta, GA. Tel: (404) 892-0321, FAX: (404) 898-9590, E-Mail: infoksaweb@kurtsalmon.com, Web Site: www.kurtsalmon.com (20)

Becker, Brian, Blethen Maine Newspapers Inc, Portland, ME. Tel: (207) 791-6650, FAX: (207) 791-6925, Web Site: www.mainetoday.com (17)

Becker, Chuck, Pasternack Enterprises Inc, Irvine, CA. Tel: (949) 261-1920, Web Site: www.pasternack.com (16)

Becker, Dena, Eddie Bauer Holdings Inc, Bellevue, WA. Tel: (425) 755-6100, Web Site: www.ediebauer.com (5)

Becker, Elaine, Atlantic Research & Consulting Inc, Boston, MA. Tel: (617) 720-0174, FAX: (617) 589-3731, E-Mail: generalmailbox@guideline.com, Web Site: www.guideline.com (30)

Becker, Jeffrey, Clients First, Westfield, NJ. Tel: (908) 232-1200, (800) 634-0040, FAX: (908) 233-8833, E-Mail: info@clientsfirst.com, Web Site: www.clientsfirst.com (27)

Becker, Jerrold L., Moultrie Manufacturing Co, Moultrie, GA. Tel: (229) 985-1312, (800) 841-8674, FAX: (229) 890-7245, Web Site: www.moultriemanufacturing.com (8)

Becker, Karly, Kable Fulfillment Services, Mount Morris, IL. Tel: (815) 734-4151, FAX: (815) 734-5228 (22)

Becker, Michael, iLoop Mobile Inc, San Jose, CA. Tel: (408) 907-3360, Web Site: www.iloopmobile.com (16)

Becker, Paul, C., Cosco Industries Inc, Chicago, IL. Tel: (708) 867-5800, (800) 323-0253, FAX: (800) 323-0275 (16)

Becker, Rich, Rich Becker & Associates/Pump-Em-Up Publishing, In Public Relations, Lenexa, KS. Tel: (913) 894-9530, FAX: (913) 894-9530, E-Mail: rbecker@kc.rr.com (20)

Becker, Richard, AllMedia Inc, Plano, TX. Tel: (469) 467-9100, FAX: (214) 291-5431, E-Mail: lmcclendon@allmediainc.com, Web Site: www.allmediainc.com (23)

Becker, Richard, The Granger Collection, New York, NY. Tel: (212) 447-1789, FAX: (212) 447-1492, Web Site: www.granger.com (38)

Becker, Robert, Telecommunications Reports International Inc, Washington, DC. Tel: (202) 312-6060, (800) 234-1660, FAX: (202) 312-6111, E-Mail: bhammond@tr.com, Web Site: www.tr.com (17)

Rich Becker & Associates/Pump-Em-Up Publishing, In Public Relations, Lenexa, KS. Tel: (913) 894-9530, FAX: (913) 894-9530, E-Mail: rbecker@kc.rr.com (20)

Beckham, Ed, Amaryllis Inc, Baton Rouge, LA. Tel: (225) 924-5560 (8)

Beckman, Andrew, Location3 Media, Denver, CO. Tel: (877) 462-9764, Web Site: www.Location3.com (32)

Beckman, John, CNA, Chicago, IL. Tel: (312) 822-5000, (800) 262-2000, E-Mail: cna_help@cna.com, Web Site: www.cna.com (15)

Beckman, Stephanie, Response ADvantage, Playa Del Rey, CA. Tel: (310) 577-0389, Web Site: www.responseadvantage.com (20)

Beckman Coulter Inc, Brea, CA. Tel: (714) 993-5321, (800) 526-3821, FAX: (800) 232-3828, Web Site: www.beckmancoulter.com (16)

Beckmann, Klaus, Beckmann Converting Inc, Amsterdam, NY. Tel: (518) 842-0073, FAX: (518) 842-0282, E-Mail: ppiusz@beckmannconverting.com, Web Site: www.beckmannconverting.com (16)

Beckmann Converting Inc, Amsterdam, NY. Tel: (518) 842-0073, FAX: (518) 842-0282, E-Mail: ppiusz@beckmannconverting.com, Web Site: www.beckmannconverting.com (16)

Becton Jr., Henry, P., WGBH Educational Foundation, Brighton, MA. Tel: (617) 300-5400, FAX: (617) 300-1026, Web Site: www.wgbh.org (1)

Bed Bath & Beyond, Farmingdale, NY. Tel: (631) 420-7050 (8)

Bedard, Tony, Frontier Natural Products Co-op, Norway, IA. Tel: (319) 227-7996, (800) 669-3275, FAX: (319) 227-7966, (800) 717-4372, E-Mail: info@frontiercoop.com, Web Site: www.frontiercoop.com (7)

Beddor, Michael, Japs-Olson Co, Saint Louis Park, MN. Tel: (952) 932-9393, (800) 548-2897, FAX: (612) 912-1900, Web Site: www.japsolson.com (27)

BeDell, Suzanne, The Dialog Corp, Morrisville, NC. Tel: (919) 804-6400, (800) 3 DIALOG, FAX: (919) 804-6410, E-Mail: customer@dialog.com, Web Site: www.dialog.com (21)

Bedford, Stacie, Gazette Communications Inc, Cedar Rapids, IA. Tel: (319) 398-8211, (800) 397-8211, FAX: (319) 368-8834, Web Site: www.gazettecommunications.com (17)

Bedford/St Martin's, Boston, MA. Tel: (617) 426-7440, FAX: (617) 426-8582, Web Site: www.bedfordstmartins.com (17)

Bedgood, Larisa, DataMentors LLC, Wesley Chapel, FL. Tel: (813) 960-7800, FAX: (813) 960-7811, E-Mail: lbedgood@datamentors.com, Web Site: www.datamentors.com (22)

Bedikian, Von, GBH Communications, Monrovia, CA. Tel: (818) 246-9900, (800) 222-5424, FAX: (818) 246-5850, E-Mail: customerservice@gbh.com, Web Site: www.gbh.com (3)

Beditz, Joseph, National Golf Foundation, Jupiter, FL. Tel: (561) 744-6006, FAX: (561) 744-6107, E-Mail: ngf@ngf.org, Web Site: www.ngf.org (1)

Bednar, R., Craig, Seattle Magazine, Seattle, WA. Tel: (206) 284-1750, (800) 637-0334, FAX: (206) 284-2550, E-Mail: customerservice@seattlemag.com, Web Site: www.seattlemag.com (17)

Bednar, Randall, S., AO Smith Corp, Milwaukee, WI. Tel: (414) 359-4000, FAX: (414) 359-4064, Web Site: www.aosmith.com (16)

Bednarz Ph.D., Shirley, Majorium, Stevens Point, WI. Tel: (715) 342-1018, (800) 654-4935, FAX: (715) 342-1118, E-Mail: sales@majorium.com, Web Site: www.letstalkselling.com (17)

Bednarz Ph.D., Timothy, Majorium, Stevens Point, WI. Tel: (715) 342-1018, (800) 654-4935, FAX: (715) 342-1118, E-Mail: sales@majorium.com, Web Site: www.letstalkselling.com (17)

Bednoff, Mitchell, E., Sage Financial Group, West Conshohocken, PA. Tel: (484) 342-4400, FAX: (484) 537-0550, E-Mail: sage@sagefinancial.com, Web Site: www.sagefinancial.com (14)

Bedwell, Judy, The Candy Factory, Newport, KY. Tel: (859) 581-4663, FAX: (859) 581-1979 (4)

Beebe, Keven, L., Alltel, Little Rock, AR. Tel: (501) 905-2590, (877) 446-3628, FAX: (501) 905-5444, Web Site: www.alltel.com (16)

Beecher, John, B., Sales Leads, Jupiter, FL. Tel: (866) 725-3753, FAX: (866) 702-5558, E-Mail: info@salesleadsinc.com, Web Site: www.salesleadsinc.com (17)

Beecher, La Verne, Sales Leads, Jupiter, FL. Tel: (866) 725-3753, FAX: (866) 702-5558, E-Mail: info@salesleadsinc.com, Web Site: www.salesleadsinc.com (17)

Beecher, Michael, Sales Leads, Jupiter, FL. Tel: (866) 725-3753, FAX: (866) 702-5558, E-Mail: info@salesleadsinc.com, Web Site: www.salesleadsinc.com (17)

Beechtree Assoc Inc, Cary, NC. Tel: (919) 852-1800, FAX: (919) 852-4400, E-Mail: jfoliano@aol.com (20)

Beegan, Paul J., B&W Press Inc, Georgetown, MA. Tel: (978) 352-6100, (877) 246-3467, FAX: (978) 352-5955, E-Mail: csr@bwpress.com, Web Site: www.bwpress.com (21)

Beegan, Russell, B&W Press Inc, Georgetown, MA. Tel: (978) 352-6100, (877) 246-3467, FAX: (978) 352-5955, E-Mail: csr@bwpress.com, Web Site: www.bwpress.com (21)

Beeks, Steve, Lions Gate Entertainment, New York, NY. Tel: (212) 577-2400, FAX: (212) 962-2872, Web Site: www.liensgatefilms.com (32)

Beemak Plastics Inc, La Mirada, CA. Tel: (310) 886-5880, (800) 421-4393, FAX: (310) 764-0330, E-Mail: info@beemak.com, Web Site: www.beemak.com (16)

Beeman Precision Airguns, Santa Fe Springs, CA. Tel: (714) 890-4800, FAX: (714) 890-4808, E-Mail: sales@beeman.com, Web Site: www.beeman.com (11)

Beene, Allan, M., American Society of Civil Engineers, Reston, VA. Tel: (703) 295-6000, (800) 548-2723, FAX: (703) 295-6343, Web Site: www.asce.org (1)

Beene, Jeff, PI Inc, Athens, TN. Tel: (423) 745-6213, FAX: (423) 745-7039, Web Site: www.pi-inc.com (16)

Beer, Mike, The Principal Financial Group, Des Moines, IA. Tel: (515) 247-5111, (800) 986-3343, FAX: (515) 246-5475, Web Site: www.principal.com (15)

Beerman, David, Moby Wrap Inc, Chico, CA. Tel: (530) 898-8200 (2)

Beesley, Brian, West Bend, West Bend, WI. Tel: (262) 334-5107, (866) 290-1851, FAX: (262) 334-6800, Web Site: www.focuselectrics.com (16)

Beever, Bob, David C Cook, Colorado Springs, CO. Tel: (719) 536-0100, (800) 323-7543, FAX: (719) 536-3232, Web Site: www.davidccook.com (17)

Beffa-Negrini, David, PC Connection, Merrimack, NH. Tel: (603) 683-2167, (800) 800-0014, FAX: (603) 683-5773, E-Mail: pr@pcconnection.com, Web Site: www.pcconnection.com, macconnection.com (22)

Begay, Lois, Indian Arts & Crafts Association, Albuquerque, NM. Tel: (505) 265-9149, FAX: (505) 265-8251, E-Mail: info@iaca.com, Web Site: www.iaca.com (1)

Beggs, Joyce, Media Horizons Inc, Norwalk, CT. Tel: (203) 857-0770, FAX: (203) 857-0296, E-Mail: mhict@mediahorizons.com, Web Site: www.mediahorizons.com (21)

Beggs, Kevin, Lions Gate Television Corp, Santa Monica, CA. Tel: (310) 449-9200, FAX: (310) 255-3870, Web Site: www.lionsgate.com (16)

Begley, Alisa, IMPACT Publishing Inc, Bradenton, FL. Tel: (941) 739-2611, (800) 4-A-NEW-ME, FAX: (941) 756-0315, E-Mail: info@impactpublishinginc.com, Web Site: www.impactpublishinginc.com (17)

Behar, Howard, Hear Music, Bellevue, WA. Tel: (425) 452-5534, E-Mail: gail@hearmusic.com, Web Site: www.hearmusic.com (3)

Behar, Howard, P., Starbucks Corp, Seattle, WA. Tel: (206) 447-1575, (800) 344-1575, FAX: (206) 447-0828, Web Site: www.starbucks.com (4)

Behavioral Science Research, Coral Gables, FL. Tel: (305) 443-2000, (800) 282-2771, FAX: (305) 448-6825 (30)

Behlen Manufacturing Co, Columbus, NE. Tel: (402) 564-3111, FAX: (402) 563-7405, E-Mail: behlen@megavision.com, Web Site: www.behlenmfg.com (16)

Behnen, Toby P., Vocational Biographies Inc, Sauk Centre, MN. Tel: (320) 352-6516, (800) 255-0752, FAX: (320) 352-5546, E-Mail: careers@vocbios.com, Web Site: www.vocbio.com (31)

Behnke, Rob, Fair Indigo, Madison, WI. Tel: (608) 824-8974, Web Site: www.fairindigo.com (2)

Behrenfeld, James R., CI Productions Inc, Addison, IL. Tel: (708) 431-2800, FAX: (630) 458-1080 (35)

Behrens, Christopher, Source Link, Miamisburg, OH. Tel: (937) 885-8000, (800) 305-9414, FAX: (937) 885-8010, E-Mail: nesbit@commdata.com, Web Site: www.sourcelink.com (28)

Behrens, Thomas, Masterworks, Poulsbo, WA. Tel: (360) 394-4300, Web Site: www.masterworks.com (1)

Bein, Arlene, Practicing Law Institute, New York, NY. Tel: (212) 824-5700, (800) 260 4PLI, FAX: (800) 321-0093, E-Mail: info@pli.edu, Web Site: www.pli.edu (16)

Beirne, Paul, Tiger Direct Inc, Miami, FL. Tel: (305) 415-2200, (800) 800-8300, FAX: (305) 415-2202, Web Site: biz.tigerdirect.com (3)

Beiser, Scott, L., Houlihan Lokey Howard & Zukin, Los Angeles, CA. Tel: (310) 553-8871, (800) 788-5300, FAX: (310) 553-2173, Web Site: www.hlhz.com (14)

Belanger, David, Community Coffee Co, Baton Rouge, LA. Tel: (225) 291-3900, (800) 525-5583, FAX: (800) 643-8199, E-Mail: ccc@communitycoffee.com, Web Site: www.communitycoffee.com (4)

Belcaro Group Inc, Greenwood Village, CO. Tel: (303) 843-0302, Web Site: www.shopathome.com (17)

Belcher, Donald D., Boys' Life & Scouting Magazines, Irving, TX. Tel: (972) 580-2000, (866) 584-6589, FAX: (972) 580-2079, Web Site: www.boyslife.org (17)

Belcher, Donald, D., Boy Scouts of America/National Supply Group, Charlotte, NC. Tel: (972) 580-2161, (800) 323-0736, E-Mail: customerservice@scoutstuff.org, Web Site: www.scoutstuff.org (1)

Belcher, Lucy, DMS Marketing Inc, Mission Viejo, CA. Tel: (949) 460-7300, Web Site: http://www.dms-marketing.com (35)

Belcher, Toni, Caterpillar Inc, Peoria, IL. Tel: (309) 675-1000, Web Site: www.cat.com (16)

Belk, H. McKay, Belk Stores Services Inc, Charlotte, NC. Tel: (704) 357-1000, FAX: (704) 357-1782, Web Site: www.belk.com (16)

Belk, John, M., Belk Stores Services Inc, Charlotte, NC. Tel: (704) 357-1000, FAX: (704) 357-1782, Web Site: www.belk.com (16)

Belk Stores Services Inc, Charlotte, NC. Tel: (704) 357-1000, FAX: (704) 357-1782, Web Site: www.belk.com (16)

Belknap, Keith, Primedia Inc, Norcross, GA. Tel: (678) 421-3000, (800) 216-1423, Web Site: www.primedia.com (31)

Bell, Alan, The Bell Group Rio Grande, Albuquerque, NM. Tel: (505) 839-3000, Web Site: www.riogrande.com (5)

Bell, Allison, Donna Salyers' Fabulous-Furs, Covington, KY. Tel: (859) 291-3300, (800) 848-4650, E-Mail: abell@fabulousfurs.com, Web Site: fabulousfurs.com (2)

Bell, Frederick, Touch of Class Catalog, Huntingburg, IN. Tel: (812) 683-3707, (800) 457-7456, FAX: (812) 683-5921, Web Site: www.touchofclasscatalog.com (8)

Bell, Gordon, LucidView, Oak Ridge, TN. Tel: (888) 582-4384, Web Site: www.lucidview.com (20)

Bell, Hugh, Rio Grande, Albuquerque, NM. Tel: (505) 839-3000, (800) 545-6566, FAX: (800) 965-2329, E-Mail: info@riogrande.com, Web Site: www.riogrande.com (16)

Bell, James, A., Boeing Co, Chicago, IL. Tel: (312) 544-2000, FAX: (312) 544-2082, Web Site: www.boeing.com (16)

Bell, James, Institute of Management & Administration (IOMA), Peterborough, NH. Tel: (800) 401-5937, FAX: (973) 622-0595 (17)

Bell, John, MMI Direct, Columbia, MD. Tel: (410) 561-1500, FAX: (410) 561-0805, Web Site: www.mmidirect.com (22)

Bell, Kevin, Lincoln Park Zoo, Chicago, IL. Tel: (312) 742-2000, FAX: (312) 742-2137, E-Mail: webmaster@lpzoo.com, Web Site: www.lpzoo.com (1)

Bell, Linda, Kendall Products/Dri-Dek, Naples, FL. Tel: (239) 643-2244, (800) 348-2398, FAX: (800) 828-4248, E-Mail: info@dri-dek.com, Web Site: www.dri-dek.com (16)

Bell, Michael, W., CIGNA International, Philadelphia, PA. Tel: (215) 761-1741, FAX: (215) 761-5515, Web Site: www.cigna.com (15)

Bell, Raymond, E., Classic Color, Broadview, IL. Tel: (708) 484-0000, FAX: (708) 344-2233, Web Site: www.classic-color.com (27)

Bell, Richard, Gates Corp, Denver, CO. Tel: (303) 744-1911, FAX: (303) 744-4000, Web Site: www.gates.com (9)

Bell, Robert, J., Business Technologies, Dubuque, IA. Tel: (563) 556-7994, (800) 451-0399, FAX: (563) 556-2512 (34)

Bell, Robert, Music Barn Inc, Niagara Falls, NY. Tel: (800) 984-0047, FAX: (905) 513-6918, E-Mail: info@themusicbarn.com, Web Site: www.themusicbarn.com (6)

Bell, Ron, Target MarkeTeam, Atlanta, GA. Tel: (770) 274-3700, FAX: (770) 274-3730, Web Site: www.tmtinc.com (35)

Bell, Stephen, H., University of Illinois Foundation, Urbana, IL. Tel: (217) 333-0810, FAX: (217) 333-5577, E-Mail: uif@uillinois.edu, Web Site: www.uif.uillinois.edu (1)

Bell & Howell Ltd, North York, ON Canada. Tel: (416) 746-2200, FAX: (416) 228-2439, Web Site: www.bellhowell.com (9)

The Bell Group Rio Grande, Albuquerque, NM. Tel: (505) 839-3000, Web Site: www.riogrande.com (5)

Bell Performance Inc, Longwood, FL. Tel: (407) 831-5021, (800) 659-2355, FAX: (407) 767-8685, E-Mail: info@bellperformance.net, Web Site: www.bellperformance.net (9)

Bellacor, Mendota Heights, MN. Tel: (651) 294-2500, (877) 723-5522, FAX: (651) 294-2595, E-Mail: customerservice@bellacor.com, Web Site: www.bellacor.com (8)

Bellantoni, Ray, Jameco Electronics, Belmont, CA. Tel: (650) 592-8097, (800) 831-4242, FAX: (650) 592-2503, (800) 237-6948, E-Mail: domestic@jameco.com, Web Site: www.jameco.com (3)

Bellardo, Louis, J., National Archives & Records Administration, College Park, MD. Tel: (301) 837-0482, (86) NARA-NARA, FAX: (301) 837-0483, Web Site: www.archives.gov (17)

Bellatone, Paul, Promotional Products Association International, Irving, TX. Tel: (972) 252-0404, FAX: (800) I-AM-PPAI, (972) 258-3004, E-Mail: membership@ppa.org, Web Site: www.ppa.org (40)

Beller, Mondy, Shop.com, Monterey, CA. Tel: (831) 647-2489, (866) 746-7005, FAX: (831) 644-9283, Web Site: www.shop.com (16)

Bellomy Research Inc, Winston Salem, NC. Tel: (336) 721-1140, FAX: (336) 721-1597, E-Mail: bellomy@interpath.com, Web Site: www.bellomyresearch.com (30)

BellTower Technologies, Greenwood Village, CO. Tel: (303) 843-0302, FAX: (303) 843-0377, Web Site: www.shopathome.com (18)

Belmont, J.F., Cosmo International, Deerfield Beach, FL. Tel: (954) 798-4500, FAX: (954) 798-4514 (16)

Belmont University, Nashville, TN. Tel: (615) 460-6000, FAX: (615) 460-6455, Web Site: www.belmont.edu (41)

Belper, Tim, Nordskog Publishing Co, Ventura, CA. Tel: (805) 642-2070, FAX: (805) 642-1862, E-Mail: pwrboatmag@aol.com, Web Site: www.nordskogpublishing.com (17)

Belski, Jeff, LaPreferida Inc, Chicago, IL. Tel: (773) 254-7200, (800) 621-5422, FAX: (773) 254-8546, Web Site: www.lapreferida.com (4)

Belth, Andrew, Alloy Media Marketing, New York, NY. Tel: (212) 244-4307, (877) 360-9688, FAX: (212) 244-4311, E-Mail: contactus@alloymerch.com, Web Site: www.alloymarketing.com (35)

Belton, Y., Marc, The Pillsbury Co, Minneapolis, MN. Tel: (763) 764-7600, (800) 775-4777, FAX: (763) 764-8330, Web Site: www.pillsbury.com (16)

Beltone, Glenview, IL. Tel: (800) 235-8663, FAX: (847) 832-3300, E-Mail: info@beltone.com, Web Site: www.beltone.com (3)

Belvoir Media Group LLC, Norwalk, CT. Tel: (203) 857-3100, (800) 424-7887, FAX: (203) 857-3103, E-Mail: customer_service@belvoir.com, Web Site: www.belvoir.com (17)

Belyea, Peter, Cablexpress Technologies, Syracuse, NY. Tel: (315) 476-3000, (800) 913-9467, FAX: (315) 455-1800, E-Mail: info@cablexpress.com, Web Site: www.CXTec.com (10)

Bemis Co Inc, Terre Haute, IN. Tel: (812) 466-2213, FAX: (812) 460-6370, E-Mail: contact@beemis.com, Web Site: www.bemis.com (34)

Benchmark Brands Inc, Norcross, GA. Tel: (770) 242-1254, Web Site: www.footsmart.com (5)

The Benchmark Co, Austin, TX. Tel: (512) 707-7500, FAX: (512) 707-7757, E-Mail: thebenc@earthlink.net, Web Site: www.thebenchmarkcompany.net (30)

Benchmark Imaging & Display, Elk Grove Village, IL. Tel: (847) 292-5150, FAX: (847) 292-5159, Web Site: www.benchmarkimaging.com (27)

Bencin, Richard, L., Richard L Bencin & Associates, Brecksville, OH. Tel: (440) 526-6726, FAX: (440) 546-1623, E-Mail: rlbencin@netzero.net, Web Site: www.rlbencin.com (20)

Richard L Bencin & Associates, Brecksville, OH. Tel: (440) 526-6726, FAX: (440) 546-1623, E-Mail: rlbencin@netzero.net, Web Site: www.rlbencin.com (20)

Bencone Uniform Connection, Winston Salem, NC. Tel: (800) 326-3261, FAX: (866) 311-8254, E-Mail: bencone1@bellsouth.net, Web Site: www.bencone.com (2)

Bendel Jr, Charles, W., Center for Professional Advancement, East Brunswick, NJ. Tel: (732) 238-1600, FAX: (732) 238-9113, E-Mail: info@cfpa.com, Web Site: www.cfpa.com (13)

Bender, A., Thomas, Cooper Surgical Inc, Trumbull, CT. Tel: (203) 601-5200, (800) 645-3670, FAX: (203) 601-1007, Web Site: www.coopersurgical.com (7)

Bender, David, A., Promotion Support Services Inc, Rock Island, IL. Tel: (309) 788-4400, FAX: (309) 788-4465, E-Mail: dbender@pss-inc.net, Web Site: www.pss-inc.net (28)

Bender, John, Recognition Systems (Dot Works), Port Washington, NY. Tel: (516) 625-5000, FAX: (516) 625-1507, E-Mail: wade@dotworks.com, Web Site: www.dotworks.com (16)

Bender, Roman, Wrisco Industries Inc, Palm Beach Gardens, FL. Tel: (561) 626-5700, (800) 627-2646, FAX: (561) 627-3574, E-Mail: sales.staff@wrisco.com, Web Site: www.wrisco.com (8)

Bender, Thomas, SW Caging Corp, Topeka, KS. Tel: (785) 232-0061, Web Site: www.swcaging.com (14)

The Bender Group, Reno, NV. Tel: (775) 788-8800, (800) 621-9402, FAX: (775) 788-8811, E-Mail: salesinfo@benderwhs.com, Web Site: www.bendergroup.com (28)

Benditt, John, Technology Review, Cambridge, MA. Tel: (617) 475-8000, FAX: (617) 258-5850, Web Site: www.technologyreview.com (17)

Bendix, Jeffrey, Medical Economics Magazine, North Olmsted, OH. Tel: (440) 243-8100, FAX: (440) 891-2735, Web Site: medicaleconomics.modernmedicine.com/about (17)

Beneal, Katie, AmericasMart Atlanta, Atlanta, GA. Tel: (404) 220-3000, FAX: (404) 220-3030, Web Site: www.americasmart.com (42)

Benedetto, Tony, NASW Assurance Services Inc, Frederick, MD. Tel: (800) 668-4274, E-Mail: zxi@naswasi.org, Web Site: www.naswinsurancetrust.org (1)

Benedict, Kennette, Bulletin of the Atomic Scientists, Chicago, IL. Tel: (773) 702-6301, FAX: (773) 980-6932, E-Mail: admin@thebulletin.org, Web Site: www.thebulletin.org (17)

Beneducci, Joseph, J., Fireman's Fund Insurance Co, Novato, CA. Tel: (415) 899-2000, FAX: (415) 899-3600, Web Site: www.firemansfund.com (14)

BenefitMall, Dallas, TX. Tel: (469) 791-3355, Web Site: www.benefitmall.com (15)

Benelli, Thomas, SCP Rapp Collins Media, New York, NY. Tel: (212) 817-6800, Web Site: www.rappcollins.com (3)

Benet Academy, Lisle, IL. Tel: (630) 719-2794, Web Site: www.benet.org (1)

Benetton USA, New York, NY. Tel: (212) 593-0290, (800) 274-7192, FAX: (212) 371-1438, E-Mail: mtaylor@bennettonusa.com, Web Site: www.benetton.com (2)

Benevides, Beth, The Catholic University of America Press, Washington, DC. Tel: (202) 319-5052, FAX: (202) 319-4985, E-Mail: cua-press@cua.edu, Web Site: www.cuapress.cua.edu (17)

Benfer, Mark, Quark Inc, Denver, CO. Tel: (303) 894-3832, Web Site: www.quark.com (34)

Benicewicz, Any, Media Source Solutions, Plantation, FL. Tel: (954) 788-0213, Web Site: www.mediasourcesolutions.com (23)

Benik, Tina, C., A T Cross Co, Lincoln, RI. Tel: (401) 333-1200, (800) 282-7677, FAX: (401) 334-2861, Web Site: www.cross.com (16)

Benjamin, Earl, Soitenly Stooges, Glendale, CA. Tel: (818) 543-0778, (800) 543-0778, FAX: (818) 543-0779, E-Mail: custserv@threestooges.com, Web Site: www.soitenlystooges.com (6)

Benjamin, Gerald, A., Henry Schein Inc, Melville, NY. Tel: (631) 843-5500, (800) 472-4346, FAX: (631) 843-5658, E-Mail: custserv@henryschein.com, Web Site: www.henryschein.com (16)

Benjamin, Heather, Transamerican Mailing, Escondido, CA. Tel: (760) 745-5343, Web Site: www.transdirect.com (20)

Benjamin, Jerry, Integrated Mail Industries Ltd, Milwaukee, WI. Tel: (414) 908-3500, FAX: (414) 449-2906, E-Mail: sales@integratedmail.com, Web Site: www.integratedmail.com (28)

Benjamin, Jim, Sterling Publishing Co Inc, New York, NY. Tel: (212) 532-7160, (800) 367-9692, FAX: (212) 213-2495, Web Site: www.sterlingpublishing.com (17)

Benjamin, Maynard, H., Envelope Manufacturers Association, Alexandria, VA. Tel: (703) 739-2200, FAX: (703) 739-2209, Web Site: www.envelope.org (1)

Benjamin, Richard, Diakon Lutheran Social Ministries, Allentown, PA. Tel: (610) 682-2145, (888) 582-2230, FAX: (610) 682-1055, E-Mail: swangerb@diakon.org, Web Site: www.diakon.org (1)

Bennack Jr, Frank, A., The Hearst Corp, New York, NY. Tel: (212) 649-2000, FAX: (212) 649-2108, Web Site: www.hearst.com/magazines/ (17)

Benne, Susan, Antiquarian Booksellers Association of America Inc, New York, NY. Tel: (212) 944-8291, FAX: (212) 944-8293, E-Mail: sbenne@abaa.org, Web Site: www.abaa.org (1)

Bennet, Philip, The Washington Post, Washington, DC. Tel: (202) 334-6000, (800) 627-1150, E-Mail: letters@washpost.com, Web Site: www.washingtonpost.com (17)

Bennett, Alan, H&R Block Inc, Kansas City, MO. Tel: (816) 572-6446, (800) 472-5625, FAX: (816) 854-8500, Web Site: www.hrblock.com (14)

Bennett, Bill, Computer Business Services Inc, Americus, GA Canada. Tel: (229) 924-4408, (866) 924-4408, FAX: (229) 924-3644, E-Mail: cdill@combusser.com, Web Site: www.combusser.com (22)

Bennett, Brian, STIR, Milwaukee, WI. Tel: (414) 278-0040, FAX: (414) 278-0390, E-Mail: brianb@stirstuff.com, Web Site: www.stirstuff.com (35)

Bennett, Frank, Clegg Industries Inc, Gardena, CA. Tel: (310) 225-3800, FAX: (800) 250-9851, E-Mail: sales@clegg.xo.com, Web Site: www.cleggonline.com (16)

Bennett, Gary, MWM Dexter Inc, Aurora, MO. Tel: (888) 833-1242, FAX: (417) 841-1040, Web Site: www.mwmdexter.com (27)

Bennett, John, Quinnipiac College, Hamden, CT. Tel: (203) 582-8600, (203) 582-8200, (800) 462-1944, FAX: (203) 281-8664, Web Site: www.quinnipiac.edu (41)

Bennett, Lynn, University of Illinois Foundation, Urbana, IL. Tel: (217) 333-0810, FAX: (217) 333-5577, E-Mail: uif@uillinois.edu, Web Site: www.uif.uillinois.edu (1)

Bennett, Mark, D., Total Training Solutions LLC, Waunakee, WI. Tel: (608) 849-5563, (800) 831-0678, FAX: (608) 849-5605, (800) 831-3776, E-Mail: kbennett@ttstrain.com, Web Site: www.ttstrain.com (5)

Bennett, Michael, Bennett Marine Video, Venice, CA. Tel: (310) 827-8064, (800) 733-8862, FAX: (310) 827-8074, E-Mail: questions@bennettmarine.com, Web Site: www.bennettmarine.com (3)

Bennett, Neysa, BennettBaker Ltd, Chicago, IL. Tel: (312) 252-8883, FAX: (312) 252-8209, E-Mail: nbennett@bennettwheelless.com, Web Site: www.bennettbaker.com (20)

Bennett, Paula, The Tog Shop Inc, Beverly, MA. Tel: (800) 342-6789, FAX: (800) 755-7557, Web Site: www.togshop.com (2)

Bennett, Richard, General Motivation Co, Grand Rapids, MI. Tel: (616) 647-3085, FAX: (616) 647-5909, E-Mail: motivate@i2k.com, Web Site: www.generalmotivation.com (33)

Bennett, Tiffany, Classic Thermographers, North Mankato, MN. Tel: (623) 582-0002, (800) 727-4200, FAX: (800) 727-4202 (10)

Bennett, Tonya, MCH Strategic Data, Sweet Springs, MO. Tel: (660) 335-6373, (800) 776-6373, FAX: (660) 335-4157, E-Mail: tonyab@mchdata.com, Web Site: www.mchdata.com (23)

Bennett, Vaneeda, American Diabetes Association, Alexandria, VA. Tel: (703) 549-1500, Web Site: www.diabetes.org (1)

Bennett Marine Video, Venice, CA. Tel: (310) 827-8064, (800) 733-8862, FAX: (310) 827-8074, E-Mail: questions@bennettmarine.com, Web Site: www.bennettmarine.com (3)

BennettBaker Ltd, Chicago, IL. Tel: (312) 252-8883, FAX: (312) 252-8209, E-Mail: nbennett@bennettwheelless.com, Web Site: www.bennettbaker.com (20)

Benoit, Michael, J., Benoit & Associates, Kankakee, IL. Tel: (815) 932-2582, FAX: (815) 932-2594, E-Mail: mbenoit@benoit-associates.com, Web Site: www.benoit-associates.com (35)

Benoit & Associates, Kankakee, IL. Tel: (815) 932-2582, FAX: (815) 932-2594, E-Mail: mbenoit@benoit-associates.com, Web Site: www.benoit-associates.com (35)

Bensing, Doug, Fulfillment Xcellence Inc (FXI), Downers Grove, IL. Tel: (630) 852-7600, FAX: (630) 852-5817, Web Site: www.fx-inc.com (28)

Bensinger, Steven, J., AIG Accident & Health, New York, NY. Tel: (212) 770-7000, (877) 638-4244, FAX: (212) 509-9705, Web Site: www.aig.com (15)

Benson, Ken, PrintWest Communications Ltd, Regina, SK Canada. Tel: (306) 525-2304, (800) 236-6438, FAX: (306) 757-2439, E-Mail: info@printwest.com, Web Site: www.printwest.com (27)

Benson, Victor, N., Holsted Marketing Inc, New York, NY. Tel: (212) 686-8537, FAX: (212) 481-0415 (35)

Bentele, Barb, Profit Potentials Inc, Hull, IA. Tel: (712) 439-1496, (800) 543-5480, FAX: (712) 439-1434, Web Site: www.profitpotentials.com (1)

Bentley, Randy, 22squared Inc, Atlanta, GA. Tel: (404) 347-8700, FAX: (404) 347-8800, Web Site: www.22squared.com (35)

Bentley College, Waltham, MA. Tel: (781) 891-2800, FAX: (781) 891-3449, Web Site: www.bentley.edu (13)

Benton, Darrell, Diversified Photo Supply Corp, Gardena, CA. Tel: (310) 328-8577, (800) 544-1609, FAX: (310) 328-8518, Web Site: www.diversifiedphoto.com (10)

Benton, Mollie, US Data Corp, Agoura Hills, CA. Tel: (818) 444-4590, Web Site: www.usdatacorp.net (23)

Benton Announcements Inc, Buffalo, NY. Tel: (716) 836-4100, FAX: (716) 836-4161 (27)

Bentz, Bob, Advanced Telecom Services Inc, Wayne, PA. Tel: (610) 688-6000, (800) 247-1287, FAX: (610) 964-9117, E-Mail: bobb@advancedtele.com, Web Site: www.advancedtele.com (29)

Benun, Ilise, The Art of Self Promotion, Hoboken, NJ. Tel: (201) 653-0783, Fax: (201) 222-2494, E-Mail: ilise@marketing-mentor.com, Web Site: www.artofselfpromotion.com (17)

Benwell Atkins, Vancouver, BC Canada. Tel: (604) 872-2326, FAX: (604) 872-4235, E-Mail: vancouver.reception@rrd.com, Web Site: rrdonnelley.com/wwwbenwell/ (21)

Benz, Jr MD, Edward J., Dana-Farber Cancer Institute, Boston, MA. Tel: (617) 632-3000, FAX: (617) 632-4070, E-Mail: suzanne_fountain@dfci.harvard.edu, Web Site: www.dana-farber.org (1)

Beran, John, R., Comerica Inc, Dallas, TX. Tel: (800) 521-1190, FAX: (925) 941-1999, Web Site: www.comerica.com (14)

Berard, Rosalie, Alfa Aesar-A Johnson Matthey Co, Ward Hill, MA. Tel: (800) 343-0660, FAX: (800) 322-4757, E-Mail: info@alfa.com, Web Site: www.alfa.com (9)

Berardino, Angela, Denver Metro Convention & Visitors Bureau, Denver, CO. Tel: (303) 892-1112, FAX: (303) 892-1636, Web Site: www.denver.org (1)

Berarducci, James, Kurt Salmon Associates Inc, Atlanta, GA. Tel: (404) 892-0321, FAX: (404) 898-9590, E-Mail: infoksaweb@kurtsalmon.com, Web Site: www.kurtsalmon.com (20)

Berean Christian Stores, West Chester, OH. Tel: (877) 405-7194, FAX: (513) 728-6975, E-Mail: customerservice@berean.com, Web Site: www.berean.com (5)

Berganti, Pat, JB Dollar Stretcher Magazine, Richfield, OH. Tel: (330) 659-3590, (800) 673-2531, FAX: (330) 659-6741, Web Site: www.jbdollar.com (31)

Bergdoll, Robert, Boston Apparel Group, Randolph, MA. Tel: (508) 583-8110, Web Site: www.bostonapparel.com (2)

Bergdorf Goodman, New York, NY. Tel: (212) 753-7300, (800) 967-3788, (800) 218-4918, FAX: (212) 872-8677, E-Mail: clientservices@bergdorfgoodman.com, Web Site: www.bergdorfgoodman.com (2)

Berge, Melissa, Atlantic Publication Group LLC, Charleston, SC. Tel: (843) 747-0025, FAX: (843) 744-0816, E-Mail: info@atlanticpublicationgrp.com, Web Site: www.atlanticpublicationgrp.com (17)

J&H Berge/The Lab Mart, South Plainfield, NJ. Tel: (908) 561-1234, FAX: (908) 561-3002, E-Mail: rgardner@labmart.com, Web Site: www.labmart.com (7)

Bergen, Peter, Weekly Reader Corp, White Plains, NY. Tel: (914) 242-4019, (914) 242-4000, (800) 446-3355, Web Site: www.weeklyreader.com (23)

Bergen, Scott, Pizza Hut Inc, Plano, TX. Tel: (972) 338-7700, (866) 298-6986, FAX: (972) 338-6869, Web Site: www.pizzahut.com (16)

Bergenfeld, Judd, Alternative Media Group, Naples, FL. Tel: (732) 741-0585, FAX: (732) 741-0489, Web Site: www.amg-global.com (31)

Bergenholtz, Thomas, Viatech Publishing Solutions Inc, Bay Shore, NY. Tel: (631) 968-8500, (800) 645-8558, FAX: (631) 968-0830, Web Site: www.viatechpub.com (16)

Berger, Charles, The Scotts Co Div of Lawn Service, Marysville, OH. Tel: (937) 644-0011, FAX: (937) 644-7261, Web Site: www.scotts.com (8)

Berger, Dave, Berger's Table Pad Co, Indianapolis, IN. Tel: (317) 631-2577, (800) 428-4567, FAX: (317) 631-2584, Web Site: www.bergerstablepads.net (8)

Berger, David, Datapoint USA Inc, San Antonio, TX. Tel: (210) 614-9977, FAX: (210) 614-2297, E-Mail: info@datapointusa.com, Web Site: www.datapointusa.com (16)

Berger, Ellie, Scholastic Inc, New York, NY. Tel: (212) 343-6100, (800) SCHOLASTIC, FAX: (212) 343-6484, Web Site: www.scholastic.com/ (17)

Berger, Joshua, American Movie Classics Holding Corp, Jericho, NY. Tel: (516) 803-3000, FAX: (516) 803-3003, Web Site: www.amctv.com (16)

Berger, Lori, Redbook Magazine, New York, NY. Tel: (212) 649-2000, (800) 888-0008, FAX: (212) 581-7605, Web Site: www.redbookmag.com (17)

Berger, Mary, University of Pennsylvania - Veterinary Medicine (Development), Philadelphia, PA. Tel: (215) 898-1480, Web Site: www.vet.upenn.edu (1)

Berger, Morry, Anthem Blue Cross Blue Shield, Saint Louis, MO. Tel: (314) 923-4444, (888) 877-9125, FAX: (314) 923-5151, E-Mail: moreinfo@bcbsmo.com, Web Site: www.bcbsmo.com (15)

Berger, Nathan, HB Communications, North Haven, CT. Tel: (203) 234-9246, (800) 243-4414, FAX: (203) 234-2013, E-Mail: info@hbcommunications.com, Web Site: www.hbcommunications.com (34)

Berger, Ralph, CenterCore Group Inc, Marked Tree, AR. Tel: (800) 686-0821, FAX: (870) 358-3330, Web Site: www.centercoregroup.com (16)

Berger, Sherri, Mary's Plant Farm & Landscaping, Hamilton, OH. Tel: (513) 894-0022, FAX: (513) 892-2053, E-Mail: marysplantfarm@zoomtown.com, Web Site: www.marysplantfarm.com (8)

Berger, Theodore, S., New York Foundation For The Arts, Brooklyn, NY. Tel: (212) 366-6900, FAX: (212) 366-1778, E-Mail: deleget@nyfa.org, Web Site: www.nyfa.org (1)

Berger, Thomas, Cross Country Computer Corp, Central Islip, NY. Tel: (631) 231-4200, Web Site: www.crosscountrycomputer.com (22)

Berger's Table Pad Co, Indianapolis, IN. Tel: (317) 631-2577, (800) 428-4567, FAX: (317) 631-2584, Web Site: www.bergerstablepads.net (8)

Bergin, Laura, Rhythm Band Inc, Fort Worth, TX. Tel: (817) 335-2561, (800) 424-4724, FAX: (800) 784-9401, E-Mail: sales@rhythmband.com, Web Site: www.rhythmband.com (11)

Bergman, Burton, Butler Specialty Co, Chicago, IL. Tel: (773) 221-1200, (800) 799-2857, FAX: (773) 221-5892, Web Site: www.butlerspecialty.net (16)

Bergman, David, Butler Specialty Co, Chicago, IL. Tel: (773) 221-1200, (800) 799-2857, FAX: (773) 221-5892, Web Site: www.butlerspecialty.net (16)

Bergman, Richard, L., Bergman Medical/Scientific/Technical Collection, Princeton, NJ. Tel: (609) 921-0749, E-Mail: information@pmiprinceton.com, Web Site: www.pmiprinceton.com (38)

Bergman, Stanley, Henry Schein Inc, Melville, NY. Tel: (631) 843-5500, (800) 472-4346, FAX: (631) 843-5658, E-Mail: custserv@henryschein.com, Web Site: www.henryschein.com (16)

Bergman, Victoria, Bergman Medical/Scientific/Technical Collection, Princeton, NJ. Tel: (609) 921-0749, E-Mail: information@pmiprinceton.com, Web Site: www.pmiprinceton.com (38)

Bergman Medical/Scientific/Technical Collection, Princeton, NJ. Tel: (609) 921-0749, E-Mail: information@pmiprinceton.com, Web Site: www.pmiprinceton.com (38)

Bergos, Jane, DHL Global Mail, Weston, FL. Tel: (954) 903-6300, (866) 616-MAIL, FAX: (954) 903-6310, E-Mail: contact@dhlglobalmail.com, Web Site: www.dhlglobalmail.com (28)

Bergsman, Barry, NTN Communications Inc, Carlsbad, CA. Tel: (760) 438-7400, (888) PLAY-NTN, (888) 752-9686, FAX: (760) 438-3505, Web Site: www.ntn.com (32)

Bergstrom, Keith, Prestwick House Inc, Clayton, DE. Tel: (302) 659-2070, Web Site: www.prestwickhouse.com (17)

Bericewicz, Amy, The Catamount Group, Southport, CT. Tel: (203) 778-4110, FAX: (203) 778-4130, E-Mail: tina@catamountgroup.net, Web Site: www.catamountgroup.net (23)

Berk II, James, L., First Media Communications Inc, Brentwood, TN. Tel: (615) 661-0826, FAX: (615) 661-4084, Web Site: www.first-media.com (16)

Berke, Sarah, General Wig Manufacturers Inc, Pompano Beach, FL. Tel: (305) 823-0600, (800) 268-7210, FAX: (314) 785-0224, E-Mail: 4service@beautytrends.com, Web Site: www.beautytrends.com (7)

Berkeley College, Paramus, NJ. Tel: (201) 291-1111 (13)

Berkery, Rosemary, T., Merrill Lynch, New York, NY. Tel: (212) 449-1000, (800) 637-7455, FAX: (212) 449-9418, Web Site: www.ml.com (14)

Berkey Brendel Sheline, Akron, OH. Tel: (330) 665-5227, FAX: (330) 665-5055, Web Site: www.servantheart.com (1)

Berkley, William, Tension Envelope Corp, Kansas City, MO. Tel: (816) 471-3800, FAX: (816) 283-1498, Web Site: www.tension.com (26)

Berko, Paul, Time Products International, Del Rio, TX. Tel: (847) 459-8885, FAX: (847) 459-8111, E-Mail: cttpi@aol.com, Web Site: www.tpi2000.com (16)

Berkobits, Joe, Colonial Redi-Record Corp, Brooklyn, NY. Tel: (718) 972-7433, (800) 637-0040, FAX: (718) 972-7438, Web Site: www.asisupplier.com/81110 (10)

Berkowitz, Roger, Legal Sea Foods Inc, Boston, MA. Tel: (617) 530-9000, (800) 343-5804, FAX: (617) 530-9649, Web Site: www.legalseafoods.com (4)

Berks, David, Executive Enterprises Inc, Hawthorne, NY. Tel: (860) 701-5900, (800) 831-8333, FAX: (800) 250-3861, (860) 701-5909, E-Mail: info@eeiconferences.com, Web Site: www.eeiconferences.com (16)

Berkshire Direct Inc, Williamstown, MA. Tel: (413) 458-1721, FAX: (413) 458-1727, E-Mail: info@berkshiredirect.com, Web Site: www.berkshiredirect.com (17)

Berkshire Record Outlet Inc, Lee, MA. Tel: (413) 243-4080, FAX: (413) 243-4340, E-Mail: broinc@berkshirerecordoutlet.com, Web Site: www2.broinc.com (3)

Berlin, Jay, Northern Tool & Equipment Inc, Burnsville, MN. Tel: (952) 894-9510, (800) 221-0516, FAX: (952) 894-1020, Web Site: www.northerntool.com (16)

Berlin Industries Inc, Carol Stream, IL. Tel: (630) 682-0600, FAX: (630) 682-3093, E-Mail: info@berlinindustries.com, Web Site: www.berlinindustries.com (27)

Berliner, Jay, MJA International, Glen Head, NY. Tel: (516) 759-1000, FAX: (516) 674-3309 (7)

Berliner, Jay, Unitron Ltd, Commack, NY. Tel: (631) 589-6666, FAX: (631) 589-6795, E-Mail: johnc@unitronusa.com, Web Site: www.unitronusa.com (9)

Berlowe, Kathy, Bert Davis Executive Search, New York, NY. Tel: (212) 838-4000, FAX: (212) 935-3291, E-Mail: info@bertdavis.com, Web Site: www.bertdavis.com (20)

Berman, Barry, CRN International Inc, Hamden, CT. Tel: (203) 288-2002, FAX: (203) 281-3291, E-Mail: info@crnradio.com, Web Site: www.crnradio.com (32)

Berman, Jeff, Warren Communications News, Washington, DC. Tel: (202) 872-9200, (800) 771-9202, FAX: (202) 318-8350, E-Mail: info@warren-news.com, Web Site: www.warren-news.com (17)

Berman, Mimi, Independent Living Aids, Jericho, NY. Tel: (516) 937-1848, (800) 537-2118, FAX: (516) 937-3906, E-Mail: techsupport@independentliving.com, Web Site: www.independentliving.com (7)

Berman, Robert S., Berman Group, Newton Center, MA. Tel: (617) 426-0870, FAX: (617) 719-1505, E-Mail: rob@bermanusa.com, Web Site: www.bermanusa.com (16)

Berman Group, Newton Center, MA. Tel: (617) 426-0870, FAX: (617) 719-1505, E-Mail: rob@bermanusa.com, Web Site: www.bermanusa.com (16)

Bernadette Business Forms Inc, O Fallon, MO. Tel: (314) 522-1700, (800) 862-7288, FAX: (314) 524-6161, Web Site: www.bbf.com (27)

Bernard, Edward, C., T Rowe Price Associates Inc, Baltimore, MD. Tel: (410) 345-2000, (800) 638-7890, FAX: (410) 986-3618, E-Mail: info@troweprice.com, Web Site: www.troweprice.com (14)

Bernard, Robert, The Limited Stores Inc, Columbus, OH. Tel: (614) 415-2000, FAX: (614) 415-2057, Web Site: www.limited.com (2)

Bernard, Ted, Savicom, San Francisco, CA. Tel: (415) 983-0990, FAX: (415) 445-9999, E-Mail: sales@savicom.net, Web Site: www.savicom.net (22)

Bernardo, Joe, Cision US Inc, Chicago, IL. Tel: (312) 922-2400, (866) 639-5087, FAX: (312) 922-3126, E-Mail: info.us@cision.com, Web Site: us.cision.com (43)

Berner, Mary, Fairchild Books, New York, NY. Tel: (212) 630-4171, (800) 932-4724, FAX: (212) 630-3868, Web Site: www.fairchildbooks.com (17)

Berner, Mary, Fairchild Publications, New York, NY. Tel: (212) 630-4000, Web Site: www.fairchildpub.com (17)

Bernheimer II, Walter, Bernheimer Associates, Wellesley, MA. Tel: (781) 237-8910, FAX: (781) 239-2932, E-Mail: wsbii@hotmail.com (20)

Bernheimer Associates, Wellesley, MA. Tel: (781) 237-8910, FAX: (781) 239-2932, E-Mail: wsbii@hotmail.com (20)

Bernier, John E., Cape Cod Cupola Co Inc, North Dartmouth, MA. Tel: (508) 994-2119, FAX: (508) 997-2511, Web Site: www.capcodcupola.com (8)

Bernstein, David, BtoB Magazine, New York, NY. Tel: (212) 210-0206, FAX: (212) 210-0422, E-Mail: aholtzman@crain.com, Web Site: www.btobonline.com (43)

Bernstein, David, Chicago Magazine, Chicago, IL. Tel: (312) 222-8999, FAX: (312) 222-0287, Web Site: www.chicagomag.com (17)

Bernstein, David, Idearc Media Corp, Dallas, TX. Tel: (972) 453-7797 (16)

Bernstein, David, SuperMedia LLC, Dallas, TX. Tel: (972) 453-7797 (31)

Bernstein, Gary, BI, Summit, NJ. Tel: (908) 722-4222, FAX: (908) 722-9199, Web Site: www.Biworldwide.com (33)

Bernstein, Marc, Graham Field Health Products Inc, Atlanta, GA. Tel: (800) 347-5678, FAX: (800) 726-0601, E-Mail: ics@grahamfield.com, Web Site: www.lumiscope.net (7)

Bernstein, Ralph, Gelco Information Network, Eden Prairie, MN. Tel: (952) 947-1500, (800) 444-6588, FAX: (952) 947-1525, Web Site: www.gelco.com (16)

Bernstein, Ronald A., Cross Marketing USA, Chicago, IL. Tel: (312) 440-3700, (866) 440-3700, FAX: (312) 943-5813, E-Mail: ronbernstein@crossmarketing.us, Web Site: www.crossmarketing.us (23)

Bernstein, Ronald, A., Marketing Incentives International Inc, Chicago, IL. Tel: (312) 440-3700, (866) 440-3700, FAX: (312) 943-5813, E-Mail: miibenefits@rcn.com, Web Site: www.mktgincentiveintl.com (33)

Bernstein-Rein Advertising, Kansas City, MO. Tel: (816) 756-0640, Web Site: www.brbrg.com (35)

Berry, Brigid, Data Partners Inc, Fort Myers, FL. Tel: (239) 267-8762, (866) 423-1818, FAX: (239) 267-9043, E-Mail: info@data-partners.com, Web Site: www.datapartners.com (22)

Berry, Burt, No Load Fund*X, San Francisco, CA. Tel: (415) 986-7979, (800) 763-8639, FAX: (415) 986-1595, Web Site: www.noloadfundx.com (14)

Berry, Diane, Coveo, Quebec, PQ Canada. Tel: (418) 263-1111, Web Site: www.coveo.com (22)

Berry, Jake, Simmons College, Boston, MA. Tel: (617) 521-2027, Web Site: www.simmons.edu (1)

Berry, Lorena, JHL Mail Marketing Inc, Stevens Point, WI. Tel: (715) 341-0581, (800) 236-0581, FAX: (715) 341-9645, E-Mail: ren@jhl.com, Web Site: www.jhl.com (28)

Berry, Lorna, August Marketing, Tequesta, FL. Tel: (561) 747-1325, Web Site: www.augustmktg.com (22)

Berry, Thomas, L., Berry Best Services Ltd, Fairfax, VA. Tel: (202) 293-4964, FAX: (202) 293-4964, E-Mail: samf@berrybest.com, Web Site: www.berrybest.com (30)

Berry Best Services Ltd, Fairfax, VA. Tel: (202) 293-4964, FAX: (202) 293-4964, E-Mail: samf@berrybest.com, Web Site: www.berrybest.com (30)

The Berry Co, Dayton, OH. Tel: (937) 296-2121, FAX: (937) 296-2011, Web Site: www.lmberry.com (35)

Berry Hill Ltd, Saint Thomas, ON Canada. Tel: (519) 631-0480, (800) 668-3072, FAX: (519) 631-8935, E-Mail: info@berryhilllimited.com, Web Site: www.berryhilllimited.com (8)

Bersani, Jamie, LimitedBrands Inc, Reynoldsburg, OH. Tel: (614) 577-5902, FAX: (614) 415-7440, Web Site: www.limitedbrands.com (16)

Berse, Leonard, Hand Assembly & Packaging Inc (HAPI), Plainview, NY. Tel: (718) 699-3400, FAX: (718) 699-3409 (28)

Berson, Lori, Berson/Dean/Stevens Inc, Westlake Village, CA. Tel: (818) 713-0134, (877) 447-0134, E-Mail: info@bersondeanstevens.com, Web Site: www.bersondeanstevens.com (35)

Berson/Dean/Stevens Inc, Westlake Village, CA. Tel: (818) 713-0134, (877) 447-0134, E-Mail: info@bersondeanstevens.com, Web Site: www.bersondeanstevens.com (35)

Bertalli, Frank, ETTSI Premiums & Incentives, Daytona Beach, FL. Tel: (386) 271-0204, Web Site: www.ettsi.com (16)

Berthiaume, Dennis, Standard Life, Montreal, PQ. Tel: (514) 499-8855, (877) 499-9555, FAX: (514) 499-4908, Web Site: www.standardlife.ca (15)

Berthiaume, Douglas, A., Waters Corp, Milford, MA. Tel: (508) 482-2000, (800) 252-4752, FAX: (508) 872-1990, Web Site: www.waters.com (15)

Bertness, Eric, Phillips Kiln Service LTD, South Sioux City, NE. Tel: (402) 494-6837, (800) 831-0876, FAX: (402) 494-6858, E-Mail: info@kilm.com, Web Site: www.kiln.com (15)

Bertoli, Gina, Windsor Vineyards, Santa Rosa, CA. Tel: (800) 741-6070, (800) 289-9463, E-Mail: webmaster@windsorvineyards.com, Web Site: www.windsorvineyards.com (15)

Bertolini, Mark, T., AETNA - Marketing Product & Communication, Hartford, CT. Tel: (860) 273-0123, (800) 872-3862, FAX: (860) 273-3971, Web Site: www.aetna.com (14)

Bertrand, Robert, Commonwealth Business Media Inc, Newark, NJ. Tel: (609) 371-7700, (800) 221-5488, FAX: (609) 371-7879, Web Site: www.cbizmedia.com (17)

Berway Visual Products Inc, Wilmington, MA. Tel: (978) 694-9195, (800) 452-0410, FAX: (978) 694-9212, E-Mail: sales@berway.com, Web Site: www.berway.com (3)

Besesparis, Ted, National Association of Professional Insurance Agents, Alexandria, VA. Tel: (703) 836-9340, FAX: (703) 836-1279, E-Mail: web@pianet.org, Web Site: www.pianet.com (1)

Besser, Barbara, Yoga Journal / Active Interest Media, San Francisco, CA. Tel: (415) 591-0555, Web Site: www.yogajournal.com (17)

Best, Anthony, J., JP Morgan Chase & Co, New York, NY. Tel: (212) 270-6000, E-Mail: jpmcinvestorrelations@jpmchase.com, Web Site: www.jpmorgan.com (14)

Best, Ellen, Eire Direct, Chicago, IL. Tel: (312) 640-4000, FAX: (312) 640-0324, E-Mail: info@eiredirect.com, Web Site: www.eiredirect.com (16)

Best, Jessica, Emfluence, Kansas City, MO. Tel: (816) 472-4455, Web Site: www.emfluence.com (21)

Best, Robert, O., Unum Corp, Portland, ME. Tel: (207) 770-2211, (800) 421-0344, FAX: (207) 770-4510, Web Site: www.unum.com (15)

Best, Tyler, A., Alamo Rent A Car, Tulsa, OK. Tel: (918) 401-6000, Web Site: www.alamo.com (16)

Best Buy, Richfield, MN. Tel: (612) 291-1000, Web Site: www.bestbuy.com (3)

Best Friends Animal Society, Kanab, UT. Tel: (435) 644-2001, Web Site: www.bestfriends.org (1)

Best ROI Lists, Boca Raton, FL. Tel: (561) 499-3201, Web Site: www.bestroilists.com (23)

Best Western International, Phoenix, AZ. Tel: (609) 957-5809, Web Site: www.bestwestern.com (19)

Besterd, John, MC Group, London, ON Canada. Tel: (519) 660-8460, FAX: (519) 660-8476, Web Site: www.themcgroup.com (35)

Bestwick, Stephen, Crabtree & Evelyn Ltd, Woodstock, CT. Tel: (860) 928-2761, (800) CRABTREE, (860) 928-0452, Web Site: www. crabtree-evelyn.com (4)

Beta Research Corp, Syosset, NY. Tel: (516) 935-3800, FAX: (516) 935-4092, E-Mail: beta@nybeta. com, Web Site: www.nybeta.com (30)

Bete, Michael, Channing L Bete Co Inc, South Deerfield, MA. Tel: (800) 477-4776, FAX: (800) 499-6464, E-Mail: custscvs@channing.bete.com, Web Site: www.channing-bete.com (17)

Channing L Bete Co Inc, South Deerfield, MA. Tel: (800) 477-4776, FAX: (800) 499-6464, E-Mail: custscvs@channing.bete.com, Web Site: www. channing-bete.com (17)

Bethel, Nalini, Bahamas Ministry of Tourism, Fort Lauderdale, FL. Tel: (954) 236-9292, Web Site: www.bahamas.com (19)

Bethesda Hospital Foundation, Boynton Beach, FL. Tel: (561) 737-7733 (1)

Bethesda List Center Inc, Bethesda, MD. Tel: (301) 986-1455, FAX: (301) 907-4870, E-Mail: info@ bethesda-list.com, Web Site: www.bethesda-list. com (24)

Better Health Fitness, Brooklyn, NY. Tel: (718) 436-4693, FAX: (718) 854-3381, Web Site: www. betterhealthfitness.com (11)

Better Homes & Gardens, New York, NY. Tel: (212) 551-7097, FAX: (212) 551-6917, E-Mail: support@bhg.com, Web Site: www.bhg.com (31)

Better Lists Inc, Stamford, CT. Tel: (203) 324-4171, FAX: (203) 358-0384, E-Mail: tim@betterlists. com, Web Site: www.betterlists.com (28)

Better Tools For Industry, Santee, CA. Tel: (619) 562-3071, FAX: (619) 562-0592, Web Site: www.bti-tool.com (9)

Betterway Books, Blue Ash, OH. Tel: (513) 531-2222, (800) 289-0963, FAX: (513) 531-4744, Web Site: www.fwpublications.com/books.asp (17)

Bettinger II, Walter, W., Charles Schwab & Co Inc, San Francisco, CA. Tel: (415) 627-7000, (800) 648-5300, FAX: (415) 421-0810, Web Site: www. schwab.com (14)

Betz, Bob, Cognis Corp, Cincinnati, OH. Tel: (513) 482-3000, FAX: (513) 482-5501, E-Mail: kathy. bollmer@cognis.com, Web Site: www.cognis-us. com (35)

Betz, Ronald, Penn Herb Co Ltd, Philadelphia, PA. Tel: (215) 632-6100, (800) 523-9971, FAX: (215) 632-7945, E-Mail: information@pennherb.com, Web Site: www.pennherb.com (7)

Betz Jr, William P., Penn Herb Co Ltd, Philadelphia, PA. Tel: (215) 632-6100, (800) 523-9971, FAX: (215) 632-7945, E-Mail: information@pennherb. com, Web Site: www.pennherb.com (7)

Beuke, Bobbie, Beuke Printing & Mailing, Cincinnati, OH. Tel: (513) 221-0008, FAX: (513) 221-0038, E-Mail: info@beuke.com, Web Site: www.beuke. com (28)

Beuke, Chuck, Beuke Printing & Mailing, Cincinnati, OH. Tel: (513) 221-0008, FAX: (513) 221-0038, E-Mail: info@beuke.com, Web Site: www.beuke. com (28)

Beuke Printing & Mailing, Cincinnati, OH. Tel: (513) 221-0008, FAX: (513) 221-0038, E-Mail: info@ beuke.com, Web Site: www.beuke.com (28)

Bevelacqua, Darcy, DB Consulting, Harrison, NY. Tel: (914) 698-2008, E-Mail: darcybev@yahoo.com (20)

Bevelacqua, Darcy, Db Marketing, Harrison, NY. Tel: (914) 698-2008 (22)

Bevevino, Rita, Whirley Drink Works, Warren, PA. Tel: (814) 723-7600, (800) 825-5575, FAX: (814) 723-3245, E-Mail: info@whirleydrinkworks.com, Web Site: www.whirleydrinkworks.com (5)

Bevilacqua, Amy, Films Media Group, New York, NY. Tel: (609) 671-1000, (800) 257-5126, FAX: (609) 671-0266, E-Mail: custserv@films.com, Web Site: www.filmsmediagroup.com (3)

Bewkes, Jeffrey, L., Time Warner Inc, New York, NY. Tel: (212) 484-8000, Web Site: www.timewarner. com (16)

Beychok, Alan, Benchmark Brands Inc, Norcross, GA. Tel: (770) 242-1254, Web Site: www.footsmart. com (5)

Beyer, John, Nathan Associates Inc, Arlington, VA. Tel: (703) 516-7700, FAX: (703) 351-6162, Web Site: www.nathaninc.com (30)

Beyond Quota LLC, Lake Forest, IL. Tel: (847) 234-9475, FAX: (847) 234-5260, E-Mail: megrinnell@ beyondquota.com, Web Site: www.beyondquota. com (35)

Bezemek, Karen, Amway Global, Ada, MI. Tel: (616) 787-6000, Web Site: www.amwayglobal.com (7)

Bhalerao, Satish, Logical Computer Selections, Short Hills, NJ. Tel: (212) 949-2290, (800) 949-2701, FAX: (212) 697-5786, E-Mail: info@logicomputer. com, Web Site: www.logicomputer.com (16)

Bharara, Vinit, Diapers.com, Jersey City, NJ. Tel: (800) 342-7377, Web Site: www.diapers.com (5)

Bhesania, Niloufer, The Kidney Foundation of Canada/Greater Ontario Branch, Hamilton, ON Canada. Tel: (800) 414-3484, FAX: (905) 318-8491, E-Mail: kidneyfoundation@bellnet.ca, Web Site: www.kidney.on.ca (1)

Bhojwani, Gary, C., Allianz Life Insurance Co of North America, Minneapolis, MN. Tel: (763) 765-6500, (800) 950-5872, Web Site: www.allianzlife. com (15)

Bhojwani, Gary, C., Fireman's Fund Insurance Co, Novato, CA. Tel: (415) 899-2000, FAX: (415) 899-3600, Web Site: www.firemansfund.com (14)

Biagini, John, F., HCI Direct, Bensalem, PA. Tel: (215) 244-9600, (888) 765-0062, FAX: (215) 244-0328, Web Site: www.silkies.com (16)

Bianucci, Deborah, BAI, Chicago, IL. Tel: (312) 683-2464, FAX: (312) 683-2373, E-Mail: info@bai.org, Web Site: www.bai.org (17)

Bibeau, Neal, Decision One, Devon, PA. Tel: (800) 767-2876, FAX: (610) 296-2910, Web Site: www. decisionone.com (34)

Bible, Geoffrey, Kraft Foods/Gevalia Kaffe, Tarrytown, NY. Tel: (914) 335-4239, Web Site: www. gevalia.com (16)

Bibler, Dean, Jaffe Brothers Natural Foods, Valley Center, CA. Tel: (760) 749-1133, (800) 548-1886, FAX: (760) 749-1282, E-Mail: jb54@worldnet.att. net, Web Site: www.organicfruitsandnuts.com (4)

Bibler, Dean, PPC, Johnston, IA. Tel: (515) 986-5070, E-Mail: sales@ppcbest.com, Web Site: www. ppcbest.com (9)

BIC Corp, Shelton, CT. Tel: (203) 783-2000, FAX: (203) 783-2081, Web Site: www.bicworld.com (16)

BIC Graphic USA, Clearwater, FL. Tel: (727) 536-7895, FAX: (800) 753-5890, Web Site: www. bicgraphic.com (33)

Bick, Israel, Bick International, Van Nuys, CA. Tel: (818) 997-6496, FAX: (818) 988-4337, E-Mail: iibick@sbcglobal.net, Web Site: www. bickinternational.com (6)

Bick International, Van Nuys, CA. Tel: (818) 997-6496, FAX: (818) 988-4337, E-Mail: iibick@ sbcglobal.net, Web Site: www.bickinternational. com (6)

Bickley, Colin, Donor Services Group, Los Angeles, CA. Tel: (310) 788-9000, (888) 474-1900, Web Site: www.donorservicesgroup.com (1)

Bickman, Barry, Arbill Safety Products, Philadelphia, PA. Tel: (215) 632-2000, (800) 523-5367, FAX: (800) 426-5808, E-Mail: orders@arbill.com, Web Site: www.arbill.com (9)

Bickman Copeland, Julie, Arbill Safety Products, Philadelphia, PA. Tel: (215) 632-2000, (800) 523-5367, FAX: (800) 426-5808, E-Mail: orders@ arbill.com, Web Site: www.arbill.com (9)

Biddle, Rick, Schultz & Williams Inc, Philadelphia, PA. Tel: (215) 625-9955, FAX: (215) 625-2701, E-Mail: mail@schultzwilliams.com, Web Site: www.sw-inc.com (1)

Biddulph, David, Market Force Corp, Newtown Square, PA. Tel: (610) 356-5220, FAX: (610) 356-5110, E-Mail: davethomas@marketforcecorp.com, Web Site: www.marketforcecorporation.com (23)

Biden, R., Hunter, National Railroad Passenger Corp, Washington, DC. Tel: (202) 906-3000, (800) USA-RAIL, FAX: (202) 906-3306, Web Site: www. amtrak.com (16)

Bidwell, Tim, Moore Medical LLC, Farmington, CT. Tel: (860) 826-3600, FAX: (860) 223-2382, Web Site: www.mooremedical.com (7)

Biegel, Bruce, Winterberry Group, New York, NY. Tel: (212) 842-6000, FAX: (212) 842-6010, E-Mail: info@winterberrygroup.com, Web Site: www.winterberrygroup.com (20)

Biehn, Doug, Blue Shield of California, San Francisco, CA. Tel: (415) 229-5000, FAX: (415) 229-5056, Web Site: www.blueshieldca.com (15)

Bielanski, Andrew S., Countrywide Financial Corp, Calabasas, CA. Tel: (818) 225-3000, FAX: (818) 225-4051, Web Site: www.countrywide.com (14)

Bielen, Richard, J., Protective Life Corp, Deerfield, IL. Tel: (847) 948-8988, (800) 323-5771, FAX: (847) 948-1156, Web Site: www.protective.com (15)

Bieler, Peter, Media Funding Corp, Malibu, CA. Tel: (310) 457-4140, FAX: (310) 774-1234, E-Mail: info@mediafunding.com, Web Site: mediafunding. com (32)

Bienen, Henry, S., Northwestern University, Evanston, IL. Tel: (847) 491-3741, FAX: (847) 491-8406, E-Mail: webmaster@northwestern.edu, Web Site: www.northwestern.edu (41)

Bienenstock, George, Fluid Metering Inc, Syosset, NY. Tel: (516) 922-6050, (800) 223-3388, FAX: (516) 624-8261, E-Mail: pumps@fmipump.com, Web Site: www.fmipump.com (15)

Bierman, Rich, Wisconsin Converting Inc, Green Bay, WI. Tel: (920) 437-6400, (800) 544-1935, FAX: (920) 436-4964, E-Mail: wci@ wisconsinconverting.com, Web Site: www. wisconsinconverting.com (26)

Bierman, Victor, NSA Technologies LLC, Akron, OH. Tel: (330) 576-4600 (9)

Biermeier, Jens, D., School of Business & Economics, Los Angeles, CA. Tel: (323) 343-2800, FAX: (323) 343-2813, Web Site: cbe.calstatela.edu (41)

Biern, Charlie, LogEtronics Corp, Sparta, NJ. Tel: (703) 912-7745, FAX: (703) 912-7610, Web Site: www.logetronics.com (23)

Biesel, Becky, Party Kits & Equestrian Gifts, Louisville, KY. Tel: (502) 425-2126, (800) 99-DERBY, FAX: (502) 425-5230, E-Mail: info@partykits. com, Web Site: www.derbygifts.com (35)

Big Brothers Big Sisters of Greater Kansas City, Kansas City, MO. Tel: (816) 561-5269, Web Site: www.bigbrothersbigsisterskc.org (1)

Bigelow, C., Bigelow Electronics, Bluffton, OH. Tel: (419) 358-7851 (3)

Bigelow Electronics, Bluffton, OH. Tel: (419) 358-7851 (3)

RC Bigelow Inc, Fairfield, CT. Tel: (203) 334-1212, Web Site: www.bigelowtea.com (4)

Biggerstaff, Patricia, Sales Development Associates Inc, Saint Louis, MO. Tel: (314) 862-8828, FAX: (314) 862-8829, E-Mail: patb@sdasti.com (21)

Biggs, John, H., Boeing Co, Chicago, IL. Tel: (312) 544-2000, FAX: (312) 544-2082, Web Site: www. boeing.com (16)

Biggs/Gilmore Communications, Kalamazoo, MI. Tel: (269) 349-7711, FAX: (269) 349-9657, E-Mail: info@biggs-gilmore.com, Web Site: www.biggs-gilmore.com (35)

Bigham, Paul, Bigham Direct & Digital, Plano, TX. Tel: (972) 801-2600, FAX: (972) 801-2649, E-Mail: pbigham@bighamagency.com, Web Site: www.bighamagency.com (35)

Bigham Direct & Digital, Plano, TX. Tel: (972) 801-2600, FAX: (972) 801-2649, E-Mail: pbigham@bighamagency.com, Web Site: www.bighamagency.com (35)

Bigley, Nichole, Primedia Inc, Norcross, GA. Tel: (678) 421-3000, (800) 216-1423, Web Site: www.primedia.com (31)

Bijoux Terner, Miami, FL. Tel: (305) 500-7500, (800) 262-3614, FAX: (305) 262-9286, E-Mail: customerservice@bijouxterner.com, Web Site: www.bijouxterner.com (16)

Bike Nashbar, Crab Orchard, WV. Tel: (800) NAS-HBAR, FAX: (877) 778-9456, E-Mail: custserv@nashbar.com, Web Site: www.bikenashbar.com (11)

The Bil-Ray Aluminum Siding Corp of Queens Inc, New Hyde Park, NY. Tel: (516) 616-4200, (800) 474-4415, FAX: (516) 616-4030, Web Site: www.homeclub.com (16)

Bilbrey, George, Return Path Inc, New York, NY. Tel: (212) 905-5500, FAX: (212) 905-5501, Web Site: www.returnpath.biz (22)

Bilbrey, John, DS Waters of North America LP, Flowery Branch, GA. Tel: (626) 585-1000, (800) 669-3402, FAX: (626) 585-8563, E-Mail: customerservice@water.com, Web Site: www.water.com (4)

Bilbrey, John, Hershey Foods Corp, Hershey, PA. Tel: (800) 454-7737, FAX: (717) 534-5204, Web Site: www.hersheygifts.com (4)

Bilby, Manda, MLS Data Management Solutions, Fort Worth, TX. Tel: (817) 804-6900, FAX: (817) 804-6999, Web Site: www.mlsc.com (22)

Biles, Steve, Invacare Supply Group, Milford, MA. Tel: (508) 429-1000, (800) 925-4792, FAX: (508) 429-1581, E-Mail: service.isg@invacare.com, Web Site: www.invacaresupplygroup.com (16)

Bilisky, Mark, Americans for Peace Now, Washington, DC. Tel: (202) 408-9898, FAX: (202) 728-1895, E-Mail: apndc@peacenow.org (1)

Bilitz, Paula, Minnesota Life, Saint Paul, MN. Tel: (651) 665-3500, (888) 237-1838, FAX: (651) 665-4488, Web Site: www.minnesotalife.com; www.securian.com (15)

Bill Me Later Inc, Timonium, MD. Tel: (443) 921-1184, Web Site: www.coporate.billmelater.com (14)

Billhardt, Gregory, Cables to Go, Moraine, OH. Tel: (937) 224-8646, (800) 506-9607, FAX: (800) 331-2841, (937) 496-2666, Web Site: www.cablestogo.com (13)

Billin Medina-Warren, Scottsdale, AZ. Tel: (972) 951-7291 (20)

Bills, David, E I DuPont De Nemours & Co, Wilmington, DE. Tel: (302) 774-1000, FAX: (302) 774-7321, Web Site: www.dupont.com (16)

Billue, Stan, Mr Fantastic LLC, Astor, FL. Tel: (407) 719-2020, E-Mail: sbillue@usa2net.net, Web Site: www.stanbillue.com (20)

Billy E Barnes, Chapel Hill, NC. Tel: (919) 942-6350, FAX: (919) 942-6350, E-Mail: bbarnes218@aol.com, Web Site: www.billybarnes.com (38)

Bilofsky, Allan, D., The List Source Inc, Cherry Hill, NJ. Tel: (856) 795-3344, FAX: (856) 795-9498 (23)

Binkley, Gregory R., The Sportsman's Guide Inc, South Saint Paul, MN. Tel: (651) 451-3030, (800) 882-2962, FAX: (651) 450-6130, E-Mail: custserv@sportsmansguide.com, Web Site: www.sportsmansguide.com (11)

Binnie, Ross, The Cleveland Orchestra, Cleveland, OH. Tel: (216) 231-7441, FAX: (216) 231-4038, Web Site: www.clevelandorchestra.com (1)

Binnie, Thomas, Sturbridge Yankee Workshop Inc, Portland, ME. Tel: (207) 774-9045, (800) 343-1144, FAX: (207) 774-2561, Web Site: www.sturbridgeyankee.com (16)

Biochlini, Brian, Pennwell Publishing, Tulsa, OK. Tel: (918) 835-3161, (800) 331-4463, E-Mail: headquarters@pennwell.com, Web Site: www.pennwell.com (17)

Biological Photo Service & Terraphotographics, Pacifica, CA. Tel: (650) 359-6219, FAX: (650) 359-6219, E-Mail: bpsterra@pacbell.net, Web Site: www.agpix.com/biologicalphoto (38)

Biomerica Inc, Irvine, CA. Tel: (949) 645-2111, FAX: (949) 722-6674, E-Mail: bmra@biomerica.com, Web Site: www.biomerica.com (7)

Biosciences-Amersham, Piscataway, NJ. Tel: (732) 457-8000, FAX: (732) 457-0557, Web Site: www.amersham.com (16)

Birchfield, Cyndy, Pontis Group, Grosse Pointe, MI. Tel: (614) 764-1274, FAX: (614) 210-0598, E-Mail: cbirchfield@pontisgroup.com, Web Site: www.pontisgroup.com (35)

Bird, Amanda, Sculptz, Feasterville Trevose, PA. Tel: (215) 494-2900, E-Mail: sdudek@sculptz.com, Web Site: www.silkies.com (2)

Bird, Andy, Disney Vacation Club, Kissimmee, FL. Tel: (407) 566-3100, (800) 500-3990, FAX: (407) 566-3393 (19)

Bird, Michael, E., ETR Associates, San Francisco, CA. Tel: (831) 438-4060, (800) 321-4407, FAX: (800) 435-8433, E-Mail: webmaster@etr.org, Web Site: www.etr.org (24)

Bird, Shelley, Fluke Biomedical, Everett, WA. Tel: (425) 347-6100, (800) 850-4608, FAX: (425) 446-5116, Web Site: www.flukebiomedical.com (16)

Birdseye, Jeff, Isuzu Motors America Inc, Anaheim, CA. Tel: (562) 229-5000, (800) 255-6727, FAX: (562) 229-5463, Web Site: www.isuzu.com (16)

Birger, Stu, Cascade Promotions Corp, Redwood City, CA. Tel: (650) 594-1757 (33)

Birney, Lori, Baltimore Magazine, Baltimore, MD. Tel: (410) 752-4200, (800) 935-0838, FAX: (410) 625-0280, E-Mail: blori@baltimoremagazine.net, Web Site: www.baltimoremagazine.net (17)

Birsh, Hope, The Maryland Saddlery Inc, Butler, MD. Tel: (410) 771-4135, (800) 428-5077, FAX: (410) 472-9722, E-Mail: mdsaddle@aol.com, Web Site: www.marylandsaddlery.com (11)

Birthday Express Inc, Bothell, WA. Tel: (425) 641-0075, FAX: (425) 641-2028, Web Site: www.birthdayexpress.com (5)

Birthday Keepsakes, Loveland, CO. Tel: (970) 669-5506, Web Site: www.bkeepsakes.com (6)

Bischmann, Joanne M., Harley-Davidson Inc, Milwaukee, WI. Tel: (414) 343-7286, FAX: (414) 343-4806, Web Site: www.harley-davidson.com (12)

Bischoff, Winfried F.W., Citigroup Inc, New York, NY. Tel: (212) 559-1000, (800) 285-3000, FAX: (212) 793-3946, Web Site: www.citigroup.com (14)

Bishop, Cameron, Telephony, Chicago, IL. Tel: (312) 595-1080, (800) 458-0479, FAX: (312) 595-0295, Web Site: www.internettelephony.com (17)

Bishop, Joanne, Patient News, Niagara Falls, NY. Tel: (705) 457-4030, (800) 667-0268, FAX: (705) 457-4067, E-Mail: jbishop@patientnews.com, Web Site: www.patientnews.com (17)

Bishop, Nick, DDB Direct Los Angeles, Los Angeles, CA. Tel: (310) 907-1500, FAX: (310) 907-1990, Web Site: www.ddbla.com (35)

Bishop, Paul, Tuttle Printing & Engraving, Rutland, VT. Tel: (802) 773-9171, (800) 776-7682, FAX: (802) 773-5785, E-Mail: info@tuttleprinting.com, Web Site: www.tuttleprinting.com (10)

Bisk/Totaltape Lists, Tampa, FL. Tel: (813) 621-6200, (800) 874-7877, FAX: (813) 627-9442, E-Mail: lists@bisk.com, Web Site: www.listpro.com (24)

Bisnaire, Jean-Paul, John Hancock Financial Services Inc, Boston, MA. Tel: (617) 572-6000, (800) 732-5543, FAX: (617) 572-6451, Web Site: www.johnhancock.com (15)

Bisset, Jeffrey, Interact Direct Marketing Inc, London, ON Canada. Tel: (519) 439-6245, Web Site: www.interactdirect.com (28)

Bissinger French Confections, Saint Louis, MO. Tel: (314) 534-2401, (800) 325-8881, FAX: (314) 534-2419, Web Site: www.bissingers.com (4)

Bisson, William T., Pensions & Investments, New York, NY. Tel: (212) 210-0100, FAX: (212) 210-0117, Web Site: www.pionline.com (17)

Bits & Pieces Inc, Lawrenceburg, IN. Tel: (866) 503-6395, FAX: (513) 354-1290, Web Site: www.bitsandpieces.com (11)

Bitstream Inc, Marlborough, MA. Tel: (617) 497-6222, Web Site: www.bitstream.com (22)

Bitter, Gay, Relevate, Springfield, VA. Tel: (703) 658-8300, (800) 523-7346, FAX: (703) 658-8301, E-Mail: sales@relevategroup.com, Web Site: www.relevategroup.com (22)

Bivins, Jackie, Executive Connections LLC, Sarasota, FL. Tel: (941) 323-8300, Web Site: www.executiveconnectionsllc.com (20)

Bixon, Herbert, Porter Wallace Corp, Toms River, NJ. Tel: (732) 505-1675, FAX: (201) 505-1632, E-Mail: inquiries@porterwallace.com, Web Site: www.porterwallace.com (33)

BIZ Journal Business Leads, Charlotte, NC. Tel: (704) 973-1273 (23)

Bizo, San Francisco, CA. Tel: (866) 497-5505, Web Site: www.bizo.com (35)

Bizzaro Rubber Stamps, Greenville, RI. Tel: (401) 231-8777, FAX: (401) 231-4770, E-Mail: bizzaroinc@earthlink.net, Web Site: www.bizzaro.com (6)

Bkir, Philipa, Baton Rouge Conventions & Visitors Bureau, Baton Rouge, LA. Tel: (225) 383-1825, (800) LA-ROUGE, FAX: (225) 346-1253, E-Mail: br@bracvb.com, Web Site: www.bracvb.com (1)

Blabolil, Richard, A., Marketing Innovators, Rosemont, IL. Tel: (847) 696-1111, (800) 543-7373, FAX: (847) 696-3194, E-Mail: info@marketinginnovators.com, Web Site: www.marketinginnovators.com (35)

Black, Bruce, Champs Software Inc, Crystal River, FL. Tel: (352) 795-2362, FAX: (352) 795-9100, E-Mail: champs@champsinc.com, Web Site: www.champsinc.com (3)

Black, Cathie, The Hearst Corp, New York, NY. Tel: (212) 649-2000, FAX: (212) 649-2108, Web Site: www.hearst.com/magazines/ (17)

Black, Cathleen, P., Hearst Magazines, New York, NY. Tel: (212) 649-2824, FAX: (212) 765-3528, Web Site: www.hearst.com/magazines (17)

Black, Eli, Decision Software Inc, Hyattsville, MD. Tel: (301) 459-9000, FAX: (301) 459-3072, E-Mail: clientservices@dsoftware.biz, Web Site: www.dsoftware.biz (22)

Black, Jennifer, Local.com, Irvine, CA. Tel: (949) 784-0800, Web Site: www.local.com (32)

Black, Jerry T., Kurt Salmon Associates Inc, Atlanta, GA. Tel: (404) 892-0321, FAX: (404) 898-9590, E-Mail: infoksaweb@kurtsalmon.com, Web Site: www.kurtsalmon.com (20)

Black, Randy, Airlines Reporting Corp, Arlington, VA. Tel: (703) 816-8135, FAX: (703) 816-8104, E-Mail: corpcom@arccorp.com, Web Site: www.arccorp.com (16)

Black, Robert, W., Kimberly-Clark Corp, Neenah, WI. Tel: (920) 721-2000, (888) 525-8388, FAX: (920) 721-7722, Web Site: www.kimberly-clark.com (16)

Black, Wahleyah, Nowetah's American Indian Store & Museum, New Portland, ME. Tel: (207) 628-4991, Web Site: www.nowetahs.webs.com (6)

Black, William, Black & Co, New York, NY. Tel: (212) 867-5533, FAX: (212) 447-0785, E-Mail: wblack6340@aol.com (20)

Black & Co, New York, NY. Tel: (212) 867-5533, FAX: (212) 447-0785, E-Mail: wblack6340@aol.com (20)

Black & Decker (US) Inc, Towson, MD. Tel: (410) 239-5000, (800) 544-6986, FAX: (410) 239-5227, Web Site: www.blackanddecker.com (16)

Black Box Corp, Lawrence, PA. Tel: (412) 873-6795, (877) 877-2269, FAX: (800) 321-0746, E-Mail: brian.kutchma@blackbox.com, Web Site: www. blackbox.com (3)

The Black Dog Tavern Co Inc, Vineyard Haven, MA. Tel: (508) 696-8182, (800) 626-1991, Web Site: www.theblackdog.com; www.theblackdogtshirt.com (2)

Black Dot Group, Chicago, IL. Tel: (815) 459-8520, FAX: (815) 459-7259, E-Mail: sales@blackdot. com, Web Site: www.blackdot.com (35)

Black Enterprise Magazine, New York, NY. Tel: (212) 242-8000, FAX: (212) 886-9618, E-Mail: corpcomm@blackenterprise.com, Web Site: www. blackenterprise.com (17)

Black Entertainment Television Inc, Washington, DC. Tel: (202) 608-2000/2006, (800) 766-0053, FAX: (202) 608-2599, Web Site: www.bet.com (16)

Black Olive Co, Chicago, IL. Tel: (312) 893-5454, FAX: (312) 276-8636, E-Mail: pittenger@ blackoliveco.com, Web Site: www.blackoliveco. com (35)

Black Star Publishing Co, White Plains, NY. Tel: (212) 679-3288, FAX: (212) 889-2052, Web Site: www.blackstar.com (38)

Blackall, Pamela, Business Automation Systems Inc, Nashville, TN. Tel: (615) 329-4585, FAX: (615) 320-0206, Web Site: www.bas-solutions.com (16)

Blackbaud Inc, Charleston, SC. Tel: (800) 443-9441 (22)

Blackburn, Betty, Safe Specialties, Kingston, TN. Tel: (865) 675-2815, (800) 695-2815, FAX: (865) 717-8249, E-Mail: black223@aol.com, Web Site: www. safespec.com (33)

Blackburn, Denise, Marketing Strategies, North Myrtle Beach, SC. Tel: (843) 692-9662, FAX: (843) 272-4913, E-Mail: pr@marketingstrategiesinc.com, Web Site: www.marketingstrategiesinc.com (35)

Blackhall, Barbara, S., Nor'east Miniature Roses Inc, Arroyo Grande, CA. Tel: (805) 426-6485, (800) 426-6485, FAX: (805) 481-7374, E-Mail: noreast@ greenheartfarms.com, Web Site: www.noreast-miniroses.com (8)

Blackman, Larry, Blue Cross Blue Shield of Louisiana, Baton Rouge, LA. Tel: (225) 295-3307, (800) 599-2583, FAX: (225) 295-2054, E-Mail: help@ bcbsla.com, Web Site: www.bcbsla.com (15)

Blackmore, David, University of Pittsburgh at Bradford, Bradford, PA. Tel: (814) 362-7500, FAX: (814) 362-5150, E-Mail: admissions@www.upb. pitt.edu, Web Site: www.upd.pitt.edu (41)

Blackstone Lists, Fort Lauderdale, FL. Tel: (954) 568-6411 (23)

Blackwell, Carl, Porta-Bote International, Mountain View, CA. Tel: (650) 961-5334, (800) 227-8882, Web Site: www.porta-bote.com (11)

Blackwell, Ron, AFL-CIO, Washington, DC. Tel: (202) 637-5000, FAX: (202) 637-5058, (202) 637-5323, Web Site: www.aflcio.org (1)

Blagman, Jack, Blagman Creative/Direct Response, Gainesville, VA. Tel: (703) 743-2493, E-Mail: jackbee21@comcast.net (20)

Blagman Creative/Direct Response, Gainesville, VA. Tel: (703) 743-2493, E-Mail: jackbee21@comcast. net (20)

Blaha, Karen, Medco Supply Co Inc, Tonawanda, NY. Tel: (716) 695-3244, (800) 556-3326, FAX: (800) 222-1934, E-Mail: sales@medcosupply.com, Web Site: www.medcosupply.com (7)

Blaine, Magreth, Blaine Window Hardware Inc, Hagerstown, MD. Tel: (301) 797-6500, (800) 678-1919, FAX: (888) 250-3960, E-Mail: info@ blainewindow.com, Web Site: www.blainewindow. com (9)

Blaine Window Hardware Inc, Hagerstown, MD. Tel: (301) 797-6500, (800) 678-1919, FAX: (888) 250-3960, E-Mail: info@blainewindow.com, Web Site: www.blainewindow.com (9)

Blair, Bruce, NutriSystem Inc, Fort Washington, PA. Tel: (215) 706-5300, (800) 321-THIN, FAX: (215) 706-5388, Web Site: www.nutrisystem.com (7)

Blair, Donald, W., Nike Inc, Beaverton, OR. Tel: (503) 671-4565, (800) 344-6543, FAX: (503) 671-6300, Web Site: www.nike.com (2)

Blair, Greg, Escort Inc, West Chester, OH. Tel: (513) 870-8500, (800) 964-3138, FAX: (513) 870-8509, E-Mail: sales@escortradar.com, Web Site: www. escortradar.com (16)

Blair Corp, Warren, PA. Tel: (814) 723-3600, (800) 458-6057, FAX: (814) 726-6123, E-Mail: blair@ blair.com, Web Site: www.blair.com (2)

DL Blair Inc, Westbury, NY. Tel: (516) 746-3700, FAX: (516) 746-3889, Web Site: www.dlblair.com (35)

William Blair & Co LLC, Chicago, IL. Tel: (312) 236-1600, (800) 621-0687, FAX: (312) 368-9418, E-Mail: info@williamblair.com, Web Site: www. williamblair.com (14)

Blaiss, Gary, ACBL, Horn Lake, MS. Tel: (901) 332-5586, FAX: (901) 398-7754, E-Mail: service@ acbl.org, Web Site: www.acbl.org (1)

Blakar Inc, Englewood, CO. Tel: (201) 672-0705, FAX: (201) 673-0725, Web Site: www.blakar.com (33)

Blake, Craig, New England Direct Marketing Association, Wellesley Hills, MA. Tel: (781) 237-1366, FAX: (781) 431-8118, E-Mail: info@nedma.com, Web Site: www.nedma.com (40)

Blake, David, Alliance of Area Business Publications, El Segundo, CA. Tel: (323) 937-5514, FAX: (323) 937-0959, E-Mail: info@bizpubs.org, Web Site: www.bizpubs.org (1)

Blake, Francis, C., The Home Depot Inc, Atlanta, GA. Tel: (770) 433-8211, (800) 430-3376, FAX: (770) 384-2356, Web Site: www.homedepot.com (16)

Blake, George, George Blake & Associates, Bradenton, FL. Tel: (941) 755-8637, E-Mail: single14all@ verizon.net (35)

George Blake & Associates, Bradenton, FL. Tel: (941) 755-8637, E-Mail: single14all@verizon.net (35)

Blakeman, Robyn, West Virginia University, Morgantown, WV. Tel: (304) 293-3505, FAX: (304) 293-3072, E-Mail: wvuwebmaster@mail.wvu.edu, Web Site: www.wvu.edu (41)

Blakemore, Claudia, The Menninger Foundation, Houston, TX. Tel: (713) 275-5000, (800) 351-9058, FAX: (713) 275-5107, Web Site: www. menningerclinic.com (1)

Blakemore, Terry, Black Box Corp, Lawrence, PA. Tel: (412) 873-6795, (877) 877-2269, FAX: (800) 321-0746, E-Mail: brian.kutchma@blackbox.com, Web Site: www.blackbox.com (3)

Blakeney, Leslie, Blakeney Design, New York, NY. Tel: (212) 243-0109, FAX: (212) 243-0109 (36)

Blakeney Design, New York, NY. Tel: (212) 243-0109, FAX: (212) 243-0109 (36)

Blanc, Doreen V., Aurora Marketing Inc, Princeton, NJ. Tel: (908) 904-1125, FAX: (908) 359-1108, E-Mail: aurora2@voicenet.com, Web Site: www. auroramarketing.net (30)

Blanchard, Clarence, Antique & Collectible Tools Inc, Pownal, ME. Tel: (207) 688-4962, FAX: (207) 688-4831, E-Mail: ceb@finetoolj.com, Web Site: www.finetoolj.com (11)

Blanchard, Paul, Arthur Blank & Co Inc, Boston, MA. Tel: (617) 325-9600, (800) 776-7333, FAX: (617) 327-1235, E-Mail: abco@abco.com, Web Site: www.arthurblank.com (27)

Blanchard, Ron, Standard Communications Corp, San Diego, CA. Tel: (858) 546-5300, (800) 745-2445, FAX: (858) 546-5301, E-Mail: satcommsales@ stdcom.com, Web Site: www.standardcomm.com (16)

Blanchard & Co Inc, New Orleans, LA. Tel: (504) 837-3010, (800) 880-4653, FAX: (504) 837-4884, Web Site: www.blanchardonline.com (16)

Blanco, Jane, Gage, Minneapolis, MN. Tel: (763) 595-5800, Web Site: www.heinrich.com (35)

Bland, Charlain, L, ZIP Mailing Services Inc, Landover, MD. Tel: (301) 386-3633, FAX: (301) 386-3637, E-Mail: zipmail@zipmailing.com, Web Site: www.zipmailing.com (28)

Bland, Delbert, Bland Farms, Glennville, GA. Tel: (912) 654-1426, (800) 843-2542, FAX: (912) 654-1330, Web Site: www.blandfarms.com (4)

Bland, Greg, G., Optronics Inc, Muskogee, OK. Tel: (918) 683-9514, (800) 364-5483, FAX: (918) 683-9517, E-Mail: sales@optronicsinc.com, Web Site: www.optronicsinc.com (11)

Bland, Murrel, W., Wyandotte West Communications Inc, Kansas City, KS. Tel: (913) 788-5565, FAX: (913) 788-9812, E-Mail: news@wyandottewest. com, Web Site: www.wyandottewest.com (17)

Bland Farms, Glennville, GA. Tel: (912) 654-1426, (800) 843-2542, FAX: (912) 654-1330, Web Site: www.blandfarms.com (4)

Blanford, Larry, Green Mountain Coffee Roasters, Inc, Waterbury, VT. Tel: (802) 244-5621, (800) 545-2326, FAX: (802) 244-5436, Web Site: www.gmcr. com (4)

Blank, Elizabeth, DATA SOLUTIONS OF AMERICA INC, Redmond, WA. Tel: (239) 540-2992, Web Site: www.dsoai.com (23)

Blank, Joshua, Pronto Post, Hialeah, FL. Tel: (305) 621-7900 (21)

Blank, Matthew, Showtime Networks Inc, New York, NY. Tel: (212) 708-1600, FAX: (212) 708-1450, Web Site: www.sho.com (16)

Blank, Stuart, Arthur Blank & Co Inc, Boston, MA. Tel: (617) 325-9600, (800) 776-7333, FAX: (617) 327-1235, E-Mail: abco@abco.com, Web Site: www.arthurblank.com (27)

Arthur Blank & Co Inc, Boston, MA. Tel: (617) 325-9600, (800) 776-7333, FAX: (617) 327-1235, E-Mail: abco@abco.com, Web Site: www. arthurblank.com (27)

Blankman, Patrick, GE Money, Alpharetta, GA. Tel: (678) 518-2403 (14)

Blase, Marta, Diebold Inc, Uniontown, OH. Tel: (330) 899-2510, (800) DIEBOLD, FAX: (330) 490-3794, E-Mail: barronp@diebold.com, Web Site: www. diebold.com (16)

Blase, Mary, Cole-Parmer Instrument Co, Vernon Hills, IL. Tel: (847) 549-7600, (800) 323-4340, FAX: (847) 247-2929, E-Mail: info@coleparmer. com, Web Site: www.coleparmer.com (16)

Blasingame, David, T., Washington University, Saint Louis, MO. Tel: (314) 935-4623, (800) 638-0700, FAX: (314) 935-7088, Web Site: www.wustl.edu (1)

Blass, Kenneth, L., Blass Communications LLC, Old Chatham, NY. Tel: (518) 766-2222, FAX: (518) 766-2445, E-Mail: kenb@blasscommunications. com, Web Site: www.blasscommunications.com (35)

Blass Communications LLC, Old Chatham, NY. Tel: (518) 766-2222, FAX: (518) 766-2445, E-Mail: kenb@blasscommunications.com, Web Site: www. blasscommunications.com (35)

Blatt, Jeff, Synapse Group Inc, Stamford, CT. Tel: (203) 595-8255, FAX: (203) 329-8237, E-Mail: webmaster@synapsemail.com, Web Site: www. synapsegroupinc.com (18)

Blatteis, Beatrice, Blatteis Communications, San Jose, CA. Tel: (901) 356-0090, Web Site: www.blatteis. com (20)

Blatteis Communications, San Jose, CA. Tel: (901) 356-0090, Web Site: www.blatteis.com (20)

Blattman, Jim, Fairfield Industries Inc, Sugar Land, TX. Tel: (281) 275-7500, (800) 231-9809, FAX: (281) 275-7550, E-Mail: jblattman@fairfield.com, Web Site: www.fairfield.com (16)

Blausey Jr., William, W., Eaton Corp, Raleigh, NC. Tel: (216) 523-4400, (800) 356-5794, FAX: (216) 523-4787, Web Site: www.eaton.com (16)

Blauvelt, Eric, Global Specialties, Wallingford, CT. Tel: (203) 272-3285, FAX: (203) 272-4330, Web Site: www.globalspecialties.com (16)

Blayne, Kevin, MSC, Woodland Hills, CA. Tel: (818) 346-1600, FAX: (818) 712-0122, Web Site: www. mscnet.com (22)

Blazek, Diane, Ball Publishing, West Chicago, IL. Tel: (630) 231-3675, FAX: (630) 231-5254, E-Mail: info@ballpublishing.com, Web Site: www. ballpublishing.com (17)

Blazucki, Dr. Joan, Warfield, MARCOR Remediation Inc, Halethorpe, MD. Tel: (410) 785-0001, (800) 547-0128, FAX: (410) 771-0348, E-Mail: info@ marcor.com, Web Site: www.marcor.com (16)

Blechman, Michelle, Chicago Association of Direct Marketing, Westmont, IL. Tel: (312) 849-2236, FAX: (312) 849-2239, E-Mail: info@cadm.org, Web Site: www.cadm.org (40)

Blehm, Jake, Spalding Laboratories Inc, Arroyo Grande, CA. Tel: (805) 489-5946, (888) 880-1579, FAX: (866) 738-9632, Web Site: www.spalding-labs.com (7)

Bleiberg, Larry, Coastal Living, Birmingham, AL. Tel: (205) 877-6007, FAX: (205) 445-8655, E-Mail: coastalliving@customersvc.com, Web Site: www. coastalliving.com (43)

Blethen Maine Newspapers Inc, Portland, ME. Tel: (207) 791-6650, FAX: (207) 791-6925, Web Site: www.mainetoday.com (17)

Bleu Marketing Solutions Inc, San Francisco, CA. Tel: (415) 345-3300, FAX: (415) 353-0299, E-Mail: helpdesk@bleumarketing.com, Web Site: www. bleumarketing.com (35)

Blevins, Teresa, F., Landmark Communications Inc, Norfolk, VA. Tel: (757) 446-2010, (800) 446-2004, FAX: (757) 446-2489, Web Site: www.landmark. com (17)

Blevins, Tim, Augsburg Fortress Publishers, Minneapolis, MN. Tel: (612) 330-3300, (800) 426-0115, FAX: (612) 330-3455, E-Mail: info@ augsburgfortress.org, Web Site: www. augsburgfortress.org (17)

Blexrud, Tom, Blexrud Direct, Spartanburg, SC. Tel: (864) 583-7399, FAX: (864) 583-7399, E-Mail: blexrud@bellsouth.net (20)

Blexrud Direct, Spartanburg, SC. Tel: (864) 583-7399, FAX: (864) 583-7399, E-Mail: blexrud@bellsouth. net (20)

Dick Blick Holdings Inc, Galesburg, IL. Tel: (309) 343-6181, FAX: (309) 343-5785, E-Mail: admin@ dickblick.com, Web Site: www.dickblick.com (16)

Bliss, Mark, Cornhusker Press, Hastings, NE. Tel: (402) 462-4141, FAX: (402) 460-4612, E-Mail: dlsales@dutton-lainson.com, Web Site: www. dutton-lainson.com (17)

Bliss World LLC, New York, NY. Tel: (212) 931-6383, Web Site: www.blissworld.com (5)

Blissliving Home, Rockville, MD. Tel: (301) 816-4224, Web Site: www.blisslivinghome.com (8)

Blitman, Joan, JRB Marketing Group, East Windsor, NJ. Tel: (301) 758-2334, FAX: (302) 348-2490, E-Mail: jrblitman@gmail.com (20)

Blitz Direct Data & Promotion, Toronto, ON Canada. Tel: (416) 922-6434, Web Site: www.cossette.com (35)

Bliwas, Ronald, A Eicoff & Co, Chicago, IL. Tel: (312) 527-7100, FAX: (312) 527-7192, E-Mail: bill.mccabe@eicoff.com, Web Site: www. eicoff.com (35)

Bloch, Christopher, SWAT Marketing Team, Grove City, PA. Tel: (412) 851-9700, FAX: (412) 291-1155, Web Site: www.swatmarketingteam.com (23)

Bloch, Henry, W., H&R Block Inc, Kansas City, MO. Tel: (816) 572-6446, (800) 472-5625, FAX: (816) 854-8500, Web Site: www.hrblock.com (14)

Bloch, Paul, Data Direct Networks (HQ), Chatsworth, CA. Tel: (818) 700-7607, (800) 837-2298, FAX: (818) 700-7601, E-Mail: info@ddn.com, Web Site: www.datadirectnet.com (3)

Block, Michael, SECO-LARM USA Inc, Irvine, CA. Tel: (949) 261-2999, (800) 662-0800, FAX: (949) 261-7326, E-Mail: info@seco-larm.com, Web Site: www.seco-larm.com (16)

Block, Mitchell, W., Direct Cinema Ltd, Santa Monica, CA. Tel: (310) 636-8200, FAX: (310) 636-8228, E-Mail: orders@directcinemalimited. com, Web Site: www.directcinema.com (35)

Block, Myrna, Basic Adhesives Inc, Clifton, NJ. Tel: (718) 497-5200, (800) 394-9310, FAX: (718) 366-1425, E-Mail: info@basicadhesives.com, Web Site: www.basicadhesives.com (9)

Block, Yale, Basic Adhesives Inc, Clifton, NJ. Tel: (718) 497-5200, (800) 394-9310, FAX: (718) 366-1425, E-Mail: info@basicadhesives.com, Web Site: www.basicadhesives.com (9)

David H Block Advertising Inc, Verona, NJ. Tel: (973) 857-3900, FAX: (973) 857-4041, Web Site: www. blockadvertising.com (35)

Blodgett, Lynn, Affiliated Computer Services Inc (ACS), Dallas, TX. Tel: (214) 841-6111, Web Site: www.acs-inc.com (22)

Blodgett, M.W., MFE Instruments, Salem, NH. Tel: (603) 893-8778, (800) 843-8011, FAX: (603) 893-8851, Web Site: www.stockeryale.com (9)

Blom, Eric, ActionPak, Scarborough, ON. Tel: (416) 321-2222, FAX: (416) 321-5286, Web Site: www. openandsave.com (21)

Blommer, Scott, FICO, Minneapolis, MN. Tel: (651) 486-1870 (22)

Bloodworth, Scott, Rhode Island Novelty, Cumberland, RI. Tel: (401) 335-3300, (800) 528-5599, FAX: (800) 448-1775, E-Mail: info@rinovelty. com, Web Site: www.rinovelty.com (16)

Bloom, Allan, Holiday Travel of America, Carlsbad, CA. Tel: (760) 431-8600, (888) 732-2479, FAX: (760) 431-3131, E-Mail: sales@htoa.com, Web Site: www.htoa.com (19)

Bloom, Carl, Carl Bloom Associates Inc, White Plains, NY. Tel: (914) 761-2800, FAX: (914) 761-2744, E-Mail: info@carlbloom.com, Web Site: www.carlbloom.com (35)

Bloom, Carl, P., Loyalty E-Marketing, White Plains, NY. Tel: (914) 761-2800, Web Site: www. carlbloom.com (35)

Bloom, Rob, Carl Bloom Associates Inc, White Plains, NY. Tel: (914) 761-2800, FAX: (914) 761-2744, E-Mail: info@carlbloom.com, Web Site: www. carlbloom.com (35)

Bloom, Robert, Business Development Solutions Inc, Cherry Hill, NJ. Tel: (856) 787-1500, Web Site: www.bdsdatabase.com (22)

Carl Bloom Associates Inc, White Plains, NY. Tel: (914) 761-2800, FAX: (914) 761-2744, E-Mail: info@carlbloom.com, Web Site: www.carlbloom. com (35)

Bloom, Hergott, Diemer, Rosenthal and Laviolette LLP, Beverly Hills, CA. Tel: (310) 859-6820, FAX: (310) 860-6820, E-Mail: sfb@bhdrl.com (20)

Bloomer, Paul, Redleaf Press, Saint Paul, MN. Tel: (651) 641-6621, (800) 423-8309, FAX: (800) 641-0115, E-Mail: jvoltz@redleafpress.org, Web Site: www.redleafpress.org (17)

Bloomin Promotions, Boulder, CO. Tel: (303) 443-3591, Web Site: www.bloominpromotions.com (25)

Bloomingdale's By Mail Ltd, New York, NY. Tel: (212) 224-7721, (800) 472-0788, FAX: (212) 715-2805, Web Site: www.bloomingdales.com (5)

Bloomingdale's Direct, New York, NY. Tel: (212) 705-2000, (866) 593-2540, FAX: (212) 705-2805, Web Site: www.bloomingdales.com (5)

Bloomquist, Conrad, Scenic Photo!, Minneapolis, MN. Tel: (612) 810-0797, E-Mail: manager@ scenicphoto.com, Web Site: www.scenicphoto.com (38)

Bloosky Interactive, Orem, UT. Tel: (888) 203-2433, FAX: (888) 465-7166, Web Site: www.bloosky. com (32)

Blowers, Richard, Society of American Magicians Inc, Parker, CO. E-Mail: rmblowers@aol.com, Web Site: www.magicsam.com (1)

BluBlocker Corp, Las Vegas, NV. Tel: (702) 597-2000, (800) BLUBLOCKER, FAX: (702) 597-2002, Web Site: www.blublocker.com (2)

Blue, Laurie, Mini City Ltd, Webster, NY. Tel: (716) 872-6560, FAX: (716) 872-4094, E-Mail: minicityus@aol.com, Web Site: www.minicityltd. com (12)

Blue Book Direct Mail & Database Service, New York, NY. Tel: (646) 746-7398, FAX: (646) 746-7434, Web Site: www.gabb.com (24)

The Blue Book of Building & Construction, Jefferson Valley, NY. Tel: (800) 431-2584, Web Site: www. thebluebook.com (17)

Blue Coral Slick 50, Houston, TX. Tel: (713) 241-6161, (800) 416-1600, FAX: (713) 241-4044, E-Mail: SCD-ConsumerSolutions@Shell.com, Web Site: www.bluecoral.com (16)

Blue Cross & Blue Shield Cobalt, Waukesha, WI. Tel: (262) 523-4020, Web Site: www.bcbsuw.org (15)

Blue Cross & Blue Shield of Florida, Jacksonville, FL. Tel: (904) 791-6111, (800) 477-3736, FAX: (904) 905-6638, E-Mail: katie.magee@bcbsfl.com, Web Site: www.bcbsfl.com (15)

Blue Cross & Blue Shield of Oklahoma, Tulsa, OK. Tel: (918) 560-3500, (800) 942-5837, E-Mail: info@bcbsok.com, Web Site: www.bcbsok.com (15)

Blue Cross & Blue Shield of South Carolina, Columbia, SC. Tel: (803) 788-0222, (800) 288-2227, FAX: (803) 736-4516, Web Site: www.bcbssc.com (15)

Blue Cross/Blue Shield of Illinois, Chicago, IL. Tel: (312) 938-6000, FAX: (312) 938-5722, Web Site: www.bcbsil.com (15)

Blue Cross Blue Shield of Louisiana, Baton Rouge, LA. Tel: (225) 295-3307, (800) 599-2583, FAX: (225) 295-2054, E-Mail: help@bcbsla.com, Web Site: www.bcbsla.com (15)

Blue Cross Blue Shield of North Carolina, Durham, NC. Tel: (800) 250-3630, Web Site: www.bcbsnc. com (15)

Blue Grass Mailing, Data & Fulfillment Services, Lexington, KY. Tel: (859) 231-7272, (800) 928-6245, FAX: (859) 259-1214, E-Mail: info@bgmailing. com, Web Site: www.bgmailing.com (28)

Blue Hill Marketing Solutions Inc, Pearl River, NY. Tel: (845) 627-6600, FAX: (845) 735-3985, Web Site: www.liftengine.com (22)

Blue Raven Technology, Wilmington, MA. Tel: (781) 778-4600, (800) 274-5343, (800) 20RAVEN, FAX: (781) 778-4848, E-Mail: sales@blueraven.com, Web Site: www.blueraven.com (3)

Blue Shield Life, San Francisco, CA. Tel: (888) 800-2742, FAX: (800) 329-2742, Web Site: www. blueshieldca.com (15)

Blue Shield of California, San Francisco, CA. Tel: (415) 229-5000, FAX: (415) 229-5056, Web Site: www.blueshieldca.com (15)

Blue Sky Factory, Baltimore, MD. Tel: (410) 230-0061, Web Site: www.blueskyfactory.com (32)

Blue Strawberry Resorts LLC, Miami Beach, FL. Tel: (756) 513-1456, (800) 873-1440, Web Site: www. bluestrawberry-resorts.com (19)

Blue Valley Tele-Marketing Inc, Home, KS. Tel: (785) 799-3500, (800) 882-0803, FAX: (785) 799-3504 (29)

Blue Vidalia, Toronto, ON Canada. Tel: (416) 572-5222, E-Mail: info@bluevidalia.ca, Web Site: www.bluevidalia.ca (35)

Bluestein, Barry, Source Communications, Hackensack, NJ. Tel: (201) 343-5222 (35)

Bluestein, Clara, Captan Associates Inc, Brick, NJ. Tel: (732) 840-1244, FAX: (732) 840-1111 (17)

Bluestem Brands, Eden Prairie, MN. Tel: (952) 656-3700, Web Site: www.fingerhut.com (16)

Bluestone Perennials Inc, Madison, OH. Tel: (440) 428-7535, (800) 852-5243, FAX: (440) 428-7198, E-Mail: bluestone@bluestoneperennials.com, Web Site: www.bluestoneperennials.com (8)

Bluewater Yachts, Mora, MN. Tel: (320) 679-3811, FAX: (320) 679-3820, E-Mail: bluewater@ncis. com, Web Site: www.bluewateryacht.com (16)

Blum, Jennifer, Salesian Missions, New Rochelle, NY. Tel: (914) 633-8344, FAX: (914) 633-7404, E-Mail: info@salesianmissions.org, Web Site: www.salesianmissions.org. (1)

Blum, Sandra J., Blum & Co LLC, Fairfield, CT. Tel: (203) 255-4813, FAX: (203) 255-3936, E-Mail: e-blum@att.net, Web Site: www.blumdirect.com (20)

Blum & Co LLC, Fairfield, CT. Tel: (203) 255-4813, FAX: (203) 255-3936, E-Mail: e-blum@att.net, Web Site: www.blumdirect.com (20)

Blumberg, Matt, Return Path Inc, New York, NY. Tel: (212) 905-5500, FAX: (212) 905-5501, Web Site: www.returnpath.biz (22)

Blumberg, Warren, Kelsey National Corp, Los Angeles, CA. Tel: (310) 390-1000, (800) 366-5656, FAX: (310) 390-3158, E-Mail: info@kelsey.com, Web Site: www.kelsey.com (15)

Blume, Rick, 21st Century Marketing, Hauppauge, NY. Tel: (631) 293-8550, FAX: (631) 293-8974, E-Mail: info@21stcm.com, Web Site: www.21stcm.com (24)

Blumenfeld, Joshua, CoverClicks LLC, New York, NY. Tel: (888) 624-1340, FAX: (212) 239-2850, E-Mail: info@coverclicksmail.com, Web Site: www.coverclicks.com (23)

Blumenfield, Arthur, BMI Fulfillment Services, Danbury, CT. Tel: (203) 546-5580, FAX: (203) 546-5575, E-Mail: barry@bmigroup.com, Web Site: www.bmigroup.com (28)

Blumenfield, Arthur, The Direct Marketing Club of New York Inc, Garden City, NY. Tel: (516) 746-6700, FAX: (516) 294-8141, E-Mail: info@dmcny.org, Web Site: www.dmcny.org (1)

Blumenfield, Barry, BMI Fulfillment Services, Danbury, CT. Tel: (203) 546-5580, FAX: (203) 546-5575, E-Mail: barry@bmigroup.com, Web Site: www.bmigroup.com (28)

Blumental, Tom, Geary's of Beverly Hills, Beverly Hills, CA. Tel: (310) 273-4741, (800) 793-6670, FAX: (310) 858-7555, Web Site: www.gearys.com (6)

Blumhos, Roy, Joys SA Inc, Hatillo, PR. Tel: (954) 426-9100, (800) 526-7148, FAX: (800) 232-9569, E-Mail: info@joyssa.com (2)

Bluner, Lelani, The Orange County Register, Santa Ana, CA. Tel: (877) 469-7344, E-Mail: customerservice@ocregister.com, Web Site: www.ocregister.com (17)

Blunt, Kenyon, SIGMA Marketing Group LLC, Rochester, NY. Tel: (585) 473-7300, (888) 277-9837, FAX: (585) 473-0332, E-Mail: mbush@sigmamarketing.com, Web Site: www.sigmamarketing.com; www.jthgearanalytics.com (Blog) (20)

Blunt, Rebecca, Graphic Arts Information Network (GAIN), Sewickley, PA. Tel: (412) 741-6860, (800) 910-4283, FAX: (412) 741-2311, E-Mail: printing@printing.org, Web Site: www.gain.net (27)

Blusk, Gloria, Spectronics Corp, Westbury, NY. Tel: (800) 274-8888, FAX: (800) 491-6868, E-Mail: vscherer@spectroline.com, Web Site: www.spectroline.com (9)

Blust, Ed, Adecco Employment Services, Melville, NY. Tel: (631) 844-7800, Web Site: www.adecco.com (20)

Bly, Bob, Bob Bly, River Vale, NJ. Tel: (201) 505-9451, FAX: (201) 573-4094, E-Mail: rwbly@bly.com, Web Site: www.bly.com (39)

Bob Bly, River Vale, NJ. Tel: (201) 505-9451, FAX: (201) 573-4094, E-Mail: rwbly@bly.com, Web Site: www.bly.com (39)

B'nai B'rith International, Washington, DC. Tel: (202) 857-6600, FAX: (202) 857-6609, E-Mail: internet@bnaibrith.org, Web Site: www.bnaibrith.org (1)

Boardman, Michael, International Coins & Currency Inc, Montpelier, VT. Tel: (802) 223-6331, FAX: (800) 229-3239, Web Site: www.iccoin.com (6)

Boardroom Inc, Stamford, CT. Tel: (203) 973-5900, FAX: (203) 967-3086, E-Mail: kseaborne@boardroom.com, Web Site: www.boardroom.com (17)

Boba, Denise, Country Sampler Group, Saint Charles, IL. Tel: (630) 377-8000, FAX: (630) 377-8194, Web Site: www.sampler.com (17)

Bobcat Co, West Fargo, ND. Tel: (701) 241-8700, FAX: (701) 241-8704, Web Site: www.bobcat.com (16)

Bobley, Mark, Bobley-Harmann Corp/GiftValues.Com, Westbury, NY. Tel: (516) 364-1800, (800) 323-1692, FAX: (516) 364-1899, E-Mail: info@bobley.com, Web Site: www.bobley.com; www.montefiorepens.com (5)

Bobley-Harmann Corp/GiftValues.Com, Westbury, NY. Tel: (516) 364-1800, (800) 323-1692, FAX: (516) 364-1899, E-Mail: info@bobley.com, Web Site: www.bobley.com; www.montefiorepens.com (5)

Bobo, Sandy, AeroGraphics, DeLand, FL. Tel: (386) 736-4793, FAX: (386) 736-9786, Web Site: www.skydivingmagazine.com (3)

Bobo, Sandy, Skydiving Magazine, DeLand, FL. Tel: (386) 736-4793, FAX: (386) 736-9786, E-Mail: admin@skydivingmagazine.com, Web Site: www.skydivingmagazine.com (17)

Boca Java, Miami, FL. Tel: (954) 949-2010, Web Site: www.bocajava.com (4)

Bock, David, Stagestep Inc, Philadelphia, PA. Tel: (267) 672-2900, (800) 523-0961, FAX: (267) 672-2914, E-Mail: stagestep@stagestep.com, Web Site: www.stagestep.com (5)

Bockus, Keith, TV Guide Magazine, New York, NY. Tel: (212) 852-7500, (800) 866-1400, Web Site: www.tvguide.com (31)

Bodaken, Bruce, Blue Shield Life, San Francisco, CA. Tel: (888) 800-2742, FAX: (800) 329-2742, Web Site: www.blueshieldca.com (15)

Bodaken, Bruce, Blue Shield of California, San Francisco, CA. Tel: (415) 229-5000, FAX: (415) 229-5056, Web Site: www.blueshieldca.com (15)

Bodden, Chris, Bodden Partners, New York, NY Canada. Tel: (212) 328-1111, Web Site: www.boddenpartners.com (35)

Bodden, Chris, Communications Plus, New York, NY. Tel: (212) 686-9570, FAX: (212) 686-9687, E-Mail: jrandolph@getcp.com, Web Site: www.boddenpartners.com (35)

Bodden Partners, New York, NY. Tel: (212) 328-1111, Web Site: www.boddenpartners.com (35)

Bodoff, Russell, Council of Better Business Bureaus - BBBOnline, Arlington, VA. Tel: (703) 276-0100, FAX: (703) 525-8277, Web Site: www.bbb.org (1)

Bodourian, Peter, Promotional Media Inc, Orange, CA. Tel: (714) 639-6590, (800) 346-5348, FAX: (714) 639-6270, E-Mail: contactus@promotionalmedia.com, Web Site: www.promotionalmedia.com (33)

Bodrato, Kathleen, Tri-Chem Inc, Belleville, NJ. Tel: (973) 751-9200, FAX: (973) 450-1057, (973) 450-1260, E-Mail: paints@trichem.com, Web Site: www.trichem.com (16)

Boduch, Bob, Christian Appalachian Project, Lexington, KY. Tel: (859) 792-3051, (866) 270-4CAP, FAX: (859) 792-6560, E-Mail: capinfo@chrisapp.org, Web Site: www.christianapp.org (1)

Body by Jake Global LLC, Los Angeles, CA. Tel: (310) 571-7101, FAX: (310) 571-7107, E-Mail: info@bodybyjake.com, Web Site: www.bodybyjake.com (16)

The Body Shop Inc, Wake Forest, NC. Tel: (919) 554-4900, (800) BODYSHOP, FAX: (919) 554-4361, Web Site: www.thebodyshop.com (7)

Bodyscapes Inc, New York, NY. Tel: (212) 243-2414, FAX: (212) 239-9058 (2)

Boeckmann, Alan, L., Burlington Northern & Santa Fe Railroad, Fort Worth, TX. Tel: (817) 878-2000, (800) 795-2673, FAX: (817) 333-7593, Web Site: www.bnsf.com (16)

Boehle, Hubert, Bauer Publishing Co, Englewood Cliffs, NJ. Tel: (201) 569-6699, FAX: (201) 510-3297, Web Site: www.bauerpublishing.com (17)

Boehmer, Ed, Starchtech, Golden Valley, MN. Tel: (763) 545-5400, (800) 597-7225, FAX: (763) 545-9450, Web Site: www.starchtech.com (16)

Boeing Co, Chicago, IL. Tel: (312) 544-2000, FAX: (312) 544-2082, Web Site: www.boeing.com (16)

Boelter, Robert, Boelter + Lincoln Marketing Communications, Milwaukee, WI. Tel: (414) 271-0101, FAX: (414) 271-1436, Web Site: www.boelterlincoln.com (35)

Boelter + Lincoln Marketing Communications, Milwaukee, WI. Tel: (414) 271-0101, FAX: (414) 271-1436, Web Site: www.boelterlincoln.com (35)

Boethner, Douglas, A, Queens College/CUNY Professional and Continuing Studies (PCS), Flushing, NY. Tel: (718) 997-5700, FAX: (718) 997-5723, E-Mail: pcs@qc.cuny.edu, Web Site: www.qc.cuny.edu/pcs (41)

Boetlcher, Jerald, Kalmbach Publishing Co, Waukesha, WI. Tel: (262) 796-8776, (800) 558-1544, FAX: (262) 796-1143, Web Site: www.kalmbach.com (17)

Boettcher, Marc, Presque Isle Wine Cellars Inc, North East, PA. Tel: (814) 725-1314, (800) 488-7492, FAX: (814) 725-2092, E-Mail: info@piwine.com, Web Site: www.piwine.com (4)

Bogan, Dan, NCR Corp, Duluth, GA. Tel: (937) 445-1936, (800) CALL-NCR, FAX: (937) 445-1682, Web Site: www.ncr.com (16)

Bogdanovic, George, Jet LithoColor Inc, Downers Grove, IL. Tel: (630) 932-9000, (800) 932-1JET, (800) 932-1538, FAX: (630) 932-9101, E-Mail: sales@jetlitho.com, Web Site: www.jetlitho.com (27)

Boggart, Neil, We Deliver America Inc, Englewood Cliffs, NJ. Tel: (201) 307-8888, FAX: (201) 307-1200, E-Mail: info@we-deliver-america.com, Web Site: www.we-deliver-america.com (31)

Boghjalian, Sarkis, ACN USA, Brooklyn, NY. Tel: (212) 334-5340, Web Site: www.churchinneed.org (1)

Boghosian, Richard, Groff DRTV, Portland, ME. Tel: (207) 415-1374, FAX: (207) 771-5320, E-Mail: regfilm@gmail.com, Web Site: www.groffvideo.com (32)

Bogle, Jack, Access Business Communications Inc, Huntington Beach, CA. Tel: (800) 675-2415, Web Site: www.abcimarketing.com (20)

Bograkos, Theresa, Mastermailer Inc, Hollywood, FL. Tel: (954) 921-0000, (800) 771-LIST, FAX: (954) 925-7900, Web Site: www.mastermailer.com (23)

Bogusky, Christine, Gardener's Eden, Merrimack, NH. Tel: (603) 888-9500, (800) 822-9600, FAX: (603) 577-8005, E-Mail: gsweeney@brookstone.com (8)

Bohannon, Louise, The Green Pond Co, Atlanta, GA. Tel: (404) 233-6343, (800) 827-7663, FAX: (404) 233-6340, E-Mail: sales@greenpond.com, Web Site: www.greenpond.com (2)

Bohn, Joyce, Mott Media LLC, Fenton, MI. Tel: (810) 714-4280, FAX: (810) 714-2077, E-Mail: info@mottmedia.com, Web Site: www.mottmedia.com (17)

Bohnert, Brad, Home Shopping Network, Saint Petersburg, FL. Tel: (727) 872-1000, FAX: (727) 571-1803, Web Site: www.hsn.com (32)

Bohr, Marianne, The Vestal Press Ltd, Lanham, MD. Tel: (301) 459-3366, (800) 462-6420, FAX: (301) 429-5746, E-Mail: sburnett@rowman.com, Web Site: www.nbnbooks.com (17)

Boise Cascade Holdings LLC, Boise, ID. Tel: (208) 384-6451, FAX: (208) 384-7189, E-Mail: mediarelations@bc.com, Web Site: www.bc.com (16)

Boisset, Jean-Charles, Buena Vista Winery, Sonoma, CA. Tel: (707) 252-7117, (800) 678-8504, FAX: (707) 252-0392, Web Site: www.buenavistawinery.com (16)

Boisson, Robert, Reno Gazette Journal, Reno, NV. Tel: (775) 788-6200, FAX: (775) 788-6563 (17)

Boisvert, Gary, Sturbridge Yankee Workshop Inc, Portland, ME. Tel: (207) 774-9045, (800) 343-1144, FAX: (207) 774-2561, Web Site: www.sturbridgeyankee.com (16)

Boivin, Melanie, Hain Celestial Group, Melville, NY. Tel: (631) 730-2200, FAX: (631) 730-2500, Web Site: www.hain-celestial.com (16)

Boklage, Julia, Hammock Publishing Inc, Nashville, TN. Tel: (615) 690-3400, FAX: (615) 690-3401, E-Mail: info@hammock.com, Web Site: www.hammock.com (17)

Bokuniewicz, Carol, Stephan Partners Inc, New York, NY. Tel: (212) 524-8583, E-Mail: george@stephenpartners.com, Web Site: www.stephanpartners.com (35)

Bolchalk, Michael, Michael Bolchalk Marketing, Tucson, AZ. Tel: (520) 745-8221, FAX: (520) 745-5540, E-Mail: michael@adwiz.com, Web Site: www.adwiz.com (35)

Michael Bolchalk Marketing, Tucson, AZ. Tel: (520) 745-8221, FAX: (520) 745-5540, E-Mail: michael@adwiz.com, Web Site: www.adwiz.com (35)

Bolcik, Veronica, Flaghouse Inc, Hasbrouck Heights, NJ. Tel: (201) 288-7600, (800) 793-7900, FAX: (800) 793-7922, E-Mail: sales@flaghouse.com, Web Site: www.flaghouse.com (5)

Boldt, Ethan, Inside Direct Mail, Philadelphia, PA. Tel: (215) 238-5300, (800) 777-8074, FAX: (215) 238-5412, E-Mail: customerservice@napco.com, Web Site: www.insidedirectmail.com (43)

Boldyrev, Serge, Kelly's Kids, Natchez, MS. Tel: (601) 442-5332, (800) 837-2066, FAX: (601) 442-4399, E-Mail: customerservice@kellyskids.com, Web Site: www.kellyskids.com (2)

Bolesky, Edward M., NEBS, Groton, MA. Tel: (978) 448-6111, (888) 823-6327, (800) 225-6380, FAX: (800) 234-4324, (978) 448-3653, E-Mail: customerservice@nebs.com, Web Site: www.nebs.com (10)

Bolgioni, Deva, M., Tuttle Printing & Engraving, Rutland, VT. Tel: (802) 773-9171, (800) 776-7682, FAX: (802) 773-5785, E-Mail: info@tuttleprinting.com, Web Site: www.tuttleprinting.com (10)

Bolind Inc, Boulder, CO. Tel: (303) 443-3142, FAX: (303) 443-9889, Web Site: www.bolind.com (16)

Bolinder, Scott, Zondervan Corp, Grand Rapids, MI. Tel: (616) 698-6900, (800) 727-3060, FAX: (616) 698-3235, Web Site: www.zondervan.com (17)

Boling, Angela, BCR Enterprises Inc, Downers Grove, IL. Tel: (630) 986-1432, (800) 227-1234, FAX: (630) 323-5324, Web Site: www.bcr.com (17)

Boling, Patricia, Replogle Globes Inc, Broadview, IL. Tel: (708) 343-0900, FAX: (708) 343-0923, E-Mail: info@replogleglobes.com, Web Site: www.replogleglobes.com (16)

Bollard, Edith, Fannie Mae, Washington, DC. Tel: (202) 752-7000, FAX: (202) 752-3808, Web Site: www.fanniemae.com (14)

Bolles, Barbara, Tri-State Advertising Co Inc, Warsaw, IN. Tel: (574) 267-5178, FAX: (574) 267-2965, E-Mail: info@tri-stateadv.com, Web Site: www.tri-stateadv.com (35)

Bolling, Jay, Roska Direct Advertising, Montgomeryville, PA. Tel: (215) 699-9200, FAX: (215) 699-9240, E-Mail: jr@roskadirect.com, Web Site: www.RoskaDirect.com (35)

Bollon, Vincent, J., Union Privilege, AFL-CIO, Washington, DC. Tel: (202) 293-5330, FAX: (202) 293-5311, Web Site: www.unionplus.org (1)

Bolton, Ted, Bolton Research Corp, Miami, FL. Tel: (305) 854-3887, FAX: (305) 854-3807, E-Mail: brcted@aol.com, Web Site: www.boltonresearch.com (30)

Bolton Research Corp, Miami, FL. Tel: (305) 854-3887, FAX: (305) 854-3807, E-Mail: brcted@aol.com, Web Site: www.boltonresearch.com (30)

The Bombay Co, Brampton, ON Canada. Tel: (877) 326-6229, E-Mail: customerservice@bombay.ca, Web Site: www.bombay.com (8)

Bommarito, Bruce, C., Nevada Commission on Tourism, Carson City, NV. Tel: (775) 687-4322, (800) NEVADA 8, FAX: (775) 687-6779, Web Site: www.travelnevada.com (1)

Bomze, Rich, Interdisciplinary Design Team, Southhampton, PA. Tel: (215) 364-5608, FAX: (215) 364-6509, E-Mail: rich.bomze@gmail.com (36)

Bon, Stacie, Javelin, Irving, TX. Tel: (972) 443-7000, E-Mail: info@javelin.mg, Web Site: javelin.mg (30)

Bon Appetit Magazine, New York, NY. Tel: (212) 286-2860, FAX: (212) 286-2536, E-Mail: paul_jowdy@bonappetit.com, Web Site: www.bonappetit.com (31)

Bonaiuto, Paul, Cygnus Business Media, Fort Atkinson, WI. Tel: (203) 227-4037, (800) 547-7377, FAX: (203) 227-4245, Web Site: www.cygnusb2b.com (17)

Bonanno, Chris, Tristar Products, Fairfield, NJ. Tel: (973) 575-5400, FAX: (973) 683-6708, E-Mail: infotp@tristarproductsinc.com, Web Site: www.tristarproductsinc.com (16)

Boncato, Joyce, Dynamic Engineering, Santa Cruz, CA. Tel: (831) 457-8891, FAX: (831) 457-4793, E-Mail: contact@penguinparty.com, Web Site: www.dyneng.com (3)

Boncher, Mark, Mar-San, Chicago, IL. Tel: (773) 583-5700, (800) 621-5582, FAX: (773) 583-1740, E-Mail: sales@mar-san.com, Web Site: www.mar-san.com (33)

Bond, Bill, Environmental Defense Fund, Washington, DC. Tel: (202) 387-3500 (1)

Bond, Carol, Carol Bond Health Foods, Liberty, TX. Tel: (800) 833-8282, Web Site: www.carolbond.com (7)

Carol Bond Health Foods, Liberty, TX. Tel: (800) 833-8282, Web Site: www.carolbond.com (7)

Bonderenko, Glen, North Shore Animal League America Inc, Port Washington, NY. Tel: (516) 883-7900, FAX: (516) 883-8256, E-Mail: donorservices@nsalamerica.org, Web Site: www.nsalamerica.org (1)

Bonelli, Anne, Gambro Inc, Lakewood, CO. Tel: (303) 232-6800, (800) 525-2623, FAX: (303) 222-6810, Web Site: www.gambro.com (16)

Boner, Rex, R., Callaway Gardens, Pine Mountain, GA. Tel: (706) 663-2281, (800) CALLAWAY, FAX: (706) 663-6812, E-Mail: info@callawaygardens.com, Web Site: www.callawaygardens.com (19)

Bongiolatti, Lee, Westgroup, Eagan, MN. Tel: (800) 344-5008, Web Site: www.westgroup.com (17)

Bonnell, Tom, O'Brien Manufacturing, Marietta, OH. Tel: (740) 374-2306, (800) 638-1901, FAX: (740) 374-5447, Web Site: www.obrienmfg.com (9)

Bonner, Chris, Delta Market Research Inc, Hatboro, PA. Tel: (215) 674-1180, FAX: (215) 674-1271, E-Mail: information@deltamarketresearch.com, Web Site: www.deltamarketresearch.com (30)

Bonner, Dave, Capgemini Americas Outsourcing, New York, NY. Tel: (212) 314-8000, FAX: (212) 314-8001 (20)

Bonner, William, AGORA Inc, Baltimore, MD. Tel: (410) 783-8499, FAX: (410) 783-8414, E-Mail: csteam@agorapublishinggroup.com, Web Site: www.agora-inc.com (17)

Bonneville Communications, Salt Lake City, UT. Tel: (801) 237-2600, (888) BONCOM, FAX: (801) 237-2614, E-Mail: bonneville@bonneville.com, Web Site: www.bonneville.com (35)

Bonnici, Madeline, Franciscan Mission Associates, Mount Vernon, NY. Tel: (914) 664-5604, FAX: (914) 664-3017, E-Mail: admin@franciscanmissionassoc.org, Web Site: www.franciscanmissionassoc.org (1)

Bonnier, Jonas, World Publications Inc, Winter Park, FL. Tel: (407) 628-4802, FAX: (407) 628-7061, Web Site: www.worldpub.net (17)

Bonsignore, Michael, R., Honeywell, Morristown, NJ. Tel: (973) 455-2000, FAX: (973) 455-4807, Web Site: www.honeywell.com (16)

Bontex, Honolulu, HI. Tel: (540) 261-2181, FAX: (540) 261-3784, E-Mail: bontex@bontex.com, Web Site: www.bontex.com (16)

Bonthius, Kevin, Marshall Fields Dept Stores, Minneapolis, MN. Tel: (612) 375-3004, Web Site: www.fields.com (5)

Bontrager, Phil, Gardens Alive! Inc, Lawrenceburg, IN. Tel: (812) 537-8665, FAX: (812) 537-5108, E-Mail: service@gardensalive.com, Web Site: www.gardens-alive.com (8)

Book, Joel, ExactTarget Inc, Indianapolis, IN. Tel: (317) 423-3928, Web Site: www.exacttarget.com (32)

Book News Inc, Portland, OR. Tel: (503) 281-9230, FAX: (503) 287-4485, E-Mail: booknews@booknews.com (43)

Book Passage Cafe, Corte Madera, CA. Tel: (415) 927-0960, (800) 999-7909, FAX: (415) 924-3838, Web Site: www.BookPassage.com (17)

Book Publishing Information Kit, Santa Barbara, CA. Tel: (805) 968-7277, (800) PARAPUB, FAX: (805) 968-1379, E-Mail: danpoynter@parapublishing.com, Web Site: www.parapublishing.com (17)

Bookbinder, Mike, Sleepy's Inc, Hicksville, NY. Tel: (516) 844-8800, (800) sleepys, FAX: (516) 844-8847, Web Site: www.sleepys.com (16)

Booker, Ellis, BtoB Magazine, New York, NY. Tel: (212) 210-0206, FAX: (212) 210-0422, E-Mail: aholtzman@crain.com, Web Site: www.btobonline.com (13)

Books on Tape, Westminster, MD. Tel: (800) 733-3000, Web Site: www.booksontape.com (17)

Bookspan, Garden City, NY. Tel: (516) 490-4561, FAX: (516) 490-4856 (13)

Boone, Jan, Corona-Lotus Inc, San Francisco, CA. Tel: (415) 956-8956, (800) 422-2924, FAX: (415) 956-4922, E-Mail: customerservice@biscoff.com, Web Site: www.biscoff.com (4)

Boone, Ken, Direct Marketing Tool Kit for Small Business, Minneapolis, MN. Tel: (612) 788-1673, E-Mail: info@nmoa.org, Web Site: www.nmoa.org/directmarketingtoolkit (43)

Boone, Matthew, Corona-Lotus Inc, San Francisco, CA. Tel: (415) 956-8956, (800) 422-2924, FAX: (415) 956-4922, E-Mail: customerservice@biscoff.com, Web Site: www.biscoff.com (4)

Boonstra, Sarah, Bluestone Perennials Inc, Madison, OH. Tel: (440) 428-7535, (800) 852-5243, FAX: (440) 428-7198, E-Mail: bluestone@bluestoneperennials.com, Web Site: www.bluestoneperennials.com (8)

Boonstra, William N., Bluestone Perennials Inc, Madison, OH. Tel: (440) 428-7535, (800) 852-5243, FAX: (440) 428-7198, E-Mail: bluestone@bluestoneperennials.com, Web Site: www.bluestoneperennials.com (8)

Bootenhoff, Margie, Vail Resorts Inc, Keystone, CO. Tel: (970) 468-2316/845-2694, FAX: (970) 453-3202, Web Site: www.keystoneresort.com (19)

Booth, Brenda, Paradysz, New York, NY. Tel: (952) 544-5121, (212) 387-0300, (800) 254-0300, FAX: (212) 387-7647, (952) 544-6320, Web Site: www.paradysz.com (23)

Booth, Lewis, Ford Motor Co, Dearborn, MI. Tel: (313) 845-8540, (800) 555-5259, FAX: (313) 845-6073, Web Site: www.ford.com (16)

Booth, William, Country Curtains Inc, Lee, MA. Tel: (413) 243-1474, (800) 456-0321, FAX: (413) 243-1067, Web Site: www.countrycurtains.com (8)

Booth Michigan, Grand Rapids, MI. Tel: (616) 222-5824, FAX: (616) 222-5318, Web Site: www.boothnewspapers.com (17)

Boothe, Paul, Ideal Industries (Canada) Corp, Ajax, ON. Tel: (905) 683-3400, (800) 824-3325, FAX: (905) 683-0209, E-Mail: nick.shkordoff@ idealindustries.com, Web Site: www.idealindustries. com (9)

Booyah Networks, Westminster, CO. Tel: (303) 426-7776, FAX: (303) 345-6700, E-Mail: support@ booyahnetworks.com, Web Site: www. booyahnetworks.com (35)

Boppe, Larry, Toter Inc, Statesville, NC. Tel: (704) 872-8171, (800) 424-0422, FAX: (704) 878-0734, E-Mail: info@toter.com, Web Site: www.toter.com (16)

Boragine, Vincent, Shape Global Technology, Sanford, ME. Tel: (207) 324-5200, (800) 627-5836, FAX: (207) 324-0875, E-Mail: info@shapeglobal.com, Web Site: www.shapenet.com (34)

Borawski, Paul, E., American Society for Quality-ASQ, Milwaukee, WI. Tel: (414) 272-8575, (800) 248-1946, FAX: (414) 272-1734, E-Mail: help@ asq.org, Web Site: www.asq.org (1)

Borbeleta Gardens, Fairbault, MN. Tel: (507) 334-2807, FAX: (507) 332-0365 (8)

Borchard, Peter, Companion Plants, Athens, OH. Tel: (740) 592-4643, FAX: (740) 593-3092, E-Mail: complants@frognet.net, Web Site: www. companionplants.com (8)

Bordas, Theresa, Intelligent Direct, Wellsboro, PA. Tel: (570) 724-7355, Web Site: www.marketmaps. com (9)

Bordeleau, Lise, Desjardins Financial Securities, Levis, PQ. Tel: (418) 838-7870, FAX: (418) 833-5985, Web Site: www. desjardinsfinancialsecurity.com (15)

Bordelon, Geraldine, Baton Rouge Conventions & Visitors Bureau, Baton Rouge, LA. Tel: (225) 383-1825, (800) LA-ROUGE, FAX: (225) 346-1253, E-Mail: br@bracvb.com, Web Site: www.bracvb. com (1)

Borden, Don, Crane Environmental, Norristown, PA. Tel: (610) 631-7700, (800) 828-2447, FAX: (610) 630-6656, E-Mail: purwater@cranenv.com, Web Site: www.cranenv.com (34)

Borden, Fran, Association of Marian Helpers, Stockbridge, MA. Tel: (413) 298-3691, Web Site: www. marian.org (1)

Borden, Leslye, PhotoEdit Inc, Costa Mesa, CA. Tel: (800) 860-2098, FAX: (800) 804-3707, E-Mail: sales@photoeditinc.com, Web Site: www. photoeditinc.com (38)

Border, Craig, Marketing Results Inc, Sicklerville, NJ. Tel: (856) 740-3334, FAX: (856) 740-3335, Web Site: www.marketingresults.net (16)

Border, Gary, A., Marketing Results Inc, Sicklerville, NJ. Tel: (856) 740-3334, FAX: (856) 740-3335, Web Site: www.marketingresults.net (16)

Borelli, Joe, Borelli Direct Marketing Inc, Kendall Park, NJ. Tel: (732) 940-1500, Web Site: www. borellidirect.com (23)

Borelli Direct Marketing Inc, Kendall Park, NJ. Tel: (732) 940-1500, Web Site: www.borellidirect.com (23)

Boren, Judi, Posh Papers, Riverside, RI. Tel: (401) 331-9873, FAX: (401) 331-2229, E-Mail: info@ poshpapersonline.com, Web Site: www. poshpapersonline.com (6)

Boreyko, B.K., Vemma Nutrition Co, Scottsdale, AZ. Tel: (800) 577-0777, FAX: (888) 314-9827, E-Mail: ms@vemma.com, Web Site: www.vemma. com (7)

Boreyko, Jason, Vemma Nutrition Co, Scottsdale, AZ. Tel: (800) 577-0777, FAX: (888) 314-9827, E-Mail: ms@vemma.com, Web Site: www.vemma. com (7)

Borgelt, Andrea, Gerber Life Insurance Co, White Plains, NY. Tel: (914) 272-4000, (800) 704-2180, FAX: (914) 272-4099, Web Site: www.gerberlife. com (15)

Borgnine, Tova, Tova Corp, West Chester, PA. Tel: (484) 701-1000, Web Site: www.beautybytova.com (7)

Boring, Troy, Thermal Product Solutions, White Deer, PA. Tel: (570) 538-7200, (800) 586-2473 (16)

Boris, John, Shutterfly, Redwood City, CA. Tel: (650) 610-5200, Web Site: www.shutterfly.com (27)

Bork, Brian, Beau Rivage Resort & Casino, Biloxi, MS. Tel: (228) 386-7150, Web Site: www. beaurivage.com (19)

Borkowski, James, Stellar Technology Inc, Amherst, NY. Tel: (800) 274-1846, FAX: (716) 250-1909, E-Mail: info@stellartech.com, Web Site: www. stellartech.com (9)

Born Free USA, Sacramento, CA. Tel: (916) 447-3085, FAX: (916) 447-3070, E-Mail: info@ bornfreeusa.org, Web Site: www.bornfreeusa.org (1)

Borneman, William, PowerDirect, Newport Beach, CA. Tel: (949) 253-3440, Web Site: www. powerdirect.net (35)

Borneo, Rudolph, J., Macy's West, San Francisco, CA. Tel: (415) 954-6089, FAX: (415) 954-6103 (16)

Boro, Albert, J., Golden Gate Transportation District, San Rafael, CA. Tel: (415) 921-5858, FAX: (415) 923-2014, Web Site: www.goldengate.org (16)

Boro, Seth, J., Thoma Cressey Bravo, Chicago, IL. Tel: (312) 777-4444, FAX: (312) 777-4445, Web Site: www.tcb.com (14)

Borower, Bryan, The List Place Inc, Charlotte, NC. Tel: (704) 672-3174, FAX: (704) 676-4755, E-Mail: bryan@thelistplace.net, Web Site: www. thelistplace.net (23)

Borowicz, Donna, Yellow Pages Association, Berkeley Heights, NJ. Tel: (908) 286-2380, (800) 336-0440, FAX: (908) 286-0620, Web Site: www. yellowpagesima.org (1)

Borowski, Patricia, A., National Association of Professional Insurance Agents, Alexandria, VA. Tel: (703) 836-9340, FAX: (703) 836-1279, E-Mail: web@pianet.org, Web Site: www.pianet.com (1)

Borowsky, Ned, S., North American Publishing Co, Philadelphia, PA. Tel: (215) 238-5300, FAX: (215) 238-5412, Web Site: www.napco.com (23)

Borowsky, Scott, C., Spectrum Retail Associates, Ardmore, PA. Tel: (610) 645-9520, (800) 570-6565, FAX: (610) 645-9524 (20)

Borowsky, Ted, Foster Manufacturing Co, Montgomeryville, PA. Tel: (215) 442-1700, (800) 523-4855, FAX: (215) 442-1313, E-Mail: information@ fostermfg.com, Web Site: www.fostermfg.com (34)

Borrero, Denira, Omnidirect, Miami Beach, FL. Tel: (800) 459-4034, Web Site: www.omnidirect.tv (35)

Borst, Margaret, Country Sampler Group, Saint Charles, IL. Tel: (630) 377-8000, FAX: (630) 377-8194, Web Site: www.sampler.com (17)

Borthwick, Sandie, Capital Insurance Group (CIG), Monterey, CA. Tel: (831) 233-5500, Web Site: www.ciginsurance.com (15)

Bortis, Linda, J., iMarlin LLC, Springfield, MO. Tel: (417) 887-7446, FAX: (417) 887-3643, E-Mail: info@imarlin.com, Web Site: www.imarlin.com (35)

Boruff, Chris, Morningstar Inc, Chicago, IL. Tel: (312) 696-6000, Web Site: www.morningstar.com (14)

Borum, Michael, Borum Photographics Inc, Nashville, TN. Tel: (615) 254-0063, (888) 254-0063, FAX: (615) 242-2334, Web Site: www.chromatics.com (37)

Borum Photographics Inc, Nashville, TN. Tel: (615) 254-0063, (888) 254-0063, FAX: (615) 242-2334, Web Site: www.chromatics.com (37)

Borysiewicz, Jeff, Corona Cigar Co, Orlando, FL. Tel: (407) 248-1212, (888) 702-4427, FAX: (407) 248-1211, E-Mail: info@coronacigar.com, Web Site: www.coronacigar.com (5)

Bosc, Joyce L., Boscobel Marketing Communications Inc, Silver Spring, MD. Tel: (301) 588-2900, E-Mail: info@boscobel.com, Web Site: www. boscobel.com (35)

Boscobel Marketing Communications Inc, Silver Spring, MD. Tel: (301) 588-2900, E-Mail: info@ boscobel.com, Web Site: www.boscobel.com (35)

Bose, Amar, G., Bose Corp, Framingham, MA. Tel: (508) 879-7330, FAX: (508) 766-7543 (3)

Bose Corp, Framingham, MA. Tel: (508) 879-7330, FAX: (508) 766-7543 (3)

Boshart, Joseph A., Cross Country Travcorps, Boca Raton, FL. Tel: (800) 530-6125, FAX: (561) 998-8533, Web Site: www.crosscountrytravcorps.com (16)

Boshoven, Steve, Foremost Insurance Group, Grand Rapids, MI. Tel: (616) 956-8241, (800) 527-3905, FAX: (800) 325-1507, Web Site: www.foremost. com (15)

Bosley, Gary, O., Marketing Solutions Group Inc, Pleasanton, CA. Tel: (510) 331-7625, E-Mail: info@marketingsolutionsgroup.biz, Web Site: www.marketingsolutionsgroup.biz (32)

Bosom Buddy Breast Forms, Boise, ID. Tel: (208) 343-9696, (800) 262-2789, FAX: (208) 343-9266, E-Mail: custserv@bosombuddy.com, Web Site: www.bosombuddy.com (7)

Bosse, John, D., Nuveen Investments, Chicago, IL. Tel: (312) 917-7700, (800) 257-8787, FAX: (312) 917-8049, Web Site: www.nuveen.com (14)

Boster, Kari, Bluewater Yachts, Mora, MN. Tel: (320) 679-3811, FAX: (320) 679-3820, E-Mail: bluewater@ncis.com, Web Site: www. bluewateryacht.com (16)

Boston, Terry, Tennessee Valley Authority, Knoxville, TN. Tel: (865) 632-2101, Web Site: www.tva.gov (16)

Boston Apparel Group, Randolph, MA. Tel: (508) 583-8110, Web Site: www.bostonapparel.com (2)

Boston Color Graphics, Billerica, MA. Tel: (978) 528-7999, (800) 767-0067, FAX: (978) 528-7609, E-Mail: sales@bostoncolorgraphics.com, Web Site: www.bostoncolorgraphics.com (27)

The Boston Co, Boston, MA. Tel: (617) 722-7000, FAX: (617) 722-7569 (14)

The Boston Consulting Group, New York, NY. Tel: (212) 446-2800 (20)

Boston Gift Show, Kennesaw, GA. Tel: (678) 285-3976, (800) 272-SHOW, FAX: (678) 285-7469, Web Site: www.bostongiftshow.com (42)

The Boston Globe, Boston, MA. Tel: (617) 929-2000, (888) MY-GLOBE, FAX: (617) 929-2606, Web Site: www.bostonglobe.com (17)

Boston Research Group, Hopkinton, MA. Tel: (508) 497-2555, FAX: (508) 497-2592, E-Mail: BRGrep@BostonResearchGroup.com, Web Site: www.bostonresearchgroup.com (30)

Boswell, Ed, The Forum Corp, Boston, MA. Tel: (617) 523-7300, (800) 367-8611, FAX: (617) 371-3300, E-Mail: forum@forum.com, Web Site: www. forum.com (20)

Bothwell, Marty, ThreeSource Fulfillment, Manteno, IL. Tel: (815) 936-1094 x4179, (888) 673-4650, FAX: (815) 936-9743, E-Mail: sandyp@ threesource.tv, Web Site: www.threesource.tv (28)

Botkin, Sanford, Tax Reduction Institute, Germantown, MD. Tel: (301) 972-3600, (800) TRI-0-TAX, FAX: (301) 972-0819, E-Mail: info@ taxreductioninstitute.com, Web Site: www. taxreductioninstitute.com (14)

Bott, Andrew, BBC Worldwide Americas Inc, New York, NY. Tel: (212) 705-9300, (800) 898-4921, FAX: (212) 888-0576, Web Site: www.bbcamerica. com (3)

Botthof, Rick, ACG/Computech Direct, Hoffman Estates, IL. Tel: (847) 843-3200, FAX: (847) 843-8060, E-Mail: info@acg-computech-direct.com, Web Site: www.acg-computech-direct.com (22)

Bottoli, Marcello, Samsonite American Tourister, Mansfield, MA. Tel: (508) 851-1400, (800) 821-6632, FAX: (508) 851-8715, E-Mail: samsonite@ casupport.ca, Web Site: www.samsonite.com (16)

Bottoli, Marcello, Samsonite Corp, Mansfield, MA. Tel: (508) 851-1400, (800) 547-BAGS, FAX: (303) 373-8715, Web Site: www.samsonite.com (16)

Bottom, Richard E., American Leads Co, Benicia, CA. Tel: (707) 747-6334, FAX: (707) 747-5323, Web Site: www.american-leads.com (23)

Bottum, Judy, Praises, Prizes & Presents, Grand Rapids, MI. Tel: (361) 851-9663, FAX: (361) 851-9663, Web Site: www.praisesprizespresents.com (5)

Botz, Jennifer, The Arizona Republic, Phoenix, AZ. Tel: (602) 444-8000, Web Site: www.azcentral.com (17)

Bouchard, Ann, Matrix Manager, Roseville, CA. Tel: (916) 783-1536, (877)-258-9037, E-Mail: info@ mymatrixmanager.com, Web Site: www. mymatrixmanager.com (28)

Boucher, Helene, Cancer Research Society, Montreal, PQ. Tel: (514) 861-9227, (888) 766-2262, FAX: (514) 861-9220, Web Site: www. CancerResearchSociety.ca (1)

Boucher, M. Adam, Wilsons Leather, Brooklyn Park, MN. Tel: (763) 391-4000, (866) 305-4704, FAX: (763) 391-4906, Web Site: www.wilsonsleather. com (2)

Bouclin, Ed, Scorecards USA, North Kingstown, RI. Tel: (401) 294-4049, (800) 553-4154, FAX: (401) 294-4076, E-Mail: sales@scorecardsusa.com, Web Site: www.scorecardsusa.com (16)

Boundless Corp, Phelps, NY. Tel: (631) 962-1500, (800) 231-5445, FAX: (631) 962-1505, E-Mail: sales@boundless.com, Web Site: www.boundless. com (16)

Bounsall, David, Four Seasons Hotels & Resorts, Toronto, ON Canada. Tel: (416) 449-1750, (800) 819-5053, FAX: (416) 441-4374, Web Site: www. fourseasons.com (19)

Bountiful Gardens, Willits, CA. Tel: (707) 459-6410, FAX: (707) 459-1925, E-Mail: bountiful@sonic. net, Web Site: www.bountifulgardens.org (8)

Bourdon, Francis, Marian Helpers Center, Stockbridge, MA. Tel: (413) 298-3691, (800) 462-7426, FAX: (413) 298-3583, Web Site: www.marian.org (1)

Bourgon, Luc, Northern Lights Direct, Chicago, IL. Tel: (312) 263-8686, FAX: (312) 624-7701, E-Mail: contact@northernlightsdirect.com, Web Site: www.northernlightsdirect.com (32)

Bourscheidt, Randall, Alliance for the Arts, New York, NY. Tel: (212) 947-6340, FAX: (212) 947-6416, E-Mail: info@allianceforarts.org, Web Site: www. nyc-arts.org (1)

Bousquet, Joyce, Reliant Data Processing, North Aurora, IL. Tel: (630) 844-4210, FAX: (630) 844-9530, E-Mail: rdpmail@aol.com (28)

Boutcher, Ann, M., Audiovox, Hauppauge, NY. Tel: (631) 231-7750, (800) 645-4994, FAX: (631) 434-3995, Web Site: www.audiovox.com (16)

Boutelle, Mark, Paslode, Vernon Hills, IL. Tel: (847) 634-1900, (800) 222-6990, FAX: (847) 634-6602, E-Mail: tech@paslode.com, Web Site: www. paslode.com (16)

Bouzari, Alex, Data Direct Networks (HQ), Chatsworth, CA. Tel: (818) 700-7607, (800) 837-2298, FAX: (818) 700-7601, E-Mail: info@ddn.com, Web Site: www.datadirectnet.com (3)

Bovasso, Robert M, Real Media Solutions, Wayne, NJ. Tel: (973) 835-7060, Web Site: www.get-realmedia.com (27)

Bovett, Debb, ACTON Group Ltd, Lincoln, NE. Tel: (402) 742-2820, FAX: (402) 470-2673, E-Mail: info@acton.com, Web Site: www.acton.com (23)

Bow, Frank, American Mail-Well Envelope Co/St Louis Div, Eureka, MO. Tel: (314) 966-2000, (800) 800-8845, FAX: (314) 966-4725, E-Mail: info@cenveo.com, Web Site: www.mail-well.com (26)

Bowater Inc, Greenville, SC. Tel: (864) 271-7733, (800) 921-3244, FAX: (864) 282-9563, E-Mail: hrsc@abitibibowater.com, Web Site: www.bowater. com (25)

Bowcut, Michael, Recreational Equipment Inc, Kent, WA. Tel: (253) 395-4803, Web Site: www.rei.com (11)

Bowden, Al, Sencore Inc, Sioux Falls, SD. Tel: (605) 339-0100, (800) SEN-CORE, FAX: (605) 339-0317, E-Mail: sales@sencore.com, Web Site: www. sencore.com (16)

Bowden, Doug, Sencore Inc, Sioux Falls, SD. Tel: (605) 339-0100, (800) SEN-CORE, FAX: (605) 339-0317, E-Mail: sales@sencore.com, Web Site: www.sencore.com (16)

Bowden, John, Conrad N Hilton College of Hotel & Restaurant Management University of Houston, Houston, TX. Tel: (713) 743-0209 (1)

Bowden, Steven, Old Vine Marketing, Napa, CA. Tel: (707) 694-9647, E-Mail: info@oldvinemarketing. com, Web Site: www.oldvinemarketing.com (22)

Bowe Bell & Howell, Durham, NC. Tel: (919) 767-6400, (800) 220-3030, E-Mail: marketing@ bowebellhowell.com, Web Site: www. bowebellhowell.com (34)

Bowen, Craig, Gift Services Inc, Vancouver, WA. Tel: (800) 379-4065, FAX: (360) 699-0597, E-Mail: corpsales@gifttree.com, Web Site: www.gifttree. com (6)

Bowen, Janie, Accutrend Data Corp, Greenwood Village, CO. Tel: (303) 488-0011, FAX: (303) 488-0133, E-Mail: info@accutrend.com, Web Site: www.accutrend.com (24)

Bowen, John, J., Johnson & Wales University, Providence, RI. Tel: (401) 598-1000, (800) DIAL-JWU, FAX: (401) 598-1833, E-Mail: admissions.pvd@ jwu.edu, Web Site: www.jwu.edu (41)

Bowen, Matt, Aloft Group, Westlake Village, CA. Tel: (805) 494-3700, Web Site: www.aloftgroup.com (33)

Bowen-Leser, Deborah, Aspen Publishers Inc, New York, NY. Tel: (800) 638-8437, FAX: (301) 417-7655, Web Site: www.aspenpublishers.com (17)

Bowens, Jaqueline, D., Children's Hospital Foundation, Washington, DC. Tel: (202) 476-3000, (800) 884-LIFE, FAX: (202) 884-5999, Web Site: www. dcchildrens.com (1)

Bower, Jay, Crossbow Group, Westport, CT. Tel: (203) 222-2244, FAX: (203) 226-7838, E-Mail: info@ crossbowgroup.com, Web Site: www. crossbowgroup.com (40)

Bower, W., Marketeers, Mission Viejo, CA. Tel: (949) 364-1669, FAX: (949) 582-0829, E-Mail: wbower@apc.net (29)

Bowers, Allen, Career Blazers, New York, NY. Tel: (212) 719-3232, FAX: (212) 221-0452 (20)

Bowers, Linda, LinguiSystems, East Moline, IL. Tel: (309) 755-2300, (800) 776-4332, FAX: (800) 577-4555, E-Mail: service@linguisystems.com, Web Site: www.linguisystems.com (17)

Bowers, Lois, A., Medical Economics Magazine, North Olmsted, OH. Tel: (440) 243-8100, FAX: (440) 891-2735, Web Site: medicaleconomics. modernmedicine.com/about (17)

Bowers, Marcia, Hyatt Legal Plans Inc, Cleveland, OH. Tel: (216) 241-0022, FAX: (216) 694-4305, Web Site: www.legalplans.com (17)

Bowers, Scott, Ghent Manufacturing Inc, Lebanon, OH. Tel: (513) 932-3445, (800) 543-0550, FAX: (513) 932-9252, E-Mail: customer_service@!ghent. com, Web Site: www.ghent.com (10)

Bowers, Thomas, M., Bowers & Associates Inc, Saint Louis, MO. Tel: (314) 963-4477, FAX: (314) 963-4483 (33)

Bowers & Associates Inc, Saint Louis, MO. Tel: (314) 963-4477, FAX: (314) 963-4483 (33)

Bowers & Merena Auctions, Irvine, CA. Tel: (949) 253-0916, (800) 458-4646, FAX: (949) 253-4091, E-Mail: auction@bowersandmerena.com, Web Site: www.bowersandmerena.com (16)

Bowers Envelope Co, Indianapolis, IN. Tel: (317) 253-4321, FAX: (317) 254-2231, Web Site: www. bowersenvelope.com (26)

The Bowery Mission, New York, NY. Tel: (212) 684-2800, Web Site: www.bowery.org (1)

Bowes, John, Behlen Manufacturing Co, Columbus, NE. Tel: (402) 564-3111, FAX: (402) 563-7405, E-Mail: behlen@megavision.com, Web Site: www. behlenmfg.com (16)

Bowick, Christopher, J., Cox Communications, Atlanta, GA. Tel: (404) 843-5000, FAX: (404) 269-2243, Web Site: www.cox.com (16)

R R Bowker, New Providence, NJ. Tel: (888) BOWKER-2 (269-5372), FAX: (908) 771-8699, Web Site: www.bowker.com (17)

Bowler, Cara, Vane & Friends, Chappaqua, NY. Tel: (914) 238-8890, E-Mail: info@vaneandfriends. com, Web Site: www.vaneandfriends.com (35)

Bowles, Crandall, C., JP Morgan Chase & Co, New York, NY. Tel: (212) 270-6000, E-Mail: jpmcinvestorrelations@jpmchase.com, Web Site: www.jpmorgan.com (14)

Bowles, Susie, Universal Security Instruments Inc, Owings Mills, MD. Tel: (410) 363-3000, FAX: (410) 363-2218, E-Mail: sales@universalsecurity. com, Web Site: www.universalsecurity.com (16)

Bowling, Mike, Access Worldwide Communications Inc, Falls Church, VA. Tel: (571) 384-7400, (800) 522-3447, FAX: (703) 531-0711, Web Site: www. accessww.com (29)

Bowman, Allyson, Merastar Insurance Co, Chattanooga, TN. Tel: (800) 637-2782, FAX: (800) 369-1430, E-Mail: merastar.assist.team@unitrindirect. com, Web Site: www.merastar.com (15)

Bowman, Bruce, Harwil Corp, Oxnard, CA. Tel: (805) 988-6800, FAX: (805) 988-6804, E-Mail: harwil@ harwil.com, Web Site: www.harwil.com (9)

Bowman, James, International Fulfillment Inc, Philadelphia, PA. Tel: (215) 638-8060, (800) 962-8080, FAX: (215) 638-8091, Web Site: www.ifionline.net (27)

Bowman, Jeffrey T., Crawford & Co, Atlanta, GA. Tel: (404) 300-1000, (800) 241-2541, FAX: (404) 300-1905, Web Site: www.crawfordandcompany. com (35)

Bowman, Jessica, SEOinhouse, Saint Charles, MO. Tel: (650) 589-8720, Web Site: www.seoinhouse. com (32)

Bowman, Leslie, Greene, Winterthur Museum & Country Estate, Wilmington, DE. Tel: (302) 888-4600, (800) 448-3883, FAX: (302) 888-4730, E-Mail: tourinfo@winterthur.org, Web Site: www. winterthur.org (6)

Bowman, Lynn, A., Harvard Pilgrim Health Care, Wellesley, MA. Tel: (617) 509-1000, FAX: (617) 509-7590, Web Site: www.harvardpilgrim.org (7)

Bowman, Nicole, Bowman Circulation Marketing, Greenwich, CT. Tel: (917) 913-6172, E-Mail: nicole@nicolebowman.com, Web Site: www. nicolebowman.com (20)

Bowman, Paul, Bowman & Partners, Roanoke, TX. Tel: (817) 431-3441, Web Site: www.bowman-partners.com (22)

Bowman & Partners, Roanoke, TX. Tel: (817) 431-3441, Web Site: www.bowman-partners.com (22)

Bowman Circulation Marketing, Greenwich, CT. Tel: (917) 913-6172, E-Mail: nicole@nicolebowman. com, Web Site: www.nicolebowman.com (20)

Bowne, William, A-1 Direct Mail Marketing Inc, Miami, FL. Tel: (305) 251-3187 (28)

BowTie Inc, Irvine, CA. Tel: (949) 855-8822, FAX: (949) 855-1850, E-Mail: mevans@bowtieinc.com, Web Site: www.animalnetwork.com (17)

Boxer, Mark, Anthem Blue Cross Blue Shield, Saint Louis, MO. Tel: (314) 923-4444, (888) 877-9125, FAX: (314) 923-5151, E-Mail: moreinfo@bcbsmo. com, Web Site: www.bcbsmo.com (15)

Boy Scouts of America/National Supply Group, Charlotte, NC. Tel: (972) 580-2161, (800) 323-0736, E-Mail: customerservice@scoutstuff.org, Web Site: www.scoutstuff.org (1)

Boyce, Shari, The Atlantic Monthly, Washington, DC. Tel: (202) 266-6000, (800) 234-2411, FAX: (202) 266-7280, Web Site: www.theatlantic.com (17)

Boyd, Emily, MediaConcepts Corp, Assonet, MA. Tel: (508) 644-3131, FAX: (508) 644-5201, E-Mail: at3@mediaconceptscorp.com, Web Site: www.mediaconceptscorp.com (35)

Boyd, Ron, Quick Draw Clip Systems Inc, Ventura, CA. Tel: (805) 644-6888, (888) 254-7797, FAX: (805) 644-7320, E-Mail: ron@clipsystems.com, Web Site: www.clipsystems.com (9)

Boyd Gaming Corp, Las Vegas, NV. Tel: (702) 792-7200, FAX: (702) 792-7313, Web Site: www.boydgaming.com (16)

Boyd Tamney Cross Inc, Wayne, PA. Tel: (610) 293-0500, FAX: (610) 687-8199, E-Mail: info@btcmarketing.com, Web Site: www.boydtamneycross.com (35)

Boyden Global Executive Search, Purchase, NY. Tel: (914) 747-0093, E-Mail: inquiry@boyden.com, Web Site: www.boyden.com (20)

Boyer, Aurelia, G., Columbia-Presbyterian Medical Center, New York, NY. Tel: (212) 305-2500, FAX: (212) 305-8023, Web Site: www.nyp.org (16)

Boyer, David, BroadVision Inc, Redwood City, CA. Tel: (650) 542-5100, FAX: (650) 364-3425, E-Mail: sales@broadvision.com, Web Site: www.broadvision.com (16)

Boyer, Herbert, W., Allergan Inc, Irvine, CA. Tel: (714) 246-4500, (800) 433-8871, FAX: (714) 246-4971, Web Site: www.allergan.com (16)

Boyer, Lisa, Lexinet Corp, Council Grove, KS. Tel: (620) 767-7000 (22)

Boyer, Phil, Aircraft Owners & Pilots Association, Frederick, MD. Tel: (301) 695-2000, (800) 872-2672, FAX: (301) 695-2375, E-Mail: aopahq@aopa.org, Web Site: www.aopa.org (1)

Boyer, Roy, Incentives America, Boulder, CO. Tel: (303) 494-8845, FAX: (303) 494-8404 (33)

Boyer de la Giroday, Eric, ING, Minneapolis, MN. Tel: (612) 342-7061, (800) 333-6965, FAX: (612) 372-5339, Web Site: www.ing.com (15)

Boylan, Philip, Touch-Base Computing, Silver Creek, GA. Tel: (706) 378-0964, E-Mail: sales@touchbase.com, Web Site: www.touchbase.com (22)

Boyle, Doug, Blue Coral Slick 50, Houston, TX. Tel: (713) 241-6161, (800) 416-1600, FAX: (713) 241-4044, E-Mail: SCD-ConsumerSolutions@Shell.com, Web Site: www.bluecoral.com (16)

Boyle, Karen, MarketMakers Group Inc, Wayne, PA. Tel: (610) 254-8924, FAX: (610) 254-9190, E-Mail: rlail@marketmakers.com, Web Site: www.marketmakersgroup.com (29)

Boyle, Lisa, C., American Marketing & Communication Corp, Hagerstown, MD. Tel: (240) 625-9225, FAX: (240) 625-9235, E-Mail: info@amcc1.com, Web Site: www.americanmarketingcc.com (20)

Boyle, Lois, J Schmid & Associates Inc, Mission, KS. Tel: (913) 236-8988, FAX: (913) 236-8987, E-Mail: info@jschmid.com, Web Site: www.jschmid.com (20)

Boyle, Lynne, Winterthur Museum & Country Estate, Wilmington, DE. Tel: (302) 888-4600, (800) 448-3883, FAX: (302) 888-4730, E-Mail: tourinfo@winterthur.org, Web Site: www.winterthur.org (6)

Boyles, Paul, A., Merastar Insurance Co, Chattanooga, TN. Tel: (800) 637-2782, FAX: (800) 369-1430, E-Mail: merastar.assist.team@unitrindirect.com, Web Site: www.merastar.com (15)

Boyles, Tom, Walt Disney Parks & Resorts, Lake Buena Vista, FL. Tel: (407) 824-2222, Web Site: www.disneyworld.com (19)

Boyles, William, R., Glidden & Boyles Inc, Mount Prospect, IL. Tel: (847) 398-5746, FAX: (847) 756-7619, E-Mail: e:marcom@gbmarcom.com, Web Site: www.glidden-boyles.com (35)

Boys & Girls Clubs of America National Headquarters, Atlanta, GA. Tel: (404) 487-5700, FAX: (404) 487-5757, (404) 815-5757, E-Mail: info@bgca.org, Web Site: www.bgca.org (1)

Boys' Life & Scouting Magazines, Irving, TX. Tel: (972) 580-2000, (866) 584-6589, FAX: (972) 580-2079, Web Site: www.boyslife.org (17)

Boysen III, Stuart, W., Hoke Communications Inc, Garden City, NY. Tel: (516) 746-6700, FAX: (516) 294-8141 (17)

Boysen, Stuart, The Direct Marketing Club of New York Inc, Garden City, NY. Tel: (516) 746-6700, FAX: (516) 294-8141, E-Mail: info@dmcny.org, Web Site: www.dmcny.org (1)

Brabender, John, A., Brabender Cox, Pittsburgh, PA. Tel: (412) 434-6320, FAX: (412) 424-6391, E-Mail: tiffany@brabendercox.com, Web Site: www.brabendercox.com (35)

Brabender Cox, Pittsburgh, PA. Tel: (412) 434-6320, FAX: (412) 424-6391, E-Mail: tiffany@brabendercox.com, Web Site: www.brabendercox.com (35)

Brach, Abe, DPC Computers, Monsey, NY. Tel: (845) 426-3790, (866) 513-CORP, FAX: (845) 426-6275, E-Mail: learnmore@salestax.com, Web Site: www.salestax.com (16)

Bracken, Johanna, Rauxa Direct, Costa Mesa, CA. Tel: (714) 427-1271, Web Site: www.rauxa.com (35)

Bracken, Lee, HR Direct, Sunrise, FL. Tel: (800) 346-1231, FAX: (800) 350-7760, Web Site: www.hrdirect.com (10)

Bradbury, John, Military Direct Marketing Inc, Poughkeepsie, NY. Tel: (845) 454-7900, FAX: (845) 454-7987 (31)

Braddon, Cynthia, The McGraw-Hill Cos, New York, NY. Tel: (212) 904-2000, (866) 436-8502, FAX: (212) 512-3840, Web Site: www.mcgraw-hill.com (17)

The Bradford Group, Niles, IL. Tel: (847) 966-2770, FAX: (847) 581-8630, Web Site: www.collectiblestoday.com (16)

Bradford Health Services, Birmingham, AL. Tel: (205) 251-7753, (800) 217-2849, Web Site: www.bradfordhealth.com (16)

Bradley, Alatia, The New Yorker Magazine, New York, NY. Tel: (212) 286-5400, FAX: (212) 286-5735, E-Mail: alatia_bradley@newyorker.com, Web Site: www.newyorker.com (17)

Bradley, Bill, Cuba Cheese Shoppe, Cuba, NY. Tel: (585) 968-3949, FAX: (716) 968-1746, Web Site: www.cubacheese.com (4)

Bradley, Christopher, W., Cuddledown Inc, Portland, ME. Tel: (207) 761-0201, (800) 323-6793, FAX: (207) 761-1948, Web Site: www.cuddledown.com (8)

Bradley, David, The Atlantic Monthly, Washington, DC. Tel: (202) 266-6000, (800) 234-2411, FAX: (202) 266-7280, Web Site: www.theatlantic.com (17)

Bradley, Denny, CCI Solutions, Olympia, WA. Tel: (360) 943-5378, (800) 426-8664, FAX: (360) 754-1566, (800) 339-TAPE, E-Mail: info@ccisolutions.com, Web Site: www.ccisolutions.com (16)

Bradley, Jeff, Cuba Cheese Shoppe, Cuba, NY. Tel: (585) 968-3949, FAX: (716) 968-1746, Web Site: www.cubacheese.com (4)

Bradley, John, F., JP Morgan Chase & Co, New York, NY. Tel: (212) 270-6000, E-Mail: jpmcinvestorrelations@jpmchase.com, Web Site: www.jpmorgan.com (14)

Bradley, Susan, V., The Peter A Tobin College of Business, Jamaica, NY. Tel: (718) 990-2600, FAX: (718) 990-1868, Web Site: www.stjohns.edu (41)

Bradley, Todd, Compaq Computer Corp, Houston, TX. Tel: (281) 370-0670, FAX: (281) 927-8835, Web Site: www.compaq.com (16)

Bradley Direct, Columbus, GA. Tel: (706) 565-2100, (866) 239-6774, (800) 241-8981, FAX: (706) 565-2132, (888) 224-7455, E-Mail: customerservice@grilllovers.com, Web Site: www.grilllovers.com (8)

Vera Bradley, Fort Wayne, IN. Tel: (800) 823-8372, Web Site: www.verabradley.com (2)

Bradpiece, Bernard, ARF Annual Convention & Research Infoplex, New York, NY. Tel: (212) 751-5656, FAX: (212) 319-5265, E-Mail: info@theARF.org, Web Site: www.theARF.org (42)

Bradpiece, Bernard, The Pennysaver Group Inc, Hanover, MD. Tel: (410) 684-2600, FAX: (410) 684-2065, Web Site: www.mdpennysaver.com (17)

Bradshaw, Brad, Nissan North America Inc, Irving, TX. Tel: (310) 532-3111, Web Site: www.nissanusa.com (16)

Brady, Cliff, Tillamook County Creamery Association, Tillamook, OR. Tel: (503) 842-4481, (800) 542-7290, FAX: (503) 842-6039, Web Site: www.tillamookcheese.com (4)

Brady, Frank, Brady Marketing Co Inc, Walnut Creek, CA. Tel: (925) 676-1300, (800) 326-6080, FAX: (925) 676-3082, E-Mail: info@bradymarketing.com, Web Site: www.bradymarketing.com (16)

Brady, Lorraine, Brady Marketing Co Inc, Walnut Creek, CA. Tel: (925) 676-1300, (800) 326-6080, FAX: (925) 676-3082, E-Mail: info@bradymarketing.com, Web Site: www.bradymarketing.com (16)

Brady, Regina, Reggie Brady Marketing Solutions LLC, Norwalk, CT. Tel: (203) 838-8138, Web Site: www.reggiebrady.com (20)

Brady, Regina, The Direct Marketing Club of New York Inc, Garden City, NY. Tel: (516) 746-6700, FAX: (516) 294-8141, E-Mail: info@dmcny.org, Web Site: www.dmcny.org (1)

Brady, Sheila, Thor Information Services Inc, Old Forge, NY. Tel: (315) 369-3872, FAX: (315) 369-2330, E-Mail: sales@thorinfo.com (23)

Brady, Stephanie, United Way Worldwide, Alexandria, VA. Tel: (703) 836-7100, Web Site: www.liveunited.org (1)

Brady Corp, Milwaukee, WI. Tel: (414) 358-6600, (800) 541-1686, FAX: (800) 292-2289, Web Site: www.bradycorp.com (16)

Brady Marketing Co Inc, Walnut Creek, CA. Tel: (925) 676-1300, (800) 326-6080, FAX: (925) 676-3082, E-Mail: info@bradymarketing.com, Web Site: www.bradymarketing.com (16)

Reggie Brady Marketing Solutions LLC, Norwalk, CT. Tel: (203) 838-8138, Web Site: www.reggiebrady.com (20)

Braghini, Amy, L., University of Illinois Foundation, Urbana, IL. Tel: (217) 333-0810, FAX: (217) 333-5577, E-Mail: uif@uillinois.edu, Web Site: www.uif.uillinois.edu (1)

Brahmam, Maya, The World Bank, Washington, DC. Tel: (202) 473-1000, FAX: (202) 477-6391, Web Site: www.worldbank.org (17)

Brahmin Leather Works, Fairhaven, MA. Tel: (508) 994-4000, (800) 229-2428, FAX: (508) 994-4153, Web Site: www.brahminusa.com (17)

Brahn, John, Diamond Marketing Solutions, Bloomingdale, IL. Tel: (630) 523-5250, FAX: (630) 523-0403, Web Site: www.dmsolutions.com (35)

Braillard II, Walter, H., Domestic Bank, Providence, RI. Tel: (401) 943-1600, (800) 566-6600, FAX: (401) 943-6708, Web Site: www.domesticbank.com (14)

Braintree Payment Solutions LLC, Chicago, IL. Tel: (773) 489-9539, Web Site: www.braintreepaymentsolutions.com (14)

Brake, Ben, Epic Research LLC, Greenville, DE. Tel: (302) 467-5445, Web Site: www.epicresearch.net (20)

Brake, Pam, Professional Creations, New Castle, IN. Tel: (765) 529-1590, (800) 428-8855, E-Mail: sales@professional-creations.com, Web Site: www. professional-creations.com (5)

Brakehorn, Mike, Merrimade Stationery Co LLC, Ansonia, CT. Tel: (800) 344-4256, FAX: (800) 883-6515, E-Mail: custserv@merrimadestationery.com, Web Site: www.merrimade.com (10)

Branaman, Lucinda, NASW Assurance Services Inc, Frederick, MD. Tel: (800) 668-4274, E-Mail: zxi@naswasi.org, Web Site: www.naswinsurancetrust. org (1)

Brancaccio, Lou, The Columbian, Vancouver, WA. Tel: (360) 694-3391, FAX: (360) 735-4503, Web Site: www.columbian.com (17)

Branch, Greg, Luxottica Retail, Mason, OH. Tel: (513) 765-6956, Web Site: www.luxottica.com (2)

Branch, Malcom, P., Delta Upsilon International Fraternity, Indianapolis, IN. Tel: (317) 875-8900, FAX: (317) 876-1629, E-Mail: ihq@deltau.org, Web Site: www.deltau.org (16)

Branch Banking & Trust Co, Wilson, NC. Tel: (252) 399-4111, FAX: (252) 246-4030 (14)

Brand New Products LLC, Chicago, IL. Tel: (773) 486-8813, Web Site: www.brandnewllc.com (4)

brandedmerchandise.ca, Peterborough, ON Canada. Tel: (705) 944-5632, (800) 461-1788, FAX: (705) 944-7500, E-Mail: info@brandedmerchandise.ca, Web Site: www.brandedmerchandise.ca (35)

Brandes, Richard, M2Media 360, Park Ridge, IL. Tel: (760) 318-7000, E-Mail: cnaughton@m2media360. com, Web Site: www.m2media360.com (17)

Brandi, JoAnna, JoAnna Brandi & Co Inc, Boca Raton, FL. Tel: (561) 279-0027, E-Mail: joanna@returnonhappiness.com, Web Site: www. returnonhappiness.com (20)

JoAnna Brandi & Co Inc, Boca Raton, FL. Tel: (561) 279-0027, E-Mail: joanna@returnonhappiness.com, Web Site: www.returnonhappiness.com (20)

Brandner, Karen, Broadmoor Hotel Inc, Colorado Springs, CO. Tel: (719) 634-7711, (866) 837-9520, FAX: (719) 577-5779, Web Site: www.broadmoor. com (19)

Brandon, Michael, SF Video Inc, San Francisco, CA. Tel: (415) 288-9400, (800) 545-5865, FAX: (415) 288-9410, E-Mail: selfservice@sfvideo.com, Web Site: www.sfvideo.com (3)

Brandon, William, Ad Infinitum Books, Mount Vernon, NY. Tel: (914) 664-5930, (800) 697-0402, FAX: (914) 664-2642, E-Mail: aibservice@adinfinitumbooks.com, Web Site: www. adinfinitumbooks.com (16)

Brandt, David, N., Cornhusker Press, Hastings, NE. Tel: (402) 462-4141, FAX: (402) 460-4612, E-Mail: dlsales@dutton-lainson.com, Web Site: www.dutton-lainson.com (17)

brandUNITY Inc, Rollingbay, WA. Tel: (206) 842-4948, E-Mail: admin@brandunity.com, Web Site: www.brandunity.com (1)

Brandywine Consulting Group Inc, West Chester, PA. Tel: (610) 696-5872, FAX: (610) 429-1954, Web Site: www.brandywineconsulting.com (17)

Brannon, Jim, Raycom Sports, Charlotte, NC. Tel: (704) 378-4456/4400, FAX: (704) 378-4465, E-Mail: whicks@raycomsports.com, Web Site: raycomsports.com (16)

Bransfield, M. Declan, Eberle & Associates Inc, McLean, VA. Tel: (703) 821-1550, FAX: (703) 821-0920, E-Mail: info@eberle1.com, Web Site: www.eberleassociates.com (1)

Bransford, Alain, Williams Worldwide Television, Santa Monica, CA. Tel: (310) 449-4506, FAX: (310) 449-4556, E-Mail: curious@williamsworldwidetv.com, Web Site: www. williamsworldwidetv.com (35)

Branstetter, Greg, Hippo Direct, Solon, OH. Tel: (440) 519-0730, FAX: (440) 519-0727, E-Mail: rapidresponse@hippodirect.com, Web Site: www. hippodirect.com (23)

Brant, Sandra, J., Brant Publications Inc, New York, NY. Tel: (212) 941-2800, FAX: (212) 941-2885, Web Site: www.interviewmagazine.com (17)

Brant Publications Inc, New York, NY. Tel: (212) 941-2800, FAX: (212) 941-2885, Web Site: www. interviewmagazine.com (17)

Brantley, Margie, Dan Dipert Travel Service Inc, Arlington, TX. Tel: (817) 543-3700, (800) 433-5335, FAX: (817) 543-3728, Web Site: www.dandipert. com (19)

Bras-Jorge, Muriel, Gems Sensors & Controls, Plainville, CT. Tel: (860) 747-3000, (800) 378-1600, FAX: (860) 747-4244, E-Mail: info@gemssensors. com, Web Site: www.gemssensors.com (9)

Brase, Jerry, Tractor Supply Co, Brentwood, TN. Tel: (615) 366-4600, (877) 872-7721, FAX: (615) 227-4608, Web Site: www.mytscstore.com (5)

Brashe Advertising Inc, Woodbury, NY. Tel: (516) 935-5544, FAX: (516) 931-1722 (35)

Brasher, Robert, P., American Printing House for the Blind, Louisville, KY. Tel: (502) 895-2405, (800) 223-1839, FAX: (502) 899-2274, E-Mail: info@aph.org, Web Site: www.aph.org (7)

Bratnober, Sarah, Popular Front Interactive Communications, Minneapolis, MN. Tel: (612) 362-0900, FAX: (612) 362-0999, E-Mail: guestlist@popularfront.com, Web Site: www.popularfront. com (35)

Brauer, Doug, Response Media, Norcross, GA. Tel: (770) 451-5478, FAX: (770) 451-4929, E-Mail: babion@responsemedia.com, Web Site: www. responsemedia.com (32)

Braun, Axel J., Safe Publications Inc, Southampton, PA. Tel: (215) 357-9049, FAX: (215) 357-5202, E-Mail: sales@safepub.com, Web Site: www. safepub.com (11)

Braun, Chris, Beemak Plastics Inc, La Mirada, CA. Tel: (310) 886-5880, (800) 421-4393, FAX: (310) 764-0330, E-Mail: info@beemak.com, Web Site: www.beemak.com (16)

Braun, Doug, Herbalife International of America Inc, Los Angeles, CA. Tel: (310) 410-9600, (866) 617-4273, FAX: (310) 258-7019, Web Site: www. herbalife.com (7)

Braun, Joel, Harris Infosource International Inc, Independence, OH. Tel: (330) 425-9000, (877) 359-6308, (800) 888-5900, (800) 748-5482, FAX: (800) 643-5997, E-Mail: customerservice@harrisinfo. com, Web Site: www.harrisinfo.com (17)

Braun, S., Tracy, National Pension Service Inc, Burlington, VT. Tel: (802) 862-3994, FAX: (802) 865-2861, E-Mail: retirementservices@people.com, Web Site: www.peoples.com/retirementservices/ (14)

Braune, Brenda, Texas Parks & Wildlife Dept, Austin, TX. Tel: (512) 389-4800, (800) 792-1112, FAX: (512) 389-8029, Web Site: www.tpwd.state.tx.us (1)

Braune, John, The Heritage Co, North Little Rock, AR. Tel: (501) 835-5000 x1142, FAX: (501) 835-5834, Web Site: www.theheritagecompany.com (29)

Braune, Sadie, University of Phoenix, Phoenix, AZ. Tel: (480) 557-1662, Web Site: www.phoenix.edu (13)

Braunert, Debbie, SoundBite Communications, Bedford, MA. Tel: (781) 359-2200, Web Site: www. soundbite.com (32)

Braunstein, Claudia, BellTower Technologies, Greenwood Village, CO. Tel: (303) 843-0302, FAX: (303) 843-0377, Web Site: www.shopathome.com (18)

Braunstein, Marc, Belcaro Group Inc, Greenwood Village, CO. Tel: (303) 843-0302, Web Site: www. shopathome.com (17)

Braunstein, Marc, BellTower Technologies, Greenwood Village, CO. Tel: (303) 843-0302, FAX: (303) 843-0377, Web Site: www.shopathome.com (18)

Braunstein, Marcia, Motion Picture & Television Fund Foundation, Woodland Hills, CA. Tel: (818) 876-1888, Web Site: www.mptvfund.org (1)

Braverman, Andy, Disney Vacation Club, Kissimmee, FL. Tel: (407) 566-3100, (800) 500-3990, FAX: (407) 566-3393 (19)

Breakey, Kelsey, Grow Communications, Coquitlam, BC Canada. Tel: (778) 822-0431, Web Site: www. growcommunications.com (35)

Breakstone, Warren, Thomson Research, Boston, MA. Tel: (617) 856-2000, Web Site: www.thomson.com/solutions/financial (14)

Breard, Jack, H., EBSCO Reception Room Subscription Services, Birmingham, AL. Tel: (205) 991-1409, (800) 527-5901, FAX: (205) 995-1621, Web Site: www.ebsco.com/errss (18)

Breashears, Vicki, National Catholic Reporter Publishing Co Inc, Kansas City, MO. Tel: (816) 531-0538, (800) 444-8910, FAX: (816) 968-2268, Web Site: www.ncronline.org (17)

Breath Appeal, Broadview, IL. Tel: (800) 300-3910, E-Mail: info@breathappeal.com, Web Site: www. breathappeal.com (35)

Breau, Shela, Bear Woods Supply Co Inc, Cornwallis, NS. Tel: (902) 638-8622, (800) 565-5066, FAX: (902) 638-8637, Web Site: www.bearwood.com, www.woodparts.ca (11)

Breazeale, Deborah, Blue Coral Slick 50, Houston, TX. Tel: (713) 241-6161, (800) 416-1600, FAX: (713) 241-4044, E-Mail: SCD-ConsumerSolutions@Shell.com, Web Site: www. bluecoral.com (16)

Brecher, Bernard, Institutional Advancement Programs Inc, Bronxville, NY. Tel: (914) 779-4092, FAX: (914) 961-4202 (1)

Breck's Bulbs, Lawrenceburg, IN. Tel: (309) 693-8600, FAX: (309) 691-9693 (8)

Bredemeier, Gay, Our365, Saint Charles, MO. Tel: (636) 946-5136, Web Site: www.growingfamily. com (37)

Bredenberg, Al, Al Bredenberg Creative Services, Bethel, CT. Tel: (203) 743-1946, E-Mail: ab@copywriter.com, Web Site: www.copywriter.com (39)

Al Bredenberg Creative Services, Bethel, CT. Tel: (203) 743-1946, E-Mail: ab@copywriter.com, Web Site: www.copywriter.com (39)

Breeden, Kenneth, R., Tennessee Valley Authority, Knoxville, TN. Tel: (865) 632-2101, Web Site: www.tva.gov (16)

Breedlove, James, Direct Mail Marketing Inc, Shreveport, LA. Tel: (318) 631-4081, FAX: (318) 621-9150, E-Mail: james_dmm@bizsport.rr.com (21)

Breen, Edward, D., Tyco Valves & Controls, Houston, TX. Tel: (713) 986-4665, (800) 343-0990, FAX: (713) 937-5466, Web Site: www.tycovalves.com (16)

Breen, Peg, New York Landmarks Conservancy, New York, NY. Tel: (212) 995-5260, FAX: (212) 995-5268, Web Site: www.nylandmarks.org (1)

Breeze, Laura, Plan USA, Warwick, RI. Tel: (401) 737-5770, (800) 556-7918, FAX: (401) 738-5608, Web Site: www.planusa.org (1)

Bregel, Larry, Strang Communications Co, Lake Mary, FL. Tel: (407) 333-0600, FAX: (407) 333-7100, E-Mail: magcustsvc@strang.com, Web Site: www. strang.com (1)

Brehm, Sharon, Stevens, American Psychological Association, Washington, DC. Tel: (202) 336-5500, (800) 374-2721, FAX: (202) 336-5568, E-Mail: order@apa.org, Web Site: www.apa.org (1)

Breidenbach, Ashley, Moto Franchise Corp, Dayton, OH. Tel: (937) 291-1900, (800) 733-6686, FAX: (937) 291-2005, E-Mail: expert@motophoto.com, Web Site: www.motophoto.com; www. portraitavenue.com (3)

Breimer, Stephen, F., Bloom, Hergott, Diemer, Rosenthal and Laviolette LLP, Beverly Hills, CA. Tel: (310) 859-6820, FAX: (310) 860-6820, E-Mail: sfb@bhdrl.com (20)

Breisinger, James, R., Kennametal Inc, Latrobe, PA. Tel: (800) 222-9327, FAX: (800) 521-3319, E-Mail: mcs-na.service@kennmetal.com, Web Site: www.kennametal.com (16)

Brekhus, Melvin, G., Texas Industries Inc, Dallas, TX. Tel: (972) 647-6700, FAX: (972) 647-3878, Web Site: www.txi.com (16)

Brekke, Bruce, Heartland America, Chaska, MN. Tel: (952) 361-3640, (800) 229-2901, FAX: (952) 368-3452, E-Mail: info@heartlandamerica.com, Web Site: www.heartlandamerica.com (3)

Brelinski, Donald, E., Grainger Parts, North Brook, IL. Tel: (847) 498-5900, FAX: (847) 498-3402, Web Site: www.grainger.com (16)

Brelsford, Dawn, Barton-Cotton, Baltimore, MD. Tel: (410) 247-4800, (800) 348-1102, FAX: (410) 536-0491, E-Mail: info@bartoncotton.com, Web Site: www.bartoncotton.com (16)

Bremer, Beverly H., Beverly Bremer Silver Shop, Atlanta, GA. Tel: (404) 261-4009, (800) 270-4009, E-Mail: sterlingsilver@worldnet.att.net, Web Site: www.beverlybremer.com (6)

Beverly Bremer Silver Shop, Atlanta, GA. Tel: (404) 261-4009, (800) 270-4009, E-Mail: sterlingsilver@worldnet.att.net, Web Site: www.beverlybremer.com (6)

Bremmer, Joe, Institute of Management & Administration (IOMA), Peterborough, NH. Tel: (800) 401-5937, FAX: (973) 622-0595 (17)

Brengle, George, The Sailing Co, Palm Coast, FL. Tel: (866) 436-2460, FAX: (401) 848-5048, Web Site: www.sailingworld.com (17)

Brennan, John, Sykes Acquisition, Newtown, PA. Tel: (800) 799-6880, Web Site: www.ictgroup.com (29)

Brennan, Kelly, McKinsey & Co, New York, NY. Tel: (212) 446-7000, FAX: (212) 446-8575, Web Site: www.mckinsey.com (20)

Brennen, Lynne, Dow Jones & Co, Princeton, NJ. Tel: (609) 520-4000, FAX: (212) 416-4348, Web Site: www.dowjones.com/corp/index.html (17)

Brennen, Steve, Journal of Commerce Group, Newark, NJ. Tel: (973) 848-7000, FAX: (973) 848-7004, Web Site: www.joc.com (17)

Brenner, Elizabeth, The News Tribune, Tacoma, WA. Tel: (253) 597-8742, E-Mail: reader.representative@thenewstribune.com, Web Site: www.thenewstribune.com (17)

Brenner, Rick, Prime, Bridgeport, CT. Tel: (203) 331-9100, (800) 873-7746, FAX: (203) 330-0123, Web Site: www.primeline.com (16)

Brenner, Stuart, SKO-Brenner-American, Baldwin, NY. Tel: (516) 771-4400, (800) 645-3390, FAX: (516) 771-7810, E-Mail: collect@skobrenner.com, Web Site: www.skobrenner.com (20)

Brentwood Benson Music Publishing, Franklin, TN. Tel: (615) 261-3400, (800) 846-7664, FAX: (615) 261-3381, E-Mail: choral@brentwoodbensonmusic.com, Web Site: www.brentwoodbenson.com (17)

Bresch, Heather, UDL Laboratories Inc, Sugar Land, TX. Tel: (281) 240-1000, (800) 231-3052, FAX: (281) 240-0002, Web Site: www.udllabs.com (7)

Breslawski, James, P., Henry Schein Inc, Melville, NY. Tel: (631) 843-5500, (800) 472-4346, FAX: (631) 843-5658, E-Mail: custserv@henryschein.com, Web Site: www.henryschein.com (16)

Breslin, Jack, G.A. Wright Direct Marketing, Denver, CO. Tel: (303) 333-4453, FAX: (303) 333-4660, E-Mail: gaming@gawright.com, Web Site: www.gawrightcasinomarketing.com (21)

Bresloff, Charles W., Recognition Products International, Easton, MD. Tel: (410) 820-0022, (800) 292-7354, FAX: (410) 820-5044, E-Mail: info@recognitionproducts.com, Web Site: www.shoprecognitionproducts.com (16)

Bretl, Jeff, Stephan Partners Inc, New York, NY. Tel: (212) 524-8583, E-Mail: george@stephenpartners.com, Web Site: www.stephanpartners.com (35)

Brett, James, Prudential Financial, Newark, NJ. Tel: (973) 802-2195, Web Site: www.prudential.com (14)

Bretta, Shawn, Da Vinci Technologies LLC, Auburn, AL. Tel: (334) 502-8925, (877) 334-4731, FAX: (208) 485-7749, E-Mail: sales@davinci.aero, Web Site: www.davincitechnologies.com (3)

Bretz, Darcy, The Middleby Corp, Elgin, IL. Tel: (847) 741-3300, FAX: (847) 741-0015, E-Mail: sales@middleby.com, Web Site: www.middleby.com (16)

Breukink, Henk, ING, Minneapolis, MN. Tel: (612) 342-7061, (800) 333-6965, FAX: (612) 372-5339, Web Site: www.ing.com (15)

Brevik, Leonard, National Association of Professional Insurance Agents, Alexandria, VA. Tel: (703) 836-9340, FAX: (703) 836-1279, E-Mail: web@pianet.org, Web Site: www.pianet.com (1)

Brewer, Flora, Rhythm Band Inc, Fort Worth, TX. Tel: (817) 335-2561, (800) 424-4724, FAX: (800) 784-9401, E-Mail: sales@rhythmband.com, Web Site: www.rhythmband.com (11)

Brewer, Hamish, JDA Software Group Inc, Scottsdale, AZ. Tel: (480) 308-3000, (800) 479-7382, FAX: (480) 308-3001, Web Site: www.jda.com (22)

Brewer, Janet, NCR Corp, Duluth, GA. Tel: (937) 445-1936, (800) CALL-NCR, FAX: (937) 445-1682, Web Site: www.ncr.com (16)

Brewster, James, Newport News, New York, NY. Tel: (800) 759-3950, Web Site: www.newport-news.com (2)

Brick, Monte, Monte Brick, Wordsmith, Melville, NY. Tel: (631) 549-9640, FAX: (631) 549-9640 (39)

Monte Brick, Wordsmith, Melville, NY. Tel: (631) 549-9640, FAX: (631) 549-9640 (39)

Brickell, Keith, Valpak Direct Marketing Systems Inc, Largo, FL. Tel: (727) 399-3000, Web Site: www.valpak.com (31)

Bricker, Laurence, Popular Front Interactive Communications, Minneapolis, MN. Tel: (612) 362-0900, FAX: (612) 362-0999, E-Mail: guestlist@popularfront.com, Web Site: www.popularfront.com (35)

Bricker, Mindy, Kay, Bulletin of the Atomic Scientists, Chicago, IL. Tel: (773) 702-6301, FAX: (773) 980-6932, E-Mail: admin@thebulletin.org, Web Site: www.thebulletin.org (17)

Brickman, Christian, A., Kimberly-Clark Corp, Neenah, WI. Tel: (920) 721-2000, (888) 525-8388, FAX: (920) 721-7722, Web Site: www.kimberly-clark.com (16)

Bridge, Ross, Stock Yards Packing Co Inc, Chicago, IL. Tel: (312) 733-6050, (877) STK-YARD, FAX: (312) 733-1746, E-Mail: customerservice@stockyards.com, Web Site: www.stockyards.com (4)

Bridge City Tool Works Inc, Portland, OR. Tel: (503) 282-6997, (800) 253-3332, FAX: (503) 287-1085, E-Mail: jjeconomaki@comcast.net, Web Site: www.bridgecitytools.com (3)

Bridges, Kevin, Callaway Gardens, Pine Mountain, GA. Tel: (706) 663-2281, (800) CALLAWAY, FAX: (706) 663-6812, E-Mail: info@callawaygardens.com, Web Site: www.callawaygardens.com (19)

Bridgestone/Firestone North American Tire LLC, Nashville, TN. Tel: (615) 937-1000, (800) 543-7522, FAX: (615) 937-3721, Web Site: www.bridgestonetire.com (16)

Bridgewell Associates, Alexandria, VA. Tel: (703) 360-6500 (29)

Bridson, Linda, Key Marketing Advantage LLC, Bethel, CT. Tel: (203) 744-9011, Web Site: www.keymarketingadvantage.com (23)

Briefings Publishing Group, Richmond, VA. Tel: (703) 567-1982, (800) 791-8699, FAX: (703) 684-2136, E-Mail: rmalvaso@douglaspublications.com, Web Site: www.briefings.com (17)

Brien, Nick, McCann Relationship Mktg, New York, NY. Tel: (646) 865-6000, FAX: (646) 487-9610, Web Site: www.mrmworldwide.com (35)

Brierley, Harold, M., Brierley & Partners, Plano, TX. Tel: (214) 760-8700, FAX: (214) 743-5511, E-Mail: bpayton@brierley.com, Web Site: www.brierley.com (35)

Brierley & Partners, Plano, TX. Tel: (214) 760-8700, FAX: (214) 743-5511, E-Mail: bpayton@brierley.com, Web Site: www.brierley.com (35)

Brigade Quartermasters Ltd, Providence, RI. Tel: (770) 428-1248, (800) 338-4327, FAX: (800) 892-2992, Web Site: www.actiongear.com (11)

Brigar Xpress Solutions, Inc, Albany, NY. Tel: (518) 438-7817, (877) 437-7817, FAX: (518) 438-0224, E-Mail: general@brigarxpress.com, Web Site: www.brigarxpress.com (28)

Briggs, Anna, C., National Humane Education Society, Charles Town, WV. Tel: (304) 725-0506, FAX: (304) 725-1523, E-Mail: nhesinformation@nhes.org, Web Site: www.nhes.org (1)

Briggs, Bill, The Source Stock Footage Library Inc, Tucson, AZ. Tel: (520) 298-4810, FAX: (520) 290-8831, E-Mail: requests@sourcefootage.com, Web Site: www.sourcefootage.com (38)

Briggs, David, Datum Timing, Test & Measurement, Beverly, MA. Tel: (978) 927-8220, FAX: (978) 927-4099, E-Mail: wriley@datum.com, Web Site: www.datum.com (9)

Briggs, Douglas, QVC Inc, West Chester, PA. Tel: (484) 701-1000, FAX: (484) 701-8500, Web Site: www.qvc.com (32)

Briggs, Krintin, Fire Light Group, White Plains, NY. Tel: (608) 441-3473, E-Mail: mincentive@aol.com, Web Site: www.incentivesmotivate.com (33)

Briggs, Maudie, Morrison Printing Co, Morristown, TN. Tel: (423) 586-4812, (800) 251-0975, FAX: (423) 586-0322, E-Mail: info@morrcom.com, Web Site: www.morrcom.com (27)

Briggs, Mike, Midwest Lists & Media, Niles, IL. Tel: (847) 966-2770, FAX: (847) 966-8630, Web Site: www.thebradfordgroup.com (23)

Briggs, Robert, The Pillsbury Co, Minneapolis, MN. Tel: (763) 764-7600, (800) 775-4777, FAX: (763) 764-8330, Web Site: www.pillsbury.com (16)

Brigham, Steven, P., Brookstone Co, Merrimack, NH. Tel: (603) 880-9500, (800) 846-3000, FAX: (603) 577-8005, E-Mail: customerservice@brookstone.com, Web Site: www.brookstone.com (3)

Bright Jr., James, J., Bristol Associates Inc, Los Angeles, CA. Tel: (310) 670-0525, FAX: (310) 670-4075, E-Mail: lfarber@bristolassoc.com, Web Site: www.bristolassoc.com (20)

Bright, Stacey, Fleet One LLC, Antioch, TN. Tel: (615) 523-6465, Web Site: www.fleetone.com (14)

Bright, Thomas R., Hitchcock Shoes Inc, Hingham, MA. Tel: (781) 749-3260, (888) 599-9433, FAX: (781) 749-3576, E-Mail: hitchcock@wideshoes.com, Web Site: www.wideshoes.com (16)

Brill, Dorothy, Synapse Group Inc, Stamford, CT. Tel: (203) 595-8255, FAX: (203) 329-8237, E-Mail: webmaster@synapsemail.com, Web Site: www.synapsegroupinc.com (18)

Brill, L, Chip, Peter Glenn Publications, Delray Beach, FL. Tel: (561) 404-4290, (888) 332-6700, FAX: (561) 892-5786, E-Mail: gregjames@pgdirect.com, Web Site: www.pgdirect.com (17)

Brilliant, Samuel, P., Hollister Inc, Libertyville, IL. Tel: (847) 680-1000, (888) 740-8999, FAX: (847) 680-2123, Web Site: www.hollister.com (16)

Brim, Alea, TransFirst Holdings Inc, Dallas, TX. Tel: (214) 453-7700, (888) 254-4137, FAX: (214) 453-7739, Web Site: www.transfirst.com (14)

Brim Electronics Inc, Lodi, NJ. Tel: (201) 796-2886, FAX: (973) 778-2792, E-Mail: info@brimelectronics.com, Web Site: www.brimelectronics.com (3)

Bringard, Mikkle, MindFireInc, Irvine, CA. Tel: (949) 474-4418w, Web Site: www.mindfireinc.com (22)

Bringham Jr., William, T., WTB Associates Inc, Wilmette, IL. Tel: (847) 251-4188 (20)

Bringham Sr., William, T., WTB Associates Inc, Wilmette, IL. Tel: (847) 251-4188 (20)

Brinker, Debbie, American Association of Critical-Care Nurses, Aliso Viejo, CA. Tel: (949) 362-2000, (800) 809-CARE, FAX: (949) 362-2020, E-Mail: info@aacn.com, Web Site: www.aacn.org (1)

Brinkerhoff, Peter, Polestar Group, West Simsbury, CT. Tel: (860) 658-4992 (20)

Brinkley, Amy, Woods, Bank of America, Charlotte, NC. Tel: (704) 386-5681, (800) 841-4000, FAX: (704) 386-6699, Web Site: www.bankofamerica.com (14)

Brinkley, Cary, Allianz Life Insurance Co of North America, Minneapolis, MN. Tel: (763) 765-6500, (800) 950-5872, Web Site: www.allianzlife.com (15)

Brinley, Steve, LIST Inc, Danbury, CT. Tel: (914) 765-0700, FAX: (914) 765-0046, E-Mail: info@l-i-s-t.com, Web Site: www.l-i-s-t.com (24)

Briones, Andrew, Interface Engineering, Portland, OR. Tel: (503) 382-2266, FAX: (503) 382-2262, E-Mail: solutions@interfaceengineering.com, Web Site: www.ieice.com (3)

Briscoe, Catie, Crabtree & Evelyn Ltd, Woodstock, CT. Tel: (860) 928-2761, (800) CRABTREE, FAX: (860) 928-0452, Web Site: www.crabtree-evelyn.com (4)

Briskin, Dennis, Catalyst Creative Services, Palo Alto, CA. Tel: (650) 325-1500, E-Mail: chief@catalystcreative.us, Web Site: www.catalystcreative.us (39)

Bristol Associates Inc, Los Angeles, CA. Tel: (310) 670-0525, FAX: (310) 670-4075, E-Mail: lfarber@bristolassoc.com, Web Site: www.bristolassoc.com (20)

Bristol-Myers Squibb Co, New York, NY. Tel: (212) 546-4000, FAX: (212) 546-9544, Web Site: www.bms.com (16)

British Columbia Automobile Association, Burnaby, BC Canada. Tel: (604) 268-5000, (800) 564-6222, FAX: (604) 268-5585, Web Site: www.bcaa.com (15)

Britton, Peter, The Write Answers Copywriting & Consulting, Blaine, WA. Tel: (888) 331-0322, Web Site: www.thewriteanswers.com (20)

Broadbent, Dave, Bushnell Outdoor Products, Overland Park, KS. Tel: (913) 752-3400, (800) 423-3537, FAX: (913) 752-3550, Web Site: www.bushnell.com (16)

Broadcast Electronics Inc, Quincy, IL. Tel: (217) 224-9600, FAX: (217) 224-9607, E-Mail: bdcast@bdcast.com, Web Site: www.bdcast.com (3)

Broadcast Media Associates, Santa Maria, CA. Tel: (805) 937-1553, E-Mail: cliffhunter@cliffhunter.com, Web Site: www.broadcastmediabroker.com (30)

Broadford & Maloney Inc, New York, NY. Tel: (212) 836-4710, FAX: (917) 322-2105, E-Mail: m.maloney@bmcorp.com, Web Site: bmcorp.com (35)

Broadhead, Robert, Elizabeth Arden Spas LLC, Stamford, CT. Tel: (203) 905-1700, FAX: (203) 905-1716, Web Site: www.reddoorspas.com (19)

Broadhead, Tim, Accountants' Supply House, Lancaster, CA. Tel: (856) 384-1144, (800) 342-5274, FAX: (800) 468-4446, Web Site: www.rapidforms.com (10)

Broadhead, Tim, Histacount & Expressions, Lancaster, CA. Tel: (800) 645-5220, FAX: (800) 332-5502, E-Mail: service@rapidforms.com, Web Site: rapidforms.com (10)

Broadhead, Tim, McBee, Lancaster, CA. Tel: (973) 263-3225, (800) 878-9443, (800) 662-2331, FAX: (973) 263-8165, E-Mail: info@mcbeeinc.com, Web Site: www.mcbeeweb.com (10)

Broadhead, Tim, Safeguard Business Systems Inc, Dallas, TX. Tel: (214) 905-3935, (800) 523-2422, FAX: (800) 439-8423, Web Site: www.gosafeguard.com (16)

Broadmoor Hotel Inc, Colorado Springs, CO. Tel: (719) 634-7711, (866) 837-9520, FAX: (719) 577-5779, Web Site: www.broadmoor.com (19)

Broadus, Robert, Broadus Advertising/Public Relations, Saint Simons Island, GA. Tel: (912) 638-0897, FAX: (912) 638-0958, E-Mail: jenniferbroadus@broadus.com, Web Site: www.broadus.com (35)

Broadus Advertising/Public Relations, Saint Simons Island, GA. Tel: (912) 638-0897, FAX: (912) 638-0958, E-Mail: jenniferbroadus@broadus.com, Web Site: www.broadus.com (35)

BroadVision Inc, Redwood City, CA. Tel: (650) 542-5100, FAX: (650) 364-3425, E-Mail: sales@broadvision.com, Web Site: www.broadvision.com (16)

Broadway Books, New York, NY. Tel: (212) 782-9644, FAX: (212) 782-8338, E-Mail: bwaypub@randomhouse.com, Web Site: www.randomhouse.com/broadway (17)

Broadway Play Publishing Inc, New York, NY. Tel: (212) 772-8334, FAX: (212) 772-8358, E-Mail: sara@broadwayplaypubl.com, Web Site: www.broadwayplaypubl.com (17)

Brobhy, Mike, International Auto Parts, Charlottesville, VA. Tel: (804) 974-7118, (800) 726-0555, FAX: (804) 973-2368, E-Mail: iap1@international-auto.com, Web Site: www.international-auto.com (12)

Brocade Communications Systems Inc, San Jose, CA. Tel: (408) 333-4300, FAX: (408) 333-8101, Web Site: www.brocade.com (16)

Brochu, Yvan, Montreal Envelope Inc, Montreal, PQ Canada. Tel: (514) 331-7110, (800) 655-2709, FAX: (514) 748-7322, E-Mail: ybrochu@enveloppe-montreal.com, Web Site: www.enveloppe-montreal.com (26)

Brock Jr, Luther, A., Luther Brock PhD, The Letter Doctor, Denton, TX. Tel: (940) 387-8058 (39)

Luther Brock PhD, The Letter Doctor, Denton, TX. Tel: (940) 387-8058 (39)

Brockett, Susan, P., Key Bank, Cleveland, OH. Tel: (216) 689-3000, (888) 539-2968, FAX: (207) 874-7044, Web Site: www.key.com (14)

Brockman, Robert, Reynolds & Reynolds Co, Houston, TX. Tel: (713) 718-1800, (800) 231-6347, FAX: (713) 718-1471, Web Site: www.reyrey.com (22)

Brockner, Tobe, Intelesure LLC, Meridian, ID. Tel: (866) 808-7366, Web Site: www.intelesure.com (29)

Phil Brodatz, Coral Gables, FL. Tel: (305) 661-5771 (37)

Broderick, Jane, Royal Bank of Canada, Toronto, ON Canada. Tel: (416) 974-5151, FAX: (416) 974-0365, Web Site: www.royalbank.com (14)

Broderick, Tom, Internet Direct Response, Inc, Fort Worth, TX. Tel: (817) 562-1506, E-Mail: operations@4idr.com, Web Site: www.4dr.com (35)

Brodeur, Alan, Direct Marketing Association of Toronto, Toronto, ON Canada. Tel: (905) 564-6616, FAX: (905) 564-6621, E-Mail: pete@themose.ca, Web Site: www.dmatoronto.org (40)

Brody, Megan, UGL Equis Corp, Chicago, IL. Tel: (312) 424-8000, FAX: (312) 424-8080, Web Site: www.equiscorp.com (16)

Broering, James, A., AcuSport Corp, Bellefontaine, OH. Tel: (937) 593-7010, FAX: (937) 592-5625, E-Mail: mwsales@acusport.com, Web Site: www.acusport.com (11)

Brogan, John, Catalyst, Rochester, NY. Tel: (585) 453-8300, (800) 836-7720, FAX: (585) 453-8360, E-Mail: info@catalystinc.com, Web Site: www.catalystinc.com (35)

Brogan, John, Global IntelliSystems, Evergreen, CO. Tel: (800) 707-7074, Web Site: www.gliq.com (22)

Brogan, Kevin, Wells Fargo, San Francisco, CA. Tel: (866) 878-5865, (800) 869-3557, FAX: (626) 312-3015, Web Site: www.wellsfargo.com (14)

Brogan, Timothy, Pharmaceutical Care Management Association, Washington, DC. Tel: (202) 207-3610, FAX: (202) 207-3623, E-Mail: info@pcmanet.org, Web Site: www.pcmanet.org (1)

Broido, Thomas, Theodore Presser Co, King Of Prussia, PA. Tel: (610) 592-1222, FAX: (610) 592-1229, E-Mail: webmaster@presser.com, Web Site: www.presser.com (17)

Brokers/Consultants Inc, Flossmoor, IL. Tel: (708) 957-2900, FAX: (708) 957-4155 (15)

Brokers International Ltd, Panora, IA. Tel: (641) 755-2775 (20)

Brokers Worldwide LLC, Folcroft, PA. Tel: (610) 461-3661, (800) MAIL-287, FAX: (610) 461-4239, E-Mail: csmith@brokersworldwide.com, Web Site: www.brokersworldwide.com (28)

Bromberg, Howard, The Flexi Group Inc, Bronx, NY. Tel: (718) 543-8699, (800) 665-8053, FAX: (718) 543-8609, E-Mail: info@flexigroup.com, Web Site: www.flexigroup.com (27)

Bromley, Ann, The Popcorn Factory, Lake Forest, IL. Tel: (847) 362-0028, (888) 216-0235, FAX: (888) 333-4595, E-Mail: service@thepopcornfactory.com, Web Site: www.thepopcornfactory.com (4)

Bromley, Ernest, Bromley Communications, San Antonio, TX. Tel: (210) 244-2000, Web Site: www.bromleyville.com (35)

Bromley, Marilyn, The Bureau of National Affairs, Inc, Arlington, VA. Tel: (703) 341-3000, (800) 372-1033, FAX: (703) 341-1688, E-Mail: mbromley@bna.com, Web Site: www.bna.com (17)

Bromley, Stan, Four Seasons Hotels & Resorts, Toronto, ON. Tel: (416) 449-1750, (800) 819-5053, FAX: (416) 441-4374, Web Site: www.fourseasons.com (19)

Bromley Communications, San Antonio, TX. Tel: (210) 244-2000, Web Site: www.bromleyville.com (35)

Brommers, Craig, Warnaco Swimwear Inc, Los Angeles, CA. Tel: (323) 726-1262, FAX: (323) 724-6931, Web Site: www.speedo.com (16)

Bronner, Wayne, Bronner's Christmas Wonderland, Frankenmuth, MI. Tel: (989) 652-9931, Web Site: www.bronners.com (6)

Bronner's Christmas Wonderland, Frankenmuth, MI. Tel: (989) 652-9931, Web Site: www.bronners.com (6)

Bronson Nutritionals LLC, Hauppauge, NY. Tel: (631) 750-0000, Web Site: www.bronsonnutritionals.com (7)

Bronstein, Philip, San Francisco Chronicle, San Francisco, CA. Tel: (415) 777-1111, FAX: (415) 536-5178, E-Mail: amatthews@sfchronicle.com, Web Site: www.sfgate.com (17)

Bronx Council on the Arts, Bronx, NY. Tel: (718) 931-9500, FAX: (718) 409-6445, E-Mail: info@bronxarts.org, Web Site: www.bronxarts.org (1)

Brook, Dan, Golden Trophy, Chicago, IL. Tel: (800) 835-6607, FAX: (800) 835-6601, E-Mail: goldentrophy@bruss.com, Web Site: www.giftsteaksonline.com (4)

Brook, Yaron, Second Renaissance Books, Irvine, CA. Tel: (860) 354-5448, (800) 729-6149, FAX: (860) 355-7161, Web Site: www.aynrandbookstore.com (17)

Brook, Yaron, The Ayn Rand Institute, Irvine, CA. Tel: (949) 222-6550, FAX: (949) 222-6558, E-Mail: mail@aynrand.org, Web Site: www.aynrand.org (1)

Brooke, Linda, H., National Audubon Society, New York, NY. Tel: (212) 979-3000, FAX: (212) 979-3188, Web Site: www.audubon.org (17)

Brooke Distributors Inc, Miami, FL. Tel: (305) 624-9752, (800) 275-8792, FAX: (305) 620-3988, E-Mail: sales@brookedms.com, Web Site: www.brooke.com (3)

Brooker, Brian, Barkley, Kansas City, MO. Tel: (816) 842-1500, Web Site: www.barkleyUS.com (35)

Brookfield Properties, Toronto, ON Canada. Tel: (416) 369-2300, FAX: (416) 369-2301, Web Site: www. brokfieldproperties.com (16)

Brookfield Zoo, Brookfield, IL. Tel: (708) 485-0263, (800) 201-0784, FAX: (708) 485-3532, Web Site: www.brookfieldzoo.org (1)

Brookhollow Cards, Rexburg, ID. Tel: (800) 822-0256, FAX: (800) 443-8847, E-Mail: service@brookhollowcards.com, Web Site: www. brookhollowcards.com (10)

Brookhurst, Bruce, Atlanta Cutlery Corp, Conyers, GA. Tel: (770) 922-3700, (800) 833-8838, FAX: (770) 760-8993, E-Mail: webmaster@atlantacutlery.com, Web Site: www.atlantacutlery.com (11)

Brooks, Erin, The Connection Contact Center Services, Burnsville, MN. Tel: (952) 948-5335, (800) 883-5777, FAX: (952) 948-5498, E-Mail: sales@the-connection.com, Web Site: www.the-connection.com (29)

Brooks, John, Black Olive Co, Chicago, IL. Tel: (312) 893-5454, FAX: (312) 276-8636, E-Mail: pittenger@blackoliveco.com, Web Site: www. blackoliveco.com (35)

Brooks, John, Western Fulfillment Management Association Inc, North Hollywood, CA. Tel: (310) 323-7220, FAX: (310) 323-7231, E-Mail: mjordan@espcomp.com, Web Site: www.wfma.org (40)

Brooks, Jonathan, Triax Data, Knoxville, TN. Tel: (865) 971-4333, Web Site: www.triaxdata.com (23)

Brooks, Lane, Food & Water Watch, Washington, DC. Tel: (202) 683-2500, Web Site: www. foodandwaterwatch.org (1)

Brooks, Mandy T., Kennesaw State University, Kennesaw, GA. Tel: (770) 423-6060, FAX: (770) 499-3261, Web Site: www.kennesaw.edu (41)

Brooks, Paul, Cole Information Services, Omaha, NE. Tel: (800) 403-5894, Web Site: www. coleinformation.com (23)

Brooks, Rod, PEMCO Insurance Cos, Seattle, WA. Tel: (206) 628-4000, (800) 467-3626, FAX: (206) 628-5886, Web Site: www.pemco.com (15)

Brooks, Ronald, E., The American Legion National Headquarters, Indianapolis, IN. Tel: (317) 630-1247, FAX: (317) 630-1369, E-Mail: acy@legion.org, Web Site: www.legion.org (1)

Brooks, Steve, Eastern Mountain Sports, Peterborough, NH. Tel: (603) 924-9571, (800) 463-6367, FAX: (603) 924-4320, Web Site: www.ems.com (16)

Brooks, Susian, Darden School Foundation Executive Foundation, Charlottesville, VA. Tel: (434) 924-3904, Web Site: www.darden.virginia.edu/execed (1)

Brooks Brothers, New York, NY. Tel: (212) 682-8800, (800) 274-1815, FAX: (212) 309-7273, Web Site: www.brooksbrothers.com (2)

Brooks Equipment Co, Charlotte, NC. Tel: (704) 596-9438, (800) 826-3473, FAX: (704) 596-1096, Web Site: www.brooksequipment.com (9)

Brooks Sports Inc, Bothell, WA. Tel: (425) 402-1632, (800) 2 BROOKS, FAX: (425) 489-1975, Web Site: www.brooksrunning.com (16)

Brookshire, Edward, CorporateRewards.com LLC, New York, NY. Tel: (212) 689-1200, Web Site: www.corporaterewards.com (35)

Brookstein, Barry, Call Compliance Inc, Glen Cove, NY. Tel: (516) 674-4545, FAX: (516) 676-2420, E-Mail: sales@callcompliance.com, Web Site: www.callcompliance.com (29)

Brookstone Co, Merrimack, NH. Tel: (603) 880-9500, (800) 846-3000, FAX: (603) 577-8005, E-Mail: customerservice@brookstone.com, Web Site: www. brookstone.com (3)

Brophy, Laura, American Appraisal Associates, Milwaukee, WI. Tel: (414) 271-7240, (800) 558-8650, FAX: (414) 225-1271, Web Site: www.american-appraisal.com (14)

Broska, Jason, CustomerLink, Duluth, MN. Tel: (218) 722-2800, (866) 245-5569, FAX: (218) 722-3287, E-Mail: info@customerlinkone.com, Web Site: www.customerlinkone.com (29)

Brosnahan, Earl, Publications International Ltd, Lincolnwood, IL. Tel: (847) 745-9299, (800) 595-8484, FAX: (847) 676-3671, Web Site: www. pubint.com (17)

Brostoff, Michael, Strategic Data Intelligence LLC, Northbrook, IL. Tel: (847) 897-5706, FAX: (847) 897-5715, E-Mail: inquiry@sdintelligence.com, Web Site: www.sdintelligence.com (22)

Brotherhood America's Oldest Winery Ltd, Washingtonville, NY. Tel: (845) 496-3661, FAX: (845) 496-8720, E-Mail: contact@brotherhoodwinery.net, Web Site: www.brotherhoodwinery.net (19)

Brothers, Alan, W., Brothers & Thompson PC, Chicago, IL. Tel: (312) 372-2909, FAX: (312) 704-6693, E-Mail: hthompson@brothersthompson.net, Web Site: www.brothersthompson.net (20)

Brothers, Ellen L., Mattel Inc, El Segundo, CA. Tel: (310) 252-2000, FAX: (310) 252-2180, Web Site: www.mattel.com (16)

Brothers, Ellen, American Girl Brands LLC, Middleton, WI. Tel: (608) 836-4848, Web Site: www. americangirl.com (6)

Brothers, Ellen, Pleasant Company, Middleton, WI. Tel: (608) 836-4848, (800) 845-0005, FAX: (608) 836-1999, Web Site: www.americangirl.com (11)

Brothers & Thompson PC, Chicago, IL. Tel: (312) 372-2909, FAX: (312) 704-6693, E-Mail: hthompson@brothersthompson.net, Web Site: www.brothersthompson.net (20)

Brotherson, Gaylen M., Mechanical Breakdown Administrators Inc, Scottsdale, AZ. Tel: (480) 860-2288, FAX: (480) 860-0425, E-Mail: gaylenb@mbadirect.com, Web Site: www.mbadirect.com (14)

Brougham, Lisa, Home Decorators Collection Inc, Hazelwood, MO. Tel: (314) 993-1516, FAX: (314) 521-5780, Web Site: www. homedecoratorscollection.com (8)

Brougher, Heather, Jenny Products Inc, Somerset, PA. Tel: (814) 445-3400, FAX: (814) 445-2280, Web Site: www.jennyproducts.com (16)

Brower, Alison, Redbook Magazine, New York, NY. Tel: (212) 649-2000, (800) 888-0008, FAX: (212) 581-7605, Web Site: www.redbookmag.com (17)

Brown II, Owsley, Brown-Forman Corp, Louisville, KY. Tel: (502) 585-1100, FAX: (502) 774-7876, E-Mail: brown-forman@b-f.com, Web Site: www. brown-forman.com (16)

Brown Jr., Harold, C., Golden Gate Transportation District, San Rafael, CA. Tel: (415) 921-5858, FAX: (415) 923-2014, Web Site: www.goldengate. org (16)

Brown, Abe, J&R Music/J&R Computer World, New York, NY. Tel: (212) 238-9000, (800) 806-1115, FAX: (212) 238-9191, Web Site: www.jandr.com (3)

Brown, Alex, Printmark, East Montpelier, VT. Tel: (802) 229-9743, FAX: (802) 229-9746, E-Mail: alex@printmark.net, Web Site: www.printmark.net (20)

Brown, B. Warren, Arthur Brown & Bro Inc, New York, NY. Tel: (212) 575-5555, (800) 772-PENS, FAX: (212) 575-5825, E-Mail: penshop@artbrown. com, Web Site: www.artbrown.com (10)

Brown, B., Brim Electronics Inc, Lodi, NJ. Tel: (201) 796-2886, FAX: (973) 778-2792, E-Mail: info@brimelectronics.com, Web Site: www. brimelectronics.com (3)

Brown, Barbara, Brown & Co, Blaine, WA. Tel: (360) 371-2489 (8)

Brown, Bart, R., Gateway Inc, Irvine, CA. Tel: (949) 471-7000, (800) 369-1409, FAX: (949) 471-7041, Web Site: www.gateway.com (3)

Brown, Bob, Las Vegas Review Journal, Las Vegas, NV. Tel: (702) 383-0211, FAX: (702) 383-4646, Web Site: www.lvrj.com (17)

Brown, Brother Anselm, Abbey of Gethsemani, New Haven, KY. Tel: (502) 549-3117, FAX: (502) 549-4124, Web Site: www.monks.org (1)

Brown, Chris, C&T Bridge Supplies, Los Alamitos, CA. Tel: (562) 598-7010, (800) 525-4718, FAX: (562) 430-8309, E-Mail: tedinlosal@aol.com (11)

Brown, Chris, National Association Broadcasters Annual Conference & Expo, Washington, DC. Tel: (202) 429-5300, (800) 622-3976, FAX: (202) 429-4199, E-Mail: nab@nab.org, Web Site: www.nab. org (42)

Brown, Craig, J., Standard Register, Dayton, OH. Tel: (937) 221-1000, (800) 755-6405, FAX: (937) 221-1239, E-Mail: julie.mcewan@standardregister.com, Web Site: www.standardregister.com (10)

Brown, David, Astral Brands LLC, Smyrna, GA. Tel: (678) 303-3088, Web Site: www.astralbrands.com (7)

Brown, Deena, E., Goodman Media Group Inc, New York, NY. Tel: (212) 262-2247, FAX: (212) 262-2278, E-Mail: jgoodman@gmgpub.com, Web Site: www.goodmanmediagroup.dev.hotresponse.com (17)

Brown, Dennis, World Kitchen Inc, Corning, NY. Tel: (607) 377-8000, (800) 999-3436, FAX: (607) 377-8946, Web Site: www.worldkitchen.com (16)

Brown, Doug, All Star Directories, Seattle, WA. Tel: (888) 404-8043, FAX: (707) 667-1524, Web Site: www.allstardirectories.com (1)

Brown, Doug, Life Works Inc, Hollywood, FL. Tel: (954) 929-8428, (888) 780-9400, FAX: (954) 925-3365, Web Site: www.healthwagon.com (20)

Brown, Douglas, Calbiochem-Novabiochem Corp, San Diego, CA. Tel: (858) 450-9600, (800) 854-3417, FAX: (858) 453-3552, E-Mail: customerservice@emdbioscience.com, Web Site: www.calbiochem. com (9)

Brown, Ed, Brown & Co, Blaine, WA. Tel: (360) 371-2489 (8)

Brown, Edward, Graham, Millipore Corp, Bedford, MA. Tel: (781) 533-6000, FAX: (781) 533-3110, Web Site: www.millipore.com (9)

Brown, Eric, Electronic Arts Inc, Redwood City, CA. Tel: (650) 628-1500, Web Site: www.ea.com (3)

Brown, Gary, Bankers Life & Casualty Co, Chicago, IL. Tel: (312) 396-6000, (800) 231-9150, Web Site: www.bankerslife.com (15)

Brown, Gene, University of Missouri/Kansas City, Kansas City, MO. Tel: (816) 235-2215, FAX: (816) 235-2312, Web Site: www.umkc.edu (41)

Brown, Greg, Brown's Omaha Plant Farms, Omaha, TX. Tel: (903) 884-2421, FAX: (903) 884-2423, E-Mail: mail@bopf.com, Web Site: www.bopf.com (8)

Brown, Gregory, Q., Motorola Inc, Montvale, NJ. Tel: (201) 949-5500, (800) 262-8509, Web Site: www. motorola.com (16)

Brown, J., Powell, Arthur Brown & Bro Inc, New York, NY. Tel: (212) 575-5555, (800) 772-PENS, FAX: (212) 575-5825, E-Mail: penshop@artbrown. com, Web Site: www.artbrown.com (10)

Brown, Janet, No Load Fund*X, San Francisco, CA. Tel: (415) 986-7979, (800) 763-8639, FAX: (415) 986-1595, Web Site: www.noloadfundx.com (14)

Brown, Jay, Greater Fort Worth Builders Association, Fort Worth, TX. Tel: (817) 284-3566, FAX: (817) 284-6465, E-Mail: info@fortworthbuilders.org, Web Site: www.forthworthbuilders.org (1)

Brown, Jeffrey, National Emblem Sales, Indianapolis, IN. Tel: (317) 630-1247, (888) 453-4466, FAX: (317) 630-1381, E-Mail: emblem@legion.org, Web Site: www.emblem.legion.org (16)

Brown, Jeffrey, The American Legion National Headquarters, Indianapolis, IN. Tel: (317) 630-1247, FAX: (317) 630-1369, E-Mail: acy@legion.org, Web Site: www.legion.org (1)

Brown, Jerry, Duggan & Brown Inc, Abington, PA. Tel: (215) 657-3400, FAX: (215) 657-6119, E-Mail: john@dugganandbrown.com (16)

Brown, Jerry, J., Duggan & Brown Inc, Barrington, IL. Tel: (847) 381-8484, FAX: (847) 381-8499 (20)

Brown, Jim, National Envelope-Midwest, Lenexa, KS. Tel: (913) 888-3282, FAX: (913) 888-8743, E-Mail: sales@natenv.com, Web Site: www. nationalenvelope.com (26)

Brown, Jody A., CACI International Inc, Arlington, VA. Tel: (703) 841-7800, FAX: (703) 841-7882, Web Site: www.caci.com (22)

Brown, Joe, L&L Management, Pasadena, CA. Tel: (626) 568-0338, FAX: (626) 568-9165 (1)

Brown, John, Fred Pryor Seminars, Mission, KS. Tel: (913) 967-8518, (800) 780-8476, FAX: (913) 967-8849, E-Mail: customerservice@pryor.com, Web Site: www.pryor.com (16)

Brown, John, Seely, Varian Medical Systems, Palo Alto, CA. Tel: (650) 493-4000, FAX: (650) 842-5196, Web Site: www.varian.com (9)

Brown, Joy, CROSSLISTS CROSS & CO INC, Bates City, MO. Tel: (816) 697-3306, FAX: (816) 697-3317, E-Mail: jmbrown@crosscompany.com, Web Site: www.crosscompany.com (23)

Brown, Kelly, Communication Resources Inc, Canton, OH. Tel: (800) 992-2144, FAX: (330) 493-3158, E-Mail: service@comresources.com, Web Site: www.comresources.com (18)

Brown, Kim, Booth Michigan, Grand Rapids, MI. Tel: (616) 222-5824, FAX: (616) 222-5318, Web Site: www.boothnewspapers.com (17)

Brown, Laura, Oxford University Press Inc, New York, NY. Tel: (212) 726-6000, FAX: (212) 726-6455, Web Site: www.oup.com/us/ (17)

Brown, Laura, WW Grainger Inc, Lake Forest, IL. Tel: (847) 535-1000, (888) 361-8649, FAX: (847) 535-9122, Web Site: www.grainger.com (9)

Brown, Laurie, Farrar Straus & Giroux Inc, New York, NY. Tel: (212) 741-6900, (800) 330-8477, FAX: (212) 633-2427, E-Mail: childrens_editorial@fsgbooks.com, Web Site: www.fsgbooks.com (17)

Brown, Malcolm, Backe Digital Brand Marketing, Radnor, PA. Tel: (610) 947-6901, E-Mail: jbacke@backemarketing.com, Web Site: www.backemarketing.com (35)

Brown, Malinda, L., Lee's Nursery, McMinnville, TN. Tel: (931) 668-4870, FAX: (931) 668-4870, E-Mail: leesnursery@blomand.net, Web Site: stores.ebay.com/Lees-Nursery (8)

Brown, Marilyn, Arthur Brown & Bro Inc, New York, NY. Tel: (212) 575-5555, (800) 772-PENS, FAX: (212) 575-5825, E-Mail: penshop@artbrown.com, Web Site: www.artbrown.com (10)

Brown, Mary Lou, MLB Associates, Lake Placid, NY. Tel: (518) 523-2371, FAX: (518) 523-9011, E-Mail: mlbassoc@aol.com, Web Site: www.mlbassociates.com (20)

Brown, Matt, Nevada Magazine, Carson City, NV. Tel: (775) 687-5416, FAX: (775) 687-6159, E-Mail: editor@nevadamagazine.com, Web Site: www.nevadamagazine.com (17)

Brown, Melanie, Jason Natural Personal Care Products, Boulder, CO. Tel: (877) 527-6601, Web Site: www.jason-natural.com (7)

Brown, Michelle, Compass Marketing Solutions, Lincoln, NE. Tel: (402) 438-3222, Web Site: www.cmsdm.com (23)

Brown, Nancy, ITT Educational Services Inc, Carmel, IN. Tel: (317) 706-9200, E-Mail: gtanner@itt-tech.edu, Web Site: www.itt-tech.edu (16)

Brown, Pamela, Liguori Publications, Liguori, MO. Tel: (636) 464-2500, (800) 325-9521, FAX: (800) 325-9526, E-Mail: liguori@liguori.org, Web Site: www.liguori.org (17)

Brown, Patte, Plan USA, Warwick, RI. Tel: (401) 737-5770, (800) 556-7918, FAX: (401) 738-5608, Web Site: www.planusa.org (1)

Brown, Peter, D., Champs Corp, Bradenton, FL. Tel: (941) 748-0577, (800) 991-6813, E-Mail: customer_service@champssports.com, Web Site: www.champssports.com (11)

Brown, Peter, G., Natural History Magazine, Durham, NC. Tel: (646) 356-6500, FAX: (646) 356-6511, E-Mail: nhmag@naturalhistorymag.com, Web Site: www.naturalhistorymag.com (17)

Brown, Richard, The Stratosphere Las Vegas, Las Vegas, NV. Tel: (702) 380-7777, (800) 998-6937, FAX: (702) 383-4755, Web Site: www.stratospherehotel.com (19)

Brown, Ronald, C., Resorts Worldwide Inc, White Plains, NY. Tel: (914) 640-8100, (800) 325-3535, FAX: (914) 640-8310, Web Site: www.starwood.com (19)

Brown, Sandi, Sandi Brown Associates, Saint Petersburg, FL. Tel: (727) 528-6980, FAX: (703) 960-4492 (35)

Brown, Sandra L., Grandma Brown's Beans Inc, Mexico, NY. Tel: (315) 963-7221, FAX: (315) 963-4072 (4)

Brown, Sharon, DM Assistance Inc, Portsmouth, NH. Tel: (603) 964-6156 (20)

Brown, Timothy, J., Princess House Inc, Taunton, MA. Tel: (508) 832-6800, (508) 823-0711, (800) 622-0039, FAX: (508) 823-5182, Web Site: www.princesshouse.com (16)

Brown, Tony, Tony Brown Productions, New York, NY. Tel: (718) 264-2226, FAX: (718) 264-1914, E-Mail: mail@tbol.net, Web Site: www.tonybrown.com (16)

Brown & Co, Blaine, WA. Tel: (360) 371-2489 (8)

Brown & Jenkins Trading Co, Cambridge, VT. Tel: (802) 862-2395, (800) 456-JAVA, FAX: (802) 863-4009, Web Site: www.brownjenkins.com (4)

Arthur Brown & Bro Inc, New York, NY. Tel: (212) 575-5555, (800) 772-PENS, FAX: (212) 575-5825, E-Mail: penshop@artbrown.com, Web Site: www.artbrown.com (10)

Brown Brothers, Sterling, PA. Tel: (570) 689-9688, FAX: (570) 689-7873, E-Mail: info@brownbrotherusa.com, Web Site: www.brownbrothersusa.com (38)

Brown-Forman Beverages Worldwide, Louisville, KY. Tel: (502) 585-1100, FAX: (502) 774-7185, E-Mail: Brown-Forman@b-f.com, Web Site: www.brown-forman.com (16)

Brown-Forman Corp, Louisville, KY. Tel: (502) 585-1100, FAX: (502) 774-7876, E-Mail: brown-forman@b-f.com, Web Site: www.brown-forman.com (16)

Matt Brown & Associates Inc, Dayton, OH. Tel: (937) 434-3949, (800) 233-3949, FAX: (937) 434-6272, E-Mail: mba@mbalists.com, Web Site: www.mbalists.com (23)

Brown Printing Co, New York, NY. Tel: (212) 782-7800, FAX: (212) 782-7878, E-Mail: contact.us@bpc.com, Web Site: www.bpc.com (27)

Sandi Brown Associates, Saint Petersburg, FL. Tel: (727) 528-6980, FAX: (703) 960-4492 (35)

Brown Shoe Co, Saint Louis, MO. Tel: (314) 854-4000, FAX: (314) 854-4274, Web Site: www.brownshoe.com (16)

Tony Brown Productions, New York, NY. Tel: (718) 264-2226, FAX: (718) 264-1914, E-Mail: mail@tbol.net, Web Site: www.tonybrown.com (16)

Brown, Van Remmen, Kanuit, Inc, El Segundo, CA. Tel: (310) 536-0777, FAX: (310) 536-0606, E-Mail: info@bvksearch.com, Web Site: www.bvksearch.com (20)

BrownCor International, Milwaukee, WI. Tel: (414) 443-9700, (800) 327-2278, FAX: (800) 343-9228, Web Site: www.bcadvantage.com (5)

Browne, Charlie, Charlie Browne Communications, Apex, NC. Tel: (919) 267-9271, FAX: (919) 267-9271, E-Mail: cbrownecom@sbcglobal.net (39)

Browne, David, Family Christian Stores, Grand Rapids, MI. Tel: (616) 554-8700, (888) 319-0319, FAX: (616) 554-8694, E-Mail: info@fcsdirect.familychristian.com, Web Site: www.familychristian.com (5)

Charlie Browne Communications, Apex, NC. Tel: (919) 267-9271, FAX: (919) 267-9271, E-Mail: cbrownecom@sbcglobal.net (39)

Brownell, Larry, Marketing Research Association, Washington, DC. Tel: (860) 682-1000, FAX: (860) 682-1010, E-Mail: email@mra-net.org, Web Site: www.mra-net.org (40)

Brownell Holly Farms, Oregon City, OR. Tel: (503) 631-7475, FAX: (503) 631-7481, E-Mail: sales@brownellhollyfarms.com, Web Site: www.brownellhollyfarms.com (6)

Brownfield, Charles, InterContinental Hotels Group, Atlanta, GA. Tel: (770) 604-2000, (877) 424-2449, FAX: (770) 604-8639, Web Site: www.ichotelsgroup.com (19)

Browning, Bruce, Magjak Printing Corp, Port Chester, NY. Tel: (914) 939-8800, Web Site: www.magjak.com (27)

Browning, Jane, Camping World Inc, Bowling Green, KY. Tel: (270) 781-2718, (800) 626-6189, FAX: (270) 796-8991, Web Site: www.campingworld.com (11)

Browning, Jim, Image Checks, Bel Air, MD. Tel: (800) 562-8768, FAX: (410) 676-8269, Web Site: www.imagechecks.com (27)

Browning, Kelly, B., American Institute for Cancer Research, Washington, DC. Tel: (202) 328-7744, (800) 843-8114, FAX: (202) 328-7226, E-Mail: aicrweb@aicr.org, Web Site: www.aicr.org (1)

Browning, Kenneth, L., Browning, Jacobson & Klein LLP, Beverly Hills, CA. Tel: (310) 247-8777, FAX: (310) 247-1827 (20)

Browning, Jacobson & Klein LLP, Beverly Hills, CA. Tel: (310) 247-8777, FAX: (310) 247-1827 (20)

Brownlee, David, Paradise Galleries, Irvine, CA. Tel: (858) 793-4000, FAX: (858) 793-3425, E-Mail: omancinelli@paradisegalleries.com, Web Site: www.paradisegalleries.com (6)

Brownrout, Todd, The Philadelphia Inquirer & Daily News, Philadelphia, PA. Tel: (215) 854-2000, FAX: (215) 854-4788, Web Site: www.phil.com/inquirer (31)

Brown's Omaha Plant Farms, Omaha, TX. Tel: (903) 884-2421, FAX: (903) 884-2423, E-Mail: mail@bopf.com, Web Site: www.bopf.com (8)

Brownstein, Rhonda, Southern Poverty Law Center, Montgomery, AL. Tel: (334) 956-8200, FAX: (334) 956-8483, Web Site: www.splcenter.org (1)

Brubaker, Steve, John Deere Credit USA, Johnston, IA. Tel: (515) 267-3000, FAX: (515) 267-3292, Web Site: www.deere.com/en_US/jdc/index.html (14)

Bruce Medical Supply, Waltham, MA. Tel: (781) 894-6262, (800) 225-8446, FAX: (781) 894-9519, E-Mail: sales@brucemedial.com, Web Site: www.brucemedical.com (7)

Bruck, David, Wendell August Forge Inc, Grove City, PA. Tel: (724) 458-8360, (800) 923-1390, FAX: (724) 458-0906, E-Mail: info@wendell.com, Web Site: www.wendellaugust.com (6)

Brucker, Randy, Cooper Communities Inc, Rogers, AR. Tel: (479) 246-6500, (800) 648-6401, FAX: (479) 855-6256, E-Mail: coopernet@ccias.com, Web Site: www.cooper-communities.com (16)

Brueckner, Renee, Association of the Miraculous Medal, Perryville, MO. Tel: (573) 547-8343, (800) 264-6279, FAX: (573) 547-1389, E-Mail: amm1@amm.org, Web Site: www.amm.org (1)

Brueggemier, Larry, Circle K Stores Inc, Akron, OH. Tel: (330) 630-6300, Web Site: www.cirlcek.com (16)

Bruffey, Teresa, Outdoor Research, Seattle, WA. Tel: (206) 467-8197, (888) 467-4327, FAX: (206) 467-0374, Web Site: www.outdoorresearch.com (11)

Bruggeman, Ronald, Golden Bison LLC, Denver, CO. Tel: (303) 962-0100, Web Site: www. highplainsbison.com (4)

Bruggeman, Ronald, Info USA City Directories, Omaha, NE. Tel: (402) 593-4500, (800) 925-4654, FAX: (402) 593-4671, E-Mail: customerservice@ infousacity.com, Web Site: www.infousacity.com (17)

Bruggeman, Ronald, infoUSA Inc, Omaha, NE. Tel: (402) 593-4500, (800) 321-0869, FAX: (402) 596-8902, Web Site: www.infousa.com (23)

Brugger, Christy, Custom Toll Free, Mill Creek, WA. Tel: (800) 933-3030, Web Site: www. customtollfree.com (5)

Brugh, Ken, Golfsmith International Inc, Austin, TX. Tel: (512) 821-4050, (800) 813-6897, FAX: (512) 837-9347, E-Mail: comments@golfsmith.com, Web Site: www.golfsmith.com (11)

Brugowicz, Andrew, A., Haworth College of Business, Kalamazoo, MI. Tel: (616) 387-6062, FAX: (616) 387-5710, E-Mail: jay.lindquist@wmich.edu, Web Site: www.hcob.wmich.edu/mktg (41)

Brulll, David, R., Trade Show Exhibitors Association, Chicago, IL. Tel: (312) 842-8732, FAX: (312) 842-8744, Web Site: www.tsea.org (42)

Bruneau, Bill, Bountiful Gardens, Willits, CA. Tel: (707) 459-6410, FAX: (707) 459-1925, E-Mail: bountiful@sonic.net, Web Site: www. bountifulgardens.org (8)

Bruner, Randall, Ghirardelli Chocolate Co, San Leandro, CA. Tel: (510) 483-6970, (800) 877-9338, FAX: (510) 297-2649, Web Site: www.ghirardelli. com (16)

Brunn, Tim, Merastar Insurance Co, Chattanooga, TN. Tel: (800) 637-2782, FAX: (800) 369-1430, E-Mail: merastar.assist.team@unitrindirect.com, Web Site: www.merastar.com (15)

Brunner, James, E., Consumer's Energy, Jackson, MI. Tel: (517) 788-0550, (800) 805-0490, FAX: (517) 788-1859, E-Mail: businesscenter@ consumerenergy.com, Web Site: www. consumersenergy.com (16)

Brunner, Pittsburgh, PA. Tel: (412) 995-9500, FAX: (412) 995-9501, Web Site: www.brunnerworks.com (35)

Bruno, Leo, Lake Shore Industries, Erie, PA. Tel: (800) 458-0463, FAX: (814) 453-4293, E-Mail: info@lsisigns.com, Web Site: www.lsisigns.com (16)

Bruno, Mike, Loctite Corp, Rocky Hill, CT. Tel: (860) 571-5100, (800) LOCTITE, (800) 562-8483, FAX: (860) 571-5465, Web Site: www.loctite.com (16)

Bruno, Robert, Microfluidics Corp, Newton, MA. Tel: (617) 969-5452, (800) 370-5452, FAX: (617) 965-1213, E-Mail: info@mfics.com, Web Site: www. microfluidicscorp.com (16)

Bruno, Shirley, Lake Shore Industries, Erie, PA. Tel: (800) 458-0463, FAX: (814) 453-4293, E-Mail: info@lsisigns.com, Web Site: www.lsisigns.com (16)

Bruno, Vincent, Vcom International Multi-Media Corp, South Hackensack, NJ. Tel: (201) 229-9800, (800) 425-4268, FAX: (800) 453-6338, E-Mail: sales@800VALIANT.com, Web Site: www. 800VALIANT.com (3)

Bruno & Ridgway Research Associates Inc, Lawrenceville, NJ. Tel: (609) 895-9889, FAX: (609) 895-6665, E-Mail: info@brunoandridgway. com, Web Site: www.brra.com (30)

Bruns, Margie, Amos Press, Inc, Sidney, OH. Tel: (937) 498-2111, FAX: (937) 498-0876, Web Site: www.amospress.com (17)

Brunsell, Bonnie, A Eicoff & Co, Chicago, IL. Tel: (312) 527-7100, FAX: (312) 527-7192, E-Mail: bill.mccabe@eicoff.com, Web Site: www. eicoff.com (35)

Brunswick, Cecile, Cecile Brunswick, New York, NY. Tel: (212) 222-2088, E-Mail: cbrunswick@nyc.rr. com, Web Site: www.cecilebrunswicknyc.com (36)

Cecile Brunswick, New York, NY. Tel: (212) 222-2088, E-Mail: cbrunswick@nyc.rr.com, Web Site: www.cecilebrunswicknyc.com (36)

Brunton, Melissa, Direct Selling Association, Washington, DC. Tel: (202) 452-8866, FAX: (202) 452-9010, E-Mail: info@dsa.org, Web Site: www.dsa. org (40)

Bruscato, Nick, Bunker Hill Auctions, Newark, IL. Tel: (630) 770-7132, E-Mail: bunkerhillauctions@ joimail.com, Web Site: www.bunkerhillauctions. com (6)

Brusco Jr., Frank, Applied Printing Technologies, Moonachie, NJ. Tel: (201) 635-9447, (888) 282-4141, FAX: (201) 896-6839, E-Mail: vpsales@ appliedprinting.com, Web Site: www. appliedprinting.com (27)

Brush, Hollis, Goodman Marketing Partners Inc, San Rafael, CA. Tel: (415) 507-9060, FAX: (415) 507-9067, E-Mail: info@goodmanmarketing.com, Web Site: www.goodmanmarketing.com (35)

Brush Fire, Cedar Knolls, NJ. Tel: (973) 871-1700, FAX: (973) 871-1717, Web Site: www. brushfireinc.com (35)

Bruu, Alyson, David C Cook, Colorado Springs, CO. Tel: (719) 536-0100, (800) 323-7543, FAX: (719) 536-3232, Web Site: www.davidccook.com (17)

Bryan, Daniel, Keith, Hale Indian River Groves Inc, Vero Beach, FL. Tel: (800) 356-7264, FAX: (877) 329-4253, E-Mail: marketing@halegroves.com, Web Site: www.hales.com (16)

Bryan, Karen, John Wiley & Sons Canada Ltd, Etobicoke, ON. Tel: (416) 236-4433, FAX: (416) 236-4448, Web Site: www.wiley.com (17)

Bryan, Nicole, The Peter A Tobin College of Business, Jamaica, NY. Tel: (718) 990-2600, FAX: (718) 990-1868, Web Site: www.stjohns.edu (41)

Bryan, Robert, Robert Bryan Ltd, Port Royal, VA. Tel: (804) 742-5555, (800) 742-8883, FAX: (804) 742-5220, E-Mail: customerservice@robertbryanltd. com, Web Site: www.robertbryanltd.com (2)

Robert Bryan Ltd, Port Royal, VA. Tel: (804) 742-5555, (800) 742-8883, FAX: (804) 742-5220, E-Mail: customerservice@robertbryanltd.com, Web Site: www.robertbryanltd.com (2)

Bryant, Andy, D., Intel Corp, Santa Clara, CA. Tel: (408) 765-8080, (800) 548-4725, FAX: (408) 765-6187, Web Site: www.intel.com (1)

Bryant, Anne, National School Boards Association Inc, Alexandria, VA. Tel: (703) 838-6722, FAX: (703) 683-7590, E-Mail: info@nsba.org, Web Site: www.nsba.org (1)

Bryant, Christine, L, American Lung Association, New York, NY. Tel: (212) 889-3370, (800) LUNGUSA, FAX: (212) 889-3375, E-Mail: info@alany.org, Web Site: www.lungusa.org (1)

Bryant, Dan, Jobscope Corp, Greenville, SC. Tel: (864) 458-3143, (800) 443-5794, FAX: (864) 234-4852, E-Mail: marketing@jobscope.com, Web Site: www.jobscope.com (16)

Bryant, Del, R., BMI, Nashville, TN. Tel: (615) 401-2000, (800) 925-8451, FAX: (615) 401-2812, E-Mail: genlic@bmi.com, Web Site: www.bmi.com (1)

Bryant, Douglas Donne, DDB Stock Photography LLC, Baton Rouge, LA. Tel: (225) 763-6235, FAX: (225) 763-6894, E-Mail: info@ddbstock. com, Web Site: www.ddbstock.com (38)

Bryant, Ed, Datum Timing, Test & Measurement, Beverly, MA. Tel: (978) 927-8220, FAX: (978) 927-4099, E-Mail: wriley@datum.com, Web Site: www.datum.com (9)

Bryant, Erin, Phoenix Learning Group Inc, Maryland Heights, MO. Tel: (314) 569-0211, (800) 221-1274, FAX: (314) 569-2834, E-Mail: dealersales@ phoenixlearninggroup.com, Web Site: www. phoenixlearninggroup.com (16)

Bryant, Jack, Concurrent Computer Corp, Duluth, GA. Tel: (678) 228-4000, (877) 978-7363, FAX: (954) 977-5580, Web Site: www.ccur.com (3)

Bryant, Jeff D., Creative Direct Marketing, Chapel Hill, NC. Tel: (919) 929-5757, E-Mail: jeffb.cdm@ mindspring.com (39)

Bryant, Scott, The Mark Group, Boca Raton, FL. Tel: (561) 241-1700, (800) 637-0152, FAX: (561) 241-1055, Web Site: www.bostonproper.com (2)

Brydels, John, Brydels Marketing LLC, Baton Rouge, LA. Tel: (225) 773-1011 (35)

Brydels Marketing LLC, Baton Rouge, LA. Tel: (225) 773-1011 (35)

Bryfonski, Dedria, Gale Research Inc, Farmington Hills, MI. Tel: (248) 699-4253, (800) 877-GALE, FAX: (313) 961-6083, Web Site: www.gale.com (17)

Brylane, Indianapolis, IN. Tel: (800) 677-0339, Web Site: www.brylanehome.com (2)

Bryson, Craig, Christian Resource Management, Orange, CA. Tel: (714) 974-0754, FAX: (714) 974-7845, E-Mail: CRMOrange@aol.com, Web Site: www.crmorange.com (22)

Bryson, Destiny, Mac Murray Petersen & Shuster LLP, New Albany, OH. Tel: (614) 939-9955, FAX: (614) 939-9955, E-Mail: dbryson@mpslawyers. com, Web Site: www.mpslawyers.com (20)

Bryson, John, E., Boeing Co, Chicago, IL. Tel: (312) 544-2000, FAX: (312) 544-2082, Web Site: www. boeing.com (16)

Bryson, Katie, Teletrack Inc, Norcross, GA. Tel: (770) 449-8809 (29)

BtoB Magazine, New York, NY. Tel: (212) 210-0206, FAX: (212) 210-0422, E-Mail: aholtzman@crain. com, Web Site: www.btobonline.com (43)

Bucco, Chickie, Katz Television Direct Response, New York, NY. Tel: (212) 424-6124, FAX: (212) 424-6130, E-Mail: chickie.bucco@katz-media.com, Web Site: www.katzdirect.com (32)

Buchert, Richard, Bauer Publishing Co, Englewood Cliffs, NJ. Tel: (201) 569-6699, FAX: (201) 510-3297, Web Site: www.bauerpublishing.com (17)

Buchingham, Madeline, Mother Jones Magazine, San Francisco, CA. Tel: (415) 321-1700, Web Site: www.motherjones.com (17)

Buchler, Bill, Improvements, West Chester, OH. Tel: (216) 591-9148, (800) 634-9484, FAX: (216) 831-4026, Web Site: www.improvementscatalog.com (8)

Buchsbaum, Bob, Dick Blick Holdings Inc, Galesburg, IL. Tel: (309) 343-6181, FAX: (309) 343-5785, E-Mail: admin@dickblick.com, Web Site: www. dickblick.com (17)

Buchsbaum, Frank, Stock Drive Products, New Hyde Park, NY. Tel: (516) 328-3300, FAX: (516) 326-8827, E-Mail: sdp-sisupport@sdp-si.com, Web Site: www.sdp.si.com (5)

Buchsbaum, Judy, Marmelstein Inc, Philadelphia, PA. Tel: (215) 925-9862, FAX: (215) 925-3889 (16)

Buchser, Rodney, H., FMS Direct, Tarzana, CA. Tel: (818) 708-7814, FAX: (818) 708-7906, Web Site: www.fmsdirect.com (16)

Buchwitz, Melody, PacNet Services Ltd, Vancouver, BC. Tel: (604) 689-0399, FAX: (604) 689-0313, E-Mail: info@pacnetservices.com, Web Site: www. pacnetservices.com (14)

Buck, Jim, Southern Emblem Co, Toast, NC. Tel: (336) 789-3348, (800) 927-0526, FAX: (336) 789-6547, Web Site: www.southernemblemco.com (5)

Buck, John D., ValueVision Media Inc, Eden Prairie, MN. Tel: (952) 943-6000, FAX: (952) 943-6711, Web Site: www.valuevisionmedia.com (32)

Buck, Nancy, Southern Emblem Co, Toast, NC. Tel: (336) 789-3348, (800) 927-0526, FAX: (336) 789-6547, Web Site: www.southernemblemco.com (5)

Buckalew, Michelle, Great-West Life, Greenwood Village, CO. Tel: (800) 537-2033, Web Site: www. greatwest.com (15)

Buckelew, Alan B., Princess Cruises (HQ), Santa Clarita, CA. Tel: (661) 753-0000, (800) Princess, FAX: (661) 284-4765, Web Site: www. princesscruises.com (19)

Buckland, Bruce, Inforonics LLC, Littleton, MA. Tel: (978) 698-7400, FAX: (978) 698-7500, E-Mail: info@inforonics.com, Web Site: www.inforonics.com (22)

Buckles, John, Marketing Consulting Services, Kingsport, TN. Tel: (423) 288-5866, FAX: (423) 288-5576 (20)

Buckley, Cali, Pennsylvania State University Press, University Park, PA. Tel: (814) 865-1327, (800) 326-9180, FAX: (814) 863-1408, Web Site: www.psupress.org (17)

Buckley, Heidi, Marketing Solutions Unlimited LLC, West Hartford, CT. Tel: (860) 523-0670, FAX: (860) 523-0675, E-Mail: info@msudirectmail.com, Web Site: www.msudirectmail.com (21)

Buckley, Jack, Incentive Associates Inc, Overland Park, KS. Tel: (913) 722-2848, FAX: (913) 722-6854, E-Mail: incentiveassociate@sbcglobal.net (33)

Buckley, Tom, Redi-Data, Fairfield, NJ. Tel: (973) 808-4500, FAX: (973) 808-5511, E-Mail: sales@redimail.com, Web Site: www.redidata.com (23)

Buckredan, Ravi, AmeriList Inc, Pomona, NY. Tel: (800) 457-2899, Web Site: www.amerilist.com (23)

Bucks County Coffee Co, Conshohocken, PA. Tel: (215) 741-1855, (800) 523-6163, FAX: (215) 741-1799, Web Site: www.buckscountycoffee.com (16)

Budco, Highland Park, MI. Tel: (313) 957-5100, Web Site: www.budco.com (35)

Budd, Tammy, Midland Lithographing Co, North Kansas City, MO. Tel: (816) 842-2224, FAX: (816) 842-4530 (27)

Budlong, Morrison, J., King Computer Services Inc, Las Cruces, NM. Tel: (818) 951-5240, FAX: (818) 353-1278, E-Mail: kingsoftware@aol.com, Web Site: www.kingcomputerservices.com (22)

Budow, Aileen, Comedy Central, New York, NY. Tel: (212) 767-8600, FAX: (212) 767-4284, Web Site: www.comedycentral.com (32)

Buena Vista Home Entertainment, Burbank, CA. Tel: (818) 560-1000, FAX: (818) 845-8728, Web Site: www.bvhe.com (3)

Buena Vista Winery, Sonoma, CA. Tel: (707) 252-7117, (800) 678-8504, FAX: (707) 252-0392, Web Site: www.buenavistawinery.com (16)

Buescher, Kent, A., Beacon Printing & Graphics Inc, Valdosta, GA. Tel: (912) 244-5634, (800) 227-7377, FAX: (912) 247-4405, Web Site: www.uspress.com (27)

Buffa, Vincent, Crane Pumps & Systems Inc, Piqua, OH. Tel: (937) 773-2442, FAX: (937) 773-2238, E-Mail: cranepumps@cranepumps.com, Web Site: www.cranepumps.com (16)

Buffkin, Craig, The Buffkin Group LLC, Franklin, TN. Tel: (615) 778-2142, E-Mail: info@thebuffkingroup.com, Web Site: www.thebuffkingroup.com (20)

The Buffkin Group LLC, Franklin, TN. Tel: (615) 778-2142, E-Mail: info@thebuffkingroup.com, Web Site: www.thebuffkingroup.com (20)

Buffo, Douglas, Leo Burnett USA, Chicago, IL. Tel: (312) 220-3200, Web Site: www.leoburnett.com (35)

Buford, C.H., Prime Access Inc, New York, NY. Tel: (212) 868-6800, FAX: (212) 868-9495, E-Mail: contact@primeaccess.net, Web Site: www.primeaccess.net (21)

Buggies Unlimited, Jacksonville, FL. Tel: (888) 444-6364, E-Mail: support@buggiesunlimited.com, Web Site: www.buggiesunlimited.com (12)

Buhler, Brian, K., Kelsey National Corp, Los Angeles, CA. Tel: (310) 390-1000, (800) 366-5656, FAX: (310) 390-3158, E-Mail: info@kelsey.com, Web Site: www.kelsey.com (15)

Buhr, Joel, First Direct Marketing LLC, Bellevue, NE. Tel: (402) 403-0000, (866) 363-9575, FAX: (402) 403-0001, E-Mail: sales@firstdirectmarketing.com, Web Site: www.firstdirectmarketing.com (23)

Buhrow, Victoria, New York Life Insurance Co/AARP, Tampa, FL. Tel: (813) 288-5500, FAX: (813) 288-5256, Web Site: www.nylaarp.com (15)

Buhrs Americas Inc, Minneapolis, MN. Tel: (763) 557-9100, FAX: (763) 557-9700, Web Site: www.buhrs.com (34)

Buice, Julie, Ranger Joe's International Military Supply, Columbus, GA. Tel: (706) 689-0082, (800) 247-4541, FAX: (706) 682-8840, E-Mail: customerservice@rangerjoes.com, Web Site: www.rangerjoes.com (2)

Buick Division General Motors Corp, Detroit, MI. Tel: (313) 556-5000, (800) 521-7300, FAX: (313) 556-5108, Web Site: www.buick.com (16)

Bulach, Rosalie, A., Name-Finders Lists Inc, Oakland, CA. Tel: (415) 955-8585, (800) 221-5009, FAX: (415) 955-8581, E-Mail: dm@namefinderslists.com, Web Site: www.namefinderslists.com (23)

Bulgrin, Artie, ARF Annual Convention & Research Infoplex, New York, NY. Tel: (212) 751-5656, FAX: (212) 319-5265, E-Mail: info@theARF.org, Web Site: www.theARF.org (42)

Bulkley Dunton Publishing Group, New York, NY. Tel: (212) 863-1800, FAX: (212) 863-1979, Web Site: www.internationalpaper.com (25)

Bull, Stephanie, The Missoulian, Missoula, MT. Tel: (406) 523-5334, FAX: (406) 523-5221, Web Site: www.missoulian.com (31)

Bull Dog Media Group Inc, Madison, SD. Tel: (605) 256-9103, Web Site: www.commissionsoup.com (20)

Bull HN Information Systems, Chelmsford, MA. Tel: (978) 294-6000, FAX: (978) 294-7999, Web Site: www.bull.com/us (16)

Bullen, Bruce, M., Harvard Pilgrim Health Care, Wellesley, MA. Tel: (617) 509-1000, FAX: (617) 509-7590, Web Site: www.harvardpilgrim.org (7)

Bulletin of the Atomic Scientists, Chicago, IL. Tel: (773) 702-6301, FAX: (773) 980-6932, E-Mail: admin@thebulletin.org, Web Site: www.thebulletin.org (17)

Bullis, William, British Columbia Automobile Association, Burnaby, BC Canada. Tel: (604) 268-5000, (800) 564-6222, FAX: (604) 268-5585, Web Site: www.bcaa.com (15)

Bullseye Database Marketing LLC, Tulsa, OK. Tel: (918) 587-1731, FAX: (918) 587-0450, E-Mail: inquiries@bullseyedm.com, Web Site: www.bullseyedm.com (35)

Bullseye Marketing Inc, Canoga Park, CA. Tel: (818) 888-8700, Web Site: www.bullseyeb2b.com (28)

BullsEye Marketing Systems LLC, West Chester, PA. Tel: (484) 356-2240, Web Site: bullseyemarketingsystems.com (35)

Bulver, Thomas, Heartland America, Chaska, MN. Tel: (952) 361-3640, (800) 229-2901, FAX: (952) 368-3452, E-Mail: info@heartlandamerica.com, Web Site: www.heartlandamerica.com (16)

Bumann, Kelly, Starz Entertainment Group, Englewood, CO. Tel: (720) 852-7700, Web Site: www.starz.com (16)

Bunch, Ed, B Bunch Co Inc, Phoenix, AZ. Tel: (602) 997-6452, FAX: (602) 997-7266, E-Mail: sales@bbunch.com, Web Site: www.bbunch.com (16)

Bunch, Max, STRATMARK, Richardson, TX. Tel: (800) 222-6070, Web Site: www.stratmark.com (1)

Bunchball, Redwood City, CA. Tel: (408) 985-2034, Web Site: www.bunchball.com (32)

Bundies, Todd, Badger Press/Photographics Inc, Kenosha, WI. Tel: (262) 658-1628, (800) 635-9773, FAX: (262) 658-0307 (27)

Bungart, Lutz, The Instrument Workshop, Ashland, OR. Tel: (541) 552-0989, (800) 442-6038, FAX: (541) 488-5846, E-Mail: shop77@fortepiano.com, Web Site: www.fortepiano.com (16)

Bungart, Martha, The Instrument Workshop, Ashland, OR. Tel: (541) 552-0989, (800) 442-6038, FAX: (541) 488-5846, E-Mail: shop77@fortepiano.com, Web Site: www.fortepiano.com (16)

Bunka, Susie, Arctic Trading Co Inc, Churchill, MB. Tel: (204) 675-8804, (800) 665-0431, FAX: (204) 675-2164, E-Mail: atcpenny@mts.net, Web Site: www.arctictradingco.com (6)

Bunker, Steven, United Envelope, Long Island City, NY. Tel: (718) 707-0700, FAX: (718) 729-8671, E-Mail: marketing@unitedenvelope.com, Web Site: www.unitedenvelope.com (26)

Bunker Hill Auctions, Newark, IL. Tel: (630) 770-7132, E-Mail: bunkerhillauctions@joimail.com, Web Site: www.bunkerhillauctions.com (6)

Bunn, John, R., BH Bunn Co, Lakeland, FL. Tel: (863) 647-1555, (800) 222-2866, FAX: (863) 686-2866, E-Mail: info@bunntyco.com, Web Site: www.bunntyco.com (34)

Bunn, Thomas W., Key Bank National Association, Albany, NY. Tel: (518) 434-4871, (800) 539-2968, Web Site: www.keybank.com (14)

Bunn, Thomas, W., Key Bank, Cleveland, OH. Tel: (216) 689-3000, (888) 539-2968, FAX: (207) 874-7044, Web Site: www.key.com (14)

BH Bunn Co, Lakeland, FL. Tel: (863) 647-1555, (800) 222-2866, FAX: (863) 686-2866, E-Mail: info@bunntyco.com, Web Site: www.bunntyco.com (34)

Bunn-O-Matic Corp, Springfield, IL. Tel: (217) 529-6601, FAX: (217) 529-6622, E-Mail: bunn@bunn.com, Web Site: www.bunn.com (16)

Bunning, Ellen, Jeroboam, San Francisco, CA. Tel: (415) 312-0198 cell, E-Mail: jeroboamster@gmail.com (38)

Bunsick, Robert, Gould Paper Corp, New York, NY. Tel: (212) 301-0000, (800) 221-3043, FAX: (212) 481-0067, Web Site: www.gouldpaper.com (25)

Bunting, Paula, Collector Books & American Quilters Society, Paducah, KY. Tel: (270) 898-6211, (800) 626-5420, FAX: (270) 898-8890, E-Mail: info@collectorbooks.com, Web Site: www.collectorbooks.com (17)

Bunzl Distribution USA, Inc, Saint Louis, MO. Tel: (314) 997-5959, (888) 997-5959, FAX: (314) 997-1405, Web Site: www.bunzldistribution.com (16)

Buote, Linda, Destinations Ireland & Great Britain, Rhinebeck, NY. Tel: (800) 832-1848, FAX: (212) 265-0154, E-Mail: info@digbtravel.com, Web Site: www.allgolftravel.com/tours (19)

Burak, Larry, Warnaco Swimwear Inc, Los Angeles, CA. Tel: (323) 726-1262, FAX: (323) 724-6931, Web Site: www.speedo.com (16)

Burak, Mitsue, GenerH, Inc, Torrance, CA. Tel: (888) 312-3443, E-Mail: info@generh.com, Web Site: www.generh.com (21)

Burbank, Dawn, Whitman Publishing LLC, Atlanta, GA. Tel: (800) 546-2995, FAX: (256) 246-1116, E-Mail: info@whitmanbooks.com, Web Site: www.whitmanbooks.com (16)

Burbeck, Darrell, Advanced Direct Marketing Inc, Loveland, CO. Tel: (970) 669-9800, (888) 553-1230, FAX: (970) 669-1920, E-Mail: sales@admimail.com (21)

Burberry, New York, NY. Tel: (212) 707-6508, Web Site: www.burberry.com (2)

Burch, Jim, East Coast Industrial Equipment & Tire, Jacksonville, FL. Tel: (904) 358-1229, (800) 874-1942, FAX: (904) 354-0888 (34)

Burchert, John, TMone, Iowa City, IA. Tel: (868) 577-2461, E-Mail: srteam@tmone.com, Web Site: www.tmone.com (29)

Burd, Carolyn, Experience In Software Inc, Berkeley, CA. Tel: (510) 644-0694, (800) 678-7008, FAX: (510) 644-4823, Web Site: www.projectkickstart.com (16)

Burd, Ethan, Alaniz - a Dmh Marketing Partners Co, Mount Pleasant, IA. Tel: (319) 385-7259, FAX: (319) 385-2825, E-Mail: info@alanizdirect.com, Web Site: www.alanizdirect.com (28)

Burd, Loretta, M., CUNA Mutual Group, Madison, WI. Tel: (608) 238-5851, (800) 356-2644, FAX: (608) 231-8839, Web Site: www.cunamutual.com (15)

Burdell, Jody, M., Children's Hospital Foundation, Washington, DC. Tel: (202) 476-3000, (800) 884-LIFE, FAX: (202) 884-5999, Web Site: www. dcchildrens.com (1)

Burden, Dave, Burden Sales Co, Lincoln, NE. Tel: (402) 474-4055, (800) 488-3407, FAX: (402) 474-5198, E-Mail: ccole@surpluscenter.com (9)

Burden, David, Surplus Center, Lincoln, NE. Tel: (402) 474-4055, (800) 488-3407, FAX: (402) 474-5198, E-Mail: customerservice1@surpluscenter. com, Web Site: www.surpluscenter.com (9)

Burden, Thomas, TBC Direct Inc, Baltimore, MD. Tel: (410) 347-7500, FAX: (410) 986-1299, E-Mail: direct@tbc.us, Web Site: www.tbcadv.us (35)

Burden Sales Co, Lincoln, NE. Tel: (402) 474-4055, (800) 488-3407, FAX: (402) 474-5198, E-Mail: ccole@surpluscenter.com (9)

Burdette, Dawn, Butler Schein Animal Health, Dublin, OH. Tel: (614) 761-9095, (888) 691-2724, FAX: (888) 329-3861, Web Site: www.butlerschein.com (16)

Burdick, Amy, Valdawn Watch Co, Long Island City, NY. Tel: (201) 807-1110, FAX: (201) 807-0228 (16)

Burdick, James, R., Gateway Inc, Irvine, CA. Tel: (949) 471-7000, (800) 369-1409, FAX: (949) 471-7041, Web Site: www.gateway.com (3)

Burdick, Walter, Swag Inc, Wichita, KS. Tel: (316) 685-3811, FAX: (316) 685-4422, E-Mail: swag@cox.net, Web Site: www.swagpromos.com (33)

The Bureau Inc, Stuart, FL. Tel: (561) 845-8400, FAX: (561) 845-7979, Web Site: www.bureauinc. com (28)

The Bureau of National Affairs, Inc, Arlington, VA. Tel: (703) 341-3000, (800) 372-1033, FAX: (703) 341-1688, E-Mail: mbromley@bna.com, Web Site: www.bna.com (17)

Bureau Van Dijk, New York, NY. Tel: (212) 797-3550, Web Site: www.bvdinfo.com (22)

Burek, John, Computer Shopper, New York, NY. Tel: (646) 472-4000, FAX: (646) 472-3912, E-Mail: feedback@computershopper.com, Web Site: www. computershopper.com (31)

Burgdoerfer, Stuart, LimitedBrands Inc, Reynoldsburg, OH. Tel: (614) 577-5902, FAX: (614) 415-7440, Web Site: www.limitedbrands.com (16)

Burger, Kent, Cooper Communities Inc, Rogers, AR. Tel: (479) 246-6500, (800) 648-6401, FAX: (479) 855-6256, E-Mail: coopernet@ccias.com, Web Site: www.cooper-communities.com (16)

Burger, Phil, Burger's Ozark Country Cured Hams Inc, California, MO. Tel: (573) 796-3134, (800) 345-5185, FAX: (573) 796-3137, E-Mail: burgers@smokehouse.com, Web Site: www. smokehouse.com (4)

Burger, Robert, Robert Burger Illustration, Stockton, NJ. Tel: (609) 397-3737, E-Mail: burgerbobz@aol. com (36)

Burger, Steve, Burger's Ozark Country Cured Hams Inc, California, MO. Tel: (573) 796-3134, (800) 345-5185, FAX: (573) 796-3137, E-Mail: burgers@smokehouse.com, Web Site: www. smokehouse.com (4)

Burger's Ozark Country Cured Hams Inc, California, MO. Tel: (573) 796-3134, (800) 345-5185, FAX: (573) 796-3137, E-Mail: burgers@smokehouse. com, Web Site: www.smokehouse.com (4)

Burgess, Bonnie, Business Promotion Ideas Inc, Tenafly, NJ. Tel: (201) 569-9777, FAX: (201) 569-2642, Web Site: www.buspromoideas.com (33)

Burgess, Janet, Amazon Drygoods, Davenport, IA. Tel: (800) 798-7979, FAX: (563) 322-4003, E-Mail: info@amazondrygoods.com, Web Site: www.amazondrygoods.com (2)

Burgess, Michael, Nightingale-Conant Corp, Niles, IL. Tel: (847) 647-0300, (800) 557-1660, FAX: (847) 647-7145, Web Site: www.nightingale.com (17)

Burgess, Peter, Media Horizons Inc, Norwalk, CT. Tel: (203) 857-0770, FAX: (203) 857-0296, E-Mail: mhict@mediahorizons.com, Web Site: www. mediahorizons.com (21)

Burghardt, Lance, Photographix, Ann Arbor, MI. FAX: (734) 476-2068, E-Mail: lkburghardt@comcast.net (37)

Burgoon, Jackie, Ambassador Press, Minneapolis, MN. Tel: (612) 521-0123, (800) 544-9112, FAX: (612) 521-4587, E-Mail: info@ambpress.com, Web Site: www.ambpress.com (27)

Burguon, Tracey, Disabled American Veterans, Cincinnati, OH. Tel: (859) 441-7300, FAX: (859) 442-2084, E-Mail: feedback@davmail.org, Web Site: www.dav.org (1)

Burk, Doreen, Ellen, Avrick Direct Inc, Santa Barbara, CA. Tel: (805) 683-6551, FAX: (805) 965-6181, E-Mail: david@avrick.com, Web Site: www. avrickdirect.com (23)

Burkarel, Rev. Msgr Paul, J.E., Our Lady of Victory Homes of Charity, Lackawanna, NY. Tel: (716) 828-9648, FAX: (716) 828-9643, E-Mail: rheist@olv-bvs.org, Web Site: www.ourladyofvictory.org (1)

Burke, Allison, Telefonix Inc, Waukegan, IL. Tel: (847) 244-4500, Web Site: www.telefonixinc.com (16)

Burke, Carol, Kayser-Roth Corp Inc, Greensboro, NC. Tel: (800) 575-3497, Web Site: www.nononsense. com (2)

Burke, E., Marketing Visions Inc, Deerfield Beach, FL. Tel: (954) 421-2002, E-Mail: marvisions@aol. com (21)

Burke, Edward, MDF Systems, Bristol, CT. Tel: (860) 584-4750, FAX: (860) 584-4759, Web Site: www. mdfsystems.com (22)

Burke, John, Weiss Research Inc, Jupiter, FL. Tel: (561) 627-3300, (877) 925-4833, FAX: (561) 625-6685, E-Mail: newbusiness@weissgroupinc.com, Web Site: www.weissgroupinc.com (17)

Burke, Peter, FLM Graphics Corp, Fairfield, NJ. Tel: (973) 575-9450, E-Mail: info@flmgraphics.com, Web Site: www.flmgraphics.com (16)

Burke, Timothy, J., Jones International Ltd, Centennial, CO. Tel: (303) 792-3111, (800) 525-7002, FAX: (303) 784-8508, E-Mail: publicrelations@jones.com, Web Site: www.jones.com (16)

Burke, Tom, TowerData, New York, NY. Tel: (646) 742-1771, Web Site: www.towerdata.com (32)

Burkett, Jeff, Advanced Direct, Greensboro, NC. Tel: (336) 299-0800, (800) 786-2812, FAX: (336) 299-2619, E-Mail: info@advdirectinc.com, Web Site: www.advdirectinc.com (21)

Burkhart, John, W., MWM Dexter Inc, Aurora, MO. Tel: (888) 833-1242, FAX: (417) 841-1040, Web Site: www.mwmdexter.com (27)

Burkholder, Laura, North American Membership Group Inc, Minnetonka, MN. Tel: (952) 936-9333, FAX: (952) 936-9755, Web Site: www.namginc. com (13)

Burkholder, Michele, ING USA Annuity & Life Ins Co, Des Moines, IA. Tel: (515) 698-7100, FAX: (515) 698-2001, Web Site: www.ing-usa.com (15)

Burkholder Flint Associates, Columbus, OH. Tel: (614) 228-2425, FAX: (614) 228-0631, E-Mail: bfa1@burkholderflint.com, Web Site: www. burkholderflint.com (35)

Burkley, Robert W., Burkley Envelope Co, Wahoo, NE. Tel: (402) 443-3010, FAX: (402) 443-4029, E-Mail: info@burkley.com, Web Site: www. burkley.com (26)

Burkley Envelope Co, Wahoo, NE. Tel: (402) 443-3010, FAX: (402) 443-4029, E-Mail: info@burkley.com, Web Site: www.burkley.com (26)

Burleson, John, Eric, KTM Sportmotorcycle USA Inc, Amherst, OH. Tel: (440) 985-3553, FAX: (440) 985-3060, Web Site: www.ktmusa.com (16)

Burley, Mark, L., Fidelity Security Life Insurance Co, Kansas City, MO. Tel: (816) 756-1060, (800) 648-8624, FAX: (816) 968-0580, E-Mail: info@fslins. com, Web Site: www.fslins.com (15)

Burley, Rick, ASK Telemarketing, Montgomery, AL. Tel: (334) 387-ASKT, FAX: (334) 387-2759, E-Mail: rburley@asktelemarketing.com, Web Site: www.asktelemarketing.com (29)

Burlington Coat Factory, Burlington, NJ. Tel: (609) 387-7800, FAX: (609) 387-7071, Web Site: www. coat.com (16)

Burlington Industries Inc, Greensboro, NC. Tel: (336) 379-2000, FAX: (336) 379-2498, Web Site: www. burlington.com (16)

Burlington Northern & Santa Fe Railroad, Fort Worth, TX. Tel: (817) 878-2000, (800) 795-2673, FAX: (817) 333-7593, Web Site: www.bnsf.com (16)

Burman, Jeff, Guarantee Trust Life Insurance Co, Glenview, IL. Tel: (847) 298-0670, FAX: (847) 298-1215, E-Mail: pr@gtlic.com, Web Site: www. gtlic.com (15)

Burman, Terry, Sterling Jewelers Inc, Akron, OH. Tel: (330) 668-5000, FAX: (330) 668-5052, E-Mail: webmaster@jewels.com, Web Site: www. sterlingjewelers.com (16)

Burn, Paul, Juvenile Diabetes Research Foundation, New York, NY. Tel: (212) 785-9500, (800) 533-CURE, FAX: (212) 785-9595, E-Mail: info@jdrf. org, Web Site: www.jdrf.org (1)

Burnett, Mark, Burnett Direct Inc, Commerce Township, MI. Tel: (248) 313-9120, E-Mail: bdisales@burnett.com, Web Site: www.burnett.com (23)

Burnett, Sheila, University Press of America Inc, Lanham, MD. Tel: (301) 459-3366, (800) 462-6420, FAX: (301) 429-5748, E-Mail: custserv@rowman. com, Web Site: www.univpress.com (17)

Burnett, Terry, Direct Marketing Association of Detroit, Royal Oak, MI. Tel: (248) 478-4888, FAX: (248) 478-6437, E-Mail: dmad@ameritech.net, Web Site: www.dmad.org (40)

Burnett Direct Inc, Commerce Township, MI. Tel: (248) 313-9120, E-Mail: bdisales@burnett.com, Web Site: www.burnett.com (23)

Leo Burnett USA, Chicago, IL. Tel: (312) 220-5959, FAX: (312) 220-3299, Web Site: www.leoburnett. com (35)

Burnett Marketing Inc, Mount Prospect, IL. Tel: (800) 837-6906, FAX: (800) 837-6978, E-Mail: burnettmkt@aol.com, Web Site: www. burnettmarketing.com (23)

Burnham, William, Soundprints, Norwalk, CT. Tel: (800) 228-7839, FAX: (203) 846-1776, E-Mail: soundprints@soundprints.com, Web Site: www. soundprints.com (6)

Burns Jr., Robert, I., Goldsmith Agio Helms, Minneapolis, MN. Tel: (612) 339-0500, FAX: (612) 339-0507, Web Site: www.agio.com (14)

Burns Sr., John, M., Burns Inc, Fall River, MA. Tel: (508) 675-0381, (800) 341-2200, FAX: (508) 677-1300, Web Site: www.burnstools.com (16)

Burns, Dr. Stephanie, Glaxo Smith Kline, Research Triangle Park, NC. Tel: (919) 483-2100, (888) 825-5249, FAX: (919) 248-8383, Web Site: www. gsk.com (16)

Burns, Jeffery, M., Burns Inc, Fall River, MA. Tel: (508) 675-0381, (800) 341-2200, FAX: (508) 677-1300, Web Site: www.burnstools.com (16)

Burns, Karen, Allstate Motor Club, South Barrington, IL. Tel: (847) 551-2300, (800) 998-8697 (13)

Burns, Kathryn, Heartland Boating Magazine, Saint Louis, MO. Tel: (314) 241-4310, (800) 366-9630, FAX: (314) 241-4207, E-Mail: info@ heartlandboating.com, Web Site: www. heartlandboating.com (17)

Burns, Kevin, Intermap Technologies, Englewood, CO. Tel: (303) 708-0955, FAX: (303) 708-0952, Web Site: www.intermap.com (32)

Burns, Mary, Barbour Publishing Inc, Uhrichsville, OH. Tel: (740) 922-6045, FAX: (740) 922-5948, (800) 220-5948, E-Mail: info@barbourbooks.com, Web Site: www.barbourbooks.com (17)

Burns, Michael, Lions Gate Entertainment, New York, NY. Tel: (212) 577-2400, FAX: (212) 962-2872, Web Site: www.liensgatefilms.com (32)

Burns, Shawn, Name Exchange, Frederick, MD. Tel: (301) 695-6140, FAX: (301) 695-5572, E-Mail: chris@nameexchange.us, Web Site: www.nameexchange.us (24)

Burns, Stephanie, A., Dow Corning Corp, Midland, MI. Tel: (989) 496-4000, (800) 248-2481, FAX: (989) 496-4572, Web Site: www.dowcorning.com (16)

Burns, Tom, Allianz Life Insurance Co of North America, Minneapolis, MN. Tel: (763) 765-6500, (800) 950-5872, Web Site: www.allianzlife.com (15)

Burns, William, Resource Publications Inc, San Jose, CA. Tel: (408) 286-8505, (888) 273-7782, FAX: (408) 287-8748, E-Mail: info@rpinet.com, Web Site: www.rpinet.com (17)

Burns Inc, Fall River, MA. Tel: (508) 675-0381, (800) 341-2200, FAX: (508) 677-1300, Web Site: www.burnstools.com (16)

Buro, Fred, A., Trump Plaza Hotel & Casino, Atlantic City, NJ. Tel: (609) 441-6000, FAX: (609) 441-7727, Web Site: www.trumpplaza.com (19)

Buroker, Andrew, B., American Heart Association, Dallas, TX. Tel: (214) 373-6300, (800) AHA-USA-1, FAX: (214) 373-3406, Web Site: www.americanheart.org (1)

W Atlee Burpee Co, Warminster, PA. Tel: (215) 674-4900, (800) 333-5808, FAX: (215) 674-4170, Web Site: www.burpee.com (8)

Burr, John, Visual Reference Publications, New York, NY. Tel: (212) 279-7000, (800) 251-4545, FAX: (212) 279-7014 (17)

Burrell, Bill, DV Burrell Seed Growers Co, Rocky Ford, CO. Tel: (719) 254-3318, (866) 254-7333, FAX: (719) 254-3319, E-Mail: burrellseeds@centurytel.net, Web Site: www.burrellseeds.us (8)

Burrell, Chet, Carefirst Blue Cross Blue Shield, Washington, DC. Tel: (202) 479-8000, FAX: (301) 470-8049, Web Site: www.carefirst.com (15)

DV Burrell Seed Growers Co, Rocky Ford, CO. Tel: (719) 254-3318, (866) 254-7333, FAX: (719) 254-3319, E-Mail: burrellseeds@centurytel.net, Web Site: www.burrellseeds.us (8)

Burress, Jefferson, DDB Direct Los Angeles, Los Angeles, CA. Tel: (310) 907-1500, FAX: (310) 907-1990, Web Site: www.ddbla.com (35)

Burris, Howard, L., Overseas Private Investment Corp (OPIC), Washington, DC. Tel: (202) 336-8400, FAX: (202) 336-7949, E-Mail: info@opic.gov, Web Site: www.opic.gov (14)

Burris, J., Mark, The Burris Agency Inc, Greensboro, NC. Tel: (336) 378-1221, FAX: (336) 378-1221, E-Mail: mburris@burris.com, Web Site: www.burris.com (35)

The Burris Agency Inc, Greensboro, NC. Tel: (336) 378-1221, FAX: (336) 378-1221, E-Mail: mburris@burris.com, Web Site: www.burris.com (35)

Burshtan, David, H., Neuberger & Berman Management, New York, NY. Tel: (212) 476-8800, (800) 877-9700, FAX: (212) 476-9090, Web Site: www.nb.com (14)

Burt, Chris, Belvoir Media Group LLC, Norwalk, CT. Tel: (203) 857-3100, (800) 424-7887, FAX: (203) 857-3103, E-Mail: customer_service@belvoir.com, Web Site: www.belvoir.com (17)

Burt, Karie, Mardev, New York, NY. Tel: (212) 584-9370, (800) 545-8517, FAX: (212) 584-9371, E-Mail: sales@mardev.com, Web Site: www.mardev.com (24)

Burtch Works LLC, Evanston, IL. Tel: (847) 328-6902, Web Site: www.burtchworks.com (20)

Burton Sr., Robert G., Cenveo Inc, Stamford, CT. Tel: (410) 633-4200, (800) 638-2850, FAX: (410) 633-1202, Web Site: www.cenveo.com (27)

Burton, Chris, Marketing Efficiency Corp, Cornelius, NC. Tel: (704) 896-5995, FAX: (704) 896-3426 (35)

Burton, Jeremy, EMC Corp, Hopkinton, MA. Tel: (888) 438-3622, Web Site: www.emc.com (16)

Burton, Tamar, Elephant Group Inc, South Plainfield, NJ. Tel: (866) 755-9008, Web Site: www.elephantgroup.com (30)

Busby, Roy, University of North Texas, Denton, TX. Tel: (940) 565-2205, Web Site: www.unt.edu/journalism (1)

Busch, Jeffrey, Island Pacific Inc, Irvine, CA. Tel: (303) 754-4700, (800) 569-1122, Web Site: www.islandpacific.com (22)

Busch, John, Lorman Education Services, Eau Claire, WI. Tel: (715) 833-3940 (1)

Busch, Robert, All-State Legal, Cranford, NJ. Tel: (908) 272-0800, (800) 222-0510, FAX: (800) 634-5184, E-Mail: sjacobs@aslegal.com, Web Site: www.aslegal.com (16)

Bush, Martha, SIGMA Marketing Group LLC, Rochester, NY. Tel: (585) 473-7300, (888) 277-9837, FAX: (585) 473-0332, E-Mail: mbush@sigmamarketing.com, Web Site: www.sigmamarketing.com; www.jthgearanalytics.com (Blog) (20)

Bush, Nancy, Riley, Lancer Label, Omaha, NE. Tel: (402) 390-9119, (800) 228-7074, FAX: (800) 344-9456, E-Mail: info@lancerlabel.com, Web Site: www.lancerlabel.com (27)

Bush, Vern, Quill Corp, Palatine, IL. Tel: (847) 634-4800, (800) 789-1331, FAX: (800) 789-6630, Web Site: www.quill.com (16)

Bush Co Inc, Fort Worth, TX. Tel: (949) 752-4210, FAX: (949) 752-4220, E-Mail: barb@bushlists.com, Web Site: www.bushlists.com (23)

Bushaw, Michael, Coast Hotels Limited, Seattle, WA. Tel: (206) 826-2700, FAX: (206) 826-2701, Web Site: www.coasthotels.com (19)

Bushee III, Richard, E., Mailing Services of Pittsburgh Inc, Freedom, PA. Tel: (724) 774-3244, (800) 876-3211, FAX: (724) 774-6996, Web Site: www.msp-pgh.com (21)

Bushnel, A.C., General Vitamin Corp, Raleigh, NC. Tel: (919) 929-5785, (800) 323-8432, FAX: (919) 929-2458, E-Mail: support@generalvitamin.com, Web Site: www.generalvitamin.com (16)

Bushnell Corporation, Overland Park, KS. Tel: (913) 752-3400, (800) 423-3537, FAX: (913) 752-3561, Web Site: www.bushnell.com (11)

Bushnell Outdoor Products, Overland Park, KS. Tel: (913) 752-3400, (800) 423-3537, FAX: (913) 752-3550, Web Site: www.bushnell.com (16)

Business Automation Systems Inc, Nashville, TN. Tel: (615) 329-4585, FAX: (615) 320-0206, Web Site: www.bas-solutions.com (16)

Business Development Solutions Inc, Cherry Hill, NJ. Tel: (856) 787-1500, Web Site: www.bdsdatabase.com (22)

Business Direct Marketing Associates Inc, Cumming, GA. Tel: (770) 888-8300, FAX: (770) 888-6482, E-Mail: bdmainc@aol.com, Web Site: www.bdmainc.com (35)

Business Extension Bureau of Texas Inc, Houston, TX. Tel: (713) 528-5568, (800) 969-5568, FAX: (713) 528-1648, E-Mail: ronr@bebtexas.com, Web Site: www.bebtexas.com (23)

Business Graphics Inc, Woodstock, IL. Tel: (815) 338-8222, (800) 435-4874, FAX: (815) 338-2652, E-Mail: busgraph@mc.net, Web Site: www.businessgraphics.com (16)

Business Mailing Center, Oxnard, CA. Tel: (805) 981-2600, (800) 882-1844, FAX: (805) 981-1180, E-Mail: answers@venturaprint.com, Web Site: www.venturaprint.com (23)

Business Marketing Association, Naperville, IL. Tel: (630) 544-5054, FAX: (630) 544-5055, E-Mail: info@marketing.org, Web Site: www.marketing.org (40)

Business Objects, Palo Alto, CA. Tel: (408) 933-6000, (888) 788-9004, Web Site: www.businessobjects.com (22)

Business Planners & Consultants Inc, New York, NY. Tel: (212) 972-1970, FAX: (212) 972-1126 (15)

Business Promotion Ideas Inc, Tenafly, NJ. Tel: (201) 569-9777, FAX: (201) 569-2642, Web Site: www.buspromoideas.com (33)

Business Publishers Inc, Durham, NC. Tel: (919) 281-0474, (800) 274-6737, FAX: (919) 544-3147, Web Site: www.bpinews.com (33)

Business Services Network, San Francisco, CA. Tel: (415) 282-8161, FAX: (415) 282-8176, E-Mail: sales@bsnc.com, Web Site: www.bsnc.com (28)

Business Technologies, Dubuque, IA. Tel: (563) 556-7994, (800) 451-0399, FAX: (563) 556-2512 (34)

BusinessOnline, San Diego, CA. Tel: (619) 699-0767, Web Site: www.businessol.com (16)

Busse, Erik, American Family Insurance Group, Madison, WI. Tel: (608) 249-2111, FAX: (608) 243-6525, E-Mail: akin1@amfam.com, Web Site: www.amfam.com (15)

Bussen, Terrance, M., Putnam Group Ltd, Trumbull, CT. Tel: (203) 452-7270, FAX: (203) 268-8071, E-Mail: info@putnamgroup.net, Web Site: putnamgroup.net (33)

Bussert, Ron, Oklahoma Dept of Commerce, Oklahoma City, OK. Tel: (405) 815-6552, (800) 879-6552, FAX: (405) 815-5344, Web Site: www.okcommerce.com (1)

Bussert, Rosemary, Datamart Direct Inc, Bloomingdale, IL. Tel: (630) 307-7100, FAX: (630) 307-8059, E-Mail: info@datamartdirect.com, Web Site: www.datamartdirect.com (27)

Bussing, Elizabeth, USA Hosts, San Francisco, CA. Tel: (415) 695-8000, (800) 368-4678, FAX: (415) 986-3668, Web Site: www.usahosts.com (19)

Bustillo, James, Blue Cross Blue Shield of Louisiana, Baton Rouge, LA. Tel: (225) 295-3307, (800) 599-2583, FAX: (225) 295-2054, E-Mail: help@bcbsla.com, Web Site: www.bcbsla.com (15)

Butcher, Andy, Strang Communications Co, Lake Mary, FL. Tel: (407) 333-0600, FAX: (407) 333-7100, E-Mail: magcustsvc@strang.com, Web Site: www.strang.com (17)

Butcher, Jane, Mother Jones Magazine, San Francisco, CA. Tel: (415) 321-1700, Web Site: www.motherjones.com (17)

Butcher, John, Sears Canada Inc, Toronto, ON. Tel: (416) 362-1711, (888) 473-2772, FAX: (613) 391-3047, E-Mail: home@sears.ca, Web Site: www.sears.ca (5)

Butcher, Quentin, Vietnam Veterans of America, Silver Spring, MD. Tel: (301) 585-4000, Web Site: www.clothingdonations.org (1)

Butera, Jay, Cedar Fresh Products, Coral Gables, FL. Tel: (305) 870-9390, Web Site: www.cedarfresh.com (16)

Buthman, Mark, A., Kimberly-Clark Corp, Neenah, WI. Tel: (920) 721-2000, (888) 525-8388, FAX: (920) 721-7722, Web Site: www.kimberly-clark.com (16)

Butkus, Raymond, ARGI - Automated Resources Group Inc, Montvale, NJ. Tel: (201) 391-1500, FAX: (201) 391-8357, Web Site: www.callargi.com (22)

Butler, Brenda, Dieste Harmel & Partners, Dallas, TX. Tel: (214) 259-8000, Web Site: www.dieste.com (35)

Butler, Brenda, Dieste, Dallas, TX. Tel: (214) 259-8000, FAX: (214) 259-8040, E-Mail: bbutler@dieste.com, Web Site: www.diesteharmel.com (35)

Butler, C., Marion, Premera Blue Cross, Spokane, WA. Tel: (425) 670-4000, (800) 422-0032, FAX: (425) 670-5853, Web Site: www.premera.com (15)

Butler, Chris, Music Sales Corp, New York, NY. Tel: (212) 254-2100, (800) 431-7187, FAX: (212) 254-2013, E-Mail: info@musicsales.com, Web Site: www.musicsales.com (17)

Butler, Doug, The Staplex Co, Brooklyn, NY. Tel: (718) 768-3333, (800) 221-0822, FAX: (718) 965-0750, E-Mail: info@staplex.com, Web Site: www.staplex.com (34)

Butler, Gary C., ADP Inc, Roseland, NJ. Tel: (973) 974-5000, (800) 225-5237, FAX: (973) 974-3334, Web Site: www.adp.com (16)

Butler, Gary L., Butler Distributing Co, Kenilworth, NJ. Tel: (908) 241-3060, FAX: (908) 298-9248, E-Mail: bwprinting@worldnet.att.net, Web Site: www.bwprinting.com (3)

Butler, James, E., Callaway Gardens, Pine Mountain, GA. Tel: (706) 663-2281, (800) CALLAWAY, FAX: (706) 663-6812, E-Mail: info@callawaygardens.com, Web Site: www.callawaygardens.com (19)

Butler, Jason, Goldleaf Data Corp, Suwanee, GA. Tel: (888) 936-3282, Web Site: www.goldleafdata.com (23)

Butler, John, M., Consumer's Energy, Jackson, MI. Tel: (517) 788-0550, (800) 805-0490, FAX: (517) 788-1859, E-Mail: businesscenter@consumerenergy.com, Web Site: www.consumersenergy.com (16)

Butler, Kim, AAVIM, Winterville, GA. Tel: (706) 742-5355, (800) 228-4689, FAX: (706) 742-7005, E-Mail: gary@aavim.com, Web Site: www.aavim.com (31)

Butler, Steven, Ideagroup Mail Service, Saint Paul, MN. Tel: (651) 490-2903, FAX: (651) 490-0728, E-Mail: ideagroup@visi.com (28)

Butler Distributing Co, Kenilworth, NJ. Tel: (908) 241-3060, FAX: (908) 298-9248, E-Mail: bwprinting@worldnet.att.net, Web Site: www.bwprinting.com (3)

Butler Schein Animal Health, Dublin, OH. Tel: (614) 761-9095, (888) 691-2724, FAX: (888) 329-3861, Web Site: www.butlerschein.com (16)

Butler Specialty Co, Chicago, IL. Tel: (773) 221-1200, (800) 799-2857, FAX: (773) 221-5892, Web Site: www.butlerspecialty.net (16)

Butler Till Media Services, Rochester, NY. Tel: (585) 473-3740, Web Site: www.butlertill.com (31)

Butt, Lisa, Ivy Tech State College, Indianapolis, IN. Tel: (317) 921-4800, (888) IVY-LINE, FAX: (317) 921-4753, Web Site: www.ivytech.edu/indianapolis (13)

H E Butt Grocery Co, San Antonio, TX. Tel: (210) 938-8357, (800) 432-3113, FAX: (210) 938-7511, Web Site: www.heb.com (16)

Butta, Thomas, V., Superstock Inc, Jacksonville, FL. Tel: (904) 565-0066, (800) 828-4545, FAX: (904) 641-4480, E-Mail: yourfriends@superstock.com, Web Site: www.superstockimages.com (38)

Butterfield Farms Inc, Rolling Hills Estates, CA. Tel: (310) 750-6160, (800) 633-2767, E-Mail: dave@gifttrading.com, Web Site: www.butterfieldfarms.com (4)

Buttigeg III, Joseph, J., Comerica Inc, Dallas, TX. Tel: (800) 521-1190, FAX: (925) 941-1999, Web Site: www.comerica.com (16)

Button, Darryl, D., Transamerica Life Insurance Co, Cedar Rapids, IA. Tel: (319) 398-8511, (800) 558-9011, FAX: (319) 369-2825, Web Site: www.transamerica.com (15)

Butts, Jim, C H Robinson Worldwide Inc, Eden Prairie, MN. Tel: (952) 937-8500, FAX: (952) 937-6740, E-Mail: info@chrobinson.com, Web Site: www.chrobinson.com (16)

Butwinick, Rich, Marketing Agencies Association Worldwide, Minneapolis, MN. Tel: (952) 922-0130, FAX: (203) 969-1499, E-Mail: keith.mccracker@maaw.org, Web Site: www.maaw.org (40)

Butz, Theodore, H., FMC Corp, Philadelphia, PA. Tel: (215) 299-6000, FAX: (215) 299-5998, Web Site: www.fmc.com (16)

Buxton, Fort Worth, TX. Tel: (817) 332-3681, Web Site: www.buxtonco.com (30)

BuyFilters.com LLC, Silverhill, AL. Tel: (866) 863-1262, Web Site: www.buyfilters.com (5)

Buyotski, Arlene, Mercury International, Avenel, NJ. Tel: (732) 396-9555, FAX: (732) 396-1492, Web Site: www.mercuryinternational.com (28)

BUYSEASONS Inc, Bothell, WA. Tel: (262) 901-2000, Web Site: www.buyseasons.com (5)

Byen, Brad, Marketing Agencies Association Worldwide, Minneapolis, MN. Tel: (952) 922-0130, FAX: (203) 969-1499, E-Mail: keith.mccracker@maaw.org, Web Site: www.maaw.org (40)

Byers, Krista, National Multiple Sclerosis Society, Denver, CO. Tel: (303) 813-1052, Web Site: www.nmss.org (1)

Byham, William, C., Development Dimensions International, Bridgeville, PA. Tel: (412) 257-0600, (800) 933-4463, FAX: (412) 220-2942, E-Mail: info@ddiworld.com, Web Site: www.ddiworld.com (16)

Bylsma PhD, Wayne, H, American College of Physicians, Washington, DC. Tel: (215) 351-2400, (800) 523-1546, FAX: (215) 351-2686, Web Site: www.acponline.org (17)

Byndon, Leah, American Speech-Language-Hearing Association, Rockville, MD. Tel: (301) 897-5700, (800) 638-8255, E-Mail: productsales@asha.org, Web Site: www.asha.org (1)

Byowner.com, Shoreham, NY. Tel: (800) BY-OWNER. FAX: (866) BY-OWNER, Web Site: www.byowner.com (35)

Byrd, Sandra, Habitat For Humanity International, Americus, GA. Tel: (229) 924-6935, FAX: (229) 924-6541, Web Site: www.habitat.org (1)

Byrne, Donal, Research in Motion Corp, Waterloo, ON Canada. Tel: (519) 888-7465, Web Site: www.rim.com (2)

Byrne, Jane, Bale Co, Providence, RI. Tel: (800) 822-5350, FAX: (401) 831-5500, Web Site: www.bale.com (16)

Byrom, Peter, Domino Amjet Inc, Gurnee, IL. Tel: (847) 244-2501, FAX: (847) 244-2645, Web Site: www.dominoamjet.com (27)

Byron, Dennis, Pioneer Hi-Bred International Inc, Johnston, IA. Tel: (515) 270-3200, FAX: (515) 270-3581, E-Mail: web.editor@pioneer.com, Web Site: www.pioneer.com (4)

Byron Plantation, Vidalia, GA. Tel: (800) 356-0171, E-Mail: greenline/byron@bellsouth.net, Web Site: www.byronplantation.com (4)

Byrum, Roberta, K., Arthritis Foundation, Atlanta, GA. Tel: (404) 872-7100, FAX: (404) 872-0457, Web Site: www.arthritis.org (1)

Byrum & Fleming, San Anselmo, CA. Tel: (415) 457-1700, Web Site: www.byrumfleming.com (23)

C

C&H Distributors LLC, Milwaukee, WI. Tel: (414) 443-1700, (888) 316-2223, FAX: (414) 443-9213, E-Mail: customerservice@chdist.com, Web Site: www.chdist.com (9)

C&S Sales Inc, Wheeling, IL. Tel: (847) 541-0710, (800) 292-7711, FAX: (847) 541-9904, E-Mail: sales@cs-sales.com, Web Site: www.cs_sales.com (9)

C&T Bridge Supplies, Los Alamitos, CA. Tel: (562) 598-7010, (800) 525-4718, FAX: (562) 430-8309, E-Mail: tedinlosal@aol.com (11)

C L & B Capital Management, Fayetteville, NY. Tel: (315) 637-0915, FAX: (413) 403-7145, Web Site: www.clbcm.com (35)

(C) Systems LLC, Edison, NJ. Tel: (732) 548-6100, Web Site: www.csystemsllc.net (22)

C-W Agencies Inc, Vancouver, BC Canada. Tel: (604) 871-3400, FAX: (604) 871-3482, E-Mail: c-wreception@c-wgroup.com, Web Site: www.c-wgroup.com (35)

CA Inc, Islandia, NY. Tel: (800) 225-5224, FAX: (631) 342-3300, E-Mail: info@ca.com, Web Site: www.ca.com (16)

CAA Auto Club & Travel Agency Inc, Thornhill, ON Canada. Tel: (519) 255-1212, (800) 564-6222, FAX: (519) 255-7379, E-Mail: info@caasco.ca, Web Site: www.central.on.caa.ca (16)

CACI International Inc, Arlington, VA. Tel: (703) 841-7800, FAX: (703) 841-7882, Web Site: www.caci.com (22)

CAIG Laboratories Inc, Poway, CA. Tel: (858) 486-8388, FAX: (858) 486-8398, E-Mail: caig123@caig.com, Web Site: www.caig.com (9)

CAM Commerce Solutions, Fountain Valley, CA. Tel: (714) 241-9241, Web Site: www.camcommerce.com (22)

CAS Design Center, North Richland Hills, TX. Tel: (817) 788-1782 (8)

CAS Inc, Omaha, NE. Tel: (402) 964-9998, (800) 524-0908 X2071, FAX: (402) 963-2103, E-Mail: sales@cas-online.com, Web Site: www.cas-online.com (23)

CBSI, Harrison, NY. Tel: (914) 381-5353, Web Site: www.cbsiservices.com (30)

CBT Direct, Tarpon Springs, FL. Tel: (727) 724-8994, (877) 872-4646, FAX: (727) 797-9143, Web Site: www.cbtdirect.com (16)

CCA Global Partners, Manchester, NH. Tel: (603) 626-0333, Web Site: www.ccaglobal.com (16)

CCC of America, Irving, TX. Tel: (214) 206-3130, (800) 935-2222, FAX: (214) 206-3134, Web Site: www.cccofamerica.com (16)

CCH Inc, Riverwoods, IL. Tel: (847) 267-7000, (888) 224-7377, Web Site: www.cch.com (17)

CCI Digital, Burbank, CA. Tel: (818) 562-6300, FAX: (818) 562-8222, Web Site: www.ccidigital.com (32)

CCI Solutions, Olympia, WA. Tel: (360) 943-5378, (800) 426-8664, FAX: (360) 754-1566, (800) 339-TAPE, E-Mail: info@ccisolutions.com, Web Site: www.ccisolutions.com (16)

CCIM Institute, Chicago, IL. Tel: (312) 321-4460, (800) 621-7027, FAX: (312) 321-4530, Web Site: www.ccim.com (1)

CCL Label, Cold Spring, KY. Tel: (859) 781-6161, (800) 422-6633, FAX: (859) 781-6339 (27)

CCMR Advertising/Marketing Communications, Kingston, NY. Tel: (845) 331-4620, FAX: (845) 331-3026, Web Site: www.gotoccmr.com (35)

CD Universe, Wallingford, CT. Tel: (203) 294-1648, Web Site: www.cduniverse.com (16)

CDI Network Inc, Naperville, IL. Tel: (708) 409-8585, FAX: (708) 409-8589, Web Site: www.cdinet.biz (27)

CDMC/Carefree Direct Marketing Corp, Carefree, AZ. Tel: (480) 488-4227, FAX: (480) 488-2841 (20)

CDMG, Torrance, CA. Tel: (310) 212-5727, FAX: (310) 212-5773, E-Mail: infomat@biz.com, Web Site: www.cdmginc.com (21)

CDMI Inc, Huntington Beach, CA. Tel: (714) 969-4064 (1)

CDMO Inc, Deer Park, NY. Tel: (631) 242-8820, FAX: (631) 242-5761, E-Mail: cdsales@cdmo.com, Web Site: www.cdmo.com (16)

CDR Fundraising Group, Bowie, MD. Tel: (301) 858-1500, FAX: (301) 858-0107, Web Site: www.cdr-nfl.com (1)

CDS Global, Des Moines, IA. Tel: (515) 247-7500, FAX: (515) 246-6882, E-Mail: dluther@cdsfulfillment.com, Web Site: www.cdsfulfillment.com (22)

CDW Computer Centers Inc, Vernon Hills, IL. Tel: (847) 465-6000, (800) 800-4239, FAX: (847) 465-3444, Web Site: www.cdw.com (3)

CDW Corp, Vernon Hills, IL. Tel: (847) 465-6000, (800) 800-4239 (16)

CGSM Inc, Wilton, CT. Tel: (203) 563-9233, FAX: (203) 563-9239, Web Site: www.cgsm.com (35)

CGT Marketing, Amityville, NY. Tel: (631) 842-4600, FAX: (631) 842-6301, Web Site: www. cgtmarketing.com (21)

CHG, Salt Lake City, UT. Tel: (801) 930-3000, (800) 453-3030, Web Site: www.comphealth.com (7)

CI Productions Inc, Addison, IL. Tel: (708) 431-2800, FAX: (630) 458-1080 (35)

CIT, Livingston, NJ. Tel: (973) 422-6040, FAX: (973) 740-5383, Web Site: www.cit.com (14)

CJ Hummul Co, Nescapeck, PA. Tel: (570) 752-0936, (800) 762-0235, FAX: (570) 752-0938, E-Mail: mail@hummul.com, Web Site: www.hummul.com (11)

CLB Media Inc, Aurora, ON Canada. Tel: (905) 727-0077, FAX: (905) 727-0017, E-Mail: km@ industrialsourcebook.com, Web Site: www. clbmedia.ca (24)

CM Consulting Services, Marshfield, MA. Tel: (781) 749-5000, FAX: (801) 749-5009, E-Mail: cmcalpine3@gmail.com (27)

CMA Awards, Don Mills, ON Canada. Tel: (416) 391-2362, FAX: (416) 441-4062, E-Mail: info@the-cma.org, Web Site: www.the-cma.org/awards (42)

CMC & Design, Rock Island, IL. Tel: (309) 786-2888, FAX: (309) 786-9887, E-Mail: cmcanddesign@aol. com (35)

CMEinfo.com, Birmingham, AL. Tel: (205) 991-9188, (800) 284-8433, FAX: (800) 284-5964, Web Site: www.cmeinfo.com (16)

CMI Direct, Montrose, CA. Tel: (951) 300-1700, FAX: (866) 723-5433, Web Site: www.cmidirect. net (15)

CMMC Market Research, Mount Freedom, NJ. Tel: (973) 989-0229, FAX: (973) 366-1185, E-Mail: dmmp@cmmcinc.com, Web Site: www.cmmcinc. com (30)

CMS Inc, Winston Salem, NC. Tel: (336) 631-2524, Web Site: www.promotionslogistics.com (14)

CMS LLC, Reston, VA. Tel: (703) 258-0000, Web Site: www.craveronline.com (1)

CNA, Chicago, IL. Tel: (312) 822-5000, (800) 262-2000, E-Mail: cna_help@cna.com, Web Site: www. cna.com (15)

CNBC-Consumer & Business Channel, Englewood Cliffs, NJ. Tel: (201) 735-2622, FAX: (201) 735-3200, Web Site: www.cnbc.com (32)

CNY Awards & Apparel Inc, New Hartford, NY. Tel: (315) 733-0931, Web Site: www.cnyapprel.com (5)

CPAC Inc, Leicester, NY. Tel: (585) 382-3223, (800) 828-6011, FAX: (585) 382-3031, E-Mail: cpacinfo@cpac.com, Web Site: www.cpac.com (16)

CPC Inc, Babylon, NY. Tel: (631) 661-6779, (800) 621-4414, FAX: (631) 661-6914, E-Mail: cpcus@ aol.com, Web Site: www.cpctours.com (19)

CPE, Chicago, IL. Tel: (312) 427-5370, FAX: (312) 427-7836, E-Mail: wgavin@cpe1.com, Web Site: www.cpe1.com (27)

CPI Card Group, Littleton, CO. Tel: (303) 973-9311, FAX: (303) 973-8420, E-Mail: mbarber@ cpicardgroup.com, Web Site: www.cpicardgroup. com (27)

CPI Corp, St Louis, MO. Tel: (314) 231-1575, (877) 763-4456, FAX: (314) 231-8150, E-Mail: feedback@cpicorp.com, Web Site: www.cpicorp. com (16)

CPM Delta 1, Inc, Dallas, TX. Tel: (214) 349-6886, (800) 627-0252, FAX: (214) 503-1557, Web Site: www.cpmdelta1.com (11)

CPO Direct Inc, Lake Forest, IL. Tel: (847) 735-7365, FAX: (847) 735-9825, E-Mail: ngoldring@ cpodirect.com, Web Site: www.cpodirect.com (35)

The CPW Group, Ronkonkoma, NY. Tel: (888) 641-7901 (28)

CRB, Chicago, IL. Tel: (312) 554-8456, (800) 621-5271, FAX: (312) 939-4135, E-Mail: info@ crbtrader.com, Web Site: www.crbtrader.com (17)

CRC Data Systems, Long Island City, NY. Tel: (718) 729-2622, E-Mail: jrafael@opinionaccess.com, Web Site: www.opinionaccess.com (22)

CRC Public Relations, Alexandria, VA. Tel: (703) 683-5004, FAX: (703) 683-1703, E-Mail: crc@ crcpublicrelations.com, Web Site: www.crc4pr.com (35)

CRK Computer Services, Southfield, MI. Tel: (248) 569-3050, FAX: (248) 569-5259, E-Mail: information@crkusa.com, Web Site: www.crkusa. com (22)

CRM Learning, Carlsbad, CA. Tel: (760) 431-9800, (800) 421-0833, FAX: (760) 931-5792, E-Mail: sales@crmlearning.com, Web Site: www. crmlearning.com (16)

CRN International Inc, Hamden, CT. Tel: (203) 288-2002, FAX: (203) 281-3291, E-Mail: info@ crnradio.com, Web Site: www.crnradio.com (32)

C.R.W. Graphics, Pennsauken, NJ. Tel: (856) 662-9111, (800) 820-3000, FAX: (856) 665-1789, E-Mail: service@crwgraphics.com, Web Site: www.crwgraphics.com (27)

CSE Inc, New Berlin, WI. Tel: (262) 786-8400, (800) 999-0001, FAX: (262) 796-2089, E-Mail: ask@ csecatalog.com, Web Site: www.csepromo.com (33)

CSG Interactive Messaging, Omaha, NE. Tel: (402) 398-4100, (800) 888-3151, FAX: (402) 398-4000, Web Site: www.prairiesys.com (29)

CSI, Conklin, NY. Tel: (607) 775-7905, Web Site: www.cleanersupply.com (16)

CSM Inc, Marietta, GA. Tel: (800) 849-6788, FAX: (770) 514-6799, E-Mail: info@csmresearch.com, Web Site: www.csmresearch.com (30)

CSPI/Nutrition Action Health Letter, Washington, DC. Tel: (202) 332-9110, FAX: (202) 265-4954, E-Mail: cspi@cspinet.org, Web Site: www.cspinet. org (17)

CSS Direct, Elkhorn, NE. Tel: (402) 359-1515, FAX: (402) 359-1516, E-Mail: custserv@cssdirect.com, Web Site: www.cssdirect.com (29)

CTA Inc, Fenton, MO. Tel: (636) 305-3100, Web Site: www.ctainc.com (5)

CTB MacMillan/McGraw-Hill, Monterey, CA. Tel: (831) 393-0700, (800) 538-9547, FAX: (831) 393-6528, E-Mail: hr@ctb.com, Web Site: www.ctb. com (16)

CTC Corp, Bennington, VT. Tel: (802) 442-6371, FAX: (802) 442-8526 (16)

CTC Teleservices, De Kalb, IL. Tel: (815) 748-4200, FAX: (630) 773-4765, Web Site: www. ctcteleservices.com (29)

CTRAC Information Solutions, Strongsville, OH. Tel: (440) 572-1000, FAX: (440) 572-3330, E-Mail: ctrac@ctrac.com, Web Site: www.ctrac.com (22)

CUES Experience Conference, Madison, WI. Tel: (608) 271-2664, (800) 252-2664, FAX: (608) 271-2303, Web Site: www.cues.org (42)

CVS Caremark, Woonsocket, RI. Tel: (401) 765-1500, FAX: (401) 769-4488, Web Site: www.cvs.com (7)

CVT Production Inc, Granger, IN. Tel: (574) 247-0647, Web Site: www.destinationfitness.com (16)

CWC Inventories Inc, Maryland Heights, MO. Tel: (314) 739-1311, FAX: (314) 739-7398, E-Mail: frankg@cwcinventories.com, Web Site: www. cwcinventories.com (33)

CX&B United Corp, Harbor City, CA. Tel: (310) 530-2102, (800) 292-8258, FAX: (310) 530-2513, E-Mail: sales@cxbunited.com, Web Site: www. cxbunited.com (33)

CXO Media Inc, Framingham, MA. Tel: (508) 872-0080, (800) 859-5478, FAX: (508) 872-0618, Web Site: www.cxo.com (17)

CYRO Industries, Parsippany, NJ. Tel: (973) 541-8000, (800) 631-5384, FAX: (973) 442-6117, (973) 442-6135, Web Site: www.cyro.com (16)

Caballero, Tony, Westlake Plastics Co, Lenni, PA. Tel: (610) 459-1000, (800) 999-1700, FAX: (610) 459-1084, Web Site: www.westlakeplastics.com (16)

Cabeen, Thomas, FPS Marketing Communications, Milford, CT. Tel: (203) 783-1940, FAX: (203) 783-1950, E-Mail: info@fpsmarketing.com, Web Site: www.fpsmarketing.com (35)

Cabela, James, Cabela's Inc, Sidney, NE. Tel: (308) 254-5505, (800) 237-4444, FAX: (308) 254-4800, Web Site: www.cabelas.com (11)

Cabela, Richard, Cabela's Inc, Sidney, NE. Tel: (308) 254-5505, (800) 237-4444, FAX: (308) 254-4800, Web Site: www.cabelas.com (11)

Cabela's Inc, Sidney, NE. Tel: (308) 254-5505, (800) 237-4444, FAX: (308) 254-4800, Web Site: www. cabelas.com (11)

Cable, Philip, E., American Science & Surplus, Niles, IL. Tel: (847) 647-0020, (800) SCI-PLUS, FAX: (847) 647-5010, E-Mail: info@sciplus.com, Web Site: www.sciplus.com (9)

Cable Car Clothiers/Robert Kirk Ltd, San Francisco, CA. Tel: (415) 397-4740, FAX: (415) 616-8998, E-Mail: info@cablecarclothiers.com, Web Site: www.cablecarclothiers.com (2)

Cable Connection, Fremont, CA. Tel: (408) 395-6700, FAX: (408) 354-3980, E-Mail: cables4u@cable-connection.com, Web Site: www.cable-connection. com (3)

Cable Direct Marketing Inc, Montville, NJ. Tel: (973) 244-0010, FAX: (973) 244-0302, E-Mail: cabledm@aol.com (31)

Cable Films & Video, Mission Hills, KS. Tel: (913) 362-2804, (800) 514-2804, FAX: (913) 362-2864, E-Mail: cablefilms@kc.rr.com, Web Site: www. onlineworld.com/movies (3)

Cable Shopping Network, Scottsdale, AZ. Tel: (480) 624-4446, Web Site: www.shopcsntv.com (16)

The Cable Show National Cable Television Association, Washington, DC. Tel: (202) 222-2300, E-Mail: webmaster@ncta.com, Web Site: www. ncta.com (42)

Cables to Go, Moraine, OH. Tel: (937) 224-8646, (800) 506-9607, FAX: (800) 331-2841, (937) 496-2666, Web Site: www.cablestogo.com (3)

Cablevision Systems Corp, Bethpage, NY. Tel: (516) 803-2300, FAX: (516) 803-3134, Web Site: www. cablevision.com (16)

Cablexpress Technologies, Syracuse, NY. Tel: (315) 476-3000, (800) 913-9467, FAX: (315) 455-1800, E-Mail: info@cablexpress.com, Web Site: www. CXTec.com (10)

Cabral Jr, Robert, M., Americraft - The Gift Brokers Inc, Wendell, MA. Tel: (978) 544-7330, (800) 866-2723, FAX: (978) 544-2771, E-Mail: info@ americraft.us, Web Site: www.americraft.us (16)

Cabral, Samuel, A., Union Privilege, AFL-CIO, Washington, DC. Tel: (202) 293-5330, FAX: (202) 293-5311, Web Site: www.unionplus.org (1)

Cabrinha, John, Mercury Media, Santa Monica, CA. Tel: (310) 451-2900, FAX: (310) 451-0180, Web Site: www.mercurymedia.com (32)

Caccavale, Michael, Pluris, Framingham, MA. Tel: (508) 663-1100, Web Site: www.plurisinc.com (22)

Cacciatore, Jerry, Quebecor World North America, North Haven, CT. Tel: (203) 288-2468, FAX: (203) 248-6478, Web Site: www.quebecorworldinc.com (27)

Caccini, Gianpaolo, CertainTeed Corp, Valley Forge, PA. Tel: (610) 341-7000/7739, (800) 233-8990, FAX: (610) 341-7777, Web Site: www.certainteed. com (16)

Cactus Mailing Company, Scottsdale, AZ. Tel: (480) 443-1442, (866) 443-1442, FAX: (480) 443-2518, E-Mail: info@cactusmailing.com, Web Site: www. cactusmailing.com (21)

Cade & Associates Advertising, Tallahassee, FL. Tel: (850) 385-0300, (800) 715-CADE, FAX: (850) 385-1165, E-Mail: webmaster@cade1.com, Web Site: www.cade1.com (35)

Cadie Products Corp, Paterson, NJ. Tel: (973) 278-8300, FAX: (973) 278-0303, E-Mail: emeyers@ cadie.com, Web Site: www.cadieproducts.com (16)

Cadieux, Dan, InfoCANADA, Mississauga, ON Canada. Tel: (866) 373-2066, FAX: (905) 306-7272, E-Mail: customerservice@infocanada.ca, Web Site: www.infocanada.ca (23)

Cadmam, Camille, Cellular One Group, Oklahoma City, OK. Tel: (509) 663-2162, (800) 545-5982, FAX: (425) 586-8451, Web Site: www.cellularone.com (16)

Cadmus Communications Corp, Richmond, VA. Tel: (804) 264-2711, FAX: (804) 262-6419, Web Site: www.cenveo.com (35)

Cady, William R., Magna Visual Inc, Saint Louis, MO. Tel: (314) 843-9000, (800) 843-3399, FAX: (314) 843-0000, E-Mail: magna@magnavisual.com, Web Site: www.magnavisual.com (9)

Caesars Atlantic City Casino/Hotel, Atlantic City, NJ. Tel: (609) 348-4411, (800) 634-6661, FAX: (609) 343-2405, Web Site: www.harrahs.com (19)

Caesars Palace, Las Vegas, NV. Tel: (702) 407-6000, (800) 634-6001, FAX: (702) 407-6037, Web Site: www.caesars.com (16)

Cafe Lango, Guilford, CT. Tel: (203) 453-1456, (800) 243-1234, FAX: (203) 453-5110, E-Mail: mail@cafelango.com, Web Site: www.audioforum.com (16)

Caffrey, Betsy, Columbia Tristar Home Video, Culver City, CA. Tel: (310) 244-4000, FAX: (310) 244-1544, Web Site: www.cthe.com (16)

Cagan, Dennis, J., TWL Knowledge Group, Carrollton, TX. Tel: (972) 309-4000, (800) 624-2272, FAX: (972) 309-5105, Web Site: www.twlk.com (3)

Cage, Lynn, Tucker Electronics Co, Garland, TX. Tel: (214) 348-8800, (887) 667-6044, FAX: (214) 348-0367, E-Mail: sales@tucker.com, Web Site: www.tucker.com (3)

Cahill, Dennis, A, ThinkDirect Marketing Group, Largo, FL. Tel: (727) 369-2700, E-Mail: info@tdmg.com, Web Site: www.tdmg.com (28)

Cahill, Rose, Savings Bank Life Insurance Co of MA (SBLI), Woburn, MA. Tel: (781) 938-3500, Web Site: www.sbli.com (15)

Cahilll, Toby, ThreeSource Fulfillment, Manteno, IL. Tel: (815) 936-1094 x4179, (888) 673-4650, FAX: (815) 936-9743, E-Mail: sandyp@threesource.tv, Web Site: www.threesource.tv (28)

Cahn, Eric, The Pin Man, Tulsa, OK. Tel: (918) 587-2405, FAX: (918) 745-2162, Web Site: www.positivepin.com (16)

Cain, Jim, Yankelovich Inc, Chapel Hill, NC. Tel: (919) 932-8600, Web Site: www.yankelovich.com (22)

Cain, John, Priests of the Sacred Heart, Hales Corners, WI. Tel: (414) 425-3383, FAX: (414) 425-5719, Web Site: www.poshusa.org (1)

Cain, Rogen, D., Bradford Health Services, Birmingham, AL. Tel: (205) 251-7753, (800) 217-2849, Web Site: www.bradfordhealth.com (16)

Cain, Tim, The Herald & Review, Decatur, IL. Tel: (217) 429-5151, FAX: (217) 421-6913, E-Mail: hrdirect@herald-review.com, Web Site: www.herald-review.com (17)

Caine, Cathy, Pacific Sportswear Co Inc, San Diego, CA. Tel: (619) 281-6688, (800) USA-8778, FAX: (619) 281-6687, E-Mail: info@pacsport.com, Web Site: www.pacsport.com (5)

Caine, Paul, T., The Cracker Box Inc, Blooming Glen, PA. Tel: (215) 443-7777, FAX: (215) 443-7777, E-Mail: walter@crackerboxkits.com, Web Site: www.crackerboxkits.com (16)

Caine, Tim, ACP - Automation Control Products, Alpharetta, GA. Tel: (678) 990-0945, FAX: (678) 990-0951, E-Mail: info@thinmanager.com, Web Site: www.thinmanager.com (16)

Caitlin, Ken, Renaissance Greeting Cards Inc, Springvale, ME. Tel: (207) 324-4153, (800) 688-9998, FAX: (207) 324-9564, E-Mail: rencards@rencards.com (5)

CakeMail Inc, Montreal, PQ Canada. Tel: (514) 316-1550, Web Site: www.cakemail.com (20)

Cakuun, Asheville, NC. Tel: (828) 225-5505, E-Mail: transformyourbrand@cakuun.com, Web Site: cakuun.com (35)

Calabrese Sr, Frank, FCL Graphics Inc, Harwood Heights, IL. Tel: (708) 867-5500, (800) 274-3380, FAX: (708) 867-7768 (27)

Calabrese, Gerald, Marketing and Product Strategy, Peabody, MA. Tel: (978) 977-2000, (800) 825-5897, FAX: (781) 238-0986, Web Site: www.lhsl.com (16)

Calandra, T.M., Starcrest Products of California Inc, Perris, CA. Tel: (909) 943-2011, FAX: (909) 943-2971, E-Mail: tmc@tstonramp.com (16)

Calbiochem-Novabiochem Corp, San Diego, CA. Tel: (858) 450-9600, (800) 854-3417, FAX: (858) 453-3552, E-Mail: customerservice@emdbioscience.com, Web Site: www.calbiochem.com (9)

Calcott, C. Reid, Educational Insights, Inc, Gardena, CA. Tel: (310) 884-2000, (888) 591-9334, FAX: (310) 886-8850, E-Mail: service@edin.com, Web Site: www.educationalinsights.com (16)

Calder, Kristin, Bethesda Hospital Foundation, Boynton Beach, FL. Tel: (561) 737-7733 (1)

Calder, Lorraine, White Flower Farm, Torrington, CT. Tel: (860) 496-9624, (800) 503-9624, FAX: (860) 496-1418, Web Site: www.whiteflowerfarm.com (8)

Calderbank, Kathy, American Stationery Co Inc, Peru, IN. Tel: (765) 473-4438, (800) 822-2577, FAX: (800) 253-9054, Web Site: www.americanstationery.com (10)

Caldwell, Doug, AstraZeneca, Wilmington, DE. Tel: (302) 866-1482, Web Site: www.astrazeneca-us.com (7)

Caldwell, Dr Robert, Hebron Academy, Hebron, ME. Tel: (207) 966-2100, Web Site: www.habronacademy.org (1)

Caldwell, Jim, Future Thunder Productions, Van Nuys, CA. Tel: (818) 986-9494, FAX: (818) 986-6644, E-Mail: jim@futurethunder.com, Web Site: www.futurethunder.com (32)

Caldwell, Joseph, Sunrise Business Products, Mineola, NY. Tel: (800) 222-7367, FAX: (631) 588-3900 (10)

Caldwell, Kathy, J., American Society of Civil Engineers, Reston, VA. Tel: (703) 295-6000, (800) 548-2723, FAX: (703) 295-6343, Web Site: www.asce.org (1)

A Caldwell List Co Inc, Norcross, GA. Tel: (770) 662-0255, (800) 241-7425, FAX: (770) 662-0351, Web Site: www.caldwell-list.com (23)

Cale, Kelley, PJT Inc, Savannah, GA. Tel: (912) 233-6220, Web Site: www.riverstreetsweets.com (4)

Cale, Kelley, River Street Sweets, Savannah, GA. Tel: (912) 234-4608, (800) 793-3876, FAX: (912) 234-1584, E-Mail: randerson@riverstreetsweets.com, Web Site: www.riverstreetsweets.com (4)

Calendar Marketing Association, Wheaton, IL. Tel: (630) 510-4500, FAX: (630) 510-4501, E-Mail: info@calendarassociation.org, Web Site: www.calendarassociation.org (1)

Calhoun, Arlene, American Biographical Institute Inc, Raleigh, NC. Tel: (919) 781-8710, FAX: (919) 781-8712, Web Site: www.abiworldwide.com (17)

Calhoun, David, L, Nielsen Business Media, New York, NY. Tel: (646) 654-4500, FAX: (646) 654-7212, E-Mail: bmcomm@nielsen.com, Web Site: www.nielsenbusinessmedia.com (16)

Calhoun, David, The Nielsen Co, New York, NY. Tel: (646) 654-5000, E-Mail: contactcommunications@nielsen.com, Web Site: www.nielsen.com (17)

Calhoun, Jim, Daystar Data Group Inc, Schaumburg, IL. Tel: (847) 202-0100, FAX: (847) 202-0107, E-Mail: sales@daystardg.com, Web Site: www.daystardg.com (22)

Calibre Press Inc, San Francisco, CA. Tel: (214) 545-3060, (800) 323-0037, FAX: (866) 225-4273, Web Site: www.calibrepress.com (17)

Calico Corners, Kennett Square, PA. Tel: (610) 444-9700, FAX: (610) 444-1221, Web Site: www.calicocorners.com (16)

Caliendo, Charlie, CSE Inc, New Berlin, WI. Tel: (262) 786-8400, (800) 999-0001, FAX: (262) 796-2089, E-Mail: ask@csecatalog.com, Web Site: www.csepromo.com (33)

California Chamber of Commerce, Sacramento, CA. Tel: (800) 331-8877, Web Site: www.calbizcentral.com (1)

California Cosmetics Corp, Tarzana, CA. Tel: (818) 225-2999, (800) 366-8243, FAX: (800) 345-7763, E-Mail: calcos@silkskin.com, Web Site: www.silkskin.com (7)

California Institute of Technology, Pasadena, CA. Tel: (626) 395-3746, FAX: (626) 795-7174, E-Mail: execedu@caltech.edu, Web Site: www.irc.caltech.edu (16)

California Mustang Parts & Accessories, City of Industry, CA. Tel: (909) 598-3383, (800) 775-0101, FAX: (909) 598-5611, E-Mail: csmustang@cal-mustang.com, Web Site: www.cal-mustang.com (16)

California Offset Printers, Glendale, CA. Tel: (818) 291-1100, (800) 280-6446, FAX: (818) 291-1190, E-Mail: info@copprints.com, Web Site: www.copprints.com (27)

California Pacific Research & New Generation, Reno, NV. Tel: (775) 829-5600, (800) 541-5703, FAX: (775) 829-5619, E-Mail: sales@newgen2000.com, Web Site: www.newgen2000.com (7)

California Society of CPA's, San Mateo, CA. Tel: (800) 922-5272, FAX: (650) 522-3009, E-Mail: info@culcpa.org, Web Site: www.calcpa.org (1)

California State Polytechnic University Business Administration Dept, San Luis Obispo, CA. Tel: (805) 756-1413, FAX: (805) 756-5057, Web Site: www.calpoly.edu (41)

California State University at Fresno, Fresno, CA. Tel: (559) 278-7830, FAX: (559) 278-8577, Web Site: www.csufresno.edu (41)

Call, Merlin, W., The Fuller Theological Seminary, Pasadena, CA. Tel: (626) 584-5200, (800) 2-FULLER, FAX: (626) 584-5449, Web Site: www.fuller.edu/cll (16)

Call Compliance Inc, Glen Cove, NY. Tel: (516) 674-4545, FAX: (516) 676-2420, E-Mail: sales@callcompliance.com, Web Site: www.callcompliance.com (29)

Call Interactive, Omaha, NE. Tel: (402) 498-7000, FAX: (402) 498-7900, Web Site: www.callit.com (29)

Callahan, Dan, O., Marketing III Direct Response, Clermont, FL. Tel: (352) 241-8040, FAX: (352) 241-4533, E-Mail: marketing35th@aol.com (35)

Callahan, David, Putt Putt Fun Centers, Winston-Salem, NC. Tel: (336) 714-3950, (866) PUTT-PUTT, FAX: (336) 714-3955, Web Site: www.puttputt.com (16)

Callahan, David, The Professional Putters Association, Winston Salem, NC. Tel: (336) 714-3950, (866) PUTT-PUTT, FAX: (336) 714-3955, Web Site: www.putt-putt.com (1)

Callahan, Linda, New Directions Publishing Corp, New York, NY. Tel: (212) 255-0230, FAX: (212) 255-0231, E-Mail: editorial@ndbooks.com, Web Site: www.ndpublishing.com (17)

Callahan, Michael, Cabela's Inc, Sidney, NE. Tel: (308) 254-5505, (800) 237-4444, FAX: (308) 254-4800, Web Site: www.cabelas.com (11)

Callahan, Ralph, W., Henderson Advertising Inc, Greenville, SC. Tel: (864) 232-5733, FAX: (864) 298-1280, Web Site: www.hendersonadv.com (35)

Callahan, Robert, F., Ziff Davis Media Inc, New York, NY. Tel: (212) 503-5100, FAX: (212) 503-5023, Web Site: www.ziffdavis.com (17)

Callahan, Tom, Smarterville Productions LLC, Elgin, IL. Tel: (800) 861-6531, FAX: (410) 843-8318, E-Mail: tom.callahan@smartville.com, Web Site: www.hooked-on-phonics.com (3)

Callari, Neil, D2: Direct, Denville, NJ. Tel: (973) 627-4410, FAX: (973) 627-3703, E-Mail: info@d2direct.com, Web Site: www.d2direct.com (35)

Callaway Gardens, Pine Mountain, GA. Tel: (706) 663-2281, (800) CALLAWAY, FAX: (706) 663-6812, E-Mail: info@callawaygardens.com, Web Site: www.callawaygardens.com (19)

Callendary, Steve, Resorts Atlantic City, Atlantic City, NJ. Tel: (609) 334-6000, (800) 336-6378, FAX: (609) 340-6349, Web Site: www.resortsac.com (19)

Calling Solutions, San Antonio, TX. Tel: (210) 822-7400, (800) 683-5500, FAX: (210) 491-1777, E-Mail: pepe@callingsolutions.com, Web Site: www.callingsolutions.com (29)

Calloway, Kevin, IJHANA, Los Angeles, CA. Tel: (213) 268-4283, (888) 421-9222, E-Mail: info@ijhana.com, Web Site: www.ijhana.com (20)

Calloway House Inc, Lancaster, PA. Tel: (717) 299-5703, (800) 233-0290, FAX: (717) 299-6754, Web Site: www.callowayhouse.com (34)

Calman, Charles, Source 4 Inc, Huntersville, NC. Tel: (704) 602-0110, (800) 541-5400, FAX: (704) 602-0119, E-Mail: source4newyork@source4.com, Web Site: www.source4.com (27)

Calmark Inc, Chicago, IL. Tel: (773) 247-7200, FAX: (773) 247-3199, E-Mail: ljakobi@calmark-inc.com, Web Site: www.clamark-inc.com (28)

Calos, Chris, American General Co, Neptune, NJ. Tel: (732) 922-7000, FAX: (732) 922-7595 (15)

Caltrider, Wayne, JC Direct Mail Inc, Groveport, OH. Tel: (614) 836-4848, FAX: (614) 836-4847, E-Mail: pwhite@wcnjcd.com (28)

Calumet Photographic Inc, Bensenville, IL. Tel: (630) 860-7447, (800) 453-2550, FAX: (800) 577-3686, E-Mail: custserv@calumetphoto.com, Web Site: www.calumetphoto.com (3)

Calvert, Lorelei, Texas Monthly, Austin, TX. Tel: (512) 320-6900, (800) 759-2000, FAX: (512) 476-9007, E-Mail: info@texasmonthly.com, Web Site: www.texasmonthly.com (17)

Calvey, Kevin, Skytel Communications Inc, Lewisville, TX. Tel: (800) 759-8737, Web Site: www.skytel.com (29)

Calvimontes, Andrew, The Envelope Connection Inc, Chicago, IL. Tel: (773) 275-3500, Web Site: www.artofbarter.com/EnvelopeConnectionProfile.html (28)

Calzaretta, Julie, Liberty Creative Solutions, Tinley Park, IL. Tel: (708) 633-7450, Web Site: www.libertycreativesolutions.com (21)

Camacho, Phillip, Bruce, Assurant Solutions Preneed Division, Atlanta, GA. Tel: (770) 763-1000, (800) PRE NEED, FAX: (770) 859-4325, Web Site: www.assurantpreneed.com (15)

Camarata, Jillian, Cooper-Atkins Corp, Middlefield, CT. Tel: (860) 347-2256, (800) 835-5011, FAX: (860) 347-5135, Web Site: www.cooper-atkins.com (34)

Cambey & West Inc, Congers, NY. Tel: (845) 267-3006, FAX: (845) 267-3503, E-Mail: info@cambeywest.com, Web Site: www.cambeywest.com (22)

Cambridge Educational, New York, NY. Tel: (800) 257-5126, FAX: (917) 339-0325, Web Site: www.filmsmediagroup.com (12)

Came, David, Marian Helpers Center, Stockbridge, MA. Tel: (413) 298-3691, (800) 462-7426, FAX: (413) 298-3583, Web Site: www.marian.org (1)

Camellia Forest Nursery, Chapel Hill, NC. Tel: (919) 968-0504, FAX: (919) 929-8971, E-Mail: camforest@aol.com, Web Site: www.camforest.com (8)

Camelot Enterprises, Bristol, WI. Tel: (262) 857-2695 (9)

Camenzind, Betty, Tender Heart Treasures, Omaha, NE. Tel: (402) 593-1313, (800) 443-1367, FAX: (402) 593-1316, E-Mail: bcamenzind@thtdesigns.com (6)

Camerlo, James, P., Dairy Farmers of America Inc, Kansas City, MO. Tel: (816) 801-6455, (888) 332-6455, FAX: (816) 801-6456, E-Mail: webmail@dfamilk.com, Web Site: www.dfamilk.com (16)

Cameron Jr, Allan, Art, Tape & Label Co, Addison, IL. Tel: (630) 543-8100, FAX: (630) 543-8153, Web Site: arttapeandlabel.com (27)

Cameron, Diane, Relaxo-Bak Inc, Anderson, IN. Tel: (765) 643-2934, (800) 527-5496, FAX: (765) 641-7448, Web Site: www.relaxobak.com (7)

Cameron, Dugald, Gardenimport Inc, Richmond Hill, ON Canada. Tel: (905) 731-1950, (800) 339-8314, FAX: (905) 731-3093, E-Mail: flower@gardenimport.com, Web Site: www.gardenimport.com (8)

Cameron, Patricia, Century Tel Enterprises Inc, Monroe, LA. Tel: (318) 388-9000, (800) 201-4102, Web Site: centurytel.com (29)

Cameron, Peter, Vermont/New Hampshire Direct Marketing Group, Woodstock, VT. Tel: (802) 457-2807, FAX: (802) 457-2807, E-Mail: vtnhmg@vtnhmg, Web Site: www.vtnhmg.org (40)

Cameron, Wade, Cameron & Co, Toronto, ON Canada. Tel: (416) 268-2326 (20)

Cameron & Co, Toronto, ON Canada. Tel: (416) 268-2326 (20)

Camille, Keith, Touch-Base Computing, Silver Creek, GA. Tel: (706) 378-0964, E-Mail: sales@touchbase.com, Web Site: www.touchbase.com (22)

Camilly, Lisa, The Akadine Press Inc, White Plains, NY. Tel: (914) 747-0777, FAX: (914) 747-0778, Web Site: www.commonreader.com (16)

Camm, Robert, J., Quadra Graphics Inc, Cherry Hill, NJ. Tel: (856) 665-4060, FAX: (856) 665-7324, E-Mail: richard.nixon@qgi.com (27)

Cammarata, Peter, Cuisinart, Stamford, CT. Tel: (203) 975-4600, FAX: (203) 975-4660, Web Site: www.cuisinart.com (16)

Camp Healthcare Inc, Jackson, MI. Tel: (517) 787-1600, (800) 492-1088, FAX: (800) 245-3765, E-Mail: info@truelife.biz, Web Site: www.camphealthcare.com (16)

Campaigns & Elections Magazine, Arlington, VA. Tel: (703) 778-4028, (800) 771-8252, FAX: (703) 778-4024, Web Site: www.campaignsandelections.com (17)

Campanaro, Sal, Modern Graphic Arts, Saint Petersburg, FL. Tel: (727) 579-1527, FAX: (727) 579-1528 (27)

Campanella, Constance, Stateside Associates, Arlington, VA. Tel: (703) 525-7466 X228 (20)

Campanelli, Joe, Sovereign Bank New England, Glastonbury, CT. Tel: (877) 768-2265, FAX: (860) 727-6517 (14)

Campbell, Anne, California Institute of Technology, Pasadena, CA. Tel: (626) 395-3746, FAX: (626) 795-7174, E-Mail: execedu@caltech.edu, Web Site: www.irc.caltech.edu (16)

Campbell, Arthur, Thermal Product Solutions, White Deer, PA. Tel: (570) 538-7200, (800) 586-2473 (16)

Campbell, Bill, Glenview State Bank, Glenview, IL. Tel: (847) 729-1900, FAX: (847) 729-5847, E-Mail: info@gsb.com, Web Site: www.gsb.com (14)

Campbell, Bill, Intuit, Mountain View, CA. Tel: (650) 944-6000, Web Site: www.inuit.com (10)

Campbell, Colin, G., The Colonial Williamsburg Foundation, Williamsburg, VA. Tel: (757) 229-1000, (757) 220-7275, (800) 761-8331, Web Site: www.williamsburgmarketplace.com (1)

Campbell, Cynthia, Office Depot, Boca Raton, FL. Tel: (561) 438-4800, (800) 937-3600, FAX: (561) 438-4001, Web Site: www.officedepot.com (16)

Campbell, Dave, Borbeleta Gardens, Fairbault, MN. Tel: (507) 334-2807, FAX: (507) 332-0365 (8)

Campbell, Dave, Projection Video Services, Springfield, VA. Tel: (703) 912-1334, (800) 377-7650, FAX: (703) 912-1350, Web Site: www.projection.com (16)

Campbell, Dave, The FX Matt Brewing Co, Utica, NY. Tel: (315) 732-0022, (800) 765-6288, FAX: (315) 624-2401, E-Mail: info@saranac.com, Web Site: www.saranac.com (4)

Campbell, David, ACCO North America, Lincolnshire, IL. Tel: (847) 541-9500, (800) 222-6462, FAX: (847) 478-0073, Web Site: www.acco.com (16)

Campbell, David, Chernoff Newman, Columbia, SC. Tel: (803) 254-8158, FAX: (803) 252-2016, E-Mail: david.campbell@cnsg.com, Web Site: www.chernoffnewman.com (35)

Campbell, David, D., Kensington Technology Group, Redwood Shores, CA. Tel: (650) 572-2700, FAX: (650) 267-2800, Web Site: www.kensington.com (16)

Campbell, Jack, Borbeleta Gardens, Fairbault, MN. Tel: (507) 334-2807, FAX: (507) 332-0365 (8)

Campbell, Jack, Gerstner Woodworks, Dayton, OH. Tel: (937) 228-1662, FAX: (937) 228-8557, E-Mail: info@gerstnerusa.com, Web Site: www.gerstnerusa.com (6)

Campbell, James P., GE Consumer & Industrial Lighting, Cleveland, OH. Tel: (216) 266-2222, (216) 266-2121, FAX: (216) 266-2930, Web Site: www.gelighting.com/na (16)

Campbell, Jeffrey, C., McKesson Corp, San Francisco, CA. Tel: (415) 983-8300, FAX: (415) 983-7160, Web Site: www.mckesson.com (7)

Campbell, Jerry, Squadron Mail Order, Carrollton, TX. Tel: (972) 242-8663, (877) 414-0434, FAX: (972) 242-3775, E-Mail: mailorder@squadron.com, Web Site: www.squadron.com (16)

Campbell, Jill, Cox Communications, Atlanta, GA. Tel: (404) 843-5000, FAX: (404) 269-2243, Web Site: www.cox.com (16)

Campbell, Marti, Creative Marketing Management, Chevy Chase, MD. Tel: (301) 650-4160, FAX: (301) 650-4161 (21)

Campbell, Michael, Anderson Direct Marketing, Poway, CA. Tel: (888) 694-5094, Web Site: www.andersondirectmarketing.com (35)

Campbell, Nancy, The Humane Society of the US, Gaithersburg, MD. Tel: (202) 452-1100, Web Site: www.hsus.org (1)

Campbell, Phillip, Nature Publishing Group, New York, NY. Tel: (212) 726-9200, FAX: (212) 696-9006, E-Mail: nature@natureny.com, Web Site: www.nature.com (17)

Campbell, Robert, H., Sunoco, Inc, Philadelphia, PA. Tel: (215) 977-3000, (800) 786-6261, FAX: (215) 977-3409, E-Mail: sunoco_online@sunoil.com, Web Site: www.sunocoinc.com (16)

Campbell, Samuel, J., Mystic Logistics, South Glastonbury, CT. Tel: (860) 659-1566, (800) 969-1566, FAX: (860) 659-1420, Web Site: www.mysticlogistics.com (35)

Campbell, Scott, The Columbian, Vancouver, WA. Tel: (360) 694-3391, FAX: (360) 735-4503, Web Site: www.columbian.com (17)

Campbell Ewald Co, Warren, MI. Tel: (586) 574-3400, FAX: (810) 575-9925, Web Site: www.campbell-ewald.com (35)

Campbell Mithun, Minneapolis, MN. Tel: (612) 347-1000, FAX: (612) 347-1515, Web Site: www.campbellmithun.com (35)

Campbell Soup Co, Camden, NJ. Tel: (856) 342-4800, (800) 257-8443, FAX: (856) 342-3878, Web Site: www.campbellsoup.com (16)

Campbell Tools Co, Springfield, OH. Tel: (937) 882-6716, FAX: (937) 882-6648, E-Mail: campbell@campbelltools.com, Web Site: www.campbelltools.com (9)

Camping World Inc, Bowling Green, KY. Tel: (270) 781-2718, (800) 626-6189, FAX: (270) 796-8991, Web Site: www.campingworld.com (11)

Campise, James, J., Quantum Color, Morton Grove, IL. Tel: (847) 967-3600, FAX: (847) 967-3610, Web Site: www.cpipress.com (27)

Campmor Inc, Mahwah, NJ. Tel: (201) 335-9064, (800) 525-4784, FAX: (201) 236-3601, Web Site: www.campmor.com (17)

Campos, Alexander, Center for Book Arts, New York, NY. Tel: (212) 481-0295, FAX: (866) 708-8994, E-Mail: info@centerforbookarts.org, Web Site: www.centerforbookarts.org (27)

Campus Dimensions Inc, Philadelphia, PA. Tel: (215) 568-1700, (800) 592-2121, FAX: (215) 568-1701, E-Mail: recruitment@cdicccc.com, Web Site: www.cdicccc.com (31)

Canada Brokerlink Insurance, Edmonton, AB Canada. Tel: (780) 474-8911, FAX: (780) 479-0573, Web Site: www.brokerlink.ca (15)

Canada Post Corp, Ottawa, ON Canada. Tel: (613) 734-8440, (866) 607-6301, FAX: (613) 734-3378, Web Site: www.canadapost.ca (16)

canadaplus.com, Windsor, ON Canada. Tel: (519) 966-3003, (877) 966-3003, FAX: (519) 966-1749, E-Mail: canadaplusinfo@canadaplus.com, Web Site: www.canadaplus.com (28)

Canadeo, Ernest, EGC Group Inc, Melville, NY. Tel: (516) 935-4944, FAX: (516) 935-7030, E-Mail: contact@egcgroup.com (35)

Canadian Blood Services, Ottawa, ON Canada. Tel: (613) 739-2300, Web Site: www.blood.ca (1)

Canadian Business, Toronto, ON Canada. Tel: (416) 596-5100, FAX: (416) 764-1200, Web Site: www.canadianbusiness.com (17)

Canadian Institute of Chartered Accountants, Toronto, ON Canada. Tel: (416) 977-3222, Web Site: www.cica.ca (1)

Canadian Marketing Association, Don Mills, ON Canada. Tel: (416) 391-2362, FAX: (416) 441-4062, E-Mail: info@the-cma.org, Web Site: www.the-cma.org (40)

Canadian Marketing Association National Convention & Trade Show, Don Mills, ON Canada. Tel: (416) 391-2362, FAX: (416) 441-4062, E-Mail: pmckenzie@the-cma.org, Web Site: www.the-cma.org (42)

Canakaris, Ronald, Montag & Caldwell Inc, Atlanta, GA. Tel: (404) 836-7100, (800) 458-5868, FAX: (404) 836-7230, Web Site: www.montag.com (14)

Canale, Vincent, J., Hertz Corp, Park Ridge, NJ. Tel: (201) 307-2000, FAX: (201) 307-2644, Web Site: www.hertz.com (19)

Cancer Fund of America Inc, Knoxville, TN. Tel: (865) 938-5281, (800) 578-5284, FAX: (865) 938-2968, Web Site: www.cfoa.org (1)

Cancer Research Society, Montreal, PQ Canada. Tel: (514) 861-9227, (888) 766-2262, FAX: (514) 861-9220, Web Site: www.CancerResearchSociety.ca (1)

Candiotti, Fred, CGT Marketing, Amityville, NY. Tel: (631) 842-4600, FAX: (631) 842-6301, Web Site: www.cgtmarketing.com (21)

Candito, Peter, Direct Marketing Tool Kit for Small Business, Minneapolis, MN. Tel: (612) 788-1673, E-Mail: info@nmoa.org, Web Site: www.nmoa.org/directmarketingtoolkit (43)

The Candy Factory, Newport, KY. Tel: (859) 581-4663, FAX: (859) 581-1979 (4)

Cane & Basket Supply Co, Los Angeles, CA. Tel: (323) 939-9644, FAX: (323) 939-7237, E-Mail: info@canebasket.com, Web Site: www.canebasket.com (8)

Canestin, Donna, J., Seton Identification Products, Branford, CT. Tel: (203) 488-8059, (800) 243-6624, FAX: (203) 488-5973, Web Site: www.seton.com (16)

Canestri, Donna, J., Champion America Inc, Branford, CT. Tel: (203) 315-1181, (877) 242-6709, FAX: (800) 336-3707, E-Mail: teamca@champion-america.com, Web Site: www.championamerica.com (10)

Canestri, Donna, J., Tricor Direct Inc/Seton, Branford, CT. Tel: (800) 243-6624, E-Mail: custsvc_setonus@seton.com, Web Site: www.seton.com (9)

Cangelose, Joe, Texas Graphic Resource, Dallas, TX. Tel: (214) 630-2800, FAX: (214) 630-0713 (27)

Cangemi, Michael, Financial Executives International, Morristown, NJ. Tel: (973) 765-1000, FAX: (973) 765-1018, Web Site: www.financialexecutives.org (1)

Cangero, Syl, Adirondack Direct, Long Island City, NY. Tel: (718) 932-4003, (800) 221-2444, FAX: (800) 477-1330, E-Mail: info@adirondackdirect.com, Web Site: www.adirondackdirect.com (10)

Canine Companions for Independence, Santa Rosa, CA. Tel: (707) 577-1700, (800) 572-2275, FAX: (707) 577-1711, E-Mail: info@cci.org, Web Site: www.caninecompanions.org (16)

The Caning Shop, Berkeley, CA. Tel: (510) 527-5010, (800) 544-3373, FAX: (510) 527-7718, Web Site: www.caning.com (11)

Canino, Jose, Argent Trading LLC, New York, NY. Tel: (212) 697-8800, FAX: (212) 697-8606, Web Site: www.Argenttrading.com (16)

Cann, Sharon, Islands Tropicals, Keaau, HI. Tel: (808) 961-0606, (800) 367-5155, FAX: (808) 966-7684, Web Site: www.islandtropicals.com (6)

Cannaday, Jim, Tony Brown Productions, New York, NY. Tel: (718) 264-2226, FAX: (718) 264-1914, E-Mail: mail@tbol.net, Web Site: www.tonybrown.com (16)

Cannella, Frank, Cannella Response Television Inc, Burlington, WI. Tel: (262) 763-4810, FAX: (262) 763-2875, E-Mail: frank@tvinfomercial.com, Web Site: www.tvinfomercial.com (32)

Cannella Response Television Inc, Burlington, WI. Tel: (262) 763-4810, FAX: (262) 763-2875, E-Mail: frank@tvinfomercial.com, Web Site: www.tvinfomercial.com (32)

Canning, Marilyn, Martindale-Hubbell, New Providence, NJ. Tel: (908) 464-6800, (800) 526-4902, FAX: (908) 771-7740 (17)

Canning Brown, Barbara, Toys "R" Us, Wayne, NJ. Tel: (973) 617-5879, FAX: (973) 617-4006, Web Site: www.toysrus.com (11)

Cannon, Colleen, F&W Publications Inc, Blue Ash, OH. Tel: (513) 531-2690, FAX: (513) 531-0293, Web Site: www.fwpublications.com (17)

Cannon, Jack, Cannon Marketing Corp, Lenexa, KS. Tel: (913) 338-3340, (800) 444-0972, FAX: (913) 273-0808, E-Mail: jack@cannonmktg.com, Web Site: www.cannonmktg.com (33)

Cannon Marketing Corp, Lenexa, KS. Tel: (913) 338-3340, (800) 444-0972, FAX: (913) 273-0808, E-Mail: jack@cannonmktg.com, Web Site: www.cannonmktg.com (33)

Canoe Ventures LLC, New York, NY. Tel: (212) 364-3600, FAX: (212) 364 3601, Web Site: www.canoe-ventures.com (32)

Canose, Gregory, Award Marketing Services LLC, Whitehouse, NJ. Tel: (908) 534-5700, FAX: (908) 534-0903, E-Mail: grcanose@aol.com, Web Site: www.awardmarketingservices.com (33)

Cantelmo, Daniel, Media Distribution Services (MDS), New York, NY. Tel: (212) 279-4800, (800) MDS-DATA, FAX: (212) 643-0576, E-Mail: services@mdsconnect.com, Web Site: www.mdsconnect.com (23)

Canter, Elaine, The List Connection Inc, Mamaroneck, NY. Tel: (914) 381-2010, FAX: (914) 381-2163 (23)

Cantler, Jan, Brooks Brothers, New York, NY. Tel: (212) 682-8800, (800) 274-1815, FAX: (212) 309-7273, Web Site: www.brooksbrothers.com (2)

Canto, Adrian, UndercoverWear Inc, Tewksbury, MA. Tel: (978) 851-8580, FAX: (978) 640-2882, E-Mail: jamiej@undercoverwear.com, Web Site: www.undercoverwear.com (2)

Canton, Mark, The American Film Institute, Los Angeles, CA. Tel: (323) 856-7600, FAX: (323) 467-4578, Web Site: www.afi.com (1)

Cantrall, Eric, McKenzie Taxidermy Supply, Granite Quarry, NC. Tel: (704) 279-7985, (800) 279-7985, Web Site: www.mckenziesp.com (16)

Cantrell, Carol, S., Parsons School of Design Human Resource Dept, New York, NY. Tel: (212) 229-5671, FAX: (212) 229-8975, E-Mail: communications@newschool.edu, Web Site: www.parsons.edu (41)

Cantrell, Christy, Alfa Insurance, Montgomery, AL. Tel: (334) 288-3900, Web Site: www.alfains.com (15)

Cantrock, Steven, ValCom Inc, Indian Rocks Beach, FL. Tel: (702) 385-9000, FAX: (702) 382-2802, Web Site: www.valcom.tv (32)

Cantu, Elsa, Megger, Dallas, TX. Tel: (214) 330-3539, Web Site: www.megger.com (16)

Canyon Marketing, Dix Hills, NY. Tel: (516) 316-7090 (7)

Canzonetta, Gina, DMB Realty Network, Scottsdale, AZ. Tel: (480) 515-0148, Web Site: www.dmbrealty.com (16)

Capalbo, Karen, Concept Media Partners, Yorktown Heights, NY. Tel: (914) 767-0032, FAX: (914) 514-1711, E-Mail: karen@conceptmediapartners.com, Web Site: www.conceptmediapartners.com (35)

Capanna, Jim, The Total Mailing System, West Deptford, NJ. Tel: (856) 628-8800, FAX: (856) 628-8810, Web Site: www.ttms.com (22)

Capano, Edward, National Review, New York, NY. Tel: (212) 679-7330, FAX: (212) 849-2852, Web Site: www.nationalreview.com (17)

Cape, Mike, xpedx Stores Division, Chicago, IL. Tel: (773) 442-6200, (800) 600-0064, FAX: (630) 628-6310, Web Site: www.epedxstores.com (25)

Cape Cod Cupola Co Inc, North Dartmouth, MA. Tel: (508) 994-2119, FAX: (508) 997-2511, Web Site: www.capcodcupola.com (8)

Capell, E Daniel, Capell & Associates, Barnegat Light, NJ. Tel: (201) 572-8774, FAX: (609) 494-7369, E-Mail: contact@capellandassociates.com, Web Site: www.capell&associates.com (20)

Capell & Associates, Barnegat Light, NJ. Tel: (201) 572-8774, FAX: (609) 494-7369, E-Mail: contact@capellandassociates.com, Web Site: www.capell&associates.com (20)

Capellas, Michael, D., First Data Merchant Services, Greenwood Village, CO. Tel: (303) 488-8000, (800) 735-3362, Web Site: www.firstdata.com (14)

Capello, Tisha, Bank Boston, Waltham, MA. Tel: (781) 788-7795, FAX: (781) 788-2513, Web Site: www.bankboston.com (14)

Caperton III, W. Gaston, The College Board, New York, NY. Tel: (212) 713-8000, FAX: (212) 713-8143, Web Site: www.collegeboard.com (1)

Capetanakis, Mike, MCDM Strategic Direct Marketing, Plainfield, IL. Tel: (815) 436-5194, FAX: (815) 439-5941 (20)

Capezio Ballet Makers Inc, Totowa, NJ. Tel: (973) 653-2093, (800) 533-1887, FAX: (800) 522-1222, E-Mail: info@balletmakers.com, Web Site: www.capeziodance.com (16)

Capezza, Joseph, C., Harvard Pilgrim Health Care, Wellesley, MA. Tel: (617) 509-1000, FAX: (617) 509-7590, Web Site: www.harvardpilgrim.org (17)

Capezzuto, John, Dalrada Financial Corp, San Diego, CA. Tel: (858) 427-8716, (877) 325-7232, FAX: (858) 277-3448, E-Mail: inquiries@dalrada.com, Web Site: www.dalrada.com (14)

Capgemini Americas Outsourcing, New York, NY. Tel: (212) 314-8000, FAX: (212) 314-8001 (20)

Capital Design, Providence, RI. Tel: (401) 270-6777, FAX: (401) 438-9360, E-Mail: info@freemiums.com, Web Site: www.freemiums.com (33)

Capital Insurance Group (CIG), Monterey, CA. Tel: (831) 233-5500, Web Site: www.ciginsurance.com (15)

Capitani, Randy, Vermont Media, West Dover, VT. Tel: (802) 464-3388, FAX: (802) 464-7255, E-Mail: vickic@vermontmedia.com, Web Site: www.dvalnews.com (35)

Capitani, Victoria, Vermont Media, West Dover, VT. Tel: (802) 464-3388, FAX: (802) 464-7255, E-Mail: vickic@vermontmedia.com, Web Site: www.dvalnews.com (35)

Capitano, Fran, Biomerica Inc, Irvine, CA. Tel: (949) 645-2111, FAX: (949) 722-6674, E-Mail: bmra@biomerica.com, Web Site: www.biomerica.com (7)

Capitol Advantage/Roll Call Group, Washington, DC. Tel: (202) 6550-6500, (800) 432-2250, E-Mail: sales@cq.com (31)

Capitol Concierge Inc, Washington, DC. Tel: (202) 223-4765, FAX: (202) 833-2287, E-Mail: onlineconcierge@capitolconcierge.com, Web Site: www.capitolconcierge.com (16)

Capitol Hill Lists, Statham, GA. Tel: (706) 546-0282 (23)

Capone, William, J., Merastar Insurance Co, Chattanooga, TN. Tel: (800) 637-2782, FAX: (800) 369-1430, E-Mail: merastar.assist.team@unitrindirect.com, Web Site: www.merastar.com (15)

Caporilli, Peter, Tidewater Workshop, Egg Harbor City, NJ. Tel: (609) 965-4000, (800) 666-8433, FAX: (609) 965-8212, Web Site: www.tidewaterworkshop.com (8)

Cappe, Mel, IRPP, Montreal, PQ Canada. Tel: (514) 985-2461, FAX: (514) 985-2559, E-Mail: irpp@irpp.org, Web Site: www.irpp.org (30)

Capps, John, E., Jarden Corp, Daleville, IN. Tel: (765) 557-3000, (800) 428-8150, FAX: (765) 281-5403, Web Site: www.jarden.com (16)

Cappuccio, Paul, T., Time Warner Inc, New York, NY. Tel: (212) 484-8000, Web Site: www.timewarner.com (16)

Capron, Phillipe, Vivendi, New York, NY. Tel: (212) 572-7000, FAX: (212) 572-1080, Web Site: www.vivendi.com (16)

Captan Associates Inc, Brick, NJ. Tel: (732) 840-1244, FAX: (732) 840-1211 (17)

Capwell, Beverly, CustomerMining, Soquel, CA. Tel: (831) 465-0890, Web Site: www.customermining.com (35)

Carabella Collection, Irvine, CA. Tel: (949) 263-2300, (800) 227-2235, FAX: (949) 263-2323, Web Site: www.carabella.com (2)

Carabini, Christina, Monex Deposit Co, Newport Beach, CA. Tel: (949) 752-1400, (800) 444-8317, FAX: (949) 752-7214, E-Mail: info@monex.com, Web Site: www.monex.com (14)

Carabini, Louis, E., Monex Deposit Co, Newport Beach, CA. Tel: (949) 752-1400, (800) 444-8317, FAX: (949) 752-7214, E-Mail: info@monex.com, Web Site: www.monex.com (14)

Carabini, Michael, Monex Deposit Co, Newport Beach, CA. Tel: (949) 752-1400, (800) 444-8317, FAX: (949) 752-7214, E-Mail: info@monex.com, Web Site: www.monex.com (14)

Caraustar, Austell, GA. Tel: (770) 948-3101, E-Mail: info@caraustar.com, Web Site: www.caraustar.com (16)

Caraustar Ashland Carton Plant, Ashland, OH. Tel: (419) 289-2666, FAX: (419) 281-5415, Web Site: www.caraustar.com (27)

Caraveo, Suzanne, FAFCO Inc, Chico, CA. Tel: (530) 332-2100, (800) 994-7652, FAX: (530) 332-2109, Web Site: www.fafco.com (16)

Carawan, Suzanne, ThePort Network, Atlanta, GA. Tel: (703) 431-2208 (32)

Carbine, Gene, Catalyst Direct Marketing/DNA, Pompton Lakes, NJ. Tel: (973) 831-4222, FAX: (973) 831-1933, E-Mail: info@catalystdm.com, Web Site: www.catalystdm.com (23)

Carbone, Becky, Book Publishing Information Kit, Santa Barbara, CA. Tel: (805) 968-7277, (800) PARAPUB, FAX: (805) 968-1379, E-Mail: danpoynter@parapublishing.com, Web Site: www.parapublishing.com (17)

Carbone, Becky, Para Publishing, Santa Barbara, CA. Tel: (805) 968-7277, (800) PARAPUB, FAX: (805) 986-1379, E-Mail: danpoynter@parapublishing.com, Web Site: www.parapublishing.com (17)

Carboni, Tamra, Louisiana State Museum, New Orleans, LA. Tel: (504) 568-6968, (800) 568-6968, FAX: (504) 568-4995, Web Site: www.lsm.crt.state.la.us (1)

Carbullido, Felix, Smith & Hawken Ltd, Novato, CA. Tel: (415) 506-3700, (800) 940-1170, FAX: (415) 506-3900, Web Site: www.smithandhawken.com (8)

Card, Richard, Mastergrip Inc, Irving, TX. Tel: (972) 554-4450, (800) 275-1100, FAX: (972) 554-1109, Web Site: www.mastergrip.com (11)

Card Sterling, Cathy, Schultz & Williams Inc, Philadelphia, PA. Tel: (215) 625-9955, FAX: (215) 625-2701, E-Mail: mail@schultzwilliams.com, Web Site: www.sw-inc.com (1)

Card Technology Inc, Hopkins, MN. Tel: (201) 845-7373, FAX: (201) 845-3337, E-Mail: info@nbstech.com, Web Site: www.nbstech.com (16)

Cardella, Thomas, L., Precision Response Corp, Plantation, FL. Tel: (954) 693-3700, FAX: (954) 693-3767, Web Site: www.prcnet.com (21)

Thomas L Cardella & Associates, Kimberton, PA. Tel: (610) 933-3822, Web Site: www.tlcassociates.com (29)

Cardello, Alberto, University of Pittsburgh at Bradford, Bradford, PA. Tel: (814) 362-7500, FAX: (814) 362-5150, E-Mail: admissions@www.upb.pitt.edu, Web Site: www.upd.pitt.edu (41)

Cardello, Joseph, MDF Systems, Bristol, CT. Tel: (860) 584-4750, FAX: (860) 584-4759, Web Site: www.mdfsystems.com (22)

Cardenas-Nolazsco, Armando, The Wedding Pages, New York, NY. Tel: (212) 219-8555, (800) 843-4983, FAX: (212) 219-1929, Web Site: www.theknot.com (16)

Cardflex Financial Services, Costa Mesa, CA. Tel: (866) 634-3044, Web Site: www.flex1.com (14)

Cardillo, Donna, The Journal News, White Plains, NY. Tel: (914) 694-9300, FAX: (914) 696-8152, Web Site: www.nyjournalnews.com (17)

Cardin, Marlene, Video Ordnance Inc, New York, NY. Tel: (212) 334-3939, (800) 377-7773, FAX: (212) 219-1969, E-Mail: info@videoordnance.com, Web Site: www.videoordnance.com (32)

Cardinal Mailing Services Ltd, Honolulu, HI. Tel: (808) 538-3884, FAX: (808) 521-1419, E-Mail: mail@cardinalservicesltd.com, Web Site: www.cardinalservicesltd.com (28)

Cardinale, Kim, CBT Direct, Tarpon Springs, FL. Tel: (727) 724-8994, (877) 872-4646, FAX: (727) 797-9143, Web Site: www.cbtdirect.com (16)

Cardona, Edward, Video Artists International, Pleasantville, NY. Tel: (914) 769-3691, (800) 477-7146, FAX: (914) 769-5407, E-Mail: orders@vaimusic.com, Web Site: www.vaimusic.com (3)

Cardone, Anthony, Standard Life, Montreal, PQ. Tel: (514) 499-8855, (877) 499-9555, FAX: (514) 499-4908, Web Site: www.standardlife.ca (15)

Cardoso, Carlos, M., Kennametal Inc, Latrobe, PA. Tel: (800) 222-9327, FAX: (800) 521-3319, E-Mail: mcs-na.service@kennmetal.com, Web Site: www.kennametal.com (16)

CardSource, Eagan, MN. Tel: (651) 686-0660, Web Site: www.cardsource.com (31)

Care2, Washington, DC. Tel: (650) 622-0860, Web Site: www.care2.com (1)

CARE USA, Atlanta, GA. Tel: (404) 979-9255, (800) 521-CARE, FAX: (404) 589-2600, E-Mail: info@care.org, Web Site: www.careusa.org (1)

CareCall Inc, Sartell, MN. Tel: (320) 253-0800, Web Site: www.arraysg.com (29)

Career Blazers, New York, NY. Tel: (212) 719-3232, FAX: (212) 221-0452 (20)

Career Education Corp, Schaumburg, IL. Tel: (847) 781-3600, Web Site: www.careered.com (1)

Carefirst Blue Cross Blue Shield, Washington, DC. Tel: (202) 479-8000, FAX: (301) 470-8049, Web Site: www.carefirst.com (15)

Careington International, Frisco, TX. Tel: (972) 335-6970, Web Site: www.careington.com (7)

Carelli, Jeanne, Cimarron Group, Hollywood, CA. Tel: (323) 337-0300, FAX: (323) 337-0333, Web Site: www.cimarrongroup.com (35)

Carendi, John, Fireman's Fund Insurance Co, Novato, CA. Tel: (415) 899-2000, FAX: (415) 899-3600, Web Site: www.firemansfund.com (14)

Carestream Health Inc, Rochester, NY. Tel: (585) 627-1800, (888) 777-2072, Web Site: www.carestreamhealth.com (7)

Carey, Albert, P., Frito-Lay, Plano, TX. Tel: (972) 334-7000, (800) 352-4477, FAX: (972) 334-2019, Web Site: www.fritolay.com (16)

Carey, Albert, P., The Quaker Oats Co, Chicago, IL. Tel: (312) 821-1000, (800) 367-6287, FAX: (312) 222-8323, Web Site: www.quakeroats.com (16)

Carey, Amy, Berkshire Direct Inc, Williamstown, MA. Tel: (413) 458-1721, FAX: (413) 458-1727, E-Mail: info@berkshiredirect.com, Web Site: www.berkshiredirect.com (17)

Carey, David, The Hearst Corp, New York, NY. Tel: (212) 649-2000, FAX: (212) 649-2108, Web Site: www.hearst.com/magazines/ (17)

Carey, Karen, AIIM International, Silver Spring, MD. Tel: (301) 587-8202, (800) 477-2446, FAX: (301) 587-2711, E-Mail: aiim@aiim.org, Web Site: www.aiim.org (1)

Carey, Peter, N., Peter N Carey & Associates Inc, Oak Brook, IL. Tel: (630) 573-4260, (877) PNCAREY, FAX: (630) 573-0529, E-Mail: pncarey1@sbcglobal.net (20)

Carey, Timothy S., New York Power Authority, Albany, NY. Tel: (518) 433-6700, Web Site: www.nypa.gov (16)

CARFAX Inc, Centreville, VA. Tel: (703) 934-2664, Web Site: www.carfax.com (12)

Carhill Enterprises Inc, Saint Louis, MO. Tel: (314) 621-7646, Web Site: www.cahillinsight.com (15)

Caribe Direct Inc, San Juan, PR. Tel: (787) 722-5188, FAX: (787) 723-6165, E-Mail: islaonline@prw.net, Web Site: www.islaonline.com (6)

Carina Associates, Croton on Hudson, NY. Tel: (914) 271-8600, FAX: (914) 271-8354 (33)

Carino, James L., Carino Nurseries, Indiana, PA. Tel: (800) 223-7075, FAX: (724) 463-3050, E-Mail: carino@carinonurseries.com, Web Site: www.carinonurseries.com (8)

Carino, Laura, Carino Nurseries, Indiana, PA. Tel: (800) 223-7075, FAX: (724) 463-3050, E-Mail: carino@carinonurseries.com, Web Site: www.carinonurseries.com (8)

Carino Nurseries, Indiana, PA. Tel: (800) 223-7075, FAX: (724) 463-3050, E-Mail: carino@carinonurseries.com, Web Site: www.carinonurseries.com (8)

Carioscia, Ursula, Bruce McGaw Graphics, Manchester Center, VT. Tel: (845) 353-8600, (888) 4BMC-GAW, FAX: (845) 353-3155, E-Mail: sales@bmcgaw.com, Web Site: www.bmcgaw.com (6)

Carkeet, Bill, Oden, Memphis, TN. Tel: (901) 578-8055, FAX: (901) 578-1911, Web Site: www.oden.com (35)

Carkhuff, Gregory, Human Resource Development Press, Amherst, MA. Tel: (413) 253-3488, (800) 822-2801, FAX: (413) 253-3490, E-Mail: info@hrdpress.com, Web Site: www.hrdpress.com (17)

Carkhuff, Robert, Human Resource Development Press, Amherst, MA. Tel: (413) 253-3488, (800) 822-2801, FAX: (413) 253-3490, E-Mail: info@hrdpress.com, Web Site: www.hrdpress.com (17)

Carley, John, St Joseph Print Thorn, Concord, ON Canada. Tel: (416) 441-1411, FAX: (416) 441-3158, Web Site: www.stjoseph.com (27)

Carlgren, Kendi, MarketAide Services Inc, Salina, KS. Tel: (785) 825-7161, (800) 204-2433, FAX: (785) 825-4697, E-Mail: kcarlgren@marketaide.com, Web Site: www.marketaide.com (21)

Carlile, D.B., Professional Print & Mail Inc, Fresno, CA. Tel: (559) 237-7468, (800) 654-7468, FAX: (559) 237-4929, E-Mail: dcarlile@printfresno.com, Web Site: www.printfresno.com (21)

Carlile, Thomas, E., Boise Cascade Holdings LLC, Boise, ID. Tel: (208) 384-6451, FAX: (208) 384-7189, E-Mail: mediarelations@bc.com, Web Site: www.bc.com (16)

Carlin, John, W., National Archives & Records Administration, College Park, MD. Tel: (301) 837-0482, (86) NARA-NARA, FAX: (301) 837-0483, Web Site: www.archives.gov (17)

Carlisle Jr., Rex, T., Deseret Book, Salt Lake City, UT. Tel: (801) 534-1515, (800) 453-4532, FAX: (801) 517-3392, Web Site: www.deseretbook.com (16)

Carlisle, Jeanette, Comsearch, Ashburn, VA. Tel: (703) 726-5500, FAX: (703) 726-5600, Web Site: www.comsearch.com (30)

Carlisle, Rex, T., Fire Mountain Gems, Grants Pass, OR. Tel: (541) 956-7890, (800) 423-2319, (800) 355-2137, FAX: (541) 470-GEMS, E-Mail: questions@firemtn.com, Web Site: www.firemtn.com (16)

Carlson, A., Oscar, American Spirit Graphics Corp, Minneapolis, MN. Tel: (612) 623-3333, FAX: (612) 623-9314, E-Mail: asgc@asgc.com, Web Site: www.asgc.com (27)

Carlson, Bob, Carlson's Gardens, Waitsfield, VT. Tel: (914) 763-5958, E-Mail: bob@carlsonsgardens.com, Web Site: www.carlsonsgardens.com (8)

Carlson, Bonnie J., Promotion Marketing Association (PMA) Inc, New York, NY. Tel: (212) 420-1100, FAX: (212) 533-7622, E-Mail: pma@pmalink.org, Web Site: www.pmalink.org (1)

Carlson, Bradley, S., IDC, Ltd, Henderson, NV. Tel: (702) 450-1000, FAX: (702) 450-1020, E-Mail: info@goidc.com, Web Site: www.goidc.com (1)

Carlson, Charles, Dow Theory Forecasts, Hammond, IN. Tel: (219) 931-6480, (800) 233-5922, FAX: (219) 931-6487, E-Mail: custserv@horizonpublishing.com, Web Site: www.dowtheory.com (17)

Carlson, Dan, Ruder Finn Inc, New York, NY. Tel: (212) 593-6400, FAX: (212) 715-1556, E-Mail: rfnewyork@ruderfinn.com, Web Site: www.ruderfinn.com (30)

Carlson, Darren, American Spirit Graphics Corp, Minneapolis, MN. Tel: (612) 623-3333, FAX: (612) 623-9314, E-Mail: asgc@asgc.com, Web Site: www.asgc.com (27)

Carlson, David, Consumer Benefit Services Inc, Naperville, IL. Tel: (630) 420-6200, (800) 657-8309, FAX: (630) 420-2294, E-Mail: dcarlson@consumerbenefit.com, Web Site: www.consumerbenefit.com (16)

Carlson, David, New Mexico State University, Las Cruces, NM. Tel: (575) 646-0111, (505) 646-3341, FAX: (505) 646-1498, Web Site: www.nmsu.edu (41)

Carlson, David, P., LaCrosse Footwear Inc, Portland, OR. Tel: (503) 262-0110, (800) 323-2668, FAX: (503) 262-0115, E-Mail: customerservice@lacrossefootwear.com, Web Site: www.lacrossefootwear.com (16)

Carlson, Julie, Heartstrings Press, Lancaster, VA. Tel: (804) 462-0884, (800) 462-0884, FAX: (716) 462-0884, E-Mail: sue@grandloving.com, Web Site: www.grandloving.com (17)

Carlson, L., Gregg, IDC, Ltd, Henderson, NV. Tel: (702) 450-1000, FAX: (702) 450-1020, E-Mail: info@goidc.com, Web Site: www.goidc.com (1)

Carlson, Lynn, Harper's Magazine, New York, NY. Tel: (212) 420-5720, FAX: (212) 260-1096, Web Site: www.harpers.org (17)

Carlson, William, Choice Hotels International, Silver Spring, MD. Tel: (301) 592-6636, (888) 770-6800, FAX: (301) 592-6157, E-Mail: ihelp@choicehotels.com, Web Site: www.choicebuys.com (16)

Carlson's Gardens, Waitsfield, VT. Tel: (914) 763-5958, E-Mail: bob@carlsonsgardens.com, Web Site: www.carlsonsgardens.com (8)

Carlton, Kay, Carlton Industries CP, La Grange, TX. Tel: (979) 242-5055, (800) 231-5988, FAX: (800) 231-5934, E-Mail: sales@carltonusa.com, Web Site: www.carltonusa.com (34)

Carlton Industries CP, La Grange, TX. Tel: (979) 242-5055, (800) 231-5988, FAX: (800) 231-5934, E-Mail: sales@carltonusa.com, Web Site: www.carltonusa.com (34)

Carlyle, Rosemarie, Barton-Cotton, Baltimore, MD. Tel: (410) 247-4800, (800) 348-1102, FAX: (410) 536-0491, E-Mail: info@bartoncotton.com, Web Site: www.bartoncotton.com (16)

Carlyle Marketing Corp, Riverwoods, IL. Tel: (847) 948-9295, FAX: (847) 948-0465, E-Mail: carlylemi@gmail.com (29)

Carmel, Douglas, Flaghouse Inc, Hasbrouck Heights, NJ. Tel: (201) 288-7600, (800) 793-7900, FAX: (800) 793-7922, E-Mail: sales@flaghouse.com, Web Site: www.flaghouse.com (5)

Carmel, George, Flaghouse Inc, Hasbrouck Heights, NJ. Tel: (201) 288-7600, (800) 793-7900, FAX: (800) 793-7922, E-Mail: sales@flaghouse.com, Web Site: www.flaghouse.com (5)

Carmichael, Greg, D., Fifth Third Bank, Cincinnati, OH. Tel: (800) 972-3030, FAX: (231) 922-4060, Web Site: www.53.com (14)

Carmichael Lynch Inc, Minneapolis, MN. Tel: (612) 334-6000, FAX: (612) 334-6101, E-Mail: roman.paluta@clynch.com, Web Site: www.carmichaellynch.com (35)

Carmody, Daniel C., Channing L Bete Co Inc, South Deerfield, MA. Tel: (800) 477-4776, FAX: (800) 499-6464, E-Mail: custscvs@channing.bete.com, Web Site: www.channing-bete.com (17)

Carnahan, Maria, The Kidney Foundation of Canada/Greater Ontario Branch, Hamilton, ON. Tel: (800) 414-3484, FAX: (905) 318-8491, E-Mail: kidneyfoundation@bellnet.ca, Web Site: www.kidney.on.ca (1)

Carneal, Jeffrey, J., Eagle Publishing, Washington, DC. Tel: (202) 216-0600, FAX: (202) 216-0612, Web Site: www.eaglepub.com (17)

The Carnegie Hall Corp, New York, NY. Tel: (212) 247-7800, FAX: (212) 373-0500, E-Mail: feedback@carnegiehall.org, Web Site: www.carnegiehall.org (35)

Carnegie Marketing Associates, Torrance, CA. Tel: (310) 540-4757, FAX: (310) 540-7407 (23)

Carney, Pete, Carney Direct Marketing, Irvine, CA. Tel: (949) 581-51000, (800) 240-3349, Web Site: www.carneydirect.com (23)

Carney, Thomas J., EF Maloney Inc, Mamaroneck, NY. Tel: (718) 549-7000, FAX: (718) 549-6320, E-Mail: efmaloney@aol.com, Web Site: www.efmaloney.com (16)

Carney Direct Marketing, Irvine, CA. Tel: (949) 581-51000, (800) 240-3349, Web Site: www.carneydirect.com (23)

Carnival Creations, Irvine, CA. Tel: (949) 833-9370, FAX: (949) 955-2078 (39)

Carnival Cruise Lines, Miami, FL. Tel: (212) 599-2600, Web Site: www.carnival.com (19)

Carnrick, Jessica, PlusMedia LLC, Danbury, CT. Tel: (203) 748-6500, FAX: (203) 748-6600, E-Mail: contact@plusme.com, Web Site: www.plusme.com (35)

Carnwath, Alison, J., PACCAR Inc, Bellevue, WA. Tel: (425) 468-7400, FAX: (425) 468-8216, Web Site: www.paccar.com (16)

Carolan, Mary, Universal Training, Lake Forest, IL. Tel: (847) 235-2170, E-Mail: information@universaltraining.com, Web Site: www.universaltraining.com (16)

Caroli, Connie, TeleManagement Search, Port Washington, NY. Tel: (516) 767-6990, FAX: (516) 767-6980, E-Mail: connie@tmrecruiters.com, Web Site: www.tmrecruiters.com (20)

Carolina Biological Supply Co, Burlington, NC. Tel: (800) 334-5551, (800) 222-7112, E-Mail: carolina@carolina.com, Web Site: www.carolina.com (9)

Carolina Exotic Gardens/CEG Nursery, Greenville, NC. Tel: (252) 758-2600, FAX: (252) 758-3252, E-Mail: cegnursery@aol.com, Web Site: www.cegnursery.com (8)

Caroll, John, Tom Snyder Productions, Watertown, MA. Tel: (617) 926-6000, (800) 342-0236, FAX: (800) 304-1254, E-Mail: ask@tomsnyder.com, Web Site: www.tomsnyder.com (16)

Carollo, Anthony, Syntellect, Phoenix, AZ. Tel: (602) 789-2800, (800) 788-9733, FAX: (602) 789-2899, Web Site: www.syntellect.com (16)

Carothers, Leslie, Environmental Law Institute, Washington, DC. Tel: (202) 939-3800, FAX: (202) 939-3868, E-Mail: law@eli.org, Web Site: www.eli.org (17)

Carp, Merlin, AEGON Direct Marketing Services Inc, Baltimore, MD. Tel: (410) 209-5617, FAX: (410) 209-5932, Web Site: www.aegondms.com (15)

Carpenter, Dave, Innovation Printing, Philadelphia, PA. Tel: (215) 969-4600, FAX: (215) 464-7664 (27)

Carpenter, Eleanor, Emperor Clock LLC, Amherst, VA. Tel: (800) 642-0011, FAX: (434) 946-1420, E-Mail: emperor@emperorclock.com, Web Site: www.emperorclock.com (16)

Carpenter, Judie, ER Carpenter, Taylor, TX. Tel: (512) 365-5833, (800) 234-9105, FAX: (512) 352-6025, Web Site: www.carpenter.com (16)

Carpenter, Kelly, National 4-H Supply Service, Chevy Chase, MD. Tel: (301) 961-2959, FAX: (301) 961-2937, E-Mail: 4hsupply@fourhcouncil.edu, Web Site: www.fourhcouncil.edu (16)

Carpenter, Kevin, Ducks Unlimited, Memphis, TN. Tel: (901) 758-3825, (800) 45DUCKS, FAX: (901) 758-3850, Web Site: www.ducks.org (1)

Carpenter, Kyle, Electrosonic, Minnetonka, MN. Tel: (952) 931-7500, FAX: (952) 938-9311, E-Mail: information@electrosonic.com, Web Site: www.electrosonic.com (32)

Carpenter, Lorelle, Dover Saddlery, Littleton, MA. Tel: (978) 952-8062, (800) 406-8204, Web Site: www.doversaddlery.com (11)

Carpenter, Michael, Michael Carpenter Photography, Springfield, VA. Tel: (703) 644-9666 (37)

Carpenter, Mike, West Bend, West Bend, WI. Tel: (262) 334-5107, (866) 290-1851, FAX: (262) 334-6800, Web Site: www.focuselectrics.com (16)

ER Carpenter, Taylor, TX. Tel: (512) 365-5833, (800) 234-9105, FAX: (512) 352-6025, Web Site: www.carpenter.com (16)

Michael Carpenter Photography, Springfield, VA. Tel: (703) 644-9666 (37)

Carqueville Graphics Inc, Streamwood, IL. Tel: (630) 837-4500, FAX: (630) 837-4510, Web Site: www.carqueville.com (27)

Carr, Alicia, Kelco Supply Co, Brooklyn Park, MN. Tel: (763) 493-1260, (800) 328-7720, FAX: (763) 493-1261, E-Mail: info@kelcosupply.com, Web Site: www.kelcosupply.com (16)

Carr, James, Family Circle Magazine Inc, New York, NY. Tel: (212) 557-6600, Web Site: www.familycircle.com (31)

Carr, John, Solo Printing, Miami, FL. Tel: (305) 594-8699, Web Site: www.soloprinting.com (27)

Carr, Tim, Creative Lift, San Francisco, CA. Tel: (415) 248-3174, Web Site: www.creativelift.net (35)

Carracino, Marilyn, Bloomingdale's By Mail Ltd, New York, NY. Tel: (212) 224-7721, (800) 472-0788, FAX: (212) 715-2805, Web Site: www.bloomingdales.com (5)

Carranza, Miguel, H E Butt Grocery Co, San Antonio, TX. Tel: (210) 938-8357, (800) 432-3113, FAX: (210) 938-7511, Web Site: www.heb.com (16)

Carrasco, Jim, Crystek Corp, Fort Myers, FL. Tel: (239) 561-3311, (800) 237-3061, FAX: (239) 561-1025, E-Mail: sales@crystek.com, Web Site: www.crystek.com (9)

Carrington, Christine, Catalogs By Lorel, King of Prussia, PA. Tel: (800) 967-2682, Web Site: www.catalogdesignstudios.com (35)

Carrizales, Nancy, Animals Animals/Earth Scenes, Chatham, NY. Tel: (518) 392-5500, (800) 392-5503, FAX: (518) 392-5550, E-Mail: info@animalsanimals.com, Web Site: www.animalsanimals.com (38)

Carroll, Allison R., Metropolis Magazine, New York, NY. Tel: (212) 627-9977, (800) 334-3046, FAX: (212) 627-9988, E-Mail: edit@metropolismag.com, Web Site: www.metropolismag.com (2)

Carroll, Brian, Carroll Enterprises Inc, Worcester, MA. Tel: (508) 770-0206, Web Site: www.sbsb.com (29)

Carroll, Ed, American Movie Classics Holding Corp, Jericho, NY. Tel: (516) 803-3000, FAX: (516) 803-3003, Web Site: www.amctv.com (16)

Carroll, Francis, R., Small Business Service Bureau Inc, Worcester, MA. Tel: (508) 756-3513, (800) 343-0939, FAX: (508) 770-0528, E-Mail: membership@sbsb.com, Web Site: www.sbsb.com (1)

Carroll, Jay, Direct Marketing Group, Eden Prairie, MN. Tel: (952) 975-5060, Web Site: www.directamsc.com (35)

Carroll, John, Hain Celestial Group, Melville, NY. Tel: (631) 730-2200, FAX: (631) 730-2500, Web Site: www.hain-celestial.com (16)

Carroll, John, Jason Natural Personal Care Products, Boulder, CO. Tel: (877) 527-6601, Web Site: www.jason-natural.com (7)

Carroll, Mike, American Fidelity Assurance Co, Oklahoma City, OK. Tel: (405) 525-6900, FAX: (405) 523-5215, Web Site: www.afadvantage.com (15)

Carroll, Ricki, New England Cheesemaking Supply Co, South Deerfield, MA. Tel: (413) 628-3808, FAX: (413) 628-4061, E-Mail: info@cheesemaking.com, Web Site: www.cheesemaking.com (4)

Carroll, Ruth, Ann, Albert S Smyth Co Inc, Timonium, MD. Tel: (410) 252-6666, (800) 638-3333, FAX: (410) 252-2355, E-Mail: smyth@albertsmyth.com, Web Site: www.albertsmyth.com (6)

Carroll, Thomas, E., Carroll Publishing, Bethesda, MD. Tel: (301) 263-9800, (800) 336-4240, FAX: (301) 263-9801, Web Site: www.carrollpub.com (17)

Carroll Enterprises Inc, Worcester, MA. Tel: (508) 770-0206, Web Site: www.sbsb.com (29)

Carroll Publishing, Bethesda, MD. Tel: (301) 263-9800, (800) 336-4240, FAX: (301) 263-9801, Web Site: www.carrollpub.com (17)

Carron, Dr Andrew, National Economic Research Associates Inc, Washington, DC. Tel: (202) 466-3510, FAX: (202) 466-3605, E-Mail: andrew.carron@nera.com, Web Site: www.nera.com (20)

Carrot-Top Industries Inc, Hillsborough, NC. Tel: (919) 732-6200, (800) 628-3524, FAX: (919) 732-5526, E-Mail: service@carrot-top.com, Web Site: www.carrot-top.com (16)

Carruthers, Albert, Memphis Net & Twine Co Inc, Memphis, TN. Tel: (901) 458-2656, (888) 674-7638, FAX: (901) 458-1601, E-Mail: fishinfo@memphisnet.net, Web Site: www.memphisnet.net (11)

Carruthers, Kevin, National Emblem Sales, Indianapolis, IN. Tel: (317) 630-1247, (888) 453-4466, FAX: (317) 630-1381, E-Mail: emblem@legion.org, Web Site: www.emblem.legion.org (16)

Carry, Ellen, Corinthian Direct, New York, NY. Tel: (212) 279-5700, FAX: (212) 239-1772, E-Mail: jonz@mediabuying.com, Web Site: www.mediabuying.com (35)

Carson, Ann, Lincoln Park Zoo, Chicago, IL. Tel: (312) 742-2000, FAX: (312) 742-2137, E-Mail: webmaster@lpzoo.com, Web Site: www.lpzoo.com (1)

Carson, David, Mailways Enterprises Inc, Crystal Lake, IL. Tel: (815) 455-4850, FAX: (815) 455-7327, E-Mail: dave@mailways.com, Web Site: www.mailways.com (28)

Carson, George, Carson & Co, Santa Ana, CA. Tel: (949) 477-9400, E-Mail: gcarson@carsonandcompany.com, Web Site: www.carsonpr.com (35)

Carson, Vernon, L., Web Direct Marketing Inc, Glenview, IL. Tel: (847) 459-0800, (877) 841-2841, FAX: (847) 459-7378, E-Mail: info@webdirectmktg.com, Web Site: www.webdirectmktg.com (35)

Carson & Co, Santa Ana, CA. Tel: (949) 477-9400, E-Mail: gcarson@carsonandcompany.com, Web Site: www.carsonpr.com (35)

Carson Pirie Scott & Co, Milwaukee, WI. Tel: (414) 347-1152, FAX: (414) 278-5748 (16)

Cartel Creativo, San Antonio, TX. Tel: (210) 892-0700, FAX: (210) 696-4299, Web Site: www.thecartel.com (35)

Carter, Brent, MoneyGram International, Dallas, TX. Tel: (800) 666-3947, Web Site: www.moneygram.com (14)

Carter, Cindy, FDAnews, Falls Church, VA. Tel: (703) 538-7600, (888) 838-5578, FAX: (703) 538-7676, E-Mail: customerservice@fdanews.com, Web Site: www.fdanews.com (17)

Carter, Colleen, Cuddledown Inc, Portland, ME. Tel: (207) 761-0201, (800) 323-6793, FAX: (207) 761-1948, Web Site: www.cuddledown.com (8)

Carter, Diane, American Horse Products, San Juan Capistrano, CA. Tel: (949) 248-5300, (800) 500-0799, FAX: (949) 248-5305, E-Mail: zjim@sbcglobal.net, Web Site: www.americanhorseproducts.com (11)

Carter, Ian, R., Hilton Hotels Corp, Mc Lean, VA. Tel: (310) 278-4321, (800) HILTONS, FAX: (310) 205-3670, Web Site: www.hilton.com (19)

Carter, James, American Horse Products, San Juan Capistrano, CA. Tel: (949) 248-5300, (800) 500-0799, FAX: (949) 248-5305, E-Mail: zjim@sbcglobal.net, Web Site: www.americanhorseproducts.com (11)

Carter, James, H., American Arbitration Association, New York, NY. Tel: (212) 716-5800, (800) 778-7879, FAX: (212) 716-5905, E-Mail: kesslerw@adr.org, Web Site: www.adr.org (1)

Carter, Jerry, Consumer Opinion Services Inc, Seattle, WA. Tel: (206) 241-6050, FAX: (206) 241-5213, E-Mail: info@cosvc.com, Web Site: www.cosvc.com (30)

Carter, Lewis, Rochling Engineered Plastics, Dallas, NC. Tel: (704) 922-7814, (800) 541-4419, FAX: (704) 922-7651, E-Mail: rep@roechling-plastics.us, Web Site: www.roechling-plastics.us (34)

Carter, Nancy, L., North Wind Picture Archives, Alfred, ME. Tel: (207) 490-1940, (800) 952-0703, FAX: (207) 490-3627, E-Mail: mail@northwindpictures.com, Web Site: www.northwindpictures.com (38)

Carter, Robert W., Uniway Management Corp, Forest Park, GA. Tel: (404) 363-6200, (888) 386-4929, FAX: (404) 363-8848, E-Mail: uniway@bellsouth.net, Web Site: www.uniway.com (16)

Carter, Robert, Communications Unlimited Inc, Richmond, VA. Tel: (804) 754-7242, E-Mail: communicationsunlimited@verizon.net (20)

Carter, Warrick, L., Columbia College Chicago, Chicago, IL. Tel: (312) 663-1600, FAX: (312) 344-0869, Web Site: www.colum.edu (41)

Carter & Holmes Inc, Newberry, SC. Tel: (803) 276-0579, FAX: (803) 276-0588, E-Mail: orchids@carterandholmes.com, Web Site: www.carterandholmes.com (8)

Harriet Carter Gifts Inc, Montgomeryville, PA. Tel: (215) 361-5100, FAX: (215) 361-1127, Web Site: www.harrietcarter.com (6)

Cartin, Kara, TARGUSinfo, Mc Lean, VA. Tel: (703) 272-6200, Web Site: www.TARGUSinfo.com (22)

Cartouche Ltd, Alexandria, VA. Tel: (703) 823-7904, (800) AT-EGYPT, FAX: (888) 283-4978, E-Mail: sales@egyptianimports.com, Web Site: www.egyptianimports.com (6)

Cartwright, Ed, Canadian Marketing Association, Don Mills, ON Canada. Tel: (416) 391-2362, FAX: (416) 441-4062, E-Mail: info@the-cma.org, Web Site: www.the-cma.org (40)

Carus, Andre, The Cricket Magazine Group, Chicago, IL. Tel: (603) 924-7209, (800) 821-0115, FAX: (815) 224-6615, E-Mail: customerservice@caruspub.com, Web Site: www.cricketmag.com (17)

Carus, Marianne, The Cricket Magazine Group, Chicago, IL. Tel: (603) 924-7209, (800) 821-0115, FAX: (815) 224-6615, E-Mail: customerservice@caruspub.com, Web Site: www.cricketmag.com (17)

Caruso Jr., Gerald, M., Goldsmith Agio Helms, Minneapolis, MN. Tel: (612) 339-0500, FAX: (612) 339-0507, Web Site: www.agio.com (14)

Caruso, Diane, Choice Media, Amherst, NH. Tel: (603) 672-3338, FAX: (603) 249-9732, E-Mail: choicemedia@comcast.net (31)

Caruso, Dominic, J., Johnson & Johnson, New Brunswick, NJ. Tel: (732) 524-0400, FAX: (732) 214-0332, Web Site: www.jnj.com (16)

Carvel Corp, Atlanta, GA. Tel: (404) 255-3250, (800) 227-8353, FAX: (404) 255-4978, Web Site: www.carvel.com (4)

Carver, Steve, The Hartford Courant, Hartford, CT. Tel: (860) 241-6200, FAX: (860) 241-3865, Web Site: www.courant.com (31)

Casablanca Express, Woodland Hills, CA. Tel: (818) 992-5100, Web Site: www.casablancaexpress.com (33)

Casabonne, Richard, J., Steck-Vaughn, Austin, TX. Tel: (512) 343-8227, (877) 866-2586, (800) 531-5015, FAX: (512) 795-3617, (877) 265-2730, E-Mail: info@steck-vaughn.com, Web Site: www.steck-vaughn.com (17)

Casaletto, Mark, Daily Commercial News & Construction Record, Markham, ON. Tel: (905) 752-5408, (800) 465-6475, FAX: (888) 396-9413, (905) 752-5450, E-Mail: dcnonl@reedbusiness.com, Web Site: www.dcnonl.com (17)

Casbarian, Archie, Arnaud's, New Orleans, LA. Tel: (504) 523-0611, (866) 230-8895, FAX: (504) 581-7908, Web Site: www.arnauds.com (16)

Casbarian, Jane, Arnaud's, New Orleans, LA. Tel: (504) 523-0611, (866) 230-8895, FAX: (504) 581-7908, Web Site: www.arnauds.com (16)

Cascade Forest Nursery, Bellevue, IA. Tel: (563) 872-3025, (800) 596-9437, FAX: (563) 872-5003, Web Site: www.cascadeforestry.com (8)

Cascade Outfitters, Boise, ID. Tel: (208) 322-4411, (800) 223-7328, FAX: (208) 322-5016, E-Mail: mail@cascadeoutfitters.com, Web Site: www.cascadeoutfitters.com (11)

Cascade Promotions Corp, Redwood City, CA. Tel: (650) 594-1757 (33)

Cascapera, Judy, Nestle USA, Glendale, CA. Tel: (818) 549-6000, (800) 225-2270, FAX: (818) 549-6952, Web Site: www.nestleusa.com (4)

Cascioli, Terry, Times Publishing Co, Erie, PA. Tel: (814) 870-1600, FAX: (814) 870-1808, E-Mail: terry.cascioli@timesnews.com (18)

Case, Cynthia, The World Bank, Washington, DC. Tel: (202) 473-1000, FAX: (202) 477-6391, Web Site: www.worldbank.org (17)

Case, David, Sweepstakes Clearinghouse, Dallas, TX. Tel: (214) 915-7100, FAX: (214) 915-7458, E-Mail: customersupport@ sweepstakesclearinghouse.com, Web Site: www. sweepstakesclearinghouse.com (16)

Case, Greg, AON Center, Chicago, IL. Tel: (312) 381-1000, FAX: (312) 381-6032, Web Site: www.aon. com (15)

Case Design Corp, Telford, PA. Tel: (215) 703-0130, (800) 847-4176, FAX: (215) 703-0139, E-Mail: sales@casedesigncorp.com, Web Site: www. casedesigncorp.com (34)

Casey Jr, Donald, M., Johnson & Johnson, New Brunswick, NJ. Tel: (732) 524-0400, FAX: (732) 214-0332, Web Site: www.jnj.com (15)

Casey, Daniel, P., Caraustar Ashland Carton Plant, Ashland, OH. Tel: (419) 289-2666, FAX: (419) 281-5415, Web Site: www.caraustar.com (27)

Casey, Larry, Marketing Connections Corp, Bedford, NH. Tel: (603) 472-8989, (800) 472-1818, FAX: (603) 472-9881, E-Mail: lcasey@mccnh.com, Web Site: www.mcciq.com (29)

Casey, Thomas, W., Washington Mutual Home Loan, Inc, Downers Grove, IL. Tel: (847) 549-6500, FAX: (847) 549-2975 (14)

Cash, Debra, L., Blanchard & Co Inc, New Orleans, LA. Tel: (504) 837-3010, (800) 880-4653, FAX: (504) 837-4884, Web Site: www.blanchardonline. com (16)

CashNetUSA, Chicago, IL. Tel: (312) 676-1583, Web Site: www.cashnetusa.com (14)

Casias, Grace, Data-Dynamix Inc, Castle Rock, CO. Tel: (720) 855-9282, (888) 314-0078, FAX: (720) 855-9099, Web Site: www.data-dynamix.com (23)

Caskey, Joan, Stonwurks, Eden Prairie, MN. Tel: (785) 526-7847, (888) 884-7881, FAX: (785) 526-7841, E-Mail: stonwurks@stonwurks.com, Web Site: www.stonwurks.com (16)

Casler, John M., The Sportsman's Guide Inc, South Saint Paul, MN. Tel: (651) 451-3030, (800) 882-2962, FAX: (651) 450-6130, E-Mail: custserv@ sportsmansguide.com, Web Site: www. sportsmansguide.com (11)

Caso, Adolph, Dante University Press, Wellesley, MA. Tel: (781) 790-1059, FAX: (781) 790-1056, E-Mail: dante@danteuniversity.org, Web Site: www.danteuniversity.com (17)

Casper, Chad, Gun Video Catalog/LMP, San Diego, CA. Tel: (858) 569-4000, (800) 942-8273, FAX: (858) 569-0505, Web Site: www.gunvideo.com; www.glockstore.com (11)

Casper, Gol, Pace Communications Inc, Greensboro, NC. Tel: (336) 378-6065, FAX: (336) 275-2864, Web Site: www.pacecommunications.com (17)

Caspersen, Daniel, Toys "R" Us, Wayne, NJ. Tel: (973) 617-5879, FAX: (973) 617-4006, Web Site: www.toysrus.com (11)

Cassaday, John, M., John Hancock Financial Services Inc, Boston, MA. Tel: (617) 572-6000, (800) 732-5543, FAX: (617) 572-6451, Web Site: www. johnhancock.com (15)

Cassell, Kristina, Boardroom Inc, Stamford, CT. Tel: (203) 973-5900, FAX: (203) 967-3086, E-Mail: kseaborne@boardroom.com, Web Site: www. boardroom.com (17)

Cassey, Ken, World Vision Inc, Federal Way, WA. Tel: (253) 815-1000, (888) 511-6548, FAX: (253) 815-3140, E-Mail: info@worldvision.org, Web Site: www.worldvision.org (1)

Cassiday, Beth, Paris Presents Inc, Gurnee, IL. Tel: (847) 263-5500, (800) 431-5723, FAX: (847) 263-5191, Web Site: www.parispresents.com (7)

Cassidy, Bill, Cassidy & Co, Eagan, MN. Tel: (651) 452-4485, FAX: (651) 452-0561, E-Mail: sarah@ cassidycompany.com, Web Site: www. cassidycompany.com (33)

Cassidy, David, Amvac Chemical Corp, Los Angeles, CA. Tel: (323) 264-3910, FAX: (323) 268-1028, Web Site: www.amvac-chemical.com (8)

Cassidy, Joseph, The Orvis Co Inc, Manchester, VT. Tel: (802) 362-3622, FAX: (802) 362-3525, Web Site: www.orvis.com (11)

Cassidy, Tom, Minnesota Multi Housing Association, Bloomington, MN. Tel: (952) 854-8500, FAX: (952) 854-3810, E-Mail: mha@mmha.com, Web Site: www.mmha.com (1)

Cassidy & Co, Eagan, MN. Tel: (651) 452-4485, FAX: (651) 452-0561, E-Mail: sarah@ cassidycompany.com, Web Site: www. cassidycompany.com (33)

Cassioli, Casey, American Eagle Outfitters, Pittsburgh, PA. Tel: (412) 432-3382, Web Site: www.ae.com (2)

Casson, Scott, American Direct Marketing Services, Dallas, TX. Tel: (214) 634-2361, (800) 527-5080, FAX: (214) 905-3829, Web Site: www.dmlist.com (23)

Castator, Jeff, James Medical Rents & Sales Inc, Fort Wayne, IN. Tel: (260) 423-9571, E-Mail: sales@ jamesmedical.com, Web Site: www.jamesmedical. net (7)

Castellvi, Frank, J., Commerce Register Inc, Midland Park, NJ. Tel: (201) 445-3000, FAX: (201) 445-5806, E-Mail: cri@comreginc.com, Web Site: www.comreginc.com (22)

Castino, Alfred, Autodesk Inc, San Rafael, CA. Tel: (415) 507-5000, FAX: (415) 507-5100, Web Site: www.autodesk.com (16)

Castle, Alan, Polyair Packaging, Chicago, IL. Tel: (773) 995-1818, (888) POLYAIR X444, FAX: (773) 995-7725, E-Mail: marketing@polyair.com, Web Site: www.polyair.com (9)

Castle, Cary, United Spinal Association, East Elmhurst, NY. Tel: (718) 803-3782, Web Site: www. unitedspinal.org (1)

Castle, Randy, The Miller Group, Dupo, IL. Tel: (636) 343-5700, (800) 325-3350, FAX: (618) 286-6202, E-Mail: info@miller-group.com, Web Site: www. multiplexdisplays.com (5)

Castleberry, John, FotoBed.com, Birmingham, AL. Tel: (888) 368-6233, E-Mail: service@fotobed. com, Web Site: www.fotobed.com (20)

Castro-Wright, Eduardo, Wal Mart Stores, Bentonville, AR. Tel: (479) 273-4000, (800) 925-6278, FAX: (479) 277-1830, Web Site: www.walmart.com (16)

Casual Living USA, Tampa, FL. Tel: (813) 884-6955, (800) 652-2948, FAX: (813) 882-4605, Web Site: www.casuallivingusa.com (6)

Casual Male Retail Group, Canton, MA. Tel: (781) 828-9300, (800) 767-0319, E-Mail: info@ casualmale.com, Web Site: www.casualmale.com (2)

Caswell-Massey Co Ltd, Edison, NJ. Tel: (732) 225-2181, (800) 326-0500, FAX: (732) 225-2385, E-Mail: info@caswellmasseyltd.com, Web Site: www.caswellmassey.com (7)

Catalano, Jim, Boundless Corp, Phelps, NY. Tel: (631) 962-1500, (800) 231-5445, FAX: (631) 962-1505, E-Mail: sales@boundless.com, Web Site: www. boundless.com (16)

The Catalog Consultancy, Vero Beach, FL. Tel: (772) 226-7740, FAX: (772) 226-7740, E-Mail: catalog321@aol.com, Web Site: www. catalogconsultant.com (20)

Catalog Design Studios, Providence, RI. Tel: (888) 409-9992, Web Site: www.catalogdesignstudios. com (34)

Catalog Marketing Group, Evanston, IL. Tel: (847) 864-8089 (20)

Catalog Media Network Inc, Evanston, IL. Tel: (847) 864-0550, FAX: (847) 864-0575, Web Site: www. thelistbank.com (23)

Catalog Music Corp, Nashville, TN. Tel: (615) 298-4338, (800) 992-4487, FAX: (615) 298-4628, Web Site: www.purecountrymusic.com (3)

Catalogs America, Gordonsville, VA. Tel: (540) 832-2253, (800) 283-4666, FAX: (540) 832-7253, E-Mail: dsayin@catalogsamerica.com, Web Site: www.catalogsamerica.com (27)

Catalogs By Lorel, King of Prussia, PA. Tel: (800) 967-2682, Web Site: www.catalogdesignstudios. com (35)

Catalogs.com, Fort Lauderdale, FL. Tel: (954) 659-9005, FAX: (954) 659-9007, Web Site: www. catalogs.com (30)

Catalyst, Rochester, NY. Tel: (585) 453-8300, (800) 836-7720, FAX: (585) 453-8360, E-Mail: info@ catalystinc.com, Web Site: www.catalystinc.com (35)

Catalyst Computer Services Inc, Los Angeles, CA. Tel: (310) 441-4300, (800) 659-2267, FAX: (310) 441-4332, E-Mail: sales@catalystsoftware.com, Web Site: www.catalystsoftware.com (32)

Catalyst Creative Services, Palo Alto, CA. Tel: (650) 325-1500, E-Mail: chief@catalystcreative.us, Web Site: www.catalystcreative.us (39)

Catalyst Direct Marketing/DNA, Pompton Lakes, NJ. Tel: (973) 831-4222, FAX: (973) 831-1933, E-Mail: info@catalystdm.com, Web Site: www. catalystdm.com (23)

Catalyst Marketing Communications Inc, Stamford, CT. Tel: (203) 348-7541, FAX: (203) 348-5688, E-Mail: b2b@catalystmc.com, Web Site: www. catalystmc.com (35)

Catalyst Marketing Group, Richmond, VA. Tel: (804) 288-9440, FAX: (804) 288-9824, E-Mail: info@ catalyst121.com, Web Site: www.catalyst121.com (35)

The Catamount Group, Southport, CT. Tel: (203) 778-4110, FAX: (203) 778-4130, E-Mail: tina@ catamountgroup.net, Web Site: www. catamountgroup.net (23)

Catanese, Samuel R., Infomercial Monitoring Service Inc, Broomall, PA. Tel: (610) 328-6902, FAX: (610) 328-6791, E-Mail: catanese@imstv.com, Web Site: www.imstv.com (20)

Catch The Wind Kite Shop, Lincoln City, OR. Tel: (541) 994-9500, (800) 227-7878, FAX: (541) 994-4766, E-Mail: catchthewindkites@yahoo.com, Web Site: www.catchthewind.com (11)

Cate, John, Alco Chemical, Chattanooga, TN. Tel: (423) 629-1405, FAX: (423) 698-8723, Web Site: www.alcochemical.com (16)

Catell, Robert B., Keyspan Energy Corp, Brooklyn, NY. Tel: (718) 403-2000, (888) 222-7359, Web Site: www.keyspanenergy.com (15)

Cater, Charles, B., Thomson West, Eagan, MN. Tel: (651) 687-7000, (800) 328-9378, FAX: (651) 687-7849, E-Mail: jeff.patrios@thomsonreuters.com, Web Site: www.thomson.com (16)

Caterpillar Inc, Peoria, IL. Tel: (309) 675-1000, Web Site: www.cat.com (16)

Caterpillar Insurance Services Corp, Nashville, TN. Tel: (615) 386-5800, Web Site: www.cat.com (15)

Cathedral Corp, Rome, NY. Tel: (315) 338-0021, (800) 698-0299, FAX: (315) 338-5874, E-Mail: sales@cathedralstewardship.com, Web Site: www. cathedralcorporation.com (21)

Catholic Charities - Brooklyn & Queens, Brooklyn, NY. Tel: (718) 722-6000, Web Site: www.ccbq.org (1)

Catholic Church Extension Society, Chicago, IL. Tel: (312) 795-6076, Web Site: www.catholicextension. org (1)

Catholic Digest, New London, CT. Tel: (800) 321-0411, E-Mail: catholicdigest@bayardinc.com, Web Site: www.catholicdigest.com (17)

Catholic Health East, Newtown Square, PA. Tel: (610) 355-2000, (877) 424-3001, FAX: (610) 271-9600, Web Site: www.che.org (1)

Catholic Relief Services, Baltimore, MD. Tel: (410) 951-7491, Web Site: www.catholicrelief.org (1)

The Catholic University of America Press, Washington, DC. Tel: (202) 319-5052, FAX: (202) 319-4985, E-Mail: cua-press@cua.edu, Web Site: www. cuapress.cua.edu (17)

Cattle Kate, Boise, ID. Tel: (208) 377-5283, (800) 332-5283, FAX: (208) 375-3827, E-Mail: cattlekate@rmisp.com, Web Site: www.cattlekate. com (2)

Catz, Safra A., Oracle Corp, Redwood Shores, CA. Tel: (650) 506-7000, (800) 633-0738, FAX: (650) 506-7200, Web Site: www.oracle.com (16)

Caudill, Robert S., Caudill & Associates Inc, Orange, CA. Tel: (714) 210-2585, FAX: (714) 210-2595, E-Mail: bobc@caudill4production.com, Web Site: www.caudill4production.com (32)

Caudill & Associates Inc, Orange, CA. Tel: (714) 210-2585, FAX: (714) 210-2595, E-Mail: bobc@caudill4production.com, Web Site: www.caudill4production.com (32)

Caufield, Scott, AllMedia Inc, Plano, TX. Tel: (469) 467-9100, FAX: (214) 291-5431, E-Mail: lmcclendon@allmediainc.com, Web Site: www.allmediainc.com (23)

Caugherty Hahn Communications, Glen Rock, NJ. Tel: (201) 251-7778, FAX: (201) 251-7779, Web Site: www.chcomm.com (20)

Caulder, Lindy, CRM Learning, Carlsbad, CA. Tel: (760) 431-9800, (800) 421-0833, FAX: (760) 931-5792, E-Mail: sales@crmlearning.com, Web Site: www.crmlearning.com (16)

Andrea B Cautela, New York, NY. Tel: (212) 577-5920 (20)

Cauton, Tamara, Creative Marketing Programs, Kansas City, MO. Tel: (816) 472-6843, (800) 373-6843, FAX: (816) 472-8184, E-Mail: getresults@cmpkc. com, Web Site: www.cmpkc.com (21)

Cavalier, Phil, Appleton Coated LLC, Combined Locks, WI. Tel: (920) 968-3999, Web Site: www. appletoncoated.com (2)

Cavallari, Ford, D., Village Software Inc, Boston, MA. Tel: (617) 695-9332, (800) 724-9332, FAX: (617) 695-1935, E-Mail: requests@villagesoft.com, Web Site: www.villagesoft.com (2)

Cavanaugh, Robert, B., JC Penney Inc, Plano, TX. Tel: (972) 431-1000, FAX: (972) 431-1977, Web Site: www.jcpenney.com (5)

Cavedo, Keith, Directory of Premium, Incentive & Travel Buyers, Richmond, VA. Tel: (804) 762-4455, (800) 223-1797, FAX: (804) 935-0271, E-Mail: amdouglas4@aol.com, Web Site: www. douglaspublications.com (43)

Cavella, Frank, South Seas Island Resort, Captiva Island, FL. Tel: (866) 565-5089, FAX: (941) 482-2470, Web Site: www.southseas.com (19)

Cavender, Art, E-Z Bowz Inc, Gatlinburg, TN. Tel: (865) 453-3060, FAX: (865) 429-3743, Web Site: www.ezbows.com (8)

Cavender, Kay, SilverPop, Atlanta, GA. Tel: (866) 745-8767, FAX: (678) 247-0501, E-Mail: info@silverpop.com, Web Site: www.silverpop.com (32)

Cavender, Lea, E-Z Bowz Inc, Gatlinburg, TN. Tel: (865) 453-3060, FAX: (865) 429-3743, Web Site: www.ezbows.com (8)

Marshall Cavendish Corp, Tarrytown, NY. Tel: (914) 332-8888, (800) 821-9881, FAX: (914) 332-1888, Web Site: www.marshallcavendish.com (17)

Caviarteria New York Inc, Astoria, NY. Tel: (212) 759-7410, (800) 422-8427, FAX: (212) 750-0358, E-Mail: info@caviarteria.com, Web Site: www. caviarteria.com (4)

Cawley, Thomas, P., Peet's Coffee & Tea Inc, Berkeley, CA. Tel: (510) 594-2100, (800) 999-2132, FAX: (510) 594-2180, E-Mail: mailorder@peets. com, Web Site: www.peets.com (4)

Frank W Cawood & Associates Inc, Peachtree City, GA. Tel: (770) 487-6307, Web Site: www.fca.com (35)

Cayce, Charles, Thomas, ARE Press, Virginia Beach, VA. Tel: (757) 491-0689, (888) 273-3400, FAX: (757) 491-0689, Web Site: www.arepress.com (1)

Caywood, Mary, Archer/Malmo, Memphis, TN. Tel: (901) 523-2000, FAX: (901) 524-5578, Web Site: www.archermalmo.com (35)

Caywood, Stacey, CCH Inc, Riverwoods, IL. Tel: (847) 267-7000, (888) 224-7377, Web Site: www. cch.com (17)

Cecala, Guy, Specialized Information Publishers Association (SIPA), Vienna, VA. Tel: (703) 992-9339, (800) 356-9302, FAX: (703) 610-9005, E-Mail: info@sipaonline.org, Web Site: www.sipaonline. com (1)

Cecchin, James, C&S Sales Inc, Wheeling, IL. Tel: (847) 541-0710, (800) 292-7711, FAX: (847) 541-9904, E-Mail: sales@cs-sales.com, Web Site: www.cs_sales.com (9)

Cecchini, Roberto, The Artists Co, New York, NY. Tel: (212) 679-7199, FAX: (212) 741-1519, E-Mail: nyc@artists-ar.com (32)

Cecil, Brad, Brad Cecil & Associates, Arlington, TX. Tel: (817) 795-8808 (1)

Cecil, Mark A, Conseco Inc, Carmel, IN. Tel: (317) 817-6100, FAX: (317) 817-2847, Web Site: www. conseco.com (15)

Cecil, Sherry, UniFirst Corp, Owensboro, KY. Tel: (270) 683-5250 X523, Web Site: www.unifirst.com (2)

Brad Cecil & Associates, Arlington, TX. Tel: (817) 795-8808 (1)

Cedar Fresh Products, Coral Gables, FL. Tel: (305) 870-9390, Web Site: www.cedarfresh.com (16)

Cedeno, Laura, Nahan Printing Inc, Saint Cloud, MN. Tel: (320) 251-7611, Web Site: www.nahan.com (27)

Cegielski, Craig, Lions Gate Television Corp, Santa Monica, CA. Tel: (310) 449-9200, FAX: (310) 255-3870, Web Site: www.lionsgate.com (16)

Cejvanovic, Amela, Veridian Credit Union, Waterloo, IA. Tel: (319) 236-5692, (800) 235-3228, FAX: (319) 833-1185, E-Mail: sarahma@veridiancu.org, Web Site: www.veridiancu.org (1)

Celebrity Endorsement Network (CEN), Calabasas, CA. Tel: (818) 225-7090, FAX: (818) 880-0898, E-Mail: info@celebrityendorsement.com, Web Site: www.celebrityendorsement.com (35)

Celentano, John, E., Bristol-Myers Squibb Co, New York, NY. Tel: (212) 546-4000, FAX: (212) 546-9544, Web Site: www.bms.com (16)

Celestial Seasonings, Boulder, CO. Tel: (303) 530-5300, (800) 434-4246, FAX: (303) 581-1249, Web Site: www.hain-celestial.com (16)

Cellular One Group, Oklahoma City, OK. Tel: (509) 663-2162, (800) 545-5982, FAX: (425) 586-8451, Web Site: www.cellularone.com (16)

Celtic Life Insurance Co, Chicago, IL. Tel: (312) 332-5401, FAX: (312) 441-0341, E-Mail: info@celtic-net.com, Web Site: www.celtic-net.com (15)

Cendrowska, Teresa, ASTM International, West Conshohocken, PA. Tel: (610) 832-9500, FAX: (610) 832-9555, E-Mail: service@astm.org, Web Site: www.astm.org (1)

Cendyn, Boca Raton, FL. Tel: (561) 750-3173, Web Site: www.cendyn.com (32)

Cengage Learning, Independence, KY. Tel: (800) 354-9706, FAX: (800) 487-8488, Web Site: www. delmar.com (17)

Cenk, William, E., WESCO, Pittsburgh, PA. Tel: (412) 454-2200, (800) 343-1201, E-Mail: info@wesco. com, Web Site: www.wescodist.com (16)

Centanni, Ross, J., Champion, Quincy, IL. Tel: (217) 222-5400, FAX: (217) 228-8260, Web Site: www. championpneumatic.com (16)

Centaur Forge LLC, Burlington, WI. Tel: (262) 763-9175, (800) 666-9175, FAX: (262) 763-8350, E-Mail: info@centaurforge.com, Web Site: www. centaurforge.com (9)

Center for Book Arts, New York, NY. Tel: (212) 481-0295, FAX: (866) 708-8994, E-Mail: info@centerforbookarts.org, Web Site: www. centerforbookarts.org (27)

Center for Creative Leadership, Greensboro, NC. Tel: (336) 545-2810, FAX: (336) 282-3284, E-Mail: info@ccl.org, Web Site: www.ccl.org (16)

The Center for eBusiness & Advanced IT, Erie, PA. Tel: (814) 898-6500, Web Site: www.ebizitpa.org (1)

Center For Information Policy Leadership, Washington, DC. Tel: (202) 778-2264, FAX: (202) 778-2201, Web Site: www.policyleaders.com (20)

Center for International Earth Science Information Network, Palisades, NY. Tel: (845) 365-8988, FAX: (845) 365-8922, E-Mail: ciesin.info@ciesin. columbia.edu, Web Site: www.ciesin.org (22)

Center for Professional Advancement, East Brunswick, NJ. Tel: (732) 238-1600, FAX: (732) 238-9113, E-Mail: info@cfpa.com, Web Site: www.cfpa.com (13)

Center for Professional Development, Tallahassee, FL. Tel: (850) 644-8004, (850) 487-1691, FAX: (850) 644-2589, Web Site: www.Learningforlife.fsu.com (16)

Center for Science in the Public Interest, Washington, DC. Tel: (202) 332-9110, FAX: (202) 265-4954, E-Mail: circ@cspinet.org, Web Site: www.cspinet. org (1)

The Center for Thanatology Research & Education Inc, Brooklyn, NY. Tel: (718) 858-3026, FAX: (718) 852-1846, E-Mail: thanatology@pipeline. com, Web Site: www.thanatology.org (23)

CenterCore Group Inc, Marked Tree, AR. Tel: (800) 686-0821, FAX: (870) 358-3330, Web Site: www. centercoregroup.com (16)

Centerpoint Energy, Minneapolis, MN. Tel: (612) 372-4664, FAX: (612) 321-4873, E-Mail: mgc-businessinformation@centerpointenergy.com, Web Site: www.minnegasco.centerpointenergy.com (16)

Centrac Inc, West Caldwell, NJ. Tel: (973) 402-0999, FAX: (973) 402-0993, E-Mail: rleeds@centrac. com, Web Site: www.centrac.com (29)

Central Letter Shop Inc, West Caldwell, NJ. Tel: (973) 808-9595, FAX: (973) 808-8339, E-Mail: lena@centrallettershop.com, Web Site: www. centrallettershop.com (23)

Central Lewmar, Clifton, NJ. Tel: (973) 622-6377, (800) 772-7301, FAX: (973) 623-4323, E-Mail: dan.watkoske@expedx.com, Web Site: www. centrallewmar.com (25)

Central National-Gottesman Inc, Purchase, NY. Tel: (914) 696-9000, FAX: (914) 696-1066, E-Mail: purchase@cng-inc.com, Web Site: www.cng-inc. com (25)

Central Pacific Bank, Honolulu, HI. Tel: (808) 544-0500, (800) 544-0500, (800) 342-8422, FAX: (808) 531-2875, Web Site: www.centralpacificbank.com (14)

Central Shippee Inc, Bloomingdale, NJ. Tel: (973) 838-1100, (800) 631-8968, FAX: (973) 838-8273, Web Site: www.centralshippee.com (16)

Central States Health & Life Co of Omaha, Omaha, NE. Tel: (402) 397-1111, (800) 826-6587, FAX: (402) 391-3772, Web Site: www.cso.com (15)

Central States Indemnity, Omaha, NE. Tel: (402) 997-8000, (402) 397-1111, (800) 445-6500, Web Site: www.csi-omaha.com (15)

Century Direct, Long Island City, NY. Tel: (212) 349-0600, FAX: (718) 349-9528, E-Mail: info@centurydirect.net, Web Site: www.centurydirect.net (28)

Century Photo, Santa Fe Springs, CA. Tel: (800) 767-0777, FAX: (714) 441-4550, Web Site: www. centuryphoto.com (10)

Century Tel Enterprises Inc, Monroe, LA. Tel: (318) 388-9000, (800) 201-4102, Web Site: centurytel. com (29)

Cenveo Color Art Inc, Eureka, MO. Tel: (314) 966-2000, FAX: (314) 966-4725, E-Mail: scott.turner@cenveo.com, Web Site: www.colorart.com (27)

Cenveo Commercial Envelope Group, Kent, WA. Tel: (206) 576-4300, (800) 347-6989, FAX: (206) 574-8013, E-Mail: info@cenveo.com, Web Site: www. cenveo.com (26)

Cenveo Inc, Stamford, CT. Tel: (410) 633-4200, (800) 638-2850, FAX: (410) 633-1202, Web Site: www.cenveo.com (27)

Cerrone, Barbara, L., Ruskin, Moscou, Faltischek, PC, Uniondale, NY. Tel: (516) 663-6600, FAX: (516) 663-6601, E-Mail: info@rmfpc.com, Web Site: www.rmfpc.com (16)

CertainTeed Corp, Valley Forge, PA. Tel: (610) 341-7000/7739, (800) 233-8990, FAX: (610) 341-7777, Web Site: www.certainteed.com (16)

Certified Lists Inc, Omaha, NE. Tel: (402) 201-2087, (866) 537-7569, FAX: (877) 655-8733, E-Mail: contact@certified-lists.com, Web Site: www.certified-lists.com (23)

Cerullo, David, INSP - The Inspirational Network, Charlotte, NC. Tel: (704) 525-9800, FAX: (704) 525-9899, E-Mail: info@insp.com, Web Site: www.insp.com (32)

Cesa, Bob, 20th Century Fox Television, Los Angeles, CA. Tel: (310) 444-8100, FAX: (310) 444-8101 (16)

Cescau, Patrick, Unilever Best Foods, Englewood Cliffs, NJ. Tel: (201) 567-8000, FAX: (201) 871-8257, E-Mail: comments@unilever.com, Web Site: www.unilever.com (16)

Cessna Aircraft Co, Wichita, KS. Tel: (316) 517-6000, FAX: (316) 517-6640, E-Mail: pmichael@cessna.textron.com, Web Site: www.cessna.com (16)

Chabin Concepts, Chico, CA. Tel: (530) 345-0364, FAX: (530) 345-6417, E-Mail: chabininc@aol.com (16)

Chabot, Andy, Cancer Research Society, Montreal, PQ. Tel: (514) 861-9227, (888) 766-2262, FAX: (514) 861-9220, Web Site: www.CancerResearchSociety.ca (1)

Chabot, Bette, Saks Fifth Avenue, New York, NY. Tel: (212) 940-5195, FAX: (212) 940-5339, Web Site: www.saksfifthavenue.com (16)

Chabot, Brian, Cape Cod Cupola Co Inc, North Dartmouth, MA. Tel: (508) 994-2119, FAX: (508) 997-2511, Web Site: www.capcodcupola.com (8)

Chace, Sharon, A., Insurance Publications Inc, Overland Park, KS. Tel: (913) 383-9191, (800) 762-3387, FAX: (913) 383-1247, E-Mail: brokerwrld@primary.net, Web Site: www.brokerworldmag.com (17)

ChaCha Mobile Answers, Carmel, IN. Tel: (317) 660-6680, Web Site: partners.chacha.com (20)

Chadda, Sanjay, Petsky Prunier LLC, New York, NY. Tel: (212) 842-6001, FAX: (212) 842-6039, Web Site: www.petskyprunier.com (14)

Chadnick, Benjamin, J., Black Star Publishing Co, White Plains, NY. Tel: (212) 679-3288, FAX: (212) 889-2052, Web Site: www.blackstar.com (38)

Chadsworth's 1-800-Columns, Wilmington, NC. Tel: (910) 763-7600, (800) 486-2118, FAX: (910) 763-3191, E-Mail: sales@columns.com, Web Site: www.columns.com (8)

Chadwick's of Boston Inc, West Bridgewater, MA. Tel: (508) 583-8110, FAX: (508) 587-3345, Web Site: www.chadwicks.com (2)

Chaffee, David, S., Chaffee & Communications, Barrington, RI. Tel: (401) 247-2300, FAX: (401) 247-2002, E-Mail: nchaffee@fullchannel.net, Web Site: www.chaffeecommunications.com (35)

Chaffee, Nancy, Chaffee & Communications, Barrington, RI. Tel: (401) 247-2300, FAX: (401) 247-2002, E-Mail: nchaffee@fullchannel.net, Web Site: www.chaffeecommunications.com (35)

Chaffee & Communications, Barrington, RI. Tel: (401) 247-2300, FAX: (401) 247-2002, E-Mail: nchaffee@fullchannel.net, Web Site: www.chaffeecommunications.com (35)

Chai, Nelson, Merrill Lynch, New York, NY. Tel: (212) 449-1000, (800) 637-7455, FAX: (212) 449-9418, Web Site: www.ml.com (14)

Chaido, Lawrence, J, Transglobal Consultants Inc, Canton, OH. Tel: (330) 477-6450, E-Mail: transglobal@earthlink.net (20)

Chaille, Susan, Arrow Co, Indianapolis, IN. Tel: (317) 692-6666, FAX: (317) 692-6769, Web Site: www.aearo.com (16)

Chaimson, David, Sony Media Software, Middleton, WI. Tel: (608) 256-3133 (3)

Chain Store Guide, Tampa, FL. Tel: (800) 927-9292, FAX: (813) 627-6882, E-Mail: info@csgis.com, Web Site: www.csgis.com (17)

Chairman's Marketing Group LLC, Princeton, NJ. Tel: (732) 745-4700 (15)

Chait, Manya, VistaPrint USA Inc, Lexington, MA. Tel: (800) 961-2075, Web Site: www.vistaprint.com (27)

Chaladoff, David, David Chaladoff Media, Fairfield, IA. Tel: (641) 472-6700, FAX: (641) 472-7736, E-Mail: david@dcimediainc.com (32)

David Chaladoff Media, Fairfield, IA. Tel: (641) 472-6700, FAX: (641) 472-7736, E-Mail: david@dcimediainc.com (32)

Chalk, W. Ken, Branch Banking & Trust Co, Wilson, NC. Tel: (252) 399-4111, FAX: (252) 246-4030 (14)

Challenge Industries Inc, Ithaca, NY. Tel: (607) 272-8990, FAX: (607) 277-7865, E-Mail: info@aboutchallenge.org, Web Site: www.aboutchallenge.org (28)

Challoner, Deborah, Avantus, Maryland Heights, MO. Tel: (314) 994-3449, Web Site: www.avantus.com (20)

Chamberlain, Chris, Idea Art Inc, Colorado Springs, CO. Tel: (615) 889-4989, (800) 433-2278, FAX: (615) 889-6731, E-Mail: customerservice@ideaart.com, Web Site: www.ideaart.com (25)

Chambers, Charles, Sara Lee Direct Home Shopping, Winston-Salem, NC. Tel: (336) 519-4400, (800) 671-5056, E-Mail: ohp.managor@onehanesplace.com, Web Site: www.onehanesplace.com (2)

Chambers, Lamar, M., Ashland Inc, Covington, KY. Tel: (859) 815-3333, Web Site: www.ashland.com (16)

Chambers, Steve, Nuance Speech Solutions, Burlington, MA. Tel: (781) 565-5000, FAX: (781) 565-5001, E-Mail: sales@speechworks.com, Web Site: www.nuance.com (16)

Chambers, Susan, United Church Homes, Marion, OH. Tel: (740) 382-4885, (800) 750-0750, FAX: (740) 382-4884, Web Site: www.unitedchurchhomes.org (1)

Chambers, Sylvia, Praises, Prizes & Presents, Grand Rapids, MI. Tel: (361) 851-9663, FAX: (361) 851-9663, Web Site: www.praisesprizespresents.com (5)

Chammah, Walid, Morgan Stanley, New York, NY. Tel: (212) 761-4000, FAX: (212) 761-0096 (14)

Champagne, Rene, R., ITT Educational Services Inc, Carmel, IN. Tel: (317) 706-9200, E-Mail: gtanner@itt-tech.edu, Web Site: www.itt-tech.edu (16)

Champion, Dr. Becky, Callaway Gardens, Pine Mountain, GA. Tel: (706) 663-2281, (800) CALLAWAY, FAX: (706) 663-6812, E-Mail: info@callawaygardens.com, Web Site: www.callawaygardens.com (19)

Champion, Ryan, Intium Services LLC, Diamond Bar, CA. Tel: (909) 743-6182, Web Site: www.intiumservices.com (32)

Champion, Quincy, IL. Tel: (217) 222-5400, FAX: (217) 228-8260, Web Site: www.championpneumatic.com (16)

Champion America Inc, Branford, CT. Tel: (203) 315-1181, (877) 242-6709, FAX: (800) 336-3707, E-Mail: teamca@champion-america.com, Web Site: www.championamerica.com (10)

Champion Printing Inc, Elsmere, KY. Tel: (513) 541-1100, (800) 543-1957, FAX: (513) 541-9398, E-Mail: cpi@championprintinginc.com, Web Site: www.championprintinginc.com (27)

Champs Corp, Bradenton, FL. Tel: (941) 748-0577, (800) 991-6813, E-Mail: customer_service@champssports.com, Web Site: www.champssports.com (11)

Champs Software Inc, Crystal River, FL. Tel: (352) 795-2362, FAX: (352) 795-9100, E-Mail: champs@champsinc.com, Web Site: www.champsinc.com (2)

Chan, Felicia, Peet's Coffee & Tea Inc, Berkeley, CA. Tel: (510) 594-2100, (800) 999-2132, FAX: (510) 594-2180, E-Mail: mailorder@peets.com, Web Site: www.peets.com (4)

Chancellor, Millicent, Landmark Graphics Corp, Houston, TX. Tel: (713) 839-2000, FAX: (713) 839-2015, E-Mail: solutions@lgc.com, Web Site: www.lgc.com (16)

Chancellor, Vicki, Sara Lee Hosiery, Winston Salem, NC. Tel: (336) 519-2711/2369, FAX: (336) 519-3254, Web Site: www.leggs.com (2)

Chandler, Chris, American Society of Media Photographers (ASMP), Philadelphia, PA. Tel: (215) 451-ASMP, FAX: (215) 451-0880, Web Site: www.asmp.org (40)

Chandler, Jim, Ingram Book Group, La Vergne, TN. Tel: (615) 793-5000, (800) 937-8000, FAX: (800) 876-0186, Web Site: www.ipage.ingrambook.com (16)

Chandler, Phyllis, Gary's Perennials, LLC, Maple Glen, PA. Tel: (215) 628-4070, (800) 898-6653, FAX: (215) 628-0216, E-Mail: roots@garysperennials.com, Web Site: www.garysperennials.com; www.perennialmarket.com (8)

Chandler, Tom, American Teleservices Association, Indianapolis, IN. Tel: (317) 816-9336, (877) 779-3974, FAX: (317) 218-0323, Web Site: www.ataconnect.org (40)

Chandronnait, Al, Custom Miniatures, Hudson, NH. Tel: (603) 882-6392 (6)

Chane, Andrew, Tools for Wellness, Oak Park, CA. Tel: (800) 456-9887, FAX: (818) 532-1775, E-Mail: info@toolsforwellness.com, Web Site: www.toolsforwellness.com (7)

Chane, Kenneth, Tools for Wellness, Oak Park, CA. Tel: (800) 456-9887, FAX: (818) 532-1775, E-Mail: info@toolsforwellness.com, Web Site: www.toolsforwellness.com (7)

Chanel Inc, New York, NY. Tel: (212) 688-5055, FAX: (212) 752-1851, Web Site: www.chanel.com (16)

Chang, Alice, Amrel, El Monte, CA. Tel: (626) 443-6818, (800) 654-9838, FAX: (626) 443-8600, E-Mail: amrel@amrel.com, Web Site: www.amrel.com (16)

Channel Neutral Marketing, Oyster Bay, NY. Tel: (516) 992-7887, FAX: (516) 983-1617, Web Site: www.channelneutralmarketing.com (35)

Channel 13 WNET Catalog Division, New York, NY. Tel: (212) 560-2000, FAX: (212) 582-3297, Web Site: www.thirteen.org (5)

Chao, Steven, USA Network, New York, NY. Tel: (212) 664-4444, FAX: (212) 664-6365, Web Site: www.usanetwork.com (32)

Chapek, Robert, Buena Vista Home Entertainment, Burbank, CA. Tel: (818) 560-1000, FAX: (818) 845-8728, Web Site: www.bvhe.com (3)

Chapel, Gary, Nightingale-Conant Corp, Niles, IL. Tel: (847) 647-0300, (800) 557-1660, FAX: (847) 647-7145, Web Site: www.nightingale.com (17)

Chapman Cubine Adams & Hussey, Arlington, VA. Tel: (703) 248-0025, Web Site: www.ahadirect.com (20)

Chappell, Robert, E., Penn Mutual, Horsham, PA. Tel: (215) 956-8083, FAX: (215) 956-8368, Web Site: www.pennmutual.com (15)

Char-Broil, Columbus, GA. Tel: (706) 571-7000, Web Site: www.charbroil.com (16)

Char-Broil Grill Lover's Catalog, Louisville, KY. Tel: (706) 565-2100, (800) 241-8981, FAX: (706) 565-2121, Web Site: www.grilllovers.com (8)

Charisma Brands LLC, Laguna Hills, CA. Tel: (949) 788-8803, Web Site: www.charismabrands.com (6)

Charity Dynamics, Austin, TX. Tel: (512) 241-0561, Web Site: www.charitydynamics.com (1)

Charles, Janice, Investors Marketing Services, Danvers, MA. Tel: (978) 774-2990, (800) 462-2551, FAX: (978) 774-4249, Web Site: www. investorsmarketing.com (14)

Charles, Rebecca, The Home Depot Inc, Atlanta, GA. Tel: (770) 433-8211, (800) 430-3376, FAX: (770) 384-2356, Web Site: www.homedepot.com (16)

Charlotte Chamber of Commerce, Charlotte, NC. Tel: (704) 378-1300, Web Site: www.boomcharlotte. com (1)

Charlton, Madison, WI. Tel: (608) 259-8004, FAX: (608) 259-8061, E-Mail: jdragisic@tcgcorp.net, Web Site: www.tcgcorp.net (29)

Charmaster Products Inc, Grand Rapids, MN. Tel: (218) 326-6786, FAX: (218) 326-1065, E-Mail: info@charmaster.com, Web Site: www.charmaster. com (8)

Charming Shoppers, Bensalem, PA. Tel: (215) 245-9100, Web Site: www.charmingshoppers.com (2)

Charnstrom, Shakopee, MN. Tel: (952) 403-0303, (800) 328-2962, FAX: (800) 916-3215, E-Mail: mail@charnstrom.com, Web Site: www.charnstrom. com (28)

Charolette Ford Trunks, Dumas, TX. Tel: (806) 934-8477, (800) 659-5614, FAX: (806) 372-3061, E-Mail: charolette@charolettefordtrunks.com, Web Site: www.charolettefordtrunks.com (11)

Charter Communications, Saint Louis, MO. Tel: (314) 965-0555, (888) 438-2427, FAX: (314) 965-9745, Web Site: www.charteroom.com (16)

Charter Direct Marketing, New York, NY. Tel: (212) 717-2770, FAX: (561) 245-7559, E-Mail: terrykollman@charterdirectmarketing.com, Web Site: www.charterdirectmarketing.com (33)

Charter One Bank, Cleveland, OH. Tel: (216) 566-5300, (877) CHARTER, (877) 242-7837, FAX: (216) 566-1465, Web Site: www.charterone.com (14)

Chartifacts, Richmond, VA. Tel: (804) 272-7120 (6)

Chartis, New York, NY. Tel: (212) 770-8013, Web Site: www.chartisinsurance.com/pcg (15)

Chasan, Alice, World Press Review, New York, NY. Tel: (212) 982-8880, Web Site: www. worldpressreview.com (18)

Chase, Carla, Chase Media Group, Yorktown Heights, NY. Tel: (914) 962-3871, FAX: (914) 962-2040, Web Site: www.chasemultimedia.com (27)

Chase, Florinda, Chase Advertising Co, Monroeville, PA. Tel: (412) 372-5980, FAX: (412) 372-6097, E-Mail: chaseadv@nb.net, Web Site: www. logomall.com/chaseadv (33)

Chase, Larry, Chase Online Marketing Strategies, New York, NY. Tel: (212) 619-4780 (35)

Chase, Paul, Financial Executives International, Morristown, NJ. Tel: (973) 765-1000, FAX: (973) 765-1018, Web Site: www.financialexecutives.org (1)

Chase, Reni, Longevity Pure Medicine, Palm Springs, CA. Tel: (800) 327-5519, FAX: (760) 329-3651, E-Mail: info@longetivtypuremedicine.com, Web Site: www.longevitypuremedicine.com (7)

Chase Advertising Co, Monroeville, PA. Tel: (412) 372-5980, FAX: (412) 372-6097, E-Mail: chaseadv@nb.net, Web Site: www.logomall.com/ chaseadv (33)

Chase Industries, Inc, Cincinnati, OH. Tel: (513) 860-5565, (800) 543-4455, FAX: (800) 245-7045, Web Site: www.chasedoors.com (16)

Chase Media Group, Yorktown Heights, NY. Tel: (914) 962-3871, FAX: (914) 962-2040, Web Site: www.chasemultimedia.com (27)

Chase Online Marketing Strategies, New York, NY. Tel: (212) 619-4780 (35)

Chasing, Hillary, J Jill Group, Inc, Quincy, MA. Tel: (617) 376-4300, (800) 642-9989, FAX: (617) 769-0177, Web Site: www.jjillgroup.com (2)

Chatelain, Elizabeth, MVI Marketing Ltd, Paso Robles, CA. Tel: (805) 459-4455, (805) 239-2994, FAX: (805) 239-2947, E-Mail: info@ mvimarketing.com, Web Site: www.mvimarketing. com (20)

Chatham, Donald, American Library Association-Publishing Services, Chicago, IL. Tel: (312) 944-6780, (800) 545-2433, FAX: (312) 280-4380, Web Site: www.ala.org (1)

Chatman, Monique, MISSCO Corp, Flowood, MS. Tel: (601) 948-8600, (800) 647-5333, FAX: (601) 987-3038 (16)

Chattanooga Shooting Supplies Inc, Chattanooga, TN. Tel: (423) 894-3007, (800) 251-4808, FAX: (423) 855-5513, Web Site: www.chattanoogashooting. com (16)

Chaturvedi, Abha, Suman Inc, Potomac, MD. Tel: (301) 461-7625, E-Mail: sales@sumaninc.com, Web Site: www.sumaninc.com (21)

Chaturvedi, Dr Anil, Suman Inc, Potomac, MD. Tel: (301) 461-7625, E-Mail: sales@sumaninc.com, Web Site: www.sumaninc.com (21)

Chaudhry-Ekinci, Lorraine, The CPW Group, Ronkonkoma, NY. Tel: (888) 641-7901 (28)

Chauduri, Robin, Atlanta Cutlery Corp, Conyers, GA. Tel: (770) 922-3700, (800) 833-8838, FAX: (770) 760-8993, E-Mail: webmaster@atlantacutlery.com, Web Site: www.atlantacutlery.com (16)

Chavannes, Danielle, Professional Photographer Magazine, Atlanta, GA. Tel: (404) 522-8600, (800) 786-6277, FAX: (404) 614-6405, E-Mail: csc@ppa. com, Web Site: www.ppa.com (17)

Chavern, David, C., US Chamber of Commerce, Washington, DC. Tel: (202) 778-6063, (800) 638-6582, FAX: (202) 887-3430, Web Site: www. uschamber.com (1)

Chavez, Robert, Hermes of Paris, New York, NY. Tel: (212) 759-7585, (800) 441-4488, FAX: (212) 644-2132 (2)

Chavez-Thompson, Linda, Union Privilege, AFL-CIO, Washington, DC. Tel: (202) 293-5330, FAX: (202) 293-5311, Web Site: www.unionplus.org (1)

Chayes, Michael, M., Stromberg Consulting, New York, NY. Tel: (646) 935-4177, (212) 812-6400, FAX: (212) 812-6300, E-Mail: info@ strombergconsulting.com, Web Site: www. strombergconsulting.com (35)

Cheak, Spencer, GameTime Inc, Fort Payne, AL. Tel: (256) 845-5610, (800) 633-2394, FAX: (256) 845-9361/2649, Web Site: www.gametime.com (11)

Cheap, Richard, A., Huntington Bancshares, Columbus, OH. Tel: (614) 480-8300, (800) 480-BANK, FAX: (614) 480-5284, Web Site: www.huntington. com (14)

Cheap Aprons, Derry, NH. Tel: (978) 689-0694, (800) 367-2374, FAX: (978) 689-2483, E-Mail: rkurman@cheapaprons.com, Web Site: www. cheapaprons.com (2)

Check Point Systems, Thorofare, NJ. Tel: (856) 848-1800, (800) 257-5540, FAX: (856) 848-0937, Web Site: www.checkpointsystems.com (34)

Checks by Phone/Checks by Web, Boynton Beach, FL. Tel: (561) 737-8700, FAX: (561) 737-5800, E-Mail: LarrySchwartz@checksbyphone.com, Web Site: www.checksbyphone.com (14)

CheckVantage, Austin, TX. Tel: (512) 442-2332, (877) 243-2501, FAX: (512) 442-5515, E-Mail: marya@ checkvantage.com, Web Site: www.checkvantage. com (14)

Chee Wah, Immee, Rogers Publishing Ltd, Toronto, ON. Tel: (416) 935-7777, FAX: (416) 935-3597, Web Site: www.rogerspublishing.ca (17)

Cheeseman, Rosanne, Times Publishing Co, Erie, PA. Tel: (814) 870-1600, FAX: (814) 870-1808, E-Mail: terry.cascioli@timesnews.com (18)

Cheever, Meg, Pittsburgh Parks Conservancy, Pittsburgh, PA. Tel: (412) 682-7275, Web Site: www. pittsburghparks.org (1)

Chefs Catalog, Colorado Springs, CO. Tel: (719) 272-2600, Web Site: www.chefscatalog.com (8)

Chehak, Gail, E., Indian Arts & Crafts Association, Albuquerque, NM. Tel: (505) 265-9149, FAX: (505) 265-8251, E-Mail: info@iaca.com, Web Site: www.iaca.com (1)

Chelsea Clock Co Inc, Chelsea, MA. Tel: (617) 884-0250, (800) 284-1778, FAX: (617) 830-0599, Web Site: www.chelseaclock.com (6)

Chem-Tainer Industries Inc, North Babylon, NY. Tel: (631) 661-8300, (800) ASK-CHEM, (800) 275-2436, FAX: (631) 661-8209, E-Mail: sales@ chemtainer.com, Web Site: www.chemtainer.com (9)

Chemical Week, New York, NY. Tel: (212) 621-4900, FAX: (212) 621-4800, E-Mail: clientservices@ chemweek.com, Web Site: www.chemweek.com (17)

Chemistri, Troy, MI. Tel: (248) 458-8300, FAX: (248) 458-8729 (35)

Chen, Dennis, Enterprex International Corp, Arcadia, CA. Tel: (626) 256-1444, FAX: (626) 256-1404, E-Mail: premium@enterprex.com, Web Site: www. enterprex.com (16)

Chen, Dr. Albert, BroadVision Inc, Redwood City, CA. Tel: (650) 542-5100, FAX: (650) 364-3425, E-Mail: sales@broadvision.com, Web Site: www. broadvision.com (16)

Chen, Dr. Pehong, BroadVision Inc, Redwood City, CA. Tel: (650) 542-5100, FAX: (650) 364-3425, E-Mail: sales@broadvision.com, Web Site: www. broadvision.com (16)

Chen, Edgar, MPS Multimedia Inc, San Mateo, CA. Tel: (650) 872-7100, FAX: (650) 872-7133, E-Mail: sales@gospg.com, Web Site: www. selectmedia.com (16)

Chen, Edward, Amrel, El Monte, CA. Tel: (626) 443-6818, (800) 654-9838, FAX: (626) 443-8600, E-Mail: amrel@amrel.com, Web Site: www.amrel. com (16)

Chen, Eric, Markwins International Corp, City of Industry, CA. Tel: (909) 595-8898, FAX: (909) 595-8820, Web Site: www.markwins.com (16)

Chen, Jim, Sun Hope Nutritional Health, Santa Monica, CA. Tel: (888) 553-5476, Web Site: www. sunhope.net (7)

Chen, Peng, Morningstar Inc, Chicago, IL. Tel: (312) 696-6000, Web Site: www.morningstar.com (14)

Chen, Robert, S., Center for International Earth Science Information Network, Palisades, NY. Tel: (845) 365-8988, FAX: (845) 365-8922, E-Mail: ciesin@ciesin.columbia.edu, Web Site: www. ciesin.org (22)

Chen, Steve, MPS Multimedia Inc, San Mateo, CA. Tel: (650) 872-7100, FAX: (650) 872-7133, E-Mail: sales@gospg.com, Web Site: www. selectmedia.com (16)

Chen, Y. C., WW Grainger Inc, Lake Forest, IL. Tel: (847) 535-1000, (888) 361-8649, FAX: (847) 535-9122, Web Site: www.grainger.com (9)

Chenault, Kenneth, I., American Express Co, New York, NY. Tel: (212) 640-2000, FAX: (212) 619-9802, Web Site: www.americanexpress.com (14)

Cheney, Kim, Redbook Magazine, New York, NY. Tel: (212) 649-2000, (800) 888-0008, FAX: (212) 581-7605, Web Site: www.redbookmag.com (17)

Cheney, Susan, Summit Marketing, Saint Louis, MO. Tel: (314) 569-3737, FAX: (314) 569-0037, E-Mail: info@summitmarketing.com, Web Site: www.summitmarketing.com (35)

Cheng, Xiangi, Boundless Corp, Phelps, NY. Tel: (631) 962-1500, (800) 231-5445, FAX: (631) 962-1505, E-Mail: sales@boundless.com, Web Site: www.boundless.com (16)

Chenoweth, Susan, Jigsaw, San Mateo, CA. Tel: (650) 235-8400, Web Site: www.jigsaw.com (24)

Cheny, Barbara, The Hyiad Group, Garden City, NY. Tel: (516) 433-3800, FAX: (516) 822-6670, Web Site: www.thehyaidgroup.com (22)

Cherhoniak, David, C., National Broadcast Finance Corp, New Haven, CT. Tel: (203) 389-6000, FAX: (203) 389-6020 (32)

Cherkis, Harvey, Brashe Advertising Inc, Woodbury, NY. Tel: (516) 935-5544, FAX: (516) 931-1722 (35)

Chermside, Brian, J, Dow Corning Corp, Midland, MI. Tel: (989) 496-4000, (800) 248-2481, FAX: (989) 496-4572, Web Site: www.dowcorning.com (16)

Chernick, Linda, Elderhostel Inc, Boston, MA. Tel: (617) 426-7788, (800) 454-5678, FAX: (617) 426-2166, Web Site: www.elderhostel.org (1)

Chernoff Newman, Columbia, SC. Tel: (803) 254-8158, FAX: (803) 252-2016, E-Mail: david. campbell@cnsg.com, Web Site: www. chernoffnewman.com (35)

Cherry, Ken, Nodine's Smokehouse, Torrington, CT. Tel: (860) 489-3213, (800) 222-2059, FAX: (860) 496-9787, E-Mail: nodinesmoke@optonline.net, Web Site: www.nodinesmokehouse.com (4)

Cherry, Linda, Z., Cherry Communications Co, Tallahassee, FL. Tel: (850) 561-3600, FAX: (850) 561-1155, E-Mail: phones@cherrycomm.com, Web Site: www.cherrycomm.com (30)

Cherry, Tom, Coptech Inc, Woburn, MA. Tel: (781) 935-2679, (800) 934-1560, FAX: (781) 935-7673, Web Site: www.coptechinc.com (16)

Cherry Brothers LLC/ Cherrydale, Quakertown, PA. Tel: (800) 570-6010, Web Site: www.cherrydale. com (1)

Cherry Communications Co, Tallahassee, FL. Tel: (850) 561-3600, FAX: (850) 561-1155, E-Mail: phones@cherrycomm.com, Web Site: www. cherrycomm.com (30)

Cherry Tree Toys Inc, Beloit, WI. Tel: (608) 314-3090, (800) 848-4363, FAX: (608) 314-3097, E-Mail: sales@cherrytreetoys.com, Web Site: www.cherrytreetoys.com (11)

Cherubini, Julian, AliMed Inc, Dedham, MA. Tel: (781) 329-2900, (800) 225-2610, FAX: (781) 329-8392, (800) 437-2966, E-Mail: info@alimed.com, Web Site: www.alimed.info (7)

Chesapeake Bay Foundation, Annapolis, MD. Tel: (410) 268-8816, Web Site: www.savethebay.cbf.org (1)

Cheskin, Redwood Shores, CA. Tel: (650) 802-2100, FAX: (650) 593-1125, E-Mail: info@cheskin.com, Web Site: www.cheskin.com (30)

Chesley, David, Interface Engineering, Portland, OR. Tel: (503) 382-2266, FAX: (503) 382-2262, E-Mail: solutions@interfaceengineering.com, Web Site: www.ieice.com (20)

Chesney, John, Creative Printing Services Inc, Des Plaines, IL. Tel: (847) 803-2800, (800) 932-2750, FAX: (847) 803-3299, E-Mail: info@creativepsi. com, Web Site: www.creativepsi.com (27)

Chessari, Jenna, REMEDY Magazine, New York, NY. Tel: (212) 695-2223, FAX: (212) 695-2936, E-Mail: info@rmedizine.com, Web Site: www. medizine.com (17)

Chester, Dan, Direct Marketing Association of Detroit, Royal Oak, MI. Tel: (248) 478-4888, FAX: (248) 478-6437, E-Mail: dmad@ameritech.net, Web Site: www.dmad.org (40)

Chestnut, Mark, Laplink Software Inc, Bellevue, WA. Tel: (425) 952-6000, (800) 527-5465, FAX: (425) 952-6002, E-Mail: marketing@laplink.com, Web Site: www.laplink.com (3)

Cheteyan II, Michael, D., ABDI, Inc Global Order Fulfillment, Leetsdale, PA. Tel: (412) 741-1142, (800) 796-6471, FAX: (412) 741-4161, E-Mail: info@abdintl.com, Web Site: www.abdintl.com (28)

Cheteyan, Judy G., ABDI, Inc Global Order Fulfillment, Leetsdale, PA. Tel: (412) 741-1142, (800) 796-6471, FAX: (412) 741-4161, E-Mail: info@ abdintl.com, Web Site: www.abdintl.com (28)

Cheung, Deborah, Institute For Natural Resources, Concord, CA. Tel: (925) 687-0860, FAX: (925) 609-2820, E-Mail: dcheung@biocorp.com (16)

Cheung, Deborah, United Systems c/o Biomed, Concord, CA. Tel: (925) 609-2820 (7)

Chevannes, Paul, Paul Chevannes, Brooklyn, NY. Tel: (718) 788-3550 (36)

Cheves, Angela, MD Anderson Cancer Center - Children's Art Project, Houston, TX. Tel: (713) 745-2575, (800) 231-1580, FAX: (713) 794-1950, E-Mail: krenner@mdanderson.org, Web Site: www. childrensart.org (1)

Chevremont-Lorenzini, Marie-Jeanne, PricewaterhouseCoopers LLP, New York, NY. Tel: (646) 471-4000, FAX: (646) 471-4444, Web Site: www.pwc. com (14)

Chew, Lewis, National Semiconductor Corp, Santa Clara, CA. Tel: (408) 721-5000, (800) 272-9959, FAX: (408) 245-0671, E-Mail: new.feedback@nsc. com, Web Site: www.national.com (14)

Chewning, Hugh, Chewning Direct Marketing, Irvine, CA. Tel: (949) 854-5401, E-Mail: hchewning@ cdmdirect.com, Web Site: www.cdmdirect.com (21)

Chewning Direct Marketing, Irvine, CA. Tel: (949) 854-5401, E-Mail: hchewning@cdmdirect.com, Web Site: www.cdmdirect.com (21)

Chhokar, Preet, NetSpend, San Mateo, CA. Web Site: www.netspend.com (14)

Chiang, Jim, Gero Vita, Costa Mesa, CA. Tel: (888) 382-9175, Web Site: www.gvi.com (16)

Chiasso, Chicago, IL. Tel: (877) CHIASSO, FAX: (312) 477-3827, Web Site: www.chiasso.com (6)

Chicago Association of Direct Marketing, Westmont, IL. Tel: (312) 849-2236, FAX: (312) 849-2239, E-Mail: info@cadm.org, Web Site: www.cadm.org (40)

Chicago Convention & Tourism Bureau, Chicago, IL. Tel: (312) 567-8500, Web Site: www. choosechicago.com (1)

Chicago Decal Co, Burr Ridge, IL. Tel: (630) 850-2122, (888) DECALS R US, (888) 332-2577, FAX: (630) 850-7177, E-Mail: sales@ chicagodecal.com, Web Site: www.chicagodecal. com (27)

Chicago Magazine, Chicago, IL. Tel: (312) 222-8999, FAX: (312) 222-0287, Web Site: www. chicagomag.com (17)

Chicago Sun-Times, Chicago, IL. Tel: (312) 321-3000, FAX: (312) 321-9655, E-Mail: jmorawez@ suntimes.com, Web Site: www.suntimes.com (31)

Chicago Tribune, Chicago, IL. Tel: (312) 222-3232, (800) 874-2863, FAX: (312) 222-2353, E-Mail: consumerservices@tribune.com, Web Site: www. chicagotribune.com (31)

Chick Harness & Supply Inc, Harrington, DE. Tel: (302) 398-4630, (800) 444-2441, FAX: (302) 398-3920, E-Mail: saddles@chicksaddlery.com, Web Site: www.chicksaddlery.com (11)

Chico's FAS Inc, Fort Myers, FL. Tel: (239) 277-6200, Web Site: www.chicos.com (2)

Chiddister, Bruce, Mailgraphics, Boulder, CO. Tel: (303) 449-4053, FAX: (303) 938-1544, E-Mail: questions@mailgraphics.com (23)

Chief Executive Magazine, Greenwich, CT. Tel: (203) 930-2700, Web Site: www.chiefexecutive.net (17)

Chief Marketer and Multichannel Merchant, New York, NY. Tel: (212) 204-4228 (17)

Chief Media, New York, NY. Tel: (212) 300-8491 (35)

Chien, Theodore, Ingenix, Reston, VA. Tel: (571) 521-7661, (800) 765-6713, FAX: (571) 521-7237, E-Mail: inform@ingenix.com, Web Site: www. ingenix.com (32)

Chilcutt, Matt, Chilcutt Direct Marketing, Oklahoma City, OK. Tel: (405) 478-7245, FAX: (405) 478-2984, Web Site: www.cdmlist.com (24)

Chilcutt, Scott R., Marketing Information Network, Edmond, OK. Tel: (405) 516-1215, FAX: (405) 516-1230, Web Site: www.minokc.com (22)

Chilcutt Direct Marketing, Oklahoma City, OK. Tel: (405) 478-7245, FAX: (405) 478-2984, Web Site: www.cdmlist.com (24)

ChildFund International, Richmond, VA. Tel: (804) 756-2700, Web Site: www.ChildFund.org (1)

Childreach US Member of Plan International, Warwick, RI. Tel: (916) 797-8707, (800) 556-7918, FAX: (916) 797-1056, Web Site: www.planusa.org (8)

Children International, Kansas City, MO. Tel: (816) 942-2000, FAX: (816) 942-3714, E-Mail: RobS@ cikc.org, Web Site: www.children.org (1)

Children of the Night, Van Nuys, CA. Tel: (818) 908-4474, (800) 551-1300, FAX: (818) 908-1468, E-Mail: llee@childrenofthenight.com, Web Site: www.childrenofthenight.org (1)

Children's Aid Society, New York, NY. Tel: (212) 949-4945, Web Site: www.childrensaidsociety.org (1)

Children's Better Health Institute, Indianapolis, IN. Tel: (317) 634-1100, FAX: (317) 684-8094, E-Mail: gjoray@tcon.net, Web Site: www.cbhi.org (1)

Children's Hospital Foundation, Washington, DC. Tel: (202) 476-3000, (800) 884-LIFE, FAX: (202) 884-5999, Web Site: www.dcchildrens.com (1)

Children's Hospital of Pittsburgh, Pittsburgh, PA. Tel: (412) 692-5325, FAX: (412) 692-7140, Web Site: www.chp.edu (1)

Children's Miracle Network, Salt Lake City, UT. Tel: (801) 214-7400, Web Site: www.cmn.org (6)

Childs, Ron, National Pen Corp, San Diego, CA. Tel: (858) 675-3000, FAX: (858) 675-3030, Web Site: www.pens.com (6)

Chiles, Dan, Watts Radiant, Springfield, MO. Tel: (417) 864-6108, (800) 276-2419, FAX: (417) 864-8161, Web Site: www.wattsheatway.com (9)

Chiles, Mike, Watts Radiant, Springfield, MO. Tel: (417) 864-6108, (800) 276-2419, FAX: (417) 864-8161, Web Site: www.wattsheatway.com (9)

China Books & Periodicals Inc, South San Francisco, CA. Tel: (650) 872-7076, (800) 818-2017, FAX: (650) 872-7808, E-Mail: info@chinabooks.com, Web Site: www.chinabooks.com (17)

ChinaStock/WorldViews, Ann Arbor, MI. Tel: (734) 996-1440, (800) 315-4462, FAX: (734) 996-1481, E-Mail: decoxphoto@aol.com, Web Site: www. denniscox.com (38)

Ching, Helen, Bamboo Cricket Service, Titusville, FL. Tel: (888) 634-7097, FAX: (646) 390-6313, E-Mail: info@bamboocricket.com, Web Site: www. bamboocricket.com (22)

Chinn, Mike, SNL Financial, Charlottesville, VA. Tel: (434) 977-1600, FAX: (434) 977-4466, E-Mail: support@sni.com, Web Site: www.snl.com (17)

Chip Peterson Photos, Saint Paul, MN. Tel: (651) 699-4286, FAX: (651) 698-7667 (38)

Chipault, Raymond, Underwood Photo Archives Inc, Woodside, CA. Tel: (650) 851-5190, FAX: (650) 851-5193, E-Mail: ray@underwoodarchives.com, Web Site: www.underwoodarchives.com (38)

Chipman, Debra, Institute for International Research Inc, New York, NY. Tel: (212) 661-3500, (800) 345-8016, FAX: (212) 599-2192, E-Mail: register@iirusa.com, Web Site: www.iir-ny.com (16)

Chirico, Emanuel, Phillips-Van Heusen Corp, New York, NY. Tel: (212) 381-3500, (800) 388-9122, FAX: (212) 381-3950, Web Site: www.pvh.com (2)

Chirokas, Steve, LSSiData, Blue Bell, PA. Tel: (610) 825-7720, (800) 210-9021, E-Mail: info@lssi.net, Web Site: www.dataserve.info (22)

Chistensen, Susan M., Direct Impact Inc, Saint Louis, MO. Tel: (314) 567-0024, FAX: (314) 567-1497, E-Mail: info@directimpactinc.com, Web Site: www.directimpactinc.com (35)

Chistoni, Walter, Media Horizons Management LLC, Norwalk, CT. Tel: (203) 857-0770, FAX: (203) 857-0296, E-Mail: info@mediahorizons.com, Web Site: www.mediahorizons.com (31)

Chittick, Denny, Insight Direct Inc, Tempe, AZ. Tel: (480) 333-3001, (800) 467-4448, FAX: (480) 902-1180, Web Site: www.insight.com (16)

Chivari, Tony, Spiegel Brands Inc, New York, NY. Tel: (800) 222-5680, Web Site: www.spiegel.com (2)

Chivari, Tony, Things Remembered, Highland Heights, OH. Tel: (440) 473-2000, (866) 902-4438, FAX: (440) 473-2018, E-Mail: customerservice@thingsremembered.com, Web Site: www.thingsremembered.com (6)

Choate, Dana, Baylor Health Care System, Dallas, TX. Tel: (214) 820-4901, (800) 4Baylor, FAX: (214) 820-7499, Web Site: www.baylorhealth.com (16)

Choate, Tim, Aptimus, San Francisco, CA. Tel: (415) 896-2123 (22)

Choate, William, USAA Alliance Services Marketing, San Antonio, TX. Tel: (210) 456-9857, FAX: (210) 498-4542, Web Site: www.usaa.com (14)

Chodosh, Ellen, Oxford University Press Inc, New York, NY. Tel: (212) 726-6000, FAX: (212) 726-6455, Web Site: www.oup.com/us/ (17)

Choice Courier Systems Inc, New York, NY. Tel: (212) 370-1999, FAX: (212) 370-0440, Web Site: www.choicecourier.com (16)

Choice Hotels International, Silver Spring, MD. Tel: (301) 592-6636, (888) 770-6800, FAX: (301) 592-6157, E-Mail: ihelp@choicehotels.com, Web Site: www.choicebuys.com (16)

Choice Magazine, Middletown, CT. Tel: (860) 347-6933, (860) 347-1387, FAX: (860) 346-8586, E-Mail: adsales@ala-choice.org, Web Site: www.ala.org/ala/acrl/acrlpubs/choice/home.cfm (31)

Choice Media, Amherst, NH. Tel: (603) 672-3338, FAX: (603) 249-9732, E-Mail: choicemedia@comcast.net (31)

Choice Point, Alpharetta, GA. Tel: (770) 752-6000, (800) 342-5339, FAX: (770) 752-6005, Web Site: www.choicepoint.com (16)

ChoiceConnex, Clearwater, FL. Tel: (727) 571-3302, Web Site: www.choiceconnex.com (29)

ChoicePoint Precision Marketing, Little Rock, AR. Tel: (978) 738-0544, (800) 937-4232, FAX: (978) 738-0582, Web Site: www.cp-pm.com (30)

Chong, Arthur, Safeco Insurance Co, Seattle, WA. Tel: (206) 545-5000, (800) 332-3226, FAX: (206) 545-5767/5651, Web Site: www.safeco.com (15)

Chong, Dr. Diane, ASM International, Materials Park, OH. Tel: (440) 338-5151, (800) 336-5152, FAX: (440) 338-4634, E-Mail: customerservice@asminternational.org, Web Site: www.asminternational.org (1)

Chopoorian, Donald, Supreme Specialty Advertising, Mount Arlington, NJ. Tel: (973) 770-8700, FAX: (973) 770-0808 (33)

Chopp, Steve, Pharmavite Corp LLC (HQ), Northridge, CA. Tel: (818) 221-6200, (800) 423-2405, FAX: (818) 221-6618, Web Site: www.pharmavite.com (16)

Chotzen, Tamar, National Audubon Society, New York, NY. Tel: (212) 979-3000, FAX: (212) 979-3188, Web Site: www.audubon.org (17)

Chou-Thompson, Mary, Interfaith Community Care, Surprise, AZ. Tel: (623) 584-4999, Web Site: www.interfaithcommunitycare.org (1)

Chouinard, Yvon, Patagonia Mail Order Inc, Reno, NV. Tel: (775) 747-1992, (800) 638-6464, FAX: (775) 747-6159, Web Site: www.patagonia.com (2)

Chow, Alan, NCR Corp, Duluth, GA. Tel: (937) 445-1936, (800) CALL-NCR, FAX: (937) 445-1682, Web Site: www.ncr.com (16)

Chow, Richard, AIFS, Stamford, CT. Tel: (203) 399-5000, Web Site: www.aifs.com (19)

Christ, Peter, Crystal Records Inc, Camas, WA. Tel: (360) 834-7022, FAX: (360) 834-9680, E-Mail: info@crystalrecords.com, Web Site: www.crystalrecords.com (3)

Christensen, Charles, Bedford/St Martin's, Boston, MA. Tel: (617) 426-7440, FAX: (617) 426-8582, Web Site: www.bedfordstmartins.com (17)

Christensen, Debbe, The Silo Inc, New Milford, CT. Tel: (860) 355-0300, (800) 353-SILO, FAX: (860) 350-5495, E-Mail: info@hunthillfarmtrust.org, Web Site: www.thesilo.com (8)

Christensen, Dickie, Leslie Jordan, Portland, OR. Tel: (503) 295-1987, (800) 935-3343, FAX: (503) 295-1989, E-Mail: sales@lesliejordan.com, Web Site: www.lesliejordan.com (2)

Christensen, Kristine, S., Equitable Life & Casualty Insurance Co, Salt Lake City, UT. Tel: (801) 579-3400, FAX: (801) 579-3789, Web Site: www.equilife.com (15)

Christensen, Leif, Manistique Papers Inc, Manistique, MI. Tel: (906) 341-2175, FAX: (906) 341-5635 (25)

Christensen, Maren, MCA/Universal Studios Inc, Universal City, CA. Tel: (818) 777-1000, FAX: (818) 866-3330, Web Site: www.universalstudios.com (3)

Christensen, Pixie, Wycliffe Bible Translators, Dallas, TX. Tel: (972) 708-7522, Web Site: www.wycliffe.org (17)

Christensen, Shirlee, Mostad & Christensen, Oak Harbor, WA. Tel: (360) 679-4164, (800) 654-1654, FAX: (360) 679-4167, E-Mail: marketing@mostad.com, Web Site: www.mostad.com (16)

Christian Appalachian Project, Lexington, KY. Tel: (859) 792-3051, (866) 270-4CAP, FAX: (859) 792-6560, E-Mail: capinfo@chrisapp.org, Web Site: www.christianapp.org (1)

Christian Book Distributors Inc, Peabody, MA. Tel: (978) 532-5300, FAX: (978) 977-5010, E-Mail: javedisian@chrbook.com, Web Site: www.chrbook.com (17)

Christian Brands, Phoenix, AZ. Tel: (602) 243-5200, (800) 521-2914, FAX: (602) 232-1855, Web Site: www.christian-brands.com (16)

Christian Broadcasting Network Inc, Virginia Beach, VA. Tel: (757) 226-3542, FAX: (757) 226-2017, Web Site: www.cbn.org (1)

Christian Children's Fund Inc, Richmond, VA. Tel: (804) 756-2700, (800) 776-6767, FAX: (804) 756-2718, Web Site: www.christianchildrensfund.org (1)

Christian Herald Association, New York, NY. Tel: (212) 684-2800, (800) BOWERY-1, FAX: (212) 684-3740, E-Mail: info@chaonline.org, Web Site: www.bowery.org (1)

Christian Relief Services Charities Inc, Alexandria, VA. Tel: (703) 317-9086, Web Site: www.christianrelief.org (1)

Christian Resource Management, Orange, CA. Tel: (714) 974-0754, FAX: (714) 974-7845, E-Mail: CRMOrange@aol.com, Web Site: www.crmorange.com (22)

The Christian Science Monitor, Boston, MA. Tel: (617) 450-2000, FAX: (617) 450-2031, Web Site: www.csmonitor.com (31)

The Christian Science Publishing Society, Boston, MA. Tel: (617) 450-2000, E-Mail: info@christianscience.com, Web Site: www.tfccs.com (17)

Christianity Today Inc, Carol Stream, IL. Tel: (630) 260-6200, FAX: (630) 260-0114, Web Site: www.christianitytoday.com (17)

Christianson, Camille, Timm Medical Technologies, Inc, Eden Prairie, MN. Tel: (952) 947-9410, (800) 438-8592, FAX: (952) 947-9411, Web Site: www.timmmedical.com (16)

Christianson, Kory, St Joseph's Indian School, Chamberlain, SD. Tel: (605) 734-3300, Web Site: www.stjo.org (1)

Christides, Stephen, Nylon Net Co, Memphis, TN. Tel: (901) 526-6500, (877) 893-6535, (800) 238-7529, FAX: (901) 526-6538, E-Mail: nylonnet@nylonnet.com, Web Site: www.nylonnet.com (11)

Christie, Stephen, Smith & Noble, Corona, CA. Tel: (909) 734-4444, (800) 248-8888, FAX: (800) 426-7780, E-Mail: contactus@smithnoble.com, Web Site: www.smithandnoble.com (8)

Christoffersen, Terry, Buck Owens' Crystal Palace, Bakersfield, CA. Tel: (661) 328-7560, FAX: (805) 328-7565, Web Site: www.buckowens.com (21)

Christopher, Gayle K., Coastal Living, Birmingham, AL. Tel: (205) 877-6007, FAX: (205) 445-8655, E-Mail: coastalliving@customersvc.com, Web Site: www.coastalliving.com (43)

Christopher, Neil, Okeefe, Marietta, GA. Tel: (973) 632-7630 (5)

Christy Jr., Donald, D., NADA Appraisal Guides, Costa Mesa, CA. Tel: (714) 556-8511, (800) 966-6232, FAX: (714) 957-0302, E-Mail: info@nadaguides.com, Web Site: www.nadaguides.com (17)

Christy, Julie, In-Sync Publications, Redondo Beach, CA. Tel: (310) 543-9045, FAX: (310) 543-9035, E-Mail: insyncpubs@aol.com, Web Site: www.insyncpubs.com (18)

Christy, Robert, In-Sync Publications, Redondo Beach, CA. Tel: (310) 543-9045, FAX: (310) 543-9035, E-Mail: insyncpubs@aol.com, Web Site: www.insyncpubs.com (18)

Chronister, Mark, MXT Card Services, LLC, New Castle, DE. Tel: (302) 323-6203, FAX: (302) 323-6219, Web Site: www.mxtcs.com (14)

Chrystie, Kim, EMC Corp, Hopkinton, MA. Tel: (888) 438-3622, Web Site: www.emc.com (16)

Chu, Selena, Queens College/CUNY Professional and Continuing Studies (PCS), Flushing, NY. Tel: (718) 997-5700, FAX: (718) 997-5723, E-Mail: pcs@qc.cuny.edu, Web Site: www.qc.cuny.edu/pcs (41)

Chua, Mark, J&H Berge/The Lab Mart, South Plainfield, NJ. Tel: (908) 561-1234, FAX: (908) 561-3002, E-Mail: rgardner@labmart.com, Web Site: www.labmart.com (7)

The Chubb Corp, Warren, NJ. Tel: (908) 903-2000, FAX: (908) 903-2027, Web Site: www.chubb.com (20)

Chugh, Ash, Epic Marketing Solutions, Halifax, NS Canada. Tel: (902) 455-5100, Web Site: www.epicmarketing.ca (22)

Chung, Irving, Waldbillig & Besteman, Madison, WI. Tel: (608) 829-0900, (800) 395-4767, FAX: (608) 829-0901, E-Mail: info@waldbest.com, Web Site: www.waldbest.com (35)

Church, Andrew G., Oneida Ltd, Oneida, NY. Tel: (315) 361-3000, (888) 263-7195, FAX: (315) 361-3700, Web Site: www.oneida.com (16)

Church, Dr. Nancy, J., State University of New York-College of Plattsburgh, Plattsburgh, NY. Tel: (518) 564-2000, FAX: (518) 564-3183, E-Mail: nancy.church@plattsburgh.edu, Web Site: www.plattsburgh.edu (41)

Church, Ellen, CMS LLC, Reston, VA. Tel: (703) 258-0000, Web Site: www.craveronline.com (1)

Church, Mark, James Medical Rents & Sales Inc, Fort Wayne, IN. Tel: (260) 423-9571, E-Mail: sales@jamesmedical.com, Web Site: www.jamesmedical.net (7)

Church Extension Plan, Salem, OR. Tel: (800) 821-1112, Web Site: www.cepnet.com (14)

Church Pension Fund, New York, NY. Tel: (866) 802-6333, Web Site: www.cpg.org (1)

Chwatsky, Ann, Ann Chwatsky Photography, Sag Harbor, NY. Tel: (212) 673-5689, FAX: (212) 673-5689, E-Mail: annphotog@aol.com, Web Site: www.annchwatskyphoto.com (37)

Ann Chwatsky Photography, Sag Harbor, NY. Tel: (212) 673-5689, FAX: (212) 673-5689, E-Mail: annphotog@aol.com, Web Site: www.annchwatskyphoto.com (37)

Chyke, Joel, Print Services Distribution Association, Chicago, IL. Tel: (703) 836-6232, (800) 336-4641, FAX: (703) 836-2241, E-Mail: psda@psda.org, Web Site: www.psda.org (1)

Ciarlo Consulting LLC, Waterbury, CT. Tel: (203) 232-6655 (20)

Cichanowski, Mike, We-No-Nah Canoe Inc, Winona, MN. Tel: (507) 454-5430, FAX: (507) 454-5448, E-Mail: info@wenonah.com, Web Site: www. wenonah.com (11)

CIDCO, Fresno, CA. Tel: (559) 497-9414, FAX: (559) 497-9435 (34)

CIGNA International, Philadelphia, PA. Tel: (215) 761-1741, FAX: (215) 761-5515, Web Site: www. cigna.com (15)

Cillo, Joanne, Tuttle Printing & Engraving, Rutland, VT. Tel: (802) 773-9171, (800) 776-7682, FAX: (802) 773-5785, E-Mail: info@tuttleprinting.com, Web Site: www.tuttleprinting.com (10)

Cimarron Group, Hollywood, CA. Tel: (323) 337-0300, FAX: (323) 337-0333, Web Site: www. cimarrongroup.com (35)

Cimini, Lou, Samsonite Corp, Mansfield, MA. Tel: (508) 851-1400, (800) 547-BAGS, FAX: (303) 373-8715, Web Site: www.samsonite.com (16)

Cimino, Camille, G., Mailorder Gardening Association, Elkridge, MD. Tel: (410) 540-9830, FAX: (410) 540-9827, Web Site: www. mailordergardening.com (1)

Cincinnati Bell Tel, Cincinnati, OH. Tel: (513) 397-9900, FAX: (513) 241-8341, Web Site: www. cincinnatibelltelephone.com (16)

Cinema World Studios, Greenpoint, NY. Tel: (718) 389-9800, FAX: (718) 389-9897, E-Mail: cinemaworldfd@verizon.net, Web Site: www. cinemaworldstudios.com (32)

Cinmar LP, West Chester, OH. Tel: (513) 603-1000, FAX: (513) 603-1020, Web Site: www.frontgate. com (8)

Cinquanti, Michael, Genium Publishing, Amsterdam, NY. Tel: (518) 842-4111, FAX: (518) 842-1843, E-Mail: sales@genium.com, Web Site: www. genium.com (17)

Cintas, Cincinnati, OH. Tel: (816) 474-7000, FAX: (816) 474-1258, Web Site: www.cintas.com (16)

Cintron, Todd, Empire Burbank Studios, Burbank, CA. Tel: (818) 840-1400, FAX: (818) 567-1062 (32)

Ciolli, Sue, Tower Hobbies/Hobbico, Champaign, IL. Tel: (217) 398-3636, (800) 637-6050, FAX: (217) 398-1104, Web Site: www.towerhobbies.com (11)

Cipolaro, Robert, Richard Bauer & Co Inc, Teaneck, NJ. Tel: (201) 692-1005, (800) 995-7881, FAX: (201) 692-8626, E-Mail: info@richardbauer.com, Web Site: www.richardbauer.com (25)

Cipolla, Jack, American Federation of Astrologers, Tempe, AZ. Tel: (480) 838-1751, (888) 301-7630, FAX: (480) 838-8293, E-Mail: afa@msn.com, Web Site: www.astrologers.com (1)

Cipriani, Bob, DS Graphics Inc, Lowell, MA. Tel: (617) 389-5350, (800) 536-8253, FAX: (617) 387-7752, E-Mail: sales@dsgraphics.com, Web Site: www.dsgraphics.com (21)

Cipriani, Stephanie, Triangle Marketing Services Inc, New York, NY. Tel: (212) 242-4040, FAX: (212) 242-1344, Web Site: www.tms-ny.com (23)

Circinus International LLC, Boston, MA. Tel: (774) 696-3517, Web Site: www.circinusinternational. com (20)

Circle K Stores Inc, Akron, OH. Tel: (330) 630-6300, Web Site: www.cirlcek.com (16)

Circulation by Phone Inc, New York, NY. Tel: (212) 557-2777 (29)

Circulation Specialists Inc, Shelton, CT. Tel: (888) 315-2472, FAX: (888) 315-2507 (20)

Cirino, Paul, Foremost Industrial Exchange, Van Nuys, CA. Tel: (818) 988-6900, FAX: (818) 787-0293 (16)

Cisco Systems Inc, San Jose, CA. Tel: (408) 526-4000, (800) 553-NETS, FAX: (408) 526-4100, Web Site: www.cisco.com (22)

Cision US Inc, Chicago, IL. Tel: (312) 922-2400, (866) 639-5087, FAX: (312) 922-3126, E-Mail: info.us@cision.com, Web Site: us.cision.com (43)

Cissna, John, L., Computermail South, Saint Petersburg, FL. Tel: (727) 579-1000, (800) 551-5478, FAX: (727) 823-5474, E-Mail: sales@

computermailsouth.com, Web Site: computermailsouth.com (23)

Cissna, Lynn, M., Computermail South, Saint Petersburg, FL. Tel: (727) 579-1000, (800) 551-5478, FAX: (727) 823-5474, E-Mail: sales@ computermailsouth.com, Web Site: computermailsouth.com (23)

Citi Cards / Citicorp Credit Services, Long Island City, NY. Tel: (718) 248-5400 (14)

Citibank, New York, NY. Tel: (212) 559-9425, (800) 285-3000, FAX: (212) 527-2318, Web Site: www. citibank.com (14)

CitiFinancial, Baltimore, MD. Tel: (410) 332-3000, (800) 995-2274, (800) 922-6235, FAX: (410) 332-3489, Web Site: www.citifinancial.com (14)

Citigroup Inc, New York, NY. Tel: (212) 559-1000, (800) 285-3000, FAX: (212) 793-3946, Web Site: www.citigroup.com (14)

Citizens Against Government Waste, Washington, DC. Tel: (202) 467-5300, (800) USA-DEBT, FAX: (202) 467-4253, E-Mail: membership@cagw.org, Web Site: www.cagw.org (1)

Citizens Bank, Dedham, MA. Tel: (603) 634-7000, FAX: (603) 634-7191, Web Site: www. citizensbank.com (14)

Citizens Republic Bank, Flint, MI. Tel: (810) 766-7651, Web Site: www.citizensbanking.com (14)

Citorino, Tom, Pennwell Publishing, Tulsa, OK. Tel: (918) 835-3161, (800) 331-4463, E-Mail: headquarters@pennwell.com, Web Site: www. pennwell.com (17)

Citrix Systems, Inc, Fort Lauderdale, FL. Tel: (954) 267-8427, Web Site: www.citrix.com (22)

Citrus Inc, Bend, OR. Tel: (541) 388-2003, FAX: (541) 388-4381, Web Site: www.citrusbegin.com (35)

City of Cerritos, Cerritos, CA. Tel: (562) 916-1319, Web Site: www.ci.cerritos.ca.us (1)

City of Hope Cancer Center, Los Angeles, CA. Tel: (626) 256-4673, Web Site: www.cityofhope.org (1)

City of LaGrange, LaGrange, GA. Tel: (706) 883-2010, FAX: (706) 883-2062, Web Site: www. lagrange-ga.org (1)

CityTwist, Boca Raton, FL. Tel: (561) 989-8480, Web Site: www.citytwist.com (32)

Civali, John, Johnny Appleseed's Inc, Beverly, MA. Tel: (978) 922-2040, (800) 767-6666, FAX: (978) 922-7001, Web Site: www.appleseeds.com (2)

Civil Service Employees Insurance Group, Walnut Creek, CA. Tel: (925) 817-6300, (415) 274-7803, (800) 282-6848, Web Site: www.cseinsurance.com (15)

Civil War Preservation Trust, Washington, DC. Tel: (202) 367-1861, Web Site: www.civilwar.org (1)

Cize, Jim, Danbury Printing & Litho Inc, Danbury, CT. Tel: (203) 792-5500, FAX: (203) 744-5633 (27)

Claiborne, Phil, Elks Magazine, Chicago, IL. Tel: (773) 755-4700, (877) 355-7624, FAX: (773) 775-4891, E-Mail: elksmag@elks.org, Web Site: www. elks.org (17)

Clairol Inc, Stamford, CT. Tel: (203) 357-5000, (800) 252-4765, FAX: (203) 357-5003, Web Site: www. clairol.com (7)

Clampitt, Donald, Clampitt Paper Co, Dallas, TX. Tel: (214) 638-3300, FAX: (214) 634-7837, E-Mail: dcrew@clampitt.com, Web Site: www.clampitt.com (16)

Clampitt Paper Co, Dallas, TX. Tel: (214) 638-3300, FAX: (214) 634-7837, E-Mail: dcrew@clampitt. com, Web Site: www.clampitt.com (16)

Clancey, Brenda, K., Transamerica Life Insurance Co, Cedar Rapids, IA. Tel: (319) 398-8511, (800) 558-9011, FAX: (319) 369-2825, Web Site: www. transamerica.com (15)

Clancey, Maura, Knowledge Networks/SRI, Roseland, NJ. Tel: (908) 497-8000, FAX: (908) 497-8001, E-Mail: mclancey@knowledgenetworks.com, Web Site: www.knowledgenetworks.com (30)

Clancy, Brenda K., Life Investors Insurance Co of America, Cedar Rapids, IA. Tel: (319) 398-8511, (800) 231-7220, FAX: (319) 369-2188, Web Site: www.lifeinvestors.com (14)

Clancy, James, R., Goldsmith Agio Helms, Minneapolis, MN. Tel: (612) 339-0500, FAX: (612) 339-0507, Web Site: www.agio.com (14)

Clapper, Jim, Belmont University, Nashville, TN. Tel: (615) 460-6000, FAX: (615) 460-6455, Web Site: www.belmont.edu (41)

Clara, Shawna, Meriks Marketers, Richfield, MN. Tel: (787) 721-0000 (3)

Clarin by Hussey Seating, North Berwick, ME. Tel: (207) 676-2271, Web Site: www.husseyseating.com (5)

Clario Analytics, Eden Prairie, MN. Tel: (952) 653-0980, (866) 849-3341, FAX: (952) 653-5900, E-Mail: sales@clarioanalytics.com, Web Site: www.clarioanalytics.com (20)

Claritas Express, Ithaca, NY. Tel: (607) 257-5757, (866) 737-7429, FAX: (607) 266-0425, E-Mail: info@claritas.com, Web Site: www.claritas.com/ express (30)

Clarity Group LLC, Chapel Hill, NC. Tel: (919) 932-6036, Web Site: www.claritygroupinc.com (20)

Clark Jr., Calvin, Clark's Corvair Parts, Inc, Shelburne Falls, MA. Tel: (413) 625-9776, FAX: (413) 625-8498, E-Mail: clarks@corvair.com, Web Site: www.corvair.com (12)

Clark, Barbara, Briefings Publishing Group, Richmond, VA. Tel: (703) 567-1982, (800) 791-8699, FAX: (703) 684-2136, E-Mail: rmalvaso@ douglaspublications.com, Web Site: www. briefings.com (17)

Clark, Bart, Suez Energy North America, Houston, TX. Tel: (713) 636-0000, FAX: (713) 636-1364, Web Site: www.tractebelpowerinc.com (16)

Clark, Bob, CPI Card Group, Littleton, CO. Tel: (303) 973-9311, FAX: (303) 973-8420, E-Mail: mbarber@cpicardgroup.com, Web Site: www. cpicardgroup.com (27)

Clark, Carine, Previo/Alteris, Lindon, UT. Tel: (801) 226-8500, (888) 252-5551, FAX: (801) 226-8506, Web Site: www.previo.com (16)

Clark, Carine, Symantec, Mountain View, CA. Tel: (408) 517-8000, FAX: (408) 517-8186, Web Site: www.symantec.com (16)

Clark, Charles, Olmsted-Kirk Paper Co, Dallas, TX. Tel: (214) 637-2220, (800) 367-6526, FAX: (214) 637-7630, E-Mail: sales@okpaper.com, Web Site: www.okpaper.com (25)

Clark, Chris, High Cotton, Birmingham, AL. Tel: (877) 838-2345, FAX: (205) 836-5587, E-Mail: sales@highscottonusa.com, Web Site: www. highcottonusa.com (28)

Clark, David, D., NutriSystem Inc, Fort Washington, PA. Tel: (215) 706-5300, (800) 321-THIN, FAX: (215) 706-5388, Web Site: www.nutrisystem.com (7)

Clark, Dennis, Fairfield Industries Inc, Sugar Land, TX. Tel: (281) 275-7500, (800) 231-9809, FAX: (281) 275-7550, E-Mail: jblattman@fairfield.com, Web Site: www.fairfield.com (16)

Clark, George, L., Rose Resnick Lighthouse for the Blind & Visually Impaired, San Francisco, CA. Tel: (415) 431-1481, FAX: (415) 863-7568, E-Mail: executive@lighthouse-sf.org, Web Site: www.lighthouse-sf.org (1)

Clark, James, JLS Mailing Services Inc, Brockton, MA. Tel: (508) 313-1050, (866) JLS-MAIL, FAX: (508) 313-1093, E-Mail: rparkinson@jlsms.com, Web Site: www.jlsms.com (28)

Clark, Jim, Clark & Clark Inc, Saint Louis, MO. Tel: (314) 994-9155, FAX: (314) 994-0573, E-Mail: jim.clark@clark-clark.net (33)

Clark, Joan, Clark's Corvair Parts, Inc, Shelburne Falls, MA. Tel: (413) 625-9776, FAX: (413) 625-8498, E-Mail: clarks@corvair.com, Web Site: www.corvair.com (12)

Clark, John, American Baseball Coaches Association, Mount Pleasant, MI. Tel: (989) 775-3300, FAX: (989) 775-3600, E-Mail: abca@abca.org, Web Site: www.abca.org (1)

Clark, Judson, Information for Public Affairs, Inc, Sacramento, CA. Tel: (916) 444-0840, (800) 726-4566, FAX: (916) 446-5369, E-Mail: info@statenet.com, Web Site: www.statenet.com (17)

Clark, Kenneth, YP Talk, Pittsburg, KS. Tel: (620) 308-6434, E-Mail: info@yptalk.com, Web Site: www.yptalk.com (31)

Clark, Kim, Suarez Corp Industries, North Canton, OH. Tel: (330) 494-5504, FAX: (330) 497-6837, E-Mail: suarez@suarez.com, Web Site: www.suarez.com (5)

Clark, Mike, Fitness Quest, Canton, OH. Tel: (330) 478-0755, (800) 321-9236, FAX: (330) 479-9213, E-Mail: customersupport@fitnessquest.com, Web Site: www.fitnessquest.com (16)

Clark, R. Kerry, Fluke Biomedical, Everett, WA. Tel: (425) 347-6100, (800) 850-4608, FAX: (425) 446-5116, Web Site: www.flukebiomedical.com (16)

Clark, Ranjana, Wachovia Bank, National Association, Charlotte, NC. Tel: (704) 590-0000, (800) WACHOVIA, FAX: (704) 427-6748 (14)

Clark, Ric, Brookfield Properties, Toronto, ON Canada. Tel: (416) 369-2300, FAX: (416) 369-2301, Web Site: www.brokfieldproperties.com (16)

Clark, Richard, Medco Health Solutions Inc, Franklin Lakes, NJ. Tel: (201) 269-3400, FAX: (201) 269-6400, Web Site: www.medco.com (7)

Clark, Richard, T., Calbiochem-Novabiochem Corp, San Diego, CA. Tel: (858) 450-9600, (800) 854-3417, FAX: (858) 453-3552, E-Mail: customerservice@emdbioscience.com, Web Site: www.calbiochem.com (9)

Clark, Richard, T., Merck & Co Inc, Whitehouse Station, NJ. Tel: (908) 423-1000, Web Site: www.merck.com (16)

Clark, Shannon, Monster Magnet, Louisville, KY. Tel: (800) 255-0234, Web Site: www.monstermagnet.com (35)

Clark, Wesley, Grainger Parts, North Brook, IL. Tel: (847) 498-5900, FAX: (847) 498-3402, Web Site: www.grainger.com (16)

Clark & Clark Inc, Saint Louis, MO. Tel: (314) 994-9155, FAX: (314) 994-0573, E-Mail: jim.clark@clark-clark.net (33)

The Clark Grave Vault Co, Columbus, OH. Tel: (614) 294-3761, FAX: (614) 299-2324, Web Site: www.clarkvault.com (16)

Clark Johnson, Sue, Reno Gazette Journal, Reno, NV. Tel: (775) 788-6200, FAX: (775) 788-6563 (17)

Clarke III, Jess, F., Jess Clarke & Sons Inc, Bradenton, FL. Tel: (941) 727-0042, FAX: (941) 753-5394, E-Mail: catalogjfc@aol.com, Web Site: www.miracleofaloe.com (35)

Clarke III, Jess, F., Miracle of Aloe, Dallas, TX. Tel: (800) 966-2563, FAX: (800) 859-9881, E-Mail: LJohnson@miracleofaloe.com, Web Site: www.miracleofaloe.com (7)

Clarke III, Jess, F., Winning Solutions Inc, Fort Worth, TX. Tel: (972) 986-5355, (866) 494-6765, E-Mail: winninginc@aol.com (7)

Clarke Jr, Jess, F., Jess Clarke & Sons Inc, Bradenton, FL. Tel: (941) 727-0042, FAX: (941) 753-5394, E-Mail: catalogjfc@aol.com, Web Site: www.miracleofaloe.com (35)

Clarke Jr, Jess, F., Winning Solutions Inc, Fort Worth, TX. Tel: (972) 986-5355, (866) 494-6765, E-Mail: winninginc@aol.com (7)

Clarke Jr., Jess, F., As Seen On PC Network, Fairfield, CT. Tel: (203) 256-9897, FAX: (203) 256-9507, E-Mail: info@asseenonpc.com, Web Site: www.asseenonpc.com (22)

Clarke Jr., Jess, F., Miracle of Aloe, Dallas, TX. Tel: (800) 966-2563, FAX: (800) 859-9881, E-Mail: LJohnson@miracleofaloe.com, Web Site: www.miracleofaloe.com (7)

Clarke, Brenda, Cancer Fund of America Inc, Knoxville, TN. Tel: (865) 938-5281, (800) 578-5284, FAX: (865) 938-2968, Web Site: www.cfoa.org (1)

Clarke, Cary, Greater Fort Worth Builders Association, Fort Worth, TX. Tel: (817) 284-3566, FAX: (817) 284-6465, E-Mail: info@fortworthbuilders.org, Web Site: www.forthworthbuilders.org (1)

Clarke, Chris, Miracle of Aloe, Dallas, TX. Tel: (800) 966-2563, FAX: (800) 859-9881, E-Mail: LJohnson@miracleofaloe.com, Web Site: www.miracleofaloe.com (7)

Clarke, Curtis, A., Duggan & Brown Inc, Abington, PA. Tel: (215) 657-3400, FAX: (215) 657-6119, E-Mail: john@dugganandbrown.com (16)

Clarke, Gwilym, Alfa Aesar-A Johnson Matthey Co, Ward Hill, MA. Tel: (800) 343-0660, FAX: (800) 322-4757, E-Mail: info@alfa.com, Web Site: www.alfa.com (9)

Clarke, Marla, Veer, Calgary, AB Canada. Tel: (403) 234-7901, Web Site: www.veer.com (16)

Clarke, Richard A., George P Clarke Advertising Inc, New York, NY. Tel: (212) 545-7400, FAX: (212) 545-7433, E-Mail: info@gpclarke.com, Web Site: gpclarke.com (35)

Clarke, Shane, B-T-B Internet Marketing Solutions, Middle Island, NY. Tel: (631) 924-3888, E-Mail: linickgroup@gmail.com, Web Site: www.linick.net; 222.asklinick.com (39)

Clarke, Tad, DM News, New York, NY. Tel: (212) 925-7300, FAX: (212) 925-8752, Web Site: www.dmnews.com (43)

Clarke, Tim, Clarke Advertising & Public Relations, Sarasota, FL. Tel: (941) 365-2710, FAX: (941) 366-4940, E-Mail: tclarke@clarkeadvertising.com, Web Site: www.clarkeadvertising.com (35)

Clarke Advertising & Public Relations, Sarasota, FL. Tel: (941) 365-2710, FAX: (941) 366-4940, E-Mail: tclarke@clarkeadvertising.com, Web Site: www.clarkeadvertising.com (35)

George P Clarke Advertising Inc, New York, NY. Tel: (212) 545-7400, FAX: (212) 545-7433, E-Mail: info@gpclarke.com, Web Site: gpclarke.com (35)

Jess Clarke & Sons Inc, Bradenton, FL. Tel: (941) 727-0042, FAX: (941) 753-5394, E-Mail: catalogjfc@aol.com, Web Site: www.miracleofaloe.com (35)

Clarken, Tom, The Hyiad Group, Garden City, NY. Tel: (516) 433-3800, FAX: (516) 822-6670, Web Site: www.thehyaidgroup.com (22)

Clark's Corvair Parts, Inc, Shelburne Falls, MA. Tel: (413) 625-9776, FAX: (413) 625-8498, E-Mail: clarks@corvair.com, Web Site: www.corvair.com (12)

Clarks of North America, Newton, MA. Tel: (617) 964-1222, (800) 925-4315, FAX: (617) 243-4213, Web Site: www.clarks.com (16)

Clarkson Eyecare, Ellisville, MO. Tel: (636) 227-2600 (5)

Classic Color, Broadview, IL. Tel: (708) 484-0000, FAX: (708) 344-2233, Web Site: www.classic-color.com (27)

Classic Motorbooks Inc, Minneapolis, MN. Tel: (715) 294-3345, (800) 826-6600, FAX: (715) 294-4448, Web Site: www.motorbooks.com (17)

Classic Thermographers, North Mankato, MN. Tel: (623) 582-0002, (800) 727-4200, FAX: (800) 727-4202 (10)

Clausen, John, Clausen Enterprises, Hendersonville, NC. Tel: (828) 777-7339, E-Mail: jhclausen@mchsi.com, Web Site: www.copy-design.com (39)

Clausen Enterprises, Hendersonville, NC. Tel: (828) 777-7339, E-Mail: jhclausen@mchsi.com, Web Site: www.copy-design.com (39)

Clavert, Pan, CRM Learning, Carlsbad, CA. Tel: (760) 431-9800, (800) 421-0833, FAX: (760) 931-5792, E-Mail: sales@crmlearning.com, Web Site: www.crmlearning.com (16)

Clawson, Angela, Texas Monthly, Austin, TX. Tel: (512) 320-6900, (800) 759-2000, FAX: (512) 476-9007, E-Mail: info@texasmonthly.com, Web Site: www.texasmonthly.com (17)

Clay, Franklin, Clay Creative Direct, Lewis Center, OH. Tel: (740) 548-0307, FAX: (740) 548-0898, E-Mail: frank@claycreativegroup.com, marketing@claycreativegroup.com, Web Site: www.claydm.com (35)

Clay, Gay, LimitedBrands Inc, Reynoldsburg, OH. Tel: (614) 577-5902, FAX: (614) 415-7440, Web Site: www.limitedbrands.com (16)

Clay, Jessica, Clay Creative Direct, Lewis Center, OH. Tel: (740) 548-0307, FAX: (740) 548-0898, E-Mail: frank@claycreativegroup.com, marketing@claycreativegroup.com, Web Site: www.claydm.com (35)

Clay, Wendy, CPAC Inc, Leicester, NY. Tel: (585) 382-3223, (800) 828-6011, FAX: (585) 382-3031, E-Mail: cpacinfo@cpac.com, Web Site: www.cpac.com (16)

Clay Creative Direct, Lewis Center, OH. Tel: (740) 548-0307, FAX: (740) 548-0898, E-Mail: frank@claycreativegroup.com, marketing@claycreativegroup.com, Web Site: www.claydm.com (35)

Clayman, Alvin, Alvin M Clayman Enterprises Inc, Kansas City, KS. Tel: (913) 384-3600, FAX: (913) 384-1227, E-Mail: bclayman@alvinclayman.com, Web Site: www.alvinmclayman.com (33)

Alvin M Clayman Enterprises Inc, Kansas City, KS. Tel: (913) 384-3600, FAX: (913) 384-1227, E-Mail: bclayman@alvinclayman.com, Web Site: www.alvinmclayman.com (33)

Claypool, Veronica, Theatre Development Fund Inc, New York, NY. Tel: (212) 912-9770, E-Mail: info@tdf.org, Web Site: www.tdf.org (1)

Clayton, Michelle, Lincoln Park Zoo, Chicago, IL. Tel: (312) 742-2000, FAX: (312) 742-2137, E-Mail: webmaster@lpzoo.com, Web Site: www.lpzoo.com (1)

AT Clayton & Co Inc, Stamford, CT. Tel: (203) 658-1200, E-Mail: webmaster@atclayton.com, Web Site: www.atclayton.com (25)

Clean Lists Associates Inc, New York, NY. Tel: (212) 551-1013, FAX: (212) 551-1107, E-Mail: cleanlists@mindspring.com (27)

Clear Visions Inc, San Antonio, TX. Tel: (210) 496-6006, FAX: (210) 496-9225, E-Mail: bidrequest@clearvisionsinc.com, Web Site: www.clearvisionsinc.com (27)

ClearOne Advantage, Columbia, MD. Tel: (443) 996-1889, Web Site: www.clearoneadvantage.com (14)

ClearSaleing Inc, Columbus, OH. Tel: (614) 448-2688, (800) 592-0463, Web Site: www.clearsaleing.com (16)

Cleary, Jeff, Catalyst, Rochester, NY. Tel: (585) 453-8300, (800) 836-7720, FAX: (585) 453-8360, E-Mail: info@catalystinc.com, Web Site: www.catalystinc.com (35)

Clegg, Kevin, Clegg Industries Inc, Gardena, CA. Tel: (310) 225-3800, FAX: (800) 250-9851, E-Mail: sales@clegg.xo.com, Web Site: www.cleggonline.com (16)

Clegg Industries Inc, Gardena, CA. Tel: (310) 225-3800, FAX: (800) 250-9851, E-Mail: sales@clegg.xo.com, Web Site: www.cleggonline.com (16)

Cleghorn, Chris, Easter Seals, Chicago, IL. Tel: (312) 726-6200, FAX: (312) 726-1494, Web Site: www.easter-seals.org (1)

Cleghorn, Chris, International Fellowship of Christians and Jews, Chicago, IL. Tel: (312) 641-7200, Web Site: www.ifcj.org (1)

Clemens, Micke, Veriad, Brea, CA. Tel: (714) 990-2700, (800) 962-0658, FAX: (800) 962-0658, E-Mail: info@veriad.com, Web Site: www.veriad.com (16)

Clemens, Stephanie, Llewellyn Publications, Woodbury, MN. Tel: (651) 291-1970, (800) 843-6666, FAX: (651) 291-1908, Web Site: www.llewellyn.com (17)

Clement, Bob, The Allied Group, Cranston, RI. Tel: (401) 946-6100, Web Site: www.thealliedgrp.com (28)

Clement, Coy, ClementDIRECT, Chapel Hill, NC. Tel: (919) 338-2853, FAX: (206) 338-2511, Web Site: www.clementdirect.com (20)

Clement, Dallas, S., Cox Communications, Atlanta, GA. Tel: (404) 843-5000, FAX: (404) 269-2243, Web Site: www.cox.com (16)

Clement, George, Clement Communications, Upper Chichester, PA. Tel: (610) 497-6800, (800) 253-6368, FAX: (610) 497-6806, E-Mail: customerservice@clement.com, Web Site: www.clement.com; www.bradycorp.com (17)

Clement, Mark, Viahealth, Rochester, NY. Tel: (585) 922-4000, (585) 922-3677, FAX: (585) 922-3929, Web Site: www.viahealth.org (16)

Clement, Stephen, H., Westpro Inc, Provo, UT. Tel: (801) 373-2525, (800) 533-3885, FAX: (801) 373-8778, E-Mail: sales@westpro.net, Web Site: westpro.net (27)

Clement Communications, Upper Chichester, PA. Tel: (610) 497-6800, (800) 253-6368, FAX: (610) 497-6806, E-Mail: customerservice@clement.com, Web Site: www.clement.com; www.bradycorp.com (17)

ClementDIRECT, Chapel Hill, NC. Tel: (919) 338-2853, FAX: (206) 338-2511, Web Site: www.clementdirect.com (20)

Clemente, Anthony, Clemente Novelties Inc, Utica, NY. Tel: (315) 732-4145, FAX: (315) 732-2251, E-Mail: clemente@6org.com (16)

Clemente Novelties Inc, Utica, NY. Tel: (315) 732-4145, FAX: (315) 732-2251, E-Mail: clemente@6org.com (16)

Clements, Mark, Mark Clements Research Inc, Mount Kisco, NY. Tel: (914) 241-1803, FAX: (914) 241-7763, E-Mail: mjfharvey@aol.com, Web Site: www.markclementsresearch.com (30)

Mark Clements Research Inc, Mount Kisco, NY. Tel: (914) 241-1803, FAX: (914) 241-7763, E-Mail: mjfharvey@aol.com, Web Site: www.markclementsresearch.com (30)

Clendenning, Bonnie, Archaeology Magazine, Long Island City, NY. Tel: (718) 472-3050, FAX: (718) 472-3051, E-Mail: production@archaeology.org, Web Site: www.archaeology.org (17)

Clendenning, Rick, INX International Ink Co, Schaumburg, IL. Tel: (800) 631-7956, FAX: (847) 969-9758, E-Mail: info@inxink.com, Web Site: www.inxinternational.com (16)

Clenney, Laura, BenefitMall, Dallas, TX. Tel: (469) 791-3355, Web Site: www.benefitmall.com (15)

Cleveland Clinic Foundation, Cleveland, OH. Tel: (216) 444-2200, Web Site: www.clevelandclinic.org (1)

Cleveland Institute of Electronics, Cleveland, OH. Tel: (216) 781-9400, FAX: (216) 781-0331, E-Mail: instruct@cie-wc.edu, Web Site: www.cie-wc.edu (13)

The Cleveland Orchestra, Cleveland, OH. Tel: (216) 231-7441, FAX: (216) 231-4038, Web Site: www.clevelandorchestra.com (1)

Clever, Al, Alpha Supply Inc, Bremerton, WA. Tel: (360) 373-3302, (800) 257-4211, FAX: (360) 377-9235 (16)

Click2Mail, Arlington, VA. Tel: (703) 521-9029, (866) 665-2787, FAX: (703) 358-8811, E-Mail: info@click2mail.com, Web Site: www.click2mail.com (20)

Clickbooth.com LLC, Sarasota, FL. Tel: (941) 483-4188, Web Site: www.integraclick.com (35)

ClickMail Marketing Inc, San Mateo, CA. Tel: (650) 653-8055, Web Site: www.clickmarketing.com (32)

ClickSpark LLC, San Francisco, CA. Tel: (800) 878-5709, E-Mail: amy@clickspark.com, Web Site: www.clickspark.com (32)

ClickSpeed, Overland Park, KS. Tel: (913) 383-1500, Web Site: www.clickspeed.com (35)

ClickSquared, Boston, MA. Tel: (781) 622-1611, (866) 402-5425, FAX: (857) 246-7645, E-Mail: info@clicksquared.com, Web Site: www.clicksquared.com (20)

ClickStream, Orland Park, IL. Tel: (949) 439-2888, Web Site: www.clickstreamtv.com (32)

ClientLogic, Nashville, TN. Tel: (615) 301-7100, E-Mail: bobfet@clientlogic.com (21)

Clients & Profits Worldwide, Oceanside, CA. Tel: (760) 945-4334, Web Site: www.clientsandprofits.com (14)

Clients First, Westfield, NJ. Tel: (908) 232-1200, (800) 634-0040, FAX: (908) 233-8833, E-Mail: info@clientsfirst.com, Web Site: www.clientsfirst.com (27)

Cliffor, Patrick, StayWell/Krames, San Bruno, CA. Tel: (650) 742-0400, FAX: (650) 244-4568, Web Site: www.staywell.com (17)

Clifford, Christina, Harlequin Enterprises Ltd, Don Mills, ON. Tel: (416) 445-5860, FAX: (416) 445-8655, E-Mail: customer_ecare@harlequin.ca, Web Site: www.eharlequin.com (17)

Clifton, Andy, Chief Executive Magazine, Greenwich, CT. Tel: (203) 930-2700, Web Site: www.chiefexecutive.net (17)

Clifton, Diane, National Council on Compensation Insurance Inc (NCCI), Boca Raton, FL. Tel: (561) 893-1000, (800) 622-4123, FAX: (561) 893-1191, Web Site: www.ncci.com (1)

Clifton, Sue, AeroGraphics, DeLand, FL. Tel: (386) 736-4793, FAX: (386) 736-9786, Web Site: www.skydivingmagazine.com (3)

Clifton, Sue, Skydiving Magazine, DeLand, FL. Tel: (386) 736-4793, FAX: (386) 736-9786, E-Mail: admin@skydivingmagazine.com, Web Site: www.skydivingmagazine.com (17)

Cliggott Publishing Co, Norwalk, CT. Tel: (203) 662-6400, (203) 661-0600, FAX: (203) 662-6420, Web Site: www.cmp.com (17)

Cline, Bill, Nationwide Graphic/Premier Print Organizations, Houston, TX. Tel: (713) 961-4700, Web Site: www.nationwidegraphics.com (27)

Cline, Ed, Careington International, Frisco, TX. Tel: (972) 335-6970, Web Site: www.careington.com (7)

Cline, Margaret, A., University of Illinois Foundation, Urbana, IL. Tel: (217) 333-0810, FAX: (217) 333-5577, E-Mail: uif@uillinois.edu, Web Site: www.uif.uillinois.edu (1)

ClingZ Inc, Rio Rancho, NM. Tel: (505) 892-2500, Web Site: www.clingz.com (17)

Clinton, Michael, A., Hearst Magazines, New York, NY. Tel: (212) 649-2824, FAX: (212) 765-3528, Web Site: www.hearst.com/magazines (17)

Clipper Magazine, Mountville, PA. Tel: (717) 569-5100, Web Site: www.clippermagazine.com (31)

Clippinger, Marni Z., Marketing Science Institute Review, Cambridge, MA. Tel: (617) 491-2060, FAX: (617) 491-2065, E-Mail: msi@msi.org, Web Site: www.msi.org (43)

Clobes, April, MSU Federal Credit Union, East Lansing, MI. Tel: (517) 333-2254, Web Site: www.msufcu.org (1)

Clock, Kirby, Mountain West Communications Inc, Hotchkiss, CO. Tel: (970) 872-2500, (800) 642-9378, FAX: (970) 872-3862, E-Mail: sales@mountainwest.com, Web Site: www.mountainwest.com (29)

Cloninger III, Kriss, American Family Life Assurance Co of Columbus (AFLAC), Columbus, GA. Tel: (706) 323-3431, (800) 992-3522, FAX: (706) 660-7446, Web Site: www.aflac.com (15)

Cloonan, James, B., American Association of Individual Investors, Chicago, IL. Tel: (312) 280-0170, FAX: (312) 280-9883, E-Mail: adam@aaii.com, Web Site: www.aaii.com (1)

The Clorox Co, Oakland, CA. Tel: (510) 271-7000, FAX: (510) 832-1463, Web Site: www.thecloroxcompany.com (16)

Close, Allyn, D., Symetra Financial, Bellevue, WA. Tel: (425) 256-8000, (800) 426-7355, FAX: (425) 256-5737, Web Site: www.symetra.com (15)

Closser, Ron, Balboa Life & Casualty, Irvine, CA. Tel: (949) 222-8000, (800) 854-6115, FAX: (949) 222-8777, Web Site: www.balboainsurance.com (15)

Clothing Solutions, Irvine, CA. Tel: (800) 336-2660, (800) 465-1981, FAX: (800) 336-6510, Web Site: www.clothingsolutions.com (2)

Clotworthy, Brian, The Information Refinery Inc, Mahwah, NJ. Tel: (201) 529-2600, (800) 529-9020, FAX: (201) 529-4030, E-Mail: info@inforefinery.com, Web Site: www.inforefinery.com (24)

Clotworthy, Gordon M., The Information Refinery Inc, Mahwah, NJ. Tel: (201) 529-2600, (800) 529-9020, FAX: (201) 529-4030, E-Mail: info@inforefinery.com, Web Site: www.inforefinery.com (24)

Clotz, Kevin, Assurant Group, New York, NY. Tel: (305) 253-2244, FAX: (305) 252-6987, Web Site: www.assurant.com (15)

Cloudt, Carole, US Historical Society, Richmond, VA. Tel: (800) 788-4478, FAX: (804) 648-0002, E-Mail: administrator@ushs.org, Web Site: www.ushs.org (16)

Clouse, Robert, Lead Me Media, Lake Worth, FL. Tel: (888) 445-3282, Web Site: www.leadmedia.com (30)

Cloutier Direct Inc, Scarborough, ME. Tel: (207) 883-9599, Web Site: www.cloutierdirect.com (28)

Clubs of America, Lakemoor, IL. Tel: (815) 363-4000, (800) CLUB-USA, FAX: (815) 363-4677, E-Mail: info@greatclubs.com, Web Site: www.clubsofamerica.com (6)

Cluett Peabody, New York, NY. Tel: (212) 984-8900, FAX: (212) 984-8910, Web Site: www.arrowshirt.com (16)

Clute, Harold, Air-Lec Industries Inc, Madison, WI. Tel: (608) 244-4754, FAX: (608) 246-7676, E-Mail: info@air-lec.com, Web Site: www.air-lec.com (16)

Clyman, Jacky, R., Cockpit USA Inc, New York, NY. Tel: (212) 575-1616, FAX: (212) 575-1636, E-Mail: jacky@cockpitusa.com, Web Site: www.cockpitusa.com (2)

Clyman, Jeff, Cockpit USA Inc, New York, NY. Tel: (212) 575-1616, FAX: (212) 575-1636, E-Mail: jacky@cockpitusa.com, Web Site: www.cockpitusa.com (2)

CO-OP PROMOTIONS, Hollywood, FL. Tel: (954) 922-2323, FAX: (954) 922-2071, E-Mail: art@co-oppromotions.com, Web Site: www.co-oppromotions.com (35)

Co-operations, Tualatin, OR. Tel: (503) 620-7977, (866) 228-6362, FAX: (503) 620-7917, E-Mail: info@fsipdx.com, Web Site: www.fsipdx.com (28)

Coach, New York, NY. Tel: (212) 594-1850, (800) 444-3611, FAX: (212) 594-1682, Web Site: www.coach.com (2)

Coalter, Rick, JA Sexauer, Elmsford, NY. Tel: (914) 472-7501, (800) 431-1872, FAX: (914) 472-5834, Web Site: www.jasmro.com (16)

Coast Hotels Limited, Seattle, WA. Tel: (206) 826-2700, FAX: (206) 826-2701, Web Site: www.coasthotels.com (19)

Coast to Coast Inc, Englewood, CO. Tel: (303) 728-2267, Web Site: www.coastresorts.com (1)

Coastal Health Train, Virginia Beach, VA. Tel: (757) 631-3142, Web Site: www.coastalhealth.com (7)

Coastal Hotel Group, Seattle, WA. Tel: (206) 388-0400, FAX: (206) 388-0401, E-Mail: info@coastalhotel.com, Web Site: www.coastalhotels.com (1)

Coastal Living, Birmingham, AL. Tel: (205) 877-6007, FAX: (205) 445-8655, E-Mail: coastalliving@customersvc.com, Web Site: www.coastalliving.com (43)

Coastal Tool & Supply, West Hartford, CT. Tel: (860) 233-8213, (877) 551-8665, FAX: (860) 233-6295, E-Mail: sales@coastaltool.com, Web Site: www. coastaltool.com (16)

Coates, Doreen, Accounting with Debits and Credits with Coates & Hutchinson PC, Odenton, MD. Tel: (800) 833-5933, FAX: (301) 912-3364, E-Mail: info@awdc.org (14)

Coats, Brian, MAR Graphics, Valmeyer, IL. Tel: (800) 851-4460, Web Site: www.margraphics.com (27)

Coats, Janet, Posty Cards Inc, Kansas City, MO. Tel: (816) 231-2323, (800) 554-5018, FAX: (888) 577-3800, E-Mail: customerservice@postycards.com, Web Site: www.postycards.com (16)

Cobalt, Seattle, WA. Tel: (206) 269-6363, Web Site: www.cobalt.com (16)

Cobb, Jerry, Kolbe Corp, Phoenix, AZ. Tel: (602) 840-9770, (800) 642-2822, FAX: (602) 952-2706, E-Mail: info@kolbe.com, Web Site: www.kolbe. com (17)

Cobbey, Robin, Cobbey & Associates Marketing Research, Carson City, NV. Tel: (775) 847-0321, (877) 433-3242, E-Mail: cobbey@cobbey.com, Web Site: www.cobbey.com (30)

Cobbey & Associates Marketing Research, Carson City, NV. Tel: (775) 847-0321, (877) 433-3242, E-Mail: cobbey@cobbey.com, Web Site: www. cobbey.com (30)

Cobblestone Publishing, Peterborough, NH. Tel: (603) 924-7209, (800) 821-0115, FAX: (603) 924-7380, E-Mail: customerservice@caruspub.com, Web Site: www.cobblestonepub.com (17)

Coble, Scott, Time Logistics Inc, Columbia, TN. Tel: (931) 540-2801, (866) 293-8463, FAX: (931) 540-2995, Web Site: www.timelogisticsinc.com (12)

The Coca-Cola Co, Atlanta, GA. Tel: (404) 676-2121, FAX: (404) 676-6792, Web Site: www.cocacola. com (16)

Cocchia, Ann, Marie, Aspen Publishers Inc, New York, NY. Tel: (800) 638-8437, FAX: (301) 417-7655, Web Site: www.aspenpublishers.com (17)

Cochran, Edmund, United Way Store, Alexandria, VA. Tel: (703) 212-6300, (800) 772-0008, FAX: (703) 212-6319, E-Mail: customerservice@unitedwaystore.com, Web Site: www. unitedwaystore.com (34)

Cochran, Gerald, D., Golden Gate Transportation District, San Rafael, CA. Tel: (415) 921-5858, FAX: (415) 923-2014, Web Site: www.goldengate.org (16)

Cochran, Randy, Symantec, Mountain View, CA. Tel: (408) 517-8000, FAX: (408) 517-8186, Web Site: www.symantec.com (16)

Cochran, Steve, MXT Card Services, LLC, New Castle, DE. Tel: (302) 323-6203, FAX: (302) 323-6219, Web Site: www.mxtcs.com (14)

Cochran, Terry, Raven's Nest Herbals, LLC, Duluth, GA. Tel: (678) 642-6691, (678) 584-0830, E-Mail: info@ravensnestherbals.com, Web Site: www. ravensnestherbals.com (7)

Cochrane, Chuck, Blethen Maine Newspapers Inc, Portland, ME. Tel: (207) 791-6650, FAX: (207) 791-6925, Web Site: www.mainetoday.com (17)

Cockpit USA Inc, New York, NY. Tel: (212) 575-1616, FAX: (212) 575-1636, E-Mail: jacky@cockpitusa.com, Web Site: www.cockpitusa.com (2)

Coco, Andrew, Knoll Group, New York, NY. Tel: (212) 343-4000, FAX: (212) 343-4180 (16)

Cocozza, Keith, Time Warner Inc, New York, NY. Tel: (212) 484-8000, Web Site: www.timewarner.com (16)

Coday, Dennis, National Catholic Reporter Publishing Co Inc, Kansas City, MO. Tel: (816) 531-0538, (800) 444-8910, FAX: (816) 968-2268, Web Site: www.ncronline.org (17)

Coe, Ben, Butler Schein Animal Health, Dublin, OH. Tel: (614) 761-9095, (888) 691-2724, FAX: (888) 329-3861, Web Site: www.butlerschein.com (16)

Coe, John M., The Sales and Marketing Institute, Scottsdale, AZ. Tel: (480) 473-5777, (888) 714-5544, FAX: (623) 979-8843, Web Site: www. b2bmarketing.com (35)

Coerper, Phil, International Filing Corp, Rockwall, TX. Tel: (800) 647-3070, FAX: (800) 633-7053, E-Mail: pcoerper@intfiling.com, Web Site: www. intfiling.com (26)

Coes, Bryce, Certified Lists Inc, Omaha, NE. Tel: (402) 201-2087, (866) 537-7569, FAX: (877) 655-8733, E-Mail: contact@certified-lists.com, Web Site: www.certified-lists.com (23)

Coffeen III, William I., Nexxlinx (HQ), Atlanta, GA. Tel: (770) 250-0349, Web Site: www.nexxlinx.com (22)

Coffeen, Steve, Las Vegas Review Journal, Las Vegas, NV. Tel: (702) 383-0211, FAX: (702) 383-4646, Web Site: www.lvrj.com (17)

Coffey, Lucia, Bookspan, Garden City, NY. Tel: (516) 490-4561, FAX: (516) 490-4856 (13)

Coffin, Christian, Doubletree Suites by Hilton, Boston, MA. Tel: (617) 783-0090, (800) 222-TREE, FAX: (617) 783-0897, E-Mail: doubletree1@hilton.com (19)

Coffin, Lew, C., Polyair Packaging, Chicago, IL. Tel: (773) 995-1818, (888) POLYAIR X444, FAX: (773) 995-7725, E-Mail: marketing@polyair.com, Web Site: www.polyair.com (9)

Coffman, Richard, Norman Control Co, Cary, IL. Tel: (847) 639-5721, FAX: (847) 639-5755, E-Mail: susan@coffmanmfg.com, Web Site: www. coffmanmfg.com (16)

Coffman, Susan, Norman Control Co, Cary, IL. Tel: (847) 639-5721, FAX: (847) 639-5755, E-Mail: susan@coffmanmfg.com, Web Site: www. coffmanmfg.com (16)

Cofield, Linda, Team Cheer, Geneseo, NY. Tel: (585) 243-8400, (585) 243-0841, (877) 243-5268, FAX: (800) 350-1562, E-Mail: custserv@teamcheer.com, Web Site: www.teamcheer.com (2)

Cofield, Randy, Team Cheer, Geneseo, NY. Tel: (585) 243-8400, (585) 243-0841, (877) 243-5268, FAX: (800) 350-1562, E-Mail: custserv@teamcheer.com, Web Site: www.teamcheer.com (2)

Cofoni, Paul, M., CACI International Inc, Arlington, VA. Tel: (703) 841-7800, FAX: (703) 841-7882, Web Site: www.caci.com (22)

Coftus, Jack, The Nielsen Co, New York, NY. Tel: (646) 654-5000, E-Mail: contactcommunications@nielsen.com, Web Site: www.nielsen.com (17)

Cogan, Stuart, A., Mega Media Associates Inc, Newport Beach, CA. Tel: (949) 673-2290, E-Mail: info@megamediaassociaes.com, Web Site: www. megamediaassociates.com (23)

Coggin, Tom, DataDirect, Atlanta, GA. Tel: (678) 530-0034, FAX: (678) 530-9563, E-Mail: info@ddirect.com, Web Site: www.ddirect.com (40)

Cogland, Don, Ad-Lib Advertising Inc, Old Bridge, NJ. Tel: (732) 679-9226, (800) 622-3542, FAX: (732) 679-9511, E-Mail: info@adlibadvertising. com, Web Site: www.adlibadvertising.com (10)

Cogley, John, Daniel Smith Inc, Seattle, WA. Tel: (206) 223-9599, (800) 426-6740, FAX: (800) 238-4065, E-Mail: sales@danielsmith.com, Web Site: www.danielsmith.com (10)

Cognis Corp, Cincinnati, OH. Tel: (513) 482-3000, FAX: (513) 482-5501, E-Mail: kathy.bollmer@cognis.com, Web Site: www.cognis-us.com (35)

CognitiveDATA Inc, Little Rock, AR. Tel: (501) 975-7580, (866) 243-7883, E-Mail: info@cognitivedata.com, Web Site: www.cognitivedata.com (22)

Cognitronics Corp, Foxboro, MA. Tel: (508) 624-7600, (888) 228-5061, FAX: (508) 624-0289, E-Mail: info@thinkengine.com, Web Site: www. cognitronics.com (34)

Cohasset Colonials, Ashburnham, MA. Tel: (978) 827-3001, (800) 288-2389, FAX: (978) 827-3227, E-Mail: cohasset@cohassetcolonials.com, Web Site: www.cohassetcolonials.com (8)

Cohen, Andrew, Exposed Brick, New York, NY. Tel: (212) 226-0060, FAX: (212) 941-8566, E-Mail: andrewc@exposedbrick.com, Web Site: www. exposedbrick.com (35)

Cohen, Arthur, Electric Media, New York, NY. Tel: (201) 461-5252 (30)

Cohen, Barbara, Kannon Consulting Inc, Chicago, IL. Tel: (312) 346-2244, FAX: (312) 346-3665, Web Site: www.kannon.com (20)

Cohen, Bob, Rio Brands, Philadelphia, PA. Tel: (215) 632-2800, FAX: (215) 824-1172 (16)

Cohen, David L., Databazaar.com, Miramar, FL. Tel: (954) 843-0483, (888) 335-3282, FAX: (954) 843-0429, E-Mail: rudy@databazaar.com, Web Site: www.databazaar.com (10)

Cohen, Dennis, Bauer Publishing Co, Englewood Cliffs, NJ. Tel: (201) 569-6699, FAX: (201) 510-3297, Web Site: www.bauerpublishing.com (17)

Cohen, Eitan, Media Stream Direct, Sherman Oaks, CA. Tel: (800) 817-8000, E-Mail: ecohen@mediastreamdirect.com, Web Site: www. mediastreamdirect.com (35)

Cohen, Eli, Polo Ralph Lauren, Lyndhurst, NJ. Tel: (212) 531-6537, (800) 377-7656, FAX: (212) 318-7690, Web Site: www.ralphlauren.com (2)

Cohen, Gail, Power Seminars, Swampscott, MA. Tel: (781) 595-9990, FAX: (781) 595-0770, Web Site: www.gailcohen.com (29)

Cohen, Hal, A-KD Mailing & Fulfillment Service, Lincolnwood, IL. Tel: (847) 673-0186, (866) 330-6245, FAX: (874) 673-0188, E-Mail: dan@kdmailing.com, Web Site: www.kdmailing.com (28)

Cohen, Harvey, Graham Field Health Products Inc, Atlanta, GA. Tel: (800) 347-5678, FAX: (800) 726-0601, E-Mail: ics@grahamfield.com, Web Site: www.lumiscope.net (7)

Cohen, Herbert, J., Cohen & Co, Brooklyn, NY. Tel: (718) 875-5065, FAX: (718) 875-5065, E-Mail: herbertjcohen@aol.com (20)

Cohen, Herbert, Platinum Press, Killingworth, CT. Tel: (860) 663-3882, FAX: (718) 825-5065, E-Mail: herbertjcohen@aol.com (20)

Cohen, Ira, IC DIRECT List Brokers, El Dorado Hills, CA. Tel: (916) 941-7605, (877) ICD-UST, FAX: (916) 941-7615, E-Mail: info@icdlist.com, Web Site: www.icdlist.com (23)

Cohen, Jeff, Teleperformance Interactive, Miami Beach, FL. Tel: (786) 437-3300, FAX: (786) 276-8452, Web Site: www.teleperformance.com (29)

Cohen, Jerry, P., Ebbets Field Flannels Inc, Seattle, WA. Tel: (206) 382-7249, FAX: (206) 382-4411, E-Mail: clubhouse@ebbets.com, Web Site: www. ebbets.com (2)

Cohen, Jill, Prospect Direct Inc, Milwaukee, WI. Tel: (414) 271-3313, (800) 624-9050, FAX: (414) 271-4244, E-Mail: info@prospect-direct.com, Web Site: www.prospect-direct.com (21)

Cohen, Lawrence, H., Alliance Bernstein, New York, NY. Tel: (212) 969-1000, (800) 962-2134, FAX: (212) 969-2229, Web Site: www.alliancebernstein. com (14)

Cohen, Leonard, Kelly, Scott & Madison Inc, Chicago, IL. Tel: (312) 977-0772, FAX: (312) 977-0874, Web Site: www.ksmmedia.com (32)

Cohen, Mark, Brooke Distributors Inc, Miami, FL. Tel: (305) 624-9752, (800) 275-8792, FAX: (305) 620-3988, E-Mail: sales@brookedms.com, Web Site: www.brooke.com (3)

Cohen, Mark, J., Rio Brands, Philadelphia, PA. Tel: (215) 632-2800, FAX: (215) 824-1172 (16)

Cohen, Michele, Society for Healthcare Strategy & Market Development, Chicago, IL. Tel: (312) 422-3888, FAX: (312) 422-4579, E-Mail: stratsoc@aha.org, Web Site: www.stratsociety.org (42)

Cohen, Ralph, New York Life Insurance Co/AARP, Tampa, FL. Tel: (813) 288-5500, FAX: (813) 288-5256, Web Site: www.nylaarp.com (15)

Cohen, Risa, Sudnow, Mailing and Fulfillment Service Association of New York, New York, NY. Tel: (212) 217-6824, (800) 394-5106, FAX: (212) 217-6824, E-Mail: info@mfsany.com, Web Site: www.mfsany.com (34)

Cohen, Rita, Magazine Publishers of America, New York, NY. Tel: (212) 872-3700, FAX: (212) 888-4217, Web Site: www.magazine.org (17)

Cohen, Sharon, Aon's Affinity Insurance Services Inc, Hatboro, PA. Tel: (215) 773-4600, Web Site: www.aon.com (15)

Cohen, Stephen, Falcon Products Inc, Newport, TN. Tel: (314) 991-9200, (800) 873-3252, FAX: (314) 991-9227, E-Mail: info@falconproducts.com, Web Site: www.falconproducts.com (16)

Cohen, Steve, List Management Services Inc, Orlando, FL. Tel: (407) 876-5544, Web Site: www.lmsonline.com (35)

Cohen, Warren, Rio Brands, Philadelphia, PA. Tel: (215) 632-2800, FAX: (215) 824-1172 (16)

Cohen, Wendy H., Newhouse School of Public Communications, Syracuse, NY. Tel: (315) 443-3611, FAX: (315) 443-4426, Web Site: newhouse.syr.edu (41)

Cohen & Co, Brooklyn, NY. Tel: (718) 875-5065, FAX: (718) 875-5065, E-Mail: herbertjcohen@aol.com (20)

Cohen Chhahira, Nancy, Coach, New York, NY. Tel: (212) 594-1850, (800) 444-3611, FAX: (212) 594-1682, Web Site: www.coach.com (2)

Cohn, Alan J., Sage Financial Group, West Conshohocken, PA. Tel: (484) 342-4400, FAX: (484) 537-0550, E-Mail: sage@sagefinancial.com, Web Site: www.sagefinancial.com (14)

Cohn, David, Sage Financial Group, West Conshohocken, PA. Tel: (484) 342-4400, FAX: (484) 537-0550, E-Mail: sage@sagefinancial.com, Web Site: www.sagefinancial.com (14)

Cohn, John, D., Rockwell Automation, Milwaukee, WI. Tel: (414) 382-2000, FAX: (414) 382-4444, Web Site: www.rockwellautomation.com (16)

Cohn, Mark A., DAMARK International Inc, La Salle, IL. Tel: (877) 326-2757, Web Site: www.damark.com (16)

Cohn, Stephen, Sage Financial Group, West Conshohocken, PA. Tel: (484) 342-4400, FAX: (484) 537-0550, E-Mail: sage@sagefinancial.com, Web Site: www.sagefinancial.com (14)

Coho, David, Univenture Inc, Marysville, OH. Tel: (937) 645-4600, Web Site: www.univenture.com (27)

Cohodes, Aaron, Precept Press, Chicago, IL. Tel: (312) 467-0580, FAX: (312) 467-9271, E-Mail: bb@bonusbooks.com, Web Site: www.bonusbooks.com (17)

Cohorts, Denver, CO. Tel: (303) 893-8600, FAX: (303) 893-8611, E-Mail: info@cohorts.com, Web Site: www.cohorts.com (35)

Coiley, Anne, Bayer Corp Consumer Care Division, Morristown, NJ. Tel: (973) 254-5000, FAX: (973) 408-8215, Web Site: www.bayercare.com (16)

Coin Laundry Association, Oakbrook Terrace, IL. Tel: (630) 963-5547, FAX: (630) 963-5864, Web Site: www.coinlaundry.org (1)

Coin World, Sidney, OH. Tel: (937) 498-0800, (800) 253-4555, FAX: (937) 498-0812, E-Mail: cwcustomerservice@coinworld.com, Web Site: www.coinworld.com (17)

Cok, Mike, Foremost Insurance Group, Grand Rapids, MI. Tel: (616) 956-8241, (800) 527-3905, FAX: (800) 325-1507, Web Site: www.foremost.com (15)

Coker, Joseph, Universal Vintage Tire Co, Hershey, PA. Tel: (717) 534-0175, (800) 233-3827, FAX: (717) 534-0719, E-Mail: sales@universaltire.com, Web Site: www.universaltire.com (11)

Coker, Murray S., Camping World Inc, Bowling Green, KY. Tel: (270) 781-2718, (800) 626-6189, FAX: (270) 796-8991, Web Site: www.campingworld.com (11)

Coker, Murray, Affinity Group Inc, Ventura, CA. Tel: (805) 667-4100, (800) 765-1912, FAX: (805) 667-4419, E-Mail: khurd@affinitygroup.com, Web Site: www.affinitygroup.com (19)

Col Voce Consulting, Exton, PA. Tel: (215) 266-2992, Web Site: www.colvoce.com (20)

Colainni, Peter, Print Services Distribution Association, Chicago, IL. Tel: (703) 836-6232, (800) 336-4641, FAX: (703) 836-2241, E-Mail: psda@psda.org, Web Site: www.psda.org (1)

Colarelli, Nick, J., Colarelli Meyer & Associates Inc, Saint Louis, MO. Tel: (314) 721-1860, (800) 459-4548, FAX: (314) 721-1992, E-Mail: cmaconsult@cmaconsult.com, Web Site: www.cmaconsult.com (20)

Colarelli Meyer & Associates Inc, Saint Louis, MO. Tel: (314) 721-1860, (800) 459-4548, FAX: (314) 721-1992, E-Mail: cmaconsult@cmaconsult.com, Web Site: www.cmaconsult.com (20)

Colassano, Laura, UNICEF, New York, NY. Tel: (212) 326-7000, Web Site: www.unicef.org (1)

Colburn, Ashley, Polaris Direct, Hooksett, NH. Tel: (603) 626-5800, E-Mail: info@polarisdirect.net, Web Site: www.polarisdirect.net (28)

Colburn, Diane, Publicis, Plano, TX. Tel: (972) 628-7500, FAX: (972) 628-7671, Web Site: www.publicis-usa.com (35)

Colby, Gordon, Voyageur Inc, Easley, SC. Tel: (802) 496-3127, (800) 311-7245, FAX: (802) 496-6247 (11)

Colca, Nick, EMED Co Inc, Buffalo, NY. Tel: (716) 626-1616, (800) 442-3633, FAX: (716) 626-1630, E-Mail: customerservice@emedco.com, Web Site: www.emedco.com (16)

Cold Spring Harbor Lab Press, Woodbury, NY. Tel: (516) 422-4100, (800) 843-4388, FAX: (516) 422-4097, E-Mail: cshpress@cshl.edu, Web Site: www.cshlpress.com (17)

Cold Stream Farm, Free Soil, MI. Tel: (231) 464-5809, E-Mail: info@coldstreamfarm.net, Web Site: www.coldstreamfarm.net (8)

Coldwater Creek, Coeur D Alene, ID. Tel: (800) 787-9196, FAX: (800) 262-0080, Web Site: www.coldwatercreek.com (2)

Cole PhD, Lorraine, YWCA of the USA, Washington, DC. Tel: (202) 467-0801, FAX: (202) 467-0802, E-Mail: info@ywca.org, Web Site: www.ywca.org (1)

Cole, Chris, Burden Sales Co, Lincoln, NE. Tel: (402) 474-4055, (800) 488-3407, FAX: (402) 474-5198, E-Mail: ccole@surpluscenter.com (9)

Cole, Chris, Surplus Center, Lincoln, NE. Tel: (402) 474-4055, (800) 488-3407, FAX: (402) 474-5198, E-Mail: customerservice1@surpluscenter.com, Web Site: www.surpluscenter.com (9)

Cole, Dawn, 1000 Islands International Tourism Council, Alexandria Bay, NY. Tel: (315) 482-2520, (800) 847-5263, (800) 456-2267, FAX: (315) 482-5906, Web Site: www.visit1000islands.com/visitorinfo/ (19)

Cole, Debra, Trump Plaza Hotel & Casino, Atlantic City, NJ. Tel: (609) 441-6000, FAX: (609) 441-7727, Web Site: www.trumpplaza.com (19)

Cole, Douglas, D., TWL Knowledge Group, Carrollton, TX. Tel: (972) 309-4000, (800) 624-2272, FAX: (972) 309-5105, Web Site: www.twlk.com (3)

Cole, Larry, Ogilvy & Mather Direct, New York, NY. Tel: (212) 237-6000, FAX: (212) 237-5123, Web Site: www.ogilvy.com (35)

Cole, Meghan, Laughlin Associates Inc, Carson City, NV. Tel: (775) 883-8484, (888) 273-8152, FAX: (775) 883-4874 (16)

Cole, Nicolas, Trinity Road LLC, Charlotte, NC. Tel: (704) 940-2240 (28)

Cole, Steven, Council of Better Business Bureaus - BBBOnline, Arlington, VA. Tel: (703) 276-0100, FAX: (703) 525-8277, Web Site: www.bbb.org (1)

Cole, Terry, Breck's Bulbs, Lawrenceburg, IN. Tel: (309) 693-8600, FAX: (309) 691-9693 (8)

Cole, Timothy H., Belvoir Media Group LLC, Norwalk, CT. Tel: (203) 857-3100, (800) 424-7887, FAX: (203) 857-3103, E-Mail: customer_service@belvoir.com, Web Site: www.belvoir.com (17)

Cole, Tom, RAZOR Transaction Building Experts, Addison, TX. Tel: (972) 663-1100, Web Site: www.razordriven.com (35)

Cole & Weber United, Seattle, WA. Tel: (206) 447-9595, Web Site: www.cwunited.com (35)

Cole Information Services, Omaha, NE. Tel: (800) 403-5894, Web Site: www.coleinformation.com (23)

Cole-Parmer Instrument Co, Vernon Hills, IL. Tel: (847) 549-7600, (800) 323-4340, FAX: (847) 247-2929, E-Mail: info@coleparmer.com, Web Site: www.coleparmer.com (16)

Coleman, Allen, Cross Country Stitching, Quakertown, PA. Tel: (215) 529-6430, (800) 231-8108, FAX: (215) 529-6434, Web Site: www.crosscountrystitching.com (16)

Coleman, Dan, John Harland Co, Decatur, GA. Tel: (770) 981-5580, (800) 723-3690, FAX: (770) 593-5367, E-Mail: jhhwebmaster@harland.net, Web Site: www.harland.net (16)

Coleman, Elizabeth, Insurance Publications Inc, Overland Park, KS. Tel: (913) 383-9191, (800) 762-3387, FAX: (913) 383-1247, E-Mail: brokerwrld@primary.net, Web Site: www.brokerworldmag.com (17)

Coleman, Frank, CBT Direct, Tarpon Springs, FL. Tel: (727) 724-8994, (877) 872-4646, FAX: (727) 797-9143, Web Site: www.cbtdirect.com (16)

Coleman, Jean, C., Integrity Music Inc, Mobile, AL. Tel: (251) 633-9000, FAX: (251) 633-5202, Web Site: www.integritymusic.com (16)

Coleman, Jon, Coleman Research Inc, Morrisville, NC. Tel: (919) 571-0000, FAX: (919) 571-9999, E-Mail: callcoleman@colemaninsights.com, Web Site: www.colemaninsights.com (30)

Coleman, Linda, Cross Country Stitching, Quakertown, PA. Tel: (215) 529-6430, (800) 231-8108, FAX: (215) 529-6434, Web Site: www.crosscountrystitching.com (17)

Coleman, Mike, Integrity Music Inc, Mobile, AL. Tel: (251) 633-9000, FAX: (251) 633-5202, Web Site: www.integritymusic.com (16)

Coleman, Milton, The Washington Post, Washington, DC. Tel: (202) 334-6000, (800) 627-1150, E-Mail: letters@washpost.com, Web Site: www.washingtonpost.com (17)

Coleman, Wes, Disney Vacation Club, Kissimmee, FL. Tel: (407) 566-3100, (800) 500-3990, FAX: (407) 566-3393 (19)

Coleman Frost LLP, Santa Monica, CA. Tel: (310) 576-7312, Web Site: www.colemanfrost.com (20)

Coleman Research Inc, Morrisville, NC. Tel: (919) 571-0000, FAX: (919) 571-9999, E-Mail: callcoleman@colemaninsights.com, Web Site: www.colemaninsights.com (30)

Cole's Appliance & Furniture Co, Chicago, IL. Tel: (773) 525-1797, FAX: (773) 525-0728 (8)

Coley, Melissa, Brookfield Properties, Toronto, ON. Tel: (416) 369-2300, FAX: (416) 369-2301, Web Site: www.brokfieldproperties.com (16)

Colfax Envelope Corp, Buffalo Grove, IL. Tel: (847) 215-1122, FAX: (847) 215-1145, Web Site: www.colfaxenv.com (26)

Colgate-Palmolive Co, New York, NY. Tel: (212) 310-2000, (800) 468-6502, FAX: (212) 310-2475, Web Site: www.colgate.com (16)

Colinear Systems, Alpharetta, GA. Tel: (770) 643-0000, (800) COLINEAR, FAX: (770) 643-0265, E-Mail: sales@colinear.com, Web Site: www.colinear.com (22)

Collamore, Thomas, US Chamber of Commerce, Washington, DC. Tel: (202) 778-6063, (800) 638-6582, FAX: (202) 887-3430, Web Site: www.uschamber.com (1)

Collard, Elijah, Reading for Education, Murfreesboro, TN. Tel: (615) 896-3800 (16)

Colle+McVoy, Minneapolis, MN. Tel: (612) 305-6000, FAX: (612) 305-6500, E-Mail: info@collemcvoy. com, Web Site: www.collemcvoy.com (35)

Collectibles Today Network, Ltd, Niles, IL. Tel: (800) 323-5577 #6, Web Site: www.collectiblestoday.com (16)

Collective - The Audience Engine, New York, NY. Tel: (646) 380-2744 (22)

Collector Books & American Quilters Society, Paducah, KY. Tel: (270) 898-6211, (800) 626-5420, FAX: (270) 898-8890, E-Mail: info@ collectorbooks.com, Web Site: www. collectorbooks.com (17)

Collector's Armoury Ltd, McDonough, GA. Tel: (703) 493-9120, FAX: (703) 493-9424, Web Site: www. collectorsarmoury.com (6)

Collector's Teapot, Kingston, NY. Tel: (845) 339-1109, (800) 724-3306, FAX: (845) 339-5530, Web Site: www.collectorsteapot.com (6)

The College Board, New York, NY. Tel: (212) 713-8000, FAX: (212) 713-8143, Web Site: www. collegeboard.com (1)

College of Business, Cincinnati, OH. Tel: (513) 556-7002, FAX: (513) 556-4891, E-Mail: business@uc. edu, Web Site: www.business.uc.edu (41)

College of Business Administration, Philadelphia, PA. Tel: (215) 895-2145, Web Site: www.drexel.edu (41)

CollegeAmerica, Salt Lake City, UT. Tel: (801) 284-7553 (1)

The Collegebound Network, Staten Island, NY. Tel: (718) 761-4800, Web Site: www.collegebound.net (32)

Collegesource Inc, San Diego, CA. Tel: (858) 560-8051, (800) 854-2670, FAX: (858) 278-8960, Web Site: www.collegesource.org (17)

Collegiate Cap & Gown, Champaign, IL. Tel: (217) 351-9500, FAX: (217) 351-9214, Web Site: www. herff-jones.com (16)

Colleluori, John, AIN Plastics Inc, Yonkers, NY. Tel: (914) 668-6800, (800) 431-2451, FAX: (914) 668-8820, Web Site: www.ainplastics.com (16)

Colleran, Jim, Wendell August Forge Inc, Grove City, PA. Tel: (724) 458-8360, (800) 923-1390, FAX: (724) 458-0906, E-Mail: info@wendell.com, Web Site: www.wendellaugust.com (6)

Colleton, Michael E., JR Tobacco/800-JR Cigar Inc, Burlington, NC. Tel: (800) 572-4427, FAX: (800) 457-3299, Web Site: www.jrcigars.com (5)

Collette Vacations, Pawtucket, RI. Tel: (401) 727-9000, FAX: (401) 727-1000, E-Mail: czesk@ collettetours.com, Web Site: www.collettevacations. com (19)

Collida, Susan, Nostrum Inc, Long Beach, CA. Tel: (562) 437-2200, Web Site: www.nostruminc.com (35)

Collider Media, Austin, TX. Tel: (512) 745-8070, Web Site: collidermedia.com (9)

Colligent, Cupertino, CA. Tel: (425) 641-1130 (30)

Collin Street Bakery, Corsicana, TX. Tel: (800) 292-7400, Web Site: www.collinstreetbakery.com (4)

Collinger, Tom, Medill IMC/Northwestern University, Evanston, IL. Tel: (847) 467-3433 (1)

Collinger, William, Collinger & Associates, Saint Louis, MO. Tel: (314) 991-8787, FAX: (314) 991-9797, E-Mail: bcmktr@aol.com (20)

Collinger & Associates, Saint Louis, MO. Tel: (314) 991-8787, FAX: (314) 991-9797, E-Mail: bcmktr@ aol.com (20)

Collingwood, Patricia, Jos A Bank Clothiers Inc, Hampstead, MD. Tel: (410) 239-2700, Web Site: www.josbank.com (2)

Collins Jr, Thomas, M., JJ Collins' Sons Inc, Woodridge, IL. Tel: (630) 960-2525, (800) 972-2296, FAX: (630) 960-7487, E-Mail: sales@jjcollins. com, Web Site: www.jjcollins.com (27)

Collins, Artie, Northern Printing Network Inc, Wheeling, IL. Tel: (847) 215-7300, FAX: (847) 215-7314, E-Mail: sales@northernprint.com, Web Site: www.northernprint.com (21)

Collins, Daniel, TMP Direct, Budd Lake, NJ. Tel: (973) 347-9400, (800) 328-2439, FAX: (973) 347-8773, E-Mail: ron.pearl@tmpwdirect.com, Web Site: www.tmpwdirect.com (29)

Collins, Daryl, Mail America Communications - a Dmh Marketing Partners Co, Forest, VA. Tel: (434) 534-8000, Web Site: www.mail-america.com (28)

Collins, Douglas, Torqmaster International, Stamford, CT. Tel: (203) 326-5945, (888) 414-4643, FAX: (203) 326-5944, E-Mail: info@torqmaster.com, Web Site: www.torqmaster.com (9)

Collins, George, C., Research & Response International, New York, NY. Tel: (212) 489-8610, FAX: (212) 262-3474, E-Mail: rrespe@bway.net, Web Site: www.rrespe.com (23)

Collins, George, J., T Rowe Price Associates Inc, Baltimore, MD. Tel: (410) 345-2000, (800) 638-7890, FAX: (410) 986-3618, E-Mail: info@troweprice. com, Web Site: www.troweprice.com (14)

Collins, Jana O., Jones & O'Malley Advertising, Toluca Lake, CA. Tel: (818) 762-8353, FAX: (818) 762-6736 (35)

Collins, Jim, Draper's & Damon's, Irvine, CA. Tel: (949) 784-3000, (800) 843-1174, FAX: (949) 784-3400, E-Mail: jilld@drapers.com, Web Site: www. drapers.com (2)

Collins, John, Marquis Awards & Specialties Inc, Powell, WY. Tel: (307) 754-2272, (800) 327-2446, FAX: (307) 754-9577, Web Site: www.rushawards. com (35)

Collins, Macolm, NCR Corp, Duluth, GA. Tel: (937) 445-1936, (800) CALL-NCR, FAX: (937) 445-1682, Web Site: www.ncr.com (16)

Collins, Melody, Collins List Exchange Inc, Henderson, NV. Tel: (702) 369-6015, Web Site: www. collinslist.com (23)

Collins, Peter, Nature Publishing Group, New York, NY. Tel: (212) 726-9200, FAX: (212) 696-9006, E-Mail: nature@natureny.com, Web Site: www. nature.com (17)

Collins, Raymond A., Brown Brothers, Sterling, PA. Tel: (570) 689-9688, FAX: (570) 689-7873, E-Mail: info@brownbrotherusa.com, Web Site: www.brownbrothersusa.com (38)

Collins, Rob, Brentwood Benson Music Publishing, Franklin, TN. Tel: (615) 261-3400, (800) 846-7664, FAX: (615) 261-3381, E-Mail: choral@ brentwoodbensonmusic.com, Web Site: www. brentwoodbenson.com (17)

Collins, Robert, T., Asbury Park Press Addresses Unlimited, Neptune, NJ. Tel: (732) 922-6000, FAX: (732) 462-3282 (21)

JJ Collins' Sons Inc, Woodridge, IL. Tel: (630) 960-2525, (800) 972-2296, FAX: (630) 960-7487, E-Mail: sales@jjcollins.com, Web Site: www. jjcollins.com (27)

Collins List Exchange Inc, Henderson, NV. Tel: (702) 369-6015, Web Site: www.collinslist.com (23)

Collis, David, Collis Curve Catalog Sales, Brownsville, TX. Tel: (210) 576-4818, (800) 298-4818, FAX: (800) 298-4818, E-Mail: brushteeth@aol. com, Web Site: www.colliscurve.com (7)

Collis Curve Catalog Sales, Brownsville, TX. Tel: (210) 576-4818, (800) 298-4818, FAX: (800) 298-4818, E-Mail: brushteeth@aol.com, Web Site: www.colliscurve.com (7)

Collom, John, Morcon Industrial Specialty Inc, Mesquite, NV. Tel: (702) 346-3447, (888) 842-7953, Web Site: www.morcon-ind.com (9)

Collova, Rob, Summit Racing Equipment, Tallmadge, OH. Tel: (330) 630-0270, FAX: (330) 630-5330, Web Site: www.summitracing.com (12)

Colman, Richard, United Systems c/o Biomed, Concord, CA. Tel: (925) 609-2820 (7)

Colombo, Deno, Vestcom Saint Louis, Earth City, MO. Tel: (314) 209-8443, (800) 264-0965, FAX: (314) 291-2195, E-Mail: sreinis@vestcom.com, Web Site: www.vestcom.com (21)

Colona, John, G., AIG Marketing, New York, NY. Tel: (212) 770-7000, (212) 770-2237, Web Site: www. agac.com (15)

The Colonial Co, Brooklyn, NY. Tel: (718) 972-7433, FAX: (718) 972-7438 (34)

Colonial Life Insurance Co Texas, Fort Worth, TX. Tel: (817) 390-2350, (888) 227-5119, FAX: (817) 390-2209, E-Mail: insurance@colonialinsurance. com, Web Site: www.colonialinsurance.com (15)

Colonial Redi-Record Corp, Brooklyn, NY. Tel: (718) 972-7433, (800) 637-0040, FAX: (718) 972-7438, Web Site: www.asisupplier.com/81110 (10)

The Colonial Williamsburg Foundation, Williamsburg, VA. Tel: (757) 229-1000, (757) 220-7275, (800) 761-8331, Web Site: www. williamsburgmarketplace.com (1)

Colonna, Robert, J., Innovative Systems Inc, Pittsburgh, PA. Tel: (412) 937-9300, (800) 622-6390, FAX: (412) 937-9309, E-Mail: info@ innovativesystems.com, Web Site: www. innovativesystems.com (22)

Color Film Media Group, Norwalk, CT. Tel: (203) 202-2929, (800) 882-1120, FAX: (203) 702-5800, E-Mail: info@colorfilm.com, Web Site: www. colorfilm.com (32)

Color Q Inc, Miamisburg, OH. Tel: (937) 866-4001, (800) 999-9818, FAX: (937) 866-4101, E-Mail: info@colorq.com, Web Site: www.colorqinc.com (27)

Colorama LLC, Sarasota, FL. Tel: (941) 378-5700, FAX: (941) 371-1844 (35)

Colorlith Corp, Providence, RI. Tel: (508) 837-6100, (800) 556-7171, FAX: (508) 677-4466, E-Mail: lep@colorlith.net, Web Site: www.colorlith.net (27)

ColorTree of Virginia Inc, Richmond, VA. Web Site: www.colortree.com (26)

Colorworks Graphics Inc, Chicago, IL. Tel: (312) 666-7642, FAX: (312) 666-0473, E-Mail: colorworks@ ameritech.net, Web Site: www.colorworksgraphics. com (34)

Colton, Bob, Steppin' Out & See America, Las Vegas, NV. Tel: (702) 798-6522, E-Mail: sales@see-america.net, Web Site: steppinoutseeamerica.com (19)

Colturi, Tom, Lucky Heart Cosmetics Inc, Memphis, TN. Tel: (901) 526-7658, (800) 283-1014, FAX: (901) 526-7660, Web Site: www.luckyheart.com (7)

Colucci, Steve, Interact Multimedia Corp, South Bend, IN. Tel: (574) 232-3400, FAX: (219) 255-6091, E-Mail: johnd@interactmultimedia.com (35)

Columbia Books, Inc, Bethesda, MD. Tel: (202) 464-1662, (888) 265-0600, FAX: (202) 464-1775, E-Mail: info@columbiabooks.com, Web Site: www.columbiabooks.com (24)

Columbia College Chicago, Chicago, IL. Tel: (312) 663-1600, FAX: (312) 344-0869, Web Site: www. colum.edu (41)

Columbia Direct Marketing Corp, Annapolis, MD. Tel: (410) 268-8881, FAX: (410) 268-8999 (35)

Columbia House, New York, NY. Tel: (212) 596-2000, Web Site: www.columbiahouse.com (24)

Columbia Journalism Review, New York, NY. Tel: (212) 854-2718, (888) 625-7782, FAX: (212) 854-8367, Web Site: www.cjr.org (17)

Columbia-Presbyterian Medical Center, New York, NY. Tel: (212) 305-2500, FAX: (212) 305-8023, Web Site: www.nyp.org (16)

Columbia Sportswear, Portland, OR. Tel: (503) 985-4203, Web Site: www.columbia.com (2)

Columbia Tristar Home Video, Culver City, CA. Tel: (310) 244-4000, FAX: (310) 244-1544, Web Site: www.cthe.com (16)

Columbia University, Annual Fund Programs, New York, NY. Tel: (212) 851-7956, Web Site: http:// giving.columbia.edu (5)

The Columbian, Vancouver, WA. Tel: (360) 694-3391, FAX: (360) 735-4503, Web Site: www.columbian. com (17)

Columbian Mutual Life Insurance Co, Binghamton, NY. Tel: (607) 724-2472, (800) 423-9765 (15)

Columbus, Shanna, Price Weber Marketing Communications Inc, Louisville, KY. Tel: (502) 499-9220, FAX: (502) 491-5593, Web Site: www.priceweber.com (35)

The Columbus Dispatch, Columbus, OH. Tel: (614) 461-5000, FAX: (614) 461-7551, E-Mail: csmith@the.dispatch.com, Web Site: www.dispatch.com (17)

Colwell, Wayne, Colwell & Salmon Communications Inc, Cresskill, NJ. Tel: (518) 482-1596, (800) 724-5318, FAX: (518) 482-1998, E-Mail: sales@colwell-salmon.com, Web Site: www.colwell-salmon.com (29)

Colwell & Salmon Communications Inc, Cresskill, NJ. Tel: (518) 482-1596, (800) 724-5318, FAX: (518) 482-1998, E-Mail: sales@colwell-salmon.com, Web Site: www.colwell-salmon.com (29)

Colyer, Mike, Ward's Natural Science, Rochester, NY. Tel: (585) 359-2502, (800) 962-2660, FAX: (585) 334-6174, E-Mail: customer_service@wardsci.com, Web Site: www.wardsci.com (34)

Com-Pak, Berlin, CT. Tel: (856) 802-1900, (856) 802-3097, E-Mail: info@com-pak.com, Web Site: www.marketpointdirect.com (28)

Com-Pak Services Inc, Moorestown, NJ. Tel: (856) 802-1900, Web Site: www.com-pak.com (28)

Comac Inc, Milpitas, CA. Tel: (408) 945-1600, (866) COMAC4U, FAX: (408) 946-1135, E-Mail: info@comac.com, Web Site: www.comac.com (28)

Comancho, Bruce, Assurant Group, New York, NY. Tel: (305) 253-2244, FAX: (305) 252-6987, Web Site: www.assurant.com (15)

Comazzi, Anthony, J., The Newman Group, Ann Arbor, MI. Tel: (734) 426-3200, FAX: (734) 426-0777, E-Mail: anewman@newman.com (3)

Combined Insurance Co of America, Glenview, IL. Tel: (847) 953-8116, (800) 490-1322, FAX: (847) 953-8070, Web Site: www.combinedinsurance.com (15)

Combs, Diane, Donna Salyers' Fabulous-Furs, Covington, KY. Tel: (859) 291-3300, (800) 848-4650, E-Mail: abell@fabulousfurs.com, Web Site: fabulousfurs.com (2)

Combs, Dorothy, Project HOPE, Millwood, VA. Tel: (540) 837-2100, Web Site: www.projecthope.org (1)

Combs, Heidi, NARAL Pro-Choice America, Washington, DC. Tel: (202) 973-3000, Web Site: www.naral.com (1)

Combs, Karen, Daydots, Fort Worth, TX. Tel: (817) 590-4500, (800) 321-3687, FAX: (800) 438-7002, E-Mail: customercare@daydots.com, Web Site: www.daydots.com (16)

Comcast Cable Communications, Philadelphia, PA. Tel: (215) 665-1700, Web Site: www.comcast.com (32)

Comdata Corp, Brentwood, TN. Tel: (615) 370-7000, (800) 266-3282, Web Site: www.comdata.com (14)

Comedy Central, New York, NY. Tel: (212) 767-8600, FAX: (212) 767-4284, Web Site: www.comedycentral.com (32)

Comerica Inc, Dallas, TX. Tel: (800) 521-1190, FAX: (925) 941-1999, Web Site: www.comerica.com (14)

Wm F Comly & Son Inc, Philadelphia, PA. Tel: (215) 634-2500, Web Site: www.comly.com (9)

Command Financial Press, New York, NY. Tel: (212) 274-6070, FAX: (212) 274-8262, E-Mail: csd@commandfinancial.com, Web Site: www.commandfinancial.com (35)

Commemorative Brands Inc, Austin, TX. Tel: (512) 444-0571, FAX: (512) 444-0065 (16)

Commerce Bancshares Inc, Saint Louis, MO. Tel: (800) 453-2265, Web Site: www.commercebank.com (14)

Commerce Register Inc, Midland Park, NJ. Tel: (201) 445-3000, FAX: (201) 445-5806, E-Mail: cri@comreginc.com, Web Site: www.comreginc.com (22)

Commercial Atlas & Marketing Guide, Skokie, IL. Tel: (800) 678-7263, FAX: (800) 934-3479, Web Site: www.randmcnally.com (43)

Commercial Data Processing Inc, Red Bank, NJ. Tel: (800) 242-3731, FAX: (973) 882-0387, E-Mail: vivieng@dataprocess.com, Web Site: www.dataprocess.com (22)

Commercial Envelope Manufacturing Co Inc, Hauppauge, NY. Tel: (631) 242-2500, FAX: (631) 242-6122, Web Site: www.commercial-envelope.com (26)

Commercial Federal Bank, Omaha, NE. Tel: (402) 554-9200, FAX: (402) 514-5304 (14)

Commercial Lithographing Co Inc, Kansas City, MO. Tel: (816) 241-2218, FAX: (816) 241-6091, E-Mail: sjohnson@commercial-lithographing.com, Web Site: www.clitho.com (31)

Commercial Mailing Lists, Framingham, MA. Tel: (508) 879-2647, (800) 875-8345, FAX: (508) 879-2911, E-Mail: bruce@commercialmailinglists.com, Web Site: www.commercialmailinglists.com (23)

Commercial Travelers Mutual Insurance Co, Utica, NY. Tel: (315) 797-5200, (800) 422-6200, FAX: (315) 797-3198, E-Mail: comtravl@commercialtravelers.com, Web Site: www.commercialtravelers.com (15)

CommercialWare Inc, Westboro, MA. Tel: (508) 655-7500, FAX: (508) 647-9495, E-Mail: info@micros-retail.com, Web Site: www.commercialware.com (22)

Commerford, Don, Consolidated Printing & Sty Co, Salina, KS. Tel: (785) 823-6356, FAX: (785) 823-9187 (35)

CommissionSoup, Madison, SD. Tel: (605) 256-9103, (866) 309-7687, FAX: (605) 256-1522, E-Mail: info@creditsoup.com, Web Site: www.commissionsoup.com (23)

Commisso, Rocco, B., Mediacom Communications Corp, Middletown, NY. Tel: (845) 695-2600, FAX: (845) 695-2699, Web Site: www.mediacomcc.com (32)

Commonwealth Business Media Inc, Newark, NJ. Tel: (609) 371-7700, (800) 221-5488, FAX: (609) 371-7879, Web Site: www.cbizmedia.com (17)

Commonwealth Lists, Fairfax, VA. Tel: (703) 273-3231, FAX: (703) 279-5970, E-Mail: info@commonwealthlists.com, Web Site: www.commonwealthlists.com (21)

Communication Concepts Inc, Ivyland, PA. Tel: (215) 672-6900, FAX: (215) 957-4362, E-Mail: info@ccgroupnet.com, Web Site: www.ccgroupnet.com (21)

Communication Creativity, Buena Vista, CO. Tel: (720) 344-4388, (800) 331-8355, FAX: (866) 685-0307, E-Mail: steve@steveheimberg.com, Web Site: www.communicationcreativity.com (17)

Communication Industries Corp, Grafton, VT. Tel: (802) 869-6500, FAX: (802) 869-6565, E-Mail: info@cicmail.com, Web Site: www.careersatcic.com (10)

Communication Logistics, Inc, Plover, WI. Tel: (715) 341-6180, FAX: (715) 341-7971, Web Site: www.comloginc.com (22)

Communication Managers, LLC, Brookfield, CT. Tel: (203) 775-4213, FAX: (203) 775-6413, E-Mail: etalian@communicationmanagers.com, Web Site: www.communicationmanagers.com (20)

Communication Resources Inc, Canton, OH. Tel: (800) 992-2144, FAX: (330) 493-3158, E-Mail: service@comresources.com, Web Site: www.comresources.com (18)

Communication Solutions LLC, Springfield, MO. Tel: (417) 862-4567, Web Site: www.comsolllc.com (29)

Communications Corp of America, Boston, VA. Tel: (540) 547-1700, FAX: (540) 547-4600, E-Mail: contact@cca.net, Web Site: www.cca.net (21)

Communications Plus, New York, NY. Tel: (212) 686-9570, FAX: (212) 686-9687, E-Mail: jrandolph@getcp.com, Web Site: www.boddenpartners.com (35)

Communications Real Laforte Inc, Montreal, PQ Canada. Tel: (514) 335-1523, (800) 836-7766, FAX: (514) 335-5981 (23)

Communications Solutions Expo, Norwalk, CT. Tel: (203) 852-6800, (877) 243-6002, FAX: (203) 853-2845, E-Mail: info@tmcnet.com, Web Site: www.tmcnet.com (42)

Communications Unlimited Inc, Richmond, VA. Tel: (804) 754-7242, E-Mail: communicationsunlimited@verizon.net (20)

Communicor, Milwaukee, WI. Tel: (414) 961-5999, FAX: (414) 961-5990, Web Site: www.communicor.com (36)

Communifx, Cranberry, PA. Tel: (724) 935-8655, Web Site: www.communifax.com (27)

The Communique Group, Parker, CO. Tel: (617) 527-2230, FAX: (617) 965-6763 (35)

Communispond Inc, East Hampton, NY. Tel: (212) 486-2300, (800) 529-5925, FAX: (212) 486-2680 (20)

Community Coffee Co, Baton Rouge, LA. Tel: (225) 291-3900, (800) 525-5583, FAX: (800) 643-8199, E-Mail: ccc@communitycoffee.com, Web Site: www.communitycoffee.com (4)

Community Direct, Mountainside, NJ. Tel: (212) 996-8222, FAX: (908) 789-2995, E-Mail: slipton@gocommunitydirect.com (35)

Community Food Bank, Tucson, AZ. Tel: (520) 622-0525, Web Site: www.communityfoodbank.org (1)

Community Newspaper Co, Needham, MA. Tel: (781) 433-6700, FAX: (781) 433-6701, E-Mail: customerservice@cnc.com, Web Site: www.nvo.com/communitynews (21)

Community Newspapers Co, Concord, MA. Tel: (978) 371-5200, FAX: (978) 371-5214, Web Site: home.wickedlocal.com (17)

COMNET Washington, Framingham, MA. Tel: (508) 879-6700, FAX: (508) 370-4325, Web Site: www.comnetexpo.com (42)

Comp USA, Inc, Miami, FL. Tel: (972) 982-4000, (800) COMP-USA, FAX: (972) 982-4030, Web Site: www.compusa.com (3)

Compact Information Systems Inc, Redmond, WA. Tel: (425) 869-1379, Web Site: www.cisdirect.com (22)

Companion Plants, Athens, OH. Tel: (740) 592-4643, FAX: (740) 593-3092, E-Mail: complants@frognet.net, Web Site: www.companionplants.com (8)

Company C, New York, NY. Tel: (212) 561-6009, FAX: (212) 260-3710, E-Mail: nnocca@companycmarketing.com, Web Site: www.companycmarketing.com (35)

The Company Store Inc, La Crosse, WI. Tel: (608) 785-1400, FAX: (608) 791-5790, Web Site: www.thecompanystore.com (16)

Compaq Computer Corp, Houston, TX. Tel: (281) 370-0670, FAX: (281) 927-8835, Web Site: www.compaq.com (16)

Compass Bank, Birmingham, AL. Tel: (205) 933-4848, (800) 239-4357, FAX: (205) 933-3702, Web Site: www.compassbank.com (14)

Compass Communications Inc, Excelsior, MN. Tel: (952) 470-2017, Web Site: www.compasscommunications.com (35)

Compass Electronics, Forest Grove, OR. Tel: (503) 357-2111, FAX: (503) 357-2111 (9)

Compass Marketing Solutions, Lincoln, NE. Tel: (402) 438-3222, Web Site: www.cmsdm.com (23)

Compass Media, Gulf Shores, AL. Tel: (251) 968-4600, Web Site: www.compassmedia.com (30)

Compassion International, Colorado Springs, CO. Tel: (800) 336-7676, Web Site: www.compassion.com (1)

CompetiScan, Chicago, IL. Tel: (312) 488-1814, Web Site: www.competiscan.com (30)

Comphealth, Salt Lake City, UT. Tel: (801) 930-3000, (800) 453-3030, FAX: (801) 930-4517, E-Mail: info@comphealth.com, Web Site: www.comphealth.com (16)

COMPITSS INC, Newbury Park, CA. Tel: (805) 823-2286, Web Site: www.compitss.com (22)

Complete Mailing Lists LLC, Bronxville, NY. Tel: (914) 771-6640, (866) 314-5478, FAX: (914) 771-6645, E-Mail: ewoolf@cml-llc.com, Web Site: www.cml-llc.com (23)

Complete Mailing Service, Toronto, ON Canada. Tel: (416) 755-7761, (888) 683-2501, FAX: (416) 755-8231, E-Mail: sales@completemailing.com, Web Site: www.completemailing.com (22)

Complete Mailing Service Inc, Santa Cruz, CA. Tel: (831) 425-5556, FAX: (831) 425-0306, Web Site: www.completemail.com (28)

Complete Mailing Solutions, Loveland, CO. Tel: (303) 761-0681, (888) 843-9937, FAX: (303) 761-7837, Web Site: www.comp-mail.com (22)

Comppon, Bob, AGORA Inc, Baltimore, MD. Tel: (410) 783-8499, FAX: (410) 783-8414, E-Mail: csteam@agorapublishinggroup.com, Web Site: www.agora-inc.com (17)

The CompTEL Annual Convention & Trade Exposition, Washington, DC. Tel: (202) 296-6650, FAX: (202) 296-7585, Web Site: www.comptel.org (42)

Compton, Carol, Country Dance and Song Society, Haydenville, MA. Tel: (413) 268-7426, FAX: (413) 268-7471, E-Mail: office@cdss.org, Web Site: www.cdss.org (1)

Compton, Jill, Protocol Services Acquisitions Corp, Sarasota, FL. Tel: (941) 906-9000, Web Site: www.protocolusa.com (20)

Compton, Kathryn, C., Mother Earth News Magazine, Topeka, KS. Tel: (785) 274-4300, (800) 678-5779, FAX: (785) 274-4305, E-Mail: bwelch@ogdenpubs.com, Web Site: www.cappers.com (17)

Compton, Larry, American Modern Insurance Group, Amelia, OH. Tel: (513) 943-7200, (800) 759-9008, FAX: (513) 947-4779, (800) 217-5150, E-Mail: customer_care@amig.com, Web Site: www.amig.com (15)

Compton, Rebecca, Access Development, Salt Lake City, UT. Tel: (801) 656-1529 (35)

Compton, Ronnie, D., AAFES, Dallas, TX. Tel: (214) 312-6700, (800) 527-6790, FAX: (214) 312-3000, Web Site: www.aafes.com (5)

Compu-Mail, Niagara Falls, NY. Tel: (716) 297-0553, (800) 255-0670, FAX: (716) 297-0822, Web Site: www.compu-mail.com (3)

Compuletter Inc, Niles, IL. Tel: (847) 647-6200, FAX: (847) 647-2309, E-Mail: directmail@compuletter.com, Web Site: www.compuletter.com (28)

Compustar, Mineola, NY. Tel: (516) 747-2510, FAX: (516) 747-4349, E-Mail: compustar@hotmail.com, Web Site: www.compustar-usa.com (3)

Computer Business Services Inc, Americus, GA. Tel: (229) 924-4408, (866) 924-4408, FAX: (229) 924-3644, E-Mail: cdill@combusser.com, Web Site: www.combusser.com (3)

Computer Dynamics Inc, Greenville, SC. Tel: (864) 627-8800, FAX: (864) 675-0106, E-Mail: CDIsales@gefanuc.com, Web Site: www.cdynamics.com (3)

Computer Shopper, New York, NY. Tel: (646) 472-4000, FAX: (646) 472-3912, E-Mail: feedback@computershopper.com, Web Site: www.computershopper.com (31)

Computer Solutions Inc, Miami, FL. Tel: (305) 558-7000, FAX: (305) 557-0003, E-Mail: mail@csiflorida.com, Web Site: www.csiflorida.com (22)

Computer Station Corp, Houston, TX. Tel: (713) 777-6860, FAX: (713) 777-3431, E-Mail: csc@computerstationcorp.com, Web Site: www.computerstationcorp.com (3)

The Computer Studio, Yonkers, NY. Tel: (914) 968-1212, FAX: (914) 968-1228, E-Mail: sales@webbusconnect.com, Web Site: www.webbusconnect.com (35)

Computerized Research & Development Inc, Granite Bay, CA. Tel: (916) 652-0497, Web Site: www.computerizedresearch.com (23)

Computermail South, Saint Petersburg, FL. Tel: (727) 579-1000, (800) 551-5478, FAX: (727) 823-5474, E-Mail: sales@computermailsouth.com, Web Site: computermailsouth.com (23)

Computers for Education, Murfreesboro, TN. Tel: (615) 896-3800, FAX: (615) 895-9041 (1)

Computerworld DataBase Div, Framingham, MA. Tel: (508) 879-0700, (800) 343-6474, FAX: (508) 875-4394, Web Site: www.computerworld.com (22)

CompuTrack, Fishers, IN. Tel: (317) 813-2222, FAX: (317) 813-2233, E-Mail: info@dgsmarketingengineers.com, Web Site: www.dgsmarketingengineers.com (35)

Comsearch, Ashburn, VA. Tel: (703) 726-5500, FAX: (703) 726-5600, Web Site: www.comsearch.com (30)

Comyn, Oliver, The Economist Newspaper NA Inc, New York, NY. Tel: (212) 554-0600, FAX: (212) 586-1191, Web Site: www.economist.com (17)

Con-Cor International, Tucson, AZ. Tel: (520) 721-8939, (888) 255-7688, FAX: (520) 721-8940, Web Site: www.con-cor.com (11)

Con-Way Freight, Ann Arbor, MI. Tel: (734) 994-6600 (12)

Con-Way Truckload, Joplin, MO. Tel: (417) 623-5229, (800) CFI-DRIVE, FAX: (417) 623-8939, E-Mail: gnichols@cfi-us.com, Web Site: www.cfi-us.com (12)

Cona, Louis, The New Yorker Magazine, New York, NY. Tel: (212) 286-5400, FAX: (212) 286-5735, E-Mail: alatia_bradley@newyorker.com, Web Site: www.newyorker.com (17)

Conant, Douglas R., Campbell Soup Co, Camden, NJ. Tel: (856) 342-4800, (800) 257-8443, FAX: (856) 342-3878, Web Site: www.campbellsoup.com (16)

Conant, Vic, Nightingale-Conant Corp, Niles, IL. Tel: (847) 647-0300, (800) 557-1660, FAX: (847) 647-7145, Web Site: www.nightingale.com (17)

Concept Communications, Nashua, NH. Tel: (603) 577-9810, Web Site: www.conceptcommusa.com (20)

Concept Communications Co, Bolingbrook, IL. Tel: (630) 829-8450, (800) 323-3524, FAX: (630) 629-8415, E-Mail: info@cstore1.com, Web Site: www.cstore1.com (16)

Concept Media Partners, Yorktown Heights, NY. Tel: (914) 767-0032, FAX: (914) 514-1711, E-Mail: karen@conceptmediapartners.com, Web Site: www.conceptmediapartners.com (35)

Concepts & Strategies Inc, Washington, DC. Tel: (202) 251-9951, FAX: (202) 478-1750, E-Mail: info@constrat.net (35)

Concepts TV Productions Inc, Boonton, NJ. Tel: (973) 331-1500, FAX: (973) 331-1550, E-Mail: collette@conceptstv.com, Web Site: www.conceptstv.com (32)

Concepts Unlimited, Broomfield, CO. Tel: (303) 449-2907, FAX: (303) 449-2967, E-Mail: conceptsunlimited@estreet.com, Web Site: www.conceptsunlimitedinc.com (35)

Concern Worldwide, New York, NY. Tel: (212) 557-8000, Web Site: /www.concernusa.org (1)

Conciatori, Glenn, Lladro USA, Moonachie, NJ. Tel: (201) 807-1177, (800) 634-9088, FAX: (201) 807-1168, E-Mail: customer-services@us.lladro.com, Web Site: www.lladro.com (16)

Concinnity Marketing & Technology Consulting Inc, Winston Salem, NC. Tel: (336) 245-4561, Web Site: www.concinnitymarketing.com (35)

Conclusive Marketing, Charlotte, NC. Tel: (615) 261-7600, (800) 346-0073, FAX: (615) 843-7244, E-Mail: info@conclusivemarketing.com, Web Site: www.conclusivemarketing.com (22)

Concord Litho, Concord, NH. Tel: (603) 225-3328, FAX: (603) 225-6120, E-Mail: print@concordlitho.com, Web Site: www.concordlitho.com (27)

Concorde Communications, Los Angeles, CA. Tel: (310) 854-4411, (800) 800-4411, FAX: (310) 854-0551, Web Site: www.concordecommunications.com (29)

Concordia Publishing House, Saint Louis, MO. Tel: (314) 268-1000, (800) 325-3040, FAX: (314) 268-1329, E-Mail: order@cph.org, Web Site: www.cph.org (17)

Concur, Redmond, WA. Tel: (425) 702-8808, Web Site: www.concur.com (22)

Concurrent Computer Corp, Duluth, GA. Tel: (678) 228-4000, (877) 978-7363, FAX: (954) 977-5580, Web Site: www.ccur.com (3)

Conde Nast, New York, NY. Tel: (212) 286-2860, FAX: (212) 880-8289, Web Site: www.conde.net (17)

Condolink, Omaha, NE. Tel: (402) 592-3525, (800) 877-9600, FAX: (402) 592-4122, E-Mail: info@condolink.com, Web Site: www.condolink.com (16)

Condon Jr., John, John Condon & Associates, Greenwich, CT. Tel: (203) 869-7006, FAX: (203) 622-1488 (20)

John Condon & Associates, Greenwich, CT. Tel: (203) 869-7006, FAX: (203) 622-1488 (20)

Condra, Bob, Porter's Camera Store Inc, Cedar Falls, IA. Tel: (319) 266-0303, (800) 553-2001, FAX: (800) 221-5329, E-Mail: bcondra@porters.com, Web Site: www.porters.com (3)

Condrin III, J. Paul, Liberty Mutual Group, Inc, Boston, MA. Tel: (617) 357-9500, (800) 837-5274, Web Site: www.libertymutual.com (15)

Condron, Christopher, The Dreyfus Corp, New York, NY. Tel: (212) 922-6000, FAX: (212) 922-8165 (14)

Coneys, Brooke, Carl Bloom Associates Inc, White Plains, NY. Tel: (914) 761-2800, FAX: (914) 761-2744, E-Mail: info@carlbloom.com, Web Site: www.carlbloom.com (35)

The Conference Board, Inc, New York, NY. Tel: (212) 759-0900, FAX: (212) 980-7014, Web Site: www.conference-board.org (16)

Conform Pacific, Lomita, CA. Tel: (800) CONFORM, FAX: (310) 496-2880, E-Mail: info@smartblock.com, Web Site: www.smartblock.com (16)

Conformer Expansion Products Inc, Great Neck, NY. Tel: (516) 504-6300, E-Mail: support@conformerinc.com, Web Site: www.conformerinc.com (26)

Conforti, Thomas, G., IHOP Corp, Glendale, CA. Tel: (818) 240-6055, FAX: (818) 553-3131, Web Site: www.ihop.com (16)

Conine, Eric, Roosevelt Paper Co, Mount Laurel, NJ. Tel: (856) 303-4200, (856) 303-4100, (800) 523-3470, FAX: (856) 642-1949, (856) 642-1950, Web Site: www.rooseveltpaper.com (25)

Conklin, Amy, Dorothy Biddle Service, Greeley, PA. Tel: (570) 226-3239, FAX: (570) 226-0349, E-Mail: info@dorothybiddle.com, Web Site: www.dorothybiddle.com (8)

Conklin, Paul, Facts On File Inc, New York, NY. Tel: (212) 967-8800, (800) 322-8755, FAX: (212) 678-3633, Web Site: www.factsonfile.com (17)

Conklin, Paul, Ferguson Publishing Co, New York, NY. Tel: (212) 613-2800, (800) 322-8755, FAX: (800) 678-3633, E-Mail: custserv@factsonfile.com, Web Site: www.fergpubco.com (17)

Conley, Helena, National Seminars Group, Shawnee Mission, KS. Tel: (913) 432-7755, (800) 258-7246, FAX: (913) 432-0824, E-Mail: cstserv@natsem.com, Web Site: www.natsem.com (16)

Conley, Michael, Design Distributors, Inc, Deer Park, NY. Tel: (631) 242-2000, FAX: (631) 242-7367, E-Mail: info@designdistributors.com, Web Site: www.designdistributors.com (21)

Conley, Olga, J Jill Group, Inc, Quincy, MA. Tel: (617) 376-4300, (800) 642-9989, FAX: (617) 769-0177, Web Site: www.jjillgroup.com (2)

Conley, Vicki, Galveston Bay Foundation, Webster, TX. Tel: (281) 332-3381, Web Site: www.galvbay.org (1)

Conlon, E., T., Mountain Craft Shop Co, Proctor, WV. Tel: (304) 455-3570, (877) 365-5869, (800) FOLK-TOY, FAX: (304) 455-1740, (866) FOLK-TOY, E-Mail: info@folktoys.com, Web Site: www.folktoys.com (11)

Conlon, Kathy, Kett Tool Co, Cincinnati, OH. Tel: (513) 271-0333, FAX: (513) 271-5318, E-Mail: info@kett-tool.com, Web Site: www.kett-tool.com (9)

Conlon, Mary, American Movie Classics Holding Corp, Jericho, NY. Tel: (516) 803-3000, FAX: (516) 803-3003, Web Site: www.amctv.com (16)

Conlon, Peggy, The Advertising Council Inc, New York, NY. Tel: (212) 922-1500, FAX: (212) 922-1676, E-Mail: info@adcouncil.org, Web Site: www.adcouncil.org (1)

Conlon, S., A., Mountain Craft Shop Co, Proctor, WV. Tel: (304) 455-3570, (877) 365-5869, (800) FOLK-TOY, FAX: (304) 455-1740, (866) FOLK-TOY, E-Mail: info@folktoys.com, Web Site: www.folktoys.com (11)

Conlon, T.J., DL Blair Inc, Westbury, NY. Tel: (516) 746-3700, FAX: (516) 746-3889, Web Site: www.dlblair.com (35)

Conmio Inc, New York, NY. Tel: (917) 583-2651, Web Site: www.conmio.com (16)

Conn, William, Simpson Electric Co, Lac Du Flambeau, WI. Tel: (715) 588-3311, FAX: (715) 588-3327, E-Mail: cservice@simpsonelectric.com, Web Site: www.simpsonelectric.com (16)

Connecticut Color, Hingham, MA. Tel: (781) 749-1005 (27)

Connecticut Marketing Associates, Wilton, CT. Tel: (203) 761-9556, FAX: (203) 761-9763 (20)

The Connection Contact Center Services, Burnsville, MN. Tel: (952) 948-5335, (800) 883-5777, FAX: (952) 948-5498, E-Mail: sales@the-connection.com, Web Site: www.the-connection.com (29)

The Connection Outsourced Call Ctr, Burnsville, MN. Tel: (800) 883-5777, Web Site: www.the-connection.com (29)

Connel, Kelly, TALX Corp, Dallas, TX. Tel: (972) 755-2100, FAX: (972) 755-2080, E-Mail: consulting@managementinsights.com, Web Site: www.managementinsights.com (20)

Connell, Colleen, GaelSong, Seattle, WA. Tel: (206) 526-8350, Web Site: www.gaelsong.com (6)

Connell Communications Inc, Peterborough, NH. Tel: (603) 924-7271, (800) 677-8847, FAX: (603) 924-7013 (17)

Connelly, Jim, Creative Teaching Press, Huntington Beach, CA. Tel: (714) 895-5047, (800) 287-8879 (17)

Connelly, John, J Edward Connelly Associates, Inc, Pittsburgh, PA. Tel: (412) 920-4100, (800) 245-6532, FAX: (412) 920-4070, Web Site: www.jeca.com (33)

Connelly, Kevin, M, SpencerStuart, Chicago, IL. Tel: (312) 822-0088, FAX: (312) 822-0116, Web Site: www.spencerstuart.com (20)

Connelly, Mike, Golf Digest Co, Wilton, CT. Tel: (203) 761-5100, FAX: (203) 371-2572, Web Site: www.golfdigest.com (17)

Connelly, Stephen, P., S Connelly & Co Inc, Annandale, MN. Tel: (320) 274-7054, E-Mail: sconco@aol.com (39)

Connelly, Wayne, DIA - Nielsen USA Inc, Moorestown, NJ. Tel: (856) 642-9700, (800) 893-6361, FAX: (856) 642-9709, Web Site: www.thomasregister.com (16)

J Edward Connelly Associates, Inc, Pittsburgh, PA. Tel: (412) 920-4100, (800) 245-6532, FAX: (412) 920-4070, Web Site: www.jeca.com (33)

S Connelly & Co Inc, Annandale, MN. Tel: (320) 274-7054, E-Mail: sconco@aol.com (39)

Conner, J., Del, Pennsylvania Firebacks, Lansdale, PA. Tel: (215) 699-0805, (888) 349-30002, FAX: (215) 699-3332, E-Mail: info@fireback.com, Web Site: www.fireback.com (8)

Connerty, Thomas, F., NutriSystem Inc, Fort Washington, PA. Tel: (215) 706-5300, (800) 321-THIN, FAX: (215) 706-5388, Web Site: www.nutrisystem.com (7)

Connex International, Danbury, CT. Tel: (800) 426-6639, FAX: (203) 731-5425, E-Mail: marketing@connexintl.com, Web Site: www.connexintl.com (22)

Conney, Frank, The Toro Consumer Div, Bloomington, MN. Tel: (952) 888-8801, (888) 384-9939, FAX: (952) 887-8258, Web Site: www.thetorocompany.com (16)

Conney Safety Products LLC, Madison, WI. Tel: (608) 271-3300, (800) 356-9100, FAX: (608) 271-3322, (800) 845-9095, E-Mail: safety@conney.com, Web Site: www.conney.com (7)

Connolly, Catherine, CM Connolly, Elk Grove, CA. Tel: (916) 897-8095, Web Site: www.cmconnolly.com (1)

Connolly, Patrick J., Williams-Sonoma Inc, San Francisco, CA. Tel: (415) 421-7900, FAX: (415) 983-9887, Web Site: www.williams-sonomainc.com (8)

Connolly, Richard, ONTIME COMPANIES, Chelsea, MA. Tel: (617) 884-8488, Web Site: www.ontimecompanies.com (28)

CM Connolly, Elk Grove, CA. Tel: (916) 897-8095, Web Site: www.cmconnolly.com (1)

Connor, Kathleen, Concur, Redmond, WA. Tel: (425) 702-8808, Web Site: www.concur.com (22)

Connor, Michael, J., MCA/Universal Studios Inc, Universal City, CA. Tel: (818) 777-1000, FAX: (818) 866-3330, Web Site: www.universalstudios.com (3)

Connor, Scott, Acurian, Horsham, PA. Tel: (215) 323-9000, Web Site: www.acurian.com (7)

Connors, Dan, Catholic Digest, New London, CT. Tel: (800) 321-0411, E-Mail: catholicdigest@bayardinc.com, Web Site: www.catholicdigest.com (17)

Connors, Martha, Technology Review, Cambridge, MA. Tel: (617) 475-8000, FAX: (617) 258-5850, Web Site: www.technologyreview.com (17)

Connors, Paul, F., Paul Connors Creative, Lake Forest, IL. Tel: (847) 295-8746 (39)

Paul Connors Creative, Lake Forest, IL. Tel: (847) 295-8746 (39)

Conor, Audrey, ACTIMAIL INC, New York, NY. Tel: (212) 245-2272, FAX: (212) 245-2523, E-Mail: actimail.usa@actimail.com, Web Site: www.actimail.com (35)

Conrad, Kathi, National Agri Marketing Conference & Exposition, Overland Park, KS. Tel: (913) 491-6500, FAX: (913) 491-6502, E-Mail: agrimktg@nama.org, Web Site: www.nama.org (42)

Conrad Direct Inc, Cresskill, NJ. Tel: (201) 567-3200, FAX: (201) 567-1530, Web Site: www.conraddirect.com (23)

Conroy, Debbie, Spirit Incentives, Fort Lauderdale, FL. Tel: (800) 860-5880, Web Site: www.spirit-incentives.com (35)

Conroy, Jennifer, Canine Companions for Independence, Santa Rosa, CA. Tel: (707) 577-1700, (800) 572-2275, FAX: (707) 577-1711, E-Mail: info@cci.org, Web Site: www.caninecompanions.org (16)

Conseco Inc, Carmel, IN. Tel: (317) 817-6100, FAX: (317) 817-2847, Web Site: www.conseco.com (15)

Conservation International, Arlington, VA. Tel: (202) 912-1285 (1)

Consolidated Electronics Inc, Dayton, OH. Tel: (800) 543-3568, FAX: (937) 252-4066, E-Mail: scoy@ceitron.com, Web Site: www.ceitron.com (3)

Consolidated Mailing Corp, Shawnee Mission, KS. Tel: (913) 262-4400, (800) 706-6245, FAX: (913) 262-7801, E-Mail: cmcmail@swbell.net, Web Site: www.consolidatedmailing.com (28)

Consolidated Market Response, Charleston, IL. Tel: (217) 348-7050, FAX: (217) 348-7060 (29)

Consolidated Plastics Co Inc, Stow, OH. Tel: (330) 425-3900, (800) 362-1000, FAX: (330) 425-3333, Web Site: www.consolidatedplastics.com (9)

Consolidated Printing & Sty Co, Salina, KS. Tel: (785) 823-6356, FAX: (785) 823-9187 (35)

Consolidated Printing Inc, Philadelphia, PA. Tel: (215) 879-1400, (800) 347-0119, FAX: (215) 879-9130, Web Site: www.condrake.com (27)

Consolidated Technologies Group LLC, Cleveland, OH. Tel: (216) 426-5328, Web Site: www.ctgadvisor.com (32)

Constant, Pete, RBS Citizens Financial Group Inc, Dedham, MA. Tel: (781) 471-1565, Web Site: www.citizensbank.com (14)

Constant Contact, Waltham, MA. Tel: (781) 472-8101, Web Site: www.constantcontact.com (32)

Constantino, Tor, Bausch & Lomb Inc, Rochester, NY. Tel: (585) 338-6000, (800) 344-8815, FAX: (585) 338-6007, Web Site: www.bausch.com (16)

Constantyn, Sarah, Blissliving Home, Rockville, MD. Tel: (301) 816-4224, Web Site: www.blisslivinghome.com (8)

Consumer Benefit Services Inc, Naperville, IL. Tel: (630) 420-6200, (800) 657-8309, FAX: (630) 420-2294, E-Mail: dcarlson@consumerbenefit.com, Web Site: www.consumerbenefit.com (16)

Consumer Credit Advocates Inc, Salt Lake City, UT. Tel: (801) 265-9333, FAX: (801) 265-9595 (16)

Consumer Focus, Plano, TX. Tel: (972) 378-9697, E-Mail: sstewart@consumerfocusco.com, Web Site: www.consumerfocusco.com (30)

Consumer Opinion Services Inc, Seattle, WA. Tel: (206) 241-6050, FAX: (206) 241-5213, E-Mail: info@cosvc.com, Web Site: www.cosvc.com (30)

Consumers Digest Inc, Deerfield, IL. Tel: (847) 607-3000, FAX: (847) 763-0200, E-Mail: postmaster@consumersdigest.com, Web Site: www.consumersdigest.com (17)

Consumer's Energy, Jackson, MI. Tel: (517) 788-0550, (800) 805-0490, FAX: (517) 788-1859, E-Mail: businesscenter@consumerenergy.com, Web Site: www.consumersenergy.com (16)

Consumers Union, Yonkers, NY. Tel: (914) 378-2000, FAX: (914) 378-2906, Web Site: www.consumerreports.org (17)

Contact Center Compliance, Santa Rosa, CA. Tel: (800) 308-0258, Web Site: www.dnc.com (22)

Contact Marketing LLC, New York, NY. Tel: (201) 530-0200, (800) 848-7501, FAX: (201) 530-2205, E-Mail: info@cmlists.com, Web Site: www.contactmarketingllc.com (23)

The Container Store, Coppell, TX. Tel: (214) 654-2000, Web Site: www.containerstore.com (8)

Conte, Joseph, M., Goldsmith Agio Helms, Minneapolis, MN. Tel: (612) 339-0500, FAX: (612) 339-0507, Web Site: www.agio.com (14)

Contempo Marketing Co, Pompano Beach, FL. Tel: (954) 978-8215, (800) 322-5089, FAX: (954) 978-8217 (23)

Continental Envelope Corp, Geneva, IL. Tel: (630) 262-8080, (800) 621-8155, FAX: (630) 262-1450, Web Site: www.continentalenvelope.com (26)

Continental Plastic Card Co, Pompano Beach, FL. Tel: (954) 794-0040, (800) 543-0670, FAX: (954) 755-4493, E-Mail: info@continentalplasticcard.com, Web Site: www.continentalplasticcard.com (27)

Continental Supply Inc, Cleveland, OH. Tel: (440) 864-6231, (800) 672-0321, FAX: (888) 672-9808 (9)

Continental Web Press Inc, Itasca, IL. Tel: (630) 773-1903, FAX: (630) 773-1909, Web Site: www.continentalweb.com (27)

Continental Western Group, Des Moines, IA. Tel: (515) 473-3000, (800) 533-0303, FAX: (515) 473-3015, Web Site: www.cwgins.com (15)

Continuing Education of the Bar (CEB), Oakland, CA. Tel: (510) 302-2000, (800) 232-3444, FAX: (510) 302-2001, Web Site: www.ceb.com (1)

Continuity Shippers Association, Woodstock, VT. Tel: (802) 672-3634 (20)

Continuum Global, San Francisco, CA. Tel: (415) 685-3301, Web Site: www.continuumglobal.com (30)

Contrino, Kathleen, The Contrino Group, Lafayette, CO. Tel: (303) 664-1290, Web Site: www.thecontrinogroup.com (20)

The Contrino Group, Lafayette, CO. Tel: (303) 664-1290, Web Site: www.thecontrinogroup.com (20)

ConvergeDirect, New York, NY. Tel: (212) 213-0111, Web Site: www.convergedirect.com (1)

Convergys Corp, Ogden, UT. Tel: (630) 668-6174, Web Site: www.convergys.com (29)

Conversa Marketing LLC, Garden City, NY. Tel: (516) 209-3822 (32)

Conversational Voice Technologies Corp, Fox Lake, IL. Tel: (847) 265-4901, (800) 994-4400, FAX: (847) 265-4915, E-Mail: sales@conservit.com, Web Site: www.conservit.com (29)

Conversen, Burlington, MA. Tel: (781) 425-1110, Web Site: www.conversen.com (35)

ConversionVoodoo.com, San Diego, CA. Tel: (858) 625-4203, Web Site: www.conversionvoodoo.com (16)

Convertible Service, San Gabriel, CA. Tel: (626) 285-2255, (800) 333-1140, FAX: (626) 285-9004, Web Site: www.convertibleparts.com (16)

Convio Inc, Austin, TX. Tel: (888) 528-9501, Web Site: www.convio.com (22)

Conway, Allen, Quality Park Products, Minneapolis, MN. Tel: (651) 645-0251, (800) 547-4252, (800) 328-2990, FAX: (800) 637-5770, (800) 701-3291, E-Mail: mktg@qualitypark.com, Web Site: www.qualitypark.com (26)

Conway, Anthony, W., Alliance of Nonprofit Mailers, Washington, DC. Tel: (202) 462-5132, FAX: (202) 462-0423, E-Mail: alliance@nonprofitmailers.org, Web Site: www.nonprofitmailers.org (40)

Conway, Arthur, DialAmerica Marketing Inc, Mahwah, NJ. Tel: (201) 327-0200, (800) 531-3131, FAX: (201) 327-4875, Web Site: www.dialamerica.com (29)

Conway, David, Eadon Ventures, Alliance, OH. Tel: (330) 418-4298 (20)

Conway, Frank, Home Loan Investment Bank, Warwick, RI. Tel: (800) 223-1700 X278, E-Mail: contactus@homeloanbank.com, Web Site: www.homeloanbank.com (14)

Conway, James, Con-Cor International, Tucson, AZ. Tel: (520) 721-8939, (888) 255-7688, FAX: (520) 721-8940, Web Site: www.con-cor.com (11)

Conway, Mike, Dow Corning Corp, Midland, MI. Tel: (989) 496-4000, (800) 248-2481, FAX: (989) 496-4572, Web Site: www.dowcorning.com (16)

Conway, William, S., Mutual of America Life Insurance Co, New York, NY. Tel: (212) 224-1600, (800) 468-3785, FAX: (212) 224-2539, Web Site: www.mutualofamerica.com (14)

Coogan, Jennie, JC Lists Co, Washington, DC. Tel: (202) 364-2705, FAX: (202) 364-2450, E-Mail: jcoogan@JClists.com (23)

Cook, Bill, Timm Medical Technologies, Inc, Eden Prairie, MN. Tel: (952) 947-9410, (800) 438-8592, FAX: (952) 947-9411, Web Site: www.timmmedical.com (16)

Cook, David T., The Christian Science Publishing Society, Boston, MA. Tel: (617) 450-2000, E-Mail: info@christianscience.com, Web Site: www.tfccs.com (17)

Cook, Gene, Mitsubishi Motor Sales of America Inc, Cypress, CA. Tel: (714) 372-6000, FAX: (714) 373-1736, Web Site: www.mitsubishicars.com (1)

Cook, Gerald, A., Hot Topic Inc, City of Industry, CA. Tel: (626) 839-4681, (800) 275-9169, FAX: (626) 839-4686, Web Site: www.hottopic.com (2)

Cook, Iam M., Colgate-Palmolive Co, New York, NY. Tel: (212) 310-2000, (800) 468-6502, FAX: (212) 310-2475, Web Site: www.colgate.com (16)

Cook, Larry, TABS Direct, Irving, TX. Tel: (281) 499-0417, (800) 231-0697, FAX: (281) 208-6081, E-Mail: tabsdirect@tabsdirect.com, Web Site: www.tabsdirect.com (21)

Cook, Linda, Warner Books, New York, NY. Tel: (212) 364-1200, FAX: (212) 522-7989, Web Site: www.twbookmark.com (17)

Cook, Peter, Concord Litho, Concord, NH. Tel: (603) 225-3328, FAX: (603) 225-6120, E-Mail: print@concordlitho.com, Web Site: www.concordlitho.com (27)

Cook, Richard, Disney Vacation Club, Kissimmee, FL. Tel: (407) 566-3100, (800) 500-3990, FAX: (407) 566-3393 (19)

Cook, Scott, Intuit, Mountain View, CA. Tel: (650) 944-6000, Web Site: www.inuit.com (10)

Cook, Tracy, InterfaceFlor LLC, La Grange, GA. Tel: (706) 882-1891, (800) 336-0225, FAX: (706) 882-0500, Web Site: www.interfaceflor.com (16)

Cook, Victoria, Playworld Systems, Lewisburg, PA. Tel: (570) 522-9800, Web Site: www.playworldsystems.com (34)

David C Cook, Colorado Springs, CO. Tel: (719) 536-0100, (800) 323-7543, FAX: (719) 536-3232, Web Site: www.davidccook.com (17)

T A Cook Consultants Inc, Raleigh, NC. Tel: (919) 510-8142, Web Site: www.tacook.com (20)

Cookbook Publishers Inc, Lenexa, KS. Tel: (913) 492-5900, (800) 227-7282, FAX: (913) 492-5947, E-Mail: info@cookbookpublishers.com, Web Site: www.cookbookpublishers.com (17)

Cooke, Allison, Atlantic Publication Group LLC, Charleston, SC. Tel: (843) 747-0025, FAX: (843) 744-0816, E-Mail: info@atlanticpublicationgrp.com, Web Site: www.atlanticpublicationgrp.com (17)

Cooke, Brent, Payless ShoeSource Inc, Topeka, KS. Tel: (785) 233-5171, Web Site: www.payless.com (2)

Cooke, Eugenia, Tuttle Printing & Engraving, Rutland, VT. Tel: (802) 773-9171, (800) 776-7682, FAX: (802) 773-5785, E-Mail: info@tuttleprinting.com, Web Site: www.tuttleprinting.com (10)

Cooke, Lauren, J Jill Group, Inc, Quincy, MA. Tel: (617) 376-4300, (800) 642-9989, FAX: (617) 769-0177, Web Site: www.jjillgroup.com (2)

Cooke, Mike, National Stationery Show, White Plains, NY. Tel: (914) 421-3200, (800) 272-SHOW, FAX: (914) 948-6180, E-Mail: cate_doyle@glmshows.com, Web Site: www.glmshows.com (42)

Cooke, Mike, New York International Gift Fair, White Plains, NY. Tel: (914) 421-3200, (800) 272-SHOW, FAX: (914) 948-6180, Web Site: www.nyigf.com (42)

Cooke, Win, Alco Chemical, Chattanooga, TN. Tel: (423) 629-1405, FAX: (423) 698-8723, Web Site: www.alcochemical.com (16)

Cooley, Bob, The FX Matt Brewing Co, Utica, NY. Tel: (315) 732-0022, (800) 765-6288, FAX: (315) 624-2401, E-Mail: info@saranac.com, Web Site: www.saranac.com (4)

Cooley, Scott, Morningstar Inc, Chicago, IL. Tel: (312) 696-6000, Web Site: www.morningstar.com (14)

Coombe, Jennifer, Majestic Products Co, Mississauga, ON. Tel: (905) 858-8010, (800) 668-5323, FAX: (905) 670-7915, Web Site: www.cfmcorp.com (16)

Cooney, Ted, brandedmerchandise.ca, Peterborough, ON Canada. Tel: (705) 944-5632, (800) 461-1788, FAX: (705) 944-7500, E-Mail: info@brandedmerchandise.ca, Web Site: www.brandedmerchandise.ca (35)

Cooper Jr., John, Cooper Communities Inc, Rogers, AR. Tel: (479) 246-6500, (800) 648-6401, FAX: (479) 855-6256, E-Mail: coopernet@ccias.com, Web Site: www.cooper-communities.com (16)

Cooper, Bob, PTI Pyramid Technologies LLC, Meriden, CT. Tel: (203) 238-0550, (888) 479-7264, FAX: (203) 634-1696, Web Site: www.pyramid-technologies.com (10)

Cooper, Bud, Fundamentals Co Inc, Bristol, VA. Tel: (800) 303-8861 (Fax), (800) 303-8861 (1)

Cooper, Caitlin, Williams Worldwide Television, Santa Monica, CA. Tel: (310) 449-4506, FAX: (310) 449-4556, E-Mail: curious@williamsworldwidetv.com, Web Site: www.williamsworldwidetv.com (35)

Cooper, Carol, D., Martindale-Hubbell, New Providence, NJ. Tel: (908) 464-6800, (800) 526-4902, FAX: (908) 771-7740 (17)

Cooper, Daniel W., Cooper Communities Inc, Rogers, AR. Tel: (479) 246-6500, (800) 648-6401, FAX: (479) 855-6256, E-Mail: coopernet@ccias.com, Web Site: www.cooper-communities.com (16)

Cooper, George, L., On-Hand Adhesives Inc, Lake Zurich, IL. Tel: (847) 437-7773, (800) 323-5158, FAX: (847) 437-8006, E-Mail: help@on-hand.com, Web Site: www.on-hand.com (16)

Cooper, Harold, TheCooperGroup, New York, NY. Tel: (212) 696-2512, Web Site: www.thecoopergroup.com (35)

Cooper, Harry, Collegesource Inc, San Diego, CA. Tel: (858) 560-8051, (800) 854-2670, FAX: (858) 278-8960, Web Site: www.collegesource.org (17)

Cooper, Joel, List Strategies Inc, New York, NY. Tel: (212) 767-1000, FAX: (212) 541-4408, E-Mail: joel@liststrategies.com, Web Site: www.liststrategies.com (23)

Cooper, Jonathan, Spectronics Corp, Westbury, NY. Tel: (800) 274-8888, FAX: (800) 491-6868, E-Mail: vscherer@spectroline.com, Web Site: www.spectroline.com (9)

Cooper, Karen, Betterway Books, Blue Ash, OH. Tel: (513) 531-2222, (800) 289-0963, FAX: (513) 531-4744, Web Site: www.fwpublications.com/books.asp (17)

Cooper, Karen, Cherry Tree Toys Inc, Beloit, WI. Tel: (608) 314-3090, (800) 848-4363, FAX: (608) 314-3097, E-Mail: sales@cherrytreetoys.com, Web Site: www.cherrytreetoys.com (11)

Cooper, Kerry, Collegesource Inc, San Diego, CA. Tel: (858) 560-8051, (800) 854-2670, FAX: (858) 278-8960, Web Site: www.collegesource.org (17)

Cooper, Leon, Home Safeguard Industries, Malibu, CA. Tel: (310) 457-5813, FAX: (310) 457-4862, E-Mail: expert@homesafeguard.com, Web Site: www.homesafeguard.com (16)

Cooper, Lisa, Ebbets Field Flannels Inc, Seattle, WA. Tel: (206) 382-7249, FAX: (206) 382-4411, E-Mail: clubhouse@ebbets.com, Web Site: www.ebbets.com (2)

Cooper, Louis, Calling Solutions, San Antonio, TX. Tel: (210) 822-7400, (800) 683-5500, FAX: (210) 491-1777, E-Mail: pepe@callingsolutions.com, Web Site: www.callingsolutions.com (29)

Cooper, Maggie, AlphaGraphics World Headquarters, Salt Lake City, UT. Tel: (801) 595-7270, (800) 955-6246, FAX: (801) 595-7271, E-Mail: contactus@alphagraphics.com, Web Site: www.alphagraphics.com (27)

Cooper, Margaret, On-Hand Adhesives Inc, Lake Zurich, IL. Tel: (847) 437-7773, (800) 323-5158, FAX: (847) 437-8006, E-Mail: help@on-hand.com, Web Site: www.on-hand.com (16)

Cooper, Michael, On-Hand Adhesives Inc, Lake Zurich, IL. Tel: (847) 437-7773, (800) 323-5158, FAX: (847) 437-8006, E-Mail: help@on-hand.com, Web Site: www.on-hand.com (16)

Cooper, Tom, Cooper & Cooper Direct Marketing, Northfield, IL. Tel: (847) 446-1123, FAX: (847) 446-1564, E-Mail: coopsdm@earthlink.net (35)

Cooper, Wayne, Specialized Information Publishers Association (SIPA), Vienna, VA. Tel: (703) 992-9339, (800) 356-9302, FAX: (703) 610-9005, E-Mail: info@sipaonline.org, Web Site: www.sipaonline.org (1)

Cooper & Cooper Direct Marketing, Northfield, IL. Tel: (847) 446-1123, FAX: (847) 446-1564, E-Mail: coopsdm@earthlink.net (35)

Cooper-Atkins Corp, Middlefield, CT. Tel: (860) 347-2256, (800) 835-5011, FAX: (860) 347-5135, Web Site: www.cooper-atkins.com (34)

Cooper Communities Inc, Rogers, AR. Tel: (479) 246-6500, (800) 648-6401, FAX: (479) 855-6256, E-Mail: coopernet@ccias.com, Web Site: www.cooper-communities.com (16)

Cooper Surgical Inc, Trumbull, CT. Tel: (203) 601-5200, (800) 645-3670, FAX: (203) 601-1007, Web Site: www.coopersurgical.com (7)

Cooper Tire & Rubber Co Inc, Findlay, OH. Tel: (419) 423-1321, (800) 854-6288, FAX: (419) 424-4212, Web Site: www.coopertire.com (16)

Cooper Vision, Fairport, NY. Tel: (585) 385-6810, (800) 341-2020, Web Site: www.coopervision.com (7)

Cooper Wight Associates Inc, Francestown, NH. Tel: (603) 547-2144 (35)

TheCooperGroup, New York, NY. Tel: (212) 696-2512, Web Site: www.thecoopergroup.com (35)

Cooperman, Allen, B., Transemantics Inc, Washington, DC. Tel: (202) 362-2505, FAX: (202) 686-5603, E-Mail: ili@transemantics.com, Web Site: www.transemantics.com (16)

Coors, Peter, H., Molson Coors Brewing Co, Denver, CO. Tel: (303) 279-6565, (800) 642-6116, FAX: (303) 277-5415, Web Site: www.molsoncoors.com (16)

Copeland, Chris, Outrider North America, Saint Louis, MO. Tel: (314) 209-1005, FAX: (314) 209-1126, Web Site: www.outrider.com (30)

Copeland, James, Center for Book Arts, New York, NY. Tel: (212) 481-0295, FAX: (866) 708-8994, E-Mail: info@centerforbookarts.org, Web Site: www.centerforbookarts.org (27)

Copeland, Lisa, Great North American Cos Inc, Dallas, TX. Tel: (972) 481-6100, (800) 527-2782, FAX: (972) 243-1637, Web Site: www.gnamerican.com (16)

Copilevitz, Errol, Copilevitz & Canter, LLC, Kansas City, MO. Tel: (816) 472-9000, FAX: (816) 472-5000, Web Site: www.copilevitz-canter.com (14)

Copilevitz & Canter, LLC, Kansas City, MO. Tel: (816) 472-9000, FAX: (816) 472-5000, Web Site: www.copilevitz-canter.com (14)

Coppa, Carol, Coppa Woodworking, Inc, San Pedro, CA. Tel: (310) 548-4142, FAX: (310) 548-6740, E-Mail: ciro@earthlink.net, Web Site: www.coppawoodworking.com (8)

Coppa, Ciro, C., Coppa Woodworking, Inc, San Pedro, CA. Tel: (310) 548-4142, FAX: (310) 548-6740, E-Mail: ciro@earthlink.net, Web Site: www.coppawoodworking.com (8)

Coppa Woodworking, Inc, San Pedro, CA. Tel: (310) 548-4142, FAX: (310) 548-6740, E-Mail: ciro@earthlink.net, Web Site: www.coppawoodworking.com (8)

Coppage, Michael, Mostad & Christensen, Oak Harbor, WA. Tel: (360) 679-4164, (800) 654-1654, FAX: (360) 679-4167, E-Mail: marketing@mostad.com, Web Site: www.mostad.com (16)

Copper Art by Morse, Claremont, NH. Tel: (603) 542-2324 (8)

Copperman, Paul, Institute of Reading Development, Novato, CA. Tel: (415) 884-8100, (800) 964-8888, FAX: (415) 382-0760, E-Mail: contactus@readingprograms.org, Web Site: www.readingprograms.org (1)

Josiah R Coppersmythe, Harwich, MA. Tel: (508) 432-8590, (800) 426-8249, FAX: (508) 432-8587, E-Mail: kethompson@jrcoppersmythe.com, Web Site: www.jrcoppersmythe.com (8)

Coptech Inc, Woburn, MA. Tel: (781) 935-2679, (800) 934-1560, FAX: (781) 935-7673, Web Site: www.coptechinc.com (16)

The Copy Pro, Oradell, NJ. Tel: (201) 986-1080, FAX: (201) 986-1170, E-Mail: thecopypro@aol.com, Web Site: www.thecopypronj.com (39)

The Copy Shoppe, Mendham, NJ. Tel: (973) 543-2679, FAX: (973) 543-2679, E-Mail: catalogistics@juno.com, Web Site: www.catalogistics.com (39)

The Copy Works, San Diego, CA. Tel: (858) 676-6757, Web Site: www.thecopyworks.com (20)

CopyDirect, Plymouth, MA. Tel: (508) 732-9900, Web Site: www.belindabrewster.com (20)

Copywriter's Council of America - (Freelancers), Middle Island, NY. Tel: (631) 924-3888, FAX: (631) 924-8555, E-Mail: cca4dmcopy@gmail.com, Web Site: www.linick.net; www.andrewlinickdirectmarketing.com (39)

Corbeille-Lepel, Pamela, Lorton Data Inc, Arden Hills, MN. Tel: (651) 203-8200, FAX: (612) 362-0299, Web Site: www.lortondata.com (22)

Corbet, Jeffrey, A., Florida Power Corp, Saint Petersburg, FL. Tel: (727) 820-5151, (800) 700-8744, FAX: (727) 384-7865, Web Site: www.progressenergy.com (16)

Corbin, Brad, Conseco Inc, Carmel, IN. Tel: (317) 817-6100, FAX: (317) 817-2847, Web Site: www.conseco.com (15)

Corbin, Dr. Stephen, B., Special Olympics International, Washington, DC. Tel: (202) 628-3630, FAX: (202) 824-0200, Web Site: www.specialolympics.org (1)

Corbin, Frank, Gambro Inc, Lakewood, CO. Tel: (303) 232-6800, (800) 525-2623, FAX: (303) 222-6810, Web Site: www.gambro.com (16)

Corbis Images, New York, NY. Tel: (212) 777-6200, FAX: (212) 375-7700, Web Site: www.corbis.com (38)

Corcillo, Jane, Jane Corcillo, Norwalk, CT. Tel: (203) 866-2008, FAX: (203) 299-0844, E-Mail: queries@corcillodirect.com, Web Site: www.corcillodirect.com (39)

Corcorah, John, Star Sprinkler Inc, Lansdale, PA. Tel: (414) 570-5000, (800) 558-5236, FAX: (414) 570-5010, Web Site: www.starsprinkler.com (9)

Corcoran, Allison, Alfa Aesar-A Johnson Matthey Co, Ward Hill, MA. Tel: (800) 343-0660, FAX: (800) 322-4757, E-Mail: info@alfa.com, Web Site: www.alfa.com (9)

Corcoran, Dan, Sales & Marketing Management Magazine, New York, NY. Tel: (800) 821-6897, FAX: (905) 470-8561, E-Mail: joyce.cooney@nielsen.com, Web Site: www.salesandmarketing.com (16)

Corcoran, Peter, N., Deloitte & Touche, Boston, MA. Tel: (617) 437-2000, FAX: (617) 437-2111, Web Site: www.deloitte.com (14)

Cordazzo, Christine, Esto Photographics Inc, Mamaroneck, NY. Tel: (914) 698-4060, FAX: (914) 698-1033, E-Mail: esto@esto.com, Web Site: www.esto.com (38)

Cordeiro, Kathy, Community Newspapers Co, Concord, MA. Tel: (978) 371-5200, FAX: (978) 371-5214, Web Site: home.wickedlocal.com (17)

Cordial, Melissa, Fallon Community Health Plan, Worcester, MA. Tel: (800) 333-2535, Web Site: www.fchp.org (1)

Cordier, Steve, Sensient Technologies, Saint Louis, MO. Tel: (314) 889-7600, (800) 325-8110, FAX: (314) 658-7318, Web Site: www.sensient-tech.com (16)

Cordova, Sally, McKee Consulting LLC, Escondido, CA. Tel: (760) 738-8200, Web Site: www.trainyourcallcenter.com (20)

Core Technologies, Boulder, CO. Tel: (614) 231-3031, (866) 624-5927, FAX: (303) 395-1474, E-Mail: support@core-tech.com, Web Site: www.mailware.com (22)

CoreBrand, New York, NY. Tel: (212) 329-3030, FAX: (212) 329-3031, E-Mail: jgregory@corebrand.com, Web Site: www.corebrand.com (35)

Corelli, Robert, Shop.com, Monterey, CA. Tel: (831) 647-2489, (866) 746-7005, FAX: (831) 644-9283, Web Site: www.shop.com (16)

COREMedia Systems Inc, Fairfield, NJ. Tel: (973) 276-0882, Web Site: www.coremedia-systems.com (22)

CoreMessagink, Lancaster, PA. Tel: (717) 207-0212, Web Site: www.cormessagink.com (39)

Coremetrics, San Mateo, CA. Tel: (877) 721-2673, Web Site: www.coremetrics.com (32)

Corenman, Nellie, Government Data Publications Inc, Washington, DC. Tel: (718) 627-0819, (800) 275-4688, FAX: (718) 998-5960, E-Mail: gdp@govdata.com, Web Site: www.govdata.com (17)

Coretto, Tony, PNT Marketing Services, Inc, Long Island City, NY. Tel: (703) 761-0291, (888) 768-2210, FAX: (914) 428-0504, E-Mail: tony@pntmarketingservices.com, Web Site: www.pntmarketingservices.com (22)

Corey, Michael P., Maine Potato Board, Presque Isle, ME. Tel: (207) 769-5061, FAX: (207) 764-4148, E-Mail: mainepotatoes@mainepotatoes.com, Web Site: www.mainepotatoes.com (1)

Corick, Diane, Huntington Associates, New York, NY. Tel: (212) 582-1870, FAX: (212) 586-3291, E-Mail: huntassoc@aol.com (35)

Corigliano, Mary, truTV, New York, NY. Tel: (212) 973-2800, FAX: (212) 973-3210, Web Site: www.trutv.com (17)

Corinthian Direct, New York, NY. Tel: (212) 279-5700, FAX: (212) 239-1772, E-Mail: jonz@mediabuying.com, Web Site: www.mediabuying.com (35)

Corley, Christina, Zones Inc, Auburn, WA. Tel: (253) 205-3000, (800) 408-9663, FAX: (425) 430-3626, E-Mail: corpsales@zones.com, Web Site: www.zones.com (3)

Cornelieus, James, M., Bristol-Myers Squibb Co, New York, NY. Tel: (212) 546-4000, FAX: (212) 546-9544, Web Site: www.bms.com (16)

Cornell, Helen, W., Champion, Quincy, IL. Tel: (217) 222-5400, FAX: (217) 228-8260, Web Site: www.championpneumatic.com (16)

Cornell Lab of Ornithology, Ithaca, NY. Tel: (607) 254-2157, (800) 843-BIRD, FAX: (607) 254-2415, E-Mail: birdslides@cornell.edu, Web Site: www.birds.cornell.edu (1)

Cornerstone Brands Inc, West Chester, OH. Tel: (513) 603-1400, Web Site: www.cornerstonebrands.com (5)

Cornerstone Business Services Inc, Council Bluffs, IA. Tel: (712) 256-4987, Web Site: www.conerstonelist.com (23)

Cornerstone Group of Companies, Toronto, ON Canada. Tel: (416) 932-9555, FAX: (416) 932-9566, E-Mail: info@cstonecanada.com, Web Site: www.cstonecanada.com (22)

Cornett, Janelle, Coastal Hotel Group, Seattle, WA. Tel: (206) 388-0400, FAX: (206) 388-0401, E-Mail: info@coastalhotel.com, Web Site: www.coastalhotels.com (1)

Cornhusker Press, Hastings, NE. Tel: (402) 462-4141, FAX: (402) 460-4612, E-Mail: dlsales@dutton-lainson.com, Web Site: www.dutton-lainson.com (17)

Cornick, Brian, Faneuil ISG, Winnipeg, MB Canada. Tel: (866) Faneuil, Web Site: www.faneuil.com (30)

Cornick, Jim, Successful Farming, Des Moines, IA. Tel: (515) 284-2143, (800) 678-2711, FAX: (515) 284-3127 (17)

Cornish, Edward, World Future Society, Bethesda, MD. Tel: (301) 656-8274, (800) 989-8274, FAX: (301) 951-0394, E-Mail: info@wfs.org, Web Site: www.wfs.org (1)

Cornish, Jefferson, World Future Society, Bethesda, MD. Tel: (301) 656-8274, (800) 989-8274, FAX: (301) 951-0394, E-Mail: info@wfs.org, Web Site: www.wfs.org (1)

Cornwell, Peter, Cornwell Data Services Inc, Paramus, NJ. Tel: (201) 261-1050, FAX: (201) 261-7569, E-Mail: jpiretra@cornwelldata.com, Web Site: www.cornwelldata.com (22)

Cornwell Data Services Inc, Paramus, NJ. Tel: (201) 261-1050, FAX: (201) 261-7569, E-Mail: jpiretra@cornwelldata.com, Web Site: www.cornwelldata.com (22)

Corona Cigar Co, Orlando, FL. Tel: (407) 248-1212, (888) 702-4427, FAX: (407) 248-1211, E-Mail: info@coronacigar.com, Web Site: www.coronacigar.com (5)

Corona-Lotus Inc, San Francisco, CA. Tel: (415) 956-8956, (800) 422-2924, FAX: (415) 956-4922, E-Mail: customerservice@biscoff.com, Web Site: www.biscoff.com (4)

Coronis, Magdalene P., Coronis Building Systems Inc, Burlington, NJ. Tel: (609) 723-2600, FAX: (609) 723-6700, E-Mail: coronis@trussframe.com, Web Site: www.trussframe.com (9)

Coronis Building Systems Inc, Burlington, NJ. Tel: (609) 723-2600, FAX: (609) 723-6700, E-Mail: coronis@trussframe.com, Web Site: www.trussframe.com (9)

Coronis Jr, Emanuel A., Coronis Building Systems Inc, Burlington, NJ. Tel: (609) 723-2600, FAX: (609) 723-6700, E-Mail: coronis@trussframe.com, Web Site: www.trussframe.com (9)

Corpora, Placido, Corpora Consulting, Bethlehem, PA. Tel: (215) 313-9229 (20)

Corpora Consulting, Bethlehem, PA. Tel: (215) 313-9229 (20)

The Corporate Communications Group, West Caldwell, NJ. Tel: (973) 386-1444, FAX: (973) 808-9740, E-Mail: useccg@corpcomm.com, Web Site: www.corpcomm.com (21)

Corporate Express, Broomfield, CO. Tel: (303) 664-2000, (888) 238-6329, Web Site: www.cexp.com (22)

Corporate Graphics Direct Marketing Solutions, Arden Hills, MN. Tel: (651) 494-1740, Web Site: www.cgids.com (22)

Corporate Incentive Solutions, Boston, MA. Tel: (301) 340-1600, (877) 244-4505, FAX: (301) 251-5887 (33)

Corporate Media Services Inc, Bloomington, MN. Tel: (952) 881-8081, E-Mail: info@corporatemediaservices.com, Web Site: corporatemediaservices.com (35)

Corporate Promotions, Nashville, TN. Tel: (615) 242-0501, FAX: (615) 256-0862, Web Site: www.promoville.com (35)

CorporateRewards.com LLC, New York, NY. Tel: (212) 689-1200, Web Site: www.corporaterewards.com (35)

Corpus, Warren, Vayan Marketing Group LLC, Boynton Beach, FL. Tel: (561) 955-9660, Web Site: www.vayan.com (23)

Corpus Christi Museum of Science & History, Corpus Christi, TX. Tel: (361) 826-4667, FAX: (361) 884-7392, Web Site: www.ccmuseum.com (1)

Corr, William, CSPI/Nutrition Action Health Letter, Washington, DC. Tel: (202) 332-9110, FAX: (202) 265-4954, E-Mail: cspi@cspinet.org, Web Site: www.cspinet.org (17)

Corral, Rafael, Argent Trading LLC, New York, NY. Tel: (212) 697-8800, FAX: (212) 697-8606, Web Site: www.Argenttrading.com (16)

Corrente-Evans, Toni, Pacific Botanicals LLC, Grants Pass, OR. Tel: (541) 479-7777, FAX: (541) 479-7780, E-Mail: pacbot1@earthlink.net, Web Site: www.pacificbotanicals.com (7)

Corrigan, Robert, A., San Francisco State University, San Francisco, CA. Tel: (415) 338-1111, FAX: (415) 338-0501, Web Site: www.sfsu.edu (41)

Corry, Thomas, P., Corry Direct Marketing LLC, Ridgefield, CT. Tel: (203) 438-1478, FAX: (203) 431-0217, E-Mail: tom@corrydirect.com, Web Site: www.corrydirect.com (20)

Corry Direct Marketing LLC, Ridgefield, CT. Tel: (203) 438-1478, FAX: (203) 431-0217, E-Mail: tom@corrydirect.com, Web Site: www.corrydirect.com (20)

CORS, Itasca, IL. Tel: (630) 250-8677, (800) 323-1352, FAX: (630) 250-7362, Web Site: www.cors.com (20)

Cortelli, Steve, Russell A Farrow Ltd, Windsor, ON. Tel: (519) 252-4415, FAX: (519) 252-0982, E-Mail: sherry.lamont@farrow.com, Web Site: www.farrow.com (16)

Cortez, Linus, Stuller, Inc, Lafayette, LA. Tel: (337) 262-7700, (800) 877-7777, FAX: (337) 981-1655, E-Mail: info@stuller.com, Web Site: www.stuller.com (2)

Cortez, Steve, Arch Telecom Inc, Austin, TX. Tel: (512) 492-0735, (800) 890-7575, FAX: (512) 495-7101, Web Site: www.archtelecom.com (16)

Corty, Andrew, P., Trend Magazines Inc, Saint Petersburg, FL. Tel: (727) 821-5800, (800) 821-5800, FAX: (727) 822-5083, E-Mail: feedback@fltrend.com, Web Site: www.floridatrend.com (17)

Cortz Inc, West Chicago, IL. Tel: (630) 876-1080, Web Site: www.intheswim.com (5)

Corwin MD, Steven, J., Columbia-Presbyterian Medical Center, New York, NY. Tel: (212) 305-2500, FAX: (212) 305-8023, Web Site: www.nyp.org (16)

Cosand, Norm, The Jackson Group, Indianapolis, IN. Tel: (888) 522-5766, Web Site: www.jacksongroup.com (35)

Cosco, John A., The Saint Francis Academy Inc, Salina, KS. Tel: (785) 825-0541, (800) 423-1342, FAX: (785) 825-2940, Web Site: www.st-francis.org (1)

Cosco Industries Inc, Chicago, IL. Tel: (708) 867-5800, (800) 323-0253, FAX: (800) 323-0275 (16)

Cosentino, Al, SK&A Information Services Inc, Irvine, CA. Tel: (949) 476-2051, (800) 752-5478, FAX: (949) 476-2168, E-Mail: skasales@skainfo.com, Web Site: www.skainfo.com (23)

Cosgrove, Jerry, Cosgrove Associates, New York, NY. Tel: (212) 888-7202, FAX: (212) 888-7201, Web Site: www.cosgrovejuro.com (14)

Cosgrove Associates, New York, NY. Tel: (212) 888-7202, FAX: (212) 888-7201, Web Site: www.cosgrovejuro.com (14)

Cosimini, Nancy, UndercoverWear Inc, Tewksbury, MA. Tel: (978) 851-8580, FAX: (978) 640-2882, E-Mail: jamiej@undercoverwear.com, Web Site: www.undercoverwear.com (2)

Cosmetique, Inc, Vernon Hills, IL. Tel: (847) 913-9099, (800) 621-8822, Web Site: www.cosmetique.com (13)

Cosmi, Anthony, Foxfire Printing & Packaging Inc, Newark, DE. Tel: (302) 368-9466, (800) 497-0516, FAX: (302) 368-9219, E-Mail: info@foxfiresigns.com, Web Site: www.foxfiresigns.com (27)

Cosmo International, Deerfield Beach, FL. Tel: (954) 798-4500, FAX: (954) 798-4514 (16)

Cossette Communications Group Inc, Quebec, PQ Canada. Tel: (418) 647-2727, FAX: (418) 647-2564, E-Mail: infomaster@cossette.com, Web Site: www.cossette.com (35)

Cost, Steven, Intergraph Corp, Madison, AL. Tel: (256) 730-2000, (800) 345-4856, FAX: (256) 730-2048, Web Site: www.intergraph.com (16)

Costa, Tamara, Metropolis Magazine, New York, NY. Tel: (212) 627-9977, (800) 334-3046, FAX: (212) 627-9988, E-Mail: edit@metropolismag.com, Web Site: www.metropolismag.com (2)

Costa, Virginie, Hermes of Paris, New York, NY. Tel: (212) 759-7585, (800) 441-4488, FAX: (212) 644-2132 (2)

Costco Wholesale, Issaquah, WA. Tel: (425) 313-8647, Web Site: www.costco.com (33)

Costello, Ellen, M., Harris Bancorp Inc, Chicago, IL. Tel: (312) 461-7961, (888) 340-BANK, FAX: (312) 461-7869, E-Mail: onlineservices@harrisbank.com, Web Site: www.harrisbank.com (14)

Costello, John, First to the Finish Inc, Carlinville, IL. Tel: (217) 854-8305, Web Site: www.firsttothefinish.com (7)

Costello, Mark, Amcat TeleProfit Inc, Oklahoma City, OK. Tel: (405) 216-8080, (800) 364-5518, FAX: (405) 216-8063, E-Mail: smart@amcat.com, Web Site: www.amcat.com (16)

Costello, Peter D., Premier Farnell Corp, Richfield, OH. Tel: (216) 525-4300, (800) 458-3222, FAX: (216) 525-4509, E-Mail: information@premierfarnell.com, Web Site: www.premierfarnell.com (16)

Costello, Richard, Amcat TeleProfit Inc, Oklahoma City, OK. Tel: (405) 216-8080, (800) 364-5518, FAX: (405) 216-8063, E-Mail: smart@amcat.com, Web Site: www.amcat.com (16)

Costopulos, Nancy, American Marketing Association, Chicago, IL. Tel: (312) 542-9000, FAX: (312) 542-9001, Web Site: www.ama.org (40)

Cote, Adrienne, AB Lambdin Inc, Hampton, VA. Tel: (800) 528-9817, FAX: (800) 221-9231, E-Mail: service@ablambdin.com (2)

Cote, Ryan, The Ballantine Corp, Wayne, NJ. Tel: (973) 305-1500, Web Site: www.ballantine.com (27)

Cote, Victoria, Invacare Continuing Care Group, Saint Louis, MO. Tel: (519) 659-1395, (800) 347-5440, FAX: (636) 519-0044, Web Site: www.invacare-ccg.com (16)

Pamela Cotrupe, Las Vegas, NV. Tel: (818) 624-0087 (20)

Cotta Transmission Co, Beloit, WI. Tel: (608) 368-5600, FAX: (608) 368-5605, E-Mail: sales@cotta.com, Web Site: www.cotta.com (16)

Cotter, Mike, Ed Voyles Hyundai Inc, Smyrna, GA. Tel: (770) 952-8881, (877) 579-0642, FAX: (770) 612-9396, Web Site: www.edvoyleshyundai.com (16)

Cotter, Pete, Motor Coach Industries International Inc, Schaumburg, IL. Tel: (847) 285-2000, (800) 624-2622, Web Site: www.mcicoach.com (16)

Cottle, Karen, Adobe Systems Inc, San Jose, CA. Tel: (408) 536-6000, (800) 833-6687, FAX: (408) 537-6000, Web Site: www.adobe.com (22)

Cotton, Eve, American Library Association-Publishing Services, Chicago, IL. Tel: (312) 944-6780, (800) 545-2433, FAX: (312) 280-4380, Web Site: www.ala.org (1)

Cottrell, Gregory, B., Caraustar, Austell, GA. Tel: (770) 948-3101, E-Mail: info@caraustar.com, Web Site: www.caraustar.com (16)

Couch, Jeanelle, Harvest Communications, Redding, CA. Tel: (800) 303-6405, FAX: (800) 926-8038, Web Site: www.harvest-communications.com (20)

Cougar Mountain Software, Boise, ID. Tel: (208) 375-4455, (800) 388-3038, FAX: (208) 375-4460, E-Mail: sales@cougarmtn.com, Web Site: www.cougarmtn.com (14)

Coughlin, Jack, Esrock Partners, Orland Park, IL. Tel: (708) 349-8400, (888) ESROCKS, FAX: (708) 349-8471, E-Mail: clay@esrock.com, Web Site: www.esrock.com (35)

Coulter, Anne, M., Legal Defense Foundation Inc, Springfield, VA. Tel: (703) 321-8501, (800) 336-3600, FAX: (703) 321-9613, E-Mail: info@nrtw.org, Web Site: www.nrtw.org (1)

Coulter, Mark, The List Emporium, Parkville, MO. Tel: (816) 505-2111, FAX: (816) 505-2112, E-Mail: listinfo@listmart.com, Web Site: www.listmart.com (23)

Council for Advancement and Support of Education (CASE), Washington, DC. Tel: (202) 328-2273, Web Site: www.case.org (1)

Council of Better Business Bureaus - BBBOnline, Arlington, VA. Tel: (703) 276-0100, FAX: (703) 525-8277, Web Site: www.bbb.org (1)

Council of Smaller Enterprises (COSE), Cincinnati, OH. Tel: (512) 455-5432, Web Site: kaobrands.com (9)

Council of Smaller Enterprises (COSE), Cleveland, OH. Tel: (216) 621-3300, Web Site: www.cose.org (1)

Council on Foreign Relations Inc, New York, NY. Tel: (212) 434-9400, FAX: (212) 861-2759, E-Mail: editor@foreignaffairs.com, Web Site: www. foreignaffairs.org (17)

Counter, John, AAA Auto Club South, Tampa, FL. Tel: (813) 289-1344, FAX: (813) 289-1340, Web Site: www.aaa.com (1)

Counter, Nicholas, International Foundation of Employee Benefit Plans, Brookfield, WI. Tel: (262) 373-7758, FAX: (262) 786-8670, Web Site: www. ifebp.org (1)

The Country Bed Shop, Ashby, MA. Tel: (978) 386-7550, FAX: (978) 386-7263, E-Mail: alan@ countrybed.com, Web Site: www.countrybed.com (16)

Country Curtains Inc, Lee, MA. Tel: (413) 243-1474, (800) 456-0321, FAX: (413) 243-1067, Web Site: www.countrycurtains.com (8)

Country Dance and Song Society, Haydenville, MA. Tel: (413) 268-7426, FAX: (413) 268-7471, E-Mail: office@cdss.org, Web Site: www.cdss.org (1)

Country Financial, Bloomington, IL. Tel: (309) 821-3000 (15)

The Country House Inc, Salisbury, MD. Tel: (410) 749-1959, (800) 331-3602, FAX: (410) 548-3224, E-Mail: web@thecountryhouse.com, Web Site: www.thecountryhouse.com (6)

Country Marketing Ltd, Ilion, NY. Tel: (315) 895-7737, FAX: (315) 895-7392, E-Mail: al@ countrymarketing.com, Web Site: www. countrymarketing.com (23)

Country Sampler Group, Saint Charles, IL. Tel: (630) 377-8000, FAX: (630) 377-8194, Web Site: www. sampler.com (17)

Countryman, Gail, Hear Music, Bellevue, WA. Tel: (425) 452-5534, E-Mail: gail@hearmusic.com, Web Site: www.hearmusic.com (3)

Countrywide Financial Corp, Calabasas, CA. Tel: (818) 225-3000, FAX: (818) 225-4051, Web Site: www.countrywide.com (14)

Counts, Jack, Glamour Shots Licensing, Oklahoma City, OK. Tel: (405) 947-8747, (888) GLAMOUR-SHOTS, FAX: (405) 951-7343, Web Site: www. glamourshots.com (16)

Courage Cards & Gifts, Golden Valley, MN. Tel: (763) 588-081, Web Site: www.couragecards.org (1)

Couri, John A., Newhouse School of Public Communications, Syracuse, NY. Tel: (315) 443-3611, FAX: (315) 443-4426, Web Site: newhouse.syr.edu (41)

Course Technology, Boston, MA. Tel: (617) 757-7900, (800) 648-7450, (800) 354-9706, FAX: (617) 487-8488, E-Mail: ed.moura@cengage.com, Web Site: www.course.com (31)

Coursesmith, Denver, CO. Tel: (303) 575-5676, FAX: (303) 575-1187, E-Mail: emailstreet@gmail.com, Web Site: www.coursesmith.com (17)

Courtenay, Adrian, DM News, New York, NY. Tel: (212) 925-7300, FAX: (212) 925-8752, Web Site: www.dmnews.com (43)

Courtenay, Watson, Impact Communications Inc, Louisville, KY. Tel: (502) 587-9084, (800) 556-9084, FAX: (502) 589-6538, E-Mail: info@impactvideo. com, Web Site: www.321impact.net (32)

Courville, Marcel, TransContinental Yorkville - O'Keefe, Etobicoke, ON Canada. Tel: (416) 741-1900, (800) 361-9690, FAX: (416) 401-2220, Web Site: www.transcontinentalprinting.com (27)

Coury, Robert, J., UDL Laboratories Inc, Sugar Land, TX. Tel: (281) 240-1000, (800) 231-3052, FAX: (281) 240-0002, Web Site: www.udllabs.com (7)

Cousins, Killian, Envelope Manufacturers Association, Alexandria, VA. Tel: (703) 739-2200, FAX: (703) 739-2209, Web Site: www.envelope.org (1)

Couture, France, Voxdata Telecom, Montreal, PQ Canada. Tel: (514) 871-1920, (800) 861-9599, FAX: (514) 871-0445, E-Mail: fcouture@voxdata. com, Web Site: www.voxdata.com (29)

Couture, Neal J, National Contract Management Association, Ashburn, VA. Tel: (571) 382-1134, (800) 344-8096, E-Mail: memberservices@ncmghq.org, Web Site: www.ncmahq.org (1)

Couture, Steven, Standard Publishing, Cincinnati, OH. Tel: (513) 931-4050, (800) 543-1301, FAX: (877) 867-5751, Web Site: www.standardpub.com (17)

Covalent Marketing, Denver, CO. Tel: (303) 588-7754, Web Site: www.covalentmarketing.com (22)

Covenant House International Headquarters, New York, NY. Tel: (212) 727-4000, (800) 999-9999, FAX: (212) 727-4992, Web Site: www. covenanthouse.org (1)

Coveo, Quebec, PQ Canada. Tel: (418) 263-1111, Web Site: www.coveo.com (22)

CoverClicks LLC, New York, NY. Tel: (888) 624-1340, FAX: (212) 239-2850, E-Mail: info@ coverclicksmail.com, Web Site: www.coverclicks. com (23)

Coverdell & Co Inc, Chicago, IL. Tel: (404) 881-2227, (800) 992-2196, FAX: (404) 881-2222, Web Site: www.coverdell.com (15)

Coverdell Canada Corporation, Montreal, PQ Canada. Tel: (514) 847-7800 (16)

Covert, David, Bank of the West, Los Angeles, CA. Tel: (509) 736-0131, Web Site: www. bankofthewest.com (14)

Covey, J., Kent, PLAS-TANKS Industries Inc, Hamilton, OH. Tel: (513) 942-3800, FAX: (513) 942-3993, E-Mail: info@plastanks.com, Web Site: www.plastanks.com (9)

Covidien International, Mansfield, MA. Tel: (508) 261-8000, (800) 962-9888, FAX: (508) 261-8105, Web Site: www.covidien.com (7)

Cowan, Rebecca, New Pig Corp, Tipton, PA. Tel: (814) 684-0101, (800) 468-4647, FAX: (814) 684-0961, E-Mail: hothogs@newpig.com, Web Site: www.newpig.com (9)

Cowdery, Clarisse, Potpourri Group Inc, Chelmsford, MA. Tel: (978) 256-4100, FAX: (978) 256-1961/ 0344, Web Site: www.potpourrigroup.com (6)

Cowell, Eugene I., Gene Cowell & Associates Inc, Alachua, FL. Tel: (352) 495-5757, FAX: (352) 495-0804, E-Mail: gcdirect@acceleration.net (35)

Gene Cowell & Associates Inc, Alachua, FL. Tel: (352) 495-5757, FAX: (352) 495-0804, E-Mail: gcdirect@acceleration.net (35)

Cowen, Peter, Memphis Net & Twine Co Inc, Memphis, TN. Tel: (901) 458-2656, (888) 674-7638, FAX: (901) 458-1601, E-Mail: fishinfo@ memphisnet.net, Web Site: www.memphisnet.net (11)

Cowley, Chuck, Jordan Direct, Phoenix, AZ. Tel: (623) 551-2728, FAX: (623) 551-2730, E-Mail: dori@jordandirect.net (23)

Cowley, Chuck, Mary Maxim Inc, Port Huron, MI. Tel: (810) 987-2000, (800) 962-9504, FAX: (810) 987-5056, E-Mail: info@marymaxim.com, Web Site: www.marymaxim.com (11)

Cox, Brian, A., ABDI, Inc Global Order Fulfillment, Leetsdale, PA. Tel: (412) 741-1142, (800) 796-6471, FAX: (412) 741-4161, E-Mail: info@abdintl. com, Web Site: www.abdintl.com (28)

Cox, Dale, Good Advertising, Memphis, TN. Tel: (901) 761-0741, (800) 325-9857, FAX: (901) 682-2568, Web Site: www.goodadvertising.com (35)

Cox, Dennis, ChinaStock/WorldViews, Ann Arbor, MI. Tel: (734) 996-1440, (800) 315-4462, FAX: (734) 996-1481, E-Mail: decoxphoto@aol.com, Web Site: www.denniscox.com (38)

Cox, Eileen, S., Cartouche Ltd, Alexandria, VA. Tel: (703) 823-7904, (800) AT-EGYPT, FAX: (888) 283-4978, E-Mail: sales@egyptianimports.com, Web Site: www.egyptianimports.com (6)

Cox, Karen, The Bradford Group, Niles, IL. Tel: (847) 966-2770, FAX: (847) 581-8630, Web Site: www. collectiblestoday.com (16)

Cox, Lincoln, Edwin Watts Golf, Fort Walton Beach, FL. Tel: (850) 244-2066, (800) 874-0146, FAX: (850) 244-5217, Web Site: www.edwinwatts.com (11)

Cox, Michelle, Briefings Publishing Group, Richmond, VA. Tel: (703) 567-1982, (800) 791-8699, FAX: (703) 684-2136, E-Mail: rmalvaso@ douglaspublications.com, Web Site: www. briefings.com (17)

Cox Communications, Atlanta, GA. Tel: (404) 843-5000, FAX: (404) 269-2243, Web Site: www.cox. com (16)

Cox Target Media/DBA Valpak, Largo, FL. Tel: (727) 399-3000, (800) 678-2743, FAX: (727) 399-3061, E-Mail: contact_sales@coxtarget.com, Web Site: www.coxdirect.com (21)

Coxon, John, Northern Illinois Consulting Inc, Libertyville, IL. Tel: (847) 828-1999, Web Site: www. cmsbusiness.com (20)

Coy, Randall, S., Communication Resources Inc, Canton, OH. Tel: (800) 992-2144, FAX: (330) 493-3158, E-Mail: service@comresources.com, Web Site: www.comresources.com (18)

Coy, Steven, S., Consolidated Electronics Inc, Dayton, OH. Tel: (800) 543-3568, FAX: (937) 252-4066, E-Mail: scoy@ceitron.com, Web Site: www. ceitron.com (3)

Coyle, John, D., Unitron Ltd, Commack, NY. Tel: (631) 589-6666, FAX: (631) 589-6795, E-Mail: johnc@unitronusa.com, Web Site: www.unitronusa. com (9)

Coyle, Maria, Union Pen Co, Hagaman, NY. Tel: (800) 846-6600, FAX: (518) 770-7018, Web Site: www.unionpen.com (5)

Coyne, Bill, Raley's Bel Air Markets, West Sacramento, CA. Tel: (916) 373-3333, FAX: (916) 373-6351, Web Site: www.raleys.com (16)

Coyne, Joan, Eclipse Marketing Services, Morristown, NJ. Tel: (800) 837-4648 (35)

Coyne American Institute, Chicago, IL. Tel: (773) 935-2520, (800) 999-5220, FAX: (773) 935-2920, Web Site: www.coyneamerican.edu (16)

Crabtree & Evelyn Ltd, Woodstock, CT. Tel: (860) 928-2761, (800) CRABTREE, FAX: (860) 928-0452, Web Site: www.crabtree-evelyn.com (4)

Cracchiolo, James, Ameriprise Financial Services Inc, Minneapolis, MN. Tel: (651) 671-3434, (612) 671-3131, (800) 386-2042, Web Site: www.ameriprise. com (14)

The Cracker Box Inc, Blooming Glen, PA. Tel: (215) 443-7777, FAX: (215) 443-7777, E-Mail: walter@ crackerboxkits.com, Web Site: www. crackerboxkits.com (16)

Craft-Diston Industries, Wichita, KS. Tel: (316) 838-4291, (800) 835-0028, FAX: (316) 838-8502, Web Site: www.craftdiston.com (16)

Craig, Becky, National Research LLC, Washington, DC. Tel: (202) 686-9350, FAX: (202) 686-7163, E-Mail: survey@nationalres.com, Web Site: www. nationalres.com (30)

Craig, Dan, Booyah Networks, Westminster, CO. Tel: (303) 426-7776, FAX: (303) 345-6700, E-Mail: support@booyahnetworks.com, Web Site: www. booyahnetworks.com (35)

Craig, David, Lowrance Electronics, Tulsa, OK. Tel: (918) 437-6881, FAX: (918) 234-1707, Web Site: www.lowrance.com (11)

Craig, Irv, Townsend Communications LLC, Kansas City, MO. Tel: (816) 361-0616, (800) 274-8867, FAX: (816) 361-6164, Web Site: www. townsendprint.com (17)

Craig, Joanna, B., Craig/Vartorella International Marketing & Advertising Inc, Camden, SC. Tel: (803) 432-4353, FAX: (803) 432-4353, E-Mail: globebiz@juno.com, Web Site: www.colasc.com/ Marketing_&_Fundraising (1)

Craig, John, Dentino Marketing, Princeton, NJ. Tel: (201) 332-1219, (800) 477-8372, FAX: (201) 332-4262, E-Mail: karl@dentinomarketing.com, Web Site: www.dentinomarketing.com (35)

Craig, John, One Hanes Place Catalog, Winston Salem, NC. Tel: (336) 519-4400, (800) 300-2600, FAX: (336) 519-0655, Web Site: www. onehanesplace.com (2)

Craig, John, Sara Lee Direct Home Shopping, Winston-Salem, NC. Tel: (336) 519-4400, (800) 671-5056, E-Mail: ohp.managor@onehanesplace. com, Web Site: www.onehanesplace.com (2)

Craig, Joycelin, Astronomical Society of the Pacific, San Francisco, CA. Tel: (415) 337-1100, (800) 335-2624, FAX: (415) 337-5205, E-Mail: service@ astrosociety.org, Web Site: www.astrosociety.org (1)

Craig, Julie, ESignal, Hayward, CA. Tel: (510) 266-6000, Web Site: www.esignal.com (14)

Craig, Peter, Fahlgren, Cincinnati, OH. Tel: (513) 241-9200, FAX: (513) 241-5982, Web Site: www. fahlgren.com (35)

Craig, Thomas, W., LTD Supply Chain, Downingtown, PA. Tel: (610) 458-3636, FAX: (610) 458-8039, E-Mail: tomc@ltdsupplychain.com, Web Site: www.ltdsupplychain.com (20)

The Ben Craig Center, Charlotte, NC. Tel: (704) 548-9113, Web Site: www.bencraigcenter.com (1)

Craig Envelope Corp, Long Island City, NY. Tel: (718) 392-9304, (888) 272-4436, FAX: (718) 937-8178, E-Mail: info@craigenvelope.com, Web Site: www.craigenvelope.com (26)

Craig/Vartorella International Marketing & Advertising Inc, Camden, SC. Tel: (803) 432-4353, FAX: (803) 432-4353, E-Mail: globebiz@juno.com, Web Site: www.colasc.com/Marketing_&_Fundraising (1)

Craik, Polly, FineLine, Winnipeg, MB Canada. Tel: (204) 942-4242, Web Site: www. finelinesolutions.com (29)

Crail, Frank, Rocky Mountain Chocolate Factory, Durango, CO. Tel: (970) 259-0554, (888) 525-2462, FAX: (970) 259-5895, E-Mail: customerservice@ rmcfusa.com, Web Site: www.rmcf.com (4)

Crain, Andrew, Tully & Holland Inc, Wellesley, MA. Tel: (781) 239-2900, FAX: (781) 239-2901, E-Mail: info@tullyandholland.com, Web Site: www.tullyandholland.com (14)

Crain, Keith, Crain Communications Inc, Detroit, MI. Tel: (313) 446-6000, FAX: (313) 446-1616, Web Site: www.crain.com (17)

Crain, Rance, Crain Communications Inc, Detroit, MI. Tel: (313) 446-6000, FAX: (313) 446-1616, Web Site: www.crain.com (17)

Crain Communications Inc, Detroit, MI. Tel: (313) 446-6000, FAX: (313) 446-1616, Web Site: www. crain.com (17)

Cram, Steve, Commonwealth Lists, Fairfax, VA. Tel: (703) 273-3231, FAX: (703) 279-5970, E-Mail: info@commonwealthlists.com, Web Site: www. commonwealthlists.com (21)

Cram, William, Prism Data Services Ltd, Mississauga, ON Canada. Tel: (905) 278-5556, FAX: (905) 278-6603, E-Mail: bill.cram@prism-data.com; sales@ prism-data.com, Web Site: www.prism-data.com (21)

Cramb, Don, Fujitsu Transaction Solutions Inc, Richardson, TX. Tel: (972) 963-2300, (800) 340-4425, Web Site: www.fujitsu.com (16)

Cramer, Gerald B., Newhouse School of Public Communications, Syracuse, NY. Tel: (315) 443-3611, FAX: (315) 443-4426, Web Site: newhouse.syr.edu (41)

Cramer, Martin, A., RBC Funds, Milwaukee, WI. Tel: (800) 422-2766, Web Site: us.rbcgam.com (14)

Cramer, Norwood, MA. Tel: (781) 278-2387, Web Site: www.crameronline.com (20)

Cramer-Krasselt, Chicago, IL. Tel: (312) 616-9600, FAX: (312) 938-3157, E-Mail: pkrivkov@c-k.com, Web Site: www.c-k.com (35)

Crandall, Roderick, Select Press, Novato, CA. Tel: (415) 209-9838, E-Mail: selectpr@aol.com (17)

Crandall, Theodore, D., Rockwell Automation, Milwaukee, WI. Tel: (414) 382-2000, FAX: (414) 382-4444, Web Site: www.rockwellautomation.com (16)

Crandall Associates Inc, Port Washington, NY. Tel: (516) 767-6800, E-Mail: joyce@crandallassociates. com, Web Site: www.crandallassociates.com (20)

Crandell, Matt, ACP - Automation Control Products, Alpharetta, GA. Tel: (678) 990-0945, FAX: (678) 990-0951, E-Mail: info@thinmanager.com, Web Site: www.thinmanager.com (16)

Crane, Andrea, Training Consultants Inc, Highland Park, IL. Tel: (847) 432-9428, FAX: (847) 432-9318, E-Mail: wetrain2@home.com (20)

Crane, Bob, Towers Watson, New York, NY. Tel: (212) 725-7550, FAX: (212) 644-7432, Web Site: www.towerswatson.com (20)

Crane, Jay, Guideline, New York, NY. Tel: (212) 645-4500, (866) GUIDELINE, FAX: (212) 645-7681, Web Site: www.findsvp.com (30)

Crane, Jennifer, Fairchild Books, New York, NY. Tel: (212) 630-4171, (800) 932-4724, FAX: (212) 630-3868, Web Site: www.fairchildbooks.com (17)

Crane, Jonathan, MCI Inc, Ashburn, VA. Tel: (703) 886-5600, FAX: (703) 885-0570 (16)

Crane, Timothy, Harris Bancorp Inc, Chicago, IL. Tel: (312) 461-7961, (888) 340-BANK, FAX: (312) 461-7869, E-Mail: onlineservices@harrisbank.com, Web Site: www.harrisbank.com (14)

Crane, Valerie, Research Communications Ltd, Canton, MA. Tel: (781) 341-1190, FAX: (781) 341-1191, E-Mail: info@researchcommunications.com (30)

Crane, William, Myllykoski North America, Norwalk, CT. Tel: (203) 229-7400, Web Site: www. myllykoski.com (25)

Crane Duplicating Service Inc, Naples, FL. Tel: (305) 280-6742, FAX: (239) 732-8415, Web Site: www. craneduplicating.com (28)

Crane Environmental, Norristown, PA. Tel: (610) 631-7700, (800) 828-2447, FAX: (610) 630-6656, E-Mail: purwater@cranenv.com, Web Site: www. cranenv.com (34)

Crane Pumps & Systems Inc, Piqua, OH. Tel: (937) 773-2442, FAX: (937) 773-2238, E-Mail: cranepumps@cranepumps.com, Web Site: www. cranepumps.com (16)

Cranford, Judith, A., Direct Selling Education Foundation, Washington, DC. Tel: (202) 452-8866, FAX: (202) 452-9015, Web Site: www.dsef.org (40)

Cranley, Edward R., Willis Music Co, Florence, KY. Tel: (859) 283-2050, (800) 354-9799, FAX: (859) 283-1784, E-Mail: ordpt@willis-music.com, Web Site: www.willismusic.com (17)

Cranley, Kevin, Willis Music Co, Florence, KY. Tel: (859) 283-2050, (800) 354-9799, FAX: (859) 283-1784, E-Mail: ordpt@willis-music.com, Web Site: www.willismusic.com (17)

Crate & Barrel, Northbrook, IL. Tel: (847) 272-2888, Web Site: www.crateandbarrell.com (8)

Cravener, Greg, Antique Electronic Supply, Tempe, AZ. Tel: (480) 820-5411, (800) 706-6789, FAX: (480) 820-4643, E-Mail: info@tubesandmore.com, Web Site: www.tubesandmore.com (3)

Cravener, Noreen, Antique Electronic Supply, Tempe, AZ. Tel: (480) 820-5411, (800) 706-6789, FAX: (480) 820-4643, E-Mail: info@tubesandmore.com, Web Site: www.tubesandmore.com (3)

Cravens, Christina, Software AG USA, Reston, VA. Tel: (703) 860-5050, (877) 724-4965, FAX: (703) 391-6975, E-Mail: info@softwareagusa.com, Web Site: www.softwareagusa.com (3)

Craver Mathews Smith & Co, Reston, VA. Tel: (703) 258-0000, FAX: (703) 258-0001, Web Site: www. craveronline.com (1)

Crawford, Jane, America, Fredericksburg, VA. Tel: (540) 658-3388, (800) 927-8277, FAX: (540) 658-3389, Web Site: www.americastore.com (6)

Crawford, Janice, Inquiry Intelligence Systems, O'Fallon, MO. Tel: (636) 281-2129, (800) 467-2329, FAX: (636) 281-1517, E-Mail: sales@ iqsalespro.com, Web Site: www.inquiry-tracking. com (22)

Crawford, John, Collin Street Bakery, Corsicana, TX. Tel: (800) 292-7400, Web Site: www. collinstreetbakery.com (4)

Crawford, Marc, Los Angeles Kings, Los Angeles, CA. Tel: (213) 742-7100, (888) KINGS-LA, FAX: (213) 742-7296, Web Site: kings.nhl.com (16)

Crawford, Thomas W., Crawford & Co, Atlanta, GA. Tel: (404) 300-1000, (800) 241-2541, FAX: (404) 300-1905, Web Site: www.crawfordandcompany. com (35)

Crawford, Thomas, J., Stewart Enterprises Inc, Jefferson, LA. Tel: (504) 729-1400, (800) 535-6017, FAX: (504) 729-1984, Web Site: www. stewartenterprises.com (16)

Crawford Advertising Associates LTD, New City, NY. Tel: (914) 946-2444, FAX: (914) 946-9236, E-Mail: crawads@aol.com, Web Site: www. crawfordadv.com (35)

Crawford & Co, Atlanta, GA. Tel: (404) 300-1000, (800) 241-2541, FAX: (404) 300-1905, Web Site: www.crawfordandcompany.com (35)

Crawshaw, Todd, Crawshaw Design, San Rafael, CA. Tel: (415) 456-5544, FAX: (415) 456-4319, E-Mail: crawshawdesign@earthlink.net, Web Site: www.crawshawdesign.com (36)

Crawshaw Design, San Rafael, CA. Tel: (415) 456-5544, FAX: (415) 456-4319, E-Mail: crawshawdesign@earthlink.net, Web Site: www. crawshawdesign.com (36)

Craycraft, Robert, M., Ashland Inc, Covington, KY. Tel: (859) 815-3333, Web Site: www.ashland.com (16)

Crayton, Gene, A., Paralyzed Veterans of America, Washington, DC. Tel: (202) 416-7636, (800) 424-8200, FAX: (202) 416-7643, E-Mail: info@pva. org, Web Site: www.pva.org (1)

Crazy Crow Trading Post, Pottsboro, TX. Tel: (903) 786-2287, (800) 786-6210, FAX: (903) 786-9059, E-Mail: info@crazycrow.com, Web Site: www. crazycrow.com (11)

Creasey Jr., F., Clay, Toys "R" Us, Wayne, NJ. Tel: (973) 617-5879, FAX: (973) 617-4006, Web Site: www.toysrus.com (11)

Createch Marketing, Montvale, NJ. Tel: (201) 326-3000, Web Site: www.createchmarketing.com (22)

Creating Results/New England, Barrington, RI. Tel: (401) 289-2500, (888) 205-8899, FAX: (401) 427-6963, E-Mail: erin@creatingresults.com, Web Site: www.creatingresults.com (35)

Creating Selling Opportunities, Houston, TX. Tel: (713) 622-6936, FAX: (713) 622-2924, E-Mail: annci@sbcglobal.net (20)

The Creative Alliance Inc, Lafayette, CO. Tel: (303) 665-8101, (888) 293-8101, FAX: (303) 665-3136, E-Mail: t@thecreativealliance.com, Web Site: www.creativealliance.com (35)

Creative Automation, Hillside, IL. Tel: (708) 449-2800, (800) 773-1588, FAX: (708) 449-3282, E-Mail: busmgr@cauto.com, Web Site: www.cauto. com (22)

Creative Awards by Lane, Elk Grove Village, IL. Tel: (847) 593-7700, FAX: (847) 593-1155, E-Mail: info@creativeawardsbylane.com, Web Site: www. creativeawardsbylane.com (33)

Creative Banner Assemblies, New Hope, MN. Tel: (763) 278-6515, Web Site: www.creativebanner. com (9)

Creative Campaigns Inc, Calabasas, CA. Tel: (818) 340-2713, FAX: (818) 337-2446, E-Mail: info@ creativecampaigns.com, Web Site: www. creativecampaigns.com (32)

Creative Catalogs Corp, Lemont, IL. Tel: (630) 783-2400, Web Site: www.personalcreations.com (6)

Creative Commerce LLC, West Chester, PA. Tel: (212) 625-1700 (35)

Creative Compliance, Chicago, IL. Tel: (916) 216-3379, E-Mail: info@creativecompliance.com, Web Site: www.creativecompliance.com (29)

Creative Copywriting, Plainfield, IL. Tel: (815) 439-9160, FAX: (815) 439-9158 (39)

Creative Direct Marketing, Chapel Hill, NC. Tel: (919) 929-5757, E-Mail: jeffb.cdm@mindspring.com (39)

Creative Freelancers Inc, Sarasota, FL. Tel: (203) 532-2924, (800) 398-9544, E-Mail: cfonline@freelancers.com, Web Site: www.freelancers.com (39)

Creative Health Products, Plymouth, MI. Tel: (734) 996-5900, (800) 742-4478, FAX: (734) 996-4650, Web Site: www.chponline.com (16)

Creative Irish Gifts, Little Rock, AR. Tel: (330) 954-1200, FAX: (330) 650-8888, E-Mail: gifts@shopirish.com, Web Site: www.shopirish.com (6)

Creative Learning Systems Inc, Longmont, CO. Tel: (800) 458-2880, FAX: (760) 546-1490, Web Site: www.clsinc.com (9)

Creative Lift, San Francisco, CA. Tel: (415) 248-3174, Web Site: www.creativelift.net (35)

Creative Mailing & Marketing, Gardena, CA. Tel: (310) 637-7100, FAX: (714) 998-9001, Web Site: www.creativemandm.com (28)

Creative Marketing Alliance Inc, Princeton Junction, NJ. Tel: (609) 799-6000, FAX: (609) 799-7032, Web Site: www.cmasolutions.com (35)

Creative Marketing Management, Chevy Chase, MD. Tel: (301) 650-4160, FAX: (301) 650-4161 (21)

Creative Marketing Programs, Kansas City, MO. Tel: (816) 472-6843, (800) 373-6843, FAX: (816) 472-8184, E-Mail: getresults@cmpkc.com, Web Site: www.cmpkc.com (21)

Creative Media Inc, Nicholasville, KY. Tel: (859) 219-9667 (35)

Creative Printing Services Inc, Des Plaines, IL. Tel: (847) 803-2800, (800) 932-2750, FAX: (847) 803-3299, E-Mail: info@creativepsi.com, Web Site: www.creativepsi.com (27)

Creative Publishing International, Minneapolis, MN. Tel: (612) 344-8100, FAX: (612) 344-8691, E-Mail: sales@creativepub.com, Web Site: www.creativepub.com (17)

Creative Strategy Inc, Chevy Chase, MD. Tel: (301) 718-4550, FAX: (301) 718-8828, E-Mail: info@creativestrategy.com, Web Site: www.creativestrategy.com (35)

Creative Synergy Inc, Germantown, MD. Tel: (301) 515-9397, Web Site: kimschwalm.com (20)

Creative Teaching Associates, Clovis, CA. Tel: (559) 291-6626, (800) 767-4282, FAX: (559) 291-2953, Web Site: www.mastercta.com (16)

Creative Teaching Press, Huntington Beach, CA. Tel: (714) 895-5047, (800) 287-8879 (17)

Creativity International, Ada, MI. Tel: (616) 956-0053, FAX: (616) 956-6957 (16)

Credicorp, Dallas, TX. Tel: (214) 915-7200, FAX: (214) 915-7415, E-Mail: support@credicorp.net, Web Site: www.credicorp.net (1)

Credit Index, Saint Cloud, MN. Tel: (973) 770-4007, FAX: (973) 770-4006, Web Site: www.ebureau.com (22)

Credit Union Executives Society, Madison, WI. Tel: (608) 271-2664, Web Site: www.cues.org (1)

Creditcards.com, Austin, TX. Tel: (512) 996-8663, Web Site: www.creditcards.com (20)

Cree, Jeff, Salt River Project, Tempe, AZ. Tel: (602) 236-5929, Web Site: www.srpnet.com (34)

Creel, John, Apothecary Products Inc, Burnsville, MN. Tel: (952) 890-1940, (800) 328-2742, FAX: (800) 328-1584, Web Site: www.apothecaryproducts.com (7)

Creel Printing of California, Costa Mesa, CA. Tel: (714) 540-7005, FAX: (714) 979-1496 (27)

Cregan, James, C., Magazine Publishers of America, New York, NY. Tel: (212) 872-3700, FAX: (212) 888-4217, Web Site: www.magazine.org (17)

Cregg, Roger, A., Del Webb, Bloomfield Hills, MI. Tel: (248) 644-7300, (888) 717-9777, FAX: (248) 433-4598, Web Site: www.delwebb.com (16)

Creighton, Beth, New York Road Runners Club, Inc, New York, NY. Tel: (212) 860-4455, (800) 405-2288, FAX: (212) 369-4704, E-Mail: webmaster@nyrr.org, Web Site: www.nyrrc.org (13)

Cremer, Francis, S., The Wisconsin Cheeseman, Sun Prairie, WI. Tel: (608) 837-5166, (800) 698-1721, FAX: (608) 837-5493, Web Site: www.wisconsincheeseman.com (4)

Cremer, Holly, The Wisconsin Cheeseman, Sun Prairie, WI. Tel: (608) 837-5166, (800) 698-1721, FAX: (608) 837-5493, Web Site: www.wisconsincheeseman.com (4)

Crescent Beach Enterprises LLC, Bohemia, NY. Tel: (631) 588-6600, FAX: (631) 588-7077, E-Mail: rjd@cbnet.com, Web Site: www.cbprod.com (32)

Crescenzo, Bob, Lancer Insurance Co, Long Beach, NY. Tel: (516) 431-4441, (800) 782-8902, FAX: (516) 889-5111, E-Mail: roneill@lancer-ins.com, Web Site: www.lancer-ins.com (15)

Crest Fruit Inc, Mission, TX. Tel: (956) 205-7300, Web Site: www.redcooper.com (4)

Crest Healthcare Supply, Dassel, MN. Tel: (800) 369-9207, (800) 328-8908, Web Site: www.cresthealthcare.com (16)

Crestline Specialties, Inc, Lewiston, ME. Tel: (207) 777-7075, (866) 488-4975, FAX: (207) 784-5038, E-Mail: info@crestline.com, Web Site: www.crestline.com (16)

Crews, Diane, L., Magna Visual Inc, Saint Louis, MO. Tel: (314) 843-9000, (800) 843-3399, FAX: (314) 843-0000, E-Mail: magna@magnavisual.com, Web Site: www.magnavisual.com (9)

Cribbs, Helen, Peerless Rattan, Plainwell, MI. Tel: (269) 685-1858, (877) 611-2263, E-Mail: sales@peerlessrattan.com, Web Site: www.peerlessrattan.com (16)

Crichton, Sarah, Farrar Straus & Giroux Inc, New York, NY. Tel: (212) 741-6900, (800) 330-8477, FAX: (212) 633-2427, E-Mail: childrens_editorial@fsgbooks.com, Web Site: www.fsgbooks.com (17)

The Cricket Magazine Group, Chicago, IL. Tel: (603) 924-7209, (800) 821-0115, FAX: (815) 224-6615, E-Mail: customerservice@caruspub.com, Web Site: www.cricketmag.com (17)

Crifasi, Camille, Greenbook Worldwide Directory of Marketing Research Companies & Services, Bradenton, FL. Tel: (212) 849-2752, (800) 792-9202, FAX: (212) 202-7920, E-Mail: info@greenbrook.org, Web Site: www.greenbook.org (43)

Crilly, John, Solarcom, Norcross, GA. Tel: (770) 449-6116, (888) SUN-DATA, FAX: (770) 448-7726, Web Site: www.solarcom.net (16)

Criscuoli, Joseph, EPI Colorspace, Gaithersburg, MD. Tel: (301) 230-2023, FAX: (301) 990-7890, E-Mail: jcriscuoli@epicolorspace.com, Web Site: www.epicolorspace.com (36)

Crispin, Porter & Bogusky, Miami, FL. Tel: (305) 859-2070, FAX: (305) 854-3419, Web Site: www.cpbgroup.com (35)

Critchlow, Paul, W., Merrill Lynch, New York, NY. Tel: (212) 449-1000, (800) 637-7455, FAX: (212) 449-9418, Web Site: www.ml.com (14)

Crittenden, Gary, American Health & Life Insurance Co, Fort Worth, TX. Tel: (817) 348-7500, (800) 995-2274, FAX: (817) 348-7553, Web Site: www.citifinancial.com (15)

Critter Mountain Wear, Crested Butte, CO. Tel: (970) 349-9326, (800) 686-9327, FAX: (978) 389-5900, E-Mail: critter@crestedbutte.net, Web Site: www.crittermountainwear.com (2)

Crocker, Gene, Carter & Holmes Inc, Newberry, SC. Tel: (803) 276-0579, FAX: (803) 276-0588, E-Mail: orchids@carterandholmes.com, Web Site: www.carterandholmes.com (8)

Croft, James, The Field Museum, Chicago, IL. Tel: (312) 665-7909, FAX: (312) 665-7101, Web Site: www.fieldmuseum.org (1)

Crohn's & Colitis Foundation of America (CCFA), New York, NY. Tel: (212) 685-3440, Web Site: www.ccfa.org (1)

Croissant, T.J., Sierra Trading Post, Cheyenne, WY. Tel: (307) 775-8050, (800) 713-4534, FAX: (307) 775-8089, Web Site: www.sierratradingpost.com (2)

Cromheecke, Todd, IMS Group II Communications, Franklin, WI. Tel: (414) 425-2080, FAX: (414) 425-6029, Web Site: www.groupii.com (21)

Crone, Annette, Collegesource Inc, San Diego, CA. Tel: (858) 560-8051, (800) 854-2670, FAX: (858) 278-8960, Web Site: www.collegesource.org (17)

Cronin, Douglas, NFocus Consulting Inc, Lancaster, OH. Tel: (740) 654-5809, Web Site: www.nfocusconsulting.com (22)

Cronin, Gary, Minuteman Press (Westchester), Elmsford, NY. Tel: (914) 347-5050, FAX: (914) 347-2563, E-Mail: gcronin@minutemanpress.com, Web Site: www.westchester.minutemanpress.com (27)

Cronin, Steve, Mercury Print & Mail Co Inc, Pawtucket, RI. Tel: (401) 724-7600, FAX: (401) 724-9920, Web Site: www.mpmri.com (28)

Cronin, W., Perry, Shelby Insurance Companies, Birmingham, AL. Tel: (800) 443-1573, FAX: (877) 837-8203, Web Site: www.vesta.com (15)

Cronin & Co, Glastonbury, CT. Tel: (860) 659-0514, Web Site: www.cronin-co.com (16)

Crook, David, Strategy Corps LLC, Brentwood, TN. Tel: (615) 221-8381, (888) 577-6933, FAX: (615) 221-8479, E-Mail: info@strategycorps.com, Web Site: www.strategycorps.com (16)

Crook, Steve, Crook & Grant Lithographers Ltd, North York, ON Canada. Tel: (416) 499-1011, FAX: (416) 499-1821 (27)

Crook, Tom, Computers for Education, Murfreesboro, TN. Tel: (615) 896-3800, FAX: (615) 895-9041 (1)

Crook & Grant Lithographers Ltd, North York, ON Canada. Tel: (416) 499-1011, FAX: (416) 499-1821 (27)

Crooks, Darhil, Esquire Magazine, New York, NY. Tel: (212) 649-2000, (800) 925-0485, FAX: (212) 265-0938, E-Mail: esquire@hearst.com, Web Site: www.esquire.com (17)

Crosbie, William, L., National Railroad Passenger Corp, Washington, DC. Tel: (202) 906-3000, (800) USA-RAIL, FAX: (202) 906-3306, Web Site: www.amtrak.com (16)

Crosby, Nancy, C., Partners Village Store, Westport, MA. Tel: (508) 636-2572, FAX: (508) 636-2529, E-Mail: info@partnersvillagestore.com, Web Site: www.partnersvillagestore.com (11)

Croshaw, Bob, Jameco Electronics, Belmont, CA. Tel: (650) 592-8097, (800) 831-4242, FAX: (650) 592-2503, (800) 237-6948, E-Mail: domestic@jameco.com, Web Site: www.jameco.com (16)

Croson, Sonny, Doorguard Systems Inc, Columbia, MD. Tel: (410) 992-5600, (800) 442-6247, FAX: (410) 992-5694, Web Site: www.doorguardsystems.com (3)

Cross, John, BJU Press, Greenville, SC. Tel: (864) 242-5100, (800) 845-5731, FAX: (800) 525-8398, (864) 271-8151, E-Mail: bjupinfo@bjupress.com, Web Site: www.bjupress.com (17)

A T Cross Co, Lincoln, RI. Tel: (401) 333-1200, (800) 282-7677, FAX: (401) 334-2861, Web Site: www.cross.com (16)

Cross Commerce Media, New York, NY. Tel: (646) 400-5095, Web Site: www.crosscommercemedia.com (35)

Cross Country Automotive Services, Medford, MA. Tel: (781) 393-9300, Web Site: www.cchs.com (16)

Cross Country Computer Corp, Central Islip, NY. Tel: (631) 231-4200, Web Site: www.crosscountrycomputer.com (22)

The Cross Country Group LLC, Medford, MA. Tel: (781) 396-3700, Web Site: www.ccgroup.com (13)

Cross Country Stitching, Quakertown, PA. Tel: (215) 529-6430, (800) 231-8108, FAX: (215) 529-6434, Web Site: www.crosscountrystitching.com (17)

Cross Country Travcorps, Boca Raton, FL. Tel: (800) 530-6125, FAX: (561) 998-8533, Web Site: www.crosscountrytravcorps.com (16)

Cross Marketing USA, Chicago, IL. Tel: (312) 440-3700, (866) 440-3700, FAX: (312) 943-5813, E-Mail: ronbernstein@crossmarketing.us, Web Site: www.crossmarketing.us (23)

Crossbow Group, Westport, CT. Tel: (203) 222-2244, FAX: (203) 226-7838, E-Mail: info@crossbowgroup.com, Web Site: www.crossbowgroup.com (40)

Crossley, Orin, Reserve National Insurance Co, Oklahoma City, OK. Tel: (405) 848-7931, Web Site: www.reservenational.com (15)

CROSSLISTS CROSS & CO INC, Bates City, MO. Tel: (816) 697-3306, FAX: (816) 697-3317, E-Mail: jmbrown@crosscompany.com, Web Site: www.crosscompany.com (23)

Crossman, Paul, G., National Fire Protection Association, Quincy, MA. Tel: (617) 770-3000, FAX: (617) 770-0700, Web Site: www.nfpa.org (1)

Crossroads Films, New York, NY. Tel: (212) 647-1300, FAX: (212) 647-9090, Web Site: www.crossroadfilms.com (32)

Crosstown Traders Inc, Tucson, AZ. Tel: (520) 745-4500 (2)

Croswhite, Brian, Nova Southeastern University - FSEHS, North Miami Beach, FL. Tel: (954) 262-8651, Web Site: www.schooloffed.nova.edu (1)

Croteu, Thomas, Newspaper Association of America, Arlington, VA. Tel: (703) 902-1600, FAX: (571) 366-1195, Web Site: www.naa.org (1)

Crouch, Gene, Tyco Valves & Controls, Houston, TX. Tel: (713) 986-4665, (800) 343-0990, FAX: (713) 937-5466, Web Site: www.tycovalves.com (16)

Crow, Timothy, M., The Home Depot Inc, Atlanta, GA. Tel: (770) 433-8211, (800) 430-3376, FAX: (770) 384-2356, Web Site: www.homedepot.com (16)

Crowder, Jerry, Bradford Health Services, Birmingham, AL. Tel: (205) 251-7753, (800) 217-2849, Web Site: www.bradfordhealth.com (16)

Crowe, Gerald, Pennsylvania Firebacks, Lansdale, PA. Tel: (215) 699-0805, (888) 349-30002, FAX: (215) 699-3332, E-Mail: info@fireback.com, Web Site: www.fireback.com (8)

Crowe, Jesse, Voice Message Broadcasting Corp, Irvine, CA. Tel: (714) 437-0600, FAX: (714) 242-1989, Web Site: www.vmbc.com (32)

Crowfoot, Jim, Creel Printing of California, Costa Mesa, CA. Tel: (714) 540-7005, FAX: (714) 979-1496 (21)

Crowley, Arthur, M., Garon Products Inc, Wall, NJ. Tel: (732) 449-1776, (800) 631-5380, FAX: (732) 449-6937, Web Site: www.garonproducts.com (16)

Crowley, Charles, PCS List & Information Technologies, Manchester, MA. Tel: (978) 532-7100, (800) 532-LIST, FAX: (978) 532-9181, E-Mail: info@pcslist.com, Web Site: www.pcslist.com (23)

Crowley, Ellen, Gale Research Inc, Farmington Hills, MI. Tel: (248) 699-4253, (800) 877-GALE, FAX: (313) 961-6083, Web Site: www.gale.com (17)

Crowley, Tara, Garon Products Inc, Wall, NJ. Tel: (732) 449-1776, (800) 631-5380, FAX: (732) 449-6937, Web Site: www.garonproducts.com (16)

Crowley, Tom, Fielder's Choice Direct, Monticello, IN. Tel: (574) 583-2741 X107, (800) 321-3177, FAX: (574) 583-CORN, Web Site: www.fielderschoicedirect.com (8)

Crowley, William, Sears Canada Inc, Toronto, ON Canada. Tel: (416) 362-1711, (888) 473-2772, FAX: (613) 391-3047, E-Mail: home@sears.ca, Web Site: www.sears.ca (5)

Crown, Eric, Insight Direct Inc, Tempe, AZ. Tel: (480) 333-3001, (800) 467-4448, FAX: (480) 902-1180, Web Site: www.insight.com (16)

Crown, Tim, A., Insight Direct Inc, Tempe, AZ. Tel: (480) 333-3001, (800) 467-4448, FAX: (480) 902-1180, Web Site: www.insight.com (16)

Crowne Plaza Chateau Le Combe, Edmonton, AB Canada. Tel: (780) 428-6611, FAX: (780) 420-8379, E-Mail: info@chateaulecombe.com, Web Site: www.chateaulecombe.com (19)

CrownPeak, Los Angeles, CA. Tel: (310) 841-5920, Web Site: www.crownpeak.com (22)

Crozier, Joan, Hooleon Corp, Melrose, NM. Tel: (928) 634-7515, (800) 937-1337, E-Mail: sales@hooleon.com, Web Site: www.hooleon.com (3)

Crozier, Robert F., Hooleon Corp, Melrose, NM. Tel: (928) 634-7515, (800) 937-1337, E-Mail: sales@hooleon.com, Web Site: www.hooleon.com (3)

Crozier, Sharon, Ruf Corp, Olathe, KS. Tel: (913) 782-8544, (800) 829-8544, FAX: (913) 782-0150, E-Mail: solutions@ruf.com, Web Site: www.ruf.com (30)

Crozzoli, Christina, Stagestep Inc, Philadelphia, PA. Tel: (267) 672-2900, (800) 523-0961, FAX: (267) 672-2914, E-Mail: stagestep@stagestep.com, Web Site: www.stagestep.com (5)

Crucius, William, Direct Print, Windham, NH. Tel: (603) 437-6831 (21)

Cruise S.C., Sr. Patricia A., Covenant House International Headquarters, New York, NY. Tel: (212) 727-4000, (800) 999-9999, FAX: (212) 727-4992, Web Site: www.covenanthouse.org (1)

Crum, John, K., American Chemical Society, Washington, DC. Tel: (202) 872-4600, (800) 227-5558, FAX: (202) 833-7716, E-Mail: service@acs.org, Web Site: www.acs.org (1)

Crumbley, Rachel, Callaway Gardens, Pine Mountain, GA. Tel: (706) 663-2281, (800) CALLAWAY, FAX: (706) 663-6812, E-Mail: info@callawaygardens.com, Web Site: www.callawaygardens.com (19)

Crump, George, Print Services Distribution Association, Chicago, IL. Tel: (703) 836-6232, (800) 336-4641, FAX: (703) 836-2241, E-Mail: psda@psda.org, Web Site: www.psda.org (1)

Crumpton, Jonathan, Brentwood Benson Music Publishing, Franklin, TN. Tel: (615) 261-3400, (800) 846-7664, FAX: (615) 261-3381, E-Mail: choral@brentwoodbensonmusic.com, Web Site: www.brentwoodbenson.com (17)

Crush Creative, Burbank, CA. Tel: (818) 842-1121, (800) 300-3686, FAX: (818) 840-0185, E-Mail: john.davies@crushcreative.com, Web Site: www.crushcreative.com (27)

Crutchfield, William, G., Crutchfield Corp, Charlottesville, VA. Tel: (434) 817-1000, (800) 955-9091, FAX: (804) 817-1010, E-Mail: administration@crutchfield.com, Web Site: www.crutchfield.com (3)

Crutchfield Corp, Charlottesville, VA. Tel: (434) 817-1000, (800) 955-9091, FAX: (804) 817-1010, E-Mail: administration@crutchfield.com, Web Site: www.crutchfield.com (3)

Cruz, Joel, Interface Engineering, Portland, OR. Tel: (503) 382-2266, FAX: (503) 382-2262, E-Mail: solutions@interfaceengineering.com, Web Site: www.ieice.com (20)

Cruz, Rey, Shasho Jones Direct Inc, New York, NY. Tel: (212) 929-2300, E-Mail: glenda@sjdirect.com, Web Site: www.sjdirect.com (20)

Crystal Records Inc, Camas, WA. Tel: (360) 834-7022, FAX: (360) 834-9680, E-Mail: info@crystalrecords.com, Web Site: www.crystalrecords.com (3)

Crystek Corp, Fort Myers, FL. Tel: (239) 561-3311, (800) 237-3061, FAX: (239) 561-1025, E-Mail: sales@crystek.com, Web Site: www.crystek.com (9)

Csipak, Dr. James, State University of New York-College of Plattsburgh, Plattsburgh, NY. Tel: (518) 564-2000, FAX: (518) 564-3183, E-Mail: nancy.church@plattsburgh.edu, Web Site: www.plattsburgh.edu (41)

Csonaki, Robert, Costco Wholesale, Issaquah, WA. Tel: (425) 313-8647, Web Site: www.costco.com (33)

Cuba Cheese Shoppe, Cuba, NY. Tel: (585) 968-3949, FAX: (716) 968-1746, Web Site: www.cubacheese.com (4)

Cucciniello, John, Direct Link Worldwide, Elizabeth, NJ. Tel: (908) 289-0703, (800) 223-7967, FAX: (908) 289-0705, E-Mail: infousa@directlink.com, Web Site: www.directlink.com (28)

Cucullu, Robert, Data Intelligence Group, Franklin, TN. Tel: (615) 595-9591, Web Site: www.wedigdata.com (22)

Cuddledown Inc, Portland, ME. Tel: (207) 761-0201, (800) 323-6793, FAX: (207) 761-1948, Web Site: www.cuddledown.com (8)

Cuisinart, Stamford, CT. Tel: (203) 975-4600, FAX: (203) 975-4660, Web Site: www.cuisinart.com (16)

Culinary Parts Unlimited, San Francisco, CA. Tel: (800) 543-7549, FAX: (415) 495-5141, Web Site: www.culinaryparts.com (16)

Cullen, Carolyn, McGruff Specialty Products Office, Amsterdam, NY. Tel: (518) 842-4388, (888) 776-7763, FAX: (800) 995-5121, E-Mail: mcgruff@spocentral.com, Web Site: www.mcgruffspo.com (16)

Cullen, D., Timothy, DelStar Technologies, Middletown, DE. Tel: (302) 378-8888, (800) 521-6713, FAX: (302) 378-4482, Web Site: www.delstarinc.com (16)

Cullinane, Sue, Direct Marketing Association of Saint Louis, Washington, MO. Tel: (866) 516-0121, FAX: (636) 239-2324, E-Mail: mparisien@mac.com, Web Site: www.dmastl.org (40)

Mary Culnan, Washington, DC. Tel: (202) 687-4031, (202) 687-0100, Web Site: www.georgetown.edu (20)

Culver, Harriet, Culver Pictures Inc, Long Island City, NY. Tel: (718) 752-9393, FAX: (718) 752-9394, Web Site: www.culverpictures.com (38)

Culver, J. Bart, Bart's Watersports, North Webster, IN. Tel: (574) 834-7666, (800) 348-5016, FAX: (574) 834-4246, E-Mail: info@barts.com, Web Site: www.bartswatersports.com (11)

Culver Pictures Inc, Long Island City, NY. Tel: (718) 752-9393, FAX: (718) 752-9394, Web Site: www.culverpictures.com (38)

Cumberland General Store Inc, Alpharetta, GA. Tel: (800) 334-4640, FAX: (678) 240-0410, E-Mail: info@cumberlandgerneral.com, Web Site: www.cumberlandgeneral.com (8)

Cumberland Woodcraft Co Inc, Carlisle, PA. Tel: (717) 243-0063, (800) 367-1884, FAX: (717) 243-6502, E-Mail: sales@cumberlandwoodcraft.com, Web Site: www.cumberlandwoodcraft.com (8)

Cumming, Ian, M., Leucadia National Corp, New York, NY. Tel: (212) 460-1900, FAX: (212) 598-4869, Web Site: www.leucadia.com (14)

Cummings, John J., John Cummings & Partners LLC, Armonk, NY. Tel: (914) 273-4691, FAX: (914) 206-3007, E-Mail: john@dbmscan.com, Web Site: www.dbmscan.com (20)

Cummings, Robert, John Cummings & Partners LLC, Armonk, NY. Tel: (914) 273-4691, FAX: (914) 206-3007, E-Mail: john@dbmscan.com, Web Site: www.dbmscan.com (20)

Cummings, Steve, Wachovia Bank, National Association, Charlotte, NC. Tel: (704) 590-0000, (800) WACHOVIA, FAX: (704) 427-6748 (14)

Cummings, Wayne, Mail Handling Services, Eden Prairie, MN. Tel: (952) 975-5000, FAX: (952) 975-5030, Web Site: www.mailhandling.com (28)

John Cummings & Partners LLC, Armonk, NY. Tel: (914) 273-4691, FAX: (914) 206-3007, E-Mail: john@dbmscan.com, Web Site: www.dbmscan.com (20)

Cumpiano, Gerardo, Caribe Direct Inc, San Juan, PR. Tel: (787) 722-5188, FAX: (787) 723-6165, E-Mail: islaonline@prw.net, Web Site: www. islaonline.com (6)

CUNA Mutual Group, Madison, WI. Tel: (608) 238-5851, (800) 356-2644, FAX: (608) 231-8839, Web Site: www.cunamutual.com (15)

CUNA - Trade Association, Madison, WI. Tel: (608) 231-4215, Web Site: www.cuna.org (1)

Cuneo, Laurence, A., Cuneo Advertising, Bloomington, MN. Tel: (952) 707-1212, FAX: (952) 707-1295, E-Mail: agency@cuneocom.com, Web Site: www.cuneocom.com (35)

Cuneo Advertising, Bloomington, MN. Tel: (952) 707-1212, FAX: (952) 707-1295, E-Mail: agency@ cuneocom.com, Web Site: www.cuneocom.com (35)

Cunningham, David, Intermap Technologies, Englewood, CO. Tel: (303) 708-0955, FAX: (303) 708-0952, Web Site: www.intermap.com (32)

Cunningham, Dr. Joseph, Blue Cross & Blue Shield of Oklahoma, Tulsa, OK. Tel: (918) 560-3500, (800) 942-5837, E-Mail: info@bcbsok.com, Web Site: www.bcbsok.com (15)

Cunningham, Gerard, Lands' End Inc, Dodgeville, WI. Tel: (608) 935-9341, (800) 963-4816, FAX: (680) 935-4831, Web Site: www.landsend.com (2)

Cunningham, Gerard, MGI Management Institute, Hawthorne, NY. Tel: (914) 428-6500, (800) 932-0191, FAX: (914) 428-0773, E-Mail: mgiusa@aol. com, Web Site: www.mgi.org (16)

Cunningham, Glenn, Thermal Product Solutions, White Deer, PA. Tel: (570) 538-7200, (800) 586-2473 (16)

Cunningham, Jack, American Period Lighting Inc, Lancaster, PA. Tel: (717) 392-5649, FAX: (717) 509-3127, E-Mail: conygham@yahoo.com, Web Site: www.americanperiod.com (8)

Cunningham, James, Alternative Media Group, Naples, FL. Tel: (732) 741-0585, FAX: (732) 741-0489, Web Site: www.amg-global.com (31)

Cunningham, James, H., Cunningham Group, Elmwood Park, IL. Tel: (708) 848-2300, (800) 962-1224, FAX: (708) 848-2174, E-Mail: cunngroup@ cg-ins.com, Web Site: www.cg-ins.com (15)

Cunningham, Thomas, WennSoft, New Berlin, WI. Tel: (262) 317-3717, Web Site: www.wennsoft.com (22)

Cunningham, Tracy, Bacompt Systems Inc, Carmel, IN. Tel: (317) 574-7474, (800) 533-7109, FAX: (317) 574-7475, E-Mail: customer.service@ bacompt.com, Web Site: www.bacompt.com (21)

Cunningham Group, Elmwood Park, IL. Tel: (708) 848-2300, (800) 962-1224, FAX: (708) 848-2174, E-Mail: cunngroup@cg-ins.com, Web Site: www. cg-ins.com (15)

Cunnyngham, Julie, Hallmark Cards Inc, Kansas City, MO. Tel: (816) 274-5111, FAX: (816) 274-7276, Web Site: www.hallmark.com (16)

Cuno, Steve, Response Agency Inc, Sandy, UT Canada. Tel: (801) 352-9100, Web Site: www. responseagency.com (35)

Curatolo, B.L., West Shore Distributors, Westlake, OH. Tel: (440) 835-5600, (800) 344-8141, FAX: (440) 835-8654, E-Mail: westshore@ameritech.net, Web Site: www.westshoreframes.com (8)

Curcio, John, Professional Training Associates Inc, Duquesne, PA. Tel: (412) 460-0266, FAX: (412) 460-0269, E-Mail: info@ptainc.com, Web Site: www.ptainc.com (17)

Curcurito, David, Esquire Magazine, New York, NY. Tel: (212) 649-2000, (800) 925-0485, FAX: (212) 265-0938, E-Mail: esquire@hearst.com, Web Site: www.esquire.com (17)

Curiale, Judy, Jupiter Images, Tucson, AZ. Tel: (520) 881-8101, (800) 764-7427, FAX: (520) 881-1841, Web Site: www.jupiterimages.com (38)

Curler, Jerry, S., Bemis Co Inc, Terre Haute, IN. Tel: (812) 466-2213, FAX: (812) 460-6370, E-Mail: contact@beemis.com, Web Site: www.bemis.com (34)

Curling, Douglas, C., Choice Point, Alpharetta, GA. Tel: (770) 752-6000, (800) 342-5339, FAX: (770) 752-6005, Web Site: www.choicepoint.com (16)

Curran, Carla, O'Currance Inc, Draper, UT. Tel: (801) 736-0500, (888) 628-7726, FAX: (801) 736-0510, E-Mail: sales@ocurrance.com, Web Site: www. ocurance.com (18)

Curran, Don, Virco Manufacturing Corp, Conway, AR. Tel: (501) 329-2901, (800) 448-4726, FAX: (800) 258-7367, E-Mail: info@virco.com, Web Site: www.virco.com (16)

Curran, Dorothy, E., Mission: A Consulting Group, Westport, CT. Tel: (203) 227-9475, FAX: (203) 227-6512, E-Mail: info@mission-consulting.com, Web Site: www.mission-consulting.com (20)

Curran, Kevin, GCC Printers, Bedford, MA. Tel: (781) 275-5800, (800) 422-7777, FAX: (781) 275-1115, (800) 442-2329, E-Mail: sales@gccprinters.com, Web Site: www.gcctech.com (10)

Curran, Martin, J., MJ Curran & Associates Inc, Sandwich, MA. Tel: (617) 247-7700, FAX: (617) 267-6429 (20)

Curran, Tara, BtoB Magazine, New York, NY. Tel: (212) 210-0206, FAX: (212) 210-0422, E-Mail: aholtzman@crain.com, Web Site: www.btobonline. com (43)

MJ Curran & Associates Inc, Sandwich, MA. Tel: (617) 247-7700, FAX: (617) 267-6429 (20)

Current USA Inc, Colorado Springs, CO. Tel: (719) 594-4100, (877) 665-4458, FAX: (719) 531-2283, Web Site: www.currentinc.com (6)

Curriculum Associates Inc, North Billerica, MA. Tel: (978) 667-8000, FAX: (978) 667-5706, E-Mail: cainfo@curriculumassociates.com, Web Site: www. curriculumassociates.com (17)

Currie, Amanda, Frontline Direct Inc, Del Mar, CA. Tel: (858) 638-1515, Web Site: www. frontlinedirect.com (23)

Currie, Brad, Mac Direct, Colmar, PA. Tel: (215) 822-5775, (800) 278-1154, FAX: (215) 822-7977, E-Mail: info@macdirect.com, Web Site: www. macdirect.com (22)

Currie, Mary, Ellen, The Right Start Inc, Denver, CO. Tel: (303) 320-8312, Web Site: www.rightstart.com (5)

Currie, Peter, Daydots, Fort Worth, TX. Tel: (817) 590-4500, (800) 321-3687, FAX: (800) 438-7002, E-Mail: customercare@daydots.com, Web Site: www.daydots.com (6)

Curry, Claire, L., The Nulman Group, Somerset, NJ. Tel: (908) 534-4041, (888) 440-3367, FAX: (908) 534-5023, E-Mail: pnulman@nulmangroup.com, Web Site: www.nulmangroup.com (35)

Curry, Pam, United Air Specialists Inc, Cincinnati, OH. Tel: (513) 891-0400, (800) 992-4422, FAX: (513) 891-4882, E-Mail: uas@uasinc.com, Web Site: www.uasinc.com (16)

Curry, Todd, Ifbyphone, Skokie, IL. Tel: (877) 295-5100, Web Site: www.ifbyphone.com (30)

Curshen, Andy, Mercury International, Avenel, NJ. Tel: (732) 396-9555, FAX: (732) 396-1492, Web Site: www.mercuryinternational.com (28)

Curtin, Brian, Enterprise Rent-A-Car, Saint Louis, MO. Tel: (314) 512-5000, Web Site: www. enterprise.com (19)

Curtin, Mary, 4Imprint Inc, Oshkosh, WI. Tel: (920) 236-7272, (888) 298-8190, (877) 446-7746, FAX: (800) 355-5043, E-Mail: administrator@4imprint. com, Web Site: www.4imprint.com (16)

Curtis, Cybil, Great Chefs Television Publishing, New Orleans, LA. Tel: (504) 581-5000, (800) 321-1499, FAX: (504) 581-1188, E-Mail: info@greatchefs. com, Web Site: www.greatchefs.com (6)

Curtis, Mary, E., Transaction Publishers, Piscataway, NJ. Tel: (732) 445-1245, FAX: (732) 748-9801, E-Mail: trans@transactionpub.com, Web Site: www.transactionpub.com (17)

Curtis, Rebecca, Veterans of Foreign Wars (VFW) of the US-National Headquarters, Kansas City, MO. Tel: (816) 756-3390, FAX: (816) 968-1149, E-Mail: info@vfw.org, Web Site: www.vfw.org (1)

Curtis, Susan, Santa Fe School of Cooking, Santa Fe, NM. Tel: (505) 983-4511, FAX: (505) 983-7540, Web Site: www.santafeschoolofcooking.com (4)

Curtis, Tim, Mid America Motorworks, Effingham, IL. Tel: (217) 347-5591, (800) 500-1500, FAX: (217) 347-2952, E-Mail: mail@mamotorworks.com, Web Site: www.mamotorworks.com (12)

Curtis 1000 Inc, Duluth, GA. Tel: (678) 380-9095, (800) 766-1007, FAX: (770) 717-1890, E-Mail: info@curtis1000.com, Web Site: www.curtis1000. com (27)

Cusack, Chris, Direct Logic Solutions, Peoria, IL. Tel: (309) 688-5500, FAX: (309) 688-5502, E-Mail: nedbarrett@direct-logic.com, Web Site: www. direct-logic.com (22)

Cusak, Tom, Enterprise Ireland, New York, NY. Tel: (212) 371-3600, FAX: (212) 371-6398, Web Site: www.enterprise-ireland.com (16)

Cushing, Kevin, AlphaGraphics World Headquarters, Salt Lake City, UT. Tel: (801) 595-7270, (800) 955-6246, FAX: (801) 595-7271, E-Mail: contactus@alphagraphics.com, Web Site: www. alphagraphics.com (27)

Cushinsky, Steven M., ACT ONE LISTS, Beverly, MA. Tel: (781) 639-1919, (800) 228-5478, FAX: (781) 639-2733, E-Mail: info@act1lists.com, Web Site: www.act1lists.com (23)

Cushman III, John C., Boys' Life & Scouting Magazines, Irving, TX. Tel: (972) 580-2000, (866) 584-6589, FAX: (972) 580-2079, Web Site: www. boyslife.org (17)

Cushman III, John, C., Boy Scouts of America/ National Supply Group, Charlotte, NC. Tel: (972) 580-2161, (800) 323-0736, E-Mail: customerservice@scoutstuff.org, Web Site: www. scoutstuff.org (1)

Cushman, Allen, Cushman Fruit Co Inc, West Palm Beach, FL. Tel: (561) 965-3535, (800) 776-2295, FAX: (561) 968-7263, E-Mail: info@honeybell. com, Web Site: www.honeybell.com (4)

Cushman, John, Cushman Fruit Co Inc, West Palm Beach, FL. Tel: (561) 965-3535, (800) 776-2295, FAX: (561) 968-7263, E-Mail: info@honeybell. com, Web Site: www.honeybell.com (4)

Cushman Fruit Co Inc, West Palm Beach, FL. Tel: (561) 965-3535, (800) 776-2295, FAX: (561) 968-7263, E-Mail: info@honeybell.com, Web Site: www.honeybell.com (4)

Custom Accessories, Niles, IL. Tel: (847) 966-6900, (800) 962-6676, FAX: (847) 966-9650, Web Site: www.causa.com (11)

Custom Direct, Joppa, MD. Tel: (410) 679-3300 (16)

Custom List Services Inc, Cape Coral, FL. Tel: (301) 497-1858, FAX: (301) 497-1858 (23)

Custom Miniatures, Hudson, NH. Tel: (603) 882-6392 (6)

Custom Toll Free, Mill Creek, WA. Tel: (800) 933-3030, Web Site: www.customtollfree.com (5)

Customer Asset Consulting Group Inc, Schaumburg, IL. Tel: (847) 805-9800, Web Site: www.cac-group.com (22)

Customer Communications Group, Lakewood, CO. Tel: (303) 986-3000, (800) 525-0313, FAX: (303) 989-4805, E-Mail: info@customer.com, Web Site: www.customer.com (35)

The Customer Connection Inc, Escondido, CA. Tel: (760) 489-8339, (800) 477-7166, FAX: (760) 489-1075, E-Mail: judd@custcon.com, Web Site: www. custcon.com (22)

Customer Growth, Blau Moritz Klang Inc, Westport, CT. Tel: (203) 226-8795, FAX: (203) 227-8601, E-Mail: josh.moritz@customer-growth.com, Web Site: www.customer-growth.com (35)

Customer Marketing Group LLC, Weston, CT. Tel: (203) 226-9845, FAX: (203) 226-9837, E-Mail: bill@4cmg.com, Web Site: www.4cmg.com (35)

Customer Portfolios LLC, Boston, MA. Tel: (617) 224-9501, Web Site: www.customerportfolios.com (22)

Customer Retention Management Group Inc, Severna Park, MD. Tel: (410) 280-1720, (888) 822-8574, FAX: (410) 280-1723 (35)

Customer Retention Solutions, Portage, MI. Tel: (269) 324-7385 (20)

CustomerFunding.com Inc, Tempe, AZ. Tel: (480) 784-1030, Web Site: www.customerfunding.com (35)

CustomerLink, Duluth, MN. Tel: (218) 722-2800, (866) 245-5569, FAX: (218) 722-3287, E-Mail: info@customerlinkone.com, Web Site: www.customerlinkone.com (29)

CustomerMining, Soquel, CA. Tel: (831) 465-0890, Web Site: www.customermining.com (35)

Custometrics Inc, Richmond Hill, ON Canada. Tel: (905) 886-4161, E-Mail: info@custometrics.ca, Web Site: www.custometrics.com (30)

Customized Newspaper Advertising, Des Moines, IA. Tel: (515) 244-2145, (800) 227-7636, FAX: (515) 244-4855, Web Site: www.cnaads.com (18)

Custus, Laura, R., World Press Review, New York, NY. Tel: (212) 982-8880, Web Site: www.worldpressreview.com (18)

Cutler, Alexander, M., Eaton Corp, Raleigh, NC. Tel: (216) 523-4400, (800) 356-5794, FAX: (216) 523-4787, Web Site: www.eaton.com (16)

Cutler, Ken, Tower Hobbies/Hobbico, Champaign, IL. Tel: (217) 398-3636, (800) 637-6050, FAX: (217) 398-1104, Web Site: www.towerhobbies.com (11)

Cutshaw, Beverly, Academic Travel Abroad Inc, Washington, DC. Tel: (202) 785-9000, (800) 556-7896, FAX: (202) 342-0317, Web Site: www.academictravel.com (19)

Cutting IV, Sam, Dakin Farm, Ferrisburgh, VT. Tel: (802) 425-3971, (800) 993-2546, FAX: (802) 425-2765, E-Mail: scutting@dakinfarm.com, Web Site: www.dakinfarm.com (4)

Cuvaison Inc, Calistoga, CA. Tel: (707) 942-6266, FAX: (707) 942-5732, E-Mail: jschuppert@cuvaison.com, Web Site: www.cuvaison.com (4)

Cyber City Teleservices Marketing Inc, Hackensack, NJ. Tel: (201) 487-1616, (800) 213-4144, E-Mail: info@cctll.com, Web Site: www.cctll.com (29)

Cyber Marketing Services, Montvale, NJ. Tel: (201) 505-1743, FAX: (201) 391-4907, E-Mail: info@crmxchange.com, Web Site: www.crmxchange.com (29)

CyberData, Hicksville, NY. Tel: (516) 942-8000, FAX: (516) 942-0800, E-Mail: info@cyberdata.com, Web Site: www.cyberdata.com (22)

CyberDefender, Los Angeles, CA. Tel: (213) 689-8631x114, Web Site: www.cyberdefender.com (22)

Cygnus Business Media, Fort Atkinson, WI. Tel: (203) 227-4037, (800) 547-7377, FAX: (203) 227-4245, Web Site: www.cygnusb2b.com (17)

Cymerys, Ed, Blue Shield Life, San Francisco, CA. Tel: (888) 800-2742, FAX: (800) 329-2742, Web Site: www.blueshieldca.com (15)

Cynthia Fields & Co (CFC), New York, NY. Tel: (212) 242-6063 (20)

Cypress Media Group, Roswell, GA. Tel: (770) 640-9918, E-Mail: info@cypressmedia.net, Web Site: www.cypressmedia.net (35)

Cyr, Mr. Tom, Nowetah's American Indian Store & Museum, New Portland, ME. Tel: (207) 628-4991, Web Site: www.nowetahs.webs.com (6)

Cyr, Mrs. Nowetah, Nowetah's American Indian Store & Museum, New Portland, ME. Tel: (207) 628-4991, Web Site: www.nowetahs.webs.com (6)

Cyril-Scott Co, Lancaster, OH. Tel: (740) 654-2112, FAX: (740) 654-7712, E-Mail: postoffice@cyrilscott.com, Web Site: www.cyrilscott.com (27)

Cystic Fibrosis Foundation, Bethesda, MD. Tel: (301) 951-4422, Web Site: www.cff.org (1)

Cytec Industries Inc, Olean, NY. Tel: (716) 372-9650, FAX: (716) 372-1594, Web Site: www.conap.com (16)

Czlonka, Michael, F., Cision US Inc, Chicago, IL. Tel: (312) 922-2400, (866) 639-5087, FAX: (312) 922-3126, E-Mail: info.us@cision.com, Web Site: us.cision.com (43)

Czubay, Kenneth, Southeast Toyota Distributors LLC, Deerfield Beach, FL. Tel: (954) 429-2000, Web Site: www.jmfamily.com (16)

Czyz, Cynthia, Champion America Inc, Branford, CT. Tel: (203) 315-1181, (877) 242-6709, FAX: (800) 336-3707, E-Mail: teamca@champion-america.com, Web Site: www.championamerica.com (10)

D

D, Elliot, Environmental Law Institute, Washington, DC. Tel: (202) 939-3800, FAX: (202) 939-3868, E-Mail: law@eli.org, Web Site: www.eli.org (17)

D&B, Parsippany, NJ. Tel: (973) 921-5500, Web Site: www.dnb.com (22)

D&B Canada, Mississauga, ON Canada. Tel: (905) 568-6000, FAX: (905) 568-6197, Web Site: www.dnb.ca (30)

D&B Sales and Marketing Solutions, Waltham, MA. Tel: (781) 672-9200, (800) 590-0065, FAX: (781) 672-9290, Web Site: www.b2bsalesandmarketing.com (22)

D&D Associates Inc, Garden City, NY. Tel: (516) 326-8800, (800) 554-0347 (22)

D&E Pharmaceuticals Inc, Farmingdale, NJ. Tel: (973) 838-8300, (800) 221-1833, FAX: (877) 838-0560, E-Mail: customerservice@dnepharm.com, Web Site: www.dnepharm.com (7)

D-J Associates, Danbury, CT. Tel: (203) 431-8777, FAX: (203) 431-3302, E-Mail: info@djassoc.com, Web Site: www.djassoc.com (23)

D2: Direct, Denville, NJ. Tel: (973) 627-4410, FAX: (973) 627-3703, E-Mail: info@d2direct.com, Web Site: www.d2direct.com (35)

D'Agostino, Chicca, Focus USA Inc, Hackensack, NJ. Tel: (201) 489-2525, FAX: (201) 489-4499, E-Mail: suzanne@focus-usa-l.com, Web Site: www.focus-usa-l.com (23)

D'Agostino, Susan, Harris Connect LLC, Brewster, NY. Tel: (800) 326-6600, Web Site: www.harrisconnect.com (1)

D'Alessandro, Dominic, John Hancock Financial Services Inc, Boston, MA. Tel: (617) 572-6000, (800) 732-5543, FAX: (617) 572-6451, Web Site: www.johnhancock.com (15)

D'Alessandro, Tiffany, Brabender Cox, Pittsburgh, PA. Tel: (412) 434-6320, FAX: (412) 424-6391, E-Mail: tiffany@brabendercox.com, Web Site: www.brabendercox.com (35)

D'Amelio, Mimi, Madison Executive Search, Ridgefield, CT. Tel: (203) 431-6565, FAX: (203) 431-6060, E-Mail: mimi@directexec.com, Web Site: www.directexec.com (20)

D'Angelo, Bruce, Diamond Marketing Solutions, Bloomingdale, IL. Tel: (630) 523-5250, FAX: (630) 523-0403, Web Site: www.dmsolutions.com (35)

D'April, Shane, Campaigns & Elections Magazine, Arlington, VA. Tel: (703) 778-4028, (800) 771-8252, FAX: (703) 778-4024, Web Site: www.campaignsandelections.com (17)

D'Auray, Terry, Orion Telescopes & Binoculars, Watsonville, CA. Tel: (831) 763-7000, (800) 447-1001, FAX: (408) 763-7017, E-Mail: sales@telescope.com, Web Site: www.telescope.com (11)

D'Aurizio, Kim, We Deliver America Inc, Englewood Cliffs, NJ. Tel: (201) 307-8888, FAX: (201) 307-1200, E-Mail: info@we-deliver-america.com, Web Site: www.we-deliver-america.com (31)

D'Micco, Daniel, Nucor Corp, Charlotte, NC. Tel: (704) 366-7000, FAX: (704) 362-4208, E-Mail: info@nucor.com, Web Site: nucor.com (16)

D'Souza, Victor, Polyair Packaging, Chicago, IL. Tel: (773) 995-1818, (888) POLYAIR X444, FAX: (773) 995-7725, E-Mail: marketing@polyair.com, Web Site: www.polyair.com (9)

DAJ Direct Inc, Costa Mesa, CA. Tel: (949) 722-0506, FAX: (949) 722-8026, Web Site: www.dajdirect.com (24)

DB Consulting, Harrison, NY. Tel: (914) 698-2008, E-Mail: darcybev@yahoo.com (20)

Db Marketing, Harrison, NY. Tel: (914) 698-2008 (22)

DBMCatalyst, Lexington, MA. Tel: (339) 227-7591 (20)

DCA, West Chester, PA. Tel: (610) 344-7488, (800) 638-6684, FAX: (610) 431-6500, E-Mail: ortho@dentalcorp.com, Web Site: www.dentalcorp.com (16)

DCI Marketing Inc, Milwaukee, WI. Tel: (414) 228-7000, (800) 284-6318, FAX: (414) 228-3411, Web Site: www.dcimarketing.com (35)

DCJ Consulting, Forest Hills, NY. Tel: (718) 575-8357 (20)

DDB Chicago, Chicago, IL. Tel: (312) 552-6000, FAX: (312) 552-2370, Web Site: www.ddbchi.com (35)

DDB Direct Los Angeles, Los Angeles, CA. Tel: (310) 907-1500, FAX: (310) 907-1990, Web Site: www.ddbla.com (35)

DDB Stock Photography LLC, Baton Rouge, LA. Tel: (225) 763-6235, FAX: (225) 763-6894, E-Mail: info@ddbstock.com, Web Site: www.ddbstock.com (38)

DEI, Minneapolis, MN. Tel: (612) 677-1505, Web Site: www.deiworksite.org (1)

DFS Group Limited, San Francisco, CA. Tel: (415) 977-2700, FAX: (415) 977-2970, Web Site: www.dfsgalleria.com (5)

D/FW Grocers Association, Carrollton, TX. Tel: (972) 353-5885, Fax: (469) 574-5252, Web Site: www.dfwga.net (1)

DHL Express, Plantation, FL. Tel: (954) 888-7000, (800) 225-5345, FAX: (954) 888-7310, Web Site: www.dhl.com (28)

DHL Global Mail, Weston, FL. Tel: (954) 903-6300, (866) 616-MAIL, FAX: (954) 903-6310, E-Mail: contact@dhlglobalmail.com, Web Site: www.dhlglobalmail.com (28)

DIA - Nielsen USA Inc, Moorestown, NJ. Tel: (856) 642-9700, (800) 893-6361, FAX: (856) 642-9709, Web Site: www.thomasregister.com (16)

DKI Direct, Montvale, NJ. Tel: (201) 391-6000, Web Site: www.dkidirect.com (35)

DKP & Associates, Inc, Skokie, IL. Tel: (847) 933-9808, E-Mail: dpearlman@dkpassociates.com, Web Site: www.dkpassociates.com (22)

D'Lights, South El Monte, CA. Tel: (818) 956-5656, FAX: (818) 956-5657, Web Site: www.dlights.com (8)

DM Assistance Inc, Portsmouth, NH. Tel: (603) 964-6156 (20)

DM Data Solutions LLC, Alexandria, VA. Tel: (703) 415-6222, Web Site: www.dmdatasolutions.com (22)

DM Info, Naperville, IL. Tel: (630) 357-0732, FAX: (630) 527-8136, E-Mail: dminfo@dmcsweeney.com (20)

DM News, New York, NY. Tel: (212) 925-7300, FAX: (212) 925-8752, Web Site: www.dmnews.com (43)

DMA (Direct Marketing Association), New York, NY. Tel: (212) 768-7277, FAX: (212) 302-6714, E-Mail: customerservice@the-dma.org, Web Site: www.the-dma.org (40)

DMA - Events-Conference Programming/Exhibitors/Speakers, New York, NY. Tel: (212) 768-7277 X1419, FAX: (212) 302-6714, E-Mail: consumer@the-dma.org, Web Site: www.the-dma.org (41)

DMA Statistical Fact Book, New York, NY. Tel: (212) 790-1500, FAX: (212) 302-6714, E-Mail: customerservice@the-dma.org, Web Site: www.the-dma.org (43)

DMB Financial, Beverly, MA. Tel: (866) 810-3210, Web Site: www.dmbfinancial.com (14)

DMB Realty Network, Scottsdale, AZ. Tel: (480) 515-0148, Web Site: www.dmbrealty.com (16)

DMC Advertising, Pewaukee, WI. Tel: (262) 523-2000, (800) 952-9165, FAX: (262) 523-2012, E-Mail: info@dmcadvertising.com, Web Site: www.dmcadvertising.com (35)

DMC Corp, Kearny, NJ. Tel: (973) 589-0606, FAX: (973) 589-8931, Web Site: www.dmc-usa.com (16)

DMG Direct Inc, Tigard, OR. Tel: (503) 579-5609, (888) 282-2122, FAX: (503) 579-4919, E-Mail: dmg@dirmarketing.com, Web Site: www.dirmarketing.com/dmginc (40)

DMG-Lists, Deer Park, NY. Tel: (631) 586-5800, FAX: (631) 586-6080, E-Mail: kathyb@dmgltd.org, Web Site: www.dmgltd.org (24)

dmh Marketing Partners - Louisville, Louisville, KY. Tel: (502) 339-6442, Web Site: www.thednrgroup.com (28)

DMN3, Houston, TX. Tel: (713) 868-3000, (800) 625-8320, FAX: (713) 868-1388, E-Mail: contact@dmn3.com, Web Site: www.dmn3.com (35)

DMRA, Mountain View, CA. Tel: (650) 650-9988, Web Site: www.dmrainc.com (22)

DMRA & Matchkey Corp, Mountain View, CA. Tel: (650) 856-9988, FAX: (650) 856-9986 (30)

DMRS Group Inc, New York, NY. Tel: (212) 590-2340, FAX: (212) 590-2341, E-Mail: bgrossman@dmrsgroup.com, Web Site: www.dmrsgroup.com (22)

DMS Insights, Dallas, TX. Tel: (972) 874-5080, (800) 409-6262, FAX: (972) 353-2450, E-Mail: info@dmsinsights.com, Web Site: www.dmsdallas.com (30)

DMSA Inc, Newfoundland, PA. Tel: (570) 676-6000 (40)

DMW Worldwide LLC, Chesterbrook, PA. Tel: (610) 407-0407, (877) 744-3699, FAX: (610) 407-9201, E-Mail: whunter@dmwdirect.com, Web Site: www.dmwdirect.com (35)

DMX-Direct, Inc, Centennial, CO. Tel: (303) 339-9300, FAX: (303) 388-6363, Web Site: www.dmx-direct.com (21)

DNP America Inc, New York, NY. Tel: (212) 503-1060, FAX: (212) 679-0613 (27)

DOM Corp, Marina Del Rey, CA. Tel: (310) 578-1164 (5)

DPC Computers, Monsey, NY. Tel: (845) 426-3790, (866) 513-CORP, FAX: (845) 426-6275, E-Mail: learnmore@salestax.com, Web Site: www.salestax.com (16)

DRG, Berne, IN. Tel: (260) 589-4000, Web Site: www.drgnetwork.com (17)

DS & A Consulting, Lexington, KY. Tel: (973) 530-4198 (20)

DS Graphics Inc, Lowell, MA. Tel: (617) 389-5350, (800) 536-8253, FAX: (617) 387-7752, E-Mail: sales@dsgraphics.com, Web Site: www.dsgraphics.com (21)

DS Waters of North America LP, Flowery Branch, GA. Tel: (626) 585-1000, (800) 669-3402, FAX: (626) 585-8563, E-Mail: customerservice@water.com, Web Site: www.water.com (4)

DST Output, South Windsor, CT. Tel: (860) 290-7337, (800) 441-7587, Web Site: www.dstoutput.com (28)

DWS Associates, Saint Paul, MN. Tel: (602) 321-6512, Web Site: www.dwstevenson.com (20)

DWS Investments Service Co, Kansas City, MO. Tel: (800) 543-5776, Web Site: www.dws-investments.com (14)

Da Costa, Debra, Direct Marketing Partners, Sacramento, CA. Tel: (916) 974-6969, (800) 909-2626, FAX: (916) 920-5156, E-Mail: info@dirmkt.com, Web Site: www.directmarketingpartners.com (29)

Da Costa, Debra, I., United Nations Federal Credit Union, Long Island City, NY. Tel: (347) 686-6000, Web Site: www.unfcu.org (1)

Da-Lite Screen Co Inc, Warsaw, IN. Tel: (574) 267-8101, (800) 622-3737, FAX: (574) 267-7804, E-Mail: info@da-lite.com, Web Site: www.da-lite.com (16)

Da Vinci Technologies LLC, Auburn, AL. Tel: (334) 502-8925, (877) 334-4731, FAX: (208) 485-7749, E-Mail: sales@davinci.aero, Web Site: www.davincitechnologies.com (3)

Dabbs, Dale, Custom Direct, Joppa, MD. Tel: (410) 679-3300 (16)

Dabbs, Karl, Tidbits Media, Montgomery, AL. Tel: (334) 290-0225, (800) 523-3096, FAX: (334) 386-0302, E-Mail: editors@tidbitsweekly.com, Web Site: www.tidbitsweekly.com (17)

Daboll, Peter, Bunchball, Redwood City, CA. Tel: (408) 985-2034, Web Site: www.bunchball.com (32)

Daboub, Leo, Cardflex Financial Services, Costa Mesa, CA. Tel: (866) 634-3044, Web Site: www.flex1.com (14)

Dabrowski, Richard C., Shaker Workshops, Ashburnham, MA. Tel: (978) 827-9900, FAX: (978) 827-6554, E-Mail: shaker9973@shakerworkshops.com, Web Site: www.shakerworkshops.com (8)

Dabrowski, Richard, Cohasset Colonials, Ashburnham, MA. Tel: (978) 827-3001, (800) 288-2389, FAX: (978) 827-3227, E-Mail: cohasset@cohassetcolonials.com, Web Site: www.cohassetcolonials.com (8)

Dachowski, Peter, CertainTeed Corp, Valley Forge, PA. Tel: (610) 341-7000/7739, (800) 233-8990, FAX: (610) 341-7777, Web Site: www.certainteed.com (16)

Dachs, David, Innovative Clip Art, York, SC. Tel: (803) 831-6727, FAX: (704) 290-2069, E-Mail: sales@innovativeclipart.com, Web Site: www.innovativeclipart.com (10)

DaCruz, Leslie, USC Viterbi School of Engineering, Los Angeles, CA. Tel: (213) 740-2502, Web Site: http://viterbi.usc.edu/ (1)

Dadarria, Robert, RAD Marketing & Cable Towns, Mount Vernon, NY. Tel: (914) 668-3563, FAX: (914) 668-4247, E-Mail: cabletowns@verizon.net (24)

Steven P d'Adolf, Oceanside, CA. Tel: (858) 451-2130, FAX: (858) 451-2130 (39)

Daedalus Books Inc, Columbia, MD. Tel: (410) 309-2700, (800) 395-2665, FAX: (410) 309-2701, Web Site: www.salebooks.com (5)

Dagestad, Mark, Schnuck Markets Inc, Saint Louis, MO. Tel: (314) 994-9900, FAX: (314) 994-4465, Web Site: www.schnucks.com (16)

Dagot, Antoine, Hilton Grand Vacations Co, Orlando, FL. Tel: (407) 521-3100, Web Site: www.hiltongrandvacations.com (19)

Dahart, Denise, Ariago Designs, Campbell, CA. Tel: (408) 668-0400, FAX: (408) 688-0401, Web Site: www.ariago.com (35)

Daher, Gerard, Speedeon Data Corp, Cleveland, OH. Tel: (440) 287-7306, Web Site: www.speedeondata.com (23)

Daher, Tonya, School Annual Publishing Co, State College, PA. Tel: (800) 436-6030, E-Mail: yearbook@schoolannual.com, Web Site: www.schoolannual.com (17)

Dahl, Roy, Crescent Beach Enterprises LLC, Bohemia, NY. Tel: (631) 588-6600, FAX: (631) 588-7077, E-Mail: rjd@cbnet.com, Web Site: www.cbprod.com (32)

Dahlberg, Peter, American Health & Life Insurance Co, Fort Worth, TX. Tel: (817) 348-7500, (800) 995-2274, FAX: (817) 348-7553, Web Site: www.citifinancial.com (15)

Dahlgren, Kent, Victor Envelope Co, Bensenville, IL. Tel: (630) 616-2750, Web Site: www.victorenvelope.com (26)

Dahlheimer, Lynda, Sense of Design Inc, Minnetonka, MN. Tel: (952) 935-8827 (36)

Dahlke, Darrel, KMA Direct Communications, Dallas, TX. Tel: (972) 244-1900, FAX: (972) 244-1901, E-Mail: sales@kma.com, Web Site: www.kma.com (1)

Dahlke, Sharon, Prairie Nursery, Westfield, WI. Tel: (608) 296-3679, (800) 476-9453, FAX: (608) 296-2741, E-Mail: webcs@prairienursery.com, Web Site: www.prairienursery.com (8)

Daigle, John, Overton's Inc, Greenville, NC. Tel: (252) 355-7600, (800) 334-6541, FAX: (252) 355-2923, E-Mail: service@overtons.com, Web Site: www.overtons.com (11)

Dail, Baljit, AON Center, Chicago, IL. Tel: (312) 381-1000, FAX: (312) 381-6032, Web Site: www.aon.com (15)

Dailey, Marc, The Columbian, Vancouver, WA. Tel: (360) 694-3391, FAX: (360) 735-4503, Web Site: www.columbian.com (17)

Daily, Andrew, P., Vail Associates Inc, Broomfield, CO. Tel: (303) 404-1800, (800) 842-8062, FAX: (303) 404-6415, Web Site: www.snow.com (19)

Daily, Francis, W., Hain Celestial Group, Melville, NY. Tel: (631) 730-2200, FAX: (631) 730-2500, Web Site: www.hain-celestial.com (16)

Daily Commercial News & Construction Record, Markham, ON Canada. Tel: (905) 752-5408, (800) 465-6475, FAX: (888) 396-9413, (905) 752-5450, E-Mail: dcnonl@reedbusiness.com, Web Site: www.dcnonl.com (17)

Daily Record & Dispatch Co, Dunn, NC. Tel: (910) 891-1234, FAX: (910) 891-5253, Web Site: www.mydailyrecord.com (17)

DaimlerChrysler Corp, Auburn Hills, MI. Tel: (248) 512-1879, Web Site: www.daimlerchrysler.com (12)

Dain Rauscher Inc, Minneapolis, MN. Tel: (612) 371-2711, FAX: (612) 373-1627, Web Site: www.dainrauscher.com (14)

Daines, Gina, Basic Research, Salt Lake City, UT. Tel: (801) 234-7000, Web Site: www.silversage.com (7)

Daintith, Stephen, Dow Jones & Co, Princeton, NJ. Tel: (609) 520-4000, FAX: (212) 416-4348, Web Site: www.dowjones.com/corp/index.html (17)

Dairy Council of California, Irvine, CA. Tel: (949) 756-7896, Web Site: www.dairycouncilofca.org (1)

Dairy Farmers of America Inc, Kansas City, MO. Tel: (816) 801-6455, (888) 332-6455, FAX: (816) 801-6456, E-Mail: webmail@dfamilk.com, Web Site: www.dfamilk.com (16)

Dairy Management Inc, Rosemont, IL. Tel: (847) 803-2000, FAX: (847) 803-2077, Web Site: www.nationaldairycouncil.org (1)

Dakar, Amber, Weiss Research Inc, Jupiter, FL. Tel: (561) 627-3300, (877) 925-4833, FAX: (561) 625-6685, E-Mail: newbusiness@weissgroupinc.com, Web Site: www.weissgroupinc.com (17)

Dakin, Jennifer, US Cellular, Chicago, IL. Tel: (773) 339-8900, Web Site: www.uscellular.com (32)

Dakin Farm, Ferrisburgh, VT. Tel: (802) 425-3971, (800) 993-2546, FAX: (802) 425-2765, E-Mail: scutting@dakinfarm.com, Web Site: www.dakinfarm.com (4)

Dakota Digital, Sioux Falls, SD. Tel: (605) 332-6513, (800) 593-4160, FAX: (605) 339-4106, E-Mail: sales@dakotadigital.com, Web Site: www.dakotadigital.com (12)

Dalco Electronics, Springboro, OH. Tel: (937) 743-8042, (800) 445-5342, FAX: (937) 743-9251, Web Site: www.dalco.com (3)

Daley, Anthony, Westcon, Tarrytown, NY. Tel: (914) 829-7000, FAX: (914) 829-7137, Web Site: www.westcon.com (16)

Daley, Kevin, Communispond Inc, East Hampton, NY. Tel: (212) 486-2300, (800) 529-5925, FAX: (212) 486-2680 (20)

Daley, Kimberly, Family Foot Care, Toms River, NJ. Tel: (732) 341-3355 (7)

Dalhoff, John, J., John Deere Consumer Products, Moline, IL. Tel: (309) 765-8000, FAX: (309) 748-0114, Web Site: www.johndeere.com (16)

Dall'Acqua, Charles, Protocol Integrated Direct Marketing, Sarasota, FL. Tel: (800) 677-2001, (800) 351-3774, FAX: (941) 906-9099, Web Site: www.protocolmarketing.com (21)

Dallas, H. James, Medtronic Inc, Minneapolis, MN. Tel: (763) 514-4000, (800) 328-2518, FAX: (763) 514-4879, Web Site: www.medtronic.com (16)

Dallum, Dan, PGI Companies Inc, Minneapolis, MN. Tel: (952) 933-5745, FAX: (952) 933-5864, E-Mail: ddallum@pgicompanies.com, Web Site: www.pgicompanies.com (27)

Dalrada Financial Corp, San Diego, CA. Tel: (858) 427-8716, (877) 325-7232, FAX: (858) 277-3448, E-Mail: inquiries@dalrada.com, Web Site: www.dalrada.com (14)

Dalton, Anne, Hanson Inc, Maumee, OH. Tel: (419) 327-6100, Web Site: www.hansoninc.com (30)

Dalton, George, D., Novo 1 Inc, Waukesha, WI. Tel: (262) 827-6400, (877) 810-7171, FAX: (262) 827-6440, Web Site: www.novo1.com (21)

Dalton, James, F., Tektronix Inc, Beaverton, OR. Tel: (503) 627-7111, (800) 833-9200, FAX: (503) 627-3247, Web Site: www.tektronix.com (16)

Dalton, John, LeadFlash, Boca Raton, FL. Tel: (561) 499-3329, Web Site: www.leadflash.com (14)

Dalton, William, The Bender Group, Reno, NV. Tel: (775) 788-8800, (800) 621-9402, FAX: (775) 788-8811, E-Mail: salesinfo@benderwhs.com, Web Site: www.bendergroup.com (28)

Daly APR, PREA, John, Jay, Daly Communications, Chevy Chase, MD. Tel: (301) 951-9110, E-Mail: speaker@johnjaydaly.com, Web Site: www.johnjaydaly.com (20)

Daly, James, P., Celtic Life Insurance Co, Chicago, IL. Tel: (312) 332-5401, FAX: (312) 441-0341, E-Mail: info@celtic-net.com, Web Site: www.celtic-net.com (15)

Daly, M., Virginia, Daly Direct Marketing, Potomac, MD. Tel: (301) 365-3201, FAX: (301) 365-7514 (39)

Daly, Michael, L., Carefirst Blue Cross Blue Shield, Washington, DC. Tel: (202) 479-8000, FAX: (301) 470-8049, Web Site: www.carefirst.com (15)

Daly, Scott, Fisher Scientific, Pittsburgh, PA. Tel: (800) 766-7000, FAX: (800) 772-7702, Web Site: www.fishersci.com (16)

Daly, Tim, Texwipe Co, Kernersville, NC. Tel: (201) 684-1800, (800) TEXWIPE, FAX: (201) 684-1801, E-Mail: info@texwipe.com, Web Site: www.texwipe.com (16)

Daly Communications, Chevy Chase, MD. Tel: (301) 951-9110, E-Mail: speaker@johnjaydaly.com, Web Site: www.johnjaydaly.com (20)

Daly Direct Marketing, Potomac, MD. Tel: (301) 365-3201, FAX: (301) 365-7514 (39)

Chet Dalzell, New York, NY. Tel: (917) 608-2251 (20)

DAMARK International Inc, La Salle, IL. Tel: (877) 326-2757, Web Site: www.damark.com (16)

Dambach, Virginia, DEI, Minneapolis, MN. Tel: (612) 677-1505, Web Site: www.deiworksite.org (1)

Damiano, Fred, Hobart & William Smith Colleges, Geneva, NY. Tel: (315) 781-3000, (800) 852-2256, FAX: (315) 781-3655, Web Site: www.hws.edu (19)

Damiano, Paula, National Association for Female Executives (NAFE), New York, NY. Tel: (800) 927-6233, E-Mail: info@nafe.com, Web Site: www.nafe.com (1)

Damilic Corp, Rockville, MD. Tel: (301) 251-2960, (800) 276-7749, FAX: (301) 251-8591, E-Mail: info@realsig.com, Web Site: www.realsig.com (15)

Daminato, Liliana, British Columbia Automobile Association, Burnaby, BC. Tel: (604) 268-5000, (800) 564-6222, FAX: (604) 268-5858, Web Site: www.bcaa.com (15)

Damman, Steve, QuantumDigital, Austin, TX. Tel: (800) 637-7373, Web Site: www.quantumdigital.com (28)

Dammann, Peter, 48HourPrint.com, Boston, MA. Tel: (800) 844-0599, Web Site: www.48hourprint.com (27)

Dammerman, Dennis, General Electric Co, Fairfield, CT. Tel: (203) 373-2211, FAX: (203) 373-3131, Web Site: www.ge.com (16)

Damore, Donald, American Student List LLC, Farmingdale, NY. Tel: (516) 248-6100, (888) 462-5600, FAX: (516) 248-6364, E-Mail: sales@studentlist.com, Web Site: www.studentlist.com (23)

Dan Smolen Direct Search LLC, Stafford, VA. Tel: (703) 835-9900, FAX: (703) 835-9966, E-Mail: dsmolen@dansmolen.com, Web Site: www.dansmolen.com (20)

Dana, Michelle, Compassion International, Colorado Springs, CO. Tel: (800) 336-7676, Web Site: www.compassion.com (1)

Dana-Farber Cancer Institute, Boston, MA. Tel: (617) 632-3000, FAX: (617) 632-4070, E-Mail: suzanne_fountain@dfci.harvard.edu, Web Site: www.dana-farber.org (1)

Danbury Printing & Litho Inc, Danbury, CT. Tel: (203) 792-5500, FAX: (203) 744-5633 (27)

Danenhauer, Greg, Parker Boiler Co, Los Angeles, CA. Tel: (323) 727-9800, FAX: (323) 722-2848, E-Mail: mleeming@parkerboiler.com, Web Site: www.parkerboiler.com (34)

Danenhauer, Sid, D., Parker Boiler Co, Los Angeles, CA. Tel: (323) 727-9800, FAX: (323) 722-2848, E-Mail: mleeming@parkerboiler.com, Web Site: www.parkerboiler.com (34)

Dang, Margaret, Bank of Hawaii, Honolulu, HI. Tel: (808) 537-8398, FAX: (808) 536-9433, Web Site: www.boh.com (14)

Daniel, Chris, Golden Trophy, Chicago, IL. Tel: (800) 835-6607, FAX: (800) 835-6601, E-Mail: goldentrophy@bruss.com, Web Site: www.giftsteaksonline.com (4)

Daniel, David, S, SpencerStuart, Chicago, IL. Tel: (312) 822-0088, FAX: (312) 822-0116, Web Site: www.spencerstuart.com (20)

Daniel, Ron, Icon Marketing Communications, Florence, KY. Tel: (859) 647-7271, FAX: (859) 647-0615, E-Mail: shawn@iconmc.com, Web Site: www.iconmc.com (21)

Daniel, Sandra, Fire Light Group, White Plains, NY. Tel: (608) 441-3473, E-Mail: mincentive@aol.com, Web Site: www.incentivesmotivate.com (33)

Daniel Gonzalez & Associates, New York, NY. Tel: (212) 682-0333 (20)

Daniels, Jeremy, L., Cornhusker Press, Hastings, NE. Tel: (402) 462-4141, FAX: (402) 460-4612, E-Mail: dlsales@dutton-lainson.com, Web Site: www.dutton-lainson.com (17)

Daniels, Leah, Zoominfo Inc, Waltham, MA. Tel: (781) 693-7500, Web Site: www.zoominfo.com (22)

Daniels, Ronald, J., University of Pennsylvania, Philadelphia, PA. Tel: (215) 898-5000, FAX: (215) 898-9659, Web Site: www.upenn.edu (1)

Daniels, Scott, SDI Marketing, Toronto, ON Canada. Tel: (949) 718-4800, (877) SDI-TEAM, FAX: (416) 674-9011, E-Mail: info@sdicapital.com, Web Site: www.sdimarketing.com (14)

Daniels, Sharon, Achieve Global, Tampa, FL. Tel: (813) 631-5500, (800) 566-0630, FAX: (813) 631-5796, Web Site: www.achieveglobal.com (16)

Daniels, Terri, CCA Global Partners, Manchester, NH. Tel: (603) 626-0333, Web Site: www.ccaglobal.com (16)

Daniels, Wendy, Diversified Investment Advisors, Harrison, NY. Tel: (914) 697-8967, FAX: (914) 697-3743, Web Site: www.divinvest.com (14)

Danielsen, Pete, MTV Networks, New York, NY. Tel: (212) 258-8000, FAX: (212) 258-8100, Web Site: www.mtv.com (32)

Danielson, R., Amerikal Products, Waukegan, IL. Tel: (847) 244-3600, FAX: (847) 244-2860, E-Mail: info@amerikal.com, Web Site: www.amerikal.com (25)

Danker, Frederick, Danker Laboratories Inc, Sarasota, FL. Tel: (800) 237-9641, FAX: (800) 665-5086, E-Mail: sales@dankerlabs.com, Web Site: www.dankerlabs.com (16)

Danker Laboratories Inc, Sarasota, FL. Tel: (800) 237-9641, FAX: (800) 665-5086, E-Mail: sales@dankerlabs.com, Web Site: www.dankerlabs.com (16)

Dansk, Bristol, PA. Tel: (914) 697-6400, (800) 326-7528, FAX: (914) 697-6464, Web Site: www.dansk.com (16)

Dante University Press, Wellesley, MA. Tel: (781) 790-1059, FAX: (781) 790-1056, E-Mail: dante@danteuniversity.org, Web Site: www.danteuniversity.com (17)

Danziger, B., Brim Electronics Inc, Lodi, NJ. Tel: (201) 796-2886, FAX: (973) 778-2792, E-Mail: info@brimelectronics.com, Web Site: www.brimelectronics.com (3)

Danziger, Robin, Educational Coin Co, Highland, NY. Tel: (845) 691-6100, Web Site: www.educationalcoin.com (16)

Dao, Rebecca, ClickMail Marketing Inc, San Mateo, CA. Tel: (650) 653-8055, Web Site: www.clickmarketing.com (32)

Dapper, G, Steven, hawkeye, Dallas, TX. Tel: (214) 749-0080, Web Site: www.hawkeyeww.com (35)

Daprile, Joseph, Premier Farnell Corp, Richfield, OH. Tel: (216) 525-4300, (800) 458-3222, FAX: (216) 525-4509, E-Mail: information@premierfarnell.com, Web Site: www.premierfarnell.com (16)

Darbee, Ricki, Smarthome, Irvine, CA. Tel: (949) 221-9200, (800) 762-7846, FAX: (949) 221-9240, E-Mail: feedback@smarthome.com, Web Site: www.smarthome.com (32)

Darby, Christian, Ronco Corp, Austin, TX. Tel: (800) 486-1806, E-Mail: customerservice@ronco.com, Web Site: www.ronco.com (15)

Darby, Jim, Super 8 Hotels Worldwide, Parsippany, NJ. Tel: (973) 428-9700, (800) 800-8000, FAX: (973) 496-7307, Web Site: www.super8.com (19)

Darby, Kristen, Marketing Research Association, Washington, DC. Tel: (860) 682-1000, FAX: (860) 682-1010, E-Mail: email@mra-net.org, Web Site: www.mra-net.org (40)

Darby, Lou, Innovative Plastic Printing Corp, Roselle, IL. Tel: (630) 665-0003, (800) 238-7686, FAX: (630) 665-7752, Web Site: www.innov8cards.com (27)

Darby, Warren, Atlantic Publication Group LLC, Charleston, SC. Tel: (843) 747-0025, FAX: (843) 744-0816, E-Mail: info@atlanticpublicationgrp.com, Web Site: www.atlanticpublicationgrp.com (17)

Darco International Inc, Huntington, WV. Tel: (304) 522-4883, Web Site: www.darcointernational.com (9)

Darden School Foundation Executive Foundation, Charlottesville, VA. Tel: (434) 924-3904, Web Site: www.darden.virginia.edu/execed (1)

Dargery, Joan, S., The Conference Board, Inc, New York, NY. Tel: (212) 759-0900, FAX: (212) 980-7014, Web Site: www.conference-board.org (16)

Darish, Nancy, E-Dialog Inc, Burlington, MA. Tel: (888) 256-7687, Web Site: www.e-dialog.com (32)

Darland, Terry, Christian Dior Perfumes, New York, NY. Tel: (212) 931-2200, FAX: (212) 931-2954, Web Site: www.dior.com (7)

Darnio, Dennis, Nordis Direct, Coral Springs, FL. Tel: (954) 323-5500, (800) 208-1169, FAX: (954) 323-0100, E-Mail: sdolan@nordisdirect.com, Web Site: www.nordisdirect.com (21)

Darooge, Bill, Baudville Inc, Grand Rapids, MI. Tel: (616) 698-0889, (800) 728-0888, FAX: (616) 698-0554, E-Mail: service@baudville.com, Web Site: www.baudville.com (16)

Darr, Anne, DeHart & Darr Associates, McLean, VA. Tel: (703) 448-1000, FAX: (703) 790-3460 (20)

Darr, Lynette, Olan Mills Inc, Chattanooga, TN. Tel: (423) 622-5141, (800) 251-6320, FAX: (423) 629-8128, Web Site: www.olanmills.com (16)

Darrah, Jason, GuideOne Insurance, West Des Moines, IA. Tel: (877) 448-4331, Web Site: www.guideone.com (15)

Darry, Gloria, Sheep Shop, Bridgton, ME. Tel: (207) 647-3548, FAX: (207) 647-3172 (5)

Darry, Richard, A., Sheep Shop, Bridgton, ME. Tel: (207) 647-3548, FAX: (207) 647-3172 (5)

Dartmouth-Hitchcock, Lebanon, NH. Tel: (603) 653-0700, Web Site: www.dmsnet.org (1)

The Dartnell Corp, Naples, FL. Tel: (585) 240-7301, (800) 447-4030, FAX: (585) 292-4392, E-Mail: customerservice@dartnellcorp.com, Web Site: www.dartnellcorp.com (17)

Daruty, Michael, MCA/Universal Studios Inc, Universal City, CA. Tel: (818) 777-1000, FAX: (818) 866-3330, Web Site: www.universalstudios.com (3)

Darwill, Hillside, IL. Tel: (708) 236-4900, Web Site: www.darwill.com (27)

Dashner, Charles, MMI Direct, Columbia, MD. Tel: (410) 561-1500, FAX: (410) 561-0805, Web Site: www.mmidirect.com (22)

Dassault Falcon Jet Corp, Little Ferry, NJ. Tel: (201) 440-6700, FAX: (201) 541-4515, Web Site: www.dassaultfalcon.com (16)

Data Analytics Corp, Plainsboro, NJ. Tel: (609) 936-899, Web Site: www.dataanalyticscorp.com (30)

The Data Base Inc, Oakhurst, NJ. Tel: (732) 531-4600, FAX: (732) 531-4798, E-Mail: don.nissim@heritagedirectdm.com, Web Site: www.heritagedirectdm.com (22)

Data Cal Corp, Gilbert, AZ. Tel: (480) 813-3100, (800) 223-0123, FAX: (480) 545-8090, E-Mail: info@datacal.com, Web Site: www.datacal.com (16)

Data Dallas Corp, Dallas, TX. Tel: (214) 638-2007, Web Site: www.ddci.net (22)

Data Dash Inc, Saint Louis, MO. Tel: (314) 832-5788, (800) 211-5988, FAX: (314) 832-5775, E-Mail: info@datadash.com, Web Site: www.datadash.com (22)

Data Direct, Morton Grove, IL. Tel: (847) 966-8327, FAX: (847) 966-8382 (28)

Data Direct Networks (HQ), Chatsworth, CA. Tel: (818) 700-7607, (800) 837-2298, FAX: (818) 700-7601, E-Mail: info@ddn.com, Web Site: www.datadirectnet.com (3)

Data-Dynamix Inc, Castle Rock, CO. Tel: (720) 855-9282, (888) 314-0078, FAX: (720) 855-9099, Web Site: www.data-dynamix.com (23)

The Data Group, Orlando, FL. Tel: (800) 262-5609, E-Mail: questions@thedatagrouponline.com, Web Site: www.thedatagrouponline.com (23)

Data Intelligence Group, Franklin, TN. Tel: (615) 595-9591, Web Site: www.wedigdata.com (22)

Data-Mail Inc, Newington, CT. Tel: (860) 666-0399, FAX: (860) 665-1226, E-Mail: brucem@data-mail.com, Web Site: www.data-mail.com (28)

Data Management & Marketing Services LLC, Broken Arrow, OK. Tel: (918) 392-0500, Web Site: www.dm-ms.net (22)

Data Management Inc, Mc Lean, VA. Tel: (703) 893-5627, (800) 334-8331, FAX: (703) 356-1698, E-Mail: info@data-management.com, Web Site: www.data-management.com (22)

Data Marketing Solutions Inc, Marblehead, MA. Tel: (781) 639-3270, Web Site: www.businesswatchnetwork.com (35)

Data-Matic Systems Co, Lansing, MI. Tel: (517) 882-4401, FAX: (517) 882-1188, Web Site: www.datamatic.net (27)

Data Partners Inc, Fort Myers, FL. Tel: (239) 267-8762, (866) 423-1818, FAX: (239) 267-9043, E-Mail: info@data-partners.com, Web Site: www.datapartners.com (22)

Data Services Direct, Parsippany, NJ. Tel: (973) 331-8101, FAX: (973) 331-8108, Web Site: www.dataservicesdirect.com (29)

Data Services Inc, Salisbury, MD. Tel: (410) 546-2206, (800) 432-4066, FAX: (410) 546-2274, Web Site: www.dataservicesinc.com (22)

DATA SOLUTIONS OF AMERICA INC, Redmond, WA. Tel: (239) 540-2992, Web Site: www.dsoai.com (23)

Data Square LLC, Wilton, CT. Tel: (203) 964-9733, E-Mail: info@datasquare.com, Web Site: www.datasquare.com (22)

Data Translation Inc, Marlborough, MA. Tel: (508) 481-3700, (800) 525-8528, FAX: (508) 481-8620, Web Site: www.datatranslation.com (34)

Data University, Lincoln, NE. Tel: (402) 742-2179, (866) 328-2848, E-Mail: info@datauniversity.com, Web Site: www.datauniversity.org (22)

The Database Centre, Fairfax, VA. Tel: (703) 359-2400, Web Site: www.databasecentre.co.uk (22)

Database Marketing Group Inc, Irvine, CA. Tel: (714) 727-0800, Web Site: www.dbmgroup.com (35)

Database Marketing Services, Guaynabo, PR. Tel: (787) 792-7005 (22)

Databazaar.com, Miramar, FL. Tel: (954) 843-0483, (888) 335-3282, FAX: (954) 843-0429, E-Mail: rudy@databazaar.com, Web Site: www.databazaar.com (10)

DataBridge Marketing Systems Corp, Montvale, NJ. Tel: (201) 664-3883, Web Site: www.Data-Bridge.org (22)

Datacard Ga-Vehren Corp, Hopkins, MN. Tel: (952) 933-1223, (800) 621-6972 x6930, FAX: (952) 931-0418, E-Mail: info@datacard.com, Web Site: www.gavehren.com (34)

DataCraft Inc, Kailua, HI. Tel: (808) 263-5583, Web Site: www.dcraftinc.com (22)

DataDirect, Atlanta, GA. Tel: (678) 530-0034, FAX: (678) 530-9563, E-Mail: info@ddirect.com, Web Site: www.ddirect.com (40)

Datahouse Inc, West Des Moines, IA. Tel: (508) 480-0012, (866) 640-3282, E-Mail: data@datahouseinc.com, Web Site: www.datahouseinc.com (23)

DataLab USA, Germantown, MD. Tel: (301) 972-1430, Web Site: www.datalabusa.com (21)

DataLever Corp, Boulder, CO. Tel: (303) 541-1515, Web Site: www.datalever.com (16)

Dataline, Princeton, NJ. Tel: (609) 452-6014, Web Site: www.datalinedata.com (23)

Datalogic Scanning, Eugene, OR. Tel: (800) 695-5700, FAX: (541) 345-7140, Web Site: www.scanning.datalogic.com (34)

DataLogix, Westminster, CO. Tel: (303) 327-1600, FAX: (303) 327-1650, Web Site: www.datalogix.com (23)

Datamann Inc, Wilder, VT. Tel: (802) 295-6600, (800) 451-4263, FAX: (802) 296-3623, Web Site: www.datamann.com (22)

Datamark Inc, Salt Lake City, UT. Tel: (801) 886-2002, (800) 279-9335, FAX: (801) 886-0102, E-Mail: info@datamark-inc.com, Web Site: www.datamark-inc.com (35)

DataMarketing Network Inc, Nashville, TN. Tel: (615) 313-7000, Web Site: www.datamarketingnetwork.com (21)

Datamart Direct Inc, Bloomingdale, IL. Tel: (630) 307-7100, FAX: (630) 307-8059, E-Mail: info@datamartdirect.com, Web Site: www.datamartdirect.com (27)

Datamatics Technologies, Burlington, MA. Tel: (781) 425-5240, FAX: (781) 425-5232, Web Site: www.datamaticstech.com (22)

Datamatx Inc, Ashland, VA. Tel: (804) 550-2513, (800) 943-5240, FAX: (804) 550-2527, Web Site: www.datamatx.com (27)

DataMentors LLC, Wesley Chapel, FL. Tel: (813) 960-7800, FAX: (813) 960-7811, E-Mail: 1bedgood@datamentors.com, Web Site: www.datamentors.com (22)

Datapoint USA Inc, San Antonio, TX. Tel: (210) 614-9977, FAX: (210) 614-2297, E-Mail: info@datapointusa.com, Web Site: www.datapointusa.com (16)

Dataprint Corp, San Mateo, CA. Tel: (650) 340-0550, (800) 227-6191, FAX: (650) 340-7028, Web Site: www.dataprint.com (34)

DataQuick, San Diego, CA. Tel: (856) 597-3100, (800) 950-9171, Web Site: www.primerasource.com (23)

Datasystem Solutions Inc, Overland Park, KS. Tel: (913) 362-6969, FAX: (913) 362-6383, E-Mail: sales@mutipub.com, Web Site: www.datasystem.com (22)

Datillo, Michael, Water's Edge Resort & Spa, Westbrook, CT. Tel: (860) 399-5901, (800) 222-5901, FAX: (860) 399-8644, Web Site: www.watersedgeresort.com (19)

Datillo, Tina, Water's Edge Resort & Spa, Westbrook, CT. Tel: (860) 399-5901, (800) 222-5901, FAX: (860) 399-8644, Web Site: www.watersedgeresort.com (19)

Datran Media, New York, NY. Tel: (212) 706-9781, Web Site: www.datranmedia.com (22)

Datt, Raj, Kennametal Inc, Latrobe, PA. Tel: (800) 222-9327, FAX: (800) 521-3319, E-Mail: mcs-na.service@kennmetal.com, Web Site: www.kennametal.com (16)

Datum Timing, Test & Measurement, Beverly, MA. Tel: (978) 927-8220, FAX: (978) 927-4099, E-Mail: wriley@datum.com, Web Site: www.datum.com (9)

Dauber, David, David Dauber & Associates, New York, NY. Tel: (212) 564-1728, FAX: (212) 208-4524, E-Mail: advancedbc@aol.com (16)

David Dauber & Associates, New York, NY. Tel: (212) 564-1728, FAX: (212) 208-4524, E-Mail: advancedbc@aol.com (16)

Daugherty, Carol, Our Designs Inc, Vancouver, WA. Tel: (859) 282-5500, (800) 382-5252, FAX: (859) 282-5508, E-Mail: sales@ourdesigns.com, Web Site: www.ourdesigns.com (16)

Daugherty, Mike, Our Designs Inc, Vancouver, WA. Tel: (859) 282-5500, (800) 382-5252, FAX: (859) 282-5508, E-Mail: sales@ourdesigns.com, Web Site: www.ourdesigns.com (16)

Daugherty, Tim, Habitat For Humanity International, Americus, GA. Tel: (229) 924-6935, FAX: (229) 924-6541, Web Site: www.habitat.org (1)

Daughton, James, Link Telemarketing Inc, Excelsior, MN. Tel: (952) 404-1609, FAX: (952) 474-0529, Web Site: www.roimark.com/link (29)

Dauman, Philippe, Viacom Inc, New York, NY. Tel: (212) 258-6000, FAX: (212) 258-6464, Web Site: www.viacom.com (16)

Davenport, Brandie, Fairytale Brownies, Phoenix, AZ. Tel: (800) 324-7982, FAX: (602) 489-5122, E-Mail: service@brownies.com, Web Site: www.brownies.com (4)

Davenport, Catherine, M., BGE Home Products & Services Inc, Baltimore, MD. Tel: (888) 243-4663, Web Site: www.bgehome.com (16)

Dave's Soda & Pet City, Agawam, MA. Tel: (413) 789-2259, Web Site: www.daveratner.com (5)

David, Christine, LO-AD Communications, Pasadena, CA. Tel: (626) 304-7750, FAX: (626) 304-2716, Web Site: www.lo-ad.com (16)

David, Joe, The Midland Co, Amelia, OH. Tel: (513) 943-7200 (15)

David, Leonard, A., Henry Schein Inc, Melville, NY. Tel: (631) 843-5500, (800) 472-4346, FAX: (631) 843-5658, E-Mail: custserv@henryschein.com, Web Site: www.henryschein.com (16)

Davidoff of Geneva Inc, Pinellas Park, FL. Tel: (203) 323-5811, (800) 328-4365, FAX: (203) 975-0090 (6)

Davidson, Bill, Harley-Davidson Inc, Milwaukee, WI. Tel: (414) 343-7286, FAX: (414) 343-4806, Web Site: www.harley-davidson.com (12)

Davidson, Brian, Association of National Advertisers Inc, New York, NY. Tel: (212) 697-5950, FAX: (212) 687-7310, Web Site: www.ana.net (40)

Davidson, Mark, Wrisco Industries Inc, Palm Beach Gardens, FL. Tel: (561) 626-5700, (800) 627-2646, FAX: (561) 627-3574, E-Mail: sales.staff@wrisco.com, Web Site: www.wrisco.com (8)

Davidson, Marla, Arthritis Foundation, Atlanta, GA. Tel: (404) 872-7100, FAX: (404) 872-0457, Web Site: www.arthritis.org (1)

Davidson, Michael, C., State Farm Insurance Cos, Bloomington, IL. Tel: (309) 766-2311, FAX: (309) 766-3621, Web Site: www.statefarm.com (15)

Davidson, Shelley, Ten Speed Press, Emeryville, CA. Tel: (510) 559-1600, (800) 841-BOOK, FAX: (510) 559-1629, E-Mail: order@tenspeed.com, Web Site: www.tenspeed.com (17)

Davidson, Terry, International Foundation of Employee Benefit Plans, Brookfield, WI. Tel: (262) 373-7758, FAX: (262) 786-8670, Web Site: www.ifebp.org (1)

Davies, Mike, PricewaterhouseCoopers LLP, New York, NY. Tel: (646) 471-4000, FAX: (646) 471-4444, Web Site: www.pwc.com (14)

Davies, Russ, IR/ARO, Bryan, OH. Tel: (419) 636-4242, (800) 495-0276, FAX: (419) 633-1674, E-Mail: russ_w_davies@irco.com, Web Site: www.arozone.com (35)

DaVinci Direct, Plymouth, MA. Tel: (508) 746-2555, FAX: (815) 301-9884, Web Site: www.davinci-direct.com (1)

Davis, Amy, Mayo Clinic, Rochester, MN. Tel: (507) 266-2511, FAX: (507) 284-0161, Web Site: www.mayoclinic.org (17)

Davis, Andrew, White Electronic Designs, Phoenix, AZ. Tel: (614) 279-6326, Web Site: www.whiteedc.com (27)

Davis, Angela, JDSU, Germantown, MD. Tel: (301) 353-1550, Web Site: www.jdsu.com (32)

Davis, Bert, Bert Davis Executive Search, New York, NY. Tel: (212) 838-4000, FAX: (212) 935-3291, E-Mail: info@bertdavis.com, Web Site: www.bertdavis.com (20)

Davis, Bob, Northern Greenhouse Sales, Neche, ND. Tel: (204) 327-5540, FAX: (204) 327-5527, E-Mail: info@northerngreenhouse.com, Web Site: www.northerngreenhouse.com (8)

Davis, Brandi, McKee & Associates Inc, Hot Springs National Park, AR. Tel: (501) 623-8833, (888) 883-4988, FAX: (501) 620-6856, E-Mail: newmoverexperts@mckeeandassociates.net, Web Site: www.newmoverexperts.com (21)

Davis, Brenda, Muscular Dystrophy Association, Tucson, AZ. Tel: (520) 529-2000, (800) 344-4863, FAX: (520) 529-5300, Web Site: www.mdausa.org (1)

Davis, Carol, Hanesbrands Inc, Winston Salem, NC. Tel: (336) 519-7460, Web Site: www.hanesbrands.com (2)

Davis, Carol, One Hanes Place Catalog, Winston Salem, NC. Tel: (336) 519-4400, (800) 300-2600, FAX: (336) 519-0655, Web Site: www.onehanesplace.com (2)

Davis, Catherine, The Container Store, Coppell, TX. Tel: (214) 654-2000, Web Site: www.containerstore.com (17)

Davis, Cathi, WRS Group Ltd, Waco, TX. Tel: (254) 776-6461, (800) 299-3366, FAX: (888) 977-7653, E-Mail: sales@wrsgroup.com, Web Site: www.wrsgroup.com (7)

Davis, Cathy, Nelson Crab Inc, Tokeland, WA. Tel: (360) 267-2911, (800) 262-0069, FAX: (360) 267-2921, E-Mail: seatreats@techline.com, Web Site: www.nelsoncrab.com (4)

Davis, Chad, Curtis 1000 Inc, Duluth, GA. Tel: (678) 380-9095, (800) 766-1007, FAX: (770) 717-1890, E-Mail: info@curtis1000.com, Web Site: www.curtis1000.com (27)

Davis, Chip, Manheim Steamroller, Omaha, NE. Tel: (402) 457-4341, FAX: (402) 457-4332, E-Mail: mailbox@amgram.com, Web Site: www.manheimsteamroller.com (3)

Davis, D., Scott, United Parcel Service, Atlanta, GA. Tel: (404) 828-6000, (800) 874-5877, FAX: (404) 828-6562, Web Site: www.ups.com (28)

Davis, Dave, Montbleu Resort Casino and Spa, Stateline, NV. Tel: (775) 588-3515, (888) 829-7630, FAX: (775) 586-2030, Web Site: www.montbleuresort.com (19)

Davis, Diane, Mott Media LLC, Fenton, MI. Tel: (810) 714-4280, FAX: (810) 714-2077, E-Mail: info@mottmedia.com, Web Site: www.mottmedia.com (17)

Davis, Don, StayWell/Krames, San Bruno, CA. Tel: (650) 742-0400, FAX: (650) 244-4568, Web Site: www.staywell.com (17)

Davis, Dorinne, S., The Davis Center, Succasunna, NJ. Tel: (862) 251-4637, FAX: (862) 251-4642, E-Mail: info@thedaviscenter.com, Web Site: www.thedaviscenter.com (16)

Davis, Dr. Jacob, A., Solitron Devices Inc, West Palm Beach, FL. Tel: (561) 848-4311, FAX: (561) 863-5946, E-Mail: sales@solitrondevices.com, Web Site: www.solitrondevices.com (16)

Davis, Dudley, Dudley's Country Kitchen, Dyersburg, TN. Tel: (901) 285-3681, (800) 242-8066, FAX: (901) 285-3638, Web Site: www.dckitchen.com (4)

Davis, Frank E., Pittman & Davis Inc, Harlingen, TX. Tel: (956) 423-2154, (800) 289-7829, FAX: (866) 329-7829, E-Mail: fruit@pittmandavis.com, Web Site: www.pittmandavis.com (4)

Davis, George, Hershey Foods Corp, Hershey, PA. Tel: (800) 454-7737, FAX: (717) 534-5204, Web Site: www.hersheygifts.com (4)

Davis, James, PMIC, Los Angeles, CA. Tel: (323) 954-0224, (800) 633-4215, FAX: (323) 954-0253, Web Site: pmiconline.stores.yahoo.net (17)

Davis, Jeffrey, L., Chadsworth's 1-800-Columns, Wilmington, NC. Tel: (910) 763-7600, (800) 486-2118, FAX: (910) 763-3191, E-Mail: sales@columns.com, Web Site: www.columns.com (8)

Davis, Jim, BJU Press, Greenville, SC. Tel: (864) 242-5100, (800) 845-5731, FAX: (800) 525-8398, (864) 271-8151, E-Mail: bjupinfo@bjupress.com, Web Site: www.bjupress.com (17)

Davis, Jim, Formsource, Lewiston, ME. Tel: (207) 782-3311, (877) 782-3311, FAX: (207) 783-0157, E-Mail: service@formsource1.com, Web Site: www.formsource1.com (27)

Davis, Jim, Thomson Reuters LPC, New York, NY. Tel: (646) 223-6890, E-Mail: lpc.americas@reuters.com, Web Site: www.loanpricing.com (14)

Davis, Ken, Christian Book Distributors Inc, Peabody, MA. Tel: (978) 532-5300, FAX: (978) 977-5010, E-Mail: javedisian@chrbook.com, Web Site: www.chrbook.com (17)

Davis, Larry, Ross-Simons, Cranston, RI. Tel: (401) 463-3100, (800) 835-0919, FAX: (401) 463-8599, Web Site: www.ross-simons.com (6)

Davis, Margaret, Northern Greenhouse Sales, Neche, ND. Tel: (204) 327-5540, FAX: (204) 327-5527, E-Mail: info@northerngreenhouse.com, Web Site: www.northerngreenhouse.com (8)

Davis, Mark, Davis Publications Inc, Worcester, MA. Tel: (508) 754-7201, (800) 533-2847, FAX: (508) 753-3834, E-Mail: contactus@davisart.com, Web Site: www.davis-art.com (17)

Davis, Martin, D., Catalog Music Corp, Nashville, TN. Tel: (615) 298-4338, (800) 992-4487, FAX: (615) 298-4628, Web Site: www.purecountrymusic.com (3)

Davis, Norma, ASM Press, Washington, DC. Tel: (202) 737-3600, (800) 546-2416, FAX: (202) 942-9342, E-Mail: books@asmusa.org, Web Site: www.asmpress.org (17)

Davis, Pam, Homesteaders Life Co, West Des Moines, IA. Tel: (515) 440-7777, (800) 477-3633, E-Mail: service@homesteaderslife.com, Web Site: www.homesteaderslife.com (15)

Davis, Peter, Gaco Western Inc, Seattle, WA. Tel: (206) 575-0450, (800) 456-4226, FAX: (206) 575-0587, E-Mail: info@gaco.com, Web Site: www.gaco.com (16)

Davis, Richard, K., US Bancorp, Minneapolis, MN. Tel: (651) 466-3000, (800) 872-2657, FAX: (612) 303-0782, Web Site: www.usbank.com (14)

Davis, Robert D., Rent-A-Center Inc, Plano, TX. Tel: (972) 801-1100, (800) 275-2996, FAX: (972) 943-0113, Web Site: www.rentacenter.com (16)

Davis, Robert, Mazda North American Operations, Irvine, CA. Tel: (949) 727-1990, (800) 222-6500, FAX: (949) 727-6101, Web Site: www.mazdausa.com (16)

Davis, Ron, Milwaukee Direct Marketing Inc, Brookfield, WI. Tel: (262) 789-2240, FAX: (262) 789-2250, E-Mail: info@milwaukeedirect.com, Web Site: www.milwaukeedirect.com (35)

Davis, Rufus, Alexian Brothers Bonaventure House, Chicago, IL. Tel: (773) 327-9921, FAX: (773) 327-9113, E-Mail: info@abam.org, Web Site: www.bonaventurehouse.org (1)

Davis, Sally, Ann, Baltimore Magazine, Baltimore, MD. Tel: (410) 752-4200, (800) 935-0838, FAX: (410) 625-0280, E-Mail: blori@baltimoremagazine.net, Web Site: www.baltimoremagazine.net (17)

Davis, Sara, Sunrise Greetings, Bloomington, IN. Tel: (812) 336-4045, (800) 457-4045, FAX: (812) 336-8712, E-Mail: info@interart.com, Web Site: www.interartdistribution.com (17)

Davis, Steve, Booth Michigan, Grand Rapids, MI. Tel: (616) 222-5824, FAX: (616) 222-5318, Web Site: www.boothnewspapers.com (17)

Davis, Timothy, The Advertising Council Inc, New York, NY. Tel: (212) 922-1500, FAX: (212) 922-1676, E-Mail: info@adcouncil.org, Web Site: www.adcouncil.org (1)

Davis, Tom, USA 800 Inc, Raytown, MO. Tel: (816) 358-1303, (800) 821-7539, FAX: (816) 358-8845, E-Mail: dlabatt@usa-800.com, Web Site: www.usa-800.com (29)

Davis & Gilbert, New York, NY. Tel: (212) 468-4800, FAX: (212) 468-4888, Web Site: www.dglaw.com (20)

Davis Art Images, Worcester, MA. Tel: (508) 754-7201, (800) 533-2847, FAX: (508) 753-3834, (508) 831-9260, E-Mail: lkeenekendrick@davisart.com, Web Site: www.davisartimages.com (38)

Bert Davis Executive Search, New York, NY. Tel: (212) 838-4000, FAX: (212) 935-3291, E-Mail: info@bertdavis.com, Web Site: www.bertdavis.com (20)

The Davis Center, Succasunna, NJ. Tel: (862) 251-4637, FAX: (862) 251-4642, E-Mail: info@thedaviscenter.com, Web Site: www.thedaviscenter.com (16)

Dick Davis Digest, Salem, MA. Tel: (978) 745-5532, FAX: (978) 745-1283, E-Mail: marketing@dickdavis.com, Web Site: www.dickdavis.com (17)

Davis Instruments Corp, Hayward, CA. Tel: (510) 732-9229, (510) 670-0589, E-Mail: info@davisnet.com, Web Site: www.davisnet.com (8)

Davis Publications Inc, Worcester, MA. Tel: (508) 754-7201, (800) 533-2847, FAX: (508) 753-3834, E-Mail: contactus@davisart.com, Web Site: www.davis-art.com (17)

Davis Sr, Edward, Pittman & Davis Inc, Harlingen, TX. Tel: (956) 423-2154, (800) 289-7829, FAX: (866) 329-7829, E-Mail: fruit@pittmandavis.com, Web Site: www.pittmandavis.com (4)

Davis-Trier, Lynn, Winterthur Museum & Country Estate, Wilmington, DE. Tel: (302) 888-4600, (800) 448-3883, FAX: (302) 888-4730, E-Mail: tourinfo@winterthur.org, Web Site: www.winterthur.org (6)

Davlin, James, A., John Deere Consumer Products, Moline, IL. Tel: (309) 765-8000, FAX: (309) 748-0114, Web Site: www.johndeere.com (16)

Davor Photo Inc, Bensalem, PA. Tel: (215) 638-2490, (800) 334-1531, FAX: (800) 724-6442, Web Site: www.davor.com (16)

Dawson, Beccie, C., Sage Software Inc, Irvine, CA. Tel: (949) 753-1222, (800) 854-3415, FAX: (949) 753-0374, Web Site: www.sagesoftware.com (16)

Dawson, David, The Herald & Review, Decatur, IL. Tel: (217) 429-5151, FAX: (217) 421-6913, E-Mail: hrdirect@herald-review.com, Web Site: www.herald-review.com (17)

Dawson, Jackie, Curriculum Associates Inc, North Billerica, MA. Tel: (978) 667-8000, FAX: (978) 667-5706, E-Mail: cainfo@curriculumassociates.com, Web Site: www.curriculumassociates.com (17)

Dawson, Ken, InfoCision Management Corp, Akron, OH. Tel: (330) 668-1400, FAX: (330) 668-1401, E-Mail: infocision@infocision.com, Web Site: www.infocision.com (29)

Dawson, Ken, Integretel Inc, San Jose, CA. Tel: (408) 362-4000, FAX: (408) 362-2795, Web Site: www.integretel.com (16)

Dawson, Luke, Herman Miller Inc, Zeeland, MI. Tel: (616) 654-3000, FAX: (616) 654-5234, E-Mail: investor@hermanmiller.com, Web Site: www.hermanmiller.com (16)

Dawson, Michelle, S., Ad Facts Inc, Cary, NC. Tel: (919) 388-3015, (800) 923-3228, E-Mail: adfacts@adfacts.com, Web Site: www.adfacts.com (30)

Dawson, Scott, School of Business Administration, Portland, OR. Tel: (503) 725-3712, FAX: (503) 725-5850, E-Mail: info@sba.pdx.edu, Web Site: www.sba.pdx.edu (41)

Dawson, Steve, Tektronix Inc, Beaverton, OR. Tel: (503) 627-7111, (800) 833-9200, FAX: (503) 627-3247, Web Site: www.tektronix.com (16)

Thomas Dawson, Palm Coast, FL. Tel: (303) 250-9000 (20)

Day, Jack, Do It Yourself Direct Marketing, Hoboken, NJ. Tel: (201) 748-6000, FAX: (201) 748-6088, E-Mail: info@wiley.com, Web Site: www.wiley.com (43)

Day, Jack, John Wiley & Sons Inc, Hoboken, NJ. Tel: (201) 748-6000, FAX: (201) 748-6088, E-Mail: info@wiley.com, Web Site: www.wiley.com (16)

Day, Rosanne, PacNet Services Ltd, Vancouver, BC Canada. Tel: (604) 689-0399, FAX: (604) 689-0313, E-Mail: info@pacnetservices.com, Web Site: www.pacnetservices.com (14)

Day Runner Direct, Sidney, NY. Tel: (800) 643-9923, FAX: (800) 643-9927, Web Site: www.dayrunner.com (10)

Day-Timers, Macungie, PA. Tel: (610) 398-1151, (800) 457-5702, (800) 225-5005, FAX: (800) 452-7398, E-Mail: connie@lomottastrategic.com, Web Site: www.daytimer.com (13)

Daya, Moaiz, Newmark Laboratories, Edison, NJ. Tel: (732) 417-1870, (800) 338-8079, FAX: (732) 225-0066, E-Mail: newmark@injersey.com (7)

Daydots, Fort Worth, TX. Tel: (817) 590-4500, (800) 321-3687, FAX: (800) 438-7002, E-Mail: customercare@daydots.com, Web Site: www.daydots.com (16)

Dayoob, Ed, Fred Meyer Jewelers Inc, Portland, OR. Tel: (503) 232-8844, (800) 457-5977, FAX: (503) 797-7616, Web Site: www.fredmeyerjewelers.com (16)

Days Inns Worldwide Inc, Parsippany, NJ. Tel: (973) 753-6000, (800) 441-1618, Web Site: www.daysinn.com (16)

Daystar Data Group Inc, Schaumburg, IL. Tel: (847) 202-0100, FAX: (847) 202-0107, E-Mail: sales@daystardg.com, Web Site: www.daystardg.com (22)

Dayton Daily News, Dayton, OH. Tel: (937) 222-5700, (888) 397-6397, FAX: (937) 225-2153, E-Mail: daytondaily@coxohio.com, Web Site: www.daytondailynews.com (18)

de Emley & Associates Inc, San Juan Capistrano, CA. Tel: (949) 493-5117, FAX: (949) 493-6382 (33)

De Grado, Joseph, DeGrado Inc, Mandeville, LA. Tel: (504) 626-5291, (800) 433-6849, FAX: (504) 626-7379, Web Site: www.orleansjewels.com (2)

de la Cueva-Peterson, Rosa Maria, Chip Peterson Photos, Saint Paul, MN. Tel: (651) 699-4286, FAX: (651) 698-7667 (38)

De La Mothe, Biekke, SickKids Foundation, Toronto, ON Canada. Tel: (416) 813-6166, Web Site: www.sickkidsfoundation.com (1)

de la Uz, Michelle, Fifth Avenue Committee, Brooklyn, NY. FAX: (718) 237-5366, Web Site: www.fifthave.org (1)

De Lacluyse, Mike, Lesman Instrument Co, Bensenville, IL. Tel: (630) 595-8400, (800) 953-7626, FAX: (630) 595-2386, E-Mail: sales@lesman.com, Web Site: www.lesman.com (9)

De Leon, Noel, City of Hope Cancer Center, Los Angeles, CA. Tel: (626) 256-4673, Web Site: www.cityofhope.org (1)

De Marco, Robert, Simmons-Boardman Publishing Corp, New York, NY. Tel: (212) 620-7200, FAX: (212) 633-1165 (17)

De Paul, Paulette, Christianity Today Inc, Carol Stream, IL. Tel: (630) 260-6200, FAX: (630) 260-0114, Web Site: www.christianitytoday.com (17)

de Rham, Abbott, de Rham & Co Inc, Dorset, VT. Tel: (802) 867-0155, (888) 867-0155, FAX: (802) 867-0361, Web Site: www.derham.com (20)

de Rham & Co Inc, Dorset, VT. Tel: (802) 867-0155, (888) 867-0155, FAX: (802) 867-0361, Web Site: www.derham.com (20)

de Solla Price, Mark, Metamorphics Media, New York, NY. Tel: (212) 924-1845, FAX: (212) 253-4053, E-Mail: info@metamorphics.com, Web Site: www.metamorphics.com (24)

De Taeye, Alain, TomTom North American, Lebanon, NH. Tel: (603) 643-0330, (800) 331-7881, FAX: (603) 653-0249, Web Site: www.tomtom.com (22)

De Turk, Nanette, P., Highmark Blue Cross Blue Shield, Pittsburgh, PA. Tel: (412) 544-7000, FAX: (412) 544-5350, Web Site: www.highmark.com (15)

De Yager, Peter W., Profit Potentials Inc, Hull, IA. Tel: (712) 439-1496, (800) 543-5480, FAX: (712) 439-1434, Web Site: www.profitpotentials.com (1)

de Young, Gary, 1000 Islands International Tourism Council, Alexandria Bay, NY. Tel: (315) 482-2520, (800) 847-5263, (800) 456-2267, FAX: (315) 482-5906, Web Site: www.visit1000islands.com/visitorinfo/ (19)

Deal, Rachelle, American Council on Exercise, San Diego, CA. Tel: (858) 279-8227, (888) 825-3636, FAX: (858) 279-8064, E-Mail: kristie.spalding@acefitness.org, Web Site: www.acefitness.org (1)

DealerTrack, New Hyde Park, NY. Tel: (866) 339-5723, Web Site: www.dealertract.com (14)

Dean, Harvey, Hearlihy & Co, Pittsburg, KS. Tel: (866) 622-1003, (800) 622-1000, FAX: (800) 443-2260, Web Site: www.hearlihy.com (17)

Dean, James, L., Colorama LLC, Sarasota, FL. Tel: (941) 378-5700, FAX: (941) 371-1844 (35)

Dean, John, S., Steelcase Inc, Grand Rapids, MI. Tel: (616) 247-2710, FAX: (616) 475-2270, Web Site: www.steelcase.com (16)

Dean, L., Marcus, Graphics International Inc, Dallas, TX. Tel: (214) 352-7565, FAX: (214) 528-0114 (27)

Dean, Richard, M., Air Force Sergeants Association, Suitland, MD. Tel: (301) 899-3500, (800) 638-0594, FAX: (301) 899-8136, E-Mail: staff@hqafsa.org, Web Site: www.hqafsa.org (1)

Dean, Stormy, L., Info USA City Directories, Omaha, NE. Tel: (402) 593-4500, (800) 925-4654, FAX: (402) 593-4671, E-Mail: customerservice@infousacity.com, Web Site: www.infousacity.com (17)

Dean & Deluca Brands Inc, Wichita, KS. Tel: (316) 683-1255, Web Site: www.deandeluca.com (4)

Deane, Silas, National Foundation for Cancer Research, Bethesda, MD. Tel: (301) 654-1250, (800) 321-CURE, FAX: (301) 654-5824, E-Mail: info@nfcr.org, Web Site: www.nfcr.org (1)

DeAngelis, Dawn, New Hampshire Public Television, Durham, NH. Tel: (603) 868-1100, E-Mail: themailbox@nhptv.org, Web Site: www.nhptv.org (32)

DeAngelo, Joseph, J., The Home Depot Inc, Atlanta, GA. Tel: (770) 433-8211, (800) 430-3376, FAX: (770) 384-2356, Web Site: www.homedepot.com (16)

Dearden, Tom, Datamark Inc, Salt Lake City, UT. Tel: (801) 886-2002, (800) 279-9335, FAX: (801) 886-0102, E-Mail: info@datamark-inc.com, Web Site: www.datamark-inc.com (35)

Deas Jr., Thomas, C., FMC Corp, Philadelphia, PA. Tel: (215) 299-6000, FAX: (215) 299-5998, Web Site: www.fmc.com (16)

Deaton, Luther, Kentucky Bankers Association, Louisville, KY. Tel: (502) 582-2453, FAX: (502) 584-6390, Web Site: www.kybanks.com (1)

Debacker, Travis, NuNaturals, Eugene, OR. Tel: (541) 344-9785, (800) 753-4372, FAX: (541) 343-0915, E-Mail: info@nunaturals.com, Web Site: www.nunaturals.com (16)

DeBellis & Ferrara, Vienna, VA. Tel: (301) 986-4499, (888) 748-2133, E-Mail: info@debellis-ferrara.com, Web Site: www.debellis-ferrara.com (35)

DeBlasio Jr, James, JD Graphic Co, Elk Grove Village, IL. Tel: (847) 364-4000, (888) 364-6216, FAX: (847) 364-4024, E-Mail: jim@jdgraphic.com, Web Site: www.jdgraphic.com (27)

Deboer, Jerry, Joseph A Bank Clothiers Inc, Hampstead, MD. Tel: (410) 239-2700, (800) 285-2265, FAX: (410) 239-5911, E-Mail: service@jos-a-bank.com, Web Site: www.josbank.com (2)

DeBow Jr., Thomas, J., DeBow Communications Ltd, New York, NY. Tel: (212) 977-8815, FAX: (212) 977-8376, E-Mail: info@debow.com, Web Site: www.debow.com (35)

Debow, Effie, Medic Alert Foundation, Turlock, CA. Tel: (209) 668-3333, (888) 633-4298, FAX: (209) 669-2495, Web Site: www.medicalert.org (1)

DeBow Communications Ltd, New York, NY. Tel: (212) 977-8815, FAX: (212) 977-8376, E-Mail: info@debow.com, Web Site: www.debow.com (35)

DeBrosse, Nancy, Projection Video Services, Springfield, VA. Tel: (703) 912-1334, (800) 377-7650, FAX: (703) 912-1350, Web Site: www.projection.com (16)

Debuque, Kenneth, Guaranty Bank, Brown Deer, WI. Tel: (414) 362-4636, (800) 235-4636, Web Site: www.guarantybank.com (14)

Debus, Liza, Tom Snyder Productions, Watertown, MA. Tel: (617) 926-6000, (800) 342-0236, FAX: (800) 304-1254, E-Mail: ask@tomsnyder.com, Web Site: www.tomsnyder.com (16)

DEC, Dawn, Kelliher Samets Volk, Burlington, VT. Tel: (802) 862-8261, FAX: (802) 863-4724, E-Mail: info@ksvc.com, Web Site: www.ksvc.com (35)

Decal Shop, Jacksonville, FL. Tel: (904) 721-3177, (800) 634-1889 (10)

DeCarlo, Frank, Tri-State Envelope Corp, Ashland, PA. Tel: (570) 875-0433, (800) 233-3102, FAX: (570) 875-0125, E-Mail: tsecny@attglobal.net, Web Site: www.tristateenvelope.com (26)

DeCarlo, Sara, FW Media, Cincinnati, OH. Tel: (513) 531-2690, Web Site: www.fwpublications.com (17)

DeCarlucci, Karen, The Wig Co, Pittsburgh, PA. Tel: (412) 221-4790, (800) 456-1788, FAX: (412) 257-8181, E-Mail: custserv@twcwigs.com (2)

DeCarlucci, Vincent, James, The Wig Co, Pittsburgh, PA. Tel: (412) 221-4790, (800) 456-1788, FAX: (412) 257-8181, E-Mail: custserv@twcwigs.com (2)

Decenzo, Georgiann, Advanstar Communications Inc, North Olmstead, OH. Tel: (440) 243-8100, (800) 225-4569, FAX: (440) 891-2740, E-Mail: info@ advanstar.com, Web Site: www.advanstarlists.com (17)

Decision Analyst Inc, Arlington, TX. Tel: (817) 640-6166, (800) 262-5974, FAX: (817) 640-6567, E-Mail: jthomas@decisionanalyst.com, Web Site: www.decisionanalyst.com (30)

Decision Demographics, Arlington, VA. Tel: (703) 931-9200, FAX: (703) 527-1448, E-Mail: tordella@decision-demographics.com, Web Site: www.decision-demographics.com (30)

Decision One, Devon, PA. Tel: (800) 767-2876, FAX: (610) 296-2910, Web Site: www.decisionone.com (34)

Decision Software Inc, Hyattsville, MD. Tel: (301) 459-9000, FAX: (301) 459-3072, E-Mail: clientservices@dsoftware.biz, Web Site: www. dsoftware.biz (22)

Deck, Nancy, Hilton Hotels Corp, Mc Lean, VA. Tel: (310) 278-4321, (800) HILTONS, FAX: (310) 205-3670, Web Site: www.hilton.com (19)

Deck the Walls Inc, Saint Peters, MO. Tel: (314) 719-8200, (866) 719-8200, FAX: (314) 719-8290, Web Site: www.deckthewalls.com (5)

Decker, Bert, Decker Communications Inc, San Francisco, CA. Tel: (877) 485-0700, FAX: (415) 543-8103, E-Mail: info@deckercommunications.com, Web Site: www.deckercommunications.com (20)

Decker, Fred, LDS Test & Measurement, Marlborough, MA. Tel: (608) 821-6600, FAX: (608) 821-6691, E-Mail: info-us@lds.spx.com, Web Site: www.lds-group.com (3)

Decker, Jack, American Printing House for the Blind, Louisville, KY. Tel: (502) 895-2405, (800) 223-1839, FAX: (502) 899-2274, E-Mail: info@aph. org, Web Site: www.aph.org (7)

Decker, Matthew, Wholesale Tool Co, Warren, MI. Tel: (800) 521-3420, FAX: (800) 521-3661, E-Mail: wtmich@aol.com, Web Site: www.wttool. com (9)

Decker Communications Inc, San Francisco, CA. Tel: (877) 485-0700, FAX: (415) 543-8103, E-Mail: info@deckercommunications.com, Web Site: www. deckercommunications.com (20)

Decko Products Inc, Sandusky, OH. Tel: (419) 626-5757, FAX: (419) 626-3135 (4)

Decorso, Bill, David H Block Advertising Inc, Verona, NJ. Tel: (973) 857-3900, FAX: (973) 857-4041, Web Site: www.blockadvertising.com (35)

DeCosmo, Joe, Chicago Association of Direct Marketing, Westmont, IL. Tel: (312) 849-2236, FAX: (312) 849-2239, E-Mail: info@cadm.org, Web Site: www.cadm.org (40)

Dedell, Suzanne, Morgan Kaufmann Publishers Inc, Burlington, MA. Tel: (781) 313-4700, E-Mail: order@mkp.com, Web Site: www.mkp.com (17)

Dederich, Katherine, Badger Press Inc, Grayslake, IL. Tel: (847) 996-1190, E-Mail: info@badgerpressinc. com, Web Site: www.badgerpressinc.com (27)

Dee, David, The Dartnell Corp, Naples, FL. Tel: (585) 240-7301, (800) 447-4030, FAX: (585) 292-4392, E-Mail: customerservice@dartnellcorp.com, Web Site: www.dartnellcorp.com (17)

Deeds, Stephen, Bowers & Merena Auctions, Irvine, CA. Tel: (949) 253-0916, (800) 458-4646, FAX: (949) 253-4091, E-Mail: auction@ bowersandmerena.com, Web Site: www. bowersandmerena.com (16)

Deere & Co Headquarters, Moline, IL. Tel: (309) 765-8000, FAX: (309) 765-5671, Web Site: www.deere. com (16)

Dees, Allen, Dees Communications/Fuller Fund Raising, Montgomery, AL. Tel: (334) 263-4436, FAX: (334) 263-4437, Web Site: www.athleticpubco.com (35)

Dees, Lee, Kendall Products/Dri-Dek, Naples, FL. Tel: (239) 643-2244, (800) 348-2398, FAX: (800) 828-4248, E-Mail: info@dri-dek.com, Web Site: www. dri-dek.com (16)

Dees, Morris, Southern Poverty Law Center, Montgomery, AL. Tel: (334) 956-8200, FAX: (334) 956-8483, Web Site: www.splcenter.org (1)

Dees Communications/Fuller Fund Raising, Montgomery, AL. Tel: (334) 263-4436, FAX: (334) 263-4437, Web Site: www.athleticpubco.com (35)

Deese, Willie, A., Calbiochem-Novabiochem Corp, San Diego, CA. Tel: (858) 450-9600, (800) 854-3417, FAX: (858) 453-3552, E-Mail: customerservice@emdbioscience.com, Web Site: www.calbiochem.com (9)

Deese, Willie, A., Merck & Co Inc, Whitehouse Station, NJ. Tel: (908) 423-1000, Web Site: www. merck.com (16)

DEFENDER Direct Inc, Indianapolis, IN. Tel: (800) 860-0303, Web Site: www.defenderdirect.com (32)

Defenders of Wildlife, Washington, DC. Tel: (202) 682-9400, Web Site: www.defenders.org (1)

Defense News Media Group, Springfield, VA. Tel: (703) 848-0490, FAX: (703) 848-0480, E-Mail: mgrant@atpco.com, Web Site: www.defensenews. com (17)

Definitely Duffy, Asheville, NC. Tel: (828) 333-5860, FAX: (866) 852-4686, E-Mail: dennis@ definitelyduffy.com, Web Site: www. definitelyduffy.com (35)

DeFrance, Tony, North American Membership Group Inc, Minnetonka, MN. Tel: (952) 936-9333, FAX: (952) 936-9755, Web Site: www.namginc.com (13)

DeFrancesco, Therese, CORS, Itasca, IL. Tel: (630) 250-8677, (800) 323-1352, FAX: (630) 250-7362, Web Site: www.cors.com (20)

DeFranco, Bobbi, Huck Spaulding Enterprises, Voorheesville, NY. Tel: (518) 768-2070, (888) 982-8866, FAX: (518) 768-2240, E-Mail: orders@ spaulding-rogers.com, Web Site: www.spaulding-rogers.com (16)

DeFrenza, Lori, Gummed Papers of America, Mc Cook, IL. Tel: (773) 650-2020, (800) 395-9000, FAX: (708) 485-8603, (800) 395-3581, E-Mail: info@labelexperts.com, Web Site: www. labelexperts.com (34)

DeGrado Inc, Mandeville, LA. Tel: (504) 626-5291, (800) 433-6849, FAX: (504) 626-7379, Web Site: www.orleansjewels.com (2)

DeHart & Darr Associates, McLean, VA. Tel: (703) 448-1000, FAX: (703) 790-3460 (20)

DeHerder, Rick, Array Marketing Group Inc, Toronto, ON Canada. Tel: (800) 295-4120, FAX: (416) 292-9759, E-Mail: info@arraymarketing.com, Web Site: www.arraymarketing.com (16)

Deighan, Janine, Troy Biologicals Inc, Troy, MI. Tel: (800) 521-0445, FAX: (248) 585-2490, E-Mail: info@troybio.com, Web Site: www.troybio.com (7)

Deis, Brian, Seiko Corp of America, Mahwah, NJ. Tel: (201) 529-5730, FAX: (201) 529-1548, Web Site: www.seiko.com (16)

Deisher, Beth, Coin World, Sidney, OH. Tel: (937) 498-0800, (800) 253-4555, FAX: (937) 498-0812, E-Mail: cwcustomerservice@coinworld.com, Web Site: www.coinworld.com (17)

Deisinger, Robert, American Technical Publishers Inc, Orland Park, IL. Tel: (708) 957-1100, (800) 323-3471, FAX: (708) 957-1101, E-Mail: service@ americantech.net, Web Site: www.go2atp.com (17)

DeJoseph, Al, C-W Agencies Inc, Vancouver, BC Canada. Tel: (604) 871-3400, FAX: (604) 871-3482, E-Mail: c-wreception@c-wgroup.com, Web Site: www.c-wgroup.com (35)

Dekel, Elie, 20th Century Fox Television, Los Angeles, CA. Tel: (310) 444-8100, FAX: (310) 444-8101 (16)

Dekkar, Tarik, AG Interactive, Cleveland, OH. Tel: (216) 889-5000, Web Site: www.aginteractive.com (32)

Dekkers, Marijn, E., Thermo Fisher Scientific I, Waltham, MA. Tel: (781) 622-1000, (800) 678-5599, FAX: (781) 622-1207, Web Site: www. thermofisher.com (9)

DeKraker, Glenn, COREMedia Systems Inc, Fairfield, NJ. Tel: (973) 276-0882, Web Site: www. coremedia-systems.com (22)

Del Cielo, Robert, The Bradford Group, Niles, IL. Tel: (847) 966-2770, FAX: (847) 581-8630, Web Site: www.collectiblestoday.com (16)

Del Enterprises, Verona, WI. Tel: (608) 845-6322, (800) 611-8045, FAX: (608) 845-3530, E-Mail: delips@tds.net, Web Site: www.delenterprises.com (33)

Del Mauro, Renee, The Suburban Chamber of Commerce, Summit, NJ. Tel: (908) 522-1700, FAX: (908) 522-9252, E-Mail: info@suburbanchambers. org, Web Site: www.suburbanchambers.org (14)

Del Monte, Ray, Wolff/SMG, Macedon, NY. Tel: (315) 986-1155, FAX: (315) 986-1161, E-Mail: rdelmonte@wolff-smg.com, Web Site: www.wolff-smg.com (28)

Del Polito, Gene A., Association for Postal Commerce, Alexandria, VA. Tel: (703) 524-0096, FAX: (703) 524-1871, Web Site: www.postcom.org (40)

Del Sindaco, Joseph M., New York Power Authority, Albany, NY. Tel: (518) 433-6700, Web Site: www. nypa.gov (16)

Del Vecchio, Claudio, Brooks Brothers, New York, NY. Tel: (212) 682-8800, (800) 274-1815, FAX: (212) 309-7273, Web Site: www.brooksbrothers. com (2)

Del Vecchio, Debra, Brooks Brothers, New York, NY. Tel: (212) 682-8800, (800) 274-1815, FAX: (212) 309-7273, Web Site: www.brooksbrothers.com (2)

Del Vecchio, Pasquale, MD&C Advertising, New Haven, CT. Tel: (203) 624-4151, FAX: (203) 401-6134, Web Site: www.mdcads.com (35)

Del Webb, Bloomfield Hills, MI. Tel: (248) 644-7300, (888) 717-9777, FAX: (248) 433-4598, Web Site: www.delwebb.com (16)

Delack, Elaine, EDMS LLC, Stanwood, WA. Tel: (360) 654-0448, (866) 222-3367, FAX: (360) 652-6199, E-Mail: info@edmsllc.com, Web Site: www. edmsllc.com (28)

DeLaney, Doreen, Balboa Life & Casualty, Irvine, CA. Tel: (949) 222-8000, (800) 854-6115, FAX: (949) 222-8777, Web Site: www.balboainsurance. com (15)

Delaney Jr., David, P., Lancer Insurance Co, Long Beach, NY. Tel: (516) 431-4441, (800) 782-8902, FAX: (516) 889-5111, E-Mail: roneill@lancer-ins. com, Web Site: www.lancer-ins.com (15)

Delaney, Chuck, Industrial Printing Co Inc, Toledo, OH. Tel: (419) 476-9101, (800) 472-9101, FAX: (800) 293-5225, E-Mail: steve.gross@cenveo.com, Web Site: www.ipcohio.com (27)

Delaney, Ezra, Nassau Community College, Garden City, NY. Tel: (516) 572-7501, E-Mail: marketing-communications@ncc.edu, Web Site: www.ncc.edu (41)

Delaney, Jay, McMaster-Carr Supply Co (HQ), Elmhurst, IL. Tel: (630) 600-3600, FAX: (630) 834-9427, E-Mail: chi.sales@mcmaster.com, Web Site: www.mcmaster.com (9)

Delaney, Karin, Birthday Keepsakes, Loveland, CO. Tel: (970) 669-5506, Web Site: www.bkeepsakes. com (6)

Delaney, Kris, Professional Photographer Magazine, Atlanta, GA. Tel: (404) 522-8600, (800) 786-6277, FAX: (404) 614-6405, E-Mail: csc@ppa.com, Web Site: www.ppa.com (17)

Delaney, Mike, National Pen Corp, San Diego, CA. Tel: (858) 675-3000, FAX: (858) 675-3030, Web Site: www.pens.com (6)

Delaney, Rory, The Pillsbury Co, Minneapolis, MN. Tel: (763) 764-7600, (800) 775-4777, FAX: (763) 764-8330, Web Site: www.pillsbury.com (16)

Delaney, Timothy, D., Lancer Insurance Co, Long Beach, NY. Tel: (516) 431-4441, (800) 782-8902, FAX: (516) 889-5111, E-Mail: roneill@lancer-ins. com, Web Site: www.lancer-ins.com (15)

Delano, Michael, The Country House Inc, Salisbury, MD. Tel: (410) 749-1959, (800) 331-3602, FAX: (410) 548-3224, E-Mail: web@thecountryhouse. com, Web Site: www.thecountryhouse.com (6)

Delauner, Trish, SRDS, Des Plaines, IL. Tel: (800) 851-7737, FAX: (847) 375-5001, Web Site: www. srds.com (17)

DeLaVergne, Ann, Ecoenvelopes, Eden Prairie, MN. Tel: (612) 605-4885, (888) 428-4364, FAX: (651) 392-8924, E-Mail: info@ecoenvelopes.com, Web Site: www.ecoenvelopes.com (20)

Delaware Investments, Philadelphia, PA. Tel: (215) 255-1200, E-Mail: service@delinvest.com, Web Site: www.delawareinvestments.com (14)

Robert DeLay, Tucson, AZ. Tel: (520) 615-8235 (20)

DeLee, Debra, Americans for Peace Now, Washington, DC. Tel: (202) 408-9898, FAX: (202) 728-1895, E-Mail: apndc@peacenow.org (1)

Deleon, Minerva, NCS, Danbury, CT. Tel: (562) 946-6900, (800) 975-6804, FAX: (800) 527-2488, Web Site: www.shopncs.com; www.ncs-apparel.com (16)

Delettre, Cecile, French Trade Office Embassy of France, New York, NY. Tel: (212) 400-2167, Web Site: www.missioneco.org (1)

delfortgroup, Atlanta, GA. Tel: (678) 325-5751, Web Site: www.paperisbetter.com (10)

Delicious Orchards, Colts Neck, NJ. Tel: (732) 462-1989, FAX: (732) 542-2111, E-Mail: info@ deliciousorchardsnj.com, Web Site: www. deliciousorchardsnj.com (4)

Delise, Susan, SSHC Inc/Radiant Heating Commercial Applications, Old Saybrook, CT. Tel: (860) 399-5434, (800) 544-5182, FAX: (860) 399-6460, (877) 675-4968, E-Mail: info@sshcinc.com, Web Site: www.sshcinc.com (9)

Delivra, Indianapolis, IN. Tel: (317) 915-9400, Web Site: www.delivra.com (32)

Dell, Michael, Janes Information Group, Alexandria, VA. Tel: (703) 683-3700, (800) 824-0768, FAX: (703) 836-0297, Web Site: www.janes.com (17)

Dell, Michael, S., Dell Computer Corp, Round Rock, TX. Tel: (512) 338-4400, FAX: (512) 283-6161, Web Site: www.dell.com (16)

Dell, Mike, Infotrends Inc, Boynton Beach, FL. Tel: (561) 732-5263, (800) 940-7991, FAX: (800) 400-7534, E-Mail: info@names.com, Web Site: www. names.com (35)

Dell Computer Corp, Round Rock, TX. Tel: (512) 338-4400, FAX: (512) 283-6161, Web Site: www. dell.com (16)

Della Bernarda, Ric, Casual Male Retail Group, Canton, MA. Tel: (781) 828-9300, (800) 767-0319, E-Mail: info@casualmale.com, Web Site: www. casualmale.com (2)

Della Penna, Michael, Conversa Marketing LLC, Garden City, NY. Tel: (516) 209-3822 (32)

Della Torre, Alex, Direct Marketing Association of Detroit, Royal Oak, MI. Tel: (248) 478-4888, FAX: (248) 478-6437, E-Mail: dmad@ameritech. net, Web Site: www.dmad.org (40)

Dellavilla, Jim, SIGMA Marketing Group LLC, Rochester, NY. Tel: (585) 473-7300, (888) 277-9837, FAX: (585) 473-0332, E-Mail: mbush@ sigmamarketing.com, Web Site: www. sigmamarketing.com; www.jthgearanalytics.com (Blog) (20)

Delmmar Communications, Cameron, MO. Tel: (816) 632-1583, (800) 872-2627, FAX: (816) 632-5107, E-Mail: sales@eradiostore.com, Web Site: www. delmmar.com (16)

Delogu, Adriana, Adriana Associates Ltd, New York, NY. Tel: (212) 719-5952, FAX: (212) 398-6414 (31)

Deloitte & Touche, Boston, MA. Tel: (617) 437-2000, FAX: (617) 437-2111, Web Site: www.deloitte.com (14)

DeLong Mailing Service, Oklahoma City, OK. Tel: (405) 272-9401 (28)

Delorme, David, DeLorme Mapping, Yarmouth, ME. Tel: (207) 846-7000, (800) 561-5105, FAX: (207) 846-7051, E-Mail: caleb.mason@delorme.com, Web Site: www.delorme.com (3)

DeLorme Mapping, Yarmouth, ME. Tel: (207) 846-7000, (800) 561-5105, FAX: (207) 846-7051, E-Mail: caleb.mason@delorme.com, Web Site: www.delorme.com (3)

DelStar Technologies, Middletown, DE. Tel: (302) 378-8888, (800) 521-6713, FAX: (302) 378-4482, Web Site: www.delstarinc.com (16)

Delta Market Research Inc, Hatboro, PA. Tel: (215) 674-1180, FAX: (215) 674-1271, E-Mail: information@deltamarketresearch.com, Web Site: www.deltamarketresearch.com (30)

Delta Tech Industries, Ontario, CA. Tel: (714) 577-8028, FAX: (714) 577-0140, E-Mail: sales@ deltatechindustries.com, Web Site: www. deltatechindustries.com (12)

Delta Upsilon International Fraternity, Indianapolis, IN. Tel: (317) 875-8900, FAX: (317) 876-1629, E-Mail: ihq@deltau.org, Web Site: www.deltau.org (16)

Delta Vacations, Fort Lauderdale, FL. Tel: (954) 522-1440, (800) 800-1504, FAX: (954) 468-4765, Web Site: www.deltavacations.com (19)

DeLuca, Jim, Western-Southern Life, Cincinnati, OH. Tel: (513) 629-1800, Web Site: www. westernsouthernlife.com (15)

DeLuca, Victoria, Ad-Lib Advertising Inc, Old Bridge, NJ. Tel: (732) 679-9226, (800) 622-3542, FAX: (732) 679-9511, E-Mail: info@adlibadvertising. com, Web Site: www.adlibadvertising.com (10)

Deluxe Corp, Shoreview, MN. Tel: (651) 490-8000, FAX: (651) 481-4163, Web Site: www.deluxe.com (27)

DeLuxe Laboratories Inc, Hollywood, CA. Tel: (323) 462-6171, FAX: (323) 960-7016, E-Mail: steven. vananda@bydeluxe.com, Web Site: www.bydeluxe. com (16)

Demakos, Mick, Kaplan Publishing, Chicago, IL. Tel: (312) 606-8905, (800) 245-2665, FAX: (312) 606-8985, E-Mail: kaplanorders@kaplan.com, Web Site: www.kaplanpublishing.com (17)

Deman, Pascal, Seton Identification Products, Branford, CT. Tel: (203) 488-8059, (800) 243-6624, FAX: (203) 488-5973, Web Site: www.seton.com (16)

Demand Telemarketing Inc, Grosse Pointe, MI. Tel: (313) 823-8598, (888) 977-2256, FAX: (313) 823-8598, E-Mail: wpatterson@create-demand.com, Web Site: www.create-demand.com (29)

Demandbase Inc, San Francisco, CA. Tel: (415) 683-2660, Web Site: www.demandbase.com (23)

DeMarco, Michelle, Pensions & Investments, New York, NY. Tel: (212) 210-0100, FAX: (212) 210-0117, Web Site: www.pionline.com (17)

DeMarie Jr., Donald, J., Masco Corp, Taylor, MI. Tel: (313) 274-7400, FAX: (313) 792-6135, E-Mail: webmaster@mascohq.com, Web Site: www.masco. com (16)

DeMartino, Angelo, ADM Productions Inc, Port Washington, NY. Tel: (516) 484-6900, (800) ADM-DIAL, FAX: (516) 621-2531, Web Site: www. admpro.com (16)

DeMartino, Anthony, ADM Productions Inc, Port Washington, NY. Tel: (516) 484-6900, (800) ADM-DIAL, FAX: (516) 621-2531, Web Site: www. admpro.com (16)

DeMartins, Paul, Medco Supply Co Inc, Tonawanda, NY. Tel: (716) 695-3244, (800) 556-3326, FAX: (800) 222-1934, E-Mail: sales@medcosupply.com, Web Site: www.medcosupply.com (7)

Demas, William, Anatomical Chart Co, Chicago, IL. Tel: (847) 679-4700, (800) 621-7500, FAX: (847) 674-0211, E-Mail: service@anatomical.com, Web Site: www.anatomical.com (7)

Dembicki, Dan, Direct Marketing Association of Detroit, Royal Oak, MI. Tel: (248) 478-4888, FAX: (248) 478-6437, E-Mail: dmad@ameritech.net, Web Site: www.dmad.org (40)

Demco Inc, Madison, WI. Tel: (608) 241-1201, FAX: (608) 241-1799, E-Mail: custserv@demco.com, Web Site: www.demco.com (10)

DeMichael, Cheryl, Tauck World Discovery, Norwalk, CT. Tel: (203) 899-6760, Web Site: www.tauck. com (19)

Demme, Robert, Micro Center, Hilliard, OH. Tel: (800) 634-3478, FAX: (614) 777-2620, E-Mail: csrs@microcenterorder.com, Web Site: www. microcenter.com (3)

Democratic Congressional Campaign Committee, Washington, DC. Tel: (202) 863-1500, FAX: (202) 485-3436, Web Site: www.dccc.com (1)

Demographic Research Co, Denver, CO. Tel: (310) 766-5590, FAX: (303) 831-9181, Web Site: www. drcmodel.com (22)

Demont, Carol, Penguin Group USA Inc, East Rutherford, NJ. Tel: (201) 909-6200, FAX: (201) 236-3381, Web Site: penguingroup.com (17)

DeMoss, Michelle, Stetson University, Deland, FL. Tel: (904) 822-7405/7406, FAX: (904) 822-7430, Web Site: www.stetson.edu (41)

DeMouy, Tasha, Gothic Arch Greenhouses Inc, Mobile, AL. Tel: (251) 432-7529, (800) 531-4769, FAX: (251) 432-2655, E-Mail: gothicarch@ comcast.net, Web Site: www. GothicArchGreenhouses.com (8)

Denault, Leo, Entergy, New Orleans, LA. Tel: (504) 576-4000, (800) ENTERGY, FAX: (504) 576-4428, Web Site: www.entergy.com (16)

Denenberg, George, Madison Sales Group, Northbrook, IL. Tel: (847) 480-2370, FAX: (847) 480-7437 (33)

Denham, Charles, R., Health Care Concepts Inc, Austin, TX. Tel: (512) 479-8508, (800) 628-4201, FAX: (512) 479-8741 (16)

Denhof, Dave, National Bulk Equipment Inc, Holland, MI. Tel: (616) 399-2220, FAX: (616) 399-7365, E-Mail: sales@nbe-inc.com, Web Site: www.nbe-inc.com (16)

Denish, Diane, Advantage Mailing Inc, Anaheim, CA. Tel: (714) 538-3881, (888) 909-6245, FAX: (714) 282-3903, Web Site: www.advantagemailinginc. com (28)

Denison, Jay, THD Inc, Lexington, MA. Tel: (781) 859-1400), Web Site: www.thdinc.com (1)

Denmark Francisco, New York, NY. Tel: (212) 444-8157, Web Site: www.dsfnyc.com (20)

Denn, David, Premier Packaging Corp, Victor, NY. Tel: (877) 924-8460, FAX: (585) 924-8753, E-Mail: info@premiercustompkg.com, Web Site: www.premiercustompkg.com (16)

Denne, Ed, Skinder-Strauss Associates, Newark, NJ. Tel: (973) 642-1440, Web Site: www.elaw.com (14)

Denning, Laura, Selman & Co, Cleveland, OH. Tel: (440) 646-9336, (800) 735-6262, FAX: (440) 646-9339, E-Mail: ldenning@selmaninsurance.com, Web Site: www.sel-co.com (15)

Dennis, Barry, Netweb/Omni LLC, Ellicott City, MD. Tel: (410) 591-1900, E-Mail: barry@netwebomni. com, Web Site: www.netwebomni.com (40)

Dennis, Daniel, Netweb/Omni LLC, Ellicott City, MD. Tel: (410) 591-1900, E-Mail: barry@netwebomni. com, Web Site: www.netwebomni.com (40)

Dennis, David, M., SBC Advertising, Columbus, OH. Tel: (614) 891-7070, FAX: (614) 891-3664, E-Mail: info@sbcadv.com, Web Site: www.sbcadv. com (35)

Dennis, Robert, J., Genesco Inc, Nashville, TN. Tel: (615) 367-7000, (888) 324-6189, FAX: (615) 367-8278, Web Site: www.genesco.com (2)

Dennis Jourdan Photography Inc, Buffalo Grove, IL. Tel: (847) 564-2570, FAX: (847) 255-5976, E-Mail: info@djphoto.com, Web Site: www. djphoto.com (37)

Dennon, G.B., Jerden Records/SpeechWorks, Redmond, WA. Tel: (425) 882-3344, (888) 401-4487, FAX: (425) 882-3494, E-Mail: jerden@aol.com, Web Site: www.soundworks.net (16)

Denny, James J., Eye Care Centers of America, San Antonio, TX. Tel: (210) 340-3531, (800) 669-1183, FAX: (210) 340-0123, E-Mail: customerservice@ visionworks.com, Web Site: www.ecca.com (7)

Denson, Charles, D., Nike Inc, Beaverton, OR. Tel: (503) 671-4565, (800) 344-6543, FAX: (503) 671-6300, Web Site: www.nike.com (2)

Denson, Russel, Reiman Publications, Greendale, WI. Tel: (414) 423-0100, (800) 344-6913, FAX: (414) 423-3840, Web Site: www.reimanpub.com (17)

Denson, Russell, Weider Publications Inc, Woodland Hills, CA. Tel: (818) 884-6800, (800) 423-5590, FAX: (818) 884-0242 (17)

Dent, Beth, AGORA Inc, Baltimore, MD. Tel: (410) 783-8499, FAX: (410) 783-8414, E-Mail: csteam@ agorapublishinggroup.com, Web Site: www.agora-inc.com (17)

Dental Economics, Tulsa, OK. Tel: (918) 835-3161, FAX: (918) 831-9804, E-Mail: kellib@pennwell. com, Web Site: www.dentaleconomics.com (24)

Dental Products Report, New York, NY. Tel: (847) 441-3700, FAX: (847) 441-3702, Web Site: www. dentalproducts.net (17)

Dentino, Karl, Dentino Marketing, Princeton, NJ. Tel: (201) 332-1219, (800) 477-8372, FAX: (201) 332-4262, E-Mail: karl@dentinomarketing.com, Web Site: www.dentinomarketing.com (35)

Dentino Marketing, Princeton, NJ. Tel: (201) 332-1219, (800) 477-8372, FAX: (201) 332-4262, E-Mail: karl@dentinomarketing.com, Web Site: www.dentinomarketing.com (35)

Denton, Mike, Formal Approach, Jefferson City, TN. Tel: (865) 475-8641, Web Site: www. formalapproach.com (2)

Denton, Neal, Alliance of Nonprofit Mailers, Washington, DC. Tel: (202) 462-5132, FAX: (202) 462-0423, E-Mail: alliance@nonprofitmailers.org, Web Site: www.nonprofitmailers.org (40)

Dentsply International, York, PA. Tel: (800) 877-0020, Web Site: www.dentsply.com (7)

Denver Metro Convention & Visitors Bureau, Denver, CO. Tel: (303) 892-1112, FAX: (303) 892-1636, Web Site: www.denver.org (1)

Denver Tax Software Inc, Littleton, CO. Tel: (303) 796-7780, (800) 326-6686, FAX: (888) 326-6686, Web Site: www.denvertax.com (16)

DePaul University, Chicago, IL. Tel: (312) 362-8000, (800) 4-DEPAUL, FAX: (312) 362-6639, E-Mail: skelly@wppost.depaul.edu, Web Site: www.depaul. edu (41)

Depeau, Jamie, TIAA-CREF, New York, NY. Tel: (212) 490-9000, FAX: (212) 916-6505, Web Site: www.tiaa-cref.org (15)

Dependable Business Forms, Villa Park, IL. Tel: (630) 530-1734, FAX: (630) 530-1789, E-Mail: j.zawaski@comcast.net, Web Site: www. dependablebusinessforms.com (27)

DeRespini, Kim, Davis Instruments Corp, Hayward, CA. Tel: (510) 732-9229, (510) 670-0589, E-Mail: info@davisnet.com, Web Site: www.davisnet.com (8)

Derke, Hanns, Advanced Machinery, New Castle, DE. Tel: (302) 322-2226, (800) 727-6553, FAX: (866) 686-1615, E-Mail: jean@advmachinery.com, Web Site: www.advmachinery.com (9)

Derke, Wolfgang, Advanced Machinery, New Castle, DE. Tel: (302) 322-2226, (800) 727-6553, FAX: (866) 686-1615, E-Mail: jean@advmachinery.com, Web Site: www.advmachinery.com (9)

Dermac Labs Inc, Salem, OR. Tel: (503) 399-8181, (800) 547-9164, FAX: (503) 581-7439, Web Site: www.touchofmink.com (16)

Dernburg, Michael, MPBS Industries, Los Angeles, CA. Tel: (323) 268-8514, (800) 421-6265, FAX: (323) 268-6305, Web Site: www.mpbs.com (16)

DeRodes, Robert, P., The Home Depot Inc, Atlanta, GA. Tel: (770) 433-8211, (800) 430-3376, FAX: (770) 384-2356, Web Site: www.homedepot.com (16)

DeRose, Donna, AccountMate Software Corp, Petaluma, CA. Tel: (415) 883-8873, FAX: (415) 883-5863, E-Mail: information@accountmate.com, Web Site: www.accountmate.com (22)

Derr, Marie, Cuvaison Inc, Calistoga, CA. Tel: (707) 942-6266, FAX: (707) 942-5732, E-Mail: jschuppert@cuvaison.com, Web Site: www. cuvaison.com (4)

Derry, Kevin, Cookbook Publishers Inc, Lenexa, KS. Tel: (913) 492-5900, (800) 227-7282, FAX: (913) 492-5947, E-Mail: info@cookbookpublishers.com, Web Site: www.cookbookpublishers.com (17)

Derry, Thomas W., Association for Financial Professionals, Bethesda, MD. Tel: (301) 907-2862, FAX: (301) 907-2864, Web Site: www.afponline.org (14)

Derry, Tom, W., Standard Directory of Advertising Agencies, New Providence, NJ. Tel: (800) 521-8110, FAX: (908) 790-5405 (43)

Derryck, Dennis, Non-Profit Management Program/ Milano - The New School of Management & Urban Policy, New York, NY. Tel: (212) 229-5400, FAX: (212) 229-5354, E-Mail: milanoadmissions@ newschool.edu, Web Site: www.newschool.edu/ milano (41)

Des Plaines Printing Co, Buffalo Grove, IL. Tel: (847) 824-1111, (800) 283-1776, FAX: (847) 824-1112, E-Mail: custserv@dppc.com, Web Site: www.dppc. com (27)

Des Prez III, John, D., John Hancock Financial Services Inc, Boston, MA. Tel: (617) 572-6000, (800) 732-5543, FAX: (617) 572-6451, Web Site: www. johnhancock.com (15)

Des Rosiers, Bert, GlaserDirect Inc, Glen Ellyn, IL. Tel: (630) 469-2075, FAX: (630) 790-5244, E-Mail: jglaser@glaserdirect.com, Web Site: www. glaserdirect.com (23)

Desai, Alka, FDAnews, Falls Church, VA. Tel: (703) 538-7600, (888) 838-5578, FAX: (703) 538-7676, E-Mail: customerservice@fdanews.com, Web Site: www.fdanews.com (17)

Desai, Sandip, Amanet, Canoga Park, CA. Tel: (818) 786-1113, FAX: (818) 786-5736, E-Mail: info@ amanet-usa.com, Web Site: www.amanet.com (16)

DeSalle, Michael, Columbia College Chicago, Chicago, IL. Tel: (312) 663-1600, FAX: (312) 344-0869, Web Site: www.colum.edu (41)

DeSantis, Helen, DeSantis Holster & Leather Goods Co, Amityville, NY. Tel: (631) 841-6300, (800) GUNHIDE, FAX: (631) 841-6320, E-Mail: contact@desantisholster.com, Web Site: www. desantisholster.com (34)

DeSantis, Susan, Who's Calling, College Station, TX. Tel: (866) 688-9300, FAX: (888) 821-4260, E-Mail: contact@whoscalling.com, Web Site: www.whoscalling.com (30)

DeSantis Holster & Leather Goods Co, Amityville, NY. Tel: (631) 841-6300, (800) GUNHIDE, FAX: (631) 841-6320, E-Mail: contact@desantisholster. com, Web Site: www.desantisholster.com (34)

Desborough, Jim, Directory of Premium, Incentive & Travel Buyers, Richmond, VA. Tel: (804) 762-4455, (800) 223-1797, FAX: (804) 935-0271, E-Mail: amdouglas4@aol.com, Web Site: www. douglaspublications.com (43)

Deseret Book, Salt Lake City, UT. Tel: (801) 534-1515, (800) 453-4532, FAX: (801) 517-3392, Web Site: www.deseretbook.com (16)

Desert Rat Truck Centers, Tucson, AZ. Tel: (520) 790-8502, (866) 444-5337, FAX: (520) 750-1918, Web Site: www.desertrat.com (12)

Design Distributors, Inc, Deer Park, NY. Tel: (631) 242-2000, FAX: (631) 242-7367, E-Mail: info@ designdistributors.com, Web Site: www. designdistributors.com (21)

Design Matters Inc!, New York, NY. Tel: (212) 560-0681, Web Site: www.designmattersinc.com (35)

Design Toscano, Inc, Elk Grove Village, IL. Tel: (847) 952-0100, (800) 525-5141, FAX: (847) 952-8992, Web Site: www.designtoscano.com (6)

DeSimone, Linda, S., Amerisure Insurance Cos, Farmington Hills, MI. Tel: (248) 615-9000, (800) 257-1900, FAX: (248) 615-8224, Web Site: www. amerisure.com (15)

Desion Conceptions, New York, NY. Tel: (212) 254-1688, FAX: (212) 533-0760, E-Mail: joel.gordon@ verizon.net, Web Site: joelgordonphotography.com (38)

DesJardin, Bonny, Jesco Industries Inc, Litchfield, MI. Tel: (517) 542-2903, (888) 463-1246, FAX: (517) 542-2501, E-Mail: jesco@jescoonline.com, Web Site: www.jescoonline.com (34)

Desjardins, Luc, Telemedia Communications US, North York, ON. Tel: (416) 733-7600, (888) 290-1466 Can., (800) 461-3773 U.S., FAX: (416) 733-3563, E-Mail: info@transcontinental.ca, Web Site: www.transcontinental.com (17)

Desjardins Financial Securities, Levis, PQ Canada. Tel: (418) 838-7870, FAX: (418) 833-5985, Web Site: www.desjardinsfinancialsecurity.com (15)

Desmond, Bevin, Morningstar Inc, Chicago, IL. Tel: (312) 696-6000, Web Site: www.morningstar.com (14)

Desrochers, Darrel, Tyco Valves & Controls, Houston, TX. Tel: (713) 986-4665, (800) 343-0990, FAX: (713) 937-5466, Web Site: www.tycovalves.com (16)

DeStefano, Gary, M., Nike Inc, Beaverton, OR. Tel: (503) 671-4565, (800) 344-6543, FAX: (503) 671-6300, Web Site: www.nike.com (2)

DeStefano, Robert, Echomax, Teaneck, NJ. Tel: (201) 837-1371, FAX: (201) 837-6142 (35)

Destination Maternity Corp, Philadelphia, PA. Tel: (215) 873-2200, Web Site: www.motherswork.com (2)

Destination Rewards, Boca Raton, FL. Tel: (561) 997-9940, (800) 242-6260, FAX: (561) 997-9945, Web Site: www.drloyalty.com (33)

Destinations Ireland & Great Britain, Rhinebeck, NY. Tel: (800) 832-1848, FAX: (212) 265-0154, E-Mail: info@digbtravel.com, Web Site: www. allgolftravel.com/tours (19)

Destrooper, Jos, Corona-Lotus Inc, San Francisco, CA. Tel: (415) 956-8956, (800) 422-2924, FAX: (415) 956-4922, E-Mail: customerservice@biscoff.com, Web Site: www.biscoff.com (4)

Details Interactive LLC, Westfield, NJ. Tel: (917) 331-0685, E-Mail: mark@detailsinteractive.com, Web Site: www.detailsinteractive.com (16)

Detman, Denise, Lester B Martin & Associates Inc, Sugar Grove, OH. Tel: (740) 746-8842, (614) 261-1722, (800) 262-1692, FAX: (614) 447-8417, (740) 746-8849, E-Mail: service@lesterbmartin.com, Web Site: www.lesterbmartin.com (33)

The Detroit Institute of Arts, Detroit, MI. Tel: (313) 833-7900, FAX: (313) 833-1390, Web Site: www. dia.org (16)

Detroit Newspapers, Detroit, MI. Tel: (313) 222-6400, FAX: (313) 222-5032, Web Site: www.freep.com (18)

Deuschle, James, Rich Products Corp, Buffalo, NY. Tel: (716) 878-8000, (800) 828-2021, FAX: (716) 878-8765, Web Site: www.richs.com (16)

Deutsch, Donny, Lowe Worldwide, New York, NY. Tel: (212) 981-7600, E-Mail: info@ loweworldwide.com, Web Site: www. loweworldwide.com (35)

Deutsch, Stanley, Mercury Envelope Co Inc, Rockville Centre, NY. Tel: (516) 678-6744, FAX: (516) 678-6764, E-Mail: mercuryenvelope@aol.com (26)

Deutsche Bank Alex Brown Inc, New York, NY. Tel: (212) 250-2500, FAX: (212) 469-5315, Web Site: www.db.com (14)

Development Dimensions International, Bridgeville, PA. Tel: (412) 257-0600, (800) 933-4463, FAX: (412) 220-2942, E-Mail: info@ddiworld.com, Web Site: www.ddiworld.com (16)

Development Resources, Saint Paul, MN. Tel: (651) 695-5558, FAX: (888) 805-1070, E-Mail: info@developmentresources.com, Web Site: www.developmentresources.com (21)

Devendran, Dave, Advance Mailing Services Inc, West Chicago, IL. Tel: (630) 293-0707, FAX: (630) 293-9268 (28)

The Devereux Group, Marblehead, MA. Tel: (781) 631-9213, FAX: (781) 639-3044, E-Mail: roeser@devereuxgroup.com, Web Site: www.devereuxgroup.com (20)

Devessa, David, Music Choice, Horsham, PA. Tel: (215) 784-5840, Web Site: www.musicchoice.com (16)

Devin, Jeff, Postal En Espanol Inc, Tampa, FL. Tel: (813) 885-8888, Web Site: www.postalenespanol.com (20)

Devincenzi, Kevin, Rapid Response Marketing, Las Vegas, NV. Tel: (702) 631-9714, (866) 997-7297, FAX: (702) 216-4038, Web Site: www.xy7.com (32)

Devine, Brian K., Petco Animal Supplies, San Diego, CA. Tel: (858) 453-7845, (877) 738-6742, FAX: (858) 453-6585, Web Site: www.petco.com (5)

Devine, Diane, Herbach & Rademan Co, Moorestown, NJ. Tel: (856) 802-0422, (800) 848-8001, FAX: (856) 802-0465, E-Mail: sales@herbach.com, Web Site: www.herbach.com (9)

Devine, Jan, Direct Impact Inc, Saint Louis, MO. Tel: (314) 567-0024, FAX: (314) 567-1497, E-Mail: info@directimpactinc.com, Web Site: www.directimpactinc.com (35)

Devine, Megan, d.trio marketing group, Minneapolis, MN. Tel: (612) 436-0323, Web Site: www.dtrio.com (35)

Devine, Michael, Philip, The Dime Savings Bank of New York FSB, Brooklyn, NY. Tel: (800) 321-3463, Web Site: www.dimewill.com (14)

Devine, Robert, Chem-Tainer Industries Inc, North Babylon, NY. Tel: (631) 661-8300, (800) ASK-CHEM, (800) 275-2436, FAX: (631) 661-8209, E-Mail: sales@chemtainer.com, Web Site: www.chemtainer.com (9)

Devitt, John, International Coins & Currency Inc, Montpelier, VT. Tel: (802) 223-6331, FAX: (800) 229-3239, Web Site: www.iccoin.com (6)

Devlin, Sherry, The Missoulian, Missoula, MT. Tel: (406) 523-5334, FAX: (406) 523-5221, Web Site: www.missoulian.com (31)

DeVoe, David, News America Publishing Inc, New York, NY. Tel: (212) 782-8000, FAX: (212) 852-7145 (17)

DeVoldre, John A., Transcat, Rochester, NY. Tel: (585) 352-9460, (800) 800-5001, FAX: (585) 352-1486, Web Site: www.transcat.com (16)

DeVore, Nancy S., Anthro Photo File, Cambridge, MA. Tel: (617) 868-4784, FAX: (617) 484-6428, Web Site: www.anthrophoto.com (38)

DeVries, Daniel, J., PC Mall, Torrance, CA. Tel: (310) 225-2600, (800) 555-MALL, Web Site: www.pcmall.com (3)

DeVries, Wes, DM Assistance Inc, Portsmouth, NH. Tel: (603) 964-6156 (20)

DeVry Inc, Oakbrook Terrace, IL. Tel: (630) 571-7700, FAX: (602) 943-4108, Web Site: www.devry.com (16)

Dew III, Matthew, J., NGL Insurance Group, Madison, WI. Tel: (608) 257-5611, (800) 548-2962, FAX: (608) 257-9340, Web Site: www.nationalguardian.com (15)

DeWalle, Allen, AAA Mid-Atlantic Insurance Groups, Wilmington, DE. Tel: (302) 299-4700, (800) 451-5921, FAX: (215) 864-5486, Web Site: www.aaamidatlantic.com (15)

DeWalt, Stacy, Learning Care Group, Novi, MI. Tel: (248) 697-9115, Web Site: www.learningcaregroup.com (16)

Dewey, Kali, McWeeney Marketing Group, Orange, CT. Tel: (203) 891-8100, (800) 272-3440, FAX: (203) 891-0775, E-Mail: george@mcweeneymarketing.com, Web Site: www.mcweeneymarketing.com (33)

DeWitt, Kathleen, JEM Research, Valparaiso, IN. Tel: (219) 464-4668, FAX: (219) 464-7011 (30)

DeWitz, Jerry, ITW Bee Leitzke, Iron Ridge, WI. Tel: (920) 625-2342, FAX: (920) 625-2643, Web Site: www.itwbeeleitzke.com (16)

Dex Direct Marketing, Lone Tree, CO. Tel: (800) 999-4630, Web Site: www.dexlist.com (31)

Dex One, Cary, NC. Tel: (919) 297-1600 (21)

Dexposito & Partners, New York, NY. Tel: (646) 747-8800, Web Site: www.dexpositoandpartners.com (35)

Dexta Corp, Napa, CA. Tel: (707) 255-2454, (800) 733-3982, FAX: (707) 255-8520, Web Site: www.dexta.com (16)

Dexter, Roger, B-T-B Internet Marketing Solutions, Middle Island, NY. Tel: (631) 924-3888, E-Mail: linickgroup@gmail.com, Web Site: www.linick.net; 222.asklinick.com (39)

Dextor, Roger, Copywriter's Council of America - (Freelancers), Middle Island, NY. Tel: (631) 924-3888, FAX: (631) 924-8555, E-Mail: cca4dmcopy@gmail.com, Web Site: www.linick.net; www.andrewlinickdirectmarketing.com (39)

Dextor, Roger, The Linick Group Inc, Middle Island, NY. Tel: (631) 924-3888, E-Mail: linickgroup@gmail.com, Web Site: www.andrewlinickdirectmarketing.com (35)

Deye, Kristen, iCrossing, Scottsdale, AZ. Tel: (480) 505-5800, FAX: (480) 505-5801 (32)

Deyling, Jim, Blue Cross & Blue Shield of South Carolina, Columbia, SC. Tel: (803) 788-0222, (800) 288-2227, FAX: (803) 736-4516, Web Site: www.bcbssc.com (15)

Deyo, Charles, Cendyn, Boca Raton, FL. Tel: (561) 750-3173, Web Site: www.cendyn.com (32)

Deyo, Russell, C., Johnson & Johnson, New Brunswick, NJ. Tel: (732) 524-0400, FAX: (732) 214-0332, Web Site: www.jnj.com (16)

DeYulis, Mark, New Pig Corp, Tipton, PA. Tel: (814) 684-0101, (800) 468-4647, FAX: (814) 684-0961, E-Mail: hothogs@newpig.com, Web Site: www.newpig.com (9)

Dharma Trading Co, Petaluma, CA. Tel: (415) 456-7657, (800) 542-5227, FAX: (415) 456-8747, E-Mail: service@dharmatrading.com, Web Site: www.dharmatrading.com (2)

Di Giovanni, Rico, Marketing Agencies Association Worldwide, Minneapolis, MN. Tel: (952) 922-0130, FAX: (203) 969-1499, E-Mail: keith.mccracker@maaw.org, Web Site: www.maaw.org (40)

Di Nicola, Robert J., Linens n' Things, Paramus, NJ. Tel: (973) 778-1300, FAX: (973) 778-0822, (973) 815-2990, Web Site: www.lnt.com (8)

Diabold, Marc, CompuTrack, Fishers, IN. Tel: (317) 813-2222, FAX: (317) 813-2233, E-Mail: info@dgsmarketingengineers.com, Web Site: www.dgsmarketingengineers.com (4)

Diagraph Corp, Saint Charles, MO. Tel: (636) 300-2000, (800) 722-1125, FAX: (636) 300-2004, E-Mail: info@diagraph.com, Web Site: www.diagraph.com (16)

Diakon Lutheran Social Ministries, Allentown, PA. Tel: (610) 682-2145, (888) 582-2230, FAX: (610) 682-1055, E-Mail: swangerb@diakon.org, Web Site: www.diakon.org (1)

Dial-A-Mattress, Hicksville, NY. Tel: (718) 472-1200, (800) 824-7777, FAX: (718) 482-6561, E-Mail: sales@mattress.com, Web Site: www.mattress.com (16)

Dial 800 LLC, Los Angeles, CA. Tel: (310) 273-9023, (800) 564-8685, Web Site: www.dial800.com (32)

DialAmerica Marketing Inc, Mahwah, NJ. Tel: (201) 327-0200, (800) 531-3131, FAX: (201) 327-4875, Web Site: www.dialamerica.com (29)

The Dialog Corp, Morrisville, NC. Tel: (919) 804-6400, (800) 3 DIALOG, FAX: (919) 804-6410, E-Mail: customer@dialog.com, Web Site: www.dialog.com (30)

Dialogue Marketing, Auburn Hills, MI. Tel: (734) 374-8400, (800) 523-5867, FAX: (248) 836-2601, Web Site: www.dialogue-marketing.com (29)

Diamond, David, A., Mutual of Omaha, Omaha, NE. Tel: (402) 342-7600, (800) 775-6000, FAX: (402) 351-2775, Web Site: www.mutualofomaha.com (15)

Diamond, Matthew, C, Alloy Media Marketing, New York, NY. Tel: (212) 244-4307, (877) 360-9688, FAX: (212) 244-4311, E-Mail: contactus@alloymerch.com, Web Site: www.alloymarketing.com (35)

Diamond, Mitch, SilverPop, Atlanta, GA. Tel: (866) 745-8767, FAX: (678) 247-0501, E-Mail: info@silverpop.com, Web Site: www.silverpop.com (32)

Diamond Envelope Corp, Aurora, IL. Tel: (630) 499-2800, FAX: (630) 499-2801 (26)

Diamond Essence, Edison, NJ. Tel: (800) 909-2525, E-Mail: info@diamondessence.com, Web Site: www.diamond-essence.com (2)

Diamond Machining Technology, Marlborough, MA. Tel: (508) 481-5944, (800) 666-4368, FAX: (508) 485-3924, Web Site: www.dmtsharp.com (9)

Diamond Marketing Solutions, Bloomingdale, IL. Tel: (630) 523-5250, FAX: (630) 523-0403, Web Site: www.dmsolutions.com (35)

Diamondback Direct - a Dmh Marketing Partners Co, Severna Park, MD. Tel: (410) 975-0001, Web Site: www.diamondbackdirect.com (35)

Diamonds By Rennie Ellen, New York, NY. Tel: (212) 869-5525, FAX: (212) 869-5526, Web Site: www.rennieellen.com (6)

Diane Publishing Co, Darby, PA. Tel: (610) 461-6200, E-Mail: hbaron@dianepublishing.net, Web Site: www.dianepublishing.net (43)

Diapers.com, Jersey City, NJ. Tel: (800) 342-7377, Web Site: www.diapers.com (5)

Dibben, David, W., Central States Health & Life Co of Omaha, Omaha, NE. Tel: (402) 397-1111, (800) 826-6587, FAX: (402) 391-3772, Web Site: www.cso.com (15)

Dibble, David, E., First Data Merchant Services, Greenwood Village, CO. Tel: (303) 488-8000, (800) 735-3362, Web Site: www.firstdata.com (14)

DiBlasi, Alfred, MetaResponse Group Inc, Deerfield Beach, FL. Tel: (954) 360-0644, FAX: (954) 360-7712, Web Site: www.metaresponse.com (23)

DiBlasi, Barbara, Marshall Fields Dept Stores, Minneapolis, MN. Tel: (612) 375-3004, Web Site: www.fields.com (5)

Diboll, Neil, Prairie Nursery, Westfield, WI. Tel: (608) 296-3679, (800) 476-9453, FAX: (608) 296-2741, E-Mail: webcs@prairienursery.com, Web Site: www.prairienursery.com (8)

DiCamillo, Gary T., Polaroid Corp, Minnetonka, MN. Tel: (781) 386-2000, (800) 765-2764, FAX: (781) 386-3263, Web Site: www.polaroid.com (16)

Dice, Chris, I-Behavior Inc, Louisville, CO. Tel: (303) 228-5000, FAX: (303) 926-1367, E-Mail: contactus@i-behavior.com, Web Site: www.i-behavior.com (23)

Dicerni, Richard, Ideal Industries (Canada) Corp, Ajax, ON. Tel: (905) 683-3400, (800) 824-3325, FAX: (905) 683-0209, E-Mail: nick.shkordoff@idealindustries.com, Web Site: www.idealindustries.com (9)

Dick, Sheri, Figi's Inc, Marshfield, WI. Tel: (715) 387-1771, (800) 422-3444, FAX: (715) 384-1129, Web Site: www.figis.com (4)

Dicker, Wendy, Durey-Libby Edible Nuts Inc, Carlstadt, NJ. Tel: (201) 939-2775, (800) 332-6887, FAX: (201) 939-0386, E-Mail: info@dureylibby. com, Web Site: www.durreylibby.com (4)

Dicker, William, Durey-Libby Edible Nuts Inc, Carlstadt, NJ. Tel: (201) 939-2775, (800) 332-6887, FAX: (201) 939-0386, E-Mail: info@dureylibby. com, Web Site: www.durreylibby.com (4)

Dickerson, David, Globe Specialty Products Inc, Millbury, MA. Tel: (508) 871-1900 (17)

Dickerson, Steve, Neopost, Carrollton, TX. Tel: (510) 489-6800, (800) 636-7678, FAX: (510) 475-6317, (510) 487-6704, Web Site: www.neopostinc.com (9)

Dickey, Chris, Barkley, Kansas City, MO. Tel: (816) 842-1500, Web Site: www.barkleyUS.com (35)

Dickinson, Martin, Environmental Law Institute, Washington, DC. Tel: (202) 939-3800, FAX: (202) 939-3868, E-Mail: law@eli.org, Web Site: www. eli.org (17)

Dickman, James G., Lewis Direct, Baltimore, MD. Tel: (410) 539-5100, FAX: (410) 539-4700 (22)

Dickson, Sally, Marketing & Media Services LLC, Warwick, RI. Tel: (401) 737-7730, Web Site: www.mmsipitv.com (30)

Dickson, Wayne, Hadley Fruit Orchards Inc, Cabazon, CA. Tel: (951) 849-4668, FAX: (951) 849-5255, Web Site: www.hadleys.com (4)

The Dico Group Inc, Toluca Lake, CA. Tel: (323) 264-2000, FAX: (323) 264-2600 (27)

DiCola, James, Urban Response LLC, Hartville, OH. Tel: (330) 877-0800, (866) 550-3501, FAX: (330) 877-0802 (17)

Dictionary of Marketing Terms, Hauppauge, NY. Tel: (631) 434-3311, (800) 645-3476, FAX: (631) 434-3723, E-Mail: barrons@barronseduc.com, Web Site: www.barronseduc.com (43)

Didactic Systems, Cranford, NJ. Tel: (908) 276-5413, FAX: (908) 276-7174, E-Mail: didacticra@aol.com (20)

Didit, Mineola, NY. Tel: (212) 631-0157, Web Site: www.did-it.com (16)

Diebel, Don, Gemini Publishing Co, Webster, TX. Tel: (281) 316-4276, E-Mail: getgirls@getgirls.com, Web Site: www.getgirls.com (17)

Diebel, Michele, Gemini Publishing Co, Webster, TX. Tel: (281) 316-4276, E-Mail: getgirls@getgirls. com, Web Site: www.getgirls.com (17)

Diebold Inc, Uniontown, OH. Tel: (330) 899-2510, (800) DIEBOLD, FAX: (330) 490-3794, E-Mail: barronp@diebold.com, Web Site: www.diebold. com (16)

Diedrich, Bill, Cables to Go, Moraine, OH. Tel: (937) 224-8646, (800) 506-9607, FAX: (800) 331-2841, (937) 496-2666, Web Site: www.cablestogo.com (3)

Diehl, Donna, High Point Insurance, Lincroft, NJ. Tel: (732) 978-6255, Web Site: www.highpointins.com (15)

Diehl, Frederick, 2-10 Home Buyers Warranty, Denver, CO. Tel: (720) 747-6000, Web Site: www.2-10.com (15)

Diehl, Irene, Strategic Data Intelligence LLC, Northbrook, IL. Tel: (847) 897-5706, FAX: (847) 897-5715, E-Mail: inquiry@sdintelligence.com, Web Site: www.sdintelligence.com (22)

Dieleman, Ann, ARAG, Des Moines, IA. Tel: (800) 247-4184, FAX: (515) 246-8710, E-Mail: service@ ARAGgroup.com, Web Site: www.araggroup.com (15)

Diem, Ruth, Hearst Magazines, New York, NY. Tel: (212) 649-2824, FAX: (212) 765-3528, Web Site: www.hearst.com/magazines (17)

Dieme, Verena, Thieme Medical Publishers Inc, New York, NY. Tel: (212) 760-0888, (800) 782-3488, FAX: (212) 947-1112, E-Mail: info@thieme.com, Web Site: www.thieme.com (17)

Diemer, Dennis, Draper's & Damon's, Irvine, CA. Tel: (949) 784-3000, (800) 843-1174, FAX: (949) 784-3400, E-Mail: jilld@drapers.com, Web Site: www.drapers.com (2)

Dier, Kelly, E., The Marmon Group LLC, Chicago, IL. Tel: (312) 372-9500, FAX: (312) 845-5305, Web Site: www.marmon.com (16)

Dierberg, James, F., First Banks Inc, Hazelwood, MO. Tel: (314) 592-5000, (800) 760-2265, Web Site: www.firstbanks.com (14)

Dierke, David, AccountMate Software Corp, Petaluma, CA. Tel: (415) 883-8873, FAX: (415) 883-5863, E-Mail: information@accountmate.com, Web Site: www.accountmate.com (22)

Diers, Michael, Old World Mouldings Inc, Bohemia, NY. Tel: (631) 563-8660, FAX: (631) 563-8815, E-Mail: mouldings@optonline.com, Web Site: www.oldworldmouldings.com (9)

Diersen, Dave, Thompson & Co Marketing Communications, Memphis, TN. Tel: (901) 527-8000, FAX: (901) 527-3697, E-Mail: info@thompson-co.com, Web Site: www.thompson-co.com (21)

Dieschbourg, Ed, Replogle Globes Inc, Broadview, IL. Tel: (708) 343-0900, FAX: (708) 343-0923, E-Mail: info@reploglobes.com, Web Site: www. reploglobes.com (16)

Dieste, Dallas, TX. Tel: (214) 259-8000, FAX: (214) 259-8040, E-Mail: bbutler@dieste.com, Web Site: www.diesteharmel.com (35)

Dieste Harmel & Partners, Dallas, TX. Tel: (214) 259-8000, Web Site: www.dieste.com (35)

Dietrich, Brian, Gaw-O'Hara Envelope Co, Western Springs, IL. Tel: (773) 638-1200, (888) 385-8439, FAX: (773) 638-1208, E-Mail: info@gawohara. com, Web Site: www.gawohara.com (26)

Dietz, Laurie, Bloomingdale's By Mail Ltd, New York, NY. Tel: (212) 224-7721, (800) 472-0788, FAX: (212) 715-2805, Web Site: www. bloomingdales.com (5)

Dietz, Lorri, American Mint LLC, Mechanicsburg, PA. Tel: (717) 458-9200, (877) 807-MINT, FAX: (717) 458-9211, E-Mail: contact@americanmint.com, Web Site: www.americanmint.com (6)

Dietz, Railen, American Management Association International, New York, NY. Tel: (212) 586-8100, (800) 262-9699, FAX: (212) 903-8168 (41)

Dietzman, Leslie, E., Family Christian Stores, Grand Rapids, MI. Tel: (616) 554-8700, (888) 319-0319, FAX: (616) 554-8694, E-Mail: info@fcsdirect. familychristian.com, Web Site: www. familychristian.com (5)

DiFebo, Val, Lowe Worldwide, New York, NY. Tel: (212) 981-7600, E-Mail: info@loweworldwide. com, Web Site: www.loweworldwide.com (35)

DigDev Direct, Deerfield Beach, FL. Tel: (954) 949-9500, Web Site: www.foundationmediagroup.com (16)

DiGeso, Amy, Estee Lauder Inc, New York, NY. Tel: (212) 572-4200, (866) 467-7363, FAX: (212) 572-3942, Web Site: www.esteelauder.com (16)

Digi International, Minnetonka, MN. Tel: (952) 912-3444, (877) 912-3444, FAX: (952) 912-4953, Web Site: www.digi.com (3)

Digi-Key Corp, Thief River Falls, MN. Tel: (218) 681-6674, (800) 344-4539, FAX: (218) 681-3380, Web Site: www.digikey.com (3)

DiGioia, Robert, DM News, New York, NY. Tel: (212) 925-7300, FAX: (212) 925-8752, Web Site: www. dmnews.com (43)

DiGiovanni, Paul, Christian Brands, Phoenix, AZ. Tel: (602) 243-5200, (800) 521-2914, FAX: (602) 232-1855, Web Site: www.christian-brands.com (16)

DiGiovanni, Tom, Christian Brands, Phoenix, AZ. Tel: (602) 243-5200, (800) 521-2914, FAX: (602) 232-1855, Web Site: www.christian-brands.com (16)

Digiovanni, Anthony, Education Management Corp, Pittsburgh, PA. Tel: (412) 995-7627, Web Site: www.edmc.edu (1)

Digispace Solutions LLC, San Diego, CA. Tel: (619) 684-6737, Web Site: www.digispace.com (35)

Digital Speech Systems, Richardson, TX. Tel: (972) 235-2999, FAX: (972) 235-3036, Web Site: www. digitalspeech.com (3)

Digital Vision Resources Group - DVRG, Overland Park, KS. Tel: (913) 754-8121, Web Site: www. dvrg.com (27)

Digitas, Boston, MA. Tel: (617) 867-1000, FAX: (617) 867-1111, E-Mail: contact@digitas.com, Web Site: www.digitas.com (35)

Dignardi, Dennis, Modular Devices, LLC, Sparta, NJ. Tel: (973) 579-7220, (800) 292-2201, FAX: (973) 579-1820, E-Mail: modulardevices@optonline.net, Web Site: www.modulardevices.biz (3)

DiGuido, Al, Zeta Interactive, New York, NY. Tel: (646) 834-9400, Web Site: www.zustek.com (32)

Dijk, Arjan, Google, New York, NY. Tel: (212) 565-0000, FAX: (212) 565-0001, Web Site: www. google.com (31)

Dik, Susan, Dik & Associates Direct Marketing, Honolulu, HI. Tel: (808) 734-8868, FAX: (808) 734-8868, E-Mail: susandik@gmail.com (35)

Dik & Associates Direct Marketing, Honolulu, HI. Tel: (808) 734-8868, FAX: (808) 734-8868, E-Mail: susandik@gmail.com (35)

Dilenschnieder, Robert, L., The Dartnell Corp, Naples, FL. Tel: (585) 240-7301, (800) 447-4030, FAX: (585) 292-4392, E-Mail: customerservice@ dartnellcorp.com, Web Site: www.dartnellcorp.com (17)

Dill, Chris, Computer Business Services Inc, Americus, GA. Tel: (229) 924-4408, (866) 924-4408, FAX: (229) 924-3644, E-Mail: cdill@combusser. com, Web Site: www.combusser.com (22)

Dill, Marcy, Technology Review, Cambridge, MA. Tel: (617) 475-8000, FAX: (617) 258-5850, Web Site: www.technologyreview.com (17)

Dillard, Amanda, LemmonTree Marketing Group, Tempe, AZ. Tel: (480) 967-1405, (888) 536-6243, FAX: (480) 967-1407, E-Mail: 7solutions@ lemmontree.com, Web Site: www.lemmontree.com (35)

Dillard, Peter, Moultrie Manufacturing Co, Moultrie, GA. Tel: (229) 985-1312, (800) 841-8674, FAX: (229) 890-7245, Web Site: www. moultriemanufacturing.com (8)

Diller, Barry, HSN Inc, Saint Petersburg, FL. Tel: (727) 872-1000, (800) 284-3100, Web Site: www. hsn.com (5)

Dillingham, William, Aspen Imaging International Inc, Cleveland, OH. Tel: (216) 881-5300, (800) 955-5555, FAX: (216) 881-8380, (800) 756-0990 (34)

Dillion, Pattie, Veratad Technologies LLC, Teaneck, NJ. Tel: (201) 510-6000, FAX: (201) 510-6036 (22)

Dillman, Frederick, Unisys, Blue Bell, PA. Tel: (215) 986-4011, (800) 874-8647, FAX: (215) 986-2312, Web Site: www.unisys.com (16)

Dillmann, Thomas, IJHANA, Los Angeles, CA. Tel: (213) 268-4283, (888) 421-9222, E-Mail: info@ ijhana.com, Web Site: www.ijhana.com (20)

Dillon, Dan, Replogle Globes Inc, Broadview, IL. Tel: (708) 343-0900, FAX: (708) 343-0923, E-Mail: info@reploglobes.com, Web Site: www. reploglobes.com (16)

Dillon, Dave, B&W Press Inc, Georgetown, MA. Tel: (978) 352-6100, (877) 246-3467, FAX: (978) 352-5955, E-Mail: csr@bwpress.com, Web Site: www. bwpress.com (21)

Dillon, David, Vermont Ski Areas Association, Montpelier, VT. Tel: (802) 223-2439, FAX: (802) 229-6917, E-Mail: info@skivermont.com, Web Site: www.skivermont.com (1)

Dillon, G., Scott, Whitaker National, Huntington, WV. Tel: (304) 525-0852, (800) 377-8721, FAX: (304) 525-0874, Web Site: www.neshold.com (16)

Dillon, Karen, INC Magazine, New York, NY. Tel: (212) 389-5377, FAX: (617) 248-8090, Web Site: www.inc.com (17)

DiLorenzo, Kathleen, National Court Reporters Association, Vienna, VA. Tel: (703) 556-6272, (800) 272-6272, FAX: (703) 556-6291, E-Mail: msic@ncrahg.org, Web Site: www.ncraonline.org (1)

Dimaio, Alicia, Special Libraries Association (SLA), Alexandria, VA. Tel: (703) 647-4900, FAX: (703) 647-4901, E-Mail: sla@sla.org, Web Site: www.sla.org (40)

DiMarizio, Jim, Mazda North American Operations, Irvine, CA. Tel: (949) 727-1990, (800) 222-6500, FAX: (949) 727-6101, Web Site: www.mazdausa.com (16)

DiMauro, Lisa, Gracewood Fruit Co, Vero Beach, FL. Tel: (772) 567-1154, E-Mail: info@gracewoodgroves.com, Web Site: www.gracewoodgroves.com (4)

The Dime Savings Bank of New York FSB, Brooklyn, NY. Tel: (800) 321-3463, Web Site: www.dimewill.com (14)

DiMichel, Anthony, Fisher-Price, East Aurora, NY. Tel: (716) 687-3300, FAX: (716) 687-3636, Web Site: www.fisherprice.com (16)

DiMino, Michael, Educational Resources, Elgin, IL. Tel: (800) 860-7004, FAX: (800) 610-5005, E-Mail: sales@edresources.com, Web Site: www.educationalresources.com (3)

Dimmock Hill Golf Course Pro Shop, Binghamton, NY. Tel: (607) 729-5511, (800) 727-5511, FAX: (607) 797-7434, Web Site: www.dimmockhill.com (11)

Dimon, James, JP Morgan Chase & Co, New York, NY. Tel: (212) 270-6000, E-Mail: jpmcinvestorrelations@jpmchase.com, Web Site: www.jpmorgan.com (14)

DiMuccio, Robert, A., Amica Insurance, Lincoln, RI. Tel: (401) 334-6000, (800) 652-6422, FAX: (401) 334-4241, Web Site: www.amica.com (15)

DineWise, Farmingdale, NY. Tel: (631) 694-1111, (800) 749-1170, FAX: (631) 694-4064, E-Mail: info@dinewise.com, Web Site: www.dinewise.com (4)

The Dingley Press, Lisbon, ME. Tel: (207) 353-4151, (800) 317-4574, FAX: (207) 353-9886, E-Mail: webrequest@dingley.com, Web Site: www.dingley.com (27)

Dingus, Teresa, CPM Delta 1, Inc, Dallas, TX. Tel: (214) 349-6886, (800) 627-0252, FAX: (214) 503-1557, Web Site: www.cpmdelta1.com (11)

Dingwerth, Jared, VastCast Media, Las Vegas, NV. Tel: (702) 221-8261, Web Site: www.vastcastmedia.com (35)

Dinn, Bill, Dinn Brothers Inc, West Springfield, MA. Tel: (413) 750-3466, (800) 628-9657, FAX: (800) 876-7497, E-Mail: sales@dinntrophy.com, Web Site: www.dinntrophy.com (16)

Dinn, Michael, Dinn Brothers Inc, West Springfield, MA. Tel: (413) 750-3466, (800) 628-9657, FAX: (800) 876-7497, E-Mail: sales@dinntrophy.com, Web Site: www.dinntrophy.com (16)

Dinn Brothers Inc, West Springfield, MA. Tel: (413) 750-3466, (800) 628-9657, FAX: (800) 876-7497, E-Mail: sales@dinntrophy.com, Web Site: www.dinntrophy.com (16)

Dinyari, Farbod, Dinyari Inc, San Jose, CA. Tel: (408) 289-5400, Web Site: www.dinyari.com (9)

Dinyari Inc, San Jose, CA. Tel: (408) 289-5400, Web Site: www.dinyari.com (9)

Christian Dior Perfumes, New York, NY. Tel: (212) 931-2200, FAX: (212) 931-2954, Web Site: www.dior.com (7)

Diorio, James, Dial 800 LLC, Los Angeles, CA. Tel: (310) 273-9023, (800) 564-8685, Web Site: www.dial800.com (32)

Dipert, Autumn, Dan Dipert Travel Service Inc, Arlington, TX. Tel: (817) 543-3700, (800) 433-5335, FAX: (817) 543-3728, Web Site: www.dandipert.com (19)

Dipert, Dan, W., Dan Dipert Travel Service Inc, Arlington, TX. Tel: (817) 543-3700, (800) 433-5335, FAX: (817) 543-3728, Web Site: www.dandipert.com (19)

Dipert, Linda, Dan Dipert Travel Service Inc, Arlington, TX. Tel: (817) 543-3700, (800) 433-5335, FAX: (817) 543-3728, Web Site: www.dandipert.com (19)

Dan Dipert Travel Service Inc, Arlington, TX. Tel: (817) 543-3700, (800) 433-5335, FAX: (817) 543-3728, Web Site: www.dandipert.com (19)

DiPiazza, Sam, PricewaterhouseCoopers LLP, New York, NY. Tel: (646) 471-4000, FAX: (646) 471-4444, Web Site: www.pwc.com (14)

DiPietro, Dave, Atlanta Cutlery Corp, Conyers, GA. Tel: (770) 922-3700, (800) 833-8838, FAX: (770) 760-8993, E-Mail: webmaster@atlantacutlery.com, Web Site: www.atlantacutlery.com (11)

DiPietro, Rose, Council of Smaller Enterprises (COSE), Cleveland, OH. Tel: (216) 621-3300, Web Site: www.cose.org (1)

DiPippo, Jerry, Our Community Phone Book, Blue Bell, PA. Tel: (610) 825-7720, (877) THE-RED-1, (877) 843-7731, FAX: (610) 825-5758, E-Mail: robynfine@community-phonebook.com, Web Site: www.communitybook.com (35)

Diradoorian, Raymond, Allergan Inc, Irvine, CA. Tel: (714) 246-4500, (800) 433-8871, FAX: (714) 246-4971, Web Site: www.allergan.com (16)

Direct Access Marketing Services Inc, Syosset, NY. Tel: (516) 364-2777, FAX: (516) 364-0644, E-Mail: info@daxcess.com, Web Site: www.daxcess.com (22)

Direct Advantage Marketing, Pittsburgh, PA. Tel: (412) 381-2300, E-Mail: information@dam.com, Web Site: www.dam.com (29)

Direct Advantage Partners, Rowayton, CT. Tel: (203) 286-7100 (20)

Direct Advertising, Holliston, MA. Tel: (508) 429-7488, E-Mail: priority@dir-adv.com, Web Site: www.dir-adv.com (35)

Direct Alliance, Tempe, AZ. Tel: (800) 546-0582, Web Site: www.directalliance.com (35)

Direct Approach, Phoenix, AZ. Tel: (602) 955-0649, FAX: (602) 955-0654, E-Mail: tbarker@directapproachlists.com, Web Site: www.directapproachlists.com (23)

Direct Auto Insurance, Nashville, TN. Tel: (615) 399-4859, Web Site: www.directgeneral.com (15)

Direct Brands Inc, New York, NY. Tel: (212) 930-4949, Web Site: www.bmgmusic.com (13)

Direct Channel Inc, West Bridgewater, MA. Tel: (508) 588-4448, FAX: (508) 588-4644, E-Mail: directch@mindspring.com, Web Site: www.directchannel.com (23)

Direct Channel LLC, Southbury, CT. Tel: (203) 262-0588, Web Site: www.directchannel.net (35)

Direct Choice Inc, Wayne, PA. Tel: (610) 995-2111, Web Site: www.directchoiceinc.com (35)

Direct Cinema Ltd, Santa Monica, CA. Tel: (310) 636-8200, FAX: (310) 636-8228, E-Mail: orders@directcinemalimited.com, Web Site: www.directcinema.com (35)

Direct Communications Corp, Rutland, VT. Tel: (802) 747-3322, FAX: (802) 747-3376, E-Mail: information@direct-com.com, Web Site: www.direct-com.com (21)

Direct Creative, Westerville, OH. Tel: (614) 882-8823, E-Mail: dean@directcreative.com, Web Site: www.directcreative.com (39)

Direct Data Capture Ltd, Huntington Station, NY. Tel: (631) 547-5500, FAX: (631) 547-6800, E-Mail: jan@datacapture.com, Web Site: www.datacapture.com (22)

Direct Dynamics LLC, Killingworth, CT. Tel: (860) 614-4816, E-Mail: info@direct-dynamics.com, Web Site: direct-dynamics.com (20)

Direct Energy, Toronto, ON Canada. Tel: (416) 758-8700, (800) 348-2999 (16)

Direct Impact Group, Needham, MA. Tel: (781) 453-2200, FAX: (781) 453-1200, E-Mail: info@directimpactgroup.com, Web Site: www.directimpactgroup.com (35)

Direct Impact Inc, Saint Louis, MO. Tel: (314) 567-0024, FAX: (314) 567-1497, E-Mail: info@directimpactinc.com, Web Site: www.directimpactinc.com (35)

Direct Link Worldwide, Elizabeth, NJ. Tel: (908) 289-0703, (800) 223-7967, FAX: (908) 289-0705, E-Mail: infousa@directlink.com, Web Site: www.directlink.com (28)

Direct List Technology Inc, Orange, CA. Tel: (714) 772-3282, (888) 772-6947, FAX: (714) 772-6947, E-Mail: apieter@directlist.com, Web Site: www.directlist.com (23)

Direct Logic Solutions, Peoria, IL. Tel: (309) 688-5500, FAX: (309) 688-5502, E-Mail: nedbarrett@direct-logic.com, Web Site: www.direct-logic.com (22)

Direct Magazine, New York, NY. Tel: (212) 204-4228, FAX: (212) 683-3986 (43)

Direct Mail Advertising Corp, Miami, FL. Tel: (305) 557-4153, (800) 683-3622, FAX: (305) 634-1896, Web Site: www.directmac.com (23)

Direct Mail Center, San Francisco, CA. Tel: (415) 252-1600, FAX: (415) 252-9100, E-Mail: dmc@directmailctr.com, Web Site: www.directmailctr.com (21)

Direct Mail Depot Inc, Piscataway, NJ. Tel: (732) 469-5900, FAX: (732) 469-8414, E-Mail: sales@directmaildepot.com, Web Site: www.directmaildepot.com (28)

Direct Mail Marketing Inc, Shreveport, LA. Tel: (318) 631-4081, FAX: (318) 621-9150, E-Mail: james_dmm@bizsport.rr.com (21)

Direct Mail of NY-Posthaste, Buchanan, NY. Tel: (914) 736-2239 (28)

Direct Mail Service Inc, Pittsburgh, PA. Tel: (412) 471-6300 (21)

Direct Mail Solutions, Henrico, VA. Tel: (804) 254-8300, Web Site: www.directmailsolutions.com (28)

Direct Mail Solutions LLC, Carol Stream, IL. Tel: (630) 653-6863, FAX: (630) 653-7144, E-Mail: support@dmspostal.com, Web Site: www.dmspostal.com (28)

Direct Mail Source, Wilmette, IL. Tel: (847) 676-3744, E-Mail: dms@directmailsource.net (28)

Direct Mail Source Inc, Scottsdale, AZ. Tel: (602) 947-1552 (23)

Direct Mail Strategy Group (DMSG), Cresskill, NJ. Tel: (201) 567-3200, (201) 567-1530, E-Mail: bschonwald@conraddirect.com, Web Site: www.conraddirect.com (31)

Direct Mail Systems, Clearwater, FL. Tel: (727) 573-1985, (800) 683-6245, FAX: (727) 573-1747, E-Mail: info@direct-mail-systems.com, Web Site: www.direct-mail-systems.com (20)

Direct Mail Trackers, Medford, NY. Tel: (631) 758-0984, E-Mail: info@dmtrackers.com, Web Site: www.dmtrackers.com (28)

Direct Market Designs Inc, Paterson, NJ. Tel: (973) 925-9600, Web Site: www.dmd-liberty.com (28)

Direct Marketers On Call Inc (DMOC), New York, NY. Tel: (212) 691-1942, FAX: (212) 924-1331, E-Mail: info@dmoc-inc.com, Web Site: www.dmoc-inc.com (20)

Direct Marketing Association, New York, NY. Tel: (212) 768-7277, Web Site: www.the-dma.org (1)

Direct Marketing Association of Detroit, Royal Oak, MI. Tel: (248) 478-4888, FAX: (248) 478-6437, E-Mail: dmad@ameritech.net, Web Site: www.dmad.org (40)

Direct Marketing Association of Northern California, Morgan Hill, CA. Tel: (800) 613-9266, FAX: (800) 613-8819, E-Mail: lbeasley@beasleydirect.com, Web Site: www.dmanc.org (40)

Direct Marketing Association of Saint Louis, Washington, MO. Tel: (866) 516-0121, FAX: (636) 239-2324, E-Mail: mparisien@mac.com, Web Site: www.dmastl.org (40)

Direct Marketing Association of Southern California, Newbury Park, CA. Tel: (818) 541-1152, FAX: (818) 541-1959, Web Site: www.ladma.org (40)

Direct Marketing Association of Toronto, Toronto, ON Canada. Tel: (905) 564-6616, FAX: (905) 564-6621, E-Mail: pete@themose.ca, Web Site: www.dmatoronto.org (40)

Direct Marketing Association of Washington, Reston, VA. Tel: (703) 689-DMAW, FAX: (703) 481-DMAW, E-Mail: info@dmaw.org, Web Site: www.dmaw.org (40)

Direct Marketing Audit Systems, Bridgeton, MO. Tel: (314) 739-7480, FAX: (314) 739-7284, Web Site: www.dmasinc.com (22)

Direct Marketing Boot Camp, Hollywood, FL. Tel: (646) 723-3230, (800) 331-7114, FAX: (954) 921-2005, E-Mail: loisgeller@loisgellermarketinggroup.com, Web Site: www.masongeller.com (41)

The Direct Marketing Club of New York Inc, Garden City, NY. Tel: (516) 746-6700, FAX: (516) 294-8141, E-Mail: info@dmcny.org, Web Site: www.dmcny.org (1)

Direct Marketing Consultant, Sharon, PA. Tel: (724) 699-0230 (20)

Direct Marketing Designs Inc, Greenwood Village, CO. Tel: (303) 649-9888, FAX: (303) 649-1917, E-Mail: info@directmarketingdesigns.com, Web Site: www.directmarketingdesigns.com (35)

Direct Marketing Digest, Minneapolis, MN. Tel: (612) 788-1673, E-Mail: info@nmoa.org, Web Site: www.nmoa.org (43)

Direct Marketing Dynamics Inc, Germantown, MD. Tel: (301) 916-3900, FAX: (301) 515-0404, E-Mail: jim@directmarketingdynamics.com, Web Site: www.directmarketingdynamics.com (35)

Direct Marketing Group, Eden Prairie, MN. Tel: (952) 975-5060, Web Site: www.directamsc.com (35)

Direct Marketing Insights Inc, Goodyear, AZ. Tel: (843) 817-7488, E-Mail: jimp@dminsights.com, Web Site: www.dminsights.com (20)

Direct Marketing International Ltd, Huntington Beach, CA. Tel: (877) 596-1919 (41)

Direct Marketing Market Place, Berkeley Heights, NJ. Tel: (908) 673-1000, (800) 473-7020, FAX: (908) 673-1179 (43)

Direct Marketing News, Markham, ON Canada. Tel: (905) 201-6600, (800) 668-1838, FAX: (905) 201-6601, E-Mail: home@dmn.ca, Web Site: www.dmn.ca (43)

Direct Marketing Partners, Sacramento, CA. Tel: (916) 974-6969, (800) 909-2626, FAX: (916) 920-5156, E-Mail: info@dirmkt.com, Web Site: www.directmarketingpartners.com (29)

Direct Marketing Publishers, Yardley, PA. Tel: (215) 321-3068, (800) 663-8387, FAX: (215) 321-9647, E-Mail: consulting@dmpublishers.com, Web Site: www.dmpublishers.com (17)

Direct Marketing Resources, Charlotte, NC. Tel: (704) 845-5890, (888) 644-4DMR, E-Mail: dan@dmresources.com, Web Site: www.dmresources.com (20)

Direct Marketing Resources Group Inc, Raleigh, NC. Tel: (919) 231-2728, (800) 517-5253, Web Site: www.improvedmarketingresults.com (20)

Direct Marketing Solutions Inc, Portland, OR. Tel: (503) 281-1400, Web Site: www.teamdms.com (35)

The Direct Marketing Specialists Inc, Chicago, IL. Tel: (312) 266-7906, FAX: (312) 266-9230, E-Mail: rwinedms@winestarmail.com (35)

Direct Marketing Strategy, Planning & Execution (Fourth Edition), Blacklick, OH. Tel: (614) 755-4152, (800) 722-4726, Web Site: www.mcgraw-hill.com (43)

Direct Marketing Tool Kit for Small Business, Minneapolis, MN. Tel: (612) 788-1673, E-Mail: info@nmoa.org, Web Site: www.nmoa.org/directmarketingtoolkit (43)

Direct Media List Management, Greenwich, CT. Tel: (203) 532-1000, FAX: (203) 532-3766, Web Site: www.directmedia.com (24)

Direct Media Millard, Peterborough, NH. Tel: (603) 924-9262, FAX: (603) 924-9420, Web Site: www.millard.com (23)

Direct Network Inc, Allentown, NJ. Tel: (732) 821-7090, FAX: (732) 821-7202, E-Mail: dirnet@verizon.net, Web Site: www.dirnetnetworklists.com (23)

Direct One Inc, Winter Park, FL. Tel: (407) 673-4500, FAX: (407) 673-4501, E-Mail: wariagno@directoneinc.com, Web Site: www.directoneinc.com (28)

Direct Options, West Chester, OH. Tel: (513) 779-4416, FAX: (513) 779-4426, E-Mail: inform@directoptions.com, Web Site: www.directoptions.com (35)

Direct Partner Solutions Inc, Flowery Branch, GA. Tel: (678) 762-9869, Web Site: www.directpartnersolutions.com (23)

Direct Partners, Marina Del Rey, CA. Tel: (310) 482-4200, FAX: (310) 482-4201, Web Site: www.directpartners.com (35)

Direct Print, Windham, NH. Tel: (603) 437-6831 (21)

Direct Resources Group, Seattle, WA. Tel: (206) 749-0001, E-Mail: results@drg.com, Web Site: www.drg.com (35)

Direct Response Academy, Austin, TX. Tel: (512) 301-5900, FAX: (512) 301-7900, E-Mail: info@dracademy.org, Web Site: www.dracademy.org (41)

Direct Response Consulting, McLean, VA. Tel: (703) 749-0010, FAX: (703) 749-0967, Web Site: www.drcs.com (17)

Direct Response Enhancements LLC, Scottsdale, AZ. Tel: (480) 451-7384, FAX: (480) 661-8460, E-Mail: drellc@aol.com, Web Site: www.dreteleconsultants.com (29)

Direct Response Insurance Administrative Services Inc (DRIASI), Chanhassen, MN. Tel: (952) 556-5600, (800) 688-0760, FAX: (952) 556-8200, E-Mail: tpa@driasi.com, Web Site: www.driasi.com (21)

Direct Response Marketing, Clearwater, FL. Tel: (727) 573-1985, (800) 683-6245, FAX: (727) 573-1747, E-Mail: drmclwr@tampabay.rr.com, Web Site: www.dmsmails.com (28)

Direct Response Marketing Inc, Palm Desert, CA. Tel: (760) 360-5900, FAX: (760) 360-7266 (32)

Direct Response Media, Wilmington, DE. Tel: (610) 995-0200, (800) 898-3761, FAX: (610) 995-0300, E-Mail: info@directresponsemedia.com, Web Site: www.directresponsemedia.com (32)

Direct Response Services, Glen Carbon, IL. Tel: (618) 288-8811, (800) 795-5478, FAX: (618) 288-3005, E-Mail: drs@drslist.com, Web Site: www.drslist.com (23)

Direct Results, West Springfield, MA. Tel: (413) 732-8310, FAX: (413) 732-8361 (21)

Direct SAT TV LLC, Southern Pines, NC. Tel: (910) 693-3042, (800) 595-4101, FAX: (866) 935-4097, Web Site: www.directsattv.com (3)

Direct Selling Association, Washington, DC. Tel: (202) 452-8866, FAX: (202) 452-9010, E-Mail: info@dsa.org, Web Site: www.dsa.org (40)

Direct Selling Education Foundation, Washington, DC. Tel: (202) 452-8866, FAX: (202) 452-9015, Web Site: www.dsef.org (40)

Direct Sports Supply, Pearisburg, VA. Tel: (540) 921-1243, (800) 456-0072, FAX: (540) 921-1475, Web Site: www.directsports.com (11)

Direct Success Communications Inc, Chester Springs, PA. Tel: (610) 321-0321, FAX: (610) 321-0322 (35)

Direct Supply Inc, Milwaukee, WI. Tel: (414) 358-2805, (800) 634-7328, FAX: (414) 358-2397, E-Mail: deardirect@directs.com, Web Site: www.directsupply.net (16)

Direct Tech Inc, Omaha, NE. Tel: (402) 895-2100, Web Site: www.direct-tech.com (34)

Direct Ventures Inc, Larchmont, NY. Tel: (914) 833-9842, FAX: (914) 834-3883, E-Mail: bsideroff@directventuresmcinc.wm (20)

DirectBuy Inc, Merrillville, IN. Tel: (219) 736-1100, FAX: (219) 755-6208, Web Site: www.ucctotalhome.com (1)

DirectConnect Group Ltd, Cleveland, OH. Tel: (216) 634-8481, Web Site: www.directgroup.com (35)

DirecTech, Maysville, KY. Tel: (866) 550-5030, E-Mail: ceo@directech.com, Web Site: www.directech.com (22)

Directions Marketing, Ann Arbor, MI. Tel: (734) 930-2820, FAX: (734) 930-9189, E-Mail: directions@directions.com.eg, Web Site: www.directions.com.eg (20)

Directives/Targeted Marketing and Communications, Plymouth, MA. Tel: (215) 546-7817, Web Site: www.directivesmarketing.com (20)

DirectMail.com, Prince Frederick, MD. Tel: (888) 690-2252, FAX: (301) 855-9810, Web Site: www.directmail.com (28)

The Directors Network, West Hartford, CT. Tel: (818) 906-0006, FAX: (818) 506-4662, Web Site: www.tdnartists.com (35)

Directory Distributing Associates Inc, Hazelwood, MO. Tel: (314) 592-8600, (800) 325-1964, FAX: (314) 592-8790, E-Mail: corporate@directrac.com, Web Site: www.ddai.com (28)

Directory of American Business & Insurance Attorneys, New York, NY. Tel: (732) 458-7788, (800) 445-7995, FAX: (732) 458-7710, E-Mail: staff@abialaw.com, Web Site: www.abialaw.com (15)

The Directory of Business Information Resources, Millerton, NY. Tel: (518) 789-8700, (800) 562-2139, FAX: (518) 789-0556, E-Mail: cstupak@greyhouse.com, Web Site: www.greyhouse.com (43)

Directory of Mail Order Catalogs, Millerton, NY. Tel: (518) 789-8700, (800) 562-2139, FAX: (518) 789-0556, E-Mail: cstupak@greyhouse.com, Web Site: www.greyhouse.com (43)

Directory of Mail Order Catalogs, Minneapolis, MN. Tel: (612) 788-1673, E-Mail: info@nmoa.org, Web Site: www.nmoa.org (43)

Directory of Major Mailers & What They Mail, Philadelphia, PA. Tel: (800) 777-8074, FAX: (215) 238-5412, E-Mail: customerservice@napco.com, Web Site: www.majormailers.com (43)

Directory of Major Malls, Nyack, NY. Tel: (845) 348-7000, (800) 898-6255, Web Site: www.shoppingcenters.com (23)

Directory of Premium, Incentive & Travel Buyers, Richmond, VA. Tel: (804) 762-4455, (800) 223-1797, FAX: (804) 935-0271, E-Mail: amdouglas4@aol.com, Web Site: www.douglaspublications.com (43)

DirectSmile LLC, Bloomfield, NJ. Tel: (973) 780-0018, Web Site: www.directsmile.com (22)

DIRECTV, El Segundo, CA. Tel: (310) 535-5000, FAX: (310) 535-5225 (16)

DiRenzo, Thomas G., Technical Marketing Group, West Caldwell, NJ. Tel: (856) 751-9585, FAX: (856) 751-9729, E-Mail: tldirenzo@aol.com, Web Site: www2.techmktgrp.com (35)

DiReso, Don, Theodore Presser Co, King Of Prussia, PA. Tel: (610) 592-1222, FAX: (610) 592-1229, E-Mail: webmaster@presser.com, Web Site: www.presser.com (17)

Direxxis Inc, Needham, MA. Tel: (781) 444-7900, Web Site: www.direxxismarketing.com (22)

DiRienzo, Robert, JC Penney Inc, Plano, TX. Tel: (972) 431-1000, FAX: (972) 431-1977, Web Site: www.jcpenney.com (5)

Dirmark Group Inc, Buford, GA. Tel: (678) 727-9677, (888) 395-6727, FAX: (800) 881-2303, E-Mail: mnewton@dirmark.com, Web Site: www. accurateleads.com (23)

DiRosa, James, R., Quartermaster Uniform & Equipment Co, Cerritos, CA. Tel: (562) 304-7300, (800) 444-8643, FAX: (562) 304-7335, Web Site: www. qmuniforms.com (2)

Diruzza, Joe, MFE Instruments, Salem, NH. Tel: (603) 893-8778, (800) 843-8011, FAX: (603) 893-8851, Web Site: www.stockeryale.com (9)

Dirxion, Saint Louis, MO. Tel: (636) 717-2300, Web Site: www.dirxion.com (16)

Disabled American Veterans, Cincinnati, OH. Tel: (859) 441-7300, FAX: (859) 442-2084, E-Mail: feedback@davmail.org, Web Site: www.dav.org (1)

Disbrow, Bill, Cox Target Media/DBA Valpak, Largo, FL. Tel: (727) 399-3000, (800) 678-2743, FAX: (727) 399-3061, E-Mail: contact_sales@coxtarget. com, Web Site: www.coxdirect.com (21)

Disbrow, Lynn, M., Institute of Real Estate Management, Chicago, IL. Tel: (312) 329-6000, (800) 837-0706, FAX: (800) 338-4736, E-Mail: custserv@ irem.org, Web Site: www.irem.org (1)

Disc Graphics Inc, Hauppauge, NY. Tel: (631) 234-1400, FAX: (631) 234-1460, E-Mail: info@ discgraphics.com, Web Site: www.discgraphics. com (27)

Disc Makers, Pennsauken, NJ. Tel: (800) 237-6666, Web Site: www.discmakers.com (3)

Disch, Thomas, R., Handi-Ramp Inc, Libertyville, IL. Tel: (847) 680-7700, (800) 876-RAMP, FAX: (847) 816-7689, E-Mail: info@handiramp.com, Web Site: www.handiramp.com (7)

DiscMail Direct Coalition, Port Washington, NY. Tel: (516) 757-6720, Web Site: http://mesalliance.org/ (40)

Discover Financial Services, Riverwoods, IL. Tel: (224) 405-3373 (14)

Discover Publications, Worthington, OH. Tel: (614) 785-1111, Web Site: www.discover.pubs.com (17)

Discovery, Eatontown, NJ. Tel: (732) 933-1899, Web Site: www.discoveryco.com (9)

Discovery Communications, New York, NY. Tel: (212) 548-5555, Web Site: www.discovery.com (32)

Discovery Communications LLC, Silver Spring, MD. Tel: (240) 662-2000, FAX: (240) 662-1868, Web Site: corporate.discovery.com (16)

Discovery Toys, Livermore, CA. Tel: (925) 606-2600, (800) 426-4777, FAX: (925) 370-0289, Web Site: www.discoverytoysinc.net (16)

Disimile, Gail, C., Beta Research Corp, Syosset, NY. Tel: (516) 935-3800, FAX: (516) 935-4092, E-Mail: beta@nybeta.com, Web Site: www.nybeta. com (30)

The Disney ABC Cable Network Group, Burbank, CA. Tel: (818) 569-7500, FAX: (818) 848-6925, Web Site: www.disneyabctv.com (32)

Disney Vacation Club, Kissimmee, FL. Tel: (407) 566-3100, (800) 500-3990, FAX: (407) 566-3393 (19)

Walt Disney Parks & Resorts, Lake Buena Vista, FL. Tel: (407) 824-2222, Web Site: www.disneyworld. com (19)

Dispatch Letter Service, New York, NY. Tel: (212) 307-5943, FAX: (212) 307-6103, Web Site: www. dispatchletterservice.com (28)

Dispensa-Matic Label Dispensers, Saint Louis, MO. Tel: (314) 231-6006, (800) 325-7303, FAX: (314) 621-1602, E-Mail: info@dispensamatic.com, Web Site: www.dispensa-matic.com (34)

Disser, David, Customer Retention Solutions, Portage, MI. Tel: (269) 324-7385 (20)

Dissette, Mark, R., Holy Cross Hospital, Fort Lauderdale, FL. Tel: (954) 771-8000, FAX: (954) 229-8597, Web Site: www.holy-cross.com (16)

Distribution Postal Co Inc, Baltimore, MD. Tel: (410) 488-1002, (800) 992-4525, FAX: (410) 488-2344, E-Mail: louishaber@distpost.com, Web Site: www. distpost.com (28)

Ditmer, Dale, Dalco Electronics, Springboro, OH. Tel: (937) 743-8042, (800) 445-5342, FAX: (937) 743-9251, Web Site: www.dalco.com (3)

Dittman, Terrie, Harcourt Educational Measurement, San Antonio, TX. Tel: (210) 299-1061, (800) 211-8378, FAX: (800) 232-1223, Web Site: www. harcourtassessment.com (17)

Dittmar, Daniel, BIC Corp, Shelton, CT. Tel: (203) 783-2000, FAX: (203) 783-2081, Web Site: www. bicworld.com (16)

Diversified Graphics Inc, Minneapolis, MN. Tel: (800) 233-7454, FAX: (612) 331-4079, Web Site: www. dgi.net (21)

Diversified Healthcare Services, Richardson, TX. Tel: (972) 238-1492, FAX: (972) 907-8283, Web Site: www.dhscorp.com (15)

Diversified Investment Advisors, Harrison, NY. Tel: (914) 697-8967, FAX: (914) 697-3743, Web Site: www.divinvest.com (14)

Diversified Photo Supply Corp, Gardena, CA. Tel: (310) 328-8577, (800) 544-1609, FAX: (310) 328-8518, Web Site: www.diversifiedphoto.com (10)

The Diversified Services Group Inc, Wayne, PA. Tel: (610) 989-1710, FAX: (610) 989-1730, E-Mail: rfgrieb@dsg-network.com, Web Site: www.dsg-network.com (20)

Divine Word Missionaries, Techny, IL. Tel: (847) 412-7233, Web Site: www.svdmissions.org (1)

Dixit, Jay, Sussex Publishers Inc, New York, NY. Tel: (212) 260-7210, FAX: (212) 260-7445, Web Site: www.blues-buster.com (17)

Dixon, Diane B., Avery Dennison Corp, Brea, CA. Tel: (714) 674-8500, (800) 462-8379, FAX: (714) 674-6929, Web Site: www.avery.com (10)

Dixon, Dick, The Pampered Pet Mart, Lisle, IL. Tel: (630) 660-0056, FAX: (630) 810-1934, E-Mail: dickdixon@aol.com, Web Site: www.dixondirect. com (35)

Dixon, J. Gordon, ARI, Orchard Hill, GA. Tel: (770) 227-8222, (800) 241-5064, FAX: (770) 227-9190, Web Site: www.halt.com (16)

Dixon, Jean, American Medical Association, Chicago, IL. Tel: (312) 464-5000, (800) 621-8335, FAX: (312) 464-4184, Web Site: www.ama-assn.org (1)

Dizon, Mark, Georgetown University Law Center/ Continuing Legal Education Div, Washington, DC. Tel: (202) 662-9890, FAX: (202) 662-9891, E-Mail: nds25@law.georgetown.edu, Web Site: www.georgetowncle.org (13)

Dlaboha, Lila, The Granger Collection, New York, NY. Tel: (212) 447-1789, FAX: (212) 447-1492, Web Site: www.granger.com (38)

DMS Marketing Inc, Mission Viejo, CA. Tel: (949) 460-7300, Web Site: http://www.dms-marketing. com (35)

Do-It Corp, South Haven, MI. Tel: (269) 637-1121, (800) 426-4822, FAX: (269) 637-7223, E-Mail: sales@do-it.com, Web Site: www.do-it.com (9)

Do It Yourself Direct Marketing, Hoboken, NJ. Tel: (201) 748-6000, FAX: (201) 748-6088, E-Mail: info@wiley.com, Web Site: www.wiley.com (43)

DoAll Co, Wheeling, IL. Tel: (847) 824-1122, (800) 92-DOALL, FAX: (847) 699-7524, E-Mail: info@ doall.com, Web Site: www.doall.com (18)

Doan, Dale, UNICEF Canada, Toronto, ON. Tel: (416) 482-4444, (800) 567-4483, FAX: (416) 487-8875, E-Mail: on.secretary@unicef.ca, Web Site: www. unicef.ca (1)

Doane, Saint Louis, MO. Tel: (314) 569-2700, (866) 647-0918, FAX: (314) 569-1083, Web Site: www. doane.com (17)

Dobbin, Daniel, Action Mailers Inc, Aston, PA. Tel: (610) 859-0500, (800) 258-5992, FAX: (610) 859-0505, Web Site: www.actionmailer.com (27)

Dobbins, Mike, Perimeter Technology Inc, Manchester, NH. Tel: (603) 645-1616, (800) 645-1650, FAX: (603) 645-1424, Web Site: www. perimetertechnology.com (34)

Dobbs, Richard, CTB MacMillan/McGraw-Hill, Monterey, CA. Tel: (831) 393-0700, (800) 538-9547, FAX: (831) 393-6528, E-Mail: hr@ctb.com, Web Site: www.ctb.com (16)

Dobin, Bruce, Reliable Mail Service Inc, Edison, NJ. Tel: (732) 346-9779, (800) 773-6338, FAX: (732) 346-9799, E-Mail: bdobin@reliablemailservice. com, Web Site: www.reliablemailservice.com (28)

Dobina, Don, MPC Louisville Promotions, Louisville, KY. Tel: (502) 451-4900, (800) 331-0989, FAX: (502) 451-5075, E-Mail: service@mpcpromotions. com, Web Site: www.mpcpromotions.com (33)

Dobkin, Jeffrey, Danielle Adams Publishing Co, Merion Station, PA. Tel: (610) 642-1000, Web Site: www.danielleadams.com (3)

Dobkin, Jeffrey, Direct Marketing Tool Kit for Small Business, Minneapolis, MN. Tel: (612) 788-1673, E-Mail: info@nmoa.org, Web Site: www.nmoa.org/ directmarketingtoolkit (43)

Dobos, Greg, MediaConcepts Corp, Assonet, MA. Tel: (508) 644-3131, FAX: (508) 644-5201, E-Mail: at3@mediaconceptscorp.com, Web Site: www. mediaconceptscorp.com (35)

Dobson, David, Kensington Technology Group, Redwood Shores, CA. Tel: (650) 572-2700, FAX: (650) 267-2800, Web Site: www.kensington.com (16)

Dobson, Jan, Florida Institute of CPA's, Tallahassee, FL. Tel: (850) 224-2727, (800) 342-3197 (FL), FAX: (850) 222-8190, E-Mail: msc@ficpa.org, Web Site: www.ficpa.org (1)

Docherty, Robert, Direct Marketing Market Place, Berkeley Heights, NJ. Tel: (908) 673-1000, (800) 473-7020, FAX: (908) 673-1179 (43)

Docherty, Robert, Marquis Who's Who LLC, Berkeley Heights, NJ. Tel: (908) 673-1000, (800) 473-7020, FAX: (908) 673-1179, E-Mail: info@ marquiswhoswho.com, Web Site: www. marquiswhoswho.com (17)

Dochtermann, Erik, Katz Dochtermann & Epstein, New York, NY. Tel: (212) 686-0006, FAX: (212) 686-6991, E-Mail: info@kdande.com, Web Site: www.kdande.com (35)

Dockeray, Tara, Fixed Address Marketing Inc, Aurora, ON Canada. Tel: (905) 750-0029, Web Site: www. fixedaddressmarketing.com (23)

Dockerman, David, Tom Snyder Productions, Watertown, MA. Tel: (617) 926-6000, (800) 342-0236, FAX: (800) 304-1254, E-Mail: ask@tomsnyder. com, Web Site: www.tomsnyder.com (16)

Dockery, Rod, Dockery House Publishing Inc, Lindale, TX. Tel: (903) 882-6900, FAX: (903) 882-6902, E-Mail: questions@dockerypublishing.com, Web Site: www.dockerypublishing.com (27)

Dockery House Publishing Inc, Lindale, TX. Tel: (903) 882-6900, FAX: (903) 882-6902, E-Mail: questions@dockerypublishing.com, Web Site: www.dockerypublishing.com (27)

Dockter, James, E., PBD Worldwide Fulfillment Services, Alpharetta, GA. Tel: (770) 442-8633, FAX: (770) 442-9742, E-Mail: sales.marketing@pbd. com, Web Site: www.pbd.com (28)

Doctor's Best Inc, San Clemente, CA. Tel: (949) 498-3628, (800) 333-6977, FAX: (800) 754-2036, (949) 498-3952, E-Mail: info@drbvitamins.com, Web Site: www.drbvitamins.com (16)

The Doctor's Co, Napa, CA. Tel: (707) 226-0176, E-Mail: info@thedoctors.com, Web Site: www. thedoctors.com (15)

Drs Foster & Smith Inc, Rhinelander, WI. Tel: (715) 369-3305, Web Site: www.drsfostersmith.com (2)

Doctors Without Borders, New York, NY. Tel: (212) 655-3767, Web Site: www.doctorswithoutborders. org (1)

Dodds Jr., William, R., The Northern Trust Co, Chicago, IL. Tel: (312) 630-6000, (888) 289-6542, FAX: (312) 630-1512, Web Site: www.ntrs.com (14)

Dodds, Diane, Rapids Wholesale Equipment, Marion, IA. Tel: (319) 447-1670, (800) 472-7431, FAX: (319) 447-1680, (800) 858-0327, E-Mail: judys@rapidswholesale.com, Web Site: www.rapidswholesale.com (16)

Dodds, Joe, Rapids Wholesale Equipment, Marion, IA. Tel: (319) 447-1670, (800) 472-7431, FAX: (319) 447-1680, (800) 858-0327, E-Mail: judys@rapidswholesale.com, Web Site: www.rapidswholesale.com (16)

Doddy, Aine, Concern Worldwide, New York, NY. Tel: (212) 557-8000, Web Site: /www.concernusa.org (1)

Dodenhoff, Steve, Syntellect, Phoenix, AZ. Tel: (602) 789-2800, (800) 788-9733, FAX: (602) 789-2899, Web Site: www.syntellect.com (16)

Dodge, Larry, Booth Michigan, Grand Rapids, MI. Tel: (616) 222-5824, FAX: (616) 222-5318, Web Site: www.boothnewspapers.com (17)

Dodson, Alisa, Country Dance and Song Society, Haydenville, MA. Tel: (413) 268-7426, FAX: (413) 268-7471, E-Mail: office@cdss.org, Web Site: www.cdss.org (1)

Dodson, David, Chattanooga Shooting Supplies Inc, Chattanooga, TN. Tel: (423) 894-3007, (800) 251-4808, FAX: (423) 855-5513, Web Site: www.chattanoogashooting.com (16)

Dodson, Gordon O., Dodson & Associates, Dallas, TX. Tel: (972) 931-1020 (20)

Dodson, Lynne, Dorothy Biddle Service, Greeley, PA. Tel: (570) 226-3239, FAX: (570) 226-0349, E-Mail: info@dorothybiddle.com, Web Site: www.dorothybiddle.com (8)

Dodson & Associates, Dallas, TX. Tel: (972) 931-1020 (20)

Doehner, George, J., Bulkley Dunton Publishing Group, New York, NY. Tel: (212) 863-1800, FAX: (212) 863-1979, Web Site: www.internationalpaper.com (25)

Doerfler, Ronald, J., The Hearst Corp, New York, NY. Tel: (212) 649-2000, FAX: (212) 649-2108, Web Site: www.hearst.com/magazines/ (17)

Doering, Tim, PNC Bank Corp, Pittsburgh, PA. Tel: (412) 762-2000/3514, (800) 422-6537, FAX: (412) 762-4482 (14)

Doerr, R., Chris, Blue Cross & Blue Shield of Florida, Jacksonville, FL. Tel: (904) 791-6111, (800) 477-3736, FAX: (904) 905-6638, E-Mail: katie.magee@bcbsfl.com, Web Site: www.bcbsfl.com (15)

Doheny II, Edward, L., P & H Mining Equipment, Milwaukee, WI. Tel: (414) 671-4400, FAX: (414) 671-7618, Web Site: www.phmining.com (16)

Doherty, Robert, B, American College of Physicians, Washington, DC. Tel: (215) 351-2400, (800) 523-1546, FAX: (215) 351-2686, Web Site: www.acponline.org (17)

Dohring, Doug, C., The Dohring Co, Glendale, CA. Tel: (818) 242-1600, FAX: (818) 649-8291, E-Mail: info@dohring.com, Web Site: www.dohring.com (30)

The Dohring Co, Glendale, CA. Tel: (818) 242-1600, FAX: (818) 649-8291, E-Mail: info@dohring.com, Web Site: www.dohring.com (30)

Doi, Tracey, C., Toyota Motor Sales USA Inc, Torrance, CA. Tel: (310) 468-4000, (800) 331-4331, FAX: (310) 468-7841, Web Site: www.toyota.com (16)

Doiel, Ron, EMED Co Inc, Buffalo, NY. Tel: (716) 626-1616, (800) 442-3633, FAX: (716) 626-1630, E-Mail: customerservice@emedco.com, Web Site: www.emedco.com (16)

Dolan, Charles F., Cablevision Systems Corp, Bethpage, NY. Tel: (516) 803-2300, FAX: (516) 803-3134, Web Site: www.cablevision.com (16)

Dolan, Denise, United Nations Foundation, Washington, DC. Tel: (202) 778-3539, Web Site: www.unfoundation.org (1)

Dolan, James L., Cablevision Systems Corp, Bethpage, NY. Tel: (516) 803-2300, FAX: (516) 803-3134, Web Site: www.cablevision.com (16)

Dolan, John P., Union Switch & Signal Inc, Pittsburgh, PA. Tel: (412) 688-2400, (800) 351-1520, FAX: (412) 688-2399, Web Site: www.switch.com (16)

Dolan, Shelley, Nordis Direct, Coral Springs, FL. Tel: (954) 323-5500, (800) 208-1169, FAX: (954) 323-0100, E-Mail: sdolan@nordisdirect.com, Web Site: www.nordisdirect.com (21)

Dolan, Tom, Westcon, Tarrytown, NY. Tel: (914) 829-7000, FAX: (914) 829-7137, Web Site: www.westcon.com (16)

Dole, Paul, KCEOC Community Action Partnership Inc, Barbourville, KY. Tel: (606) 546-3152, Web Site: kceoc.com (1)

Dole Fresh Flowers, Miami, FL. Tel: (305) 925-7900, Web Site: www.dole.com (8)

Domagala, Richard, Mystic Logistics, South Glastonbury, CT. Tel: (860) 659-1566, (800) 969-1566, FAX: (860) 659-1420, Web Site: www.mysticlogistics.com (35)

Doman, Mark, Credit Index, Saint Cloud, MN. Tel: (973) 770-4007, FAX: (973) 770-4006, Web Site: www.ebureau.com (22)

Domanico, Ronald, J., Caraustar, Austell, GA. Tel: (770) 948-3101, E-Mail: info@caraustar.com, Web Site: www.caraustar.com (16)

Domanico, Tom, FCB HealthCare & ProHealth, New York, NY. Tel: (212) 672-2300, FAX: (212) 672-2301 (3)

Dome Printing, Sacramento, CA. Tel: (800) 343-3139 (27)

Domeck, Brian, C., The Progressive Corp, Mayfield Village, OH. Tel: (440) 461-5000, (800) PRO-GRESSIVE, (800) 776-4737, FAX: (800) 456-6590, Web Site: www.progressive.com (15)

Domestic Bank, Providence, RI. Tel: (401) 943-1600, (800) 566-6600, FAX: (401) 943-6708, Web Site: www.domesticbank.com (14)

Domingo, Placida, Washington National Opera, Washington, DC. Tel: (202) 295-2400, (800) US-OPERA, FAX: (202) 295-2460, E-Mail: mail@dc-opera.org, Web Site: www.dc-opera.org (16)

Dominick, Don, George Sterne Agency Inc, Fallbrook, CA. Tel: (760) 432-6913, (800) 772-8174, FAX: (760) 432-9570, E-Mail: mim@georgesterneagency.com, Web Site: www.georgesterneagency.com (23)

Dominick, Lynne, Woman's Day Special Interest Publications, New York, NY. Tel: (212) 767-6000, FAX: (212) 767-5612, Web Site: www.womensday.com (17)

Dominick, Philip, S., Jet LithoColor Inc, Downers Grove, IL. Tel: (630) 932-9000, (800) 932-1JET, (800) 932-1538, FAX: (630) 932-9101, E-Mail: sales@jetlitho.com, Web Site: www.jetlitho.com (27)

Dominion Retail Inc, Richmond, VA. Tel: (804) 819-2268, Web Site: www.dom.com (16)

Domino Amjet Inc, Gurnee, IL. Tel: (847) 244-2501, FAX: (847) 244-2645, Web Site: www.dominoamjet.com (27)

Domorski, Paul, EMS Technologies, Norcross, GA. Tel: (770) 263-9200, FAX: (770) 447-4405, Web Site: www.ems-t.com (16)

Domtar Inc, Fort Mill, SC. Tel: (803) 802-8283, FAX: (810) 982-7124, Web Site: www.domtar.com (25)

Domville, Sara, Betterway Books, Blue Ash, OH. Tel: (513) 531-2222, (800) 289-0963, FAX: (513) 531-4744, Web Site: www.fwpublications.com/books.asp (17)

Don, Robert, E., Edward Don & Co, North Riverside, IL. Tel: (708) 442-9400, (800) 777-4366, FAX: (708) 442-0436, Web Site: www.don.com (16)

Don, Steven, R., Edward Don & Co, North Riverside, IL. Tel: (708) 442-9400, (800) 777-4366, FAX: (708) 442-0436, Web Site: www.don.com (16)

Edward Don & Co, North Riverside, IL. Tel: (708) 442-9400, (800) 777-4366, FAX: (708) 442-0436, Web Site: www.don.com (16)

Donahoe, Ed, Donahoe Purohit Miller Advertising, Chicago, IL. Tel: (312) 341-8100, FAX: (312) 341-8119, Web Site: www.dpmadvert.com (35)

Donahoe Purohit Miller Advertising, Chicago, IL. Tel: (312) 341-8100, FAX: (312) 341-8119, Web Site: www.dpmadvert.com (35)

Donahue, Christopher, Rapid City Journal, Rapid City, SD. Tel: (605) 394-8300, FAX: (605) 394-8462, E-Mail: classifieds@rapidcityjournal.com, Web Site: www.rapidcityjournal.com (18)

Donahue, J. Christopher, Federated Investors Co, Pittsburgh, PA. Tel: (412) 288-1900, (800) 341-7400, FAX: (412) 288-1171, Web Site: www.federatedinvestors.com (14)

Donahue, Mark, Replacements Ltd, Greensboro, NC. Tel: (336) 697-3000, (800) REPLACE, FAX: (336) 697-3100, E-Mail: mark.donahue@replacements.com, Web Site: www.replacements.com (8)

Donahue, Michael, D., American Association of Advertising Agencies, New York, NY. Tel: (212) 682-2500, FAX: (212) 682-8391, Web Site: www.aaaa.org (40)

Donald, Arnold, Juvenile Diabetes Research Foundation, New York, NY. Tel: (212) 785-9500, (800) 533-CURE, FAX: (212) 785-9595, E-Mail: info@jdrf.org, Web Site: www.jdrf.org (1)

Donald, James, L., Starbucks Corp, Seattle, WA. Tel: (206) 447-1575, (800) 344-1575, FAX: (206) 447-0828, Web Site: www.starbucks.com (4)

Donald, Jim, Hear Music, Bellevue, WA. Tel: (425) 452-5534, E-Mail: gail@hearmusic.com, Web Site: www.hearmusic.com (3)

Donaldson, Jerry, L., Fostoria Industries Inc, Johnson City, TN. Tel: (419) 435-9201, (800) 495-4525, FAX: (419) 435-0842, E-Mail: email@fostoriaindustries.com, Web Site: www.fostoriaindustries.com (9)

Donaldson, Rich, LL Bean Inc, Freeport, ME. Tel: (207) 865-4761, (800) 441-5713, FAX: (207) 552-3080, Web Site: www.llbean.com (2)

Donaldson, Samantha, Federal Citizen Information Center, Pueblo, CO. Tel: (888) 8-PUEBLO, FAX: (719) 948-9724, E-Mail: catalog.pueblo@gsa.gov, Web Site: www.pueblo.gsa.gov (5)

Donatelli, David, A., EMC Corp, Hopkinton, MA. Tel: (888) 438-3622, Web Site: www.emc.com (16)

Donato, Thomas, Nielsen Trade Dimensions, Wilton, CT. Tel: (203) 222-5750, (800) 291-0410, FAX: (203) 222-5701, E-Mail: tradedimensions.info@nielsen.com, Web Site: www.tradedimensions.com (17)

Donelly, Carol, Plan USA, Warwick, RI. Tel: (401) 737-5770, (800) 556-7918, FAX: (401) 738-5608, Web Site: www.planusa.org (1)

Doner Direct, Baltimore, MD. Tel: (248) 354-9700, FAX: (248) 827-0880 (21)

Donihe Graphics Inc, Kingsport, TN. Tel: (423) 246-2800, (800) 251-0337, FAX: (423) 246-7025, Web Site: www.champion-industries.com (27)

Donikian, Claudine, Pentera Inc, Indianapolis, IN. Tel: (617) 277-5033, Web Site: www.pentera.com (28)

Donio, Father Frank, Pallottine Center for Apostolic Causes Inc/St Jude Shrine, Baltimore, MD. Tel: (410) 685-6026, (877) 278-5833, FAX: (410) 234-1459, E-Mail: info@stjudeshrine.org, Web Site: www.stjudeshrine.org (1)

Donlon, J.P., Chief Executive Magazine, Greenwich, CT. Tel: (203) 930-2700, Web Site: www.chiefexecutive.net (17)

Donnelley Marketing, Pearl River, NY. Tel: (201) 476-2300, FAX: (201) 476-2151, Web Site: www.infousa.com (23)

RR Donnelley & Sons Co, Chicago, IL. Tel: (312) 326-8000, FAX: (312) 326-7156, Web Site: www.rrdonnelly.com (31)

Donnelly, Christopher, Geiger Donnelly Marketing LLC, Foxboro, MA. Tel: (508) 549-0909, FAX: (508) 549-0916 (35)

Donnelly, Louise, Marketrac Inc, Westbury, NY. Tel: (516) 365-4330, FAX: (516) 365-5789 (20)

Donnelly, Michael, J., Maritz, Fenton, MO. Tel: (636) 827-4246, FAX: (636) 827-8929, Web Site: www.maritz.com (35)

Donnelly, Michael, Life-Study Fellowship Foundation Inc, Darien, CT. Tel: (203) 655-1436, FAX: (203) 655-1392, Web Site: www.lifestudyfellowship.com (17)

Donnelly, Michael, Starcrest Products of California Inc, Perris, CA. Tel: (909) 943-2011, FAX: (909) 943-2971, E-Mail: tmc@tstonramp.com (16)

Donoghue, Jerry, Asheville Compassionate Communication Center, Asheville, NC. Tel: (828) 252-0538, E-Mail: jerry@ashevilleccc.com, Web Site: ashevilleccc.com (13)

Donoghue, Marlene, Creative Health Products, Plymouth, MI. Tel: (734) 996-5900, (800) 742-4478, FAX: (734) 996-4650, Web Site: www.chponline.com (16)

Donoghue, W.C., Creative Health Products, Plymouth, MI. Tel: (734) 996-5900, (800) 742-4478, FAX: (734) 996-4650, Web Site: www.chponline.com (16)

Donohoe, Marina, Enterprise Ireland, New York, NY. Tel: (212) 371-3600, FAX: (212) 371-6398, Web Site: www.enterprise-ireland.com (16)

Donohoe, Mary, National Geographic Society, Washington, DC. Tel: (202) 857-7311, (800) NGS-LINE, FAX: (202) 457-8200, Web Site: www.nationalgeographic.com (17)

Donohue, GE, DeBellis & Ferrara, Vienna, VA. Tel: (301) 986-4499, (888) 748-2133, E-Mail: info@debellis-ferrara.com, Web Site: www.debellis-ferrara.com (35)

Donohue, Margaret, The Tog Shop Inc, Beverly, MA. Tel: (800) 342-6789, FAX: (800) 755-7557, Web Site: www.togshop.com (2)

Donohue, Thomas J., US Chamber of Commerce, Washington, DC. Tel: (202) 778-6063, (800) 638-6582, FAX: (202) 887-3430, Web Site: www.uschamber.com (1)

Donor Services Group, Los Angeles, CA. Tel: (310) 788-9000, (888) 474-1900, Web Site: www.donorservicesgroup.com (1)

Donoso, Hernan, Brotherhood America's Oldest Winery Ltd, Washingtonville, NY. Tel: (845) 496-3661, FAX: (845) 496-8720, E-Mail: contact@brotherhoodwinery.net, Web Site: www.brotherhoodwinery.net (19)

Donovan Jr., William, Donovan Advertising, Lititz, PA. Tel: (717) 560-1333, FAX: (717) 560-2034, Web Site: www.donovanadv.com (35)

Donovan, Randi, The Law Offices of James Sokolove, Wellesley Hills, MA. Tel: (617) 742-0696, Web Site: www.jimsokolove.com (14)

Donovan, Sheila, Global DM Solutions, Boonton, NJ. Tel: (973) 402-2205, (866) 402-2205, FAX: (973) 402-2305, E-Mail: contact@globaldmsolutions.com, Web Site: www.globaldmsolutions.com (23)

Donovan Advertising, Lititz, PA. Tel: (717) 560-1333, FAX: (717) 560-2034, Web Site: www.donovanadv.com (35)

Doolan, Victor, H., Volvo Cars of North America, Northvale, NJ. Tel: (201) 768-7300, (800) 458-1552, E-Mail: customercare@volvocars.com, Web Site: www.volvocars.com (16)

Dooley, Craig, The Merchandise Mart, Chicago, IL. Tel: (312) 527-4141, (800) 677-6278, Web Site: www.merchandisemart.com (42)

Dooley, Richard, Society of American Magicians Inc, Parker, CO. E-Mail: rmblowers@aol.com, Web Site: www.magicsam.com (1)

Dooley, Robert, Global Computer Corp, Port Washington, NY. Tel: (516) 625-4300, (888) 845-6225, FAX: (516) 625-4072, Web Site: www.globalcomputer.com (3)

Dooley, Thomas, E., Viacom Inc, New York, NY. Tel: (212) 258-6000, FAX: (212) 258-6464, Web Site: www.viacom.com (16)

Doolittle, John, M, Nortel Networks Corp, Mississauga, ON Canada. Tel: (905) 863-7000, (888) 901-7286, Web Site: www.nortel.com (34)

Doombos, Chris, David C Cook, Colorado Springs, CO. Tel: (719) 536-0100, (800) 323-7543, FAX: (719) 536-3232, Web Site: www.davidccook.com (17)

Doonan, Judith, A & A Research, Kalispell, MT. Tel: (406) 752-7857 (30)

Doonan, Lynn, Affinion Group Inc, Stamford, CT. Tel: (203) 956-1176, Web Site: www.affiniongroup.com (16)

Doorguard Systems Inc, Columbia, MD. Tel: (410) 992-5600, (800) 442-6247, FAX: (410) 992-5694, Web Site: www.doorguardsystems.com (3)

Dopp, Liz, Rochester Institute of Technology, Rochester, NY. Tel: (585) 475-7436, Web Site: www.rit.edu (1)

Doran, Barbara, H., Doran & Forgacs Inc, West Chester, PA. Tel: (610) 344-0570, FAX: (610) 344-7203 (35)

Doran & Forgacs Inc, West Chester, PA. Tel: (610) 344-0570, FAX: (610) 344-7203 (35)

Dordick, Sy, Web Direct Marketing Inc, Glenview, IL. Tel: (847) 459-0800, (877) 841-2841, FAX: (847) 459-7378, E-Mail: info@webdirectmktg.com, Web Site: www.webdirectmktg.com (35)

Doremus & Co, New York, NY. Tel: (212) 366-3000, FAX: (212) 366-3060, E-Mail: anderson@doremus.com, Web Site: www.doremus.com (35)

Doren, Andre, AVD Marketing, Hollywood, FL. Tel: (954) 410-9000, Web Site: www.avdmarketing.com (20)

Doretti, Dirk J., Clubs of America, Lakemoor, IL. Tel: (815) 363-4000, (800) CLUB-USA, FAX: (815) 363-4677, E-Mail: info@greatclubs.com, Web Site: www.clubsofamerica.com (6)

Doretti, Douglas M., Clubs of America, Lakemoor, IL. Tel: (815) 363-4000, (800) CLUB-USA, FAX: (815) 363-4677, E-Mail: info@greatclubs.com, Web Site: www.clubsofamerica.com (6)

Dorew, Kim, Lamkin Corp, San Diego, CA. Tel: (619) 661-7090, (800) 642-7755, FAX: (619) 661-0014, E-Mail: info@lamkingrips.com, Web Site: www.lamkingrips.com (11)

Dorian, Michael, FTD Group Inc, Downers Grove, IL. Tel: (630) 719-7800, (800) 788-9000, FAX: (630) 719-6170, E-Mail: ftdmemberservices@ftdi.com, Web Site: www.ftdi.com (29)

Dorman, David, AT&T, Bedminster, NJ. Tel: (800) 222-0300, FAX: (908) 532-1675, Web Site: www.att.com (16)

Dorman, Robin, Boss, A T Cross Co, Lincoln, RI. Tel: (401) 333-1200, (800) 282-7677, FAX: (401) 334-2861, Web Site: www.cross.com (16)

Dorn, Brian, Edward G Dorn & Associates Inc, Geneva, IL. Tel: (630) 232-2010, FAX: (630) 232-2033, Web Site: www.egdinc.com (35)

Edward G Dorn & Associates Inc, Geneva, IL. Tel: (630) 232-2010, FAX: (630) 232-2033, Web Site: www.egdinc.com (35)

Dorothy Biddle Service, Greeley, PA. Tel: (570) 226-3239, FAX: (570) 226-0349, E-Mail: info@dorothybiddle.com, Web Site: www.dorothybiddle.com (3)

Dorothy's Ruffled Originals Inc, Wilmington, NC. Tel: (910) 686-8087, (800) 367-6849, FAX: (910) 686-2958, E-Mail: curtains@dorothysoriginals.com, Web Site: www.dorothysoriginals.com (8)

Dorr, Marjorie, Anthem Blue Cross Blue Shield, North Haven, CT. Tel: (203) 239-8381, (800) 545-0948, FAX: (203) 985-7918, Web Site: www.anthem.com (15)

Dorsman, Peter, A., Standard Register, Dayton, OH. Tel: (937) 221-1000, (800) 755-6405, FAX: (937) 221-1239, E-Mail: julie.mcewan@standardregister.com, Web Site: www.standardregister.com (10)

Doster, Steven, American General Life & Accident Insurance, Nashville, TN. Tel: (615) 749-1000, (800) 888-2452, Web Site: www.agla.com (15)

DotJe, John, US Data Corp, Omaha, NE. Tel: (402) 502-5623, (888) 578-3282, FAX: (402) 502-5623, Web Site: www.usdatacorporation.com (29)

Dotomi Inc, Chicago, IL. Tel: (312) 588-3600, Web Site: www.dotomi.com (32)

Dotson, Sandy, Integrated Marketing Technology Inc, San Francisco, CA. Tel: (415) 699-2280, FAX: (917) 591-5333, E-Mail: information@imtnetwork.com, Web Site: www.imtnetwork.com (22)

Double Envelope, Gainesville, FL. Tel: (800) 543-5275, Web Site: www.double-envelope.com (26)

Doubleday Direct, Scarborough, ON Canada. Tel: (416) 977-7891, FAX: (416) 977-8707 (13)

Doubletree Suites by Hilton, Boston, MA. Tel: (617) 783-0090, (800) 222-TREE, FAX: (617) 783-0897, E-Mail: doubletree1@hilton.com (19)

DoubleVerify, New York, NY. Tel: (212) 631-2111, Web Site: www.doubleverify.com (9)

Doucette, Donald, S., Ivy Tech State College, Indianapolis, IN. Tel: (317) 921-4800, (888) IVY-LINE, FAX: (317) 921-4753, Web Site: www.ivytech.edu/indianapolis (13)

Dougan, Sally, Bert Davis Executive Search, New York, NY. Tel: (212) 838-4000, FAX: (212) 935-3291, E-Mail: info@bertdavis.com, Web Site: www.bertdavis.com (20)

Dougherty, David, F., Convergys Corp, Ogden, UT. Tel: (630) 668-6174, Web Site: www.convergys.com (29)

Dougherty, Kevin, Marian Helpers Center, Stockbridge, MA. Tel: (413) 298-3691, (800) 462-7426, FAX: (413) 298-3583, Web Site: www.marian.org (1)

Dougherty, Kris, Delivra, Indianapolis, IN. Tel: (317) 915-9400, Web Site: www.delivra.com (32)

Dougherty, Paul, Premier Packaging Corp, Victor, NY. Tel: (877) 924-8460, FAX: (585) 924-8753, E-Mail: info@premiercustompkg.com, Web Site: www.premiercustompkg.com (16)

Dougherty, Thomas, HealthRight International, New York, NY. Tel: (212) 226-9890, Web Site: www.healthright.org (1)

Douglas, Brad, Direct Resources Group, Seattle, WA. Tel: (206) 749-0001, E-Mail: results@drg.com, Web Site: www.drg.com (35)

Douglas, Brad, Hacker Group Inc, Seattle, WA. Tel: (206) 805-1500, E-Mail: info@hackergroup.com, Web Site: www.hackergroup.com (35)

Douglas, Brian, Association of Energy Engineers, Atlanta, GA. Tel: (770) 447-5083 x210, FAX: (770) 446-3969, E-Mail: info@aeecenter.org, Web Site: www.aeecenter.org (40)

Douglas, Dean, Sterling Fluid Systems, Indianapolis, IN. Tel: (317) 925-9661, (800) 879-0182, FAX: (317) 924-7388, Web Site: www.peerlesspump.com (16)

Douglas, Jaime, The Black Dog Tavern Co Inc, Vineyard Haven, MA. Tel: (508) 696-8182, (800) 626-1991, Web Site: www.theblackdog.com; www.theblackdogtshirt.com (2)

Douglas, Nina, The Iams Co, Dayton, OH. Tel: (937) 898-7387, (800) 675-3849, FAX: (937) 264-7264, Web Site: www.iams.com (16)

Douglas, Robert, S., The Black Dog Tavern Co Inc, Vineyard Haven, MA. Tel: (508) 696-8182, (800) 626-1991, Web Site: www.theblackdog.com; www.theblackdogtshirt.com (2)

Douglas Press Inc, Bellwood, IL. Tel: (708) 547-8400, (800) 323-0705, FAX: (708) 547-0296, Web Site: www.douglaspress.com (16)

Douglas Shaw & Associates, Naperville, IL. Tel: (630) 562-1321, Web Site: www.douglasshaw.com (1)

Douglass, David, M., Photoworks, Cleveland, OH. Tel: (206) 281-1390, (800) PHOTOWORKS, FAX: (206) 284-5357, E-Mail: info@photoworks.com, Web Site: www.photoworks.com (16)

Doumas, Mike, FP Mailing Solutions, Addison, IL. Tel: (800) 341-6052, FAX: (630) 693-0626, Web Site: www.fp-usa.com (34)

Douthat, Annette, AllBrands.com Sewing Machine Superstore, Baton Rouge, LA. Tel: (225) 923-1285, (866) 255-2726, FAX: (225) 923-1261, E-Mail: info@allbrands.com, Web Site: www.allbrands.com (11)

Douthat, John, M., AllBrands.com Sewing Machine Superstore, Baton Rouge, LA. Tel: (225) 923-1285, (866) 255-2726, FAX: (225) 923-1261, E-Mail: info@allbrands.com, Web Site: www.allbrands.com (11)

Dover Publications Inc, Mineola, NY. Tel: (516) 294-7000, (800) 223-3130, FAX: (516) 873-1401, Web Site: www.doverpublications.com (17)

Dover Saddlery, Littleton, MA. Tel: (978) 952-8062, (800) 406-8204, Web Site: www.doversaddlery.com (11)

Dovetail, Littleton, CO. Tel: (303) 904-4771, FAX: (303) 904-4776, E-Mail: welcome@dovetailnet. com, Web Site: www.dovetailnet.com (22)

Dovetail Art & Design Inc, Dover, OH. Tel: (303) 987-9300, Web Site: www.dovetailart.com (20)

Dow, John, Special Olympics International, Washington, DC. Tel: (202) 628-3630, FAX: (202) 824-0200, Web Site: www.specialolympics.org (1)

Dow, Roger, Travel Industry Association, Washington, DC. Tel: (202) 408-8422, FAX: (202) 408-1255, E-Mail: feedback@tia.org, Web Site: www.tia.org (1)

Dow Chemical USA, Midland, MI. Tel: (989) 636-1000, (800) 447-4369, FAX: (989) 832-1465, E-Mail: jadams@dow.com, Web Site: www.dow. com (16)

Dow Corning Corp, Midland, MI. Tel: (989) 496-4000, (800) 248-2481, FAX: (989) 496-4572, Web Site: www.dowcorning.com (16)

Dow Jones & Co, Princeton, NJ. Tel: (609) 520-4000, FAX: (212) 416-4348, Web Site: www.dowjones. com/corp/index.html (17)

Dow Theory Forecasts, Hammond, IN. Tel: (219) 931-6480, (800) 233-5922, FAX: (219) 931-6487, E-Mail: custserv@horizonpublishing.com, Web Site: www.dowtheory.com (17)

Dowd, Patricia, Patricia Dowd Inc, Atascadero, CA. Tel: (805) 985-8243, E-Mail: pdowd@pdisearch. com, Web Site: www.pdisearch.com (20)

Patricia Dowd Inc, Atascadero, CA. Tel: (805) 985-8243, E-Mail: pdowd@pdisearch.com, Web Site: www.pdisearch.com (20)

Dowdell Jr, Rodger, B., American Power Conversion Corp, West Kingston, RI. Tel: (401) 789-5735, (800) 788-2208, FAX: (401) 789-3710, E-Mail: public.relations@apcc.com, Web Site: www.apcc. com (3)

Dowden, C. James, Alliance of Area Business Publications, El Segundo, CA. Tel: (323) 937-5514, FAX: (323) 937-0959, E-Mail: info@bizpubs.org, Web Site: www.bizpubs.org (1)

Dowdy, Mark, Wholesale Tool Co, Warren, MI. Tel: (800) 521-3420, FAX: (800) 521-3661, E-Mail: wtmich@aol.com, Web Site: www.wttool.com (9)

Dowis, Mark, Paralyzed Veterans of America, Washington, DC. Tel: (202) 416-7636, (800) 424-8200, FAX: (202) 416-7643, E-Mail: info@pva.org, Web Site: www.pva.org (1)

Dowling, Bernadette, M., Data Services Inc, Salisbury, MD. Tel: (410) 546-2206, (800) 432-4066, FAX: (410) 546-2274, Web Site: www.dataservicesinc. com (22)

Dowling, Jack, Westbeth Gallery, New York, NY. Tel: (212) 989-4650 (36)

Dowling, Melissa, Multichannel Merchant Magazine, Stamford, CT. Tel: (203) 358-4386, FAX: (203) 358-5823, E-Mail: melissa.dowling@penton.com, Web Site: www.multichannelmerchant.com (31)

Dowling, Stephen, Sani Serv, Mooresville, IN. Tel: (317) 831-7030, FAX: (317) 381-7036, Web Site: www.saniserv.com (16)

Dowling, Steven A., Pearson Education, Upper Saddle River, NJ. Tel: (201) 236-7000, FAX: (201) 236-3290, E-Mail: communications@pearsoned.com, Web Site: www.pearsoned.com (17)

Down Home Comforts, Windsor, CT. Tel: (860) 830-0606, (860) 688-3780, Web Site: downhomecomforts.com (8)

Downey, Janie, New England Mail Order Association, Scarborough, ME. Tel: (207) 885-0090, (860) 691-1260, FAX: (207) 885-0097, Web Site: www. nemoa.org (40)

Downie Jr., Leonard, The Washington Post, Washington, DC. Tel: (202) 334-6000, (800) 627-1150, E-Mail: letters@washpost.com, Web Site: www. washingtonpost.com (17)

Downing, Jonathan, The Ad Farm, Ottawa Hills, OH. Tel: (419) 720-5676, Web Site: www.theadfarm. com (20)

Downing, Tom, Random House Direct Marketing, New York, NY. Tel: (212) 572-4985, (800) 678-5681, FAX: (212) 572-6018, Web Site: www. randomhousedirect.com (17)

Downs, Lorraine, Planet Cotton, Gaithersburg, MD. Tel: (301) 948-0400, FAX: (301) 948-9031, Web Site: www.planetcotton.com (2)

Downton, Charles, E., Delta Upsilon International Fraternity, Indianapolis, IN. Tel: (317) 875-8900, FAX: (317) 876-1629, E-Mail: ihq@deltau.org, Web Site: www.deltau.org (16)

Doyle Jr, Joseph, D., The Doyle Group Inc, Ponte Vedra Beach, FL. Tel: (904) 285-6020, FAX: (904) 285-9944 (31)

Doyle Jr., Donald, W., Blanchard & Co Inc, New Orleans, LA. Tel: (504) 837-3010, (800) 880-4653, FAX: (504) 837-4884, Web Site: www. blanchardonline.com (16)

Doyle, A., Alfreda's Film Works, Denver, CO. Tel: (303) 575-5676, FAX: (303) 575-1187, E-Mail: emailstreet@gmail.com, Web Site: www. gumbomedia.com (17)

Doyle, A., Be Somebody Be Yourself, Denver, CO. Tel: (303) 575-5676, FAX: (303) 575-1187, E-Mail: emailstreet@gmail.com, Web Site: www. besomebodybeyourself.com (35)

Doyle, A., Coursesmith, Denver, CO. Tel: (303) 575-5676, FAX: (303) 575-1187, E-Mail: emailstreet@ gmail.com, Web Site: www.coursesmith.com (17)

Doyle, A., Prosperity And Profits Unlimited Distribution Services, Denver, CO. Tel: (303) 575-5676, FAX: (303) 575-1187, E-Mail: emailstreet@gmail. com, Web Site: www. prosperityandprofitsunlimited.com (16)

Doyle, A., Story Time Stories That Rhyme, Denver, CO. Tel: (303) 575-5676, FAX: (303) 575-1187, E-Mail: emailstreet@gmail.com, Web Site: www. storytimestoriesthatrhyme.com (17)

Doyle, A., Thimband, Denver, CO. Tel: (303) 575-5676, FAX: (303) 575-1187, E-Mail: email@ contentprovidermedia.info (17)

Doyle, Bill, Mullen, Boston, MA. Tel: (978) 468-1155, Web Site: www.mullen.com (35)

Doyle, Corbette, AON Center, Chicago, IL. Tel: (312) 381-1000, FAX: (312) 381-6032, Web Site: www. aon.com (17)

Doyle, Daniel, S., Mal Warwick Associates, Berkeley, CA. Tel: (510) 843-8888, FAX: (510) 843-0142, E-Mail: info@malwarwick.com, Web Site: www. malwarwick.com (1)

Doyle, Gene, Creative Media Inc, Nicholasville, KY. Tel: (859) 219-9667 (35)

Doyle, Hugh, The Services Group (TSG), Arlington, VA. Tel: (703) 528-7444, FAX: (703) 522-2329, E-Mail: tsg@tsginc.com, Web Site: www.tsginc. com (20)

Doyle, Jack, Amergent, Peabody, MA. Tel: (800) 370-7500, Web Site: www.amergent.com (1)

Doyle, John, Universal Training, Lake Forest, IL. Tel: (847) 235-2170, E-Mail: information@ universaltraining.com, Web Site: www. universaltraining.com (16)

Doyle, Patrick, Barton & Cooney, Burlington, NJ. Tel: (609) 747-9300, FAX: (609) 747-9700, E-Mail: pmdoyle@bartoncooney.com, Web Site: www. bartoncooney.com (28)

Doyle, Paul, Newspaper Association of America, Arlington, VA. Tel: (703) 902-1600, FAX: (571) 366-1195, Web Site: www.naa.org (1)

The Doyle Group Inc, Ponte Vedra Beach, FL. Tel: (904) 285-6020, FAX: (904) 285-9944 (31)

Dozier, Alan, Beltone, Glenview, IL. Tel: (800) 235-8663, FAX: (847) 832-3300, E-Mail: info@ beltone.com, Web Site: www.beltone.com (3)

Dozier Equipment International, Milwaukee, WI. Tel: (800) 251-1234, FAX: (800) 336-6608, Web Site: www.dozierequip.com (9)

Dr Jays, New York, NY. Tel: (212) 334-7999, Web Site: drjays.com (2)

Dr Leonard's Healthcare Corp, Edison, NJ. Tel: (732) 225-0100, FAX: (732) 225-0302, Web Site: www. doctorleonard.com (7)

Draeger, Paul, Center for Creative Leadership, Greensboro, NC. Tel: (336) 545-2810, FAX: (336) 282-3284, E-Mail: info@ccl.org, Web Site: www.ccl. org (16)

Draft, Howard, Draftfcb Chicago (HQ), Chicago, IL. Tel: (312) 425-5000, FAX: (312) 425-5010, E-Mail: linda.liming@draftfcb.com, Web Site: www.draftfcb.com (35)

Draftfcb Chicago (HQ), Chicago, IL. Tel: (312) 425-5000, FAX: (312) 425-5010, E-Mail: linda. liming@draftfcb.com, Web Site: www.draftfcb.com (35)

Dragich, John, Dragich Auto Literature, Princeton, MN. Tel: (763) 389-8600, FAX: (763) 389-8222, E-Mail: mail@dragich.com, Web Site: www. dragich.com (16)

Dragich Auto Literature, Princeton, MN. Tel: (763) 389-8600, FAX: (763) 389-8222, E-Mail: mail@ dragich.com, Web Site: www.dragich.com (16)

Dragin, Stephen, Allyn & Bacon, Upper Saddle River, NJ. Tel: (617) 848-7216, FAX: (781) 455-1220 (17)

Dragisic, John, Charlton, Madison, WI. Tel: (608) 259-8004, FAX: (608) 259-8061, E-Mail: jdragisic@tcgcorp.net, Web Site: www.tcgcorp.net (29)

Dragonette, Rob, Barton-Cotton, Baltimore, MD. Tel: (410) 247-4800, (800) 348-1102, FAX: (410) 536-0491, E-Mail: info@bartoncotton.com, Web Site: www.bartoncotton.com (16)

Dragoon, John, Novell Inc, Waltham, MA. Tel: (801) 861-4272, (800) 529-3400, FAX: (781) 464-8100, E-Mail: crc@novell.com, Web Site: www.novell. com (22)

Drake, Chuck, Crane Pumps & Systems Inc, Piqua, OH. Tel: (937) 773-2442, FAX: (937) 773-2238, E-Mail: cranepumps@cranepumps.com, Web Site: www.cranepumps.com (16)

Drake, Gavin, Quark Inc, Denver, CO. Tel: (303) 894-3832, Web Site: www.quark.com (34)

Drake, Glenn, Tupperware, Orlando, FL. Tel: (407) 826-5050, (800) 366-3800, FAX: (407) 826-8874, Web Site: www.tupperware.com (16)

Drake, O., Burtch, American Association of Advertising Agencies, New York, NY. Tel: (212) 682-2500, FAX: (212) 682-8391, Web Site: www.aaaa.org (40)

Drake, Perry, Drake Direct, New York, NY. Tel: (212) 759-1225, FAX: (212) 759-9756, E-Mail: Rhonda@DrakeDirect.com, Web Site: www. drakedirect.com (22)

Drake, Rhonda, Knehans, Drake Direct, New York, NY. Tel: (212) 759-1225, FAX: (212) 759-9756, E-Mail: Rhonda@DrakeDirect.com, Web Site: www.drakedirect.com (22)

Drake Direct, New York, NY. Tel: (212) 759-1225, FAX: (212) 759-9756, E-Mail: Rhonda@ DrakeDirect.com, Web Site: www.drakedirect.com (22)

Dranikoff, Lee, American Securities Capital Partners, New York, NY. Tel: (212) 476-8000, Web Site: www.american-securities.com (15)

Drapeau, Anne, VistaPrint USA Inc, Lexington, MA. Tel: (800) 961-2075, Web Site: www.vistaprint.com (27)

Draper, John, Mead Westvaco Consumer & Office Products, Dayton, OH. Tel: (937) 222-6323, (800) 345-6323, FAX: (937) 495-3192, Web Site: www.mead.com (10)

Draper, Mike, Pastime Publications Inc, Denver, CO. Tel: (303) 534-7867, (888) 650-8665, FAX: (630) 214-7600, E-Mail: post@pastimecompany.com, Web Site: www.pastimecompany.com (17)

Draper's & Damon's, Irvine, CA. Tel: (949) 784-3000, (800) 843-1174, FAX: (949) 784-3400, E-Mail: jilld@drapers.com, Web Site: www.drapers.com (2)

Drapkin, Lisa, American Express Co, New York, NY. Tel: (212) 640-2000, FAX: (212) 619-9802, Web Site: www.americanexpress.com (14)

Draught, Eric, J., Unitrin, Chicago, IL. Tel: (312) 661-4600, (800) 733-7366, FAX: (312) 494-6995, Web Site: www.unitrin.com (15)

Drawing Board Inc, Waynesboro, PA. Tel: (301) 739-4487, (800) 527-9530, FAX: (800) 253-1838, E-Mail: customerservice@drawingboard.com, Web Site: www.drawingboard.com (16)

Drayer, Scott, Paul Fredrick Menstyle, Fleetwood, PA. Tel: (610) 944-0909, (800) 247-1417, FAX: (610) 944-6452, E-Mail: custserv@menstyle.com, Web Site: www.paulfredricks.com (27)

Drayton, John, University of Oklahoma Press, Norman, OK. Tel: (800) 627-7377, FAX: (405) 364-5798, Web Site: www.oupress.com (17)

Dream Products Inc, Chatsworth, CA. Tel: (818) 773-4233, Web Site: www.dreamproducts.net (5)

Dreher, Gary, Advanced Mail Inc, Eau Claire, WI. Tel: (715) 839-8801, FAX: (715) 839-8906, Web Site: www.amailinc.com (28)

Dreher, Lincoln, Hansen Corp, Princeton, IN. Tel: (812) 385-3415, FAX: (812) 385-3013, E-Mail: sales@hansen-motor.com, Web Site: www.hansen-motor.com (16)

Dreis & Krump Manufacturing Co, Peotone, IL. Tel: (708) 258-1200, FAX: (708) 258-9682, E-Mail: chicago@dreis-krump.com, Web Site: www.dreis-krump.com (16)

Dreishpoon Ph.D., Douglas, The Gallery Shop, Buffalo, NY. Tel: (716) 882-8700 X258, FAX: (716) 882-1958, E-Mail: gallshop@albrightknox.org, Web Site: www.albrightknox.org (6)

Dreller, Mike, Falcon Products Inc, Newport, TN. Tel: (314) 991-9200, (800) 873-3252, FAX: (314) 991-9227, E-Mail: info@falconproducts.com, Web Site: www.falconproducts.com (16)

Dremann, Alex, Redwood City Seed Co, Redwood City, CA. Tel: (650) 325-7333, FAX: (650) 325-4056, Web Site: www.ecoseeds.com (8)

Dremann, Craig, C., Redwood City Seed Co, Redwood City, CA. Tel: (650) 325-7333, FAX: (650) 325-4056, Web Site: www.ecoseeds.com (8)

Dremann, Sue, Redwood City Seed Co, Redwood City, CA. Tel: (650) 325-7333, FAX: (650) 325-4056, Web Site: www.ecoseeds.com (8)

Drenning, Ronald, First Marketing Co, Pompano Beach, FL. Tel: (954) 979-0700, FAX: (954) 971-4707, Web Site: www.first-marketing.com (31)

Dresden, Phillip, Dresden Direct Inc, Palm Beach Gardens, FL. Tel: (561) 622-3400, Web Site: www.dresdendirect.com (23)

Dresden Direct Inc, Palm Beach Gardens, FL. Tel: (561) 622-3400, Web Site: www.dresdendirect.com (23)

Dreska, Bill, Direct Channel LLC, Southbury, CT. Tel: (203) 262-0588, Web Site: www.directchannel.net (35)

Dresser, Mark, American 3B Scientific, Tucker, GA. Tel: (770) 492-9111, Web Site: www.a3bs.com (16)

Dresser, Mark, Sportime International, Norcross, GA. Tel: (770) 449-5700, (800) 283-5700, FAX: (770) 510-7290, E-Mail: orders@sportime.com, Web Site: www.sportime.com (11)

Drevlow, Lauren, American Spirit Graphics Corp, Minneapolis, MN. Tel: (612) 623-3333, FAX: (612) 623-9314, E-Mail: asgc@asgc.com, Web Site: www.asgc.com (27)

Drew, Colleen, Draper's & Damon's, Irvine, CA. Tel: (949) 784-3000, (800) 843-1174, FAX: (949) 784-3400, E-Mail: jilld@drapers.com, Web Site: www.drapers.com (2)

Drew, Michael, Professional Binding Products Inc, Thousand Oaks, CA. Tel: (800) 545-9413, (800) 443-7557, E-Mail: sales@probinding.com, Web Site: www.probinding.com (16)

Drew, Mike, Telect Inc, Liberty Lake, WA. Tel: (509) 926-6000, FAX: (509) 926-8915, E-Mail: getinfo@telect.com, Web Site: www.telect.com (16)

Drewes, Alyssa, Bodyscapes Inc, New York, NY. Tel: (212) 243-2414, FAX: (212) 239-9058 (2)

Drewes, Henrietta, Bodyscapes Inc, New York, NY. Tel: (212) 243-2414, FAX: (212) 239-9058 (2)

Drewes, William, Bodyscapes Inc, New York, NY. Tel: (212) 243-2414, FAX: (212) 239-9058 (2)

Drexel, George, Industrial Arts & Graphics, Middleburg, VA. Tel: (540) 687-6770, (866) 324-7746, FAX: (215) 765-6625 (27)

Drexel University (Goodwin College of Professional Studies), Philadelphia, PA. E-Mail: goodwin@drexel.edu, Web Site: www.drexel.edu/goodwin (16)

The Dreyfus Corp, New York, NY. Tel: (212) 922-6000, FAX: (212) 922-8165 (14)

Dreyfuss, Sharon, LED Signs, Stockbridge, MI. Tel: (954) 771-5488, FAX: (954) 267-0551, Web Site: www.finest.com (23)

Dreymann, Daniel, Goodmail Systems Inc, San Francisco, CA. Tel: (877) 650-6505, Web Site: www.goodmailsystems.com (32)

Drinko, J. Randall, Cleveland Institute of Electronics, Cleveland, OH. Tel: (216) 781-9400, FAX: (216) 781-0331, E-Mail: instruct@cie-wc.edu, Web Site: www.cie-wc.edu (13)

Drinnan, Faith, The Oyster Group, Dartmouth, NS Canada. Tel: (877) 405-4858, E-Mail: fdrinnan@theoystergroup.ca, Web Site: www.theoystergroup.ca (22)

Driscoll, Dan, September Productions, Nantucket, MA. Tel: (508) 332-3577, FAX: (508) 228-3853, E-Mail: info@september.com, Web Site: www.september.com (32)

Driscoll, Linda, Communications Solutions Expo, Norwalk, CT. Tel: (203) 852-6800, (877) 243-6002, FAX: (203) 853-2845, E-Mail: info@tmcnet.com, Web Site: www.tmcnet.com (42)

Driscoll Label Co Inc, East Hanover, NJ. Tel: (973) 575-8492, FAX: (800) 342-1195, (973) 575-8345, E-Mail: info@driscolllabel.com, Web Site: www.driscolllabel.com (27)

Dritz, Michael A., Newhouse School of Public Communications, Syracuse, NY. Tel: (315) 443-3611, FAX: (315) 443-4426, Web Site: newhouse.syr.edu (41)

Driver, Carrie, Foundation of FirstHealth, Pinehurst, NC. Tel: (910) 695-7500, Web Site: www.firsthealth.org/foundation (1)

Driver, Louann, Global Demand Publishing Inc, Jacksonville, NC. Tel: (910) 937-0562, FAX: (910) 455-1937, E-Mail: globaldemandpublishing@yahoo.com (22)

Drobenko, John, Caviarteria New York Inc, Astoria, NY. Tel: (212) 759-7410, (800) 422-8427, FAX: (212) 750-0358, E-Mail: info@caviarteria.com, Web Site: www.caviarteria.com (4)

Drolet, Danielle, Bayard Inc, New London, CT. Tel: (860) 437-3012, Web Site: www.bayard-inc.com (31)

Drolet, Patricia, Corpus Christi Museum of Science & History, Corpus Christi, TX. Tel: (361) 826-4667, FAX: (361) 884-7392, Web Site: www.ccmuseum.com (1)

Droll Yankees Inc, Foster, RI. Tel: (860) 799-8980, (800) 352-9164, FAX: (860) 779-8938, E-Mail: jen@drollyankees.com, Web Site: www.drollyankees.com (8)

Drosdick, John G., Sunoco, Inc, Philadelphia, PA. Tel: (215) 977-3000, (800) 786-6261, FAX: (215) 977-3409, E-Mail: sunoco_online@sunoil.com, Web Site: www.sunocoinc.com (16)

Droutman, Andrew, GCC Printers, Bedford, MA. Tel: (781) 275-5800, (800) 422-7777, FAX: (781) 275-1115, (800) 442-2329, E-Mail: sales@gccprinters.com, Web Site: www.gcctech.com (10)

Drozd, Ann, Marie, Beber Silverstein Group, Miami, FL. Tel: (305) 856-9800, (800) ASKBEBR, FAX: (305) 854-7686, E-Mail: jennifer@thinkbsq.com, Web Site: www.thinkbsq.com (35)

Drozdenko, Ronald, Western Connecticut State University, Danbury, CT. Tel: (203) 837-8200, FAX: (203) 837-8527, E-Mail: hills@wcsu.edu, Web Site: www.wcsu.edu (41)

Drucker, Charles, Fifth Third Bank, Cincinnati, OH. Tel: (800) 972-3030, FAX: (231) 922-4060, Web Site: www.53.com (14)

Drucker, Rick, Northern Printing Network Inc, Wheeling, IL. Tel: (847) 215-7300, FAX: (847) 215-7314, E-Mail: sales@northernprint.com, Web Site: www.northernprint.com (21)

Druckman, Lauren, Gulbenkian Swim Inc, Danbury, CT. Tel: (203) 790-0800, (800) 431-2586, FAX: (203) 791-1449, Web Site: www.gulbenkianswim.com (33)

Drug Information Association, Horsham, PA. Tel: (215) 442-6124, Web Site: www.diahome.org (1)

Drug Policy Alliance, New York, NY. Tel: (212) 613-8020, FAX: (212) 613-8021, E-Mail: nyc@drugpolicy.org, Web Site: www.drugpolicy.org (1)

Drum, Jason, Voxdata Telecom, Montreal, PQ. Tel: (514) 871-1920, (800) 861-9599, FAX: (514) 871-0445, E-Mail: fcouture@voxdata.com, Web Site: www.voxdata.com (29)

Drumbeat Indian Arts Inc, Phoenix, AZ. Tel: (602) 266-4823, (800) 895-4859, FAX: (602) 265-2402, E-Mail: info@drumbeatindianarts.com, Web Site: www.drumbeatindianarts.com (6)

Drumm, Robert, General Tours/TBI Tours, Keene, NH. Tel: (603) 357-5033, (800) 221-2216, FAX: (603) 357-4548, E-Mail: info@generaltours.com, Web Site: www.generaltours.com (19)

Drumm, Wesley, Nesco American Harvest, Two Rivers, WI. Tel: (920) 793-1368, (800) 288-4545, FAX: (920) 794-3161, Web Site: www.nesco.com (32)

Drummond, Jim, Conclusive Marketing, Charlotte, NC. Tel: (615) 261-7600, (800) 346-0073, FAX: (615) 843-7244, E-Mail: info@conclusivemarketing.com, Web Site: www.conclusivemarketing.com (22)

Drury, Tom, Lab Safety Supply Inc, Janesville, WI. Tel: (608) 754-2345, (800) 356-2855, FAX: (800) 543-9910, Web Site: www.labsafety.com (5)

Druskin, Robert, Citigroup Inc, New York, NY. Tel: (212) 559-1000, (800) 285-3000, FAX: (212) 793-3946, Web Site: www.citigroup.com (14)

Drybrough, Ralph, MeritDirect, White Plains, NY. Tel: (914) 368-1000, Web Site: www.meritdirect.com (23)

Drysdale, Ross, Arrowhead Mountain Spring Water, Wilkes Barre, PA. Tel: (800) 873-7775, Web Site: www.arrowheadwater.com (16)

DS Direct Communications, Redondo Beach, CA. Tel: (310) 540-4313 (23)

d.trio marketing group, Minneapolis, MN. Tel: (612) 436-0323, Web Site: www.dtrio.com (35)

Du Clos, David, XL Environmental, Exton, PA. Tel: (610) 968-9500, (800) 327-1414, FAX: (610) 458-9109, E-Mail: webinfo.xli@xlgroup.com, Web Site: www.xlenvironmental.com (15)

The Du-Rite Group Inc, Englewood, NJ. Tel: (201) 387-7000, FAX: (201) 385-8513, E-Mail: information@duriteconstruction.com, Web Site: www.duriteconstruction.com (16)

Duaybes, LeighAnn, NCP Solutions, Birmingham, AL. Tel: (250) 849-5200, Web Site: www.ncprint.com (21)

Dubasek, J., Adams Manufacturing Co, Cleveland, OH. Tel: (216) 587-6801, FAX: (216) 587-6807, E-Mail: adamsx@att.net, Web Site: www.adamsmanufacturing.com (9)

Dubin, Burt, Personal Achievement Institute, Kingman, AZ. Tel: (928) 753-7546, (800) 321-1225, FAX: (928) 753-7554, E-Mail: burt@burtdubin.com, Web Site: www.speakingbizsuccess.com (17)

Dubin, Howard, S., Manufacturers-News Inc, Evanston, IL. Tel: (847) 864-7000, (888) 752-5200, FAX: (847) 332-1100, E-Mail: hdubin@manufacturersnews.com, Web Site: www.manufacturersnews.com (23)

Dubin, Thomas, G., Manufacturers-News Inc, Evanston, IL. Tel: (847) 864-7000, (888) 752-5200, FAX: (847) 332-1100, E-Mail: hdubin@manufacturersnews.com, Web Site: www.manufacturersnews.com (23)

DuBois, Molly, M., C H Robinson Worldwide Inc, Eden Prairie, MN. Tel: (952) 937-8500, FAX: (952) 937-6740, E-Mail: info@chrobinson.com, Web Site: www.chrobinson.com (16)

DuBose, Michael, Vertis Media & Marketing Services, Baltimore, MD. Tel: (410) 528-9800, (800) 577-8371, E-Mail: Info@VertisInc.com, Web Site: www.vertisinc.com (28)

Dubose, Edwin, Colonial Life Insurance Co Texas, Fort Worth, TX. Tel: (817) 390-2350, (888) 227-5119, FAX: (817) 390-2209, E-Mail: insurance@colonialinsurance.com, Web Site: www.colonialinsurance.com (15)

Dubow, Craig, A., Gannett Co Inc, Mc Lean, VA. Tel: (703) 854-6000, FAX: (703) 854-2046, E-Mail: gcishare@gannett.com, Web Site: www.gannett.com (16)

Dubrow, Andrea, Wathne Ltd, New York, NY. Tel: (212) 757-3001, FAX: (212) 757-2448 (2)

Dubrow, Lee, Straw Hat Cooperative Corp, San Ramon, CA. Tel: (925) 837-3400, FAX: (925) 820-1080, E-Mail: info@strawhatpizza.com, Web Site: www.strawhatpizza.com (16)

Ducatelli, Tom, Zones Inc, Auburn, WA. Tel: (253) 205-3000, (800) 408-9663, FAX: (425) 430-3626, E-Mail: corpsales@zones.com, Web Site: www.zones.com (3)

Duccilli, Steve, ST Media Group International, Cincinnati, OH. Tel: (513) 421-2050, (800) 925-1110, FAX: (513) 421-5144, E-Mail: customer@stmediagroup.com, Web Site: www.signweb.com (17)

DuChateau, Brandan, Jones Publishing Inc, Iola, WI. Tel: (715) 445-5000, (800) 331-0038, FAX: (715) 445-4053, E-Mail: jonespub@jonespublishing.com, Web Site: www.jonespublishing.com (17)

Duchene, Mark, AIG Marketing, New York, NY. Tel: (212) 770-7000, (212) 770-2237, Web Site: www.agac.com (15)

Ducic, David, Sierra Scientific Inc, Phoenix, AZ. Tel: (602) 256-0540, FAX: (602) 252-1972, Web Site: www.value-tek.com (9)

Ducks Unlimited, Memphis, TN. Tel: (901) 758-3825, (800) 45DUCKS, FAX: (901) 758-3850, Web Site: www.ducks.org (1)

Ducktrap River Fish Farm, Belfast, ME. Tel: (207) 338-6280, (800) 828-3825, FAX: (207) 338-9020, E-Mail: smoked@ducktrap.com, Web Site: www.ducktrap.com (4)

Duckworth, Alison, Antique Rose Emporium, Brenham, TX. Tel: (800) 441-0002, FAX: (979) 836-0928, E-Mail: roses@industyinet.com, Web Site: www.weareroses.com (8)

Duclos, Lorraine, PDQ Post Group, Surrey, BC Canada. Tel: (604) 888-0676, (888) 998-9878, FAX: (604) 888-4467, E-Mail: lorraine@pdqpostgroup.com, Web Site: www.pdqpostgroup.com (21)

Duda, Donald, Methode Electronics Inc, Chicago, IL. Tel: (708) 867-6777, FAX: (708) 867-6999, E-Mail: info@methode.com, Web Site: www.methode.com (9)

Dudek, Andrew, Telcordia Technologies, Piscataway, NJ. Tel: (732) 699-2000, FAX: (973) 829-2458, Web Site: www.telcordia.com (16)

Dudek, Sue, Sculptz, Feasterville Trevose, PA. Tel: (215) 494-2900, E-Mail: sdudek@sculptz.com, Web Site: www.silkies.com (2)

Dudley, Frank, Guideline Washington DC, Washington, DC. Tel: (703) 312-6004, (866) GUIDELINE, E-Mail: fdudley@guideline.com, Web Site: www.guideline.com (30)

Dudley, Staci, The Iams Co, Dayton, OH. Tel: (937) 898-7387, (800) 675-3849, FAX: (937) 264-7264, Web Site: www.iams.com (16)

Dudley, Steve, Midwest Premiums & Promotions, Leawood, KS. Tel: (913) 383-9333, FAX: (913) 383-9555, E-Mail: dudleymidwestpremiums@yahoo.com (33)

Dudley's Country Kitchen, Dyersburg, TN. Tel: (901) 285-3681, (800) 242-8066, FAX: (901) 285-3638, Web Site: www.dckitchen.com (4)

Dudnyk Advertising & Public Relations, Horsham, PA. Tel: (215) 443-9406, (800) 438-3695, E-Mail: fpowers@dudnyk.com, Web Site: www.dudnyk.com (35)

Duerr, John, Spectronics Corp, Westbury, NY. Tel: (800) 274-8888, FAX: (800) 491-6868, E-Mail: vscherer@spectroline.com, Web Site: www.spectroline.com (9)

Duff, Dale B., DB Duff & Associates, Arlee, MT. Tel: (724) 224-5513, FAX: (724) 224-5186 (35)

Duff, Stephen D., F.M. Howell & Co, Elmira, NY. Tel: (607) 734-6291, FAX: (607) 735-0464, E-Mail: best@howellpkg.com, Web Site: www.howellpkg.com (16)

DB Duff & Associates, Arlee, MT. Tel: (724) 224-5513, FAX: (724) 224-5186 (35)

Duffey, Petrosky & Co, Farmington Hills, MI. Tel: (248) 489-8300, FAX: (248) 994-1600, E-Mail: info@dp-company.com, Web Site: www.dp-company.com (35)

Dufford, Donn, Dufford Marketing, Pasadena, CA. Tel: (626) 665-2268, E-Mail: donnduff@aol.com (21)

Dufford Marketing, Pasadena, CA. Tel: (626) 665-2268, E-Mail: donnduff@aol.com (21)

Duffy, Brian, Lea & Perrins Inc, Fair Lawn, NJ. Tel: (201) 791-1600, FAX: (201) 791-8945, Web Site: www.leaperrins.com (16)

Duffy, Dennis, Definitely Duffy, Asheville, NC. Tel: (828) 333-5860, FAX: (866) 852-4686, E-Mail: dennis@definitelyduffy.com, Web Site: www.definitelyduffy.com (35)

Duffy, James, P., Vertrue Inc, Norwalk, CT. Tel: (203) 324-7635, FAX: (203) 674-7080, Web Site: www.vertrue.com (13)

Duffy, Jean, DeBellis & Ferrara, Vienna, VA. Tel: (301) 986-4499, (888) 748-2133, E-Mail: info@debellis-ferrara.com, Web Site: www.debellis-ferrara.com (35)

Duffy, Michael, Paymentech, Salem, NH. Tel: (603) 896-6000, FAX: (603) 896-8717, Web Site: www.paymentech.com (14)

Duffy, Mike, Norman Rockwell Museum, Stockbridge, MA. Tel: (413) 298-4100, (800) 742-9450, FAX: (413) 298-4144, E-Mail: emazzer@nrm.org, Web Site: www.nrm.org (16)

Duffy, Shannon, Jigsaw, San Mateo, CA. Tel: (650) 235-8400, Web Site: www.jigsaw.com (24)

Duffy, Steve, Wells Lamont Industry Group, Niles, IL. Tel: (847) 647-8200, (800) 247-3295, FAX: (847) 470-1026, Web Site: www.wellslamontindustry.com (34)

Duffy, William, iKnowtion LLC, Burlington, MA. Tel: (781) 494-9989, Web Site: www.iknowtion.com (20)

Dufresne, Jim, Worcester Envelope, Auburn, MA. Tel: (800) 343-1398, FAX: (508) 832-3796, Web Site: www.worcester-envelope.com (26)

Dugan, William, Publishing Fulfillment Consulting LLC, Brewster, NY. Tel: (845) 278-2800, Web Site: www.fulfillmentconsulting.com (20)

Dugas Jr., Richard, J., Del Webb, Bloomfield Hills, MI. Tel: (248) 644-7300, (888) 717-9777, FAX: (248) 433-4598, Web Site: www.delwebb.com (16)

Dugas, Denis, Army Times Publishing Co, Springfield, VA. Tel: (703) 750-9000, (800) 336-4590, FAX: (703) 750-8129, E-Mail: cust-svc@atpco.com, Web Site: www.armytimes.com (17)

Duggan, John, P., Duggan & Brown Inc, Abington, PA. Tel: (215) 657-3400, FAX: (215) 657-6119, E-Mail: john@dugganandbrown.com (16)

Duggan & Brown Inc, Barrington, IL. Tel: (847) 381-8484, FAX: (847) 381-8499 (20)

Duggan & Brown Inc, Abington, PA. Tel: (215) 657-3400, FAX: (215) 657-6119, E-Mail: john@dugganandbrown.com (16)

Duggan-Josephs, Kathy, D-J Associates, Danbury, CT. Tel: (203) 431-8777, FAX: (203) 431-3302, E-Mail: info@djassoc.com, Web Site: www.djassoc.com (23)

Dukat, Gregory, Ventyx, Atlanta, GA. Tel: (770) 952-8444, (800) 868-0497, FAX: (770) 955-2977, E-Mail: support@ventyx.com, Web Site: www.ventyx.com (16)

Duke, Marlies, New England Mail Order Association, Scarborough, ME. Tel: (207) 885-0090, (860) 691-1260, FAX: (207) 885-0097, Web Site: www.nemoa.org (40)

Duke, Michael, Terry, Wal Mart Stores, Bentonville, AR. Tel: (479) 273-4000, (800) 925-6278, FAX: (479) 277-1830, Web Site: www.walmart.com (16)

Dukky, Mandeville, LA. Tel: (985) 626-5155, E-Mail: info@dukky.com, Web Site: www.dukky.com (32)

Dullea, John, As We Change, Oshkosh, WI. Tel: (619) 213-2200, (800) 993-0192, FAX: (619) 213-2253, E-Mail: help@aswechange.com, Web Site: www.aswechange.com (7)

Duluth Trading Co Inc, Belleville, WI. Tel: (800) 505-8888, FAX: (888) 950-3199, E-Mail: customerservice@duluthtrading.com, Web Site: www.duluthtrading.com (8)

Dunbar, Yolanda, Frederick's of Hollywood Group Inc, Los Angeles, CA. Tel: (323) 466-5151, (800) 323-9525, FAX: (323) 464-5149, Web Site: www.fredericks.com (2)

Dunbart, Gary, Miller Harness Co, Westford, MA. Tel: (800) 784-5831, E-Mail: customerservice@millerharness.com, Web Site: www.millerharness.com (11)

Duncan, Bill, Maxon Furniture Inc, Muscatine, IA. Tel: (253) 395-4139, Web Site: www.maxonfurniture.com (10)

Duncan, Candace, Alliance Defense Fund, Scottsdale, AZ. Tel: (480) 444-0020, Web Site: www.telladf.org (1)

Duncan, David, Civil War Preservation Trust, Washington, DC. Tel: (202) 367-1861, Web Site: www.civilwar.org (1)

Duncan, George, Duncan Direct Associates, Peterborough, NH. Tel: (603) 924-3121, FAX: (603) 924-8511, E-Mail: duncandirect@pobox.com, Web Site: www.duncandirect.com (39)

Duncan, J., Robert, Duncan Aviation, Lincoln, NE. Tel: (402) 475-2611, (800) 228-4277, FAX: (402) 475-5541, Web Site: www.duncanaviation.com (16)

Duncan, Mallory, National Retail Federation Inc, Washington, DC. Tel: (202) 783-7971, (800) 673-4692, FAX: (202) 737-2849, E-Mail: webmaster@nrf.com, Web Site: www.nrf.com (1)

Duncan, Richard, Loews Hotels, New York, NY. Tel: (212) 521-2000, (866) 563-9792, FAX: (212) 545-2714, Web Site: www.loewshotels.com (19)

Duncan Aviation, Lincoln, NE. Tel: (402) 475-2611, (800) 228-4277, FAX: (402) 475-5541, Web Site: www.duncanaviation.com (16)

Duncan Direct Associates, Peterborough, NH. Tel: (603) 924-3121, FAX: (603) 924-8511, E-Mail: duncandirect@pobox.com, Web Site: www.duncandirect.com (39)

Duncan Thompson, John, Cotta Transmission Co, Beloit, WI. Tel: (608) 368-5600, FAX: (608) 368-5605, E-Mail: sales@cotta.com, Web Site: www.cotta.com (16)

Duncanson, Donald M., Dynacolor Graphics Inc, Hialeah, FL. Tel: (305) 625-5388, (800) 624-8840, FAX: (305) 888-9903, E-Mail: dmail@dynacolor.com, Web Site: www.dynacolor.com (27)

Duncomb, Andrew, Tony Stone Images, Chicago, IL. Tel: (800) 234-7880, FAX: (312) 922-9075, Web Site: www.getty-images.com (38)

Duncraft Inc, Concord, NH. Tel: (603) 224-0200, (800) 593-5656, FAX: (603) 226-3735, E-Mail: info@duncraft.com, Web Site: www.duncraft.com (16)

Dundee Internet Services Inc, Azalia, MI. Tel: (734) 529-5331, Web Site: mailing-list-services.com/dundee.net (22)

Dunetz, Janet, Promark Direct Marketing Concepts Inc, Hackensack, NJ. Tel: (201) 489-0532, (800) 776-6275, FAX: (201) 489-2680, E-Mail: jdunetz@promarkdirectmarketing.com (21)

Dungan, David N., AnswerThink Inc, Miami, FL. Tel: (305) 375-8005, FAX: (305) 379-8810, Web Site: www.answerthink.com (35)

Dungan, Virginia, B, National Humane Education Society, Charles Town, WV. Tel: (304) 725-0506, FAX: (304) 725-1523, E-Mail: nhesinformation@nhes.org, Web Site: www.nhes.org (1)

Dunham, Lisa, Smithsonian Enterprises, New York, NY. Tel: (212) 916-1300, (800) 766-2149, FAX: (212) 490-0058, E-Mail: email@simag.si.edu, Web Site: www.smithsonianmag.com (16)

Dunham, Paul, Pace Inc, Annapolis Junction, MD. Tel: (910) 695-7223, FAX: (910) 944-1724, Web Site: www.paceworldwide.com/index.asp (16)

Dunham, Rick, Dunham & Co, Plano, TX. Tel: (469) 454-0100 (1)

Dunham, Sandra, Pace Inc, Annapolis Junction, MD. Tel: (910) 695-7223, FAX: (910) 944-1724, Web Site: www.paceworldwide.com/index.asp (16)

Dunham & Co, Plano, TX. Tel: (469) 454-0100 (1)

Dunhill, Andy, Dunhill International List Co Inc, Boca Raton, FL. Tel: (561) 998-7800, (800) 386-4455, FAX: (561) 998-7880, E-Mail: sales@dunhills.com, Web Site: www.dunhills.com (23)

Dunhill, Cindy, Dunhill International List Co Inc, Boca Raton, FL. Tel: (561) 998-7800, (800) 386-4455, FAX: (561) 998-7880, E-Mail: sales@dunhills.com, Web Site: www.dunhills.com (23)

Dunhill, Robert, Dunhill International List Co Inc, Boca Raton, FL. Tel: (561) 998-7800, (800) 386-4455, FAX: (561) 998-7880, E-Mail: sales@dunhills.com, Web Site: www.dunhills.com (23)

Hugo Dunhill Mailing Lists Inc, New Rochelle, NY. Tel: (212) 213-9300, (800) 611-0557, FAX: (212) 213-9245, E-Mail: info@hdml.com, Web Site: www.hdml.com (23)

Dunhill International List Co Inc, Boca Raton, FL. Tel: (561) 998-7800, (800) 386-4455, FAX: (561) 998-7880, E-Mail: sales@dunhills.com, Web Site: www.dunhills.com (23)

Dunlad, Jennifer, American Red Cross, Washington, DC. Tel: (703) 303-5000 X5, (800) RED-CROSS, Web Site: www.redcross.org (1)

Dunlap, Al, Sunbeam, Boca Raton, FL. Tel: (561) 912-4100, FAX: (561) 912-4567, Web Site: www.sunbeam.com (16)

Dunlap, Dennis, American Marketing Association, Chicago, IL. Tel: (312) 542-9000, FAX: (312) 542-9001, Web Site: www.ama.org (40)

Dunlap, Dennis, L., Business Marketing Association, Naperville, IL. Tel: (630) 544-5054, FAX: (630) 544-5055, E-Mail: info@marketing.org, Web Site: www.marketing.org (40)

Dunlap, Dennis, L., Winter Marketing Educators' Conference, Chicago, IL. Tel: (312) 542-9000, (800) 262-1150, FAX: (312) 542-9001, E-Mail: info@ama.org, Web Site: www.ama.org (42)

Dunlap, Larry, E., Fostoria Industries Inc, Johnson City, TN. Tel: (419) 435-9201, (800) 495-4525, FAX: (419) 435-0842, E-Mail: email@fostoriaindustries.com, Web Site: www.fostoriaindustries.com (9)

Dunleavey, Jennifer, Direct Selling Association, Washington, DC. Tel: (202) 452-8866, FAX: (202) 452-9010, E-Mail: info@dsa.org, Web Site: www.dsa.org (40)

Dunleavy, John, California Society of CPA's, San Mateo, CA. Tel: (800) 922-5272, FAX: (650) 522-3009, E-Mail: info@culcpa.org, Web Site: www.calcpa.org (1)

Dunn, Anna, Marie, AMD Research & Marketing LLC, Safety Harbor, FL. Tel: (727) 409-1087, Web Site: www.amdresearch-marketing.com (30)

Dunn, Dennis, Growing Child, Inc, West Lafayette, IN. Tel: (765) 464-0920, (800) 927-7289, FAX: (765) 423-4495, E-Mail: service@growingchild.com, Web Site: www.growingchild.com (17)

Dunn, Gregory, W., Gifts Corp, Barrie, ON. Tel: (905) 670-1126, (800) 565-3130, FAX: (905) 670-1127, E-Mail: customerservice@regal.ca, Web Site: www.regalgreetings.com (6)

Dunn, James, The New York Times Co, New York, NY. Tel: (212) 556-3881, FAX: (212) 556-7389, Web Site: www.nytimes.com (17)

Dunn, John, ADM Productions Inc, Port Washington, NY. Tel: (516) 484-6900, (800) ADM-DIAL, FAX: (516) 621-2531, Web Site: www.admpro.com (16)

Dunn, Maureen, H., Tennessee Valley Authority, Knoxville, TN. Tel: (865) 632-2101, Web Site: www.tva.gov (16)

Dunn, Michael, M., Duncraft Inc, Concord, NH. Tel: (603) 224-0200, (800) 593-5656, FAX: (603) 226-3735, E-Mail: info@duncraft.com, Web Site: www.duncraft.com (16)

Dunn, Sharon, Duncraft Inc, Concord, NH. Tel: (603) 224-0200, (800) 593-5656, FAX: (603) 226-3735, E-Mail: info@duncraft.com, Web Site: www.duncraft.com (16)

Dunn, Stephen, DUNN DATA Co Inc, Brewster, NY. Tel: (845) 278-1200, Web Site: www.dunndataco.com (23)

Dunn, Vincent, G., Levenger, Delray Beach, FL. Tel: (561) 276-2436, (800) 677-8034, FAX: (561) 266-2181, E-Mail: orders@levenger.com, Web Site: www.levenger.com (5)

DUNN DATA Co Inc, Brewster, NY. Tel: (845) 278-1200, Web Site: www.dunndataco.com (23)

Dunne, Joseph, TigerDirect.ca, Richmond Hill, ON Canada. Tel: (888) 771-9999, (800) 800-8300, FAX: (905) 482-3134, Web Site: www.tigerdirect.ca (3)

Dunnes, Elaine, McBee, Lancaster, CA. Tel: (973) 263-3225, (800) 878-9443, (800) 662-2331, FAX: (973) 263-8165, E-Mail: info@mcbeeinc.com, Web Site: www.mcbeeweb.com (10)

Dunning, Jack, E., Dunnings Diversified LLC, Cave Creek, AZ. Tel: (480) 585-5230, FAX: (480) 585-4565, E-Mail: jack.dundiv@cox.net (23)

Dunnings Diversified LLC, Cave Creek, AZ. Tel: (480) 585-5230, FAX: (480) 585-4565, E-Mail: jack.dundiv@cox.net (23)

Dunphy, Peter, Doctor's Best Inc, San Clemente, CA. Tel: (949) 498-3628, (800) 333-6977, FAX: (800) 754-2036, (949) 498-3952, E-Mail: info@drbvitamins.com, Web Site: www.drbvitamins.com (16)

Dunsmore, Joe, Digi International, Minnetonka, MN. Tel: (952) 912-3444, (877) 912-3444, FAX: (952) 912-4953, Web Site: www.digi.com (3)

Dupli Envelope & Graphics Corp, Syracuse, NY. Tel: (315) 472-1316, (800) 724-2477, FAX: (315) 422-3637, Web Site: www.duplionline.com (26)

Duplication Factory Inc, Chaska, MN. Tel: (952) 448-9912, (800) 279-2009, FAX: (952) 448-3983, E-Mail: info@duplicationfactory.com, Web Site: www.duplicationfactory.com (31)

Dupon, Davy, Almore International Inc, Portland, OR. Tel: (503) 643-6633, (800) 547-1511, FAX: (503) 643-9748, E-Mail: info@almore.com, Web Site: www.almore.com (7)

Dupont Color Proofing, Wilmington, DE. Tel: (800) 345-9999, FAX: (302) 892-8030, Web Site: www.dupont.com/proofing (27)

E I DuPont De Nemours & Co, Wilmington, DE. Tel: (302) 774-1000, FAX: (302) 774-7321, Web Site: www.dupont.com (16)

Dupuis, Frank J., Your Man Tours, El Segundo, CA. Tel: (310) 649-3820, FAX: (310) 649-2118, E-Mail: ymt@earthlink.net, Web Site: www.ymtvacations.com (19)

Dupuis, Sharon, Photri Images LLC, Fairfax, VA. Tel: (703) 978-0129, E-Mail: info@photriimages.com, Web Site: www.photriimages.com (38)

Duques, Henry C., Unisys, Blue Bell, PA. Tel: (215) 986-4011, (800) 874-8647, FAX: (215) 986-2312, Web Site: www.unisys.com (16)

Duques, Henry, C., First Data Corp, Greenwood Village, CO. Tel: (303) 488-8000, (800) 735-3362, Web Site: www.firstdata.com (28)

Duracell, Bethel, CT. Tel: (203) 796-4000, FAX: (203) 207-7842, Web Site: www.duracell.com (16)

Durand, Bob, Atlantic Publication Group LLC, Charleston, SC. Tel: (843) 747-0025, FAX: (843) 744-0816, E-Mail: info@atlanticpublicationgrp.com, Web Site: www.atlanticpublicationgrp.com (17)

Durante, Tony, Charter Direct Marketing, New York, NY. Tel: (212) 717-2770, FAX: (561) 245-7559, E-Mail: terrykollman@charterdirectmarketing.com, Web Site: www.charterdirectmarketing.com (35)

Durasol Corp, Amesbury, MA. Tel: (978) 388-2020, (800) 370-0683, FAX: (978) 388-9762, Web Site: www.durasolcorp.com (34)

Durate, Bernarda, 21st Century Insurance, Woodland Hills, CA. Tel: (818) 704-3700, FAX: (818) 226-1198, E-Mail: executiveoffice@21st.com, Web Site: www.21st.com (15)

Durey-Libby Edible Nuts Inc, Carlstadt, NJ. Tel: (201) 939-2775, (800) 332-6887, FAX: (201) 939-0386, E-Mail: info@dureylibby.com, Web Site: www.durreylibby.com (4)

The Durham Manufacturing Co, Durham, CT. Tel: (860) 349-3427, (800) 243-3774, FAX: (800) 782-5499, (860) 349-8572, E-Mail: info@durhammfg.com, Web Site: www.durhammfg.com (16)

Durian, Bogdan, Delta Tech Industries, Ontario, CA. Tel: (714) 577-8028, FAX: (714) 577-0140, E-Mail: sales@deltatechindustries.com, Web Site: www.deltatechindustries.com (16)

During, Kimberly, WinterSilks LLC, Warren, PA. Tel: (904) 645-6000, Web Site: www.wintersilks.com (2)

Durio, Belle, Louisiana Nursery, Opelousas, LA. Tel: (337) 948-3696, FAX: (337) 942-6404, Web Site: www.dvrionursery.com (8)

Durio, Dalton, Louisiana Nursery, Opelousas, LA. Tel: (337) 948-3696, FAX: (337) 942-6404, Web Site: www.dvrionursery.com (8)

Durio, Ken, Louisiana Nursery, Opelousas, LA. Tel: (337) 948-3696, FAX: (337) 942-6404, Web Site: www.dvrionursery.com (8)

Durler, Berit, N., Zoological Society of San Diego, San Diego, CA. Tel: (619) 231-1515, FAX: (619) 557-3937, Web Site: www.sandiegozoo.com (1)

Durley, Dale, H., American Tax Associates Inc, Columbus, OH. Tel: (614) 443-5343, FAX: (614) 443-0279 (20)

Durrah, Elaine, Reliance Electric, Fort Smith, AR. Tel: (479) 646-4711, FAX: (479) 648-5792, E-Mail: smtraylor@powersystems.rockwell.com, Web Site: www.reliance.com (9)

Durrett, Dan, B Shackman & Co Inc, Galesburg, MI. Tel: (269) 484-1000, (800) 221-7656, FAX: (269) 484-1010, Web Site: www.shackman.com (6)

Durrett, Jason, B Shackman & Co Inc, Galesburg, MI. Tel: (269) 484-1000, (800) 221-7656, FAX: (269) 484-1010, Web Site: www.shackman.com (6)

Durrett, Johanna, B Shackman & Co Inc, Galesburg, MI. Tel: (269) 484-1000, (800) 221-7656, FAX: (269) 484-1010, Web Site: www.shackman.com (6)

Durs, Don, Stile-Tile Like Metal Roofing, Sellersburg, IN. Tel: (812) 246-1866, (800) 999-7777, FAX: (800) 477-9318, (800) 944-6884, Web Site: www.mtsales.com (9)

Dursi, Bonnie, Hotline List Corp, New York, NY. Tel: (212) 840-8135, FAX: (212) 840-8139 (23)

Dutch Gardens, Burlington, VT. Tel: (802) 660-3500, (800) 950-4470, FAX: (800) 551-6712, E-Mail: info@dutchgardens.com, Web Site: www.dutchgardens.com (8)

Duval, Christopher, McCabe & Duval Advertising, Portland, ME. Tel: (207) 773-4538, (800) 603-6069, FAX: (207) 773-7245, Web Site: www.mccabe-duval.com (35)

Duval, Dennis, American Spirit Mailing, Howard Lake, MN. Tel: (320) 543-3737, FAX: (320) 543-3228, E-Mail: asgc@asgc-mail.com, Web Site: www.asgc.com (28)

Dvorak, Kathleen, Richardson Electronics Ltd, Lafox, IL. Tel: (630) 208-2200, FAX: (630) 208-2550, E-Mail: edg@rell.com, Web Site: www.rell.com (16)

Dvoskin, Diane, American Society for Training & Development, Alexandria, VA. Tel: (703) 683-8100, (800) NAT-ASTD, FAX: (703) 683-8103, Web Site: www.astd.org (1)

Dworman, Steven, Infomercial Marketing Report, Beverly Hills, CA. Tel: (310) 826-8810, FAX: (310) 826-0097, E-Mail: clarkkent@aol.com (32)

Dwyer, Barbara, Knollwood Groves at Cushman's, West Palm Beach, FL. Tel: (561) 734-4800, (800) 222-9696, FAX: (800) 776-4329, E-Mail: sales@knollwoodgroves.com, Web Site: www.knollwoodgroves.com (4)

The Dwyer Group, Waco, TX. Tel: (254) 759-5850, Web Site: www.dwyergroup.com (16)

Dwyer Instruments Inc, Michigan City, IN. Tel: (219) 879-8868, Web Site: www.dwyer-inst.com (16)

Dwyre, Loretta, Luster Care Products, Saint Louis, MO. Tel: (636) 272-1885, (800) 291-5223, FAX: (636) 272-1869, Web Site: www.lusterlace.com (16)

DX Engineering, Akron, OH. Tel: (800) 777-0703, FAX: (330) 572-3279, E-Mail: info@comteksystems.com, Web Site: www.comteksystems.com (16)

Dyck, A.R., Poker Player, Sherman Oaks, CA. Tel: (310) 674-3365, FAX: (310) 674-3205, E-Mail: ard@gamblingtimes.com, Web Site: www.gamblingtimes.com (17)

Dydacomp Development Corp, Parsippany, NJ. Tel: (973) 237-9415, (800) 858-3666, FAX: (973) 237-9043, E-Mail: sales@dydacomp.com, Web Site: www.dydacomp.com (22)

Dye, Kim, Nu-Parr Swimwear, Phoenix, AZ. Tel: (602) 279-4044, (800) 230-7277, FAX: (602) 212-2636, E-Mail: info@nu-parr.com, Web Site: www.nu-parr.com (2)

Dyer, Christopher, ListAbility Inc, Venice, FL. Tel: (866) 446-2055, (800) 626-6500, Web Site: www.listability.com (23)

Dyer, Deb, Cuddledown Inc, Portland, ME. Tel: (207) 761-0201, (800) 323-6793, FAX: (207) 761-1948, Web Site: www.cuddledown.com (8)

Dyer, Esther, R., National Medical Fellowships, New York, NY. Tel: (212) 483-8880, FAX: (212) 483-8897, Web Site: www.nfm-online.org (1)

Dyess, Carl, D., International Specialized Book Services Inc, Portland, OR. Tel: (503) 287-3093, (800) 944-6190, FAX: (503) 280-8832, E-Mail: isbs_sales@isbs.com, Web Site: www.isbscatalog.com (16)

Dykstra, Michael, Hyphos360 Inc, Clearwater, FL. Tel: (727) 532-0700, (800) 733-1817, FAX: (727) 524-3424, Web Site: www.hyphos360.com (21)

Dykun, L, Ventriloquist Voice Solutions International Inc, Mississauga, ON. Tel: (866) 446-0860, E-Mail: info@vvsii.com, Web Site: www.vvsii.com (29)

Dylla, H. Frederick, American Institute of Physics, Melville, NY. Tel: (516) 576-2200, (800) 892-8259, FAX: (516) 576-2374, E-Mail: aipinfo@aip.org, Web Site: www.aip.org (17)

Dynacolor Graphics Inc, Hialeah, FL. Tel: (305) 625-5388, (800) 624-8840, FAX: (305) 888-9903, E-Mail: dmail@dynacolor.com, Web Site: www.dynacolor.com (27)

Dynamic Development Co, Mission Viejo, CA. Tel: (949) 768-5798, E-Mail: antiwear@dynamicdevelopment.com, Web Site: www.dynamicdevelopment.com (12)

Dynamic Engineering, Santa Cruz, CA. Tel: (831) 457-8891, FAX: (831) 457-4793, E-Mail: contact@penguinparty.com, Web Site: www.dyneng.com (3)

Dynamic Graphics, Indianapolis, IN. Tel: (317) 328-2555, Web Site: www.dgiink.com (27)

Dynamics Research Corp, Andover, MA. Tel: (978) 475-9090, (800) 522-4321, FAX: (978) 475-8205, Web Site: www.drc.com (16)

Dyon, Allen, DMRA, Mountain View, CA. Tel: (650) 650-9988, Web Site: www.dmrainc.com (22)

Dysert, Scott, Liebert Corp, Columbus, OH. Tel: (614) 841-6700, (800) LIEBERT, FAX: (614) 841-6022, Web Site: www.liebert.com (16)

Dyson, Gregory, ICMA Retirement Corp, Washington, DC. Tel: (202) 962-4600, (800) 669-7400, FAX: (202) 962-4601, E-Mail: investorservices@icmarc.org, Web Site: www.icmarc.org (14)

Dyson, Peter, American Society of Media Photographers (ASMP), Philadelphia, PA. Tel: (215) 451-ASMP, FAX: (215) 451-0880, Web Site: www.asmp.org (40)

Dziurman, Mark, Dziurman Dzign Inc, Clawson, MI. Tel: (248) 288-8800 X1, FAX: (248) 288-8804, E-Mail: dziurman@dzdzign.com, Web Site: www.dzdzign.com (35)

Dziurman Dzign Inc, Clawson, MI. Tel: (248) 288-8800 X1, FAX: (248) 288-8804, E-Mail: dziurman@dzdzign.com, Web Site: www.dzdzign.com (35)

Dzvonik, Michael, Grizzard Advertising, Glendale, CA. Tel: (818) 325-4892, (800) 241-9351, FAX: (818) 543-1308, Web Site: www.grizzard.com (35)

E

E&D Web Printing Inc, Rochelle, IL. Tel: (708) 656-6600, (800) 323-5733, FAX: (708) 656-8390, E-Mail: info@eanddweb.com, Web Site: www.eanddweb.com (27)

E&M Advertising Inc, New York, NY. Tel: (212) 981-5901, FAX: (212) 981-2121, E-Mail: mmedico@emadv.com, Web Site: www.emadv.com (35)

E & M Media Group Inc, New York, NY. Tel: (212) 455-0107, Web Site: www.emtvsales.com (35)

E-Centives Inc, Bethesda, MD. Tel: (240) 333-6100, (877) 323-6848, FAX: (240) 333-6250, E-Mail: sales@e-centives.com, Web Site: www.e-centives.com (32)

E-Dialog Inc, Burlington, MA. Tel: (888) 256-7687, Web Site: www.e-dialog.com (32)

E! Entertainment Television, Los Angeles, CA. Tel: (323) 937-3408, FAX: (323) 954-2660, Web Site: www.eonline.com (32)

E Hille, Angler's Supply House, Williamsport, PA. Tel: (570) 323-7564, (800) 326-6612, FAX: (570) 323-9995, Web Site: www.anglersupplyhouse.com (11)

E Media Advantage, Livingston, NJ. Tel: (917) 994-3685, FAX: (973) 455-1312, E-Mail: tnevitt@emediaadvantage.com, Web Site: emediaadvantage.com (20)

E-Miles.com, Dallas, TX. Tel: (214) 757-4700, Web Site: www.e-miles.com (19)

e-Pipeconnection, Evansville, IN. Tel: (812) 474-4529, (800) 262-4300, FAX: (812) 474-4531, E-Mail: sales@e-pipeconnection.com, Web Site: www.e-pipeconnection.com (9)

E-Z Bowz Inc, Gatlinburg, TN. Tel: (865) 453-3060, FAX: (865) 429-3743, Web Site: www.ezbows.com (8)

E-Z-EM Inc, Melville, NY. Tel: (516) 333-8230, (800) 544-4624, FAX: (516) 333-8278, E-Mail: webmaster@ezem.com, Web Site: www.ezem.com (7)

EBA Wholesale Corp, Brooklyn, NY. Tel: (718) 253-4700, (866) 2 ASK EBA, FAX: (718) 253-9232, Web Site: www.shopeba.com (3)

EBM Direct Marketing Services LLC, Port Washington, NY. Tel: (516) 874-7839, Web Site: www.ebmdirectmarketing.com (20)

EBSCO Reception Room Subscription Services, Birmingham, AL. Tel: (205) 991-1409, (800) 527-5901, FAX: (205) 995-1621, Web Site: www.ebsco.com/errss (18)

ECHO - Electronic Clearing House Inc, Woodland Hills, CA. Tel: (805) 419-8700, Web Site: www.echo-inc.com (14)

EDC Publishing, Tulsa, OK. Tel: (918) 622-4522, (800) 475-4522, FAX: (800) 747-4509, Web Site: www.edcpub.com (17)

EDMS LLC, Stanwood, WA. Tel: (360) 654-0448, (866) 222-3367, FAX: (360) 652-6199, E-Mail: info@edmsllc.com, Web Site: www.edmsllc.com (28)

eFootage, Pasadena, CA. Tel: (626) 395-9593, FAX: (626) 395-5394, E-Mail: info@efootage.com, Web Site: www.efootage.com (38)

EGC Group Inc, Melville, NY. Tel: (516) 935-4944, FAX: (516) 935-7030, E-Mail: contact@egcgroup.com (35)

EMAK Worldwide, Chicago, IL. Tel: (323) 932-4300, E-Mail: jim.holbrook@emak.com, Web Site: www.emak.com (33)

EMC Corp, Hopkinton, MA. Tel: (888) 438-3622, Web Site: www.emc.com (16)

EMED Co Inc, Buffalo, NY. Tel: (716) 626-1616, (800) 442-3633, FAX: (716) 626-1630, E-Mail: customerservice@emedco.com, Web Site: www.emedco.com (16)

EMI Strategic Marketing Inc, Boston, MA. Tel: (617) 451-9451, FAX: (617) 451-1193, E-Mail: cedlund@emiboston.com, Web Site: www.emiboston.com (35)

EMS Technologies, Norcross, GA. Tel: (770) 263-9200, FAX: (770) 447-4405, Web Site: www.ems-t.com (16)

EOS International Inc, Carlsbad, CA. Tel: (760) 431-8400, (800) 876-5484, FAX: (760) 431-8448, Web Site: www.eosintl.com (5)

EPI Colorspace, Gaithersburg, MD. Tel: (301) 230-2023, FAX: (301) 990-7890, E-Mail: jcriscuoli@epicolorspace.com, Web Site: www.epicolorspace.com (36)

ERS Direct Marketing, Thousand Oaks, CA. Tel: (805) 499-1129, FAX: (805) 499-3189, E-Mail: eileen@ersdirect.com, Web Site: www.ersdirect.com (21)

ESA - A Sandy Alexander Co, Clifton, NJ. Tel: (973) 470-8100, Web Site: www.tbccolor.com (32)

ESL Federal Credit Union, Rochester, NY. Tel: (585) 336-1000, (800) 848-2265, FAX: (585) 336-1138, Web Site: www.esl.org (14)

ESP Printing & Mailing Inc, Boise, ID. Tel: (800) 338-6789, FAX: (208) 345-4765, E-Mail: data@espmap.com (28)

ESPN, New York, NY. Tel: (212) 456-4995 (5)

ETI Sales Support, Valhalla, NY. Tel: (914) 747-3030, (800) 466-4384, FAX: (914) 747-3466, E-Mail: info@etisales.com, Web Site: www.etisales.com (29)

ETR Associates, San Francisco, CA. Tel: (831) 438-4060, (800) 321-4407, FAX: (800) 435-8433, E-Mail: webmaster@etr.org, Web Site: www.etr.org (24)

ETS Inc, Indianapolis, IN. Tel: (317) 290-8982, (800) 228-6292, FAX: (317) 329-4630, E-Mail: info@etstsan.com, Web Site: www.etstans.com (7)

ETTSI Premiums & Incentives, Daytona Beach, FL. Tel: (386) 271-0204, Web Site: www.ettsi.com (16)

EU Services, Rockville, MD. Tel: (301) 424-3300, (800) 230-3362, FAX: (301) 424-3696, Web Site: www.euservices.com (21)

EWA & Miniature Cars USA Inc, Berkeley Heights, NJ. Tel: (732) 424-7811, (800) 392-4454, FAX: (732) 424-7814, E-Mail: ewa@ewacars.com (11)

EXL, Jersey City, NJ. Tel: (201) 748-4729 (16)

The EZ-Forms Co, Kerrville, TX. Tel: (281) 667-4414, FAX: (281) 667-4415, E-Mail: ezformscontactus@gmail.com, Web Site: www.ez-forms.com (21)

Eadon Ventures, Alliance, OH. Tel: (330) 418-4298 (20)

Eagle, Denise, ZCard North America, New York, NY. Tel: (212) 797-3450, Web Site: www.zcard.com (31)

Eagle Asset Management Inc, Saint Petersburg, FL. Tel: (727) 573-2453, FAX: (727) 573-8020, Web Site: www.eagleasset.com (14)

Eagle Claw Fishing Tackle, Denver, CO. Tel: (303) 321-1481, FAX: (303) 321-4750, E-Mail: info@eagleclaw.com, Web Site: www.eagleclaw.com (11)

Eagle Marketing Services Inc, San Diego, CA. Tel: (619) 223-1273, (800) 548-5858, FAX: (727) 803-0512, E-Mail: gettunedin@eaglemarketing.com, Web Site: www.eaglemarketing.com (35)

Eagle Publishing, Washington, DC. Tel: (202) 216-0600, FAX: (202) 216-0612, Web Site: www.eaglepub.com (17)

Eagle:xm, Denver, CO. Tel: (303) 320-5411, (800) 426-5376, FAX: (303) 393-6884, E-Mail: bettersolutions@eaglexm.com, Web Site: www.eaglexm.com (21)

Eaker, Dean, Wired Assets Data Corp, Greenwich, CT. Tel: (203) 340-2316, Web Site: www.wiredassets.com (22)

Earhart, Mike, Bunchball, Redwood City, CA. Tel: (408) 985-2034, Web Site: www.bunchball.com (32)

Earl, Rachel, St Labre Indian School, Ashland, MT. Tel: (406) 784-4500, Web Site: www.stlabre.org (1)

Earlywine, Lisa, World Publications Inc, Winter Park, FL. Tel: (407) 628-4802, FAX: (407) 628-7061, Web Site: www.worldpub.net (17)

Earnest, Don, Calumet Photographic Inc, Bensenville, IL. Tel: (630) 860-7447, (800) 453-2550, FAX: (800) 577-3686, E-Mail: custserv@calumetphoto.com, Web Site: www.calumetphoto.com (3)

Earthrise, Irvine, CA. Tel: (949) 623-9980, FAX: (949) 623-0990, E-Mail: info@earthrise.com, Web Site: www.earthrise.com (16)

East Coast Industrial Equipment & Tire, Jacksonville, FL. Tel: (904) 358-1229, (800) 874-1942, FAX: (904) 354-0888 (34)

Eastbay Running Store Inc, Wausau, WI. Tel: (715) 845-5538, (800) 826-2205, FAX: (715) 261-9500, Web Site: www.eastbay.com (2)

Easter Seals, Chicago, IL. Tel: (312) 726-6200, FAX: (312) 726-1494, Web Site: www.easter-seals.org (1)

Easterday, Vickie, Burkholder Flint Associates, Columbus, OH. Tel: (614) 228-2425, FAX: (614) 228-0631, E-Mail: bfa1@burkholderflint.com, Web Site: www.burkholderflint.com (35)

Eastern Bank, Lynn, MA. Tel: (800) EASTERN, Web Site: www.easternbank.com (14)

Eastern Collection Corp, Sag Harbor, NY. Tel: (631) 563-2112, (800) 243-1204, FAX: (631) 563-2471, E-Mail: ecc1626@aol.com (20)

Eastern Michigan University, Ypsilanti, MI. Tel: (734) 487-1849, FAX: (734) 484-1151, Web Site: www.emich.edu (16)

Eastern Mountain Sports, Peterborough, NH. Tel: (603) 924-9571, (800) 463-6367, FAX: (603) 924-4320, Web Site: www.ems.com (16)

Easthill Group Inc, Pottstown, PA. Tel: (610) 323-9099, (610) 323-9063, (610) 323-2200, (888) 869-4433, (800) 345-1178, FAX: (610) 323-6268, Web Site: www.eastwoodcompany.com (12)

Eastlan Ratings, Sisters, OR. Tel: (877) 886-3320, FAX: (541) 318-4646, E-Mail: info@eastlanratings.com, Web Site: www.eastlanratings.com (30)

Eastman, David, Agency.com, New York, NY. Tel: (212) 358-2600, FAX: (212) 358-2604, Web Site: www.agency.com (20)

Eastman Chemical Co, Kingsport, TN. Tel: (800) 695-4322, Web Site: www.eatman.com (16)

Eastman Kodak Co, Rochester, NY. Tel: (585) 724-0251, (800) 698-3324, FAX: (585) 724-1089, Web Site: www.kodak.com (27)

Eastman Vidal, Jill, 1-800-Flowers.com, Carle Place, NY. Tel: (516) 237-6000, Web Site: www.1800flowers.com (16)

Easton, David, David Easton Inc, New York, NY. Tel: (212) 334-3820, FAX: (212) 334-3821, Web Site: www.davideastoninc.com (16)

David Easton Inc, New York, NY. Tel: (212) 334-3820, FAX: (212) 334-3821, Web Site: www.davideastoninc.com (16)

Eastwood, Michael, Time Communications, Saint Paul, MN. Tel: (800) 486-8581, FAX: (612) 298-1945, E-Mail: info@timecommunications.biz, Web Site: www.timecommunications.biz (29)

Easy Analytic Software Inc, Fresh Meadows, NY. Tel: (718) 740-7930, Web Site: www.easidemographics.com (22)

Easy Color Printing, San Leandro, CA. Tel: (510) 580-6500, FAX: (510) 580-6570, Web Site: www.easycolorprinting.com (35)

EasyLink Services International Corp, Piscataway, NJ. Tel: (800) 828-7115, FAX: (732) 652-3810, E-Mail: sales@easylink.com, Web Site: www.easylink.com (16)

Eaton, Amy, Pinnacle Orchards, Maumee, OH. Tel: (419) 893-7611, (800) 442-5671, FAX: (419) 893-0164, Web Site: www.pinnacleorchards.com (4)

Eaton, Jon, International Marine, Camden, ME. Tel: (207) 236-4837, FAX: (207) 236-6314, Web Site: www.internationalmarine.com (17)

Eaton Corp, Raleigh, NC. Tel: (216) 523-4400, (800) 356-5794, FAX: (216) 523-4787, Web Site: www.eaton.com (16)

Ebanks, Michele, Essence Communications Inc, New York, NY. Tel: (212) 522-1212, FAX: (212) 921-5173, Web Site: www.essence.com (17)

Ebay, San Jose, CA. Tel: (408) 376-7400, Web Site: www.ebay.com (16)

Ebbesen, Samuel, E., Overseas Private Investment Corp (OPIC), Washington, DC. Tel: (202) 336-8400, FAX: (202) 336-7949, E-Mail: info@opic.gov, Web Site: www.opic.gov (11)

Ebbets Field Flannels Inc, Seattle, WA. Tel: (206) 382-7249, FAX: (206) 382-4411, E-Mail: clubhouse@ebbets.com, Web Site: www.ebbets.com (2)

Ebel, Greg, 4Imprint Inc, Oshkosh, WI. Tel: (920) 236-7272, (888) 298-8190, (877) 446-7746, FAX: (800) 355-5043, E-Mail: administrator@4imprint.com, Web Site: www.4imprint.com (16)

Ebeling, Sean, Edward Jones, Des Peres, MO Canada. Tel: (314) 515-2000, Web Site: www.edwardjones.com (14)

Eberle, Bruce, Eberle Communications Group Inc, McLean, VA. Tel: (703) 893-1095, FAX: (703) 821-0920, Web Site: www.eberleassociates.com (35)

Eberle, Bruce, W., Eberle & Associates Inc, McLean, VA. Tel: (703) 821-1550, FAX: (703) 821-0920, E-Mail: info@eberle1.com, Web Site: www.eberleassociates.com (1)

Eberle, Terry, Florida Today, Melbourne, FL. Tel: (321) 242-3500, (877) 424-0156, FAX: (321) 242-3729, Web Site: www.floridatoday.com (17)

Eberle & Associates Inc, McLean, VA. Tel: (703) 821-1550, FAX: (703) 821-0920, E-Mail: info@eberle1.com, Web Site: www.eberleassociates.com (1)

Eberle Communications Group Inc, McLean, VA. Tel: (703) 893-1095, FAX: (703) 821-0920, Web Site: www.eberleassociates.com (35)

Eberlein, Gail, K., Direct Response Enhancements LLC, Scottsdale, AZ. Tel: (480) 451-7384, FAX: (480) 661-8460, E-Mail: drellc@aol.com, Web Site: www.dreteleconsultants.com (29)

Ebersole, Del, Ebersole Lapidary Supply Inc, Wichita, KS. Tel: (316) 945-4771, (877) EBERSOLE, FAX: (316) 945-4773, E-Mail: ebersolerocks@sbcglobal.net, Web Site: www.ebersolelapidary.com (11)

Ebersole, Len, Ebersole Lapidary Supply Inc, Wichita, KS. Tel: (316) 945-4771, (877) EBERSOLE, FAX: (316) 945-4773, E-Mail: ebersolerocks@sbcglobal.net, Web Site: www.ebersolelapidary.com (11)

Ebersole Lapidary Supply Inc, Wichita, KS. Tel: (316) 945-4771, (877) EBERSOLE, FAX: (316) 945-4773, E-Mail: ebersolerocks@sbcglobal.net, Web Site: www.ebersolelapidary.com (11)

Ebert, Ann, Cumberland General Store Inc, Alpharetta, GA. Tel: (800) 334-4640, FAX: (678) 240-0410, E-Mail: info@cumberlandgerneral.com, Web Site: www.cumberlandgeneral.com (8)

Ebling, Ken, MDE Marketing, Mahwah, NJ. Tel: (201) 891-7010, Web Site: www.wdemarketing.com (16)

eBureau LLC, Saint Cloud, MN. Tel: (320) 534-5000, Web Site: www.ebureau.com (22)

Echnologist Scrub Tech, Mesquite, TX. Tel: (520) 208-6314 (34)

Echo Data, Coatesville, PA. Tel: (610) 466-2100, (800) 511-3870, FAX: (610) 466-2110, E-Mail: sroberts@echodata.com, Web Site: www.echodata.com (22)

Echohard, John-Louis, The Nature Conservancy, Arlington, VA. Tel: (703) 841-5300, (800) 628-6860, FAX: (703) 841-1283, E-Mail: magazine@tnc.org, Web Site: www.nature.org (1)

Echols, Terumi, Christianity Today Inc, Carol Stream, IL. Tel: (630) 260-6200, FAX: (630) 260-0114, Web Site: www.christianitytoday.com (17)

Echols, Tracy, MISSCO Corp, Flowood, MS. Tel: (601) 948-8600, (800) 647-5333, FAX: (601) 987-3038 (16)

Echomax, Teaneck, NJ. Tel: (201) 837-1371, FAX: (201) 837-6142 (35)

Echotouch Corp, Austin, TX. Tel: (512) 327-5638, Web Site: www.echotouch.com (20)

Eck, Robert, Beeman Precision Airguns, Santa Fe Springs, CA. Tel: (714) 890-4800, FAX: (714) 890-4808, E-Mail: sales@beeman.com, Web Site: www.beeman.com (11)

Eckankar, Minneapolis, MN. Tel: (612) 544-3001, (800) 327-5113, FAX: (612) 474-1127, Web Site: www.eckankar.org (17)

Eckels, Jeff, e-Pipeconnection, Evansville, IN. Tel: (812) 474-4529, (800) 262-4300, FAX: (812) 474-4531, E-Mail: sales@e-pipeconnection.com, Web Site: www.e-pipeconnection.com (9)

Eckenard, Lynn, LevLane Advertising, Philadelphia, PA. Tel: (215) 825-9600, FAX: (215) 825-9601 (35)

Ecker, William, D., The Hartz Mountain Corp, Secaucus, NJ. Tel: (201) 271-4800, (800) 275-1414, FAX: (201) 271-0068, Web Site: www.hartz.com (16)

Eckert, Joanne, truTV, New York, NY. Tel: (212) 973-2800, FAX: (212) 973-3210, Web Site: www.trutv.com (17)

Eckert, Mark, JLG Industries Inc, McConnellsburg, PA. Tel: (717) 485-5161, (877) JLG-SELL, FAX: (717) 485-6417, E-Mail: comments@jlg.com, Web Site: www.jlg.com (16)

Eckert, Robert A., Fisher-Price, East Aurora, NY. Tel: (716) 687-3300, FAX: (716) 687-3636, Web Site: www.fisherprice.com (16)

Eckert, Robert, A., Mattel Inc, El Segundo, CA. Tel: (310) 252-2000, FAX: (310) 252-2180, Web Site: www.mattel.com (16)

Ecklers, Titusville, FL. Tel: (888) 787-3626, (800) 284-3906, E-Mail: custsvc@ecklers.net, Web Site: www.ecklers.com (12)

Eckman, Jamie, Brookhollow Cards, Rexburg, ID. Tel: (800) 822-0256, FAX: (800) 443-8847, E-Mail: service@brookhollowcards.com, Web Site: www.brookhollowcards.com (10)

Eckmann, Juergen, Nautilus Inc, Vancouver, WA. Tel: (360) 859-2900, (800) 675-0171, FAX: (360) 694-2755, Web Site: www.nautilus.com (11)

Eckstein, Stacy, Gun Video Catalog/LMP, San Diego, CA. Tel: (858) 569-4000, (800) 942-8273, FAX: (858) 569-0505, Web Site: www.gunvideo.com; www.glockstore.com (11)

Eckweiler, Tania, SmartReply Inc, Irvine, CA. Tel: (949) 340-0700, Web Site: www.smartreply.com (29)

Eclipse Direct Marketing, Mineola, NY. Tel: (212) 931-8344, FAX: (212) 931-8377, E-Mail: jkaiser@eclipsedm.com, Web Site: www.eclipsedm.com (23)

Eclipse Marketing Services, Morristown, NJ. Tel: (800) 837-4648 (35)

Ecoenvelopes, Eden Prairie, MN. Tel: (612) 605-4885, (888) 428-4364, FAX: (651) 392-8924, E-Mail: info@ecoenvelopes.com, Web Site: www.ecoenvelopes.com (20)

Ecolab Professional Products, Saint Paul, MN. Tel: (651) 293-4248, FAX: (651) 225-3025, E-Mail: ecolabs@ecolabs.com, Web Site: www.ecolab.com (16)

Ecological Fibers Inc, Lunenburg, MA. Tel: (978) 537-0003, FAX: (978) 537-2238, E-Mail: jquill@ecofibers.com (25)

Economaki, John, Bridge City Tool Works Inc, Portland, OR. Tel: (503) 282-6997, (800) 253-3332, FAX: (503) 287-1085, E-Mail: jjeconomaki@comcast.net, Web Site: www.bridgecitytools.com (9)

The Economist Newspaper NA Inc, New York, NY. Tel: (212) 554-0600, FAX: (212) 586-1191, Web Site: www.economist.com (17)

Economy Handicrafts, Brooklyn, NY. Tel: (718) 431-9300, (800) 216-1601, FAX: (718) 431-9309, Web Site: www.vanguardcrafts.com (16)

The Edbraham Group, Westbrook, CT. Tel: (860) 664-4120, Web Site: www.theedbrahamgroup.com (20)

Edbrooke, Shirley, The Edbraham Group, Westbrook, CT. Tel: (860) 664-4120, Web Site: www.theedbrahamgroup.com (20)

Eddings, Chris, Alliance of Area Business Publications, El Segundo, CA. Tel: (323) 937-5514, FAX: (323) 937-0959, E-Mail: info@bizpubs.org, Web Site: www.bizpubs.org (1)

Eddington, Pam, Sheridan Books Inc, Chelsea, MI. Tel: (734) 662-3291, (734) 475-9145, (800) 999-BOOK, FAX: (734) 475-7337, E-Mail: info@sheridanbooks.com, Web Site: www.sheridanbooks.com (27)

Eddy, George, Heinrich Marketing, Denver, CO. Tel: (303) 233-8660, (800) 356-5036, FAX: (303) 239-5352, E-Mail: georgeeddy@heinrich.com, Web Site: www.heinrich.com (35)

Edelman, Barbara, A., Gebbie Press Inc, New Paltz, NY. Tel: (845) 255-7560, FAX: (888) 345-2790, E-Mail: gebbiepress@pipeline.com, Web Site: www.gebbieinc.com (17)

Edelman, Barbara, All-In-One Directory, New Paltz, NY. Tel: (845) 255-7560, FAX: (888) 345-2790, E-Mail: gebbiepress@pipeline.com, Web Site: www.gebbieinc.com (43)

Edelman, Daniel, H., Macy's West, San Francisco, CA. Tel: (415) 954-6089, FAX: (415) 954-6103 (16)

Edelman, Glenn, Wine Enthusiast Cos, Mount Kisco, NY. Tel: (914) 345-9463, (800) 356-8466, FAX: (914) 345-3129, Web Site: www.wineenthusiast.com (4)

Edelman, Robert, Edelman Direct Marketing Inc, Great Neck, NY. Tel: (516) 829-9398 (20)

Edelman, Scott, A., KCET, Los Angeles, CA. Tel: (323) 666-6500, FAX: (323) 953-5661, E-Mail: viewerservices@kcet.org, Web Site: www.kcet.org (1)

Edelman Direct Marketing Inc, Great Neck, NY. Tel: (516) 829-9398 (20)

Edelmann Scott Inc, Richmond, VA. Tel: (804) 643-1931, FAX: (804) 643-1934, E-Mail: dickscott@edelmannscott.com, Web Site: www.edelmannscott.com (35)

Edelson, Larry, Weiss Research Inc, Jupiter, FL. Tel: (561) 627-3300, (877) 925-4833, FAX: (561) 625-6685, E-Mail: newbusiness@weissgroupinc.com, Web Site: www.weissgroupinc.com (17)

Edelstein, Steven, J., Fosdick Fulfillment Corp, Wallingford, CT. Tel: (203) 269-0211, (800) 759-5588, FAX: (203) 679-3290, E-Mail: sales@fosdickcorp.com, Web Site: www.fosdickfulfillment.com (28)

Edelstone, Charles, Dassault Falcon Jet Corp, Little Ferry, NJ. Tel: (201) 440-6700, FAX: (201) 541-4515, Web Site: www.dassaultfalcon.com (16)

Eden, Maria, B., Direct Response Media, Wilmington, DE. Tel: (610) 995-0200, (800) 898-3761, FAX: (610) 995-0300, E-Mail: info@directresponsemedia.com, Web Site: www.directresponsemedia.com (32)

Edgar, Donna, Eastern Mountain Sports, Peterborough, NH. Tel: (603) 924-9571, (800) 463-6367, FAX: (603) 924-4320, Web Site: www.ems.com (16)

Edge Teleservices, Inc, Oak Lawn, IL. Tel: (708) 857-5000, (800) 394-2323, FAX: (708) 857-5029, E-Mail: contactme@edgeteleservices.com, Web Site: www.edgeteleservices.com (29)

EdgeMark Partners Inc, Glen Allen, VA. Tel: (804) 967-2000, Web Site: www.edgemarkpartners.com (35)

Edgerton, Brendan, Crutchfield Corp, Charlottesville, VA. Tel: (434) 817-1000, (800) 955-9091, FAX: (804) 817-1010, E-Mail: administration@crutchfield.com, Web Site: www.crutchfield.com (3)

Edible Landscaping, Afton, VA. Tel: (434) 361-9134, (800) 524-4156, FAX: (434) 361-1916, E-Mail: info@ediblelandscaping.com, Web Site: www.eat-it.com (8)

Edison Electric Institute, Washington, DC. Tel: (202) 508-5000, FAX: (202) 508-5096, Web Site: www.eei.org (1)

Editorial Code & Data Inc, Walled Lake, MI. Tel: (248) 926-5187, FAX: (248) 926-6047, E-Mail: Monique@marketsize.com, Web Site: www.marketsize.com (30)

Editorial Freelance Association, New York, NY. Tel: (212) 929-5400, (866) 929-5400, FAX: (212) 929-5439, E-Mail: office@the-efa.org, Web Site: www.the-efa.org (31)

Editorial Projects in Education Inc, Bethesda, MD. Tel: (301) 280-3100, (800) 346-1834, FAX: (301) 280-3250, Web Site: www.edweek.org (17)

Editors Press Inc, Hyattsville, MD. Tel: (301) 853-4900, (888) 853-4900, FAX: (301) 853-4961, Web Site: www.edpress.com (27)

Edlund, Campbell, EMI Strategic Marketing Inc, Boston, MA. Tel: (617) 451-9451, FAX: (617) 451-1193, E-Mail: cedlund@emiboston.com, Web Site: www.emiboston.com (35)

Edman, Jeff, PC World, San Francisco, CA. Tel: (415) 243-0500, FAX: (415) 442-1891, Web Site: www.pcworld.com (17)

Edmonds, Lynn, S., LW Robbins Associates, Holliston, MA. Tel: (508) 893-0210, (800) 229-5972, FAX: (508) 893-0212, E-Mail: ppapsador@lwra.com, Web Site: www.lwra.com (1)

Edmonds, Mel, MISSCO Corp, Flowood, MS. Tel: (601) 948-8600, (800) 647-5333, FAX: (601) 987-3038 (16)

Edmonds, Thomas, Edmonds Associates Inc, Vienna, VA. Tel: (703) 448-8221, (703) 448-8000, Web Site: www.edmondsassociates.com (35)

Edmonds Associates Inc, Vienna, VA. Tel: (703) 448-8221, (703) 448-8000, Web Site: www.edmondsassociates.com (35)

Edmund, Marisa, Edmund Optics Inc, Barrington, NJ. Tel: (856) 573-6250, (800) 363-1992, FAX: (856) 573-6295, E-Mail: sales@edmundoptic.com, Web Site: www.edmundoptics.com (9)

Edmund, Robert M., Edmund Optics Inc, Barrington, NJ. Tel: (856) 573-6250, (800) 363-1992, FAX: (856) 573-6295, E-Mail: sales@edmundoptic.com, Web Site: www.edmundoptics.com (9)

Edmund Optics Inc, Barrington, NJ. Tel: (856) 573-6250, (800) 363-1992, FAX: (856) 573-6295, E-Mail: sales@edmundoptic.com, Web Site: www.edmundoptics.com (9)

Edo Interactive, Nashville, TN. Tel: (615) 297-6080, Web Site: www.edointeractive.com (16)

Edroy Products Co Inc, Nyack, NY. Tel: (845) 358-6600, (800) 233-8803, FAX: (845) 358-4098, E-Mail: sales@edroyproducts.com, Web Site: www.edroyproducts.com (16)

Edsall, Jr. Robert, Sun Harvest Citrus, Fort Myers, FL. Tel: (239) 768-2686, (800) 743-1480, FAX: (239) 768-9255, E-Mail: info@sunharvestcitrus.com, Web Site: www.SunHarvestCitrus.com (6)

Edson, B. Montgomery, Guarantee Trust Life Insurance Co, Glenview, IL. Tel: (847) 298-0670, FAX: (847) 298-1215, E-Mail: pr@gtlic.com, Web Site: www.gtlic.com (15)

Educate, Eric, J., Fair Isaac Corp, Minneapolis, MN. Tel: (612) 758-5200, E-Mail: info@fairisaac.com, Web Site: www.fairisaac.com (22)

Education Direct, Scranton, PA. Tel: (570) 342-7701, FAX: (570) 961-4851, Web Site: www.educationdirect.com (16)

Education Dynamics LLC, Hoboken, NJ. Tel: (201) 377-3001 (30)

Education Management Corp, Pittsburgh, PA. Tel: (412) 995-7627, Web Site: www.edmc.edu (1)

Educational Coin Co, Highland, NY. Tel: (845) 691-6100, Web Site: www.educationalcoin.com (16)

Educational First Steps, Dallas, TX. Tel: (214) 824-7940), Web Site: educationalfirststeps.org (1)

Educational Insights, Inc, Gardena, CA. Tel: (310) 884-2000, (888) 591-9334, FAX: (310) 886-8850, E-Mail: service@edin.com, Web Site: www.educationalinsights.com (16)

Educational Lists Services Inc, Downers Grove, IL. Tel: (630) 968-1290, FAX: (630) 968-6010, E-Mail: jquinn@educationallist.com, Web Site: www.educationallist.com (24)

Educational Resources, Elgin, IL. Tel: (800) 860-7004, FAX: (800) 610-5005, E-Mail: sales@edresources. com, Web Site: www.educationalresources.com (3)

Educational Testing Service, Princeton, NJ. Tel: (609) 683-2292, FAX: (609) 734-5410, Web Site: www. ets.org (16)

Educators Progress Service Inc, Randolph, WI. Tel: (920) 326-3126, (888) 951-4469, Web Site: www. freeteachingaids.com (17)

EduTrek, Salt Lake City, UT. Tel: (801) 716-3924, Web Site: edutrek.com (16)

Edwards III, Samuel, W., S Wallace Edwards & Sons Inc, Surry, VA. Tel: (757) 294-3121, (800) 290-9213, FAX: (757) 294-5378, E-Mail: info@ virginiatraditions.com, Web Site: www. virginiatraditions.com (4)

Edwards, Ashley, IZEA, Orlando, FL. Tel: (321) 332-6830, Web Site: www.izea.com (20)

Edwards, Barrie, Music Sales Corp, New York, NY. Tel: (212) 254-2100, (800) 431-7187, FAX: (212) 254-2013, E-Mail: info@musicsales.com, Web Site: www.musicsales.com (17)

Edwards, Brenda, TNS Intersearch, White Plains, NY. Tel: (914) 684-6100, FAX: (914) 684-6078, Web Site: www.tns-global.com (30)

Edwards, Chris, Winetasting.com, Napa, CA. Tel: (800) 435-2225, FAX: (707) 252-0268, Web Site: www.geerwade.com (4)

Edwards, Cynthia, Targetbase, Irving, TX. Tel: (972) 506-3400, (800) 446-6603, FAX: (972) 506-3505, E-Mail: info@targetbase.com, Web Site: www. targetbase.com (35)

Edwards, Darrell, HCI Direct, Bensalem, PA. Tel: (215) 244-9600, (888) 765-0062, FAX: (215) 244-0328, Web Site: www.silkies.com (16)

Edwards, V, Gard Communications, Portland, OR. Tel: (503) 221-0100, FAX: (503) 226-4854, Web Site: www.gardcommunications.com (35)

Edwards, Virginia, B., Editorial Projects in Education Inc, Bethesda, MD. Tel: (301) 280-3100, (800) 346-1834, FAX: (301) 280-3250, Web Site: www. edweek.org (17)

S Wallace Edwards & Sons Inc, Surry, VA. Tel: (757) 294-3121, (800) 290-9213, FAX: (757) 294-5378, E-Mail: info@virginiatraditions.com, Web Site: www.virginiatraditions.com (4)

Edwards Sakach, Deborah, American Historic Inns Inc, Dana Point, CA. Tel: (949) 497-2232, (800) 397-4667, FAX: (949) 497-9228, E-Mail: comments@iloveinns.com, Web Site: www. iloveinns.com (17)

Edwards-Pullin, Jan, Publication Fulfillment Svcs, Cypress, CA. Tel: (714) 226-9785, FAX: (714) 226-9733, E-Mail: janpullin@pfsmag.com, Web Site: www.pfsmag.com (20)

Edwin Watts Golf, Fort Walton Beach, FL. Tel: (850) 244-2066, (800) 874-0146, FAX: (850) 244-5217, Web Site: www.edwinwatts.com (11)

Eechambadi, Naras, Quaero Corp, Charlotte, NC. Tel: (877) 570-2199, Web Site: www.quaero.com (22)

Eek, Randy, Advanced Business Teleservices, Inc, Talent, OR. Tel: (800) 866-9220, FAX: (541) 535-6942, E-Mail: randy@abtc.com, Web Site: www. abtc.com (29)

Eenigenburg, Jill, Eenigenburg & Co, Bellevue, WA. Tel: (425) 649-0777, FAX: (425) 649-0719 (35)

Eenigenburg & Co, Bellevue, WA. Tel: (425) 649-0777, FAX: (425) 649-0719 (35)

Effective Marketing Associates, Inc, West Linn, OR. Tel: (503) 657-5859, FAX: (503) 657-5886, Web Site: www.e-m-a.com (20)

Effective Promotions Inc, Fort Johnson, NY. Tel: (518) 274-0291, (888) 467-3514, FAX: (518) 274-0290, Web Site: www.efpromotions.com (16)

Effrem, Debbie, Wood Carvers Supply Inc, Englewood, FL. Tel: (941) 698-0123, (800) 284-6229, FAX: (941) 698-0329, E-Mail: info@ woodcarverssupply.com, Web Site: www. woodcarverssupply.com (9)

Effrem, Timothy, Wood Carvers Supply Inc, Englewood, FL. Tel: (941) 698-0123, (800) 284-6229, FAX: (941) 698-0329, E-Mail: info@ woodcarverssupply.com, Web Site: www. woodcarverssupply.com (9)

Effron, Mark, TitanTV Media, Cedar Rapids, IA. Tel: (319) 365-5597, (800) 365-7629, FAX: (319) 365-5694, E-Mail: mktg@titantv.com, Web Site: www. titantv.com (20)

Efston, Irene, Efstonscience Inc, Toronto, ON. Tel: (416) 787-4581, (888) 777-5255, FAX: (416) 787-5140, E-Mail: info@escience.ca, Web Site: www.e-sci.com (3)

Efston, Nick, Efstonscience Inc, Toronto, ON Canada. Tel: (416) 787-4581, (888) 777-5255, FAX: (416) 787-5140, E-Mail: info@escience.ca, Web Site: www.e-sci.com (3)

Efstonscience Inc, Toronto, ON Canada. Tel: (416) 787-4581, (888) 777-5255, FAX: (416) 787-5140, E-Mail: info@escience.ca, Web Site: www.e-sci. com (3)

Egan, Dean, Roosevelt Paper Co, Mount Laurel, NJ. Tel: (856) 303-4200, (856) 303-4100, (800) 523-3470, FAX: (856) 642-1949, (856) 642-1950, Web Site: www.rooseveltpaper.com (25)

Egan, Michael, Delta Vacations, Fort Lauderdale, FL. Tel: (954) 522-1440, (800) 800-1504, FAX: (954) 468-4765, Web Site: www.deltavacations.com (19)

Egan, Richard, York Label, Omaha, NE. Tel: (402) 829-4594, FAX: (402) 445-4282, Web Site: www. yorklabel.com (27)

Egan, Shane, Phoenix Learning Group Inc, Maryland Heights, MO. Tel: (314) 569-0211, (800) 221-1274, FAX: (314) 569-2834, E-Mail: dealersales@ phoenixlearninggroup.com, Web Site: www. phoenixlearninggroup.com (16)

Egan, Veronica, Intellidyn Corp, Hingham, MA. Tel: (781) 741-5503, (866) 773-5756, FAX: (631) 390-0458, E-Mail: kmf@intellidyn.com, Web Site: www.intellidyn.com (22)

Egger, Terrence C.Z., The Plain Dealer, Cleveland, OH. Tel: (216) 999-5000, FAX: (216) 999-6356, Web Site: www.plaindealer.com (18)

Egger, Terry, St Louis Post-Dispatch, Saint Louis, MO. Tel: (314) 340-8000, (800) 365-0820, FAX: (314) 340-3140, Web Site: www.postnet.com (17)

Eggleston, Jim, Cole Information Services, Omaha, NE. Tel: (800) 403-5894, Web Site: www. coleinformation.com (23)

Eggs by Byrd, Wappapello, MO. Tel: (573) 222-7999, (800) 235-EGGS, FAX: (573) 222-8009, E-Mail: eggsbybyrd@dishmail.net (10)

Ehlers, Christy, Sally Beauty Supply LLC, Denton, TX. Tel: (940) 898-7500, (800) 275-7255, Web Site: www.sallybeauty.com (7)

Ehmann, Elizabeh, Petsky Prunier LLC, New York, NY. Tel: (212) 842-6001, FAX: (212) 842-6039, Web Site: www.petskyprunier.com (14)

Ehmke, L.A., BFS Credit Services Co, Brook Park, OH. Tel: (216) 362-5094, FAX: (216) 362-5236, E-Mail: lupinettijim@bfsusa.com (16)

Ehringer, Ann, KCET, Los Angeles, CA. Tel: (323) 666-6500, FAX: (323) 953-5661, E-Mail: viewerservices@kcet.org, Web Site: www.kcet.org (1)

Ehrlich, Jeffrey, Fulfillment Plus Inc, Holtsville, NY. Tel: (631) 758-8300, FAX: (631) 758-8360, E-Mail: jeff.ehrlich@fulfillmentplusny.com, Web Site: www.fulfillmentplusny.com (28)

Ehrnrooth, Henrik, JP Management Consulting (North America) Inc, New York, NY. Tel: (914) 332-4000, FAX: (914) 332-4411 (30)

Eichinger, Marilynne, Informal Education Products, Milwaukie, OR. Tel: (503) 794-7100, (888) 444-5500, FAX: (503) 794-7111, E-Mail: sales@ museumtour.com, Web Site: www.museumtour.com (11)

Eichten, Ed, Eichten's Hidden Acres, Center City, MN. Tel: (651) 257-4752, FAX: (651) 257-6286, E-Mail: eichtens@frontiernet.net, Web Site: www. specialtycheese.com (4)

Eichten-Carlson, Eileen, Eichten's Hidden Acres, Center City, MN. Tel: (651) 257-4752, FAX: (651) 257-6286, E-Mail: eichtens@frontiernet.net, Web Site: www.specialtycheese.com (4)

Eichten's Hidden Acres, Center City, MN. Tel: (651) 257-4752, FAX: (651) 257-6286, E-Mail: eichtens@frontiernet.net, Web Site: www. specialtycheese.com (4)

A Eicoff & Co, Chicago, IL. Tel: (312) 527-7100, FAX: (312) 527-7192, E-Mail: bill.mccabe@eicoff. com, Web Site: www.eicoff.com (35)

Eidel, Zeneth, Eidel Marketing Communication Corp, Briarcliff Manor, NY. Tel: (914) 762-4985, FAX: (914) 762-4986 (35)

Eidel Marketing Communication Corp, Briarcliff Manor, NY. Tel: (914) 762-4985, FAX: (914) 762-4986 (35)

Eiger, Neil, Projector-Recorder Belt Corp, Oceanside, NY. Tel: (516) 536-5000, (800) 645-2202, FAX: (516) 764-5747, (800) 645-2200, E-Mail: sales@ russellind.com, Web Site: www.russellind.com (3)

800 Call KC, Kansas City, MO. Tel: (816) 231-4321, (800) 722-5554, FAX: (816) 241-2743, E-Mail: sales@call-kc.com, Web Site: www.call-kc.com (29)

800 Response, Burlington, VT. Tel: (802) 860-0378, (800) NEW-SALES, FAX: (800) NEW-ORDER, E-Mail: sales@800response.com, Web Site: www. 800response.com (32)

802 Creative Partners Inc, Bethel, VT. Tel: (802) 234-9755, FAX: (802) 234-6719, E-Mail: info@ 802creative.com, Web Site: www.802creative.com (35)

89 Degrees, Burlington, MA. Tel: (781) 221-5400, Web Site: www.89degrees.com (9)

Eike, Ron, Omaha Steaks Inc, Omaha, NE. Tel: (402) 597-3000, FAX: (402) 597-8252, E-Mail: info@ omahasteaks.com, Web Site: www.omahasteaks. com (4)

Eilenberger's Bakery Inc, Palestine, TX. Tel: (903) 729-2253, (800) 831-2544, FAX: (903) 723-2915, Web Site: www.eilenbergerbakery.com (4)

Eince, Richard, Fowler's Chocolates Inc, Buffalo, NY. Tel: (716) 877-9983, (800) 824-2263, FAX: (716) 877-9959, E-Mail: customerservice@ fowlerschocolates.com, Web Site: www. fowlerschocolates.com (4)

Einhaus, Brian, ClickSpark LLC, San Francisco, CA. Tel: (800) 878-5709, E-Mail: amy@clickspark. com, Web Site: www.clickspark.com (32)

Einhorn, Stephen, Einhorn Associates Inc, Milwaukee, WI. Tel: (414) 453-4488, FAX: (414) 453-4831, Web Site: www.einhornassociates.com (20)

Einhorn, Stephen, I., SECO Financial Services Inc, Mount Laurel, NJ. Tel: (856) 273-0050, (800) 898-SECO, FAX: (856) 273-9228, Web Site: www. secofinancial.com (23)

Einhorn Associates Inc, Milwaukee, WI. Tel: (414) 453-4488, FAX: (414) 453-4831, Web Site: www. einhornassociates.com (20)

Einstein, Peter, Sage Communications, Hudson, MA. Tel: (978) 567-8888, Web Site: www. sagecommunications.com (35)

Eire Direct, Chicago, IL. Tel: (312) 640-4000, FAX: (312) 640-0324, E-Mail: info@eiredirect.com, Web Site: www.eiredirect.com (16)

Eiseman Jr, William, US Tape & Label Corp, Saint Louis, MO. Tel: (314) 824-4444, (800) 569-1906, FAX: (314) 824-4400, E-Mail: harrisonc@ustl. com, Web Site: www.ustl.com (27)

Eisenberg, Geoffrey A., West Marine Inc, Watsonville, CA. Tel: (831) 761-4825, (800) BOATING, (800) 262-8464, FAX: (831) 768-5000, E-Mail: customercare@westmarine.com, Web Site: www. westmarine.com (11)

Eisenberg, Jeff, Mercury Commerce Inc, Westbury, NY. Tel: (212) 307-7001, FAX: (646) 219-3982, E-Mail: contact@mercury-commerce.com, Web Site: www.mercury-commerce.com (22)

Eisenberg, Ken, S., Industrial Marketing Associates, Cranford, NJ. Tel: (908) 276-4256, E-Mail: ken@industrialmarketingassociates.com, Web Site: www.industrialmarketingassociates.com (30)

Eisenbrown, Steven, A., Rockwell Automation, Milwaukee, WI. Tel: (414) 382-2000, FAX: (414) 382-4444, Web Site: www.rockwellautomation.com (16)

Eisenhauer, Elizabeth, Down Home Comforts, Windsor, CT. Tel: (860) 830-0606, (860) 688-3780, Web Site: downhomecomforts.com (8)

Ejupi, Jim, Allstate Motor Club, South Barrington, IL. Tel: (847) 551-2300, (800) 998-8697 (13)

Ekberg, Daniel, Diamond Machining Technology, Marlborough, MA. Tel: (508) 481-5944, (800) 666-4368, FAX: (508) 485-3924, Web Site: www.dmtsharp.com (9)

Ekroth, Chad, CommissionSoup, Madison, SD. Tel: (605) 256-9103, (866) 309-7687, FAX: (605) 256-1522, E-Mail: info@creditsoup.com, Web Site: www.commissionsoup.com (23)

Ekstrom, Lars, Goldsmith Agio Helms, Minneapolis, MN. Tel: (612) 339-0500, FAX: (612) 339-0507, Web Site: www.agio.com (14)

Elam, Mike, Continental Western Group, Des Moines, IA. Tel: (515) 473-3000, (800) 533-0303, FAX: (515) 473-3015, Web Site: www.cwgins.com (15)

Elbel, Tim, Esco Corp, Portland, OR. Tel: (503) 228-2141, FAX: (503) 778-6682, Web Site: www.escocorp.com (16)

Elbert, Lynn, Klahowya Native American & Nature Gift Shop, Bandon, OR. Tel: (541) 347-5099, FAX: (541) 347-4132 (6)

Elbing, Steve, Service Litho Print Inc, Oshkosh, WI. Tel: (920) 231-3060, (800) 544-1493, FAX: (920) 231-1272, E-Mail: slp@service-litho.com (27)

Elcom International Inc, Norwood, MA. Tel: (781) 440-3333, FAX: (781) 762-1540, Web Site: www.elcom.com (22)

Elder, Bonny, Gift Services Inc, Vancouver, WA. Tel: (800) 379-4065, FAX: (360) 699-0597, E-Mail: corpsales@gifttree.com, Web Site: www.gifttree.com (6)

Elderhostel, Inc, Boston, MA. Tel: (617) 426-7788, (800) 454-5678, FAX: (617) 426-2166, Web Site: www.elderhostel.org (1)

Elderly Instruments, Lansing, MI. Tel: (517) 372-7890, (888) 473-5810, FAX: (517) 372-5155, E-Mail: elderly@elderly.com, Web Site: www.elderly.com (5)

Electric Insurance Co, Beverly, MA. Tel: (978) 921-2080, (800) 227-2757, FAX: (978) 524-5583, E-Mail: sales@electricinsurance.com, Web Site: www.electricinsurance.com (15)

Electric Media, New York, NY. Tel: (201) 461-5252 (30)

Electronic Arts Inc, Redwood City, CA. Tel: (650) 628-1500, Web Site: www.ea.com (3)

Electronic Retailing Association, Washington, DC. Tel: (703) 841-1751, FAX: (703) 841-1860, E-Mail: askera@retailing.org, Web Site: www.retailing.org (42)

Electrosonic, Minnetonka, MN. Tel: (952) 931-7500, FAX: (952) 938-9311, E-Mail: information@electrosonic.com, Web Site: www.electrosonic.com (32)

ElectroWarmth Products LLC, Danville, OH. Tel: (740) 599-7222, (800) 990-4622, FAX: (740) 599-6848, E-Mail: sales@electrowarmth.com, Web Site: www.electrowarmth.com (8)

Elemental Scientific LLC, Appleton, WI. Tel: (920) 882-1277, E-Mail: info@elementalscientific.net (9)

Elephant Group Inc, South Plainfield, NJ. Tel: (866) 755-9008, Web Site: www.elephantgroup.com (30)

Eleven Inc, San Francisco, CA. Tel: (415) 707-1111, Web Site: www.eleveninc.com (35)

Edward Elgar Publishing Inc, Northampton, MA. Tel: (413) 584-5551, FAX: (413) 584-9933, E-Mail: sales@e-elgar.com, Web Site: www.e-elgar.com (17)

Eli Journals, Durham, NC. Tel: (585) 203-5248, (800) 223-8720, FAX: (585) 292-4392, Web Site: www.elijournals.com (16)

JS Eliezer Associates Inc, Stamford, CT. Tel: (203) 658-1300 (20)

Elinsky, Sherry, United States Tennis Association, White Plains, NY. Tel: (914) 696-7156, Web Site: www.usta.com (1)

Elisman, Boris, Kensington Technology Group, Redwood Shores, CA. Tel: (650) 572-2700, FAX: (650) 267-2800, Web Site: www.kensington.com (16)

Elite Debit, Sun Valley, CA. Tel: (435) 688-0634 X302, Web Site: www.elitedebit.com (14)

Elite Promotions, Highland Park, IL. Tel: (773) 282-0338, FAX: (773) 282-9081, E-Mail: mike@elitepromotions.com, Web Site: www.elitepromotions.com (33)

Elite Sportswear LP, Reading, PA. Tel: (610) 921-1469, (800) 345-4087, FAX: (610) 921-0208, E-Mail: gkelite@gkelite.com, Web Site: www.gk-elitesportswear.com (2)

Elkhart Cases, Elkhart, IN. Tel: (574) 295-7700, (800) 582-0319, FAX: (574) 295-7761, E-Mail: elkcases@aol.com (2)

Elkin, Robert, Palm Coast Data LLC, Palm Coast, FL. Tel: (386) 445-4662, FAX: (386) 445-2728, Web Site: www.palmcoastd.com (28)

Elkins, Dave, Zumbox, Westlake Village, CA. Tel: (818) 707-7400, Web Site: www.zumbox.com (21)

Elkins, Doris, G&S Packing Co Inc, Weirsdale, FL. Tel: (352) 821-2251, (800) 949-9074, FAX: (352) 821-5000, Web Site: www.gspacking.com (16)

Elkins, James, The Legal Studies Forum, Morgantown, WV. Tel: (304) 293-7354, FAX: (304) 293-6891, E-Mail: jelkins@labs.net (1)

Elkins, Kenneth, J., BMI, Nashville, TN. Tel: (615) 401-2000, (800) 925-8451, FAX: (615) 401-2812, E-Mail: genlic@bmi.com, Web Site: www.bmi.com (1)

Elkon, Idan, Graphnet Inc, New York, NY. Tel: (212) 994-1100, (800) 327-1800, FAX: (212) 994-1188, E-Mail: custsvc@graphnet.com, Web Site: www.graphnet.com (28)

Elkon, Yaakov, Graphnet Inc, New York, NY. Tel: (212) 994-1100, (800) 327-1800, FAX: (212) 994-1188, E-Mail: custsvc@graphnet.com, Web Site: www.graphnet.com (28)

Elks Magazine, Chicago, IL. Tel: (773) 755-4700, (877) 355-7624, FAX: (773) 775-4891, E-Mail: elksmag@elks.org, Web Site: www.elks.org (17)

Ellal, Greg, Professional Cutlery Direct, North Branford, CT. Tel: (203) 871-1000, FAX: (203) 871-1010, E-Mail: terri@cutlery.com, Web Site: www.cutlery.com (4)

Ellen, Rennie, Diamonds By Rennie Ellen, New York, NY. Tel: (212) 869-5525, FAX: (212) 869-5526, Web Site: www.rennieellen.com (6)

Ellerbusch, Michael, Ellerbusch Instrument Co, Cincinnati, OH. Tel: (513) 641-1800, (800) 582-2644, FAX: (513) 641-4360, E-Mail: info@ellerbusch.com, Web Site: www.ellerbusch.com (9)

Ellerbusch Instrument Co, Cincinnati, OH. Tel: (513) 641-1800, (800) 582-2644, FAX: (513) 641-4360, E-Mail: info@ellerbusch.com, Web Site: www.ellerbusch.com (9)

Ellett, Bob, The RYTEX Co, Peru, IN. Tel: (317) 872-8553, (800) 277-5458, FAX: (317) 872-8535, (800) 329-1669, Web Site: www.rytex.com (10)

Ellett, John, n Fusion Group, Austin, TX. Tel: (512) 716-7000, FAX: (512) 716-7001, Web Site: www.nfusion.com (35)

Elliot, Kristina, The Copy Pro, Oradell, NJ. Tel: (201) 986-1080, FAX: (201) 986-1170, E-Mail: thecopypro@aol.com, Web Site: www.thecopypronj.com (39)

Elliot, Robin, Parkinson's Disease Foundation, New York, NY. Tel: (212) 923-4700, (800) 457-6676, FAX: (212) 923-4778, Web Site: www.pdf.org (1)

Elliott, Bob, Aerovox Inc, New Bedford, MA. Tel: (508) 994-9661, (888) AEROVOX, FAX: (508) 995-3000, E-Mail: sales1@aerovox.com, Web Site: www.aerovox.com (16)

Elliott, James, W., Western Graphics, Lemon Grove, CA. Tel: (619) 668-4736, FAX: (619) 668-4742, E-Mail: jim@westerngraphics.org, Web Site: www.westerngraphics.org (21)

Elliott, John, Elliott Marketing Group Inc, Pittsburgh, PA. Tel: (412) 831-1183 (22)

Elliott, Richard, M., Medical Marketing Service Inc, Wood Dale, IL. Tel: (630) 477-1559, (800) 633-5478, FAX: (630) 350-1896, E-Mail: t-nugent@mmslists.com, Web Site: www.mmslists.com (24)

Elliott, Stacy, Weiss, Your Choice Or Mine, San Mateo, CA. Tel: (650) 340-7959, FAX: (650) 340-0449 (16)

Elliott, Thomas, Your Choice Or Mine, San Mateo, CA. Tel: (650) 340-7959, FAX: (650) 340-0449 (16)

Elliott Marketing Group Inc, Pittsburgh, PA. Tel: (412) 831-1183 (22)

Ellis, Arthur, The Soap Factory, Bedford, MA. Tel: (781) 275-8363, E-Mail: soapfac@verizon.net, Web Site: www.alcasoft.com/soapfact/ (7)

Ellis, Lynda, Capitol Concierge Inc, Washington, DC. Tel: (202) 223-4765, FAX: (202) 833-2287, E-Mail: onlineconcierge@capitolconcierge.com, Web Site: www.capitolconcierge.com (16)

Ellis, Marianne, DDB Direct Los Angeles, Los Angeles, CA. Tel: (310) 907-1500, FAX: (310) 907-1990, Web Site: www.ddbla.com (35)

Ellis, Marietta, The Soap Factory, Bedford, MA. Tel: (781) 275-8363, E-Mail: soapfac@verizon.net, Web Site: www.alcasoft.com/soapfact/ (7)

Ellis, Pete, Spa-Finder Inc, New York, NY. Tel: (212) 924-6800, (800) ALL-SPAS, FAX: (212) 924-7240, Web Site: www.spafinder.com (7)

Ellis, Richard, Getty Images, Seattle, WA. Tel: (206) 925-5018, (800) 462-4379, Web Site: www.gettyimages.com (38)

Ellis, Susie, Spa-Finder Inc, New York, NY. Tel: (212) 924-6800, (800) ALL-SPAS, FAX: (212) 924-7240, Web Site: www.spafinder.com (7)

Ellis, Thomas, Priester Pecan Co Inc, Fort Deposit, AL. Tel: (334) 227-4301, Web Site: www.priesters.com (4)

Ellis, Tim, Volkswagen Group of America Inc, Auburn Hills, MI. Tel: (248) 754-5000, FAX: (248) 754-4930, Web Site: www.vw.com (16)

Ellis Systems Corp, Lake Forest, IL. Tel: (847) 371-0200, (800) 253-5547, FAX: (847) 371-0202, E-Mail: tom@ellisfiling.com, Web Site: www.ellismh.com (9)

Ellison, Larry, Oracle Corp, Redwood Shores, CA. Tel: (650) 506-7000, (800) 633-0738, FAX: (650) 506-7200, Web Site: www.oracle.com (16)

Ellsworth, Robert, K., Hook & Hackle Co Inc, Homestead, PA. Tel: (800) 652-8342, FAX: (412) 476-8639, E-Mail: ron@hookhack.com, Web Site: www.hookhack.com (11)

Elmers Products Inc, Westerville, OH. Tel: (614) 985-2600, (800) 848-9400, FAX: (614) 985-2605, E-Mail: comments@elmers.com, Web Site: www.elmers.com (25)

Elmore, Michael, G., Ace Hardware Corp, Oak Brook, IL. Tel: (630) 990-6600, FAX: (630) 990-6838, Web Site: www.acehardware.com (16)

Elmstrom, Paul V., CPC Inc, Babylon, NY. Tel: (631) 661-6779, (800) 621-4414, FAX: (631) 661-6914, E-Mail: cpcus@aol.com, Web Site: www.cpctours.com (19)

Elmwood Spa, Toronto, ON Canada. Tel: (416) 964-4515, Web Site: www.elmwoodspa.com (19)

Eloqua Corp, Vienna, VA. Tel: (416) 864-0440, Web Site: www.eloqua.com (22)

Elouazzani, Kenza, Ken Elo, Montreal, PQ Canada. Tel: (514) 926-6945 (20)

Elseth, Chad, The JM Group Inc, San Antonio, TX. Tel: (210) 637-0404, FAX: (210) 637-0081 (28)

Elsevier, New York, NY. Tel: (212) 989-5800, FAX: (212) 633-3990, Web Site: www.elsevier.com (17)

Elter, Kathy, Walter Karl Inc, Pearl River, NY. Tel: (845) 620-0700, FAX: (845) 620-1885, E-Mail: info@walterkarl.infousa.com, Web Site: www.walterkarl.com (22)

Elverding, Peter, ING, Minneapolis, MN. Tel: (612) 342-7061, (800) 333-6965, FAX: (612) 372-5339, Web Site: www.ing.com (15)

Ely, Alan, UNICEF Canada, Toronto, ON Canada. Tel: (416) 482-4444, (800) 567-4483, FAX: (416) 487-8875, E-Mail: on.secretary@unicef.ca, Web Site: www.unicef.ca (1)

ElZayn, Haytehm, National Administrative Service Co LLC, Dublin, OH. Tel: (614) 358-1500 (29)

Emailogics Inc/Emailbrain, Vancouver, WA. Tel: (866) 873-3019, Web Site: www.emailbrain.com (20)

Emailvision, New York, NY. Tel: (212) 257-6018, Web Site: www.emailvision.com (22)

Emanuelli, Joe, Mergent Inc, Fort Mill, SC. Tel: (800) 342-5647, Web Site: www.mergent.com (14)

eMarketing Strategy Group, New York, NY. Tel: (212) 679-6486, Web Site: www.ruthstevens.com (20)

Embassy Digital, Oakville, ON Canada. Tel: (905) 829-9969, (888) 477-8629, FAX: (905) 829-9429, E-Mail: info@embassydigital.com, Web Site: www.embassydigital.com (27)

Emberson, Dick, America's Call Center, Jacksonville, FL. Tel: (904) 224-2000, (800) 598-2580, FAX: (904) 737-1107, E-Mail: info@webcallusa.com, Web Site: www.webcallusa.com (29)

Embke, Tia, NBI Inc, Eau Claire, WI. Tel: (715) 835-8525, Web Site: www.nbi-sems.com (1)

Emblem & Badge Inc, Johnston, RI. Tel: (401) 365-1265, (800) 875-5444, FAX: (401) 365-1263, E-Mail: sales@recognition.com, Web Site: www.recognition.com (6)

Embrace Home Loans, Middletown, RI. Tel: (401) 846-3100, Web Site: www.afsitfinance.com (14)

Embrey, Michael T., FunME Events, Dekalb, IL. Tel: (800) 386-6321, FAX: (815) 787-3100, E-Mail: funMEevents@aol.com, Web Site: www.funMEevents.com (20)

Emergency Essentials Inc, Orem, UT. Tel: (801) 222-9596, FAX: (801) 222-9598, E-Mail: webmaster@beprepared.com, Web Site: www.beprepared.com (16)

Emerging Marketing, Columbus, OH. Tel: (614) 923-6000 X229, FAX: (614) 424-6200, E-Mail: chris@360em.com, Web Site: www.emergingmarketing.com (35)

Emerson, Paul, Ingenix, Reston, VA. Tel: (571) 521-7661, (800) 765-6713, FAX: (571) 521-7237, E-Mail: inform@ingenix.com, Web Site: www.ingenix.com (32)

Emerson Ecologics, Bedford, NH. Tel: (603) 656-9778 (7)

Emery Jr., Sidney, W., MTS Systems Corp, Eden Prairie, MN. Tel: (952) 937-4000, (800) 328-2255, FAX: (952) 937-4515, E-Mail: info@mts.com, Web Site: www.mts.com (16)

Emery, Jack, ESA - A Sandy Alexander Co, Clifton, NJ. Tel: (973) 470-8100, Web Site: www.tbccolor.com (32)

Emfluence, Kansas City, MO. Tel: (816) 472-4455, Web Site: www.emfluence.com (21)

Emigrant Savings Bank, New York, NY. Tel: (212) 850-4521, (800) EMIGRANT, FAX: (212) 850-4372, Web Site: www.emigrant.com (14)

Emisare, Greensboro, NC. Tel: (336) 378-0510, Web Site: www.emisare.com (32)

Emkes, Mark, Bridgestone/Firestone North American Tire LLC, Nashville, TN. Tel: (615) 937-1000, (800) 543-7522, FAX: (615) 937-3721, Web Site: www.bridgestonetire.com (16)

Emley, Fredi Thorndike, de Emley & Associates Inc, San Juan Capistrano, CA. Tel: (949) 493-5117, FAX: (949) 493-6382 (33)

Emma, James, P., Nova Communications Inc, Geneva, IL. Tel: (630) 377-1889, (800) 816-6682, FAX: (630) 377-1899, E-Mail: sales@novacominc.com, Web Site: www.novacominc.com (35)

Emmons, Linda, Everfast Inc, Kennett Square, PA. Tel: (610) 444-9700, Web Site: www.calicocorners.com (8)

Emond, Gary, GRP Funding LLC, Springfield, MA. Tel: (877) 571-7999, Web Site: www.grpfunding.com (14)

Emonds, Lisa, Fire Mountain Gems, Grants Pass, OR. Tel: (541) 956-7890, (800) 423-2319, (800) 355-2137, FAX: (541) 470-GEMS, E-Mail: questions@firemtn.com, Web Site: www.firemtn.com (16)

Emory-Walker, Patricia, tangerine direct - a service of archer malmo, Memphis, TN. Tel: (901) 523-2000, Web Site: www.archermalmo.com (35)

Emperor Clock LLC, Amherst, VA. Tel: (800) 642-0011, FAX: (434) 946-1420, E-Mail: emperor@emperorclock.com, Web Site: www.emperorclock.com (16)

Empire Blue Cross & Blue Shield, New York, NY. Tel: (212) 476-1000, (877) 476-7111, FAX: (212) 476-1281, Web Site: www.empireblue.com (15)

Empire Burbank Studios, Burbank, CA. Tel: (818) 840-1400, FAX: (818) 567-1062 (32)

Empire City Casino at Yonkers Raceway, Yonkers, NY. Tel: (914) 968-4200, Web Site: www.empirecitygaming.com (19)

Empire Coffee & Tea Co, New York, NY. Tel: (212) 268-1220, (800) 262-5908, E-Mail: owners@empirecoffeetea.com, Web Site: www.empirecoffeetea.com (4)

Empire Imports Inc, Amherst, MA. Tel: (413) 256-4917, (800) 544-4744, FAX: (413) 256-4645, E-Mail: info@empireimports.com, Web Site: www.empireimports.com (34)

Empire Scientific, Deer Park, NY. Tel: (631) 595-9206, (800) 645-7220, FAX: (631) 595-9384, (800) 343-5733, E-Mail: sales@empirescientific.com, Web Site: www.empirescientific.com (16)

Employers Group, El Segundo, CA. Tel: (800) 748-8484, Web Site: www.employersgroup.com (20)

EMPLOYERS Insurance, Reno, NV. Tel: (775) 327-2677, Web Site: www.employers.com (15)

Employment Publishing Inc, Wayne, PA. Tel: (610) 975-4539, FAX: (610) 687-7860, E-Mail: jfanning@employment911.com (17)

Emrick, John, Norm Thompson Outfitters Inc, Hillsboro, OR. Tel: (503) 614-4600, (800) 547-1160, FAX: (503) 614-4599, Web Site: www.normthompson.com (2)

Emslie, Scott, G., Sunshine Glassworks Ltd, Buffalo, NY. Tel: (716) 668-2918, (800) 828-7159, FAX: (716) 668-2932, E-Mail: info23@sunshineglass.com, Web Site: www.sunshineglass.com (11)

En ESPANOL Publishing Group LLC, Beverly Hills, CA. Tel: (310) 248-2680 (17)

Encircle, Miami, FL. Tel: (305) 592-7800, FAX: (305) 470-2660, E-Mail: merchantservices@encirclepayments.com, Web Site: www.insta-check.com (14)

Enco Manufacturing Co, Fernley, NV. Tel: (775) 788-7175, (800) 873-3626, FAX: (800) 965-5857, E-Mail: milanesp@use-enco.com, Web Site: www.use-enco.com (9)

Encore Marketing International, Lanham, MD. Tel: (301) 459-8020, (800) 846-9398, FAX: (301) 731-0525, E-Mail: customerservice@encoremarketing.com, Web Site: www.encoremarketing.com (16)

Encyclopaedia Britannica Inc, Chicago, IL. Tel: (312) 347-7319, (800) 323-1229, FAX: (312) 347-7225 (17)

Ende, John, Argent Trading LLC, New York, NY. Tel: (212) 697-8800, FAX: (212) 697-8606, Web Site: www.Argenttrading.com (16)

Endsley, Terry, M., Navistar, Warrenville, IL. Tel: (630) 753-5804, (800) 448-7825, FAX: (630) 753-2303, Web Site: www.navistar.com (16)

Energizer Battery Co Inc, Saint Louis, MO. Tel: (314) 985-2000, (800) 383-7323, FAX: (636) 733-4001, Web Site: www.energizer.com (16)

Enerpac, Menomonee Falls, WI. Tel: (262) 781-6600, (800) 433-2766, FAX: (262) 781-1028, Web Site: www.enerpac.com (16)

Enertex Marketing, New York, NY. Tel: (212) 532-3115, FAX: (212) 532-1878, E-Mail: info@enertexmarketing.com, Web Site: www.enertexmarketing.com (22)

Eng, Suzanne, Smithsonian Enterprises, New York, NY. Tel: (212) 916-1300, (800) 766-2149, FAX: (212) 490-0058, E-Mail: email@simag.si.edu, Web Site: www.smithsonianmag.com (17)

Engagenextgen LLC, Mound, MN. Tel: (952) 905-4474 (20)

Engauge Direct, Atlanta, GA. Tel: (404) 601-4332, (804) 363-5715, Web Site: www.engauge.com (35)

Engel, Dorothy, Seybold Publications, Gilbertsville, PA. Tel: (610) 327-3958, (888) 544-7104, FAX: (888) 463-4814, E-Mail: molly@thejossgroup, Web Site: www.seyboldreports.com (17)

Engel, Geraldine, American Civil Liberties Union Foundation, New York, NY. Tel: (212) 549-2600, Web Site: www.aclu.org (1)

Engel, Jannie, The New Yorker Magazine, New York, NY. Tel: (212) 286-5400, FAX: (212) 286-5735, E-Mail: alatia_bradley@newyorker.com, Web Site: www.newyorker.com (17)

Engel, John, D., Donna Salyers' Fabulous-Furs, Covington, KY. Tel: (859) 291-3300, (800) 848-4650, E-Mail: abell@fabulousfurs.com, Web Site: fabulousfurs.com (2)

Engel, John, J., WESCO, Pittsburgh, PA. Tel: (412) 454-2200, (800) 343-1201, E-Mail: info@wesco.com, Web Site: www.wescodist.com (16)

Engel, Laura, Angel Sales Inc, Chicago, IL. Tel: (773) 883-8858, FAX: (773) 883-8889, E-Mail: info@angelsales.com, Web Site: www.angelsales.com (31)

Engel, Robert, Angel Sales Inc, Chicago, IL. Tel: (773) 883-8858, FAX: (773) 883-8889, E-Mail: info@angelsales.com, Web Site: www.angelsales.com (31)

Engelhorn, Lorinda, American Horse Products, San Juan Capistrano, CA. Tel: (949) 248-5300, (800) 500-0799, FAX: (949) 248-5305, E-Mail: zjim@sbcglobal.net, Web Site: www.americanhorseproducts.com (11)

Engh, Rohn, PhotoSource International, Osceola, WI. Tel: (715) 248-3800, X27, (800) 223-3860, FAX: (715) 248-3800, E-Mail: info@photosource.com, Web Site: www.photosource.com (38)

Engineering Services & Products Co, South Windsor, CT. Tel: (860) 528-1119, (800) 835-7877, FAX: (800) 457-8887, Web Site: www.teksupply.com (9)

England, Andrew, J., MillerCoors LLC, Chicago, IL. Tel: (800) 645-5376, Web Site: www.millercoors.com (4)

Englander, Robert, Belvoir Media Group LLC, Norwalk, CT. Tel: (203) 857-3100, (800) 424-7887, FAX: (203) 857-3103, E-Mail: customer_service@belvoir.com, Web Site: www.belvoir.com (17)

English, Brittany, Columbia Books, Inc, Bethesda, MD. Tel: (202) 464-1662, (888) 265-0600, FAX: (202) 464-1775, E-Mail: info@columbiabooks.com, Web Site: www.columbiabooks.com (24)

English, Catherine, American Library Association-Publishing Services, Chicago, IL. Tel: (312) 944-6780, (800) 545-2433, FAX: (312) 280-4380, Web Site: www.ala.org (1)

English, Glenn, National Rural Electric Cooperative Association, Arlington, VA. Tel: (703) 907-5500, FAX: (703) 907-5528, Web Site: www.nreca.org (1)

English, Jeffrey, Empire Scientific, Deer Park, NY. Tel: (631) 595-9206, (800) 645-7220, FAX: (631) 595-9384, (800) 343-5733, E-Mail: sales@empirescientific.com, Web Site: www.empirescientific.com (16)

English, Katherine, The Houston Chronicle, Houston, TX. Tel: (713) 362-7171, Web Site: www.houstonchronicle.com (31)

English, William, Scope 1, Kalamazoo, MI. Tel: (269) 323-1333, Web Site: www.scope 1.com (16)

Engstrom, Erik, Elsevier, New York, NY. Tel: (212) 989-5800, FAX: (212) 633-3990, Web Site: www.elsevier.com (17)

Engstrom, John, Database Marketing Group Inc, Irvine, CA. Tel: (714) 727-0800, Web Site: www.dbmgroup.com (35)

Enke, Roger, Action-AD, Bettendorf, IA. Tel: (563) 355-9581, FAX: (563) 355-9586 (35)

ENMAX Corp, Calgary, AB Canada. Tel: (403) 514-3122, Web Site: www.enmax.com (9)

Ennis Inc, Midlothian, TX. Tel: (972) 775-9801, (800) 962-0944, FAX: (800) 645-8339, Web Site: www.ennis.com (16)

Enos, Jim, Pennwell Publishing, Tulsa, OK. Tel: (918) 835-3161, (800) 331-4463, E-Mail: headquarters@pennwell.com, Web Site: www.pennwell.com (17)

Ensign, Chris, AT&T Language Line Services, Monterey, CA. Tel: (831) 648-5861, (877) 886-3885, FAX: (800) 821-9040, E-Mail: wecare@languageline.com, Web Site: www.languageline.com (29)

Ensor, P., Richard, Institutional Investor Inc, New York, NY. Tel: (212) 224-3300, FAX: (212) 224-3592, Web Site: www.institutionalinvestor.com (17)

Entergy, New Orleans, LA. Tel: (504) 576-4000, (800) ENTERGY, FAX: (504) 576-4428, Web Site: www.entergy.com (16)

Enterprex International Corp, Arcadia, CA. Tel: (626) 256-1444, FAX: (626) 256-1404, E-Mail: premium@enterprex.com, Web Site: www.enterprex.com (16)

Enterprise Ireland, New York, NY. Tel: (212) 371-3600, FAX: (212) 371-6398, Web Site: www.enterprise-ireland.com (16)

Enterprise Rent-A-Car, Saint Louis, MO. Tel: (314) 512-5000, Web Site: www.enterprise.com (19)

Carol Enters List Co Inc, Fairfax, VA. Tel: (703) 425-0052, FAX: (703) 425-0056, E-Mail: listmanagement@carolenters.com, Web Site: www.carolenterslists.com (23)

Entertainment Music Marketing Corp, Baldwin, NY. Tel: (631) 243-0600, FAX: (631) 243-0605, E-Mail: emmcmusic@aol.com, Web Site: www.emmcmusic.com (16)

Entertainment Publications Inc, Troy, MI. Tel: (248) 404-1000, (888) 231-SAVE, FAX: (248) 404-1915, Web Site: www.entertainment.com (31)

ENTIERA, Minneapolis, MN. Tel: (866) 387-4271, Web Site: www.entiera.com (22)

Entrepreneur Media Inc, Irvine, CA. Tel: (949) 261-2325, (800) 274-6229, FAX: (949) 261-0234, Web Site: www.entrepreneur.com (17)

Entrepreneur Partners, Philadelphia, PA. Tel: (267) 322-7000, Web Site: www.epfunds.com (14)

The Envelope Connection Inc, Chicago, IL. Tel: (773) 275-3500, Web Site: www.artofbarter.com/EnvelopeConnectionProfile.html (28)

The Envelope Man Plus, Kansas City, MO. Tel: (816) 474-5555, (800) 597-1099, FAX: (816) 221-3700, E-Mail: sales@envelopeman.com, Web Site: www.envelopeman.com (16)

Envelope Manufacturers Association, Alexandria, VA. Tel: (703) 739-2200, FAX: (703) 739-2209, Web Site: www.envelope.org (1)

Envelope Products Group, Springfield, MA. Tel: (413) 736-7211, (888) 715-6641, (800) 628-9265, FAX: (413) 787-9749, E-Mail: envelopes@meadwestvaco.com, Web Site: www.meadwestvaco.com/envelopeprod.nsf (26)

Environmental Defense Fund, Washington, DC. Tel: (202) 387-3500 (1)

Environmental Law Institute, Washington, DC. Tel: (202) 939-3800, FAX: (202) 939-3868, E-Mail: law@eli.org, Web Site: www.eli.org (17)

Environmental Research Associates, Princeton, NJ. Tel: (609) 683-4860, FAX: (609) 683-8398 (30)

Envision, Newport, RI. Tel: (401) 619-1500, (800) 524-8238, FAX: (401) 619-0130, E-Mail: envision@att.net, Web Site: www.envision-stock.com (38)

Eperformax Inc, Thompsons Station, TN. Tel: (901) 751-4800, (888) 384-7004, FAX: (901) 751-4805, E-Mail: info0609@eperformax.com, Web Site: www.eperformax.com (29)

Epic Marketing Solutions, Halifax, NS Canada. Tel: (902) 455-5100, Web Site: www.epicmarketing.ca (22)

Epic Media Group, New York, NY. Tel: (212) 308-8509, Web Site: www.epicadvertising.com (30)

Epic Research LLC, Greenville, DE. Tel: (302) 467-5445, Web Site: www.epicresearch.net (20)

Epilepsy Foundation, Landover, MD. Tel: (301) 459-3700, (800) 332-1000, FAX: (301) 577-9056, E-Mail: postmaster@efa.org, Web Site: www.efa.org (1)

Episcopal Relief & Development, New York, NY. Tel: (212) 922-5129, Web Site: www.er-d.org (1)

Epp, Helmut, P., DePaul University, Chicago, IL. Tel: (312) 362-8000, (800) 4-DEPAUL, FAX: (312) 362-6639, E-Mail: skelly@wppost.depaul.edu, Web Site: www.depaul.edu (41)

Epperson, Christine, The Virginia Diner Inc, Wakefield, VA. Tel: (757) 899-6213, (888) 823-4637, FAX: (757) 899-2281, E-Mail: vadiner@vadiner.com, Web Site: www.vadiner.com (4)

Epperson, Will, MAX Federal Credit Union, Montgomery, AL. Tel: (334) 260-2600, (800) 776-6776, FAX: (334) 270-0921, Web Site: www.mymax.com (14)

Eppinger, Nick, AAA Mid-Atlantic Insurance Groups, Wilmington, DE. Tel: (302) 299-4700, (800) 451-5921, FAX: (215) 864-5486, Web Site: www.aaamidatlantic.com (15)

Epps, Monique, Van, Booth Michigan, Grand Rapids, MI. Tel: (616) 222-5824, FAX: (616) 222-5318, Web Site: www.boothnewspapers.com (17)

Epsilon, Irving, TX. Tel: (972) 582-9600, (800) 309-0505, FAX: (972) 582-9700, E-Mail: info@epsilon.com, Web Site: www.epsilon.com (22)

Epson America, Long Beach, CA. Tel: (562) 981-3840, (800) 873-7766, FAX: (562) 290-5220, Web Site: www.epson.com (10)

Epstein, Arthur, Antares Information Tech, Chadds Ford, PA. Tel: (631) 234-5700, (800) 330-2579, FAX: (631) 234-5472, E-Mail: steve@antares-iti.com, Web Site: www.antares-iti.com (21)

Epstein, Barbara, Nyrev Inc, New York, NY. Tel: (212) 757-8070, FAX: (212) 333-5374, E-Mail: mail@nybooks.com, Web Site: www.nybooks.com (17)

Epstein, David, National Association of Professional Insurance Agents, Alexandria, VA. Tel: (703) 836-9340, FAX: (703) 836-1279, E-Mail: web@pianet.org, Web Site: www.pianet.com (1)

Epstein, David, Novartis Pharmaceuticals Corp, East Hanover, NJ. Tel: (862) 778-6914, FAX: (973) 781-8119, Web Site: www.pharma.us.novartis.com (7)

Epstein, John, Direct Results, West Springfield, MA. Tel: (413) 732-8310, FAX: (413) 732-8361 (21)

Epton, Terrence, J., USA Hosts, San Francisco, CA. Tel: (415) 695-8000, (800) 368-4678, FAX: (415) 986-3668, Web Site: www.usahosts.com (19)

Equifax, Atlanta, GA. Tel: (248) 603-3000, (888) 202-4025, FAX: (248) 603-3085, Web Site: www.equifax.com (23)

Equifax Credit Information Services Inc, Atlanta, GA. Tel: (404) 885-8000, (800) 685-5000, FAX: (404) 885-8988, Web Site: www.equifax.com (20)

Equifax Database Marketing, Wakefield, MA. Tel: (781) 246-0040, (800) 660-5125, FAX: (781) 246-3720, E-Mail: monica.baker@equifax.com (22)

Equifax Marketing Services, Atlanta, GA. Tel: (800) 466-5897, Web Site: www.equifax.com/consumer/marketing (23)

Equitable Life & Casualty Insurance Co, Salt Lake City, UT. Tel: (801) 579-3400, FAX: (801) 579-3789, Web Site: www.equilife.com (15)

Equity Management Inc, San Diego, CA. Tel: (858) 558-2500, FAX: (858) 558-2547, Web Site: www.equitymanagementinc.com (20)

Equity Residential Properties, Chicago, IL. Tel: (312) 474-1300, FAX: (312) 474-8703, E-Mail: mgraycraddock@eqr.com, Web Site: www.eqr.com (20)

Erdahl, Randy, Clario Analytics, Eden Prairie, MN. Tel: (952) 653-0980, (866) 849-3341, FAX: (952) 653-5900, E-Mail: sales@clarioanalytics.com, Web Site: www.clarioanalytics.com (20)

Erdman, Amy, Cliggott Publishing Co, Norwalk, CT. Tel: (203) 662-6400, (203) 661-0600, FAX: (203) 662-6420, Web Site: www.cmp.com (17)

Erdo, Peter, Graves Lapidary Co, Pompano Beach, FL. Tel: (954) 960-0300, (800) 327-9103, FAX: (954) 960-0301, E-Mail: sales@gravescompany.com, Web Site: www.gravescompany.com (9)

Erdo, Victoria, Graves Lapidary Co, Pompano Beach, FL. Tel: (954) 960-0300, (800) 327-9103, FAX: (954) 960-0301, E-Mail: sales@gravescompany.com, Web Site: www.gravescompany.com (9)

Erdos & Morgan Inc, Syosset, NY. Tel: (516) 935-6959, FAX: (516) 935-4040, E-Mail: info@erdosmorgan.com, Web Site: www.erdosmorgan.com (30)

Erehig, Dick, Kaye-Smith, Renton, WA. Tel: (425) 228-8600, (800) 822-9987, FAX: (425) 226-4312, E-Mail: info@kayesmith.com, Web Site: www.kayesmith.com (21)

Erickson, Jodie, Power Music, Salt Lake City, UT. Tel: (801) 292-2418, (800) 777-BEAT, FAX: (801) 292-2462, Web Site: www.powermusic.com (16)

Erickson, Peter H., Hall-Erickson Inc, Westmont, IL. Tel: (630) 434-7779, FAX: (630) 434-1216 (16)

Erickson, Terri, L., J Peterman Co, Lexington, KY. Tel: (888) 647-2555, FAX: (859) 254-0869, Web Site: www.jpeterman.com (5)

Erickson, Tom, Northern Tool & Equipment Inc, Burnsville, MN. Tel: (952) 894-9510, (800) 221-0516, FAX: (952) 894-1020, Web Site: www.northerntool.com (16)

Erikson, Gordon, M., Smith & Hawken Ltd, Novato, CA. Tel: (415) 506-3700, (800) 940-1170, FAX: (415) 506-3900, Web Site: www.smithandhawken.com (8)

Erikson, John, R., American Capital, Bethesda, MD. Tel: (301) 951-6122, FAX: (301) 654-6714, E-Mail: info@americancapital.com, Web Site: www.americancapital.com (15)

Erkes, Ronald D., Ronald D Erkes & Associates, Glencoe, IL. Tel: (847) 835-1867, FAX: (847) 835-9233 (35)

Ronald D Erkes & Associates, Glencoe, IL. Tel: (847) 835-1867, FAX: (847) 835-9233 (35)

Erlandson, Barbara, Erlandson Associates, Leesburg, VA. Tel: (703) 669-0889, E-Mail: bgerlandso@aol.com (20)

Erlandson, Greg, Our Sunday Visitor Publishing, Huntington, IN. Tel: (260) 356-8400, (800) 348-2440, FAX: (260) 356-8472, E-Mail: athomas@osv.com, Web Site: www.osv.com (17)

Erlandson Associates, Leesburg, VA. Tel: (703) 669-0889, E-Mail: bgerlandso@aol.com (20)

Erlewine, Dan, Stewart-MacDonald, Athens, OH. Tel: (740) 592-3021, (800) 848-2273, FAX: (740) 593-7922, E-Mail: hostetler@stewmac.com, Web Site: www.stewmac.com (16)

Erlich, Gary, Erlich Communications, San Diego, CA. Tel: (858) 780-9595, FAX: (858) 780-2922, E-Mail: gde@erlcomm.com (32)

Erlich Communications, San Diego, CA. Tel: (858) 780-9595, FAX: (858) 780-2922, E-Mail: gde@erlcomm.com (32)

Erna, Christine, J., New England Direct Marketing Association, Wellesley Hills, MA. Tel: (781) 237-1366, FAX: (781) 431-8118, E-Mail: info@nedma.com, Web Site: www.nedma.com (40)

Ernan Roman Direct Marketing Corp, Little Neck, NY. Tel: (718) 225-4151, FAX: (718) 225-4889, E-Mail: ernan@erdm.com, Web Site: www.erdm.com (20)

Ernst, Connie, P., Stewart Enterprises Inc, Jefferson, LA. Tel: (504) 729-1400, (800) 535-6017, FAX: (504) 729-1984, Web Site: www.stewartenterprises.com (16)

Ernst, Roger, Case Design Corp, Telford, PA. Tel: (215) 703-0130, (800) 847-4176, FAX: (215) 703-0139, E-Mail: sales@casedesigncorp.com, Web Site: www.casedesigncorp.com (34)

Ernst & Young LLP, New York, NY. Tel: (212) 773-6146, FAX: (312) 879-4000, Web Site: www.ey.com (20)

Erskine, John, Creative Awards by Lane, Elk Grove Village, IL. Tel: (847) 593-7700, FAX: (847) 593-1155, E-Mail: info@creativeawardsbylane.com, Web Site: www.creativeawardsbylane.com (33)

Ertel, Louis, Foote-Jones/Illinois Gear, Aberdeen, SD. Tel: (605) 225-0360, FAX: (605) 225-0567, Web Site: www.footejones.com (16)

Erwin, Dave, National Envelope Corp, Ennis, TX. Tel: (800) 696-0409, Web Site: www.nationalenvelope.com (26)

Erwin, Richard, Ames Specialty Packaging & Digital Print, Somerville, MA. Tel: (617) 776-3360, (800) 521-2637, FAX: (617) 623-8895, E-Mail: info@amespage.com, Web Site: www.amespage.com (26)

Erwin, Tanyalee, The News Tribune, Tacoma, WA. Tel: (253) 597-8742, E-Mail: reader.representative@thenewstribune.com, Web Site: www.thenewstribune.com (17)

Esco Corp, Portland, OR. Tel: (503) 228-2141, FAX: (503) 778-6682, Web Site: www.escocorp.com (16)

Escoe, Steven, Facts 'n Figures, Sherman Oaks, CA. Tel: (661) 222-2278, (818) 986-6600, FAX: (661) 222-2287, Web Site: www.factsnfiguresinc.com (30)

Escort Inc, West Chester, OH. Tel: (513) 870-8500, (800) 964-3138, FAX: (513) 870-8509, E-Mail: sales@escortradar.com, Web Site: www.escortradar.com (16)

Eshelman, David, DeLorme Mapping, Yarmouth, ME. Tel: (207) 846-7000, (800) 561-5105, FAX: (207) 846-7051, E-Mail: caleb.mason@delorme.com, Web Site: www.delorme.com (3)

ESignal, Hayward, CA. Tel: (510) 266-6000, Web Site: www.esignal.com (14)

Eskin, Elliot B., Pro/Phase Marketing Inc, Eden Prairie, MN. Tel: (952) 974-1100, (866) 876-2737, FAX: (952) 974-7874, E-Mail: inquiry@repeatrewards.com, Web Site: www.ppmi.com (21)

Esler, Susan, B., Ashland Inc, Covington, KY. Tel: (859) 815-3333, Web Site: www.ashland.com (16)

Espinola, Jill, Morgan Kaufmann Publishers Inc, Burlington, MA. Tel: (781) 313-4700, E-Mail: order@mkp.com, Web Site: www.mkp.com (17)

Esposito, Chris, Four Seasons Sunrooms, Holbrook, NY. Tel: (631) 563-4000, FAX: (631) 563-4010 (8)

Esposito, Joe, Four Seasons Sunrooms, Holbrook, NY. Tel: (631) 563-4000, FAX: (631) 563-4010 (8)

Esprit Line Co Ltd - USA, Greenwich, CT. Tel: (203) 629-5124 (16)

Esquire Magazine, New York, NY. Tel: (212) 649-2000, (800) 925-0485, FAX: (212) 265-0938, E-Mail: esquire@hearst.com, Web Site: www.esquire.com (17)

ESRI, Redlands, CA. Tel: (909) 793-2853, Web Site: www.esri.com (22)

Esrock Partners, Orland Park, IL. Tel: (708) 349-8400, (888) ESROCKS, FAX: (708) 349-8471, E-Mail: clay@esrock.com, Web Site: www.esrock.com (35)

Esselte Americas, Melville, NY. Tel: (631) 675-5700, (800) 645-6051, FAX: (631) 622-1970, Web Site: www.curtis.com (16)

Essence Communications Inc, New York, NY. Tel: (212) 522-1212, FAX: (212) 921-5173, Web Site: www.essence.com (17)

Essential Products Co Inc, New York, NY. Tel: (212) 344-4288 (7)

Esser, Frank, Vivendi, New York, NY. Tel: (212) 572-7000, FAX: (212) 572-1080, Web Site: www.vivendi.com (16)

Esser, Patrick, J., Cox Communications, Atlanta, GA Canada. Tel: (404) 843-5000, FAX: (404) 269-2243, Web Site: www.cox.com (16)

Esser, Paul, The Wisconsin Cheeseman, Sun Prairie, WI. Tel: (608) 837-5166, (800) 698-1721, FAX: (608) 837-5493, Web Site: www.wisconsincheeseman.com (4)

Essex Printing Co Inc, Croton On Hudson, NY. Tel: (212) 688-4720, (800) 443-9113, FAX: (212) 308-2764, E-Mail: essexptg@aol.com, Web Site: www.essex-printing.com (27)

Estabrook, A.G., Fred B Estabrook Co Inc, New Hampton, NH. Tel: (603) 744-6316 (21)

Fred B Estabrook Co Inc, New Hampton, NH. Tel: (603) 744-6316 (21)

Estee Lauder Inc, New York, NY. Tel: (212) 572-4200, (866) 467-7363, FAX: (212) 572-3942, Web Site: www.esteelauder.com (16)

Estee Marketing Group Inc, New Rochelle, NY. Tel: (914) 235-7080, FAX: (914) 235-6518, E-Mail: info@esteemarketing.com, Web Site: www.esteemarketing.com (24)

Estepa, Jim, Journeys, Nashville, TN. Tel: (615) 367-8000, (888) 324-6356, FAX: (615) 367-8123, Web Site: www.journeys.com (2)

Esterly, Diana, E., Speed-Mat, Biddeford, ME. Tel: (207) 294-4358, (800) 882-7017, FAX: (207) 882-9279, E-Mail: info@speedmat.com, Web Site: www.speed-mat.com (16)

Esterly, Harry, F., Speed-Mat, Biddeford, ME. Tel: (207) 294-4358, (800) 882-7017, FAX: (207) 882-9279, E-Mail: info@speedmat.com, Web Site: www.speed-mat.com (16)

Esterow, Judith, Art News Magazine, New York, NY. Tel: (212) 398-1690, FAX: (212) 819-0394, E-Mail: info@artnews.com, Web Site: www.artnewsonline.com (17)

Esterow, Milton, Art News Magazine, New York, NY. Tel: (212) 398-1690, FAX: (212) 819-0394, E-Mail: info@artnews.com, Web Site: www.artnewsonline.com (17)

Estes Ph.D., Carroll, L., National Committee to Preserve Social Security & Medicare, Washington, DC. Tel: (202) 216-0420, (800) 966-1935, FAX: (202) 216-0446, E-Mail: kreard@ncpssm.org, Web Site: www.ncpssm.org (1)

Estes Industries, Penrose, CO. Tel: (719) 372-6565, FAX: (719) 372-3419, Web Site: www.estesrockets.com (11)

Estka, Robert J., Special Markets Sales Co, Indianapolis, IN. Tel: (317) 595-6587, FAX: (317) 595-9853, E-Mail: info@specialmkts.com, Web Site: www.specialmkts.com (33)

Esto Photographics Inc, Mamaroneck, NY. Tel: (914) 698-4060, FAX: (914) 698-1033, E-Mail: esto@esto.com, Web Site: www.esto.com (38)

eStock Photo, Long Island City, NY. Tel: (212) 689-5580, (800) 284-3399, FAX: (212) 545-1185, E-Mail: sales@estockphoto.com, Web Site: www.estockphoto.com (38)

Estok, Marcy, SAE International, Warrendale, PA. Tel: (724) 776-4841, Web Site: www.sae.org (6)

eTargetMedia.com Inc, Coconut Creek, FL. Tel: (954) 480-8470, (888) 805-3282, FAX: (954) 480-8489, E-Mail: info@etargetmedia.com, Web Site: www.etargetmedia.com (32)

Etchworld, Hawthorne, NJ. Tel: (973) 423-4002, (800) 872-3458, FAX: (973) 427-8823, Web Site: www.etchworld.com (11)

Etech Inc, Lufkin, TX. Tel: (936) 633-9333, Web Site: www.effectiveteleservices.com (29)

Ethel M Chocolates Inc, Henderson, NV. Tel: (702) 458-8864, (800) 471-0352, FAX: (800) 392-2587, E-Mail: chocolatier@ethelm.com, Web Site: www.ethelm.com (4)

Ethell, Judy, A., Bearingpoint Inc, Montvale, NJ. Tel: (201) 307-7000, FAX: (201) 505-3765, Web Site: www.bearingpoint.com (14)

Ethen, Troy, Taymark Inc, White Bear Lake, MN. Tel: (651) 426-1667, (800) 479-2043, FAX: (651) 426-0275, Web Site: www.mninternational.com (1)

Ethier, Mark, Improvements, West Chester, OH. Tel: (216) 591-9148, (800) 634-9484, FAX: (216) 831-4026, Web Site: www.improvementscatalog.com (8)

Ethnic Technologies LLC, South Hackensack, NJ. Tel: (201) 440-8923, (866) 333-8324, FAX: (201) 440-2168, E-Mail: candace@ethnictechnologies.com, Web Site: www.ethnictechnologies.com (23)

Ethyl Corp, Richmond, VA. Tel: (804) 788-5000, FAX: (804) 788-5688, Web Site: www.ethyl.com (16)

Ettelson, John, R., William Blair & Co LLC, Chicago, IL. Tel: (312) 236-1600, (800) 621-0687, FAX: (312) 368-9418, E-Mail: info@williamblair.com, Web Site: www.williamblair.com (14)

Ettinger, Nora, Cornell Lab of Ornithology, Ithaca, NY. Tel: (607) 254-2157, (800) 843-BIRD, FAX: (607) 254-2415, E-Mail: birdslides@cornell.edu, Web Site: www.birds.cornell.edu (1)

Etzcorn, Janis L., Landscape Forms Inc, Kalamazoo, MI. Tel: (616) 381-0490, (800) 430-6209, FAX: (616) 381-3455, E-Mail: specify@landscapeforms.com, Web Site: www.landscapeforms.com (16)

Euro RSCG Worldwide, New York, NY. Tel: (212) 886-2000, FAX: (212) 886-2016, Web Site: www.eurorscg.com (35)

Evans, Carl, Eagle Marketing Services Inc, San Diego, CA. Tel: (619) 223-1273, (800) 548-5858, FAX: (727) 803-0512, E-Mail: gettunedin@eaglemarketing.com, Web Site: www.eaglemarketing.com (35)

Evans, Carol, Working Mother, New York, NY. Tel: (212) 221-9595, FAX: (212) 219-7448, Web Site: www.workingmother.com (31)

Evans, Catherine, Ball Publishing, West Chicago, IL. Tel: (630) 231-3675, FAX: (630) 231-5254, E-Mail: info@ballpublishing.com, Web Site: www.ballpublishing.com (17)

Evans, David, Food for the Hungry Inc, Phoenix, AZ. Tel: (480) 998-3100, (800) 248-6437, FAX: (480) 998-4806, E-Mail: hunger@fh.org, Web Site: www.fh.org (1)

Evans, Dennis, Cookbook Publishers Inc, Lenexa, KS. Tel: (913) 492-5900, (800) 227-7282, FAX: (913) 492-5947, E-Mail: info@cookbookpublishers.com, Web Site: www.cookbookpublishers.com (17)

Evans, Gary, USA TODAY, Mc Lean, VA. Tel: (703) 854-3400, (800) 872-0001, E-Mail: accuracy@usatoday.com, Web Site: www.usatoday.com (17)

Evans, Glenn, RG Barry Corp, Pickerington, OH. FAX: (614) 866-9787, E-Mail: sales@rgbarry.com, Web Site: www.rgbarry.com (2)

Evans, Gregory, P., Indium Corp of America, Clinton, NY. Tel: (315) 853-4900, (800) 446-3486, FAX: (800) 221-5759, E-Mail: askus@indium.com, Web Site: www.indium.com (16)

Evans, James, P., Doubletree Suites by Hilton, Boston, MA. Tel: (617) 783-0090, (800) 222-TREE, FAX: (617) 783-0897, E-Mail: doubletree1@hilton.com (19)

Evans, Janet, American Biographical Institute Inc, Raleigh, NC. Tel: (919) 781-8710, FAX: (919) 781-8712, Web Site: www.abiworldwide.com (17)

Evans, John, British Columbia Automobile Association, Burnaby, BC. Tel: (604) 268-5000, (800) 564-6222, FAX: (604) 268-5585, Web Site: www.bcaa.com (15)

Evans, John, SilverState Marketing Solutions, Las Vegas, NV. Tel: (702) 489-2124, Web Site: www. silverstateprintmail.com (28)

Evans, Julie, Omaha Steaks Inc, Omaha, NE. Tel: (402) 597-3000, FAX: (402) 597-8252, E-Mail: info@omahasteaks.com, Web Site: www. omahasteaks.com (4)

Evans, Kris, Mary Elizabeth Granger & Associates Inc, Baltimore, MD. Tel: (410) 842-1170, (800) 296-5157, FAX: (410) 842-1185, E-Mail: bonnie@ maryegranger.com, Web Site: www.maryegranger. com (23)

Evans, Lee, RG Barry Corp, Pickerington, OH. FAX: (614) 866-9787, E-Mail: sales@rgbarry.com, Web Site: www.rgbarry.com (2)

Evans, Lori, Lorton Data Inc, Arden Hills, MN. Tel: (651) 203-8200, FAX: (612) 362-0299, Web Site: www.lortondata.com (22)

Evans, Lynn, Haynes & Partners Communications Inc, Indianapolis, IN. Tel: (317) 860-3000, FAX: (317) 860-3001, E-Mail: levans@hp-inc.com, Web Site: www.hp-inc.com (35)

Evans, Marge, Annie's Attic LLC, Big Sandy, TX. Tel: (903) 636-4303, FAX: (903) 636-4088, Web Site: www.anniesattic.com (11)

Evans, Michael, BowTie Inc, Irvine, CA. Tel: (949) 855-8822, FAX: (949) 855-1850, E-Mail: mevans@bowtieinc.com, Web Site: www. animalnetwork.com (17)

Evans, N., Sedlak, Highland Hills, OH. Tel: (216) 206-4700, FAX: (216) 206-4840, E-Mail: info@ jasedlak.com, Web Site: www.jasedlak.com (20)

Evans, Pamela, BAM! Direct Inc, Suwanee, GA. Tel: (678) 947-1943, Web Site: www.bamdirect.com (35)

Evans, Robert, Liberty Life Insurance Co, Greenville, SC. Tel: (864) 609-8111, (800) 344-5834 (Mktg), FAX: (864) 609-4411, Web Site: www.libertycorp. com (15)

Evans, Ronald, W., Interex, Amesbury, MA. Tel: (978) 388-8755, (800) INTEREX, FAX: (978) 388-8747, Web Site: www.interexexhibits.com (17)

Evans, Steve, Scott Sign Systems Inc, Sarasota, FL. Tel: (941) 355-5171, (800) 237-9447, FAX: (941) 351-1787, E-Mail: mail@scottssigns.com, Web Site: www.scottssigns.com (16)

Evans, Tana, Columbia Tristar Home Video, Culver City, CA. Tel: (310) 244-4000, FAX: (310) 244-1544, Web Site: www.cthe.com (16)

Evans, Tony, Lorton Data Inc, Arden Hills, MN. Tel: (651) 203-8200, FAX: (612) 362-0299, Web Site: www.lortondata.com (22)

Evans-Lombe, Nick, Getty Images, Seattle, WA. Tel: (206) 925-5018, (800) 462-4379, Web Site: www. gettyimages.com (38)

Evensen, Nancy, North American Membership Group Inc, Minnetonka, MN. Tel: (952) 936-9333, FAX: (952) 936-9755, Web Site: www.namginc.com (13)

Event 360 Inc, Chicago, IL. Tel: (773) 247-5360, Web Site: www.event360.com (1)

Eventful Inc, San Diego, CA. Tel: (858) 754-3004, Web Site: www.eventful.com (19)

Everest, Christi, DeLong Mailing Service, Oklahoma City, OK. Tel: (405) 272-9401 (28)

Everett, John, Utilities Supply Corp, Woburn, MA. Tel: (781) 395-9023, (800) 343-7555, FAX: (781) 395-2329, (800) 232-8726, E-Mail: jge@fwwebb. com, Web Site: www.uscosupply.com (16)

Everett, Tony, Doner Direct, Baltimore, MD. Tel: (248) 354-9700, FAX: (248) 827-0880 (21)

Everex Computer Systems Inc, Fremont, CA. Tel: (866) 850-8835, (800) 383-7391, FAX: (510) 683-2186, E-Mail: customerservice@everex.com, Web Site: www.everex.com (16)

Everfast Inc, Kennett Square, PA. Tel: (610) 444-9700, Web Site: www.calicocorners.com (8)

Evergreen Enterprises Inc, Richmond, VA. Tel: (804) 231-1800, Web Site: www.myevergreen.com (8)

Evergreen Marketing, Seneca, SC. Tel: (864) 882-1170, FAX: (864) 882-1112, E-Mail: evawn@ evergreenmarketing.com, Web Site: www. evergreenmarketing.com (23)

Everly, Joseph, W., Amtelco, McFarland, WI. Tel: (608) 838-4194, (800) 356-9148, FAX: (608) 838-8367, E-Mail: info@amtelco.com, Web Site: www. amtelco.com (16)

Evernden, Marlene, AMI Instore, Framingham, MA. Tel: (508) 652-0200, (877) 652-0200, FAX: (508) 652-0101, E-Mail: info@advancemarketing.com, Web Site: www.advancemarketing.com (31)

Everton, Marsha, Pfaltzgraff Co, York, PA. Tel: (717) 852-2211, (800) 999-2811, FAX: (800) 717-2481, E-Mail: service@pfaltzgraff.com, Web Site: www. pfaltzgraff.com (8)

Everyday Media, Garrison, NY. Tel: (845) 788-3900, FAX: (212) 481-7800, Web Site: www. everydaymedia.com (31)

Ewald, Robert, Silicon Graphics Inc, Fremont, CA. Tel: (510) 933-8300, Web Site: www.sgi.com (16)

eWay Direct, Southport, CT. Tel: (888) 655-0464, Web Site: www.ewaydirect.com (32)

Ewen, David, EMED Co Inc, Buffalo, NY. Tel: (716) 626-1616, (800) 442-3633, FAX: (716) 626-1630, E-Mail: customerservice@emedco.com, Web Site: www.emedco.com (16)

Ewer, Marilyn, MKE Enterprises, North Reading, MA. Tel: (978) 664-3877, FAX: (978) 664-2835, E-Mail: mke@theworld.com, Web Site: www.mke-enterprises.com (35)

Ewing, Dr. John H., American Mathematical Society, Providence, RI. Tel: (401) 455-4000, (800) 321-4267, FAX: (401) 331-3842, E-Mail: ams@ams. org, Web Site: www.ams.org (17)

Ewing, Tom, Educational Testing Service, Princeton, NJ. Tel: (609) 683-2292, FAX: (609) 734-5410, Web Site: www.ets.org (16)

Ewing, William, D., The Foxon Co, Providence, RI. Tel: (401) 421-2386, (800) 556-6943, FAX: (401) 421-8996 (27)

Ewing Galloway Inc, Oceanside, NY. Tel: (516) 764-8620, E-Mail: ewinggalloway@aol.com, Web Site: www.indexstock.com (38)

ExactTarget Inc, Indianapolis, IN. Tel: (317) 423-3928, Web Site: www.exacttarget.com (32)

Excalibur Enterprises Inc, Winston Salem, NC. Tel: (336) 744-5000, (800) 441-4193, FAX: (336) 767-8257, E-Mail: info@excaliburmail.com, Web Site: www.excaliburmail.com (28)

Excelligence Learning Corp, Monterey, CA. Tel: (831) 333-2000, Web Site: www.excelligencelearning. com (5)

Excelsior Direct, Lancaster, PA. Tel: (717) 399-3550, FAX: (717) 399-3200 (35)

Executive Buying Corp, Naperville, IL. Tel: (630) 420-6200, FAX: (630) 420-2294, Web Site: www. consumerbenefit.com (33)

Executive Connections LLC, Sarasota, FL. Tel: (941) 323-8300, Web Site: www.executiveconnectionsllc. com (20)

Executive Enterprises Inc, Hawthorne, NY. Tel: (860) 701-5900, (800) 831-8333, FAX: (800) 250-3861, (860) 701-5909, E-Mail: info@eeiconferences.com, Web Site: www.eeiconferences.com (16)

Executive Protection Products Inc, Napa, CA. Tel: (707) 253-7142, FAX: (707) 253-7149, E-Mail: services@epsecuritysolutions.com, Web Site: epsecuritysolutions.com (16)

Executive Search International, Newton, MA. Tel: (617) 527-8787, E-Mail: info@execsearchintl.com, Web Site: www.execsearchintl.com (20)

Exhibitgroup/Giltspur, Hodgkins, IL. Tel: (972) 538-3031, (800) 843-3944, Web Site: www.e-g.com (30)

Exhibitrac Direct Marketing, Las Vegas, NV. Tel: (303) 988-6601, FAX: (303) 988-6602, E-Mail: sales@exhibitrac.com, Web Site: www.exhibitrac. com (23)

Expedia Inc, Bellevue, WA. Tel: (425) 679-7200, Web Site: www.expedia.com (19)

Experian, Costa Mesa, CA. Tel: (714) 830-7000, (888) EXPERIAN, Web Site: www.experian.com (30)

Experian Simmons, New York, NY. Tel: (212) 471-2850, FAX: (212) 471-2940, E-Mail: ellenr@smrb. com, Web Site: www.smrb.com (30)

Experience In Software Inc, Berkeley, CA. Tel: (510) 644-0694, (800) 678-7008, FAX: (510) 644-3823, Web Site: www.projectkickstart.com (16)

Exposed Brick, New York, NY. Tel: (212) 226-0060, FAX: (212) 941-8566, E-Mail: andrewc@ exposedbrick.com, Web Site: www.exposedbrick. com (35)

Express LLC, Columbus, OH. Tel: (614) 415-4282, Web Site: www.expressfashion.com (2)

Expressions Custom Furniture, Hickory, NC. Tel: (828) 328-1851, FAX: (828) 328-2176, Web Site: www.expressionsfurniture.com (16)

Exum, Ashe B., Happy Jack Inc, Snow Hill, NC. Tel: (252) 747-2911, (800) 326-5225, FAX: (252) 747-4111, E-Mail: happyjack@happyjackinc.com, Web Site: www.happyjackinc.com (11)

Exum, Joe, Happy Jack Inc, Snow Hill, NC. Tel: (252) 747-2911, (800) 326-5225, FAX: (252) 747-4111, E-Mail: happyjack@happyjackinc.com, Web Site: www.happyjackinc.com (11)

Ey, Fred, FocalPoint Marketing LLC, Metuchen, NJ. Tel: (877) 252-4305, Web Site: www.nipgroup.com (35)

Eye Care Centers of America, San Antonio, TX. Tel: (210) 340-3531, (800) 669-1183, FAX: (210) 340-0123, E-Mail: customerservice@visionworks.com, Web Site: www.ecca.com (7)

Eyeglass Service Industries, Lynbrook, NY. Tel: (516) 599-1135, FAX: (516) 599-4825 (2)

Euro RSCG 4D Worldwide, San Francisco, CA. Tel: (415) 345-7700, FAX: (415) 345-7701 (35)

F

F&W Publications Inc, Blue Ash, OH. Tel: (513) 531-2690, FAX: (513) 531-0293, Web Site: www. fwpublications.com (17)

F P International, Redwood City, CA. Tel: (650) 261-5300, (800) 866-9946, FAX: (650) 361-1713, Web Site: www.fpintl.com (16)

The FX Matt Brewing Co, Utica, NY. Tel: (315) 732-0022, (800) 765-6288, FAX: (315) 624-2401, E-Mail: info@saranac.com, Web Site: www. saranac.com (4)

FAFCO Inc, Chico, CA. Tel: (530) 332-2100, (800) 994-7652, FAX: (530) 332-2109, Web Site: www. fafco.com (16)

FAO Schwarz, New York, NY. Tel: (212) 644-9400, (800) 426-TOYS, FAX: (212) 688-6053, Web Site: www.fao.com (11)

FCB HealthCare & ProHealth, New York, NY. Tel: (212) 672-2300, FAX: (212) 672-2301 (35)

FCIA Management Co Inc, New York, NY. Tel: (212) 885-1500, FAX: (212) 885-1535, E-Mail: service@ fcia.com, Web Site: www.fcia.com (15)

FCL Graphics Inc, Harwood Heights, IL. Tel: (708) 867-5500, (800) 274-3380, FAX: (708) 867-7768 (27)

FDAnews, Falls Church, VA. Tel: (703) 538-7600, (888) 838-5578, FAX: (703) 538-7676, E-Mail: customerservice@fdanews.com, Web Site: www. fdanews.com (17)

FG Companies, Wayzata, MN. Tel: (952) 540-4901, Web Site: www.fgcompanies.com (22)

FGI Research, Chapel Hill, NC. Tel: (919) 929-7759, FAX: (919) 932-8829, E-Mail: info@fgiresearch. com, Web Site: www.fgiresearch.com (35)

FICO, Minneapolis, MN. Tel: (651) 486-1870 (22)

FIU Online, Miami, FL. Tel: (305) 348-8489 (1)

FJ Associates LLC, Wilmington, NC. Tel: (910) 452-2643, FAX: (630) 982-1056 (23)

FKM, Houston, TX. Tel: (713) 862-5100, FAX: (713) 869-6560, E-Mail: rklein@fkmagency.com, Web Site: www.fkmagency.com (35)

FLM Graphics Corp, Fairfield, NJ. Tel: (973) 575-9450, E-Mail: info@flmgraphics.com, Web Site: www.flmgraphics.com (16)

FMC Corp, Philadelphia, PA. Tel: (215) 299-6000, FAX: (215) 299-5998, Web Site: www.fmc.com (16)

FMP Direct Inc, Scottsdale, AZ. Tel: (847) 816-1919, (800) 995-3343, FAX: (847) 816-1969, E-Mail: info@fmpdirect.com, Web Site: www.fmpdirect.com (21)

FMS Direct, Tarzana, CA. Tel: (818) 708-7814, FAX: (818) 708-7906, Web Site: www.fmsdirect.com (35)

FNC INC, Oxford, MS. Tel: (662) 236-8254, Web Site: www.fncinc.com (14)

FP Mailing Solutions, Addison, IL. Tel: (800) 341-6052, FAX: (630) 693-0626, Web Site: www.fp-usa.com (34)

FPS Marketing Communications, Milford, CT. Tel: (203) 783-1940, FAX: (203) 783-1950, E-Mail: info@fpsmarketing.com, Web Site: www.fpsmarketing.com (35)

FT Publications Inc, New York, NY. Tel: (212) 641-6500, FAX: (212) 641-6544, E-Mail: adsales@ft.com, Web Site: www.ft.com (17)

FTD Florist Transworld Delivery, Downers Grove, IL. Tel: (630) 719-7756, (800) SEND-FTD, Web Site: www.ftd.com (16)

FTD Group Inc, Downers Grove, IL. Tel: (630) 719-7800, (800) 788-9000, FAX: (630) 719-6170, E-Mail: ftdmemberservices@ftdi.com, Web Site: www.ftdi.com (29)

FW Media, Cincinnati, OH. Tel: (513) 531-2690, Web Site: www.fwpublications.com (17)

Fabbro, Ron, SC Direct, West Bridgewater, MA. Tel: (800) 343-9695, Web Site: www.scdirect.com (2)

Fabian, Roger, J., ASM International, Materials Park, OH. Tel: (440) 338-5151, (800) 336-5152, FAX: (440) 338-4634, E-Mail: customerservice@asminternational.org, Web Site: www.asminternational.org (1)

Fabiano, Lisa, MVBMS EURO RSCG, New York, NY. Tel: (212) 886-2000, FAX: (212) 886-2016, E-Mail: northamerica@eurorscg.com, Web Site: www.eurorscg.com (35)

Facts 'n Figures, Sherman Oaks, CA. Tel: (661) 222-2278, (818) 986-6600, FAX: (661) 222-2287, Web Site: www.factsnfiguresinc.com (30)

Facts On File Inc, New York, NY. Tel: (212) 967-8800, (800) 322-8755, FAX: (212) 678-3633, Web Site: www.factsonfile.com (17)

Fadel, Mitchell, Rent-A-Center Inc, Plano, TX. Tel: (972) 801-1100, (800) 275-2996, FAX: (972) 943-0113, Web Site: www.rentacenter.com (16)

Fagan, Charles, E., Polo Ralph Lauren, Lyndhurst, NJ. Tel: (212) 531-6537, (800) 377-7656, FAX: (212) 318-7690, Web Site: www.ralphlauren.com (2)

Fagan, John, Penguin Putnam Inc, New York, NY. Tel: (212) 366-2000, FAX: (212) 366-2278, Web Site: www.penguinputnam.com (17)

Fagan, Ray, Hatchett & Fagan Direct, Birmingham, AL. Tel: (205) 458-8200, Web Site: www.hfdirect.com (35)

Fahey, John, National Geographic Society, Washington, DC. Tel: (202) 857-7311, (800) NGS-LINE, FAX: (202) 457-8200, Web Site: www.nationalgeographic.com (17)

Fahlbeck, Dale, D., Elkhart Cases, Elkhart, IN. Tel: (574) 295-7700, (800) 582-0319, FAX: (574) 295-7761, E-Mail: elkcases@aol.com (2)

Fahlgren, Cincinnati, OH. Tel: (513) 241-9200, FAX: (513) 241-5982, Web Site: www.fahlgren.com (35)

Fahmie, Tom, Commercial Data Processing Inc, Red Bank, NJ. Tel: (800) 242-3731, FAX: (973) 882-0387, E-Mail: vivieng@dataprocess.com, Web Site: www.dataprocess.com (22)

Fain, Bruce, Pacific Botanicals LLC, Grants Pass, OR. Tel: (541) 479-7777, FAX: (541) 479-7780, E-Mail: pacbot1@earthlink.net, Web Site: www.pacificbotanicals.com (7)

Fain, Deborah, Infomorphosis/Marketing Solutions, New York, NY. Tel: (212) 366-6216, FAX: (212) 255-4784, E-Mail: dfain@nyc.rr.com (20)

Fainman, Burt, Butler Specialty Co, Chicago, IL. Tel: (773) 221-1200, (800) 799-2857, FAX: (773) 221-5892, Web Site: www.butlerspecialty.net (16)

Fainstein, Boris, Medco Health Solutions Inc, Franklin Lakes, NJ. Tel: (201) 269-3400, FAX: (201) 269-6400, Web Site: www.medco.com (7)

Faintreny, Eric, Chadwick's of Boston Inc, West Bridgewater, MA. Tel: (508) 583-8110, FAX: (508) 587-3345, Web Site: www.chadwicks.com (2)

Fair, Pamela, J., Southern California Gas Co, Anaheim, CA. Tel: (714) 634-3054, (800) 427-2200, FAX: (714) 937-7712, E-Mail: Tjavid@socalgas.com, Web Site: www.socalgas.com (1)

Fair Indigo, Madison, WI. Tel: (608) 824-8974, Web Site: www.fairindigo.com (2)

Fair Isaac Corp, Minneapolis, MN. Tel: (612) 758-5200, E-Mail: info@fairisaac.com, Web Site: www.fairisaac.com (22)

Fairbanks, John F., NEBS, Groton, MA. Tel: (978) 448-6111, (888) 823-6327, (800) 225-6380, FAX: (800) 234-4324, (978) 448-3653, E-Mail: customerservice@nebs.com, Web Site: www.nebs.com (10)

Fairbanks, John, Accountants' Supply House, Lancaster, CA. Tel: (856) 384-1144, (800) 342-5274, FAX: (800) 468-4446, Web Site: www.rapidforms.com (10)

Fairbanks, John, McBee, Lancaster, CA. Tel: (973) 263-3225, (800) 878-9443, (800) 662-2331, FAX: (973) 263-8165, E-Mail: info@mcbeeinc.com, Web Site: www.mcbeeweb.com (10)

Fairbrother, Jay, P., Direct Advantage Marketing, Pittsburgh, PA. Tel: (412) 381-2300, E-Mail: information@dam.com, Web Site: www.dam.com (29)

Fairchild, Nancy, Air Chek Inc, Naples, NC. Tel: (828) 684-0893, (800) AIR-CHEK, FAX: (828) 684-8498, Web Site: www.radon.com (9)

Fairchild Books, New York, NY. Tel: (212) 630-4171, (800) 932-4724, FAX: (212) 630-3868, Web Site: www.fairchildbooks.com (17)

Fairchild Publications, New York, NY. Tel: (212) 630-4000, Web Site: www.fairchildpub.com (17)

Fairclough, Ann, XDM Corp, San Francisco, CA. Tel: (415) 989-3000, FAX: (925) 934-0599, E-Mail: info@xdm.com, Web Site: www.xdm.com (21)

Faire Harbour Limited, Scituate, MA. Tel: (781) 545-2465, FAX: (781) 545-2465 (5)

Fairfield, Bill, infoGROUP, Omaha, NE. Tel: (800) 555-5335 X4541, Web Site: www.infoUSA.com (23)

Fairfield Industries Inc, Sugar Land, TX. Tel: (281) 275-7500, (800) 231-9809, FAX: (281) 275-7550, E-Mail: jblattman@fairfield.com, Web Site: www.fairfield.com (16)

Fairfield Marketing Group Inc, Easton, CT. Tel: (203) 261-5585 X205, (203) 261-5568, FAX: (203) 261-0884, E-Mail: ed@fairfieldmarketing.com, Web Site: www.fairfieldmarketing.com (22)

Fairman, Mark, Potpourri Group Inc, Chelmsford, MA. Tel: (978) 256-4100, FAX: (978) 256-1961/0344, Web Site: www.potpourrigroup.com (6)

Fairytale Brownies, Phoenix, AZ. Tel: (800) 324-7982, FAX: (602) 489-5122, E-Mail: service@brownies.com, Web Site: www.brownies.com (4)

Faison, Ralph E., Andrew Wireless Solutions, Westchester, IL. Tel: (800) 349-5444, Web Site: www.andrew.com (16)

Falato, Rory, Chase Industries, Inc, Cincinnati, OH. Tel: (513) 860-5565, (800) 543-4455, FAX: (800) 245-7045, Web Site: www.chasedoors.com (16)

Falchuk, Evan, Doctor's Best Inc, San Clemente, CA. Tel: (949) 498-3628, (800) 333-6977, FAX: (800) 754-2036, (949) 498-3952, E-Mail: info@drbvitamins.com, Web Site: www.drbvitamins.com (16)

Falcon Products Inc, Newport, TN. Tel: (314) 991-9200, (800) 873-3252, FAX: (314) 991-9227, E-Mail: info@falconproducts.com, Web Site: www.falconproducts.com (16)

Falcon Safety Products, Branchburg, NJ. Tel: (908) 707-4900, FAX: (908) 707-8855, Web Site: www.falconsafety.com (16)

Falcone, Joseph, Taylor Gifts Inc, Paoli, PA. Tel: (610) 725-1122, FAX: (610) 725-1144, Web Site: www.taylorgifts.com (8)

Falcone, Robert, S., Nautilus Inc, Vancouver, WA. Tel: (360) 859-2900, (800) 675-0171, FAX: (360) 694-2755, Web Site: www.nautilus.com (11)

Falconer, Lynn, CDMG, Torrance, CA. Tel: (310) 212-5727, FAX: (310) 212-5773, E-Mail: infomat@biz.com, Web Site: www.cdmginc.com (21)

Falk, Lisa, American Hotel Register Co, Vernon Hills, IL. Tel: (708) 743-4163, FAX: (708) 564-5797, Web Site: www.americanhotel.com (23)

Falk, Steve, Westminster International, Richmond Hill, ON Canada. Tel: (416) 494-6245, FAX: (905) 771-9349 (21)

Falk, Thomas, J., Kimberly-Clark Corp, Neenah, WI. Tel: (920) 721-2000, (888) 525-8388, FAX: (920) 721-7722, Web Site: www.kimberly-clark.com (16)

Falkson, Michael, ETI Sales Support, Valhalla, NY. Tel: (914) 747-3030, (800) 466-4384, FAX: (914) 747-3466, E-Mail: info@etisales.com, Web Site: www.etisales.com (29)

Fallis, Charles, National Active & Retired Federal Employees Association, Alexandria, VA. Tel: (703) 838-7760, (800) 456-8410, FAX: (703) 838-7785, Web Site: www.narfe.org (1)

Fallon III, John, A., Eastern Michigan University, Ypsilanti, MI. Tel: (734) 487-1849, FAX: (734) 484-1151, Web Site: www.emich.edu (16)

Fallon, Art, Houston Direct Marketing Association, Houston, TX. Tel: (281) 931-8883, FAX: (281) 820-4023, Web Site: www.houstondma.org (40)

Fallon, Nancy, Spectrum Systems Inc, Fairfax, VA. Tel: (703) 591-7400 X217, (800) 929-3781, FAX: (703) 591-9780, E-Mail: spectrum@spectrum-systems.com, Web Site: www.spectrum-systems.com (34)

Fallon, Padraic, M., Institutional Investor Inc, New York, NY. Tel: (212) 224-3300, FAX: (212) 224-3592, Web Site: www.institutionalinvestor.com (17)

Fallon, Minneapolis, MN. Tel: (612) 758-2345, FAX: (612) 758-2346, Web Site: www.fallon.com (35)

Fallon Community Health Plan, Worcester, MA. Tel: (800) 333-2535, Web Site: www.fchp.org (1)

R Falls Agency, Minneapolis, MN. Tel: (612) 872-6372, (800) 339-1119, FAX: (612) 872-1018, E-Mail: info@fallsagency.com, Web Site: www.fallsagency.com (35)

Falor, John, American Bronzing Co, Columbus, OH. Tel: (614) 252-7388, (800) 423-5678, FAX: (614) 252-4602, E-Mail: bronzeinfo@bronshoe.com, Web Site: www.abcbronze.com (16)

Faltischek, Michael, Ruskin, Moscou, Faltischek, PC, Uniondale, NY. Tel: (516) 663-6600, FAX: (516) 663-6601, E-Mail: info@rmfpc.com, Web Site: www.rmfpc.com (16)

Falzone, Mary Ann, Falzone & Associates LLC, Sellersville, PA. Tel: (215) 822-8941 (29)

Falzone, Paul, Together, Dallas, TX. Tel: (972) 407-1609, (800) 678-DATE, FAX: (972) 407-0082, Web Site: www.togetherdating.com (16)

Falzone & Associates LLC, Sellersville, PA. Tel: (215) 822-8941 (29)

Family Album, Kinzers, PA. Tel: (717) 442-0220, FAX: (717) 442-7904, E-Mail: rarebooks@pobox.com (6)

Family Christian Stores, Grand Rapids, MI. Tel: (616) 554-8700, (888) 319-0319, FAX: (616) 554-8694, E-Mail: info@fcsdirect.familychristian.com, Web Site: www.familychristian.com (5)

Family Circle Magazine Inc, New York, NY. Tel: (212) 557-6600, Web Site: www.familycircle.com (31)

Family Foot Care, Toms River, NJ. Tel: (732) 341-3355 (7)

The Family Handyman, Eagan, MN. Tel: (651) 454-9200, FAX: (651) 994-2250 (17)

Famous Smoke Shop Inc, Easton, PA. Tel: (610) 559-7000, (800) 672-5544, FAX: (610) 559-7170, E-Mail: info@famous-smoke.com, Web Site: www.famous-smoke.com (16)

Fancher, David, Cooper Vision, Fairport, NY. Tel: (585) 385-6810, (800) 341-2020, Web Site: www.coopervision.com (7)

Fancy Fronds, Gold Bar, WA. Tel: (360) 793-1472, FAX: (360) 793-4243, E-Mail: judith@fancyfronds.com, Web Site: www.fancyfronds.com (8)

Fanelli, Dr. Sean, A., Nassau Community College, Garden City, NY. Tel: (516) 572-7501, E-Mail: marketing-communications@ncc.edu, Web Site: www.ncc.edu (41)

The Faneuil Group, Winnipeg, MB Canada. Tel: (204) 934-1900, (866) FANEUIL, FAX: (617) 742-3666, Web Site: www.faneuil.com (29)

Faneuil ISG, Winnipeg, MB Canada. Tel: (866) Faneuil, Web Site: www.faneuil.com (30)

Fankhauser, Brent, Data-Dynamix Inc, Castle Rock, CO. Tel: (720) 855-9282, (888) 314-0078, FAX: (720) 855-9099, Web Site: www.data-dynamix.com (23)

Fannie Mae, Washington, DC. Tel: (202) 752-7000, FAX: (202) 752-3808, Web Site: www.fanniemae.com (14)

Fannin, Jake, Employment Publishing Inc, Wayne, PA. Tel: (610) 975-4539, FAX: (610) 687-7860, E-Mail: jfanning@employment911.com (17)

Fanolis, George, C., Fosdick Fulfillment Corp, Wallingford, CT. Tel: (203) 269-0211, (800) 759-5588, FAX: (203) 679-3290, E-Mail: sales@fosdickcorp.com, Web Site: www.fosdickfulfillment.com (28)

Fansworth, Bob, GameTime Inc, Fort Payne, AL. Tel: (256) 845-5610, (800) 633-2394, FAX: (256) 845-9361/2649, Web Site: www.gametime.com (11)

Fantle, Susan, The Copy Works, San Diego, CA. Tel: (858) 676-6757, Web Site: www.thecopyworks.com (20)

Far West Media Services, Long Beach, CA. Tel: (562) 496-3342, FAX: (562) 496-4329, Web Site: www.farwestmedia.com (32)

Faraci, John V., International Paper, Memphis, TN. Tel: (901) 419-9000, (800) 207-4003, Web Site: www.internationalpaper.com (16)

Faraci, Philip J., Eastman Kodak Co, Rochester, NY. Tel: (585) 724-0251, (800) 698-3324, FAX: (585) 724-1089, Web Site: www.kodak.com (27)

Faragi, Francine, The First Occupational Center of New Jersey, Orange, NJ. Tel: (973) 672-5800, FAX: (973) 672-0065, E-Mail: ocnj@ocnj.org, Web Site: www.ocnj.org (28)

Farah, Rogen, N., Polo Ralph Lauren, Lyndhurst, NJ. Tel: (212) 531-6537, (800) 377-7656, FAX: (212) 318-7690, Web Site: www.ralphlauren.com (2)

Farber, Naomi, Conde Nast, New York, NY. Tel: (212) 286-2860, FAX: (212) 880-8289, Web Site: www.conde.net (17)

Farber, Steve, Triangle Printers Inc, Skokie, IL. Tel: (847) 675-3700, FAX: (847) 674-1230, E-Mail: blevin@triangleprinters.com, Web Site: www.triangleprinters.com (27)

Fargo, Linda, Bergdorf Goodman, New York, NY. Tel: (212) 753-7300, (800) 967-3788, (800) 218-4918, FAX: (212) 872-8677, E-Mail: clientservices@bergdorfgoodman.com, Web Site: www.bergdorfgoodman.com (2)

Faris Jr, Robert, L., Faris Mailing Inc, Indianapolis, IN. Tel: (317) 246-3315, FAX: (317) 246-3330, E-Mail: farismailing@iquest.net, Web Site: farismailing.com (28)

Faris, Bill, Avatar Studios, Saint Louis, MO. Tel: (314) 533-2242, FAX: (314) 533-3349, Web Site: www.avatar-studios.com (32)

Faris Mailing Inc, Indianapolis, IN. Tel: (317) 246-3315, FAX: (317) 246-3330, E-Mail: farismailing@iquest.net, Web Site: farismailing.com (28)

Farley, Ed, Ashrae Learning Institute, Atlanta, GA. Tel: (404) 636-8400, (800) 527-4723, FAX: (404) 321-5478, E-Mail: ashrae@ashrae.org, Web Site: www.ashrae.org (31)

Farley, Ed, Unisource Worldwide, Inc, Norcross, GA. Tel: (770) 447-9000, (800) 864-7687, FAX: (770) 729-0385, Web Site: www.unisourcelink.com (25)

Farley, Richard, Marshall Cavendish Corp, Tarrytown, NY. Tel: (914) 332-8888, (800) 821-9881, FAX: (914) 332-1888, Web Site: www.marshallcavendish.com (17)

Farley, Steve, The Bombay Co, Brampton, ON. Tel: (877) 326-6229, E-Mail: customerservice@bombay.ca, Web Site: www.bombay.com (8)

Farley, Tom, Brookfield Properties, Toronto, ON. Tel: (416) 369-2300, FAX: (416) 369-2301, Web Site: www.brokfieldproperties.com (16)

Farm Bureau Insurance, Lansing, MI. Tel: (517) 323-7000, (800) 292-2680, FAX: (517) 327-0208, Web Site: www.farmbureauinsurance-mi.com (15)

Farm Home Offices, Richfield, MN. Tel: (612) 920-0907, (800) 788-7218, FAX: (866) 404-0257, Web Site: www.sylvette.com (10)

Farm Journal Inc, Philadelphia, PA. Tel: (215) 557-8937, FAX: (215) 568-4238 (17)

Farm Market iD, Westmont, IL. Tel: (630) 654-5700, (800) 313-4778, FAX: (630) 654-4470, Web Site: www.farmmarketid.com (23)

Farm Progress Co, Saint Charles, IL. Tel: (630) 690-5600, FAX: (630) 462-2202, E-Mail: dwilson@farmprogress.com, Web Site: www.farmprogress.com (17)

Farmer, Gary, AAVIM, Winterville, GA. Tel: (706) 742-5355, (800) 228-4689, FAX: (706) 742-7005, E-Mail: gary@aavim.com, Web Site: www.aavim.com (31)

Farmer, Jody, Creditcards.com, Austin, TX. Tel: (512) 996-8663, Web Site: www.creditcards.com (20)

Farmer, Lisa, Daily Record & Dispatch Co, Dunn, NC. Tel: (910) 891-1234, FAX: (910) 891-5253, Web Site: www.mydailyrecord.com (17)

Farmer, Maryann, Magna-Tel Inc, Cape Girardeau, MO. Tel: (573) 334-3096, FAX: (573) 335-1715, Web Site: www.magna.tel.com (5)

Farmers Insurance, Los Angeles, CA. Tel: (410) 366-1000, (410) 338-1633, (800) 327-6377, FAX: (410) 554-1926, Web Site: www.farmers.com (15)

Farnsworth, Carolyn, Bantam Dell Publishing Group Inc, New York, NY. Tel: (212) 782-9000, FAX: (212) 940-7381, Web Site: www.randomhouse.com/bantamdell (17)

Farnsworth, Susan, CARE USA, Atlanta, GA. Tel: (404) 979-9255, (800) 521-CARE, FAX: (404) 589-2600, E-Mail: info@care.org, Web Site: www.careusa.org (1)

Farooq, Omar, CIT, Livingston, NJ. Tel: (973) 422-6040, FAX: (973) 740-5383, Web Site: www.cit.com (14)

Farr, Kevin M., Fisher-Price, East Aurora, NY. Tel: (716) 687-3300, FAX: (716) 687-3636, Web Site: www.fisherprice.com (16)

Farr, Mike, JIST Publishing, Saint Paul, MN. Tel: (800) 648-5478, FAX: (800) 547-8329, E-Mail: info@jist.com, Web Site: www.jist.com (17)

Farr-Jones, Stephen, ADM Marketing, Burbank, CA. Tel: (888) 800-1001 (20)

Farrar Straus & Giroux Inc, New York, NY. Tel: (212) 741-6900, (800) 330-8477, FAX: (212) 633-2427, E-Mail: childrens_editorial@fsgbooks.com, Web Site: www.fsgbooks.com (17)

Farrell Sr., James, H., American Preferred Reader's Service Inc, Fort Lauderdale, FL. Tel: (954) 489-2443, FAX: (954) 492-2343, E-Mail: jfarrell@amerpref.com, Web Site: www.amerpref.com (18)

Farrell, Caryn, American Preferred Reader's Service Inc, Fort Lauderdale, FL. Tel: (954) 489-2443, FAX: (954) 492-2343, E-Mail: jfarrell@amerpref.com, Web Site: www.amerpref.com (18)

Farrell, Christine, Suntrust Banks Inc, Atlanta, GA. Tel: (404) 588-7914, (800) 786-8787, FAX: (404) 532-0550, E-Mail: emmett.harmon@suntrust.com, Web Site: www.suntrust.com (14)

Farrell, Lawrence, Sunstar, Chicago, IL. Tel: (773) 777-4000, FAX: (773) 777-1417, E-Mail: dominico@sunstar.com, Web Site: www.sunstar.com (16)

Farren, David, Right On Computer Software, Greenlawn, NY. E-Mail: riteonsoft@aol.com, Web Site: rightonprograms.com (3)

Farrey, Ronald, Unique Data Services Inc, Downers Grove, IL. Tel: (630) 968-6000, Web Site: www.uniquedata.com (28)

Farrington, Katharine, Affinity Federal Credit Union, Basking Ridge, NJ. Tel: (908) 860-7306, Web Site: www.affinityfcu.org (1)

Farrington Transportation, Bolingbrook, IL. Tel: (630) 783-9200 (12)

Farrow, John, Russell A Farrow Ltd, Windsor, ON. Tel: (519) 252-4415, FAX: (519) 252-0982, E-Mail: sherry.lamont@farrow.com, Web Site: www.farrow.com (16)

Farrow, Rick, Russell A Farrow Ltd, Windsor, ON Canada. Tel: (519) 252-4415, FAX: (519) 252-0982, E-Mail: sherry.lamont@farrow.com, Web Site: www.farrow.com (16)

Russell A Farrow Ltd, Windsor, ON Canada. Tel: (519) 252-4415, FAX: (519) 252-0982, E-Mail: sherry.lamont@farrow.com, Web Site: www.farrow.com (16)

Farstar, Frisco, TX. Tel: (214) 649-0422, Web Site: http://www.wedontplayfair.com (35)

Fasano, Patricia A., Fasano & Associates, Beverly Hills, CA. Tel: (818) 728-9030, FAX: (818) 728-9070, E-Mail: pfasano@fasano-accoc.com, Web Site: www.fasano-assoc.com (23)

Fasano & Associates, Beverly Hills, CA. Tel: (818) 728-9030, FAX: (818) 728-9070, E-Mail: pfasano@fasano-accoc.com, Web Site: www.fasano-assoc.com (23)

Fashion Institute of Technology Library, New York, NY. Tel: (212) 217-4346, Web Site: www.fitnyc.edu (1)

Fasking, Greg, Infinity Insurance Co, Birmingham, AL. Tel: (800) 527-5412, Web Site: www.infinityauto.com (15)

Fasnacht, Jill, Howell, American College of Physician Executives, Tampa, FL. Tel: (813) 287-2000, (800) 562-8088, FAX: (813) 287-8993, E-Mail: acpe@acpe.org, Web Site: www.acpe.org (1)

Faso, Lawrence, eFootage, Pasadena, CA. Tel: (626) 395-9593, FAX: (626) 395-5394, E-Mail: info@efootage.com, Web Site: www.efootage.com (38)

Faso, Steven, Brand New Products LLC, Chicago, IL. Tel: (773) 486-8813, Web Site: www.brandnewllc.com (4)

Fasola, Ken, Humana Inc, Louisville, KY. Tel: (502) 580-5005, FAX: (502) 580-3141, Web Site: www.humana.com (7)

Fasolv, Mark, Ballard Designs, Atlanta, GA. Tel: (404) 352-8486, (800) 367-2775, FAX: (404) 352-1660, Web Site: www.ballarddesigns.com (8)

Fasseel, Jeff, Advertising Network Solutions, Lake Orion, MI. Tel: (248) 475-7881, Web Site: www.adnetworksolutions.com (20)

Fassett, Sean, American Movie Classics Holding Corp, Jericho, NY. Tel: (516) 803-3000, FAX: (516) 803-3003, Web Site: www.amctv.com (16)

Fasson Roll Div, Mentor, OH. Tel: (440) 354-7900, FAX: (440) 358-4712, (440) 358-6025, Web Site: www.fasson.com (16)

Fastlicht, Michaelle, En ESPANOL Publishing Group LLC, Beverly Hills, CA. Tel: (310) 248-2680 (17)

Father Flanagan's Boy's Home, Boys Town, NE. Tel: (402) 498-1934, FAX: (402) 498-1969, Web Site: www.boystown.org (1)

Fathers of St Edmund Southern Missions Inc, Selma, AL. Tel: (334) 872-2359, FAX: (334) 875-8189, E-Mail: jm1428@aol.com, Web Site: www.edmunditemissions.org (1)

Fatt, Rory, Firepower Marketing Inc, Blaine, WA. Tel: (604) 940-6900, Web Site: www.roryfatt.com (35)

FatWallet, Beloit, WI. Tel: (815) 877-8992, Web Site: www.fatwallet.com (14)

Faughnan, Adam, ReputationDefender, Redwood City, CA. Tel: (650) 241-7491, (888) 720-3332, E-Mail: helpdesk@reputation.com, Web Site: www.reputationdefender.com (32)

Faulhaber, Glen, G-Plex Direct Mail, Holtsville, NY. Tel: (631) 447-9500, Web Site: www.g-plex.net (28)

Faulkner, Dave, Strongwell, Bristol, VA. Tel: (276) 645-8000, FAX: (276) 645-8132, E-Mail: gbarefoot@strongwell.com, Web Site: www.strongwell.com (9)

Faultless Starch/Bon Ami Co, Kansas City, MO. Tel: (816) 842-1230, FAX: (816) 842-3417, E-Mail: info@faultless.com, Web Site: www.faultless.com (16)

Fauntleroy, Walter, Fauntleroy Supply Co/Wing Supply, Greenville, KY. Tel: (270) 338-5866, (800) 388-9464, FAX: (270) 338-0057, Web Site: www.wingsupply.com (11)

Fauntleroy Supply Co/Wing Supply, Greenville, KY. Tel: (270) 338-5866, (800) 388-9464, FAX: (270) 338-0057, Web Site: www.wingsupply.com (11)

Faust, Doug, Masterpiece Studios Inc, Mankato, MN. Tel: (507) 388-8788, (800) 447-0219, FAX: (507) 344-4606, E-Mail: masterpiecestudios@masterpiecestudios.com, Web Site: www.masterpiecestudios.com (16)

Faust, Richard, Membership Cards Only LLC, Vienna, VA. Tel: (800) 772-2737, Web Site: wwww.membershipcards.com (27)

Favata, Jennifer, Butler Till Media Services, Rochester, NY. Tel: (585) 473-3740, Web Site: www.butlertill.com (31)

Fawaz, Marwan, Charter Communications, Saint Louis, MO. Tel: (314) 965-0555, (888) 438-2427, FAX: (314) 965-9745, Web Site: www.charteroom.com (16)

Fay, Bill, Amos Press, Inc, Sidney, OH. Tel: (937) 498-2111, FAX: (937) 498-0876, Web Site: www.amospress.com (17)

Fay, Preston, Technekes LLC, Charlotte, NC. Tel: (704) 342-2900, FAX: (704) 342-2975, Web Site: www.technekes.com (22)

Fay, Sharen, E., Alliance Bernstein, New York, NY. Tel: (212) 969-1000, (800) 962-2134, FAX: (212) 969-2229, Web Site: www.alliancebernstein.com (14)

Fayad, John, Concept Communications, Nashua, NH. Tel: (603) 577-9810, Web Site: www.conceptcommusa.com (20)

Fazer, Bernard, The Hamilton Group Ltd Inc, Jacksonville, FL. Tel: (904) 279-1300, FAX: (904) 279-1414, Web Site: www.collectibletoday.com (16)

Fazey, Milli, KET, Lexington, KY. Tel: (859) 258-7000, (800) 432-0951, FAX: (606) 258-7396, E-Mail: rgriffin@ket.org, Web Site: www.ket.org (17)

Fazio, Robert, Goldline International, Santa Monica, CA. Tel: (310) 587-1420, (800) 827-4653, FAX: (310) 319-0265, E-Mail: president@goldlinecoins.com, Web Site: www.goldlinecoins.com (14)

Fazzio, James, Boston Research Group, Hopkinton, MA. Tel: (508) 497-2555, FAX: (508) 497-2592, E-Mail: BRGrep@BostonResearchGroup.com, Web Site: www.bostonresearchgroup.com (30)

Fearon, Richard, H., Eaton Corp, Raleigh, NC. Tel: (216) 523-4400, (800) 356-5794, FAX: (216) 523-4787, Web Site: www.eaton.com (16)

Feasel, Joanne, Airomat Corp, Fort Wayne, IN. Tel: (260) 747-7408, (800) 348-4905, FAX: (260) 747-7409, E-Mail: airomat@airomat.com, Web Site: www.mymatting.com (16)

Feder, Ted, Art Resource Inc, New York, NY. Tel: (212) 505-8700, FAX: (212) 505-2053, E-Mail: requests@artres.com, Web Site: www.artres.com (38)

Federal Citizen Information Center, Pueblo, CO. Tel: (888) 8-PUEBLO, FAX: (719) 948-9724, E-Mail: catalog.pueblo@gsa.gov, Web Site: www.pueblo.gsa.gov (5)

Federal Direct, Clifton, NJ. Tel: (973) 667-9800, Web Site: www.feddirect.com (27)

Federal Envelope Co, Bensenville, IL. Tel: (630) 595-2000, FAX: (630) 595-1212, E-Mail: postmaster@federalenvelope.com, Web Site: www.federalenvelope.com (26)

Federal Express, Memphis, TN. Tel: (901) 369-3600, FAX: (901) 395-5082, Web Site: www.fedex.com (16)

Federal Home Loan Mortgage Corp (Freddie Mac), McLean, VA. Tel: (703) 903-2000, (800) 424-5401, Web Site: www.freddiemac.com (14)

Federated Investors Co, Pittsburgh, PA. Tel: (412) 288-1900, (800) 341-7400, FAX: (412) 288-1171, Web Site: www.federatedinvestors.com (14)

Federici, Theresa, Franciscan Mission Associates, Mount Vernon, NY. Tel: (914) 664-5604, FAX: (914) 664-3017, E-Mail: admin@franciscanmissionassoc.org, Web Site: www.franciscanmissionassoc.org (1)

Federman, Robyn, Catalyst, Rochester, NY. Tel: (585) 453-8300, (800) 836-7720, FAX: (585) 453-8360, E-Mail: info@catalystinc.com, Web Site: www.catalystinc.com (35)

FedEx Ground, Coraopolis, PA. Tel: (412) 269-1000, (800) 762-3725, FAX: (412) 747-4295, Web Site: www.fedex.com/us/ground/main (28)

Fedus, Gary, Mitchell Graphics Inc, Petoskey, MI. Tel: (231) 347-4635, (800) 583-9401, FAX: (231) 347-9255, E-Mail: info@mitchellgraphics.com, Web Site: www.mitchellgraphics.com (27)

Feed the Children, Oklahoma City, OK. Tel: (800) 627-4556, Web Site: www.feedthechildren.org (1)

FEEDING AMERICA, Chicago, IL. Tel: (312) 263-2303, Web Site: www.secondharvest.org (1)

Feeley, Heather, ARF Annual Convention & Research Infoplex, New York, NY. Tel: (212) 751-5656, FAX: (212) 319-5265, E-Mail: info@theARF.org, Web Site: www.theARF.org (42)

Feeney, Kevin, Unisource Worldwide, Inc, Norcross, GA. Tel: (770) 447-9000, (800) 864-7687, FAX: (770) 729-0385, Web Site: www.unisourcelink.com (25)

Fegley, Kent, Accountants' Supply House, Lancaster, CA. Tel: (856) 384-1144, (800) 342-5274, FAX: (800) 468-4446, Web Site: www.rapidforms.com (10)

Fehlner, John, Neighborhood Cleaners Association International, New York, NY. Tel: (212) 967-3002, (800) 888-1622, FAX: (212) 967-2240, E-Mail: info@nca-i.com, Web Site: www.nca-i.com (1)

Feierbend, Janel, Book Passage Cafe, Corte Madera, CA. Tel: (415) 927-0960, (800) 999-7909, FAX: (415) 924-3838, Web Site: www.BookPassage.com (17)

Feige, Bob, Massachusetts Horticultural Society, Wellesley, MA. Tel: (617) 933-4929, (617) 933-4900, FAX: (617) 933-4901, E-Mail: hort_line@masshort.org, Web Site: www.masshort.org (1)

Feiler, William, Amvac Chemical Corp, Los Angeles, CA. Tel: (323) 264-3910, FAX: (323) 268-1028, Web Site: www.amvac-chemical.com (8)

Feinberg, Bob, Stephan Partners Inc, New York, NY. Tel: (212) 524-8583, E-Mail: george@stephenpartners.com, Web Site: www.stephanpartners.com (35)

Feinberg, Kenneth, R., Washington National Opera, Washington, DC. Tel: (202) 295-2400, (800) US-OPERA, FAX: (202) 295-2460, E-Mail: mail@dc-opera.org, Web Site: www.dc-opera.org (16)

Feinberg, Stan, SF Video Inc, San Francisco, CA. Tel: (415) 288-9400, (800) 545-5865, FAX: (415) 288-9410, E-Mail: selfservice@sfvideo.com, Web Site: www.sfvideo.com (3)

Feinberg, Steven, SF Video Inc, San Francisco, CA. Tel: (415) 288-9400, (800) 545-5865, FAX: (415) 288-9410, E-Mail: selfservice@sfvideo.com, Web Site: www.sfvideo.com (3)

Feiner, Donna, The Advertising Council Inc, New York, NY. Tel: (212) 922-1500, FAX: (212) 922-1676, E-Mail: info@adcouncil.org, Web Site: www.adcouncil.org (1)

Feingold, Ben, Columbia Tristar Home Video, Culver City, CA. Tel: (310) 244-4000, FAX: (310) 244-1544, Web Site: www.cthe.com (16)

Feingold, David, Emigrant Savings Bank, New York, NY. Tel: (212) 850-4521, (800) EMIGRANT, FAX: (212) 850-4372, Web Site: www.emigrant.com (14)

Feingold, Reenie, Visual Horizons, Rochester, NY. Tel: (585) 424-5300, (800) 424-1011, FAX: (800) 424-5411, E-Mail: cs@visualhorizons.com, Web Site: www.visualhorizons.com (16)

Feingold, Stanley, Z., Visual Horizons, Rochester, NY. Tel: (585) 424-5300, (800) 424-1011, FAX: (800) 424-5411, E-Mail: cs@visualhorizons.com, Web Site: www.visualhorizons.com (16)

Feinour, Kenneth, Diakon Lutheran Social Ministries, Allentown, PA. Tel: (610) 682-2145, (888) 582-2230, FAX: (610) 682-1055, E-Mail: swangerb@diakon.org, Web Site: www.diakon.org (1)

Feinsod, Joan, Graphik Dimensions Ltd, High Point, NC. Tel: (336) 887-3500, (800) 221-0262, FAX: (336) 887-3773, E-Mail: customercare@pictureframes.com, Web Site: www.pictureframes.com (14)

Feinson, Jim, Gardener's Supply Co, Burlington, VT. Tel: (802) 660-3500, (888) 833-1412, FAX: (802) 660-3501, E-Mail: info@gardeners.com, Web Site: www.gardeners.com (8)

Feinstein, Barbara, Right On Computer Software, Greenlawn, NY. E-Mail: riteonsoft@aol.com, Web Site: rightonprograms.com (3)

Feinstein, Don, Right On Computer Software, Greenlawn, NY. E-Mail: riteonsoft@aol.com, Web Site: rightonprograms.com (3)

Feinstein, Peter, Higher Power Marketing, Phoenix, AZ. Tel: (480) 837-3580, (888) 922-3580, FAX: (480) 837-3589, E-Mail: info@hpowermarketing.com, Web Site: www.hpowermarketing.com (30)

Felco Printing & Mailing, Kansas City, MO. Tel: (816) 421-5164, (800) 467-0805, FAX: (816) 421-1607, E-Mail: felco@felco.net, Web Site: www.felco.net (27)

Feldberg, Harley, Avnet Inc, Phoenix, AZ. Tel: (480) 643-2000, FAX: (480) 643-7240, Web Site: www.avnet.com (16)

Feldbush, A.F., A&M Direct Mail Service Inc, San Dimas, CA. Tel: (909) 599-3905, (909) 579-0111, (800) 735-3905, FAX: (909) 599-3516, E-Mail: mail@amdirectmail.com (28)

Feldman, Harvey, A., Harvey Associates-Direct Marketing Solutions, Cresskill, NJ. Tel: (201) 962-8463, E-Mail: harveyfnj@optonline.net (3)

Feldman, Jeffrey, Media Directions Inc, Woodcliff Lake, NJ. Tel: (201) 930-4949, FAX: (201) 930-9229, E-Mail: mail@media-directions.com, Web Site: www.media-directions.com (23)

Feldman, Jerome, I., General Physics Corp, Elkridge, MD. Tel: (410) 379-3600, (800) 727-6677, FAX: (410) 540-5302, E-Mail: info@gpworldwide.com, Web Site: www.gpworldwide.com (16)

Feldman, Joel, Zenith Direct, New York, NY. Tel: (212) 859-5100, Web Site: www.zodirect.com (35)

Feldman, Martin, J, Mark Clements Research Inc, Mount Kisco, NY. Tel: (914) 241-1803, FAX: (914) 241-7763, E-Mail: mjfharvey@aol.com, Web Site: www.markclementsresearch.com (30)

Feldman, Rich, Source Marketing, Norwalk, CT. Tel: (203) 222-2741, FAX: (203) 291-4010, E-Mail: bardes@source-marketing.com, Web Site: www.source-marketing.com (35)

Feldman, Roger S., Feldman & Associates Inc, Northfield, IL. Tel: (847) 784-0404, FAX: (847) 784-0664, E-Mail: rfeldman@feldmans.net (35)

Feldman, Samuel, Samuel Feldman, New York, NY. Tel: (212) 362-9517, E-Mail: samuelfeldman@verizon.net (39)

Feldman & Associates Inc, Northfield, IL. Tel: (847) 784-0404, FAX: (847) 784-0664, E-Mail: rfeldman@feldmans.net (35)

Samuel Feldman, New York, NY. Tel: (212) 362-9517, E-Mail: samuelfeldman@verizon.net (39)

Feldstein, Eric, A., GMAC Insurance, Atlanta, GA. Tel: (314) 493-8000, (800) GMAC-123, FAX: (314) 493-8114, Web Site: www.gmacinsurance.com (15)

Felke, Kathryn, IMPACT International Marketing, Lake Havasu City, AZ. Tel: (866) 389-0798, E-Mail: salesinfo@imgroup.com, Web Site: www.imgroup.com (35)

Felmer, Tom, Brady Corp, Milwaukee, WI. Tel: (414) 358-6600, (800) 541-1686, FAX: (800) 292-2289, Web Site: www.bradycorp.com (16)

Felsenthal, Bob, BtoB Magazine, New York, NY. Tel: (212) 210-0206, FAX: (212) 210-0422, E-Mail: aholtzman@crain.com, Web Site: www.btobonline.com (43)

Felshman, Tamara, Gilson Co Inc, Lewis Center, OH. Tel: (740) 548-7298, (800) 444-1508, FAX: (740) 548-5314, E-Mail: sales@gilsonco.com, Web Site: www.globalgilson.com (9)

Felsing, Myles, RedEnvelope Inc, San Diego, CA. Tel: (619) 528-4888, (877) 733-3683, Web Site: www.redenvelope.com (6)

Feltheimer, John, Lions Gate Entertainment, New York, NY. Tel: (212) 577-2400, FAX: (212) 962-2872, Web Site: www.liensgatefilms.com (32)

Fencik, George, George Fencik Associates, Point Pleasant, NJ. Tel: (732) 295-8092, (800) 443-6743, FAX: (732) 295-1729, E-Mail: gfencik@aol.com (16)

George Fencik Associates, Point Pleasant, NJ. Tel: (732) 295-8092, (800) 443-6743, FAX: (732) 295-1729, E-Mail: gfencik@aol.com (16)

Fendler, Stephen, CM Almy & Son Inc, Greenwich, CT. Tel: (203) 552-7600, FAX: (203) 552-7605, E-Mail: almyaccess@almy.com, Web Site: www.almy.com (5)

Feng, Pia, P., Peppermill Marketing Inc, Los Angeles, CA. Tel: (310) 659-8900, (877) 600-7775, FAX: (310) 659-8901, E-Mail: inquiry@peppermillmarketing.com, Web Site: www.peppermillmarketing.com (23)

Fenkel, William R., Styled Packaging LLC, Philadelphia, PA. Tel: (610) 529-4122, FAX: (610) 520-9662, E-Mail: bill@styledpackaging.com, Web Site: www.styledpackaging.com (34)

Fennessey, Kevin, Pernod Ricard USA, Purchase, NY. Tel: (914) 848-4800, Web Site: www.pernod-ricard-usa.com (16)

Fenske, Tom, Fenske Media Corp, Rapid City, SD. Tel: (605) 343-6070, (800) 821-6343, FAX: (605) 348-2108, E-Mail: tomf@fenskemedia.com, Web Site: www.fenskemedia.com (34)

Fenske Media Corp, Rapid City, SD. Tel: (605) 343-6070, (800) 821-6343, FAX: (605) 348-2108, E-Mail: tomf@fenskemedia.com, Web Site: www.fenskemedia.com (34)

Fenwick, Katherine, CNA, Chicago, IL. Tel: (312) 822-5000, (800) 262-2000, E-Mail: cna_help@cna.com, Web Site: www.cna.com (15)

Ferari, William, Forecast Direct Marketing Group, Pittsburgh, PA. Tel: (412) 481-5699, FAX: (412) 481-0872, E-Mail: forecast@sgi.net (21)

Ferber, Elizabeth, Fifth Avenue Committee, Brooklyn, NY. FAX: (718) 237-5366, Web Site: www.fifthave.org (1)

Ferentinos, John, Qualco, Inc, Passaic, NJ. Tel: (973) 473-1222, (800) 289-2567, FAX: (973) 473-0535, E-Mail: feedback@qualco.com, Web Site: www.qualco.com (8)

Ferentinos, Thomas, Qualco, Inc, Passaic, NJ. Tel: (973) 473-1222, (800) 289-2567, FAX: (973) 473-0535, E-Mail: feedback@qualco.com, Web Site: www.qualco.com (8)

Ferguson, Daniel, Universal Engineering Corp, Cedar Rapids, IA. Tel: (319) 365-0441, (800) 366-2051, FAX: (319) 369-5440, E-Mail: info@universalcrusher.com, Web Site: www.universalcrusher.com (16)

Ferguson, Frank, E., Curriculum Associates Inc, North Billerica, MA. Tel: (978) 667-8000, FAX: (978) 667-5706, E-Mail: cainfo@curriculumassociates.com, Web Site: www.curriculumassociates.com (17)

Ferguson, Jack, PC Connection, Merrimack, NH. Tel: (603) 683-2167, (800) 800-0014, FAX: (603) 683-5773, E-Mail: pr@pcconnection.com, Web Site: www.pcconnection.com, macconnection.com (22)

Ferguson Publishing Co, New York, NY. Tel: (212) 613-2800, (800) 322-8755, FAX: (800) 678-3633, E-Mail: custserv@factsonfile.com, Web Site: www.fergpubco.com (17)

Ferillo, Charles, Ferillo & Associates, Columbia, SC. Tel: (803) 771-6106, FAX: (803) 799-8019 (35)

Ferillo & Associates, Columbia, SC. Tel: (803) 771-6106, FAX: (803) 799-8019 (35)

Fernandez, Christina, B., National Humane Education Society, Charles Town, WV. Tel: (304) 725-0506, FAX: (304) 725-1523, E-Mail: nhesinformation@nhes.org, Web Site: www.nhes.org (1)

Fernandez, James, Tiffany & Co, New York, NY. Tel: (212) 755-8000, FAX: (212) 320-7550, Web Site: www.tiffany.com (6)

Fernandez, Raul, Proxicom, Reston, VA. Tel: (703) 262-3200, FAX: (703) 262-3201, Web Site: www.proxicom.com (32)

Ferrara, Kellie, Stewart Enterprises Inc, Jefferson, LA. Tel: (504) 729-1400, (800) 535-6017, FAX: (504) 729-1984, Web Site: www.stewartenterprises.com (16)

Ferrara, Michael C., Microfluidics Corp, Newton, MA. Tel: (617) 969-5452, (800) 370-5452, FAX: (617) 965-1213, E-Mail: info@mfics.com, Web Site: www.microfluidicscorp.com (16)

Ferrara Bakery & Cafe Inc, New York, NY. Tel: (212) 226-6150, FAX: (212) 226-0667, E-Mail: information@ferraracafe.com, Web Site: www.ferraracafe.com (4)

Ferrari, Nick, Erdos & Morgan Inc, Syosset, NY. Tel: (516) 935-6959, FAX: (516) 935-4040, E-Mail: info@erdosmorgan.com, Web Site: www.erdosmorgan.com (30)

Ferrato, Jim, Protocol Integrated Direct Marketing, Sarasota, FL. Tel: (800) 677-2001, (800) 351-3774, FAX: (941) 906-9099, Web Site: www.protocolmarketing.com (21)

Ferrer, Alberto, The Vidal Partnership, New York, NY. Tel: (646) 356-6600, FAX: (212) 661-7650, Web Site: www.vidalpartnership.com (35)

Ferres, Stephanie, Motherwear, Holyoke, MA. Tel: (413) 586-1978, (800) 950-2500, FAX: (413) 532-4058, E-Mail: customerservice@motherwear.com, Web Site: www.motherwear.com (2)

Ferrin, Lynn, Select Comfort Corp, Minneapolis, MN. Tel: (763) 551-7000, (888) 411-2188, FAX: (763) 551-7826, Web Site: www.selectcomfort.com (16)

Ferrini, John, JF Direct Marketing Inc, Ossining, NY. Tel: (914) 762-8633, FAX: (914) 762-9247, E-Mail: jfdirect@bestweb.net, Web Site: www.jfdirectmarketing.com (23)

Ferrise, Sam, Baldwin Filters, Kearney, NE. Tel: (308) 234-1951, (800) 822-5394, FAX: (800) 828-4453, E-Mail: info@baldwinfilter.com, Web Site: www.baldwinfilter.com (16)

Ferruzza, Gene, Communifx, Cranberry, PA. Tel: (724) 935-8655, Web Site: www.communifax.com (27)

Fertig, Dennis, Consumers Digest Inc, Deerfield, IL. Tel: (847) 607-3000, FAX: (847) 763-0200, E-Mail: postmaster@consumersdigest.com, Web Site: www.consumersdigest.com (17)

Festa, Fred, W R Grace & Co, Columbia, MD. Tel: (410) 531-4000, FAX: (410) 531-4367, Web Site: www.grace.com (16)

Fetherston, Jim, Hess Print Solutions, Kent, OH. Tel: (330) 677-3353, FAX: (330) 677-8256, E-Mail: sshowerman@hessprintsolutions.com, Web Site: www.thepressofohio.com (27)

Fetherstonhaugh, Brian, OgilvyOne Worldwide, New York, NY. Tel: (212) 237-6000, Web Site: www.ogilvy-canada.com (35)

Fetner, John, Kellyco Metal Detector Distributors, Winter Springs, FL. Tel: (407) 699-8700, (800) 327-9697, FAX: (407) 695-6671, E-Mail: customerservice@kellycodetectors.com, Web Site: www.kellycodetectors.com (11)

Fetter Label, Louisville, KY. Tel: (502) 634-4771, (800) 234-4771, FAX: (502) 634-3587, E-Mail: info@fettergroup.com (27)

Feuss, Linda, C H Robinson Worldwide Inc, Eden Prairie, MN. Tel: (952) 937-8500, FAX: (952) 937-6740, E-Mail: info@chrobinson.com, Web Site: www.chrobinson.com (16)

Fewell, Mike, Passport International Ltd, North Charleston, SC. Tel: (843) 881-8690, (800) 606-1383, FAX: (843) 881-6247, E-Mail: csv@passportintl.com, Web Site: www.passportintl.com (2)

Fick, Stephen, Kirshenbaum, Bond & Partners, New York, NY. Tel: (212) 633-0080, FAX: (212) 463-8643, E-Mail: press@kb.com, Web Site: www.kb.com (35)

Ficke, Randy, Associated Premium Corp, Cincinnati, OH. Tel: (513) 679-4444, FAX: (513) 679-4447, Web Site: www.associatedpremium.com (33)

Fiddler's Rock Communications Inc, McLean, VA. Tel: (703) 406-1500, FAX: (703) 406-1595, Web Site: www.frmktg.com (33)

The Fidelis Group Inc, Little Ferry, NJ. Tel: (410) 721-3450, Web Site: www.thefidelisgroup.net (22)

Fidelity Investments, Boston, MA. Tel: (617) 563-7000, (800) 343-3548, FAX: (617) 476-6150, Web Site: www.fidelity.com (14)

Fidelity Security Life Insurance Co, Kansas City, MO. Tel: (816) 756-1060, (800) 648-8624, FAX: (816) 968-0580, E-Mail: info@fslins.com, Web Site: www.fslins.com (15)

Fiedler, Maryanne, Voice Systems Engineering Inc, Langhorne, PA. Tel: (215) 953-8568, Web Site: www.vseinc.com (32)

Field, David, National Trust for Historic Preservation, Washington, DC. Tel: (202) 588-6124, Web Site: www.nationaltrust.org (1)

Field, Jessamy, Howard Rice Nemerovski Canady Falk & Rabkin, San Francisco, CA. Tel: (415) 464-1000, Web Site: www.howardrice.com (14)

Field, Kenneth, W., Continental Web Press Inc, Itasca, IL. Tel: (630) 773-1903, FAX: (630) 773-1909, Web Site: www.continentalweb.com (27)

The Field Companies Inc, Watertown, MA. Tel: (617) 926-5550, (800) 346-6552, FAX: (617) 924-9011, E-Mail: info@fieldcompanies.com, Web Site: www.fieldcompanies.com (21)

The Field Museum, Chicago, IL. Tel: (312) 665-7909, FAX: (312) 665-7101, Web Site: www. fieldmuseum.org (1)

Fielder, Lynn, Planned Parenthood Mar Monte, San Jose, CA. Tel: (408) 287-7532, FAX: (408) 971-6935, Web Site: www.plannedparenthood.org (1)

Fielder's Choice Direct, Monticello, IN. Tel: (574) 583-2741 X107, (800) 321-3177, FAX: (574) 583-CORN, Web Site: www.fielderschoicedirect.com (8)

Fielding, Jennifer, Electric Insurance Co, Beverly, MA. Tel: (978) 921-2080, (800) 227-2757, FAX: (978) 524-5583, E-Mail: sales@electricinsurance. com, Web Site: www.electricinsurance.com (15)

Fiedler, David L., ESL Federal Credit Union, Rochester, NY. Tel: (585) 336-1000, (800) 848-2265, FAX: (585) 336-1138, Web Site: www.esl.org (14)

Fields, Cindy, Cynthia Fields & Co (CFC), New York, NY. Tel: (212) 242-6063 (20)

Fields, Joan, Mailworks Inc, Freeport, ME. Tel: (207) 865-1477, FAX: (207) 865-1479, E-Mail: mailwks@aol.com, Web Site: www.mailworks.net (1)

Fieldstone Gardens Inc, Vassalboro, ME. Tel: (207) 923-3836, FAX: (207) 923-3836, E-Mail: info@ fieldstonegardens.com, Web Site: www. fieldstonegardens.com (8)

Fienberg, Debra, Douglas Press Inc, Bellwood, IL. Tel: (708) 547-8400, (800) 323-0705, FAX: (708) 547-0296, Web Site: www.douglaspress.com (16)

Fienberg, Frank, Douglas Press Inc, Bellwood, IL. Tel: (708) 547-8400, (800) 323-0705, FAX: (708) 547-0296, Web Site: www.douglaspress.com (16)

Fiengold, Reenie, Store Smart Express/Visual Horizons, Rochester, NY. Tel: (585) 424-5300, (800) 424-1011, FAX: (585) 424-1064, E-Mail: cs@ storesmart.com, Web Site: www.storesmart.com (16)

Fiengold, Stan, Store Smart Express/Visual Horizons, Rochester, NY. Tel: (585) 424-5300, (800) 424-1011, FAX: (585) 424-1064, E-Mail: cs@ storesmart.com, Web Site: www.storesmart.com (16)

Fierko, Ed, Osmonics Inc, Minnetonka, MN. Tel: (952) 264-3937, (800) 605-6698, FAX: (952) 536-3301, Web Site: www.osmonics.com (16)

Fifth Avenue Committee, Brooklyn, NY. FAX: (718) 237-5366, Web Site: www.fifthave.org (1)

Fifth Gear, Indianapolis, IN. Tel: (317) 631-0907, Web Site: www.sigma-micro.com (22)

Fifth Third Bank, Cincinnati, OH. Tel: (800) 972-3030, FAX: (231) 922-4060, Web Site: www.53. com (14)

Figi's Inc, Marshfield, WI. Tel: (715) 387-1771, (800) 422-3444, FAX: (715) 384-1129, Web Site: www. figis.com (4)

Figler, Jeff, Jefferson Mailing Lists, Poway, CA. Tel: (858) 679-1233, FAX: (858) 679-1279 (23)

Figliulo, Mark, TBWA/Chiat/Day Inc, New York, NY. Tel: (212) 804-1000, FAX: (212) 804-1200, E-Mail: jamie.gallo@tbwachiat.com, Web Site: www.tbwachiat.com (35)

Figuccio, Jim, Hatteras, Tinton Falls, NJ. Tel: (732) 223-9888, Web Site: www.hatteraspc.com (27)

Figurs*, Toronto, ON Canada. Tel: (416) 826-9083 (20)

Figurski, Dan, Educational Resources, Elgin, IL. Tel: (800) 860-7004, FAX: (800) 610-5005, E-Mail: sales@edresources.com, Web Site: www. educationalresources.com (3)

FileMaker Inc, Santa Clara, CA. Tel: (408) 987-7347, Web Site: www.filemaker.com (22)

Filene's Basement, Secaucus, NJ. Tel: (617) 348-7000, FAX: (617) 357-2596 (16)

Fili-Krushel, Patricia, Time Warner Inc, New York, NY. Tel: (212) 484-8000, Web Site: www. timewarner.com (16)

Filipopoulas, Anna, Direct Energy, Toronto, ON Canada. Tel: (416) 758-8700, (800) 348-2999 (16)

Filkins, Dan, Aerovox Inc, New Bedford, MA. Tel: (508) 994-9661, (888) AEROVOX, FAX: (508) 995-3000, E-Mail: sales1@aerovox.com, Web Site: www.aerovox.com (16)

Filla, Tom, Houston Direct Marketing Association, Houston, TX. Tel: (281) 931-8883, FAX: (281) 820-4023, Web Site: www.houstondma.org (40)

Filmore, Charles, Rickert, Unity School of Christianity, Unity Village, MO. Tel: (816) 254-3550, FAX: (816) 251-3554, E-Mail: unity@unityonline.org, Web Site: www.unityonline.org (17)

Films Media Group, New York, NY. Tel: (609) 671-1000, (800) 257-5126, FAX: (609) 671-0266, E-Mail: custserv@films.com, Web Site: www. filmsmediagroup.com (3)

Fimmano, Frank, J., Aon Consulting New York, New York, NY. Tel: (212) 792-9759, (212) 792-9700, (212) 441-2000, FAX: (212) 792-9720, E-Mail: garry_sullivan@aoncons.com (15)

Fimpler Jr., William, Cane & Basket Supply Co, Los Angeles, CA. Tel: (323) 939-9644, FAX: (323) 939-7237, E-Mail: info@canebasket.com, Web Site: www.canebasket.com (8)

Fimpler, William, L., Cane & Basket Supply Co, Los Angeles, CA. Tel: (323) 939-9644, FAX: (323) 939-7237, E-Mail: info@canebasket.com, Web Site: www.canebasket.com (8)

Fina, George, Michael C Fina, New York, NY. Tel: (212) 557-2500, Web Site: www.michaelcfina.com (6)

Michael C Fina, New York, NY. Tel: (212) 557-2500, Web Site: www.michaelcfina.com (6)

Financial Executives International, Morristown, NJ. Tel: (973) 765-1000, FAX: (973) 765-1018, Web Site: www.financialexecutives.org (1)

Financial Publishing Co, South Bend, IN. Tel: (800) 247-3214, FAX: (574) 243-6060, Web Site: www. financial-publishing.com (17)

Financial Services International Corp, Seattle, WA. Tel: (206) 386-5475, FAX: (206) 654-0499 (14)

Financial Times, New York, NY. Tel: (212) 641-6500, Web Site: www.ft.com (17)

Finch, Kip, Vertrue Inc, Norwalk, CT. Tel: (203) 324-7635, FAX: (203) 674-7080, Web Site: www. vertrue.com (13)

Finch Paper, Glens Falls, NY. Tel: (518) 793-2541, (800) 833-9983, FAX: (518) 743-9656, E-Mail: amcdowell@finchpaper.com, Web Site: www. finchpaper.com (25)

Finck, Bill, Finck Cigar Co, San Antonio, TX. Tel: (210) 341-8888, (800) 221-0638, FAX: (210) 341-8890, E-Mail: info@finckcigar.com, Web Site: www.finckcigar.com (5)

Finck Cigar Co, San Antonio, TX. Tel: (210) 341-8888, (800) 221-0638, FAX: (210) 341-8890, E-Mail: info@finckcigar.com, Web Site: www. finckcigar.com (5)

Finck Jr, Bill, Finck Cigar Co, San Antonio, TX. Tel: (210) 341-8888, (800) 221-0638, FAX: (210) 341-8890, E-Mail: info@finckcigar.com, Web Site: www.finckcigar.com (5)

Findley, Jean, University of Pennsylvania, Philadelphia, PA. Tel: (215) 898-5000, FAX: (215) 898-9659, Web Site: www.upenn.edu (1)

Fine, Alan, Marvel Entertainment Inc, New York, NY. Tel: (212) 576-4000, FAX: (847) 579-1277, Web Site: www.marvel.com (31)

Fine Architectural Metalsmiths, Chester, NY. Tel: (845) 651-7550, FAX: (845) 651-7857, Web Site: www.iceforge.com (1)

Finelight Inc, Louisville, KY. Tel: (502) 589-5896, E-Mail: info@finelight.com, Web Site: www. finelight.com (35)

FineLine, Winnipeg, MB Canada. Tel: (204) 942-4242, Web Site: www.finelinesolutions.com (29)

Finerty, Judith, E., Finerty & Wolfe Advertising Inc, Chicago, IL. Tel: (773) 348-3918, FAX: (773) 348-5873, Web Site: www.finertyandwolfe.com (35)

Finerty & Wolfe Advertising Inc, Chicago, IL. Tel: (773) 348-3918, FAX: (773) 348-5873, Web Site: www.finertyandwolfe.com (35)

Finishing Plus, Inc, Chicago, IL. Tel: (773) 523-5510, FAX: (773) 523-9155, E-Mail: info@finishingplus. com, Web Site: www.finishingplus.com (28)

Fink, Barry, American Century Investments, Kansas City, MO. Tel: (816) 531-5575, (800) 345-2021, FAX: (816) 340-7962, Web Site: www. americancentury.com (14)

Fink, Gregg, PNC Bank Corp, Pittsburgh, PA. Tel: (412) 762-2000/3514, (800) 422-6537, FAX: (412) 762-4482 (14)

Fink, Lisa, Institute of Reading Development, Novato, CA. Tel: (415) 884-8100, (800) 964-8888, FAX: (415) 382-0760, E-Mail: contactus@ readingprograms.org, Web Site: www. readingprograms.org (1)

Fink, Mary Ann, Missouri Landscape & Nursery Association, Bowling Green, MO. Tel: (636) 542-1234, E-Mail: admin@mlng.org, Web Site: www. mlna.org (1)

Finke, Evan, Specialty Store Services Inc, Des Plaines, IL. Tel: (847) 470-7000, (888) 441-4440, FAX: (847) 470-5355, Web Site: www. specialtystoreservices.com (16)

Finke, Malcom, Specialty Store Services Inc, Des Plaines, IL. Tel: (847) 470-7000, (888) 441-4440, FAX: (847) 470-5355, Web Site: www. specialtystoreservices.com (16)

Finkelstein, James, A., Direct Marketing Market Place, Berkeley Heights, NJ. Tel: (908) 673-1000, (800) 473-7020, FAX: (908) 673-1179 (43)

Finkelstein, James, A., Marquis Who's Who LLC, Berkeley Heights, NJ. Tel: (908) 673-1000, (800) 473-7020, FAX: (908) 673-1179, E-Mail: info@ marquiswhoswho.com, Web Site: www. marquiswhoswho.com (17)

Finkelstein, James, A., Thomson Financial, New York, NY. Tel: (212) 803-8200, FAX: (212) 843-9608 (17)

Finkelstein, Steven, Carnival Creations, Irvine, CA. Tel: (949) 833-9370, FAX: (949) 955-2078 (39)

Finken, Jan, IQ Marketing, Excelsior, MN. Tel: (952) 897-7300, FAX: (952) 820-8041, Web Site: www. iqmarketing.com (21)

Finlaysonitsj, Richard, Overton's Inc, Greenville, NC. Tel: (252) 355-7600, (800) 334-6541, FAX: (252) 355-2923, E-Mail: service@overtons.com, Web Site: www.overtons.com (11)

Finley, Guy, MESA, Port Washington, NY. Tel: (516) 767-6720, Web Site: www.mesalliance.org/ (22)

Finley Products Inc, Lancaster, PA. Tel: (717) 735-8200, (888) 626-5301, FAX: (717) 735-8210, E-Mail: fininfo@finleyproducts.com, Web Site: www.2X4basics.com (16)

Finn, Jack, Destination Rewards, Boca Raton, FL. Tel: (561) 997-9940, (800) 242-6260, FAX: (561) 997-9945, Web Site: www.drloyalty.com (33)

Finn, Linda, Nordstrom Inc, Seattle, WA. Tel: (206) 303-2301, FAX: (206) 373-3198 (2)

Finn, Mickey, Destination Rewards, Boca Raton, FL. Tel: (561) 997-9940, (800) 242-6260, FAX: (561) 997-9945, Web Site: www.drloyalty.com (33)

Finn, Patrick, Results Producers, Los Angeles, CA. Tel: (213) 481-7400, FAX: (213) 481-7474, E-Mail: info@resultsproducers.com, Web Site: www.resultsproducers.com (32)

Finn, Robert, WW Grainger Inc, Lake Forest, IL. Tel: (847) 535-1000, (888) 361-8649, FAX: (847) 535-9122, Web Site: www.grainger.com (9)

Finnegan, Jackie, MCH Strategic Data, Sweet Springs, MO. Tel: (660) 335-6373, (800) 776-6373, FAX: (660) 335-4157, E-Mail: tonyab@mchdata.com, Web Site: www.mchdata.com (23)

Finnegan, Ray, A+ Letter Service, Lakewood, NJ. Tel: (732) 905-2010, FAX: (732) 905-4662, E-Mail: aplus@aplusletter.com, Web Site: www.aplusletters. com (28)

Finnegan, Ro, Rockler Woodworking & Hardware, Medina, MN. Tel: (763) 478-8201, (800) 279-4441, FAX: (763) 478-8393, E-Mail: info@rockler.com, Web Site: www.rockler.com (8)

Finnegan, Jr, John H., The Hope Co Inc, Bridgeton, MO. Tel: (314) 739-7254, (800) 325-4026, FAX: (314) 739-7786, E-Mail: info@hopecompany.com (16)

Finnegan, Sr, John, H., The Hope Co Inc, Bridgeton, MO. Tel: (314) 739-7254, (800) 325-4026, FAX: (314) 739-7786, E-Mail: info@hopecompany.com (16)

Finney, Gary, Virido LLC, Scottsdale, AZ. Tel: (480) 419-9063, Web Site: www.virido.com (29)

Finney, Julie, United Wire Service, Peoria, IL. Tel: (309) 689-6160, FAX: (309) 689-6488, E-Mail: julie.finney@choicepoint.com, Web Site: www.unitedwire.net (28)

Fiore, Dave, Balfour, Austin, TX. Tel: (512) 444-0571, FAX: (512) 440-1138, Web Site: www.artcarved.com (16)

Fiore, Stacia, Digispace Solutions LLC, San Diego, CA. Tel: (619) 684-6737, Web Site: www.digispace.com (35)

Fiorella's Jack Stack Barbecue, Kansas City, MO. Tel: (816) 452-1185, Web Site: www.jackstackbbq.com (21)

Fiorello, Vince, FLM Graphics Corp, Fairfield, NJ. Tel: (973) 575-9450, E-Mail: info@flmgraphics.com, Web Site: www.flmgraphics.com (16)

Fiorentino, Lisa, University of Pittsburgh at Bradford, Bradford, PA. Tel: (814) 362-7500, FAX: (814) 362-5150, E-Mail: admissions@www.upb.pitt.edu, Web Site: www.upd.pitt.edu (41)

Fire Light Group, White Plains, NY. Tel: (608) 441-3473, E-Mail: mincentive@aol.com, Web Site: www.incentivesmotivate.com (33)

Fire Mountain Gems, Grants Pass, OR. Tel: (541) 956-7890, (800) 423-2319, (800) 355-2137, FAX: (541) 470-GEMS, E-Mail: questions@firemtn.com, Web Site: www.firemtn.com (16)

Firebrand Group, Las Vegas, NV. Tel: (877) 776-4771, Web Site: www.firebrandgroup.biz (23)

FireFly, Honolulu, HI. Tel: (808) 545-2122, FAX: (808) 535-1655, Web Site: www.fireflyhawaii.com (21)

Fireman's Fund Insurance Co, Novato, CA. Tel: (415) 899-2000, FAX: (415) 899-3600, Web Site: www.firemansfund.com (14)

Firepower Marketing Inc, Blaine, WA. Tel: (604) 940-6900, Web Site: www.roryfatt.com (35)

Firestone, Jim, Xerox Corp, Rochester, NY. Tel: (716) 423-5090, FAX: (716) 423-5479, Web Site: www.xerox.com (16)

First, Doug, The Wisconsin Cheeseman, Sun Prairie, WI. Tel: (608) 837-5166, (800) 698-1721, FAX: (608) 837-5493, Web Site: www.wisconsincheeseman.com (4)

First Advantage Membership Services, Poway, CA. Tel: (619) 938-6803 (14)

First American CoreLogic, Santa Ana, CA. Tel: (866) 774-3282, Web Site: www.facorelogic.com (30)

First American Printing & Direct Mail, Ocean Springs, MS. Tel: (228) 875-8199, (800) 967-2637, FAX: (228) 875-8198, E-Mail: sales@fapdm.com, Web Site: www.fapdm.com (21)

First Banks Inc, Hazelwood, MO. Tel: (314) 592-5000, (800) 760-2265, Web Site: www.firstbanks.com (14)

First Class Direct Inc, Loveland, CO. Tel: (970) 613-0608, Web Site: www.firstclassdirect.com (21)

First Cyber Services, Omaha, NE. Tel: (402) 330-3222, (888) 977-3222, FAX: (402) 330-3444, E-Mail: cat@1csinc.com, Web Site: www.firstcyberserv.com (31)

First Data Corp, Greenwood Village, CO. Tel: (303) 488-8000, (800) 735-3362, Web Site: www.firstdata.com (28)

First Data Merchant Services, Greenwood Village, CO. Tel: (303) 488-8000, (800) 735-3362, Web Site: www.firstdata.com (14)

First Direct Corp, Hopewell Junction, NY. Tel: (845) 221-3800, (800) 935-4386, E-Mail: info@1stdirect.com, Web Site: www.1stdirect.com (35)

First Direct Marketing LLC, Bellevue, NE. Tel: (402) 403-0000, (866) 363-9575, FAX: (402) 403-0001, E-Mail: sales@firstdirectmarketing.com, Web Site: www.firstdirectmarketing.com (23)

First Hawaiian Bank, Honolulu, HI. Tel: (808) 525-6273, (888) 844-4444, FAX: (808) 525-5798, E-Mail: bfarias@fhb.com, Web Site: www.fhb.com (14)

First Marketing Co, Pompano Beach, FL. Tel: (954) 979-0700, FAX: (954) 971-4707, Web Site: www.first-marketing.com (31)

First Media Communications Inc, Brentwood, TN. Tel: (615) 661-0826, FAX: (615) 661-4084, Web Site: www.first-media.com (16)

First Merit Bank (HQ), Akron, OH. Tel: (330) 996-6300, (888) 554-4362, Web Site: www.firstmerit.com (14)

First National Information Network, Burbank, CA. Tel: (855) 909-6800, FAX: (818) 558-6663, E-Mail: info@fnin.com, Web Site: www.fnin.com (30)

First National List Service Inc, Chicago, IL. Tel: (773) 509-1266, (888) 621-5548, FAX: (773) 509-1277, E-Mail: firstnl@sbcglobal.net (23)

The First Occupational Center of New Jersey, Orange, NJ. Tel: (973) 672-5800, FAX: (973) 672-0065, E-Mail: ocnj@ocnj.org, Web Site: www.ocnj.org (28)

First of Omaha Merchant Processing, Omaha, NE. Tel: (402) 341-0500, (800) 228-2443 (20)

First Tennessee Bank, Memphis, TN. Tel: (901) 523-4547, Web Site: www.firsttennessee.com (14)

First to the Finish Inc, Carlinville, IL. Tel: (217) 854-8305, Web Site: www.firsttothefinish.com (7)

First Wave Technologies, Atlanta, GA. Tel: (770) 431-1200, FAX: (770) 431-1201 (22)

FirstGroup America, Cincinnati, OH. Tel: (513) 419-8635, Web Site: www.firstgroupamerica.com (12)

F1rstmark Inc, Campton, NH. Tel: (603) 726-4800, (800) 729-2600, FAX: (603) 726-4840, E-Mail: info@firstmark.com, Web Site: www.firstmark.com (23)

Fischbein, Stephen, Just Packaging Inc, South Plainfield, NJ. Tel: (908) 753-6700, FAX: (908) 753-6709, E-Mail: sfischbein@justpackaging.com, Web Site: www.justpackaging.com (28)

Fischer, Crystal, AccuData Integrated Marketing, Fort Myers, FL. Tel: (239) 425-4400, (800) 732-3440, FAX: (239) 425-4401, E-Mail: info@accudata.com, Web Site: www.accudata.com (23)

Fischer, George, CA Inc, Islandia, NY. Tel: (800) 225-5224, FAX: (631) 342-3300, E-Mail: info@ca.com, Web Site: www.ca.com (16)

Fischer, John, SalesLeadsTv (Federal Union Inc), Boca Raton, FL. Tel: (561) 981-8777, (800) 590-5323, FAX: (561) 981-8786, E-Mail: contact_us@salesleads.tv, Web Site: www.salesleads.tv (23)

Fischer, Timothy, National Association for Printing Leadership, East Rutherford, NJ. Tel: (201) 634-9600, (800) 642-6275, FAX: (201) 634-0324, Web Site: www.napl.org (1)

Carl Fischer Music, New York, NY. Tel: (212) 777-0900, (800) 762-2328, FAX: (212) 477-6996, E-Mail: cf-info@carlfischer.com, Web Site: www.carlfischer.com (17)

Fiserv, Norcross, GA. Tel: (678) 375-3000, Web Site: www.checkfreecorp.com (14)

Fish, Randy, Holiday Travel of America, Carlsbad, CA. Tel: (760) 431-8600, (888) 732-2479, FAX: (760) 431-3131, E-Mail: sales@htoa.com, Web Site: www.htoa.com (19)

Fish, Robin, Rauxa Direct, Costa Mesa, CA. Tel: (714) 427-1271, Web Site: www.rauxa.com (35)

Fish-Rogers, Laura, Universal Media Syndicate Inc, Canton, OH. Tel: (330) 966-9000, Web Site: www.uni-syn.com (35)

Fishbein, Larry, The Kiplinger Washington Editors Inc, Washington, DC. Tel: (202) 887-6400, (800) 544-0155, FAX: (202) 496-1817, Web Site: www.kiplinger.com (17)

Fisher, Christopher, Broadmoor Hotel Inc, Colorado Springs, CO. Tel: (719) 634-7711, (866) 837-9520, FAX: (719) 577-5779, Web Site: www.broadmoor.com (19)

Fisher, Dave, Bunzl Distribution USA, Inc, Saint Louis, MO. Tel: (314) 997-5959, (888) 997-5959, FAX: (314) 997-1405, Web Site: www.bunzldistribution.com (16)

Fisher, George, Oral Roberts University, Tulsa, OK. Tel: (918) 495-6161, FAX: (918) 495-6222, E-Mail: admissions@oru.edu, Web Site: www.oru.edu (1)

Fisher, James, B., Innovative Marketing Services Inc, Houston, TX. Tel: (281) 398-0321, (800) 231-4678, FAX: (281) 398-0679, E-Mail: mfisher@imstcorp.com, Web Site: www.imstcorp.com (30)

Fisher, Jerry, T., Charter Communications, Saint Louis, MO. Tel: (314) 965-0555, (888) 438-2427, FAX: (314) 965-9745, Web Site: www.charteroom.com (16)

Fisher, Joseph C., Interdata, Sanibel, FL. Tel: (941) 472-1119, FAX: (941) 472-4272, E-Mail: jfisher435@aol.com, Web Site: www.interdata.org (30)

Fisher, Mark, Biomerica Inc, Irvine, CA. Tel: (949) 645-2111, FAX: (949) 722-6674, E-Mail: bmra@biomerica.com, Web Site: www.biomerica.com (7)

Fisher, Mark, NextScreen LLC, Austin, TX. Tel: (512) 892-8682, Web Site: www.avguide.com (17)

Fisher, Megan, River Street Sweets, Savannah, GA. Tel: (912) 234-4608, (800) 793-3876, FAX: (912) 234-1584, E-Mail: randerson@riverstreetsweets.com, Web Site: www.riverstreetsweets.com (4)

Fisher, Michael, Print Services Distribution Association, Chicago, IL. Tel: (703) 836-6232, (800) 336-4641, FAX: (703) 836-2241, E-Mail: psda@psda.org, Web Site: www.psda.org (1)

Fisher, Nigel, UNICEF Canada, Toronto, ON. Tel: (416) 482-4444, (800) 567-4483, FAX: (416) 487-8875, E-Mail: on.secretary@unicef.ca, Web Site: www.unicef.ca (1)

Fisher, Patti, Sea Bear, Anacortes, WA. Tel: (360) 293-4661, (800) 645-3474, FAX: (888) 487-6427, Web Site: www.seabear.com (16)

Fisher, Peter, Gaylord Entertainment Co, Nashville, TN. Tel: (615) 316-6000, Web Site: www.gaylordentertainment.com (19)

Fisher, Robin, Telesystems Marketing Inc, Houston, TX. Tel: (713) 784-3439, (800) 622-0190, FAX: (713) 780-5974, E-Mail: kimberly@nwpros.com, Web Site: www.telesystemsmarketing.com (29)

Fisher, Stefani, Van Groesbeck & Co, Richmond, VA. Tel: (804) 285-3176, Web Site: www.vangroesbeckco.com (1)

Fisher, Steven, R., Communications Corp of America, Boston, VA. Tel: (540) 547-1700, FAX: (540) 547-4600, E-Mail: contact@cca.net, Web Site: www.cca.net (21)

Fisher, Wiley, Fiorella's Jack Stack Barbecue, Kansas City, MO. Tel: (816) 452-1185, Web Site: www.jackstackbbq.com (21)

Fisher Group Inc, Hiawatha, IA. Tel: (319) 393-5405, FAX: (319) 393-2738, E-Mail: info@fishergroup.com, Web Site: www.fishergroup.com (27)

Fisher Investments, Woodside, CA. Tel: (650) 851-3334, Web Site: www.fi.com (14)

Fisher-Price, East Aurora, NY. Tel: (716) 687-3300, FAX: (716) 687-3636, Web Site: www.fisherprice.com (16)

Fisher Scientific, Pittsburgh, PA. Tel: (800) 766-7000, FAX: (800) 772-7702, Web Site: www.fishersci.com (16)

Fiske, David, Massachusetts Horticultural Society, Wellesley, MA. Tel: (617) 933-4929, (617) 933-4900, FAX: (617) 933-4901, E-Mail: hort_line@masshort.org, Web Site: www.masshort.org (1)

Fitch, Renee, The Silo Inc, New Milford, CT. Tel: (860) 355-0300, (800) 353-SILO, FAX: (860) 350-5495, E-Mail: info@hunthillfarmtrust.org, Web Site: www.thesilo.com (8)

Fite, Stephanie, Henry Wurst Inc, North Kansas City, MO. Tel: (816) 842-3113, FAX: (816) 472-6221, E-Mail: info@henrywurst.com, Web Site: www.henrywurst.com (27)

Fitness Quest, Canton, OH. Tel: (330) 478-0755, (800) 321-9236, FAX: (330) 479-9213, E-Mail: customersupport@fitnessquest.com, Web Site: www.fitnessquest.com (16)

Fitness Systems Manufacturing Corp, Sinking Spring, PA. Tel: (610) 670-0135, (800) 822-9995, E-Mail: vitaminout@aol.com, Web Site: www.fitness-systems.net (7)

Fitness USA Super Centers, West Bloomfield, MI. Tel: (248) 737-7200, (800) GET-FIT-1, FAX: (248) 932-3300, Web Site: www.fitnessusa.com (16)

Fitter International Inc, Calgary, AB Canada. Tel: (800) 348-8371, FAX: (866) 250-8824, E-Mail: sales2@fitter1.com, Web Site: www.fitter1.com (1)

Fitzgerald + Co, Atlanta, GA. Tel: (404) 504-6900, FAX: (404) 239-0548, E-Mail: dave.fitzgerald@fitzco.com, Web Site: www.fitzco.com (35)

Fitzgerald Sr, James, Rand Material Handling Equipment Co Inc, Janesville, WI. Tel: (401) 751-7657, (800) 366-2300, FAX: (800) 755-7263, E-Mail: cs@randmh.com, Web Site: www.randmh.com (16)

Fitzgerald, David, Fitzgerald + Co, Atlanta, GA. Tel: (404) 504-6900, FAX: (404) 239-0548, E-Mail: dave.fitzgerald@fitzco.com, Web Site: www.fitzco.com (35)

Fitzgerald, Gary, T., Meister Media Worldwide, Willoughby, OH. Tel: (440) 942-2000, (800) 572-7740, FAX: (440) 975-3447, E-Mail: info@meistermedia.com, Web Site: www.meistermedia.com (17)

Fitzgerald, James, AirTran Airways, Atlanta, GA. Tel: (678) 254-7459, Web Site: www.airtran.com (19)

Fitzgerald, James, Taradel LLC, Glen Allen, VA. Tel: (804) 364-8444, Web Site: www.taradel.com (31)

Fitzgerald, Jim, Calmark Inc, Chicago, IL. Tel: (773) 247-7200, FAX: (773) 247-3199, E-Mail: ljakobi@calmark-inc.com, Web Site: www.clamark-inc.com (28)

Fitzgerald, Patrick, Buena Vista Home Entertainment, Burbank, CA. Tel: (818) 560-1000, FAX: (818) 845-8728, Web Site: www.bvhe.com (3)

Fitzgerald, Rob, Walter Karl Inc, Pearl River, NY. Tel: (845) 620-0700, FAX: (845) 620-1885, E-Mail: info@walterkarl.infousa.com, Web Site: www.walterkarl.com (22)

Fitzgerald, Robert, J., Hampden Papers Inc, Holyoke, MA. Tel: (413) 536-1000, FAX: (413) 532-9161 (25)

Fitzgerald, Timothy J., The Middleby Corp, Elgin, IL. Tel: (847) 741-3300, FAX: (847) 741-0015, E-Mail: sales@middleby.com, Web Site: www.middleby.com (16)

FitzGibbon, Jim, Four Seasons Hotels & Resorts, Toronto, ON. Tel: (416) 449-1750, (800) 819-5053, FAX: (416) 441-4374, Web Site: www.fourseasons.com (19)

Fitzgibbons, Ruth, Richards Partners, Dallas, TX. Tel: (214) 891-5700, FAX: (214) 891-3515, E-Mail: ruth_fitzgibbons@richards.com, Web Site: www.richardspartners.com (35)

Fitzmorris, Andy, First Cyber Services, Omaha, NE. Tel: (402) 330-3222, (888) 977-3222, FAX: (402) 330-3444, E-Mail: cat@1csinc.com, Web Site: www.firstcyberserv.com (31)

Fitzpatrick, Bea, Orient Expressed Imports Inc, New Orleans, LA. Tel: (888) 856-3948, FAX: (504) 899-5566, E-Mail: orient@orientexpressed.com, Web Site: www.orientexpressed.com (2)

Fitzpatrick, J., Kevin, Helzberg Diamonds, North Kansas City, MO. Tel: (816) 842-7780, (800) HELZBURG, FAX: (816) 480-0294, Web Site: www.helzberg.com (16)

Fitzpatrick, J., Michael, Rohm & Haas Co, Philadelphia, PA. Tel: (215) 592-3000, (877) 288-5881, FAX: (215) 592-3377, Web Site: www.rohmhess.com (16)

Fitzpatrick, Jane, Country Curtains Inc, Lee, MA. Tel: (413) 243-1474, (800) 456-0321, FAX: (413) 243-1067, Web Site: www.countrycurtains.com (8)

Fitzpatrick, John, Cornell Lab of Ornithology, Ithaca, NY. Tel: (607) 254-2157, (800) 843-BIRD, FAX: (607) 254-2415, E-Mail: birdslides@cornell.edu, Web Site: www.birds.cornell.edu (1)

5Metacom, Carmel, IN. Tel: (317) 580-7540, FAX: (317) 580-7550, E-Mail: mail@5metacom.com, Web Site: www.5metacom.com (35)

501 Post, Austin, TX. Tel: (512) 476-3876, FAX: (512) 477-3912, E-Mail: godwyer@501studios.com, Web Site: www.501post.com (32)

Fixed Address Marketing Inc, Aurora, ON Canada. Tel: (905) 750-0029, Web Site: www.fixedaddressmarketing.com (23)

Fixel, Gary, Spectronics Corp, Westbury, NY. Tel: (800) 274-8888, FAX: (800) 491-6868, E-Mail: vscherer@spectroline.com, Web Site: www.spectroline.com (9)

Flach, Bill, Clario Analytics, Eden Prairie, MN. Tel: (952) 653-0980, (866) 849-3341, FAX: (952) 653-5900, E-Mail: sales@clarioanalytics.com, Web Site: www.clarioanalytics.com (20)

Flagg, Russell, E., Flagg Management Inc, New York, NY. Tel: (212) 286-0333, FAX: (212) 286-0086, E-Mail: flaggmgmt@msn.com, Web Site: www.flaggmgmt.com (41)

Flagg Management Inc, New York, NY. Tel: (212) 286-0333, FAX: (212) 286-0086, E-Mail: flaggmgmt@msn.com, Web Site: www.flaggmgmt.com (41)

Flaghouse Inc, Hasbrouck Heights, NJ. Tel: (201) 288-7600, (800) 793-7900, FAX: (800) 793-7922, E-Mail: sales@flaghouse.com, Web Site: www.flaghouse.com (5)

Flaherty, Brendan, Warrior Custom Golf Inc, Irvine, CA. Tel: (949) 699-2499, Web Site: www.warriorcustomgolf.com (11)

Flaherty, Dennis, Victory Corps, New Hope, MN. Tel: (763) 561-5600, (800) 328-6120, FAX: (763) 561-8523, E-Mail: cs@victorycorps.com, Web Site: www.victorycorps.com (16)

Flaherty, Jim, NBTY Inc, Ronkonkoma, NY. Tel: (631) 200-2000, FAX: (631) 567-7148, Web Site: www.nbty.com (7)

Flaherty, Lee F., Flair Communications Agency Inc, Chicago, IL. Tel: (312) 943-5959, (800) 621-8317, FAX: (312) 943-0881, E-Mail: lflaherty@flairagency.com, Web Site: www.flairpromo.com (35)

Flaherty, Pamela, M., American Health & Life Insurance Co, Fort Worth, TX. Tel: (817) 348-7500, (800) 995-2274, FAX: (817) 348-7553, Web Site: www.citifinancial.com (15)

Flair Communications Agency Inc, Chicago, IL. Tel: (312) 943-5959, (800) 621-8317, FAX: (312) 943-0881, E-Mail: lflaherty@flairagency.com, Web Site: www.flairpromo.com (35)

Flamm, Joseph, D., Flamm Advertising Inc, Great Neck, NY. Tel: (516) 466-2090 (35)

Flamm Advertising Inc, Great Neck, NY. Tel: (516) 466-2090 (35)

Flanagan, Bryan, Zig Ziglar Corp, Plano, TX. Tel: (972) 233-9191, (800) 527-0306, FAX: (469) 321-7556, E-Mail: info@ziglar.com, Web Site: www.zigziglar.com (16)

Flanagan, John F., Goodheart-Willcox Publisher, Tinley Park, IL. Tel: (708) 687-5000, (800) 323-0440, FAX: (708) 687-3900, E-Mail: custserv@g-w.com, Web Site: www.g-w.com (17)

Flanagan, Kathy, Aspen Publishers Inc, New York, NY. Tel: (800) 638-8437, FAX: (301) 417-7655, Web Site: www.aspenpublishers.com (17)

Flanagan, Sandy, APW-Wright Line, Worcester, MA. Tel: (508) 852-4300, (800) 225-7348, FAX: (508) 852-3060, Web Site: www.wrightline.com (16)

Flannery, Ann, Legal Sea Foods Inc, Boston, MA. Tel: (617) 530-9000, (800) 343-5804, FAX: (617) 530-9649, Web Site: www.legalseafoods.com (4)

Flannery, Caimin, Caimin Flannery & Associates, Naperville, IL. Tel: (630) 236-1955 (14)

Flannery, Donald, Maine Potato Board, Presque Isle, ME. Tel: (207) 769-5061, FAX: (207) 764-4148, E-Mail: mainepotatoes@mainepotatoes.com, Web Site: www.mainepotatoes.com (1)

Flannery, Michael, D., Redwood Partners Ltd, New York, NY. Tel: (212) 843-8585, FAX: (212) 843-9093, E-Mail: info@redwoodpartners.com, Web Site: www.redwoodpartners.com (20)

Caimin Flannery & Associates, Naperville, IL. Tel: (630) 236-1955 (14)

FlarePath LLC, New York, NY. Tel: (212) 927-1296 (20)

Flaten, Don D., International Direct Media Co & Information Publishing Co, San Francisco, CA. Tel: (415) 661-4730, E-Mail: infopubsf@aol.com, Web Site: www.bookwormproductions.com (17)

Flater, Kerry, Nutritional Research Associates Inc, South Whitley, IN. Tel: (260) 723-4931, (800) 456-4931, FAX: (260) 723-6297, E-Mail: info@nrfeeds.com, Web Site: www.nrfeeds.com (16)

Flatow, Mike, Sara Lee Hosiery, Winston Salem, NC. Tel: (336) 519-2711/2369, FAX: (336) 519-3254, Web Site: www.leggs.com (2)

Flatz, Sheila, University of Minnesota, Saint Paul, MN. Tel: (612) 625-0256, Web Site: www.cce.umn.edu (1)

Flaxenburg, Eric, French Creek Sheep & Wool Co Inc, Elverson, PA. Tel: (610) 286-5700, (800) 977-4337, FAX: (610) 286-0324, E-Mail: info@frenchcreeksw.com, Web Site: www.frenchcreeksw.com (2)

Flaxenburg, Jean, French Creek Sheep & Wool Co Inc, Elverson, PA. Tel: (610) 286-5700, (800) 977-4337, FAX: (610) 286-0324, E-Mail: info@frenchcreeksw.com, Web Site: www.frenchcreeksw.com (2)

Flaxman, Jon, Compaq Computer Corp, Houston, TX. Tel: (281) 370-0670, FAX: (281) 927-8835, Web Site: www.compaq.com (16)

Fleck, Steve, Jofco Inc, Jasper, IN. Tel: (812) 482-5154, (800) 23-JOFCO, FAX: (812) 634-2392, E-Mail: furniture@jofco.com, Web Site: www.jofco.com (16)

Fleet One LLC, Antioch, TN. Tel: (615) 523-6465, Web Site: www.fleetone.com (14)

Fleischer, Kathie, Intellidyn Corp, Hingham, MA. Tel: (781) 741-5503, (866) 773-5756, FAX: (631) 390-0458, E-Mail: kmf@intellidyn.com, Web Site: www.intellidyn.com (22)

Fleischer, Lee, A., University of Pennsylvania, Philadelphia, PA. Tel: (215) 898-5000, FAX: (215) 898-9659, Web Site: www.upenn.edu (1)

Fleischman, Virginia, VMF Inc, Washington, DC. Tel: (202) 966-3361, FAX: (202) 362-8409, E-Mail: veflei@aol.com (20)

Fleischmann, John, Potpourri Group Inc, Chelmsford, MA. Tel: (978) 256-4100, FAX: (978) 256-1961/0344, Web Site: www.potpourrigroup.com (6)

Fleischner, Michael, H., Peterson's, Lawrenceville, NJ. Tel: (609) 896-1800, FAX: (609) 896-1811, E-Mail: custsvc@petersons.com, Web Site: www.petersons.com (17)

Fleming, Alan, B., Las Vegas Review Journal, Las Vegas, NV. Tel: (702) 383-0211, FAX: (702) 383-4646, Web Site: www.lvrj.com (17)

Fleming, Connie, Oakstone Publishing LLC, Birmingham, AL. Tel: (205) 991-5188, (800) 952-0690, FAX: (205) 995-4656, Web Site: www.oakstonepublishing.com (17)

Fleming, Katherin, Chief Executive Magazine, Greenwich, CT. Tel: (203) 930-2700, Web Site: www.chiefexecutive.net (17)

Fleming, Mark, School Specialty Inc, Greenville, WI. Tel: (920) 734-5712, (888) 388-3224, FAX: (920) 734-5112, E-Mail: info@schoolspecialty.com, Web Site: www.schoolspecialty.com (16)

Fleming, Michele, Precision Mailing Solutions, Huntsville, AL. Tel: (256) 852-1963, FAX: (256) 852-1963, E-Mail: precisionmailing@mchsi.com (23)

Fleming, Richard, Harbour Bay Inc, Suffern, NY. Tel: (845) 368-2857, FAX: (845) 368-2349 (16)

Fleming, Robert, Byrum & Fleming, San Anselmo, CA. Tel: (415) 457-1700, Web Site: www.byrumfleming.com (23)

Fleming, Robert, L., Chick Harness & Supply Inc, Harrington, DE. Tel: (302) 398-4630, (800) 444-2441, FAX: (302) 398-3920, E-Mail: saddles@chicksaddlery.com, Web Site: www.chicksaddlery.com (11)

Fleming, Scott, Replacements Ltd, Greensboro, NC. Tel: (336) 697-3000, (800) REPLACE, FAX: (336) 697-3100, E-Mail: mark.donahue@replacements.com, Web Site: www.replacements.com (8)

Fleming, Steve, RedEnvelope Inc, San Diego, CA. Tel: (619) 528-4888, (877) 733-3683, Web Site: www.redenvelope.com (6)

Fletcher, Bill, The Right Lists Ltd, Clarksville, MD. Tel: (410) 531-0467, Web Site: www.rightlists.com (23)

Fletcher, Grant, Rastar, Salt Lake City, UT. Tel: (801) 973-6720, Web Site: www.rastek.com (35)

Fletcher, Jay, Food Chemical News, Arlington, VA. Tel: (202) 887-6320, (888) 732-7070, FAX: (202) 887-6335, E-Mail: cs@foodregulation.com, Web Site: www.foodchemicalnews.com (17)

Fletcher, Katy R., Gardens Of The Blue Ridge Inc, Pineola, NC. Tel: (828) 733-2417, FAX: (828) 733-8894, E-Mail: gardensblueridge@boone.net, Web Site: www.gardensoftheblueridge.com (8)

Fletcher, Keith, Florida Direct Marketing Association, Tamarac, FL. Tel: (786) 357-3275, E-Mail: president@fdma.org, Web Site: www.fdma.org (40)

Fletcher, Kelly, Shop At Home LLC, Knoxville, TN. Tel: (615) 263-8000, (866) 366-4010, E-Mail: public.relations@jtv.com, Web Site: www.shopathometv.com (32)

Fletcher, Patricia, PeterAlex Media Corp, Charlotte, NC. Tel: (704) 947-9082, (888) 818-3849, FAX: (704) 947-9083, E-Mail: info@peteralex.com, Web Site: www.peteralex.com (35)

Fletcher, Paul H., Gardens Of The Blue Ridge Inc, Pineola, NC. Tel: (828) 733-2417, FAX: (828) 733-8894, E-Mail: gardensblueridge@boone.net, Web Site: www.gardensoftheblueridge.com (8)

Fletcher, Robyn P., Gardens Of The Blue Ridge Inc, Pineola, NC. Tel: (828) 733-2417, FAX: (828) 733-8894, E-Mail: gardensblueridge@boone.net, Web Site: www.gardensoftheblueridge.com (8)

Fletcher, Sarah, Catalog Design Studios, Providence, RI. Tel: (888) 409-9992, Web Site: www.catalogdesignstudios.com (21)

Fletcher, William U., Fletcher Direct, Cary, NC. Tel: (919) 460-9513, FAX: (240) 757-1110, E-Mail: billf@fletcherdirect.com (35)

Fletcher, William, E., Diamond Machining Technology, Marlborough, MA. Tel: (508) 481-5944, (800) 666-4368, FAX: (508) 485-3924, E-Mail: www.dmtsharp.com (9)

Fletcher Direct, Cary, NC. Tel: (919) 460-9513, FAX: (240) 757-1110, E-Mail: billf@fletcherdirect.com (35)

Flex Products, Carlstadt, NJ. Tel: (201) 933-3030, (800) 526-6273, FAX: (201) 933-2396, E-Mail: info@flex-products.com, Web Site: www.flex-products.com (34)

FLEXcon, Spencer, MA. Tel: (508) 885-8200, Web Site: www.flexcon.com (16)

The Flexi Group Inc, Bronx, NY. Tel: (718) 543-8699, (800) 665-8053, FAX: (718) 543-8609, E-Mail: info@flexigroup.com, Web Site: www.flexigroup.com (27)

Flick, Kenneth E., Omega Research & Development, Douglasville, GA. Tel: (770) 942-9876, (800) 554-4053, Web Site: www.caralarm.com (12)

Flicker, John, National Audubon Society, New York, NY. Tel: (212) 979-3000, FAX: (212) 979-3188, Web Site: www.audubon.org (17)

Flickinger, Richard, Flickinger's Nursery, Sagamore, PA. Tel: (800) 368-7381, FAX: (724) 783-6528, Web Site: www.flicknursery.com (8)

Flickinger, Thomas, Flickinger's Nursery, Sagamore, PA. Tel: (800) 368-7381, FAX: (724) 783-6528, Web Site: www.flicknursery.com (8)

Flickinger's Nursery, Sagamore, PA. Tel: (800) 368-7381, FAX: (724) 783-6528, Web Site: www.flicknursery.com (8)

Flight Form Cases Inc, Bedford Park, IL. Tel: (708) 458-8989, (800) 657-1199, FAX: (708) 458-9023, E-Mail: info@caseguys.net, Web Site: www.flightform.com (9)

The Flinchbaugh Co Inc, Manchester, PA. Tel: (717) 266-2202, FAX: (717) 266-7055, E-Mail: flinchbaugh@blazenet.net, Web Site: www.flinchbaugh.com (16)

Flint Communications, Fargo, ND. Tel: (701) 237-4850, FAX: (701) 234-9680, Web Site: www.flintcom.com (35)

Flom, Robert, Win Craft Inc, Winona, MN. Tel: (507) 454-5510, (800) 533-8100, FAX: (507) 454-6403, Web Site: www.wincraftschool.com (5)

Flood, Bill, Upstart, Madison, WI. Tel: (920) 563-9571, FAX: (800) 448-5828, Web Site: www.highsmith.com (5)

Flora, Carlin, Sussex Publishers Inc, New York, NY. Tel: (212) 260-7210, FAX: (212) 260-7445, Web Site: www.blues-buster.com (17)

Florence, David, W., Direct Media List Management, Greenwich, CT. Tel: (203) 532-1000, FAX: (203) 532-3766, Web Site: www.directmedia.com (24)

Flores, Eduardo, CustomerFunding.com Inc, Tempe, AZ. Tel: (480) 784-1030, Web Site: www.customerfunding.com (35)

Flores, Eliezer, Action Direct Inc, Miami, FL. Tel: (305) 969-0056, E-Mail: info@action-direct.com, Web Site: www.action-direct.com (11)

Flores, J.O., Action Direct Inc, Miami, FL. Tel: (305) 969-0056, E-Mail: info@action-direct.com, Web Site: www.action-direct.com (11)

Flores, Johnny, San Antonio Express-News, San Antonio, TX. Tel: (210) 250-2601, Web Site: www.express-news.net (35)

Flores, Omar, Action Direct Inc, Miami, FL. Tel: (305) 969-0056, E-Mail: info@action-direct.com, Web Site: www.action-direct.com (11)

Flores, Peter, P., Texas Parks & Wildlife Dept, Austin, TX. Tel: (512) 389-4800, (800) 792-1112, FAX: (512) 389-8029, Web Site: www.tpwd.state.tx.us (1)

Flores, Robert, Luster Care Products, Saint Louis, MO. Tel: (636) 272-1885, (800) 291-5223, FAX: (636) 272-1869, Web Site: www.lusterlace.com (16)

Floria, Jenny, Gillette Children's Specialty Healthcare, Saint Paul, MN. Tel: (651) 229-1726, Web Site: www.gillettechildrens.org (1)

Florian, Beth, Florian Tools, Southington, CT. Tel: (860) 628-9643, (800) 275-3618, FAX: (860) 628-6036, E-Mail: sales@floriantools.com, Web Site: www.floriantools.com (8)

Florian, Jared, What on Earth, Hudson, OH. Tel: (330) 963-6554, (800) 945-2552, FAX: (800) 950-9569, Web Site: www.whatonearthcatalog.com (5)

Florian, Judy, Florian Tools, Southington, CT. Tel: (860) 628-9643, (800) 275-3618, FAX: (860) 628-6036, E-Mail: sales@floriantools.com, Web Site: www.floriantools.com (8)

Florian, Nathaniel, Florian Tools, Southington, CT. Tel: (860) 628-9643, (800) 275-3618, FAX: (860) 628-6036, E-Mail: sales@floriantools.com, Web Site: www.floriantools.com (8)

Florian, Sean, E., Florian Tools, Southington, CT. Tel: (860) 628-9643, (800) 275-3618, FAX: (860) 628-6036, E-Mail: sales@floriantools.com, Web Site: www.floriantools.com (8)

Florian Tools, Southington, CT. Tel: (860) 628-9643, (800) 275-3618, FAX: (860) 628-6036, E-Mail: sales@floriantools.com, Web Site: www.floriantools.com (8)

Florida A&M University, Tallahassee, FL. Tel: (850) 599-3718, FAX: (850) 599-3086 (16)

Florida Credit Union, Gainesville, FL. Tel: (352) 377-4141, Web Site: www.flcu.org (14)

Florida Direct Marketing Association, Tamarac, FL. Tel: (786) 357-3275, E-Mail: president@fdma.org, Web Site: www.fdma.org (40)

Florida Gift Fruit Shippers Association, Orlando, FL. Tel: (407) 295-1491, FAX: (407) 290-0918, Web Site: www.fgfsa.com (1)

Florida Institute of CPA's, Tallahassee, FL. Tel: (850) 224-2727, (800) 342-3197 (FL), FAX: (850) 222-8190, E-Mail: msc@ficpa.org, Web Site: www.ficpa.org (1)

Florida Power & Light Co, Miami, FL. Tel: (305) 552-3552, (800) 468-8243, FAX: (305) 552-2487, Web Site: www.fpl.com (16)

Florida Power Corp, Saint Petersburg, FL. Tel: (727) 820-5151, (800) 700-8744, FAX: (727) 384-7865, Web Site: www.progressenergy.com (16)

Florida Today, Melbourne, FL. Tel: (321) 242-3500, (877) 424-0156, FAX: (321) 242-3729, Web Site: www.floridatoday.com (17)

Florin, Dave, The Hiebing Group, Madison, WI. Tel: (608) 256-6357, FAX: (608) 256-0693, E-Mail: ideas@hiebing.com, Web Site: www.hiebing.com (35)

Flory III, Curtis B., Zircon Co Inc, Salem, MA. Tel: (978) 741-7000, FAX: (978) 532-0012 (22)

Flowers, Michael, Rascal, Sewell, NJ. Tel: (856) 468-1000, (800) 662-4548, FAX: (856) 468-3426, Web Site: www.electricmobility.com (7)

Flowers, Robb, Hobart & William Smith Colleges, Geneva, NY. Tel: (315) 781-3000, (800) 852-2256, FAX: (315) 781-3655, Web Site: www.hws.edu (19)

Floyd, Craig, National Law Enforcement Officers Memorial Fund, Washington, DC. Tel: (202) 737-3400, Web Site: www.nleomf.com (1)

Floyd, Elson, S., University of Missouri, Columbia, MO. Tel: (573) 882-6333, (800) 856-2181, FAX: (573) 882-2721, E-Mail: visitus@missouri.edu, Web Site: www.missouri.edu (41)

Fluid Metering Inc, Syosset, NY. Tel: (516) 922-6050, (800) 223-3388, FAX: (516) 624-8261, E-Mail: pumps@fmipump.com, Web Site: www.fmipump.com (16)

Fluke, John, M., PACCAR Inc, Bellevue, WA. Tel: (425) 468-7400, FAX: (425) 468-8216, Web Site: www.paccar.com (16)

Fluke Biomedical, Everett, WA. Tel: (425) 347-6100, (800) 850-4608, FAX: (425) 446-5116, Web Site: www.flukebiomedical.com (16)

Flynn, Jack, Tann Selective Communications Inc, Richmond Hill, ON Canada. Tel: (905) 881-1030, FAX: (416) 881-1035 (21)

Flynn, Jim, Hult Fritz Matuszak Associates, Peoria, IL. Tel: (309) 673-8191, FAX: (309) 674-5530, E-Mail: jflynn@hfma.com, Web Site: www.hfma.com (35)

Flynn, Kris, LO-AD Communications, Pasadena, CA. Tel: (626) 304-7750, FAX: (626) 304-2716, Web Site: www.lo-ad.com (16)

Flynn, Liz, Marsh US Consumer, Urbandale, IA. Tel: (515) 365-6102 (15)

Flynn, Marcella, E., PRIORITY Data Systems Inc, Omaha, NE. Tel: (402) 592-2550, (877) 273-7774, FAX: (402) 592-5052, E-Mail: sales@pdomaha.com, Web Site: www.priority-data.com (22)

Flynn, Pat, Bentley College, Waltham, MA. Tel: (781) 891-2800, FAX: (781) 891-3449, Web Site: www.bentley.edu (13)

Flynn, Terry, Hello Direct, Nashua, NH. Tel: (408) 972-1990, (800) 435-5634, FAX: (408) 972-8155, Web Site: www.hello-direct.com (16)

Flynn, William, J., Mutual of America Life Insurance Co, New York, NY. Tel: (212) 224-1600, (800) 468-3785, FAX: (212) 224-2539, Web Site: www.mutualofamerica.com (14)

FocalPoint Marketing LLC, Metuchen, NJ. Tel: (877) 252-4305, Web Site: www.nipgroup.com (35)

Focus Direct - a Dmh Marketing Partners Co, San Antonio, TX. Tel: (210) 247-1634, (800) 299-9185, FAX: (210) 247-1691, Web Site: www.focusdirect.com (28)

Focus on the ROI, Massapequa Park, NY. Tel: (917) 620-1838 (20)

Focus Plus Inc, New York, NY. Tel: (212) 675-0142, (800) 340-8846, FAX: (212) 645-3171, E-Mail: info@focusplusny.com, Web Site: www.focusplusny.com (30)

Focus USA Inc, Hackensack, NJ. Tel: (201) 489-2525, FAX: (201) 489-4499, E-Mail: suzanne@focus-usa-l.com, Web Site: www.focus-usa-l.com (23)

Fogarty, Michael, Kokopelli Communications Group Inc, Chicago, IL. Tel: (312) 726-5656, Web Site: www.kcgi.net (35)

Fogel, Bob, Uniforms & Scrubs.com, Ballwin, MO. Tel: (636) 391-9200, FAX: (636) 391-9205, E-Mail: questions@uniformsandscrubs.com, Web Site: www.whiteswanscrubs.com (7)

Fogel, Henry, League of American Orchestras, New York, NY. Tel: (212) 262-5161, FAX: (212) 262-5198, Web Site: www.symphony.org; www.americanorchestras.org (1)

Foggle, Glen, American Century Investments, Kansas City, MO. Tel: (816) 531-5575, (800) 345-2021, FAX: (816) 340-7962, Web Site: www.americancentury.com (14)

Foilmania, Miami, FL. Tel: (305) 854-8525, Web Site: www.foilmania.com (27)

Fojtik, Carl, The Motivation Show, Westmont, IL. Tel: (630) 434-7779, (800) 752-6312, FAX: (630) 434-1216, E-Mail: moti@heiexpo.com, Web Site: www.motivationshow.com (42)

Folder Factory Inc, Mount Jackson, VA. Tel: (540) 984-8852, (800) 296-4321, FAX: (540) 477-9677, E-Mail: webmaster@folders.com, Web Site: www.folders.com (27)

Foley, Kevin, ACCENT Marketing Services LLC, Jeffersonville, IN. Tel: (812) 206-6200, Web Site: www.accentonline.com (20)

Foley, Kevin, S., Business Planners & Consultants Inc, New York, NY. Tel: (212) 972-1970, FAX: (212) 972-1126 (15)

Foley, Nick, Home Planners, Tucson, AZ. Tel: (520) 297-8200, FAX: (520) 297-6219, E-Mail: sales@homeplanners.com, Web Site: www.homeplanners.com (17)

Foley, Nick, The Media Crew, Orlando, FL. Tel: (407) 839-0390, Web Site: www.themediacrew.com (35)

Foley, Rich, Cengage Learning, Independence, KY. Tel: (800) 354-9706, FAX: (800) 487-8488, Web Site: www.delmar.com (17)

Foley, Rich, Thomson-Gale, Farmington Hills, MI. Tel: (800) 877-4253, FAX: (877) 363-4253, Web Site: www.galegroup.com (17)

Folia, Karl, Leader Direct Marketing Ltd, Surrey, BC Canada. Tel: (604) 542-2026, FAX: (604) 542-2090, E-Mail: listinfo@leaderdirect.ca, Web Site: www.theleadergroup.ca (21)

Foliano, Jay, Beechtree Assoc Inc, Cary, NC. Tel: (919) 852-1800, FAX: (919) 852-4400, E-Mail: jfoliano@aol.com (20)

Folkerth, John, R., Shopsmith Inc, Dayton, OH. Tel: (937) 898-6070, (800) 543-7586, FAX: (937) 890-5197, Web Site: www.shopsmith.com (16)

Folkerth, Robert, Shopsmith Inc, Dayton, OH. Tel: (937) 898-6070, (800) 543-7586, FAX: (937) 890-5197, Web Site: www.shopsmith.com (16)

Folkes, Sally, General Binding Corp, Northbrook, IL. Tel: (800) 723-4000, FAX: (800) 952-1166, (847) 272-1389, Web Site: www.gbc.com (10)

Folks, Valerie, USC Marshall School of Business Dept of Marketing, Los Angeles, CA. Tel: (213) 740-5033, FAX: (213) 740-7828, E-Mail: dennis.rook@marshall.usc.edu (41)

Folkwein, Kristy, Dow Corning Corp, Midland, MI. Tel: (989) 496-4000, (800) 248-2481, FAX: (989) 496-4572, Web Site: www.dowcorning.com (16)

Follett, Charles, Dow Theory Forecasts, Hammond, IN. Tel: (219) 931-6480, (800) 233-5922, FAX: (219) 931-6487, E-Mail: custserv@horizonpublishing.com, Web Site: www.dowtheory.com (17)

Follett Library Resources, McHenry, IL. Tel: (815) 759-1700, (800) 435-6170, FAX: (800) 852-5458, E-Mail: custserv@flr.follett.com, Web Site: www.flr.follett.com (16)

Follo, James, M., The New York Times Co, New York, NY. Tel: (212) 556-3881, FAX: (212) 556-7389, Web Site: www.nytimes.com (17)

Folta, Carl, D., Viacom Inc, New York, NY. Tel: (212) 258-6000, FAX: (212) 258-6464, Web Site: www.viacom.com (16)

Foltz, John, Corporate Media Services Inc, Bloomington, MN. Tel: (952) 881-8081, E-Mail: info@corporatemediaservices.com, Web Site: corporatemediaservices.com (35)

Fonner, Pat, Esco Corp, Portland, OR. Tel: (503) 228-2141, FAX: (503) 778-6682, Web Site: www.escocorp.com (16)

Fonseca, Clemencia, Hitachi Data Systems, Irvine, CA. Tel: (408) 970-1000, Web Site: www.hds.com (22)

Fontaine, Chantal, Promotional Product Professionals of Canada, Saint-Laurent, PQ. Tel: (514) 489-5359, FAX: (514) 489-7760, (800) 489-8741, E-Mail: gladys@pppc.ca, Web Site: www.pppc.ca (1)

Fontaine, Richard, Martha Stewart Living Omnimedia, New York, NY. Tel: (212) 827-8000, Web Site: www.marthastewart.com (17)

Fontana, Christine, MM Batch, Westhampton Beach, NY. Tel: (212) 737-0700, FAX: (212) 454-1124, E-Mail: christine@bannerdirect.com, Web Site: www.bannerdirect.com (35)

Fontana, Paula, Executive Connections LLC, Sarasota, FL. Tel: (941) 323-8300, Web Site: www.executiveconnectionsllc.com (20)

Fontanes, A. Alexander, Liberty Mutual Group, Inc, Boston, MA. Tel: (617) 357-9500, (800) 837-5274, Web Site: www.libertymutual.com (15)

Fontenot, Marie, Data-Dynamix Inc, Castle Rock, CO. Tel: (720) 855-9282, (888) 314-0078, FAX: (720) 855-9099, Web Site: www.data-dynamix.com (23)

Fontes, Chris, Clement Communications, Upper Chichester, PA. Tel: (610) 497-6800, (800) 253-6368, FAX: (610) 497-6806, E-Mail: customerservice@clement.com, Web Site: www.clement.com; www.bradycorp.com (17)

Food & Water Watch, Washington, DC. Tel: (202) 683-2500, Web Site: www.foodandwaterwatch.org (1)

Food Chemical News, Arlington, VA. Tel: (202) 887-6320, (888) 732-7070, FAX: (202) 887-6335, E-Mail: cs@foodregulation.com, Web Site: www.foodchemicalnews.com (17)

Food for the Hungry Inc, Phoenix, AZ. Tel: (480) 998-3100, (800) 248-6437, FAX: (480) 998-4806, E-Mail: hunger@fh.org, Web Site: www.fh.org (1)

Food for the Poor Inc, Coconut Creek, FL. Tel: (954) 427-2222, Web Site: www.foodforthepoor.com (1)

Food Marketing Institute (FMI), Arlington, VA. Tel: (202) 452-8444, FAX: (202) 429-4519, E-Mail: fmi@fmi.org, Web Site: www.fmi.org (40)

Foor, Jessa, National Association of Federal Credit Unions, Arlington, VA. Tel: (800) 336-4644, Web Site: www.nafcu.org (14)

Foos, Brian, ST Media Group International, Cincinnati, OH. Tel: (513) 421-2050, (800) 925-1110, FAX: (513) 421-5144, E-Mail: customer@stmediagroup.com, Web Site: www.signweb.com (17)

Foote, William, USG Corp, Chicago, IL. Tel: (312) 436-4000, (800) 621-9622, FAX: (312) 672-4093, Web Site: www.usg.com (34)

Foote, Francisco & Co, West Caldwell, NJ. Tel: (973) 226-1212, FAX: (973) 226-3409 (1)

Foote-Jones/Illinois Gear, Aberdeen, SD. Tel: (605) 225-0360, FAX: (605) 225-0567, Web Site: www.footejones.com (16)

Forbes, Betty, Christian Children's Fund Inc, Richmond, VA. Tel: (804) 756-2700, (800) 776-6767, FAX: (804) 756-2718, Web Site: www.christianchildrensfund.org (1)

Forbes, Elroy, Houston Direct Marketing Association, Houston, TX. Tel: (281) 931-8883, FAX: (281) 820-4023, Web Site: www.houstondma.org (40)

Forbes, Glenn S., Mayo Clinic, Rochester, MN. Tel: (507) 266-2511, FAX: (507) 284-0161, Web Site: www.mayoclinic.org (17)

Forbes Inc, New York, NY. Tel: (212) 620-2200, FAX: (212) 620-2245, Web Site: www.forbesinc.com (17)

Forchon, Stephen, Response Innovations Inc, Toronto, ON Canada. Tel: (416) 368-6217 (35)

Ford, Charolette, Charolette Ford Trunks, Dumas, TX. Tel: (806) 934-8477, (800) 659-5614, FAX: (806) 372-3061, E-Mail: charolette@charoletteford trunks.com, Web Site: www.charolettefordtrunks.com (11)

Ford, Freeman A., FAFCO Inc, Chico, CA. Tel: (530) 332-2100, (800) 994-7652, FAX: (530) 332-2109, Web Site: www.fafco.com (16)

Ford, Jon, Paladin Press, Boulder, CO. Tel: (303) 443-7250, (800) 392-2400, FAX: (303) 442-8741, E-Mail: service@paladin-press.com, Web Site: www.paladin-press.com (17)

Ford, Linda, Virginia Port Authority, Norfolk, VA. Tel: (757) 683-8000, (800) 446-8098, FAX: (757) 683-2897, Web Site: www.portofvirginia.com (16)

Ford, Marshall, Sage Software Inc, Irvine, CA. Tel: (949) 753-1222, (800) 854-3415, FAX: (949) 753-0374, Web Site: www.sagesoftware.com (16)

Ford, Michael, H., Des Plaines Printing Co, Buffalo Grove, IL. Tel: (847) 824-1111, (800) 283-1776, FAX: (847) 824-1112, E-Mail: custserv@dppc.com, Web Site: www.dppc.com (27)

Ford, Mike, Simplex Grinnell, Westminster, MA. Tel: (978) 731-2500, (800) SIMPLEX, FAX: (978) 731-7856, Web Site: www.simplexgrinnel.com (16)

Ford, Rod, CognitiveDATA Inc, Little Rock, AR. Tel: (501) 975-7580, (866) 243-7883, E-Mail: info@cognitivedata.com, Web Site: www.cognitivedata.com (22)

Ford, Scott, T., Alltel, Little Rock, AR. Tel: (501) 905-2590, (877) 446-3628, FAX: (501) 905-5444, Web Site: www.alltel.com (16)

Ford, Tim, JC Whitney, Chicago, IL. Tel: (312) 431-6000, FAX: (312) 431-5650, Web Site: www.jcwhitney.com (12)

Ford, Tony, Alfa CTP Systems, Tewksbury, MA. Tel: (603) 689-1101, FAX: (603) 689-1197, Web Site: www.alfactp.com (10)

Ford, William, Clay, Ford Motor Co, Dearborn, MI. Tel: (313) 845-8540, (800) 555-5259, FAX: (313) 845-6073, Web Site: www.ford.com (16)

Ford Foundation Office of Communications, New York, NY. Tel: (212) 573-5169, E-Mail: office-of-communications@fordfound.org, Web Site: www.fordfound.org (5)

Ford Motor Co, Dearborn, MI. Tel: (313) 845-8540, (800) 555-5259, FAX: (313) 845-6073, Web Site: www.ford.com (16)

Forde, Joan, Midwest Direct Marketing Association Inc, Saint Paul, MN. Tel: (651) 999-5351, FAX: (651) 917-1835, E-Mail: mdma@mdma.org, Web Site: www.mdma.org (40)

Forde, Joan, US Bank, Minneapolis, MN. Tel: (612) 973-1111, Web Site: www.usbank.com (14)

Fordham University Graduate School of Business Administration, New York, NY. Tel: (212) 636-6200, (800) 825-4422, FAX: (212) 636-7076, Web Site: www.fordham.edu (41)

Forecast Direct Marketing Group, Pittsburgh, PA. Tel: (412) 481-5699, FAX: (412) 481-0872, E-Mail: forecast@sgi.net (21)

Forecaster Publishing Co Inc, Tarzana, CA. Tel: (818) 345-4421 (14)

Foreman, Bart, Group 3 Marketing, Wayzata, MN. Tel: (952) 475-3269, (888) 571-6554, FAX: (952) 449-0403, E-Mail: info@group3marketing.com, Web Site: www.group3marketing.com (20)

Foreman, Melissa, Bill Me Later Inc, Timonium, MD. Tel: (443) 921-1184, Web Site: www.coporate. billmelater.com (14)

Foreman, Melissa, PayPal Inc, Timonium, MD. Tel: (443) 921-1184, Web Site: www.corporate. billmelater.com (14)

Foremaster, Cindy, Laitram Machinery, Harahan, LA. Tel: (504) 733-6000, FAX: (504) 733-6111 (16)

Foremost Industrial Exchange, Van Nuys, CA. Tel: (818) 988-6900, FAX: (818) 787-0293 (16)

Foremost Insurance Group, Grand Rapids, MI. Tel: (616) 956-8241, (800) 527-3905, FAX: (800) 325-1507, Web Site: www.foremost.com (15)

Foremost Packaging, Rancho Cucamonga, CA. Tel: (909) 941-1713, FAX: (909) 941-4092, E-Mail: foremost.mail@verizon.net, Web Site: www. foremostpackaging.com (27)

ForeSee Results Inc, Ann Arbor, MI. Tel: (734) 205-2600, Web Site: www.foreseeresults.com (30)

Forest Envelope Co, Lisle, IL. Tel: (630) 515-1200 (26)

Foresters, Toronto, ON Canada. Tel: (416) 467-2544, Web Site: www.foresters.com (15)

Forestry Suppliers Inc, Jackson, MS. Tel: (601) 354-3565, (800) 543-4203, FAX: (601) 292-0165, E-Mail: fsi@forestry-suppliers.com, Web Site: www.forestry-suppliers.com (9)

Forethought Financial Services Inc, Batesville, IN. Tel: (812) 934-7139, (800) 331-8853, FAX: (812) 934-8560, Web Site: www.forethought.com (15)

Form House Inc, Skokie, IL. Tel: (708) 594-7300, FAX: (708) 594-7390, E-Mail: ktalbot@ theformhouse.com, Web Site: www.theformhouse. com (28)

Formal Approach, Jefferson City, TN. Tel: (865) 475-8641, Web Site: www.formalapproach.com (2)

Forman, Charles, M2Media 360, Park Ridge, IL. Tel: (760) 318-7000, E-Mail: cnaughton@m2media360. com, Web Site: www.m2media360.com (17)

Forman, William, E., Commercial Mailing Lists, Framingham, MA. Tel: (508) 879-2647, (800) 875-8345, FAX: (508) 879-2911, E-Mail: bruce@ commercialmailinglists.com, Web Site: www. commercialmailinglists.com (23)

Formica, Lisa, Philadelphia Direct Marketing Association Inc, Havertown, PA. Tel: (215) 473-1668, FAX: (215) 477-1109, E-Mail: contact@the-pdma. org, Web Site: www.the-pdma.org (40)

Formsource, Lewiston, ME. Tel: (207) 782-3311, (877) 782-3311, FAX: (207) 783-0157, E-Mail: service@formsource1.com, Web Site: www. formsource1.com (27)

Forquer, M., William, Open Text Inc, Waterloo, ON. Tel: (519) 888-9933, (800) 499-6544, FAX: (519) 888-0677, E-Mail: support@opentext.com, Web Site: www.opentext.com (16)

Forrest, Caswell, Klondike Marketing Inc, Boulder, CO. Tel: (720) 406-1177, (888) 395-5438, FAX: (888) 395-5438, Web Site: www. klondikemarketing.com (35)

Forrester, Jalayne, Sunset Magazine, Menlo Park, CA. Tel: (650) 321-3600, FAX: (650) 328-6215 (17)

Forrister, Brad, M Lee Smith Publishers LLC, Brentwood, TN. Tel: (615) 373-7517, (800) 274-6774, FAX: (615) 373-5183, E-Mail: custserv@ mleesmith.com, Web Site: www.mleesmith.com (27)

Forster, Margaret, Nestle Purina/Checkmark Communications, Saint Louis, MO. Tel: (314) 982-1000, FAX: (314) 982-3580, Web Site: www.purina.com (35)

Forster, Marshall, Columbia Tristar Home Video, Culver City, CA. Tel: (310) 244-4000, FAX: (310) 244-1544, Web Site: www.cthe.com (16)

Forsyth, John, Wellmark Blue Cross & Blue Shield of Iowa, Des Moines, IA. Tel: (515) 245-4500, FAX: (515) 323-7722, Web Site: www.wellmark.com (15)

Forsythe, Michael, CNY Awards & Apparel Inc, New Hartford, NY. Tel: (315) 733-0931, Web Site: www.cnyapprel.com (5)

Fort Group, Ridgefield Park, NJ. Tel: (201) 445-0202, FAX: (201) 445-0626, Web Site: www.fortgroup. com (35)

Fort Hays State University, Hays, KS. Tel: (785) 628-FHSU, FAX: (785) 628-4046, Web Site: www. fhsu.edu (41)

Forte, Deborah, A, Scholastic Inc, New York, NY. Tel: (212) 343-6100, (800) SCHOLASTIC, FAX: (212) 343-6484, Web Site: www.scholastic.com/ (17)

Fortent, Miami, FL. Tel: (305) 530-0500, (800) 232-3652, FAX: (305) 530-9434, Web Site: www. fortent.com (31)

Fortin, Dana, Advanced Financial Services, Middletown, RI. Tel: (401) 846-3100, Web Site: www. afsfitfinance.com (14)

Fortin, Dana, Embrace Home Loans, Middletown, RI. Tel: (401) 846-3100, Web Site: www. afsfitfinance.com (14)

Fortunato, Joseph, General Nutrition Corp, Pittsburgh, PA. Tel: (412) 288-4600, (877) GNC-4700, FAX: (412) 402-7218, Web Site: www.gnc.com (7)

48HourPrint.com, Boston, MA. Tel: (800) 844-0599, Web Site: www.48hourprint.com (27)

The Forum Corp, Boston, MA. Tel: (617) 523-7300, (800) 367-8611, FAX: (617) 371-3300, E-Mail: forum@forum.com, Web Site: www.forum.com (20)

Forum Publishing Co, Centerport, NY. Tel: (631) 754-5000, (800) 635-7654, FAX: (631) 754-0630, E-Mail: forumpublishing@aol.com, Web Site: www.forum123.com (17)

Fosdick Fulfillment Corp, Wallingford, CT. Tel: (203) 269-0211, (800) 759-5588, FAX: (203) 679-3290, E-Mail: sales@fosdickcorp.com, Web Site: www. fosdickfulfillment.com (28)

Fosdyck, Vicki, Direct One Inc, Winter Park, FL. Tel: (407) 673-4500, FAX: (407) 673-4501, E-Mail: wariagno@directoneinc.com, Web Site: www. directoneinc.com (28)

Foshay, Molly, Sappi Fine Paper North America, Boston, MA. Tel: (617) 423-7300, FAX: (617) 423-5494, Web Site: www.sappi.com (25)

Fosina, Jim, Fosina Marketing Group Inc, Danbury, CT. Tel: (203) 790-0013 (35)

Fosina Marketing Group Inc, Danbury, CT. Tel: (203) 790-0013 (35)

Fossil, Richardson, TX. Tel: (469) 587-2628, Web Site: www.fossil.com (2)

Stephen Fossler Co Inc, Des Plaines, IL. Tel: (800) 762-0030, FAX: (800) 424-9292, E-Mail: customerservice@fossler.com, Web Site: sfc. stephen-fossler.com (27)

Fossum, Polly, Victory Corps, New Hope, MN. Tel: (763) 561-5600, (800) 328-6120, FAX: (763) 561-8523, E-Mail: cs@victorycorps.com, Web Site: www.victorycorps.com (16)

Foster, Betsy, Whole Foods Market Inc, Austin, TX. Tel: (512) 477-4455, FAX: (512) 482-7000, Web Site: www.wholefoodsmarket.com (4)

Foster, Bradley, R., Country Dance and Song Society, Haydenville, MA. Tel: (413) 268-7426, FAX: (413) 268-7471, E-Mail: office@cdss.org, Web Site: www.cdss.org (1)

Foster, Daniel, Oakton Community College, Des Plaines, IL. Tel: (847) 635-1600, FAX: (847) 635-1706, Web Site: www.oakton.edu (41)

Foster, David, Weider Publications Inc, Woodland Hills, CA. Tel: (818) 884-6800, (800) 423-5590, FAX: (818) 884-0242 (17)

Foster, Frank, Medals of America, Fountain Inn, SC. Tel: (864) 862-0635, (800) 308-0849, FAX: (800) 407-8640, E-Mail: medals@usmedals.com, Web Site: www.usmedals.com (6)

Foster, George, Foster Direct, Lafayette, LA. Tel: (337) 235-1848, FAX: (337) 237-7246, E-Mail: gfoster@fostermarketing.com, Web Site: www. fostermarketing.com (35)

Foster, Kim, Reno Gazette Journal, Reno, NV. Tel: (775) 788-6200, FAX: (775) 788-6563 (17)

Foster, Lee, Foster Travel Publishing, Berkeley, CA. Tel: (510) 549-2202, FAX: (510) 549-1131, E-Mail: lee@fostertravel.com, Web Site: www. fostertravel.com (38)

Foster, Leo, Campbell Tools Co, Springfield, OH. Tel: (937) 882-6716, FAX: (937) 882-6648, E-Mail: campbell@campbelltools.com, Web Site: www. campbelltools.com (16)

Foster, Linda, Medals of America, Fountain Inn, SC. Tel: (864) 862-0635, (800) 308-0849, FAX: (800) 407-8640, E-Mail: medals@usmedals.com, Web Site: www.usmedals.com (6)

Foster, Liz, Integrated Alliance Limited Partnership, Denton, TX. Tel: (940) 565-9415, FAX: (940) 383-1876, E-Mail: ryoung@integratedalliance.com, Web Site: www.integratedalliance.com (29)

Foster, Marshal, Columbia Tristar Home Video, Culver City, CA. Tel: (310) 244-4000, FAX: (310) 244-1544, Web Site: www.cthe.com (16)

Foster, Mary, Sylvan Learning Centers, Baltimore, MD. Tel: (410) 843-8000, FAX: (410) 843-8057, Web Site: www.educate.com (16)

Foster, Todd, Intelligencer Printing Co, Lancaster, PA. Tel: (717) 291-3100, (800) 233-0107, FAX: (717) 569-2643, Web Site: www.intellprinting.com (27)

Foster, William, K., FMC Corp, Philadelphia, PA. Tel: (215) 299-6000, FAX: (215) 299-5998, Web Site: www.fmc.com (16)

Foster Direct, Lafayette, LA. Tel: (337) 235-1848, FAX: (337) 237-7246, E-Mail: gfoster@ fostermarketing.com, Web Site: www. fostermarketing.com (35)

Foster Manufacturing Co, Montgomeryville, PA. Tel: (215) 442-1700, (800) 523-4855, FAX: (215) 442-1313, E-Mail: information@fostermfg.com, Web Site: www.fostermfg.com (34)

Foster Travel Publishing, Berkeley, CA. Tel: (510) 549-2202, FAX: (510) 549-1131, E-Mail: lee@ fostertravel.com, Web Site: www.fostertravel.com (38)

Foster-Cheek, Kaye, Johnson & Johnson, New Brunswick, NJ. Tel: (732) 524-0400, FAX: (732) 214-0332, Web Site: www.jnj.com (16)

Fostoria Industries Inc, Johnson City, TN. Tel: (419) 435-9201, (800) 495-4525, FAX: (419) 435-0842, E-Mail: email@fostoriaindustries.com, Web Site: www.fostoriaindustries.com (9)

Fotch, Katherine, System Pavers, Newport Beach, CA. Tel: (949) 263-8300, Web Site: www.systempavers. com (16)

Foth, Ted, Red Rock Marketing Group LLC, Las Vegas, NV. Tel: (702) 944-9604, FAX: (702) 838-9673, E-Mail: info@redrockmarketing.net, Web Site: www.redrockmarketing.net (35)

FotoBed.com, Birmingham, AL. Tel: (888) 368-6233, E-Mail: service@fotobed.com, Web Site: www.fotobed.com (20)

Foulston, Matthew, Mazda North American Operations, Irvine, CA. Tel: (949) 727-1990, (800) 222-6500, FAX: (949) 727-6101, Web Site: www.mazdausa.com (16)

Foundation Fighting Blindness, Columbia, MD. Tel: (410) 423-0600, Web Site: www.fightblindness.org (1)

Foundation for Chiropractic Education & Research, Norwalk, IA. Tel: (515) 282-7118 (1)

Foundation Media Group, Deerfield Beach, FL. Tel: (954) 949-9500, (800) 873-5137, FAX: (954) 337-0251, Web Site: www.foundationmediagroup.com (35)

Foundation of FirstHealth, Pinehurst, NC. Tel: (910) 695-7500, Web Site: www.firsthealth.org/foundation (1)

Founder, Jeanniey, Mullen, Zinio Systems Inc, San Francisco, CA. Tel: (415) 494-2700, FAX: (415) 494-2701, Web Site: www.zinio.com (31)

Fountain, Suzanne, Dana-Farber Cancer Institute, Boston, MA. Tel: (617) 632-3000, FAX: (617) 632-4070, E-Mail: suzanne_fountain@dfci.harvard.edu, Web Site: www.dana-farber.org (1)

Four Corners Direct Inc, Sarasota, FL. Tel: (941) 364-8585 (16)

Four Directions Media, Oneida, NY. Tel: (315) 829-8316, Web Site: www.fourdirectionsinc.com (17)

4Imprint Inc, Oshkosh, WI. Tel: (920) 236-7272, (888) 298-8190, (877) 446-7746, FAX: (800) 355-5043, E-Mail: administrator@4imprint.com, Web Site: www.4imprint.com (16)

Four Seasons Hotels & Resorts, Toronto, ON Canada. Tel: (416) 449-1750, (800) 819-5053, FAX: (416) 441-4374, Web Site: www.fourseasons.com (19)

Four Seasons Sunrooms, Holbrook, NY. Tel: (631) 563-4000, FAX: (631) 563-4010 (8)

Four Star Marketing Inc, Lincolnwood, IL. Tel: (800) 888-2991, FAX: (847) 679-6449, E-Mail: sales@conventionbags.com, Web Site: www.conventionbags.com (33)

Four Wheel Drive Hardware LLC, Columbiana, OH. Tel: (330) 482-4733, FAX: (330) 482-5035, E-Mail: info@4wd.com, Web Site: www.4wd.com (12)

Fourshee, Coleman, Klingspor's Woodworking Shop, Hickory, NC. Tel: (828) 326-WOOD, (800) 228-0000, FAX: (828) 327-4634, E-Mail: sales@woodworkingshop.com, Web Site: www.woodworkingshop.com (9)

Fouse, Mel, Mustek Inc, Tustin, CA. Tel: (949) 790-3800, FAX: (949) 788-3670, Web Site: www.mustek.com (3)

Fowkes, Dale, Health Freedom Nutrition LLC, Reno, NV. Tel: (775) 324-2050, Web Site: www.hfn-usa.com (7)

Fowkes, Rick, Kett Tool Co, Cincinnati, OH. Tel: (513) 271-0333, FAX: (513) 271-5318, E-Mail: info@kett-tool.com, Web Site: www.kett-tool.com (9)

Fowler, David, Marketfish Inc, Seattle, WA. Tel: (206) 905-1090, FAX: (206) 694-2564, Web Site: www.marketfish.com (23)

Fowler, Jeff, Decision Software Inc, Hyattsville, MD. Tel: (301) 459-9000, FAX: (301) 459-3072, E-Mail: clientservices@dsoftware.biz, Web Site: www.dsoftware.biz (22)

Fowler, Jim, Jigsaw, San Mateo, CA. Tel: (650) 235-8400, Web Site: www.jigsaw.com (24)

Fowler, Peggy, Queen Bee Gardens, Lovell, WY. Tel: (307) 548-2543, (800) 225-7553, FAX: (307) 548-6721, E-Mail: queenbee@tctwest.net, Web Site: queenbeegardens.com (4)

Fowler, Richard C., Market Focus Inc, Evanston, IL. Tel: (847) 328-2900, FAX: (847) 328-8121 (30)

Fowler, Richard, M., Texas Industries Inc, Dallas, TX. Tel: (972) 647-6700, FAX: (972) 647-3878, Web Site: www.txi.com (16)

Fowler, Steve, Houston Direct Marketing Association, Houston, TX. Tel: (281) 931-8883, FAX: (281) 820-4023, Web Site: www.houstondma.org (40)

Fowler's Chocolates Inc, Buffalo, NY. Tel: (716) 877-9983, (800) 824-2263, FAX: (716) 877-9959, E-Mail: customerservice@fowlerschocolates.com, Web Site: www.fowlerschocolates.com (4)

Fox, Allison, The Bradford Group, Niles, IL. Tel: (847) 966-2770, FAX: (847) 581-8630, Web Site: www.collectiblestoday.com (16)

Fox, Bill, Arcade Marketing, Inc, Chattanooga, TN. Tel: (423) 624-3301, FAX: (423) 622-4635 (27)

Fox, Jeffrey, H., Alltel, Little Rock, AR. Tel: (501) 905-2590, (877) 446-3628, FAX: (501) 905-5444, Web Site: www.alltel.com (16)

Fox, John, Northern Printing Network Inc, Wheeling, IL. Tel: (847) 215-7300, FAX: (847) 215-7314, E-Mail: sales@northernprint.com, Web Site: www.northernprint.com (21)

Fox, Joseph M., Fox Media Services, Natick, MA. Tel: (508) 655-5665, (800) 369-2327, FAX: (419) 715-5628, E-Mail: joe@foxmediaservices.com, Web Site: www.foxmediaservices.com (32)

Fox, Ken, Berry Hill Ltd, Saint Thomas, ON Canada. Tel: (519) 631-0480, (800) 668-3072, FAX: (519) 631-8935, E-Mail: info@berryhilllimited.com, Web Site: www.berryhilllimited.com (8)

Fox, Larry, Larry Fox & Co Ltd, Valley Stream, NY. Tel: (516) 791-7929, (800) 397-7923, FAX: (516) 791-1022, E-Mail: larry@larryfox.com, Web Site: www.larryfox.com (16)

Fox, Marlys, Fox Associates Inc, Chicago, IL. Tel: (312) 644-3888, FAX: (312) 644-8718, Web Site: www.foxrep.com (31)

Fox, Michael, J., Rogers Publishing Ltd, Toronto, ON. Tel: (416) 935-7777, FAX: (416) 935-3597, Web Site: www.rogerspublishing.ca (17)

Fox, Mitchell, Golf Digest Co, Wilton, CT. Tel: (203) 761-5100, FAX: (203) 371-2572, Web Site: www.golfdigest.com (17)

Fox, Peggy, New Directions Publishing Corp, New York, NY. Tel: (212) 255-0230, FAX: (212) 255-0231, E-Mail: editorial@ndbooks.com, Web Site: www.ndpublishing.com (17)

Fox, Rich, Rich Fox & Associates Inc, Carmel Valley, CA. Tel: (831) 659-1123 (1)

Fox, Steve, PC World, San Francisco, CA. Tel: (415) 243-0500, FAX: (415) 442-1891, Web Site: www.pcworld.com (17)

Fox, Thomas, National Catholic Reporter Publishing Co Inc, Kansas City, MO. Tel: (816) 531-0538, (800) 444-8910, FAX: (816) 968-2268, Web Site: www.ncronline.org (17)

Fox Associates Inc, Chicago, IL. Tel: (312) 644-3888, FAX: (312) 644-8718, Web Site: www.foxrep.com (31)

Fox Chase Cancer Center, Philadelphia, PA. Tel: (215) 728-6900, (888) FOXCHASE, FAX: (215) 728-2594, Web Site: www.fccc.edu (1)

Larry Fox & Co Ltd, Valley Stream, NY. Tel: (516) 791-7929, (800) 397-7923, FAX: (516) 791-1022, E-Mail: larry@larryfox.com, Web Site: www.larryfox.com (16)

Fox Lite, Inc, Fairborn, OH. Tel: (937) 864-1966, FAX: (937) 864-7010, E-Mail: doug@foxlite.com, Web Site: www.foxlite.com (9)

Fox Media Services, Natick, MA. Tel: (508) 655-5665, (800) 369-2327, FAX: (419) 715-5628, E-Mail: joe@foxmediaservices.com, Web Site: www.foxmediaservices.com (32)

Rich Fox & Associates Inc, Carmel Valley, CA. Tel: (831) 659-1123 (1)

Fox River Paper Co, Appleton, WI. Tel: (920) 733-7341, (800) 558-8327, FAX: (920) 733-2975, E-Mail: info@foxriverpaper.com, Web Site: www.foxriverpaper.com (27)

Fox Valley Systems Inc, Cary, IL. Tel: (847) 639-5744, (800) 323-4770, FAX: (847) 639-8190, Web Site: www.foxpaint.com (9)

Foxfire Printing & Packaging Inc, Newark, DE. Tel: (302) 368-9466, (800) 497-0516, FAX: (302) 368-9219, E-Mail: info@foxfiresigns.com, Web Site: www.foxfiresigns.com (27)

Foxhall Corp, McLean, VA. Tel: (703) 749-3126 (20)

Foxhall Corporation, McLean, VA. Tel: (703) 749-3126 (20)

The Foxon Co, Providence, RI. Tel: (401) 421-2386, (800) 556-6943, FAX: (401) 421-8996 (27)

Foxx, Lucia M., Ronell Clock Co, Grants Pass, OR. Tel: (541) 471-0194, (800) 334-0135, FAX: (541) 471-0099, Web Site: www.ronellclock.com (5)

Foy, David, T., Symetra Financial, Bellevue, WA. Tel: (425) 256-8000, (800) 426-7355, FAX: (425) 256-5737, Web Site: www.symetra.com (15)

Foy, Jim, Aspect Softwear, Chelmsford, MA. Tel: (978) 250-7900, FAX: (978) 244-7410, E-Mail: info@aspect.com, Web Site: www.aspect.com (29)

Frack, Joseph, Society of Financial Service Professionals, Newtown Square, PA. Tel: (610) 526-2500, FAX: (610) 527-1499, Web Site: www.financialpro.org (1)

Fractal Analytics, Jersey City, NJ. Tel: (201) 633-8728, Web Site: www.fractalanalytics.com (35)

Fradkin, Steven, L., The Northern Trust Co, Chicago, IL. Tel: (312) 630-6000, (888) 289-6542, FAX: (312) 630-1512, Web Site: www.ntrs.com (14)

Fraenkel, Sallie, Spa-Finder Inc, New York, NY. Tel: (212) 924-6800, (800) ALL-SPAS, FAX: (212) 924-7240, Web Site: www.spafinder.com (7)

Fragal, Ray, Direct Mail Service Inc, Pittsburgh, PA. Tel: (412) 471-6300 (21)

Fragman, Claude, Americ Disc, Drummondville, PQ Canada. Tel: (800) 263-0419, FAX: (819) 478-4575, Web Site: www.americdisc.com (33)

Fragrance International Inc, Youngstown, OH. Tel: (330) 747-3341, (888) 547-8355, FAX: (330) 747-3343, Web Site: www.kisstell.com (16)

Frahman, Dennis, Sage Software Inc, Irvine, CA. Tel: (949) 753-1222, (800) 854-3415, FAX: (949) 753-0374, Web Site: www.sagesoftware.com (16)

Fraim, William, L., AcuSport Corp, Bellefontaine, OH. Tel: (937) 593-7010, FAX: (937) 592-5625, E-Mail: mwsales@acusport.com, Web Site: www.acusport.com (11)

Frain, Kevin, M., BarnesandNoble.com, New York, NY. Tel: (212) 414-6000, (800) THE-BOOK, FAX: (212) 414-6140, E-Mail: service@barnesandnoble.com, Web Site: www.barnesandnoble.com (16)

Fraiser, Mike, Promotion Fulfillment Ctr, Camanche, IA. Tel: (563) 259-0105, (800) 493-7063, FAX: (563) 259-0110, E-Mail: info@pfcfulfills.com, Web Site: www.pfcfulfills.com (28)

Fraizer, Michael, D., Genworth Financial Inc, Richmond, VA. Tel: (804) 281-6000, (888) 436-9678, FAX: (804) 662-2414, Web Site: www.genworth.com (14)

Francais, Eric, Walter Karl Inc, Pearl River, NY. Tel: (845) 620-0700, FAX: (845) 620-1885, E-Mail: info@walterkarl.infousa.com, Web Site: www.walterkarl.com (22)

Francesco, John, Di, Gump's By Mail Inc, San Francisco, CA. Tel: (415) 982-1616, (800) 882-8055, FAX: (800) 984-9361, Web Site: www.gumpsbymail.com (6)

Francese, Tom, Novell Inc, Waltham, MA. Tel: (801) 861-4272, (800) 529-3400, FAX: (781) 464-8100, E-Mail: crc@novell.com, Web Site: www.novell.com (22)

Franch, John, Cygnus Business Media, Fort Atkinson, WI. Tel: (203) 227-4037, (800) 547-7377, FAX: (203) 227-4245, Web Site: www.cygnusb2b.com (17)

Franchino, Michael, Peppermill Marketing Inc, Los Angeles, CA. Tel: (310) 659-8900, (877) 600-7775, FAX: (310) 659-8901, E-Mail: inquiry@peppermillmarketing.com, Web Site: www.peppermillmarketing.com (23)

Franchise Services Inc, Mission Viejo, CA. Tel: (949) 282-3800, Web Site: www.pip.com (27)

Franchot, Michael, Summit Industries Inc, Marietta, GA. Tel: (770) 590-0600, (800) 241-6996, FAX: (770) 590-0714, E-Mail: info@summitinds.com, Web Site: www.summitinds.com (5)

Francis, Merle, Blue Cross Blue Shield of Louisiana, Baton Rouge, LA. Tel: (225) 295-3307, (800) 599-2583, FAX: (225) 295-2054, E-Mail: help@bcbsla.com, Web Site: www.bcbsla.com (15)

Francis, Nancy, Ideas To Go Inc, Minneapolis, MN. Tel: (612) 331-1570, FAX: (612) 331-1602, E-Mail: cebert@ideastogo.com, Web Site: www.ideastogo.com (30)

Francis, Philip L., PetSmart Inc, Phoenix, AZ. Tel: (623) 587-2009, (800) 738-1385, FAX: (623) 580-6183, Web Site: www.petsmart.com (5)

Francis, Philip L., State Line Tack Inc, Phoenix, AZ. Tel: (623) 580-6100, (800) 228-9208, FAX: (623) 580-6183, E-Mail: customerservice@statelinetack.com, Web Site: www.statelinetack.com (16)

Francis, Ron, Wire Works, Chester, PA. Tel: (610) 485-1981, (800) 292-1940, Web Site: www.wire-works.com (9)

Francis, Scott, Photographer's Market, Blue Ash, OH. Tel: (513) 531-2690, FAX: (513) 531-2686, E-Mail: photomarket@fwpubs.com, Web Site: www.photographersmarket.com (43)

Francis, Susanne, Spinneybeck Enterprises, Getzville, NY. Tel: (716) 446-2380, (800) 482-7777, FAX: (716) 446-2396, E-Mail: sales@spinneybeck.com, Web Site: www.spinneybeck.com (16)

Franciscan Friars of the Atonement - Graymoor, Garrison, NY. Tel: (845) 424-3671, FAX: (845) 424-2168, E-Mail: info@atonementfriars.org, Web Site: www.atonementfriars.org (1)

Franciscan Mission Associates, Mount Vernon, NY. Tel: (914) 664-5604, FAX: (914) 664-3017, E-Mail: admin@franciscanmissionassoc.org, Web Site: www.franciscanmissionassoc.org (1)

Francisco, Peter W., Foote, Francisco & Co, West Caldwell, NJ. Tel: (973) 226-1212, FAX: (973) 226-3409 (1)

Franco, Adolfo, Direct Selling Association, Washington, DC. Tel: (202) 452-8866, FAX: (202) 452-9010, E-Mail: info@dsa.org, Web Site: www.dsa.org (40)

Franco, Lawrence, D&B Canada, Mississauga, ON. Tel: (905) 568-6000, FAX: (905) 568-6197, Web Site: www.dnb.ca (30)

Franco, Lynn, The Conference Board, Inc, New York, NY. Tel: (212) 759-0900, FAX: (212) 980-7014, Web Site: www.conference-board.org (16)

Frank, Harley, Admiral Packaging Inc, Providence, RI. Tel: (800) 262-0027, FAX: (401) 331-1910, Web Site: www.admiralpkg.com (26)

Frank, Terry, Bunzl Distribution USA, Inc, Saint Louis, MO. Tel: (314) 997-5959, (888) 997-5959, FAX: (314) 997-1405, Web Site: www.bunzldistribution.com (16)

Frank Joseph, Chevy Chase, MD. Tel: (301) 656-8753, E-Mail: mr.dm@verizon.net (39)

Frank Mobility Systems Inc, Oakdale, PA. Tel: (888) 426-8581, FAX: (724) 695-3710, E-Mail: info@lfrankmobility.com, Web Site: www.lifestandusa.com (34)

Frank Siteman Photography, Winchester, MA. Tel: (781) 729-3747, E-Mail: frank@franksiteman.com, Web Site: www.franksiteman.com (37)

Frankel, Dr. Ellen, The Jewish Publication Society, Philadelphia, PA. Tel: (215) 832-0600, (800) 234-3151, FAX: (215) 568-2017, E-Mail: jewishbook@jewishpub.org, Web Site: www.jewishpub.org (17)

Frankel, Mark, American Medical Association, Chicago, IL. Tel: (312) 464-5000, (800) 621-8335, FAX: (312) 464-4184, Web Site: www.ama-assn.org (1)

Frankel, Rich, CMEinfo.com, Birmingham, AL. Tel: (205) 991-9188, (800) 284-8433, FAX: (800) 284-5964, Web Site: www.cmeinfo.com (16)

Frankfort, Lou, Coach, New York, NY. Tel: (212) 594-1850, (800) 444-3611, FAX: (212) 594-1682, Web Site: www.coach.com (2)

Frankhouse, Dale, Adventure Creations Inc, Costa Mesa, CA. Tel: (949) 515-3600, FAX: (949) 515-3933, E-Mail: sales@adv-creations.com, Web Site: www.adv-creations.com (16)

Frankio, Phil, Speakers Guild Inc, Sandwich, MA. Tel: (508) 888-6702, (800) 343-4530, FAX: (508) 888-6771, E-Mail: info@speakersguild.com, Web Site: www.speakersguild.com (16)

Franklin Dr., E., Bernard, Delta Upsilon International Fraternity, Indianapolis, IN. Tel: (317) 875-8900, FAX: (317) 876-1629, E-Mail: ihq@deltau.org, Web Site: www.deltau.org (16)

Franklin, Bob, San Francisco Bay Area Rapid Transit District (BART), Oakland, CA. Tel: (510) 464-6000, FAX: (510) 464-7103, Web Site: www.bart.gov (16)

Franklin, Cal, TN Marketing, Wayzata, MN. Tel: (763) 577-1216, Web Site: www.tnmarketing.com (35)

Franklin, Jack, Paralyzed Veterans of America, Washington, DC. Tel: (202) 416-7636, (800) 424-8200, FAX: (202) 416-7643, E-Mail: info@pva.org, Web Site: www.pva.org (1)

Franklin, Julie, The Iams Co, Dayton, OH. Tel: (937) 898-7387, (800) 675-3849, FAX: (937) 264-7264, Web Site: www.iams.com (16)

Franklin, Leonard, G., Franklin & Welker Direct Marketing Services, Miami, FL. Tel: (305) 758-6690, FAX: (305) 758-9399 (30)

Franklin, Lindley, FCIA Management Co Inc, New York, NY. Tel: (212) 885-1500, FAX: (212) 885-1535, E-Mail: service@fcia.com, Web Site: www.fcia.com (15)

Franklin, Martin, E., Jarden Corp, Daleville, IN. Tel: (765) 557-3000, (800) 428-8150, FAX: (765) 281-5403, Web Site: www.jarden.com (16)

Franklin, Rebecca, Gibson Auer LLC, Victor, ID. Tel: (208) 787-2153, E-Mail: helpdesk@galabs.com, Web Site: www.galabs.com (7)

Franklin, Robert, McFarland & Co Inc Publishers, Jefferson, NC. Tel: (336) 246-4460, (800) 253-2187, FAX: (336) 246-5018, E-Mail: info@mcfarlandpub.com, Web Site: www.mcfarlandpub.com (17)

Franklin, Roger, Franklin Advertising Inc, Blakely, GA. Tel: (229) 723-3665, FAX: (407) 386-6666, E-Mail: franklinad@aol.com, Web Site: www.franklinadv.com (35)

Franklin, Rusty, Sellstrom Manufacturing Co, Palatine, IL. Tel: (847) 358-2000, (800) 323-7402, FAX: (847) 358-8564, E-Mail: sellstrom@sellstrom.com, Web Site: www.sellstrom.com (16)

Franklin Advertising Inc, Blakely, GA. Tel: (229) 723-3665, FAX: (407) 386-6666, E-Mail: franklinad@aol.com, Web Site: www.franklinadv.com (35)

Franklin & Welker Direct Marketing Services, Miami, FL. Tel: (305) 758-6690, FAX: (305) 758-9399 (30)

Franklin Estimating Systems, Woods Cross, UT. Tel: (801) 303-6083, (800) 346-7363, FAX: (801) 303-4540, E-Mail: management@franklinestimating.com, Web Site: www.fesys.com (17)

The Franklin Mint, Exton, PA. Tel: (610) 497-4800, (800) THE-MINT, FAX: (610) 497-4956, E-Mail: info@franklinmint.com, Web Site: www.franklinmint.com (16)

Fran's Basket House, Inc, Succasunna, NJ. Tel: (973) 584-2230, (800) 372-6799, FAX: (973) 584-7446, E-Mail: inquiry@franswicker.com, Web Site: www.franswicker.com (8)

Fran's Gifts to Go, Myrtle Beach, SC. Tel: (843) 445-2625, (800) 476-6887, E-Mail: customerservice@fransgiftstogo.com, Web Site: www.fransgiftstogo.com (4)

Franz, Kevin, Intelligencer Printing Co, Lancaster, PA. Tel: (717) 291-3100, (800) 233-0107, FAX: (717) 569-2643, Web Site: www.intellprinting.com (27)

Franzblau, R.M., Thompson Cigar Co, Tampa, FL. Tel: (813) 884-6344, (800) 237-2559, FAX: (813) 882-4605, Web Site: www.thompsoncigar.com (6)

Franzblau, Robert, Casual Living USA, Tampa, FL. Tel: (813) 884-6955, (800) 652-2948, FAX: (813) 882-4605, Web Site: www.casuallivingusa.com (6)

Franzen, Tim, American Spirit Graphics Corp, Minneapolis, MN. Tel: (612) 623-3333, FAX: (612) 623-9314, E-Mail: asgc@asgc.com, Web Site: www.asgc.com (27)

Franzen, Tim, Harris Bancorp Inc, Chicago, IL. Tel: (312) 461-7961, (888) 340-BANK, FAX: (312) 461-7869, E-Mail: onlineservices@harrisbank.com, Web Site: www.harrisbank.com (14)

Frappier, Renee, PacNet Services Ltd, Vancouver, BC. Tel: (604) 689-0399, FAX: (604) 689-0313, E-Mail: info@pacnetservices.com, Web Site: www.pacnetservices.com (14)

Frary, Stephen, R., Oriental Trading Co Inc, Omaha, NE. Tel: (402) 596-1200, (800) 875-8480, FAX: (402) 331-3873, Web Site: www.oriental.com (5)

Fraser Papers Inc, Madawaska, ME. Tel: (203) 705-2800, FAX: (203) 705-2801 (25)

Fratoni, Doreen, Jaypro Sports, Waterford, CT. Tel: (860) 447-3001, (800) 243-0533, FAX: (800) 988-3363, E-Mail: info@jaypro.com, Web Site: www.jaypro.com (11)

Frattaroli, Brian, Intromark Inc, Pittsburgh, PA. Tel: (412) 288-1300, (800) 851-6030 X1368, FAX: (412) 338-0497, E-Mail: licensing@intromark.com (16)

Fraud & Theft Information Bureau, Boynton Beach, FL. Tel: (561) 737-8700, FAX: (561) 737-5800, E-Mail: sales@fraudandtheft.com, Web Site: www.fraudandtheftinfo.com (43)

Frausto, Ernie, NestFamily.com, Coppell, TX. Tel: (972) 402-7100, (800) 596-7386, FAX: (972) 629-7181, Web Site: www.nestfamily.com (3)

Frayne, Heather, Direct Marketers On Call Inc (DMOC), New York, NY. Tel: (212) 691-1942, FAX: (212) 924-1331, E-Mail: info@dmoc-inc.com, Web Site: www.dmoc-inc.com (20)

Frazelle, Raye, Jackson, Chadsworth's 1-800-Columns, Wilmington, NC. Tel: (910) 763-7600, (800) 486-2118, FAX: (910) 763-3191, E-Mail: sales@columns.com, Web Site: www.columns.com (8)

Frazier, David, R., David R Frazier Photolibrary Inc, Boise, ID. Tel: (208) 342-9250, (800) 342-3283, FAX: (208) 342-2307, E-Mail: dave@drfphoto.com, Web Site: www.drfphoto.com (38)

Frazier, Gary, USC Marshall School of Business Dept of Marketing, Los Angeles, CA. Tel: (213) 740-5033, FAX: (213) 740-7828, E-Mail: dennis.rook@marshall.usc.edu (41)

Frazier, Kenneth, C., Merck & Co Inc, Whitehouse Station, NJ. Tel: (908) 423-1000, Web Site: www.merck.com (16)

Frazier, Richard, Volunteers of America, Alexandria, VA. Tel: (703) 341-5000, Web Site: www.volunteersofamerica.org (1)

David R Frazier Photolibrary Inc, Boise, ID. Tel: (208) 342-9250, (800) 342-3283, FAX: (208) 342-2307, E-Mail: dave@drfphoto.com, Web Site: www.drfphoto.com (38)

Frazzini, Maria, Washington Gas Energy Services, Herndon, VA. Tel: (703) 793-7500, Web Site: www.wges.com (16)

Frechette, Peter, L., Patterson Dental, Saint Paul, MN. Tel: (651) 686-1600, (800) 328-5536, FAX: (651) 686-9331, Web Site: www.pattersondental.com (10)

Fredel, Alfred, Carl Fischer Music, New York, NY. Tel: (212) 777-0900, (800) 762-2328, FAX: (212) 477-6996, E-Mail: cf-info@carlfischer.com, Web Site: www.carlfischer.com (17)

Frederick, Aaron, Alfa Aesar-A Johnson Matthey Co, Ward Hill, MA. Tel: (800) 343-0660, FAX: (800) 322-4757, E-Mail: info@alfa.com, Web Site: www.alfa.com (9)

Frederick, Sherman, R., Las Vegas Review Journal, Las Vegas, NV. Tel: (702) 383-0211, FAX: (702) 383-4646, Web Site: www.lvrj.com (17)

Frederick's of Hollywood Group Inc, Los Angeles, CA. Tel: (323) 466-5151, (800) 323-9525, FAX: (323) 464-5149, Web Site: www.fredericks.com (2)

Frederickson, Flemming, Laitram Machinery, Harahan, LA. Tel: (504) 733-6000, FAX: (504) 733-6111 (16)

Paul Fredrick Menstyle, Fleetwood, PA. Tel: (610) 944-0909, (800) 247-1417, FAX: (610) 944-6452, E-Mail: custserv@menstyle.com, Web Site: www.paulfredricks.com (2)

Freed, Bernie, 925 Business Furniture, Kensington, MD. Tel: (800) 525-0302, FAX: (302) 349-4587, E-Mail: bjfreed@erols.com, Web Site: www.natcofurniture.com (34)

Freed, Larry, ForeSee Results Inc, Ann Arbor, MI. Tel: (734) 205-2600, Web Site: www.foreseeresults.com (30)

Freedman, Christlin, Fire Mountain Gems, Grants Pass, OR. Tel: (541) 956-7890, (800) 423-2319, (800) 355-2137, FAX: (541) 470-GEMS, E-Mail: questions@firemtn.com, Web Site: www.firemtn.com (16)

Freedman, Glenn, LIST Inc, Danbury, CT. Tel: (914) 765-0700, FAX: (914) 765-0046, E-Mail: info@l-i-s-t.com, Web Site: www.l-i-s-t.com (24)

Freedman, Jack, Paul Stuart, New York, NY. Tel: (212) 682-0320, FAX: (212) 983-5871, E-Mail: info@paulstuart.com, Web Site: www.paulstuart.com (2)

Freedman, Karl, Ashworth University, Norcross, GA. Tel: (770) 729-8400, (800) 957-5412, FAX: (770) 729-9294, E-Mail: info@ashworthuniversity.edu, Web Site: www.ashworthuniversity.edu (13)

Freedman, Mark, The Company Store Inc, La Crosse, WI. Tel: (608) 785-1400, FAX: (608) 791-5790, Web Site: www.thecompanystore.com (16)

Freedman, Stuart, Fire Mountain Gems, Grants Pass, OR. Tel: (541) 956-7890, (800) 423-2319, (800) 355-2137, FAX: (541) 470-GEMS, E-Mail: questions@firemtn.com, Web Site: www.firemtn.com (16)

Freedom Graphic Systems Inc, Milton, WI. Tel: (608) 868-7007, (800) 334-3540, FAX: (608) 868-7006, E-Mail: information@fgs.com, Web Site: www.freedomgraphicsystems.com (28)

Freel, Michael, Polyair Packaging, Chicago, IL. Tel: (773) 995-1818, (888) POLYAIR X444, FAX: (773) 995-7725, E-Mail: marketing@polyair.com, Web Site: www.polyair.com (9)

Freeman, Barry D., Goldsmith Agio Helms, Minneapolis, MN. Tel: (612) 339-0500, FAX: (612) 339-0507, Web Site: www.agio.com (14)

Freeman, Irving, Kipp Brothers Inc, Greenfield, IN. Tel: (317) 634-5507, (800) 428-1153, FAX: (800) 832-5477, E-Mail: toys@kippbro.com (33)

Freeman, Jack, The Keystone Equities Group, Oaks, PA. Tel: (610) 415-6300, (800) 715-9905, FAX: (610) 415-6328, Web Site: www.keystoneequities.com (20)

Freeman, Lawrence, Value Line Publishing Inc, New York, NY. Tel: (212) 907-1500, FAX: (212) 818-9747, Web Site: www.valueline.com (17)

Freeman, Lawrence, Vanderbilt Advertising, New York, NY. Tel: (212) 907-1500, FAX: (212) 907-1914, Web Site: www.valueline.com (14)

Freeman, Russell, Coyne American Institute, Chicago, IL. Tel: (773) 935-2520, (800) 999-5220, FAX: (773) 935-2920, Web Site: www.coyneamerican.edu (16)

Freeman Decorating Co, Kearny, NJ. Tel: (201) 998-6006 (16)

Freeport Music Inc, Farmingville, NY. Tel: (631) 549-4108, (888) 549-4108, E-Mail: sales@musicalinstruments.com; sales@freeportmusic.com, Web Site: www.musicalinstruments.com (11)

Freese, Walt, Celestial Seasonings, Boulder, CO. Tel: (303) 530-5300, (800) 434-4246, FAX: (303) 581-1249, Web Site: www.hain-celestial.com (16)

Freestate, Donna, REGIT Inc, Glen Ellyn, IL. Tel: (630) 495-1500, (800) 537-9786, FAX: (630) 495-1611, E-Mail: regit@regitinc.com, Web Site: www.regitinc.com (15)

Freestyle Photographic Supplies, Los Angeles, CA. Tel: (323) 660-3640, Web Site: www.freestylephoto.biz (5)

Frehner, Jeff, Pacific Cycle Inc, Madison, WI. Tel: (608) 268-2468, (800) 724-9466, FAX: (847) 236-3692, (847) 573-0602, E-Mail: info@pacificcycle.com, Web Site: www.pacificcycle.com (16)

Freidman, Joseph, J&R Music/J&R Computer World, New York, NY. Tel: (212) 238-9000, (800) 806-1115, FAX: (212) 238-9191, Web Site: www.jandr.com (3)

Freidman, Rachelle, J&R Music/J&R Computer World, New York, NY. Tel: (212) 238-9000, (800) 806-1115, FAX: (212) 238-9191, Web Site: www.jandr.com (3)

Freidus, Marc, Victor Machinery Exchange, Brooklyn, NY. Tel: (800) 723-5359, E-Mail: sales@victornet.com, Web Site: www.victornet.com (9)

Freifeld, Lorrie, Sales & Marketing Management Magazine, New York, NY. Tel: (800) 821-6897, FAX: (905) 470-8561, E-Mail: joyce.cooney@nielsen.com, Web Site: www.salesandmarketing.com (16)

Freitaq, Randal, J., Lincoln Financial Group, Radnor, PA. Tel: (215) 448-1400, (877) 275-5462, FAX: (215) 448-3962, Web Site: www.lfg.com (15)

French Jr., R., Reid, Intergraph Corp, Madison, AL. Tel: (256) 730-2000, (800) 345-4856, FAX: (256) 730-2048, Web Site: www.intergraph.com (16)

French, Don, The Source Stock Footage Library Inc, Tucson, AZ. Tel: (520) 298-4810, FAX: (520) 290-8831, E-Mail: requests@sourcefootage.com, Web Site: www.sourcefootage.com (38)

French, Ian, Northern Lights Direct, Chicago, IL. Tel: (312) 263-8686, FAX: (312) 624-7701, E-Mail: contact@northernlightsdirect.com, Web Site: www.northernlightsdirect.com (32)

French, Sandy, Northern Lights Direct, Chicago, IL. Tel: (312) 263-8686, FAX: (312) 624-7701, E-Mail: contact@northernlightsdirect.com, Web Site: www.northernlightsdirect.com (32)

French Creek Sheep & Wool Co Inc, Elverson, PA. Tel: (610) 286-5700, (800) 977-4337, FAX: (610) 286-0324, E-Mail: info@frenchcreeksw.com, Web Site: www.frenchcreeksw.com (2)

French Trade Office Embassy of France, New York, NY. Tel: (212) 400-2167, Web Site: www.missioneco.org (1)

Frenkel, Lev, Digital Speech Systems, Richardson, TX. Tel: (972) 235-2999, FAX: (972) 235-3036, Web Site: www.digitalspeech.com (3)

Frenz, Thomas R., List Advisor Inc, Farmingdale, NY. Tel: (631) 777-2900, FAX: (631) 777-3050 (23)

FreshAddress Inc, Newton, MA. Tel: (617) 965-4500, (800) 321-3009, FAX: (617) 965-4551, Web Site: www.freshaddress.com (22)

FreshDirect, Long Island City, NY. Tel: (718) 928-1531 (5)

Fresno Oxygen, Fresno, CA. Tel: (559) 233-6684, (800) 404-9353, FAX: (559) 233-4206, E-Mail: info@fresnooxygen.com, Web Site: www.fresnooxygen.com (9)

Fretz Jr., William, B., The Keystone Equities Group, Oaks, PA. Tel: (610) 415-6300, (800) 715-9905, FAX: (610) 415-6328, Web Site: www.keystoneequities.com (20)

Fretz, Deborah, M., Sunoco, Inc, Philadelphia, PA. Tel: (215) 977-3000, (800) 786-6261, FAX: (215) 977-3409, E-Mail: sunoco_online@sunoil.com, Web Site: www.sunocoinc.com (16)

Fretz, L., Keith, The Keystone Equities Group, Oaks, PA. Tel: (610) 415-6300, (800) 715-9905, FAX: (610) 415-6328, Web Site: www.keystoneequities.com (20)

Freund, Ronald, Midpoint National Inc, Kansas City, KS. Tel: (913) 362-7400, (800) 228-4321, FAX: (913) 362-7401, E-Mail: info@midpt.com, Web Site: www.midpointorderfulfillment.com (28)

Frey, Edward, Arcelor Mittal, Coatesville, PA. Tel: (610) 383-2000, FAX: (610) 383-5036, Web Site: www.arcelormittal.com (16)

Frey, Scott, PossibleNOW Inc, Duluth, GA. Tel: (770) 255-1020, Web Site: www.dncsolution.com (22)

Freyd, William, IDC, Ltd, Henderson, NV. Tel: (702) 450-1000, FAX: (702) 450-1020, E-Mail: info@goidc.com, Web Site: www.goidc.com (1)

Fricke, Heinz, Washington National Opera, Washington, DC. Tel: (202) 295-2400, (800) US-OPERA, FAX: (202) 295-2460, E-Mail: mail@dc-opera.org, Web Site: www.dc-opera.org (16)

Frid, Peter, A., New Hampshire Public Television, Durham, NH. Tel: (603) 868-1100, E-Mail: themailbox@nhptv.org, Web Site: www.nhptv.org (32)

Friday, Denise, S., AMA Insurance Agency Inc, Chicago, IL. Tel: (312) 464-2425, (800) 458-5736, FAX: (312) 419-5096, Web Site: www.amainsure.com (15)

Friday Report, Garden City, NY. Tel: (516) 746-6700, FAX: (516) 294-8141 (43)

Fried-Cassorla Communications Inc, Melrose Park, PA. Tel: (215) 635-5189, FAX: (215) 635-0461, E-Mail: albert@fried-cas.com, Web Site: www.fried-cas.com (35)

Fried-Cassorla, Albert, Fried-Cassorla Communications Inc, Melrose Park, PA. Tel: (215) 635-5189, FAX: (215) 635-0461, E-Mail: albert@fried-cas.com, Web Site: www.fried-cas.com (35)

Friedberg, Joyce, Campbell Soup Co, Camden, NJ. Tel: (856) 342-4800, (800) 257-8443, FAX: (856) 342-3878, Web Site: www.campbellsoup.com (16)

Friedberg, Richard, Shelburne Co, Taneytown, MD. Tel: (410) 876-5902, FAX: (410) 876-4612, Web Site: www.zoysiafarms.com (8)

Friedel, Mike, Amtelco, McFarland, WI. Tel: (608) 838-4194, (800) 356-9148, FAX: (608) 838-8367, E-Mail: info@amtelco.com, Web Site: www.amtelco.com (16)

Friedenberg, Michael, CXO Media Inc, Framingham, MA. Tel: (508) 872-0080, (800) 859-5478, FAX: (508) 872-0618, Web Site: www.cxo.com (17)

Friedhoff, Ed, Flex Products, Carlstadt, NJ. Tel: (201) 933-3030, (800) 526-6273, FAX: (201) 933-2396, E-Mail: info@flex-products.com, Web Site: www.flex-products.com (34)

Friedland, Abbot, The Scholar's Bookshelf, Princeton, NJ. Tel: (609) 395-6933, FAX: (609) 395-0755, E-Mail: books@scholarsbookshelf.com, Web Site: www.scholarsbookshelf.com (5)

Friedland, Jay, Guideline Research Corp, New York, NY. Tel: (212) 947-5140, FAX: (212) 629-0061, Web Site: www.guidelineresearch.com (30)

Friedland, Jim, McMaster-Carr Supply Co (HQ), Elmhurst, IL. Tel: (630) 600-3600, FAX: (630) 834-9427, E-Mail: chi.sales@mcmaster.com, Web Site: www.mcmaster.com (9)

Friedlander, David H., Vitamin Power Inc, Hauppauge, NY. Tel: (516) 378-0900, (800) 645-6567, FAX: (516) 378-0919, E-Mail: vitpower@aol.com, Web Site: www.vitaminpower.com (7)

Friedlander, Edward, Vitamin Power Inc, Hauppauge, NY. Tel: (516) 378-0900, (800) 645-6567, FAX: (516) 378-0919, E-Mail: vitpower@aol.com, Web Site: www.vitaminpower.com (7)

Friedle, Ronald, Publishers Diversified Mail Service Inc, Milwaukee, WI. Tel: (414) 354-1423, FAX: (414) 354-9338, E-Mail: webmaster@ publishersmail.com, Web Site: www. publishersmail.com (21)

Friedman, Donald R., CA Inc, Islandia, NY. Tel: (800) 225-5224, FAX: (631) 342-3300, E-Mail: info@ca. com, Web Site: www.ca.com (16)

Friedman, Douglas, Lions Gate Television Corp, Santa Monica, CA. Tel: (310) 449-9200, FAX: (310) 255-3870, Web Site: www.lionsgate.com (16)

Friedman, Jane, HarperCollins, New York, NY. Tel: (212) 207-7000, (800) 242-7737, FAX: (212) 207-7145, Web Site: www.harpercollins.com (17)

Friedman, Lance, Kraft Foods/Gevalia Kaffe, Tarrytown, NY. Tel: (914) 335-4239, Web Site: www. gevalia.com (16)

Friedman, Marvin, Better Health Fitness, Brooklyn, NY. Tel: (718) 436-4693, FAX: (718) 854-3381, Web Site: www.betterhealthfitness.com (11)

Friedman, Neil, Mattel Inc, El Segundo, CA. Tel: (310) 252-2000, FAX: (310) 252-2180, Web Site: www.mattel.com (16)

A I Friedman Inc, New York, NY. Tel: (212) 243-9000, (800) 204-6352, FAX: (212) 929-7320, Web Site: www.aifriedman.com (10)

Jonathan Friedman, Hollywood, FL. Tel: (954) 416-3419 (20)

Friedman Marketing Svcs, Harrison, NY. Tel: (914) 698-9591, FAX: (914) 698-0485, E-Mail: paula. wynne@gfk.com, Web Site: www.friedmanmktg. com (30)

Friedrich, Dennis, Brookfield Properties, Toronto, ON. Tel: (416) 369-2300, FAX: (416) 369-2301, Web Site: www.brokfieldproperties.com (16)

Friend, R., Douglas, National Court Reporters Association, Vienna, VA. Tel: (703) 556-6272, (800) 272-6272, FAX: (703) 556-6291, E-Mail: msic@ ncrahg.org, Web Site: www.ncraonline.org (1)

Friendly, Ian, R., General Mills Inc, Minneapolis, MN. Tel: (763) 764-7600, FAX: (763) 764-7384, Web Site: www.generalmills.com (8)

Friendman, Linda, E! Entertainment Television, Los Angeles, CA. Tel: (323) 937-3408, FAX: (323) 954-2660, Web Site: www.eonline.com (32)

Friesen, Patricia, Pat Friesen & Co LLC, Leawood, KS. Tel: (913) 341-1211, FAX: (913) 341-4343, Web Site: www.patfriesen.com (36)

Friesen, Rod, Truitt Brothers Inc, Salem, OR. Tel: (503) 362-3674, (800) 547-8712, FAX: (503) 588-2868, E-Mail: truittbrothers@truittbros.com, Web Site: www.truittbros.com (16)

Pat Friesen & Co LLC, Leawood, KS. Tel: (913) 341-1211, FAX: (913) 341-4343, Web Site: www. patfriesen.com (36)

Frigon, Lloyd, Stonwurks, Eden Prairie, MN. Tel: (785) 526-7847, (888) 884-7881, FAX: (785) 526-7841, E-Mail: stonwurks@stonwurks.com, Web Site: www.stonwurks.com (16)

Frigstad, David, Frost & Sullivan Inc, Mountain View, CA. Tel: (877) 690-3329, (877) 463-7678, FAX: (877) 690-3329, E-Mail: myfrost@frost.com, Web Site: www.frost.com (30)

Frisen, Lisa, Winnipeg Art Gallery, Winnipeg, MB. Tel: (204) 786-6641, FAX: (204) 788-4998, E-Mail: inquiries@wag.mb.ca, Web Site: www. wag.mb.ca (1)

Frishman, P.J., RocketWear, New York, NY. Tel: (212) 977-9227, Web Site: www.rocketwear.net (2)

Frith, Russell, Lawn Doctor Inc, Holmdel, NJ. Tel: (732) 946-0029, (800) 631-5660, FAX: (732) 946-9089, Web Site: www.lawndoctor.com (16)

Frith, Scott, Lawn Doctor Inc, Holmdel, NJ. Tel: (732) 946-0029, (800) 631-5660, FAX: (732) 946-9089, Web Site: www.lawndoctor.com (16)

Frito-Lay, Plano, TX. Tel: (972) 334-7000, (800) 352-4477, FAX: (972) 334-2019, Web Site: www. fritolay.com (16)

Fritz, Catherine, Insurance Publications Inc, Overland Park, KS. Tel: (913) 383-9191, (800) 762-3387, FAX: (913) 383-1247, E-Mail: brokerwrld@ primary.net, Web Site: www.brokerworldmag.com (17)

Fritz, Gerard, Novastock Photo Agency, Matthews, NC. Tel: (704) 847-6185, (888) 894-8622, FAX: (704) 841-8181, E-Mail: novastock@aol.com, Web Site: www.creativeshake.com/novastock (38)

Fritz, Mike, Estes Industries, Penrose, CO. Tel: (719) 372-6565, FAX: (719) 372-3419, Web Site: www. estesrockets.com (11)

Froelich, Vern, Web Graphics, Naples, FL. Tel: (239) 775-2295 (27)

Froese, Garth, PacificEast, Sumas, WA. Tel: (800) 665-8400, Web Site: www.pacificeast.com (22)

Frog Tool Co Ltd, Dixon, IL. Tel: (815) 288-3811, E-Mail: info@frogwoodtools.com, Web Site: www. frogwoodtools.com (11)

Frojd, Tim, Martin Williams Advertising, Minneapolis, MN. Tel: (612) 342-9739, FAX: (612) 342-9700, Web Site: www.martinwilliams.com (35)

Fromm, Allan, An-Ser Services, Green Bay, WI. Tel: (920) 490-7000, (800) 723-0000, E-Mail: allanf@ anser.com, Web Site: www.anser.com (29)

Fromm, Ronald, Brown Shoe Co, Saint Louis, MO. Tel: (314) 854-4000, FAX: (314) 854-4274, Web Site: www.brownshoe.com (16)

Front Porch Inc, Sonora, CA. Tel: (209) 288-5500, Web Site: www.frontporch.com (35)

Frontier Communications, Stamford, CT. Tel: (203) 614-5600, Web Site: www.czn.com (29)

Frontier Corp, Rochester, NY. Tel: (716) 777-1000, Web Site: www.frontieronline.com (16)

Frontier Natural Products Co-op, Norway, IA. Tel: (319) 227-7996, (800) 669-3275, FAX: (319) 227-7966, (800) 717-4372, E-Mail: info@frontiercoop. com, Web Site: www.frontiercoop.com (7)

Frontline Data Group, Vienna, VA. Tel: (703) 734-5700) (23)

Frontline Direct Inc, Del Mar, CA. Tel: (858) 638-1515, Web Site: www.frontlinedirect.com (23)

Frost & Sullivan Inc, Mountain View, CA. Tel: (877) 690-3329, (877) 463-7678, FAX: (877) 690-3329, E-Mail: myfrost@frost.com, Web Site: www.frost. com (30)

Frost Bank, San Antonio, TX. Tel: (210) 220-5155, Web Site: www.frostbank.com (14)

Frozies, Melba, Names in the Mail Inc, Dallas, TX. Tel: (972) 681-5701, (800) 688-5701, FAX: (972) 681-5786, E-Mail: nimnames@att.net (23)

Fruech, Leo H., Cascade Forest Nursery, Bellevue, IA. Tel: (563) 872-3025, (800) 596-9437, FAX: (563) 872-5003, Web Site: www.cascadeforestry.com (8)

Fruechte, Christine, Colle+McVoy, Minneapolis, MN. Tel: (612) 305-6000, FAX: (612) 305-6500, E-Mail: info@collemcvoy.com, Web Site: www. collemcvoy.com (35)

Fruge, David, Smith & Noble, Corona, CA. Tel: (909) 734-4444, (800) 248-8888, FAX: (800) 426-7780, E-Mail: contactus@smithnoble.com, Web Site: www.smithandnoble.com (8)

Fruland, Ann, The Merchandise Mart, Chicago, IL. Tel: (312) 527-4141, (800) 677-6278, Web Site: www.merchandisemart.com (42)

Frustieri, Jim, DataBridge Marketing Systems Corp, Montvale, NJ. Tel: (201) 664-3883, Web Site: www.Data-Bridge.org (22)

Fruth, Steve, Fostoria Industries Inc, Johnson City, TN. Tel: (419) 435-9201, (800) 495-4525, FAX: (419) 435-0842, E-Mail: email@fostoriaindustries. com, Web Site: www.fostoriaindustries.com (9)

Fry, Carl, Craft-Diston Industries, Wichita, KS. Tel: (316) 838-4291, (800) 835-0028, FAX: (316) 838-8502, Web Site: www.craftdiston.com (16)

Fry, Jacki, Jon-Don, Roselle, IL. Tel: (800) 556-6366, Web Site: www.jondon.com (34)

Fry Communciations Inc, Mechanicsburg, PA. Tel: (717) 766-0211 (27)

Fry Consultants Inc, Atlanta, GA. Tel: (770) 226-8888, FAX: (770) 226-8899, E-Mail: mail@ fryconsultants.com, Web Site: www.fryconsultants. com (30)

Fry Inc, Ann Arbor, MI. Tel: (415) 896-5300 X221, FAX: (741) 741-0906, E-Mail: mbriggs@frymulti. com, Web Site: www.fry.com (3)

Frye, Frederick, A., Zoological Society of San Diego, San Diego, CA. Tel: (619) 231-1515, FAX: (619) 557-3937, Web Site: www.sandiegozoo.org (1)

Fryer, William, R., SBDP Corp, Cincinnati, OH. Tel: (513) 871-7019, FAX: (513) 871-0134, E-Mail: info@sbdp.com, Web Site: www.sbdp.com (22)

Fryling, Gregory, A., Cooper Surgical Inc, Trumbull, CT. Tel: (203) 601-5200, (800) 645-3670, FAX: (203) 601-1007, Web Site: www.coopersurgical. com (7)

Fubins, Marc, Communications Solutions Expo, Norwalk, CT. Tel: (203) 852-6800, (877) 243-6002, FAX: (203) 853-2845, E-Mail: info@tmcnet.com, Web Site: www.tmcnet.com (42)

Fuchs, Steve, True North Inc, New York, NY. Tel: (212) 557-4202, Web Site: www.truenorthinc.com (35)

Fucich, Mark, Tyco Valves & Controls, Houston, TX. Tel: (713) 986-4665, (800) 343-0990, FAX: (713) 937-5466, Web Site: www.tycovalves.com (16)

Fuersich, Lawrence, Visual Reference Publications, New York, NY. Tel: (212) 279-7000, (800) 251-4545, FAX: (212) 279-7014 (17)

Fugate, Lisa, First Data Corp, Greenwood Village, CO. Tel: (303) 488-8000, (800) 735-3362, Web Site: www.firstdata.com (28)

Fugiel, Dave, Nimlok, Niles, IL. Tel: (847) 647-1012, (800) 233-8870, FAX: (847) 647-2044, E-Mail: info@nimlok.com, Web Site: www.nimlok.com (16)

Fuji Photo Film USA, Valhalla, NY. Tel: (914) 789-8100, (800) 755-3854, FAX: (914) 789-8295, Web Site: www.fujifilmusa.com (16)

Fujii, Ted, Mark James & Associates Inc, Oswego, IL. Tel: (630) 548-8100, FAX: (630) 548-6107, E-Mail: info@markjamesassociates.com, Web Site: www.markjamesassociates.com/contact.html (16)

Fujii Communications Inc, Lincolnwood, IL. Tel: (847) 677-0542, FAX: (847) 677-0523, E-Mail: fujiicom@flash.net (35)

Fujii Falcone, Laurie, Fujii Communications Inc, Lincolnwood, IL. Tel: (847) 677-0542, FAX: (847) 677-0523, E-Mail: fujiicom@flash.net (35)

Fujisankei Communications International Inc, New York, NY. Tel: (212) 753-8100, FAX: (212) 702-0420, Web Site: www.fujisankei.com (32)

Fujita, Victor, IMC Direct, Honolulu, HI. Tel: (808) 545-1680, FAX: (808) 528-4293 (35)

Fujitsu Computer Systems, Sunnyvale, CA. Tel: (408) 746-6000, (800) 538-8460, FAX: (408) 992-2674, E-Mail: solutions@us.fujitsu.com, Web Site: www. fujitsu.com (22)

Fujitsu Transaction Solutions Inc, Richardson, TX. Tel: (972) 963-2300, (800) 340-4425, Web Site: www.fujitsu.com (16)

Fukagawa, Mikako, Potpourri Group Inc, Chelmsford, MA. Tel: (978) 256-4100, FAX: (978) 256-1961/0344, Web Site: www.potpourrigroup.com (6)

Fukakusa, Jancie, R., RBC Dain Rauscher, Boston, MA. Tel: (617) 725-2000, FAX: (617) 725-1393, Web Site: www.rbcdainrauscher.com (14)

Fukasawa, Kenji, Nihon Keizai Shimbun America Inc, New York, NY. Tel: (212) 261-6230, FAX: (212) 261-6239, Web Site: www.nikkeius.com (17)

Fulcrum, New York, NY. Tel: (888) 245-9450 (22)

Fulcrum Publishing, Golden, CO. Tel: (303) 277-1623, (800) 992-2908, FAX: (303) 279-7111, Web Site: www.fulcrum-books.com (17)

Fulfillment Express Inc, Pico Rivera, CA. Tel: (562) 948-4400, (800) 700-9295, FAX: (562) 948-4459, E-Mail: information@fex.com, Web Site: www.fex. com (28)

Fulfillment Plus Inc, Holtsville, NY. Tel: (631) 758-8300, FAX: (631) 758-8360, E-Mail: jeff.ehrlich@fulfillmentplusny.com, Web Site: www.fulfillmentplusny.com (28)

Fulfillment Xcellence Inc (FXI), Downers Grove, IL. Tel: (630) 852-7600, FAX: (630) 852-5817, Web Site: www.fx-inc.com (28)

Fulham, Paul, Zachry Associates Inc, Abilene, TX. Tel: (325) 677-1342, E-Mail: pfulham@zachryinc.com, Web Site: www.zachryinc.com (28)

Fuller, Linda, Habitat For Humanity International, Americus, GA. Tel: (229) 924-6935, FAX: (229) 924-6541, Web Site: www.habitat.org (1)

Fuller, Millard, Habitat For Humanity International, Americus, GA. Tel: (229) 924-6935, FAX: (229) 924-6541, Web Site: www.habitat.org (1)

Fuller, Steve, LL Bean Inc, Freeport, ME. Tel: (207) 865-4761, (800) 441-5713, FAX: (207) 552-3080, Web Site: www.llbean.com (2)

Fuller, Tara, OSRAM Sylvania, Danvers, MA. Tel: (978) 750-2210, Web Site: www.sylvania.com (16)

Fuller, Tony F., Rent-A-Center Inc, Plano, TX. Tel: (972) 801-1100, (800) 275-2996, FAX: (972) 943-0113, Web Site: www.rentacenter.com (16)

The Fuller Brush Co, Great Bend, KS. Tel: (800) 522-0499, FAX: (620) 792-1906, E-Mail: info@fuller.com, Web Site: www.fuller.com (5)

The Fuller Theological Seminary, Pasadena, CA. Tel: (626) 584-5200, (800) 2-FULLER, FAX: (626) 584-5449, Web Site: www.fuller.edu/cll (16)

Fullington, Robert, LOTSolutions, Jacksonville, FL. Tel: (904) 350-9660, Web Site: www.lotsolutions.com (14)

Fullmer, John, H., MyPoints.Com Inc, San Francisco, CA. Tel: (415) 856-0877, FAX: (415) 615-1122, E-Mail: memberservices@mypoints.com, Web Site: www.mypoints.com (35)

Fulton, Sharon, Travelclick, Schaumburg, IL. Tel: (847) 585-5016 (19)

Funasaki, Mark, Fred Meyer Jewelers Inc, Portland, OR. Tel: (503) 232-8844, (800) 457-5977, FAX: (503) 797-7616, Web Site: www.fredmeyerjewelers.com (16)

Funches, Venessa, Auburn University at Montgomery, Montgomery, AL. Tel: (334) 244-3621, (800) 227-2649, FAX: (334) 244-3826, Web Site: www.aum.edu (41)

Fund, Ken, Creative Publishing International, Minneapolis, MN. Tel: (612) 344-8100, FAX: (612) 344-8691, E-Mail: sales@creativepub.com, Web Site: www.creativepub.com (17)

Fund for Public Interest Research, Washington, DC. Tel: (202) 546-3965, Web Site: www.ffpir.org (1)

Fund Raising Management, Garden City, NY. Tel: (516) 746-6700, FAX: (516) 294-8141 (43)

Fundamental Photographs, New York, NY. Tel: (212) 473-5770, FAX: (212) 228-5059, E-Mail: mail@fphoto.com, Web Site: www.fphoto.com (38)

Fundamentals Co Inc, Bristol, VA. Tel: (800) 303-8861 (Fax), (800) 303-8861 (1)

FunME Events, Dekalb, IL. Tel: (800) 386-6321, FAX: (815) 787-3100, E-Mail: funMEevents@aol.com, Web Site: www.funMEevents.com (43)

Funo, Yukitoshi, Toyota Motor Sales USA Inc, Torrance, CA. Tel: (310) 468-4000, (800) 331-4331, FAX: (310) 468-7841, Web Site: www.toyota.com (16)

Fuqua, Mike, SIGMA Marketing Group LLC, Rochester, NY. Tel: (585) 473-7300, (888) 277-9837, FAX: (585) 473-0332, E-Mail: mbush@sigmamarketing.com, Web Site: www.sigmamarketing.com; www.jthgearanalytics.com (Blog) (20)

Furbush III, Douglas, D., Affinity Marketing Group, Wellesley Hills, MA. Tel: (781) 239-9310, FAX: (781) 239-9645, E-Mail: info@affinitymg.com, Web Site: www.affinitymg.com (24)

Furgiuele, Joseph, Furgiuele & Co Inc, Crestwood, NY. Tel: (914) 793-0045, FAX: (914) 779-6447, E-Mail: fci@fcidms.com, Web Site: www.fcidms.com (20)

Furgiuele & Co Inc, Crestwood, NY. Tel: (914) 793-0045, FAX: (914) 779-6447, E-Mail: fci@fcidms.com, Web Site: www.fcidms.com (20)

Furlo, L., Morley Companies, Saginaw, MI. Tel: (989) 791-2550, (800) 336-5554, FAX: (989) 792-1002, E-Mail: info@morleynet.com, Web Site: www.morleynet.com (33)

Furlong, Mark F., Marshall & Ilsley Corp, Milwaukee, WI. Tel: (414) 765-7801, FAX: (414) 765-7899, Web Site: www.micorp.com (14)

Furlong-Weber, Maureen, The Peter A Tobin College of Business, Jamaica, NY. Tel: (718) 990-2600, FAX: (718) 990-1868, Web Site: www.stjohns.edu (41)

Furman, Alan, Alan Furman & Co, Rockville, MD. Tel: (202) 397-8463, (800) 654-7184, FAX: (301) 881-0810, E-Mail: watches@alanfurman.com, Web Site: www.alanfurman.com (2)

Alan Furman & Co, Rockville, MD. Tel: (202) 397-8463, (800) 654-7184, FAX: (301) 881-0810, E-Mail: watches@alanfurman.com, Web Site: www.alanfurman.com (2)

Furman Roth Advertising, New York, NY. Tel: (212) 687-2300, FAX: (212) 687-0858, Web Site: www.furmanroth.com (35)

Furnia, Joseph, Intelitec, Granby, MA. Tel: (413) 467-7420, FAX: (413) 467-9476, E-Mail: info@intelitec.com, Web Site: www.intelitec.com (23)

Furrier, Jack, Desert Rat Truck Centers, Tucson, AZ. Tel: (520) 790-8502, (866) 444-5337, FAX: (520) 750-1918, Web Site: www.desertrat.com (12)

Furrier, Mike, Desert Rat Truck Centers, Tucson, AZ. Tel: (520) 790-8502, (866) 444-5337, FAX: (520) 750-1918, Web Site: www.desertrat.com (12)

Furrier, Tracy, Synapse Group Inc, Stamford, CT. Tel: (203) 595-8255, FAX: (203) 329-8237, E-Mail: webmaster@synapsemail.com, Web Site: www.synapsegroupinc.com (18)

Furuseth, Peter, Dain Rauscher Inc, Minneapolis, MN. Tel: (612) 371-2711, FAX: (612) 373-1627, Web Site: www.dainrauscher.com (14)

Fuss, Eduardo, Eduardo Fuss, Santa Fe, NM. Tel: (505) 424-0304, FAX: (505) 424-0602 (37)

Eduardo Fuss, Santa Fe, NM. Tel: (505) 424-0304, FAX: (505) 424-0602 (37)

Fuston, Kay, Coastal Living, Birmingham, AL. Tel: (205) 877-6007, FAX: (205) 445-8655, E-Mail: coastalliving@customersvc.com, Web Site: www.coastalliving.com (43)

Future Thunder Productions, Van Nuys, CA. Tel: (818) 986-9494, FAX: (818) 986-6644, E-Mail: jim@futurethunder.com, Web Site: www.futurethunder.com (32)

G

G&A Marketing, Milford, OH. Tel: (513) 965-6301, (800) 688-1370, E-Mail: info@gamarketing.com, Web Site: www.gamarketing.com (35)

G&S Packing Co Inc, Weirsdale, FL. Tel: (352) 821-2251, (800) 949-9074, FAX: (352) 821-5000, Web Site: www.gspacking.com (16)

G H Bass & Co, New York, NY. Tel: (212) 381-3900, FAX: (212) 381-3950, Web Site: www.pvh.com (16)

G-Neil Direct Mail, Sunrise, FL. Tel: (800) 999-9111, FAX: (954) 851-1264, E-Mail: tcs@gneil.com, Web Site: www.gneil.com (10)

G-Plex Direct Mail, Holtsville, NY. Tel: (631) 447-9500, Web Site: www.g-plex.net (16)

G2 Promotional Marketing, New York, NY. Tel: (212) 537-3700, FAX: (203) 352-0798, Web Site: www.g2pm.com (16)

G2 Worldwide, New York, NY. Tel: (212) 537-3700, Web Site: www.g2dd.com (35)

GBE Plus, Hartford, CT. Tel: (860) 727-9100, (800) 842-0139, FAX: (860) 527-6041, Web Site: www.gbeplus.com (26)

GBH Communications, Monrovia, CA. Tel: (818) 246-9900, (800) 222-5424, FAX: (818) 246-5850, E-Mail: customerservice@gbh.com, Web Site: www.gbh.com (3)

GC Direct, Seattle, WA. Tel: (206) 262-1999, Web Site: www.gcdirect.com (35)

GC Services, Houston, TX. Tel: (713) 777-4441, FAX: (713) 776-6535, E-Mail: marketing.communications@gcserv.com, Web Site: www.gcserv.com (20)

GCC Printers, Bedford, MA. Tel: (781) 275-5800, (800) 422-7777, FAX: (781) 275-1115, (800) 442-2329, E-Mail: sales@gccprinters.com, Web Site: www.gcctech.com (10)

GE Canada, Mississauga, ON Canada. Tel: (905) 858-5100, Web Site: www.ge.com/canada (9)

GE Consumer & Industrial Lighting, Cleveland, OH. Tel: (216) 266-2222, (216) 266-2121, FAX: (216) 266-2930, Web Site: www.gelighting.com/na (16)

GE Money, Alpharetta, GA. Tel: (678) 518-2403 (14)

GE Partnership Marketing Group, Schaumburg, IL. Tel: (847) 605-3000, FAX: (847) 605-7368, Web Site: www.gepmg.com (14)

GEICO Direct, Washington, DC. Tel: (301) 986-2842, (800) 841-3000, FAX: (301) 986-2068, Web Site: www.geico.com (15)

GFK Custom Research North America, New York, NY. Tel: (212) 240-5300, (800) 274-3577, FAX: (212) 240-5353, E-Mail: info@gfkamerica.com, Web Site: www.gfkamerica.com (30)

GG Direct, Portland, ME. Tel: (207) 772-0414, FAX: (207) 871-1444, E-Mail: info@ggdirect.com, Web Site: www.ggdirect.com (21)

GHW Associates, Lake Suzy, FL. Tel: (941) 625-4293, E-Mail: ghw@ghw-associates.com, Web Site: www.ghw-associates.com (35)

GIE Import Export Corp, Columbus, OH. Tel: (614) 888-5850, FAX: (614) 436-0723 (33)

GKV, Baltimore, MD. Tel: (410) 539-5400, FAX: (410) 234-2441, E-Mail: newbusiness@gkv.com, Web Site: www.gvk.com (35)

GLM Communications, New York, NY. Tel: (212) 929-1300, FAX: (212) 929-9574, Web Site: www.glmcommunications.com (31)

GM Customer Relationship Management, Detroit, MI. Tel: (313) 667-2621 (35)

GMAC Insurance, Atlanta, GA. Tel: (314) 493-8000, (800) GMAC-123, FAX: (314) 493-8114, Web Site: www.gmacinsurance.com (15)

GMC Software Technology Inc, Charlestown, MA. Tel: (617) 712-1200, Web Site: www.gmc.net (22)

GMG Productions Inc, Roslyn, NY. Tel: (516) 482-0022, FAX: (516) 482-0097, Web Site: www.gmgproductions.com (3)

GMI Distribution, Somerset, NJ. Tel: (732) 846-4800, FAX: (732) 846-4709, E-Mail: keith@gmidistribution.com, Web Site: www.gmidistribution.com (28)

GN Netcom, Nashua, NH. Tel: (603) 598-1100, (800) 345-8639, FAX: (603) 598-1122, Web Site: www.jabra.com (16)

The GRI Marketing Group Inc, Trumbull, CT. Tel: (203) 261-3337, (800) 356-4890, FAX: (203) 261-1113, E-Mail: bsnider@gridirect.com, Web Site: www.gridirect.com (35)

GRP Funding LLC, Springfield, MA. Tel: (877) 571-7999, Web Site: www.grpfunding.com (14)

GS Direct Inc, Eden Prairie, MN. Tel: (952) 942-6115, (800) 234-3729, FAX: (952) 942-0216, Web Site: www.gsdirect.net (34)

GS Marketing, Houston, TX. Tel: (713) 580-3900, FAX: (713) 580-5950, E-Mail: angie.sherrell@gsmarketing.com, Web Site: www.gsmarketing.com (21)

GSD&M Idea City, Austin, TX. Tel: (512) 242-4736, Web Site: www.gsdm.com (35)

GSI Commerce, Pacoima, CA. Tel: (818) 834-8800, (800) 244-7371, FAX: (818) 834-8840, Web Site: www.gsicommerce.com (21)

GSP Marketing Services, Chicago, IL. Tel: (312) 944-3000, FAX: (312) 944-8587, E-Mail: mikes@gspmarketing.com, Web Site: www.gspmarketing.com (35)

GTM Sportswear, Manhattan, KS. Tel: (800) 336-4486, Web Site: www.gtmsportswear.com (2)

GWR Wealth Management, Omaha, NE. Tel: (402) 496-7200, FAX: (402) 496-0378, Web Site: www.gwrwealth.com (14)

GXS Corp, Gaithersburg, MD. Tel: (301) 340-4000, (800) 560-4347, FAX: (301) 340-5299, Web Site: www.gxs.com (30)

Gabay, Heny, Super 8 Hotels Worldwide, Parsippany, NJ. Tel: (973) 428-9700, (800) 800-8000, FAX: (973) 496-7307, Web Site: www.super8.com (19)

Gabel, Phil, Thomson Financial, New York, NY. Tel: (212) 803-8200, FAX: (212) 843-9608 (17)

Gabor, Lisa, American Express Publishing Corp, New York, NY. Tel: (212) 382-5600, (888) 461-6180, FAX: (212) 827-6496, E-Mail: aepc@custmersvc.com, Web Site: www.amexpub.com (17)

Gabriel Group, Earth City, MO. Tel: (314) 743-5700, FAX: (314) 576-5573, E-Mail: sales@gabrielgr.com, Web Site: www.gabrielgr.com (21)

Gabrielson, Charles, USA Weekend, New York, NY. Tel: (800) 487-4956, FAX: (703) 854-2122, Web Site: www.usaweekend.com (31)

Gaches, Greg, Cable Connection, Fremont, CA. Tel: (408) 395-6700, FAX: (408) 354-3980, E-Mail: cables4u@cable-connection.com, Web Site: www.cable-connection.com (3)

Gaco Western Inc, Seattle, WA. Tel: (206) 575-0450, (800) 456-4226, FAX: (206) 575-0587, E-Mail: info@gaco.com, Web Site: www.gaco.com (16)

Gadbut, Albert, AcquireWEB Inc, Foster City, CA. Tel: (650) 212-2233, Web Site: www.acquireWEB.com (22)

Gaddis, Evan, R., National Electrical Manufacturers Association (NEMA), Rosslyn, VA. Tel: (703) 841-3200, FAX: (703) 841-5900, E-Mail: communications@nema.org, Web Site: www.nema.org (34)

Gady, Wendy, Pohaku Inc, Kailua, HI. Tel: (319) 653-2569, Web Site: www.gopohaku.com (20)

Gaebe, Morris, J.W., Johnson & Wales University, Providence, RI. Tel: (401) 598-1000, (800) DIAL-JWU, FAX: (401) 598-1833, E-Mail: admissions.pvd@jwu.edu, Web Site: www.jwu.edu (41)

GaelSong, Seattle, WA. Tel: (206) 526-8350, Web Site: www.gaelsong.com (6)

Gaffney, Julie, The Arizona Direct Marketing Association, Scottsdale, AZ. Tel: (480) 970-8643, FAX: (480) 893-1157, E-Mail: julie@brownies.com, Web Site: www.azdma.org (40)

Gage, Minneapolis, MN. Tel: (763) 595-5800, Web Site: www.heinrich.com (35)

Gagliardo, Coleen, Gaylord Brothers, Syracuse, NY. Tel: (315) 634-8440, Web Site: www.gaylord.com (16)

Gagne, Gaetan, L'Entraide Assurance, Quebec, PQ Canada. Tel: (418) 658-0663, FAX: (418) 658-5065, E-Mail: service@lentraide.com, Web Site: www.lentraide.com (15)

Gagne, Patrick, Komunik, Montreal, PQ Canada. Tel: (514) 904-0710, Web Site: www.komunik.com (20)

Gagnon, Rik, White Cap Wholesale Contractors Supplies, Costa Mesa, CA. Tel: (800) 944-8322, FAX: (866) 791-8396, E-Mail: customerservice@whitecap.com, Web Site: www.whitecapdirect.com (16)

Gahm, Gordon, Kitchen Kompact Inc, Jeffersonville, IN. Tel: (812) 282-6681, FAX: (812) 282-7880, E-Mail: webmaster@kitchenkompact.com, Web Site: www.kitchenkompact.com (8)

Gahm, Phillip, Kitchen Kompact Inc, Jeffersonville, IN. Tel: (812) 282-6681, FAX: (812) 282-7880, E-Mail: webmaster@kitchenkompact.com, Web Site: www.kitchenkompact.com (8)

Gahm, Walter, Kitchen Kompact Inc, Jeffersonville, IN. Tel: (812) 282-6681, FAX: (812) 282-7880, E-Mail: webmaster@kitchenkompact.com, Web Site: www.kitchenkompact.com (8)

Gaiam Inc, Boulder, CO. Tel: (877) 989-6321, Web Site: life.gaiam.com (9)

Gaier, Mark, RR Donnelley Response Marketing Services, Downers Grove, IL. Tel: (800) 722-9001, FAX: (630) 322-6270, Web Site: www.rms.rrd.com (31)

Gaige, Marianne, W., Cathedral Corp, Rome, NY. Tel: (315) 338-0021, (800) 698-0299, FAX: (315) 338-5874, E-Mail: sales@cathedralstewardship.com, Web Site: www.cathedralcorporation.com (21)

Gaines, Tammy, The United Methodist Publishing House, Nashville, TN. Tel: (615) 749-6000, (800) 672-1789, FAX: (615) 749-6417, E-Mail: productsandservices@umpublishing.com, Web Site: www.umpublishing.com (17)

Gaines, Virginia, KET, Lexington, KY. Tel: (859) 258-7000, (800) 432-0951, FAX: (606) 258-7396, E-Mail: rgriffin@ket.org, Web Site: www.ket.org (17)

Gaippe, Gordon, August Home Publishing Co, Des Moines, IA. Tel: (515) 875-7000, FAX: (515) 282-6741, E-Mail: ask@workbenchmag.com, Web Site: www.augusthome.com (17)

Gaito, Kathleen, Catholic Digest, New London, CT. Tel: (800) 321-0411, E-Mail: catholicdigest@bayardinc.com, Web Site: www.catholicdigest.com (17)

Galanty, Mark, Galanty & Co Inc, Santa Monica, CA. Tel: (310) 451-2525, FAX: (310) 451-5020, E-Mail: galanty@ix.netcom (35)

Galanty & Co Inc, Santa Monica, CA. Tel: (310) 451-2525, FAX: (310) 451-5020, E-Mail: galanty@ix.netcom (35)

Galassi, Jonathan, Farrar Straus & Giroux Inc, New York, NY. Tel: (212) 741-6900, (800) 330-8477, FAX: (212) 633-2427, E-Mail: childrens_editorial@fsgbooks.com, Web Site: www.fsgbooks.com (17)

Galbornetti, Christina, V12 Group, Red Bank, NJ. Tel: (732) 842-1001, Web Site: www.v12group.com (23)

Galbraith, Dianne, Klahowya Native American & Nature Gift Shop, Bandon, OR. Tel: (541) 347-5099, FAX: (541) 347-4132 (6)

Galbraith, Robert, Union Switch & Signal Inc, Pittsburgh, PA. Tel: (412) 688-2400, (800) 351-1520, FAX: (412) 688-2399, Web Site: www.switch.com (16)

Galbreath, Diane, White Cap Wholesale Contractors Supplies, Costa Mesa, CA. Tel: (800) 944-8322, FAX: (866) 791-8396, E-Mail: customerservice@whitecap.com, Web Site: www.whitecapdirect.com (16)

Gale, Laura, United Stationers, Deerfield, IL. Tel: (847) 627-7000, Web Site: www.unitedstationers.com (23)

Gale, Wayne, Stokes Seeds Inc, Buffalo, NY. Tel: (716) 695-6980, (800) 396-9238, FAX: (888) 834-3334, Web Site: www.stokeseeds.com (8)

Gale Research Inc, Farmington Hills, MI. Tel: (248) 699-4253, (800) 877-GALE, FAX: (313) 961-6083, Web Site: www.gale.com (17)

Galen Williams Landscaping & Garden Design, East Hampton, NY. Tel: (631) 324-6220, FAX: (631) 329-3684 (16)

Galer, Mike, Amigo Mobility International Inc, Bridgeport, MI. Tel: (989) 777-0910, (800) 692-6446, FAX: (989) 777-8184, E-Mail: info@myamigo.com, Web Site: www.myamigo.com (16)

Galgano, Brenda, A&P, Montvale, NJ. Tel: (201) 573-9700, (866) 44 FRESH, FAX: (201) 505-3054, E-Mail: apcustomerrel@aptea.com, Web Site: www.aptea.com (16)

Gallagher, Kelly, R R Bowker, New Providence, NJ. Tel: (888) BOWKER-2 (269-5372), FAX: (908) 771-8699, Web Site: www.bowker.com (17)

Gallagher, Kevin, Body by Jake Global LLC, Los Angeles, CA. Tel: (310) 571-7101, FAX: (310) 571-7107, E-Mail: info@bodybyjake.com, Web Site: www.bodybyjake.com (16)

Gallagher, Kevin, Merchant E-Solutions, Redwood City, CA. Tel: (678) 493-8853 (14)

Gallagher, Patricia, Liberty Fund Inc, Indianapolis, IN. Tel: (317) 842-0880, Web Site: www.libertyfund.org (1)

Gallagher, R.F., Hampton Marketing Corp, Medford, NY. Tel: (516) 924-1335, (800) 229-1019, FAX: (516) 924-1669, Web Site: www.hamptonstamp.com (16)

Gallagher, Ronald T., Hampton Marketing Corp, Medford, NY. Tel: (516) 924-1335, (800) 229-1019, FAX: (516) 924-1669, Web Site: www.hamptonstamp.com (16)

Gallagher, Shay, The Bradford Group, Niles, IL. Tel: (847) 966-2770, FAX: (847) 581-8630, Web Site: www.collectiblestoday.com (16)

Gallagher, Steven, Hampton Marketing Corp, Medford, NY. Tel: (516) 924-1335, (800) 229-1019, FAX: (516) 924-1669, Web Site: www.hamptonstamp.com (16)

Gallagher de Meij, Kathy, Children's Aid Society, New York, NY. Tel: (212) 949-4945, Web Site: www.childrensaidsociety.org (1)

Gallaher, John, American Mailing Service Inc, Ashland, KY. Tel: (606) 329-2741, (800) 678-8384, FAX: (606) 325-8558, Web Site: www.thegallahergroup.com (28)

Gallarneau, Cliff, Lion Apparel, Dayton, OH. Tel: (937) 898-1949, (800) 548-6614, FAX: (937) 913-5667, Web Site: www.lionapparel.com (2)

Gallatin, David, Mailing Specialists Inc, Greensburg, PA. Tel: (724) 832-3840, (888) 216-1056, FAX: (724) 832-8419, E-Mail: sales@mailmsi.com, Web Site: www.mailmsi.com (28)

Galle, Kenneth, Veratad Technologies LLC, Teaneck, NJ. Tel: (201) 510-6000, FAX: (201) 510-6036 (22)

Gallery of Cats, Valencia, CA. Tel: (818) 782-6264, E-Mail: helpdesk@galleryofcats.com, Web Site: www.galleryofcats.com (6)

The Gallery Shop, Buffalo, NY. Tel: (716) 882-8700 X258, FAX: (716) 882-1958, E-Mail: gallshop@albrightknox.org, Web Site: www.albrightknox.org (6)

Gallick, Joe, Penske Logistics, Reading, PA. Tel: (610) 775-6000, (800) 529-6531, FAX: (610) 775-6432, Web Site: www.penskelogistics.com (16)

Gallimore, Dave, Encore Marketing International, Lanham, MD. Tel: (301) 459-8020, (800) 846-9398, FAX: (301) 731-0525, E-Mail: customerservice@encoremarketing.com, Web Site: www.encoremarketing.com (16)

Galling, Debbie, SA-SO/Time Wise, Arlington, TX. Tel: (972) 641-4911, (800) 523-8060, FAX: (972) 660-5684, E-Mail: info@sa-so.com, Web Site: www.sa-so.com (33)

Gallion, Karen, Sunset Magazine, Menlo Park, CA. Tel: (650) 321-3600, FAX: (650) 328-6215 (17)

Gallo, Anthony, Association for Postal Commerce, Alexandria, VA. Tel: (703) 524-0096, FAX: (703) 524-1871, Web Site: www.postcom.org (40)

Gallo, Diane, Diane Gallo Associates, Gilbertsville, NY. Tel: (607) 783-2386, E-Mail: dgallo@stny.rr.com, Web Site: www.dianegallo.com (39)

Gallo, Jamie, TBWA/Chiat/Day Inc, New York, NY. Tel: (212) 804-1000, FAX: (212) 804-1200, E-Mail: jamie.gallo@tbwachiat.com, Web Site: www.tbwachiat.com (35)

Gallo, Jennifer, Investors Marketing Services, Danvers, MA. Tel: (978) 774-2990, (800) 462-2551, FAX: (978) 774-4249, Web Site: www. investorsmarketing.com (14)

Gallo, Mark, Magellan's Catalog, Santa Barbara, CA. Tel: (800) 962-4943, FAX: (800) 962-4940, E-Mail: sales@magellans.com, Web Site: www. magellans.com (5)

Diane Gallo Associates, Gilbertsville, NY. Tel: (607) 783-2386, E-Mail: dgallo@stny.rr.com, Web Site: www.dianegallo.com (39)

Gallogly, Meg, Media Mart, Falls Church, VA. Tel: (703) 905-4532, FAX: (703) 905-8097, E-Mail: mgallogly@media-mart.com, Web Site: www. media-mart.com (24)

Galloway, Elisa, Galloway Research Service, San Antonio, TX. Tel: (210) 734-4346, FAX: (210) 732-4500, E-Mail: lbrazel@gallowayresearch.com, Web Site: www.gallowayresearch.com (30)

Galloway, John, The Atlantic Monthly, Washington, DC. Tel: (202) 266-6000, (800) 234-2411, FAX: (202) 266-7280, Web Site: www.theatlantic.com (17)

Galloway, Mary, The Virginia Diner Inc, Wakefield, VA. Tel: (757) 899-6213, (888) 823-4637, FAX: (757) 899-2281, E-Mail: vadiner@vadiner.com, Web Site: www.vadiner.com (4)

Galloway Farms, Miami, FL. Tel: (305) 274-7472, FAX: (305) 274-3233, E-Mail: galloway_inc@ bellsouth.net, Web Site: www.gallowayform.com (8)

Galloway Research Service, San Antonio, TX. Tel: (210) 734-4346, FAX: (210) 732-4500, E-Mail: lbrazel@gallowayresearch.com, Web Site: www. gallowayresearch.com (30)

Gall's Inc, Lexington, KY. Tel: (859) 266-7227, (800) 477-7766, FAX: (859) 268-5954, E-Mail: helpdesk@galls.com, Web Site: www.galls.com (16)

Gallup Inter-tribal Indian Ceremonial, Gallup, NM. Tel: (505) 863-3896, FAX: (505) 863-9168, E-Mail: ceremonial@cnetco.com, Web Site: www. indianceremonial.com (1)

Galonek, Brian, A., All Star Premium Products Inc, Fiskdale, MA. Tel: (508) 347-7672, (800) 526-8629, FAX: (508) 347-5404, E-Mail: sales@ incentiveusa.com, Web Site: www.incentiveusa. com (33)

Galub, Jack, Jack Galub, New York, NY. Tel: (212) 737-9013 (39)

Jack Galub, New York, NY. Tel: (212) 737-9013 (39)

Galveston Bay Foundation, Webster, TX. Tel: (281) 332-3381, Web Site: www.galvbay.org (1)

Galvin, Kevin, Galvin Associates Inc, Marstons Mills, MA. Tel: (508) 420-8100, FAX: (508) 420-1973, E-Mail: info-1@galvinassociates.com, Web Site: www.galvinassociates.com (22)

Galvin Associates Inc, Marstons Mills, MA. Tel: (508) 420-8100, FAX: (508) 420-1973, E-Mail: info-1@ galvinassociates.com, Web Site: www. galvinassociates.com (22)

Gambrell, Michael, R., Dow Chemical USA, Midland, MI. Tel: (989) 636-1000, (800) 447-4369, FAX: (989) 832-1465, E-Mail: jadams@dow.com, Web Site: www.dow.com (16)

Gambro Inc, Lakewood, CO. Tel: (303) 232-6800, (800) 525-2623, FAX: (303) 222-6810, Web Site: www.gambro.com (16)

Game Show Placements Ltd, Hollywood, CA. Tel: (323) 874-7818, E-Mail: gsp@ix.netcom.com, Web Site: www.gspltd.com (35)

GameTime Inc, Fort Payne, AL. Tel: (256) 845-5610, (800) 633-2394, FAX: (256) 845-9361/2649, Web Site: www.gametime.com (11)

Gamino, Linda, UGL Equis Corp, Chicago, IL. Tel: (312) 424-8000, FAX: (312) 424-8080, Web Site: www.equiscorp.com (16)

Gamma Photo Labs LLC, Chicago, IL. Tel: (312) 337-0022, FAX: (312) 337-3753, Web Site: www. photobition.com (16)

Gammon, Larry, New York Easter Seal Society, New York, NY. Tel: (312) 726-6200, (212) 943-4364, (800) 221-6827, FAX: (212) 695-4807, (312) 726-4258, Web Site: ny.easterseals.com (1)

Gandolfi, Margie, New York Blood Center Inc, New York, NY. Tel: (212) 570-3000, (800) 933-2566, FAX: (212) 570-3195, Web Site: www. nybloodcenter.org (1)

Gangemi, Dr. Richard, Viahealth, Rochester, NY. Tel: (585) 922-4000, (585) 922-3677, FAX: (585) 922-3929, Web Site: www.viahealth.org (16)

Gangi, Paul A., Harris Publishing, Brewster, NY. Tel: (800) 326-6600, FAX: (914) 287-2144, E-Mail: moreinfo@harrisconnect.com, Web Site: www. bcharrispub.com (35)

Gangloff, Deborah, American Forests, Washington, DC. Tel: (202) 737-1944, FAX: (202) 737-2457, E-Mail: info@amfor.org, Web Site: www. americanforests.org (1)

Gannett Co Inc, Mc Lean, VA. Tel: (703) 854-6000, FAX: (703) 854-2046, E-Mail: gcishare@gannett. com, Web Site: www.gannett.com (16)

Gannett Direct Marketing Services Inc, Louisville, KY. Tel: (502) 454-6660, (800) 345-5654, FAX: (502) 459-7479, Web Site: www.gdms.com (21)

Gannon, Kevin, T., Robert A Stanger & Co Inc, Shrewsbury, NJ. Tel: (732) 389-3600, FAX: (732) 389-1751, E-Mail: info@rastanger.com, Web Site: www.rastanger.com (14)

Gansert, Carey, San Diego Direct Marketing Association, San Diego, CA. Tel: (858) 503-1471, E-Mail: webmaster@sddma.org, Web Site: www.sddma.org (40)

Gant, Russell, Supelco Inc, Bellefonte, PA. Tel: (814) 359-3441, (800) 359-3041, FAX: (814) 359-3044, E-Mail: supelco@sial.com, Web Site: www.sigma-aldrich.com (16)

Ganz, David, L., Relationship1, Rye, NY. Tel: (914) 921-4400, E-Mail: marketing@relationship1.com, Web Site: www.relationship1.com (21)

Garber, Ann, Market Square Communications Inc, Stevens Point, WI. Tel: (715) 344-4609, FAX: (715) 344-6885 (20)

Garber, Gregg, D., Bonneville Communications, Salt Lake City, UT. Tel: (801) 237-2600, (888) BON-COM, FAX: (801) 237-2614, E-Mail: bonneville@ bonneville.com, Web Site: www.bonneville.com (35)

Garcia, A.L., Advertising Mailers Inc, Edison, NJ. Tel: (732) 225-3404, (800) 427-8513, FAX: (732) 225-7429, E-Mail: admailers@aol.com (28)

Garcia, Candie, Clampitt Paper Co, Dallas, TX. Tel: (214) 638-3300, FAX: (214) 634-7837, E-Mail: dcrew@clampitt.com, Web Site: www.clampitt.com (16)

Garcia, Erika, Blue Strawberry Resorts LLC, Miami Beach, FL. Tel: (756) 513-1456, (800) 873-1440, Web Site: www.bluestrawberry-resorts.com (19)

Garcia, Joanne, John Sutherland & Associates, San Diego, CA. Tel: (858) 535-1139, (800) 545-9591, FAX: (858) 535-9124 (15)

Garcia, Jonathan, PFE Inc, Irvine, CA. Tel: (949) 417-0330, FAX: (949) 417-0331, Web Site: www. pfeinc.com (34)

Garcia, Norman, Name-Finders Lists Inc, Oakland, CA. Tel: (415) 955-8585, (800) 221-5009, FAX: (415) 955-8581, E-Mail: dm@namefinderslists. com, Web Site: www.namefinderslists.com (23)

Garcia, Rosalie, Walter Karl Inc, Pearl River, NY. Tel: (845) 620-0700, FAX: (845) 620-1885, E-Mail: info@walterkarl.infousa.com, Web Site: www. walterkarl.com (22)

Gard Communications, Portland, OR. Tel: (503) 221-0100, FAX: (503) 226-4854, Web Site: www. gardcommunications.com (35)

Gardella, Patricia, Gardella & Co, Atlanta, GA. Tel: (404) 355-1005, FAX: (404) 355-4888, E-Mail: gardellastudio@comcast.com (21)

Gardella & Co, Atlanta, GA. Tel: (404) 355-1005, FAX: (404) 355-4888, E-Mail: gardellastudio@ comcast.com (21)

Garden Botanika Inc, Saint Louis, MO. Tel: (425) 881-9603, (800) 968-7842, FAX: (425) 869-6235, Web Site: www.gardenbotanika.com (7)

Garden Perennials, Wayne, NE. Tel: (402) 375-3615, (888) 375-3615, Web Site: www.gardenperennials. net (8)

Gardener's Eden, Merrimack, NH. Tel: (603) 888-9500, (800) 822-9600, FAX: (603) 577-8005, E-Mail: gsweeney@brookstone.com (8)

Gardener's Supply Co, Burlington, VT. Tel: (802) 660-3500, (888) 833-1412, FAX: (802) 660-3501, E-Mail: info@gardeners.com, Web Site: www. gardeners.com (8)

Gardenimport Inc, Richmond Hill, ON Canada. Tel: (905) 731-1950, (800) 339-8314, FAX: (905) 731-3093, E-Mail: flower@gardenimport.com, Web Site: www.gardenimport.com (8)

Gardens Alive! Inc, Lawrenceburg, IN. Tel: (812) 537-8665, FAX: (812) 537-5108, E-Mail: service@ gardensalive.com, Web Site: www.gardens-alive. com (8)

Gardens Of The Blue Ridge Inc, Pineola, NC. Tel: (828) 733-2417, FAX: (828) 733-8894, E-Mail: gardensblueridge@boone.net, Web Site: www. gardensoftheblueridge.com (8)

Garder, Dimitri, Global-Z International Inc, Bennington, VT. Tel: (802) 445-1011, FAX: (802) 445-1016, E-Mail: info@globalz.com, Web Site: www. globalz.com (22)

Gardineer, Vaughn, UNICOR- Services Business Group, Washington, DC. Tel: (202) 305-3500, Web Site: www.unicor.gov/services (28)

Gardner, David, The Motley Fool, Alexandria, VA. FAX: (703) 254-1999, E-Mail: cs@fool.com, Web Site: www.Fool.com (14)

Gardner, John, Integrative Logic LLC, Lawrenceville, GA. Tel: (678) 638-2600, Web Site: www. integrativelogic.com (30)

Gardner, Mark, Sappi Fine Paper North America, Boston, MA. Tel: (617) 423-7300, FAX: (617) 423-5494, Web Site: www.sappi.com (25)

Gardner, Melanie, University of Southern Mississippi, Hattiesburg, MS. Tel: (601) 266-4734, Web Site: www.usm.edu (1)

Gardner, Mickey, Current USA Inc, Colorado Springs, CO. Tel: (719) 594-4100, (877) 665-4458, FAX: (719) 531-2283, Web Site: www.currentinc.com (6)

Gardner, Nancy, TechniServe Inc, Troy, MI. Tel: (248) 989-0100, FAX: (248) 989-0111, E-Mail: info@ techni-serve.com, Web Site: www.techni-serve.com (22)

Gardner, Robert, J&H Berge/The Lab Mart, South Plainfield, NJ. Tel: (908) 561-1234, FAX: (908) 561-3002, E-Mail: rgardner@labmart.com, Web Site: www.labmart.com (7)

Gardner, Robert, US Postal Service-Library, Washington, DC. Tel: (202) 268-2904, FAX: (202) 268-6436, Web Site: www.usps.com (28)

Gardner, Steve, NCS Learn, Trabuco Canyon, CA. Tel: (949) 766-1068, Web Site: www.ncslearn.com (16)

Gardner, Tom, The Motley Fool, Alexandria, VA. FAX: (703) 254-1999, E-Mail: cs@fool.com, Web Site: www.Fool.com (14)

Gardune, Christena, Koeppel Direct, Dallas, TX. Tel: (972) 732-6110, FAX: (972) 248-2759, E-Mail: pkoeppel@koeppelinc.com, Web Site: www. koeppeldirect.com (32)

Garelick, Sheila, Brylane, Indianapolis, IN. Tel: (800) 677-0339, Web Site: www.brylanehome.com (2)

Garfinkel, Dean, Call Compliance Inc, Glen Cove, NY. Tel: (516) 674-4545, FAX: (516) 676-2420, E-Mail: sales@callcompliance.com, Web Site: www.callcompliance.com (29)

Garfinkel, Dean, Quality Contact Solutions Inc, Aurora, NE. Tel: (402) 210-2692, (866) 963-2889, FAX: (402) 210-2692, E-Mail: info@

qualitycontactsolutions.com, Web Site: www.
qualitycontactsolutions.com (29)

Garfinkel Andrews, Alison, Call Compliance Inc, Glen
Cove, NY. Tel: (516) 674-4545, FAX: (516) 676-
2420, E-Mail: sales@callcompliance.com, Web
Site: www.callcompliance.com (29)

Garile, Giovanni, Martin Worldwide Inc, Oak Park,
CA. Tel: (888) 694-5478, Web Site: www.
martinworldwide.net (23)

Garland, Amy, Blue Sky Factory, Baltimore, MD. Tel:
(410) 230-0061, Web Site: www.blueskyfactory.
com (32)

Garlinghouse Co, Beaufort, SC. Tel: (703) 547-4115,
(800) 235-5700, FAX: (703) 222-9705, Web Site:
www.familyhomeplans.com (17)

Garner, David, Sitel, Nashville, TN. Tel: (615) 301-
7100, (866) 95-SITEL, E-Mail: pr-na@sitel.com,
Web Site: www.sitel.com (23)

Garner, Emily, Quality Education Data (QED), Shelton, CT. Tel: (203) 926-4800, (800) 333-8802,
E-Mail: mdrinfor@dnb.com, Web Site: www.
schooldata.com (23)

Garner, J, Kenneth, Who's Who - The MFSA Buyers'
Guide to Blue Ribbon Mailing Services, Alexandria, VA. Tel: (703) 836-9200, FAX: (703) 548-
8204, E-Mail: masa-mail@masa.org, Web Site:
www.mfsanet.org (43)

Garner, J., Kenneth, Mailing & Fulfillment Service
Association (MFSA), Alexandria, VA. Tel: (703)
836-9200, (800) 333-6272, FAX: (703) 548-8204,
E-Mail: mfsa-mail@mfsanet.org, Web Site: www.
mfsanet.org (40)

Garner, Stephen, B., Effective Marketing Associates,
Inc, West Linn, OR. Tel: (503) 657-5859, FAX:
(503) 657-5886, Web Site: www.e-m-a.com (20)

Garner, Steve, JIST Publishing, Saint Paul, MN. Tel:
(800) 648-5478, FAX: (800) 547-8329, E-Mail:
info@jist.com, Web Site: www.jist.com (17)

Garnet Hill Inc, Franconia, NH. Tel: (603) 823-5545,
FAX: (603) 823-7034, Web Site: www.garnethill.
com (2)

Garnett, Doug, Atomic Direct LLC, Portland, OR. Tel:
(503) 296-6131, Web Site: www.atomicdirect.com
(35)

Garnier, Jean-Pierre, Glaxo Smith Kline, Research
Triangle Park, NC. Tel: (919) 483-2100, (888)
825-5249, FAX: (919) 248-8383, Web Site: www.
gsk.com (16)

Garofalo, Regina, Anheuser-Busch Inc Promotional
Products Group, Shelton, CT. Tel: (800) 742-5283,
Web Site: www.budshop.com (6)

Garon Products Inc, Wall, NJ. Tel: (732) 449-1776,
(800) 631-5380, FAX: (732) 449-6937, Web Site:
www.garonproducts.com (16)

Garone, Jennifer, Microsoft Corp, Redmond, WA. Tel:
(425) 882-8080, FAX: (425) 936-7329, Web Site:
www.microsoft.com (22)

Garret, Desta, Nordskog Publishing Co, Ventura, CA.
Tel: (805) 642-2070, FAX: (805) 642-1862,
E-Mail: pwrboatmag@aol.com, Web Site: www.
nordskogpublishing.com (17)

Garreton, Catalina, Nimblefish Technologies, San
Francisco, CA. Tel: (415) 247-7000, Web Site:
www.nimblefish.com (30)

Garrett, Audrey, Winfield Marketing Corp, Chicago,
IL. Tel: (773) 743-8784, FAX: (440) 764-4871
(31)

Garrett, Evelyn, The Dreyfus Corp, New York, NY.
Tel: (212) 922-6000, FAX: (212) 922-8165 (14)

Garrett, Mark, Adobe Systems Inc, San Jose, CA. Tel:
(408) 536-6000, (800) 833-6687, FAX: (408) 537-
6000, Web Site: www.adobe.com (22)

Garrett, Patrick, Sickafus Sheepskins, Strausstown,
PA. Tel: (610) 488-1782, (888) 751-1300, FAX:
(610) 488-1576, E-Mail: pat@patgarrett.com, Web
Site: www.sheepcoat.com (2)

Garrett, Scott, Beckman Coulter Inc, Brea, CA. Tel:
(714) 993-5321, (800) 526-3821, FAX: (800) 232-
3828, Web Site: www.beckmancoulter.com (16)

Garris, Robert, Aerosoles, Edison, NJ. Tel: (732) 985-
6900, FAX: (732) 985-3697, E-Mail: bgarris@
aerosoles.com, Web Site: www.aerosoles.com (2)

Garrison, Beth, Hearlihy & Co, Pittsburg, KS. Tel:
(866) 622-1003, (800) 622-1000, FAX: (800) 443-
2260, Web Site: www.hearlihy.com (17)

Garrison, Glenn, Mr G's Enterprises, Fort Worth, TX.
Tel: (817) 831-3501, FAX: (817) 831-0638,
E-Mail: mrgs@mrgusa.com, Web Site: www.
mrgusa.com (16)

Garrison, Neal, Oliver of Adrian Inc, Adrian, MI. Tel:
(517) 263-2132, (877) 668-0885, FAX: (517) 265-
8698, E-Mail: info@oliverinstrument.com, Web
Site: www.oliverofadrian.com (16)

Garrison, Stanley, M., Choice Point, Alpharetta, GA.
Tel: (770) 752-6000, (800) 342-5339, FAX: (770)
752-6005, Web Site: www.choicepoint.com (16)

Garriss, Steve, Compass Electronics, Forest Grove,
OR. Tel: (503) 357-2111, FAX: (503) 357-2111 (9)

Garritano, Joe, Penn Garritano Direct Response Marketing, Minneapolis, MN. Tel: (612) 333-3775,
FAX: (612) 333-3775, Web Site: www.
penngarritano.com (35)

Garrity, William, E., Consumer's Energy, Jackson, MI.
Tel: (517) 788-0550, (800) 805-0490, FAX: (517)
788-1859, E-Mail: businesscenter@
consumerenergy.com, Web Site: www.
consumersenergy.com (16)

Garrow, Ron, National Mail Advertising Inc, Houston,
TX. Tel: (713) 869-8551, FAX: (713) 868-5743,
E-Mail: sales@nationalmail.com, Web Site: www.
nationalmail.com (28)

Garrubbo, Edwin, Creative Commerce LLC, West
Chester, PA. Tel: (212) 625-1700 (35)

Garson Jr., Walter, Walter Garson Jr & Associates Inc,
Bensalem, PA. Tel: (215) 245-6610, FAX: (215)
245-0281, E-Mail: walt@garsonmail.com (28)

Walter Garson Jr & Associates Inc, Bensalem, PA.
Tel: (215) 245-6610, FAX: (215) 245-0281,
E-Mail: walt@garsonmail.com (28)

Garstecki, Jay, Quantum Group, Morton Grove, IL.
Tel: (847) 967-3600, Web Site: www.
quantumgroup.com (35)

Garten, Wayne, Hanover Direct Inc, Weehawken, NJ.
Tel: (201) 863-7300, FAX: (201) 272-3280, Web
Site: www.hanoverdirect.com (5)

Gartenberg, David, Selltel Inc, Brick, NJ. Tel: (732)
920-8700, (888) 840-9481, FAX: (732) 903-0836,
E-Mail: info@nationalprotection.com (29)

Gartner Inc, San Jose, CA. Tel: (408) 468-8000, (800)
419-3282, FAX: (408) 954-1780, E-Mail: tom.
mccall@gartner.com, Web Site: www.gartner.com
(20)

Garvan Communications Inc, Locust Valley, NY. Tel:
(516) 827-4000, FAX: (516) 827-4001, Web Site:
www.garvan.com (35)

Garver Advertising Service Inc, New York, NY. Tel:
(212) 371-3325, E-Mail: garverads@aol.com (35)

Garvey Jr., Ed, J., The Garvey Group, Niles, IL. Tel:
(847) 647-1900, FAX: (847) 647-6550, E-Mail:
info@thegarveygroup.com, Web Site: www.
thegarveygroup.com (27)

Garvey, Lee, Click2Mail, Arlington, VA. Tel: (703)
521-9029, (866) 665-2787, FAX: (703) 358-8811,
E-Mail: info@click2mail.com, Web Site: www.
click2mail.com (20)

The Garvey Group, Niles, IL. Tel: (847) 647-1900,
FAX: (847) 647-6550, E-Mail: info@
thegarveygroup.com, Web Site: www.
thegarveygroup.com (27)

Garwood, Amber, NewPage Corp, Miamisburg, OH.
Tel: (937) 242-9068, (877) 855-7243, FAX: (937)
242-9327, Web Site: www.newpagecorp.com (25)

Gary's Perennials, LLC, Maple Glen, PA. Tel: (215)
628-4070, (800) 898-6653, FAX: (215) 628-0216,
E-Mail: roots@garysperennials.com, Web Site:
www.garysperennials.com; www.perennialmarket.
com (8)

Garza, Jose, Marvin Envelope & Paper Co, Wheeling,
IL. Tel: (773) 489-3300, (800) 227-0011, FAX:
(773) 489-4783, E-Mail: marvinenvelope@aol.com
(27)

Garza, Linda, Pecan Producers International, Corsicana, TX. Tel: (903) 872-1337, (800) 732-2648,
FAX: (903) 874-7143 (4)

Gasaway, Sharilyn, Alltel, Little Rock, AR. Tel: (501)
905-2590, (877) 446-3628, FAX: (501) 905-5444,
Web Site: www.alltel.com (16)

GasPedal, Chicago, IL. Tel: (312) 932-9000, Web Site:
www.gaspedal.net (20)

Gasperment, Sophie, The Body Shop Inc, Wake Forest, NC. Tel: (919) 554-4900, (800) BODYSHOP,
FAX: (919) 554-4361, Web Site: www.
thebodyshop.com (7)

Gass, Bill, Fielder's Choice Direct, Monticello, IN.
Tel: (574) 583-2741 X107, (800) 321-3177, FAX:
(574) 583-CORN, Web Site: www.
fielderschoicedirect.com (8)

Gast, Ann, Anheuser-Busch Inc Promotional Products
Group, Shelton, CT. Tel: (800) 742-5283, Web
Site: www.budshop.com (6)

Gatehouse, Michelle, Lifestyle Change Communications, Kennesaw, GA. Tel: (770) 218-8200, (800)
411-5771, FAX: (770) 218-8211, E-Mail: experts@
lifestylechange.com, Web Site: www.
lifestylechange.com (24)

Gately, Jerry, Direct Mail Solutions LLC, Carol
Stream, IL. Tel: (630) 653-6863, FAX: (630) 653-
7144, E-Mail: support@dmspostal.com, Web Site:
www.dmspostal.com (28)

Gates, Greg, Manning Materials, Birdsboro, PA. Tel:
(610) 385-6797, (800) 445-1719, FAX: (610) 385-
7524, E-Mail: mmsupport@manningmaterials.com,
Web Site: www.manningmaterials.com (16)

Gates, Jim, BuyFilters.com LLC, Silverhill, AL. Tel:
(866) 863-1262, Web Site: www.buyfilters.com (5)

Gates, Robert, Gates Marketing, Atlanta, GA. Tel:
(770) 455-9662, FAX: (770) 455-8785 (22)

Gates, Robert, VF Imagewear, Nashville, TN. Tel:
(615) 565-5000, (800) 733-5271, Web Site: www.
vfimagewear.com (16)

Gates Corp, Denver, CO. Tel: (303) 744-1911, FAX:
(303) 744-4000, Web Site: www.gates.com (9)

Gates Marketing, Atlanta, GA. Tel: (770) 455-9662,
FAX: (770) 455-8785 (22)

Gateskill, Russ, Garnet Hill Inc, Franconia, NH. Tel:
(603) 823-5545, FAX: (603) 823-7034, Web Site:
www.garnethill.com (2)

Gateway Bank and Trust, Raleigh, NC. Tel: (919)
865-3869, Web Site: www.gatewaybankandtrust.
com (14)

Gateway Inc, Irvine, CA. Tel: (949) 471-7000, (800)
369-1409, FAX: (949) 471-7041, Web Site: www.
gateway.com (3)

The Gateway Learning Corp, Irvine, CA. Tel: (714)
429-2223, (800) 222-3334, FAX: (714) 338-2525
(16)

Gatlin, Greg, ADT Worldwide, Boca Raton, FL. Tel:
(561) 988-3600, FAX: (561) 988-3673, Web Site:
www.tycofireandsecurity.com (16)

Gatsch, Mary, E., Peterson's, Lawrenceville, NJ. Tel:
(609) 896-1800, FAX: (609) 896-1811, E-Mail:
custsvc@petersons.com, Web Site: www.petersons.
com (17)

Gatti, William, A., Bookspan, Garden City, NY. Tel:
(516) 490-4561, FAX: (516) 490-4856 (13)

Gaudet, Mark, B&W Press Inc, Georgetown, MA. Tel:
(978) 352-6100, (877) 246-3467, FAX: (978) 352-
5955, E-Mail: csr@bwpress.com, Web Site: www.
bwpress.com (21)

Gault, Marc, G., Marc G Gault Advertising & Marketing Consulting, Stone Mountain, GA. Tel: (770)
938-0781 (35)

Marc G Gault Advertising & Marketing Consulting,
Stone Mountain, GA. Tel: (770) 938-0781 (35)

Gavales, Lisa, Bloomingdale's Direct, New York, NY.
Tel: (212) 705-2000, (866) 593-2540, FAX: (212)
705-2805, Web Site: www.bloomingdales.com (16)

Gavelek, Mike, Sunburst Technology, Elgin, IL. Tel: (914) 747-3310, FAX: (914) 747-4109, E-Mail: service@nysunburst.com, Web Site: www.sunburst.com (17)

Gavin, Patrick, JW Jung Seed Co, Randolph, WI. Tel: (920) 326-3121, (800) 297-3123, FAX: (920) 326-5769, E-Mail: info@jungseed.com, Web Site: www.jungseed.com (8)

Gavin, William, CPE, Chicago, IL. Tel: (312) 427-5370, FAX: (312) 427-7836, E-Mail: wgavin@cpe1.com, Web Site: www.cpe1.com (27)

Gavinson, Pat, New Mexico State University, Las Cruces, NM. Tel: (575) 646-0111, (505) 646-3341, FAX: (505) 646-1498, Web Site: www.nmsu.edu (41)

Gaw-O'Hara Envelope Co, Western Springs, IL. Tel: (773) 638-1200, (888) 385-8439, FAX: (773) 638-1208, E-Mail: info@gawohara.com, Web Site: www.gawohara.com (26)

Gay, Brian, Champs Software Inc, Crystal River, FL. Tel: (352) 795-2362, FAX: (352) 795-9100, E-Mail: champs@champsinc.com, Web Site: www.champsinc.com (3)

Gay Men's Health Crisis, New York, NY. Tel: (212) 367-1000, FAX: (212) 367-1220, E-Mail: webmaster@gmhc.org, Web Site: www.gmhc.org (1)

Gayle III, Norman, W., Shelby Insurance Companies, Birmingham, AL. Tel: (800) 443-1573, FAX: (877) 837-8203, Web Site: www.vesta.com (15)

Gayle M.D., M.P.H., Helene, D., CARE USA, Atlanta, GA. Tel: (404) 979-9255, (800) 521-CARE, FAX: (404) 589-2600, E-Mail: info@care.org, Web Site: www.careusa.org (1)

Gaylord, Amy, Westlake Plastics Co, Lenni, PA. Tel: (610) 459-1000, (800) 999-1700, FAX: (610) 459-1084, Web Site: www.westlakeplastics.com (16)

Gaylord, Jeremy, P., Gaylord Communications Unlimited, Bridgewater, VT. Tel: (802) 672-6200, FAX: (802) 672-6226 (35)

Gaylord Brothers, Syracuse, NY. Tel: (315) 634-8440, Web Site: www.gaylord.com (16)

Gaylord Communications Unlimited, Bridgewater, VT. Tel: (802) 672-6200, FAX: (802) 672-6226 (35)

Gaylord Entertainment Co, Nashville, TN. Tel: (615) 316-6000, Web Site: www.gaylordentertainment.com (19)

Gaynor, Paul, Market Focus Direct, Markham, ON Canada. Tel: (905) 477-0801, FAX: (905) 477-4473, E-Mail: info@market-focus.com, Web Site: www.market-focus.com (28)

Gazette Communications Inc, Cedar Rapids, IA. Tel: (319) 398-8211, (800) 397-8211, FAX: (319) 368-8834, Web Site: www.gazettecommunications.com (17)

Gazette Direct Marketing Co, Cedar Rapids, IA. Tel: (319) 399-5997, FAX: (319) 399-5998, Web Site: www.gazette.com (20)

Gazzale, Bob, The American Film Institute, Los Angeles, CA. Tel: (323) 856-7600, FAX: (323) 467-4578, Web Site: www.afi.com (1)

Gazzolo, Glenn, The Popcorn Factory, Lake Forest, IL. Tel: (847) 362-0028, (888) 216-0235, FAX: (888) 333-4595, E-Mail: service@thepopcornfactory.com, Web Site: www.thepopcornfactory.com (4)

Gearen, Mark D., Hobart & William Smith Colleges, Geneva, NY. Tel: (315) 781-3000, (800) 852-2256, FAX: (315) 781-3655, Web Site: www.hws.edu (19)

Geary, Pamela, Western Pennsylvania Conservancy, Pittsburgh, PA. Tel: (412) 288-2777, Web Site: www.paconserve.org (1)

Geary's of Beverly Hills, Beverly Hills, CA. Tel: (310) 273-4741, (800) 793-6670, FAX: (310) 858-7555, Web Site: www.gearys.com (6)

Gebarowski, Fred, ISA-The Instrumentation Systems & Automation Society, Research Triangle Park, NC. Tel: (919) 549-8411, FAX: (919) 549-8288, E-Mail: info@isa.org, Web Site: www.isa.org (1)

Gebauer, Ruediger, Springer Science & Business Media LLC, New York, NY. Tel: (212) 460-1500, FAX: (212) 473-6272, Web Site: www.springer-ny.com (17)

Gebbie, Mark, All-In-One Directory, New Paltz, NY. Tel: (845) 255-7560, FAX: (888) 345-2790, E-Mail: gebbiepress@pipeline.com, Web Site: www.gebbieinc.com (43)

Gebbie, Mark, Gebbie Press Inc, New Paltz, NY. Tel: (845) 255-7560, FAX: (888) 345-2790, E-Mail: gebbiepress@pipeline.com, Web Site: www.gebbieinc.com (17)

Gebbie Press Inc, New Paltz, NY. Tel: (845) 255-7560, FAX: (888) 345-2790, E-Mail: gebbiepress@pipeline.com, Web Site: www.gebbieinc.com (17)

Gebert, Richard, Grant Thornton LLP, Philadelphia, PA. Tel: (215) 561-4200, FAX: (215) 561-1066, Web Site: www.grantthornton.com (20)

Gebhardt, George E., Eye Care Centers of America, San Antonio, TX. Tel: (210) 340-3531, (800) 669-1183, FAX: (210) 340-0123, E-Mail: customerservice@visionworks.com, Web Site: www.ecca.com (7)

Gebhart, Karen, Aircraft Owners & Pilots Association, Frederick, MD. Tel: (301) 695-2000, (800) 872-2672, FAX: (301) 695-2375, E-Mail: aopahq@aopa.org, Web Site: www.aopa.org (1)

Gebhart, Walter, M., Phillips Kiln Service LTD, South Sioux City, NE. Tel: (402) 494-6837, (800) 831-0876, FAX: (402) 494-6858, E-Mail: info@kilm.com, Web Site: www.kiln.com (17)

Gedeon, Harvey, Estee Lauder Inc, New York, NY. Tel: (212) 572-4200, (866) 467-7363, FAX: (212) 572-3942, Web Site: www.esteelauder.com (16)

Gedney, Karen, Karen Gedney Communications, Brooklyn, NY. Tel: (718) 680-1627, FAX: (917) 591-5547, E-Mail: kg@karengedney.com, Web Site: www.karengedney.com (35)

Karen Gedney Communications, Brooklyn, NY. Tel: (718) 680-1627, FAX: (917) 591-5547, E-Mail: kg@karengedney.com, Web Site: www.karengedney.com (35)

Geer, David, Listmasters Direct Mail Services, Bensalem, PA. Tel: (215) 633-8200, (800) 234-5478, FAX: (215) 633-8209, E-Mail: sales@listmastersdirect.com, Web Site: www.listmastersdirect.com (23)

Gegax, Tom, CSPI/Nutrition Action Health Letter, Washington, DC. Tel: (202) 332-9110, FAX: (202) 265-4954, E-Mail: cspi@cspinet.org, Web Site: www.cspinet.org (17)

Gehner, Scott, Parcel Insurance Plan Inc, Saint Louis, MO. Tel: (314) 692-0300, (800) 325-7390, FAX: (314) 692-7598, E-Mail: office@pipinsure.com, Web Site: www.pipinsure.com (15)

Gehringer, Richard, Oxford University Press Inc, New York, NY. Tel: (212) 726-6000, FAX: (212) 726-6455, Web Site: www.oup.com/us/ (17)

Geiger, Eugene, Geiger Brothers, Lewiston, ME. Tel: (207) 755-2000, FAX: (207) 755-2422, E-Mail: ggeiger@geiger.com, Web Site: www.geiger.com (33)

Geiger, Kevin, Standard Buying Service Ltd, New York, NY. Tel: (212) 686-6800, FAX: (212) 532-4102, E-Mail: info@sbspromo.com, Web Site: www.standardbuying.com (33)

Geiger, Larry, American Management Association, New York, NY. Tel: (212) 586-8100, FAX: (212) 903-8186, Web Site: www.amanet.org (1)

Geiger, Steve, Curtis 1000 Inc, Duluth, GA. Tel: (678) 380-9095, (800) 766-1007, FAX: (770) 717-1890, E-Mail: info@curtis1000.com, Web Site: www.curtis1000.com (27)

Geiger Brothers, Lewiston, ME. Tel: (207) 755-2000, FAX: (207) 755-2422, E-Mail: ggeiger@geiger.com, Web Site: www.geiger.com (33)

Geiger Donnelly Marketing LLC, Foxboro, MA. Tel: (508) 549-0909, FAX: (508) 549-0916 (35)

Geilenkrichen, Katie, Vente Inc, Omaha, NE. Tel: (402) 898-6800, (877) 899-9691, FAX: (402) 334-4829, Web Site: www.venteinc.com (30)

Gelco Information Network, Eden Prairie, MN. Tel: (952) 947-1500, (800) 444-6588, FAX: (952) 947-1525, Web Site: www.gelco.com (16)

Gelderman Group Inc, Brookfield, CT. Tel: (203) 740-9000, FAX: (203) 702-7096, E-Mail: geldermangroup@earthlink.net (23)

Gelinas, R. Gerald, Thousand Trails LP, Chicago, IL. Tel: (214) 618-7200, (800) 205-0606, FAX: (214) 618-7324, Web Site: www.1000trails.com (16)

Geller, Allan, Visions Marketing Services, Lancaster, PA. Tel: (717) 381-2100, (800) 222-1577, FAX: (717) 295-8020, Web Site: www.wecloseloans.com (29)

Geller, Lois, Direct Marketing Boot Camp, Hollywood, FL. Tel: (646) 723-3230, (800) 331-7114, FAX: (954) 921-2005, E-Mail: loisgeller@loisgellermarketinggroup.com, Web Site: www.masongeller.com (41)

Geller, Lois, Lois Geller Marketing Group, Hollywood, FL. Tel: (646) 723-3231, FAX: (954) 921-2005, E-Mail: loisgeller@loisgellermarketinggroup.com, Web Site: www.loisgellermarketinggroup.com (35)

David Geller Associates, New York, NY. Tel: (212) 455-0100, FAX: (212) 455-0164 (31)

Lois Geller Marketing Group, Hollywood, FL. Tel: (646) 723-3231, FAX: (954) 921-2005, E-Mail: loisgeller@loisgellermarketinggroup.com, Web Site: www.loisgellermarketinggroup.com (35)

Geltner, Sharon, Mark James & Associates Inc, Oswego, IL. Tel: (630) 548-8100, FAX: (630) 548-6107, E-Mail: info@markjamesassociates.com, Web Site: www.markjamesassociates.com/contact.html (16)

Gemalto Inc, Montgomeryville, PA. Tel: (215) 390-2000, E-Mail: us.sales@gemalto.com, Web Site: www.gemalto.com (16)

Gemello, John, M., San Francisco State University, San Francisco, CA. Tel: (415) 338-1111, FAX: (415) 338-0501, Web Site: www.sfsu.edu (41)

Gemini Publishing Co, Webster, TX. Tel: (281) 316-4276, E-Mail: getgirls@getgirls.com, Web Site: www.getgirls.com (17)

Gems Sensors & Controls, Plainville, CT. Tel: (860) 747-3000, (800) 378-1600, FAX: (860) 747-4244, E-Mail: info@gemssensors.com, Web Site: www.gemssensors.com (9)

Genada Imports, Teaneck, NJ. Tel: (973) 569-9660, FAX: (973) 569-9660 (8)

Gendelev, Boris, Wheaton Group, Chapel Hill, NC. Tel: (919) 969-8859, FAX: (425) 675-6014, E-Mail: jim.wheaton@wheatongroup.com, Web Site: www.wheatongroup.com (22)

Gendreau, Ronald, R., The Hartford Financial Services Inc, Southington, CT. Tel: (860) 843-8070, (860) 547-5000, FAX: (860) 547-2680, Web Site: www.thehartford.com (15)

Gendron, George, INC Magazine, New York, NY. Tel: (212) 389-5377, FAX: (617) 248-8090, Web Site: www.inc.com (17)

General Binding Corp, Northbrook, IL. Tel: (800) 723-4000, FAX: (800) 952-1166, (847) 272-1389, Web Site: www.gbc.com (10)

General Electric Co, Fairfield, CT. Tel: (203) 373-2211, FAX: (203) 373-3131, Web Site: www.ge.com (16)

General Growth Properties, Chicago, IL. Tel: (312) 960-5413, Web Site: www.generalgrowth.com (5)

General Mills Inc, Minneapolis, MN. Tel: (763) 764-7600, FAX: (763) 764-7384, Web Site: www.generalmills.com (8)

General Motivation Co, Grand Rapids, MI. Tel: (616) 647-3085, FAX: (616) 647-5909, E-Mail: motivate@i2k.com, Web Site: www.generalmotivation.com (33)

General Nutrition Corp, Pittsburgh, PA. Tel: (412) 288-4600, (877) GNC-4700, FAX: (412) 402-7218, Web Site: www.gnc.com (7)

General Pencil Co Inc, Jersey City, NJ. Tel: (201) 653-5351, FAX: (201) 653-2298, E-Mail: info@ generalpencil.com, Web Site: www.generalpencil. com (16)

General Physics Corp, Elkridge, MD. Tel: (410) 379-3600, (800) 727-6677, FAX: (410) 540-5302, E-Mail: info@gpworldwide.com, Web Site: www. gpworldwide.com (16)

General Printers, Oshawa, ON Canada. Tel: (416) 490-6000, (888) 718-6600, FAX: (905) 436-0813, E-Mail: thornley@generalprinters.com, Web Site: www.generalprinters.com (27)

General Tours/TBI Tours, Keene, NH. Tel: (603) 357-5033, (800) 221-2216, FAX: (603) 357-4548, E-Mail: info@generaltours.com, Web Site: www. generaltours.com (19)

General Vitamin Corp, Raleigh, NC. Tel: (919) 929-5785, (800) 323-8432, FAX: (919) 929-2458, E-Mail: support@generalvitamin.com, Web Site: www.generalvitamin.com (16)

General Wig Manufacturers Inc, Pompano Beach, FL. Tel: (305) 823-0600, (800) 268-7210, FAX: (314) 785-0224, E-Mail: 4service@beautytrends.com, Web Site: www.beautytrends.com (7)

Genereaux, Scott, Data Direct Networks (HQ), Chatsworth, CA. Tel: (818) 700-7607, (800) 837-2298, FAX: (818) 700-7601, E-Mail: info@ddn.com, Web Site: www.datadirectnet.com (13)

GenerH, Inc, Torrance, CA. Tel: (888) 312-3443, E-Mail: info@generh.com, Web Site: www.generh. com (21)

Genesco Inc, Nashville, TN. Tel: (615) 367-7000, (888) 324-6189, FAX: (615) 367-8278, Web Site: www.genesco.com (2)

GENESYS Sampling Systems, Horsham, PA. Tel: (215) 653-7100, (800) 336-7674, FAX: (215) 653-7115, E-Mail: info@m-s-g.com, Web Site: www. m-s-g.com (30)

Genetica DNA Laboratories Inc, Cincinnati, OH. Tel: (513) 985-9777, (800) 433-6848, FAX: (513) 985-9983, Web Site: www.genetica.com (16)

Genick, Michael, National Postal Forum, Fairfax, VA. Tel: (703) 218-5015, FAX: (703) 218-5020, E-Mail: info@npf.org, Web Site: www.npf.org (42)

Genium Publishing, Amsterdam, NY. Tel: (518) 842-4111, FAX: (518) 842-1843, E-Mail: sales@ genium.com, Web Site: www.genium.com (17)

Gennera Knab & Co, Burbank, CA. Tel: (312) 337-2010, FAX: (312) 337-2433, E-Mail: cleveland-office@priva.com, Web Site: www.priva.com (35)

Genovese, Anthony, DaVinci Direct, Plymouth, MA. Tel: (508) 746-2555, FAX: (815) 301-9884, Web Site: www.davinci-direct.com (1)

Genovese, Kristin, Paramount Lists Inc, Erie, PA. Tel: (814) 459-8787, (800) 723-5478, FAX: (814) 459-1398, Web Site: www.paramountlists.com (23)

Genovese, Tina, Gulf Coast List Service, Tampa, FL. Tel: (813) 962-3594, FAX: (813) 907-8463, E-Mail: tg@gulfcoastlist.com (23)

Gent, Sir Christopher, Glaxo Smith Kline, Research Triangle Park, NC. Tel: (919) 483-2100, (888) 825-5249, FAX: (919) 248-8383, Web Site: www. gsk.com (16)

Gentile, Dave, Folder Factory Inc, Mount Jackson, VA. Tel: (540) 984-8852, (800) 296-4321, FAX: (540) 477-9677, E-Mail: webmaster@folders.com, Web Site: www.folders.com (27)

Gentile, Pam, RG Barry Corp, Pickerington, OH. FAX: (614) 866-9787, E-Mail: sales@rgbarry.com, Web Site: www.rgbarry.com (27)

Gentner, Steve, Verso Paper, Memphis, TN. Tel: (901) 369-4241, Web Site: www.versopaper.com (25)

Gentry, Bern, L., The Pin Man, Tulsa, OK. Tel: (918) 587-2405, FAX: (918) 745-2162, Web Site: www. positivepin.com (16)

Gentry, Julie, Richardson Electronics Ltd, Lafox, IL. Tel: (630) 208-2200, FAX: (630) 208-2550, E-Mail: edg@rell.com, Web Site: www.rell.com (16)

Gentry, Marilyn, American Institute for Cancer Research, Washington, DC. Tel: (202) 328-7744, (800) 843-8114, FAX: (202) 328-7226, E-Mail: aicrweb@aicr.org, Web Site: www.aicr.org (1)

Gentry, Michelle, The Pin Man, Tulsa, OK. Tel: (918) 587-2405, FAX: (918) 745-2162, Web Site: www. positivepin.com (16)

Genworth Financial Inc, Richmond, VA. Tel: (804) 281-6000, (888) 436-9678, FAX: (804) 662-2414, Web Site: www.genworth.com (14)

George, Bill, Synergy Arts Interactive, Asheville, NC. Tel: (914) 997-7222, FAX: (914) 997-8893, E-Mail: bgeorge@synergyarts.com, Web Site: www.synergyarts.com (36)

George, Chris, Interactive Marketing Group Inc, Allendale, NJ. Tel: (201) 327-0974, FAX: (201) 327-3596, E-Mail: info@imgusa.com, Web Site: www. imgusa.com/index.aspx (21)

George, Julie, Emperor Clock LLC, Amherst, VA. Tel: (800) 642-0011, FAX: (434) 946-1420, E-Mail: emperor@emperorclock.com, Web Site: www. emperorclock.com (16)

George, K.A., Interactive Marketing Group Inc, Allendale, NJ. Tel: (201) 327-0974, FAX: (201) 327-3596, E-Mail: info@imgusa.com, Web Site: www. imgusa.com/index.aspx (21)

George, Michael, Consolidated Printing Inc, Philadelphia, PA. Tel: (215) 879-1400, (800) 347-0119, FAX: (215) 879-9130, Web Site: www.condrake. com (27)

George, Michael, QDirect, West Chester, PA. Tel: (484) 701-1000, FAX: (484) 701-1599, Web Site: www.qdirect.com (32)

George, Rick, Vidi Emi Inc, San Leandro, CA. Tel: (510) 667-9999, FAX: (510) 352-9999, E-Mail: info@vidiemi.com, Web Site: www.vidiemi.com (32)

George, Ron, Mail Communications, Novato, CA. Tel: (415) 883-2383, FAX: (415) 883-3238, E-Mail: george@mailcomusa.com, Web Site: www. mailcomusa.com (28)

George, William, Partners Health, Philadelphia, PA. Tel: (215) 849-9600, (800) 553-0784, E-Mail: sroberts@healthpart.com, Web Site: www. healthpart.com (15)

Georgetown University Law Center/Continuing Legal Education Div, Washington, DC. Tel: (202) 662-9890, FAX: (202) 662-9891, E-Mail: nds25@law. georgetown.edu, Web Site: www.georgetowncle.org (13)

Georgetown University McDonough School of Business, Washington, DC. Tel: (202) 687-4591, Web Site: www.msb.edu (1)

Georgia Institute of Technology, Atlanta, GA. Tel: (404) 385-3500, Web Site: www.dlpe.gatech.edu (1)

Georgia-Pacific Corp LLC, Atlanta, GA. Tel: (404) 652-4000, Web Site: www.gp.com (25)

Georgia Power, Atlanta, GA. Tel: (404) 506-3440 (16)

Geoscape, Miami, FL. Tel: (305) 860-1460, Web Site: www.geoscape.com (22)

Gerald, Bernadette, Berway Visual Products Inc, Wilmington, MA. Tel: (978) 694-9195, (800) 452-0410, FAX: (978) 694-9212, E-Mail: sales@ berway.com, Web Site: www.berway.com (3)

Gerald, Michael, Berway Visual Products Inc, Wilmington, MA. Tel: (978) 694-9195, (800) 452-0410, FAX: (978) 694-9212, E-Mail: sales@berway.com, Web Site: www.berway.com (3)

Gerber, Audrey, A., DFS Group Limited, San Francisco, CA. Tel: (415) 977-2700, FAX: (415) 977-2970, Web Site: www.dfsgalleria.com (5)

Gerber, William, J., TD Ameritrade Holding Corp, Omaha, NE. Tel: (402) 331-7856, (800) 237-8692, FAX: (402) 597-7789, Web Site: www.amtd.com (35)

Gerber Garment Technology Inc, Tolland, CT. Tel: (860) 871-8082, FAX: (860) 871-6007, E-Mail: info@gerbertechnology.com, Web Site: www. gerbertechnology.com (34)

Gerber Life Insurance Co, White Plains, NY. Tel: (914) 272-4000, (800) 704-2180, FAX: (914) 272-4099, Web Site: www.gerberlife.com (15)

Gerber Products Co, Fremont, MI. Tel: (231) 928-2000, (800) 443-7237, Web Site: www.gerber.com (16)

Gerchen, Gary, Midland Marketing Group, Saint Joseph, MO. Tel: (816) 261-9007, FAX: (816) 233-0859, E-Mail: info@midlandmarketinggroup.com, Web Site: www.midlandmarketinggroup.com (16)

Gerdes, Scott, Tender Heart Treasures, Omaha, NE. Tel: (402) 593-1313, (800) 443-1367, FAX: (402) 593-1316, E-Mail: bcamenzind@thtdesigns.com (6)

Gerfen, Mike, Biggs/Gilmore Communications, Kalamazoo, MI. Tel: (269) 349-7711, FAX: (269) 349-9657, E-Mail: info@biggs-gilmore.com, Web Site: www.biggs-gilmore.com (35)

Gerhardt, Carl, Allegra Network, LLC, Plymouth, MI. Tel: (248) 596-8600, FAX: (248) 596-8601, Web Site: www2.allegranetwork.com (27)

Gerhardt, Mike, Impact Ratings Inc, Newtown, PA. Tel: (610) 353-8311, FAX: (610) 353-8344 (30)

Gerhold, John, Yenkin-Majestic, Columbus, OH. Tel: (614) 253-8511, FAX: (614) 253-6327 (16)

Geringer, Steven, Association for Computing Machinery (ACM), New York, NY. Tel: (212) 869-7440, FAX: (212) 944-1318, Web Site: www.acm.org (1)

Germain, Steven, BJ's Wholesale Club Inc, Westborough, MA. Tel: (508) 651-7400, FAX: (508) 651-6167, Web Site: www.bjs.com (13)

German, Sarah, XL Environmental, Exton, PA. Tel: (610) 968-9500, (800) 327-1414, FAX: (610) 458-9109, E-Mail: webinfo.xli@xlgroup.com, Web Site: www.xlenvironmental.com (15)

Gero Vita, Costa Mesa, CA. Tel: (888) 382-9175, Web Site: www.gvi.com (16)

Gerrard, Larry, Woodcraft Supply Corp LLC, Parkersburg, WV. Tel: (304) 422-5412, (800) 344-3348, FAX: (304) 422-5417, Web Site: www.woodcraft. com (9)

Gershon, Bill, Bill Gershon Marketing Communications, Skokie, IL. Tel: (847) 676-9452, FAX: (847) 674-7205, E-Mail: gershcom@yahoo.com (39)

Gershon, Edwin, M., National 4-H Supply Service, Chevy Chase, MD. Tel: (301) 961-2959, FAX: (301) 961-2937, E-Mail: 4hsupply@fourhcouncil. edu, Web Site: www.fourhcouncil.edu (16)

Bill Gershon Marketing Communications, Skokie, IL. Tel: (847) 676-9452, FAX: (847) 674-7205, E-Mail: gershcom@yahoo.com (39)

Gersie, Michael, H., The Principal Financial Group, Des Moines, IA. Tel: (515) 247-5111, (800) 986-3343, FAX: (515) 246-5475, Web Site: www. principal.com (15)

Gerstner Woodworks, Dayton, OH. Tel: (937) 228-1662, FAX: (937) 228-8557, E-Mail: info@ gerstnerusa.com, Web Site: www.gerstnerusa.com (6)

Gerten, Nick, Meyer Associates Teleservices, Saint Cloud, MN. Tel: (320) 259-4000, (800) 676-9233, FAX: (320) 259-4044, E-Mail: info@callmeyer. com, Web Site: www.callmeyer.com (29)

Gerth, Michael, AAFES, Dallas, TX. Tel: (214) 312-6700, (800) 527-6790, FAX: (214) 312-3000, Web Site: www.aafes.com (5)

Gervasi, Carole, The Collegebound Network, Staten Island, NY. Tel: (718) 761-4800, Web Site: www. collegebound.net (32)

Gesele, Bill, Brown Printing Co, New York, NY. Tel: (212) 782-7800, FAX: (212) 782-7878, E-Mail: contact.us@bpc.com, Web Site: www.bpc.com (27)

Geshkovich, Michelle, FAO Schwarz, New York, NY. Tel: (212) 644-9400, (800) 426-TOYS, FAX: (212) 688-6053, Web Site: www.fao.com (11)

Gesualdo, Thomas, A., Delicious Orchards, Colts Neck, NJ. Tel: (732) 462-1989, FAX: (732) 542-2111, E-Mail: info@deliciousorchardsnj.com, Web Site: www.deliciousorchardsnj.com (4)

Get Seen Media Group, Los Angeles, CA. Tel: (323) 424-4669, Web Site: www.getseenmedia.com (16)

Getko Direct Response, Coral Springs, FL. Tel: (800) 642-8732, FAX: (954) 320-7565, E-Mail: gdrservices@getkodirect.com, Web Site: www.getkodirect.com (24)

Getronics, Tewksbury, MA. Tel: (978) 625-5000, Web Site: www.getronics.com (16)

Getty, Mark, Getty Images, Seattle, WA. Tel: (206) 925-5018, (800) 462-4379, Web Site: www.gettyimages.com (38)

Getty, Mark, The Image Bank, New York, NY. Tel: (646) 613-4000, FAX: (646) 613-4601, Web Site: www.gettyimages.com (38)

Getty Images, Seattle, WA. Tel: (206) 925-5018, (800) 462-4379, Web Site: www.gettyimages.com (38)

Gevicchi, Paul, Suez Energy North America, Houston, TX. Tel: (713) 636-0000, FAX: (713) 636-1364, Web Site: www.tractebelpowerinc.com (16)

Gevorkian, Cindy, Knott's Berry Farm Foods, Buena Park, CA. Tel: (714) 220-5200, (800) 877-6887, FAX: (714) 220-5150, Web Site: www.knotts.com (4)

Geyer, Jeff, Truitt Brothers Inc, Salem, OR. Tel: (503) 362-3674, (800) 547-8712, FAX: (503) 588-2868, E-Mail: truittbrothers@truittbros.com, Web Site: www.truittbros.com (16)

Geyres, Philippe, Oberthur Card Systems, Chantilly, VA. Tel: (703) 263-0100, FAX: (703) 263-0503, E-Mail: info@oberthurcs.com, Web Site: www.oberthurcs.com (28)

Gfeller, Robert, J., Lowe's Companies Inc, Mooresville, NC. Tel: (704) 758-1000, FAX: (336) 651-4766, Web Site: www.lowes.com (8)

Ghent Manufacturing Inc, Lebanon, OH. Tel: (513) 932-3445, (800) 543-0550, FAX: (513) 932-9252, E-Mail: customer_service@!ghent.com, Web Site: www.ghent.com (10)

Ghirardelli Chocolate Co, San Leandro, CA. Tel: (510) 483-6970, (800) 877-9338, FAX: (510) 297-2649, Web Site: www.ghirardelli.com (16)

Ghort, Michael, Retrieval Masters Creditors Bureau Inc, Elmsford, NY. Tel: (914) 592-0055, (800) 666-8097, FAX: (914) 345-5023, E-Mail: info@retrievalmasters.com, Web Site: www.retrievalmasters.com (20)

Ghuman, Donna, Marketlinc, Saskatoon, SK Canada. Tel: (306) 956-7000, FAX: (306) 668-5812, E-Mail: info@marketlinc.com, Web Site: www.marketlinc.com (29)

Giamalva, Peter, Resort Condominiums International Inc, Carmel, IN. Tel: (317) 876-1692, FAX: (317) 871-9699, Web Site: www.rci.com (19)

Giambruno, John, Planned Parenthood Mar Monte, San Jose, CA. Tel: (408) 287-7532, FAX: (408) 971-6935, Web Site: www.plannedparenthood.org (1)

Giammasi, Stella, Thirteen/WNET, New York, NY. FAX: (212) 560-1314, Web Site: www.thirteen.org (1)

Gianfagna, Jean, M., Gianfagna Strategic Marketing Inc, Westlake, OH. Tel: (440) 808-4700, FAX: (440) 808-4707, E-Mail: tellmemore@gianfagnamarketing.com, Web Site: www.gianfagnamarketing.com (35)

Gianfagna Strategic Marketing Inc, Westlake, OH. Tel: (440) 808-4700, FAX: (440) 808-4707, E-Mail: tellmemore@gianfagnamarketing.com, Web Site: www.gianfagnamarketing.com (35)

Gianni, Patrice, Marketing Results Inc, Sicklerville, NJ. Tel: (856) 740-3334, FAX: (856) 740-3335, Web Site: www.marketingresults.net (16)

Gianopulos, Frank, Audio Editions Books-on-Cassette & CD, Auburn, CA. Tel: (800) 231-4261, FAX: (800) 882-1840, E-Mail: info@audioeditions.com, Web Site: www.audioeditions.com (3)

Giaramita, Eileen, GreatLists.com, Dulles, VA. Tel: (703) 821-8130, (800) 296-0888, FAX: (703) 821-8243, E-Mail: info@greatlists.com, Web Site: www.greatlists.com (23)

Gibas, Jeff, OlympPak, Minneapolis, MN. Tel: (763) 504-5400, (800) 967-1705, FAX: (763) 504-5401, E-Mail: jgibas@olympak.com, Web Site: www.olympak.com (27)

Gibb, Tara, United Business Media, Manhasset, NY. Tel: (516) 562-5000, Web Site: www.ubmtechnology.com (17)

Gibbens, Dan, The Scooter Store, New Braunfels, TX. Tel: (830) 608-9200 (7)

Gibbons, Courtney, MasterCard Worldwide, Purchase, NY. Tel: (914) 249-2000, (800) 622-7747, FAX: (914) 249-4220, Web Site: www.mastercard.com (14)

Gibbons, Raymond, J., American Heart Association, Dallas, TX. Tel: (214) 373-6300, (800) AHA-USA-1, FAX: (214) 373-3406, Web Site: www.americanheart.org (1)

Gibbs, Brad, Plattform Advertising, Lenexa, KS. Tel: (913) 254-6000, (800) 279-9988, FAX: (913) 538-5078, E-Mail: info@plattformad.com, Web Site: www.plattformad.com (35)

Gibbs, David, Pizza Hut Inc, Plano, TX. Tel: (972) 338-7700, (866) 298-6986, FAX: (972) 338-6869, Web Site: www.pizzahut.com (16)

Gibbs, Michael, Astronomical Society of the Pacific, San Francisco, CA. Tel: (415) 337-1100, (800) 335-2624, FAX: (415) 337-5205, E-Mail: service@astrosociety.org, Web Site: www.astrosociety.org (1)

Gibbs, Sheilah, Fifth Avenue Committee, Brooklyn, NY. FAX: (718) 237-5366, Web Site: www.fifthave.org (1)

Gibson, C., American Association for Justice, Washington, DC. Tel: (202) 965-3500, (800) 424-2725, FAX: (202) 625-7313, Web Site: www.justice.org (1)

Gibson, Carol, National Jewish Health, Denver, CO. Tel: (303) 398-1070, (800) 222-LUNG, (800) 423, FAX: (303) 398-1663, E-Mail: trubeyp@njhealth.org, Web Site: www.njhealth.org (21)

Gibson, Frank, A., Memphis Net & Twine Co Inc, Memphis, TN. Tel: (901) 458-2656, (888) 674-7638, FAX: (901) 458-1601, E-Mail: fishinfo@memphisnet.net, Web Site: www.memphisnet.net (11)

Gibson, George, Walker Publishing Co Inc, New York, NY. Tel: (212) 727-8300, (800) 289-2553, FAX: (212) 727-0984 (17)

Gibson, Jeannine, Infocus Marketing Inc, Warrenton, VA. Tel: (540) 428-3240, Web Site: www.infocuslists.com (23)

Gibson, John, Landmark Graphics Corp, Houston, TX. Tel: (713) 839-2000, FAX: (713) 839-2015, E-Mail: solutions@lgc.com, Web Site: www.lgc.com (16)

Gibson, Katherine, TAPPI (Technical Association of the Pulp & Paper Industry), Norcross, GA. Tel: (678) 642-66, (800) 332-8686, FAX: (770) 446-6947, E-Mail: webmaster@tappi.org, Web Site: www.tappi.org (1)

Gibson, Mark, AccuTrade Inc, Bellevue, NE. Tel: (800) 882-4887, FAX: (816) 243-3762, E-Mail: info@accutrade.com (14)

Gibson, Mark, Compass Bank, Birmingham, AL. Tel: (205) 933-4848, (800) 239-4357, FAX: (205) 933-3702, Web Site: www.compassbank.com (14)

Gibson, Paul, CCH Inc, Riverwoods, IL. Tel: (847) 267-7000, (888) 224-7377, Web Site: www.cch.com (17)

Gibson, Steve, E., Gibson Direct Inc, Coppell, TX. Tel: (972) 462-7580, FAX: (972) 304-9202 (20)

Gibson, Tom, Ross-Simons, Cranston, RI. Tel: (401) 463-3100, (800) 835-0919, FAX: (401) 463-8599, Web Site: www.ross-simons.com (6)

Gibson Auer LLC, Victor, ID. Tel: (208) 787-2153, E-Mail: helpdesk@galabs.com, Web Site: www.galabs.com (7)

Gibson Direct Inc, Coppell, TX. Tel: (972) 462-7580, FAX: (972) 304-9202 (20)

Gidish, Rebecca, Eye Care Centers of America, San Antonio, TX. Tel: (210) 340-3531, (800) 669-1183, FAX: (210) 340-0123, E-Mail: customerservice@visionworks.com, Web Site: www.ecca.com (7)

Gierhart, Wanda, The Limited Stores Inc, Columbus, OH. Tel: (614) 415-2000, FAX: (614) 415-2057, Web Site: www.limited.com (2)

Gieseler, Tim J., Orion Telescopes & Binoculars, Watsonville, CA. Tel: (831) 763-7000, (800) 447-1001, FAX: (408) 763-7017, E-Mail: sales@telescope.com, Web Site: www.telescope.com (11)

Gieselman, Dave, Blue Cross/Blue Shield of Illinois, Chicago, IL. Tel: (312) 938-6000, FAX: (312) 938-5722, Web Site: www.bcbsil.com (15)

Giesler, Gary, AmeriMark Holdings LLC, Cleveland, OH. Tel: (440) 325-2000, FAX: (440) 234-8925, Web Site: www.amerimark.com (7)

Giesler, Michael, F., FMC Corp, Philadelphia, PA. Tel: (215) 299-6000, FAX: (215) 299-5998, Web Site: www.fmc.com (16)

Giesmann, Jean, New England Mail Order Association, Scarborough, ME. Tel: (207) 885-0090, (860) 691-1260, FAX: (207) 885-0097, Web Site: www.nemoa.org (40)

Giffney, Karin, Discover Financial Services, Riverwoods, IL. Tel: (224) 405-3373 (14)

Gifford, William, Philip Morris USA Inc, Richmond, VA. Tel: (804) 274-2000, FAX: (804) 484-8231, Web Site: www.philipmorrisusa.com (16)

Gift Services Inc, Vancouver, WA. Tel: (800) 379-4065, FAX: (360) 699-0597, E-Mail: corpsales@gifttree.com, Web Site: www.gifttree.com (6)

Gifts Corp, Barrie, ON Canada. Tel: (905) 670-1126, (800) 565-3130, FAX: (905) 670-1127, E-Mail: customerservice@regal.ca, Web Site: www.regalgreetings.com (6)

Gil, Frank, New Win Publishing Inc, El Monte, CA. Tel: (626) 448-3448, FAX: (626) 602-3817, E-Mail: info@AcademicLearningCompany.com, Web Site: www.newwinpublishing.com (17)

Gilany, Barry, J., Zurich, Schaumburg, IL. Tel: (847) 605-3712, (800) 382-2150, FAX: (847) 605-6403, Web Site: www.zurichna.com (15)

Gilbert, Bob, Intrasight, Scottsdale, AZ. Tel: (480) 603-9400, FAX: (480) 603-9460, Web Site: www.intrasightmarketing.com (35)

Gilbert, Christian, The Jackson Laboratory JAX Research Systems, Bar Harbor, ME. Tel: (800) 422-6423, Web Site: www.jax.org/jaxmice (1)

Gilbert, Eric, Upbeat Inc, Saint Louis, MO. Tel: (314) 535-5005, (800) 325-3047, FAX: (314) 535-4419, E-Mail: custservice@upbeat.com, Web Site: www.upbeat.com (9)

Gilbert, Ernest, Video Artists International, Pleasantville, NY. Tel: (914) 769-3691, (800) 477-7146, FAX: (914) 769-5407, E-Mail: orders@vaimusic.com, Web Site: www.vaimusic.com (3)

Gilbert, Mike, GC Direct, Seattle, WA. Tel: (206) 262-1999, Web Site: www.gcdirect.com (35)

Gilbert, Steven, Affinitas Corp, Omaha, NE. Tel: (402) 397-7077, (800) 369-6495, FAX: (402) 397-7576, Web Site: www.affinitas.net (29)

Gilboyne, Mark, T., Westwood Publishing Co, Glendale, CA. Tel: (818) 242-1159, FAX: (818) 247-9379 (17)

Gilchrist, Sherry, Taylor, New England Direct Marketing Association, Wellesley Hills, MA. Tel: (781) 237-1366, FAX: (781) 431-8118, E-Mail: info@nedma.com, Web Site: www.nedma.com (40)

Gilchrist & Partners, Boston, MA. Tel: (617) 314-4096, (866) 617-5070 (20)

Giles, Jane, Cambey & West Inc, Congers, NY. Tel: (845) 267-3006, FAX: (845) 267-3503, E-Mail: info@cambeywest.com, Web Site: www.cambeywest.com (22)

Gilkey, Gregg, Consolidated Plastics Co Inc, Stow, OH. Tel: (330) 425-3900, (800) 362-1000, FAX: (330) 425-3333, Web Site: www. consolidatedplastics.com (9)

Gillespie, Richard, J., Gillespie, Lawrenceville, NJ. Tel: (609) 895-0200, FAX: (609) 895-0222, Web Site: www.gillespie.com (35)

Gillespie, Lawrenceville, NJ. Tel: (609) 895-0200, FAX: (609) 895-0222, Web Site: www.gillespie. com (35)

Gillespie Magazine Marketing & Publishing, Lawrenceville, NJ. Tel: (609) 895-0200, FAX: (609) 895-0222, Web Site: www.gillespie.com (20)

Gillette Children's Specialty Healthcare, Saint Paul, MN. Tel: (651) 229-1726, Web Site: www. gillettechildrens.org (1)

Gilliam, Jeff, Toter Inc, Statesville, NC. Tel: (704) 872-8171, (800) 424-0422, FAX: (704) 878-0734, E-Mail: info@toter.com, Web Site: www.toter.com (16)

Gillien, Wayne, Ruud Lighting Inc, Racine, WI. Tel: (262) 886-1900, (800) 236-7000, FAX: (800) 236-7500, E-Mail: sales@ruudlighting.com, Web Site: www.ruudlighting.com (9)

Gilligan, Edward, American Express Co, New York, NY. Tel: (212) 640-2000, FAX: (212) 619-9802, Web Site: www.americanexpress.com (14)

Gilligan, Tom, Daily Record & Dispatch Co, Dunn, NC. Tel: (910) 891-1234, FAX: (910) 891-5253, Web Site: www.mydailyrecord.com (17)

Gilliland, Mike, Airlines Reporting Corp, Arlington, VA. Tel: (703) 816-8135, FAX: (703) 816-8104, E-Mail: corpcom@arccorp.com, Web Site: www. arccorp.com (16)

Gilliom Manufacturing Inc, Saint Charles, MO. Tel: (636) 724-1812, FAX: (314) 723-0080 (8)

Gillis Odelbo, Catherine, Morningstar Inc, Chicago, IL. Tel: (312) 696-6000, Web Site: www. morningstar.com (14)

Gillogly, Bridget, Robert J Matthews Co, Massillon, OH. Tel: (330) 834-3000, (800) 321-0235, FAX: (330) 830-2762, Web Site: www.pbsanimalhealth. com (7)

Gillooly, Edward, BJ's Wholesale Club Inc, Westborough, MA. Tel: (508) 651-7400, FAX: (508) 651-6167, Web Site: www.bjs.com (13)

Gillund, Laura, C H Robinson Worldwide Inc, Eden Prairie, MN. Tel: (952) 937-8500, FAX: (952) 937-6740, E-Mail: info@chrobinson.com, Web Site: www.chrobinson.com (16)

Gilman, Robert, Gilman's Lapidary Supply, Hellertown, PA. Tel: (610) 838-8767, FAX: (610) 838-2961, E-Mail: info@lostcave.com, Web Site: www. lostcave.com (11)

Gilman's Lapidary Supply, Hellertown, PA. Tel: (610) 838-8767, FAX: (610) 838-2961, E-Mail: info@ lostcave.com, Web Site: www.lostcave.com (11)

Gilner, Paul, Life Extension Foundation, Fort Lauderdale, FL. Tel: (954) 766-8433, (800) 678-8989, FAX: (954) 771-2827, E-Mail: info@lef.org, Web Site: www.lef.org (7)

Gilroy, Maureen, OfficeMax Inc, Naperville, IL. Tel: (630) 864-5809, (800) 661-5931, Web Site: www. officemax.com (10)

Gilson, Rob, Imperial Supplies, Green Bay, WI. Tel: (920) 494-5403, (800) 558-2808, FAX: (800) 553-8769, Web Site: www.imperialsupplies.com (16)

Gilson Co Inc, Lewis Center, OH. Tel: (740) 548-7298, (800) 444-1508, FAX: (740) 548-5314, E-Mail: sales@gilsonco.com, Web Site: www. globalgilson.com (7)

Gimbel, Diane, Gimbels of Maine Inc, Boothbay Harbor, ME. Tel: (207) 633-5088, FAX: (207) 633-5128, Web Site: www.gimbelscollectibles.com (6)

Gimbel, Mark S., Gimbels of Maine Inc, Boothbay Harbor, ME. Tel: (207) 633-5088, FAX: (207) 633-5128, Web Site: www.gimbelscollectibles.com (6)

Gimbels of Maine Inc, Boothbay Harbor, ME. Tel: (207) 633-5088, FAX: (207) 633-5128, Web Site: www.gimbelscollectibles.com (6)

Gimlin, Hal F., Omni Farm, West Jefferson, NC. Tel: (336) 982-3475, (800) TREE-FARM, FAX: (336) 982-4163, E-Mail: omnifarm@omnifarm.com, Web Site: www.omnifarm.com (16)

Gincel, Sherry, Air Ambulance Network Inc, Palm Harbor, FL. Tel: (727) 934-3999, (800) 327-1966, FAX: (727) 937-0276, Web Site: www. airambulancenetwork.com (16)

Ginger, Andrew R., Snap-on Inc, Kenosha, WI. Tel: (262) 656-5200, (800) 866-5748, (800) 786-6600, FAX: (262) 656-5577, Web Site: www.snapon.com (9)

Ginsberg, Ari, Contact Marketing LLC, New York, NY. Tel: (201) 530-0200, (800) 848-7501, FAX: (201) 530-2205, E-Mail: info@cmlists.com, Web Site: www.contactmarketingllc.com (23)

Ginsberg, Frank, CWC Inventories Inc, Maryland Heights, MO. Tel: (314) 739-1311, FAX: (314) 739-7398, E-Mail: frankg@cwcinventories.com, Web Site: www.cwcinventories.com (33)

Ginsberg O'Sullivan, Susan, TransitCenter Inc, New York, NY. Tel: (212) 329-2000, Web Site: www. transitcenter.com (1)

Ginsburg, Gerry, L., Ginsburg Global, Stamford, CT. Tel: (203) 359-2420, FAX: (203) 325-4443, E-Mail: gerry@ginsburgglobal.com, Web Site: www.ginsburgglobal.com (24)

Ginsburg, Richard, Protection One Inc, Lawrence, KS. Tel: (785) 856-5500, (800) GET-HELP, Web Site: www.protectionone.com (16)

Ginsburg Global, Stamford, CT. Tel: (203) 359-2420, FAX: (203) 325-4443, E-Mail: gerry@ ginsburgglobal.com, Web Site: www. ginsburgglobal.com (24)

Ginzburg, Mitchell, TRANZACT, Fort Lee, NJ Canada. Tel: (201) 461-5665, Web Site: www. tranzact.net (35)

Gioga, Doug, Hyatt Hotels Corp, Chicago, IL. Tel: (312) 750-1234, FAX: (312) 780-5289, Web Site: www.hyatt.com (16)

Gioia, Joyce, L., The Herman Group, Austin, TX. Tel: (336) 210-3547, E-Mail: info@hermangroup.com, Web Site: www.hermangroup.com (20)

Gion, Ron, Impressions Unlimited Inc, Deerfield, IL. Tel: (630) 705-6464, FAX: (630) 705-1598, E-Mail: info@impressionsunltd.com, Web Site: www.impressionsunltd.com (27)

Giordano, Pat, Hampshire Agency, Great Neck, NY. Tel: (516) 466-3814, FAX: (516) 466-0910 (14)

Giorgio, Michael R., Suarez Corp Industries, North Canton, OH. Tel: (330) 494-5504, FAX: (330) 497-6837, E-Mail: suarez@suarez.com, Web Site: www.suarez.com (5)

Giovanetti, Rego, ASM International, Materials Park, OH. Tel: (440) 338-5151, (800) 336-5152, FAX: (440) 338-4634, E-Mail: customerservice@ asminternational.org, Web Site: www. asminternational.org (1)

Girard, Donald, Experian, Costa Mesa, CA. Tel: (714) 830-7000, (888) EXPERIAN, Web Site: www. experian.com (30)

Girardi, Robert, SofTrek Corp, Amherst, NY. Tel: (800) 442-9211, Web Site: www.softrek.com (22)

Giresi, Mark, A., LimitedBrands Inc, Reynoldsburg, OH. Tel: (614) 577-5902, FAX: (614) 415-7440, Web Site: www.limitedbrands.com (16)

Girl Scouts of the USA, New York, NY. Tel: (212) 852-8009, Web Site: www.girlscouts.org (1)

Giroux, David, Seton Identification Products, Branford, CT. Tel: (203) 488-8059, (800) 243-6624, FAX: (203) 488-5973, Web Site: www.seton.com (16)

Giroux, Nathalie, Cancer Research Society, Montreal, PQ. Tel: (514) 861-9227, (888) 766-2262, FAX: (514) 861-9220, Web Site: www. CancerResearchSociety.ca (1)

Giroux, Stephen, L., National Community Pharmacists Association, Alexandria, VA. Tel: (703) 683-8200, (800) 544-7447, FAX: (703) 683-3619, E-Mail: info@ncpanet.org, Web Site: www.ncpanet.org (1)

Girsky, Stephen, J., Buick Division General Motors Corp, Detroit, MI. Tel: (313) 556-5000, (800) 521-7300, FAX: (313) 556-5108, Web Site: www. buick.com (16)

Gisel Jr., William G., Rich Products Corp, Buffalo, NY. Tel: (716) 878-8000, (800) 828-2021, FAX: (716) 878-8765, Web Site: www.richs.com (16)

Gish, Dale, Gish, Sherwood & Friends Inc, Nashville, TN. Tel: (615) 385-1100, (800) 241-3325, FAX: (615) 783-0500, Web Site: www.gish.com (35)

Gish, Sherwood & Friends Inc, Nashville, TN. Tel: (615) 385-1100, (800) 241-3325, FAX: (615) 783-0500, Web Site: www.gish.com (35)

Gitlin, Saul, Kang & Lee Advertising Inc/K&L Direct, New York, NY. Tel: (212) 375-8111, FAX: (212) 375-8255, E-Mail: info@kanglee.com, Web Site: www.kanglee.com (35)

Gitlitz Consulting, Washington, DC. Tel: (202) 965-6185 (35)

Gittus, Kathleen, Nancy's Notions LLC, Beaver Dam, WI. Tel: (920) 887-0391, (800) 833-0690, FAX: (800) 255-8119, E-Mail: comments@ nancysnotions.com, Web Site: www.nancysnotions. com (11)

Giufre, Tina, Sun Harvest Citrus, Fort Myers, FL. Tel: (239) 768-2686, (800) 743-1480, FAX: (239) 768-9255, E-Mail: info@sunharvestcitrus.com, Web Site: www.SunHarvestCitrus.com (6)

Giugni, June, Cosmetique, Inc, Vernon Hills, IL. Tel: (847) 913-9099, (800) 621-8822, Web Site: www. cosmetique.com (13)

Givens, Michele, Editorial Projects in Education Inc, Bethesda, MD. Tel: (301) 280-3100, (800) 346-1834, FAX: (301) 280-3250, Web Site: www. edweek.org (17)

Giza, Dennis, F., Columbia Journalism Review, New York, NY. Tel: (212) 854-2718, (888) 625-7782, FAX: (212) 854-8367, Web Site: www.cjr.org (17)

Gjestvang, Terri, L., The Marketing Advantage Inc, Little Rock, AR. Tel: (501) 954-7771, FAX: (501) 954-7879, E-Mail: central_reservations@tmae.net, Web Site: www.freevacations.com (21)

Gladden, Ray, Carolina Biological Supply Co, Burlington, NC. Tel: (800) 334-5551, (800) 222-7112, E-Mail: carolina@carolina.com, Web Site: www. carolina.com (9)

Glader, Bonita, OAG Worldwide, Downers Grove, IL. Tel: (630) 515-5300, FAX: (630) 515-5301, E-Mail: custsvc@oag.com, Web Site: www.oag. com (17)

Glahn, Ted, Solarcom, Norcross, GA. Tel: (770) 449-6116, (888) SUN-DATA, FAX: (770) 448-7726, Web Site: www.solarcom.net (16)

Glamour Shots Licensing, Oklahoma City, OK. Tel: (405) 947-8747, (888) GLAMOUR-SHOTS, FAX: (405) 951-7343, Web Site: www.glamourshots.com (16)

Glancy, Paul, JetSpring, Richmond, VA. Tel: (877) 695-3834, Web Site: www.jetspring.com (30)

Glas-Col, Terre Haute, IN. Tel: (812) 235-6167, FAX: (812) 234-6975, Web Site: www.i-2-r.com (16)

Glasco, Doug, EdgeMark Partners Inc, Glen Allen, VA. Tel: (804) 967-2000, Web Site: www. edgemarkpartners.com (35)

Glaser, Alvin B., Essex Printing Co Inc, Croton On Hudson, NY. Tel: (212) 688-4720, (800) 443-9113, FAX: (212) 308-2764, E-Mail: essexptg@aol.com, Web Site: www.essex-printing.com (27)

Glaser, Ed, ColorTree of Virginia Inc, Richmond, VA. Web Site: www.colortree.com (26)

Glaser, Joseph, GlaserDirect Inc, Glen Ellyn, IL. Tel: (630) 469-2075, FAX: (630) 790-5244, E-Mail: jglaser@glaserdirect.com, Web Site: www. glaserdirect.com (23)

Glaser, Steve, A., Steve A Glaser Communications Services, Champaign, IL. Tel: (217) 351-0981, FAX: (217) 351-0981, E-Mail: steve@sagcs.net, Web Site: www.sags.net (39)

Steve A Glaser Communications Services, Champaign, IL. Tel: (217) 351-0981, FAX: (217) 351-0981, E-Mail: steve@sagcs.net, Web Site: www.sags.net (39)

GlaserDirect Inc, Glen Ellyn, IL. Tel: (630) 469-2075, FAX: (630) 790-5244, E-Mail: jglaser@glaserdirect.com, Web Site: www.glaserdirect.com (23)

Glass, Bill, WearGuard Corp, Norwell, MA. Tel: (781) 871-4100, (800) 388-3300, FAX: (781) 871-2639, Web Site: www.wearguard.com (2)

Glass, Dennis, R., Lincoln Financial Group, Radnor, PA. Tel: (215) 448-1400, (877) 275-5462, FAX: (215) 448-3962, Web Site: www.lfg.com (15)

Glass, Dennis, Scorecards USA, North Kingstown, RI. Tel: (401) 294-4049, (800) 553-4154, FAX: (401) 294-4076, E-Mail: sales@scorecardsusa.com, Web Site: www.scorecardsusa.com (16)

Glass, Howard, Interactive Response Technologies Inc, Fort Lauderdale, FL. Tel: (954) 484-4973, (800) 700-3033, FAX: (954) 484-0818, E-Mail: hglass@callcenter.com, Web Site: www.callcenter.com (29)

Glass, Kelly, Affinity Express, Elgin, IL. Tel: (847) 930-3200, FAX: (847) 930-3299, E-Mail: kellyg@affinityexpress.com, Web Site: www.affinityexpress.com (16)

Glass, Peter, Peter Glass Photography, East Hartford, CT. Tel: (860) 528-8559, E-Mail: peter@peterglass.com, Web Site: www.peterglass.com (37)

Glass, Russell, Bizo, San Francisco, CA. Tel: (866) 497-5505, Web Site: www.bizo.com (35)

Peter Glass Photography, East Hartford, CT. Tel: (860) 528-8559, E-Mail: peter@peterglass.com, Web Site: www.peterglass.com (37)

Glasscock, Larry, C., Anthem Corporate Communications, Indianapolis, IN. Tel: (207) 822-7000, FAX: (207) 822-7741, Web Site: www.anthem.com (15)

Glassman, Hilary E., Frontier Corp, Rochester, NY. Tel: (716) 777-1000, Web Site: www.frontieronline.com (16)

Glassman, Neil, Broadcast Electronics Inc, Quincy, IL. Tel: (217) 224-9600, FAX: (217) 224-9607, E-Mail: bdcast@bdcast.com, Web Site: www.bdcast.com (3)

Glastris, Paul, The Washington Monthly Co, Washington, DC. Tel: (202) 393-5155, FAX: (202) 393-2444, E-Mail: editors@washingtonmonthly.com, Web Site: www.washingtonmonthly.com (17)

Glatfelter II, George H., Glatfelter, York, PA. Tel: (717) 225-4711, (866) 744-7380, FAX: (717) 225-6834, E-Mail: info@glatfelter.com, Web Site: www.glatfelter.com (25)

Glatfelter, York, PA. Tel: (717) 225-4711, (866) 744-7380, FAX: (717) 225-6834, E-Mail: info@glatfelter.com, Web Site: www.glatfelter.com (25)

Glauberman, Jay, Malco Products Inc, Barberton, OH. Tel: (330) 753-0361, (800) 253-2526, FAX: (330) 753-2025, Web Site: www.malcopro.com (16)

Glauberman, Stuart, Malco Products Inc, Barberton, OH. Tel: (330) 753-0361, (800) 253-2526, FAX: (330) 753-2025, Web Site: www.malcopro.com (16)

Glaxo Smith Kline, Research Triangle Park, NC. Tel: (919) 483-2100, (888) 825-5249, FAX: (919) 248-8383, Web Site: www.gsk.com (16)

Glazebrook, Tonya, Medic Alert Foundation, Turlock, CA. Tel: (209) 668-3333, (888) 633-4298, FAX: (209) 669-2495, Web Site: www.medicalert.org (1)

Glazer, William, Glazer-Kennedy Insider Circle, Chicago, IL. Tel: (410) 825-8600, Web Site: www.dankennedy.com (20)

Glazer-Kennedy Insider Circle, Chicago, IL. Tel: (410) 825-8600, Web Site: www.dankennedy.com (20)

Gleason, John P., Portland Cement Association, Skokie, IL. Tel: (847) 966-6200, FAX: (847) 966-9781, Web Site: www.cement.org (1)

Gleeson, Kathleen, A., Response Insurance, Scranton, PA. Tel: (203) 634-7255, (800) 518-2984, FAX: (203) 634-7319, E-Mail: webcs@response.com, Web Site: www.response.com (15)

Glen, Ron, Direct Marketing News, Markham, ON. Tel: (905) 201-6600, (800) 668-1838, FAX: (905) 201-6601, E-Mail: home@dmn.ca, Web Site: www.dmn.ca (43)

Glen, T, Michael, Federal Express, Memphis, TN. Tel: (901) 369-3600, FAX: (901) 395-5082, Web Site: www.fedex.com (16)

Glengarry Marketing, Austin, TX. Tel: (800) 883-1924 (20)

Glenn, Don, The Vane Brothers Co, Baltimore, MD. Tel: (410) 631-5096, FAX: (410) 631-7781, E-Mail: webmaster@vanebros.com, Web Site: www.vanebros.com (16)

Glenn, J., Thomas, Ace Hardware Corp, Oak Brook, IL. Tel: (630) 990-6600, FAX: (630) 990-6838, Web Site: www.acehardware.com (16)

Peter Glenn Publications, Delray Beach, FL. Tel: (561) 404-4290, (888) 332-6700, FAX: (561) 892-5786, E-Mail: gregjames@pgdirect.com, Web Site: www.pgdirect.com (17)

Glenne, Tabitha, ALSAC - St. Jude, Memphis, TN. Tel: (901) 495-3300, FAX: (901) 495-3103, Web Site: www.stjude.org (1)

Glens Falls Hospital Foundation, Glens Falls, NY. FAX: (518) 926-7012, Web Site: www.glensfallshospital.org (1)

Glenview Capital Management, New York, NY. Tel: (212) 812-4700 (14)

Glenview State Bank, Glenview, IL. Tel: (847) 729-1900, FAX: (847) 729-5847, E-Mail: info@gsb.com, Web Site: www.gsb.com (24)

Glerum, Matt, Sportif Mail Order Inc, Sparks, NV. Tel: (775) 359-6400, (800) 776-7843, FAX: (800) 776-3291, Web Site: www.sportif.com (2)

Glick, Abbey, Sunshine Farm & Gardens, Renick, WV. Tel: (304) 497-2208, FAX: (304) 497-2698, E-Mail: barry@sunfarm.com, Web Site: www.sunfarm.com (8)

Glick, Angie, Sunshine Farm & Gardens, Renick, WV. Tel: (304) 497-2208, FAX: (304) 497-2698, E-Mail: barry@sunfarm.com, Web Site: www.sunfarm.com (8)

Glick, Art, Almost Heaven Group, Renick, WV. Tel: (304) 645-2310, FAX: (304) 497-2698, E-Mail: art@almostheaven.net, Web Site: www.almostheaven.net (16)

Glick, Barry, Sunshine Farm & Gardens, Renick, WV. Tel: (304) 497-2208, FAX: (304) 497-2698, E-Mail: barry@sunfarm.com, Web Site: www.sunfarm.com (8)

Glick, Charles, Unum Corp, Portland, ME. Tel: (207) 770-2211, (800) 421-0344, FAX: (207) 770-4510, Web Site: www.unum.com (15)

Glick, Leonard, S., GIE Import Export Corp, Columbus, OH. Tel: (614) 888-5850, FAX: (614) 436-0723 (33)

Glick, Zak, Sunshine Farm & Gardens, Renick, WV. Tel: (304) 497-2208, FAX: (304) 497-2698, E-Mail: barry@sunfarm.com, Web Site: www.sunfarm.com (8)

Glickman, Bob, Harbor Freight Tools, Camarillo, CA. Tel: (805) 445-4791, (800) 423-2567, FAX: (800) 445-4925, Web Site: www.harborfreight.com (9)

Glickman, James, Glickman Research Associates/GRA Focus Center, Northvale, NJ. Tel: (201) 767-8888, (800) 334-3978, FAX: (201) 767-6933, E-Mail: j.glickman@glickmanresearch.com, Web Site: www.glickmanresearch.com (30)

Glickman Research Associates/GRA Focus Center, Northvale, NJ. Tel: (201) 767-8888, (800) 334-3978, FAX: (201) 767-6933, E-Mail: j.glickman@glickmanresearch.com, Web Site: www.glickmanresearch.com (30)

Glicksman, Russell, The Beam Group, Gladwyne, PA. Tel: (215) 988-2100, FAX: (215) 988-1558, Web Site: www.beamgroup.com (20)

Glidden & Boyles Inc, Mount Prospect, IL. Tel: (847) 398-5746, FAX: (847) 756-7619, E-Mail: e:marcom@gbmarcom.com, Web Site: www.glidden-boyles.com (35)

Glimm, Prof. James G., American Mathematical Society, Providence, RI. Tel: (401) 455-4000, (800) 321-4267, FAX: (401) 331-3842, E-Mail: ams@ams.org, Web Site: www.ams.org (17)

Glisan, George, The Hickory Printing Group, Conover, NC. Tel: (828) 465-3431, (800) 442-5679, FAX: (828) 465-2517, E-Mail: gglisan@hickoryprinting.com, Web Site: www.hickoryprinting.com (27)

Global Business Information Services Inc (GLOBIS), Chicago, IL. Tel: (773) 220-4000, Web Site: www.glo-bis.com (23)

Global Computer Corp, Port Washington, NY. Tel: (516) 625-4300, (888) 845-6225, FAX: (516) 625-4072, Web Site: www.globalcomputer.com (3)

Global Computer Supplies, Port Washington, NY. Tel: (732) 264-8200, (800) 446-9662, FAX: (732) 888-8316, Web Site: www.globalcomputer.com (34)

Global Crossing Telecom Inc, Florham Park, NJ. Tel: (800) 466-4600, FAX: (973) 937-0100, E-Mail: iccc@globalcrossing.com, Web Site: www.globalcrossing.com (29)

Global Demand Publishing Inc, Jacksonville, NC. Tel: (910) 937-0562, FAX: (910) 455-1937, E-Mail: globaldemandpublishing@yahoo.com (18)

Global DM Solutions, Boonton, NJ. Tel: (973) 402-2205, (866) 402-2205, FAX: (973) 402-2305, E-Mail: contact@globaldmsolutions.com, Web Site: www.globaldmsolutions.com (23)

Global Equipment Co Inc, Port Washington, NY. Tel: (516) 484-3100, (888) 978-7759, FAX: (516) 608-7111, Web Site: www.globalindustrial.com (9)

Global Infomercial Services Inc, Burr Ridge, IL. Tel: (708) 229-2424, FAX: (708) 229-2407, E-Mail: info@giservices.tv, Web Site: www.giservices.tv (34)

Global IntelliSystems, Evergreen, CO. Tel: (800) 707-7074, Web Site: www.gliq.com (22)

Global Marketing Group Ltd, New York, NY. Tel: (212) 247-6060, FAX: (212) 586-5446, E-Mail: kimglobal@aol.com, Web Site: www.gmgsolution.com (20)

Global Response Corp, Margate, FL. Tel: (954) 973-7300, (800) 537-8000, FAX: (954) 968-9862, E-Mail: wendys@globalresponse.com, Web Site: www.globalresponse.com (29)

Global Specialties, Wallingford, CT. Tel: (203) 272-3285, FAX: (203) 272-4330, Web Site: www.globalspecialties.com (16)

Global Turnkey Systems Inc, Parsippany, NJ. Tel: (973) 331-1010, FAX: (973) 331-0042, E-Mail: sales@gtsystems.com, Web Site: www.gtsystems.com (22)

Global Village Marketing & Data Services Inc, Cheyenne, WY. Tel: (425) 829-9060, Web Site: www.globalvillagemktg.com (41)

Global Ware Solutions, Redwood City, CA. Tel: (650) 363-2200, (800) 469-7500, FAX: (650) 599-3280, E-Mail: sales@gwsmail.com, Web Site: www.globalwaresolutions.com (22)

Global-Z International Inc, Bennington, VT. Tel: (802) 445-1011, FAX: (802) 445-1016, E-Mail: info@globalz.com, Web Site: www.globalz.com (22)

Globalization Partners, Mc Lean, VA. Tel: (703) 268-2193 (35)

Globe Marketing Systems, Coral Springs, FL. Tel: (954) 753-7173, (800) 382-9013, FAX: (954) 741-1369, Web Site: www.globemarketingsystems.com (21)

Globe Photos Inc, West Islip, NY. Tel: (212) 645-9292, FAX: (212) 627-8932 (38)

Globe Specialty Products Inc, Millbury, MA. Tel: (508) 871-1900 (17)

Globe Ticket & Label Co, Lombard, IL. Tel: (404) 762-9711, (800) 523-5968, FAX: (404) 762-7019, Web Site: www.globeticket.com (16)

Globel Direct, Calgary, AB Canada. Tel: (403) 531-6500, (800) 551-5721, FAX: (403) 531-6560, E-Mail: jr.richardson@globel.com, Web Site: www.globel.com (28)

Globus, Betty, InterMedia Advertising, Encino, CA. Tel: (818) 995-1455, FAX: (818) 995-7115, Web Site: www.intermedia-advertising.com (35)

Glosser, Roy J., American Locker Security Systems Inc, Coppell, TX. Tel: (817) 329-1600, (800) 828-9118, E-Mail: info@americanlocker.com, Web Site: www.americanlocker.com (16)

Glotfelty, Richard, C., Paralyzed Veterans of America, Washington, DC. Tel: (202) 416-7636, (800) 424-8200, FAX: (202) 416-7643, E-Mail: info@pva. org, Web Site: www.pva.org (1)

Glouatts, John, Tristar Products, Fairfield, NJ. Tel: (973) 575-5400, FAX: (973) 683-6708, E-Mail: infotp@tristarproductsinc.com, Web Site: www. tristarproductsinc.com (16)

Glovsky, Staci, Vitamin Research Products, Carson City, NV. Tel: (775) 884-8205, Web Site: www.vrp. com (7)

Glowracki, Joey, The Sporting News Publishing Co, Charlotte, NC. Tel: (704) 973-1546, (800) 443-1886, FAX: (704) 973-1552, Web Site: www. sportingnews.com (17)

Glynn Denney, Barbara, Arizona Highways Magazine, Phoenix, AZ. Tel: (602) 712-2200, FAX: (602) 254-4505, E-Mail: editor@arizonahighways.com, Web Site: www.arizonahighways.com (17)

Gnames Media Group, Grapevine, TX. Tel: (972) 871-2828, FAX: (972) 871-2929, E-Mail: info@ gnames.com, Web Site: www.gnames.com (23)

Go, Robert, Air Power USA, Los Angeles, CA. Tel: (310) 641-0830, (888) 888-8231, FAX: (310) 641-8515, Web Site: www.airpowerusa.com (12)

Go Ahead Vacations, Cambridge, MA. Tel: (617) 619-1000, (800) 242-4686, FAX: (617) 619-1001, E-Mail: goahead@et.com, Web Site: www. goaheadvacations.com (16)

Go Promos, Gloversville, NY. Tel: (800) 523-9909, FAX: (800) 523-3292, E-Mail: customerservice@ gopromos.com, Web Site: www.gopromos.com (5)

Gobberdiel, Jim, University of Illinois Foundation, Urbana, IL. Tel: (217) 333-0810, FAX: (217) 333-5577, E-Mail: uif@uillinois.edu, Web Site: www. uif.uillinois.edu (1)

Goddard, Doug, Gamma Photo Labs LLC, Chicago, IL. Tel: (312) 337-0022, FAX: (312) 337-3753, Web Site: www.photobition.com (16)

Goddard, Jeffrey, TVA Productions Inc (The Video Agency), Studio City, CA. Tel: (818) 505-8300, (888) 322-4296, FAX: (818) 505-8370, E-Mail: info@tvaproductions.com, Web Site: www. tvaproductions.com (35)

Goddard, Jerry, Goddard Manufacturing Co, Logan, KS. Tel: (785) 689-4341, (800) 536-4341, E-Mail: jerry@spiral-staircases.com, Web Site: www.spiral-staircases.com (8)

Goddard Manufacturing Co, Logan, KS. Tel: (785) 689-4341, (800) 536-4341, E-Mail: jerry@spiral-staircases.com, Web Site: www.spiral-staircases. com (8)

Godfrey III, William, A., Dow Jones & Co, Princeton, NJ. Tel: (609) 520-4000, FAX: (212) 416-4348, Web Site: www.dowjones.com/corp/index.html (17)

Godfrey, Patty, L., Insurance Publications Inc, Overland Park, KS. Tel: (913) 383-9191, (800) 762-3387, FAX: (913) 383-1247, E-Mail: brokerwrld@ primary.net, Web Site: www.brokerworldmag.com (17)

Godin, Gary, MFE Instruments, Salem, NH. Tel: (603) 893-8778, (800) 843-8011, FAX: (603) 893-8851, Web Site: www.stockeryale.com (9)

Godiva Chocolatier, New York, NY. Tel: (212) 984-5977, Web Site: www.godiva.com (4)

Godlasky, Thomas C., Aviva USA Corp, Des Moines, IA. Tel: (515) 362-3600, FAX: (800) 531-0038, Web Site: www.avivausa.com (14)

Godlewski, Rob, Powr-Flite, a Tacony Co, Fort Worth, TX. Tel: (800) 880-2913, Web Site: www. powrflite.com (9)

Godshall, Kenneth, Magazine Publishers of America, New York, NY. Tel: (212) 872-3700, FAX: (212) 888-4217, Web Site: www.magazine.org (17)

Godsil, Mark, J&J Commerce, Galesburg, IL. Tel: (309) 344-2950, Web Site: www.jjdog.com (5)

Goede, Michael, American Mint LLC, Mechanicsburg, PA. Tel: (717) 458-9200, (877) 807-MINT, FAX: (717) 458-9211, E-Mail: contact@americanmint. com, Web Site: www.americanmint.com (6)

Goergens, D.C., West End Diving Centers Inc, Bridgeton, MO. Tel: (314) 209-7200, E-Mail: info@ westenddiving.com, Web Site: www.2dive.com (35)

Goertz, Elene, American Society of Media Photographers (ASMP), Philadelphia, PA. Tel: (215) 451-ASMP, FAX: (215) 451-0880, Web Site: www. asmp.org (40)

Goethel, Mike, Demco Inc, Madison, WI. Tel: (608) 241-1201, FAX: (608) 241-1799, E-Mail: custserv@demco.com, Web Site: www.demco.com (10)

Goff, Isaac, Dharma Trading Co, Petaluma, CA. Tel: (415) 456-7657, (800) 542-5227, FAX: (415) 456-8747, E-Mail: service@dharmatrading.com, Web Site: www.dharmatrading.com (2)

Goffin, Michael, Marketfish Inc, Seattle, WA. Tel: (206) 905-1090, FAX: (206) 694-2564, Web Site: www.marketfish.com (23)

Goggin, Mark W., Golden State Envelopes, Thousand Oaks, CA. Tel: (818) 865-7940, (800) 252-7600, FAX: (818) 865-0012, E-Mail: answers@golden-state-env.com, Web Site: www.golden-state-env. com (26)

Goggins, Colleen, Johnson & Johnson, New Brunswick, NJ. Tel: (732) 524-0400, FAX: (732) 214-0332, Web Site: www.jnj.com (16)

Gogoel, Michael, BYK-Gardner USA, Columbia, MD. Tel: (310) 483-6500, Web Site: www.byk.com (16)

Gogue, Jay, Auburn University at Montgomery, Montgomery, AL. Tel: (334) 244-3621, (800) 227-2649, FAX: (334) 244-3826, Web Site: www.aum.edu (41)

Gohn Brothers, Middlebury, IN. Tel: (219) 825-2400, (800) 595-0031, Web Site: www.gohnbrothers.com (5)

Goings, Rick, Tupperware, Orlando, FL. Tel: (407) 826-5050, (800) 366-3800, FAX: (407) 826-8874, Web Site: www.tupperware.com (16)

Gokey, Tim, H&R Block Inc, Kansas City, MO. Tel: (816) 572-6446, (800) 472-5625, FAX: (816) 854-8500, Web Site: www.hrblock.com (14)

Golberg, Meg, AIIM International, Silver Spring, MD. Tel: (301) 587-8202, (800) 477-2446, FAX: (301) 587-2711, E-Mail: aiim@aiim.org, Web Site: www. aiim.org (1)

Gold, David, WearGuard Corp, Norwell, MA. Tel: (781) 871-4100, (800) 388-3300, FAX: (781) 871-2639, Web Site: www.wearguard.com (2)

Gold, Erika, F., Hammond World Atlas Corp, New York, NY. Tel: (908) 206-1300, (800) 526-4953, FAX: (908) 206-1104, E-Mail: erika@ hammondmap.com, Web Site: www.hammondmap. com (17)

Gold, James, J, Neiman-Marcus Group, Dallas, TX. Tel: (214) 743-7600, (888) 888-4757, FAX: (214) 573-5320, Web Site: www.neimanmarcus.com (8)

Gold, Keith, Flaghouse Inc, Hasbrouck Heights, NJ. Tel: (201) 288-7600, (800) 793-7900, FAX: (800) 793-7922, E-Mail: sales@flaghouse.com, Web Site: www.flaghouse.com (5)

Gold, L.T., Nightingale Resources, Cold Spring, NY. Tel: (718) 338-3976, (212) 753-5383, (800) 953-9929 (17)

Gold, Stephen, National Electrical Manufacturers Association (NEMA), Rosslyn, VA. Tel: (703) 841-3200, FAX: (703) 841-5900, E-Mail: communications@nema.org, Web Site: www.nema. org (34)

Barbara Gold, New York, NY. Tel: (917) 750-4038 (20)

Gold Line Connector Inc, West Redding, CT. Tel: (203) 938-2588, FAX: (203) 938-8740, E-Mail: sales@gold-line.com, Web Site: www.gold-line. com (3)

Gold Medal Hair Products Inc, Farmingdale, NY. Tel: (516) 378-6900, (800) 324-7136, FAX: (516) 378-0168, E-Mail: customerservice@goldmedalhair. com, Web Site: www.goldmedalhair.com (7)

Gold Medal Products Co, Cincinnati, OH. Tel: (513) 769-7676, (800) 543-0862, FAX: (800) 542-1496, E-Mail: info@gmpopcorn.com, Web Site: www. gmpopcorn.com (16)

Goldberg, Andrew, Publishers Clearing House, Port Washington, NY. Tel: (516) 883-5432, FAX: (516) 767-4567, E-Mail: cirving@pch.com, Web Site: www.pch.com (18)

Goldberg, Bernard, A., Direct Marketing Publishers, Yardley, PA. Tel: (215) 321-3068, (800) 663-8387, FAX: (215) 321-9647, E-Mail: consulting@ dmpublishers.com, Web Site: www.dmpublishers. com (17)

Goldberg, Dan, A-KD Mailing & Fulfillment Service, Lincolnwood, IL. Tel: (847) 673-0186, (866) 330-6245, FAX: (874) 673-0188, E-Mail: dan@ kdmailing.com, Web Site: www.kdmailing.com (28)

Goldberg, Marc, S., Advertising Idea Stores, Ardmore, PA. Tel: (610) 642-1990, FAX: (610) 649-5593, E-Mail: uniongoods@msn.com, Web Site: www. uniongoods.com (35)

Goldberg, Marilyn, Museum Masters Inc, New York, NY. Tel: (917) 273-8710, (212) 360-7100, FAX: (212) 360-7102, E-Mail: MMIMarilyn@aol.com, Web Site: www.museummasters.com (16)

Goldberg, Michele, Peter Pan Bus Lines Inc, Springfield, MA. Tel: (413) 781-2900, (800) 343-9999, FAX: (413) 746-8671, E-Mail: info@peterpanbus. com, Web Site: www.peterpanbus.com (19)

Goldberg, Richard, AsiaEXP, Miami, FL. Tel: (305) 675-5969, Web Site: www.asiaexp.com (16)

Goldberg, Scott, L., Bankers Life & Casualty Co, Chicago, IL. Tel: (312) 396-6000, (800) 231-9150, Web Site: www.bankerslife.com (15)

Goldberg, Stanley, R., Hampshire Agency, Great Neck, NY. Tel: (516) 466-3814, FAX: (516) 466-0910 (14)

Goldberg, Steve, Media Recruiting Group Inc, Irvington, NY. Tel: (914) 591-5511, FAX: (914) 591-8911, E-Mail: resume@mediarecruiting.com, Web Site: www.mediarecruiting.com (20)

Goldberg, Stuart, Informed Sources Inc, Plainview, NY. Tel: (800) 201-6060, FAX: (516) 576-0249, E-Mail: info@informed-sources.com, Web Site: www.informed-sources.com (30)

Goldbrenner, Joseph, The Goldmark Group Inc, Clifton, NJ. Tel: (973) 777-5720, (800) 632-9632, FAX: (973) 777-2390, E-Mail: info@ goldmarkgroup.com, Web Site: www. goldmarkgroup.com (35)

Goldem, Shane, Greater Fort Worth Builders Association, Fort Worth, TX. Tel: (817) 284-3566, FAX: (817) 284-6465, E-Mail: info@fortworthbuilders. org, Web Site: www.forthworthbuilders.org (1)

Golden, Don, Action Communications Inc, Boca Raton, FL. Tel: (561) 995-1995, (800) 558-5085, FAX: (561) 995-1990 (27)

Golden, Ed, Ed Golden & Associates, Austin, TX. Tel: (512) 458-8222, FAX: (512) 454-3536 (20)

Golden, John, CNA, Chicago, IL. Tel: (312) 822-5000, (800) 262-1000, E-Mail: cna_help@cna.com, Web Site: www.cna.com (15)

Golden, John, Charter Direct Marketing, New York, NY. Tel: (212) 717-2770, FAX: (561) 245-7559, E-Mail: terrykollman@charterdirectmarketing.com, Web Site: www.charterdirectmarketing.com (35)

Golden, Lawrence, RSVP Publications, Tampa, FL. Tel: (813) 960-7787, Web Site: www. MailToTheAffluent.com (31)

Golden, Michael, Stephen Gould Paper Co Inc, Whippany, NJ. Tel: (973) 428-1500, FAX: (973) 428-5274, Web Site: www.stephengould.com (27)

Golden Bear Golf Inc, North Palm Beach, FL. Tel: (561) 626-3900, FAX: (561) 626-4104, Web Site: www.nicklaus.com (16)

Golden Bison LLC, Denver, CO. Tel: (303) 962-0100, Web Site: www.highplainsbison.com (4)

Ed Golden & Associates, Austin, TX. Tel: (512) 458-8222, FAX: (512) 454-3536 (20)

Golden Fleece Designs Inc, Burbank, CA. Tel: (818) 848-7724, FAX: (818) 566-7100, Web Site: www.mandonia.com (16)

Golden Gate Transportation District, San Rafael, CA. Tel: (415) 921-5858, FAX: (415) 923-2014, Web Site: www.goldengate.org (16)

Golden Key International Honour Society, Atlanta, GA. Tel: (404) 377-2400, Web Site: www.goldenkey.org (1)

Golden Millennium Productions Inc, Pasadena, CA. Tel: (818) 500-1099, E-Mail: info@goldenproductions.com, Web Site: www.goldenproductions.com (32)

Golden River Fruit Co, Vero Beach, FL. Tel: (772) 562-4502, FAX: (772) 562-9747 (4)

Golden Rule Insurance Co, Indianapolis, IN. Tel: (317) 297-4123, FAX: (317) 297-0908, Web Site: www.goldenrule.com (15)

Golden State Envelopes, Thousand Oaks, CA. Tel: (818) 865-7940, (800) 252-7600, FAX: (818) 865-0012, E-Mail: answers@golden-state-env.com, Web Site: www.golden-state-env.com (26)

Golden Trophy, Chicago, IL. Tel: (800) 835-6607, FAX: (800) 835-6601, E-Mail: goldentrophy@bruss.com, Web Site: www.giftsteaksonline.com (4)

Goldenberg, Norman, Terminix International, The Trugreen Companies, Memphis, TN. Tel: (901) 766-1105, Web Site: www.trugreenchemlawn.com (16)

Goldfarb, Debra, Institute Lists/IOMA, Peterborough, NH. Tel: (973) 718-4766, FAX: (973) 622-0595, E-Mail: lists@institutelists.com, Web Site: www.institutelists.com (24)

Goldfarb, Donna, Unilever Best Foods, Englewood Cliffs, NJ. Tel: (201) 567-8000, FAX: (201) 871-8257, E-Mail: comments@unilever.com, Web Site: www.unilever.com (16)

Goldfarb, Eric, Bearingpoint Inc, Montvale, NJ. Tel: (201) 307-7000, FAX: (201) 505-3765, Web Site: www.bearingpoint.com (14)

Goldfarb, Jeff, A I Friedman Inc, New York, NY. Tel: (212) 243-9000, (800) 204-6352, FAX: (212) 929-7320, Web Site: www.aifriedman.com (10)

Goldfarb, Stuart, Columbia House, New York, NY. Tel: (212) 596-2000, Web Site: www.columbiahouse.com (4)

Goldfedder, Judd, The Customer Connection Inc, Escondido, CA. Tel: (760) 489-8339, (800) 477-7166, FAX: (760) 489-1075, E-Mail: judd@custcon.com, Web Site: www.custcon.com (22)

Goldklank, Mitchell, Direct Mail Depot Inc, Piscataway, NJ. Tel: (732) 469-5900, FAX: (732) 469-8414, E-Mail: sales@directmaildepot.com, Web Site: www.directmaildepot.com (28)

Goldleaf Data Corp, Suwanee, GA. Tel: (888) 936-3282, Web Site: www.goldleafdata.com (23)

Goldline International, Santa Monica, CA. Tel: (310) 587-1420, (800) 827-4653, FAX: (310) 319-0265, E-Mail: president@goldlinecoins.com, Web Site: www.goldlinecoins.com (14)

Goldman, Michael, Boys' Life & Scouting Magazines, Irving, TX. Tel: (972) 580-2000, (866) 584-6589, FAX: (972) 580-2079, Web Site: www.boyslife.org (17)

Goldman, Phyllis B., Monkeyshines Publishers, Greensboro, NC. FAX: (336) 292-6999, E-Mail: mkshines@nr.infi.net, Web Site: www.monkeyshinespublishers.com (17)

Goldman, Richard, CompetiScan, Chicago, IL. Tel: (312) 488-1814, Web Site: www.competiscan.com (30)

Goldman, Rick, Dream Products Inc, Chatsworth, CA. Tel: (818) 773-4233, Web Site: www.dreamproducts.net (5)

The Goldmark Group Inc, Clifton, NJ. Tel: (973) 777-5720, (800) 632-9632, FAX: (973) 777-2390, E-Mail: info@goldmarkgroup.com, Web Site: www.goldmarkgroup.com (35)

Goldner, Mark, Parker Steel Co, Toledo, OH. Tel: (419) 473-2481, (800) 333-4140, FAX: (419) 471-2655, Web Site: www.metricmetal.com (16)

Goldner, Paul, Parker Steel Co, Toledo, OH. Tel: (419) 473-2481, (800) 333-4140, FAX: (419) 471-2655, Web Site: www.metricmetal.com (16)

Goldner, Sharon, Parker Steel Co, Toledo, OH. Tel: (419) 473-2481, (800) 333-4140, FAX: (419) 471-2655, Web Site: www.metricmetal.com (16)

Goldsberry, John, P., Gateway Inc, Irvine, CA. Tel: (949) 471-7000, (800) 369-1409, FAX: (949) 471-7041, Web Site: www.gateway.com (3)

Goldschein, Perry, SRB Marketing Inc, New Paltz, NY. Tel: (866) 210-1183, Web Site: www.srbmarketing.com (30)

Goldshein, Sandy, Sandy Goldshein Associates Inc, New York, NY. Tel: (212) 366-5105, Web Site: www.sgany.com (35)

Goldsher, Barry, Engineering Services & Products Co, South Windsor, CT. Tel: (860) 528-1119, (800) 835-7877, FAX: (800) 457-8887, Web Site: www.teksupply.com (9)

Goldsmith, Richard, The Horah Group, Pleasantville, NY. Tel: (914) 495-3200, FAX: (914) 769-8802, E-Mail: dgoldsmith@horah.com, Web Site: www.horah.com (21)

Goldsmith, Robert, Oriental Trading Co Inc, Omaha, NE. Tel: (402) 596-1200, (800) 875-8480, FAX: (402) 331-3873, Web Site: www.oriental.com (5)

Goldsmith, Sr. Dave, Oriental Trading Co Inc, Omaha, NE. Tel: (402) 596-1200, (800) 875-8480, FAX: (402) 331-3873, Web Site: www.oriental.com (5)

Goldsmith Agio Helms, Minneapolis, MN. Tel: (612) 339-0500, FAX: (612) 339-0507, Web Site: www.agio.com (14)

Goldstein, Alan J., The Computer Studio, Yonkers, NY. Tel: (914) 968-1212, FAX: (914) 968-1228, E-Mail: sales@webbusconnect.com, Web Site: www.webbusconnect.com (35)

Goldstein, Ben, Ben Loeb Inc, Fairfield, NJ. Tel: (973) 882-9022, (800) 854-8275, FAX: (973) 882-8647, Web Site: www.bsloeb.com (33)

Goldstein, Cary, Blue Cross/Blue Shield of Illinois, Chicago, IL. Tel: (312) 938-6000, FAX: (312) 938-5722, Web Site: www.bcbsil.com (15)

Goldstein, David, Jerry's Artarama, Raleigh, NC. Tel: (919) 878-8478, (800) U-ARTIST, FAX: (919) 873-9565, E-Mail: micah@jerrysartarama.com, Web Site: www.jerrysartarama.com (10)

Goldstein, Debra, LH Management, Hartsdale, NY. Tel: (914) 285-3456, FAX: (914) 285-3450, E-Mail: lh@leonhenryinc.com, Web Site: www.leonhenryinc.com (24)

Goldstein, Ira, Jerry's Artarama, Raleigh, NC. Tel: (919) 878-8478, (800) U-ARTIST, FAX: (919) 873-9565, E-Mail: micah@jerrysartarama.com, Web Site: www.jerrysartarama.com (10)

Goldstein, Jeff, IDMS Inc, Melville, NY. Tel: (631) 249-7744, (800) 582-5831, FAX: (631) 249-4425, E-Mail: sales@idmsinc.com, Web Site: www.idmsinc.com (16)

Goldstein, Jennifer, Publications International Ltd, Lincolnwood, IL. Tel: (847) 745-9299, (800) 595-8484, FAX: (847) 676-3671, Web Site: www.pubint.com (17)

Goldstein, Jeremy, Navitar Inc, Rochester, NY. Tel: (585) 359-4000, FAX: (585) 359-4999, E-Mail: info@navitar.com, Web Site: www.navitar.com (16)

Goldstein, Josh, Data Direct Networks (HQ), Chatsworth, CA. Tel: (818) 700-7607, (800) 837-2298, FAX: (818) 700-7601, E-Mail: info@ddn.com, Web Site: www.datadirectnet.com (3)

Goldstein, Leslie, IDMS Inc, Melville, NY. Tel: (631) 249-7744, (800) 582-5831, FAX: (631) 249-4425, E-Mail: sales@idmsinc.com, Web Site: www.idmsinc.com (16)

Goldstein, Marc, Profile Mailing Service Inc, Syosset, NY. Tel: (516) 802-3974 (16)

Goldstein, Mike, Islands Tropicals, Keaau, HI. Tel: (808) 961-0606, (800) 367-5155, FAX: (808) 966-7684, Web Site: www.islandtropicals.com (6)

Goldstein, Nancy, A La Carte, Chicago, IL. Tel: (773) 745-5900, (800) 723-2370, FAX: (773) 237-3075, E-Mail: info@alacarteline.com, Web Site: www.alacarteline.com (16)

Goldstein, Patricia, Emigrant Savings Bank, New York, NY. Tel: (212) 850-4521, (800) EMIGRANT, FAX: (212) 850-4372, Web Site: www.emigrant.com (14)

Goldstein, Sheldon, Vcom International Multi-Media Corp, South Hackensack, NJ. Tel: (201) 229-9800, (800) 425-4268, FAX: (800) 453-6338, E-Mail: sales@800VALIANT.com, Web Site: www.800VALIANT.com (3)

Goldston, Georgie, Health Affairs, Bethesda, MD. Tel: (301) 656-7401, FAX: (301) 654-2845, Web Site: www.healthaffairs.org (17)

Goldstone, Jerry A., BCR Enterprises Inc, Downers Grove, IL. Tel: (630) 986-1432, (800) 227-1234, FAX: (630) 323-5324, Web Site: www.bcr.com (17)

Goldsworth, Carroll, Taubenpost Inc, Lake Forest, CA. Tel: (949) 770-3233, FAX: (949) 380-3940, E-Mail: info@taubenpost.com, Web Site: www.taubenpost.com (28)

Goldwasser, Dawn, Renton's Inc, Centennial, CO. Tel: (303) 865-7025, (800) 365-6644, E-Mail: info@rentons.com, Web Site: www.rentons.com (10)

Golf Card International, Englewood, CO. Tel: (800) 321-8269, FAX: (303) 792-7332, Web Site: www.golfcard.com (1)

Golf Digest Co, Wilton, CT. Tel: (203) 761-5100, FAX: (203) 371-2572, Web Site: www.golfdigest.com (17)

Golf Haus, Lansing, MI. Tel: (517) 482-8842, FAX: (517) 482-8843 (11)

Golfsmith International Inc, Austin, TX. Tel: (512) 821-4050, (800) 813-6897, FAX: (512) 837-9347, E-Mail: comments@golfsmith.com, Web Site: www.golfsmith.com (11)

Gollaher, Greg, Polynesian Cultural Center, Honolulu, HI. Tel: (808) 293-3333, (800) 367-7060, FAX: (888) 722-7339, E-Mail: internetrez@polynesia.com, Web Site: www.polynesia.com (16)

Gomez, Cynthia, The Dartnell Corp, Naples, FL. Tel: (585) 240-7301, (800) 447-4030, FAX: (585) 292-4392, E-Mail: customerservice@dartnellcorp.com, Web Site: www.dartnellcorp.com (17)

Gonier, Dennis, E., DMS Insights, Dallas, TX. Tel: (972) 874-5080, (800) 409-6262, FAX: (972) 353-2450, E-Mail: info@dmsinsights.com, Web Site: www.dmsdallas.com (30)

Gonsalves, Mark, DirectBuy Inc, Merrillville, IN. Tel: (219) 736-1100, FAX: (219) 755-6208, Web Site: www.ucctotalhome.com (1)

Gonzales, Kimberly, AGIA Insurance Services, Carpinteria, CA. Tel: (805) 566-9191, FAX: (805) 566-1887, Web Site: www.agia.com (15)

Gonzales, Scott, Three Georges and the Nuthouse, Mobile, AL. Tel: (334) 433-1689, FAX: (334) 433-3364, E-Mail: sales@threegeorges.com, Web Site: www.threegeorges.com (16)

Gonzales, Siobhan, Three Georges and the Nuthouse, Mobile, AL. Tel: (334) 433-1689, FAX: (334) 433-3364, E-Mail: sales@threegeorges.com, Web Site: www.threegeorges.com (16)

Gonzales, Steven, Affina, Peoria, IL. Tel: (309) 685-5901, (877) 4 AFFINA, Web Site: www.affina.com (30)

Gonzalez, Carlos, MFP&W Promotions Direct, San Juan, PR. Tel: (787) 781-1616, FAX: (787) 793-5355, Web Site: www.jwtworld.com (35)

Gonzalez, Daniel, Daniel Gonzalez & Associates, New York, NY. Tel: (212) 682-0333 (20)

Gonzalez, Jane, Collis Curve Catalog Sales, Brownsville, TX. Tel: (210) 576-4818, (800) 298-4818, FAX: (800) 298-4818, E-Mail: brushteeth@aol.com, Web Site: www.colliscurve.com (7)

Gonzalez, Saul, Con-Way Truckload, Joplin, MO. Tel: (417) 623-5229, (800) CFI-DRIVE, FAX: (417) 623-8939, E-Mail: gnichols@cfi-us.com, Web Site: www.cfi-us.com (12)

Good, Kyle, Scholastic Inc, New York, NY. Tel: (212) 343-6100, (800) SCHOLASTIC, FAX: (212) 343-6484, Web Site: www.scholastic.com/ (17)

Good Advertising, Memphis, TN. Tel: (901) 761-0741, (800) 325-9857, FAX: (901) 682-2568, Web Site: www.goodadvertising.com (35)

Good Directions Co Inc, Danbury, CT. Tel: (203) 743-3775, FAX: (203) 743-5226, E-Mail: sales@good-directions.com, Web Site: www.good-directions.com (8)

The Jane Goodall Institute, Arlington, VA. Tel: (703) 682-9220, Web Site: www.janegoodall.org (1)

Goodell, Jackie, Diagraph Corp, Saint Charles, MO. Tel: (636) 300-2000, (800) 722-1125, FAX: (636) 300-2004, E-Mail: info@diagraph.com, Web Site: www.diagraph.com (16)

Gooden, H, James, American Lung Association, New York, NY. Tel: (212) 889-3370, (800) LUNGUSA, FAX: (212) 889-3375, E-Mail: info@alany.org, Web Site: www.lungusa.org (1)

Goodenough, Ryan, American Institute for Economic Research, Great Barrington, MA. Tel: (413) 528-1216, (888) 528-1216, E-Mail: info@aier.org, Web Site: www.aier.org (1)

Goodfader, Joel, AMI Instore, Framingham, MA. Tel: (508) 652-0200, (877) 652-0200, FAX: (508) 652-0101, E-Mail: info@advancemarketing.com, Web Site: www.advancemarketing.com (31)

Goodheart-Willcox Publisher, Tinley Park, IL. Tel: (708) 687-5000, (800) 323-0440, FAX: (708) 687-3900, E-Mail: custserv@g-w.com, Web Site: www.g-w.com (17)

Goodin, Stephanie, Gold Medal Products Co, Cincinnati, OH. Tel: (513) 769-7676, (800) 543-0862, FAX: (800) 542-1496, E-Mail: info@gmpopcorn.com, Web Site: www.gmpopcorn.com (16)

Goodkind, Dan, Goodkind & Goodkind Direct Inc, Arcata, CA. Tel: (712) 347-6114, (800) 690-9342, FAX: (712) 347-5754, E-Mail: mail@goodkind.com, Web Site: www.goodkind.com (28)

Goodkind, Kathi, Goodkind & Goodkind Direct Inc, Arcata, CA. Tel: (712) 347-6114, (800) 690-9342, FAX: (712) 347-5754, E-Mail: mail@goodkind.com, Web Site: www.goodkind.com (28)

Goodkind & Goodkind Direct Inc, Arcata, CA. Tel: (712) 347-6114, (800) 690-9342, FAX: (712) 347-5754, E-Mail: mail@goodkind.com, Web Site: www.goodkind.com (28)

Goodloe, Shantae, Federal Citizen Information Center, Pueblo, CO. Tel: (888) 8-PUEBLO, FAX: (719) 948-9724, E-Mail: catalog.pueblo@gsa.gov, Web Site: www.pueblo.gsa.gov (5)

Goodmail Systems Inc, San Francisco, CA. Tel: (877) 650-6505, Web Site: www.goodmailsystems.com (32)

Goodman, Alyce, Lillian Vernon Corp, Colorado Springs, CO. Tel: (757) 427-7923, FAX: (757) 427-7819, E-Mail: publicrelations@lillianvernon.com, Web Site: www.lillianvernon.com (6)

Goodman, Carolyn, Goodman Marketing Partners Inc, San Rafael, CA. Tel: (415) 507-9060, FAX: (415) 507-9067, E-Mail: info@goodmanmarketing.com, Web Site: www.goodmanmarketing.com (35)

Goodman, Eleanor, Pennsylvania State University Press, University Park, PA. Tel: (814) 865-1327, (800) 326-9180, FAX: (814) 863-1408, Web Site: www.psupress.org (17)

Goodman, Eric, Transamerica Occidental Life Co, Los Angeles, CA. Tel: (213) 742-3111, FAX: (213) 741-6623, Web Site: www.transamerica.com (15)

Goodman, Jason, Goodman Media Group Inc, New York, NY. Tel: (212) 262-2247, FAX: (212) 262-2278, E-Mail: jgoodman@gmgpub.com, Web Site: www.goodmanmediagroup.dev.hotresponse.com (17)

Goodman, John, Helzberg Diamonds, North Kansas City, MO. Tel: (816) 842-7780, (800) HELZBURG, FAX: (816) 480-0294, Web Site: www.helzberg.com (16)

Goodman, John, Technical Assistance Research Programs (TARP), Arlington, VA. Tel: (703) 524-1456, FAX: (703) 524-6374, Web Site: www.tarp.com (20)

Goodman, Kim, Tom Snyder Productions, Watertown, MA. Tel: (617) 926-6000, (800) 342-0236, FAX: (800) 304-1254, E-Mail: ask@tomsnyder.com, Web Site: www.tomsnyder.com (16)

Goodman, Meg, PCG, Inc, Batavia, IL. Tel: (630) 482-9300, FAX: (630) 454-3750, E-Mail: sasmith@pcgnow.com, Web Site: www.pcgnow.com (20)

Goodman, Michael, Shepard's Inc, Bethel, CT. Tel: (203) 830-8300, (800) 243-0993, FAX: (203) 830-8389, Web Site: www.shepardsinc.com (22)

Goodman, Susan, Goodman & Co, New York, NY. Tel: (212) 579-0020, Web Site: www.goodmancompany.com (20)

Goodman, Will, Guidance Associates, Mount Kisco, NY. Tel: (914) 666-4100, (800) 431-1242, FAX: (914) 666-5319, E-Mail: willg1961@gmail.com, Web Site: www.guidanceassociates.com (31)

Goodman & Co, New York, NY. Tel: (212) 579-0020, Web Site: www.goodmancompany.com (20)

Goodman Marketing Partners Inc, San Rafael, CA. Tel: (415) 507-9060, FAX: (415) 507-9067, E-Mail: info@goodmanmarketing.com, Web Site: www.goodmanmarketing.com (35)

Goodman Media Group Inc, New York, NY. Tel: (212) 262-2247, FAX: (212) 262-2278, E-Mail: jgoodman@gmgpub.com, Web Site: www.goodmanmediagroup.dev.hotresponse.com (17)

Goodrich, Jon, E., Gould & Goodrich, Lillington, NC. Tel: (910) 893-2071, (800) 277-0732, FAX: (910) 893-4742, E-Mail: service@gouldusa.com, Web Site: www.gouldusa.com (2)

Goodrick, Stephen, O., Legal Defense Foundation Inc, Springfield, VA. Tel: (703) 321-8501, (800) 336-3600, FAX: (703) 321-9613, E-Mail: info@nrtw.org, Web Site: www.nrtw.org (1)

Goodroe, J., Glenn, White Point Leads Group LLC, Gulf Breeze, FL. Tel: (850) 934-5577, Web Site: www.whitepointleads.com (29)

Goodvin, Grant, Heart Thoughts Inc, Wichita, KS. Tel: (316) 688-5781, (800) 524-2229, FAX: (316) 687-2846, Web Site: www.heart-thoughts.com (27)

Goodway Group, Jenkintown, PA. Tel: (215) 887-5700, FAX: (215) 881-2239, E-Mail: david@goodwaygroup.com, Web Site: www.goodwaygroup.com (35)

Goodwick, David, Leverage Marketing Group, Newtown, CT. Tel: (203) 426-1267, FAX: (203) 426-5934, E-Mail: info@leverage-marketing.com, Web Site: www.leverage-marketing.com (35)

Goodwill Industries of San Francisco, San Francisco, CA. Tel: (415) 575-2101, FAX: (415) 575-2170, Web Site: www.sfgoodwill.org (1)

Goodwin, Greg, Maus & Hoffman Inc, Fort Lauderdale, FL. Tel: (954) 463-1200, Web Site: www.mausandhoffman.com (2)

Goodwin, Jeff, EOS International Inc, Carlsbad, CA. Tel: (760) 431-8400, (800) 876-5484, FAX: (760) 431-8448, Web Site: www.eosintl.com (5)

Goodwin, William, M., WESCO, Pittsburgh, PA. Tel: (412) 454-2200, (800) 343-1201, E-Mail: info@wesco.com, Web Site: www.wescodist.com (16)

Goodyear Tire & Rubber Co, Akron, OH. Tel: (330) 796-3250, Web Site: www.goodyear.com (16)

Google, New York, NY. Tel: (212) 565-0000, FAX: (212) 565-0001, Web Site: www.google.com (31)

Goolara LLC, Alameda, CA. Tel: (510) 522-800, Web Site: www.goolara.com (32)

Gorchels, Linda, University of Wisconsin-Madison School of Business Executive Education, Madison, WI. Tel: (608) 441-7357 (1)

Gorday, Virginia, AMC Inc, Atlanta, GA. Tel: (404) 220-2000, FAX: (404) 220-3030 (2)

Gordon, Alan, R., Iroquois Products, Chicago, IL. Tel: (773) 436-3900, (800) 453-3355, FAX: (773) 436-4908, E-Mail: sales@iroquoisproducts.com, Web Site: www.iroquoisproducts.com (10)

Gordon, Andrew, Direct Impact Group, Needham, MA. Tel: (781) 453-2200, FAX: (781) 453-1200, E-Mail: info@directimpactgroup.com, Web Site: www.directimpactgroup.com (35)

Gordon, Christopher, Accountants' Supply House, Lancaster, CA. Tel: (856) 384-1144, (800) 342-5274, FAX: (800) 468-4446, Web Site: www.rapidforms.com (10)

Gordon, Clifford, DoAll Co, Wheeling, IL. Tel: (847) 824-1122, (800) 92-DOALL, FAX: (847) 699-7524, E-Mail: info@doall.com, Web Site: www.doall.com (16)

Gordon, Don, CDW Computer Centers Inc, Vernon Hills, IL. Tel: (847) 465-6000, (800) 800-4239, FAX: (847) 465-3444, Web Site: www.cdw.com (3)

Gordon, Joel, Desion Conceptions, New York, NY. Tel: (212) 254-1688, FAX: (212) 533-0760, E-Mail: joel.gordon@verizon.net, Web Site: joelgordonphotography.com (38)

Gordon, Joel, Joel Gordon Photography, New York, NY. Tel: (212) 254-1688, E-Mail: joel.gordon@verizon.net, Web Site: joelgordonphotography.com (38)

Gordon, Keith, GMI Distribution, Somerset, NJ. Tel: (732) 846-4800, FAX: (732) 846-4709, E-Mail: keith@gmidistribution.com, Web Site: www.gmidistribution.com (28)

Gordon, Keith, Gordon Management Inc, Somerset, NJ. Tel: (732) 846-4800, FAX: (732) 846-4709, E-Mail: keith@gmidistribution.com, Web Site: www.gmidistribution.com (28)

Gordon, Kenneth, Gordon Management Inc, Somerset, NJ. Tel: (732) 846-4800, FAX: (732) 846-4709, E-Mail: keith@gmidistribution.com, Web Site: www.gmidistribution.com (28)

Gordon, Nancy, HAVE Inc, Hudson, NY. Tel: (518) 828-2000, (800) 999-HAVE (4283), FAX: (518) 828-2008, E-Mail: kstein@haveinc.com, Web Site: www.haveinc.com (3)

Gordon, Rafi, Baseline FT, Los Angeles, CA. Tel: (310) 393-9999, (212) 254-8235, (800) 242-7546, FAX: (212) 529-3330, E-Mail: info@baseline.hollywood.com, Web Site: www.baseline.hollywood.com (17)

Gordon, Tinka, Ghirardelli Chocolate Co, San Leandro, CA. Tel: (510) 483-6970, (800) 877-9338, FAX: (510) 297-2649, Web Site: www.ghirardelli.com (16)

Alan Gordon Enterprises, Hollywood, CA. Tel: (323) 466-3561, FAX: (323) 871-2193, E-Mail: info@alangordon.com, Web Site: www.alangordon.com (32)

Joel Gordon Photography, New York, NY. Tel: (212) 254-1688, E-Mail: joel.gordon@verizon.net, Web Site: www.joelgordonphotography.com (38)

Gordon Management Inc, Somerset, NJ. Tel: (732) 846-4800, FAX: (732) 846-4709, E-Mail: keith@gmidistribution.com, Web Site: www.gmidistribution.com (28)

Gore, Les, Executive Search International, Newton, MA. Tel: (617) 527-8787, E-Mail: info@ execsearchintl.com, Web Site: www.execsearchintl. com (20)

WL Gore & Associates Inc, Newark, DE. Tel: (410) 506-7787, (888) 914-4673, E-Mail: info@wlgore. com, Web Site: www.wlgore.com (2)

Gorelick, Jamie, S., Fannie Mae, Washington, DC. Tel: (202) 752-7000, FAX: (202) 752-3808, Web Site: www.fanniemae.com (14)

Gorey, Michael, K., Bridgestone/Firestone North American Tire LLC, Nashville, TN. Tel: (615) 937-1000, (800) 543-7522, FAX: (615) 937-3721, Web Site: www.bridgestonetire.com (16)

Gorges, Lynn, Battleground Antiques Inc, New Bern, NC. Tel: (252) 636-3039, FAX: (252) 637-1862, E-Mail: tarheelrebel2000@aol.com, Web Site: www.civilwarantiques.com (6)

Gorges, William, D., Battleground Antiques Inc, New Bern, NC. Tel: (252) 636-3039, FAX: (252) 637-1862, E-Mail: tarheelrebel2000@aol.com, Web Site: www.civilwarantiques.com (6)

Gorgonne, Tom, Magnet LLC, Washington, MO. Tel: (636) 239-5661, (800) 458-9457, FAX: (636) 239-4490, E-Mail: contactus@themagnetgroup.com, Web Site: www.magnetllc.com (2)

Gorham, Phyllis, Call Compliance Inc, Glen Cove, NY. Tel: (516) 674-4545, FAX: (516) 676-2420, E-Mail: sales@callcompliance.com, Web Site: www.callcompliance.com (29)

Gorham's Inc, Springfield, IL. Tel: (217) 544-1727, (800) 500-3949, FAX: (217) 544-1623, E-Mail: gorhams@gorhams.com, Web Site: www.gorhams. com (33)

Gorlenkova, Elaine, Opus Inc, Lititz, PA. Tel: (717) 626-2125, (800) 800-1819, FAX: (717) 626-1912, E-Mail: opususa@woodstream.com, Web Site: www.opususa.com (8)

Gorman, James, P., Morgan Stanley, New York, NY. Tel: (212) 761-4000, FAX: (212) 761-0096 (14)

Gorman, Kathleen, A., RBC Funds, Milwaukee, WI. Tel: (800) 422-2766, Web Site: us.rbcgam.com (14)

Gorman, Leon, LL Bean Inc, Freeport, ME. Tel: (207) 865-4761, (800) 441-5713, FAX: (207) 552-3080, Web Site: www.llbean.com (2)

Gornitsky, Rhonda, International Masters Publishers Inc, Montoursville, PA. Tel: (800) 570-5718, E-Mail: customerservice@imp-usa.com, Web Site: www.imponline.com (17)

Goroff, Mark, Breath Appeal, Broadview, IL. Tel: (800) 300-3910, E-Mail: info@breathappeal.com, Web Site: www.breathappeal.com (35)

Gorr, Gwynne, The Franklin Mint, Exton, PA. Tel: (610) 497-4800, (800) THE-MINT, FAX: (610) 497-4956, E-Mail: info@franklinmint.com, Web Site: www.franklinmint.com (16)

Gorsky, Alex, Johnson & Johnson, New Brunswick, NJ. Tel: (732) 524-0400, FAX: (732) 214-0332, Web Site: www.jnj.com (16)

Gorsuch, David, Gorsuch Ltd, Vail, CO. Tel: (970) 476-2294, (800) 525-9808, FAX: (970) 476-4323, Web Site: www.gorsuchltd.com (2)

Gorsuch, Gary, Mercury International Trading, North Attleboro, MA. Tel: (508) 699-9000, FAX: (508) 699-9088, Web Site: www.mercuryfootwear.com (2)

Gorsuch, Renie, Gorsuch Ltd, Vail, CO. Tel: (970) 476-2294, (800) 525-9808, FAX: (970) 476-4323, Web Site: www.gorsuchltd.com (2)

Gorsuch Ltd, Vail, CO. Tel: (970) 476-2294, (800) 525-9808, FAX: (970) 476-4323, Web Site: www. gorsuchltd.com (2)

Gorvine, Tara, Edward Elgar Publishing Inc, Northampton, MA. Tel: (413) 584-5551, FAX: (413) 584-9933, E-Mail: sales@e-elgar.com, Web Site: www.e-elgar.com (17)

Goss International, Durham, NH. Tel: (603) 749-6600, FAX: (603) 750-6860, Web Site: www. gossinternational.com (27)

Gosse, Jonathan, American Technical Publishers Inc, Orland Park, IL. Tel: (708) 957-1100, (800) 323-3471, FAX: (708) 957-1101, E-Mail: service@ americantech.net, Web Site: www.go2atp.com (17)

Gosselin, Nick, VistaPrint USA Inc, Lexington, MA. Tel: (800) 961-2075, Web Site: www.vistaprint. com (27)

Gossett, Elaine, Imagemakers Marketing Inc, Marietta, GA. Tel: (770) 926-9552, FAX: (770) 926-9558, Web Site: www.imagemakersmarketing.com (21)

Gossett, Jon, Minnesota Public Radio, Saint Paul, MN. Tel: (651) 290-1500, (800) 228-7123, FAX: (651) 290-1260, E-Mail: mail@mpr.org, Web Site: www.mpr.org (1)

Gossler, Eric, Gossler Farms Nursery, Springfield, OR. Tel: (541) 746-3922, FAX: (541) 744-7924, Web Site: www.gosslerfarms.com (8)

Gossler, Marjory, Gossler Farms Nursery, Springfield, OR. Tel: (541) 746-3922, FAX: (541) 744-7924, Web Site: www.gosslerfarms.com (8)

Gossler, Roger, Gossler Farms Nursery, Springfield, OR. Tel: (541) 746-3922, FAX: (541) 744-7924, Web Site: www.gosslerfarms.com (8)

Gossler Farms Nursery, Springfield, OR. Tel: (541) 746-3922, FAX: (541) 744-7924, Web Site: www. gosslerfarms.com (8)

Gossman, Bill, Advanced Software Applications, Bridgeville, PA. Tel: (412) 220-9300, E-Mail: asa@ asacorp.com, Web Site: www.asacorp.com (22)

Gostic, Julia, Sweepstakes Clearinghouse, Dallas, TX. Tel: (214) 915-7100, FAX: (214) 915-7458, E-Mail: customersupport@ sweepstakesclearinghouse.com, Web Site: www. sweepstakesclearinghouse.com (16)

Gotbetter, Amy, Direct Marketers On Call Inc (DMOC), New York, NY. Tel: (212) 691-1942, FAX: (212) 924-1331, E-Mail: info@dmoc-inc. com, Web Site: www.dmoc-inc.com (20)

Gotfredson, Mike, Road Runner Sports Inc, San Diego, CA. Tel: (858) 974-4200, (800) 636-3560, FAX: (800) 453-5443, Web Site: www. roadrunnersports.com (11)

Gothic Arch Greenhouses Inc, Mobile, AL. Tel: (251) 432-7529, (800) 531-4769, FAX: (251) 432-2655, E-Mail: gothicarch@comcast.net, Web Site: www. GothicArchGreenhouses.com (8)

Gottehrer, Rita, Better Health Fitness, Brooklyn, NY. Tel: (718) 436-4693, FAX: (718) 854-3381, Web Site: www.betterhealthfitness.com (11)

Gottesmann, Patricia, Cablevision Systems Corp, Bethpage, NY. Tel: (516) 803-2300, FAX: (516) 803-3134, Web Site: www.cablevision.com (16)

Gottfried, Glenn, Infolure, Phoenix, AZ. Tel: (602) 308-6700, FAX: (602) 308-6801, E-Mail: glenn. gottfried@infolure.com, Web Site: www.infolure. com (22)

Gottlieb, Richard, Directory of Mail Order Catalogs, Millerton, NY. Tel: (518) 789-8700, (800) 562-2139, FAX: (518) 789-0556, E-Mail: cstupak@ greyhouse.com, Web Site: www.greyhouse.com (43)

Gottlieb, Richard, Grey House Publishing, Amenia, NY. Tel: (518) 789-8700, (800) 562-2139, FAX: (518) 789-0556, E-Mail: books@greyhouse.com, Web Site: www.greyhouse.com (43)

Gottlieb, Richard, The Directory of Business Information Resources, Millerton, NY. Tel: (518) 789-8700, (800) 562-2139, FAX: (518) 789-0556, E-Mail: cstupak@greyhouse.com, Web Site: www. greyhouse.com (43)

Gottung, Lizanne, C., Kimberly-Clark Corp, Neenah, WI. Tel: (920) 721-2000, (888) 525-8388, FAX: (920) 721-7722, Web Site: www.kimberly-clark. com (16)

Gotwald, Bruce, C., Ethyl Corp, Richmond, VA. Tel: (804) 788-5000, FAX: (804) 788-5688, Web Site: www.ethyl.com (16)

Gotwald, Thomas, E., Ethyl Corp, Richmond, VA. Tel: (804) 788-5000, FAX: (804) 788-5688, Web Site: www.ethyl.com (16)

Goudeseune, Scott, American Council on Exercise, San Diego, CA. Tel: (858) 279-8227, (888) 825-3636, FAX: (858) 279-8064, E-Mail: kristie. spalding@acefitness.org, Web Site: www. acefitness.org (1)

Goudis, Richard, Herbalife International of America Inc, Los Angeles, CA. Tel: (310) 410-9600, (866) 617-4273, FAX: (310) 258-7019, Web Site: www. herbalife.com (7)

Gough, Al, Cablexpress Technologies, Syracuse, NY. Tel: (315) 476-3000, (800) 913-9467, FAX: (315) 455-1800, E-Mail: info@cablexpress.com, Web Site: www.CXTec.com (10)

Gouhin, Patrick, ISA-The Instrumentation Systems & Automation Society, Research Triangle Park, NC. Tel: (919) 549-8411, FAX: (919) 549-8288, E-Mail: info@isa.org, Web Site: www.isa.org (1)

Gould, A., Michael, Eastlan Ratings, Sisters, OR. Tel: (877) 886-3320, FAX: (541) 318-4646, E-Mail: info@eastlanratings.com, Web Site: www. eastlanratings.com (30)

Gould, C.W.D., Broadway Play Publishing Inc, New York, NY. Tel: (212) 772-8334, FAX: (212) 772-8358, E-Mail: sara@broadwayplaypubl.com, Web Site: www.broadwayplaypubl.com (17)

Gould, Carolyn, Directives/Targeted Marketing and Communications, Plymouth, MA. Tel: (215) 546-7817, Web Site: www.directivesmarketing.com (20)

Gould, David, Thermo Pro, Duluth, GA. Tel: (678) 475-1647, (800) 523-5542, FAX: (678) 475-1747, Web Site: www.thermopro.com (16)

Gould, Jerry, Conrad Direct Inc, Cresskill, NJ. Tel: (201) 567-3200, FAX: (201) 567-1530, Web Site: www.conraddirect.com (23)

Gould, K.J., Covidien International, Mansfield, MA. Tel: (508) 261-8000, (800) 962-9888, FAX: (508) 261-8105, Web Site: www.covidien.com (7)

Gould, Marston, All Star Directories, Seattle, WA. Tel: (888) 404-8043, FAX: (707) 667-1524, Web Site: www.allstardirectories.com (13)

Gould, Michael L., Thermo Pro, Duluth, GA. Tel: (678) 475-1647, (800) 523-5542, FAX: (678) 475-1747, Web Site: www.thermopro.com (16)

Gould, Michael, Bloomingdale's Direct, New York, NY. Tel: (212) 705-2000, (866) 593-2540, FAX: (212) 705-2805, Web Site: www.bloomingdales. com (16)

Gould, Phyllis, Gould & Goodrich, Lillington, NC. Tel: (910) 893-2071, (800) 277-0732, FAX: (910) 893-4742, E-Mail: service@gouldusa.com, Web Site: www.gouldusa.com (2)

Gould, Rick, Ohio Envelope Manufacturing Co, Cleveland, OH. Tel: (216) 267-2920, (800) 989-0336, FAX: (216) 267-1765, E-Mail: mgmt@ ohioenvelope.com, Web Site: www.ohioenvelope. com (24)

Gould, Robert, Gould & Goodrich, Lillington, NC. Tel: (910) 893-2071, (800) 277-0732, FAX: (910) 893-4742, E-Mail: service@gouldusa.com, Web Site: www.gouldusa.com (2)

Gould & Goodrich, Lillington, NC. Tel: (910) 893-2071, (800) 277-0732, FAX: (910) 893-4742, E-Mail: service@gouldusa.com, Web Site: www. gouldusa.com (2)

Gould Paper Corp, New York, NY. Tel: (212) 301-0000, (800) 221-3043, FAX: (212) 481-0067, Web Site: www.gouldpaper.com (25)

Stephen Gould Paper Co Inc, Whippany, NJ. Tel: (973) 428-1500, FAX: (973) 428-5274, Web Site: www.stephengould.com (27)

Gourlay, John, American Craft Council, Minneapolis, MN. Tel: (212) 274-0630, FAX: (212) 274-0650, E-Mail: council@craftcouncil.org, Web Site: www. craftcouncil.org (17)

Gourley, Bob, The Gourley Group, San Pedro, CA. Tel: (310) 519-1324, (888) 656-1324, FAX: (310) 519-9323, E-Mail: issuestoday@yahoo.com, Web Site: www.issuestodayradio.com (32)

The Gourley Group, San Pedro, CA. Tel: (310) 519-1324, (888) 656-1324, FAX: (310) 519-9323, E-Mail: issuestoday@yahoo.com, Web Site: www.issuestodayradio.com (32)

Gouwens, Robert, R., LaPreferida Inc, Chicago, IL. Tel: (773) 254-7200, (800) 621-5422, FAX: (773) 254-8546, Web Site: www.lapreferida.com (4)

Governing Magazine, Washington, DC. Tel: (202) 862-8802, Web Site: www.governing.com (17)

Government Data Publications Inc, Washington, DC. Tel: (718) 627-0819, (800) 275-4688, FAX: (718) 998-5960, E-Mail: gdp@govdata.com, Web Site: www.govdata.com (17)

Government of India Tourist Office, New York, NY. Tel: (212) 586-4901, (800) 953-9399, FAX: (212) 582-3274, Web Site: www.incredibleindia.org (1)

Government Technology Services Inc, Herndon, VA. Tel: (703) 502-2000, (800) 234-GTSI, FAX: (703) 222-5218, Web Site: www.gtsi.com (16)

Gow, Frank, Audio Classics Ltd, Vestal, NY. Tel: (607) 766-3501, FAX: (607) 766-3502, E-Mail: steve@audioclassics.com, Web Site: www.audioclassics.com (3)

Gozenbach, Dawnelle, USAA Alliance Services Marketing, San Antonio, TX. Tel: (210) 456-9857, FAX: (210) 498-4542, Web Site: www.usaa.com (14)

Grabczak, Natalie, Air France, New York, NY. Tel: (212) 830-4000, FAX: (212) 830-4244, Web Site: www.airfrance.fr.com (16)

Grabin, Bill, Renaissance Greeting Cards Inc, Springvale, ME. Tel: (207) 324-4153, (800) 688-9998, FAX: (207) 324-9564, E-Mail: rencards@rencards.com (5)

Grabowski, Jim, Hasco First Photo, Saint Charles, MO. Tel: (636) 946-5115, FAX: (636) 946-7148, Web Site: www.growingfamily.com (16)

Grace, Alfred, Polynesian Cultural Center, Honolulu, HI. Tel: (808) 293-3333, (800) 367-7060, FAX: (888) 722-7339, E-Mail: internetrez@polynesia.com, Web Site: www.polynesia.com (16)

Grace Nathan & Associates, Chicago, IL. Tel: (847) 763-1174 (33)

W R Grace & Co, Columbia, MD. Tel: (410) 531-4000, FAX: (410) 531-4367, Web Site: www.grace.com (16)

Graceland, Memphis, TN. Tel: (901) 332-3322, (800) 238-2010, FAX: (901) 344-3120, Web Site: www.elvis.com (6)

Gracewood Fruit Co, Vero Beach, FL. Tel: (772) 567-1154, E-Mail: info@gracewoodgroves.com, Web Site: www.gracewoodgroves.com (4)

Graci, Joseph, Sleepy's Inc, Hicksville, NY. Tel: (516) 844-8800, (800) sleepys, FAX: (516) 844-8847, Web Site: www.sleepys.com (16)

Graddick Weir, Mirian, Calbiochem-Novabiochem Corp, San Diego, CA. Tel: (858) 450-9600, (800) 854-3417, FAX: (858) 453-3552, E-Mail: customerservice@emdbioscience.com, Web Site: www.calbiochem.com (9)

Grade Finders Inc, Exton, PA. Tel: (610) 524-7070, FAX: (610) 524-8912, E-Mail: info@gradefinders.com, Web Site: www.gradefinders.com (17)

Graduate Management Admission Council, Reston, VA. Tel: (703) 668-9813, Web Site: www.mba.com (20)

Graduate School USDA, Washington, DC. Tel: (202) 314-3300, FAX: (202) 690-6577, E-Mail: pubaffairs@grad.usda.gov, Web Site: www.grad.usda.gov (1)

Graebner, Carol, H&R Block Inc, Kansas City, MO. Tel: (816) 572-6446, (800) 472-5625, FAX: (816) 854-8500, Web Site: www.hrblock.com (14)

Graf, Francine, Choice Magazine, Middletown, CT. Tel: (860) 347-6933, (860) 347-1387, FAX: (860) 346-8586, E-Mail: adsales@ala-choice.org, Web Site: www.ala.org/ala/acrl/acrlpubs/choice/home.cfm (31)

Grafek Direct, Syracuse, NY. Tel: (315) 422-4732, (800) 724-2477, FAX: (315) 425-9624, E-Mail: grafek@duplionline.com, Web Site: www.duplionline.com (27)

Grafica Group, Morristown, NJ. Tel: (973) 309-7500, FAX: (973) 309-7501, E-Mail: info@grafica.com, Web Site: www.grafica.com (35)

Grafton, Barb, Pfaltzgraff Co, York, PA. Tel: (717) 852-2211, (800) 999-2811, FAX: (800) 717-2481, E-Mail: service@pfaltzgraff.com, Web Site: www.pfaltzgraff.com (8)

Gragg, Sam, Teradata Corp, Miamisburg, OH. Tel: (937) 242-4800, Web Site: www.teradata.com (22)

Gragg Advertising, Kansas City, MO. Tel: (816) 931-0050, Web Site: www.graggadv.com (35)

Graham, Bill, CAA Auto Club & Travel Agency Inc, Thornhill, ON Canada. Tel: (519) 255-1212, (800) 564-6222, FAX: (519) 255-7379, E-Mail: info@caasco.ca, Web Site: www.central.on.caa.ca (1)

Graham, Billy, Billy Graham Evangelistic Association, Charlotte, NC. Tel: (704) 401-2491, (877) 2-GRAHAM, Web Site: www.billygraham.org (1)

Graham, Dan, The Berry Co, Dayton, OH. Tel: (937) 296-2121, FAX: (937) 296-2011, Web Site: www.lmberry.com (35)

Graham, Donald, E., The Washington Post, Washington, DC. Tel: (202) 334-6000, (800) 627-1150, E-Mail: letters@washpost.com, Web Site: www.washingtonpost.com (17)

Graham, Franklin, Billy Graham Evangelistic Association, Charlotte, NC. Tel: (704) 401-2491, (877) 2-GRAHAM, Web Site: www.billygraham.org (1)

Graham, Gary, Burlington Coat Factory, Burlington, NJ. Tel: (609) 387-7800, FAX: (609) 387-7071, Web Site: www.coat.com (16)

Graham, Jennifer, Dirxion, Saint Louis, MO. Tel: (636) 717-2300, Web Site: www.dirxion.com (16)

Graham, Jessica, Visa USA, Foster City, CA. Tel: (650) 432-3200, FAX: (650) 432-2875, Web Site: www.visa.com (14)

Graham, Marianne, The Hamilton Collection, Jacksonville, FL. Tel: (904) 279-1300, (866) 323-5577, FAX: (904) 279-1495, Web Site: www.hamiltoncollection.com (6)

Graham, Mark, Data University, Lincoln, NE. Tel: (402) 742-2179, (866) 328-2848, E-Mail: info@datauniversity.com, Web Site: www.datauniversity.org (22)

Graham, Mary, Thomas Nelson, Inc, Nashville, TN. Tel: (615) 889-9000, (800) 251-4000, FAX: (615) 889-5940, Web Site: www.thomasnelson.com (17)

Graham, Patricia, Knowledge Networks/SRI, Roseland, NJ. Tel: (908) 497-8000, FAX: (908) 497-8001, E-Mail: mclancey@knowledgenetworks.com, Web Site: www.knowledgenetworks.com (30)

Graham, Ronald, M., Ennis Inc, Midlothian, TX. Tel: (972) 775-9801, (800) 962-0944, FAX: (800) 645-8339, Web Site: www.ennis.com (16)

Graham, Tom, Mutual of Omaha, Omaha, NE. Tel: (402) 342-7600, (800) 775-6000, FAX: (402) 351-2775, Web Site: www.mutualofomaha.com (15)

Billy Graham Evangelistic Association, Charlotte, NC. Tel: (704) 401-2491, (877) 2-GRAHAM, Web Site: www.billygraham.org (1)

Graham Field Health Products Inc, Atlanta, GA. Tel: (800) 347-5678, FAX: (800) 726-0601, E-Mail: ics@grahamfield.com, Web Site: www.lumiscope.net (7)

Grainger Parts, North Brook, IL. Tel: (847) 498-5900, FAX: (847) 498-3402, Web Site: www.grainger.com (16)

WW Grainger Inc, Lake Forest, IL. Tel: (847) 535-1000, (888) 361-8649, FAX: (847) 535-9122, Web Site: www.grainger.com (9)

Gramma's Graphics Inc, Lancaster, VA. Tel: (804) 462-0884, FAX: (804) 462-0884, E-Mail: sunprints@grandloving.com, Web Site: www.bubblink.com/donnelly (36)

Grammer, Jill, American Name Services Inc, Orem, UT. Tel: (801) 235-8061, (800) 434-1851, FAX: (801) 764-0613, E-Mail: sales@americannameservices.com, Web Site: www.americannameservices.com (23)

Granados, Patricia, Triton College, River Grove, IL. Tel: (708) 456-0300, FAX: (708) 583-3121, Web Site: www.triton.edu (16)

Granchos, Louis, The Gallery Shop, Buffalo, NY. Tel: (716) 882-8700 X258, FAX: (716) 882-1958, E-Mail: gallshop@albrightknox.org, Web Site: www.albrightknox.org (6)

Grand Canyon Association, Flagstaff, AZ. Tel: (928) 863-3876, Web Site: www.grandcanyon.org (1)

Grand Canyon University, Phoenix, AZ. Tel: (602) 639-6277, Web Site: www.gcu.edu (13)

Grand Circle Travel, Boston, MA. Tel: (617) 350-7500, (800) 959-0405, FAX: (617) 346-6030, Web Site: www.gct.com (19)

Grand Pacific Resorts, Carlsbad, CA. Tel: (760) 827-4101, Web Site: www.grandpacificresorts.com (19)

Grandma Brown's Beans Inc, Mexico, NY. Tel: (315) 963-7221, FAX: (315) 963-4072 (4)

Granet, Peter, Cision US Inc, Chicago, IL. Tel: (312) 922-2400, (866) 639-5087, FAX: (312) 922-3126, E-Mail: info.us@cision.com, Web Site: us.cision.com (43)

Grange, Carey, Murad Inc, El Segundo, CA. Tel: (310) 726-0600, Web Site: www.murad.com (7)

Granger, David, Esquire Magazine, New York, NY. Tel: (212) 649-2000, (800) 925-0485, FAX: (212) 265-0938, E-Mail: esquire@hearst.com, Web Site: www.esquire.com (17)

Granger, Mary, E., Mary Elizabeth Granger & Associates Inc, Baltimore, MD. Tel: (410) 842-1170, (800) 296-5157, FAX: (410) 842-1185, E-Mail: bonnie@maryegranger.com, Web Site: www.maryegranger.com (23)

The Granger Collection, New York, NY. Tel: (212) 447-1789, FAX: (212) 447-1492, Web Site: www.granger.com (38)

Mary Elizabeth Granger & Associates Inc, Baltimore, MD. Tel: (410) 842-1170, (800) 296-5157, FAX: (410) 842-1185, E-Mail: bonnie@maryegranger.com, Web Site: www.maryegranger.com (23)

Grann, Phyllis, Penguin Publishing Group, New York, NY. Tel: (212) 366-2000, FAX: (212) 366-2952, Web Site: www.penguinputnam.com (17)

Grano, Joseph, UBS Wealth Management US, Weehawken, NJ. Tel: (201) 352-3000, (888) 279-3343, FAX: (201) 617-8589, Web Site: www.ubs.com/financialservicesinc (14)

Grant Jr., W. King, KEH.com, Smyrna, GA. Tel: (770) 333-4200, (800) 342-5534, FAX: (770) 333-4242, E-Mail: sales@keh.com, Web Site: www.keh.com (16)

Grant, Carl, US Chamber of Commerce, Washington, DC. Tel: (202) 778-6063, (800) 638-6582, FAX: (202) 887-3430, Web Site: www.uschamber.com (1)

Grant, Eric, The Washington Post, Washington, DC. Tel: (202) 334-6000, (800) 627-1150, E-Mail: letters@washpost.com, Web Site: www.washingtonpost.com (17)

Grant, Gerald, SMY Media Inc, Chicago, IL. Tel: (312) 621-9600, FAX: (312) 621-0924, E-Mail: info@smymedia.com, Web Site: www.smymedia.com (32)

Grant, Hallie, Sailrite Enterprises, Inc, Columbia City, IN. Tel: (260) 693-2242, (800) 348-2769, FAX: (260) 693-2246, E-Mail: sailrite@sailrite.com, Web Site: www.sailrite.com (11)

Grant, Kent, Academy of Psychic Arts & Sciences, Dallas, TX. Tel: (214) 219-2020, FAX: (214) 599-0040, E-Mail: academy@psychic2020.com (5)

Grant, Matthew, Sailrite Enterprises, Inc, Columbia City, IN. Tel: (260) 693-2242, (800) 348-2769, FAX: (260) 693-2246, E-Mail: sailrite@sailrite.com, Web Site: www.sailrite.com (11)

Grant, Maurice, Defense News Media Group, Springfield, VA. Tel: (703) 848-0490, FAX: (703) 848-0480, E-Mail: mgrant@atpco.com, Web Site: www.defensenews.com (17)

Grant, Mike, Reed Exhibitions, Norwalk, CT. Tel: (203) 840-4800, (888) 745-7644, FAX: (203) 840-5805, E-Mail: dhalter@reedexpo.com, Web Site: www.readerexpo.com (16)

Grant's Mailing Services Inc, Mississauga, ON Canada. Tel: (905) 624-9082, FAX: (905) 624-0007, E-Mail: info@grants-mailing.ca, Web Site: www.grants-mailing.ca (27)

Granum, Patricia, Co-operations, Tualatin, OR. Tel: (503) 620-7977, (866) 228-6362, FAX: (503) 620-7917, E-Mail: info@fsipdx.com, Web Site: www.fsipdx.com (28)

The Graph Co, Vineland, NJ. Tel: (856) 825-9199, FAX: (856) 825-5573, E-Mail: graphco2@verizon.net (14)

Graphic Arts Blue Book/AF Lewis Marketing, New York, NY. Tel: (646) 746-7429, FAX: (212) 519-7434, Web Site: www.gabb.com (24)

Graphic Arts Blue Book Online, Oak Brook, IL. Tel: (630) 288-8333, (800) 323-4958, Web Site: www.gammag.com (43)

Graphic Arts Center, Garland, TX. Tel: (972) 271-0591, (800) 865-7086, FAX: (972) 271-8392 (27)

Graphic Arts Information Network (GAIN), Sewickley, PA. Tel: (412) 741-6860, (800) 910-4283, FAX: (412) 741-2311, E-Mail: printing@printing.org, Web Site: www.gain.net (27)

Graphic Communications Center, Appleton, WI. Tel: (920) 733-4483, (800) 422-3696, FAX: (920) 733-1700 (27)

Graphic Communications Holdings Inc, Hudson, OH. Tel: (330) 650-5522, E-Mail: info@graphiccommunications.com, Web Site: www.graphiccommunications.com (25)

Graphic Converting Inc, Elmhurst, IL. Tel: (630) 758-4100, (800) 447-1935, FAX: (630) 833-1058, E-Mail: sales@graphicconverting.com, Web Site: www.graphicconverting.com (36)

Graphics International Inc, Dallas, TX. Tel: (214) 352-7565, FAX: (214) 528-0114 (27)

Graphik Dimensions Ltd, High Point, NC. Tel: (336) 887-3500, (800) 221-0262, FAX: (336) 887-3773, E-Mail: customercare@pictureframes.com, Web Site: www.pictureframes.com (16)

Graphnet Inc, New York, NY. Tel: (212) 994-1100, (800) 327-1800, FAX: (212) 994-1188, E-Mail: custsvc@graphnet.com, Web Site: www.graphnet.com (28)

Grasee, Mike, Pleasant Company, Middleton, WI. Tel: (608) 836-4848, (800) 845-0005, FAX: (608) 836-1999, Web Site: www.americangirl.com (11)

Grassman, Paul, Oakton Community College, Des Plaines, IL. Tel: (847) 635-1600, FAX: (847) 635-1706, Web Site: www.oakton.edu (41)

Grassmyer, Bill, MediaTree, Parsippany, NJ. Tel: (800) 475-8703, FAX: (973) 781-1071, E-Mail: sales@mediatreegroup.com, Web Site: www.mediatreegroup.com (27)

Gration, Laurence, Association for Facilities Engineering, Herndon, VA. Tel: (571) 203-7171, FAX: (571) 766-2142, E-Mail: info@afe.org, Web Site: www.afe.org (1)

Grau, Thomas, Independent Insurance Agents & Brokers of America, Alexandria, VA. Tel: (703) 683-4422, (800) 221-7917, FAX: (703) 683-7556, E-Mail: info@iiaba.org, Web Site: www.iiaba.org (1)

Grausam, Michael, Thermal Product Solutions, White Deer, PA. Tel: (570) 538-7200, (800) 586-2473 (16)

Grause, Corey, American Church Lists Inc, Omaha, NE. Tel: (402) 596-8905, (888) 733-1812, FAX: (402) 596-8907, E-Mail: americanchurchlists@infousa.com, Web Site: www.americanchurchlists.com (24)

Graves Sr., Earl, G., Black Enterprise Magazine, New York, NY. Tel: (212) 242-8000, FAX: (212) 886-9618, E-Mail: corpcomm@blackenterprise.com, Web Site: www.blackenterprise.com (17)

Graves, Bill, American Trucking Association, Arlington, VA. Tel: (703) 838-1700, FAX: (800) 254-2571, E-Mail: atamembership@trucking.org, Web Site: www.truckline.com (1)

Graves, Earl, "Butch", Black Enterprise Magazine, New York, NY. Tel: (212) 242-8000, FAX: (212) 886-9618, E-Mail: corpcomm@blackenterprise.com, Web Site: www.blackenterprise.com (17)

Graves, Jeffrey, B., Sedlak, Highland Hills, OH. Tel: (216) 206-4700, FAX: (216) 206-4840, E-Mail: info@jasedlak.com, Web Site: www.jasedlak.com (20)

Graves, John, Ashworth University, Norcross, GA. Tel: (770) 729-8400, (800) 957-5412, FAX: (770) 729-9294, E-Mail: info@ashworthuniversity.edu, Web Site: www.ashworthuniversity.edu (13)

Graves, Mark, Cole-Parmer Instrument Co, Vernon Hills, IL. Tel: (847) 549-7600, (800) 323-4340, FAX: (847) 247-2929, E-Mail: info@coleparmer.com, Web Site: www.coleparmer.com (16)

Graves, Michael, Black Enterprise Magazine, New York, NY. Tel: (212) 242-8000, FAX: (212) 886-9618, E-Mail: corpcomm@blackenterprise.com, Web Site: www.blackenterprise.com (17)

Graves Lapidary Co, Pompano Beach, FL. Tel: (954) 960-0300, (800) 327-9103, FAX: (954) 960-0301, E-Mail: sales@gravescompany.com, Web Site: www.gravescompany.com (9)

Gravitt, Mark, Raven's Nest Herbals, LLC, Duluth, GA. Tel: (678) 642-6691, (678) 584-0830, E-Mail: info@ravensnestherbals.com, Web Site: www.ravensnestherbals.com (7)

Gray, Chris, Zillner Marketing Communications Inc, Lenexa, KS. Tel: (913) 599-3230, Web Site: www.zillner.com (35)

Gray, Donna, Melitta USA, Clearwater, FL. Tel: (727) 535-2111, Web Site: www.melitta.com (4)

Gray, Edna, ETS Inc, Indianapolis, IN. Tel: (317) 290-8982, (800) 228-6292, FAX: (317) 329-4630, E-Mail: info@etstsan.com, Web Site: www.etstans.com (7)

Gray, Gerald, American Forests, Washington, DC. Tel: (202) 737-1944, FAX: (202) 737-2457, E-Mail: info@amfor.org, Web Site: www.americanforests.org (1)

Gray, Jeff, R., Gray & Graham Inc, Westport, CT. Tel: (203) 227-3900, FAX: (203) 227-3593, Web Site: www.graygraham.com (35)

Gray, Jonathon, Direct Alliance, Tempe, AZ. Tel: (800) 546-0582, Web Site: www.directalliance.com (35)

Gray, Michael, W., Marketing & Promotions Group, Ridgewood, NJ. Tel: (201) 251-8339, FAX: (201) 251-8340, Web Site: www.promowave.com (35)

Gray, Nancy, R., American Chemical Society, Washington, DC. Tel: (202) 872-4600, (800) 227-5558, FAX: (202) 833-7716, E-Mail: service@acs.org, Web Site: www.acs.org (1)

Gray, Richard, F., Arich Corp, New York, NY. Tel: (212) 247-1800, FAX: (212) 247-2231, Web Site: www.arichinc.com (20)

Gray, Robert A., The Gray Printing Co, Fostoria, OH. Tel: (419) 435-6638 (27)

Gray, Robert, C., Highmark Blue Cross Blue Shield, Pittsburgh, PA. Tel: (412) 544-7000, FAX: (412) 544-5350, Web Site: www.highmark.com (15)

Gray, Roger, GKV, Baltimore, MD. Tel: (410) 539-5400, FAX: (410) 234-2441, E-Mail: newbusiness@gkv.com, Web Site: www.gvk.com (35)

Gray, Stephen, The Christian Science Monitor, Boston, MA. Tel: (617) 450-2000, FAX: (617) 450-2031, Web Site: www.csmonitor.com (31)

Gray, Trevor, ETS Inc, Indianapolis, IN. Tel: (317) 290-8982, (800) 228-6292, FAX: (317) 329-4630, E-Mail: info@etstsan.com, Web Site: www.etstans.com (7)

Gray & Graham Inc, Westport, CT. Tel: (203) 227-3900, FAX: (203) 227-3593, Web Site: www.graygraham.com (35)

Gray Craddock, Mary, Equity Residential Properties, Chicago, IL. Tel: (312) 474-1300, FAX: (312) 474-8703, E-Mail: mgraycraddock@eqr.com, Web Site: www.eqr.com (20)

The Gray Printing Co, Fostoria, OH. Tel: (419) 435-6638 (27)

Graycar, Edward, W., Physicians Mutual Insurance Co, Omaha, NE. Tel: (402) 633-1604, (888) 932-7642, FAX: (402) 633-1604, Web Site: www.physiciansmutual.com (15)

Grayer, John, Kaplan Publishing, Chicago, IL. Tel: (312) 606-8905, (800) 245-2665, FAX: (312) 606-8985, E-Mail: kaplanorders@kaplan.com, Web Site: www.kaplanpublishing.com (17)

GrayHair Software, Mount Laurel, NJ. Web Site: www.grayhairsoftware.com (22)

Grayson, David, American Fine Paper Co, Appleton, WI. Tel: (920) 733-6100, (800) 458-5446, FAX: (920) 380-8711, E-Mail: found@americanfinepaper.com, Web Site: www.americanfinepaper.com (25)

Grayson-Marston, Kathryn, CXO Media Inc, Framingham, MA. Tel: (508) 872-0080, (800) 859-5478, FAX: (508) 872-0618, Web Site: www.cxo.com (17)

Graziani, Cheryl, Bay Manufacturing, Milan, OH. Tel: (419) 499-4602, FAX: (419) 499-4603, Web Site: www.baymfg.com (16)

Greaney, Dennis, Mary Kay Cosmetics Inc, Addison, TX. Tel: (972) 687-6300, (800) MARY KAY, FAX: (972) 687-1611, Web Site: www.marykay.com (16)

The Great Amarillo Directory, Amarillo, TX. Tel: (806) 353-5155, FAX: (806) 359-2974, Web Site: www.worldpages.com (17)

The Great Books Foundation, Chicago, IL. Tel: (312) 332-5870, Web Site: www.greatbooks.org (1)

Great Chefs Television Publishing, New Orleans, LA. Tel: (504) 581-5000, (800) 321-1499, FAX: (504) 581-1188, E-Mail: info@greatchefs.com, Web Site: www.greatchefs.com (15)

Great Ideas Inc/CSP, Highland Park, IL. Tel: (847) 432-9060, (800) 611-5515, FAX: (800) 956-4443, E-Mail: sales@greatideasinc.com, Web Site: www.greatideasinc.com (33)

Great Lakes Fulfillment Inc, Erie, PA. Tel: (814) 456-2175, (800) 964-5478, FAX: (814) 455-1942, E-Mail: info@greatlakeslists.com, Web Site: www.greatlakeslists.com (23)

Great Lakes Integrated, Cleveland, OH. Tel: (216) 651-1500, (800) 745-4846, FAX: (216) 651-8311, E-Mail: bbemer@glintergrated.com, Web Site: www.gll.com (27)

Great North American Cos Inc, Dallas, TX. Tel: (972) 481-6100, (800) 527-2782, FAX: (972) 243-1637, Web Site: www.gnamerican.com (16)

Great-West Life, Greenwood Village, CO. Tel: (800) 537-2033, Web Site: www.greatwest.com (15)

Great Western Bank, Sioux Falls, SD. Tel: (605) 334-2545, Web Site: greatwesternbank.com (14)

Greater Fort Worth Builders Association, Fort Worth, TX. Tel: (817) 284-3566, FAX: (817) 284-6465, E-Mail: info@fortworthbuilders.org, Web Site: www.forthworthbuilders.org (1)

GreatLists.com, Dulles, VA. Tel: (703) 821-8130, (800) 296-0888, FAX: (703) 821-8243, E-Mail: info@greatlists.com, Web Site: www.greatlists.com (23)

Greber, Brian, Weyerhaeuser Co, Federal Way, WA. Tel: (253) 924-2345, (800) 525-5440, FAX: (253) 924-2685, Web Site: www.wy.com (25)

Grech, Paul, A., Dispatch Letter Service, New York, NY. Tel: (212) 307-5943, FAX: (212) 307-6103, Web Site: www.dispatchletterservice.com (28)

Grech, Stephen, Dispatch Letter Service, New York, NY. Tel: (212) 307-5943, FAX: (212) 307-6103, Web Site: www.dispatchletterservice.com (28)

Greco Jr., John, A., DMA (Direct Marketing Association), New York, NY. Tel: (212) 768-7277, FAX: (212) 302-6714, E-Mail: customerservice@the-dma.org, Web Site: www.the-dma.org (40)

Green Jr., Robert, A., The Verdi Group Inc, Pittsford, NY. Tel: (585) 381-4275, FAX: (585) 381-4293, E-Mail: info@theverdigroup.com, Web Site: www.theverdigroup.com (35)

Green, Barry, Hooleon Corp, Melrose, NM. Tel: (928) 634-7515, (800) 937-1337, E-Mail: sales@hooleon.com, Web Site: www.hooleon.com (3)

Green, Charles, Thomas Computer Corp, Orlando, FL. Tel: (407) 855-2020, (800) 621-3906, FAX: (407) 426-2805, E-Mail: hildap@thomascompute.com, Web Site: www.thomascomputer.com (16)

Green, David I., Results Advertising Inc, Hasbrouck Heights, NJ. Tel: (201) 288-7888, FAX: (201) 288-5112, E-Mail: info@resultsinc.com, Web Site: www.resultsinc.com (35)

Green, Jessica, A., Keeneland Association Inc, Lexington, KY. Tel: (859) 254-3412, (800) 456-3412, FAX: (859) 255-2484, Web Site: www.keeneland.com (16)

Green, Jim, Customer Retention Management Group Inc, Severna Park, MD. Tel: (410) 280-1720, (888) 822-8574, FAX: (410) 280-1723 (35)

Green, Jim, JL Green & Associates, Oxford, NC. Tel: (919) 693-3713 (39)

Green, John, Automated Graphic Systems Inc, White Plains, MD. Tel: (301) 843-1800, (800) 678-8760, FAX: (301) 843-6339, E-Mail: info@ags.com, Web Site: www.ags.com (31)

Green, John, The Journal News, White Plains, NY. Tel: (914) 694-9300, FAX: (914) 696-8152, Web Site: www.nyjournalnews.com (17)

Green, Kevin, Lillian Vernon Corp, Colorado Springs, CO. Tel: (757) 427-7923, FAX: (757) 427-7819, E-Mail: publicrelations@lillianvernon.com, Web Site: www.lillianvernon.com (6)

Green, Lori, Peruvian Connection Ltd, Tonganoxie, KS. Tel: (913) 845-2450, Web Site: www.peruvianconnection.com (2)

Green, Michael, E., DMRA & Matchkey Corp, Mountain View, CA. Tel: (650) 856-9988, FAX: (650) 856-9986 (30)

Green, Richard, Dalrada Financial Corp, San Diego, CA. Tel: (858) 427-8716, (877) 325-7232, FAX: (858) 277-3448, E-Mail: inquiries@dalrada.com, Web Site: www.dalrada.com (14)

Green, Rick, Newsday, Melville, NY. Tel: (631) 843-2020, FAX: (631) 843-5424, Web Site: www.newsday.com (17)

Green, Stanley, Thomas Computer Corp, Orlando, FL. Tel: (407) 855-2020, (800) 621-3906, FAX: (407) 426-2805, E-Mail: hildap@thomascompute.com, Web Site: www.thomascomputer.com (16)

Green, Susan, Sunburst Technology, Elgin, IL. Tel: (914) 747-3310, FAX: (914) 747-4109, E-Mail: service@nysunburst.com, Web Site: www.sunburst.com (17)

Green, Tara, Sunburst Technology, Elgin, IL. Tel: (914) 747-3310, FAX: (914) 747-4109, E-Mail: service@nysunburst.com, Web Site: www.sunburst.com (17)

JL Green & Associates, Oxford, NC. Tel: (919) 693-3713 (39)

Green Mountain Coffee Roasters, Inc, Waterbury, VT. Tel: (802) 244-5621, (800) 545-2326, FAX: (802) 244-5436, Web Site: www.gmcr.com (4)

The Green Pond Co, Atlanta, GA. Tel: (404) 233-6343, (800) 827-7663, FAX: (404) 233-6340, E-Mail: sales@greenpond.com, Web Site: www.greenpond.com (2)

Green River Trading Co, Millerton, NY. Tel: (518) 789-3311 (8)

Greenawalt, Andy, Cole-Parmer Instrument Co, Vernon Hills, IL. Tel: (847) 549-7600, (800) 323-4340, FAX: (847) 247-2929, E-Mail: info@coleparmer.com, Web Site: www.coleparmer.com (16)

Greenbaum, Julie, A., Getko Direct Response, Coral Springs, FL. Tel: (800) 642-8732, FAX: (954) 320-7565, E-Mail: gdrservices@getkodirect.com, Web Site: www.getkodirect.com (24)

Greenbaum, Julie, HomeData, Santa Barbara, CA. Tel: (516) 605-0451, (800) 628-9456, FAX: (516) 605-0455, E-Mail: info@homedata.com, Web Site: www.homedata.com (24)

Greenberg, Laura, Norman Hecht Research Inc, Syosset, NY. Tel: (516) 496-8866, FAX: (516) 496-8165, E-Mail: nhr@normanhechtresearch.com, Web Site: www.normanhechtresearch.com (30)

Greenberg, Mark, Showtime Networks Inc, New York, NY. Tel: (212) 708-1600, FAX: (212) 708-1450, Web Site: www.sho.com (16)

Greenberg, Martin, Greenberg Consulting, Somers, NY. Tel: (914) 669-8588, FAX: (914) 669-8888, E-Mail: mgreenb@sover.net (39)

Greenberg, Randy, Greene an RMG Direct Co, Lincolnshire, IL. Tel: (847) 948-7400, (800) 356-1300 x1809, FAX: (847) 948-0400, Web Site: www.rmgdirectinc.com (29)

Greenberg Consulting, Somers, NY. Tel: (914) 669-8588, FAX: (914) 669-8888, E-Mail: mgreenb@sover.net (39)

Greenbook Worldwide Directory of Marketing Research Companies & Services, Bradenton, FL. Tel: (212) 849-2752, (800) 792-9202, FAX: (212) 202-7920, E-Mail: info@greenbrook.org, Web Site: www.greenbook.org (43)

Greenburg, Eric, Life Line Screening, Independence, OH. Tel: (216) 581-6556, Web Site: www.lifelinescreening.com (7)

Greene, Barry, Hearst Business Communications, Uniondale, NY. Tel: (516) 227-1300, FAX: (516) 227-1901 (24)

Greene, Dan, NEC Group Inc, Burbank, CA. Tel: (818) 909-9963, Web Site: www.thehomeshow.com (32)

Greene, Henry, Specialized Information Publishers Association (SIPA), Vienna, VA. Tel: (703) 992-9339, (800) 356-9302, FAX: (703) 610-9005, E-Mail: info@sipaonline.org, Web Site: www.sipaonline.com (1)

Greene, Joseph, Bernstein-Rein Advertising, Kansas City, MO. Tel: (816) 756-0640, Web Site: www.brbrg.com (35)

Greene, Ken, Days Inns Worldwide Inc, Parsippany, NJ. Tel: (973) 753-6000, (800) 441-1618, Web Site: www.daysinn.com (16)

Greene, Lisa, Specialized Fundraising Services, Spartanburg, SC. Tel: (864) 579-7755, Web Site: www.specializedfundraising.net (23)

Greene, Ted, United Security Products Inc, Poway, CA. Tel: (858) 413-0149, (800) 227-1592, FAX: (858) 413-0124, E-Mail: usp@unitedsecurity.com, Web Site: www.unitedsecurity.com (16)

Greene an RMG Direct Co, Lincolnshire, IL. Tel: (847) 948-7400, (800) 356-1300 x1809, FAX: (847) 948-0400, Web Site: www.rmgdirectinc.com (29)

Greenfield, David, W., Kennametal Inc, Latrobe, PA. Tel: (800) 222-9327, FAX: (800) 521-3319, E-Mail: mcs-na.service@kennmetal.com, Web Site: www.kennametal.com (16)

Greenfield, Gary, GXS Corp, Gaithersburg, MD. Tel: (301) 340-4000, (800) 560-4347, FAX: (301) 340-5299, Web Site: www.gxs.com (30)

Greenfield, Joan, Joan Greenfield Creative, Jamaica Plain, MA. Tel: (617) 983-2055, FAX: (617) 983-2056, E-Mail: jgcreative@aol.com (39)

Greenfield, Tamna, International Specialized Book Services Inc, Portland, OR. Tel: (503) 287-3093, (800) 944-6190, FAX: (503) 280-8832, E-Mail: isbs_sales@isbs.com, Web Site: www.isbscatalog.com (16)

Joan Greenfield Creative, Jamaica Plain, MA. Tel: (617) 983-2055, FAX: (617) 983-2056, E-Mail: jgcreative@aol.com (39)

Greenglass, Cyndi, Diamond Marketing Solutions, Bloomingdale, IL. Tel: (630) 523-5250, FAX: (630) 523-0403, Web Site: www.dmsolutions.com (35)

GreenPath Sustainability Consultants, New City, NY. Tel: (914) 980-8346 (20)

Greenpeace USA, Washington, DC. Tel: (202) 462-1177, Web Site: www.greenpeace.org (40)

Greenspan, Richard, National Court Reporters Association, Vienna, VA. Tel: (703) 556-6272, (800) 272-6272, FAX: (703) 556-6291, E-Mail: msic@ncrahg.org, Web Site: www.ncraonline.org (1)

Greenstein, David, Marshall Domestics LLC, West Warwick, RI. Tel: (401) 821-8760, (800) 556-7440, FAX: (401) 821-2230, E-Mail: marshalldomestics@verizon.net, Web Site: www.marshalldomestics.com (5)

Greenstein, Judith, Editorial Freelance Association, New York, NY. Tel: (212) 929-5400, (866) 929-5400, FAX: (212) 929-5439, E-Mail: office@the-efa.org, Web Site: www.the-efa.org (31)

Greenwalt, Steve, NCP Solutions, Birmingham, AL. Tel: (250) 849-5200, Web Site: www.ncprint.com (21)

Greenwood, Alex, Spectra Merchandising International Inc, Chicago, IL. Tel: (773) 202-8408, FAX: (773) 202-8409 (16)

Greenwood, Sara, Spa-Finder Inc, New York, NY. Tel: (212) 924-6800, (800) ALL-SPAS, FAX: (212) 924-7240, Web Site: www.spafinder.com (7)

Greenwood Publishing Group Inc, Portsmouth, NH. Tel: (203) 226-3571, FAX: (203) 222-1502, E-Mail: sales@greenwood.com, Web Site: www.greenwood.com (17)

Greer, Harold, Greer Gardens, Eugene, OR. Tel: (541) 686-8266, (800) 548-0111, FAX: (541) 686-0910, E-Mail: orders@greergardens.com, Web Site: www.greergardens.com (8)

Greer Gardens, Eugene, OR. Tel: (541) 686-8266, (800) 548-0111, FAX: (541) 686-0910, E-Mail: orders@greergardens.com, Web Site: www.greergardens.com (8)

Grefe, Richard, American Institute of Graphic Arts (AIGA), New York, NY. Tel: (212) 807-1990, FAX: (212) 807-1799, E-Mail: grefe@aiga.org, Web Site: www.aiga.org (40)

Gregitis, David, Patriot Communications LLC, Wayne, PA. Tel: (610) 225-0100, FAX: (610) 687-3835 (32)

Gregor, Jeff, TNT (Turner Network Television LP), Atlanta, GA. Tel: (404) 827-1700, E-Mail: tnt@turner.com, Web Site: www.tnt.tv (32)

Gregory, James, CoreBrand, New York, NY. Tel: (212) 329-3030, FAX: (212) 329-3031, E-Mail: jgregory@corebrand.com, Web Site: www.corebrand.com (35)

Gregory, Roy, NextScreen LLC, Austin, TX. Tel: (512) 892-8682, Web Site: www.avguide.com (17)

Gregory, Scott, Triggerfish Marketing, San Francisco, CA. Tel: (415) 671-4699, Web Site: www.triggerfish.com (30)

Gregory, Sheri, Sheri Gregory Inc, Dobbs Ferry, NY. Tel: (914) 693-2499, FAX: (914) 693-2393, E-Mail: sgi.inc@verizon.net, Web Site: www.puffaliciouspoufs.com (33)

Sheri Gregory Inc, Dobbs Ferry, NY. Tel: (914) 693-2499, FAX: (914) 693-2393, E-Mail: sgi.inc@verizon.net, Web Site: www.puffaliciouspoufs.com (33)

Greif, Jim, Banner & Greif Ltd, New York, NY. Tel: (212) 847-0010, FAX: (212) 949-9806 (35)

Greig, Paul G., First Merit Bank (HQ), Akron, OH. Tel: (330) 996-6300, (888) 554-4362, Web Site: www.firstmerit.com (14)

Greig, W., George, William Blair & Co LLC, Chicago, IL. Tel: (312) 236-1600, (800) 621-0687, FAX: (312) 368-9418, E-Mail: info@williamblair.com, Web Site: www.williamblair.com (14)

Gremillion, Rob, Tribune Co, Chicago, IL. Tel: (312) 222-9100, FAX: (312) 222-1573, Web Site: www.tribune.com (17)

Gremmel, Patricia, Drexel University (Goodwin College of Professional Studies), Philadelphia, PA. E-Mail: goodwin@drexel.edu, Web Site: www.drexel.edu/goodwin (16)

Grenesko, Donald, C., Tribune Co, Chicago, IL. Tel: (312) 222-9100, FAX: (312) 222-1573, Web Site: www.tribune.com (17)

Gressett, Wayne, Harcourt Educational Measurement, San Antonio, TX. Tel: (210) 299-1061, (800) 211-8378, FAX: (800) 232-1223, Web Site: www.harcourtassessment.com (17)

Gretschel, Gerry, List America, Washington, DC. Tel: (202) 298-9206, (202) 298-8030, FAX: (202) 244-4999, (202) 244-7294, Web Site: www.mdg.nc.org (23)

Gretschel, W., Michael, Market Development Group Inc, Washington, DC. Tel: (202) 298-8030, FAX: (202) 244-4999, Web Site: www.mdginc.org (1)

Gretter, Blair, MidAmerica Lists Inc, Cedar Rapids, IA. Tel: (800) 747-5900, FAX: (888) 312-5478, E-Mail: sales@malists.com, Web Site: www.malists.com (23)

Greving, Robert, C., Unum Corp, Portland, ME. Tel: (207) 770-2211, (800) 421-0344, FAX: (207) 770-4510, Web Site: www.unum.com (15)

Grey, Chris, Emigrant Savings Bank, New York, NY. Tel: (212) 850-4521, (800) EMIGRANT, FAX: (212) 850-4372, Web Site: www.emigrant.com (14)

Grey Birch Group LLC, Irvington, NY. Tel: (914) 479-5088, Web Site: www.greybirch.com (20)

Grey Healthcare Group, New York, NY. Tel: (212) 886-3000, FAX: (212) 886-3297, E-Mail: info@ghgroup.com, Web Site: www.ghgroup.com (35)

Grey House Publishing, Amenia, NY. Tel: (518) 789-8700, (800) 562-2139, FAX: (518) 789-0556, E-Mail: books@greyhouse.com, Web Site: www.greyhouse.com (43)

Greystone Graphics, Kansas City, MO. Tel: (913) 342-1393, (800) 458-7407, FAX: (913) 621-4856, E-Mail: info@greystonegraphics.com, Web Site: www.greystonegraphics.com (27)

Greystone Services Inc, Beverly, MA. Tel: (978) 535-9185, FAX: (978) 535-7826, E-Mail: greystone@gstone.biz (35)

Gribble, George, IPD Printing & Distributing Inc, Atlanta, GA. Tel: (770) 458-6351, FAX: (770) 454-6236 (27)

Gribble, James, Direct Marketing Dynamics Inc, Germantown, MD. Tel: (301) 916-3900, FAX: (301) 515-0404, E-Mail: jim@directmarketingdynamics.com, Web Site: www.directmarketingdynamics.com (35)

Gridley, Linda, Gridley & Co LLC, New York, NY. Tel: (212) 400-9720, Web Site: www.gridleyco.com (14)

Gridley & Co LLC, New York, NY. Tel: (212) 400-9720, Web Site: www.gridleyco.com (14)

Grieb, Robert F., The Diversified Services Group Inc, Wayne, PA. Tel: (610) 989-1710, FAX: (610) 989-1730, E-Mail: rfgrieb@dsg-network.com, Web Site: www.dsg-network.com (20)

Grier, Monica, Triangle Printers Inc, Skokie, IL. Tel: (847) 675-3700, FAX: (847) 674-1230, E-Mail: blevin@triangleprinters.com, Web Site: www.triangleprinters.com (27)

Griesen, Thomas, Rohlik Specialties Co, Bloomfield Hills, MI. Tel: (248) 858-8880, FAX: (248) 858-7323 (33)

Griesmer, Rosemary, Equifax Marketing Services, Atlanta, GA. Tel: (800) 466-5897, Web Site: www.equifax.com/consumer/marketing (23)

Griffen, Neil, JAM Communications, Washington, DC. Tel: (202) 986-4750, FAX: (202) 232-9146, E-Mail: neil@jamagency.com, Web Site: www.jamagency.com (35)

Griffin, Danielle, North Shore Animal League America Inc, Port Washington, NY. Tel: (516) 883-7900, FAX: (516) 883-8256, E-Mail: donorservices@nsalamerica.org, Web Site: www.nsalamerica.org (17)

Griffin, Jack, Meredith Corp, Des Moines, IA. Tel: (515) 284-3000, FAX: (515) 284-2700, Web Site: www.meredith.com (17)

Griffin, Jean, Warner Books, New York, NY. Tel: (212) 364-1200, FAX: (212) 522-7989, Web Site: www.twbookmark.com (17)

Griffin, Mary Ellen, Pernod Ricard USA, Purchase, NY. Tel: (914) 848-4800, Web Site: www.pernod-ricard-usa.com (16)

Griffin, Ms. Danielle, Epilepsy Foundation, Landover, MD. Tel: (301) 459-3700, (800) 332-1000, FAX: (301) 577-9056, E-Mail: postmaster@efa.org, Web Site: www.efa.org (1)

Griffin, Peter, Esquire Magazine, New York, NY. Tel: (212) 649-2000, (800) 925-0485, FAX: (212) 265-0938, E-Mail: esquire@hearst.com, Web Site: www.esquire.com (17)

Griffin, Raymond, Scan Optics Inc, Manchester, CT. Tel: (860) 645-7878, (800) 745-6001, FAX: (860) 645-7995, E-Mail: info@scanoptics.com, Web Site: www.scanoptics.com (16)

Griffin, Ron, KET, Lexington, KY. Tel: (859) 258-7000, (800) 432-0951, FAX: (606) 258-7396, E-Mail: rgriffin@ket.org, Web Site: www.ket.org (17)

Griffith, Andrew, Sage Software Inc, Irvine, CA. Tel: (949) 753-1222, (800) 854-3415, FAX: (949) 753-0374, Web Site: www.sagesoftware.com (16)

Griffith, Bill, Nationwide Displays Inc, Ronkonkoma, NY. Tel: (631) 467-2034, FAX: (631) 467-2079, E-Mail: info@nationwidedisplays.com, Web Site: www.nationwidedisplays.com (16)

Griffith, Kimberly, Young Pecan Co, Florence, SC. Tel: (843) 662-8591, (800) 829-6864, FAX: (843) 664-2344, E-Mail: sales@youngpecan.com, Web Site: www.youngpecan.com (4)

Griffith, Nancy, Aviation Book Co, Seattle, WA. Tel: (206) 767-5232, FAX: (206) 763-3428, E-Mail: sales@aviationbook.com, Web Site: www.aviationbook.com (17)

Griffith, Ray, A., Ace Hardware Corp, Oak Brook, IL. Tel: (630) 990-6600, FAX: (630) 990-6838, Web Site: www.acehardware.com (16)

Griffith, Richard, Commercial Travelers Mutual Insurance Co, Utica, NY. Tel: (315) 797-5200, (800) 422-6200, FAX: (315) 797-3198, E-Mail: comtravl@commercialtravelers.com, Web Site: www.commercialtravelers.com (15)

Griffith, Scott, Voyageur Inc, Easley, SC. Tel: (802) 496-3127, (800) 311-7245, FAX: (802) 496-6247 (11)

Griffith, Steve, Nationwide Displays Inc, Ronkonkoma, NY. Tel: (631) 467-2034, FAX: (631) 467-2079, E-Mail: info@nationwidedisplays.com, Web Site: www.nationwidedisplays.com (16)

Griffiths, William, D., Eberle & Associates Inc, McLean, VA. Tel: (703) 821-1550, FAX: (703) 821-0920, E-Mail: info@eberle1.com, Web Site: www.eberleassociates.com (1)

Griggs, Brent, Protective Life Corp, Deerfield, IL. Tel: (847) 948-8988, (800) 323-5771, FAX: (847) 948-1156, Web Site: www.protective.com (15)

Grijalva, Arthur, Adwest Mailers Inc, Northridge, CA. Tel: (818) 982-3720, FAX: (818) 982-3786, E-Mail: sales@adwest.com, Web Site: www.adwest.com (28)

Grijalva, Frank, Adwest Mailers Inc, Northridge, CA. Tel: (818) 982-3720, FAX: (818) 982-3786, E-Mail: sales@adwest.com, Web Site: www.adwest.com (28)

Grill, John, WorleyParsons, Reading, PA. Tel: (610) 855-2000, FAX: (610) 885-2001, Web Site: www.worleyparsons.com (16)

Grillos, John, Oxford University Press Inc, New York, NY. Tel: (212) 726-6000, FAX: (212) 726-6455, Web Site: www.oup.com/us/ (17)

Grimes, Brian, Plastic Graphic, Wauconda, IL. Tel: (847) 487-2030, FAX: (847) 487-2050, E-Mail: bgrimespgc@sbcglobal.net, Web Site: www.plasticgraphic.com (27)

Grimes, Gary, S., Grimes Seeds and Plants, Concord, OH. Tel: (800) 241-7333, FAX: (440) 352-1800, Web Site: www.grimesseeds.com (8)

Grimes Seeds and Plants, Concord, OH. Tel: (800) 241-7333, FAX: (440) 352-1800, Web Site: www.grimesseeds.com (8)

Grimm, Foster, Video Artists International, Pleasantville, NY. Tel: (914) 769-3691, (800) 477-7146, FAX: (914) 769-5407, E-Mail: orders@vaimusic.com, Web Site: www.vaimusic.com (3)

Grimmett, Jerry, Collin Street Bakery, Corsicana, TX. Tel: (800) 292-7400, Web Site: www.collinstreetbakery.com (4)

Grindle, Dan, ElectroWarmth Products LLC, Danville, OH. Tel: (740) 599-7222, (800) 990-4622, FAX: (740) 599-6848, E-Mail: sales@electrowarmth.com, Web Site: www.electrowarmth.com (8)

Grindle, Larry, ElectroWarmth Products LLC, Danville, OH. Tel: (740) 599-7222, (800) 990-4622, FAX: (740) 599-6848, E-Mail: sales@electrowarmth.com, Web Site: www.electrowarmth.com (8)

Grinnell, Maureen, Eddy, Beyond Quota LLC, Lake Forest, IL. Tel: (847) 234-9475, FAX: (847) 234-5260, E-Mail: megrinnell@beyondquota.com, Web Site: www.beyondquota.com (35)

Grissom, Kathleen, Luzier Personalized Cosmetics, Kansas City, MO. Tel: (816) 531-8338, (800) 821-6632, FAX: (816) 531-6979, Web Site: www.luzier.com (7)

Griswald, Marlee, Patagonia Mail Order Inc, Reno, NV. Tel: (775) 747-1992, (800) 638-6464, FAX: (775) 747-6159, Web Site: www.patagonia.com (2)

Griswell, J., Barry, The Principal Financial Group, Des Moines, IA. Tel: (515) 247-5111, (800) 986-3343, FAX: (515) 246-5475, Web Site: www.principal.com (15)

Gritzmacher, John, Herrschners Inc, Stevens Point, WI. Tel: (715) 341-4554, (800) 441-0838, FAX: (715) 341-2250, E-Mail: customerservice@herrschners.com, Web Site: www.herrschners.com (11)

Grizzard, Chip, Grizzard Communications Group Inc, Atlanta, GA. Tel: (404) 522-8330, Web Site: www.grizzard.com (35)

Grizzard Advertising, Glendale, CA. Tel: (818) 325-4892, (800) 241-9351, FAX: (818) 543-1308, Web Site: www.grizzard.com (35)

Grizzard Communications Group Inc, Atlanta, GA. Tel: (404) 522-8330, Web Site: www.grizzard.com (35)

Grizzly Industrial Inc, Bellingham, WA. Tel: (360) 647-0801, (800) 523-4777, FAX: (360) 671-8375, E-Mail: csr@grizzly.com, Web Site: www.grizzly.com (9)

Grodd, Clifford, Paul Stuart, New York, NY. Tel: (212) 682-0320, FAX: (212) 983-5871, E-Mail: info@paulstuart.com, Web Site: www.paulstuart.com (2)

Grodecki, Lawrence, McFayden/McConnell, Brandon, MB Canada. Tel: (800) 205-7111, FAX: (877) 625-1888, Web Site: www.mcfayden.com (8)

Grodsky, Mark, Rich Brands, Phoenix, AZ. Tel: (602) 889-4800, (877) 856-1753, FAX: (602) 889-4830, E-Mail: sales@esscentualbrands.com, Web Site: esscentualbrands.com (16)

Groeninger, Steve, Magnaflux, Glenview, IL. Tel: (847) 657-5300, FAX: (847) 657-5388, Web Site: www.magnaflux.com (16)

Van Groesbeck & Co, Richmond, VA. Tel: (804) 285-3176, Web Site: www.vangroesbeckco.com (1)

Groetsch, Dave, Stolle Machinery LLC, Centennial, CO. Tel: (303) 708-9044, (800) 228-4593, FAX: (303) 708-9045, E-Mail: cmd.info@stollemachinery.com, Web Site: www.stollemachinery.com (34)

Groff, Reginald, Groff DRTV, Portland, ME. Tel: (207) 415-1374, FAX: (207) 771-5320, E-Mail: regfilm@gmail.com, Web Site: www.groffvideo.com (32)

Groff DRTV, Portland, ME. Tel: (207) 415-1374, FAX: (207) 771-5320, E-Mail: regfilm@gmail.com, Web Site: www.groffvideo.com (32)

Grogan, John, MBI Direct Mail, Deland, FL. Tel: (386) 736-9998, Web Site: www.directmail-mbi.com (28)

Grolier Publishing, Danbury, CT. Tel: (203) 797-3500, (800) 621-1115, FAX: (203) 797-3720, Web Site: www.grolier.com (17)

Gromek, Joseph, Warnaco, New York, NY. Tel: (212) 287-8207, FAX: (212) 682-7368, E-Mail: contactus@warnaco.com, Web Site: www.warnaco.com (2)

Groom, Judy, Computerized Research & Development Inc, Granite Bay, CA. Tel: (916) 652-0497, Web Site: www.computerizedresearch.com (23)

Grosch, Greg, White Cap Wholesale Contractors Supplies, Costa Mesa, CA. Tel: (800) 944-8322, FAX: (866) 791-8396, E-Mail: customerservice@whitecap.com, Web Site: www.whitecapdirect.com (16)

Gross, Adam, The Jordan Edmiston Group Inc, New York, NY. Tel: (212) 754-0710, Web Site: www.jegi.com (14)

Gross, Art, Day-Timers, Macungie, PA. Tel: (610) 398-1151, (800) 457-5702, (800) 225-5005, FAX: (800) 452-7398, E-Mail: connie@lomottastrategic.com, Web Site: www.daytimer.com (13)

Gross, Larry, Carolina Biological Supply Co, Burlington, NC. Tel: (800) 334-5551, (800) 222-7112, E-Mail: carolina@carolina.com, Web Site: www.carolina.com (9)

Gross, Martin, Martin Gross & Friends, New York, NY. Tel: (212) 689-0772, FAX: (212) 481-0552, E-Mail: grossdirect@aol.com (39)

Gross, Shirley, Image Direct, Los Angeles, CA. Tel: (310) 312-4884 (32)

Gross-Goldberg, Luella, ING, Minneapolis, MN. Tel: (612) 342-7061, (800) 333-6965, FAX: (612) 372-5339, Web Site: www.ing.com (15)

Grossblatt, Harvey B., Universal Security Instruments Inc, Owings Mills, MD. Tel: (410) 363-3000, FAX: (410) 363-2218, E-Mail: sales@universalsecurity.com, Web Site: www.universalsecurity.com (16)

Grossman M.D., Robert, I., New York University Medical Center, New York, NY. Tel: (212) 263-7800, FAX: (212) 263-8426, Web Site: www.med.nyu.edu (1)

Grossman, Bernice, DMRS Group Inc, New York, NY. Tel: (212) 590-2340, FAX: (212) 590-2341, E-Mail: bgrossman@dmrsgroup.com, Web Site: www.dmrsgroup.com (22)

Grossman, Gordon W., Gordon W Grossman Inc, Pound Ridge, NY. Tel: (914) 238-9387, FAX: (914) 238-1635 (20)

Grossman, Henry, Henry Grossman, New York, NY. Tel: (212) 580-7751 (37)

Grossman, Martin, A., ITT Educational Services Inc, Carmel, IN. Tel: (317) 706-9200, E-Mail: gtanner@itt-tech.edu, Web Site: www.itt-tech.edu (16)

Grossman, Mindy, F., Improvements, West Chester, OH. Tel: (216) 591-9148, (800) 634-9484, FAX: (216) 831-4026, Web Site: www.improvementscatalog.com (8)

Grossman, Mindy, HSN Inc, Saint Petersburg, FL. Tel: (727) 872-1000, (800) 284-3100, Web Site: www.hsn.com (5)

Gordon W Grossman Inc, Pound Ridge, NY. Tel: (914) 238-9387, FAX: (914) 238-1635 (20)

Henry Grossman, New York, NY. Tel: (212) 580-7751 (37)

Grosvenor, Gilbert, National Geographic Society, Washington, DC. Tel: (202) 857-7311, (800) NGS-LINE, FAX: (202) 457-8200, Web Site: www.nationalgeographic.com (17)

Grotell, Al, Al Grotell, Underwater Photography, New York, NY. Tel: (212) 349-3165, FAX: (212) 349-4363 (38)

Al Grotell, Underwater Photography, New York, NY. Tel: (212) 349-3165, FAX: (212) 349-4363 (38)

Grothe, Chris, Prism Marketing Group, Schaller, IA. Tel: (800) 862-4827, FAX: (712) 275-4855, E-Mail: cjgrothe@schallertel.net, Web Site: www.prismktg.com (29)

Ground Truth, New York, NY. Tel: (212) 851-4000 (21)

Grounds, Deborah, Financial Publishing Co, South Bend, IN. Tel: (800) 247-3214, FAX: (574) 243-6060, Web Site: www.financial-publishing.com (17)

Group f/64, Winston-Salem, NC. Tel: (336) 748-8272, FAX: (336) 748-8780 (20)

Group M Inc, Nyack, NY. Tel: (201) 227-0747, E-Mail: gmi.prm@gmail.com, Web Site: www.groupm.org (35)

Group Mojo, Portland, OR. Tel: (503) 493-2242, FAX: (503) 493-2246, E-Mail: sam@mojops.com, Web Site: www.groupmojo.com (32)

Group O Inc, Milan, IL. Tel: (309) 736-8300, Web Site: www.groupo.com (30)

Group 1 Software Inc, Lanham, MD. Tel: (301) 731-2300, (888) 413-6763, FAX: (301) 731-0360, E-Mail: info@g1.com, Web Site: www.g1.com (22)

Group 3 Marketing, Wayzata, MN. Tel: (952) 475-3269, (888) 571-6554, FAX: (952) 449-0403, E-Mail: info@group3marketing.com, Web Site: www.group3marketing.com (20)

Group2Marketing, Medford, OR. Tel: (541) 734-2565, Web Site: www.group2marketing.net (29)

GroupLevinson, Philadelphia, PA. Tel: (215) 627-3030, Web Site: grouplevinson.com (35)

GroupM Direct, New York, NY. Tel: (212) 474-0830, Web Site: www.groupm.com (35)

Grove, Judy A., Grove Enterprises Inc, Brasstown, NC. Tel: (828) 837-9200, (800) 438-8155, FAX: (828) 837-2216, E-Mail: judy@grove-ent.com, Web Site: www.grove-ent.com (16)

Grove, Laurel, Rapid City Journal, Rapid City, SD. Tel: (605) 394-8300, FAX: (605) 394-8462, E-Mail: classifieds@rapidcityjournal.com, Web Site: www.rapidcityjournal.com (18)

Grove, Robert, Grove Enterprises Inc, Brasstown, NC. Tel: (828) 837-9200, (800) 438-8155, FAX: (828) 837-2216, E-Mail: judy@grove-ent.com, Web Site: www.grove-ent.com (16)

Grove Communications, Crystal Lake, IL. Tel: (312) 884-0270, FAX: (312) 884-0275, Web Site: www.grovecommunications.com (35)

Grove Enterprises Inc, Brasstown, NC. Tel: (828) 837-9200, (800) 438-8155, FAX: (828) 837-2216, E-Mail: judy@grove-ent.com, Web Site: www.grove-ent.com (16)

Groveman, George, Audio-Digest Foundation, Glendale, CA. Tel: (818) 240-7500, (800) 423-2308, FAX: (818) 240-7379, Web Site: www.audio-digest.org (1)

Grover, John, Grover Co, Mesa, AZ. Tel: (480) 827-8011, FAX: (480) 827-8014 (16)

Grover, Rande, Grover Co, Mesa, AZ. Tel: (480) 827-8011, FAX: (480) 827-8014 (16)

Grover Co, Mesa, AZ. Tel: (480) 827-8011, FAX: (480) 827-8014 (16)

Groves, David, PHE Inc, Hillsborough, NC. Tel: (919) 644-8100, (800) 293-4654, FAX: (919) 644-8150, E-Mail: custserv@adameve.com (5)

Grow Communications, Coquitlam, BC Canada. Tel: (778) 822-0431, Web Site: www.growcommunications.com (35)

Grower's Supply Co, Dexter, MI. Tel: (734) 426-5852, FAX: (734) 426-5750, E-Mail: growers@grower-supply.com, Web Site: www.growerssupplycompany.com (8)

Growing Child, Inc, West Lafayette, IN. Tel: (765) 464-0920, (800) 927-7289, FAX: (765) 423-4495, E-Mail: service@growingchild.com, Web Site: www.growingchild.com (17)

Growing Family Portraits, Seattle, WA. Tel: (206) 587-0333, Web Site: www.silversand.com (16)

Growth Platforms Institute, Wilton, CT. Tel: (203) 529-0500, E-Mail: info@growthplatforms.org, Web Site: www.growthplatforms.org (20)

Grozier, Scott A., State Line Tack Inc, Phoenix, AZ. Tel: (623) 580-6100, (800) 228-9208, FAX: (623) 580-6183, E-Mail: customerservice@statelinetack.com, Web Site: www.statelinetack.com (16)

Gruaz, Bruno, DoAll Co, Wheeling, IL. Tel: (847) 824-1122, (800) 92-DOALL, FAX: (847) 699-7524, E-Mail: info@doall.com, Web Site: www.doall.com (16)

Gruber, Andrew, JS Eliezer Associates Inc, Stamford, CT. Tel: (203) 658-1300 (20)

Gruber, David, Fran's Basket House, Inc, Succasunna, NJ. Tel: (973) 584-2230, (800) 372-6799, FAX: (973) 584-7446, E-Mail: inquiry@franswicker.com, Web Site: www.franswicker.com (8)

Gruber, Donna, Queens College/CUNY Professional and Continuing Studies (PCS), Flushing, NY. Tel: (718) 997-5700, FAX: (718) 997-5723, E-Mail: pcs@qc.cuny.edu, Web Site: www.qc.cuny.edu/pcs (41)

Gruber, J.H., Gruber & Allison Inc, Boynton Beach, FL. Tel: (561) 752-9960, FAX: (561) 752-0085 (17)

Gruber, John, Wenner Media LLC, New York, NY. Tel: (212) 484-1616, FAX: (212) 484-1713 (17)

Gruber, Philip, Inkwell Inc, Cresco, PA. Tel: (570) 595-3344, E-Mail: philip@inkwellinc.com (36)

Gruber & Allison Inc, Boynton Beach, FL. Tel: (561) 752-9960, FAX: (561) 752-0085 (17)

Grubman, James, Media Printing Corp, Pompano Beach, FL. Tel: (954) 984-7300, FAX: (954) 888-8542 (27)

Grucci, Vincent, CGT Marketing, Amityville, NY. Tel: (631) 842-4600, FAX: (631) 842-6301, Web Site: www.cgtmarketing.com (21)

Grudnowski, Tom, Sara Isaac, Saint Paul, MN. Tel: (651) 482-8593, FAX: (651) 481-8077, Web Site: www.saraisaac.com (22)

Grudy, J., Lee, Strang Communications Co, Lake Mary, FL. Tel: (407) 333-0600, FAX: (407) 333-7100, E-Mail: magcustsvc@strang.com, Web Site: www.strang.com (17)

Grunebach, Steve, PRO Chemical & Dye Inc, Fall River, MA. Tel: (508) 676-3838, FAX: (508) 676-3980, Web Site: www.prochemicalanddye.com (10)

Grunsten, Richard, GSP Marketing Services, Chicago, IL. Tel: (312) 944-3000, FAX: (312) 944-8587, E-Mail: mikes@gspmarketing.com, Web Site: www.gspmarketing.com (35)

Gruppo, Claire, Gruppo Levey & Co, New York, NY. Tel: (212) 697-5753, FAX: (212) 949-7294, E-Mail: info@glconline.com, Web Site: www.glconline.com (14)

Gruppo Levey & Co, New York, NY. Tel: (212) 697-5753, FAX: (212) 949-7294, E-Mail: info@glconline.com, Web Site: www.glconline.com (14)

Grzelewski, Robert, Grove Communications, Crystal Lake, IL. Tel: (312) 884-0270, FAX: (312) 884-0275, Web Site: www.grovecommunications.com (35)

Grzywa, Tom, The Miller Group, Dupo, IL. Tel: (636) 343-5700, (800) 325-3350, FAX: (618) 286-6202, E-Mail: info@miller-group.com, Web Site: www. multiplexdisplays.com (5)

Guarantee Trust Life Insurance Co, Glenview, IL. Tel: (847) 299-0670, FAX: (847) 298-1215, E-Mail: pr@gtlic.com, Web Site: www.gtlic.com (15)

Guaranty Bank, Brown Deer, WI. Tel: (414) 362-4636, (800) 235-4636, Web Site: www.guarantybank.com (14)

Guarderas, Darwin, Direct Market Designs Inc, Paterson, NJ. Tel: (973) 925-9600, Web Site: www. dmd-liberty.com (28)

Guarderas, Ligia, Liberty Envelope Inc, Paterson, NJ. Tel: (973) 546-5600, FAX: (973) 546-4721 (26)

The Guardian Life Insurance Co, New York, NY. Tel: (212) 598-8000, Web Site: www.guardianlife.com (15)

Guarrera, F., J., Trans Union Corp, Chicago, IL. Tel: (312) 258-1717, (800) 335-9888, FAX: (312) 466-8385, Web Site: www.transunion.com (14)

Guastaferro, Denny, The Pennysaver Group Inc, Hanover, MD. Tel: (410) 684-2600, FAX: (410) 684-2065, Web Site: www.mdpennysaver.com (17)

Gudat, Sandra, Customer Communications Group, Lakewood, CO. Tel: (303) 986-3000, (800) 525-0313, FAX: (303) 989-4805, E-Mail: info@ customer.com, Web Site: www.customer.com (35)

Guercio, Alfred, Ulano Corp, Brooklyn, NY. Tel: (718) 237-4700, (800) 221-0616, FAX: (718) 802-1119, E-Mail: ulano@ulano.com, Web Site: www. ulano.com (34)

Guerra Jr., Michael, J., Benton Announcements Inc, Buffalo, NY. Tel: (716) 836-4100, FAX: (716) 836-4161 (27)

Guerra Sr., Michael, J., Benton Announcements Inc, Buffalo, NY. Tel: (716) 836-4100, FAX: (716) 836-4161 (27)

Guerra, Maria, Crystek Corp, Fort Myers, FL. Tel: (239) 561-3311, (800) 237-3061, FAX: (239) 561-1025, E-Mail: sales@crystek.com, Web Site: www. crystek.com (9)

Guerra, Philip, J., Benton Announcements Inc, Buffalo, NY. Tel: (716) 836-4100, FAX: (716) 836-4161 (27)

Guerrero, Penny, Greenbook Worldwide Directory of Marketing Research Companies & Services, Bradenton, FL. Tel: (212) 849-2752, (800) 792-9202, FAX: (212) 202-7920, E-Mail: info@ greenbrook.org, Web Site: www.greenbook.org (43)

Guerriero, Tracy, Thurston Moore Country Ltd, Madison, TN. Tel: (615) 868-7448, FAX: (615) 868-3738 (16)

Guertin, Timothy, E., Varian Medical Systems, Palo Alto, CA. Tel: (650) 493-4000, FAX: (650) 842-5196, Web Site: www.varian.com (9)

Guess, Erica, Boston Gift Show, Kennesaw, GA. Tel: (678) 285-3976, (800) 272-SHOW, FAX: (678) 285-7469, Web Site: www.bostongiftshow.com (42)

Guest, Gregory, Georgia-Pacific Corp LLC, Atlanta, GA. Tel: (404) 652-4000, Web Site: www.gp.com (25)

Guevara, Mario, BIC Corp, Shelton, CT. Tel: (203) 783-2000, FAX: (203) 783-2081, Web Site: www. bicworld.com (16)

Gugalal, Dave, Sandy Corp, Troy, MI. Tel: (800) 733-4739, FAX: (248) 729-4701, E-Mail: info@ sandycorp.com, Web Site: www.sandycorp.com (16)

Guice, Rev. Gregory, Unity School of Christianity, Unity Village, MO. Tel: (816) 254-3550, FAX: (816) 251-3554, E-Mail: unity@unityonline.org, Web Site: www.unityonline.org (17)

Guida, Kent, Houston Direct Marketing Association, Houston, TX. Tel: (281) 931-8883, FAX: (281) 820-4023, Web Site: www.houstondma.org (40)

Guidance Associates, Mount Kisco, NY. Tel: (914) 666-4100, (800) 431-1242, FAX: (914) 666-5319, E-Mail: willg1961@gmail.com, Web Site: www. guidanceassociates.com (31)

Guide to American & International Directories, Delray Beach, FL. Tel: (561) 367-3799, FAX: (561) 451-0803, E-Mail: bkleinpub@aol.com (43)

Guideline, New York, NY. Tel: (212) 645-4500, (866) GUIDELINE, FAX: (212) 645-7681, Web Site: www.findsvp.com (30)

Guideline Research Corp, New York, NY. Tel: (212) 947-5140, FAX: (212) 629-0061, Web Site: www. guidelineresearch.com (30)

Guideline Washington DC, Washington, DC. Tel: (703) 312-6004, (866) GUIDELINE, E-Mail: fdudley@guideline.com, Web Site: www.guideline. com (30)

GuideOne Insurance, West Des Moines, IA. Tel: (877) 448-4331, Web Site: www.guideone.com (15)

Guideposts, Danbury, CT. Tel: (845) 225-3681, FAX: (845) 228-2056, Web Site: www.guideposts.org (1)

Guiding Eyes for the Blind, Yorktown Heights, NY. Tel: (914) 245-4042, (800) 942-0149, FAX: (914) 245-1609, Web Site: www.guidingeyes.org (16)

Guido III, Umberto, Peter Glenn Publications, Delray Beach, FL. Tel: (561) 404-4290, (888) 332-6700, FAX: (561) 892-5786, E-Mail: gregjames@ pgdirect.com, Web Site: www.pgdirect.com (17)

Guignon III, Paul, C., The Envelope Man Plus, Kansas City, MO. Tel: (816) 474-5555, (800) 597-1099, FAX: (816) 221-3700, E-Mail: sales@ envelopeman.com, Web Site: www.envelopeman. com (26)

Guild, Joshua, Sierra Scientific Inc, Phoenix, AZ. Tel: (602) 256-0540, FAX: (602) 252-1972, Web Site: www.value-tek.com (9)

The Guild Co, Philadelphia, PA. Tel: (201) 750-3222, FAX: (201) 750-4961, E-Mail: mmi-guild@ mailmkt.com, Web Site: www.mailmkt.com (23)

The Guild Inc, Madison, WI. Tel: (608) 257-2590, Web Site: www.guild.com (8)

Guilford Publications Inc, New York, NY. Tel: (212) 431-9800, (800) 365-7006, FAX: (212) 966-6708, E-Mail: info@guilford.com, Web Site: www. guilford.com (17)

Guiliano, Edward, School of Management, Old Westbury, NY. Tel: (516) 686-1000, (800) 345-NYIT, (800) 345-6948, Web Site: www.nyit.edu (41)

Guiliano, Vincent, Valassis, Windsor, CT. Tel: (860) 285-6100, FAX: (203) 845-5338, Web Site: www. valassis.com (31)

Guinasso, Vick, DHL Express, Plantation, FL. Tel: (954) 888-7000, (800) 225-5345, FAX: (954) 888-7310, Web Site: www.dhl.com (28)

Guiney, Alice, Things Remembered, Highland Heights, OH. Tel: (440) 473-2000, (866) 902-4438, FAX: (440) 473-2018, E-Mail: customerservice@ thingsremembered.com, Web Site: www. thingsremembered.com (6)

Gujral, Robert, AMVETS National Service Foundation, Lanham, MD. Tel: (301) 459-6181, (877) 726-8387, FAX: (301) 459-5578, Web Site: www. amvets.org (1)

Gulam, Ray, MARKOTS, Menlo Park, CA. Tel: (925) 240-0093, Web Site: www.markots.com (35)

Gulbenkian Jr., Ed, Gulbenkian Swim Inc, Danbury, CT. Tel: (203) 790-0800, (800) 431-2586, FAX: (203) 791-1449, Web Site: www.gulbenkianswim. com (33)

Gulbenkian Swim Inc, Danbury, CT. Tel: (203) 790-0800, (800) 431-2586, FAX: (203) 791-1449, Web Site: www.gulbenkianswim.com (33)

Gulden, Dan, Outdoor Research, Seattle, WA. Tel: (206) 467-8197, (888) 467-4327, FAX: (206) 467-0374, Web Site: www.outdoorresearch.com (11)

Gulf Coast Data Supply Inc, Milton, FL. Tel: (850) 994-7042, (800) 226-DISK, FAX: (850) 479-4441, Web Site: www.gulfdata.com (3)

Gulf Coast List Service, Tampa, FL. Tel: (813) 962-3594, FAX: (813) 907-8463, E-Mail: tg@ gulfcoastlist.com (23)

Gulf Publishing Co, Houston, TX. Tel: (713) 529-4301, FAX: (713) 520-4433, E-Mail: publications@gulfpub.com, Web Site: www. gulfpub.com (17)

Gulfstream Aircraft Inc, Savannah, GA. Tel: (912) 965-5300, FAX: (912) 965-3775, E-Mail: info@ gulfstream.com, Web Site: www.gulfstream.com (16)

Guliano, Neil, Petco Animal Supplies, San Diego, CA. Tel: (858) 453-7845, (877) 738-6742, FAX: (858) 453-6585, Web Site: www.petco.com (5)

Gullette, Fred, Book News Inc, Portland, OR. Tel: (503) 281-9230, FAX: (503) 287-4485, E-Mail: booknews@booknews.com (43)

Gulley, Rick, Zoological Society of San Diego, San Diego, CA. Tel: (619) 231-1515, FAX: (619) 557-3937, Web Site: www.sandiegozoo.org (1)

Gullickson, Michael, Jaypro Sports, Waterford, CT. Tel: (860) 447-3001, (800) 243-0533, FAX: (800) 988-3363, E-Mail: info@jaypro.com, Web Site: www.jaypro.com (11)

Gulmi, James, S., Genesco Inc, Nashville, TN. Tel: (615) 367-7000, (888) 324-6189, FAX: (615) 367-8278, Web Site: www.genesco.com (2)

Gumas, John, Gumas Advertising, San Francisco, CA. Tel: (415) 621-7575, FAX: (415) 255-8804, E-Mail: jgumas@gumas.com, Web Site: www. gumas.com (35)

Gumas Advertising, San Francisco, CA. Tel: (415) 621-7575, FAX: (415) 255-8804, E-Mail: jgumas@ gumas.com, Web Site: www.gumas.com (35)

Gumbert, Jerry, Audience Research & Development, Fort Worth, TX. Tel: (817) 924-6922, FAX: (817) 924-7539, E-Mail: jgumbert@ar-d.com, Web Site: www.ar-d.com (20)

Gumbleton, Mary, Clare, Concepts & Strategies Inc, Washington, DC. Tel: (202) 251-9951, FAX: (202) 478-1750, E-Mail: info@constrat.net (35)

Gummed Papers of America, Mc Cook, IL. Tel: (773) 650-2020, (800) 395-9000, FAX: (708) 485-8603, (800) 395-3581, E-Mail: info@labelexperts.com, Web Site: www.labelexperts.com (34)

Gummesson, Charlotte, Teleperformance Canada, Toronto, ON. Tel: (416) 922-3519, Web Site: www. teleperformance.ca (35)

Gump's By Mail Inc, San Francisco, CA. Tel: (415) 982-1616, (800) 882-8055, FAX: (800) 984-9361, Web Site: www.gumpsbymail.com (6)

Gun Video Catalog/LMP, San Diego, CA. Tel: (858) 569-4000, (800) 942-8273, FAX: (858) 569-0505, Web Site: www.gunvideo.com; www.glockstore. com (11)

Gunasekaram, Kishan, The Helicopter Group, Richmond Hill, ON Canada. Tel: (905) 731-2440, Web Site: www.thehelicoptergroup.com (28)

Gund, Agnes, The Museum of Modern Art, New York, NY. Tel: (212) 708-9400, FAX: (212) 333-1123, E-Mail: info@moma.org, Web Site: www.moma. org (5)

Gundersen, Jeff, Executive Connections LLC, Sarasota, FL. Tel: (941) 323-8300, Web Site: www. executiveconnectionsllc.com (20)

Gundersen, Steven, Gundersen Partners LLC, New York, NY. Tel: (212) 677-7660, FAX: (212) 358-0275, Web Site: www.gundersenpartners.com (20)

Gundersen Partners LLC, New York, NY. Tel: (212) 677-7660, FAX: (212) 358-0275, Web Site: www. gundersenpartners.com (20)

Gunleikscrud, Hans, Helly-Hansen, Auburn, WA. Tel: (800) 435-5901, FAX: (425) 649-3740, E-Mail: webmaster@hellyhansen.com, Web Site: www. hellyhansen.com (16)

Gunning, Pat, G&A Marketing, Milford, OH. Tel: (513) 965-6301, (800) 688-1370, E-Mail: info@ gamarketing.com, Web Site: www.gamarketing. com (35)

Gunst, Richard, M., The Quaker Oats Co, Chicago, IL. Tel: (312) 821-1000, (800) 367-6287, FAX: (312) 222-8323, Web Site: www.quakeroats.com (16)

Gunther, Kirk, IPS - Sendero Corp, Norcross, GA. Tel: (770) 409-0047, (800) 879-1996, FAX: (770) 409-1735, E-Mail: sales@ips-sendero.com, Web Site: www.ips-sendero.com (14)

Guntick, Michael, Alternative Marketing Solutions Inc, Phoenixville, PA. Tel: (610) 783-1320, FAX: (610) 783-1324, E-Mail: guntick@amsolutions. com, Web Site: www.amsolutions.com (21)

Gupta, Raj, L., Rohm & Haas Co, Philadelphia, PA. Tel: (215) 592-3000, (877) 288-5881, FAX: (215) 592-3377, Web Site: www.rohmhess.com (16)

Gupta, Vin, American Business Directories, Omaha, NE. Tel: (402) 593-4600, (800) 555-6124, FAX: (402) 596-0475, Web Site: www.infousa.com (43)

Gupta, Vinod, American Medical Information Inc, Omaha, NE. Tel: (402) 593-4500, (866) 241-9044, FAX: (402) 331-1505, E-Mail: support@drlists. com, Web Site: americanmedicalinfo.com (24)

Gupta, Vinod, Info USA City Directories, Omaha, NE. Tel: (402) 593-4500, (800) 925-4654, FAX: (402) 593-4671, E-Mail: customerservice@infousacity. com, Web Site: www.infousacity.com (17)

Gupta, Vinod, New Business USA, Omaha, NE. Tel: (800) 321-0869, FAX: (402) 331-0176, E-Mail: help@infousa.com, Web Site: www.infousa.com (23)

Gurgol, Margaret, Nestle Purina/Checkmark Communications, Saint Louis, MO. Tel: (314) 982-1000, FAX: (314) 982-3580, Web Site: www.purina.com (35)

Gurien, Alan, Nassau Community College, Garden City, NY. Tel: (516) 572-7501, E-Mail: marketing-communications@ncc.edu, Web Site: www.ncc.edu (41)

Gurin, Joel, Consumers Union, Yonkers, NY. Tel: (914) 378-2000, FAX: (914) 378-2906, Web Site: www.consumerreports.org (17)

Gurley, Wayne, Allegiant Direct Inc, Brentwood, TN. Tel: (615) 373-2042, FAX: (615) 373-2099, E-Mail: welcome@allegiantdirect.com, Web Site: www.allegiantdirect.com (35)

Gurn, Jim, MRI Norwalk, Pompano Beach, FL. Tel: (203) 926-1200, FAX: (203) 926-1211, E-Mail: jbgurn@mricoastalgroup.com, Web Site: www. mricoastalgroup.com (20)

Gurney, Larry, Fitness USA Super Centers, West Bloomfield, MI. Tel: (248) 737-7200, (800) GET-FIT-1, FAX: (248) 932-3300, Web Site: www. fitnessusa.com (16)

Gurshaney, Naren, K., ADT Worldwide, Boca Raton, FL. Tel: (561) 988-3600, FAX: (561) 988-3673, Web Site: www.tycofireandsecurity.com (16)

Gurtman, Arthur, GMG Productions Inc, Roslyn, NY. Tel: (516) 482-0022, FAX: (516) 482-0097, Web Site: www.gmgproductions.com (3)

Gurtman, Bernard, GMG Productions Inc, Roslyn, NY. Tel: (516) 482-0022, FAX: (516) 482-0097, Web Site: www.gmgproductions.com (3)

Gurtner, Thomas, Four Seasons Hotels & Resorts, Toronto, ON. Tel: (416) 449-1750, (800) 819-5053, FAX: (416) 441-4374, Web Site: www.fourseasons. com (19)

Gurzap, Ayse, Team Nash Inc, East Hampton, NY. Tel: (646) 497-0297, (631) 267-3385, E-Mail: results@ teamnash.com, Web Site: www.teamnash.com (35)

Guse, Hazel, Audio Editions Books-on-Cassette & CD, Auburn, CA. Tel: (800) 231-4261, FAX: (800) 882-1840, E-Mail: info@audioeditions.com, Web Site: www.audioeditions.com (3)

Guseinov, Gary, CyberDefender, Los Angeles, CA. Tel: (213) 689-8631x114, Web Site: www. cyberdefender.com (22)

Gusfield, Edward, Time Products International, Del Rio, TX. Tel: (847) 459-8885, FAX: (847) 459-8111, E-Mail: cttpi@aol.com, Web Site: www. tpi2000.com (16)

Gust, Daniel, Triplex, Washington, DC. Tel: (202) 887-8001, (866) 872-8099, FAX: (202) 887-8008, E-Mail: info@tdmc.com, Web Site: www.tdmc.com (22)

Gust, David, American Health & Safety Inc, Stoughton, WI. Tel: (630) 413-5662, (800) 522-7554, FAX: (800) 326-3245, Web Site: www.ahsafety. com (16)

Gustafsson, Magnus, Aerosoles, Edison, NJ. Tel: (732) 985-6900, FAX: (732) 985-3697, E-Mail: bgarris@ aerosoles.com, Web Site: www.aerosoles.com (2)

Gustavson, John, CMA Awards, Don Mills, ON Canada. Tel: (416) 391-2362, FAX: (416) 441-4062, E-Mail: info@the-cma.org, Web Site: www. the-cma.org/awards (42)

Gutai, Beatrice, Jafra Cosmetics International Inc, Westlake Village, CA. Tel: (805) 557-1889, (800) 551-2345, Web Site: www.jafra.com (7)

Guthrie, Bill, Brown Printing Co, New York, NY. Tel: (212) 782-7800, FAX: (212) 782-7878, E-Mail: contact.us@bpc.com, Web Site: www.bpc.com (27)

Guthrie, Mary, Cornell Lab of Ornithology, Ithaca, NY. Tel: (607) 254-2157, (800) 843-BIRD, FAX: (607) 254-2415, E-Mail: birdslides@cornell.edu, Web Site: www.birds.cornell.edu (1)

Guthrie, Mary, National Postal Forum, Fairfax, VA. Tel: (703) 218-5015, FAX: (703) 218-5020, E-Mail: info@npf.org, Web Site: www.npf.org (42)

Guthy-Renker Corp, Palm Desert, CA. Tel: (760) 773-9022, (800) 274-4910, FAX: (760) 773-9016, Web Site: www.guthy-renker.com (32)

Gutierrez, Mario, Nielsen Trade Dimensions, Wilton, CT. Tel: (203) 222-5750, (800) 291-0410, FAX: (203) 222-5701, E-Mail: tradedimensions.info@ nielsen.com, Web Site: www.tradedimensions.com (17)

Gutman, Amy, University of Pennsylvania, Philadelphia, PA. Tel: (215) 898-5000, FAX: (215) 898-9659, Web Site: www.upenn.edu (1)

Gutman, Luisa, Holy Cross Hospital, Fort Lauderdale, FL. Tel: (954) 771-8000, FAX: (954) 229-8597, Web Site: www.holy-cross.com (16)

Guttenberg, Edward, Foremost Industrial Exchange, Van Nuys, CA. Tel: (818) 988-6900, FAX: (818) 787-0293 (16)

Guttosch, Bob, Cole-Parmer Instrument Co, Vernon Hills, IL. Tel: (847) 549-7600, (800) 323-4340, FAX: (847) 247-2929, E-Mail: info@coleparmer. com, Web Site: www.coleparmer.com (16)

Guy, Dana, International Crystal Manufacturing Co, Oklahoma City, OK. Tel: (405) 236-3741, (800) 252-6780, FAX: (405) 235-1904, E-Mail: info@ icmfg.com, Web Site: www.icmfg.com (16)

Guyer, Ann, PCS List & Information Technologies, Manchester, MA. Tel: (978) 532-7100, (800) 532-LIST, FAX: (978) 532-9181, E-Mail: info@pcslist. com, Web Site: www.pcslist.com (23)

Guyer, Douglas, International Direct Response Inc, Berwyn, PA. Tel: (610) 993-0500, FAX: (610) 993-9938, E-Mail: idr@idronline.com, Web Site: www.idronline.com (23)

Guzman, Angela, Democratic Congressional Campaign Committee, Washington, DC. Tel: (202) 863-1500, FAX: (202) 485-3436, Web Site: www.dccc.org (1)

Guzman, Emanuel, Cengage Learning, Independence, KY. Tel: (800) 354-9706, FAX: (800) 487-8488, Web Site: www.delmar.com (17)

Guzman, Sergio, United Farm Workers of America, AFL-CIO, Keene, CA. Tel: (661) 823-6158, FAX: (661) 823-6177, E-Mail: execoffice@ufw.org, Web Site: www.ufw.org (1)

Gwaltney, John, Forestry Suppliers Inc, Jackson, MS. Tel: (601) 354-3565, (800) 543-4203, FAX: (601) 292-0165, E-Mail: fsi@forestry-suppliers.com, Web Site: www.forestry-suppliers.com (9)

The Gymboree Corp, San Francisco, CA. Tel: (877) 449-6932, Web Site: www.gymboree.com (2)

H

H & H Graphics, Lancaster, PA. Tel: (717) 393-3941, Web Site: www.hhgraphicsgroup.com (31)

H&M Associates, Danbury, CT. Tel: (203) 748-8248, FAX: (203) 792-9555 (33)

H&R Block Inc, Kansas City, MO. Tel: (816) 572-6446, (800) 472-5625, FAX: (816) 854-8500, Web Site: www.hrblock.com (14)

HR Direct Inc, Fairfield, IA. Tel: (641) 472-7188, FAX: (641) 472-5729, E-Mail: info@hrdirect.net, Web Site: www.hrdirect.net (23)

HB Communications, North Haven, CT. Tel: (203) 234-9246, (800) 243-4414, FAX: (203) 234-2013, E-Mail: info@hbcommunications.com, Web Site: www.hbcommunications.com (34)

HB Distributors, Chatsworth, CA. Tel: (818) 882-0000, (800) 266-3478, FAX: (818) 700-1808, Web Site: www.hddistributors.com (34)

HCI Direct, Bensalem, PA. Tel: (215) 244-9600, (888) 765-0062, FAX: (215) 244-0328, Web Site: www. silkies.com (16)

HD Supply, San Diego, CA. Tel: (858) 831-2000 (34)

HDA Inc, Saint Louis, MO. Tel: (314) 770-2222, (800) 533-4350, FAX: (314) 770-1454, E-Mail: plans@hdainc.com, Web Site: www.designamerica. com (17)

HDI Group, San Francisco, CA. Tel: (415) 794-3320, Web Site: www.hobbsdirect.com (20)

The Herald & Review, Decatur, IL. Tel: (217) 429-5151, FAX: (217) 421-6913, E-Mail: hrdirect@ herald-review.com, Web Site: www.herald-review. com (17)

HHC Direct, San Diego, CA. Tel: (800) 358-8765, FAX: (619) 220-0988, Web Site: www.hhcdirect. com (35)

HK Systems Inc, New Berlin, WI. Tel: (262) 860-7000, (800) HK SYSTEMS, FAX: (262) 860-7010, E-Mail: hkinfo@hksystems.com, Web Site: www. hksystems.com (34)

HMI Marketing, Brooklyn Park, MN. Tel: (800) 468-4144, FAX: (800) 468-8814, Web Site: www. hmimarketing.com (7)

HP Indigo & Inkjet Press Solutions, Scottsdale, AZ. Tel: (404) 427-7418 (16)

HR Direct, Sunrise, FL. Tel: (800) 346-1231, FAX: (800) 350-7760, Web Site: www.hrdirect.com (10)

HSBC Bank USA, NA, Buffalo, NY. Tel: (716) 841-2424, FAX: (716) 841-5391, Web Site: www. banking.us.hsbc.com (14)

HSN Inc, Saint Petersburg, FL. Tel: (727) 872-1000, (800) 284-3100, Web Site: www.hsn.com (5)

HSP Direct, Herndon, VA. Tel: (703) 793-3220, FAX: (703) 793-3221, Web Site: www.hspdirect.com (1)

Haaland, Mark, Telpro Inc, Grand Forks, ND. Tel: (701) 775-0551, FAX: (701) 775-0629 (9)

Haank, Derk, Springer Science & Business Media LLC, New York, NY. Tel: (212) 460-1500, FAX: (212) 473-6272, Web Site: www.springer-ny.com (17)

Haas, Mike, Guarantee Trust Life Insurance Co, Glenview, IL. Tel: (847) 298-0670, FAX: (847) 298-1215, E-Mail: pr@gtlic.com, Web Site: www.gtlic. com (15)

Haas, Pam, The Direct Marketing Club of New York Inc, Garden City, NY. Tel: (516) 746-6700, FAX: (516) 294-8141, E-Mail: info@dmcny.org, Web Site: www.dmcny.org (1)

Haas, Robert, D., Levi Strauss & Co, San Francisco, CA. Tel: (415) 501-6000, FAX: (415) 501-7112, Web Site: www.levistrauss.com (16)

Haband Co Inc, Oakland, NJ. Tel: (201) 651-1000, FAX: (201) 405-7777, Web Site: www.haband.com (2)

Habbee, John, The NH Broadcaster, Lowell, MA. Tel: (978) 458-7100, Web Site: www.nhbroadcaster.com (31)

Haber, Barry, Cuisinart, Stamford, CT. Tel: (203) 975-4600, FAX: (203) 975-4660, Web Site: www. cuisinart.com (16)

Haber, Jon, American Association for Justice, Washington, DC. Tel: (202) 965-3500, (800) 424-2725, FAX: (202) 625-7313, Web Site: www.justice.org (1)

Haber, Louis, Distribution Postal Co Inc, Baltimore, MD. Tel: (410) 488-1002, (800) 992-4525, FAX: (410) 488-2344, E-Mail: louishaber@distpost.com, Web Site: www.distpost.com (28)

Haber, Renee, Laughlin/Constable, Chicago, IL. Tel: (312) 422-5900, FAX: (312) 422-5901, Web Site: www.laughlin.com (35)

Haberman, Fern, The Dico Group Inc, Toluca Lake, CA. Tel: (323) 264-2000, FAX: (323) 264-2600 (27)

Habing, Cheryl, Mid America Designs Inc, Effingham, IL. Tel: (217) 540-4200, (800) 350-4543, FAX: (217) 540-4800, E-Mail: mail@mamotorworks. com, Web Site: www.mamotorworks.com (12)

Habitat For Humanity International, Americus, GA. Tel: (229) 924-6935, FAX: (229) 924-6541, Web Site: www.habitat.org (1)

Habyan, Bonnie, Arbor Commercial Mortgage, Union-dale, NY. Tel: (516) 229-6615, Web Site: www. thearbornet.com (14)

Habzda, Jim, Geiger Brothers, Lewiston, ME. Tel: (207) 755-2000, FAX: (207) 755-2422, E-Mail: ggeiger@geiger.com, Web Site: www.geiger.com (33)

Hachenburg, Candy, Dunhill International List Co Inc, Boca Raton, FL. Tel: (561) 998-7800, (800) 386-4455, FAX: (561) 998-7880, E-Mail: sales@ dunhills.com, Web Site: www.dunhills.com (23)

Hachette Filipacchi List Management, New York, NY. Tel: (212) 767-6677, FAX: (212) 767-5605, Web Site: www.hfmuslists.com (17)

Hack, Brian, Stephan Partners Inc, New York, NY. Tel: (212) 524-8583, E-Mail: george@ stephenpartners.com, Web Site: www. stephanpartners.com (35)

Hack, Rob, Oneida Ltd, Oneida, NY. Tel: (315) 361-3000, (888) 263-7195, FAX: (315) 361-3700, Web Site: www.oneida.com (16)

Hacker, Allison, International Sign Association Inter-national Convention, Alexandria, VA. Tel: (703) 836-4012, (866) WHY-SIGN, FAX: (703) 836-8353, Web Site: www.signs.org (42)

Hacker, Steven, IAEE Annual Meeting and Exhibition, Dallas, TX. Tel: (972) 458-8002, FAX: (972) 458-8119, E-Mail: info@iaee.com, Web Site: www. iaee.com (42)

Hacker Group Inc, Seattle, WA. Tel: (206) 805-1500, E-Mail: info@hackergroup.com, Web Site: www. hackergroup.com (35)

Hackett, Emily, T., The Internet Alliance, Washington, DC. Tel: (202) 861-2476, FAX: (202) 955-8081, E-Mail: info@internetalliance.org, Web Site: www. internetalliance.org (40)

Hackett, James, P., Steelcase Inc, Grand Rapids, MI. Tel: (616) 247-2710, FAX: (616) 475-2270, Web Site: www.steelcase.com (16)

Hadaway, David, Altair Data Resources, Franklin, TN. Tel: (615) 468-6800, (866) 261-4695, FAX: (615) 468-6878, E-Mail: info@altairdata.com, Web Site: www.altairdata.com (23)

Haddox, Darryl, Magnet LLC, Washington, MO. Tel: (636) 239-5661, (800) 458-9457, FAX: (636) 239-4490, E-Mail: contactus@themagnetgroup.com, Web Site: www.magnetllc.com (16)

Hadeed, Charles P., Transcat, Rochester, NY. Tel: (585) 352-9460, (800) 800-5001, FAX: (585) 352-1486, Web Site: www.transcat.com (16)

Hadley Fruit Orchards Inc, Cabazon, CA. Tel: (951) 849-4668, FAX: (951) 849-5255, Web Site: www. hadleys.com (4)

Haefling, Karen, Key Bank, Cleveland, OH. Tel: (216) 689-3000, (888) 539-2968, FAX: (207) 874-7044, Web Site: www.key.com (14)

Haefner, Bob, Stellar Technology Inc, Amherst, NY. Tel: (800) 274-1846, FAX: (716) 250-1909, E-Mail: info@stellartech.com, Web Site: www. stellartech.com (9)

Hafer, Matthew, HSP Direct, Herndon, VA. Tel: (703) 793-3220, FAX: (703) 793-3221, Web Site: www. hspdirect.com (1)

Hafford, Patrick, The Christian Science Publishing Society, Boston, MA. Tel: (617) 450-2000, E-Mail: info@christianscience.com, Web Site: www.tfccs. com (17)

Hagadasn, Becky, The Catamount Group, Southport, CT. Tel: (203) 778-4110, FAX: (203) 778-4130, E-Mail: tina@catamountgroup.net, Web Site: www. catamountgroup.net (23)

Hagadone Printing Co, Honolulu, HI. Tel: (808) 847-5310, (800) 491-4888, FAX: (808) 841-0094, E-Mail: sales@hagadoneprinting.com, Web Site: www.hagadoneprinting.com (27)

Hagale, Jim, Bass Pro Shops, Springfield, MO. Tel: (417) 873-5000, FAX: (417) 873-5882, Web Site: www.basspro.com (11)

Hagan, Michael, J., NutriSystem Inc, Fort Washington, PA. Tel: (215) 706-5300, (800) 321-THIN, FAX: (215) 706-5388, Web Site: www.nutrisystem.com (7)

Hagedorn, James, The Scotts Co Div of Lawn Service, Marysville, OH. Tel: (937) 644-0011, FAX: (937) 644-7261, Web Site: www.scotts.com (8)

Hagedorn, Jim, Scotts-Sierra Horticultural, Marysville, OH. Tel: (888) 270-3714, Web Site: www. scottscompany.com (16)

Hagee, Lisa, NCO Financial Systems, Horsham, PA. Tel: (215) 441-3000, (800) 220-2274, FAX: (215) 441-3923, E-Mail: marketing@ncogroup.com, Web Site: www.ncogroup.com (29)

Hagemeyer - North America, Charleston, SC. Tel: (843) 745-2400, FAX: (843) 745-6942, E-Mail: info@hagemeyerna.com, Web Site: www. hagemeyerna.com (16)

Hagen, Larry, Miller Stockman, Denver, CO. Tel: (303) 428-5696, FAX: (303) 430-1130 (2)

Hagen, Lisa, Elizabeth Arden Spas LLC, Stamford, CT. Tel: (203) 905-1700, FAX: (203) 905-1716, Web Site: www.reddoorspas.com (19)

Hagen, Paulette, Agco Spra-Coup, Duluth, GA. Tel: (320) 231-9400, FAX: (320) 231-9413, Web Site: www.agcocorp.com (16)

Hagen, Vickie, Omaha Creative Group Inc, Omaha, NE. Tel: (800) 228-2778, Web Site: www. omahasteaks.com (4)

Hagen, Vickie, Omaha Steaks Inc, Omaha, NE. Tel: (402) 597-3000, FAX: (402) 597-8252, E-Mail: info@omahasteaks.com, Web Site: www. omahasteaks.com (4)

Hageny, Colin, Business Marketing Association, Na-perville, IL. Tel: (630) 544-5054, FAX: (630) 544-5055, E-Mail: info@marketing.org, Web Site: www.marketing.org (40)

Hageny, Colin, Marketing News, Chicago, IL. Tel: (312) 542-9000, (800) 262-1150, FAX: (312) 542-9001, E-Mail: news@ama.org, Web Site: www. ama.org (43)

Hagerman, Douglas, M., Rockwell Automation, Mil-waukee, WI. Tel: (414) 382-2000, FAX: (414) 382-4444, Web Site: www.rockwellautomation.com (16)

Haggerty, Greg, Telecom Inc, Oakland, CA. Tel: (510) 873-8283, (800) 243-3101, FAX: (510) 873-8293, Web Site: www.telecominc.com (29)

Haggerty, Jim, Quark Inc, Denver, CO. Tel: (303) 894-3832, Web Site: www.quark.com (34)

Haggerty, Margaret, Adirondack Direct, Long Island City, NY. Tel: (718) 932-4003, (800) 221-2444, FAX: (800) 477-1330, E-Mail: info@ adirondackdirect.com, Web Site: www. adirondackdirect.com (10)

Haggerty, Michael, Physicians Planning Association Services, Deerfield Beach, FL. Tel: (954) 571-1877, (800) 221-2168, FAX: (954) 571-8582, E-Mail: insurance@assnservices.com, Web Site: www.physiciansplanning.com (16)

Haggstrom, Don, Russ Reid Co, Pasadena, CA. Tel: (626) 449-6100, FAX: (626) 449-6190, E-Mail: info@russreid.com, Web Site: www.russreid.com (35)

Hagie, John, Hagie Manufacturing Co, Clarion, IA. Tel: (515) 532-2861, (800) 247-4885, FAX: (515) 532-3553, E-Mail: info@hagie.com, Web Site: www.hagie.com (9)

Hagie Manufacturing Co, Clarion, IA. Tel: (515) 532-2861, (800) 247-4885, FAX: (515) 532-3553, E-Mail: info@hagie.com, Web Site: www.hagie. com (9)

Hagood, Louis, Oxbridge Communications Inc, New York, NY. Tel: (212) 741-0231, (800) 955-0231, FAX: (212) 633-2938, E-Mail: custserv@oxbridge. com, Web Site: www.mediafinder.com; www. oxbridge.com (30)

Hagood, Patricia, Oxbridge Communications Inc, New York, NY. Tel: (212) 741-0231, (800) 955-0231, FAX: (212) 633-2938, E-Mail: custserv@oxbridge. com, Web Site: www.mediafinder.com; www. oxbridge.com (30)

Hahn, Charles, J., Dow Chemical USA, Midland, MI. Tel: (989) 636-1000, (800) 447-4369, FAX: (989) 832-1465, E-Mail: jadams@dow.com, Web Site: www.dow.com (16)

Hahn, Fred, E., Hahn, Crane & Associates Advertising Inc, San Diego, CA. Tel: (858) 581-8561 (35)

Hahn, Lisa, C., Caugherty Hahn Communications, Glen Rock, NJ. Tel: (201) 251-7778, FAX: (201) 251-7779, Web Site: www.chcomm.com (16)

Hahn, Mark, FLM Graphics Corp, Fairfield, NJ. Tel: (973) 575-9450, E-Mail: info@flmgraphics.com, Web Site: www.flmgraphics.com (16)

Hahn, Crane & Associates Advertising Inc, San Diego, CA. Tel: (858) 581-8561 (35)

Hahs, Jennifer, Martin Williams Advertising, Minne-apolis, MN. Tel: (612) 342-9739, FAX: (612) 342-9700, Web Site: www.martinwilliams.com (35)

Haid, Brittany, MGM MIRAGE, Las Vegas, NV. Tel: (702) 693-8005, Web Site: www.mirageresorts.com (19)

Haight, Bill, Magna Publications Inc, Madison, WI. Tel: (608) 246-3580, FAX: (608) 246-3597, Web Site: www.magnapubs.com (17)

Hailey, V., Ann, LimitedBrands Inc, Reynoldsburg, OH. Tel: (614) 577-5902, FAX: (614) 415-7440, Web Site: www.limitedbrands.com (16)

Hain Celestial Group, Melville, NY. Tel: (631) 730-2200, FAX: (631) 730-2500, Web Site: www.hain-celestial.com (16)

Haines, Ken, Raycom Sports, Charlotte, NC. Tel: (704) 378-4456/4400, FAX: (704) 378-4465, E-Mail: whicks@raycomsports.com, Web Site: raycomsports.com (16)

Haining, Kevin, Direct Mail Trackers, Medford, NY. Tel: (631) 758-0984, E-Mail: info@dmtrackers. com, Web Site: www.dmtrackers.com (28)

Hajek, Ron, Jim Mersfelder & Associates Inc, Cleve-land, OH. Tel: (216) 574-9009, FAX: (216) 574-9721, Web Site: www.jma-usa.com (33)

Haker, Paul, Markgraf & Wells Marketing, Minneapo-lis, MN. Tel: (612) 870-8550 (35)

Hal Levy & Associates, High Falls, NY. Tel: (845) 687-4400 (20)

Halbur, Jim, Farm Home Offices, Richfield, MN. Tel: (612) 920-0907, (800) 788-7218, FAX: (866) 404-0257, Web Site: www.sylvette.com (10)

Haldy, Joe, Gazette Direct Marketing Co, Cedar Rap-ids, IA. Tel: (319) 399-5997, FAX: (319) 399-5998, Web Site: www.gazette.com (20)

Hale III, Stephen, Hale Indian River Groves Inc, Vero Beach, FL. Tel: (800) 356-7264, FAX: (877) 329-4253, E-Mail: marketing@halegroves.com, Web Site: www.hales.com (16)

Hale, Houston, Zouire, Overland Park, KS. Tel: (913) 384-6888, (800) 346-8991, FAX: (913) 384-5757, E-Mail: info@zouire.com, Web Site: www.zouire. com (33)

Hale, Michael, MT&L Card Products & Fulfillment Services, Nashville, TN. Tel: (615) 254-9471, Web Site: www.mtlcard.com (28)

Hale, Robert, Shipping Solutions, Eagan, MN. Tel: (651) 905-1727, (888) 890-7447, FAX: (651) 905-1827, E-Mail: info@shipsolutions.com, Web Site: www.shipsolutions.com (16)

Hale Indian River Groves Inc, Vero Beach, FL. Tel: (800) 356-7264, FAX: (877) 329-4253, E-Mail: marketing@halegroves.com, Web Site: www.hales.com (16)

Haley, Roy, W., WESCO, Pittsburgh, PA. Tel: (412) 454-2200, (800) 343-1201, E-Mail: info@wesco.com, Web Site: www.wescodist.com (16)

Robert Half International Inc, Menlo Park, CA. Tel: (650) 234-6000, FAX: (650) 234-6930, E-Mail: webmaster@rhi.com, Web Site: www.rhii.com (20)

Halkyard, Jonathan, S., Harrah's Marketing, Reno, NV. Tel: (775) 786-3232, FAX: (775) 722-2815, Web Site: www.harrahsreno.com (16)

Halkyard, Jonathon, S., Caesars Palace, Las Vegas, NV. Tel: (702) 407-6000, (800) 634-6001, FAX: (702) 407-6037, Web Site: www.caesars.com (16)

Hall Jr, O. B., Grayson, Regions, Birmingham, AL. Tel: (205) 326-5262, FAX: (205) 326-4072, Web Site: www.regions.com (14)

Hall, Anthony, ASH Recruitment Solutions, Exeter, NH. Tel: (603) 778-8888, E-Mail: t.hall@ashrecruit.com, Web Site: www.ashrecruit.com (20)

Hall, Brian, Westgroup, Eagan, MN. Tel: (800) 344-5008, Web Site: www.westgroup.com (17)

Hall, Bruce, C., Petco Animal Supplies, San Diego, CA. Tel: (858) 453-7845, (877) 738-6742, FAX: (858) 453-6585, Web Site: www.petco.com (5)

Hall, Douglas, B., Richard Saunders International, Cincinnati, OH. Tel: (513) 271-9911, FAX: (513) 271-9966, E-Mail: doug@eurekaranch.com, Web Site: www.eurekaranch.com (20)

Hall, Elizabeth, Haymarket Group Ltd, New York, NY. Tel: (212) 239-0855, FAX: (212) 967-4184, Web Site: www.chocalatiermagazine.com (17)

Hall, Erin, Thermal Product Solutions, White Deer, PA. Tel: (570) 538-7200, (800) 586-2473 (16)

Hall, Garrett, The Added Touch, Niagara Falls, NY. Tel: (905) 828-4041, (888) AD-TOUCH, FAX: (905) 338-1486, E-Mail: addedtouch@gmail.com, Web Site: www.addedtouch.com (28)

Hall, Jan, Partners Village Store, Westport, MA. Tel: (508) 636-2572, FAX: (508) 636-2529, E-Mail: info@partnersvillagestore.com, Web Site: www.partnersvillagestore.com (11)

Hall, Jason, TMone, Iowa City, IA. Tel: (868) 577-2461, E-Mail: srteam@tmone.com, Web Site: www.tmone.com (29)

Hall, Les, Reynolds & Reynolds Co, Houston, TX. Tel: (713) 718-1800, (800) 231-6347, FAX: (713) 718-1471, Web Site: www.reyrey.com (22)

Hall, Mary, Physical Therapy Institute Inc, Poway, CA. Tel: (858) 485-7103 (16)

Hall, Michael, E., Fidelity Security Life Insurance Co, Kansas City, MO. Tel: (816) 756-1060, (800) 648-8624, FAX: (816) 968-0580, E-Mail: info@fslins.com, Web Site: www.fslins.com (15)

Hall, Paul, Mastery Marketing Group, Dublin, OH. Tel: (703) 938-0101, (203) 544-8997, (800) MKT-0121, FAX: (203) 544-8397, (703) 938-0144, E-Mail: info@masterymg.com, Web Site: www.masterymktgrp.com (20)

Hall, Scott, UPM North America, Westmont, IL. Tel: (630) 850-3310, (866) 300-4175, FAX: (630) 850-3510, Web Site: www.upm-kymmene.com (25)

Hall, Stephen, Smith & Noble, Corona, CA. Tel: (909) 734-4444, (800) 248-8888, FAX: (800) 426-7780, E-Mail: contactus@smithnoble.com, Web Site: www.smithandnoble.com (8)

Hall, Tom, City of LaGrange, LaGrange, GA. Tel: (706) 883-2010, FAX: (706) 883-2062, Web Site: www.lagrange-ga.org (1)

Hall-Erickson Inc, Westmont, IL. Tel: (630) 434-7779, FAX: (630) 434-1216 (16)

Halla, Brian, National Semiconductor Corp, Santa Clara, CA. Tel: (408) 721-5000, (800) 272-9959, FAX: (408) 245-0671, E-Mail: new.feedback@nsc.com, Web Site: www.national.com (16)

Hallacy, Gene, Mower & Associates, Charlotte, NC. Tel: (704) 375-0123, FAX: (704) 375-0222, Web Site: www.mower.com (35)

Hallard, Karen, Literary Market Place, New Providence, NJ. Tel: (800) 409-4929, FAX: (908) 219-0192, E-Mail: khallard@infotoday.com, Web Site: www.literarymarketplace.com (43)

Halleak Jr., Joseph, Neighborhood Cleaners Association International, New York, NY. Tel: (212) 967-3002, (800) 888-1622, FAX: (212) 967-2240, E-Mail: info@nca-i.com, Web Site: www.nca-i.com (1)

Hallelujah Acres, Shelby, NC. Tel: (704) 481-1700, Web Site: www.hacres.com (5)

Haller, Lou, Ampersand Press, Port Townsend, WA. Tel: (360) 379-5187, (800) 624-4263, FAX: (360) 379-0324, E-Mail: info@ampersandpress.com, Web Site: www.ampersandpress.com (11)

Haller, Maureen, Easter Seals, Chicago, IL. Tel: (312) 726-6200, FAX: (312) 726-1494, Web Site: www.easter-seals.org (1)

Hallett, David, L., Goldsmith Agio Helms, Minneapolis, MN. Tel: (612) 339-0500, FAX: (612) 339-0507, Web Site: www.agio.com (14)

Halligan, Katy, Potpourri Group Inc, Chelmsford, MA. Tel: (978) 256-4100, FAX: (978) 256-1961/0344, Web Site: www.potpourrigroup.com (6)

Halliwell, Gary, NetProspex Inc, Waltham, MA. Tel: (888) 826-4877, E-Mail: sales@netprospex.com, Web Site: www.netprospex.com (22)

Hallmark, Adrian, M., Volkswagen Group of America Inc, Auburn Hills, MI. Tel: (248) 754-5000, FAX: (248) 754-4930, Web Site: www.vw.com (16)

Hallmark Cards Inc, Kansas City, MO. Tel: (816) 274-5111, FAX: (816) 274-7276, Web Site: www.hallmark.com (16)

Hallock, Andy, Hubert Co, Harrison, OH. Tel: (513) 367-8767, (800) 543-7374, FAX: (513) 367-8823, Web Site: www.hubert.com (16)

Halls Sr., Donald, J., Halls Kansas City, Kansas City, MO. Tel: (816) 274-8111, (800) 624-4034, FAX: (816) 545-2121, Web Site: www.hallskc.com (16)

Halls Kansas City, Kansas City, MO. Tel: (816) 274-8111, (800) 624-4034, FAX: (816) 545-2121, Web Site: www.hallskc.com (16)

Halo Branded Solutions, Sterling, IL. Tel: (877) 592-4256, (866) 840-6401, FAX: (815) 632-6900, E-Mail: moreinfo@haloleewayne.com, Web Site: www.haloleewayne.com (33)

HALO/Lee Wayne, Sterling, IL. Tel: (815) 632-0980, (866) 840-6401, FAX: (815) 632-6900, E-Mail: moreinfo@leewayne.com, Web Site: www.leewayne.com (16)

Halogen Response Media, New York, NY. Tel: (212) 468-4000, Web Site: www.halogenresponse.com (31)

Halporn, Roberta, The Center for Thanatology Research & Education Inc, Brooklyn, NY. Tel: (718) 858-3026, FAX: (718) 852-1846, E-Mail: thanatology@pipeline.com, Web Site: www.thanatology.org (23)

Halsom Home Care Inc, Centerville, OH. Tel: (937) 438-6600, (800) 345-5438, FAX: (937) 438-6620, E-Mail: main@halsom.com, Web Site: www.halsom.com (16)

Halstead, Karen, Eleven Inc, San Francisco, CA. Tel: (415) 707-1111, Web Site: www.eleveninc.com (35)

Halter, Denise, Reed Exhibitions, Norwalk, CT. Tel: (203) 840-4800, (888) 745-7644, FAX: (203) 840-5805, E-Mail: dhalter@reedexpo.com, Web Site: www.readerexpo.com (16)

Halverson, Glen, Vemma Nutrition Co, Scottsdale, AZ. Tel: (800) 577-0777, FAX: (888) 314-9827, E-Mail: ms@vemma.com, Web Site: www.vemma.com (7)

Halvorson, Larry, R., Impulse Inc, Las Vegas, NV. Tel: (702) 948-1100, (800) 328-0184, FAX: (702) 948-1104 (3)

Halvorson, Michael, Impulse Inc, Las Vegas, NV. Tel: (702) 948-1100, (800) 328-0184, FAX: (702) 948-1104 (3)

Halvorsrude, Ken, Doctor's Best Inc, San Clemente, CA. Tel: (949) 498-3628, (800) 333-6977, FAX: (800) 754-2036, (949) 498-3952, E-Mail: info@drbvitamins.com, Web Site: www.drbvitamins.com (16)

Hamakor Judaica Inc, Niles, IL. Tel: (847) 966-4040, (800) 426-2567, FAX: (847) 966-4033, E-Mail: service@ewishource.com, Web Site: www.jewishsource.com (5)

Hamann, Beth, Smart Practice, Phoenix, AZ. Tel: (800) 522-0800, FAX: (800) 522-8329, E-Mail: info@smartpractice.com, Web Site: www.smartpractice.com (17)

Hamann, Dr. Curt, Smart Practice, Phoenix, AZ. Tel: (800) 522-0800, FAX: (800) 522-8329, E-Mail: info@smartpractice.com, Web Site: www.smartpractice.com (17)

Hambleton, Kristin, Neolane, Newton, MA. Tel: (617) 467-6760, Web Site: www.neolane.com (22)

Hamburger, Daniel, DeVry Inc, Oakbrook Terrace, IL. Tel: (630) 571-7700, FAX: (602) 943-4108, Web Site: www.devry.com (16)

Hamerman, Felicia, United Business Media, Manhasset, NY. Tel: (516) 562-5000, Web Site: www.ubmtechnology.com (17)

Hamil, John, Sovereign Bank New England, Glastonbury, CT. Tel: (877) 768-2265, FAX: (860) 727-6517 (14)

Hamilton, Bill, Florida Power & Light Co, Miami, FL. Tel: (305) 552-3552, (800) 468-8243, FAX: (305) 552-2487, Web Site: www.fpl.com (16)

Hamilton, Bruce, Country Dance and Song Society, Haydenville, MA. Tel: (413) 268-7426, FAX: (413) 268-7471, E-Mail: office@cdss.org, Web Site: www.cdss.org (1)

Hamilton, Dana, L., Fidelity Security Life Insurance Co, Kansas City, MO. Tel: (816) 756-1060, (800) 648-8624, FAX: (816) 968-0580, E-Mail: info@fslins.com, Web Site: www.fslins.com (15)

Hamilton, David, Brant Publications Inc, New York, NY. Tel: (212) 941-2800, FAX: (212) 941-2885, Web Site: www.interviewmagazine.com (17)

Hamilton, John, Service Web Offset Corp, Chicago, IL. Tel: (312) 567-7000, (800) 621-1567, FAX: (312) 567-9121, E-Mail: jhamilton@swoc.com, Web Site: www.swoc.com (27)

Hamilton, Kyle, American Church Inc, Youngstown, OH. Tel: (330) 758-4545, (800) 250-7112, FAX: (800) 763-8772, E-Mail: sales@americanchurch.com, Web Site: www.americanchurch.com (26)

Hamilton, Laura, B., MTS Systems Corp, Eden Prairie, MN. Tel: (952) 937-4000, (800) 328-2255, FAX: (952) 937-4515, E-Mail: info@mts.com, Web Site: www.mts.com (16)

Hamilton, Richard, University of Missouri/Kansas City, Kansas City, MO. Tel: (816) 235-2215, FAX: (816) 235-2312, Web Site: www.umkc.edu (41)

Hamilton, Susan, A&P, Montvale, NJ. Tel: (201) 573-9700, (866) 44 FRESH, FAX: (201) 505-3054, E-Mail: apcustomerrel@aptea.com, Web Site: www.aptea.com (16)

Hamilton Beach/Proctor-Silex Inc, Glen Allen, VA. Tel: (804) 273-9777, FAX: (804) 527-7142, Web Site: www.hambeach.com (16)

Hamilton Campaigns, Washington, DC. Tel: (202) 686-5900, FAX: (202) 686-7080, E-Mail: info@hamiltoncampaigns.com, Web Site: www.hamiltoncampaigns.com (30)

The Hamilton Collection, Jacksonville, FL. Tel: (904) 279-1300, (866) 323-5577, FAX: (904) 279-1495, Web Site: www.hamiltoncollection.com (6)

Hamilton Contact Center Services, Aurora, NE. Tel: (402) 694-4343, (800) 972-3237, FAX: (402) 694-4433, Web Site: www.hamiltontm.com (29)

The Hamilton Group Ltd Inc, Jacksonville, FL. Tel: (904) 279-1300, FAX: (904) 279-1414, Web Site: www.collectibletoday.com (16)

Hamilton Sorter Co, Fairfield, OH. Tel: (513) 870-4400, (800) 503-9966, FAX: (800) 503-9963, E-Mail: sstreight@hamiltonsorter.com, Web Site: www.hamiltonsorter.com (34)

Hamilton Watch, Weehawken, NJ. Tel: (201) 271-1400, (800) 243-8463, Web Site: www.hamiltonwatches.com (16)

Hamlin, Pam, Arnold Brand Response, Toronto, ON. Tel: (416) 355-5009, Web Site: www.arnoldworldwide.com (35)

Hamm, David, Schawk DesPlaines, Des Plaines, IL. Tel: (847) 296-6000, (800) 629-1909, FAX: (847) 296-4694, Web Site: www.schawk.com (27)

Hamm, Don, Assurant Health, Milwaukee, WI. Tel: (414) 244-0658, (800) 800-1212, FAX: (414) 224-0472, Web Site: www.assuranthealth.com (15)

Hamm, Jack, Christian Appalachian Project, Lexington, KY. Tel: (859) 792-3051, (866) 270-4CAP, FAX: (859) 792-6560, E-Mail: capinfo@chrisapp.org, Web Site: www.christianapp.org (1)

Hammacher Schlemmer, New York, NY. Tel: (847) 581-8600, (800) 233-4800, FAX: (847) 581-8616, Web Site: www.hammacher.com (16)

Hamman, Robert, SCA Promotions Inc, Dallas, TX. Tel: (214) 860-3700, (888) 860-3700, FAX: (214) 860-3723, E-Mail: scainfo@scapromo.com, Web Site: www.scapromo.com (15)

Hammar, Mark, Total Data Solutions, North Andover, MA. Tel: (978) 686-2311, Web Site: www.ttldatasolutions.com (23)

Hammelman, David, H., GameTime Inc, Fort Payne, AL. Tel: (256) 845-5610, (800) 633-2394, FAX: (256) 845-9361/2649, Web Site: www.gametime.com (11)

Hammer, Bonnie, Sci-Fi Channel, New York, NY. Tel: (212) 413-5000, FAX: (212) 413-6509, Web Site: www.scifi.com (32)

Hammergren, John, H., McKesson Corp, San Francisco, CA. Tel: (415) 983-8300, FAX: (415) 983-7160, Web Site: www.mckesson.com (7)

Hammersley, John, Eclipse Direct Marketing, Mineola, NY. Tel: (212) 931-8344, FAX: (212) 931-8377, E-Mail: jkaiser@eclipsedm.com, Web Site: www.eclipsedm.com (23)

Hammilton, Dennis, LO-AD Communications, Pasadena, CA. Tel: (626) 304-7750, FAX: (626) 304-2716, Web Site: www.lo-ad.com (16)

Hammock, Statton, Network Solutions LLC, Herndon, VA. Tel: (703) 668-4600, Web Site: www.networksolutions.com (32)

Hammock Publishing Inc, Nashville, TN. Tel: (615) 690-3400, FAX: (615) 690-3401, E-Mail: info@hammock.com, Web Site: www.hammock.com (17)

Hammond, Brian, Telecommunications Reports International Inc, Washington, DC. Tel: (202) 312-6060, (800) 234-1660, FAX: (202) 312-6111, E-Mail: bhammond@tr.com, Web Site: www.tr.com (17)

Hammond, Holly, Gnames Media Group, Grapevine, TX. Tel: (972) 871-2828, FAX: (972) 871-2929, E-Mail: info@gnames.com, Web Site: www.gnames.com (23)

Hammond, Stacy, NASW Assurance Services Inc, Frederick, MD. Tel: (800) 668-4274, E-Mail: zxi@naswasi.org, Web Site: www.naswinsurancetrust.org (1)

Hammond, Stevan, Allied Marketing Group Inc, Dallas, TX. Tel: (214) 915-7000, FAX: (214) 905-5133, E-Mail: support@alliedmarketinggroup.com, Web Site: www.alliedmarketinggroup.com (21)

Hammond, Steven, Sweepstakes Clearinghouse, Dallas, TX. Tel: (214) 915-7100, FAX: (214) 915-7458, E-Mail: customersupport@sweepstakesclearinghouse.com, Web Site: www.sweepstakesclearinghouse.com (16)

Hammond Paradigm Communications Group, Cincinnati, OH. Tel: (513) 381-7100, (800) 898-4121, FAX: (513) 381-8756, Web Site: www.hammondcg.com (35)

Hammond World Atlas Corp, New York, NY. Tel: (908) 206-1300, (800) 526-4953, FAX: (908) 206-1104, E-Mail: erika@hammondmap.com, Web Site: www.hammondmap.com (17)

Hammonds, Lisa, Medcom Inc, Cypress, CA. Tel: (800) 877-1443, FAX: (714) 891-3140, E-Mail: lhammonds@medcominc.com, Web Site: www.medcominc.com (17)

Hammonds, Tim, Food Marketing Institute (FMI), Arlington, VA. Tel: (202) 452-8444, FAX: (202) 429-4519, E-Mail: fmi@fmi.org, Web Site: www.fmi.org (40)

Hampden Papers Inc, Holyoke, MA. Tel: (413) 536-1000, FAX: (413) 532-9161 (25)

Hampshire Agency, Great Neck, NY. Tel: (516) 466-3814, FAX: (516) 466-0910 (14)

Hampshire Pewter Co, Wolfeboro, NH. Tel: (603) 569-4944, (800) 639-7704, FAX: (603) 569-4524, E-Mail: gifts@hampshirepewter.com, Web Site: www.hampshirepewter.com (6)

Hampton, Gerald, New Mexico State University, Las Cruces, NM. Tel: (575) 646-0111, (505) 646-3311, FAX: (505) 646-1498, Web Site: www.nmsu.edu (41)

Hampton, Mark, Sheplers Catalog Sales Inc, Wichita, KS. Tel: (316) 946-3838, (800) 835-4004, FAX: (316) 946-3729, Web Site: www.sheplers.com (2)

Hampton, Renee, Booth Michigan, Grand Rapids, MI. Tel: (616) 222-5824, FAX: (616) 222-5318, Web Site: www.boothnewspapers.com (17)

Hampton, William, B., Colonial Life Insurance Co Texas, Fort Worth, TX. Tel: (817) 390-2350, (888) 227-5119, FAX: (817) 390-2209, E-Mail: insurance@colonialinsurance.com, Web Site: www.colonialinsurance.com (15)

Hampton Marketing Corp, Medford, NY. Tel: (516) 924-1335, (800) 229-1019, FAX: (516) 924-1669, Web Site: www.hamptonstamp.com (16)

Hamric, Kevin, Creative Publishing International, Minneapolis, MN. Tel: (612) 344-8100, FAX: (612) 344-8691, E-Mail: sales@creativepub.com, Web Site: www.creativepub.com (17)

Hamsa, William, R., Physicians Mutual Insurance Co, Omaha, NE. Tel: (402) 633-1604, (888) 932-7642, FAX: (402) 633-1604, Web Site: www.physiciansmutual.com (15)

Hana, Sandy, Wag/Aero Group, Lyons, WI. Tel: (262) 763-9586, (800) 558-6868, FAX: (262) 763-7595, E-Mail: wagaero-sales@wagaero.com, Web Site: www.wagaero.com (16)

Hancock, Claire, Quark Inc, Denver, CO. Tel: (303) 894-3832, Web Site: www.quark.com (34)

Hancock, Harley, D., Input Systems Inc, Paramount, CA. Tel: (562) 634-1170, (800) 327-9337, FAX: (562) 634-0993, E-Mail: info@sweepssoftware.com, Web Site: www.sweepssoftware.com (22)

Hancock, John, Gerber Garment Technology Inc, Tolland, CT. Tel: (860) 871-8082, FAX: (860) 871-6007, E-Mail: info@gerbertechnology.com, Web Site: www.gerbertechnology.com (34)

Hancock, Scott, A., International City/County Management Association, Washington, DC. Tel: (202) 289-ICMA, FAX: (202) 962-3500, E-Mail: customerservice@icma.org, Web Site: www.icma.org (1)

Hand Assembly & Packaging Inc (HAPI), Plainview, NY. Tel: (718) 699-3400, FAX: (718) 699-3409 (28)

Handeland, Stacy, Victory Corps, New Hope, MN. Tel: (763) 561-5600, (800) 328-6120, FAX: (763) 561-8523, E-Mail: cs@victorycorps.com, Web Site: www.victorycorps.com (16)

Handi-Ramp Inc, Libertyville, IL. Tel: (847) 680-7700, (800) 876-RAMP, FAX: (847) 816-7689, E-Mail: info@handiramp.com, Web Site: www.handiramp.com (7)

Handley, Greg, Datum Timing, Test & Measurement, Beverly, MA. Tel: (978) 927-8220, FAX: (978) 927-4099, E-Mail: wriley@datum.com, Web Site: www.datum.com (9)

Handley, Mark, International Crystal Manufacturing Co, Oklahoma City, OK. Tel: (405) 236-3741, (800) 252-6780, FAX: (405) 235-1904, E-Mail: info@icmfg.com, Web Site: www.icmfg.com (16)

Handy Store Fixtures Inc, Newark, NJ. Tel: (973) 242-1600, (800) 631-4280, FAX: (973) 642-6222, Web Site: www.handystorefixtures.com (16)

Hanesbrands Inc, Winston Salem, NC. Tel: (336) 519-7460, Web Site: www.hanesbrands.com (2)

Hanfling, Renita, Amacom Books, New York, NY. Tel: (212) 903-8376, FAX: (212) 903-8083, E-Mail: customerservice@amanet.org, Web Site: www.amacombooks.org (17)

Hang, Sherry, Yeck Brothers Co, Dayton, OH. Tel: (937) 294-4000, (800) 417-2767, FAX: (937) 294-6985, E-Mail: byeck@yeck.com, Web Site: www.yeck.com (35)

Hanik, Michael, J., Total Care, Rockville, MD. Tel: (301) 251-2061, (800) 334-3802, FAX: (301) 251-5891, E-Mail: totalcare@sprintmail.com, Web Site: www.totalmedinc.com (7)

Hanika, Mike, Culinary Parts Unlimited, San Francisco, CA. Tel: (800) 543-7549, FAX: (415) 495-5141, Web Site: www.culinaryparts.com (16)

Hanisko, Gail, Charter One Bank, Cleveland, OH. Tel: (216) 566-5300, (877) CHARTER, (877) 242-7837, FAX: (216) 566-1465, Web Site: www.charterone.com (14)

Hanley, Tom, Smith Hanley Associates, Southport, CT. Tel: (203) 319-4300, (888) 221-2900, FAX: (203) 319-4320, Web Site: www.smithhanley.com (20)

Hanley Wood LLC, Washington, DC. Tel: (202) 452-0800, FAX: (202) 785-1974, Web Site: www.hanleywood.com (16)

Hanna Instruments Inc, Woonsocket, RI. Tel: (401) 765-7500, (800) 426-6287, FAX: (401) 765-7575, E-Mail: custsvc@hannainst.com, Web Site: www.hannainst.com (16)

Hannah, Jerome, Penn Herb Co Ltd, Philadelphia, PA. Tel: (215) 632-6100, (800) 523-9971, FAX: (215) 632-7945, E-Mail: information@pennherb.com, Web Site: www.pennherb.com (16)

Hannah, Marcia, CertainTeed Corp, Valley Forge, PA. Tel: (610) 341-7000/7739, (800) 233-8990, FAX: (610) 341-7777, Web Site: www.certainteed.com (16)

Hannasch, Brian, Circle K Stores Inc, Akron, OH. Tel: (330) 630-6300, Web Site: www.cirlcek.com (16)

Hannecke Display Systems Inc, Boonton, NJ. Tel: (973) 335-0434, FAX: (973) 335-1274, E-Mail: info.usa@hannecke.com, Web Site: www.hannecke.com (27)

Hanner, Lizzie, American Society of Interior Designers, Washington, DC. Tel: (202) 546-3480, FAX: (202) 546-3240, E-Mail: asid@asid.org, Web Site: www.asid.org (1)

Hannigan, Lawrence, New York Blood Center Inc, New York, NY. Tel: (212) 570-3000, (800) 933-2566, FAX: (212) 570-3195, Web Site: www.nybloodcenter.org (1)

Hannon, Bridget, GWR Wealth Management, Omaha, NE. Tel: (402) 496-7200, FAX: (402) 496-0378, Web Site: www.gwrwealth.com (14)

Hanobik, Raymond, G., Hanobik Communications, Coraopolis, PA. Tel: (412) 264-3077, FAX: (412) 264-0321 (35)

Hanobik Communications, Coraopolis, PA. Tel: (412) 264-3077, FAX: (412) 264-0321 (35)

Hanorof, Debbie, Hofstra University, Hempstead, NY. Tel: (516) 463-7200, FAX: (516) 463-4833, E-Mail: ccepa@hofstra.edu, Web Site: ccepa.hofstra.edu (41)

Hanover Direct Inc, Weehawken, NJ. Tel: (201) 863-7300, FAX: (201) 272-3280, Web Site: www.hanoverdirect.com (5)

The Hanover Shoe Co, Newton, MA. Tel: (617) 964-1222, FAX: (617) 243-4210, Web Site: www.clarks.com (16)

Hanrahan, Don, Dick Davis Digest, Salem, MA. Tel: (978) 745-5532, FAX: (978) 745-1283, E-Mail: marketing@dickdavis.com, Web Site: www.dickdavis.com (17)

Hans, Paul, Genium Publishing, Amsterdam, NY. Tel: (518) 842-4111, FAX: (518) 842-1843, E-Mail: sales@genium.com, Web Site: www.genium.com (17)

Hanscomb, Neil, Atlantic Spice Co, North Truro, MA. Tel: (508) 487-6100, (800) 316-7965, FAX: (508) 487-2550, E-Mail: mark@atlanticspice.com, Web Site: www.atlanticspice.com (4)

Hansee, Donna, WILD Flavors Inc, Erlanger, KY. Tel: (859) 342-3600, Web Site: www.wildflavors.com (4)

Hansell, Raymond, Marastar Communications, Wayne, PA. Tel: (610) 902-0080, FAX: (610) 902-0600, E-Mail: info@marastar.com, Web Site: www.marastar.com (13)

Hansen, Becky, Travel Planners Inc, New York, NY. Tel: (212) 532-1660, (800) 221-3531, FAX: (212) 779-6102, Web Site: www.tphousing.com (19)

Hansen, Eric, American Society of Interior Designers, Washington, DC. Tel: (202) 546-3480, FAX: (202) 546-3240, E-Mail: asid@asid.org, Web Site: www.asid.org (1)

Hansen, John, Davis Instruments Corp, Hayward, CA. Tel: (510) 732-9229, (510) 670-0589, E-Mail: info@davisnet.com, Web Site: www.davisnet.com (8)

Hansen, Marcia A., Senior Publishers Media Group, San Diego, CA. Tel: (858) 272-9023, (800) 727-3646, FAX: (858) 272-7275, E-Mail: marcia@spmg.com, Web Site: www.spmg.com (31)

Hansen, Mark, Horace Mann Educators Corp, Springfield, IL. Tel: (217) 789-2500, FAX: (217) 788-5161, Web Site: www.horacemann.com (15)

Hansen, Marty, Alexian Brothers Bonaventure House, Chicago, IL. Tel: (773) 327-9921, FAX: (773) 327-9113, E-Mail: info@abam.org, Web Site: www.bonaventurehouse.org (1)

Hansen, Michael, Calendar Marketing Association, Wheaton, IL. Tel: (630) 510-4500, FAX: (630) 510-4501, E-Mail: info@calendarassociation.org, Web Site: www.calendarassociation.org (1)

Hansen, Michael, Elsevier, New York, NY. Tel: (212) 989-5800, FAX: (212) 633-3990, Web Site: www.elsevier.com (17)

Hansen, Michael, R., Lone Star Web Inc, Dallas, TX. Tel: (214) 443-2200, FAX: (214) 630-4364, E-Mail: jerry@lonestarweb.com, Web Site: www.lonestarweb.com (27)

Hansen, Michael, The Psychological Corp, San Antonio, TX. Tel: (800) 211-8378, FAX: (800) 232-1223, Web Site: www.psychcorp.com (17)

Hansen, Mike, Amateur Electronic Supply LLC, Milwaukee, WI. Tel: (414) 558-0333, (800) 558-0411, FAX: (414) 358-3337, Web Site: www.aesham.com (16)

Hansen, Ray, Forestry Suppliers Inc, Jackson, MS. Tel: (601) 354-3565, (800) 543-4203, FAX: (601) 292-0165, E-Mail: fsi@forestry-suppliers.com, Web Site: www.forestry-suppliers.com (9)

Hansen, Richard, A., The Keystone Equities Group, Oaks, PA. Tel: (610) 415-6300, (800) 715-9905, FAX: (610) 415-6328, Web Site: www.keystoneequities.com (20)

Hansen, Robert, D., Dow Corning Corp, Midland, MI. Tel: (989) 496-4000, (800) 248-2481, FAX: (989) 496-4572, Web Site: www.dowcorning.com (16)

Hansen, Scott, Harland Financial Solutions Inc, Lake Mary, FL. Tel: (407) 804-6600, (800) 815-5592, FAX: (407) 829-6702, Web Site: www.harlandfinancialsolutions.com (16)

Hansen, Tracy, Nahan Printing Inc, Saint Cloud, MN. Tel: (320) 251-7611, Web Site: www.nahan.com (27)

Chris Hansen, New Berlin, WI. Tel: (414) 607-5700, FAX: (414) 607-5704, Web Site: www.chr-hansen.com (16)

Hansen Corp, Princeton, IN. Tel: (812) 385-3415, FAX: (812) 385-3013, E-Mail: sales@hansen-motor.com, Web Site: www.hansen-motor.com (16)

Hanson, Cynthia, Infolure, Phoenix, AZ. Tel: (602) 308-6700, FAX: (602) 308-6801, E-Mail: glenn.gottfried@infolure.com, Web Site: www.infolure.com (22)

Hanson, Elizabeth, Drexel University (Goodwin College of Professional Studies), Philadelphia, PA. E-Mail: goodwin@drexel.edu, Web Site: www.drexel.edu/goodwin (16)

Hanson, James, L., Mutual of Omaha, Omaha, NE. Tel: (402) 342-7600, (800) 775-6000, FAX: (402) 351-2775, Web Site: www.mutualofomaha.com (15)

Hanson, John, P & H Mining Equipment, Milwaukee, WI. Tel: (414) 671-4400, FAX: (414) 671-7618, Web Site: www.phmining.com (16)

Hanson, Robert, Levi Strauss & Co, San Francisco, CA. Tel: (415) 501-6000, FAX: (415) 501-7112, Web Site: www.levistrauss.com (16)

Hanson Inc, Maumee, OH. Tel: (419) 327-6100, Web Site: www.hansoninc.com (30)

Hansraj, Bharat, Omega Direct Response Inc, Richmond Hill, ON Canada. Tel: (905) 482-2340, FAX: (905) 482-9721, E-Mail: odrsales@omegadirect.com, Web Site: www.omegadirect.com (29)

Hanton, Carl, The World Bank, Washington, DC. Tel: (202) 473-1000, FAX: (202) 477-6391, Web Site: www.worldbank.org (17)

Hanway, H., Edward, CIGNA International, Philadelphia, PA. Tel: (215) 761-1741, FAX: (215) 761-5515, Web Site: www.cigna.com (15)

Hapoienu, Spencer, Insight Out of Chaos, New York, NY. Tel: (212) 935-0044, Web Site: www.iooc.com (22)

Happy Jack Inc, Snow Hill, NC. Tel: (252) 747-2911, (800) 326-5225, FAX: (252) 747-4111, E-Mail: happyjack@happyjackinc.com, Web Site: www.happyjackinc.com (11)

Happy Trails Resort, Surprise, AZ. Tel: (623) 584-0066, FAX: (623) 546-2968, E-Mail: happytrails@uccinc.net, Web Site: www.htresort.com (19)

Har Court Inc, Orlando, FL. Tel: (407) 345-2000, FAX: (407) 345-1052 (17)

Hara, Carolyn, Hawaiian Host Inc, Honolulu, HI. Tel: (808) 848-0500, Web Site: www.hawaiianhost.com (4)

Harbach, Ed, Bearingpoint Inc, Montvale, NJ. Tel: (201) 307-7000, FAX: (201) 505-3765, Web Site: www.bearingpoint.com (14)

Harber, Bruce, B., Winmill & Co, New York, NY. Tel: (212) 785-0900, (800) 400-MIDAS, FAX: (212) 363-1100, E-Mail: info@midasfunds.com, Web Site: www.midasfunds.com (14)

Harbin, Ben, LifeWay Christian Resources, Nashville, TN. Tel: (615) 251-5822, Web Site: www.lifeway.com (1)

Harbin, Roger, F., Symetra Financial, Bellevue, WA. Tel: (425) 256-8000, (800) 426-7355, FAX: (425) 256-5737, Web Site: www.symetra.com (15)

Harbison, Tom, ClientLogic, Nashville, TN. Tel: (615) 301-7100, E-Mail: bobfet@clientlogic.com (21)

Harbor Freight Tools, Camarillo, CA. Tel: (805) 445-4791, (800) 423-2567, FAX: (800) 445-4925, Web Site: www.harborfreight.com (9)

Harbour Bay Inc, Suffern, NY. Tel: (845) 368-2857, FAX: (845) 368-2349 (16)

Harcourt Educational Measurement, San Antonio, TX. Tel: (210) 299-1061, (800) 211-8378, FAX: (800) 232-1223, Web Site: www.harcourtassessment.com (17)

Hardenbergh, David, Rural Alaska Community Action Program Inc, Anchorage, AK. Tel: (907) 279-2511, FAX: (907) 278-2309, Web Site: www.ruralcap.com (1)

Hardin, Joe, SRDS, Des Plaines, IL. Tel: (800) 851-7737, FAX: (847) 375-5001, Web Site: www.srds.com (17)

Harding, Carol, KozaK Auto Drywash Inc, Batavia, NY. Tel: (716) 343-8111, (800) 237-9927, FAX: (585) 343-3732, E-Mail: info@kozak.com, Web Site: www.dryautowash.com (16)

Harding, Craig, Direct Tech Inc, Omaha, NE. Tel: (402) 895-2100, Web Site: www.direct-tech.com (34)

Harding, Edward R., KozaK Auto Drywash Inc, Batavia, NY. Tel: (716) 343-8111, (800) 237-9927, FAX: (585) 343-3732, E-Mail: info@kozak.com, Web Site: www.dryautowash.com (16)

Harding, Joyce, The Detroit Institute of Arts, Detroit, MI. Tel: (313) 833-7900, FAX: (313) 833-1390, Web Site: www.dia.org (16)

Harding, Kathleen, Balmar Inc, Falls Church, VA. Tel: (703) 289-9000, FAX: (703) 289-9143, E-Mail: marketing@balmar.com, Web Site: www.balmar.com (27)

Harding, Robin, Juvenile Diabetes Research Foundation, New York, NY. Tel: (212) 785-9500, (800) 533-CURE, FAX: (212) 785-9595, E-Mail: info@jdrf.org, Web Site: www.jdrf.org (1)

Harding, Shawn, Infinity Direct Inc, Plymouth, MN. Tel: (763) 559-1111, Web Site: www.infinitydirect.com (35)

Harding, Susan, Prime Media Equine Group, Gaithersburg, MD. Tel: (301) 977-3900, FAX: (301) 990-9015, Web Site: www.equisearch.com (17)

Hardy, Cary, American Numismatic Association, Colorado Springs, CO. Tel: (719) 632-2646, Web Site: www.money.org (1)

Hardy, Darren, Success Magazine, Lake Dallas, TX. Tel: (800) 570-6414, Web Site: www.successmagazine.com (43)

Hardy, Robert, C., Uniway Management Corp, Forest Park, GA. Tel: (404) 363-6200, (888) 386-4929, FAX: (404) 363-8848, E-Mail: uniway@bellsouth.net, Web Site: www.uniway.com (16)

Hare, David, New England List Services Inc, Danville, VT. Tel: (802) 684-1179, (877) 252-2100, FAX: (802) 684-2113, E-Mail: dave@nelists.com, Web Site: www.nelists.com (23)

Hare, Loralee, Telerx, Horsham, PA. Tel: (800) 2TEL-ERX, Web Site: www.telerx.com (29)

Hare, Susan, Sunrise Greetings, Bloomington, IN. Tel: (812) 336-4045, (800) 457-4045, FAX: (812) 336-8712, E-Mail: info@interart.com, Web Site: www.interartdistribution.com (17)

Haren, Jack, Mohawk, Cohoes, NY. Tel: (518) 237-1740, (800) 843-6455, FAX: (518) 237-7394, E-Mail: info@mohawkpaper.com, Web Site: www.mohawkconnects.com (25)

Harenski, Hallie, MetLife International, Long Island City, NY. Tel: (212) 578-3128 (15)

Harff, Todd, Creating Results/New England, Barrington, RI. Tel: (401) 289-2500, (888) 205-8899, FAX: (401) 427-6963, E-Mail: erin@creatingresults.com, Web Site: www.creatingresults.com (35)

Hargis, Eric, Epilepsy Foundation, Landover, MD. Tel: (301) 459-3700, (800) 332-1000, FAX: (301) 577-9056, E-Mail: postmaster@efa.org, Web Site: www.efa.org (1)

Hargis, Kenny, Venture Encoding Service Inc, Fort Worth, TX. Tel: (817) 283-9500, FAX: (817) 868-1705, E-Mail: sales@venture-encoding.com, Web Site: www.venture-encoding.com (27)

Hargreaves, David, David Hargreaves Ltd, Hopewell Junction, NY. Tel: (516) 944-9443, FAX: (516) 944-5825, E-Mail: dhltd@optonline.net (33)

Hargreaves, Linda, Lotions & Lace, Riverside, CA. Tel: (909) 686-5223, FAX: (909) 686-5765, E-Mail: linda@ez-access.com, Web Site: www.sexyvideos.com (2)

Hargreaves, Ray, Lotions & Lace, Riverside, CA. Tel: (909) 686-5223, FAX: (909) 686-5765, E-Mail: linda@ez-access.com, Web Site: www.sexyvideos. com (2)

David Hargreaves Ltd, Hopewell Junction, NY. Tel: (516) 944-9443, FAX: (516) 944-5825, E-Mail: dhltd@optonline.net (33)

Hargrove, Anne, Neighborhood Cleaners Association International, New York, NY. Tel: (212) 967-3002, (800) 888-1622, FAX: (212) 967-2240, E-Mail: info@nca-i.com, Web Site: www.nca-i.com (1)

Harkin, Emilie, Council on Foreign Relations Inc, New York, NY. Tel: (212) 434-9400, FAX: (212) 861-2759, E-Mail: editor@foreignaffairs.com, Web Site: www.foreignaffairs.org (17)

Harland, Brent, Consolidated Plastics Co Inc, Stow, OH. Tel: (330) 425-3900, (800) 362-1000, FAX: (330) 425-3333, Web Site: www. consolidatedplastics.com (9)

Harland Clarke Marketing Services, Decatur, GA. Tel: (866) 609-8609, Web Site: www.harlandclarke.com (31)

Harland Financial Solutions Inc, Lake Mary, FL. Tel: (407) 804-6600, (800) 815-5592, FAX: (407) 829-6702, Web Site: www. harlandfinancialsolutions.com (16)

John Harland Co, Decatur, GA. Tel: (770) 981-5580, (800) 723-3690, FAX: (770) 593-5367, E-Mail: jhhwebmaster@harland.net, Web Site: www. harland.net (16)

Harlequin Enterprises Ltd, Don Mills, ON Canada. Tel: (416) 445-5860, FAX: (416) 445-8655, E-Mail: customer_ecare@harlequin.ca, Web Site: www.eharlequin.com (17)

Harley-Davidson Inc, Milwaukee, WI. Tel: (414) 343-7286, FAX: (414) 343-4806, Web Site: www. harley-davidson.com (12)

Harling Marketing Inc, Kirkland, PQ Canada. Tel: (514) 695-1430, FAX: (514) 695-0530, E-Mail: info@harlingdirect.com, Web Site: www. harlingdirect.com (21)

Harlow, Kevin, ICS Marketing Support Services, Lansing, MI. Tel: (517) 394-1890, (888) 394-1890, FAX: (517) 394-7408, E-Mail: sales@icshq.com, Web Site: www.icshq.com (21)

Harman's Cheese & Country Store Inc, Sugar Hill, NH. Tel: (603) 823-8000, E-Mail: cheese@ harmanscheese.com, Web Site: www. HarmansCheese.com (4)

Harmelin, Joanne, Harmelin Direct, Bala Cynwyd, PA. Tel: (610) 668-7900, FAX: (610) 668-9257, E-Mail: president@harmelin.com, Web Site: www. harmelin.com (32)

Harmelin Direct, Bala Cynwyd, PA. Tel: (610) 668-7900, FAX: (610) 668-9257, E-Mail: president@ harmelin.com, Web Site: www.harmelin.com (32)

Harmon, Emmett, Suntrust Banks Inc, Atlanta, GA. Tel: (404) 588-7914, (800) 786-8787, FAX: (404) 532-0550, E-Mail: emmett.harmon@suntrust.com, Web Site: www.suntrust.com (14)

Harmon, Raymond, W., Hasco First Photo, Saint Charles, MO. Tel: (636) 946-5115, FAX: (636) 946-7148, Web Site: www.growingfamily.com (16)

Harmon-Schmitt, Kelly, Fallon, Minneapolis, MN. Tel: (612) 758-2345, FAX: (612) 758-2346, Web Site: www.fallon.com (35)

Harnetiaux, Tom, Nevco Scoreboard Co, Greenville, IL. Tel: (618) 664-0360, (800) 851-4040, FAX: (618) 664-0398, E-Mail: sales@nevcoscoreboards. com, Web Site: www.nevcoscoreboards.com (16)

Harnum, Gary, International Mailing Solutions LLC, Burlington, MA. Tel: (718) 376-5000, Web Site: www.mailims.com (28)

Harold Walter Siebens School of Business, Storm Lake, IA. Tel: (712) 749-2410, (800) 383-2821, FAX: (712) 749-2037, Web Site: www2.bvu.edu/ academics/business (41)

Harp, Katherine, Paragon Printing & Mailing, Austin, TX. Tel: (512) 821-0222, FAX: (512) 821-0200, E-Mail: paragon@paragonprinting.com, Web Site: paragonprinting.com (23)

Harper, Bill, Vegetarian Times, El Segundo, CA. Tel: (310) 356-4100, FAX: (310) 356-4110, Web Site: www.vegetariantimes.com (31)

Harper, Kathy, Standard Register, Dayton, OH. Tel: (937) 221-1000, (800) 755-6405, FAX: (937) 221-1239, E-Mail: julie.mcewan@standardregister.com, Web Site: www.standardregister.com (10)

Harper, Kellie, Merrick Bank, South Jordan, UT. Tel: (801) 545-6647, Web Site: www.merrickbank.com (14)

Harper College, Palatine, IL. Tel: (847) 925-6000, Web Site: www.harpercollege.com (1)

HarperCollins, New York, NY. Tel: (212) 207-7000, (800) 242-7737, FAX: (212) 207-7145, Web Site: www.harpercollins.com (17)

Harper's Magazine, New York, NY. Tel: (212) 420-5720, FAX: (212) 260-1096, Web Site: www. harpers.org (17)

Harrah's Entertainment Inc, Las Vegas, NV. Tel: (702) 407-6000, FAX: (702) 407-6499, (702) 407-6500, Web Site: www.harrahs.com (19)

Harrah's Marketing, Reno, NV. Tel: (775) 786-3232, FAX: (775) 722-2815, Web Site: www.harrahsreno. com (16)

Harraman, Brad, E-Miles.com, Dallas, TX. Tel: (214) 757-4700, Web Site: www.e-miles.com (19)

Harransky, Charles, Squadron Mail Order, Carrollton, TX. Tel: (972) 242-8663, (877) 414-0434, FAX: (972) 242-3775, E-Mail: mailorder@squadron.com, Web Site: www.squadron.com (16)

Harrel, William, College of Business Administration, Philadelphia, PA. Tel: (215) 895-2145, Web Site: www.drexel.edu (41)

Harrell, Henry H., Universal Corp, Richmond, VA. Tel: (804) 359-9311, FAX: (804) 254-3582, Web Site: www.universalcorp.com (16)

Harrell, Suzanne, Center for Professional Development, Tallahassee, FL. Tel: (850) 644-8004, (850) 487-1691, FAX: (850) 644-2589, Web Site: www. Learningforlife.fsu.com (16)

Harriman, Dann, Saunders Manufacturing Co Inc, Readfield, ME. Tel: (207) 685-3385, (800) 341-4674, FAX: (207) 685-9918, E-Mail: jsherwood@ saunders-usa.com, Web Site: www.saunders-usa. com (16)

Harrington, Jerry, Pioneer Hi-Bred International Inc, Johnston, IA. Tel: (515) 270-3200, FAX: (515) 270-3581, E-Mail: web.editor@pioneer.com, Web Site: www.pioneer.com (4)

Harrington, Jessica, Schultz & Williams Inc, Philadelphia, PA. Tel: (215) 625-9955, FAX: (215) 625-2701, E-Mail: mail@schultzwilliams.com, Web Site: www.sw-inc.com (1)

Harrington, Judy, B., Partners Health, Philadelphia, PA. Tel: (215) 849-9600, (800) 553-0784, E-Mail: sroberts@healthpart.com, Web Site: www. healthpart.com (15)

Harrington, Nancy, Newsmax Media Inc, West Palm Beach, FL. Tel: (888) 766-7542, E-Mail: sales@ newsmax.com, Web Site: www.newsmax.com/ advertise (24)

Harrington, Paul, Reebok International Ltd, Canton, MA. Tel: (781) 401-5000, (800) 843-4444, FAX: (781) 401-4402, Web Site: www.reebok.com (2)

Harrington, Tara, Direct Auto Insurance, Nashville, TN. Tel: (615) 399-4859, Web Site: www. directgeneral.com (15)

Harrington's of Vermont Inc, Richmond, VT. Tel: (802) 434-7500, FAX: (802) 434-3166, E-Mail: info@harringtonham.com, Web Site: www. harringtonham.com (4)

Harris II, J., Robert, JRH Marketing Services Inc, New York, NY. Tel: (718) 786-9640, FAX: (718) 786-9642, E-Mail: office@ jrhmarketingservices.com, Web Site: www. jrhmarketingservices.com (30)

Harris Jr., Henry, E., Kenmore Stamp Co, Milford, NH. Tel: (603) 673-1745, (800) 225-5059, FAX: (603) 673-3222, Web Site: www.kenmorestamp. com (6)

Harris, Amina, Moon Shine Trading Co, Woodland, CA. Tel: (530) 668-0660, (800) 678-1226, FAX: (530) 668-6061, E-Mail: store@moonshinetrading. com, Web Site: www.moonshinetrading.com (4)

Harris, Arlene, Boy Scouts of America/National Supply Group, Charlotte, NC. Tel: (972) 580-2161, (800) 323-0736, E-Mail: customerservice@ scoutstuff.org, Web Site: www.scoutstuff.org (1)

Harris, Benjamin, C., Unicall International Inc, Fairlawn, OH. Tel: (330) 864-9364, FAX: (330) 864-9367, E-Mail: harrisb@unicallinc.com, Web Site: www.unicallinc.com (29)

Harris, Benjamin, Lunarcow Design, Akron, OH. Tel: (330) 253-9000, (800) 594-9620, FAX: (330) 253-9001, E-Mail: info@lunarcow.com, Web Site: www.lunarcow.com (35)

Harris, Bill, AAA Mid-Atlantic Insurance Groups, Wilmington, DE. Tel: (302) 299-4700, (800) 451-5921, FAX: (215) 864-5486, Web Site: www. aaamidatlantic.com (15)

Harris, Bob, Hot Sauce Harry's, North Port, FL. Tel: (214) 902-8552, (800) 588-8979, FAX: (214) 956-9885, E-Mail: info@hotsauceharrys.com, Web Site: www.hotsauceharrys.com (4)

Harris, Bob, Society of Manufacturing Engineers, Dearborn, MI. Tel: (313) 425-3000, (800) 733-4763, FAX: (313) 425-3400, E-Mail: communications@sme.org, Web Site: www.sme.org (1)

Harris, Brian, Gates Corp, Denver, CO. Tel: (303) 744-1911, FAX: (303) 744-4000, Web Site: www. gates.com (9)

Harris, Brian, Mary Maxim Inc, Port Huron, MI. Tel: (810) 987-2000, (800) 962-9504, FAX: (810) 987-5056, E-Mail: info@marymaxim.com, Web Site: www.marymaxim.com (11)

Harris, Brian, Paradigm Promotions LLC, San Francisco, CA. Tel: (415) 387-2158, FAX: (415) 387-2185, E-Mail: brian@brianharris.com, Web Site: www.paradigmpromotions.com (35)

Harris, Charles, Natural History Magazine, Durham, NC. Tel: (646) 356-6500, FAX: (646) 356-6511, E-Mail: nhmag@naturalhistorymag.com, Web Site: www.naturalhistorymag.com (17)

Harris, Conrad, Consumers Union, Yonkers, NY. Tel: (914) 378-2000, FAX: (914) 378-2906, Web Site: www.consumerreports.org (17)

Harris, Cy, Prime Graphics Inc, Wood Dale, IL. Tel: (630) 227-1300, FAX: (630) 227-1823, E-Mail: moreinfo@primegraphicsinc.com, Web Site: www. primegraphicsinc.com (27)

Harris, H., Michael, Aldata, Saint Paul, MN. Tel: (952) 432-6900, FAX: (952) 432-7064, E-Mail: mharris@aldata.com, Web Site: www.aldata.com (23)

Harris, Helaine, Daedalus Books Inc, Columbia, MD. Tel: (410) 309-2700, (800) 395-2665, FAX: (410) 309-2701, Web Site: www.salebooks.com (5)

Harris, Howard, Eagle:xm, Denver, CO. Tel: (303) 320-5411, (800) 426-5376, FAX: (303) 393-6884, E-Mail: bettersolutions@eaglexm.com, Web Site: www.eaglexm.com (21)

Harris, Janet, I., Harris Marketing Inc, Indianapolis, IN. Tel: (317) 251-9729, E-Mail: hmdataindy@ msn.com, Web Site: www.listsandmail.com (23)

Harris, Jay, Mother Jones Magazine, San Francisco, CA. Tel: (415) 321-1700, Web Site: www. motherjones.com (17)

Harris, Jay, San Jose Mercury News, San Jose, CA. Tel: (408) 920-5000, FAX: (408) 271-3690, Web Site: www.bayarea.com (17)

Harris, Judy L., Films Media Group, New York, NY. Tel: (609) 671-1000, (800) 257-5126, FAX: (609) 671-0266, E-Mail: custserv@films.com, Web Site: www.filmsmediagroup.com (3)

Harris, Ken, Mrs Beasley's & Miss Grace Lemon Cake Co, Los Angeles, CA. Tel: (800) 710-7742, FAX: (310) 668-2148, E-Mail: general@mrsbeasleys.com, Web Site: www.mrsbeasleys.com (4)

Harris, Mark, Wolfe Publishing Co Inc, Prescott, AZ. Tel: (928) 445-7810, (800) 899-7810, FAX: (928) 778-5124, E-Mail: wolfepub@riflemag.com, Web Site: www.riflemagazine.com (17)

Harris, Michelle, Our Data Works Inc, Lewisville, TX. Tel: (469) 546-3000, (800) 268-2505, FAX: (469) 546-3013, E-Mail: info@ourdataworks.com, Web Site: www.ourdataworks.com (29)

Harris, Renee, New York University/Center for Marketing, New York, NY. Tel: (212) 998-0500, FAX: (212) 995-4006, E-Mail: mkt@stern.nyu.edu, Web Site: w4.stern.nyu.edu/marketing (41)

Harris, Rod, US Foodservice, Rosemont, IL. Tel: (410) 312-7100, FAX: (410) 312-7167, Web Site: www.usfoodservice.com (4)

Harris, Steve, Concordia Publishing House, Saint Louis, MO. Tel: (314) 268-1000, (800) 325-3040, FAX: (314) 268-1329, E-Mail: order@cph.org, Web Site: www.cph.org (17)

Harris, Steven, Cable Shopping Network, Scottsdale, AZ. Tel: (480) 624-4446, Web Site: www.shopcsntv.com (16)

Harris, Steven, H&R Block Inc, Kansas City, MO. Tel: (816) 572-6446, (800) 472-5625, FAX: (816) 854-8500, Web Site: www.hrblock.com (14)

Harris, William, K., Bernard C Harris Publishing Co Inc, Brewster, NY. Tel: (800) 326-6600, FAX: (845) 940-0801, E-Mail: moreinfo@harrisconnect.com, Web Site: www.bcharrispub.com (29)

Harris Bancorp Inc, Chicago, IL. Tel: (312) 461-7961, (888) 340-BANK, FAX: (312) 461-7869, E-Mail: onlineservices@harrisbank.com, Web Site: www.harrisbank.com (14)

Bernard C Harris Publishing Co Inc, Brewster, NY. Tel: (800) 326-6600, FAX: (845) 940-0801, E-Mail: moreinfo@harrisconnect.com, Web Site: www.bcharrispub.com (29)

Harris Connect LLC, Brewster, NY. Tel: (800) 326-6600, Web Site: www.harrisconnect.com (1)

Harris Corp, Melbourne, FL. Tel: (407) 727-9100, FAX: (407) 726-5427 (16)

Harris Direct, Canoga Park, CA. Tel: (818) 222-3470 x102, Web Site: www.harris-direct.org (1)

Harris Infosource International Inc, Independence, OH. Tel: (330) 425-9000, (877) 359-6308, (800) 888-5900, (800) 748-5482, FAX: (800) 643-5997, E-Mail: customerservice@harrisinfo.com, Web Site: www.harrisinfo.com (17)

Harris Interactive, New York, NY. Tel: (585) 272-8400, (800) 866-7655, FAX: (585) 272-8680, E-Mail: info@harrisinteractive.com, Web Site: www.harrisinteractive.com (30)

Harris Marketing Group, Birmingham, MI. Tel: (248) 723-6300, FAX: (248) 723-6301, E-Mail: info@harris-hmg.com, Web Site: www.harris-hmg.com (35)

Harris Marketing Inc, Indianapolis, IN. Tel: (317) 251-9729, E-Mail: hmdataindy@msn.com, Web Site: www.listsandmail.com (23)

Harris Publishing, Brewster, NY. Tel: (800) 326-6600, FAX: (914) 287-2144, E-Mail: moreinfo@harrisconnect.com, Web Site: www.bcharrispub.com (35)

Harrison, Ashton, Shades of Light, Richmond, VA. Tel: (804) 288-3235, (877) 288-5029, FAX: (804) 288-5029, E-Mail: visitor@shadesoflight.com, Web Site: www.shadesoflight.com (8)

Harrison, Colleen, First American CoreLogic, Santa Ana, CA. Tel: (866) 774-3282, Web Site: www.facorelogic.com (30)

Harrison, Gregory, Franklin Estimating Systems, Woods Cross, UT. Tel: (801) 303-6083, (800) 346-7363, FAX: (801) 303-4540, E-Mail: management@franklinestimating.com, Web Site: www.fesys.com (17)

Harrison, Jeffrey, S., Blue Raven Technology, Wilmington, MA. Tel: (781) 778-4600, (800) 274-5343, (800) 20RAVEN, FAX: (781) 778-4848, E-Mail: sales@blueraven.com, Web Site: www.blueraven.com (3)

Harrison, John, J., The Keystone Equities Group, Oaks, PA. Tel: (610) 415-6300, (800) 715-9905, FAX: (610) 415-6328, Web Site: www.keystoneequities.com (20)

Harrison, Mary, E., Mary's Plant Farm & Landscaping, Hamilton, OH. Tel: (513) 894-0022, FAX: (513) 892-2053, E-Mail: marysplantfarm@zoomtown.com, Web Site: www.marysplantfarm.com (8)

Harrison, Sam, Linett & Harrison, Union, NJ. Tel: (908) 686-0606, FAX: (908) 686-0623, E-Mail: sharrison@linettandharrison.com, Web Site: www.linettandharrison.com (35)

Harrower, M. Colletta, Armento Inc, Buffalo, NY. Tel: (716) 875-2423, (866) 276-3686, FAX: (716) 875-8011, E-Mail: armento@aol.com, Web Site: www.armento-columbarium.com (5)

Harry & David Holdings Inc, Medford, OR. Tel: (541) 864-2500, (800) 345-5655, FAX: (541) 864-2742 (4)

Harsh, Bruce, US Department of Commerce, Washington, DC. Tel: (202) 482-4582 (1)

Hart, Ann, Weaver, Temple University, Philadelphia, PA. Tel: (215) 204-7282, FAX: (215) 204-4554, Web Site: www.sbm.temple.edu (41)

Hart, Clare, Info USA, Omaha, NE. Tel: (800) 321-0869, E-Mail: help@infousa.com, Web Site: www.infousa.com (23)

Hart, Julie, Teachers' Discovery, Auburn Hills, MI. Tel: (248) 340-7220, FAX: (248) 340-7212 (5)

Hart, Karl, Wendell August Forge Inc, Grove City, PA. Tel: (724) 458-8360, (800) 923-1390, FAX: (724) 458-0906, E-Mail: info@wendell.com, Web Site: www.wendellaugust.com (6)

Hart, Lora Lee, Trigon Blue Cross/Blue Shield, Roanoke, VA. Tel: (540) 853-5000, (800) 553-3164, FAX: (540) 853-3053, Web Site: www.trigon.com (15)

Hart, Patti, Times Union, Albany, NY. Tel: (518) 454-5694, FAX: (518) 454-5628, Web Site: www.timesunion.com (18)

Hart, Rachel, Seattle Magazine, Seattle, WA. Tel: (206) 284-1750, (800) 637-0334, FAX: (206) 284-2550, E-Mail: customerservice@seattlemag.com, Web Site: www.seattlemag.com (17)

Hart, Sue, IPD Co Inc, Portland, OR. Tel: (503) 257-7500, (800) 444-6473, FAX: (503) 257-7596, E-Mail: info@ipdusa.com, Web Site: www.ipdusa.com (12)

Harte, Chris, Star Tribune, Minneapolis, MN. Tel: (612) 673-4000, FAX: (612) 673-4359, E-Mail: charte@startribune.com, Web Site: www.startribunecompany.com (17)

Harte-Hanks, Austin, TX. Tel: (512) 434-1100, (800) 456-9748, FAX: (512) 244-9222, Web Site: www.harte-hanks.com (22)

Hartford, Betsey, Signature Communications, Milton, MA. Tel: (617) 642-1300, FAX: (617) 696-2144, E-Mail: info@signaturecom.com, Web Site: www.signaturecom.com (21)

Hartford, Jeff, Audience Development, Norwalk, CT. Tel: (203) 854-6730, FAX: (203) 854-6735, E-Mail: inolan@red7media.com, Web Site: www.audiencedevelopment.com (43)

Hartford, Owen, Signature Communications, Milton, MA. Tel: (617) 642-1300, FAX: (617) 696-2144, E-Mail: info@signaturecom.com, Web Site: www.signaturecom.com (21)

The Hartford Courant, Hartford, CT. Tel: (860) 241-6200, FAX: (860) 241-3865, Web Site: www.courant.com (31)

The Hartford Financial Services Inc, Southington, CT. Tel: (860) 843-8070, (860) 547-5000, FAX: (860) 547-2680, Web Site: www.thehartford.com (15)

Hartgill, Richard, Nature Publishing Group, New York, NY. Tel: (212) 726-9200, FAX: (212) 696-9006, E-Mail: nature@natureny.com, Web Site: www.nature.com (17)

Hartigan, Bridget, The Catamount Group, Southport, CT. Tel: (203) 778-4110, FAX: (203) 778-4130, E-Mail: tina@catamountgroup.net, Web Site: www.catamountgroup.net (23)

Hartle, Charles, Rod's Western Palace, Columbus, OH. Tel: (614) 268-8200, (800) 325-8508, FAX: (800) 330-7637, E-Mail: rods@rods.com, Web Site: www.rods.com (2)

Hartle, Scott, Rod's Western Palace, Columbus, OH. Tel: (614) 268-8200, (800) 325-8508, FAX: (800) 330-7637, E-Mail: rods@rods.com, Web Site: www.rods.com (2)

Hartless, Frank, Starcrest Products of California Inc, Perris, CA. Tel: (909) 943-2011, FAX: (909) 943-2971, E-Mail: tmc@tstonramp.com (16)

Hartley Data Service Inc, Glenview, IL. Tel: (847) 724-9280, (800) 433-2796, FAX: (847) 729-2199, Web Site: www.hartleydata.com (22)

Hartlieb, Leslie, ETS Inc, Indianapolis, IN. Tel: (317) 290-8982, (800) 228-6292, FAX: (317) 329-4630, E-Mail: info@etstsan.com, Web Site: www.etstans.com (7)

Hartman, Bobbie, FirstGroup America, Cincinnati, OH. Tel: (513) 419-8635, Web Site: www.firstgroupamerica.com (12)

Hartman, Carolyn, Kraftbilt, Tulsa, OK. Tel: (918) 628-1260, (800) 331-7290, FAX: (918) 632-7371, Web Site: www.kraftbilt.com (10)

Hartman, Elizabeth, Elizabeth Hartman, Syosset, NY. Tel: (516) 650-8862 (20)

Elizabeth Hartman, Syosset, NY. Tel: (516) 650-8862 (20)

Hartnack, Richard, C., US Bancorp, Minneapolis, MN. Tel: (651) 466-3000, (800) 872-2657, FAX: (612) 303-0782, Web Site: www.usbank.com (14)

Hartnett, John, Thomson Reuters, New York, NY. Tel: (212) 367-6300, (800) 950-1216, FAX: (212) 367-6301, Web Site: www.riahome.com (17)

Hartnett, Mark, Formsource, Lewiston, ME. Tel: (207) 782-3311, (877) 782-3311, FAX: (207) 783-0157, E-Mail: service@formsource1.com, Web Site: www.formsource1.com (27)

Hartnett, Vincent, Penske Logistics, Reading, PA. Tel: (610) 775-6000, (800) 529-6531, FAX: (610) 775-6432, Web Site: www.penskelogistics.com (16)

Hartsaw, Teresa, Eperformax Inc, Thompsons Station, TN. Tel: (901) 751-4800, (888) 384-7004, FAX: (901) 751-4805, E-Mail: info0609@eperformax.com, Web Site: www.eperformax.com (29)

Hartwig, Vicky, Leslie Jordan, Portland, OR. Tel: (503) 295-1987, (800) 935-3343, FAX: (503) 295-1989, E-Mail: sales@lesliejordan.com, Web Site: www.lesliejordan.com (2)

The Harty Press Inc, New Haven, CT. Tel: (203) 562-5112, (800) 654-0562, FAX: (203) 782-9168, E-Mail: gplatt@hartynet.com, Web Site: www.hartynet.com (21)

The Hartz Mountain Corp, Secaucus, NJ. Tel: (201) 271-4800, (800) 275-1414, FAX: (201) 271-0068, Web Site: www.hartz.com (16)

Hartzell, Skip, The Mark Group, Boca Raton, FL. Tel: (561) 241-1700, (800) 637-0152, FAX: (561) 241-1055, Web Site: www.bostonproper.com (2)

Harvard Business Review, Watertown, MA. Tel: (617) 783-7400, FAX: (617) 783-7664, Web Site: www.hbsp.harvard.edu (17)

Harvard Business School - Executive Education, Boston, MA. Tel: (617) 496-2193, Web Site: www.exed.hbs.edu (1)

Harvard Business School Publishing, Boston, MA. Tel: (617) 783-7400, Web Site: www.harvardbusiness.org (17)

Harvard Pilgrim Health Care, Wellesley, MA. Tel: (617) 509-1000, FAX: (617) 509-7590, Web Site: www.harvardpilgrim.org (7)

Harvard Square Records, Round Rock, TX. Tel: (877) 465-7669, E-Mail: LPnow@yahoo.com, Web Site: www.lpnow.com (3)

Harvatine, John, Creative Publishing International, Minneapolis, MN. Tel: (612) 344-8100, FAX: (612) 344-8691, E-Mail: sales@creativepub.com, Web Site: www.creativepub.com (17)

Harvest Communications, Redding, CA. Tel: (800) 303-6405, FAX: (800) 926-8038, Web Site: www. harvest-communications.com (20)

Harvey, Duanne, Tucker Electronics Co, Garland, TX. Tel: (214) 348-8800, (887) 667-6044, FAX: (214) 348-0367, E-Mail: sales@tucker.com, Web Site: www.tucker.com (3)

Harvey, Gavin, In Demand, New York, NY. Tel: (646) 486-1010, FAX: (646) 486-0855, Web Site: www. indemand.com (32)

Harvey, Katherine, Curriculum Associates Inc, North Billerica, MA. Tel: (978) 667-8000, FAX: (978) 667-5706, E-Mail: cainfo@curriculumassociates. com, Web Site: www.curriculumassociates.com (17)

Harvey, Kathy, Potpourri Group Inc, Chelmsford, MA. Tel: (978) 256-4100, FAX: (978) 256-1961/0344, Web Site: www.potpourrigroup.com (6)

Harvey, Peter, E., Intellidyn Corp, Hingham, MA. Tel: (781) 741-5503, (866) 773-5756, FAX: (631) 390-0458, E-Mail: kmf@intellidyn.com, Web Site: www.intellidyn.com (22)

Harvey Associates-Direct Marketing Solutions, Cresskill, NJ. Tel: (201) 962-8463, E-Mail: harveyfnj@optonline.net (35)

Harwell, Lane, Alliance for the Arts, New York, NY. Tel: (212) 947-6340, FAX: (212) 947-6416, E-Mail: info@allianceforarts.org, Web Site: www. nyc-arts.org (1)

Harwil Corp, Oxnard, CA. Tel: (805) 988-6800, FAX: (805) 988-6804, E-Mail: harwil@harwil.com, Web Site: www.harwil.com (1)

Harwood, Thomas, A., Mutual of America Life Insurance Co, New York, NY. Tel: (212) 224-1600, (800) 468-3785, FAX: (212) 224-2539, Web Site: www.mutualofamerica.com (14)

Hasbro Inc, Pawtucket, RI. Tel: (401) 727-5000, (800) 242-7276, FAX: (401) 727-5121, Web Site: www. hasbro.com (11)

Hasco First Photo, Saint Charles, MO. Tel: (636) 946-5115, FAX: (636) 946-7148, Web Site: www. growingfamily.com (16)

Hasen, Jeff, HipCricket Inc, Kirkland, WA. Tel: (425) 452-1111, Web Site: www.hipcricket.com (16)

Hasler Mailing Systems and Solutions, Milford, CT. Tel: (203) 301-3400, (800) 995-2035, FAX: (203) 301-2600, E-Mail: info@haslerinc.com, Web Site: www.haslerinc.com (34)

Hassenfeld, Alan, Hasbro Inc, Pawtucket, RI. Tel: (401) 727-5000, (800) 242-7276, FAX: (401) 727-5121, Web Site: www.hasbro.com (11)

Hassler, Sharon, Cumberland General Store Inc, Alpharetta, GA. Tel: (800) 334-4640, FAX: (678) 240-0410, E-Mail: info@cumberlandgerneral.com, Web Site: www.cumberlandgeneral.com (8)

Hastings, Lorraine, BP Rice & Co, El Segundo, CA. Tel: (562) 926-5861, FAX: (562) 404-7130, E-Mail: info@bprco.com, Web Site: www.bprco. com (35)

Hastings, Lyn, Random House Direct Marketing, New York, NY. Tel: (212) 572-4985, (800) 678-5681, FAX: (212) 572-6018, Web Site: www. randomhousedirect.com (17)

Hastings, William, Academic Management Services, Boston, MA. Tel: (508) 235-2900, (800) 891-4203, FAX: (508) 235-2991, E-Mail: info@amsweb.com, Web Site: www.amsweb.com (14)

Hatanaka, Hirofumi, Teikoku Databank America Inc, New York, NY. Tel: (212) 421-9805, FAX: (212) 421-9806, E-Mail: info@teikoku.com, Web Site: www.teikoku.com (24)

Hatch, Denny, Denny Hatch Associates Inc, Philadelphia, PA. Tel: (215) 627-9103, FAX: (215) 627-6610, E-Mail: dennyhatch@yahoo.com, Web Site: www.dennyhatch.com (20)

Hatch, Mark, Honeywell Wintress Controls, Acton, MA. Tel: (978) 264-9550, (800) 333-3282, FAX: (978) 263-0630, Web Site: www.wintress.com (16)

Hatch, Peggy, Target Marketing Group, Philadelphia, PA. Tel: (215) 238-5300, Web Site: www. targetonline.com (31)

Hatch, Peggy, Target Marketing Magazine, Philadelphia, PA. Tel: (215) 238-5300, (800) 777-8074, FAX: (215) 238-5270, Web Site: www. targetmarketingmag.com (43)

Denny Hatch Associates Inc, Philadelphia, PA. Tel: (215) 627-9103, FAX: (215) 627-6610, E-Mail: dennyhatch@yahoo.com, Web Site: www. dennyhatch.com (20)

Hatchell, David, David C Cook, Colorado Springs, CO. Tel: (719) 536-0100, (800) 323-7543, FAX: (719) 536-3232, Web Site: www.davidccook.com (17)

Hatchett & Fagan Direct, Birmingham, AL. Tel: (205) 458-8200, Web Site: www.hfdirect.com (35)

Hatchholdings LLC, Plano, TX. Tel: (214) 505-4697 (20)

Hatfield, David, Energizer Battery Co Inc, Saint Louis, MO. Tel: (314) 985-2000, (800) 383-7323, FAX: (636) 733-4001, Web Site: www.energizer. com (16)

Hatfield, Scott, Cox Communications, Atlanta, GA. Tel: (404) 843-5000, FAX: (404) 269-2243, Web Site: www.cox.com (16)

Hathaway, Diane, M., Recycled Software Inc, Palm Springs, CA. Tel: (760) 655-5666, (800) 851-2425, FAX: (702) 323-5333, E-Mail: diane@ recycledsoftware.com, Web Site: www. recycledsoftware.com (3)

Hathaway, Jim, Grafica Group, Morristown, NJ. Tel: (973) 309-7500, FAX: (973) 309-7501, E-Mail: info@grafica.com, Web Site: www.grafica.com (35)

Hathaway, Misty, Mayo Clinic, Rochester, MN. Tel: (507) 266-2511, FAX: (507) 284-0161, Web Site: www.mayoclinic.org (17)

Hatlestad, Tim, CCIM Institute, Chicago, IL. Tel: (312) 321-4460, (800) 621-7027, FAX: (312) 321-4530, Web Site: www.ccim.com (1)

Hattara, Jeffrey, J., Datacard Ga-Vehren Corp, Hopkins, MN. Tel: (952) 933-1223, (800) 621-6972 x6930, FAX: (952) 931-0418, E-Mail: info@ datacard.com, Web Site: www.gavehren.com (34)

Hatteras, Tinton Falls, NJ. Tel: (732) 223-9888, Web Site: www.hatterascpc.com (27)

Hattersly, Gavin, MillerCoors LLC, Chicago, IL. Tel: (800) 645-5376, Web Site: www.millercoors.com (4)

Hatton-Brown Publishers Inc, Montgomery, AL. Tel: (334) 834-1170, FAX: (334) 834-4525, E-Mail: webman@hattonbrown.com, Web Site: www. hattonbrown.com (17)

Haub, Christian, A&P, Montvale, NJ. Tel: (201) 573-9700, (866) 44 FRESH, FAX: (201) 505-3054, E-Mail: apcustomerrel@aptea.com, Web Site: www.aptea.com (1)

Hauemeyer III, Horace, Metropolis Magazine, New York, NY. Tel: (212) 627-9977, (800) 334-3046, FAX: (212) 627-9988, E-Mail: edit@ metropolismag.com, Web Site: www. metropolismag.com (2)

Hauge, James, PPC, Johnston, IA. Tel: (515) 986-5070, E-Mail: sales@ppcbest.com, Web Site: www. ppcbest.com (9)

Haugen, Erik, Tribune Direct Marketing, Northlake, IL. Tel: (708) 836-2712, Web Site: www. tribunedirect.com (28)

Haugen, Janet B., Unisys, Blue Bell, PA. Tel: (215) 986-4011, (800) 874-8647, FAX: (215) 986-2312, Web Site: www.unisys.com (16)

Haugland, Henry, WebReply.com Inc, Natick, MA. Tel: (508) 318-4600, Web Site: www.webreply.com (35)

Haukins, Mike, Finelight Inc, Louisville, KY. Tel: (502) 589-5896, E-Mail: info@finelight.com, Web Site: www.finelight.com (35)

Haun, James, Oleda & Co Inc, Fort Worth, TX. Tel: (817) 731-1147, (800) 731-4247, FAX: (817) 731-1149, E-Mail: oleda@oleda.com, Web Site: www. oleda.com (16)

Haus, Jennifer, Songbird Hearing Inc, Princeton Junction, NJ. Tel: (732) 828-8300, Web Site: www. songbirdhearing.com (7)

Haus, Lisa, Associated Integrated Marketing, Wichita, KS. Tel: (316) 683-4691, Web Site: www. meetassociated.com (35)

Hausbeck, Janet, Amigo Mobility International Inc, Bridgeport, MI. Tel: (989) 777-0910, (800) 692-6446, FAX: (989) 777-8184, E-Mail: info@ myamigo.com, Web Site: www.myamigo.com (16)

Hauser, Barry, Hauser List Services, NMIS, East Meadow, NY. Tel: (516) 935-8603, FAX: (516) 935-8626, E-Mail: david@hausernet.com, Web Site: www.hausertrack.com (20)

Hauser, David, Hauser List Services, NMIS, East Meadow, NY. Tel: (516) 935-8603, FAX: (516) 935-8626, E-Mail: david@hausernet.com, Web Site: www.hausertrack.com (20)

Hauser, Laura, Moritt, Hock, Hamroff & Horowitz, Garden City, NY. Tel: (516) 873-2000, FAX: (516) 873-2010, E-Mail: lhauser@morritthock.com, Web Site: www.moritthock.com (16)

Hauser, Leela, Bureau Van Dijk, New York, NY. Tel: (212) 797-3550, Web Site: www.bvdinfo.com (22)

Hauser List Services, NMIS, East Meadow, NY. Tel: (516) 935-8603, FAX: (516) 935-8626, E-Mail: david@hausernet.com, Web Site: www.hausertrack. com (20)

Hausrath, David, L., Ashland Inc, Covington, KY. Tel: (859) 815-3333, Web Site: www.ashland.com (16)

Havard, Linda, Playboy Enterprises Inc, Beverly Hills, CA. Tel: (310) 860-1215, Web Site: www. playboyenterprises.com (17)

HAVE Inc, Hudson, NY. Tel: (518) 828-2000, (800) 999-HAVE (4283), FAX: (518) 828-2008, E-Mail: kstein@haveinc.com, Web Site: www.haveinc.com (3)

Havel's Inc, Cincinnati, OH. Tel: (800) 638-4770 (7)

Havens, Gary, The Family Handyman, Eagan, MN. Tel: (651) 454-9200, FAX: (651) 994-2250 (17)

Havens, Rob, The Newman Group, Ann Arbor, MI. Tel: (734) 426-3200, FAX: (734) 426-0777, E-Mail: anewman@newman.com (4)

Havranek, Alan, D., Old World Mouldings Inc, Bohemia, NY. Tel: (631) 563-8660, FAX: (631) 563-8815, E-Mail: mouldings@optonline.com, Web Site: www.oldworldmouldings.com (9)

Havro, Tina, Indoor Gardening Supplies, Dexter, MI. Tel: (734) 426-9080, (800) 823-5740, FAX: (866) 823-4978, Web Site: www.indoorgardensupplies. com (8)

Hawaiian Host Inc, Honolulu, HI. Tel: (808) 848-0500, Web Site: www.hawaiianhost.com (4)

Hawco, Steven, Lego Direct Marketing, Enfield, CT. Tel: (860) 749-2291, FAX: (860) FAX-LEGO, Web Site: www.lego.com (11)

Hawk, Jeffrey, A., American Trim, Lima, OH. Tel: (419) 228-1145, FAX: (419) 996-4850, E-Mail: sales@amtrim.com, Web Site: www.amtrim.com (9)

hawkeye, Dallas, TX. Tel: (214) 749-0080, Web Site: www.hawkeyeww.com (35)

Hawkins, Arlene, Tom Snyder Productions, Watertown, MA. Tel: (617) 926-6000, (800) 342-0236, FAX: (800) 304-1254, E-Mail: ask@tomsnyder. com, Web Site: www.tomsnyder.com (16)

Hawkins, Jeanne, Advisor Media Inc, San Diego, CA. Tel: (858) 278-5600, FAX: (858) 278-5600, Web Site: www.advisor.com (23)

Hawkins, Jim, Florida A&M University, Tallahassee, FL. Tel: (850) 599-3718, FAX: (850) 599-3086 (16)

Hawkins, Terri, Suntrust Banks Inc, Atlanta, GA. Tel: (404) 588-7914, (800) 786-8787, FAX: (404) 532-0550, E-Mail: emmett.harmon@suntrust.com, Web Site: www.suntrust.com (14)

Hawkins III, William A., Medtronic Inc, Minneapolis, MN. Tel: (763) 514-4000, (800) 328-2518, FAX: (763) 514-4879, Web Site: www.medtronic.com (16)

Haworth College of Business, Kalamazoo, MI. Tel: (616) 387-6062, FAX: (616) 387-5710, E-Mail: jay.lindquist@wmich.edu, Web Site: www.hcob.wmich.edu/mktg (41)

Haworth Inc, Holland, MI. Tel: (616) 393-3000, (800) 344-2600, FAX: (616) 393-1570, Web Site: www.haworth.com (34)

Hawthorne, Amy, ReachForce, Austin, TX. Tel: (512) 327-9000, FAX: (512) 327-9090, E-Mail: info@reachforce.com, Web Site: www.reachforce.com (23)

Hawthorne, David, HR Direct Inc, Fairfield, IA. Tel: (641) 472-7188, FAX: (641) 472-5729, E-Mail: info@hrdirect.net, Web Site: www.hrdirect.net (23)

Hawthorne, Timothy, R., Hawthorne Direct Inc, Fairfield, IA. Tel: (641) 472-3800, FAX: (641) 472-6043, E-Mail: drtv@hawthornedirect.com, Web Site: www.hawthornedirect.com (35)

Hawthorne Direct Inc, Fairfield, IA. Tel: (641) 472-3800, FAX: (641) 472-6043, E-Mail: drtv@hawthornedirect.com, Web Site: www.hawthornedirect.com (35)

Hay, Gary, W., Cessna Aircraft Co, Wichita, KS. Tel: (316) 517-6000, FAX: (316) 517-6640, E-Mail: pmichael@cessna.textron.com, Web Site: www.cessna.com (16)

Hayde, Edward, Maryknoll Fathers & Brothers, Maryknoll, NY. Tel: (914) 941-7590, (888) 627-9566, FAX: (914) 944-3613, E-Mail: mkweb@maryknoll.org, Web Site: www.maryknoll.org (1)

Hayden, Deborah, Houston Direct Marketing Association, Houston, TX. Tel: (281) 931-8883, FAX: (281) 820-4023, Web Site: www.houstondma.org (40)

Hayden, Deborah, Pacific Lists Inc, Oakland, CA. Tel: (415) 945-9450, FAX: (415) 945-9451, E-Mail: listinfo@pacificlists.com, Web Site: www.pacificlists.com (23)

Hayden, John, American Modern Insurance Group, Amelia, OH. Tel: (513) 943-7200, (800) 759-9008, FAX: (513) 947-4779, (800) 217-5150, E-Mail: customer_care@amig.com, Web Site: www.amig.com (15)

Hayden, Michael, Redi-Data, Fairfield, NJ. Tel: (973) 808-4500, FAX: (973) 808-5511, E-Mail: sales@redimail.com, Web Site: www.redidata.com (23)

Haydock, John, Crutchfield Corp, Charlottesville, VA. Tel: (434) 817-1000, (800) 955-9091, FAX: (804) 817-1010, E-Mail: administration@crutchfield.com, Web Site: www.crutchfield.com (3)

Haydu, Lucy, Marketing Research Association, Washington, DC. Tel: (860) 682-1000, FAX: (860) 682-1010, E-Mail: email@mra-net.org, Web Site: www.mra-net.org (40)

Hayducky, Deb, McWeeney Marketing Group, Orange, CT. Tel: (203) 891-8100, (800) 272-3440, FAX: (203) 891-0775, E-Mail: george@mcweeneymarketing.com, Web Site: www.mcweeneymarketing.com (33)

Hayes Jr., George, Active Graphics Inc, Cicero, IL. Tel: (312) 733-4343, FAX: (312) 733-4614, E-Mail: info@activegraphics.net, Web Site: www.activegraphics.net (21)

Hayes, Dana, Harlequin Enterprises Ltd, Don Mills, ON Canada. Tel: (416) 445-5860, FAX: (416) 445-8655, E-Mail: customer_ecare@harlequin.ca, Web Site: www.eharlequin.com (17)

Hayes, Gwen, Elmwood Spa, Toronto, ON Canada. Tel: (416) 964-4515, Web Site: www.elmwoodspa.com (19)

Hayes, Joseph, SRDS, Des Plaines, IL. Tel: (800) 851-7737, FAX: (847) 375-5001, Web Site: www.srds.com (17)

Hayes, Kevin, Methode Electronics Inc, Chicago, IL. Tel: (708) 867-6777, FAX: (708) 867-6999, E-Mail: info@methode.com, Web Site: www.methode.com (9)

Hayes, Lisa, Menardi Mikropul LLC, Trenton, SC. Tel: (803) 663-6551, (800) 321-3218, FAX: (803) 663-4029, E-Mail: info@menardifilters.com, Web Site: www.menardifilters.com (16)

Hayes, M.C., DX Engineering, Akron, OH. Tel: (800) 777-0703, FAX: (330) 572-3279, E-Mail: info@comteksystems.com, Web Site: www.comteksystems.com (16)

Hayes, Mary, LEC Ltd, Chicago, IL. Tel: (312) 670-0077, Web Site: www.lecltd.com (35)

Hayes, Mary, S., Hearst Direct Response Advertising Sales, New York, NY. Tel: (212) 649-2920, Web Site: www.hearst.com (31)

Hayes, Ron, Convertible Service, San Gabriel, CA. Tel: (626) 285-2255, (800) 333-1140, FAX: (626) 285-9004, Web Site: www.convertibleparts.com (16)

Hayes, Steve, Omaha Print, Omaha, NE. Tel: (402) 734-4400, (800) 369-0033, FAX: (402) 734-7492, E-Mail: shayes@omahaprint.com, Web Site: www.omahaprint.com (21)

Hayes, Thomas J., DX Engineering, Akron, OH. Tel: (800) 777-0703, FAX: (330) 572-3279, E-Mail: info@comteksystems.com, Web Site: www.comteksystems.com (16)

Haymarket Group Ltd, New York, NY. Tel: (212) 239-0855, FAX: (212) 967-4184, Web Site: www.chocalatiermagazine.com (17)

Haynes, Janet, Bell, Alabama State University/College of Business Administration, Montgomery, AL. Tel: (334) 229-4124, FAX: (334) 229-4870, E-Mail: pvaughn@alasu.edu, Web Site: www.cobanetworks.com (41)

Haynes, John, Pete Rickard Inc, Cobleskill, NY. Tel: (518) 234-2731, (800) 282-5663, FAX: (518) 234-2454, E-Mail: info@peterickard.com, Web Site: www.peterickard.com (11)

Haynes, Matt, CSS Direct, Elkhorn, NE. Tel: (402) 359-1515, FAX: (402) 359-1516, E-Mail: custserv@cssdirect.com, Web Site: www.cssdirect.com (29)

Haynes, Phil, Haynes Marketing Network, Macon, GA. Tel: (912) 742-5266, Web Site: www.haynesmarketing.com (35)

Haynes, Shawn, Markwins International Corp, City of Industry, CA. Tel: (909) 595-8898, FAX: (909) 595-8820, Web Site: www.markwins.com (16)

Haynes & Partners Communications Inc, Indianapolis, IN. Tel: (317) 860-3000, FAX: (317) 860-3001, E-Mail: levans@hp-inc.com, Web Site: www.hp-inc.com (35)

Haynes Marketing Network, Macon, GA. Tel: (912) 742-5266, Web Site: www.haynesmarketing.com (35)

Hays, Lisa, Team Nash Inc, East Hampton, NY. Tel: (646) 497-0297, (631) 267-3385, E-Mail: results@teamnash.com, Web Site: www.teamnash.com (35)

Hays International Mailing Services, Edgewater, NJ. Tel: (201) 307-8888, E-Mail: ltucker@haysmailing.com, Web Site: www.haysmailing.com (28)

Hayward, Al, Pacific Propeller Inc, Kent, WA. Tel: (253) 872-7767, (800) 722-7767, FAX: (253) 872-7221, E-Mail: jheikke@pacprop.com, Web Site: www.pacificpropeller.com (16)

Hayzlett, Jeff, Kodak Graphic Communications, Rochester, NY. Tel: (800) 944-6171, Web Site: www.kpgraphics.com (27)

Hazelden, Center City, MN. Tel: (651) 213-4200, (800) 257-7810, FAX: (651) 213-4411, E-Mail: info@hazelden.org, Web Site: www.hazelden.org (7)

Hazen, Rick, Circle K Stores Inc, Akron, OH. Tel: (330) 630-6300, Web Site: www.cirlcek.com (16)

He, Xiaohong, Quinnipiac College, Hamden, CT. Tel: (203) 582-8600, (203) 582-8200, (800) 462-1944, FAX: (203) 281-8664, Web Site: www.quinnipiac.edu (41)

Health Affairs, Bethesda, MD. Tel: (301) 656-7401, FAX: (301) 654-2845, Web Site: www.healthaffairs.org (17)

Health Alliance Plan, Detroit, MI. Tel: (248) 443-1075, FAX: (248) 443-8851, E-Mail: alandin1@hapcorp.org, Web Site: www.hapcorp.org (15)

Health Care Concepts Inc, Austin, TX. Tel: (512) 479-8508, (800) 628-4201, FAX: (512) 479-8741 (16)

Health Care Logistics, Circleville, OH. Tel: (800) 848-1633, Web Site: www.healthcarelogistics.com (16)

Health Freedom Nutrition LLC, Reno, NV. Tel: (775) 324-2050, Web Site: www.hfn-usa.com (7)

Health International Corp, Saint Petersburg, FL. Tel: (800) 780-6744, FAX: (727) 595-6456, Web Site: www.tonylittle.com (32)

Health O Meter, Alsip, IL. Tel: (708) 377-0600, (800) 815-6615, FAX: (708) 377-0601, E-Mail: HomProCS@homscales.com, Web Site: www.homscales.com (16)

HealthPlan Services, Tampa, FL. Tel: (813) 289-1000, (800) 545-6441, Web Site: www.healthplan.com (15)

Health Sciences Consortium, Chapel Hill, NC. Tel: (919) 942-8731, FAX: (919) 942-3689, E-Mail: tony.penta@edtsi.com, Web Site: www.healthsciencesconsortium.org (17)

Healthcare Communications Group, El Segundo, CA. Tel: (310) 606-5703, (800) 504-0933, FAX: (310) 606-5705, E-Mail: fkilpatrick@hcg.com, Web Site: www.hcg.com (32)

Healthcare Data Solutions, Foothill Ranch, CA. Tel: (949) 421-5971, Web Site: www.healthcaredatasolutions.com (23)

HealthCare Insight, South Jordan, UT. Tel: (801) 285-5800, Web Site: www.hcinsight.com (35)

Healthfest, Edison, NJ. Tel: (732) 225-0100 (5)

HealthInfo Direct, Schaumburg, IL. Tel: (630) 936-9465 (20)

HealthRight International, New York, NY. Tel: (212) 226-9890, Web Site: www.healthright.org (1)

The Healthy Back Store, Beltsville, MD. Tel: (703) 339-1700, (800) 4 MY BACK, FAX: (703) 339-0671, E-Mail: service@healthyback.com, Web Site: www.healthyback.com (16)

Healthy Directions LLC, Potomac, MD. Tel: (301) 340-7788, Web Site: www.healthydirections.com (34)

Healy, Amy, Perlik, Yellow Pages Association, Berkeley Heights, NJ. Tel: (908) 286-2380, (800) 336-0440, FAX: (908) 286-0620, Web Site: www.yellowpagesima.org (1)

Healy, Gigi, The Right Start Inc, Denver, CO. Tel: (303) 320-8312, Web Site: www.rightstart.com (5)

Healy, John, Dydacomp Development Corp, Parsippany, NJ. Tel: (973) 237-9415, (800) 858-3666, FAX: (973) 237-9043, E-Mail: sales@dydacomp.com, Web Site: www.dydacomp.com (22)

Healy List Marketing, Danvers, MA. Tel: (978) 578-1868 (23)

Hear Music, Bellevue, WA. Tel: (425) 452-5534, E-Mail: gail@hearmusic.com, Web Site: www.hearmusic.com (3)

Heard, Melissa, Sellstrom Manufacturing Co, Palatine, IL. Tel: (847) 358-2000, (800) 323-7402, FAX: (847) 358-8564, E-Mail: sellstrom@sellstrom.com, Web Site: www.sellstrom.com (16)

Hearlihy, Sandra, Hearlihy & Co, Pittsburg, KS. Tel: (866) 622-1003, (800) 622-1000, FAX: (800) 443-2260, Web Site: www.hearlihy.com (17)

Hearlihy & Co, Pittsburg, KS. Tel: (866) 622-1003, (800) 622-1000, FAX: (800) 443-2260, Web Site: www.hearlihy.com (17)

Hearst, George, R., The Hearst Corp, New York, NY. Tel: (212) 649-2000, FAX: (212) 649-2108, Web Site: www.hearst.com/magazines/ (17)

Hearst Business Communications, Uniondale, NY. Tel: (516) 227-1300, FAX: (516) 227-1901 (24)

The Hearst Corp, New York, NY. Tel: (212) 649-2000, FAX: (212) 649-2108, Web Site: www.hearst.com/magazines/ (17)

Hearst Direct Response Advertising Sales, New York, NY. Tel: (212) 649-2920, Web Site: www.hearst.com (31)

Hearst Magazines, New York, NY. Tel: (212) 649-2824, FAX: (212) 765-3528, Web Site: www.hearst.com/magazines (17)

Heart Thoughts Inc, Wichita, KS. Tel: (316) 688-5781, (800) 524-2229, FAX: (316) 687-2846, Web Site: www.heart-thoughts.com (27)

Hearthside Quilts & Supplies, Hinesburg, VT. Tel: (802) 482-7800, (800) 451-3533, FAX: (802) 482-7803, E-Mail: hearthsidequilts@att.net, Web Site: www.hearthsidequilts.com (11)

Heartland America, Chaska, MN. Tel: (952) 361-3640, (800) 229-2901, FAX: (952) 368-3452, E-Mail: info@heartlandamerica.com, Web Site: www.heartlandamerica.com (3)

Heartland Boating Magazine, Saint Louis, MO. Tel: (314) 241-4310, (800) 366-9630, FAX: (314) 241-4207, E-Mail: info@heartlandboating.com, Web Site: www.heartlandboating.com (17)

Heartstrings Press, Lancaster, VA. Tel: (804) 462-0884, (800) 462-0884, FAX: (716) 462-0884, E-Mail: sue@grandloving.com, Web Site: www.grandloving.com (17)

Heath, Barb, Klockit, Lake Geneva, WI. Tel: (262) 248-7000, (800) 556-2548, FAX: (262) 248-9899, E-Mail: klockit@klockit.com, Web Site: www.klockit.com (6)

Heath, David, Redleaf Press, Saint Paul, MN. Tel: (651) 641-6621, (800) 423-8309, FAX: (800) 641-0115, E-Mail: jvoltz@redleafpress.org, Web Site: www.redleafpress.org (17)

Heath, Gary, Gambro Inc, Lakewood, CO. Tel: (303) 232-6800, (800) 525-2623, FAX: (303) 222-6810, Web Site: www.gambro.com (16)

Heath, Jinger, L., Beauticontrol Cosmetics Inc, Carrollton, TX. Tel: (972) 458-0601, (800) BEAUTI-1, FAX: (972) 458-6904, E-Mail: clientservices@beauticontrol.com, Web Site: www.beauticontrol.com (16)

Heath, Ralph, Ovation Marketing, La Crosse, WI. Tel: (608) 785-2460, FAX: (608) 785-2496 (35)

Heath Kit Co, Saint Joseph, MI. Tel: (269) 925-6000, (800) 253-0570, FAX: (269) 925-2898, E-Mail: info@heathkit.com, Web Site: www.heathkit.com (3)

Heatherington, Stacy, National League for Nursing, New York, NY. Tel: (212) 363-5555, (800) 669-1656, FAX: (212) 812-0391, E-Mail: generalinfo@nln.org, Web Site: www.nln.org (1)

Heaton, Amy, Pfaelzer Brothers, Maumee, OH. Tel: (419) 893-7611, (800) 345-9290, FAX: (419) 893-0164, Web Site: www.phaelzerbrothers.com (16)

Heator, Marty, Schoolcraft College, Livonia, MI. Tel: (734) 462-4417, Web Site: www.schoolcraft.edu (1)

Heaven & Earth, Virginia Beach, VA. Tel: (757) 420-3576, E-Mail: teamkr8@heavenandearth.hrcoxmail.com, Web Site: www.heavenandearth.com (5)

Heavy Rotation, Milwaukee, WI. Tel: (414) 384-5200, (800) 886-4759, FAX: (414) 434-9318, E-Mail: info@holoubekstudios.com, Web Site: heavytees.com (27)

Hebb, Walter, General Binding Corp, Northbrook, IL. Tel: (800) 723-4000, FAX: (800) 952-1166, (847) 272-1389, Web Site: www.gbc.com (10)

Hebden, William, Hebden Direct, Philadelphia, PA. Tel: (215) 923-3891, E-Mail: hebdendirect@comcast.net (39)

Hebden Direct, Philadelphia, PA. Tel: (215) 923-3891, E-Mail: hebdendirect@comcast.net (39)

Hebert Jr., Curt, L., Entergy, New Orleans, LA. Tel: (504) 576-4000, (800) ENTERGY, FAX: (504) 576-4428, Web Site: www.entergy.com (16)

Hebert, Brian, Association for Computing Machinery (ACM), New York, NY. Tel: (212) 869-7440, FAX: (212) 944-1318, Web Site: www.acm.org (1)

Hebert, James, Paymentech, Salem, NH. Tel: (603) 896-6000, FAX: (603) 896-8717, Web Site: www.paymentech.com (14)

Hebron Academy, Hebron, ME. Tel: (207) 966-2100, Web Site: www.habronacademy.org (1)

Hecht, Brian, Kikucall, New York, NY. Tel: (646) 747-1078, Web Site: www.kikucall.com (3)

Hecht, Donald, L., Mailco Inc, Wayne, NJ. Tel: (973) 777-9500, FAX: (973) 777-5469, E-Mail: marvin@mailcoinc.com, Web Site: www.mailcoinc.com (28)

Hecht, Larry M., Hecht Rubber Corp, Jacksonville, FL. Tel: (904) 731-3401, (800) 872-3401, FAX: (904) 730-0066, Web Site: www.hechtrubber.com (16)

Hecht, Stuart, Hecht Rubber Corp, Jacksonville, FL. Tel: (904) 731-3401, (800) 872-3401, FAX: (904) 730-0066, Web Site: www.hechtrubber.com (16)

Norman Hecht Research Inc, Syosset, NY. Tel: (516) 496-8866, FAX: (516) 496-8165, E-Mail: nhr@normanhechtresearch.com, Web Site: www.normanhechtresearch.com (30)

Hecht Rubber Corp, Jacksonville, FL. Tel: (904) 731-3401, (800) 872-3401, FAX: (904) 730-0066, Web Site: www.hechtrubber.com (16)

Heck, Doug, Suarez Corp Industries, North Canton, OH. Tel: (330) 494-5504, FAX: (330) 497-6837, E-Mail: suarez@suarez.com, Web Site: www.suarez.com (5)

Heck, Julie, Patterson Dental, Saint Paul, MN. Tel: (651) 686-1600, (800) 328-5536, FAX: (651) 686-9331, Web Site: www.pattersondental.com (10)

Heck, Julie, Skyline Displays, Saint Paul, MN. Tel: (651) 234-6634, Web Site: www.skyline.com (5)

Heck, Kirby, Current USA Inc, Colorado Springs, CO. Tel: (719) 594-4100, (877) 665-4458, FAX: (719) 531-2283, Web Site: www.currentinc.com (6)

Heckelman, Daniel, H., B'nai B'rith International, Washington, DC. Tel: (202) 857-6600, FAX: (202) 857-6609, E-Mail: internet@bnaibrith.org, Web Site: www.bnaibrith.org (1)

Hecker, Helen, Twin Peaks Press, Vancouver, WA. Tel: (360) 694-2462, (800) 637-2256, FAX: (360) 696-3210, E-Mail: info@twinpeakspress.com, Web Site: www.twinpeakspress.com (24)

Heckman, Peter H., Horace Mann Educators Corp, Springfield, IL. Tel: (217) 789-2500, FAX: (217) 788-5161, Web Site: www.horacemann.com (15)

Hedden, Andrew, S, Scholastic Inc, New York, NY. Tel: (212) 343-6100, (800) SCHOLASTIC, FAX: (212) 343-6484, Web Site: www.scholastic.com/ (17)

Hederman, Rea, Nyrev Inc, New York, NY. Tel: (212) 757-8070, FAX: (212) 333-5374, E-Mail: mail@nybooks.com, Web Site: www.nybooks.com (17)

Hedlund, Greg, Charnstrom, Shakopee, MN. Tel: (952) 403-0303, (800) 328-2962, FAX: (800) 916-3215, E-Mail: mail@charnstrom.com, Web Site: www.charnstrom.com (28)

Heffel, Ruth, Fort Hays State University, Hays, KS. Tel: (785) 628-FHSU, FAX: (785) 628-4046, Web Site: www.fhsu.edu (41)

Heffernan, Richard, Penguin Publishing Group, New York, NY. Tel: (212) 366-2000, FAX: (212) 366-2952, Web Site: www.penguinputnam.com (17)

Hefner, Christie, Playboy Enterprises Inc, Beverly Hills, CA. Tel: (310) 860-1215, Web Site: www.playboyenterprises.com (17)

Heggen, Arthur, Safeware, The Insurance Agency Inc, Columbus, OH. Tel: (614) 781-1492, (800) 800-1492, FAX: (614) 781-0559, E-Mail: service@safeware.com, Web Site: www.safeware.com (15)

Hegner, Mike, Chase Industries, Inc, Cincinnati, OH. Tel: (513) 860-5565, (800) 543-4455, FAX: (800) 245-7045, Web Site: www.chasedoors.com (16)

Hegtherwick, Gilbert, Angel Records, New York, NY. Tel: (212) 786-8600, FAX: (212) 253-3119, Web Site: www.angelrecords.com (3)

Hegy-Martin, Nancy, Essence Communications Inc, New York, NY. Tel: (212) 522-1212, FAX: (212) 921-5173, Web Site: www.essence.com (17)

Heid, Francis, Advanstar Communications Inc, North Olmstead, OH. Tel: (440) 243-8100, (800) 225-4569, FAX: (440) 891-2740, E-Mail: info@advanstar.com, Web Site: www.advanstarlists.com (17)

Heidemann, Rob, Daydots, Fort Worth, TX. Tel: (817) 590-4500, (800) 321-3687, FAX: (800) 438-7002, E-Mail: customercare@daydots.com, Web Site: www.daydots.com (16)

Heiden, Mark, Point To Point Marketing Inc, Fort Collins, CO. Tel: (970) 472-0131, Web Site: www.ptpmarketing.com (35)

Heiderer, F., Cody, Marketing Economics Inc, Chicago, IL. Tel: (312) 642-2188, FAX: (312) 642-3091, E-Mail: codyh@meimedia.com, Web Site: www.meimedia.com (23)

Heikke, Jeff, Pacific Propeller Inc, Kent, WA. Tel: (253) 872-7767, (800) 722-7767, FAX: (253) 872-7221, E-Mail: jheikke@pacprop.com, Web Site: www.pacificpropeller.com (16)

Heiland, Chris, Sierra Scientific Inc, Phoenix, AZ. Tel: (602) 256-0540, FAX: (602) 252-1972, Web Site: www.value-tek.com (9)

Heiland, George, Sierra Scientific Inc, Phoenix, AZ. Tel: (602) 256-0540, FAX: (602) 252-1972, Web Site: www.value-tek.com (9)

Heiland, Greg, Sierra Scientific Inc, Phoenix, AZ. Tel: (602) 256-0540, FAX: (602) 252-1972, Web Site: www.value-tek.com (9)

Heilhecker, Bill, SIG Pack Inc Doboy Div, New Richmond, WI. Tel: (715) 246-6511, FAX: (715) 246-6539, Web Site: www.doboy.com (34)

Grant Heilman Photography Inc, Lititz, PA. Tel: (717) 626-0296, (800) 622-2046, FAX: (717) 626-0971, E-Mail: info@heilmanphoto.com, Web Site: www.heilmanphoto.com (38)

Heim, Tamara, L., Thomas Nelson, Inc, Nashville, TN. Tel: (615) 889-9000, (800) 251-4000, FAX: (615) 889-5940, Web Site: www.thomasnelson.com (17)

Heim, Wolf, Zotos International, Darien, CT. Tel: (203) 655-8911, (800) 242-WAVE, (800) 242-9283, FAX: (203) 656-7890, E-Mail: HumanResources@zotosintl.com, Web Site: www.zotos.com (16)

Heimberg, Steve, Communication Creativity, Buena Vista, CO. Tel: (720) 344-4388, (800) 331-8355, FAX: (866) 685-0307, E-Mail: steve@steveheimberg.com, Web Site: www.communicationcreativity.com (17)

Heimerman, Jon, Eagle Publishing, Washington, DC. Tel: (202) 216-0600, FAX: (202) 216-0612, Web Site: www.eaglepub.com (17)

Hein, Linda, Redleaf Press, Saint Paul, MN. Tel: (651) 641-6621, (800) 423-8309, FAX: (800) 641-0115, E-Mail: jvoltz@redleafpress.org, Web Site: www.redleafpress.org (17)

Hein, Lisa, California Chamber of Commerce, Sacramento, CA. Tel: (800) 331-8877, Web Site: www.calbizcentral.com (1)

Hein, Meredith, Advanta Corp, Spring House, PA. Tel: (215) 657-4000, (800) 255-0022, Web Site: www.advanta.com (14)

Heinlein, James, ALSTOM Signaling Inc, West Henrietta, NY. Tel: (585) 279-2228, Web Site: www.alstomsignalingsolutions.com (16)

Heinlen, Chuck, Paslode, Vernon Hills, IL. Tel: (847) 634-1900, (800) 222-6990, FAX: (847) 634-6602, E-Mail: tech@paslode.com, Web Site: www.paslode.com (16)

Heinrich Marketing, Denver, CO. Tel: (303) 233-8660, (800) 356-5036, FAX: (303) 239-5352, E-Mail: georgeeddy@heinrich.com, Web Site: www.heinrich.com (35)

Heinstein, Michael, Art.com, Emeryville, CA. Tel: (510) 879-4700, Web Site: www.art.com (8)

Heiser, Alexander, Flint Communications, Fargo, ND. Tel: (701) 237-4850, FAX: (701) 234-9680, Web Site: www.flintcom.com (35)

Heiss, Beth, Lerner Publishing Group, Minneapolis, MN. Tel: (612) 332-3344, (800) 328-4929, FAX: (800) 332-1132, E-Mail: info@lernerbooks.com, Web Site: www.lernerbooks.com (17)

Heisser, Barbara, Active Network Media & Marketing, San Diego, CA. Tel: (858) 964-6064, (877) 228-4808, Web Site: www.activemarketinggroup.com (23)

Heist, Richard, L., Our Lady of Victory Homes of Charity, Lackawanna, NY. Tel: (716) 828-9648, FAX: (716) 828-9643, E-Mail: rheist@olv-bvs.org, Web Site: www.ourladyofvictory.org (1)

Heisz, Deborah, Success Magazine, Lake Dallas, TX. Tel: (800) 570-6414, Web Site: www.successmagazine.com (43)

Heitman, Christopher, J., Pegasus Auto Racing Supplies Inc, New Berlin, WI. Tel: (262) 317-1234, (800) 688-6946, FAX: (262) 317-1201, E-Mail: info@pegasusautoracing.com, Web Site: www.pegasusautoracing.com (12)

Helbing, Scott, Dell Computer Corp, Round Rock, TX. Tel: (512) 338-4400, (512) 283-6161, Web Site: www.dell.com (16)

Held, Lori, Trout Unlimited, Arlington, VA. Tel: (703) 522-0200, Web Site: www.tu.org (1)

Heldref Publications, Washington, DC. Tel: (215) 625-8900, (202) 296-6267, FAX: (202) 296-5149, Web Site: www.heldref.org (17)

Helf, Judith, New York Philharmonic, New York, NY. Tel: (212) 875-5691, Web Site: www.newyorkphilharmonic.org (1)

Helias, Scott, Raritan Inc, Somerset, NJ. Tel: (732) 764-8886, Web Site: www.raritan.com (22)

The Helicopter Group, Richmond Hill, ON Canada. Tel: (905) 731-2440, Web Site: www.thehelicoptergroup.com (28)

Heller, Andrew M., W C Heller & Co, Montpelier, OH. Tel: (419) 485-3176, FAX: (419) 485-8694 (16)

Heller, Christian, Harris Infosource International Inc, Independence, OH. Tel: (330) 425-9000, (877) 359-6308, (800) 888-5900, (800) 748-5482, FAX: (800) 643-5997, E-Mail: customerservice@harrisinfo.com, Web Site: www.harrisinfo.com (17)

Heller, Gary, Alfax Wholesale Furniture Inc, Farmers Branch, TX. Tel: (212) 947-9560, (800) 221-5710, FAX: (212) 947-4734, Web Site: www.alfaxfurniture.com (33)

Heller, R.L., W C Heller & Co, Montpelier, OH. Tel: (419) 485-3176, FAX: (419) 485-8694 (16)

Heller, Scott, Communication Industries Corp, Grafton, VT. Tel: (802) 869-6500, FAX: (802) 869-6565, E-Mail: info@cicmail.com, Web Site: www.careersatcic.com (10)

Heller Financial, Chicago, IL. Tel: (312) 441-7000, FAX: (312) 441-7367, Web Site: www.hellerfin.com (14)

W C Heller & Co, Montpelier, OH. Tel: (419) 485-3176, FAX: (419) 485-8694 (16)

Walter E Heller College of Business Administration, Chicago, IL. Tel: (312) 281-3293, FAX: (312) 281-3290, Web Site: www.roosevelt.edu (41)

Hellinga, Jeff, Trans Union Corp, Chicago, IL. Tel: (312) 258-1717, (800) 335-9888, FAX: (312) 466-8385, Web Site: www.transunion.com (14)

Hello Direct, Nashua, NH. Tel: (408) 972-1990, (800) 435-5634, FAX: (408) 972-8155, Web Site: www.hello-direct.com (16)

Helly-Hansen, Auburn, WA. Tel: (800) 435-5901, FAX: (425) 649-3740, E-Mail: webmaster@hellyhansen.com, Web Site: www.hellyhansen.com (16)

Helm, Sally, The Sailing Co, Palm Coast, FL. Tel: (866) 436-2460, FAX: (401) 848-5048, Web Site: www.sailingworld.com (17)

Helman, Andy, Helman Group Ltd, Oxnard, CA. Tel: (805) 487-7772, FAX: (805) 487-9975, E-Mail: barryh@helmangroup.com, Web Site: www.helmangroup.com (16)

Helman, Barry, Helman Group Ltd, Oxnard, CA. Tel: (805) 487-7772, FAX: (805) 487-9975, E-Mail: barryh@helmangroup.com, Web Site: www.helmangroup.com (16)

Helman Group Ltd, Oxnard, CA. Tel: (805) 487-7772, FAX: (805) 487-9975, E-Mail: barryh@helmangroup.com, Web Site: www.helmangroup.com (16)

Helmer, Dan, Wilton Armetale, Mount Joy, PA. Tel: (717) 653-4444, (800) 553-2048, FAX: (717) 653-6573, E-Mail: cservice@armetale.com, Web Site: www.armetale.com (16)

Helmers, Cathy, Peter Li Education Group, Dayton, OH. Tel: (937) 293-1415, (800) 523-4625, FAX: (937) 293-1310, Web Site: www.peterli.com (17)

Helms, Jack, P., Goldsmith Agio Helms, Minneapolis, MN. Tel: (612) 339-0500, FAX: (612) 339-0507, Web Site: www.agio.com (14)

Helsley, James, Houston Direct Marketing Association, Houston, TX. Tel: (281) 931-8883, FAX: (281) 820-4023, Web Site: www.houstondma.org (40)

Helsley, Tom, Automated Mailing Systems Corp, Dallas, TX. Tel: (972) 869-2844, (800) 527-1668, FAX: (972) 869-2735, E-Mail: amsco@amscodallas.com (34)

Heltzer, John, Protocol, Sarasota, FL. Tel: (800) 800-8627, FAX: (203) 271-4970, Web Site: www.protocolmarketing.com (29)

Helzberg Diamonds, North Kansas City, MO. Tel: (816) 842-7780, (800) HELZBURG, FAX: (816) 480-0294, Web Site: www.helzberg.com (16)

Hemisphere Marketing, Kansas City, MO. Tel: (816) 444-5439, Web Site: www.hemispheremarketing.com (20)

Hemmings, Robert, Hemmings IV Direct, Pasadena, CA. Tel: (626) 796-7188 (35)

Hemmings IV Direct, Pasadena, CA. Tel: (626) 796-7188 (35)

Hemmings Motor News, Bennington, VT. Tel: (800) 227-4373, FAX: (802) 447-9631, Web Site: www.hmn.com (17)

Hemmingson, John, Esco Corp, Portland, OR. Tel: (503) 228-2141, FAX: (503) 778-6682, Web Site: www.escocorp.com (16)

Hen, Sam, Unicom Electric Inc, Walnut, CA. Tel: (626) 964-7873, (800) 346-6668, FAX: (626) 964-7880, E-Mail: info@unicomlink.com, Web Site: www.unicomlink.com (16)

Hendell, Reuben, MRM Worldwide, New York, NY. Tel: (646) 865-6230, Web Site: www.mrmworldwide.com (35)

Henderson III, J., Sherman, The CompTEL Annual Convention & Trade Exposition, Washington, DC. Tel: (202) 296-6650, FAX: (202) 296-7585, Web Site: www.comptel.org (42)

Henderson, Ann, Nevada Magazine, Carson City, NV. Tel: (775) 687-5416, FAX: (775) 687-6159, E-Mail: editor@nevadamagazine.com, Web Site: www.nevadamagazine.com (17)

Henderson, David L., American Locker Security Systems Inc, Coppell, TX. Tel: (817) 329-1600, (800) 828-9118, E-Mail: info@americanlocker.com, Web Site: www.americanlocker.com (16)

Henderson, Frederick, A., Buick Division General Motors Corp, Detroit, MI. Tel: (313) 556-5000, (800) 521-7300, FAX: (313) 556-5108, Web Site: www.buick.com (16)

Henderson, George, Burlington Industries Inc, Greensboro, NC. Tel: (336) 379-2000, FAX: (336) 379-2498, Web Site: www.burlington.com (17)

Henderson, Lynn, O., Doane, Saint Louis, MO. Tel: (314) 569-2700, (866) 647-0918, FAX: (314) 569-1083, Web Site: www.doane.com (17)

Henderson, Rick, American Speech-Language-Hearing Association, Rockville, MD. Tel: (301) 897-5700, (800) 638-8255, E-Mail: productsales@asha.org, Web Site: www.asha.org (1)

Henderson, Ruth, The Silo Inc, New Milford, CT. Tel: (860) 355-0300, (800) 353-SILO, FAX: (860) 350-5495, E-Mail: info@hunthillfarmtrust.org, Web Site: www.thesilo.com (8)

Henderson Advertising Inc, Greenville, SC. Tel: (864) 232-5733, FAX: (864) 298-1280, Web Site: www.hendersonadv.com (35)

Hendley, Audrey, American Express Co, New York, NY. Tel: (212) 640-2000, FAX: (212) 619-9802, Web Site: www.americanexpress.com (14)

Hendrick, Jacqueline, LearnCom HR Consulting & Training, Irvine, CA. Tel: (515) 440-0890, (800) 698-8263, FAX: (515) 221-3149, E-Mail: nhartline@learncom.com, Web Site: www.learncomhr.com (16)

Hendricks, John, Discovery Communications LLC, Silver Spring, MD. Tel: (240) 662-2000, FAX: (240) 662-1868, Web Site: corporate.discovery.com (16)

Hendricks, John, The Learning Channel, Silver Spring, MD. Tel: (240) 662-2000, Web Site: tlc.discovery.com (32)

Hendricks, Todd, ASPCA, New York, NY. Tel: (212) 876-7700, Web Site: www.aspca.org (1)

Hendricks, Virgil, Mid West Floor Co Inc, Saint Louis, MO. Tel: (314) 647-6060, FAX: (314) 647-9189, E-Mail: sales@mid-westfloor.com, Web Site: www.mid-westfloor.com (16)

Hendrickson, Ray, Christian Book Distributors Inc, Peabody, MA. Tel: (978) 532-5300, FAX: (978) 977-5010, E-Mail: javedisian@chrbook.com, Web Site: www.chrbook.com (17)

Hendrix, Christian, Meister Media Worldwide, Willoughby, OH. Tel: (440) 942-2000, (800) 572-7740, FAX: (440) 975-3447, E-Mail: info@meistermedia.com, Web Site: www.meistermedia.com (17)

Hendrix, Darrell, Milwaukee Electric Tool Corp, Brookfield, WI. Tel: (262) 781-3600, (800) 414-6527, FAX: (262) 781-3611, (800) 638-9582, Web Site: www.mil-electric-tool.com (16)

Hendrix, Lucy, Magnets 4 Media, Washington, MO. Tel: (843) 216-6665, (800) 642-6384, FAX: (636) 390-5147, E-Mail: sales@magnets4media.com, Web Site: www.magnets4media.com (30)

Hendryx, Carolyn, Ebersole Lapidary Supply Inc, Wichita, KS. Tel: (316) 945-4771, (877) EBERSOLE, FAX: (316) 945-4773, E-Mail: ebersolerocks@sbcglobal.net, Web Site: www.ebersolelapidary.com (11)

Heneberry, David, David Heneberry Associates, West Grove, PA. Tel: (203) 778-0692, FAX: (203) 778-0699 (20)

David Heneberry Associates, West Grove, PA. Tel: (203) 778-0692, FAX: (203) 778-0699 (20)

Henke, Jack, Henke & Associates Inc, Cedarburg, WI. Tel: (262) 375-9090, FAX: (262) 375-2262, E-Mail: jhenke@henkeinc.com, Web Site: www.henkeinc.com (35)

Henke & Associates Inc, Cedarburg, WI. Tel: (262) 375-9090, FAX: (262) 375-2262, E-Mail: jhenke@henkeinc.com, Web Site: www.henkeinc.com (35)

Henkel, Andrew, Johnson & Quin Inc, Niles, IL. Tel: (847) 588-4800, FAX: (847) 647-6949, E-Mail: jqinfo@j-quin.com, Web Site: www.j-quin.com (28)

Henkel, Dave, Johnson & Quin Inc, Niles, IL. Tel: (847) 588-4800, FAX: (847) 647-6949, E-Mail: jqinfo@j-quin.com, Web Site: www.j-quin.com (28)

Henkel, Jerry, Direct Communications Corp, Rutland, VT. Tel: (802) 747-3322, FAX: (802) 747-3376, E-Mail: information@direct-com.com, Web Site: www.direct-com.com (21)

Henley, Jeffrey O., Oracle Corp, Redwood Shores, CA. Tel: (650) 506-7000, (800) 633-0738, FAX: (650) 506-7200, Web Site: www.oracle.com (14)

Hennagin, David, GSD&M Idea City, Austin, TX. Tel: (512) 242-4736, Web Site: www.gsdm.com (35)

Hennenfent, Ken, American Teleservices Association, Indianapolis, IN. Tel: (317) 816-9336, (877) 779-3974, FAX: (317) 218-0323, Web Site: www.ataconnect.org (40)

Hennerberg, Gary, Hennerberg Group Inc, Colleyville, TX. Tel: (817) 318-8100, E-Mail: gary@hennerberg.com, Web Site: www.hennerberg.com (35)

Hennerberg Group Inc, Colleyville, TX. Tel: (817) 318-8100, E-Mail: gary@hennerberg.com, Web Site: www.hennerberg.com (35)

Hennessey, Edward, Littleton Coin Co Inc, Littleton, NH. Tel: (603) 444-5386, FAX: (603) 444-0121, E-Mail: jhennessey@littletoncoin.com, Web Site: www.littletoncoin.com (6)

Hennig, Ryan, Miles Kimball Co, Oshkosh, WI. Tel: (920) 231-3800, FAX: (920) 231-0422, Web Site: www.mileskimball.com (6)

Henning, David, NSB Group, Pointe-Claire, PQ Canada. Tel: (514) 426-0822, E-Mail: infona@nsbgroup.com, Web Site: www.nsbgroup.com (22)

Henning, Richard, Edward Elgar Publishing Inc, Northampton, MA. Tel: (413) 584-5551, FAX: (413) 584-9933, E-Mail: sales@e-elgar.com, Web Site: www.e-elgar.com (17)

Henningfield, Mary Pat, Wag/Aero Group, Lyons, WI. Tel: (262) 763-9586, (800) 558-6868, FAX: (262) 763-7595, E-Mail: wagaero-sales@wagaero.com, Web Site: www.wagaero.com (16)

Henricks, Susan, Arbor Capital 1, Omaha, NE. Tel: (402) 991-4962 (14)

Henricson, C., Robert, New England Life Insurance Co, Boston, MA. Tel: (617) 578-2000, FAX: (617) 536-2393, Web Site: www.nefn.metlife.com (15)

Henry, Barbara, Indianapolis Newspapers Inc, Indianapolis, IN. Tel: (317) 444-4444, FAX: (317) 633-9414, Web Site: www.indystar.com (17)

Henry, Bill, TomTom North American, Lebanon, NH. Tel: (603) 643-0330, (800) 331-7881, FAX: (603) 653-0249, Web Site: www.tomtom.com (22)

Henry, Gail, Leon Henry Inc, Hartsdale, NY. Tel: (914) 285-3456, FAX: (914) 285-3450, E-Mail: lh@leonhenryinc.com, Web Site: www.leonhenryinc.com (23)

Henry, Holly, W., National Community Pharmacists Association, Alexandria, VA. Tel: (703) 683-8200, (800) 544-7447, FAX: (703) 683-3619, E-Mail: info@ncpanet.org, Web Site: www.ncpanet.org (1)

Henry, Kevin, Dental Economics, Tulsa, OK. Tel: (918) 835-3161, FAX: (918) 831-9804, E-Mail: kellib@pennwell.com, Web Site: www.dentaleconomics.com (24)

Henry, Leon, Leon Henry Inc, Hartsdale, NY. Tel: (914) 285-3456, FAX: (914) 285-3450, E-Mail: lh@leonhenryinc.com, Web Site: www.leonhenryinc.com (23)

Henry, Lynn, LH Management, Hartsdale, NY. Tel: (914) 285-3456, FAX: (914) 285-3450, E-Mail: lh@leonhenryinc.com, Web Site: www.leonhenryinc.com (24)

Henry, Lynn, Leon Henry Inc, Hartsdale, NY. Tel: (914) 285-3456, FAX: (914) 285-3450, E-Mail: lh@leonhenryinc.com, Web Site: www.leonhenryinc.com (23)

Henry, Mark, Direct Marketing News, Markham, ON Canada. Tel: (905) 201-6600, (800) 668-1838, FAX: (905) 201-6601, E-Mail: home@dmn.ca, Web Site: www.dmn.ca (43)

Henry, Peter, O'Keefe Henry Direct Inc, Deerfield, IL. Tel: (847) 681-9200, FAX: (847) 681-9299, Web Site: www.okeefehenrydirect.com (20)

Henry, Thelma, LH Management, Hartsdale, NY. Tel: (914) 285-3456, FAX: (914) 285-3450, E-Mail: lh@leonhenryinc.com, Web Site: www.leonhenryinc.com (24)

Leon Henry Inc, Hartsdale, NY. Tel: (914) 285-3456, FAX: (914) 285-3450, E-Mail: lh@leonhenryinc.com, Web Site: www.leonhenryinc.com (23)

Hensley, Robert, Joseph A Bank Clothiers Inc, Hampstead, MD. Tel: (410) 239-2700, (800) 285-2265, FAX: (410) 239-5911, E-Mail: service@jos-a-bank.com, Web Site: www.josbank.com (2)

Henson, Jim, Ellerbusch Instrument Co, Cincinnati, OH. Tel: (513) 641-1800, (800) 582-2644, FAX: (513) 641-4360, E-Mail: info@ellerbusch.com, Web Site: www.ellerbusch.com (9)

Henthorn, Lisa, PartnerData LLC, Evanston, IL. Tel: (847) 733-0819 (30)

Herb, Ike, Hickory Farms, Maumee, OH. Tel: (419) 893-7611, (800) 822-4438, FAX: (419) 893-0164, Web Site: www.hickoryfarms.com (4)

Herb, Ike, Pfaelzer Brothers, Maumee, OH. Tel: (419) 893-7611, (800) 345-9290, FAX: (419) 893-0164, Web Site: www.phaelzerbrothers.com (16)

Herb, Ike, Pinnacle Orchards, Maumee, OH. Tel: (419) 893-7611, (800) 442-5671, FAX: (419) 893-0164, Web Site: www.pinnacleorchards.com (4)

Herb, Sandy, Meyer Decorative Surfaces Inc, Atlanta, GA. Tel: (404) 699-3900, (800) 776-3900, FAX: (404) 699-3914, Web Site: www.meyerdeco.com (8)

Herbach & Rademan Co, Moorestown, NJ. Tel: (856) 802-0422, (800) 848-8001, FAX: (856) 802-0465, E-Mail: sales@herbach.com, Web Site: www.herbach.com (9)

Herbalife International of America Inc, Los Angeles, CA. Tel: (310) 410-9600, (866) 617-4273, FAX: (310) 258-7019, Web Site: www.herbalife.com (7)

Herber, Paul, L., ASM International, Materials Park, OH. Tel: (440) 338-5151, (800) 336-5152, FAX: (440) 338-4634, E-Mail: customerservice@asminternational.org, Web Site: www.asminternational.org (1)

Herbert, Alan, F., Hollister Inc, Libertyville, IL. Tel: (847) 680-1000, (888) 740-8999, FAX: (847) 680-2123, Web Site: www.hollister.com (16)

Herbert, Anthony, Kappa Publishing Group, Blue Bell, PA. Tel: (215) 643-6385, FAX: (215) 628-3571, Web Site: www.kappapublishing.com (17)

Herbert, Pat, Omni Farm, West Jefferson, NC. Tel: (336) 982-3475, (800) TREE-FARM, FAX: (336) 982-4163, E-Mail: omnifarm@omnifarm.com, Web Site: www.omnifarm.com (16)

Herbert, Paul, Kappa Publishing Group, Blue Bell, PA. Tel: (215) 643-6385, FAX: (215) 628-3571, Web Site: www.kappapublishing.com (17)

Herceg, Lisa, National Association of Realtors, Chicago, IL. Tel: (312) 329-8526, Web Site: www.realtors.org (1)

Herchig, Suzette, Edison Electric Institute, Washington, DC. Tel: (202) 508-5000, FAX: (202) 508-5096, Web Site: www.eei.org (1)

Hercky, Peter, Hercky-Pasqua-Herman, Roselle Park, NJ. Tel: (908) 241-9474, FAX: (908) 241-8961, E-Mail: hercky@hph-comm.com (35)

Hercky-Pasqua-Herman, Roselle Park, NJ. Tel: (908) 241-9474, FAX: (908) 241-8961, E-Mail: hercky@hph-comm.com (35)

The Heritage Co, North Little Rock, AR. Tel: (501) 835-5000 x1142, FAX: (501) 835-5834, Web Site: www.theheritagecompany.com (29)

Heritage Direct, Oakhurst, NJ. Tel: (732) 531-2212, FAX: (732) 531-4798, Web Site: www.actionmarkets.com (22)

Herklots, Michael, Davidoff of Geneva Inc, Pinellas Park, FL. Tel: (203) 323-5811, (800) 328-4365, FAX: (203) 975-0090 (6)

Herlofsky, Peter, J., International City/County Management Association, Washington, DC. Tel: (202) 289-ICMA, FAX: (202) 962-3500, E-Mail: customerservice@icma.org, Web Site: www.icma.org (1)

Herman, Aaron, M., Latest Products Corp, Woodbury, NY. Tel: (516) 367-4700, (800) 288-3547, FAX: (516) 367-4714, E-Mail: info@latestprod.com, Web Site: www.latestprod.com (7)

Herman, Dave, Dansk, Bristol, PA. Tel: (914) 697-6400, (800) 326-7528, FAX: (914) 697-6464, Web Site: www.dansk.com (16)

Herman, Edie, Warren Communications News, Washington, DC. Tel: (202) 872-9200, (800) 771-9202, FAX: (202) 318-8350, E-Mail: info@warren-news.com, Web Site: www.warren-news.com (17)

Herman, Rhonda, McFarland & Co Inc Publishers, Jefferson, NC. Tel: (336) 246-4460, (800) 253-2187, FAX: (336) 246-5018, E-Mail: info@mcfarlandpub.com, Web Site: www.mcfarlandpub.com (17)

Herman, Robert, North American Communications Inc (East), Duncansville, PA. Tel: (814) 696-3553, (800) 624-1533, FAX: (814) 696-1180, E-Mail: info@nacmail.com, Web Site: www.nacmail.com (26)

Herman, Susan, Segerdahl Graphics, Wheeling, IL. Tel: (847) 850-8800, FAX: (773) 477-2051 (27)

The Herman Group, Austin, TX. Tel: (336) 210-3547, E-Mail: info@hermangroup.com, Web Site: www.hermangroup.com (20)

Herman Miller Inc, Zeeland, MI. Tel: (616) 654-3000, FAX: (616) 654-5234, E-Mail: investor@hermanmiller.com, Web Site: www.hermanmiller.com (16)

Hermann, Patricia, Advantage Marketing Group, Elk Grove Village, IL. Tel: (847) 952-2100, FAX: (847) 952-3348, Web Site: www.goamg.com (28)

Hermann, Scott, First Advantage Membership Services, Poway, CA. Tel: (619) 938-6803 (14)

Hermes, Charles, R., Cornhusker Press, Hastings, NE. Tel: (402) 462-4141, FAX: (402) 460-4612, E-Mail: dlsales@dutton-lainson.com, Web Site: www.dutton-lainson.com (17)

Hermes of Paris, New York, NY. Tel: (212) 759-7585, (800) 441-4488, FAX: (212) 644-2132 (2)

Hernandez, Bris, Elks Magazine, Chicago, IL. Tel: (773) 755-4700, (877) 355-7624, FAX: (773) 775-4891, E-Mail: elksmag@elks.org, Web Site: www.elks.org (17)

Hernandez, Fred, Modern Postcard, Carlsbad, CA. Tel: (800) 959-8365, Web Site: www.modernpostcard.com (10)

Hernandez, Maureen, PPS - Packaging Printing Specialists, Saint Charles, IL. Tel: (630) 513-8060, (877) 573-8060, FAX: (630) 513-8062, E-Mail: pps@ppsofil.com, Web Site: www.PPSofIL.com (27)

Hernandez, Robert, Golden Millennium Productions Inc, Pasadena, CA. Tel: (818) 500-1099, E-Mail: info@goldenproductions.com, Web Site: www.goldenproductions.com (32)

Hernandez, Robert, M., USX, Pittsburgh, PA. Tel: (412) 433-1121, E-Mail: webmaster@usx.com, Web Site: www.usx.com (16)

Hernandez, Tom, Specific Media Inc, Irvine, CA. E-Mail: info@specificmedia.com, Web Site: www.specificmedia.com (35)

Hernandez, William, H., Safti First, San Francisco, CA. Tel: (415) 824-4900, (888) 653-3333, FAX: (415) 824-5900, (888) 653-4444, E-Mail: info@safti.com, Web Site: www.safti.com (16)

Herndon, Lisa, M., Catch The Wind Kite Shop, Lincoln City, OR. Tel: (541) 994-9500, (800) 227-7878, FAX: (541) 994-4766, E-Mail: catchthewindkites@yahoo.com, Web Site: www.catchthewind.com (11)

Herntier, John, Charnstrom, Shakopee, MN. Tel: (952) 403-0303, (800) 328-2962, FAX: (800) 916-3215, E-Mail: mail@charnstrom.com, Web Site: www. charnstrom.com (28)

Herold-Martinez, Kelly, XPO, Torrance, CA. Tel: (310) 784-8485, Web Site: www.xpomail.com (28)

Heroux, Dr. Lise, State University of New York-College of Plattsburgh, Plattsburgh, NY. Tel: (518) 564-2000, FAX: (518) 564-3183, E-Mail: nancy. church@plattsburgh.edu, Web Site: www. plattsburgh.edu (41)

Herr, Edwin, Herr Foods Inc, Nottingham, PA. Tel: (610) 932-9330, (800) 344-3777, FAX: (610) 932-2137, E-Mail: info@herrs.com, Web Site: www. herrfoods.com (16)

Herr, James, Herr Foods Inc, Nottingham, PA. Tel: (610) 932-9330, (800) 344-3777, FAX: (610) 932-2137, E-Mail: info@herrs.com, Web Site: www. herrfoods.com (16)

Herr Foods Inc, Nottingham, PA. Tel: (610) 932-9330, (800) 344-3777, FAX: (610) 932-2137, E-Mail: info@herrs.com, Web Site: www.herrfoods.com (16)

Herre, Tom, Referee Enterprises, Franksville, WI. Tel: (262) 632-8855, FAX: (262) 632-5460, E-Mail: questions@referee.com, Web Site: www.referee. com (1)

Herrera, Maurice, Hugo Dunhill Mailing Lists Inc, New Rochelle, NY. Tel: (212) 213-9300, (800) 611-0557, FAX: (212) 213-9245, E-Mail: info@ hdml.com, Web Site: www.hdml.com (23)

Herrera, Richard, U-Haul International, Phoenix, AZ. Tel: (602) 263-6011, (800) GO-UHAUL, FAX: (602) 263-6598, Web Site: www.uhaul.com (16)

Herres, Gen, USAA, San Antonio, TX. Tel: (512) 498-6524, FAX: (512) 498-8000 (15)

Herres, Robert T., USAA Alliance Services Marketing, San Antonio, TX. Tel: (210) 456-9857, FAX: (210) 498-4542, Web Site: www.usaa.com (14)

Herrick, Gregory, Historic Aviation, Minneapolis, MN. Tel: (651) 635-0100, (800) 225-5575, FAX: (651) 635-0700, E-Mail: info@historicaviation.com, Web Site: www.historicaviation.com (12)

Herrin, Donna, M., American Association of Critical-Care Nurses, Aliso Viejo, CA. Tel: (949) 362-2000, (800) 809-CARE, FAX: (949) 362-2020, E-Mail: info@aacn.com, Web Site: www.aacn.org (1)

Herrington, Lee, R., Herrington, Londonderry, NH. Tel: (603) 437-1600, (800) 903-2878, FAX: (603) 437-1340, (603) 437-3492, E-Mail: customerservice@herringtoncatalog.com, Web Site: www.herringtoncatalog.com (16)

Herrington, Londonderry, NH. Tel: (603) 437-1600, (800) 903-2878, FAX: (603) 437-1340, (603) 437-3492, E-Mail: customerservice@herringtoncatalog. com, Web Site: www.herringtoncatalog.com (16)

Ned Herrmann Group, Lake Lure, NC. Tel: (828) 625-9153, Web Site: www.hbdi.com (35)

Herrmann-Nehdi, Ann, Ned Herrmann Group, Lake Lure, NC. Tel: (828) 625-9153, Web Site: www. hbdi.com (35)

Herrschners Inc, Stevens Point, WI. Tel: (715) 341-4554, (800) 441-0838, FAX: (715) 341-2250, E-Mail: customerservice@herrschners.com, Web Site: www.herrschners.com (11)

Hersant, Kristin, Strongmail Systems Inc, Redwood City, CA. Tel: (800) 971-0380, Web Site: www. strongmail.com (32)

Herschend Family Entertainment, Branson, MO. Tel: (417) 338-3810, FAX: (417) 338-8144, Web Site: www.silverdollarcity.com (5)

Hersh, Anita K., Lister Butler Inc, New York, NY. Tel: (212) 951-6100, FAX: (212) 481-0230, Web Site: www.listerbutler.com (20)

Hersh, Bob, Lefty's Corner, Clarks Summit, PA. Tel: (570) 586-LEFT, (570) 586-5338, FAX: (570) 585-2906, E-Mail: info@leftyscorner.com, Web Site: www.leftyscorner.com (6)

Hersh, Dale, Lefty's Corner, Clarks Summit, PA. Tel: (570) 586-LEFT, (570) 586-5338, FAX: (570) 585-2906, E-Mail: info@leftyscorner.com, Web Site: www.leftyscorner.com (6)

Hersh, Randi, Ultra Direct Marketing Inc, Jackson, NJ. Tel: (732) 364-8337, (800) 365-8587, FAX: (732) 364-9598, E-Mail: contact@ultradirect.com, Web Site: www.ultradirect.com (16)

Hershberger, Julia, Sustainable Forestry Initiative Inc, Washington, DC. Tel: (202) 596-3450, FAX: (202) 596-3451, E-Mail: info@sfiprogram.org, Web Site: www.sfiprogram.org (1)

Hershey, Douglas, New Pig Corp, Tipton, PA. Tel: (814) 684-0101, (800) 468-4647, FAX: (814) 684-0961, E-Mail: hothogs@newpig.com, Web Site: www.newpig.com (9)

Hershey Foods Corp, Hershey, PA. Tel: (800) 454-7737, FAX: (717) 534-5204, Web Site: www. hersheygifts.com (4)

Hershey Park, Hershey, PA. Tel: (717) 534-3149, (800) HERSHEY, E-Mail: info@hersheypa.com, Web Site: www.hersheypark.com (19)

Hershey's Mail Order, Hershey, PA. Tel: (717) 534-7381, (800) 544-1347, FAX: (717) 534-7947, E-Mail: hersheygiftsinfo@hersheys.com, Web Site: www.hersheygifts.com (4)

Hershman, Robert, American Library Association-Publishing Services, Chicago, IL. Tel: (312) 944-6780, (800) 545-2433, FAX: (312) 280-4380, Web Site: www.ala.org (1)

Hersum, A.R., AAI, Hopkinton, MA. Tel: (508) 544-1250, (877) 866-8500, FAX: (508) 544-1253, E-Mail: info@aai-agency.com, Web Site: www.aai-agency.com (35)

Hersum, Mark, AAI, Hopkinton, MA. Tel: (508) 544-1250, (877) 866-8500, FAX: (508) 544-1253, E-Mail: info@aai-agency.com, Web Site: www.aai-agency.com (35)

Hertz, Eugene, Diapers.com, Jersey City, NJ. Tel: (800) 342-7377, Web Site: www.diapers.com (5)

Hertz, Gerald, Genada Imports, Teaneck, NJ. Tel: (973) 569-9660, FAX: (973) 569-9660 (8)

Hertz, Steve, Antares Information Tech, Chadds Ford, PA. Tel: (631) 234-5700, (800) 330-2579, FAX: (631) 234-5472, E-Mail: steve@antares-iti.com, Web Site: www.antares-iti.com (21)

Hertz Corp, Park Ridge, NJ. Tel: (201) 307-2000, FAX: (201) 307-2644, Web Site: www.hertz.com (19)

Hervieu, Philippe, Yves Rocher North America Inc, Longueuil, PQ Canada. Tel: (450) 442-9555, Web Site: www.yvesrocherusa.com (7)

Herzer, David, G., Delta Upsilon International Fraternity, Indianapolis, IN. Tel: (317) 875-8900, FAX: (317) 876-1629, E-Mail: ihq@deltau.org, Web Site: www.deltau.org (16)

Herzog, Sylviane, Concorde Communications, Los Angeles, CA. Tel: (310) 854-4411, (800) 800-4411, FAX: (310) 854-0551, Web Site: www. concordecommunications.com (29)

Hesemann, Ted, Herrschners Inc, Stevens Point, WI. Tel: (715) 341-4554, (800) 441-0838, FAX: (715) 341-2250, E-Mail: customerservice@herrschners. com, Web Site: www.herrschners.com (11)

Heslop, Julian, Glaxo Smith Kline, Research Triangle Park, NC. Tel: (919) 483-2100, (888) 825-5249, FAX: (919) 248-8383, Web Site: www.gsk.com (16)

Hess, Carol, Political Resources, Lake Worth, FL. Tel: (800) 423-2677, FAX: (561) 533-0104, E-Mail: info@politicalresources.com, Web Site: www. politicalresources.com (23)

Hess, Richard, E., Pennrich, Waterford, PA. Tel: (814) 866-2412, FAX: (814) 864-3908 (23)

Hess, Sara, Farm Progress Co, Saint Charles, IL. Tel: (630) 690-5600, FAX: (630) 462-2202, E-Mail: dwilson@farmprogress.com, Web Site: www. farmprogress.com (17)

Hess Print Solutions, Kent, OH. Tel: (330) 677-3353, FAX: (330) 677-8256, E-Mail: sshowerman@ hessprintsolutions.com, Web Site: www. thepressofohio.com (27)

Hesse, Dan, Sprint PCS, Overland Park, KS. Tel: (800) 927-2199, Web Site: www.sprintpcs.com (16)

Hester, Walter, Maui Jim Inc, Peoria, IL. Tel: (309) 691-3700, FAX: (309) 683-2202, Web Site: www. mauijim.com (16)

Hestermann, Francine, Fort Hays State University, Hays, KS. Tel: (785) 628-FHSU, FAX: (785) 628-4046, Web Site: www.fhsu.edu (41)

Hesters, Grady, Audio Editions Books-on-Cassette & CD, Auburn, CA. Tel: (800) 231-4261, FAX: (800) 882-1840, E-Mail: info@audioeditions.com, Web Site: www.audioeditions.com (3)

Heston, Charlton, National Rifle Association of America, Fairfax, VA. Tel: (703) 267-1000, (800) 672-3888, FAX: (703) 267-3957, E-Mail: nra. contact@nra.org, Web Site: www.nra.org (1)

Heth, Todd, Cuvaison Inc, Calistoga, CA. Tel: (707) 942-6266, FAX: (707) 942-5732, E-Mail: jschuppert@cuvaison.com, Web Site: www. cuvaison.com (4)

Hetzuer, Frances, E., Amigo Mobility International Inc, Bridgeport, MI. Tel: (989) 777-0910, (800) 692-6446, FAX: (989) 777-8184, E-Mail: info@ myamigo.com, Web Site: www.myamigo.com (16)

Hewlett-Packard Co, Palo Alto, CA. Tel: (650) 857-1501, (800) 752-0900, FAX: (650) 857-5518, Web Site: www.hp.com (16)

Heydendael, Arthur, G., America Direct Book Service Custom Publishing, Ossining, NY. Tel: (914) 271-3640, FAX: (914) 271-3641, E-Mail: info@ americadirectbook.com, Web Site: www. americadirectbook.com (17)

Heyer, Bill, Heyer Corp, Roselle, IL. Tel: (708) 398-7646, FAX: (866) 542-9858, E-Mail: info@ heyerco.com, Web Site: www.heyerco.com (34)

Heyer Corp, Roselle, IL. Tel: (708) 398-7646, FAX: (866) 542-9858, E-Mail: info@heyerco.com, Web Site: www.heyerco.com (34)

Heyes, Peter B., Frontier Corp, Rochester, NY. Tel: (716) 777-1000, Web Site: www.frontieronline.com (16)

Heyman, Bruce, Window Coverings Exchange, North Plainfield, NJ. Tel: (908) 755-4700 (8)

Heynes, Bill, A-KD Mailing & Fulfillment Service, Lincolnwood, IL. Tel: (847) 673-0186, (866) 330-6245, FAX: (874) 673-0188, E-Mail: dan@ kdmailing.com, Web Site: www.kdmailing.com (28)

Hi-C Production, New Hyde Park, NY. Tel: (516) 746-2142, FAX: (516) 294-1964, E-Mail: haponte435@ aol.com (27)

Hi-Tech Marketing Solutions, Pompano Beach, FL. Tel: (954) 784-3830, Web Site: www.coastmailers. com (27)

Hiban, Michael, Omega List Co, McLean, VA. Tel: (703) 821-1890, FAX: (703) 821-8794, E-Mail: mhiban@omegalist.com, Web Site: www.omegalist. com (23)

Hibbard, Timothy, A., WESCO, Pittsburgh, PA. Tel: (412) 454-2200, (800) 343-1201, E-Mail: info@ wesco.com, Web Site: www.wescodist.com (16)

The Hibbert Group, Trenton, NJ. Tel: (609) 394-7500, (800) 545-4747, FAX: (609) 695-6553, Web Site: www.hibbertco.com (28)

Hibbs Jr, Ralph, L, American College of Physicians, Washington, DC. Tel: (215) 351-2400, (800) 523-1546, FAX: (215) 351-2686, Web Site: www. acponline.org (17)

Hickey, Dan, Better Homes & Gardens, New York, NY. Tel: (212) 551-7097, FAX: (212) 551-6917, E-Mail: support@bhg.com, Web Site: www.bhg. com (31)

Hickey, Jim, Planet Cotton, Gaithersburg, MD. Tel: (301) 948-0400, FAX: (301) 948-9031, Web Site: www.planetcotton.com (2)

Hickey, Mark, Telephony, Chicago, IL. Tel: (312) 595-1080, (800) 458-0479, FAX: (312) 595-0295, Web Site: www.internettelephony.com (17)

Hickey, Mike, 802 Creative Partners Inc, Bethel, VT. Tel: (802) 234-9755, FAX: (802) 234-6719, E-Mail: info@802creative.com, Web Site: www.802creative.com (35)

Hickman, Del, Multi-Level Marketing International Association (MLMIA), Irvine, CA. Tel: (949) 854-0484, FAX: (949) 854-7687, E-Mail: info@mlmia.com, Web Site: www.mlmia.com/ (1)

Hickner, Joe, Woodwind & Brasswind Inc, Indianapolis, IN. Tel: (574) 251-3500, (800) 348-5003, FAX: (574) 251-3501, Web Site: www.wwbw.com (5)

Hickory Farms, Maumee, OH. Tel: (419) 893-7611, (800) 822-4438, FAX: (419) 893-0164, Web Site: www.hickoryfarms.com (4)

The Hickory Printing Group, Conover, NC. Tel: (828) 465-3431, (800) 442-5679, FAX: (828) 465-2517, E-Mail: gglisan@hickoryprinting.com, Web Site: www.hickoryprinting.com (27)

Hicks, Barbara, Houston Direct Marketing Association, Houston, TX. Tel: (281) 931-8883, FAX: (281) 820-4023, Web Site: www.houstondma.org (40)

Hicks, Deborah, A., Harvard Pilgrim Health Care, Wellesley, MA. Tel: (617) 509-1000, FAX: (617) 509-7590, Web Site: www.harvardpilgrim.org (7)

Hicks, Gunner, Allied Printing Services Inc, Manchester, CT. Tel: (860) 643-1101, (800) 225-8777, (800) 224-8894, FAX: (860) 643-9723, E-Mail: allied@alliedprinting.com, Web Site: www.alliedprinting.com (27)

Hicks, James, Trigon Blue Cross/Blue Shield, Roanoke, VA. Tel: (540) 853-5000, (800) 553-3164, FAX: (540) 853-3053, Web Site: www.trigon.com (15)

Hicks, Jeff, Crispin, Porter & Bogusky, Miami, FL. Tel: (305) 859-2070, FAX: (305) 854-3419, Web Site: www.cpbgroup.com (35)

Hicks, Kenneth, JC Penney Inc, Plano, TX. Tel: (972) 431-1000, FAX: (972) 431-1977, Web Site: www.jcpenney.com (5)

Hicks, Randy, Solarcom, Norcross, GA. Tel: (770) 449-6116, (888) SUN-DATA, FAX: (770) 448-7726, Web Site: www.solarcom.net (16)

Hicks, Robert, admail.net/List Media, Aurora, OH. Tel: (330) 995-0864, FAX: (330) 995-0873, E-Mail: sales@admail.net, Web Site: www.admail.net (32)

Hicks, Tyler, G., How I Grossed More Than $1 Million in Direct Mail Order Starting with Little Cash & Less Know How, Rockville Centre, NY. Tel: (516) 766-5850, (800) 323-0548, FAX: (516) 766-5919, Web Site: www.iwsmoney.com (43)

Hidalgo, Jerry, Parker Steel Co, Toledo, OH. Tel: (419) 473-2481, (800) 333-4140, FAX: (419) 471-2655, Web Site: www.metricmetal.com (16)

Hiebert, Crystal, Winnipeg Art Gallery, Winnipeg, MB. Tel: (204) 786-6641, FAX: (204) 788-4998, E-Mail: inquiries@wag.mb.ca, Web Site: www.wag.mb.ca (1)

The Hiebing Group, Madison, WI. Tel: (608) 256-6357, FAX: (608) 256-0693, E-Mail: ideas@hiebing.com, Web Site: www.hiebing.com (35)

Hier, Marlene, Simon Wiesenthal Center, Los Angeles, CA. Tel: (310) 553-9036, Web Site: wiesenthal.com (1)

Hietikko, Donna, Mary Maxim Inc, Port Huron, MI. Tel: (810) 987-2000, (800) 962-9504, FAX: (810) 987-5056, E-Mail: info@marymaxim.com, Web Site: www.marymaxim.com (11)

Higgins, Mark, BCC Software Inc, Rochester, NY. Tel: (585) 272-9130, (800) 453-3130, FAX: (585) 340-8850, Web Site: www.bccsoftware.com (22)

Higgins, Patrick, Roche Pharmaceuticals, Nutley, NJ. Tel: (973) 235-5000, FAX: (973) 235-7605, Web Site: www.rocheusa.com (7)

Higgins, Shaun, The Spokesman-Review, Spokane, WA. Tel: (509) 459-5060, FAX: (509) 459-5083, E-Mail: shaunh@spokesman.com, Web Site: www.spokane.net (17)

Higgins, Thomas, The College Board, New York, NY. Tel: (212) 713-8000, FAX: (212) 713-8143, Web Site: www.collegeboard.com (1)

High Cotton, Birmingham, AL. Tel: (877) 838-2345, FAX: (205) 836-5587, E-Mail: sales@highscottonusa.com, Web Site: www.highcottonusa.com (28)

High Note Media Inc, Chicago, IL. Tel: (773) 980-6873, Web Site: www.highnotemedia.com (20)

High Octane Communications, San Rafael, CA. Tel: (415) 256-9369, FAX: (415) 256-8988, E-Mail: chris@hocadvertising.com, Web Site: www.hocadvertising.com (35)

High Point Insurance, Lincroft, NJ. Tel: (732) 978-6255, Web Site: www.highpointins.com (15)

Highby, Dennis, Cabela's Inc, Sidney, NE. Tel: (308) 254-5505, (800) 237-4444, FAX: (308) 254-4800, Web Site: www.cabelas.com (11)

Higher Power Marketing, Phoenix, AZ. Tel: (480) 837-3580, (888) 922-3580, FAX: (480) 837-3589, E-Mail: info@hpowermarketing.com, Web Site: www.hpowermarketing.com (35)

Highley, Jay, ChaCha Mobile Answers, Carmel, IN. Tel: (317) 660-6680, Web Site: partners.chacha.com (20)

Highlights For Children, Columbus, OH. Tel: (614) 487-2601, (800) 848-8922, FAX: (614) 487-2700, Web Site: www.highlights.com (17)

Highmark Blue Cross Blue Shield, Pittsburgh, PA. Tel: (412) 544-7000, FAX: (412) 544-5350, Web Site: www.highmark.com (15)

HighScope Educational Research Foundation, Ypsilanti, MI. Tel: (734) 485-2000, (800) 40-PRESS, FAX: (734) 485-0704, E-Mail: lschweinhart@highscope.org, Web Site: www.highscope.org (17)

Higley, Karen, Fluke Biomedical, Everett, WA. Tel: (425) 347-6100, (800) 850-4608, FAX: (425) 446-5116, Web Site: www.flukebiomedical.com (16)

Higman, Rebecca, Network for Good, Bethesda, MD. Tel: (240) 482-3211, Web Site: www.networkforgood.org (1)

Hijkoop, Franz, The Quaker Oats Co, Chicago, IL. Tel: (312) 821-1000, (800) 367-6287, FAX: (312) 222-8323, Web Site: www.quakeroats.com (16)

Hilbert, Greg, S&S Worldwide, Colchester, CT. Tel: (860) 537-3451, (800) 288-9941, FAX: (860) 537-2866, E-Mail: cservice@ssww.com, Web Site: www.ssww.com (17)

Hilbert, Stan, Telect Inc, Liberty Lake, WA. Tel: (509) 926-6000, FAX: (509) 926-8915, E-Mail: getinfo@telect.com, Web Site: www.telect.com (16)

Hilburt, Laura, Sure Fit Inc, Alburtis, PA. Tel: (610) 264-7300, Web Site: www.surefit.com (8)

Hildebrand, Scott, Engauge Direct, Atlanta, GA. Tel: (404) 601-4332, (804) 363-5715, Web Site: www.engauge.com (35)

Hile, Deborah, Prestige Mailing Lists Inc, Van Nuys, CA. Tel: (818) 374-1320, FAX: (818) 374-1344, E-Mail: Debbie@prestigemaillists.com, Web Site: www.prestigemailinglists.com (24)

Tommy Hilfiger, New York, NY. Tel: (212) 548-1368, Web Site: www.tommy.com (2)

Hilfman, Deborah, New York International Gift Fair, White Plains, NY. Tel: (914) 421-3200, (800) 272-SHOW, FAX: (914) 948-6180, Web Site: www.nyigf.com (42)

Hilger, Joe, G-Neil Direct Mail, Sunrise, FL. Tel: (800) 999-9111, FAX: (954) 851-1264, E-Mail: tcs@gneil.com, Web Site: www.gneil.com (10)

Hilkemann, Aaron, C., Duncan Aviation, Lincoln, NE. Tel: (402) 475-2611, (800) 228-4277, FAX: (402) 475-5541, Web Site: www.duncanaviation.com (16)

Hilkert, Tom, Merchandising Equipment Group (MEG), Cambridge City, IN. Tel: (765) 478-3141, (800) 645-3315, FAX: (765) 478-4439, E-Mail: meginfo@megfixtures.com, Web Site: www.megfixtures.com (34)

Hill, Andrea, Rio Grande, Albuquerque, NM. Tel: (505) 839-3000, (800) 545-6566, FAX: (800) 965-2329, E-Mail: info@riogrande.com, Web Site: www.riogrande.com (16)

Hill, Barb, Townsend Communications LLC, Kansas City, MO. Tel: (816) 361-0616, (800) 274-8867, FAX: (816) 361-6164, Web Site: www.townsendprint.com (17)

Hill, Benjamin, BW Hill & Associates LLC, Oak Park, IL. Tel: (800) 431-3183, Web Site: www.bwhillassociates.com (30)

Hill, Chris, A., Sprint PCS, Overland Park, KS. Tel: (800) 927-2199, Web Site: www.sprintpcs.com (16)

Hill, Connie, American Direct Marketing Services, Dallas, TX. Tel: (214) 634-2361, (800) 527-5080, FAX: (214) 905-3829, Web Site: www.dmlist.com (23)

Hill, Constance, TFC Inc, Napa, CA. Tel: (707) 224-6161, Web Site: www.tfcinc.com (27)

Hill, David, Perfection Tip Co/Camping Products Co, Long Beach, CA. Tel: (562) 491-0076, (800) 525-4835, FAX: (562) 435-7599 (16)

Hill, Dr. Marjorie, Gay Men's Health Crisis, New York, NY. Tel: (212) 367-1000, FAX: (212) 367-1220, E-Mail: webmaster@gmhc.org, Web Site: www.gmhc.org (1)

Hill, Gregory, Titan Manufacturing, Holbrook, MA. Tel: (781) 767-1963, Web Site: www.americantitan.com (34)

Hill, Jim, The Psychological Corp, San Antonio, TX. Tel: (800) 211-8378, FAX: (800) 232-1223, Web Site: www.psychcorp.com (17)

Hill, Judith, Tillamook County Creamery Association, Tillamook, OR. Tel: (503) 842-4481, (800) 542-7290, FAX: (503) 842-6039, Web Site: www.tillamookcheese.com (4)

Hill, Lorne, Supremex Inc, La Salle, PQ Canada. Tel: (514) 595-0555, Web Site: www.supremex.com (26)

Hill, Richard, Rent Mother Nature, Cambridge, MA. Tel: (617) 868-5059, (800) 232-4048, FAX: (617) 868-5861, Web Site: www.rentmothernature.com (4)

Hill, Steven, Eagle Asset Management Inc, Saint Petersburg, FL. Tel: (727) 573-2453, FAX: (727) 573-8020, Web Site: www.eagleasset.com (14)

Hill, Tom, Micro Plastics Inc, Flippin, AR. Tel: (870) 453-2261, (800) 466-1467, FAX: (870) 453-8676, E-Mail: mpsales@microplastics.com, Web Site: www.microplastics.com (16)

Hill, Wally, CMA Awards, Don Mills, ON. Tel: (416) 391-2362, FAX: (416) 441-4062, E-Mail: info@the-cma.org, Web Site: www.the-cma.org/awards (42)

BW Hill & Associates LLC, Oak Park, IL. Tel: (800) 431-3183, Web Site: www.bwhillassociates.com (30)

Hill Holliday, Boston, MA. Tel: (617) 366-4000, Web Site: www.hhcc.com (35)

James J Hill Reference Library, Saint Paul, MN. Tel: (651) 265-5500, Web Site: www.jjhill.org (1)

Hill Mailing & Printing of Florida Inc, Brandon, FL. Tel: (813) 258-5220 (21)

Hilleary, Rick, RealData Services Inc, Glenwood Springs, CO. Tel: (970) 945-2456, FAX: (970) 945-5356, E-Mail: rick@realdataservices.com, Web Site: www.realdataservices.com (22)

Hillimire, Jeff, Engauge Direct, Atlanta, GA. Tel: (404) 601-4332, (804) 363-5715, Web Site: www.engauge.com (35)

Hillin, Andrew, Carhill Enterprises Inc, Saint Louis, MO. Tel: (314) 621-7646, Web Site: www.cahillinsight.com (15)

Hillis, Jay, Wildlife Education Ltd, Park Hills, KY. Tel: (858) 513-7600, FAX: (858) 513-7660, E-Mail: animals@zoobooks.com, Web Site: www.zoobooks.com (17)

Hillis, John, StatSoft Inc, Tulsa, OK. Tel: (918) 749-1119, FAX: (918) 749-2217, E-Mail: info@statsoft.com, Web Site: www.statsoft.com (9)

Hillis, Robert, J., Direct Supply Inc, Milwaukee, WI. Tel: (414) 358-2805, (800) 634-7328, FAX: (414) 358-2397, E-Mail: deardirect@directs.com, Web Site: www.directsupply.net (16)

Hillman, Ginger, Fairchild Books, New York, NY. Tel: (212) 630-4171, (800) 932-4724, FAX: (212) 630-3868, Web Site: www.fairchildbooks.com (17)

Hillside Wire Cloth Co, Bloomfield, NJ. Tel: (973) 751-3131, (800) 826-7395, FAX: (973) 470-8183, E-Mail: info@hillsidewirecloth.com, Web Site: www.hillsidewirecloth.com (9)

Diana Hils, Houston, TX. Tel: (713) 546-4550 (5)

Hilsheimer, Lawrence, A., Nationwide Mutual Insurance Co, Columbus, OH. Tel: (614) 249-7111, (800) 882-2822, FAX: (614) 854-3676, Web Site: www.nationwide.com (15)

Hiltenbrand, Danny, Graceland, Memphis, TN. Tel: (901) 332-3322, (800) 238-2010, FAX: (901) 344-3120, Web Site: www.elvis.com (6)

Hilti North America, Tulsa, OK. Tel: (918) 252-6000, Web Site: www.hilti.com (34)

Hilton, Larry, Spectrum Chemicals & Laboratory Products, Gardena, CA. Tel: (310) 516-8000, Web Site: www.spectrumchemical.com (16)

Hilton, Scott, Diapers.com, Jersey City, NJ. Tel: (800) 342-7377, Web Site: www.diapers.com (5)

Conrad N Hilton College of Hotel & Restaurant Management University of Houston, Houston, TX. Tel: (713) 743-0209 (1)

Hilton Grand Vacations Co, Orlando, FL. Tel: (407) 521-3100, Web Site: www.hiltongrandvacations.com (19)

Hilton HHonors Worldwide, McLean, VA. Tel: (703) 883-1000, Web Site: www.hilton.com (16)

Hilton Hotels Corp, Mc Lean, VA. Tel: (310) 278-4321, (800) HILTONS, FAX: (310) 205-3670, Web Site: www.hilton.com (19)

Himan, Dennis, P., The Toro Consumer Div, Bloomington, MN. Tel: (952) 888-8801, (888) 384-9939, FAX: (952) 887-8258, Web Site: www.thetorocompany.com (16)

Himmel Jr., Keith, L., J Peterman Co, Lexington, KY. Tel: (888) 647-2555, FAX: (859) 254-0869, Web Site: www.jpeterman.com (5)

HIMSS, Chicago, IL. Tel: (312) 664-4467, Web Site: www.himss.org (1)

Hinaga, Steven, DataCraft Inc, Kailua, HI. Tel: (808) 263-5583, Web Site: www.dcraftinc.com (22)

Hinda Incentives, Chicago, IL. Tel: (773) 890-5900, (800) 621-4412, FAX: (773) 890-4606, E-Mail: contact@hinda.com, Web Site: www.hinda.com (33)

Hindman, W.J., Industrial Marketing Services, Elk Grove Village, IL. Tel: (847) 258-8850, FAX: (847) 593-0462, E-Mail: whindman@imscomm.com (35)

Hinds, Ossie, Cornerstone Group of Companies, Toronto, ON Canada. Tel: (416) 932-9555, FAX: (416) 932-9566, E-Mail: info@cstonecanada.com, Web Site: www.cstonecanada.com (22)

Hinds, Tim, American Recreation Products Inc, Saint Louis, MO. Tel: (314) 576-8000, FAX: (314) 576-8072 (11)

Hines, Chris, American Kidney Fund, Rockville, MD. Tel: (301) 881-3052, Web Site: www.kidneyfund.org (1)

Hines, Thomas, A., JJ Keller & Associates Inc, Neenah, WI. Tel: (920) 722-2848, (800) 327-6868, FAX: (800) 727-7516, E-Mail: thines@jjkeller.com, Web Site: www.jjkeller.com/jjk (16)

Hing, Kevin, Danker Laboratories Inc, Sarasota, FL. Tel: (800) 237-9641, FAX: (800) 665-5086, E-Mail: sales@dankerlabs.com, Web Site: www.dankerlabs.com (16)

Hinkle, April, Brumley, Texas Monthly, Austin, TX. Tel: (512) 320-6900, (800) 759-2000, FAX: (512) 476-9007, E-Mail: info@texasmonthly.com, Web Site: www.texasmonthly.com (17)

Hinkle, Richard, Broadcast Electronics Inc, Quincy, IL. Tel: (217) 224-9600, FAX: (217) 224-9607, E-Mail: bdcast@bdcast.com, Web Site: www.bdcast.com (3)

Hinnant, Keith, Cystic Fibrosis Foundation, Bethesda, MD. Tel: (301) 951-4422, Web Site: www.cff.org (1)

Hinrichs, Joe, Ford Motor Co, Dearborn, MI. Tel: (313) 845-8540, (800) 555-5259, FAX: (313) 845-6073, Web Site: www.ford.com (16)

Hinrichs, Melissa, Quality Contact Solutions Inc, Aurora, NE. Tel: (402) 210-2692, (866) 963-2889, FAX: (402) 210-2692, E-Mail: info@qualitycontactsolutions.com, Web Site: www.qualitycontactsolutions.com (29)

Hintelmann, Lisa, Esquire Magazine, New York, NY. Tel: (212) 649-2000, (800) 925-0485, FAX: (212) 265-0938, E-Mail: esquire@hearst.com, Web Site: www.esquire.com (17)

Hinton, Jason, Concepts & Strategies Inc, Washington, DC. Tel: (202) 251-9951, FAX: (202) 478-1750, E-Mail: info@constrat.net (35)

Hinton, Leslie, F., Dow Jones & Co, Princeton, NJ. Tel: (609) 520-4000, FAX: (212) 416-4348, Web Site: www.dowjones.com/corp/index.html (17)

Hinton, Patricia, Ansar Inc, Thompsons Station, TN. Tel: (615) 368-2025, Web Site: www.ansarinc.com (1)

HipCricket Inc, Kirkland, WA. Tel: (425) 452-1111, Web Site: www.hipcricket.com (16)

Hippo Direct, Solon, OH. Tel: (440) 519-0730, FAX: (440) 519-0727, E-Mail: rapidresponse@hippodirect.com, Web Site: www.hippodirect.com (23)

Hireko Golf, City of Industry, CA. Tel: (800) 367-8912, FAX: (888) 367-8912, E-Mail: support@hirekogolf.com, Web Site: www.hireko.com (11)

Hirsch, Angela, American Nicaraguan Foundation, Miami, FL. Tel: (305) 374-3391, Web Site: www.aidnicaragua.org (1)

Hirsch, Harvey, Media Consultants, Lyndhurst, NJ. Tel: (201) 933-2015, FAX: (201) 933-6314, E-Mail: hlhirsch@earthlink.net, Web Site: www.mediaconsultants.net (35)

Hirshberg, Eric, Lowe Worldwide, New York, NY. Tel: (212) 981-7600, E-Mail: info@loweworldwide.com, Web Site: www.loweworldwide.com (35)

Hirson, Mona, Weingeroff Enterprises Inc, Cranston, RI. Tel: (401) 467-2200, FAX: (401) 785-1320, Web Site: www.weingeroff.com (16)

Hirst, Steve, Calibre Press Inc, San Francisco, CA. Tel: (214) 545-3060, (800) 323-0037, FAX: (866) 225-4273, Web Site: www.calibrepress.com (17)

Hislop, Reid, MapInfo, Canada, Toronto, ON Canada. Tel: (416) 594-5200, (800) 268-3282, FAX: (416) 594-5201, E-Mail: canada.sales@mapinfo.com, Web Site: www.mapinfo.com (24)

Hislop, Thomas, P., Golden Bear Golf Inc, North Palm Beach, FL. Tel: (561) 626-3900, FAX: (561) 626-4104, Web Site: www.nicklaus.com (16)

Histacount & Expressions, Lancaster, CA. Tel: (800) 645-5220, FAX: (800) 332-5502, E-Mail: service@rapidforms.com, Web Site: www.rapidforms.com (10)

Historic Aviation, Minneapolis, MN. Tel: (651) 635-0100, (800) 225-5575, FAX: (651) 635-0700, E-Mail: info@historicaviation.com, Web Site: www.historicaviation.com (12)

Historical Replications Inc, Jackson, MS. Tel: (601) 981-8743, (800) 426-5628, FAX: (601) 981-8185, E-Mail: info@historicaldesigns.com, Web Site: www.historicaldesigns.com (8)

The Historical Research Center International Inc, Boynton Beach, FL. Tel: (561) 732-5263, (800) 985-9956, FAX: (561) 940-7991, E-Mail: custsvc@names.com, Web Site: www.historicalresearchcenter.net (16)

The History Book Club Inc, Mechanicsburg, PA. Tel: (718) 918-2665, E-Mail: paula.batson@dgna.com, Web Site: www.historybookclub.com (13)

History (Reference & Preservation) Division, Annapolis, MD. Tel: (410) 268-6110, (800) 233-8764, FAX: (410) 571-7940, E-Mail: dsheehan@usni.org, Web Site: www.usni.org (38)

Hitachi Data Systems, Irvine, CA. Tel: (408) 970-1000, Web Site: www.hds.com (22)

Hitchcock Shoes Inc, Hingham, MA. Tel: (781) 749-3260, (888) 599-9433, FAX: (781) 749-3576, E-Mail: hitchcock@wideshoes.com, Web Site: www.wideshoes.com (2)

Hitchins, William E., The Hitchins Corp, Canoga Park, CA. Tel: (818) 715-0510, FAX: (818) 715-0510 (35)

The Hitchins Corp, Canoga Park, CA. Tel: (818) 715-0510, FAX: (818) 715-0510 (35)

Hladky, Joe F., Gazette Communications Inc, Cedar Rapids, IA. Tel: (319) 398-8211, (800) 397-8211, FAX: (319) 368-8834, Web Site: www.gazettecommunications.com (17)

Hlavac, Randy, Marketing Synergy Inc, Naperville, IL. Tel: (630) 328-9550, FAX: (630) 328-9553, E-Mail: RHlavac@MSINetwork.com, Web Site: www.msinetwork.com (30)

Hnatek, Richard, Falcon Products Inc, Newport, TN. Tel: (314) 991-9200, (800) 873-3252, FAX: (314) 991-9227, E-Mail: info@falconproducts.com, Web Site: www.falconproducts.com (16)

Ho, Florence, Wyndham Hotel Group, Parsippany, NJ. Tel: (973) 753-8925, Web Site: www.cendant.com (19)

Ho, Monica, TMP Directional Marketing, Waukesha, WI. Tel: (212) 351-7595, Web Site: www.tmpdm.com (30)

Ho, Vincent, VGH Solutions, Markham, ON Canada. Tel: (905) 471-4735, FAX: (905) 471-2608 (7)

Hoag, William, J., The Marketing Advantage Inc, Little Rock, AR. Tel: (501) 954-7771, FAX: (501) 954-7879, E-Mail: central_reservations@tmae.net, Web Site: www.freevacations.com (21)

Hoaglin, Tom, Huntington Bancshares, Columbus, OH. Tel: (614) 480-8300, (800) 480-BANK, FAX: (614) 480-5284, Web Site: www.huntington.com (14)

Hoard, Christine A., Glens Falls Hospital Foundation, Glens Falls, NY. FAX: (518) 926-7012, Web Site: www.glensfallshospital.org (1)

Hoarty, Thomas, Microfluidics Corp, Newton, MA. Tel: (617) 969-5452, (800) 370-5452, FAX: (617) 965-1213, E-Mail: info@mfics.com, Web Site: www.microfluidicscorp.com (16)

Hobart, Danielle, Mystic Logistics, South Glastonbury, CT. Tel: (860) 659-1566, (800) 969-1566, FAX: (860) 659-1420, Web Site: www.mysticlogistics.com (35)

Hobart & William Smith Colleges, Geneva, NY. Tel: (315) 781-3000, (800) 852-2256, FAX: (315) 781-3655, Web Site: www.hws.edu (19)

Hobbs, David, InterfaceFlor LLC, La Grange, GA. Tel: (706) 882-1891, (800) 336-0225, FAX: (706) 882-0500, Web Site: www.interfaceflor.com (16)

Hobbs, Kevin, Affinity Group Inc, Ventura, CA. Tel: (805) 667-4100, (800) 765-1912, FAX: (805) 667-4419, E-Mail: khurd@affinitygroup.com, Web Site: www.affinitygroup.com (19)

Hobbs, Michele, HDI Group, San Francisco, CA. Tel: (415) 794-3320, Web Site: www.hobbsdirect.com (20)

Hobbs, Stephanie, Yellow Pages Association, Berkeley Heights, NJ. Tel: (908) 286-2380, (800) 336-0440, FAX: (908) 286-0620, Web Site: www.yellowpagesima.org (1)

Hobbs, Woodson, Phoenix Technologies Ltd, Milpitas, CA. Tel: (408) 570-1000, (800) 677-7305, FAX: (408) 570-1001, Web Site: www.phoenix.com (22)

Hobby Builders Supply, Atlanta, GA. Tel: (770) 242-1498, (800) 223-7171, FAX: (770) 242-1497, (800) 926-6464, Web Site: www.miniatures.com (11)

Hobby Surplus Sales, New Britain, CT. Tel: (860) 223-0600, (800) 233-0872, FAX: (860) 225-5316, E-Mail: amatohobby@sbcglobal.net, Web Site: www.hobbysurplus.com (11)

Hobday, Sean, Zones Inc, Auburn, WA. Tel: (253) 205-3000, (800) 408-9663, FAX: (425) 430-3626, E-Mail: corpsales@zones.com, Web Site: www.zones.com (3)

Hobson, Paul, The Stratosphere Las Vegas, Las Vegas, NV. Tel: (702) 380-7777, (800) 998-6937, FAX: (702) 383-4755, Web Site: www.stratospherehotel.com (19)

Hobsons, Cincinnati, OH. Tel: (513) 985-4186, Web Site: www.hobsons.com (16)

Hochberg, Fred P., Non-Profit Management Program/Milano - The New School of Management & Urban Policy, New York, NY. Tel: (212) 229-5400, FAX: (212) 229-5354, E-Mail: milanoadmissions@newschool.edu, Web Site: www.newschool.edu/milano (41)

Hochhauser, Hal, Shakespeare Mailing Service, New York, NY. Tel: (212) 560-8958, E-Mail: support@shakespearemailing.com, Web Site: www.shakespearemailing.com (28)

Hochman, Alan, Carina Associates, Croton on Hudson, NY. Tel: (914) 271-8600, FAX: (914) 271-8354 (33)

Hochman, Karen, Ad Hoc Marketing Resources Inc, New York, NY. Tel: (212) 595-1800, FAX: (212) 656-1860, E-Mail: adhocmrktg@aol.com, Web Site: www.members.aol.com/adhocmrktg (20)

Hock, Alan, Moritt, Hock, Hamroff & Horowitz, Garden City, NY. Tel: (516) 873-2000, FAX: (516) 873-2010, E-Mail: lhauser@morritthock.com, Web Site: www.morritthock.com (16)

Hock, Jackie, Eagle Claw Fishing Tackle, Denver, CO. Tel: (303) 321-1481, FAX: (303) 321-4750, E-Mail: info@eagleclaw.com, Web Site: www.eagleclaw.com (11)

Hockaday, Ira, Hallmark Cards Inc, Kansas City, MO. Tel: (816) 274-5111, FAX: (816) 274-7276, Web Site: www.hallmark.com (16)

Hodes, Chuck, Hodes Photography, Buffalo Grove, IL. Tel: (847) 215-3939, E-Mail: hodesphotography@comcast.net, Web Site: www.hodesphotography.com (37)

Hodes Photography, Buffalo Grove, IL. Tel: (847) 215-3939, E-Mail: hodesphotography@comcast.net, Web Site: www.hodesphotography.com (37)

Hodge, Jenny, American Modern Insurance Group, Amelia, OH. Tel: (513) 943-7200, (800) 759-9008, FAX: (513) 947-4779, (800) 217-5150, E-Mail: customer_care@amig.com, Web Site: www.amig.com (15)

Hodges, Charles, E., TAPPI (Technical Association of the Pulp & Paper Industry), Norcross, GA. Tel: (678) 642-66, (800) 332-8686, FAX: (770) 446-6947, E-Mail: webmaster@tappi.org, Web Site: www.tappi.org (1)

Hodges, G., Tommy, American Trucking Association, Arlington, VA. Tel: (703) 838-1700, FAX: (800) 254-2571, E-Mail: atamembership@trucking.org, Web Site: www.truckline.com (1)

Hodges, Keith, National Community Pharmacists Association, Alexandria, VA. Tel: (703) 683-8200, (800) 544-7447, FAX: (703) 683-3619, E-Mail: info@ncpanet.org, Web Site: www.ncpanet.org (1)

Hodges, Richard, Johnny Appleseed's Inc, Beverly, MA. Tel: (978) 922-2040, (800) 767-6666, FAX: (978) 922-7001, Web Site: www.appleseeds.com (2)

Hodgkins, Rebecca, Cramer, Norwood, MA. Tel: (781) 278-2387, Web Site: www.crameronline.com (20)

Hodgson, Daniel, Crutchfield Corp, Charlottesville, VA. Tel: (434) 817-1000, (800) 955-9091, FAX: (804) 817-1010, E-Mail: administration@crutchfield.com, Web Site: www.crutchfield.com (3)

Hodson, Nancy, Cold Spring Harbor Lab Press, Woodbury, NY. Tel: (516) 422-4100, (800) 843-4388, FAX: (516) 422-4097, E-Mail: cshpress@cshl.edu, Web Site: www.cshlpress.com (17)

Hoeg, Krystyna, T., Sunlife of Canada, Wellesley Hills, MA. Tel: (781) 237-6030, (800) SUNLIFE, FAX: (781) 446-1779, Web Site: www.sunlife-usa.com (15)

Hoeg, Thomas, E., Amerisure Insurance Cos, Farmington Hills, MI. Tel: (248) 615-9000, (800) 257-1900, FAX: (248) 615-8224, Web Site: www.amerisure.com (15)

Hoenle, Ralph, Johnson Smith Co, Bradenton, FL. Tel: (941) 747-5566, Web Site: www.johnsonsmith.com (5)

Hoerres, Peg, Smith Hanley Associates, Southport, CT. Tel: (203) 319-4300, (888) 221-2900, FAX: (203) 319-4320, Web Site: www.smithhanley.com (20)

Hoetger, William, Mott Media LLC, Fenton, MI. Tel: (810) 714-4280, FAX: (810) 714-2077, E-Mail: info@mottmedia.com, Web Site: www.mottmedia.com (17)

Hofer, Thomas W., Spring-Green Lawn Care Corp, Plainfield, IL. Tel: (815) 436-8777, FAX: (815) 436-9056, Web Site: www.spring-green.com (16)

Hoff, Clay, House of Eyes II, Greensboro, NC. Tel: (336) 852-7107, FAX: (336) 854-0311 (2)

Hoff, Don, American Slide-Chart Corp, Carol Stream, IL. Tel: (630) 665-3333, (800) 323-4433, FAX: (630) 665-3491, E-Mail: info2@americanslidechart.com, Web Site: www.americanslidechart.com (27)

Hoff, Don, Perrygraf, Carol Stream, IL. Tel: (630) 665-3333, (800) 323-4433, FAX: (630) 665-3491, E-Mail: info2@americanperrygraf.com, Web Site: www.perrygraf.com (16)

Hoff, Jeff, House of Eyes II, Greensboro, NC. Tel: (336) 852-7107, FAX: (336) 854-0311 (2)

Hoff, Jennifer, Hoff Communications Inc, Lansdowne, PA. Tel: (610) 623-2091, E-Mail: service@hoffcomm.com, Web Site: www.hoffcommunications.com (35)

Hoff, Jennifer, Houston Direct Marketing Association, Houston, TX. Tel: (281) 931-8883, FAX: (281) 820-4023, Web Site: www.houstondma.org (40)

Hoff, Tammy, House of Eyes II, Greensboro, NC. Tel: (336) 852-7107, FAX: (336) 854-0311 (2)

Hoff Communications Inc, Lansdowne, PA. Tel: (610) 623-2091, E-Mail: service@hoffcomm.com, Web Site: www.hoffcommunications.com (35)

Hoffman, Carrie, TV Guide Magazine, New York, NY. Tel: (212) 852-7500, (800) 866-1400, Web Site: www.tvguide.com (31)

Hoffman, David, Fitness Systems Manufacturing Corp, Sinking Spring, PA. Tel: (610) 670-0135, (800) 822-9995, E-Mail: vitaminout@aol.com, Web Site: www.fitness-systems.net (7)

Hoffman, Donna, Association for Postal Commerce, Alexandria, VA. Tel: (703) 524-0096, FAX: (703) 524-1871, Web Site: www.postcom.org (40)

Hoffman, James, The Patio, Murrieta, CA. Tel: (909) 304-0460 (8)

Hoffman, Jeff, The Chubb Corp, Warren, NJ. Tel: (908) 903-2000, FAX: (908) 903-2027, Web Site: www.chubb.com (20)

Hoffman, Lance, CRC Data Systems, Long Island City, NY. Tel: (718) 729-2622, E-Mail: jrafael@opinionaccess.com, Web Site: www.opinionaccess.com (12)

Hoffman, Mark, CNBC-Consumer & Business Channel, Englewood Cliffs, NJ. Tel: (201) 735-2622, FAX: (201) 735-3200, Web Site: www.cnbc.com (32)

Hoffman, Mark, Corporate Express, Broomfield, CO. Tel: (303) 664-2000, (888) 238-6329, Web Site: www.cexp.com (22)

Hoffman, Mary, Oakstone Publishing LLC, Birmingham, AL. Tel: (205) 991-5188, (800) 952-0690, FAX: (205) 995-4656, Web Site: www.oakstonepublishing.com (17)

Hoffman, Michael, Hoffman Mint, Fort Lauderdale, FL. Tel: (831) 625-5333, (800) 227-5813, FAX: (831) 649-3318, E-Mail: sales@hoffmanmint.com, Web Site: www.hoffmanmint.com (6)

Hoffman, Mike, The Toro Consumer Div, Bloomington, MN. Tel: (952) 888-8801, (888) 384-9939, FAX: (952) 887-8258, Web Site: www.thetorocompany.com (16)

Hoffman, Philip, Brylane, Indianapolis, IN. Tel: (800) 677-0339, Web Site: www.brylanehome.com (2)

Hoffman, Rowe, Kett Tool Co, Cincinnati, OH. Tel: (513) 271-0333, FAX: (513) 271-5318, E-Mail: info@kett-tool.com, Web Site: www.kett-tool.com (9)

Deborah Hoffman Copywriting, Corrales, NM. Tel: (505) 440-8725 (20)

Hoffman Mint, Fort Lauderdale, FL. Tel: (831) 625-5333, (800) 227-5813, FAX: (831) 649-3318, E-Mail: sales@hoffmanmint.com, Web Site: www.hoffmanmint.com (6)

Hofmann, Sheryl, Time/System, Chicopee, MA. Tel: (800) 637-9942, FAX: (800) 269-3075, E-Mail: customerservice@timesystem.us, Web Site: www.timesystem.us (16)

Hofmann, Thomas W., Sunoco, Inc, Philadelphia, PA. Tel: (215) 977-3000, (800) 786-6261, FAX: (215) 977-3409, E-Mail: sunoco_online@sunoil.com, Web Site: www.sunocoinc.com (16)

Hofstra University, Hempstead, NY. Tel: (516) 463-7200, FAX: (516) 463-4833, E-Mail: ccepa@hofstra.edu, Web Site: ccepa.hofstra.edu (41)

Hoga, Takashi, Fujisankei Communications International Inc, New York, NY. Tel: (212) 753-8100, FAX: (212) 702-0420, Web Site: www.fujisankei.com (32)

Hogan, Barbara-Jean, Bethesda List Center Inc, Bethesda, MD. Tel: (301) 986-1455, FAX: (301) 907-4870, E-Mail: info@bethesda-list.com, Web Site: www.bethesda-list.com (24)

Hogan, David, National Retail Federation Inc, Washington, DC. Tel: (202) 783-7971, (800) 673-4692, FAX: (202) 737-2849, E-Mail: webmaster@nrf.com, Web Site: www.nrf.com (1)

Hogan, Douglas, W., JP Hogan & Co, Knoxville, TN. Tel: (865) 546-7661, FAX: (865) 523-7300, E-Mail: dhogan@thehogancompany.net, Web Site: www.thehogancompany.net (35)

Hogan, Jack, LifeScript, Mission Viejo, CA. Tel: (949) 454-0422, Web Site: www.lifescript.com (7)

Hogan, James, HSP Direct, Herndon, VA. Tel: (703) 793-3220, FAX: (703) 793-3221, Web Site: www.hspdirect.com (1)

Hogan, Joe, Biosciences-Amersham, Piscataway, NJ. Tel: (732) 457-8000, FAX: (732) 457-0557, Web Site: www.amersham.com (16)

Hogan, Julie, DMA - Events-Conference Programming/Exhibitors/Speakers, New York, NY. Tel: (212) 768-7277 X1419, FAX: (212) 302-6714, E-Mail: consumer@the-dma.org, Web Site: www.the-dma.org (41)

Hogan, Randi, ActionAid, Washington, DC. Tel: (202) 835-1240, Web Site: www.actionaidusa.org (1)

JP Hogan & Co, Knoxville, TN. Tel: (865) 546-7661, FAX: (865) 523-7300, E-Mail: dhogan@thehogancompany.net, Web Site: www.thehogancompany.net (35)

Hogard Business Services Inc, Bradley, IL. Tel: (815) 932-1835, FAX: (815) 932-4793, E-Mail: hogards@att.net, Web Site: www.hogardbusinessservices.com (28)

Hogsett, Scott, Shakespeare Co, Columbia, SC. Tel: (803) 754-7000, (800) 347-3759, FAX: (803) 754-7342, Web Site: www.shakespeare-fishing.com (11)

Hohler, Robert, Robert Hohler Associates, Boston, MA. Tel: (617) 531-0010, FAX: (617) 531-0015, E-Mail: hohassoc@aol.com (35)

Robert Hohler Associates, Boston, MA. Tel: (617) 531-0010, FAX: (617) 531-0015, E-Mail: hohassoc@aol.com (35)

Hoing, Jim, Omaha Vaccine Co, Omaha, NE. Tel: (402) 731-9600, (800) 367-4444, FAX: (800) 242-9447, E-Mail: customerservice@OmahaVaccine.com, Web Site: www.omahavaccine.com (16)

Hoke III, Henry, Reed, Hoke Communications Inc, Garden City, NY. Tel: (516) 746-6700, FAX: (516) 294-8141 (17)

Hoke, Henry, Fund Raising Management, Garden City, NY. Tel: (516) 746-6700, FAX: (516) 294-8141 (43)

Hoke Communications Inc, Garden City, NY. Tel: (516) 746-6700, FAX: (516) 294-8141 (17)

Holbrook, Jim, EMAK Worldwide, Chicago, IL. Tel: (323) 932-4300, E-Mail: jim.holbrook@emak.com, Web Site: www.emak.com (33)

Holbrook, Kevin, Boca Java, Miami, FL. Tel: (954) 949-2010, Web Site: www.bocajava.com (4)

Holden Dr., John, AAAS/Science, Washington, DC. Tel: (202) 326-6400, FAX: (202) 371-9526, E-Mail: webmaster@aaas.org, Web Site: www.aaas.org (1)

Holden, Alfred C., Fordham University Graduate School of Business Administration, New York, NY. Tel: (212) 636-6200, (800) 825-4422, FAX: (212) 636-7076, Web Site: www.fordham.edu (41)

Holden, Betsy, Kraft Foods/Gevalia Kaffe, Tarrytown, NY. Tel: (914) 335-4239, Web Site: www.gevalia.com (16)

Holden, Pam, Acxiom Co, Marlton, NJ. Tel: (800) 635-5833, FAX: (856) 988-6662 (23)

Holden, Stan, Holden Copywriting, Deerfield, IL. Tel: (847) 236-0669, E-Mail: holdendm@aol.com (39)

Holden, Win, Arizona Highways Magazine, Phoenix, AZ. Tel: (602) 712-2200, FAX: (602) 254-4505, E-Mail: editor@arizonahighways.com, Web Site: www.arizonahighways.com (17)

Holden Copywriting, Deerfield, IL. Tel: (847) 236-0669, E-Mail: holdendm@aol.com (39)

Holden-Bache, Adam, Mass Transmit, Charlotte, NC. Tel: (704) 248-8817, Web Site: www.masstransmit.com (32)

Holecek, Mark, American Marketing Systems Inc, Burr Ridge, IL. Tel: (630) 382-1000, FAX: (630) 325-0825, E-Mail: studentservices@thepei.com, Web Site: www.amsdirect.com (35)

Holecek, Mark, S., AMS Direct, Burr Ridge, IL. Tel: (630) 382-1000, FAX: (630) 325-0825, Web Site: www.amsdirect.com (13)

Holian, Janet, VistaPrint USA Inc, Lexington, MA. Tel: (800) 961-2075, Web Site: www.vistaprint.com (27)

Holiber, William, D., US News & World Report, New York, NY. Tel: (212) 916-7360, FAX: (212) 643-7842, Web Site: www.usnews.com (17)

Holiday Travel of America, Carlsbad, CA. Tel: (760) 431-8600, (888) 732-2479, FAX: (760) 431-3131, E-Mail: sales@htoa.com, Web Site: www.htoa.com (19)

Holiday Vacations, Eau Claire, WI. Tel: (715) 834-5555, (800) 826-2266, FAX: (715) 834-8554, E-Mail: info@holidayvacations.net, Web Site: www.holidayvacations.net (19)

Holl, David B., Mary Kay Cosmetics Inc, Addison, TX. Tel: (972) 687-6300, (800) MARY KAY, FAX: (972) 687-1611, Web Site: www.marykay.com (16)

Holland, Angela, Suntrust Banks Inc, Atlanta, GA. Tel: (404) 588-7914, (800) 786-8787, FAX: (404) 532-0550, E-Mail: emmett.harmon@suntrust.com, Web Site: www.suntrust.com (14)

Holland, Deborah, St Petersburg/Clearwater Area CVB, Clearwater, FL. Tel: (727) 464-7200, Web Site: www.floridasbeach.com (1)

Holland, Hillary, K., Winterthur Museum & Country Estate, Wilmington, DE. Tel: (302) 888-4600, (800) 448-3883, FAX: (302) 888-4730, E-Mail: tourinfo@winterthur.org, Web Site: www.winterthur.org (6)

Holland, James A., Libertyville Saddle Shop Inc, Libertyville, IL. Tel: (847) 362-0570, FAX: (847) 680-3200, E-Mail: info@saddleshop.com, Web Site: www.saddleshop.com (11)

Holland, Jeff, Vertical Media Group, Fort Lee, NJ. Tel: (201) 245-7935 (20)

Holland, Julie, Holland Wildflower Farm, Elkins, AR. Tel: (501) 643-2622, (800) 684-3734, FAX: (501) 643-2249, E-Mail: hwildflowerfarm@yahoo.com, Web Site: www.hwildflower.com (8)

Holland, Mike, Byron Plantation, Vidalia, GA. Tel: (800) 356-0171, E-Mail: greenline/byron@bellsouth.net, Web Site: www.byronplantation.com (4)

Holland Wildflower Farm, Elkins, AR. Tel: (501) 643-2622, (800) 684-3734, FAX: (501) 643-2249, E-Mail: hwildflowerfarm@yahoo.com, Web Site: www.hwildflower.com (8)

Hollandbaek, Michael, Ducktrap River Fish Farm, Belfast, ME. Tel: (207) 338-6280, (800) 828-3825, FAX: (207) 338-9020, E-Mail: smoked@ducktrap.com, Web Site: www.ducktrap.com (4)

Hollander, Bruce, Don Jagoda Associates Inc, Melville, NY. Tel: (631) 454-1800, FAX: (631) 454-1834, E-Mail: information@dja.com, Web Site: www.dja.com (35)

Hollander, Bruce, Innovative Packaging of Westchester, Spring Valley, NY. Tel: (845) 364-9500 (26)

Hollander, Ken, Kenneth Hollander Associates Inc, Mendocino, CA. Tel: (707) 962-1648, FAX: (707) 962-1635 (30)

Kenneth Hollander Associates Inc, Mendocino, CA. Tel: (707) 962-1648, FAX: (707) 962-1635 (30)

Hollars, W., Michael, Hansen Corp, Princeton, IN. Tel: (812) 385-3415, FAX: (812) 385-3013, E-Mail: sales@hansen-motor.com, Web Site: www.hansen-motor.com (16)

Hollenbeck, Nancy, Hollenbeck Productions, Seattle, WA. Tel: (206) 592-1800, FAX: (206) 592-9199, E-Mail: pixhot@aol.com, Web Site: www.hollenbeckproductions.com (37)

Hollenbeck Productions, Seattle, WA. Tel: (206) 592-1800, FAX: (206) 592-9199, E-Mail: pixhot@aol.com, Web Site: www.hollenbeckproductions.com (37)

Hollenstein, Mike, Duluth Trading Co Inc, Belleville, WI. Tel: (800) 505-8888, FAX: (888) 950-3199, E-Mail: customerservice@duluthtrading.com, Web Site: www.duluthtrading.com (8)

Holley, Jeffrey, D., CUNA Mutual Group, Madison, WI. Tel: (608) 238-5851, (800) 356-2644, FAX: (608) 231-8839, Web Site: www.cunamutual.com (15)

Hollfelder, Jack, Business Marketing Association, Naperville, IL. Tel: (630) 544-5054, FAX: (630) 544-5055, E-Mail: info@marketing.org, Web Site: www.marketing.org (40)

Hollfelder, Jack, Marketing News, Chicago, IL. Tel: (312) 542-9000, (800) 262-1150, FAX: (312) 542-9001, E-Mail: news@ama.org, Web Site: www.ama.org (14)

Holliday, Chad, Dupont Color Proofing, Wilmington, DE. Tel: (800) 345-9999, FAX: (302) 892-8030, Web Site: www.dupont.com/proofing (27)

Holliday, Charles, E I DuPont De Nemours & Co, Wilmington, DE. Tel: (302) 774-1000, FAX: (302) 774-7321, Web Site: www.dupont.com (16)

Hollinger, Mark, Discovery Communications LLC, Silver Spring, MD. Tel: (240) 662-2000, FAX: (240) 662-1868, Web Site: corporate.discovery.com (16)

Hollingworth, Steve, CARE USA, Atlanta, GA. Tel: (404) 979-9255, (800) 521-CARE, FAX: (404) 589-2600, E-Mail: info@care.org, Web Site: www.careusa.org (1)

Hollister, Brent, Sears Canada Inc, Toronto, ON. Tel: (416) 362-1711, (888) 473-2772, FAX: (613) 391-3047, E-Mail: home@sears.ca, Web Site: www.sears.ca (5)

Hollister, Dean, Martindale-Hubbell, New Providence, NJ. Tel: (908) 464-6800, (800) 526-4902, FAX: (908) 771-7740 (17)

Hollister, Glenn, Ideal Industries Inc, Sycamore, IL. Tel: (815) 895-5181, (800) 435-0705, FAX: (815) 895-4800, E-Mail: ideal_industries@idealindustries.com, Web Site: www.idealindustries.com (16)

Hollister, Joyce, Nevada Magazine, Carson City, NV. Tel: (775) 687-5416, FAX: (775) 687-6159, E-Mail: editor@nevadamagazine.com, Web Site: www.nevadamagazine.com (17)

Hollister Inc, Libertyville, IL. Tel: (847) 680-1000, (888) 740-8999, FAX: (847) 680-2123, Web Site: www.hollister.com (16)

Hollomon, R., Scott, Collin Street Bakery, Corsicana, TX. Tel: (800) 292-7400, Web Site: www.collinstreetbakery.com (4)

Holloway, J., David, American Technical Publishers Inc, Orland Park, IL. Tel: (708) 957-1100, (800) 323-3471, FAX: (708) 957-1101, E-Mail: service@americantech.net, Web Site: www.go2atp.com (17)

Holloway, Judy, The Suburban Chamber of Commerce, Summit, NJ. Tel: (908) 522-1700, FAX: (908) 522-9252, E-Mail: info@suburbanchambers.org, Web Site: www.suburbanchambers.org (14)

Hollums, Sheila, Direct Advantage Marketing, Pittsburgh, PA. Tel: (412) 381-2300, E-Mail: information@dam.com, Web Site: www.dam.com (29)

Hollywood Film Archive, Los Angeles, CA. Tel: (323) 655-4968, Web Site: www.hfarchive.com (17)

Holmes IV, Owen, M., Carter & Holmes Inc, Newberry, SC. Tel: (803) 276-0579, FAX: (803) 276-0588, E-Mail: orchids@carterandholmes.com, Web Site: www.carterandholmes.com (8)

Holmes, Barry, Accurate Marketing Systems, River Edge, NJ. Tel: (201) 265-5198 (22)

Holmes, Carol, Edwards, The Scotts Co Div of Lawn Service, Marysville, OH. Tel: (937) 644-0011, FAX: (937) 644-7261, Web Site: www.scotts.com (8)

Holmes, Cheryl, Black Entertainment Television Inc, Washington, DC. Tel: (202) 608-2000/2006, (800) 766-0053, FAX: (202) 608-2599, Web Site: www.bet.com (16)

Holmes, Gary, The Nielsen Co, New York, NY. Tel: (646) 654-5000, E-Mail: contactcommunications@nielsen.com, Web Site: www.nielsen.com (17)

Holmes, Heather, Technology Review, Cambridge, MA. Tel: (617) 475-8000, FAX: (617) 258-5850, Web Site: www.technologyreview.com (17)

Holmes, Mary, Garden Botanika Inc, Saint Louis, MO. Tel: (425) 881-9603, (800) 968-7842, FAX: (425) 869-6235, Web Site: www.gardenbotanika.com (7)

Holmgren, Dale, Oakwood Homes Corp, Greensboro, NC. Tel: (336) 664-2400, (800) 822-0633, FAX: (336) 315-3249, Web Site: www.oakwoodhomes.com (16)

Holoubek, Brian, Heavy Rotation, Milwaukee, WI. Tel: (414) 384-5200, (800) 886-4759, FAX: (414) 434-9318, E-Mail: info@holoubekstudios.com, Web Site: heavytees.com (27)

Holowacz, Phillip, Unadilla Laminated Products, Unadilla, NY. Tel: (607) 369-9341, FAX: (607) 369-3608, E-Mail: info@unalam.com, Web Site: www.unalam.com (16)

Holson Jr., Richard S., Guarantee Trust Life Insurance Co, Glenview, IL. Tel: (847) 298-0670, FAX: (847) 298-1215, E-Mail: pr@gtlic.com, Web Site: www.gtlic.com (15)

Holsted Marketing Inc, New York, NY. Tel: (212) 686-8537, FAX: (212) 481-0415 (35)

Holston, Michael, J., Compaq Computer Corp, Houston, TX. Tel: (281) 370-0670, FAX: (281) 927-8835, Web Site: www.compaq.com (16)

Holt, Jo, Louisville Direct Marketing Association, Louisville, KY. Tel: (888) 392-1941, E-Mail: ldmacontact@ldma.org, Web Site: www.ldma.org (40)

Holt Baker, Arlene, AFL-CIO, Washington, DC. Tel: (202) 637-5000, FAX: (202) 637-5058, (202) 637-5323, Web Site: www.aflcio.org (1)

Holtscheider, Rev. Dennis, H., DePaul University, Chicago, IL. Tel: (312) 362-8000, (800) 4-DEPAUL, FAX: (312) 362-6639, E-Mail: skelly@wppost. depaul.edu, Web Site: www.depaul.edu (41)

Holtsoi, Gary, Gallup Inter-tribal Indian Ceremonial, Gallup, NM. Tel: (505) 863-3896, FAX: (505) 863-9168, E-Mail: ceremonial@cnetco.com, Web Site: www.indianceremonial.com (1)

Holtzman, Mark, Nor1, Sunnyvale, CA. Tel: (408) 852-9248, Web Site: www.nor1.com (32)

Holy Cross Hospital, Fort Lauderdale, FL. Tel: (954) 771-8000, FAX: (954) 229-8597, Web Site: www. holy-cross.com (16)

Holzberg, Michael, Abacus Communications, Manchester, NH. Tel: (800) 888-3188, FAX: (603) 645-5093, E-Mail: michael@call-centers.com, Web Site: www.callabacus.com (29)

Homan, Benjamin, Food for the Hungry Inc, Phoenix, AZ. Tel: (480) 998-3100, (800) 248-6437, FAX: (480) 998-4806, E-Mail: hunger@fh.org, Web Site: www.fh.org (1)

Homan, Tammy, Jones Publishing Inc, Iola, WI. Tel: (715) 445-5000, (800) 331-0038, FAX: (715) 445-4053, E-Mail: jonespub@jonespublishing.com, Web Site: www.jonespublishing.com (17)

Home Decorators Collection Inc, Hazelwood, MO. Tel: (314) 993-1516, FAX: (314) 521-5780, Web Site: www.homedecoratorscollection.com (8)

The Home Depot Inc, Atlanta, GA. Tel: (770) 433-8211, (800) 430-3376, FAX: (770) 384-2356, Web Site: www.homedepot.com (16)

Home Interiors & Gifts Inc, Carrollton, TX. Tel: (972) 695-1000, FAX: (972) 695-1112 (16)

Home Loan Investment Bank, Warwick, RI. Tel: (800) 223-1700 X278, E-Mail: contactus@ homeloanbank.com, Web Site: www. homeloanbank.com (14)

Home 123 Mortgage, Riverwoods, IL. Tel: (888) 215-0080, E-Mail: info@home123.com, Web Site: www.home123.com (14)

Home Owner Data Services Inc, Lawrenceville, GA. Tel: (770) 925-9000, FAX: (770) 925-8977, E-Mail: hdsi@newhomedata.net, Web Site: www. newhomedata.net (23)

Home Planners, Tucson, AZ. Tel: (520) 297-8200, FAX: (520) 297-6219, E-Mail: sales@ homeplanners.com, Web Site: www.homeplanners. com (17)

Home Safeguard Industries, Malibu, CA. Tel: (310) 457-5813, FAX: (310) 457-4862, E-Mail: expert@ homesafeguard.com, Web Site: www. homesafeguard.com (9)

Home-Sew Inc, Bethlehem, PA. Tel: (610) 867-3833, (800) 344-4739, FAX: (610) 867-9717, Web Site: www.homesew.com (11)

Home Shopping Network, Saint Petersburg, FL. Tel: (727) 872-1000, FAX: (727) 571-1803, Web Site: www.hsn.com (32)

HomeAway.com Inc, Austin, TX. Tel: (512) 782-0805, (877) 228-3145, Web Site: www.homeaway.com (19)

Homecraft Veneer & Woodworker Supply, Youngstown, PA. Tel: (724) 537-8435, (800) 796-6348, FAX: (724) 537-0543, E-Mail: woodman@ homecraftveneer.com, Web Site: www. homecraftveneer.com (8)

HomeData, Santa Barbara, CA. Tel: (516) 605-0451, (800) 628-9456, FAX: (516) 605-0455, E-Mail: info@homedata.com, Web Site: www.homedata. com (24)

Homeowners Marketing Services Inc, North Hollywood, CA. Tel: (818) 506-1507, (800) 232-2134, FAX: (818) 505-9729, (818) 506-4110, E-Mail: lists@homeown.org, Web Site: www.homeown.org (23)

Homer, Michael, Psion Teklogix Inc, Mississauga, ON. Tel: (905) 813-9900, (800) 322-3437, E-Mail: ptinfo@psion.com, Web Site: www.psionteklogix. com (3)

Homes, Suzanne, Networking Alternatives for Publishers, Retailers & Artists, Inc, Eastsound, WA. Tel: (360) 376-2702, (800) 367-1907, FAX: (360) 376-2704, E-Mail: futureweb@rockisland.com (40)

Homespun Tapes Music Instruction, Woodstock, NY. Tel: (845) 246-2550, (800) 338-2737, FAX: (845) 246-5282, E-Mail: info@homespuntapes.com, Web Site: www.homespuntapes.com (3)

Homesteaders Life Co, West Des Moines, IA. Tel: (515) 440-7777, (800) 477-3633, E-Mail: service@ homesteaderslife.com, Web Site: www. homesteaderslife.com (15)

Honaker, L., Michael, American Psychological Association, Washington, DC. Tel: (202) 336-5500, (800) 374-2721, FAX: (202) 336-5568, E-Mail: order@apa.org, Web Site: www.apa.org (1)

The HoneyBaked Ham Co, Holland, OH. Tel: (419) 868-6400, E-Mail: info@honeybaked.com, Web Site: www.honeybaked.com (4)

Honeywell, Morristown, NJ. Tel: (973) 455-2000, FAX: (973) 455-4807, Web Site: www.honeywell. com (16)

Honeywell Wintress Controls, Acton, MA. Tel: (978) 264-9550, (800) 333-3282, FAX: (978) 263-0630, Web Site: www.wintress.com (16)

Hood, Andy, The Newman Group, Ann Arbor, MI. Tel: (734) 426-3200, FAX: (734) 426-0777, E-Mail: anewman@newman.com (3)

Hood, George, The Salvation Army National Headquarters, Alexandria, VA. Tel: (703) 684-5500, Web Site: www.salvationarmyusa.org (1)

Hood, Kim, American Fidelity Assurance Co, Oklahoma City, OK. Tel: (405) 525-6900, FAX: (405) 523-5215, Web Site: www.afadvantage.com (15)

Hood, Mark, E., Brown Shoe Co, Saint Louis, MO. Tel: (314) 854-4000, FAX: (314) 854-4274, Web Site: www.brownshoe.com (16)

Hood, Shawn, Sherman Specialty Toy Co Inc, Jericho, NY. Tel: (516) 861-6420, (516) 546-7400, (800) 645-6513, FAX: (516) 861-1033, (800) 853-8697, E-Mail: orders@shermanspecialty.com, Web Site: www.shermanspecialty.com (16)

Hoody, Mike, Central States Indemnity, Omaha, NE. Tel: (402) 997-8000, (402) 397-1111, (800) 445-6500, Web Site: www.csi-omaha.com (15)

Hook & Hackle Co Inc, Homestead, PA. Tel: (800) 652-8342, FAX: (412) 476-8639, E-Mail: ron@ hookhack.com, Web Site: www.hookhack.com (11)

Hooker, Betty, Wendover Associates Inc, Greensboro, NC. Tel: (336) 299-6611, FAX: (336) 292-4261 (35)

Hooker, Stan, Midland Paper, Wheeling, IL. Tel: (847) 777-2700, (800) 323-8522, FAX: (847) 777-2552, E-Mail: whl@midlandpaper.com, Web Site: www. midlandpaper.com (25)

Hooleon Corp, Melrose, NM. Tel: (928) 634-7515, (800) 937-1337, E-Mail: sales@hooleon.com, Web Site: www.hooleon.com (3)

Hooper, Ann, Lathem Time Corp, Atlanta, GA. Tel: (404) 691-0400, (800) 241-4990, FAX: (404) 696-6048, Web Site: www.lathem.com (16)

Hooper, Jeff, Coin Laundry Association, Oakbrook Terrace, IL. Tel: (630) 963-5547, FAX: (630) 963-5864, Web Site: www.coinlaundry.org (1)

Hoops, Rev. Christian, Nordskog Publishing Co, Ventura, CA. Tel: (805) 642-2070, FAX: (805) 642-1862, E-Mail: pwrboatmag@aol.com, Web Site: www.nordskogpublishing.com (17)

Hoover, David, R., Hoover's Mfg Co, Peru, IL. Tel: (815) 223-1159, (888) 333-1499, FAX: (815) 223-1499, Web Site: www.hmchonors.com (2)

Hoover, R., Larry, Huntington Bancshares, Columbus, OH. Tel: (614) 480-8300, (800) 480-BANK, FAX: (614) 480-5284, Web Site: www.huntington.com (14)

Hoover's, Austin, TX. Tel: (512) 374-4500 (22)

Hoover's Mfg Co, Peru, IL. Tel: (815) 223-1159, (888) 333-1499, FAX: (815) 223-1499, Web Site: www.hmchonors.com (2)

Hope, Dave, American Crane & Equipment Corp, Douglassville, PA. Tel: (610) 385-6061, (877) 877-6778, FAX: (610) 385-3191/4876, E-Mail: info@ americancrane.com, Web Site: www.americancrane. com (16)

The Hope Co Inc, Bridgeton, MO. Tel: (314) 739-7254, (800) 325-4026, FAX: (314) 739-7786, E-Mail: info@hopecompany.com (16)

Hopkins Jr., George, E., The Maine Connection, Portland, ME. Tel: (207) 780-4355, FAX: (207) 780-4239, E-Mail: ghopkins@midcoast.com (27)

Hopkins, Jerry, Innovative List Marketing Inc, Fairfax, VA. Tel: (703) 425-5356, Web Site: www.ilmlists. com (23)

Hopkins, Jerry, Texas Refinery Corp, Fort Worth, TX. Tel: (817) 332-1161, FAX: (817) 336-8441, E-Mail: jhopkins@texasrefinery.com, Web Site: www.texasrefinery.com (9)

Hopkins, Katharine, First Tennessee Bank, Memphis, TN. Tel: (901) 523-4547, Web Site: www. firsttennessee.com (14)

Hopkins, Lisa, Sybase Inc, Dublin, CA. Tel: (925) 236-5000, Web Site: www.sybase.com/product/ datawarehousing (22)

Hopkins, Mark, Fox Lite, Inc, Fairborn, OH. Tel: (937) 864-1966, FAX: (937) 864-7010, E-Mail: doug@foxlite.com, Web Site: www.foxlite.com (9)

Hopkins, Rick, Love To Learn Inc, Salem, UT. Tel: (801) 423-2009, (888) 771-1034, FAX: (801) 423-9188, E-Mail: customerservice@lovetolearn.net, Web Site: www.lovetolearn.net (5)

Hopkins, Robert, Direct Mail Solutions LLC, Carol Stream, IL. Tel: (630) 653-6863, FAX: (630) 653-7144, E-Mail: support@dmspostal.com, Web Site: www.dmspostal.com (28)

Hopkins, Rusty, Directory of Premium, Incentive & Travel Buyers, Richmond, VA. Tel: (804) 762-4455, (800) 223-1797, FAX: (804) 935-0271, E-Mail: amdouglas4@aol.com, Web Site: www. douglaspublications.com (43)

Hopkins Medical Products, Baltimore, MD. Tel: (410) 484-2036, (800) 835-1995, FAX: (410) 484-4036, E-Mail: customerservice@hopkinsmedical.net, Web Site: www.hopkinsmedicalproducts.com (7)

Hoplamazian, Mark, Hyatt Hotels Corp, Chicago, IL. Tel: (312) 750-1234, FAX: (312) 780-5289, Web Site: www.hyatt.com (16)

Hopp, Jeff, Ripon Printers, Ripon, WI. Tel: (920) 748-3136, (800) 321-3136, FAX: (920) 748-3741, E-Mail: info@riponprinters.com, Web Site: www. riponprinters.com (27)

Hopp, Jeffrey, Leslie Shoe Co Inc, Rogers City, MI. Tel: (989) 734-4030, (800) 716-8617, E-Mail: info@sexyshoes.com, Web Site: www.sexyshoes. com (2)

Hopple, Richard, V., Guideposts, Danbury, CT. Tel: (845) 225-3681, FAX: (845) 228-2056, Web Site: www.guideposts.org (1)

Hopson, Andy, Noble, Chicago, IL. Tel: (312) 670-2900, FAX: (312) 670-7420, Web Site: www. noble.net (35)

Hoquest, Karen, M., Ann Taylor Inc, New York, NY. Tel: (212) 457-2075, (800) FAX-ANN, FAX: (800) DIAL-ANN, Web Site: www.anninc.com (2)

Hoquet, Karen, M., Macy's Marketing, New York, NY. Tel: (212) 695-4400, FAX: (212) 494-1517, Web Site: www.macys.com (16)

Horace Mann Educators Corp, Springfield, IL. Tel: (217) 789-2500, FAX: (217) 788-5161, Web Site: www.horacemann.com (15)

The Horah Group, Pleasantville, NY. Tel: (914) 495-3200, FAX: (914) 769-8802, E-Mail: dgoldsmith@horah.com, Web Site: www.horah.com (21)

Horder, Lisa, LIST Inc, Danbury, CT. Tel: (914) 765-0700, FAX: (914) 765-0046, E-Mail: info@l-i-s-t.com, Web Site: www.l-i-s-t.com (24)

Horizon Lists, Bronx, NY. Tel: (845) 300-4932, Web Site: www.horizonlists.com (23)

Horizon Paper Co Inc, Stamford, CT. Tel: (203) 358-0855, (866) 358-0855, FAX: (203) 358-0828, Web Site: www.horizonpaper.com (25)

Hormel Foods Corp, Austin, MN. Tel: (507) 437-5611, (800) 523-4635, FAX: (507) 437-5158, Web Site: www.hormel.com (16)

Horn, Alan F., Warner Bros, Burbank, CA. Tel: (818) 954-6000, Web Site: www.warnerbros.com (3)

Horn, Sue, Victoria's Secret Catalogue, Columbus, OH. FAX: (614) 337-5075, Web Site: www.victoriassecret.com (2)

Horn, Theresa, 21st Century Marketing, Hauppauge, NY. Tel: (631) 293-8550, FAX: (631) 293-8974, E-Mail: info@21stcm.com, Web Site: www.21stcm.com (24)

Horn Packaging Corp, Lancaster, MA. Tel: (978) 772-0290, (800) 832-7020, FAX: (978) 772-4611, E-Mail: mccarthy@horncorp.com, Web Site: www.hornpackaging.com (5)

Hornberger, Jim, Golf Haus, Lansing, MI. Tel: (517) 482-8842, FAX: (517) 482-8843 (11)

Hornbuster, Louis, Mel Bay Publications Inc, Pacific, MO. Tel: (800) 8-MELBAY, FAX: (636) 257-5062, E-Mail: email@melbay.com, Web Site: www.melbay.com (17)

Horner, Jane, DCI Marketing Inc, Milwaukee, WI. Tel: (414) 228-7000, (800) 284-6318, FAX: (414) 228-3411, Web Site: www.dcimarketing.com (35)

Horning, Roxanne, V., Gannett Co Inc, Mc Lean, VA. Tel: (703) 854-6000, FAX: (703) 854-2046, E-Mail: gcishare@gannett.com, Web Site: www.gannett.com (16)

Hornstein, Lee, (C) Systems LLC, Edison, NJ. Tel: (732) 548-6100, Web Site: www.csystemsllc.net (22)

Hornstein, Scott, Ernan Roman Direct Marketing Corp, Little Neck, NY. Tel: (718) 225-4151, FAX: (718) 225-4889, E-Mail: ernan@erdm.com, Web Site: www.erdm.com (20)

Horowitz, Aaron, Cosmetique, Inc, Vernon Hills, IL. Tel: (847) 913-9099, (800) 621-8822, Web Site: www.cosmetique.com (13)

Horowitz, Robert, David K Horowitz Studio Inc, Philadelphia, PA. Tel: (215) 765-3600, FAX: (215) 763-1056 (37)

David K Horowitz Studio Inc, Philadelphia, PA. Tel: (215) 765-3600, FAX: (215) 763-1056 (37)

Horticulture Magazine, Blue Ash, OH. Tel: (513) 531-2690, FAX: (513) 891-7153, Web Site: www.hortmag.com (17)

Horton, Dave, Doubletree Suites by Hilton, Boston, MA. Tel: (617) 783-0090, (800) 222-TREE, FAX: (617) 783-0897, E-Mail: doubletree1@hilton.com (19)

Horton, Juana I, Horton Interpreting Inc, Providence, RI. Tel: (401) 331-4798, (800) 345-2135, FAX: (401) 331-2822, Web Site: www.language-link.com (30)

Horton, Terri, Cookbook Publishers Inc, Lenexa, KS. Tel: (913) 492-5900, (800) 227-7282, FAX: (913) 492-5947, E-Mail: info@cookbookpublishers.com, Web Site: www.cookbookpublishers.com (17)

Horton Interpreting Inc, Providence, RI. Tel: (401) 331-4798, (800) 345-2135, FAX: (401) 331-2822, Web Site: www.language-link.com (30)

Horvath, Deborah, Washington Mutual Home Loan, Inc, Downers Grove, IL. Tel: (847) 549-6500, FAX: (847) 549-2975 (14)

Horwitz, Allen, IClimber Inc, Burbank, CA. Tel: (818) 567-3030, Web Site: www.iclimber.com (16)

Horwitz, Allen, Submit Express, Burbank, CA. Tel: (818) 567-3030, Web Site: www.iclimber.com (32)

Hoskins, Marla, The Response Shop Inc, La Jolla, CA. Tel: (858) 456-6180, FAX: (858) 456-5090, E-Mail: marla@responseshop.com, Web Site: www.responseshop.com (35)

Hoslins, Marla, The Testimonial Wrangler, La Jolla, CA. Tel: (858) 735-7646 (35)

Hosseini, Hossein, Avery Dennison Corp, Brea, CA. Tel: (714) 674-8500, (800) 462-8379, FAX: (714) 674-6929, Web Site: www.avery.com (10)

Hostetler, Jay, Stewart-MacDonald, Athens, OH. Tel: (740) 592-3021, (800) 848-2273, FAX: (740) 593-7922, E-Mail: hostetler@stewmac.com, Web Site: www.stewmac.com (16)

Hostetter Jr., Amos, B., WGBH Educational Foundation, Brighton, MA. Tel: (617) 300-5400, FAX: (617) 300-1026, Web Site: www.wgbh.org (1)

Hot Sauce Harry's, North Port, FL. Tel: (214) 902-8552, (800) 588-8979, FAX: (214) 956-9885, E-Mail: info@hotsauceharrys.com, Web Site: www.hotsauceharrys.com (4)

Hot Topic Inc, City of Industry, CA. Tel: (626) 839-4681, (800) 275-9169, FAX: (626) 839-4686, Web Site: www.hottopic.com (2)

Hotaling, Veronica, Syracuse University, Syracuse, NY. Tel: (315) 443-4944, Web Site: syr.edu (1)

Hotline List Corp, New York, NY. Tel: (212) 840-8135, FAX: (212) 840-8139 (23)

Hotton, George, Theodore Presser Co, King Of Prussia, PA. Tel: (610) 592-1222, FAX: (610) 592-1229, E-Mail: webmaster@presser.com, Web Site: www.presser.com (17)

Hou, Alex, American Research Corp, El Monte, CA. Tel: (626) 284-1904, (800) FIND-ARC, (800) 346-3272, FAX: (626) 284-4213, E-Mail: arcinfo@800findarc.com, Web Site: www.800findarc.com (3)

Houhlne, Tim, WS Live LLC, Dubuque, IA. Tel: (563) 582-9501, (800) 582-9501, FAX: (563) 582-2003, Web Site: www.wslive.com (29)

Houlihan, Dennis, Roland Products Inc, Los Angeles, CA. Tel: (323) 731-1111, FAX: (323) 731-9585, E-Mail: salesinfo@rolandinc.com, Web Site: www.rolandinc.com (16)

Houlihan, Mary, Anheuser-Busch Inc Promotional Products Group, Shelton, CT. Tel: (800) 742-5283, Web Site: www.budshop.com (6)

Houlihan Lokey Howard & Zukin, Los Angeles, CA. Tel: (310) 553-8871, (800) 788-5300, FAX: (310) 553-2173, Web Site: www.hlhz.com (14)

House, Dave, Brocade Communications Systems Inc, San Jose, CA. Tel: (408) 333-4300, FAX: (408) 333-8101, Web Site: www.brocade.com (16)

House, Gwen, Potpourri Group Inc, Chelmsford, MA. Tel: (978) 256-4100, FAX: (978) 256-1961/0344, Web Site: www.potpourrigroup.com (6)

House, Laurie, Martha M House Furniture, Montgomery, AL. Tel: (334) 264-3558, (800) 225-4195, FAX: (334) 262-2610, Web Site: www.marthahouse.com (8)

House, Martha, M., Martha M House Furniture, Montgomery, AL. Tel: (334) 264-3558, (800) 225-4195, FAX: (334) 262-2610, Web Site: www.marthahouse.com (8)

House, Tom, LT Associates, Rio Verde, AZ. Tel: (952) 943-9790, FAX: (952) 943-9794, E-Mail: thouse2az@aol.com, Web Site: www.ltapromotions.net (33)

House, William, C., Martha M House Furniture, Montgomery, AL. Tel: (334) 264-3558, (800) 225-4195, FAX: (334) 262-2610, Web Site: www.marthahouse.com (8)

Martha M House Furniture, Montgomery, AL. Tel: (334) 264-3558, (800) 225-4195, FAX: (334) 262-2610, Web Site: www.marthahouse.com (8)

House of Eyes II, Greensboro, NC. Tel: (336) 852-7107, FAX: (336) 854-0311 (2)

House of Marketing Research, Pasadena, CA. Tel: (626) 486-1400, FAX: (626) 486-1404, Web Site: www.hmr-research.com (30)

House of Oldies, New York, NY. Tel: (212) 243-0500, FAX: (212) 989-1697, E-Mail: rabramson@houseofoldies.com, Web Site: www.houseofoldies.com (6)

House of Onyx, Inc, Greenville, KY. Tel: (270) 338-2363, (800) 844-3100, FAX: (270) 338-9605, E-Mail: sales@houseofonyx.com, Web Site: www.houseofonyx.com (6)

House of Orange, Brentwood Bay, BC Canada. Tel: (866) 401-9174, FAX: (250) 652-8673, E-Mail: houseoforange@shaw.ca, Web Site: www.houseoforange.biz (2)

House of Wesley Inc, Bloomington, IL. Tel: (309) 663-9551, FAX: (309) 663-6691, Web Site: www.houseofwesley.com (8)

House Party Inc, Irvington, NY. Tel: (720) 496-2500, (888) 591-1678, E-Mail: help@houseparty.com, Web Site: www.houseparty.com (30)

Housely, James, Facts On File Inc, New York, NY. Tel: (212) 967-8800, (800) 322-8755, FAX: (212) 678-3633, Web Site: www.factsonfile.com (17)

Houseworth, Tom, Liguori Publications, Liguori, MO. Tel: (636) 464-2500, (800) 325-9521, FAX: (800) 325-9526, E-Mail: liguori@liguori.org, Web Site: www.liguori.org (17)

Housley, James, Cambridge Educational, New York, NY. Tel: (800) 257-5126, FAX: (917) 339-0325, Web Site: www.filmsmediagroup.com (12)

Houss, Joseph, Interstate EDP & Direct Mail Center Inc, Brooklyn, NY. Tel: (718) 965-2500, FAX: (718) 965-2504, E-Mail: info@interstateedp.com, Web Site: www.interstateedp.com (28)

Houss, Max, Interstate EDP & Direct Mail Center Inc, Brooklyn, NY. Tel: (718) 965-2500, FAX: (718) 965-2504, E-Mail: info@interstateedp.com, Web Site: www.interstateedp.com (28)

Houston, Michelle, LENSER, San Rafael, CA. Tel: (415) 446-2500, E-Mail: carol@lenser.com, Web Site: www.lenser.com (35)

The Houston Chronicle, Houston, TX. Tel: (713) 362-7171, Web Site: www.houstonchronicle.com (31)

Houston Direct Marketing Association, Houston, TX. Tel: (281) 931-8883, FAX: (281) 820-4023, Web Site: www.houstondma.org (40)

Houvener, Jim, Quebecor World Midland, Midland, MI. Tel: (989) 496-3333, (800) 448-4288, FAX: (989) 496-1921, Web Site: www.quebecorworldinc.com (27)

Hovan, Nadine, Practicing Law Institute, New York, NY. Tel: (212) 824-5700, (800) 260 4PLI, FAX: (800) 321-0093, E-Mail: info@pli.edu, Web Site: www.pli.edu (16)

Hovespain, Ronald, W., Novell Inc, Waltham, MA. Tel: (801) 861-4272, (800) 529-3400, FAX: (781) 464-8100, E-Mail: crc@novell.com, Web Site: www.novell.com (22)

Hovey, Kim, Premiere Global Services Inc, Atlanta, GA. Tel: (404) 262-8400, (800) 546-1541, FAX: (913) 661-9042, Web Site: www.PGiConnect.com (22)

How I Grossed More Than $1 Million in Direct Mail Order Starting with Little Cash & Less Know How, Rockville Centre, NY. Tel: (516) 766-5850, (800) 323-0548, FAX: (516) 766-5919, Web Site: www.iwsmoney.com (43)

Howard, A., Air-Scent International, Pittsburgh, PA. Tel: (800) 247-0770, FAX: (412) 252-2000, E-Mail: laura@aromaresource.com, Web Site: www.airscent.com (16)

Howard, Bonnie, Citigroup Inc, New York, NY. Tel: (212) 559-1000, (800) 285-3000, FAX: (212) 793-3946, Web Site: www.citigroup.com (14)

Howard, Cherene, Pennsylvania State University Press, University Park, PA. Tel: (814) 865-1327, (800) 326-9180, FAX: (814) 863-1408, Web Site: www.psupress.org (17)

Howard, Elaine, Army Times Publishing Co, Springfield, VA. Tel: (703) 750-9000, (800) 336-4590, FAX: (703) 750-8129, E-Mail: cust-svc@atpco.com, Web Site: www.armytimes.com (17)

Howard, Jerry, National Association of Home Builders, Washington, DC. Tel: (202) 266-8200, (800) 368-5242, FAX: (202) 266-8400, Web Site: www. nahb.org (24)

Howard, Marilyn, Creative Freelancers Inc, Sarasota, FL. Tel: (203) 532-2924, (800) 398-9544, E-Mail: cfonline@freelancers.com, Web Site: www. freelancers.com (39)

Howard, Peter, Staples Inc, Framingham, MA. Tel: (508) 253-5000, FAX: (508) 253-7803, Web Site: www.staples.com (10)

Howard, Stephen, P., Insurance Publications Inc, Overland Park, KS. Tel: (913) 383-9191, (800) 762-3387, FAX: (913) 383-1247, E-Mail: brokerwrld@ primary.net, Web Site: www.brokerworldmag.com (17)

Howard, Susan, American General Life Insurance Co, Houston, TX. Tel: (713) 522-1111, FAX: (713) 522-8531, Web Site: www.aglife.com (15)

Howard, Vicki, Christianity Today Inc, Carol Stream, IL. Tel: (630) 260-6200, FAX: (630) 260-0114, Web Site: www.christianitytoday.com (17)

Howard Rice Nemerovski Canady Falk & Rabkin, San Francisco, CA. Tel: (415) 464-1000, Web Site: www.howardrice.com (14)

Howard-Sloan-Koller Group, New York, NY. Tel: (212) 661-5250, FAX: (212) 557-9178, E-Mail: ekoller@hsksearch.com, Web Site: www.hsksearch. com (20)

Howard-Greene, Dan, California State Polytechnic University Business Administration Dept, San Luis Obispo, CA. Tel: (805) 756-1413, FAX: (805) 756-5057, Web Site: www.calpoly.edu (41)

Howatt, Tom, Wausau Paper Mills Co, Brokaw, WI. Tel: (715) 675-3361, FAX: (715) 675-5181, Web Site: www.wausaupaper.com (25)

Howe III, Rick, Saint Mary's Paper Corp, Wheaton, IL. Tel: (630) 668-6279, FAX: (630) 668-6292, Web Site: www.stmarys-paper.com (25)

Howe, Keith, Echnologist Scrub Tech, Mesquite, TX. Tel: (520) 208-6314 (34)

Howell, Arthur, Summit Industries Inc, Marietta, GA. Tel: (770) 590-0600, (800) 241-6996, FAX: (770) 590-0714, E-Mail: info@summitinds.com, Web Site: www.summitinds.com (5)

Howell, Brian, The Columbus Dispatch, Columbus, OH. Tel: (614) 461-5000, FAX: (614) 461-7551, E-Mail: csmith@the.dispatch.com, Web Site: www. dispatch.com (17)

Howell, George, F.M. Howell & Co, Elmira, NY. Tel: (607) 734-6291, FAX: (607) 735-0464, E-Mail: best@howellpkg.com, Web Site: www.howellpkg. com (16)

Howell, Nelson, American Society for Training & Development, Alexandria, VA. Tel: (703) 683-8100, (800) NAT-ASTD, FAX: (703) 683-8103, Web Site: www.astd.org (1)

Howell, Stephen, The Nature Conservancy, Arlington, VA. Tel: (703) 841-5300, (800) 628-6860, FAX: (703) 841-1283, E-Mail: magazine@tnc.org, Web Site: www.nature.org (1)

F.M. Howell & Co, Elmira, NY. Tel: (607) 734-6291, FAX: (607) 735-0464, E-Mail: best@howellpkg. com, Web Site: www.howellpkg.com (16)

Howell Marketing Services, Elmira, NY. Tel: (607) 734-6291, FAX: (607) 734-6759, E-Mail: gl@ howellmarketingservices.com, Web Site: www. howellmarketingservices.com (28)

Howland, MaryAnne, Ibis Communications Inc, Nashville, TN. Tel: (615) 777-1900, FAX: (615) 777-1906, E-Mail: mhowland@ibiscommunications. com, Web Site: www.ibiscommunications.com (35)

Howlett, Dick, Army Times Publishing Co, Springfield, VA. Tel: (703) 750-9000, (800) 336-4590, FAX: (703) 750-8129, E-Mail: cust-svc@atpco. com, Web Site: www.armytimes.com (17)

Howley, Nicolas, Marathon Norco Aerospace Inc, Waco, TX. Tel: (254) 776-0650, FAX: (254) 776-6558, Web Site: www.mptc.com (16)

Howse, Jennifer, March of Dimes Birth Defects Foundation, White Plains, NY. Tel: (914) 428-7100, FAX: (914) 428-8203, Web Site: www.modimes. org (1)

Hoy, Douglas, Fox Lite, Inc, Fairborn, OH. Tel: (937) 864-1966, FAX: (937) 864-7010, E-Mail: doug@ foxlite.com, Web Site: www.foxlite.com (9)

Hoy, Stephanie, Direct Mail Solutions, Henrico, VA. Tel: (804) 254-8300, Web Site: www. directmailsolutions.com (28)

Hoye, Steve, FT Publications Inc, New York, NY. Tel: (212) 641-6500, FAX: (212) 641-6544, E-Mail: adsales@ft.com, Web Site: www.ft.com (17)

Hoyt, Coleman W., Coleman W Hoyt Consultant, Woodstock, VT. Tel: (802) 672-3634, FAX: (802) 672-5116, E-Mail: cwhoyt@vermontel.net (20)

Hoyt, Coleman, Continuity Shippers Association, Woodstock, VT. Tel: (802) 672-3634 (20)

Coleman W Hoyt Consultant, Woodstock, VT. Tel: (802) 672-3634, FAX: (802) 672-5116, E-Mail: cwhoyt@vermontel.net (20)

Hrabak, DeAnne, Vita-Mix Corp, Cleveland, OH. Tel: (440) 235-4840, (800) VITA-MIX, FAX: (440) 235-3726, E-Mail: service@vitamix.com, Web Site: www.vitamix.com (16)

Hradel, Craig, Cold Stream Farm, Free Soil, MI. Tel: (231) 464-5809, E-Mail: info@coldstreamfarm.net, Web Site: www.coldstreamfarm.net (8)

Hren, Eddie, Martin Worldwide Inc, Oak Park, CA. Tel: (888) 694-5478, Web Site: www. martinworldwide.net (23)

Hritzak, Adam, ClearSaleing Inc, Columbus, OH. Tel: (614) 448-2688, (800) 592-0463, Web Site: www. clearsaleing.com (16)

Hron, Ihor, North American Co for Life & Health Insurance, Chicago, IL. Tel: (312) 648-7600, (800) 800-3656, FAX: (614) 365-9209, Web Site: www. nacolah.com (15)

Hrubes, Jessica, CUES Experience Conference, Madison, WI. Tel: (608) 271-2664, (800) 252-2664, FAX: (608) 271-2303, Web Site: www.cues.org (42)

Hrubes, Jessica, Credit Union Executives Society, Madison, WI. Tel: (608) 271-2664, Web Site: www.cues.org (1)

Hsu, Charles, J., Retawmatic Corp, Flushing, NY. Tel: (718) 886-0502 (9)

Hsu, Dr William, Y., Kennametal Inc, Latrobe, PA. Tel: (800) 222-9327, FAX: (800) 521-3319, E-Mail: mcs-na.service@kennmetal.com, Web Site: www.kennametal.com (16)

Hsu, Julie, Markwins International Corp, City of Industry, CA. Tel: (909) 595-8898, FAX: (909) 595-8820, Web Site: www.markwins.com (16)

Huard, Benoit, Telemedia Communications US, North York, ON. Tel: (416) 733-7600, (888) 290-1466 Can., (800) 461-3773 U.S., FAX: (416) 733-3563, E-Mail: info@transcontinental.ca, Web Site: www. transcontinental.com (17)

Hubbard, Kristi, Beauticontrol Cosmetics Inc, Carrollton, TX. Tel: (972) 458-0601, (800) BEAUTI-1, FAX: (972) 458-6904, E-Mail: clientservices@ beauticontrol.com, Web Site: www.beauticontrol. com (16)

Hubbart, Susan, Ricci Lee Hubbart Associates Inc, Cupertino, CA. Tel: (408) 725-1242, FAX: (408) 716-2704, E-Mail: susan@riccilee.com, Web Site: www.riccilee.com (16)

HubCast Inc, Wakefield, MA. Tel: (781) 221-7200, Web Site: www.hubeast.com (27)

Huber, Fred, Heldref Publications, Washington, DC. Tel: (215) 625-8900, (202) 296-6267, FAX: (202) 296-5149, Web Site: www.heldref.org (17)

Huber, Ray, Population Connection, Washington, DC. Tel: (202) 332-2200, Web Site: www. populationconnection.net (1)

Huber, Tom, Smithsonian Enterprises, New York, NY. Tel: (212) 916-1300, (800) 766-2149, FAX: (212) 490-0058, E-Mail: email@simag.si.edu, Web Site: www.smithsonianmag.com (17)

Hubert, Dick, Videoware Corp, Rye Brook, NY. Tel: (914) 937-6007, FAX: (914) 937-6414, E-Mail: info@videoware.com, Web Site: www.videoware. com (35)

Hubert, Don, Money Mailer LLC, Garden Grove, CA. Tel: (714) 889-1590, Web Site: www.moneymailer. net (31)

Hubert Co, Harrison, OH. Tel: (513) 367-8767, (800) 543-7374, FAX: (513) 367-8823, Web Site: www. hubert.com (16)

Hubler, Olivette, Olivette Hubler Graphics Inc, Dallas, TX. Tel: (214) 941-9444 (36)

Olivette Hubler Graphics Inc, Dallas, TX. Tel: (214) 941-9444 (36)

Hubner, Donald, A., Central Shippee Inc, Bloomingdale, NJ. Tel: (973) 838-1100, (800) 631-8968, FAX: (973) 838-8273, Web Site: www. centralshippee.com (16)

Hubner, Eric, Central Shippee Inc, Bloomingdale, NJ. Tel: (973) 838-1100, (800) 631-8968, FAX: (973) 838-8273, Web Site: www.centralshippee.com (16)

Huck, Brian, Day-Timers, Macungie, PA. Tel: (610) 398-1151, (800) 457-5702, (800) 225-5005, (800) 452-7398, E-Mail: connie@lomottastrategic. com, Web Site: www.daytimer.com (13)

Huck, Gabe, CCC of America, Irving, TX. Tel: (214) 206-3130, (800) 935-2222, FAX: (214) 206-3134, Web Site: www.cccofamerica.com (16)

Huckabay, David, Rapid Color Printing, Las Vegas, NV. Tel: (702) 792-6055, FAX: (702) 792-1437, Web Site: www.rapidocolor.com (27)

Hudak, Kevin, Cuisinart, Stamford, CT. Tel: (203) 975-4600, FAX: (203) 975-4660, Web Site: www. cuisinart.com (16)

Hudak, Tim, PC Ontario Fund, Toronto, ON Canada. Tel: (416) 861-3085, (416) 861-0020, (800) 903-6453, FAX: (416) 861-1760, (416) 861-9593, E-Mail: comments@ontariopc.net, Web Site: www. ontariopc.com (1)

Huddelston, Tari, Ethel M Chocolates Inc, Henderson, NV. Tel: (702) 458-8864, (800) 471-0352, FAX: (800) 392-2587, E-Mail: chocolatier@ethelm.com, Web Site: www.ethelm.com (4)

Huddleston, Jono, DataMarketing Network Inc, Nashville, TN. Tel: (615) 313-7000, Web Site: www. datamarketingnetwork.com (21)

Hudelist, Erwin, Hagadone Printing Co, Honolulu, HI. Tel: (808) 847-5310, (800) 491-4888, FAX: (808) 841-0094, E-Mail: sales@hagadoneprinting.com, Web Site: www.hagadoneprinting.com (27)

Hudetz, Frank, Solar Communications, Wheaton, IL. Tel: (630) 983-1400, (800) 890-6906, FAX: (630) 983-6125, Web Site: www.solarcommunications. com (31)

Hudock, Terry, Sound Beach Marketing Partners LLC, Old Greenwich, CT. Tel: (203) 698-0708, FAX: (203) 698-0712, E-Mail: thudock@ soundbeachmarketing.com, Web Site: www. soundbeachmarketing.com (23)

Hudson, Ann, Royal Canin, Saint Charles, MO Canada. Tel: (636) 926-0003, Web Site: www. royalcanin.us (16)

Hudson, Carol, CARE USA, Atlanta, GA. Tel: (404) 979-9255, (800) 521-CARE, FAX: (404) 589-2600, E-Mail: info@care.org, Web Site: www.careusa.org (1)

Hudson, Corey, Canine Companions for Independence, Santa Rosa, CA. Tel: (707) 577-1700, (800) 572-2275, FAX: (707) 577-1711, E-Mail: info@cci.org, Web Site: www.caninecompanions.org (16)

Hudson, Kyle, Creative Learning Systems Inc, Longmont, CO. Tel: (800) 458-2880, FAX: (760) 546-1490, Web Site: www.clsinc.com (9)

Hudson, Paul H., Roberts Communications Inc, Rochester, NY. Tel: (716) 325-6000, FAX: (716) 325-6001, Web Site: www.robertscomm.com (35)

Hudson, Philip, Graduate School USDA, Washington, DC. Tel: (202) 314-3300, FAX: (202) 690-6577, E-Mail: pubaffairs@grad.usda.gov, Web Site: www. grad.usda.gov (1)

Huelsbeck, David, Uniforms & Scrubs.com, Ballwin, MO. Tel: (636) 391-9200, FAX: (636) 391-9205, E-Mail: questions@uniformsandscrubs.com, Web Site: www.whiteswanscrubs.com (7)

Huerta, Elmer, E., American Cancer Society, Atlanta, GA. Tel: (404) 471-5852, (800) ACS-2345, FAX: (404) 982-3677, Web Site: www.cancer.org (1)

Hueter, Joan, Accuracy in Media Inc, Washington, DC. Tel: (202) 364-4401, FAX: (202) 364-4098, E-Mail: info@aim.org, Web Site: www.aim.org (1)

Huey, Craig, A., CDMG, Torrance, CA. Tel: (310) 212-5727, FAX: (310) 212-5773, E-Mail: infomat@biz.com, Web Site: www.cdmginc.com (21)

Huey, Rodney, Blue Cross & Blue Shield of Oklahoma, Tulsa, OK. Tel: (918) 560-3500, (800) 942-5837, E-Mail: info@bcbsok.com, Web Site: www. bcbsok.com (15)

Huff, Bill, Augsburg Fortress Publishers, Minneapolis, MN. Tel: (612) 330-3300, (800) 426-0115, FAX: (612) 330-3455, E-Mail: info@augsburgfortress. org, Web Site: www.augsburgfortress.org (17)

Huff, James, B., Universal Security Instruments Inc, Owings Mills, MD. Tel: (410) 363-3000, FAX: (410) 363-2218, E-Mail: sales@universalsecurity. com, Web Site: www.universalsecurity.com (16)

Huff, Jamie, Progressive Impressions International, Bloomington, IL. Tel: (309) 664-0444, Web Site: www.whateverittakes.com (35)

Huff, Rita, RPM Direct LLC, Lambertville, NJ. Tel: (609) 566-7150, Web Site: www.r4pm.com (35)

Huffman, Cindy, REI-Recreational Equipment Inc, Kent, WA. Tel: (253) 891-2500, (800) 426-4840, FAX: (253) 891-2523, Web Site: www.rei.com (11)

Huge Jr., James, F., Council on Foreign Relations Inc, New York, NY. Tel: (212) 434-9400, FAX: (212) 861-2759, E-Mail: editor@foreignaffairs.com, Web Site: www.foreignaffairs.org (17)

Hugg, Bill, William B Hugg Enterprise Inc Swim Wear & Accessories, Ambler, PA. Tel: (215) 646-5544, (800) 255-7946, FAX: (215) 646-1280, E-Mail: wbhswim@aol.com, Web Site: www. 800allswim.com (11)

William B Hugg Enterprise Inc Swim Wear & Accessories, Ambler, PA. Tel: (215) 646-5544, (800) 255-7946, FAX: (215) 646-1280, E-Mail: wbhswim@aol.com, Web Site: www.800allswim. com (11)

Huggett, Kevin, Northern Tool & Equipment Inc, Burnsville, MN. Tel: (952) 894-9510, (800) 221-0516, FAX: (952) 894-1020, Web Site: www. northerntool.com (16)

Huggins, Liz, Harcourt Educational Measurement, San Antonio, TX. Tel: (210) 299-1061, (800) 211-8378, FAX: (800) 232-1223, Web Site: www. harcourtassessment.com (17)

Hughery, Byron, Direct Response Consulting, McLean, VA. Tel: (703) 749-0010, FAX: (703) 749-0967, Web Site: www.drcs.com (17)

Hughes, Bob, Direct Marketing Association of Southern California, Newbury Park, CA. Tel: (818) 541-1152, FAX: (818) 541-1959, Web Site: www. ladma.org (40)

Hughes, Duff, The Vane Brothers Co, Baltimore, MD. Tel: (410) 631-5096, FAX: (410) 631-7781, E-Mail: webmaster@vanebros.com, Web Site: www.vanebros.com (16)

Hughes, Elaine, A., EA Hughes & Co, New York, NY. Tel: (212) 689-4600, FAX: (212) 689-4975, E-Mail: hr@eahughes.com, Web Site: www. eahughes.com (20)

Hughes, Holly, A&B Equipment Co, Fort Worth, TX. Tel: (817) 332-8361, (800) 426-0683, FAX: (817) 332-8430, Web Site: www.abequipmentcompany. com (16)

Hughes, Kristy, DirectBuy Inc, Merrillville, IN. Tel: (219) 736-1100, FAX: (219) 755-6208, Web Site: www.ucctotalhome.com (1)

Hughes, Leslie, Corbis Images, New York, NY. Tel: (212) 777-6200, FAX: (212) 375-7700, Web Site: www.corbis.com (38)

Hughes, Mike, Market-Ability Inc, Lafayette, CA. Tel: (925) 299-7900, (800) 434-6275, FAX: (925) 284-2331, Web Site: www.market-ability.net (35)

Hughes, Mike, Safeco Insurance Co, Seattle, WA. Tel: (206) 545-5000, (800) 332-3226, FAX: (206) 545-5767/5651, Web Site: www.safeco.com (15)

Hughes, Sandra, The Procter & Gamble Co, Cincinnati, OH. Tel: (513) 983-4224, (800) 742-6253, FAX: (513) 983-9369, Web Site: www.pg.com (16)

Hughes, Tony, The Order Fulfillment Group, Zionsville, IN. Tel: (317) 733-7755, FAX: (317) 733-8799, E-Mail: thughes@tofg.com, Web Site: www. tofg.com (28)

EA Hughes & Co, New York, NY. Tel: (212) 689-4600, FAX: (212) 689-4975, E-Mail: hr@ eahughes.com, Web Site: www.eahughes.com (20)

The Hughes Group Inc, Saint Louis, MO. Tel: (314) 571-6300, FAX: (314) 862-1616, E-Mail: jschnurbusch@hughes-stl.com, Web Site: www. hughesgroup.com (35)

Hughey, Bryon, Foxhall Corporation, McLean, VA. Tel: (703) 749-3126 (20)

Hughey, Byron, Foxhall Corp, McLean, VA. Tel: (703) 749-3126 (20)

Hughson, Dean, Wimmer's Meat Products Inc, West Point, NE. Tel: (402) 372-2437, (800) 358-0761, FAX: (402) 372-5659, Web Site: www. wimmersmeats.com (4)

Hui, Alan, Easy Color Printing, San Leandro, CA. Tel: (510) 580-6500, FAX: (510) 580-6570, Web Site: www.easycolorprinting.com (35)

Hui, Jackie, Johnson Rauhoff Inc, Saint Joseph, MI. Tel: (269) 428-3377, (800) 572-3996, FAX: (269) 428-3312, Web Site: www.johnsonrauhoff.com (35)

Huisingh, Rosemary, LinguiSystems, East Moline, IL. Tel: (309) 755-2300, (800) 776-4332, FAX: (800) 577-4555, E-Mail: service@linguisystems.com, Web Site: www.linguisystems.com (17)

Hull, Lucy, M., Selltel Inc, Brick, NJ. Tel: (732) 920-8700, (888) 840-9481, FAX: (732) 903-0836, E-Mail: info@nationalprotection.com (29)

Hulon, Wade, Anritsu Co, Morgan Hill, CA. Tel: (408) 778-2000, (800) 267-4878, FAX: (408) 776-1744, Web Site: www.us.anritsu.com (16)

Hulse, Chris, Madison Direct Marketing Ltd, Stamford, CT. Tel: (203) 653-3200, FAX: (203) 316-0518, Web Site: www.madisondm.com (31)

Hult Fritz Matuszak Associates, Peoria, IL. Tel: (309) 673-8191, FAX: (309) 674-5530, E-Mail: jflynn@ hfma.com, Web Site: www.hfma.com (35)

Hultin, Linnet, Atlantic Spice Co, North Truro, MA. Tel: (508) 487-6100, (800) 316-7965, FAX: (508) 487-2550, E-Mail: mark@atlanticspice.com, Web Site: www.atlanticspice.com (4)

Human Resource Development Press, Amherst, MA. Tel: (413) 253-3488, (800) 822-2801, FAX: (413) 253-3490, E-Mail: info@hrdpress.com, Web Site: www.hrdpress.com (17)

Human Rights Campaign, Washington, DC. Tel: (202) 216-1500, Web Site: www.hrc.org (40)

Humana Inc, Louisville, KY. Tel: (502) 580-5005, FAX: (502) 580-3141, Web Site: www.humana. com (7)

The Humane Society of the US, Gaithersburg, MD. Tel: (202) 452-1100, Web Site: www.hsus.org (1)

Humbert, Dave, Current USA Inc, Colorado Springs, CO. Tel: (719) 594-4100, (877) 665-4458, FAX: (719) 531-2283, Web Site: www.currentinc.com (6)

Hummel, John, Hummel Integrated Marketing Solutions, Union, NJ. Tel: (908) 688-5300, FAX: (908) 688-6020, E-Mail: hummelmlg@aol.com (21)

Hummel Integrated Marketing Solutions, Union, NJ. Tel: (908) 688-5300, FAX: (908) 688-6020, E-Mail: hummelmlg@aol.com (21)

Humphrey, Clint, Quebecor-World Infiniti, Enfield, CT. Tel: (860) 741-0150, (800) 221-6052, FAX: (860) 741-2553, E-Mail: clint.humphrey@ quebecorworld.com, Web Site: www. infinitigraphics.com (27)

Humphries, Melita, Schermer Pecans, Glennville, GA. Tel: (800) 841-3403, E-Mail: information@ schermerpecans.com, Web Site: www.pecantreats. com (4)

Hund, Thomas, N., Burlington Northern & Santa Fe Railroad, Fort Worth, TX. Tel: (817) 878-2000, (800) 795-2673, FAX: (817) 333-7593, Web Site: www.bnsf.com (16)

Hungerford, William, Strategic Software Systems LLC, Richmond, VA. Tel: (804) 288-8827x110, Web Site: www.sss1.com (22)

Hungsberg, Jill, Marshall Fields Dept Stores, Minneapolis, MN. Tel: (612) 375-3004, Web Site: www. fields.com (5)

Hunnewell, Tim, MarketerNet LLC, Chicago, IL. Tel: (312) 775-9320, (888) 443-3684, FAX: (312) 775-9328, E-Mail: info@marketernet.com, Web Site: www.marketernet.com (22)

Hunnicutt, David, Wellness Councils of America, Omaha, NE. Tel: (402) 827-3590, FAX: (402) 827-3594, E-Mail: wellworkplace@welcoa.org, Web Site: www.welcoa.org (1)

Hunt, Brian, Hunt Marketing Group, Seattle, WA. Tel: (206) 447-5665, Web Site: www.hmgseattle.com (35)

Hunt, C, Ventriloquist Voice Solutions International Inc, Mississauga, ON. Tel: (866) 446-0860, E-Mail: info@vvsii.com, Web Site: www.vvsii.com (29)

Hunt, Catherine, T., American Chemical Society, Washington, DC. Tel: (202) 872-4600, (800) 227-5558, FAX: (202) 833-7716, E-Mail: service@acs. org, Web Site: www.acs.org (1)

Hunt, Clark, Kansas City Chiefs, Kansas City, MO. Tel: (816) 920-9300, (888) 99-CHIEFS, FAX: (816) 923-4719, Web Site: www.kcchiefs.com (16)

Hunt, Dan, Mason Companies Inc, Chippewa Falls, WI. Tel: (715) 723-1871, (800) 826-7030, FAX: (715) 720-4247, Web Site: www. masoncompaniesinc.com (2)

Hunt, F., Randal, Aerovox Inc, New Bedford, MA. Tel: (508) 994-9661, (888) AEROVOX, FAX: (508) 995-3000, E-Mail: sales1@aerovox.com, Web Site: www.aerovox.com (16)

Hunt, J., Ventriloquist Voice Solutions International Inc, Mississauga, ON Canada. Tel: (866) 446-0860, E-Mail: info@vvsii.com, Web Site: www.vvsii.com (29)

Hunt, James, E., Winmill & Co, New York, NY. Tel: (212) 785-0900, (800) 400-MIDAS, FAX: (212) 363-1100, E-Mail: info@midasfunds.com, Web Site: www.midasfunds.com (14)

Hunt, Lorraine, Nevada Commission on Tourism, Carson City, NV. Tel: (775) 687-4322, (800) NEVADA 8, FAX: (775) 687-6779, Web Site: www. travelnevada.com (1)

Hunt, Robert, New Day Marketing Ltd, Santa Barbara, CA. Tel: (805) 965-7833, FAX: (805) 965-1284, Web Site: www.newdaymarketing.com (35)

Hunt Marketing Group, Seattle, WA. Tel: (206) 447-5665, Web Site: www.hmgseattle.com (35)

Hunter, Barbara, Air Ambulance Network Inc, Palm Harbor, FL. Tel: (727) 934-3999, (800) 327-1966, FAX: (727) 937-0276, Web Site: www. airambulancenetwork.com (16)

Hunter, Christine, F., The Metropolitan Opera, New York, NY. Tel: (212) 799-3100, (212) 362-6000, FAX: (212) 870-7695, Web Site: www.metopera. org (1)

Hunter, Clifford, M., Broadcast Media Associates, Santa Maria, CA. Tel: (805) 937-1553, E-Mail: cliffhunter@cliffhunter.com, Web Site: www. broadcastmediabroker.com (30)

Hunter, Jennifer, Scott's Directories, Don Mills, ON Canada. Tel: (416) 442-2010, (800) 408-9431, FAX: (416) 442-2078, E-Mail: sales@scottsinfo.com, Web Site: www.scottsinfo.com (31)

Hunter, Joyce, Miller Stockman, Denver, CO. Tel: (303) 428-5696, FAX: (303) 430-1130 (2)

Hunter, Richard, Air Ambulance Network Inc, Palm Harbor, FL. Tel: (727) 934-3999, (800) 327-1966, FAX: (727) 937-0276, Web Site: www.airambulancenetwork.com (16)

Hunter, Rick, Color Q Inc, Miamisburg, OH. Tel: (937) 866-4001, (800) 999-9818, FAX: (937) 866-4101, E-Mail: info@colorq.com, Web Site: www.colorqinc.com (27)

Hunter, Robert, Lewis Cleaning Systems, Kiel, WI. Tel: (920) 894-2293, FAX: (920) 894-7029, Web Site: www.lewissonics.com (34)

Hunter, Timothy, Key Computer Service of Chelsea, New York, NY. Tel: (212) 206-8060, FAX: (212) 206-8398 (28)

Hunter, Victor, Hunter Business Group LLC, Milwaukee, WI. Tel: (414) 203-8060, (800) 423-4010, FAX: (414) 203-8225, E-Mail: hunter@hunterbusiness.com, Web Site: www.hunterbusiness.com (20)

Hunter, Warren, DMW Worldwide LLC, Chesterbrook, PA. Tel: (610) 407-0407, (877) 744-3699, FAX: (610) 407-9201, E-Mail: whunter@dmwdirect.com, Web Site: www.dmwdirect.com (35)

Hunter, Willard M., Prime Graphics Inc, Wood Dale, IL. Tel: (630) 227-1300, FAX: (630) 227-1823, E-Mail: moreinfo@primegraphicsinc.com, Web Site: www.primegraphicsinc.com (27)

Hunter, William, Smithfield Packing Co Inc, Smithfield, VA. Tel: (757) 357-4321, FAX: (757) 357-1339, E-Mail: information@smithfieldfoods.com, Web Site: www.smithfieldfoods.com (16)

Hunter Business Group LLC, Milwaukee, WI. Tel: (414) 203-8060, (800) 423-4010, FAX: (414) 203-8225, E-Mail: hunter@hunterbusiness.com, Web Site: www.hunterbusiness.com (20)

Huntington, Patricia, S., Huntington Associates, New York, NY. Tel: (212) 582-1870, FAX: (212) 586-3291, E-Mail: huntassoc@aol.com (16)

Huntington Associates, New York, NY. Tel: (212) 582-1870, FAX: (212) 586-3291, E-Mail: huntassoc@aol.com (35)

Huntington Bancshares, Columbus, OH. Tel: (614) 480-8300, (800) 480-BANK, FAX: (614) 480-5284, Web Site: www.huntington.com (14)

Huntoon, Keith, Blue Hill Marketing Solutions Inc, Pearl River, NY. Tel: (845) 627-6600, FAX: (845) 735-3985, Web Site: www.liftengine.com (22)

Huntsinger & Jeffer Inc, Richmond, VA. Tel: (804) 266-2499, FAX: (804) 266-8563, E-Mail: vickil@huntsinger-jeffer.com, Web Site: www.huntsinger-jeffer.com (21)

Hupp, Dennis, Direct Marketing Audit Systems, Bridgeton, MO. Tel: (314) 739-7480, FAX: (314) 739-7284, Web Site: www.dmasinc.com (22)

Hurd, Mark, Compaq Computer Corp, Houston, TX. Tel: (281) 370-0670, FAX: (281) 927-8835, Web Site: www.compaq.com (16)

Hurd, Mark, V., Hewlett-Packard Co, Palo Alto, CA. Tel: (650) 857-1501, (800) 752-0900, FAX: (650) 857-5518, Web Site: www.hp.com (16)

Hurletron Inc, Libertyville, IL. Tel: (847) 680-7022, FAX: (847) 680-7338, Web Site: www.hurletron.com (34)

Hurley, Cheryl, The Library of America, New York, NY. Tel: (212) 308-3360, (800) 964-5778, FAX: (212) 750-8352, E-Mail: info@loa.org, Web Site: www.loa.org (13)

Hurley, Gerry, Vertex Inc, Berwyn, PA. Tel: (610) 640-4200, (800) 355-3500, FAX: (610) 640-5892, Web Site: www.vertexinc.com (16)

Hurley, Jack, Direct Mail Advertising Corp, Miami, FL. Tel: (305) 557-4153, (800) 683-3622, FAX: (305) 634-1896, Web Site: www.directmac.com (23)

Hurley, Tom, DMW Worldwide LLC, Chesterbrook, PA. Tel: (610) 407-0407, (877) 744-3699, FAX: (610) 407-9201, E-Mail: whunter@dmwdirect.com, Web Site: www.dmwdirect.com (35)

Hurteau, Claudia, Roseberry Direct List Management & Brokerage, Elon, NC. Tel: (336) 532-1000, Web Site: www.roseberrydirect.com (23)

Hurvitz, David, Leadership Directories Inc, New York, NY. Tel: (212) 627-4140, FAX: (212) 645-0931, E-Mail: info@leadershipdirectories.com, Web Site: www.leadershipdirectories.com (17)

Hurwitz, Marty, MVI Marketing Ltd, Paso Robles, CA. Tel: (805) 459-4455, (805) 239-2994, FAX: (805) 239-2947, E-Mail: info@mvimarketing.com, Web Site: www.mvimarketing.com (20)

Huse, Paul, Joyce Meyer Ministries, Fenton, MO. Tel: (636) 349-0303, Web Site: www.joycemeyer.org (1)

Husky Envelope Products, Walled Lake, MI. Tel: (248) 624-7070, FAX: (248) 624-5990, E-Mail: bmuehl@huskyenvelope.com, Web Site: www.huskyenvelope.com (26)

Huslen, Gregory, US Playing Card Co, Erlanger, KY. Tel: (513) 396-5700, (800) 542-7430, FAX: (513) 392-5879 (16)

Husnik, Sarah, Periscope Inc, Minneapolis, MN. Tel: (612) 339-0663, (800) 339-2103, FAX: (612) 339-0600, E-Mail: bill@ps-mpls.com, Web Site: www.periscope.com (35)

Hussey, James, Chapman Cubine Adams & Hussey, Arlington, VA. Tel: (703) 248-0025, Web Site: www.ahadirect.com (20)

Hussey, Jay, Baldwin Filters, Kearney, NE. Tel: (308) 234-1951, (800) 822-5394, FAX: (800) 828-4453, E-Mail: info@baldwinfilter.com, Web Site: www.baldwinfilter.com (16)

Hussey, Mary Jo, Wikco Industries Inc, Casa Grande, AZ. Tel: (520) 316-0446, FAX: (520) 316-0446, E-Mail: sales@wikco.com, Web Site: www.wikco.com (5)

Hussey, Michael, E., AMS Direct, Burr Ridge, IL. Tel: (630) 382-1000, FAX: (630) 325-0825, Web Site: www.amsdirect.com (13)

Hussey, Mike, Wikco Industries Inc, Casa Grande, AZ. Tel: (520) 316-0446, FAX: (520) 316-0446, E-Mail: sales@wikco.com, Web Site: www.wikco.com (5)

Hustad, Shannin, Classic Thermographers, North Mankato, MN. Tel: (623) 582-0002, (800) 727-4200, FAX: (800) 727-4202 (10)

Hutchins, Traver, REMEDY Magazine, New York, NY. Tel: (212) 695-2223, FAX: (212) 695-2936, E-Mail: info@rmedizine.com, Web Site: www.medizine.com (17)

Hutchinson, Gary, WRS Group Ltd, Waco, TX. Tel: (254) 776-6461, (800) 299-3366, FAX: (888) 977-7653, E-Mail: sales@wrsgroup.com, Web Site: www.wrsgroup.com (7)

Hutchinson, Harold, Harwil Corp, Oxnard, CA. Tel: (805) 988-6800, FAX: (805) 988-6804, E-Mail: harwil@harwil.com, Web Site: www.harwil.com (9)

Hutchinson, R., Kenneth, University of Missouri, Columbia, MO. Tel: (573) 882-6333, (800) 856-2181, FAX: (573) 882-2721, E-Mail: visitus@missouri.edu, Web Site: www.missouri.edu (41)

Hutchinson, Teeni, Southern Poverty Law Center, Montgomery, AL. Tel: (334) 956-8200, FAX: (334) 956-8483, Web Site: www.splcenter.org (1)

Hutchinson, Theresa, Accounting with Debits and Credits with Coates & Hutchinson PC, Odenton, MD. Tel: (800) 833-5933, FAX: (301) 912-3364, E-Mail: info@awdc.org (14)

Hutchison, Kristi, Big Brothers Big Sisters of Greater Kansas City, Kansas City, MO. Tel: (816) 561-5269, Web Site: www.bigbrothersbigsisterskc.org (1)

Hutchisson, Rachel, Blackbaud Inc, Charleston, SC. Tel: (800) 443-9441 (22)

Hutney, Beverly, The Stelter Co, Des Moines, IA. Tel: (800) 331-6881 (20)

Hutsen, Yogi, Coastal Hotel Group, Seattle, WA. Tel: (206) 388-0400, FAX: (206) 388-0401, E-Mail: info@coastalhotel.com, Web Site: www.coastalhotels.com (1)

Hutson, Darryl, A, InteliSpend, Fenton, MO. Tel: (636) 226-2000, Web Site: intelispend.com (35)

Huttlin, Donald, BBF Integrated Solutions, Largo, FL. Tel: (800) 666-8082, Web Site: www.bbfprinting.com (27)

Huvar, Jeff, The Print Box Inc, Brooklyn, NY. Tel: (212) 741-1381, (800) 546-4011, FAX: (212) 463-9071, E-Mail: info@promobrands.com, Web Site: www.promobrands.com (33)

Huxta, Wendy, Current USA Inc, Colorado Springs, CO. Tel: (719) 594-4100, (877) 665-4458, FAX: (719) 531-2283, Web Site: www.currentinc.com (6)

Huyser, Karen, Thorndike Press, Waterville, ME. Tel: (207) 859-1000, (800) 223-1244, E-Mail: gale.salesassistance@cengage.com, Web Site: www.galegroup.com (17)

Hwang, Lawrence, SECO-LARM USA Inc, Irvine, CA. Tel: (949) 261-2999, (800) 662-0800, FAX: (949) 261-7326, E-Mail: info@seco-larm.com, Web Site: www.seco-larm.com (16)

Hy Cite Corp, Madison, WI. Tel: (608) 273-3373, (800) 279-3373, FAX: (608) 273-0936, Web Site: www.hycite.com (16)

HY-KO Products Co, Northfield, OH. Tel: (330) 467-7446, Web Site: www.hy-ko.com (16)

Hyatt, Michael, S., Thomas Nelson, Inc, Nashville, TN. Tel: (615) 889-9000, (800) 251-4000, FAX: (615) 889-5940, Web Site: www.thomasnelson.com (17)

Hyatt Fruit Co, Vero Beach, FL. Tel: (772) 567-3766, (866) 991-8889, FAX: (772) 567-0973, Web Site: www.hyattfruitco.com (4)

Hyatt Hotels Corp, Chicago, IL. Tel: (312) 750-1234, FAX: (312) 780-5289, Web Site: www.hyatt.com (16)

Hyatt Legal Plans Inc, Cleveland, OH. Tel: (216) 241-0022, FAX: (216) 694-4305, Web Site: www.legalplans.com (16)

Hyder Jr., James, W., Fetter Label, Louisville, KY. Tel: (502) 634-4771, (800) 234-4771, FAX: (502) 634-3587, E-Mail: info@fettergroup.com (27)

Hydra Group LLC, Los Angeles, CA. Tel: (310) 526-6680, FAX: (310) 526-6682, Web Site: www.hydragroup.com (9)

Hygienic Fabrics & Filters Inc, Sheboygan, WI. Tel: (920) 457-7383, (800) 876-2009, FAX: (920) 457-2558, Web Site: www.hyfab.com (16)

The Hyiad Group, Garden City, NY. Tel: (516) 433-3800, FAX: (516) 822-6670, Web Site: www.thehyaidgroup.com (22)

Hylton, Annie, City of Cerritos, Cerritos, CA. Tel: (562) 916-1319, Web Site: www.ci.cerritos.ca.us (1)

Hylton, Christa, USA Weekend, New York, NY. Tel: (800) 487-4956, FAX: (703) 854-2122, Web Site: www.usaweekend.com (31)

Hyman, Mike, New Mexico State University, Las Cruces, NM. Tel: (575) 646-0111, (505) 646-3341, FAX: (505) 646-1498, Web Site: www.nmsu.edu (41)

Hyman's, Hanahan, SC. Tel: (843) 571-7870, (800) 354-9626, FAX: (843) 571-7575, E-Mail: support@hymans.com, Web Site: www.hymans.com (2)

Hyme, Mier, Hyman's, Hanahan, SC. Tel: (843) 571-7870, (800) 354-9626, FAX: (843) 571-7575, E-Mail: support@hymans.com, Web Site: www.hymans.com (2)

Hynes, Tom, Ellis Systems Corp, Lake Forest, IL. Tel: (847) 371-0200, (800) 253-5547, FAX: (847) 371-0202, E-Mail: tom@ellisfiling.com, Web Site: www.ellismh.com (9)

Hyphos360 Inc, Clearwater, FL. Tel: (727) 532-0700, (800) 733-1817, FAX: (727) 524-3424, Web Site: www.hyphos360.com (21)

I

I-Behavior Inc, Louisville, CO. Tel: (303) 228-5000, FAX: (303) 926-1367, E-Mail: contactus@i-behavior.com, Web Site: www.i-behavior.com (23)

IAEE Annual Meeting and Exhibition, Dallas, TX. Tel: (972) 458-8002, FAX: (972) 458-8119, E-Mail: info@iaee.com, Web Site: www.iaee.com (42)

IBM Corp, Armonk, NY. Tel: (914) 765-1900, FAX: (914) 765-6633, Web Site: www.ibm.com (16)

IBux, Chico, CA. Tel: (530) 895-0431 (23)

IC DIRECT List Brokers, El Dorado Hills, CA. Tel: (916) 941-7605, (877) ICD-UST, FAX: (916) 941-7615, E-Mail: info@icdlist.com, Web Site: www.icdlist.com (23)

IC System Inc, Saint Paul, MN. Tel: (651) 483-0585, (800) 245-8875, FAX: (651) 481-6363, E-Mail: promo@icsystem.com, Web Site: www.icsystem.com (21)

ICIS Inc, Upper Black Eddy, PA. Tel: (610) 982-0429, E-Mail: icis@ptdprolog.net, Web Site: www.icisjewelry.com (2)

ICMA Retirement Corp, Washington, DC. Tel: (202) 962-4600, (800) 669-7400, FAX: (202) 962-4601, E-Mail: investorservices@icmarc.org, Web Site: www.icmarc.org (14)

ICOM Information & Communications Inc, Toronto, ON Canada. Tel: (416) 297-4058, (800) 603-4555, FAX: (416) 297-7084, E-Mail: info@i-com.com, Web Site: www.i-com.com (23)

ICS Audio Video Supply Inc, Phoenix, AZ. Tel: (602) 242-9207 (3)

ICS Corp, Philadelphia, PA. Tel: (888) 223-2840, FAX: (215) 634-1522, E-Mail: info@ics-corporation.com, Web Site: www.ics-corporation.com (21)

ICS Marketing Support Services, Lansing, MI. Tel: (517) 394-1890, (888) 394-1890, FAX: (517) 394-7408, E-Mail: sales@icshq.com, Web Site: www.icshq.com (21)

ICT Group Inc, Tampa, FL. Tel: (215) 757-0200, (800) 799-6880, Web Site: www.ictgroup.com (29)

IDC, Ltd, Henderson, NV. Tel: (702) 450-1000, FAX: (702) 450-1020, E-Mail: info@goidc.com, Web Site: www.goidc.com (1)

IDG List Services, Framingham, MA. Tel: (888) 434-5478, FAX: (508) 370-0020, Web Site: www.idglist.com (24)

IDMS Inc, Melville, NY. Tel: (631) 249-7744, (800) 582-5831, FAX: (631) 249-4425, E-Mail: sales@idmsinc.com, Web Site: www.idmsinc.com (16)

The IDT Group, Philadelphia, PA. Tel: (215) 487-4420, FAX: (215) 487-3110, Web Site: www.idthospitality.com (22)

IEEE/Spectrum Magazine, New York, NY. Tel: (212) 419-7768, FAX: (212) 419-7589, E-Mail: i.rodriguez@ieee.org, Web Site: www.spectrum.ieee.org (24)

The IEI Corp, Princeton, NJ. Tel: (609) 987-2700, FAX: (609) 987-2703 (6)

Ifbyphone, Skokie, IL. Tel: (877) 295-5100, Web Site: www.ifbyphone.com (30)

IHFRA, High Point, NC. Tel: (336) 889-3920, FAX: (336) 464-2125, E-Mail: ihfra@ihfra.org, Web Site: www.ihfra.org (23)

IHOP Corp, Glendale, CA. Tel: (818) 240-6055, FAX: (818) 553-3131, Web Site: www.ihop.com (16)

IHS Inc, Englewood, CO. Tel: (303) 790-0600, (800) 525-7052, FAX: (303) 754-3940, E-Mail: customer.support@ihs.com, Web Site: www.ihs.com (17)

IJHANA, Los Angeles, CA. Tel: (213) 268-4283, (888) 421-9222, E-Mail: info@ijhana.com, Web Site: www.ijhana.com (20)

IMC Direct, Honolulu, HI. Tel: (808) 545-1680, FAX: (808) 528-4293 (35)

IMC - Multi Media Marketing, Jenkintown, PA. Tel: (215) 887-5700 X107, FAX: (215) 887-7076, E-Mail: berylwolk@aol.com, Web Site: berylsworld.com (31)

IMN, Waltham, MA. Tel: (781) 890-4700, Web Site: www.imninc.com (32)

IMS Group II Communications, Franklin, WI. Tel: (414) 425-2080, FAX: (414) 425-6029, Web Site: www.groupii.com (21)

IMSI/Design LLC, Novato, CA. Tel: (415) 483-8000, (800) 833-4674, FAX: (415) 884-9023, Web Site: www.imsisoft.com (34)

IMV, Des Plaines, IL. Tel: (847) 297-1404, FAX: (847) 297-5010, E-Mail: sales@imvinfo.com, Web Site: www.imvlimited.com (20)

INC Magazine, New York, NY. Tel: (212) 389-5377, FAX: (617) 248-8090, Web Site: www.inc.com (17)

ING, Minneapolis, MN. Tel: (612) 342-7061, (800) 333-6965, FAX: (612) 372-5339, Web Site: www.ing.com (15)

ING USA Annuity & Life Ins Co, Des Moines, IA. Tel: (515) 698-7100, FAX: (515) 698-2001, Web Site: www.ing-usa.com (15)

INPEX, Pittsburgh, PA. Tel: (412) 288-1343, (412) 288-1300, (888) 544-6739, (888) 54-INPEX, FAX: (412) 288-4546, E-Mail: info@inpex.com, Web Site: www.inpex.com (42)

INX International Ink Co, Schaumburg, IL. Tel: (800) 631-7956, FAX: (847) 969-9758, E-Mail: info@inxink.com, Web Site: www.inxinternational.com (16)

IPD Co Inc, Portland, OR. Tel: (503) 257-7500, (800) 444-6473, FAX: (503) 257-7596, E-Mail: info@ipdusa.com, Web Site: www.ipdusa.com (12)

IPD Printing & Distributing Inc, Atlanta, GA. Tel: (770) 458-6351, FAX: (770) 454-6236 (27)

IPG, New York, NY. Tel: (646) 229-2255 (20)

IPS - Sendero Corp, Norcross, GA. Tel: (770) 409-0047, (800) 879-1996, FAX: (770) 409-1735, E-Mail: sales@ips-sendero.com, Web Site: www.ips-sendero.com (14)

IQ Marketing, Excelsior, MN. Tel: (952) 897-7300, FAX: (952) 820-8041, Web Site: www.iqmarketing.com (21)

IR/ARO, Bryan, OH. Tel: (419) 636-4242, (800) 495-0276, FAX: (419) 633-1674, E-Mail: russ_w_davies@irco.com, Web Site: www.arozone.com (13)

IRPP, Montreal, PQ Canada. Tel: (514) 985-2461, FAX: (514) 985-2559, E-Mail: irpp@irpp.org, Web Site: www.irpp.org (30)

ISA-The Instrumentation Systems & Automation Society, Research Triangle Park, NC. Tel: (919) 549-8411, FAX: (919) 549-8288, E-Mail: info@isa.org, Web Site: www.isa.org (1)

ITAGroup, West Des Moines, IA. Tel: (515) 224-3400, (800) 257-1985, FAX: (515) 224-3589, Web Site: www.itagroup.com (33)

ITT Educational Services Inc, Carmel, IN. Tel: (317) 706-9200, E-Mail: gtanner@itt-tech.edu, Web Site: www.itt-tech.edu (16)

ITW Bee Leitzke, Iron Ridge, WI. Tel: (920) 625-2342, FAX: (920) 625-2643, Web Site: www.itwbeeleitzke.com (16)

ITW Vortec, Cincinnati, OH. Tel: (513) 891-7474, (800) 441-7475, FAX: (513) 891-4092, E-Mail: techsupport@vortec.com, Web Site: www.vortec.com (16)

IWCO Direct, Chanhassen, MN. Tel: (952) 474-0961, FAX: (952) 474-6467 (21)

IZEA, Orlando, FL. Tel: (321) 332-6830, Web Site: www.izea.com (20)

Iacinelli, Joseph, Standard Life, Montreal, PQ Canada. Tel: (514) 499-8855, (877) 499-9555, FAX: (514) 499-4908, Web Site: www.standardlife.ca (15)

Iacobacci, Charlene, Jaz Holdings LLC, Liberty Corner, NJ. Tel: (973) 574-7600, (800) 999-9554, FAX: (973) 944-5073, E-Mail: webmaster@regentbook.com, Web Site: www.regentbook.com (16)

The Iams Co, Dayton, OH. Tel: (937) 898-7387, (800) 675-3849, FAX: (937) 264-7264, Web Site: www.iams.com (16)

Ian, Grant, Pioneer Hi-Bred International Inc, Johnston, IA. Tel: (515) 270-3200, FAX: (515) 270-3581, E-Mail: web.editor@pioneer.com, Web Site: www.pioneer.com (4)

Iannaccone, Dominick, Advertising Distributors of America Inc, Hauppauge, NY. Tel: (631) 231-5700, FAX: (631) 434-1063 (21)

Iannini, Robert, E., Information Unlimited Inc, Amherst, NH. Tel: (603) 673-4730, (800) 221-1705, FAX: (603) 672-5406, E-Mail: wako2@xtdl.com, Web Site: www.amazing1.com (11)

Ianoello, Angelo, Con-Way Truckload, Joplin, MO. Tel: (417) 623-5229, (800) CFI-DRIVE, FAX: (417) 623-8939, E-Mail: gnichols@cfi-us.com, Web Site: www.cfi-us.com (12)

Iarocci, Joe, CARE USA, Atlanta, GA. Tel: (404) 979-9255, (800) 521-CARE, FAX: (404) 589-2600, E-Mail: info@care.org, Web Site: www.careusa.org (1)

Iazzetto, Joe, Unicom Marketing Group Inc, Broadview, IL. Tel: (312) 738-1404, FAX: (312) 738-1405, E-Mail: info@unicommarketing.com, Web Site: www.unicommarketing.com (35)

Ibanez, Maria, Society of American Magicians Inc, Parker, CO. E-Mail: rmblowers@aol.com, Web Site: www.magicsam.com (1)

Ibis Communications Inc, Nashville, TN. Tel: (615) 777-1900, FAX: (615) 777-1906, E-Mail: mhowland@ibiscommunications.com, Web Site: www.ibiscommunications.com (35)

IBSDirect, King of Prussia, PA. Tel: (610) 265-8210, Web Site: www.ibsdm.com (27)

Ice, Carl, R., Burlington Northern & Santa Fe Railroad, Fort Worth, TX. Tel: (817) 878-2000, (800) 795-2673, FAX: (817) 333-7593, Web Site: www.bnsf.com (16)

Ickes, Erin, Message Systems, Columbia, MD. Tel: (410) 872-4910, (877) 887-3031, FAX: (410) 872-4912, E-Mail: information@messagesystems.com, Web Site: www.messagesystems.com (32)

IClimber Inc, Burbank, CA. Tel: (818) 567-3030, Web Site: www.iclimber.com (16)

The Icon, Los Angeles, CA. Tel: (323) 933-1666, E-Mail: icon@iconia.com, Web Site: www.iconia.com (37)

Icon Marketing Communications, Florence, KY. Tel: (859) 647-7271, FAX: (859) 647-0615, E-Mail: shawn@iconmc.com, Web Site: www.iconmc.com (21)

Icon Media Direct Inc, Van Nuys, CA. Tel: (818) 995-6400, FAX: (818) 995-6405, E-Mail: info@iconmediadirect.com, Web Site: www.iconmediadirect.com (35)

iContact, Morrisville, NC. Tel: (866) 803-9462, Web Site: www.icontact.com (32)

iCrossing, Scottsdale, AZ. Tel: (480) 505-5800, FAX: (480) 505-5801 (32)

Ida, Doreen, Nestle USA, Glendale, CA. Tel: (818) 549-6000, (800) 225-2270, FAX: (818) 549-6952, Web Site: www.nestleusa.com (4)

Idea Art Inc, Colorado Springs, CO. Tel: (615) 889-4989, (800) 433-2278, FAX: (615) 889-6731, E-Mail: customerservice@ideaart.com, Web Site: www.ideaart.com (25)

The Idea Club.com(TM) & Dumas Martin Consulting, Pomona, CA. Tel: (909) 620-4772, FAX: (909) 629-4739, E-Mail: theideaclub@peoplepc.com, Web Site: www.incorpman.com (16)

I/D/E/A Inc, Caldwell, ID. Tel: (208) 459-6357, (800) 635-9261, FAX: (208) 459-6484, Web Site: www.relyonidea.com (16)

IdeaOverTen LLC, Allentown, PA. Tel: (610) 437-4340, (866) 864-2836, FAX: (866) 414-6165, E-Mail: marketing@ideaover10.com, Web Site: www.ideaover10.com (35)

Ideagroup Mail Service, Saint Paul, MN. Tel: (651) 490-2903, FAX: (651) 490-0728, E-Mail: ideagroup@visi.com (28)

Ideal Images, Glastonbury, CT. Tel: (860) 633-8600, FAX: (860) 659-3235 (38)

Ideal Industries (Canada) Corp, Ajax, ON Canada. Tel: (905) 683-3400, (800) 824-3325, FAX: (905) 683-0209, E-Mail: nick.shkordoff@idealindustries.com, Web Site: www.idealindustries.com (9)

Ideal Industries Inc, Sycamore, IL. Tel: (815) 895-5181, (800) 435-0705, FAX: (815) 895-4800, E-Mail: ideal_industries@idealindustries.com, Web Site: www.idealindustries.com (16)

Idealliance, Alexandria, VA. Tel: (703) 837-1070, FAX: (703) 837-1072 (40)

Ideals Publications Inc, Nashville, TN. Tel: (615) 333-0478, FAX: (615) 781-1447, Web Site: www.idealspublications.com (17)

Idearc Media Corp, Dallas, TX. Tel: (972) 453-7797 (16)

Ideas Companies Inc, Naperville, IL. Tel: (630) 357-7522, (800) 323-5656, FAX: (630) 357-7538 (33)

Ideas in SEO, Miami, FL. Tel: (786) 280-6051 (20)

Ideas To Go Inc, Minneapolis, MN. Tel: (612) 331-1570, FAX: (612) 331-1602, E-Mail: cebert@ideastogo.com, Web Site: www.ideastogo.com (30)

Idol, Kelly, Relevate, Springfield, VA. Tel: (703) 658-8300, (800) 523-7346, FAX: (703) 658-8301, E-Mail: sales@relevategroup.com, Web Site: www.relevategroup.com (22)

Idowu, Olajire, Narrow Way, Lafayette, CA. Tel: (925) 283-4074 (6)

Igeli, Claire, The Washington Monthly Co, Washington, DC. Tel: (202) 393-5155, FAX: (202) 393-2444, E-Mail: editors@washingtonmonthly.com, Web Site: www.washingtonmonthly.com (17)

Iglehart, John, Health Affairs, Bethesda, MD. Tel: (301) 656-7401, FAX: (301) 654-2845, Web Site: www.healthaffairs.org (17)

The Ignition Network, Chicago, IL. Tel: (312) 420-4398, Web Site: www.theignitionnetwork.com (35)

iKnowtion LLC, Burlington, MA. Tel: (781) 494-9989, Web Site: www.iknowtion.com (20)

Ikon Communications Consultants Inc, Wellesley, MA. Tel: (781) 237-6060, FAX: (781) 235-3504 (35)

iLoop Mobile Inc, San Jose, CA. Tel: (408) 907-3360, Web Site: www.iloopmobile.com (16)

Iltis, Carolee E., Ford Foundation Office of Communications, New York, NY. Tel: (212) 573-5169, E-Mail: office-of-communications@fordfound.org, Web Site: www.fordfound.org (5)

The Image Bank, New York, NY. Tel: (646) 613-4000, FAX: (646) 613-4601, Web Site: www.gettyimages.com (38)

Image Checks, Bel Air, MD. Tel: (800) 562-8768, FAX: (410) 676-8269, Web Site: www.imagechecks.com (27)

Image Direct, Los Angeles, CA. Tel: (310) 312-4884 (32)

Image Photos/Clemens Kalischer, Stockbridge, MA. Tel: (413) 298-5500, FAX: (413) 298-5500, E-Mail: inform@bcn.net (38)

The Image Works Inc, Woodstock, NY. Tel: (845) 679-8500, (800) 475-8801, FAX: (845) 679-0606, E-Mail: info@theimageworks.com, Web Site: www.theimageworks.com (38)

Imagemakers Marketing Inc, Marietta, GA. Tel: (770) 926-9552, FAX: (770) 926-9558, Web Site: www.imagemakersmarketing.com (21)

Imagestate, New York, NY. Tel: (212) 982-1915, FAX: (212) 725-1241, E-Mail: photo@internationalstock.com (37)

Imagination Works, Trumbull, CT. Tel: (203) 377-1747, FAX: (203) 377-7401, E-Mail: jim@imaginationworks.net, Web Site: www.imaginationworks.net (20)

Imagine Fulfillment Services, Torrance, CA. Tel: (310) 217-4610, FAX: (310) 217-9632, E-Mail: andya@imaginefulfillment.com, Web Site: www.imaginefulfillment.com (28)

Imagine 360 Marketing, New York, NY. Tel: (212) 313-9616, Web Site: www.i360m.com (20)

Imahara, Alan, Imahara Associates Inc, Fremont, CA. Tel: (510) 742-3289, FAX: (510) 742-3289, E-Mail: imahara@aol.com, Web Site: www.imahara.com (35)

Imahara Associates Inc, Fremont, CA. Tel: (510) 742-3289, FAX: (510) 742-3289, E-Mail: imahara@aol.com, Web Site: www.imahara.com (35)

iMarketing LTD Inc, Princeton, NJ. Tel: (609) 921-0400, FAX: (609) 921-0491, E-Mail: info@imarketingltd.com, Web Site: www.imarketingltd.com (35)

iMarketing Solutions Group Inc, Milwaukee, WI. Tel: (414) 224-0701, (800) 879-0076, FAX: (414) 224-0943, Web Site: imarketingsolutionsgroup.com (29)

iMarlin LLC, Springfield, MO. Tel: (417) 887-7446, FAX: (417) 887-3643, E-Mail: info@imarlin.com, Web Site: www.imarlin.com (35)

Imber, Jane, Dictionary of Marketing Terms, Hauppauge, NY. Tel: (631) 434-3311, (800) 645-3476, FAX: (631) 434-3723, E-Mail: barrons@barronseduc.com, Web Site: www.barronseduc.com (43)

Imber, Jane, Gorsuch Ltd, Vail, CO. Tel: (970) 476-2294, (800) 525-9808, FAX: (970) 476-4323, Web Site: www.gorsuchltd.com (2)

Imbriani, Jennifer, Jenco Productions Inc, San Bernardino, CA. Tel: (909) 381-9453, Web Site: www.jencoproductions.com (28)

Imbrilc, Lydia, List Process Co Inc, New York, NY. Tel: (212) 517-8550, FAX: (212) 517-9728, Web Site: www.listprocesscompany.com (23)

Imbrogno, Karen, Insurance.com, Solon, OH. Tel: (440) 715-0075, Web Site: www.insurance.com (15)

Imig, Gary, Sierra Trading Post, Cheyenne, WY. Tel: (307) 775-8050, (800) 713-4534, FAX: (307) 775-8089, Web Site: www.sierratradingpost.com (2)

Imler, Dan, Tension Envelope Corp, Kansas City, MO. Tel: (816) 471-3800, FAX: (816) 283-1498, Web Site: www.tension.com (26)

Immelt, Jeffrey, R., GE Partnership Marketing Group, Schaumburg, IL. Tel: (847) 605-3000, FAX: (847) 605-7368, Web Site: www.gepmg.com (14)

Immergluck, Phillip, S., PSI Marketing Consultants Inc, Des Plaines, IL. Tel: (773) 878-0800, (800) 933-4774, FAX: (773) 878-4219 (29)

Impact Communications Inc, Louisville, KY. Tel: (502) 587-9084, (800) 556-9084, FAX: (502) 589-6538, E-Mail: info@impactvideo.com, Web Site: www.321impact.net (32)

IMPACT International Marketing, Lake Havasu City, AZ. Tel: (866) 389-0798, E-Mail: salesinfo@imgroup.com, Web Site: www.imgroup.com (35)

Impact Mailing, Minneapolis, MN. Tel: (612) 521-6245, FAX: (612) 521-1349, E-Mail: sales@impactmailing.com, Web Site: www.impactmailing.com (28)

IMPACT Publishing Inc, Bradenton, FL. Tel: (941) 739-2611, (800) 4-A-NEW-ME, FAX: (941) 756-0315, E-Mail: info@impactpublishinginc.com, Web Site: www.impactpublishinginc.com (17)

Impact Ratings Inc, Newtown, PA. Tel: (610) 353-8311, FAX: (610) 353-8344 (30)

Impact Sales Inc, Cedar Rapids, IA. Tel: (319) 363-2641, FAX: (319) 362-5481 (33)

Imperial Supplies, Green Bay, WI. Tel: (920) 494-5403, (800) 558-2808, FAX: (800) 553-8769, Web Site: www.imperialsupplies.com (16)

Impressions Direct, Saint Louis, MO. Tel: (314) 951-2100, Web Site: www.impressions-direct.com (28)

Impressions Unlimited Inc, Deerfield, IL. Tel: (630) 705-6464, FAX: (630) 705-1598, E-Mail: info@impressionsunltd.com, Web Site: www.impressionsunltd.com (27)

Improvements, West Chester, OH. Tel: (216) 591-9148, (800) 634-9484, FAX: (216) 831-4026, Web Site: www.improvementscatalog.com (28)

Impulse Inc, Las Vegas, NV. Tel: (702) 948-1100, (800) 328-0184, FAX: (702) 948-1104 (3)

Imtek, Bridgeport, NJ. Tel: (800) 346-8354, FAX: (856) 467-8967, Web Site: www.imtek.com (27)

In Demand, New York, NY. Tel: (646) 486-1010, FAX: (646) 486-0855, Web Site: www.indemand.com (32)

In-Sync Publications, Redondo Beach, CA. Tel: (310) 543-9045, FAX: (310) 543-9035, E-Mail: insyncpubs@aol.com, Web Site: www.insyncpubs.com (18)

In Touch Ministries, Atlanta, GA. Tel: (770) 451-1001), Web Site: www.intouch.org (1)

Inami, Tamotsu, Teikoku Databank America Inc, New York, NY. Tel: (212) 421-9805, FAX: (212) 421-9806, E-Mail: info@teikoku.com, Web Site: www.teikoku.com (24)

Incentive Associates Inc, Overland Park, KS. Tel: (913) 722-2848, FAX: (913) 722-6854, E-Mail: incentiveassociate@sbcglobal.net (33)

Incentive Manufacturers Representatives Association (IMRA), Naperville, IL. Tel: (630) 369-7786, FAX: (630) 369-3773, E-Mail: tom@imraorg.net, Web Site: www.imraorg.net (40)

Incentives America, Boulder, CO. Tel: (303) 494-8845, FAX: (303) 494-8404 (33)

Incept Corp, Canton, OH. Tel: (330) 649-8000, Web Site: www.inceptcorp.com (29)

Inchcoombe, Steven, Nature Publishing Group, New York, NY. Tel: (212) 726-9200, FAX: (212) 696-9006, E-Mail: nature@natureny.com, Web Site: www.nature.com (17)

Indenbaum, Laurie, Rubber Stamps of America, Dublin, NH. Tel: (800) 553-5031, FAX: (603) 563-8102, E-Mail: stampusa@verizon.net, Web Site: www.stampusa.com (1)

Independent Consultant, Saint Paul, MN. Tel: (612) 239-6572 (20)

Independent Insurance Agents & Brokers of America, Alexandria, VA. Tel: (703) 683-4422, (800) 221-7917, FAX: (703) 683-7556, E-Mail: info@iiaba.org, Web Site: www.iiaba.org (1)

Independent Living Aids, Jericho, NY. Tel: (516) 937-1848, (800) 537-2118, FAX: (516) 937-3906, E-Mail: techsupport@independentliving.com, Web Site: www.independentliving.com (7)

Inderbitzen, Robert, American Radio Relay League, Newington, CT. Tel: (860) 594-0200, Web Site: www.arrl.org (1)

Indian Arts & Crafts Association, Albuquerque, NM. Tel: (505) 265-9149, FAX: (505) 265-8251, E-Mail: info@iaca.com, Web Site: www.iaca.com (1)

Indian House Records & Tapes, Taos, NM. Tel: (575) 776-2953, (800) 748-0522, FAX: (575) 776-2804, E-Mail: music@indianhouse.com, Web Site: www.indianhouse.com (3)

Indianapolis Motor Speedway, Indianapolis, IN. Tel: (317) 492-6700, Web Site: www.indianapolismotorspeedway.com (19)

Indianapolis Newspapers Inc, Indianapolis, IN. Tel: (317) 444-4444, FAX: (317) 633-9414, Web Site: www.indystar.com (17)

Indium Corp of America, Clinton, NY. Tel: (315) 853-4900, (800) 446-3486, FAX: (800) 221-5759, E-Mail: askus@indium.com, Web Site: www.indium.com (16)

Indoor Gardening Supplies, Dexter, MI. Tel: (734) 426-9080, (800) 823-5740, FAX: (866) 823-4978, Web Site: www.indoorgardensupplies.com (8)

Indrigo, Peter I., Unitron Ltd, Commack, NY. Tel: (631) 589-6666, FAX: (631) 589-6795, E-Mail: johnc@unitronusa.com, Web Site: www.unitronusa.com (9)

Indros Group, Brooklyn, NY. Tel: (866) 463-7671, Web Site: www.easypurl.com (35)

Indus-Tool, Chicago, IL. Tel: (312) 226-2473, (800) 662-5021, FAX: (312) 226-2480, E-Mail: sales@indus-tool.com, Web Site: www.indus-tool.com (12)

Industrial Arts & Graphics, Middleburg, VA. Tel: (540) 687-6770, (866) 324-7746, FAX: (215) 765-6625 (27)

Industrial Instruments & Supplies Inc, Southampton, PA. Tel: (215) 396-0822, (800) 523-6079, FAX: (215) 396-0833, E-Mail: customerservice@iisusa.com, Web Site: www.iisusa.com (9)

Industrial Marketing Associates, Cranford, NJ. Tel: (908) 276-4256, E-Mail: ken@industrialmarketingassociates.com, Web Site: www.industrialmarketingassociates.com (30)

Industrial Marketing Services, Elk Grove Village, IL. Tel: (847) 258-8850, FAX: (847) 593-0462, E-Mail: whindman@imscomm.com (35)

Industrial Printing Co Inc, Toledo, OH. Tel: (419) 476-9101, (800) 472-9101, FAX: (800) 293-5225, E-Mail: steve.gross@cenveo.com, Web Site: www.ipcohio.com (27)

Industrial Uniform Co Inc, Wichita, KS. Tel: (316) 264-2871, (800) 333-3666, FAX: (316) 264-2708, E-Mail: uniform@industrialuniform.com, Web Site: www.industrialuniform.com (2)

Infantino, Bob, The Hanover Shoe Co, Newton, MA. Tel: (617) 964-1222, FAX: (617) 243-4210, Web Site: www.clarks.com (16)

Infinian Corp, Los Altos, CA. Tel: (415) 260-8142, Web Site: www.infinian.com (29)

Infinite Media, White Plains, NY. Tel: (914) 949-1547, FAX: (914) 949-1605, E-Mail: mail@infinite-media.com, Web Site: www.infinite-media.com (23)

Infinity Direct Inc, Plymouth, MN. Tel: (763) 559-1111, Web Site: www.infinitydirect.com (35)

Infinity Insurance Co, Birmingham, AL. Tel: (800) 527-5412, Web Site: www.infinityauto.com (15)

Infinity Trading Co Inc, Spring, TX. Tel: (281) 931-8000, FAX: (281) 931-8139, E-Mail: sales@infinitytradingcompany.com, Web Site: www.infinitytradingcompany.com (34)

Influence Inc, Hamilton, OH. Tel: (513) 825-8600, FAX: (513) 825-9213, E-Mail: info@influenceinc.com, Web Site: www.influenceinc.com (35)

Influent Inc, Dublin, OH. Tel: (614) 280-1600, (800) 856-6768, FAX: (614) 280-1610, E-Mail: info@influentinc.com, Web Site: www.influentinc.com (29)

Info Direct, Huntsville, AL. Tel: (256) 534-5478, (800) 239-5478, FAX: (256) 536-0705, E-Mail: dklib@hiway.net, Web Site: www.infodirectlists.com (23)

Info USA, Omaha, NE. Tel: (800) 321-0869, E-Mail: help@infousa.com, Web Site: www.infousa.com (23)

Info USA City Directories, Omaha, NE. Tel: (402) 593-4500, (800) 925-4654, FAX: (402) 593-4671, E-Mail: customerservice@infousacity.com, Web Site: www.infousacity.com (17)

Info USA Services Group, Pearl River, NY. Tel: (201) 476-2000, (888) 322-5323, FAX: (201) 476-2301, Web Site: www.infousa.com (23)

InfoCANADA, Mississauga, ON Canada. Tel: (866) 373-2066, FAX: (905) 306-7272, E-Mail: customerservice@infocanada.ca, Web Site: www.infocanada.ca (23)

InfoCision Management Corp, Akron, OH. Tel: (330) 668-1400, FAX: (330) 668-1401, E-Mail: infocision@infocision.com, Web Site: www.infocision.com (29)

Infocore Inc, Carlsbad, CA. Tel: (760) 607-2500, FAX: (760) 607-2505, E-Mail: bstewart@infocoreinc.com, Web Site: www.infocoreinc.com (23)

Infocus Marketing Inc, Warrenton, VA. Tel: (540) 428-3240, Web Site: www.infocuslists.com (23)

infoGROUP, Omaha, NE. Tel: (800) 555-5335 X4541, Web Site: www.infoUSA.com (23)

Infolure, Phoenix, AZ. Tel: (602) 308-6700, FAX: (602) 308-6801, E-Mail: glenn.gottfried@infolure.com, Web Site: www.infolure.com (22)

Infomart, Dallas, TX. Tel: (214) 800-8000, FAX: (214) 800-8100, Web Site: www.infomartusa.com (16)

Infomercial Marketing Report, Beverly Hills, CA. Tel: (310) 826-8810, FAX: (310) 826-0097, E-Mail: clarkkent@aol.com (32)

Infomercial Monitoring Service Inc, Broomall, PA. Tel: (610) 328-6902, FAX: (610) 328-6791, E-Mail: catanese@imstv.com, Web Site: www.imstv.com (20)

Infomercial Sales Inc, Las Vegas, NV. Tel: (702) 253-0433, FAX: (702) 871-0759, Web Site: www.infomercialsalesinc.com (32)

Infomercial Solutions Inc, Agoura Hills, CA. Tel: (818) 879-1140, FAX: (818) 879-1148, E-Mail: david@infomercialsolutions.com, Web Site: www.infomercialsolutions.com (32)

Infomorphosis/Marketing Solutions, New York, NY. Tel: (212) 366-6216, FAX: (212) 255-4784, E-Mail: dfain@nyc.rr.com (20)

Infor, Alpharetta, GA. Tel: (864) 422-5310, Web Site: www.infor.com (22)

Informal Education Products, Milwaukie, OR. Tel: (503) 794-7100, (888) 444-5500, FAX: (503) 794-7111, E-Mail: sales@museumtour.com, Web Site: www.museumtour.com (11)

Information Command Inc, Chicago, IL. Tel: (312) 245-1111, (800) 376-6654, FAX: (312) 245-1128, E-Mail: gon@phonebiz2000.com, Web Site: www.info2u.com (22)

The Information Engine, Bradenton, FL. Tel: (904) 645-6000, Web Site: www.informationeng.com (22)

Information for Public Affairs, Inc, Sacramento, CA. Tel: (916) 444-0840, (800) 726-4566, FAX: (916) 446-5369, E-Mail: info@statenet.com, Web Site: www.statenet.com (17)

The Information Refinery Inc, Mahwah, NJ. Tel: (201) 529-2600, (800) 529-9020, FAX: (201) 529-4030, E-Mail: info@inforefinery.com, Web Site: www.inforefinery.com (24)

Information Resources Inc, Chicago, IL. Tel: (312) 726-1221, Web Site: www.infores.com (30)

Information Sources Inc, Walnut Creek, CA. Tel: (510) 525-6220, FAX: (510) 525-1568, Web Site: www.tectrends.com (22)

Information Unlimited Inc, Amherst, NH. Tel: (603) 673-4730, (800) 221-1705, FAX: (603) 672-5406, E-Mail: wako2@xtdl.com, Web Site: www.amazing1.com (11)

Informed Sources Inc, Plainview, NY. Tel: (800) 201-6060, FAX: (516) 576-0249, E-Mail: info@informed-sources.com, Web Site: www.informed-sources.com (30)

Inforonics LLC, Littleton, MA. Tel: (978) 698-7400, FAX: (978) 698-7500, E-Mail: info@inforonics.com, Web Site: www.inforonics.com (22)

InfoSource Inc, Oviedo, FL. Tel: (407) 796-5200, (800) 393-4636, FAX: (407) 796-5190, E-Mail: isisale@howtomaster.com, Web Site: www.infosourcelearning.com (3)

Infotrends Inc, Boynton Beach, FL. Tel: (561) 732-5263, (800) 940-7991, FAX: (800) 400-7534, E-Mail: info@names.com, Web Site: www.names.com (34)

infoUSA Inc, Omaha, NE. Tel: (402) 593-4500, (800) 321-0869, FAX: (402) 596-8902, Web Site: www.infousa.com (23)

Infutor Data Solutions, Minooka, IL. Tel: (815) 467-0601, Web Site: www.infutor.com (23)

Ingber, Ellen, Larry Fox & Co Ltd, Valley Stream, NY. Tel: (516) 791-7929, (800) 397-7923, FAX: (516) 791-1022, E-Mail: larry@larryfox.com, Web Site: www.larryfox.com (16)

Ingebritson, Britt, Williamson-Dickie Manufacturing Co, Fort Worth, TX. Tel: (800) 336-7201, FAX: (817) 877-5027, E-Mail: customerservice@dickies.com, Web Site: www.dickies.com (2)

Ingenix, Reston, VA. Tel: (571) 521-7661, (800) 765-6713, FAX: (571) 521-7237, E-Mail: inform@ingenix.com, Web Site: www.ingenix.com (32)

Ingersoll, John, Farmers Insurance, Los Angeles, CA. Tel: (410) 366-1000, (410) 338-1633, (800) 327-6377, FAX: (410) 554-1926, Web Site: www.farmers.com (15)

Inglis, David, Toyota Racing Development USA Inc, Costa Mesa, CA. Tel: (714) 444-1188, FAX: (714) 444-0339, Web Site: www.trdusa.com (34)

Inglis, John, Cold Spring Harbor Lab Press, Woodbury, NY. Tel: (516) 422-4100, (800) 843-4388, FAX: (516) 422-4097, E-Mail: cshpress@cshl.edu, Web Site: www.cshlpress.com (17)

Ingram, Ardith, Business Automation Systems Inc, Nashville, TN. Tel: (615) 329-4585, FAX: (615) 320-0206, Web Site: www.bas-solutions.com (16)

Ingram, Barbara, Solarcom, Norcross, GA. Tel: (770) 449-6116, (888) SUN-DATA, FAX: (770) 448-7726, Web Site: www.solarcom.net (16)

Ingram, Chip, Walk Thru The Bible Ministries Inc, Atlanta, GA. Tel: (770) 458-9300, Web Site: www.walkthru.org (1)

Ingram, Debbie, PPS - Packaging Printing Specialists, Saint Charles, IL. Tel: (630) 513-8060, (877) 573-8060, FAX: (630) 513-8062, E-Mail: pps@ppsofil.com, Web Site: www.PPSofIL.com (27)

Ingram, Mark, A., CSPI/Nutrition Action Health Letter, Washington, DC. Tel: (202) 332-9110, FAX: (202) 265-4954, E-Mail: cspi@cspinet.org, Web Site: www.cspinet.org (17)

Ingram, Raymond, E., Business Automation Systems Inc, Nashville, TN. Tel: (615) 329-4585, FAX: (615) 320-0206, Web Site: www.bas-solutions.com (16)

Ingram Book Group, La Vergne, TN. Tel: (615) 793-5000, (800) 937-8000, FAX: (800) 876-0186, Web Site: www.ipage.ingrambook.com (16)

Ingwersen, Mary, Sylvan Learning Centers, Baltimore, MD. Tel: (410) 843-8000, FAX: (410) 843-8057, Web Site: www.educate.com (16)

Initiative Media Worldwide, New York, NY. Tel: (212) 605-7000, FAX: (212) 605-7200, Web Site: www.initiativemedia.com (32)

The Inkpen, Pembroke Pines, FL. Tel: (954) 450-9220, FAX: (305) 624-5126, Web Site: www.theinkpen.com (27)

Inkwell Inc, Cresco, PA. Tel: (570) 595-3344, E-Mail: philip@inkwellinc.com (36)

Inland Press, Detroit, MI. Tel: (313) 961-6000, FAX: (313) 961-7817, Web Site: www.inlandpress.com (27)

Inman, Christopher, Art.com, Emeryville, CA. Tel: (510) 879-4700, Web Site: www.art.com (8)

Inman, Hilary, Communications Solutions Expo, Norwalk, CT. Tel: (203) 852-6800, (877) 243-6002, FAX: (203) 853-2845, E-Mail: info@tmcnet.com, Web Site: www.tmcnet.com (42)

Inmar, Winston-Salem, NC. Tel: (336) 631-2524, FAX: (336) 770-3470, E-Mail: ibizdev@inmar.com, Web Site: www.promotionslogistics.com (14)

Innis Maggiore Group Inc, Canton, OH. Tel: (330) 492-5500, FAX: (330) 492-5568, E-Mail: dick@innismaggiore.com, Web Site: www.innismaggiore.com (35)

Innotrac Corp, Duluth, GA. Tel: (678) 584-4000, FAX: (678) 475-5840, Web Site: www.innotrac.com (28)

Innovation Printing, Philadelphia, PA. Tel: (215) 969-4600, FAX: (215) 464-7664 (27)

Innovative Clip Art, York, SC. Tel: (803) 831-6727, FAX: (704) 290-2069, E-Mail: sales@innovativeclipart.com, Web Site: innovativeclipart.com (10)

Innovative Concepts, Hicksville, NY. Tel: (516) 479-2200, (800) 631-0209, FAX: (516) 479-2215, E-Mail: info@ic-mr.com, Web Site: www.ic-mr.com (30)

Innovative Industries Inc, Carthage, MO. Tel: (417) 358-6891, (800) 344-7467, FAX: (417) 358-1849, E-Mail: info@innovativeindustries.com, Web Site: www.innovativeindustries.com (28)

Innovative List Marketing Inc, Fairfax, VA. Tel: (703) 425-5356, Web Site: www.ilmlists.com (23)

Innovative Marketing Direct Inc, Tampa, FL. Tel: (813) 873-7909, FAX: (813) 873-7918, Web Site: www.innovativedirectmail.com (21)

Innovative Marketing Services Inc, Houston, TX. Tel: (281) 398-0321, (800) 231-4678, FAX: (281) 398-0679, E-Mail: mfisher@imstcorp.com, Web Site: www.imstcorp.com (30)

Innovative Marketing Solutions LLC, Bangor, ME. Tel: (207) 262-6233, Web Site: www.imsmaine.net (29)

Innovative Packaging of Westchester, Spring Valley, NY. Tel: (845) 364-9500 (26)

Innovative Plastic Printing Corp, Roselle, IL. Tel: (630) 665-0003, (800) 238-7686, FAX: (630) 665-7752, Web Site: www.innov8cards.com (27)

Innovative Systems Inc, Pittsburgh, PA. Tel: (412) 937-9300, (800) 622-6390, FAX: (412) 937-9309, E-Mail: info@innovativesystems.com, Web Site: www.innovativesystems.com (22)

Innovyx Inc, Seattle, WA. Tel: (212) 817-6900, Web Site: www.innovyx.com (32)

Input Systems Inc, Paramount, CA. Tel: (562) 634-1170, (800) 327-9337, FAX: (562) 634-0993, E-Mail: info@sweepssoftware.com, Web Site: www.sweepssoftware.com (22)

Inquiry Intelligence Systems, O'Fallon, MO. Tel: (636) 281-2129, (800) 467-2329, FAX: (636) 281-1517, E-Mail: sales@iqsalespro.com, Web Site: www.inquiry-tracking.com (22)

Insel, Richard, A., Juvenile Diabetes Research Foundation, New York, NY. Tel: (212) 785-9500, (800) 533-CURE, FAX: (212) 785-9595, E-Mail: info@jdrf.org, Web Site: www.jdrf.org (1)

Insetta, Bob, Arcelor Mittal, Coatesville, PA. Tel: (610) 383-2000, FAX: (610) 383-5036, Web Site: www.arcelormittal.com (16)

Inside Direct Mail, Philadelphia, PA. Tel: (215) 238-5300, (800) 777-8074, FAX: (215) 238-5412, E-Mail: customservice@napco.com, Web Site: www.insidedirectmail.com (43)

Insight Direct Inc, Tempe, AZ. Tel: (480) 333-3001, (800) 467-4448, FAX: (480) 902-1180, Web Site: www.insight.com (16)

Insight Out of Chaos, New York, NY. Tel: (212) 935-0044, Web Site: www.iooc.com (22)

INSP - The Inspirational Network, Charlotte, NC. Tel: (704) 525-9800, FAX: (704) 525-9899, E-Mail: info@insp.com, Web Site: www.insp.com (32)

The Inspiration Networks, Indian Land, SC. Tel: (704) 561-7872, Web Site: www.insptoday.com (1)

Institute for International Research Inc, New York, NY. Tel: (212) 661-3500, (800) 345-8016, FAX: (212) 599-2192, E-Mail: register@iirusa.com, Web Site: www.iir-ny.com (16)

Institute For Natural Resources, Concord, CA. Tel: (925) 687-0860, FAX: (925) 609-2820, E-Mail: dcheung@biocorp.com (16)

Institute for Student Achievement, Carle Place, NY. Tel: (516) 812-6700, Web Site: www.studentachievement.org (1)

Institute Lists/IOMA, Peterborough, NH. Tel: (973) 718-4766, FAX: (973) 622-0595, E-Mail: lists@institutelists.com, Web Site: www.institutelists.com (24)

Institute of Business Forecasting, Great Neck, NY. Tel: (516) 504-7576, Web Site: www.ibf.org (1)

Institute of Management Accountants Inc, Montvale, NJ. Tel: (201) 573-9000, (800) 638-4427, FAX: (201) 474-1600, E-Mail: ima@imanet.org, Web Site: www.imanet.org (1)

Institute of Management & Administration (IOMA), Peterborough, NH. Tel: (800) 401-5937, FAX: (973) 622-0595 (17)

Institute of Reading Development, Novato, CA. Tel: (415) 884-8100, (800) 964-8888, FAX: (415) 382-0760, E-Mail: contactus@readingprograms.org, Web Site: www.readingprograms.org (1)

Institute of Real Estate Management, Chicago, IL. Tel: (312) 329-6000, (800) 837-0706, FAX: (800) 338-4736, E-Mail: custserv@irem.org, Web Site: www.irem.org (1)

Institutional Advancement Programs Inc, Bronxville, NY. Tel: (914) 779-4092, FAX: (914) 961-4202 (1)

Institutional Investor Inc, New York, NY. Tel: (212) 224-3300, FAX: (212) 224-3592, Web Site: www.institutionalinvestor.com (17)

Institutional Real Estate Inc, San Ramon, CA. Tel: (925) 244-0500, FAX: (925) 244-0520, Web Site: www.irei.com (17)

Instructor's Choice Dancewear, Massapequa Park, NY. Tel: (516) 799-7010, FAX: (516) 799-7993, E-Mail: customerservice@instructorschoice.com, Web Site: www.instructorschoice.com (2)

The Instrument Workshop, Ashland, OR. Tel: (541) 552-0989, (800) 442-6038, FAX: (541) 488-5846, E-Mail: shop77@fortepiano.com, Web Site: www.fortepiano.com (16)

Insurance.com, Solon, OH. Tel: (440) 715-0075, Web Site: www.insurance.com (15)

Insurance Publications Inc, Overland Park, KS. Tel: (913) 383-9191, (800) 762-3387, FAX: (913) 383-1247, E-Mail: brokerwrld@primary.net, Web Site: www.brokerworldmag.com (17)

Intagio Trading Network, San Francisco, CA. Tel: (415) 247-9500, FAX: (415) 543-0375, Web Site: www.intagio.com (32)

Integer Group, Des Moines, IA. Tel: (515) 288-7910, FAX: (515) 288-8439, E-Mail: fmaher@integermidwest.com, Web Site: www.integer.com (35)

Integrated Advertising Inc, Jacksonville, FL. Tel: (904) 296-1700, E-Mail: mary@integratedadvertising.com (35)

Integrated Alliance Limited Partnership, Denton, TX. Tel: (940) 565-9415, FAX: (940) 383-1876, E-Mail: ryoung@integratedalliance.com, Web Site: www.integratedalliance.com (29)

Integrated Business Services Inc, Lake Forest, IL. Tel: (847) 735-1690, Web Site: www.medbase200.com (22)

Integrated Direct Marketing, Reston, VA. Tel: (703) 547-4961, E-Mail: info@integrated-dm.com, Web Site: www.integrated-dm.com (23)

Integrated Mail Industries Ltd, Milwaukee, WI. Tel: (414) 908-3500, FAX: (414) 449-2906, E-Mail: sales@integratedmail.com, Web Site: www.integratedmail.com (28)

Integrated Marketing Solutions (IMS), Ashland, NE. Tel: (402) 486-3151, FAX: (402) 486-3161 (20)

Integrated Marketing Technology Inc, San Francisco, CA. Tel: (415) 699-2280, FAX: (917) 591-5333, E-Mail: information@imtnetwork.com, Web Site: www.imtnetwork.com (22)

Integrated Messaging Inc, Winnipeg, MB Canada. Tel: (204) 786-7630, (800) 561-3734, FAX: (204) 786-7718, E-Mail: sales@imi.mb.ca, Web Site: www.imi.mb.ca (29)

Integrated Print & Graphics, South Elgin, IL. Tel: (847) 695-6777, Web Site: www.ipandginc.com (27)

Integrated Product Development Group, Chicago, IL. Web Site: www.integratedpdg.com (1)

Integrative Logic LLC, Lawrenceville, GA. Tel: (678) 638-2600, Web Site: www.integrativelogic.com (30)

Integretel Inc, San Jose, CA. Tel: (408) 362-4000, FAX: (408) 362-2795, Web Site: www.integretel.com (16)

Integrity Music Inc, Mobile, AL. Tel: (251) 633-9000, FAX: (251) 633-5202, Web Site: www.integritymusic.com (16)

Intel Corp, Santa Clara, CA. Tel: (408) 765-8080, (800) 548-4725, FAX: (408) 765-6187, Web Site: www.intel.com (16)

Intelesure LLC, Meridian, ID. Tel: (866) 808-7366, Web Site: www.intelesure.com (29)

InteliSpend, Fenton, MO. Tel: (636) 226-2000, Web Site: intelispend.com (35)

InteliSpend Prepaid Solutions, Fenton, MO. Tel: (636) 226-2000, Web Site: www.aeis.com (5)

InteliTarget, Winchester, VA. Tel: (540) 409-4801, Web Site: www.intelitarget.com (29)

Intelitec, Granby, MA. Tel: (413) 467-7420, FAX: (413) 467-9476, E-Mail: info@intelitec.com, Web Site: www.intelitec.com (23)

Intelius Inc, Bellevue, WA. Tel: (425) 974-6100, Web Site: www.intelius.com (22)

Intellidyn Corp, Hingham, MA. Tel: (781) 741-5503, (866) 773-5756, FAX: (631) 390-0458, E-Mail: kmf@intellidyn.com, Web Site: www.intellidyn.com (22)

Intelligencer Printing Co, Lancaster, PA. Tel: (717) 291-3100, (800) 233-0107, FAX: (717) 569-2643, Web Site: www.intellprinting.com (27)

Intelligent Direct, Wellsboro, PA. Tel: (570) 724-7355, Web Site: www.marketmaps.com (9)

IntelliQuote Insurance Services, El Dorado Hills, CA. Tel: (800) 543-3467, Web Site: www.intelliquote.com (15)

Inter Direct USA, Houston, TX. Tel: (281) 497-7606, FAX: (281) 497-7616, E-Mail: scotthaney@interdirectusa.com, Web Site: www.interdirectusa.com (21)

Inter-Media Marketing Solutions, West Chester, PA. Tel: (800) 835-3466, FAX: (610) 429-5137, Web Site: www.intermediamarketing.com (29)

Inter7 Internet Technologies Inc, Galena, IL. Tel: (815) 776-9465, Web Site: www.inter7.com (3)

Interact Direct Marketing Inc, London, ON Canada. Tel: (519) 439-6245, Web Site: www.interactdirect.com (28)

Interact Multimedia Corp, South Bend, IN. Tel: (574) 232-3400, FAX: (219) 255-6091, E-Mail: johnd@interactmultimedia.com (35)

Interactive Marketing Group Inc, Allendale, NJ. Tel: (201) 327-0974, FAX: (201) 327-3596, E-Mail: info@imgusa.com, Web Site: www.imgusa.com/index.aspx (21)

Interactive Marketing Institute, Richmond, VA. Tel: (800) 925-5308, Web Site: www.imi.vcu.edu (41)

Interactive Marketing Solutions, Stamford, CT. Tel: (203) 653-2746 (22)

Interactive Response Technologies Inc, Fort Lauderdale, FL. Tel: (954) 484-4973, (800) 700-3033, FAX: (954) 484-0818, E-Mail: hglass@callcenter.com, Web Site: www.callcenter.com (29)

Interactive Search Group, Cleveland, OH. Tel: (216) 255-3388, Web Site: www.isgstaffingnow.com (20)

InterContinental Hotels Group, Atlanta, GA. Tel: (770) 604-2000, (877) 424-2449, FAX: (770) 604-8639, Web Site: www.ichotelsgroup.com (19)

Interdata, Sanibel, FL. Tel: (941) 472-1119, FAX: (941) 472-4272, E-Mail: jfisher435@aol.com, Web Site: www.interdata.com (30)

Interdisciplinary Design Team, Southhampton, PA. Tel: (215) 364-5608, FAX: (215) 364-6509, E-Mail: rich.bomze@gmail.com (36)

Interex, Amesbury, MA. Tel: (978) 388-8755, (800) INTEREX, FAX: (978) 388-8747, Web Site: www.interexhibits.com (17)

Interface Engineering, Portland, OR. Tel: (503) 382-2266, FAX: (503) 382-2262, E-Mail: solutions@interfaceengineering.com, Web Site: www.ieice.com (20)

InterfaceFlor LLC, La Grange, GA. Tel: (706) 882-1891, (800) 336-0225, FAX: (706) 882-0500, Web Site: www.interfaceflor.com (16)

The Interfaith Alliance, Washington, DC. Tel: (202) 639-6370, Web Site: www.interfaithalliance.org (1)

Interfaith Community Care, Surprise, AZ. Tel: (623) 584-4999, Web Site: www. interfaithcommunitycare.org (1)

Intergraph Corp, Madison, AL. Tel: (256) 730-2000, (800) 345-4856, FAX: (256) 730-2048, Web Site: www.intergraph.com (16)

Interior Concepts Corp, Spring Lake, MI. Tel: (616) 842-5550, (800) 678-5550, FAX: (616) 842-7122, Web Site: www.interiorconcepts.com (34)

Interline Creative Group Inc, Palatine, IL. Tel: (847) 358-4848, FAX: (847) 358-8089, E-Mail: info@ interlinegroup.com, Web Site: www.interlinegroup. com (35)

Intermap Technologies, Englewood, CO. Tel: (303) 708-0955, FAX: (303) 708-0952, Web Site: www. intermap.com (32)

InterMedia Advertising, Encino, CA. Tel: (818) 995-1455, FAX: (818) 995-7115, Web Site: www. intermedia-advertising.com (35)

Intermedia Consultants Inc, Princeton, NJ. Tel: (609) 430-8460, Web Site: http://iprintmedia.com (35)

InterMedia Outdoors Inc, New York, NY. Tel: (212) 852-6600 (31)

International Academy - Compounding Pharmacists, Missouri City, TX. Tel: (281) 933-8400, Web Site: www.iacprx.org (1)

International Advertising Association, New York, NY. Tel: (212) 557-1133, FAX: (212) 983-0455, E-Mail: membership@iaaglobal.com, Web Site: www.iaaglobal.org (1)

International Auto Parts, Charlottesville, VA. Tel: (804) 974-7118, (800) 726-0555, FAX: (804) 973-2368, E-Mail: iap1@international-auto.com, Web Site: www.international-auto.com (12)

International Bible Society, Colorado Springs, CO. Tel: (719) 488-9200, FAX: (719) 867-2812, Web Site: www.ibs.org (1)

International City/County Management Association, Washington, DC. Tel: (202) 289-ICMA, FAX: (202) 962-3500, E-Mail: customerservice@icma. org, Web Site: www.icma.org (1)

International Coins & Currency Inc, Montpelier, VT. Tel: (802) 223-6331, FAX: (800) 229-3239, Web Site: www.iccoin.com (6)

International Collectors Society, Camden, NY. Tel: (800) 606-3490, FAX: (410) 998-9707, E-Mail: info@mysticstamp.com, Web Site: www.icsnow. com (6)

International Corp, Hasbrouck Heights, NJ. Tel: (201) 203-3083, Web Site: www.datadirectsolutions.com (20)

International Crystal Manufacturing Co, Oklahoma City, OK. Tel: (405) 236-3741, (800) 252-6780, FAX: (405) 235-1904, E-Mail: info@icmfg.com, Web Site: www.icmfg.com (16)

International Currency LLC, Beaumont, TX. Tel: (409) 866-0588 (11)

International Data Management - a Dmh Marketing Partners Co, Akron, OH. Tel: (330) 869-8500, Web Site: www.idmi.com (22)

International Direct Marketing Consultants Inc, Dallas, TX. Tel: (214) 443-9494, FAX: (214) 443-9512, E-Mail: billmcnutt@charter.net, Web Site: www. dmtrademissions.com (20)

International Direct Media Co & Information Publishing Co, San Francisco, CA. Tel: (415) 661-4730, E-Mail: infopubsf@aol.com, Web Site: www. bookwormproductions.com (17)

International Direct Response Inc, Berwyn, PA. Tel: (610) 993-0500, FAX: (610) 993-9938, E-Mail: idr@idronline.com, Web Site: www.idronline.com (23)

International Direct Response Services Ltd, Delta, BC Canada. Tel: (604) 951-6855, Web Site: www. idrs.ca (28)

International Fellowship of Christians and Jews, Chicago, IL. Tel: (312) 641-7200, Web Site: www.ifcj. org (1)

International Filing Corp, Rockwall, TX. Tel: (800) 647-3070, FAX: (800) 633-7053, E-Mail: pcoerper@intfiling.com, Web Site: www. intfiling.com (26)

International Foundation of Employee Benefit Plans, Brookfield, WI. Tel: (262) 373-7758, FAX: (262) 786-8670, Web Site: www.ifebp.org (1)

International Fulfillment Inc, Philadelphia, PA. Tel: (215) 638-8060, (800) 962-8080, FAX: (215) 638-8091, Web Site: www.ifionline.net (27)

International Fund for Animal Welfare, Yarmouth Port, MA. Tel: (508) 744-2000, Web Site: www.ifaw.org (1)

International Gamco Inc, Omaha, NE. Tel: (402) 571-2449, (800) 524-2626, FAX: (402) 571-7941, E-Mail: mark.stevens@intlgamco.com, Web Site: www.intlgamco.com (31)

International Irrigation Systems, Niagara Falls, NY. Tel: (905) 688-4090, (877) IRRIGRO, FAX: (905) 688-4093, E-Mail: info@irrigro.com, Web Site: www.irrigro.com (8)

International Mailing Solutions LLC, Burlington, MA. Tel: (718) 376-5000, Web Site: www.mailims.com (28)

International Manufacturing Co, Whitesburg, GA. Tel: (770) 834-2094, FAX: (770) 834-2096, E-Mail: textilenterprise@aol.net (8)

International Marine, Camden, ME. Tel: (207) 236-4837, FAX: (207) 236-6314, Web Site: www. internationalmarine.com (17)

International Marketing Partners Ltd, Los Angeles, CA. Tel: (310) 665-1155, FAX: (310) 665-1155, E-Mail: info@intermarketingonline.com (35)

International Masters Publishers Inc, Montoursville, PA. Tel: (800) 570-5718, E-Mail: customerservice@imp-usa.com, Web Site: www. imponline.com (17)

International Newspaper Network, Moline, IL. Tel: (309) 743-0800, (800) 293-9576, FAX: (309) 743-0830, E-Mail: info@TownNews.com, Web Site: www.townnews.com (32)

International Paper, Memphis, TN. Tel: (901) 419-9000, (800) 207-4003, Web Site: www. internationalpaper.com (16)

International Planned Parenthood Federation Western Hemisphere Region Inc, New York, NY. Tel: (212) 248-6400, (866) IPPFWHR, FAX: (212) 248-2441, E-Mail: info@ippfwhr.org, Web Site: www. ippfwhr.org (1)

International Prepaid Communications Association, Washington, DC. Tel: (202) 544-4448, FAX: (202) 547-7417 (40)

International Resource Management Co, Bedford, TX. Tel: (817) 861-9191, FAX: (817) 277-0868, E-Mail: james@irmco.net, Web Site: www.irmco. net (20)

International Sign Association, Alexandria, VA. Tel: (703) 836-4012, FAX: (703) 836-8353, Web Site: www.signs.org (42)

International Sign Association International Convention, Alexandria, VA. Tel: (703) 836-4012, (866) WHY-SIGN, FAX: (703) 836-8353, Web Site: www.signs.org (42)

International Society for Technology in Education, Eugene, OR. Tel: (541) 349-7575, Web Site: www. iste.org (1)

International Specialized Book Services Inc, Portland, OR. Tel: (503) 287-3093, (800) 944-6190, FAX: (503) 280-8832, E-Mail: isbs_sales@isbs.com, Web Site: www.isbscatalog.com (16)

International Wine Accessories Inc, Wichita, KS. Tel: (214) 349-6097, (800) 527-4072, FAX: (214) 349-8712, E-Mail: customerservice@iwawine.com, Web Site: www.iwawine.com (4)

The Internet Alliance, Washington, DC. Tel: (202) 861-2476, FAX: (202) 955-8081, E-Mail: info@ internetalliance.org, Web Site: www. internetalliance.org (40)

Internet Direct Response, Inc, Fort Worth, TX. Tel: (817) 562-1506, E-Mail: operations@4idr.com, Web Site: www.4dr.com (35)

Interprint Web & Sheetfed, Clearwater, FL. Tel: (727) 531-8957, (800) 749-5152, FAX: (727) 536-0647, E-Mail: customerservice@printerusa.com, Web Site: www.printerusa.com (27)

The Interprovincial Group, Scarborough, ON Canada. Tel: (416) 283-5555, FAX: (416) 283-6643, E-Mail: info@interprovincialgroup.com, Web Site: www.interprovincialgroup.com (21)

Interrante, Steve, Freeport Music Inc, Farmingville, NY. Tel: (631) 549-4108, (888) 549-4108, E-Mail: sales@musicalinstruments.com; sales@ freeportmusic.com, Web Site: www. musicalinstruments.com (11)

Intersections, Chantilly, VA. Tel: (703) 488-6100, Web Site: www.charteredmarketing.com (14)

Interstate EDP & Direct Mail Center Inc, Brooklyn, NY. Tel: (718) 965-2500, FAX: (718) 965-2504, E-Mail: info@interstateedp.com, Web Site: www. interstateedp.com (28)

Interstate Printing Co, Omaha, NE. Tel: (402) 341-8028, (800) 788-4177, FAX: (402) 341-6168, E-Mail: printer@interstateprinting.com, Web Site: www.interstateprinting.com (27)

InterTrend Communications Inc, Long Beach, CA. Tel: (562) 733-1852, Web Site: www.intertrend. com (35)

Interval International, South Miami, FL. Tel: (305) 925-7019, Web Site: www.intervalworld.com (35)

Interwood Direct, Toronto, ON Canada. Tel: (888) 275-5205, Web Site: www.interwood.com (8)

Intium Services LLC, Diamond Bar, CA. Tel: (909) 743-6182, Web Site: www.intiumservices.com (32)

Intra Business Systems Inc, South Bend, IN. Tel: (574) 257-7940, FAX: (574) 257-7944, E-Mail: info@intrabusinesssystems.com, Web Site: www. intrabusinesssystems.com (16)

Intrasight, Scottsdale, AZ. Tel: (480) 603-9400, FAX: (480) 603-9460, Web Site: www. intrasightmarketing.com (35)

Intravartolo, Jill, Kansas City Direct Marketing Association, Kansas City, MO. Tel: (816) 561-5323, FAX: (816) 561-1991, E-Mail: info@kcdma.org, Web Site: www.kcdma.org (40)

Intregila, Mark, King Teleservices, New York, NY. Tel: (718) 361-4100, (800) 817-5468, E-Mail: info@king-teleservices.com, Web Site: www.king-teleservices.com (29)

Intrepid Distributors Inc, Mississauga, ON Canada. Tel: (905) 607-5170, (800) 263-6011, FAX: (800) 361-6307, E-Mail: sales@intrepid.on.ca, Web Site: www.intrepid.on.ca (33)

Intromark Inc, Pittsburgh, PA. Tel: (412) 288-1300, (800) 851-6030 X1368, FAX: (412) 338-0497, E-Mail: licensing@intromark.com (16)

Intuit, Mountain View, CA. Tel: (650) 944-6000, Web Site: www.inuit.com (10)

Invacare Continuing Care Group, Saint Louis, MO. Tel: (519) 659-1395, (800) 347-5440, FAX: (636) 519-0044, Web Site: www.invacare-ccg.com (16)

Invacare Supply Group, Milford, MA. Tel: (508) 429-1000, (800) 225-4792, FAX: (508) 429-1581, E-Mail: service.isg@invacare.com, Web Site: www.invacaresupplygroup.com (16)

InvestorPlace Media LLC, Rockville, MD. Tel: (800) 219-8592, Web Site: www.investorplace.com (24)

Investors Alliance Inc, Pompano Beach, FL. Tel: (800) 490-6627, E-Mail: info@powerinvestor.com, Web Site: www.powerinvestor.com (24)

Investors Marketing Services, Danvers, MA. Tel: (978) 774-2990, (800) 462-2551, FAX: (978) 774-4249, Web Site: www.investorsmarketing.com (14)

Invitation Hotline, Manalapan, NJ. Tel: (732) 536-9115, (800) 800-4355, FAX: (732) 972-4875, E-Mail: info@invitationhotline.com, Web Site: www.invitationhotline.com (27)

Involve Social, Fremont, CA. Tel: (510) 396-3941, Web Site: www.involvesocial.com (1)

INWAVE Internet, Janesville, WI. Tel: (888) 469-2831, FAX: (608) 752-8981, Web Site: www.inwave.com (16)

Iomega Corp, Roy, UT. Tel: (801) 332-1000, (888) 446-6342, FAX: (801) 332-3158, Web Site: www.iomega.com (16)

Ion Exhibits, Itasca, IL. Tel: (630) 285-9500, FAX: (630) 235-9501, E-Mail: info@ionexhibits.com, Web Site: www.ionexhibits.com (36)

Ion Media Networks Inc, West Palm Beach, FL. Tel: (561) 659-4122, (800) 646-7296, FAX: (561) 659-4252, Web Site: www.ionmedia.tv (32)

Iosca, Phil, Hanna Andersson Corp, Portland, OR. Tel: (503) 242-0920, (800) 222-0544, FAX: (503) 321-5289, Web Site: www.hannaandersson.com (2)

Iowa Medical Society, West Des Moines, IA. Tel: (515) 223-1401, FAX: (515) 223-0590, Web Site: www.iowamedical.org (1)

Iowa Student Loan Liquidity Corp, West Des Moines, IA. Tel: (515) 243-5626, Web Site: www.studentloan.org (1)

IPacesetters, Montvale, NJ. Tel: (201) 391-1500, Web Site: www.ipacesetters.com (22)

Ipema, Tim, Unity School of Christianity, Unity Village, MO. Tel: (816) 254-3550, FAX: (816) 251-3554, E-Mail: unity@unityonline.org, Web Site: www.unityonline.org (17)

Ipsos-ASI Inc, Norwalk, CT. Tel: (203) 840-3400, FAX: (203) 840-3450, E-Mail: info@ipsos-asi.com, Web Site: www.ipsos-asi.com (30)

Ipswitch Inc, Lexington, MA. Tel: (781) 676-5700, Web Site: www.whatsupgold.com (22)

Irani, Zack, Biomerica Inc, Irvine, CA. Tel: (949) 645-2111, FAX: (949) 722-6674, E-Mail: bmra@biomerica.com, Web Site: www.biomerica.com (7)

Iris Marketing, Bel Air, MD. Tel: (443) 742-1232 (20)

Iroquois Products, Chicago, IL. Tel: (773) 436-3900, (800) 453-3355, FAX: (773) 436-4908, E-Mail: sales@iroquoisproducts.com, Web Site: www.iroquoisproducts.com (10)

Irresistible Ink Inc, Duluth, MN. Tel: (218) 336-4200, (800) 543-8396, Web Site: www.irresistibleink.com (28)

Irvin, Gayle, Society for Healthcare Strategy & Market Development, Chicago, IL. Tel: (312) 422-3888, FAX: (312) 422-4579, E-Mail: stratsoc@aha.org, Web Site: www.stratsociety.org (42)

Irvine, Donald, Accuracy in Media Inc, Washington, DC. Tel: (202) 364-4401, FAX: (202) 364-4098, E-Mail: info@aim.org, Web Site: www.aim.org (1)

Irving, Mark, Atlantic Spice Co, North Truro, MA. Tel: (508) 487-6100, (800) 316-7965, FAX: (508) 487-2550, E-Mail: mark@atlanticspice.com, Web Site: www.atlanticspice.com (4)

Irwin, Dave, The Allant Group, Naperville, IL. Tel: (800) 367-7311, FAX: (630) 355-3090, E-Mail: dirwin@allantgroup.com, Web Site: www.allantgroup.com (22)

Irwin, Dr. Paul, American Bible Society, New York, NY. Tel: (212) 408-1200, FAX: (212) 408-1264, Web Site: www.americanbible.org (1)

Irwin, Jim, Aircraft Spruce & Specialty Co, Corona, CA. Tel: (909) 372-9555, (877) 4-Spruce, FAX: (909) 372-0555, E-Mail: info@aircraft-spruce.com, Web Site: www.aircraft-spruce.com (12)

Irwin, Nanci, Aircraft Spruce & Specialty Co, Corona, CA. Tel: (909) 372-9555, (877) 4-Spruce, FAX: (909) 372-0555, E-Mail: info@aircraft-spruce.com, Web Site: www.aircraft-spruce.com (12)

Isaac, Marty, Webloyalty.com, Norwalk, CT. Tel: (203) 846-3300, Web Site: www.webloyalty.com (32)

Isaac, Steve, Interactive Marketing Institute, Richmond, VA. Tel: (800) 925-5308, Web Site: www.imi.vcu.edu (41)

Isaac, Steven, Education Dynamics LLC, Hoboken, NJ. Tel: (201) 377-3001 (30)

Isaacs, Robert, C, Stanley Home Products, Great Bend, KS. Tel: (620) 792-1711, (800) 628-9032, Web Site: www.shponline.com (8)

Isaacs, Tony, Indian House Records & Tapes, Taos, NM. Tel: (575) 776-2953, (800) 748-0522, FAX: (575) 776-2804, E-Mail: music@indianhouse.com, Web Site: www.indianhouse.com (3)

Isaacson, Kay, Banana Republic, Grove City, OH. Tel: (888) 277-8953, FAX: (888) 906-2465, Web Site: www.bananarepublic.com (2)

Isacson, Alan, AB Isacson Associates Inc, New York, NY. Tel: (212) 529-4500, FAX: (212) 529-4442, Web Site: www.abipr.com (2)

AB Isacson Associates Inc, New York, NY. Tel: (212) 529-4500, FAX: (212) 529-4442, Web Site: www.abipr.com (35)

Isdell, E. Neville, The Coca-Cola Co, Atlanta, GA. Tel: (404) 676-2121, FAX: (404) 676-6792, Web Site: www.cocacola.com (16)

Ishii, Shin, Itochu Chemicals America Inc, White Plains, NY. Tel: (914) 333-7800, (800) 423-6870, FAX: (914) 333-7848, Web Site: www.itochu-sc.com (16)

Island Pacific Inc, Irvine, CA. Tel: (303) 754-4700, (800) 569-1122, Web Site: www.islandpacific.com (22)

Islands Tropicals, Keaau, HI. Tel: (808) 961-0606, (800) 367-5155, FAX: (808) 966-7684, Web Site: www.islandtropicals.com (6)

Isler, Adam, PNT Marketing Services, Inc, Long Island City, NY. Tel: (703) 761-0291, (888) 768-2210, FAX: (914) 428-0504, E-Mail: tony@pntmarketingservices.com, Web Site: www.pntmarketingservices.com (22)

Israel, James A., John Deere Credit USA, Johnston, IA. Tel: (515) 267-3000, FAX: (515) 267-3292, Web Site: www.deere.com/en_US/jdc/index.html (14)

Israel, Lillian, Association for Computing Machinery (ACM), New York, NY. Tel: (212) 869-7440, FAX: (212) 944-1318, Web Site: www.acm.org (1)

Israel, Walter, Durasol Corp, Amesbury, MA. Tel: (978) 388-2020, (800) 370-0683, FAX: (978) 388-9762, Web Site: www.durasolcorp.com (34)

Issues & Answers Network Inc, Virginia Beach, VA. Tel: (757) 456-1100, FAX: (757) 456-0377, E-Mail: info@issans.com, Web Site: www.issans.com (30)

Istock, Verne, Bank One, Chicago, IL. Tel: (888) 963-4000, (866) 265-1727, (800) 452-3141, Web Site: www.bankone.com (14)

Isuzu Motors America Inc, Anaheim, CA. Tel: (562) 229-5000, (800) 255-6727, FAX: (562) 229-5463, Web Site: www.isuzu.com (16)

Itochu Chemicals America Inc, White Plains, NY. Tel: (914) 333-7800, (800) 423-6870, FAX: (914) 333-7848, Web Site: www.itochu-sc.com (16)

Ittner, George, Newport News, New York, NY. Tel: (800) 759-3950, Web Site: www.newport-news.com (2)

Ivancic, Dennis, World Vision Canada, Mississauga, ON Canada. Tel: (905) 565-6200 X2173, Web Site: www.worldvision.ca (1)

Ivanov, Sergey, Heldref Publications, Washington, DC. Tel: (215) 625-8900, (202) 296-6267, FAX: (202) 296-5149, Web Site: www.heldref.org (17)

Iverson, Ann, C., Creating Selling Opportunities, Houston, TX. Tel: (713) 622-6936, FAX: (713) 622-2924, E-Mail: annci@sbcglobal.net (20)

Iverson, Dodi, Direct Response Insurance Administrative Services Inc (DRIASI), Chanhassen, MN. Tel: (952) 556-5600, (800) 688-0760, FAX: (952) 556-8200, E-Mail: tpa@driasi.com, Web Site: www.driasi.com (21)

Ives, Debi, S., Wildlife Education Ltd, Park Hills, KY. Tel: (858) 513-7600, FAX: (858) 513-7660, E-Mail: animals@zoobooks.com, Web Site: www.zoobooks.com (17)

Ivie, Flower Mound, TX. Tel: (972) 899-5000 (35)

IVisionMobile Inc, Chatsworth, CA. Tel: (866) 655-5302, Web Site: www.ivisionmobile.com (35)

Ivy Tech State College, Indianapolis, IN. Tel: (317) 921-4800, (888) IVY-LINE, FAX: (317) 921-4753, Web Site: www.ivytech.edu/indianapolis (13)

Iyengar, Sriram, ChoiceConnex, Clearwater, FL. Tel: (727) 571-3302, Web Site: www.choiceconnex.com (29)

Izenstark, Debra, Direct Mail Source, Wilmette, IL. Tel: (847) 676-3744, E-Mail: dms@directmailsource.net (28)

Izoz, Steve, Wathne Ltd, New York, NY. Tel: (212) 757-3001, FAX: (212) 757-2448 (2)

J

J&L Concepts Inc, Valdosta, GA. Tel: (800) 346-5083, FAX: (912) 247-2468, E-Mail: promo@jlconcepts.com, Web Site: www.jlconcepts.com (33)

J&L Industrial Supply, Southfield, MI. Tel: (734) 458-7000, (800) 521-9520, FAX: (734) 261-0352, Web Site: www.jlindustrial.com (9)

J&R Music/J&R Computer World, New York, NY. Tel: (212) 238-9000, (800) 806-1115, FAX: (212) 238-9191, Web Site: www.jandr.com (3)

J&J Commerce, Galesburg, IL. Tel: (309) 344-2950, Web Site: www.jjdog.com (5)

J&P Cycles, Anamosa, IA. Tel: (319) 462-4819, Web Site: www.j-pcycles.com (12)

JB Dollar Stretcher Magazine, Richfield, OH. Tel: (330) 659-3590, (800) 673-2531, FAX: (330) 659-6741, Web Site: www.jbdollar.com (31)

JC Direct Mail Inc, Groveport, OH. Tel: (614) 836-4848, FAX: (614) 836-4847, E-Mail: pwhite@wcnjcd.com (28)

JC Lists Co, Washington, DC. Tel: (202) 364-2705, FAX: (202) 364-2450, E-Mail: jcoogan@JClists.com (23)

JC Penney Inc, Plano, TX. Tel: (972) 431-1000, FAX: (972) 431-1977, Web Site: www.jcpenney.com (5)

JC Penney Telemarketing Inc, Milwaukee, WI. Tel: (262) 792-5504, (800) 323-4343, FAX: (262) 792-5598, Web Site: www.jcpenney.com (29)

JC Whitney, Chicago, IL. Tel: (312) 431-6000, FAX: (312) 431-5650, Web Site: www.jcwhitney.com (12)

JD Graphic Co, Elk Grove Village, IL. Tel: (847) 364-4000, (888) 364-6216, FAX: (847) 364-4024, E-Mail: jim@jdgraphic.com, Web Site: www.jdgraphic.com (27)

JDR Microdevices, Mountain View, CA. Tel: (408) 494-1400, (800) 538-5000, FAX: (800) 538-5005, E-Mail: sales@jdr.com, Web Site: www.jdr.com (3)

JDSU, Germantown, MD. Tel: (301) 353-1550, Web Site: www.jdsu.com (32)

JEM Research, Valparaiso, IN. Tel: (219) 464-4668, FAX: (219) 464-7011 (30)

JF Direct Marketing Inc, Ossining, NY. Tel: (914) 762-8633, FAX: (914) 762-9247, E-Mail: jfdirect@bestweb.net, Web Site: www.jfdirectmarketing.com (23)

JHL Mail Marketing Inc, Stevens Point, WI. Tel: (715) 341-0581, (800) 236-0581, FAX: (715) 341-9645, E-Mail: ren@jhl.com, Web Site: www.jhl.com (28)

JIST Publishing, Saint Paul, MN. Tel: (800) 648-5478, FAX: (800) 547-8329, E-Mail: info@jist.com, Web Site: www.jist.com (17)

JJI International Inc, Cranston, RI. Tel: (401) 732-8668, (866) 732-8668, FAX: (401) 732-8778, E-Mail: info@jjiinternational.com, Web Site: www.jjiinternational.com (35)

JK Associates LLC, Palo Alto, CA. Tel: (650) 838-9816, FAX: (650) 838-9867, Web Site: www.jk-associates.com (20)

JLG Industries Inc, McConnellsburg, PA. Tel: (717) 485-5161, (877) JLG-SELL, FAX: (717) 485-6417, E-Mail: comments@jlg.com, Web Site: www.jlg.com (16)

JLMC, New York, NY. Tel: (917) 476-3072 (20)

JLS Mailing Services Inc, Brockton, MA. Tel: (508) 313-1050, (866) JLS-MAIL, FAX: (508) 313-1093, E-Mail: rparkinson@jlsms.com, Web Site: www. jlsms.com (28)

The JM Group Inc, San Antonio, TX. Tel: (210) 637-0404, FAX: (210) 637-0081 (28)

Jos A Bank Clothiers Inc, Hampstead, MD. Tel: (410) 239-2700, Web Site: www.josbank.com (2)

JP Management Consulting (North America) Inc, New York, NY. Tel: (914) 332-4000, FAX: (914) 332-4411 (30)

JP Morgan Chase & Co, New York, NY. Tel: (212) 270-6000, E-Mail: jpmcinvestorrelations@ jpmchase.com, Web Site: www.jpmorgan.com (14)

JR Direct Response International Inc, Delta, BC Canada. Tel: (604) 940-0277, FAX: (604) 946-1419, E-Mail: tammythackray@jrdirect.com, Web Site: www.jrdirect.com (23)

JR Tobacco/800-JR Cigar Inc, Burlington, NC. Tel: (800) 572-4427, FAX: (800) 457-3299, Web Site: www.jrcigars.com (5)

JRB Marketing Group, East Windsor, NJ. Tel: (301) 758-2334, FAX: (302) 348-2490, E-Mail: jrblitman@gmail.com (20)

JRH Marketing Services Inc, New York, NY. Tel: (718) 786-9640, FAX: (718) 786-9642, E-Mail: office@jrhmarketingservices.com, Web Site: www. jrhmarketingservices.com (30)

JS Direct Address Limited, North Vancouver, BC Canada. Tel: (604) 987-1282, FAX: (604) 987-1283 (23)

JSA Creative Services LLC, Chicago, IL. Tel: (773) 772-3445, FAX: (773) 772-3446, E-Mail: jsacreative@comcast.net, Web Site: www. jsacreative.com (39)

JSR Advertising Corp, New York, NY. Tel: (212) 995-1661, E-Mail: jsr@nyc.rr.com, Web Site: www. quantmethod.com (35)

JT International, Teaneck, NJ. Tel: (201) 871-1210, Web Site: www.jti.com (16)

JVW Direct, Pittsburgh, PA. Tel: (412) 241-5920, FAX: (412) 241-5850, E-Mail: john@jvwdirect. com (35)

JWT Inside, Santa Monica, CA. Tel: (310) 309-8282, (877) 665-8768, FAX: (310) 309-8283, E-Mail: conversations@jwtinside.com, Web Site: www. jwtworks.com (35)

JZ Marketing, Lehigh Acres, FL. Tel: (239) 693-7567, Web Site: www.jzmktg.com (20)

Jabowski, James, R., Deere & Co Headquarters, Moline, IL. Tel: (309) 765-8000, FAX: (309) 765-5671, Web Site: www.deere.com (16)

Jaccard, Walter B., Thousand Trails LP, Chicago, IL. Tel: (214) 618-7200, (800) 205-0606, FAX: (214) 618-7324, Web Site: www.1000trails.com (16)

Jach, Kevin, Goldsmith Agio Helms, Minneapolis, MN. Tel: (612) 339-0500, FAX: (612) 339-0507, Web Site: www.agio.com (14)

Jack Schecterson visualmarketing Consultants, Little Neck, NY. Tel: (718) 225-3536 (20)

Jackman, Michael, DeLuxe Laboratories Inc, Hollywood, CA. Tel: (323) 462-6171, FAX: (323) 960-7016, E-Mail: steven.vananda@bydeluxe.com, Web Site: www.bydeluxe.com (16)

Jackmen, Glenn, NCS, Danbury, CT. Tel: (562) 946-6900, (800) 975-6804, FAX: (800) 527-2488, Web Site: www.shopncs.com; www.ncs-apparel.com (16)

Jackson, Ann, Rockler Woodworking & Hardware, Medina, MN. Tel: (763) 478-8201, (800) 279-4441, FAX: (763) 478-8393, E-Mail: info@rockler. com, Web Site: www.rockler.com (8)

Jackson, Barbara, Animal Health Express, Inc, Tucson, AZ. Tel: (520) 888-0294, (800) 533-8115, FAX: (520) 888-0297, (800) 437-9898, E-Mail: info@ animalhealthexpress.com, Web Site: www. animalhealthexpress.com (5)

Jackson, Blair, Bloosky Interactive, Orem, UT. Tel: (888) 203-2433, FAX: (888) 465-7166, Web Site: www.bloosky.com (32)

Jackson, Bruce, USA Direct Inc, York, PA. Tel: (717) 852-1000, (800) 441-1850, FAX: (717) 852-1030, Web Site: www.usamailnow.com (21)

Jackson, Carolyn, UCEA, Boston, MA. Tel: (617) 738-6410, FAX: (617) 734-1452, Web Site: www. revike.org (1)

Jackson, Dolores, Woman's Missionary Union, Birmingham, AL. Tel: (205) 991-8100, FAX: (205) 991-4990, E-Mail: email@wmu.org, Web Site: www.wmu.org (17)

Jackson, Donald, R., The Jackson Consulting Group Ltd, Middletown, DE. Tel: (302) 378-0218, (866) 450-7005, FAX: (302) 378-0219, E-Mail: djack98489@aol.com, Web Site: www.jcg-ltd.com (20)

Jackson, John, Real Goods Trading Corp, San Rafael, CA. Tel: (707) 542-2600, (888) 567-6527, Web Site: www.realgoods.com (5)

Jackson, John, T., Paralyzed Veterans of America, Washington, DC. Tel: (202) 416-7636, (800) 424-8200, FAX: (202) 416-7643, E-Mail: info@pva. org, Web Site: www.pva.org (1)

Jackson, Kathryn E., Response Design Corp, Ocean City, NJ. Tel: (609) 601-5866, (800) 366-4732, FAX: (609) 788-3619, E-Mail: rdc@ responsedesign.com, Web Site: www. responsedesign.com (20)

Jackson, Marianne, Blue Shield Life, San Francisco, CA. Tel: (888) 800-2742, FAX: (800) 329-2742, Web Site: www.blueshieldca.com (15)

Jackson, Nigel, D., Intermap Technologies, Englewood, CO. Tel: (303) 708-0955, FAX: (303) 708-0952, Web Site: www.intermap.com (32)

Jackson, Patricia, Regnery Publishing, Washington, DC. Tel: (202) 216-0600, FAX: (202) 216-0612, Web Site: www.regnery.com (17)

Jackson, Regina, Warner Press, Anderson, IN. Tel: (765) 644-7721, (800) 741-7721, FAX: (765) 640-8005, E-Mail: wporders@warnerpress.org, Web Site: www.warnerpress.com (17)

Jackson, Sid, Baton Rouge Conventions & Visitors Bureau, Baton Rouge, LA. Tel: (225) 383-1825, (800) LA-ROUGE, FAX: (225) 346-1253, E-Mail: br@bracvb.com, Web Site: www.bracvb.com (1)

Jackson, Tasha, Marketing Research Association, Washington, DC. Tel: (860) 682-1000, FAX: (860) 682-1010, E-Mail: email@mra-net.org, Web Site: www.mra-net.org (40)

Jackson, Tim, Animal Health Express, Inc, Tucson, AZ. Tel: (520) 888-0294, (800) 533-8115, FAX: (520) 888-0297, (800) 437-9898, E-Mail: info@ animalhealthexpress.com, Web Site: www. animalhealthexpress.com (5)

Jackson, Tyrone, W., School of Business & Economics, Los Angeles, CA. Tel: (323) 343-2800, FAX: (323) 343-2813, Web Site: cbe.calstatela.edu (41)

Jackson, Wendy, Redirect Relationship Marketing, Salt Lake City, UT. Tel: (801) 453-0100, Web Site: www.redirectnow.com (35)

The Jackson Consulting Group Ltd, Middletown, DE. Tel: (302) 378-0218, (866) 450-7005, FAX: (302) 378-0219, E-Mail: djack98489@aol.com, Web Site: www.jcg-ltd.com (20)

The Jackson Group, Indianapolis, IN. Tel: (888) 522-5766, Web Site: www.jacksongroup.com (35)

The Jackson Laboratory JAX Research Systems, Bar Harbor, ME. Tel: (800) 422-6423, Web Site: www. jax.org/jaxmice (1)

Jacob, Dabney, Orient Expressed Imports Inc, New Orleans, LA. Tel: (888) 856-3948, FAX: (504) 899-5566, E-Mail: orient@orientexpressed.com, Web Site: www.orientexpressed.com (2)

Jacobs, Andrew, Influent Inc, Dublin, OH. Tel: (614) 280-1600, (800) 856-6768, FAX: (614) 280-1610, E-Mail: info@influentinc.com, Web Site: www. influentinc.com (29)

Jacobs, Daniel, DAJ Direct Inc, Costa Mesa, CA. Tel: (949) 722-0506, FAX: (949) 722-8026, Web Site: www.dajdirect.com (24)

Jacobs, David, Koeppel Direct, Dallas, TX. Tel: (972) 732-6110, FAX: (972) 248-2759, E-Mail: pkoeppel@koeppelinc.com, Web Site: www. koeppeldirect.com (32)

Jacobs, Ed, Wind River Group, Akron, OH. Tel: (330) 644-7774, FAX: (330) 645-2045 (20)

Jacobs, Frank, Falcon Products Inc, Newport, TN. Tel: (314) 991-9200, (800) 873-3252, FAX: (314) 991-9227, E-Mail: info@falconproducts.com, Web Site: www.falconproducts.com (16)

Jacobs, Jeremy, Campaigns & Elections Magazine, Arlington, VA. Tel: (703) 778-4028, (800) 771-8252, FAX: (703) 778-4024, Web Site: www. campaignsandelections.com (17)

Jacobs, Leonard, Kalmed Dental Products Inc, Marietta, GA. Tel: (770) 971-8815, (800) 322-8815, FAX: (770) 509-8823, E-Mail: sales@kalmed.com, Web Site: www.kalmed.com (7)

Jacobs, Michael, Harry N Abrams Inc, New York, NY. Tel: (212) 206-7715, FAX: (212) 645-8437, Web Site: www.hnabooks.com (17)

Jacobs, Norman, Lakeside Publishing Co LLC, Evanston, IL. Tel: (847) 491-6440, FAX: (847) 491-0459, E-Mail: cs@centurysports.net, Web Site: www.centurysports.net (17)

Jacobs, Richard, P., Eaton Corp, Raleigh, NC. Tel: (216) 523-4400, (800) 356-5794, FAX: (216) 523-4787, Web Site: www.eaton.com (16)

Jacobs, Robin, House Party Inc, Irvington, NY. Tel: (720) 496-2500, (888) 591-1678, E-Mail: help@ houseparty.com, Web Site: www.houseparty.com (30)

Jacobs, Ron, Jacobs & Clevenger Inc, Chicago, IL. Tel: (312) 894-3000, FAX: (312) 645-9825, E-Mail: mail@jacobsclevenger.com, Web Site: www.jacobsclevenger.com (35)

Jacobs, Sheldon, No Load Fund Investor, Brentwood, TN. Tel: (800) 706-6364, FAX: (800) 785-9212, E-Mail: NoLoad@mleesmith.com, Web Site: www. noloadfundinvestor.com (14)

Jacobs, Steve, AdPack/ITOCHU International Inc, New York, NY. Tel: (212) 818-8000, Web Site: www.adpackusa.com (25)

Jacobs, Tom, Reliable Racing Supply, Queensbury, NY. Tel: (518) 793-5677, FAX: (518) 793-6491, Web Site: www.reliableracing.com (11)

Jacobs & Clevenger Inc, Chicago, IL. Tel: (312) 894-3000, FAX: (312) 645-9825, E-Mail: mail@ jacobsclevenger.com, Web Site: www. jacobsclevenger.com (35)

Jacobsen Ph.D., Gary, A., Jacobsen Lenticular Tool & Cylinder Engraving Technologies Co (Jacotech), Itasca, IL. Tel: (630) 467-0900, FAX: (630) 467-0900, E-Mail: gj@jacotech.com, Web Site: www. jacotech.com; www.lenticlearlens.com (34)

Jacobsen, Harlan, Single Scene News, Tempe, AZ. Tel: (480) 945-6746, FAX: (480) 945-6746, E-Mail: publisher@azsinglescene.com, Web Site: www.azsinglescene.com (17)

Jacobsen, Janet, Single Scene News, Tempe, AZ. Tel: (480) 945-6746, FAX: (480) 945-6746, E-Mail: publisher@azsinglescene.com, Web Site: www. azsinglescene.com (17)

Jacobsen, Jeff, Single Scene News, Tempe, AZ. Tel: (480) 945-6746, FAX: (480) 945-6746, E-Mail: publisher@azsinglescene.com, Web Site: www. azsinglescene.com (17)

Jacobsen, Michael, Diebold Inc, Uniontown, OH. Tel: (330) 899-2510, (800) DIEBOLD, FAX: (330) 490-3794, E-Mail: barronp@diebold.com, Web Site: www.diebold.com (16)

Jacobsen Lenticular Tool & Cylinder Engraving Technologies Co (Jacotech), Itasca, IL. Tel: (630) 467-0900, FAX: (630) 467-0900, E-Mail: gj@jacotech. com, Web Site: www.jacotech.com; www. lenticlearlens.com (34)

Jacobsohn, Richard, H., Jacobsohn Consulting Associates, Highland Park, IL. Tel: (312) 543-3330, E-Mail: jacobsohnr@aol.com (20)

Jacobsohn Consulting Associates, Highland Park, IL. Tel: (312) 543-3330, E-Mail: jacobsohnr@aol.com (20)

Jacobson Ph.D., Michael, F., CSPI/Nutrition Action Health Letter, Washington, DC. Tel: (202) 332-9110, FAX: (202) 265-4954, E-Mail: cspi@cspinet.org, Web Site: www.cspinet.org (17)

Jacobson, Cathy, Carson Pirie Scott & Co, Milwaukee, WI. Tel: (414) 347-1152, FAX: (414) 278-5748 (16)

Jacobson, Kevin, HD Supply, San Diego, CA. Tel: (858) 831-2000 (34)

Jacobson, Michael, Center for Science in the Public Interest, Washington, DC. Tel: (202) 332-9110, FAX: (202) 265-4954, E-Mail: circ@cspinet.org, Web Site: www.cspinet.org (1)

Jacobson, Mitchell, MSC Industrial Supply Co, Melville, NY. Tel: (516) 812-2000, (800) 645-7270, FAX: (800) 255-5067, E-Mail: executive@mscdirect.com, Web Site: www.mscdirect.com (9)

Jacobson, Ted, Polynesian Cultural Center, Honolulu, HI. Tel: (808) 293-3333, (800) 367-7060, FAX: (888) 722-7339, E-Mail: internetrez@polynesia.com, Web Site: www.polynesia.com (16)

Jacoby, Stefan, Volkswagen Group of America Inc, Auburn Hills, MI. Tel: (248) 754-5000, FAX: (248) 754-4930, Web Site: www.vw.com (16)

Jacona, Patricia, Vanguard, Valley Forge, PA. Tel: (610) 648-6000, Web Site: www.vanguard.com (14)

Jacops, Randall, Artemis International Solutions Corp, Austin, TX. Tel: (512) 874-3030, (800) 477-6648, FAX: (512) 874-8900, Web Site: www.aisc.com (22)

Jacques, Ingrid, Hugo Dunhill Mailing Lists Inc, New Rochelle, NY. Tel: (212) 213-9300, (800) 611-0557, FAX: (212) 213-9245, E-Mail: info@hdml.com, Web Site: www.hdml.com (23)

Jaeck, Glenn, Ty Pac, Baldwinsville, NY. Tel: (315) 638-9431, (800) 356-8964, FAX: (315) 638-9433, E-Mail: ty-pac@hotmail.com (34)

Jaeger, Jo-Anne, C., Beauticontrol Cosmetics Inc, Carrollton, TX. Tel: (972) 458-0601, (800) BEAUTI-1, FAX: (972) 458-6904, E-Mail: clientservices@beauticontrol.com, Web Site: www.beauticontrol.com (16)

Jaehnert, Frank, M., Brady Corp, Milwaukee, WI. Tel: (414) 358-6600, (800) 541-1686, FAX: (800) 292-2289, Web Site: www.bradycorp.com (16)

Jaff Marketing Group Inc, Spring, TX. Tel: (281) 353-0004, FAX: (281) 288-0970 (16)

Jaffe, Jay, M., Actuarial Enterprises Ltd, Chicago, IL. Tel: (312) 397-0099, E-Mail: jay@actentltd.com (20)

Jaffe, Michael, Michael Jaffe Stamps Inc/Brookman Stamp Co, Vancouver, WA. Tel: (360) 695-6161, (800) 782-6770, FAX: (360) 695-1616, E-Mail: mjaffe@brookmanstamps.com, Web Site: www.brookmanstamps.com (6)

Jaffe Brothers Natural Foods, Valley Center, CA. Tel: (760) 749-1133, (800) 548-1886, FAX: (760) 749-1282, E-Mail: jb54@worldnet.att.net, Web Site: www.organicfruitsandnuts.com (4)

Michael Jaffe Stamps Inc/Brookman Stamp Co, Vancouver, WA. Tel: (360) 695-6161, (800) 782-6770, FAX: (360) 695-1616, E-Mail: mjaffe@brookmanstamps.com, Web Site: www.brookmanstamps.com (6)

Jaffee, Larry, Promo Magazine, New York, NY. Tel: (203) 358-9900, (800) 927-5007, FAX: (203) 358-5816, E-Mail: larry.jaffee@penton.com, Web Site: www.promomagazine.com (17)

Jafra Cosmetics International Inc, Westlake Village, CA. Tel: (805) 557-1889, (800) 551-2345, Web Site: www.jafra.com (7)

Jagoda, Don, Don Jagoda Associates Inc, Melville, NY. Tel: (631) 454-1800, FAX: (631) 454-1834, E-Mail: information@dja.com, Web Site: www.dja.com (35)

Don Jagoda Associates Inc, Melville, NY. Tel: (631) 454-1800, FAX: (631) 454-1834, E-Mail: information@dja.com, Web Site: www.dja.com (35)

Jahn, Martin, Paslode, Vernon Hills, IL. Tel: (847) 634-1900, (800) 222-6990, FAX: (847) 634-6602, E-Mail: tech@paslode.com, Web Site: www.paslode.com (16)

Jain, Vivek, Fluke Biomedical, Everett, WA. Tel: (425) 347-6100, (800) 850-4608, FAX: (425) 446-5116, Web Site: www.flukebiomedical.com (16)

Jaitlin, Geraldine, Cold Spring Harbor Lab Press, Woodbury, NY. Tel: (516) 422-4100, (800) 843-4388, FAX: (516) 422-4097, E-Mail: cshpress@cshl.edu, Web Site: www.cshlpress.com (17)

JAK Productions, Atlanta, GA. Tel: (770) 612-1386, FAX: (770) 612-9163, E-Mail: jkeller2@ix.netcom.com (29)

Jalili, Houshang, Carabella Collection, Irvine, CA. Tel: (949) 263-2300, (800) 227-2235, FAX: (949) 263-2323, Web Site: www.carabella.com (2)

Jalili, Monir, Carabella Collection, Irvine, CA. Tel: (949) 263-2300, (800) 227-2235, FAX: (949) 263-2323, Web Site: www.carabella.com (2)

JAM Communications, Washington, DC. Tel: (202) 986-4750, FAX: (202) 232-9146, E-Mail: neil@jamagency.com, Web Site: www.jamagency.com (35)

Jamax Direct LLC, Englewood Cliffs, NJ. Tel: (201) 569-4540 (23)

Jameco Electronics, Belmont, CA. Tel: (650) 592-8097, (800) 831-4242, FAX: (650) 592-2503, (800) 237-6948, E-Mail: domestic@jameco.com, Web Site: www.jameco.com (3)

James, Ashton, Kelly's Kids, Natchez, MS. Tel: (601) 442-5332, (800) 837-2066, FAX: (601) 442-4399, E-Mail: customerservice@kellyskids.com, Web Site: www.kellyskids.com (2)

James, Barbara, Howell Marketing Services, Elmira, NY. Tel: (607) 734-6291, FAX: (607) 734-6759, E-Mail: gl@howellmarketingservices.com, Web Site: www.howellmarketingservices.com (28)

James, Carrie, Infocore Inc, Carlsbad, CA. Tel: (760) 607-2500, FAX: (760) 607-2505, E-Mail: bstewart@infocoreinc.com, Web Site: www.infocoreinc.com (23)

James, Dana, Bissinger French Confections, Saint Louis, MO. Tel: (314) 534-2401, (800) 325-8881, FAX: (314) 534-2419, Web Site: www.bissingers.com (4)

James, Daniel, E., Carolina Biological Supply Co, Burlington, NC. Tel: (800) 334-5551, (800) 222-7112, E-Mail: carolina@carolina.com, Web Site: www.carolina.com (9)

James, Diane, CAIG Laboratories Inc, Poway, CA. Tel: (858) 486-8388, FAX: (858) 486-8398, E-Mail: caig123@caig.com, Web Site: www.caig.com (9)

James, Donald, M., Vulcan Materials Co, Birmingham, AL. Tel: (205) 298-3000, FAX: (205) 298-2960, Web Site: www.vulcanmaterials.com (16)

James, Glenn, Renaissance Learning, Wisconsin Rapids, WI. Tel: (715) 424-3636, (800) 338-4204, FAX: (715) 424-4242, E-Mail: answers@renlearn.com, Web Site: www.renlearn.com (5)

James, Gregory, Peter Glenn Publications, Delray Beach, FL. Tel: (561) 404-4290, (888) 332-6700, FAX: (561) 892-5786, E-Mail: gregjames@pgdirect.com, Web Site: www.pgdirect.com (17)

James, Jerry, The CompTEL Annual Convention & Trade Exposition, Washington, DC. Tel: (202) 296-6650, FAX: (202) 296-7585, Web Site: www.comptel.org (42)

James, Juanita, The History Book Club Inc, Mechanicsburg, PA. Tel: (718) 918-2665, E-Mail: paula.batson@dgna.com, Web Site: www.historybookclub.com (13)

James, Laura, A., Golf Card International, Englewood, CO. Tel: (800) 321-8269, FAX: (303) 792-7332, Web Site: www.golfcard.com (1)

James, Lynn, Kelly's Kids, Natchez, MS. Tel: (601) 442-5332, (800) 837-2066, FAX: (601) 442-4399, E-Mail: customerservice@kellyskids.com, Web Site: www.kellyskids.com (2)

James, Mike, James Medical Rents & Sales Inc, Fort Wayne, IN. Tel: (260) 423-9571, E-Mail: sales@jamesmedical.com, Web Site: www.jamesmedical.net (7)

James, Rich, Ideal Images, Glastonbury, CT. Tel: (860) 633-8600, FAX: (860) 659-3235 (38)

James, Rich, New England Stock Photo, Glastonbury, CT. FAX: (860) 659-3235 (38)

James, Richard L., DOM Corp, Marina Del Rey, CA. Tel: (310) 578-1164 (5)

James, Robert, Balboa Life & Casualty, Irvine, CA. Tel: (949) 222-8000, (800) 854-6115, FAX: (949) 222-8777, Web Site: www.balboainsurance.com (15)

James, Robert, M., Kross Inc, Santa Clarita, CA. Tel: (661) 284-3557, (800) 456-3699, FAX: (661) 257-1914, Web Site: www.krosskits.com (16)

James, Sandra, James Medical Rents & Sales Inc, Fort Wayne, IN. Tel: (260) 423-9571, E-Mail: sales@jamesmedical.com, Web Site: www.jamesmedical.net (7)

James, Tiffany, UndercoverWear Inc, Tewksbury, MA. Tel: (978) 851-8580, FAX: (978) 640-2882, E-Mail: jamiej@undercoverwear.com, Web Site: www.undercoverwear.com (2)

James, Todd, Haworth Inc, Holland, MI. Tel: (616) 393-3000, (800) 344-2600, FAX: (616) 393-1570, Web Site: www.haworth.com (34)

James, Victoria, Victoria James Executive Search Inc, South Kent, CT. Tel: (203) 750-8838 X101, FAX: (203) 547-6284, E-Mail: vjames@victoriajames.com, Web Site: www.victoriajames.com (20)

James, Victoria, Women in Direct Marketing International, New York, NY. Tel: (516) 746-6700, FAX: (516) 294-8141, Web Site: www.wdmi.org (40)

James, Walter, UndercoverWear Inc, Tewksbury, MA. Tel: (978) 851-8580, FAX: (978) 640-2882, E-Mail: jamiej@undercoverwear.com, Web Site: www.undercoverwear.com (2)

James Medical Rents & Sales Inc, Fort Wayne, IN. Tel: (260) 423-9571, E-Mail: sales@jamesmedical.com, Web Site: www.jamesmedical.net (7)

Robert James Co Inc, Moody, AL. Tel: (205) 640-7081, (800) 633-8296, FAX: (205) 640-7087 (10)

Victoria James Executive Search Inc, South Kent, CT. Tel: (203) 750-8838 X101, FAX: (203) 547-6284, E-Mail: vjames@victoriajames.com, Web Site: www.victoriajames.com (20)

James-Gilboe, Lynda, Gale Research Inc, Farmington Hills, MI. Tel: (248) 699-4253, (800) 877-GALE, FAX: (313) 961-6083, Web Site: www.gale.com (17)

Jameson, Piper, Lincoln Educational Services, West Orange, NJ. Tel: (973) 736-9340 (13)

Jamgochian, Bryan, MeadWestvaco, Springfield, MA. Tel: (888) 715-6641, Web Site: www.mwvenvelopes.com (26)

Jamieson, Charles, Affinity4, Norfolk, VA. Tel: (757) 465-4602, Web Site: www.affinity4.com (16)

Herbert L Jamison & Co LLC, West Orange, NJ. Tel: (973) 731-0806, (800) JAMISON, (800) 526-4766, FAX: (973) 731-3035, Web Site: www.jamisongroup.com (15)

Jamitkowski, Jamie, UndercoverWear Inc, Tewksbury, MA. Tel: (978) 851-8580, FAX: (978) 640-2882, E-Mail: jamiej@undercoverwear.com, Web Site: www.undercoverwear.com (2)

Jan Associates, Oakland, CA. Tel: (510) 530-6180 (7)

Janc, Ken, Lorex Inc, Elk River, MN. Tel: (763) 441-0055, Web Site: www.lorexinc.com (35)

Jandron, Paul, Invacare Supply Group, Milford, MA. Tel: (508) 429-1000, (800) 225-4792, FAX: (508) 429-1581, E-Mail: service.isg@invacare.com, Web Site: www.invacaresupplygroup.com (16)

Jane Corcillo, Norwalk, CT. Tel: (203) 866-2008, FAX: (203) 299-0844, E-Mail: queries@corcillodirect.com, Web Site: www.corcillodirect.com (39)

Janes Information Group, Alexandria, VA. Tel: (703) 683-3700, (800) 824-0768, FAX: (703) 836-0297, Web Site: www.janes.com (17)

Jania, Alan, Diamond Envelope Corp, Aurora, IL. Tel: (630) 499-2800, FAX: (630) 499-2801 (26)

Janice's LLC, Hartford, CT. Tel: (860) 523-4479, FAX: (860) 523-4178, E-Mail: dlerner@janices.com, Web Site: www.janices.com (8)

Janicki, Harry, Nomadics Tipi Makers, Bend, OR. Tel: (541) 389-3980, FAX: (541) 389-3980, Web Site: www.tipi.com (11)

Jankay, James, Emailvision, New York, NY. Tel: (212) 257-6018, Web Site: www.emailvision.com (22)

Jankey, Molly, Andrea Electronics Corp, Bohemia, NY. Tel: (631) 719-1800, (800) 442-7787, FAX: (631) 719-1950, Web Site: www.andreaelectronics.com (16)

Jankowski, Kim, Automotive Headphones, Sterling Heights, MI. Tel: (586) 292-6166 (16)

Jann, Bill, Media Dynamics LLC, Greenwich, CT. Tel: (203) 531-6600, FAX: (203) 531-6661, E-Mail: bjann@mediadynamx.com, Web Site: www.Media-Dynamics.com (31)

Jannotta, Edgar, D., William Blair & Co LLC, Chicago, IL. Tel: (312) 236-1600, (800) 621-0687, FAX: (312) 368-9418, E-Mail: info@williamblair.com, Web Site: www.williamblair.com (14)

Janos, Edward, H., Support Plus, Hudson, OH. Tel: (508) 359-2910, (800) 229-2910, FAX: (508) 359-0139, E-Mail: cs@supportplus.com, Web Site: www.supportplus.com (7)

Janos, Eloise, Support Plus, Hudson, OH. Tel: (508) 359-2910, (800) 229-2910, FAX: (508) 359-0139, E-Mail: cs@supportplus.com, Web Site: www.supportplus.com (7)

Janszen, Robert, Amity Unlimited Inc, Cincinnati, OH. Tel: (513) 554-4500, FAX: (513) 554-0450, Web Site: www.amityunlimited.com (28)

Jantz Supply Koval Knives, Davis, OK. Tel: (580) 369-2316, (800) 351-8900, FAX: (580) 369-3082, Web Site: www.knifemaking.com (9)

Japinga, Ronald, West Marine Inc, Watsonville, CA. Tel: (831) 761-4825, (800) BOATING, (800) 262-8464, FAX: (831) 768-5000, E-Mail: customercare@westmarine.com, Web Site: www.westmarine.com (11)

Japs-Olson Co, Saint Louis Park, MN. Tel: (952) 932-9393, (800) 548-2897, FAX: (612) 912-1900, Web Site: www.japsolson.com (27)

Jarashow, Daniel, Campmor Inc, Mahwah, NJ. Tel: (201) 335-9064, (800) 525-4784, FAX: (201) 236-3601, Web Site: www.campmor.com (17)

Jarashow, Morton, Campmor Inc, Mahwah, NJ. Tel: (201) 335-9064, (800) 525-4784, FAX: (201) 236-3601, Web Site: www.campmor.com (17)

Jarden Corp, Daleville, IN. Tel: (765) 557-3000, (800) 428-8150, FAX: (765) 281-5403, Web Site: www.jarden.com (16)

Jardine, Richard, Haney, The Carnegie Hall Corp, New York, NY. Tel: (212) 247-7800, FAX: (212) 373-0500, E-Mail: feedback@carnegiehall.org, Web Site: www.carnegiehall.org (35)

Jaromin, Christina, iContact, Morrisville, NC. Tel: (866) 803-9462, Web Site: www.icontact.com (32)

Jaros, Karin, The Morton Arboretum, Lisle, IL. Tel: (630) 968-0074, Web Site: www.mortonarb.org (1)

Jarr, Robert, Communicor, Milwaukee, WI. Tel: (414) 961-5999, FAX: (414) 961-5990, Web Site: www.communicor.com (36)

Jarrett Jr., William, S., Goldsmith Agio Helms, Minneapolis, MN. Tel: (612) 339-0500, FAX: (612) 339-0507, Web Site: www.agio.com (14)

Jarvis, Mike, Chain Store Guide, Tampa, FL. Tel: (800) 927-9292, FAX: (813) 627-6882, E-Mail: info@csgis.com, Web Site: www.csgis.com (17)

Jarvis, Sidney A., Advertising Mailers Inc, Edison, NJ. Tel: (732) 225-3404, (800) 427-8513, FAX: (732) 225-7429, E-Mail: admailers@aol.com (28)

Jarymiszyn, Phil, PNT Marketing Services, Inc, Long Island City, NY. Tel: (703) 761-0291, (888) 768-2210, FAX: (914) 428-0504, E-Mail: tony@pntmarketingservices.com, Web Site: www.pntmarketingservices.com (22)

Jasek Enterprises, Westlake Village, CA. Tel: (805) 379-2871, FAX: (805) 379-9839 (20)

Jason, Debra, The Write Direction, Boulder, CO. Tel: (808) 635-8031, E-Mail: debra@writedirection.com, Web Site: www.writedirection.com (39)

Jason, Tracey, Nielsen Trade Dimensions, Wilton, CT. Tel: (203) 222-5750, (800) 291-0410, FAX: (203) 222-5701, E-Mail: tradedimensions.info@nielsen.com, Web Site: www.tradedimensions.com (17)

Jason Natural Personal Care Products, Boulder, CO. Tel: (877) 527-6601, Web Site: www.jason-natural.com (7)

Jasper, Robert, G., Marketing Horizons Inc, Saint Louis, MO. Tel: (314) 432-1957, (800) 669-0839, FAX: (314) 432-7014, E-Mail: jkramer@mhorizons.com (30)

Jastrem, John, Exhibitgroup/Giltspur, Hodgkins, IL. Tel: (972) 538-3031, (800) 843-3944, Web Site: www.e-g.com (30)

Jauzapaitis, Stephen, Arbus Capital Ltd, Schaumburg, IL. Tel: (847) 290-9600, FAX: (847) 290-9601 (16)

Javelin, Irving, TX. Tel: (972) 443-7000, E-Mail: info@javelin.mg, Web Site: javelin.mg (30)

Javid, Tina, Southern California Gas Co, Anaheim, CA. Tel: (714) 634-3054, (800) 427-2200, FAX: (714) 937-7712, E-Mail: Tjavid@socalgas.com, Web Site: www.socalgas.com (1)

Jaworski, Don, Brocade Communications Systems Inc, San Jose, CA. Tel: (408) 333-4300, FAX: (408) 333-8101, Web Site: www.brocade.com (16)

Jaworski, Michele, Michele Jaworski, Ramsey, NJ. Tel: (201) 825-6932 (31)

Michele Jaworski, Ramsey, NJ. Tel: (201) 825-6932 (31)

Jayne, Fairman, Sandy Mush Herb Nursery, Leicester, NC. Tel: (828) 683-2014, E-Mail: info@sandymushherbs.com, Web Site: www.sandymushherbs.com (8)

Jayne, Kate, Sandy Mush Herb Nursery, Leicester, NC. Tel: (828) 683-2014, E-Mail: info@sandymushherbs.com, Web Site: www.sandymushherbs.com (8)

Jaypro Sports, Waterford, CT. Tel: (860) 447-3001, (800) 243-0533, FAX: (800) 988-3363, E-Mail: info@jaypro.com, Web Site: www.jaypro.com (11)

Jaz Holdings LLC, Liberty Corner, NJ. Tel: (973) 574-7600, (800) 999-9554, FAX: (973) 944-5073, E-Mail: webmaster@regentbook.com, Web Site: www.regentbook.com (16)

Jazzercise Inc, Carlsbad, CA. Tel: (760) 476-1750, (800) FIT IS IT, FAX: (760) 602-7180, E-Mail: info@jazzercise.com, Web Site: www.jazzercise.com (2)

JazzTimes Magazine Inc, Quincy, MA. Tel: (617) 706-9110, FAX: (617) 536-0102, E-Mail: info@jazztimes.com, Web Site: www.jazztimes.com (17)

JDA Software Group Inc, Scottsdale, AZ. Tel: (480) 308-3000, (800) 479-7382, FAX: (480) 308-3001, Web Site: www.jda.com (22)

Jedele, Mary, Sue, Marketing/Media Dynamics Inc, Harpers Ferry, WV. Tel: (304) 725-1119 (20)

Jeffers, Dorothy, Jeffers & Co, Dothan, AL. Tel: (334) 793-6257, (800) 533-3377, FAX: (334) 793-5179, Web Site: www.1800jeffers.com (5)

Jeffers, Ruth, Jeffers & Co, Dothan, AL. Tel: (334) 793-6257, (800) 533-3377, FAX: (334) 793-5179, Web Site: www.1800jeffers.com (5)

Jeffers & Co, Dothan, AL. Tel: (334) 793-6257, (800) 533-3377, FAX: (334) 793-5179, Web Site: www.1800jeffers.com (5)

Jefferson Mailing Lists, Poway, CA. Tel: (858) 679-1233, FAX: (858) 679-1279 (23)

Jefferson National, Louisville, KY. Tel: (502) 587-3853, Web Site: www.jeffnat.com (14)

Jeffery, Gary, The Popcorn Factory, Lake Forest, IL. Tel: (847) 362-0028, (888) 216-0235, FAX: (888) 333-4595, E-Mail: service@thepopcornfactory.com, Web Site: www.thepopcornfactory.com (4)

Jeffery, Jeannie, Butler Schein Animal Health, Dublin, OH. Tel: (614) 761-9095, (888) 691-2724, FAX: (888) 329-3861, Web Site: www.butlerschein.com (16)

Jeffrey, John, The Wisconsin Cheeseman, Sun Prairie, WI. Tel: (608) 837-5166, (800) 698-1721, FAX: (608) 837-5493, Web Site: www.wisconsincheeseman.com (4)

Jeffrey Lant Associates Inc, Cambridge, MA. Tel: (617) 547-6372, FAX: (617) 547-0061, E-Mail: drjlant@worldprofit.com, Web Site: www.worldprofit.com (5)

Jeffries, Bill, CTA Inc, Fenton, MO. Tel: (636) 305-3100, Web Site: www.ctainc.com (5)

Jellison, Bob, PAPYRUS, Fairfield, CA. Tel: (707) 428-0200, Web Site: www.papyrusonline.com (5)

Jenc, Jack, McArdle Printing Co Inc, Upper Marlboro, MD. Tel: (301) 390-8500, FAX: (301) 390-8052, Web Site: www.mcardleprinting.com (27)

Jenco Productions Inc, San Bernardino, CA. Tel: (909) 381-9453, Web Site: www.jencoproductions.com (28)

Jenkin, Tom, Caesars Palace, Las Vegas, NV. Tel: (702) 407-6000, (800) 634-6001, FAX: (702) 407-6037, Web Site: www.caesars.com (16)

Jenkin, Tom, Harrah's Marketing, Reno, NV. Tel: (775) 786-3232, FAX: (775) 722-2815, Web Site: www.harrahsreno.com (16)

Jenkings, Gregory, The Flinchbaugh Co Inc, Manchester, PA. Tel: (717) 266-2202, FAX: (717) 266-7055, E-Mail: flinchbaugh@blazenet.net, Web Site: www.flinchbaugh.com (16)

Jenkins, Ben, Wachovia Bank, National Association, Charlotte, NC. Tel: (704) 590-0000, (800) WACHOVIA, FAX: (704) 427-6748 (14)

Jenkins, James, R., John Deere Consumer Products, Moline, IL. Tel: (309) 765-8000, FAX: (309) 748-0114, Web Site: www.johndeere.com (16)

Jenkins, Larry, Levenger, Delray Beach, FL. Tel: (561) 276-2436, (800) 677-8034, FAX: (561) 266-2181, E-Mail: orders@levenger.com, Web Site: www.levenger.com (5)

Jenkins, Michael, MarketLeverage, Lake Mary, FL. Tel: (407) 805-8800, Web Site: www.precisionplaymedia.com (22)

Jenkins, Michael, Precision Play Media / MarketLeverage, Lake Mary, FL. Tel: (407) 805-8800, Web Site: www.precisionplaymedia.com (22)

Jenkins, P., Thomas, Open Text Inc, Waterloo, ON Canada. Tel: (519) 888-9933, (800) 499-6544, FAX: (519) 888-0677, E-Mail: support@opentext.com, Web Site: www.opentext.com (16)

Jenkins, Tracy, Lending Tree/Home Loan Center, Charlotte, NC. Tel: (704) 541-5351, Web Site: www.lendingtree.com (14)

Jenks, Mack, Gerber Products Co, Fremont, MI. Tel: (231) 928-2000, (800) 443-7237, Web Site: www.gerber.com (16)

Jenks, Tom, BBM Canada Inc, Don Mills, ON. Tel: (416) 445-9800, FAX: (416) 445-8644, E-Mail: info@bbm.ca, Web Site: www.bbm.ca (30)

Jenks, William, Safeco Insurance Co, Seattle, WA. Tel: (206) 545-5000, (800) 332-3226, FAX: (206) 545-5767/5651, Web Site: www.safeco.com (15)

Jenloz, Claude, The Renovator's Supply Inc, Millers Falls, MA. Tel: (413) 423-3300, (800) 659-2211, FAX: (413) 423-3800, E-Mail: customercare@rensup.com, Web Site: www.rensup.com (5)

Jennemann, Mark, Bullseye Database Marketing LLC, Tulsa, OK. Tel: (918) 587-1731, FAX: (918) 587-0450, E-Mail: inquiries@bullseyedm.com, Web Site: www.bullseyedm.com (35)

Jenner, Brian, Brian Jenner Inc, Pasco, WA. Tel: (509) 735-2172, FAX: (509) 783-8042 (6)

Brian Jenner Inc, Pasco, WA. Tel: (509) 735-2172, FAX: (509) 783-8042 (6)

Jenney, Noreen, S., Celebrity Endorsement Network (CEN), Calabasas, CA. Tel: (818) 225-7090, FAX: (818) 880-0898, E-Mail: info@celebrityendorsement.com, Web Site: www.celebrityendorsement.com (35)

Jennings, Karen, George W Park Seed Co Inc, Greenwood, SC. Tel: (864) 223-8555, (864) 223-7333, FAX: (864) 941-4206, E-Mail: info@parkseed.com, Web Site: www.parkseed.com (8)

Jennings, Vince, National Mail/Marketing Corp, Broomall, PA. Tel: (610) 544-8200, FAX: (610) 544-1819, Web Site: www.natlmail.com (20)

Jenny Products Inc, Somerset, PA. Tel: (814) 445-3400, FAX: (814) 445-2280, Web Site: www.jennyproducts.com (16)

Jensen, Jeff, Specialized Association Services, Irving, TX. Tel: (469) 524-5122, E-Mail: hvincent@1sas.com, Web Site: www.1sas.com (1)

Jensen, Jeffrey, J., National Motor Club of America Inc, Irving, TX. Tel: (972) 999-4400, (800) 523-4582, FAX: (972) 999-4405, Web Site: www.nmca.com (1)

Jensen, Jim, F P International, Redwood City, CA. Tel: (650) 261-5300, (800) 866-9946, FAX: (650) 361-1713, Web Site: www.fpintl.com (16)

Jensen, Kenneth, R., Coast to Coast Inc, Englewood, CO. Tel: (303) 728-2267, Web Site: www.coastresorts.com (1)

Jensen, Peter, Quark Inc, Denver, CO. Tel: (303) 894-3832, Web Site: www.quark.com (34)

Jensen, Rodger, Oriental Trading Co Inc, Omaha, NE. Tel: (402) 596-1200, (800) 875-8480, FAX: (402) 331-3873, Web Site: www.oriental.com (5)

Jensen, Stephan, Direct Resources Group, Seattle, WA. Tel: (206) 749-0001, E-Mail: results@drg.com, Web Site: www.drg.com (35)

Jensen, Victoria, Credicorp, Dallas, TX. Tel: (214) 915-7200, FAX: (214) 915-7415, E-Mail: support@credicorp.net, Web Site: www.credicorp.net (1)

Jensen, William, T., Methode Electronics Inc, Chicago, IL. Tel: (708) 867-6777, FAX: (708) 867-6999, E-Mail: info@methode.com, Web Site: www.methode.com (9)

Jenson, David, Oliver Russell & Associates, Boise, ID. Tel: (208) 344-1734, FAX: (208) 344-1211, Web Site: www.oliverrussell.com (35)

Jeppesen, Englewood, CO. Tel: (303) 799-9090, Web Site: www.jeppesen.com (22)

Jerchower, Barbara, Williams, Caliri, Miller & Otley, Wayne, NJ. Tel: (973) 694-0800, FAX: (973) 694-0302, Web Site: www.wcmolaw.com (20)

Jerden Records/SpeechWorks, Redmond, WA. Tel: (425) 882-3344, (888) 401-4487, FAX: (425) 882-3494, E-Mail: jerden@aol.com, Web Site: www.soundworks.net (16)

Jerick, Marty, ICS Marketing Support Services, Lansing, MI. Tel: (517) 394-1890, (888) 394-1890, FAX: (517) 394-7408, E-Mail: sales@icshq.com, Web Site: www.icshq.com (21)

Jeroboam, San Francisco, CA. Tel: (415) 312-0198 cell, E-Mail: jeroboamster@gmail.com (38)

Jerome, Al, KCET, Los Angeles, CA. Tel: (323) 666-6500, FAX: (323) 953-5661, E-Mail: viewerservices@kcet.org, Web Site: www.kcet.org (1)

Jerry's Artarama, Raleigh, NC. Tel: (919) 878-8478, (800) U-ARTIST, FAX: (919) 873-9565, E-Mail: micah@jerrysartarama.com, Web Site: www.jerrysartarama.com (10)

Jersey Printing Associates Inc, Atlantic Highlands, NJ. Tel: (732) 872-9654, FAX: (732) 872-9309, E-Mail: sales@jerseyprinting.com, Web Site: www.jerseyprinting.com (27)

Jesco Industries Inc, Litchfield, MI. Tel: (517) 542-2903, (888) 463-1246, FAX: (517) 542-2501, E-Mail: jesco@jescoonline.com, Web Site: www.jescoonline.com (34)

Jeske, Doug, the meyocks group, West Des Moines, IA. Tel: (515) 225-1200, FAX: (515) 225-6400, E-Mail: dougjeske@areyoubrave.com, Web Site: www.areyoubrave.com (35)

Jeske, Paula, J., Schawk, Des Plaines, IL. Tel: (847) 827-9494, FAX: (847) 827-1264, Web Site: www.schawk.com (35)

Jessee, Lance H., Posty Cards Inc, Kansas City, MO. Tel: (816) 231-2323, (800) 554-5018, FAX: (888) 577-3800, E-Mail: customerservice@postycards.com, Web Site: www.postycards.com (16)

Jessup, Bill, Psion Teklogix Inc, Mississauga, ON. Tel: (905) 813-9900, (800) 322-3437, E-Mail: ptinfo@psion.com, Web Site: www.psionteklogix.com (3)

Jet LithoColor Inc, Downers Grove, IL. Tel: (630) 932-9000, (800) 932-1JET, (800) 932-1538, FAX: (630) 932-9101, E-Mail: sales@jetlitho.com, Web Site: www.jetlitho.com (27)

JetSpring, Richmond, VA. Tel: (877) 695-3834, Web Site: www.jetspring.com (30)

Jewell, Jan, Birthday Express Inc, Bothell, WA. Tel: (425) 641-0075, FAX: (425) 641-2028, Web Site: www.birthdayexpress.com (5)

Jewett, Dwight, Globe Marketing Systems, Coral Springs, FL. Tel: (954) 753-7173, (800) 382-9013, FAX: (954) 741-1369, Web Site: www.globemarketingsystems.com (21)

Jewett, Rebecca, Windward Group, Shelburne, VT. Tel: (802) 985-3631, Web Site: www.windwardgroup.us (20)

The Jewish Federation of Greater Washington, Rockville, MD. Tel: (301) 230-7261, Web Site: www.shalomdc.org (1)

The Jewish Publication Society, Philadelphia, PA. Tel: (215) 832-0600, (800) 234-3151, FAX: (215) 568-2017, E-Mail: jewishbook@jewishpub.org, Web Site: www.jewishpub.org (17)

Jewison, Phil, Daystar Data Group Inc, Schaumburg, IL. Tel: (847) 202-0100, FAX: (847) 202-0107, E-Mail: sales@daystardg.com, Web Site: www.daystardg.com (22)

Jeworski, Dwain, Lois Geller Marketing Group, Hollywood, FL. Tel: (646) 723-3231, FAX: (954) 921-2005, E-Mail: loisgeller@loisgellermarketinggroup.com, Web Site: www.loisgellermarketinggroup.com (35)

Jigsaw, San Mateo, CA. Tel: (650) 235-8400, Web Site: www.jigsaw.com (24)

J Jill Group, Inc, Quincy, MA. Tel: (617) 376-4300, (800) 642-9989, FAX: (617) 769-0177, Web Site: www.jjillgroup.com (2)

Jillian, Louise, Go Ahead Vacations, Cambridge, MA. Tel: (617) 619-1000, (800) 242-4686, FAX: (617) 619-1001, E-Mail: goahead@et.com, Web Site: www.goaheadvacations.com (16)

Jilling, John, Eagle Claw Fishing Tackle, Denver, CO. Tel: (303) 321-1481, FAX: (303) 321-4750, E-Mail: info@eagleclaw.com, Web Site: www.eagleclaw.com (11)

Jimenez, Selena, KHL Engineered Packaging Solutions, Buena Park, CA. Tel: (714) 690-6361 (16)

Jimenez, Terry, A., Newsday, Melville, NY. Tel: (631) 843-2020, FAX: (631) 843-5424, Web Site: www.newsday.com (17)

Jin, Yuangie, Boundless Corp, Phelps, NY. Tel: (631) 962-1500, (800) 231-5445, FAX: (631) 962-1505, E-Mail: sales@boundless.com, Web Site: www.boundless.com (16)

Jiwa, ick, Omega Direct Response Inc, Richmond Hill, ON. Tel: (905) 482-2340, FAX: (905) 482-9721, E-Mail: odrsales@omegadirect.com, Web Site: www.omegadirect.com (29)

Joakins, Melody, The Ken Roberts Co, Daphne, AL. Tel: (541) 955-2867, FAX: (541) 955-2730, Web Site: www.kenroberts.com (5)

Jobs, Steve, Apple Computer Inc, Cupertino, CA. Tel: (408) 996-1010, FAX: (408) 996-0275, Web Site: www.apple.com (16)

Jobscope Corp, Greenville, SC. Tel: (864) 458-3143, (800) 443-5794, FAX: (864) 234-4852, E-Mail: marketing@jobscope.com, Web Site: www.jobscope.com (16)

Jobse, Tracey, Progressive Distribution Services Inc, Grand Rapids, MI. Tel: (616) 957-5900, (800) 304-3699, FAX: (616) 957-2990, E-Mail: sales@progressive-commerce.com, Web Site: www.prodist.com (28)

Jobson, James, Rigden Inc, Boulder, CO. Tel: (303) 442-8190, FAX: (303) 442-8686, E-Mail: rigden@rigden.com, Web Site: www.rigden.com (22)

Jockey International Global Inc, Kenosha, WI. Tel: (262) 658-8111 (2)

Jodie, Kregg, Mary Kay Cosmetics Inc, Addison, TX. Tel: (972) 687-6300, (800) MARY KAY, FAX: (972) 687-1611, Web Site: www.marykay.com (16)

Jofco Inc, Jasper, IN. Tel: (812) 482-5114, (800) 23-JOFCO, FAX: (812) 634-2392, E-Mail: furniture@jofco.com, Web Site: www.jofco.com (16)

Joffe, Karen, Public Issues Management, Piedmont, CA. Tel: (510) 654-9114, FAX: (510) 654-0196 (20)

Joffe, Rodney, Whitehat Inc, Tempe, AZ. Tel: (480) 858-9000, FAX: (480) 858-9001, Web Site: www.whitehat.com (32)

Joffrey Long Consultants, Granada Hills, CA. Tel: (818) 635-1777, Web Site: www.southwestbancorp.com (20)

Joggerst, Patrick, Telcordia Technologies, Piscataway, NJ. Tel: (732) 699-2000, FAX: (973) 829-2458, Web Site: www.telcordia.com (16)

John, Douglas, Christian Herald Association, New York, NY. Tel: (212) 684-2800, (800) BOWERY-1, FAX: (212) 684-3740, E-Mail: info@chaonline.org, Web Site: www.bowery.org (1)

John, Roxanne, Institute for International Research Inc, New York, NY. Tel: (212) 661-3500, (800) 345-8016, FAX: (212) 599-2192, E-Mail: register@iirusa.com, Web Site: www.iir-ny.com (16)

John, Thomas, Actividentity Corp, Fremont, CA. Tel: (510) 574-0100, (800) 529-9499, FAX: (510) 574-0101, Web Site: www.actividentity.com (32)

John Deere Consumer Products, Moline, IL. Tel: (309) 765-8000, FAX: (309) 748-0114, Web Site: www.johndeere.com (16)

John Deere Credit USA, Johnston, IA. Tel: (515) 267-3000, FAX: (515) 267-3292, Web Site: www.deere.com/en_US/jdc/index.html (14)

John Hancock Financial Services Inc, Boston, MA. Tel: (617) 572-6000, (800) 732-5543, FAX: (617) 572-6451, Web Site: www.johnhancock.com (15)

John Hancock Retirement Plan Services, Toronto, ON Canada. Tel: (416) 852-1035, Web Site: www.jhancock.com (14)

John Henry Packaging, Lansing, MI. Tel: (707) 778-1250, (800) 327-5997, FAX: (707) 762-1253, Web Site: www.jhpackaging.com (27)

Johnny Appleseed's Inc, Beverly, MA. Tel: (978) 922-2040, (800) 767-6666, FAX: (978) 922-7001, Web Site: www.appleseeds.com (2)

Johns, John E., Protective Life Insurance Co, Birmingham, AL. Tel: (205) 268-1000, (800) 866-3555, FAX: (205) 868-3086, Web Site: www.protective.com (1)

Johns, John, D., Protective Life Corp, Deerfield, IL. Tel: (847) 948-8988, (800) 323-5771, FAX: (847) 948-1156, Web Site: www.protective.com (15)

Johns, Ken, Brunner, Pittsburgh, PA. Tel: (412) 995-9500, FAX: (412) 995-9501, Web Site: www.brunnerworks.com (35)

Johns, Mickey, Wyandotte West Communications Inc, Kansas City, KS. Tel: (913) 788-5565, FAX: (913) 788-9812, E-Mail: news@wyandottewest.com, Web Site: www.wyandottewest.com (17)

Johns, Steve, Print Mailers Inc, Houston, TX. Tel: (832) 201-2000, (800) 656-8883, FAX: (832) 201-2001, E-Mail: steve@pminet.com, Web Site: www.pminet.com (21)

Johnson, Alan, Gulf Coast Data Supply Inc, Milton, FL. Tel: (850) 994-7042, (800) 226-DISK, FAX: (850) 479-4441, Web Site: www.gulfdata.com (3)

Johnson, Allen, Westhoff Machine Co, Saint Louis, MO. Tel: (314) 963-7130, (800) 364-0280, FAX: (800) 324-1942, E-Mail: mail@westhoffinc.com, Web Site: www.westhoffinc.com (9)

Johnson, Arthur, C., ABA/BMA Trust Wealth Management and Marketing Conference, Washington, DC. Tel: (202) 663-5000, (800) BANKERS, FAX: (202) 828-4540, E-Mail: custserv@aba.com, Web Site: www.aba.com (42)

Johnson, Barbara, CRN International Inc, Hamden, CT. Tel: (203) 288-2002, FAX: (203) 281-3291, E-Mail: info@crnradio.com, Web Site: www.crnradio.com (32)

Johnson, Billy, R., The American Legion National Headquarters, Indianapolis, IN. Tel: (317) 630-1247, FAX: (317) 630-1369, E-Mail: acy@legion.org, Web Site: www.legion.org (1)

Johnson, Bob, Parker Boiler Co, Los Angeles, CA. Tel: (323) 727-9800, FAX: (323) 722-2848, E-Mail: mleeming@parkerboiler.com, Web Site: www.parkerboiler.com (34)

Johnson, Brenda, Mays Mission for the Handicapped Inc, Heber Springs, AR. Tel: (501) 362-7526, (888) 503-7955, FAX: (501) 362-7529, E-Mail: sniehaus@maysmission.org, Web Site: www.maysmission.org (27)

Johnson, Brett, Optronics Inc, Muskogee, OK. Tel: (918) 683-9514, (800) 364-5483, FAX: (918) 683-9517, E-Mail: sales@optronicsinc.com, Web Site: www.optronicsinc.com (11)

Johnson, Bruce, W., Strata Marketing Inc, Chicago, IL. Tel: (312) 222-1555, FAX: (312) 222-2510, Web Site: www.stratag.com (30)

Johnson, Bud, FAO Schwarz, New York, NY. Tel: (212) 644-9400, (800) 426-TOYS, FAX: (212) 688-6053, Web Site: www.fao.com (11)

Johnson, Carolyn, M., Protective Life Corp, Deerfield, IL. Tel: (847) 948-8988, (800) 323-5771, FAX: (847) 948-1156, Web Site: www.protective.com (15)

Johnson, Cea Jay, Stick-Em Up Inc, Pleasanton, CA. Tel: (925) 426-1040, FAX: (925) 426-1085, E-Mail: stickemup@trivalley.com, Web Site: www.stickemup.com (5)

Johnson, Chris, Jostens, Inc, Minneapolis, MN. Tel: (952) 830-3300, FAX: (952) 830-3293, Web Site: www.jostens.com (16)

Johnson, Christopher, C., Roberts Stock/Classic Stock, Philadelphia, PA. Tel: (213) 386-4600, (800) 786-6300, FAX: (213) 365-7171, E-Mail: aspstockpix@earthlink.net, Web Site: www.americanstockphotos.com (38)

Johnson, Colin, Symetra Financial, Bellevue, WA. Tel: (425) 256-8000, (800) 426-7355, FAX: (425) 256-5737, Web Site: www.symetra.com (15)

Johnson, Craig, Musician's Friend, Westlake Village, CA. Tel: (541) 772-5173, Web Site: www.musiciansfriend.com (5)

Johnson, Dan, Team Cheer, Geneseo, NY. Tel: (585) 243-8400, (585) 243-0841, (877) 243-5268, FAX: (800) 350-1562, E-Mail: custserv@teamcheer.com, Web Site: www.teamcheer.com (2)

Johnson, Danielle, National Contract Management Association, Ashburn, VA. Tel: (571) 382-1134, (800) 344-8096, E-Mail: memberservices@ncmghq.org, Web Site: www.ncmahq.org (1)

Johnson, Darin, HealthCare Insight, South Jordan, UT. Tel: (801) 285-5800, Web Site: www.hcinsight.com (35)

Johnson, David, Live Design, New York, NY. Tel: (212) 204-4268, FAX: (212) 204-4291, Web Site: livedesignonline.com (17)

Johnson, David, M., The Hartford Financial Services Inc, Southington, CT. Tel: (860) 843-8070, (860) 547-5000, FAX: (860) 547-2680, Web Site: www.thehartford.com (15)

Johnson, David, Sax Arts & Crafts, Appleton, WI. Tel: (800) 558-6696, FAX: (800) 328-4729, E-Mail: info@saxarts.com, Web Site: www.saxarts.com (10)

Johnson, David, School Specialty Inc, Greenville, WI. Tel: (920) 734-5712, (888) 388-3224, FAX: (920) 734-5112, E-Mail: info@schoolspecialty.com, Web Site: www.schoolspecialty.com (16)

Johnson, David, Tova Corp, West Chester, PA. Tel: (484) 701-1000, Web Site: www.beautybytova.com (7)

Johnson, Dick, Eastbay Running Store Inc, Wausau, WI. Tel: (715) 845-5538, (800) 826-2205, FAX: (715) 261-9500, Web Site: www.eastbay.com (2)

Johnson, Ed, House of Orange, Brentwood Bay, BC Canada. Tel: (866) 401-9174, FAX: (250) 652-8673, E-Mail: houseoforange@shaw.ca, Web Site: www.houseoforange.biz (2)

Johnson, Edward C., Fidelity Investments, Boston, MA. Tel: (617) 563-7000, (800) 343-3548, FAX: (617) 476-6150, Web Site: www.fidelity.com (14)

Johnson, Edward, Dynamics Research Corp, Andover, MA. Tel: (978) 475-9090, (800) 522-4321, FAX: (978) 475-8205, Web Site: www.drc.com (16)

Johnson, Eric, Hy Cite Corp, Madison, WI. Tel: (608) 273-3373, (800) 279-3373, FAX: (608) 273-0936, Web Site: www.hycite.com (16)

Johnson, Eric, Neuberger & Berman Management, New York, NY. Tel: (212) 476-8800, (800) 877-9700, FAX: (212) 476-9090, Web Site: www.nb.com (14)

Johnson, Eric, The Orvis Co Inc, Manchester, VT. Tel: (802) 362-3622, FAX: (802) 362-3525, Web Site: www.orvis.com (11)

Johnson, Eric, Win Craft Inc, Winona, MN. Tel: (507) 454-5510, (800) 533-8100, FAX: (507) 454-6403, Web Site: www.wincraftschool.com (5)

Johnson, F.B., Gramma's Graphics Inc, Lancaster, VA. Tel: (804) 462-0884, FAX: (804) 462-0884, E-Mail: sunprints@grandloving.com, Web Site: www.bubblink.com/donnelly (36)

Johnson, F.B., Heartstrings Press, Lancaster, VA. Tel: (804) 462-0884, (800) 462-0884, FAX: (716) 462-0884, E-Mail: sue@grandloving.com, Web Site: www.grandloving.com (17)

Johnson, Fred, CUES Experience Conference, Madison, WI. Tel: (608) 271-2664, (800) 252-2664, FAX: (608) 271-2303, Web Site: www.cues.org (42)

Johnson, Gary, D., Patterson Dental, Saint Paul, MN. Tel: (651) 686-1600, (800) 328-5536, FAX: (651) 686-9331, Web Site: www.pattersondental.com (10)

Johnson, Gary, Vertrue Inc, Norwalk, CT. Tel: (203) 324-7635, FAX: (203) 674-7080, Web Site: www.vertrue.com (13)

Johnson, Geoffrey, Chicago Magazine, Chicago, IL. Tel: (312) 222-8999, FAX: (312) 222-0287, Web Site: www.chicagomag.com (17)

Johnson, Grady, Alliance of Area Business Publications, El Segundo, CA. Tel: (323) 937-5514, FAX: (323) 937-0959, E-Mail: info@bizpubs.org, Web Site: www.bizpubs.org (1)

Johnson, Grant, A., Johnson Direct LLC, Brookfield, WI. Tel: (262) 782-2750, (800) 710-2750, FAX: (262) 782-2751, E-Mail: info@johnsondirect.com, Web Site: www.johnsondirect.com (1)

Johnson, James W., Automation Mailing & Shipping Solutions Inc, Cleveland, OH. Tel: (216) 241-4487, (800) 883-7935, FAX: (216) 241-5918, E-Mail: service@mailshipsolutions.com, Web Site: www.mailshipsolutions.com (16)

Johnson, James, E., International Resource Management Co, Bedford, TX. Tel: (817) 861-9191, FAX: (817) 277-0868, E-Mail: james@irmco.net, Web Site: www.irmco.net (20)

Johnson, James, K., Alloy Media Marketing, New York, NY. Tel: (212) 244-4307, (877) 360-9688, FAX: (212) 244-4311, E-Mail: contactus@alloymerch.com, Web Site: www.alloymarketing.com (35)

Johnson, James, Safeware, The Insurance Agency Inc, Columbus, OH. Tel: (614) 781-1492, (800) 800-1492, FAX: (614) 781-0559, E-Mail: service@safeware.com, Web Site: www.safeware.com (15)

Johnson, Janice, Westhoff, Westhoff Machine Co, Saint Louis, MO. Tel: (314) 963-7130, (800) 364-0280, FAX: (800) 324-1942, E-Mail: mail@westhoffinc.com, Web Site: www.westhoffinc.com (9)

Johnson, Jeff, NTP Distribution, Wilsonville, OR. Tel: (503) 570-0171, Web Site: www.ntpdistribution.com (34)

Johnson, Jim, Cable Connection, Fremont, CA. Tel: (408) 395-6700, FAX: (408) 354-3980, E-Mail: cables4u@cable-connection.com, Web Site: www.cable-connection.com (3)

Johnson, Jim, Liberty Orchards Co Inc, Cashmere, WA. Tel: (509) 782-2191, (800) 888-5696, FAX: (509) 782-1487, E-Mail: service@libertyorchards.com, Web Site: www.libertyorchards.com (16)

Johnson, Jim, Movie Central, Toronto, ON. Tel: (416) 479-6784, E-Mail: info@moviecentral.ca, Web Site: www.moviecentral.ca (32)

Johnson, Jim, Solarcom, Norcross, GA. Tel: (770) 449-6116, (888) SUN-DATA, FAX: (770) 448-7726, Web Site: www.solarcom.net (16)

Johnson, Joel, W., Hormel Foods Corp, Austin, MN. Tel: (507) 437-5611, (800) 523-4635, FAX: (507) 437-5158, Web Site: www.hormel.com (16)

Johnson, John, Campbell Soup Co, Camden, NJ. Tel: (856) 342-4800, (800) 257-8443, FAX: (856) 342-3878, Web Site: www.campbellsoup.com (16)

Johnson, John, Holy Cross Hospital, Fort Lauderdale, FL. Tel: (954) 771-8000, FAX: (954) 229-8597, Web Site: www.holy-cross.com (16)

Johnson, Ken, Position Technologies Inc, Saint Charles, IL. Tel: (630) 262-5300, FAX: (630) 232-2998, Web Site: www.positiontech.com (16)

Johnson, Kent, S., Highlights For Children, Columbus, OH. Tel: (614) 487-2601, (800) 848-8922, FAX: (614) 487-2700, Web Site: www.highlights.com (17)

Johnson, Kevin, Straw Hat Cooperative Corp, San Ramon, CA. Tel: (925) 837-3400, FAX: (925) 820-1080, E-Mail: info@strawhatpizza.com, Web Site: www.strawhatpizza.com (16)

Johnson, Kris, LemmonTree Marketing Group, Tempe, AZ. Tel: (480) 967-1405, (888) 536-6243, FAX: (480) 967-1407, E-Mail: 7solutions@lemmontree.com, Web Site: www.lemmontree.com (35)

Johnson, Mark, E., Mark Everett Johnson Inc, Carlisle, PA. Tel: (603) 465-3888, FAX: (603) 465-3889, E-Mail: mark@copy.pro (39)

Johnson, Mark, PPS - Packaging Printing Specialists, Saint Charles, IL. Tel: (630) 513-8060, (877) 573-8060, FAX: (630) 513-8062, E-Mail: pps@ppsofil.com, Web Site: www.PPSofIL.com (27)

Johnson, Michael, O., Herbalife International of America Inc, Los Angeles, CA. Tel: (310) 410-9600, (866) 617-4273, FAX: (310) 258-7019, Web Site: www.herbalife.com (7)

Johnson, Michael, The Washingtonian, Washington, DC. Tel: (202) 296-3600, E-Mail: editorial@washingtonian.com, Web Site: www.washingtonian.com (17)

Johnson, Paul, LinguiSystems, East Moline, IL. Tel: (309) 755-2300, (800) 776-4332, FAX: (800) 577-4555, E-Mail: service@linguisystems.com, Web Site: www.linguisystems.com (17)

Johnson, Ralph, Lake County Press Inc, Waukegan, IL. Tel: (847) 336-4333 (27)

Johnson, Randal, A., Typed Letters Corp, Mount Pleasant, IA. Tel: (316) 729-9093, FAX: (316) 729-9933, E-Mail: janet@typeletters.com, Web Site: www.typedletters.com (21)

Johnson, Rich, American Student Marketing LLC, Highland Park, IL. Tel: (847) 432-4329, Web Site: www.asmdm.com (23)

Johnson, Richard, Washington National Opera, Washington, DC. Tel: (202) 295-2400, (800) US-OPERA, FAX: (202) 295-2460, E-Mail: mail@dc-opera.org, Web Site: www.dc-opera.org (16)

Johnson, Rob, Missouri Landscape & Nursery Association, Bowling Green, MO. Tel: (636) 542-1234, E-Mail: admin@mlng.org, Web Site: www.mlna.org (1)

Johnson, Rudd, Bisk/Totaltape Lists, Tampa, FL. Tel: (813) 621-6200, (800) 874-7877, FAX: (813) 627-9442, E-Mail: lists@bisk.com, Web Site: www.listpro.com (24)

Johnson, Scott, Dakota Digital, Sioux Falls, SD. Tel: (605) 332-6513, (800) 593-4160, FAX: (605) 339-4106, E-Mail: sales@dakotadigital.com, Web Site: www.dakotadigital.com (12)

Johnson, Scott, Relevate, Springfield, VA. Tel: (703) 658-8300, (800) 523-7346, FAX: (703) 658-8301, E-Mail: sales@relevategroup.com, Web Site: www.relevategroup.com (22)

Johnson, Sharon, Three Sixty Inc, Chicago, IL. Tel: (312) 255-0360, FAX: (312) 255-1932, E-Mail: 360@360-communications.com, Web Site: www.360-communications.com (35)

Johnson, Sheree, Nicholson Kovac Inc, Kansas City, MO. Tel: (816) 842-8881, FAX: (816) 842-6340, E-Mail: nk@nicholsonkovac.com, Web Site: www.nkhw.com (35)

Johnson, Sonia, Waytek, Chanhassen, MN. Tel: (952) 465-0431, Web Site: www.waytekwire.com (16)

Johnson, Sue, Heartstrings Press, Lancaster, VA. Tel: (804) 462-0884, (800) 462-0884, FAX: (716) 462-0884, E-Mail: sue@grandloving.com, Web Site: www.grandloving.com (17)

Johnson, Sue, Hobby Builders Supply, Atlanta, GA. Tel: (770) 242-1498, (800) 223-7171, FAX: (770) 242-1497, (800) 926-6464, Web Site: www.miniatures.com (11)

Johnson, Susan, Gramma's Graphics Inc, Lancaster, VA. Tel: (804) 462-0884, FAX: (804) 462-0884, E-Mail: sunprints@grandloving.com, Web Site: www.bubblink.com/donnelly (36)

Johnson, Tom, E-Z-EM Inc, Melville, NY. Tel: (516) 333-8230, (800) 544-4624, FAX: (516) 333-8278, E-Mail: webmaster@ezem.com, Web Site: www.ezem.com (7)

Johnson, Wayne, The Pennysaver Group Inc, Hanover, MD. Tel: (410) 684-2600, FAX: (410) 684-2065, Web Site: www.mdpennysaver.com (17)

Johnson, William, A., Dial-A-Mattress, Hicksville, NY. Tel: (718) 472-1200, (800) 824-7777, FAX: (718) 482-6561, E-Mail: sales@mattress.com, Web Site: www.mattress.com (16)

Johnson & Johnson, New Brunswick, NJ. Tel: (732) 524-0400, FAX: (732) 214-0332, Web Site: www.jnj.com (16)

Johnson & Quin Inc, Niles, IL. Tel: (847) 588-4800, FAX: (847) 647-6949, E-Mail: jqinfo@j-quin.com, Web Site: www.j-quin.com (28)

Johnson & Wales University, Providence, RI. Tel: (401) 598-1000, (800) DIAL-JWU, FAX: (401) 598-1833, E-Mail: admissions.pvd@jwu.edu, Web Site: www.jwu.edu (41)

Johnson Direct LLC, Brookfield, WI. Tel: (262) 782-2750, (800) 710-2750, FAX: (262) 782-2751, E-Mail: info@johnsondirect.com, Web Site: www.johnsondirect.com (35)

Mark Everett Johnson Inc, Carlisle, PA. Tel: (603) 465-3888, FAX: (603) 465-3889, E-Mail: mark@copy.pro (39)

Johnson Rauhoff Inc, Saint Joseph, MI. Tel: (269) 428-3377, (800) 523-7996, FAX: (269) 428-3312, Web Site: www.johnsonrauhoff.com (35)

Johnson Smith Co, Bradenton, FL. Tel: (941) 747-5566, Web Site: www.johnsonsmith.com (5)

Johnson Wilshire Distributors Service Corp, Santa Fe Springs, CA. Tel: (562) 777-0088, (800) 922-2456, FAX: (562) 777-0099, (800) 993-9699, E-Mail: jwigloves@aol.com, Web Site: www.johnsonwilshire.com (34)

Johnsong, Kirk, Longevity Network Ltd, Henderson, NV. Tel: (702) 454-7000, (800) 242-1000, FAX: (702) 435-4786, Web Site: www.longevitynetwork.com (7)

Johnsos, Judith, Business Graphics Inc, Woodstock, IL. Tel: (815) 338-8222, (800) 435-4874, FAX: (815) 338-2652, E-Mail: busgraph@mc.net, Web Site: www.businessgraphics.com (16)

Johnsos, Luke, Business Graphics Inc, Woodstock, IL. Tel: (815) 338-8222, (800) 435-4874, FAX: (815) 338-2652, E-Mail: busgraph@mc.net, Web Site: www.businessgraphics.com (16)

Johnsten, Christine, Wysong Corp, Midland, MI. Tel: (989) 631-0009, (800) 748-0188, FAX: (989) 631-8801, E-Mail: wysong@wysong.net, Web Site: www.wysong.net (7)

Johnston Jr., John, Pete Rickard Inc, Cobleskill, NY. Tel: (518) 234-2731, (800) 282-5663, FAX: (518) 234-2454, E-Mail: info@peterickard.com, Web Site: www.peterickard.com (11)

Johnston, Andrew, Publishers Computer Corp, New Milford, NJ. Tel: (201) 261-3700, FAX: (201) 261-9110, E-Mail: mail@publisherscomputer.com, Web Site: www.publisherscomputer.com (22)

Johnston, Charlie, Nevada Magazine, Carson City, NV. Tel: (775) 687-5416, FAX: (775) 687-6159, E-Mail: editor@nevadamagazine.com, Web Site: www.nevadamagazine.com (17)

Johnston, Howard, American Megatrends Inc, Norcross, GA. Tel: (770) 246-8600, (800) 828-9264, FAX: (770) 246-8790, Web Site: www.ami.com (3)

Johnston, Kristi, Bert Davis Executive Search, New York, NY. Tel: (212) 838-4000, FAX: (212) 935-3291, E-Mail: info@bertdavis.com, Web Site: www.bertdavis.com (20)

Johnston, Steve, The National Underwriter Co, Erlanger, KY. Tel: (800) 543-0874, FAX: (856) 692-2246, E-Mail: customerservice@nuco.com, Web Site: www.nuco.com (17)

Joiner, Suzanne, FEEDING AMERICA, Chicago, IL. Tel: (312) 263-2303, Web Site: www.secondharvest.org (1)

Joint Commission, Oakbrook Terrace, IL. Tel: (630) 792-5000, Web Site: www.jcaho.org (1)

Jolly, Kamal, Kuwait Airways Corp, Fort Lee, NJ. Tel: (201) 582-9222, (800) 4-KUWAIT, FAX: (212) 659-4270, E-Mail: nyc@kuwait-airways.com, Web Site: www.kuwait-airways.com (19)

Jon-Don, Roselle, IL. Tel: (800) 556-6366, Web Site: www.jondon.com (34)

JonCas PostExperts Inc, Ville Saint Laurent, PQ Canada. Tel: (514) 333-7480, FAX: (514) 332-6915, E-Mail: sherif.zaky@quebecorworld.com, Web Site: www.postexperts.com (23)

Jondal, Dan, Sea Bear, Anacortes, WA. Tel: (360) 293-4661, (800) 645-3474, FAX: (888) 487-6427, Web Site: www.seabear.com (16)

Jones Jr, Milton, H., Bank of America, Charlotte, NC. Tel: (704) 386-5681, (800) 841-4000, FAX: (704) 386-6699, Web Site: www.bankofamerica.com (14)

Jones, Aaron, Western Data Services Inc, Carlsbad, NM. Tel: (505) 234-2927, FAX: (505) 234-9637, E-Mail: directmail@wdsi.net, Web Site: www.wdsi.net (35)

Jones, Amy, Zig Ziglar Corp, Plano, TX. Tel: (972) 233-9191, (800) 527-0306, FAX: (469) 321-7556, E-Mail: info@ziglar.com, Web Site: www.zigziglar.com (16)

Jones, Benjamin, Fancy Fronds, Gold Bar, WA. Tel: (360) 793-1472, FAX: (360) 793-4243, E-Mail: judith@fancyfronds.com, Web Site: www.fancyfronds.com (8)

Jones, Bill, First Class Direct Inc, Loveland, CO. Tel: (970) 613-0608, Web Site: www.firstclassdirect.com (21)

Jones, Bill, Harris Infosource International Inc, Independence, OH. Tel: (330) 425-9000, (877) 359-6308, (800) 888-5900, (800) 748-5482, FAX: (800) 643-5997, E-Mail: customerservice@harrisinfo.com, Web Site: www.harrisinfo.com (17)

Jones, Bob, Parker Boiler Co, Los Angeles, CA. Tel: (323) 727-9800, FAX: (323) 722-2848, E-Mail: mleeming@parkerboiler.com, Web Site: www.parkerboiler.com (34)

Jones, Brad, Jazzercise Inc, Carlsbad, CA. Tel: (760) 476-1750, (800) FIT IS IT, FAX: (760) 602-7180, E-Mail: info@jazzercise.com, Web Site: www.jazzercise.com (2)

Jones, Collin, Institutional Investor Inc, New York, NY. Tel: (212) 224-3300, FAX: (212) 224-3592, Web Site: www.institutionalinvestor.com (17)

Jones, Dale, Agco Spra-Coup, Duluth, GA. Tel: (320) 231-9400, FAX: (320) 231-9413, Web Site: www.agcocorp.com (16)

Jones, Dana, Tandy Leather Co, Fort Worth, TX. Tel: (817) 872-3200, FAX: (817) 496-7859, E-Mail: tlfhelp@tandyleather.com, Web Site: www.tandyleatherfactory.com (11)

Jones, David, A., Marlin P Jones & Associates Inc, Lake Park, FL. Tel: (561) 848-8236, (800) 652-6733, FAX: (561) 844-8764, E-Mail: mpja@mpja.com, Web Site: www.mpja.com (3)

Jones, David, Euro RSCG Worldwide, New York, NY. Tel: (212) 886-2000, FAX: (212) 886-2016, Web Site: www.eurorscg.com (35)

Jones, Dr. Robert, New York Blood Center Inc, New York, NY. Tel: (212) 570-3000, (800) 933-2566, FAX: (212) 570-3195, Web Site: www.nybloodcenter.org (1)

Jones, Elizabeth, Safeguard Business Systems Inc, Dallas, TX. Tel: (214) 905-3935, (800) 523-2422, FAX: (800) 439-8423, Web Site: www.gosafeguard.com (16)

Jones, F., Macy, EMI Strategic Marketing Inc, Boston, MA. Tel: (617) 451-9451, FAX: (617) 451-1193, E-Mail: cedlund@emiboston.com, Web Site: www.emiboston.com (35)

Jones, Fred, Quality Products Inc, Columbus, MS. Tel: (662) 328-1477, (800) 647-1057, FAX: (800) 824-8510, E-Mail: kshep@classroomsupply.com, Web Site: www.classroomsupply.com (10)

Jones, Glen, Jones International Ltd, Centennial, CO. Tel: (303) 792-3111, (800) 525-7002, FAX: (303) 784-8508, E-Mail: publicrelations@jones.com, Web Site: www.jones.com (16)

Jones, Glen, Product Information Network, Englewood, CO. Tel: (303) 792-3111, (800) 525-7002, FAX: (303) 784-8549, Web Site: www.pinnet.com (32)

Jones, Glen, Vulcan Information Packaging, Vincent, AL. Tel: (205) 672-2241, (800) 633-4526, FAX: (205) 672-1276, Web Site: www.vulcan-online.com (16)

Jones, Greg, China Books & Periodicals Inc, South San Francisco, CA. Tel: (650) 872-7076, (800) 818-2017, FAX: (650) 872-7808, E-Mail: info@chinabooks.com, Web Site: www.chinabooks.com (17)

Jones, Gregory, P., Gilbert H Wild & Son Inc, Reeds, MO. Tel: (417) 548-3514, FAX: (417) 548-6831, Web Site: www.gilberthwild.com (8)

Jones, H, Doug, Pontis Group, Grosse Pointe, MI. Tel: (614) 764-1274, FAX: (614) 210-0598, E-Mail: cbirchfield@pontisgroup.com, Web Site: www.pontisgroup.com (35)

Jones, Janis L., Harrah's Entertainment Inc, Las Vegas, NV. Tel: (702) 407-6000, FAX: (702) 407-6499, (702) 407-6500, Web Site: www.harrahs.com (19)

Jones, Jennifer, CARE USA, Atlanta, GA. Tel: (404) 979-9255, (800) 521-CARE, FAX: (404) 589-2600, E-Mail: info@care.org, Web Site: www.careusa.org (1)

Jones, Jennifer, Hyatt Fruit Co, Vero Beach, FL. Tel: (772) 567-3766, (866) 991-8889, FAX: (772) 567-0973, Web Site: www.hyattfruitco.com (4)

Jones, Jerry, Kappler Protective Apparel & Fabrics, Guntersville, AL. Tel: (256) 505-4005, (800) 600-4019, FAX: (256) 505-4151, E-Mail: usa@kappler.com, Web Site: www.kappler.com (2)

Jones, Jerry, Partners Marketing Inc, Saint Charles, IL. Tel: (630) 524-9901, FAX: (630) 524-9909, E-Mail: georgeb@partnersmarketing.com, Web Site: www.partnersmarketing.com (22)

Jones, Jerry, Twin City Engraving/Premier Promotions, Saint Joseph, MI. Tel: (616) 983-0601, (800) 222-7752, FAX: (616) 983-3571, Web Site: www.premierpromos.com (33)

Jones, Jim, Edward Don & Co, North Riverside, IL. Tel: (708) 442-9400, (800) 777-4366, FAX: (708) 442-0436, Web Site: www.don.com (16)

Jones, Joe, Jones Publishing Inc, Iola, WI. Tel: (715) 445-5000, (800) 331-0038, FAX: (715) 445-4053, E-Mail: jonespub@jonespublishing.com, Web Site: www.jonespublishing.com (17)

Jones, John, W., Deck the Walls Inc, Saint Peters, MO. Tel: (314) 719-8200, (866) 719-8200, FAX: (314) 719-8290, Web Site: www.deckthewalls.com (5)

Jones, Judith, Fancy Fronds, Gold Bar, WA. Tel: (360) 793-1472, FAX: (360) 793-4243, E-Mail: judith@fancyfronds.com, Web Site: www.fancyfronds.com (8)

Jones, K.C., Pacific Media Exchange, Berkeley, CA. Tel: (510) 528-9181, FAX: (510) 528-3449, E-Mail: pacificmedia@comcast.net, Web Site: www.pacificmediaexchange.com (35)

Jones, Kathleen, Lopez Negrete Communications, Houston, TX. Tel: (713) 877-8777, FAX: (713) 877-8796, E-Mail: LNCmailbox@lopeznegrete.com, Web Site: www.lopeznegrete.com (35)

Jones, Kelly, Premera Blue Cross, Spokane, WA. Tel: (425) 670-4000, (800) 422-0032, FAX: (425) 670-5853, Web Site: www.premera.com (15)

Jones, Kelly, Telect Inc, Liberty Lake, WA. Tel: (509) 926-6000, FAX: (509) 926-8915, E-Mail: getinfo@telect.com, Web Site: www.telect.com (16)

Jones, Malcolm, Colgate-Palmolive Co, New York, NY. Tel: (212) 310-2000, (800) 468-6502, FAX: (212) 310-2475, Web Site: www.colgate.com (16)

Jones, Marlin, L., Marlin P Jones & Associates Inc, Lake Park, FL. Tel: (561) 848-8236, (800) 652-6733, FAX: (561) 844-8764, E-Mail: mpja@mpja.com, Web Site: www.mpja.com (3)

Jones, Marlin, P., Marlin P Jones & Associates Inc, Lake Park, FL. Tel: (561) 848-8236, (800) 652-6733, FAX: (561) 844-8764, E-Mail: mpja@mpja.com, Web Site: www.mpja.com (3)

Jones, Murray, BC & Associates Representatives Inc, Fate, TX. Tel: (972) 722-7365, (800) 275-1298, FAX: (972) 722-7714, E-Mail: terri@bcincentives.com, Web Site: www.bcincentives.com (33)

Jones, Paul, W., AO Smith Corp, Milwaukee, WI. Tel: (414) 359-4000, FAX: (414) 359-4064, Web Site: www.aosmith.com (16)

Jones, Renee, American Clearinghouse Inc, Louisville, KY. Tel: (800) 944-6361, Web Site: www.americanclearinghouse.com (23)

Jones, Richard, F., Fidelity Security Life Insurance Co, Kansas City, MO. Tel: (816) 756-1060, (800) 648-8624, FAX: (816) 968-0580, E-Mail: info@fslins.com, Web Site: www.fslins.com (15)

Jones, Robert, T., National Alliance of Business, Washington, DC. Tel: (202) 289-2888, (800) 787-2448 (1)

Jones, Russell, League of American Orchestras, New York, NY. Tel: (212) 262-5161, FAX: (212) 262-5198, Web Site: www.symphony.org; www.americanorchestras.org (1)

Jones, Sarah, Jones School Supply Co Inc, Irmo, SC. Tel: (803) 772-3796, FAX: (800) 942-5921, Web Site: www.jonesawards.com (6)

Jones, Sherri, TKL Interactive, The Colony, TX. Tel: (972) 370-7878, (800) 789-3893, FAX: (972) 370-7879, Web Site: www.tklinteractive.com (23)

Jones, Steve, Golfsmith International Inc, Austin, TX. Tel: (512) 821-4050, (800) 813-6897, FAX: (512) 837-9347, E-Mail: comments@golfsmith.com, Web Site: www.golfsmith.com (11)

Jones, Steve, Maple Grove Farms of Vermont Inc, Saint Johnsbury, VT. Tel: (802) 748-5141, FAX: (802) 748-9647, E-Mail: maple@maplegrove.com, Web Site: www.maplegrove.com (4)

Jones, Steven, D., Fieldstone Gardens Inc, Vassalboro, ME. Tel: (207) 923-3836, FAX: (207) 923-3836, E-Mail: info@fieldstonegardens.com, Web Site: www.fieldstonegardens.com (8)

Jones, Susan, K., Susan K Jones & Associates, Grand Rapids, MI. Tel: (616) 458-0305, E-Mail: sjones9200@aol.com (39)

Jones, Terri, L., BC & Associates Representatives Inc, Fate, TX. Tel: (972) 722-7365, (800) 275-1298, FAX: (972) 722-7714, E-Mail: terri@bcincentives.com, Web Site: www.bcincentives.com (33)

Jones, Tom, Infomart, Dallas, TX. Tel: (214) 800-8000, FAX: (214) 800-8100, Web Site: www.infomartusa.com (16)

Jones, Tom, Ingram Book Group, La Vergne, TN. Tel: (615) 793-5000, (800) 937-8000, FAX: (800) 876-0186, Web Site: www.ipage.ingrambook.com (16)

Jones, Tom, R., Hyatt Fruit Co, Vero Beach, FL. Tel: (772) 567-3766, (866) 991-8889, FAX: (772) 567-0973, Web Site: www.hyattfruitco.com (4)

Jones, Tom, Sportime International, Norcross, GA. Tel: (770) 449-5700, (800) 283-5700, FAX: (770) 510-7290, E-Mail: orders@sportime.com, Web Site: www.sportime.com (11)

Jones, Tylie, Tylie Jones & Associates, Burbank, CA. Tel: (800) 922-0662, E-Mail: tylie@tylie.com, Web Site: www.tylie.com (32)

Jones, William, B., The Virginia Diner Inc, Wakefield, VA. Tel: (757) 899-6213, (888) 823-4637, FAX: (757) 899-2281, E-Mail: vadiner@vadiner.com, Web Site: www.vadiner.com (4)

Jones & O'Malley Advertising, Toluca Lake, CA. Tel: (818) 762-8353, FAX: (818) 762-6736 (35)

Jones & Thomas Inc, Decatur, IL. Tel: (217) 423-1889, FAX: (217) 425-0680, E-Mail: bill@jonesthomas.com, Web Site: www.jonesthomas.com (35)

Edward Jones, Des Peres, MO. Tel: (314) 515-2000, Web Site: www.edwardjones.com (14)

Jones International Ltd, Centennial, CO. Tel: (303) 792-3111, (800) 525-7002, FAX: (303) 784-8508, E-Mail: publicrelations@jones.com, Web Site: www.jones.com (16)

Marlin P Jones & Associates Inc, Lake Park, FL. Tel: (561) 848-8236, (800) 652-6733, FAX: (561) 844-8764, E-Mail: mpja@mpja.com, Web Site: www.mpja.com (3)

Jones Publishing Inc, Iola, WI. Tel: (715) 445-5000, (800) 331-0038, FAX: (715) 445-4053, E-Mail: jonespub@jonespublishing.com, Web Site: www.jonespublishing.com (17)

Jones School Supply Co Inc, Irmo, SC. Tel: (803) 772-3796, FAX: (800) 942-5921, Web Site: www.jonesawards.com (6)

Susan K Jones & Associates, Grand Rapids, MI. Tel: (616) 458-0305, E-Mail: sjones9200@aol.com (39)

Tylie Jones & Associates, Burbank, CA. Tel: (800) 922-0662, E-Mail: tylie@tylie.com, Web Site: www.tylie.com (32)

Jonesi, Dave, C&S Sales Inc, Wheeling, IL. Tel: (847) 541-0710, (800) 292-7711, FAX: (847) 541-9904, E-Mail: sales@cs-sales.com, Web Site: www.cs_sales.com (9)

Joop, Peter, Infocore Inc, Carlsbad, CA. Tel: (760) 607-2500, FAX: (760) 607-2505, E-Mail: bstewart@infocoreinc.com, Web Site: www.infocoreinc.com (23)

Joos, David, W., Consumer's Energy, Jackson, MI. Tel: (517) 788-0550, (800) 805-0490, FAX: (517) 788-1859, E-Mail: businesscenter@consumerenergy.com, Web Site: www.consumersenergy.com (16)

Joray, Gregory, M., Children's Better Health Institute, Indianapolis, IN. Tel: (317) 634-1100, FAX: (317) 684-8094, E-Mail: gjoray@tcon.net, Web Site: www.cbhi.org (1)

Jordan, Jack, Creative Mailing & Marketing, Gardena, CA. Tel: (310) 637-7100, FAX: (714) 998-9001, Web Site: www.creativemandm.com (28)

Jordan, Jack, Engineering Services & Products Co, South Windsor, CT. Tel: (860) 528-1119, (800) 835-7877, FAX: (800) 457-8887, Web Site: www.teksupply.com (9)

Jordan, Jacqueline, E., Envelope Manufacturers Association, Alexandria, VA. Tel: (703) 739-2200, FAX: (703) 739-2209, Web Site: www.envelope.org (1)

Jordan, Leslie, Leslie Jordan, Portland, OR. Tel: (503) 295-1987, (800) 935-3343, FAX: (503) 295-1989, E-Mail: sales@lesliejordan.com, Web Site: www.lesliejordan.com (2)

Jordan, Michael, Western Fulfillment Management Association Inc, North Hollywood, CA. Tel: (310) 323-7220, FAX: (310) 323-7231, E-Mail: mjordan@espcomp.com, Web Site: www.wfma.org (40)

Jordan, Peter, CRM Learning, Carlsbad, CA. Tel: (760) 431-9800, (800) 421-0833, FAX: (760) 931-5792, E-Mail: sales@crmlearning.com, Web Site: www.crmlearning.com (16)

Jordan, Philip, CTC Corp, Bennington, VT. Tel: (802) 442-6371, FAX: (802) 442-8526 (16)

Jordan, Todd, Rappahannock Electric Cooperative, Fredericksburg, VA. Tel: (540) 898-8500, Web Site: www.myrec.coop (1)

Jordan Direct, Phoenix, AZ. Tel: (623) 551-2728, FAX: (623) 551-2730, E-Mail: dori@jordandirect.net (23)

The Jordan Edmiston Group Inc, New York, NY. Tel: (212) 754-0710, Web Site: www.jegi.com (14)

Jorgensen, Robert, The Adcentive Group Inc, San Diego, CA. Tel: (858) 278-9200, FAX: (858) 278-9079, E-Mail: info@adcentive.com, Web Site: www.adcentive.com (35)

Jorgovan, Mike, Complete Mailing Lists LLC, Bronxville, NY. Tel: (914) 771-6640, (866) 314-5478, FAX: (914) 771-6645, E-Mail: ewoolf@cml-llc.com, Web Site: www.cml-llc.com (23)

Josen, Bob, Things Deco, New York, NY. Tel: (212) 362-8961, E-Mail: thingsdeco@hotmail.com, Web Site: www.thingsdeco.com (6)

Joseph Jr., Robert, H., Alliance Bernstein, New York, NY. Tel: (212) 969-1000, (800) 962-2134, FAX: (212) 969-2229, Web Site: www.alliancebernstein.com (14)

Joseph, Brian, National Motor Club of America Inc, Irving, TX. Tel: (972) 999-4400, (800) 523-4582, FAX: (972) 999-4405, Web Site: www.nmca.com (1)

Joseph, David, ACTIMAIL`INC, New York, NY. Tel: (212) 245-2272, FAX: (212) 245-2523, E-Mail: actimail.usa@actimail.com, Web Site: www.actimail.com (35)

Joseph, Father, Marian Helpers Center, Stockbridge, MA. Tel: (413) 298-3691, (800) 462-7426, FAX: (413) 298-3583, Web Site: www.marian.org (1)

Joseph, Frank, Frank Joseph, Chevy Chase, MD. Tel: (301) 656-8753, E-Mail: mr.dm@verizon.net (39)

Joseph, Jacqueline, American Marketing Solutions LLC, Uniontown, PA. Tel: (724) 437-3707 (5)

Joseph, James, E., Oneida Ltd, Oneida, NY. Tel: (315) 361-3000, (888) 263-7195, FAX: (315) 361-3700, Web Site: www.oneida.com (16)

Joseph, Patricia, Advanstar Communications Inc, North Olmstead, OH. Tel: (440) 243-8100, (800) 225-4569, FAX: (440) 891-2740, E-Mail: info@advanstar.com, Web Site: www.advanstarlists.com (17)

Josephs, Richard, Lissan Computing Co Inc, Ridgefield, CT. Tel: (203) 431-8755, FAX: (203) 431-3302, E-Mail: info@lissan.com, Web Site: www.lissan.com (22)

Josephson, Joseph P., Magnaplan Corp, Champlain, NY. Tel: (518) 298-8404, (800) 361-1192, FAX: (518) 298-2368, E-Mail: info@visualplanning.com, Web Site: www.visualplanning.com (10)

Joshi, Vyomesh, Hewlett-Packard Co, Palo Alto, CA. Tel: (650) 857-1501, (800) 752-0900, FAX: (650) 857-5518, Web Site: www.hp.com (16)

Joslin, Jeffrey L., Joslin Photo Puzzle Co, Southampton, PA. Tel: (215) 357-8346, FAX: (215) 357-0307, E-Mail: 2832@comcast.net, Web Site: www.jigsawpuzzle.com (16)

Joslin, Marcia S., Joslin Photo Puzzle Co, Southampton, PA. Tel: (215) 357-8346, FAX: (215) 357-0307, E-Mail: 2832@comcast.net, Web Site: www.jigsawpuzzle.com (16)

Joslin Photo Puzzle Co, Southampton, PA. Tel: (215) 357-8346, FAX: (215) 357-0307, E-Mail: 2832@comcast.net, Web Site: www.jigsawpuzzle.com (16)

Jossey-Bass Inc Publishers, San Francisco, CA. Tel: (415) 433-1740, FAX: (415) 433-0499, E-Mail: webperson@jbp.com, Web Site: www.josseybass.com (17)

Jost, Kenneth, Redstone Federal Credit Union, Huntsville, AL. Tel: (256) 837-6110, Web Site: www.redfcu.org (1)

Josten, Bruce, US Chamber of Commerce, Washington, DC. Tel: (202) 778-6063, (800) 638-6582, FAX: (202) 887-3430, Web Site: www.uschamber.com (1)

Jostens, Inc, Minneapolis, MN. Tel: (952) 830-3300, FAX: (952) 830-3293, Web Site: www.jostens.com (16)

Jourdan, Dennis, Dennis Jourdan Photography Inc, Buffalo Grove, IL. Tel: (847) 564-2570, FAX: (847) 255-5976, E-Mail: info@djphoto.com, Web Site: www.djphoto.com (37)

The Journal News, White Plains, NY. Tel: (914) 694-9300, FAX: (914) 696-8152, Web Site: www.nyjournalnews.com (17)

Journal of Commerce Group, Newark, NJ. Tel: (973) 848-7000, FAX: (973) 848-7004, Web Site: www.joc.com (17)

Journal of Marketing Research, Chicago, IL. Tel: (312) 542-9000, (800) AMA-1150, FAX: (312) 542-9001, E-Mail: info@ama.org, Web Site: www.marketingpower.org (43)

Journal Star, Peoria, IL. Tel: (309) 686-3026, FAX: (309) 686-3265, Web Site: www.pjstar.com (17)

Journey, R. Bruce, Technology Review, Cambridge, MA. Tel: (617) 475-8000, FAX: (617) 258-5850, Web Site: www.technologyreview.com (17)

Journeys, Nashville, TN. Tel: (615) 367-8000, (888) 324-6356, FAX: (615) 367-8123, Web Site: www.journeys.com (2)

Jovanelly, Linda, Marshall & Swift, Los Angeles, CA. Tel: (213) 683-9000, FAX: (213) 683-9010, Web Site: www.marshallswift.com (17)

Jow, Annie, Computer Station Corp, Houston, TX. Tel: (713) 777-6860, FAX: (713) 777-3431, E-Mail: csc@computerstationcorp.com, Web Site: www.computerstationcorp.com (3)

Jow, Tsong (Jeff), Computer Station Corp, Houston, TX. Tel: (713) 777-6860, FAX: (713) 777-3431, E-Mail: csc@computerstationcorp.com, Web Site: www.computerstationcorp.com (3)

Jowdy, Paul, Bon Appetit Magazine, New York, NY. Tel: (212) 286-2860, FAX: (212) 286-2536, E-Mail: paul_jowdy@bonappetit.com, Web Site: www.bonappetit.com (31)

Joy, Susan, Journeys, Nashville, TN. Tel: (615) 367-8000, (888) 324-6356, FAX: (615) 367-8123, Web Site: www.journeys.com (2)

Joyce, Cindy, Lab Safety Supply Inc, Janesville, WI. Tel: (608) 754-2345, (800) 356-2855, FAX: (800) 543-9910, Web Site: www.labsafety.com (5)

Joyce, Kathy, St Louis Post-Dispatch, Saint Louis, MO. Tel: (314) 340-8000, (800) 365-0820, FAX: (314) 340-3140, Web Site: www.postnet.com (17)

Joyce, Leon, Carolina Biological Supply Co, Burlington, NC. Tel: (800) 334-5551, (800) 222-7112, E-Mail: carolina@carolina.com, Web Site: www.carolina.com (9)

Joyce, Tom, Beckman Coulter Inc, Brea, CA. Tel: (714) 993-5321, (800) 526-3821, FAX: (800) 232-3828, Web Site: www.beckmancoulter.com (16)

Joyner, Robert B., Horace Mann Educators Corp, Springfield, IL. Tel: (217) 789-2500, FAX: (217) 788-5161, Web Site: www.horacemann.com (15)

Joys SA Inc, Hatillo, PR. Tel: (954) 426-9100, (800) 526-7148, FAX: (800) 232-9569, E-Mail: info@joyssa.com (2)

Juba, Mark, Best Buy, Richfield, MN. Tel: (612) 291-1000, Web Site: www.bestbuy.com (3)

Judd Ph.D., Vaughn, C., Auburn University at Montgomery, Montgomery, AL. Tel: (334) 244-3621, (800) 227-2649, FAX: (334) 244-3826, Web Site: www.aum.edu (41)

Judelson, Andrew, Sports Illustrated Picture Sales, New York, NY. FAX: (212) 522-0102, E-Mail: andrew_judelson@timeinc.com (38)

Judge, Bob, Edelmann Scott Inc, Richmond, VA. Tel: (804) 643-1931, FAX: (804) 643-1934, E-Mail: dickscott@edelmannscott.com, Web Site: www.edelmannscott.com (35)

Judge, Tom, Direct Marketing Partners, Sacramento, CA. Tel: (916) 974-6969, (800) 909-2626, FAX: (916) 920-5156, E-Mail: info@dirmkt.com, Web Site: www.directmarketingpartners.com (29)

Judkins, Jennifer, Convio Inc, Austin, TX. Tel: (888) 528-9501, Web Site: www.convio.com (22)

Juenger, Lisa, American Ostomy Supply, Earth City, MO. Tel: (314) 291-2900, (800) 858-5858, FAX: (800) 545-0065 (16)

Juergens, Jennifer, Sales & Marketing Management Magazine, New York, NY. Tel: (800) 821-6897, FAX: (905) 470-8561, E-Mail: joyce.cooney@nielsen.com, Web Site: www.salesandmarketing.com (16)

Juge, Richard, E., CCIM Institute, Chicago, IL. Tel: (312) 321-4460, (800) 621-7027, FAX: (312) 321-4530, Web Site: www.ccim.com (1)

Jukes, Terence, Ability Commerce, Delray Beach, FL. Tel: (561) 330-3151, Web Site: www.abilitycommerce.com (20)

Jukes, Terry, Logicnology Inc, Sunrise, FL. Tel: (954) 851-1200, FAX: (954) 846-8552 (22)

Jule, Thomas, Rapidforms Inc, Lancaster, CA. Tel: (856) 384-1144, (800) 257-8354, FAX: (856) 384-1697, Web Site: www.rapidforms.com (27)

Jule, Tom, Accountants' Supply House, Lancaster, CA. Tel: (856) 384-1144, (800) 342-5274, FAX: (800) 468-4446, Web Site: www.rapidforms.com (10)

Julian, Joan, Encyclopaedia Britannica Inc, Chicago, IL. Tel: (312) 347-7319, (800) 323-1229, FAX: (312) 347-7225 (17)

Julian, Paul, C., McKesson Corp, San Francisco, CA. Tel: (415) 983-8300, FAX: (415) 983-7160, Web Site: www.mckesson.com (7)

Jump Technologies Inc, Eagan, MN. Tel: (651) 287-6000, Web Site: www.jumptech.com (32)

Jung, Pat, Surdell & Partners, Omaha, NE. Tel: (402) 501-7488, (800) 733-7765, FAX: (402) 733-2083, E-Mail: dsurdell@surdellpartners.com, Web Site: www.surdellpartners.com (27)

JW Jung Seed Co, Randolph, WI. Tel: (920) 326-3121, (800) 297-3123, FAX: (920) 326-5769, E-Mail: info@jungseed.com, Web Site: www.jungseed.com (8)

Jungle Consulting, Colorado Springs, CO. Tel: (702) 596-4366 (20)

Junior's Cheesecake, Brooklyn, NY. Tel: (718) 852-5257, (800) 458-6467, FAX: (718) 260-9849, E-Mail: info@juniorscheesecake.com, Web Site: www.juniorscheesecake.com (16)

Junius, Daniel M., NEBS, Groton, MA. Tel: (978) 448-6111, (888) 823-6327, (800) 225-6380, FAX: (800) 234-4324, (978) 448-3653, E-Mail: customerservice@nebs.com, Web Site: www.nebs.com (10)

Jupiter Images, Tucson, AZ. Tel: (520) 881-8101, (800) 764-7427, FAX: (520) 881-1841, Web Site: www.jupiterimages.com (38)

Jupiterimages Corp, Peoria, IL. Tel: (312) 980-6111, (800) 764-7427, Web Site: www.jupiterimages.com (36)

Jurgena, R., Mail Advertising Services Inc, Darnestown, MD. Tel: (301) 762-9015 (28)

Jurgensen, Jerry, G., Nationwide Mutual Insurance Co, Columbus, OH. Tel: (614) 249-7111, (800) 882-2822, FAX: (614) 854-3676, Web Site: www.nationwide.com (15)

Jurick, Jeffrey, S., IWCO Direct, Chanhassen, MN. Tel: (952) 474-0961, FAX: (952) 474-6467 (21)

Juskiw, Susan, The Senior Source, Valley Cottage, NY. Tel: (800) 882-9930, FAX: (845) 358-8772, Web Site: www.theseniorsource.com (23)

Just Packaging Inc, South Plainfield, NJ. Tel: (908) 753-6700, FAX: (908) 753-6709, E-Mail: sfischbein@justpackaging.com, Web Site: www.justpackaging.com (28)

Justice, Martha, Premier IMS, Houston, TX. Tel: (713) 222-8871, FAX: (713) 222-0334, E-Mail: norm2@mailplex.com, Web Site: www.premiercompany.com (21)

Justin Discount Boots & Cowboy Outfitters, Justin, TX. Tel: (940) 648-2797, FAX: (940) 648-3282, Web Site: www.justinboots.com (2)

Justman, Mark, A., Portland Cement Association, Skokie, IL. Tel: (847) 966-6200, FAX: (847) 966-9781, Web Site: www.cement.org (1)

JustThinkIncorporated, Sherwood Park, AB Canada. Tel: (780) 416-0244 (16)

Juvenile Diabetes Research Foundation, New York, NY. Tel: (212) 785-9500, (800) 533-CURE, FAX: (212) 785-9595, E-Mail: info@jdrf.org, Web Site: www.jdrf.org (1)

K

K-D Lamp Co, Andover, OH. Tel: (440) 293-4064, FAX: (440) 293-4591, E-Mail: admin@atc-lighting-plastics.com, Web Site: www.k-dlamp.com (12)

K-Log, Zion, IL. Tel: (847) 872-6611, Web Site: www.k-log.com (8)

K-tel International, Golden Valley, MN. Tel: (204) 889-5430, (800) 665-5021, FAX: (612) 559-6803, Web Site: www.ktel.com (16)

KAR Graphics, Mashpee, MA. Tel: (508) 539-9270, (800) 760-5192, FAX: (508) 539-1108, E-Mail: hoop@cape.com, Web Site: www.hoophouse.com (8)

KBM Group, Richardson, TX. Tel: (972) 664-3600, FAX: (972) 664-3656, E-Mail: info@knowledgebasemarketing.com, Web Site: www.kbm1.com (22)

KCEOC Community Action Partnership Inc, Barbourville, KY. Tel: (606) 546-3152, Web Site: kceoc.com (1)

KCET, Los Angeles, CA. Tel: (323) 666-6500, FAX: (323) 953-5661, E-Mail: viewerservices@kcet.org, Web Site: www.kcet.org (1)

KCI Communications Inc, Falls Church, VA. Tel: (703) 394-4931, FAX: (703) 905-8100, Web Site: www.kci-com.com (17)

KCMS, Upper Marlboro, MD. Tel: (301) 853-1300, FAX: (301) 853-1390, Web Site: www.kcms.com (21)

KEH.com, Smyrna, GA. Tel: (770) 333-4200, (800) 342-5534, FAX: (770) 333-4242, E-Mail: sales@keh.com, Web Site: www.keh.com (16)

KET, Lexington, KY. Tel: (859) 258-7000, (800) 432-0951, FAX: (606) 258-7396, E-Mail: rgriffin@ket.org, Web Site: www.ket.org (17)

KHL Engineered Packaging Solutions, Buena Park, CA. Tel: (714) 690-6361 (16)

KICU-TV, San Jose, CA. Tel: (408) 953-3636, FAX: (408) 953-3610, Web Site: www.ktvu.com (32)

KMA Direct Communications, Dallas, TX. Tel: (972) 244-1900, FAX: (972) 244-1901, E-Mail: sales@kma.com, Web Site: www.kma.com (1)

KNG Inc, Nampa, ID. Tel: (208) 318-0188, Web Site: www.kng.com (34)

KPBS FM/TV, San Diego, CA. Tel: (619) 594-1515, Web Site: www.kpbs.org (1)

KPR, New York, NY. Tel: (212) 856-8400, FAX: (212) 856-8660, Web Site: www.kprny.com (35)

KTM Sportmotorcycle USA Inc, Amherst, OH. Tel: (440) 985-3553, FAX: (440) 985-3060, Web Site: www.ktmusa.com (16)

KTVU Retail Services, Oakland, CA. Tel: (510) 874-0228, FAX: (510) 874-0229, Web Site: www.ktvu.com (32)

KV Vet Supply Co, Inc, David City, NE. Tel: (402) 367-6047, Web Site: www.kvvet.com (5)

KWHY-TV Channel 22, Burbank, CA. Tel: (213) 344-3700, E-Mail: info@canal22.tv, Web Site: www.kwhy.com (32)

KXEN, San Francisco, CA. Tel: (415) 904-4160, Web Site: www.kxen.com (22)

KZS Advertising, Smithtown, NY. Tel: (651) 348-1440, FAX: (631) 348-1449, Web Site: www.kzsadvertising.com (35)

Kabakow, Ed, Media People Inc, New York, NY. Tel: (212) 779-7172, FAX: (212) 779-7248, Web Site: www.mediapeople.com (31)

Kabakow, James, Media Horizons Inc, Norwalk, CT. Tel: (203) 857-0770, FAX: (203) 857-0296, E-Mail: mhict@mediahorizons.com, Web Site: www.mediahorizons.com (21)

Kabat, Kevin, T., Fifth Third Bank, Cincinnati, OH. Tel: (800) 972-3030, FAX: (231) 922-4060, Web Site: www.53.com (14)

Kable Fulfillment Services, Mount Morris, IL. Tel: (815) 734-4151, FAX: (815) 734-5228 (22)

Kachain, Harry, Graphic Communications Center, Appleton, WI. Tel: (920) 733-4483, (800) 422-3696, FAX: (920) 733-1700 (27)

Kackley, Brent, Rootblast International, Canton, OH. Tel: (330) 453-5828, FAX: (330) 453-5170, Web Site: www.rootblast.cc (32)

Kaczkowski, Mark, Kraft Foods/Gevalia Kaffe, Tarrytown, NY. Tel: (914) 335-4239, Web Site: www.gevalia.com (16)

Kaczynski, Mark, Nissan Motor Acceptance Corp, Irving, TX. Tel: (800) 647-7261, Web Site: www.nissanusa.com (14)

Kadant Johnson Inc, Three Rivers, MI. Tel: (269) 278-1715, FAX: (269) 279-5980, Web Site: www.kadantjohnson.com (16)

Kaenel, Bob, Sunrise Medical Inc, Boulder, CO. Tel: (303) 218-4500, (800) 333-4000, FAX: (303) 218-4949, Web Site: www.sunrisemedical.com (16)

Kagel, David, Magnet LLC, Washington, MO. Tel: (636) 239-5661, (800) 458-9457, FAX: (636) 239-4490, E-Mail: contactus@themagnetgroup.com, Web Site: www.magnetllc.com (16)

Kahan, Ronald, Ariss Kahan Database Marketing Group Inc, Englewood, CO. Tel: (303) 368-9800, FAX: (720) 274-5000, E-Mail: info@dbmktg.com, Web Site: www.arisskahan.com (35)

Ariss Kahan Database Marketing Group Inc, Englewood, CO. Tel: (303) 368-9800, FAX: (720) 274-5000, E-Mail: info@dbmktg.com, Web Site: www.arisskahan.com (35)

Kahana, Yoram, Shooting Star International, Hollywood, CA. Tel: (323) 469-2020, FAX: (323) 464-0880, Web Site: www.shootingstaragency.com (38)

Kahl, Jean, Securitec Publications, Germantown, WI. Tel: (262) 532-4000, (800) 783-2145, FAX: (262) 532-4001, E-Mail: securitec@securitec.com (7)

Kahle, Rita, D., Ace Hardware Corp, Oak Brook, IL. Tel: (630) 990-6600, FAX: (630) 990-6838, Web Site: www.acehardware.com (16)

Kahler, Michael, E., Poly One Corp, Avon Lake, OH. Tel: (440) 930-1000, (866) POLY-ONE, FAX: (440) 930-1428, Web Site: www.polyone.com (16)

Kahlow, Thad, BusinessOnline, San Diego, CA. Tel: (619) 699-0767, Web Site: www.businessol.com (16)

Kahn, Ellis, Media Response Inc, Hollywood, FL. Tel: (954) 967-9899, (888) 801-9899, FAX: (954) 967-9321, E-Mail: info@media-response.com, Web Site: www.media-response.com (35)

Kahn, Harold, D., DWS Investments Service Co, Kansas City, MO. Tel: (800) 543-5776, Web Site: www.dws-investments.com (14)

Kahn, Kenneth, The Dartnell Corp, Naples, FL. Tel: (585) 240-7301, (800) 447-4030, FAX: (585) 292-4392, E-Mail: customerservice@dartnellcorp.com, Web Site: www.dartnellcorp.com (17)

Kahn, Stephen, Stark Brothers Fulfillment Services, Louisiana, MO. Tel: (573) 754-5511, (800) 325-4180, FAX: (573) 754-5290, E-Mail: info@starkbros.com, Web Site: www.starkbros.com (8)

Kahn, Vicky, truTV, New York, NY. Tel: (212) 973-2800, FAX: (212) 973-3210, Web Site: www.trutv.com (17)

Kahren, John, Sterling Fluid Systems, Indianapolis, IN. Tel: (317) 925-9661, (800) 879-0182, FAX: (317) 924-7388, Web Site: www.peerlesspump.com (16)

Kahwaty, Patti, Penton Learning Systems Inc, New York, NY. Tel: (212) 885-2700, FAX: (212) 885-2703, E-Mail: info@iqpc.com, Web Site: www.iqpc.com (16)

Kaigler, Denise, Reebok International Ltd, Canton, MA. Tel: (781) 401-5000, (800) 843-4444, FAX: (781) 401-4402, Web Site: www.reebok.com (2)

Kail, Marilyn, Marc USA, Pittsburgh, PA. Tel: (412) 562-2015, FAX: (412) 562-2022, Web Site: www.marcusa.com (35)

Kaill, David, Photoworks, Cleveland, OH. Tel: (206) 281-1390, (800) PHOTOWORKS, FAX: (206) 284-5357, E-Mail: info@photoworks.com, Web Site: www.photoworks.com (16)

Kaines, Ellen, National Bulk Equipment Inc, Holland, MI. Tel: (616) 399-2220, FAX: (616) 399-7365, E-Mail: sales@nbe-inc.com, Web Site: www.nbe-inc.com (16)

Kaiser, Bonnie, Printing + Quick Copy, Philadelphia, PA. Tel: (215) 331-5999 (27)

Kaiser, Ed, Polyline LLC, Elmhurst, IL. Tel: (630) 993-2700, (800) 701-3865, FAX: (800) 816-3330, Web Site: www.polylinecorp.com (3)

Kaiser, Gina, Florida Today, Melbourne, FL. Tel: (321) 242-3500, (877) 424-0156, FAX: (321) 242-3729, Web Site: www.floridatoday.com (17)

Kaiser, Jane, Eclipse Direct Marketing, Mineola, NY. Tel: (212) 931-8344, FAX: (212) 931-8377, E-Mail: jkaiser@eclipsedm.com, Web Site: www.eclipsedm.com (23)

Kaiser, Joseph, B., USI Affinity, Philadelphia, PA. Tel: (610) 833-2876, (800) 625-2876, FAX: (610) 265-2876, E-Mail: info@usiaffinity.com, Web Site: www.brcorp.com (15)

Kaiser, Peter, The Kaiser Group Inc, Waukesha, WI. Tel: (262) 544-4971, FAX: (262) 544-6271, Web Site: www.kaisergrp.com (20)

Kaiser, Ray, Polyline LLC, Elmhurst, IL. Tel: (630) 993-2700, (800) 701-3865, FAX: (800) 816-3330, Web Site: www.polylinecorp.com (3)

Kaiser, Winfried, Champion, Quincy, IL. Tel: (217) 222-5400, FAX: (217) 228-8260, Web Site: www.championpneumatic.com (16)

Kaiser Foundation Health Plan of the Mid-Atlantic States Inc, Rockville, MD. Tel: (301) 816-5641, Web Site: kp.org (1)

The Kaiser Group Inc, Waukesha, WI. Tel: (262) 544-4971, FAX: (262) 544-6271, Web Site: www.kaisergrp.com (20)

Kaitz, James A., Association for Financial Professionals, Bethesda, MD. Tel: (301) 907-2862, FAX: (301) 907-2864, Web Site: www.afponline.org (14)

Kakalik, John, Western Connecticut State University, Danbury, CT. Tel: (203) 837-8200, FAX: (203) 837-8527, E-Mail: hills@wcsu.edu, Web Site: www.wcsu.edu (41)

Kalafa, Victor, Cross Country Travcorps, Boca Raton, FL. Tel: (800) 530-6125, FAX: (561) 998-8533, Web Site: www.crosscountrytravcorps.com (16)

Kalb, Ben, Ben Kalb Productions, Las Vegas, NV. Tel: (702) 871-8787, FAX: (702) 597-0741, E-Mail: benkalb@benkalbproductions.com, Web Site: www.benkalbproductions.com (32)

Ben Kalb Productions, Las Vegas, NV. Tel: (702) 871-8787, FAX: (702) 597-0741, E-Mail: benkalb@benkalbproductions.com, Web Site: www.benkalbproductions.com (32)

Kalian, Dennis, The Roblin Group Inc, White Plains, NY. Tel: (914) 686-7221, FAX: (914) 372-1028, E-Mail: freethingsusa@yahoo.com, Web Site: www.freethingsusa.com (17)

Kalian, Linda, The Roblin Group Inc, White Plains, NY. Tel: (914) 686-7221, FAX: (914) 372-1028, E-Mail: freethingsusa@yahoo.com, Web Site: www.freethingsusa.com (17)

Kalian, Robert, The Roblin Group Inc, White Plains, NY. Tel: (914) 686-7221, FAX: (914) 372-1028, E-Mail: freethingsusa@yahoo.com, Web Site: www.freethingsusa.com (17)

Kalinka, John, Foremost Insurance Group, Grand Rapids, MI. Tel: (616) 956-8241, (800) 527-3905, FAX: (800) 325-1507, Web Site: www.foremost.com (15)

Kalischer, Clemens, Image Photos/Clemens Kalischer, Stockbridge, MA. Tel: (413) 298-5500, FAX: (413) 298-5500, E-Mail: inform@bcn.net (38)

Kalish, Kurt, Magnets 4 Media, Washington, MO. Tel: (843) 216-6665, (800) 642-6384, FAX: (636) 390-5147, E-Mail: sales@magnets4media.com, Web Site: www.magnets4media.com (30)

Kallenberg, Jim, MPBS Industries, Los Angeles, CA. Tel: (323) 268-8514, (800) 421-6265, FAX: (323) 268-6305, Web Site: www.mpbs.com (16)

Kallet, Stephen, The List Authority Inc, Westwood, NJ. Tel: (201) 666-0100 (24)

Kalmbach Publishing Co, Waukesha, WI. Tel: (262) 796-8776, (800) 558-1544, FAX: (262) 796-1143, Web Site: www.kalmbach.com (17)

Kalmed Dental Products Inc, Marietta, GA. Tel: (770) 971-8815, (800) 322-8815, FAX: (770) 509-8823, E-Mail: sales@kalmed.com, Web Site: www.kalmed.com (7)

Kalra-ali, Sonia, Daily Commercial News & Construction Record, Markham, ON. Tel: (905) 752-5408, (800) 465-6475, FAX: (888) 396-9413, (905) 752-5450, E-Mail: dcnonl@reedbusiness.com, Web Site: www.dcnonl.com (17)

Kalt, Bernard, School Annual Publishing Co, State College, PA. Tel: (800) 436-6030, E-Mail: yearbook@schoolannual.com, Web Site: www.schoolannual.com (17)

Kalter, Dr. Marjorie, New York University, New York, NY. Tel: (212) 992-3221, Web Site: www.scps.nyu.edu (1)

Kalunian, Shannon, Mitsubishi Motor Sales of America Inc, Cypress, CA. Tel: (714) 372-6000, FAX: (714) 373-1736, Web Site: www.mitsubishicars.com (1)

Kam, Karl, International Advertising Association, New York, NY. Tel: (212) 557-1133, FAX: (212) 983-0455, E-Mail: membership@iaaglobal.com, Web Site: www.iaaglobal.org (1)

Kamenz, Ina, B., Thermo Fisher Scientific I, Waltham, MA. Tel: (781) 622-1000, (800) 678-5599, FAX: (781) 622-1207, Web Site: www.thermofisher.com (9)

Kamgar, Fred, Smith & Noble, Corona, CA. Tel: (909) 734-4444, (800) 248-8888, FAX: (800) 426-7780, E-Mail: contactus@smithnoble.com, Web Site: www.smithandnoble.com (8)

Kamil, Harvey, Puritan's Pride, Ronkonkoma, NY. Tel: (631) 567-9500, FAX: (631) 471-5693, E-Mail: info@puritan.com, Web Site: www.puritan.com (7)

Kamin, John, V., Forecaster Publishing Co Inc, Tarzana, CA. Tel: (818) 345-4421 (14)

Kamp, Lorraine, Suarez Corp Industries, North Canton, OH. Tel: (330) 494-5504, FAX: (330) 497-6837, E-Mail: suarez@suarez.com, Web Site: www.suarez.com (5)

Kampars, John, Intra Business Systems Inc, South Bend, IN. Tel: (574) 257-7940, FAX: (574) 257-7944, E-Mail: info@intrabusinesssystems.com, Web Site: www.intrabusinesssystems.com (16)

Kampfer, Thomas, Iomega Corp, Roy, UT. Tel: (801) 332-1000, (888) 446-6342, FAX: (801) 332-3158, Web Site: www.iomega.com (16)

Kan, David, Mustek Inc, Tustin, CA. Tel: (949) 790-3800, FAX: (949) 788-3670, Web Site: www.mustek.com (3)

Kananowicz, Cheryl, DST Output, South Windsor, CT. Tel: (860) 290-7337, (800) 441-7587, Web Site: www.dstoutput.com (28)

Kandrach, Chuck, The Plain Dealer, Cleveland, OH. Tel: (216) 999-5000, FAX: (216) 999-6356, Web Site: www.plaindealer.com (18)

Kane, Bob, McBee, Lancaster, CA. Tel: (973) 263-3225, (800) 878-9443, (800) 662-2331, FAX: (973) 263-8165, E-Mail: info@mcbeeinc.com, Web Site: www.mcbeeweb.com (10)

Kane, Rachel, Perennial Pleasures Nursery, East Hardwick, VT. Tel: (802) 472-5104, FAX: (802) 472-6572, E-Mail: annex@perennialpleasures.net, Web Site: www.antiqueplants.com (8)

Kaneda, Hiroo, Sunstar, Chicago, IL. Tel: (773) 777-4000, FAX: (773) 777-1417, E-Mail: dominico@sunstar.com, Web Site: www.sunstar.com (16)

Kaneshiro, June, Bank of Hawaii, Honolulu, HI. Tel: (808) 537-8398, FAX: (808) 536-9433, Web Site: www.boh.com (14)

Kaneva, Nadia, Iris Shokoff Associates, New York, NY. Tel: (212) 295-9191, FAX: (212) 293-3779 (31)

Kaney, Howard, West Bend, West Bend, WI. Tel: (262) 334-5107, (866) 290-1851, FAX: (262) 334-6800, Web Site: www.focuselectrics.com (16)

Kanfer, Ronald, Response Dynamics Inc, Vienna, VA. Tel: (703) 442-7595, FAX: (703) 790-8564 (35)

Kang & Lee Advertising Inc/K&L Brief, New York, NY. Tel: (212) 375-8111, FAX: (212) 375-8255, E-Mail: info@kanglee.com, Web Site: www.kanglee.com (35)

Kangaju, Eustace, Temple University, Philadelphia, PA. Tel: (215) 204-7282, FAX: (215) 204-4554, Web Site: www.sbm.temple.edu (41)

Kanganis, George T., FTD Group Inc, Downers Grove, IL. Tel: (630) 719-7800, (800) 788-9000, FAX: (630) 719-6170, E-Mail: ftdmemberservices@ftdi.com, Web Site: www.ftdi.com (29)

Kani, Brick, Creative Learning Systems Inc, Longmont, CO. Tel: (800) 458-2880, FAX: (760) 546-1490, Web Site: www.clsinc.com (9)

Kannan, Victor, American Megatrends Inc, Norcross, GA. Tel: (770) 246-8600, (800) 828-9264, FAX: (770) 246-8790, Web Site: www.ami.com (3)

Kannett, Jeff, Irving Kannett & Associates Inc, Morton Grove, IL. Tel: (847) 965-8810, FAX: (847) 965-8826, Web Site: www.kannett.com (33)

Irving Kannett & Associates Inc, Morton Grove, IL. Tel: (847) 965-8810, FAX: (847) 965-8826, Web Site: www.kannett.com (33)

Kannon Consulting Inc, Chicago, IL. Tel: (312) 346-2244, FAX: (312) 346-3665, Web Site: www.kannon.com (20)

Kano Laboratories, Nashville, TN. Tel: (615) 833-4101, (800) 311-3374, FAX: (615) 833-5790, Web Site: www.kanolabs.com (16)

Kanodia, Rahul, L., Datamatics Technologies, Burlington, MA. Tel: (781) 425-5240, FAX: (781) 425-5232, Web Site: www.datamaticstech.com (22)

Kansas City Chiefs, Kansas City, MO. Tel: (816) 920-9300, (888) 99-CHIEFS, FAX: (816) 923-4719, Web Site: www.kcchiefs.com (16)

Kansas City Direct Marketing Association, Kansas City, MO. Tel: (816) 561-5323, FAX: (816) 561-1991, E-Mail: info@kcdma.org, Web Site: www.kcdma.org (40)

Kansas State University Division of Continuing Education, Manhattan, KS. Tel: (785) 532-5888, Web Site: www.dce.ksu.edu (41)

Kanter, David, AccuList Inc, Ventura, CA. Tel: (805) 644-1966, Web Site: www.acculist.com (23)

Kantor, Russell, Tamrac Inc, Chatsworth, CA. Tel: (818) 407-9500, Web Site: www.tamrac.com (2)

Kantrowitz, Jonathan, Queue Inc, Stratford, CT. Tel: (203) 335-0906, (800) 232-2224, FAX: (800) 775-2729, E-Mail: jdk@queueinc.com, Web Site: www.qworkbooks.com (17)

Kao, An-Chian, Village Software Inc, Boston, MA. Tel: (617) 695-9332, (800) 724-9332, FAX: (617) 695-1935, E-Mail: requests@villagesoft.com, Web Site: www.villagesoft.com (3)

Kao, Richard, H., School of Business & Economics, Los Angeles, CA. Tel: (323) 343-2800, FAX: (323) 343-2813, Web Site: cbe.calstatela.edu (41)

Kao Brands, Cincinnati, OH. Tel: (512) 455-5432, Web Site: www.kaobrands.com (9)

Kapelke, Steve, Columbia College Chicago, Chicago, IL. Tel: (312) 663-1600, FAX: (312) 344-0869, Web Site: www.colum.edu (41)

Kaplan, Bill, FreshAddress Inc, Newton, MA. Tel: (617) 965-4500, (800) 321-3009, FAX: (617) 965-4551, Web Site: www.freshaddress.com (22)

Kaplan, Bo, Toys To Grow On, Carson, CA. Tel: (310) 537-8600, (800) 874-4242, FAX: (800) 537-5403, E-Mail: toyinfo@toystogrowon.com, Web Site: www.ttgo.com (11)

Kaplan, Charles, Toys To Grow On, Carson, CA. Tel: (310) 537-8600, (800) 874-4242, FAX: (800) 537-5403, E-Mail: toyinfo@toystogrowon.com, Web Site: www.ttgo.com (11)

Kaplan, David, Tafford Uniforms, Montgomeryville, PA. Tel: (215) 643-9666, E-Mail: customerservice@tafford.com, Web Site: www.tafford.com (2)

Kaplan, Joel, S., B'nai B'rith International, Washington, DC. Tel: (202) 857-6600, FAX: (202) 857-6609, E-Mail: internet@bnaibrith.org, Web Site: www.bnaibrith.org (1)

Kaplan, Jon, E., TeleDevelopment Services Inc, Richfield, OH. Tel: (330) 659-4441, FAX: (330) 659-4442, E-Mail: jkaplan@teledevelopment.com, Web Site: www.teledevelopment.com (20)

Kaplan, Larry, Tele Business USA, Northbrook, IL. Tel: (847) 480-1560, FAX: (847) 897-4120, Web Site: www.tbiz.com (29)

Kaplan, Leon, ABCO Inc, Dallas, TX. Tel: (214) 565-5250, Web Site: www.abcoinc.com (20)

Kaplan, Louis, Fran's Basket House, Inc, Succasunna, NJ. Tel: (973) 584-2230, (800) 372-6799, FAX: (973) 584-7446, E-Mail: inquiry@franswicker.com, Web Site: www.franswicker.com (8)

Kaplan, Michael, Toys To Grow On, Carson, CA. Tel: (310) 537-8600, (800) 874-4242, FAX: (800) 537-5403, E-Mail: toyinfo@toystogrowon.com, Web Site: www.ttgo.com (11)

Kaplan, Stuart R., US Games Systems Inc, Stamford, CT. Tel: (203) 353-8400, (800) 544-2637, FAX: (203) 353-8431, Web Site: www.usgamesinc.com (11)

Kaplan Inc, New York, NY. Tel: (212) 492-5800, (800) 527-8378, FAX: (212) 492-5933, Web Site: www.kaplan.com (16)

Kaplan Publishing, Chicago, IL. Tel: (312) 606-8905, (800) 245-2665, FAX: (312) 606-8985, E-Mail: kaplanorders@kaplan.com, Web Site: www.kaplanpublishing.com (17)

Kaplan Test Prep & Admissions, New York, NY. Tel: (212) 997-5800, Web Site: www.kaptest.com (1)

Kaporis, Kathy, Taylor Capital Group, Inc, Rosemont, IL. Tel: (847) 653-7978, FAX: (847) 653-7890, E-Mail: investor.relations@coletaylor.com, Web Site: www.taylorcapitalgroup.com (14)

Kapotes, Jim, The Lifestyle Marketing Corp, Glen Rock, NJ. Tel: (201) 670-7985, FAX: (201) 251-2443 (35)

Kappa Publishing Group, Blue Bell, PA. Tel: (215) 643-6385, FAX: (215) 628-3571, Web Site: www.kappapublishing.com (17)

Kappa Studios, Burbank, CA. Tel: (818) 843-3400, FAX: (818) 559-2418, E-Mail: info@kappastudios.com, Web Site: www.kappastudios.com (32)

Kappelman, Peter, Land O' Lakes Inc, Arden Hills, MN. Tel: (651) 481-2222, (800) 328-9680, FAX: (651) 481-2000, Web Site: www.landolakes.com (16)

Kappler, George, Kappler Protective Apparel & Fabrics, Guntersville, AL. Tel: (256) 505-4005, (800) 600-4019, FAX: (256) 505-4151, E-Mail: usa@kappler.com, Web Site: www.kappler.com (2)

Kappler Protective Apparel & Fabrics, Guntersville, AL. Tel: (256) 505-4005, (800) 600-4019, FAX: (256) 505-4151, E-Mail: usa@kappler.com, Web Site: www.kappler.com (2)

Kapur, Rajeev, Smarthome, Irvine, CA. Tel: (949) 221-9200, (800) 762-7846, FAX: (949) 221-9240, E-Mail: feedback@smarthome.com, Web Site: www.smarthome.com (32)

Kapur, Sundeep, Vermont/New Hampshire Direct Marketing Group, Woodstock, VT. Tel: (802) 457-2807, FAX: (802) 457-2807, E-Mail: vtnhmg@vtnhmg, Web Site: www.vtnhmg.org (40)

Karaban, Glenn, Karaban Labiner Associates, New York, NY. Tel: (212) 840-0660, FAX: (212) 944-1884, E-Mail: gkaraban@klapublishing.com, Web Site: www.klapublishing.com (31)

Karaban Labiner Associates, New York, NY. Tel: (212) 840-0660, FAX: (212) 944-1884, E-Mail: gkaraban@klapublishing.com, Web Site: www.klapublishing.com (31)

Karasea Inc, Hastings On Hudson, NY. Tel: (914) 646-4481 (35)

Karasz, Larry, Data Cal Corp, Gilbert, AZ. Tel: (480) 813-3100, (800) 223-0123, FAX: (480) 545-8090, E-Mail: info@datacal.com, Web Site: www.datacal.com (16)

Karcy, Bob, VIEW Video Inc/Arcadia Entertainment Corp, Saugerties, NY. Tel: (845) 246-9955, FAX: (845) 246-9966, E-Mail: sales@view.com, Web Site: www.view.com (16)

Kardash, William J., Columbia Direct Marketing Corp, Annapolis, MD. Tel: (410) 268-8881, FAX: (410) 268-8999 (35)

Kari, Ross, Safeco Insurance Co, Seattle, WA. Tel: (206) 545-5000, (800) 332-3226, FAX: (206) 545-5767/5651, Web Site: www.safeco.com (15)

Karl, Bob, New Customer Acquisition, Medford, OR. Tel: (541) 779-9999, FAX: (541) 779-1935, E-Mail: bobk@postage-exempt.com (31)

Walter Karl Inc, Pearl River, NY. Tel: (845) 620-0700, FAX: (845) 620-1885, E-Mail: info@walterkarl.infousa.com, Web Site: www.walterkarl.com (22)

Karlen, Cindi, Karlen Design, San Luis Obispo, CA. Tel: (805) 541-6561, E-Mail: info@karlendesign.com, Web Site: www.karlendesign.com (35)

Karlen Design, San Luis Obispo, CA. Tel: (805) 541-6561, E-Mail: info@karlendesign.com, Web Site: www.karlendesign.com (35)

Karlstad Flom, Linda, Midwest Technology Products & Services, Sioux City, IA. Tel: (712) 252-3601, (800) 831-5904, FAX: (800) 258-7054, E-Mail: web@midwesttechnology.com, Web Site: www.midwesttechnology.com (9)

Karmele, Gerald, Freestyle Photographic Supplies, Los Angeles, CA. Tel: (323) 660-3640, Web Site: www.freestylephoto.biz (5)

Karnan, Parker, Brooks Sports Inc, Bothell, WA. Tel: (425) 402-1632, (800) 2 BROOKS, FAX: (425) 489-1975, Web Site: www.brooksrunning.com (16)

Karol Media, Wilkes-Barre, PA. Tel: (570) 822-8899, (800) 526-4773, FAX: (570) 822-8226, Web Site: www.karolmedia.com (28)

Karow, Al, TruGreen/ChemLawn, Lewis Center, OH. Tel: (614) 846-1800, (800) TRUE-GREEN, FAX: (614) 431-0155, Web Site: www.trugreen.com (16)

Karp, Dan, Wyse Direct, Cleveland, OH. Tel: (216) 696-2427, FAX: (216) 736-4440, Web Site: www.wysedirect.com (35)

Karpowicz, Paul, Meredith Corp, Des Moines, IA. Tel: (515) 284-3000, FAX: (515) 284-2700, Web Site: www.meredith.com (17)

Karren, Boyd, Oliver Russell & Associates, Boise, ID. Tel: (208) 344-1734, FAX: (208) 344-1211, Web Site: www.oliverrussell.com (35)

Karschner, Christi, Bowling, Tender Heart Treasures, Omaha, NE. Tel: (402) 593-1313, (800) 443-1367, FAX: (402) 593-1316, E-Mail: bcamenzind@thtdesigns.com (6)

Karstedt, Chris, Bowers & Merena Auctions, Irvine, CA. Tel: (949) 253-0916, (800) 458-4646, FAX: (949) 253-4091, E-Mail: auction@bowersandmerena.com, Web Site: www.bowersandmerena.com (16)

Karten, Stuart, Stuart Karten Design, Marina Del Rey, CA. Tel: (310) 827-8722, FAX: (310) 821-4492, Web Site: www.kartendesign.com (36)

Kartsounes, George, Manufacturers-News Inc, Evanston, IL. Tel: (847) 864-7000, (888) 752-5200, FAX: (847) 332-1100, E-Mail: hdubin@manufacturersnews.com, Web Site: www.manufacturersnews.com (23)

Kartsounes, Scott, Manufacturers-News Inc, Evanston, IL. Tel: (847) 864-7000, (888) 752-5200, FAX: (847) 332-1100, E-Mail: hdubin@manufacturersnews.com, Web Site: www.manufacturersnews.com (23)

Kartychak, Darr, Intermedia Consultants Inc, Princeton, NJ. Tel: (609) 430-8460, Web Site: http://iprintmedia.com (35)

Kasander, Bonnie, Encore Marketing International, Lanham, MD. Tel: (301) 459-8020, (800) 846-9398, FAX: (301) 731-0525, E-Mail: customerservice@encoremarketing.com, Web Site: www.encoremarketing.com (16)

Kasanders, Paul, Visible Computer Supply Corp, Saint Charles, IL. Tel: (630) 377-2586, (800) 323-0628, FAX: (800) 233-2016, Web Site: www.wallace.com (16)

Kashan, Robert, L.P. THEBAULT CO., Parsippany, NJ. Tel: (973) 884-1300, FAX: (973) 952-8296, Web Site: www.earthcolor.com (27)

Kasower, Adam, Mighty Net Inc, Calabasas, CA. Tel: (818) 407-4620, FAX: (818) 407-4630, E-Mail: info@mightynet.com, Web Site: www.mightynet.com (35)

Kasp, Gladys, Promotional Product Professionals of Canada, Saint-Laurent, PQ. Tel: (514) 489-5359, FAX: (514) 489-7760, (800) 489-8741, E-Mail: gladys@pppc.ca, Web Site: www.pppc.ca (1)

Kasper, Joan, National Association for Printing Leadership, East Rutherford, NJ. Tel: (201) 634-9600, (800) 642-6275, FAX: (201) 634-0324, Web Site: www.napl.org (1)

Kasper, Robert, Informed Sources Inc, Plainview, NY. Tel: (800) 201-6060, FAX: (516) 576-0249, E-Mail: info@informed-sources.com, Web Site: www.informed-sources.com (30)

Kassel, Norman, Nationwide Beauty & Barber Supply, Syracuse, NY. Tel: (315) 446-9026, FAX: (315) 446-8943, E-Mail: sales@nationwidebeauty.com, Web Site: www.nationwidebeauty.com (16)

Kassel, Richard, Nationwide Beauty & Barber Supply, Syracuse, NY. Tel: (315) 446-9026, FAX: (315) 446-8943, E-Mail: sales@nationwidebeauty.com, Web Site: www.nationwidebeauty.com (16)

Kasten, Alan, United States Bronze Sign Co Inc, New Hyde Park, NY. Tel: (516) 352-5155, FAX: (516) 352-1761, Web Site: www.usbronze.com (1)

Kasten, Peter, United States Bronze Sign Co Inc, New Hyde Park, NY. Tel: (516) 352-5155, FAX: (516) 352-1761, Web Site: www.usbronze.com (1)

Kastning, Tracy, Saunders Manufacturing Co Inc, Readfield, ME. Tel: (207) 685-3385, (800) 341-4674, FAX: (207) 685-9918, E-Mail: jsherwood@saunders-usa.com, Web Site: www.saunders-usa.com (16)

Katalin, Spencer, Spear Engineering Co, Colorado Springs, CO. Tel: (719) 471-9850 (16)

Katchian, Sonia, Photo Shuttle Japan, Chapel Hill, NC. Tel: (919) 967-1585, E-Mail: sonia@photoshuttle.com, Web Site: www.photoshuttle.com (37)

Katchur, Bryan J., Woodcraft Supply Corp LLC, Parkersburg, WV. Tel: (304) 422-5412, (800) 344-3348, FAX: (304) 422-5417, Web Site: www.woodcraft.com (9)

Katkin, Eli, HHC Direct, San Diego, CA. Tel: (800) 358-8765, FAX: (619) 220-0988, Web Site: www.hhcdirect.com (35)

Katner, Katherine, J., DKP & Associates, Inc, Skokie, IL. Tel: (847) 933-9808, E-Mail: dpearlman@dkpassociates.com, Web Site: www.dkpassociates.com (22)

Kato, Hisatoyo, Fuji Photo Film USA, Valhalla, NY. Tel: (914) 789-8100, (800) 755-3854, FAX: (914) 789-8295, Web Site: www.fujifilmusa.com (16)

Katri, Cindy, Pitney Bowes International Mail Services, Newark, NJ. Tel: (800) 521-0080, FAX: (973) 368-6301, E-Mail: marketing@pb.com, Web Site: www.intmail.com (28)

Katsuyoshi, Dan, Roland Products Inc, Los Angeles, CA. Tel: (323) 731-1111, FAX: (323) 731-9585, E-Mail: salesinfo@rolandinc.com, Web Site: www.rolandinc.com (16)

Katt, Heather, Allergan Inc, Irvine, CA. Tel: (714) 246-4500, (800) 433-8871, FAX: (714) 246-4971, Web Site: www.allergan.com (16)

Katz, Andrew, Nice Lines Direct Mail, Norristown, PA. Tel: (610) 279-1100, (888) 815-NICE, FAX: (610) 279-7800, Web Site: www.nicelines.com (21)

Katz, Andrew, PetEdge, Beverly, MA. Tel: (978) 998-8100, (800) 738-3343, FAX: (978) 887-8499, E-Mail: support@petedge.com, Web Site: www.petedge.com (16)

Katz, Ed, Choice Courier Systems Inc, New York, NY. Tel: (212) 370-1999, FAX: (212) 370-0440, Web Site: www.choicecourier.com (16)

Katz, Josef, Trump University, New York, NY. Web Site: www.trumpuniversity.com (13)

Katz, Karen, Neiman-Marcus Group, Dallas, TX. Tel: (214) 743-7600, (888) 888-4757, FAX: (214) 573-5320, Web Site: www.neimanmarcus.com (8)

Katz, Leslie, American Speech-Language-Hearing Association, Rockville, MD. Tel: (301) 897-5700, (800) 638-8255, E-Mail: productsales@asha.org, Web Site: www.asha.org (1)

Katz, Michael, Choice Courier Systems Inc, New York, NY. Tel: (212) 370-1999, FAX: (212) 370-0440, Web Site: www.choicecourier.com (16)

Katz, Mory, Response Insurance, Scranton, PA. Tel: (203) 634-7255, (800) 518-2984, FAX: (203) 634-7319, E-Mail: webcs@response.com, Web Site: www.response.com (15)

Katz, Paul, PartyLite Gifts Inc, Plymouth, MA. Tel: (508) 830-3100, FAX: (508) 830-0026, Web Site: www.partylite.com (8)

Katz, Robert, Easy Analytic Software Inc, Fresh Meadows, NY. Tel: (718) 740-7930, Web Site: www.easidemographics.com (22)

Katz, Stan, ACBL, Horn Lake, MS. Tel: (901) 332-5586, FAX: (901) 398-7754, E-Mail: service@acbl.org, Web Site: www.acbl.org (1)

Katz Dochtermann & Epstein, New York, NY. Tel: (212) 686-0006, FAX: (212) 686-6991, E-Mail: info@kdande.com, Web Site: www.kdande.com (35)

Katz Television Direct Response, New York, NY. Tel: (212) 424-6124, FAX: (212) 424-6130, E-Mail: chickie.bucco@katz-media.com, Web Site: www.katzdirect.com (32)

Katzenberg, Jeffrey, Motion Picture & Television Fund Foundation, Woodland Hills, CA. Tel: (818) 876-1888, Web Site: www.mptvfund.org (1)

Kaufman, Jay, Paragon Laboratories, Torrance, CA. Tel: (310) 370-1563, (800) 231-3670, FAX: (310) 370-7354, E-Mail: sales@paragonlabsusa.com, Web Site: www.paragonlabsusa.com (16)

Kaufman, Julie, The Popcorn Factory, Lake Forest, IL. Tel: (847) 362-0028, (888) 216-0235, FAX: (888) 333-4595, E-Mail: service@thepopcornfactory.com, Web Site: www.thepopcornfactory.com (4)

Kaufman, Kenneth, A., Omni Print Inc, Lanham, MD. Tel: (301) 731-7000, FAX: (301) 731-7001, E-Mail: info@omniprint.net, Web Site: www.omniprint.net (27)

Kaufman, Lois, Environmental Research Associates, Princeton, NJ. Tel: (609) 683-4860, FAX: (609) 683-8398 (30)

Kaufman, Pete, Valentine Research Inc, Cincinnati, OH. Tel: (513) 984-8900, (800) 331-3030, FAX: (513) 984-8976, E-Mail: sales@valentine1.com, Web Site: www.valentine1.com (16)

Kaufman, Richard, Paragon Laboratories, Torrance, CA. Tel: (310) 370-1563, (800) 231-3670, FAX: (310) 370-7354, E-Mail: sales@paragonlabsusa.com, Web Site: www.paragonlabsusa.com (16)

Kaufman, Steve, People for the American Way, Washington, DC. Tel: (202) 467-2352, Web Site: www.pfaw.org (1)

Kaufmann, Dave, Denver Tax Software Inc, Littleton, CO. Tel: (303) 796-7780, (800) 326-6686, FAX: (888) 326-6686, Web Site: www.denvertax.com (16)

Kaul, Ajay, Lenovo, Morrisville, NC. Tel: (919) 257-6315, Web Site: www.uslenovo.com (3)

Kaupanger, Jonathan, International Sign Association International Convention, Alexandria, VA. Tel: (703) 836-4012, (866) WHY-SIGN, FAX: (703) 836-8353, Web Site: www.signs.org (42)

Kaupe, Chris, Tully & Holland Inc, Wellesley, MA. Tel: (781) 239-2900, FAX: (781) 239-2901, E-Mail: info@tullyandholland.com, Web Site: www.tullyandholland.com (14)

Kauppila, John, Duncan Aviation, Lincoln, NE. Tel: (402) 475-2611, (800) 228-4277, FAX: (402) 475-5541, Web Site: www.duncanaviation.com (16)

Kavanagh, Kim, Potpourri Group Inc, Chelmsford, MA. Tel: (978) 256-4100, FAX: (978) 256-1961/0344, Web Site: www.potpourrigroup.com (6)

Kavanaugh, Bridget, M., Crain Communications Inc, Detroit, MI. Tel: (313) 446-6000, FAX: (313) 446-1616, Web Site: www.crain.com (17)

Kavensky, Jodie, CMC & Design, Rock Island, IL. Tel: (309) 786-2888, FAX: (309) 786-9887, E-Mail: cmcanddesign@aol.com (35)

Kawa, Chet, Alco Chemical, Chattanooga, TN. Tel: (423) 629-1405, FAX: (423) 698-8723, Web Site: www.alcochemical.com (16)

Kawalek, Polly, B., The Quaker Oats Co, Chicago, IL. Tel: (312) 821-1000, (800) 367-6287, FAX: (312) 222-8323, Web Site: www.quakeroats.com (16)

Kay, Ian, Janes Information Group, Alexandria, VA. Tel: (703) 683-3700, (800) 824-0768, FAX: (703) 836-0297, Web Site: www.janes.com (17)

Kaye, Paul, I/D/E/A Inc, Caldwell, ID. Tel: (208) 459-6357, (800) 635-9261, FAX: (208) 459-6484, Web Site: www.relyonidea.com (16)

Kaye, Paula, New Income Sources, Hermosa Beach, CA. Tel: (310) 376-9238, (800) 288-7058, FAX: (310) 376-9258, E-Mail: pk@nisdm.com (21)

Kaye, Sandy, Porta-Bote International, Mountain View, CA. Tel: (650) 961-5334, (800) 227-8882, Web Site: www.porta-bote.com (11)

Kaye-Smith, Renton, WA. Tel: (425) 228-8600, (800) 822-9987, FAX: (425) 226-4312, E-Mail: info@ kayesmith.com, Web Site: www.kayesmith.com (21)

Kaylor, Dan, Kaylor's School Supply, Albertville, AL. Tel: (256) 878-1200, (800) 239-9999, FAX: (800) 239-9998, E-Mail: sales@kaylorsinc.com, Web Site: www.kaylorsinc.com (16)

Kaylor, Jesse, Kaylor's School Supply, Albertville, AL. Tel: (256) 878-1200, (800) 239-9999, FAX: (800) 239-9998, E-Mail: sales@kaylorsinc.com, Web Site: www.kaylorsinc.com (16)

Kaylor, Tom, WRS Group Ltd, Waco, TX. Tel: (254) 776-6461, (800) 299-3366, FAX: (888) 977-7653, E-Mail: sales@wrsgroup.com, Web Site: www. wrsgroup.com (7)

Kaylor's School Supply, Albertville, AL. Tel: (256) 878-1200, (800) 239-9999, FAX: (800) 239-9998, E-Mail: sales@kaylorsinc.com, Web Site: www. kaylorsinc.com (16)

Kayne, Catherine, Kayne & Son Custom Hardware Inc, Candler, NC. Tel: (828) 667-8868, FAX: (828) 665-8303, E-Mail: kaynehdwe@charter.net, Web Site: www.customforgedhardware.com (8)

Kayne, David, Kayne & Son Custom Hardware Inc, Candler, NC. Tel: (828) 667-8868, FAX: (828) 665-8303, E-Mail: kaynehdwe@charter.net, Web Site: www.customforgedhardware.com (8)

Kayne, Shirley, Kayne & Son Custom Hardware Inc, Candler, NC. Tel: (828) 667-8868, FAX: (828) 665-8303, E-Mail: kaynehdwe@charter.net, Web Site: www.customforgedhardware.com (8)

Kayne, Steve, Kayne & Son Custom Hardware Inc, Candler, NC. Tel: (828) 667-8868, FAX: (828) 665-8303, E-Mail: kaynehdwe@charter.net, Web Site: www.customforgedhardware.com (8)

Kayne & Son Custom Hardware Inc, Candler, NC. Tel: (828) 667-8868, FAX: (828) 665-8303, E-Mail: kaynehdwe@charter.net, Web Site: www. customforgedhardware.com (8)

Kaynes Jr., Robert, American Bronzing Co, Columbus, OH. Tel: (614) 252-7388, (800) 423-5678, FAX: (614) 252-4602, E-Mail: bronzeinfo@bronshoe. com, Web Site: www.abcbronze.com (16)

Kayser-Roth Corp Inc, Greensboro, NC. Tel: (800) 575-3497, Web Site: www.nononsense.com (2)

Kazantzakis, Nikos, San Francisco State University, San Francisco, CA. Tel: (415) 338-1111, FAX: (415) 338-0501, Web Site: www.sfsu.edu (41)

Keane Jr., John, Life-Study Fellowship Foundation Inc, Darien, CT. Tel: (203) 655-1436, FAX: (203) 655-1392, Web Site: www.lifestudyfellowship.com (17)

Keane, Amy, Dorothy Biddle Service, Greeley, PA. Tel: (570) 226-3239, FAX: (570) 226-0349, E-Mail: info@dorothybiddle.com, Web Site: www. dorothybiddle.com (8)

Keane, Marylee, American Marketing Association/ New York Chapter, New York, NY. Tel: (212) 687-3280, FAX: (212) 557-9242, E-Mail: mlkeane@ nyama.org, Web Site: www.nyama.org (40)

Keane, Michael, Life-Study Fellowship Foundation Inc, Darien, CT. Tel: (203) 655-1436, FAX: (203) 655-1392, Web Site: www.lifestudyfellowship.com (17)

Keane, Robert, VistaPrint USA Inc, Lexington, MA. Tel: (800) 961-2075, Web Site: www.vistaprint. com (27)

Kearney, Jim, Eire Direct, Chicago, IL. Tel: (312) 640-4000, FAX: (312) 640-0324, E-Mail: info@ eiredirect.com, Web Site: www.eiredirect.com (16)

Kearney, Louisa, D., World Press Review, New York, NY. Tel: (212) 982-8880, Web Site: www. worldpressreview.com (16)

Kearns, Bill, Clement Communications, Upper Chichester, PA. Tel: (610) 497-6800, (800) 253-6368, FAX: (610) 497-6806, E-Mail: customerservice@ clement.com, Web Site: www.clement.com; www. bradycorp.com (17)

Kearns, Kim, Cablevision Systems Corp, Bethpage, NY. Tel: (516) 803-2300, FAX: (516) 803-3134, Web Site: www.cablevision.com (16)

Keary, Wayne, Automotive Forms, Baltimore, MD. Tel: (410) 285-3700, FAX: (410) 284-8418, E-Mail: sales@autoforms.com, Web Site: www. autoforms.com (16)

Keary, Wayne, Keary Advertising Co Inc, Baltimore, MD. Tel: (410) 285-3700, (800) 428-5429, FAX: (410) 284-8418, E-Mail: wayne@keary.com, Web Site: www.keary.com (35)

Keary Advertising Co Inc, Baltimore, MD. Tel: (410) 285-3700, (800) 428-5429, FAX: (410) 284-8418, E-Mail: wayne@keary.com, Web Site: www.keary. com (35)

Keating, Cheryl, Mailing Source, Costa Mesa, CA. Tel: (949) 722-9391 (28)

Keating Magee Advertising, New Orleans, LA. Tel: (504) 299-8000, FAX: (504) 525-6647, E-Mail: jmagee@keatingmagee.com, Web Site: www. keatingmagee.com (35)

Keaton, Earl, Saunders Military Insignia, Naples, FL. Tel: (239) 298-8228, (800) 442-3133, FAX: (239) 774-3323, E-Mail: info@saundersinsignia.com, Web Site: www.saundersinsignia.com (6)

Keats, Steven, Macromark Inc, Brewster, NY. Tel: (845) 230-6300, FAX: (845) 278-0650, E-Mail: david@macromark.com, Web Site: www. macromark.com (23)

Kee, Gilbert, Promotional Products Fulfillment & Distribution Ltd, Whitby, ON Canada. Tel: (905) 668-5060, (800) 263-4678, FAX: (800) 993-0543, E-Mail: sales@ppfd.com, Web Site: www.ppfd.com (22)

Keefe, Donald, J., American Printing House for the Blind, Louisville, KY. Tel: (502) 895-2405, (800) 223-1839, FAX: (502) 899-2274, E-Mail: info@ aph.org, Web Site: www.aph.org (7)

Keefe, Mark, PrimeNet, Clearwater, FL. Tel: (651) 405-4000, FAX: (651) 405-4100, Web Site: www. pnms.com (22)

Keefhaver, Joe, Wyandotte West Communications Inc, Kansas City, KS. Tel: (913) 788-5565, FAX: (913) 788-9812, E-Mail: news@wyandottewest.com, Web Site: www.wyandottewest.com (17)

Keegan, Robert J., Goodyear Tire & Rubber Co, Akron, OH. Tel: (330) 796-3250, Web Site: www. goodyear.com (16)

Keehn, Dennis, The Keehn Co, Pound Ridge, NY. Tel: (914) 764-8591, FAX: (914) 764-5388, E-Mail: dkeehnco@optonline.net (35)

The Keehn Co, Pound Ridge, NY. Tel: (914) 764-8591, FAX: (914) 764-5388, E-Mail: dkeehnco@ optonline.net (35)

Keely, William, G., Whitaker National, Huntington, WV. Tel: (304) 525-0852, (800) 377-8721, FAX: (304) 525-0874, Web Site: www.neshold.com (16)

Keeman, Deb, Stream International, Wellesley, MA. Tel: (781) 304-1800, (888) 264-5834, FAX: (781) 575-6999, Web Site: www.stream.com (16)

Keenan, Anne, USI Affinity, Philadelphia, PA. Tel: (610) 833-2876, (800) 625-2876, FAX: (610) 265-2876, E-Mail: info@usiaffinity.com, Web Site: www.brcorp.com (15)

Keenan, Jack, L., Tele Resources Inc, Duluth, MN. Tel: (888) 698-8787 X114, FAX: (218) 724-2466, E-Mail: mark.swanson@teleresources.net, Web Site: www.teleresources.net (29)

Keenan, John, Anthem Marketing, Chicago, IL. Tel: (312) 441-0382 (22)

Keene, Michael, The John Roberts Co, Minneapolis, MN. Tel: (763) 755-5500, (800) 551-1534, FAX: (763) 755-0394, E-Mail: jfoster@johnroberts.com, Web Site: www.johnroberts.com (28)

Keene-Kendrick, Lydia, Davis Art Images, Worcester, MA. Tel: (508) 754-7201, (800) 533-2847, FAX: (508) 753-3834, (508) 831-9260, E-Mail: lkeenekendrick@davisart.com, Web Site: www. davisartimages.com (38)

Keeneland Association Inc, Lexington, KY. Tel: (859) 254-3412, (800) 456-3412, FAX: (859) 255-2484, Web Site: www.keeneland.com (16)

Keeney, Tyler, Who's Who - The MFSA Buyers' Guide to Blue Ribbon Mailing Services, Alexandria, VA. Tel: (703) 836-9200, FAX: (703) 548-8204, E-Mail: masa-mail@masa.org, Web Site: www.mfsanet.org (43)

Keessen, Robert, H., Scott Publications, Inc, Muskegon, MI. Tel: (248) 477-6650, (800) 458-8237, FAX: (248) 477-6795, E-Mail: contactus@ scottpublications.com, Web Site: www. scottpublications.com (17)

Keffer, Thomas, Oppenheimer Funds, New York, NY. Tel: (212) 323-0200, FAX: (212) 323-0493, Web Site: www.oppenheimerfunds.com (14)

Kehoe, Debra, Daniel Smith Inc, Seattle, WA. Tel: (206) 223-9599, (800) 426-6740, FAX: (800) 238-4065, E-Mail: sales@danielsmith.com, Web Site: www.danielsmith.com (10)

Kehoe, John, Trinity Direct, Butler, NJ. Tel: (973) 283-3600, Web Site: www.trinitydirect.net (23)

Keifer, Joy, Babyshoe.com, Hendersonville, NC. Tel: (828) 697-5811, (800) 543-8566, FAX: (828) 697-5815, E-Mail: info@babyshoe.com, Web Site: www.babyshoe.com (6)

Keiffner, John, ETS Inc, Indianapolis, IN. Tel: (317) 290-8982, (800) 228-6292, FAX: (317) 329-4630, E-Mail: info@etstsan.com, Web Site: www.etstans. com (7)

Keiler & Co, Farmington, CT. Tel: (860) 677-8821, FAX: (860) 676-8164, E-Mail: newbiz@keiler. com, Web Site: www.keiler.com (35)

Keilitz, Dave, American Baseball Coaches Association, Mount Pleasant, MI. Tel: (989) 775-3300, FAX: (989) 775-3600, E-Mail: abca@abca.org, Web Site: www.abca.org (1)

Keir, Gerald J., First Hawaiian Bank, Honolulu, HI. Tel: (808) 525-6273, (888) 844-4444, FAX: (808) 525-5798, E-Mail: bfarias@fhb.com, Web Site: www.fhb.com (14)

Keiser, Lauren, Carl Fischer Music, New York, NY. Tel: (212) 777-0900, (800) 762-2328, FAX: (212) 477-6996, E-Mail: cf-info@carlfischer.com, Web Site: www.carlfischer.com (17)

Keith MD, Stephen, N., National Medical Fellowships, New York, NY. Tel: (212) 483-8880, FAX: (212) 483-8897, Web Site: www.nfm-online.org (1)

Keith, Jason, VistaPrint USA Inc, Lexington, MA. Tel: (800) 961-2075, Web Site: www.vistaprint.com (27)

Kelco Supply Co, Brooklyn Park, MN. Tel: (763) 493-1260, (800) 328-7720, FAX: (763) 493-1261, E-Mail: info@kelcosupply.com, Web Site: www. kelcosupply.com (16)

Keleher, David, Dynamics Research Corp, Andover, MA. Tel: (978) 475-9090, (800) 522-4321, FAX: (978) 475-8205, Web Site: www.drc.com (16)

Kelenc, Maria, The Production Partners, Toronto, ON Canada. Tel: (416) 504-5071, FAX: (416) 504-7390, Web Site: www.cfacommunications.com (32)

Kelleher, Patrick, Genworth Financial Inc, Richmond, VA. Tel: (804) 281-6000, (888) 436-9678, FAX: (804) 662-2414, Web Site: www.genworth.com (14)

Kelleher, Richard, Doubletree Suites by Hilton, Boston, MA. Tel: (617) 783-0090, (800) 222-TREE, FAX: (617) 783-0897, E-Mail: doubletree1@hilton. com (19)

Kellen, Mike, Assurant Health, Milwaukee, WI. Tel: (414) 244-0658, (800) 800-1212, FAX: (414) 224-0472, Web Site: www.assuranthealth.com (15)

Kellenberger, Dan, Cadie Products Corp, Paterson, NJ. Tel: (973) 278-8300, FAX: (973) 278-0303, E-Mail: emeyers@cadie.com, Web Site: www. cadieproducts.com (16)

Keller Jr., Kenneth, C., Motorola Inc, Montvale, NJ. Tel: (201) 949-5500, (800) 262-8509, Web Site: www.motorola.com (16)

Keller, Alex, Association for Facilities Engineering, Herndon, VA. Tel: (571) 203-7171, FAX: (571) 766-2142, E-Mail: info@afe.org, Web Site: www. afe.org (1)

Keller, Barb, We Deliver America Inc, Englewood Cliffs, NJ. Tel: (201) 307-8888, (800) 307-1200, E-Mail: info@we-deliver-america.com, Web Site: www.we-deliver-america.com (31)

Keller, Jack, JAK Productions, Atlanta, GA. Tel: (770) 612-1386, FAX: (770) 612-9163, E-Mail: jkeller2@ix.netcom.com (29)

Keller, James, JJ Keller & Associates Inc, Neenah, WI. Tel: (920) 722-2848, (800) 327-6868, FAX: (800) 727-7516, E-Mail: thines@jjkeller.com, Web Site: www.jjkeller.com/jjk (16)

Keller, Joel, San Francisco Bay Area Rapid Transit District (BART), Oakland, CA. Tel: (510) 464-6000, FAX: (510) 464-7103, Web Site: www.bart. gov (16)

Keller, Robert, JJ Keller & Associates Inc, Neenah, WI. Tel: (920) 722-2848, (800) 327-6868, FAX: (800) 727-7516, E-Mail: thines@jjkeller.com, Web Site: www.jjkeller.com/jjk (16)

Keller, Scott, Solar Components Corp, Manchester, NH. Tel: (603) 668-8186, FAX: (603) 668-1783, Web Site: www.solar-components.com (9)

Keller, Steven, Assurant Health, Milwaukee, WI. Tel: (414) 244-0658, (800) 800-1212, FAX: (414) 224-0472, Web Site: www.assuranthealth.com (15)

Keller Crescent Co, Greensboro, NC. Tel: (508) 478-7641, FAX: (508) 634-3709, Web Site: www. kellercrescent.com (35)

JJ Keller & Associates Inc, Neenah, WI. Tel: (920) 722-2848, (800) 327-6868, FAX: (800) 727-7516, E-Mail: thines@jjkeller.com, Web Site: www. jjkeller.com/jjk (16)

Kellerhals, Ken, Bissinger French Confections, Saint Louis, MO. Tel: (314) 534-2401, (800) 325-8881, FAX: (314) 534-2419, Web Site: www.bissingers. com (4)

Kelley, Barbara M., Bausch & Lomb Inc, Rochester, NY. Tel: (585) 338-6000, (800) 344-8815, FAX: (585) 338-6007, Web Site: www.bausch.com (16)

Kelley, Dana, CMI Direct, Montrose, CA. Tel: (951) 300-1700, FAX: (866) 723-5433, Web Site: www. cmidirect.net (15)

Kelley, Jeff, Direct Media Millard, Peterborough, NH. Tel: (603) 924-9262, FAX: (603) 924-9420, Web Site: www.millard.com (23)

Kelley, Lawrence, California State Polytechnic University Business Administration Dept, San Luis Obispo, CA. Tel: (805) 756-1413, FAX: (805) 756-5057, Web Site: www.calpoly.edu (41)

Kelley, Leigh, Anne, Regions, Birmingham, AL. Tel: (205) 326-5262, FAX: (205) 326-4072, Web Site: www.regions.com (14)

Kelley, Susan, Kelley Swofford Roy Inc, Miami, FL. Tel: (305) 444-0004, (800) 537-5565, FAX: (305) 444-9057, E-Mail: skelley@ksrteam.com, Web Site: www.kelleyswoffordroy.com (35)

Kelley, Thomas J., New York Power Authority, Albany, NY. Tel: (518) 433-6700, Web Site: www. nypa.gov (16)

Kelley Swofford Roy Inc, Miami, FL. Tel: (305) 444-0004, (800) 537-5565, FAX: (305) 444-9057, E-Mail: skelley@ksrteam.com, Web Site: www. kelleyswoffordroy.com (35)

Kelliher Samets Volk, Burlington, VT. Tel: (802) 862-8261, FAX: (802) 863-4724, E-Mail: info@ksvc. com, Web Site: www.ksvc.com (35)

Kellog, David, Council on Foreign Relations Inc, New York, NY. Tel: (212) 434-9400, FAX: (212) 861-2759, E-Mail: editor@foreignaffairs.com, Web Site: www.foreignaffairs.org (17)

Kelly, Brent J., Marshall & Ilsley Corp, Milwaukee, WI. Tel: (414) 765-7801, FAX: (414) 765-7899, Web Site: www.micorp.com (14)

Kelly, David, AnalyticsIQ Inc, Atlanta, GA. Tel: (770) 407-8855, Web Site: www.analytics-iq.com (30)

Kelly, David, DMA (Direct Marketing Association), New York, NY. Tel: (212) 768-7277, FAX: (212) 302-6714, E-Mail: customerservice@the-dma.org, Web Site: www.the-dma.org (40)

Kelly, Ed, American Express Publishing Corp, New York, NY. Tel: (212) 382-5600, (888) 461-6180, FAX: (212) 827-6496, E-Mail: aepc@custmersvc. com, Web Site: www.amexpub.com (17)

Kelly, Edmund, F., Liberty Mutual Group, Inc, Boston, MA. Tel: (617) 357-9500, (800) 837-5274, Web Site: www.libertymutual.com (15)

Kelly, Fran, Arnold Worldwide, Boston, MA. Tel: (617) 587-8000, FAX: (617) 587-8070, Web Site: www.arnoldworldwide.com (35)

Kelly, Gene, Executive Protection Products Inc, Napa, CA. Tel: (707) 253-7142, FAX: (707) 253-7149, E-Mail: services@epsecuritysolutions.com, Web Site: epsecuritysolutions.com (16)

Kelly, John, McWeeney Marketing Group, Orange, CT. Tel: (203) 891-8100, (800) 272-3440, FAX: (203) 891-0775, E-Mail: george@ mcweeneymarketing.com, Web Site: www. mcweeneymarketing.com (33)

Kelly, John, Recording for the Blind & Dyslexic Inc, Princeton, NJ. Tel: (609) 452-0606, (800) 221-4792, FAX: (609) 520-7996, E-Mail: info@rfbd. org, Web Site: www.rfbd.org (16)

Kelly, Judith, B., Alpha List Marketing Inc, Marietta, GA. Tel: (404) 995-7049, (800) 822-2902, FAX: (404) 601-0826, E-Mail: info@alphalistmarketing. com (23)

Kelly, Karla, Electronic Retailing Association, Washington, DC. Tel: (703) 841-1751, FAX: (703) 841-1860, E-Mail: askera@retailing.org, Web Site: www.retailing.org (42)

Kelly, Kevin, P., Farm Bureau Insurance, Lansing, MI. Tel: (517) 323-7000, (800) 292-2680, FAX: (517) 327-0208, Web Site: www.farmbureauinsurance-mi. com (15)

Kelly, Kevin, V., Volkswagen Group of America Inc, Auburn Hills, MI. Tel: (248) 754-5000, FAX: (248) 754-4930, Web Site: www.vw.com (16)

Kelly, Laraine, Institute of Management & Administration (IOMA), Peterborough, NH. Tel: (800) 401-5937, FAX: (973) 622-0595 (17)

Kelly, Maggie, American Bankers Association, Washington, DC. Tel: (202) 789-0300, (800) BANK-ERS, FAX: (202) 296-9258, Web Site: www.aba. com (1)

Kelly, Mara, Loehmann's, Bronx, NY. Tel: (718) 409-2000, Web Site: www.loehmanns.com (2)

Kelly, Maureen, C., The Suburban Chamber of Commerce, Summit, NJ. Tel: (908) 522-1700, FAX: (908) 522-9252, E-Mail: info@suburbanchambers. org, Web Site: www.suburbanchambers.org (14)

Kelly, Michael, Editors Press Inc, Hyattsville, MD. Tel: (301) 853-4900, (888) 853-4900, FAX: (301) 853-4961, Web Site: www.edpress.com (27)

Kelly, Patricia, MM Batch, Westhampton Beach, NY. Tel: (212) 737-0700, FAX: (212) 454-1124, E-Mail: christine@bannerdirect.com, Web Site: www.bannerdirect.com (35)

Kelly, Patrick, The Company Store Inc, La Crosse, WI. Tel: (608) 785-1400, FAX: (608) 791-5790, Web Site: www.thecompanystore.com (16)

Kelly, Rob, Earthrise, Irvine, CA. Tel: (949) 623-0980, FAX: (949) 623-0990, E-Mail: info@earthrise.com, Web Site: www.earthrise.com (16)

Kelly, Thomas, Hawthorne Direct Inc, Fairfield, IA. Tel: (641) 472-3800, FAX: (641) 472-6043, E-Mail: drtv@hawthornedirect.com, Web Site: www.hawthornedirect.com (16)

Kelly, Thomas, New York Life Insurance Co/AARP, Tampa, FL. Tel: (813) 288-5500, FAX: (813) 288-5256, Web Site: www.nylaarp.com (15)

Kelly, William M., Alloyd Brands, Dekalb, IL. Tel: (815) 756-8451, (800) 756-7639, FAX: (815) 756-5187/9192, Web Site: www.alloyd.com (16)

Kelly, William, J., HCI Direct, Bensalem, PA. Tel: (215) 244-9600, (888) 765-0062, FAX: (215) 244-0328, Web Site: www.silkies.com (16)

Kelly, Scott & Madison Inc, Chicago, IL. Tel: (312) 977-0772, FAX: (312) 977-0874, Web Site: www. ksmmedia.com (32)

Kelly-Radford Ph.D., Lily, M., Center for Creative Leadership, Greensboro, NC. Tel: (336) 545-2810, FAX: (336) 282-3284, E-Mail: info@ccl.org, Web Site: www.ccl.org (16)

Kellyco Metal Detector Distributors, Winter Springs, FL. Tel: (407) 699-8700, (800) 327-9697, FAX: (407) 695-6671, E-Mail: customerservice@ kellycodetectors.com, Web Site: www. kellycodetectors.com (11)

Kelly's Kids, Natchez, MS. Tel: (601) 442-5332, (800) 837-2066, FAX: (601) 442-4399, E-Mail: customerservice@kellyskids.com, Web Site: www. kellyskids.com (2)

Kelsey, Mark, Kelsey National Corp, Los Angeles, CA. Tel: (310) 390-1000, (800) 366-5656, FAX: (310) 390-3158, E-Mail: info@kelsey.com, Web Site: www.kelsey.com (15)

Kelsey, Meg, City of LaGrange, LaGrange, GA. Tel: (706) 883-2010, FAX: (706) 883-2062, Web Site: www.lagrange-ga.org (1)

Kelsey, Van, Kelsey National Corp, Los Angeles, CA. Tel: (310) 390-1000, (800) 366-5656, FAX: (310) 390-3158, E-Mail: info@kelsey.com, Web Site: www.kelsey.com (15)

Kelsey III, Van, Kelsey National Corp, Los Angeles, CA. Tel: (310) 390-1000, (800) 366-5656, FAX: (310) 390-3158, E-Mail: info@kelsey.com, Web Site: www.kelsey.com (15)

Kelsey National Corp, Los Angeles, CA. Tel: (310) 390-1000, (800) 366-5656, FAX: (310) 390-3158, E-Mail: info@kelsey.com, Web Site: www.kelsey. com (15)

Keltner, Thomas, C., Hilton Hotels Corp, Mc Lean, VA. Tel: (310) 278-4321, (800) HILTONS, FAX: (310) 205-3670, Web Site: www.hilton.com (19)

Kemmitz, Greg, Skypoint Communications Inc, Loretto, MN. Tel: (763) 548-2600, FAX: (763) 548-2610, E-Mail: info@skypoint.com, Web Site: www.skypoint.com (16)

Kemp, Gil, Home Decorators Collection Inc, Hazelwood, MO. Tel: (314) 993-1516, FAX: (314) 521-5780, Web Site: www.homedecoratorscollection. com (8)

Kemp, Jennifer, Bluestem Brands, Eden Prairie, MN. Tel: (952) 656-3700, Web Site: www.fingerhut.com (16)

Kemp, Jim, Collector's Armoury Ltd, McDonough, GA. Tel: (703) 493-9120, FAX: (703) 493-9424, Web Site: www.collectorsarmoury.com (6)

Kemper, David, W., Washington University, Saint Louis, MO. Tel: (314) 935-4623, (800) 638-0700, FAX: (314) 935-7088, Web Site: www.wustl.edu (1)

Kemper, Jane, PESI LLC, Eau Claire, WI. Tel: (800) 844-8260, FAX: (800) 554-9775, E-Mail: info@ pesi.com, Web Site: www.pesi.com (17)

Kemper, Kimberly, Texas Farm Bureau Insurance Cos, Waco, TX. Tel: (254) 751-2688, Web Site: www. txfb-ins.com (15)

Kemper, Mike, Associated Materials, Cuyahoga Falls, OH. Tel: (330) 922-2182, Web Site: www.alside. com (8)

Ken Elo, Montreal, PQ Canada. Tel: (514) 926-6945 (20)

Kendall Products/Dri-Dek, Naples, FL. Tel: (239) 643-2244, (800) 348-2398, FAX: (800) 828-4248, E-Mail: info@dri-dek.com, Web Site: www.dri-dek.com (16)

Kender, Richard, N., Merck & Co Inc, Whitehouse Station, NJ. Tel: (908) 423-1000, Web Site: www. merck.com (16)

Kendrick, Carl, Bass Pro Shops, Springfield, MO. Tel: (417) 873-5000, FAX: (417) 873-5882, Web Site: www.basspro.com (11)

Kendrick, David, Interior Concepts Corp, Spring Lake, MI. Tel: (616) 842-5550, (800) 678-5550, FAX: (616) 842-7122, Web Site: www.interiorconcepts. com (34)

Kening, Phillip, Beacon Marketing Group, Galloway, NJ. Tel: (609) 677-4776, Web Site: www. beaconmktg.com (35)

Keniston, Kimberly, Alfa Aesar-A Johnson Matthey Co, Ward Hill, MA. Tel: (800) 343-0660, FAX: (800) 322-4757, E-Mail: info@alfa.com, Web Site: www.alfa.com (9)

Kenmore Stamp Co, Milford, NH. Tel: (603) 673-1745, (800) 225-5059, FAX: (603) 673-3222, Web Site: www.kenmorestamp.com (6)

Kennametal Inc, Latrobe, PA. Tel: (800) 222-9327, FAX: (800) 521-3319, E-Mail: mcs-na.service@ kennmetal.com, Web Site: www.kennametal.com (16)

Kennedy, Alan, Tupperware, Orlando, FL. Tel: (407) 826-5050, (800) 366-3800, FAX: (407) 826-8874, Web Site: www.tupperware.com (16)

Kennedy, Ben, Proven Prospects Inc, Hermosa Beach, CA. Tel: (805) 448-6253, Web Site: www. provemprospects.com (20)

Kennedy, Boyd, Texas Parks & Wildlife Dept, Austin, TX. Tel: (512) 389-4800, (800) 792-1112, FAX: (512) 389-8029, Web Site: www.tpwd.state.tx.us (1)

Kennedy, Bryan, Epsilon, Irving, TX. Tel: (972) 582-9600, (800) 309-0505, FAX: (972) 582-9700, E-Mail: info@epsilon.com, Web Site: www. epsilon.com (22)

Kennedy, Candace, Ethnic Technologies LLC, South Hackensack, NJ. Tel: (201) 440-8923, (866) 333-8324, FAX: (201) 440-2168, E-Mail: candace@ ethnictechnologies.com, Web Site: www. ethnictechnologies.com (23)

Kennedy, Chris, CUNA Mutual Group, Madison, WI. Tel: (608) 238-5851, (800) 356-2644, FAX: (608) 231-8839, Web Site: www.cunamutual.com (15)

Kennedy, Chris, The Merchandise Mart, Chicago, IL. Tel: (312) 527-4141, (800) 677-6278, Web Site: www.merchandisemart.com (42)

Kennedy, Dan, Annie's Attic LLC, Big Sandy, TX. Tel: (903) 636-4303, FAX: (903) 636-4088, Web Site: www.anniesattic.com (11)

Kennedy, Dan, S., Kennedy Inner Circle, Phoenix, AZ. Tel: (602) 269-3111, FAX: (602) 269-3113 (20)

Kennedy, Daniel, W., Whitehorse Gear, Center Conway, NH. Tel: (603) 356-6556, FAX: (603) 356-6590, E-Mail: customerservice@whitehorsepress. com, Web Site: www.whitehorsepress.com (11)

Kennedy, Deborah, Channel Neutral Marketing, Oyster Bay, NY. Tel: (516) 992-7887, FAX: (516) 983-1617, Web Site: www.channelneutralmarketing.com (35)

Kennedy, Edward, Bausch & Lomb Inc, Rochester, NY. Tel: (585) 338-6000, (800) 344-8815, FAX: (585) 338-6007, Web Site: www.bausch.com (16)

Kennedy, Hank, Amacom Books, New York, NY. Tel: (212) 903-8376, FAX: (212) 903-8083, E-Mail: customerservice@amanet.org, Web Site: www. amacombooks.org (17)

Kennedy, James A.C., T Rowe Price Associates Inc, Baltimore, MD. Tel: (410) 345-2000, (800) 638-7890, FAX: (410) 986-3618, E-Mail: info@ troweprice.com, Web Site: www.troweprice.com (14)

Kennedy, James, Scientific Games Canada, Montreal, PQ Canada. Tel: (514) 254-3000, FAX: (514) 254-1411, Web Site: www.scientificgames.com (27)

Kennedy, Judith, M., Whitehorse Gear, Center Conway, NH. Tel: (603) 356-6556, FAX: (603) 356-6590, E-Mail: customerservice@whitehorsepress. com, Web Site: www.whitehorsepress.com (11)

Kennedy, Thomas, C., Alamo Rent A Car, Tulsa, OK. Tel: (918) 401-6000, Web Site: www.alamo.com (16)

Kennedy, Thomas, Covenant House International Headquarters, New York, NY. Tel: (212) 727-4000, (800) 999-9999, FAX: (212) 727-4992, Web Site: www.covenanthouse.org (1)

Kennedy, Tracy, Suntrust Banks Inc, Atlanta, GA. Tel: (404) 588-7914, (800) 786-8787, FAX: (404) 532-0550, E-Mail: emmett.harmon@suntrust.com, Web Site: www.suntrust.com (14)

Kennedy Inner Circle, Phoenix, AZ. Tel: (602) 269-3111, FAX: (602) 269-3113 (20)

Kennel, James, DMX-Direct, Inc, Centennial, CO. Tel: (303) 339-9300, FAX: (303) 388-6363, Web Site: www.dmx-direct.com (21)

Kennel Vet, Laurel, DE. Tel: (302) 875-7111, (800) 782-0627, FAX: (302) 269-3986, E-Mail: info@ petmarket.com, Web Site: www.kennelvet.com (11)

Judith Kennerk, Princeton Junction, NJ. Tel: (609) 240-2876 (20)

Kennesaw State University, Kennesaw, GA. Tel: (770) 423-6060, FAX: (770) 499-3261, Web Site: www. kennesaw.edu (41)

Kenneth, Renee, David Sams Industries Inc/TV First, Agoura Hills, CA. Tel: (818) 707-7022, FAX: (818) 707-8130, E-Mail: customerservice@ samsdirect.com, Web Site: www.tvfirst.com (35)

Kenney, John, Esquire Magazine, New York, NY. Tel: (212) 649-2000, (800) 925-0485, FAX: (212) 265-0938, E-Mail: esquire@hearst.com, Web Site: www.esquire.com (17)

Kenney, Philip M., Hopkins Medical Products, Baltimore, MD. Tel: (410) 484-2036, (800) 835-1995, FAX: (410) 484-4036, E-Mail: customerservice@ hopkinsmedical.net, Web Site: www. hopkinsmedicalproducts.com (7)

Kenney, Rick, ST&P Marketing Communications Inc, Fairlawn, OH. Tel: (330) 668-1932, FAX: (330) 668-2078, Web Site: www.stpinc.com (35)

Kenney, Robert, Kenney Marketing & Advertising Inc, King of Prussia, PA. Tel: (610) 341-0430, FAX: (610) 341-0480, E-Mail: info@kmaphl.com, Web Site: www.kmaphl.com (35)

Kenney Marketing & Advertising Inc, King of Prussia, PA. Tel: (610) 341-0430, FAX: (610) 341-0480, E-Mail: info@kmaphl.com, Web Site: www. kmaphl.com (35)

Kensey, John, Vance Industries Inc, Niles, IL. Tel: (847) 375-8900, FAX: (847) 375-6818, E-Mail: vance@vanceind.com, Web Site: www.vanceind. com (16)

Kensington Publishing Corp, New York, NY. Tel: (212) 407-1500, (800) 221-2647, FAX: (212) 407-1590, Web Site: www.kensingtonbooks.com (17)

Kensington Technology Group, Redwood Shores, CA. Tel: (650) 572-2700, FAX: (650) 267-2800, Web Site: www.kensington.com (16)

Kent, Allan, F., Veterans of Foreign Wars (VFW) of the US-National Headquarters, Kansas City, MO. Tel: (816) 756-3390, FAX: (816) 968-1149, E-Mail: info@vfw.org, Web Site: www.vfw.org (1)

Kent, Evan, APC By Schneider Electric, West Kingston, RI. Tel: (401) 789-5735, Web Site: www.apc. com (34)

Kent, Mary, The Great Books Foundation, Chicago, IL. Tel: (312) 332-5870, Web Site: www. greatbooks.org (1)

Kent, Muhtar, The Coca-Cola Co, Atlanta, GA. Tel: (404) 676-2121, FAX: (404) 676-6792, Web Site: www.cocacola.com (16)

Kent, Richard, Lakeside Publishing Co LLC, Evanston, IL. Tel: (847) 491-6440, FAX: (847) 491-0459, E-Mail: cs@centurysports.net, Web Site: www.centurysports.net (17)

Kent, Steve, F&W Publications Inc, Blue Ash, OH. Tel: (513) 531-2690, FAX: (513) 531-0293, Web Site: www.fwpublications.com (17)

Kentucky Bankers Association, Louisville, KY. Tel: (502) 582-2453, FAX: (502) 584-6390, Web Site: www.kybanks.com (1)

Kenworthy, John, Kenworthy Marketing & Promotional Products, Columbia, SC. Tel: (803) 765-2222, (800) JKE-IDEA, FAX: (803) 765-2121, Web Site: www.discountpromotions.com (35)

Kenworthy Marketing & Promotional Products, Columbia, SC. Tel: (803) 765-2222, (800) JKE-IDEA, FAX: (803) 765-2121, Web Site: www. discountpromotions.com (35)

Kenzer, Mark, Pacific Spirit Corp, Forest Grove, OR. Tel: (503) 357-1566, (800) 634-9057, FAX: (503) 357-1699, Web Site: www.pacificspiritcatalogs.com (6)

Kenzer, Robert, Kenzer Group, LLC, New York, NY. Tel: (212) 308-4300, FAX: (917) 534-6280, E-Mail: info@kenzergroup.com, Web Site: kenzergroup.com (20)

Kenzer Group, LLC, New York, NY. Tel: (212) 308-4300, FAX: (917) 534-6280, E-Mail: info@ kenzergroup.com, Web Site: kenzergroup.com (20)

Keough, Michael, J., Caraustar, Austell, GA. Tel: (770) 948-3101, E-Mail: info@caraustar.com, Web Site: www.caraustar.com (16)

Kepler II, David, E., Dow Chemical USA, Midland, MI. Tel: (989) 636-1000, (800) 447-4369, FAX: (989) 832-1465, E-Mail: jadams@dow.com, Web Site: www.dow.com (16)

Keplinger, Teresa, The Columbian, Vancouver, WA. Tel: (360) 694-3391, FAX: (360) 735-4503, Web Site: www.columbian.com (17)

Ker, Fred, New Zealand Tourism Board, Santa Monica, CA. Tel: (310) 857-2213, FAX: (310) 395-5453, E-Mail: nzinfo@nztb.govt.nz, Web Site: www.purenz.com (19)

Kerber, Art, Green River Trading Co, Millerton, NY. Tel: (518) 789-3311 (8)

Kerber, Charles, A., Unique Data Services Inc, Downers Grove, IL. Tel: (630) 968-6000, Web Site: www.uniquedata.com (28)

Kerber, Cheryl, New York Findings, Fresh Meadows, NY. Tel: (212) 925-5745, FAX: (212) 925-5870, E-Mail: nyfindings@aol.com, Web Site: www. newyorkfindings.com (6)

Kerber, Sidney, The Catalog Consultancy, Vero Beach, FL. Tel: (772) 226-7740, FAX: (772) 226-7740, E-Mail: catalog321@aol.com, Web Site: www. catalogconsultant.com (20)

Kerckhoff III, Arthur, F., Gabriel Group, Earth City, MO. Tel: (314) 743-5700, FAX: (314) 576-5573, E-Mail: sales@gabrielgr.com, Web Site: www. gabrielgr.com (21)

Kerekes, Kaye, Bunker Hill Auctions, Newark, IL. Tel: (630) 770-7132, E-Mail: bunkerhillauctions@ joimail.com, Web Site: www.bunkerhillauctions. com (6)

Kerley, Tracy, Entrepreneur Media Inc, Irvine, CA. Tel: (949) 261-2325, (800) 274-6229, FAX: (949) 261-0234, Web Site: www.entrepreneur.com (17)

Kerman, Ashley, Inmar, Winston-Salem, NC. Tel: (336) 631-2524, FAX: (336) 770-3470, E-Mail: ibizdev@inmar.com, Web Site: www. promotionslogistics.com (14)

Kern, Dan, Main Street Direct, New York, NY. Tel: (212) 779-3000, FAX: (212) 779-3061, E-Mail: jkern@mainstreetdirect.com, Web Site: www. mainstreetdirect.com (31)

Kern, Louise, Global Business Information Services Inc (GLOBIS), Chicago, IL. Tel: (773) 220-4000, Web Site: www.glo-bis.com (23)

Kern, Russell, Kern Direct Marketing, Woodland Hills, CA. Tel: (818) 703-8775, FAX: (818) 703-8458, Web Site: www.kerndirect.com (35)

Kern, Russell, The Kern Organization, Woodland Hills, CA. Tel: (818) 703-8775, Web Site: www. kerndirect.com (35)

Kern Direct Marketing, Woodland Hills, CA. Tel: (818) 703-8775, FAX: (818) 703-8458, Web Site: www.kerndirect.com (35)

The Kern Organization, Woodland Hills, CA. Tel: (818) 703-8775, Web Site: www.kerndirect.com (35)

Kerner, Kevin, Harte-Hanks, Austin, TX. Tel: (512) 434-1100, (800) 456-9748, FAX: (512) 244-9222, Web Site: www.harte-hanks.com (22)

Kerr, David, Sunlife of Canada, Wellesley Hills, MA. Tel: (781) 237-6030, (800) SUNLIFE, FAX: (781) 446-1779, Web Site: www.sunlife-usa.com (15)

Kerr, Dorothy, Dorothy Kerr & Associates, Milwaukee, WI. Tel: (414) 228-0335, FAX: (414) 228-0337 (20)

Kerr, Mary Ann, TMP Direct, Budd Lake, NJ. Tel: (973) 347-9400, (800) 328-2439, FAX: (973) 347-8773, E-Mail: ron.pearl@tmpwdirect.com, Web Site: www.tmpwdirect.com (29)

Dorothy Kerr & Associates, Milwaukee, WI. Tel: (414) 228-0335, FAX: (414) 228-0337 (20)

Kerr-Hays Co, Ligonier, PA. Tel: (724) 238-6694, FAX: (724) 238-7440 (16)

Kerrick, DeAnna, Safeco Insurance Co, Seattle, WA. Tel: (206) 545-5000, (800) 332-3226, FAX: (206) 545-5767/5651, Web Site: www.safeco.com (15)

Kerry, Tony, Script to Screen Inc, Santa Ana, CA. Tel: (714) 558-3971, (800) 453-0003, FAX: (714) 558-1759, E-Mail: newbusiness@scripttoscreen.com, Web Site: www.scripttoscreen.com (32)

Kersey, Tammy, The Colonial Williamsburg Foundation, Williamsburg, VA. Tel: (757) 229-1000, (757) 220-7275, (800) 761-8331, Web Site: www.williamsburgmarketplace.com (1)

Kersh, Russell, E., Sunbeam, Boca Raton, FL. Tel: (561) 912-4100, FAX: (561) 912-4567, Web Site: www.sunbeam.com (16)

Kersten, Jim, Hess Print Solutions, Kent, OH. Tel: (330) 677-3353, FAX: (330) 677-8256, E-Mail: sshowerman@hessprintsolutions.com, Web Site: www.thepressofohio.com (27)

Kerwin, Jim, Jim Kerwin Freelance Copywriter, Naples, FL. Tel: (239) 597-4445, E-Mail: jwkerwin@mac.com (39)

Jim Kerwin Freelance Copywriter, Naples, FL. Tel: (239) 597-4445, E-Mail: jwkerwin@mac.com (39)

Keshner, Maurice, Cinema World Studios, Greenpoint, NY. Tel: (718) 389-9800, FAX: (718) 389-9897, E-Mail: cinemaworldfd@verizon.net, Web Site: www.cinemaworldstudios.com (32)

Kesman, Thomas, Harris Bancorp Inc, Chicago, IL. Tel: (312) 461-7961, (888) 340-BANK, FAX: (312) 461-7869, E-Mail: onlineservices@harrisbank.com, Web Site: www.harrisbank.com (14)

Kessel, Barry, RTC Relationship Marketing, Washington, DC. Tel: (202) 625-2111, FAX: (202) 424-7900, Web Site: www.rtcrm.com (35)

Kessler, Michelle, Uncle Ben's Inc, Greenville, MS. Tel: (662) 335-8000, (800) 548-6253, (800) 54-UNCLE, FAX: (662) 378-4370, E-Mail: info@unclebens.com, Web Site: www.unclebens.com (4)

Kessler, Rev. Mathew J., Liguori Publications, Liguori, MO. Tel: (636) 464-2500, (800) 325-9521, FAX: (800) 325-9526, E-Mail: liguori@liguori.org, Web Site: www.liguori.org (17)

Kessler, Steve, Home Decorators Collection Inc, Hazelwood, MO. Tel: (314) 993-1516, FAX: (314) 521-5780, Web Site: www.homedecoratorscollection.com (8)

Kestenbaum, Jeff, AIG Accident & Health, New York, NY. Tel: (212) 770-7000, (877) 638-4244, FAX: (212) 509-9705, Web Site: www.aig.com (15)

Kester, David, Kester's Wild Game Food Nurseries Inc, Omro, WI. Tel: (920) 685-2929, (800) 558-8815, FAX: (920) 685-6727, E-Mail: pkester@vbe.com, Web Site: www.kestersnursery.com (8)

Kester, Patricia, Kester's Wild Game Food Nurseries Inc, Omro, WI. Tel: (920) 685-2929, (800) 558-8815, FAX: (920) 685-6727, E-Mail: pkester@vbe.com, Web Site: www.kestersnursery.com (8)

Kester's Wild Game Food Nurseries Inc, Omro, WI. Tel: (920) 685-2929, (800) 558-8815, FAX: (920) 685-6727, E-Mail: pkester@vbe.com, Web Site: www.kestersnursery.com (8)

Kestler, George, AmeriCall Group Inc, Naperville, IL. Tel: (630) 955-9100, (800) 688-0078, FAX: (630) 955-9955, E-Mail: sales@americallgroup.com, Web Site: www.americallgroup.com (29)

Kestnbaum, Kate, KesTry, Chicago, IL. Tel: (312) 664-6060, FAX: (312) 664-6059, E-Mail: kkestnbaum@earthlink.net (20)

KesTry, Chicago, IL. Tel: (312) 664-6060, FAX: (312) 664-6059, E-Mail: kkestnbaum@earthlink.net (20)

Ketchel, Kim, Jones International Ltd, Centennial, CO. Tel: (303) 792-3111, (800) 525-7002, FAX: (303) 784-8508, E-Mail: publicrelations@jones.com, Web Site: www.jones.com (16)

Ketchiff, David, Charles F Beardsley Advertising, Avon, CT. Tel: (860) 676-0256, FAX: (860) 674-1917, E-Mail: charles.beardsley@snet.net (35)

Ketchum, New York, NY. Tel: (646) 935-3900, FAX: (646) 935-4482, E-Mail: editor@ketchum.com, Web Site: www.ketchum.com (35)

Ketonis, Philip, Hachette Filipacchi List Management, New York, NY. Tel: (212) 767-6677, FAX: (212) 767-5605, Web Site: www.hfmuslists.com (17)

Kett Tool Co, Cincinnati, OH. Tel: (513) 271-0333, FAX: (513) 271-5318, E-Mail: info@kett-tool.com, Web Site: www.kett-tool.com (9)

Ketterer, Robert, HDA Inc, Saint Louis, MO. Tel: (314) 770-2222, (800) 533-4350, FAX: (314) 770-1454, E-Mail: plans@hdainc.com, Web Site: www.designamerica.com (17)

Ketterman, Ken, Zimmerman Irrigation Inc, Biglerville, PA. Tel: (717) 337-2727, (800) 452-5699, FAX: (717) 337-1785, E-Mail: info@trikl-eez.com, Web Site: www.trickl-eez.com (16)

Kettwig, Kay A., Osmonics Inc, Minnetonka, MN. Tel: (952) 264-3937, (800) 605-6698, FAX: (952) 536-3301, Web Site: www.osmonics.com (16)

Ketzner, Beth, NameBank International LLC, Baltimore, MD. Tel: (410) 783-8460, FAX: (410) 783-8464, E-Mail: beth@namebank.com, Web Site: www.namebank.com (23)

Keuler, Jean, Society of the Divine Savior, New Holstein, WI. Tel: (920) 898-4201 (1)

Kewley, Jeanne, Impact Sales Inc, Cedar Rapids, IA. Tel: (319) 363-2641, FAX: (319) 362-5481 (33)

Key, Scott, Janes Information Group, Alexandria, VA. Tel: (703) 683-3700, (800) 824-0768, FAX: (703) 836-0297, Web Site: www.janes.com (17)

Key Bank, Cleveland, OH. Tel: (216) 689-3000, (888) 539-2968, FAX: (207) 874-7044, Web Site: www.key.com (14)

Key Bank National Association, Albany, NY. Tel: (518) 434-4871, (800) 539-2968, Web Site: www.keybank.com (14)

Key Communications Inc, Garrisonville, VA. Tel: (540) 720-5584, FAX: (540) 720-5687, E-Mail: usglass@aol.com, Web Site: www.key-com.com (17)

Key Computer Service of Chelsea, New York, NY. Tel: (212) 206-8060, FAX: (212) 206-8398 (28)

Key Mail Group of Companies, Buffalo, NY. Tel: (800) 863-3128, Web Site: www.key-mail.com (28)

Key Marketing Advantage LLC, Bethel, CT. Tel: (203) 744-9011, Web Site: www.keymarketingadvantage.com (23)

Key West Aloe Holdings LLC, Fort Lauderdale, FL. Tel: (305) 883-3166, FAX: (305) 883-3185, Web Site: www.keywestaloe.com (16)

Keyboard Workshop, Medford, OR. Tel: (541) 664-7052, FAX: (541) 664-7052, E-Mail: duane@playpiano.com, Web Site: www.playpiano.com (17)

Keyes, Norman, Grant's Mailing Services Inc, Mississauga, ON Canada. Tel: (905) 624-9082, FAX: (905) 624-0007, E-Mail: info@grants-mailing.ca, Web Site: www.grants-mailing.ca (27)

Keyes, Thomas, D., Protective Life Corp, Deerfield, IL. Tel: (847) 948-8988, (800) 323-5771, FAX: (847) 948-1156, Web Site: www.protective.com (15)

Keylor, Randy, Integrated Alliance Limited Partnership, Denton, TX. Tel: (940) 565-9415, FAX: (940) 383-1876, E-Mail: ryoung@integratedalliance.com, Web Site: www.integratedalliance.com (29)

Keyser, Richard L., WW Grainger Inc, Lake Forest, IL. Tel: (847) 535-1000, (888) 361-8649, FAX: (847) 535-9122, Web Site: www.grainger.com (9)

Keyspan Energy Corp, Brooklyn, NY. Tel: (718) 403-2000, (888) 222-7359, Web Site: www.keyspanenergy.com (16)

The Keystone Equities Group, Oaks, PA. Tel: (610) 415-6300, (800) 715-9905, FAX: (610) 415-6328, Web Site: www.keystoneequities.com (20)

Keystone Press Agency Inc, Montreal, PQ Canada. Tel: (514) 482-5312, (877) 482-5312, FAX: (514) 483-9005, E-Mail: pictures@keystonepressagency.com, Web Site: www.ketstonepressagency.com (38)

Keystone Promotions Inc, Little Egg Harbor, NJ. Tel: (908) 688-6713, FAX: (908) 688-6645, E-Mail: mgunther_kpi@msn.com, Web Site: www.keystonepromotionsinc.com (27)

Kforce Inc, Tampa, FL. Tel: (813) 552-2394, Web Site: www.kforce.com (20)

Khachoian, Ani, Soitenly Stooges, Glendale, CA. Tel: (818) 543-0778, (800) 543-0778, FAX: (818) 543-0779, E-Mail: custserv@threestooges.com, Web Site: www.soitenlystooges.com (6)

Khalil, Nicholas, Check Point Systems, Thorofare, NJ. Tel: (856) 848-1800, (800) 257-5540, FAX: (856) 848-0937, Web Site: www.checkpointsystems.com (34)

Khalsa, P.S., NAM Mailing Lists, Santa Cruz, NM. Tel: (505) 753-5086, FAX: (505) 753-9249, E-Mail: nam@newmexico.com (24)

Khanna, Vinit, OKS-Ameridial Inc, Bala Cynwyd, PA. Tel: (610) 667-3000, FAX: (610) 667-3002, E-Mail: info@oksgroup.com, Web Site: www.oksameridial.com (23)

Kheradpir, Shaygan, Verizon Communications Inc, New York, NY. Tel: (212) 395-1000, (800) 621-9900, FAX: (212) 571-1897, Web Site: www.verizon.com (3)

Khouri, Dan, Unique Mailing Services Inc, Bolingbrook, IL. Tel: (630) 739-4848, FAX: (630) 783-1838, E-Mail: info@uniqmail.com, Web Site: www.uniqmail.com (28)

Khubani, A.J., Telebrands Corp, Fairfield, NJ. Tel: (973) 244-0300, FAX: (973) 244-0233, Web Site: www.telebrands.com (21)

Khulusi, Frank, PC Mall, Torrance, CA. Tel: (310) 225-2600, (800) 555-MALL, Web Site: www.pcmall.com (3)

Kibble, Wayne, Alco Chemical, Chattanooga, TN. Tel: (423) 629-1405, FAX: (423) 698-8723, Web Site: www.alcochemical.com (16)

Kibler, Tom, Whirlpool Corp, Benton Harbor, MI. Tel: (616) 923-5000, FAX: (616) 923-2759, Web Site: www.whirlpoolcorp.com (16)

KickApps Corp, New York, NY. Tel: (212) 730-4558, Web Site: www.kickapps.com (32)

Kid Stuff Marketing, Inc, Topeka, KS. Tel: (785) 862-3707, (800) 677-4712, FAX: (785) 862-0070, E-Mail: info@kidstuff.com, Web Site: www.kidsstuff.com (33)

Kidder, Tim, Adknowledge, Kansas City, MO. Tel: (816) 931-1771, Web Site: www.adknowledge.com (32)

The Kidney Foundation of Canada/Greater Ontario Branch, Hamilton, ON Canada. Tel: (800) 414-3484, FAX: (905) 318-8491, E-Mail: kidneyfoundation@bellnet.ca, Web Site: www.kidney.on.ca (1)

Kiecker, Pamela, Interactive Marketing Institute, Richmond, VA. Tel: (800) 925-5308, Web Site: www.imi.vcu.edu (41)

Kiely, Leo, MillerCoors LLC, Chicago, IL. Tel: (800) 645-5376, Web Site: www.millercoors.com (4)

Kiely, Leo, Molson Coors Brewing Co, Denver, CO. Tel: (303) 279-6565, (800) 642-6116, FAX: (303) 277-5415, Web Site: www.molsoncoors.com (16)

Kiener, Martin, SCICOM Data Services Ltd, Minnetonka, MN. Tel: (952) 933-4200, (800) 488-9087, FAX: (952) 936-4132, Web Site: www.scicom.com (22)

Kieran, David, First National Information Network, Burbank, CA. Tel: (855) 909-6800, FAX: (818) 558-6663, E-Mail: info@fnin.com, Web Site: www.fnin.com (30)

Kieschnick, Michael, Working Assets, San Francisco, CA. Tel: (800) 668-9253, FAX: (415) 371-1046, Web Site: www.workingassets.com (16)

Kihm, Carolyn, Guiding Eyes for the Blind, Yorktown Heights, NY. Tel: (914) 245-4042, (800) 942-0149, FAX: (914) 245-1609, Web Site: www.guidingeyes.org (16)

Kijewski, Thomas, Greene an RMG Direct Co, Lincolnshire, IL. Tel: (847) 948-7400, (800) 356-1300 x1809, FAX: (847) 948-0400, Web Site: www.rmgdirectinc.com (29)

Kikucall, New York, NY. Tel: (646) 747-1078, Web Site: www.kikucall.com (3)

Kilawee, Barbara, Houston Direct Marketing Association, Houston, TX. Tel: (281) 931-8883, FAX: (281) 820-4023, Web Site: www.houstondma.org (40)

Kilberry, William, Tempco Electric Heater Corp, Wood Dale, IL. Tel: (630) 350-2252, (800) 323-6859, FAX: (630) 350-0232, E-Mail: dpadlo@tempco.com, Web Site: www.tempco.com (9)

Kilcullen, Patrick, The Gallery Shop, Buffalo, NY. Tel: (716) 882-8700 X258, FAX: (716) 882-1958, E-Mail: gallshop@albrightknox.org, Web Site: www.albrightknox.org (6)

Kileen, Kieran, Marketing Agencies Association Worldwide, Minneapolis, MN. Tel: (952) 922-0130, FAX: (203) 969-1499, E-Mail: keith.mccracker@maaw.org, Web Site: www.maaw.org (40)

Kilgannon, Rena, Kilgannon, Atlanta, GA. Tel: (404) 876-2800, FAX: (404) 876-2830, E-Mail: contact@kilgannon.com, Web Site: www.kilgannon.com (35)

Kilgannon, Atlanta, GA. Tel: (404) 876-2800, FAX: (404) 876-2830, E-Mail: contact@kilgannon.com, Web Site: www.kilgannon.com (35)

Kilgore, Paul, Capitol Hill Lists, Statham, GA. Tel: (706) 546-0282 (23)

Kilgore, Tom, Tennessee Valley Authority, Knoxville, TN. Tel: (865) 632-2101, Web Site: www.tva.gov (16)

Killeen, Patrick, Progressive Energy Corp, San Marcos, CA. Tel: (760) 727-2906, (800) 525-8624, FAX: (760) 727-0947, E-Mail: patrickkilleen@cox.net (5)

Killen, John, Win Craft Inc, Winona, MN. Tel: (507) 454-5510, (800) 533-8100, FAX: (507) 454-6403, Web Site: www.wincraftschool.com (5)

Killian, Bob, Killian & Co, Chicago, IL. Tel: (312) 836-0050, E-Mail: bob@killianadvertising.com, Web Site: www.killianadvertising.com (35)

Killian, Tammy, Micro Plastics Inc, Flippin, AR. Tel: (870) 453-2261, (800) 466-1467, FAX: (870) 453-8676, E-Mail: mpsales@microplastics.com, Web Site: www.microplastics.com (16)

Killian & Co, Chicago, IL. Tel: (312) 836-0050, E-Mail: bob@killianadvertising.com, Web Site: www.killianadvertising.com (35)

Killinger, Kerry, Washington Mutual Home Loan, Inc, Downers Grove, IL. Tel: (847) 549-6500, FAX: (847) 549-2975 (14)

Killingstad, Chris, TENNANT Co, Minneapolis, MN. Tel: (763) 540-1200, (800) 553-8033, FAX: (763) 513-2142, E-Mail: info@tennantco.com, Web Site: www.tennantco.com (34)

Kilner, Patricia, California Society of CPA's, San Mateo, CA. Tel: (800) 922-5272, FAX: (650) 522-3009, E-Mail: info@culcpa.org, Web Site: www.calcpa.org (1)

Kilpatrick, Frank, S., Healthcare Communications Group, El Segundo, CA. Tel: (310) 606-5703, (800) 504-0933, FAX: (310) 606-5705, E-Mail: fkilpatrick@hcg.com, Web Site: www.hcg.com (32)

Kim, Grace, ABC Carpet & Home, New York, NY. Tel: (212) 473-3000, (800) 888-RUGS, FAX: (212) 777-3713, Web Site: www.abccarpet.com (8)

Kim, Jeanny, Smithsonian Institution, Washington, DC. Tel: (202) 357-2700, Web Site: www.si.edu (6)

Kim, Joanne, Roland Products Inc, Los Angeles, CA. Tel: (323) 731-1111, FAX: (323) 731-9585, E-Mail: salesinfo@rolandinc.com, Web Site: www.rolandinc.com (16)

Kim, Yoan, Longevity Network Ltd, Henderson, NV. Tel: (702) 454-7000, (800) 242-1000, FAX: (702) 435-4786, Web Site: www.longevitynetwork.com (7)

Kim, Younjee, Ace Communications, Garden City, NY. Tel: (718) 458-3800, (800) 468-7667, FAX: (516) 872-8156, Web Site: www.aceav.com (3)

Kimball, Dan, B&W Press Inc, Georgetown, MA. Tel: (978) 352-6100, (877) 246-3467, FAX: (978) 352-5955, E-Mail: csr@bwpress.com, Web Site: www.bwpress.com (21)

Kimball, John, Newspaper Association of America, Arlington, VA. Tel: (703) 902-1600, FAX: (571) 366-1195, Web Site: www.naa.org (1)

Kimball, Stephen, Stephen Kimball DM Copywriting, Cedar Hills, UT. Tel: (801) 796-7234, FAX: (801) 796-5799, E-Mail: stephen@skcopywriting.com, Web Site: www.skcopywriting.com (39)

Miles Kimball Co, Oshkosh, WI. Tel: (920) 231-3800, FAX: (920) 231-0422, Web Site: www.mileskimball.com (6)

Stephen Kimball DM Copywriting, Cedar Hills, UT. Tel: (801) 796-7234, FAX: (801) 796-5799, E-Mail: stephen@skcopywriting.com, Web Site: www.skcopywriting.com (39)

Kimberlin, Kelly, Franchise Services Inc, Mission Viejo, CA. Tel: (949) 282-3800, Web Site: www.pip.com (27)

Kimberly-Clark Corp, Neenah, WI. Tel: (920) 721-2000, (888) 525-8388, FAX: (920) 721-7722, Web Site: www.kimberly-clark.com (16)

Kimble, Gertrude, Kimbo Educational, Long Branch, NJ. Tel: (732) 229-4949, (800) 848-6099 (NM), (800) 631-2187 (NJ), FAX: (732) 870-3340, E-Mail: kimboed@aol.com, Web Site: www.kimboed.com (17)

Kimble, James, Kimbo Educational, Long Branch, NJ. Tel: (732) 229-4949, (800) 848-6099 (NM), (800) 631-2187 (NJ), FAX: (732) 870-3340, E-Mail: kimboed@aol.com, Web Site: www.kimboed.com (17)

Kimble, Jeffrey, Kimbo Educational, Long Branch, NJ. Tel: (732) 229-4949, (800) 848-6099 (NM), (800) 631-2187 (NJ), FAX: (732) 870-3340, E-Mail: kimboed@aol.com, Web Site: www.kimboed.com (17)

Kimbo Educational, Long Branch, NJ. Tel: (732) 229-4949, (800) 848-6099 (NM), (800) 631-2187 (NJ), FAX: (732) 870-3340, E-Mail: kimboed@aol.com, Web Site: www.kimboed.com (17)

Kimbrough, John, Sheshunoff Information Services Inc, Austin, TX. Tel: (800) 456-2340, Web Site: www.sheshunoff.com (14)

Kimmerling Hoveling, Pamela, Rola-Kimmerling Associates, New York, NY. Tel: (646) 367-4815, FAX: (646) 367-4901, E-Mail: p_kimhov@rkadv.com, Web Site: www.rkadv.com (35)

Kimura, Lori, Milici Valenti Ng Pack, Honolulu, HI. Tel: (808) 536-0881, FAX: (808) 529-6208, E-Mail: info@mvnp.com, Web Site: www.mvnp.com (35)

Kincaid, Jeff, Creative Printing Services Inc, Des Plaines, IL. Tel: (847) 803-2800, (800) 932-2750, FAX: (847) 803-3299, E-Mail: info@creativepsi.com, Web Site: www.creativepsi.com (27)

Kincaid, Judith, W., JK Associates LLC, Palo Alto, CA. Tel: (650) 838-9816, FAX: (650) 838-9867, Web Site: www.jk-associates.com (20)

Kincheloe, Michael, Karol Media, Wilkes-Barre, PA. Tel: (570) 822-8899, (800) 526-4773, FAX: (570) 822-8226, Web Site: www.karolmedia.com (28)

Kind, John, Masterpiece Studios Inc, Mankato, MN. Tel: (507) 388-8788, (800) 447-0219, FAX: (507) 344-4606, E-Mail: masterpiecestudios@masterpiecestudios.com, Web Site: www.masterpiecestudios.com (16)

Kindler, Jeffrey, B., Pfizer Inc, New York, NY. Tel: (212) 733-2323, Web Site: www.pfizer.com (16)

Kinerk, Niles, Gardens Alive! Inc, Lawrenceburg, IN. Tel: (812) 537-8665, FAX: (812) 537-5108, E-Mail: service@gardensalive.com, Web Site: www.gardens-alive.com (8)

King, Allen, Universal Corp, Richmond, VA. Tel: (804) 359-9311, FAX: (804) 254-3582, Web Site: www.universalcorp.com (16)

King, Allison, FDAnews, Falls Church, VA. Tel: (703) 538-7600, (888) 838-5578, FAX: (703) 538-7676, E-Mail: customerservice@fdanews.com, Web Site: www.fdanews.com (17)

King, Andy, American Family Insurance Group, Madison, WI. Tel: (608) 249-2111, FAX: (608) 243-6525, E-Mail: akin1@amfam.com, Web Site: www.amfam.com (15)

King, Cathy, King Direct Marketing Inc, Daytona Beach, FL. Tel: (386) 788-8925, FAX: (386) 761-0234 (33)

King, David, Fulcrum, New York, NY. Tel: (888) 245-9450 (22)

King, Donna, Sturm, Rosenburg, King & Co, Chicago, IL. Tel: (312) 943-1881, FAX: (312) 943-2346, Web Site: www.sturmads.com (35)

King, Gyr, Bruce McGaw Graphics, Manchester Center, VT. Tel: (845) 353-8600, (888) 4BMCGAW, FAX: (845) 353-3155, E-Mail: sales@bmcgaw.com, Web Site: www.bmcgaw.com (6)

King, Jim, King Printing Solutions, New Tazewell, TN. Tel: (423) 626-7700, (800) 251-9236, FAX: (423) 526-5225, E-Mail: sales@kbfcorp.com, Web Site: www.kbfcorp.com (27)

King, Karen, Homesteaders Life Co, West Des Moines, IA. Tel: (515) 440-7777, (800) 477-3633, E-Mail: service@homesteaderslife.com, Web Site: www.homesteaderslife.com (15)

King, Kelly S., Branch Banking & Trust Co, Wilson, NC. Tel: (252) 399-4111, FAX: (252) 246-4030 (14)

King, Kevin, Year One Inc, Braselton, GA. Tel: (706) 658-2140, FAX: (706) 654-5355, E-Mail: info@yearone.com, Web Site: www.yearone.com (16)

King, Leanne, Mervyn's, Pleasanton, CA. Tel: (510) 727-3000, (800) 480-5014, FAX: (510) 727-5851, Web Site: www.mervyns.com (16)

King, Mark, Texwipe Co, Kernersville, NC. Tel: (201) 684-1800, (800) TEXWIPE, FAX: (201) 684-1801, E-Mail: info@texwipe.com, Web Site: www.texwipe.com (16)

King, Mike, Year One Inc, Braselton, GA. Tel: (706) 658-2140, FAX: (706) 654-5355, E-Mail: info@yearone.com, Web Site: www.yearone.com (16)

King, Rick, Showtime Networks Inc, New York, NY. Tel: (212) 708-1600, FAX: (212) 708-1450, Web Site: www.sho.com (16)

King, Roger, King World Productions Inc, New York, NY. Tel: (212) 315-4000, Web Site: www.kingworld.com (32)

King, William, Strategy Corps LLC, Brentwood, TN. Tel: (615) 221-8381, (888) 577-6933, FAX: (615) 221-8479, E-Mail: info@strategycorps.com, Web Site: www.strategycorps.com (16)

King Computer Services Inc, Las Cruces, NM. Tel: (818) 951-5240, FAX: (818) 353-1278, E-Mail: kingsoftware@aol.com, Web Site: www. kingcomputerservices.com (22)

King Direct Marketing Inc, Daytona Beach, FL. Tel: (386) 788-8925, FAX: (386) 761-0234 (33)

King Features, New York, NY. Tel: (212) 455-4000, FAX: (212) 682-8332 (17)

King Pharmaceuticals, Inc, Bristol, TN. Tel: (423) 989-8000, (888) 840-5370, FAX: (423) 274-8677, Web Site: www.kingpharm.com (7)

King Printing Solutions, New Tazewell, TN. Tel: (423) 626-7700, (800) 251-9236, FAX: (423) 526-5225, E-Mail: sales@kbfcorp.com, Web Site: www. kbfcorp.com (27)

King Ranch Saddle Shop, Kingsville, TX. Tel: (361) 595-1424, (800) 282-KING, FAX: (361) 595-1011, E-Mail: krsaddleshop@king-ranch.com, Web Site: www.krsaddleshop.com (8)

King Teleservices, New York, NY. Tel: (718) 361-4100, (800) 817-5468, E-Mail: info@king-teleservices.com, Web Site: www.king-teleservices. com (29)

King World CBS, Santa Monica, CA. Tel: (310) 264-3300, Web Site: www.kingworld.com (32)

King World Productions Inc, New York, NY. Tel: (212) 315-4000, Web Site: www.kingworld.com (32)

Kingery, John, F., Kingery Printing Co, Effingham, IL. Tel: (217) 347-5151, FAX: (217) 540-5400, Web Site: www.kingeryprinting.com (27)

Kingery Printing Co, Effingham, IL. Tel: (217) 347-5151, FAX: (217) 540-5400, Web Site: www. kingeryprinting.com (27)

Kingrey, Connie, Minnesota Multi Housing Association, Bloomington, MN. Tel: (952) 854-8500, FAX: (952) 854-3810, E-Mail: mha@mmha.com, Web Site: www.mmha.com (1)

King's Chandelier Co, Eden, NC. Tel: (336) 623-6188, FAX: (336) 627-9935, E-Mail: crystal@chandelier. com, Web Site: www.chandelier.com (6)

Kingsbury, Bridget, Ann, Barker Specialty Co, Cheshire, CT. Tel: (203) 272-2222, (800) BARK-ERS, (800) 227-5377, FAX: (203) 272-2727, Web Site: www.barkerspecialty.com (33)

Kingsley North Inc, Norway, MI. Tel: (906) 563-9228, (800) 338-9280, FAX: (906) 563-7143, E-Mail: sales@kingsleynorth.com, Web Site: www. kingsleynorth.com (11)

Kinman, Eric, Veridian Credit Union, Waterloo, IA. Tel: (319) 236-5692, (800) 235-3228, FAX: (319) 833-1185, E-Mail: sarahma@veridiancu.org, Web Site: www.veridiancu.org (1)

Kinnan, R., Douglas, Amerisure Insurance Cos, Farmington Hills, MI. Tel: (248) 615-9000, (800) 257-1900, FAX: (248) 615-8224, Web Site: www. amerisure.com (1)

Kinnel, Sarah, DataLogix, Westminster, CO. Tel: (303) 327-1600, FAX: (303) 327-1650, Web Site: www. datalogix.com (23)

Kinney, J.D., MediaGraphics, Eau Claire, WI. Tel: (751) 590-4488, (866) 324-1658, E-Mail: mediagraphics@devkinney.com, Web Site: www. devkinney.com (35)

Kintz, Bruce, G., Concordia Publishing House, Saint Louis, MO. Tel: (314) 268-1000, (800) 325-3040, FAX: (314) 268-1329, E-Mail: order@cph.org, Web Site: www.cph.org (17)

Kiper, Kevin, Excelligence Learning Corp, Monterey, CA. Tel: (831) 333-2000, Web Site: www. excelligencelearning.com (5)

Kiphart, Richard, P., William Blair & Co LLC, Chicago, IL. Tel: (312) 236-1600, (800) 621-0687, FAX: (312) 368-9418, E-Mail: info@williamblair. com, Web Site: www.williamblair.com (14)

Kiplinger, Knight, A., The Kiplinger Washington Editors Inc, Washington, DC. Tel: (202) 887-6400, (800) 544-0155, FAX: (202) 496-1817, Web Site: www.kiplinger.com (17)

The Kiplinger Washington Editors Inc, Washington, DC. Tel: (202) 887-6400, (800) 544-0155, FAX: (202) 496-1817, Web Site: www.kiplinger.com (17)

Kipp Brothers Inc, Greenfield, IN. Tel: (317) 634-5507, (800) 428-1153, FAX: (800) 832-5477, E-Mail: toys@kippbro.com (33)

Kipplinger, Todd, L., The Kiplinger Washington Editors Inc, Washington, DC. Tel: (202) 887-6400, (800) 544-0155, FAX: (202) 496-1817, Web Site: www.kiplinger.com (17)

Kirbey, Kevin, Amsterdam Printing, Amsterdam, NY. Tel: (518) 842-6000, (800) 203-9917, FAX: (518) 843-5204, E-Mail: customerservice@ amsterdamprinting.com, Web Site: www. amsterdamprinting.com (16)

Kirby, Kent, Adnet USA, Arlington Heights, IL. Tel: (847) 483-5300, FAX: (773) 304-2700, Web Site: www.adnet.us (16)

Kirby, Kevin, Go Promos, Gloversville, NY. Tel: (800) 523-9909, FAX: (800) 523-3292, E-Mail: customerservice@gopromos.com, Web Site: www. gopromos.com (5)

Kirby, Kevin, K-D Lamp Co, Andover, OH. Tel: (440) 293-4064, FAX: (440) 293-4591, E-Mail: admin@ atc-lighting-plastics.com, Web Site: www.k-dlamp. com (12)

Kirches, Debra, R., Partners Health, Philadelphia, PA. Tel: (215) 849-9600, (800) 553-0784, E-Mail: sroberts@healthpart.com, Web Site: www. healthpart.com (1)

Kirchoff, Karin, Defenders of Wildlife, Washington, DC. Tel: (202) 682-9400, Web Site: www. defenders.org (1)

Kirchwehm, Michael, HDA Inc, Saint Louis, MO. Tel: (314) 770-2222, (800) 533-4350, FAX: (314) 770-1454, E-Mail: plans@hdainc.com, Web Site: www. designamerica.com (17)

Kirejczyk, Cynthia, F., A-T Surgical Manufacturing Co, Holyoke, MA. Tel: (413) 532-4551, (800) 225-2023, FAX: (413) 532-0826, E-Mail: atsmci@a-surgical.com, Web Site: www.atsurgical.com (2)

Kirejczyk, Eugene P., A-T Surgical Manufacturing Co, Holyoke, MA. Tel: (413) 532-4551, (800) 225-2023, FAX: (413) 532-0826, E-Mail: atsmci@a-surgical.com, Web Site: www.atsurgical.com (2)

Kirk, Matt, ClickSpeed, Overland Park, KS. Tel: (913) 383-1500, Web Site: www.clickspeed.com (35)

Kirkeng, Peggy, Chicago Tribune, Chicago, IL. Tel: (312) 222-3232, (800) 874-2863, FAX: (312) 222-2353, E-Mail: consumerservices@tribune.com, Web Site: www.chicagotribune.com (31)

Kirkham, John, A., Open Text Inc, Waterloo, ON. Tel: (519) 888-9933, (800) 499-6544, FAX: (519) 888-0677, E-Mail: support@opentext.com, Web Site: www.opentext.com (16)

Kirkland, John, MLS Data Management Solutions, Fort Worth, TX. Tel: (817) 804-6900, FAX: (817) 804-6999, Web Site: www.mlsc.com (22)

Kirkland, Ronald, E., American Family Life Assurance Co of Columbus (AFLAC), Columbus, GA. Tel: (706) 323-3431, (800) 992-3522, FAX: (706) 660-7446, Web Site: www.aflac.com (15)

Kirkpatrick, Brad, Rhythm Band Inc, Fort Worth, TX. Tel: (817) 335-2561, (800) 424-4724, FAX: (800) 784-9401, E-Mail: sales@rhythmband.com, Web Site: www.rhythmband.com (11)

Kirkpatrick, Douglas, Heldref Publications, Washington, DC. Tel: (215) 625-8900, (202) 296-6267, FAX: (202) 296-5149, Web Site: www.heldref.org (17)

Kirkpatrick, Will, Will Kirkpatrick Shorebird Decoys Inc, Hudson, MA. Tel: (978) 562-7841, FAX: (978) 562-3514, E-Mail: wekdecoys@aol.com, Web Site: www.kirkpatrickdecoys.com (6)

Will Kirkpatrick Shorebird Decoys Inc, Hudson, MA. Tel: (978) 562-7841, FAX: (978) 562-3514, E-Mail: wekdecoys@aol.com, Web Site: www. kirkpatrickdecoys.com (6)

Kirsch, Herbert, AAA BEST Mailing Lists Inc, Tucson, AZ. Tel: (520) 885-0400, (800) 692-2378, FAX: (520) 885-3100, E-Mail: best@bestmailing. com, Web Site: www.bestmailing.com (23)

Kirsch, Karen, J., AAA BEST Mailing Lists Inc, Tucson, AZ. Tel: (520) 885-0400, (800) 692-2378, FAX: (520) 885-3100, E-Mail: best@bestmailing. com, Web Site: www.bestmailing.com (23)

Kirscher, Elizabeth, Morningstar Inc, Chicago, IL. Tel: (312) 696-6000, Web Site: www.morningstar.com (14)

Kirschner, Mark, LinkShare Corp, New York, NY. Tel: (646) 654-6000, Web Site: www.linkshare.com (32)

Kirshbaum, Laurence, Warner Books, New York, NY. Tel: (212) 364-1200, FAX: (212) 522-7989, Web Site: www.twbookmark.com (17)

Kirshenbaum, Bond & Partners, New York, NY. Tel: (212) 633-0080, FAX: (212) 463-8643, E-Mail: press@kb.com, Web Site: www.kb.com (35)

Kirsner, Laura, Helzberg Diamonds, North Kansas City, MO. Tel: (816) 842-7780, (800) HELZBURG, FAX: (816) 480-0294, Web Site: www.helzberg.com (16)

Kiser, Anita, I/D/E/A Inc, Caldwell, ID. Tel: (208) 459-6357, (800) 635-9261, FAX: (208) 459-6484, Web Site: www.relyonidea.com (16)

Kislik, Liz, Liz Kislik Associates LLC, Rockville Centre, NY. Tel: (516) 568-2932, FAX: (516) 568-2936, Web Site: www.lizkislik.com (20)

Liz Kislik Associates LLC, Rockville Centre, NY. Tel: (516) 568-2932, FAX: (516) 568-2936, Web Site: www.lizkislik.com (20)

Kistler-Tiffany Companies LLC, Berwyn, PA. Tel: (610) 722-3300, (866) 250-5413, Web Site: www. ktadv.com (20)

Kitajima, Yoshitoshi, DNP America Inc, New York, NY. Tel: (212) 503-1060, FAX: (212) 679-0613 (27)

Kitchen Kompact Inc, Jeffersonville, IN. Tel: (812) 282-6681, FAX: (812) 282-7880, E-Mail: webmaster@kitchenkompact.com, Web Site: www. kitchenkompact.com (8)

Kitchener, Beth, Webloyalty.com, Norwalk, CT. Tel: (203) 846-3300, Web Site: www.webloyalty.com (32)

Kitt, Lonnie, QC Supply LLC, Schuyler, NE. Tel: (402) 352-3167, Web Site: www.qcsupply.com (16)

Kittner, Alyse, Society for Healthcare Strategy & Market Development, Chicago, IL. Tel: (312) 422-3888, FAX: (312) 422-4579, E-Mail: stratsoc@aha. org, Web Site: www.stratsociety.org (42)

Kives, Philip, K-tel International, Golden Valley, MN. Tel: (204) 889-5430, (800) 665-5021, FAX: (612) 559-6803, Web Site: www.ktel.com (16)

Kizer, John, Central States Indemnity, Omaha, NE. Tel: (402) 997-8000, (402) 397-1111, (800) 445-6500, Web Site: www.csi-omaha.com (15)

Kizer, Richard, T., Central States Health & Life Co of Omaha, Omaha, NE. Tel: (402) 397-1111, (800) 826-6587, FAX: (402) 391-3772, Web Site: www. cso.com (15)

Kizer, T., Edward, Central States Health & Life Co of Omaha, Omaha, NE. Tel: (402) 397-1111, (800) 826-6587, FAX: (402) 391-3772, Web Site: www. cso.com (15)

Klahowya Native American & Nature Gift Shop, Bandon, OR. Tel: (541) 347-5099, FAX: (541) 347-4132 (6)

Klan, Frank G., Color Q Inc, Miamisburg, OH. Tel: (937) 866-4001, (800) 999-9818, FAX: (937) 866-4101, E-Mail: info@colorq.com, Web Site: www. colorqinc.com (27)

Klang, Peggy, Student Marketing Group Inc, Lynbrook, NY. Tel: (516) 593-8877, Web Site: www. studentmarketing.net (23)

Klapmeier, Jolie, Bluewater Yachts, Mora, MN. Tel: (320) 679-3811, FAX: (320) 679-3820, E-Mail: bluewater@ncis.com, Web Site: www. bluewateryacht.com (16)

Klapmeier, Steve, Bluewater Yachts, Mora, MN. Tel: (320) 679-3811, FAX: (320) 679-3820, E-Mail: bluewater@ncis.com, Web Site: www. bluewateryacht.com (16)

Klar, Rick, Equitable Life & Casualty Insurance Co, Salt Lake City, UT. Tel: (801) 579-3400, FAX: (801) 579-3789, Web Site: www.equilife.com (15)

Klatell, James, Campaigns & Elections Magazine, Arlington, VA. Tel: (703) 778-4028, (800) 771-8252, FAX: (703) 778-4024, Web Site: www. campaignsandelections.com (17)

Klayko, Michael, Brocade Communications Systems Inc, San Jose, CA. Tel: (408) 333-4300, FAX: (408) 333-8101, Web Site: www.brocade.com (16)

Klebe, Tim, K-Log, Zion, IL. Tel: (847) 872-6611, Web Site: www.k-log.com (8)

Kleeger, Neil L., Gallery of Cats, Valencia, CA. Tel: (818) 782-6264, E-Mail: helpdesk@galleryofcats. com, Web Site: www.galleryofcats.com (6)

Kleeman, Alan, A.S. Kleeman & Associates, Duluth, GA. Tel: (770) 752-0500, FAX: (770) 752-0066 (20)

A.S. Kleeman & Associates, Duluth, GA. Tel: (770) 752-0500, FAX: (770) 752-0066 (20)

Kleen, Tom, Stratford Hall, North Mankato, MN. Tel: (708) 496-4908, (800) 628-9028, FAX: (708) 496-8058, E-Mail: stratfordhall@myprinter.com, Web Site: www.stratfordhall.com (10)

Klehm, Peter, Western Fulfillment Management Association Inc, North Hollywood, CA. Tel: (310) 323-7220, FAX: (310) 323-7231, E-Mail: mjordan@ espcomp.com, Web Site: www.wfma.org (40)

Klein, Abraham, M, M&M Health Care Apparel Co, Brooklyn, NY. Tel: (800) 221-8929, E-Mail: fashionease@aol.com (2)

Klein, Al, Louisville Direct Marketing Association, Louisville, KY. Tel: (888) 392-1941, E-Mail: ldmacontact@ldma.org, Web Site: www.ldma.org (40)

Klein, Andy, US Tax Shield, Encino, CA. Tel: (877) 929-3535, Web Site: www.ustaxshield.com (14)

Klein, Bernard, B Klein Publications, Delray Beach, FL. Tel: (561) 496-3316, FAX: (561) 496-5546, E-Mail: bkleinpub@aol.com (17)

Klein, Bernard, Guide to American & International Directories, Delray Beach, FL. Tel: (561) 367-3799, FAX: (561) 451-0803, E-Mail: bkleinpub@ aol.com (43)

Klein, Bernard, Mail Order Business Directory, Boca Raton, FL. Tel: (561) 367-3799, FAX: (561) 451-0803, E-Mail: bkleinpub@aol.com (43)

Klein, Betty, B Klein Publications, Delray Beach, FL. Tel: (561) 496-3316, FAX: (561) 496-5546, E-Mail: bkleinpub@aol.com (17)

Klein, Bob, Corinthian Direct, New York, NY. Tel: (212) 279-5700, FAX: (212) 239-1772, E-Mail: jonz@mediabuying.com, Web Site: www. mediabuying.com (35)

Klein, Dave, Hurletron Inc, Libertyville, IL. Tel: (847) 680-7022, FAX: (847) 680-7338, Web Site: www. hurletron.com (34)

Klein, David, Advertising Age, New York, NY. Tel: (212) 210-0100, FAX: (212) 210-0111, Web Site: www.crain.com (43)

Klein, David, Auto Anything, San Diego, CA. Tel: (858) 569-8111, (800) 874-8888, FAX: (858) 569-8503, E-Mail: customerservice@autoanything.com, Web Site: www.autoanything.com (34)

Klein, David, Macromark Inc, Brewster, NY. Tel: (845) 230-6300, FAX: (845) 278-0650, E-Mail: david@macromark.com, Web Site: www. macromark.com (23)

Klein, Debbie, Arizona Highways Magazine, Phoenix, AZ. Tel: (602) 712-2200, FAX: (602) 254-4505, E-Mail: editor@arizonahighways.com, Web Site: www.arizonahighways.com (17)

Klein, Hans, Hannecke Display Systems Inc, Boonton, NJ. Tel: (973) 335-0434, FAX: (973) 335-1274, E-Mail: info.usa@hannecke.com, Web Site: www. hannecke.com (27)

Klein, Howard, Lanmark Group Inc, West Long Branch, NJ. Tel: (732) 389-4500, FAX: (732) 389-4998, E-Mail: info@lanmarkgroup.com, Web Site: www.lanmarkgroup.com (35)

Klein, Jonathan, Getty Images, Seattle, WA. Tel: (206) 925-5018, (800) 462-4379, Web Site: www. gettyimages.com (38)

Klein, Lawrence, Thought Technology Ltd, Montreal, PQ. Tel: (514) 489-8251, (800) 361-3651, FAX: (514) 489-8255, E-Mail: lawrence@ thoughttechnology.com, Web Site: www. thoughttechnology.com (16)

Klein, Michael, Cable Direct Marketing Inc, Montville, NJ. Tel: (973) 244-0010, FAX: (973) 244-0302, E-Mail: cabledm@aol.com (31)

Klein, Paul, Rich Products Corp, Buffalo, NY. Tel: (716) 878-8000, (800) 828-2021, FAX: (716) 878-8765, Web Site: www.richs.com (16)

Klein, Rich, FKM, Houston, TX. Tel: (713) 862-5100, FAX: (713) 869-6560, E-Mail: rklein@fkmagency. com, Web Site: www.fkmagency.com (35)

Klein, Stephanie, Higher Power Marketing, Phoenix, AZ. Tel: (480) 837-3580, (888) 922-3580, FAX: (480) 837-3589, E-Mail: info@hpowermarketing. com, Web Site: www.hpowermarketing.com (30)

Klein, Stephen, Encore Marketing International, Lanham, MD. Tel: (301) 459-8020, (800) 846-9398, FAX: (301) 731-0525, E-Mail: customerservice@ encoremarketing.com, Web Site: www. encoremarketing.com (16)

Klein, Steve, Wolf Blumberg Krody Inc, Cincinnati, OH. Tel: (513) 784-0066, FAX: (513) 784-0986, E-Mail: sklein@wbk.com, Web Site: www.wbk. com (35)

Klein, Susan, Walt Klein & Associates Inc, Denver, CO. Tel: (303) 298-8015, FAX: (303) 298-8194, Web Site: www.wka.com (35)

Klein, Walt, Walt Klein & Associates Inc, Denver, CO. Tel: (303) 298-8015, FAX: (303) 298-8194, Web Site: www.wka.com (35)

B Klein Publications, Delray Beach, FL. Tel: (561) 496-3316, FAX: (561) 496-5546, E-Mail: bkleinpub@aol.com (17)

Calvin Klein Cosmetics Co, New York, NY. Tel: (212) 759-8888, FAX: (212) 479-4399 (7)

Walt Klein & Associates Inc, Denver, CO. Tel: (303) 298-8015, FAX: (303) 298-8194, Web Site: www. wka.com (35)

Kleiner, Madeline, A., Hilton Hotels Corp, Mc Lean, VA. Tel: (310) 278-4321, (800) HILTONS, FAX: (310) 205-3670, Web Site: www.hilton.com (19)

Kleinfeld, Neil, Growth Platforms Institute, Wilton, CT. Tel: (203) 529-0500, E-Mail: info@ growthplatforms.org, Web Site: www. growthplatforms.org (20)

Kleinfelter, Mary Ann, L-Com Inc, Andover, MA. Tel: (978) 682-6936, Web Site: www.L-com.com (22)

Kleinrock, Margaret, Renaissance Greeting Cards Inc, Springvale, ME. Tel: (207) 324-4153, (800) 688-9998, FAX: (207) 324-9564, E-Mail: rencards@ rencards.com (5)

Kleinrock, Randy, Renaissance Greeting Cards Inc, Springvale, ME. Tel: (207) 324-4153, (800) 688-9998, FAX: (207) 324-9564, E-Mail: rencards@ rencards.com (5)

Kleinschmidt, Roxann, Vocational Biographies Inc, Sauk Centre, MN. Tel: (320) 352-6516, (800) 255-0752, FAX: (320) 352-5546, E-Mail: careers@ vocbios.com, Web Site: www.vocbio.com (31)

Klemtner Advertising Inc, New York, NY. Tel: (212) 463-3400, FAX: (212) 463-3541 (35)

Klenman, Anne, TVA Productions Inc (The Video Agency), Studio City, CA. Tel: (818) 505-8300, (888) 322-4296, FAX: (818) 505-8370, E-Mail: info@tvaproductions.com, Web Site: www. tvaproductions.com (35)

Klibanoff, Daniel, Info Direct, Huntsville, AL. Tel: (256) 534-5478, (800) 239-5478, FAX: (256) 536-0705, E-Mail: dklib@hiway.net, Web Site: www. infodirectlists.com (23)

Klieman, Lisa, Innovyx Inc, Seattle, WA. Tel: (212) 817-6900, Web Site: www.innovyx.com (32)

Klien, Ann, The Trumpet Club, New York, NY. Tel: (212) 343-6100, FAX: (212) 343-7709, Web Site: www.scholastic.com (17)

Kline, Carnie, Halls Kansas City, Kansas City, MO. Tel: (816) 274-8111, (800) 624-4034, FAX: (816) 545-2121, Web Site: www.hallskc.com (16)

Kline, Kim, Euro RSCG 4D Worldwide, San Francisco, CA. Tel: (415) 345-7700, FAX: (415) 345-7701 (35)

Kline, Robert H., US Historical Society, Richmond, VA. Tel: (800) 788-4478, FAX: (804) 648-0002, E-Mail: administrator@ushs.org, Web Site: www. ushs.org (16)

Klingaman, Paul, Suarez Corp Industries, North Canton, OH. Tel: (330) 494-5504, FAX: (330) 497-6837, E-Mail: suarez@suarez.com, Web Site: www.suarez.com (5)

Klingel, Stephen, J., National Council on Compensation Insurance Inc (NCCI), Boca Raton, FL. Tel: (561) 893-1000, (800) 622-4123, FAX: (561) 893-1191, Web Site: www.ncci.com (1)

Klinger, Randy, Hollister Inc, Libertyville, IL. Tel: (847) 680-1000, (888) 740-8999, FAX: (847) 680-2123, Web Site: www.hollister.com (16)

Klinger, Scott, allconnect, Atlanta, GA. Tel: (404) 260-2449, Web Site: www.allconnect.com (32)

Klingspor, Christoph, Ambient Shapes Inc, Hickory, NC. Tel: (800) 438-2244, FAX: (800) 872-2005, E-Mail: sales@ambientshapes.com, Web Site: www.ambientshapes.com (7)

Klingspor, Christoph, Klingspor's Woodworking Shop, Hickory, NC. Tel: (828) 326-WOOD, (800) 228-0000, FAX: (828) 327-4634, E-Mail: sales@ woodworkingshop.com, Web Site: www. woodworkingshop.com (9)

Klingspor, Rosemarie, Ambient Shapes Inc, Hickory, NC. Tel: (800) 438-2244, FAX: (800) 872-2005, E-Mail: sales@ambientshapes.com, Web Site: www.ambientshapes.com (7)

Klingspor's Woodworking Shop, Hickory, NC. Tel: (828) 326-WOOD, (800) 228-0000, FAX: (828) 327-4634, E-Mail: sales@woodworkingshop.com, Web Site: www.woodworkingshop.com (9)

Klinkenberg, R.B., Harrington's of Vermont Inc, Richmond, VT. Tel: (802) 434-7500, FAX: (802) 434-3166, E-Mail: info@harringtonham.com, Web Site: www.harringtonham.com (4)

Klippel, John, H., Arthritis Foundation, Atlanta, GA. Tel: (404) 872-7100, FAX: (404) 872-0457, Web Site: www.arthritis.org (1)

Klise, Molly, Thomas Klise/Crimson Multimedia, Mystic, CT. Tel: (800) 937-0092, FAX: (860) 536-5141, E-Mail: info@crimsoninc.com, Web Site: www.crimsoninc.com (16)

Klitzner, Alan, Klitzner Industries, Providence, RI. Tel: (401) 751-7500, (800) 556-6860, FAX: (800) 556-3199, E-Mail: info@klitzner.com, Web Site: www.klitzner.com; www.providenceline.com (6)

Klitzner, Dean, Klitzner Industries, Providence, RI. Tel: (401) 751-7500, (800) 556-6860, FAX: (800) 556-3199, E-Mail: info@klitzner.com, Web Site: www.klitzner.com; www.providenceline.com (6)

Klitzner Industries, Providence, RI. Tel: (401) 751-7500, (800) 556-6860, FAX: (800) 556-3199, E-Mail: info@klitzner.com, Web Site: www. klitzner.com; www.providenceline.com (6)

Klockit, Lake Geneva, WI. Tel: (262) 248-7000, (800) 556-2548, FAX: (262) 248-9899, E-Mail: klockit@ klockit.com, Web Site: www.klockit.com (6)

Kloke, Gretchen, Starwood Hotels & Resorts, Stamford, CT. Tel: (914) 640-8268, FAX: (914) 640-8310, Web Site: www.starwoodhotels.com (19)

Klondike Marketing Inc, Boulder, CO. Tel: (720) 406-1177, (888) 395-5438, FAX: (888) 395-5438, Web Site: www.klondikemarketing.com (35)

Klonowski, Len, American Recreation Products Inc, Saint Louis, MO. Tel: (314) 576-8000, FAX: (314) 576-8072 (11)

Klopman, William, A., Burlington Industries Inc, Greensboro, NC. Tel: (336) 379-2000, FAX: (336) 379-2498, Web Site: www.burlington.com (16)

Kloss, Linda, L., American Health Information Management Association, Chicago, IL. Tel: (312) 233-1100, FAX: (312) 233-1090, E-Mail: info@ahima.org, Web Site: www.ahima.org (1)

Klotzman, Bruce, Our Data Works Inc, Lewisville, TX. Tel: (469) 546-3000, (800) 268-2505, FAX: (469) 546-3013, E-Mail: info@ourdataworks.com, Web Site: www.ourdataworks.com (29)

Kluger, Joel, Sunbelt Media Service, Chapel Hill, NC. Tel: (919) 967-7174, FAX: (919) 967-6050 (32)

Klumack, Barbara, Donnelley Marketing, Pearl River, NY. Tel: (201) 476-2300, FAX: (201) 476-2151, Web Site: www.infousa.com (23)

Klune, Andy, Syntellect, Phoenix, AZ. Tel: (602) 789-2800, (800) 788-9733, FAX: (602) 789-2899, Web Site: www.syntellect.com (16)

Knab, Michael, Gennera Knab & Co, Burbank, CA. Tel: (312) 337-2010, FAX: (312) 337-2433, E-Mail: cleveland-office@priva.com, Web Site: www.priva.com (35)

Knapp, John, CIDCO, Fresno, CA. Tel: (559) 497-9414, FAX: (559) 497-9435 (34)

Knapp, Judith, A., Andrew Associates Inc, Enfield, CT. Tel: (860) 253-0000, FAX: (860) 741-0850, Web Site: www.andrewmail.com (23)

Knapp, Kathy, S&S Worldwide, Colchester, CT. Tel: (860) 537-3451, (800) 288-9941, FAX: (860) 537-2866, E-Mail: cservice@ssww.com, Web Site: www.ssww.com (11)

Knapstein, Michael, Waldbillig & Besteman, Madison, WI. Tel: (608) 829-0900, (800) 395-4767, FAX: (608) 829-0901, E-Mail: info@waldbest.com, Web Site: www.waldbest.com (35)

Knechtal, Brad, Richardson Electronics Ltd, Lafox, IL. Tel: (630) 208-2200, FAX: (630) 208-2550, E-Mail: edg@rell.com, Web Site: www.rell.com (16)

Kneeland, Tim, Life Investors Insurance Co of America, Cedar Rapids, IA. Tel: (319) 398-8511, (800) 231-7220, FAX: (319) 369-2188, Web Site: www.lifeinvestors.com (14)

Kneib, Gina, DMW Worldwide LLC, Chesterbrook, PA. Tel: (610) 407-0407, (877) 744-3699, FAX: (610) 407-9201, E-Mail: whunter@dmwdirect.com, Web Site: www.dmwdirect.com (35)

Kneip, Maggie, Harry N Abrams Inc, New York, NY. Tel: (212) 206-7715, FAX: (212) 645-8437, Web Site: www.hnabooks.com (17)

Knight, Darrell, Message Technologies Inc, Atlanta, GA. Tel: (770) 240-8000, (800) 868-3684, FAX: (770) 240-7474, E-Mail: info@messagetech.com, Web Site: www.messagetech.com (30)

Knight, David E., Hatton-Brown Publishers Inc, Montgomery, AL. Tel: (334) 834-1170, FAX: (334) 834-4525, E-Mail: webman@hattonbrown.com, Web Site: www.hattonbrown.com (17)

Knight, Fred, BCR Enterprises Inc, Downers Grove, IL. Tel: (630) 986-1432, (800) 227-1234, FAX: (630) 323-5324, Web Site: www.bcr.com (17)

Knight, Jeff, International Currency LLC, Beaumont, TX. Tel: (409) 866-0588 (11)

Knight, Phil, Nike Inc, Beaverton, OR. Tel: (503) 671-4565, (800) 344-6543, FAX: (503) 671-6300, Web Site: www.nike.com (2)

Knight, Susan, E., MTS Systems Corp, Eden Prairie, MN. Tel: (952) 937-4000, (800) 328-2255, FAX: (952) 937-4515, E-Mail: info@mts.com, Web Site: www.mts.com (16)

Knight, Timothy, P., Newsday, Melville, NY. Tel: (631) 843-2020, FAX: (631) 843-5424, Web Site: www.newsday.com (17)

Knoblich, Ed, Smithfield Packing Co Inc, Smithfield, VA. Tel: (757) 357-4321, FAX: (757) 357-1339, E-Mail: information@smithfieldfoods.com, Web Site: www.smithfieldfoods.com (16)

Knobloch, Karen, National Retail Federation Inc, Washington, DC. Tel: (202) 783-7971, (800) 673-4692, FAX: (202) 737-2849, E-Mail: webmaster@nrf.com, Web Site: www.nrf.com (1)

Knodel, Todd, CommissionSoup, Madison, SD. Tel: (605) 256-9103, (866) 309-7687, FAX: (605) 256-1522, E-Mail: info@creditsoup.com, Web Site: www.commissionsoup.com (23)

Knoesel, John, N., Commercial Envelope Manufacturing Co Inc, Hauppauge, NY. Tel: (631) 242-2500, FAX: (631) 242-6122, Web Site: www.commercial-envelope.com (26)

Knoll, David, E., Sunoco, Inc, Philadelphia, PA. Tel: (215) 977-3000, (800) 786-6261, FAX: (215) 977-3409, E-Mail: sunoco_online@sunoil.com, Web Site: www.sunocoinc.com (16)

Knoll Group, New York, NY. Tel: (212) 343-4000, FAX: (212) 343-4180 (16)

Knollwood Groves at Cushman's, West Palm Beach, FL. Tel: (561) 734-4800, (800) 222-9696, FAX: (800) 776-4329, E-Mail: sales@knollwoodgroves.com, Web Site: www.knollwoodgroves.com (4)

Knoop, Brian, Victory Corps, New Hope, MN. Tel: (763) 561-5600, (800) 328-6120, FAX: (763) 561-8523, E-Mail: cs@victorycorps.com, Web Site: www.victorycorps.com (16)

Knope, Matt, Prakken Publications Inc, Ann Arbor, MI. Tel: (734) 975-2800, (800) 530-9673, FAX: (734) 975-2787, E-Mail: vanessa@techdirections.com, Web Site: www.eddigest.com; www.techdirections.com (17)

Knoplol, Terry, Upbeat Inc, Saint Louis, MO. Tel: (314) 535-5005, (800) 325-3047, FAX: (314) 535-4419, E-Mail: custservice@upbeat.com, Web Site: www.upbeat.com (9)

Knorre, Michael J., Northwest Direct Inc, Bellevue, WA. Tel: (425) 643-7917, Web Site: www.nwdirectmarketing.com (35)

Knott's Berry Farm Foods, Buena Park, CA. Tel: (714) 220-5200, (800) 877-6887, FAX: (714) 220-5150, Web Site: www.knotts.com (4)

Knowledge Networks/SRI, Roseland, NJ. Tel: (908) 497-8000, FAX: (908) 497-8001, E-Mail: mclancey@knowledgenetworks.com, Web Site: www.knowledgenetworks.com (30)

Knowles, Milana, Spa-Finder Inc, New York, NY. Tel: (212) 924-6800, (800) ALL-SPAS, FAX: (212) 924-7240, Web Site: www.spafinder.com (7)

Knox, Doug, Tyndale House Publishers, Carol Stream, IL. Tel: (630) 668-8300, FAX: (630) 668-3245 (17)

Knudsen, Larry, Camp Healthcare Inc, Jackson, MI. Tel: (517) 787-1600, (800) 492-1088, FAX: (800) 245-3765, E-Mail: info@truelife.biz, Web Site: www.camphealthcare.com (16)

Knutson, Daniel, E., Land O' Lakes Inc, Arden Hills, MN. Tel: (651) 481-2222, (800) 328-9680, FAX: (651) 481-2000, Web Site: www.landolakes.com (16)

Knutson, Ronald, J., Ace Hardware Corp, Oak Brook, IL. Tel: (630) 990-6600, FAX: (630) 990-6838, Web Site: www.acehardware.com (16)

Koach, Gail, Brown-Forman Beverages Worldwide, Louisville, KY. Tel: (502) 585-1100, FAX: (502) 774-7185, E-Mail: Brown-Forman@b-f.com, Web Site: www.brown-forman.com (16)

Kobek, Bob, American Teleservices Association, Indianapolis, IN. Tel: (317) 816-9336, (877) 779-3974, FAX: (317) 218-0323, Web Site: www.ataconnect.org (40)

Kobel, Richard, American Institute of Physics, Melville, NY. Tel: (516) 576-2200, (800) 892-8259, FAX: (516) 576-2374, E-Mail: aipinfo@aip.org, Web Site: www.aip.org (17)

Kobie Marketing Inc, Saint Petersburg, FL. Tel: (727) 822-5353, (800) 821-7892, FAX: (727) 822-5265, Web Site: www.kobie.com (35)

Kobil, Jeff, LDS Group Inc, New York, NY. Tel: (646) 390-5702, FAX: (646) 390-5715, E-Mail: rvergara@ldsgroupinc.com, Web Site: www.ldsgroupinc.com (23)

Kobs, Jim, Kobs Strategic Consulting, Chicago, IL. Tel: (312) 938-4430, FAX: (847) 934-1194, E-Mail: kobs4ksc@aol.com (20)

Kobs Strategic Consulting, Chicago, IL. Tel: (312) 938-4430, FAX: (847) 934-1194, E-Mail: kobs4ksc@aol.com (20)

Kobuszewski Jr., Frank, Cablexpress Technologies, Syracuse, NY. Tel: (315) 476-3000, (800) 913-9467, FAX: (315) 455-1800, E-Mail: info@cablexpress.com, Web Site: www.CXTec.com (10)

Koch, Amelia, Chesapeake Bay Foundation, Annapolis, MD. Tel: (410) 268-8816, Web Site: www.savethebay.cbf.org (1)

Koch, Douglas, Brown Shoe Co, Saint Louis, MO. Tel: (314) 854-4000, FAX: (314) 854-4274, Web Site: www.brownshoe.com (16)

Koch, Jeremy, Magazine Publishers of America, New York, NY. Tel: (212) 872-3700, FAX: (212) 888-4217, Web Site: www.magazine.org (17)

Kochar, Father Joseph, Pallottine Center for Apostolic Causes Inc/St Jude Shrine, Baltimore, MD. Tel: (410) 685-6026, (877) 278-5833, FAX: (410) 234-1459, E-Mail: info@stjudeshrine.org, Web Site: www.stjudeshrine.org (1)

Kochberg, Keith, iMarketing LTD Inc, Princeton, NJ. Tel: (609) 921-0400, FAX: (609) 921-0491, E-Mail: info@imarketingltd.com, Web Site: www.imarketingltd.com (35)

Kochevar, John, J., Kochevar Research Associates, Charlestown, MA. Tel: (617) 242-4332, FAX: (617) 242-8009, E-Mail: kra@bigfoot.com, Web Site: www.kochevarresearch.com (20)

Kochevar Research Associates, Charlestown, MA. Tel: (617) 242-4332, FAX: (617) 242-8009, E-Mail: kra@bigfoot.com, Web Site: www.kochevarresearch.com (20)

Kocurek, Richard, Critter Mountain Wear, Crested Butte, CO. Tel: (970) 349-9326, (800) 686-9327, FAX: (978) 389-5900, E-Mail: critter@crestedbutte.net, Web Site: www.crittermountainwear.com (2)

Kodak, Skip, Lego Direct Marketing, Enfield, CT. Tel: (860) 749-2291, FAX: (860) FAX-LEGO, Web Site: www.lego.com (11)

Kodak Graphic Communications, Rochester, NY. Tel: (800) 944-6171, Web Site: www.kpgraphics.com (27)

Koechling, William, William Koechling Photography, Wheaton, IL. Tel: (630) 665-4379, Web Site: www.koechlingphoto.com (37)

William Koechling Photography, Wheaton, IL. Tel: (630) 665-4379, Web Site: www.koechlingphoto.com (37)

Koehl, Emmy, Skullduggery, Anaheim, CA. Tel: (714) 777-6425, (800) 3 FOSSIL, FAX: (714) 832-1215, Web Site: www.skullduggery.com (16)

Koehl, Peter, Skullduggery, Anaheim, CA. Tel: (714) 777-6425, (800) 3 FOSSIL, FAX: (714) 832-1215, Web Site: www.skullduggery.com (16)

Koehler, James, Micro Center, Hilliard, OH. Tel: (800) 634-3478, FAX: (614) 777-2620, E-Mail: csrs@microcenterorder.com, Web Site: www.microcenter.com (3)

Koeppel, Peter, Koeppel Direct, Dallas, TX. Tel: (972) 732-6110, FAX: (972) 248-2759, E-Mail: pkoeppel@koeppelinc.com, Web Site: www.koeppeldirect.com (32)

Koeppel Direct, Dallas, TX. Tel: (972) 732-6110, FAX: (972) 248-2759, E-Mail: pkoeppel@koeppelinc.com, Web Site: www.koeppeldirect.com (32)

Koeppl, James, Apothecary Products Inc, Burnsville, MN. Tel: (952) 890-1940, (800) 328-2742, FAX: (800) 328-1584, Web Site: www.apothecaryproducts.com (7)

Koeze, Jeff, Koeze Co, Grand Rapids, MI. Tel: (800) 555-9688, E-Mail: service@koezedirect.com, Web Site: www.koeze.com (16)

Koeze Co, Grand Rapids, MI. Tel: (800) 555-9688, E-Mail: service@koezedirect.com, Web Site: www.koeze.com (16)

Koga, Hiro, ACTON Group Ltd, Lincoln, NE. Tel: (402) 742-2820, FAX: (402) 470-2673, E-Mail: info@acton.com, Web Site: www.acton.com (23)

Kogler, Clare, Jordan Whitney Inc, Tustin, CA. Tel: (714) 832-3353, FAX: (714) 832-4422, E-Mail: info@jwgreensheet.com, Web Site: www. jwgreensheet.com (32)

Kogler, John, Jordan Whitney Inc, Tustin, CA. Tel: (714) 832-3353, FAX: (714) 832-4422, E-Mail: info@jwgreensheet.com, Web Site: www. jwgreensheet.com (32)

Kohler, C. Bart, Hubert Co, Harrison, OH. Tel: (513) 367-8767, (800) 543-7374, FAX: (513) 367-8823, Web Site: www.hubert.com (16)

Kohn, Andrew, Hyatt Legal Plans Inc, Cleveland, OH. Tel: (216) 241-0022, FAX: (216) 694-4305, Web Site: www.legalplans.com (16)

Kohomvan, Jeremy, New York Easter Seal Society, New York, NY. Tel: (312) 726-6200, (212) 943-4364, (800) 221-6827, FAX: (212) 695-4807, (312) 726-4258, Web Site: ny.easterseals.com (1)

Kohrs, Sherry, CPI Corp, St Louis, MO. Tel: (314) 231-1575, (877) 763-4456, FAX: (314) 231-8150, E-Mail: feedback@cpicorp.com, Web Site: www. cpicorp.com (16)

Kohut, Carleen, National Retail Federation Inc, Washington, DC. Tel: (202) 783-7971, (800) 673-4692, FAX: (202) 737-2849, E-Mail: webmaster@nrf. com, Web Site: www.nrf.com (1)

Kohut, Dr James, Youngstown State University, Youngstown, OH. Tel: (330) 742-3064, Web Site: www.ysu.edu (41)

Koivisto, Mark, Product to Market LLC, Cokato, MN. Tel: (320) 286-9997 (20)

Kokopelli Communications Group Inc, Chicago, IL. Tel: (312) 726-5656, Web Site: www.kcgi.net (35)

Kolakowski, Gene, Murphy Bed Co Inc, Farmingdale, NY. Tel: (631) 420-4330, (800) 845-2337, FAX: (631) 420-4337, E-Mail: info@ murphybedcompany.com, Web Site: www. murphybedcompany.com (8)

Kolbe, David, Kolbe Corp, Phoenix, AZ. Tel: (602) 840-9770, (800) 642-2822, FAX: (602) 952-2706, E-Mail: info@kolbe.com, Web Site: www.kolbe. com (17)

Kolbe, Kathryn, Kolbe Corp, Phoenix, AZ. Tel: (602) 840-9770, (800) 642-2822, FAX: (602) 952-2706, E-Mail: info@kolbe.com, Web Site: www.kolbe. com (17)

Kolbe Corp, Phoenix, AZ. Tel: (602) 840-9770, (800) 642-2822, FAX: (602) 952-2706, E-Mail: info@ kolbe.com, Web Site: www.kolbe.com (17)

Kolbrener, Tom, St Louis Slot Machine Co, Saint Louis, MO. Tel: (314) 432-1699, E-Mail: stlslot@ earthlink.net, Web Site: www.stlouisslot.com (6)

Kolier, Mark, CGSM Inc, Wilton, CT. Tel: (203) 563-9233, FAX: (203) 563-9239, Web Site: www.cgsm. com (35)

Kolinsky, Jay, MALM Chemical Corp, Pound Ridge, NY. Tel: (914) 764-5775, FAX: (914) 764-5386, E-Mail: custserv1@malms.com, Web Site: www. malms.com (16)

Kolke, Cynthia, A., Whitewing Labs, Granada Hills, CA. Tel: (800) 950-3030, FAX: (818) 240-2785, E-Mail: service@whitewing.com, Web Site: www. whitewing.com (20)

Koll, Thomas, Laplink Software Inc, Bellevue, WA. Tel: (425) 952-6000, (800) 527-5465, FAX: (425) 952-6002, E-Mail: marketing@laplink.com, Web Site: www.laplink.com (3)

Koller Jr., Edward, R., Howard-Sloan-Koller Group, New York, NY. Tel: (212) 661-5250, FAX: (212) 557-9178, E-Mail: ekoller@hsksearch.com, Web Site: www.hsksearch.com (20)

Kollias, George, Kollias & Associates, Chicago, IL. Tel: (312) 857-7707 (35)

Kollias & Associates, Chicago, IL. Tel: (312) 857-7707 (35)

Kollin, Cheryl, American Forests, Washington, DC. Tel: (202) 737-1944, FAX: (202) 737-2457, E-Mail: info@amfor.org, Web Site: www. americanforests.org (1)

Kollman, Terry, Charter Direct Marketing, New York, NY. Tel: (212) 717-2770, FAX: (561) 245-7559, E-Mail: terrykollman@charterdirectmarketing.com, Web Site: www.charterdirectmarketing.com (35)

Kollmann, Carol, Mailing Lists Plus Inc, Bellevue, WA. Tel: (425) 451-3335, (877) 339-4584, FAX: (425) 646-4485, E-Mail: info@mailinglistsplus. com, Web Site: www.mailinglistsplus.com (21)

Kolowsky, Donald, Christian Herald Association, New York, NY. Tel: (212) 684-2800, (800) BOWERY-1, FAX: (212) 684-3740, E-Mail: info@chaonline.org, Web Site: www.bowery.org (1)

Kolpon, Jay, Bayer Corp Consumer Care Division, Morristown, NJ. Tel: (973) 254-5000, FAX: (973) 408-8215, Web Site: www.bayercare.com (16)

Koltonuk, David, SAF Financial Services Inc, Schaumburg, IL. Tel: (800) 323-3000, FAX: (847) 310-8969 (27)

Komara, Vanessa, Hilti North America, Tulsa, OK. Tel: (918) 252-6000, Web Site: www.hilti.com (34)

Susan G Komen for the Cure, Dallas, TX. Tel: (972) 855-1600, Web Site: www.komen.org (1)

Komori, Shingetaka, Fuji Photo Film USA, Valhalla, NY. Tel: (914) 789-8100, (800) 755-3854, FAX: (914) 789-8295, Web Site: www.fujifilmusa.com (16)

Komunik, Montreal, PQ Canada. Tel: (514) 904-0710, Web Site: www.komunik.com (20)

Konalczyk, Philip, J Jill Group, Inc, Quincy, MA. Tel: (617) 376-4300, (800) 642-9989, FAX: (617) 769-0177, Web Site: www.jjillgroup.com (2)

Konecky, Sean, William S Konecky Associates Inc, Old Saybrook, CT. Tel: (860) 388-0878, FAX: (860) 388-0273 (17)

Konecky, William, William S Konecky Associates Inc, Old Saybrook, CT. Tel: (860) 388-0878, FAX: (860) 388-0273 (17)

William S Konecky Associates Inc, Old Saybrook, CT. Tel: (860) 388-0878, FAX: (860) 388-0273 (17)

Konecny, Buddy, Seashore Vacations, Hilton Head Island, SC. Tel: (843) 785-2191, (800) 845-0077, FAX: (843) 785-6450, E-Mail: seashorehhi@ hargray.com, Web Site: www.seashorehhi.com (19)

Konicov, Susanne, IMPACT Publishing Inc, Bradenton, FL. Tel: (941) 739-2611, (800) 4-A-NEW-ME, FAX: (941) 756-0315, E-Mail: info@ impactpublishinginc.com, Web Site: www. impactpublishinginc.com (17)

Konik, Stan, Konik & Co Inc, Skokie, IL. Tel: (847) 933-1800, FAX: (847) 933-1818, E-Mail: stan@ konik.com, Web Site: www.konik.com (33)

Konik & Co Inc, Skokie, IL. Tel: (847) 933-1800, FAX: (847) 933-1818, E-Mail: stan@konik.com, Web Site: www.konik.com (33)

Konkle, Glen, Equity Management Inc, San Diego, CA. Tel: (858) 558-2500, FAX: (858) 558-2547, Web Site: www.equitymanagementinc.com (20)

Kontzias, Olga, Fairchild Books, New York, NY. Tel: (212) 630-4171, (800) 932-4724, FAX: (212) 630-3868, Web Site: www.fairchildbooks.com (17)

Koob, Robert, California State Polytechnic University Business Administration Dept, San Luis Obispo, CA. Tel: (805) 756-1413, FAX: (805) 756-5057, Web Site: www.calpoly.edu (41)

Koogle, Margaret, Lilypons Water Gardens, Adamstown, MD. Tel: (301) 874-3763, (800) 999-5459, FAX: (301) 874-2959, Web Site: www.lilypons. com (8)

Koolish, Dan, Hartley Data Service Inc, Glenview, IL. Tel: (847) 724-9280, (800) 433-2796, FAX: (847) 729-2199, Web Site: www.hartleydata.com (22)

Koolish, Ruth, Information Sources Inc, Walnut Creek, CA. Tel: (510) 525-6220, FAX: (510) 525-1568, Web Site: www.tectrends.com (22)

Kools, Joe, Jones Publishing Inc, Iola, WI. Tel: (715) 445-5000, (800) 331-0038, FAX: (715) 445-4053, E-Mail: jonespub@jonespublishing.com, Web Site: www.jonespublishing.com (17)

Koosha, Sandra, Gracewood Fruit Co, Vero Beach, FL. Tel: (772) 567-1154, E-Mail: info@ gracewoodgroves.com, Web Site: www. gracewoodgroves.com (4)

Koper, Jennifer, Anderson Niebuhr & Associates Inc, Arden Hills, MN. Tel: (651) 486-8712, (800) 678-5577, FAX: (651) 486-0536, E-Mail: info@ana-inc.com, Web Site: www.ana-inc.com (30)

Kopf, Ken, KZS Advertising, Smithtown, NY. Tel: (651) 348-1440, FAX: (631) 348-1449, Web Site: www.kzsadvertising.com (35)

Kopischke, Julia, The Los Angeles Convention & Visitors Bureau, Los Angeles, CA. Tel: (213) 624-7300, (800) 366-6116, FAX: (213) 627-9746, Web Site: discoverlosangeles.com (19)

Kopp, David, Dydacomp Development Corp, Parsippany, NJ. Tel: (973) 237-9415, (800) 858-3666, FAX: (973) 237-9043, E-Mail: sales@dydacomp. com, Web Site: www.dydacomp.com (22)

Korab, Holly, University of Illinois College of LAS, Office of Advancement, Champaign, IL. Tel: (217) 333-7108, Web Site: www.las.uiuc.edu (1)

Koran, Bob, United Communications Group, Gaithersburg, MD. Tel: (301) 287-2700, FAX: (301) 816-8945, E-Mail: webmaster@ucg.com, Web Site: www.ucg.com (17)

Koren, Daniella, DKI Direct, Montvale, NJ. Tel: (201) 391-6000, Web Site: www.dkidirect.com (35)

Korgman, Max, Touchpoint Data Solutions, Cumming, GA. Tel: (770) 886-8611, Web Site: www. touchpointdata.com (23)

Korn, Gail, Garden Perennials, Wayne, NE. Tel: (402) 375-3615, (888) 375-3615, Web Site: www. gardenperennials.net (8)

Korowitz, Bill, Magnet LLC, Washington, MO. Tel: (636) 239-5661, (800) 458-9457, FAX: (636) 239-4490, E-Mail: contactus@themagnetgroup.com, Web Site: www.magnetllc.com (16)

Korsmeyer, Mark, Dairy Farmers of America Inc, Kansas City, MO. Tel: (816) 801-6455, (888) 332-6455, FAX: (816) 801-6456, E-Mail: webmail@ dfamilk.com, Web Site: www.dfamilk.com (16)

Korwin, Richard, M., Wideband by Kars, New Rochelle, NY. Tel: (212) 691-9000, FAX: (212) 691-9835, E-Mail: info@widebandjewelry.com, Web Site: www.widebandjewelry.com (16)

Korzak, J.T., Mid-Central Printing & Mailing Inc, Wilmette, IL. Tel: (847) 251-4040, FAX: (847) 251-8615, E-Mail: mcpm@mcpm.com, Web Site: www.mcpm.com (28)

Kosh, Mitchell, A., Polo Ralph Lauren, Lyndhurst, NJ. Tel: (212) 531-6537, (800) 377-7656, FAX: (212) 318-7690, Web Site: www.ralphlauren.com (2)

Koskinen, Brenda, Johnny Appleseed's Inc, Beverly, MA. Tel: (978) 922-2040, (800) 767-6666, FAX: (978) 922-7001, Web Site: www.appleseeds.com (2)

Kosloff, David, Roosevelt Paper Co, Mount Laurel, NJ. Tel: (856) 303-4200, (856) 303-4100, (800) 523-3470, FAX: (856) 642-1949, (856) 642-1950, Web Site: www.rooseveltpaper.com (25)

Kosloff, Ted, Roosevelt Paper Co, Mount Laurel, NJ. Tel: (856) 303-4200, (856) 303-4100, (800) 523-3470, FAX: (856) 642-1949, (856) 642-1950, Web Site: www.rooseveltpaper.com (25)

Koslowski, Patrice, The Dreyfus Corp, New York, NY. Tel: (212) 922-6000, FAX: (212) 922-8165 (14)

Kostelini, Charles, Bontex, Honolulu, HI. Tel: (540) 261-2181, FAX: (540) 261-3784, E-Mail: bontex@ bontex.com, Web Site: www.bontex.com (16)

Kostelni, J.C., Bontex, Honolulu, HI. Tel: (540) 261-2181, FAX: (540) 261-3784, E-Mail: bontex@ bontex.com, Web Site: www.bontex.com (16)

Koszuta, Jeff, Rainbow Graphics Inc, Mundelein, IL. Tel: (847) 824-9600, Web Site: www.rainbowgraphics.com (27)

Kotch, Michael, Quadrant Engineering Plastic Products, Reading, PA. Tel: (610) 320-6600, (800) 366-0300, FAX: (610) 320-6868, Web Site: www.quadrantepp.com (16)

Kotcher, Ray, Ketchum, New York, NY. Tel: (646) 935-3900, FAX: (646) 935-4482, E-Mail: editor@ketchum.com, Web Site: www.ketchum.com (35)

Kotlarz, Corey, The Connection Contact Center Services, Burnsville, MN. Tel: (952) 948-5335, (800) 883-5777, FAX: (952) 948-5498, E-Mail: sales@the-connection.com, Web Site: www.the-connection.com (29)

Kottler, Anne, Sage Communications, Hudson, MA. Tel: (978) 567-8888, Web Site: www.sagecommunications.com (35)

Kottler, Josef, Sage Communications, Hudson, MA. Tel: (978) 567-8888, Web Site: www.sagecommunications.com (35)

Kotula, Donald, L., Northern Tool & Equipment Inc, Burnsville, MN. Tel: (952) 894-9510, (800) 221-0516, FAX: (952) 894-1020, Web Site: www.northerntool.com (16)

Kotulka, Frank, S., Data-Matic Systems Co, Lansing, MI. Tel: (517) 882-4401, FAX: (517) 882-1188, Web Site: www.datamatic.net (27)

Koubek, Randy, Thomson Financial, New York, NY. Tel: (212) 803-8200, FAX: (212) 843-9608 (17)

Kounalakis, Markos, The Washington Monthly Co, Washington, DC. Tel: (202) 393-5155, FAX: (202) 393-2444, E-Mail: editors@washingtonmonthly.com, Web Site: www.washingtonmonthly.com (17)

Kourtis, Spyro, Hacker Group Inc, Seattle, WA. Tel: (206) 805-1500, E-Mail: info@hackergroup.com, Web Site: www.hackergroup.com (35)

Koury, Conny, Baker & Taylor Inc, Charlotte, NC. Tel: (704) 998-3100, (800) 775-1800, FAX: (704) 998-3316, E-Mail: btinfo@btol.com, Web Site: www.btol.com (16)

Kouyoumjian, Charles, H., Blue Raven Technology, Wilmington, MA. Tel: (781) 778-4600, (800) 274-5343, (800) 20RAVEN, FAX: (781) 778-4848, E-Mail: sales@blueraven.com, Web Site: www.blueraven.com (3)

Kouzmanoff, Catherine, Inter7 Internet Technologies Inc, Galena, IL. Tel: (815) 776-9465, Web Site: www.inter7.com (3)

Kovac, Pete, Nicholson Kovac Inc, Kansas City, MO. Tel: (816) 842-8881, FAX: (816) 842-6340, E-Mail: nk@nicholsonkovac.com, Web Site: www.nkhw.com (35)

Kovach, David, Kistler-Tiffany Companies LLC, Berwyn, PA. Tel: (610) 722-3300, (866) 250-5413, Web Site: www.ktadv.com (20)

Koval, Judy, Jantz Supply Koval Knives, Davis, OK. Tel: (580) 369-2316, (800) 351-8900, FAX: (580) 369-3082, Web Site: www.knifemaking.com (9)

Koval, Mick, Jantz Supply Koval Knives, Davis, OK. Tel: (580) 369-2316, (800) 351-8900, FAX: (580) 369-3082, Web Site: www.knifemaking.com (9)

Kovar, Joe, SECO-LARM USA Inc, Irvine, CA. Tel: (949) 261-2999, (800) 662-0800, FAX: (949) 261-7326, E-Mail: info@seco-larm.com, Web Site: www.seco-larm.com (16)

Kovarik, Allen, D., AD-Sells Inc, Lisle, IL. Tel: (630) 241-0090 (33)

Kovatch, Michael, Contact Center Compliance, Santa Rosa, CA. Tel: (800) 308-0258, Web Site: www.dnc.com (22)

Kowal, David, Harrah's Entertainment Inc, Las Vegas, NV. Tel: (702) 407-6000, FAX: (702) 407-6499, (702) 407-6500, Web Site: www.harrahs.com (19)

Kowal, G., Paul, Kowal & Associates Inc, Cambridge, MA. Tel: (617) 577-0700, FAX: (617) 577-0500, E-Mail: pkowal@kowalassociates.com, Web Site: www.kowalassociates.com (20)

Kowal & Associates Inc, Cambridge, MA. Tel: (617) 577-0700, FAX: (617) 577-0500, E-Mail: pkowal@kowalassociates.com, Web Site: www.kowalassociates.com (20)

Kowalawski, Brian, Great Lakes Fulfillment Inc, Erie, PA. Tel: (814) 456-2175, (800) 964-5478, FAX: (814) 455-1942, E-Mail: info@greatlakeslists.com, Web Site: www.greatlakeslists.com (23)

Kowalczyk, Mike, Valassis, Windsor, CT. Tel: (860) 285-6100, FAX: (203) 845-5338, Web Site: www.valassis.com (31)

Kowalski, Anita, C&H Distributors LLC, Milwaukee, WI. Tel: (414) 443-1700, (888) 316-2223, FAX: (414) 443-9213, E-Mail: customerservice@chdist.com, Web Site: www.chdist.com (9)

Kowalski, Ed, The United Methodist Publishing House, Nashville, TN. Tel: (615) 749-6000, (800) 672-1789, FAX: (615) 749-6417, E-Mail: productsandservices@umpublishing.com, Web Site: www.umpublishing.com (17)

Kowalsky, George, Response Insurance, Scranton, PA. Tel: (203) 634-7255, (800) 518-2984, FAX: (203) 634-7319, E-Mail: webcs@response.com, Web Site: www.response.com (15)

Kowkabany, Bruce, Core Technologies, Boulder, CO. Tel: (614) 231-3031, (866) 624-5927, FAX: (303) 395-1474, E-Mail: support@core-tech.com, Web Site: www.mailware.com (22)

Kowolaski, Mike, Tiffany & Co, New York, NY. Tel: (212) 755-8000, FAX: (212) 320-7550, Web Site: www.tiffany.com (6)

Koye, Dennis, Source Communications, Hackensack, NJ. Tel: (201) 343-5222 (35)

KozaK Auto Drywash Inc, Batavia, NY. Tel: (716) 343-8111, (800) 237-9927, FAX: (585) 343-3732, E-Mail: info@kozak.com, Web Site: www.dryautowash.com (16)

Kozeliski, Jon, Star Silkscreeen Design Inc, Decatur, IL. Tel: (217) 877-0804, FAX: (217) 877-0843 (2)

Koziara, Tanya, Con-Way Freight, Ann Arbor, MI. Tel: (734) 994-6600 (12)

Kozma, Alicia, Crohn's & Colitis Foundation of America (CCFA), New York, NY. Tel: (212) 685-3440, Web Site: www.ccfa.org (1)

Kozoman, Robert, L., DePaul University, Chicago, IL. Tel: (312) 362-8000, (800) 4-DEPAUL, FAX: (312) 362-6639, E-Mail: skelly@wppost.depaul.edu, Web Site: www.depaul.edu (41)

Kozyrski, Elena, Atlantic Publication Group LLC, Charleston, SC. Tel: (843) 747-0025, FAX: (843) 744-0816, E-Mail: info@atlanticpublicationgrp.com, Web Site: www.atlanticpublicationgrp.com (17)

Kraetzer, Kenneth, CBSI, Harrison, NY. Tel: (914) 381-5353, Web Site: www.cbsiservices.com (30)

Kraft, Larry, Digi International, Minnetonka, MN. Tel: (952) 912-3444, (877) 912-3444, FAX: (952) 912-4953, Web Site: www.digi.com (3)

Kraft, Lyle, Plattform Advertising, Lenexa, KS. Tel: (913) 254-6000, (800) 279-9988, FAX: (913) 538-5078, E-Mail: info@plattformad.com, Web Site: www.plattformad.com (35)

Kraft, Melissa, Comcast Cable Communications, Philadelphia, PA. Tel: (215) 665-1700, Web Site: www.comcast.com (32)

Kraft, Steven, Automation Research Inc, Columbus, OH. Tel: (614) 538-1507 (22)

Kraft Foods/Gevalia Kaffe, Tarrytown, NY. Tel: (914) 335-4239, Web Site: www.gevalia.com (16)

Kraftbilt, Tulsa, OK. Tel: (918) 628-1260, (800) 331-7290, FAX: (918) 632-7371, Web Site: www.kraftbilt.com (10)

Kragen, Ken, Kragen & Co, Beverly Hills, CA. Tel: (310) 854-4400, (877) 808-0698, FAX: (310) 854-0238, E-Mail: kenkragen@aol.com, Web Site: www.partsamerica.com (32)

Kragen & Co, Beverly Hills, CA. Tel: (310) 854-4400, (877) 808-0698, FAX: (310) 854-0238, E-Mail: kenkragen@aol.com, Web Site: www.partsamerica.com (32)

Krakora, Kevin, J., Diebold Inc, Uniontown, OH. Tel: (330) 899-2510, (800) DIEBOLD, FAX: (330) 490-3794, E-Mail: barronp@diebold.com, Web Site: www.diebold.com (16)

Kramer, Carl, Gilson Co Inc, Lewis Center, OH. Tel: (740) 548-7298, (800) 444-1508, FAX: (740) 548-5314, E-Mail: sales@gilsonco.com, Web Site: www.globalgilson.com (16)

Kramer, David, A., The Marketing Agency LLC, Fort Lauderdale, FL. Tel: (954) 771-1177, FAX: (866) 379-5788, E-Mail: marketing@themarketingagency.com, Web Site: www.themarketingagency.com (35)

Kramer, Eileen, Editorial Freelance Association, New York, NY. Tel: (212) 929-5400, (866) 929-5400, FAX: (212) 929-5439, E-Mail: office@the-efa.org, Web Site: www.the-efa.org (31)

Kramer, Gordon M, Continental Plastic Card Co, Pompano Beach, FL. Tel: (954) 794-0040, (800) 543-0670, FAX: (954) 755-4493, E-Mail: info@continentalplasticcard.com, Web Site: www.continentalplasticcard.com (27)

Kramer, Lyn, Kramer & Associates, Cincinnati, OH. Tel: (513) 792-5700, (800) 281-1400, FAX: (513) 792-5709, E-Mail: eservice@kramerandassociates.com, Web Site: www.kramerandassociates.com (20)

Kramer, Richard J, Goodyear Tire & Rubber Co, Akron, OH. Tel: (330) 796-3250, Web Site: www.goodyear.com (16)

Kramer, Ross, Listrak, Lititz, PA. Tel: (717) 627-4528, Web Site: www.listrak.com (32)

Kramer, Tom, Wildseed Farms, Fredericksburg, TX. Tel: (830) 990-8080, (800) 848-0078, FAX: (830) 990-8090, E-Mail: orders1@wildseedfarms.com, Web Site: www.wildseedfarms.com (8)

Kramer & Associates, Cincinnati, OH. Tel: (513) 792-5700, (800) 281-1400, FAX: (513) 792-5709, E-Mail: eservice@kramerandassociates.com, Web Site: www.kramerandassociates.com (20)

Krames - Staywell, Yardley, PA. Tel: (267) 685-2500, Web Site: www.krames.com (7)

Krampf, Larry, Marke Communications Inc, New York, NY. Tel: (212) 201-0600, (800) 716-2753, FAX: (212) 213-0785, Web Site: www.marke.com (35)

Krane, Hillary, K., Levi Strauss & Co, San Francisco, CA. Tel: (415) 501-6000, FAX: (415) 501-7112, Web Site: www.levistrauss.com (16)

Kraner, Matt, The Plain Dealer, Cleveland, OH. Tel: (216) 999-5000, FAX: (216) 999-6356, Web Site: www.plaindealer.com (18)

Kraner, Matthew, G., St Louis Post-Dispatch, Saint Louis, MO. Tel: (314) 340-8000, (800) 365-0820, FAX: (314) 340-3140, Web Site: www.postnet.com (17)

Kranjac, Paulette, List Process Co Inc, New York, NY. Tel: (212) 517-8550, FAX: (212) 517-9728, Web Site: www.listprocesscompany.com (23)

Kranzberg, Ken, Tricor Braun, Woodridge, IL. Tel: (708) 385-9333, FAX: (708) 385-3015, Web Site: www.tricorbraun.com (16)

Krapf, Eric, BCR Enterprises Inc, Downers Grove, IL. Tel: (630) 986-1432, (800) 227-1234, FAX: (630) 323-5324, Web Site: www.bcr.com (17)

Krapf, Wallace, Magnatag Visable Systems, Macedon, NY. Tel: (315) 986-3033, FAX: (315) 986-4000, Web Site: www.magnatag.com (16)

Krasner, Martin, P., TCJC, New York, NY. Tel: (212) 268-4100, FAX: (212) 268-4209 (2)

Krasney, Barry, Cole's Appliance & Furniture Co, Chicago, IL. Tel: (773) 525-1797, FAX: (773) 525-0728 (8)

Krasnow, Heather, AccuData Integrated Marketing, Fort Myers, FL. Tel: (239) 425-4400, (800) 732-3440, FAX: (239) 425-4401, E-Mail: info@accudata.com, Web Site: www.accudata.com (23)

Krassin, Ron, Zotos International, Darien, CT. Tel: (203) 655-8911, (800) 242-WAVE, (800) 242-9283, FAX: (203) 656-7890, E-Mail: HumanResources@zotosintl.com, Web Site: www.zotos.com (16)

Kratovil, Jonathan, The Pond-Ekberg Co, Chicopee, MA. Tel: (413) 594-7511, (800) 225-7511, FAX: (413) 594-2179, E-Mail: sales@pond-ekberg.com, Web Site: www.pondekberg.com (27)

Kraus, Donald R., The Clorox Co, Oakland, CA. Tel: (510) 271-7000, FAX: (510) 832-1463, Web Site: www.thecloroxcompany.com (16)

Kraus, Ed, EC Kraus Home Wine & Beer Making Supplies, Independence, MO. Tel: (816) 254-7448, (800) 353-1906, FAX: (816) 254-7051, E-Mail: customerservice@eckraus.com, Web Site: www.eckraus.com (4)

Kraus, Eric, A., Covidien International, Mansfield, MA. Tel: (508) 261-8000, (800) 962-9888, FAX: (508) 261-8105, Web Site: www.covidien.com (7)

Kraus, Steve, Olan Mills Inc, Chattanooga, TN. Tel: (423) 622-5141, (800) 251-6320, FAX: (423) 629-8128, Web Site: www.olanmills.com (16)

EC Kraus Home Wine & Beer Making Supplies, Independence, MO. Tel: (816) 254-7448, (800) 353-1906, FAX: (816) 254-7051, E-Mail: customerservice@eckraus.com, Web Site: www.eckraus.com (4)

Krause, Dorothy, L., Marketplace of the Master Inc, Rockford, IL. Tel: (815) 874-1733, (800) 621-1255, FAX: (815) 874-4351, E-Mail: marketplace@marketplaceofthemaster.com, Web Site: www.marketplaceofthemaster.com (5)

Krause, Richard, C., Marketplace of the Master Inc, Rockford, IL. Tel: (815) 874-1733, (800) 621-1255, FAX: (815) 874-4351, E-Mail: marketplace@marketplaceofthemaster.com, Web Site: www.marketplaceofthemaster.com (5)

Krause Publications Inc, Iola, WI. Tel: (715) 445-2214, FAX: (715) 445-4087, E-Mail: info@krause.com, Web Site: www.krause.com (17)

Krauss, Julianne, The Hartz Mountain Corp, Secaucus, NJ. Tel: (201) 271-4800, (800) 275-1414, FAX: (201) 271-0068, Web Site: www.hartz.com (16)

Krauss, Michael, Authentic Designs Colonial and Early American Lighting Fixtures Inc, West Rupert, VT. Tel: (802) 394-7713, (800) 844-9416, FAX: (802) 394-2422, E-Mail: mail@authenticdesigns.com, Web Site: www.authenticdesigns.com (8)

Kravetz, David, Fairytale Brownies, Phoenix, AZ. Tel: (800) 324-7982, FAX: (602) 489-5122, E-Mail: service@brownies.com, Web Site: www.brownies.com (4)

Kravis, Marie, Josee, The Museum of Modern Art, New York, NY. Tel: (212) 708-9400, FAX: (212) 333-1123, E-Mail: info@moma.org, Web Site: www.moma.org (5)

Kravitsky, Charles, Fireman's Fund Insurance Co, Novato, CA. Tel: (415) 899-2000, FAX: (415) 899-3600, Web Site: www.firemansfund.com (14)

Krawchuk, Barry, America's Call Center, Jacksonville, FL. Tel: (904) 224-2000, (800) 598-2580, FAX: (904) 737-1107, E-Mail: info@webcallusa.com, Web Site: www.webcallusa.com (29)

Krawitz, Natalie, R., University of Missouri, Columbia, MO. Tel: (573) 882-6333, (800) 856-2181, FAX: (573) 882-2721, E-Mail: visitus@missouri.edu, Web Site: www.missouri.edu (41)

Krear, J. David, National Committee to Preserve Social Security & Medicare, Washington, DC. Tel: (202) 216-0420, (800) 966-1935, FAX: (202) 216-0446, E-Mail: kreard@ncpssm.org, Web Site: www.ncpssm.org (1)

Kreber, Frank, Kreber Graphics Inc, Columbus, OH. Tel: (614) 529-5701, (800) 777-3501, FAX: (614) 777-4890, E-Mail: info@kreber.com, Web Site: www.kreber.com (27)

Kreber Graphics Inc, Columbus, OH. Tel: (614) 529-5701, (800) 777-3501, FAX: (614) 777-4890, E-Mail: info@kreber.com, Web Site: www.kreber.com (27)

Kreczko, Alan, J., The Hartford Financial Services Inc, Southington, CT. Tel: (860) 843-8070, (860) 547-5000, FAX: (860) 547-2680, Web Site: www.thehartford.com (15)

Kreg Tool Co, Huxley, IA. Tel: (515) 597-6400, Web Site: www.kregtool.com (16)

Kreichman, Harris, eTargetMedia.com Inc, Coconut Creek, FL. Tel: (954) 480-8470, (888) 805-3282, FAX: (954) 480-8489, E-Mail: info@etargetmedia.com, Web Site: www.etargetmedia.com (32)

Kreicker, Clayton, R., Tri-State Advertising Co Inc, Warsaw, IN. Tel: (574) 267-5178, FAX: (574) 267-2965, E-Mail: info@tri-stateadv.com, Web Site: www.tri-stateadv.com (35)

Kreiman, David, Glenview State Bank, Glenview, IL. Tel: (847) 729-1900, FAX: (847) 729-5847, E-Mail: info@gsb.com, Web Site: www.gsb.com (14)

Krein, Erick, Markertek Video Supply, Saugerties, NY. Tel: (845) 246-3036, (800) 522-2025, FAX: (847) 246-1757, E-Mail: sales@markertek.com, Web Site: www.markertek.com (3)

Krejci, Allan, Hormel Foods Corp, Austin, MN. Tel: (507) 437-5611, (800) 523-4635, FAX: (507) 437-5158, Web Site: www.hormel.com (16)

Kremer, Frank, Summit Racing Equipment, Tallmadge, OH. Tel: (330) 630-0270, FAX: (330) 630-5330, Web Site: www.summitracing.com (12)

Kremer, John, 1001 Ways to Market Your Books, Taos, NM. Tel: (575) 751-3398, FAX: (575) 751-3100, E-Mail: info@bookmarket.com, Web Site: www.bookmarket.com (43)

Kremer, John, Open Horizons, Taos, NM. Tel: (575) 751-3398, FAX: (575) 751-3100, E-Mail: info@bookmarket.com, Web Site: www.bookmarket.com (39)

Kremp, Dave, ITW Vortec, Cincinnati, OH. Tel: (513) 891-7474, (800) 441-7475, FAX: (513) 891-4092, E-Mail: techsupport@vortec.com, Web Site: www.vortec.com (16)

Kress, Bob, Bell Performance Inc, Longwood, FL. Tel: (407) 831-5021, (800) 659-2355, FAX: (407) 767-8685, E-Mail: info@bellperformance.net, Web Site: www.bellperformance.net (9)

Kress, Staci, American Customer Care Inc, Bristol, CT. Tel: (866) 400-6886, Web Site: www.americancustomercare.com (29)

Kresser, David, Gift Services Inc, Vancouver, WA. Tel: (800) 379-4065, FAX: (360) 699-0597, E-Mail: corpsales@gifttree.com, Web Site: www.gifttree.com (5)

Kretchmer, Gary, Target & Response Inc, Chicago, IL. Tel: (312) 321-0500, FAX: (312) 321-0051, Web Site: www.target-response.com (5)

Kretschmann, Fred, Kennel Vet, Laurel, DE. Tel: (302) 875-7111, (800) 782-0627, FAX: (302) 269-3986, E-Mail: info@petmarket.com, Web Site: www.kennelvet.com (11)

Kretschmann, Meryl, Kennel Vet, Laurel, DE. Tel: (302) 875-7111, (800) 782-0627, FAX: (302) 269-3986, E-Mail: info@petmarket.com, Web Site: www.kennelvet.com (11)

Kretschmer, Diane, Continuing Education of the Bar (CEB), Oakland, CA. Tel: (510) 302-2000, (800) 232-3444, FAX: (510) 302-2001, Web Site: www.ceb.com (1)

Kricensky, Nori, Smith & Hawken Ltd, Novato, CA. Tel: (415) 506-3700, (800) 940-1170, FAX: (415) 506-3900, Web Site: www.smithandhawken.com (8)

Krieger, Lisa, Winn Devon, Richmond, BC Canada. Tel: (206) 763-9544, (800) 875-4150, FAX: (206) 762-1389, Web Site: www.winndevon.com (17)

Krieger, Lou, Poker Player, Sherman Oaks, CA. Tel: (310) 674-3365, FAX: (310) 674-3205, E-Mail: ard@gamblingtimes.com, Web Site: www.gamblingtimes.com (17)

Krieger, Niki, Winn Devon, Richmond, BC. Tel: (206) 763-9544, (800) 875-4150, FAX: (206) 762-1389, Web Site: www.winndevon.com (17)

Kriete, Edward, Hasbro Inc, Pawtucket, RI. Tel: (401) 727-5000, (800) 242-7276, FAX: (401) 727-5121, Web Site: www.hasbro.com (11)

Krill, Kay, Ann Taylor Inc, New York, NY. Tel: (212) 457-2075, (800) FAX-ANN, FAX: (800) DIAL-ANN, Web Site: www.anninc.com (2)

Krings, Jack, CPI Corp, St Louis, MO. Tel: (314) 231-1575, (877) 763-4456, FAX: (314) 231-8150, E-Mail: feedback@cpicorp.com, Web Site: www.cpicorp.com (16)

Krisel, Ross, Prosodie Interactive, Plantation, FL. Tel: (954) 671-6500, (866) 776-7634, FAX: (954) 915-0567, E-Mail: info@prosodiemail.com, Web Site: www.ivrinc.com (29)

Kristo, Bryce, INX International Ink Co, Schaumburg, IL. Tel: (800) 631-7956, FAX: (847) 969-9758, E-Mail: info@inxink.com, Web Site: www.inxinternational.com (16)

Kritzeck, Paul, Crest Healthcare Supply, Dassel, MN. Tel: (800) 369-9207, (800) 328-8908, Web Site: www.cresthealthcare.com (16)

Krivkovich, Peter, Cramer-Krasselt, Chicago, IL. Tel: (312) 616-9600, FAX: (312) 938-3157, E-Mail: pkrivkov@c-k.com, Web Site: www.c-k.com (35)

Krivoruchka, Mark, W., Cooper Tire & Rubber Co Inc, Findlay, OH. Tel: (419) 423-1321, (800) 854-6288, FAX: (419) 424-4212, Web Site: www.coopertire.com (16)

Krivsky, Emmett, Backyard Gardening, Tiger, GA. Tel: (706) 782-4224, (800) 681-3962, FAX: (800) 311-9539, E-Mail: info@yardzone.com, Web Site: www.yardzone.com (8)

Krizek, Paul, Christian Relief Services Charities Inc, Alexandria, VA. Tel: (703) 317-9086, Web Site: www.christianrelief.org (1)

Krna, Rick, Professional Direct Marketing & Mailing List Inc, Boca Raton, FL. Tel: (561) 241-4414, (800) 777-5478, FAX: (561) 241-5878, E-Mail: pdm@pdmm.info, Web Site: www.pdmm.us (23)

Kroeger, Dan, Gold Medal Products Co, Cincinnati, OH. Tel: (513) 769-7676, (800) 543-0862, FAX: (800) 542-1496, E-Mail: info@gmpopcorn.com, Web Site: www.gmpopcorn.com (16)

The Kroger Co, Cincinnati, OH. Tel: (513) 762-4000, Web Site: www.kroger.com (4)

Kroll, Gretchen, Tripar International Inc, Roselle, IL. Tel: (630) 980-5100, (800) 222-1142, FAX: (800) 648-9015, E-Mail: sales@tripar.com, Web Site: www.tripar.com (28)

Kroll, Leland, Kroll Direct Marketing Inc, Plainsboro, NJ. Tel: (609) 275-2900, FAX: (609) 275-6606, E-Mail: lee@krolldirect.com, Web Site: www.krolldirect.com (23)

Kroll, Woodrow, Back to the Bible, Lincoln, NE. Tel: (402) 464-7200, (800) 811-2397, FAX: (402) 464-7474, E-Mail: info@backtothebible.org, Web Site: www.backtothebible.org (5)

Kroll Direct Marketing Inc, Plainsboro, NJ. Tel: (609) 275-2900, FAX: (609) 275-6606, E-Mail: lee@krolldirect.com, Web Site: www.krolldirect.com (23)

Kromer, Bob, The New Piper Aircraft Inc, Vero Beach, FL. Tel: (772) 567-4361, FAX: (772) 978-6573, E-Mail: marketing@piper.com, Web Site: www.newpiper.com (16)

Krone, Philip, Productive Strategies Inc, Northfield, IL. Tel: (847) 446-0008, FAX: (847) 446-0211, E-Mail: pkrone@productivestrategies.com, Web Site: www.productivestrategies.com (20)

Kronrad, Robert, All Star Carts & Vehicles, Bay Shore, NY. Tel: (631) 666-5252, (800) 831-3166, FAX: (631) 666-1319, Web Site: www.allstarcarts.com (16)

Kronrad, Stephen, All Star Carts & Vehicles, Bay Shore, NY. Tel: (631) 666-5252, (800) 831-3166, FAX: (631) 666-1319, Web Site: www.allstarcarts.com (16)

Kropp, Joann, Walter Karl Inc, Pearl River, NY. Tel: (845) 620-0700, FAX: (845) 620-1885, E-Mail: info@walterkarl.infousa.com, Web Site: www.walterkarl.com (22)

Kropp, Mike, Kropp Enterprises, Kissimmee, FL. Tel: (407) 566-9276, FAX: (407) 566-9276 (2)

Kropp Enterprises, Kissimmee, FL. Tel: (407) 566-9276, FAX: (407) 566-9276 (2)

Kross Inc, Santa Clarita, CA. Tel: (661) 284-3557, (800) 456-3699, FAX: (661) 257-1914, Web Site: www.krosskits.com (16)

Krosser, Stuart, Sherman Specialty Toy Co Inc, Jericho, NY. Tel: (516) 861-6420, (516) 546-7400, (800) 645-6513, FAX: (516) 861-1033, (800) 853-8697, E-Mail: orders@shermanspecialty.com, Web Site: www.shermanspecialty.com (16)

Kroth, Laura, Coastal Hotel Group, Seattle, WA. Tel: (206) 388-0400, FAX: (206) 388-0401, E-Mail: info@coastalhotel.com, Web Site: www.coastalhotels.com (1)

Krott, Joseph, P., Sunoco, Inc, Philadelphia, PA. Tel: (215) 977-3000, (800) 786-6261, FAX: (215) 977-3409, E-Mail: sunoco_online@sunoil.com, Web Site: www.sunocoinc.com (16)

Kroupa, Ivan, Kadant Johnson Inc, Three Rivers, MI. Tel: (269) 278-1715, FAX: (269) 279-5980, Web Site: www.kadantjohnson.com (16)

Krow, Gary, Comdata Corp, Brentwood, TN. Tel: (615) 370-7000, (800) 266-3282, Web Site: www.comdata.com (14)

Kruckeberg, Lloyd, Shopguide.com, Amarillo, TX. Tel: (806) 351-0005, FAX: (806) 351-0059, E-Mail: info@shopguide.com, Web Site: www.shopguide.com (27)

Kruczlnicki, David G., Glens Falls Hospital Foundation, Glens Falls, NY. FAX: (518) 926-7012, Web Site: www.glensfallshospital.org (1)

Krueger, Eugene, C., National Fulfillment Services, Holmes, PA. Tel: (610) 532-4700, (800) NFS-1306, FAX: (610) 586-3232, E-Mail: tkrueger@nfsrv.com, Web Site: www.nfsrv.com (28)

Krueger, Jim, Figi's Inc, Marshfield, WI. Tel: (715) 387-1771, (800) 422-3444, FAX: (715) 384-1129, Web Site: www.figis.com (4)

Krueger, Thomas, National Fulfillment Services, Holmes, PA. Tel: (610) 532-4700, (800) NFS-1306, FAX: (610) 586-3232, E-Mail: tkrueger@nfsrv.com, Web Site: www.nfsrv.com (28)

Krug, E, Herbert, Herbert Krug & Associates Inc, Evanston, IL. Tel: (847) 864-0550, FAX: (847) 864-0575 (20)

Krug, E. Herbert, Catalog Marketing Group, Evanston, IL. Tel: (847) 864-8089 (20)

Krug, E. Herbert, Catalog Media Network Inc, Evanston, IL. Tel: (847) 864-0550, FAX: (847) 864-0575, Web Site: www.thelistbank.com (23)

Krug, E. Herbert, The List Bank, Evanston, IL. Tel: (847) 864-0550, FAX: (847) 864-0575, E-Mail: catalogmed@aol.com, Web Site: www.thelistbank.com (24)

Krug, Kelly, Visa USA, Foster City, CA. Tel: (650) 432-3200, FAX: (650) 432-2875, Web Site: www.visa.com (14)

Herbert Krug & Associates Inc, Evanston, IL. Tel: (847) 864-0550, FAX: (847) 864-0575 (20)

Kruggel, James, C., The Catholic University of America Press, Washington, DC. Tel: (202) 319-5052, FAX: (202) 319-4985, E-Mail: cua-press@cua.edu, Web Site: www.cuapress.cua.edu (17)

Krupa, Charles, Haynes & Partners Communications Inc, Indianapolis, IN. Tel: (317) 860-3000, FAX: (317) 860-3001, E-Mail: levans@hp-inc.com, Web Site: www.hp-inc.com (35)

Krupp, Steven, J&H Berge/The Lab Mart, South Plainfield, NJ. Tel: (908) 561-1234, FAX: (908) 561-3002, E-Mail: rgardner@labmart.com, Web Site: www.labmart.com (7)

Kruse, Daniel, J., Kruse Asset Management, San Antonio, TX. Tel: (210) 499-0777, (800) 952-1973, FAX: (210) 499-4217, E-Mail: sales@kruseasset.com, Web Site: www.kruseasset.com (35)

Kruse Asset Management, San Antonio, TX. Tel: (210) 499-0777, (800) 952-1973, FAX: (210) 499-4217, E-Mail: sales@kruseasset.com, Web Site: www.kruseasset.com (35)

Krutzberg, Keith, Epson America, Long Beach, CA. Tel: (562) 981-3840, (800) 873-7766, FAX: (562) 290-5220, Web Site: www.epson.com (10)

Kruysman, Gretchen, Thomas Moser Cabinetmakers, Freeport, ME. Tel: (207) 865-4519, (800) 708-9041, FAX: (207) 865-6539, E-Mail: freeportshowroom@thosmoser.com, Web Site: www.thosmoser.com (35)

Kryl, Susan, Kryl & Co Inc, Chicago, IL. Tel: (312) 641-0338, FAX: (312) 641-0314, E-Mail: info@krylandco.com, Web Site: www.krylandco.com (35)

Kryl & Co Inc, Chicago, IL. Tel: (312) 641-0338, FAX: (312) 641-0314, E-Mail: info@krylandco.com, Web Site: www.krylandco.com (35)

Kuamoo, Misty, Micro Center, Hilliard, OH. Tel: (800) 634-3478, FAX: (614) 777-2620, E-Mail: csrs@microcenterorder.com, Web Site: www.microcenter.com (3)

Kubach, Douglas G., Pearson Education, Upper Saddle River, NJ. Tel: (201) 236-7000, FAX: (201) 236-3290, E-Mail: communications@pearsoned.com, Web Site: www.pearsoned.com (17)

Kubanka, Stefanie, CoreBrand, New York, NY. Tel: (212) 329-3030, FAX: (212) 329-3031, E-Mail: jgregory@corebrand.com, Web Site: www.corebrand.com (35)

Kubic, Joe, Adcom Communications, Cleveland, OH. Tel: (216) 574-9100, FAX: (216) 574-6131, E-Mail: adcom@adcom1.com, Web Site: www.adcom1.com (35)

Kubik, Keith, ClickStream, Orland Park, IL. Tel: (949) 439-2888, Web Site: www.clickstreamtv.com (32)

Kubis, Thaddeus, NAK Marketing & Communications, New York, NY. Tel: (212) 505-9290, Web Site: www.nakcomm.com (20)

Kuczer, Ronald, Maverick Ventures Product Line, Chesterfield, MO. Tel: (636) 537-4656, (800) 467-4656, FAX: (636) 537-4657, E-Mail: hang10cd@aol.com, Web Site: www.hang10cd.com (5)

Kuehn, Dr Alfred A., Management Science Associates Inc, Pittsburgh, PA. Tel: (412) 362-2000, (800) MSA-INFO, FAX: (412) 363-5598, E-Mail: info@msa.com, Web Site: www.msa.com (20)

Kuehn, Mary, K-tel International, Golden Valley, MN. Tel: (204) 889-5430, (800) 665-5021, FAX: (612) 559-6803, Web Site: www.ktel.com (16)

Kuendig, John, Ryan IDirect, Wilton, CT. Tel: (203) 210-3000, FAX: (203) 210-7926, Web Site: www.ryanpartnership.com (35)

Kuester, Dennis J., Marshall & Ilsley Corp, Milwaukee, WI. Tel: (414) 765-7801, FAX: (414) 765-7899, Web Site: www.micorp.com (14)

Kugel, Moshe, 3 Gen Co, Brooklyn, NY. Tel: (718) 773-3388, FAX: (718) 467-0843 (23)

Kugler, Larry, The Millard Group, Lincolnwood, IL. Tel: (847) 674-4100, (800) 339-6876, FAX: (847) 677-0790, E-Mail: sales@millardgroup.com, Web Site: www.millardgroup.com (16)

Kuhlman, Paul, Acme Tools, Grand Forks, ND. Tel: (701) 746-2881, Web Site: www.acmetoolcrib.com (8)

Kuhn, Brent, BKV Inc, Atlanta, GA. Tel: (404) 233-0332, FAX: (404) 233-0302, E-Mail: sylviam@bkv.com, Web Site: www.bkv.com (35)

Kuhn, Whitey, Kuhn & Wittenborn Inc, Kansas City, MO. Tel: (816) 471-7888, FAX: (816) 471-7530, E-Mail: humanresources@kuhnwitt.com, Web Site: www.kuhnwitt.com (35)

Kuhn & Wittenborn Inc, Kansas City, MO. Tel: (816) 471-7888, FAX: (816) 471-7530, E-Mail: humanresources@kuhnwitt.com, Web Site: www.kuhnwitt.com (35)

Kuhr, Jim, The FX Matt Brewing Co, Utica, NY. Tel: (315) 732-0022, (800) 765-6288, FAX: (315) 624-2401, E-Mail: info@saranac.com, Web Site: www.saranac.com (4)

Kula, Mike, Falcon Products Inc, Newport, TN. Tel: (314) 991-9200, (800) 873-3252, FAX: (314) 991-9227, E-Mail: info@falconproducts.com, Web Site: www.falconproducts.com (16)

Kulczycki, Bill, Patagonia Mail Order Inc, Reno, NV. Tel: (775) 747-1992, (800) 638-6464, FAX: (775) 747-6159, Web Site: www.patagonia.com (2)

Kulick, John, Eckankar, Minneapolis, MN. Tel: (612) 544-3001, (800) 327-5113, FAX: (612) 474-1127, Web Site: www.eckankar.org (17)

Kulikowski, Frederick, R, Commercial Federal Bank, Omaha, NE. Tel: (402) 554-9200, FAX: (402) 514-5304 (14)

Kulp, Dale, GENESYS Sampling Systems, Horsham, PA. Tel: (215) 653-7100, (800) 336-7674, FAX: (215) 653-7115, E-Mail: info@m-s-g.com, Web Site: www.m-s-g.com (30)

Kuman, Peg, Relevate, Springfield, VA. Tel: (703) 658-8300, (800) 523-7346, FAX: (703) 658-8301, E-Mail: sales@relevategroup.com, Web Site: www.relevategroup.com (22)

Kumar, Raj, Data Square LLC, Wilton, CT. Tel: (203) 964-9733, E-Mail: info@datasquare.com, Web Site: www.datasquare.com (22)

Kummer, Lisa, Wilsons Leather, Brooklyn Park, MN. Tel: (763) 391-4000, (866) 305-4704, FAX: (763) 391-4906, Web Site: www.wilsonsleather.com (2)

Kummunt, Alexander, K., National Railroad Passenger Corp, Washington, DC. Tel: (202) 906-3000, (800) USA-RAIL, FAX: (202) 906-3306, Web Site: www.amtrak.com (16)

Kundahl, Dr. Edward, IdeaOverTen LLC, Allentown, PA. Tel: (610) 437-4340, (866) 864-2836, FAX: (866) 414-6165, E-Mail: marketing@ideaover10.com, Web Site: www.ideaover10.com (35)

Kunert, Del, Concurrent Computer Corp, Duluth, GA. Tel: (678) 228-4000, (877) 978-7363, FAX: (954) 977-5580, Web Site: www.ccur.com (3)

Kunihiro, Jim, ServiceMaster Co, Memphis, TN. Tel: (901) 766-1400, (901) 597-8502, (888) 937-3783, (866) 782-6787, FAX: (901) 766-1491, Web Site: www.servicemaster.com (8)

Kunkel, Peter, Diversified Investment Advisors, Harrison, NY. Tel: (914) 697-8967, FAX: (914) 697-3743, Web Site: www.divinvest.com (14)

Kuntz, Ray, American Trucking Association, Arlington, VA. Tel: (703) 838-1700, FAX: (800) 254-2571, E-Mail: atamembership@trucking.org, Web Site: www.truckline.com (1)

Kunz, Heidi, Blue Shield Life, San Francisco, CA. Tel: (888) 800-2742, FAX: (800) 329-2742, Web Site: www.blueshieldca.com (14)

Kunze, Mary, A., Advanced Concepts Inc, Milwaukee, WI. Tel: (414) 362-9640, FAX: (414) 362-9646, E-Mail: info@advanced-concepts.com, Web Site: www.advanced-concepts.com (22)

Kuo, John, W., Varian Medical Systems, Palo Alto, CA. Tel: (650) 493-4000, FAX: (650) 842-5196, Web Site: www.varian.com (9)

Kupperman, Dennis, RB Toy Design Inc, Glenview, IL. Tel: (847) 577-5683, FAX: (847) 272-4034, E-Mail: info@rbtoydesign.com, Web Site: www.rbtoy.com (33)

Kupshe, Ken, Woodcraft Supply Corp LLC, Parkersburg, WV. Tel: (304) 422-5412, (800) 344-3348, FAX: (304) 422-5417, Web Site: www.woodcraft.com (9)

Kurant, Gloria, L., Kurant Direct Inc, New York, NY. Tel: (212) 866-0770, FAX: (212) 866-0806, E-Mail: gkurant@aol.com, Web Site: www.kurantdirect.com (29)

Kurant Direct Inc, New York, NY. Tel: (212) 866-0770, FAX: (212) 866-0806, E-Mail: gkurant@aol.com, Web Site: www.kurantdirect.com (29)

Kuras, Laura, Thomas Business Lists, New York, NY. Tel: (212) 695-0500, FAX: (212) 290-7362, E-Mail: contact@thomaspublishing.com, Web Site: www.thomaspublishing.com (24)

Kurkow, Richard, M, SpencerStuart, Chicago, IL. Tel: (312) 822-0088, FAX: (312) 822-0116, Web Site: www.spencerstuart.com (22)

Kurland, James, The Communique Group, Parker, CO. Tel: (617) 527-2230, FAX: (617) 965-6763 (35)

Kurman, Rick, Cheap Aprons, Derry, NH. Tel: (978) 689-0694, (800) 367-2374, FAX: (978) 689-2483, E-Mail: rkurman@cheapaprons.com, Web Site: www.cheapaprons.com (2)

Kurnett, Dierdre, DeLuxe Laboratories Inc, Hollywood, CA. Tel: (323) 462-6171, FAX: (323) 960-7016, E-Mail: steven.vananda@bydeluxe.com, Web Site: www.bydeluxe.com (16)

Kurpiel, Martin, Creative Automation, Hillside, IL. Tel: (708) 449-2800, (800) 773-1588, FAX: (708) 449-3282, E-Mail: busmgr@cauto.com, Web Site: www.cauto.com (22)

Kurpius, Gary, L., Veterans of Foreign Wars (VFW) of the US-National Headquarters, Kansas City, MO. Tel: (816) 756-3390, FAX: (816) 968-1149, E-Mail: info@vfw.org, Web Site: www.vfw.org (1)

Kurth, Jesse, Sigma Micro LLC, Indianapolis, IN. Tel: (317) 631-0907, (800) 383-4421, FAX: (317) 631-6585, Web Site: www.sigma-micro.com (21)

Kurtz, Brian, Boardroom Inc, Stamford, CT. Tel: (203) 973-5900, FAX: (203) 967-3086, E-Mail: kseaborne@boardroom.com, Web Site: www.boardroom.com (17)

Kurtz, Craig, Red Edge Labs LLC, Aliso Viejo, CA. Tel: (800) 931-1055, Web Site: www.rededgelabs.com (35)

Kurtz, Jill, Our Sunday Visitor Publishing, Huntington, IN. Tel: (260) 356-8400, (800) 348-2440, FAX: (260) 356-8472, E-Mail: athomas@osv.com, Web Site: www.osv.com (17)

Kurtz, Max, Ztek Co, Lexington, KY. Tel: (859) 281-1611, (800) 247-1603, FAX: (859) 281-1521, E-Mail: cs@ztek.com, Web Site: www.ztek.com (3)

Kurtz, Michael, Manchester Farms Inc, Columbia, SC. Tel: (803) 469-2588, (800) 845-0421, FAX: (803) 469-8637, E-Mail: customerservice@manchesterfarms.com, Web Site: www.manchesterfarms.com (4)

Kurtzweil, Jerry, Publications International Ltd, Lincolnwood, IL. Tel: (847) 745-9299, (800) 595-8484, FAX: (847) 676-3671, Web Site: www.pubint.com (17)

Kurz, George, J., The HoneyBaked Ham Co, Holland, OH. Tel: (419) 868-6400, E-Mail: info@honeybaked.com, Web Site: www.honeybaked.com (4)

Kuse, Allan, RSC The Quality Measurement Co, Evansville, IN. Tel: (812) 425-4562, FAX: (812) 425-2844 (30)

Kusek, Kristan, Heath Kit Co, Saint Joseph, MI. Tel: (269) 925-6000, (800) 253-0570, FAX: (269) 925-2898, E-Mail: info@heathkit.com, Web Site: www.heathkit.com (3)

Kushner, Alexander, M., Jasek Enterprises, Westlake Village, CA. Tel: (805) 379-2871, FAX: (805) 379-9839 (20)

Kushner, Paul, RMA-The Risk Management Association, Philadelphia, PA. Tel: (215) 446-4000, FAX: (215) 446-4101, E-Mail: customers@rmahq.org, Web Site: www.rmahq.org (1)

Kust, Mike, Aimia, Minneapolis, MN. Tel: (763) 445-3453, FAX: (763) 496-3453, Web Site: www.carlsonmarketing.com (35)

Kuster, Bradley S., Continental Western Group, Des Moines, IA. Tel: (515) 473-3000, (800) 533-0303, FAX: (515) 473-3015, Web Site: www.cwgins.com (15)

Kustz, Heidi, Alliance of Nonprofit Mailers, Washington, DC. Tel: (202) 462-5132, FAX: (202) 462-0423, E-Mail: alliance@nonprofitmailers.org, Web Site: www.nonprofitmailers.org (40)

Kutasovic, Paul, School of Management, Old Westbury, NY. Tel: (516) 686-1000, (800) 345-NYIT, (800) 345-6948, Web Site: www.nyit.edu (41)

Kutchma, Brian, Black Box Corp, Lawrence, PA. Tel: (412) 873-6795, (877) 877-2269, FAX: (800) 321-0746, E-Mail: brian.kutchma@blackbox.com, Web Site: www.blackbox.com (3)

Kutza, Patricia, Patricia Kutza Co, Vallejo, CA. Tel: (707) 552-0442, E-Mail: pkutza@pacbell.net (2)

Patricia Kutza Co, Vallejo, CA. Tel: (707) 552-0442, E-Mail: pkutza@pacbell.net (2)

Kuvacevich, Richard, Wells Fargo, San Francisco, CA. Tel: (866) 878-5865, (800) 869-3557, FAX: (626) 312-3015, Web Site: www.wellsfargo.com (14)

Kuwait Airways Corp, Fort Lee, NJ. Tel: (201) 582-9222, (800) 4-KUWAIT, FAX: (212) 659-4270, E-Mail: nyc@kuwait-airways.com, Web Site: www.kuwait-airways.com (19)

Kuzins, Matt, Matt & Kumpany Kuzins, Sacramento, CA. Tel: (916) 446-2008, FAX: (916) 446-5302, E-Mail: matt@kuzins.com (1)

Kwak, Soomi, Canadian Business, Toronto, ON Canada. Tel: (416) 596-5100, FAX: (416) 764-1200, Web Site: www.canadianbusiness.com (17)

Kwant, Kimberly, Entertainment Publications Inc, Troy, MI. Tel: (248) 404-1000, (888) 231-SAVE, FAX: (248) 404-1915, Web Site: www.entertainment.com (31)

Kwik-File, Sheboygan, WI. Tel: (763) 572-1980, (800) 822-8037, FAX: (763) 572-0168, Web Site: www.mayline.com (27)

Kwok, Herbert, Time Products International, Del Rio, TX. Tel: (847) 459-8885, FAX: (847) 459-8111, E-Mail: cttpi@aol.com, Web Site: www.tpi2000.com (16)

Kyp Systems Inc, New York, NY. Tel: (212) 551-7878, FAX: (917) 591-1514, E-Mail: steves@kyp.com, Web Site: www.ikyp.com (35)

L

L & E Meridian, Springfield, VA. Tel: (703) 913-0300, (800) 555-1556, FAX: (703) 913-7052, E-Mail: pmaaseide@l-e.com, Web Site: www.l-e.com (21)

L&L Management, Pasadena, CA. Tel: (626) 568-0338, FAX: (626) 568-9165 (16)

L-Com Inc, Andover, MA. Tel: (978) 682-6936, Web Site: www.L-com.com (22)

L6 Holdings Corp, Duluth, GA. Tel: (678) 957-0511 (14)

L3 Virtual Solutions LLC, Marengo, OH. Tel: (740) 625-6535, Web Site: www.l3vs.com (20)

LCA Vision, Cincinnati, OH. Tel: (513) 792-9292, FAX: (513) 792-5620, Web Site: www.lasikplus.com (41)

LCH Direct Inc, Waltham, MA. Tel: (978) 664-2900, FAX: (978) 664-4812, E-Mail: info@lchdirect.com, Web Site: www.lchdirect.com (35)

LDS Group Inc, New York, NY. Tel: (646) 390-5702, FAX: (646) 390-5715, E-Mail: rvergara@ldsgroupinc.com, Web Site: www.ldsgroupinc.com (23)

LDS Test & Measurement, Marlborough, MA. Tel: (608) 821-6600, FAX: (608) 821-6691, E-Mail: info-us@lds.spx.com, Web Site: www.lds-group.com (3)

LEC Ltd, Chicago, IL. Tel: (312) 670-0077, Web Site: www.lecltd.com (35)

LED Signs, Stockbridge, MI. Tel: (954) 771-5488, FAX: (954) 267-0551, Web Site: www.finest.com (23)

LGP GEM LTD, New York, NY. Tel: (212) 840-2510, FAX: (212) 302-6182, E-Mail: sales@lgpltd.com, Web Site: www.lgpltd.com (16)

LH Management, Hartsdale, NY. Tel: (914) 285-3456, FAX: (914) 285-3450, E-Mail: lh@leonhenryinc.com, Web Site: www.leonhenryinc.com (24)

LHH & F Inc, Hillsdale, NY. Tel: (518) 325-4000, (800) 955-1129 (35)

LIM College, New York, NY. Tel: (212) 752-1530, Web Site: www.limcollege.edu (1)

LIMRA International, Windsor, CT. Tel: (860) 688-3358, Web Site: www.limra.com (1)

LKH&S Inc, Chicago, IL. Tel: (312) 595-0200, FAX: (312) 595-0300, E-Mail: lkhs@lkhs.com, Web Site: www.lkhs.com (35)

LLR/Research, Haverhill, MA. Tel: (978) 374-0931, FAX: (978) 374-1008 (38)

LMC Direct, Ottawa, ON Canada. Tel: (613) 521-8181, FAX: (613) 521-3015 (23)

LN Marketing Associates, Emerald Hills, CA. Tel: (650) 368-7181 (20)

L.P. THEBAULT CO., Parsippany, NJ. Tel: (973) 884-1300, FAX: (973) 952-8296, Web Site: www.earthcolor.com (27)

LPL, Scottsdale, AZ. Tel: (480) 457-2007, Web Site: www.lifelock.com (21)

LS Direct Marketing, Suffern, NY. Tel: (845) 357-1238, E-Mail: info@ls-direct.com, Web Site: www.ls-direct.com (23)

LS Records, Madison, TN. Tel: (615) 868-7171, FAX: (615) 860-7665, E-Mail: ls654@home.com, Web Site: www.cristylane.com (17)

LSC Marketing, Little Rock, AR. Tel: (501) 374-2332, (866) LSC-MKGT, FAX: (501) 372-6570, Web Site: www.lscmarketing.com (28)

LSSiData, Blue Bell, PA. Tel: (610) 825-7720, (800) 210-9021, E-Mail: info@lssi.net, Web Site: www.dataserve.info (22)

LT Associates, Rio Verde, AZ. Tel: (952) 943-9790, FAX: (952) 943-9794, E-Mail: thouse2az@aol.com, Web Site: www.ltapromotions.net (33)

LTD Supply Chain, Downingtown, PA. Tel: (610) 458-3636, FAX: (610) 458-8039, E-Mail: tomc@ltdsupplychain.com, Web Site: www.ltdsupplychain.com (20)

La Bar, Gaile, Mail Movers & Mailing Services, Upper Darby, PA. Tel: (610) 888-6969, (610) 734-1220, FAX: (610) 734-1200, E-Mail: mailmovers@rcn.com, Web Site: www.mailmoversandmore.com (22)

La Bine, Ronald, C., Premier Print and Service Group Inc, Chicago, IL. Tel: (312) 648-2266, (800) 648-3677, FAX: (312) 648-1361, E-Mail: blabin@premierprint.com, Web Site: www.premierprint.com (21)

La Charite, Father Roger, J., Fathers of St Edmund Southern Missions Inc, Selma, AL. Tel: (334) 872-2359, FAX: (334) 875-8189, E-Mail: jm1428@aol.com, Web Site: www.edmunditemissions.org (1)

La Forgia, John, Mayo Clinic, Rochester, MN. Tel: (507) 266-2511, FAX: (507) 284-0161, Web Site: www.mayoclinic.org (17)

La Forgia, Robert, M., Hilton Hotels Corp, Mc Lean, VA. Tel: (310) 278-4321, (800) HILTONS, FAX: (310) 205-3670, Web Site: www.hilton.com (19)

La Penta, George, Weichert Co, Morris Plains, NJ. Tel: (973) 397-8516, Web Site: www.weichert.com (14)

Lab Safety Supply Inc, Janesville, WI. Tel: (608) 754-2345, (800) 356-2855, FAX: (800) 543-9910, Web Site: www.labsafety.com (5)

Laba, Larry, SOAR Inflatables, Healdsburg, CA. Tel: (707) 433-5599, FAX: (707) 433-4499, E-Mail: sales@soar1.com, Web Site: www.soar1.com (11)

Laban, Rick, Gold Medal Hair Products Inc, Farmingdale, NY. Tel: (516) 378-6900, (800) 324-7136, FAX: (516) 378-0168, E-Mail: customerservice@goldmedalhair.com, Web Site: www.goldmedalhair.com (7)

Labels West Inc, Woodinville, WA. Tel: (425) 486-8484, (800) 540-3009, FAX: (425) 486-8488, Web Site: www.labelswest.com (27)

Laben, Gary, KBM Group, Richardson, TX. Tel: (972) 664-3600, FAX: (972) 664-3656, E-Mail: info@ knowledgebasemarketing.com, Web Site: www. kbm1.com (22)

Laben, Gary, Wunderman, New York, NY. Tel: (212) 941-3000, FAX: (212) 888-7520, Web Site: www. wunderman.com (35)

LaBonia, Michael, Star Tribune, Minneapolis, MN. Tel: (612) 673-4000, FAX: (612) 673-4359, E-Mail: charte@startribune.com, Web Site: www. startribunecompany.com (17)

Labonowski, Christine, D'Lights, South El Monte, CA. Tel: (818) 956-5656, FAX: (818) 956-5657, Web Site: www.dlights.com (8)

LaBorde, Charles, Vector Marketing Corp, Olean, NY. Tel: (716) 373-6141, FAX: (716) 373-6145, Web Site: www.cutco.com (5)

Labrake, Mike, Amigo Mobility International Inc, Bridgeport, MI. Tel: (989) 777-0910, (800) 692-6446, FAX: (989) 777-8184, E-Mail: info@ myamigo.com, Web Site: www.myamigo.com (16)

LaBree, Lela, PhotoSource International, Osceola, WI. Tel: (715) 248-3800, X27, (800) 223-3860, FAX: (715) 248-3800, E-Mail: info@photosource.com, Web Site: www.photosource.com (38)

Labry III, Edward, A., First Data Merchant Services, Greenwood Village, CO. Tel: (303) 488-8000, (800) 735-3362, Web Site: www.firstdata.com (14)

Labs, Rick, C L & B Capital Management, Fayetteville, NY. Tel: (315) 637-0915, FAX: (413) 403-7145, Web Site: www.clbcm.com (35)

The Lacek Group, Minneapolis, MN. Tel: (612) 359-3700, FAX: (612) 359-9395, E-Mail: info@lacek. com, Web Site: www.lacek.com (35)

Lacey, James, MassMutual Financial Group, Springfield, MA. Tel: (413) 788-8411, FAX: (413) 744-8889, E-Mail: name@www.massmutual.com, Web Site: www.massmutual.com (15)

Lachman, Deborah F., Anthem Blue Cross, Westlake Village, CA. Tel: (805) 557-6655, (800) 333-0912, FAX: (800) 557-6872, Web Site: www.bluecrossca. com (15)

Lachnicht, Cheslie, A Caldwell List Co Inc, Norcross, GA. Tel: (770) 662-0255, (800) 241-7425, FAX: (770) 662-0351, Web Site: www.caldwell-list.com (23)

LaCivita, Steven, University of Chicago GSB, Chicago, IL. Tel: (312) 464-8733, Web Site: www. chicagoexec.net (1)

Lack, Marily, Anatomical Chart Co, Chicago, IL. Tel: (847) 679-4700, (800) 621-7500, FAX: (847) 674-0211, E-Mail: service@anatomical.com, Web Site: www.anatomical.com (7)

LaCour, John, DMN3, Houston, TX. Tel: (713) 868-3000, (800) 625-8320, FAX: (713) 868-1388, E-Mail: contact@dmn3.com, Web Site: www. dmn3.com (35)

LaCour, Paula, Magic Seasonings Mail Order, New Orleans, LA. Tel: (504) 731-3590, (800) 457-2857, FAX: (504) 731-3576, E-Mail: jlm@chefpaul.com, Web Site: www.chefpaul.com (4)

LaCrosse Footwear Inc, Portland, OR. Tel: (503) 262-0110, (800) 323-2668, FAX: (503) 262-0115, E-Mail: customerservice@lacrossefootwear.com, Web Site: www.lacrossefootwear.com (16)

Lacy, Alan, J., Sears, Roebuck & Co, Hoffman Estates, IL. Tel: (847) 286-2500, FAX: (847) 286-7829, Web Site: www.sears.com (16)

Lacy, Andy, Quality Education Data (QED), Shelton, CT. Tel: (203) 926-4800, (800) 333-8802, E-Mail: mdrinfor@dnb.com, Web Site: www.schooldata. com (23)

Lacy, Stephen, M., Meredith Corp, Des Moines, IA. Tel: (515) 284-3000, FAX: (515) 284-2700, Web Site: www.meredith.com (17)

Ladd, Jack, W., Ladd Associates Inc, San Francisco, CA. Tel: (415) 921-1001, FAX: (415) 921-2311, E-Mail: info@laddassociates.com, Web Site: laddassociates.com (20)

Ladd, Robert, Charter Communications, Saint Louis, MO. Tel: (314) 965-0555, (888) 438-2427, FAX: (314) 965-9745, Web Site: www.charteroom.com (16)

Ladd Associates Inc, San Francisco, CA. Tel: (415) 921-1001, FAX: (415) 921-2311, E-Mail: info@ laddassociates.com, Web Site: laddassociates.com (20)

Ladden, Bernice, Women in Direct Marketing International, New York, NY. Tel: (516) 746-6700, FAX: (516) 294-8141, Web Site: www.wdmi.org (40)

Ladiuala, Sajjad, S., Neuberger & Berman Management, New York, NY. Tel: (212) 476-8800, (800) 877-9700, FAX: (212) 476-9090, Web Site: www. nb.com (14)

Ladner, Robert, Behavioral Science Research, Coral Gables, FL. Tel: (305) 443-2000, (800) 282-2771, FAX: (305) 448-6825 (30)

Ladouceur, Mark, Drawing Board Inc, Waynesboro, PA. Tel: (301) 739-4487, (800) 527-9530, FAX: (800) 253-1838, E-Mail: customerservice@ drawingboard.com, Web Site: www.drawingboard. com (16)

Ladouceur, Mark, Medco Supply Co Inc, Tonawanda, NY. Tel: (716) 695-3244, (800) 556-3326, FAX: (800) 222-1934, E-Mail: sales@medcosupply.com, Web Site: www.medcosupply.com (7)

The LadyBug Co, Berry Creek, CA. Tel: (530) 589-5227, FAX: (530) 589-4639 (8)

Laerdal Medical, Wappingers Falls, NY. Tel: (877) 523-7325, Web Site: www.laerdal.com (34)

LaFemina, Peter, Coastal Hotel Group, Seattle, WA. Tel: (206) 388-0400, FAX: (206) 388-0401, E-Mail: name@coastalhotel.com, Web Site: www. coastalhotels.com (1)

Lafferty, Alex, Lafferty Equipment Manufacturing Inc, North Little Rock, AR. Tel: (501) 851-2820, (800) 999-2820, FAX: (501) 851-3719, E-Mail: webmaster@laffertyequipment.com, Web Site: www.laffertyequipment.com (9)

Lafferty, Drew, Lafferty Equipment Manufacturing Inc, North Little Rock, AR. Tel: (501) 851-2820, (800) 999-2820, FAX: (501) 851-3719, E-Mail: webmaster@laffertyequipment.com, Web Site: www.laffertyequipment.com (9)

Lafferty Equipment Manufacturing Inc, North Little Rock, AR. Tel: (501) 851-2820, (800) 999-2820, FAX: (501) 851-3719, E-Mail: webmaster@ laffertyequipment.com, Web Site: www. laffertyequipment.com (9)

Laffin, Joyce, FLEXcon, Spencer, MA. Tel: (508) 885-8200, Web Site: www.flexcon.com (16)

Lafley, A. G., The Iams Co, Dayton, OH. Tel: (937) 898-7387, (800) 675-3849, FAX: (937) 264-7264, Web Site: www.iams.com (16)

Lafley, Alan, G., The Procter & Gamble Co, Cincinnati, OH. Tel: (513) 983-4224, (800) 742-6253, FAX: (513) 983-9369, Web Site: www.pg.com (16)

LaForet, Lou, Spring, Mississauga, ON Canada. Tel: (905) 678-2770, (888) 624-5327, FAX: (905) 678-9788, E-Mail: lou.laforet@springglobalmail.com, Web Site: www.springglobalmail.com (21)

Laforte, Real, Communications Real Laforte Inc, Montreal, PQ Canada. Tel: (514) 335-1523, (800) 836-7766, FAX: (514) 335-5981 (23)

LaFrance, Nina, Crain Communications Inc, Detroit, MI. Tel: (313) 446-6000, FAX: (313) 446-1616, Web Site: www.crain.com (17)

LaFrance, Nina, Forbes Inc, New York, NY. Tel: (212) 620-2200, FAX: (212) 620-2245, Web Site: www. forbesinc.com (17)

LaFrenier, Douglas, American Institute of Physics, Melville, NY. Tel: (516) 576-2200, (800) 892-8259, FAX: (516) 576-2374, E-Mail: aipinfo@aip. org, Web Site: www.aip.org (17)

Lage MAS, Paul, Norwood Promotional Products, Clearwater, FL. Tel: (317) 275-2500, (800) 959-9138, FAX: (317) 275-2570, Web Site: www. norwood.com (16)

Lageman, Malia, Cardinal Mailing Services Ltd, Honolulu, HI. Tel: (808) 538-3884, (808) 521-1419, E-Mail: mail@cardinalservicesltd.com, Web Site: www.cardinalservicesltd.com (28)

Lagerlof, John, Paasche Airbrush Co, Chicago, IL. Tel: (773) 867-9191, FAX: (773) 867-9198, E-Mail: info@paascheairbrush.com, Web Site: www.paascheairbrush.com (10)

Lagerlof, Patricia, Paasche Airbrush Co, Chicago, IL. Tel: (773) 867-9191, FAX: (773) 867-9198, E-Mail: info@paascheairbrush.com, Web Site: www.paascheairbrush.com (10)

LaGona, Lorraine, Cooper Vision, Fairport, NY. Tel: (585) 385-6810, (800) 341-2020, Web Site: www. coopervision.com (7)

Lahey, John, L., Quinnipiac College, Hamden, CT. Tel: (203) 582-8600, (203) 582-8200, (800) 462-1944, FAX: (203) 281-8664, Web Site: www. quinnipiac.edu (41)

Lahey Clinic, Burlington, MA. Tel: (781) 744-5100, Web Site: www.lahey.org (1)

Laiken, Thomas, Hygienic Fabrics & Filters Inc, Sheboygan, WI. Tel: (920) 457-7383, (800) 876-2009, FAX: (920) 457-2558, Web Site: www.hyfab.com (16)

Lail, Robert, MarketMakers Group Inc, Wayne, PA. Tel: (610) 254-8924, FAX: (610) 254-9190, E-Mail: rlail@marketmakers.com, Web Site: www. marketmakersgroup.com (29)

Laine, Jimmy, Wakefield Peanut Co, Wakefield, VA. Tel: (757) 899-5481, (800) 803-1309, FAX: (757) 899-7604, Web Site: www.wakefieldpeanutco.com (4)

Laing, Don, Special Olympics International, Washington, DC. Tel: (202) 628-3630, FAX: (202) 824-0200, Web Site: www.specialolympics.org (1)

Laing, James M., James M Laing & Associates, Chanhassen, MN. Tel: (952) 474-1138 (21)

James M Laing & Associates, Chanhassen, MN. Tel: (952) 474-1138 (21)

Lair, Robert, G., Oil & Gas Journal, Tulsa, OK. Tel: (918) 835-3161, (800) 331-4463, FAX: (918) 832-9497, Web Site: www.pennwell.com; www.ogj.com (17)

Laird, Cal, Veriad, Brea, CA. Tel: (714) 990-2700, (800) 962-0658, FAX: (800) 962-0658, E-Mail: info@veriad.com, Web Site: www.veriad.com (16)

Laird, Katie, Sutherland Global Services, Pittsford, NY. Tel: (585) 586-5757, (800) 388-4557, FAX: (585) 419-2418, E-Mail: katie-laird@suth.com, Web Site: www.suth.com (35)

Laitram Machinery, Harahan, LA. Tel: (504) 733-6000, FAX: (504) 733-6111 (16)

Lake, Jeff, Duncan Aviation, Lincoln, NE. Tel: (402) 475-2611, (800) 228-4277, FAX: (402) 475-5541, Web Site: www.duncanaviation.com (16)

Lake, Larry, Western River Expeditions, Salt Lake City, UT. Tel: (801) 942-6669, (866) 904-1160, FAX: (801) 942-8514, Web Site: www. westernriver.com (19)

Lake, Leslie, Marshall & Swift, Los Angeles, CA. Tel: (213) 683-9000, FAX: (213) 683-9010, Web Site: www.marshallswift.com (17)

Lake, Ryan, Lake Group Media Inc, Armonk, NY. Tel: (914) 925-2400, FAX: (914) 925-2499, E-Mail: joerobinson@lakegroupmedia.com, Web Site: www.lakegroupmedia.com (23)

Lake, Steve, R., Connecticut Marketing Associates, Wilton, CT. Tel: (203) 761-9556, FAX: (203) 761-9763 (20)

Lake County Press Inc, Waukegan, IL. Tel: (847) 336-4333 (27)

Lake Group Media Inc, Armonk, NY. Tel: (914) 925-2400, FAX: (914) 925-2499, E-Mail: joerobinson@ lakegroupmedia.com, Web Site: www. lakegroupmedia.com (23)

Lake Shore Industries, Erie, PA. Tel: (800) 458-0463, FAX: (814) 453-4293, E-Mail: info@lsisigns.com, Web Site: www.lsisigns.com (16)

Lakely, Dedra, Dynamic Engineering, Santa Cruz, CA. Tel: (831) 457-8891, FAX: (831) 457-4793, E-Mail: contact@penguinparty.com, Web Site: www.dyneng.com (3)

Lakeside Publishing Co LLC, Evanston, IL. Tel: (847) 491-6440, FAX: (847) 491-0459, E-Mail: cs@centurysports.net, Web Site: www.centurysports.net (17)

The Lakeville Journal LLC, Lakeville, CT. Tel: (860) 435-9873, FAX: (860) 435-4802 (37)

Lakewood Products LLC, Suamico, WI. Tel: (920) 361-7717, (800) 872-8458, FAX: (920) 361-7719, E-Mail: info@lakewoodproducts.com, Web Site: www.lakewoodproducts.com (11)

Lakos, Tom, Koeze Co, Grand Rapids, MI. Tel: (800) 555-9688, E-Mail: service@koezedirect.com, Web Site: www.koeze.com (16)

Lakshmanan, Al, COMPITSS INC, Newbury Park, CA. Tel: (805) 823-2286, Web Site: www.compitss.com (22)

Lakshmi-Ratan Ph D., Ramesh, A., DMA (Direct Marketing Association), New York, NY. Tel: (212) 768-7277, FAX: (212) 302-6714, E-Mail: customerservice@the-dma.org, Web Site: www.the-dma.org (40)

Lal, Jagdish, Kuwait Airways Corp, Fort Lee, NJ. Tel: (201) 582-9222, (800) 4-KUWAIT, FAX: (212) 659-4270, E-Mail: nyc@kuwait-airways.com, Web Site: www.kuwait-airways.com (19)

Lala, Jo Anne, Sunbeam, Boca Raton, FL. Tel: (561) 912-4100, FAX: (561) 912-4567, Web Site: www.sunbeam.com (16)

Lalji, Firoz, Zones Inc, Auburn, WA. Tel: (253) 205-3000, (800) 408-9663, FAX: (425) 430-3626, E-Mail: corpsales@zones.com, Web Site: www.zones.com (3)

Lally, Eugene, F., Dynamic Development Co, Mission Viejo, CA. Tel: (949) 768-5798, E-Mail: antiwear@dynamicdevelopment.com, Web Site: www.dynamicdevelopment.com (12)

Lalyk, Casey, Navitar Inc, Rochester, NY. Tel: (585) 359-4000, FAX: (585) 359-4999, E-Mail: info@navitar.com, Web Site: www.navitar.com (16)

Lamar, Craig, Leslie Jordan, Portland, OR. Tel: (503) 295-1987, (800) 935-3343, FAX: (503) 295-1989, E-Mail: sales@lesliejordan.com, Web Site: www.lesliejordan.com (2)

Lamb, Anthony, Chem-Tainer Industries Inc, North Babylon, NY. Tel: (631) 661-8300, (800) ASK-CHEM, (800) 275-2436, FAX: (631) 661-8209, E-Mail: sales@chemtainer.com, Web Site: www.chemtainer.com (9)

Lamb, Jerry, CCI Solutions, Olympia, WA. Tel: (360) 943-5378, (800) 426-8664, FAX: (360) 754-1566, (800) 339-TAPE, E-Mail: info@ccisolutions.com, Web Site: www.ccisolutions.com (16)

AB Lambdin Inc, Hampton, VA. Tel: (800) 528-9817, FAX: (800) 221-9231, E-Mail: service@ablambdin.com (2)

Lambert, Carole, A., Brookstone Co, Merrimack, NH. Tel: (603) 880-9500, (800) 846-3000, FAX: (603) 577-8005, E-Mail: customerservice@brookstone.com, Web Site: www.brookstone.com (3)

Lambert, Dean, Homesteaders Life Co, West Des Moines, IA. Tel: (515) 440-7777, (800) 477-3633, E-Mail: service@homesteaderslife.com, Web Site: www.homesteaderslife.com (15)

Lambert, Frank, ACTON Group Ltd, Lincoln, NE. Tel: (402) 742-2820, FAX: (402) 470-2673, E-Mail: info@acton.com, Web Site: www.acton.com (23)

Lambert, Jon, ACTON Group Ltd, Lincoln, NE. Tel: (402) 742-2820, FAX: (402) 470-2673, E-Mail: info@acton.com, Web Site: www.acton.com (23)

Lambert, Robert, Belmont University, Nashville, TN. Tel: (615) 460-6000, FAX: (615) 460-6455, Web Site: www.belmont.edu (41)

Lambert, Steve, Nissan Motor Acceptance Corp, Irving, TX. Tel: (800) 647-7261, Web Site: www.nissanusa.com (14)

Lambert, Timothy, Unisys, Blue Bell, PA. Tel: (215) 986-4011, (800) 874-8647, FAX: (215) 986-2312, Web Site: www.unisys.com (16)

Lambertucci, Donna, NutriSystem Inc, Fort Washington, PA. Tel: (215) 706-5300, (800) 321-THIN, FAX: (215) 706-5388, Web Site: www.nutrisystem.com (7)

Lambeth Jr., George, S., Golden River Fruit Co, Vero Beach, FL. Tel: (772) 562-4502, FAX: (772) 562-9747 (4)

Lamel, Ira, J., Hain Celestial Group, Melville, NY. Tel: (631) 730-2200, FAX: (631) 730-2500, Web Site: www.hain-celestial.com (16)

Lamel, Ira, J., Jason Natural Personal Care Products, Boulder, CO. Tel: (877) 527-6601, Web Site: www.jason-natural.com (14)

Lamentino, Lisa, Oppenheimer Funds, New York, NY. Tel: (212) 323-0200, FAX: (212) 323-0493, Web Site: www.oppenheimerfunds.com (14)

Lamere, David, The Boston Co, Boston, MA. Tel: (617) 722-7000, FAX: (617) 722-7569 (14)

Laminex Inc, Fort Mill, SC. Tel: (704) 679-4170, (800) 438-8850, FAX: (704) 679-8453, Web Site: www.laminex.com (16)

Lamirand, Jim, NRS, Decatur, TX. Tel: (940) 393-7009, Web Site: www.nrsworld.com (11)

Lamkin, Bob, Lamkin Corp, San Diego, CA. Tel: (619) 661-7090, (800) 642-7755, FAX: (619) 661-0014, E-Mail: info@lamkingrips.com, Web Site: www.lamkingrips.com (11)

Lamkin Corp, San Diego, CA. Tel: (619) 661-7090, (800) 642-7755, FAX: (619) 661-0014, E-Mail: info@lamkingrips.com, Web Site: www.lamkingrips.com (11)

Lammerding, Edward, Information for Public Affairs, Inc, Sacramento, CA. Tel: (916) 444-0840, (800) 726-4566, FAX: (916) 446-5369, E-Mail: info@statenet.com, Web Site: www.statenet.com (17)

Lammers, Jennifer, RBC Funds, Milwaukee, WI. Tel: (800) 422-2766, Web Site: us.rbcgam.com (14)

Lamond, Eric, Soitenly Stooges, Glendale, CA. Tel: (818) 543-0778, (800) 543-0778, FAX: (818) 543-0779, E-Mail: custserv@threestooges.com, Web Site: www.soitenlystooges.com (6)

Lamontagne, Lark, L3 Virtual Solutions LLC, Marengo, OH. Tel: (740) 625-6535, Web Site: www.l3vs.com (11)

LaMotta, Connie, LaMotta Strategic Communications Inc, Congers, NY. Tel: (845) 358-6301, Web Site: www.lamottastrategic.com (20)

LaMotta Strategic Communications Inc, Congers, NY. Tel: (845) 358-6301, Web Site: www.lamottastrategic.com (20)

Lampariello, Vincent, Maison Glass Delicacies, Jersey City, NJ. Tel: (212) 755-3316, (800) 822-5564, E-Mail: info@maisonglass.com, Web Site: www.maisonglass.com (4)

Lamparter, William, PrintCom Consulting Group, Waxhaw, NC. Tel: (704) 843-5350, FAX: (704) 843-5352, E-Mail: printcom@aol.com (20)

Lampe, Jeanne, Miller Printing, Springfield, OH. Tel: (937) 325-5503, (877) 325-5503, FAX: (937) 324-5697, Web Site: www.miller-printing.com (27)

Lampert, Edward, S., Sears Home Improvement Products Inc, Longwood, FL. Tel: (407) 767-0990, (877) 840-7126, FAX: (407) 831-1848, Web Site: www.searshomepro.com (16)

Lan, Erlene, Mountain West Supply Co, Scottsdale, AZ. Tel: (602) 971-1200, (800) 528-6169, FAX: (602) 996-5077 (3)

Lancaster, Rich, AccuData Integrated Marketing, Fort Myers, FL. Tel: (239) 425-4400, (800) 732-3440, FAX: (239) 425-4401, E-Mail: info@accudata.com, Web Site: www.accudata.com (23)

Lance, Howard, L., Harris Corp, Melbourne, FL. Tel: (407) 727-9100, FAX: (407) 726-5427 (16)

Lance, Maureen, MSC Lists, Santa Barbara, CA. Tel: (805) 967-4955, FAX: (805) 964-1702, E-Mail: kingstock@juno.com (24)

Lancer Insurance Co, Long Beach, NY. Tel: (516) 431-4441, (800) 782-8902, FAX: (516) 889-5111, E-Mail: roneill@lancer-ins.com, Web Site: www.lancer-ins.com (15)

Lancer Label, Omaha, NE. Tel: (402) 390-9119, (800) 228-7074, FAX: (800) 344-9456, E-Mail: info@lancerlabel.com, Web Site: www.lancerlabel.com (27)

Lancino, Kristin, Music Sales Corp, New York, NY. Tel: (212) 254-2100, (800) 431-7187, FAX: (212) 254-2013, E-Mail: info@musicsales.com, Web Site: www.musicsales.com (17)

Land O' Lakes Inc, Arden Hills, MN. Tel: (651) 481-2222, (800) 328-9680, FAX: (651) 481-2000, Web Site: www.landolakes.com (16)

LandaJob, Kansas City, MO. Tel: (816) 523-1881, (800) 931-8806, FAX: (816) 523-1876, E-Mail: adstaff@landajobnow.com, Web Site: www.landajobnow.com (20)

Landau, Jeanne, 800 Response, Burlington, VT. Tel: (802) 860-0378, (800) NEW-SALES, FAX: (800) NEW-ORDER, E-Mail: sales@800response.com, Web Site: www.800response.com (32)

Landauer, Jeramy, Landauer Corp, Urbandale, IA. Tel: (515) 287-2144, (800) 557-2144, FAX: (515) 276-5102, E-Mail: info@landauercorp.com, Web Site: www.landauercorp.com (17)

Landauer Corp, Urbandale, IA. Tel: (515) 287-2144, (800) 557-2144, FAX: (515) 276-5102, E-Mail: info@landauercorp.com, Web Site: www.landauercorp.com (17)

Landino, Anita, Health Alliance Plan, Detroit, MI. Tel: (248) 443-1075, FAX: (248) 443-8851, E-Mail: alandin1@hapcorp.org, Web Site: www.hapcorp.org (15)

Landis, Clint, Frontier Natural Products Co-op, Norway, IA. Tel: (319) 227-7996, (800) 669-3275, FAX: (319) 227-7966, (800) 717-4372, E-Mail: info@frontiercoop.com, Web Site: www.frontiercoop.com (7)

Landmark Communications Inc, Norfolk, VA. Tel: (757) 446-2010, (800) 446-2004, FAX: (757) 446-2489, Web Site: www.landmark.com (17)

Landmark Graphics Corp, Houston, TX. Tel: (713) 839-2000, FAX: (713) 839-2015, E-Mail: solutions@lgc.com, Web Site: www.lgc.com (16)

Landrum, Kyle, Exhibitrac Direct Marketing, Las Vegas, NV. Tel: (303) 988-6601, FAX: (303) 988-6602, E-Mail: sales@exhibitrac.com, Web Site: www.exhibitrac.com (23)

Landry, Lisa, Legal Sea Foods Inc, Boston, MA. Tel: (617) 530-9000, (800) 343-5804, FAX: (617) 530-9649, Web Site: www.legalseafoods.com (4)

Lands' End Inc, Dodgeville, WI. Tel: (608) 935-9341, (800) 963-4816, FAX: (680) 935-4831, Web Site: www.landsend.com (2)

Landscape Forms Inc, Kalamazoo, MI. Tel: (616) 381-0490, (800) 430-6209, FAX: (616) 381-3455, E-Mail: specify@landscapeforms.com, Web Site: www.landscapeforms.com (1)

Lane, Jamie, Wpromote Inc, El Segundo, CA. Tel: (310) 421-4844, Web Site: www.wpromote.com (30)

Lane, John, American Student Assistance, Boston, MA. Tel: (800) 999-9000, Web Site: www.amsa.com (1)

Lane, Katrina, Harrah's Entertainment Inc, Las Vegas, NV. Tel: (702) 407-6000, FAX: (702) 407-6499, (702) 407-6500, Web Site: www.harrahs.com (19)

Lane, Robert, L., Kaplan Publishing, Chicago, IL. Tel: (312) 606-8905, (800) 245-2665, FAX: (312) 606-8985, E-Mail: kaplanorders@kaplan.com, Web Site: www.kaplanpublishing.com (17)

Lane, Robert, W., Deere & Co Headquarters, Moline, IL. Tel: (309) 765-8000, FAX: (309) 765-5671, Web Site: www.deere.com (16)

Lane, Robert, W., John Deere Consumer Products, Moline, IL. Tel: (309) 765-8000, FAX: (309) 748-0114, Web Site: www.johndeere.com (16)

Lanese, Michael, ClearSaleing Inc, Columbus, OH. Tel: (614) 448-2688, (800) 592-0463, Web Site: www.clearsaleing.com (16)

Lang, Jim, Imagination Works, Trumbull, CT. Tel: (203) 377-1747, FAX: (203) 377-7401, E-Mail: jim@imaginationworks.net, Web Site: www. imaginationworks.net (20)

Lang, John, Epson America, Long Beach, CA. Tel: (562) 981-3840, (800) 873-7766, FAX: (562) 290-5220, Web Site: www.epson.com (10)

Lang, Laura, Digitas, Boston, MA. Tel: (617) 867-1000, FAX: (617) 867-1111, E-Mail: contact@ digitas.com, Web Site: www.digitas.com (35)

Lang, Noah, ReputationDefender, Redwood City, CA. Tel: (650) 241-7491, (888) 720-3332, E-Mail: helpdesk@reputation.com, Web Site: www. reputationdefender.com (32)

Lang, Sharon, Dharma Trading Co, Petaluma, CA. Tel: (415) 456-7657, (800) 542-5227, FAX: (415) 456-8747, E-Mail: service@dharmatrading.com, Web Site: www.dharmatrading.com (2)

Langdon, John, J., Hickory Farms, Maumee, OH. Tel: (419) 893-7611, (800) 822-4438, FAX: (419) 893-0164, Web Site: www.hickoryfarms.com (4)

Langdon, John, J., Pfaelzer Brothers, Maumee, OH. Tel: (419) 893-7611, (800) 345-9290, FAX: (419) 893-0164, Web Site: www.phaelzerbrothers.com (16)

Langdon, John, J., Pinnacle Orchards, Maumee, OH. Tel: (419) 893-7611, (800) 442-5671, FAX: (419) 893-0164, Web Site: www.pinnacleorchards.com (4)

Langdon, Scott, Nationwide Card Services Inc, Memphis, TN. Tel: (901) 383-4405, Web Site: www. nationwidecardservices.com (35)

Lange, Mark, CVT Production Inc, Granger, IN. Tel: (574) 247-0647, Web Site: www. destinationfitness.com (16)

Langel, Sharon, Gerber Life Insurance Co, White Plains, NY. Tel: (914) 272-4000, (800) 704-2180, FAX: (914) 272-4099, Web Site: www.gerberlife. com (15)

Langer, Steven, Abbott, Langer Association Surveys, Washington, DC. Tel: (877) 210-6563, FAX: (877) 239-2457, E-Mail: info@abbott-langer.com, Web Site: www.abbott-langer.com (17)

Langevin, Erin, Langevin Learning Services, Ottawa, ON Canada. Tel: (613) 288-3064, Web Site: www. langevin.com (40)

Langevin Learning Services, Ottawa, ON Canada. Tel: (613) 288-3064, Web Site: www.langevin.com (40)

Langhoff, Linda, Dex Direct Marketing, Lone Tree, CO. Tel: (800) 999-4630, Web Site: www.dexlist. com (31)

Langhorne, Andrew, iMarketing Solutions Group Inc, Milwaukee, WI. Tel: (414) 224-0701, (800) 879-0076, FAX: (414) 224-0943, Web Site: imarketingsolutionsgroup.com (29)

Langlois, Ken, Collegiate Cap & Gown, Champaign, IL. Tel: (217) 351-9500, FAX: (217) 351-9214, Web Site: www.herff-jones.com (16)

Langon, Tom, The Bil-Ray Aluminum Siding Corp of Queens Inc, New Hyde Park, NY. Tel: (516) 616-4200, (800) 474-4415, FAX: (516) 616-4030, Web Site: www.homeclub.com (16)

Lankin, Frances, United Way of Greater Toronto, Toronto, ON Canada. Tel: (416) 777-2001, FAX: (416) 777-0962, Web Site: www.unitedwaytoronto. com (1)

Lanmark Group Inc, West Long Branch, NJ. Tel: (732) 389-4500, FAX: (732) 389-4998, E-Mail: info@lanmarkgroup.com, Web Site: www. lanmarkgroup.com (35)

Lannon, Larry, Telephony, Chicago, IL. Tel: (312) 595-1080, (800) 458-0479, FAX: (312) 595-0295, Web Site: www.internettelephony.com (17)

Lant, Jeffrey, Jeffrey Lant Associates Inc, Cambridge, MA. Tel: (617) 547-6372, FAX: (617) 547-0061, E-Mail: drjlant@worldprofit.com, Web Site: www. worldprofit.com (5)

Lant, Jeffrey, Sure-Fire Business Success Catalog, Cambridge, MA. Tel: (617) 547-6372, FAX: (617) 547-0061, E-Mail: drjlant@worldprofit.com, Web Site: www.worldprofit.com (17)

Lant, Jim, Turtle Bay Management Co Inc, Virginia Beach, VA. Tel: (757) 422-2760, FAX: (757) 422-1434, E-Mail: jimlant@turtlebaymanagement.com, Web Site: www.turtlebaymanagement.com (20)

Lantos, Phyllis, R. F., Columbia-Presbyterian Medical Center, New York, NY. Tel: (212) 305-2500, FAX: (212) 305-8023, Web Site: www.nyp.org (16)

Lanzi, Nickolas, Direct Choice Inc, Wayne, PA. Tel: (610) 995-2111, Web Site: www.directchoiceinc. com (35)

Lapedes, Richard, Lion Apparel, Dayton, OH. Tel: (937) 898-1949, (800) 548-6614, FAX: (937) 913-5667, Web Site: www.lionapparel.com (2)

LaPierre, Wayne, National Rifle Association of America, Fairfax, VA. Tel: (703) 267-1000, (800) 672-3888, FAX: (703) 267-3957, E-Mail: nra. contact@nra.org, Web Site: www.nra.org (1)

Lapin, Jeff, F&W Publications Inc, Blue Ash, OH. Tel: (513) 531-2690, FAX: (513) 531-0293, Web Site: www.fwpublications.com (17)

Lapin, Phil, Falcon Safety Products, Branchburg, NJ. Tel: (908) 707-4900, FAX: (908) 707-8855, Web Site: www.falconsafety.com (16)

Laplink Software Inc, Bellevue, WA. Tel: (425) 952-6000, (800) 527-5465, FAX: (425) 952-6002, E-Mail: marketing@laplink.com, Web Site: www. laplink.com (3)

LaPlume, Joseph, Domestic Bank, Providence, RI. Tel: (401) 943-1600, (800) 566-6600, FAX: (401) 943-6708, Web Site: www.domesticbank.com (14)

Lapointe, Bruce, Amateur Electronic Supply LLC, Milwaukee, WI. Tel: (414) 558-0333, (800) 558-0411, FAX: (414) 358-3337, Web Site: www. aesham.com (16)

Laporta, Matt, Response Unlimited, Waynesboro, VA. Tel: (540) 943-6721, FAX: (540) 943-0841, E-Mail: info@ru-lists.com, Web Site: www. responseunlimited.com (23)

LaPreferida Inc, Chicago, IL. Tel: (773) 254-7200, (800) 621-5422, FAX: (773) 254-8546, Web Site: www.lapreferida.com (4)

LaRamee, Dr. Pierre, M., International Planned Parenthood Federation Western Hemisphere Region Inc, New York, NY. Tel: (212) 248-6400, (866) IPPFWHR, FAX: (212) 248-2441, E-Mail: info@ ippfwhr.org, Web Site: www.ippfwhr.org (1)

Laran Communications Inc, Winfield, IL. Tel: (630) 690-2141, FAX: (630) 690-2143, Web Site: www. web-ads.com (16)

Larance, Rhonda, Jeppesen, Englewood, CO. Tel: (303) 799-9090, Web Site: www.jeppesen.com (22)

Lardino, Frank, Investors Alliance Inc, Pompano Beach, FL. Tel: (800) 490-6627, E-Mail: info@ powerinvestor.com, Web Site: www.powerinvestor. com (1)

Largiader, Jeff, Lifeboat Distribution, Shrewsbury, NJ. Tel: (732) 389-8950, FAX: (732) 389-9227, Web Site: www.programmersparadise.com (16)

Largie LLC, Riverton, NJ. Tel: (609) 870-8187 (35)

Larino, Tracie, ALC Inc, Princeton, NJ. Tel: (609) 580-2800, (800) ALC-LIST, FAX: (609) 580-2888, E-Mail: info@alc.com, Web Site: www.alc.com (23)

Lark in the Morning, Mendocino, CA. Tel: (707) 964-5569, FAX: (707) 964-1979, E-Mail: info@ larkinam.com, Web Site: www.larkinthemorning. com (5)

Larkey, Michael, Linens n' Things, Paramus, NJ. Tel: (973) 778-1300, FAX: (973) 778-0822, (973) 815-2990, Web Site: www.lnt.com (8)

Larkin, Edward, Speakers Guild Inc, Sandwich, MA. Tel: (508) 888-6702, (800) 343-4530, FAX: (508) 888-6771, E-Mail: info@speakersguild.com, Web Site: www.speakersguild.com (16)

Larkin, Jane, Alliance of Area Business Publications, El Segundo, CA. Tel: (323) 937-5514, FAX: (323) 937-0959, E-Mail: info@bizpubs.org, Web Site: www.bizpubs.org (1)

Larkin, Morgan, HomeAway.com Inc, Austin, TX. Tel: (512) 782-0805, (877) 228-3145, Web Site: www. homeaway.com (19)

Larkwood Group LLC, Oakland, CA. Tel: (510) 444-7766 (1)

Larlee, Dan, Harland Financial Solutions Inc, Lake Mary, FL. Tel: (407) 804-6600, (800) 815-5592, FAX: (407) 829-6702, Web Site: www. harlandfinancialsolutions.com (16)

Larmon, Patrick, Bunzl Distribution USA, Inc, Saint Louis, MO. Tel: (314) 997-5959, (888) 997-5959, FAX: (314) 997-1405, Web Site: www. bunzldistribution.com (16)

Laroche, Emmanuel, Sensory Consumer Science, Teterboro, NJ. Tel: (201) 462-2389, Web Site: www.symrise.com (7)

Larsen, Beth, Thrivent Financial for Lutherans, Appleton, WI. Tel: (920) 734-5721, (800) 847-4836, FAX: (920) 730-4781, E-Mail: mail@thrivent.com, Web Site: www.thrivent.com (14)

Larsen, Dana, Ace Hardware Corp, Oak Brook, IL. Tel: (630) 990-6600, FAX: (630) 990-6838, Web Site: www.acehardware.com (16)

Larsen, Edward, Talbots, Hingham, MA. Tel: (781) 749-7600, (800) 825-2687, FAX: (781) 741-4369, Web Site: www.talbots.com (2)

Larsen Andras, Trina, College of Business Administration, Philadelphia, PA. Tel: (215) 895-2145, Web Site: www.drexel.edu (41)

Larson, Aaron M., Continental Western Group, Des Moines, IA. Tel: (515) 473-3000, (800) 533-0303, FAX: (515) 473-3015, Web Site: www.cwgins.com (15)

Larson, Chris, Ligonier Ministries, Lake Mary, FL. Tel: (407) 333-4244, (800) 435-4343, FAX: (407) 333-4377, Web Site: www.ligonier.org (5)

Larson, Dave, Brooks Sports Inc, Bothell, WA. Tel: (425) 402-1632, (800) 2 BROOKS, FAX: (425) 489-1975, Web Site: www.brooksrunning.com (16)

Larson, David, Taymark Inc, White Bear Lake, MN. Tel: (651) 426-1667, (800) 479-2043, FAX: (651) 426-0275, Web Site: www.mninternational.com (1)

Larson, John, Escort Inc, West Chester, OH. Tel: (513) 870-8500, (800) 964-3138, FAX: (513) 870-8509, E-Mail: sales@escortradar.com, Web Site: www. escortradar.com (16)

Larson, John, NGL Insurance Group, Madison, WI. Tel: (608) 257-5611, (800) 548-2962, FAX: (608) 257-9340, Web Site: www.nationalguardian.com (15)

Larson, Kristi, Charlton, Madison, WI. Tel: (608) 259-8004, FAX: (608) 259-8061, E-Mail: jdragisic@ tcgcorp.net, Web Site: www.tcgcorp.net (29)

Larson, Lisa, Midwest Direct Marketing Association Inc, Saint Paul, MN. Tel: (651) 999-5351, FAX: (651) 917-1835, E-Mail: mdma@mdma.org, Web Site: www.mdma.org (40)

Larson, Mark A., Digi-Key Corp, Thief River Falls, MN. Tel: (218) 681-6674, (800) 344-4539, FAX: (218) 681-3380, Web Site: www.digikey.com (3)

Larson, Rich, United Air Specialists Inc, Cincinnati, OH. Tel: (513) 891-0400, (800) 992-4422, FAX: (513) 891-4882, E-Mail: uas@uasinc.com, Web Site: www.uasinc.com (16)

Larson, Russell, Kalmbach Publishing Co, Waukesha, WI. Tel: (262) 796-8776, (800) 558-1544, FAX: (262) 796-1143, Web Site: www.kalmbach.com (17)

Larson, Scott, Strategic Marketing Services, Eagan, MN. Tel: (651) 456-0100, E-Mail: sms@ fishnet.com (16)

Larson, Timothy M., Jostens, Inc, Minneapolis, MN. Tel: (952) 830-3300, FAX: (952) 830-3293, Web Site: www.jostens.com (16)

LaRue, Jack, Thomson Tax & Accounting, Dexter, MI. Tel: (800) 968-8900, FAX: (734) 426-3750, E-Mail: jack.larue@thomson.com, Web Site: www.cs.thomson.com (22)

Las Vegas Review Journal, Las Vegas, NV. Tel: (702) 383-0211, FAX: (702) 383-4646, Web Site: www.lvrj.com (17)

Laschinger, Mary, xpedx, Loveland, OH. Tel: (513) 965-2900, FAX: (513) 965-2849, Web Site: www.xpedx.com (25)

Laser Label Technologies Inc, Stow, OH. Tel: (800) 882-4050, FAX: (800) 395-4721, E-Mail: sales@lltproducts.com, Web Site: www.lltproducts.com (10)

Lasermax Roll Systems, Billerica, MA. Tel: (978) 608-0500, FAX: (978) 608-0558, Web Site: www.lasermaxroll.com (27)

Lashmit, Mary Kay, Daily Record & Dispatch Co, Dunn, NC. Tel: (910) 891-1234, FAX: (910) 891-5253, Web Site: www.mydailyrecord.com (17)

Lasky, William, J., JLG Industries Inc, McConnellsburg, PA. Tel: (717) 485-5161, (877) JLG-SELL, FAX: (717) 485-6417, E-Mail: comments@jlg.com, Web Site: www.jlg.com (16)

Lassin, Gary, Harriet Carter Gifts Inc, Montgomeryville, PA. Tel: (215) 361-5100, FAX: (215) 361-1127, Web Site: www.harrietcarter.com (6)

Lassin, Ronald, P., Harriet Carter Gifts Inc, Montgomeryville, PA. Tel: (215) 361-5100, FAX: (215) 361-1127, Web Site: www.harrietcarter.com (6)

Lassus, Don, WorleyParsons, Reading, PA. Tel: (610) 855-2000, FAX: (610) 885-2001, Web Site: www.worleyparsons.com (16)

Last, Bruce, At Last Naturals, North Salem, NY. Tel: (800) 527-8123, FAX: (914) 747-3791, E-Mail: info@atlastnaturals.com, Web Site: www.atlastnaturals.com (7)

Last, Ray, At Last Naturals, North Salem, NY. Tel: (800) 527-8123, FAX: (914) 747-3791, E-Mail: info@atlastnaturals.com, Web Site: www.atlastnaturals.com (7)

Last, Zane, At Last Naturals, North Salem, NY. Tel: (800) 527-8123, FAX: (914) 747-3791, E-Mail: info@atlastnaturals.com, Web Site: www.atlastnaturals.com (7)

Laster, Larry, J., Intergraph Corp, Madison, AL. Tel: (256) 730-2000, (800) 345-4856, FAX: (256) 730-2048, Web Site: www.intergraph.com (16)

Laswell, Bette, BDL Homeware, Glendale, AZ. Tel: (623) 572-5038, (800) BDL-4BDL, FAX: (623) 572-5082 (3)

Latest Products Corp, Woodbury, NY. Tel: (516) 367-4700, (800) 288-3547, FAX: (516) 367-4714, E-Mail: info@latestprod.com, Web Site: www.latestprod.com (7)

Lathem, William, Lathem Time Corp, Atlanta, GA. Tel: (404) 691-0400, (800) 241-4990, FAX: (404) 696-6048, Web Site: www.lathem.com (16)

Lathem Time Corp, Atlanta, GA. Tel: (404) 691-0400, (800) 241-4990, FAX: (404) 696-6048, Web Site: www.lathem.com (16)

Latimer, Lisa, Helman Group Ltd, Oxnard, CA. Tel: (805) 487-7772, FAX: (805) 487-9975, E-Mail: barryh@helmangroup.com, Web Site: www.helmangroup.com (16)

Latimer, Shawn, Hadley Fruit Orchards Inc, Cabazon, CA. Tel: (951) 849-4668, FAX: (951) 849-5255, Web Site: www.hadleys.com (4)

Latimer, Wallace, Edmund Optics Inc, Barrington, NJ. Tel: (856) 573-6250, (800) 363-1992, FAX: (856) 573-6295, E-Mail: sales@edmundoptic.com, Web Site: www.edmundoptics.com (9)

Latin Force Group LLC, Miami, FL. Tel: (305) 860-1460, FAX: (305) 860-6161, Web Site: www.latinforce.com (22)

Latin-Pak, Chesterfield, MO. Tel: (636) 536-5344, (800) 625-4283, FAX: (636) 536-9456, E-Mail: latinpak@latinpak.com, Web Site: www.latinpak.com (35)

LatinLists, Miami, FL. Tel: (954) 302-1795, Web Site: www.latinlists.net (23)

Latko, Chris, Webb Designs Inc, El Cajon, CA. Tel: (619) 596-6400, (800) 262-9322, FAX: (619) 596-4511, E-Mail: awebb@webbshade.com, Web Site: www.webbshade.com (16)

LaToure, Jonna, Aviva USA Corp, Des Moines, IA. Tel: (515) 362-3600, FAX: (800) 531-0038, Web Site: www.avivausa.com (14)

Latzer, Kristin, MCRB Fulfillment Corp, Westlake Village, CA. Tel: (818) 407-4300, (800) 942-MCRB, FAX: (818) 407-0248, E-Mail: sallen@mcrb.com, Web Site: www.mcrb.com (28)

Laubacker, Matt, Publishers Circulation Fulfillment Inc, Pensacola, FL. Tel: (850) 475-2000 (32)

Laudadio, Kathy, Brush Fire, Cedar Knolls, NJ. Tel: (973) 871-1700, FAX: (973) 871-1717, Web Site: www.brushfireinc.com (35)

Lauder, Aerin, Estee Lauder Inc, New York, NY. Tel: (212) 572-4200, (866) 467-7363, FAX: (212) 572-3942, Web Site: www.esteelauder.com (16)

Lauder, William, Estee Lauder Inc, New York, NY. Tel: (212) 572-4200, (866) 467-7363, FAX: (212) 572-3942, Web Site: www.esteelauder.com (16)

Lauer, Henning, Bauer Publishing Co, Englewood Cliffs, NJ. Tel: (201) 569-6699, FAX: (201) 510-3297, Web Site: www.bauerpublishing.com (17)

Lauer, John, N., Diebold Inc, Uniontown, OH. Tel: (330) 899-2510, (800) DIEBOLD, FAX: (330) 490-3794, E-Mail: barronp@diebold.com, Web Site: www.diebold.com (16)

Laufer, Al, Nature Trade Center, Naples, FL. Tel: (239) 592-7611, Web Site: www.naturerx.com (21)

Laufer, Amy, Kimbo Educational, Long Branch, NJ. Tel: (732) 229-4949, (800) 848-6099 (NM), (800) 631-2187 (NJ), FAX: (732) 870-3340, E-Mail: kimboed@aol.com, Web Site: www.kimboed.com (17)

Laufer, Eli, MRV Communications, Chatsworth, CA. Tel: (818) 773-0900, FAX: (818) 773-0906, Web Site: www.mrv.com (3)

Laufer, Prakash, Motherwear, Holyoke, MA. Tel: (413) 586-1978, (800) 950-2500, FAX: (413) 532-4058, E-Mail: customerservice@motherwear.com, Web Site: www.motherwear.com (2)

Laughlin, Lewis E., Laughlin Associates Inc, Carson City, NV. Tel: (775) 883-8484, (888) 273-8152, FAX: (775) 883-4874 (16)

Laughlin, Sarah, Hyatt Hotels Corp, Chicago, IL. Tel: (312) 750-1234, FAX: (312) 780-5289, Web Site: www.hyatt.com (16)

Laughlin Associates Inc, Carson City, NV. Tel: (775) 883-8484, (888) 273-8152, FAX: (775) 883-4874 (16)

Laughlin/Constable, Chicago, IL. Tel: (312) 422-5900, FAX: (312) 422-5901, Web Site: www.laughlin.com (35)

Laughner, Carol, Level 5 Communications Inc, Dublin, NH. Tel: (603) 563-1631, FAX: (603) 563-8912, Web Site: www.deskeng.com (32)

Laumeister, Bruce, CTC Corp, Bennington, VT. Tel: (802) 442-6371, FAX: (802) 442-8526 (16)

Launer, John, Crest Fruit Inc, Mission, TX. Tel: (956) 205-7300, Web Site: www.redcooper.com (4)

Launer, John, Red Cooper, Mission, TX. Tel: (800) 825-8531, FAX: (956) 205-7331, Web Site: www.redcooper.com (4)

Launey, Robert, E., LHH & F Inc, Hillsdale, NY. Tel: (518) 325-4000, (800) 955-1129 (35)

Laura, Timothy, On-Demand Mail Services, Auburn Hills, MI. Tel: (888) 954-6245, Web Site: www.odmailservices.com (28)

Laurello, David, J., Stratus Technologies, Maynard, MA. Tel: (978) 461-7000, (800) 787-2887, FAX: (978) 461-3670, Web Site: www.stratus.com (16)

Lauren, Ralph, Polo Ralph Lauren, Lyndhurst, NJ. Tel: (212) 531-6537, (800) 377-7656, FAX: (212) 318-7690, Web Site: www.ralphlauren.com (2)

Laurendeau, Alain, Cancer Research Society, Montreal, PQ Canada. Tel: (514) 861-9227, (888) 766-2262, FAX: (514) 861-9220, Web Site: www.CancerResearchSociety.ca (1)

Laurent, Louie, ZLR Ignition, Des Moines, IA. Tel: (515) 244-4456, FAX: (515) 244-5749, Web Site: www.zlr.com (35)

Lauridsen, Jeff, Direct One Inc, Winter Park, FL. Tel: (407) 673-4500, FAX: (407) 673-4501, E-Mail: wariagno@directoneinc.com, Web Site: www.directoneinc.com (28)

Lautenschlager DVM, Craig, Pine Castle Animal Hospital, Orlando, FL. Tel: (407) 855-5010 (16)

Lauterbach, Shane, Mail Advertising Supply Co Inc, Sussex, WI. Tel: (262) 549-1730, (800) 558-2126, FAX: (800) 784-2591 (25)

Lauth, Kurt, Home Loan Investment Bank, Warwick, RI. Tel: (800) 223-1700 X278, E-Mail: contactus@homeloanbank.com, Web Site: www.homeloanbank.com (14)

Lautman Maska Neill & Co, Washington, DC. Tel: (202) 296-9660, Web Site: www.lautmandc.com (1)

Lautt, Larry, Crest Healthcare Supply, Dassel, MN. Tel: (800) 369-9207, (800) 328-8908, Web Site: www.cresthealthcare.com (16)

Lautzenhiser, Gary, G., Aristokraft Inc, Jasper, IN. Tel: (812) 482-2527, FAX: (812) 482-9872, Web Site: www.aristokraft.com (16)

Laux, Don, Medco Supply Co Inc, Tonawanda, NY. Tel: (716) 695-3244, (800) 556-3326, FAX: (800) 222-1934, E-Mail: sales@medcosupply.com, Web Site: www.medcosupply.com (7)

Lavau, Pascal, Cesbron, Brylane, Indianapolis, IN. Tel: (800) 677-0339, Web Site: www.brylanehome.com (2)

Laven, Ava, Laven & Loeb Inc, Beachwood, OH. Tel: (623) 217-2101, (216) 291-3483, E-Mail: alaven@lavenandloeb.com; vtaylor@lavenandloeb.com, Web Site: www.lavenandloeb.com (20)

Laven, Marc, The Gymboree Corp, San Francisco, CA. Tel: (877) 449-6932, Web Site: www.gymboree.com (2)

Laven & Loeb Inc, Beachwood, OH. Tel: (623) 217-2101, (216) 291-3483, E-Mail: alaven@lavenandloeb.com; vtaylor@lavenandloeb.com, Web Site: www.lavenandloeb.com (20)

Lavey, John, Hammock Publishing Inc, Nashville, TN. Tel: (615) 690-3400, FAX: (615) 690-3401, E-Mail: info@hammock.com, Web Site: www.hammock.com (17)

Lavin, John, Destination Rewards, Boca Raton, FL. Tel: (561) 997-9940, (800) 242-6260, FAX: (561) 997-9945, Web Site: www.drloyalty.com (33)

Lavoie, Daniel, The Hartford Financial Services Inc, Southington, CT. Tel: (860) 843-8070, (860) 547-5000, FAX: (860) 547-2680, Web Site: www.thehartford.com (15)

Law, Howard, W., Sporty's Preferred Living, Batavia, OH. Tel: (513) 735-9000, (800) 776-7897, FAX: (800) 543-8633, Web Site: www.sportys.com (5)

Law, Lauren, Baylor Health Care System, Dallas, TX. Tel: (214) 820-4901, (800) 4Baylor, FAX: (214) 820-7499, Web Site: www.baylorhealth.com (16)

Law, Merry, WorldVu LLC, Baltimore, MD. Tel: (410) 522-4223, FAX: (410) 522-4233, E-Mail: info@worldvu.com, Web Site: www.worldvu.com (17)

The Law Offices of James Sokolove, Wellesley Hills, MA. Tel: (617) 742-0696, Web Site: www.jimsokolove.com (14)

Richard Law, Deer Park, NY. Tel: (917) 267-8293 (20)

Lawce, Rich, MSC Metalworking, Melville, NY. Tel: (516) 812-2000, (800) 521-9520, E-Mail: inquiry@rutlandtool.com, Web Site: www.rutlandtool.com (34)

Lawitzen, Bruce, First of Omaha Merchant Processing, Omaha, NE Canada. Tel: (402) 341-0500, (800) 228-2443 (20)

Lawler, Kathleen A., Harley-Davidson Inc, Milwaukee, WI. Tel: (414) 343-7286, FAX: (414) 343-4806, Web Site: www.harley-davidson.com (12)

Lawler, Veronica, The Los Angeles Lakers Inc, El Segundo, CA. Tel: (310) 426-6000, FAX: (310) 426-6115, E-Mail: vlawlor@la-lakers.com, Web Site: www.nba.com/lakers (11)

Lawless, Robert, J., McCormick & Co Inc, Hunt Valley, MD. Tel: (410) 771-7301, (800) 474-7742, FAX: (410) 527-6337, Web Site: www.mccormick.com (4)

Lawlor, Janet, Licensing Industry Merchandisers' Association (LIMA), New York, NY. Tel: (212) 244-1944, FAX: (212) 563-6552, E-Mail: info@licensing.org, Web Site: www.licensing.org (40)

Lawlor, Jennifer, INPEX, Pittsburgh, PA. Tel: (412) 288-1343, (412) 288-1300, (888) 544-6739, (888) 54-INPEX, FAX: (412) 288-4546, E-Mail: info@inpex.com, Web Site: www.inpex.com (42)

Lawn Doctor Inc, Holmdel, NJ. Tel: (732) 946-0029, (800) 631-5660, FAX: (732) 946-9089, Web Site: www.lawndoctor.com (16)

Lawrence, Daren, McFeely's Square Drive Screws, Madison, WI. Tel: (434) 846-2729, (800) 443-7937, FAX: (804) 847-7136, E-Mail: tech@mcfeelys.com, Web Site: www.mcfeelys.com (16)

Lawrence, Derek, Fulcrum Publishing, Golden, CO. Tel: (303) 277-1623, (800) 992-2908, FAX: (303) 279-7111, Web Site: www.fulcrum-books.com (17)

Lawrence, E., Michael, Lawrence Direct Marketing Inc, Warrenton, VA. Tel: (540) 349-9278, FAX: (540) 347-7885 (23)

Lawrence, Gary, Lift Outreach, Richland Hills, TX. Tel: (817) 658-2980 (1)

Lawrence, Jim, Bellacor, Mendota Heights, MN. Tel: (651) 294-2500, (877) 723-5522, FAX: (651) 294-2595, E-Mail: customerservice@bellacor.com, Web Site: www.bellacor.com (8)

Lawrence, Jim, Galloway Farms, Miami, FL. Tel: (305) 274-7472, FAX: (305) 274-3233, E-Mail: galloway_inc@bellsouth.net, Web Site: www.gallowayform.com (8)

Lawrence, Paula, Governing Magazine, Washington, DC. Tel: (202) 862-8802, Web Site: www.governing.com (17)

Lawrence, Regina, Forecaster Publishing Co Inc, Tarzana, CA. Tel: (818) 345-4421 (14)

Lawrence, Robyn, Griggs, Mother Earth News Magazine, Topeka, KS. Tel: (785) 274-4300, (800) 678-5779, FAX: (785) 274-4305, E-Mail: bwelch@ogdenpubs.com, Web Site: www.cappers.com (17)

Lawrence Direct Marketing Inc, Warrenton, VA. Tel: (540) 349-9278, FAX: (540) 347-7885 (23)

Lawrence-Longo, Sue, Stratus Technologies, Maynard, MA. Tel: (978) 461-7000, (800) 787-2887, FAX: (978) 461-3670, Web Site: www.stratus.com (16)

Lawson, Bill, Linguistic Systems Inc, Cambridge, MA. Tel: (877) 654-5006, FAX: (617) 528-7491, E-Mail: info@linguist.com, Web Site: www.linguist.com (27)

Lawson, Keith, Market Builder Inc, Mesa, AZ. Tel: (480) 641-6200, FAX: (480) 641-6239, E-Mail: info@themarketbuilder.com, Web Site: www.themarketbuilder.com (21)

Lawson, Kelli, BET Services, Washington, DC. Tel: (202) 608-2000, (800) 626-9911, FAX: (202) 635-3761, Web Site: www.bet.com (32)

Lawson, Roger, Allan, Fidelity Investments, Boston, MA. Tel: (617) 563-7000, (800) 343-3548, FAX: (617) 476-6150, Web Site: www.fidelity.com (14)

Lawson, Ron, National Technical Information Service, Alexandria, VA. Tel: (703) 605-6000, FAX: (703) 605-6900, Web Site: www.ntis.gov (17)

Lawson, Vance, Thomas Nelson, Inc, Nashville, TN. Tel: (615) 889-9000, (800) 251-4000, FAX: (615) 889-5940, Web Site: www.thomasnelson.com (17)

Lawyer, Jeff, Huck Spaulding Enterprises, Voorheesville, NY. Tel: (518) 768-2070, (888) 982-8866, FAX: (518) 768-2240, E-Mail: orders@spaulding-rogers.com, Web Site: www.spaulding-rogers.com (16)

Lawyer, William, Huck Spaulding Enterprises, Voorheesville, NY. Tel: (518) 768-2070, (888) 982-8866, FAX: (518) 768-2240, E-Mail: orders@spaulding-rogers.com, Web Site: www.spaulding-rogers.com (16)

Lawyers & Judges Publishing Co Inc, Tucson, AZ. Tel: (520) 323-1500, FAX: (520) 323-0055, E-Mail: sales@lawyersandjudges.com, Web Site: www.lawyersandjudges.com (23)

Lawyers Diary and Manual, Newark, NJ. Tel: (208) 762-5403, (800) 444-4041, FAX: (973) 242-1905, E-Mail: mail@lawdiary.com, Web Site: www.lawdiary.com (24)

Lawyer's Weekly Publications, Boston, MA. Tel: (617) 451-7300, FAX: (617) 451-0132, Web Site: www.lawyersweekly.com (17)

Lay, Terry L., School Specialty Inc, Greenville, WI. Tel: (920) 734-5712, (888) 388-3224, FAX: (920) 734-5112, E-Mail: info@schoolspecialty.com, Web Site: www.schoolspecialty.com (16)

Laya, Bonnie, Corpus Christi Museum of Science & History, Corpus Christi, TX. Tel: (361) 826-4667, FAX: (361) 884-7392, Web Site: www.ccmuseum.com (1)

Layock, Pamela, Harlequin Enterprises Ltd, Don Mills, ON. Tel: (416) 445-5860, FAX: (416) 445-8655, E-Mail: customer_ecare@harlequin.ca, Web Site: www.eharlequin.com (17)

Layton, Les, Whitney Worldwide Inc, Saint Paul, MN. Tel: (651) 748-5000, (800) 597-0227, FAX: (651) 748-4000, Web Site: www.whitneyworld.com (20)

Lazar, Chaim, Net 60 LLC, New York, NY. Tel: (201) 833-9003, FAX: (201) 336-9088, E-Mail: chaim@net60.com, Web Site: www.net60.com (23)

Lazar, Elysa, Lazar Media Group Inc, Charleston, SC. Tel: (877) 579-0222, FAX: (843) 577-5542, E-Mail: email@lazarshopping.com, Web Site: www.lazarmedia.com (17)

Lazar Media Group Inc, Charleston, SC. Tel: (877) 579-0222, FAX: (843) 577-5542, E-Mail: email@lazarshopping.com, Web Site: www.lazarmedia.com (17)

Lazardi, Stephanie, Emailogics Inc/Emailbrain, Vancouver, WA. Tel: (866) 873-3019, Web Site: www.emailbrain.com (20)

Lazarus, Janet, Horticulture Magazine, Blue Ash, OH. Tel: (513) 531-2690, FAX: (513) 891-7153, Web Site: www.hortmag.com (17)

Lazarus, Warren S., Lazarus Marketing, Oceanside, NY. Tel: (516) 678-5107, FAX: (516) 766-3160, E-Mail: warrenl@lazmkt.com, Web Site: www.lazarusmarketing.com (21)

Lazarus, Warren, Lazarus Fulfillment House, Oceanside, NY. Tel: (516) 678-5107, (212) 431-3337, FAX: (516) 766-3160, Web Site: www.lazarusmarketing.com (28)

Lazarus Fulfillment House, Oceanside, NY. Tel: (516) 678-5107, (212) 431-3337, FAX: (516) 766-3160, Web Site: www.lazarusmarketing.com (28)

Lazarus Marketing, Oceanside, NY. Tel: (516) 678-5107, FAX: (516) 766-3160, E-Mail: warrenl@lazmkt.com, Web Site: www.lazarusmarketing.com (21)

Lazkani, Nancy, Icon Media Direct Inc, Van Nuys, CA. Tel: (818) 995-6400, FAX: (818) 995-6405, E-Mail: info@iconmediadirect.com, Web Site: www.iconmediadirect.com (35)

Lazverini, Doug, Wallace Targeted Communications, Saint Charles, IL. Tel: (630) 313-7000, FAX: (630) 377-4622, Web Site: www.wallace.com (27)

Lazydays RV Center, Seffner, FL. Tel: (813) 246-4333, Web Site: www.lazydays.com (12)

Le, Nhien, Unisfair, Menlo Park, CA. Tel: (866) 354-4030, Web Site: www.unisfair.com (20)

Le Bell, Andre, Bentley College, Waltham, MA. Tel: (781) 891-2800, FAX: (781) 891-3449, Web Site: www.bentley.edu (13)

Le Jardin Du Gourmet, Saint Johnsbury Center, VT. Tel: (802) 748-1446, FAX: (802) 748-9592, E-Mail: orderdesk@artisticgardens.com, Web Site: www.artisticgardens.com (8)

Le Poin, Charles, G., The Bil-Ray Aluminum Siding Corp of Queens Inc, New Hyde Park, NY. Tel: (516) 616-4200, (800) 474-4415, FAX: (516) 616-4030, Web Site: www.homeclub.com (16)

Lea & Perrins Inc, Fair Lawn, NJ. Tel: (201) 791-1600, FAX: (201) 791-8945, Web Site: www.leaperrins.com (16)

Leach, Ron, Shutterbug, Titusville, FL. Tel: (321) 269-3212, FAX: (321) 255-3146, Web Site: www.shutterbug.net (17)

Lead Gen Media Group, Staten Island, NY. Tel: (718) 215-2233, Web Site: leadgenmediagroup.com (23)

Lead Me Media, Lake Worth, FL. Tel: (888) 445-3282, Web Site: www.leadmedia.com (30)

LeadCreations.Com LLC, Coral Gables, FL. Tel: (305) 851-8110, Web Site: www.leadcreations.com (23)

Leader, Thomas, Simmons-Boardman Publishing Corp, New York, NY. Tel: (212) 620-7200, FAX: (212) 633-1165 (17)

Leader Direct Marketing Ltd, Surrey, BC Canada. Tel: (604) 542-2026, FAX: (604) 542-2090, E-Mail: listinfo@leaderdirect.ca, Web Site: www.theleadergroup.ca (21)

Leadership Directories Inc, New York, NY. Tel: (212) 627-4140, FAX: (212) 645-0931, E-Mail: info@leadershipdirectories.com, Web Site: www.leadershipdirectories.com (17)

Leadership Software Corp, Nyack, NY. Tel: (845) 358-0406, (800) 872-0068, FAX: (845) 358-0359, E-Mail: info@leadersoft.com, Web Site: www.leadersoft.com (16)

LeadFlash, Boca Raton, FL. Tel: (561) 499-3329, Web Site: www.leadflash.com (14)

LeadPile, Phoenix, AZ. Tel: (602) 909-9890, Web Site: www.leadpile.com (23)

Leads-Plus Inc, Killarney, FL. Tel: (800) 548-4571, E-Mail: eurekaman43@hotmail.com, Web Site: www.salesprospectingexpert.com (20)

League of American Orchestras, New York, NY. Tel: (212) 262-5161, FAX: (212) 262-5198, Web Site: www.symphony.org; www.americanorchestras.org (1)

Leahey, Beth, Orlando/ Orange County Convention & Visitor's Bureau, Orlando, FL. Tel: (407) 541-4239, Web Site: visitorlando.com (19)

Leahy, James, American Hotel Register Co, Vernon Hills, IL. Tel: (708) 743-4163, FAX: (708) 564-5797, Web Site: www.americanhotel.com (23)

Leahy, Michael, BCR Enterprises Inc, Downers Grove, IL. Tel: (630) 986-1432, (800) 227-1234, FAX: (630) 323-5324, Web Site: www.bcr.com (17)

Leanin' Tree Inc, Boulder, CO. Tel: (303) 530-7768, (800) 525-0656, FAX: (303) 530-5124, E-Mail: info@leanintree.com, Web Site: www.leanintree.com (4)

Leapfrog Online, Evanston, IL. Tel: (847) 492-1968, Web Site: www.leapfrogonline.com (35)

Leaps & Bounds LLC, Fort Lee, NJ. Tel: (201) 947-5459 (20)

LearnCom HR Consulting & Training, Irvine, CA. Tel: (515) 440-0890, (800) 698-8263, FAX: (515) 221-3149, E-Mail: nhartline@learncom.com, Web Site: www.learncomhr.com (16)

Learning Care Group, Novi, MI. Tel: (248) 697-9115, Web Site: www.learningcaregroup.com (16)

The Learning Channel, Silver Spring, MD. Tel: (240) 662-2000, Web Site: tlc.discovery.com (32)

Learning Communications LLC, Irvine, CA. Tel: (800) 622-3610, FAX: (949) 727-4323, E-Mail: sales@learncom.com, Web Site: www.learncom.com (16)

Learning Resources Institute, Downers Grove, IL. Tel: (630) 963-0398 (20)

Learning Seed, Chicago, IL. Tel: (800) 634-4941, Web Site: www.learningseed.com (3)

Leasure, G. Mark, Ghent Manufacturing Inc, Lebanon, OH. Tel: (513) 932-3445, (800) 543-0550, FAX: (513) 932-9252, E-Mail: customer_service@!ghent.com, Web Site: www.ghent.com (10)

Leasure, George, Ghent Manufacturing Inc, Lebanon, OH. Tel: (513) 932-3445, (800) 543-0550, FAX: (513) 932-9252, E-Mail: customer_service@!ghent.com, Web Site: www.ghent.com (10)

Leather Unlimited Corp, Belgium, WI. Tel: (920) 994-9464, (800) 993-2889, FAX: (920) 994-4099, E-Mail: leatherunltd@yahoo.com, Web Site: www.leatherunltd.com (2)

Leatherman, Barth, ITW Bee Leitzke, Iron Ridge, WI. Tel: (920) 625-2342, FAX: (920) 625-2643, Web Site: www.itwbeeleitzke.com (16)

Leathers, Tammi, The Union Labor Life Insurance Co, Silver Spring, MD. Tel: (202) 962-2945, FAX: (202) 962-8429, E-Mail: info@ullico.com, Web Site: www.unioncare.com (15)

Leavens, Donald, National Electrical Manufacturers Association (NEMA), Rosslyn, VA. Tel: (703) 841-3200, FAX: (703) 841-5900, E-Mail: communications@nema.org, Web Site: www.nema.org (34)

Leaver, Marcus, E., Sterling Publishing Co Inc, New York, NY. Tel: (212) 532-7160, (800) 367-9692, FAX: (212) 213-2495, Web Site: www.sterlingpublishing.com (17)

Leavitt, Russell, Timberline Total Solutions LLC, Omaha, NE. Tel: (402) 397-6945, (877) 575-2255, FAX: (402) 255-5045, E-Mail: rleavitt@timberlinesolutions.com (29)

Leber, Ward, Time Motion Tools, Poway, CA. Tel: (800) 779-8170, FAX: (800) 779-8171, Web Site: www.timemotion.com (9)

LeBow, Bennett, New Valley, Miami, FL. Tel: (305) 579-8000, FAX: (305) 579-8001, Web Site: www.newvalley.com (28)

LeCates, Jeff, Bamboo Cricket Service, Titusville, FL. Tel: (888) 634-7097, FAX: (646) 390-6313, E-Mail: info@bamboocricket.com, Web Site: www.bamboocricket.com (22)

Lechner, Andrew, TWL Knowledge Group, Carrollton, TX. Tel: (972) 309-4000, (800) 624-2272, FAX: (972) 309-5105, Web Site: www.twlk.com (3)

Lechner, James, E., Clothing Solutions, Irvine, CA. Tel: (800) 336-2660, (800) 465-1981, FAX: (800) 336-6510, Web Site: www.clothingsolutions.com (2)

Leck, Brian, Allen, Matkins, Leck, Gamble & Mallory, Los Angeles, CA. Tel: (213) 622-5555, FAX: (213) 620-8816, E-Mail: communications@allenmatkins.com, Web Site: www.allenmatkins.com (20)

Lecker, Barb, American Speech-Language-Hearing Association, Rockville, MD. Tel: (301) 897-5700, (800) 638-8255, E-Mail: productsales@asha.org, Web Site: www.asha.org (1)

LeClaire, Dominic, USADATA Inc, New York, NY. Tel: (212) 679-1411, Web Site: www.usadata.com (23)

Leder, Julie, Datamart Direct Inc, Bloomingdale, IL. Tel: (630) 307-7100, FAX: (630) 307-8059, E-Mail: info@datamartdirect.com, Web Site: www.datamartdirect.com (27)

Lederer, Melissa, Q Interactive, Chicago, IL. Tel: (312) 977-0390, (888) 729-6465, FAX: (312) 224-5001, E-Mail: solutions@qinteractive.com, Web Site: www.qinteractive.com (40)

Lederman, Fred, B., Focus Direct - a Dmh Marketing Partners Co, San Antonio, TX. Tel: (210) 247-1634, (800) 299-9185, FAX: (210) 247-1691, Web Site: www.focusdirect.com (28)

Ledford, Tony, Watts Radiant, Springfield, MO. Tel: (417) 864-6108, (800) 276-2419, FAX: (417) 864-8161, Web Site: www.wattsheatway.com (9)

Ledsinger Jr., Charles, Choice Hotels International, Silver Spring, MD. Tel: (301) 592-6636, (888) 770-6800, FAX: (301) 592-6157, E-Mail: ihelp@choicehotels.com, Web Site: www.choicebuys.com (16)

Leduc, Laura, Voicelogic, Toronto, ON Canada. Tel: (888) 552-8858, Web Site: www.voicelogic.com (29)

Lee, Albert, Marshall Cavendish Corp, Tarrytown, NY. Tel: (914) 332-8888, (800) 821-9881, FAX: (914) 332-1888, Web Site: www.marshallcavendish.com (17)

Lee, Andy, Alorica Inc, Chino, CA. Tel: (909) 606-3600, (866) 256-7422, FAX: (909) 606-7708, E-Mail: info@alorica.com, Web Site: www.alorica.com (29)

Lee, Brad, National Mail Order Association (NMOA), Minneapolis, MN. Tel: (612) 788-1673, E-Mail: info@nmoa.org, Web Site: www.nmoa.org (40)

Lee, Bruce, K., Fifth Third Bank, Cincinnati, OH. Tel: (800) 972-3030, FAX: (231) 922-4060, Web Site: www.53.com (14)

Lee, Cassandra, North American Mailing Technologies Inc, Lawrenceville, GA. Tel: (770) 962-5833 (22)

Lee, Chau, Regitar USA Inc, Montgomery, AL. Tel: (334) 244-1885, (877) 734-4827, FAX: (334) 244-1901, E-Mail: info@regitar.com, Web Site: www.regitar.com (9)

Lee, Cyndi, RMI Direct Marketing Inc, Danbury, CT. Tel: (203) 798-0448, FAX: (203) 778-6130, E-Mail: info@rmidirect.com, Web Site: www.rmidirect.com (23)

Lee, Cyndi, The Direct Marketing Club of New York Inc, Garden City, NY. Tel: (516) 746-6700, FAX: (516) 294-8141, E-Mail: info@dmcny.org, Web Site: www.dmcny.org (1)

Lee, Dale, ISA-The Instrumentation Systems & Automation Society, Research Triangle Park, NC. Tel: (919) 549-8411, FAX: (919) 549-8288, E-Mail: info@isa.org, Web Site: www.isa.org (1)

Lee, David, F&W Publications Inc, Blue Ash, OH. Tel: (513) 531-2690, FAX: (513) 531-0293, Web Site: www.fwpublications.com (17)

Lee, Dr. Lois, Children of the Night, Van Nuys, CA. Tel: (818) 908-4474, (800) 551-1300, FAX: (818) 908-1468, E-Mail: llee@childrenofthenight.com, Web Site: www.childrenofthenight.org (1)

Lee, Edar, Mercury Media, Santa Monica, CA. Tel: (310) 451-2900, FAX: (310) 451-0180, Web Site: www.mercurymedia.com (32)

Lee, Freddy, S., School of Business & Economics, Los Angeles, CA. Tel: (323) 343-2800, FAX: (323) 343-2813, Web Site: cbe.calstatela.edu (41)

Lee, Granville, R., Brownell Holly Farms, Oregon City, OR. Tel: (503) 631-7475, FAX: (503) 631-7481, E-Mail: sales@brownellhollyfarms.com, Web Site: www.brownellhollyfarms.com (6)

Lee, Jack, ANDREWS WHARTON INC, Commack, NY. Tel: (631) 470-4546 (35)

Lee, Jane, Lillian Vernon Corp, Colorado Springs, CO. Tel: (757) 427-7923, FAX: (757) 427-7819, E-Mail: publicrelations@lillianvernon.com, Web Site: www.lillianvernon.com (1)

Lee, Jeff, People's United Bank, Bridgeport, CT. Tel: (203) 338-7171, Web Site: www.peoples.com (14)

Lee, Jenny, Brownell Holly Farms, Oregon City, OR. Tel: (503) 631-7475, FAX: (503) 631-7481, E-Mail: sales@brownellhollyfarms.com, Web Site: www.brownellhollyfarms.com (6)

Lee, Jonathan, The CompTEL Annual Convention & Trade Exposition, Washington, DC. Tel: (202) 296-6650, FAX: (202) 296-7585, Web Site: www.comptel.org (42)

Lee, Keith, 3D Mail Results, Kent, WA. FAX: (853) 859-7300 (5)

Lee, Ken, Michael Wiese Productions, Studio City, CA. Tel: (818) 379-8799, (800) 833-5738, FAX: (818) 986-3408, Web Site: www.mwp.com (17)

Lee, Kevin, Didit, Mineola, NY. Tel: (212) 631-0157, Web Site: www.did-it.com (16)

Lee, Lauren, Brownell Holly Farms, Oregon City, OR. Tel: (503) 631-7475, FAX: (503) 631-7481, E-Mail: sales@brownellhollyfarms.com, Web Site: www.brownellhollyfarms.com (6)

Lee, Margaret, B., Oakton Community College, Des Plaines, IL. Tel: (847) 635-1600, FAX: (847) 635-1706, Web Site: www.oakton.edu (41)

Lee, Michael, International Advertising Association, New York, NY. Tel: (212) 557-1133, FAX: (212) 983-0455, E-Mail: membership@iaaglobal.com, Web Site: www.iaaglobal.org (1)

Lee, Randy, GBH Communications, Monrovia, CA. Tel: (818) 246-9900, (800) 222-5424, FAX: (818) 246-5850, E-Mail: customerservice@gbh.com, Web Site: www.gbh.com (3)

Lee, Robert, S., Hill Mailing & Printing of Florida Inc, Brandon, FL. Tel: (813) 258-5220 (21)

Lee, Thomas P., Territorial Newspapers, Tucson, AZ. Tel: (520) 294-1200, FAX: (520) 294-4040, Web Site: www.azbiz.com (17)

Lee-Fong, Christopher, UNICEF Canada, Toronto, ON. Tel: (416) 482-4444, (800) 567-4483, FAX: (416) 487-8875, E-Mail: on.secretary@unicef.ca, Web Site: www.unicef.ca (1)

Leeds, Bob, Global Equipment Co Inc, Port Washington, NY. Tel: (516) 484-3100, (888) 978-7759, FAX: (516) 608-7111, Web Site: www.globalindustrial.com (9)

Leeds, Bruce, Global Equipment Co Inc, Port Washington, NY. Tel: (516) 484-3100, (888) 978-7759, FAX: (516) 608-7111, Web Site: www.globalindustrial.com (9)

Leeds, Bruce, Tiger Direct Inc, Miami, FL. Tel: (305) 415-2200, (800) 800-8300, FAX: (305) 415-2202, Web Site: biz.tigerdirect.com (3)

Leeds, Richard, Comp USA, Inc, Miami, FL. Tel: (972) 982-4000, (800) COMP-USA, FAX: (972) 982-4030, Web Site: www.compusa.com (3)

Leeds, Richard, Global Computer Corp, Port Washington, NY. Tel: (516) 625-4300, (888) 845-6225, FAX: (516) 625-4072, Web Site: www.globalcomputer.com (3)

Leeds, Richard, Global Equipment Co Inc, Port Washington, NY. Tel: (516) 484-3100, (888) 978-7759, FAX: (516) 608-7111, Web Site: www.globalindustrial.com (9)

Leeds, Richard, Systemax Inc, Port Washington, NY. Tel: (516) 608-7000, FAX: (516) 6208-7001, Web Site: www.systemax.com (16)

Leeds, Richard, Tiger Direct Inc, Miami, FL. Tel: (305) 415-2200, (800) 800-8300, FAX: (305) 415-2202, Web Site: biz.tigerdirect.com (3)

Leeds, Robert, Tiger Direct Inc, Miami, FL. Tel: (305) 415-2200, (800) 800-8300, FAX: (305) 415-2202, Web Site: biz.tigerdirect.com (3)

Leeds, Ronald, Centrac Inc, West Caldwell, NJ. Tel: (973) 402-0999, FAX: (973) 402-0993, E-Mail: rleeds@centrac.com, Web Site: www.centrac.com (29)

Leeming, Michael, J., Parker Boiler Co, Los Angeles, CA. Tel: (323) 727-9800, FAX: (323) 722-2848, E-Mail: mleeming@parkerboiler.com, Web Site: www.parkerboiler.com (34)

Leerentueld, Rudi, Kadant Johnson Inc, Three Rivers, MI. Tel: (269) 278-1715, FAX: (269) 279-5980, Web Site: www.kadantjohnson.com (16)

Lee's Nursery, McMinnville, TN. Tel: (931) 668-4870, FAX: (931) 668-4870, E-Mail: leesnursery@blomand.net, Web Site: stores.ebay.com/Lees-Nursery (8)

Leesi, John-Peter, Astro Air, LP, Jacksonville, TX. Tel: (903) 586-3691, FAX: (903) 589-8094, E-Mail: sales@astroair.com, Web Site: www.astroair.com (9)

Lefavre, Hadia, The Scotts Co Div of Lawn Service, Marysville, OH. Tel: (937) 644-0011, FAX: (937) 644-7261, Web Site: www.scotts.com (8)

Lefcort, Henry, J., Round Lake Publishing Co, Trumbull, CT. Tel: (203) 459-8484, Web Site: www.letterworks.com (17)

LeFebvre, Dustin, Specialty Print Communications, Niles, IL. Tel: (847) 588-2580, Web Site: www. specialtyprintcomm.com (27)

Lefferts, Coni, PCI, Keyport, NJ. Tel: (732) 335-3700, (888) 826-1646, FAX: (732) 264-9313, E-Mail: conil@packaging-usa.com, Web Site: www. packaging-usa.com (35)

Lefkowitz, Herb, We Deliver America Inc, Englewood Cliffs, NJ. Tel: (201) 307-8888, FAX: (201) 307-1200, E-Mail: info@we-deliver-america.com, Web Site: www.we-deliver-america.com (31)

LeFort, Mike, Rapid City Journal, Rapid City, SD. Tel: (605) 394-8300, FAX: (605) 394-8462, E-Mail: classifieds@rapidcityjournal.com, Web Site: www.rapidcityjournal.com (18)

Lefton Jr., Al, Paul, Al Paul Lefton Co Inc, Philadelphia, PA. Tel: (215) 923-9600, FAX: (215) 351-4298, Web Site: www.lefton.com (35)

Al Paul Lefton Co Inc, Philadelphia, PA. Tel: (215) 923-9600, FAX: (215) 351-4298, Web Site: www. lefton.com (35)

Lefty's Corner, Clarks Summit, PA. Tel: (570) 586-LEFT, (570) 586-5338, FAX: (570) 585-2906, E-Mail: info@leftyscorner.com, Web Site: www. leftyscorner.com (6)

Legal Defense Foundation Inc, Springfield, VA. Tel: (703) 321-8501, (800) 336-3600, FAX: (703) 321-9613, E-Mail: info@nrtw.org, Web Site: www.nrtw. org (1)

Legal Sea Foods Inc, Boston, MA. Tel: (617) 530-9000, (800) 343-5804, FAX: (617) 530-9649, Web Site: www.legalseafoods.com (4)

The Legal Studies Forum, Morgantown, WV. Tel: (304) 293-7354, FAX: (304) 293-6891, E-Mail: jelkins@labs.net (1)

Legaspi, Liza, InterTrend Communications Inc, Long Beach, CA. Tel: (562) 733-1852, Web Site: www. intertrend.com (35)

LeGault, Sharon, Cooper-Atkins Corp, Middlefield, CT. Tel: (860) 347-2256, (800) 835-5011, FAX: (860) 347-5135, Web Site: www.cooper-atkins.com (34)

Legendre, Derek, CARFAX Inc, Centreville, VA. Tel: (703) 934-2664, Web Site: www.carfax.com (12)

Legere, John, Global Crossing Telecom Inc, Florham Park, NJ. Tel: (800) 466-4600, FAX: (973) 937-0100, E-Mail: iccc@globalcrossing.com, Web Site: www.globalcrossing.com (29)

Legge, Dorri, Partners Village Store, Westport, MA. Tel: (508) 636-2572, FAX: (508) 636-2529, E-Mail: info@partnersvillagestore.com, Web Site: www.partnersvillagestore.com (11)

Lego Direct Marketing, Enfield, CT. Tel: (860) 749-2291, FAX: (860) FAX-LEGO, Web Site: www. lego.com (11)

Legrand Hart, Denver, CO. Tel: (303) 298-8470, FAX: (303) 298-8570, Web Site: www.legrandhart.com (20)

Legrand-Hart, DeeDee, Legrand Hart, Denver, CO. Tel: (303) 298-8470, FAX: (303) 298-8570, Web Site: www.legrandhart.com (20)

Lehere, Kim, MWM Dexter Inc, Aurora, MO. Tel: (888) 833-1242, FAX: (417) 841-1040, Web Site: www.mwmdexter.com (27)

Lehigh Direct, Broadview, IL. Tel: (708) 681-3612, FAX: (708) 681-4694, Web Site: www.lehighdirect. com (27)

Lehman, Galen, Lehman's, Dalton, OH. Tel: (330) 857-5757, (877) 438-5346, FAX: (330) 857-5785, E-Mail: info@lehmans.com, Web Site: www. lehmans.com (8)

Lehman, Glenda, Lehman's, Dalton, OH. Tel: (330) 857-5757, (877) 438-5346, FAX: (330) 857-5785, E-Mail: info@lehmans.com, Web Site: www. lehmans.com (8)

Lehman, Jay, Lehman's, Dalton, OH. Tel: (330) 857-5757, (877) 438-5346, FAX: (330) 857-5785, E-Mail: info@lehmans.com, Web Site: www. lehmans.com (8)

Lehman, Timothy J., Thrivent Financial for Lutherans, Appleton, WI. Tel: (920) 734-5721, (800) 847-4836, FAX: (920) 730-4781, E-Mail: mail@ thrivent.com, Web Site: www.thrivent.com (14)

Lehmann, Bill, Jones & Thomas Inc, Decatur, IL. Tel: (217) 423-1889, FAX: (217) 425-0680, E-Mail: bill@jonesthomas.com, Web Site: www. jonesthomas.com (35)

Lehman's, Dalton, OH. Tel: (330) 857-5757, (877) 438-5346, FAX: (330) 857-5785, E-Mail: info@ lehmans.com, Web Site: www.lehmans.com (8)

Lehmen, Ed, Initiative Media Worldwide, New York, NY. Tel: (212) 605-7000, FAX: (212) 605-7200, Web Site: www.initiativemedia.com (32)

Lehmen, Ted, Ted's Promotions Inc, Baldwin, GA. Tel: (770) 972-8081, FAX: (770) 573-3141, E-Mail: ted@tedspromotions.com, Web Site: www. tedspromotions.com (33)

Leibowitz, Teri, Leibowitz Market Research Associates Inc, Charlotte, NC. Tel: (704) 357-1961, FAX: (704) 357-1965, E-Mail: info@leibowitz-research. com, Web Site: www.leibowitz-research.com (30)

Leibowitz Market Research Associates Inc, Charlotte, NC. Tel: (704) 357-1961, FAX: (704) 357-1965, E-Mail: info@leibowitz-research.com, Web Site: www.leibowitz-research.com (30)

Leichtling, Scott, Newark Electronics, Chicago, IL. Tel: (773) 784-5100, (800) 4-Newark, FAX: (888) 551-4801, E-Mail: webmaster@newark.com, Web Site: www.newark.com (3)

Leide, Dominic, The Office Gurus, Seminole, FL. Tel: (727) 803-7114, Web Site: www.theofficegurus.com (29)

Leigh, Kevin, M., The Keystone Equities Group, Oaks, PA. Tel: (610) 415-6300, (800) 715-9905, FAX: (610) 415-6328, Web Site: www. keystoneequities.com (20)

Lein, Chuck, Stuller, Inc, Lafayette, LA. Tel: (337) 262-7700, (800) 877-7777, FAX: (337) 981-1655, E-Mail: info@stuller.com, Web Site: www.stuller. com (2)

Leininger, Len, JC Penney Telemarketing Inc, Milwaukee, WI. Tel: (262) 792-5504, (800) 323-4343, FAX: (262) 792-5598, Web Site: www.jcpenney. com (29)

Leinweber, Tabetha, Susan G Komen for the Cure, Dallas, TX. Tel: (972) 855-1600, Web Site: www. komen.org (1)

Leiss, Daniel, Jenny Products Inc, Somerset, PA. Tel: (814) 445-3400, FAX: (814) 445-2280, Web Site: www.jennyproducts.com (16)

Leiss, Peter, Jenny Products Inc, Somerset, PA. Tel: (814) 445-3400, FAX: (814) 445-2280, Web Site: www.jennyproducts.com (16)

Leisure Arts Inc, Little Rock, AR. Tel: (501) 868-8800, Web Site: www.leisurearts.com (17)

Leitstein, Robert, Halls Kansas City, Kansas City, MO. Tel: (816) 274-8111, (800) 624-4034, FAX: (816) 545-2121, Web Site: www.hallskc.com (16)

Leitzell, Melissa, Golden Key International Honour Society, Atlanta, GA. Tel: (404) 377-2400, Web Site: www.goldenkey.org (1)

Leiwekei, Timothy, J., Los Angeles Kings, Los Angeles, CA. Tel: (213) 742-7100, (888) KINGS-LA, FAX: (213) 742-7296, Web Site: kings.nhl.com (16)

Lemasters, Craig, Assurant Solutions Preneed Division, Atlanta, GA. Tel: (770) 763-1000, (800) PRE NEED, FAX: (770) 859-4325, Web Site: www. assurantpreneed.com (15)

Lemay, Frankye, Sunnyland Farms Inc, Albany, GA. Tel: (229) 436-5654, (800) 999-2488, FAX: (229) 888-8332, Web Site: www.sunnylandfarms.com (4)

Lemee, Brian, D., Lemee's Inc, Bridgewater, MA. Tel: (508) 697-2672, E-Mail: slemeephot@aol.com, Web Site: www.lemeesfireplace.com (8)

Lemee, Ruth E., Lemee's Inc, Bridgewater, MA. Tel: (508) 697-2672, E-Mail: slemeephot@aol.com, Web Site: www.lemeesfireplace.com (8)

Lemee, Susan, Lemee's Inc, Bridgewater, MA. Tel: (508) 697-2672, E-Mail: slemeephot@aol.com, Web Site: www.lemeesfireplace.com (8)

Lemee's Inc, Bridgewater, MA. Tel: (508) 697-2672, E-Mail: slemeephot@aol.com, Web Site: www. lemeesfireplace.com (8)

Lemer, Troy, Booyah Networks, Westminster, CO. Tel: (303) 426-7776, FAX: (303) 345-6700, E-Mail: support@booyahnetworks.com, Web Site: www. booyahnetworks.com (35)

Lemmon, Nicolette, LemmonTree Marketing Group, Tempe, AZ. Tel: (480) 967-1405, (888) 536-6243, FAX: (480) 967-1407, E-Mail: 7solutions@ lemmontree.com, Web Site: www.lemmontree.com (35)

LemmonTree Marketing Group, Tempe, AZ. Tel: (480) 967-1405, (888) 536-6243, FAX: (480) 967-1407, E-Mail: 7solutions@lemmontree.com, Web Site: www.lemmontree.com (35)

Lemonis, Marcus, Camping World Inc, Bowling Green, KY. Tel: (270) 781-2718, (800) 626-6189, FAX: (270) 796-8991, Web Site: www. campingworld.com (11)

Lemonis, Marcus, Woodall Publishing Co LP, Ventura, CA. Tel: (805) 667-4100, (800) 323-9076, FAX: (805) 667-4468, Web Site: www.woodalls.com (17)

Lemp, John, Clickbooth.com LLC, Sarasota, FL. Tel: (941) 483-4188, Web Site: www.integraclick.com (35)

Lemsky, James, R., Jason Natural Personal Care Products, Boulder, CO. Tel: (877) 527-6601, Web Site: www.jason-natural.com (7)

Len, Charles, NestFamily.com, Coppell, TX. Tel: (972) 402-7100, (800) 596-7386, FAX: (972) 629-7181, Web Site: www.nestfamily.com (3)

Lendhart, Alfonso E., McGruff Specialty Products Office, Amsterdam, NY. Tel: (518) 842-4388, (888) 776-7763, FAX: (800) 995-5121, E-Mail: mcgruff@spocentral.com, Web Site: www. mcgruffspo.com (16)

Lending Tree/Home Loan Center, Charlotte, NC. Tel: (704) 541-5351, Web Site: www.lendingtree.com (14)

Lenhart, Larry, F P International, Redwood City, CA. Tel: (650) 261-5300, (800) 866-9946, FAX: (650) 361-1713, Web Site: www.fpintl.com (16)

Lenich, William, MELDISCO, Mahwah, NJ. Tel: (201) 934-2000, FAX: (201) 934-2570, Web Site: www.meldisco.com (16)

Lennertz, Carl, HarperCollins, New York, NY. Tel: (212) 207-7000, (800) 242-7737, FAX: (212) 207-7145, Web Site: www.harpercollins.com (17)

Lenovo, Morrisville, NC. Tel: (919) 257-6315, Web Site: www.uslenovo.com (3)

Lenox, Jim, Manchester Farms Inc, Columbia, SC. Tel: (803) 469-2588, (800) 845-0421, FAX: (803) 469-8637, E-Mail: customerservice@ manchesterfarms.com, Web Site: www. manchesterfarms.com (4)

Lenox Group Inc, Bristol, PA. Tel: (267) 525-7800, (800) 223-4311, Web Site: www.lenox.com (6)

Lensch, Deb, KV Vet Supply Co, Inc, David City, NE. Tel: (402) 367-6047, Web Site: www.kvvet.com (5)

Lenser, John, LENSER, San Rafael, CA. Tel: (415) 446-2500, E-Mail: carol@lenser.com, Web Site: www.lenser.com (35)

LENSER, San Rafael, CA. Tel: (415) 446-2500, E-Mail: carol@lenser.com, Web Site: www.lenser. com (35)

Lent, Max, Max Lent Communications, Webster, NY. Tel: (585) 670-9707, E-Mail: max@maxlent.com, Web Site: www.maxlent.com (39)

Max Lent Communications, Webster, NY. Tel: (585) 670-9707, E-Mail: max@maxlent.com, Web Site: www.maxlent.com (39)

L'Entraide Assurance, Quebec, PQ Canada. Tel: (418) 658-0663, FAX: (418) 658-5065, E-Mail: service@ lentraide.com, Web Site: www.lentraide.com (15)

Lentz, James, Toyota Motor Sales USA Inc, Torrance, CA. Tel: (310) 468-4000, (800) 331-4331, FAX: (310) 468-7841, Web Site: www.toyota.com (16)

Lenzen, David, Presentation Packaging, Minneapolis, MN. Tel: (763) 540-9544, (800) 818-2698, FAX: (763) 540-9522, Web Site: www. presentationpackaging.com (35)

Leo Burnett Detroit, Troy, MI. Tel: (248) 458-8331, FAX: (248) 458-8736, Web Site: www.leoburnett. com (35)

Leo Burnett USA, Chicago, IL. Tel: (312) 220-3200, Web Site: www.leoburnett.com (35)

Leonard, J., Wayne, Entergy, New Orleans, LA. Tel: (504) 576-4000, (800) ENTERGY, FAX: (504) 576-4428, Web Site: www.entergy.com (16)

Leonard, John, Lucent Direct Catalog, New Providence, NJ. Tel: (908) 582-8500, (908) 582-3000, (800) 4-LUCENT, E-Mail: execoffice@alcatel-lucent.com, Web Site: www.alcatel-lucent.com (3)

Leonard, Linda, Facts On File Inc, New York, NY. Tel: (212) 967-8800, (800) 322-8755, FAX: (212) 678-3633, Web Site: www.factsonfile.com (17)

Leonard, Mark, The Faneuil Group, Winnipeg, MB Canada. Tel: (204) 934-1900, (866) FANEUIL, FAX: (617) 742-3666, Web Site: www.faneuil.com (29)

Leonard, Sara, E., Federal Home Loan Mortgage Corp (Freddie Mac), McLean, VA. Tel: (703) 903-2000, (800) 424-5401, Web Site: www.freddiemac.com (14)

AM Leonard Inc, Piqua, OH. Tel: (937) 773-2694, (800) 543-8955, FAX: (800) 433-0633, (937) 773-9993, E-Mail: info@amleo.com, Web Site: www. amleo.com (8)

Hal Leonard Corp, Milwaukee, WI. Tel: (414) 774-3630, FAX: (414) 774-3259, Web Site: www. halleonard.com (17)

Leonardi, John, Brush Fire, Cedar Knolls, NJ. Tel: (973) 871-1700, FAX: (973) 871-1717, Web Site: www.brushfireinc.com (35)

Leonards Jr., Stew, Stew Leonard's, Norwalk, CT. Tel: (203) 847-7214, FAX: (203) 847-1488, Web Site: www.stewleonards.com (4)

Leone, Paul, Magnet LLC, Washington, MO. Tel: (636) 239-5661, (800) 458-9457, FAX: (636) 239-4490, E-Mail: contactus@themagnetgroup.com, Web Site: www.magnetllc.com (16)

Leonhardt, Cathy, Peter J Solomon Co, New York, NY. Tel: (212) 508-1600, Web Site: www.pjsc.com (14)

Leonhardt, Patti, Miller Harness Co, Westford, MA. Tel: (800) 784-5831, E-Mail: customerservice@ millerharness.com, Web Site: www.millerharness. com (11)

Leopold Jr., Augie, Augie Leopold Advertising Specialties, Metairie, LA. Tel: (504) 836-0525, FAX: (504) 836-2396, E-Mail: aleopold@bellsouth.net (33)

Leopold, Gary, Irma S Mann Strategic Marketing Inc, Boston, MA. Tel: (617) 353-1822, FAX: (617) 266-1890, Web Site: www.irmamann.com (35)

Augie Leopold Advertising Specialties, Metairie, LA. Tel: (504) 836-0525, FAX: (504) 836-2396, E-Mail: aleopold@bellsouth.net (33)

Lepore, Peter, Ferrara Bakery & Cafe Inc, New York, NY. Tel: (212) 226-6150, FAX: (212) 226-0667, E-Mail: information@ferraracafe.com, Web Site: www.ferraracafe.com (4)

Lepoutre, Richard, Statware, Centerbrook, CT. Tel: (860) 767-9000, FAX: (860) 767-3145, E-Mail: info@statware.net, Web Site: www.powerlist.com (16)

Lerner, Adam, Lerner Publishing Group, Minneapolis, MN. Tel: (612) 332-3344, (800) 328-4929, FAX: (800) 332-1132, E-Mail: info@lernerbooks.com, Web Site: www.lernerbooks.com (17)

Lerner, David, Janice's LLC, Hartford, CT. Tel: (860) 523-4479, FAX: (860) 523-4178, E-Mail: dlerner@ janices.com, Web Site: www.janices.com (8)

Lerner, Harry, Lerner Publishing Group, Minneapolis, MN. Tel: (612) 332-3344, (800) 328-4929, FAX: (800) 332-1132, E-Mail: info@lernerbooks.com, Web Site: www.lernerbooks.com (17)

Lerner Publishing Group, Minneapolis, MN. Tel: (612) 332-3344, (800) 328-4929, FAX: (800) 332-1132, E-Mail: info@lernerbooks.com, Web Site: www. lernerbooks.com (17)

LeRoach, Robert, Ion Media Networks Inc, West Palm Beach, FL. Tel: (561) 659-4122, (800) 646-7296, FAX: (561) 659-4252, Web Site: www.ionmedia.tv (32)

Lerose, Robert, Lerose Copywriting, Uniondale, NY. Tel: (516) 486-0472, FAX: (516) 486-0386, E-Mail: robertler@optonline.net, Web Site: www. robertlerose.com (39)

Lerose, Robert, Robert Lerose, Uniondale, NY. Tel: (516) 486-0472, FAX: (516) 486-0386, E-Mail: robertler@optonline.net, Web Site: www. robertlerose.com (39)

Lerose Copywriting, Uniondale, NY. Tel: (516) 486-0472, FAX: (516) 486-0386, E-Mail: robertler@ optonline.net, Web Site: www.robertlerose.com (39)

Robert Lerose, Uniondale, NY. Tel: (516) 486-0472, FAX: (516) 486-0386, E-Mail: robertler@ optonline.net, Web Site: www.robertlerose.com (39)

Lesch, Sigrid, Thieme Medical Publishers Inc, New York, NY. Tel: (212) 760-0888, (800) 782-3488, FAX: (212) 947-1112, E-Mail: info@thieme.com, Web Site: www.thieme.com (17)

Lesh, Dawn, New York University/Center for Marketing, New York, NY. Tel: (212) 998-0500, FAX: (212) 995-4006, E-Mail: mkt@stern.nyu.edu, Web Site: w4.stern.nyu.edu/marketing (41)

LeShay, David, Theatre Development Fund Inc, New York, NY. Tel: (212) 912-9770, E-Mail: info@tdf. org, Web Site: www.tdf.org (1)

Leshinsky, Barbara, The Advertising Council Inc, New York, NY. Tel: (212) 922-1500, FAX: (212) 922-1676, E-Mail: info@adcouncil.org, Web Site: www.adcouncil.org (1)

Leshner Dr., Alan, I., AAAS/Science, Washington, DC. Tel: (202) 326-6400, FAX: (202) 371-9526, E-Mail: webmaster@aaas.org, Web Site: www. aaas.org (1)

Leshner, Leigh, Venture Entertainment Group, Sherman Oaks, CA. Tel: (800) 981-8433, FAX: (818) 981-3466, E-Mail: venture818@aol.com, Web Site: www.venture818.com (3)

Lesjak, Catherine, A., Hewlett-Packard Co, Palo Alto, CA. Tel: (650) 857-1501, (800) 752-0900, FAX: (650) 857-5518, Web Site: www.hp.com (16)

Lesjak, Cathie, Compaq Computer Corp, Houston, TX. Tel: (281) 370-0670, (281) 927-8835, Web Site: www.compaq.com (16)

Lesko, Edward, Reb Storage Systems International, Chicago, IL. Tel: (773) 252-0400, (800) 252-5955, FAX: (773) 252-0303, E-Mail: sales@rebsteel.com, Web Site: www.industrialebuy.com (9)

Lesko, Tom, Reb Storage Systems International, Chicago, IL. Tel: (773) 252-0400, (800) 252-5955, FAX: (773) 252-0303, E-Mail: sales@rebsteel.com, Web Site: www.industrialebuy.com (9)

Leslie Jordan, Portland, OR. Tel: (503) 295-1987, (800) 935-3343, FAX: (503) 295-1989, E-Mail: sales@lesliejordan.com, Web Site: www. lesliejordan.com (2)

Leslie Shoe Co Inc, Rogers City, MI. Tel: (989) 734-4030, (800) 716-8617, E-Mail: info@sexyshoes. com, Web Site: www.sexyshoes.com (2)

Lesman Instrument Co, Bensenville, IL. Tel: (630) 595-8400, (800) 953-7626, FAX: (630) 595-2386, E-Mail: sales@lesman.com, Web Site: www. lesman.com (9)

Lesnar, K.A., Western Web Printing, Sioux Falls, SD. Tel: (605) 339-2383, (888) 855-4563, FAX: (605) 339-1523, E-Mail: info@westernwebprinting.com, Web Site: www.westernwebprinting.com (27)

Lesniak, David, Imtek, Bridgeport, NJ. Tel: (800) 346-8354, FAX: (856) 467-8967, Web Site: www. imtek.com (27)

Lesonsky, Rieva, Entrepreneur Media Inc, Irvine, CA. Tel: (949) 261-2325, (800) 274-6229, FAX: (949) 261-0234, Web Site: www.entrepreneur.com (17)

Lesperance, Tracy, Born Free USA, Sacramento, CA. Tel: (916) 447-3085, FAX: (916) 447-3070, E-Mail: info@bornfreeusa.org, Web Site: www. bornfreeusa.org (1)

Lessin, Carol, Charmaster Products Inc, Grand Rapids, MN. Tel: (218) 326-6786, FAX: (218) 326-1065, E-Mail: info@charmaster.com, Web Site: www. charmaster.com (8)

Lessin, Larry, Charmaster Products Inc, Grand Rapids, MN. Tel: (218) 326-6786, FAX: (218) 326-1065, E-Mail: info@charmaster.com, Web Site: www. charmaster.com (8)

Lester, Robert, Parlay International, Walnut Creek, CA. Tel: (510) 601-1000, FAX: (510) 601-1008, E-Mail: info@parlay.com, Web Site: www.parlay. com (17)

Lester, Victoria, Huntsinger & Jeffer Inc, Richmond, VA. Tel: (804) 266-2499, FAX: (804) 266-8563, E-Mail: vickil@huntsinger-jeffer.com, Web Site: www.huntsinger-jeffer.com (21)

Lester, W. Howard, Williams-Sonoma Inc, San Francisco, CA. Tel: (415) 421-7900, FAX: (415) 983-9887, Web Site: www.williams-sonomainc.com (8)

Lester Inc, Branford, CT. Tel: (203) 488-5265, (800) 999-5265, FAX: (203) 483-0408, Web Site: www. lesterusa.com (29)

Lethers, Alan, America's Finest Pet Doors, San Luis Obispo, CA. Tel: (805) 781-7700 X201, (800) 826-2871, FAX: (805) 781-9734, E-Mail: alan@ petdoors.com, Web Site: www.petdoors.com (16)

The Letter Shop Inc, Pittsburgh, PA. Tel: (412) 882-6200, FAX: (412) 882-7200, E-Mail: info@ lettershopcanton.com (28)

Lettergraphics Inc, Syracuse, NY. Tel: (315) 476-8328, FAX: (315) 476-1818, E-Mail: nancyo@ broadviewnet.net, Web Site: lettergraphics.net (28)

Lettig, Mary, Lou, Ultradent Products Inc, South Jordan, UT. Tel: (801) 572-4200, Web Site: www. ultradent.com (7)

Letts, Phillip, Intagio Trading Network, San Francisco, CA. Tel: (415) 247-9500, FAX: (415) 543-0375, Web Site: www.intagio.com (32)

Leucadia National Corp, New York, NY. Tel: (212) 460-1900, FAX: (212) 598-4869, Web Site: www. leucadia.com (14)

The Leukemia & Lymphoma Society, White Plains, NY. Tel: (914) 949-5213 (1)

Lev, Bruce, Lev & Berlin, Norwalk, CT. Tel: (203) 838-8500, (800) 377-4508, FAX: (203) 854-1652, E-Mail: info@levberlin.com, Web Site: www. levberlin.com (20)

Lev & Berlin, Norwalk, CT. Tel: (203) 838-8500, (800) 377-4508, FAX: (203) 854-1652, E-Mail: info@levberlin.com, Web Site: www.levberlin.com (20)

Leveen, Lori, Levenger, Delray Beach, FL. Tel: (561) 276-2436, (800) 677-8034, FAX: (561) 266-2181, E-Mail: orders@levenger.com, Web Site: www. levenger.com (5)

Leveen, Steve, Levenger, Delray Beach, FL. Tel: (561) 276-2436, (800) 677-8034, FAX: (561) 266-2181, E-Mail: orders@levenger.com, Web Site: www. levenger.com (5)

Level 5 Communications Inc, Dublin, NH. Tel: (603) 563-1631, FAX: (603) 563-8912, Web Site: www. deskeng.com (32)

Levenger, Delray Beach, FL. Tel: (561) 276-2436, (800) 677-8034, FAX: (561) 266-2181, E-Mail: orders@levenger.com, Web Site: www.levenger. com (5)

Levenson, Bruce, United Communications Group, Gaithersburg, MD. Tel: (301) 287-2700, FAX: (301) 816-8945, E-Mail: webmaster@ucg.com, Web Site: www.ucg.com (17)

Levenson, Stanley, R., Levenson & Brinker Public Relations, Dallas, TX. Tel: (214) 932-6076, (214) 880-0200, FAX: (214) 880-0628, E-Mail: s.levenson@levensonbrinkerpr.com, Web Site: www.levensonbrinkerpr.com (35)

Levenson & Brinker Public Relations, Dallas, TX. Tel: (214) 932-6076, (214) 880-0200, FAX: (214) 880-0628, E-Mail: s.levenson@levensonbrinkerpr.com, Web Site: www.levensonbrinkerpr.com (35)

Leverage Marketing Group, Newtown, CT. Tel: (203) 426-1267, FAX: (203) 426-5934, E-Mail: info@leverage-marketing.com, Web Site: www.leverage-marketing.com (35)

Leverte, Robert, J., Leverte Associates Inc, Mahwah, NJ. Tel: (203) 221-4900, FAX: (203) 221-4901, E-Mail: rleverte@leverte.com, Web Site: www.leverte.com (35)

Leverte Associates Inc, Mahwah, NJ. Tel: (203) 221-4900, FAX: (203) 221-4901, E-Mail: rleverte@leverte.com, Web Site: www.leverte.com (35)

Levey, Hugh, Gruppo Levey & Co, New York, NY. Tel: (212) 697-5753, FAX: (212) 949-7294, E-Mail: info@glconline.com, Web Site: www.glconline.com (14)

Levey, Tom, RadioShack Corp, Fort Worth, TX. Tel: (817) 415-2010, FAX: (817) 415-2647, Web Site: www.radioshack.com (3)

Levi, Michael, Ion Exhibits, Itasca, IL. Tel: (630) 285-9500, FAX: (630) 235-9501, E-Mail: info@ionexhibits.com, Web Site: www.ionexhibits.com (36)

Levi Strauss & Co, San Francisco, CA. Tel: (415) 501-6000, FAX: (415) 501-7112, Web Site: www.levistrauss.com (2)

Levigne, Patrick, National Rural Electric Cooperative Association, Arlington, VA. Tel: (703) 907-5500, FAX: (703) 907-5528, Web Site: www.nreca.org (1)

Levin Jr., Joseph, J., Southern Poverty Law Center, Montgomery, AL. Tel: (334) 956-8200, FAX: (334) 956-8483, Web Site: www.splcenter.org (1)

Levin, Barb, Triangle Printers Inc, Skokie, IL. Tel: (847) 675-3700, FAX: (847) 674-1230, E-Mail: blevin@triangleprinters.com, Web Site: www.triangleprinters.com (27)

Levin, Cliff, The Healthy Back Store, Beltsville, MD. Tel: (703) 339-1700, (800) 4 MY BACK, FAX: (703) 339-0671, E-Mail: service@healthyback.com, Web Site: www.healthyback.com (16)

Levin, Irwin, Social Studies School Service, Culver City, CA. Tel: (310) 839-2436, (800) 421-4246, FAX: (310) 839-2249, (800) 944-5432, E-Mail: access@socialstudies.com, Web Site: www.socialstudies.com (16)

Levin, Jerry, Sunbeam, Boca Raton, FL. Tel: (561) 912-4100, FAX: (561) 912-4567, Web Site: www.sunbeam.com (16)

Levine, Arthur, Anne Klein, New York, NY. Tel: (212) 536-9000, FAX: (212) 536-9000 (16)

Levine, Bruce, Smart Marketing, Dix Hills, NY. Tel: (631) 254-5259, FAX: (631) 254-4814, E-Mail: info@smartmarket.com, Web Site: www.smartmarket.com (35)

Levine, Ed, Sussex Publishers Inc, New York, NY. Tel: (212) 260-7210, FAX: (212) 260-7445, Web Site: www.blues-buster.com (17)

Levine, Glenn, List Team, Sherman Oaks, CA. Tel: (818) 986-1166, Web Site: www.listteam.com (23)

Levine, James, The Metropolitan Opera, New York, NY. Tel: (212) 799-3100, (212) 362-6000, FAX: (212) 870-7695, Web Site: www.metopera.org (1)

Levine, Jeff, Tele Business USA, Northbrook, IL. Tel: (847) 480-1560, FAX: (847) 897-4120, Web Site: www.tbiz.com (29)

Levine, Joshua, H., Mentor Corp, Santa Barbara, CA. Tel: (805) 879-6000, (800) 525-0245, FAX: (805) 964-2712, Web Site: www.mentorcorp.com (16)

Levine, Marty, Webb Mason, Hunt Valley, MD. Tel: (410) 785-1111, Web Site: www.webbmason.com (20)

Levine, Matthew, Research To Prevent Blindness Inc, New York, NY. Tel: (212) 752-4333, (800) 621-0026, FAX: (212) 688-6231, E-Mail: inforequest@rpbusa.org, Web Site: www.rpbusa.org (1)

Levine, Phil, Ethel M Chocolates Inc, Henderson, NV. Tel: (702) 458-8864, (800) 471-0352, FAX: (800) 392-2587, E-Mail: chocolatier@ethelm.com, Web Site: www.ethelm.com (4)

Levine, Russell, Zoe Marketing, San Diego, CA. Tel: (858) 408-1700 (20)

Levine, William, J., The MEDIA Organization Inc, Woodbury, NY. Tel: (516) 496-2577, FAX: (516) 496-3331 (23)

Levinson, Janine, The Hyiad Group, Garden City, NY. Tel: (516) 433-3800, FAX: (516) 822-6670, Web Site: www.thehyaidgroup.com (22)

Levinson, Leo, GroupLevinson, Philadelphia, PA. Tel: (215) 627-3030, Web Site: grouplevinson.com (35)

Levinson, Richard, The Hyiad Group, Garden City, NY. Tel: (516) 433-3800, FAX: (516) 822-6670, Web Site: www.thehyaidgroup.com (22)

Levison, Michael, ReMark USA, Minnetonka, MN. Tel: (952) 938-4699, FAX: (952) 988-8500, E-Mail: jessica.sbragia@remarkgroup.com, Web Site: www.remarkamericas.com (15)

Levitan, Peter, Citrus Inc, Bend, OR. Tel: (541) 388-2003, FAX: (541) 388-4381, Web Site: www.citrusbegin.com (35)

Levitt, Rachelle, ULI-The Urban Land Institute, Washington, DC. Tel: (202) 624-7000, FAX: (202) 624-7140, Web Site: www.uli.org (1)

Levitz, Bill, Argent Trading LLC, New York, NY. Tel: (212) 697-8800, FAX: (212) 697-8606, Web Site: www.Argenttrading.com (16)

LevLane Advertising, Philadelphia, PA. Tel: (215) 825-9600, FAX: (215) 825-9601 (35)

Levy, Brad, Fragrance International Inc, Youngstown, OH. Tel: (330) 747-3341, (888) 547-8355, FAX: (330) 747-3343, Web Site: www.kisstell.com (16)

Levy, David, Singer Direct, New York, NY. Tel: (212) 209-1900, Web Site: www.singerdirect.com (23)

Levy, Debra A., Key Communications Inc, Garrisonville, VA. Tel: (540) 720-5584, FAX: (540) 720-5687, E-Mail: usglass@aol.com, Web Site: www.key-com.com (17)

Levy, Hal, Hal Levy & Associates, High Falls, NY. Tel: (845) 687-4400 (20)

Levy, James, P., Steck-Vaughn, Austin, TX. Tel: (512) 343-8227, (877) 866-2586, (800) 531-5015, FAX: (512) 795-3617, (877) 265-2730, E-Mail: info@steck-vaughn.com, Web Site: www.steck-vaughn.com (17)

Levy, Jean, Bernard, Vivendi, New York, NY. Tel: (212) 572-7000, FAX: (212) 572-1080, Web Site: www.vivendi.com (16)

Levy, Judy, Fragrance International Inc, Youngstown, OH. Tel: (330) 747-3341, (888) 547-8355, FAX: (330) 747-3343, Web Site: www.kisstell.com (16)

Levy, Karen, Karen Levy Calligraphy, New York, NY. Tel: (212) 472-1669 (36)

Levy, Lester, A., NCH Corp, Dallas, TX. Tel: (972) 438-0211, FAX: (972) 438-0186, Web Site: www.nch.com (34)

Levy, Mark, Federal Citizen Information Center, Pueblo, CO. Tel: (888) 8-PUEBLO, FAX: (719) 948-9724, E-Mail: catalog.pueblo@gsa.gov, Web Site: www.pueblo.gsa.gov (5)

Levy, Michael R., Texas Monthly, Austin, TX. Tel: (512) 320-6900, (800) 759-2000, FAX: (512) 476-9007, E-Mail: info@texasmonthly.com, Web Site: www.texasmonthly.com (17)

Levy, Richard, Varian Medical Systems, Palo Alto, CA. Tel: (650) 493-4000, FAX: (650) 842-5196, Web Site: www.varian.com (9)

Levy, Robert, Tele Business USA, Northbrook, IL. Tel: (847) 480-1560, FAX: (847) 897-4120, Web Site: www.tbiz.com (29)

Levy, Steve, NEA's Member Benefits Corp, Gaithersburg, MD. Tel: (301) 251-9600, FAX: (301) 527-8210, Web Site: www.neamb.com (1)

Levy, Yoav, Phototake/The Creative Link, New York, NY. Tel: (212) 736-2525, (800) 542-3686, FAX: (212) 736-1919, E-Mail: photoinfo@phototakeusa.com, Web Site: www.phototakeusa.com (38)

Karen Levy Calligraphy, New York, NY. Tel: (212) 472-1669 (36)

Lewallen, Brian, Muscle Dynamics Fitness Network Inc, Santa Fe Springs, CA. Tel: (310) 323-9055, (800) 544-2944, FAX: (310) 323-7608, E-Mail: info@muscledynamics.com, Web Site: www.maxicam.com (32)

Lewark, Larry, A., Macy's Marketing, New York, NY. Tel: (212) 695-4400, FAX: (212) 494-1517, Web Site: www.macys.com (16)

Lewien, Gary, Hamilton Contact Center Services, Aurora, NE. Tel: (402) 694-4343, (800) 972-3237, FAX: (402) 694-4433, Web Site: www.hamiltontm.com (29)

Lewin, Bart, American Marketing Association/New York Chapter, New York, NY. Tel: (212) 687-3280, FAX: (212) 557-9242, E-Mail: mlkeane@nyama.org, Web Site: www.nyama.org (40)

Lewin, Stanton, LKH&S Inc, Chicago, IL. Tel: (312) 595-0200, FAX: (312) 595-0300, E-Mail: lkhs@lkhs.com, Web Site: www.lkhs.com (35)

Lewinter, Mel, Motown Records, New York, NY. Tel: (212) 373-0750, FAX: (212) 489-9096, Web Site: www.motown.com (3)

Lewis Jr., Morgan, Medical Economics Magazine, North Olmsted, OH. Tel: (440) 243-8100, FAX: (440) 891-2735, Web Site: medicaleconomics.modernmedicine.com/about (17)

Lewis MD, Phillip, J., Rohm & Haas Co, Philadelphia, PA. Tel: (215) 592-3000, (877) 288-5881, FAX: (215) 592-3377, Web Site: www.rohmhess.com (16)

Lewis, Allan, Grand Circle Travel, Boston, MA. Tel: (617) 350-7500, (800) 959-0405, FAX: (617) 346-6030, Web Site: www.gct.com (19)

Lewis, Barbara, Women in Direct Marketing International, New York, NY. Tel: (516) 746-6700, FAX: (516) 294-8141, Web Site: www.wdmi.org (40)

Lewis, Brian, Movie/Entertainment Book Club, Washington, DC. Tel: (800) 879-3270, FAX: (202) 216-0614, E-Mail: meb@eaglepub.com (13)

Lewis, Charles, J., Creativity International, Ada, MI. Tel: (616) 956-0053, FAX: (616) 956-6957 (16)

Lewis, Charlotte, House of Onyx, Inc, Greenville, KY. Tel: (270) 338-2363, (800) 844-3100, FAX: (270) 338-9605, E-Mail: sales@houseofonyx.com, Web Site: www.houseofonyx.com (6)

Lewis, David, F&W Publications Inc, Blue Ash, OH. Tel: (513) 531-2690, FAX: (513) 531-0293, Web Site: www.fwpublications.com (17)

Lewis, Dwight, Beemak Plastics Inc, La Mirada, CA. Tel: (310) 886-5880, (800) 421-4393, FAX: (310) 764-0330, E-Mail: info@beemak.com, Web Site: www.beemak.com (16)

Lewis, Edward, Essence Communications Inc, New York, NY. Tel: (212) 522-1212, FAX: (212) 921-5173, Web Site: www.essence.com (17)

Lewis, Evawn, R., Evergreen Marketing, Seneca, SC. Tel: (864) 882-1170, FAX: (864) 882-1112, E-Mail: evawn@evergreenmarketing.com, Web Site: www.evergreenmarketing.com (23)

Lewis, Harriet, Grand Circle Travel, Boston, MA. Tel: (617) 350-7500, (800) 959-0405, FAX: (617) 346-6030, Web Site: www.gct.com (19)

Lewis, Herschell, Gordon, Lewis Enterprises, Pompano Beach, FL. Tel: (954) 782-1750, FAX: (954) 785-3391, E-Mail: hglewis1@aol.com; hgl@herschellgordonlewis.com, Web Site: www.herschellgordonlewis.com (39)

Lewis, Janet, USA TODAY, Mc Lean, VA. Tel: (703) 854-3400, (800) 872-0001, E-Mail: accuracy@usatoday.com, Web Site: www.usatoday.com (17)

Lewis, Jean, Think Ink, Bothell, WA. Tel: (425) 778-1935, (800) 778-1935, E-Mail: jean.lewis1@comcast.net, Web Site: www.thinkink.net (10)

Lewis, John, ACNielsen, New York, NY. Tel: (646) 654-5000, FAX: (646) 654-5002, E-Mail: globalc@nielsen.com, Web Site: www.acnielsen.com (30)

Lewis, Jonathan, Landmark Graphics Corp, Houston, TX. Tel: (713) 839-2000, FAX: (713) 839-2015, E-Mail: solutions@lgc.com, Web Site: www.lgc.com (16)

Lewis, Judy, American Counseling Association, Broken Arrow, OK. Tel: (703) 823-6862, FAX: (703) 823-0252, E-Mail: webmaster@counseling.org, Web Site: www.counseling.org (1)

Lewis, Kenneth, D., Bank of America, Charlotte, NC. Tel: (704) 386-5681, (800) 841-4000, FAX: (704) 386-6699, Web Site: www.bankofamerica.com (14)

Lewis, Mark, G., The St John Associates Inc, Bronx, NY. Tel: (718) 655-2500, FAX: (718) 655-0295, E-Mail: stjmail@aol.com, Web Site: www.stjohn1.com (21)

Lewis, Mark, Lewis Direct Inc, Superior, CO. Tel: (303) 494-0730, FAX: (303) 494-0729, E-Mail: lewismails@aol.com, Web Site: www.lewis-direct.com (23)

Lewis, Peter, B., The Progressive Corp, Mayfield Village, OH. Tel: (440) 461-5000, (800) PROGRESSIVE, (800) 776-4737, FAX: (800) 456-6590, Web Site: www.progressive.com (15)

Lewis, Ray, Response Resources, Destrehan, LA. Tel: (985) 725-0162, FAX: (504) 764-2839 (35)

Lewis, Rev. Beth, A., Augsburg Fortress Publishers, Minneapolis, MN. Tel: (612) 330-3300, (800) 426-0115, FAX: (612) 330-3455, E-Mail: info@augsburgfortress.org, Web Site: www.augsburgfortress.org (17)

Lewis, Roger, Commercial Federal Bank, Omaha, NE. Tel: (402) 554-9200, FAX: (402) 514-5304 (14)

Lewis, Sean, P., Elcom International Inc, Norwood, MA. Tel: (781) 440-3333, FAX: (781) 762-1540, Web Site: www.elcom.com (22)

Lewis, Sheri, Creativity International, Ada, MI. Tel: (616) 956-0053, FAX: (616) 956-6957 (16)

Lewis, Steve, The Directors Network, West Hartford, CT. Tel: (818) 906-0006, FAX: (818) 506-4662, Web Site: www.tdnartists.com (35)

Lewis Cleaning Systems, Kiel, WI. Tel: (920) 894-2293, FAX: (920) 894-7029, Web Site: www.lewissonics.com (34)

Lewis Direct, Baltimore, MD. Tel: (410) 539-5100, FAX: (410) 539-4700 (22)

Lewis Direct Inc, Superior, CO. Tel: (303) 494-0730, FAX: (303) 494-0729, E-Mail: lewismails@aol.com, Web Site: www.lewis-direct.com (23)

Lewis Enterprises, Pompano Beach, FL. Tel: (954) 782-1750, FAX: (954) 785-3391, E-Mail: hglewis1@aol.com; hgl@herschellgordonlewis.com, Web Site: www.herschellgordonlewis.com (39)

Lewison, Dale, University of Akron, Akron, OH. Tel: (330) 972-5758 (1)

Lewtan, Douglas, Lewtan Industries Corp, Hartford, CT. Tel: (860) 278-9800, FAX: (860) 278-9019, E-Mail: lewtan@snet.net, Web Site: www.lewtan8.com (33)

Lewtan Industries Corp, Hartford, CT. Tel: (860) 278-9800, FAX: (860) 278-9019, E-Mail: lewtan@snet.net, Web Site: www.lewtan8.com (33)

Lexinet Corp, Council Grove, KS. Tel: (620) 767-7000 (22)

Lexington Luggage Limited, New York, NY. Tel: (212) 223-0698, (800) 822-0404, FAX: (212) 753-3298, E-Mail: sales@lexingtonluggage.com, Web Site: www.lexingtonluggage.com (19)

Lexis Nexis Matthew Bender, Albany, NY. Tel: (518) 487-3000, (800) 424-4200, E-Mail: lexisnexis@matthewbender, Web Site: www.bender.lexisnexis.com (17)

LexisNexis, Miamisburg, OH. Tel: (937) 865-6800, (800) 227-9597, (800) 227-4908, FAX: (800) 348-2609, E-Mail: pr@lexisnexis.com, Web Site: www.lexisnexis.com (16)

LexisNexis Risk & Information Analytics, Bellevue, WA. Tel: (908) 673-2648, Web Site: http://risk.lexisnexis.com (23)

Lexus Division of Toyota, Torrance, CA. Tel: (213) 328-2075 (12)

Leyden, David, Alert Marketing, Glen Ellyn, IL. Tel: (630) 790-0386, Web Site: www.alertmarketing.com (28)

Leyrer, D., Conclusive Marketing, Charlotte, NC. Tel: (615) 261-7600, (800) 346-0073, FAX: (615) 843-7244, E-Mail: info@conclusivemarketing.com, Web Site: www.conclusivemarketing.com (22)

Li, Peter, Peter Li Education Group, Dayton, OH. Tel: (937) 293-1415, (800) 523-4625, FAX: (937) 293-1310, Web Site: www.peterli.com (17)

Li, Richard, P., Demographic Research Co, Denver, CO. Tel: (310) 766-5590, FAX: (303) 831-9181, Web Site: www.drcmodel.com (22)

Peter Li Education Group, Dayton, OH. Tel: (937) 293-1415, (800) 523-4625, FAX: (937) 293-1310, Web Site: www.peterli.com (17)

Liantonio, Collette, Concepts TV Productions Inc, Boonton, NJ. Tel: (973) 331-1500, FAX: (973) 331-1550, E-Mail: collette@conceptstv.com, Web Site: www.conceptstv.com (32)

Liao, Sheila, Air Power USA, Los Angeles, CA. Tel: (310) 641-0830, (888) 888-8231, FAX: (310) 641-8515, Web Site: www.airpowerusa.com (12)

Liberty Creative Solutions, Tinley Park, IL. Tel: (708) 633-7450, Web Site: www.libertycreativesolutions.com (21)

Liberty Envelope Inc, Paterson, NJ. Tel: (973) 546-5600, FAX: (973) 546-4721 (26)

Liberty Fund Inc, Indianapolis, IN. Tel: (317) 842-0880, Web Site: www.libertyfund.org (1)

Liberty Life Insurance Co, Greenville, SC. Tel: (864) 609-8111, (800) 344-5834 (Mktg), FAX: (864) 609-4411, Web Site: www.libertycorp.com (15)

Liberty Mutual Group, Inc, Boston, MA. Tel: (617) 357-9500, (800) 837-5274, Web Site: www.libertymutual.com (15)

Liberty Orchards Co Inc, Cashmere, WA. Tel: (509) 782-2191, (800) 888-5696, FAX: (509) 782-1487, E-Mail: service@libertyorchards.com, Web Site: www.libertyorchards.com (16)

Liberty Tax Service, Virginia Beach, VA. Tel: (757) 493-8855 X8115 (14)

Liberty Tree Network, Oakland, CA. Tel: (510) 568-6047, (800) 927-8733, FAX: (510) 568-6040, E-Mail: info@liberty-tree.com, Web Site: www.liberty-tree.org (5)

Libertyville Saddle Shop Inc, Libertyville, IL. Tel: (847) 362-0570, FAX: (847) 680-3200, E-Mail: info@saddleshop.com, Web Site: www.saddleshop.com (11)

Libey, Donald, R., Libey-Concordia, Cherry Hill, NJ. Tel: (877) 903-9448, FAX: (856) 885-5068, E-Mail: libey@libey.com, Web Site: www.libey.com (20)

Libey-Concordia, Cherry Hill, NJ. Tel: (877) 903-9448, FAX: (856) 885-5068, E-Mail: libey@libey.com, Web Site: www.libey.com (20)

The Library of America, New York, NY. Tel: (212) 308-3360, (800) 964-5778, FAX: (212) 750-8352, E-Mail: info@loa.org, Web Site: www.loa.org (13)

Licata, Bill, LCH Direct Inc, Waltham, MA. Tel: (978) 664-2900, FAX: (978) 664-4812, E-Mail: info@lchdirect.com, Web Site: www.lchdirect.com (35)

Licensing Industry Merchandisers' Association (LIMA), New York, NY. Tel: (212) 244-1944, FAX: (212) 563-6552, E-Mail: info@licensing.org, Web Site: www.licensing.org (40)

Lichter, Andrew, Bradley Direct, Columbus, GA. Tel: (706) 565-2100, (866) 239-6774, (800) 241-8981, FAX: (706) 565-2132, (888) 224-7455, E-Mail: customerservice@grilllovers.com, Web Site: www.grilllovers.com (8)

Lichter, Leslie, UJA/Federation of New York, New York, NY. Tel: (212) 980-1000, FAX: (212) 785-9321, Web Site: www.ujafedny.org (1)

Liebenson, Sid, Marketing Highway, Deerfield, IL. Tel: (312) 502-3732, E-Mail: info@marketinghighway.com, Web Site: www.marketinghighway.com (20)

Lieber, Mitchell, A., Lieber & Associates, Chicago, IL. Tel: (773) 325-9400, FAX: (773) 325-0621, E-Mail: info@lieberandassociates.com, Web Site: www.lieberandassociates.com (29)

Lieber & Associates, Chicago, IL. Tel: (773) 325-9400, FAX: (773) 325-0621, E-Mail: info@lieberandassociates.com, Web Site: www.lieberandassociates.com (29)

Lieberfarb, Richard, Scan Optics Inc, Manchester, CT. Tel: (860) 645-7878, (800) 745-6001, FAX: (860) 645-7995, E-Mail: info@scanoptics.com, Web Site: www.scanoptics.com (16)

Lieberman, Barry, Advantage Plus Marketing Group, Aliso Viejo, CA. Tel: (714) 573-7300, (800) 432-9466, FAX: (714) 573-7301, E-Mail: info@apmg.com, Web Site: www.apmg.com (30)

Lieberman, David, Dalrada Financial Corp, San Diego, CA. Tel: (858) 427-8716, (877) 325-7232, FAX: (858) 277-3448, E-Mail: inquiries@dalrada.com, Web Site: www.dalrada.com (14)

Lieberman, Gerald, B&G Lieberman Co Inc, Charlotte, NC. Tel: (704) 376-0717, (800) 438-0346, FAX: (800) 248-2696, E-Mail: bgl@bglieberman.com, Web Site: www.bglieberman.com (16)

Lieberman, Gerald, M., Alliance Bernstein, New York, NY. Tel: (212) 969-1000, (800) 962-2134, FAX: (212) 969-2229, Web Site: www.alliancebernstein.com (14)

Lieberman, Larry, B&G Lieberman Co Inc, Charlotte, NC. Tel: (704) 376-0717, (800) 438-0346, FAX: (800) 248-2696, E-Mail: bgl@bglieberman.com, Web Site: www.bglieberman.com (16)

Lieberman, Lenny, Lieberman Productions, San Francisco, CA. Tel: (415) 955-0855, FAX: (415) 955-0822 (32)

Lieberman, Robert, Jay, All-Ways Advertising Co, Bloomfield, NJ. Tel: (973) 338-0700, (800) 255-9291, FAX: (973) 338-1410, Web Site: www.all-waysadvertising.com (33)

Lieberman, Ron, Family Album, Kinzers, PA. Tel: (717) 442-0220, FAX: (717) 442-7904, E-Mail: rarebooks@pobox.com (6)

Lieberman Productions, San Francisco, CA. Tel: (415) 955-0855, FAX: (415) 955-0822 (32)

Liebert Corp, Columbus, OH. Tel: (614) 841-6700, (800) LIEBERT, FAX: (614) 841-6022, Web Site: www.liebert.com (16)

Liebling, Donald, Brant Publications Inc, New York, NY. Tel: (212) 941-2800, FAX: (212) 941-2885, Web Site: www.interviewmagazine.com (17)

Liebowitz, Stuart, Physicians Planning Association Services, Deerfield Beach, FL. Tel: (954) 571-1877, (800) 221-2168, FAX: (954) 571-8582, E-Mail: insurance@assnservices.com, Web Site: www.physiciansplanning.com (16)

Liedel, Christopher, A., National Geographic Society, Washington, DC. Tel: (202) 857-7311, (800) NGS-LINE, FAX: (202) 457-8200, Web Site: www.nationalgeographic.com (17)

Life Extension Foundation, Fort Lauderdale, FL. Tel: (954) 766-8433, (800) 678-8989, FAX: (954) 771-2827, E-Mail: info@lef.org, Web Site: www.lef.org (7)

Life Fitness, Schiller Park, IL. Tel: (847) 288-3300, (800) 735-3867, FAX: (847) 288-3703, E-Mail: webmaster@lifefitness.com, Web Site: www.lifefitness.com (11)

Life Investors Insurance Co of America, Cedar Rapids, IA. Tel: (319) 398-8511, (800) 231-7220, FAX: (319) 369-2188, Web Site: www.lifeinvestors.com (14)

Life Line Screening, Independence, OH. Tel: (216) 581-6556, Web Site: www.lifelinescreening.com (7)

Life-Study Fellowship Foundation Inc, Darien, CT. Tel: (203) 655-1436, FAX: (203) 655-1392, Web Site: www.lifestudyfellowship.com (17)

Life Technologies, Grand Island, NY. Tel: (800) 955-6288, FAX: (800) 331-2286, E-Mail: catalog@lifetech.com, Web Site: www.lifetechnologies.com (9)

Life Works Inc, Hollywood, FL. Tel: (954) 929-8428, (888) 780-9400, FAX: (954) 925-3365, Web Site: www.healthwagon.com (20)

Lifeboat Distribution, Shrewsbury, NJ. Tel: (732) 389-8950, FAX: (732) 389-9227, Web Site: www.programmersparadise.com (16)

LifeLock, Tempe, AZ. Tel: (480) 457-2007, Web Site: www.lifelock.com (16)

LifeScript, Mission Viejo, CA. Tel: (949) 454-0422, Web Site: www.lifescript.com (7)

Lifestyle Change Communications, Kennesaw, GA. Tel: (770) 218-8200, (800) 411-5771, FAX: (770) 218-8211, E-Mail: experts@lifestylechange.com, Web Site: www.lifestylechange.com (24)

The Lifestyle Marketing Corp, Glen Rock, NJ. Tel: (201) 670-7985, FAX: (201) 251-2443 (35)

Lifetime Brands Inc, Garden City, NY. Tel: (516) 683-6000, FAX: (516) 683-6161, E-Mail: postmaster@brands.com, Web Site: www.lifetimebrands.com (8)

Lifetips, Boston, MA. Tel: (617) 886-9001, Web Site: www.lifetips.com (16)

LifeWay Christian Resources, Nashville, TN. Tel: (615) 251-5822, Web Site: www.lifeway.com (1)

Lift Outreach, Richland Hills, TX. Tel: (817) 658-2980 (1)

Lifton, Charles, Contempo Marketing Co, Pompano Beach, FL. Tel: (954) 978-8215, (800) 322-5089, FAX: (954) 978-8217 (23)

Lifynski, Maj Ernest, Centaur Forge LLC, Burlington, WI. Tel: (262) 763-9175, (800) 666-9175, FAX: (262) 763-8350, E-Mail: info@centaurforge.com, Web Site: www.centaurforge.com (9)

Liggett-Stashower Direct, Cleveland, OH. Tel: (216) 348-8500, (800) 877-4573, FAX: (216) 736-8118, E-Mail: mnylander@liggett.com, Web Site: www.liggett.com (35)

Light, Arnold, H., Fire Light Group, White Plains, NY. Tel: (608) 441-3473, E-Mail: mincentive@aol.com, Web Site: www.incentivesmotivate.com (33)

Light, Mark, Sterling Jewelers Inc, Akron, OH. Tel: (330) 668-5000, FAX: (330) 668-5052, E-Mail: webmaster@jewels.com, Web Site: www.sterlingjewelers.com (16)

Light Sources Inc, Virginia Beach, VA. Tel: (757) 424-8636, (800) 882-8834, FAX: (757) 424-6186, E-Mail: lightsources@earthlink.net, Web Site: www.lightsourcesinc.com (16)

Lighthouse List Co, Pompano Beach, FL. Tel: (954) 489-3008, (800) 684-2180, FAX: (954) 489-0850, E-Mail: mtlistdude@aol.com, Web Site: www.lighthouselist.com (16)

Lightman, Steve, Crosstown Traders Inc, Tucson, AZ. Tel: (520) 745-4500 (2)

Ligonier Ministries, Lake Mary, FL. Tel: (407) 333-4244, (800) 435-4343, FAX: (407) 333-4377, Web Site: www.ligonier.org (5)

Liguori Publications, Liguori, MO. Tel: (636) 464-2500, (800) 325-9521, FAX: (800) 325-9526, E-Mail: liguori@liguori.org, Web Site: www.liguori.org (17)

Liguory, Tom, National Pen Corp, San Diego, CA. Tel: (858) 675-3000, FAX: (858) 675-3030, Web Site: www.pens.com (2)

Ligurotis, Nora, TargetCom Inc, Chicago, IL. Tel: (312) 822-1100, FAX: (312) 822-9628, E-Mail: tcomcontact@targetcom.com, Web Site: www.targetcom.com (35)

Lijewski, Carl, Mason Companies Inc, Chippewa Falls, WI. Tel: (715) 723-1871, (800) 826-7030, FAX: (715) 720-4247, Web Site: www.masoncompaniesinc.com (2)

Likoff, Laurie, Facts On File Inc, New York, NY. Tel: (212) 967-8800, (800) 322-8755, FAX: (212) 678-3633, Web Site: www.factsonfile.com (17)

Lile, Katie, Har Court Inc, Orlando, FL. Tel: (407) 345-2000, FAX: (407) 345-1052 (17)

Lilienthal, Brad, Kreg Tool Co, Huxley, IA. Tel: (515) 597-6400, Web Site: www.kregtool.com (16)

Lilienthal, Stephen, CNA, Chicago, IL. Tel: (312) 822-5000, (800) 262-2000, E-Mail: cna_help@cna.com, Web Site: www.cna.com (15)

Lillian Vernon Corp, Colorado Springs, CO. Tel: (757) 427-7923, FAX: (757) 427-7819, E-Mail: publicrelations@lillianvernon.com, Web Site: www.lillianvernon.com (6)

Lillie, James, E., Jarden Corp, Daleville, IN. Tel: (765) 557-3000, (800) 428-8150, FAX: (765) 281-5403, Web Site: www.jarden.com (16)

Lilly, Sam, Learning Resources Institute, Downers Grove, IL. Tel: (630) 963-0398 (20)

Lilly, Scott, Kendall Products/Dri-Dek, Naples, FL. Tel: (239) 643-2244, (800) 348-2398, FAX: (800) 828-4248, E-Mail: info@dri-dek.com, Web Site: www.dri-dek.com (16)

Lilypons Water Gardens, Adamstown, MD. Tel: (301) 874-3763, (800) 999-5459, FAX: (301) 874-2959, Web Site: www.lilypons.com (8)

Lim, Jason, Halogen Response Media, New York, NY. Tel: (212) 468-4000, Web Site: www.halogenresponse.com (31)

Limes, Dale, HALO/Lee Wayne, Sterling, IL. Tel: (815) 632-0980, (866) 840-6401, FAX: (815) 632-6900, E-Mail: moreinfo@leewayne.com, Web Site: www.leewayne.com (16)

The Limited Stores Inc, Columbus, OH. Tel: (614) 415-2000, FAX: (614) 415-2057, Web Site: www.limited.com (2)

LimitedBrands Inc, Reynoldsburg, OH. Tel: (614) 577-5902, FAX: (614) 415-7440, Web Site: www.limitedbrands.com (16)

Lin, John, Everex Computer Systems Inc, Fremont, CA. Tel: (866) 850-8835, (800) 383-7391, FAX: (510) 683-2186, E-Mail: customerservice@everex.com, Web Site: www.everex.com (16)

Lin Terry, Paterson, NJ. Tel: (973) 345-6677, FAX: (973) 345-5551, E-Mail: linterry@aol.com, Web Site: www.linterry.com (6)

Linchitz, Joel, Joel Linchitz Consulting Services/Phone for Success, New York, NY. Tel: (212) 431-6700, FAX: (212) 865-2008, E-Mail: phoneforsuccess@compuserve.com, Web Site: www.callcenter-salestraining.com/index.php (29)

Joel Linchitz Consulting Services/Phone for Success, New York, NY. Tel: (212) 431-6700, FAX: (212) 865-2008, E-Mail: phoneforsuccess@compuserve.com, Web Site: www.callcenter-salestraining.com/index.php (29)

Lincoln Educational Services, West Orange, NJ. Tel: (973) 736-9340 (13)

Lincoln Financial Group, Radnor, PA. Tel: (215) 448-1400, (877) 275-5462, FAX: (215) 448-3962, Web Site: www.lfg.com (15)

Lincoln Park Zoo, Chicago, IL. Tel: (312) 742-2000, FAX: (312) 742-2137, E-Mail: webmaster@lpzoo.com, Web Site: www.lpzoo.com (1)

Lincoln Picture Studio, Dayton, OH. Tel: (937) 439-9633 (38)

Lind, Louise, T., Lindustries Inc, Weston, MA. Tel: (781) 237-8177 (8)

Lind, Willard, H., Lindustries Inc, Weston, MA. Tel: (781) 237-8177 (8)

Lindauer, Jennifer, Citi Cards / Citicorp Credit Services, Long Island City, NY. Tel: (718) 248-5400 (14)

Lindberg, Greg, Business Publishers Inc, Durham, NC. Tel: (919) 281-0474, (800) 274-6737, FAX: (919) 544-3147, Web Site: www.bpinews.com (17)

Lindberg, Greg, Eli Journals, Durham, NC. Tel: (585) 203-5248, (800) 223-8720, FAX: (585) 292-4392, Web Site: www.elijournals.com (16)

Lindeke, Bruce F., Bolind Inc, Boulder, CO. Tel: (303) 443-3142, FAX: (303) 443-9889, Web Site: www.bolind.com (16)

Lindemann, Robert E., Stock Drive Products, New Hyde Park, NY. Tel: (516) 328-3300, FAX: (516) 326-8827, E-Mail: sdp-sisupport@sdp-si.com, Web Site: www.sdp.si.com (5)

Linden, Carmelita, Divine Word Missionaries, Techny, IL. Tel: (847) 412-7233, Web Site: www.svdmissions.org (1)

Linden, Shira, PromoWriting, Trumbull, CT. Tel: (203) 371-0654, E-Mail: shira@promowriting.com, Web Site: www.promowriting.com (35)

Linder, Ryan, Olson & Co, Minneapolis, MN. Tel: (612) 215-9800, FAX: (612) 215-9801, E-Mail: info@oco.com, Web Site: www.oco.com (35)

Linderman, Martha, Playboy Enterprises Inc, Beverly Hills, CA. Tel: (310) 860-1215, Web Site: www.playboyenterprises.com (17)

Lindner, Bill, Center for Professional Development, Tallahassee, FL. Tel: (850) 644-8004, (850) 487-1691, FAX: (850) 644-2589, Web Site: www.Learningforlife.fsu.com (16)

Lindner, James, Mitchell International, San Diego, CA. Tel: (858) 368-7000, FAX: (858) 238-9111, Web Site: www.mitchell.com (17)

Lindquist, Jay D., Haworth College of Business, Kalamazoo, MI. Tel: (616) 387-6062, FAX: (616) 387-5710, E-Mail: jay.lindquist@wmich.edu, Web Site: www.hcob.wmich.edu/mktg (41)

Lindsay, Tillman, Shield Healthcare, Valencia, CA. Tel: (661) 294-4200, (800) 228-7150, FAX: (661) 294-1043, Web Site: www.shieldhealthcare.com (7)

Lindsey, David, DEFENDER Direct Inc, Indianapolis, IN. Tel: (800) 860-0303, Web Site: www.defenderdirect.com (12)

Lindsey, John, L., Thomas Marketing Information Center, New York, NY. Tel: (212) 695-0500, FAX: (212) 290-7362, E-Mail: contact@thomaspublishing.com, Web Site: www.thomaspublishing.com (30)

Lindsey, Suzanna, Sur La Table, Seattle, WA. Tel: (206) 682-7175, FAX: (206) 682-1026 (8)

Lindustries Inc, Weston, MA. Tel: (781) 237-8177 (8)

Lindwall, Jared, The Bender Group, Reno, NV. Tel: (775) 788-8800, (800) 621-9402, FAX: (775) 788-8811, E-Mail: salesinfo@benderwhs.com, Web Site: www.bendergroup.com (28)

Linen, Worth, WLA Inc, New York, NY. Tel: (212) 584-1810 (20)

Linens n' Things, Paramus, NJ. Tel: (973) 778-1300, FAX: (973) 778-0822, (973) 815-2990, Web Site: www.lnt.com (8)

Lines, Corin, AdPack/ITOCHU International Inc, New York, NY. Tel: (212) 818-8000, Web Site: www.adpackusa.com (25)

Linett & Harrison, Union, NJ. Tel: (908) 686-0606, FAX: (908) 686-0623, E-Mail: sharrison@linettandharrison.com, Web Site: www.linettandharrison.com (35)

Ling, Liu, Marshall Cavendish Corp, Tarrytown, NY. Tel: (914) 332-8888, (800) 821-9881, FAX: (914) 332-1888, Web Site: www.marshallcavendish.com (17)

Lingau, Daniel, Crossroads Films, New York, NY. Tel: (212) 647-1300, FAX: (212) 647-9090, Web Site: www.crossroadfilms.com (32)

Linguistic Systems Inc, Cambridge, MA. Tel: (877) 654-5006, FAX: (617) 528-7491, E-Mail: info@linguist.com, Web Site: www.linguist.com (27)

LinguiSystems, East Moline, IL. Tel: (309) 755-2300, (800) 776-4332, FAX: (800) 577-4555, E-Mail: service@linguisystems.com, Web Site: www.linguisystems.com (17)

Linick, Dr Andrew, S., The Author's, Writer's & Information Book/Video Publisher's Advice-Line, Middle Island, NY. Tel: (631) 924-3888, (631) 775-6075, FAX: (631) 924-8555, E-Mail:

andrewlinick@gmail.com; linickgroup@gmail.com, Web Site: andrewlinickdirectmarketing.com; www. asklinick.com (20)

Linick, Dr. Andrew, S., Andrew S Linick PhD-The Copyologist (R), Middle Island, NY. Tel: (631) 924-3888, (631) 775-6075, FAX: (631) 924-8555, E-Mail: andrewlinick@gmail.com; andrew@ asklinick.com, Web Site: www. andrewlinickdirectmarketing.com; www.asklinick. com (39)

Linick, Dr. Andrew, The Linick Group Inc, Middle Island, NY. Tel: (631) 924-3888, E-Mail: linickgroup@gmail.com, Web Site: www. andrewlinickdirectmarketing.com (35)

Andrew S Linick PhD-The Copyologist (R), Middle Island, NY. Tel: (631) 924-3888, (631) 775-6075, FAX: (631) 924-8555, E-Mail: andrewlinick@ gmail.com; andrew@asklinick.com, Web Site: www.andrewlinickdirectmarketing.com; www. asklinick.com (39)

The Linick Group Inc, Middle Island, NY. Tel: (631) 924-3888, E-Mail: linickgroup@gmail.com, Web Site: www.andrewlinickdirectmarketing.com (35)

Link, Nina, Magazine Publishers of America, New York, NY. Tel: (212) 872-3700, FAX: (212) 888-4217, Web Site: www.magazine.org (17)

Link Telemarketing Inc, Excelsior, MN. Tel: (952) 404-1609, FAX: (952) 474-0529, Web Site: www. roimark.com/link (29)

Linkin, Gerald, Linkin Communications, Los Angeles, CA. Tel: (310) 391-1288 (35)

Linkin Communications, Los Angeles, CA. Tel: (310) 391-1288 (35)

Links Magazine, Hilton Head Island, SC. Tel: (843) 842-6200, FAX: (843) 842-6233, Web Site: www. linksmagazine.com (17)

LinkShare Corp, New York, NY. Tel: (646) 654-6000, Web Site: www.linkshare.com (32)

LinkWorth, Lewisville, TX. Tel: (214) 440-3901, Web Site: www.linkworth.com (32)

Linnemann, Mavis, Inside Direct Mail, Philadelphia, PA. Tel: (215) 238-5300, (800) 777-8074, FAX: (215) 238-5412, E-Mail: customerservice@napco. com, Web Site: www.insidedirectmail.com (43)

Linse, Mark, MGM Mailing Lists, South Sandwich, MA. Tel: (508) 539-1300, (800) 660-5322, FAX: (508) 539-0700 (23)

Lintner, Connie, Delmmar Communications, Cameron, MO. Tel: (816) 632-1583, (800) 872-2627, FAX: (816) 632-5107, E-Mail: sales@eradiostore.com, Web Site: www.delmmar.com (16)

Linton, D.B., The Linton Co, Darien, GA. Tel: (912) 638-3538, (800) 841-0200, FAX: (912) 437-3195, E-Mail: cinfo@davientel.net, Web Site: www. lintonlabels.com (34)

The Linton Co, Darien, GA. Tel: (912) 638-3538, (800) 841-0200, FAX: (912) 437-3195, E-Mail: cinfo@davientel.net, Web Site: www.lintonlabels. com (34)

Linville, Larry, The United Methodist Publishing House, Nashville, TN. Tel: (615) 749-6000, (800) 672-1789, FAX: (615) 749-6417, E-Mail: productsandservices@umpublishing.org, Web Site: www.umpublishing.com (17)

Linzer, Daniel, H., Northwestern University, Evanston, IL. Tel: (847) 491-3741, FAX: (847) 491-8406, E-Mail: webmaster@northwestern.edu, Web Site: www.northwestern.edu (41)

Linzer, Howard, Macromark Inc, Brewster, NY. Tel: (845) 230-6300, FAX: (845) 278-0650, E-Mail: david@macromark.com, Web Site: www. macromark.com (23)

Liodice, Robert, Association of National Advertisers Inc, New York, NY. Tel: (212) 697-5950, FAX: (212) 687-7310, Web Site: www.ana.net (40)

Lion Apparel, Dayton, OH. Tel: (937) 898-1949, (800) 548-6614, FAX: (937) 913-5667, Web Site: www. lionapparel.com (2)

Lions Gate Entertainment, New York, NY. Tel: (212) 577-2400, FAX: (212) 962-2872, Web Site: www. liensgatefilms.com (32)

Lions Gate Television Corp, Santa Monica, CA. Tel: (310) 449-9200, FAX: (310) 255-3870, Web Site: www.lionsgate.com (16)

Lion's Share Marketing Group, Inc, Houston, TX. Tel: (713) 686-4252, Web Site: www.lionsshare.com (20)

Lioon, Douglas L., Advanced Medical Nutrition Inc, Pittsburgh, PA. Tel: (412) 494-0100, (800) 879-2664, (800) 437-8888, FAX: (888) 245-4440, Web Site: www.douglaslabs.com (7)

Lipic, Steve, Lipic's Recognition, Saint Louis, MO. Tel: (314) 775-2500, (800) 771-4640, FAX: (314) 775-2501, E-Mail: lipic@lipic.com, Web Site: www.lipics.com (33)

Lipic's Recognition, Saint Louis, MO. Tel: (314) 775-2500, (800) 771-4640, FAX: (314) 775-2501, E-Mail: lipic@lipic.com, Web Site: www.lipics. com (33)

Lipman, Nathaniel, J., The Affinion Group, Franklin, TN. Tel: (610) 933-3645, (800) 251-2148, FAX: (610) 933-7744, Web Site: www.affiniongroup.com (35)

Lipper, Martin, J., RBC Dain Rauscher, Boston, MA. Tel: (617) 725-2000, FAX: (617) 725-1393, Web Site: www.rbcdainrauscher.com (14)

Lippert, Jerry, Nelson-Jameson Inc, Marshfield, WI. Tel: (715) 387-1151, (800) 826-8302, FAX: (715) 387-8746, E-Mail: sales@nelsonjameson.com, Web Site: www.nelsonjameson.com (9)

Lippincott, Williams & Wilkins, Baltimore, MD. Tel: (410) 528-4000, (800) 638-0672, FAX: (410) 528-8597, E-Mail: customerservice@lww.com, Web Site: www.lww.com (17)

Lipske, Donald, E., Del Enterprises, Verona, WI. Tel: (608) 845-6322, (800) 611-8045, FAX: (608) 845-3530, E-Mail: delips@tds.net, Web Site: www. delenterprises.com (33)

Lipsky, Mark, Radio Direct Response, Media, PA. Tel: (610) 892-7300, FAX: (610) 892-1899, E-Mail: info@radiodirect.com, Web Site: www.radiodirect. com (35)

Lipson, David, Peak Impact Inc, Ottawa, ON Canada. Tel: (613) 592-3100, Web Site: www.peakimpact. com (14)

Lipton, E. Trina, E Trina Lipton, New York, NY. Tel: (917) 327-6886, (212) 674-5558, FAX: (212) 674-3523, E-Mail: trinalipton@hotmail.com (37)

Lipton, Shelly, Community Direct, Mountainside, NJ. Tel: (212) 996-8222, FAX: (212) 789-2995, E-Mail: slipton@gocommunitydirect.com (35)

E Trina Lipton, New York, NY. Tel: (917) 327-6886, (212) 674-5558, FAX: (212) 674-3523, E-Mail: trinalipton@hotmail.com (37)

Liquid Focus Direct LLC, Bridgeport, CT. Tel: (203) 635-4382, Web Site: www.liquidfocus.com (32)

Liquori, Dorothy, Women in Direct Marketing International, New York, NY. Tel: (516) 746-6700, FAX: (516) 294-8141, Web Site: www.wdmi.org (40)

Lisicki, George, Veterans of Foreign Wars (VFW) of the US-National Headquarters, Kansas City, MO. Tel: (816) 756-3390, FAX: (816) 968-1149, E-Mail: info@vfw.org, Web Site: www.vfw.org (1)

Lisicki, Thomas, D., The Stash Tea Catalog, Tigard, OR. Tel: (800) 547-1514, FAX: (503) 684-4424, E-Mail: stash@stashtea.com, Web Site: www. stashtea.com (4)

Liska, Tommy, Clampitt Paper Co, Dallas, TX. Tel: (214) 638-3300, FAX: (214) 634-7837, E-Mail: dcrew@clampitt.com, Web Site: www.clampitt.com (16)

Liskey, Keith, Strongwell, Bristol, VA. Tel: (276) 645-8000, FAX: (276) 645-8132, E-Mail: gbarefoot@ strongwell.com, Web Site: www.strongwell.com (9)

Liss, Jeffrey, A Liss & Co Inc, Woodside, NY. Tel: (718) 728-0600, (800) 221-0938, FAX: (718) 728-1227, E-Mail: alissco@aol.com (16)

Liss, Jerold, A Liss & Co Inc, Woodside, NY. Tel: (718) 728-0600, (800) 221-0938, FAX: (718) 728-1227, E-Mail: alissco@aol.com (16)

A Liss & Co Inc, Woodside, NY. Tel: (718) 728-0600, (800) 221-0938, FAX: (718) 728-1227, E-Mail: alissco@aol.com (16)

Nancy Liss, New York, NY. Tel: (646) 418-5000 (20)

Lissan Computing Co Inc, Ridgefield, CT. Tel: (203) 431-8755, FAX: (203) 431-3302, E-Mail: info@ lissan.com, Web Site: www.lissan.com (22)

List Advisor Inc, Farmingdale, NY. Tel: (631) 777-2900, FAX: (631) 777-3050 (23)

List Alliance Inc, Alamo, CA. Tel: (925) 820-3151, E-Mail: info@listalliance.com, Web Site: www. listalliance.com (23)

List America, Washington, DC. Tel: (202) 298-9206, (202) 298-8030, FAX: (202) 244-4999, (202) 244-7294, Web Site: www.mdg.nc.org (23)

The List Authority Inc, Westwood, NJ. Tel: (201) 666-0100 (24)

The List Bank, Evanston, IL. Tel: (847) 864-0550, FAX: (847) 864-0575, E-Mail: catalogmed@aol. com, Web Site: www.thelistbank.com (24)

List Connection Inc, Simpsonville, SC. Tel: (864) 962-0761, Web Site: www.listconnection.net (23)

The List Connection Inc, Mamaroneck, NY. Tel: (914) 381-2010, FAX: (914) 381-2163 (23)

The List Emporium, Parkville, MO. Tel: (816) 505-2111, FAX: (816) 505-2112, E-Mail: listinfo@ listmart.com, Web Site: www.listmart.com (23)

LIST Inc, Danbury, CT. Tel: (914) 765-0700, FAX: (914) 765-0046, E-Mail: info@l-i-s-t.com, Web Site: www.l-i-s-t.com (24)

List Locators & Managers, Overland Park, KS. Tel: (913) 338-5055, (800) 487-8720, FAX: (913) 338-5055 (23)

List Management Center, Hightstown, NJ. Tel: (609) 426-5695, FAX: (609) 426-5096, E-Mail: renee_krug@mcgraw-hill.com, Web Site: www. mcgraw-hill.com (24)

List Management Services Inc, Orlando, FL. Tel: (407) 876-5544, Web Site: www.lmsonline.com (35)

List Marketing Group Inc, Cleveland, OH. Tel: (216) 990-2000, Web Site: www.listmarketinggroup.com (23)

The List Place Inc, Charlotte, NC. Tel: (704) 672-3174, FAX: (704) 676-4755, E-Mail: bryan@ thelistplace.net, Web Site: www.thelistplace.net (23)

List Pro of America, San Diego, CA. Tel: (858) 483-1410, FAX: (858) 270-6669, Web Site: www. swmall.com (23)

List Process Co Inc, New York, NY. Tel: (212) 517-8550, FAX: (212) 517-9728, Web Site: www. listprocesscompany.com (23)

List Service Direct Inc, Leonia, NJ. Tel: (201) 585-1447, (800) 371-5487, FAX: (201) 585-1732, E-Mail: info@listservicedirect.com, Web Site: www.listservicedirect.com (23)

List Services Fundraising, Bethel, CT. Tel: (203) 743-2600, Web Site: www.listservices.com (23)

The List Source Inc, Cherry Hill, NJ. Tel: (856) 795-3344, FAX: (856) 795-9498 (23)

List Strategies Inc, New York, NY. Tel: (212) 767-1000, FAX: (212) 541-4408, E-Mail: joel@ liststrategies.com, Web Site: www.liststrategies. com (23)

List Team, Sherman Oaks, CA. Tel: (818) 986-1166, Web Site: www.listteam.com (23)

ListAbility Inc, Venice, FL. Tel: (866) 446-2055, (800) 626-6500, Web Site: www.listability.com (23)

Listening Library Inc, Random House Audio, New York, NY. Tel: (800) 726-0600, FAX: (800) 454-0606, Web Site: www.randomhouse.com/audio (3)

Lister Butler Inc, New York, NY. Tel: (212) 951-6100, FAX: (212) 481-0230, Web Site: www.listerbutler. com (20)

ListK, Atlanta, GA. Tel: (800) 600-3389, FAX: (800) 878-2489, Web Site: www.listk.com (32)

Listman, Deb, The Franklin Mint, Exton, PA. Tel: (610) 497-4800, (800) THE-MINT, FAX: (610) 497-4956, E-Mail: info@franklinmint.com, Web Site: www.franklinmint.com (16)

Listmasters Direct Mail Services, Bensalem, PA. Tel: (215) 633-8200, (800) 234-5478, FAX: (215) 633-8209, E-Mail: sales@listmastersdirect.com, Web Site: www.listmastersdirect.com (23)

Listrak, Lititz, PA. Tel: (717) 627-4528, Web Site: www.listrak.com (32)

LISTS Inc, Jacksonville, FL. Tel: (904) 733-6106, (800) 805-5478, FAX: (904) 730-7540, Web Site: www.lists-inc.com (23)

Literary Market Place, New Providence, NJ. Tel: (800) 409-4929, FAX: (908) 219-0192, E-Mail: khallard@infotoday.com, Web Site: www.literarymarketplace.com (43)

Lithia Motors Inc, Medford, OR. Tel: (541) 774-7602 (12)

Litho-Web Inc, Etobicoke, ON Canada. Tel: (416) 674-8899, (800) 490-6688, FAX: (416) 674-8537, E-Mail: inquiry@lithoweb.ca, Web Site: www.lithoweb.ca (27)

Litle, Tim, Litle & Co, Lowell, MA. Tel: (978) 275-6500, Web Site: www.litle.com (14)

Litle & Co, Lowell, MA. Tel: (978) 275-6500, Web Site: www.litle.com (14)

Litrides, Lindy, CoreMessagink, Lancaster, PA. Tel: (717) 207-0212, Web Site: www.cormessagink.com (39)

Litt M.D., Andrew, W., New York University Medical Center, New York, NY. Tel: (212) 263-7800, FAX: (212) 263-8426, Web Site: www.med.nyu.edu (1)

Little II, George, F., National Stationery Show, White Plains, NY. Tel: (914) 421-3200, (800) 272-SHOW, FAX: (914) 948-6180, E-Mail: cate_doyle@glmshows.com, Web Site: www.glmshows.com (42)

Little II, George, F., New York International Gift Fair, White Plains, NY. Tel: (914) 421-3200, (800) 272-SHOW, FAX: (914) 948-6180, Web Site: www.nyigf.com (42)

Little, Chris, Successful Farming, Des Moines, IA. Tel: (515) 284-2143, (800) 678-2711, FAX: (515) 284-3127 (17)

Little, John, Blue Cross & Blue Shield of South Carolina, Columbia, SC. Tel: (803) 788-0222, (800) 288-2227, FAX: (803) 736-4516, Web Site: www.bcbssc.com (15)

Little, Michael, D., Christian Broadcasting Network Inc, Virginia Beach, VA. Tel: (757) 226-3542, FAX: (757) 226-2017, Web Site: www.cbn.org (1)

Little, Randy, PFI Western Stores Inc, Springfield, MO. Tel: (417) 889-2668, (800) 222-4734, FAX: (417) 889-7204, E-Mail: pfi.@pfiwestern.com, Web Site: www.pfiwestern.com (2)

Little, Rita, Bed Bath & Beyond, Farmingdale, NY. Tel: (631) 420-7050 (8)

Little, Tony, Health International Corp, Saint Petersburg, FL. Tel: (800) 780-6744, FAX: (727) 595-6456, Web Site: www.tonylittle.com (32)

Little & King Co LLC, Great Neck, NY. Tel: (516) 377-1377 X12, FAX: (212) 575-0739, E-Mail: lkinfo@littleandking.com, Web Site: www.littleandking.com (35)

Arthur D Little Inc, Boston, MA. Tel: (617) 532-9550, FAX: (617) 261-6630, Web Site: www.adlittle-us.com (20)

Littlefield, Gloriane, Harland Clarke Marketing Services, Decatur, GA. Tel: (866) 609-8609, Web Site: www.harlandclarke.com (31)

Littleton, Jeff, Ashrae Learning Institute, Atlanta, GA. Tel: (404) 636-8400, (800) 527-4723, FAX: (404) 321-5478, E-Mail: ashrae@ashrae.org, Web Site: www.ashrae.org (31)

Littleton, Tim, Chefs Catalog, Colorado Springs, CO. Tel: (719) 272-2600, Web Site: www.chefscatalog.com (8)

Littleton Coin Co Inc, Littleton, NH. Tel: (603) 444-5386, FAX: (603) 444-0121, E-Mail: jhennessey@littletoncoin.com, Web Site: www.littletoncoin.com (6)

Litvinoff, Marc, C., Guideline, New York, NY. Tel: (212) 645-4500, (866) GUIDELINE, FAX: (212) 645-7681, Web Site: www.findsvp.com (30)

Litzky, Fred, Catalyst Direct Marketing/DNA, Pompton Lakes, NJ. Tel: (973) 831-4222, FAX: (973) 831-1933, E-Mail: info@catalystdm.com, Web Site: www.catalystdm.com (23)

Liu, David, The Wedding Pages, New York, NY. Tel: (212) 219-8555, (800) 843-4983, FAX: (212) 219-1929, Web Site: www.theknot.com (16)

Live Design, New York, NY. Tel: (212) 204-4268, FAX: (212) 204-4291, Web Site: livedesignonline.com (17)

Live Nation, Beverly Hills, CA. Tel: (310) 598-4100, Web Site: www.livenation.com (19)

Lively, Mike, Direct Sports Supply, Pearisburg, VA. Tel: (540) 921-1243, (800) 456-0072, FAX: (540) 921-1475, Web Site: www.directsports.com (11)

LiveOps Inc, Santa Clara, CA. Tel: (408) 844-2400, Web Site: www.liveops.com (29)

Liveris, Andrew, Dow Chemical USA, Midland, MI. Tel: (989) 636-1000, (800) 447-4369, FAX: (989) 832-1465, E-Mail: jadams@dow.com, Web Site: www.dow.com (16)

Livermore, Arnold, Blue Cross & Blue Shield of Florida, Jacksonville, FL. Tel: (904) 791-6111, (800) 477-3736, FAX: (904) 905-6638, E-Mail: katie.magee@bcbsfl.com, Web Site: www.bcbsfl.com (15)

Livernoche, Craig, DineWise, Farmingdale, NY. Tel: (631) 694-1111, (800) 749-1170, FAX: (631) 694-4064, E-Mail: info@dinewise.com, Web Site: www.dinewise.com (4)

Livingston Jr., Fin, Finley Products Inc, Lancaster, PA. Tel: (717) 735-8200, (888) 626-5301, FAX: (717) 735-8210, E-Mail: fininfo@finleyproducts.com, Web Site: www.2X4basics.com (16)

Livingston, Howard, Finley Products Inc, Lancaster, PA. Tel: (717) 735-8200, (888) 626-5301, FAX: (717) 735-8210, E-Mail: fininfo@finleyproducts.com, Web Site: www.2X4basics.com (16)

Lizama, George, Production Solutions, Vienna, VA. Tel: (703) 734-5700 (20)

Lizotte, Mike, American Meadows Inc & Vermont Wild Flowers Farm, Williston, VT. Tel: (802) 985-9455, (877) 309-7333, FAX: (802) 985-9268, E-Mail: erin@americanmeadows.com, Web Site: www.americanmeadows.com (8)

Lladro Dolz, Jose, Lladro USA, Moonachie, NJ. Tel: (201) 807-1177, (800) 634-9088, FAX: (201) 807-1168, E-Mail: customer-services@us.lladro.com, Web Site: www.lladro.com (16)

Lladro USA, Moonachie, NJ. Tel: (201) 807-1177, (800) 634-9088, FAX: (201) 807-1168, E-Mail: customer-services@us.lladro.com, Web Site: www.lladro.com (16)

Llewelin, Charlie, Texas Monthly, Austin, TX. Tel: (512) 320-6900, (800) 759-2000, FAX: (512) 476-9007, E-Mail: info@texasmonthly.com, Web Site: www.texasmonthly.com (17)

Llewellyn Publications, Woodbury, MN. Tel: (651) 291-1970, (800) 843-6666, FAX: (651) 291-1908, Web Site: www.llewellyn.com (17)

Llorens, John, Arch Telecom Inc, Austin, TX. Tel: (512) 492-0735, (800) 890-7575, FAX: (512) 495-7101, Web Site: www.archtelecom.com (16)

Lloyd, Dan, Frontier Natural Products Co-op, Norway, IA. Tel: (319) 227-7996, (800) 669-3275, FAX: (319) 227-7966, (800) 717-4372, E-Mail: info@frontiercoop.com, Web Site: www.frontiercoop.com (7)

Lloyd, Larry, Innovative Industries Inc, Carthage, MO. Tel: (417) 358-6891, (800) 344-7467, FAX: (417) 358-1849, E-Mail: info@innovativeindustries.com, Web Site: www.innovativeindustries.com (28)

Lloyd, Marie, Sauve, Stephen Thomas, Toronto, ON. Tel: (416) 690-8801, FAX: (416) 690-7256, E-Mail: mail@stephenthomas.ca, Web Site: www.stephenthomas.ca (1)

Lloyd, Nancy, Day Runner Direct, Sidney, NY. Tel: (800) 643-9923, FAX: (800) 643-9927, Web Site: www.dayrunner.com (10)

Lloyd, Steve, Direct Marketing News, Markham, ON. Tel: (905) 201-6600, (800) 668-1838, FAX: (905) 201-6601, E-Mail: home@dmn.ca, Web Site: www.dmn.ca (43)

Lloyd, Tracie, KV Vet Supply Co, Inc, David City, NE. Tel: (402) 367-6047, Web Site: www.kvvet.com (5)

Lloyd-Martin, Heather, SuccessWorks Search Marketing Inc, West Linn, OR. Tel: (503) 922-3627, Web Site: www.seocopywriting.com (32)

Lo, Jeffrey, Unicom Electric Inc, Walnut, CA. Tel: (626) 964-7873, (800) 346-6668, FAX: (626) 964-7880, E-Mail: info@unicomlink.com, Web Site: www.unicomlink.com (16)

LO-AD Communications, Pasadena, CA. Tel: (626) 304-7750, FAX: (626) 304-2716, Web Site: www.lo-ad.com (16)

Lo Giudice, Carolyn, LinguiSystems, East Moline, IL. Tel: (309) 755-2300, (800) 776-4332, FAX: (800) 577-4555, E-Mail: service@linguisystems.com, Web Site: www.linguisystems.com (17)

Lo Ink Specialties, Kennebunkport, ME. Tel: (207) 967-9110, (800) 777-6471, FAX: (800) 895-6465, E-Mail: rwatson@loink.com, Web Site: www.loink.com (16)

Lobascio, Frank, Herbach & Rademan Co, Moorestown, NJ. Tel: (856) 802-0422, (800) 848-8001, FAX: (856) 802-0465, E-Mail: sales@herbach.com, Web Site: www.herbach.com (9)

Lobeck, William, Alamo Rent A Car, Tulsa, OK. Tel: (918) 401-6000, Web Site: www.alamo.com (16)

Lobel, Leonard, Government Data Publications Inc, Washington, DC. Tel: (718) 627-0819, (800) 275-4688, FAX: (718) 998-5960, E-Mail: gdp@govdata.com, Web Site: www.govdata.com (17)

Lobel, Siegfried, Government Data Publications Inc, Washington, DC. Tel: (718) 627-0819, (800) 275-4688, FAX: (718) 998-5960, E-Mail: gdp@govdata.com, Web Site: www.govdata.com (17)

Local.com, Irvine, CA. Tel: (949) 784-0800, Web Site: www.local.com (32)

Local Government Federal Credit Union, Raleigh, NC. Tel: (919) 755-0534, Web Site: www.lgfcu.org (14)

Location Sound Corp, North Hollywood, CA. Tel: (818) 980-9891, (800) 228-4429, FAX: (818) 980-9911, E-Mail: information@locationsound.com, Web Site: www.locationsound.com (3)

Location3 Media, Denver, CO. Tel: (877) 462-9764, Web Site: www.Location3.com (32)

Lockard, Pam, DMN3, Houston, TX. Tel: (713) 868-3000, (800) 625-8320, FAX: (713) 868-1388, E-Mail: contact@dmn3.com, Web Site: www.dmn3.com (35)

Lockard & Wechsler, Irvington, NY. Tel: (914) 591-6600 (35)

Lockhart Industries Inc, Dallas, TX. Tel: (214) 348-1422, Web Site: www.lockhartadvantage.com (9)

Lockheed Martin Corp, Bethesda, MD. Tel: (301) 897-6000 (16)

Lockwood, Lisa, Marketing Research Association, Washington, DC. Tel: (860) 682-1000, FAX: (860) 682-1010, E-Mail: email@mra-net.org, Web Site: www.mra-net.org (40)

Locreille, Daniela, Hobsons, Cincinnati, OH. Tel: (513) 985-4186, Web Site: www.hobsons.com (16)

Loctite Corp, Rocky Hill, CT. Tel: (860) 571-5100, (800) LOCTITE, (800) 562-8483, FAX: (860) 571-5465, Web Site: www.loctite.com (16)

Loden, Jim, Comp USA, Inc, Miami, FL. Tel: (972) 982-4000, (800) COMP-USA, FAX: (972) 982-4030, Web Site: www.compusa.com (3)

Lodewick, Therese, Integrated Marketing Technology Inc, San Francisco, CA. Tel: (415) 699-2280, FAX: (917) 591-5333, E-Mail: information@imtnetwork. com, Web Site: www.imtnetwork.com (22)

Loeb, Michael, Synapse Group Inc, Stamford, CT. Tel: (203) 595-8255, FAX: (203) 329-8237, E-Mail: webmaster@synapsemail.com, Web Site: www. synapsegroupinc.com (18)

Loeb, Richard, Laven & Loeb Inc, Beachwood, OH. Tel: (623) 217-2101, (216) 291-3483, E-Mail: alaven@lavenandloeb.com; vtaylor@lavenandloeb. com, Web Site: www.lavenandloeb.com (20)

Loeb & Loeb Inc, New York, NY. Tel: (212) 407-4000, Web Site: www.loeb.com (20)

Ben Loeb Inc, Fairfield, NJ. Tel: (973) 882-9022, (800) 854-8275, FAX: (973) 882-8647, Web Site: www.bsloeb.com (33)

Loeding, Deborah, V., The HW Wilson Co, Bronx, NY. Tel: (718) 588-8400, (800) 367-6770, FAX: (800) 590-1617, E-Mail: custserv@hwwilson.com, Web Site: www.hwwilson.com (17)

Loeffler, Mary, AllMedia Inc, Plano, TX. Tel: (469) 467-9100, FAX: (214) 291-5431, E-Mail: lmcclendon@allmediainc.com, Web Site: www. allmediainc.com (23)

Loeffler, Mary, The Granger Collection, New York, NY. Tel: (212) 447-1789, FAX: (212) 447-1492, Web Site: www.granger.com (38)

Loehmann's, Bronx, NY. Tel: (718) 409-2000, Web Site: www.loehmanns.com (2)

Loews Hotels, New York, NY. Tel: (212) 521-2000, (866) 563-9792, FAX: (212) 545-2714, Web Site: www.loewshotels.com (19)

Loflin, Stephen, National Society of Collegiate Scholars, Washington, DC. Tel: (202) 265-9000, Web Site: www.nscs.org (1)

Lofquist, John, J, Take 5 Solutions LLC, Boca Raton, FL. Tel: (561) 819-5555, (866) 861-8862, FAX: (561) 819-0245, E-Mail: sales@take5s.com, Web Site: www.take5solutions.com (30)

Logan, Barbara, Hammock Publishing Inc, Nashville, TN. Tel: (615) 690-3400, FAX: (615) 690-3401, E-Mail: info@hammock.com, Web Site: www. hammock.com (17)

Logan, Denise, White Mane Publishing Co Inc, Shippensburg, PA. Tel: (717) 532-2237, (888) 948-6263, FAX: (717) 532-6110, E-Mail: marketing@ whitemane.com, Web Site: www.whitemane.com (17)

LogEtronics Corp, Sparta, NJ. Tel: (703) 912-7745, FAX: (703) 912-7610, Web Site: www.logetronics. com (34)

Loggia, Joe, Advanstar Communications Inc, North Olmsted, OH. Tel: (440) 243-8100, (800) 225-4569, FAX: (440) 891-2740, E-Mail: info@ advanstar.com, Web Site: www.advanstarlists.com (17)

Logical Computer Selections, Short Hills, NJ. Tel: (212) 949-2290, (800) 949-2701, FAX: (212) 697-5786, E-Mail: info@logicomputer.com, Web Site: www.logicomputer.com (16)

Logicnology Inc, Sunrise, FL. Tel: (954) 851-1200, FAX: (954) 846-8552 (22)

Lohkemper, Mark, CAIG Laboratories Inc, Poway, CA. Tel: (858) 486-8388, FAX: (858) 486-8398, E-Mail: caig123@caig.com, Web Site: www.caig. com (9)

Lohner, Mike, Home Interiors & Gifts Inc, Carrollton, TX. Tel: (972) 695-1000, FAX: (972) 695-1112 (16)

Loizzo, Larry, AW Direct Inc, Madison, WI. Tel: (860) 828-7800, (800) 243-3194, FAX: (800) 828-9678, E-Mail: contactus@awdirect.com, Web Site: www.awdirect.com (12)

Loizzo, Larry, Lab Safety Supply Inc, Janesville, WI. Tel: (608) 754-2345, (800) 356-2855, FAX: (800) 543-9910, Web Site: www.labsafety.com (17)

Lojacono, Joseph, Valmark Associates LLC, Buffalo, NY. Tel: (716) 893-1494, Web Site: www. valmarkassociates.com (35)

Loken, Ted, Sight Marketing, Minneapolis, MN. Tel: (651) 379-4059, Web Site: www.sightmarketing. com (30)

Lokis, Marianna, Adirondack Direct, Long Island City, NY. Tel: (718) 932-4003, (800) 221-2444, FAX: (800) 477-1330, E-Mail: info@adirondackdirect. com, Web Site: www.adirondackdirect.com (10)

Lombard, Gary, Woodcraft Supply Corp LLC, Parkersburg, WV. Tel: (304) 422-5412, (800) 344-3348, FAX: (304) 422-5417, Web Site: www.woodcraft. com (9)

Lombard, John, Bowe Bell & Howell, Durham, NC. Tel: (919) 767-6400, (800) 220-3030, E-Mail: marketing@bowebellhowell.com, Web Site: www. bowebellhowell.com (34)

Lombardi, Michael, Lombardi Publishing Corp, Vaughan, ON Canada. Tel: (905) 760-9929, Web Site: www.lombardipublishing.com (17)

Lombardi Publishing Corp, Vaughan, ON Canada. Tel: (905) 760-9929, Web Site: www. lombardipublishing.com (17)

Lombardo, Anthony, A., E-Z-EM Inc, Melville, NY. Tel: (516) 333-8230, (800) 544-4624, FAX: (516) 333-8278, E-Mail: webmaster@ezem.com, Web Site: www.ezem.com (7)

Lombardo, Doug, ThinkDirect Marketing Group, Largo, FL. Tel: (727) 369-2700, E-Mail: info@ tdmg.com, Web Site: www.tdmg.com (28)

Lombardo, Katherine, Kurt Salmon Associates Inc, Atlanta, GA. Tel: (404) 892-0321, FAX: (404) 898-9590, E-Mail: infoksaweb@kurtsalmon.com, Web Site: www.kurtsalmon.com (20)

Lombardo, Philip, J., National Association Broadcasters Annual Conference & Expo, Washington, DC. Tel: (202) 429-5300, (800) 622-3976, FAX: (202) 429-4199, E-Mail: nab@nab.org, Web Site: www. nab.org (42)

Lombari, Dean, Los Angeles Kings, Los Angeles, CA. Tel: (213) 742-7100, (888) KINGS-LA, FAX: (213) 742-7296, Web Site: kings.nhl.com (16)

London, Jennifer, SPSS Inc, Chicago, IL. Tel: (312) 651-3000, (800) 543-2185, FAX: (312) 651-3690, E-Mail: sales@spss.com, Web Site: www.spss.com (22)

Lone Star Web Inc, Dallas, TX. Tel: (214) 443-2200, FAX: (214) 630-4364, E-Mail: jerry@lonestarweb. com, Web Site: www.lonestarweb.com (27)

Lonergan, Daniel, L6 Holdings Corp, Duluth, GA. Tel: (678) 957-0511 (14)

Lonergan, Pat, Newmark Laboratories, Edison, NJ. Tel: (732) 417-1870, (800) 338-8079, FAX: (732) 225-0066, E-Mail: newmark@injersey.com (7)

Long, Alecia, Louisiana State Museum, New Orleans, LA. Tel: (504) 568-6968, (800) 568-6968, FAX: (504) 568-4995, Web Site: www.lsm.crt.state.la.us (1)

Long, David, H., Liberty Mutual Group, Inc, Boston, MA. Tel: (617) 357-9500, (800) 837-5274, Web Site: www.libertymutual.com (15)

Long, Emily, Net-Results, Golden, CO. Tel: (303) 771-2552, Web Site: www.net-results.com (32)

Long, Erik, Pfaelzer Brothers, Maumee, OH. Tel: (419) 893-7611, (800) 345-9290, FAX: (419) 893-0164, Web Site: www.phaelzerbrothers.com (16)

Long, Erik, Pinnacle Orchards, Maumee, OH. Tel: (419) 893-7611, (800) 442-5671, FAX: (419) 893-0164, Web Site: www.pinnacleorchards.com (4)

Long, Ginny, Moen Inc, North Olmsted, OH. Tel: (440) 962-2000, Web Site: www.moen.com (16)

Long, Jay, Nordstrom Inc, Seattle, WA. Tel: (206) 303-2301, FAX: (206) 373-3198 (2)

Long, Jeffrey, T., Sigma Micro LLC, Indianapolis, IN. Tel: (317) 631-0907, (800) 383-4421, FAX: (317) 631-6585, Web Site: www.sigma-micro.com (21)

Long, Jill, Felco Printing & Mailing, Kansas City, MO. Tel: (816) 421-5164, (800) 467-0805, FAX: (816) 421-1607, E-Mail: felco@felco.net, Web Site: www.felco.net (27)

Long, Joffrey, Joffrey Long Consultants, Granada Hills, CA. Tel: (818) 635-1777, Web Site: www. southwestbancorp.com (20)

Long, Joffrey, Southwest Consultants, Granada Hills, CA. Tel: (818) 635-1777, Web Site: www. southwestbancorp.com (20)

Long, Larry, CPM Delta 1, Inc, Dallas, TX. Tel: (214) 349-6886, (800) 627-0252, FAX: (214) 503-1557, Web Site: www.cpmdelta1.com (11)

Long, Laurie, Creative Teaching Associates, Clovis, CA. Tel: (559) 291-6626, (800) 767-4282, FAX: (559) 291-2953, Web Site: www.mastercta.com (16)

Long, Paul, Kappa Studios, Burbank, CA. Tel: (818) 843-3400, FAX: (818) 559-2418, E-Mail: info@ kappastudios.com, Web Site: www.kappastudios. com (32)

Long, Peter, E., MCH Strategic Data, Sweet Springs, MO. Tel: (660) 335-6373, (800) 776-6373, FAX: (660) 335-4157, E-Mail: tonyab@mchdata.com, Web Site: www.mchdata.com (23)

Long, Richard, USG Corp, Chicago, IL. Tel: (312) 436-4000, (800) 621-9622, FAX: (312) 672-4093, Web Site: www.usg.com (34)

Long, Ron, Pinkerton Security & Investigation Services, Parsippany, NJ. Tel: (973) 397-2276, (800) 724-1616, FAX: (973) 397-2491, Web Site: www. ci-pinkerton.com (16)

Long, Roy, Long's Electronics Inc, Irondale, AL. Tel: (205) 956-6767, (800) 633-3410, FAX: (800) 633-2530, E-Mail: info@longselectronics.com, Web Site: www.longselectronics.com (3)

Long, Tim, Laminex Inc, Fort Mill, SC. Tel: (704) 679-4170, (800) 438-8850, FAX: (704) 679-8453, Web Site: www.laminex.com (16)

Long, Tom, MillerCoors LLC, Chicago, IL. Tel: (800) 645-5376, Web Site: www.millercoors.com (4)

Long, Wendy, Da-Lite Screen Co Inc, Warsaw, IN. Tel: (574) 267-8101, (800) 622-3737, FAX: (574) 267-7804, E-Mail: info@da-lite.com, Web Site: www.da-lite.com (16)

Long & Foster Insurance, Chantilly, VA. Tel: (703) 278-1426 (15)

Longevity Network Ltd, Henderson, NV. Tel: (702) 454-7000, (800) 242-1000, FAX: (702) 435-4786, Web Site: www.longevitynetwork.com (7)

Longevity Pure Medicine, Palm Springs, CA. Tel: (800) 327-5519, FAX: (760) 329-3651, E-Mail: info@longetivtypuremedicine.com, Web Site: www.longevitypuremedicine.com (7)

Longley, Steve, TPG Direct Inc, Philadelphia, PA. Tel: (215) 592-8303, Web Site: www.tpgadvertising. com (35)

Longo, Al, Publicity Inc, Mansfield, MA. Tel: (617) 367-3555, FAX: (617) 367-3557 (35)

Longo, Anthony, Rainbow Art Glass, Wall, NJ. Tel: (732) 681-6003, (800) 526-2356, FAX: (732) 681-4984, E-Mail: info@rainbowartglass.com, Web Site: www.rainbowartglass.com (16)

Longo, Charles M., Rainbow Art Glass, Wall, NJ. Tel: (732) 681-6003, (800) 526-2356, FAX: (732) 681-4984, E-Mail: info@rainbowartglass.com, Web Site: www.rainbowartglass.com (16)

Long's Electronics Inc, Irondale, AL. Tel: (205) 956-6767, (800) 633-3410, FAX: (800) 633-2530, E-Mail: info@longselectronics.com, Web Site: www.longselectronics.com (3)

Longseth, Ann, Veridian Credit Union, Waterloo, IA. Tel: (319) 236-5692, (800) 235-3228, FAX: (319) 833-1185, E-Mail: sarahma@veridiancu.org, Web Site: www.veridiancu.org (1)

Longsworth, Kathy, Phoenix Learning Group Inc, Maryland Heights, MO. Tel: (314) 569-0211, (800) 221-1274, FAX: (314) 569-2834, E-Mail: dealersales@phoenixlearninggroup.com, Web Site: www.phoenixlearninggroup.com (16)

Longview Fibre Co, Longview, WA. Tel: (360) 425-1550, FAX: (360) 230-5135, E-Mail: info@ longviewfibre.com, Web Site: www.longfibre.com (25)

Longwell, Mark, Carino Nurseries, Indiana, PA. Tel: (800) 223-7075, FAX: (724) 463-3050, E-Mail: carino@carinonurseries.com, Web Site: www.carinonurseries.com (8)

Lonis, Diane, Crate & Barrel, Northbrook, IL. Tel: (847) 272-2888, Web Site: www.crateandbarrell.com (8)

Lonsdale, Marty, World Vision Inc, Federal Way, WA. Tel: (253) 815-1000, (888) 511-6548, FAX: (253) 815-3140, E-Mail: info@worldvision.org, Web Site: www.worldvision.org (1)

Loomis, Daniel, Crystek Corp, Fort Myers, FL. Tel: (239) 561-3311, (800) 237-3061, FAX: (239) 561-1025, E-Mail: sales@crystek.com, Web Site: www.crystek.com (9)

Loosbrock, Lou, Longview Fibre Co, Longview, WA. Tel: (360) 425-1550, FAX: (360) 230-5135, E-Mail: info@longviewfibre.com, Web Site: www.longfibre.com (25)

LoParco, Melissa, A., Catalyst Marketing Communications Inc, Stamford, CT. Tel: (203) 348-7541, FAX: (203) 348-5688, E-Mail: b2b@catalystmc.com, Web Site: www.catalystmc.com (35)

Lopes, Philip, MPBS Industries, Los Angeles, CA. Tel: (323) 268-8514, (800) 421-6265, FAX: (323) 268-6305, Web Site: www.mpbs.com (16)

Lopez, Adelmo S., Blair Corp, Warren, PA. Tel: (814) 723-3600, (800) 458-6057, FAX: (814) 726-6123, E-Mail: blair@blair.com, Web Site: www.blair.com (2)

Lopez, Alexander, Open Systems Services, Miami, FL. Tel: (305) 541-1970 (20)

Lopez, Elisa, Avis World Headquarters, Parsippany, NJ. Tel: (973) 496-3500, Web Site: www.avis.com (19)

Lopez, Mary, T., Integrated Advertising Inc, Jacksonville, FL. Tel: (904) 296-1700, E-Mail: mary@integratedadvertising.com (35)

Lopez, William, Xpectrum Marketing Group, San Diego, CA. Tel: (858) 277-0079, FAX: (858) 277-0076, E-Mail: info@xpectrummg.com, Web Site: www.xpectrummg.com (35)

Lopez, Yolanda, GenerH, Inc, Torrance, CA. Tel: (888) 312-3443, E-Mail: info@generh.com, Web Site: www.generh.com (21)

Lopez Negrete, Alex, Lopez Negrete Communications, Houston, TX. Tel: (713) 877-8777, FAX: (713) 877-8796, E-Mail: LNCmailbox@lopeznegrete.com, Web Site: www.lopeznegrete.com (35)

Lopez Negrete Communications, Houston, TX. Tel: (713) 877-8777, FAX: (713) 877-8796, E-Mail: LNCmailbox@lopeznegrete.com, Web Site: www.lopeznegrete.com (35)

Lopez-Cepero, Lianne, Response Mine Interactive, Atlanta, GA. Tel: (404) 233-0370, Web Site: www.responsemine.com (35)

Loporto, Santo, AXA Equitable, New York, NY. Tel: (212) 554-1234, (212) 314-2956, Web Site: www.axaonline.com (15)

Loppnow, Donald, M., Eastern Michigan University, Ypsilanti, MI. Tel: (734) 487-1849, FAX: (734) 484-1151, Web Site: www.emich.edu (16)

LoPresti, Michael, TNF, Toronto, ON Canada. Tel: (416) 924-5751, FAX: (416) 923-7085, Web Site: www.tnf-cf.com (30)

Lorczak, Margaret, US News & World Report, New York, NY. Tel: (212) 916-7360, FAX: (212) 643-7842, Web Site: www.usnews.com (17)

Lord, Albert, L., SLM Corp, Reston, VA. Tel: (703) 810-3000, FAX: (703) 984-5042, Web Site: www.salliemae.com (16)

LoRe, Linda, Frederick's of Hollywood Group Inc, Los Angeles, CA. Tel: (323) 466-5151, (800) 323-9525, FAX: (323) 464-5149, Web Site: www.fredericks.com (2)

Lore, Marc, Diapers.com, Jersey City, NJ. Tel: (800) 342-7377, Web Site: www.diapers.com (5)

Lorenz, Gary, Cenveo Color Art Inc, Eureka, MO. Tel: (314) 966-2000, FAX: (314) 966-4725, E-Mail: scott.turner@cenveo.com, Web Site: www.colorart.com (27)

Lorenzen, Andreas, Stibo Systems, Kennesaw, GA. Tel: (770) 425-3282, Web Site: www.stibocatalog.com (22)

Lorex Inc, Elk River, MN. Tel: (763) 441-0055, Web Site: www.lorexinc.com (35)

Lorillard Tobacco Co, Greensboro, NC. Tel: (336) 335-7000, (888) 818-3304, FAX: (336) 373-6917, E-Mail: externalaffairs@lorrilard.com, Web Site: www.lorillard.net (16)

Lorman Education Services, Eau Claire, WI. Tel: (715) 833-3940 (1)

Lorton Data Inc, Arden Hills, MN. Tel: (651) 203-8200, FAX: (612) 362-0299, Web Site: www.lortondata.com (22)

Lortz Direct Marketing Inc, Omaha, NE. Tel: (800) 366-7686, Web Site: www.lortzdirect.com (35)

The Los Angeles Convention & Visitors Bureau, Los Angeles, CA. Tel: (213) 624-7300, (800) 366-6116, FAX: (213) 627-9746, Web Site: discoverlosangeles.com (19)

Los Angeles Kings, Los Angeles, CA. Tel: (213) 742-7100, (888) KINGS-LA, FAX: (213) 742-7296, Web Site: kings.nhl.com (16)

The Los Angeles Lakers Inc, El Segundo, CA. Tel: (310) 426-6000, FAX: (310) 426-6115, E-Mail: vlawlor@la-lakers.com, Web Site: www.nba.com/lakers (11)

Los Angeles Times, Los Angeles, CA. Tel: (213) 237-5000, (800) 528-4637, FAX: (213) 237-7679, E-Mail: rob.barrett@latimes.com, Web Site: www.latimes.com (31)

Losee, Kendra, National University, La Jolla, CA. Tel: (800) 628-8648, Web Site: www.nu.edu (1)

Lotame Solutions, Columbia, MD. Tel: (410) 379-2195, Web Site: www.lotame.com (22)

Lotan, Noam, MRV Communications, Chatsworth, CA. Tel: (818) 773-0900, FAX: (818) 773-0906, Web Site: www.mrv.com (3)

Loth, Susan, M., Disabled American Veterans, Cincinnati, OH. Tel: (859) 441-7300, FAX: (859) 442-2084, E-Mail: feedback@davmail.org, Web Site: www.dav.org (1)

Lothman, Martin, Four Corners Direct Inc, Sarasota, FL. Tel: (941) 364-8585 (16)

Lotions & Lace, Riverside, CA. Tel: (909) 686-5223, FAX: (909) 686-5765, E-Mail: linda@ez-access.com, Web Site: www.sexyvideos.com (2)

LOTSolutions, Jacksonville, FL. Tel: (904) 350-9660, Web Site: www.lotsolutions.com (14)

Lott, Edward, ABC Clio, Santa Barbara, CA. Tel: (805) 968-1911, FAX: (805) 685-9685, E-Mail: elott@abc/clio.com, Web Site: www.abc-clio.com (17)

Lotti, Michael, Business Marketing Association, Naperville, IL. Tel: (630) 544-5054, FAX: (630) 544-5055, E-Mail: info@marketing.org, Web Site: www.marketing.org (40)

Lotti, Michael, Marketing News, Chicago, IL. Tel: (312) 542-9000, (800) 262-1150, FAX: (312) 542-9001, E-Mail: news@ama.org, Web Site: www.ama.org (43)

Loucks, Grant, Alan Gordon Enterprises, Hollywood, CA. Tel: (323) 466-3561, FAX: (323) 871-2193, E-Mail: info@alangordon.com, Web Site: www.alangordon.com (32)

Louderback, John, JLG Industries Inc, McConnellsburg, PA. Tel: (717) 485-5161, (877) JLG-SELL, FAX: (717) 485-6417, E-Mail: comments@jlg.com, Web Site: www.jlg.com (16)

Loughran, Judy, Da-Lite Screen Co Inc, Warsaw, IN. Tel: (574) 267-8101, (800) 622-3737, FAX: (574) 267-7804, E-Mail: info@da-lite.com, Web Site: www.da-lite.com (16)

Louisiana Nursery, Opelousas, LA. Tel: (337) 948-3696, FAX: (337) 942-6404, Web Site: www.dvrionursery.com (8)

Louisiana State Museum, New Orleans, LA. Tel: (504) 568-6968, (800) 568-6968, FAX: (504) 568-4995, Web Site: www.lsm.crt.state.la.us (1)

Louisville Direct Marketing Association, Louisville, KY. Tel: (888) 392-1941, E-Mail: ldmacontact@ldma.org, Web Site: www.ldma.org (40)

Lounsbury, Jon, B., Play Fair Toys, Boulder, CO. Tel: (303) 444-7502, (800) 824-7255, FAX: (303) 440-3393, E-Mail: service@playfairtoys.com, Web Site: www.playfairtoys.com (11)

Lounsbury, Susan S., Play Fair Toys, Boulder, CO. Tel: (303) 444-7502, (800) 824-7255, FAX: (303) 440-3393, E-Mail: service@playfairtoys.com, Web Site: www.playfairtoys.com (11)

Loury, John, Advanced Marketing Direct, Buffalo, NY. Tel: (800) 696-7567, Web Site: www.amdirect.com (28)

Love, Christopher, E&D Web Printing Inc, Rochelle, IL. Tel: (708) 656-6600, (800) 323-5733, FAX: (708) 656-8390, E-Mail: info@eanddweb.com, Web Site: www.eanddweb.com (27)

Love, Kathi, Mediamark Research Inc, New York, NY. Tel: (212) 884-9200, (800) 310-3305, FAX: (212) 884-9339, Web Site: www.mediamark.com (30)

Love, Mike, Love Envelopes Inc, Dallas, TX. Tel: (214) 637-5900, (800) 569-5683, FAX: (214) 951-0469, E-Mail: sales.dallas@loveenvelopes.com, Web Site: www.loveenvelopes.com (26)

Love Envelopes Inc, Dallas, TX. Tel: (214) 637-5900, (800) 569-5683, FAX: (214) 951-0469, E-Mail: sales.dallas@loveenvelopes.com, Web Site: www.loveenvelopes.com (26)

Love To Learn Inc, Salem, UT. Tel: (801) 423-2009, (888) 771-1034, FAX: (801) 423-9188, E-Mail: customerservice@lovetolearn.net, Web Site: www.lovetolearn.net (5)

Lovejoy, Scott, Renaissance Greeting Cards Inc, Springvale, ME. Tel: (207) 324-4153, (800) 688-9998, FAX: (207) 324-9564, E-Mail: rencards@rencards.com (5)

Lovelace-Young, Kim, Missouri Landscape & Nursery Association, Bowling Green, MO. Tel: (636) 542-1234, E-Mail: admin@mlng.org, Web Site: www.mlna.org (1)

Loveless, Joshua, Cancer Fund of America Inc, Knoxville, TN. Tel: (865) 938-5281, (800) 578-5284, FAX: (865) 938-2968, Web Site: www.cfoa.org (1)

Lovelets, Bobby, Greater Fort Worth Builders Association, Fort Worth, TX. Tel: (817) 284-3566, FAX: (817) 284-6465, E-Mail: info@fortworthbuilders.org, Web Site: www.forthworthbuilders.org (1)

Lovell III, Lawrence, L., Louisiana State Museum, New Orleans, LA. Tel: (504) 568-6968, (800) 568-6968, FAX: (504) 568-4995, Web Site: www.lsm.crt.state.la.us (1)

Lovell, John, John Lovell Communication Services, Portland, ME. Tel: (207) 774-0232, FAX: (207) 774-0232 (39)

Lovell, Sara, Pilot Direct, Norfolk, VA. Tel: (757) 446-2874, Web Site: www.pilotdirect.com (35)

John Lovell Communication Services, Portland, ME. Tel: (207) 774-0232, FAX: (207) 774-0232 (39)

Lovely, Rich, ADT Worldwide, Boca Raton, FL. Tel: (561) 988-3600, FAX: (561) 988-3673, Web Site: www.tycofireandsecurity.com (16)

Lovely, Richard, J., Rohm & Haas Co, Philadelphia, PA. Tel: (215) 592-3000, (877) 288-5881, FAX: (215) 592-3377, Web Site: www.rohmhess.com (16)

Loveman, Gary, Caesars Palace, Las Vegas, NV. Tel: (702) 407-6000, (800) 634-6001, FAX: (702) 407-6037, Web Site: www.caesars.com (16)

Loveman, Gary, Harrah's Marketing, Reno, NV. Tel: (775) 786-3232, FAX: (775) 722-2815, Web Site: www.harrahsreno.com (16)

Loves Travel Stops & Country Stores, Oklahoma City, OK. Tel: (405) 242-2490, Web Site: www.loves.com (5)

Lovett, Gary, California Mustang Parts & Accessories, City of Industry, CA. Tel: (909) 598-3383, (800) 775-0101, FAX: (909) 598-5611, E-Mail: csmustang@cal-mustang.com, Web Site: www.cal-mustang.com (16)

Lovett, Michael, J., Charter Communications, Saint Louis, MO. Tel: (314) 965-0555, (888) 438-2427, FAX: (314) 965-9745, Web Site: www.charteroom.com (16)

Lovett, Mike, Ingram Book Group, La Vergne, TN. Tel: (615) 793-5000, (800) 937-8000, FAX: (800) 876-0186, Web Site: www.ipage.ingrambook.com (16)

Loving Promises & More, Longview, WA. Tel: (360) 425-8466, (800) 999-6909 (16)

Lovins, David, Banker & Tradesman, Boston, MA. Tel: (617) 428-5100, FAX: (617) 428-5119, E-Mail: dmoore@thewarrengroup.com, Web Site: www.thewarrengroup.com (17)

Lovisone, Rick, America, Fredericksburg, VA. Tel: (540) 658-3388, (800) 927-8277, FAX: (540) 658-3389, Web Site: www.americastore.com (6)

Low, Gary, M., Metro Speedgear, Livingston, NJ. Tel: (908) 286-1886, (800) 777-4453, FAX: (908) 286-0002, E-Mail: info@speedgear.com, Web Site: www.speedgear.com (11)

Low, Tanya, PointOne Graphics Inc, Toronto, ON Canada. Tel: (416) 255-8202, Web Site: www.point-one.com (27)

Lowan, Keith, Sprint PCS, Overland Park, KS. Tel: (800) 927-2199, Web Site: www.sprintpcs.com (16)

Lowdon, Davidson, C., CRB, Chicago, IL. Tel: (312) 554-8456, (800) 621-5271, FAX: (312) 939-4135, E-Mail: info@crbtrader.com, Web Site: www.crbtrader.com (17)

Lowe, Carol, See's Candies Inc, Carson, CA. Tel: (800) 347-7337, Web Site: www.sees.com (4)

Lowe, Chris, Dial 800 LLC, Los Angeles, CA. Tel: (310) 273-9023, (800) 564-8685, Web Site: www.dial800.com (32)

Lowe, Linda, Fox Chase Cancer Center, Philadelphia, PA. Tel: (215) 728-6900, (888) FOXCHASE, FAX: (215) 728-2594, Web Site: www.fccc.edu (1)

Lowe, Robert, R, American Society on Aging, San Francisco, CA. Tel: (415) 974-9600, (800) 537-9728, FAX: (415) 974-0300, E-Mail: info@asaging.org, Web Site: www.asaging.org (1)

Lowe Worldwide, New York, NY. Tel: (212) 981-7600, E-Mail: info@loweworldwide.com, Web Site: www.loweworldwide.com (35)

Lower II, Louis G., Horace Mann Educators Corp, Springfield, IL. Tel: (217) 789-2500, FAX: (217) 788-5161, Web Site: www.horacemann.com (15)

Lowery, Linda, Photographic Society of America Inc (PSA), Oklahoma City, OK. Tel: (405) 843-1437, FAX: (405) 843-1438, E-Mail: HQ@psa-photo.org, Web Site: www.psa-photo.org (40)

Lowe's Companies Inc, Mooresville, NC. Tel: (704) 758-1000, FAX: (336) 651-4766, Web Site: www.lowes.com (8)

Lowitz, Jennifer, Frederick's of Hollywood Group Inc, Los Angeles, CA. Tel: (323) 466-5151, (800) 323-9525, FAX: (323) 464-5149, Web Site: www.fredericks.com (2)

Lowman, Diane, Smithsonian Enterprises, New York, NY. Tel: (212) 916-1300, (800) 766-2149, FAX: (212) 490-0058, E-Mail: email@simag.si.edu, Web Site: www.smithsonianmag.com (17)

Lowman, Paul, Case Design Corp, Telford, PA. Tel: (215) 703-0130, (800) 847-4176, FAX: (215) 703-0139, E-Mail: sales@casedesigncorp.com, Web Site: www.casedesigncorp.com (34)

Lowman, Suzanne, Iowa Student Loan Liquidity Corp, West Des Moines, IA. Tel: (515) 243-5626, Web Site: www.studentloan.org (1)

Lowman, W.M., CYRO Industries, Parsippany, NJ. Tel: (973) 541-8000, (800) 631-5384, FAX: (973) 442-6117, (973) 442-6135, Web Site: www.cyro.com (16)

Lownds, Don, Pacific Propeller Inc, Kent, WA. Tel: (253) 872-7767, (800) 722-7767, FAX: (253) 872-7221, E-Mail: jheikke@pacprop.com, Web Site: www.pacificpropeller.com (16)

Lownstein, Tim, Stress Market, Port Angeles, WA. Tel: (360) 457-9223, (800) 578-7377, FAX: (360) 457-9466, E-Mail: info@stressmarket.com, Web Site: www.stressmarket.com (17)

Lowrance, Darrell, Lowrance Electronics, Tulsa, OK. Tel: (918) 437-6881, FAX: (918) 234-1707, Web Site: www.lowrance.com (11)

Lowrance Electronics, Tulsa, OK. Tel: (918) 437-6881, FAX: (918) 234-1707, Web Site: www.lowrance.com (11)

Lowrie, Doug, Datum Timing, Test & Measurement, Beverly, MA. Tel: (978) 927-8220, FAX: (978) 927-4099, E-Mail: wriley@datum.com, Web Site: www.datum.com (9)

Lowry, Bruce, Pro CD Inc, Omaha, NE. Tel: (800) 992-3766, FAX: (402) 750-0020 (17)

Lowry, Glen, D., The Museum of Modern Art, New York, NY. Tel: (212) 708-9400, FAX: (212) 333-1123, E-Mail: info@moma.org, Web Site: www.moma.org (5)

Lowry, Richard, National Review, New York, NY. Tel: (212) 679-7330, FAX: (212) 849-2852, Web Site: www.nationalreview.com (17)

Lowry, William, Country Sampler Group, Saint Charles, IL. Tel: (630) 377-8000, FAX: (630) 377-8194, Web Site: www.sampler.com (17)

Loyalty E-Marketing, White Plains, NY. Tel: (914) 761-2800, Web Site: www.carlbloom.com (35)

LoyaltyOne, Marblehead, MA. Tel: (781) 990-8844, Web Site: www.speechrep.com (17)

LoyaltyOne, Toronto, ON Canada. Tel: (416) 228-6500, Web Site: www.loyalty.com; www.airmiles.ca (22)

Loyaltyworks Inc, Atlanta, GA. Tel: (678) 539-5000, (800) 844-5000, FAX: (678) 539-5173, Web Site: www.loyaltyworks.com (21)

Loyd, Rick, Collector Books & American Quilters Society, Paducah, KY. Tel: (270) 898-6211, (800) 626-5420, FAX: (270) 898-8890, E-Mail: info@collectorbooks.com, Web Site: www.collectorbooks.com (17)

Loyle, Harry D., Moto Franchise Corp, Dayton, OH. Tel: (937) 291-1900, (800) 733-6686, FAX: (937) 291-2005, E-Mail: expert@motophoto.com, Web Site: www.motophoto.com; www.portraitavenue.com (3)

Loyola University Chicago, Chicago, IL. Tel: (312) 915-8900, Web Site: www.luc.edu (1)

Lubarsky, Gary, New England Direct Marketing Association, Wellesley Hills, MA. Tel: (781) 237-1366, FAX: (781) 431-8118, E-Mail: info@nedma.com, Web Site: www.nedma.com (40)

Lubell, Mark, Magnum Photos Inc, New York, NY. Tel: (212) 929-6000, FAX: (212) 929-9325, E-Mail: photography@magnumphotos.com, Web Site: www.magnumphotos.com (38)

Lubovitz, Arye, Tabline Data Services Inc, New York, NY. Tel: (212) 695-4873, FAX: (212) 629-4423 (30)

Lubrano, Sharon, R R Bowker, New Providence, NJ. Tel: (888) BOWKER-2 (269-5372), FAX: (908) 771-8699, Web Site: www.bowker.com (17)

Lubs, John, Mason Companies Inc, Chippewa Falls, WI. Tel: (715) 723-1871, (800) 826-7030, FAX: (715) 720-4247, Web Site: www.masoncompaniesinc.com (2)

Luca, Ray, LogEtronics Corp, Sparta, NJ. Tel: (703) 912-7745, FAX: (703) 912-7610, Web Site: www.logetronics.com (34)

Lucanish, James, O'Neil Data Systems Inc, Los Angeles, CA. Tel: (310) 448-6400, Web Site: www.oneildata.com (27)

Lucas, Brian, Gifts Corp, Barrie, ON. Tel: (905) 670-1126, (800) 565-3130, FAX: (905) 670-1127, E-Mail: customerservice@regal.ca, Web Site: www.regalgreetings.com (6)

Lucas, David, Vance, Intergraph Corp, Madison, AL. Tel: (256) 730-2000, (800) 345-4856, FAX: (256) 730-2048, Web Site: www.intergraph.com (16)

Lucas, Ned, Lucas & Associates, Montebello, CA. Tel: (323) 728-7899 (29)

Lucas, Wonya, Y., Discovery Communications LLC, Silver Spring, MD. Tel: (240) 662-2000, FAX: (240) 662-1868, Web Site: corporate.discovery.com (16)

Lucas & Associates, Montebello, CA. Tel: (323) 728-7899 (29)

Lucci, Marysue, Marastar Communications, Wayne, PA. Tel: (610) 902-0080, FAX: (610) 902-0600, E-Mail: info@marastar.com, Web Site: www.marastar.com (13)

Luce, Elizabeth, Sugarbush Farm Inc, Woodstock, VT. Tel: (802) 457-1757, (800) 281-1757, FAX: (802) 457-3269, E-Mail: contact@sugarbushfarm.com, Web Site: www.sugarbushfarm.com (4)

Luce, Linda, Quick Draw Clip Systems Inc, Ventura, CA. Tel: (805) 644-6888, (888) 254-7797, FAX: (805) 644-7320, E-Mail: ron@clipsystems.com, Web Site: www.clipsystems.com (9)

Luce Corp, Hamden, CT. Tel: (203) 787-0281, FAX: (203) 230-2753 (16)

Lucent Direct Catalog, New Providence, NJ. Tel: (908) 582-8500, (908) 582-3000, (800) 4-LUCENT, E-Mail: execoffice@alcatel-lucent.com, Web Site: www.alcatel-lucent.com (3)

Lucero, Dyan, Jafra Cosmetics International Inc, Westlake Village, CA. Tel: (805) 557-1889, (800) 551-2345, Web Site: www.jafra.com (7)

Lucey, Jack, Jack Lucey Art & Illustration, San Rafael, CA. Tel: (415) 453-3172, E-Mail: clucey1@sbcglobal.net (36)

Jack Lucey Art & Illustration, San Rafael, CA. Tel: (415) 453-3172, E-Mail: clucey1@sbcglobal.net (36)

LucidView, Oak Ridge, TN. Tel: (888) 582-4384, Web Site: www.lucidview.com (20)

Luciono, Mark, MGI Management Institute, Hawthorne, NY. Tel: (914) 428-6500, (800) 932-0191, FAX: (914) 428-0773, E-Mail: mgiusa@aol.com, Web Site: www.mgi.org (16)

Luck, Joel, Wasserman Uniform Co, Fort Lauderdale, FL. Tel: (614) 279-8888, (614) 279-7000, (800) 848-3576, FAX: (614) 464-0416, (800) 204-0416, E-Mail: custserv@wassermanuniform.com, Web Site: www.wassermanuniform.com (2)

Lucky Heart Cosmetics Inc, Memphis, TN. Tel: (901) 526-7658, (800) 283-1014, FAX: (901) 526-7660, Web Site: www.luckyheart.com (7)

Ludgin, Robert, S., Coastal Tool & Supply, West Hartford, CT. Tel: (860) 233-8213, (877) 551-8665, FAX: (860) 233-6295, E-Mail: sales@coastaltool.com, Web Site: www.coastaltool.com (16)

Ludwick, Suzanne, BBS & Associates, Akron, OH. Tel: (330) 665-5227, Web Site: www.servantheart.com (1)

Ludwig, David, Thomson Financial, New York, NY. Tel: (212) 803-8200, FAX: (212) 843-9608 (17)

Luebbehusen, Gene, Jofco Inc, Jasper, IN. Tel: (812) 482-5154, (800) 23-JOFCO, FAX: (812) 634-2392, E-Mail: furniture@jofco.com, Web Site: www.jofco.com (16)

Luebke, Michele, American Society for Quality-ASQ, Milwaukee, WI. Tel: (414) 272-8575, (800) 248-1946, FAX: (414) 272-1734, E-Mail: help@asq.org, Web Site: www.asq.org (1)

Lueken, Sharon, Abbey Press, Saint Meinrad, IN. Tel: (812) 357-8011, FAX: (812) 357-8388, Web Site: www.abbeypress.com (6)

Lufrano, Robert, I., Blue Cross & Blue Shield of Florida, Jacksonville, FL. Tel: (904) 791-6111, (800) 477-3736, FAX: (904) 905-6638, E-Mail: katie.magee@bcbsfl.com, Web Site: www.bcbsfl.com (15)

Lufthansa German Airlines, East Meadow, NY. Tel: (516) 296-9416, FAX: (516) 296-9386, Web Site: www.lufthansa-usa.com (19)

Luggage Base, Nipomo, CA. Tel: (805) 929-8191, (888) 832-1201, FAX: (805) 929-8192, E-Mail: service@luggagebase.com, Web Site: www.luggagebase.com (16)

Lukacs, Mark, NewPage Corp, Miamisburg, OH. Tel: (937) 242-9068, (877) 855-7243, FAX: (937) 242-9327, Web Site: www.newpagecorp.com (25)

Luke, Teresa, Card Technology Inc, Hopkins, MN. Tel: (201) 845-7373, FAX: (201) 845-3337, E-Mail: info@nbstech.com, Web Site: www.nbstech.com (16)

Luke, Warren, K., ABA/BMA Trust Wealth Management and Marketing Conference, Washington, DC. Tel: (202) 663-5000, (800) BANKERS, FAX: (202) 828-4540, E-Mail: custserv@aba.com, Web Site: www.aba.com (42)

Lukoskie, Katherine, Bolind Inc, Boulder, CO. Tel: (303) 443-3142, FAX: (303) 443-9889, Web Site: www.bolind.com (16)

Lumpkin, Richard, A., Consolidated Market Response, Charleston, IL. Tel: (217) 348-7050, FAX: (217) 348-7060 (29)

Lunarcow Design, Akron, OH. Tel: (330) 253-9000, (800) 594-9620, FAX: (330) 253-9001, E-Mail: info@lunarcow.com, Web Site: www.lunarcow.com (35)

Lund, Barbara, Informal Education Products, Milwaukie, OR. Tel: (503) 794-7100, (888) 444-5500, FAX: (503) 794-7111, E-Mail: sales@museumtour.com, Web Site: www.museumtour.com (11)

Lund, Kimberly, Nestle USA, Glendale, CA. Tel: (818) 549-6000, (800) 225-2270, FAX: (818) 549-6952, Web Site: www.nestleusa.com (4)

Lund, Peder, C., Paladin Press, Boulder, CO. Tel: (303) 443-7250, (800) 392-2400, FAX: (303) 442-8741, E-Mail: service@paladin-press.com, Web Site: www.paladin-press.com (17)

Lund, Sharon, R Falls Agency, Minneapolis, MN. Tel: (612) 872-6372, (800) 339-1119, FAX: (612) 872-1018, E-Mail: info@fallsagency.com, Web Site: www.fallsagency.com (35)

Lundberg, Theodore, E., Life-Study Fellowship Foundation Inc, Darien, CT. Tel: (203) 655-1436, FAX: (203) 655-1392, Web Site: www.lifestudyfellowship.com (17)

Lundberg, Wendell, Lundberg Family Farms, Richvale, CA. Tel: (530) 882-4551, FAX: (530) 882-4500, E-Mail: info@lundberg.com, Web Site: www.lundberg.com (16)

Lundberg Family Farms, Richvale, CA. Tel: (530) 882-4551, FAX: (530) 882-4500, E-Mail: info@lundberg.com, Web Site: www.lundberg.com (16)

Lunden, Denise, S., Software Marketing Associates Inc, Rocky Hill, CT. Tel: (860) 721-8929, FAX: (860) 257-9679, E-Mail: sma@sma-promail.com, Web Site: www.sma-promail.com (22)

Lunderman, William H., Colgate-Palmolive Co, New York, NY. Tel: (212) 310-2000, (800) 468-6502, FAX: (212) 310-2475, Web Site: www.colgate.com (16)

Lundgren, Drew, CAS Inc, Omaha, NE. Tel: (402) 964-9998, (800) 524-0908 X2071, FAX: (402) 963-2103, E-Mail: sales@cas-online.com, Web Site: www.cas-online.com (23)

Lundgren, Terry, J., Ann Taylor Inc, New York, NY. Tel: (212) 457-2075, (800) FAX-ANN, FAX: (800) DIAL-ANN, Web Site: www.anninc.com (2)

Lundgren, Terry, J., Macy's Marketing, New York, NY. Tel: (212) 695-4400, FAX: (212) 494-1517, Web Site: www.macys.com (16)

Lundin, Richard, Da-Lite Screen Co Inc, Warsaw, IN. Tel: (574) 267-8101, (800) 622-3737, FAX: (574) 267-7804, E-Mail: info@da-lite.com, Web Site: www.da-lite.com (16)

Lundmark Advertising & Design Inc, Kansas City, MO. Tel: (816) 842-5236, FAX: (816) 221-7175, Web Site: www.lundonline.net (35)

Lundstrom, Stephen, D., Rees Associates Inc, Des Moines, IA. Tel: (515) 243-2127, FAX: (515) 243-1026, Web Site: www.reesassociates.com (28)

Lundy, Kathy, Charnstrom, Shakopee, MN. Tel: (952) 403-0303, (800) 328-2962, FAX: (800) 916-3215, E-Mail: mail@charnstrom.com, Web Site: www.charnstrom.com (28)

Lunenschloss, John, T., Air-Lec Industries Inc, Madison, WI. Tel: (608) 244-4743, FAX: (608) 246-7676, E-Mail: info@air-lec.com, Web Site: www.air-lec.com (16)

Lung, Richard, Stew Leonard's, Norwalk, CT. Tel: (203) 847-7214, FAX: (203) 847-1488, Web Site: www.stewleonards.com (4)

Lunick, Stuart, Thermal Product Solutions, White Deer, PA. Tel: (570) 538-7200, (800) 586-2473 (16)

Lunt, Jim, Data Cal Corp, Gilbert, AZ. Tel: (480) 813-3100, (800) 223-0123, FAX: (480) 545-8090, E-Mail: info@datacal.com, Web Site: www.datacal.com (16)

Lupinetti, Jim, BFS Credit Services Co, Brook Park, OH. Tel: (216) 362-5094, FAX: (216) 362-5236, E-Mail: lupinettijim@bfsusa.com (16)

Lure-Craft, Lagrange, IN. Tel: (260) 463-2687, (800) 925-9088, FAX: (260) 463-8383, E-Mail: kimstraley@lurecraft.com, Web Site: www.lurecraft.com (11)

Lurrie, Wendy, G2 Worldwide, New York, NY. Tel: (212) 537-3700, Web Site: www.g2dd.com (35)

Luse, Bob, Sears Home Improvement Products Inc, Longwood, FL. Tel: (407) 767-0990, (877) 840-7126, FAX: (407) 831-1848, Web Site: www.searshomepro.com (16)

Lussier, Gary, Christian Book Distributors Inc, Peabody, MA. Tel: (978) 532-5300, FAX: (978) 977-5010, E-Mail: javedisian@chrbook.com, Web Site: www.chrbook.com (17)

Lustbader, Todd, Winston Marketing Group, Elk Grove Village, IL. Tel: (847) 350-5800 (8)

Luster Care Products, Saint Louis, MO. Tel: (636) 272-1885, (800) 291-5223, FAX: (636) 272-1869, Web Site: www.lusterlace.com (16)

Lustigman, Andrew, The Lustigman Firm P C, New York, NY. Tel: (212) 683-9180, FAX: (212) 683-9181, E-Mail: andy@lfirm.com, Web Site: www.lustigmanfirm.com (35)

Lustigman, Sheldon, The Lustigman Firm P C, New York, NY. Tel: (212) 683-9180, FAX: (212) 683-9181, E-Mail: andy@lfirm.com, Web Site: www.lustigmanfirm.com (35)

The Lustigman Firm P C, New York, NY. Tel: (212) 683-9180, FAX: (212) 683-9181, E-Mail: andy@lfirm.com, Web Site: www.lustigmanfirm.com (35)

Luter III, Joseph, W., Smithfield Packing Co Inc, Smithfield, VA. Tel: (757) 357-4321, FAX: (757) 357-1339, E-Mail: information@smithfieldfoods.com, Web Site: www.smithfieldfoods.com (16)

Luterman, Gerald, Keyspan Energy Corp, Brooklyn, NY. Tel: (718) 403-2000, (888) 222-7359, Web Site: www.keyspanenergy.com (16)

Luther, Dennis, CDS Global, Des Moines, IA. Tel: (515) 247-7500, FAX: (515) 246-6882, E-Mail: dluther@cdsfulfillment.com, Web Site: www.cdsfulfillment.com (22)

Luther, John, M., Gracewood Fruit Co, Vero Beach, FL. Tel: (772) 567-1154, E-Mail: info@gracewoodgroves.com, Web Site: www.gracewoodgroves.com (4)

Lutheran Church Extension Fund - Missouri Synod, Saint Louis, MO. Tel: (800) 843-5233, FAX: (314) 996-1131, Web Site: www.lcef.org (1)

Luttrell, Wayne, Tri-Media Marketing Services Inc, Wilmette, IL. Tel: (800) 874-4062, Web Site: www.trimediaonline.com (23)

Lutz, Robert, A., Buick Division General Motors Corp, Detroit, MI. Tel: (313) 556-5000, (800) 521-7300, FAX: (313) 556-5108, Web Site: www.buick.com (16)

Luukko, Peter, Wachovia Center, Philadelphia, PA. Tel: (215) 336-3600, FAX: (215) 389-9518, E-Mail: info@comcast-spectacor.com, Web Site: www.comcast-spectacor.com (16)

Lux, David, P., RBC Funds, Milwaukee, WI. Tel: (800) 422-2766, Web Site: us.rbcgam.com (14)

Lux, Robert, Federal Home Loan Mortgage Corp (Freddie Mac), McLean, VA. Tel: (703) 903-2000, (800) 424-5401, Web Site: www.freddiemac.com (16)

Luxeder, Tom, The Taunton Press, Newtown, CT. Tel: (203) 426-8171, (800) 477-8727, FAX: (203) 426-3434, Web Site: www.taunton.com (17)

Luxottica Retail, Mason, OH. Tel: (513) 765-6956, Web Site: www.luxottica.com (2)

Luzi, Armin, Thetford Corp, Ann Arbor, MI. Tel: (734) 769-6000, (800) 543-1219, FAX: (734) 769-2023, Web Site: www.thetford.com (16)

Luzier Personalized Cosmetics, Kansas City, MO. Tel: (816) 531-8338, (800) 821-6632, FAX: (816) 531-6979, Web Site: www.luzier.com (7)

Lyash, Jeffrey, J., Florida Power Corp, Saint Petersburg, FL. Tel: (727) 820-5151, (800) 700-8744, FAX: (727) 384-7865, Web Site: www.progressenergy.com (16)

Lyden, Kevin, UPM North America, Westmont, IL. Tel: (630) 850-3310, (866) 300-4175, FAX: (630) 850-3510, Web Site: www.upm-kymmene.com (25)

Lyke, Andy, Ripon Printers, Ripon, WI. Tel: (920) 748-3136, (800) 321-3136, FAX: (920) 748-3741, E-Mail: info@riponprinters.com, Web Site: www.riponprinters.com (27)

Lyman, David, H., The Maine Photographic Workshops, Rockport, ME. Tel: (207) 236-8581, (877) 577-7700, FAX: (207) 236-2558, E-Mail: info@theworkshops.com, Web Site: www.theworkshops.com (16)

Lyman, Donald, ADT Worldwide, Boca Raton, FL. Tel: (561) 988-3600, FAX: (561) 988-3673, Web Site: www.tycofireandsecurity.com (16)

Lyman, Jim, Edward Don & Co, North Riverside, IL. Tel: (708) 442-9400, (800) 777-4366, FAX: (708) 442-0436, Web Site: www.don.com (16)

Lynah, Susan, Bland Farms, Glennville, GA. Tel: (912) 654-1426, (800) 843-2542, FAX: (912) 654-1330, Web Site: www.blandfarms.com (4)

Lynam, Joe, Integretel Inc, San Jose, CA. Tel: (408) 362-4000, FAX: (408) 362-2795, Web Site: www.integretel.com (16)

Lynch Ph.D., William F., Drexel University (Goodwin College of Professional Studies), Philadelphia, PA. E-Mail: goodwin@drexel.edu, Web Site: www.drexel.edu/goodwin (16)

Lynch, Bob, South-Western Publishing, Madison, OH. Tel: (513) 299-1000, FAX: (513) 527-6992 (17)

Lynch, Brunny, The Leukemia & Lymphoma Society, White Plains, NY. Tel: (914) 949-5213 (1)

Lynch, Chris, New England Journal of Medicine, Waltham, MA. Tel: (781) 893-3800, FAX: (781) 893-7729, Web Site: www.nejm.org (17)

Lynch, Mike, MELDISCO, Mahwah, NJ. Tel: (201) 934-2000, FAX: (201) 934-2570, Web Site: www.meldisco.com (16)

Lynch, Neil, P., Aristokraft Inc, Jasper, IN. Tel: (812) 482-2527, FAX: (812) 482-9872, Web Site: www.aristokraft.com (16)

Lynch, Peter, Warner Bros, Burbank, CA. Tel: (818) 954-6000, Web Site: www.warnerbros.com (3)

Lynch, Philip, Brown-Forman Corp, Louisville, KY. Tel: (502) 585-1100, FAX: (502) 774-7876, E-Mail: brown-forman@b-f.com, Web Site: www.brown-forman.com (16)

Lynn, Don, State Farm Insurance Cos, Bloomington, IL. Tel: (309) 766-2311, FAX: (309) 766-3621, Web Site: www.statefarm.com (15)

Lynn, Nancy, Kennel Vet, Laurel, DE. Tel: (302) 875-7111, (800) 782-0627, FAX: (302) 269-3986, E-Mail: info@petmarket.com, Web Site: www.kennelvet.com (11)

Lynn-Shiflett, Cheryl, The National Restaurant Association Educational Foundation, Chicago, IL. Tel: (312) 715-1010, FAX: (312) 583-9767 (1)

Lynner, Terry, A., Goldsmith Agio Helms, Minneapolis, MN. Tel: (612) 339-0500, FAX: (612) 339-0507, Web Site: www.agio.com (14)

Lyon, Glenn, S., J Peterman Co, Lexington, KY. Tel: (888) 647-2555, FAX: (859) 254-0869, Web Site: www.jpeterman.com (5)

Lyon, Patty, Signature Styles LLC, New York, NY. Tel: (800) 443-4856, FAX: (902) 862-5063 (2)

Lyon, Sharon, Lion's Share Marketing Group, Inc, Houston, TX. Tel: (713) 686-4252, Web Site: www.lionsshare.com (20)

Lyons, Amy, L., Specialists Marketing Services Inc, Hasbrouck Heights, NJ. Tel: (201) 865-5800, FAX: (201) 288-4295, E-Mail: listinfo@specialistsms.com, Web Site: www.specialistsms.com (23)

Lyons, Jed, E., University Press of America Inc, Lanham, MD. Tel: (301) 459-3366, (800) 462-6420, FAX: (301) 429-5748, E-Mail: custserv@rowman.com, Web Site: www.univpress.com (17)

Lyons, Jim, Rapp Collins Worldwide, New York, NY. Tel: (212) 817-6800, FAX: (212) 686-7047, Web Site: www.rappcollins.com (35)

Lyons, Richard, Cellular One Group, Oklahoma City, OK. Tel: (509) 663-2162, (800) 545-5982, FAX: (425) 586-8451, Web Site: www.cellularone.com (16)

Lyons-Tarr, Kevin, 4Imprint Inc, Oshkosh, WI. Tel: (920) 236-7272, (888) 298-8190, (877) 446-7746, FAX: (800) 355-5043, E-Mail: administrator@4imprint.com, Web Site: www.4imprint.com (16)

Lyris Inc, Emeryville, CA. Tel: (510) 844-1551, (800) 768-2929, FAX: (510) 844-1598, E-Mail: sales@lyris.com, Web Site: www.lyris.com (32)

Lytle, Ken, Merastar Insurance Co, Chattanooga, TN. Tel: (800) 637-2782, FAX: (800) 369-1430, E-Mail: merastar.assist.team@unitrindirect.com, Web Site: www.merastar.com (15)

Steve Lytle, Chicago, IL. Tel: (312) 894-7000 (20)

M

M&M Health Care Apparel Co, Brooklyn, NY. Tel: (800) 221-8929, E-Mail: fashionease@aol.com (2)

M R Group Inc, Plymouth, MN. Tel: (763) 550-0760, FAX: (763) 550-0760, E-Mail: webmaster@mrgrp.com, Web Site: www.mrgrp.com (33)

M'Guinness, Jim, Jim M'Guinness Design, Los Altos, CA. Tel: (650) 967-3811 (36)

M2Media 360, Park Ridge, IL. Tel: (760) 318-7000, E-Mail: cnaughton@m2media360.com, Web Site: www.m2media360.com (17)

MAR Graphics, Valmeyer, IL. Tel: (800) 851-4460, Web Site: www.margraphics.com (27)

MBI Direct Mail, Deland, FL. Tel: (386) 736-9998, Web Site: www.directmail-mbi.com (23)

MBI Inc, Norwalk, CT. Tel: (203) 853-2000, E-Mail: webmail@mbi-inc.com, Web Site: www.mbi-inc.com (16)

MBS, Melville, NY. Tel: (631) 851-5000, Web Site: www.mbsinsight.com (22)

MC Group, London, ON Canada. Tel: (519) 660-8460, FAX: (519) 660-8476, Web Site: www.themcgroup.com (35)

MCA/Universal Studios Inc, Universal City, CA. Tel: (818) 777-1000, FAX: (818) 866-3330, Web Site: www.universalstudios.com (3)

MCCS, Mason, OH. Tel: (513) 573-2284, FAX: (513) 573-2197, Web Site: www.federated.com (14)

MCDM Strategic Direct Marketing, Plainfield, IL. Tel: (815) 436-5194, FAX: (815) 439-5941 (20)

MCH Strategic Data, Sweet Springs, MO. Tel: (660) 335-6373, (800) 776-6373, FAX: (660) 335-4157, E-Mail: tonyab@mchdata.com, Web Site: www.mchdata.com (23)

MCI Inc, Ashburn, VA. Tel: (703) 886-5600, FAX: (703) 885-0570 (16)

MCRB Fulfillment Corp, Westlake Village, CA. Tel: (818) 407-4300, (800) 942-MCRB, FAX: (818) 407-0248, E-Mail: sallen@mcrb.com, Web Site: www.mcrb.com (28)

MD&C Advertising, New Haven, CT. Tel: (203) 624-4151, FAX: (203) 401-6134, Web Site: www.mdcads.com (35)

MDE Marketing, Mahwah, NJ. Tel: (201) 891-7010, Web Site: www.wdemarketing.com (16)

MDF Systems, Bristol, CT. Tel: (860) 584-4750, FAX: (860) 584-4759, Web Site: www.mdfsystems.com (22)

MDI Lists, Weston, FL. Tel: (954) 384-1557, FAX: (954) 389-0939, Web Site: www.mdilists.com (23)

MDR, Sunrise, FL. Tel: (954) 845-9500, (800) 327-4660, FAX: (954) 845-9505, E-Mail: customerservice@mdr.org, Web Site: www.mdr.org (7)

MESA, Port Washington, NY. Tel: (516) 767-6720, Web Site: www.mesalliance.org/ (22)

MFE Instruments, Salem, NH. Tel: (603) 893-8778, (800) 843-8011, FAX: (603) 893-8851, Web Site: www.stockeryale.com (9)

MFP&W Promotions Direct, San Juan, PR. Tel: (787) 781-1616, FAX: (787) 793-5355, Web Site: www.jwtworld.com (35)

MFS Investment Management, Boston, MA. Tel: (617) 954-6249, Web Site: www.mfs.com (14)

MGI Management Institute, Hawthorne, NY. Tel: (914) 428-6500, (800) 932-0191, FAX: (914) 428-0773, E-Mail: mgiusa@aol.com, Web Site: www.mgi.org (16)

MGM Grand Detroit, Detroit, MI. Tel: (877) 888-2121, Web Site: www.mgmgrand.com/det (16)

MGM Mailing Lists, South Sandwich, MA. Tel: (508) 539-1300, (800) 660-5322, FAX: (508) 539-0700 (23)

MGM MIRAGE, Las Vegas, NV. Tel: (702) 693-8005, Web Site: www.mirageresorts.com (19)

MGP Direct Inc, Fulton, MD. Tel: (410) 531-0383, FAX: (410) 531-8142, E-Mail: roberta@mgpdirect.com, Web Site: www.mgpdirect.com (35)

MI-T-M Corp, Peosta, IA. Tel: (863) 556-7484, Web Site: www.mitm.com (9)

MJA International, Glen Head, NY. Tel: (516) 759-1000, FAX: (516) 674-3309 (7)

MJM Incentives Inc, Rochester, NY. Tel: (585) 424-6720, FAX: (585) 424-4387, E-Mail: cmeier@mjmincentives.com, Web Site: www.mjmincentives.com (33)

MKE Enterprises, North Reading, MA. Tel: (978) 664-3877, FAX: (978) 664-2835, E-Mail: mke@theworld.com, Web Site: www.mke-enterprises.com (35)

MKS Marketing Inc, Austin, TX. Tel: (512) 263-8017, (800) 544-8989, FAX: (402) 333-9610, E-Mail: info@telemarketingoutsource.com, Web Site: www.telemarketingoutsource.com (29)

MLB Associates, Lake Placid, NY. Tel: (518) 523-2371, FAX: (518) 523-9011, E-Mail: mlbassoc@aol.com, Web Site: www.mlbassociates.com (9)

MLS Data Management Solutions, Fort Worth, TX. Tel: (817) 804-6900, FAX: (817) 804-6999, Web Site: www.mlsc.com (22)

MM Batch, Westhampton Beach, NY. Tel: (212) 737-0700, FAX: (212) 454-1124, E-Mail: christine@bannerdirect.com, Web Site: www.bannerdirect.com (35)

MMI Direct, Columbia, MD. Tel: (410) 561-1500, FAX: (410) 561-0805, Web Site: www.mmidirect.com (22)

MMS Education, Newtown, PA. Tel: (215) 579-8590 (5)

MPBS Industries, Los Angeles, CA. Tel: (323) 268-8514, (800) 421-6265, FAX: (323) 268-6305, Web Site: www.mpbs.com (16)

MPC Louisville Promotions, Louisville, KY. Tel: (502) 451-4900, (800) 331-0989, FAX: (502) 451-5075, E-Mail: service@mpcpromotions.com, Web Site: www.mpcpromotions.com (33)

MPS Multimedia Inc, San Mateo, CA. Tel: (650) 872-7100, FAX: (650) 872-7133, E-Mail: sales@gospg.com, Web Site: www.selectmedia.com (16)

The MR Group Inc, Charleston, SC. Tel: (843) 402-0566, FAX: (843) 852-9051, E-Mail: mgm@themrgroup.com, Web Site: www.themrgroup.com (9)

MRC Marketing Inc, Saint Paul, MN. Tel: (612) 759-2069, E-Mail: info@mrcmarketing.com, Web Site: www.mrcmarketing.com (21)

MRI Norwalk, Pompano Beach, FL. Tel: (203) 926-1200, FAX: (203) 926-1211, E-Mail: jbgurn@mricoastalgroup.com, Web Site: www.mricoastalgroup.com (20)

MRM Worldwide, New York, NY. Tel: (646) 865-6230, Web Site: www.mrmworldwide.com (35)

MRV Communications, Chatsworth, CA. Tel: (818) 773-0900, FAX: (818) 773-0906, Web Site: www.mrv.com (3)

MRW Communications, Hingham, MA. Tel: (781) 740-4525, FAX: (718) 926-0371, E-Mail: jim@mrwinc.com, Web Site: www.mrwinc.com (35)

MSC, Woodland Hills, CA. Tel: (818) 346-1600, FAX: (818) 712-0122, Web Site: www.mscnet.com (22)

MSC Industrial Supply Co, Melville, NY. Tel: (516) 812-2000, (800) 645-7270, FAX: (800) 255-5067, E-Mail: executive@mscdirect.com, Web Site: www.mscdirect.com (9)

MSC Lists, Santa Barbara, CA. Tel: (805) 967-4955, FAX: (805) 964-1702, E-Mail: kingstock@juno.com (24)

MSI List Marketing, Palatine, IL. Tel: (847) 934-1111, FAX: (847) 890-6700, E-Mail: jeff@msilist.com, Web Site: www.msilist.com (23)

The MSR Group, Omaha, NE. Tel: (402) 392-0755, (800) 737-0755, FAX: (402) 392-1068, E-Mail: info@theMSRgroup.com, Web Site: www.theMSRgroup.com (30)

MSU Federal Credit Union, East Lansing, MI. Tel: (517) 333-2254, Web Site: www.msufcu.org (1)

MT&L Card Products & Fulfillment Services, Nashville, TN. Tel: (615) 254-9471, Web Site: www.mtlcard.com (28)

MTI Information Technologies LLC, Langhorne, PA. Tel: (267) 569-2400, Web Site: www.mtiadvantage.com (30)

MTS Publishing, Naperville, IL. Tel: (630) 955-9750, (800) 332-4655, FAX: (630) 955-9787, E-Mail: info@mtspbl.com, Web Site: www.mtspbl.com (17)

MTS Systems Corp, Eden Prairie, MN. Tel: (952) 937-4000, (800) 328-2255, FAX: (952) 937-4515, E-Mail: info@mts.com, Web Site: www.mts.com (16)

MVBMS EURO RSCG, New York, NY. Tel: (212) 886-2000, FAX: (212) 886-2016, E-Mail: northamerica@eurorscg.com, Web Site: www.eurorscg.com (35)

MVI Marketing Ltd, Paso Robles, CA. Tel: (805) 459-4455, (805) 239-2994, FAX: (805) 239-2947, E-Mail: info@mvimarketing.com, Web Site: www.mvimarketing.com (20)

MVS Mailers Inc, Bohemia, NY. Tel: (800) 641-7917, FAX: (631) 699-0101, E-Mail: muraco@mvsmailers.com, Web Site: www.mvsmailers.com (28)

MXT Card Services, LLC, New Castle, DE. Tel: (302) 323-6203, FAX: (302) 323-6219, Web Site: www.mxtcs.com (14)

Ma, Lysi, Sussex Publishers Inc, New York, NY. Tel: (212) 260-7210, FAX: (212) 260-7445, Web Site: www.blues-buster.com (17)

Ma, Priscilla, The Smile Train, New York, NY. Tel: (212) 689-9199, Web Site: www.smiletrain.org (1)

Ma, Yale, Everex Computer Systems Inc, Fremont, CA. Tel: (866) 850-8835, (800) 383-7391, FAX: (510) 683-2186, E-Mail: customerservice@everex.com, Web Site: www.everex.com (16)

Maag, Alan, Avnet Inc, Phoenix, AZ. Tel: (480) 643-2000, FAX: (480) 643-7240, Web Site: www.avnet.com (16)

Maas, Joe, Financial Services International Corp, Seattle, WA. Tel: (206) 386-5475, FAX: (206) 654-0499 (14)

Maaseide, Peter, L & E Meridian, Springfield, VA. Tel: (703) 913-0300, (800) 555-1556, FAX: (703) 913-7052, E-Mail: pmaaseide@l-e.com, Web Site: www.l-e.com (21)

Mac Direct, Colmar, PA. Tel: (215) 822-5775, (800) 278-1154, FAX: (215) 822-7977, E-Mail: info@macdirect.com, Web Site: www.macdirect.com (22)

Mac McIntosh Inc, North Kingstown, RI. Tel: (401) 294-7730, (800) 944-5553, FAX: (401) 679-0176, E-Mail: info@sales-lead-experts.com, Web Site: www.sales-lead-experts.com (20)

Mac Murray, Helen, Mac Murray Petersen & Shuster LLP, New Albany, OH. Tel: (614) 939-9955, FAX: (614) 939-9955, E-Mail: dbryson@mpslawyers.com, Web Site: www.mpslawyers.com (20)

Mac Murray Petersen & Shuster LLP, New Albany, OH. Tel: (614) 939-9955, FAX: (614) 939-9955, E-Mail: dbryson@mpslawyers.com, Web Site: www.mpslawyers.com (20)

Mac Pac Inc, Pembroke, MA. Tel: (781) 826-6900, FAX: (781) 826-6880, E-Mail: jsargeant@macpacinc.com, Web Site: www.macpacinc.com (26)

MacArthur, John R., Harper's Magazine, New York, NY. Tel: (212) 420-5720, FAX: (212) 260-1096, Web Site: www.harpers.org (17)

Macartney III, William, N., Indium Corp of America, Clinton, NY. Tel: (315) 853-4900, (800) 446-3486, FAX: (800) 221-5759, E-Mail: askus@indium.com, Web Site: www.indium.com (16)

MacAskill, Karolyn, James J Hill Reference Library, Saint Paul, MN. Tel: (651) 265-5500, Web Site: www.jjhill.org (1)

MacCleary, Randy, Liebert Corp, Columbus, OH. Tel: (614) 841-6700, (800) LIEBERT, FAX: (614) 841-6022, Web Site: www.liebert.com (16)

MacCormack, Charles, Save the Children Federation Inc, Westport, CT. Tel: (203) 221-4000, (800) 728-3843, FAX: (203) 222-1067, E-Mail: twebster@savethechildren.org, Web Site: www.savethechildren.org (1)

MacCurrach, Augie, Customer Portfolios LLC, Boston, MA. Tel: (617) 224-9501, Web Site: www.customerportfolios.com (22)

MacDonald, Bill, Stewart-MacDonald, Athens, OH. Tel: (740) 592-3021, (800) 848-2273, FAX: (740) 593-7922, E-Mail: hostetler@stewmac.com, Web Site: www.stewmac.com (16)

MacDonald, John, Sony DADC, New York, NY. Tel: (212) 833-8000, Web Site: www.sonydadc.com (3)

MacDonald, Scott, Print Products International, Annapolis Junction, MD. Tel: (910) 695-7223, FAX: (910) 944-1724, Web Site: www.paceworldwide.com (9)

MacDowell, Richard, Mac Pac Inc, Pembroke, MA. Tel: (781) 826-6900, FAX: (781) 826-6880, E-Mail: jsargeant@macpacinc.com, Web Site: www.macpacinc.com (26)

Macfarlan, M. Reid, Arquest Inc, Millstone Twp, NJ. Tel: (609) 395-9500, (888) ARQUEST, (888) 270-8378, FAX: (609) 395-9778, Web Site: www.arquest.com (16)

Machalek, Jon, Machalek Communications, Burnsville, MN. Tel: (952) 736-8000, (800) 846-5520, FAX: (886) 490-8834, E-Mail: publisher@machalek.com, Web Site: www.machalek.com (31)

Machalek Communications, Burnsville, MN. Tel: (952) 736-8000, (800) 846-5520, FAX: (886) 490-8834, E-Mail: publisher@machalek.com, Web Site: www.machalek.com (31)

Machleit Ph.D., Karen A., College of Business, Cincinnati, OH. Tel: (513) 556-7002, FAX: (513) 556-4891, E-Mail: business@uc.edu, Web Site: www.business.uc.edu (41)

MacIntosh, Ann, MacIntosh Survey Center, East Providence, RI. Tel: (401) 438-8330, FAX: (401) 434-9219, E-Mail: macsurvey@aol.com (30)

MacIntosh Survey Center, East Providence, RI. Tel: (401) 438-8330, FAX: (401) 434-9219, E-Mail: macsurvey@aol.com (30)

MacIntyre, Ron, Do-It Corp, South Haven, MI. Tel: (269) 637-1121, (800) 426-4822, FAX: (269) 637-7223, E-Mail: sales@do-it.com, Web Site: www.do-it.com (9)

Mack Jr., Michael, J., Deere & Co Headquarters, Moline, IL. Tel: (309) 765-8000, FAX: (309) 765-5671, Web Site: www.deere.com (16)

Mack, Ed, Fine Architectural Metalsmiths, Chester, NY. Tel: (845) 651-7550, FAX: (845) 651-7857, Web Site: www.iceforge.com (16)

Mack, John, J., Columbia-Presbyterian Medical Center, New York, NY. Tel: (212) 305-2500, FAX: (212) 305-8023, Web Site: www.nyp.org (16)

Mack, John, J., Morgan Stanley, New York, NY. Tel: (212) 761-4000, FAX: (212) 761-0096 (14)

Mack, Odell, PM Productions, Los Angeles, CA. Tel: (310) 559-3127, FAX: (310) 559-3168, E-Mail: odellmack@hotmail.com, Web Site: wwwmyvideozationnetwork.com (32)

Mack, Rhoda Weber, Fine Architectural Metalsmiths, Chester, NY. Tel: (845) 651-7550, FAX: (845) 651-7857, Web Site: www.iceforge.com (16)

Mack, Robin, Creative Health Products, Plymouth, MI. Tel: (734) 996-5900, (800) 742-4478, FAX: (734) 996-4650, Web Site: www.chponline.com (16)

Mack, Timothy C., World Future Society, Bethesda, MD. Tel: (301) 656-8274, (800) 989-8274, FAX: (301) 951-0394, E-Mail: info@wfs.org, Web Site: www.wfs.org (1)

MackayMitchell Envelope Co, Minneapolis, MN. Tel: (800) 622-5299, Web Site: www.mackayenvelope.com (26)

Macke Sr., Joseph, D., Macke Bindery Inc, Cincinnati, OH. Tel: (513) 771-7500, FAX: (531) 771-3830, Web Site: www.mackebrothers.com (28)

Macke Bindery Inc, Cincinnati, OH. Tel: (513) 771-7500, FAX: (531) 771-3830, Web Site: www.mackebrothers.com (28)

MacKenzie, Dan, Blue Cross/Blue Shield of Illinois, Chicago, IL. Tel: (312) 938-6000, FAX: (312) 938-5722, Web Site: www.bcbsil.com (15)

MacKenzie, Leslie, Directory of Mail Order Catalogs, Millerton, NY. Tel: (518) 789-8700, (800) 562-2139, FAX: (518) 789-0556, E-Mail: cstupak@greyhouse.com, Web Site: www.greyhouse.com (43)

MacKenzie, Leslie, Grey House Publishing, Amenia, NY. Tel: (518) 789-8700, (800) 562-2139, FAX: (518) 789-0556, E-Mail: books@greyhouse.com, Web Site: www.greyhouse.com (43)

MacKenzie, Leslie, The Directory of Business Information Resources, Millerton, NY. Tel: (518) 789-8700, (800) 562-2139, FAX: (518) 789-0556, E-Mail: cstupak@greyhouse.com, Web Site: www.greyhouse.com (43)

Mackenzie Andersen, Susan, Andersen Design, East Boothbay, ME. Tel: (207) 350-4057, (866) 711-8421, E-Mail: studio@andersenstudio.com, Web Site: www.andersenstudio.com (33)

Mackey, Jim, MarketerNet LLC, Chicago, IL. Tel: (312) 775-9320, (888) 443-3684, FAX: (312) 775-9328, E-Mail: info@marketernet.com, Web Site: www.marketernet.com (22)

MacKinnon, Don, Hear Music, Bellevue, WA. Tel: (425) 452-5534, E-Mail: gail@hearmusic.com, Web Site: www.hearmusic.com (3)

MacKinnon, Kelli, Marquis Who's Who LLC, Berkeley Heights, NJ. Tel: (908) 673-1000, (800) 473-7020, FAX: (908) 673-1179, E-Mail: info@marquiswhoswho.com, Web Site: www.marquiswhoswho.com (17)

Mackinnon, Elinor, Anthem Blue Cross, Westlake Village, CA. Tel: (805) 557-6655, (800) 333-0912, FAX: (800) 557-6872, Web Site: www.bluecrossca.com (15)

Macko, Deb, Raybuck Autobody Parts, Punxsutawney, PA. Tel: (814) 938-5248, FAX: (814) 938-4250, E-Mail: service@raybuck.com, Web Site: www.raybuck.com (12)

Macko, Terry, World Wildlife Fund, Washington, DC. Tel: (202) 293-4800, Web Site: www.worldwildlife.org (1)

Mackrell, William, Pitney Bowes of Canada Limited, Mississauga, ON Canada. Tel: (905) 219-3000, (866) 669-6627, FAX: (905) 219-3826, Web Site: www.pitneybowes.ca (34)

MacLaren McCann, Toronto, ON Canada. Tel: (416) 594-6000, FAX: (416) 643-7026, Web Site: www.maclaren.com (35)

MacLeod, Charles, Sanna Mattson MacLeod, Smithtown, NY. Tel: (631) 265-5160, FAX: (631) 265-5185, E-Mail: info@smmadagency.com, Web Site: www.smmadagency.com (35)

MacLeod, Jim, BBM Canada Inc, Don Mills, ON Canada. Tel: (416) 445-9800, FAX: (416) 445-8644, E-Mail: info@bbm.ca, Web Site: www.bbm.ca (30)

MacLeod, Valerie, Gale Research Inc, Farmington Hills, MI. Tel: (248) 699-4253, (800) 877-GALE, FAX: (313) 961-6083, Web Site: www.gale.com (17)

Macleod, Donald, National Semiconductor Corp, Santa Clara, CA. Tel: (408) 721-5000, (800) 272-9959, FAX: (408) 245-0671, E-Mail: new.feedback@nsc.com, Web Site: www.national.com (16)

Maclure, Jennifer, Vail Associates Inc, Broomfield, CO. Tel: (303) 404-1800, (800) 842-8062, FAX: (303) 404-6415, Web Site: www.snow.com (19)

MacNabb, Amy, Infocore Inc, Carlsbad, CA. Tel: (760) 607-2500, FAX: (760) 607-2505, E-Mail: bstewart@infocoreinc.com, Web Site: www.infocoreinc.com (23)

MacNicholl, Tina, The Catamount Group, Southport, CT. Tel: (203) 778-4110, FAX: (203) 778-4130, E-Mail: tina@catamountgroup.net, Web Site: www.catamountgroup.net (23)

Macomber, Mark, E., ABA/BMA Trust Wealth Management and Marketing Conference, Washington, DC. Tel: (202) 663-5000, (800) BANKERS, FAX: (202) 828-4540, E-Mail: custserv@aba.com, Web Site: www.aba.com (42)

MACORP Print Group, Souderton, PA. Tel: (215) 703-0500, (877) 4MACORP, FAX: (215) 703-0501, E-Mail: info@4macorp.com, Web Site: www.4macorp.com (27)

Macourek, Peter, Rose Electronics, Houston, TX. Tel: (281) 933-7673, (800) 333-9343, FAX: (281) 933-0044, E-Mail: sales@rose.com, Web Site: www.rose.com (3)

MacPhee Marketing Communications, Toronto, ON Canada. Tel: (416) 868-1370 (35)

MacPherson, Lori, Buena Vista Home Entertainment, Burbank, CA. Tel: (818) 560-1000, FAX: (818) 845-8728, Web Site: www.bvhe.com (3)

Macromark Inc, Brewster, NY. Tel: (845) 230-6300, FAX: (845) 278-0650, E-Mail: david@macromark.com, Web Site: www.macromark.com (23)

MacRostie, Don, Stewart-MacDonald, Athens, OH. Tel: (740) 592-3021, (800) 848-2273, FAX: (740) 593-7922, E-Mail: hostetler@stewmac.com, Web Site: www.stewmac.com (16)

Macy's, City Of Industry, CA. Tel: (323) 227-2000, FAX: (323) 227-2774, Web Site: www.federated-fds.com (5)

Macy's Marketing, New York, NY. Tel: (212) 695-4400, FAX: (212) 494-1517, Web Site: www.macys.com (16)

Macy's West, San Francisco, CA. Tel: (415) 954-6089, FAX: (415) 954-6103 (16)

Madara, Steve, Liebert Corp, Columbus, OH. Tel: (614) 841-6700, (800) LIEBERT, FAX: (614) 841-6022, Web Site: www.liebert.com (16)

Maddocks, Andy, In Touch Ministries, Atlanta, GA. Tel: (770) 451-1001, Web Site: www.intouch.org (1)

Maddox, Jeff, Jobscope Corp, Greenville, SC. Tel: (864) 458-3143, (800) 443-5794, FAX: (864) 234-4852, E-Mail: marketing@jobscope.com, Web Site: www.jobscope.com (16)

Madison, Paula, National Medical Fellowships, New York, NY. Tel: (212) 483-8880, FAX: (212) 483-8897, Web Site: www.nfm-online.org (1)

Madison Direct Marketing Ltd, Stamford, CT. Tel: (203) 653-3200, FAX: (203) 316-0518, Web Site: www.madisondm.com (31)

Madison Executive Search, Ridgefield, CT. Tel: (203) 431-6565, FAX: (203) 431-6060, E-Mail: mimi@directexec.com, Web Site: www.directexec.com (20)

Madison Sales Group, Northbrook, IL. Tel: (847) 480-2370, FAX: (847) 480-7437 (33)

Madisonavegifts.com, Watertown, NY. Tel: (315) 779-9228, (866) 421-1744, E-Mail: magsales@madisonavegifts.com, Web Site: www.madisonavegifts.com (6)

Madonna, Wendy, A., Penn Mutual, Horsham, PA. Tel: (215) 956-8083, FAX: (215) 956-8368, Web Site: www.pennmutual.com (15)

Madorin, Harry, American Association of Individual Investors, Chicago, IL. Tel: (312) 280-0170, FAX: (312) 280-9883, E-Mail: adam@aaii.com, Web Site: www.aaii.com (1)

Madorsky, Michelle, University of California Irvine Extension, Irvine, CA. Tel: (949) 824-5413, Web Site: extension.uci.edu (1)

Madrigal, Molly, The Sharper Image, New York, NY. Tel: (415) 445-6000, (800) 344-5555, FAX: (800) 552-2525, E-Mail: info@sharperimage.com, Web Site: www.sharperimage.com (6)

Maduras, Randy, Brotherhood America's Oldest Winery Ltd, Washingtonville, NY. Tel: (845) 496-3661, FAX: (845) 496-8720, E-Mail: contact@brotherhoodwinery.net, Web Site: www.brotherhoodwinery.net (19)

Maffucci, Nancy, Wunderman, New York, NY. Tel: (212) 941-3000, FAX: (212) 888-7520, Web Site: www.wunderman.com (35)

Magagna, John, P., MACORP Print Group, Souderton, PA. Tel: (215) 703-0500, (877) 4MACORP, FAX: (215) 703-0501, E-Mail: info@4macorp.com, Web Site: www.4macorp.com (27)

Magazine Publishers of America, New York, NY. Tel: (212) 872-3700, FAX: (212) 888-4217, Web Site: www.magazine.org (17)

Magda, Bobby, Lawn Doctor Inc, Holmdel, NJ. Tel: (732) 946-0029, (800) 631-5660, FAX: (732) 946-9089, Web Site: www.lawndoctor.com (16)

Magee, Jennifer Keating, Keating Magee Advertising, New Orleans, LA. Tel: (504) 299-8000, FAX: (504) 525-6647, E-Mail: jmagee@keatingmagee.com, Web Site: www.keatingmagee.com (35)

Magee, Larry, Bridgestone/Firestone North American Tire LLC, Nashville, TN. Tel: (615) 937-1000, (800) 543-7522, FAX: (615) 937-3721, Web Site: www.bridgestonetire.com (16)

Magee, Monique, Darnay, Editorial Code & Data Inc, Walled Lake, MI. Tel: (248) 926-5187, FAX: (248) 926-6047, E-Mail: Monique@marketsize.com, Web Site: www.marketsize.com (30)

Magee, Tim B., PAC Worldwide, Redmond, WA. Tel: (425) 885-9330, (800) 535-0039, FAX: (425) 885-2934, Web Site: www.pac.com (26)

Magellan's Catalog, Santa Barbara, CA. Tel: (800) 962-4943, FAX: (800) 962-4940, E-Mail: sales@magellans.com, Web Site: www.magellans.com (5)

Magento, Culver City, CA. Tel: (310) 367-5334, Web Site: www.magento.com (22)

Maggio, Steven, J., DaVinci Direct, Plymouth, MA. Tel: (508) 746-2555, FAX: (815) 301-9884, Web Site: www.davinci-direct.com (1)

Maggiore, Dick, Innis Maggiore Group Inc, Canton, OH. Tel: (330) 492-5500, FAX: (330) 492-5568, E-Mail: dick@innismaggiore.com, Web Site: www.innismaggiore.com (35)

Magiathlin, Peter, MBI Inc, Norwalk, CT. Tel: (203) 853-2000, E-Mail: webmail@mbi-inc.com, Web Site: www.mbi-inc.com (16)

Magic Seasonings Mail Order, New Orleans, LA. Tel: (504) 731-3590, (800) 457-2857, FAX: (504) 731-3576, E-Mail: jlm@chefpaul.com, Web Site: www.chefpaul.com (4)

Frank N Magid Associates Inc, Marion, IA. Tel: (319) 377-7345, FAX: (319) 377-5861, E-Mail: mailIA@magid.com, Web Site: www.magid.com (30)

Magidson, Jay, Statistical Innovations Inc, Belmont, MA. Tel: (617) 489-4490, FAX: (617) 489-4499, E-Mail: statisticalinnovations@gmail.com, Web Site: www.statisticalinnovations.com (20)

Magill, Lenny, Gun Video Catalog/LMP, San Diego, CA. Tel: (858) 569-4000, (800) 942-8273, FAX: (858) 569-0505, Web Site: www.gunvideo.com; www.glockstore.com (11)

Magill, Michael, D., Ennis Inc, Midlothian, TX. Tel: (972) 775-9801, (800) 962-0944, FAX: (800) 645-8339, Web Site: www.ennis.com (16)

Maginnis, John, Blue Cross Blue Shield of Louisiana, Baton Rouge, LA. Tel: (225) 295-3307, (800) 599-2583, FAX: (225) 295-2054, E-Mail: help@bcbsla.com, Web Site: www.bcbsla.com (15)

Magjak Printing Corp, Port Chester, NY. Tel: (914) 939-8800, Web Site: www.magjak.com (27)

Magley, Janet, Tidewater Workshop, Egg Harbor City, NJ. Tel: (609) 965-4000, (800) 666-8433, FAX: (609) 965-8212, Web Site: www.tidewaterworkshop.com (8)

The Magna Group, Glen Rock, NJ. Tel: (201) 652-8600, Web Site: www.themagnagroup.com (35)

Magna Publications Inc, Madison, WI. Tel: (608) 246-3580, FAX: (608) 246-3597, Web Site: www.magnapubs.com (17)

Magna-Tel Inc, Cape Girardeau, MO. Tel: (573) 334-3096, FAX: (573) 335-1715, Web Site: www.magna.tel.com (5)

Magna Visual Inc, Saint Louis, MO. Tel: (314) 843-9000, (800) 843-3399, FAX: (314) 843-0000, E-Mail: magna@magnavisual.com, Web Site: www.magnavisual.com (9)

Magnaflux, Glenview, IL. Tel: (847) 657-5300, FAX: (847) 657-5388, Web Site: www.magnaflux.com (16)

Magnani, Greg, Sales Service/America Inc, Alexandria, VA. Tel: (703) 813-2400 (16)

Magnaplan Corp, Champlain, NY. Tel: (518) 298-8404, (800) 361-1192, FAX: (518) 298-2368, E-Mail: info@visualplanning.com, Web Site: www.visualplanning.com (10)

Magnatag Visable Systems, Macedon, NY. Tel: (315) 986-3033, FAX: (315) 986-4000, Web Site: www.magnatag.com (16)

Magnet LLC, Washington, MO. Tel: (636) 239-5661, (800) 458-9457, FAX: (636) 239-4490, E-Mail: contactus@themagnetgroup.com, Web Site: www.magnetllc.com (16)

Magnets 4 Media, Washington, MO. Tel: (843) 216-6665, (800) 642-6384, FAX: (636) 390-5147, E-Mail: sales@magnets4media.com, Web Site: www.magnets4media.com (22)

Magnets USA, Roanoke, VA. Tel: (540) 857-3045, Web Site: www.magnetsusa.com (30)

The Magni Co Inc, McKinney, TX. Tel: (972) 540-2050, (800) 645-9199, FAX: (972) 540-1057, E-Mail: sales@magnico.com, Web Site: www.magnico.com; www.magnilife.com (16)

Magnolia Hall, Jasper, GA. Tel: (404) 351-1910, (866) 410-2755, FAX: (404) 351-2151, E-Mail: belvedere@magnoliahall.com, Web Site: www.magnoliahall.com (8)

Magnum Photos Inc, New York, NY. Tel: (212) 929-6000, FAX: (212) 929-9325, E-Mail: photography@magnumphotos.com, Web Site: www.magnumphotos.com (38)

Magnuson, Eric, Active Network Media & Marketing, San Diego, CA. Tel: (858) 964-6064, (877) 228-4808, Web Site: www.activemarketinggroup.com (23)

Maguire, Michael, Structural Graphics, Essex, CT. Tel: (860) 767-2661, Web Site: www.structuralgraphics.com (27)

Maguire, William, Peninsular Printing of Daytona Beach Inc, Ormond Beach, FL. Tel: (386) 274-4837, FAX: (386) 274-5023, E-Mail: penprint@bellsouth.net, Web Site: www.peninsularprinting.com (27)

Mahaffey, Lisa, AXA Equitable, New York, NY. Tel: (212) 554-1234, (212) 314-2956, Web Site: www.axaonline.com (15)

Mahan, Bart, Buggies Unlimited, Jacksonville, FL. Tel: (888) 444-6364, E-Mail: support@buggiesunlimited.com, Web Site: www.buggiesunlimited.com (12)

Mahan, Kathryn, Brooks Equipment Co, Charlotte, NC. Tel: (704) 596-9438, (800) 826-3473, FAX: (704) 596-1096, Web Site: www.brooksequipment.com (9)

Mahar, Brendan, PacNet Services Ltd, Vancouver, BC. Tel: (604) 689-0399, FAX: (604) 689-0313, E-Mail: info@pacnetservices.com, Web Site: www.pacnetservices.com (14)

Mahar Kerr, Molly, Vermont Ski Areas Association, Montpelier, VT. Tel: (802) 223-2439, FAX: (802) 229-6917, E-Mail: info@skivermont.com, Web Site: www.skivermont.com (14)

Maher, Frank, Integer Group, Des Moines, IA. Tel: (515) 288-7910, FAX: (515) 288-8439, E-Mail: fmaher@integermidwest.com, Web Site: www.integer.com (35)

Maher, Hamilton, BtoB Magazine, New York, NY. Tel: (212) 210-0206, FAX: (212) 210-0422, E-Mail: aholtzman@crain.com, Web Site: www.btobonline.com (43)

Maher, Lawrence, M., Veterans of Foreign Wars (VFW) of the US-National Headquarters, Kansas City, MO. Tel: (816) 756-3390, FAX: (816) 968-1149, E-Mail: info@vfw.org, Web Site: www.vfw.org (1)

Maher, Mark, Web Graphics, Glens Falls, NY. Tel: (518) 792-6501, (800) 833-8863, FAX: (518) 792-9353, (800) 833-8861, E-Mail: marketing@printatweb.com, Web Site: www.printatweb.com (27)

Mahler, Hugh, F., Wolf Envelope Co, Birmingham, MI. Tel: (248) 687-2745, (800) 466-WOLF, FAX: (248) 687-2751, Web Site: www.wolfenvelope.com (26)

Mahlstedt, Pete, Trumble Greetings, Boulder, CO. Tel: (800) 525-0656, FAX: (303) 530-5124, E-Mail: info@leanintree.com, Web Site: www.leanintree.com (6)

Mahon Egen, Maureen, Warner Books, New York, NY. Tel: (212) 364-1200, FAX: (212) 522-7989, Web Site: www.twbookmark.com (17)

Mahoney, Erin, Washington Lists Inc, McLean, VA. Tel: (703) 749-3110, FAX: (703) 749-0960, E-Mail: emahoney@washingtonlists.com, Web Site: www.washingtonlists.com (23)

Mahoney, Kevin, F., A T Cross Co, Lincoln, RI. Tel: (401) 333-1200, (800) 282-7677, FAX: (401) 334-2861, Web Site: www.cross.com (16)

Mahoney, Sharron, Conde Nast, New York, NY. Tel: (212) 286-2860, FAX: (212) 880-8289, Web Site: www.conde.net (17)

Mahoney, Tom, ITAGroup, West Des Moines, IA. Tel: (515) 224-3400, (800) 257-1985, FAX: (515) 224-3589, Web Site: www.itagroup.com (33)

Maiden, James, Long & Foster Insurance, Chantilly, VA. Tel: (703) 278-1426 (15)

Maidenform Inc, Iselin, NJ. Tel: (732) 621-2281, Web Site: www.maidenform.com (2)

Maier, Bruno, Pacific Cycle Inc, Madison, WI. Tel: (608) 268-2468, (800) 724-9466, FAX: (847) 236-3692, (847) 573-0602, E-Mail: info@pacificcycle. com, Web Site: www.pacificcycle.com (16)

Maier, Jim, Baron/Barclay Bridge Supplies, Louisville, KY. Tel: (502) 426-0410, (800) 274-2221, FAX: (502) 426-2044, E-Mail: baronbarclay@ baronbarclay.com, Web Site: www.baronbarclay. com (11)

Maier, Kelley, Ingram Book Group, La Vergne, TN. Tel: (615) 793-5000, (800) 937-8000, FAX: (800) 876-0186, Web Site: www.ipage.ingrambook.com (16)

Maier, Steven, Direct Mail Strategy Group (DMSG), Cresskill, NJ. Tel: (201) 567-3200, FAX: (201) 567-1530, E-Mail: bschonwald@conraddirect.com, Web Site: www.conraddirect.com (31)

Mail Advertising Corp, Fort Worth, TX. Tel: (817) 390-7726, FAX: (817) 390-7223, E-Mail: wjjohnson@star-telegram.com, Web Site: www. macus.com (28)

Mail Advertising Services Inc, Darnestown, MD. Tel: (301) 762-9015 (28)

Mail Advertising Supply Co Inc, Sussex, WI. Tel: (262) 549-1730, (800) 558-2126, FAX: (800) 784-2591 (25)

Mail America, Wheeling, WV. Tel: (304) 242-8081, Web Site: www.mailamerica.com (35)

Mail America Communications - a Dmh Marketing Partners Co, Forest, VA. Tel: (434) 534-8000, Web Site: www.mail-america.com (28)

Mail Boxes Etc, San Diego, CA. Tel: (858) 455-8800, FAX: (858) 546-7488, Web Site: www.mbe.com (28)

Mail Communications, Novato, CA. Tel: (415) 883-2383, FAX: (415) 883-3238, E-Mail: george@ mailcomusa.com, Web Site: www.mailcomusa.com (28)

Mail Computer Service, West Bridgewater, MA. Tel: (508) 584-6490, (800) 640-8530, FAX: (508) 584-2890 (21)

Mail Enterprises LLC, Birmingham, AL. Tel: (205) 595-4945, (800) 595-4945, FAX: (205) 595-4943, Web Site: www.mailent.com (21)

Mail Handling Services, Eden Prairie, MN. Tel: (952) 975-5000, FAX: (952) 975-5030, Web Site: www. mailhandling.com (28)

Mail Management Enterprises, Seaford, DE. Tel: (410) 883-3224, FAX: (410) 883-3392, E-Mail: mailmgt@aol.com, Web Site: www. mailmanagemententerprises.com (20)

Mail Movers & Mailing Services, Upper Darby, PA. Tel: (610) 888-6969, (610) 734-1220, FAX: (610) 734-1200, E-Mail: mailmovers@rcn.com, Web Site: www.mailmoversandmore.com (22)

Mail Order Business, Dubuque, IA. Tel: (319) 589-1000 X1076, (800) 772-9165, FAX: (319) 589-1046, Web Site: www.kendallhunt.com (43)

Mail Order Business Directory, Boca Raton, FL. Tel: (561) 367-3799, FAX: (561) 451-0803, E-Mail: bkleinpub@aol.com (43)

Mail Order Media & Marketing Inc, Fuquay Varina, NC. Tel: (203) 254-9390, FAX: (203) 254-3253, E-Mail: mailordermedia2000@yahoo.com (35)

The Mail Room Inc, Colorado Springs, CO. Tel: (719) 636-1303, (888) 686-1303, FAX: (719) 636-1814, E-Mail: wpowell@themailroominc.com, Web Site: www.themailroominc.com (28)

Mail-Well Envelope, Jersey City, NJ. Tel: (201) 434-2100, (800) 526-3020, E-Mail: info@cenveo.com, Web Site: www.mail-well.com (26)

MailBlazer, Santa Ana, CA. Tel: (714) 662-5396, Web Site: www.mailblazer.com (27)

The Mailbox of Ithaca Inc, Ithaca, NY. Tel: (607) 257-3865, (800) 382-6348, FAX: (607) 266-0508, E-Mail: mailbox@lightlink.com, Web Site: www. mailboxofithaca.com (28)

Mailco Inc, Wayne, NJ. Tel: (973) 777-9500, FAX: (973) 777-5469, E-Mail: marvin@mailcoinc.com, Web Site: www.mailcoinc.com (28)

Mailer's Software, Rancho Santa Margarita, CA. Tel: (949) 858-3000, (800) 635-4772, FAX: (949) 589-5211, Web Site: www.mailerssoftware.com (22)

Mailgraphics, Boulder, CO. Tel: (303) 449-4053, FAX: (303) 938-1544, E-Mail: questions@mailgraphics. com (23)

Mailing & Fulfillment Service Association (MFSA), Alexandria, VA. Tel: (703) 836-9200, (800) 333-6272, FAX: (703) 548-8204, E-Mail: mfsa-mail@ mfsanet.org, Web Site: www.mfsanet.org (40)

Mailing and Fulfillment Service Association of New York, New York, NY. Tel: (212) 217-6824, (800) 394-5106, FAX: (212) 217-6824, E-Mail: info@ mfsany.com, Web Site: www.mfsany.com (34)

The Mailing House Inc, Bell, CA. Tel: (323) 262-6000, FAX: (323) 262-6622, E-Mail: tmh4mail@ themailinghouse.com, Web Site: www. themailinghouse.com (28)

Mailing Lists Plus Inc, Bellevue, WA. Tel: (425) 451-3335, (877) 339-4584, FAX: (425) 646-4485, E-Mail: info@mailinglistsplus.com, Web Site: www.mailinglistsplus.com (21)

Mailing Services of Pittsburgh Inc, Freedom, PA. Tel: (724) 774-3244, (800) 876-3211, FAX: (724) 774-6996, Web Site: www.msp-pgh.com (21)

Mailing Source, Costa Mesa, CA. Tel: (949) 722-9391 (28)

Mailing Specialists Inc, Greensburg, PA. Tel: (724) 832-3840, (888) 216-1056, FAX: (724) 832-8419, E-Mail: sales@mailmsi.com, Web Site: www. mailmsi.com (28)

Mailmaster Corp, Jonesboro, AR. Tel: (870) 972-8845, (800) 551-7018, FAX: (870) 972-0877, E-Mail: info@mail-master.com, Web Site: www.mail-master.com (28)

Mailmen Inc, Hauppauge, NY. Tel: (631) 582-6900, FAX: (631) 582-6948, E-Mail: getresults@ mailmeninc.com, Web Site: www.mailmeninc.com (28)

Mailorder Gardening Association, Elkridge, MD. Tel: (410) 540-9830, FAX: (410) 540-9827, Web Site: www.mailordergardening.com (1)

Mailways Enterprises Inc, Crystal Lake, IL. Tel: (815) 455-4850, FAX: (815) 455-7327, E-Mail: dave@ mailways.com, Web Site: www.mailways.com (28)

Mailworks Inc, Freeport, ME. Tel: (207) 865-1477, FAX: (207) 865-1479, E-Mail: mailwks@aol.com, Web Site: www.mailworks.net (1)

Main, Barbara, Texas Refinery Corp, Fort Worth, TX. Tel: (817) 332-1161, FAX: (817) 336-8441, E-Mail: jhopkins@texasrefinery.com, Web Site: www.texasrefinery.com (9)

Main, Bill, Landscape Forms Inc, Kalamazoo, MI. Tel: (616) 381-0490, (800) 430-6209, FAX: (616) 381-3455, E-Mail: specify@landscapeforms.com, Web Site: www.landscapeforms.com (16)

Main Street Direct, New York, NY. Tel: (212) 779-3000, FAX: (212) 779-3061, E-Mail: jkern@ mainstreetdirect.com, Web Site: www. mainstreetdirect.com (31)

Maine, James, T., Automated Equipment Service Inc, Poughkeepsie, NY. Tel: (845) 452-2100, (800) 468-4068, FAX: (845) 485-8221, E-Mail: info@ aesmailpro.com, Web Site: www.aesmailpro.com (34)

The Maine Connection, Portland, ME. Tel: (207) 780-4355, FAX: (207) 780-4239, E-Mail: ghopkins@ midcoast.com (27)

The Maine Photographic Workshops, Rockport, ME. Tel: (207) 236-8581, (877) 577-7704, FAX: (207) 236-2558, E-Mail: info@theworkshops.com, Web Site: www.theworkshops.com (16)

Maine Potato Board, Presque Isle, ME. Tel: (207) 769-5061, FAX: (207) 764-4148, E-Mail: mainepotatoes@mainepotatoes.com, Web Site: www.mainepotatoes.com (1)

Maingi, Shailesh, Supelco Inc, Bellefonte, PA. Tel: (814) 359-3441, (800) 359-3041, FAX: (814) 359-3044, E-Mail: supelco@sial.com, Web Site: www. sigma-aldrich.com (16)

Mainprice, Rena, Lone Star Web Inc, Dallas, TX. Tel: (214) 443-2200, FAX: (214) 630-4364, E-Mail: jerry@lonestarweb.com, Web Site: www. lonestarweb.com (27)

Maison Glass Delicacies, Jersey City, NJ. Tel: (212) 755-3316, (800) 822-5564, E-Mail: info@ maisonglass.com, Web Site: www.maisonglass.com (4)

Maites, Alan, Robinson & Maites Inc, Chicago, IL. Tel: (312) 372-9333, FAX: (312) 372-0682, E-Mail: amaites@robinsonmaites.com, Web Site: www.robinsonmaites.com (35)

Majestic Marketing Inc, Corona, CA. Tel: (951) 280-2400, Web Site: www.bagmasters.com (35)

Majestic Products Co, Mississauga, ON Canada. Tel: (905) 858-8010, (800) 668-5323, FAX: (905) 670-7915, Web Site: www.cfmcorp.com (16)

Majorium, Stevens Point, WI. Tel: (715) 342-1018, (800) 654-4935, FAX: (715) 342-1118, E-Mail: sales@majorium.com, Web Site: www. letstalkselling.com (17)

Maka, Ted, Shape LLC, Addison, IL. Tel: (630) 620-8394, (800) 367-5811, FAX: (630) 620-0784, E-Mail: sales@shapellc.com, Web Site: www. shapellc.com (3)

Make-A-Wish Foundation of America, Phoenix, AZ. Tel: (602) 279-9474, FAX: (602) 279-0855, Web Site: www.wish.org (1)

Making It Big, Cotati, CA. Tel: (707) 795-1995, (877) 644-1995, FAX: (707) 795-4874, E-Mail: mib@ makingitbig.com, Web Site: www.makingitbig.com (2)

Makofsky, Bob, Conformer Expansion Products Inc, Great Neck, NY. Tel: (516) 504-6300, E-Mail: support@conformerinc.com, Web Site: www. conformerinc.com (26)

Makofsky, Marvin, Conformer Expansion Products Inc, Great Neck, NY. Tel: (516) 504-6300, E-Mail: support@conformerinc.com, Web Site: www. conformerinc.com (26)

Malafi, Elizabeth, Ferguson Publishing Co, New York, NY. Tel: (212) 613-2800, (800) 322-8755, FAX: (800) 678-3633, E-Mail: custserv@factsonfile.com, Web Site: www.fergpubco.com (17)

Malamed, David, Jamax Direct LLC, Englewood Cliffs, NJ. Tel: (201) 569-4540 (23)

Maland, Tim, Nevada Commission on Tourism, Carson City, NV. Tel: (775) 687-4322, (800) NEVADA 8, FAX: (775) 687-6779, Web Site: www. travelnevada.com (1)

Malco Products Inc, Barberton, OH. Tel: (330) 753-0361, (800) 253-2526, FAX: (330) 753-2025, Web Site: www.malcopro.com (16)

Maldonado, Shelley, The Reggio Register Co Inc, Leominster, MA. Tel: (978) 870-1020, (800) 880-3090, FAX: (978) 870-1030, E-Mail: reggio@ reggioregister.com, Web Site: www.reggioregister. com (8)

Male, Jane, Kansas City Direct Marketing Association, Kansas City, MO. Tel: (816) 561-5323, FAX: (816) 561-1991, E-Mail: info@kcdma.org, Web Site: www.kcdma.org (40)

Malek, Kenneth, Ken Malek Associates Inc, Yardley, PA. Tel: (215) 579-2070, FAX: (215) 860-3498, Web Site: www.kenmalek.com (20)

Ken Malek Associates Inc, Yardley, PA. Tel: (215) 579-2070, FAX: (215) 860-3498, Web Site: www. kenmalek.com (20)

Malewicki, Rob, Lab Safety Supply Inc, Janesville, WI. Tel: (608) 754-2345, (800) 356-2855, FAX: (800) 543-9910, Web Site: www.labsafety.com (5)

Malik, Rajiv, UDL Laboratories Inc, Sugar Land, TX. Tel: (281) 240-1000, (800) 231-3052, FAX: (281) 240-0002, Web Site: www.udllabs.com (7)

Malin, Ira, Travel Planners Inc, New York, NY. Tel: (212) 532-1660, (800) 221-3531, FAX: (212) 779-6102, Web Site: www.tphousing.com (19)

Malin, Linda, Barton & Cooney, Burlington, NJ. Tel: (609) 747-9300, FAX: (609) 747-9700, E-Mail: pmdoyle@bartoncooney.com, Web Site: www. bartoncooney.com (28)

Malkani, Shirin, Ziff Davis Media Inc, New York, NY. Tel: (212) 503-5100, FAX: (212) 503-5023, Web Site: www.ziffdavis.com (17)

Mallardi, Mark J., Educational Insights, Inc, Gardena, CA. Tel: (310) 884-2000, (888) 591-9334, FAX: (310) 886-8850, E-Mail: service@edin.com, Web Site: www.educationalinsights.com (16)

Mallette, Ken, Oxfam America, Boston, MA. Tel: (617) 482-1211, (800) 776-9326, FAX: (617) 728-2594, E-Mail: kmallette@oxfamamerica.org, Web Site: www.oxfamamerica.org (1)

Malley, Kenneth, Medco Health Solutions Inc, Franklin Lakes, NJ. Tel: (201) 269-3400, FAX: (201) 269-6400, Web Site: www.medco.com (7)

Mallie, Tina, Zurich, Schaumburg, IL. Tel: (847) 605-3712, (800) 382-2150, FAX: (847) 605-6403, Web Site: www.zurichna.com (15)

Mallin, Ed, Donnelley Marketing, Pearl River, NY. Tel: (201) 476-2300, FAX: (201) 476-2151, Web Site: www.infousa.com (23)

Mallin, Edward, C., Info USA Services Group, Pearl River, NY. Tel: (201) 476-2000, (888) 322-5323, FAX: (201) 476-2301, Web Site: www.infousa.com (23)

Mallof, Joseph T., World Kitchen Inc, Corning, NY. Tel: (607) 377-8000, (800) 999-3436, FAX: (607) 377-8946, Web Site: www.worldkitchen.com (16)

Mallory, Linda, Harriet Carter Gifts Inc, Montgomeryville, PA. Tel: (215) 361-5100, FAX: (215) 361-1127, Web Site: www.harrietcarter.com (6)

Malloy, Dennis, New Hampshire Public Television, Durham, NH. Tel: (603) 868-1100, E-Mail: themailbox@nhptv.org, Web Site: www.nhptv.org (32)

Malloy, Lawrence, State Line Tack Inc, Phoenix, AZ. Tel: (623) 580-6100, (800) 228-9208, FAX: (623) 580-6183, E-Mail: customerservice@statelinetack. com, Web Site: www.statelinetack.com (16)

MALM Chemical Corp, Pound Ridge, NY. Tel: (914) 764-5775, FAX: (914) 764-5386, E-Mail: custserv1@malms.com, Web Site: www.malms. com (16)

Malone, Dr Beverly, National League for Nursing, New York, NY. Tel: (212) 363-5555, (800) 669-1656, FAX: (212) 812-0391, E-Mail: generalinfo@ nln.org, Web Site: www.nln.org (1)

Malone, Gayle, TALX Corp, Dallas, TX. Tel: (972) 755-2100, FAX: (972) 755-2080, E-Mail: consulting@managementinsights.com, Web Site: www.managementinsights.com (16)

Malone, John, Thousand Trails LP, Chicago, IL. Tel: (214) 618-7200, (800) 205-0606, FAX: (214) 618-7324, Web Site: www.1000trails.com (16)

Malone, Joseph J., Horace Mann Educators Corp, Springfield, IL. Tel: (217) 789-2500, FAX: (217) 788-5161, Web Site: www.horacemann.com (15)

Malone, Mark, Lowe's Companies Inc, Mooresville, NC. Tel: (704) 758-1000, FAX: (336) 651-4766, Web Site: www.lowes.com (8)

Malone, Mary, Orient Expressed Imports Inc, New Orleans, LA. Tel: (888) 856-3948, FAX: (504) 899-5566, E-Mail: orient@orientexpressed.com, Web Site: www.orientexpressed.com (2)

Malone, Tim, Mohawk Lifts, Amsterdam, NY. Tel: (518) 842-1431, (800) 833-2006, FAX: (518) 842-1289, E-Mail: rwells@mohawklifts.com, Web Site: www.mohawklifts.com (9)

Maloney, Antoinette, The Maloney Group, New York, NY. Tel: (212) 777-6655, FAX: (212) 777-6600 (16)

Maloney, E. F., EF Maloney Inc, Mamaroneck, NY. Tel: (718) 549-7000, FAX: (718) 549-6320, E-Mail: efmaloney@aol.com, Web Site: www. efmaloney.com (16)

Maloney, Julie, Broadford & Maloney Inc, New York, NY. Tel: (212) 836-4710, FAX: (917) 322-2105, E-Mail: m.maloney@bmcorp.com, Web Site: bmcorp.com (35)

Maloney, Peter, Potpourri Group Inc, Chelmsford, MA. Tel: (978) 256-4100, FAX: (978) 256-1961/0344, Web Site: www.potpourrigroup.com (6)

Maloney, R J, The Weather Channel, New York, NY. Tel: (212) 856-5200, FAX: (212) 856-5215, Web Site: www.weather.com (32)

Maloney, Scott, Smart Practice, Phoenix, AZ. Tel: (800) 522-0800, FAX: (800) 522-8329, E-Mail: info@smartpractice.com, Web Site: www. smartpractice.com (17)

Maloney, Sean, M., Intel Corp, Santa Clara, CA. Tel: (408) 765-8080, (800) 548-4725, FAX: (408) 765-6187, Web Site: www.intel.com (16)

Maloney, Terry, Isuzu Motors America Inc, Anaheim, CA. Tel: (562) 229-5000, (800) 255-6727, FAX: (562) 229-5463, Web Site: www.isuzu.com (16)

Maloney, Theresa, National Review, New York, NY. Tel: (212) 679-7330, FAX: (212) 849-2852, Web Site: www.nationalreview.com (17)

Maloney, Tom, Aramark Uniform Services, Burbank, CA. Tel: (818) 953-2022, Web Site: www.aramark-uniform.com (2)

EF Maloney Inc, Mamaroneck, NY. Tel: (718) 549-7000, FAX: (718) 549-6320, E-Mail: efmaloney@ aol.com, Web Site: www.efmaloney.com (16)

The Maloney Group, New York, NY. Tel: (212) 777-6655, FAX: (212) 777-6600 (16)

Maloof, George, New England Life Insurance Co, Boston, MA. Tel: (617) 578-2000, FAX: (617) 536-2393, Web Site: www.nefn.metlife.com (15)

Malordy, Jody, Metropolitan Museum of Art, New York, NY. Tel: (212) 879-5500, FAX: (718) 628-5485, Web Site: www.metmuseum.org/store (8)

Maloy, Judith, Polaris Direct, Hooksett, NH. Tel: (603) 626-5800, E-Mail: info@polarisdirect.net, Web Site: www.polarisdirect.net (28)

Malvaso, Rebekah, Briefings Publishing Group, Richmond, VA. Tel: (703) 567-1982, (800) 791-8699, FAX: (703) 684-2136, E-Mail: rmalvaso@ douglaspublications.com, Web Site: www. briefings.com (17)

Malys, Marcia, MediaWorks Advertising & Marketing Inc, Ormond Beach, FL. Tel: (407) 909-1903, E-Mail: mmalys@cfl.rr.com, Web Site: www. mediaworksusa.com (21)

Mammel, Kevin, Quark Inc, Denver, CO. Tel: (303) 894-3832, Web Site: www.quark.com (34)

Management Science Associates Inc, Pittsburgh, PA. Tel: (412) 362-2000, (800) MSA-INFO, FAX: (412) 363-5598, E-Mail: info@msa.com, Web Site: www.msa.com (20)

Mancelli, Vincent, UDL Laboratories Inc, Sugar Land, TX. Tel: (281) 240-1000, (800) 231-3052, FAX: (281) 240-0002, Web Site: www.udllabs.com (7)

Manchester Farms Inc, Columbia, SC. Tel: (803) 469-2588, (800) 845-0421, FAX: (803) 469-8637, E-Mail: customerservice@manchesterfarms.com, Web Site: www.manchesterfarms.com (4)

Manchikatla, Lavanya, REWAY Inc, Miramar, FL. Tel: (954) 205-1996, Web Site: www.rewayconsulting. com (22)

Mancinelli, Ozzie, Paradise Galleries, Irvine, CA. Tel: (858) 793-4000, FAX: (858) 793-3425, E-Mail: omancinelli@paradisegalleries.com, Web Site: www.paradisegalleries.com (6)

Mancini, John, AIIM International, Silver Spring, MD. Tel: (301) 587-8202, (800) 477-2446, FAX: (301) 587-2711, E-Mail: aiim@aiim.org, Web Site: www. aiim.org (1)

Mancoma Inc, Davenport, IA. Tel: (563) 323-6245, FAX: (563) 323-0804, E-Mail: b.mangan@ mancoma.com (23)

Mancuso, Leslie, Chase Media Group, Yorktown Heights, NY. Tel: (914) 962-3871, FAX: (914) 962-2040, Web Site: www.chasemultimedia.com (27)

Mancuso, Lisa, Fisher-Price, East Aurora, NY. Tel: (716) 687-3300, FAX: (716) 687-3636, Web Site: www.fisherprice.com (16)

Mancuso, Paulanne, Calvin Klein Cosmetics Co, New York, NY. Tel: (212) 759-8888, FAX: (212) 479-4399 (7)

Mancuso, Steve, DMC Corp, Kearny, NJ. Tel: (973) 589-0606, FAX: (973) 589-8931, Web Site: www. dmc-usa.com (16)

Mandel, Leonard, LMC Direct, Ottawa, ON Canada. Tel: (613) 521-8181, FAX: (613) 521-3015 (23)

Mandel, Leslie, The Rich List Co, Wainscott, NY. Tel: (212) 737-8917, FAX: (212) 861-5384, E-Mail: richlistco@aol.com, Web Site: www.richlist.com (24)

Mandel, Rick, Mandel Co, Milwaukee, WI. Tel: (414) 271-6970, (800) 888-6970, FAX: (414) 271-1254, E-Mail: rick.mandel@mandelcompany.com, Web Site: www.mandelcompany.com (27)

Mandel Co, Milwaukee, WI. Tel: (414) 271-6970, (800) 888-6970, FAX: (414) 271-1254, E-Mail: rick.mandel@mandelcompany.com, Web Site: www.mandelcompany.com (27)

Mandelbaum, Howard, Photofest, New York, NY. Tel: (212) 633-6330, FAX: (212) 366-9062, E-Mail: requests@photofestnyc.com (38)

Mandell, Andrew, J., Data-Mail Inc, Newington, CT. Tel: (860) 666-0399, FAX: (860) 665-1226, E-Mail: brucem@data-mail.com, Web Site: www. data-mail.com (28)

Mandell, Mark, Data-Mail Inc, Newington, CT. Tel: (860) 666-0399, FAX: (860) 665-1226, E-Mail: brucem@data-mail.com, Web Site: www.data-mail. com (28)

Manderfield, Ellen, Rockler Woodworking & Hardware, Medina, MN. Tel: (763) 478-8201, (800) 279-4441, FAX: (763) 478-8393, E-Mail: info@ rockler.com, Web Site: www.rockler.com (8)

Mandia, Mark, DMW Worldwide LLC, Chesterbrook, PA. Tel: (610) 407-0407, (877) 744-3699, FAX: (610) 407-9201, E-Mail: whunter@dmwdirect.com, Web Site: www.dmwdirect.com (35)

Mane Solutions, New York, NY. Tel: (212) 736-0306, FAX: (212) 239-2039 (16)

Maneto, Jim, Hemmings Motor News, Bennington, VT. Tel: (800) 227-4373, FAX: (802) 447-9631, Web Site: www.hmn.com (17)

Manetti, Louis, Polyair Packaging, Chicago, IL. Tel: (773) 995-1818, (888) POLYAIR X444, FAX: (773) 995-7725, E-Mail: marketing@polyair.com, Web Site: www.polyair.com (9)

Maneval, Judy, Sanky Communications Inc, New York, NY. Tel: (212) 868-4300, Web Site: www. sankyinc.com (1)

Manfredi, Bill, Wunderman, New York, NY. Tel: (212) 941-3000, FAX: (212) 888-7520, Web Site: www. wunderman.com (35)

Mangan, Benjamin, W., Mancoma Inc, Davenport, IA. Tel: (563) 323-6245, FAX: (563) 323-0804, E-Mail: b.mangan@mancoma.com (23)

Mangano, Domenic, J., Village Coin Shop, Plaistow, NH. Tel: (603) 382-5492/7151, FAX: (603) 382-5682, E-Mail: don@villagecoin.com, Web Site: www.villagecoin.com (6)

Mangano, Frank, American Student List LLC, Farmingdale, NY. Tel: (516) 248-6100, (888) 462-5600, FAX: (516) 248-6364, E-Mail: sales@studentlist. com, Web Site: www.studentlist.com (23)

Mangialardi, Frank, Post Linx Corp, Scarborough, ON Canada. Tel: (416) 752-8100, FAX: (416) 752-8239, Web Site: www.postlinx.com (28)

Mangieri, Christopher, J., Mangieri/Hull Solutions LLC, Sandy Hook, CT. Tel: (203) 270-4800, FAX: (203) 270-4815, E-Mail: chris@mhrecruiters.com, Web Site: www.mhrecruiters.com (20)

Mangieri/Hull Solutions LLC, Sandy Hook, CT. Tel: (203) 270-4800, FAX: (203) 270-4815, E-Mail: chris@mhrecruiters.com, Web Site: www. mhrecruiters.com (20)

Mangone, David, TVA Productions Inc (The Video Agency), Studio City, CA. Tel: (818) 505-8300, (888) 322-4296, FAX: (818) 505-8370, E-Mail: info@tvaproductions.com, Web Site: www.tvaproductions.com (35)

Mangrich, Gerry, Universal Engineering Corp, Cedar Rapids, IA. Tel: (319) 365-0441, (800) 366-2051, FAX: (319) 369-5440, E-Mail: info@universalcrusher.com, Web Site: www.universalcrusher.com (3)

Manhattan College, Bronx, NY. Tel: (718) 862-7285, Web Site: www.manhattan.edu (1)

Manhattan Media Services Inc, New York, NY. Tel: (212) 808-4077, FAX: (212) 808-4080, E-Mail: mmorello@manhmedia.com, Web Site: www.manhmedia.com (21)

Manheim Steamroller, Omaha, NE. Tel: (402) 457-4341, FAX: (402) 457-4332, E-Mail: mailbox@amgram.com, Web Site: www.manheimsteamroller.com (3)

Manheimer, Heidi, Shiseido Cosmetics America, New York, NY. Tel: (212) 805-2300, FAX: (212) 688-0109, Web Site: www.sca.shiseido.com (7)

Manis, Lee, American Bible Society, New York, NY. Tel: (212) 408-1200, FAX: (212) 408-1264, Web Site: www.americanbible.org (1)

Manistique Papers Inc, Manistique, MI. Tel: (906) 341-2175, FAX: (906) 341-5635 (25)

Manko, Janet, The Lakeville Journal LLC, Lakeville, CT. Tel: (860) 435-9873, FAX: (860) 435-4802 (37)

Manley, Eugene, Manley & Associates Inc, Woodridge, IL. Tel: (630) 963-1123, FAX: (630) 963-1124 (35)

Manley & Associates Inc, Woodridge, IL. Tel: (630) 963-1123, FAX: (630) 963-1124 (35)

Mann Jr., Robert, Accenture, Boston, MA. Tel: (617) 488-4000, FAX: (617) 488-4001, Web Site: www.accenture.com (20)

Mann, David, Professional Marketing Associates, Mount Pleasant, SC. Tel: (843) 971-8150, FAX: (843) 971-8159 (33)

Mann, John, Datamann Inc, Wilder, VT. Tel: (802) 295-6600, (800) 451-4263, FAX: (802) 296-3623, Web Site: www.datamann.com (22)

Mann, Judith, S., Capital Design, Providence, RI. Tel: (401) 270-6777, FAX: (401) 438-9360, E-Mail: info@freemiums.com, Web Site: www.freemiums.com (33)

Irma S Mann Strategic Marketing Inc, Boston, MA. Tel: (617) 353-1822, FAX: (617) 266-1890, Web Site: www.irmamann.com (35)

Manna, Christina, Association of National Advertisers Inc, New York, NY. Tel: (212) 697-5950, FAX: (212) 687-7310, Web Site: www.ana.net (40)

Mannarino, Melanie, Redbook Magazine, New York, NY. Tel: (212) 649-2000, (800) 888-0008, FAX: (212) 581-7605, Web Site: www.redbookmag.com (17)

Mannatt, Wendy, Paladin Press, Boulder, CO. Tel: (303) 443-7250, (800) 392-2400, FAX: (303) 442-8741, E-Mail: service@paladin-press.com, Web Site: www.paladin-press.com (17)

Mannello Jr., Louis, J., Zurich, Schaumburg, IL. Tel: (847) 605-3712, (800) 382-2150, FAX: (847) 605-6403, Web Site: www.zurichna.com (15)

Manning, Frederick, J., Celtic Life Insurance Co, Chicago, IL. Tel: (312) 332-5401, FAX: (312) 441-0341, E-Mail: info@celtic-net.com, Web Site: www.celtic-net.com (15)

Manning, Gay, Datasystem Solutions Inc, Overland Park, KS. Tel: (913) 362-6969, FAX: (913) 362-6383, E-Mail: sales@mutipub.com, Web Site: www.datasystem.com (22)

Manning, James, Astronomical Society of the Pacific, San Francisco, CA. Tel: (415) 337-1100, (800) 335-2624, FAX: (415) 337-5205, E-Mail: service@astrosociety.org, Web Site: www.astrosociety.org (1)

Manning, Jeannene, Finelight Inc, Louisville, KY. Tel: (502) 589-5896, E-Mail: info@finelight.com, Web Site: www.finelight.com (35)

Manning, Jennifer, Country Financial, Bloomington, IL. Tel: (309) 821-3000 (15)

Manning, Kenneth, P., Sensient Technologies, Saint Louis, MO. Tel: (314) 889-7600, (800) 325-8110, FAX: (314) 658-7318, Web Site: www.sensient-tech.com (16)

Manning, Kimberly, Cronin & Co, Glastonbury, CT. Tel: (860) 659-0514, Web Site: www.cronin-co.com (16)

Manning, Mike, Manning Media International, Mc Kinney, TX. Tel: (972) 562-6960, Web Site: www.manningmedia.com (23)

Manning, Paul, Springer Science & Business Media LLC, New York, NY. Tel: (212) 460-1500, FAX: (212) 473-6272, Web Site: www.springer-ny.com (17)

Manning Materials, Birdsboro, PA. Tel: (610) 385-6797, (800) 445-1719, FAX: (610) 385-7524, E-Mail: mmsupport@manningmaterials.com, Web Site: www.manningmaterials.com (16)

Manning Media International, Mc Kinney, TX. Tel: (972) 562-6960, Web Site: www.manningmedia.com (23)

Mannion, Meg, Emerging Marketing, Columbus, OH. Tel: (614) 923-6000 X229, FAX: (614) 424-6200, E-Mail: chris@360em.com, Web Site: www.emergingmarketing.com (35)

Manns, Tinisha, Denver Metro Convention & Visitors Bureau, Denver, CO. Tel: (303) 892-1112, FAX: (303) 892-1636, Web Site: www.denver.org (1)

Mano, Barry, Referee Enterprises, Franksville, WI. Tel: (262) 632-8855, FAX: (262) 632-5460, E-Mail: questions@referee.com, Web Site: www.referee.com (1)

Manoogian, Richard, A., Masco Corp, Taylor, MI. Tel: (313) 274-7400, FAX: (313) 792-6135, E-Mail: webmaster@mascohq.com, Web Site: www.masco.com (16)

Manos, John, Consumers Digest Inc, Deerfield, IL. Tel: (847) 607-3000, FAX: (847) 763-0200, E-Mail: postmaster@consumersdigest.com, Web Site: www.consumersdigest.com (17)

Manos, Steve, Kadant Johnson Inc, Three Rivers, MI. Tel: (269) 278-1715, FAX: (269) 279-5980, Web Site: www.kadantjohnson.com (16)

Manos, Wayne, Cold Spring Harbor Lab Press, Woodbury, NY. Tel: (516) 422-4100, (800) 843-4388, FAX: (516) 422-4097, E-Mail: cshpress@cshl.edu, Web Site: www.cshlpress.com (17)

Manseau, Andrea, PEP Direct, Wilton, NH. Tel: (603) 654-6141, Web Site: www.pep-direct.com (21)

Mansfield, Edward, The Washingtonian, Washington, DC. Tel: (202) 296-3600, E-Mail: editorial@washingtonian.com, Web Site: www.washingtonian.com (17)

Mansfield, John, The Durham Manufacturing Co, Durham, CT. Tel: (860) 349-3427, (800) 243-3774, FAX: (800) 782-5499, (860) 349-8572, E-Mail: info@durhammfg.com, Web Site: www.durhammfg.com (16)

Manson, Jeffrey, Western Psychological Services, Torrance, CA. Tel: (310) 478-2061, (800) 648-8857, FAX: (310)) 478-7838, E-Mail: marketing@wpspublish.com, Web Site: www.wpspublish.com (16)

Mansueto, Joe, Morningstar Inc, Chicago, IL. Tel: (312) 696-6000, Web Site: www.morningstar.com (14)

Mantica, Karen, Local Government Federal Credit Union, Raleigh, NC. Tel: (919) 755-0534, Web Site: www.lgfcu.org (14)

Mantych, Christine, Stark Brothers Nurseries & Orchards, Louisiana, MO. Tel: (573) 754-8800, (800) 325-4180, E-Mail: info@starkbros.com, Web Site: www.starkbros.com (8)

Mantz, James, Mercy Home for Boys & Girls, Chicago, IL. Tel: (312) 738-7560, Web Site: www.mercyhome.org (1)

Mantz, Macia, Informal Education Products, Milwaukie, OR. Tel: (503) 794-7100, (888) 444-5500, FAX: (503) 794-7111, E-Mail: sales@museumtour.com, Web Site: www.museumtour.com (11)

Manufacturers-News Inc, Evanston, IL. Tel: (847) 864-7000, (888) 752-5200, FAX: (847) 332-1100, E-Mail: hdubin@manufacturersnews.com, Web Site: www.manufacturersnews.com (23)

Manulife Financial Inc, Toronto, ON Canada. Tel: (416) 229-4515, (800) 387-0990, FAX: (416) 229-3028, Web Site: www.manulife.com (15)

Manus, Morty, Alfred Publishing Co Inc, Van Nuys, CA. Tel: (818) 891-5999, (800) 292-6122, FAX: (818) 895-5301, E-Mail: sales@alfred.com, Web Site: www.alfred.com (17)

Manus, Ron, Alfred Publishing Co Inc, Van Nuys, CA. Tel: (818) 891-5999, (800) 292-6122, FAX: (818) 895-5301, E-Mail: sales@alfred.com, Web Site: www.alfred.com (17)

Manus, Steven, Alfred Publishing Co Inc, Van Nuys, CA. Tel: (818) 891-5999, (800) 292-6122, FAX: (818) 895-5301, E-Mail: sales@alfred.com, Web Site: www.alfred.com (17)

Manville, Sheryl, American Family Life Assurance Co of Columbus (AFLAC), Columbus, GA. Tel: (706) 323-3431, (800) 992-3522, FAX: (706) 660-7446, Web Site: www.aflac.com (15)

Manypenny, Tiena, Dean & Deluca Brands Inc, Wichita, KS. Tel: (316) 683-1255, Web Site: www.deandeluca.com (4)

Manzee, William, Eastern Mountain Sports, Peterborough, NH. Tel: (603) 924-9571, (800) 463-6367, FAX: (603) 924-4320, Web Site: www.ems.com (16)

Manzi, Jim, P., Thermo Fisher Scientific I, Waltham, MA. Tel: (781) 622-1000, (800) 678-5599, FAX: (781) 622-1207, Web Site: www.thermofisher.com (9)

MAP International, Brunswick, GA. Tel: (912) 265-6010, (800) 225-8550, FAX: (912) 265-6170, Web Site: www.map.org (1)

Mapes, Ann, Drs Foster & Smith Inc, Rhinelander, WI. Tel: (715) 369-3305, Web Site: www.drsfostersmith.com (2)

Mapes, Christopher, L., AO Smith Corp, Milwaukee, WI. Tel: (414) 359-4000, FAX: (414) 359-4064, Web Site: www.aosmith.com (16)

MapInfo, Canada, Toronto, ON Canada. Tel: (416) 594-5200, (800) 268-3282, FAX: (416) 594-5201, E-Mail: canada.sales@mapinfo.com, Web Site: www.mapinfo.com (24)

Maple Grove Farms of Vermont Inc, Saint Johnsbury, VT. Tel: (802) 748-5141, FAX: (802) 748-9647, E-Mail: maple@maplegrove.com, Web Site: www.maplegrove.com (4)

Mapping Analytics, Rochester, NY. Tel: (585) 271-6490, (877) 893-6490, FAX: (585) 271-1132, E-Mail: sales@mappinganalytics.com, Web Site: www.mappinganalytics.com (20)

Mar, Sandy, LiveOps Inc, Santa Clara, CA. Tel: (408) 844-2400, Web Site: www.liveops.com (29)

Mar-San, Chicago, IL. Tel: (773) 583-5700, (800) 621-5582, FAX: (773) 583-1740, E-Mail: sales@mar-san.com, Web Site: www.mar-san.com (33)

Mara, Thomas, Leucadia National Corp, New York, NY. Tel: (212) 460-1900, FAX: (212) 598-4869, Web Site: www.leucadia.com (14)

Maradonna, Bonnie, Winterthur Museum & Country Estate, Wilmington, DE. Tel: (302) 888-4600, (800) 448-3883, FAX: (302) 888-4730, E-Mail: tourinfo@winterthur.org, Web Site: www.winterthur.org (6)

Marastar Communications, Wayne, PA. Tel: (610) 902-0080, FAX: (610) 902-0600, E-Mail: info@marastar.com, Web Site: www.marastar.com (13)

Marathon Norco Aerospace Inc, Waco, TX. Tel: (254) 776-0650, FAX: (254) 776-6558, Web Site: www. mptc.com (16)

Marber, Allen, Walter E Heller College of Business Administration, Chicago, IL. Tel: (312) 281-3293, FAX: (312) 281-3290, Web Site: www.roosevelt. edu (41)

Marc USA, Pittsburgh, PA. Tel: (412) 562-2015, FAX: (412) 562-2022, Web Site: www.marcusa.com (35)

Marcantonio, Mike, Allegra Network, LLC, Plymouth, MI. Tel: (248) 596-8600, FAX: (248) 596-8601, Web Site: www2.allegranetwork.com (27)

Marcario, Robert, W., National Rifle Association of America, Fairfax, VA. Tel: (703) 267-1000, (800) 672-3888, FAX: (703) 267-3957, E-Mail: nra. contact@nra.org, Web Site: www.nra.org (1)

March of Dimes Birth Defects Foundation, White Plains, NY. Tel: (914) 428-7100, FAX: (914) 428-8203, Web Site: www.modimes.org (1)

Marchese, David, Marchese Communications Inc, Marina Del Rey, CA. Tel: (213) 533-6444, (213) 399-5999, (866) 441-8086, E-Mail: david@ marchesecommunications.com, Web Site: www. marchesecommunications.com (35)

Marchese, Joseph, WS Ponton Inc, Pittsburgh, PA. Tel: (412) 782-2360, (800) 628-7806, FAX: (412) 782-1109, E-Mail: joseph@wsponton.com, Web Site: www.wsponton.com (23)

Marchese Communications Inc, Marina Del Rey, CA. Tel: (213) 533-6444, (213) 399-5999, (866) 441-8086, E-Mail: david@marchesecommunications. com, Web Site: www.marchesecommunications. com (35)

Marchetti, Karen, J, Strategic Marketing and Advertising Inc, Carlsbad, CA. Tel: (760) 930-6123, E-Mail: dmservices@smaresource.com, Web Site: www.responsefx.com (35)

Marciniak, Lori, Heath Kit Co, Saint Joseph, MI. Tel: (269) 925-6000, (800) 253-0570, FAX: (269) 925-2898, E-Mail: info@heathkit.com, Web Site: www. heathkit.com (3)

Marco, Barbara, Marco Data Service, De Soto, MO. Tel: (636) 337-3109, FAX: (636) 586-1938 (22)

Marco Data Service, De Soto, MO. Tel: (636) 337-3109, FAX: (636) 586-1938 (22)

Marco Sales & Incentives Ltd, Brantford, ON Canada. Tel: (519) 751-2227, (888) 636-6161, FAX: (519) 751-0561, E-Mail: sales@themarcocorporation. com, Web Site: www.themarcocorporation.com (28)

MarCom Technologies, Kelowna, BC Canada. Tel: (250) 868-9352, FAX: (250) 868-9362 (29)

MARCOR Remediation Inc, Halethorpe, MD. Tel: (410) 785-0001, (800) 547-0128, FAX: (410) 771-0348, E-Mail: info@marcor.com, Web Site: www. marcor.com (16)

Marcott, Mary, NOVO1, Fort Worth, TX. Tel: (817) 355-6899, FAX: (817) 355-8505, Web Site: www. novo1.com (29)

Marcoux, Remi, Telemedia Communications US, North York, ON Canada. Tel: (416) 733-7600, (888) 290-1466 Can., (800) 461-3773 U.S., FAX: (416) 733-3563, E-Mail: info@transcontinental.ca, Web Site: www.transcontinental.com (17)

Marcoux, Remi, Trans Continental Inc, Montreal, PQ Canada. Tel: (514) 954-4000, FAX: (514) 954-4016, Web Site: www.transcontinental-gtc.com (31)

Marcus, Bruce, D., The McGraw-Hill Cos, New York, NY. Tel: (212) 904-2000, (866) 436-8502, FAX: (212) 512-3840, Web Site: www.mcgraw-hill.com (17)

Marcus, Joan, Lester Inc, Branford, CT. Tel: (203) 488-5265, (800) 999-5265, FAX: (203) 483-0408, Web Site: www.lesterusa.com (29)

Marcus, Madeline, Cablevision Systems Corp, Bethpage, NY. Tel: (516) 803-2300, FAX: (516) 803-3134, Web Site: www.cablevision.com (16)

Marcus, Steven, Marcus Productions Inc, Fort Lauderdale, FL. Tel: (954) 922-9166, E-Mail: steve@ marcusproductions.com, Web Site: www. marcusproductions.com (32)

Marcus Productions Inc, Fort Lauderdale, FL. Tel: (954) 922-9166, E-Mail: steve@ marcusproductions.com, Web Site: www. marcusproductions.com (32)

Mardak, Keith, Hal Leonard Corp, Milwaukee, WI. Tel: (414) 774-3630, FAX: (414) 774-3259, Web Site: www.halleonard.com (17)

Marden-Kane Inc, Garden City, NY. Tel: (516) 365-3999, FAX: (516) 365-5250, E-Mail: expert@ mardenkane.com, Web Site: www.mardenkane.com (35)

Mardev, New York, NY. Tel: (212) 584-9370, (800) 545-8517, FAX: (212) 584-9371, E-Mail: sales@ mardev.com, Web Site: www.mardev.com (24)

Mardev-DM2, Lombard, IL. Tel: (800) 323-4958, FAX: (303) 265-5457, E-Mail: info@mardevdm2. com, Web Site: www.mardevdm2.com (24)

Mardiron Optics, Stoneham, MA. Tel: (781) 938-8339, FAX: (781) 938-8339, Web Site: www. mardironooptics.com (11)

Mardirosian, K. Greg, Mardiron Optics, Stoneham, MA. Tel: (781) 938-8339, FAX: (781) 938-8339, Web Site: www.mardironooptics.com (11)

Marecek, Douglas, Integrated Print & Graphics, South Elgin, IL. Tel: (847) 695-6777, Web Site: www. ipandginc.com (27)

Margalit, Shlomo, MRV Communications, Chatsworth, CA. Tel: (818) 773-0900, FAX: (818) 773-0906, Web Site: www.mrv.com (3)

Margolies, Mervyn, Merjo Advertising & Sales Promotions Co, Owings Mills, MD. Tel: (410) 345-9000, FAX: (410) 345-9002, E-Mail: merjoadv@ qis.net, Web Site: www.promoplace.com/merjo (33)

Margolin, Leslie, Anthem Blue Cross, Westlake Village, CA. Tel: (805) 557-6655, (800) 333-0912, FAX: (800) 557-6872, Web Site: www.bluecrossca. com (15)

Margolis, John, D., Northwestern University, Evanston, IL. Tel: (847) 491-3741, FAX: (847) 491-8406, E-Mail: webmaster@northwestern.edu, Web Site: www.northwestern.edu (41)

Margro, Thomas, E., San Francisco Bay Area Rapid Transit District (BART), Oakland, CA. Tel: (510) 464-6000, FAX: (510) 464-7103, Web Site: www. bart.gov (16)

Margulies, Jacob, Continental Envelope Corp, Geneva, IL. Tel: (630) 262-8080, (800) 621-8155, FAX: (630) 262-1450, Web Site: www. continentalenvelope.com (26)

Marian Helpers Center, Stockbridge, MA. Tel: (413) 298-3691, (800) 462-7426, FAX: (413) 298-3583, Web Site: www.marian.org (1)

Marianacci, Thomas, Media Resource Group Inc, Mount Kisco, NY. Tel: (914) 471-4448, FAX: (914) 244-4458, Web Site: www.mrginc.com (31)

Mariano, Joseph, Direct Selling Association, Washington, DC. Tel: (202) 452-8866, FAX: (202) 452-9010, E-Mail: info@dsa.org, Web Site: www.dsa. org (40)

Marie, Ruth, Association of Energy Engineers, Atlanta, GA. Tel: (770) 447-5083 x210, FAX: (770) 446-3969, E-Mail: info@aeecenter.org, Web Site: www.aeecenter.org (40)

Marimac Inc, Montreal, PQ Canada. Tel: (514) 725-7600, FAX: (514) 376-0801, Web Site: www. marimac.com (8)

Marinea, Phil, Levi Strauss & Co, San Francisco, CA. Tel: (415) 501-6000, FAX: (415) 501-7112, Web Site: www.levistrauss.com (16)

Marinkovich, David, DHL Global Mail, Weston, FL. Tel: (954) 903-6300, (866) 616-MAIL, FAX: (954) 903-6310, E-Mail: contact@dhlglobalmail.com, Web Site: www.dhlglobalmail.com (28)

Marino, Anne, Shiseido Cosmetics America, New York, NY. Tel: (212) 805-2300, FAX: (212) 688-0109, Web Site: www.sca.shiseido.com (7)

Marino, Edward, J., Presstek Inc, Hudson, NH. Tel: (800) 422-3616 (34)

Marino, Felicia, Instructor's Choice Dancewear, Massapequa Park, NY. Tel: (516) 799-7010, FAX: (516) 799-7993, E-Mail: customerservice@ instructorschoice.com, Web Site: www. instructorschoice.com (2)

Marino, Glenn, Premier Packaging Corp, Victor, NY. Tel: (877) 924-8460, FAX: (585) 924-8753, E-Mail: info@premiercustompkg.com, Web Site: www.premiercustompkg.com (16)

Marino, Glenn, Tucker Printers, Henrietta, NY. Tel: (585) 359-3030, Web Site: www.tuckerprinters.com (27)

Marino, Pamela, Choice Magazine, Middletown, CT. Tel: (860) 347-6933, (860) 347-1387, FAX: (860) 346-8586, E-Mail: adsales@ala-choice.org, Web Site: www.ala.org/ala/acrl/acrlpubs/choice/home. cfm (31)

Marion, Ed, The EZ-Forms Co, Kerrville, TX. Tel: (281) 667-4414, FAX: (281) 667-4415, E-Mail: ezformscontactus@gmail.com, Web Site: www.ez-forms.com (21)

Maris West & Baker, Jackson, MS. Tel: (601) 977-9200, FAX: (601) 977-9257, Web Site: www.mwb. com (35)

Maritz, Fenton, MO. Tel: (636) 827-4246, FAX: (636) 827-8929, Web Site: www.maritz.com (35)

Marjon, Steven, Shutterfly, Redwood City, CA. Tel: (650) 610-5200, Web Site: www.shutterfly.com (27)

The Mark Group, Boca Raton, FL. Tel: (561) 241-1700, (800) 637-0152, FAX: (561) 241-1055, Web Site: www.bostonproper.com (2)

Mark James & Associates Inc, Oswego, IL. Tel: (630) 548-8100, FAX: (630) 548-6107, E-Mail: info@ markjamesassociates.com, Web Site: www. markjamesassociates.com/contact.html (16)

Marke Communications Inc, New York, NY. Tel: (212) 201-0600, (800) 716-2753, FAX: (212) 213-0785, Web Site: www.marke.com (35)

Markertek Video Supply, Saugerties, NY. Tel: (845) 246-3036, (800) 522-2025, FAX: (847) 246-1757, E-Mail: sales@markertek.com, Web Site: www. markertek.com (3)

Markese, John D., American Association of Individual Investors, Chicago, IL. Tel: (312) 280-0170, FAX: (312) 280-9883, E-Mail: adam@aaii.com, Web Site: www.aaii.com (1)

Market-Ability Inc, Lafayette, CA. Tel: (925) 299-7900, (800) 434-6275, FAX: (925) 284-2331, Web Site: www.market-ability.net (35)

Market Approach Consulting, Lorena, TX. Tel: (254) 857-7017, Web Site: www.marketapproach.net (23)

Market Builder Inc, Mesa, AZ. Tel: (480) 641-6200, FAX: (480) 641-6239, E-Mail: info@ themarketbuilder.com, Web Site: www. themarketbuilder.com (21)

Market Data Retrieval, Shelton, CT. Tel: (203) 926-4800, (800) 333-8802, FAX: (203) 929-5253, E-Mail: mdrinfo@dnb.com, Web Site: www. schooldata.com (23)

Market Development Group Inc, Washington, DC. Tel: (202) 298-8030, FAX: (202) 244-4999, Web Site: www.mdginc.org (1)

Market Discovery Group, Roslyn, NY. Tel: (516) 365-8555, E-Mail: schiffmanl@aol.com (30)

Market Focus Direct, Markham, ON Canada. Tel: (905) 477-0801, FAX: (905) 477-4473, E-Mail: info@market-focus.com, Web Site: www.market-focus.com (28)

Market Focus Inc, Evanston, IL. Tel: (847) 328-2900, FAX: (847) 328-8121 (30)

Market Force Corp, Newtown Square, PA. Tel: (610) 356-5220, FAX: (610) 356-5110, E-Mail: davethomas@marketforcecorp.com, Web Site: www.marketforcecorporation.com (23)

Market Incentives Corp, Frazer, PA. Tel: (610) 644-5700, (800) 486-8881, FAX: (610) 889-9636, E-Mail: micpa@marketincentives.com, Web Site: www.marketincentives.com (33)

Market Probe International Inc, New York, NY. Tel: (212) 725-7676, FAX: (212) 725-7529, E-Mail: info@marketprobeint.com, Web Site: www.marketprobeint.com (30)

Market Recognition, Boxborough, MA. Tel: (978) 314-0127, Web Site: www.marketrecognition.com (20)

Market Response International, South Orleans, MA. Tel: (508) 240-1877, FAX: (508) 945-4010, E-Mail: rmiller@capecod.net, Web Site: www.millerinternational.com (30)

MARKET SHARE, Bradenton, FL. Tel: (941) 794-6059, FAX: (941) 794-6059, E-Mail: rsouthwick@tampabay.rr.com (23)

Market Square Communications Inc, Stevens Point, WI. Tel: (715) 344-4609, FAX: (715) 344-6885 (20)

Market Street Lists Inc, Exeter, NH. Tel: (603) 772-6666, (888) 675-LIST, FAX: (603) 772-0184, E-Mail: info@market-street.com, Web Site: www.market-street.com (23)

MarketAide Services Inc, Salina, KS. Tel: (785) 825-7161, (800) 204-2433, FAX: (785) 825-4697, E-Mail: kcarlgren@marketaide.com, Web Site: www.marketaide.com (21)

Marketeers, Mission Viejo, CA. Tel: (949) 364-1669, FAX: (949) 582-0829, E-Mail: wbower@apc.net (29)

MarketerNet LLC, Chicago, IL. Tel: (312) 775-9320, (888) 443-3684, FAX: (312) 775-9328, E-Mail: info@marketernet.com, Web Site: www.marketernet.com (22)

Marketfish Inc, Seattle, WA. Tel: (206) 905-1090, FAX: (206) 694-2564, Web Site: www.marketfish.com (23)

The Marketing Advantage Inc, Little Rock, AR. Tel: (501) 954-7771, FAX: (501) 954-7879, E-Mail: central_reservations@tmae.net, Web Site: www.freevacations.com (21)

Marketing Advents, Alexandria, VA. Tel: (703) 706-0387, FAX: (703) 836-2181, E-Mail: info@dmaw.org, Web Site: www.dmaw.org (43)

Marketing Agencies Association Worldwide, Minneapolis, MN. Tel: (952) 922-0130, FAX: (203) 969-1499, E-Mail: keith.mccracker@maaw.org, Web Site: www.maaw.org (40)

The Marketing Agency LLC, Fort Lauderdale, FL. Tel: (954) 771-1177, FAX: (866) 379-5788, E-Mail: marketing@themarketingagency.com, Web Site: www.themarketingagency.com (35)

The Marketing Alliance, Fairfield, CT. Tel: (203) 254-0474 (20)

Marketing & Media Services LLC, Warwick, RI. Tel: (401) 737-7730, Web Site: www.mmsipitv.com (30)

Marketing and Product Strategy, Peabody, MA. Tel: (978) 977-2000, (800) 825-5897, FAX: (781) 238-0986, Web Site: www.lhsl.com (16)

Marketing & Promotions Group, Ridgewood, NJ. Tel: (201) 251-8339, FAX: (201) 251-8340, Web Site: www.promowave.com (35)

Marketing Communication Resource Inc, Willoughby, OH. Tel: (440) 484-3010, FAX: (440) 484-3020 (28)

Marketing Connections Corp, Bedford, NH. Tel: (603) 472-8989, (800) 472-1818, FAX: (603) 472-9881, E-Mail: lcasey@mccnh.com, Web Site: www.mcciq.com (29)

Marketing Consulting Services, Kingsport, TN. Tel: (423) 288-5866, FAX: (423) 288-5576 (20)

Marketing Direct Inc, Saint Louis, MO. Tel: (314) 590-8300, FAX: (314) 966-5632, E-Mail: dbarnes@marketingdirect.com, Web Site: www.marketingdirect.com (35)

Marketing Economics Inc, Chicago, IL. Tel: (312) 642-2188, FAX: (312) 642-3091, E-Mail: codyh@meimedia.com, Web Site: www.meimedia.com (23)

Marketing Efficiency Corp, Cornelius, NC. Tel: (704) 896-5995, FAX: (704) 896-3426 (35)

Marketing General Inc, Alexandria, VA. Tel: (703) 739-1000, (800) 644-6646, FAX: (703) 549-6057, E-Mail: info@marketinggeneral.com, Web Site: www.marketinggeneral.com (35)

Marketing Highway, Deerfield, IL. Tel: (312) 502-3732, E-Mail: info@marketinghighway.com, Web Site: www.marketinghighway.com (20)

Marketing Horizons Inc, Saint Louis, MO. Tel: (314) 432-1957, (800) 669-0839, FAX: (314) 432-7014, E-Mail: jkramer@mhorizons.com (30)

Marketing Incentives International Inc, Chicago, IL. Tel: (312) 440-3700, (866) 440-3700, FAX: (312) 943-5813, E-Mail: miibenefits@rcn.com, Web Site: www.mktgincentiveintl.com (33)

Marketing Information Network, Edmond, OK. Tel: (405) 516-1215, FAX: (405) 516-1230, Web Site: www.minokc.com (22)

Marketing Innovators, Rosemont, IL. Tel: (847) 696-1111, (800) 543-7373, FAX: (847) 696-3194, E-Mail: info@marketinginnovators.com, Web Site: www.marketinginnovators.com (35)

The Marketing Machine, Irvine, CA. Tel: (949) 733-3778, (949) 733-1778, FAX: (949) 559-6993, E-Mail: request@the-marketing-machine.com, Web Site: www.mktgmach.com (39)

Marketing/Media Dynamics Inc, Harpers Ferry, WV. Tel: (304) 725-1119 (20)

Marketing News, Chicago, IL. Tel: (312) 542-9000, (800) 262-1150, FAX: (312) 542-9001, E-Mail: news@ama.org, Web Site: www.ama.org (43)

Marketing1by1 LLC, Fairfax, VA. Tel: (703) 934-6020, Web Site: marketing1by1.com (22)

Marketing Out-of-the-Box Inc, Chicago, IL. Tel: (847) 588-8100, (888) 588-8100, FAX: (847) 294-0706, E-Mail: possibilities@motb.com, Web Site: motb.com (35)

The Marketing Place, Sun Valley, CA. Tel: (818) 834-8500, FAX: (818) 834-8511, E-Mail: mktgplace@aol.com, Web Site: wwwthemarketingplace.com (23)

Marketing Research Association, Washington, DC. Tel: (860) 682-1000, FAX: (860) 682-1010, E-Mail: email@mra-net.org, Web Site: www.mra-net.org (40)

Marketing Resources Network Inc, Marina Del Rey, CA. Tel: (310) 459-2271, FAX: (310) 459-2287 (32)

Marketing Results Inc, Sicklerville, NJ. Tel: (856) 740-3334, FAX: (856) 740-3335, Web Site: www.marketingresults.net (16)

Marketing Science Institute Review, Cambridge, MA. Tel: (617) 491-2060, FAX: (617) 491-2065, E-Mail: msi@msi.org, Web Site: www.msi.org (43)

Marketing Signals Group, Frisco, TX. Tel: (386) 761-4840, Web Site: www.movesignals.com (23)

Marketing Solutions, Lathrup Village, MI. Tel: (248) 443-5252, FAX: (248) 443-5252 (20)

Marketing Solutions Group Inc, Pleasanton, CA. Tel: (510) 331-7625, E-Mail: info@marketingsolutionsgroup.biz, Web Site: www.marketingsolutionsgroup.biz (32)

Marketing Solutions Now Inc, Roswell, GA. Tel: (770) 777-4121, Web Site: www.marketingsolutionsnow.com (23)

Marketing Solutions Unlimited LLC, West Hartford, CT. Tel: (860) 523-0670, FAX: (860) 523-0675, E-Mail: info@msudirectmail.com, Web Site: www.msudirectmail.com (21)

The Marketing Store, Lombard, IL. Tel: (630) 693-1400, Web Site: www.themarketingstore.com (35)

Marketing Strategies, North Myrtle Beach, SC. Tel: (843) 692-9662, FAX: (843) 272-4913, E-Mail: pr@marketingstrategiesinc.com, Web Site: www.marketingstrategiesinc.com (35)

Marketing Synergy Inc, Naperville, IL. Tel: (630) 328-9550, FAX: (630) 328-9553, E-Mail: RHlavac@MSINetwork.com, Web Site: www.msinetwork.com (30)

Marketing Systems Analysis, Ventnor, NJ. Tel: (609) 487-9340, FAX: (866) 214-3208, E-Mail: ernie@schell.com, Web Site: www.schell.com (20)

Marketing III Direct Response, Clermont, FL. Tel: (352) 241-8040, FAX: (352) 241-4533, E-Mail: marketing35th@aol.com (35)

Marketing Visions Inc, Deerfield Beach, FL. Tel: (954) 421-2002, E-Mail: marvisions@aol.com (21)

Marketing Visions Inc, Tarrytown, NY. Tel: (914) 631-3900, FAX: (914) 631-3003, E-Mail: marvisions@aol.com (35)

Marketing Works Inc, Los Angeles, CA. Tel: (323) 436-2000, FAX: (213) 382-7538, E-Mail: marketingwork@mediaone.net, Web Site: www.mworks-inc.com (32)

MarketLeverage, Lake Mary, FL. Tel: (407) 805-8800, Web Site: www.precisionplaymedia.com (22)

Marketlinc, Saskatoon, SK Canada. Tel: (306) 956-7000, FAX: (306) 668-5812, E-Mail: info@marketlinc.com, Web Site: www.marketlinc.com (29)

MarketMakers Group Inc, Wayne, PA. Tel: (610) 254-8924, FAX: (610) 254-9190, E-Mail: rlail@marketmakers.com, Web Site: www.marketmakersgroup.com (29)

MarketNet Services LLC, Spring Lake, MI. Tel: (616) 847-7992, Web Site: www.marketnet1.com (22)

The MarketPlace Group Inc, Norwood, MA. Tel: (781) 762-6600, FAX: (781) 762-1300 (31)

Marketplace of the Master Inc, Rockford, IL. Tel: (815) 874-1733, (800) 621-1255, FAX: (815) 874-4351, E-Mail: marketplace@marketplaceofthemaster.com, Web Site: www.marketplaceofthemaster.com (5)

MarketPower Direct Marketing, Atlanta, GA. Tel: (404) 433-5555, E-Mail: joel@marketpoweronline.com, Web Site: www.marketpoweronline.com (35)

Marketrac Inc, Westbury, NY. Tel: (516) 365-4330, FAX: (516) 365-5789 (20)

Marketry Inc, Bellevue, WA. Tel: (425) 451-1262, (800) 346-2013, FAX: (425) 451-1941, E-Mail: greg@marketry.com, Web Site: www.marketry.com (23)

MarketSense, Burr Ridge, IL. Tel: (630) 654-0170, Web Site: www.market-sense.com (35)

Marketshare Publications Inc, Overland Park, KS. Tel: (913) 338-3360, (800) 488-8051, FAX: (913) 217-2895, Web Site: www.marketsharepubs.com (17)

Marketsmith Inc, Parsippany, NJ. Tel: (973) 889-0006, Web Site: www.marketsmithinc.com (21)

MarketVision Research Inc, Cincinnati, OH. Tel: (513) 791-3100, FAX: (513) 794-3500, E-Mail: jpinnell@mv-research.com, Web Site: www.marketvisionresearch.com (30)

Markey, Krislynne, Trade Show Exhibitors Association, Chicago, IL. Tel: (312) 842-8732, FAX: (312) 842-8744, Web Site: www.tsea.org (42)

Markgraf, Richard J., Markgraf & Wells Marketing, Minneapolis, MN. Tel: (612) 870-8550 (35)

Markgraf & Wells Marketing, Minneapolis, MN. Tel: (612) 870-8550 (35)

Markham, Ann, Communication Creativity, Buena Vista, CO. Tel: (720) 344-4388, (800) 331-8355, FAX: (866) 685-0307, E-Mail: steve@steveheimberg.com, Web Site: www.communicationcreativity.com (17)

Markham, Elizabeth, Focus Plus Inc, New York, NY. Tel: (212) 675-0142, (800) 340-8846, FAX: (212) 645-3171, E-Mail: info@focusplusny.com, Web Site: www.focusplusny.com (30)

Marking Specialists Group, Buffalo Grove, IL. Tel: (847) 793-8100, (800) 678-8073, FAX: (847) 793-8109, E-Mail: info@marking-specialists.com, Web Site: www.marking-specialists.com (27)

Markinson, Brian, A., King Pharmaceuticals, Inc, Bristol, TN. Tel: (423) 989-8000, (888) 840-5370, FAX: (423) 274-8677, Web Site: www.kingpharm. com (7)

Markley, H.J., Deere & Co Headquarters, Moline, IL. Tel: (309) 765-8000, FAX: (309) 765-5671, Web Site: www.deere.com (16)

Markley, H.J., John Deere Consumer Products, Moline, IL. Tel: (309) 765-8000, FAX: (309) 748-0114, Web Site: www.johndeere.com (16)

Markley, Lyn, Frito-Lay, Plano, TX. Tel: (972) 334-7000, (800) 352-4477, FAX: (972) 334-2019, Web Site: www.fritolay.com (16)

MARKOTS, Menlo Park, CA. Tel: (925) 240-0093, Web Site: www.markots.com (35)

Marks, Dan, ServiceMaster Co, Memphis, TN. Tel: (901) 766-1400, (901) 597-8502, (888) 937-3783, (866) 782-6787, FAX: (901) 766-1491, Web Site: www.servicemaster.com (8)

Marks, Fred, Direct Marketing Market Place, Berkeley Heights, NJ. Tel: (908) 673-1000, (800) 473-7020, FAX: (908) 673-1179 (43)

Marks, Fred, Marquis Who's Who LLC, Berkeley Heights, NJ. Tel: (908) 673-1000, (800) 473-7020, FAX: (908) 673-1179, E-Mail: info@ marquiswhoswho.com, Web Site: www. marquiswhoswho.com (17)

Marks, Peter, Maris West & Baker, Jackson, MS. Tel: (601) 977-9200, FAX: (601) 977-9257, Web Site: www.mwb.com (35)

Marks, Suzanne, Pasadena Advertising, Pasadena, CA. Tel: (626) 584-0011, Web Site: www. pasadenaadvertising.com (35)

Marks, Ted, Fowler's Chocolates Inc, Buffalo, NY. Tel: (716) 877-9983, (800) 824-2263, FAX: (716) 877-9959, E-Mail: customerservice@ fowlerschocolates.com, Web Site: www. fowlerschocolates.com (4)

Marks, Valerie, Linett & Harrison, Union, NJ. Tel: (908) 686-0606, FAX: (908) 686-0623, E-Mail: sharrison@linettandharrison.com, Web Site: www. linettandharrison.com (35)

Markson, Mitch, Edelman Direct Marketing Inc, Great Neck, NY. Tel: (516) 829-9398 (20)

Markson Scientific LLC, Henderson, NC. Tel: (808) 791-0490, (800) 528-5114, FAX: (800) 858-2243, E-Mail: sales@markson.com, Web Site: www. markson.com (9)

Markwell, D.G., MAX Federal Credit Union, Montgomery, AL. Tel: (334) 260-2600, (800) 776-6776, FAX: (334) 270-0921, Web Site: www.mymax.com (14)

Markwins International Corp, City of Industry, CA. Tel: (909) 595-8898, FAX: (909) 595-8820, Web Site: www.markwins.com (16)

Marlow, Bruce, W., 21st Century Insurance, Woodland Hills, CA. Tel: (818) 704-3700, FAX: (818) 226-1198, E-Mail: executiveoffice@21st.com, Web Site: www.21st.com (16)

Marlowe, Anthony, TMone, Iowa City, IA. Tel: (868) 577-2461, E-Mail: srteam@tmone.com, Web Site: www.tmone.com (29)

Marlowe, John, W., Markson Scientific LLC, Henderson, NC. Tel: (808) 791-0490, (800) 528-5114, FAX: (800) 858-2243, E-Mail: sales@markson. com, Web Site: www.markson.com (9)

Marmelstein Inc, Philadelphia, PA. Tel: (215) 925-9862, FAX: (215) 925-3889 (16)

Marmion, Sally, Leadership Software Corp, Nyack, NY. Tel: (845) 358-0406, (800) 872-0068, FAX: (845) 358-0359, E-Mail: info@leadersoft.com, Web Site: www.leadersoft.com (16)

Marmitt, Sandy, Burtch Works LLC, Evanston, IL. Tel: (847) 328-6902, Web Site: www.burtchworks. com (20)

The Marmon Group LLC, Chicago, IL. Tel: (312) 372-9500, FAX: (312) 845-5305, Web Site: www. marmon.com (16)

Marnell, Thomas, J., Marnell Database Marketing, Chicago, IL. Tel: (312) 944-3511 (20)

Marnell Database Marketing, Chicago, IL. Tel: (312) 944-3511 (20)

Marogni, Aldo, California Society of CPA's, San Mateo, CA. Tel: (800) 922-5272, FAX: (650) 522-3009, E-Mail: info@culcpa.org, Web Site: www. calcpa.org (1)

Maron Esq., Lawrence, New Jersey Institute for Continuing Legal Education, New Brunswick, NJ. Tel: (732) 249-5100, Web Site: www.njicle.com (1)

Marquardt, Roche & Partners, Stamford, CT. Tel: (203) 327-0890, FAX: (203) 353-8487, E-Mail: ideas@mrp-website.com, Web Site: www.mrp-website.com (35)

Marquilis, Bill, Lifetime Brands Inc, Garden City, NY. Tel: (516) 683-6000, FAX: (516) 683-6161, E-Mail: postmaster@brands.com, Web Site: www. lifetimebrands.com (8)

Marquis, Nancy, Sales Magic Inc, Boynton Beach, FL. Tel: (561) 732-5263, (800) 940-7991, FAX: (561) 375-9413, Web Site: www.names.com (32)

Marquis, Steve, Visible Results USA Inc, Overland Park, KS. Tel: (913) 851-9400, FAX: (913) 851-0628, E-Mail: info@visibleresults.com, Web Site: www.visibleresults.com (32)

Marquis Awards & Specialties Inc, Powell, WY. Tel: (307) 754-2272, (800) 327-2446, FAX: (307) 754-9577, Web Site: www.rushawards.com (35)

Marquis Who's Who LLC, Berkeley Heights, NJ. Tel: (908) 673-1000, (800) 473-7020, FAX: (908) 673-1179, E-Mail: info@marquiswhoswho.com, Web Site: www.marquiswhoswho.com (17)

Marra, Thomas, M., The Hartford Financial Services Inc, Southington, CT. Tel: (860) 843-8070, (860) 547-5000, FAX: (860) 547-2680, Web Site: www. thehartford.com (15)

Marrachi, Tom, Aircraft Spruce & Specialty Co, Corona, CA. Tel: (909) 372-9555, (877) 4-Spruce, FAX: (909) 372-0555, E-Mail: info@aircraft-spruce.com, Web Site: www.aircraft-spruce.com (12)

Marrah, John, Profit Center Software Inc, Port Washington, NY. Tel: (516) 414-6300, (888) 446-6240, FAX: (516) 414-6304, E-Mail: jmarrah@ profitcenter.com, Web Site: www.profitcenter.com (22)

Marriott Jr., J.W., Marriott International Inc, Washington, DC. Tel: (301) 380-3000, (301) 380-1791, E-Mail: internet.customer.care@marriott.com, Web Site: www.marriott.com (19)

Marriott International Inc, Washington, DC. Tel: (301) 380-3000, (301) 380-1791, E-Mail: internet. customer.care@marriott.com, Web Site: www. marriott.com (19)

Marriott Ownership Resorts Sales & Marketing, Orlando, FL. Tel: (407) 206-6000, (800) 850-6674, FAX: (407) 851-1304 (19)

Marrocco, Tracy, Penn Mutual, Horsham, PA. Tel: (215) 956-8083, FAX: (215) 956-8368, Web Site: www.pennmutual.com (15)

Marron, Donald, B., The Museum of Modern Art, New York, NY. Tel: (212) 708-9400, FAX: (212) 333-1123, E-Mail: info@moma.org, Web Site: www.moma.org (5)

Marrow, Michael, P., APAC Customer Services Inc, Bannockburn, IL. Tel: (847) 374-4980, (800) 688-7687, FAX: (847) 236-5453, Web Site: www. apaccustomerservices.com (29)

Marrs, Donald, International Marketing Partners Ltd, Los Angeles, CA. Tel: (310) 665-1155, FAX: (310) 665-1155, E-Mail: info@intermarketingonline.com (35)

Mars Research, Fort Lauderdale, FL. Tel: (954) 771-7725, (877) 755-2805, FAX: (954) 771-8824, E-Mail: ron@marsresearch.com, Web Site: www. marsresearch.com (30)

Mars-Povietti, Laura, Grey House Publishing, Amenia, NY. Tel: (518) 789-8700, (800) 562-2139, FAX: (518) 789-0556, E-Mail: books@greyhouse.com, Web Site: www.greyhouse.com (43)

Marsh, Danielle, Chief Executive Magazine, Greenwich, CT. Tel: (203) 930-2700, Web Site: www. chiefexecutive.net (17)

Marsh, Jeffrey, Littleton Coin Co Inc, Littleton, NH. Tel: (603) 444-5386, FAX: (603) 444-0121, E-Mail: jhennessey@littletoncoin.com, Web Site: www.littletoncoin.com (6)

Marsh, Ronald, K., Audience Identification Inc, Lisle, IL. Tel: (630) 435-0460, FAX: (630) 435-0470, E-Mail: rmarsh@audienceid.com (22)

Marsh Affinity Group Services, Chicago, IL. Tel: (800) 621-3008, Web Site: www.seaburychicago. com (15)

Marsh US Consumer, Urbandale, IA. Tel: (515) 365-6102 (15)

Marshall Sr., James, Epson America, Long Beach, CA. Tel: (562) 981-3840, (800) 873-7766, FAX: (562) 290-5220, Web Site: www.epson.com (10)

Marshall, Beth, AM Leonard Inc, Piqua, OH. Tel: (937) 773-2694, (800) 543-8955, FAX: (800) 433-0633, (937) 773-9993, E-Mail: info@amleo.com, Web Site: www.amleo.com (8)

Marshall, Cindy, Pace Communications Inc, Greensboro, NC. Tel: (336) 378-6065, FAX: (336) 275-2864, Web Site: www.pacecommunications.com (17)

Marshall, Craig A., Marshall Marketing & Communications Inc, Pittsburgh, PA. Tel: (412) 914-0970, FAX: (412) 914-0971, Web Site: www.mm-c.com (30)

Marshall, David, Chiasso, Chicago, IL. Tel: (877) CHIASSO, FAX: (312) 477-3827, Web Site: www. chiasso.com (6)

Marshall, Era, C., Smithsonian Institution, Washington, DC. Tel: (202) 357-2700, Web Site: www.si. edu (6)

Marshall, Janice, USAA Alliance Services Marketing, San Antonio, TX. Tel: (210) 456-9857, FAX: (210) 498-4542, Web Site: www.usaa.com (14)

Marshall, Kathy, Chain Store Guide, Tampa, FL. Tel: (800) 927-9292, FAX: (813) 627-6882, E-Mail: info@csgis.com, Web Site: www.csgis.com (17)

Marshall, Kenneth, Camping World Inc, Bowling Green, KY. Tel: (270) 781-2718, (800) 626-6189, FAX: (270) 796-8991, Web Site: www. campingworld.com (11)

Marshall, Kim, Lorenza, Denver Metro Convention & Visitors Bureau, Denver, CO. Tel: (303) 892-1112, FAX: (303) 892-1636, Web Site: www.denver.org (1)

Marshall, Peter, D2: Direct, Denville, NJ. Tel: (973) 627-4410, FAX: (973) 627-3703, E-Mail: info@ d2direct.com, Web Site: www.d2direct.com (35)

Marshall, Tom, Bowers Envelope Co, Indianapolis, IN. Tel: (317) 253-4321, FAX: (317) 254-2231, Web Site: www.bowersenvelope.com (26)

Marshall & Ilsley Corp, Milwaukee, WI. Tel: (414) 765-7801, FAX: (414) 765-7899, Web Site: www. micorp.com (14)

Marshall & Swift, Los Angeles, CA. Tel: (213) 683-9000, FAX: (213) 683-9010, Web Site: www. marshallswift.com (17)

Marshall Domestics LLC, West Warwick, RI. Tel: (401) 821-8760, (800) 556-7440, FAX: (401) 821-2230, E-Mail: marshalldomestics@verizon.net, Web Site: www.marshalldomestics.com (5)

Marshall Fields Dept Stores, Minneapolis, MN. Tel: (612) 375-3004, Web Site: www.fields.com (5)

Marshall Marketing & Communications Inc, Pittsburgh, PA. Tel: (412) 914-0970, FAX: (412) 914-0971, Web Site: www.mm-c.com (30)

Marshik, Kelly, Sense of Design Inc, Minnetonka, MN. Tel: (952) 935-8827 (36)

Marsicano, Denise, Frederick's of Hollywood Group Inc, Los Angeles, CA. Tel: (323) 466-5151, (800) 323-9525, FAX: (323) 464-5149, Web Site: www. fredericks.com (2)

Marsicano, Linda, Playboy Enterprises Inc, Beverly Hills, CA. Tel: (310) 860-1215, Web Site: www. playboyenterprises.com (17)

Marszalek, Lewis, R., Celtic Life Insurance Co, Chicago, IL. Tel: (312) 332-5401, FAX: (312) 441-0341, E-Mail: info@celtic-net.com, Web Site: www.celtic-net.com (15)

Martel, David, Harbor Freight Tools, Camarillo, CA. Tel: (805) 445-4791, (800) 423-2567, FAX: (800) 445-4925, Web Site: www.harborfreight.com (9)

Martens, Chris, NextScreen LLC, Austin, TX. Tel: (512) 892-8682, Web Site: www.avguide.com (17)

Martens, Lisa, Everyday Media, Garrison, NY. Tel: (845) 788-3900, FAX: (212) 481-7800, Web Site: www.everydaymedia.com (31)

Marth, William, Teva Pharmaceuticals USA, North Wales, PA. Tel: (215) 591-3000, (888) TEVAUSA, FAX: (215) 591-8600, Web Site: www.tevausa.com (7)

Martha, Geoffrey, Medtronic Inc, Minneapolis, MN. Tel: (763) 514-4000, (800) 328-2518, FAX: (763) 514-4879, Web Site: www.medtronic.com (16)

Martin Jr., Dumas, The Idea Club.com(TM) & Dumas Martin Consulting, Pomona, CA. Tel: (909) 620-4772, FAX: (909) 629-4739, E-Mail: theideaclub@peoplepc.com, Web Site: www.incorpman.com (16)

Martin Jr., Rodney, O., American General Life Insurance Co, Houston, TX. Tel: (713) 522-1111, FAX: (713) 522-8531, Web Site: www.aglife.com (15)

Martin, Beverly, Libertyville Saddle Shop Inc, Libertyville, IL. Tel: (847) 362-0570, FAX: (847) 680-3200, E-Mail: info@saddleshop.com, Web Site: www.saddleshop.com (11)

Martin, Bill, Century Photo, Santa Fe Springs, CA. Tel: (800) 767-0777, FAX: (714) 441-4550, Web Site: www.centuryphoto.com (10)

Martin, Bob, Bike Nashbar, Crab Orchard, WV. Tel: (800) NAS-HBAR, FAX: (877) 778-9456, E-Mail: custserv@nashbar.com, Web Site: www.bikenashbar.com (11)

Martin, Bob, Louisiana State Museum, New Orleans, LA. Tel: (504) 568-6968, (800) 568-6968, FAX: (504) 568-4995, Web Site: www.lsm.crt.state.la.us (1)

Martin, Claire, Promotional Product Professionals of Canada, Saint-Laurent, PQ Canada. Tel: (514) 489-5359, FAX: (514) 489-7760, (800) 489-8741, E-Mail: gladys@pppc.ca, Web Site: www.pppc.ca (1)

Martin, Don, Bloomin Promotions, Boulder, CO. Tel: (303) 443-3591, Web Site: www.bloominpromotions.com (25)

Martin, Greg, Libertyville Saddle Shop Inc, Libertyville, IL. Tel: (847) 362-0570, FAX: (847) 680-3200, E-Mail: info@saddleshop.com, Web Site: www.saddleshop.com (11)

Martin, Jack L., Libertyville Saddle Shop Inc, Libertyville, IL. Tel: (847) 362-0570, FAX: (847) 680-3200, E-Mail: info@saddleshop.com, Web Site: www.saddleshop.com (11)

Martin, Jean, Center for Professional Development, Tallahassee, FL. Tel: (850) 644-8004, (850) 487-1691, FAX: (850) 644-2589, Web Site: www.Learningforlife.fsu.com (16)

Martin, Joan, Brahmin Leather Works, Fairhaven, MA. Tel: (508) 994-4000, (800) 229-2428, FAX: (508) 994-4153, Web Site: www.brahminusa.com (16)

Martin, Joe, Monster Magnet, Louisville, KY. Tel: (800) 255-0234, Web Site: www.monstermagnet.com (16)

Martin, John, K., Time Warner Inc, New York, NY. Tel: (212) 484-8000, Web Site: www.timewarner.com (16)

Martin, Jonathan, Telecom Inc, Oakland, CA. Tel: (510) 873-8283, (800) 243-3101, FAX: (510) 873-8293, Web Site: www.telecominc.com (29)

Martin, Kristina, M., West Virginia University, Morgantown, WV. Tel: (304) 293-3505, FAX: (304) 293-3072, E-Mail: wvuwebmaster@mail.wvu.edu, Web Site: www.wvu.edu (41)

Martin, Larry, T., St Louis Post-Dispatch, Saint Louis, MO. Tel: (314) 340-8000, (800) 365-0820, FAX: (314) 340-3140, Web Site: www.postnet.com (17)

Martin, Linda, Mary Elizabeth Granger & Associates Inc, Baltimore, MD. Tel: (410) 842-1170, (800) 296-5157, FAX: (410) 842-1185, E-Mail: bonnie@maryegranger.com, Web Site: www.maryegranger.com (23)

Martin, Louise, Psion Teklogix Inc, Mississauga, ON Canada. Tel: (905) 813-9900, (800) 322-3437, E-Mail: ptinfo@psion.com, Web Site: www.psionteklogix.com (3)

Martin, Murray, D., Pitney Bowes Software Systems, Stamford, CT. Tel: (800) 624-5377, Web Site: www.pitneybowes.com (22)

Martin, Patrick, C., Saint Gregory Group, Cincinnati, OH. Tel: (513) 769-8440, FAX: (513) 769-1640, E-Mail: pmartin@stgregory.com, Web Site: www.stgregory.com (35)

Martin, Paul, MSC Metalworking, Melville, NY. Tel: (516) 812-2000, (800) 521-9520, E-Mail: inquiry@rutlandtool.com, Web Site: www.rutlandtool.com (34)

Martin, Rebecca, Oneupweb, Traverse City, MI. Tel: (231) 922-9977, (877) 568-7477, FAX: (231) 922-9966, E-Mail: info@oneupweb.com, Web Site: www.oneupweb.com (35)

Martin, Richard, Goodwill Industries of San Francisco, San Francisco, CA. Tel: (415) 575-2101, FAX: (415) 575-2170, Web Site: www.sfgoodwill.org (1)

Martin, Robert, Marco Sales & Incentives Ltd, Brantford, ON Canada. Tel: (519) 751-2227, (888) 636-6161, FAX: (519) 751-0561, E-Mail: sales@themarcocorporation.com, Web Site: www.themarcocorporation.com (28)

Martin, Robert, World Book Inc, Chicago, IL. Tel: (312) 729-5800, (800) 255-1750, FAX: (312) 729-5600, Web Site: www.worldbook.com (17)

Martin, Robert, WorleyParsons, Reading, PA. Tel: (610) 855-2000, FAX: (610) 885-2001, Web Site: www.worleyparsons.com (16)

Martin, Scott, Data Partners Inc, Fort Myers, FL. Tel: (239) 267-8762, (866) 423-1818, FAX: (239) 267-9043, E-Mail: info@data-partners.com, Web Site: www.datapartners.com (22)

Martin, Steve, J., TruGreen/ChemLawn, Lewis Center, OH. Tel: (614) 846-1800, (800) TRUE-GREEN, FAX: (614) 431-0155, Web Site: www.trugreen.com (16)

Martin, Steve, Libertyville Saddle Shop Inc, Libertyville, IL. Tel: (847) 362-0570, FAX: (847) 680-3200, E-Mail: info@saddleshop.com, Web Site: www.saddleshop.com (11)

Martin, Steven, ServiceMaster Co, Memphis, TN. Tel: (901) 766-1400, (901) 597-8502, (888) 937-3783, (866) 782-6787, FAX: (901) 766-1491, Web Site: www.servicemaster.com (8)

Martin, Tad, Cross Commerce Media, New York, NY. Tel: (646) 400-5095, Web Site: www.crosscommercemedia.com (35)

Martin, Thomas, P., Rutland Products, Rutland, VT. Tel: (802) 775-5519, FAX: (802) 775-5262, E-Mail: sales@rutland.com, Web Site: www.rutland.com (16)

Martin, Thomas, ValCom Inc, Indian Rocks Beach, FL. Tel: (702) 385-9000, FAX: (702) 382-2802, Web Site: www.valcom.tv (32)

Martin, William, R., Brahmin Leather Works, Fairhaven, MA. Tel: (508) 994-4000, (800) 229-2428, FAX: (508) 994-4153, Web Site: www.brahminusa.com (16)

The Martin Agency, Richmond, VA. Tel: (804) 698-8000, FAX: (804) 698-8001, Web Site: www.martinagency.com (35)

Martin Gross & Friends, New York, NY. Tel: (212) 689-0772, FAX: (212) 481-0552, E-Mail: grossdirect@aol.com (39)

Lester B Martin & Associates Inc, Sugar Grove, OH. Tel: (740) 746-8842, (614) 261-1722, (800) 262-1692, FAX: (614) 447-8417, (740) 746-8849, E-Mail: service@lesterbmartin.com, Web Site: www.lesterbmartin.com (33)

Martin Thomas International, Barrington, RI. Tel: (401) 245-8500, FAX: (401) 245-0694, E-Mail: contact@martinthomas.com, Web Site: www.martinthomas.com (35)

Martin Williams Advertising, Minneapolis, MN. Tel: (612) 342-9739, FAX: (612) 342-9700, Web Site: www.martinwilliams.com (35)

Martin Worldwide Inc, Oak Park, CA. Tel: (888) 694-5478, Web Site: www.martinworldwide.net (23)

Martindale-Hubbell, New Providence, NJ. Tel: (908) 464-6800, (800) 526-4902, FAX: (908) 771-7740 (17)

Martineau, Catherine, Martineau & Associates, Menlo Park, CA. Tel: (650) 326-5030, FAX: (650) 329-0883 (20)

Martineau, Christian, Standard Life, Montreal, PQ. Tel: (514) 499-8855, (877) 499-9555, FAX: (514) 499-4908, Web Site: www.standardlife.ca (15)

Martineau & Associates, Menlo Park, CA. Tel: (650) 326-5030, FAX: (650) 329-0883 (20)

Martinek, Paul, J., Lawyer's Weekly Publications, Boston, MA. Tel: (617) 451-7300, FAX: (617) 451-0132, Web Site: www.lawyersweekly.com (17)

Martinez, Arthur, Sears Home Improvement Products Inc, Longwood, FL. Tel: (407) 767-0990, (877) 840-7126, FAX: (407) 831-1848, Web Site: www.searshomepro.com (16)

Martinez, Felipe, Cosmo International, Deerfield Beach, FL. Tel: (954) 798-4500, FAX: (954) 798-4514 (16)

Martinez, Mereille, Native American Rights Fund, Boulder, CO. Tel: (303) 447-8760, Web Site: www.narf.org (1)

Martinez, Nubia, International Advertising Association, New York, NY. Tel: (212) 557-1133, FAX: (212) 983-0455, E-Mail: membership@iaaglobal.com, Web Site: www.iaaglobal.org (1)

Martinez, Yemil, Institute for International Research Inc, New York, NY. Tel: (212) 661-3500, (800) 345-8016, FAX: (212) 599-2192, E-Mail: register@iirusa.com, Web Site: www.iir-ny.com (16)

Martini, Robert, Americansource Bergan, Chesterbrook, PA. Tel: (610) 727-7000, (800) 829-3132, E-Mail: info@amerisourcebergan.com, Web Site: www.amerisourcebergan.com (7)

Martino, David, Martino & Binzer, Farmington, CT. Tel: (860) 678-4300, Web Site: www.goodbait.com (35)

Martino, Rick, Bearingpoint Inc, Montvale, NJ. Tel: (201) 307-7000, FAX: (201) 505-3765, Web Site: www.bearingpoint.com (14)

Martino, Rocco, Guideposts, Danbury, CT. Tel: (845) 225-3681, FAX: (845) 228-2056, Web Site: www.guideposts.org (1)

Martino & Binzer, Farmington, CT. Tel: (860) 678-4300, Web Site: www.goodbait.com (35)

Martins, Tim, Barbour Publishing Inc, Uhrichsville, OH. Tel: (740) 922-6045, FAX: (740) 922-5948, (800) 220-5948, E-Mail: info@barbourbooks.com, Web Site: www.barbourbooks.com (17)

Martire, Frank, R., NuEdge Systems, Brown Deer, WI. Tel: (800) 236-3282, Web Site: www.nuedgesystems.com (20)

Martone, Anthony, Trump Plaza Hotel & Casino, Atlantic City, NJ. Tel: (609) 441-6000, FAX: (609) 441-7727, Web Site: www.trumpplaza.com (19)

Martone, S. Michael, ADP Inc, Roseland, NJ. Tel: (973) 974-5000, (800) 225-5237, FAX: (973) 974-3334, Web Site: www.adp.com (16)

Martorano, Ben, AmeriCall Group Inc, Naperville, IL. Tel: (630) 955-9100, (800) 688-0078, FAX: (630) 955-9955, E-Mail: sales@americallgroup.com, Web Site: www.americallgroup.com (29)

Martore, Gracia, C., Gannett Co Inc, Mc Lean, VA. Tel: (703) 854-6000, FAX: (703) 854-2046, E-Mail: gcishare@gannett.com, Web Site: www.gannett.com (16)

Martt, Joan, Cooper Vision, Fairport, NY. Tel: (585) 385-6810, (800) 341-2020, Web Site: www. coopervision.com (7)

Martucci, James, American Association of Advertising Agencies, New York, NY. Tel: (212) 682-2500, FAX: (212) 682-8391, Web Site: www.aaaa.org (40)

Martyn, Linda, GBE Plus, Hartford, CT. Tel: (860) 727-9100, (800) 842-0139, FAX: (860) 527-6041, Web Site: www.gbeplus.com (26)

Marvel, Hunter, M., Marvel Associates, Old Greenwich, CT. Tel: (203) 637-4777 (20)

Marvel Associates, Old Greenwich, CT. Tel: (203) 637-4777 (20)

Marvel Entertainment Inc, New York, NY. Tel: (212) 576-4000, FAX: (847) 579-1277, Web Site: www. marvel.com (31)

Marvin Envelope & Paper Co, Wheeling, IL. Tel: (773) 489-3300, (800) 227-0011, FAX: (773) 489-4783, E-Mail: marvinenvelope@aol.com (27)

Marvoak, Dian, Benetton USA, New York, NY. Tel: (212) 593-0290, (800) 274-7192, FAX: (212) 371-1438, E-Mail: mtaylor@bennettonusa.com, Web Site: www.benetton.com (2)

Marx, Tom, The Marx Group, San Rafael, CA. Tel: (415) 453-0844, FAX: (415) 451-0166, E-Mail: info@themarxgrp.com, Web Site: www. themarxgrp.com (35)

The Marx Group, San Rafael, CA. Tel: (415) 453-0844, FAX: (415) 451-0166, E-Mail: info@ themarxgrp.com, Web Site: www.themarxgrp.com (35)

Mary Kay Cosmetics Inc, Addison, TX. Tel: (972) 687-6300, (800) MARY KAY, FAX: (972) 687-1611, Web Site: www.marykay.com (16)

Mary of Puddin Hill Inc, Greenville, TX. Tel: (903) 455-2651, (800) 545-8889, FAX: (903) 455-4522, E-Mail: customerservice@puddinhill.com, Web Site: www.puddinhill.com (16)

Maryknoll Fathers & Brothers, Maryknoll, NY. Tel: (914) 941-7590, (888) 627-9566, FAX: (914) 944-3613, E-Mail: mkweb@maryknoll.org, Web Site: www.maryknoll.org (1)

The Maryland Saddlery Inc, Butler, MD. Tel: (410) 771-4135, (800) 428-5077, FAX: (410) 472-9722, E-Mail: mdsaddle@aol.com, Web Site: www. marylandsaddlery.com (11)

Mary's Plant Farm & Landscaping, Hamilton, OH. Tel: (513) 894-0022, FAX: (513) 892-2053, E-Mail: marysplantfarm@zoomtown.com, Web Site: www.marysplantfarm.com (8)

T Marzetti Co Inc, Columbus, OH. Tel: (614) 846-2232, FAX: (614) 848-8330, Web Site: www. marzetti.com (4)

Mas, Greg, Falcon Safety Products, Branchburg, NJ. Tel: (908) 707-4900, FAX: (908) 707-8855, Web Site: www.falconsafety.com (4)

Mascari, Tom, Reliance Electric, Fort Smith, AR. Tel: (479) 646-4711, FAX: (479) 648-5792, E-Mail: smtraylor@powersystems.rockwell.com, Web Site: www.reliance.com (9)

Masco Corp, Taylor, MI. Tel: (313) 274-7400, FAX: (313) 792-6135, E-Mail: webmaster@mascohq. com, Web Site: www.masco.com (16)

Mascolo, Anna, Marie, Nassau Community College, Garden City, NY. Tel: (516) 572-7501, E-Mail: marketing-communications@ncc.edu, Web Site: www.ncc.edu (41)

Masiello, Jennifer, Droll Yankees Inc, Foster, RI. Tel: (860) 799-8980, (800) 352-9164, FAX: (860) 779-8938, E-Mail: jen@drollyankees.com, Web Site: www.drollyankees.com (8)

Maska, Lisa, Lautman Maska Neill & Co, Washington, DC. Tel: (202) 296-9660, Web Site: www. lautmandc.com (1)

Maskalunas, Scott, A., Thoma Cressey Bravo, Chicago, IL. Tel: (312) 777-4444, FAX: (312) 777-4445, Web Site: www.tcb.com (14)

Mason, Caleb, DeLorme Mapping, Yarmouth, ME. Tel: (207) 846-7000, (800) 561-5105, FAX: (207) 846-7051, E-Mail: caleb.mason@delorme.com, Web Site: www.delorme.com (3)

Mason, Janice, L., NAPR - National Association of Publishers Representatives, Kansas City, KS. Tel: (913) 708-8344, FAX: (913) 708-8618, E-Mail: napr@naprassoc.com, Web Site: www.naprassoc. com (35)

Mason, Lawrence D., Goodyear Tire & Rubber Co, Akron, OH. Tel: (330) 796-3250, Web Site: www. goodyear.com (16)

Mason, Marvin, D., C&H Distributors LLC, Milwaukee, WI. Tel: (414) 443-1700, (888) 316-2223, FAX: (414) 443-9213, E-Mail: customerservice@ chdist.com, Web Site: www.chdist.com (9)

Mason, Neil, Direct Access Marketing Services Inc, Syosset, NY. Tel: (516) 364-2777, FAX: (516) 364-0644, E-Mail: info@daxcess.com, Web Site: www.daxcess.com (22)

Mason, Renee, Ashworth University, Norcross, GA. Tel: (770) 729-8400, (800) 957-5412, FAX: (770) 729-9294, E-Mail: info@ashworthuniversity.edu, Web Site: www.ashworthuniversity.edu (13)

Mason, William, R., American Greetings Corp, Cleveland, OH. Tel: (216) 252-7300, FAX: (216) 252-6777 (16)

Mason Companies Inc, Chippewa Falls, WI. Tel: (715) 723-1871, (800) 826-7030, FAX: (715) 720-4247, Web Site: www.masoncompaniesinc.com (2)

George Mason University School of Management, Fairfax, VA. Tel: (703) 993-1871 (1)

WB Mason Co, New York, NY. Tel: (888) 926-2766, Web Site: www.wbmason.com (16)

Masood, Faheem, ESL Federal Credit Union, Rochester, NY. Tel: (585) 336-1000, (800) 848-2265, FAX: (585) 336-1138, Web Site: www.esl.org (14)

Mass Transmit, Charlotte, NC. Tel: (704) 248-8817, Web Site: www.masstransmit.com (32)

Massa, Art, ACNielsen, Schaumburg, IL. Tel: (847) 605-5000, FAX: (847) 605-2000, E-Mail: mkarr@ datamartdirect.com, Web Site: www.datamartdirect. com (30)

Massa, Gerald, L., GLM Communications, New York, NY. Tel: (212) 929-1300, FAX: (212) 929-9574, Web Site: www.glmcommunications.com (31)

Massa, Ronald, E., AO Smith Corp, Milwaukee, WI. Tel: (414) 359-4000, FAX: (414) 359-4064, Web Site: www.aosmith.com (16)

Massachusetts Horticultural Society, Wellesley, MA. Tel: (617) 933-4929, (617) 933-4900, FAX: (617) 933-4901, E-Mail: hort_line@masshort.org, Web Site: www.masshort.org (1)

Massari, Wayne, CTC Corp, Bennington, VT. Tel: (802) 442-6371, FAX: (802) 442-8526 (16)

Masscot Internet Inc, West Yarmouth, MA. Tel: (508) 778-6320, (877) 627-7268, FAX: (888) 884-9960, E-Mail: admin@masscot.net, Web Site: www. masscothosting.com (21)

Massengill, Mathew, Western Digital Corp, Irvine, CA. Tel: (949) 672-7000, FAX: (949) 672-7837, Web Site: www.westerndigital.com (22)

Massey, Richard, Alltel, Little Rock, AR. Tel: (501) 905-2590, (877) 446-3628, FAX: (501) 905-5444, Web Site: www.alltel.com (16)

Massey, Ron, Mary of Puddin Hill Inc, Greenville, TX. Tel: (903) 455-2651, (800) 545-8889, FAX: (903) 455-4522, E-Mail: customerservice@ puddinhill.com, Web Site: www.puddinhill.com (16)

Massmann, Cal, Tractor Supply Co, Brentwood, TN. Tel: (615) 366-4600, (877) 872-7721, FAX: (615) 227-4608, Web Site: www.mytscstore.com (5)

MassMutual Financial Group, Springfield, MA. Tel: (413) 788-8411, FAX: (413) 744-8889, E-Mail: name@www.massmutual.com, Web Site: www. massmutual.com (15)

Masten, Steve, Masten Publishing Systems, Chesterfield, MO. Tel: (636) 527-1810, (800) 616-9476, E-Mail: steve@mastensystems.com, Web Site: www.mastensystems.com (20)

Masten Publishing Systems, Chesterfield, MO. Tel: (636) 527-1810, (800) 616-9476, E-Mail: steve@ mastensystems.com, Web Site: www. mastensystems.com (20)

MasterCard Worldwide, Purchase, NY. Tel: (914) 249-2000, (800) 622-7747, FAX: (914) 249-4220, Web Site: www.mastercard.com (14)

Mastergrip Inc, Irving, TX. Tel: (972) 554-4450, (800) 275-1100, FAX: (972) 554-1109, Web Site: www. mastergrip.com (11)

Mastermailer Inc, Hollywood, FL. Tel: (954) 921-0000, (800) 771-LIST, FAX: (954) 925-7900, Web Site: www.mastermailer.com (23)

Masterpiece Studios Inc, Mankato, MN. Tel: (507) 388-8788, (800) 447-0219, FAX: (507) 344-4606, E-Mail: masterpiecestudios@masterpiecestudios. com, Web Site: www.masterpiecestudios.com (16)

Mastervision Inc, New York, NY. Tel: (212) 879-0448, (800) 876-0091, FAX: (212) 744-3560, E-Mail: stadin1@aol.com, Web Site: www.mastervision. com (16)

Masterworks, Poulsbo, WA. Tel: (360) 394-4300, Web Site: www.masterworks.com (1)

Mastery Marketing Group, Dublin, OH. Tel: (703) 938-0101, (203) 544-8997, (800) MKT-0121, FAX: (203) 544-8397, (703) 938-0144, E-Mail: info@ masterymg.com, Web Site: www.masterymktgrp. com (20)

Mastrangelo, Donna, IBSDirect, King of Prussia, PA. Tel: (610) 265-8210, Web Site: www.ibsdm.com (27)

Mastria, Louis, Canoe Ventures LLC, New York, NY. Tel: (212) 364-3600, FAX: (212) 364 3601, Web Site: www.canoe-ventures.com (32)

Mastrippolito, Amy, Brunner, Pittsburgh, PA. Tel: (412) 995-9500, FAX: (412) 995-9501, Web Site: www.brunnerworks.com (35)

Mastropole, Anthony, Crystek Corp, Fort Myers, FL. Tel: (239) 561-3311, (800) 237-3061, FAX: (239) 561-1025, E-Mail: sales@crystek.com, Web Site: www.crystek.com (9)

Masucci, Richard, Prompt Mailers Inc, Staten Island, NY. Tel: (718) 447-6206, FAX: (718) 981-7333, E-Mail: info@promptmailers.com, Web Site: www. promptmailers.com (28)

Masuda, Noboru, Sunstar, Chicago, IL. Tel: (773) 777-4000, FAX: (773) 777-1417, E-Mail: dominico@ sunstar.com, Web Site: www.sunstar.com (16)

Mathai, Suresh, Continuum Global, San Francisco, CA. Tel: (415) 685-3301, Web Site: www. continuumglobal.com (30)

Matheis, Dennis, Anthem Blue Cross Blue Shield, Saint Louis, MO. Tel: (314) 923-4444, (888) 877-9125, FAX: (314) 923-5151, E-Mail: moreinfo@ bcbsmo.com, Web Site: www.bcbsmo.com (15)

Matherly, Jeana, The Herald & Review, Decatur, IL. Tel: (217) 429-5151, FAX: (217) 421-6913, E-Mail: hrdirect@herald-review.com, Web Site: www.herald-review.com (17)

Mathews, Kate, African Wildlife Foundation, Washington, DC. Tel: (202) 939-3333, Web Site: www. awf.org (1)

Mathews, Mich, Microsoft Corp, Redmond, WA. Tel: (425) 882-8080, FAX: (425) 936-7329, Web Site: www.microsoft.com (22)

Mathieson, David, Brady Corp, Milwaukee, WI. Tel: (414) 358-6600, (800) 541-1686, FAX: (800) 292-2289, Web Site: www.bradycorp.com (16)

Mathieu, Bernard, National Envelope Corp, Ennis, TX. Tel: (800) 696-0409, Web Site: www. nationalenvelope.com (26)

Mathis, Catherine, J., The New York Times Co, New York, NY. Tel: (212) 556-3881, FAX: (212) 556-7389, Web Site: www.nytimes.com (17)

Mathis, Mike, SKM Group, Depew, NY. Tel: (716) 989-3200, FAX: (716) 989-3220, E-Mail: info@skmgroup.com, Web Site: www.skmgroup.com (35)

Mathis, Stuart, Mail Boxes Etc, San Diego, CA. Tel: (858) 455-8800, FAX: (858) 546-7488, Web Site: www.mbe.com (28)

Mathot, Sarah, Dairy Council of California, Irvine, CA. Tel: (949) 756-7896, Web Site: www.dairycouncilofca.org (1)

Matloff, Robert, Guilford Publications Inc, New York, NY. Tel: (212) 431-9800, (800) 365-7006, FAX: (212) 966-6708, E-Mail: info@guilford.com, Web Site: www.guilford.com (17)

Matrix, Miami Beach, FL. Tel: (305) 865-7000, FAX: (305) 864-3114 (30)

Matrix Manager, Roseville, CA. Tel: (916) 783-1536, (877)-258-9037, E-Mail: info@mymatrixmanager.com, Web Site: www.mymatrixmanager.com (28)

Matsuda, Tetsu, Seiko Corp of America, Mahwah, NJ. Tel: (201) 529-5730, FAX: (201) 529-1548, Web Site: www.seiko.com (16)

Matt Sr., J., Kemper, Dupli Envelope & Graphics Corp, Syracuse, NY. Tel: (315) 472-1316, (800) 724-2477, FAX: (315) 422-3637, Web Site: www.duplionline.com (26)

Matt, Fred, The FX Matt Brewing Co, Utica, NY. Tel: (315) 732-0022, (800) 765-6288, FAX: (315) 624-2401, E-Mail: info@saranac.com, Web Site: www.saranac.com (4)

Matt, Kemper, J., Grafek Direct, Syracuse, NY. Tel: (315) 422-4732, (800) 724-2477, FAX: (315) 425-9624, E-Mail: grafek@duplionline.com, Web Site: www.duplionline.com (27)

Matt, Nicolas, O., The FX Matt Brewing Co, Utica, NY. Tel: (315) 732-0022, (800) 765-6288, FAX: (315) 624-2401, E-Mail: info@saranac.com, Web Site: www.saranac.com (4)

Matt & Kumpany Kuzins, Sacramento, CA. Tel: (916) 446-2008, FAX: (916) 446-5302, E-Mail: matt@kuzins.com (1)

Matte, Larry, Cyber Marketing Services, Montvale, NJ. Tel: (201) 505-1743, FAX: (201) 391-4907, E-Mail: info@crmxchange.com, Web Site: www.crmxchange.com (29)

Mattel Inc, El Segundo, CA. Tel: (310) 252-2000, FAX: (310) 252-2180, Web Site: www.mattel.com (16)

Mattern, Bill, American Business Directories, Omaha, NE. Tel: (402) 593-4600, (800) 555-6124, FAX: (402) 596-0475, Web Site: www.infousa.com (43)

Matthes, Hans, GBH Communications, Monrovia, CA. Tel: (818) 246-9900, (800) 222-5424, FAX: (818) 246-5850, E-Mail: customerservice@gbh.com, Web Site: www.gbh.com (3)

Matthes, Mark, Duncan Aviation, Lincoln, NE. Tel: (402) 475-2611, (800) 228-4277, FAX: (402) 475-5541, Web Site: www.duncanaviation.com (16)

Matthew, Abe, Custom Accessories, Niles, IL. Tel: (847) 966-6900, (800) 962-6676, FAX: (847) 966-9650, Web Site: www.causa.com (11)

Matthew, Ken, Custom Accessories, Niles, IL. Tel: (847) 966-6900, (800) 962-6676, FAX: (847) 966-9650, Web Site: www.causa.com (11)

Matthew, Norman, Custom Accessories, Niles, IL. Tel: (847) 966-6900, (800) 962-6676, FAX: (847) 966-9650, Web Site: www.causa.com (11)

Matthews, Allen, San Francisco Chronicle, San Francisco, CA. Tel: (415) 777-1111, FAX: (415) 536-5178, E-Mail: amatthews@sfchronicle.com, Web Site: www.sfgate.com (17)

Matthews, Bill, Super Coups, East Taunton, MA. Tel: (508) 977-2000, (800) 626-2620, FAX: (508) 977-0644, Web Site: www.supercoups.com (26)

Matthews, Blaine, Matthews 1812 House Inc, Cornwall Bridge, CT. Tel: (860) 672-0149, (800) 662-1812, FAX: (860) 672-1812, E-Mail: info@matthews1812house.com, Web Site: www.matthews1812house.com (4)

Matthews, Craig G., Keyspan Energy Corp, Brooklyn, NY. Tel: (718) 403-2000, (888) 222-7359, Web Site: www.keyspanenergy.com (16)

Matthews, Deanna, Matthews 1812 House Inc, Cornwall Bridge, CT. Tel: (860) 672-0149, (800) 662-1812, FAX: (860) 672-1812, E-Mail: info@matthews1812house.com, Web Site: www.matthews1812house.com (4)

Matthews, J., Daniel, Robert J Matthews Co, Massillon, OH. Tel: (330) 834-3000, (800) 321-0235, FAX: (330) 830-2762, Web Site: www.pbsanimalhealth.com (7)

Matthews, Michael, Bloomingdale's By Mail Ltd, New York, NY. Tel: (212) 224-7721, (800) 472-0788, FAX: (212) 715-2805, Web Site: www.bloomingdales.com (5)

Matthews 1812 House Inc, Cornwall Bridge, CT. Tel: (860) 672-0149, (800) 662-1812, FAX: (860) 672-1812, E-Mail: info@matthews1812house.com, Web Site: www.matthews1812house.com (4)

Robert J Matthews Co, Massillon, OH. Tel: (330) 834-3000, (800) 321-0235, FAX: (330) 830-2762, Web Site: www.pbsanimalhealth.com (7)

Mattys, Gerry, Timm Medical Technologies, Inc, Eden Prairie, MN. Tel: (952) 947-9410, (800) 438-8592, FAX: (952) 947-9411, Web Site: www.timmmedical.com (16)

Matzell, Tom, MRW Communications, Hingham, MA. Tel: (781) 740-4525, FAX: (718) 926-0371, E-Mail: jim@mrwinc.com, Web Site: www.mrwinc.com (35)

Matzke, Chris, ICMA Retirement Corp, Washington, DC. Tel: (202) 962-4600, (800) 669-7400, FAX: (202) 962-4601, E-Mail: investorservices@icmarc.org, Web Site: www.icmarc.org (14)

Mauer, John, Gems Sensors & Controls, Plainville, CT. Tel: (860) 747-3000, (800) 378-1600, FAX: (860) 747-4244, E-Mail: info@gemssensors.com, Web Site: www.gemssensors.com (9)

Maui Jim Inc, Peoria, IL. Tel: (309) 691-3700, FAX: (309) 683-2202, Web Site: www.mauijim.com (16)

Maul, Terry, Wimmer's Meat Products Inc, West Point, NE. Tel: (402) 372-2437, (800) 358-0761, FAX: (402) 372-5659, Web Site: www.wimmersmeats.com (4)

Maull, Howard, Rose Resnick Lighthouse for the Blind & Visually Impaired, San Francisco, CA. Tel: (415) 431-1481, FAX: (415) 863-7568, E-Mail: executive@lighthouse-sf.org, Web Site: www.lighthouse-sf.org (1)

Maumee, George, Lesman Instrument Co, Bensenville, IL. Tel: (630) 595-8400, (800) 953-7626, FAX: (630) 595-2386, E-Mail: sales@lesman.com, Web Site: www.lesman.com (9)

Maunder, Jackie, The Missoulian, Missoula, MT. Tel: (406) 523-5334, FAX: (406) 523-5221, Web Site: www.missoulian.com (31)

Maurer, Karmen, McKnight's Long-Term Care News, Northfield, IL. Tel: (847) 784-8706, (800) 558-1703, FAX: (847) 784-9346, E-Mail: mltcn-webmaster@mltcn.com, Web Site: www.mcknightsonline.com (17)

Maurer, Myron, The Merchandise Mart, Chicago, IL. Tel: (312) 527-4141, (800) 677-6278, Web Site: www.merchandisemart.com (42)

Maurer, Ron, Falcon Safety Products, Branchburg, NJ. Tel: (908) 707-4900, FAX: (908) 707-8855, Web Site: www.falconsafety.com (16)

Maurice, Carl, Magnaplan Corp, Champlain, NY. Tel: (518) 298-8404, (800) 361-1192, FAX: (518) 298-2368, E-Mail: info@visualplanning.com, Web Site: www.visualplanning.com (10)

Mauro, Grace, BOC Gases, Murray Hill, NJ. Tel: (908) 464-8100, (800) 262-4273, FAX: (410) 749-4073, E-Mail: info@linde.com, Web Site: www.boc-gases.com (16)

Maus & Hoffman Inc, Fort Lauderdale, FL. Tel: (954) 463-1200, Web Site: www.mausandhoffman.com (2)

Mauss, James, Estes Industries, Penrose, CO. Tel: (719) 372-6565, FAX: (719) 372-3419, Web Site: www.estesrockets.com (11)

Mavel, James, C., Scan Optics Inc, Manchester, CT. Tel: (860) 645-7878, (800) 645-6001, FAX: (860) 645-7995, E-Mail: info@scanoptics.com, Web Site: www.scanoptics.com (16)

Maverick Ventures Product Line, Chesterfield, MO. Tel: (636) 537-4656, (800) 467-4656, FAX: (636) 537-4657, E-Mail: hang10cd@aol.com, Web Site: www.hang10cd.com (5)

Mavis, Todd, Mitchell International, San Diego, CA. Tel: (858) 368-7000, FAX: (858) 238-9111, Web Site: www.mitchell.com (17)

MAX Federal Credit Union, Montgomery, AL. Tel: (334) 260-2600, (800) 776-6776, FAX: (334) 270-0921, Web Site: www.mymax.com (14)

Maxim Direct, Greensboro, NC. Tel: (336) 841-6892, FAX: (336) 886-1655, Web Site: www.maximdirect.com (35)

Mary Maxim Inc, Port Huron, MI. Tel: (810) 987-2000, (800) 962-9504, FAX: (810) 987-5056, E-Mail: info@marymaxim.com, Web Site: www.marymaxim.com (11)

Maxon Furniture Inc, Muscatine, IA. Tel: (253) 395-4139, Web Site: www.maxonfurniture.com (10)

Maxwell, Joanne Dutcher, Ideas Companies Inc, Naperville, IL. Tel: (630) 357-7522, (800) 323-5656, FAX: (630) 357-7538 (33)

Maxwell & Miller Marketing Communications, Kalamazoo, MI. Tel: (269) 382-4060 x26, FAX: (269) 382-0504, E-Mail: info@maxwellandmiller.com, Web Site: www.maxwellandmiller.com (35)

May, Alison, RedEnvelope Inc, San Diego, CA. Tel: (619) 528-4888, (877) 733-3683, Web Site: www.redenvelope.com (6)

May, Carl, W., Biological Photo Service & Terraphotographics, Pacifica, CA. Tel: (650) 359-6219, FAX: (650) 359-6219, E-Mail: bpsterra@pacbell.net, Web Site: www.agpix.com/biologicalphoto (38)

May, Christy, Strategic Planning Marketing Scouting & Sales, Foxboro, MA. Tel: (781) 215-5117, (866) 638-5323, FAX: (774) 215-5117, E-Mail: cmay@dmcommunications.com, Web Site: www.dmcommunications.com (35)

May, Kenneth, Resort Condominiums International Inc, Carmel, IN. Tel: (317) 876-1692, FAX: (317) 871-9699, Web Site: www.rci.com (19)

May, Kevin, Links Magazine, Hilton Head Island, SC. Tel: (843) 842-6200, FAX: (843) 842-6233, Web Site: www.linksmagazine.com (17)

May, Larry, Direct Media Millard, Peterborough, NH. Tel: (603) 924-9262, FAX: (603) 924-9420, Web Site: www.millard.com (23)

May, Linda, The Vestal Press Ltd, Lanham, MD. Tel: (301) 459-3366, (800) 462-6420, FAX: (301) 429-5746, E-Mail: sburnett@rowman.com, Web Site: www.nbnbooks.com (17)

May, Mark, Shopsmith Inc, Dayton, OH. Tel: (937) 898-6070, (800) 543-7586, FAX: (937) 890-5197, Web Site: www.shopsmith.com (10)

May, Michael, C., Federal Home Loan Mortgage Corp (Freddie Mac), McLean, VA. Tel: (703) 903-2000, (800) 424-5401, Web Site: www.freddiemac.com (14)

Mayer, Barry, D., Harvard Square Records, Round Rock, TX. Tel: (877) 465-7669, E-Mail: LPnow@yahoo.com, Web Site: www.lpnow.com (3)

Mayer, Bob, IMSI/Design LLC, Novato, CA. Tel: (415) 483-8000, (800) 833-4674, FAX: (415) 884-9023, Web Site: www.imsisoft.com (34)

Mayer, David, Butterfield Farms Inc, Rolling Hills Estates, CA. Tel: (310) 750-6160, (800) 633-2767, E-Mail: dave@gifttrading.com, Web Site: www.butterfieldfarms.com (4)

Mayer, James, Viking Pump Inc, Cedar Falls, IA. Tel: (319) 266-1741, FAX: (319) 273-8157, E-Mail: info@vikingpump.com, Web Site: www.vikingpump.com (16)

Mayer, Jerry, The Inkpen, Pembroke Pines, FL. Tel: (954) 450-9220, FAX: (305) 624-5126, Web Site: www.theinkpen.com (27)

Mayer, Jonathan, Cedar Fresh Products, Coral Gables, FL. Tel: (305) 870-9390, Web Site: www. cedarfresh.com (16)

Mayer, Kevin, Disney Vacation Club, Kissimmee, FL. Tel: (407) 566-3100, (800) 500-3990, FAX: (407) 566-3393 (19)

Mayer, Margery, W, Scholastic Inc, New York, NY. Tel: (212) 343-6100, (800) SCHOLASTIC, FAX: (212) 343-6484, Web Site: www.scholastic.com/ (17)

Mayer, Mark, Peter A Mayer Advertising Inc, New Orleans, LA. Tel: (504) 581-7191, Web Site: www. peteramayer.com (35)

Mayer, Mike, Frank Mayer & Associates Inc, Grafton, WI. Tel: (262) 377-4700, (800) 837-1232, FAX: (262) 377-3449, E-Mail: dave.zoerb@frankmayer. com, Web Site: www.frankmayer.com (35)

Mayer, Russel, P., Biosciences-Amersham, Piscataway, NJ. Tel: (732) 457-8000, FAX: (732) 457-0557, Web Site: www.amersham.com (16)

Frank Mayer & Associates Inc, Grafton, WI. Tel: (262) 377-4700, (800) 837-1232, FAX: (262) 377-3449, E-Mail: dave.zoerb@frankmayer.com, Web Site: www.frankmayer.com (35)

Peter A Mayer Advertising Inc, New Orleans, LA. Tel: (504) 581-7191, Web Site: www.peteramayer.com (35)

Mayes, Steve, Spirit Direct Marketing Services, Houston, TX. Tel: (281) 496-5614 (23)

Mayfield, Ken, National Mailroom Service Inc, Knoxville, TN. Tel: (866) 862-4141, FAX: (800) 231-4141, E-Mail: info@nationalmailroom.com, Web Site: www.nationalmailroom.com (35)

Mayfield, Tammi, Aon Innovative Solutions, Chicago, IL. Tel: (303) 279-2900, FAX: (303) 216-1732, Web Site: www.aon.com (16)

Maynard, Amy, Highlights For Children, Columbus, OH. Tel: (614) 487-2601, (800) 848-8922, FAX: (614) 487-2700, Web Site: www.highlights.com (17)

Maynard, Bruce, Amica Insurance, Lincoln, RI. Tel: (401) 334-6000, (800) 652-6422, FAX: (401) 334-4241, Web Site: www.amica.com (15)

Maynard, Mark, Crutchfield Corp, Charlottesville, VA. Tel: (434) 817-1000, (800) 955-9091, FAX: (804) 817-1010, E-Mail: administration@crutchfield.com, Web Site: www.crutchfield.com (3)

Mayne, Clifton P., Mayne Associates, Lafayette, CA. Tel: (925) 284-8500, FAX: (925) 284-8502 (39)

Mayne Associates, Lafayette, CA. Tel: (925) 284-8500, FAX: (925) 284-8502 (39)

Mayo, Forrest, Mayo Marketing Ideas, Torrance, CA. Tel: (310) 517-9272, FAX: (310) 517-9279 (35)

Mayo Clinic, Rochester, MN. Tel: (507) 266-2511, FAX: (507) 284-0161, Web Site: www.mayoclinic. org (17)

Mayo Marketing Ideas, Torrance, CA. Tel: (310) 517-9272, FAX: (310) 517-9279 (35)

Mays, Crystal, Computer Business Services Inc, Americus, GA. Tel: (229) 924-4408, (866) 924-4408, FAX: (229) 924-3644, E-Mail: cdill@ combusser.com, Web Site: www.combusser.com (22)

Mays Mission for the Handicapped Inc, Heber Springs, AR. Tel: (501) 362-7526, (888) 503-7955, FAX: (501) 362-7529, E-Mail: sniehaus@ maysmission.org, Web Site: www.maysmission.org (27)

Mayton Jr., James, L., United Investors Life Insurance Co, Birmingham, AL. Tel: (205) 325-4300, (800) 288-2722, FAX: (205) 325-4157, Web Site: www. uilic.com (15)

Mazda North American Operations, Irvine, CA. Tel: (949) 727-1990, (800) 222-6500, FAX: (949) 727-6101, Web Site: www.mazdausa.com (16)

Mazeau, Dr. Jean-Fierre, Steuben Glass, New York, NY. Tel: (607) 974-8659, (800) STEUBEN, FAX: (607) 974-8441, E-Mail: info@steuben.com, Web Site: www.steuben.com (6)

Mazlish, Tony, The Healthy Back Store, Beltsville, MD. Tel: (703) 339-1700, (800) 4 MY BACK, FAX: (703) 339-0671, E-Mail: service@ healthyback.com, Web Site: www.healthyback.com (16)

Mazzaschi, Michael, Stock Boston LLC, Brookline, MA. Tel: (617) 266-2300, FAX: (617) 277-0502, E-Mail: requests@stockboston.com, Web Site: www.stockboston.com (38)

Mazzer, Ellen S., Norman Rockwell Museum, Stock-bridge, MA. Tel: (413) 298-4100, (800) 742-9450, FAX: (413) 298-4144, E-Mail: emazzer@nrm.org, Web Site: www.nrm.org (16)

Mazzone Jr, Michael, R., Mazzone Marketing Group LLC, Brooklyn, NY. Tel: (718) 369-0001, (866) 928-5478, FAX: (718) 369-0099, E-Mail: info@ mazzonemarketinggroup.com, Web Site: www. mazzonemarketinggroup.com (23)

Mazzone Marketing Group LLC, Brooklyn, NY. Tel: (718) 369-0001, (866) 928-5478, FAX: (718) 369-0099, E-Mail: info@mazzonemarketinggroup.com, Web Site: www.mazzonemarketinggroup.com (23)

Mazzuca, Robert, Boy Scouts of America/National Supply Group, Charlotte, NC. Tel: (972) 580-2161, (800) 323-0736, E-Mail: customerservice@ scoutstuff.org, Web Site: www.scoutstuff.org (1)

Mc Abee, Ronald, G., Vulcan Materials Co, Birmingham, AL. Tel: (205) 298-3000, FAX: (205) 298-2960, Web Site: www.vulcanmaterials.com (16)

Mc Carthy, Charlie, Tetley USA Inc, Montvale, NJ. Tel: (203) 929-9200, (800) 728-0084, FAX: (203) 926-0876, Web Site: www.tetleyusa.com (16)

Mc Hugh, Robert, W., Champs Corp, Bradenton, FL. Tel: (941) 748-0577, (800) 991-6813, E-Mail: customer_service@champssports.com, Web Site: www.champssports.com (11)

McAdams, Joe, TL Enterprises Inc, Ventura, CA. Tel: (805) 667-4100, FAX: (805) 667-4419 (17)

McAdams, Sharon, HB Distributors, Chatsworth, CA. Tel: (818) 882-0000, (800) 266-3478, FAX: (818) 700-1808, Web Site: www.hddistributors.com (34)

McAfee, Lynn, D., Lynn McAfee, North Hollywood, CA. Tel: (818) 763-0227 (37)

McAfee, Rob, Sani Serv, Mooresville, IN. Tel: (317) 831-7030, FAX: (317) 381-7036, Web Site: www. saniserv.com (16)

Lynn McAfee, North Hollywood, CA. Tel: (818) 763-0227 (37)

McAlister, James, The Marketing Alliance, Fairfield, CT. Tel: (203) 254-0474 (20)

McAllister, Michael, PM Consulting Corp, Fairfax, VA. FAX: (703) 272-1500, Web Site: www.ecnext. com (20)

McAllister, Stephen, Design Matters Inc!, New York, NY. Tel: (212) 560-0681, Web Site: www. designmattersinc.com (35)

McAlpine, Charles, M., CM Consulting Services, Marshfield, MA. Tel: (781) 749-5000, FAX: (801) 749-5009, E-Mail: cmcalpine3@gmail.com (27)

McArdle Printing Co Inc, Upper Marlboro, MD. Tel: (301) 390-8500, FAX: (301) 390-8052, Web Site: www.mcardleprinting.com (27)

McAtee, Angie, Southwest Publishing & Mailing Corp, Topeka, KS. Tel: (785) 233-5662, Web Site: www.swpks.com (28)

McBee, Richard, Tektronix Inc, Beaverton, OR. Tel: (503) 627-7111, (800) 833-9200, FAX: (503) 627-3247, Web Site: www.tektronix.com (16)

McBee, Lancaster, CA. Tel: (973) 263-3225, (800) 878-9443, (800) 662-2331, FAX: (973) 263-8165, E-Mail: info@mcbeeinc.com, Web Site: www. mcbeeweb.com (10)

McBee Associates Inc, Wayne, PA. Tel: (610) 964-9680, Web Site: www.mcbeeassociates.com (20)

McBeth, Susan, Harley-Davidson Inc, Milwaukee, WI. Tel: (414) 343-7286, FAX: (414) 343-4806, Web Site: www.harley-davidson.com (12)

McBride, Dave, Sara Lee Hosiery, Winston Salem, NC. Tel: (336) 519-2711/2369, FAX: (336) 519-3254, Web Site: www.leggs.com (2)

McBride, John, L., Magic Seasonings Mail Order, New Orleans, LA. Tel: (504) 731-3590, (800) 457-2857, FAX: (504) 731-3576, E-Mail: jlm@ chefpaul.com, Web Site: www.chefpaul.com (4)

McBride, Kenneth, Mane Solutions, New York, NY. Tel: (212) 736-0306, FAX: (212) 239-2039 (16)

McBride, Mary, WB Mason Co, New York, NY. Tel: (888) 926-2766, Web Site: www.wbmason.com (16)

McBride, Shawn, Magic Seasonings Mail Order, New Orleans, LA. Tel: (504) 731-3590, (800) 457-2857, FAX: (504) 731-3576, E-Mail: jlm@chefpaul.com, Web Site: www.chefpaul.com (4)

McBurney, Susan, Wake Forest University Baptist Medical Center, Winston Salem, NC. Tel: (336) 716-4665, Web Site: www.wfubmc.edu (1)

McCabe, Edward, Gruppo Levey & Co, New York, NY. Tel: (212) 697-5753, FAX: (212) 949-7294, E-Mail: info@glconline.com, Web Site: www. glconline.com (14)

McCabe, Leslie, Orange Leap, Dallas, TX. Tel: (972) 220-0341, Web Site: www.orangeleap.com (1)

McCabe, Lisa, Bulletin of the Atomic Scientists, Chicago, IL. Tel: (773) 702-6301, FAX: (773) 980-6932, E-Mail: admin@thebulletin.org, Web Site: www.thebulletin.org (1)

McCabe, Randy, Orange Leap, Dallas, TX. Tel: (972) 220-0341, Web Site: www.orangeleap.com (1)

McCabe, Rebekah, Chanel Inc, New York, NY. Tel: (212) 688-5055, FAX: (212) 752-1851, Web Site: www.chanel.com (16)

McCabe, Tom, KMA Direct Communications, Dallas, TX. Tel: (972) 244-1900, FAX: (972) 244-1901, E-Mail: sales@kma.com, Web Site: www.kma.com (1)

McCabe & Duval Advertising, Portland, ME. Tel: (207) 773-4538, (800) 603-6069, FAX: (207) 773-7245, Web Site: www.mccabe-duval.com (35)

McCaffrey III, Neil, T., McCaffrey Enterprises, Fort Collins, CO. Tel: (970) 493-4840, FAX: (970) 493-8781 (21)

McCaffrey, Jim, Turner Broadcasting System Inc, Atlanta, GA. Tel: (404) 827-1700, FAX: (404) 827-1575, Web Site: www.turner.com (32)

McCaffrey, Mary Ann, Mullen & McCaffrey Direct Response, East Hampton, NY. Tel: (631) 324-4265, FAX: (631) 324-2135, E-Mail: mullenmccaffrey@ aol.com, Web Site: www.mullenandmccaffrey.com (35)

McCaffrey Enterprises, Fort Collins, CO. Tel: (970) 493-4840, FAX: (970) 493-8781 (21)

McCalip, Maggie, Swanson Health Products, Fargo, ND. Tel: (701) 356-2800, (800) 824-4491, FAX: (800) 726-7691, E-Mail: customercare@ swansonvitamins.com, Web Site: www. swansonvitamins.com (35)

McCall, Bruce, Guaranty Bank, Brown Deer, WI. Tel: (414) 362-4636, (800) 235-4636, Web Site: www. guarantybank.com (14)

McCall, Claire, S., Genesco Inc, Nashville, TN. Tel: (615) 367-7000, (888) 324-6189, FAX: (615) 367-8278, Web Site: www.genesco.com (2)

McCall, Josh, The Jack Morton Co, Chicago, IL. Tel: (312) 274-6060, FAX: (312) 274-6061, E-Mail: experience@jackmorton.com, Web Site: www. jackmorton.com (35)

McCall, Susan, The Peter A Tobin College of Business, Jamaica, NY. Tel: (718) 990-2600, FAX: (718) 990-1868, Web Site: www.stjohns.edu (41)

McCall, Tom, Gartner Inc, San Jose, CA. Tel: (408) 468-8000, (800) 419-3282, FAX: (408) 954-1780, E-Mail: tom.mccall@gartner.com, Web Site: www. gartner.com (20)

McCallen, Joan, ICMA Retirement Corp, Washington, DC. Tel: (202) 962-4600, (800) 669-7400, FAX: (202) 962-4601, E-Mail: investorservices@icmarc. org, Web Site: www.icmarc.org (14)

McCann Relationship Mktg, New York, NY. Tel: (646) 865-6000, FAX: (646) 487-9610, Web Site: www. mrmworldwide.com (35)

McCarney, Laurie, Bank of Hawaii, Honolulu, HI. Tel: (808) 537-8398, FAX: (808) 536-9433, Web Site: www.boh.com (14)

McCarter Jr., John, W., The Field Museum, Chicago, IL. Tel: (312) 665-7909, FAX: (312) 665-7101, Web Site: www.fieldmuseum.org (1)

McCarter, John, Saatchi & Saatchi Canada, Toronto, ON Canada. Tel: (416) 359-9595, FAX: (416) 866-8485, Web Site: www.saatchi.ca (21)

McCarthy, Daniel J., Frontier Corp, Rochester, NY. Tel: (716) 777-1000, Web Site: www. frontieronline.com (16)

McCarthy, Dr. Kevin, Tangent Media LLC, Atlanta, GA. Tel: (404) 444-2357, Web Site: www. tangentmedia.us (30)

McCarthy, Karen, Little & King Co LLC, Great Neck, NY. Tel: (516) 377-1377 X12, FAX: (212) 575-0739, E-Mail: lkinfo@littleandking.com, Web Site: www.littleandking.com (35)

McCarthy, Kari, Learning Seed, Chicago, IL. Tel: (800) 634-4941, Web Site: www.learningseed.com (3)

McCarthy, Kathryn, Biosciences-Amersham, Piscataway, NJ. Tel: (732) 457-8000, FAX: (732) 457-0557, Web Site: www.amersham.com (14)

McCarthy, Kevin, P., Unum Corp, Portland, ME. Tel: (207) 770-2211, (800) 421-0344, FAX: (207) 770-4510, Web Site: www.unum.com (15)

McCarthy, Margaret, AETNA - Marketing Product & Communication, Hartford, CT. Tel: (860) 273-0123, (800) 872-3862, FAX: (860) 273-3971, Web Site: www.aetna.com (14)

McCarthy, Michael, JC Whitney, Chicago, IL. Tel: (312) 431-6000, FAX: (312) 431-5650, Web Site: www.jcwhitney.com (12)

McCarthy, Michael, McCarthy Media Group Inc, Monroe, WI. Tel: (608) 837-4343, (800) 410-5352, FAX: (608) 837-5006, E-Mail: lists@ mccarthymediagroup.com, Web Site: www. mccarthymediagroup.com (23)

McCarthy, Mike, Sears Home Improvement Products Inc, Longwood, FL. Tel: (407) 767-0990, (877) 840-7126, FAX: (407) 831-1848, Web Site: www. searshomepro.com (16)

McCarthy, P.J., PJ McCarthy & Associates Inc, Downers Grove, IL. Tel: (630) 969-3532, FAX: (630) 969-3565, E-Mail: KDicola@aol.com (23)

McCarthy, Patrick, Fairchild Publications, New York, NY. Tel: (212) 630-4000, Web Site: www. fairchildpub.com (17)

McCarthy, Peter, Duplication Factory Inc, Chaska, MN. Tel: (952) 448-9912, (800) 279-2009, FAX: (952) 448-3983, E-Mail: info@duplicationfactory. com, Web Site: www.duplicationfactory.com (31)

McCarthy, R., Patrick, Chemistri, Troy, MI. Tel: (248) 458-8300, FAX: (248) 458-8729 (35)

McCarthy, Robert, McCarthy & King Marketing Inc, Milford, MA. Tel: (508) 473-8643, FAX: (508) 473-7294, Web Site: www.mccarthyandking.com (35)

McCarthy, Terrance, M., First Banks Inc, Hazelwood, MO. Tel: (314) 592-5000, (800) 760-2265, Web Site: www.firstbanks.com (14)

McCarthy, Thomas, International Marine, Camden, ME. Tel: (207) 236-4837, FAX: (207) 236-6314, Web Site: www.internationalmarine.com (17)

McCarthy & King Marketing Inc, Milford, MA. Tel: (508) 473-8643, FAX: (508) 473-7294, Web Site: www.mccarthyandking.com (35)

McCarthy DiCola, Kathleen, PJ McCarthy & Associates Inc, Downers Grove, IL. Tel: (630) 969-3532, FAX: (630) 969-3565, E-Mail: KDicola@aol.com (23)

McCarthy Media Group Inc, Monroe, WI. Tel: (608) 837-4343, (800) 410-5352, FAX: (608) 837-5006, E-Mail: lists@mccarthymediagroup.com, Web Site: www.mccarthymediagroup.com (23)

PJ McCarthy & Associates Inc, Downers Grove, IL. Tel: (630) 969-3532, FAX: (630) 969-3565, E-Mail: KDicola@aol.com (23)

McCarthy Schroeder, Megan, PJ McCarthy & Associates Inc, Downers Grove, IL. Tel: (630) 969-3532, FAX: (630) 969-3565, E-Mail: KDicola@aol.com (23)

McCarty, Joyce, American Stationery Co Inc, Peru, IN. Tel: (765) 473-4438, (800) 822-2577, FAX: (800) 253-9054, Web Site: www. americanstationery.com (10)

McCaskey, Raymond, Blue Cross/Blue Shield of Illinois, Chicago, IL. Tel: (312) 938-6000, FAX: (312) 938-5722, Web Site: www.bcbsil.com (15)

McCassney, Jim, The Wig Co, Pittsburgh, PA. Tel: (412) 221-4790, (800) 456-1788, FAX: (412) 257-8181, E-Mail: custserv@twcwigs.com (2)

McCauley, Frank, AETNA - Marketing Product & Communication, Hartford, CT. Tel: (860) 273-0123, (800) 872-3862, FAX: (860) 273-3971, Web Site: www.aetna.com (14)

McCauley, Katie, Indianapolis Motor Speedway, Indianapolis, IN. Tel: (317) 492-6700, Web Site: www. indianapolismotorspeedway.com (19)

McCauley, Pat, Direct Mail Source Inc, Scottsdale, AZ. Tel: (602) 947-1552 (23)

McClain, Katie, State Street Global Advisors, Boston, MA. Tel: (617) 664-2618, Web Site: www.ssga. com (14)

McClanahan, David, M., Centerpoint Energy, Minneapolis, MN. Tel: (612) 372-4664, FAX: (612) 321-4873, E-Mail: mgc-businessinformation@ centerpointenergy.com, Web Site: www. minnegasco.centerpointenergy.com (16)

McClarin, Robert, Protection One Inc, Lawrence, KS. Tel: (785) 856-5500, (800) GET-HELP, Web Site: www.protectionone.com (16)

McClatchy Co, Sacramento, CA. Tel: (916) 321-1855, FAX: (916) 321-1869, Web Site: www.mcclatchy. com (17)

McClellan, Greg, MAX Federal Credit Union, Montgomery, AL. Tel: (334) 260-2600, (800) 776-6776, FAX: (334) 270-0921, Web Site: www.mymax.com (14)

McClellan, Michael, Plexus Marketing Group Inc, Atlanta, GA. Tel: (770) 390-9692, (800) 9-PLEXUS, FAX: (770) 390-9693, Web Site: www.plexusmarketing.com (20)

McClellan, Michael, Propay, Lehi, UT. Tel: (801) 341-5647, Web Site: www.propay.com (14)

McClelland, E.L., Cyril-Scott Co, Lancaster, OH. Tel: (740) 654-2112, FAX: (740) 654-7712, E-Mail: postoffice@cyrilscott.com, Web Site: www. cyrilscott.com (27)

McClendon, Charles, Casablanca Express, Woodland Hills, CA. Tel: (818) 992-5100, Web Site: www. casablancaexpress.com (33)

McClendon, Laura, AllMedia Inc, Plano, TX. Tel: (469) 467-9100, FAX: (214) 291-5431, E-Mail: lmcclendon@allmediainc.com, Web Site: www. allmediainc.com (23)

McClendon, Mark, Do-It Corp, South Haven, MI. Tel: (269) 637-1121, (800) 426-4822, FAX: (269) 637-7223, E-Mail: sales@do-it.com, Web Site: www. do-it.com (9)

McCloud, Fern, Appalachian Nurseries, Inc, Chambersburg, PA. Tel: (717) 597-0066, (877) 743-4733, E-Mail: info@appnursery.com, Web Site: www. appnursery.com (8)

McCloud, Lisa, Bunn-O-Matic Corp, Springfield, IL. Tel: (217) 529-6601, FAX: (217) 529-6622, E-Mail: bunn@bunn.com, Web Site: www.bunn. com (16)

McCloud, Tom, Appalachian Nurseries, Inc, Chambersburg, PA. Tel: (717) 597-0066, (877) 743-4733, E-Mail: info@appnursery.com, Web Site: www. appnursery.com (8)

McClure, Brian, Echotouch Corp, Austin, TX. Tel: (512) 327-5638, Web Site: www.echotouch.com (20)

McClure, Charles, CCIM Institute, Chicago, IL. Tel: (312) 321-4460, (800) 621-7027, FAX: (312) 321-4530, Web Site: www.ccim.com (1)

McClure, Kenneth A., USAA, San Antonio, TX. Tel: (512) 498-6524, FAX: (512) 498-8000 (15)

McClure & Zimmerman, Randolph, WI. Tel: (800) 883-6998, FAX: (800) 374-6120, Web Site: www. mzbulb.com (8)

McCluskey, Malcolm, List Services Fundraising, Bethel, CT. Tel: (203) 743-2600, Web Site: www. listservices.com (23)

McCollister, Mark, R., TAPPI (Technical Association of the Pulp & Paper Industry), Norcross, GA. Tel: (678) 642-66, (800) 332-8686, FAX: (770) 446-6947, E-Mail: webmaster@tappi.org, Web Site: www.tappi.org (1)

McCollom, Marc, R., Sovereign Bank New England, Glastonbury, CT. Tel: (877) 768-2265, FAX: (860) 727-6517 (14)

McCollum Jr., William, R., Tennessee Valley Authority, Knoxville, TN. Tel: (865) 632-2101, Web Site: www.tva.gov (1)

McConnell, Bringier, Bart's Watersports, North Webster, IN. Tel: (574) 834-7666, (800) 348-5016, FAX: (574) 834-4246, E-Mail: info@barts.com, Web Site: www.bartswatersports.com (11)

McConnell, John, Journal Star, Peoria, IL. Tel: (309) 686-3026, FAX: (309) 686-3265, Web Site: www. pjstar.com (17)

McConnell, Marilyn, AIDC (American International Distribution Corp), Williston, VT. Tel: (800) 678-2432, FAX: (802) 864-7626, E-Mail: jmacon@ aidcvt.com, Web Site: www.aidcvt.com (22)

McConnell, Mike, Nissan Motor Acceptance Corp, Irving, TX. Tel: (800) 647-7261, Web Site: www. nissanusa.com (14)

McConnell, Patrick, Daily Commercial News & Construction Record, Markham, ON Canada. Tel: (905) 752-5408, (800) 465-6475, FAX: (888) 396-9413, (905) 752-5450, E-Mail: dcnonl@ reedbusiness.com, Web Site: www.dcnonl.com (17)

McConnell, Sari, Conformer Expansion Products Inc, Great Neck, NY. Tel: (516) 504-6300, E-Mail: support@conformerinc.com, Web Site: www. conformerinc.com (26)

McCord, Ted, Wasserman Uniform Co, Fort Lauderdale, FL. Tel: (614) 279-8888, (614) 279-7000, (800) 848-3576, FAX: (614) 464-0416, (800) 204-0416, E-Mail: custserv@wassermanuniform.com, Web Site: www.wassermanuniform.com (2)

McCormack, Jill, American Society for Training & Development, Alexandria, VA. Tel: (703) 683-8100, (800) NAT-ASTD, FAX: (703) 683-8103, Web Site: www.astd.org (1)

McCormack, Kenneth, Halls Kansas City, Kansas City, MO. Tel: (816) 274-8111, (800) 624-4034, FAX: (816) 545-2121, Web Site: www.hallskc.com (16)

McCormack, Robert, Gall's Inc, Lexington, KY. Tel: (859) 266-7227, (800) 477-7766, FAX: (859) 268-5954, E-Mail: help-desk@galls.com, Web Site: www.galls.com (16)

McCormick, Amy, The CompTEL Annual Convention & Trade Exposition, Washington, DC. Tel: (202) 296-6650, FAX: (202) 296-7585, Web Site: www. comptel.org (42)

McCormick, Chris, Starkey Laboratories, Eden Prairie, MN. Tel: (952) 941-6401, Web Site: www.starkey. com (16)

McCormick, Christopher, LL Bean Inc, Freeport, ME. Tel: (207) 865-4761, (800) 441-5713, FAX: (207) 552-3080, Web Site: www.llbean.com (2)

McCormick, John, National Business Furniture Inc, Milwaukee, WI. Tel: (414) 276-8511, (800) 558-1010, FAX: (414) 276-8371, Web Site: www. nationalbusinessfurniture.com (10)

McCormick, Larry, Tidewater Direct LLC, Centreville, MD. Tel: (410) 758-1500, FAX: (410) 758-2478, Web Site: www.tidewaterdirect.com (27)

McCormick, Mary, National Business Furniture Inc, Milwaukee, WI. Tel: (414) 276-8511, (800) 558-1010, FAX: (414) 276-8371, Web Site: www. nationalbusinessfurniture.com (10)

McCormick, Mike, Direct Marketing Boot Camp, Hollywood, FL. Tel: (646) 723-3230, (800) 331-7114, FAX: (954) 921-2005, E-Mail: loisgeller@ loisgellermarketinggroup.com, Web Site: www. masongeller.com (41)

McCormick, Rachel, BBC Direct Mktg Svcs, Shamong, NJ. Tel: (877) 786-4389, FAX: (609) 268-9939, E-Mail: csr@bbcglobal.com, Web Site: www.bbcglobal.com (20)

McCormick, Steven, J., The Nature Conservancy, Arlington, VA. Tel: (703) 841-5300, (800) 628-6860, FAX: (703) 841-1283, E-Mail: magazine@tnc.org, Web Site: www.nature.org (1)

McCormick & Co Inc, Hunt Valley, MD. Tel: (410) 771-7301, (800) 474-7742, FAX: (410) 527-6337, Web Site: www.mccormick.com (4)

McCormick-Armstrong Co Inc, Wichita, KS. Tel: (316) 264-1363, (800) 733-1363, FAX: (316) 263-4511, E-Mail: sales@mccormickarmstrong.com, Web Site: www.mccormickarmstrong.com (27)

McCourt, Michelle, Parks, Atmosphere BBDO, New York, NY. Tel: (212) 827-2500, FAX: (212) 827-2525, Web Site: www.atmospherebbdo.com (35)

McCourt Label Co, Lewis Run, PA. Tel: (800) 458-2390, Web Site: www..mccourtlabel.com (27)

McCoy, Gary, The Marx Group, San Rafael, CA. Tel: (415) 453-0844, FAX: (415) 451-0166, E-Mail: info@themarxgrp.com, Web Site: www. themarxgrp.com (35)

McCoy, Jane, Chilcutt Direct Marketing, Oklahoma City, OK. Tel: (405) 478-7245, FAX: (405) 478-2984, Web Site: www.cdmlist.com (24)

McCoy, Jennifer, OccuNomix, Port Jefferson Station, NY. Tel: (631) 791-1912, Web Site: www. occunomix.com (34)

McCoy, Sheri, S., Johnson & Johnson, New Brunswick, NJ. Tel: (732) 524-0400, FAX: (732) 214-0332, Web Site: www.jnj.com (16)

McCracken, Robert, MTI Information Technologies LLC, Langhorne, PA. Tel: (267) 569-2400, Web Site: www.mtiadvantage.com (30)

McCreight, David, Lands' End Inc, Dodgeville, WI. Tel: (608) 935-9341, (800) 963-4816, FAX: (680) 935-4831, Web Site: www.landsend.com (2)

McCreight, Tim, American Institute of Chemical Engineers, New York, NY. Tel: (203) 702-7660, (800) 242-4363, FAX: (203) 775-5177, E-Mail: xpress@ aiche.org, Web Site: www.aiche.org (1)

McCrum, David, Thousand Trails LP, Chicago, IL. Tel: (214) 618-7200, (800) 205-0606, FAX: (214) 618-7324, Web Site: www.1000trails.com (16)

McCubbin, Gene, Pop Labs Inc, Houston, TX. Tel: (713) 243-4500, Web Site: www.poplabs.com (35)

McCue, Laura, Hanna Andersson Corp, Portland, OR. Tel: (503) 242-0920, (800) 222-0544, FAX: (503) 321-5289, Web Site: www.hannaandersson.com (2)

McCue, Michael, Sales & Marketing Management Magazine, New York, NY. Tel: (800) 821-6897, FAX: (905) 470-8561, E-Mail: joyce.cooney@ nielsen.com, Web Site: www.salesandmarketing. com (16)

McCulley, Karen, CPAC Inc, Leicester, NY. Tel: (585) 382-3223, (800) 828-6011, FAX: (585) 382-3031, E-Mail: cpacinfo@cpac.com, Web Site: www.cpac. com (16)

McCullough Jr., Frank, New York Power Authority, Albany, NY. Tel: (518) 433-6700, Web Site: www. nypa.gov (16)

McCullough, Alan, J., Homecraft Veneer & Woodworker Supply, Youngstown, PA. Tel: (724) 537-8435, (800) 796-6348, FAX: (724) 537-0543, E-Mail: woodman@homecraftveneer.com, Web Site: www.homecraftveneer.com (8)

McCullough, Gordon, American Heart Association, Dallas, TX. Tel: (214) 373-6300, (800) AHA-USA-1, FAX: (214) 373-3406, Web Site: www. americanheart.org (1)

McCune, Thomas, Navitar Inc, Rochester, NY. Tel: (585) 359-4000, FAX: (585) 359-4999, E-Mail: info@navitar.com, Web Site: www.navitar.com (16)

McCurry, Kristin, MINDset Direct, Arlington, VA. Tel: (703) 538-6463, Web Site: www.mindsetdirect.com (1)

McDermott Jr., James, E., Amica Insurance, Lincoln, RI. Tel: (401) 334-6000, (800) 652-6422, FAX: (401) 334-4241, Web Site: www.amica.com (15)

McDermott, Deborah, Covidien International, Mansfield, MA. Tel: (508) 261-8000, (800) 962-9888, FAX: (508) 261-8105, Web Site: www.covidien. com (7)

McDermott, Janet, Ewing Galloway Inc, Oceanside, NY. Tel: (516) 764-8620, E-Mail: ewinggalloway@ aol.com, Web Site: www.indexstock.com (38)

McDonald, B., McDonald Enterprises Ltd, Vienna, VA. Tel: (703) 813-6040, FAX: (703) 847-9662 (35)

McDonald, Dan, Marketing Solutions Now Inc, Roswell, GA. Tel: (770) 777-4121, Web Site: www.marketingsolutionsnow.com (23)

McDonald, Debbie, Bowers & Merena Auctions, Irvine, CA. Tel: (949) 253-0916, (800) 458-4646, FAX: (949) 253-4091, E-Mail: auction@ bowersandmerena.com, Web Site: www. bowersandmerena.com (16)

McDonald, J., T., MarketNet Services LLC, Spring Lake, MI. Tel: (616) 847-7992, Web Site: www. marketnet1.com (22)

McDonald, Jane, Institute of Real Estate Management, Chicago, IL. Tel: (312) 329-6000, (800) 837-0706, FAX: (800) 338-4736, E-Mail: custserv@irem.org, Web Site: www.irem.org (1)

McDonald, Jean, Nordstrom Inc, Seattle, WA. Tel: (206) 303-2301, FAX: (206) 373-3198 (2)

McDonald, John, Masscot Internet Inc, West Yarmouth, MA. Tel: (508) 778-6320, (877) 627-7268, FAX: (888) 884-9960, E-Mail: admin@ masscot.net, Web Site: www.masscothosting.com (21)

McDonald, Joseph, The Field Companies Inc, Watertown, MA. Tel: (617) 926-5550, (800) 346-6552, FAX: (617) 924-9011, E-Mail: info@ fieldcompanies.com, Web Site: www. fieldcompanies.com (21)

McDonald, Marjorie, McDonald Obsolete Parts Co, Rockport, IN. Tel: (812) 359-4965, FAX: (812) 359-5555, E-Mail: parts@mcdonaldparts.com, Web Site: www.mcdonaldparts.com (16)

McDonald, Maureen, Institute of Reading Development, Novato, CA. Tel: (415) 884-8100, (800) 964-8888, FAX: (415) 382-0760, E-Mail: contactus@readingprograms.org, Web Site: www. readingprograms.org (1)

McDonald, Robert, McDonald Obsolete Parts Co, Rockport, IN. Tel: (812) 359-4965, FAX: (812) 359-5555, E-Mail: parts@mcdonaldparts.com, Web Site: www.mcdonaldparts.com (16)

McDonald, Will, McDonald Obsolete Parts Co, Rockport, IN. Tel: (812) 359-4965, FAX: (812) 359-5555, E-Mail: parts@mcdonaldparts.com, Web Site: www.mcdonaldparts.com (16)

McDonald Enterprises Ltd, Vienna, VA. Tel: (703) 813-6040, FAX: (703) 847-9662 (35)

McDonald Obsolete Parts Co, Rockport, IN. Tel: (812) 359-4965, FAX: (812) 359-5555, E-Mail: parts@ mcdonaldparts.com, Web Site: www. mcdonaldparts.com (16)

Shannon McDonald, New York, NY. Tel: (917) 838-2057 (20)

McDonnell, Mark, Facts On File Inc, New York, NY. Tel: (212) 967-8800, (800) 322-8755, FAX: (212) 678-3633, Web Site: www.factsonfile.com (17)

McDonnell, Sue, K, Dow Corning Corp, Midland, MI. Tel: (989) 496-4000, (800) 248-2481, FAX: (989) 496-4572, Web Site: www.dowcorning.com (16)

McDonough, Bill, Telephony, Chicago, IL. Tel: (312) 595-1080, (800) 458-0479, FAX: (312) 595-0295, Web Site: www.internettelephony.com (17)

McDonough, Cindy L., Harold Walter Siebens School of Business, Storm Lake, IA. Tel: (712) 749-2410, (800) 383-2821, FAX: (712) 749-2037, Web Site: www2.bvu.edu/academics/business (41)

McDonough, Matthew, J., TNT International Express, Melville, NY. Tel: (800) 558-5555 (28)

McDougal Littell, Evanston, IL. Tel: (847) 869-2300, FAX: (847) 869-0841, Web Site: www. mcdougallittell.com (17)

McDowell, Anthony T., Finch Paper, Glens Falls, NY. Tel: (518) 793-2541, (800) 833-9983, FAX: (518) 743-9656, E-Mail: amcdowell@finchpaper.com, Web Site: www.finchpaper.com (25)

McDowell, Kelly, AB Lambdin Inc, Hampton, VA. Tel: (800) 528-9817, FAX: (800) 221-9231, E-Mail: service@ablambdin.com (12)

McDowell, Robert, L., Olan Mills Inc, Chattanooga, TN. Tel: (423) 622-5141, (800) 251-6320, FAX: (423) 629-8128, Web Site: www.olanmills.com (16)

McDowell, Shirley, A., CAS Design Center, North Richland Hills, TX. Tel: (817) 788-1782 (8)

McDowell, T. J., Neutron Industries, Phoenix, AZ. Tel: (602) 864-0090, (888) 712-7127, FAX: (602) 357-3996, (877) 646-7337, E-Mail: questions@ neutronindustries.com, Web Site: www. neutronindustries.com (16)

McDowell, Tom, F., CAS Design Center, North Richland Hills, TX. Tel: (817) 788-1782 (8)

McDuel, Regina, Higher Power Marketing, Phoenix, AZ. Tel: (480) 837-3580, (888) 922-3580, FAX: (480) 837-3589, E-Mail: info@hpowermarketing. com, Web Site: www.hpowermarketing.com (30)

McElhany, Ryan, Texas Farm Bureau Insurance Companies, Waxahachie, TX. Tel: (972) 825-4842, Web Site: www.sagu.edu (1)

McElheney, J., Ronald, North Carolina Electric Membership Corp, Raleigh, NC. Tel: (919) 872-0800, (800) 662-8835, FAX: (919) 645-3410, E-Mail: info@ncemcs.com, Web Site: www.ncemcs.com (30)

McElroy, Evan, Boys & Girls Clubs of America National Headquarters, Atlanta, GA. Tel: (404) 487-5700, FAX: (404) 487-5757, (404) 815-5757, E-Mail: info@bgca.org, Web Site: www.bgca.org (1)

McElroy, I.D., Psion Teklogix Inc, Mississauga, ON. Tel: (905) 813-9900, (800) 322-3437, E-Mail: ptinfo@psion.com, Web Site: www.psionteklogix. com (3)

McElroy, Kevin, Marketing Results Inc, Sicklerville, NJ. Tel: (856) 740-3334, FAX: (856) 740-3335, Web Site: www.marketingresults.net (16)

McElveen-Hunter, Bonnie, Pace Communications Inc, Greensboro, NC. Tel: (336) 378-6065, FAX: (336) 275-2864, Web Site: www.pacecommunications. com (17)

McEntee, Elliott, C., National Automated Clearing House Association, Herndon, VA. Tel: (703) 561-1100, FAX: (703) 787-0996, Web Site: www. nacha.org (1)

McEwan, Julie, Standard Register, Dayton, OH. Tel: (937) 221-1000, (800) 755-6405, FAX: (937) 221-1239, E-Mail: julie.mcewan@standardregister.com, Web Site: www.standardregister.com (10)

McEwen, Janice, Clarks of North America, Newton, MA. Tel: (617) 964-1222, (800) 925-4315, FAX: (617) 243-4213, Web Site: www.clarks.com (16)

McFadden, Michael, F., Goldsmith Agio Helms, Minneapolis, MN. Tel: (612) 339-0500, FAX: (612) 339-0507, Web Site: www.agio.com (14)

McFadden, Ronald, Zones Inc, Auburn, WA. Tel: (253) 205-3000, (800) 408-9663, FAX: (425) 430-3626, E-Mail: corpsales@zones.com, Web Site: www.zones.com (3)

McFarland, Ruth, Cision US Inc, Chicago, IL. Tel: (312) 922-2400, (866) 639-5087, FAX: (312) 922-3126, E-Mail: info.us@cision.com, Web Site: us.cision.com (43)

McFarland & Co Inc Publishers, Jefferson, NC. Tel: (336) 246-4460, (800) 253-2187, FAX: (336) 246-5018, E-Mail: info@mcfarlandpub.com, Web Site: www.mcfarlandpub.com (17)

McFarlend, Dave, Tax Management Inc, Bethesda, MD. Tel: (202) 452-4200, FAX: (202) 496-6013 (17)

McFayden/McConnell, Brandon, MB Canada. Tel: (800) 205-7111, FAX: (877) 625-1888, Web Site: www.mcfayden.com (8)

McFeely, Katlyn, American Foundation for the Blind Inc, New York, NY. Tel: (212) 502-7600, FAX: (212) 502-7777, E-Mail: afbinfo@afb.org, Web Site: www.afb.org/afb (1)

McFeely's Square Drive Screws, Madison, WI. Tel: (434) 846-2729, (800) 443-7937, FAX: (804) 847-7136, E-Mail: tech@mcfeelys.com, Web Site: www.mcfeelys.com (16)

McFeeters, Paul, J., Open Text Inc, Waterloo, ON. Tel: (519) 888-9933, (800) 499-6544, FAX: (519) 888-0677, E-Mail: support@opentext.com, Web Site: www.opentext.com (16)

McFeetors, Raymond, L., Great-West Life, Greenwood Village, CO. Tel: (800) 537-2033, Web Site: www.greatwest.com (15)

McGahey, Thomas, S., High Cotton, Birmingham, AL. Tel: (877) 838-2345, FAX: (205) 836-5587, E-Mail: sales@highscottonusa.com, Web Site: www.highcottonusa.com (28)

McGarry, Andrew, ULTA Salon Cosmetics Fragrance, Romeoville, IL. Tel: (630) 226-0020 (7)

McGaw, Nancy, Bruce McGaw Graphics, Manchester Center, VT. Tel: (845) 353-8600, (888) 4BMC-GAW, FAX: (845) 353-3155, E-Mail: sales@bmcgaw.com, Web Site: www.bmcgaw.com (6)

Bruce McGaw Graphics, Manchester Center, VT. Tel: (845) 353-8600, (888) 4BMCGAW, FAX: (845) 353-3155, E-Mail: sales@bmcgaw.com, Web Site: www.bmcgaw.com (6)

McGee, Bill, Savicom, San Francisco, CA. Tel: (415) 983-0990, FAX: (415) 445-9999, E-Mail: sales@savicom.net, Web Site: www.savicom.net (22)

McGee, Donald, Ultimate Office, Farmingdale, NJ. Tel: (732) 780-6911, (800) 631-2233, FAX: (732) 780-9833, Web Site: www.ultoffice.com (16)

McGee, Vickie, Where 2 Get It Inc, Anaheim, CA. Tel: (888) 377-2767, Web Site: www.where2getit.com (30)

McGhee, Heather, Petco Animal Supplies, San Diego, CA. Tel: (858) 453-7845, (877) 738-6742, FAX: (858) 453-6585, Web Site: www.petco.com (5)

McGill, Lee, Eagle Claw Fishing Tackle, Denver, CO. Tel: (303) 321-1481, FAX: (303) 321-4750, E-Mail: info@eagleclaw.com, Web Site: www.eagleclaw.com (11)

McGilvray, Lana, Datran Media, New York, NY. Tel: (212) 706-9781, Web Site: www.datranmedia.com (22)

McGilvray, Lana, Skylist, Austin, TX. Tel: (877) 250-2922, FAX: (512) 857-0368, E-Mail: sales@skylist.com, Web Site: www.skylist.net (32)

McGinley, James, W., Methode Electronics Inc, Chicago, IL. Tel: (708) 867-6777, FAX: (708) 867-6999, E-Mail: info@methode.com, Web Site: www.methode.com (9)

McGinley, Patty, Arrowhead Mountain Spring Water, Wilkes Barre, PA. Tel: (800) 873-7775, Web Site: www.arrowheadwater.com (16)

McGinley, Thomas, Equifax Database Marketing, Wakefield, MA. Tel: (781) 246-0040, (800) 660-5125, FAX: (781) 246-3720, E-Mail: monica.baker@equifax.com (22)

McGinnis Jr., A.J., Simmons-Boardman Publishing Corp, New York, NY. Tel: (212) 620-7200, FAX: (212) 633-1165 (17)

McGinty, James, J., Hot Topic Inc, City of Industry, CA. Tel: (626) 839-4681, (800) 275-9169, FAX: (626) 839-4686, Web Site: www.hottopic.com (2)

McGoey, Michael, Blanchard & Co Inc, New Orleans, LA. Tel: (504) 837-3010, (800) 880-4653, FAX: (504) 837-4884, Web Site: www.blanchardonline.com (16)

McGonagle, David, J., The Catholic University of America Press, Washington, DC. Tel: (202) 319-5052, FAX: (202) 319-4985, E-Mail: cua-press@cua.edu, Web Site: www.cuapress.cua.edu (17)

McGonigle, Kristie, CGSM Inc, Wilton, CT. Tel: (203) 563-9233, FAX: (203) 563-9239, Web Site: www.cgsm.com (35)

McGovern, Chris, Emerging Marketing, Columbus, OH. Tel: (614) 923-6000 X229, FAX: (614) 424-6200, E-Mail: chris@360em.com, Web Site: www.emergingmarketing.com (35)

McGovern, John, C., Progressive Distribution Services Inc, Grand Rapids, MI. Tel: (616) 957-5900, (800) 304-3699, FAX: (616) 957-2990, E-Mail: sales@progressive-commerce.com, Web Site: www.prodist.com (28)

McGovern, Ken, Com-Pak, Berlin, CT. Tel: (856) 802-1900, (856) 802-3097, E-Mail: info@com-pak.com, Web Site: www.marketpointdirect.com (28)

McGovern, Lisa, InfoSource Inc, Oviedo, FL. Tel: (407) 796-5200, (800) 393-4636, FAX: (407) 796-5190, E-Mail: isisale@howtomaster.com, Web Site: www.infosourcelearning.com (3)

McGowan, Chris, Los Angeles Kings, Los Angeles, CA. Tel: (213) 742-7100, (888) KINGS-LA, FAX: (213) 742-7296, Web Site: kings.nhl.com (16)

McGowan, Jim, The Missoulian, Missoula, MT. Tel: (406) 523-5334, FAX: (406) 523-5221, Web Site: www.missoulian.com (31)

Mcgowan, Mark, Online Print Solutions, San Francisco, CA. Tel: (415) 651-4157, Web Site: www.onlineprintsolutions.com (32)

McGrady, Laura, Cafe Lango, Guilford, CT. Tel: (203) 453-1456, (800) 243-1234, FAX: (203) 453-5110, E-Mail: mail@cafelango.com, Web Site: www.audioforum.com (16)

McGrath, Christopher, Bliss World LLC, New York, NY. Tel: (212) 931-6383, Web Site: www.blissworld.com (5)

McGrath, Jack, Brigar Xpress Solutions, Inc, Albany, NY. Tel: (518) 438-7817, (877) 437-7817, FAX: (518) 438-0224, E-Mail: general@brigarxpress.com, Web Site: www.brigarxpress.com (28)

McGrath, John, The Offset House Inc, Essex Junction, VT. Tel: (802) 878-4440, FAX: (802) 879-4865, Web Site: www.offsethouse.com (27)

McGrath, Joseph W., Unisys, Blue Bell, PA. Tel: (215) 986-4011, (800) 874-8647, FAX: (215) 986-2312, Web Site: www.unisys.com (16)

McGrath, Kevin, The Offset House Inc, Essex Junction, VT. Tel: (802) 878-4440, FAX: (802) 879-4865, Web Site: www.offsethouse.com (27)

McGrath, Monica, Ultimate Products Inc, Chula Vista, CA. Tel: (813) 881-1575, (800) 477-4287, FAX: (813) 881-1831, E-Mail: office@ultimatehat.com, Web Site: www.ultimatehat.com (16)

McGrath, Timothy, PC Connection, Merrimack, NH. Tel: (603) 683-2167, (800) 800-0014, FAX: (603) 683-5773, E-Mail: pr@pcconnection.com, Web Site: www.pcconnection.com, macconnection.com (22)

McGraw III, Harold, W., The McGraw-Hill Cos, New York, NY. Tel: (212) 904-2000, (866) 436-8502, FAX: (212) 512-3840, Web Site: www.mcgraw-hill.com (17)

The McGraw-Hill Cos, New York, NY. Tel: (212) 904-2000, (866) 436-8502, FAX: (212) 512-3840, Web Site: www.mcgraw-hill.com (17)

McGregor, David, TigerDirect.ca, Richmond Hill, ON. Tel: (888) 771-9999, (800) 800-8300, FAX: (905) 482-3134, Web Site: www.tigerdirect.ca (3)

McGrew, Pat, Eastman Kodak Co, Rochester, NY. Tel: (585) 724-0251, (800) 698-3324, FAX: (585) 724-1089, Web Site: www.kodak.com (17)

McGruff Specialty Products Office, Amsterdam, NY. Tel: (518) 842-4388, (888) 776-7763, FAX: (800) 995-5121, E-Mail: mcgruff@spocentral.com, Web Site: www.mcgruffspo.com (17)

McGuiness, Anna, Hagemeyer - North America, Charleston, SC. Tel: (843) 745-2400, FAX: (843) 745-6942, E-Mail: info@hagemeyerna.com, Web Site: www.hagemeyerna.com (16)

McGuinness, Peter, J., Issues & Answers Network Inc, Virginia Beach, VA. Tel: (757) 456-1100, FAX: (757) 456-0377, E-Mail: info@issans.com, Web Site: www.issans.com (30)

McGuire, Dan, St Louis Post-Dispatch, Saint Louis, MO. Tel: (314) 340-8000, (800) 365-0820, FAX: (314) 340-3140, Web Site: www.postnet.com (17)

McGuire, Deb, Bay Manufacturing, Milan, OH. Tel: (419) 499-4602, FAX: (419) 499-4603, Web Site: www.baymfg.com (16)

McGuire, Ingrid, Ernst & Young LLP, New York, NY. Tel: (212) 773-6146, FAX: (312) 879-4000, Web Site: www.ey.com (20)

McGuire, M.J., Bay Manufacturing, Milan, OH. Tel: (419) 499-4602, FAX: (419) 499-4603, Web Site: www.baymfg.com (16)

McGuire, Marilyn, Networking Alternatives for Publishers, Retailers & Artists, Inc, Eastsound, WA. Tel: (360) 376-2702, (800) 367-1907, FAX: (360) 376-2704, E-Mail: futureweb@rockisland.com (40)

McGuire, Michael, Corona-Lotus Inc, San Francisco, CA. Tel: (415) 956-8956, (800) 422-2924, FAX: (415) 956-4922, E-Mail: customerservice@biscoff.com, Web Site: www.biscoff.com (24)

McGuire, Susan, Indian Arts & Crafts Association, Albuquerque, NM. Tel: (505) 265-9149, FAX: (505) 265-8251, E-Mail: info@iaca.com, Web Site: www.iaca.com (1)

McHaney, Eric, Grand Canyon University, Phoenix, AZ. Tel: (602) 639-6277, Web Site: www.gcu.edu (13)

McHugh, Daniel, National Institute for Trial Advocacy (NITA), Boulder, CO. Tel: (800) 225-6482, Web Site: www.nita.org (1)

McHugh, Mark, Valassis Canada, Toronto, ON Canada. Tel: (416) 259-3600, Web Site: www.valassis.com (35)

McHugh, Pam, Mintel International, Chicago, IL. Tel: (312) 932-0500, Web Site: www.comperemedia.com (30)

McHugh, Stephen, The Original Honey Baked Ham Co of the East, Marblehead, MA. Tel: (781) 639-2200, Web Site: www.honeybakedmailorder.com (4)

McIlquham, John, The NonProfit Times, Morris Plains, NJ. Tel: (973) 401-0202, FAX: (973) 401-0404, Web Site: www.nptimes.com (17)

McIlvaine, Robert, The McIlvaine Co, Northbrook, IL. Tel: (847) 784-0012, FAX: (847) 784-0061, E-Mail: editor@mcilvainecompany.com, Web Site: www.mcilvainecompany.com (30)

The McIlvaine Co, Northbrook, IL. Tel: (847) 784-0012, FAX: (847) 784-0061, E-Mail: editor@mcilvainecompany.com, Web Site: www.mcilvainecompany.com (30)

McIntosh, Bruce, D., Portland Cement Association, Skokie, IL. Tel: (847) 966-6200, FAX: (847) 966-9781, Web Site: www.cement.org (1)

McIntosh, Damian, Thoma Cressey Bravo, Chicago, IL. Tel: (312) 777-4444, FAX: (312) 777-4445, Web Site: www.tcb.com (14)

McIntosh, M.H., Mac McIntosh Inc, North Kingstown, RI. Tel: (401) 294-7730, (800) 944-5553, FAX: (401) 679-0176, E-Mail: info@sales-lead-experts.com, Web Site: www.sales-lead-experts.com (20)

McIntosh, Madeline, Books on Tape, Westminster, MD. Tel: (800) 733-3000, Web Site: www. booksontape.com (17)

McIntosh, Robert, Creative Learning Systems Inc, Longmont, CO. Tel: (800) 458-2880, FAX: (760) 546-1490, Web Site: www.clsinc.com (9)

McIntyre, Bill, Allegra Network, LLC, Plymouth, MI. Tel: (248) 596-8600, FAX: (248) 596-8601, Web Site: www2.allegranetwork.com (27)

McIntyre, Mary, Beth, Win-Win Giving, West Newton, MA. Tel: (617) 645-5479 (1)

McIntyre, Susan, McIntyre Direct, Portland, OR. Tel: (503) 286-1400, FAX: (503) 286-7622, Web Site: www.mcintyredirect.com (21)

McIntyre, Tom, Dr Leonard's Healthcare Corp, Edison, NJ. Tel: (732) 225-0100, FAX: (732) 225-0302, Web Site: www.doctorleonard.com (7)

McIntyre Direct, Portland, OR. Tel: (503) 286-1400, FAX: (503) 286-7622, Web Site: www. mcintyredirect.com (21)

McIsaac, Susan, United Way of Greater Toronto, Toronto, ON. Tel: (416) 777-2001, FAX: (416) 777-0962, Web Site: www.unitedwaytoronto.com (1)

McKay, Patricia, A., Office Depot, Boca Raton, FL. Tel: (561) 438-4800, (800) 937-3600, FAX: (561) 438-4001, Web Site: www.officedepot.com (16)

McKay, Scott, J., Genworth Financial Inc, Richmond, VA. Tel: (804) 281-6000, (888) 436-9678, FAX: (804) 662-2414, Web Site: www.genworth.com (14)

McKean, Brian, Tom Snyder Productions, Watertown, MA. Tel: (617) 926-6000, (800) 342-0236, FAX: (800) 304-1254, E-Mail: ask@tomsnyder.com, Web Site: www.tomsnyder.com (16)

McKean, Lauri, Uncharted Country Publishing, Madison, WI. Tel: (575) 776-3470, E-Mail: ucp@ taichihealth.com, Web Site: www.taichihealth.com (17)

McKee, David, ALSAC - St. Jude, Memphis, TN. Tel: (901) 495-3300, FAX: (901) 495-3103, Web Site: www.stjude.org (1)

McKee, David, Annie's Attic LLC, Big Sandy, TX. Tel: (903) 636-4303, FAX: (903) 636-4088, Web Site: www.anniesattic.com (11)

McKee, David, DRG, Berne, IN. Tel: (260) 589-4000, Web Site: www.drgnetwork.com (17)

McKee, Marie, Steuben Glass, New York, NY. Tel: (607) 974-8659, (800) STEUBEN, FAX: (607) 974-8441, E-Mail: info@steuben.com, Web Site: www.steuben.com (6)

McKee, Patrick, Challenge Industries Inc, Ithaca, NY. Tel: (607) 272-8990, FAX: (607) 277-7865, E-Mail: info@aboutchallenge.org, Web Site: aboutchallenge.org (28)

McKee, Rev. Daun, Diakon Lutheran Social Ministries, Allentown, PA. Tel: (610) 682-2145, (888) 582-2230, FAX: (610) 682-1055, E-Mail: swangerb@diakon.org, Web Site: www.diakon.org (1)

McKee & Associates Inc, Hot Springs National Park, AR. Tel: (501) 623-8833, (888) 883-4988, FAX: (501) 620-6856, E-Mail: newmoverexperts@ mckeeandassociates.net, Web Site: www. newmoverexperts.com (21)

McKee Consulting LLC, Escondido, CA. Tel: (760) 738-8200, Web Site: www.trainyourcallcenter.com (20)

McKenna, Elizabeth, Westlake Plastics Co, Lenni, PA. Tel: (610) 459-1000, (800) 999-1700, FAX: (610) 459-1084, Web Site: www.westlakeplastics.com (16)

McKenna, Gwen, Mountain Press Publishing Co, Missoula, MT. Tel: (406) 728-1900, (800) 234-5308, FAX: (406) 728-1635, E-Mail: info@mtnpress. com, Web Site: www.mountain-press.com (17)

McKenna, John, Siemens IT Solutions & Services Inc, Norwalk, CT. Tel: (203) 642-2300, FAX: (203) 642-2399, Web Site: www.it-solutions.usa.siemens. com (16)

McKenna, Linda, Credit Index, Saint Cloud, MN. Tel: (973) 770-4007, FAX: (973) 770-4006, Web Site: www.ebureau.com (22)

McKenna, Lore, Baker Corp, Seal Beach, CA. Tel: (562) 430-6262 (16)

McKenna, Mark, Putnam Investments, Canton, MA. Tel: (617) 292-1000, (800) 225-1581, FAX: (617) 292-1683, Web Site: www.putnam.com (14)

McKenna, Michael, Editorial Projects in Education Inc, Bethesda, MD. Tel: (301) 280-3100, (800) 346-1834, FAX: (301) 280-3250, Web Site: www. edweek.org (17)

McKenna, Shawn, Juvenile Diabetes Research Foundation, New York, NY. Tel: (212) 785-9500, (800) 533-CURE, FAX: (212) 785-9595, E-Mail: info@ jdrf.org, Web Site: www.jdrf.org (1)

McKensie, Lynn, PC Connection, Merrimack, NH. Tel: (603) 683-2167, (800) 800-0014, FAX: (603) 683-5773, E-Mail: pr@pcconnection.com, Web Site: www.pcconnection.com, macconnection.com (22)

McKenzie, Barry, McKenzie Taxidermy Supply, Granite Quarry, NC. Tel: (704) 279-7985, (800) 279-7985, Web Site: www.mckenziesp.com (16)

McKenzie, David, Sun Harvest Citrus, Fort Myers, FL. Tel: (239) 768-2686, (800) 743-1480, FAX: (239) 768-9255, E-Mail: info@sunharvestcitrus. com, Web Site: www.SunHarvestCitrus.com (6)

McKenzie, Don, SourceLink, Itasca, IL. Tel: (866) 947-6872, Web Site: www.sourcelink.com (20)

McKenzie, E., Communication Concepts Inc, Ivyland, PA. Tel: (215) 672-6900, FAX: (215) 957-4362, E-Mail: info@ccgroupnet.com, Web Site: www. ccgroupnet.com (21)

McKenzie, Kevin, McKenzie Taxidermy Supply, Granite Quarry, NC. Tel: (704) 279-7985, (800) 279-7985, Web Site: www.mckenziesp.com (16)

McKenzie, Sandy, Sun Harvest Citrus, Fort Myers, FL. Tel: (239) 768-2686, (800) 743-1480, FAX: (239) 768-9255, E-Mail: info@sunharvestcitrus. com, Web Site: www.SunHarvestCitrus.com (6)

McKenzie Taxidermy Supply, Granite Quarry, NC. Tel: (704) 279-7985, (800) 279-7985, Web Site: www.mckenziesp.com (16)

McKeon, Brian, Timberland.com, Stratham, NH. Tel: (603) 772-9500, Web Site: www.Timberland.com (16)

McKeon, David, C&H Distributors LLC, Milwaukee, WI. Tel: (414) 443-1700, (888) 316-2223, FAX: (414) 443-9213, E-Mail: customerservice@chdist. com, Web Site: www.chdist.com (9)

McKesson Corp, San Francisco, CA. Tel: (415) 983-8300, FAX: (415) 983-7160, Web Site: www. mckesson.com (7)

McKinley, Bill, Benchmark Imaging & Display, Elk Grove Village, IL. Tel: (847) 292-5150, FAX: (847) 292-5159, Web Site: www. benchmarkimaging.com (27)

McKinley, Tracey, Rogers Publishing Ltd, Toronto, ON. Tel: (416) 935-7777, FAX: (416) 935-3597, Web Site: www.rogerspublishing.ca (17)

McKinnell, Henry, A., Pfizer Inc, New York, NY. Tel: (212) 733-2323, Web Site: www.pfizer.com (16)

McKinney, J., Bruce, Hershey Park, Hershey, PA. Tel: (717) 534-3149, (800) HERSHEY, E-Mail: info@ hersheypa.com, Web Site: www.hersheypark.com (19)

McKinney, William, E., Customer Marketing Group LLC, Weston, CT. Tel: (203) 226-9845, FAX: (203) 226-9837, E-Mail: bill@4cmg.com, Web Site: www.4cmg.com (35)

McKinnie, Pam, Concepts Unlimited, Broomfield, CO. Tel: (303) 449-2907, FAX: (303) 449-2967, E-Mail: conceptsunlimited@estreet.com, Web Site: www.conceptsunlimitedinc.com (35)

McKinsey & Co, New York, NY. Tel: (212) 446-7000, FAX: (212) 446-8575, Web Site: www.mckinsey. com (20)

McKinstry, Anne, Missouri Landscape & Nursery Association, Bowling Green, MO. Tel: (636) 542-1234, E-Mail: admin@mlng.org, Web Site: www. mlna.org (1)

McKnight, Andy, Tri-Chem Inc, Belleville, NJ. Tel: (973) 751-9200, FAX: (973) 450-1057, (973) 450-1260, E-Mail: paints@trichem.com, Web Site: www.trichem.com (16)

McKnight's Long-Term Care News, Northfield, IL. Tel: (847) 784-8706, (800) 558-1703, FAX: (847) 784-9346, E-Mail: mltcn-webmaster@mltcn.com, Web Site: www.mcknightsonline.com (17)

McLachlan, Neil, Mead Westvaco Consumer & Office Products, Dayton, OH. Tel: (937) 222-6323, (800) 345-6323, FAX: (937) 495-3192, Web Site: www. mead.com (10)

McLain, Craig, American Solutions for Business, Glenwood, MN. Tel: (320) 634-5471, FAX: (320) 634-5265, Web Site: www.americanbus.com (25)

Mclancon, Jeff, Video Artists International, Pleasantville, NY. Tel: (914) 769-3691, (800) 477-7146, FAX: (914) 769-5407, E-Mail: orders@vaimusic. com, Web Site: www.vaimusic.com (3)

McLauchlin, Jay, HealthPlan Services, Tampa, FL. Tel: (813) 289-1000, (800) 545-6441, Web Site: www.healthplan.com (15)

McLaughlin, Andy, Specialized Information Publishers Association (SIPA), Vienna, VA. Tel: (703) 992-9339, (800) 356-9302, FAX: (703) 610-9005, E-Mail: info@sipaonline.org, Web Site: www. sipaonline.com (1)

McLaughlin, Elizabeth, M., Hot Topic Inc, City of Industry, CA. Tel: (626) 839-4681, (800) 275-9169, FAX: (626) 839-4686, Web Site: www. hottopic.com (2)

McLaughlin, Joe, John Alden Life Insurance Co/North Star Marketing, Duluth, GA. Tel: (678) 473-1211, (800) 768-6288, FAX: (678) 473-9573, Web Site: www.nstarmarketing.com (15)

McLaughlin, Shari, Automotive Forms, Baltimore, MD. Tel: (410) 285-3700, FAX: (410) 284-8418, E-Mail: sales@autoforms.com, Web Site: www. autoforms.com (16)

McLaughlin, Theresa, Citizens Bank, Dedham, MA. Tel: (603) 634-7000, FAX: (603) 634-7191, Web Site: www.citizensbank.com (14)

McLaughlin, Todd, The Association of Fundraising Professionals, Arlington, VA. Tel: (800) 666-3863, Web Site: www.afpnet.org (1)

McLaughlin, Tom, E-Z-EM Inc, Melville, NY. Tel: (516) 333-8230, (800) 544-4624, FAX: (516) 333-8278, E-Mail: webmaster@ezem.com, Web Site: www.ezem.com (7)

McLaughlin, William, Select Comfort Corp, Minneapolis, MN. Tel: (763) 551-7000, (888) 411-2188, FAX: (763) 551-7826, Web Site: www. selectcomfort.com (16)

McLean, Donna, National Railroad Passenger Corp, Washington, DC. Tel: (202) 906-3000, (800) USA-RAIL, FAX: (202) 906-3306, Web Site: www. amtrak.com (16)

McLean, Mark, Market Approach Consulting, Lorena, TX. Tel: (254) 857-7017, Web Site: www. marketapproach.net (23)

McLeod, Al, California State University at Fresno, Fresno, CA. Tel: (559) 278-7830, FAX: (559) 278-8577, Web Site: www.csufresno.edu (41)

McLoughlin, Jacqueline, Advertising Research Foundation, New York, NY. Tel: (212) 751-5656, FAX: (212) 319-5265, E-Mail: info@thearf.org, Web Site: www.thearf.org (40)

McLuster, Linda, Recognition Systems (Dot Works), Port Washington, NY. Tel: (516) 625-5000, FAX: (516) 625-1507, E-Mail: wade@dotworks.com, Web Site: www.dotworks.com (16)

McMahen, Nancy, National Rural Electric Cooperative Association, Arlington, VA. Tel: (703) 907-5500, FAX: (703) 907-5528, Web Site: www.nreca.org (1)

McMahon, Bill, K-tel International, Golden Valley, MN. Tel: (204) 889-5430, (800) 665-5021, FAX: (612) 559-6803, Web Site: www.ktel.com (16)

McMahon, Bill, Nautilus Inc, Vancouver, WA. Tel: (360) 859-2900, (800) 675-0171, FAX: (360) 694-2755, Web Site: www.nautilus.com (11)

McMahon, Pat, One Point, Scranton, PA. Tel: (570) 342-0737, (800) 526-4460, FAX: (570) 343-6361, Web Site: www.opoffice.com (10)

McManis, James, NetHawk Interactive, Emeryville, CA. Tel: (510) 595-2220, Web Site: www.nethawk.net (23)

McManus, Donna, NestFamily.com, Coppell, TX. Tel: (972) 402-7100, (800) 596-7386, FAX: (972) 629-7181, Web Site: www.nestfamily.com (3)

McMaster, Eileen, Anne Klein, New York, NY. Tel: (212) 536-9000, FAX: (212) 536-9000 (16)

McMaster-Carr Supply Co (HQ), Elmhurst, IL. Tel: (630) 600-3600, FAX: (630) 834-9427, E-Mail: chi.sales@mcmaster.com, Web Site: www.mcmaster.com (9)

McMeekin, Bruce, New England Direct Marketing Association, Wellesley Hills, MA. Tel: (781) 237-1366, FAX: (781) 431-8118, E-Mail: info@nedma.com, Web Site: www.nedma.com (40)

McMeekin, Nancy M., Oakstone Publishing LLC, Birmingham, AL. Tel: (205) 991-5188, (800) 952-0690, FAX: (205) 995-4656, Web Site: www.oakstonepublishing.com (17)

McMenamin, John, Princeton Book Co Publishers, Hightstown, NJ. Tel: (609) 426-0602, (800) 220-7149, FAX: (609) 426-1344, E-Mail: pbc@dancehorizons.com, Web Site: www.dancehorizons.com (17)

McMillan, Michael, The Connection Contact Center Services, Burnsville, MN. Tel: (952) 948-5335, (800) 883-5777, FAX: (952) 948-5498, E-Mail: sales@the-connection.com, Web Site: www.the-connection.com (29)

McMillan, Michelle, Mardev-DM2, Lombard, IL. Tel: (800) 323-4958, FAX: (303) 265-5457, E-Mail: info@mardevdm2.com, Web Site: www.mardevdm2.com (24)

McMillan, Sheri, Microbiz Corp, Fountain Valley, CA. Tel: (201) 785-1311, (800) 726-3282, FAX: (201) 758-1568, E-Mail: info@microbiz.com, Web Site: www.microbiz.com (3)

McMorrow, Patrick, J., Tuttle Printing & Engraving, Rutland, VT. Tel: (802) 773-9171, (800) 776-7682, FAX: (802) 773-5785, E-Mail: info@tuttleprinting.com, Web Site: www.tuttleprinting.com (10)

McMullan, Theresa, SkyMall Inc, Phoenix, AZ. Tel: (602) 254-9777, (800) SKY-MALL, FAX: (602) 254-6075, Web Site: www.skymall.com (17)

Mcmullen, James, Tillamook County Creamery Association, Tillamook, OR. Tel: (503) 842-4481, (800) 542-7290, FAX: (503) 842-6039, Web Site: www.tillamookcheese.com (4)

McMurry Inc, Phoenix, AZ. Tel: (602) 395-5850, Web Site: www.mcmurry.com (17)

McMurtry, Laramie, Mailmaster Corp, Jonesboro, AR. Tel: (870) 972-8845, (800) 551-7018, FAX: (870) 972-0877, E-Mail: info@mail-master.com, Web Site: www.mail-master.com (28)

McNabb, Mike, Fran's Gifts to Go, Myrtle Beach, SC. Tel: (843) 445-2625, (800) 476-6887, E-Mail: customerservice@fransgiftstogo.com, Web Site: www.fransgiftstogo.com (4)

McNair, Nick, Bradley Direct, Columbus, GA. Tel: (706) 565-2100, (866) 239-6774, (800) 241-8981, FAX: (706) 565-2132, (888) 224-7455, E-Mail: customerservice@grilllovers.com, Web Site: www.grilllovers.com (8)

McNair lll, James D., Garlinghouse Co, Beaufort, SC. Tel: (703) 547-4115, (800) 235-5700, FAX: (703) 222-9705, Web Site: www.familyhomeplans.com (17)

McNally, Edward, M., Morris James Hitchens & Williams, Wilmington, DE. Tel: (302) 888-6800, FAX: (302) 571-1750, Web Site: www.morrisjames.com (20)

McNamara, Brian, International Sign Association, Alexandria, VA. Tel: (703) 836-4012, FAX: (703) 836-8353, Web Site: www.signs.org (42)

McNamara, Jim, McNamara & Associates, Van Nuys, CA. Tel: (818) 907-6212, E-Mail: jim@mcdrtv.com, Web Site: www.mcdrtv.com (39)

McNamara, John, One Call Systems Inc, Baden, PA. Tel: (412) 415-5000, (800) 845-9945, FAX: (412) 415-5023, E-Mail: jmcnamara@1-call.com, Web Site: www.1-call.com (29)

McNamara, Keith, Fujitsu Transaction Solutions Inc, Richardson, TX. Tel: (972) 963-2300, (800) 340-4425, Web Site: www.fujitsu.com (16)

McNamara, Thomas, Quattro Direct LLC, Berwyn, PA. Tel: (610) 993-0070, Web Site: www.quattrodirect.com (35)

McNamara, Tim, C., Boyden Global Executive Search, Purchase, NY. Tel: (914) 747-0093, E-Mail: inquiry@boyden.com, Web Site: www.boyden.com (20)

McNamara & Associates, Van Nuys, CA. Tel: (818) 907-6212, E-Mail: jim@mcdrtv.com, Web Site: www.mcdrtv.com (39)

McNamera, Michael, Key Bank, Cleveland, OH. Tel: (216) 689-3000, (888) 539-2968, FAX: (207) 874-7044, Web Site: www.key.com (14)

McNaughton, Stanley W., PEMCO Insurance Cos, Seattle, WA. Tel: (206) 628-4000, (800) 467-3626, FAX: (206) 628-5886, Web Site: www.pemco.com (15)

McNeff, John, Nova DM, Dunmore, PA. Tel: (570) 342-8668 (35)

McNeil, James, BAI, Chicago, IL. Tel: (312) 683-2464, FAX: (312) 683-2373, E-Mail: info@bai.org, Web Site: www.bai.org (17)

McNeil, Thomas, DineWise, Farmingdale, NY. Tel: (631) 694-1111, (800) 749-1170, FAX: (631) 694-4064, E-Mail: info@dinewise.com, Web Site: www.dinewise.com (4)

Mcneil, Keith, Catch The Wind Kite Shop, Lincoln City, OR. Tel: (541) 994-9500, (800) 227-7878, FAX: (541) 994-4766, E-Mail: catchthewindkites@yahoo.com, Web Site: www.catchthewind.com (11)

McNerney Jr., W., James, Boeing Co, Chicago, IL. Tel: (312) 544-2000, FAX: (312) 544-2082, Web Site: www.boeing.com (16)

McNerney, Patrick, PJ McNerney & Associates Inc, Cincinnati, OH. Tel: (513) 825-5547, FAX: (513) 825-5601, E-Mail: tim@pjmcnerney.com, Web Site: www.pjmcnerney.com (28)

PJ McNerney & Associates Inc, Cincinnati, OH. Tel: (513) 825-5547, FAX: (513) 825-5601, E-Mail: tim@pjmcnerney.com, Web Site: www.pjmcnerney.com (28)

McNicholas, Christine, Q Interactive, Chicago, IL. Tel: (312) 977-0390, (888) 729-6465, FAX: (312) 224-5001, E-Mail: solutions@qinteractive.com, Web Site: www.qinteractive.com (40)

McNichols Co, Tampa, FL. Tel: (813) 282-3828, FAX: (813) 288-9342, E-Mail: sales@mcnichols.com, Web Site: www.mcnichols.com (16)

McNitt, Peter, B., Harris Bancorp Inc, Chicago, IL. Tel: (312) 461-7961, (888) 340-BANK, FAX: (312) 461-7869, E-Mail: onlineservices@harrisbank.com, Web Site: www.harrisbank.com (14)

McNulty, Despina, Kappa Publishing Group, Blue Bell, PA. Tel: (215) 643-6385, FAX: (215) 628-3571, Web Site: www.kappapublishing.com (17)

McNutt III, William, International Direct Marketing Consultants Inc, Dallas, TX. Tel: (214) 443-9494, FAX: (214) 443-9512, E-Mail: billmcnutt@charter.net, Web Site: www.dmtrademissions.com (20)

McNutt, L. William, Collin Street Bakery, Corsicana, TX. Tel: (800) 292-7400, Web Site: www.collinstreetbakery.com (4)

McNutt, Robert, P., Collin Street Bakery, Corsicana, TX. Tel: (800) 292-7400, Web Site: www.collinstreetbakery.com (4)

McPeak, Jacquelyn, Mail Management Enterprises, Seaford, DE. Tel: (410) 883-3224, FAX: (410) 883-3392, E-Mail: mailmgt@aol.com, Web Site: www.mailmanagemententerprises.com (20)

McPhedrain, Rusty, Mary Maxim Inc, Port Huron, MI. Tel: (810) 987-2000, (800) 962-9504, FAX: (810) 987-5056, E-Mail: info@marymaxim.com, Web Site: www.marymaxim.com (11)

McPherson, M., Peter, Dow Jones & Co, Princeton, NJ. Tel: (609) 520-4000, FAX: (212) 416-4348, Web Site: www.dowjones.com/corp/index.html (17)

McPherson, Richard, McPherson Associates Inc, Malvern, PA. Tel: (610) 640-1555, Web Site: www.mcphersonassociates.com (1)

McPherson Associates Inc, Malvern, PA. Tel: (610) 640-1555, Web Site: www.mcphersonassociates.com (1)

McQuade, Eugene, M., Federal Home Loan Mortgage Corp (Freddie Mac), McLean, VA. Tel: (703) 903-2000, (800) 424-5401, Web Site: www.freddiemac.com (14)

McQueen, Penny, Finelight Inc, Louisville, KY. Tel: (502) 589-5896, E-Mail: info@finelight.com, Web Site: www.finelight.com (35)

McQuitty, Shaun, New Mexico State University, Las Cruces, NM. Tel: (575) 646-0111, (505) 646-3341, FAX: (505) 646-1498, Web Site: www.nmsu.edu (41)

McRuer, Jerry, Direct Partners, Marina Del Rey, CA. Tel: (310) 482-4200, FAX: (310) 482-4201, Web Site: www.directpartners.com (35)

McSlarrow, Kyle, The Cable Show National Cable Television Association, Washington, DC. Tel: (202) 222-2300, E-Mail: webmaster@ncta.com, Web Site: www.ncta.com (42)

McSlasrow, Kyle, National Cable & Telecommunications Association, Washington, DC. Tel: (202) 222-2300, FAX: (202) 775-3675, Web Site: www.ncta.com (40)

McSpadden, Joe, BBS Chicago, Chicago, IL. Tel: (312) 326-8000, Web Site: www.rrdonnelley.com (31)

McStocker, Kim, Smith Hanley Associates, Southport, CT. Tel: (203) 319-4300, (888) 221-2900, FAX: (203) 319-4320, Web Site: www.smithhanley.com (20)

McStravick, John, ADT Worldwide, Boca Raton, FL. Tel: (561) 988-3600, FAX: (561) 988-3673, Web Site: www.tycofireandsecurity.com (16)

McSwain, Pam, Parker Systems Inc, Chesapeake, VA. Tel: (757) 485-2955, (866) 472-7537, FAX: (757) 487-5872, E-Mail: info@parkersystemsinc.com, Web Site: www.parkersystemsinc.com (16)

McSweeney, David, DM Info, Naperville, IL. Tel: (630) 357-0732, FAX: (630) 527-8136, E-Mail: dminfo@dmcsweeney.com (20)

McTaggart, Tanya, McBee Associates Inc, Wayne, PA. Tel: (610) 964-9680, Web Site: www.mcbeeassociates.com (20)

McVay, Barry, Panoptic Enterprises, Burke, VA. Tel: (703) 451-5953, (800) 594-4766, FAX: (703) 451-5953, E-Mail: panoptic@fedgovcontracts.com, Web Site: www.fedgovcontracts.com (17)

McVay, Tim, KTVU Retail Services, Oakland, CA. Tel: (510) 874-0228, FAX: (510) 874-0229, Web Site: www.ktvu.com (32)

McVay, Vivina, Panoptic Enterprises, Burke, VA. Tel: (703) 451-5953, (800) 594-4766, FAX: (703) 451-5953, E-Mail: panoptic@fedgovcontracts.com, Web Site: www.fedgovcontracts.com (17)

McVey, Alicia, UPMC Health Plan, Pittsburgh, PA. Tel: (412) 454-3469, Web Site: www.upmchealthplan.com (1)

McVicker, Earl, D., ABA/BMA Trust Wealth Management and Marketing Conference, Washington, DC. Tel: (202) 663-5000, (800) BANKERS, FAX: (202) 828-4540, E-Mail: custserv@aba.com, Web Site: www.aba.com (42)

McVoy, Marilyn, Stickers 'N' Stuff Inc, Louisville, CO. Tel: (303) 661-0200, E-Mail: sales@stickersnstuff.com, Web Site: www.stickersnstuff.biz (6)

McWeeney, George, McWeeney Marketing Group, Orange, CT. Tel: (203) 891-8100, (800) 272-3440, FAX: (203) 891-0775, E-Mail: george@mcweeneymarketing.com, Web Site: www.mcweeneymarketing.com (33)

McWeeney Marketing Group, Orange, CT. Tel: (203) 891-8100, (800) 272-3440, FAX: (203) 891-0775, E-Mail: george@mcweeneymarketing.com, Web Site: www.mcweeneymarketing.com (33)

McWhorter, Anthony, United Investors Life Insurance Co, Birmingham, AL. Tel: (205) 325-4300, (800) 288-2722, FAX: (205) 325-4157, Web Site: www.uilic.com (15)

McWilliams, Beth, Happy Trails Resort, Surprise, AZ. Tel: (623) 584-0066, FAX: (623) 546-2968, E-Mail: happytrails@uccinc.net, Web Site: www.htresort.com (19)

McWilliams, Bruce, Teachers' Discovery, Auburn Hills, MI. Tel: (248) 340-7220, FAX: (248) 340-7212 (5)

Mead, Robert M, AETNA - Marketing Product & Communication, Hartford, CT. Tel: (860) 273-0123, (800) 872-3862, FAX: (860) 273-3971, Web Site: www.aetna.com (14)

Mead Fine Paper Division, Sidney, NY. Tel: (800) 936-9811, Web Site: www.mead.com (25)

Mead Johnson Co, Evansville, IN. Tel: (812) 429-5204, Web Site: www.MeadJohnson.com (7)

Mead Westvaco Consumer & Office Products, Dayton, OH. Tel: (937) 222-6323, (800) 345-6323, FAX: (937) 495-3192, Web Site: www.mead.com (10)

Meader, Kelly J., Glens Falls Hospital Foundation, Glens Falls, NY. FAX: (518) 926-7012, Web Site: www.glensfallshospital.org (1)

Meadors, Alyce, The United Methodist Publishing House, Nashville, TN. Tel: (615) 749-6000, (800) 672-1789, FAX: (615) 749-6417, E-Mail: productsandservices@umpublishing.com, Web Site: www.umpublishing.com (17)

Meadowcroft, Lisa, African Medical & Research Foundation Inc (AMREF USA), New York, NY. Tel: (212) 768-2440, Web Site: www.amref.org (1)

Meadowcroft, William, D., Nautilus Inc, Vancouver, WA. Tel: (360) 859-2900, (800) 675-0171, FAX: (360) 694-2755, Web Site: www.nautilus.com (11)

Meadows, Marc, Meadows Design Office, Washington, DC. Tel: (202) 966-6007, FAX: (202) 966-6733, E-Mail: mdo@mdomedia.com, Web Site: www.mdomedia.com (35)

Meadows Design Office, Washington, DC. Tel: (202) 966-6007, FAX: (202) 966-6733, E-Mail: mdo@mdomedia.com, Web Site: www.mdomedia.com (35)

MeadWestvaco, Springfield, MA. Tel: (888) 715-6641, Web Site: www.mwvenvelopes.com (26)

Meakem, Glen, Surplus Record, Chicago, IL. Tel: (312) 372-9077, (800) 622-5449, FAX: (312) 372-6537, E-Mail: surplus@surplusrecord.com, Web Site: www.surplusrecord.com (17)

Means, Chris, Chattanooga Shooting Supplies Inc, Chattanooga, TN. Tel: (423) 894-3007, (800) 251-4808, FAX: (423) 855-5513, Web Site: www.chattanoogashooting.com (16)

Meany, Susan, SKM Group, Depew, NY. Tel: (716) 989-3200, FAX: (716) 989-3220, E-Mail: info@skmgroup.com, Web Site: www.skmgroup.com (35)

Mechanical Breakdown Administrators Inc, Scottsdale, AZ. Tel: (480) 860-2288, FAX: (480) 860-0425, E-Mail: gaylenb@mbadirect.com, Web Site: www.mbadirect.com (14)

Meckler, Allan, Jupiterimages Corp, Peoria, IL. Tel: (312) 980-6111, (800) 764-7427, Web Site: www.jupiterimages.com (36)

Meckley, David, Wilton Armetale, Mount Joy, PA. Tel: (717) 653-4444, (800) 553-2048, FAX: (717) 653-6573, E-Mail: cservice@armetale.com, Web Site: www.armetale.com (16)

Medals of America, Fountain Inn, SC. Tel: (864) 862-0635, (800) 308-0849, FAX: (800) 407-8640, E-Mail: medals@usmedals.com, Web Site: www.usmedals.com (6)

Medavante, Hamilton, NJ. Tel: (609) 528-9413, Web Site: www.metavante.com (20)

Medco Health Solutions Inc, Franklin Lakes, NJ. Tel: (201) 269-3400, FAX: (201) 269-6400, Web Site: www.medco.com (7)

Medco Insurance Co, Omaha, NE. Tel: (800) 228-6080, E-Mail: clientservices@gomedico.com, Web Site: www.gomedico.com (15)

Medco Supply Co Inc, Tonawanda, NY. Tel: (716) 695-3244, (800) 556-3326, FAX: (800) 222-1934, E-Mail: sales@medcosupply.com, Web Site: www.medcosupply.com (7)

Medcom Inc, Cypress, CA. Tel: (800) 877-1443, FAX: (714) 891-3140, E-Mail: lhammonds@medcominc.com, Web Site: www.medcominc.com (17)

Media Consultants, Lyndhurst, NJ. Tel: (201) 933-2015, FAX: (201) 933-6314, E-Mail: hlhirsch@earthlink.net, Web Site: www.mediaconsultants.net (35)

Media Consultants Inc, Bayside, NY. Tel: (718) 423-6300, FAX: (718) 428-7482, E-Mail: mediaconsults@aol.com (32)

The Media Crew, Orlando, FL. Tel: (407) 839-0390, Web Site: www.themediacrew.com (35)

Media Directions Inc, Woodcliff Lake, NJ. Tel: (201) 930-4949, FAX: (201) 930-9229, E-Mail: mail@media-directions.com, Web Site: www.media-directions.com (23)

Media Distribution Services (MDS), New York, NY. Tel: (212) 279-4800, (800) MDS-DATA, FAX: (212) 643-0576, E-Mail: services@mdsconnect.com, Web Site: www.mdsconnect.com (23)

Media Dynamics LLC, Greenwich, CT. Tel: (203) 531-6600, FAX: (203) 531-6661, E-Mail: bjann@mediadynamx.com, Web Site: www.Media-Dynamics.com (31)

Media Funding Corp, Malibu, CA. Tel: (310) 457-4140, FAX: (310) 774-1234, E-Mail: info@mediafunding.com, Web Site: mediafunding.com (32)

Media Horizons Inc, Norwalk, CT. Tel: (203) 857-0770, FAX: (203) 857-0296, E-Mail: mhict@mediahorizons.com, Web Site: www.mediahorizons.com (21)

Media Horizons Management LLC, Norwalk, CT. Tel: (203) 857-0770, FAX: (203) 857-0296, E-Mail: info@mediahorizons.com, Web Site: www.mediahorizons.com (31)

Media Link Communications, New York, NY. Tel: (212) 674-8843, FAX: (212) 260-8489, E-Mail: mlinkcom@aol.com, Web Site: www.getprinted.com (27)

Media Management & Magnetics Inc, Menomonee Falls, WI. Tel: (262) 251-5511, (800) 242-2090, FAX: (262) 251-4737, E-Mail: medmgt@computersupplypeople.com, Web Site: www.computersupplypeople.com (3)

Media Management Services Inc, Newton, PA. Tel: (215) 579-8590, (800) 523-5948, FAX: (215) 579-8589, Web Site: www.mmseducation.com (20)

Media Mart, Falls Church, VA. Tel: (703) 905-4532, FAX: (703) 905-8097, E-Mail: mgallogly@media-mart.com, Web Site: www.media-mart.com (24)

Media Monitors Inc, White Plains, NY. Tel: (914) 428-5971, FAX: (914) 428-4541, E-Mail: jselig@mediamonitors.com, Web Site: www.mediamonitors.com (30)

The MEDIA Organization Inc, Woodbury, NY. Tel: (516) 496-2577, FAX: (516) 496-3331 (23)

Media People Inc, New York, NY. Tel: (212) 779-7172, FAX: (212) 779-7248, Web Site: www.mediapeople.com (31)

Media Printing Corp, Pompano Beach, FL. Tel: (954) 984-7300, FAX: (954) 888-8542 (27)

Media Recruiting Group Inc, Irvington, NY. Tel: (914) 591-5511, FAX: (914) 591-8911, E-Mail: resume@mediarecruiting.com, Web Site: www.mediarecruiting.com (20)

Media Resource Group Inc, Mount Kisco, NY. Tel: (914) 471-4448, FAX: (914) 244-4458, Web Site: www.mrginc.com (31)

Media Response Inc, Hollywood, FL. Tel: (954) 967-9899, (888) 801-9899, FAX: (954) 967-9321, E-Mail: info@media-response.com, Web Site: www.media-response.com (35)

Media Source Solutions, Plantation, FL. Tel: (954) 788-0213, Web Site: www.mediasourcesolutions.com (23)

Media Space Solutions, Norwalk, CT. Tel: (203) 849-8855, (888) 672-2100, FAX: (203) 849-5946, E-Mail: nsb@mindspring.com, Web Site: www.mediaspacesolutions.com (31)

Media Stream Direct, Sherman Oaks, CA. Tel: (800) 817-8000, E-Mail: ecohen@mediastreamdirect.com, Web Site: www.mediastreamdirect.com (35)

Media Two, Baltimore, MD. Tel: (410) 828-0120, FAX: (410) 825-1002, Web Site: www.mediatwo.com (17)

Mediacom Communications Corp, Middletown, NY. Tel: (845) 695-2600, FAX: (845) 695-2699, Web Site: www.mediacomcc.com (32)

MediaConcepts Corp, Assonet, MA. Tel: (508) 644-3131, FAX: (508) 644-5201, E-Mail: at3@mediaconceptscorp.com, Web Site: www.mediaconceptscorp.com (35)

MediaGraphics, Eau Claire, WI. Tel: (751) 590-4488, (866) 324-1658, E-Mail: mediagraphics@devkinney.com, Web Site: www.devkinney.com (35)

Mediamark Research Inc, New York, NY. Tel: (212) 884-9200, (800) 310-3305, FAX: (212) 884-9339, Web Site: www.mediamark.com (30)

MediaTree, Parsippany, NJ. Tel: (800) 475-8703, FAX: (973) 781-1071, E-Mail: sales@mediatreegroup.com, Web Site: www.mediatreegroup.com (27)

MediaWorks Advertising & Marketing Inc, Ormond Beach, FL. Tel: (407) 909-1903, E-Mail: mmalys@cfl.rr.com, Web Site: www.mediaworksusa.com (21)

Medibadge Inc, Omaha, NE. Tel: (402) 571-1800, (800) 228-0040, FAX: (800) 546-1072, E-Mail: stan@medibadge.com, Web Site: www.medibadge.com (5)

Medic Alert Foundation, Turlock, CA. Tel: (209) 668-3333, (888) 633-4298, FAX: (209) 669-2495, Web Site: www.medicalert.org (1)

Medical Arts Press, Minneapolis, MN. Tel: (763) 493-7300, (800) 328-2179, FAX: (800) 328-0023, Web Site: www.medicalartspress.com (27)

Medical Economics Magazine, North Olmsted, OH. Tel: (440) 243-8100, FAX: (440) 891-2735, Web Site: medicaleconomics.modernmedicine.com/about (17)

Medical Group Management Association (MGMA), Englewood, CO. Tel: (303) 799-1111, FAX: (303) 643-4439, E-Mail: marketing@mgma.com, Web Site: www.mgma.com (1)

Medical Letter Inc, New Rochelle, NY. Tel: (914) 235-0500, Web Site: www.medicalletter.org (1)

Medical Marketing Service Inc, Wood Dale, IL. Tel: (630) 477-1559, (800) 633-5478, FAX: (630) 350-1896, E-Mail: t-nugent@mmslists.com, Web Site: www.mmslists.com (24)

Medico, Michael, L., E&M Advertising Inc, New York, NY. Tel: (212) 981-5901, FAX: (212) 981-2121, E-Mail: mmedico@emadv.com, Web Site: www.emadv.com (35)

Medicx Media Solutions, Scottsdale, AZ. Tel: (480) 614-0060, Web Site: www.medicxmedia.com (23)

Medifast Inc, Owings Mills, MD. Tel: (410) 504-8222, Web Site: www.medifastdiet.com (4)

Medill IMC/Northwestern University, Evanston, IL. Tel: (847) 467-3433 (1)

Medina, Jill, Draper's & Damon's, Irvine, CA. Tel: (949) 784-3000, (800) 843-1174, FAX: (949) 784-3400, E-Mail: jilld@drapers.com, Web Site: www.drapers.com (2)

Medina, John, CYRO Industries, Parsippany, NJ. Tel: (973) 541-8000, (800) 631-5384, FAX: (973) 442-6117, (973) 442-6135, Web Site: www.cyro.com (16)

Medina, Kurt, Medina Associates, Rose Valley, PA. Tel: (610) 565-8836, FAX: (610) 565-8184, E-Mail: kurtmedina@aol.com, Web Site: www.medinaassociates.com (20)

Medina Associates, Rose Valley, PA. Tel: (610) 565-8836, FAX: (610) 565-8184, E-Mail: kurtmedina@aol.com, Web Site: www.medinaassociates.com (20)

Medina-Warren, Billin, Billin Medina-Warren, Scottsdale, AZ. Tel: (972) 951-7291 (20)

Meditz, Howard, Marquardt, Roche & Partners, Stamford, CT. Tel: (203) 327-0890, FAX: (203) 353-8487, E-Mail: ideas@mrp-website.com, Web Site: www.mrp-website.com (35)

Medlin, Connie, Babyshoe.com, Hendersonville, NC. Tel: (828) 697-5811, (800) 543-8566, FAX: (828) 697-5815, E-Mail: info@babyshoe.com, Web Site: www.babyshoe.com (6)

Medtronic Inc, Minneapolis, MN. Tel: (763) 514-4000, (800) 328-2518, FAX: (763) 514-4879, Web Site: www.medtronic.com (16)

Meek, Gary, E., Houlihan Lokey Howard & Zukin, Los Angeles, CA. Tel: (310) 553-8871, (800) 788-5300, FAX: (310) 553-2173, Web Site: www.hlhz.com (14)

Meeker, Bob, Preferred Communications, Butner, NC. Tel: (919) 575-4600, (877) 589-9800, Web Site: www.satstar.com (24)

Meeks, Matt, GameTime Inc, Fort Payne, AL. Tel: (256) 845-5610, (800) 633-2394, FAX: (256) 845-9361/2649, Web Site: www.gametime.com (11)

Meelia, Richard J., Covidien International, Mansfield, MA. Tel: (508) 261-8000, (800) 962-9888, FAX: (508) 261-8105, Web Site: www.covidien.com (7)

Meemic Insurance Co, Auburn Hills, MI. Tel: (888) 463-3642, Web Site: www.meemic.com (15)

Meerdink, Tod, Eastbay Running Store Inc, Wausau, WI. Tel: (715) 845-5538, (800) 826-2205, FAX: (715) 261-9500, Web Site: www.eastbay.com (2)

Mega Media Associates Inc, Newport Beach, CA. Tel: (949) 673-2290, E-Mail: info@megamediaassociaes.com, Web Site: www.megamediaassociates.com (23)

Megger, Dallas, TX. Tel: (214) 330-3539, Web Site: www.megger.com (16)

Megna, Jay, Life Fitness, Schiller Park, IL. Tel: (847) 288-3300, (800) 735-3867, FAX: (847) 288-3703, E-Mail: webmaster@lifefitness.com, Web Site: www.lifefitness.com (11)

Megna, Richard, Fundamental Photographs, New York, NY. Tel: (212) 473-5770, FAX: (212) 228-5059, E-Mail: mail@fphoto.com, Web Site: www.fphoto.com (38)

Meguiar, Barry, Meguiar's Inc, Irvine, CA. Tel: (949) 752-8000, (800) 347-5700, FAX: (949) 752-6659, Web Site: www.meguiars.com (16)

Meguiar's Inc, Irvine, CA. Tel: (949) 752-8000, (800) 347-5700, FAX: (949) 752-6659, Web Site: www.meguiars.com (16)

Mehendale, T., Intrepid Distributors Inc, Mississauga, ON Canada. Tel: (905) 607-5170, (800) 263-6011, FAX: (800) 361-6307, E-Mail: sales@intrepid.on.ca, Web Site: www.intrepid.on.ca (33)

Mehren, William, Priority Systems Inc, Grayslake, IL. Tel: (773) 539-1884, (800) 330-3448, FAX: (773) 539-1755, E-Mail: sbender@priority.com, Web Site: www.priority.com (21)

Mehrlander, Carmie, The Bombay Co, Brampton, ON Canada. Tel: (877) 326-6229, E-Mail: customerservice@bombay.ca, Web Site: www.bombay.com (8)

Mehta, Bobby, Trans Union Corp, Chicago, IL. Tel: (312) 258-1717, (800) 335-9888, FAX: (312) 466-8385, Web Site: www.transunion.com (14)

Mehta, Krishna, EXL, Jersey City, NJ. Tel: (201) 748-4729 (16)

Meich, John, H., High Cotton, Birmingham, AL. Tel: (877) 838-2345, FAX: (205) 836-5587, E-Mail: sales@highcottonusa.com, Web Site: www.highcottonusa.com (28)

Meier, Bob, NASCO, Fort Atkinson, WI. Tel: (920) 563-2446, FAX: (920) 563-8296, E-Mail: info@nasco.com, Web Site: www.enasco.com (5)

Meier, Manuela, Cobblestone Publishing, Peterborough, NH. Tel: (603) 924-7209, (800) 821-0115, FAX: (603) 924-7380, E-Mail: customerservice@caruspub.com, Web Site: www.cobblestonepub.com (17)

Meier, Rich, O'Connell Meier LLC, Alexandria, VA. Tel: (703) 635-2893, (866) 391-1415, FAX: (703) 739-0478, E-Mail: info@omdirect.com, Web Site: www.omdirect.com (21)

Meifi, Mike, Champs Software Inc, Crystal River, FL. Tel: (352) 795-2362, FAX: (352) 795-9100, E-Mail: champs@champsinc.com, Web Site: www.champsinc.com (3)

Meinen, Mary, Wag/Aero Group, Lyons, WI. Tel: (262) 763-9586, (800) 558-6868, FAX: (262) 763-7595, E-Mail: wagaero-sales@wagaero.com, Web Site: www.wagaero.com (16)

Meinhardt, Jim, Hal Leonard Corp, Milwaukee, WI. Tel: (414) 774-3630, FAX: (414) 774-3259, Web Site: www.halleonard.com (17)

Meisel, Eric, Turncraft Clocks Inc, Spring Park, MN. Tel: (952) 471-9573, (800) 544-1711, FAX: (952) 471-8579, E-Mail: office@meiselwoodhobby.com, Web Site: www.meiselwoodhobby.com (6)

Meisel, Greg, Turncraft Clocks Inc, Spring Park, MN. Tel: (952) 471-9573, (800) 544-1711, FAX: (952) 471-8579, E-Mail: office@meiselwoodhobby.com, Web Site: www.meiselwoodhobby.com (6)

Meisel, Paul, Turncraft Clocks Inc, Spring Park, MN. Tel: (952) 471-9573, (800) 544-1711, FAX: (952) 471-8579, E-Mail: office@meiselwoodhobby.com, Web Site: www.meiselwoodhobby.com (6)

Meister, Eileen, Sporting Clays Ltd, Titusville, FL. Tel: (321) 268-5010, FAX: (321) 267-7216, E-Mail: sales@sportingclays.net, Web Site: www.sportingclays.net (17)

Meister Media Worldwide, Willoughby, OH. Tel: (440) 942-2000, (800) 572-7740, FAX: (440) 975-3447, E-Mail: info@meistermedia.com, Web Site: www.meistermedia.com (17)

Meixner, Michael, canadaplus.com, Windsor, ON Canada. Tel: (519) 966-3003, (877) 966-3003, FAX: (519) 966-1749, E-Mail: canadaplusinfo@canadaplus.com, Web Site: www.canadaplus.com (28)

Mel, Rod, Higher Power Marketing, Phoenix, AZ. Tel: (480) 837-3580, (888) 922-3580, FAX: (480) 837-3589, E-Mail: info@hpowermarketing.com, Web Site: www.hpowermarketing.com (30)

Melancon, Barry C., American Institute of CPAs, New York, NY. Tel: (212) 596-6200, (888) 777-7077, FAX: (212) 596-6213, Web Site: www.aicpa.org (1)

Melancon, Donald, J., Shopguide.com, Amarillo, TX. Tel: (806) 351-0005, FAX: (806) 351-0059, E-Mail: info@shopguide.com, Web Site: www.shopguide.com (27)

Melancon, Serena, USA Hosts, San Francisco, CA. Tel: (415) 695-8000, (800) 368-4678, FAX: (415) 986-3668, Web Site: www.usahosts.com (19)

Melani, Kenneth, R., Highmark Blue Cross Blue Shield, Pittsburgh, PA. Tel: (412) 544-7000, FAX: (412) 544-5350, Web Site: www.highmark.com (15)

Melaniphy Jr, John, Melaniphy & Associates, Inc, Chicago, IL. Tel: (773) 467-1212, FAX: (773) 774-0454, E-Mail: jmelaniphy@melaniphy.com, Web Site: www.melaniphy.com (8)

Melaniphy Sr, John, Melaniphy & Associates, Inc, Chicago, IL. Tel: (773) 467-1212, FAX: (773) 774-0454, E-Mail: jmelaniphy@melaniphy.com, Web Site: www.melaniphy.com (8)

Melaniphy & Associates, Inc, Chicago, IL. Tel: (773) 467-1212, FAX: (773) 774-0454, E-Mail: jmelaniphy@melaniphy.com, Web Site: www.melaniphy.com (8)

MELDISCO, Mahwah, NJ. Tel: (201) 934-2000, FAX: (201) 934-2570, Web Site: www.meldisco.com (16)

Melgoza, Cesar, Geoscape, Miami, FL. Tel: (305) 860-1460, Web Site: www.geoscape.com (22)

Melgoza, Cesar, M., Latin Force Group LLC, Miami, FL. Tel: (305) 860-1460, FAX: (305) 860-6161, Web Site: www.latinforce.com (22)

Melikian, Harry, The Vantage Group Inc, Boston, MA. Tel: (617) 878-6000, FAX: (617) 878-6156, Web Site: www.vantagetravel.com (14)

Meling, Sara, Meling & Associates, West Rutland, VT. Tel: (802) 774-1030 (23)

Meling & Associates, West Rutland, VT. Tel: (802) 774-1030 (23)

Melingagio APR, John, Father Flanagan's Boy's Home, Boys Town, NE. Tel: (402) 498-1934, FAX: (402) 498-1969, Web Site: www.boystown.org (1)

Melissa, Ray, Mailer's Software, Rancho Santa Margarita, CA. Tel: (949) 858-3000, (800) 635-4772, FAX: (949) 589-5211, Web Site: www.mailerssoftware.com (22)

Melissa, Raymond, Melissa Data Corp, Rancho Santa Margarita, CA. Tel: (949) 589-5200, (800) 800-6245, FAX: (949) 589-5211, E-Mail: sales@melissadata.com, Web Site: www.melissadata.com (22)

Melissa Data Corp, Rancho Santa Margarita, CA. Tel: (949) 589-5200, (800) 800-6245, FAX: (949) 589-5211, E-Mail: sales@melissadata.com, Web Site: www.melissadata.com (22)

Melitta USA, Clearwater, FL. Tel: (727) 535-2111, Web Site: www.melitta.com (4)

Mellen, Charles, S., A T Cross Co, Lincoln, RI. Tel: (401) 333-1200, (800) 282-7677, FAX: (401) 334-2861, Web Site: www.cross.com (16)

Mellon, Laurie, Consumers Union, Yonkers, NY. Tel: (914) 378-2000, FAX: (914) 378-2906, Web Site: www.consumerreports.org (17)

Melnick, David, Siquis Ltd, Baltimore, MD. Tel: (410) 323-4800, FAX: (410) 323-4113, Web Site: www.siquis.com (35)

Melnick, Steven, 20th Century Fox Television, Los Angeles, CA. Tel: (310) 444-8100, FAX: (310) 444-8101 (16)

Melton, Carol, A., Time Warner Inc, New York, NY. Tel: (212) 484-8000, Web Site: www.timewarner.com (16)

Melton, James, C., Baker & Taylor Inc, Charlotte, NC. Tel: (704) 998-3100, (800) 775-1800, FAX: (704) 998-3316, E-Mail: btinfo@btol.com, Web Site: www.btol.com (16)

Melton, Jarvis, Dover Publications Inc, Mineola, NY. Tel: (516) 294-7000, (800) 223-3130, FAX: (516) 873-1401, Web Site: www.doverpublications.com (17)

Melton, Scott, NAACP (National Association for the Advancement of Colored People), Baltimore, MD. Tel: (410) 580-5617, Web Site: www.naacp.org (1)

Meltzer, Barry, Institute For Natural Resources, Concord, CA. Tel: (925) 687-0860, FAX: (925) 609-2820, E-Mail: dcheung@biocorp.com (16)

Meltzer, Barry, San Francisco Herb & Natural Food Co, Fremont, CA. Tel: (510) 770-1215, (800) 227-2830, FAX: (510) 770-9021, E-Mail: customerservice@herbspicetea.com, Web Site: www.herbspicetea.com (4)

Meltzer, Dorit, Teva Pharmaceuticals USA, North Wales, PA. Tel: (215) 591-3000, (888) TEVAUSA, FAX: (215) 591-8600, Web Site: www.tevausa.com (7)

Meltzer, Jeff, Meltzer Media Productions, New York, NY. Tel: (212) 868-4600, FAX: (212) 302-6175, E-Mail: jeffmeltzer@earthlink.net (35)

Meltzer, Steve, Stephan Partners Inc, New York, NY. Tel: (212) 524-8583, E-Mail: george@ stephenpartners.com, Web Site: www. stephanpartners.com (35)

Meltzer Media Productions, New York, NY. Tel: (212) 868-4600, FAX: (212) 302-6175, E-Mail: jeffmeltzer@earthlink.net (35)

Melucci, Giulia, Harper's Magazine, New York, NY. Tel: (212) 420-5720, FAX: (212) 260-1096, Web Site: www.harpers.org (17)

Melville, Lori, American Horse Products, San Juan Capistrano, CA. Tel: (949) 248-5300, (800) 500-0799, FAX: (949) 248-5305, E-Mail: zjim@ sbcglobal.net, Web Site: www. americanhorseproducts.com (11)

Melynis, Indre, Guilford Publications Inc, New York, NY. Tel: (212) 431-9800, (800) 365-7006, FAX: (212) 966-6708, E-Mail: info@guilford.com, Web Site: www.guilford.com (17)

Membership Cards Only LLC, Vienna, VA. Tel: (800) 772-2737, Web Site: wwww.membershipcards.com (27)

Memorial Sloan Kettering Cancer Center, New York, NY. Tel: (646) 227-3528, Web Site: www.mskcc. org (1)

Memphis Net & Twine Co Inc, Memphis, TN. Tel: (901) 458-2656, (888) 674-7638, FAX: (901) 458-1601, E-Mail: fishinfo@memphisnet.net, Web Site: www.memphisnet.net (11)

Menadier, Jim, InteliSpend, Fenton, MO. Tel: (636) 226-2000, Web Site: intelispend.com (35)

Menardi Mikropul LLC, Trenton, SC. Tel: (803) 663-6551, (800) 321-3218, FAX: (803) 663-4029, E-Mail: info@menardifilters.com, Web Site: www. menardifilters.com (16)

Menconi, Ron, Mail Computer Service, West Bridge-water, MA. Tel: (508) 584-6490, (800) 640-8530, FAX: (508) 584-2890 (21)

Mendelsohn, Bruce, Marketing Research Association, Washington, DC. Tel: (860) 682-1000, FAX: (860) 682-1010, E-Mail: email@mra-net.org, Web Site: www.mra-net.org (40)

Mendelson, Peter, Gerber Life Insurance Co, White Plains, NY. Tel: (914) 272-4000, (800) 704-2180, FAX: (914) 272-4099, Web Site: www.gerberlife. com (15)

Mendes, Andre, Special Olympics International, Wash-ington, DC. Tel: (202) 628-3630, FAX: (202) 824-0200, Web Site: www.specialolympics.org (1)

Mendez, Anthony, Trophyland USA Inc, Hialeah, FL. Tel: (305) 823-4830, (800) 327-5820, FAX: (305) 823-4836, E-Mail: info@trophyland.com, Web Site: www.trophyland.com (5)

Mendlik, Steven, Oriental Trading Co Inc, Omaha, NE. Tel: (402) 596-1200, (800) 875-8480, FAX: (402) 331-3873, Web Site: www.oriental.com (5)

Mendoza, Javier, AvMed Health Plan Inc, Miami, FL. Tel: (305) 671-5437, Web Site: www.avmed.org (1)

Mennella, John, Chemical Week, New York, NY. Tel: (212) 621-4900, FAX: (212) 621-4800, E-Mail: clientservices@chemweek.com, Web Site: www. chemweek.com (17)

The Menninger Foundation, Houston, TX. Tel: (713) 275-5000, (800) 351-9058, FAX: (713) 275-5107, Web Site: www.menningerclinic.com (1)

Menoudakos, Toni, Mail Order Media & Marketing Inc, Fuquay Varina, NC. Tel: (203) 254-9390, FAX: (203) 254-3253, E-Mail: mailordermedia2000@yahoo.com (35)

Mense, D., Craig, CNA, Chicago, IL. Tel: (312) 822-5000, (800) 262-2000, E-Mail: cna_help@cna.com, Web Site: www.cna.com (15)

Mensing, Jon, AllMedia Inc, Plano, TX. Tel: (469) 467-9100, FAX: (214) 291-5431, E-Mail: lmcclendon@allmediainc.com, Web Site: www. allmediainc.com (23)

Mento, Lynn, AARP, Washington, DC. Tel: (202) 434-2277, Web Site: www.aarp.org (1)

Mentor Corp, Santa Barbara, CA. Tel: (805) 879-6000, (800) 525-0245, FAX: (805) 964-2712, Web Site: www.mentorcorp.com (16)

Mentoring Minds, Tyler, TX. Tel: (903) 509-4002 (17)

Menzel, Michelle, Technicolor, Camarillo, CA. Tel: (805) 445-1122, (800) 732-4555, FAX: (805) 445-4280, E-Mail: info@technicolor.com, Web Site: www.technicolor.com (21)

Meola, Rocco J., The First Occupational Center of New Jersey, Orange, NJ. Tel: (973) 672-5800, FAX: (973) 672-0065, E-Mail: ocnj@ocnj.org, Web Site: www.ocnj.org (28)

Merastar Insurance Co, Chattanooga, TN. Tel: (800) 637-2782, FAX: (800) 369-1430, E-Mail: merastar. assist.team@unitrindirect.com, Web Site: www. merastar.com (15)

Mercatante, Mary, Thomson-Gale, Farmington Hills, MI. Tel: (800) 877-4253, FAX: (877) 363-4253, Web Site: www.galegroup.com (17)

Merchandise Group, Los Angeles, CA. Tel: (310) 481-7300, (800) 421-4511, FAX: (310) 481-1900, E-Mail: adsales@merchandisegroup.com, Web Site: www.merchandisegroup.com (42)

The Merchandise Mart, Chicago, IL. Tel: (312) 527-4141, (800) 677-6278, Web Site: www. merchandisemart.com (42)

Merchandising Equipment Group (MEG), Cambridge City, IN. Tel: (765) 478-3141, (800) 645-3315, FAX: (765) 478-4439, E-Mail: meginfo@ megfixtures.com, Web Site: www.megfixtures.com (34)

Merchant E-Solutions, Redwood City, CA. Tel: (678) 493-8853 (14)

Merck & Co Inc, Whitehouse Station, NJ. Tel: (908) 423-1000, Web Site: www.merck.com (16)

Mercury Commerce Inc, Westbury, NY. Tel: (212) 307-7001, FAX: (646) 219-3982, E-Mail: contact@ mercury-commerce.com, Web Site: www.mercury-commerce.com (22)

Mercury Envelope Co Inc, Rockville Centre, NY. Tel: (516) 678-6744, FAX: (516) 678-6764, E-Mail: mercuryenvelope@aol.com (26)

Mercury International, Avenel, NJ. Tel: (732) 396-9555, FAX: (732) 396-1492, Web Site: www. mercuryinternational.com (28)

Mercury International Trading, North Attleboro, MA. Tel: (508) 699-9000, FAX: (508) 699-9088, Web Site: www.mercuryfootwear.com (2)

Mercury Media, Santa Monica, CA. Tel: (310) 451-2900, FAX: (310) 451-0180, Web Site: www. mercurymedia.com (32)

Mercury Print & Mail Co Inc, Pawtucket, RI. Tel: (401) 724-7600, FAX: (401) 724-9920, Web Site: www.mpmri.com (28)

Mercy Home for Boys & Girls, Chicago, IL. Tel: (312) 738-7560, Web Site: www.mercyhome.org (1)

Meredith, Rick, Premier Direct Marketing Inc, Louis-ville, KY. Tel: (502) 367-6441, (800) 737-0205, FAX: (502) 361-2961, E-Mail: rmeredith@ premierdm.net, Web Site: www.premierdm.net (28)

Meredith, Sandra, World Wide Mailers, Windsor, ON Canada. Tel: (519) 254-6245, FAX: (519) 254-2608, E-Mail: tab@worldwidemailers.com, Web Site: www.worldwidemailers.com (28)

Meredith, Thomas, J., Motorola Inc, Montvale, NJ. Tel: (201) 949-5500, (800) 262-8509, Web Site: www.motorola.com (16)

Meredith Corp, Des Moines, IA. Tel: (515) 284-3000, FAX: (515) 284-2700, Web Site: www.meredith. com (17)

Mergent Inc, Fort Mill, SC. Tel: (800) 342-5647, Web Site: www.mergent.com (14)

The Merging Technologies Group LLC, Hauppauge, NY. Tel: (631) 435-2955, FAX: (631) 952-0664, E-Mail: info@mt-group.com, Web Site: www.mt-group.com (23)

Mergner, Lee, JazzTimes Magazine Inc, Quincy, MA. Tel: (617) 706-9110, FAX: (617) 536-0102, E-Mail: info@jazztimes.com, Web Site: www. jazztimes.com (17)

Meriks Gifts, San Diego, CA. Tel: (787) 721-0000 (6)

Meriks Inc, Baltimore, MD. Tel: (787) 721-0000 (3)

Meriks Marketers, Richfield, MN. Tel: (787) 721-0000 (3)

Meriks Mayan Chocolaterie, Washington, DC. Tel: (787) 721-0000 (27)

Meriks Partners, Tucson, AZ. Tel: (413) 243-0857 (10)

Merisel, New York, NY. Tel: (212) 594-4800, FAX: (212) 594-4488, E-Mail: corp@merisel.com, Web Site: www.merisel.com (16)

Merit Industries Inc, Georgetown, TX. Tel: (512) 863-8541, (800) 637-4823, FAX: (512) 863-9861 (33)

MeritDirect, White Plains, NY. Tel: (914) 368-1000, Web Site: www.meritdirect.com (23)

Merjo Advertising & Sales Promotions Co, Owings Mills, MD. Tel: (410) 345-9000, FAX: (410) 345-9002, E-Mail: merjoadv@qis.net, Web Site: www. promoplace.com/merjo (33)

Merkel-Sobotta, Eric, Springer Science & Business Media LLC, New York, NY. Tel: (212) 460-1500, FAX: (212) 473-6272, Web Site: www.springer-ny. com (17)

Merkle Inc, Columbia, MD. Tel: (443) 542-4000, (877) 9MERKLE, Web Site: www.merkleinc.com (22)

Merkley, David, B., Sears Canada Inc, Toronto, ON. Tel: (416) 362-1711, (888) 473-2772, FAX: (613) 391-3047, E-Mail: home@sears.ca, Web Site: www.sears.ca (5)

Merkur, Lawrence, Winslow Publishing, Toronto, ON. Tel: (416) 789-4733, E-Mail: winslow@interlog. com, Web Site: www.winslowpublishing.com (17)

Merlo, Larry, J., CVS Caremark, Woonsocket, RI. Tel: (401) 765-1500, FAX: (401) 769-4488, Web Site: www.cvs.com (7)

Merrell, A., Kent, Merrell Remington & Associates, Salt Lake City, UT. Tel: (801) 975-0109, (800) 347-7468, FAX: (801) 975-0107, Web Site: www. merrellremington.com (35)

Merrell, Halley, A., American Chemical Society, Washington, DC. Tel: (202) 872-4600, (800) 227-5558, FAX: (202) 833-7716, E-Mail: service@acs. org, Web Site: www.acs.org (1)

Merrell Remington & Associates, Salt Lake City, UT. Tel: (801) 975-0109, (800) 347-7468, FAX: (801) 975-0107, Web Site: www.merrellremington.com (35)

Merriam, Lloyd, Colinear Systems, Alpharetta, GA. Tel: (770) 643-0000, (800) COLINEAR, FAX: (770) 643-0265, E-Mail: sales@colinear.com, Web Site: www.colinear.com (22)

Merrick Bank, South Jordan, UT. Tel: (801) 545-6647, Web Site: www.merrickbank.com (14)

Merrill, Richard, Golden Rule Insurance Co, India-napolis, IN. Tel: (317) 297-4123, FAX: (317) 297-0908, Web Site: www.goldenrule.com (15)

Merrill, April, ProSource, Houston, TX. Tel: (713) 667-3690, FAX: (713) 660-9629, Web Site: www. prosourcedev.com (20)

Merrill, Brian, Western River Expeditions, Salt Lake City, UT. Tel: (801) 942-6669, (866) 904-1160, FAX: (801) 942-8514, Web Site: www. westernriver.com (19)

Merrill, Dean, International Bible Society, Colorado Springs, CO. Tel: (719) 488-9200, FAX: (719) 867-2812, Web Site: www.ibs.org (1)

Merrill, Lee, Ann, Spalding Laboratories Inc, Arroyo Grande, CA. Tel: (805) 489-5946, (888) 880-1579, FAX: (866) 738-9632, Web Site: www.spalding-labs.com (7)

Merrill, Rick, Promotional Products Association International, Irving, TX. Tel: (972) 252-0404, FAX: (800) I-AM-PPAI, (972) 258-3004, E-Mail: membership@ppa.org, Web Site: www.ppa.org (40)

Merrill, Stephanie, COMNET Washington, Framingham, MA. Tel: (508) 879-6700, FAX: (508) 370-4325, Web Site: www.comnetexpo.com (42)

Merrill Corp, Saint Cloud, MN. Tel: (320) 656-5000, FAX: (320) 656-5163 (18)

Merrill Lynch, New York, NY. Tel: (212) 449-1000, (800) 637-7455, FAX: (212) 449-9418, Web Site: www.ml.com (14)

Merrimack College, North Andover, MA. Tel: (978) 837-5154, E-Mail: denise.tuccelli@merrimack.edu, Web Site: www.merrimack.edu (41)

Merrimade Stationery Co LLC, Ansonia, CT. Tel: (800) 344-4256, FAX: (800) 883-6515, E-Mail: custserv@merrimadestationery.com, Web Site: www.merrimade.com (10)

Merritt, Mark, Pharmaceutical Care Management Association, Washington, DC. Tel: (202) 207-3610, FAX: (202) 207-3623, E-Mail: info@pcmanet.org, Web Site: www.pcmanet.org (1)

Merry, Rod, DAMARK International Inc, La Salle, IL. Tel: (877) 326-2757, Web Site: www.damark.com (16)

Merryfield, Zoann, Hallmark Cards Inc, Kansas City, MO. Tel: (816) 274-5111, FAX: (816) 274-7276, Web Site: www.hallmark.com (16)

Mersco Medical, Pierre, SD. Tel: (605) 224-6687, (800) 234-1881, FAX: (605) 322-1801 (16)

Jim Mersfelder & Associates Inc, Cleveland, OH. Tel: (216) 574-9009, FAX: (216) 574-9721, Web Site: www.jma-usa.com (33)

Mershad, Richard, M., Micro Center, Hilliard, OH. Tel: (800) 634-3478, FAX: (614) 777-2620, E-Mail: csrs@microcenterorder.com, Web Site: www.microcenter.com (3)

Merszei, Geoffrey, E., Dow Chemical USA, Midland, MI. Tel: (989) 636-1000, (800) 447-4369, FAX: (989) 832-1465, E-Mail: jadams@dow.com, Web Site: www.dow.com (16)

Merti, Betty, Walch Publishing, Portland, ME. Tel: (207) 772-2846, (800) 558-2846, FAX: (207) 772-3105, E-Mail: customerservice@walch.com, Web Site: www.walch.com (17)

Merton, Jeff, Harley-Davidson Inc, Milwaukee, WI. Tel: (414) 343-7286, FAX: (414) 343-4806, Web Site: www.harley-davidson.com (12)

Mertz, Howard, W., Relationship1, Rye, NY. Tel: (914) 921-4400, E-Mail: marketing@relationship1. com, Web Site: www.relationship1.com (21)

Mertz, Tom, TradeNet Publishing Inc, Gardner, KS. Tel: (800) 884-7301, Web Site: www. tradenetonline.com (35)

Mertzel, Kenneth, Balboa Life & Casualty, Irvine, CA. Tel: (949) 222-8000, (800) 854-6115, FAX: (949) 222-8777, Web Site: www.balboainsurance.com (15)

Mervyn's, Pleasanton, CA. Tel: (510) 727-3000, (800) 480-5014, FAX: (510) 727-5851, Web Site: www. mervyns.com (16)

The Mesa Group, West Palm Beach, FL. Tel: (212) 645-9666, (888) 637-2477, FAX: (212) 243-0564, E-Mail: info@mesagrp.com, Web Site: www. mesagrp.com (35)

Mesci, Mark, Burlington Coat Factory, Burlington, NJ. Tel: (609) 387-7800, FAX: (609) 387-7071, Web Site: www.coat.com (16)

Mesher, Page, Off the Wall Magnetics LLC, Portland, OR. Tel: (800) 337-2637, Web Site: www. 4thefridge.com (16)

Message Systems, Columbia, MD. Tel: (410) 872-4910, (877) 887-3031, FAX: (410) 872-4912, E-Mail: information@messagesystems.com, Web Site: www.messagesystems.com (32)

Message Technologies Inc, Atlanta, GA. Tel: (770) 240-8000, (800) 868-3684, FAX: (770) 240-7474, E-Mail: info@messagetech.com, Web Site: www. messagetech.com (30)

Messelt, Jen, Bushnell Outdoor Products, Overland Park, KS. Tel: (913) 752-3400, (800) 423-3537, FAX: (913) 752-3550, Web Site: www.bushnell. com (16)

Messer, Jerry, Data Services Inc, Salisbury, MD. Tel: (410) 546-2206, (800) 432-4066, FAX: (410) 546-2274, Web Site: www.dataservicesinc.com (22)

Messick, William, L., Delta Upsilon International Fraternity, Indianapolis, IN. Tel: (317) 875-8900, FAX: (317) 876-1629, E-Mail: ihq@deltau.org, Web Site: www.deltau.org (16)

Messier, Earle, Thomas, Southern Flavoring Co Inc, Bedford, VA. Tel: (540) 586-8565, (800) 765-8565, FAX: (540) 586-8568, E-Mail: tom@ southernflavoring.com, Web Site: www. southernflavoring.com (16)

Messier, John, P., Southern Flavoring Co Inc, Bedford, VA. Tel: (540) 586-8565, (800) 765-8565, FAX: (540) 586-8568, E-Mail: tom@southernflavoring. com, Web Site: www.southernflavoring.com (16)

Messina, Lori, Access Direct Systems Inc, Farmingdale, NY. Tel: (631) 420-0700, Web Site: www. accessdirect.com (28)

Messinger, William, Hillside Wire Cloth Co, Bloomfield, NJ. Tel: (973) 751-3131, (800) 826-7395, FAX: (973) 470-8183, E-Mail: info@ hillsidewirecloth.com, Web Site: www. hillsidewirecloth.com (9)

Messmer Jr, Harold, M., Robert Half International Inc, Menlo Park, CA. Tel: (650) 234-6000, FAX: (650) 234-6930, E-Mail: webmaster@rhi.com, Web Site: www.rhii.com (20)

Messmer, Max, Accountemps, Menlo Park, CA. Tel: (650) 234-6000, (800) 803-8367, FAX: (650) 234-6998, Web Site: www.accountemps.com (16)

Messner, Joe, Bushnell Outdoor Products, Overland Park, KS. Tel: (913) 752-3400, (800) 423-3537, FAX: (913) 752-3550, Web Site: www.bushnell. com (16)

Mestas, Richard, Datahouse Inc, West Des Moines, IA. Tel: (508) 480-0012, (866) 640-3282, E-Mail: data@datahouseinc.com, Web Site: www. datahouseinc.com (23)

Metamorphics Media, New York, NY. Tel: (212) 924-1845, FAX: (212) 253-4053, E-Mail: info@ metamorphics.com, Web Site: www.metamorphics. com (24)

MetaResponse Group Inc, Deerfield Beach, FL. Tel: (954) 360-0644, FAX: (954) 360-7712, Web Site: www.metaresponse.com (23)

Metcalfe, Mark, Overton's Inc, Greenville, NC. Tel: (252) 355-7600, (800) 334-6541, FAX: (252) 355-2923, E-Mail: service@overtons.com, Web Site: www.overtons.com (11)

Metcalfe, Susan, Dr Leonard's Healthcare Corp, Edison, NJ. Tel: (732) 225-0100, FAX: (732) 225-0302, Web Site: www.doctorleonard.com (7)

Methode Electronics Inc, Chicago, IL. Tel: (708) 867-6777, FAX: (708) 867-6999, E-Mail: info@ methode.com, Web Site: www.methode.com (9)

MetLife International, Long Island City, NY. Tel: (212) 578-3128 (15)

Metrics Marketing, Westlake, OH. Tel: (440) 331-1688, Web Site: www.precisiondialogue.com (35)

Metro Speedgear, Livingston, NJ. Tel: (908) 286-1886, (800) 777-4453, FAX: (908) 286-0002, E-Mail: info@speedgear.com, Web Site: www.speedgear. com (11)

Metropolis Magazine, New York, NY. Tel: (212) 627-9977, (800) 334-3046, FAX: (212) 627-9988, E-Mail: edit@metropolismag.com, Web Site: www. metropolismag.com (2)

Metropolitan Graphic Arts, Mundelein, IL. Tel: (847) 566-9502, FAX: (847) 566-9519, Web Site: www. mgaprinting.com (27)

Metropolitan Museum of Art, New York, NY. Tel: (212) 879-5500, FAX: (718) 628-5485, Web Site: www.metmuseum.org/store (8)

Metropolitan Newspaper Advertising Services Inc, New York, NY. Tel: (212) 689-8200, FAX: (212) 532-1710, E-Mail: getinfo@metrosn.com, Web Site: www.metrosn.com (31)

The Metropolitan Opera, New York, NY. Tel: (212) 799-3100, (212) 362-6000, FAX: (212) 870-7695, Web Site: www.metopera.org (1)

Metropolitan Property & Casualty Ins, Warwick, RI. Tel: (401) 827-2104 (15)

Metso Minerals/WS Tyler, Waukesha, WI. Tel: (803) 699-4200, (262) 717-2500, FAX: (262) 717-2501, E-Mail: minerals.info.csr@metso.com, Web Site: www.metsominerals.com (16)

Mettler, Robert, L., Macy's West, San Francisco, CA. Tel: (415) 954-6089, FAX: (415) 954-6103 (16)

Metz, Don, Health Affairs, Bethesda, MD. Tel: (301) 656-7401, FAX: (301) 654-2845, Web Site: www. healthaffairs.org (17)

Metzger, Dave, Pacific Botanicals LLC, Grants Pass, OR. Tel: (541) 479-7777, FAX: (541) 479-7780, E-Mail: pacbot1@earthlink.net, Web Site: www. pacificbotanicals.com (7)

Metzger, John, A&P, Montvale, NJ. Tel: (201) 573-9700, (866) 44 FRESH, FAX: (201) 505-3054, E-Mail: apcustomerrel@aptea.com, Web Site: www.aptea.com (16)

Metzger, Thomas, Citizens Bank, Dedham, MA. Tel: (603) 634-7000, FAX: (603) 634-7191, Web Site: www.citizensbank.com (14)

Metzler, Paul, The Professional Golfers' Association of America, Palm Beach Gardens, FL. Tel: (561) 624-8400, Web Site: www.pga.com (1)

Metzner, Raymond, KV Vet Supply Co, Inc, David City, NE. Tel: (402) 367-6047, Web Site: www. kvvet.com (5)

Meudt, Mark, West Corp, Omaha, NE. Tel: (800) 841-9000, FAX: (402) 963-1602, E-Mail: sales@west. com, Web Site: www.west.com (20)

Mewhirter, Jack, HALO/Lee Wayne, Sterling, IL. Tel: (815) 632-0980, (866) 840-6401, FAX: (815) 632-6900, E-Mail: moreinfo@leewayne.com, Web Site: www.leewayne.com (16)

Meyer III, Henry, L., Key Bank, Cleveland, OH. Tel: (216) 689-3000, (888) 539-2968, FAX: (207) 874-7044, Web Site: www.key.com (14)

Meyer, Barry M., Warner Bros, Burbank, CA. Tel: (818) 954-6000, Web Site: www.warnerbros.com (3)

Meyer, Bill, Adpress Inc, New York, NY. Tel: (212) 679-1710, FAX: (212) 532-9508, E-Mail: adpressinc@aol.com, Web Site: www.adpressinc. com (23)

Meyer, Chris, Partminer, Centennial, CO. Tel: (303) 200-5500, FAX: (303) 754-3940, Web Site: www. partminer.com (17)

Meyer, David, Dairy Farmers of America Inc, Kansas City, MO. Tel: (816) 801-6455, (888) 332-6455, FAX: (816) 801-6456, E-Mail: webmail@dfamilk. com, Web Site: www.dfamilk.com (16)

Meyer, Dennis, L., Meyer Partners, Schaumburg, IL. Tel: (630) 339-3930, (800) 676-4176, FAX: (630) 339-3939, E-Mail: info@meyerpartners.com, Web Site: www.meyerpartners.com (17)

Meyer, Gordon, eBureau LLC, Saint Cloud, MN. Tel: (320) 534-5000, Web Site: www.ebureau.com (22)

Meyer, Gregory, American Forests, Washington, DC. Tel: (202) 737-1944, FAX: (202) 737-2457, E-Mail: info@amfor.org, Web Site: www. americanforests.org (1)

Meyer, Jeff, Parker Steel Co, Toledo, OH. Tel: (419) 473-2481, (800) 333-4140, FAX: (419) 471-2655, Web Site: www.metricmetal.com (16)

Meyer, John, Angler's Catalog Co, Eagle, ID. Tel: (208) 378-9536, (800) 657-8040, FAX: (208) 735-8758, E-Mail: sales@anglers-catalog.com, Web Site: www.anglers-catalog.com (11)

Meyer, John, The B&F System Inc, Dallas, TX. Tel: (214) 333-2111, FAX: (214) 333-2137, E-Mail: service@bnfusa.com, Web Site: www.bnfusa.com (33)

Meyer, Kirk, Stonwurks, Eden Prairie, MN. Tel: (785) 526-7847, (888) 884-7881, FAX: (785) 526-7841, E-Mail: stonwurks@stonwurks.com, Web Site: www.stonwurks.com (16)

Meyer, Lawrence R, Meyer Associates Teleservices, Saint Cloud, MN. Tel: (320) 259-4000, (800) 676-9233, FAX: (320) 259-4044, E-Mail: info@callmeyer.com, Web Site: www.callmeyer.com (29)

Meyer, Marcia, BarterNews, Laguna Niguel, CA. Tel: (949) 831-0607, FAX: (949) 831-9378, E-Mail: bmeyer@barternews.com, Web Site: www.barternews.com (17)

Meyer, Robert, B., BarterNews, Laguna Niguel, CA. Tel: (949) 831-0607, FAX: (949) 831-9378, E-Mail: bmeyer@barternews.com, Web Site: www.barternews.com (17)

Meyer, Ron, MCA/Universal Studios Inc, Universal City, CA. Tel: (818) 777-1000, FAX: (818) 866-3330, Web Site: www.universalstudios.com (3)

Meyer Associates Teleservices, Saint Cloud, MN. Tel: (320) 259-4000, (800) 676-9233, FAX: (320) 259-4044, E-Mail: info@callmeyer.com, Web Site: www.callmeyer.com (29)

Meyer Decorative Surfaces Inc, Atlanta, GA. Tel: (404) 699-3900, (800) 776-3900, FAX: (404) 699-3914, Web Site: www.meyerdeco.com (8)

Fred Meyer Jewelers Inc, Portland, OR. Tel: (503) 232-8844, (800) 457-5977, FAX: (503) 797-7616, Web Site: www.fredmeyerjewelers.com (16)

Meyer Fulfillment, Stratford, CT. Tel: (203) 375-5801, (800) 873-6393, E-Mail: vdarish@meyerfulfillment.com, Web Site: www.meyerfulfillment.com (28)

Joyce Meyer Ministries, Fenton, MO. Tel: (636) 349-0303, Web Site: www.joycemeyer.org (1)

Meyer Partners, Schaumburg, IL. Tel: (630) 339-3930, (800) 676-4176, FAX: (630) 339-3939, E-Mail: info@meyerpartners.com, Web Site: www.meyerpartners.com (1)

Meyering, Kelly, The Blue Book of Building & Construction, Jefferson Valley, NY. Tel: (800) 431-2584, Web Site: www.thebluebook.com (17)

Meyers, Edwin, W., Cadie Products Corp, Paterson, NJ. Tel: (973) 278-8300, FAX: (973) 278-0303, E-Mail: emeyers@cadie.com, Web Site: www.cadieproducts.com (16)

Meyers, Kenneth, Cadie Products Corp, Paterson, NJ. Tel: (973) 278-8300, FAX: (973) 278-0303, E-Mail: emeyers@cadie.com, Web Site: www.cadieproducts.com (16)

Meyers, Peter, ICOM Information & Communications Inc, Toronto, ON Canada. Tel: (416) 297-4058, (800) 603-4555, FAX: (416) 297-7084, E-Mail: info@i-com.com, Web Site: www.i-com.com (23)

Meyers, Phil, Summit Industries Inc, Marietta, GA. Tel: (770) 590-0600, (800) 241-6996, FAX: (770) 590-0714, E-Mail: info@summitinds.com, Web Site: www.summitinds.com (5)

Meyers, Rich, Vitamin Specialties Co, Freehold, NJ. Tel: (732) 308-3000, FAX: (732) 683-1622, Web Site: www.ivcinc.com (7)

Meyers, Sarah, ArtNetwork-Artworld Mailing Lists, Nevada City, CA. Tel: (530) 478-0920, (800) 383-0677, FAX: (530) 470-0256, E-Mail: info@artmarketing.com, Web Site: www.artmarketing.com (23)

Meyers, Vaughn, Penguin Party Products, Campbell, CA. Tel: (408) 377-1303, FAX: (408) 377-6319, Web Site: www.penguinparty.com (5)

Meylan Corp, Montclair, NJ. Tel: (973) 744-6400, (888) 769-9667, FAX: (973) 744-1011, E-Mail: meylan1@aol.com, Web Site: www.meylan.com/home.html (9)

Meyn, Betty, BMI Home Decorating, Spring Grove, IL. Tel: (815) 675-3703, FAX: (815) 675-3703, E-Mail: bmigroup@aol.com (16)

Meyn, George, BMI Home Decorating, Spring Grove, IL. Tel: (815) 675-3703, FAX: (815) 675-3703, E-Mail: bmigroup@aol.com (16)

the meyocks group, West Des Moines, IA. Tel: (515) 225-1200, FAX: (515) 225-6400, E-Mail: dougjeske@areyoubrave.com, Web Site: www.areyoubrave.com (35)

Mezzalingua, Daniel N., Newhouse School of Public Communications, Syracuse, NY. Tel: (315) 443-3611, FAX: (315) 443-4426, Web Site: newhouse.syr.edu (41)

Jim M'Guinness Design, Los Altos, CA. Tel: (650) 967-3811 (36)

The Miami Herald Media Co, Miami, FL. Tel: (305) 350-2111 (17)

Miami Valley Marketing Group Inc, Dayton, OH. Tel: (937) 299-1825, FAX: (937) 299-9967, E-Mail: tomnorwalk@aol.com (35)

Micca, Father Louis, Pallottine Center for Apostolic Causes Inc/St Jude Shrine, Baltimore, MD. Tel: (410) 685-6026, (877) 278-5833, FAX: (410) 234-1459, E-Mail: info@stjudeshrine.org, Web Site: www.stjudeshrine.org (1)

Michaels, Benjamin, Preferred Premium & Fulfillment Corp, Deerfield, IL. Tel: (847) 677-3080, FAX: (847) 564-5738 (33)

Michaels, Mike, Studio M Productions Unlimited, Los Angeles, CA. Tel: (213) 389-7372, (888) 389-7372 (32)

Michaels, Randy, Tribune Co, Chicago, IL. Tel: (312) 222-9100, FAX: (312) 222-1573, Web Site: www.tribune.com (17)

Michael's, Irving, TX. Tel: (972) 409-1300, FAX: (972) 409-1551, Web Site: www.michaels.com (11)

John Michaels Associates Inc, Newington, CT. Tel: (860) 666-1414, FAX: (860) 666-1515, E-Mail: john@jmalogos.com, Web Site: www.johnmichaelinc.com (33)

Michaelson, Gregg, Rodale Inc, Emmaus, PA. Tel: (610) 967-5171, FAX: (610) 967-8963, Web Site: www.rodale.com (17)

Michaelson, Michael, Rainwater Associates Inc, New York, NY. Tel: (212) 861-2856, FAX: (212) 861-1729, E-Mail: rainwine@aol.com (20)

Michalski, Jim, Edmund Optics Inc, Barrington, NJ. Tel: (856) 573-6250, (800) 363-1992, FAX: (856) 573-6295, E-Mail: sales@edmundoptic.com, Web Site: www.edmundoptics.com (9)

Michaud, Charles, PCI Paper Conversions Inc, Syracuse, NY. Tel: (315) 437-1641, FAX: (315) 437-3634, E-Mail: sales@padmaker.com, Web Site: www.padmaker.com (27)

Michaud, Christie, Atlantic Publication Group LLC, Charleston, SC. Tel: (843) 747-0025, FAX: (843) 744-0816, E-Mail: info@atlanticpublicationgrp.com, Web Site: www.atlanticpublicationgrp.com (17)

Michaud, Jay, Brown & Jenkins Trading Co, Cambridge, VT. Tel: (802) 862-2395, (800) 456-JAVA, FAX: (802) 863-4009, Web Site: www.brownjenkins.com (4)

Michaud, Joe, Blethen Maine Newspapers Inc, Portland, ME. Tel: (207) 791-6650, FAX: (207) 791-6925, Web Site: www.mainetoday.com (17)

Michaud, Lynn, Troy Biologicals Inc, Troy, MI. Tel: (800) 521-0445, FAX: (248) 585-2490, E-Mail: info@troybio.com, Web Site: www.troybio.com (7)

Michaud, Maria, TD Bank NA, Falmouth, ME. Tel: (207) 770-2196, Web Site: www.tdbanknorth.com (14)

Michaux, Michael, Ingenix, Reston, VA. Tel: (571) 521-7661, (800) 765-6713, FAX: (571) 521-7237, E-Mail: inform@ingenix.com, Web Site: www.ingenix.com (32)

Michel, Bill, Eddie Bauer, Groveport, OH. Tel: (425) 882-6100, (800) 426-8020, FAX: (425) 556-7696, Web Site: www.eddiebauer.com (2)

Michel, Bill, Michel Consulting, Bend, OR. Tel: (541) 633-7838 (20)

Michel, Philip, M., Cessna Aircraft Co, Wichita, KS. Tel: (316) 517-6000, FAX: (316) 517-6640, E-Mail: pmichael@cessna.textron.com, Web Site: www.cessna.com (16)

Michel Consulting, Bend, OR. Tel: (541) 633-7838 (20)

Michelson, James, A., Simons-Michelson-Zieve Inc (SMZ), Troy, MI. Tel: (248) 362-4242, FAX: (248) 362-2014, Web Site: www.smz.com (35)

Michigan Apple Committee, Lansing, MI. Tel: (517) 669-8353, (800) 456-2753, FAX: (517) 669-9506, E-Mail: staff@michiganapples.com, Web Site: www.michiganapples.com (1)

Mickey, Bill, Audience Development, Norwalk, CT. Tel: (203) 854-6730, FAX: (203) 854-6735, E-Mail: inolan@red7media.com, Web Site: www.audiencedevelopment.com (43)

Mickwee, Ann, Mickwee Group Inc, Newark, CA. Tel: (510) 651-6522, FAX: (510) 770-9682, E-Mail: info@generatemarketing.com, Web Site: www.generatemarketing.com (16)

Mickwee, Ron, Mickwee Group Inc, Newark, CA. Tel: (510) 651-6522, FAX: (510) 770-9682, E-Mail: info@generatemarketing.com, Web Site: www.generatemarketing.com (16)

Mickwee Group Inc, Newark, CA. Tel: (510) 651-6522, FAX: (510) 770-9682, E-Mail: info@generatemarketing.com, Web Site: www.generatemarketing.com (16)

Micro Center, Hilliard, OH. Tel: (800) 634-3478, FAX: (614) 777-2620, E-Mail: csrs@microcenterorder.com, Web Site: www.microcenter.com (3)

Micro Plastics Inc, Flippin, AR. Tel: (870) 453-2261, (800) 466-1467, FAX: (870) 453-8676, E-Mail: mpsales@microplastics.com, Web Site: www.microplastics.com (16)

Microbiz Corp, Fountain Valley, CA. Tel: (201) 785-1311, (800) 726-3282, FAX: (201) 758-1568, E-Mail: info@microbiz.com, Web Site: www.microbiz.com (3)

Microfluidics Corp, Newton, MA. Tel: (617) 969-5452, (800) 370-5452, FAX: (617) 965-1213, E-Mail: info@mfics.com, Web Site: www.microfluidicscorp.com (16)

Micron Corp, Norwood, MA. Tel: (781) 769-5771, (800) 456-0734, FAX: (781) 762-3531, E-Mail: info@microncorp.com, Web Site: www.microncorp.com (16)

Microsoft Corp, Redmond, WA. Tel: (425) 882-8080, FAX: (425) 936-7329, Web Site: www.microsoft.com (22)

Microvideo Learning Systems, Inc, New York, NY. Tel: (403) 233-9411, (800) 231-4021, FAX: (800) 879-6857, E-Mail: info@microvideo.com, Web Site: www.microvideo.com (3)

Mid America Designs Inc, Effingham, IL. Tel: (217) 540-4200, (800) 350-4543, FAX: (217) 540-4800, E-Mail: mail@mamotorworks.com, Web Site: www.mamotorworks.com (12)

Mid America Direct Marketing Association, Omaha, NE. Tel: (402) 964-8444, FAX: (402) 964-8484, Web Site: www.madma.org (40)

Mid America Motorworks, Effingham, IL. Tel: (217) 347-5591, (800) 500-1500, FAX: (217) 347-2952, E-Mail: mail@mamotorworks.com, Web Site: www.mamotorworks.com (12)

Mid-Central Printing & Mailing Inc, Wilmette, IL. Tel: (847) 251-4040, FAX: (847) 251-8615, E-Mail: mcpm@mcpm.com, Web Site: www.mcpm.com (28)

Mid West Floor Co Inc, Saint Louis, MO. Tel: (314) 647-6060, FAX: (314) 647-9189, E-Mail: sales@mid-westfloor.com, Web Site: www.mid-westfloor.com (16)

MidAmerica Lists Inc, Cedar Rapids, IA. Tel: (800) 747-5900, FAX: (888) 312-5478, E-Mail: sales@malists.com, Web Site: www.malists.com (23)

Midco Call Center Services, Sioux Falls, SD. Tel: (605) 330-4125, (800) 843-8800, FAX: (605) 357-5414, Web Site: www.midcocall.com (29)

Midcontinent Financial Center Inc, Columbia, MO. Tel: (573) 443-6002, Web Site: www.americanmutualloans.com (14)

Middendorf, Sandra, Augsburg Fortress Publishers, Minneapolis, MN. Tel: (612) 330-3300, (800) 426-0115, FAX: (612) 330-3455, E-Mail: info@augsburgfortress.org, Web Site: www.augsburgfortress.org (17)

The Middleby Corp, Elgin, IL. Tel: (847) 741-3300, FAX: (847) 741-0015, E-Mail: sales@middleby.com, Web Site: www.middleby.com (16)

The Midland Co, Amelia, OH. Tel: (513) 943-7200 (15)

Midland Lithographing Co, North Kansas City, MO. Tel: (816) 842-2224, FAX: (816) 842-4530 (27)

Midland Marketing Group, Saint Joseph, MO. Tel: (816) 261-9007, FAX: (816) 233-0859, E-Mail: info@midlandmarketinggroup.com, Web Site: www.midlandmarketinggroup.com (16)

Midland Paper, Wheeling, IL. Tel: (847) 777-2700, (800) 323-8522, FAX: (847) 777-2552, E-Mail: whl@midlandpaper.com, Web Site: www.midlandpaper.com (25)

Midolo, John, Viahealth, Rochester, NY. Tel: (585) 922-4000, (585) 922-3677, FAX: (585) 922-3929, Web Site: www.viahealth.org (16)

Midpoint National Inc, Kansas City, KS. Tel: (913) 362-7400, (800) 228-4321, FAX: (913) 362-7401, E-Mail: info@midpt.com, Web Site: www.midpointorderfulfillment.com (28)

Midwest Center for Stress & Anxiety Inc, Oak Harbor, OH. Tel: (419) 898-4357, (800) 611-0857, FAX: (419) 898-0669, Web Site: www.stresscenter.com (7)

Midwest Direct Marketing Association Inc, Saint Paul, MN. Tel: (651) 999-5351, FAX: (651) 917-1835, E-Mail: mdma@mdma.org, Web Site: www.mdma.org (40)

Midwest Direct Marketing Inc, Spring Hill, KS. Tel: (913) 686-2220, E-Mail: info@midwestdm.com, Web Site: www.midwestdm.com (21)

Midwest Lists & Media, Niles, IL. Tel: (847) 966-2770, FAX: (847) 966-8630, Web Site: www.thebradfordgroup.com (16)

Midwest Premiums & Promotions, Leawood, KS. Tel: (913) 383-9333, FAX: (913) 383-9555, E-Mail: dudleymidwestpremiums@yahoo.com (33)

Midwest Publishing Inc, Phoenix, AZ. Tel: (602) 943-1244, FAX: (602) 331-0702 (17)

Midwest Technology Products & Services, Sioux City, IA. Tel: (712) 252-3601, (800) 831-5904, FAX: (800) 258-7054, E-Mail: web@midwesttechnology.com, Web Site: www.midwesttechnology.com (9)

Mielke, Thomas, J., Kimberly-Clark Corp, Neenah, WI. Tel: (920) 721-2000, (888) 525-8388, FAX: (920) 721-7722, Web Site: www.kimberly-clark.com (16)

Miers, Charles, Rizzoli International Publications Inc, New York, NY. Tel: (212) 387-3400, FAX: (212) 387-3535 (17)

Mighty Net Inc, Calabasas, CA. Tel: (818) 407-4620, FAX: (818) 407-4630, E-Mail: info@mightynet.com, Web Site: www.mightynet.com (16)

Miglautsch, John, Miglautsch Marketing Inc, Hartland, WI. Tel: (262) 369-3900, FAX: (262) 369-3915, E-Mail: info@migmar.com, Web Site: www.migmar.com (20)

Miglautsch Marketing Inc, Hartland, WI. Tel: (262) 369-3900, FAX: (262) 369-3915, E-Mail: info@migmar.com, Web Site: www.migmar.com (20)

Mihalek, Ron, Zimmerman Irrigation Inc, Biglerville, PA. Tel: (717) 337-2727, (800) 452-5699, FAX: (717) 337-1785, E-Mail: info@trikl-eez.com, Web Site: www.trickl-eez.com (16)

Mihalko, Kristin, School of Business Administration, Portland, OR. Tel: (503) 725-3712, FAX: (503) 725-5850, E-Mail: info@sba.pdx.edu, Web Site: www.sba.pdx.edu (41)

Mihoerck, Grace, Carino Nurseries, Indiana, PA. Tel: (800) 223-7075, FAX: (724) 463-3050, E-Mail: carino@carinonurseries.com, Web Site: www.carinonurseries.com (8)

Mikhael, Kamel, Padulo Integrated, Toronto, ON Canada. Tel: (416) 966-4000, (800) 454-5321, FAX: (416) 966-4012, E-Mail: rpadulo@padulo.ca, Web Site: www.padulo.ca (35)

Miklius, Ray, Broadcast Electronics Inc, Quincy, IL. Tel: (217) 224-9600, FAX: (217) 224-9607, E-Mail: bdcast@bdcast.com, Web Site: www.bdcast.com (3)

Mikola, Gary, Society of Manufacturing Engineers, Dearborn, MI. Tel: (313) 425-3000, (800) 733-4763, FAX: (313) 425-3400, E-Mail: communications@sme.org, Web Site: www.sme.org (1)

Mikos, Wayne, Courage Cards & Gifts, Golden Valley, MN. Tel: (763) 588-081, Web Site: www.couragecards.org (1)

Milam, Dolores, Stratford Hall, North Mankato, MN. Tel: (708) 496-4908, (800) 628-9028, FAX: (708) 496-8058, E-Mail: stratfordhall@myprinter.com, Web Site: www.stratfordhall.com (10)

Milanesi, Perry, Enco Manufacturing Co, Fernley, NV. Tel: (775) 788-7175, (800) 873-3626, FAX: (800) 965-5857, E-Mail: milanesp@use-enco.com, Web Site: www.use-enco.com (9)

Milani, Louis, J., Consumers Union, Yonkers, NY. Tel: (914) 378-2000, FAX: (914) 378-2906, Web Site: www.consumerreports.org (17)

Milano, Denise, Veriad, Brea, CA. Tel: (714) 990-2700, (800) 962-0658, FAX: (800) 962-0658, E-Mail: info@veriad.com, Web Site: www.veriad.com (16)

Milberg, Fran, FJ Associates LLC, Wilmington, NC. Tel: (910) 452-2643, FAX: (630) 982-1056 (23)

Milberg, Jeffrey, A., Milberg Penn *International, Mount Kisco, NY. Tel: (914) 241-0858, (914) 239-4300, E-Mail: contact@mpioutsourcing.com, Web Site: www.mpioutsourcing.com (29)

Milberg, Jeffrey, FJ Associates LLC, Wilmington, NC. Tel: (910) 452-2643, FAX: (630) 982-1056 (23)

Milberg Penn *International, Mount Kisco, NY. Tel: (914) 241-0858, (914) 239-4300, E-Mail: contact@mpioutsourcing.com, Web Site: www.mpioutsourcing.com (29)

Miles, Pamela, Ducks Unlimited, Memphis, TN. Tel: (901) 758-3825, (800) 45DUCKS, FAX: (901) 758-3850, Web Site: www.ducks.org (1)

Milford, Kent, CLB Media Inc, Aurora, ON Canada. Tel: (905) 727-0077, FAX: (905) 727-0017, E-Mail: km@industrialsourcebook.com, Web Site: www.clbmedia.ca (24)

Milici Valenti Ng Pack, Honolulu, HI. Tel: (808) 536-0881, FAX: (808) 529-6208, E-Mail: info@mvnp.com, Web Site: www.mvnp.com (35)

Military Direct Marketing Inc, Poughkeepsie, NY. Tel: (845) 454-7900, FAX: (845) 454-7987 (31)

Military Officers Association of America, Alexandria, VA. Tel: (703) 838-8144, Web Site: www.moaa.org (1)

Military Order of the Purple Heart Svc, Annandale, VA. Tel: (703) 256-6139 (1)

The Millard Group, Lincolnwood, IL. Tel: (847) 674-4100, (800) 339-6876, FAX: (847) 677-0790, E-Mail: sales@millardgroup.com, Web Site: www.millardgroup.com (16)

Millcraft of Michigan, Livonia, MI. Tel: (734) 266-3710, (800) 482-0556, FAX: (734) 266-3705, Web Site: www.millcraft.com (25)

Miller III, Henry L., Key Bank National Association, Albany, NY. Tel: (518) 434-4871, (800) 539-2968, Web Site: www.keybank.com (14)

Miller, Adrian, Adrian Miller Direct Marketing, Port Washington, NY. Tel: (516) 767-9288, E-Mail: amiller@adrianmiller.com, Web Site: www.adrianmiller.com (20)

Miller, Alex, R., Svoboda Collins LLC, Chicago, IL. Tel: (312) 267-8750, FAX: (312) 267-6025, E-Mail: info@svoco.com, Web Site: www.svoco.com (5)

Miller, Allyn, Flair Communications Agency Inc, Chicago, IL. Tel: (312) 943-5959, (800) 621-8317, FAX: (312) 943-0881, E-Mail: lflaherty@flairagency.com, Web Site: www.flairpromo.com (35)

Miller, Bill, Eagle Claw Fishing Tackle, Denver, CO. Tel: (303) 321-1481, FAX: (303) 321-4750, E-Mail: info@eagleclaw.com, Web Site: www.eagleclaw.com (11)

Miller, Bill, Portland Rescue Mission, Portland, OR. Tel: (503) 906-7605, Web Site: www.portlandrescuemission.org (1)

Miller, Brittney, Manchester Farms Inc, Columbia, SC. Tel: (803) 469-2588, (800) 845-0421, FAX: (803) 469-8637, E-Mail: customerservice@manchesterfarms.com, Web Site: www.manchesterfarms.com (4)

Miller, Bruce, World Publications Inc, Winter Park, FL. Tel: (407) 628-4802, FAX: (407) 628-7061, Web Site: www.worldpub.net (17)

Miller, Chandra, Lucky Heart Cosmetics Inc, Memphis, TN. Tel: (901) 526-7658, (800) 283-1014, FAX: (901) 526-7660, Web Site: www.luckyheart.com (7)

Miller, Charles, Key Bank National Association, Albany, NY. Tel: (518) 434-4871, (800) 539-2968, Web Site: www.keybank.com (14)

Miller, Chris, Canada Brokerlink Insurance, Edmonton, AB Canada. Tel: (780) 474-8911, FAX: (780) 479-0573, Web Site: www.brokerlink.ca (15)

Miller, Dan, North American Co for Life & Health Insurance, Chicago, IL. Tel: (312) 648-7600, (800) 800-3656, FAX: (614) 365-9209, Web Site: www.nacolah.com (15)

Miller, Dan, Transit Treasure Inc, New York, NY. Tel: (646) 706-1001, Web Site: www.transittreasure.com (12)

Miller, David J., JE Miller Nurseries Inc, Canandaigua, NY. Tel: (585) 396-2647, (800) 836-9630, FAX: (585) 396-2154, E-Mail: jmiller@millernurseries.com, Web Site: www.millernurseries.com (8)

Miller, David, Safeguard Business Systems Inc, Dallas, TX. Tel: (214) 905-3935, (800) 523-2422, FAX: (800) 439-8423, Web Site: www.gosafeguard.com (16)

Miller, Doug, Boston Gift Show, Kennesaw, GA. Tel: (678) 285-3976, (800) 272-SHOW, FAX: (678) 285-7469, Web Site: www.bostongiftshow.com (42)

Miller, Ellen, Marian Helpers Center, Stockbridge, MA. Tel: (413) 298-3691, (800) 462-7426, FAX: (413) 298-3583, Web Site: www.marian.org (1)

Miller, F., Milton, Ashworth University, Norcross, GA. Tel: (770) 729-8400, (800) 957-5412, FAX: (770) 729-9294, E-Mail: info@ashworthuniversity.edu, Web Site: www.ashworthuniversity.edu (13)

Miller, Gail, American Kennel Club, New York, NY. Tel: (212) 696-8200, FAX: (212) 696-8217, (212) 696-8299, Web Site: www.akc.org (17)

Miller, Garth, Rexcraft Wedding Invitations, Rexburg, ID. Tel: (208) 359-1000, (800) 635-3898, FAX: (800) 826-2712, E-Mail: cs@rexcraft.com, Web Site: www.rexcraft.com (16)

Miller, George R., JE Miller Nurseries Inc, Canandaigua, NY. Tel: (585) 396-2647, (800) 836-9630, FAX: (585) 396-2154, E-Mail: jmiller@millernurseries.com, Web Site: www.millernurseries.com (8)

Miller, Greg, Gold Line Connector Inc, West Redding, CT. Tel: (203) 938-2588, FAX: (203) 938-8740, E-Mail: sales@gold-line.com, Web Site: www.gold-line.com (3)

Miller, Greg, Maxwell & Miller Marketing Communications, Kalamazoo, MI. Tel: (269) 382-4060 x26, FAX: (269) 382-0504, E-Mail: info@maxwellandmiller.com, Web Site: www.maxwellandmiller.com (35)

Miller, Herbert, Cable Films & Video, Mission Hills, KS. Tel: (913) 362-2804, (800) 514-2804, FAX: (913) 362-2864, E-Mail: cablefilms@kc.rr.com, Web Site: www.onlineworld.com/movies (3)

Miller, Jay, Peter Pauls Nurseries, Canandaigua, NY. Tel: (716) 394-7397, FAX: (716) 394-4122, E-Mail: ippnurse@eznet.net (8)

Miller, Jeff, Fox River Paper Co, Appleton, WI. Tel: (920) 733-7341, (800) 558-8327, FAX: (920) 733-2975, E-Mail: info@foxriverpaper.com, Web Site: www.foxriverpaper.com (27)

Miller, Jim, Rubbermaid Inc, Fairlawn, OH. Tel: (888) 895-2110, (866) 271-9249, E-Mail: info@rubbermaid.com, Web Site: www.rubbermaid.com (8)

Miller, John, Clario Analytics, Eden Prairie, MN. Tel: (952) 653-0980, (866) 849-3341, FAX: (952) 653-5900, E-Mail: sales@clarioanalytics.com, Web Site: www.clarioanalytics.com (20)

Miller, John, E., JE Miller Nurseries Inc, Canandaigua, NY. Tel: (585) 396-2647, (800) 836-9630, FAX: (585) 396-2154, E-Mail: jmiller@millernurseries.com, Web Site: www.millernurseries.com (8)

Miller, John, West Farm Foods (Branch), Caldwell, ID. Tel: (208) 459-3687, FAX: (208) 459-9135, Web Site: www.westfarm.com (16)

Miller, Jonathon, America Online Inc, Dulles, VA. Tel: (703) 265-1000 (32)

Miller, Joseph, Miller Advertising Inc, Edison, NJ. Tel: (732) 494-5611, FAX: (732) 494-6075 (36)

Miller, Judy, S&G Business Associates Inc, Elkhart, IN. Tel: (574) 295-0163 (23)

Miller, Justin, American Family Insurance Group, Madison, WI. Tel: (608) 249-2111, FAX: (608) 243-6525, E-Mail: akin1@amfam.com, Web Site: www.amfam.com (15)

Miller, Kay, Catholic Health East, Newtown Square, PA. Tel: (610) 355-2000, (877) 424-3001, FAX: (610) 271-9600, Web Site: www.che.org (1)

Miller, Kenneth, Global Marketing Group Ltd, New York, NY. Tel: (212) 247-6060, FAX: (212) 586-5446, E-Mail: kimglobal@aol.com, Web Site: www.gmgsolution.com (20)

Miller, Larry, Corinthian Direct, New York, NY. Tel: (212) 279-5700, FAX: (212) 239-1772, E-Mail: jonz@mediabuying.com, Web Site: www.mediabuying.com (35)

Miller, Laura, Educational Testing Service, Princeton, NJ. Tel: (609) 683-2292, FAX: (609) 734-5410, Web Site: www.ets.org (16)

Miller, Linda, Condolink, Omaha, NE. Tel: (402) 592-3525, (800) 877-9600, FAX: (402) 592-4122, E-Mail: info@condolink.com, Web Site: www.condolink.com (16)

Miller, Linda, The Washington Monthly Co, Washington, DC. Tel: (202) 393-5155, FAX: (202) 393-2444, E-Mail: editors@washingtonmonthly.com, Web Site: www.washingtonmonthly.com (17)

Miller, Marj, Gold Line Connector Inc, West Redding, CT. Tel: (203) 938-2588, FAX: (203) 938-8740, E-Mail: sales@gold-line.com, Web Site: www.gold-line.com (3)

Miller, Mark, Ecolab Professional Products, Saint Paul, MN. Tel: (651) 293-4248, FAX: (651) 225-3025, E-Mail: ecolabs@ecolabs.com, Web Site: www.ecolab.com (16)

Miller, Martin, Gold Line Connector Inc, West Redding, CT. Tel: (203) 938-2588, FAX: (203) 938-8740, E-Mail: sales@gold-line.com, Web Site: www.gold-line.com (3)

Miller, Mary L., PetSmart Inc, Phoenix, AZ. Tel: (623) 587-2009, (800) 738-1385, FAX: (623) 580-6183, Web Site: www.petsmart.com (5)

Miller, Meredith, Natural History Magazine, Durham, NC. Tel: (646) 356-6500, FAX: (646) 356-6511, E-Mail: nhmag@naturalhistorymag.com, Web Site: www.naturalhistorymag.com (17)

Miller, Nicholas, Kyp Systems Inc, New York, NY. Tel: (212) 551-7878, FAX: (917) 591-1514, E-Mail: steves@kyp.com, Web Site: www.ikyp.com (35)

Miller, Nikki, GTM Sportswear, Manhattan, KS. Tel: (800) 336-4486, Web Site: www.gtmsportswear.com (2)

Miller, Pamela, Sunset Magazine, Menlo Park, CA. Tel: (650) 321-3600, FAX: (650) 328-6215 (17)

Miller, Patty, Sylvan Learning Centers, Baltimore, MD. Tel: (410) 843-8000, FAX: (410) 843-8057, Web Site: www.educate.com (16)

Miller, Paul, Cornell Lab of Ornithology, Ithaca, NY. Tel: (607) 254-2157, (800) 843-BIRD, FAX: (607) 254-2415, E-Mail: birdslides@cornell.edu, Web Site: www.birds.cornell.edu (1)

Miller, Paula, Cablexpress Technologies, Syracuse, NY. Tel: (315) 476-3000, (800) 913-9467, FAX: (315) 455-1800, E-Mail: info@cablexpress.com, Web Site: www.CXTec.com (10)

Miller, Pete, Lasermax Roll Systems, Billerica, MA. Tel: (978) 608-0500, FAX: (978) 608-0558, Web Site: www.lasermaxroll.com (27)

Miller, Peter, A., AIDC (American International Distribution Corp), Williston, VT. Tel: (800) 678-2432, FAX: (802) 864-7626, E-Mail: jmacon@aidcvt.com, Web Site: www.aidcvt.com (22)

Miller, Philip D., Alternate Marketing Networks Inc, Hudsonville, MI. Tel: (616) 662-6420, FAX: (616) 662-6422, Web Site: www.altmarket.com (28)

Miller, Renee, The Miller Group Advertising, Los Angeles, CA. Tel: (310) 442-0101, FAX: (310) 442-0107, E-Mail: TMGConnect@millergroup.net, Web Site: www.millergroup.net (35)

Miller, Richard, N., Market Response International, South Orleans, MA. Tel: (508) 240-1877, FAX: (508) 945-4010, E-Mail: rmiller@capecod.net, Web Site: www.millerinternational.com (30)

Miller, Robert, Marriott Ownership Resorts Sales & Marketing, Orlando, FL. Tel: (407) 206-6000, (800) 850-6674, FAX: (407) 851-1304 (19)

Miller, Robert, Precise Media Services Inc, Ontario, CA. Tel: (908) 481-3305, (800) 444-4217, FAX: (908) 481-3405, Web Site: www.precisemedia.com (27)

Miller, Roger, Osmonics Inc, Minnetonka, MN. Tel: (952) 264-3937, (800) 605-6698, FAX: (952) 536-3301, Web Site: www.osmonics.com (16)

Miller, Ron, US Cavalry, Radcliff, KY. Tel: (270) 351-1164, FAX: (270) 352-0266, E-Mail: hq@uscavalry.com, Web Site: www.uscavalry.com (6)

Miller, Scott, GMAC Insurance, Atlanta, GA. Tel: (314) 493-8000, (800) GMAC-123, FAX: (314) 493-8114, Web Site: www.gmacinsurance.com (15)

Miller, Scott, Heller Financial, Chicago, IL. Tel: (312) 441-7000, FAX: (312) 441-7367, Web Site: www.hellerfin.com (14)

Miller, Scott, Integrated Product Development Group, Chicago, IL. Web Site: www.integratedpdg.com (1)

Miller, Scott, Media Directions Inc, Woodcliff Lake, NJ. Tel: (201) 930-4949, FAX: (201) 930-9229, E-Mail: mail@media-directions.com, Web Site: www.media-directions.com (1)

Miller, Seth, L., The Mark Group, Boca Raton, FL. Tel: (561) 241-1700, (800) 637-0152, FAX: (561) 241-1055, Web Site: www.bostonproper.com (2)

Miller, Sharon, Arbill Safety Products, Philadelphia, PA. Tel: (215) 632-2000, (800) 523-5367, FAX: (800) 426-5808, E-Mail: orders@arbill.com, Web Site: www.arbill.com (9)

Miller, Stephanie, Raycom Sports, Charlotte, NC. Tel: (704) 378-4456/4400, FAX: (704) 378-4465, E-Mail: whicks@raycomsports.com, Web Site: raycomsports.com (16)

Miller, Steve, Miller Direct Inc, Fort Mill, SC. Tel: (803) 548-6900, FAX: (803) 548-8701 (31)

Miller, Steve, PEMCO Insurance Cos, Seattle, WA. Tel: (206) 628-4000, (800) 467-3626, FAX: (206) 628-5886, Web Site: www.pemco.com (15)

Miller, Thomas, Plan USA, Warwick, RI. Tel: (401) 737-5770, (800) 556-7918, FAX: (401) 738-5608, Web Site: www.planusa.org (1)

Miller, Ward, Avon Products Inc, New York, NY. Tel: (212) 282-7000, (800) 367-2866, FAX: (212) 282-6225, Web Site: www.avon.com (7)

Miller, Wendy, US Fund for UNICEF, New York, NY. Tel: (212) 686-5522, FAX: (212) 779-1679, Web Site: www.unicefusa.org (6)

Miller, William L., Kid Stuff Marketing, Inc, Topeka, KS. Tel: (785) 862-3707, (800) 677-4712, FAX: (785) 862-0070, E-Mail: info@kidstuff.com, Web Site: www.kidsstuff.com (33)

Miller, William, Meister Media Worldwide, Willoughby, OH. Tel: (440) 942-2000, (800) 572-7740, FAX: (440) 975-3447, E-Mail: info@meistermedia.com, Web Site: www.meistermedia.com (17)

Miller, William, Naval Institute Press, Annapolis, MD. Tel: (410) 268-6110, (800) 233-8764, FAX: (410) 571-1703, E-Mail: webmaster@usni.org, Web Site: www.usni.org/navalinstitutepress (17)

Adrian Miller Direct Marketing, Port Washington, NY. Tel: (516) 767-9288, E-Mail: amiller@adrianmiller.com, Web Site: www.adrianmiller.com (20)

Miller Advertising Inc, Edison, NJ. Tel: (732) 494-5611, FAX: (732) 494-6075 (36)

Miller Direct Inc, Fort Mill, SC. Tel: (803) 548-6900, FAX: (803) 548-8701 (31)

The Miller Group, Dupo, IL. Tel: (636) 343-5700, (800) 325-3350, FAX: (618) 286-6202, E-Mail: info@miller-group.com, Web Site: www.multiplexdisplays.com (5)

The Miller Group Advertising, Los Angeles, CA. Tel: (310) 442-0101, FAX: (310) 442-0107, E-Mail: TMGConnect@millergroup.net, Web Site: www.millergroup.net (35)

Miller Harness Co, Westford, MA. Tel: (800) 784-5831, E-Mail: customerservice@millerharness.com, Web Site: www.millerharness.com (11)

JE Miller Nurseries Inc, Canandaigua, NY. Tel: (585) 396-2647, (800) 836-9630, FAX: (585) 396-2154, E-Mail: jmiller@millernurseries.com, Web Site: www.millernurseries.com (8)

Miller Printing, Springfield, OH. Tel: (937) 325-5503, (877) 325-5503, FAX: (937) 324-5697, Web Site: www.miller-printing.com (27)

Miller Rollman, Jane, Development Dimensions International, Bridgeville, PA. Tel: (412) 257-0600, (800) 933-4463, FAX: (412) 220-2942, E-Mail: info@ddiworld.com, Web Site: www.ddiworld.com (16)

Miller Stockman, Denver, CO. Tel: (303) 428-5696, FAX: (303) 430-1130 (2)

Miller-Carlson, Tamela, American Indian College Fund, Denver, CO. Tel: (303) 426-8900, Web Site: www.collegefund.org (1)

MillerCoors LLC, Chicago, IL. Tel: (800) 645-5376, Web Site: www.millercoors.com (4)

Miller's First Insurance Companies, Alton, IL. Tel: (618) 463-3636, (800) 558-0500, FAX: (618) 463-3614, Web Site: www.millersfirst.com (15)

Millions By Marketing Inc, Mendham, NJ. Tel: (973) 222-0011, Web Site: www.millionsbymarketing.com (22)

Milliorn, Mike, Daydots, Fort Worth, TX. Tel: (817) 590-4500, (800) 321-3687, FAX: (800) 438-7002, E-Mail: customercare@daydots.com, Web Site: www.daydots.com (16)

Millipore Corp, Bedford, MA. Tel: (781) 533-6000, FAX: (781) 533-3110, Web Site: www.millipore.com (9)

Millis, Michael, E., Northwestern University, Evanston, IL. Tel: (847) 491-3741, FAX: (847) 491-8406, E-Mail: webmaster@northwestern.edu, Web Site: www.northwestern.edu (41)

Mills, John, AmMed Direct, Antioch, TN. Tel: (615) 941-3900, Web Site: www.ammeddirect.com (7)

Mills, Larry, Action Mailers Inc, Aston, PA. Tel: (610) 859-0500, (800) 258-5992, FAX: (610) 859-0505, Web Site: www.actionmailer.com (27)

Mills, Mark, Progressive Communications, Lake Mary, FL. Tel: (407) 333-9500, FAX: (407) 333-7979, E-Mail: info@progressivecommunications.com, Web Site: www.progressivecommunications.com (21)

Mills, Nancy, Upbeat Inc, Saint Louis, MO. Tel: (314) 535-5005, (800) 325-3047, FAX: (314) 535-4419, E-Mail: custservice@upbeat.com, Web Site: www. upbeat.com (9)

Mills, Ossie, The Inspiration Networks, Indian Land, SC. Tel: (704) 561-7872, Web Site: www. insptoday.com (1)

Mills, Rebecca, Combined Insurance Co of America, Glenview, IL. Tel: (847) 953-8116, (800) 490-1322, FAX: (847) 953-8070, Web Site: www. combinedinsurance.com (15)

Milman, Fred, Fred Milman Associates, Glen Cove, NY. Tel: (516) 625-8075, FAX: (516) 625-5927, E-Mail: fmilman@compuserve.com (20)

Fred Milman Associates, Glen Cove, NY. Tel: (516) 625-8075, FAX: (516) 625-5927, E-Mail: fmilman@compuserve.com (20)

Milne, Tibby, McGruff Specialty Products Office, Amsterdam, NY. Tel: (518) 842-4388, (888) 776-7763, FAX: (800) 995-5121, E-Mail: mcgruff@ spocentral.com, Web Site: www.mcgruffspo.com (16)

Milnor, George, Miller's First Insurance Companies, Alton, IL. Tel: (618) 463-3636, (800) 558-0500, FAX: (618) 463-3614, Web Site: www. millersfirst.com (15)

Milrod, Jane, Milrod Executive Search, Princeton, NJ. Tel: (609) 683-8787, FAX: (609) 683-8221 (20)

Milrod Executive Search, Princeton, NJ. Tel: (609) 683-8787, FAX: (609) 683-8221 (20)

Milstein, Howard, P., Emigrant Savings Bank, New York, NY. Tel: (212) 850-4521, (800) EMI-GRANT, FAX: (212) 850-4372, Web Site: www. emigrant.com (14)

Milwaukee Direct Marketing Inc, Brookfield, WI. Tel: (262) 789-2240, FAX: (262) 789-2250, E-Mail: info@milwaukeedirect.com, Web Site: www. milwaukeedirect.com (35)

Milwaukee Electric Tool Corp, Brookfield, WI. Tel: (262) 781-3600, (800) 414-6527, FAX: (262) 781-3611, (800) 638-9582, Web Site: www.mil-electric-tool.com (16)

MIMAARTS LLC, New York, NY. Tel: (212) 584-1810 (20)

Mims, John, Thomson, Carrollton, TX. Tel: (972) 250-7000, Web Site: www.thomson.com (34)

Minac, Elaine, Minacs Worldwide, Farmington Hills, MI. Tel: (416) 380-3800, FAX: (416) 380-3830, E-Mail: info@minacs.com, Web Site: www.minacs. com (29)

Minacs Worldwide, Farmington Hills, MI. Tel: (416) 380-3800, FAX: (416) 380-3830, E-Mail: info@ minacs.com, Web Site: www.minacs.com (29)

Minardi, Eduardo, Bridgestone/Firestone North American Tire LLC, Nashville, TN. Tel: (615) 937-1000, (800) 543-7522, FAX: (615) 937-3721, Web Site: www.bridgestonetire.com (16)

Minasian, Stan, Animal Fund, San Francisco, CA. Tel: (415) 775-4636, E-Mail: delphinus@aol.com, Web Site: www.animalfund.org (9)

Minchak Jr, Robert J., JB Dollar Stretcher Magazine, Richfield, OH. Tel: (330) 659-3590, (800) 673-2531, FAX: (330) 659-6741, Web Site: www. jbdollar.com (31)

Minchew, Brian, Cables to Go, Moraine, OH. Tel: (937) 224-8646, (800) 506-9607, FAX: (800) 331-2841, (937) 496-2666, Web Site: www.cablestogo. com (3)

Minden, Larry, Minden Pictures, Watsonville, CA. Tel: (831) 761-3600, (888) 825-0641, FAX: (831) 761-3233, E-Mail: info@mindenpictures.com, Web Site: www.mindenpictures.com (38)

Minden Pictures, Watsonville, CA. Tel: (831) 761-3600, (888) 825-0641, FAX: (831) 761-3233, E-Mail: info@mindenpictures.com, Web Site: www.mindenpictures.com (38)

MindFireInc, Irvine, CA. Tel: (949) 474-4418w, Web Site: www.mindfireinc.com (22)

MINDset Direct, Arlington, VA. Tel: (703) 538-6463, Web Site: www.mindsetdirect.com (1)

Mineo, Frank P., Jafra Cosmetics International Inc, Westlake Village, CA. Tel: (805) 557-1889, (800) 551-2345, Web Site: www.jafra.com (7)

Miner, Gary, StatSoft Inc, Tulsa, OK. Tel: (918) 749-1119, FAX: (918) 749-2217, E-Mail: info@statsoft. com, Web Site: www.statsoft.com (9)

Minetto, Neil, Laplink Software Inc, Bellevue, WA. Tel: (425) 952-6000, (800) 527-5465, FAX: (425) 952-6002, E-Mail: marketing@laplink.com, Web Site: www.laplink.com (3)

Mini City Ltd, Webster, NY. Tel: (716) 872-6560, FAX: (716) 872-4094, E-Mail: minicityus@aol. com, Web Site: www.minicityltd.com (12)

Minitab Inc, State College, PA. Tel: (814) 238-3280, (800) 448-3555, FAX: (814) 238-4383, E-Mail: sales@minitab.com, Web Site: www.minitab.com (16)

Minix, Phil, Reiman Publications, Greendale, WI. Tel: (414) 423-0100, (800) 344-6913, FAX: (414) 423-3840, Web Site: www.reimanpub.com (17)

Minnesota Life, Saint Paul, MN. Tel: (651) 665-3500, (888) 237-1838, FAX: (651) 665-4488, Web Site: www.minnesotalife.com; www.securian.com (15)

Minnesota Multi Housing Association, Bloomington, MN. Tel: (952) 854-8500, FAX: (952) 854-3810, E-Mail: mha@mmha.com, Web Site: www.mmha. com (1)

Minnesota Public Radio, Saint Paul, MN. Tel: (651) 290-1500, (800) 228-7123, FAX: (651) 290-1260, E-Mail: mail@mpr.org, Web Site: www.mpr.org (1)

Minnetonka By Mail, Bronx, NY. FAX: (718) 885-3500, E-Mail: eileenlwagner@email.msn.com (2)

Minor, Marion, M2Media 360, Park Ridge, IL. Tel: (760) 318-7000, E-Mail: cnaughton@m2media360. com, Web Site: www.m2media360.com (17)

Mintel International, Chicago, IL. Tel: (312) 932-0500, Web Site: www.comperemedia.com (30)

Minton, D.R., Carolina Exotic Gardens/CEG Nursery, Greenville, NC. Tel: (252) 758-2600, FAX: (252) 758-3252, E-Mail: cegnursery@aol.com, Web Site: www.cegnursery.com (8)

Minton, Sherry, American Heart Association, Dallas, TX. Tel: (214) 373-6300, (800) AHA-USA-1, FAX: (214) 373-3406, Web Site: www. americanheart.org (1)

Mintz, Paul, Porta-Bote International, Mountain View, CA. Tel: (650) 961-5334, (800) 227-8882, Web Site: www.porta-bote.com (11)

Minuteman Press (Westchester), Elmsford, NY. Tel: (914) 347-5050, FAX: (914) 347-2563, E-Mail: gcronin@minutemanpress.com, Web Site: www. westchester.minutemanpress.com (27)

Mirabal, Alisa, Marketing Results Inc, Sicklerville, NJ. Tel: (856) 740-3334, FAX: (856) 740-3335, Web Site: www.marketingresults.net (16)

Mirabello, Rhianna, US Games Systems Inc, Stamford, CT. Tel: (203) 353-8400, (800) 544-2637, FAX: (203) 353-8431, Web Site: www.usgamesinc. com (11)

Mirabille, Peter, TSI, Albany, NY. Tel: (518) 463-5555, FAX: (518) 463-4504, E-Mail: tsi@capital. net, Web Site: www.tsidrivers.com (20)

Miracle Ear, Minneapolis, MN. Tel: (877) 268-4264, FAX: (763) 268-4365, Web Site: www.miracle-ear. com (14)

Miracle of Aloe, Dallas, TX. Tel: (800) 966-2563, FAX: (800) 859-9881, E-Mail: LJohnson@ miracleofaloe.com, Web Site: www.miracleofaloe. com (7)

Miranda, Alban, DWS Investments Service Co, Kansas City, MO. Tel: (800) 543-5776, Web Site: www.dws-investments.com (14)

Mirbach, H.W., Crossbow Group, Westport, CT. Tel: (203) 222-2244, FAX: (203) 226-7838, E-Mail: info@crossbowgroup.com, Web Site: www. crossbowgroup.com (40)

Mirchandani, Keith, Tristar Products, Fairfield, NJ. Tel: (973) 575-5400, FAX: (973) 683-6708, E-Mail: infotp@tristarproductsinc.com, Web Site: www.tristarproductsinc.com (16)

Mirly, Rev. Ray, Lutheran Church Extension Fund - Missouri Synod, Saint Louis, MO. Tel: (800) 843-5233, FAX: (314) 996-1131, Web Site: www.lcef. org (1)

Mirman, Richard E., Harrah's Entertainment Inc, Las Vegas, NV. Tel: (702) 407-6000, FAX: (702) 407-6499, (702) 407-6500, Web Site: www.harrahs.com (19)

Misa, Donna, Dataprint Corp, San Mateo, CA. Tel: (650) 340-0550, (800) 227-6191, FAX: (650) 340-7028, Web Site: www.dataprint.com (34)

Misener, Paul, Amazon.com, Washington, DC. Tel: (202) 347-7390 (16)

Mishica, Alicia, Specialized Mailing Services Inc, Huntington Beach, CA. Tel: (714) 274-2284, E-Mail: info@specializedmailing.com, Web Site: www.specializedmailing.com (28)

Misischia, Frank, L., FLM Graphics Corp, Fairfield, NJ. Tel: (973) 575-9450, E-Mail: info@ flmgraphics.com, Web Site: www.flmgraphics.com (16)

Miskovsky, Andrea, MBS, Melville, NY. Tel: (631) 851-5000, Web Site: www.mbsinsight.com (22)

Misniak, Paul, Career Education Corp, Schaumburg, IL. Tel: (847) 781-3600, Web Site: www.careered. com (1)

MISSCO Corp, Flowood, MS. Tel: (601) 948-8600, (800) 647-5333, FAX: (601) 987-3038 (16)

Missett, Judi, Shepphard, Jazzercise Inc, Carlsbad, CA. Tel: (760) 476-1750, (800) FIT IS IT, FAX: (760) 602-7180, E-Mail: info@jazzercise.com, Web Site: www.jazzercise.com (2)

Missett, Kathy, Jazzercise Inc, Carlsbad, CA. Tel: (760) 476-1750, (800) FIT IS IT, FAX: (760) 602-7180, E-Mail: info@jazzercise.com, Web Site: www.jazzercise.com (2)

Mission: A Consulting Group, Westport, CT. Tel: (203) 227-9475, FAX: (203) 227-6512, E-Mail: info@mission-consulting.com, Web Site: www. mission-consulting.com (20)

Missionary Society of St Columban, Saint Columbans, NE. Tel: (402) 291-1920, Web Site: www. columban.org (1)

The Missoulian, Missoula, MT. Tel: (406) 523-5334, FAX: (406) 523-5221, Web Site: www.missoulian. com (31)

Missouri Landscape & Nursery Association, Bowling Green, MO. Tel: (636) 542-1234, E-Mail: admin@ mlng.org, Web Site: www.mlna.org (1)

Missouri Life Inc, Boonville, MO. Tel: (660) 882-9898, (800) 492-2593, FAX: (660) 882-9899, E-Mail: info@missourilife.com, Web Site: www. missourilife.com (17)

Mr Fantastic LLC, Astor, FL. Tel: (407) 719-2020, E-Mail: sbillue@usa2net.net, Web Site: www. stanbillue.com (20)

Mr G's Enterprises, Fort Worth, TX. Tel: (817) 831-3501, FAX: (817) 831-0638, E-Mail: mrgs@ mrgusa.com, Web Site: www.mrgusa.com (16)

Mr Wash Car Wash, Kensington, MD. Tel: (301) 933-4858, Web Site: www.mrwash.com (16)

Mitchel, Ted, Montbleu Resort Casino and Spa, Stateline, NV. Tel: (775) 588-3515, (888) 829-7630, FAX: (775) 586-2030, Web Site: www. montbleuresort.com (19)

Mitchel, Thomas, Las Vegas Review Journal, Las Vegas, NV. Tel: (702) 383-0211, FAX: (702) 383-4646, Web Site: www.lvrj.com (17)

Mitchell, Bob, Replogle Globes Inc, Broadview, IL. Tel: (708) 343-0900, FAX: (708) 343-0923, E-Mail: info@replogleglobes.com, Web Site: www. replogleglobes.com (16)

Mitchell, Chuck, Consumers Digest Inc, Deerfield, IL. Tel: (847) 607-3000, FAX: (847) 763-0200, E-Mail: postmaster@consumersdigest.com, Web Site: www.consumersdigest.com (17)

Mitchell, Fenton, CX&B United Corp, Harbor City, CA. Tel: (310) 530-2102, (800) 292-8258, FAX: (310) 530-2513, E-Mail: sales@cxbunited.com, Web Site: www.cxbunited.com (33)

Mitchell, Jim, Convergys Corp, Ogden, UT. Tel: (630) 668-6174, Web Site: www.convergys.com (29)

Mitchell, Jim, Lexis Nexis Matthew Bender, Albany, NY. Tel: (518) 487-3000, (800) 424-4200, E-Mail: lexisnexis@matthewbender, Web Site: www. bender.lexisnexis.com (17)

Mitchell, Lee, Thoma Cressey Bravo, Chicago, IL. Tel: (312) 777-4444, FAX: (312) 777-4445, Web Site: www.tcb.com (14)

Mitchell, Lisa, A., Hagemeyer - North America, Charleston, SC. Tel: (843) 745-2400, FAX: (843) 745-6942, E-Mail: info@hagemeyerna.com, Web Site: www.hagemeyerna.com (16)

Mitchell, Mark, INWAVE Internet, Janesville, WI. Tel: (888) 469-2831, FAX: (608) 752-8981, Web Site: www.inwave.com (16)

Mitchell, Michael, G., Cognitronics Corp, Foxboro, MA. Tel: (508) 624-7600, (888) 228-5061, FAX: (508) 624-0289, E-Mail: info@thinkengine.com, Web Site: www.cognitronics.com (34)

Mitchell, Patricia, J., Americraft - The Gift Brokers Inc, Wendell, MA. Tel: (978) 544-7330, (800) 866-2723, FAX: (978) 544-2771, E-Mail: info@ americraft.us, Web Site: www.americraft.us (16)

Mitchell, Patty, Pennsylvania State University Press, University Park, PA. Tel: (814) 865-1327, (800) 326-9180, FAX: (814) 863-1408, Web Site: www. psupress.org (17)

Mitchell, Rod, CX&B United Corp, Harbor City, CA. Tel: (310) 530-2102, (800) 292-8258, FAX: (310) 530-2513, E-Mail: sales@cxbunited.com, Web Site: www.cxbunited.com (33)

Mitchell, Terry, CitiFinancial, Baltimore, MD. Tel: (410) 332-3000, (800) 995-2274, (800) 922-6235, FAX: (410) 332-3489, Web Site: www. citifinancial.com (14)

Mitchell, William, E., Arrow Advantage, Eden Prairie, MN. Tel: (952) 906-7100, (800) 833-3557, FAX: (952) 906-7135, Web Site: www.arrow.com (3)

Mitchell & Resnikoff/Weightman, Elkins Park, PA. Tel: (215) 635-1000, FAX: (215) 635-6542, E-Mail: info@mitch-res.com, Web Site: www. Mitch-Res.com (35)

Mitchell Graphics Inc, Petoskey, MI. Tel: (231) 347-4635, (800) 583-9401, FAX: (231) 347-9255, E-Mail: info@mitchellgraphics.com, Web Site: www.mitchellgraphics.com (27)

Mitchell International, San Diego, CA. Tel: (858) 368-7000, FAX: (858) 238-9111, Web Site: www. mitchell.com (17)

Mitelman, Bonnie, Anti-Defamation League, New York, NY. Tel: (212) 885-5870, Web Site: www. adl.org (1)

Mitera, Mark-Christopher, HH Backer Associates Inc, Chicago, IL. Tel: (312) 578-1818, FAX: (312) 578-1819, E-Mail: hhbacker@hhbacker.com, Web Site: www.hhbacker.com (17)

Mitrani, Amy, Food Chemical News, Arlington, VA. Tel: (202) 887-6320, (888) 732-7070, FAX: (202) 887-6335, E-Mail: cs@foodregulation.com, Web Site: www.foodchemicalnews.com (17)

Mitschele, George, Bernadette Business Forms Inc, O Fallon, MO. Tel: (314) 522-1700, (800) 862-7288, FAX: (314) 524-6161, Web Site: www.bbf.com (27)

Mitson, Les, W., Nilodor Inc, Bolivar, OH. Tel: (330) 874-1017, (800) 443-4321, FAX: (330) 874-3366, E-Mail: info@nilodor.com, Web Site: www.nilodor. com (16)

Mitsubishi Digital Electronics America Inc, Irvine, CA. Tel: (949) 465-6000, FAX: (949) 859-4770, Web Site: www.mitsubishi-tv.com (3)

Mitsubishi Motor Sales of America Inc, Cypress, CA. Tel: (714) 372-6000, FAX: (714) 373-1736, Web Site: www.mitsubishicars.com (1)

Mitsui, Ken, Methode Electronics Inc, Chicago, IL. Tel: (708) 867-6777, FAX: (708) 867-6999, E-Mail: info@methode.com, Web Site: www. methode.com (9)

Frank Mittermeier Inc, Bronx, NY. Tel: (718) 828-3843, (800) 360-3843, FAX: (718) 518-7233, E-Mail: info@dastrausa.com, Web Site: www. dastrausa.com (11)

Mittlestadt, Mitchell, Imperial Supplies, Green Bay, WI. Tel: (920) 494-5403, (800) 558-2808, FAX: (800) 553-8769, Web Site: www.imperialsupplies. com (16)

Miville, Mark, Solar Components Corp, Manchester, NH. Tel: (603) 668-8186, FAX: (603) 668-1783, Web Site: www.solar-components.com (9)

Mix, Mark, A., Legal Defense Foundation Inc, Springfield, VA. Tel: (703) 321-8501, (800) 336-3600, FAX: (703) 321-9613, E-Mail: info@nrtw.org, Web Site: www.nrtw.org (1)

Miyares Jr, Marcelino, GenerH, Inc, Torrance, CA. Tel: (888) 312-3443, E-Mail: info@generh.com, Web Site: www.generh.com (21)

Mlotek, Mark, E., Henry Schein Inc, Melville, NY. Tel: (631) 843-5500, (800) 472-4346, FAX: (631) 843-5658, E-Mail: custserv@henryschein.com, Web Site: www.henryschein.com (16)

Moat, Jeff, Canadian Blood Services, Ottawa, ON Canada. Tel: (613) 739-2300, Web Site: www. blood.ca (1)

Mobed, Rohnington, IHS Inc, Englewood, CO. Tel: (303) 790-0600, (800) 525-7052, FAX: (303) 754-3940, E-Mail: customer.support@ihs.com, Web Site: www.ihs.com (17)

Mobile Fusion, Lakewood, CO. Tel: (720) 963-8000, (800) 431-8556, Web Site: www.mobile-fusion.com (16)

Moby Wrap Inc, Chico, CA. Tel: (530) 898-8200 (2)

Mochalski, Cynthia, American Family Insurance Group, Madison, WI. Tel: (608) 249-2111, FAX: (608) 243-6525, E-Mail: akin1@amfam.com, Web Site: www.amfam.com (15)

Modany, Kevin, M., ITT Educational Services Inc, Carmel, IN. Tel: (317) 706-9200, E-Mail: gtanner@itt-tech.edu, Web Site: www.itt-tech.edu (16)

Modek, Matt, Cotta Transmission Co, Beloit, WI. Tel: (608) 368-5600, FAX: (608) 368-5605, E-Mail: sales@cotta.com, Web Site: www.cotta.com (16)

Modem Media, Stamford, CT. Tel: (203) 299-7000, FAX: (203) 299-7060, Web Site: www. modemmedia.com (35)

Modern Graphic Arts, Saint Petersburg, FL. Tel: (727) 579-1527, FAX: (727) 579-1528 (27)

Modern Information Services Inc, Statesville, NC. Tel: (704) 872-1020 (27)

Modern Mail, Newark, DE. Tel: (302) 391-1200, Web Site: www.triggermarketing.com (20)

Modern Postcard, Carlsbad, CA. Tel: (800) 959-8365, Web Site: www.modernpostcard.com (10)

ModernAd Media LLC, Deerfield Beach, FL. Tel: (561) 750-5131 X206, Web Site: www.modernad. com (40)

Modernage Custom Digital Imaging Labs, New York, NY. Tel: (212) 997-1800, (800) 997-2510, FAX: (212) 869-4796, E-Mail: info@modernage.com, Web Site: www.modernage.com (16)

Modlin, Cliff, Marking Specialists Group, Buffalo Grove, IL. Tel: (847) 793-8100, (800) 678-8073, FAX: (847) 793-8109, E-Mail: info@marking-specialists.com, Web Site: www.marking-specialists.com (27)

Modular Devices, LLC, Sparta, NJ. Tel: (973) 579-7220, (800) 292-2201, FAX: (973) 579-1820, E-Mail: modulardevices@optonline.net, Web Site: www.modulardevices.biz (3)

Modular Mailing Systems, Tampa, FL. Tel: (305) 826-9077, (800) 881-MAIL, E-Mail: sales@ modularmailing.com, Web Site: www. modularmailing.com (34)

Moede, Paul, International Bible Society, Colorado Springs, CO. Tel: (719) 488-9200, FAX: (719) 867-2812, Web Site: www.ibs.org (1)

Moeller, Jim, Serenity, Maria Stein, OH. Tel: (419) 925-1215, (800) 869-1684, FAX: (419) 925-1216, E-Mail: serenity@bright.net, Web Site: www. serenitymusic.com (17)

Moen Inc, North Olmsted, OH. Tel: (440) 962-2000, Web Site: www.moen.com (1)

Mogren, Todd, Coastal Tool & Supply, West Hartford, CT. Tel: (860) 233-8213, (877) 551-8665, FAX: (860) 233-6295, E-Mail: sales@coastaltool.com, Web Site: www.coastaltool.com (16)

Mohan-Neill, Sumaria, Walter E Heller College of Business Administration, Chicago, IL. Tel: (312) 281-3293, FAX: (312) 281-3290, Web Site: www. roosevelt.edu (41)

Mohawk, Cohoes, NY. Tel: (518) 237-1740, (800) 843-6455, FAX: (518) 237-7394, E-Mail: info@ mohawkpaper.com, Web Site: www. mohawkconnects.com (25)

Mohawk Lifts, Amsterdam, NY. Tel: (518) 842-1431, (800) 833-2006, FAX: (518) 842-1289, E-Mail: rwells@mohawklifts.com, Web Site: www. mohawklifts.com (9)

Mohney, Ron A., Moto Franchise Corp, Dayton, OH. Tel: (937) 291-1900, (800) 733-6686, FAX: (937) 291-2005, E-Mail: expert@motophoto.com, Web Site: www.motophoto.com; www.portraitavenue. com (3)

Mohr, Eric, EBM Direct Marketing Services LLC, Port Washington, NY. Tel: (516) 874-7839, Web Site: www.ebmdirectmarketing.com (20)

Mohr, Richard, Intermap Technologies, Englewood, CO. Tel: (303) 708-0955, FAX: (303) 708-0952, Web Site: www.intermap.com (32)

Moir, Doug, Sportif Mail Order Inc, Sparks, NV. Tel: (775) 359-6400, (800) 776-7843, FAX: (800) 776-3291, Web Site: www.sportif.com (2)

Mokover, Peter, Spectrum Research, Ventnor City, NJ. Tel: (609) 822-0056, E-Mail: peter@ spectrumresearch.com (30)

Moldenhauer, Walter, Texas Parks & Wildlife Dept, Austin, TX. Tel: (512) 389-4800, (800) 792-1112, FAX: (512) 389-8029, Web Site: www.tpwd.state. tx.us (1)

Molinari, Alfred, Data Translation Inc, Marlborough, MA. Tel: (508) 481-3700, (800) 525-8528, FAX: (508) 481-8620, Web Site: www.datatranslation. com (34)

Moll, Gary, American Forests, Washington, DC. Tel: (202) 737-1944, FAX: (202) 737-2457, E-Mail: info@amfor.org, Web Site: www.americanforests. org (1)

Moller, Stacy, Stickertape, Nesconset, NY. Tel: (800) 811-2891, FAX: (800) 727-5577, E-Mail: CustomerService@stickertape.com, Web Site: www.stickertape.com (27)

Mollica, Celia, Manhattan Media Services Inc, New York, NY. Tel: (212) 808-4077, FAX: (212) 808-4080, E-Mail: mmorello@manhmedia.com, Web Site: www.manhmedia.com (21)

Molloy, Lawrence, PetSmart Inc, Phoenix, AZ. Tel: (623) 587-2009, (800) 738-1385, FAX: (623) 580-6183, Web Site: www.petsmart.com (5)

Molnar, Carole, Dentino Marketing, Princeton, NJ. Tel: (201) 332-1219, (800) 477-8372, FAX: (201) 332-4262, E-Mail: karl@dentinomarketing.com, Web Site: www.dentinomarketing.com (35)

Molson, Eric, H., Molson Coors Brewing Co, Denver, CO. Tel: (303) 279-6565, (800) 642-6116, FAX: (303) 277-5415, Web Site: www.molsoncoors.com (16)

Molson Coors Brewing Co, Denver, CO. Tel: (303) 279-6565, (800) 642-6116, FAX: (303) 277-5415, Web Site: www.molsoncoors.com (16)

Mon, Donald, American Health Information Management Association, Chicago, IL. Tel: (312) 233-1100, FAX: (312) 233-1090, E-Mail: info@ahima.org, Web Site: www.ahima.org (1)

Monaco, Katherine, T., CPC Inc, Babylon, NY. Tel: (631) 661-6779, (800) 621-4414, FAX: (631) 661-6914, E-Mail: cpcus@aol.com, Web Site: www.cpctours.com (19)

Monaco, Rosemarie, Group M Inc, Nyack, NY. Tel: (201) 227-0747, E-Mail: gmi.prm@gmail.com, Web Site: www.groupm.org (35)

Monaco, Vince, The Monaco Group, Santa Ana, CA. Tel: (714) 505-5180, FAX: (714) 505-5187, E-Mail: service@monaco.com, Web Site: www.monacogroup.com (27)

The Monaco Group, Santa Ana, CA. Tel: (714) 505-5180, FAX: (714) 505-5187, E-Mail: service@monaco.com, Web Site: www.monacogroup.com (27)

Monadnock Paper Mills Inc, Bennington, NH. Tel: (603) 588-3311, (800) 221-2159, FAX: (603) 588-3158, Web Site: www.monadnockpaper.com (25)

Monast, Jane, Mohawk, Cohoes, NY. Tel: (518) 237-1740, (800) 843-6455, FAX: (518) 237-7394, E-Mail: info@mohawkpaper.com, Web Site: www.mohawkconnects.com (25)

Monastra, A.J., Wrisco Industries Inc, Palm Beach Gardens, FL. Tel: (561) 626-5700, (800) 627-2646, FAX: (561) 627-3574, E-Mail: sales.staff@wrisco.com, Web Site: www.wrisco.com (8)

Monastra, Steve, Wrisco Industries Inc, Palm Beach Gardens, FL. Tel: (561) 626-5700, (800) 627-2646, FAX: (561) 627-3574, E-Mail: sales.staff@wrisco.com, Web Site: www.wrisco.com (8)

Mondello, Mike, Sea Bear, Anacortes, WA. Tel: (360) 293-4661, (800) 645-3474, FAX: (888) 487-6427, Web Site: www.seabear.com (16)

Mondloch, Ben, Gale Research Inc, Farmington Hills, MI. Tel: (248) 699-4253, (800) 877-GALE, FAX: (313) 961-6083, Web Site: www.gale.com (17)

Monestero, Andrew, Zim-American Israeli Shipping Co Inc, Staten Island, NY. Tel: (718) 313-1950, Web Site: www.zim.com (16)

Monetti, Kathy, Pleasant Company, Middleton, WI. Tel: (608) 836-4848, (800) 845-0005, FAX: (608) 836-1999, Web Site: www.americangirl.com (11)

Monex Deposit Co, Newport Beach, CA. Tel: (949) 752-1400, (800) 444-8317, FAX: (949) 752-7214, E-Mail: info@monex.com, Web Site: www.monex.com (14)

Money Mailer Direct Marketing, Garden Grove, CA. Tel: (800) 416-1713, Web Site: www.moneymailerdirect.com (35)

Money Mailer LLC, Garden Grove, CA. Tel: (714) 889-1590, Web Site: www.moneymailer.net (31)

MoneyGram International, Dallas, TX. Tel: (800) 666-3947, Web Site: www.moneygram.com (14)

Monfradi Dunn, JoAnne, Alliant, Brewster, NY. Tel: (845) 276-2600, Web Site: www.alliantdata.com (22)

Monfrini, Bob, Australian Tourist Commission, Los Angeles, CA. Tel: (310) 695-3200, Web Site: www.australia.com (16)

Monk, Mike, Alpha Dog Marketing Inc, Lincoln, NE. Tel: (402) 486-0668, Web Site: www.alphadogmktg.com (1)

Monkeyshines Publishers, Greensboro, NC. FAX: (336) 292-6999, E-Mail: mkshines@nr.infi.net, Web Site: www.monkeyshinespublishers.com (17)

Monks, Tom, The Hyiad Group, Garden City, NY. Tel: (516) 433-3800, FAX: (516) 822-6670, Web Site: www.thehyaidgroup.com (22)

Monroe, Bill, Customized Newspaper Advertising, Des Moines, IA. Tel: (515) 244-2145, (800) 227-7636, FAX: (515) 244-4855, Web Site: www.cnaads.com (18)

Monroe, Jerry, Towne Allpoints Communications, Santa Ana, CA. Tel: (714) 540-3095, (800) 243-8099, FAX: (714) 540-4192, E-Mail: info@towne.com, Web Site: www.towne.com (21)

Monroe, Matt, n Fusion Group, Austin, TX. Tel: (512) 716-7000, FAX: (512) 716-7001, Web Site: www.nfusion.com (35)

Monroy, Gerardo, Bankers Life & Casualty Co, Chicago, IL. Tel: (312) 396-6000, (800) 231-9150, Web Site: www.bankerslife.com (15)

Monsees, Gregg, Peters, Putnam Rolling Ladder Co Inc, New York, NY. Tel: (212) 226-5147, FAX: (212) 941-1836, E-Mail: putnam1905@aol.com, Web Site: www.putnamrollingladder.com (5)

Monserrat, K. Robin, Florida Power & Light Co, Miami, FL. Tel: (305) 552-3552, (800) 468-8243, FAX: (305) 552-2487, Web Site: www.fpl.com (16)

Monson, Barbara, M., Envelope Manufacturers Association, Alexandria, VA. Tel: (703) 739-2200, FAX: (703) 739-2209, Web Site: www.envelope.org (1)

Monster Magnet, Louisville, KY. Tel: (800) 255-0234, Web Site: www.monstermagnet.com (35)

Monster Worldwide, Maynard, MA. Tel: (888) MONSTER, Web Site: www.monster.com (20)

Montag & Caldwell Inc, Atlanta, GA. Tel: (404) 836-7100, (800) 458-5868, FAX: (404) 836-7230, Web Site: www.montag.com (14)

Montague, Larry, N., TAPPI (Technical Association of the Pulp & Paper Industry), Norcross, GA. Tel: (678) 642-66, (800) 332-8686, FAX: (770) 446-6947, E-Mail: webmaster@tappi.org, Web Site: www.tappi.org (1)

Montalao, Debbie, The Hamilton Group Ltd Inc, Jacksonville, FL. Tel: (904) 279-1300, FAX: (904) 279-1414, Web Site: www.collectibletoday.com (16)

Montalvo, David, Active Web Group, Hauppauge, NY. Tel: (800) 978-3417, FAX: (800) 719-4402, E-Mail: info@activewebgroup.com, Web Site: www.activewebgroup.com (9)

Montandon, John, L., Phoenix Data Processing, Westmont, IL. Tel: (630) 654-4400, FAX: (630) 654-4470, E-Mail: sales@phoenixdataprocessing.com, Web Site: www.phoenixdataprocessing.com (22)

Montbleu Resort Casino and Spa, Stateline, NV. Tel: (775) 588-3515, (888) 829-7630, FAX: (775) 586-2030, Web Site: www.montbleuresort.com (19)

Montegrande, Antoinette, Phoenix Learning Group Inc, Maryland Heights, MO. Tel: (314) 569-0211, (800) 221-1274, FAX: (314) 569-2834, E-Mail: dealersales@phoenixlearninggroup.com, Web Site: www.phoenixlearninggroup.com (16)

Monteith, Timothy, J., Masco Corp, Taylor, MI. Tel: (313) 274-7400, FAX: (313) 792-6135, E-Mail: webmaster@mascohq.com, Web Site: www.masco.com (16)

Montepaula, Tillian, Meriks Partners, Tucson, AZ. Tel: (413) 243-0857 (10)

Montes, Nisley, Torqmaster International, Stamford, CT. Tel: (203) 326-5945, (888) 414-4643, FAX: (203) 326-5944, E-Mail: info@torqmaster.com, Web Site: www.torqmaster.com (9)

Montgomery, Clifford, Vivitar Corp, Tempe, AZ. Tel: (800) 592-9541, FAX: (909) 348-6390, Web Site: www.vivitar.com (16)

Montgomery, Keith, Kaiser Foundation Health Plan of the Mid-Atlantic States Inc, Rockville, MD. Tel: (301) 816-5641, Web Site: kp.org (1)

Montgomery, Nancy, RJ Reynolds Tobacco Co, Winston Salem, NC. Tel: (336) 741-5111 (16)

Montreal Envelope Inc, Montreal, PQ Canada. Tel: (514) 331-7110, (800) 655-2709, FAX: (514) 748-7322, E-Mail: ybrochu@enveloppe-montreal.com, Web Site: www.enveloppe-montreal.com (26)

Montross, David, UGL Equis Corp, Chicago, IL. Tel: (312) 424-8000, FAX: (312) 424-8080, Web Site: www.equiscorp.com (16)

Moody, J., Ward, Astronomical Society of the Pacific, San Francisco, CA. Tel: (415) 337-1100, (800) 335-2624, FAX: (415) 337-5205, E-Mail: service@astrosociety.org, Web Site: www.astrosociety.org (1)

Moody, Jessica, Directory of Mail Order Catalogs, Millerton, NY. Tel: (518) 789-8700, (800) 562-2139, FAX: (518) 789-0556, E-Mail: cstupak@greyhouse.com, Web Site: www.greyhouse.com (43)

Moody, Jessica, Grey House Publishing, Amenia, NY. Tel: (518) 789-8700, (800) 562-2139, FAX: (518) 789-0556, E-Mail: books@greyhouse.com, Web Site: www.greyhouse.com (43)

Moody, Jessica, The Directory of Business Information Resources, Millerton, NY. Tel: (518) 789-8700, (800) 562-2139, FAX: (518) 789-0556, E-Mail: cstupak@greyhouse.com, Web Site: www.greyhouse.com (43)

Moody, Robin, Daedalus Books Inc, Columbia, MD. Tel: (410) 309-2700, (800) 395-2665, FAX: (410) 309-2701, Web Site: www.salebooks.com (5)

Moog, Matthew, Q Interactive, Chicago, IL. Tel: (312) 977-0390, (888) 729-6465, FAX: (312) 224-5001, E-Mail: solutions@qinteractive.com, Web Site: www.qinteractive.com (40)

Moomau, Bud, Vet Vax, Tonganoxie, KS. Tel: (913) 845-3760, (800) 369-8297, FAX: (913) 845-9472, E-Mail: sales@vetvax.com (11)

Moon, Jo, Janes Information Group, Alexandria, VA. Tel: (703) 683-3700, (800) 824-0768, FAX: (703) 836-0297, Web Site: www.janes.com (17)

Moon, Samuel, Air Power USA, Los Angeles, CA. Tel: (310) 641-0830, (888) 888-8231, FAX: (310) 641-8515, Web Site: www.airpowerusa.com (12)

Moon Shine Trading Co, Woodland, CA. Tel: (530) 668-0660, (800) 678-1226, FAX: (530) 668-6061, E-Mail: store@moonshinetrading.com, Web Site: www.moonshinetrading.com (4)

Moonan, Joan, The Hibbert Group, Trenton, NJ. Tel: (609) 394-7500, (800) 545-4747, FAX: (609) 695-6553, Web Site: www.hibbertco.com (28)

Mooney, Beth E., Key Bank National Association, Albany, NY. Tel: (518) 434-4871, (800) 539-2968, Web Site: www.keybank.com (14)

Mooney, John, Delta Vacations, Fort Lauderdale, FL. Tel: (954) 522-1440, (800) 800-1504, FAX: (954) 468-4765, Web Site: www.deltavacations.com (19)

Mooney, Patricia, New & Unique Videos, San Diego, CA. Tel: (619) 644-3001, (619) 644-3000, E-Mail: info@newuniquevideos.com, Web Site: www.newuniquevideos.com (3)

Moore, Allie, Newport Creative Communications, Duxbury, MA. Tel: (781) 934-1414, Web Site: www.newportcreative.com (1)

Moore, Angie, Arthritis Foundation, Atlanta, GA. Tel: (404) 872-7100, FAX: (404) 872-0457, Web Site: www.arthritis.org (1)

Moore, Charles, Charles Moore Associates Inc, Southampton, PA. Tel: (215) 355-6084, FAX: (215) 364-2212, E-Mail: cmadirectmail@yahoo.com, Web Site: www.cmadirectmail.com (24)

Moore, Christopher, International Data Management - a Dmh Marketing Partners Co, Akron, OH. Tel: (330) 869-8500, Web Site: www.idmi.com (22)

Moore, Deborah, Banker & Tradesman, Boston, MA. Tel: (617) 428-5100, FAX: (617) 428-5119, E-Mail: dmoore@thewarrengroup.com, Web Site: www.thewarrengroup.com (17)

Moore, Delia, American Family Life Assurance Co of Columbus (AFLAC), Columbus, GA. Tel: (706) 323-3431, (800) 992-3522, FAX: (706) 660-7446, Web Site: www.aflac.com (15)

Moore, Diane, Windstar Cruises, Seattle, WA. Tel: (206) 292-9606, (800) 258-SAIL, FAX: (206) 340-0975, E-Mail: info@windstarcruises.com, Web Site: www.windstarcruises.com (19)

Moore, Eileen, National Contract Management Association, Ashburn, VA. Tel: (571) 382-1134, (800) 344-8096, E-Mail: memberservices@ncmghq.org, Web Site: www.ncmahq.org (1)

Moore, Gary, Jungle Consulting, Colorado Springs, CO. Tel: (702) 596-4366 (20)

Moore, James, Leo Burnett Detroit, Troy, MI. Tel: (248) 458-8331, FAX: (248) 458-8736, Web Site: www.leoburnett.com (35)

Moore, Jan, S., Direct Options, West Chester, OH. Tel: (513) 779-4416, FAX: (513) 779-4426, E-Mail: inform@directoptions.com, Web Site: www. directoptions.com (35)

Moore, Jim, SanSegal Sportswear (HQ), Sandy, UT. Tel: (801) 566-3248, (800) 338-6048, FAX: (801) 566-3350, E-Mail: sansegal@sansegal.com, Web Site: www.sansegal.com (2)

Moore, John, Collegiate Cap & Gown, Champaign, IL. Tel: (217) 351-9500, FAX: (217) 351-9214, Web Site: www.herff-jones.com (16)

Moore, Kate, Facts On File Inc, New York, NY. Tel: (212) 967-8800, (800) 322-8755, FAX: (212) 678-3633, Web Site: www.factsonfile.com (17)

Moore, Kevin, Indium Corp of America, Clinton, NY. Tel: (315) 853-4900, (800) 446-3486, FAX: (800) 221-5759, E-Mail: askus@indium.com, Web Site: www.indium.com (16)

Moore, Lester W.B., Polynesian Cultural Center, Honolulu, HI. Tel: (808) 293-3333, (800) 367-7060, FAX: (888) 722-7339, E-Mail: internetrez@ polynesia.com, Web Site: www.polynesia.com (16)

Moore, Marc, Blue Cross Blue Shield of North Carolina, Durham, NC. Tel: (800) 250-3630, Web Site: www.bcbsnc.com (15)

Moore, Marcia, Rees Associates Inc, Des Moines, IA. Tel: (515) 243-2127, FAX: (515) 243-1026, Web Site: www.reesassociates.com (28)

Moore, Margot, Murphy, New England Mail Order Association, Scarborough, ME. Tel: (207) 885-0090, (860) 691-1260, FAX: (207) 885-0097, Web Site: www.nemoa.org (40)

Moore, Mark, TeleDirect International Inc, Scottsdale, AZ. Tel: (480) 585-6464, (800) 531-6440, FAX: (480) 585-3373, Web Site: www.tdirect.com (29)

Moore, Mark, e-Pipeconnection, Evansville, IN. Tel: (812) 474-4529, (800) 262-4300, FAX: (812) 474-4531, E-Mail: sales@e-pipeconnection.com, Web Site: www.e-pipeconnection.com (9)

Moore, Pamela, Prakken Publications Inc, Ann Arbor, MI. Tel: (734) 975-2800, (800) 530-9673, FAX: (734) 975-2787, E-Mail: vanessa@techdirections. com, Web Site: www.eddigest.com; www. techdirections.com (17)

Moore, Ralph, S., Sequoia Nursery, Fresno, CA. Tel: (559) 732-0309, FAX: (559) 732-0192, E-Mail: seqnursery@aol.com, Web Site: www. sequoianursery.com (8)

Moore, Ray, George W Park Seed Co Inc, Greenwood, SC. Tel: (864) 223-8555, (864) 223-7333, FAX: (864) 941-4206, E-Mail: info@parkseed. com, Web Site: www.parkseed.com (8)

Moore, Robert J., Bausch & Lomb Inc, Rochester, NY. Tel: (585) 338-6000, (800) 344-8815, FAX: (585) 338-6007, Web Site: www.bausch.com (16)

Moore, Robert, The Dingley Press, Lisbon, ME. Tel: (207) 353-4151, (800) 317-4574, FAX: (207) 353-9886, E-Mail: webrequest@dingley.com, Web Site: www.dingley.com (27)

Moore, Scott, SC Direct, West Bridgewater, MA. Tel: (800) 343-9695, Web Site: www.scdirect.com (2)

Moore, Steven D.R., Stream International, Wellesley, MA. Tel: (781) 304-1800, (888) 264-5834, FAX: (781) 575-6999, Web Site: www.stream.com (16)

Moore, Thurston, Thurston Moore Country Ltd, Madison, TN. Tel: (615) 868-7448, FAX: (615) 868-3738 (16)

Charles Moore Associates Inc, Southampton, PA. Tel: (215) 355-6084, FAX: (215) 364-2212, E-Mail: cmadirectmail@yahoo.com, Web Site: www. cmadirectmail.com (24)

Moore Medical LLC, Farmington, CT. Tel: (860) 826-3600, FAX: (860) 223-2382, Web Site: www. mooremedical.com (7)

Thurston Moore Country Ltd, Madison, TN. Tel: (615) 868-7448, FAX: (615) 868-3738 (16)

Moorhead, Douglas P., Presque Isle Wine Cellars Inc, North East, PA. Tel: (814) 725-1314, (800) 488-7492, FAX: (814) 725-2092, E-Mail: info@piwine. com, Web Site: www.piwine.com (4)

Moosmann, Art, Fireman's Fund Insurance Co, Novato, CA. Tel: (415) 899-2000, FAX: (415) 899-3600, Web Site: www.firemansfund.com (14)

Mopsik, Eugene, American Society of Media Photographers (ASMP), Philadelphia, PA. Tel: (215) 451-ASMP, FAX: (215) 451-0880, Web Site: www. asmp.org (40)

Mora, Chuck, Bamboo Cricket Service, Titusville, FL. Tel: (888) 634-7097, FAX: (646) 390-6313, E-Mail: info@bamboocricket.com, Web Site: www. bamboocricket.com (22)

Mora, Jake, R2C Group, Portland, OR. Tel: (503) 222-0025, Web Site: www.r2cgroup.com (35)

Mora, John, M., Creative Copywriting, Plainfield, IL. Tel: (815) 439-9160, FAX: (815) 439-9158 (39)

Mora, Michaela, Relevant Insights LLC, Euless, TX. Tel: (817) 545-8017 (30)

Morales, Angelo, Frank Mittermeier Inc, Bronx, NY. Tel: (718) 828-3843, (800) 360-3843, FAX: (718) 518-7233, E-Mail: info@dastrausa.com, Web Site: www.dastrausa.com (11)

Morales, Rose, King Ranch Saddle Shop, Kingsville, TX. Tel: (361) 595-1424, (800) 282-KING, FAX: (361) 595-1011, E-Mail: krsaddleshop@king-ranch. com, Web Site: www.krsaddleshop.com (8)

Moran, Adam, Macromark Inc, Brewster, NY. Tel: (845) 230-6300, FAX: (845) 278-0650, E-Mail: david@macromark.com, Web Site: www. macromark.com (23)

Moran, Dan, Rock-Tred Corp, Waukegan, IL. Tel: (847) 673-8200, (800) 762-8733, FAX: (847) 679-6665, Web Site: www.rocktred.com (9)

Moran, Dori, Pacific Botanicals LLC, Grants Pass, OR. Tel: (541) 479-7777, FAX: (541) 479-7780, E-Mail: pacbot1@earthlink.net, Web Site: www. pacificbotanicals.com (7)

Moran, Geri, Burberry, New York, NY. Tel: (212) 707-6508, Web Site: www.burberry.com (2)

Moran, Jackie, Trophyland USA Inc, Hialeah, FL. Tel: (305) 823-4830, (800) 327-5820, FAX: (305) 823-4836, E-Mail: info@trophyland.com, Web Site: www.trophyland.com (5)

Moran, Jennifer, Weiss Research Inc, Jupiter, FL. Tel: (561) 627-3300, (877) 925-4833, FAX: (561) 625-6685, E-Mail: newbusiness@weissgroupinc.com, Web Site: www.weissgroupinc.com (17)

Moran, Kevin, Central States Indemnity, Omaha, NE. Tel: (402) 997-8000, (402) 397-1111, (800) 445-6500, Web Site: www.csi-omaha.com (15)

Moran, Lynn, Ethel M Chocolates Inc, Henderson, NV. Tel: (702) 458-8864, (800) 471-0352, FAX: (800) 392-2587, E-Mail: chocolatier@ethelm.com, Web Site: www.ethelm.com (4)

Moran, Lynn, Savitz, Los Angeles, CA. Tel: (310) 642-4799, FAX: (310) 642-7795, E-Mail: lmoran@ savitzfieldandfocus.com, Web Site: www. savitzfieldandfocus.com (20)

Moran, Robert F., PetSmart Inc, Phoenix, AZ. Tel: (623) 587-2009, (800) 738-1385, FAX: (623) 580-6183, Web Site: www.petsmart.com (5)

Moran, Robert F., State Line Tack Inc, Phoenix, AZ. Tel: (623) 580-6100, (800) 228-9208, FAX: (623) 580-6183, E-Mail: customerservice@statelinetack. com, Web Site: www.statelinetack.com (16)

Moran, Ron, Moran Direct Inc, Houston, TX. Tel: (713) 880-3725, FAX: (713) 263-7647, E-Mail: rmoran@morandirect.com, Web Site: www. morandirect.com (20)

Moran, Thomas, J., Mutual of America Life Insurance Co, New York, NY. Tel: (212) 224-1600, (800) 468-3785, FAX: (212) 224-2539, Web Site: www. mutualofamerica.com (14)

Moran, Thomas, West Marine Inc, Watsonville, CA. Tel: (831) 761-4825, (800) BOATING, (800) 262-8464, FAX: (831) 768-5000, E-Mail: customercare@westmarine.com, Web Site: www. westmarine.com (11)

Moran, Tom, Thomson West, Eagan, MN. Tel: (651) 687-7000, (800) 328-9378, FAX: (651) 687-7849, E-Mail: jeff.patrios@thomsonreuters.com, Web Site: www.thomson.com (17)

Moran Direct Inc, Houston, TX. Tel: (713) 880-3725, FAX: (713) 263-7647, E-Mail: rmoran@ morandirect.com, Web Site: www.morandirect.com (20)

Morano, Vince, Markertek Video Supply, Saugerties, NY. Tel: (845) 246-3036, (800) 522-2025, FAX: (847) 246-1757, E-Mail: sales@markertek.com, Web Site: www.markertek.com (3)

Morantz, Stan, S Morantz Inc, Philadelphia, PA. Tel: (215) 969-0266, (800) 695-4522, FAX: (215) 969-0566, E-Mail: info@morantz.com, Web Site: www. morantz.com (34)

S Morantz Inc, Philadelphia, PA. Tel: (215) 969-0266, (800) 695-4522, FAX: (215) 969-0566, E-Mail: info@morantz.com, Web Site: www.morantz.com (34)

Morassut, Paolo, CAA Auto Club & Travel Agency Inc, Thornhill, ON. Tel: (519) 255-1212, (800) 564-6222, FAX: (519) 255-7379, E-Mail: info@ caasco.ca, Web Site: www.central.on.caa.ca (1)

Morawez, Joy, Chicago Sun-Times, Chicago, IL. Tel: (312) 321-3000, FAX: (312) 321-9655, E-Mail: jmorawez@suntimes.com, Web Site: www. suntimes.com (31)

Morcon Industrial Specialty Inc, Mesquite, NV. Tel: (702) 346-3447, (888) 842-7953, Web Site: www. morcon-ind.com (9)

Morecroft, Michael, J., Hamilton Beach/Proctor-Silex Inc, Glen Allen, VA. Tel: (804) 273-9777, FAX: (804) 527-7142, Web Site: www.hambeach.com (16)

Morehouse, Ted, Emigrant Savings Bank, New York, NY. Tel: (212) 850-4521, (800) EMIGRANT, FAX: (212) 850-4372, Web Site: www.emigrant. com (14)

Morel, Daniel, Wunderman, New York, NY. Tel: (212) 941-3000, FAX: (212) 888-7520, Web Site: www. wunderman.com (35)

Morel, Xavier, ACTIMAIL INC, New York, NY. Tel: (212) 245-2272, FAX: (212) 245-2523, E-Mail: actimail.usa@actimail.com, Web Site: www. actimail.com (35)

Morelli, Michael, Littleton Coin Co Inc, Littleton, NH. Tel: (603) 444-5386, FAX: (603) 444-0121, E-Mail: jhennessey@littletoncoin.com, Web Site: www.littletoncoin.com (6)

Morelli, Stephen, Ruud Lighting Inc, Racine, WI. Tel: (262) 886-1900, (800) 236-7000, FAX: (800) 236-7500, E-Mail: sales@ruudlighting.com, Web Site: www.ruudlighting.com (9)

Morello, Marianna, Manhattan Media Services Inc, New York, NY. Tel: (212) 808-4077, FAX: (212) 808-4080, E-Mail: mmorello@manhmedia.com, Web Site: www.manhmedia.com (21)

MoreMedia Direct Inc, Miami Beach, FL. Tel: (305) 672-9793, E-Mail: info@moremediadirect.com, Web Site: www.moremediadirect.com (35)

Moreno, Victoria, Blue Coral Slick 50, Houston, TX. Tel: (713) 241-6161, (800) 416-1600, FAX: (713) 241-4044, E-Mail: SCD-ConsumerSolutions@ Shell.com, Web Site: www.bluecoral.com (16)

Moresi, John, Impressions Direct, Saint Louis, MO. Tel: (314) 951-2100, Web Site: www.impressions-direct.com (28)

Moret, Pam, Thrivent Financial for Lutherans, Appleton, WI. Tel: (920) 734-5721, (800) 847-4836, FAX: (920) 730-4781, E-Mail: mail@thrivent.com, Web Site: www.thrivent.com (14)

Jacques Moret Inc, New York, NY. Tel: (212) 354-2400, FAX: (212) 354-5544, E-Mail: info@moret. com, Web Site: www.moret.com (16)

MoreVisibility, Boca Raton, FL. Tel: (561) 620-9682, Web Site: www.morevisibility.com (32)

Morfidis, Erifili, Teleperformance Canada, Toronto, ON Canada. Tel: (416) 922-3519, Web Site: www.teleperformance.ca (35)

Morgan, Alan, Alan Morgan & Associates Inc, Jacksonville, FL. Tel: (904) 262-1316, FAX: (904) 880-6182, E-Mail: amorgan@alanmorgan.com, Web Site: www.alanmorgan.com (29)

Morgan, Bob, Bob Morgan Woodworking Supplies Inc, Westport, KY. Tel: (502) 265-0954, E-Mail: bmorgan@insightbb.com, Web Site: www.morganwood.com (8)

Morgan, Charles, Acxiom Corp, Little Rock, AR. Tel: (501) 342-1000, Web Site: www.acxiom.com (22)

Morgan, David, G., American Society of Civil Engineers, Reston, VA. Tel: (703) 295-6000, (800) 548-2723, FAX: (703) 295-6343, Web Site: www.asce.org (1)

Morgan, Edward, H., Christian Herald Association, New York, NY. Tel: (212) 684-2800, (800) BOWERY-1, FAX: (212) 684-3740, E-Mail: info@chaonline.org, Web Site: www.bowery.org (1)

Morgan, Joe, Standard Register, Dayton, OH. Tel: (937) 221-1000, (800) 755-6405, FAX: (937) 221-1239, E-Mail: julie.mcewan@standardregister.com, Web Site: www.standardregister.com (10)

Morgan, John, Association of Coupon Professionals, Drexel Hill, PA. Tel: (610) 789-1478, FAX: (610) 789-5309, E-Mail: john.morgan@acp-hq.org, Web Site: www.couponpros.org (40)

Morgan, Melanie, Community Food Bank, Tucson, AZ. Tel: (520) 622-0525, Web Site: www.communityfoodbank.org (1)

Morgan, Paul, Nationwide Yellow Pages Service, Hackettstown, NJ. Tel: (973) 765-9600, (800) 526-2718, FAX: (973) 765-0004, E-Mail: info@nationwideyp.com, Web Site: www.nationwideyp.com (35)

Morgan, Robert, ASTM International, West Conshohocken, PA. Tel: (610) 832-9500, FAX: (610) 832-9555, E-Mail: service@astm.org, Web Site: www.astm.org (1)

Morgan, Sue, Lynn, National Court Reporters Association, Vienna, VA. Tel: (703) 556-6272, (800) 272-6272, FAX: (703) 556-6291, E-Mail: msic@ncrahg.org, Web Site: www.ncraonline.org (1)

Morgan, Tim, H., United America Advertising Inc, Enid, OK. Tel: (580) 233-7200, FAX: (580) 548-8432 (29)

Morgan, Tracey, TBC Direct Inc, Baltimore, MD. Tel: (410) 347-7500, FAX: (410) 986-1299, E-Mail: direct@tbc.us, Web Site: www.tbcadv.us (35)

Morgan, Willy, The NonProfit Times, Morris Plains, NJ. Tel: (973) 401-0202, FAX: (973) 401-0404, Web Site: www.nptimes.com (17)

Alan Morgan & Associates Inc, Jacksonville, FL. Tel: (904) 262-1316, FAX: (904) 880-6182, E-Mail: amorgan@alanmorgan.com, Web Site: www.alanmorgan.com (29)

Bob Morgan Woodworking Supplies Inc, Westport, KY. Tel: (502) 265-0954, E-Mail: bmorgan@insightbb.com, Web Site: www.morganwood.com (8)

Morgan Kaufmann Publishers Inc, Burlington, MA. Tel: (781) 313-4700, E-Mail: order@mkp.com, Web Site: www.mkp.com (17)

Morgan Stanley, New York, NY. Tel: (212) 761-4000, FAX: (212) 761-0096 (14)

Morgano, Anthony, American Express Publishing Corp, New York, NY. Tel: (212) 382-5600, (888) 461-6180, FAX: (212) 827-6496, E-Mail: aepc@custmersvc.com, Web Site: www.amexpub.com (17)

Moriarty, Ann, G2 Promotional Marketing, New York, NY. Tel: (212) 537-3700, FAX: (203) 352-0798, Web Site: www.g2pm.com (16)

Morin, Georges, Cossette Communications Group Inc, Quebec, PQ Canada. Tel: (418) 647-2727, FAX: (418) 647-2564, E-Mail: infomaster@cossette.com, Web Site: www.cossette.com (35)

Morin, Matt, Reliable Technologies Inc, Manchester, NH. Tel: (603) 644-2528, (800) 346-7890, FAX: (603) 627-5553, Web Site: www.tei-imaging.com (16)

Morin, Richard, Bell Performance Inc, Longwood, FL. Tel: (407) 831-5021, (800) 659-2355, FAX: (407) 767-8685, E-Mail: info@bellperformance.net, Web Site: www.bellperformance.net (9)

Morio, Jason, ReachForce, Austin, TX. Tel: (512) 327-9000, FAX: (512) 327-9090, E-Mail: info@reachforce.com, Web Site: www.reachforce.com (23)

Morisada, Ikuo, Mitsubishi Digital Electronics America Inc, Irvine, CA. Tel: (949) 465-6000, FAX: (949) 859-4770, Web Site: www.mitsubishi-tv.com (3)

Morishita, Leroy, M., San Francisco State University, San Francisco, CA. Tel: (415) 338-1111, FAX: (415) 338-0501, Web Site: www.sfsu.edu (41)

Moritani, Hitoshi, Noevir Direct Marketing Inc, Montvale, NJ. Tel: (201) 391-0001, (800) 872-8888, FAX: (201) 391-1740, E-Mail: marketing@noevirusa.com, Web Site: www.noevir.com (7)

Moritt, Neil J., Moritt, Hock, Hamroff & Horowitz, Garden City, NY. Tel: (516) 873-2000, FAX: (516) 873-2010, E-Mail: lhauser@morritthock.com, Web Site: www.moritthock.com (16)

Moritt, Hock, Hamroff & Horowitz, Garden City, NY. Tel: (516) 873-2000, FAX: (516) 873-2010, E-Mail: lhauser@morritthock.com, Web Site: www.moritthock.com (16)

Moritz, Joshua, Customer Growth, Blau Moritz Klang Inc, Westport, CT. Tel: (203) 226-8795, FAX: (203) 227-8601, E-Mail: josh.moritz@customer-growth.com, Web Site: www.customer-growth.com (35)

Morkes, Rhonda, Morkes Chocolates, Palatine, IL. Tel: (847) 359-3454, FAX: (847) 359-3553, E-Mail: yummy@morkeschocolates.com, Web Site: www.morkeschocolates.com (4)

Morkes Chocolates, Palatine, IL. Tel: (847) 359-3454, FAX: (847) 359-3553, E-Mail: yummy@morkeschocolates.com, Web Site: www.morkeschocolates.com (4)

Morley Companies, Saginaw, MI. Tel: (989) 791-2550, (800) 336-5554, FAX: (989) 792-1002, E-Mail: info@morleynet.com, Web Site: www.morleynet.com (33)

Morneau, Doug, Rhino Marketing Inc, Los Angeles, CA. Tel: (604) 472-3240, (877) 605-7022, FAX: (604) 637-5619, Web Site: www.rhino.ca (20)

Morningstar, Renee, Campbell Tools Co, Springfield, OH. Tel: (937) 882-6716, FAX: (937) 882-6648, E-Mail: campbell@campbelltools.com, Web Site: www.campbelltools.com (9)

Morningstar Inc, Chicago, IL. Tel: (312) 696-6000, Web Site: www.morningstar.com (14)

Moroney, Richard, Dow Theory Forecasts, Hammond, IN. Tel: (219) 931-6480, (800) 233-5922, FAX: (219) 931-6487, E-Mail: custserv@horizonpublishing.com, Web Site: www.dowtheory.com (17)

Moroz, Michael, DAMARK International Inc, La Salle, IL. Tel: (877) 326-2757, Web Site: www.damark.com (16)

Morpace Inc, Farmington Hills, MI. Tel: (248) 737-5300, FAX: (248) 737-5326, E-Mail: information@morpace.com, Web Site: www.morpace.com (30)

Morphy, Martha, National Archives & Records Administration, College Park, MD. Tel: (301) 837-0482, (86) NARA-NARA, FAX: (301) 837-0483, Web Site: www.archives.gov (17)

Morra, Marion, E., American Cancer Society, Atlanta, GA. Tel: (404) 471-5852, (800) ACS-2345, FAX: (404) 982-3677, Web Site: www.cancer.org (1)

Morra, Vincent, Whitaker National, Huntington, WV. Tel: (304) 525-0852, (800) 377-8721, FAX: (304) 525-0874, Web Site: www.neshold.com (16)

Morrell, Allen, Simmons-Boardman Publishing Corp, New York, NY. Tel: (212) 620-7200, FAX: (212) 633-1165 (17)

Morris IV, William, S., Morris Communications Corp, Augusta, GA. Tel: (706) 724-0851, FAX: (706) 722-0011, Web Site: www.morris.com (31)

Morris, Angela, M., Hamilton Contact Center Services, Aurora, NE. Tel: (402) 694-4343, (800) 972-3237, FAX: (402) 694-4433, Web Site: www.hamiltontm.com (29)

Morris, Angela, Quality Contact Solutions Inc, Aurora, NE. Tel: (402) 210-2692, (866) 963-2889, FAX: (402) 210-2692, E-Mail: info@qualitycontactsolutions.com, Web Site: www.qualitycontactsolutions.com (29)

Morris, Bill, American Teleservices Association, Indianapolis, IN. Tel: (317) 816-9336, (877) 779-3974, FAX: (317) 218-0323, Web Site: www.ataconnect.org (40)

Morris, Brad, Morris Group Inc, Windsor, CT. Tel: (860) 687-3475, FAX: (860) 687-3476, E-Mail: jmorris_lee@morris-lee.com, Web Site: www.morrisgroupinc.com (35)

Morris, Cheri, Morris & Fellows, Atlanta, GA. Tel: (404) 250-0225 (20)

Morris, Dianne, The Sperry & Hutchinson Co Inc, Delray Beach, FL. Tel: (561) 454-7621, FAX: (561) 265-2493, E-Mail: mediarelations@shsolutions.com, Web Site: www.greenpoints.com (6)

Morris, Donna, Adobe Systems Inc, San Jose, CA. Tel: (408) 536-6000, (800) 833-6687, FAX: (408) 537-6000, Web Site: www.adobe.com (22)

Morris, Doug, Vivendi, New York, NY. Tel: (212) 572-7000, FAX: (212) 572-1080, Web Site: www.vivendi.com (16)

Morris, Dwight A., Carrot-Top Industries Inc, Hillsborough, NC. Tel: (919) 732-6200, (800) 628-3524, FAX: (919) 732-5526, E-Mail: service@carrot-top.com, Web Site: www.carrot-top.com (16)

Morris, Greg, Millions By Marketing Inc, Mendham, NJ. Tel: (973) 222-0011, Web Site: www.millionsbymarketing.com (22)

Morris, Harvey, Chicago Convention & Tourism Bureau, Chicago, IL. Tel: (312) 567-8500, Web Site: www.choosechicago.com (1)

Morris, James, Direct Marketing Designs Inc, Greenwood Village, CO. Tel: (303) 649-9888, FAX: (303) 649-1917, E-Mail: info@directmarketingdesigns.com, Web Site: www.directmarketingdesigns.com (35)

Morris, Janet, Ranger Joe's International Military Supply, Columbus, GA. Tel: (706) 689-0082, (800) 247-4541, FAX: (706) 682-8840, E-Mail: customerservice@rangerjoes.com, Web Site: www.rangerjoes.com (2)

Morris, Jeff, New Hampshire Public Television, Durham, NH. Tel: (603) 868-1100, E-Mail: themailbox@nhptv.org, Web Site: www.nhptv.org (32)

Morris, John, Bass Pro Shops, Springfield, MO. Tel: (417) 873-5000, FAX: (417) 873-5882, Web Site: www.basspro.com (11)

Morris, Kevin, The Pond-Ekberg Co, Chicopee, MA. Tel: (413) 594-7511, (800) 225-7511, FAX: (413) 594-2179, E-Mail: sales@pond-ekberg.com, Web Site: www.pondekberg.com (27)

Morris, Larry, Bontex, Honolulu, HI. Tel: (540) 261-2181, FAX: (540) 261-3784, E-Mail: bontex@bontex.com, Web Site: www.bontex.com (16)

Morris, Liz, Polo Ralph Lauren, Lyndhurst, NJ. Tel: (212) 531-6537, (800) 377-7656, FAX: (212) 318-7690, Web Site: www.ralphlauren.com (2)

Morris, Rick, CCI Digital, Burbank, CA. Tel: (818) 562-6300, FAX: (818) 562-8222, Web Site: www.ccidigital.com (32)

Morris, Shawn, National Auto Warranty, Wentzville, MO. Tel: (800) 649-1620 (16)

Morris, Steve, Advanstar Communications Inc, North Olmstead, OH. Tel: (440) 243-8100, (800) 225-4569, FAX: (440) 891-2740, E-Mail: info@advanstar.com, Web Site: www.advanstarlists.com (17)

Morris, Steve, The Arbitron Co, New York, NY. Tel: (212) 887-1314, FAX: (212) 887-1558, Web Site: www.arbitron.com (30)

Morris, Thomas, E., TWL Knowledge Group, Carrollton, TX. Tel: (972) 309-4000, (800) 624-2272, FAX: (972) 309-5105, Web Site: www.twlk.com (3)

Morris, Thomas, W., The Cleveland Orchestra, Cleveland, OH. Tel: (216) 231-7441, FAX: (216) 231-4038, Web Site: www.clevelandorchestra.com (1)

Morris, Tom, Stile-Tile Like Metal Roofing, Sellersburg, IN. Tel: (812) 246-1866, (800) 999-7777, FAX: (800) 477-9318, (800) 944-6884, Web Site: www.mtsales.com (9)

Morris & Fellows, Atlanta, GA. Tel: (404) 250-0225 (20)

Morris Communications Corp, Augusta, GA. Tel: (706) 724-0851, FAX: (706) 722-0011, Web Site: www.morris.com (31)

Morris Group Inc, Windsor, CT. Tel: (860) 687-3475, FAX: (860) 687-3476, E-Mail: jmorris_lee@morris-lee.com, Web Site: www.morrisgroupinc.com (35)

Morris James Hitchens & Williams, Wilmington, DE. Tel: (302) 888-6800, FAX: (302) 571-1750, Web Site: www.morrisjames.com (20)

Morris Visitors Publications LLC, Augusta, GA. Tel: (305) 892-6644, FAX: (305) 892-1005, E-Mail: mvpcustomerservice@morris.com, Web Site: www.morrisvisitorpublications.com (17)

Morrison, Andrew, RFM Broadcasting, New Rochelle, NY. Tel: (914) 633-0725, FAX: (914) 206-4144, E-Mail: andrew@rfmitv.com (35)

Morrison, James G., Association of Marian Helpers, Stockbridge, MA. Tel: (413) 298-3691, Web Site: www.marian.org (1)

Morrison, Ken, P., Doane, Saint Louis, MO. Tel: (314) 569-2700, (866) 647-0918, FAX: (314) 569-1083, Web Site: www.doane.com (17)

Morrison, Lindsay, H, SRDS, Des Plaines, IL. Tel: (800) 851-7737, FAX: (847) 375-5001, Web Site: www.srds.com (17)

Morrison, Patricia, B., Motorola Inc, Montvale, NJ. Tel: (201) 949-5500, (800) 262-8509, Web Site: www.motorola.com (16)

Morrison, Robert, S., The Quaker Oats Co, Chicago, IL. Tel: (312) 821-1000, (800) 367-6287, FAX: (312) 222-8323, Web Site: www.quakeroats.com (16)

Morrison, Sylvia, Cleveland Clinic Foundation, Cleveland, OH. Tel: (216) 444-2200, Web Site: www.clevelandclinic.org (1)

Morrison Printing Co, Morristown, TN. Tel: (423) 586-4812, (800) 251-0975, FAX: (423) 586-0322, E-Mail: info@morrcom.com, Web Site: www.morrcom.com (27)

Morrissey, Raymond, Franciscan Friars of the Atonement - Graymoor, Garrison, NY. Tel: (845) 424-3671, FAX: (845) 424-2168, E-Mail: info@atonementfriars.org, Web Site: www.atonementfriars.org (1)

Morrow, Barry, Alitalia, New York, NY. Tel: (800) 223-5730, FAX: (212) 903-3568, E-Mail: customer.relationsnyc@alitalia.it, Web Site: www.alitalia.com (19)

Morrow, Bill, Crain Communications Inc, Detroit, MI. Tel: (313) 446-6000, FAX: (313) 446-1616, Web Site: www.crain.com (17)

Morrow, Christopher, Christopher Morrow Photography, Port Saint Lucie, FL. Tel: (845) 325-1233, E-Mail: chris@chrismorrow.com, Web Site: www.chrismorrow.com (37)

Morrow, Elizabeth, Diamondback Direct - a Dmh Marketing Partners Co, Severna Park, MD. Tel: (410) 975-0001, Web Site: www.diamondbackdirect.com (35)

Morrow, Joel, Mobile Fusion, Lakewood, CO. Tel: (720) 963-8000, (800) 431-8556, Web Site: www.mobile-fusion.com (16)

Morrow, Kris, Diversified Graphics Inc, Minneapolis, MN. Tel: (800) 233-7454, FAX: (612) 331-4079, Web Site: www.dgi.net (21)

Morrow, Teri, Appalachian Mountain Club, Boston, MA. Tel: (617) 523-0655, Web Site: www.outdoors.com (1)

Christopher Morrow Photography, Port Saint Lucie, FL. Tel: (845) 325-1233, E-Mail: chris@chrismorrow.com, Web Site: www.chrismorrow.com (37)

Morrows, Bruce, Skypoint Communications Inc, Loretto, MN. Tel: (763) 548-2600, FAX: (763) 548-2610, E-Mail: info@skypoint.com, Web Site: www.skypoint.com (16)

Morse, David, New American Dimensions, Los Angeles, CA. Tel: (310) 670-6800 (20)

Morse, Larry, Quill Corp, Palatine, IL. Tel: (847) 634-4800, (800) 789-1331, FAX: (800) 789-6630, Web Site: www.quill.com (16)

Morse, Stephen, Copper Art by Morse, Claremont, NH. Tel: (603) 542-2324 (8)

Morten, James, E., Interprint Web & Sheetfed, Clearwater, FL. Tel: (727) 531-8957, (800) 749-5152, FAX: (727) 536-0647, E-Mail: customerservice@printerusa.com, Web Site: www.printerusa.com (27)

Mortimer Spiller Co Inc, Buffalo, NY. Tel: (716) 834-0860 (33)

Mortland, Shirley, A., Hitchcock Shoes Inc, Hingham, MA. Tel: (781) 749-3260, (888) 599-9433, FAX: (781) 749-3576, E-Mail: hitchcock@wideshoes.com, Web Site: www.wideshoes.com (2)

Morton, Larry, Hal Leonard Corp, Milwaukee, WI. Tel: (414) 774-3630, FAX: (414) 774-3259, Web Site: www.halleonard.com (17)

Morton, Mark, The Newman Group, Ann Arbor, MI. Tel: (734) 426-3200, FAX: (734) 426-0777, E-Mail: anewman@newman.com (3)

Morton, Sue, Data Dash Inc, Saint Louis, MO. Tel: (314) 832-5788, (800) 211-5988, FAX: (314) 832-5775, E-Mail: info@datadash.com, Web Site: www.datadash.com (22)

Morton Advertising Inc, New York, NY. Tel: (212) 465-2250, FAX: (212) 465-1575, E-Mail: don@mortonad.com, Web Site: www.mortonad.com (35)

The Morton Arboretum, Lisle, IL. Tel: (630) 968-0074, Web Site: www.mortonarb.org (1)

The Jack Morton Co, Chicago, IL. Tel: (312) 274-6060, FAX: (312) 274-6061, E-Mail: experience@jackmorton.com, Web Site: www.jackmorton.com (35)

Mosbacher Jr., Robert, Overseas Private Investment Corp (OPIC), Washington, DC. Tel: (202) 336-8400, FAX: (202) 336-7949, E-Mail: info@opic.gov, Web Site: www.opic.gov (14)

Moscetti, Franco, Miracle Ear, Minneapolis, MN. Tel: (877) 268-4264, FAX: (763) 268-4365, Web Site: www.miracle-ear.com (16)

Moser, Dave, Perfect Plastic Printing Corp, Saint Charles, IL. Tel: (630) 584-1600, FAX: (630) 584-0648, E-Mail: ppp@perfectplastic.com, Web Site: www.perfectplastic.com (27)

Thomas Moser Cabinetmakers, Freeport, ME. Tel: (207) 865-4519, (800) 708-9041, FAX: (207) 865-6539, E-Mail: freeportshowroom@thosmoser.com, Web Site: www.thosmoser.com (16)

Moses, James, Elderhostel Inc, Boston, MA. Tel: (617) 426-7788, (800) 454-5678, FAX: (617) 426-2166, Web Site: www.elderhostel.org (1)

Mosher, Adam, Tuttle, Wallingford, CT. Tel: (203) 949-4290, (800) 882-7511, FAX: (203) 949-4288, Web Site: www.tuttlecatalog.com (2)

Mosher, Ben, Tuttle, Wallingford, CT. Tel: (203) 949-4290, (800) 882-7511, FAX: (203) 949-4288, Web Site: www.tuttlecatalog.com (2)

Mosher, Fred, Associated Photo, Florence, KY. Tel: (859) 344-1460, (800) 727-2580, FAX: (859) 282-0032 (16)

Mosher, George, Alfax Wholesale Furniture Inc, Farmers Branch, TX. Tel: (212) 947-9560, (800) 221-5710, FAX: (212) 947-4734, Web Site: www.alfaxfurniture.com (33)

Mosier, Andrew, Mead Johnson Co, Evansville, IN. Tel: (812) 429-5204, Web Site: www.MeadJohnson.com (7)

Mosinski, Joseph, National Foundation for Cancer Research, Bethesda, MD. Tel: (301) 654-1250, (800) 321-CURE, FAX: (301) 654-5824, E-Mail: info@nfcr.org, Web Site: www.nfcr.org (1)

Moskowitz, Paul, Pizza Hut Inc, Plano, TX. Tel: (972) 338-7700, (866) 298-6986, FAX: (972) 338-6869, Web Site: www.pizzahut.com (16)

Mosley, Ben, Bencone Uniform Connection, Winston Salem, NC. Tel: (800) 326-3261, FAX: (866) 311-8254, E-Mail: bencone1@bellsouth.net, Web Site: www.bencone.com (2)

Mosley, John, Sheplers Catalog Sales Inc, Wichita, KS. Tel: (316) 946-3838, (800) 835-4004, FAX: (316) 946-3729, Web Site: www.sheplers.com (2)

Mosley, Sanders, Bencone Uniform Connection, Winston Salem, NC. Tel: (800) 326-3261, FAX: (866) 311-8254, E-Mail: bencone1@bellsouth.net, Web Site: www.bencone.com (2)

Mosley, Troy, Sportsmith LLC, Tulsa, OK. Tel: (918) 307-2446, Web Site: www.sportsmith.net (11)

Moss, Bryan, Gulfstream Aircraft Inc, Savannah, GA. Tel: (912) 965-5300, FAX: (912) 965-3775, E-Mail: info@gulfstream.com, Web Site: www.gulfstream.com (16)

Moss, Danny, Greater Fort Worth Builders Association, Fort Worth, TX. Tel: (817) 284-3566, FAX: (817) 284-6465, E-Mail: info@fortworthbuilders.org, Web Site: www.forthworthbuilders.org (1)

Moss, Susan, FireFly, Honolulu, HI. Tel: (808) 545-2122, FAX: (808) 535-1655, Web Site: www.fireflyhawaii.com (21)

Moss, Will, Four Star Marketing Inc, Lincolnwood, IL. Tel: (800) 888-2991, FAX: (847) 679-6449, E-Mail: sales@conventionbags.com, Web Site: www.conventionbags.com (33)

Mosses, Michael, Community Newspaper Co, Needham, MA. Tel: (781) 433-6700, FAX: (781) 433-6701, E-Mail: customerservice@cnc.com, Web Site: www.nvo.com/communitynews (21)

Mostad, Arvid, Mostad & Christensen, Oak Harbor, WA. Tel: (360) 679-4164, (800) 654-1654, FAX: (360) 679-4167, E-Mail: marketing@mostad.com, Web Site: www.mostad.com (16)

Mostad & Christensen, Oak Harbor, WA. Tel: (360) 679-4164, (800) 654-1654, FAX: (360) 679-4167, E-Mail: marketing@mostad.com, Web Site: www.mostad.com (16)

Mosterion, Kiki, Argent Trading LLC, New York, NY. Tel: (212) 697-8800, FAX: (212) 697-8606, Web Site: www.Argenttrading.com (16)

Motameni, Dr. Reza, California State University at Fresno, Fresno, CA. Tel: (559) 278-7830, FAX: (559) 278-8577, Web Site: www.csufresno.edu (41)

Mother Earth News Magazine, Topeka, KS. Tel: (785) 274-4300, (800) 678-5779, FAX: (785) 274-4305, E-Mail: bwelch@ogdenpubs.com, Web Site: www.cappers.com (17)

Mother Jones Magazine, San Francisco, CA. Tel: (415) 321-1700, Web Site: www.motherjones.com (17)

Motherhead, Ivan, UMI Publications Inc, Charlotte, NC. Tel: (800) 747-9287, FAX: (704) 374-0729, E-Mail: info@umipub.com, Web Site: www.umipub.com (17)

Motherwear, Holyoke, MA. Tel: (413) 586-1978, (800) 950-2500, FAX: (413) 532-4058, E-Mail: customerservice@motherwear.com, Web Site: www.motherwear.com (2)

Motient Communications, Reston, VA. Tel: (847) 478-4330, (800) 752-2672, FAX: (703) 758-6111 (16)

Motion Picture & Television Fund Foundation, Woodland Hills, CA. Tel: (818) 876-1888, Web Site: www.mptvfund.org (1)

The Motivation Show, Westmont, IL. Tel: (630) 434-7779, (800) 752-6312, FAX: (630) 434-1216, E-Mail: moti@heiexpo.com, Web Site: www.motivationshow.com (42)

The Motley Fool, Alexandria, VA. FAX: (703) 254-1999, E-Mail: cs@fool.com, Web Site: www.Fool.com (14)

Moto, Nick, Hazelden, Center City, MN. Tel: (651) 213-4200, (800) 257-7810, FAX: (651) 213-4411, E-Mail: info@hazelden.org, Web Site: www.hazelden.org (7)

Moto Franchise Corp, Dayton, OH. Tel: (937) 291-1900, (800) 733-6686, FAX: (937) 291-2005, E-Mail: expert@motophoto.com, Web Site: www.motophoto.com; www.portraitavenue.com (3)

Motor Coach Industries International Inc, Schaumburg, IL. Tel: (847) 285-2000, (800) 624-2622, Web Site: www.mcicoach.com (16)

Motorola Inc, Montvale, NJ. Tel: (201) 949-5500, (800) 262-8509, Web Site: www.motorola.com (16)

Motown Records, New York, NY. Tel: (212) 373-0750, FAX: (212) 489-9096, Web Site: www.motown.com (3)

Mott, Eric, Lyris Inc, Emeryville, CA. Tel: (510) 844-1551, (800) 768-2929, FAX: (510) 844-1598, E-Mail: sales@lyris.com, Web Site: www.lyris.com (32)

Mott, Joyce, L., Fathers of St Edmund Southern Missions Inc, Selma, AL. Tel: (334) 872-2359, FAX: (334) 875-8189, E-Mail: jm1428@aol.com, Web Site: www.edmunditemissions.org (1)

Mott, Randall, D., Hewlett-Packard Co, Palo Alto, CA. Tel: (650) 857-1501, (800) 752-0900, FAX: (650) 857-5518, Web Site: www.hp.com (16)

Mott Media LLC, Fenton, MI. Tel: (810) 714-4280, FAX: (810) 714-2077, E-Mail: info@mottmedia.com, Web Site: www.mottmedia.com (17)

Motta, Sharon, Management Science Associates Inc, Pittsburgh, PA. Tel: (412) 362-2000, (800) MSA-INFO, FAX: (412) 363-5598, E-Mail: info@msa.com, Web Site: www.msa.com (20)

Moulton, Garth, Jigsaw, San Mateo, CA. Tel: (650) 235-8400, Web Site: www.jigsaw.com (24)

Moultrie, Armida, Ross Metals, New York, NY. Tel: (212) 869-1407, (800) 654-ROSS (16)

Moultrie Manufacturing Co, Moultrie, GA. Tel: (229) 985-1312, (800) 841-8674, FAX: (229) 890-7245, Web Site: www.moultriemanufacturing.com (8)

Mount, Clyde, 3PL Worldwide Inc, Milford, CT. Tel: (203) 567-1099, Web Site: www.3plworldwide.com (28)

Mount, Portia, Center for Creative Leadership, Greensboro, NC. Tel: (336) 545-2810, FAX: (336) 282-3284, E-Mail: info@ccl.org, Web Site: www.ccl.org (16)

Mount, Tenny, Eagle Claw Fishing Tackle, Denver, CO. Tel: (303) 321-1481, FAX: (303) 321-4750, E-Mail: info@eagleclaw.com, Web Site: www.eagleclaw.com (11)

Mountain Craft Shop Co, Proctor, WV. Tel: (304) 455-3570, (877) 365-5869, (800) FOLK-TOY, FAX: (304) 455-1740, (866) FOLK-TOY, E-Mail: info@folktoys.com, Web Site: www.folktoys.com (11)

Mountain Press Publishing Co, Missoula, MT. Tel: (406) 728-1900, (800) 234-5308, FAX: (406) 728-1635, E-Mail: info@mtnpress.com, Web Site: www.mountain-press.com (17)

Mountain West Communications Inc, Hotchkiss, CO. Tel: (970) 872-2500, (800) 642-9378, FAX: (970) 872-3862, E-Mail: sales@mountainwest.com, Web Site: www.mountainwest.com (29)

Mountain West Supply Co, Scottsdale, AZ. Tel: (602) 971-1200, (800) 528-6169, FAX: (602) 996-5077 (3)

Moura, Ed, Course Technology, Boston, MA. Tel: (617) 757-7900, (800) 648-7450, (800) 354-9706, FAX: (617) 487-8488, E-Mail: ed.moura@cengage.com, Web Site: www.course.com (31)

Mouring, Veronica, AEGON Direct Marketing Services Inc, Baltimore, MD. Tel: (410) 209-5617, FAX: (410) 209-5932, Web Site: www.aegondms.com (15)

Mouse, Chris, Burger's Ozark Country Cured Hams Inc, California, MO. Tel: (573) 796-3134, (800) 345-5185, FAX: (573) 796-3137, E-Mail: burgers@smokehouse.com, Web Site: www.smokehouse.com (4)

Moussavi, Michele, KXEN, San Francisco, CA. Tel: (415) 904-4160, Web Site: www.kxen.com (22)

Mousseau, Bradley, PC Connection, Merrimack, NH. Tel: (603) 683-2167, (800) 800-0014, FAX: (603) 683-5773, E-Mail: pr@pcconnection.com, Web Site: www.pcconnection.com, macconnection.com (22)

Mousseau, Heather, Winnipeg Art Gallery, Winnipeg, MB Canada. Tel: (204) 786-6641, FAX: (204) 788-4998, E-Mail: inquiries@wag.mb.ca, Web Site: www.wag.mb.ca (1)

Mouw, Richard, W., The Fuller Theological Seminary, Pasadena, CA. Tel: (626) 584-5200, (800) 2-FULLER, FAX: (626) 584-5449, Web Site: www.fuller.edu/cll (16)

Mouzakis, Andrea, Reed Smith Hall Dickler Advertising & Law Marketing Group, New York, NY. Tel: (212) 549-0377, FAX: (212) 521-5450, Web Site: www.reedsmith.com (20)

Movada Media Inc, Winnipeg, MB Canada. Tel: (204) 284-9000, Web Site: www.movadamedia.com (5)

Movie Central, Toronto, ON Canada. Tel: (416) 479-6784, E-Mail: info@moviecentral.ca, Web Site: www.moviecentral.ca (32)

Movie/Entertainment Book Club, Washington, DC. Tel: (800) 879-3270, FAX: (202) 216-0614, E-Mail: meb@eaglepub.com (13)

Mowell, Larry, Cotta Transmission Co, Beloit, WI. Tel: (608) 368-5600, FAX: (608) 368-5605, E-Mail: sales@cotta.com, Web Site: www.cotta.com (16)

Mowen, Ginny, Red Hill Corp, Gettysburg, PA. Tel: (717) 337-3038, (800) 822-4003, FAX: (717) 337-0732, E-Mail: custserv@supergrit.com, Web Site: www.supergrit.com (34)

Mower, Eric, Eric Mower & Associates, Rochester, NY. Tel: (585) 385-2000, Web Site: www.mower.com (35)

Mower & Associates, Charlotte, NC. Tel: (704) 375-0123, FAX: (704) 375-0222, Web Site: www.mower.com (35)

Eric Mower & Associates, Rochester, NY. Tel: (585) 385-2000, Web Site: www.mower.com (35)

Mowrey-Reise, Mary, Bethesda List Center Inc, Bethesda, MD. Tel: (301) 986-1455, FAX: (301) 907-4870, E-Mail: info@bethesda-list.com, Web Site: www.bethesda-list.com (24)

Moyen, Luc, Brocade Communications Systems Inc, San Jose, CA. Tel: (408) 333-4300, FAX: (408) 333-8101, Web Site: www.brocade.com (16)

Moyer, Barry, Litho-Web Inc, Etobicoke, ON Canada. Tel: (416) 674-8899, (800) 490-6688, FAX: (416) 674-8537, E-Mail: inquiry@lithoweb.ca, Web Site: www.lithoweb.ca (27)

Moyer, Bruce, Direct Marketing Association of Detroit, Royal Oak, MI. Tel: (248) 478-4888, FAX: (248) 478-6437, E-Mail: dmad@ameritech.net, Web Site: www.dmad.org (40)

Moyer, Bruce, S., Directions Marketing, Ann Arbor, MI. Tel: (734) 930-2820, FAX: (734) 930-9189, E-Mail: directions@directions.com.eg, Web Site: www.directions.com.eg (20)

Moyer, Chuck, Conney Safety Products LLC, Madison, WI. Tel: (608) 271-3300, (800) 356-9100, FAX: (608) 271-3322, (800) 845-9095, E-Mail: safety@conney.com, Web Site: www.conney.com (7)

Moyer, Louise, Penske Logistics, Reading, PA. Tel: (610) 775-6000, (800) 529-6531, FAX: (610) 775-6432, Web Site: www.penskelogistics.com (16)

Moyer, Mark, D., Ziff Davis Media Inc, New York, NY. Tel: (212) 503-5100, FAX: (212) 503-5023, Web Site: www.ziffdavis.com (17)

Moyer, Todd, Trump Marina Hotel & Casino, Atlantic City, NJ. Tel: (609) 441-2000, FAX: (609) 340-5107, Web Site: www.trumpmarina.com (19)

Moyinhan, Thomas, F., Brookstone Co, Merrimack, NH. Tel: (603) 880-9500, (800) 846-3000, FAX: (603) 577-8005, E-Mail: customerservice@brookstone.com, Web Site: www.brookstone.com (3)

Moylan, John, J., Golden Gate Transportation District, San Rafael, CA. Tel: (415) 921-5858, FAX: (415) 923-2014, Web Site: www.goldengate.org (16)

Moyle, Shep, Shindigz, South Whitley, IN. Tel: (219) 723-5171, (800) 314-8736, FAX: (219) 723-6976, E-Mail: csr@shindigz.com, Web Site: www.shindigz.com (27)

Moyle, Wendy, Shindigz, South Whitley, IN. Tel: (219) 723-5171, (800) 314-8736, FAX: (219) 723-6976, E-Mail: csr@shindigz.com, Web Site: www.shindigz.com (27)

Moynier, Bob, Keystone Press Agency Inc, Montreal, PQ Canada. Tel: (514) 482-5312, (877) 482-5312, FAX: (514) 483-9005, E-Mail: pictures@keystonepressagency.com, Web Site: www.ketstonepressagency.com (38)

Mozillo, Angelo R., Countrywide Financial Corp, Calabasas, CA. Tel: (818) 225-3000, FAX: (818) 225-4051, Web Site: www.countrywide.com (14)

Mrs Beasley's & Miss Grace Lemon Cake Co, Los Angeles, CA. Tel: (800) 710-7742, FAX: (310) 668-2148, E-Mail: general@mrsbeasleys.com, Web Site: www.mrsbeasleys.com (4)

MSC Metalworking, Melville, NY. Tel: (516) 812-2000, (800) 521-9520, E-Mail: inquiry@rutlandtool.com, Web Site: www.rutlandtool.com (34)

MSW Research, Lake Success, NY. Tel: (516) 394-6000, FAX: (516) 394-6001, E-Mail: mail@mswresearch.com, Web Site: www.mswresearch.com (30)

MTV Networks, New York, NY. Tel: (212) 258-8000, FAX: (212) 258-8100, Web Site: www.mtv.com (32)

Mucci, Robert, A., NGL Insurance Group, Madison, WI. Tel: (608) 257-5611, (800) 548-2962, FAX: (608) 257-9340, Web Site: www.nationalguardian.com (15)

Muckler, Jeff, Direct Logic Solutions, Peoria, IL. Tel: (309) 688-5500, FAX: (309) 688-5502, E-Mail: nedbarrett@direct-logic.com, Web Site: www.direct-logic.com (22)

Mudd, Daniel, H., Fannie Mae, Washington, DC. Tel: (202) 752-7000, FAX: (202) 752-3808, Web Site: www.fanniemae.com (14)

Mudditt, Alison, Academy of Marketing Science Journal, Thousand Oaks, CA. Tel: (805) 499-0721, FAX: (800) 583-2665, (805) 499-0871, Web Site: www.sagepub.com (43)

Mudge, Chris, Customized Newspaper Advertising, Des Moines, IA. Tel: (515) 244-2145, (800) 227-7636, FAX: (515) 244-4855, Web Site: www.cnaads.com (18)

Muehl, Bob, Husky Envelope Products, Walled Lake, MI. Tel: (248) 624-7070, FAX: (248) 624-5990, E-Mail: bmuehl@huskyenvelope.com, Web Site: www.huskyenvelope.com (26)

Mueke, Diane, Seastrom Manufacturing Co Inc, Twin Falls, ID. Tel: (208) 737-4300, (800) 634-2356, FAX: (208) 734-7222, E-Mail: info@seastrom-mfg.com, Web Site: www.seastrom-mfg.com (3)

Mueller, Carol, Duluth Trading Co Inc, Belleville, WI. Tel: (800) 505-8888, FAX: (888) 950-3199, E-Mail: customerservice@duluthtrading.com, Web Site: www.duluthtrading.com (8)

Mueller, Eduard R., Qwest, Denver, CO. Tel: (303) 992-1400, (800) 603-6000, FAX: (303) 896-8515, Web Site: www.qwest.com (20)

Mueller, Joan, Brush Fire, Cedar Knolls, NJ. Tel: (973) 871-1700, FAX: (973) 871-1717, Web Site: www.brushfireinc.com (35)

Mueller, Lee, Coyne American Institute, Chicago, IL. Tel: (773) 935-2520, (800) 999-5220, FAX: (773) 935-2920, Web Site: www.coyneamerican.edu (16)

Mueller, Leo, SunPorch Structures Inc, Westport, CT. Tel: (203) 454-0040, (866) 919-9620, FAX: (203) 454-0020, E-Mail: leo@sunporch.com, Web Site: www.sunporch.com (8)

Mueller, Michael, Triangle Printers Inc, Skokie, IL. Tel: (847) 675-3700, FAX: (847) 674-1230, E-Mail: blevin@triangleprinters.com, Web Site: www.triangleprinters.com (27)

Mueller, Roger, P., RPM Industries Inc, Auburn, NY. Tel: (315) 255-1105, (800) 669-3676, FAX: (315) 252-1167, Web Site: www.rpmdisplays.com (33)

Mueller, Stacy, The Missoulian, Missoula, MT. Tel: (406) 523-5334, FAX: (406) 523-5221, Web Site: www.missoulian.com (31)

Mueller, Stephanie, Demco Inc, Madison, WI. Tel: (608) 241-1201, FAX: (608) 241-1799, E-Mail: custserv@demco.com, Web Site: www.demco.com (10)

Mufflin, Mark, Diversified Investment Advisors, Harrison, NY. Tel: (914) 697-8967, FAX: (914) 697-3743, Web Site: www.divinvest.com (14)

Muir, Bob, Chase Industries, Inc, Cincinnati, OH. Tel: (513) 860-5565, (800) 543-4455, FAX: (800) 245-7045, Web Site: www.chasedoors.com (16)

Muir, Stan, Harland Financial Solutions Inc, Lake Mary, FL. Tel: (407) 804-6600, (800) 815-5592, FAX: (407) 829-6702, Web Site: www.harlandfinancialsolutions.com (16)

Muir, William, F., GMAC Insurance, Atlanta, GA. Tel: (314) 493-8000, (800) GMAC-123, FAX: (314) 493-8114, Web Site: www.gmacinsurance.com (15)

Muirheid, Willard, Tower Hobbies/Hobbico, Champaign, IL. Tel: (217) 398-3636, (800) 637-6050, FAX: (217) 398-1104, Web Site: www.towerhobbies.com (11)

Mukai, Akira, Isuzu Motors America Inc, Anaheim, CA. Tel: (562) 229-5000, (800) 255-6727, FAX: (562) 229-5463, Web Site: www.isuzu.com (16)

Mulally, Alan, Ford Motor Co, Dearborn, MI. Tel: (313) 845-8540, (800) 555-5259, FAX: (313) 845-6073, Web Site: www.ford.com (16)

Mulcahy, J., Patrick, Energizer Battery Co Inc, Saint Louis, MO. Tel: (314) 985-2000, (800) 383-7323, FAX: (636) 733-4001, Web Site: www.energizer.com (16)

Mulcahy, Kathleen, Promotion Marketing Association (PMA) Inc, New York, NY. Tel: (212) 420-1100, FAX: (212) 533-7622, E-Mail: pma@pmalink.org, Web Site: www.pmalink.org (1)

Mulder, Don, Anritsu Co, Morgan Hill, CA. Tel: (408) 778-2000, (800) 267-4878, FAX: (408) 776-1744, Web Site: www.us.anritsu.com (16)

Muldoon, Katie, Muldoon & Baer Inc, Palm Beach Gardens, FL. Tel: (561) 630-0999, FAX: (561) 630-9466, Web Site: www.muldoonandbaer.com (20)

Muldoon & Baer Inc, Palm Beach Gardens, FL. Tel: (561) 630-0999, FAX: (561) 630-9466, Web Site: www.muldoonandbaer.com (20)

Mule, Ann C., Sunoco, Inc, Philadelphia, PA. Tel: (215) 977-3000, (800) 786-6261, FAX: (215) 977-3409, E-Mail: sunoco_online@sunoil.com, Web Site: www.sunocoinc.com (16)

Mulherin, Pat, KEH.com, Smyrna, GA. Tel: (770) 333-4200, (800) 342-5534, FAX: (770) 333-4242, E-Mail: sales@keh.com, Web Site: www.keh.com (16)

Mull, Dennis, Fujitsu Computer Systems, Sunnyvale, CA. Tel: (408) 746-6000, (800) 538-8460, FAX: (408) 992-2674, E-Mail: solutions@us.fujitsu.com, Web Site: www.fujitsu.com (22)

Mullan, June, Hofstra University, Hempstead, NY. Tel: (516) 463-7200, FAX: (516) 463-4833, E-Mail: ccepa@hofstra.edu, Web Site: ccepa.hofstra.edu (41)

Mullaney, Amber, Jefferson National, Louisville, KY. Tel: (502) 587-3853, Web Site: www.jeffnat.com (14)

Mullen, Jennifer, INPEX, Pittsburgh, PA. Tel: (412) 288-1343, (412) 288-1300, (888) 544-6739, (888) 54-INPEX, FAX: (412) 288-4546, E-Mail: info@inpex.com, Web Site: www.inpex.com (42)

Mullen, Joan, Creative Compliance, Chicago, IL. Tel: (916) 216-3379, E-Mail: info@creativecompliance.com, Web Site: www.creativecompliance.com (29)

Mullen, Micah, Jerry's Artarama, Raleigh, NC. Tel: (919) 878-8478, (800) U-ARTIST, FAX: (919) 873-9565, E-Mail: micah@jerrysartarama.com, Web Site: www.jerrysartarama.com (10)

Mullen, Tracy, National Retail Federation Inc, Washington, DC. Tel: (202) 783-7971, (800) 673-4692, FAX: (202) 737-2849, E-Mail: webmaster@nrf.com, Web Site: www.nrf.com (1)

Mullen, Boston, MA. Tel: (978) 468-1155, Web Site: www.mullen.com (35)

Mullen & McCaffrey Direct Response, East Hampton, NY. Tel: (631) 324-4265, FAX: (631) 324-2135, E-Mail: mullenmccaffrey@aol.com, Web Site: www.mullenandmccaffrey.com (35)

Muller, Fred, Card Technology Inc, Hopkins, MN. Tel: (201) 845-7373, FAX: (201) 845-3337, E-Mail: info@nbstech.com, Web Site: www.nbstech.com (16)

Mullis, Jeff, e-Pipeconnection, Evansville, IN. Tel: (812) 474-4529, (800) 262-4300, FAX: (812) 474-4531, E-Mail: sales@e-pipeconnection.com, Web Site: www.e-pipeconnection.com (9)

Mullis, Rick, Aristokraft Inc, Jasper, IN. Tel: (812) 482-2527, FAX: (812) 482-9872, Web Site: www.aristokraft.com (16)

Mulloy, Gary, ADVO Inc, Windsor, CT. Tel: (860) 285-6100, FAX: (860) 285-1567, Web Site: www.advo.com (21)

Multi-Level Marketing International Association (MLMIA), Irvine, CA. Tel: (949) 854-0484, FAX: (949) 854-7687, E-Mail: info@mlmia.com, Web Site: www.mlmia.com/ (1)

Multi-Media Publishing & Packaging Inc, Panorama City, CA. Tel: (818) 341-7484, (800) 982-8138, FAX: (818) 341-2807, E-Mail: sales@mmppinc.com, Web Site: www.mmppinc.com (27)

Multichannel Merchant Magazine, Stamford, CT. Tel: (203) 358-4386, FAX: (203) 358-5823, E-Mail: melissa.dowling@penton.com, Web Site: www.multichannelmerchant.com (31)

Multiple Sclerosis Association of America, Cherry Hill, NJ. Tel: (856) 488-4500, Web Site: www.msaa.com (1)

MultiView, Irving, TX. Tel: (972) 402-7056 (1)

Mummert, Hallie, Inside Direct Mail, Philadelphia, PA. Tel: (215) 238-5300, (800) 777-8074, FAX: (215) 238-5412, E-Mail: customerservice@napco.com, Web Site: www.insidedirectmail.com (43)

Mummert, Hallie, Target Marketing Magazine, Philadelphia, PA. Tel: (215) 238-5300, (800) 777-8074, FAX: (215) 238-5270, Web Site: www.targetmarketingmag.com (43)

Mummert, Michele, Dentsply International, York, PA. Tel: (800) 877-0020, Web Site: www.dentsply.com (7)

Mumper, Melanie, Taylor Nelson Sofres Intersearch, Horsham, PA. Tel: (419) 725-8560, E-Mail: info@intersearch.tnsofres.com, Web Site: www.intersearch.tnsofres.com (30)

Munce, Don, National Research Center for College & University Admissions, Lees Summit, MO. Tel: (816) 525-2201, Web Site: www.nrccua.org (1)

Munch, Dr. James, Wright State University, Dayton, OH. Tel: (937) 775-3047, FAX: (513) 775-3952, E-Mail: teresa.stelmat@wright.edu, Web Site: www.wright.edu/business/acad/marketing (41)

Munford, Gregory, BMD, Alexandria, VA. Tel: (703) 549-3500, Web Site: www.b-m-d.com (35)

Munn, Sallly, Council of Better Business Bureaus - BBBOnline, Arlington, VA. Tel: (703) 276-0100, FAX: (703) 525-8277, Web Site: www.bbb.org (1)

Munoz, Julio, ADRA International, Silver Spring, MD. Tel: (301) 680-6373, Web Site: www.adra.org (1)

Munroe, Dwight, Theodore Presser Co, King Of Prussia, PA. Tel: (610) 592-1222, FAX: (610) 592-1229, E-Mail: webmaster@presser.com, Web Site: www.presser.com (17)

Munson, Brenda, Rose Electronics, Houston, TX. Tel: (281) 933-7673, (800) 333-9343, FAX: (281) 933-0044, E-Mail: sales@rose.com, Web Site: www.rose.com (3)

Muoio, Michael, Lillian Vernon Corp, Colorado Springs, CO. Tel: (757) 427-7923, FAX: (757) 427-7819, E-Mail: publicrelations@lillianvernon.com, Web Site: www.lillianvernon.com (6)

Murabito, John, M., CIGNA International, Philadelphia, PA. Tel: (215) 761-1741, FAX: (215) 761-5515, Web Site: www.cigna.com (15)

Murach, Mike, Mike Murach & Associates Inc, Fresno, CA. Tel: (559) 440-9071, (800) 221-5528, FAX: (559) 440-0963, E-Mail: murachbooks@murach.com, Web Site: www.murach.com (17)

Mike Murach & Associates Inc, Fresno, CA. Tel: (559) 440-9071, (800) 221-5528, FAX: (559) 440-0963, E-Mail: murachbooks@murach.com, Web Site: www.murach.com (17)

Muraco, Steven, MVS Mailers Inc, Bohemia, NY. Tel: (800) 641-7917, FAX: (631) 699-0101, E-Mail: muraco@mvsmailers.com, Web Site: www.mvsmailers.com (28)

Murad Inc, El Segundo, CA. Tel: (310) 726-0600, Web Site: www.murad.com (7)

Muratore, Robert, KPR, New York, NY. Tel: (212) 856-8400, FAX: (212) 856-8660, Web Site: www.kprny.com (35)

Murder by Mail, West Tisbury, MA. Tel: (617) 670-9400, (508) 693-5205, FAX: (508) 693-7997, E-Mail: info@murderbymail.com, Web Site: www.murderbymail.com (1)

Murdoch, K. Rupert, News America Publishing Inc, New York, NY. Tel: (212) 782-8000, FAX: (212) 852-7145 (17)

Murdoch, K., Rupert, News America Marketing, New York, NY. Tel: (212) 852-8000, (800) 462-0852, FAX: (212) 575-5845, Web Site: www.newsamerica.com (31)

Murph, Eleanora, O., The Idea Club.com(TM) & Dumas Martin Consulting, Pomona, CA. Tel: (909) 620-4772, FAX: (909) 629-4739, E-Mail: theideaclub@peoplepc.com, Web Site: www.incorpman.com (16)

Murphy, Barbara, BKV, Overland Park, KS. Tel: (913) 648-8333, FAX: (913) 648-5024, Web Site: www.bkv.com (35)

Murphy, C. Joe, Scott's Dog Supply Inc, Indianapolis, IN. Tel: (317) 222-5382, (800) 966-3647, FAX: (317) 298-7284, E-Mail: cmurphy154@aol.com, Web Site: www.scottsdog.com (11)

Murphy, Clark, W., Murphy Bed Co Inc, Farmingdale, NY. Tel: (631) 420-4330, (800) 845-2337, FAX: (631) 420-4337, E-Mail: info@murphybedcompany.com, Web Site: www.murphybedcompany.com (8)

Murphy, Dan, Partminer, Centennial, CO. Tel: (303) 200-5500, FAX: (303) 754-3940, Web Site: www.partminer.com (17)

Murphy, Elaine, Kimbo Educational, Long Branch, NJ. Tel: (732) 229-4949, (800) 848-6099 (NM), (800) 631-2187 (NJ), FAX: (732) 870-3340, E-Mail: kimboed@aol.com, Web Site: www.kimboed.com (17)

Murphy, Gerry, Enterprise Ireland, New York, NY. Tel: (212) 371-3600, FAX: (212) 371-6398, Web Site: www.enterprise-ireland.com (16)

Murphy, James, Viking Pump Inc, Cedar Falls, IA. Tel: (319) 266-1741, FAX: (319) 273-8157, E-Mail: info@vikingpump.com, Web Site: www. vikingpump.com (16)

Murphy, John, J., Craft-Diston Industries, Wichita, KS. Tel: (316) 838-4291, (800) 835-0028, FAX: (316) 838-8502, Web Site: www.craftdiston.com (16)

Murphy, John, M., Home Loan Investment Bank, Warwick, RI. Tel: (800) 223-1700 X278, E-Mail: contactus@homeloanbank.com, Web Site: www. homeloanbank.com (14)

Murphy, Jon, First American Printing & Direct Mail, Ocean Springs, MS. Tel: (228) 875-8199, (800) 967-2637, FAX: (228) 875-8198, E-Mail: sales@ fapdm.com, Web Site: www.fapdm.com (21)

Murphy, Ken, Alliance Data, Plano, TX. Tel: (972) 348-5100, Web Site: www.alliancedata.com (28)

Murphy, Lisa, Live Design, New York, NY. Tel: (212) 204-4268, FAX: (212) 204-4291, Web Site: livedesignonline.com (17)

Murphy, Liz, RedEngine Digital, Mc Lean, VA. Tel: (703) 556-6951, Web Site: www.redenginedigital. com (20)

Murphy, Marion, GroupM Direct, New York, NY. Tel: (212) 474-0830, Web Site: www.groupm.com (35)

Murphy, Mark, J., Advantage List Marketing Inc, Holliston, MA. Tel: (508) 429-4400, FAX: (508) 429-7117 (23)

Murphy, Mary, Ellen, UJA/Federation of New York, New York, NY. Tel: (212) 980-1000, FAX: (212) 785-9321, Web Site: www.ujafedny.org (1)

Murphy, Matt, Coast Hotels Limited, Seattle, WA. Tel: (206) 826-2700, FAX: (206) 826-2701, Web Site: www.coasthotels.com (19)

Murphy, Michael, Edith Roman Associates Inc, Pearl River, NY. Tel: (845) 620-9000, (800) 223-2194, FAX: (845) 620-9035 (23)

Murphy, Michael, J., MJM Incentives Inc, Rochester, NY. Tel: (585) 424-6720, FAX: (585) 424-4387, E-Mail: cmeier@mjmincentives.com, Web Site: www.mjmincentives.com (33)

Murphy, Michael, Pearl Insurance Group LLC, Peoria Heights, IL. Tel: (309) 688-9000, Web Site: www. pearlinsurance.com (15)

Murphy, Patricia, Modular Devices, LLC, Sparta, NJ. Tel: (973) 579-7220, (800) 292-2201, FAX: (973) 579-1820, E-Mail: modulardevices@optonline.net, Web Site: www.modulardevices.biz (3)

Murphy, Patrick, Gems Sensors & Controls, Plainville, CT. Tel: (860) 747-3000, (800) 378-1600, FAX: (860) 747-4244, E-Mail: info@gemssensors.com, Web Site: www.gemssensors.com (9)

Murphy, Patty, Webster Bank, Waterbury, CT. Tel: (203) 578-2460, FAX: (203) 754-5939, Web Site: www.websterbank.com (14)

Murphy, Robert, E., California Pacific Research & New Generation, Reno, NV. Tel: (775) 829-5600, (800) 541-5703, FAX: (775) 829-5619, E-Mail: sales@newgen2000.com, Web Site: www. newgen2000.com (7)

Murphy, Steven, Rodale Inc, Emmaus, PA. Tel: (610) 967-5171, FAX: (610) 967-8963, Web Site: www. rodale.com (17)

Murphy, Terry, M., AO Smith Corp, Milwaukee, WI. Tel: (414) 359-4000, FAX: (414) 359-4064, Web Site: www.aosmith.com (1)

Murphy Bed Co Inc, Farmingdale, NY. Tel: (631) 420-4330, (800) 845-2337, FAX: (631) 420-4337, E-Mail: info@murphybedcompany.com, Web Site: www.murphybedcompany.com (8)

Murphy Brian, Sheila, SCA Promotions Inc, Dallas, TX. Tel: (214) 860-3700, (888) 860-3700, FAX: (214) 860-3723, E-Mail: scainfo@scapromo.com, Web Site: www.scapromo.com (15)

Murray, Burk, Digi International, Minnetonka, MN. Tel: (952) 912-3444, (877) 912-3444, FAX: (952) 912-4953, Web Site: www.digi.com (3)

Murray, Charles, F., CMI Direct, Montrose, CA. Tel: (951) 300-1700, FAX: (866) 723-5433, Web Site: www.cmidirect.net (15)

Murray, Darcy, Empire City Casino at Yonkers Raceway, Yonkers, NY. Tel: (914) 968-4200, Web Site: www.empirecitygaming.com (19)

Murray, David, Spectrum Data, Oregon, IL. Tel: (815) 732-6567 (22)

Murray, Gail, San Francisco Bay Area Rapid Transit District (BART), Oakland, CA. Tel: (510) 464-6000, FAX: (510) 464-7103, Web Site: www.bart. gov (16)

Murray, George, Sterling Jewelers Inc, Akron, OH. Tel: (330) 668-5000, FAX: (330) 668-5052, E-Mail: webmaster@jewels.com, Web Site: www. sterlingjewelers.com (16)

Murray, Jeffrey, Sencore Inc, Sioux Falls, SD. Tel: (605) 339-0100, (800) SEN-CORE, FAX: (605) 339-0317, E-Mail: sales@sencore.com, Web Site: www.sencore.com (16)

Murray, John, Newspaper Association of America, Arlington, VA. Tel: (703) 902-1600, FAX: (571) 366-1195, Web Site: www.naa.org (1)

Murray, Kim, L., Vision Media, Modesto, CA. Tel: (209) 526-6500, FAX: (209) 522-2100, E-Mail: info@visionmediatv.com, Web Site: www. visionmediatv.com (35)

Murray, Lori, North Shore Animal League America Inc, Port Washington, NY. Tel: (516) 883-7900, FAX: (516) 883-8256, E-Mail: donorservices@ nsalamerica.org, Web Site: www.nsalamerica.org (1)

Murray, Marilyn, National Luggage Dealers Association, Glenview, IL. Tel: (847) 998-6869, FAX: (847) 998-6884, E-Mail: inquiry@nlda.com, Web Site: www.nlda.com (1)

Murray, Mike, TMA Direct, Reston, VA. Tel: (703) 547-4940, Web Site: www.tmalist.com (23)

Murray, Mike, The MR Group Inc, Charleston, SC. Tel: (843) 402-0566, FAX: (843) 852-9051, E-Mail: mgm@themrgroup.com, Web Site: www. themrgroup.com (9)

Murray, Mike, Tony Murray & Associates, Fairfax, VA. Tel: (703) 425-5356, (800) 783-6400, FAX: (703) 425-4537 (23)

Murray, Robert J., NEBS, Groton, MA. Tel: (978) 448-6111, (888) 823-6327, (800) 225-6380, FAX: (800) 234-4324, (978) 448-3653, E-Mail: customerservice@nebs.com, Web Site: www.nebs. com (10)

Murray, Robert, P., AAA Southern New England, Providence, RI. Tel: (401) 868-2005, FAX: (401) 868-2085, Web Site: www.aaa.com (1)

Murray, Shannon, MD Anderson Cancer Center - Children's Art Project, Houston, TX. Tel: (713) 745-2575, (800) 231-1580, FAX: (713) 794-1950, E-Mail: krenner@mdanderson.org, Web Site: www. childrensart.org (1)

Murray, Susan, Short Sizes Inc, Northfield, OH. Tel: (440) 605-1000, (800) 272-9000, FAX: (440) 605-1065, E-Mail: orders@shortsizesinc.com, Web Site: www.shortsizesinc.com (2)

Murray, Thomas, InterContinental Hotels Group, Atlanta, GA. Tel: (770) 604-2000, (877) 424-2449, FAX: (770) 604-8639, Web Site: www. ichotelsgroup.com (19)

Murray, Virginia, Active Parenting, Marietta, GA. Tel: (770) 429-0565, (800) 825-0060, (800) 235-7755, FAX: (770) 429-0334, E-Mail: cservice@ activeparenting.com, Web Site: www. activeparenting.com (17)

Tony Murray & Associates, Fairfax, VA. Tel: (703) 425-5356, (800) 783-6400, FAX: (703) 425-4537 (23)

Muscle Dynamics Fitness Network Inc, Santa Fe Springs, CA. Tel: (310) 323-9055, (800) 544-2944, FAX: (310) 323-7608, E-Mail: info@ muscledynamics.com, Web Site: www.maxicam. com (32)

Muscular Dystrophy Association, Tucson, AZ. Tel: (520) 529-2000, (800) 344-4863, FAX: (520) 529-5300, Web Site: www.mdausa.org (1)

Muselman, Arthur, K., Annie's Attic LLC, Big Sandy, TX. Tel: (903) 636-4303, FAX: (903) 636-4088, Web Site: www.anniesattic.com (11)

Museum Masters Inc, New York, NY. Tel: (917) 273-8710, (212) 360-7100, FAX: (212) 360-7102, E-Mail: MMIMarilyn@aol.com, Web Site: www. museummasters.com (16)

The Museum of Modern Art, New York, NY. Tel: (212) 708-9400, FAX: (212) 333-1123, E-Mail: info@moma.org, Web Site: www.moma.org (5)

Musgrave, Michael, K., Western Printing Machinery (WPM), Schiller Park, IL. Tel: (847) 678-1740, FAX: (847) 678-6176, E-Mail: info@wpm.com, Web Site: www.wpm.com (34)

Musgrove, Linda, Tri-Chem Inc, Belleville, NJ. Tel: (973) 751-9200, FAX: (973) 450-1057, (973) 450-1260, E-Mail: paints@trichem.com, Web Site: www.trichem.com (16)

Music Barn Inc, Niagara Falls, NY. Tel: (800) 984-0047, FAX: (905) 513-6918, E-Mail: info@ themusicbarn.com, Web Site: www.themusicbarn. com (6)

Music Choice, Horsham, PA. Tel: (215) 784-5840, Web Site: www.musicchoice.com (16)

Music Sales Corp, New York, NY. Tel: (212) 254-2100, (800) 431-7187, FAX: (212) 254-2013, E-Mail: info@musicsales.com, Web Site: www. musicsales.com (17)

Music Treasures Co, Richmond, VA. Tel: (804) 730-8800, (800) 666-7565, FAX: (888) MUSIC-TC, E-Mail: musict@musictreasures.com, Web Site: www.musictreasures.com (16)

Musician's Friend, Westlake Village, CA. Tel: (541) 772-5173, Web Site: www.musiciansfriend.com (5)

Muskegon Power Tool Corp, North Muskegon, MI. Tel: (231) 766-2194, (800) 635-5465, FAX: (231) 766-3846 (16)

Mustafa, Frank, Get Seen Media Group, Los Angeles, CA. Tel: (323) 424-4669, Web Site: www. getseenmedia.com (16)

Mustek Inc, Tustin, CA. Tel: (949) 790-3800, FAX: (949) 788-3670, Web Site: www.mustek.com (3)

Mustich Jr, James, The Akadine Press Inc, White Plains, NY. Tel: (914) 747-0777, FAX: (914) 747-0778, Web Site: www.commonreader.com (16)

Musto, Ken, Brush Fire, Cedar Knolls, NJ. Tel: (973) 871-1700, FAX: (973) 871-1717, Web Site: www. brushfireinc.com (35)

Muth, Kevin, Professional Direct Marketing & Mailing List Inc, Boca Raton, FL. Tel: (561) 241-4414, (800) 777-5478, FAX: (561) 241-5878, E-Mail: pdm@pdmm.info, Web Site: www.pdmm.us (23)

Mutual of America Life Insurance Co, New York, NY. Tel: (212) 224-1600, (800) 468-3785, FAX: (212) 224-2539, Web Site: www.mutualofamerica.com (14)

Mutual of Omaha, Omaha, NE. Tel: (402) 342-7600, (800) 775-6000, FAX: (402) 351-2775, Web Site: www.mutualofomaha.com (15)

Muyskens, James, L., Queens College/CUNY Professional and Continuing Studies (PCS), Flushing, NY. Tel: (718) 997-5700, FAX: (718) 997-5723, E-Mail: pcs@qc.cuny.edu, Web Site: www.qc.cuny. edu/pcs (41)

Muzzy, Peter, QED Marketing Inc, Central Islip, NY. Tel: (631) 851-4254 (22)

MWM Dexter Inc, Aurora, MO. Tel: (888) 833-1242, FAX: (417) 841-1040, Web Site: www.mwmdexter. com (27)

MxEnergy Inc, Stamford, CT. Tel: (203) 356-1318, Web Site: www.mxenergy.com (1)

My Mailing Service, Inc, Atlanta, GA. Tel: (404) 321-6222, E-Mail: info@mymailingservice.com, Web Site: www.mymailingservice.com (23)

Myers, Bill, Diagraph Corp, Saint Charles, MO. Tel: (636) 300-2000, (800) 722-1125, FAX: (636) 300-2004, E-Mail: info@diagraph.com, Web Site: www.diagraph.com (16)

Myers, Diana, Save the Children Federation Inc, Westport, CT. Tel: (203) 221-4000, (800) 728-3843, FAX: (203) 222-1067, E-Mail: twebster@savethechildren.org, Web Site: www.savethechildren.org (1)

Myers, Douglas, G., Zoological Society of San Diego, San Diego, CA. Tel: (619) 231-1515, FAX: (619) 557-3937, Web Site: www.sandiegozoo.org (1)

Myers, Hal, K., Thought Technology Ltd, Montreal, PQ Canada. Tel: (514) 489-8251, (800) 361-3651, FAX: (514) 489-8255, E-Mail: lawrence@thoughttechnology.com, Web Site: www.thoughttechnology.com (16)

Myers, James M., Petco Animal Supplies, San Diego, CA. Tel: (858) 453-7845, (877) 738-6742, FAX: (858) 453-6585, Web Site: www.petco.com (5)

Myers, John, A-Mark Inc, Dresher, PA. Tel: (215) 886-4740, FAX: (215) 886-4749 (15)

Myers, Martha, Northeast Hinge Distributors Inc, Hollis, NH. Tel: (603) 465-3244, (800) 882-0120, FAX: (603) 465-3313, E-Mail: nehinge@nehinge.com, Web Site: www.nehinge.com (9)

Myers, Mary, Wag/Aero Group, Lyons, WI. Tel: (262) 763-9586, (800) 558-6868, FAX: (262) 763-7595, E-Mail: wagaero-sales@wagaero.com, Web Site: www.wagaero.com (16)

Myers, Matt, Sylvan Learning Centers, Baltimore, MD. Tel: (410) 843-8000, FAX: (410) 843-8057, Web Site: www.educate.com (16)

Myers, Paul, Valley Forge Tape & Label Co Inc, Exton, PA. Tel: (610) 524-8900, (800) 345-1323, FAX: (610) 524-8906, E-Mail: vfsales@vftl.com, Web Site: www.vftl.com (27)

Myers, Peter, Myers, Myers & Adams Advertising Inc, Fort Lauderdale, FL. Tel: (954) 523-6262, FAX: (954) 523-3517, E-Mail: pete@mmanda.com, Web Site: www.mmanda.com (21)

Myers, Myers & Adams Advertising Inc, Fort Lauderdale, FL. Tel: (954) 523-6262, FAX: (954) 523-3517, E-Mail: pete@mmanda.com, Web Site: www.mmanda.com (35)

Myhran, Brooks, D., Goldsmith Agio Helms, Minneapolis, MN. Tel: (612) 339-0500, FAX: (612) 339-0507, Web Site: www.agio.com (14)

Myint, Viraya, Manhattan Media Services Inc, New York, NY. Tel: (212) 808-4077, FAX: (212) 808-4080, E-Mail: mmorello@manhmedia.com, Web Site: www.manhmedia.com (21)

Mylan, Mark, Hill Holliday, Boston, MA. Tel: (617) 366-4000, Web Site: www.hhcc.com (35)

Mylenek, Bob, Group2Marketing, Medford, OR. Tel: (541) 734-2565, Web Site: www.group2marketing.net (29)

Myllykoski North America, Norwalk, CT. Tel: (203) 229-7400, Web Site: www.myllykoski.com (25)

MyPoints.Com Inc, San Francisco, CA. Tel: (415) 856-0877, FAX: (415) 615-1122, E-Mail: memberservices@mypoints.com, Web Site: www.mypoints.com (35)

Myriad Systems Inc, Oklahoma City, OK. Tel: (405) 478-9000, (866) 505-1730, FAX: (405) 478-8315, Web Site: www.myriadsystems.com (22)

Myron Corp, Maywood, NJ. Tel: (201) 843-6464, (877) 803-3358, FAX: (201) 843-8390, Web Site: www.myron.com (16)

Myroniak, Tom, Specialty Equipment Market Association, Diamond Bar, CA. Tel: (909) 396-0289, Web Site: www.sema.org (1)

Mystic Logistics, South Glastonbury, CT. Tel: (860) 659-1566, (800) 969-1566, FAX: (860) 659-1420, Web Site: www.mysticlogistics.com (35)

Mystic Seaport Museum Stores, Mystic, CT. Tel: (860) 572-5315, (860) 572-0711, FAX: (860) 572-5324, Web Site: www.mysticseaport.org (6)

Mystic Stamp Co Inc, Camden, NY. Tel: (866) 660-7147, FAX: (800) 385-4919, E-Mail: info@mysticstamp.com, Web Site: www.mysticstamp.com (16)

N

n Fusion Group, Austin, TX. Tel: (512) 716-7000, FAX: (512) 716-7001, Web Site: www.nfusion.com (35)

NAACP (National Association for the Advancement of Colored People), Baltimore, MD. Tel: (410) 580-5617, Web Site: www.naacp.org (1)

NAM Mailing Lists, Santa Cruz, NM. Tel: (505) 753-5086, FAX: (505) 753-9249, E-Mail: nam@newmexico.com (24)

NAPR - National Association of Publishers Representatives, Kansas City, KS. Tel: (913) 708-8344, FAX: (913) 708-8618, E-Mail: napr@naprassoc.com, Web Site: www.naprassoc.com (35)

NARAL Pro-Choice America, Washington, DC. Tel: (202) 973-3000, Web Site: www.naral.com (1)

NASA Federal Credit Union, Upper Marlboro, MD. Tel: (301) 249-1800, Web Site: www.nasafcu.com (1)

NASCO, Fort Atkinson, WI. Tel: (920) 563-2446, FAX: (920) 563-8296, E-Mail: info@nasco.com, Web Site: www.enasco.com (5)

NASW Assurance Services Inc, Frederick, MD. Tel: (800) 668-4274, E-Mail: zxi@naswasi.org, Web Site: www.naswinsurancetrust.org (1)

NAVTEQ, Chicago, IL. Tel: (312) 780-1989 (35)

NBI Inc, Eau Claire, WI. Tel: (715) 835-8525, Web Site: www.nbi-sems.com (1)

NBTY Inc, Ronkonkoma, NY. Tel: (631) 200-2000, FAX: (631) 567-7148, Web Site: www.nbty.com (7)

NCH Corp, Dallas, TX. Tel: (972) 438-0211, FAX: (972) 438-0186, Web Site: www.nch.com (34)

NCO Financial Systems, Horsham, PA. Tel: (215) 441-3000, (800) 220-2274, FAX: (215) 441-3923, E-Mail: marketing@ncogroup.com, Web Site: www.ncogroup.com (29)

NCP Solutions, Birmingham, AL. Tel: (250) 849-5200, Web Site: www.ncprint.com (21)

NCP Solutions, Reston, VA. Tel: (703) 438-6000, (800) 822-9919, FAX: (703) 438-3570, Web Site: www.nwf.org (17)

NCR Corp, Duluth, GA. Tel: (937) 445-1936, (800) CALL-NCR, FAX: (937) 445-1682, Web Site: www.ncr.com (16)

NCRI List Management, Englewood Cliffs, NJ. Tel: (201) 541-9500, FAX: (201) 541-1944, E-Mail: info@ncrilists.com, Web Site: www.ncrilists.com (23)

NCS, Danbury, CT. Tel: (562) 946-6900, (800) 975-6804, FAX: (800) 527-2488, Web Site: www.shopncs.com; www.ncs-apparel.com (16)

NCS Learn, Trabuco Canyon, CA. Tel: (949) 766-1068, Web Site: www.ncslearn.com (16)

NEA's Member Benefits Corp, Gaithersburg, MD. Tel: (301) 251-9600, FAX: (301) 527-8210, Web Site: www.neamb.com (1)

NEBS, Groton, MA. Tel: (978) 448-6111, (888) 823-6327, (800) 225-6380, (800) 234-4324, (978) 448-3653, E-Mail: customerservice@nebs.com, Web Site: www.nebs.com (10)

NEC Group Inc, Burbank, CA. Tel: (818) 909-9963, Web Site: www.thehomeshow.com (32)

NETC, Boston, MA. Tel: (617) 725-0044 (5)

NFIB - National Federation of Independent Business, Nashville, TN. Tel: (615) 872-5800, Web Site: www.nfib.com (1)

NGL Insurance Group, Madison, WI. Tel: (608) 257-5611, (800) 548-2962, FAX: (608) 257-9340, Web Site: www.nationalguardian.com (15)

The NH Broadcaster, Lowell, MA. Tel: (978) 458-7100, Web Site: www.nhbroadcaster.com (31)

NNE Marketing, Concord, MA. Tel: (617) 429-7999, Web Site: www.nnemarketing.com (1)

The NPD Group Inc, Port Washington, NY. Tel: (516) 625-0700, FAX: (516) 625-2444, Web Site: www.npd.com (30)

NPI, Fort Worth, TX. Tel: (214) 634-2288, FAX: (682) 503-8214, E-Mail: sales@npisorters.com, Web Site: www.npisorters.com (16)

NRS, Decatur, TX. Tel: (940) 393-7009, Web Site: www.nrsworld.com (11)

NSA Technologies LLC, Akron, OH. Tel: (330) 576-4600 (9)

NSB Group, Pointe-Claire, PQ Canada. Tel: (514) 426-0822, E-Mail: infona@nsbgroup.com, Web Site: www.nsbgroup.com (22)

NTL Institute, Arlington, VA. Tel: (703) 548-8840, (800) 277-4685, FAX: (703) 684-1256, E-Mail: info@ntl.org, Web Site: www.ntl.org (1)

NTN Communications Inc, Carlsbad, CA. Tel: (760) 438-7400, (888) PLAY-NTN, (888) 752-9686, FAX: (760) 438-3505, Web Site: www.ntn.com (32)

NTP Distribution, Wilsonville, OR. Tel: (503) 570-0171, Web Site: www.ntpdistribution.com (34)

NYSARC, Inc, Delmar, NY. Tel: (518) 439-8311, FAX: (518) 439-1893, E-Mail: info@nysarc.org, Web Site: www.nysarc.org (1)

Nabel MD, Elizabeth, ACP Medicine, Hamilton, ON Canada. Tel: (905) 522-8526, (855) 647-6511, FAX: (905) 522-9273, E-Mail: acpmedicine@deckerpublishing.com, Web Site: acpmedicine.com (17)

Nabers Jr, Drayton, Protective Life Insurance Co, Birmingham, AL. Tel: (205) 268-1000, (800) 866-3555, FAX: (205) 868-3086, Web Site: www.protective.com (15)

Nabinger, Susan, Country Marketing Ltd, Ilion, NY. Tel: (315) 895-7737, FAX: (315) 895-7392, E-Mail: al@countrymarketing.com, Web Site: www.countrymarketing.com (23)

Nabipoor, Omid, Interface Engineering, Portland, OR. Tel: (503) 382-2266, FAX: (503) 382-2262, E-Mail: solutions@interfaceengineering.com, Web Site: www.ieice.com (20)

Naccarato, Vincent, Wilton Industries Inc, Woodridge, IL. Tel: (630) 963-1818, (800) 794-5866, FAX: (630) 963-7196, E-Mail: info@wilton.com, Web Site: www.wilton.com (16)

Nachemin, Farley, Gump's By Mail Inc, San Francisco, CA. Tel: (415) 982-1616, (800) 882-8055, FAX: (800) 984-9361, Web Site: www.gumpsbymail.com (6)

Nachtsheim, Stephen P., Deluxe Corp, Shoreview, MN. Tel: (651) 490-8000, FAX: (651) 481-4163, Web Site: www.deluxe.com (27)

NADA Appraisal Guides, Costa Mesa, CA. Tel: (714) 556-8511, (800) 966-6232, FAX: (714) 957-0302, E-Mail: info@nadaguides.com, Web Site: www.nadaguides.com (17)

Nadelmann, Ethan, Drug Policy Alliance, New York, NY. Tel: (212) 613-8020, FAX: (212) 613-8021, E-Mail: nyc@drugpolicy.org, Web Site: www.drugpolicy.org (1)

Nadler, Pegg, Pegg Nadler Associates Inc, New York, NY. Tel: (212) 861-0846 (22)

Nadler, Pegg, The Direct Marketing Club of New York Inc, Garden City, NY. Tel: (516) 746-6700, FAX: (516) 294-8141, E-Mail: info@dmcny.org, Web Site: www.dmcny.org (1)

Naergaard, Leif, Chris Hansen, New Berlin, WI. Tel: (414) 607-5700, FAX: (414) 607-5704, Web Site: www.chr-hansen.com (16)

Nafzinger, Roy, 800 Call KC, Kansas City, MO. Tel: (816) 231-4321, (800) 722-5554, FAX: (816) 241-2743, E-Mail: sales@call-kc.com, Web Site: www.call-kc.com (29)

Nagarajan, Sree, Colligent, Cupertino, CA. Tel: (425) 641-1130 (30)

Nagel, Jan, Christian Herald Association, New York, NY. Tel: (212) 684-2800, (800) BOWERY-1, FAX: (212) 684-3740, E-Mail: info@chaonline.org, Web Site: www.bowery.org (1)

Naggiar, Caroline, Tiffany & Co, New York, NY. Tel: (212) 755-8000, FAX: (212) 320-7550, Web Site: www.tiffany.com (6)

Nagle, Glenn, Think Shapes Mail, Tampa, FL. Tel: (813) 885-2225, (800) 889-4406, Web Site: www.jigsawprinting.com (27)

Nagourney, Donald, School of Management, Old Westbury, NY. Tel: (516) 686-1000, (800) 345-NYIT, (800) 345-6948, Web Site: www.nyit.edu (41)

Nagourney, Marvin, D&D Associates Inc, Garden City, NY. Tel: (516) 326-8800, (800) 554-0347 (22)

Nagy, Kathy, Strategy Network, Plymouth, MI. Tel: (734) 464-8100, FAX: (734) 464-4133, E-Mail: info@strategynetwork.com, Web Site: www.strategy-network.com (35)

Nahan Printing Inc, Saint Cloud, MN. Tel: (320) 251-7611, Web Site: www.nahan.com (27)

Nahley Fleishman, Susan, Warner Bros, Burbank, CA. Tel: (818) 954-6000, Web Site: www.warnerbros.com (3)

NAK Marketing & Communications, New York, NY. Tel: (212) 505-9290, Web Site: www.nakcomm.com (20)

Nakagawa, Randy, Grand Pacific Resorts, Carlsbad, CA. Tel: (760) 827-4101, Web Site: www.grandpacificresorts.com (19)

Nakashima, Alison, Schoolwise Press, San Francisco, CA. Tel: (415) 337-7971, (800) 247-8443 x 202, FAX: (415) 337-1146, E-Mail: info@schoolwisepress.com, Web Site: www.schoolwisepress.com (17)

Nallon, Jane, Oliver Russell & Associates, Boise, ID. Tel: (208) 344-1734, FAX: (208) 344-1211, Web Site: www.oliverrussell.com (35)

Name Exchange, Frederick, MD. Tel: (301) 695-6140, FAX: (301) 695-5572, E-Mail: chris@nameexchange.us, Web Site: www.nameexchange.us (24)

Name-Finders Lists Inc, Oakland, CA. Tel: (415) 955-8585, (800) 221-5009, FAX: (415) 955-8581, E-Mail: dm@namefinderslists.com, Web Site: www.namefinderslists.com (23)

NameBank International LLC, Baltimore, MD. Tel: (410) 783-8460, FAX: (410) 783-8464, E-Mail: beth@namebank.com, Web Site: www.namebank.com (23)

Namenson, Jared, Institute of Reading Development, Novato, CA. Tel: (415) 884-8100, (800) 964-8888, FAX: (415) 382-0760, E-Mail: contactus@readingprograms.org, Web Site: www.readingprograms.org (1)

Names in the Mail Inc, Dallas, TX. Tel: (972) 681-5701, (800) 688-5701, FAX: (972) 681-5786, E-Mail: nimnames@att.net (23)

Names in the News, Oakland, CA. Tel: (415) 989-3350, FAX: (415) 433-7796, E-Mail: name@nincal.com, Web Site: www.nincal.com (23)

Namken, Darin, Bull Dog Media Group Inc, Madison, SD. Tel: (605) 256-9103, Web Site: www.commissionsoup.com (20)

Namken, Darin, CommissionSoup, Madison, SD. Tel: (605) 256-9103, (866) 309-7687, FAX: (605) 256-1522, E-Mail: info@creditsoup.com, Web Site: www.commissionsoup.com (23)

Nancy's Notions LLC, Beaver Dam, WI. Tel: (920) 887-0391, (800) 833-0690, FAX: (800) 255-8119, E-Mail: comments@nancysnotions.com, Web Site: www.nancysnotions.com (11)

Nandkeolyar, Shelley, Norm Thompson Outfitters Inc, Hillsboro, OR. Tel: (503) 614-4600, (800) 547-1160, FAX: (503) 614-4599, Web Site: www.normthompson.com (2)

Nangle, Kevin, Reiman Publications, Greendale, WI. Tel: (414) 423-0100, (800) 344-6913, FAX: (414) 423-3840, Web Site: www.reimanpub.com (17)

Nanus, Jeff, AAA Umbrella Co Inc, Northvale, NJ. Tel: (201) 784-3242, (800) 426-7446, FAX: (201) 226-0041, Web Site: www.aaaumbrella.com (16)

Napalitno, Val, Petry Television Inc, New York, NY. Tel: (212) 230-5600, FAX: (323) 655-2862, E-Mail: info@petrymedia.com, Web Site: www.petrymedia.com (32)

Napier, Elizabeth, Tully & Holland Inc, Wellesley, MA. Tel: (781) 239-2900, FAX: (781) 239-2901, E-Mail: info@tullyandholland.com, Web Site: www.tullyandholland.com (14)

Napiorkowski, George, Mail-Well Envelope, Jersey City, NJ. Tel: (201) 434-2100, (800) 526-3020, E-Mail: info@cenveo.com, Web Site: www.mail-well.com (26)

Napoli, Michele, Women in Direct Marketing International, New York, NY. Tel: (516) 746-6700, FAX: (516) 294-8141, Web Site: www.wdmi.org (40)

Napolitano, Robert, St Joseph's College, Brooklyn, NY. Tel: (718) 399-1223, Web Site: www.sjcny.edu (1)

NAR Productions, Barryville, NY. Tel: (845) 557-8713, FAX: (845) 557-6770, E-Mail: info@aodceus.com, Web Site: www.aodceus.com (17)

Narayen, Shantanu, Adobe Systems Inc, San Jose, CA. Tel: (408) 536-6000, (800) 833-6687, FAX: (408) 537-6000, Web Site: www.adobe.com (22)

Nardo, Martino, Hanna Instruments Inc, Woonsocket, RI. Tel: (401) 765-7500, (800) 426-6287, FAX: (401) 765-7575, E-Mail: custsvc@hannainst.com, Web Site: www.hannainst.com (16)

Nardo, Pamela, Hanna Instruments Inc, Woonsocket, RI. Tel: (401) 765-7500, (800) 426-6287, FAX: (401) 765-7575, E-Mail: custsvc@hannainst.com, Web Site: www.hannainst.com (16)

Narrow Way, Lafayette, CA. Tel: (925) 283-4074 (6)

Nash, Bill, LaPreferida Inc, Chicago, IL. Tel: (773) 254-7200, (800) 621-5422, FAX: (773) 254-8546, Web Site: www.lapreferida.com (4)

Nash, Edward, Direct Marketing Strategy, Planning & Execution (Fourth Edition), Blacklick, OH. Tel: (614) 755-4152, (800) 722-4726, Web Site: www.mcgraw-hill.com (43)

Nash, Edward, Team Nash Inc, East Hampton, NY. Tel: (646) 497-0297, (631) 267-3385, E-Mail: results@teamnash.com, Web Site: www.teamnash.com (35)

Nash, Lisa, LN Marketing Associates, Emerald Hills, CA. Tel: (650) 368-7181 (20)

Nasif, Teresa, S., Federal Citizen Information Center, Pueblo, CO. Tel: (888) 8-PUEBLO, FAX: (719) 948-9724, E-Mail: catalog.pueblo@gsa.gov, Web Site: www.pueblo.gsa.gov (5)

Nassar, Paul, Marimac Inc, Montreal, PQ Canada. Tel: (514) 725-7600, FAX: (514) 376-0801, Web Site: www.marimac.com (8)

Nassau Broadcasting Co, Princeton, NJ. Tel: (609) 419-0300, (800) 248-WPST, FAX: (609) 915-9778, E-Mail: lrios@wpst.com, Web Site: www.wpst.com (32)

Nassau Community College, Garden City, NY. Tel: (516) 572-7501, E-Mail: marketing-communications@ncc.edu, Web Site: www.ncc.edu (41)

Nassetta, Christopher, Hilton Hotels Corp, Mc Lean, VA. Tel: (310) 278-4321, (800) HILTONS, FAX: (310) 205-3670, Web Site: www.hilton.com (19)

Nasta, Frank, A., Applied Info Group, Kenilworth, NJ. Tel: (908) 241-7007, Web Site: www.appliedinfogroup.com (22)

Nat Com Marketing, Miami, FL. Tel: (786) 425-0028, FAX: (786) 425-0067, E-Mail: info@natcom-marketing.com, Web Site: www.natcom-marketing.com (33)

Natale Jr., John, A., Urbani Truffles USA Corp, New York, NY. Tel: (212) 247-8800, FAX: (212) 247-8900, E-Mail: info@urbani.com, Web Site: www.urbanitartufi.com (4)

Natale, Patrick, J., American Society of Civil Engineers, Reston, VA. Tel: (703) 295-6000, (800) 548-2723, FAX: (703) 295-6343, Web Site: www.asce.org (1)

Natcom Inc, Bixby, OK. Tel: (918) 491-6100, (800) 554-1999, FAX: (918) 491-9410, E-Mail: cs@natcom-publications.com, Web Site: www.natcom-publications.com (17)

Nathan, Grace, Grace Nathan & Associates, Chicago, IL. Tel: (847) 763-1174 (33)

Nathan, Jan, Publishers Marketing Association (PMA), Manhattan Beach, CA. Tel: (310) 372-2732, FAX: (310) 374-3342, E-Mail: info@pma-online.org, Web Site: www.pma-online.org (40)

Nathan Associates Inc, Arlington, VA. Tel: (703) 516-7700, FAX: (703) 351-6162, Web Site: www.nathaninc.com (30)

Nathanson, Alice, Uncle Ben's Inc, Greenville, MS. Tel: (662) 335-8000, (800) 548-6253, (800) 54-UNCLE, FAX: (662) 378-4370, E-Mail: info@unclebens.com, Web Site: www.unclebens.com (4)

National A-1 Advertising Inc, Philadelphia, PA. Tel: (215) 418-2700, (800) 245-4647, FAX: (215) 627-4026, Web Site: www.nationala-1.com (35)

National Active & Retired Federal Employees Association, Alexandria, VA. Tel: (703) 838-7760, (800) 456-8410, FAX: (703) 838-7785, Web Site: www.narfe.org (1)

National Administrative Service Co LLC, Dublin, OH. Tel: (614) 358-1500 (29)

National Agri Marketing Conference & Exposition, Overland Park, KS. Tel: (913) 491-6500, FAX: (913) 491-6502, E-Mail: agrimktg@nama.org, Web Site: www.nama.org (42)

National Alliance of Business, Washington, DC. Tel: (202) 289-2888, (800) 787-2448 (1)

National Archives & Records Administration, College Park, MD. Tel: (301) 837-0482, (86) NARA-NARA, FAX: (301) 837-0483, Web Site: www.archives.gov (17)

National Association Broadcasters Annual Conference & Expo, Washington, DC. Tel: (202) 429-5300, (800) 622-3976, FAX: (202) 429-4199, E-Mail: nab@nab.org, Web Site: www.nab.org (42)

National Association for Female Executives (NAFE), New York, NY. Tel: (800) 927-6233, E-Mail: info@nafe.com, Web Site: www.nafe.com (1)

National Association for Printing Leadership, East Rutherford, NJ. Tel: (201) 634-9600, (800) 642-6275, FAX: (201) 634-0324, Web Site: www.napl.org (1)

National Association of Federal Credit Unions, Arlington, VA. Tel: (800) 336-4644, Web Site: www.nafcu.org (14)

National Association of Home Builders, Washington, DC. Tel: (202) 266-8200, (800) 368-5242, FAX: (202) 266-8400, Web Site: www.nahb.org (24)

National Association of Professional Insurance Agents, Alexandria, VA. Tel: (703) 836-9340, FAX: (703) 836-1279, E-Mail: web@pianet.org, Web Site: www.pianet.com (1)

National Association of Realtors, Chicago, IL. Tel: (312) 329-8526, Web Site: www.realtors.org (1)

National Audubon Society, New York, NY. Tel: (212) 979-3000, FAX: (212) 979-3188, Web Site: www.audubon.org (17)

National Auto Warranty, Wentzville, MO. Tel: (800) 649-1620 (16)

National Automated Clearing House Association, Herndon, VA. Tel: (703) 561-1100, FAX: (703) 787-0996, Web Site: www.nacha.org (1)

National Basketball Association, Secaucus, NJ. Tel: (212) 407-8000, FAX: (212) 826-0579, Web Site: www.nba.com (1)

National Broadcast Finance Corp, New Haven, CT. Tel: (203) 389-6000, FAX: (203) 389-6020 (32)

National Bulk Equipment Inc, Holland, MI. Tel: (616) 399-2220, FAX: (616) 399-7365, E-Mail: sales@nbe-inc.com, Web Site: www.nbe-inc.com (16)

National Business Furniture Inc, Milwaukee, WI. Tel: (414) 276-8511, (800) 558-1010, FAX: (414) 276-8371, Web Site: www.nationalbusinessfurniture.com (10)

National Cable & Telecommunications Association, Washington, DC. Tel: (202) 222-2300, FAX: (202) 775-3675, Web Site: www.ncta.com (40)

National Cable Communications, New York, NY. Tel: (212) 548-3300, FAX: (212) 519-0099, Web Site: www.spotcable.com (32)

National Catholic Reporter Publishing Co Inc, Kansas City, MO. Tel: (816) 531-0538, (800) 444-8910, FAX: (816) 968-2268, Web Site: www.ncronline.org (17)

National City Bank, Cleveland, OH. Tel: (216) 222-2000, (800) 622-8100, FAX: (216) 222-9359, Web Site: www.nationalcity.com (14)

National Committee to Preserve Social Security & Medicare, Washington, DC. Tel: (202) 216-0420, (800) 966-1935, FAX: (202) 216-0446, E-Mail: kreard@ncpssm.org, Web Site: www.ncpssm.org (1)

National Community Pharmacists Association, Alexandria, VA. Tel: (703) 683-8200, (800) 544-7447, FAX: (703) 683-3619, E-Mail: info@ncpanet.org, Web Site: www.ncpanet.org (1)

National Contract Management Association, Ashburn, VA. Tel: (571) 382-1134, (800) 344-8096, E-Mail: memberservices@ncmghq.org, Web Site: www.ncmahq.org (1)

National Council on Compensation Insurance Inc (NCCI), Boca Raton, FL. Tel: (561) 893-1000, (800) 622-4123, FAX: (561) 893-1191, Web Site: www.ncci.com (1)

National Court Reporters Association, Vienna, VA. Tel: (703) 556-6272, (800) 272-6272, FAX: (703) 556-6291, E-Mail: msic@ncrahg.org, Web Site: www.ncraonline.org (1)

National Crime Prevention Council, Amsterdam, NY. Tel: (518) 842-4388, (888) 776-7763, FAX: (800) 995-5121, E-Mail: mcgruff@spocentral.com, Web Site: www.mcgruffspo.com (17)

National Defense Industrial Association, Arlington, VA. Tel: (703) 522-1820, FAX: (703) 522-1885, Web Site: www.ndia.org (1)

National Economic Research Associates Inc, Washington, DC. Tel: (202) 466-3510, FAX: (202) 466-3605, E-Mail: andrew.carron@nera.com, Web Site: www.nera.com (20)

National Electrical Manufacturers Association (NEMA), Rosslyn, VA. Tel: (703) 841-3200, FAX: (703) 841-5900, E-Mail: communications@nema.org, Web Site: www.nema.org (34)

National Emblem Sales, Indianapolis, IN. Tel: (317) 630-1247, (888) 453-4466, FAX: (317) 630-1381, E-Mail: emblem@legion.org, Web Site: www.emblem.legion.org (16)

National Enquirer, Boca Raton, FL. Tel: (561) 989-1221, Web Site: www.nationalenquirer.com (17)

National Envelope Advertising Co Inc, Meadowbrook, PA. Tel: (215) 887-8496, FAX: (215) 887-2652 (26)

National Envelope Corp, Ennis, TX. Tel: (800) 696-0409, Web Site: www.nationalenvelope.com (26)

National Envelope-Midwest, Lenexa, KS. Tel: (913) 888-3282, FAX: (913) 888-8743, E-Mail: sales@natenv.com, Web Site: www.nationalenvelope.com (26)

National Fire Protection Association, Quincy, MA. Tel: (617) 770-3000, FAX: (617) 770-0700, Web Site: www.nfpa.org (1)

National Foundation for Cancer Research, Bethesda, MD. Tel: (301) 654-1250, (800) 321-CURE, FAX: (301) 654-5824, E-Mail: info@nfcr.org, Web Site: www.nfcr.org (1)

National 4-H Supply Service, Chevy Chase, MD. Tel: (301) 961-2959, FAX: (301) 961-2937, E-Mail: 4hsupply@fourhcouncil.edu, Web Site: www.fourhcouncil.edu (16)

National Fulfillment Services, Holmes, PA. Tel: (610) 532-4700, (800) NFS-1306, FAX: (610) 586-3232, E-Mail: tkrueger@nfsrv.com, Web Site: www.nfsrv.com (28)

National Fundraising Lists, Bowie, MD. Tel: (410) 721-5700, FAX: (410) 721-5795, E-Mail: info@nflists.com, Web Site: www.nflists.com (23)

National Gallery of Art Gift Shop, Washington, DC. Tel: (202) 842-6466, (800) 697-9350, FAX: (202) 842-4043, Web Site: www.nga.gov (16)

National Geographic Society, Washington, DC. Tel: (202) 857-7311, (800) NGS-LINE, FAX: (202) 457-8200, Web Site: www.nationalgeographic.com (17)

National Golf Foundation, Jupiter, FL. Tel: (561) 744-6006, FAX: (561) 744-6107, E-Mail: ngf@ngf.org, Web Site: www.ngf.org (1)

National Graphics Inc, North Branford, CT. Tel: (203) 481-2351, FAX: (203) 483-0256 (27)

National Hardware Show, Norwalk, CT. Tel: (203) 840-5622, (888) 425-9377, FAX: (203) 840-9622, E-Mail: inquiry@hardware.reedexpo.com, Web Site: www.nationalhardwareshow.com (42)

National Humane Education Society, Charles Town, WV. Tel: (304) 725-0506, FAX: (304) 725-1523, E-Mail: nhesinformation@nhes.org, Web Site: www.nhes.org (1)

National Institute for Trial Advocacy (NITA), Boulder, CO. Tel: (800) 225-6482, Web Site: www.nita.org (1)

National Jewish Health, Denver, CO. Tel: (303) 398-1070, (800) 222-LUNG, FAX: (303) 398-1663, E-Mail: trubeyp@njhealth.org, Web Site: www.njhealth.org (1)

National Journal Group, Washington, DC. Tel: (202) 266-7541 (17)

National Law Enforcement Officers Memorial Fund, Washington, DC. Tel: (202) 737-3400, Web Site: www.nleomf.com (1)

National League for Nursing, New York, NY. Tel: (212) 363-5555, (800) 669-1656, FAX: (212) 812-0391, E-Mail: generalinfo@nln.org, Web Site: www.nln.org (1)

National Luggage Dealers Association, Glenview, IL. Tel: (847) 998-6869, FAX: (847) 998-6884, E-Mail: inquiry@nlda.com, Web Site: www.nlda.com (1)

National Mail Advertising Inc, Houston, TX. Tel: (713) 869-8551, FAX: (713) 868-5743, E-Mail: sales@nationalmail.com, Web Site: www.nationalmail.com (28)

National Mail Graphics Corp, Exton, PA. Tel: (610) 524-1600, FAX: (610) 524-7638, E-Mail: jsikorski@nmgcorp.com, Web Site: www.nmgcorp.com (27)

National Mail-It Inc, Shreveport, LA. Tel: (318) 683-0093, Web Site: www.nationalmailit.com (27)

National Mail/Marketing Corp, Broomall, PA. Tel: (610) 544-8200, FAX: (610) 544-1819, Web Site: www.natlmail.com (20)

National Mail Order Association (NMOA), Minneapolis, MN. Tel: (612) 788-1673, E-Mail: info@nmoa.org, Web Site: www.nmoa.org (40)

National Mailroom Service Inc, Knoxville, TN. Tel: (866) 862-4141, FAX: (800) 231-4141, E-Mail: info@nationalmailroom.com, Web Site: www.nationalmailroom.com (35)

National Medical Fellowships, New York, NY. Tel: (212) 483-8880, FAX: (212) 483-8897, Web Site: www.nfm-online.org (1)

National Motor Club of America Inc, Irving, TX. Tel: (972) 999-4400, (800) 523-4582, FAX: (972) 999-4405, Web Site: www.nmca.com (1)

National Multiple Sclerosis Society, Denver, CO. Tel: (303) 813-1052, Web Site: www.nmss.org (1)

National Osteoporosis Foundation, Washington, DC. Tel: (202) 721-6346, Web Site: www.nof.org (1)

National Parkinson Foundation, Miami, FL. Tel: (800) 937-4545, Web Site: www.parkinson.org (1)

National Pen Corp, San Diego, CA. Tel: (858) 675-3000, FAX: (858) 675-3030, Web Site: www.pens.com (6)

National Pension Service Inc, Burlington, VT. Tel: (802) 862-3994, FAX: (802) 865-2861, E-Mail: retirementservices@people.com, Web Site: www.peoples.com/retirementservices/ (14)

National Postal Forum, Fairfax, VA. Tel: (703) 218-5015, FAX: (703) 218-5020, E-Mail: info@npf.org, Web Site: www.npf.org (42)

National Railroad Passenger Corp, Washington, DC. Tel: (202) 906-3000, (800) USA-RAIL, FAX: (202) 906-3306, Web Site: www.amtrak.com (16)

National Relief Charities, Elkwood, VA. Tel: (540) 825-5950 (1)

National Research Center for College & University Admissions, Lees Summit, MO. Tel: (816) 525-2201, Web Site: www.nrccua.org (1)

National Research LLC, Washington, DC. Tel: (202) 686-9350, FAX: (202) 686-7163, E-Mail: survey@nationalres.com, Web Site: www.nationalres.com (30)

The National Restaurant Association Educational Foundation, Chicago, IL. Tel: (312) 715-1010, FAX: (312) 583-9767 (1)

National Retail Federation Inc, Washington, DC. Tel: (202) 783-7971, (800) 673-4692, FAX: (202) 737-2849, E-Mail: webmaster@nrf.com, Web Site: www.nrf.com (1)

National Review, New York, NY. Tel: (212) 679-7330, FAX: (212) 849-2852, Web Site: www.nationalreview.com (17)

National Rifle Association of America, Fairfax, VA. Tel: (703) 267-1000, (800) 672-3888, FAX: (703) 267-3957, E-Mail: nra.contact@nra.org, Web Site: www.nra.org (1)

National Rural Electric Cooperative Association, Arlington, VA. Tel: (703) 907-5500, FAX: (703) 907-5528, Web Site: www.nreca.org (1)

National School Boards Association Inc, Alexandria, VA. Tel: (703) 838-6722, FAX: (703) 683-7590, E-Mail: info@nsba.org, Web Site: www.nsba.org (1)

National Semiconductor Corp, Santa Clara, CA. Tel: (408) 721-5000, (800) 272-9959, FAX: (408) 245-0671, E-Mail: new.feedback@nsc.com, Web Site: www.national.com (16)

National Seminars Group, Shawnee Mission, KS. Tel: (913) 432-7755, (800) 258-7246, FAX: (913) 432-0824, E-Mail: cstserv@natsem.com, Web Site: www.natsem.com (16)

National Society of Collegiate Scholars, Washington, DC. Tel: (202) 265-9000, Web Site: www.nscs.org (1)

National Stationery Show, White Plains, NY. Tel: (914) 421-3200, (800) 272-SHOW, FAX: (914) 948-6180, E-Mail: cate_doyle@glmshows.com, Web Site: www.glmshows.com (42)

National Systems Corp, Chicago, IL. Tel: (312) 855-1000, FAX: (312) 222-1605, E-Mail: support@nationalsystems.com, Web Site: www.nationalsystems.com (29)

National Technical Information Service, Alexandria, VA. Tel: (703) 605-6000, FAX: (703) 605-6900, Web Site: www.ntis.gov (17)

National Trust for Historic Preservation, Washington, DC. Tel: (202) 588-6124, Web Site: www.nationaltrust.org (1)

The National Underwriter Co, Erlanger, KY. Tel: (800) 543-0874, FAX: (856) 692-2246, E-Mail: customerservice@nuco.com, Web Site: www.nuco.com (17)

National University, La Jolla, CA. Tel: (800) 628-8648, Web Site: www.nu.edu (1)

National Wholesale Co Inc, Lexington, NC. Tel: (336) 248-5904, (800) 480-4673, FAX: (336) 248-2880, E-Mail: customerservice@shopnational.com, Web Site: www.shopnational.com (2)

National Wildlife Federation, Reston, VA. Tel: (703) 438-6000, Web Site: www.nwf.org (1)

Nationwide Beauty & Barber Supply, Syracuse, NY. Tel: (315) 446-9026, FAX: (315) 446-8943, E-Mail: sales@nationwidebeauty.com, Web Site: www.nationwidebeauty.com (16)

Nationwide Card Services Inc, Memphis, TN. Tel: (901) 383-4405, Web Site: www.nationwidecardservices.com (35)

Nationwide Displays Inc, Ronkonkoma, NY. Tel: (631) 467-2034, FAX: (631) 467-2079, E-Mail: info@nationwidedisplays.com, Web Site: www.nationwidedisplays.com (16)

Nationwide Graphic/Premier Print Organizations, Houston, TX. Tel: (713) 961-4700, Web Site: www.nationwidegraphics.com (27)

Nationwide Mutual Insurance Co, Columbus, OH. Tel: (614) 249-7111, (800) 882-2822, FAX: (614) 854-3676, Web Site: www.nationwide.com (15)

Nationwide Yellow Pages Service, Hackettstown, NJ. Tel: (973) 765-9600, (800) 526-2718, FAX: (973) 765-0004, E-Mail: info@nationwideyp.com, Web Site: www.nationwideyp.com (35)

Native American Heritage Associations, Front Royal, VA. Tel: (540) 636-1020, Web Site: www.naha-inc.org (1)

Native American Rights Fund, Boulder, CO. Tel: (303) 447-8760, Web Site: www.narf.org (1)

Natural Essentials Inc, Streetsboro, OH. Tel: (330) 562-8022, (888) 968-7220, FAX: (330) 562-8022, E-Mail: questions@naturalessentials.com, Web Site: www.naturalessentials.com (5)

Natural History Magazine, Durham, NC. Tel: (646) 356-6500, FAX: (646) 356-6511, E-Mail: nhmag@naturalhistorymag.com, Web Site: www.naturalhistorymag.com (17)

The Nature Conservancy, Arlington, VA. Tel: (703) 841-5300, (800) 628-6860, FAX: (703) 841-1283, E-Mail: magazine@tnc.org, Web Site: www.nature.org (1)

Nature Publishing Group, New York, NY. Tel: (212) 726-9200, FAX: (212) 696-9006, E-Mail: nature@natureny.com, Web Site: www.nature.com (17)

Nature Trade Center, Naples, FL. Tel: (239) 592-7611, Web Site: www.naturerx.com (21)

Naturmed, Camp Verde, AZ. Tel: (800) 218-1378, Web Site: www.ivlproducts.com (7)

Naughton, Cheryl, M2Media 360, Park Ridge, IL. Tel: (760) 318-7000, E-Mail: cnaughton@m2media360.com, Web Site: www.m2media360.com (17)

Nauman, Barbara, Providence Journal Telemarketing, Providence, RI. Tel: (401) 277-7000, FAX: (401) 277-8046, E-Mail: bnauman@projo.com, Web Site: www.projo.com (27)

Nautilus Inc, Vancouver, WA. Tel: (360) 859-2900, (800) 675-0171, FAX: (360) 694-2755, Web Site: www.nautilus.com (11)

Naval Institute Press, Annapolis, MD. Tel: (410) 268-6110, (800) 233-8764, FAX: (410) 571-1703, E-Mail: webmaster@usni.org, Web Site: www.usni.org/navalinstitutepress (17)

Navistar Inc, Warrenville, IL. Tel: (630) 753-5804, (800) 448-7825, FAX: (630) 753-2303, Web Site: www.navistar.com (16)

Navitar Inc, Rochester, NY. Tel: (585) 359-4000, FAX: (585) 359-4999, E-Mail: info@navitar.com, Web Site: www.navitar.com (7)

Navy Federal Credit Union, Vienna, VA. Tel: (703) 206-4245, Web Site: www.navyfederal.org (14)

Nawrot, Dan, Okun Brothers Shoes Inc, Kalamazoo, MI. Tel: (269) 342-1536, (800) 433-6344, FAX: (269) 383-3401 (2)

Naylor Inc, Gainesville, FL. Tel: (404) 739-7280, Web Site: www.naylorinc.com (27)

Neagoe, Dan, CRK Computer Services, Southfield, MI. Tel: (248) 569-3050, FAX: (248) 569-5259, E-Mail: information@crkusa.com, Web Site: www.crkusa.com (22)

Neal, Carl, R., Amica Insurance, Lincoln, RI. Tel: (401) 334-6000, (800) 652-6422, FAX: (401) 334-4241, Web Site: www.amica.com (15)

Neal, Diane, Mervyn's, Pleasanton, CA. Tel: (510) 727-3000, (800) 480-5014, FAX: (510) 727-5851, Web Site: www.mervyns.com (16)

Neal, Janell, H E Butt Grocery Co, San Antonio, TX. Tel: (210) 938-8357, (800) 432-3113, FAX: (210) 938-7511, Web Site: www.heb.com (16)

Neal, Michael, A., GE Partnership Marketing Group, Schaumburg, IL. Tel: (847) 605-3000, FAX: (847) 605-7368, Web Site: www.gepmg.com (14)

Nealis, Nora, Neighborhood Cleaners Association International, New York, NY. Tel: (212) 967-3002, (800) 888-1622, FAX: (212) 967-2240, E-Mail: info@nca-i.com, Web Site: www.nca-i.com (1)

Nealy, Nila, Black Olive Co, Chicago, IL. Tel: (312) 893-5454, FAX: (312) 276-8636, E-Mail: pittenger@blackoliveco.com, Web Site: www.blackoliveco.com (35)

Nealy, Steve, Black Olive Co, Chicago, IL. Tel: (312) 893-5454, FAX: (312) 276-8636, E-Mail: pittenger@blackoliveco.com, Web Site: www.blackoliveco.com (35)

Neanth, Greg, Gifts Corp, Barrie, ON. Tel: (905) 670-1126, (800) 565-3130, FAX: (905) 670-1127, E-Mail: customerservice@regal.ca, Web Site: www.regalgreetings.com (6)

Neary, Amy, John Alden Life Insurance Co/North Star Marketing, Duluth, GA. Tel: (678) 473-1211, (800) 768-6288, FAX: (678) 473-9573, Web Site: www.nstarmarketing.com (15)

Neary, Daniel, P., Mutual of Omaha, Omaha, NE. Tel: (402) 342-7600, (800) 775-6000, FAX: (402) 351-2775, Web Site: www.mutualofomaha.com (15)

Neary, Kevin, Prime Media Equine Group, Gaithersburg, MD. Tel: (301) 977-3900, FAX: (301) 990-9015, Web Site: www.equisearch.com (17)

Neat Co, Philadelphia, PA. Tel: (866) 632-8732, Web Site: neatco.com (22)

Nebel, Randy, Longview Fibre Co, Longview, WA. Tel: (360) 425-1550, FAX: (360) 230-5135, E-Mail: info@longviewfibre.com, Web Site: www.longfibre.com (25)

Neckes, Mark, Johnson & Wales University, Providence, RI. Tel: (401) 598-1000, (800) DIAL-JWU, FAX: (401) 598-1833, E-Mail: admissions.pvd@jwu.edu, Web Site: www.jwu.edu (41)

Neejer, Kevin, CNY Awards & Apparel Inc, New Hartford, NY. Tel: (315) 733-0931, Web Site: www.cnyapprel.com (5)

Neekin, Jim, MVBMS EURO RSCG, New York, NY. Tel: (212) 886-2000, FAX: (212) 886-2016, E-Mail: northamerica@eurorscg.com, Web Site: www.eurorscg.com (35)

Neely, Stacie, Bosom Buddy Breast Forms, Boise, ID. Tel: (208) 343-9696, (800) 262-2789, FAX: (208) 343-9266, E-Mail: custserv@bosombuddy.com, Web Site: www.bosombuddy.com (7)

Neff, R.L., International Irrigation Systems, Niagara Falls, NY. Tel: (905) 688-4090, (877) IRRIGRO, FAX: (905) 688-4093, E-Mail: info@irrigro.com, Web Site: www.irrigro.com (8)

Negri, Paul, T., Dover Publications Inc, Mineola, NY. Tel: (516) 294-7000, (800) 223-3130, FAX: (516) 873-1401, Web Site: www.doverpublications.com (17)

Nehmer, Kathy, Educators Progress Service Inc, Randolph, WI. Tel: (920) 326-3126, (888) 951-4469, Web Site: www.freeteachingaids.com (17)

Neibauer, Nathan, Neibauer Press, Warminster, PA. Tel: (215) 322-6200, (800) 322-6203, FAX: (215) 322-2495, E-Mail: sales@neibauer.com, Web Site: www.neibauer.com (27)

Neibauer, Ruth, Neibauer Press, Warminster, PA. Tel: (215) 322-6200, (800) 322-6203, FAX: (215) 322-2495, E-Mail: sales@neibauer.com, Web Site: www.neibauer.com (27)

Neibauer Press, Warminster, PA. Tel: (215) 322-6200, (800) 322-6203, FAX: (215) 322-2495, E-Mail: sales@neibauer.com, Web Site: www.neibauer.com (27)

Neighborhood Cleaners Association International, New York, NY. Tel: (212) 967-3002, (800) 888-1622, FAX: (212) 967-2240, E-Mail: info@nca-i.com, Web Site: www.nca-i.com (1)

Neighborhood Greetings, Millersville, PA. Tel: (717) 871-9053, (800) 332-9200, FAX: (717) 871-9053, E-Mail: info@neighborhoodgreetings.net, Web Site: www.neighborhoodgreetings.net (23)

Neil, Steven, M., Cooper Surgical Inc, Trumbull, CT. Tel: (203) 601-5200, (800) 645-3670, FAX: (203) 601-1007, Web Site: www.coopersurgical.com (7)

Neill, Tiffany, Lautman Maska Neill & Co, Washington, DC. Tel: (202) 296-9660, Web Site: www.lautmandc.com (1)

Neiman, Kathy, Fort Hays State University, Hays, KS. Tel: (785) 628-FHSU, FAX: (785) 628-4046, Web Site: www.fhsu.edu (41)

Neiman, Tom, Stock Montage Inc, Chicago, IL. Tel: (773) 637-9790, (800) 404-0425, FAX: (773) 637-9794, E-Mail: mail@stockmontage.com, Web Site: www.stockmontage.com (38)

Neiman-Marcus Group, Dallas, TX. Tel: (214) 743-7600, (888) 888-4757, FAX: (214) 573-5320, Web Site: www.neimanmarcus.com (8)

Neimer, Dave, VF Imagewear, Nashville, TN. Tel: (615) 565-5000, (800) 733-5271, Web Site: www.vfimagewear.com (2)

Neiner, Jean, StayWell/Krames, San Bruno, CA. Tel: (650) 742-0400, FAX: (650) 244-4568, Web Site: www.staywell.com (17)

Nelis, Angie, Roche Diagnostics Corp, Indianapolis, IN. Tel: (317) 521-2000, Web Site: www.accu-chek.com (7)

Nelles, William, A., Monex Deposit Co, Newport Beach, CA. Tel: (949) 752-1400, (800) 444-8317, FAX: (949) 752-7214, E-Mail: info@monex.com, Web Site: www.monex.com (14)

Nelson, Brian, Trancos Inc, Pleasanton, CA. Tel: (650) 364-3110, Web Site: www.trancos.com (16)

Nelson, Carl, A., Pastime Publications Inc, Denver, CO. Tel: (303) 534-7867, (888) 650-8665, FAX: (630) 214-7600, E-Mail: post@pastimecompany.com, Web Site: www.pastimecompany.com (17)

Nelson, David, Bankers Life & Casualty Co, Chicago, IL. Tel: (312) 396-6000, (800) 231-9150, Web Site: www.bankerslife.com (15)

Nelson, Dean, Prime Media Equine Group, Gaithersburg, MD. Tel: (301) 977-3900, FAX: (301) 990-9015, Web Site: www.equisearch.com (17)

Nelson, Dean, Primedia Inc, Norcross, GA. Tel: (678) 421-3000, (800) 216-1423, Web Site: www.primedia.com (31)

Nelson, Donald, C., SGD Golf Co, Tallmadge, OH. Tel: (330) 745-4400, (800) 321-3411, FAX: (330) 745-4420, (888) 299-4240, Web Site: www.sgdgolf.com (34)

Nelson, Erik, PackStream LLC, Louisville, KY. Tel: (502) 552-9624, Web Site: www.packstream.com (20)

Nelson, Howard C., Omar's Touch Therapy, Madison, WI. Tel: (608) 658-6718, E-Mail: omar@omarstouch.com, Web Site: www.omarstouch.com (23)

Nelson, John, Nelson-Jameson Inc, Marshfield, WI. Tel: (715) 387-1151, (800) 826-8302, FAX: (715) 387-8746, E-Mail: sales@nelsonjameson.com, Web Site: www.nelsonjameson.com (9)

Nelson, Judy, Creative Catalogs Corp, Lemont, IL. Tel: (630) 783-2400, Web Site: www.personalcreations.com (6)

Nelson, Judy, Personal Creations, Lemont, IL. Tel: (630) 783-2400, (866) 834-7695, Web Site: www.personalcreations.com (6)

Nelson, Kristi, Nelson Crab Inc, Tokeland, WA. Tel: (360) 267-2911, (800) 262-0069, FAX: (360) 267-2921, E-Mail: seatreats@techline.com, Web Site: www.nelsoncrab.com (4)

Nelson, Paul, Paul Nelson Direct Marketing, Santa Monica, CA. Tel: (310) 392-9533 (20)

Nelson, Scott, Collector's Armoury Ltd, McDonough, GA. Tel: (703) 493-9120, FAX: (703) 493-9424, Web Site: www.collectorsarmoury.com (6)

Nelson, Scott, R., Bobcat Co, West Fargo, ND. Tel: (701) 241-8700, FAX: (701) 241-8704, Web Site: www.bobcat.com (16)

Nelson, Shana, Missett, Jazzercise Inc, Carlsbad, CA. Tel: (760) 476-1750, (800) FIT IS IT, FAX: (760) 602-7180, E-Mail: info@jazzercise.com, Web Site: www.jazzercise.com (2)

Nelson, Terry, The Guild Inc, Madison, WI. Tel: (608) 257-2590, Web Site: www.guild.com (8)

Nelson, Todd, Kwik-File, Sheboygan, WI. Tel: (763) 572-1980, (800) 822-8037, FAX: (763) 572-0168, Web Site: www.mayline.com (27)

Nelson, Todd, The Herald & Review, Decatur, IL. Tel: (217) 429-5151, FAX: (217) 421-6913, E-Mail: hrdirect@herald-review.com, Web Site: www.herald-review.com (17)

Nelson, Tom, Collector's Armoury Ltd, McDonough, GA. Tel: (703) 493-9120, FAX: (703) 493-9424, Web Site: www.collectorsarmoury.com (6)

Nelson Crab Inc, Tokeland, WA. Tel: (360) 267-2911, (800) 262-0069, FAX: (360) 267-2921, E-Mail: seatreats@techline.com, Web Site: www.nelsoncrab.com (4)

Nelson-Jameson Inc, Marshfield, WI. Tel: (715) 387-1151, (800) 826-8302, FAX: (715) 387-8746, E-Mail: sales@nelsonjameson.com, Web Site: www.nelsonjameson.com (9)

Paul Nelson Direct Marketing, Santa Monica, CA. Tel: (310) 392-9533 (20)

Thomas Nelson, Inc, Nashville, TN. Tel: (615) 889-9000, (800) 251-4000, FAX: (615) 889-5940, Web Site: www.thomasnelson.com (17)

Neo-Tech Publishing Co, Henderson, NV. Tel: (702) 891-0303, FAX: (702) 795-8393 (17)

Neolane, Newton, MA. Tel: (617) 467-6760, Web Site: www.neolane.com (22)

Neopost, Carrollton, TX. Tel: (510) 489-6800, (800) 636-7678, FAX: (510) 475-6317, (510) 487-6704, Web Site: www.neopostinc.com (9)

Nesbitt, Mark, TNS Media Intelligence, New York, NY. Tel: (212) 991-6000, FAX: (212) 991-6010, Web Site: www.tns-mi.com (32)

Nesco American Harvest, Two Rivers, WI. Tel: (920) 793-1368, (800) 288-4545, FAX: (920) 794-3161, Web Site: www.nesco.com (32)

Ness, Antonia, Gruppo Levey & Co, New York, NY. Tel: (212) 697-5753, FAX: (212) 949-7294, E-Mail: info@glconline.com, Web Site: www.glconline.com (14)

Ness, Greg, SUNDOG, Fargo, ND. Tel: (701) 235-5525, (888) 9-SUNDOG, FAX: (701) 235-8941, Web Site: www.sundog.net (35)

Nessim, Linda, The Princeton Review, Scranton, PA. Tel: (212) 874-8282, FAX: (212) 874-0775, E-Mail: helpme@review.com, Web Site: www.review.com (16)

NestFamily.com, Coppell, TX. Tel: (972) 402-7100, (800) 596-7386, FAX: (972) 629-7181, Web Site: www.nestfamily.com (3)

Nestle Clinical Nutrition Co, Hopkins, MN. Tel: (877) 463-7853, (800) 284-9488, FAX: (877) 563-7853, Web Site: www.nestle-nutrition.com (16)

Nestle Purina/Checkmark Communications, Saint Louis, MO. Tel: (314) 982-1000, FAX: (314) 982-3580, Web Site: www.purina.com (35)

Nestle USA, Glendale, CA. Tel: (818) 549-6000, (800) 225-2270, FAX: (818) 549-6952, Web Site: www.nestleusa.com (4)

Net-Results, Golden, CO. Tel: (303) 771-2552, Web Site: www.net-results.com (32)

Net 60 LLC, New York, NY. Tel: (201) 833-9003, FAX: (201) 336-9088, E-Mail: chaim@net60.com, Web Site: www.net60.com (23)

NetHawk Interactive, Emeryville, CA. Tel: (510) 595-2220, Web Site: www.nethawk.net (23)

NetProspex Inc, Waltham, MA. Tel: (888) 826-4877, E-Mail: sales@netprospex.com, Web Site: www.netprospex.com (22)

NetSpend, San Mateo, CA. Web Site: www.netspend.com (14)

Nettesheim, Matt, Emergency Essentials Inc, Orem, UT. Tel: (801) 222-9596, FAX: (801) 222-9598, E-Mail: webmaster@beprepared.com, Web Site: www.beprepared.com (16)

Netweb/Omni LLC, Ellicott City, MD. Tel: (410) 591-1900, E-Mail: barry@netwebomni.com, Web Site: www.netwebomni.com (40)

Network for Good, Bethesda, MD. Tel: (240) 482-3211, Web Site: www.networkforgood.org (1)

Network Solutions LLC, Herndon, VA. Tel: (703) 668-4600, Web Site: www.networksolutions.com (32)

Network Tel Services Inc, Woodland Hills, CA. Tel: (818) 992-4300, (800) 727-6874, FAX: (818) 992-8415, Web Site: www.nts.net (16)

Networking Alternatives for Publishers, Retailers & Artists, Inc, Eastsound, WA. Tel: (360) 376-2702, (800) 367-1907, FAX: (360) 376-2704, E-Mail: futureweb@rockisland.com (40)

Neuberger, Scott, Infocore Inc, Carlsbad, CA. Tel: (760) 607-2500, FAX: (760) 607-2505, E-Mail: bstewart@infocoreinc.com, Web Site: www.infocoreinc.com (23)

Neuberger & Berman Management, New York, NY. Tel: (212) 476-8800, (800) 877-9700, FAX: (212) 476-9090, Web Site: www.nb.com (14)

Neufeld, Dan, Lin Terry, Paterson, NJ. Tel: (973) 345-6677, FAX: (973) 345-5551, E-Mail: linterry@aol.com, Web Site: www.linterry.com (6)

Neukranz, Richard, K., Richard K Neukranz Associates, Jacksonville, FL. Tel: (904) 998-1201, FAX: (904) 998-1579, E-Mail: rneukranz@bellsouth.net (39)

Richard K Neukranz Associates, Jacksonville, FL. Tel: (904) 998-1201, FAX: (904) 998-1579, E-Mail: rneukranz@bellsouth.net (39)

Neuman, Morris, SpeechSoft Inc, Armonk, NY. Tel: (914) 273-5560, (800) 878-8117, E-Mail: sales@speechsoft.com, Web Site: www.speechsoft.com (29)

Neustar Inc, Sterling, VA. Tel: (571) 434-5400, Web Site: www.tcpacompliance.us (29)

Neustein, Barry, Poly-Flex Corp, Edgewood, NY. Tel: (631) 586-9500, FAX: (631) 586-6631, E-Mail: info@poly-flexcorp.com, Web Site: www.poly-flexcorp.com (26)

Neutron Industries, Phoenix, AZ. Tel: (602) 864-0090, (888) 712-7127, FAX: (602) 357-3996, (877) 646-7337, E-Mail: questions@neutronindustries.com, Web Site: www.neutronindustries.com (16)

Nevada Commission on Tourism, Carson City, NV. Tel: (775) 687-4322, (800) NEVADA 8, FAX: (775) 687-6779, Web Site: www.travelnevada.com (1)

Nevada Magazine, Carson City, NV. Tel: (775) 687-5416, FAX: (775) 687-6159, E-Mail: editor@nevadamagazine.com, Web Site: www.nevadamagazine.com (17)

Nevard, Stephen, One On One Advertising Inc, New Haven, CT. Tel: (203) 562-6259, FAX: (203) 789-1253 (35)

Nevco Scoreboard Co, Greenville, IL. Tel: (618) 664-0360, (800) 851-4040, FAX: (618) 664-0398, E-Mail: sales@nevcoscoreboards.com, Web Site: www.nevcoscoreboards.com (16)

Nevels, James, Hershey Foods Corp, Hershey, PA. Tel: (800) 454-7737, FAX: (717) 534-5204, Web Site: www.hersheygifts.com (4)

Neville, Shawn, MELDISCO, Mahwah, NJ. Tel: (201) 934-2000, FAX: (201) 934-2570, Web Site: www.meldisco.com (16)

Nevin, Darius, G., Protection One Inc, Lawrence, KS. Tel: (785) 856-5500, (800) GET-HELP, Web Site: www.protectionone.com (16)

Nevinger, MG, Nevco Scoreboard Co, Greenville, IL. Tel: (618) 664-0360, (800) 851-4040, FAX: (618) 664-0398, E-Mail: sales@nevcoscoreboards.com, Web Site: www.nevcoscoreboards.com (16)

Nevitt, Toni, E Media Advantage, Livingston, NJ. Tel: (917) 994-3685, FAX: (973) 455-1312, E-Mail: tnevitt@emediaadvantage.com, Web Site: emediaadvantage.com (20)

New, David, Americansource Bergan, Chesterbrook, PA. Tel: (610) 727-7000, (800) 829-3132, E-Mail: info@amerisourcebergan.com, Web Site: www.amerisourcebergan.com (7)

New American Dimensions, Los Angeles, CA. Tel: (310) 670-6800 (20)

New & Unique Videos, San Diego, CA. Tel: (619) 644-3001, (619) 644-3000, E-Mail: info@newuniquevideos.com, Web Site: www.newuniquevideos.com (3)

New Business USA, Omaha, NE. Tel: (800) 321-0869, FAX: (402) 331-0176, E-Mail: help@infousa.com, Web Site: www.infousa.com (16)

New Customer Acquisition, Medford, OR. Tel: (541) 779-9999, FAX: (541) 779-1935, E-Mail: bobk@postage-exempt.com (31)

NEW Customer Service Companies Inc, Sterling, VA. Tel: (703) 707-1582, Web Site: www.newcorp.com (20)

New Day Marketing Ltd, Santa Barbara, CA. Tel: (805) 965-7833, FAX: (805) 965-1284, Web Site: www.newdaymarketing.com (35)

New Directions Publishing Corp, New York, NY. Tel: (212) 255-0230, FAX: (212) 255-0231, E-Mail: editorial@ndbooks.com, Web Site: www.ndpublishing.com (17)

New England Cheesemaking Supply Co, South Deerfield, MA. Tel: (413) 628-3808, FAX: (413) 628-4061, E-Mail: info@cheesemaking.com, Web Site: www.cheesemaking.com (4)

New England Direct Marketing Association, Wellesley Hills, MA. Tel: (781) 237-1366, FAX: (781) 431-8118, E-Mail: info@nedma.com, Web Site: www.nedma.com (40)

New England Journal of Medicine, Waltham, MA. Tel: (781) 893-3800, FAX: (781) 893-7729, Web Site: www.nejm.org (17)

New England Life Insurance Co, Boston, MA. Tel: (617) 578-2000, FAX: (617) 536-2393, Web Site: www.nefn.metlife.com (15)

New England List Services Inc, Danville, VT. Tel: (802) 684-1179, (877) 252-2100, FAX: (802) 684-2113, E-Mail: dave@nelists.com, Web Site: www.nelists.com (23)

New England Mail Order Association, Scarborough, ME. Tel: (207) 885-0090, (860) 691-1260, FAX: (207) 885-0097, Web Site: www.nemoa.org (40)

New England Stock Photo, Glastonbury, CT. FAX: (860) 659-3235 (38)

New Hampshire Public Television, Durham, NH. Tel: (603) 868-1100, E-Mail: themailbox@nhptv.org, Web Site: www.nhptv.org (32)

New Hermes Inc, Duluth, GA. Tel: (770) 623-0331, (800) 843-7637, FAX: (800) 533-7637, E-Mail: sales@gravograph-newhermes.com, Web Site: www.gravograph.com/usa/government/index.php (34)

New Income Sources, Hermosa Beach, CA. Tel: (310) 376-9238, (800) 288-7058, FAX: (310) 376-9258, E-Mail: pk@nisdm.com (21)

New Jersey Institute for Continuing Legal Education, New Brunswick, NJ. Tel: (732) 249-5100, Web Site: www.njicle.com (1)

Nexx Group Inc, Fort Myers, FL. Tel: (239) 225-1516, (800) 566-1183, FAX: (239) 288-4968, Web Site: www.nexxagroup.com (23)

Nexxlinx (HQ), Atlanta, GA. Tel: (770) 250-0349, Web Site: www.nexxlinx.com (22)

Nezwek, Joe, F P International, Redwood City, CA. Tel: (650) 261-5300, (800) 866-9946, FAX: (650) 361-1713, Web Site: www.fpintl.com (16)

NFocus Consulting Inc, Lancaster, OH. Tel: (740) 654-5809, Web Site: www.nfocusconsulting.com (22)

Ng, Pamela, Teleflora, Los Angeles, CA. Tel: (310) 966-3586, Web Site: www.teleflora.com (16)

Ng, S. K., WMG USA Inc, New York, NY. Tel: (212) 278-0066, E-Mail: business@wmg-group.com, Web Site: www.wmg-group.com (28)

Nguyen, Nam, TDC Direct, Mississauga, ON Canada. Tel: (905) 564-6616, FAX: (905) 564-6621, E-Mail: nam@tdcdirect.com, Web Site: www.tdcdirect.com (21)

Nguyen, Tiffany, San Francisco Herb & Natural Food Co, Fremont, CA. Tel: (510) 770-1215, (800) 227-2830, FAX: (510) 770-9021, E-Mail: customerservice@herbspicetea.com, Web Site: www.herbspicetea.com (4)

Niaura, Matt, Engineering Services & Products Co, South Windsor, CT. Tel: (860) 528-1119, (800) 835-7877, FAX: (800) 457-8887, Web Site: www.teksupply.com (9)

Niblock, Robert, A., Lowe's Companies Inc, Mooresville, NC. Tel: (704) 758-1000, FAX: (336) 651-4766, Web Site: www.lowes.com (8)

Nice Lines Direct Mail, Norristown, PA. Tel: (610) 279-1100, (888) 815-NICE, FAX: (610) 279-7800, Web Site: www.nicelines.com (21)

Nicely, Olza, M., GEICO Direct, Washington, DC. Tel: (301) 986-2842, (800) 841-3000, FAX: (301) 986-2068, Web Site: www.geico.com (15)

Nicholas, J. K., Chelsea Clock Co Inc, Chelsea, MA. Tel: (617) 884-0250, (800) 284-1778, FAX: (617) 830-0599, Web Site: www.chelseaclock.com (6)

Nicholich, Mike, Tech Image, Buffalo Grove, IL. Tel: (847) 279-0022, (888) 4-TECH-PR, FAX: (847) 279-8922, E-Mail: info@techimage.com, Web Site: www.techimage.com (35)

Nichols Ph.D, Judith E., Covenant House International Headquarters, New York, NY. Tel: (212) 727-4000, (800) 999-9999, FAX: (212) 727-4992, Web Site: www.covenanthouse.org (1)

Nichols, Gaylord, California Institute of Technology, Pasadena, CA. Tel: (626) 395-3746, FAX: (626) 795-7174, E-Mail: execedu@caltech.edu, Web Site: www.irc.caltech.edu (16)

Nichols, Su-Liu, Newspaper Association of America, Arlington, VA. Tel: (703) 902-1600, FAX: (571) 366-1195, Web Site: www.naa.org (1)

Nichols, Thomas, B., Blue Grass Mailing, Data & Fulfillment Services, Lexington, KY. Tel: (859) 231-7272, (800) 928-6245, FAX: (859) 259-1214, E-Mail: info@bgmailing.com, Web Site: www.bgmailing.com (28)

Nicholson, James, B., Amerisure Insurance Cos, Farmington Hills, MI. Tel: (248) 615-9000, (800) 257-1900, FAX: (248) 615-8224, Web Site: www.amerisure.com (15)

Nicholson, Nick, Keeneland Association Inc, Lexington, KY. Tel: (859) 254-3412, (800) 456-3412, FAX: (859) 255-2484, Web Site: www.keeneland.com (16)

Nicholson Kovac Inc, Kansas City, MO. Tel: (816) 842-8881, FAX: (816) 842-6340, E-Mail: nk@nicholsonkovac.com, Web Site: www.nkhw.com (35)

Nichtawitz, Anthony, Caswell-Massey Co Ltd, Edison, NJ. Tel: (732) 225-2181, (800) 326-0500, FAX: (732) 225-2385, E-Mail: info@caswellmasseyltd.com, Web Site: www.caswellmassey.com (7)

Nichting, Thomas, CSG Interactive Messaging, Omaha, NE. Tel: (402) 398-4100, (800) 888-3151, FAX: (402) 398-4000, Web Site: www.prairiesys.com (29)

Nichting, Tom, Call Interactive, Omaha, NE. Tel: (402) 498-7000, FAX: (402) 498-7900, Web Site: www.callit.com (29)

Nickel, Jeff, TrueSense Marketing, Freedom, PA. Tel: (877) 878-6584, Web Site: www.truesense.com (35)

Nickel, Steve, Back to the Bible, Lincoln, NE. Tel: (402) 464-7200, (800) 811-2397, FAX: (402) 464-7474, E-Mail: info@backtothebible.org, Web Site: www.backtothebible.org (5)

Nickerson, Greg, Bader Rutter & Associates, Brookfield, WI. Tel: (262) 784-7200, FAX: (262) 938-5595, Web Site: www.baderrutter.com (35)

Nicklaus, Jack, Golden Bear Golf Inc, North Palm Beach, FL. Tel: (561) 626-3900, FAX: (561) 626-4104, Web Site: www.nicklaus.com (16)

Nicksic, John, John Nicksic, Santa Fe, NM. Tel: (505) 983-7656, FAX: (505) 983-7159, E-Mail: nicksic@mindspring.com (39)

John Nicksic, Santa Fe, NM. Tel: (505) 983-7656, FAX: (505) 983-7159, E-Mail: nicksic@mindspring.com (39)

Nicolichuk, Michael, Arrowhead Mountain Spring Water, Wilkes Barre, PA. Tel: (800) 873-7775, Web Site: www.arrowheadwater.com (16)

Nicolin, Magnus, Esselte Americas, Melville, NY. Tel: (631) 675-5700, (800) 645-6051, FAX: (631) 622-1970, Web Site: www.curtis.com (16)

Nicols, Virginia, The Marketing Machine, Irvine, CA. Tel: (949) 733-3778, (949) 733-1778, FAX: (949) 559-6993, E-Mail: request@the-marketing-machine.com, Web Site: www.mktgmach.com (39)

Nieberding, Paul, Lexus Division of Toyota, Torrance, CA. Tel: (213) 328-2075 (12)

Niehaus, Sherry, Mays Mission for the Handicapped Inc, Heber Springs, AR. Tel: (501) 362-7526, (888) 503-7955, FAX: (501) 362-7529, E-Mail: sniehaus@maysmission.org, Web Site: www.maysmission.org (27)

Nielsen, Jane, Frito-Lay, Plano, TX. Tel: (972) 334-7000, (800) 352-4477, FAX: (972) 334-2019, Web Site: www.fritolay.com (16)

Nielsen, New York, NY. Tel: (703) 488-2700, (800) 765-7615, FAX: (703) 488-2800, E-Mail: bmcomm@nielsen.com, Web Site: www.nielsenbusinessmedia.com (42)

Nielsen Business Media, New York, NY. Tel: (646) 654-4500, FAX: (646) 654-7212, E-Mail: bmcomm@nielsen.com, Web Site: www.nielsenbusinessmedia.com (16)

Nielsen Claritas, San Diego, CA. Tel: (800) 866-6520, Web Site: www.claritas.com (30)

The Nielsen Co, New York, NY. Tel: (646) 654-5000, E-Mail: contactcommunications@nielsen.com, Web Site: www.nielsen.com (17)

Nielsen Media Research, Inc, New York, NY. Tel: (646) 654-8300, Web Site: en-us.nielsen.com (30)

Nielsen Trade Dimensions, Wilton, CT. Tel: (203) 222-5750, (800) 291-0410, FAX: (203) 222-5701, E-Mail: tradedimensions.info@nielsen.com, Web Site: www.tradedimensions.com (17)

Niemeyer, W. Phil, NASCO, Fort Atkinson, WI. Tel: (920) 563-2446, FAX: (920) 563-8296, E-Mail: info@nasco.com, Web Site: www.enasco.com (5)

Niemir, Chris, InfoSource Inc, Oviedo, FL. Tel: (407) 796-5200, (800) 393-4636, FAX: (407) 796-5190, E-Mail: isisale@howtomaster.com, Web Site: www.infosourcelearning.com (3)

Nierenberg, Roy A., Experience In Software Inc, Berkeley, CA. Tel: (510) 644-0694, (800) 678-7008, FAX: (510) 644-3823, Web Site: www.projectkickstart.com (16)

Nieto, Cassie, Progressive Distribution Services Inc, Grand Rapids, MI. Tel: (616) 957-5900, (800) 304-3699, FAX: (616) 957-2990, E-Mail: sales@progressive-commerce.com, Web Site: www.prodist.com (28)

Niggemeyer, W.F., Decko Products Inc, Sandusky, OH. Tel: (419) 626-5757, FAX: (419) 626-3135 (4)

Niggli, David, FAO Schwarz, New York, NY. Tel: (212) 644-9400, (800) 426-TOYS, FAX: (212) 688-6053, Web Site: www.fao.com (11)

Niggli, Michael, R., Southern California Gas Co, Anaheim, CA. Tel: (714) 634-3054, (800) 427-2200, FAX: (714) 937-7712, E-Mail: Tjavid@socalgas.com, Web Site: www.socalgas.com (1)

Nightingale-Conant Corp, Niles, IL. Tel: (847) 647-0300, (800) 557-1660, FAX: (847) 647-7145, Web Site: www.nightingale.com (17)

Nightingale Resources, Cold Spring, NY. Tel: (718) 338-3976, (212) 753-5383, (800) 953-9929 (17)

Nigro, Judy, Penn Mutual, Horsham, PA. Tel: (215) 956-8083, FAX: (215) 956-8368, Web Site: www.pennmutual.com (15)

Nigro, Lynne, Direct Marketing Consultant, Sharon, PA. Tel: (724) 699-0230 (20)

NigroNewMedia, Hermitage, PA. Tel: (724) 699-0230 (20)

Nihon Keizai Shimbun America Inc, New York, NY. Tel: (212) 261-6230, FAX: (212) 261-6239, Web Site: www.nikkeius.com (17)

Nike Inc, Beaverton, OR. Tel: (503) 671-4565, (800) 344-6543, FAX: (503) 671-6300, Web Site: www.nike.com (2)

Nikitas, Steve, Berkshire Record Outlet Inc, Lee, MA. Tel: (413) 243-4080, FAX: (413) 243-4340, E-Mail: broinc@berkshirerecordoutlet.com, Web Site: www2.broinc.com (39)

Niles, Matt, Starchtech, Golden Valley, MN. Tel: (763) 545-5400, (800) 597-7225, FAX: (763) 545-9450, Web Site: www.starchtech.com (16)

Nilodor Inc, Bolivar, OH. Tel: (330) 874-1017, (800) 443-4321, FAX: (330) 874-3366, E-Mail: info@nilodor.com, Web Site: www.nilodor.com (16)

Nimblefish Technologies, San Francisco, CA. Tel: (415) 247-7000, Web Site: www.nimblefish.com (30)

Nimlok, Niles, IL. Tel: (847) 647-1012, (800) 233-8870, FAX: (847) 647-2044, E-Mail: info@nimlok.com, Web Site: www.nimlok.com (16)

Nimmo, Andrew, C., The MarketPlace Group Inc, Norwood, MA. Tel: (781) 762-6600, FAX: (781) 762-1300 (31)

925 Business Furniture, Kensington, MD. Tel: (800) 525-0302, FAX: (302) 349-4587, E-Mail: bjfreed@erols.com, Web Site: www.natcofurniture.com (16)

Ninomiya, Aki, Mitsubishi Digital Electronics America Inc, Irvine, CA. Tel: (949) 465-6000, FAX: (949) 859-4770, Web Site: www.mitsubishi-tv.com (16)

Nishimori, Seiji, Shiseido Cosmetics America, New York, NY. Tel: (212) 805-2300, FAX: (212) 688-0109, Web Site: www.sca.shiseido.com (7)

Nishiyama, Asahiko, Bridgestone/Firestone North American Tire LLC, Nashville, TN. Tel: (615) 937-1000, (800) 543-7522, FAX: (615) 937-3721, Web Site: www.bridgestonetire.com (16)

Nisivocci, Kathy, American General Co, Neptune, NJ. Tel: (732) 922-7000, FAX: (732) 922-7595 (15)

Nissan Motor Acceptance Corp, Irving, TX. Tel: (800) 647-7261, Web Site: www.nissanusa.com (14)

Nissan North America Inc, Irving, TX. Tel: (310) 532-3111, Web Site: www.nissanusa.com (16)

Nissim, Donald, Heritage Direct, Oakhurst, NJ. Tel: (732) 531-2212, FAX: (732) 531-4798, Web Site: www.actionmarkets.com (22)

Nissim, Donald, The Data Base Inc, Oakhurst, NJ. Tel: (732) 531-4600, FAX: (732) 531-4798, E-Mail: don.nissim@heritagedirectdm.com, Web Site: www.heritagedirectdm.com (22)

Nixle LLC, Westfield, NJ. Tel: (856) 427-9000, Web Site: www.nixle.com (35)

Nixon, Gordon, RBC Dain Rauscher, Boston, MA. Tel: (617) 725-2000, FAX: (617) 725-1393, Web Site: www.rbcdainrauscher.com (14)

Nixon, Richard, R., Quadra Graphics Inc, Cherry Hill, NJ. Tel: (856) 665-4060, FAX: (856) 665-7324, E-Mail: richard.nixon@qgi.com (27)

Niyazov, Solomon, Profit Center Software Inc, Port Washington, NY. Tel: (516) 414-6300, (888) 446-6240, FAX: (516) 414-6304, E-Mail: jmarrah@profitcenter.com, Web Site: www.profitcenter.com (22)

No Fault Sports Products, Houston, TX. Tel: (713) 683-7101, (800) 462-7766, FAX: (713) 683-7103, E-Mail: nofaultsports@comcast.net, Web Site: www.nofaultsports.com (11)

No Load Fund Investor, Brentwood, TN. Tel: (800) 706-6364, FAX: (800) 785-9212, E-Mail: NoLoad@mleesmith.com, Web Site: www.noloadfundinvestor.com (14)

No Load Fund*X, San Francisco, CA. Tel: (415) 986-7979, (800) 763-8639, FAX: (415) 986-1595, Web Site: www.noloadfundx.com (14)

Noah, David, M., Shipping Solutions, Eagan, MN. Tel: (651) 905-1727, (888) 890-7447, FAX: (651) 905-1827, E-Mail: info@shipsolutions.com, Web Site: www.shipsolutions.com (16)

Nober, Roger, Burlington Northern & Santa Fe Railroad, Fort Worth, TX. Tel: (817) 878-2000, (800) 795-2673, FAX: (817) 333-7593, Web Site: www.bnsf.com (16)

Nobile, Lou, CityTwist, Boca Raton, FL. Tel: (561) 989-8480, Web Site: www.citytwist.com (32)

Noble, Larry, T Marzetti Co Inc, Columbus, OH. Tel: (614) 846-2232, FAX: (614) 848-8330, Web Site: www.marzetti.com (4)

Noble, Nancy, International Fund for Animal Welfare, Yarmouth Port, MA. Tel: (508) 744-2000, Web Site: www.ifaw.org (1)

Noble, Terry, Apothecary Products Inc, Burnsville, MN. Tel: (952) 890-1940, (800) 328-2742, FAX: (800) 328-1584, Web Site: www.apothecaryproducts.com (7)

Noble, Chicago, IL. Tel: (312) 670-2900, FAX: (312) 670-7420, Web Site: www.noble.net (35)

Nocca, Nick, Company C, New York, NY. Tel: (212) 561-6009, FAX: (212) 260-3710, E-Mail: nnocca@companycmarketing.com, Web Site: www.companycmarketing.com (35)

Nodine, Ronald, Nodine's Smokehouse, Torrington, CT. Tel: (860) 489-3213, (800) 222-2059, FAX: (860) 496-9787, E-Mail: nodinesmoke@optonline.net, Web Site: www.nodinesmokehouse.com (4)

Nodine's Smokehouse, Torrington, CT. Tel: (860) 489-3213, (800) 222-2059, FAX: (860) 496-9787, E-Mail: nodinesmoke@optonline.net, Web Site: www.nodinesmokehouse.com (4)

Noe, Diane, BT Americas, New York, NY. Tel: (646) 487-7400, (800) 331-4568, FAX: (646) 487-3370, Web Site: www.btglobalservices.com (22)

Noe, Dorothy C., Dorothy's Ruffled Originals Inc, Wilmington, NC. Tel: (910) 686-8087, (800) 367-6849, FAX: (910) 686-2958, E-Mail: curtains@dorothysoriginals.com, Web Site: www.dorothysoriginals.com (8)

Noe, James B., Dorothy's Ruffled Originals Inc, Wilmington, NC. Tel: (910) 686-8087, (800) 367-6849, FAX: (910) 686-2958, E-Mail: curtains@dorothysoriginals.com, Web Site: www.dorothysoriginals.com (8)

Noevir Direct Marketing Inc, Montvale, NJ. Tel: (201) 391-0001, (800) 872-8888, FAX: (201) 391-1740, E-Mail: marketing@noevirusa.com, Web Site: www.noevir.com (7)

Nojowitz, Rabbi Dovid, Torah Umesorah Publications, Brooklyn, NY. Tel: (212) 227-1000, E-Mail: umesorah@aol.com, Web Site: torah-umesorah.com (5)

Nokes, Jon, Smart Inventions Inc, Paramount, CA. Tel: (562) 272-1416, (800) 275-7494, FAX: (562) 272-1423, E-Mail: customerservice@smartinventions.com, Web Site: www.smartinventions.com (32)

Nolan, Irene, Audience Development, Norwalk, CT. Tel: (203) 854-6730, FAX: (203) 854-6735, E-Mail: inolan@red7media.com, Web Site: www.audiencedevelopment.com (43)

Nolan, Kevin, Aegis Communications, Irving, TX. Tel: (972) 830-1800, (800) 332-0266, FAX: (972) 830-1801, E-Mail: info@aegisglobal.com, Web Site: www.aegiscomgroup.com (29)

Nolan, Peter, Commercial Atlas & Marketing Guide, Skokie, IL. Tel: (800) 678-7263, FAX: (800) 934-3479, Web Site: www.randmcnally.com (43)

Nolan, Russ, North American Membership Group Inc, Minnetonka, MN. Tel: (952) 936-9333, FAX: (952) 936-9755, Web Site: www.namginc.com (13)

Nomadics Tipi Makers, Bend, OR. Tel: (541) 389-3980, FAX: (541) 389-3980, Web Site: www.tipi.com (13)

Non-Profit Management Program/Milano - The New School of Management & Urban Policy, New York, NY. Tel: (212) 229-5400, FAX: (212) 229-5354, E-Mail: milanoadmissions@newschool.edu, Web Site: www.newschool.edu/milano (41)

The NonProfit Times, Morris Plains, NJ. Tel: (973) 401-0202, FAX: (973) 401-0404, Web Site: www.nptimes.com (17)

Noonan, Charles, Boston Color Graphics, Billerica, MA. Tel: (978) 528-7999, (800) 767-0067, FAX: (978) 528-7609, E-Mail: sales@bostoncolorgraphics.com, Web Site: www.bostoncolorgraphics.com (27)

Noonan, Jack, SPSS Inc, Chicago, IL. Tel: (312) 651-3000, (800) 543-2185, FAX: (312) 651-3690, E-Mail: sales@spss.com, Web Site: www.spss.com (22)

Noonan, Jim, Media Management & Magnetics Inc, Menomonee Falls, WI. Tel: (262) 251-5511, (800) 242-2090, FAX: (262) 251-4737, E-Mail: medmgt@computersupplypeople.com, Web Site: www.computersupplypeople.com (3)

Noonan, Laura, 800 Response, Burlington, VT. Tel: (802) 860-0378, (800) NEW-SALES, FAX: (800) NEW-ORDER, E-Mail: sales@800response.com, Web Site: www.800response.com (32)

Nor1, Sunnyvale, CA. Tel: (408) 852-9248, Web Site: www.nor1.com (32)

Nordahl, Bennie, International Masters Publishers Inc, Montoursville, PA. Tel: (800) 570-5718, E-Mail: customerservice@imp-usa.com, Web Site: www.imponline.com (17)

Norderhaug, Mike, Assurant Health, Milwaukee, WI. Tel: (414) 244-0658, (800) 800-1212, FAX: (414) 224-0472, Web Site: www.assuranthealth.com (15)

Nordis Direct, Coral Springs, FL. Tel: (954) 323-5500, (800) 208-1169, FAX: (954) 323-0100, E-Mail: sdolan@nordisdirect.com, Web Site: www.nordisdirect.com (21)

Nordloh, Christopher, L., Lt Moses Willard Inc, Milford, OH. Tel: (513) 248-5500, (800) 621-8956, FAX: (513) 831-0548, E-Mail: info@ltmoses.com, Web Site: www.ltmoses.com (16)

Nordskog, Jerry, Nordskog Publishing Co, Ventura, CA. Tel: (805) 642-2070, FAX: (805) 642-1862, E-Mail: pwrboatmag@aol.com, Web Site: www.nordskogpublishing.com (17)

Nordskog Publishing Co, Ventura, CA. Tel: (805) 642-2070, FAX: (805) 642-1862, E-Mail: pwrboatmag@aol.com, Web Site: www.nordskogpublishing.com (17)

Nordstrand, Barry, J., Solutran, Plymouth, MN. Tel: (763) 559-2225, (888) 765-8872, FAX: (763) 559-8872, E-Mail: solutions@solutran.com, Web Site: www.solutran.com (20)

Nordstrom, Daniel, J., Outdoor Research, Seattle, WA. Tel: (206) 467-8197, (888) 467-4327, FAX: (206) 467-0374, Web Site: www.outdoorresearch.com (11)

Nordstrom Inc, Seattle, WA. Tel: (206) 303-2301, FAX: (206) 373-3198 (2)

Nor'east Miniature Roses Inc, Arroyo Grande, CA. Tel: (805) 426-6485, (800) 426-6485, FAX: (805) 481-7374, E-Mail: noreast@greenheartfarms.com, Web Site: www.noreast-miniroses.com (8)

Noren, Leif, E., CRC Public Relations, Alexandria, VA. Tel: (703) 683-5004, FAX: (703) 683-1703, E-Mail: crc@crcpublicrelations.com, Web Site: www.crc4pr.com (35)

Norheim, Oddvar, American Crane & Equipment Corp, Douglassville, PA. Tel: (610) 385-6061, (877) 877-6778, FAX: (610) 385-3191/4876, E-Mail: info@americancrane.com, Web Site: www.americancrane.com (16)

Norin, Miles, AGORA Inc, Baltimore, MD. Tel: (410) 783-8499, FAX: (410) 783-8414, E-Mail: csteam@agorapublishinggroup.com, Web Site: www.agora-inc.com (17)

Norinski, Dave, American Color, Irving, TX. Tel: (602) 333-1000, FAX: (602) 333-1099, Web Site: www.amcolor.com (27)

Norman Jr., John, C., Personnel Policy Service Inc, Louisville, KY. Tel: (502) 899-5102, (800) 437-3735, FAX: (800) 755-7011, E-Mail: info@ppspublishers.com, Web Site: www.ppspublishers.com (17)

Norman, Larry, M., Transamerica Life Insurance Co, Cedar Rapids, IA. Tel: (319) 398-8511, (800) 558-9011, FAX: (319) 369-2825, Web Site: www.transamerica.com (15)

Norman, Linda, UCEA, Boston, MA. Tel: (617) 738-6410, FAX: (617) 734-1452, Web Site: www.revike.org (1)

Norman, Margaret, KET, Lexington, KY. Tel: (859) 258-7000, (800) 432-0951, FAX: (606) 258-7396, E-Mail: rgriffin@ket.org, Web Site: www.ket.org (17)

Norman, Roberta, Dick Davis Digest, Salem, MA. Tel: (978) 745-5532, FAX: (978) 745-1283, E-Mail: marketing@dickdavis.com, Web Site: www.dickdavis.com (17)

Norman, Vickie, L., Robertson Mailing List Co, Leesburg, VA. Tel: (703) 726-2822, (800) 788-4564, FAX: (703) 726-9882, E-Mail: vnorman@rmlc.net, Web Site: www.rmlc.net (23)

Norman Control Co, Cary, IL. Tel: (847) 639-5721, FAX: (847) 639-5755, E-Mail: susan@coffmanmfg.com, Web Site: www.coffmanmfg.com (16)

Norman Rockwell Museum, Stockbridge, MA. Tel: (413) 298-4100, (800) 742-9450, FAX: (413) 298-4144, E-Mail: emazzer@nrm.org, Web Site: www.nrm.org (16)

Noronha, Wilbert, Trans Union Corp, Chicago, IL. Tel: (312) 258-1717, (800) 335-9888, FAX: (312) 466-8385, Web Site: www.transunion.com (14)

Norquist, Tom, GameTime Inc, Fort Payne, AL. Tel: (256) 845-5610, (800) 633-2394, FAX: (256) 845-9361/2649, Web Site: www.gametime.com (11)

Norris, Gerri, 3D Mail Results, Kent, WA. FAX: (853) 859-7300 (5)

Norris, Greg, Goss International, Durham, NH. Tel: (603) 749-6600, FAX: (603) 750-6860, Web Site: www.gossinternational.com (27)

Norris, Gwen, Danker Laboratories Inc, Sarasota, FL. Tel: (800) 237-9641, FAX: (800) 665-5086, E-Mail: sales@dankerlabs.com, Web Site: www.dankerlabs.com (16)

Norris, John, New Hermes Inc, Duluth, GA. Tel: (770) 623-0331, (800) 843-7637, FAX: (800) 533-7637, E-Mail: sales@gravograph-newhermes.com, Web Site: www.gravograph.com/usa/government/index.php (34)

Norris, Lauren, Liz Kislik Associates LLC, Rockville Centre, NY. Tel: (516) 568-2932, FAX: (516) 568-2936, Web Site: www.lizkislik.com (20)

Norris, Patsy, Village Interiors Carpet One, Newton, NC. Tel: (828) 465-6818, FAX: (828) 465-1864, E-Mail: sales@carpet-one.net, Web Site: www.carpetone.com/village (8)

Norris, Robert, E., Village Interiors Carpet One, Newton, NC. Tel: (828) 465-6818, FAX: (828) 465-1864, E-Mail: sales@carpet-one.net, Web Site: www.carpetone.com/village (8)

Norscot Group, Mequon, WI. Tel: (262) 241-3313, (800) 653-3313, FAX: (262) 241-4904, Web Site: www.norscot.com (5)

Norse, Nathan, Nourse Farms, South Deerfield, MA. Tel: (413) 665-2658, FAX: (413) 665-7888, E-Mail: info@noursefarms.com, Web Site: www.noursefarms.com (8)

Norseng, Michael, Esquire Magazine, New York, NY. Tel: (212) 649-2000, (800) 925-0485, FAX: (212) 265-0938, E-Mail: esquire@hearst.com, Web Site: www.esquire.com (17)

Nortel Networks Corp, Mississauga, ON Canada. Tel: (905) 863-7000, (888) 901-7286, Web Site: www.nortel.com (34)

North, Adam, News Marketing Canada, Toronto, ON Canada. Tel: (416) 775-3000, FAX: (416) 775-3055, E-Mail: spetkovich@newsmarketing.ca, Web Site: www.newsmarketing.ca (20)

North, Jack, W., State Farm Insurance Cos, Bloomington, IL. Tel: (309) 766-2311, FAX: (309) 766-3621, Web Site: www.statefarm.com (15)

North America Life Insurance Co, Austin, TX. Tel: (512) 347-1835, Web Site: www.nagrp.com (15)

North American Communications, Armonk, NY. Tel: (914) 273-8620, FAX: (914) 273-3135, E-Mail: info@nacmail.com, Web Site: www.nacmail.com (21)

North American Communications Inc (East), Duncansville, PA. Tel: (814) 696-3553, (800) 624-1533, FAX: (814) 696-1180, E-Mail: info@nacmail.com, Web Site: www.nacmail.com (26)

North American Co for Life & Health Insurance, Chicago, IL. Tel: (312) 648-7600, (800) 800-3656, FAX: (614) 365-9209, Web Site: www.nacolah.com (15)

North American Mailing Technologies Inc, Lawrenceville, GA. Tel: (770) 962-5833 (22)

North American Membership Group Inc, Minnetonka, MN. Tel: (952) 936-9333, FAX: (952) 936-9755, Web Site: www.namginc.com (13)

North American Publishing Co, Philadelphia, PA. Tel: (215) 238-5300, FAX: (215) 238-5412, Web Site: www.napco.com (23)

North Carolina Electric Membership Corp, Raleigh, NC. Tel: (919) 872-0800, (800) 662-8835, FAX: (919) 645-3410, E-Mail: info@ncemcs.com, Web Site: www.ncemcs.com (30)

North Point Resources, Alpharetta, GA. Tel: (678) 892-5000, Web Site: www.northpointstore.org (1)

North Shore Animal League America Inc, Port Washington, NY. Tel: (516) 883-7900, FAX: (516) 883-8256, E-Mail: donorservices@nsalamerica.org, Web Site: www.nsalamerica.org (1)

North Wind Picture Archives, Alfred, ME. Tel: (207) 490-1940, (800) 952-0703, FAX: (207) 490-3627, E-Mail: mail@northwindpictures.com, Web Site: www.northwindpictures.com (1)

North-Rudin, Bill, Drug Policy Alliance, New York, NY. Tel: (212) 613-8020, FAX: (212) 613-8021, E-Mail: nyc@drugpolicy.org, Web Site: www.drugpolicy.org (1)

Northeast Hinge Distributors Inc, Hollis, NH. Tel: (603) 465-3244, (800) 882-0120, FAX: (603) 465-3313, E-Mail: nehinge@nehinge.com, Web Site: www.nehinge.com (1)

Northeimer, John, Universal Vintage Tire Co, Hershey, PA. Tel: (717) 534-0175, (800) 233-3827, FAX: (717) 534-0719, E-Mail: sales@universaltire.com, Web Site: www.universaltire.com (11)

Northern Cross, Lecompton, KS. Tel: (785) 887-6010, (800) 625-7233, FAX: (785) 887-6263 (16)

Northern Greenhouse Sales, Neche, ND. Tel: (204) 327-5540, FAX: (204) 327-5527, E-Mail: info@northerngreenhouse.com, Web Site: www.northerngreenhouse.com (8)

Northern Illinois Consulting Inc, Libertyville, IL. Tel: (847) 828-1999, Web Site: www.cmsbusiness.com (20)

Northern Kentucky University, Highland Heights, KY. Tel: (859) 572-5220, (800) 637-9948, FAX: (859) 572-6177, Web Site: www.nku.edu (41)

Northern Lights Direct, Chicago, IL. Tel: (312) 263-8686, FAX: (312) 624-7701, E-Mail: contact@northernlightsdirect.com, Web Site: www.northernlightsdirect.com (32)

Northern Printing Network Inc, Wheeling, IL. Tel: (847) 215-7300, FAX: (847) 215-7314, E-Mail: sales@northernprint.com, Web Site: www.northernprint.com (21)

Northern Response (International) Ltd, Toronto, ON Canada. Tel: (905) 737-6698, (866) 584-1694, FAX: (905) 737-0099, E-Mail: general@nresponse.com, Web Site: www.shopnorthern.com (22)

Northern Safety Co Inc, Utica, NY. Tel: (315) 793-4900, Web Site: www.northernsafety.com (16)

Northern Tool & Equipment Inc, Burnsville, MN. Tel: (952) 894-9510, (800) 221-0516, FAX: (952) 894-1020, Web Site: www.northerntool.com (16)

The Northern Trust Co, Chicago, IL. Tel: (312) 630-6000, (888) 289-6542, FAX: (312) 630-1512, Web Site: www.ntrs.com (14)

Northlich, Cincinnati, OH. Tel: (513) 421-8840, FAX: (513) 287-1858, E-Mail: northlich@northlich.com, Web Site: www.northlich.com (35)

Northrop, Edward, S., Mentor Corp, Santa Barbara, CA. Tel: (805) 879-6000, (800) 525-0245, FAX: (805) 964-2712, Web Site: www.mentorcorp.com (16)

Northrop, James, Princess House Inc, Taunton, MA. Tel: (508) 832-6800, (508) 823-0711, (800) 622-0039, FAX: (508) 823-5182, Web Site: www.princesshouse.com (16)

Northwest Direct Inc, Bellevue, WA. Tel: (425) 643-7917, Web Site: www.nwdirectmarketing.com (35)

Northwest Laboratories, Seattle, WA. Tel: (206) 763-6252, FAX: (206) 763-3949, Web Site: www.nwlabs.net (9)

Northwest Mailing Service Inc, Chicago, IL. Tel: (773) 237-2264, Web Site: www.nwmail.com (28)

Northwestern Mutual, Milwaukee, WI. Tel: (414) 271-1444, Web Site: www.northwesternmutual.com (14)

Northwestern University, Evanston, IL. Tel: (847) 491-3741, FAX: (847) 491-8406, E-Mail: webmaster@northwestern.edu, Web Site: www.northwestern.edu (41)

Norton, David W., Harrah's Entertainment Inc, Las Vegas, NV. Tel: (702) 407-6000, FAX: (702) 407-6499, (702) 407-6500, Web Site: www.harrahs.com (19)

Norton, Jeff, Missionary Society of St Columban, Saint Columbans, NE. Tel: (402) 291-1920, Web Site: www.columban.org (1)

Norton, Jeffrey, Cafe Lango, Guilford, CT. Tel: (203) 453-1456, (800) 243-1234, FAX: (203) 453-5110, E-Mail: mail@cafelango.com, Web Site: www.audioforum.com (16)

Norton, Jennifer, Brant Publications Inc, New York, NY. Tel: (212) 941-2800, FAX: (212) 941-2885, Web Site: www.interviewmagazine.com (17)

Norton, Negley, Yellow Pages Association, Berkeley Heights, NJ. Tel: (908) 286-2380, (800) 336-0440, FAX: (908) 286-0620, Web Site: www.yellowpagesima.org (1)

Norton, Pat, Active Web Group, Hauppauge, NY. Tel: (800) 978-3417, FAX: (800) 719-4402, E-Mail: info@activewebgroup.com, Web Site: www.activewebgroup.com (9)

Norton, Richard, National Golf Foundation, Jupiter, FL. Tel: (561) 744-6006, FAX: (561) 744-6107, E-Mail: ngf@ngf.org, Web Site: www.ngf.org (1)

Norton, Robert, FTD Florist Transworld Delivery, Downers Grove, IL. Tel: (630) 719-7756, (800) SEND-FTD, Web Site: www.ftd.com (16)

Norton, Robert, W., Scientific Marketing Services Inc, Landisville, NJ. Tel: (856) 697-1257, FAX: (856) 697-9639, E-Mail: info@smsmktg.com, Web Site: www.smsmktg.com (35)

Norton, Ronnie, Ventyx, Atlanta, GA. Tel: (770) 952-8444, (800) 868-0497, FAX: (770) 955-2977, E-Mail: support@ventyx.com, Web Site: www.ventyx.com (16)

Norton, Steve, Concurrent Computer Corp, Duluth, GA. Tel: (678) 228-4000, (877) 978-7363, FAX: (954) 977-5580, Web Site: www.ccur.com (3)

Norton Moffatt, Laurie, Norman Rockwell Museum, Stockbridge, MA. Tel: (413) 298-4100, (800) 742-9450, FAX: (413) 298-4144, E-Mail: emazzer@nrm.org, Web Site: www.nrm.org (16)

Norwalk, Thomas S., Miami Valley Marketing Group Inc, Dayton, OH. Tel: (937) 299-1825, FAX: (937) 299-9967, E-Mail: tomnorwalk@aol.com (35)

Norwood Promotional Products, Clearwater, FL. Tel: (317) 275-2500, (800) 959-9138, FAX: (317) 275-2570, Web Site: www.norwood.com (16)

Nosbusch, Keith, Rockwell Automation, Milwaukee, WI. Tel: (414) 382-2000, FAX: (414) 382-4444, Web Site: www.rockwellautomation.com (16)

Nostradamus Advertising, New York, NY. Tel: (212) 581-1362, E-Mail: nos@nostradamus.net, Web Site: www.nostradamus.net (36)

Nostrum Inc, Long Beach, CA. Tel: (562) 437-2200, Web Site: www.nostruminc.com (35)

Notaro, Heather, Merrimack College, North Andover, MA. Tel: (978) 837-5154, E-Mail: denise.tuccelli@merrimack.edu, Web Site: www.merrimack.edu (41)

Nourse Farms, South Deerfield, MA. Tel: (413) 665-2658, FAX: (413) 665-7888, E-Mail: info@noursefarms.com, Web Site: www.noursefarms.com (8)

Nova Communications Inc, Geneva, IL. Tel: (630) 377-1889, (800) 816-6682, FAX: (630) 377-1899, E-Mail: sales@novacominc.com, Web Site: www.novacominc.com (35)

Nova DM, Dunmore, PA. Tel: (570) 342-8668 (35)

Nova Power Marketing, Phoenix, AZ. Tel: (602) 558-7540, FAX: (602) 926-8351, E-Mail: novamarkdm@cox.net, Web Site: www.novamarkdm.com (35)

Nova Southeastern University - FSEHS, North Miami Beach, FL. Tel: (954) 262-8651, Web Site: www.schoolofed.nova.edu (1)

Novack, Janette, National Seminars Group, Shawnee Mission, KS. Tel: (913) 432-7755, (800) 258-7246, FAX: (913) 432-0824, E-Mail: cstserv@natsem.com, Web Site: www.natsem.com (16)

Novak, Joseph, BFC, Batavia, IL. Tel: (630) 879-9240, Web Site: www.bfcprint.com (28)

Novak, Mike, AmeriCall Group Inc, Naperville, IL. Tel: (630) 955-9100, (800) 688-0078, FAX: (630) 955-9955, E-Mail: sales@americallgroup.com, Web Site: www.americallgroup.com (29)

Novak, Patty, Battery Pros Inc, Horseshoe Beach, FL. Tel: (352) 498-2477, (800) 451-7171, FAX: (352) 498-2482, E-Mail: sales@probattery.com, Web Site: www.probattery.com (9)

Novartis Pharmaceuticals Corp, East Hanover, NJ. Tel: (862) 778-6914, FAX: (973) 781-8119, Web Site: www.pharma.us.novartis.com (7)

Novastock Photo Agency, Matthews, NC. Tel: (704) 847-6185, (888) 894-8622, FAX: (704) 841-8181, E-Mail: novastock@aol.com, Web Site: www.creativeshake.com/novastock (38)

Novell Inc, Waltham, MA. Tel: (801) 861-4272, (800) 529-3400, FAX: (781) 464-8100, E-Mail: crc@novell.com, Web Site: www.novell.com (22)

Novelli, Bob, Anthem Blue Cross, Westlake Village, CA. Tel: (805) 557-6655, (800) 333-0912, FAX: (800) 557-6872, Web Site: www.bluecrossca.com (15)

Novelli, Bob, Blue Shield Life, San Francisco, CA. Tel: (888) 800-2742, FAX: (800) 329-2742, Web Site: www.blueshieldca.com (15)

NOVO1, Fort Worth, TX. Tel: (817) 355-6899, FAX: (817) 355-8505, Web Site: www.novo1.com (29)

Novo 1 Inc, Waukesha, WI. Tel: (262) 827-6400, (877) 810-7171, FAX: (262) 827-6440, Web Site: www.novo1.com (21)

Novus Media Inc, Plymouth, MN. Tel: (612) 758-8600, Web Site: www.npmnetwork.com (31)

Nowak, Jeffrey, G., DMC Advertising, Pewaukee, WI. Tel: (262) 523-2000, (800) 952-9165, FAX: (262) 523-2012, E-Mail: info@dmcadvertising.com, Web Site: www.dmcadvertising.com (35)

Nowakowski, James, A., Interline Creative Group Inc, Palatine, IL. Tel: (847) 358-4848, FAX: (847) 358-8089, E-Mail: info@interlinegroup.com, Web Site: www.interlinegroup.com (35)

Nowell's Inc, San Rafael, CA. Tel: (415) 332-4933, FAX: (415) 332-4936, E-Mail: contact@nowellslighting.com, Web Site: www.nowellslighting.com (8)

Nowers, Suzanne, Cole, Nexus Direct, Virginia Beach, VA. Tel: (757) 340-5960, (800) 965-0577, FAX: (757) 340-5980, E-Mail: info@nexusdirect.com, Web Site: www.nexusdirect.com (35)

Nowetah's American Indian Store & Museum, New Portland, ME. Tel: (207) 628-4991, Web Site: www.nowetahs.webs.com (6)

Nowicki, Joe, Herman Miller Inc, Zeeland, MI. Tel: (616) 654-3000, FAX: (616) 654-5234, E-Mail: investor@hermanmiller.com, Web Site: www.hermanmiller.com (16)

Nowicki, Michele, San Diego Direct Marketing Association, San Diego, CA. Tel: (858) 503-1471, E-Mail: webmaster@sddma.org, Web Site: www.sddma.org (40)

Nowinski, Christine, Farrell, HH Backer Associates Inc, Chicago, IL. Tel: (312) 578-1818, FAX: (312) 578-1819, E-Mail: hhbacker@hhbacker.com, Web Site: www.hhbacker.com (17)

Nowworthy, Eddis, Benwell Atkins, Vancouver, BC Canada. Tel: (604) 872-2326, FAX: (604) 872-4235, E-Mail: vancouver.reception@rrd.com, Web Site: www.rrdonnelley.com/wwwbenwell/ (21)

Noyes, Al, Walch Publishing, Portland, ME. Tel: (207) 772-2846, (800) 558-2846, FAX: (207) 772-3105, E-Mail: customerservice@walch.com, Web Site: www.walch.com (17)

Noyes, Erik, China Books & Periodicals Inc, South San Francisco, CA. Tel: (650) 872-7076, (800) 818-2017, FAX: (650) 872-7808, E-Mail: info@chinabooks.com, Web Site: www.chinabooks.com (17)

Nu-Parr Swimwear, Phoenix, AZ. Tel: (602) 279-4044, (800) 230-7277, FAX: (602) 212-2636, E-Mail: info@nu-parr.com, Web Site: www.nu-parr.com (2)

Nuance Speech Solutions, Burlington, MA. Tel: (781) 565-5000, FAX: (781) 565-5001, E-Mail: sales@speechworks.com, Web Site: www.nuance.com (17)

Nuckolls, Jeannie, Mountain Press Publishing Co, Missoula, MT. Tel: (406) 728-1900, (800) 234-5308, FAX: (406) 728-1635, E-Mail: info@mtnpress.com, Web Site: www.mountain-press.com (17)

Nuclear Plant Journal, Downers Grove, IL. Tel: (630) 858-6161, FAX: (630) 852-8787, Web Site: www.nuclearplantjournal.com (17)

Nucor Corp, Charlotte, NC. Tel: (704) 366-7000, FAX: (704) 362-4208, E-Mail: info@nucor.com, Web Site: nucor.com (16)

NuEdge Systems, Brown Deer, WI. Tel: (800) 236-3282, Web Site: www.nuedgesystems.com (20)

Nugent, Jack, BJ's Wholesale Club Inc, Westborough, MA. Tel: (508) 651-7400, FAX: (508) 651-6167, Web Site: www.bjs.com (13)

Nugent, Terence, J., Medical Marketing Service Inc, Wood Dale, IL. Tel: (630) 477-1559, (800) 633-5478, FAX: (630) 350-1896, E-Mail: t-nugent@mmslists.com, Web Site: www.mmslists.com (24)

Nulman, Philip, R., The Nulman Group, Somerset, NJ. Tel: (908) 534-4041, (888) 440-3367, FAX: (908) 534-5023, E-Mail: pnulman@nulmangroup.com, Web Site: www.nulmangroup.com (35)

The Nulman Group, Somerset, NJ. Tel: (908) 534-4041, (888) 440-3367, FAX: (908) 534-5023, E-Mail: pnulman@nulmangroup.com, Web Site: www.nulmangroup.com (35)

NuNaturals, Eugene, OR. Tel: (541) 344-9785, (800) 753-4372, FAX: (541) 343-0915, E-Mail: info@nunaturals.com, Web Site: www.nunaturals.com (16)

Nunes, Luis, PPI Benefit Solutions, Wallingford, CT. Tel: (888) 674-0046, FAX: (203) 468-9886, E-Mail: clientservices@ppibenefits.com, Web Site: www.ppibenefits.com (15)

Nunez, Jesse, KWHY-TV Channel 22, Burbank, CA. Tel: (213) 344-3700, E-Mail: info@canal22.tv, Web Site: www.kwhy.com (32)

Nurn, Charles, Sterling Publishing Co Inc, New York, NY. Tel: (212) 532-7160, (800) 367-9692, FAX: (212) 213-2495, Web Site: www.sterlingpublishing.com (17)

Nurnberg, Charles, G., Sterling Publishing Co Inc, New York, NY. Tel: (212) 532-7160, (800) 367-9692, FAX: (212) 213-2495, Web Site: www.sterlingpublishing.com (17)

Nuss, Robert, L., Drumbeat Indian Arts Inc, Phoenix, AZ. Tel: (602) 266-4823, (800) 895-4859, FAX: (602) 265-2402, E-Mail: info@drumbeatindianarts.com, Web Site: www.drumbeatindianarts.com (6)

Nussbaum, Becky, SA-SO/Time Wise, Arlington, TX. Tel: (972) 641-4911, (800) 523-8060, FAX: (972) 660-5684, E-Mail: info@sa-so.com, Web Site: www.sa-so.com (33)

Nussbaum, Becky, Sa-So, Arlington, TX. Tel: (972) 641-4911, (800) 752-4294, FAX: (972) 660-3684, E-Mail: info@sa-so.com, Web Site: www.sa-so.com (16)

Nussbaum, David, Direct Network Inc, Allentown, NJ. Tel: (732) 821-7090, FAX: (732) 821-7202, E-Mail: dirnet@verizon.net, Web Site: www.dirnetworklists.com (23)

Nussbaum, Joe, Sa-So, Arlington, TX. Tel: (972) 641-4911, (800) 752-4294, FAX: (972) 660-3684, E-Mail: info@sa-so.com, Web Site: www.sa-so.com (16)

Nussbaum, Nathan, Nat Nussbaum & Associates Inc, Coral Springs, FL. Tel: (954) 345-9131, FAX: (954) 345-0786, E-Mail: nlnmktg@aol.com (16)

Nussbaum, Stephen, Cold Spring Harbor Lab Press, Woodbury, NY. Tel: (516) 422-4100, (800) 843-4388, FAX: (516) 422-4097, E-Mail: cshpress@cshl.edu, Web Site: www.cshlpress.com (17)

Nat Nussbaum & Associates Inc, Coral Springs, FL. Tel: (954) 345-9131, FAX: (954) 345-0786, E-Mail: nlnmktg@aol.com (16)

NuStats Inc, West Lake Hills, TX. Tel: (512) 306-9065, (800) 44-STATS, FAX: (512) 306-9065, Web Site: www.nustats.com (30)

Nuti, Bill, NCR Corp, Duluth, GA. Tel: (937) 445-1936, (800) CALL-NCR, FAX: (937) 445-1682, Web Site: www.ncr.com (16)

NutraOrigin, Lake Success, NY. Tel: (516) 858-0301, Web Site: www.nutraorigin.com (7)

Nutri-Health Supplements, Cottonwood, AZ. Tel: (928) 340-5400 (7)

NutriSystem Inc, Fort Washington, PA. Tel: (215) 706-5300, (800) 321-THIN, FAX: (215) 706-5388, Web Site: www.nutrisystem.com (7)

Nutritional Research Associates Inc, South Whitley, IN. Tel: (260) 723-4931, (800) 456-4931, FAX: (260) 723-6297, E-Mail: info@nrfeeds.com, Web Site: www.nrfeeds.com (16)

Nutting, Lori, J., Military Direct Marketing Inc, Poughkeepsie, NY. Tel: (845) 454-7900, FAX: (845) 454-7987 (31)

Nuveen Investments, Chicago, IL. Tel: (312) 917-7700, (800) 257-8787, FAX: (312) 917-8049, Web Site: www.nuveen.com (14)

Nyce, James, ARF Annual Convention & Research Infoplex, New York, NY. Tel: (212) 751-5656, FAX: (212) 319-5265, E-Mail: info@theARF.org, Web Site: www.theARF.org (42)

Nye, John, Zimmerman Irrigation Inc, Biglerville, PA. Tel: (717) 337-2727, (800) 452-5699, FAX: (717) 337-1785, E-Mail: info@trikl-eez.com, Web Site: www.trickl-eez.com (16)

Nye, Sandra, Zimmerman Irrigation Inc, Biglerville, PA. Tel: (717) 337-2727, (800) 452-5699, FAX: (717) 337-1785, E-Mail: info@trikl-eez.com, Web Site: www.trickl-eez.com (16)

Nyenauis, Michael, MAP International, Brunswick, GA. Tel: (912) 265-6010, (800) 225-8550, FAX: (912) 265-6170, Web Site: www.map.org (1)

Nylander, Mark, Liggett-Stashower Direct, Cleveland, OH. Tel: (216) 348-8500, (800) 877-4573, FAX: (216) 736-8118, E-Mail: mnylander@liggett.com, Web Site: www.liggett.com (35)

Nylon Net Co, Memphis, TN. Tel: (901) 526-6500, (877) 893-6535, (800) 238-7529, FAX: (901) 526-6538, E-Mail: nylonnet@nylonnet.com, Web Site: www.nylonnet.com (11)

Nyrev Inc, New York, NY. Tel: (212) 757-8070, FAX: (212) 333-5374, E-Mail: mail@nybooks.com, Web Site: www.nybooks.com (17)

Nystrom, Peggy, Superior Real Estate Supply, Phoenix, AZ. Tel: (623) 516-9202, (800) 234-0095, FAX: (623) 516-9209, E-Mail: sales@superiorrealestatesupply.com, Web Site: www.superiorrealestate.com (10)

Nyugen, Tuong, Gero Vita, Costa Mesa, CA. Tel: (888) 382-9175, Web Site: www.gvi.com (16)

O

O' Donnell, Richard, Research Institute America, Carrollton, TX. Tel: (972) 250-7000, (800) 950-1216, Web Site: www.ria.thompson.com (14)

O' Handy III, Edward, Charter One Bank, Cleveland, OH. Tel: (216) 566-5300, (877) CHARTER, (877) 242-7837, FAX: (216) 566-1465, Web Site: www.charterone.com (14)

O'Brien, Andrew, Golden Bear Golf Inc, North Palm Beach, FL. Tel: (561) 626-3900, FAX: (561) 626-4104, Web Site: www.nicklaus.com (16)

O'Brien, Chris, Go Ahead Vacations, Cambridge, MA. Tel: (617) 619-1000, (800) 242-4686, FAX: (617) 619-1001, E-Mail: goahead@et.com, Web Site: www.goaheadvacations.com (17)

O'Brien, Clinton, Care2, Washington, DC. Tel: (650) 622-0860, Web Site: www.care2.com (1)

O'Brien, Declan, Destinations Ireland & Great Britain, Rhinebeck, NY. Tel: (800) 832-1848, FAX: (212) 265-0154, E-Mail: info@digbtravel.com, Web Site: www.allgolftravel.com/tours (19)

O'Brien, Diane, List Pro of America, San Diego, CA. Tel: (858) 483-1410, FAX: (858) 270-6669, Web Site: www.swmall.com (23)

O'Brien, Edward, J., Gump's By Mail Inc, San Francisco, CA. Tel: (415) 982-1616, (800) 882-8055, FAX: (800) 984-9361, Web Site: www.gumpsbymail.com (6)

O'Brien, James, J., Ashland Inc, Covington, KY. Tel: (859) 815-3333, Web Site: www.ashland.com (16)

O'Brien, James, Print Management Partners, Des Plaines, IL. Tel: (847) 699-2999, Web Site: www.ourpartners.com (27)

O'Brien, Kenneth, E., RR Donnelley & Sons Co, Chicago, IL. Tel: (312) 326-8000, FAX: (312) 326-7156, Web Site: www.rrdonnelly.com (31)

O'Brien, Kevin, O'Brien Document Solutions, Bartlett, IL. Tel: (630) 830-0990, FAX: (630) 830-0062, E-Mail: obrien_info@obinc.com, Web Site: www.obinc.com (27)

O'Brien, Patricia, M., Effective Promotions Inc, Fort Johnson, NY. Tel: (518) 274-0291, (888) 467-3514, FAX: (518) 274-0290, Web Site: www.efpromotions.com (16)

O'Brien, Robert, Time Customer Service Inc, Tampa, FL. Tel: (813) 878-6100, (800) 723-NCOA, FAX: (813) 878-6452, Web Site: www.timecustomerservice.com (22)

O'Brien, Tom, PNC Bank Corp, Pittsburgh, PA. Tel: (412) 762-2000/3514, (800) 422-6537, FAX: (412) 762-4482 (14)

O'Callahan, Patrice, Marketing III Direct Response, Clermont, FL. Tel: (352) 241-8040, FAX: (352) 241-4533, E-Mail: marketing35th@aol.com (35)

O'Connell, Bob, Vanguard Direct, New York, NY. Tel: (212) 736-0770, FAX: (212) 736-8305, Web Site: www.vanguarddirect.com (35)

O'Connell, Joseph, M., Leather Unlimited Corp, Belgium, WI. Tel: (920) 994-9464, (800) 993-2889, FAX: (920) 994-4099, E-Mail: leatherunltd@yahoo.com, Web Site: www.leatherunltd.com (2)

O'Connell, Kevin, LSSiData, Blue Bell, PA. Tel: (610) 825-7720, (800) 210-9021, E-Mail: info@lssi.net, Web Site: www.dataserve.info (22)

O'Connell, Lynn, O'Connell Meier LLC, Alexandria, VA. Tel: (703) 635-2893, (866) 391-1415, FAX: (703) 739-0478, E-Mail: info@omdirect.com, Web Site: www.omdirect.com (21)

O'Connell, Maureen, Scholastic Inc, New York, NY. Tel: (212) 343-6100, (800) SCHOLASTIC, FAX: (212) 343-6484, Web Site: www.scholastic.com/ (17)

O'Connell, Patricia C., Leather Unlimited Corp, Belgium, WI. Tel: (920) 994-9464, (800) 993-2889, FAX: (920) 994-4099, E-Mail: leatherunltd@yahoo.com, Web Site: www.leatherunltd.com (2)

O'Connell, Robert, Print Services Distribution Association, Chicago, IL. Tel: (703) 836-6232, (800) 336-4641, FAX: (703) 836-2241, E-Mail: psda@psda.org, Web Site: www.psda.org (1)

O'Connell, Stacy, Intagio Trading Network, San Francisco, CA. Tel: (415) 247-9500, FAX: (415) 543-0375, Web Site: www.intagio.com (32)

O'Connor, Barbara, Yahoo Inc, New York, NY. Tel: (212) 381-6829 (32)

O'Connor, Diane, Creative Irish Gifts, Little Rock, AR. Tel: (330) 954-1200, FAX: (330) 650-8888, E-Mail: gifts@shopirish.com, Web Site: www.shopirish.com (6)

O'Connor, Donald, Tully & Holland Inc, Wellesley, MA. Tel: (781) 239-2900, FAX: (781) 239-2901, E-Mail: info@tullyandholland.com, Web Site: www.tullyandholland.com (14)

O'Connor, Jerry, Diversified Healthcare Services, Richardson, TX. Tel: (972) 238-1492, FAX: (972) 907-8283, Web Site: www.dhscorp.com (15)

O'Connor, John C., JVW Direct, Pittsburgh, PA. Tel: (412) 241-5920, FAX: (412) 241-5850, E-Mail: john@jvwdirect.com (35)

O'Connor, John, McKnight's Long-Term Care News, Northfield, IL. Tel: (847) 784-8706, (800) 558-1703, FAX: (847) 784-9346, E-Mail: mltcnwebmaster@mltcn.com, Web Site: www.mcknightsonline.com (17)

O'Connor, Jr. Thomas, D., Mohawk, Cohoes, NY. Tel: (518) 237-1740, (800) 843-6455, FAX: (518) 237-7394, E-Mail: info@mohawkpaper.com, Web Site: www.mohawkconnects.com (25)

O'Connor, Karne, Blethen Maine Newspapers Inc, Portland, ME. Tel: (207) 791-6650, FAX: (207) 791-6925, Web Site: www.mainetoday.com (17)

O'Connor, Michael, St Joseph Communications, Concord, ON Canada. Tel: (905) 660-3111, FAX: (905) 669-1972, Web Site: www.stjoseph.com (27)

O'Connor, Patrick, Michigan Apple Committee, Lansing, MI. Tel: (517) 669-8353, (800) 456-2753, FAX: (517) 669-9506, E-Mail: staff@michiganapples.com, Web Site: www.michiganapples.com (1)

O'Connor, Robert, Creative Irish Gifts, Little Rock, AR. Tel: (330) 954-1200, FAX: (330) 650-8888, E-Mail: gifts@shopirish.com, Web Site: www.shopirish.com (6)

O'Connor, Tom, Springs Global Inc, New York, NY. Tel: (888) 926-7888, Web Site: www.springs.com (16)

O'Connor-Vos, Lynn, Grey Healthcare Group, New York, NY. Tel: (212) 886-3000, FAX: (212) 886-3297, E-Mail: info@ghgroup.com, Web Site: www.ghgroup.com (35)

O'Dea, Patrick, J., Peet's Coffee & Tea Inc, Berkeley, CA. Tel: (510) 594-2100, (800) 999-2132, FAX: (510) 594-2180, E-Mail: mailorder@peets.com, Web Site: www.peets.com (4)

O'Dell, Paul, J., The Software Labs Inc, Bellevue, WA. Tel: (425) 653-2432, FAX: (425) 643-8090, Web Site: www.softwarelabs.com (3)

O'Donnell, Bonnie, Grand Canyon Association, Flagstaff, AZ. Tel: (928) 863-3876, Web Site: www.grandcanyon.org (1)

O'Donnell, Linda, Web Direct Marketing Inc, Glenview, IL. Tel: (847) 459-0800, (877) 841-2841, FAX: (847) 459-7378, E-Mail: info@webdirectmktg.com, Web Site: www.webdirectmktg.com (35)

O'Donnell, Tim, Lundberg Family Farms, Richvale, CA. Tel: (530) 882-4551, FAX: (530) 882-4500, E-Mail: info@lundberg.com, Web Site: www.lundberg.com (16)

O'Donovan, Barry, Random House Children's Books, New York, NY. Tel: (212) 782-9000, (800) 726-0600, Web Site: www.randomhouse.com/kids (13)

O'Drobinak, Larry, UGL Equis Corp, Chicago, IL. Tel: (312) 424-8000, FAX: (312) 424-8080, Web Site: www.equiscorp.com (16)

O'Dwyer, George, 501 Post, Austin, TX. Tel: (512) 476-3876, FAX: (512) 477-3912, E-Mail: godwyer@501studios.com, Web Site: www.501post.com (32)

O'Dwyer, Jack, O'Dwyers Directory of Public Relations Firms, New York, NY. Tel: (212) 679-2471, (866) 395-7710, FAX: (212) 683-2750, E-Mail: john@odwyerpr.com, Web Site: www.odwyerpr.com (43)

O'Grady, Matt, Nielsen Claritas, San Diego, CA. Tel: (800) 866-6520, Web Site: www.claritas.com (30)

O'Halleran, Michael, AON Center, Chicago, IL. Tel: (312) 381-1000, FAX: (312) 381-6032, Web Site: www.aon.com (15)

O'Halloran, Kevin, Tiffany & Co, New York, NY. Tel: (212) 755-8000, FAX: (212) 320-7550, Web Site: www.tiffany.com (6)

O'Halloran, Mark, O'Halloran Advertising, Westport, CT. Tel: (203) 571-6203 (39)

O'Halloran, Patrick, ENTIERA, Minneapolis, MN. Tel: (866) 387-4271, Web Site: www.entiera.com (22)

O'Hara, Arthur, Olympia Sales Inc, Enfield, CT. Tel: (860) 749-0751, (800) 338-9992, FAX: (860) 814-4451, E-Mail: info@olympiasales.net, Web Site: www.olympiasales.us (16)

O'Hara, Gerry, Marquardt, Roche & Partners, Stamford, CT. Tel: (203) 327-0890, FAX: (203) 353-8487, E-Mail: ideas@mrp-website.com, Web Site: www.mrp-website.com (35)

O'Hara, Joseph M., Moto Franchise Corp, Dayton, OH. Tel: (937) 291-1900, (800) 733-6686, FAX: (937) 291-2005, E-Mail: expert@motophoto.com, Web Site: www.motophoto.com; www.portraitavenue.com (3)

O'Hara, Stephen, M., Angelica Image Apparel, Saint Louis, MO. Tel: (314) 854-3800, (800) 235-8410, Web Site: www.angelica.com (16)

O'Hara, Thomas, A., Olympia Sales Inc, Enfield, CT. Tel: (860) 749-0751, (800) 338-9992, FAX: (860) 814-4451, E-Mail: info@olympiasales.net, Web Site: www.olympiasales.us (16)

O'Keefe, Carolyn, P., IHOP Corp, Glendale, CA. Tel: (818) 240-6055, FAX: (818) 553-3131, Web Site: www.ihop.com (16)

O'Keefe, Gianna, Ruud Lighting Inc, Racine, WI. Tel: (262) 886-1900, (800) 236-7000, FAX: (800) 236-7500, E-Mail: sales@ruudlighting.com, Web Site: www.ruudlighting.com (9)

O'Keefe, Kelly, Centerpoint Energy, Minneapolis, MN. Tel: (612) 372-4664, FAX: (612) 321-4873, E-Mail: mgc-businessinformation@centerpointenergy.com, Web Site: www.minnegasco.centerpointenergy.com (16)

O'Keefe, William, Safti First, San Francisco, CA. Tel: (415) 824-4900, (888) 653-3333, FAX: (415) 824-5900, (888) 653-4444, E-Mail: info@safti.com, Web Site: www.safti.com (16)

O'Keeffe Jr., William, Safti First, San Francisco, CA. Tel: (415) 824-4900, (888) 653-3333, FAX: (415) 824-5900, (888) 653-4444, E-Mail: info@safti.com, Web Site: www.safti.com (16)

O'Keeffe, Kathryn, Safti First, San Francisco, CA. Tel: (415) 824-4900, (888) 653-3333, FAX: (415) 824-5900, (888) 653-4444, E-Mail: info@safti.com, Web Site: www.safti.com (16)

O'Leary, David, American General Life & Accident Insurance, Nashville, TN. Tel: (615) 749-1000, (800) 888-2452, Web Site: www.agla.com (15)

O'Looney, Michael, Merrill Lynch, New York, NY. Tel: (212) 449-1000, (800) 637-7455, FAX: (212) 449-9418, Web Site: www.ml.com (14)

O'Malley, John, Harland Financial Solutions Inc, Lake Mary, FL. Tel: (407) 804-6600, (800) 815-5592, FAX: (407) 829-6702, Web Site: www.harlandfinancialsolutions.com (16)

O'Malley, John, P., Westcon, Tarrytown, NY. Tel: (914) 829-7000, FAX: (914) 829-7137, Web Site: www.westcon.com (16)

O'Malley, Lorie, DWS Investments Service Co, Kansas City, MO. Tel: (800) 543-5776, Web Site: www.dws-investments.com (14)

O'Malley, Thomas, American Dermatological Corp, Miami, FL. Tel: (305) 573-0763, (888) 573-0763, FAX: (305) 573-1704, E-Mail: info@dermatique.com, Web Site: www.dermatique.com (16)

O'Malley, William, J., American Dermatological Corp, Miami, FL. Tel: (305) 573-0763, (888) 573-0763, FAX: (305) 573-1704, E-Mail: info@dermatique.com, Web Site: www.dermatique.com (16)

O'Neil, George, F., Home Owner Data Services Inc, Lawrenceville, GA. Tel: (770) 925-9000, FAX: (770) 925-8977, E-Mail: hdsi@newhomedata.net, Web Site: www.newhomedata.net (23)

O'Neil, Laurence, Society for Human Resource Management, Alexandria, VA. Tel: (703) 548-3440, (800) 283-SHRM, FAX: (703) 535-6490, E-Mail: shrmstore@shrm.org, Web Site: www.shrm.org (1)

O'Neil, Mark, The NH Broadcaster, Lowell, MA. Tel: (978) 458-7100, Web Site: www.nhbroadcaster.com (31)

O'Neil, Michael, Bank of Hawaii, Honolulu, HI. Tel: (808) 537-8398, FAX: (808) 536-9433, Web Site: www.boh.com (14)

O'Neil, Michael, Mentor Corp, Santa Barbara, CA. Tel: (805) 879-6000, (800) 525-0245, FAX: (805) 964-2712, Web Site: www.mentorcorp.com (16)

O'Neil, Robert, J., International City/County Management Association, Washington, DC. Tel: (202) 289-ICMA, FAX: (202) 962-3500, E-Mail: customerservice@icma.org, Web Site: www.icma.org (1)

O'Neil, Susan, Bamboo Cricket, West Palm Beach, FL. Tel: (561) 768-7968, (800) 260-8050, FAX: (561) 653-3990, Web Site: www.bamboocricket. com (32)

O'Neill, Kathleen, American Lung Association, New York, NY. Tel: (212) 889-3370, (800) LUNGUSA, FAX: (212) 889-3375, E-Mail: info@alany.org, Web Site: www.lungusa.org (1)

O'Neill, Katie, Fulcrum Publishing, Golden, CO. Tel: (303) 277-1623, (800) 992-2908, FAX: (303) 279-7111, Web Site: www.fulcrum-books.com (17)

O'Neill, Paul, Direct Channel Inc, West Bridgewater, MA. Tel: (508) 588-4448, FAX: (508) 588-4644, E-Mail: directch@mindspring.com, Web Site: www.directchannel.com (23)

O'Neill, Randy, Lancer Insurance Co, Long Beach, NY. Tel: (516) 431-4441, (800) 782-8902, FAX: (516) 889-5111, E-Mail: roneill@lancer-ins.com, Web Site: www.lancer-ins.com (15)

O'Neill, Rita, O'Neill Marketing Co, Fairfax, VA. Tel: (703) 934-0272, Web Site: www.oneillmarketing. com (23)

O'Neill, Rob, The Angler's Den, Pawling, NY. Tel: (845) 855-5182, E-Mail: flyfish@anglersden.net, Web Site: www.anglersden.net (11)

O'Neill, Thomas, Harry Winston Inc, New York, NY. Tel: (212) 245-2000, FAX: (212) 489-0016, E-Mail: hw@harrywinston.com, Web Site: www. harry-winston.com (16)

O'Quinn-Humphries, Shelly, Jones School Supply Co Inc, Irmo, SC. Tel: (803) 772-3796, FAX: (800) 942-5921, Web Site: www.jonesawards.com (6)

O'Reilly, Kathleen, CSPI/Nutrition Action Health Letter, Washington, DC. Tel: (202) 332-9110, FAX: (202) 265-4954, E-Mail: cspi@cspinet.org, Web Site: www.cspinet.org (17)

O'Reilly, Matt, Ace Communications, Garden City, NY. Tel: (718) 458-3800, (800) 468-7667, FAX: (516) 872-8156, Web Site: www.aceav.com (3)

O'Reilly, Priscilla, Grand Circle Travel, Boston, MA. Tel: (617) 350-7500, (800) 959-0405, FAX: (617) 346-6030, Web Site: www.gct.com (19)

O'Rorke, Elizabeth, The Economist Newspaper NA Inc, New York, NY. Tel: (212) 554-0600, FAX: (212) 586-1191, Web Site: www.economist.com (17)

O'Rourke, Betsy, Days Inns Worldwide Inc, Parsippany, NJ. Tel: (973) 753-6000, (800) 441-1618, Web Site: www.daysinn.com (16)

O'Rourke, Jeanne, Massachusetts Horticultural Society, Wellesley, MA. Tel: (617) 933-4929, (617) 933-4900, FAX: (617) 933-4901, E-Mail: hort_line@masshort.org, Web Site: www.masshort. org (1)

O'Rourke, Tom, O'Rourke Hospitality Marketing LLC, Newburyport, MA. Tel: (978) 465-5955, Web Site: www.orourkehospitality.com (35)

O'Shea, Barbara, Penguin Publishing Group, New York, NY. Tel: (212) 366-2000, FAX: (212) 366-2952, Web Site: www.penguinputnam.com (17)

O'Shea, Christopher, Accellos Inc, Colorado Springs, CO. Tel: (719) 433-7000, Web Site: www.accellos. com (12)

O'Sullivan, James, J., Mazda North American Operations, Irvine, CA. Tel: (949) 727-1990, (800) 222-6500, FAX: (949) 727-6101, Web Site: www. mazdausa.com (1)

O'Sullivan, Joan, Marsh Affinity Group Services, Chicago, IL. Tel: (800) 621-3008, Web Site: www. seaburychicago.com (15)

O'Sullivan, Karin, Innovative Systems Inc, Pittsburgh, PA. Tel: (412) 937-9300, (800) 622-6390, FAX: (412) 937-9309, E-Mail: info@innovativesystems. com, Web Site: www.innovativesystems.com (22)

O'Toole, Brian, Crane Pumps & Systems Inc, Piqua, OH. Tel: (937) 773-2442, FAX: (937) 773-2238, E-Mail: cranepumps@cranepumps.com, Web Site: www.cranepumps.com (16)

O'Toole, David, Thomson Reuters, New York, NY. Tel: (212) 367-6300, (800) 950-1216, FAX: (212) 367-6301, Web Site: www.riahome.com (17)

O'Toole, James, Websource & Paper Corp, Norcross, GA. Tel: (212) 255-1600, FAX: (212) 463-7095, Web Site: www.websource-paper.com (25)

O2 Consulting Inc, Atlanta, GA. Tel: (404) 384-3990 (22)

O2K1, New York, NY. Tel: (646) 839-6254, Web Site: www.02kl.com (35)

OAG Worldwide, Downers Grove, IL. Tel: (630) 515-5300, FAX: (630) 515-5301, E-Mail: custsvc@oag. com, Web Site: www.oag.com (17)

OKS-Ameridial Inc, Bala Cynwyd, PA. Tel: (610) 667-3000, FAX: (610) 667-3002, E-Mail: info@ oksgroup.com, Web Site: www.oksameridial.com (29)

OMP, Washington, DC. Tel: (202) 467-0048, Web Site: www.ompdirect.com (1)

OMSI Inc, Belleville, IL. Tel: (618) 398-7640, Web Site: www.oblatesusa.org (1)

ORC Macro International, New York, NY. Tel: (212) 941-5555, FAX: (212) 941-7031, E-Mail: info@ icfi.com, Web Site: www.icfi.com (30)

ORC ProTel LLC, Lansing, IL. Tel: (708) 418-7413, FAX: (708) 418-7457, Web Site: www.orcprotel. com (29)

OSG Billing, Englewood, NJ. Tel: (201) 871-1100, Web Site: www.osgbilling.com (20)

OSRAM Sylvania, Danvers, MA. Tel: (978) 750-2210, Web Site: www.sylvania.com (16)

OTM Partners, Arlington, VA. Tel: (800) 759-2244, Web Site: www.otmpartners.biz (35)

Oak Knoll Limited Liability Co, South Salem, NY. Tel: (914) 533-0208 (20)

Oakes, Fred, Elks Magazine, Chicago, IL. Tel: (773) 755-4700, (877) 355-7624, FAX: (773) 775-4891, E-Mail: elksmag@elks.org, Web Site: www.elks. org (17)

Oakes, Joe, DM News, New York, NY. Tel: (212) 925-7300, FAX: (212) 925-8752, Web Site: www. dmnews.com (43)

Oakes, Katie, SCA Direct, Fairfax, VA. Tel: (703) 293-6339, Web Site: www.scadirect.com (1)

Oakes, Marvin, Wilton Industries Inc, Woodridge, IL. Tel: (630) 963-1818, (800) 794-5866, FAX: (630) 963-7196, E-Mail: info@wilton.com, Web Site: www.wilton.com (16)

Oakley, Michele, Vector Marketing Corp, Olean, NY. Tel: (716) 373-6141, FAX: (716) 373-6145, Web Site: www.cutco.com (5)

Oakley Inc, Foothill Ranch, CA. Tel: (949) 829-0991, Web Site: www.oakley.com (2)

Oakstone Publishing LLC, Birmingham, AL. Tel: (205) 991-5188, (800) 952-0690, FAX: (205) 995-4656, Web Site: www.oakstonepublishing.com (17)

Oakton Community College, Des Plaines, IL. Tel: (847) 635-1600, FAX: (847) 635-1706, Web Site: www.oakton.edu (41)

Oakwood Homes Corp, Greensboro, NC. Tel: (336) 664-2400, (800) 822-0633, FAX: (336) 315-3249, Web Site: www.oakwoodhomes.com (16)

Oates, Richard, Zig Ziglar Corp, Plano, TX. Tel: (972) 233-9191, (800) 527-0306, FAX: (469) 321-7556, E-Mail: info@ziglar.com, Web Site: www.zigziglar. com (16)

Oberg, Michael, Reed/Harris, Portland, OR. Tel: (503) 224-1812, (800) 238-1812, FAX: (503) 223-8283, E-Mail: info@reedharris.com, Web Site: www. reedharris.com (21)

Oberman, Aaron, Omeda, Northbrook, IL. Tel: (847) 564-8900, Web Site: www.omeda.com (22)

Obermier, Beanie, William-Neil Associates, Sidney, NE. Tel: (800) 216-2214, FAX: (308) 254-6102, Web Site: www.william-neil.com (24)

Obernier, Robert, B., Horizon Paper Co Inc, Stamford, CT. Tel: (203) 358-0855, (866) 358-0855, FAX: (203) 358-0828, Web Site: www.horizonpaper.com (25)

Oberski, Mark, FlarePath LLC, New York, NY. Tel: (212) 927-1296 (20)

Oberstein, Howard, The Marketing Place, Sun Valley, CA. Tel: (818) 834-8500, FAX: (818) 834-8511, E-Mail: mktgplace@aol.com, Web Site: wwwthemarketingplace.com (23)

Oberthur Card Systems, Chantilly, VA. Tel: (703) 263-0100, FAX: (703) 263-0503, E-Mail: info@ oberthurcs.com, Web Site: www.oberthurcs.com (28)

Oblate Missions, San Antonio, TX. Tel: (210) 736-1685, FAX: (210) 736-1314 (1)

O'Brien Document Solutions, Bartlett, IL. Tel: (630) 830-0990, FAX: (630) 830-0062, E-Mail: obrien_info@obinc.com, Web Site: www.obinc. com (27)

O'Brien Manufacturing, Marietta, OH. Tel: (740) 374-2306, (800) 638-1901, FAX: (740) 374-5447, Web Site: www.obrienmfg.com (9)

The Occasions Group, North Mankato, MN. Tel: (507) 625-6464 (16)

Occhiat, Thomas, Progressive Direct Marketing, Depew, NY. Tel: (716) 681-6848, (800) 344-7593, FAX: (716) 681-9173, Web Site: www.pdmny.com (35)

OccuNomix, Port Jefferson Station, NY. Tel: (631) 791-1912, Web Site: www.occunomix.com (34)

OCE North America Inc, Boca Raton, FL. Tel: (561) 997-3100, (800) 523-5444, FAX: (561) 998-9160, Web Site: www.oceproductionprinting.com (34)

Ocean Conservancy, Washington, DC. Tel: (202) 429-5609, Web Site: www.oceanconservancy.org (1)

Ocello, Carmen, Direct Mail Depot Inc, Piscataway, NJ. Tel: (732) 469-5900, FAX: (732) 469-8414, E-Mail: sales@directmaildepot.com, Web Site: www.directmaildepot.com (28)

Ochsenbein, Roland, Greenwood Publishing Group Inc, Portsmouth, NH. Tel: (203) 226-3571, FAX: (203) 222-1502, E-Mail: sales@greenwood.com, Web Site: www.greenwood.com (17)

O'Connell Meier LLC, Alexandria, VA. Tel: (703) 635-2893, (866) 391-1415, FAX: (703) 739-0478, E-Mail: info@omdirect.com, Web Site: www. omdirect.com (21)

O'Currance Inc, Draper, UT. Tel: (801) 736-0500, (888) 628-7726, FAX: (801) 736-0510, E-Mail: sales@ocurrance.com, Web Site: www.ocurance. com (18)

Oda, Frances, Mitsubishi Motor Sales of America Inc, Cypress, CA. Tel: (714) 372-6000, FAX: (714) 373-1736, Web Site: www.mitsubishicars.com (1)

Odden, Lee, TopRank Online Marketing, Mound, MN. Tel: (952) 400-0194, Web Site: www. toprankresults.com (32)

Odell, Patricia, Promo Magazine, New York, NY. Tel: (203) 358-9900, (800) 927-5007, FAX: (203) 358-5816, E-Mail: larry.jaffee@penton.com, Web Site: www.promomagazine.com (17)

Odell, Simms & Associates Inc, Falls Church, VA. Tel: (703) 903-9797, FAX: (703) 903-8850, E-Mail: webmaster@odellsimms.com, Web Site: www.odellsimms.com (35)

Oden, Memphis, TN. Tel: (901) 578-8055, FAX: (901) 578-1911, Web Site: www.oden.com (35)

Odland, Mary, National Business Furniture Inc, Milwaukee, WI. Tel: (414) 276-8511, (800) 558-1010, FAX: (414) 276-8371, Web Site: www. nationalbusinessfurniture.com (10)

Odle, David, Hyman's, Hanahan, SC. Tel: (843) 571-7870, (800) 354-9626, FAX: (843) 571-7575, E-Mail: support@hymans.com, Web Site: www. hymans.com (2)

Odlum, Canie, Washington National Opera, Washington, DC. Tel: (202) 295-2400, (800) US-OPERA, FAX: (202) 295-2460, E-Mail: mail@dc-opera.org, Web Site: www.dc-opera.org (16)

Odom, Bill, Manchester Farms Inc, Columbia, SC. Tel: (803) 469-2588, (800) 845-0421, FAX: (803) 469-8637, E-Mail: customerservice@manchesterfarms.com, Web Site: www.manchesterfarms.com (4)

Odom, Diane, FP Mailing Solutions, Addison, IL. Tel: (800) 341-6052, FAX: (630) 693-0626, Web Site: www.fp-usa.com (34)

Odom, Steve, Manchester Farms Inc, Columbia, SC. Tel: (803) 469-2588, (800) 845-0421, FAX: (803) 469-8637, E-Mail: customerservice@manchesterfarms.com, Web Site: www.manchesterfarms.com (4)

O'Dwyers Directory of Public Relations Firms, New York, NY. Tel: (212) 679-2471, (866) 395-7710, FAX: (212) 683-2750, E-Mail: john@odwyerpr.com, Web Site: www.odwyerpr.com (43)

Oechsle, H., Hohn, Partminer, Centennial, CO. Tel: (303) 200-5500, FAX: (303) 754-3940, Web Site: www.partminer.com (17)

Oechsle, H., John, IHS Inc, Englewood, CO. Tel: (303) 790-0600, (800) 525-7052, FAX: (303) 754-3940, E-Mail: customer.support@ihs.com, Web Site: www.ihs.com (17)

Oerthing, Laurie, Laitram Machinery, Harahan, LA. Tel: (504) 733-6000, FAX: (504) 733-6111 (16)

Off the Wall Magnetics LLC, Portland, OR. Tel: (800) 337-2637, Web Site: www.4thefridge.com (16)

Office Depot, Boca Raton, FL. Tel: (561) 438-4800, (800) 937-3600, FAX: (561) 438-4001, Web Site: www.officedepot.com (16)

Office Express Inc, Evanston, IL. Tel: (888) 526-8438, FAX: (773) 341-7322, E-Mail: sales@envelopesexpress.com, Web Site: www.envelopesexpress.com (26)

The Office Gurus, Seminole, FL. Tel: (727) 803-7114, Web Site: www.theofficegurus.com (29)

officefurniture.com, Milwaukee, WI. Tel: (414) 272-6080, (800) 933-0053, FAX: (414) 272-0248, (800) 468-1526, Web Site: www.officefurniture.com (8)

OfficeMax Inc, Naperville, IL. Tel: (630) 864-5809, (800) 661-5931, Web Site: www.officemax.com (10)

Official Offset Corp, Amityville, NY. Tel: (631) 957-8500 (27)

The Offset House Inc, Essex Junction, VT. Tel: (802) 878-4440, FAX: (802) 879-4865, Web Site: www.offsethouse.com (27)

Ogarrio, Andrea, Rose Resnick Lighthouse for the Blind & Visually Impaired, San Francisco, CA. Tel: (415) 431-1481, FAX: (415) 863-7568, E-Mail: executive@lighthouse-sf.org, Web Site: www.lighthouse-sf.org (1)

Ogilvy & Mather Direct, New York, NY. Tel: (212) 237-6000, FAX: (212) 237-5123, Web Site: www.ogilvy.com (35)

OgilvyOne Worldwide, New York, NY. Tel: (212) 237-6000, Web Site: www.ogilvy-canada.com (35)

Oglander, Allen H., Dispensa-Matic Label Dispensers, Saint Louis, MO. Tel: (314) 231-6006, (800) 325-7303, FAX: (314) 621-1602, E-Mail: info@dispensamatic.com, Web Site: www.dispensa-matic.com (34)

Ogren, Rhonda, Llewellyn Publications, Woodbury, MN. Tel: (651) 291-1970, (800) 843-6666, FAX: (651) 291-1908, Web Site: www.llewellyn.com (17)

Oh, Tom, Smithsonian Institution, Washington, DC. Tel: (202) 357-2700, Web Site: www.si.edu (6)

O'Halloran Advertising, Westport, CT. Tel: (203) 571-6203 (39)

Ohio Envelope Manufacturing Co, Cleveland, OH. Tel: (216) 267-2920, (800) 989-0336, FAX: (216) 267-1765, E-Mail: mgmt@ohioenvelope.com, Web Site: www.ohioenvelope.com (26)

Ohlmann, Walter, The Ohlmann Group Direct, Dayton, OH. Tel: (937) 278-0681, FAX: (937) 277-1723, E-Mail: info@ohlmanngroup.com, Web Site: www.ohlmanngroup.com (35)

The Ohlmann Group Direct, Dayton, OH. Tel: (937) 278-0681, FAX: (937) 277-1723, E-Mail: info@ohlmanngroup.com, Web Site: www.ohlmanngroup.com (35)

Oil & Gas Journal, Tulsa, OK. Tel: (918) 835-3161, (800) 331-4463, FAX: (918) 832-9497, Web Site: www.pennwell.com; www.ogj.com (17)

Okas, Daisy L., American Kennel Club, New York, NY. Tel: (212) 696-8200, FAX: (212) 696-8217, (212) 696-8299, Web Site: www.akc.org (17)

Okeefe, Marietta, GA. Tel: (973) 632-7630 (5)

O'Keefe Henry Direct Inc, Deerfield, IL. Tel: (847) 681-9200, FAX: (847) 681-9299, Web Site: www.okeefehenrydirect.com (20)

Oklahoma Dept of Commerce, Oklahoma City, OK. Tel: (405) 815-6552, (800) 879-6552, FAX: (405) 815-5344, Web Site: www.okcommerce.com (1)

Okun Brothers Shoes Inc, Kalamazoo, MI. Tel: (269) 342-1536, (800) 433-6344, FAX: (269) 383-3401 (2)

Olafsson, Olaf, Time Warner Inc, New York, NY. Tel: (212) 484-8000, Web Site: www.timewarner.com (16)

Olan Mills Inc, Chattanooga, TN. Tel: (423) 622-5141, (800) 251-6320, FAX: (423) 629-8128, Web Site: www.olanmills.com (16)

Oland, Steve, Office Depot, Boca Raton, FL. Tel: (561) 438-4800, (800) 937-3600, FAX: (561) 438-4001, Web Site: www.officedepot.com (16)

Olbres, Tamara, C., Interex, Amesbury, MA. Tel: (978) 388-8755, (800) INTEREX, FAX: (978) 388-8747, Web Site: www.interexhibits.com (17)

Old Vine Marketing, Napa, CA. Tel: (707) 694-9647, E-Mail: info@oldvinemarketing.com, Web Site: www.oldvinemarketing.com (22)

Old World Ind, Northbrook, IL. Tel: (847) 559-2137, Web Site: www.oldworldind.com (34)

Old World Mouldings Inc, Bohemia, NY. Tel: (631) 563-8660, FAX: (631) 563-8815, E-Mail: mouldings@optonline.com, Web Site: www.oldworldmouldings.com (9)

Oldenkamp, Rick, Midwest Technology Products & Services, Sioux City, IA. Tel: (712) 252-3601, (800) 831-5904, FAX: (800) 258-7054, E-Mail: web@midwesttechnology.com, Web Site: www.midwesttechnology.com (9)

Oldham, Lisa, Specialized Products Co, Southlake, TX. Tel: (817) 329-6647, (800) 866-5353, FAX: (800) 234-8286, E-Mail: spc@specialized.net, Web Site: www.specialized.net (16)

Olding, Robert, Damilic Corp, Rockville, MD. Tel: (301) 251-2960, (800) 276-7749, FAX: (301) 251-8591, E-Mail: info@realsig.com, Web Site: www.realsig.com (16)

Oleda & Co Inc, Fort Worth, TX. Tel: (817) 731-1147, (800) 731-4247, FAX: (817) 731-1149, E-Mail: oleda@oleda.com, Web Site: www.oleda.com (16)

Oles Envelope Corp, Baltimore, MD. Tel: (410) 243-1520, (800) 822-6537, FAX: (410) 366-7022, Web Site: www.olesenvelope.com (26)

Olesuk, Frank, D., Olesuk Financial Services, McHenry, IL. Tel: (815) 363-0808, FAX: (815) 363-0843, E-Mail: folesuk@sagepointadvisor.com, Web Site: www.olesukfinancialservices.com (14)

Olesuk, Karlene, M., Olesuk Financial Services, McHenry, IL. Tel: (815) 363-0808, FAX: (815) 363-0843, E-Mail: folesuk@sagepointadvisor.com, Web Site: www.olesukfinancialservices.com (14)

Olesuk, Patricia, S., Olesuk Financial Services, McHenry, IL. Tel: (815) 363-0808, FAX: (815) 363-0843, E-Mail: folesuk@sagepointadvisor.com, Web Site: www.olesukfinancialservices.com (14)

Olesuk Financial Services, McHenry, IL. Tel: (815) 363-0808, FAX: (815) 363-0843, E-Mail: folesuk@sagepointadvisor.com, Web Site: www.olesukfinancialservices.com (14)

Oliver, Deborah, International Marine, Camden, ME. Tel: (207) 236-4837, FAX: (207) 236-6314, Web Site: www.internationalmarine.com (17)

Oliver, Francois, Telemedia Communications US, North York, ON. Tel: (416) 733-7600, (888) 290-1466 Can., (800) 461-3773 U.S., FAX: (416) 733-3563, E-Mail: info@transcontinental.ca, Web Site: www.transcontinental.com (17)

Oliver, Michael, O., Brady Corp, Milwaukee, WI. Tel: (414) 358-6600, (800) 541-1686, FAX: (800) 292-2289, Web Site: www.bradycorp.com (17)

Oliver, Susan, Cornerstone Group of Companies, Toronto, ON. Tel: (416) 932-9555, FAX: (416) 932-9566, E-Mail: info@cstonecanada.com, Web Site: www.cstonecanada.com (22)

Oliver, Tim, Tensar International Corporation, Alpharetta, GA. Tel: (404) 250-1290, Web Site: www.tensarcorp.com (16)

Oliver of Adrian Inc, Adrian, MI. Tel: (517) 263-2132, (877) 668-0885, FAX: (517) 265-8698, E-Mail: info@oliverinstrument.com, Web Site: www.oliverofadrian.com (16)

Oliver Russell & Associates, Boise, ID. Tel: (208) 344-1734, FAX: (208) 344-1211, Web Site: www.oliverrussell.com (35)

Oliver Wyman, New York, NY. Tel: (212) 541-8100, (212) 345-8000, Web Site: www.oliverwyman.com (14)

Oliveri, Ann, ULI-The Urban Land Institute, Washington, DC. Tel: (202) 624-7000, FAX: (202) 624-7140, Web Site: www.uli.org (1)

Oller, Janet, Herschend Family Entertainment, Branson, MO. Tel: (417) 338-3810, FAX: (417) 338-8144, Web Site: www.silverdollarcity.com (5)

Olmstead, C., Elvan, David C Cook, Colorado Springs, CO. Tel: (719) 536-0100, (800) 323-7543, FAX: (719) 536-3232, Web Site: www.davidccook.com (17)

Olmsted, Dick, Farm Market iD, Westmont, IL. Tel: (630) 654-5700, (800) 313-4778, FAX: (630) 654-4470, Web Site: www.farmmarketid.com (23)

Olmsted-Kirk Paper Co, Dallas, TX. Tel: (214) 637-2220, (800) 367-6526, FAX: (214) 637-7630, E-Mail: sales@okpaper.com, Web Site: www.okpaper.com (25)

Olrich, Scott, Responsys, San Bruno, CA. Tel: (650) 745-1700, Web Site: www.responsys.com (20)

Olsen, Christina, Sunset Magazine, Menlo Park, CA. Tel: (650) 321-3600, FAX: (650) 328-6215 (17)

Olsen, Kelsey, Quality Contact Solutions Inc, Aurora, NE. Tel: (402) 210-2692, (866) 963-2889, FAX: (402) 210-2692, E-Mail: info@qualitycontactsolutions.com, Web Site: www.qualitycontactsolutions.com (29)

Olsen, Paul, Olsen's Mill Direct, Oshkosh, WI. Tel: (800) 537-4979, (800) 452-3699, FAX: (920) 426-6369, E-Mail: sales@olsensmilldirect.com (2)

Olsen, Peter, Listening Library Inc, Random House Audio, New York, NY. Tel: (800) 726-0600, FAX: (800) 454-0606, Web Site: www.randomhouse.com/audio (3)

Olsen, Richard, J., RJ Olsen Inc, Natick, MA. Tel: (508) 647-3777, FAX: (508) 647-6777, E-Mail: dickolsen@aol.com (30)

Olsen's Mill Direct, Oshkosh, WI. Tel: (800) 537-4979, (800) 452-3699, FAX: (920) 426-6369, E-Mail: sales@olsensmilldirect.com (2)

Olshefsky, Jim, ASTM International, West Conshohocken, PA. Tel: (610) 832-9500, FAX: (610) 832-9555, E-Mail: service@astm.org, Web Site: www.astm.org (1)

Olson, John, Olson & Co, Minneapolis, MN. Tel: (612) 215-9800, FAX: (612) 215-9801, E-Mail: info@oco.com, Web Site: www.oco.com (35)

Olson, Karen, Allegra Print & Imaging - East, Louisville, KY. Tel: (502) 895-1530, Web Site: www.allegra-east.com (27)

Olson, Karol, Union Privilege, AFL-CIO, Washington, DC. Tel: (202) 293-5330, FAX: (202) 293-5311, Web Site: www.unionplus.org (1)

Olson, Peter, Premiere Global Services Inc, Atlanta, GA. Tel: (404) 262-8400, (800) 546-1541, FAX: (913) 661-9042, Web Site: www.PGiConnect.com (22)

Olson, Rick, PESI LLC, Eau Claire, WI. Tel: (800) 844-8260, FAX: (800) 554-9775, E-Mail: info@pesi.com, Web Site: www.pesi.com (17)

Olson, Sande, Rose Electronics, Houston, TX. Tel: (281) 933-7673, (800) 333-9343, FAX: (281) 933-0044, E-Mail: sales@rose.com, Web Site: www.rose.com (3)

Olson, Sandra, S., TeleRep, Glen Burnie, MD. Tel: (800) 638-2000, FAX: (410) 761-3357, Web Site: www.telerep.com (29)

Olson, Thomas D., Triton College, River Grove, IL. Tel: (708) 456-0300, FAX: (708) 583-3121, Web Site: www.triton.edu (16)

Olson, William, Vertrue Inc, Norwalk, CT. Tel: (203) 324-7635, FAX: (203) 674-7080, Web Site: www.vertrue.com (13)

Olson & Co, Minneapolis, MN. Tel: (612) 215-9800, FAX: (612) 215-9801, E-Mail: info@oco.com, Web Site: www.oco.com (35)

OlymPak, Minneapolis, MN. Tel: (763) 504-5400, (800) 967-1705, FAX: (763) 504-5401, E-Mail: jgibas@olympak.com, Web Site: www.olympak.com (27)

Olympia Sales Inc, Enfield, CT. Tel: (860) 749-0751, (800) 338-9992, FAX: (860) 814-4451, E-Mail: info@olympiasales.net, Web Site: www.olympiasales.us (16)

Olzer, Timothy, O2 Consulting Inc, Atlanta, GA. Tel: (404) 384-3990 (22)

Omaha Creative Group Inc, Omaha, NE. Tel: (800) 228-2778, Web Site: www.omahasteaks.com (4)

Omaha Fixture International, Omaha, NE. Tel: (402) 592-3720, (800) 531-6627, FAX: (402) 593-5716, (800) 531-6627, Web Site: www.omahafixture.com (8)

Omaha Print, Omaha, NE. Tel: (402) 734-4400, (800) 369-0033, FAX: (402) 734-7492, E-Mail: shayes@omahaprint.com, Web Site: www.omahaprint.com (21)

Omaha Steaks Inc, Omaha, NE. Tel: (402) 597-3000, FAX: (402) 597-8252, E-Mail: info@omahasteaks.com, Web Site: www.omahasteaks.com (4)

Omaha Vaccine Co, Omaha, NE. Tel: (402) 731-9600, (800) 367-4444, FAX: (800) 242-9447, E-Mail: customerservice@OmahaVaccine.com, Web Site: www.omahavaccine.com (16)

Oman, Greg, SCICOM Data Services Ltd, Minnetonka, MN. Tel: (952) 933-4200, (800) 488-9087, FAX: (952) 936-4132, Web Site: www.scicom.com (22)

Omar's Touch Therapy, Madison, WI. Tel: (608) 658-6718, E-Mail: omar@omarstouch.com, Web Site: www.omarstouch.com (23)

Omeda, Northbrook, IL. Tel: (847) 564-8900, Web Site: www.omeda.com (22)

Omega Direct Response Inc, Richmond Hill, ON Canada. Tel: (905) 482-2340, FAX: (905) 482-9721, E-Mail: odrsales@omegadirect.com, Web Site: www.omegadirect.com (29)

Omega List Co, McLean, VA. Tel: (703) 821-1890, FAX: (703) 821-8794, E-Mail: mhiban@omegalist.com, Web Site: www.omegalist.com (23)

Omega Mobile, San Francisco, CA. Tel: (415) 596-6342, Web Site: www.omegamobile.com (29)

Omega Research & Development, Douglasville, GA. Tel: (770) 942-9876, (800) 554-4053, Web Site: www.caralarm.com (12)

Omega Studios, Elgin, IL. Tel: (972) 444-8556, FAX: (972) 444-8559, E-Mail: omegastudios@rrd.com, Web Site: www.omega-studios.com (37)

Omni Farm, West Jefferson, NC. Tel: (336) 982-3475, (800) TREE-FARM, FAX: (336) 982-4163, E-Mail: omnifarm@omnifarm.com, Web Site: www.omnifarm.com (16)

Omni Print Inc, Lanham, MD. Tel: (301) 731-7000, FAX: (301) 731-7001, E-Mail: info@omniprint.net, Web Site: www.omniprint.net (27)

Omnicom Media Group Direct, New York, NY. Tel: (212) 590-7012 (35)

Omnidirect, Miami Beach, FL. Tel: (800) 459-4034, Web Site: www.omnidirect.tv (35)

Omnigraphics Inc, Aston, PA. Tel: (610) 461-3548, (800) 234-1340, FAX: (800) 875-1340, E-Mail: info@omnigraphics.com, Web Site: www.omnigraphics.com (17)

On-Demand Mail Services, Auburn Hills, MI. Tel: (888) 954-6245, Web Site: www.odmailservices.com (28)

On-Hand Adhesives Inc, Lake Zurich, IL. Tel: (847) 437-7773, (800) 323-5158, FAX: (847) 437-8006, E-Mail: help@on-hand.com, Web Site: www.on-hand.com (16)

On-Line Technologies Inc, Scarborough, ME. Tel: (207) 396-5172, (207) 396-5101, Web Site: www.on-linetechnologies.com (31)

OnBrand24, Beverly, MA. Tel: (855) 662-7263 (29)

One Call Systems Inc, Baden, PA. Tel: (412) 415-5000, (800) 845-9945, FAX: (412) 415-5023, E-Mail: jmcnamara@1-call.com, Web Site: www.1-call.com (29)

1-800-Contacts, Orem, UT. Tel: (800) CONTACTS, FAX: (801) 924-9000, Web Site: www.1800contacts.com (7)

1-800-DialWord.com, Boone, NC. Tel: (800) DIAL-WORD, FAX: (877) 329-3627, Web Site: www.1800dialword.com (29)

1-800-Flowers.com, Carle Place, NY. Tel: (516) 237-6000, Web Site: www.1800flowers.com (16)

One Hanes Place Catalog, Winston Salem, NC. Tel: (336) 519-4400, (800) 300-2600, FAX: (336) 519-0655, Web Site: www.onehanesplace.com (2)

100% Real Estate Inc, Orlando, FL. Tel: (800) 454-3422, E-Mail: rcs@100percentflorida.com, Web Site: www.100percentflorida.com (16)

One On One Advertising Inc, New Haven, CT. Tel: (203) 562-6259, FAX: (203) 789-1253 (35)

One Point, Scranton, PA. Tel: (570) 342-0737, (800) 526-4460, FAX: (570) 343-6361, Web Site: www.opoffice.com (10)

1000 Islands International Tourism Council, Alexandria Bay, NY. Tel: (315) 482-2520, (800) 847-5263, (800) 456-2267, FAX: (315) 482-5906, Web Site: www.visit1000islands.com/visitorinfo/ (19)

1to1 Media, Stamford, CT. Tel: (203) 642-5121, FAX: (203) 316-5121, (203) 642-5126, Web Site: www.1to1media.com (35)

One World Projects, Batavia, NY. Tel: (585) 343-4490, FAX: (585) 344-3551, E-Mail: sales@oneworldprojects.com, Web Site: www.oneworldprojects.com (6)

One World Telecom, Miami, FL. Tel: (786) 664-6100 x6672, Web Site: www.nopin.us (29)

1001 Ways to Market Your Books, Taos, NM. Tel: (575) 751-3398, FAX: (575) 751-3100, E-Mail: info@bookmarket.com, Web Site: www.bookmarket.com (43)

Oneida Ltd, Oneida, NY. Tel: (315) 361-3000, (888) 263-7195, FAX: (315) 361-3700, Web Site: www.oneida.com (16)

O'Neil Data Systems Inc, Los Angeles, CA. Tel: (310) 448-6400, Web Site: www.oneildata.com (27)

O'Neill Marketing Co, Fairfax, VA. Tel: (703) 934-0272, Web Site: www.oneillmarketing.com (23)

Oneupweb, Traverse City, MI. Tel: (231) 922-9977, (877) 568-7477, FAX: (231) 922-9966, E-Mail: info@oneupweb.com, Web Site: www.oneupweb.com (35)

Online Print Solutions, San Francisco, CA. Tel: (415) 651-4157, Web Site: www.onlineprintsolutions.com (32)

ONTIME COMPANIES, Chelsea, MA. Tel: (617) 884-8488, Web Site: www.ontimecompanies.com (28)

OnTrac, Phoenix, AZ. Tel: (602) 333-4417, (800) 334-5000 (28)

Onuschak, John, Flaghouse Inc, Hasbrouck Heights, NJ. Tel: (201) 288-7600, (800) 793-7900, FAX: (800) 793-7922, E-Mail: sales@flaghouse.com, Web Site: www.flaghouse.com (5)

Onyx Productions Inc, Los Angeles, CA. Tel: (323) 692-9830, FAX: (323) 692-9832, E-Mail: info@onyxprod.com, Web Site: www.onyxprod.com (32)

Oomingmak Musk Ox Producers Cooperative, Anchorage, AK. Tel: (907) 272-9225, (888) 360-9665, FAX: (907) 258-4225, E-Mail: oomingmak@qiviut.com, Web Site: www.qiviut.com (6)

Oommen, Sherry, McKnight's Long-Term Care News, Northfield, IL. Tel: (847) 784-8706, (800) 558-1703, FAX: (847) 784-9346, E-Mail: mltcn-webmaster@mltcn.com, Web Site: www.mcknightsonline.com (17)

Open Horizons, Taos, NM. Tel: (575) 751-3398, FAX: (575) 751-3100, E-Mail: info@bookmarket.com, Web Site: www.bookmarket.com (39)

Open Systems Services, Miami, FL. Tel: (305) 541-1970 (20)

Open Text Inc, Waterloo, ON Canada. Tel: (519) 888-9933, (800) 499-6544, FAX: (519) 888-0677, E-Mail: support@opentext.com, Web Site: www.opentext.com (16)

Operation Smile Inc, Norfolk, VA. Tel: (757) 321-7645, Web Site: www.operationsmile.org (1)

Opex Corp, Moorestown, NJ. Tel: (856) 727-1100, FAX: (856) 727-1955, Web Site: www.opex.com (34)

Opiela, Paul, International Auto Parts, Charlottesville, VA. Tel: (804) 974-7118, (800) 726-0555, FAX: (804) 973-2368, E-Mail: iap1@international-auto.com, Web Site: www.international-auto.com (12)

OPIN Systems Inc, Bloomington, MN. Tel: (651) 994-6555, (800) 888-1804, FAX: (651) 994-7828, E-Mail: judywy@opin.com, Web Site: www.opin.com (22)

Oppenheim, Ellen, Magazine Publishers of America, New York, NY. Tel: (212) 872-3700, FAX: (212) 888-4217, Web Site: www.magazine.org (17)

Oppenheimer Funds, New York, NY. Tel: (212) 323-0200, FAX: (212) 323-0493, Web Site: www.oppenheimerfunds.com (14)

Oppito, Gary, Escort Inc, West Chester, OH. Tel: (513) 870-8500, (800) 964-3138, FAX: (513) 870-8509, E-Mail: sales@escortradar.com, Web Site: www.escortradar.com (16)

Oprison, Rich, General Nutrition Corp, Pittsburgh, PA. Tel: (412) 288-4600, (877) GNC-4700, FAX: (412) 402-7218, Web Site: www.gnc.com (7)

Opryland, Nashville, TN. Tel: (615) 889-1000, FAX: (615) 871-7741, E-Mail: info@gaylordhotels.com, Web Site: www.oprylandhotels.com (16)

Optimum Group, Cincinnati, OH. Tel: (513) 577-7000, FAX: (513) 577-7099, E-Mail: info@coactivemarketing.com, Web Site: www.getcoactive.com (21)

Optronics Inc, Muskogee, OK. Tel: (918) 683-9514, (800) 364-5483, FAX: (918) 683-9517, E-Mail: sales@optronicsinc.com, Web Site: www.optronicsinc.com (11)

Opus Inc, Lititz, PA. Tel: (717) 626-2125, (800) 800-1819, FAX: (717) 626-1912, E-Mail: opususa@woodstream.com, Web Site: www.opususa.com (8)

Oracle Corp, Redwood Shores, CA. Tel: (650) 506-7000, (800) 633-0738, FAX: (650) 506-7200, Web Site: www.oracle.com (16)

Oral Roberts University, Tulsa, OK. Tel: (918) 495-6161, FAX: (918) 495-6222, E-Mail: admissions@oru.edu, Web Site: www.oru.edu (1)

The Orange County Register, Santa Ana, CA. Tel: (877) 469-7344, E-Mail: customerservice@ocregister.com, Web Site: www.ocregister.com (17)

Orange Leap, Dallas, TX. Tel: (972) 220-0341, Web Site: www.orangeleap.com (1)

Orbis Books, Maryknoll, NY. Tel: (914) 941-7636 X2576, (800) 258-5838, FAX: (914) 941-7005, E-Mail: orbisbooks@maryknoll.org, Web Site: www.orbisbooks.com (17)

Orbit Manufacturing Co, Perkasie, PA. Tel: (215) 453-9228, (888) 895-0958, FAX: (215) 257-7399, Web Site: www.orbitmfg.com (9)

Orchard Supply Hardware, San Jose, CA. Tel: (408) 281-3500, FAX: (408) 225-0388, Web Site: www.osh.com (16)

Orcholski, Heidi, Direct Response Insurance Administrative Services Inc (DRIASI), Chanhassen, MN. Tel: (952) 556-5600, (800) 688-0760, FAX: (952) 556-8200, E-Mail: tpa@driasi.com, Web Site: www.driasi.com (21)

Ordenza Marketing Group Inc, Burnaby, BC Canada. Tel: (604) 451-1414, Web Site: www.odenza.com (35)

The Order Fulfillment Group, Zionsville, IN. Tel: (317) 733-7755, FAX: (317) 733-8799, E-Mail: thughes@tofg.com, Web Site: www.tofg.com (28)

Oregon Freeze Dry Inc, Albany, OR. Tel: (541) 926-6001, FAX: (541) 967-6527, Web Site: www.ofd.com (4)

Orenstein, Robert, International Wine Accessories Inc, Wichita, KS. Tel: (214) 349-6097, (800) 527-4072, FAX: (214) 349-8712, E-Mail: customerservice@iwawine.com, Web Site: www.iwawine.com (4)

Orenstein, Scott, H., G H Bass & Co, New York, NY. Tel: (212) 381-3900, FAX: (212) 381-3950, Web Site: www.pvh.com (16)

Glen Orenstein, Merrick, NY. Tel: (516) 359-8785 (20)

Orf, Robert, S., DataMentors LLC, Wesley Chapel, FL. Tel: (813) 960-7800, FAX: (813) 960-7811, E-Mail: 1bedgood@datamentors.com, Web Site: www.datamentors.com (22)

Organ, Denise, D&E Pharmaceuticals Inc, Farmingdale, NJ. Tel: (973) 838-8300, (800) 221-1833, FAX: (877) 838-0560, E-Mail: customerservice@dnepharm.com, Web Site: www.dnepharm.com (7)

Organ, Eric, D&E Pharmaceuticals Inc, Farmingdale, NJ. Tel: (973) 838-8300, (800) 221-1833, FAX: (877) 838-0560, E-Mail: customerservice@dnepharm.com, Web Site: www.dnepharm.com (7)

Orgler, Joel, Tri-State Envelope Corp, Ashland, PA. Tel: (570) 875-0433, (800) 233-3102, FAX: (570) 875-0125, E-Mail: tsecny@attglobal.net, Web Site: www.tristateenvelope.com (26)

Orgler, Thomas, Northwest Mailing Service Inc, Chicago, IL. Tel: (773) 237-2264, Web Site: www.nwmail.com (28)

Orient Expressed Imports Inc, New Orleans, LA. Tel: (888) 856-3948, FAX: (504) 899-5566, E-Mail: orient@orientexpressed.com, Web Site: www.orientexpressed.com (2)

Oriental Trading Co Inc, Omaha, NE. Tel: (402) 596-1200, (800) 875-8480, FAX: (402) 331-3873, Web Site: www.oriental.com (5)

The Original Honey Baked Ham Co of the East, Marblehead, MA. Tel: (781) 639-2200, Web Site: www.honeybakedmailorder.com (4)

Orina, Nann, CheckVantage, Austin, TX. Tel: (512) 442-2332, (877) 243-2501, FAX: (512) 442-5515, E-Mail: marya@checkvantage.com, Web Site: www.checkvantage.com (14)

Orion, Federal Way, WA. Tel: (253) 661-7805, Web Site: www.orionworks.org (1)

Orion Telescopes & Binoculars, Watsonville, CA. Tel: (831) 763-7000, (800) 447-1001, FAX: (408) 763-7017, E-Mail: sales@telescope.com, Web Site: www.telescope.com (11)

Orisek, Martin, Concept Communications Co, Bolingbrook, IL. Tel: (630) 829-8450, (800) 323-3524, FAX: (630) 629-8415, E-Mail: info@cstore1.com, Web Site: www.cstore1.com (16)

Orisek, Rudolf, Concept Communications Co, Bolingbrook, IL. Tel: (630) 829-8450, (800) 323-3524, FAX: (630) 629-8415, E-Mail: info@cstore1.com, Web Site: www.cstore1.com (16)

Orisek, Tim, Concept Communications Co, Bolingbrook, IL. Tel: (630) 829-8450, (800) 323-3524, FAX: (630) 629-8415, E-Mail: info@cstore1.com, Web Site: www.cstore1.com (16)

Orlando, John, Millcraft of Michigan, Livonia, MI. Tel: (734) 266-3710, (800) 482-0556, FAX: (734) 266-3705, Web Site: www.millcraft.com (25)

Orlando, Joseph, A., Leucadia National Corp, New York, NY. Tel: (212) 460-1900, FAX: (212) 598-4869, Web Site: www.leucadia.com (14)

Orlando/ Orange County Convention & Visitor's Bureau, Orlando, FL. Tel: (407) 541-4239, Web Site: visitorlando.com (19)

Orlick, Abe, Davor Photo Inc, Bensalem, PA. Tel: (215) 638-2490, (800) 334-1531, FAX: (800) 724-6442, Web Site: www.davor.com (16)

Orlie, Christopher, E., High Octane Communications, San Rafael, CA. Tel: (415) 256-9369, FAX: (415) 256-8988, E-Mail: chris@hocadvertising.com, Web Site: www.hocadvertising.com (35)

Orloff, Brad, United Retail Inc, Rochelle Park, NJ. Tel: (201) 845-0880, Web Site: www.avenue.com (2)

Orme, Alison, Crabtree & Evelyn Ltd, Woodstock, CT. Tel: (860) 928-2761, (800) CRABTREE, FAX: (860) 928-0452, Web Site: www.crabtree-evelyn.com (4)

Orme, Tom, Alpha Supply Inc, Bremerton, WA. Tel: (360) 373-3302, (800) 257-4211, FAX: (360) 377-9235 (16)

Ormsby, Thomas, Indian Arts & Crafts Association, Albuquerque, NM. Tel: (505) 265-9149, FAX: (505) 265-8251, E-Mail: info@iaca.com, Web Site: www.iaca.com (1)

Ornela de Lemos, Anne, R, American Society on Aging, San Francisco, CA. Tel: (415) 974-9600, (800) 537-9728, FAX: (415) 974-0300, E-Mail: info@asaging.org, Web Site: www.asaging.org (1)

Orner, Lita, The Vestal Press Ltd, Lanham, MD. Tel: (301) 459-3366, (800) 462-6420, FAX: (301) 429-5746, E-Mail: sburnett@rowman.com, Web Site: www.nbnbooks.com (17)

O'Rourke Hospitality Marketing LLC, Newburyport, MA. Tel: (978) 465-5955, Web Site: www.orourkehospitality.com (35)

Orr, Dwight, W., Creative Marketing Programs, Kansas City, MO. Tel: (816) 472-6843, (800) 373-6843, FAX: (816) 472-8184, E-Mail: getresults@cmpkc.com, Web Site: www.cmpkc.com (21)

Orr, Ken, ICS Marketing Support Services, Lansing, MI. Tel: (517) 394-1890, (888) 394-1890, FAX: (517) 394-7408, E-Mail: sales@icshq.com, Web Site: www.icshq.com (21)

Orr, Marjorie, Alexian Brothers Bonaventure House, Chicago, IL. Tel: (773) 327-9921, FAX: (773) 327-9113, E-Mail: info@abam.org, Web Site: www.bonaventurehouse.org (1)

Ort-Mabry, Catherine, American College of Cardiology, Washington, DC. Tel: (202) 375-6426, Web Site: www.acc.org (1)

Orthocofski, Dave, MacPhee Marketing Communications, Toronto, ON Canada. Tel: (416) 868-1370 (35)

Ortman, Ross, Dakota Digital, Sioux Falls, SD. Tel: (605) 332-6513, (800) 593-4160, FAX: (605) 339-4106, E-Mail: sales@dakotadigital.com, Web Site: www.dakotadigital.com (12)

The Orvis Co Inc, Manchester, VT. Tel: (802) 362-3622, FAX: (802) 362-3525, Web Site: www.orvis.com (11)

Osborn, Kenneth, Liquid Focus Direct LLC, Bridgeport, CT. Tel: (203) 635-4382, Web Site: www.liquidfocus.com (32)

Osborn, Michael, Catalyst, Rochester, NY. Tel: (585) 453-8300, (800) 836-7720, FAX: (585) 453-8360, E-Mail: info@catalystinc.com, Web Site: www.catalystinc.com (35)

Osborn, Nancy, Lettergraphics Inc, Syracuse, NY. Tel: (315) 476-8328, FAX: (315) 476-1818, E-Mail: nancyo@broadviewnet.net, Web Site: lettergraphics.net (28)

Osborne, Amy, Chadsworth's 1-800-Columns, Wilmington, NC. Tel: (910) 763-7600, (800) 486-2118, FAX: (910) 763-3191, E-Mail: sales@columns.com, Web Site: www.columns.com (8)

Osborne, Richard, M., USA Direct Inc, York, PA. Tel: (717) 852-1000, (800) 441-1850, FAX: (717) 852-1030, Web Site: www.usamailnow.com (21)

Osborne, W., Jeffrey, WorleyParsons, Reading, PA. Tel: (610) 855-2000, FAX: (610) 885-2001, Web Site: www.worleyparsons.com (16)

Osborne, William, The Northern Trust Co, Chicago, IL. Tel: (312) 630-6000, (888) 289-6542, FAX: (312) 630-1512, Web Site: www.ntrs.com (14)

Osbourne, Ronald, W., Sunlife of Canada, Wellesley Hills, MA. Tel: (781) 237-6030, (800) SUNLIFE, FAX: (781) 446-1779, Web Site: www.sunlife-usa.com (15)

Oscarson, Stephen, AmeriCall Group Inc, Naperville, IL. Tel: (630) 955-9100, (800) 688-0078, FAX: (630) 955-9955, E-Mail: sales@americallgroup.com, Web Site: www.americallgroup.com (29)

Oseth, Todd, Intermap Technologies, Englewood, CO. Tel: (303) 708-0955, FAX: (303) 708-0952, Web Site: www.intermap.com (32)

Oslund, Gordon, J., Shady Oaks Nursery, LLC, Waseca, MN. Tel: (507) 835-5033, FAX: (507) 835-8772, E-Mail: shadyoaks@shadyoaks.com, Web Site: www.shadyoaks.com (8)

Osmon, Roy, Spectrum Communication Services Inc, Brookfield, WI. Tel: (262) 821-8400, (800) 701-3559, FAX: (262) 821-1492, E-Mail: sales@spectrumcomm.com, Web Site: www.spectrumcomm.com (29)

Osmonics Inc, Minnetonka, MN. Tel: (952) 264-3937, (800) 605-6698, FAX: (952) 536-3301, Web Site: www.osmonics.com (16)

Ossa, Pamela, Anda Inc, Weston, FL. Tel: (954) 217-4144, Web Site: www.andanet.com (7)

Ossoff, Richard, M., Specialized Information Publishers Association (SIPA), Vienna, VA. Tel: (703) 992-9339, (800) 356-9302, FAX: (703) 610-9005, E-Mail: info@sipaonline.org, Web Site: www.sipaonline.com (1)

Ostendorf, Dan, Lincoln Picture Studio, Dayton, OH. Tel: (937) 439-9633 (38)

Oster, Gary, Travel Industry Association, Washington, DC. Tel: (202) 408-8422, FAX: (202) 408-1255, E-Mail: feedback@tia.org, Web Site: www.tia.org (1)

Oster, Michelle, Cattle Kate, Boise, ID. Tel: (208) 377-5283, (800) 332-5283, FAX: (208) 375-3827, E-Mail: cattlekate@rmisp.com, Web Site: www.cattlekate.com (2)

Osterberg, Jon, PEMCO Insurance Cos, Seattle, WA. Tel: (206) 628-4000, (800) 467-3626, FAX: (206) 628-5886, Web Site: www.pemco.com (15)

Osterday, Andrew, Premiere Global Services Inc, Atlanta, GA. Tel: (404) 262-8400, (800) 546-1541, FAX: (913) 661-9042, Web Site: www.PGiConnect.com (22)

Osterloh, Don, Grizzly Industrial Inc, Bellingham, WA. Tel: (360) 647-0801, (800) 523-4777, FAX: (360) 671-8375, E-Mail: csr@grizzly.com, Web Site: www.grizzly.com (9)

Ostertag, Robert, BJT Management Group, Ada, MI. Tel: (616) 682-0369, Web Site: www.bjtmgt.com (20)

Ostling, Jack, Nassau Community College, Garden City, NY. Tel: (516) 572-7501, E-Mail: marketing-communications@ncc.edu, Web Site: www.ncc.edu (41)

Ostrager, Gary, Macy's, City Of Industry, CA. Tel: (323) 227-2000, FAX: (323) 227-2774, Web Site: www.federated-fds.com (5)

Ostrom, Rachael, Aveda Corp, Minneapolis, MN. Tel: (763) 951-4201, Web Site: www.aveda.com (7)

Ostrov, Gerald M., Bausch & Lomb Inc, Rochester, NY. Tel: (585) 338-6000, (800) 344-8815, FAX: (585) 338-6007, Web Site: www.bausch.com (16)

Ostrusina, Edward, Flight Form Cases Inc, Bedford Park, IL Canada. Tel: (708) 458-8989, (800) 657-1199, FAX: (708) 458-9023, E-Mail: info@caseguys.net, Web Site: www.flightform.com (9)

Oswell, Audrey, Resorts Atlantic City, Atlantic City, NJ. Tel: (609) 334-6000, (609) 336-6378, FAX: (609) 340-6349, Web Site: www.resortsac.com (19)

Otani, Noboru, Esprit Line Co Ltd - USA, Greenwich, CT. Tel: (203) 629-5124 (16)

Otellini, Paul, S., Intel Corp, Santa Clara, CA. Tel: (408) 765-8080, (800) 548-4725, FAX: (408) 765-6187, Web Site: www.intel.com (16)

The Other List Co Inc, Matawan, NJ. Tel: (732) 591-1180, FAX: (732) 591-8472 (23)

Otillio, Dana, Society of Petroleum Engineers, Richardson, TX. Tel: (972) 952-9393, Web Site: www.spe.org (1)

OTOlabs LLC, Charlestown, MA. Tel: (617) 236-8400, Web Site: www.otolabs.com (30)

Otting, Joseph, M., US Bancorp, Minneapolis, MN. Tel: (651) 466-3000, (800) 872-2657, FAX: (612) 303-0782, Web Site: www.usbank.com (14)

Ottman, Louis, S., Simplicity Pattern Co Inc/Style Patterns Ltd/New Look English Pattern Co Ltd, New York, NY. Tel: (212) 372-0500, (888) 588-2700, FAX: (212) 372-0628, E-Mail: info@simplicitypatt.com, Web Site: www.simplicitypatt.com (8)

Otto, Eddie, TXU Energy, Irving, TX. Tel: (972) 868-8345, Web Site: www.txu.com (16)

Otto Environmental Systems of North America, Charlotte, NC. Tel: (704) 588-9191, (800) 227-5885, FAX: (704) 588-5250, E-Mail: info@otto-usa.com, Web Site: www.otto-usa.com (16)

Ottolenghi, Arturo, M., Red Hill Corp, Gettysburg, PA. Tel: (717) 337-3038, (800) 822-4003, FAX: (717) 337-0732, E-Mail: custserv@supergrit.com, Web Site: www.supergrit.com (34)

Otuteye, Godfred, Money Mailer Direct Marketing, Garden Grove, CA. Tel: (800) 416-1713, Web Site: www.moneymailerdirect.com (35)

Our Community Phone Book, Blue Bell, PA. Tel: (610) 825-7720, (877) THE-RED-1, (877) 843-7731, FAX: (610) 825-5758, E-Mail: robynfine@community-phonebook.com, Web Site: www.communitybook.com (35)

Our Data Works Inc, Lewisville, TX. Tel: (469) 546-3000, (800) 268-2505, FAX: (469) 546-3013, E-Mail: info@ourdataworks.com, Web Site: www.ourdataworks.com (29)

Our Designs Inc, Vancouver, WA. Tel: (859) 282-5500, (800) 382-5252, FAX: (859) 282-5508, E-Mail: sales@ourdesigns.com, Web Site: www.ourdesigns.com (16)

Our Lady of Victory Homes of Charity, Lackawanna, NY. Tel: (716) 828-9648, FAX: (716) 828-9643, E-Mail: rheist@olv-bvs.org, Web Site: www.ourladyofvictory.org (1)

Our Sunday Visitor Publishing, Huntington, IN. Tel: (260) 356-8400, (800) 348-2440, FAX: (260) 356-8472, E-Mail: athomas@osv.com, Web Site: www.osv.com (17)

Our365, Saint Charles, MO. Tel: (636) 946-5136, Web Site: www.growingfamily.com (37)

Outdoor Research, Seattle, WA. Tel: (206) 467-8197, (888) 467-4327, FAX: (206) 467-0374, Web Site: www.outdoorresearch.com (11)

Outlook Group Corp, Neenah, WI. Tel: (920) 722-2333, FAX: (920) 727-8529, E-Mail: path@outlookgroup.com, Web Site: www.outlookgroup.com (27)

Outrider North America, Saint Louis, MO. Tel: (314) 209-1005, FAX: (314) 209-1126, Web Site: www.outrider.com (30)

Outsource America Inc, Bradenton, FL. Tel: (800) 729-5694, FAX: (441) 746-3595, E-Mail: sales@oaiworld.com, Web Site: www.oaiworld.com (24)

Outsourcing Solutions Inc, Chesterfield, MO. Tel: (847) 419-1790, FAX: (847) 419-1818 (20)

Ovation Marketing, La Crosse, WI. Tel: (608) 785-2460, FAX: (608) 785-2496 (35)

Ovative/Group LLC, Minneapolis, MN. Tel: (612) 886-1010, Web Site: www.ovative.com (20)

Overseas Private Investment Corp (OPIC), Washington, DC. Tel: (202) 336-8400, FAX: (202) 336-7949, E-Mail: info@opic.gov, Web Site: www.opic.gov (14)

Overton's Inc, Greenville, NC. Tel: (252) 355-7600, (800) 334-6541, FAX: (252) 355-2923, E-Mail: service@overtons.com, Web Site: www.overtons.com (11)

Oviatt, Greg, Barnes & Noble Direct, New York, NY. Tel: (212) 414-6000, FAX: (212) 414-6171, Web Site: www.barnesandnoble.com (23)

Owen, Ford, Ames Taping Tool System Inc, Stone Mountain, GA. Tel: (770) 243-2647, FAX: (770) 243-2658, Web Site: www.amestools.com (9)

Owen, J.D., Boys' Life & Scouting Magazines, Irving, TX. Tel: (972) 580-2000, (866) 584-6589, FAX: (972) 580-2079, Web Site: www.boyslife.org (17)

Owen, Kathy, Bucks County Coffee Co, Conshohocken, PA. Tel: (215) 741-1855, (800) 523-6163, FAX: (215) 741-1799, Web Site: www.buckscountycoffee.com (16)

Owen, Richard B., Adtron Inc, Bloomington, IL. Tel: (309) 662-1221, FAX: (309) 663-6691 (35)

Owen, Richard, House of Wesley Inc, Bloomington, IL. Tel: (309) 663-9551, FAX: (309) 663-6691, Web Site: www.houseofwesley.com (8)

Owen, Rodger, R., Bucks County Coffee Co, Conshohocken, PA. Tel: (215) 741-1855, (800) 523-6163, FAX: (215) 741-1799, Web Site: www.buckscountycoffee.com (16)

Owens, Alexandra, American Society of Journalists & Authors Directory, New York, NY. Tel: (212) 997-0947, FAX: (212) 768-7414, E-Mail: asjany@ibm.net (43)

Owens, Andy, 1-800-DialWord.com, Boone, NC. Tel: (800) DIALWORD, FAX: (877) 329-3627, Web Site: www.1800dialword.com (29)

Owens, Beth, Townsend Communications LLC, Kansas City, MO. Tel: (816) 361-0616, (800) 274-8867, FAX: (816) 361-6164, Web Site: www.townsendprint.com (17)

Owens, Betsy, Commercial Atlas & Marketing Guide, Skokie, IL. Tel: (800) 678-7263, (800) 934-3479, Web Site: www.randmcnally.com (43)

Owens, Michael, Coverdell & Co Inc, Chicago, IL. Tel: (404) 881-2227, (800) 992-2196, FAX: (404) 881-2222, Web Site: www.coverdell.com (15)

Owens, Robert, W., Sunoco, Inc, Philadelphia, PA. Tel: (215) 977-3000, (800) 786-6261, FAX: (215) 977-3409, E-Mail: sunoco_online@sunoil.com, Web Site: www.sunocoinc.com (16)

Owens, Tracey, O2K1, New York, NY. Tel: (646) 839-6254, Web Site: www.02kl.com (35)

Owens, Tracy, Association of National Advertisers Inc, New York, NY. Tel: (212) 697-5950, FAX: (212) 687-7310, Web Site: www.ana.net (40)

Buck Owens' Crystal Palace, Bakersfield, CA. Tel: (661) 328-7560, FAX: (805) 328-7565, Web Site: www.buckowens.com (21)

Oxbridge Communications Inc, New York, NY. Tel: (212) 741-0231, (800) 955-0231, FAX: (212) 633-2938, E-Mail: custserv@oxbridge.com, Web Site: www.mediafinder.com; www.oxbridge.com (30)

Oxfam America, Boston, MA. Tel: (617) 482-1211, (800) 776-9326, FAX: (617) 728-2594, E-Mail: kmallette@oxfamamerica.org, Web Site: www.oxfamamerica.org (1)

Oxford, Dave, Activision Value, Eden Prairie, MN. Tel: (952) 918-9400, FAX: (952) 918-9560 (16)

Oxford Health Plans, Inc, Trumbull, CT. Tel: (800) 889-7658, FAX: (203) 459-6464, E-Mail: info@speedmat.com, Web Site: www.oxhp.com (15)

Oxford University Press Inc, New York, NY. Tel: (212) 726-6000, FAX: (212) 726-6455, Web Site: www.oup.com/us/ (17)

Oyamatsu, Keiko, Teikoku Databank America Inc, New York, NY. Tel: (212) 421-9805, FAX: (212) 421-9806, E-Mail: info@teikoku.com, Web Site: www.teikoku.com (24)

The Oyster Group, Dartmouth, NS Canada. Tel: (877) 405-4858, E-Mail: fdrinnan@theoystergroup.ca, Web Site: www.theoystergroup.ca (22)

Ozgen, Gus, Peppermill Marketing Inc, Los Angeles, CA. Tel: (310) 659-8900, (877) 600-7775, FAX: (310) 659-8901, E-Mail: inquiry@peppermillmarketing.com, Web Site: www.peppermillmarketing.com (23)

Ozmina, Tracy A., Academy of Marketing Science Journal, Thousand Oaks, CA. Tel: (805) 499-0721, FAX: (800) 583-2665, (805) 499-0871, Web Site: www.sagepub.com (43)

P

P & H Mining Equipment, Milwaukee, WI. Tel: (414) 671-4400, FAX: (414) 671-7618, Web Site: www.phmining.com (16)

PAC Worldwide, Redmond, WA. Tel: (425) 885-9330, (800) 535-0039, FAX: (425) 885-2934, Web Site: www.pac.com (26)

PBD Worldwide Fulfillment Services, Alpharetta, GA. Tel: (770) 442-8633, FAX: (770) 442-9742, E-Mail: sales.marketing@pbd.com, Web Site: www.pbd.com (28)

PBM Graphics, Greensboro, NC. Tel: (336) 664-5800, (800) 849-8200, FAX: (336) 931-0965, Web Site: www.pbmgraphics.com (28)

PBS Distribution, Arlington, VA. Tel: (703) 739-5085, Web Site: shoppbs.org (3)

PC Connection, Merrimack, NH. Tel: (603) 683-2167, (800) 800-0014, FAX: (603) 683-5773, E-Mail: pr@pcconnection.com, Web Site: www.pcconnection.com, macconnection.com (22)

PC Mall, Torrance, CA. Tel: (310) 225-2600, (800) 555-MALL, Web Site: www.pcmall.com (3)

PC/Nametag Inc, Verona, WI. Tel: (608) 845-1850, (800) 233-9767, E-Mail: sales@pcnametag.com, Web Site: www.pcnametag.com (16)

PC Ontario Fund, Toronto, ON Canada. Tel: (416) 861-3085, (416) 861-0020, (800) 903-6453, FAX: (416) 861-1760, (416) 861-9593, E-Mail: comments@ontariopc.net, Web Site: www.ontariopc.com (1)

PC World, San Francisco, CA. Tel: (415) 243-0500, FAX: (415) 442-1891, Web Site: www.pcworld.com (17)

PCCW Teleservices, Dublin, OH. Tel: (614) 280-1600, Web Site: www.influentinc.com (29)

PCG, Inc, Batavia, IL. Tel: (630) 482-9300, FAX: (630) 454-3750, E-Mail: sasmith@pcgnow.com, Web Site: www.pcgnow.com (20)

PCI, Keyport, NJ. Tel: (732) 335-3700, (888) 826-1646, FAX: (732) 264-9313, E-Mail: conil@packaging-usa.com, Web Site: www.packaging-usa.com (35)

PCI Paper Conversions Inc, Syracuse, NY. Tel: (315) 437-1641, FAX: (315) 437-3634, E-Mail: sales@padmaker.com, Web Site: www.padmaker.com (27)

PCS List & Information Technologies, Manchester, MA. Tel: (978) 532-7100, (800) 532-LIST, FAX: (978) 532-9181, E-Mail: info@pcslist.com, Web Site: www.pcslist.com (23)

PDQ Post Group, Surrey, BC Canada. Tel: (604) 888-0676, (888) 998-9878, FAX: (604) 888-4467, E-Mail: lorraine@pdqpostgroup.com, Web Site: www.pdqpostgroup.com (21)

PDS International Mail Service, Hauppauge, NY. Tel: (631) 815-1750, Web Site: www.pdsmail.com; www.internationalmail.com (28)

PEP Direct, Wilton, NH. Tel: (603) 654-6141, Web Site: www.pep-direct.com (21)

PESI LLC, Eau Claire, WI. Tel: (800) 844-8260, FAX: (800) 554-9775, E-Mail: info@pesi.com, Web Site: www.pesi.com (17)

PFE Inc, Irvine, CA. Tel: (949) 417-0330, FAX: (949) 417-0331, Web Site: www.pfeinc.com (34)

PFI Western Stores Inc, Springfield, MO. Tel: (417) 889-2668, (800) 222-4734, FAX: (417) 889-7204, E-Mail: pfi.@pfiwestern.com, Web Site: www.pfiwestern.com (2)

PGI Companies Inc, Minneapolis, MN. Tel: (952) 933-5745, FAX: (952) 933-5864, E-Mail: ddallum@pgicompanies.com, Web Site: www.pgicompanies.com (27)

PHE Inc, Hillsborough, NC. Tel: (919) 644-8100, (800) 293-4654, FAX: (919) 644-8150, E-Mail: custserv@adameve.com (5)

PI Inc, Athens, TN. Tel: (423) 745-6213, FAX: (423) 745-7039, Web Site: www.pi-inc.com (16)

PJT Inc, Savannah, GA. Tel: (912) 233-6220, Web Site: www.riverstreetsweets.com (4)

PM Consulting Corp, Fairfax, VA. FAX: (703) 272-1500, Web Site: www.ecnext.com (20)

PM Productions, Los Angeles, CA. Tel: (310) 559-3127, FAX: (310) 559-3168, E-Mail: odellmack@hotmail.com, Web Site: wwwmyvideozationnetwork.com (32)

PMDS Inc, Annapolis Junction, MD. Tel: (301) 604-3305 (28)

PMG, Columbia, MD. Tel: (410) 290-0667, Web Site: www.pmgdirect.net (20)

PMH/Caramanning, Farmington Hills, MI. Tel: (248) 488-5300, FAX: (248) 488-5363, E-Mail: marketing@pmh.com, Web Site: www.pmh.com (35)

PMIC, Los Angeles, CA. Tel: (323) 954-0224, (800) 633-4215, FAX: (323) 954-0253, Web Site: pmiconline.stores.yahoo.net (17)

PNC Bank Corp, Pittsburgh, PA. Tel: (412) 762-2000/3514, (800) 422-6537, FAX: (412) 762-4482 (14)

PNC Global Investment Servicing, Lynnfield, MA. Tel: (781) 477-4124, Web Site: www.pnc.com (14)

PNT Marketing Services, Inc, Long Island City, NY. Tel: (703) 761-0291, (888) 768-2210, FAX: (914) 428-0504, E-Mail: tony@pntmarketingservices.com, Web Site: www.pntmarketingservices.com (22)

POPAI-The Global Association for Marketing at-Retail, Chicago, IL. Tel: (312)-863-2900, FAX: (312) 229-1152, Web Site: www.popai.com (40)

PPC, Johnston, IA. Tel: (515) 986-5070, E-Mail: sales@ppcbest.com, Web Site: www.ppcbest.com (9)

PPI Benefit Solutions, Wallingford, CT. Tel: (888) 674-0046, FAX: (203) 468-9886, E-Mail: clientservices@ppibenefits.com, Web Site: www.ppibenefits.com (15)

PPN INC, Holbrook, MA. Tel: (781) 767-5776, (800) 289-4776, FAX: (781) 767-4776, E-Mail: customer.service@ppninc.com, Web Site: www.ppninc.com (7)

PPS - Packaging Printing Specialists, Saint Charles, IL. Tel: (630) 513-8060, (877) 573-8060, FAX: (630) 513-8062, E-Mail: pps@ppsofil.com, Web Site: www.PPSofIL.com (27)

Precise Media Services Inc, Ontario, CA. Tel: (908) 481-3305, (800) 444-4217, FAX: (908) 481-3405, Web Site: www.precisemedia.com (27)

PSA, Buffalo Grove, IL. Tel: (847) 478-6000, Web Site: www.psa.com (27)

PSI Marketing Consultants Inc, Des Plaines, IL. Tel: (773) 878-0800, (800) 933-4774, FAX: (773) 878-4219 (29)

PTC, Needham, MA. Tel: (781) 370-5000, Web Site: www.ptc.com (22)

PTI Pyramid Technologies LLC, Meriden, CT. Tel: (203) 238-0550, (888) 479-7264, FAX: (203) 634-1696, Web Site: www.pyramid-technologies.com (10)

PVC Plastics Co, Evansville, IN. Tel: (812) 476-3592, (800) 782-7527, FAX: (812) 474-4531 (16)

Paasche, Carl, Woodcrafters Lumber Sales Inc, Portland, OR. Tel: (503) 231-0226, (800) 777-3709, FAX: (503) 232-0511, E-Mail: spen@worldnet.att.net, Web Site: www.woodcrafters.us (9)

Paasche Airbrush Co, Chicago, IL. Tel: (773) 867-9191, FAX: (773) 867-9198, E-Mail: info@paascheairbrush.com, Web Site: www.paascheairbrush.com (10)

PACCAR Inc, Bellevue, WA. Tel: (425) 468-7400, FAX: (425) 468-8216, Web Site: www.paccar.com (16)

Pace, Barry, Cortz Inc, West Chicago, IL. Tel: (630) 876-1080, Web Site: www.intheswim.com (5)

Pace, Bernadette, Hearst Magazines, New York, NY. Tel: (212) 649-2824, FAX: (212) 765-3528, Web Site: www.hearst.com/magazines (17)

Pace, David, A., Starbucks Corp, Seattle, WA. Tel: (206) 447-1575, (800) 344-1575, FAX: (206) 447-0828, Web Site: www.starbucks.com (4)

Pace Communications Inc, Greensboro, NC. Tel: (336) 378-6065, FAX: (336) 275-2864, Web Site: www.pacecommunications.com (17)

Pace Inc, Annapolis Junction, MD. Tel: (910) 695-7223, FAX: (910) 944-1724, Web Site: www.paceworldwide.com/index.asp (16)

Pace University - Div of Enrollment Mgmt, New York, NY. Tel: (212) 346-1781, (866) 722-3338, FAX: (212) 346-1821, Web Site: www.pace.edu/pace/ (16)

Pacer, Leonard, A., Central States Health & Life Co of Omaha, Omaha, NE. Tel: (402) 397-1111, (800) 826-6587, FAX: (402) 391-3772, Web Site: www.cso.com (15)

Pachmayr Ltd, Middletown, CT. Tel: (800) 225-9626, FAX: (860) 632-1699, Web Site: www.lymanproducts.com (11)

Pacific Botanicals LLC, Grants Pass, OR. Tel: (541) 479-7777, FAX: (541) 479-7780, E-Mail: pacbot1@earthlink.net, Web Site: www.pacificbotanicals.com (7)

Pacific Cycle Inc, Madison, WI. Tel: (608) 268-2468, (800) 724-9466, FAX: (847) 236-3692, (847) 573-0602, E-Mail: info@pacificcycle.com, Web Site: www.pacificcycle.com (16)

Pacific Lists Inc, Oakland, CA. Tel: (415) 945-9450, FAX: (415) 945-9451, E-Mail: listinfo@pacificlists.com, Web Site: www.pacificlists.com (23)

Pacific Media Exchange, Berkeley, CA. Tel: (510) 528-9181, FAX: (510) 528-3449, E-Mail: pacificmedia@comcast.net, Web Site: www.pacificmediaexchange.com (35)

Pacific Propeller Inc, Kent, WA. Tel: (253) 872-7767, (800) 722-7767, FAX: (253) 872-7221, E-Mail: jheikke@pacprop.com, Web Site: www.pacificpropeller.com (16)

Pacific Spirit Corp, Forest Grove, OR. Tel: (503) 357-1566, (800) 634-9057, FAX: (503) 357-1699, Web Site: www.pacificspiritcatalogs.com (6)

Pacific Sportswear Co Inc, San Diego, CA. Tel: (619) 281-6688, (800) USA-8778, FAX: (619) 281-6687, E-Mail: info@pacsport.com, Web Site: www.pacsport.com (5)

PacificEast, Sumas, WA. Tel: (800) 665-8400, Web Site: www.pacificeast.com (22)

Pacino, Al, The American Film Institute, Los Angeles, CA. Tel: (323) 856-7600, FAX: (323) 467-4578, Web Site: www.afi.com (1)

Pacitti, Peter, DeLuxe Laboratories Inc, Hollywood, CA. Tel: (323) 462-6171, FAX: (323) 960-7016, E-Mail: steven.vananda@bydeluxe.com, Web Site: www.bydeluxe.com (16)

Pack, Jamie, Gillespie Magazine Marketing & Publishing, Lawrenceville, NJ. Tel: (609) 895-0200, FAX: (609) 895-0222, Web Site: www.gillespie.com (20)

Packer, Donna, Packer List Inc, Washington, DC. Tel: (202) 546-1889, FAX: (202) 546-1897, E-Mail: listpacker@aol.com (23)

Packer, Sharon, American Civil Defense Association, Draper, UT. Tel: (800) 501-0077, FAX: (800) 403-1369, E-Mail: info@tacda.org, Web Site: www.tacda.org (16)

Packer List Inc, Washington, DC. Tel: (202) 546-1889, FAX: (202) 546-1897, E-Mail: listpacker@aol.com (23)

Packham, Maura, Worldcolor, Atlanta, GA. Tel: (770) 936-7100, Web Site: www.worldcolor.com (27)

PackStream LLC, Louisville, KY. Tel: (502) 552-9624, Web Site: www.packstream.com (20)

PacNet Services Ltd, Vancouver, BC Canada. Tel: (604) 689-0399, FAX: (604) 689-0313, E-Mail: info@pacnetservices.com, Web Site: www.pacnetservices.com (14)

Pactiv Corp, Lake Forest, IL. Tel: (847) 482-2000, (800) 828-2850, FAX: (847) 482-4738, Web Site: www.pactiv.com (26)

Paczkowski, Walter, Data Analytics Corp, Plainsboro, NJ. Tel: (609) 936-899, Web Site: www.dataanalyticscorp.com (30)

Paddock, N.E., Association of Desk-Top Publishers (AD-TP), San Diego, CA. Tel: (619) 563-9714, FAX: (619) 280-3778 (40)

Paddon, Sherry, Team Cheer, Geneseo, NY. Tel: (585) 243-8400, (585) 243-0841, (877) 243-5268, FAX: (800) 350-1562, E-Mail: custserv@teamcheer.com, Web Site: www.teamcheer.com (2)

Padgett, Alisa, Weiss Research Inc, Jupiter, FL. Tel: (561) 627-3300, (877) 925-4833, FAX: (561) 625-6685, E-Mail: newbusiness@weissgroupinc.com, Web Site: www.weissgroupinc.com (17)

Padgett, Anne, The Press & Standard, Walterboro, SC. Tel: (843) 549-2586, Web Site: colletontoday.com (31)

Padgett, Larry, Concordia Publishing House, Saint Louis, MO. Tel: (314) 268-1000, (800) 325-3040, FAX: (314) 268-1329, E-Mail: order@cph.org, Web Site: www.cph.org (17)

Padgitt, James L., Direct Marketing Insights Inc, Goodyear, AZ. Tel: (843) 817-7488, E-Mail: jimp@dminsights.com, Web Site: www.dminsights.com (20)

Padlo, Dennis, C., Tempco Electric Heater Corp, Wood Dale, IL. Tel: (630) 350-2252, (800) 323-6859, FAX: (630) 350-0232, E-Mail: dpadlo@tempco.com, Web Site: www.tempco.com (9)

Padou, Abigail, The Catholic University of America Press, Washington, DC. Tel: (202) 319-5052, FAX: (202) 319-4985, E-Mail: cua-press@cua.edu, Web Site: www.cuapress.cua.edu (17)

Padulo, Richard, Padulo Integrated, Toronto, ON. Tel: (416) 966-4000, (800) 454-5321, FAX: (416) 966-4012, E-Mail: rpadulo@padulo.ca, Web Site: www.padulo.ca (35)

Padulo Integrated, Toronto, ON Canada. Tel: (416) 966-4000, (800) 454-5321, FAX: (416) 966-4012, E-Mail: rpadulo@padulo.ca, Web Site: www.padulo.ca (35)

Page Jr, Henry, C., Ethyl Corp, Richmond, VA. Tel: (804) 788-5000, FAX: (804) 788-5688, Web Site: www.ethyl.com (16)

Page, Bob, Replacements Ltd, Greensboro, NC. Tel: (336) 697-3000, (800) REPLACE, FAX: (336) 697-3100, E-Mail: mark.donahue@replacements.com, Web Site: www.replacements.com (8)

Page, Graeme, Alzheimer Society of Canada, Toronto, ON Canada. Tel: (416) 488-8772, (800) 616-8816, FAX: (416) 488-3778, E-Mail: gpage@alzheimer.ca, Web Site: www.alzheimer.ca (1)

Page, John, Wachovia Center, Philadelphia, PA. Tel: (215) 336-3600, FAX: (215) 389-9518, E-Mail: info@comcast-spectacor.com, Web Site: www.comcast-spectacor.com (16)

Pagnam, Julia, Luce Corp, Hamden, CT. Tel: (203) 787-0281, FAX: (203) 230-2753 (16)

Pagnam, Mary, Luce Corp, Hamden, CT. Tel: (203) 787-0281, FAX: (203) 230-2753 (16)

Pagnam, Timothy, F., Luce Corp, Hamden, CT. Tel: (203) 787-0281, FAX: (203) 230-2753 (16)

Pagos Haller, Stacy, American Health Assistance Foundation, Clarksburg, MD. Tel: (301) 948-3224 (1)

Paige, Jacqueline, Smith Hanley Associates, Southport, CT. Tel: (203) 319-4300, (888) 221-2900, FAX: (203) 319-4320, Web Site: www.smithhanley.com (20)

Paige, William, H., New England Journal of Medicine, Waltham, MA. Tel: (781) 893-3800, FAX: (781) 893-7729, Web Site: www.nejm.org (17)

Paillot, Nicolas, BIC Graphic USA, Clearwater, FL. Tel: (727) 536-7895, FAX: (800) 753-5890, Web Site: www.bicgraphic.com (33)

Paine, Kathy, Liberty Orchards Co Inc, Cashmere, WA. Tel: (509) 782-2191, (800) 888-5696, FAX: (509) 782-1487, E-Mail: service@libertyorchards. com, Web Site: www.libertyorchards.com (16)

Paine, Susan, Share Group Inc, Newton, MA. Tel: (617) 629-4500, FAX: (617) 629-4510, E-Mail: info@sharegroup.com, Web Site: www.sharegroup. com (29)

Painter, John, Foremost Packaging, Rancho Cucamonga, CA. Tel: (909) 941-1713, FAX: (909) 941-4092, E-Mail: foremost.mail@verizon.net, Web Site: www.foremostpackaging.com (27)

Pake, Dana, All Star Directories, Seattle, WA. Tel: (888) 404-8043, FAX: (707) 667-1524, Web Site: www.allstardirectories.com (17)

PAL Health Technology, Pekin, IL. Tel: (309) 347-8785, (800) 223-2957, FAX: (309) 477-4456, Web Site: www.palhealth.com (16)

Paladin Press, Boulder, CO. Tel: (303) 443-7250, (800) 392-2400, FAX: (303) 442-8741, E-Mail: service@paladin-press.com, Web Site: www. paladin-press.com (17)

Paladino, Stephen, IWCO Direct, Chanhassen, MN. Tel: (952) 474-0961, FAX: (952) 474-6467 (21)

Palagiano, Vincent, F., The Dime Savings Bank of New York FSB, Brooklyn, NY. Tel: (800) 321-3463, Web Site: www.dimewill.com (14)

Palange, Caitlin, Potpourri Group Inc, Chelmsford, MA. Tel: (978) 256-4100, FAX: (978) 256-1961/0344, Web Site: www.potpourrigroup.com (6)

Palecek, Jane, Mother Jones Magazine, San Francisco, CA. Tel: (415) 321-1700, Web Site: www. motherjones.com (17)

Paley, William, Texwipe Co, Kernersville, NC. Tel: (201) 684-1800, (800) TEXWIPE, FAX: (201) 684-1801, E-Mail: info@texwipe.com, Web Site: www.texwipe.com (16)

Pallottine Center for Apostolic Causes Inc/St Jude Shrine, Baltimore, MD. Tel: (410) 685-6026, (877) 278-5833, FAX: (410) 234-1459, E-Mail: info@stjudeshrine.org, Web Site: www.stjudeshrine.org (1)

Palm, Joan, The Travelers Insurance Cos, Hartford, CT. Tel: (860) 277-8252, (651) 317-2685, FAX: (860) 954-7691, Web Site: www.travelers.com (15)

Palm Coast Data LLC, Palm Coast, FL. Tel: (386) 445-4662, FAX: (386) 445-2728, Web Site: www. palmcoastd.com (28)

Palmer, Anthony, J., Kimberly-Clark Corp, Neenah, WI. Tel: (920) 721-2000, (888) 525-8388, FAX: (920) 721-7722, Web Site: www.kimberly-clark. com (16)

Palmer, Dawn, Color Film Media Group, Norwalk, CT. Tel: (203) 202-2929, (800) 882-1120, FAX: (203) 702-5800, E-Mail: info@colorfilm.com, Web Site: www.colorfilm.com (32)

Palmer, Graham, Telcordia Technologies, Piscataway, NJ. Tel: (732) 699-2000, FAX: (973) 829-2458, Web Site: www.telcordia.com (16)

Palmer, Greg, Reid Supply Co, Muskegon, MI. Tel: (231) 777-3951, (800) 253-0421, FAX: (231) 767-3882, E-Mail: mail@reidsupply.com, Web Site: www.reidsupply.com (16)

Palmer, Michael, Association of National Advertisers Inc, New York, NY. Tel: (212) 697-5950, FAX: (212) 687-7310, Web Site: www.ana.net (40)

Palmer, Paul, Lehigh Direct, Broadview, IL. Tel: (708) 681-3612, FAX: (708) 681-4694, Web Site: www. lehighdirect.com (27)

Palmer, Rona, Woodwind & Brasswind Inc, Indianapolis, IN. Tel: (574) 251-3500, (800) 348-5003, FAX: (574) 251-3501, Web Site: www.wwbw.com (5)

Palmore, Roderick, General Mills Inc, Minneapolis, MN. Tel: (763) 764-7600, FAX: (763) 764-7384, Web Site: www.generalmills.com (8)

Palombo, Joe, Ventriloquist Voice Solutions International Inc, Mississauga, ON. Tel: (866) 446-0860, E-Mail: info@vvsii.com, Web Site: www.vvsii.com (29)

Palozola, Nancy, Tailwinds Inc, Mill Valley, CA. Tel: (415) 927-4242, (800) TAILWIND, FAX: (415) 927-0199, E-Mail: service@tailwinds.com, Web Site: www.tailwinds.com (6)

Paluta, Roman, Carmichael Lynch Inc, Minneapolis, MN. Tel: (612) 334-6000, FAX: (612) 334-6101, E-Mail: roman.paluta@clynch.com, Web Site: www.carmichaellynch.com (35)

Pampano, Paul, Meriks Mayan Chocolaterie, Washington, DC. Tel: (787) 721-0000 (27)

The Pampered Pet Mart, Lisle, IL. Tel: (630) 660-0056, FAX: (630) 810-1934, E-Mail: dickdixon@aol.com, Web Site: www.dixondirect.com (35)

Pamperin, Theodore, ACP American Catalog Partnerships LLC, Summit, NJ. Tel: (908) 598-1947 (20)

Pan Pacific Hotel & Resorts America, Seattle, WA. Tel: (206) 264-8111, (877) 324-4856, FAX: (206) 654-5049, Web Site: www.panpacific.com (19)

Pandit, Vikram, Citibank, New York, NY. Tel: (212) 559-9425, (800) 285-3000, FAX: (212) 527-2318, Web Site: www.citibank.com (14)

Pandit, Vikram, S., Citigroup Inc, New York, NY. Tel: (212) 559-1000, (800) 285-3000, FAX: (212) 793-3946, Web Site: www.citigroup.com (14)

Panfili, David, Location Sound Corp, North Hollywood, CA. Tel: (818) 980-9891, (800) 228-4429, FAX: (818) 980-9911, E-Mail: information@locationsound.com, Web Site: www.locationsound.com (3)

Pang, David, Johnson Wilshire Distributors Service Corp, Santa Fe Springs, CA. Tel: (562) 777-0088, (800) 922-2456, FAX: (562) 777-0099, (800) 993-9699, E-Mail: jwigloves@aol.com, Web Site: www.johnsonwilshire.com (34)

Pangborn, Dominic, Pangborn Design Ltd, Detroit, MI. Tel: (313) 259-3400, FAX: (313) 259-5690, E-Mail: info@pangborndesign.com, Web Site: www.pangborndesign.com (36)

Pangborn Design Ltd, Detroit, MI. Tel: (313) 259-3400, FAX: (313) 259-5690, E-Mail: info@pangborndesign.com, Web Site: www. pangborndesign.com (36)

Pango Pango Swimwear Corp, Pompano Beach, FL. Tel: (954) 786-0255, (800) 858-9431, FAX: (954) 786-7745, E-Mail: pango_swimwear@bellsouth. net, Web Site: www.pango-pangoswimwear.com (2)

Panho, Jim, American Locker Security Systems Inc, Coppell, TX. Tel: (817) 329-1600, (800) 828-9118, E-Mail: info@americanlocker.com, Web Site: www.americanlocker.com (16)

Panke M.D.; Ph.D., Elizabeth, Genetica DNA Laboratories Inc, Cincinnati, OH. Tel: (513) 985-9777, (800) 433-6848, FAX: (513) 985-9983, Web Site: www.genetica.com (16)

Panoptic Enterprises, Burke, VA. Tel: (703) 451-5953, (800) 594-4766, FAX: (703) 451-5953, E-Mail: panoptic@fedgovcontracts.com, Web Site: www. fedgovcontracts.com (17)

Panos, Matthew, Food for the Hungry Inc, Phoenix, AZ. Tel: (480) 998-3100, (800) 248-6437, FAX: (480) 998-4806, E-Mail: hunger@fh.org, Web Site: www.fh.org (1)

Panousis, Mary, Ellen, WL Gore & Associates Inc, Newark, DE. Tel: (410) 506-7787, (888) 914-4673, E-Mail: info@wlgore.com, Web Site: www.wlgore. com (2)

Paolucci, Joanne, Jacques Moret Inc, New York, NY. Tel: (212) 354-2400, FAX: (212) 354-5544, E-Mail: info@moret.com, Web Site: www.moret. com (16)

Papa, John, J., John Michaels Associates Inc, Newington, CT. Tel: (860) 666-1414, FAX: (860) 666-1515, E-Mail: john@jmalogos.com, Web Site: www.johnmichaelinc.com (33)

Papa John's International, Louisville, KY. Tel: (502) 261-7272, Web Site: www.papajohns.com (4)

Papalia, John, Statlistics, Danbury, CT. Tel: (203) 778-8700, Web Site: www.statlistics.com (23)

Papamarcos Ph.D., Steven, D., The Peter A Tobin College of Business, Jamaica, NY. Tel: (718) 990-2600, FAX: (718) 990-1868, Web Site: www. stjohns.edu (41)

Paparozzi, Andrew, D., National Association for Printing Leadership, East Rutherford, NJ. Tel: (201) 634-9600, (800) 642-6275, FAX: (201) 634-0324, Web Site: www.napl.org (1)

Papier, Alison, The Economist Newspaper NA Inc, New York, NY. Tel: (212) 554-0600, FAX: (212) 586-1191, Web Site: www.economist.com (17)

Papillion Times Group, Bellevue, NE. Tel: (402) 339-3331, (877) 476-4237, FAX: (402) 537-2997, E-Mail: advertising@papilliontimes.com, Web Site: www.papilliontimes.com (31)

Pappas, Andy, Relevate, Springfield, VA. Tel: (703) 658-8300, (800) 523-7346, FAX: (703) 658-8301, E-Mail: sales@relevategroup.com, Web Site: www. relevategroup.com (22)

Pappas, Julie, Remington College, Heathrow, FL. Tel: (407) 562-5691, Web Site: www.remingtoncollege. edu (13)

Pappas, Milton, Redcats USA, New York, NY. Tel: (212) 613-9500, Web Site: www.brylane.com (2)

Pappas, Susan, F., Pappas MacDonnell Inc, Southport, CT. Tel: (203) 254-1944, FAX: (203) 256-8232, E-Mail: info@pappasmacdonnell.com, Web Site: www.pappasmacdonnell.com (35)

Pappas MacDonnell Inc, Southport, CT. Tel: (203) 254-1944, FAX: (203) 256-8232, E-Mail: info@pappasmacdonnell.com, Web Site: www. pappasmacdonnell.com (35)

Papsadore, Polly, LW Robbins Associates, Holliston, MA. Tel: (508) 893-0210, (800) 229-5972, FAX: (508) 893-0212, E-Mail: ppapsador@lwra.com, Web Site: www.lwra.com (1)

Papson, Donald, Hershey's Mail Order, Hershey, PA. Tel: (717) 534-7381, (800) 544-1347, FAX: (717) 534-7947, E-Mail: hersheygiftsinfo@hersheys.com, Web Site: www.hersheygifts.com (4)

PAPYRUS, Fairfield, CA. Tel: (707) 428-0200, Web Site: www.papyrusonline.com (5)

Para Publishing, Santa Barbara, CA. Tel: (805) 968-7277, (800) PARAPUB, FAX: (805) 986-1379, E-Mail: danpoynter@parapublishing.com, Web Site: www.parapublishing.com (17)

Parade Publications, New York, NY. Tel: (212) 450-7000, FAX: (212) 450-7284, Web Site: www. parade.com (31)

Paradigm Promotions LLC, San Francisco, CA. Tel: (415) 387-2158, FAX: (415) 387-2185, E-Mail: brian@brianharris.com, Web Site: www. paradigmpromotions.com (35)

Paradis, Judy, Crestline Specialties, Inc, Lewiston, ME. Tel: (207) 777-7075, (866) 488-4975, FAX: (207) 784-5038, E-Mail: info@crestline.com, Web Site: www.crestline.com (16)

Paradis, Stacie, US News & World Report, New York, NY. Tel: (212) 916-7360, FAX: (212) 643-7842, Web Site: www.usnews.com (17)

Paradise Galleries, Irvine, CA. Tel: (858) 793-4000, FAX: (858) 793-3425, E-Mail: omancinelli@paradisegalleries.com, Web Site: www. paradisegalleries.com (6)

Paradysz, Chris, Paradysz, New York, NY. Tel: (952) 544-5121, (212) 387-0300, (800) 254-0300, FAX: (212) 387-7647, (952) 544-6320, Web Site: www.paradysz.com (23)

Paradysz, New York, NY. Tel: (952) 544-5121, (212) 387-0300, (800) 254-0300, FAX: (212) 387-7647, (952) 544-6320, Web Site: www.paradysz.com (23)

Paragon Laboratories, Torrance, CA. Tel: (310) 370-1563, (800) 231-3670, FAX: (310) 370-7354, E-Mail: sales@paragonlabsusa.com, Web Site: www.paragonlabsusa.com (16)

Paragon Media Strategies, Denver, CO. Tel: (303) 922-5600, FAX: (303) 922-1589, E-Mail: info@paragonmediastrategies.com, Web Site: www.paragonmediastrategies.com (30)

Paragon Printing & Mailing, Austin, TX. Tel: (512) 821-0222, FAX: (512) 821-0200, E-Mail: paragon@paragonprinting.com, Web Site: paragonprinting.com (23)

Paralyzed Veterans of America, Washington, DC. Tel: (202) 416-7636, (800) 424-8200, FAX: (202) 416-7643, E-Mail: info@pva.org, Web Site: www.pva.org (1)

Paramount Lists Inc, Erie, PA. Tel: (814) 459-8787, (800) 723-5478, FAX: (814) 459-1398, Web Site: www.paramountlists.com (23)

Parasco, Barbara, Balducci Enterprises Inc, Germantown, MD. Tel: (240) 403-2440, FAX: (240) 403-2520 (16)

Parcel Insurance Plan Inc, Saint Louis, MO. Tel: (314) 692-0300, (800) 325-7390, FAX: (314) 692-7598, E-Mail: office@pipinsure.com, Web Site: www.pipinsure.com (15)

Pardes MD, Herbert, Columbia-Presbyterian Medical Center, New York, NY. Tel: (212) 305-2500, FAX: (212) 305-8023, Web Site: www.nyp.org (16)

Pardini, Kara, Crawford & Co, Atlanta, GA. Tel: (404) 300-1000, (800) 241-2541, FAX: (404) 300-1905, Web Site: www.crawfordandcompany.com (35)

Pardue, Bill, LexisNexis, Miamisburg, OH. Tel: (937) 865-6800, (800) 227-9597, (800) 227-4908, FAX: (800) 348-2609, E-Mail: pr@lexisnexis.com, Web Site: www.lexisnexis.com (16)

Parent, Lorrie, Polaroid Corp, Minnetonka, MN. Tel: (781) 386-2000, (800) 765-2764, FAX: (781) 386-3263, Web Site: www.polaroid.com (16)

Parenting Concepts Inc, Murrieta, CA. Tel: (951) 672-1131, (800) 727-3683, E-Mail: babyslings@aol.com, Web Site: www.parentingconcepts.com (2)

Paresky, Susan S., Dana-Farber Cancer Institute, Boston, MA. Tel: (617) 632-3000, FAX: (617) 632-4070, E-Mail: suzanne_fountain@dfci.harvard.edu, Web Site: www.dana-farber.org (1)

Parham, John, J&P Cycles, Anamosa, IA. Tel: (319) 462-4819, Web Site: www.j-pcycles.com (12)

Parikh, Sachin, Suntel Inc, Hamden, CT. Tel: (203) 287-9114, FAX: (203) 248-3883, E-Mail: info@suntelinc.com, Web Site: www.suntelinc.com (22)

Paris Presents Inc, Gurnee, IL. Tel: (847) 263-5500, (800) 431-5723, FAX: (847) 263-5191, Web Site: www.parispresents.com (7)

Parise Marketing Group, Millwood, NY. Tel: (914) 941-7467, FAX: (914) 941-7931, Web Site: www.parise.com (35)

Parish, Glen, Virco Manufacturing Corp, Conway, AR. Tel: (501) 329-2901, (800) 448-4726, FAX: (800) 258-7367, E-Mail: info@virco.com, Web Site: www.virco.com (16)

Parish, James Robert, James Robert Parish Consulting, Studio City, CA. Tel: (818) 753-9455, FAX: (818) 505-6509, E-Mail: jrparish@sbcglobal.net, Web Site: www.jamesrobertparish.com (20)

James Robert Parish Consulting, Studio City, CA. Tel: (818) 753-9455, FAX: (818) 505-6509, E-Mail: jrparish@sbcglobal.net, Web Site: www.jamesrobertparish.com (20)

Parisi, Linda, Roche Pharmaceuticals, Nutley, NJ. Tel: (973) 235-5000, FAX: (973) 235-7605, Web Site: www.rocheusa.com (7)

Parisien, Maurice R., Direct Marketing Association of Saint Louis, Washington, MO. Tel: (866) 516-0121, FAX: (636) 239-2324, E-Mail: mparisien@mac.com, Web Site: www.dmastl.org (40)

Park, Cynthia, Kang & Lee Advertising Inc/K&L Direct, New York, NY. Tel: (212) 375-8111, FAX: (212) 375-8255, E-Mail: info@kanglee.com, Web Site: www.kanglee.com (35)

Park, Ernest, Select Comfort Corp, Minneapolis, MN. Tel: (763) 551-7000, (888) 411-2188, FAX: (763) 551-7826, Web Site: www.selectcomfort.com (16)

Park, Hunter, Jobscope Corp, Greenville, SC. Tel: (864) 458-3143, (800) 443-5794, FAX: (864) 234-4852, E-Mail: marketing@jobscope.com, Web Site: www.jobscope.com (16)

Park, Jaemin, Ghirardelli Chocolate Co, San Leandro, CA. Tel: (510) 483-6970, (800) 877-9338, FAX: (510) 297-2649, Web Site: www.ghirardelli.com (16)

Park, Susan, LoyaltyOne, Toronto, ON Canada. Tel: (416) 228-6500, Web Site: www.loyalty.com; www.airmiles.ca (22)

George W Park Seed Co Inc, Greenwood, SC. Tel: (864) 223-8555, (864) 223-7333, FAX: (864) 941-4206, E-Mail: info@parkseed.com, Web Site: www.parkseed.com (8)

Parke-Bell, Carla, Touch of Class Catalog, Huntingburg, IN. Tel: (812) 683-3707, (800) 457-7456, FAX: (812) 683-5921, Web Site: www.touchofclasscatalog.com (8)

Parker, Alyce, Caesars Atlantic City Casino/Hotel, Atlantic City, NJ. Tel: (609) 348-4411, (800) 634-6661, FAX: (609) 343-2405, Web Site: www.harrahs.com (19)

Parker, Cyrus, Power & Tel Supply, Randolph, VT. Tel: (800) 451-4381, FAX: (802) 234-5006, E-Mail: cablesales@ptsupply.com, Web Site: www.ptsupply.com/enterprise (16)

Parker, Elissa, Environmental Law Institute, Washington, DC. Tel: (202) 939-3800, FAX: (202) 939-3868, E-Mail: law@eli.org, Web Site: www.eli.org (17)

Parker, Elizabeth, Caribe Direct Inc, San Juan, PR. Tel: (787) 722-5188, FAX: (787) 723-6165, E-Mail: islaonline@prw.net, Web Site: www.islaonline.com (6)

Parker, Ellen, Parker Systems Inc, Chesapeake, VA. Tel: (757) 485-2955, (866) 472-7537, FAX: (757) 487-5872, E-Mail: info@parkersystemsinc.com, Web Site: www.parkersystemsinc.com (16)

Parker, George, Krames - Staywell, Yardley, PA. Tel: (267) 685-2500, Web Site: www.krames.com (7)

Parker, James, A., MRC Marketing Inc, Saint Paul, MN. Tel: (612) 759-2069, E-Mail: info@mrcmarketing.com, Web Site: www.mrcmarketing.com (21)

Parker, Janet, N., Society for Human Resource Management, Alexandria, VA. Tel: (703) 548-3440, (800) 283-SHRM, FAX: (703) 535-6490, E-Mail: shrmstore@shrm.org, Web Site: www.shrm.org (1)

Parker, John, Parker Systems Inc, Chesapeake, VA. Tel: (757) 485-2955, (866) 472-7537, FAX: (757) 487-5872, E-Mail: info@parkersystemsinc.com, Web Site: www.parkersystemsinc.com (16)

Parker, Mark, Nike Inc, Beaverton, OR. Tel: (503) 671-4565, (800) 344-6543, FAX: (503) 671-6300, Web Site: www.nike.com (2)

Parker, Melissa, Hermes of Paris, New York, NY. Tel: (212) 759-7585, (800) 441-4488, FAX: (212) 644-2132 (2)

Parker, Michael, ITW Vortec, Cincinnati, OH. Tel: (513) 891-7474, (800) 441-7475, FAX: (513) 891-4092, E-Mail: techsupport@vortec.com, Web Site: www.vortec.com (16)

Parker, Raymond, Scan Optics Inc, Manchester, CT. Tel: (860) 645-7878, (800) 745-6001, FAX: (860) 645-7995, E-Mail: info@scanoptics.com, Web Site: www.scanoptics.com (16)

Parker, Richard, Bauer Publishing Co, Englewood Cliffs, NJ. Tel: (201) 569-6699, FAX: (201) 510-3297, Web Site: www.bauerpublishing.com (17)

Parker, Tim, Classic Motorbooks Inc, Minneapolis, MN. Tel: (715) 294-3345, (800) 826-6600, FAX: (715) 294-4448, Web Site: www.motorbooks.com (17)

Parker, Tim, Quayside Publishing Group/MBI Publishing, Minneapolis, MN. Tel: (715) 294-3345, (800) 826-6600, FAX: (715) 294-4448, Web Site: www.motorbooks.com (17)

Parker Boiler Co, Los Angeles, CA. Tel: (323) 727-9800, FAX: (323) 722-2848, E-Mail: mleeming@parkerboiler.com, Web Site: www.parkerboiler.com (34)

Parker Hannifin Corp, Cleveland, OH. Tel: (216) 896-2490, Web Site: www.parker.com (9)

Parker Software, Orlando, FL. Tel: (800) 680-7712, Web Site: www.parker-software.com (22)

Parker Steel Co, Toledo, OH. Tel: (419) 473-2481, (800) 333-4140, FAX: (419) 471-2655, Web Site: www.metricmetal.com (16)

Parker Systems Inc, Chesapeake, VA. Tel: (757) 485-2955, (866) 472-7537, FAX: (757) 487-5872, E-Mail: info@parkersystemsinc.com, Web Site: www.parkersystemsinc.com (16)

Parkes, Bill, n Fusion Group, Austin, TX. Tel: (512) 716-7000, FAX: (512) 716-7001, Web Site: www.nfusion.com (35)

Parkinson, Carol, Naval Institute Press, Annapolis, MD. Tel: (410) 268-6110, (800) 233-8764, FAX: (410) 571-1703, E-Mail: webmaster@usni.org, Web Site: www.usni.org/navalinstitutepress (17)

Parkinson, Ron, JLS Mailing Services Inc, Brockton, MA. Tel: (508) 313-1050, (866) JLS-MAIL, FAX: (508) 313-1093, E-Mail: rparkinson@jlsms.com, Web Site: www.jlsms.com (28)

Parkinson's Disease Foundation, New York, NY. Tel: (212) 923-4700, (800) 457-6676, FAX: (212) 923-4778, Web Site: www.pdf.org (1)

Parks, Ben, General Physics Corp, Elkridge, MD. Tel: (410) 379-3600, (800) 727-6677, FAX: (410) 540-5302, E-Mail: info@gpworldwide.com, Web Site: www.gpworldwide.com (16)

Parks, Bob, Sport Supply Group, Dallas, TX. Tel: (972) 484-9484, FAX: (972) 247-0650, Web Site: www.sportsupplygroup.com (11)

Parks, David, Camellia Forest Nursery, Chapel Hill, NC. Tel: (919) 968-0504, FAX: (919) 929-8971, E-Mail: camforest@aol.com, Web Site: www.camforest.com (8)

Parks, Kai-Mei, Camellia Forest Nursery, Chapel Hill, NC. Tel: (919) 968-0504, FAX: (919) 929-8971, E-Mail: camforest@aol.com, Web Site: www.camforest.com (8)

Parks, Kathy, IHFRA, High Point, NC. Tel: (336) 889-3920, FAX: (336) 464-2125, E-Mail: ihfra@ihfra.org, Web Site: www.ihfra.org (23)

Parks, Kent, NASCO, Fort Atkinson, WI. Tel: (920) 563-2446, FAX: (920) 563-8296, E-Mail: info@nasco.com, Web Site: www.enasco.com (5)

Parlay International, Walnut Creek, CA. Tel: (510) 601-1000, FAX: (510) 601-1008, E-Mail: info@parlay.com, Web Site: www.parlay.com (17)

Parmelee, James, Parmelee Associates, Arlington, VA. Tel: (703) 502-0161 (35)

Parmelee Associates, Arlington, VA. Tel: (703) 502-0161 (35)

Parmer, Jean, Marie, Parmer Books, San Diego, CA. Tel: (619) 287-0693, E-Mail: parmerbook@aol.com, Web Site: www.parmerbook.com (6)

Parmer Books, San Diego, CA. Tel: (619) 287-0693, E-Mail: parmerbook@aol.com, Web Site: www.parmerbook.com (6)

Parnell, Bill, Datalogic Scanning, Eugene, OR. Tel: (800) 695-5700, FAX: (541) 345-7140, Web Site: www.scanning.datalogic.com (34)

Parquet, Tremayne, American Association of University Women, Washington, DC. Tel: (202) 725-7611, Web Site: www.aauw.org (1)

Parr, Steve, Prime Media Equine Group, Gaithersburg, MD. Tel: (301) 977-3900, FAX: (301) 990-9015, Web Site: www.equisearch.com (17)

Parr Rud, C Olivia, Data Square LLC, Wilton, CT. Tel: (203) 964-9733, E-Mail: info@datasquare.com, Web Site: www.datasquare.com (22)

Parrell, Jerry, F., Alamo Rent A Car, Tulsa, OK. Tel: (918) 401-6000, Web Site: www.alamo.com (16)

Parrella, Lenny, Gardener's Eden, Merrimack, NH. Tel: (603) 888-9500, (800) 822-9600, FAX: (603) 577-8005, E-Mail: gsweeney@brookstone.com (8)

Parrett, William, G., Deloitte & Touche, Boston, MA. Tel: (617) 437-2000, FAX: (617) 437-2111, Web Site: www.deloitte.com (14)

Parrish, J., Perfection Tip Co/Camping Products Co, Long Beach, CA. Tel: (562) 491-0076, (800) 525-4835, FAX: (562) 435-7599 (16)

Parrish, Selina, Kentucky Bankers Association, Louisville, KY. Tel: (502) 582-2453, FAX: (502) 584-6390, Web Site: www.kybanks.com (1)

Parrott, Bob, Jobscope Corp, Greenville, SC. Tel: (864) 458-3143, (800) 443-5794, FAX: (864) 234-4852, E-Mail: marketing@jobscope.com, Web Site: www.jobscope.com (16)

Parrott, Christina, American Family Insurance Group, Madison, WI. Tel: (608) 249-2111, FAX: (608) 243-6525, E-Mail: akin1@amfam.com, Web Site: www.amfam.com (15)

Parry, David, T., Academic Travel Abroad Inc, Washington, DC. Tel: (202) 785-9000, (800) 556-7896, FAX: (202) 342-0317, Web Site: www.academictravel.com (19)

Parry, Jim, Stephan Partners Inc, New York, NY. Tel: (212) 524-8583, E-Mail: george@stephenpartners.com, Web Site: www.stephanpartners.com (35)

Parry, Lisa, Burger's Ozark Country Cured Hams Inc, California, MO. Tel: (573) 796-3134, (800) 345-5185, FAX: (573) 796-3137, E-Mail: burgers@smokehouse.com, Web Site: www.smokehouse.com (4)

Parshall, Mary Ann, Premier Data Group, Camarillo, CA. Tel: (805) 445-7522, FAX: (805) 445-8876, Web Site: www.premierdatagroup.com (23)

Parshall, Mary, Ann, Premier Data Solution, Camarillo, CA. Tel: (805) 987-2789, (800) 537-3282, (800) 333-DATA, FAX: (800) 333-6974, E-Mail: info@premierdatasolution.com, Web Site: www.premierdatasolution.com (23)

Parsons, Ben, Support Systems International Corp, Richmond, CA. Tel: (510) 234-9090, (800) 777-6269, FAX: (510) 233-8888, E-Mail: info@support-systems-intl.com, Web Site: www.support-systems-intl.com (3)

Parsons School of Design Human Resource Dept, New York, NY. Tel: (212) 229-5671, FAX: (212) 229-8975, E-Mail: communications@newschool.edu, Web Site: www.parsons.edu (41)

Partain, Katherine, Military Officers Association of America, Alexandria, VA. Tel: (703) 838-8144, Web Site: www.moaa.org (1)

Partis, Kathy, Brush Fire, Cedar Knolls, NJ. Tel: (973) 871-1700, FAX: (973) 871-1717, Web Site: www.brushfireinc.com (35)

Partminer, Centennial, CO. Tel: (303) 200-5500, FAX: (303) 754-3940, Web Site: www.partminer.com (17)

PartnerData LLC, Evanston, IL. Tel: (847) 733-0819 (30)

Partners for Incentives, Cleveland, OH. Tel: (216) 881-3000, (800) 292-7371, FAX: (216) 881-7413, Web Site: www.pfi-awards.com (33)

Partners Health, Philadelphia, PA. Tel: (215) 849-9600, (800) 553-0784, E-Mail: sroberts@healthpart.com, Web Site: www.healthpart.com (15)

Partners Marketing Inc, Saint Charles, IL. Tel: (630) 524-9901, FAX: (630) 524-9909, E-Mail: georgeb@partnersmarketing.com, Web Site: www.partnersmarketing.com (22)

Partners Village Store, Westport, MA. Tel: (508) 636-2572, FAX: (508) 636-2529, E-Mail: info@partnersvillagestore.com, Web Site: www.partnersvillagestore.com (11)

Partoll, Kimberly, America Online Inc, Dulles, VA. Tel: (703) 265-1000 (32)

Parts Express, Springboro, OH. Tel: (937) 743-3000, (800) 338-0531, FAX: (937) 743-1677, E-Mail: sales@parts-express.com, Web Site: www.partsexpress.com (3)

Parts Place Inc, Auburn Hills, MI. Tel: (248) 373-2300, (888) 432-3548, FAX: (248) 373-5950, Web Site: www.partsplaceinc.com (12)

Party Kits & Equestrian Gifts, Louisville, KY. Tel: (502) 425-2126, (800) 99-DERBY, FAX: (502) 425-5230, E-Mail: info@partykits.com, Web Site: www.derbygifts.com (6)

PartyLite Gifts Inc, Plymouth, MA. Tel: (508) 830-3100, FAX: (508) 830-0026, Web Site: www.partylite.com (8)

Parulekar, Suneil, National Semiconductor Corp, Santa Clara, CA. Tel: (408) 721-5000, (800) 272-9959, FAX: (408) 245-0671, E-Mail: new.feedback@nsc.com, Web Site: www.national.com (16)

Paruzynski, Dan, C&H Distributors LLC, Milwaukee, WI. Tel: (414) 443-1700, (888) 316-2223, FAX: (414) 443-9213, E-Mail: customerservice@chdist.com, Web Site: www.chdist.com (9)

Parvin, Pat, Action In Mailing, Montgomery, AL. Tel: (334) 286-4667, (800) 277-6245, FAX: (334) 286-6008, E-Mail: info@actioninmailing.com, Web Site: www.actioninmailing.com (21)

Pasadena Advertising, Pasadena, CA. Tel: (626) 584-0011, Web Site: www.pasadenaadvertising.com (35)

Paschal, Allen, Thomson-Gale, Farmington Hills, MI. Tel: (800) 877-4253, FAX: (877) 363-4253, Web Site: www.galegroup.com (17)

Pasckvale, Alexandria, OSG Billing, Englewood, NJ. Tel: (201) 871-1100, Web Site: www.osgbilling.com (20)

Pascoe, Eric, Bell & Howell Ltd, North York, ON. Tel: (416) 746-2200, FAX: (416) 228-2439, Web Site: www.bellhowell.com (9)

Pascoe, Michelle, Warnaco Swimwear Inc, Los Angeles, CA. Tel: (323) 726-1262, FAX: (323) 724-6931, Web Site: www.speedo.com (16)

Pashia, Gale, The Service Center LTD, Houston, TX. Tel: (713) 690-8175, FAX: (713) 690-6844, Web Site: www.calltsc.com (28)

Pashko, Sue, Envision, Newport, RI. Tel: (401) 619-1500, (800) 524-8238, FAX: (401) 619-0130, E-Mail: envision@att.net, Web Site: www.envision-stock.com (38)

Paslode, Vernon Hills, IL. Tel: (847) 634-1900, (800) 222-6990, FAX: (847) 634-6602, E-Mail: tech@paslode.com, Web Site: www.paslode.com (16)

Paslov, Eugene, T., Harcourt Educational Measurement, San Antonio, TX. Tel: (210) 299-1061, (800) 211-8378, FAX: (800) 232-1223, Web Site: www.harcourtassessment.com (17)

Passoff, Alissa, Bruce McGaw Graphics, Manchester Center, VT. Tel: (845) 353-8600, (888) 4BMC-GAW, FAX: (845) 353-3155, E-Mail: sales@bmcgaw.com, Web Site: www.bmcgaw.com (6)

Passon, Gary, Network Tel Services Inc, Woodland Hills, CA. Tel: (818) 992-4300, (800) 727-6874, FAX: (818) 992-8415, Web Site: www.nts.net (16)

Passport International Ltd, North Charleston, SC. Tel: (843) 881-8690, (800) 606-1383, FAX: (843) 881-6247, E-Mail: csv@passportintl.com, Web Site: www.passportintl.com (2)

Pasternack Enterprises Inc, Irvine, CA. Tel: (949) 261-1920, Web Site: www.pasternack.com (16)

Pastime Publications Inc, Denver, CO. Tel: (303) 534-7867, (888) 650-8665, FAX: (630) 214-7600, E-Mail: post@pastimecompany.com, Web Site: www.pastimecompany.com (17)

Paszkiewic, Elizabeth, StatSoft Inc, Tulsa, OK. Tel: (918) 749-1119, FAX: (918) 749-2217, E-Mail: info@statsoft.com, Web Site: www.statsoft.com (9)

Patagonia, Ventura, CA. Tel: (805) 643-8616, Web Site: www.patagonia.com (2)

Patagonia Mail Order Inc, Reno, NV. Tel: (775) 747-1992, (800) 638-6464, FAX: (775) 747-6159, Web Site: www.patagonia.com (2)

Pate, A.M., Texas Refinery Corp, Fort Worth, TX. Tel: (817) 332-1161, FAX: (817) 336-8441, E-Mail: jhopkins@texasrefinery.com, Web Site: www.texasrefinery.com (9)

Pate Sr, Ronald O., VF Imagewear, Nashville, TN. Tel: (615) 565-5000, (800) 733-5271, Web Site: www.vfimagewear.com (2)

Patel, Nalin, Key West Aloe Holdings LLC, Fort Lauderdale, FL. Tel: (305) 883-3166, FAX: (305) 883-3185, Web Site: www.keywestaloe.com (16)

Patel, Praibhuling, Affinity Group Inc, Ventura, CA. Tel: (805) 667-4100, (800) 765-1912, FAX: (805) 667-4419, E-Mail: khurd@affinitygroup.com, Web Site: www.affinitygroup.com (19)

Patella, Tony, Prudent Publishing Co, Ridgefield Park, NJ. Tel: (201) 641-7900, FAX: (800) 772-1144 (16)

Patenaude, Jason, The Cricket Magazine Group, Chicago, IL. Tel: (603) 924-7209, (800) 821-0115, FAX: (815) 224-6615, E-Mail: customerservice@caruspub.com, Web Site: www.cricketmag.com (17)

Paterson, David, J., Bowater Inc, Greenville, SC. Tel: (864) 271-7733, (800) 921-3244, FAX: (864) 282-9563, E-Mail: hrsc@abitibibowater.com, Web Site: www.bowater.com (17)

Paterson, Graham, Cougar Mountain Software, Boise, ID. Tel: (208) 375-4455, (800) 388-3038, FAX: (208) 375-4460, E-Mail: sales@cougarmtn.com, Web Site: www.cougarmtn.com (14)

Paterson, Jill, Allianz Life Insurance Co of North America, Minneapolis, MN. Tel: (763) 765-6500, (800) 950-5872, Web Site: www.allianzlife.com (15)

Paterson, Russell, The Merging Technologies Group LLC, Hauppauge, NY. Tel: (631) 435-2955, FAX: (631) 952-0664, E-Mail: info@mt-group.com, Web Site: www.mt-group.com (23)

Path to Purchase Institute, Skokie, IL. Tel: (847) 675-7400, Web Site: www.p2pi.org (17)

Patient News, Niagara Falls, NY. Tel: (705) 457-4030, (800) 667-0268, FAX: (705) 457-4067, E-Mail: jbishop@patientnews.com, Web Site: www.patientnews.com (17)

Patino, Paul, Meriks Mayan Chocolaterie, Washington, DC. Tel: (787) 721-0000 (27)

The Patio, Murrieta, CA. Tel: (909) 304-0460 (8)

Patmore, Kimberly, S., First Data Merchant Services, Greenwood Village, CO. Tel: (303) 488-8000, (800) 735-3362, Web Site: www.firstdata.com (14)

Patneau, John, Graphic Communications Holdings Inc, Hudson, OH. Tel: (330) 650-5522, E-Mail: info@graphiccommunications.com, Web Site: www.graphiccommunications.com (25)

Patota, Anne, Guilford Publications Inc, New York, NY. Tel: (212) 431-9800, (800) 365-7006, FAX: (212) 966-6708, E-Mail: info@guilford.com, Web Site: www.guilford.com (17)

Patrick, Barbara, Tax Management Inc, Bethesda, MD. Tel: (202) 452-4200, FAX: (202) 496-6013 (17)

Patrick, Jodi, Glynn, Magna Publications Inc, Madison, WI. Tel: (608) 246-3580, FAX: (608) 246-3597, Web Site: www.magnapubs.com (17)

Patrick, Kenneth, Artisanal LLC, Holicong, PA. Tel: (215) 862-8000, FAX: (215) 862-8008, E-Mail: info@artisanaldesign.com, Web Site: www.artisanaldesign.com (8)

Patrios, Jeff, Thomson West, Eagan, MN. Tel: (651) 687-7000, (800) 328-9378, FAX: (651) 687-7849, E-Mail: jeff.patrios@thomsonreuters.com, Web Site: www.thomson.com (17)

Patriot Communications LLC, Wayne, PA. Tel: (610) 225-0100, FAX: (610) 687-3835 (32)

Patrone, Mary Jane, The Boston Globe, Boston, MA. Tel: (617) 929-2000, (888) MY-GLOBE, FAX: (617) 929-2606, Web Site: www.bostonglobe.com (17)

Patsley, Pam, Paymentech, Salem, NH. Tel: (603) 896-6000, FAX: (603) 896-8717, Web Site: www. paymentech.com (14)

Patsuno, Paul, Invacare Supply Group, Milford, MA. Tel: (508) 429-1000, (800) 225-4792, FAX: (508) 429-1581, E-Mail: service.isg@invacare.com, Web Site: www.invacaresupplygroup.com (16)

Patten, Charles, R., Colfax Envelope Corp, Buffalo Grove, IL. Tel: (847) 215-1122, FAX: (847) 215-1145, Web Site: www.colfaxenv.com (26)

Patterson, David, John Deere Credit USA, Johnston, IA. Tel: (515) 267-3000, FAX: (515) 267-3292, Web Site: www.deere.com/en_US/jdc/index.html (14)

Patterson, Ewan, DDB Chicago, Chicago, IL. Tel: (312) 552-6000, FAX: (312) 552-2370, Web Site: www.ddbchi.com (35)

Patterson, Herbert, The Durham Manufacturing Co, Durham, CT. Tel: (860) 349-3427, (800) 243-3774, FAX: (800) 782-5499, (860) 349-8572, E-Mail: info@durhammfg.com, Web Site: www. durhammfg.com (16)

Patterson, James, F., Nationwide Mutual Insurance Co, Columbus, OH. Tel: (614) 249-7111, (800) 882-2822, FAX: (614) 854-3676, Web Site: www. nationwide.com (15)

Patterson, Judith, Pets United LLC, Hazleton, PA. Tel: (570) 384-5555, (800) 738-7877, FAX: (570) 384-2500, E-Mail: customerservice@petsupplies.com, Web Site: www.allpets.com (5)

Patterson, Patty, Institute of Management & Administration (IOMA), Peterborough, NH. Tel: (800) 401-5937, FAX: (973) 622-0595 (17)

Patterson, R., Thomas Scientific, Swedesboro, NJ. Tel: (800) 345-2100, FAX: (856) 467-3087, E-Mail: value@thomassci.com, Web Site: www.thomassci. com (9)

Patterson, Richard, The Durham Manufacturing Co, Durham, CT. Tel: (860) 349-3427, (800) 243-3774, FAX: (800) 782-5499, (860) 349-8572, E-Mail: info@durhammfg.com, Web Site: www. durhammfg.com (16)

Patterson, Rick, Disabled American Veterans, Cincinnati, OH. Tel: (859) 441-7300, FAX: (859) 442-2084, E-Mail: feedback@davmail.org, Web Site: www.dav.org (1)

Patterson, Solon P., Montag & Caldwell Inc, Atlanta, GA. Tel: (404) 836-7100, (800) 458-5868, FAX: (404) 836-7230, Web Site: www.montag.com (14)

Patterson, Steve, Trends International LLC, Indianapolis, IN. Tel: (317) 388-1212, (800) 354-4639, FAX: (317) 388-1414, E-Mail: info@trendsinternational. com, Web Site: www.trendsinternational.com (38)

Patterson, Stuart, Nuance Speech Solutions, Burlington, MA. Tel: (781) 565-5000, FAX: (781) 565-5001, E-Mail: sales@speechworks.com, Web Site: www.nuance.com (16)

Patterson, William, Demand Telemarketing Inc, Grosse Pointe, MI. Tel: (313) 823-8598, (888) 977-2256, FAX: (313) 823-8598, E-Mail: wpatterson@create-demand.com, Web Site: www.create-demand.com (29)

Patterson Dental, Saint Paul, MN. Tel: (651) 686-1600, (800) 328-5536, FAX: (651) 686-9331, Web Site: www.pattersondental.com (10)

Patton, David, Brahmin Leather Works, Fairhaven, MA. Tel: (508) 994-4000, (800) 229-2428, FAX: (508) 994-4153, Web Site: www.brahminusa.com (16)

Patton, Jerry, V., Uniformed Services Benefit Association, Overland Park, KS. Tel: (800) 368-7021, Web Site: www.usba.com (15)

Patton, Lewis, UMI Publications Inc, Charlotte, NC. Tel: (800) 747-9287, FAX: (704) 374-0729, E-Mail: info@umipub.com, Web Site: www. umipub.com (17)

Pauker, Andy, Microbiz Corp, Fountain Valley, CA. Tel: (201) 785-1311, (800) 726-3282, FAX: (201) 758-1568, E-Mail: info@microbiz.com, Web Site: www.microbiz.com (3)

Paul, Amy, HSP Direct, Herndon, VA. Tel: (703) 793-3220, FAX: (703) 793-3221, Web Site: www. hspdirect.com (1)

Paul, Carl F., Golfsmith International Inc, Austin, TX. Tel: (512) 821-4050, (800) 813-6897, FAX: (512) 837-9347, E-Mail: comments@golfsmith.com, Web Site: www.golfsmith.com (11)

Paul, Christopher, S., Fiddler's Rock Communications Inc, McLean, VA. Tel: (703) 406-1500, FAX: (703) 406-1595, Web Site: www.frmktg.com (33)

Paul, Frank C., Golfsmith International Inc, Austin, TX. Tel: (512) 821-4050, (800) 813-6897, FAX: (512) 837-9347, E-Mail: comments@golfsmith. com, Web Site: www.golfsmith.com (11)

Paul, Gary, American Association for Justice, Washington, DC. Tel: (202) 965-3500, (800) 424-2725, FAX: (202) 625-7313, Web Site: www.justice.org (1)

Paul, John, AAA Southern New England, Providence, RI. Tel: (401) 868-2005, FAX: (401) 868-2085, Web Site: www.aaa.com (1)

Paul, Kenneth, M., Institute of Real Estate Management, Chicago, IL. Tel: (312) 329-6000, (800) 837-0706, FAX: (800) 338-4736, E-Mail: custserv@ irem.org, Web Site: www.irem.org (1)

Paul, Rakesh, J., Gump's By Mail Inc, San Francisco, CA. Tel: (415) 982-1616, (800) 882-8055, FAX: (800) 984-9361, Web Site: www.gumpsbymail.com (6)

Paul Chevannes, Brooklyn, NY. Tel: (718) 788-3550 (36)

Paul, Hastings, Janofsky & Walker LLP, New York, NY. Tel: (212) 318-6037, FAX: (212) 319-4090, E-Mail: robertsherman@paulhastings.com, Web Site: www.paulhastings.com (20)

Pauley, Dana, Trumble Greetings, Boulder, CO. Tel: (800) 525-0656, FAX: (303) 530-5124, E-Mail: info@leanintree.com, Web Site: www.leanintree. com (6)

Paulino, Frank, Official Offset Corp, Amityville, NY. Tel: (631) 957-8500 (27)

Paullin, James, Selling Solutions Inc, Atlanta, GA. Tel: (404) 261-4966, FAX: (404) 264-1767, E-Mail: information@selsol.com, Web Site: www. selsol.com (35)

Paullin, William, Selling Solutions Inc, Atlanta, GA. Tel: (404) 261-4966, FAX: (404) 264-1767, E-Mail: information@selsol.com, Web Site: www. selsol.com (35)

Paulson, Tim, Augsburg Fortress Publishers, Minneapolis, MN. Tel: (612) 330-3300, (800) 426-0115, FAX: (612) 330-3455, E-Mail: info@ augsburgfortress.org, Web Site: www. augsburgfortress.org (17)

Paulus, Holly, Nexx Group Inc, Fort Myers, FL. Tel: (239) 225-1516, (800) 566-1183, FAX: (239) 288-4968, Web Site: www.nexxagroup.com (23)

Paupore, Daniel, Kingsley North Inc, Norway, MI. Tel: (906) 563-9228, (800) 338-9280, FAX: (906) 563-7143, E-Mail: sales@kingsleynorth.com, Web Site: www.kingsleynorth.com (11)

Paupore, Mark, Kingsley North Inc, Norway, MI. Tel: (906) 563-9228, (800) 338-9280, FAX: (906) 563-7143, E-Mail: sales@kingsleynorth.com, Web Site: www.kingsleynorth.com (11)

Paust, Christine, Texas Children's Hospital, Houston, TX. Tel: (832) 824-2936, Web Site: www. texaschildrenshospital.org (1)

Pavely, Richard W., CMMC Market Research, Mount Freedom, NJ. Tel: (973) 989-0229, FAX: (973) 366-1185, E-Mail: dmmp@cmmcinc.com, Web Site: www.cmmcinc.com (30)

Pavlides, Pavlos, Astro Air, LP, Jacksonville, TX. Tel: (903) 586-3691, FAX: (903) 589-8094, E-Mail: sales@astroair.com, Web Site: www.astroair.com (9)

Pavlish, Mike, Profit Boosters Copywriting, Aurora, OH. Tel: (330) 963-0330, FAX: (330) 562-2446, E-Mail: mikepavlish@profitboosterscopy.com, Web Site: www.profitboosterscopy.com (39)

Pavloff, Susan, Coverdell & Co Inc, Chicago, IL. Tel: (404) 881-2227, (800) 992-2196, FAX: (404) 881-2222, Web Site: www.coverdell.com (15)

Pawlak, Nicole, Women's Sports Foundation, East Meadow, NY. Tel: (516) 542-4700, Web Site: www.womenssportsfoundation.org (1)

Paxton, James, Medical Group Management Association (MGMA), Englewood, CO. Tel: (303) 799-1111, FAX: (303) 643-4439, E-Mail: marketing@ mgma.com, Web Site: www.mgma.com (1)

Paxton, Valerie, Insight Direct Inc, Tempe, AZ. Tel: (480) 333-3001, (800) 467-4448, FAX: (480) 902-1180, Web Site: www.insight.com (16)

Payless ShoeSource Inc, Topeka, KS. Tel: (785) 233-5171, Web Site: www.payless.com (2)

Paylor, Craig, JLG Industries Inc, McConnellsburg, PA. Tel: (717) 485-5161, (877) JLG-SELL, FAX: (717) 485-6417, E-Mail: comments@jlg.com, Web Site: www.jlg.com (16)

Payment, Meg, Kelly's Kids, Natchez, MS. Tel: (601) 442-5332, (800) 837-2066, FAX: (601) 442-4399, E-Mail: customerservice@kellyskids.com, Web Site: www.kellyskids.com (2)

Paymentech, Salem, NH. Tel: (603) 896-6000, FAX: (603) 896-8717, Web Site: www.paymentech.com (14)

Payne, Dale, SanSegal Sportswear (HQ), Sandy, UT. Tel: (801) 566-3248, (800) 338-6048, FAX: (801) 566-3350, E-Mail: sansegal@sansegal.com, Web Site: www.sansegal.com (2)

Payne, Ellen, List Locators & Managers, Overland Park, KS. Tel: (913) 338-5055, (800) 487-8720, FAX: (913) 338-5055 (23)

Payne, Howard, L., Marketshare Publications Inc, Overland Park, KS. Tel: (913) 338-3360, (800) 488-8051, FAX: (913) 217-2895, Web Site: www. marketsharepubs.com (17)

Payne, Kim, Primedia Inc, Norcross, GA. Tel: (678) 421-3000, (800) 216-1423, Web Site: www. primedia.com (31)

PayPal Inc, Timonium, MD. Tel: (443) 921-1184, Web Site: www.corporate.billmelater.com (14)

Payton, Billy, Brierley & Partners, Plano, TX. Tel: (214) 760-8700, FAX: (214) 743-5511, E-Mail: bpayton@brierley.com, Web Site: www.brierley. com (35)

Peachtree Data Inc, Duluth, GA. Tel: (678) 987-4600, Web Site: www.peachtreedata.com (22)

Peacock, Ken, Forestry Suppliers Inc, Jackson, MS. Tel: (601) 354-3565, (800) 543-4203, FAX: (601) 292-0165, E-Mail: fsi@forestry-suppliers.com, Web Site: www.forestry-suppliers.com (9)

Peak Computer Systems, Belleville, IL. Tel: (618) 398-5612, E-Mail: info@peaknet.net, Web Site: www.peaknet.net (22)

Peak Impact Inc, Ottawa, ON Canada. Tel: (613) 592-3100, Web Site: www.peakimpact.com (14)

Pearce, Walter, KCI Communications Inc, Falls Church, VA. Tel: (703) 394-4931, FAX: (703) 905-8100, Web Site: www.kci-com.com (17)

Pearl, Ron, TMP Direct, Budd Lake, NJ. Tel: (973) 347-9400, (800) 328-2439, FAX: (973) 347-8773, E-Mail: ron.pearl@tmpwdirect.com, Web Site: www.tmpwdirect.com (29)

Pearl Insurance Group LLC, Peoria Heights, IL. Tel: (309) 688-9000, Web Site: www.pearlinsurance. com (15)

Pearlman, Deborah, E., DKP & Associates, Inc, Skokie, IL. Tel: (847) 933-9808, E-Mail: dpearlman@dkpassociates.com, Web Site: www. dkpassociates.com (22)

Pearson, Anita, OMP, Washington, DC. Tel: (202) 467-0048, Web Site: www.ompdirect.com (1)

Pearson, David, Lahey Clinic, Burlington, MA. Tel: (781) 744-5100, Web Site: www.lahey.org (1)

Pearson, Harry, NextScreen LLC, Austin, TX. Tel: (512) 892-8682, Web Site: www.avguide.com (17)

Pearson, Kenneth, ASTM International, West Conshohocken, PA. Tel: (610) 832-9500, FAX: (610) 832-9555, E-Mail: service@astm.org, Web Site: www. astm.org (1)

Pearson, Rebecca, Travel Industry Association, Washington, DC. Tel: (202) 408-8422, FAX: (202) 408-1255, E-Mail: feedback@tia.org, Web Site: www. tia.org (1)

Pearson Education, Upper Saddle River, NJ. Tel: (201) 236-7000, FAX: (201) 236-3290, E-Mail: communications@pearsoned.com, Web Site: www. pearsoned.com (17)

Pease, Alan, The Country Bed Shop, Ashby, MA. Tel: (978) 386-7550, FAX: (978) 386-7263, E-Mail: alan@countrybed.com, Web Site: www.countrybed. com (16)

Pease, John, Global Specialties, Wallingford, CT. Tel: (203) 272-3285, FAX: (203) 272-4330, Web Site: www.globalspecialties.com (16)

Pecan Producers International, Corsicana, TX. Tel: (903) 872-1337, (800) 732-2648, FAX: (903) 874-7143 (4)

Pecher, Dick, Preferred Advertising Inc, Ballwin, MO. Tel: (314) 298-8555, (800) 289-7858, FAX: (314) 298-8557, E-Mail: websales@preferredadvertising. com, Web Site: www.preferredadvertising.com (33)

Peck, Thomas, H., US News & World Report, New York, NY. Tel: (212) 916-7360, FAX: (212) 643-7842, Web Site: www.usnews.com (17)

Peck Rock Associates, Bristol, RI. Tel: (401) 253-9307, FAX: (401) 254-0424, E-Mail: pra@aol.com, Web Site: www.peckrock.com (33)

Pecker, David, National Enquirer, Boca Raton, FL. Tel: (561) 989-1221, Web Site: www. nationalenquirer.com (17)

Peckham, Suzanne, Prakken Publications Inc, Ann Arbor, MI. Tel: (734) 975-2800, (800) 530-9673, FAX: (734) 975-2787, E-Mail: vanessa@ techdirections.com, Web Site: www.eddigest.com; www.techdirections.com (17)

Pectol, Don, Emergency Essentials Inc, Orem, UT. Tel: (801) 222-9596, FAX: (801) 222-9598, E-Mail: webmaster@beprepared.com, Web Site: www.beprepared.com (16)

Peddicord, Kathleen, AGORA Inc, Baltimore, MD. Tel: (410) 783-8499, FAX: (410) 783-8414, E-Mail: csteam@agorapublishinggroup.com, Web Site: www.agora-inc.com (17)

Pedersen, Amy, Morgan Kaufmann Publishers Inc, Burlington, MA. Tel: (781) 313-4700, E-Mail: order@mkp.com, Web Site: www.mkp.com (17)

Pedersen, Ron, S&H Solutions, Delray Beach, FL. Tel: (561) 454-7600, FAX: (561) 265-2493, E-Mail: customerservice@shsolutions.com, Web Site: www.shsolutions.com (35)

Pederson, Jeffrey, TAB Boards International Inc, Westminster, CO. Tel: (303) 839-1200, FAX: (303) 839-0012, Web Site: www.tabboards.com (14)

Pedlow, John, Broadcast Electronics Inc, Quincy, IL. Tel: (217) 224-9600, FAX: (217) 224-9607, E-Mail: bdcast@bdcast.com, Web Site: www. bdcast.com (3)

Pedone, Michael, F., Pedone, New York, NY. Tel: (212) 627-3300, FAX: (212) 627-3388, E-Mail: info@pedone.com, Web Site: www.pedonepartners. com (35)

Pedone, New York, NY. Tel: (212) 627-3300, FAX: (212) 627-3388, E-Mail: info@pedone.com, Web Site: www.pedonepartners.com (35)

Pedreiro, Anna, AC Pedreiro, Morganville, NJ. Tel: (732) 598-6766 (27)

Pedrick, Ray, Mohawk Lifts, Amsterdam, NY. Tel: (518) 842-1431, (800) 833-2006, FAX: (518) 842-1289, E-Mail: rwells@mohawklifts.com, Web Site: www.mohawklifts.com (9)

Pedroni, Karen, M., HH Backer Associates Inc, Chicago, IL. Tel: (312) 578-1818, FAX: (312) 578-1819, E-Mail: hhbacker@hhbacker.com, Web Site: www.hhbacker.com (17)

Pedtke, Richard, F., Bobcat Co, West Fargo, ND. Tel: (701) 241-8700, FAX: (701) 241-8704, Web Site: www.bobcat.com (16)

Peel, Jim, Texas Refinery Corp, Fort Worth, TX. Tel: (817) 332-1161, FAX: (817) 336-8441, E-Mail: jhopkins@texasrefinery.com, Web Site: www. texasrefinery.com (9)

Peerless Rattan, Plainwell, MI. Tel: (269) 685-1858, (877) 611-2263, E-Mail: sales@peerlessrattan.com, Web Site: www.peerlessrattan.com (16)

Peeters, Geert, Suez Energy North America, Houston, TX. Tel: (713) 636-0000, FAX: (713) 636-1364, Web Site: www.tractebelpowerinc.com (16)

Peet's Coffee & Tea Inc, Berkeley, CA. Tel: (510) 594-2100, (800) 999-2132, FAX: (510) 594-2180, E-Mail: mailorder@peets.com, Web Site: www. peets.com (16)

Pefanis, Peter, J., Protection One Inc, Lawrence, KS. Tel: (785) 856-5500, (800) GET-HELP, Web Site: www.protectionone.com (16)

Peffers, Kathryn, Penny Wise Office Products, Bowie, MD. Tel: (301) 805-7733, (800) 942-3311, FAX: (800) 622-4411, Web Site: www.penny-wise.com (10)

Pegasus Auto Racing Supplies Inc, New Berlin, WI. Tel: (262) 317-1234, (800) 688-6946, FAX: (262) 317-1201, E-Mail: info@pegasusautoracing.com, Web Site: www.pegasusautoracing.com (12)

Pegg Nadler Associates Inc, New York, NY. Tel: (212) 861-0846 (22)

Pegran, Ron, McFeely's Square Drive Screws, Madison, WI. Tel: (434) 846-2729, (800) 443-7937, FAX: (804) 847-7136, E-Mail: tech@mcfeelys. com, Web Site: www.mcfeelys.com (16)

Peha, Jamie, Seattle Magazine, Seattle, WA. Tel: (206) 284-1750, (800) 637-0334, FAX: (206) 284-2550, E-Mail: customerservice@seattlemag.com, Web Site: www.seattlemag.com (17)

Peirce, Jean-Marie, Trumble Greetings, Boulder, CO. Tel: (800) 525-0656, FAX: (303) 530-5124, E-Mail: info@leanintree.com, Web Site: www. leanintree.com (2)

Peixotto, Bob, LL Bean Inc, Freeport, ME. Tel: (207) 865-4761, (800) 441-5713, FAX: (207) 552-3080, Web Site: www.llbean.com (2)

Pekarek, Jim, Cornerstone Brands Inc, West Chester, OH. Tel: (513) 603-1400, Web Site: www. cornerstonebrands.com (5)

Pelfrey, Jody, Data Partners Inc, Fort Myers, FL. Tel: (239) 267-8762, (866) 423-1818, FAX: (239) 267-9043, E-Mail: info@data-partners.com, Web Site: www.datapartners.com (22)

Pelland, Michael, AIDC (American International Distribution Corp), Williston, VT. Tel: (800) 678-2432, FAX: (802) 864-7626, E-Mail: jmacon@ aidcvt.com, Web Site: www.aidcvt.com (22)

Pellegrino, A. Robert, Breck's Bulbs, Lawrenceburg, IN. Tel: (309) 693-8600, FAX: (309) 691-9693 (8)

Pellegrino, Gary, Natural Essentials Inc, Streetsboro, OH. Tel: (330) 562-8022, (888) 968-7220, FAX: (330) 562-8022, E-Mail: questions@ naturalessentials.com, Web Site: www. naturalessentials.com (5)

Pellegrino, Louis, Profile Coverage Corp, Melville, NY. Tel: (631) 981-7600, FAX: (631) 981-7681, E-Mail: info@profileinsure.com, Web Site: www. profileinsure.com (15)

Pelletier, Tom, Tom Pelletier, Patchogue, NY. Tel: (631) 569-5552, FAX: (413) 825-7968, E-Mail: tom@tompelletier.com, Web Site: www. tompelletier.com (39)

Tom Pelletier, Patchogue, NY. Tel: (631) 569-5552, FAX: (413) 825-7968, E-Mail: tom@tompelletier. com, Web Site: www.tompelletier.com (39)

Pellitteri, Marcia, Creative Campaigns Inc, Calabasas, CA. Tel: (818) 340-2713, FAX: (818) 337-2446, E-Mail: info@creativecampaigns.com, Web Site: www.creativecampaigns.com (32)

PEMCO Insurance Cos, Seattle, WA. Tel: (206) 628-4000, (800) 467-3626, FAX: (206) 628-5886, Web Site: www.pemco.com (15)

Penberthy, Stephen, Woodcrafters Lumber Sales Inc, Portland, OR. Tel: (503) 231-0226, (800) 777-3709, FAX: (503) 232-0511, E-Mail: spen@ worldnet.att.net, Web Site: www.woodcrafters.us (9)

Pence, Dennis, Coldwater Creek, Coeur D Alene, ID. Tel: (800) 787-9196, FAX: (800) 262-0080, Web Site: www.coldwatercreek.com (2)

Pendell, Don, Don Pendell & Associates, Dayton, OH. Tel: (937) 254-4210 (39)

Don Pendell & Associates, Dayton, OH. Tel: (937) 254-4210 (39)

Pendergast, Jane, The Tog Shop Inc, Beverly, MA. Tel: (800) 342-6789, FAX: (800) 755-7557, Web Site: www.togshop.com (2)

Penders, Jim, Command Financial Press, New York, NY. Tel: (212) 274-6070, FAX: (212) 274-8262, E-Mail: csd@commandfinancial.com, Web Site: www.commandfinancial.com (35)

Penegar, James, BIZ Journal Business Leads, Charlotte, NC. Tel: (704) 973-1273 (23)

Pengra, Molly, USA Hosts, San Francisco, CA. Tel: (415) 695-8000, (800) 368-4678, FAX: (415) 986-3668, Web Site: www.usahosts.com (19)

Penguin Group USA Inc, East Rutherford, NJ. Tel: (201) 909-6200, FAX: (201) 236-3381, Web Site: penguingroup.com (17)

Penguin Party Products, Campbell, CA. Tel: (408) 377-1303, FAX: (408) 377-6319, Web Site: www. penguinparty.com (5)

Penguin Publishing Group, New York, NY. Tel: (212) 366-2000, FAX: (212) 366-2952, Web Site: www. penguinputnam.com (17)

Penguin Putnam Inc, New York, NY. Tel: (212) 366-2000, FAX: (212) 366-2278, Web Site: www. penguinputnam.com (17)

Peninsular Printing of Daytona Beach Inc, Ormond Beach, FL. Tel: (386) 274-4837, FAX: (386) 274-5023, E-Mail: penprint@bellsouth.net, Web Site: www.peninsularprinting.com (27)

Penisson, Rene, Vivendi, New York, NY. Tel: (212) 572-7000, FAX: (212) 572-1080, Web Site: www. vivendi.com (17)

Penko, John, American General Co, Neptune, NJ. Tel: (732) 922-7000, FAX: (732) 922-7595 (15)

Penn, Jeff, Eastbay Running Store Inc, Wausau, WI. Tel: (715) 845-5538, (800) 826-2205, FAX: (715) 261-9500, Web Site: www.eastbay.com (2)

Penn, Richard, E., Milberg Penn *International, Mount Kisco, NY. Tel: (914) 241-0858, (914) 239-4300, E-Mail: contact@mpioutsourcing.com, Web Site: www.mpioutsourcing.com (29)

Penn, Steve, Penn Garritano Direct Response Marketing, Minneapolis, MN. Tel: (612) 333-3775, FAX: (612) 333-3775, Web Site: www.penngarritano.com (35)

Penn, Yael, Imagine 360 Marketing, New York, NY. Tel: (212) 313-9616, Web Site: www.i360m.com (20)

Penn Garritano Direct Response Marketing, Minneapolis, MN. Tel: (612) 333-3775, FAX: (612) 333-3775, Web Site: www.penngarritano.com (35)

Penn Herb Co Ltd, Philadelphia, PA. Tel: (215) 632-6100, (800) 523-9971, FAX: (215) 632-7945, E-Mail: information@pennherb.com, Web Site: www.pennherb.com (7)

Penn Industries Inc, Cerritos, CA. Tel: (562) 926-0455, FAX: (562) 926-8955, Web Site: www. pennlitho.com (27)

Penn Mutual, Horsham, PA. Tel: (215) 956-8083, FAX: (215) 956-8368, Web Site: www.pennmutual. com (15)

Penn State Hazleton, Hazleton, PA. Tel: (570) 450-3175, Web Site: www.hn.psu.edu (1)

Pennell, Dave, Malco Products Inc, Barberton, OH. Tel: (330) 753-0361, (800) 253-2526, FAX: (330) 753-2025, Web Site: www.malcopro.com (16)

Pennington, Eric, Carrot-Top Industries Inc, Hillsborough, NC. Tel: (919) 732-6200, (800) 628-3524, FAX: (919) 732-5526, E-Mail: service@carrot-top. com, Web Site: www.carrot-top.com (16)

Pennington, Hal, Genesco Inc, Nashville, TN. Tel: (615) 367-7000, (888) 324-6189, FAX: (615) 367-8278, Web Site: www.genesco.com (2)

Pennington, Roger, Direct Mail Systems, Clearwater, FL. Tel: (727) 573-1985, (800) 683-6245, FAX: (727) 573-1747, E-Mail: info@direct-mail-systems. com, Web Site: www.direct-mail-systems.com (20)

Pennington, Roger, Direct Response Marketing, Clearwater, FL. Tel: (727) 573-1985, (800) 683-6245, FAX: (727) 573-1747, E-Mail: drmclwr@ tampabay.rr.com, Web Site: www.dmsmails.com (28)

Pennington, Terry, Ennis Inc, Midlothian, TX. Tel: (972) 775-9801, (800) 962-0944, FAX: (800) 645-8339, Web Site: www.ennis.com (16)

Pennrich, Waterford, PA. Tel: (814) 866-2412, FAX: (814) 864-3908 (23)

Pennstreet Bakery, Grand Rapids, MI. Tel: (616) 241-2583, (800) 84-CAKES, FAX: (616) 241-6332, Web Site: www.pennstreet.com (16)

Pennsylvania Firebacks, Lansdale, PA. Tel: (215) 699-0805, (888) 349-30002, FAX: (215) 699-3332, E-Mail: info@fireback.com, Web Site: www. fireback.com (16)

Pennsylvania State University Press, University Park, PA. Tel: (814) 865-1327, (800) 326-9180, FAX: (814) 863-1408, Web Site: www.psupress.org (17)

PennWell Lists, Tulsa, OK. Tel: (918) 835-3161, (800) 331-4463, FAX: (918) 831-9497, Web Site: www. pennwell.com (24)

Pennwell Publishing, Tulsa, OK. Tel: (918) 835-3161, (800) 331-4463, E-Mail: headquarters@pennwell. com, Web Site: www.pennwell.com (17)

Penny, Phil, Belvoir Media Group LLC, Norwalk, CT. Tel: (203) 857-3100, (800) 424-7887, FAX: (203) 857-3103, E-Mail: customer_service@belvoir.com, Web Site: www.belvoir.com (17)

Penny Wise Office Products, Bowie, MD. Tel: (301) 805-7733, (800) 942-3311, FAX: (800) 622-4411, Web Site: www.penny-wise.com (10)

Pennypacker, Barry, L., Champion, Quincy, IL. Tel: (217) 222-5400, FAX: (217) 228-8260, Web Site: www.championpneumatic.com (16)

The Pennysaver Group Inc, Hanover, MD. Tel: (410) 684-2600, FAX: (410) 684-2065, Web Site: www. mdpennysaver.com (17)

Penrose, Amy, ClickSpark LLC, San Francisco, CA. Tel: (800) 878-5709, E-Mail: amy@clickspark. com, Web Site: www.clickspark.com (32)

Pensions & Investments, New York, NY. Tel: (212) 210-0100, FAX: (212) 210-0117, Web Site: www. pionline.com (17)

Penske Logistics, Reading, PA. Tel: (610) 775-6000, (800) 529-6531, FAX: (610) 775-6432, Web Site: www.penskelogistics.com (16)

Penta, Tony, Health Sciences Consortium, Chapel Hill, NC. Tel: (919) 942-8731, FAX: (919) 942-3689, E-Mail: tony.penta@edtsi.com, Web Site: www. healthsciencesconsortium.org (17)

Penta Edd, Frank, B., Health Sciences Consortium, Chapel Hill, NC. Tel: (919) 942-8731, FAX: (919) 942-3689, E-Mail: tony.penta@edtsi.com, Web Site: www.healthsciencesconsortium.org (17)

Pente, Bob, The PENTE Corp, Toronto, ON Canada. Tel: (416) 214-2014, FAX: (416) 214-1202, Web Site: www.wiredpente.com (35)

The PENTE Corp, Toronto, ON Canada. Tel: (416) 214-2014, FAX: (416) 214-1202, Web Site: www. wiredpente.com (35)

Pentera Inc, Indianapolis, IN. Tel: (617) 277-5033, Web Site: www.pentera.com (1)

Penton Learning Systems Inc, New York, NY. Tel: (212) 885-2700, FAX: (212) 885-2703, E-Mail: info@iqpc.com, Web Site: www.iqpc.com (16)

People for the American Way, Washington, DC. Tel: (202) 467-2352, Web Site: www.pfaw.org (1)

Peoples, Jeffrey, Window Book Inc, Cambridge, MA. Tel: (617) 441-3500, Web Site: www.windowbook. com (22)

Peoples Benefit Life Insurance Co, Exton, PA. Tel: (610) 648-5000, FAX: (610) 648-5348 (15)

People's United Bank, Bridgeport, CT. Tel: (203) 338-7171, Web Site: www.peoples.com (14)

Pepe, Greg, Media People Inc, New York, NY. Tel: (212) 779-7172, FAX: (212) 779-7248, Web Site: www.mediapeople.com (31)

Pepper, Charlie, Tinsley Tool Supply Inc, Powell, TN. Tel: (865) 681-9633, FAX: (865) 982-1655, E-Mail: gene@tinsleytool.com, Web Site: www. tinsleytool.com (9)

Pepper, Ginger, Morris & Fellows, Atlanta, GA. Tel: (404) 250-0225 (20)

Pepper, Jeff, Foremost Insurance Group, Grand Rapids, MI. Tel: (616) 956-8241, (800) 527-3905, FAX: (800) 325-1507, Web Site: www.foremost. com (15)

Peppermill Marketing Inc, Los Angeles, CA. Tel: (310) 659-8900, (877) 600-7775, FAX: (310) 659-8901, E-Mail: inquiry@peppermillmarketing.com, Web Site: www.peppermillmarketing.com (23)

Peppers, Don, 1to1 Media, Stamford, CT. Tel: (203) 642-5121, FAX: (203) 316-5121, (203) 642-5126, Web Site: www.1to1media.com (35)

Peragine-Krauss, Maria, Authentic Designs Colonial and Early American Lighting Fixtures Inc, West Rupert, VT. Tel: (802) 394-7713, (800) 844-9416, FAX: (802) 394-2422, E-Mail: mail@ authenticdesigns.com, Web Site: www. authenticdesigns.com (8)

Perciasepe, Robert, National Audubon Society, New York, NY. Tel: (212) 979-3000, FAX: (212) 979-3188, Web Site: www.audubon.org (17)

Percipio Media, LLC, Cambridge, MA. Tel: (617) 995-7855 (20)

Percy-Dove, Anna, Blitz Direct Data & Promotion, Toronto, ON Canada. Tel: (416) 922-6434, Web Site: www.cossette.com (35)

Perdiew, James R., James R Perdiew & Co, Barrington, IL. Tel: (847) 842-8525, FAX: (847) 842-8518, E-Mail: jrpco@perdiew.com, Web Site: www.perdiew.com (20)

James R Perdiew & Co, Barrington, IL. Tel: (847) 842-8525, FAX: (847) 842-8518, E-Mail: jrpco@ perdiew.com, Web Site: www.perdiew.com (20)

Perea, Lawrence, UGL Equis Corp, Chicago, IL. Tel: (312) 424-8000, FAX: (312) 424-8080, Web Site: www.equiscorp.com (16)

Perennial Pleasures Nursery, East Hardwick, VT. Tel: (802) 472-5104, FAX: (802) 472-6572, E-Mail: annex@perennialpleasures.net, Web Site: www. antiqueplants.com (8)

Peressutti, Gian-Carlo, RR Donnelley & Sons Co, Chicago, IL. Tel: (312) 326-8000, FAX: (312) 326-7156, Web Site: www.rrdonnelly.com (31)

Perez, Antonio M., Eastman Kodak Co, Rochester, NY. Tel: (585) 724-0251, (800) 698-3324, FAX: (585) 724-1089, Web Site: www.kodak.com (27)

Perez, David, B., Gambro Inc, Lakewood, CO. Tel: (303) 232-6800, (800) 525-2623, FAX: (303) 222-6810, Web Site: www.gambro.com (16)

Perez, Javier, Estee Lauder Inc, New York, NY. Tel: (212) 572-4200, (866) 467-7363, FAX: (212) 572-3942, Web Site: www.esteelauder.com (16)

Perez, Paul, American Appraisal Associates, Milwaukee, WI. Tel: (414) 271-7240, (800) 558-8650, FAX: (414) 225-1271, Web Site: www.american-appraisal.com (14)

Perfall, Clay, Archway Marketing Services, Rogers, MN. Tel: (763) 428-3300, (866) 779-9855 X1933, FAX: (763) 488-6803, E-Mail: sales@archway. com, Web Site: www.archway.com (28)

Perfect Plastic Printing Corp, Saint Charles, IL. Tel: (630) 584-1600, FAX: (630) 584-0648, E-Mail: ppp@perfectplastic.com, Web Site: www. perfectplastic.com (27)

Perfection Tip Co/Camping Products Co, Long Beach, CA. Tel: (562) 491-0076, (800) 525-4835, FAX: (562) 435-7599 (16)

Perfit, Stephen, CCIM Institute, Chicago, IL. Tel: (312) 321-4460, (800) 621-7027, FAX: (312) 321-4530, Web Site: www.ccim.com (1)

Performance Direct Inc, Atlanta, GA. Tel: (678) 608-2820, (800) 869-2300, FAX: (404) 869-2547, E-Mail: info@performancede.com (22)

Performance Media Solutions Inc & TrueWorx Inc, Las Vegas, NV. Tel: (866) 827-7077 (16)

Performance Printing/ Optigraphics, Dallas, TX. Tel: (214) 665-1038, (800) 662-2813, FAX: (214) 665-1090, Web Site: www.performancecompanies.com (27)

Perger, Rebecca, Marketing Results Inc, Sicklerville, NJ. Tel: (856) 740-3334, FAX: (856) 740-3335, Web Site: www.marketingresults.net (16)

Periatt, Jeffrey, A., Auburn University at Montgomery, Montgomery, AL. Tel: (334) 244-3621, (800) 227-2649, FAX: (334) 244-3826, Web Site: www.aum. edu (41)

Perimeter Technology Inc, Manchester, NH. Tel: (603) 645-1616, (800) 645-1650, FAX: (603) 645-1424, Web Site: www.perimetertechnology.com (34)

Perina, Kaja, Sussex Publishers Inc, New York, NY. Tel: (212) 260-7210, FAX: (212) 260-7445, Web Site: www.blues-buster.com (17)

Periodical Publisher's Service Bureau Inc, Sandusky, OH. Tel: (419) 626-0623, (800) 220-1247, FAX: (419) 626-4576, Web Site: www.ppsb.com (18)

Periscope Inc, Minneapolis, MN. Tel: (612) 339-0663, (800) 339-2103, FAX: (612) 339-0600, E-Mail: bill@ps-mpls.com, Web Site: www.periscope.com (35)

Perkins, Lara, Capitol Advantage/Roll Call Group, Washington, DC. Tel: (202) 6550-6500, (800) 432-2250, E-Mail: sales@cq.com (31)

Perkins, Leigh, H., The Orvis Co Inc, Manchester, VT. Tel: (802) 362-3622, FAX: (802) 362-3525, Web Site: www.orvis.com (11)

Perkins, Pat, Keller Crescent Co, Greensboro, NC. Tel: (508) 478-7641, FAX: (508) 634-3709, Web Site: www.kellercrescent.com (16)

Perkins, Patty, Directory of Major Mailers & What They Mail, Philadelphia, PA. Tel: (800) 777-8074, FAX: (215) 238-5412, E-Mail: customerservice@ napco.com, Web Site: www.majormailers.com (43)

Perkins, Patty, Inside Direct Mail, Philadelphia, PA. Tel: (215) 238-5300, (800) 777-8074, FAX: (215) 238-5412, E-Mail: customservice@napco.com, Web Site: www.insidedirectmail.com (43)

Perkins, Perk, The Orvis Co Inc, Manchester, VT. Tel: (802) 362-3622, FAX: (802) 362-3525, Web Site: www.orvis.com (11)

Perkins, Sarah, Pangborn Design Ltd, Detroit, MI. Tel: (313) 259-3400, FAX: (313) 259-5690, E-Mail: info@pangborndesign.com, Web Site: www. pangborndesign.com (36)

Perkins, Terry, Peter Li Education Group, Dayton, OH. Tel: (937) 293-1415, (800) 523-4625, FAX: (937) 293-1310, Web Site: www.peterli.com (17)

Perlick, Gary, Renkim Corp, Southgate, MI. Tel: (734) 374-8300, FAX: (734) 374-8323, E-Mail: info@ renkim.com, Web Site: www.renkim.com (22)

Perlman, Rita, US Chamber of Commerce, Washington, DC. Tel: (202) 778-6063, (800) 638-6582, FAX: (202) 887-3430, Web Site: www.uschamber.com (1)

Perlman, Victor, American Society of Media Photographers (ASMP), Philadelphia, PA. Tel: (215) 451-ASMP, FAX: (215) 451-0880, Web Site: www.asmp.org (40)

Perlmutter, David, Intel Corp, Santa Clara, CA. Tel: (408) 765-8080, (800) 548-4725, FAX: (408) 765-6187, Web Site: www.intel.com (16)

Perlstein, Joshua, Response Media, Norcross, GA. Tel: (770) 451-5478, FAX: (770) 451-4929, E-Mail: babion@responsemedia.com, Web Site: www.responsemedia.com (32)

Perlstein, Keith, Response Media, Norcross, GA. Tel: (770) 451-5478, FAX: (770) 451-4929, E-Mail: babion@responsemedia.com, Web Site: www.responsemedia.com (32)

Perlstein, Steve, Mohawk Lifts, Amsterdam, NY. Tel: (518) 842-1431, (800) 833-2006, FAX: (518) 842-1289, E-Mail: rwells@mohawklifts.com, Web Site: www.mohawklifts.com (9)

Pernick, Sandy, Creative Compliance, Chicago, IL. Tel: (916) 216-3379, E-Mail: info@creativecompliance.com, Web Site: www.creativecompliance.com (29)

S Pernick & Associates, Wilmette, IL. Tel: (847) 256-0115 (20)

Pernod Ricard USA, Purchase, NY. Tel: (914) 848-4800, Web Site: www.pernod-ricard-usa.com (16)

Peros, Jim, IHOP Corp, Glendale, CA. Tel: (818) 240-6055, FAX: (818) 553-3131, Web Site: www.ihop.com (16)

Perra, Wayne, Weight Watchers International, New York, NY. Tel: (516) 390-1400, FAX: (516) 390-1302, Web Site: www.weight-watchers.com (16)

Perrella, Ronald, Ron Perrella DRS (DR Specialists), Laguna Niguel, CA. Tel: (949) 495-7661, FAX: (949) 495-7660, E-Mail: rperrdrs@aol.com, Web Site: www.ronperrelladrs.com (35)

Perret, Jan, Technology Marketing Corp/TMC, Norwalk, CT. Tel: (203) 852-6800, (800) 243-6002, FAX: (203) 953-2845, E-Mail: tmc@tmcnet.com, Web Site: www.tmcnet.com (29)

Perrott, M., Ward, Madison Executive Search, Ridgefield, CT. Tel: (203) 431-6565, FAX: (203) 431-6060, E-Mail: mimi@directexec.com, Web Site: www.directexec.com (20)

Perry, Jason, Majestic Products Co, Mississauga, ON. Tel: (905) 858-8010, (800) 668-5323, FAX: (905) 670-7915, Web Site: www.cfmcorp.com (16)

Perry, Les, Seiko Corp of America, Mahwah, NJ. Tel: (201) 529-5730, FAX: (201) 529-1548, Web Site: www.seiko.com (16)

Perry, Rick, Lippincott, Williams & Wilkins, Baltimore, MD. Tel: (410) 528-4000, (800) 638-0672, FAX: (410) 528-8597, E-Mail: customerservice@lww.com, Web Site: www.lww.com (17)

Perry, Russell, Oklahoma Dept of Commerce, Oklahoma City, OK. Tel: (405) 815-6552, (800) 879-6552, FAX: (405) 815-5344, Web Site: www.okcommerce.com (1)

Perry, Scott, Bankers Life & Casualty Co, Chicago, IL. Tel: (312) 396-6000, (800) 231-9150, Web Site: www.bankerslife.com (15)

Perry, Scott, The Herald & Review, Decatur, IL. Tel: (217) 429-5151, FAX: (217) 421-6913, E-Mail: hrdirect@herald-review.com, Web Site: www.herald-review.com (17)

Perry, Wayne, Moultrie Manufacturing Co, Moultrie, GA. Tel: (229) 985-1312, (800) 841-8674, FAX: (229) 890-7245, Web Site: www.moultriemanufacturing.com (8)

Perrygraf, Carol Stream, IL. Tel: (630) 665-3333, (800) 323-4433, FAX: (630) 665-3491, E-Mail: info2@americanperrygraf.com, Web Site: www.perrygraf.com (16)

Perryman, Glen, Indianapolis Newspapers Inc, Indianapolis, IN. Tel: (317) 444-4444, FAX: (317) 633-9414, Web Site: www.indystar.com (17)

Persiani, Maurice, List Management Center, Hightstown, NJ. Tel: (609) 426-5695, FAX: (609) 426-5096, E-Mail: renee_krug@mcgraw-hill.com, Web Site: www.mcgraw-hill.com (24)

Person to Person Marketing LLC, Riverdale, NJ. Tel: (973) 835-8112, FAX: (973) 835-8525, E-Mail: sales@persontopersondirect.com, Web Site: www.persontopersondirect.com (29)

Personal Achievement Institute, Kingman, AZ. Tel: (928) 753-7546, (800) 321-1225, FAX: (928) 753-7554, E-Mail: burt@burtdubin.com, Web Site: www.speakingbizsuccess.com (17)

Personal Creations, Lemont, IL. Tel: (630) 783-2400, (866) 834-7695, Web Site: www.personalcreations.com (6)

Personnel Policy Service Inc, Louisville, KY. Tel: (502) 899-5102, (800) 437-3735, FAX: (800) 755-7011, E-Mail: info@ppspublishers.com, Web Site: www.ppspublishers.com (17)

Persson, Richard, RJ Persson Enterprises Inc, Montrose, CO. Tel: (303) 249-6000, FAX: (303) 249-0800 (16)

RJ Persson Enterprises Inc, Montrose, CO. Tel: (303) 249-6000, FAX: (303) 249-0800 (16)

Perusse, Edward, Home-Sew Inc, Bethlehem, PA. Tel: (610) 867-3833, (800) 344-4739, FAX: (610) 867-9717, Web Site: www.homesew.com (11)

Perusse, Lucy, Home-Sew Inc, Bethlehem, PA. Tel: (610) 867-3833, (800) 344-4739, FAX: (610) 867-9717, Web Site: www.homesew.com (11)

Perutz, Simon, Nimlok, Niles, IL. Tel: (847) 647-1012, (800) 233-8870, FAX: (847) 647-2044, E-Mail: info@nimlok.com, Web Site: www.nimlok.com (14)

Peruvian Connection Ltd, Tonganoxie, KS. Tel: (913) 845-2450, Web Site: www.peruvianconnection.com (2)

Pervin, Dan, University of Chicago Press, Chicago, IL. Tel: (773) 702-7700, FAX: (773) 702-9756, Web Site: www.press.uchicago.edu (17)

Pesce, William, Austin & Williams, Hauppauge, NY. Tel: (631) 231-6600, (888) 281-9200, FAX: (212) 434-7022, E-Mail: info@austin-williams.com, Web Site: www.austin-williams.com (21)

Pesce, William, J., Do It Yourself Direct Marketing, Hoboken, NJ. Tel: (201) 748-6000, FAX: (201) 748-6088, E-Mail: info@wiley.com, Web Site: www.wiley.com (43)

Pesce, William, J., John Wiley & Sons Inc, Hoboken, NJ. Tel: (201) 748-6000, FAX: (201) 748-6088, E-Mail: info@wiley.com, Web Site: www.wiley.com (17)

Peschke, Donald, August Home Publishing Co, Des Moines, IA. Tel: (515) 875-7000, FAX: (515) 282-6741, E-Mail: ask@workbenchmag.com, Web Site: www.augusthome.com (17)

Peskin, Kenny, International Sign Association International Convention, Alexandria, VA. Tel: (703) 836-4012, (866) WHY-SIGN, FAX: (703) 836-8353, Web Site: www.signs.org (42)

Peskowitz, Ed, United Communications Group, Gaithersburg, MD. Tel: (301) 287-2700, FAX: (301) 816-8945, E-Mail: webmaster@ucg.com, Web Site: www.ucg.com (17)

Pestarino, Bart, Sentinel Peak LLC, Redmond, WA. Tel: (360) 293-7271, Web Site: www.sentinel-peak.com (20)

Pestka, John, Bunzl Distribution USA, Inc, Saint Louis, MO. Tel: (314) 997-5959, (888) 997-5959, FAX: (314) 997-1405, Web Site: www.bunzldistribution.com (16)

Petco Animal Supplies, San Diego, CA. Tel: (858) 453-7845, (877) 738-6742, FAX: (858) 453-6585, Web Site: www.petco.com (5)

PetEdge, Beverly, MA. Tel: (978) 998-8100, (800) 738-3343, FAX: (978) 887-8499, E-Mail: support@petedge.com, Web Site: www.petedge.com (16)

Peter, Eugene W., Interstate Printing Co, Omaha, NE. Tel: (402) 341-8028, (800) 788-4177, FAX: (402) 341-6168, E-Mail: printer@interstateprinting.com, Web Site: www.interstateprinting.com (27)

Peter N Carey & Associates Inc, Oak Brook, IL. Tel: (630) 573-4260, (877) PNCAREY, FAX: (630) 573-0529, E-Mail: pncarey1@sbcglobal.net (20)

Peter Pan Bus Lines Inc, Springfield, MA. Tel: (413) 781-2900, (800) 343-9999, FAX: (413) 746-8671, E-Mail: info@peterpanbus.com, Web Site: www.peterpanbus.com (19)

Peter Pauls Nurseries, Canandaigua, NY. Tel: (716) 394-7397, FAX: (716) 394-4122, E-Mail: ippnurse@eznet.net (8)

PeterAlex Media Corp, Charlotte, NC. Tel: (704) 947-9082, (888) 818-3849, FAX: (704) 947-9083, E-Mail: info@peteralex.com, Web Site: www.peteralex.com (35)

J Peterman Co, Lexington, KY. Tel: (888) 647-2555, FAX: (859) 254-0869, Web Site: www.jpeterman.com (5)

Peters, Anelda, National Association of Professional Insurance Agents, Alexandria, VA. Tel: (703) 836-9340, FAX: (703) 836-1279, E-Mail: web@pianet.org, Web Site: www.pianet.com (1)

Peters, Charles M., Gazette Communications Inc, Cedar Rapids, IA. Tel: (319) 398-8211, (800) 397-8211, FAX: (319) 368-8834, Web Site: www.gazettecommunications.com (17)

Peters, David, Sellstrom Manufacturing Co, Palatine, IL. Tel: (847) 358-2000, (800) 323-7402, FAX: (847) 358-8564, E-Mail: sellstrom@sellstrom.com, Web Site: www.sellstrom.com (16)

Peters, Ed, Four Wheel Drive Hardware LLC, Columbiana, OH. Tel: (330) 482-4733, FAX: (330) 482-5035, E-Mail: info@4wd.com, Web Site: www.4wd.com (12)

Peters, Geoffrey, CDR Fundraising Group, Bowie, MD. Tel: (301) 858-1500, FAX: (301) 858-0107, Web Site: www.cdr-nfl.com (1)

Peters, Jenny, Premier Farnell Corp, Richfield, OH. Tel: (216) 525-4300, (800) 458-3222, FAX: (216) 525-4509, E-Mail: information@premierfarnell.com, Web Site: www.premierfarnell.com (16)

Peters, Kathy, Magna-Tel Inc, Cape Girardeau, MO. Tel: (573) 334-3096, FAX: (573) 335-1715, Web Site: www.magna.tel.com (5)

Peters, Lauren, B., Champs Corp, Bradenton, FL. Tel: (941) 748-0577, (800) 991-6813, E-Mail: customer_service@champssports.com, Web Site: www.champssports.com (11)

Peters, Mary, National Railroad Passenger Corp, Washington, DC. Tel: (202) 906-3000, (800) USA-RAIL, FAX: (202) 906-3306, Web Site: www.amtrak.com (16)

Peters, Pam, Airomat Corp, Fort Wayne, IN. Tel: (260) 747-7408, (800) 348-4905, FAX: (260) 747-7409, E-Mail: airomat@airomat.com, Web Site: www.mymatting.com (16)

Peters, Robert J., T O Printing & Mailing Services, Westlake Village, CA. Tel: (818) 991-0068 (23)

Peters, Sam, Specialty Envelope Inc, Cincinnati, OH. Tel: (513) 542-4700, (800) 288-8884, FAX: (513) 542-5260, E-Mail: info@specialtyenvelope.com, Web Site: www.specialtyenvelope.com (26)

Peters, Scott, Regions, Birmingham, AL. Tel: (205) 326-5262, FAX: (205) 326-4072, Web Site: www.regions.com (14)

Petersen, Kenneth, Direct Response Services, Glen Carbon, IL. Tel: (618) 288-8811, (800) 795-5478, FAX: (618) 288-3005, E-Mail: drs@drslist.com, Web Site: www.drslist.com (23)

Petersmark, Frank, L., Amerisure Insurance Cos, Farmington Hills, MI. Tel: (248) 615-9000, (800) 257-1900, FAX: (248) 615-8224, Web Site: www.amerisure.com (15)

Peterson Jr., Chester, Sunshine Unlimited Inc, Lindsborg, KS. Tel: (785) 227-3880, FAX: (785) 227-3880, E-Mail: cpeterjr@aol.com, Web Site: www.sunshine-unlimited.com (9)

Peterson, Anne M., World Innovators Inc, Roxbury, CT. Tel: (860) 210-8088, FAX: (860) 210-7829, E-Mail: apeterson@worldinnovators.com, Web Site: www.worldinnovators.com (24)

Peterson, Britt, Cole & Weber United, Seattle, WA. Tel: (206) 447-9595, Web Site: www.cwunited.com (35)

Peterson, Carl, Kansas City Chiefs, Kansas City, MO. Tel: (816) 920-9300, (888) 99-CHIEFS, FAX: (816) 923-4719, Web Site: www.kcchiefs.com (16)

Peterson, Chris, Integrated Marketing Solutions (IMS), Ashland, NE. Tel: (402) 486-3151, FAX: (402) 486-3161 (20)

Peterson, Cynthia, WRS Group Ltd, Waco, TX. Tel: (254) 776-6461, (800) 299-3366, FAX: (888) 977-7653, E-Mail: sales@wrsgroup.com, Web Site: www.wrsgroup.com (7)

Peterson, Deborah, Motient Communications, Reston, VA. Tel: (847) 478-4330, (800) 752-2672, FAX: (703) 758-6111 (16)

Peterson, George, C., AutoPacific Inc, Tustin, CA. Tel: (714) 838-4234, FAX: (714) 838-4260, Web Site: www.autopacific.com (30)

Peterson, Gretchen, Hanna Andersson Corp, Portland, OR. Tel: (503) 242-0920, (800) 222-0544, FAX: (503) 321-5289, Web Site: www.hannaandersson.com (2)

Peterson, Jason, Interactive Search Group, Cleveland, OH. Tel: (216) 255-3388, Web Site: www.isgstaffingnow.com (20)

Peterson, Joan, Davis Instruments Corp, Hayward, CA. Tel: (510) 732-9229, (510) 670-0589, E-Mail: info@davisnet.com, Web Site: www.davisnet.com (8)

Peterson, John, Ligonier Ministries, Lake Mary, FL. Tel: (407) 333-4244, (800) 435-4343, FAX: (407) 333-4377, Web Site: www.ligonier.org (5)

Peterson, John, TransFirst Holdings Inc, Dallas, TX. Tel: (214) 453-7700, (888) 254-4137, FAX: (214) 453-7739, Web Site: www.transfirst.com (14)

Peterson, Kathleen, Flynn, American Association for Justice, Washington, DC. Tel: (202) 965-3500, (800) 424-2725, FAX: (202) 625-7313, Web Site: www.justice.org (1)

Peterson, Kurt, Nilodor Inc, Bolivar, OH. Tel: (330) 874-1017, (800) 443-4321, FAX: (330) 874-3366, E-Mail: info@nilodor.com, Web Site: www.nilodor.com (16)

Peterson, Michelle, Aircraft Owners & Pilots Association, Frederick, MD. Tel: (301) 695-2000, (800) 872-2672, FAX: (301) 695-2375, E-Mail: aopahq@aopa.org, Web Site: www.aopa.org (1)

Peterson, Robin, Midwest Technology Products & Services, Sioux City, IA. Tel: (712) 252-3601, (800) 831-5904, FAX: (800) 258-7054, E-Mail: web@midwesttechnology.com, Web Site: www.midwesttechnology.com (9)

Peterson, Robin, New Mexico State University, Las Cruces, NM. Tel: (575) 646-0111, (505) 646-3341, FAX: (505) 646-1498, Web Site: www.nmsu.edu (41)

Peterson, Scott, First Direct Marketing LLC, Bellevue, NE. Tel: (402) 403-0000, (866) 363-9575, FAX: (402) 403-0001, E-Mail: sales@firstdirectmarketing.com, Web Site: www.firstdirectmarketing.com (23)

Peterson, Scott, Summit Racing Equipment, Tallmadge, OH. Tel: (330) 630-0270, FAX: (330) 630-5330, Web Site: www.summitracing.com (12)

Peterson, Timothy, NutraOrigin, Lake Success, NY. Tel: (516) 858-0301, Web Site: www.nutraorigin.com (7)

Peterson's, Lawrenceville, NJ. Tel: (609) 896-1800, FAX: (609) 896-1811, E-Mail: custsvc@petersons.com, Web Site: www.petersons.com (17)

Petra Industries, Edmond, OK. Tel: (405) 216-2100, Web Site: www.patra.com (34)

Petras, Michael B., GE Consumer & Industrial Lighting, Cleveland, OH. Tel: (216) 266-2222, (216) 266-2121, FAX: (216) 266-2930, Web Site: www.gelighting.com/na (16)

Petrea, Barry, Goodyear Tire & Rubber Co, Akron, OH. Tel: (330) 796-3250, Web Site: www.goodyear.com (16)

Petren, Carol, Ann, CIGNA International, Philadelphia, PA. Tel: (215) 761-1741, FAX: (215) 761-5515, Web Site: www.cigna.com (15)

Petro, Tom, JD Power Associates, Westlake Village, CA. Tel: (805) 418-8000, (888) 537-6937, FAX: (805) 418-8900, E-Mail: information@jdpa.com, Web Site: www.jdpower.com (30)

Petrocelli, Elaine, Book Passage Cafe, Corte Madera, CA. Tel: (415) 927-0960, (800) 999-7909, FAX: (415) 924-3838, Web Site: www.BookPassage.com (17)

Petroff, Chris, Gold Medal Products Co, Cincinnati, OH. Tel: (513) 769-7676, (800) 543-0862, FAX: (800) 542-1496, E-Mail: info@gmpopcorn.com, Web Site: www.gmpopcorn.com (16)

Petrone, Joanne, Blue Hill Marketing Solutions Inc, Pearl River, NY. Tel: (845) 627-6600, FAX: (845) 735-3985, Web Site: www.liftengine.com (22)

Petrosky, Mark, Duffey, Petrosky & Co, Farmington Hills, MI. Tel: (248) 489-8300, FAX: (248) 994-1600, E-Mail: info@dp-company.com, Web Site: www.dp-company.com (35)

Petrov, Bobbi, California Society of CPA's, San Mateo, CA. Tel: (800) 922-5272, FAX: (650) 522-3009, E-Mail: info@culcpa.org, Web Site: www.calcpa.org (1)

Petruzzelli, Diane, Grolier Publishing, Danbury, CT. Tel: (203) 797-3500, (800) 621-1115, FAX: (203) 797-3720, Web Site: www.grolier.com (17)

Petry Television Inc, New York, NY. Tel: (212) 230-5600, FAX: (323) 655-2862, E-Mail: info@petrymedia.com, Web Site: www.petrymedia.com (32)

Pets United LLC, Hazleton, PA. Tel: (570) 384-5555, (800) 738-7877, FAX: (570) 384-2500, E-Mail: customerservice@petsupplies.com, Web Site: www.allpets.com (13)

Petsky, Michael, Petsky Prunier LLC, New York, NY. Tel: (212) 842-6001, FAX: (212) 842-6039, Web Site: www.petskyprunier.com (14)

Petsky Prunier LLC, New York, NY. Tel: (212) 842-6001, FAX: (212) 842-6039, Web Site: www.petskyprunier.com (14)

PetSmart Inc, Phoenix, AZ. Tel: (623) 587-2009, (800) 738-1385, FAX: (623) 580-6183, Web Site: www.petsmart.com (5)

Pettenger, Roger, Prima-Nelson Printing Inc, Glenview, IL. Tel: (847) 729-8410, FAX: (847) 244-1421 (21)

Pettersen, Brian, Paasche Airbrush Co, Chicago, IL. Tel: (773) 867-9191, FAX: (773) 867-9198, E-Mail: info@paascheairbrush.com, Web Site: www.paascheairbrush.com (10)

Petty, Richard, Power Music, Salt Lake City, UT. Tel: (801) 292-2418, (800) 777-BEAT, FAX: (801) 292-2462, Web Site: www.powermusic.com (16)

Petty, Warren, Parsons School of Design Human Resource Dept, New York, NY. Tel: (212) 229-5671, FAX: (212) 229-8975, E-Mail: communications@newschool.edu, Web Site: www.parsons.edu (41)

Pew III, Robert, C., Steelcase Inc, Grand Rapids, MI. Tel: (616) 247-2710, FAX: (616) 475-2270, Web Site: www.steelcase.com (16)

Pfaelzer Brothers, Maumee, OH. Tel: (419) 893-7611, (800) 345-9290, FAX: (419) 893-0164, Web Site: www.phaelzerbrothers.com (16)

Pfaf, Sherry, National Agri Marketing Conference & Exposition, Overland Park, KS. Tel: (913) 491-6500, FAX: (913) 491-6502, E-Mail: agrimktg@nama.org, Web Site: www.nama.org (42)

Pfaltzgraff Co, York, PA. Tel: (717) 852-2211, (800) 999-2811, FAX: (800) 717-2481, E-Mail: service@pfaltzgraff.com, Web Site: www.pfaltzgraff.com (8)

Pfeffer, Adam, B., American Association of Individual Investors, Chicago, IL. Tel: (312) 280-0170, FAX: (312) 280-9883, E-Mail: adam@aaii.com, Web Site: www.aaii.com (1)

Pfeifer, Rick, American Trim, Lima, OH. Tel: (419) 228-1145, FAX: (419) 996-4850, E-Mail: sales@amtrim.com, Web Site: www.amtrim.com (9)

Pfeiffer, William, E., Commercial Lithographing Co Inc, Kansas City, MO. Tel: (816) 241-2218, FAX: (816) 241-6091, E-Mail: sjohnson@commercial-lithographing.com, Web Site: www.clitho.com (31)

Pfiefer, Marty, Light Sources Inc, Virginia Beach, VA. Tel: (757) 424-8636, (800) 882-8834, FAX: (757) 424-6186, E-Mail: lightsources@earthlink.net, Web Site: www.lightsourcesinc.com (16)

Pfister, Jim, PennWell Lists, Tulsa, OK. Tel: (918) 835-3161, (800) 331-4463, FAX: (918) 831-9497, Web Site: www.pennwell.com (24)

Pfizer Inc, New York, NY. Tel: (212) 733-2323, Web Site: www.pfizer.com (16)

Pflanzer, Carl, EWA & Miniature Cars USA Inc, Berkeley Heights, NJ. Tel: (732) 424-7811, (800) 392-4454, FAX: (732) 424-7814, E-Mail: ewa@ewacars.com (11)

Pfund, Katie, Heldref Publications, Washington, DC. Tel: (215) 625-8900, (202) 296-6267, FAX: (202) 296-5149, Web Site: www.heldref.org (17)

Pharmaceutical Care Management Association, Washington, DC. Tel: (202) 207-3610, FAX: (202) 207-3623, E-Mail: info@pcmanet.org, Web Site: www.pcmanet.org (1)

PharmArt, Circleville, OH. Tel: (860) 932-8588, (800) 848-1633, FAX: (800) 477-2923, Web Site: www.healthcarelogistics.com/Pharmart (6)

Pharmavite Corp LLC (HQ), Northridge, CA. Tel: (818) 221-6200, (800) 423-2405, FAX: (818) 221-6618, Web Site: www.pharmavite.com (16)

Pharris, Walt, Fairfield Industries Inc, Sugar Land, TX. Tel: (281) 275-7500, (800) 231-9809, FAX: (281) 275-7550, E-Mail: jblattman@fairfield.com, Web Site: www.fairfield.com (16)

Phelan, Mike, TransFirst ePayment Services, Omaha, NE. Tel: (888) 541-9800, Web Site: epay.transfirst.com (14)

Phelps, Craig, Amica Insurance, Lincoln, RI. Tel: (401) 334-6000, (800) 652-6422, FAX: (401) 334-4241, Web Site: www.amica.com (15)

Phelps, Steven, M., NGL Insurance Group, Madison, WI. Tel: (608) 257-5611, (800) 548-2962, FAX: (608) 257-9340, Web Site: www.nationalguardian.com (15)

The Philadelphia Contributorship Insurance Co, Philadelphia, PA. Tel: (215) 627-1752, (800) 346-9229, E-Mail: info@contributorship.com, Web Site: www.contributorship.com (15)

Philadelphia Direct Marketing Association Inc, Havertown, PA. Tel: (215) 473-1668, FAX: (215) 477-1109, E-Mail: contact@the-pdma.org, Web Site: www.the-pdma.org (40)

The Philadelphia Inquirer & Daily News, Philadelphia, PA. Tel: (215) 854-2000, FAX: (215) 854-4788, Web Site: www.phil.com/inquirer (31)

Philadelphia Museum of Art, Philadelphia, PA. Tel: (215) 684-7840, Web Site: www.philamuseum.org (1)

Philip Morris USA Inc, Richmond, VA. Tel: (804) 274-2000, FAX: (804) 484-8231, Web Site: www.philipmorrisusa.com (16)

Philips, Richard, Houlihan Lokey Howard & Zukin, Los Angeles, CA. Tel: (310) 553-8871, (800) 788-5300, FAX: (310) 553-2173, Web Site: www.hlhz.com (14)

Philips Lifeline, Framingham, MA. Tel: (508) 988-1533, Web Site: www.lifelinesys.com (7)

Phillips, Al, Progressive Business Publications, Malvern, PA. Tel: (610) 695-8600, (800) 220-5000, FAX: (610) 647-8089, E-Mail: customer_service@pbp.com, Web Site: www.pbp.com (17)

Phillips, Carol, Promotional Product Professionals of Canada, Saint-Laurent, PQ. Tel: (514) 489-5359, FAX: (514) 489-7760, (800) 489-8741, E-Mail: gladys@pppc.ca, Web Site: www.pppc.ca (1)

Phillips, Cathy, Publishers Press Inc, Shepherdsville, KY. Tel: (502) 955-6526, Web Site: www.pubpress.com (27)

Phillips, Dale, W., Methode Electronics Inc, Chicago, IL. Tel: (708) 867-6777, FAX: (708) 867-6999, E-Mail: info@methode.com, Web Site: www.methode.com (9)

Phillips, Dennis, Hamilton Watch, Weehawken, NJ. Tel: (201) 271-1400, (800) 243-8463, Web Site: www.hamiltonwatches.com (16)

Phillips, Don, Morningstar Inc, Chicago, IL. Tel: (312) 696-6000, Web Site: www.morningstar.com (14)

Phillips, Glenna, Direct Marketing Association of Saint Louis, Washington, MO. Tel: (866) 516-0121, FAX: (636) 239-2324, E-Mail: mparisien@mac.com, Web Site: www.dmastl.org (40)

Phillips, Gordon B., Seedburo Equipment Co, Des Plaines, IL. Tel: (312) 738-3700, (800) 284-5779, FAX: (312) 738-5329, E-Mail: sales@seedburo.com, Web Site: www.seedburo.com (8)

Phillips, John, Sisk Fulfillment Service Inc, Federalsburg, MD. Tel: (410) 754-8141, FAX: (410) 754-8223, Web Site: www.siskfulfillment.com (22)

Phillips, Larry, Foremost Industrial Exchange, Van Nuys, CA. Tel: (818) 988-6900, FAX: (818) 787-0293 (16)

Phillips, Lisa, Faith, Random House Direct Marketing, New York, NY. Tel: (212) 572-4985, (800) 678-5681, FAX: (212) 572-6018, Web Site: www.randomhousedirect.com (17)

Phillips, Marc, C., Promotional Product Professionals of Canada, Saint-Laurent, PQ. Tel: (514) 489-5359, FAX: (514) 489-7760, (800) 489-8741, E-Mail: gladys@pppc.ca, Web Site: www.pppc.ca (1)

Phillips, Nick, American Baseball Coaches Association, Mount Pleasant, MI. Tel: (989) 775-3300, FAX: (989) 775-3600, E-Mail: abca@abca.org, Web Site: www.abca.org (1)

Phillips, Scott, APS Technologies, Hillsboro, OR. Tel: (503) 844-4500, (800) 233-7550, FAX: (503) 844-4508, E-Mail: sales@lacie.com, Web Site: www.lacie.com (35)

Phillips, Thomas, J., InvestorPlace Media LLC, Rockville, MD. Tel: (800) 219-8592, Web Site: www.investorplace.com (24)

Phillips, Thomas, L., Eagle Publishing, Washington, DC. Tel: (202) 216-0600, FAX: (202) 216-0612, Web Site: www.eaglepub.com (17)

Phillips, Tina, Phillips Direct Marketing Group, Scottsdale, AZ. Tel: (480) 368-7200 X224, FAX: (480) 368-7222, E-Mail: tina@pdmg.tv, Web Site: www.pdldrtv.com (35)

Phillips Direct Marketing Group, Scottsdale, AZ. Tel: (480) 368-7200 X224, FAX: (480) 368-7222, E-Mail: tina@pdmg.tv, Web Site: www.pdldrtv.com (35)

Phillips Kiln Service LTD, South Sioux City, NE. Tel: (402) 494-6837, (800) 831-0876, FAX: (402) 494-6858, E-Mail: info@kilm.com, Web Site: www.kiln.com (16)

Phillips-Van Heusen Corp, New York, NY. Tel: (212) 381-3500, (800) 388-9122, FAX: (212) 381-3950, Web Site: www.pvh.com (2)

Phinn, Cynthia, Orion Telescopes & Binoculars, Watsonville, CA. Tel: (831) 763-7000, (800) 447-1001, FAX: (408) 763-7017, E-Mail: sales@telescope.com, Web Site: www.telescope.com (11)

Phipps, Cynthia, The Animal Medical Center, New York, NY. Tel: (212) 838-8100, FAX: (212) 832-9630, Web Site: www.amcny.org (16)

Phoenix Data Processing, Westmont, IL. Tel: (630) 654-4400, FAX: (630) 654-4470, E-Mail: sales@phoenixdataprocessing.com, Web Site: www.phoenixdataprocessing.com (22)

Phoenix Learning Group Inc, Maryland Heights, MO. Tel: (314) 569-0211, (800) 221-1274, FAX: (314) 569-2834, E-Mail: dealersales@phoenixlearninggroup.com, Web Site: www.phoenixlearninggroup.com (16)

Phoenix Marketing Group Ltd, Georgetown, CT. Tel: (203) 762-8665, FAX: (203) 762-8285 (21)

Phoenix Marketing International, Horsham, PA. Tel: (215) 392-0264, Web Site: www.phoenixmi.com (30)

Phoenix Poke Boats Inc, McKee, KY. Tel: (606) 965-2803, E-Mail: pokeboat@pokeboat.com, Web Site: www.pokeboat.com (16)

Phoenix Technologies Ltd, Milpitas, CA. Tel: (408) 570-1000, (800) 677-7305, FAX: (408) 570-1001, Web Site: www.phoenix.com (22)

Phomsopha, Sam, TechniServe Inc, Troy, MI. Tel: (248) 989-0100, FAX: (248) 989-0111, E-Mail: info@techni-serve.com, Web Site: www.techni-serve.com (22)

Phone Bank Systems Inc, East Lansing, MI. Tel: (517) 332-1500, FAX: (517) 332-1514, E-Mail: rusha@phonebanks.com, Web Site: www.phonebanks.com (1)

Photo Researchers Inc, New York, NY. Tel: (212) 758-3420, (800) 833-9033, FAX: (212) 355-0731, E-Mail: info@photoresearchers.com, Web Site: www.photoresearchers.com (38)

Photo Shuttle Japan, Chapel Hill, NC. Tel: (919) 967-1585, E-Mail: sonia@photoshuttle.com, Web Site: www.photoshuttle.com (37)

PhotoEdit Inc, Costa Mesa, CA. Tel: (800) 860-2098, FAX: (800) 804-3707, E-Mail: sales@photoeditinc.com, Web Site: www.photoeditinc.com (38)

Photofest, New York, NY. Tel: (212) 633-6330, FAX: (212) 366-9062, E-Mail: requests@photofestnyc.com (38)

Photographer's Formulary Inc, Condon, MT. Tel: (406) 754-2891, (800) 922-5255, FAX: (406) 754-2896, E-Mail: formulary@blackfoot.net, Web Site: www.photoformulary.com (9)

Photographer's Market, Blue Ash, OH. Tel: (513) 531-2690, FAX: (513) 531-2686, E-Mail: photomarket@fwpubs.com, Web Site: www.photographersmarket.com (43)

Photographic Society of America Inc (PSA), Oklahoma City, OK. Tel: (405) 843-1437, FAX: (405) 843-1438, E-Mail: HQ@psa-photo.org, Web Site: www.psa-photo.org (40)

Photographix, Ann Arbor, MI. FAX: (734) 476-2068, E-Mail: lkburghardt@comcast.net (37)

PhotoSource International, Osceola, WI. Tel: (715) 248-3800, X27, (800) 223-3860, FAX: (715) 248-3800, E-Mail: info@photosource.com, Web Site: www.photosource.com (38)

PhotoStamps.com, Los Angeles, CA. Tel: (310) 482-5800, Web Site: www.photostamps.com (5)

Phototake/The Creative Link, New York, NY. Tel: (212) 736-2525, (800) 542-3686, FAX: (212) 736-1919, E-Mail: photoinfo@phototakeusa.com, Web Site: www.phototakeusa.com (38)

Photoworks, Cleveland, OH. Tel: (206) 281-1390, (800) PHOTOWORKS, FAX: (206) 284-5357, E-Mail: info@photoworks.com, Web Site: www.photoworks.com (16)

Photri Images LLC, Fairfax, VA. Tel: (703) 978-0129, E-Mail: info@photriimages.com, Web Site: www.photriimages.com (38)

Physical Therapy Institute Inc, Poway, CA. Tel: (858) 485-7103 (16)

Physicians Mutual Insurance Co, Omaha, NE. Tel: (402) 633-1604, (888) 932-7642, FAX: (402) 633-1604, Web Site: www.physiciansmutual.com (15)

Physicians Planning Association Services, Deerfield Beach, FL. Tel: (954) 571-1877, (800) 221-2168, FAX: (954) 571-8582, E-Mail: insurance@assnservices.com, Web Site: www.physiciansplanning.com (16)

Piccinno, Patrick, J., IHOP Corp, Glendale, CA. Tel: (818) 240-6055, FAX: (818) 553-3131, Web Site: www.ihop.com (16)

Piccolo, Mara, Marimac Inc, Montreal, PQ. Tel: (514) 725-7600, FAX: (514) 376-0801, Web Site: www.marimac.com (8)

Pichotta, Nicholas, J., Cooper Surgical Inc, Trumbull, CT. Tel: (203) 601-5200, (800) 645-3670, FAX: (203) 601-1007, Web Site: www.coopersurgical.com (7)

Pick, Robert, Father Flanagan's Boy's Home, Boys Town, NE. Tel: (402) 498-1934, FAX: (402) 498-1969, Web Site: www.boystown.org (1)

Pickard, J., Adam, Georgia Power, Atlanta, GA. Tel: (404) 506-3440 (16)

Pickelle, Curtis, Practice Builders, Irvine, CA. Tel: (714) 751-7960, (800) 679-1262, FAX: (714) 751-7801, E-Mail: info@practicebuilders.com, Web Site: www.practicebuilders.com (35)

Picket, Jenny, National Agri Marketing Conference & Exposition, Overland Park, KS. Tel: (913) 491-6500, FAX: (913) 491-6502, E-Mail: agrimktg@nama.org, Web Site: www.nama.org (42)

Pickett, David, Interface Engineering, Portland, OR. Tel: (503) 382-2266, FAX: (503) 382-2262, E-Mail: solutions@interfaceengineering.com, Web Site: www.ieice.com (20)

Picknelly, Peter A., Peter Pan Bus Lines Inc, Springfield, MA. Tel: (413) 781-2900, (800) 343-9999, FAX: (413) 746-8671, E-Mail: info@peterpanbus.com, Web Site: www.peterpanbus.com (19)

Pickwoad, Lauren, Safeguard Business Systems Inc, Dallas, TX. Tel: (214) 905-3935, (800) 523-2422, FAX: (800) 439-8423, Web Site: www.gosafeguard.com (16)

Picon, Michael, Redbook Magazine, New York, NY. Tel: (212) 649-2000, (800) 888-0008, FAX: (212) 581-7605, Web Site: www.redbookmag.com (17)

Picone, Terrence, Etchworld, Hawthorne, NJ. Tel: (973) 423-4002, (800) 872-3458, FAX: (973) 427-8823, Web Site: www.etchworld.com (11)

Piecka, Rosalyn, MM Batch, Westhampton Beach, NY. Tel: (212) 737-0700, FAX: (212) 454-1124, E-Mail: christine@bannerdirect.com, Web Site: www.bannerdirect.com (35)

Pier 1 Imports Inc, Fort Worth, TX. Tel: (817) 252-8000, Web Site: www.pier1.com (8)

Pierce, Christopher, A., The Dingley Press, Lisbon, ME. Tel: (207) 353-4151, (800) 317-4574, FAX: (207) 353-9886, E-Mail: webrequest@dingley.com, Web Site: www.dingley.com (27)

Pierce, Kelly, Armento Inc, Buffalo, NY. Tel: (716) 875-2423, (866) 276-3686, FAX: (716) 875-8011, E-Mail: armento@aol.com, Web Site: www.armento-columbarium.com (5)

Pierce, Larry, Colorlith Corp, Providence, RI. Tel: (508) 837-6100, (800) 556-7171, FAX: (508) 677-4466, E-Mail: lep@colorlith.net, Web Site: www.colorlith.net (27)

Pierce, Lea, Lea Pierce Direct Response Strategy & Execution, Santa Rosa, CA. Tel: (707) 571-1586, (800) 932-4748, E-Mail: info@leapierce.com, Web Site: www.leapierce.com (39)

Pierce, Robert, Armento Inc, Buffalo, NY. Tel: (716) 875-2423, (866) 276-3686, FAX: (716) 875-8011, E-Mail: armento@aol.com, Web Site: www.armento-columbarium.com (5)

Lea Pierce Direct Response Strategy & Execution, Santa Rosa, CA. Tel: (707) 571-1586, (800) 932-4748, E-Mail: info@leapierce.com, Web Site: www.leapierce.com (39)

Pierer, Stefan, KTM Sportmotorcycle USA Inc, Amherst, OH. Tel: (440) 985-3553, FAX: (440) 985-3060, Web Site: www.ktmusa.com (16)

Pierson, Alan, Land O' Lakes Inc, Arden Hills, MN. Tel: (651) 481-2222, (800) 328-9680, FAX: (651) 481-2000, Web Site: www.landolakes.com (16)

Pierson, Dave, CPI Corp, St Louis, MO. Tel: (314) 231-1575, (877) 763-4456, FAX: (314) 231-8150, E-Mail: feedback@cpicorp.com, Web Site: www.cpicorp.com (16)

Pierzynski, Ed, Thomas Scientific, Swedesboro, NJ. Tel: (800) 345-2100, FAX: (856) 467-3087, E-Mail: value@thomassci.com, Web Site: www.thomassci.com (9)

Pieter, Andy, Direct List Technology Inc, Orange, CA. Tel: (714) 772-3282, (888) 772-6947, FAX: (714) 772-6947, E-Mail: apieter@directlist.com, Web Site: www.directlist.com (23)

Pietranton, Arlene, American Speech-Language-Hearing Association, Rockville, MD. Tel: (301) 897-5700, (800) 638-8255, E-Mail: productsales@asha.org, Web Site: www.asha.org (1)

Pietsch, Gary L., Selkirk Press, Sandpoint, ID. Tel: (208) 263-7523, FAX: (208) 263-2229, E-Mail: selkirkpress@nidlink.com (27)

Pifke, Robert, Visa USA, Foster City, CA. Tel: (650) 432-3200, FAX: (650) 432-2875, Web Site: www.visa.com (14)

Piggott, Mark, C., PACCAR Inc, Bellevue, WA. Tel: (425) 468-7400, FAX: (425) 468-8216, Web Site: www.paccar.com (16)

Pike, Debbie, AFA Service Corp, Atlanta, GA. Tel: (404) 262-2729, (404) 237-2964, Web Site: www.arbys.com (16)

Pike, Dorothy, A., Pike Communications Inc, Beverly, MA. Tel: (978) 524-8777, (800) 331-7453, FAX: (978) 524-8585, E-Mail: info@pikecommunications.com, Web Site: www.pikecommunications.com (35)

Pike, Gerry, DMSA Inc, Newfoundland, PA. Tel: (570) 676-6000 (40)

Pike Communications Inc, Beverly, MA. Tel: (978) 524-8777, (800) 331-7453, FAX: (978) 524-8585, E-Mail: info@pikecommunications.com, Web Site: www.pikecommunications.com (35)

Pilani's Live in Style, Egg Harbor Township, NJ. Tel: (609) 927-4686, (800) 537-1832, FAX: (609) 927-5686, E-Mail: sihart@aol.com (2)

Pilgrim Printed Promotional Plastics, Brockton, MA. Tel: (508) 436-6300, (800) 343-7810, FAX: (508) 580-3542, E-Mail: pilgrimsales@pilgrimplastics.com, Web Site: www.pilgrimplastics.com (27)

Piller, Herbert, Merit Industries Inc, Georgetown, TX. Tel: (512) 863-8541, (800) 637-4823, FAX: (512) 863-9861 (33)

The Pillsbury Co, Minneapolis, MN. Tel: (763) 764-7600, (800) 775-4777, FAX: (763) 764-8330, Web Site: www.pillsbury.com (16)

Pillsbury Winthrop Shaw Pittman LLP, Los Angeles, CA. Tel: (213) 488-7100, Web Site: www.pillsburywinthrop.com (20)

Pilot Direct, Norfolk, VA. Tel: (757) 446-2874, Web Site: www.pilotdirect.com (35)

The Pin Man, Tulsa, OK. Tel: (918) 587-2405, FAX: (918) 745-2162, Web Site: www.positivepin.com (16)

Pinchuk, Nicholas T., Snap-on Inc, Kenosha, WI. Tel: (262) 656-5200, (800) 866-5748, (800) 786-6600, FAX: (262) 656-5577, Web Site: www.snapon.com (9)

Pincus, Walter, Handy Store Fixtures Inc, Newark, NJ. Tel: (973) 242-1600, (800) 631-4280, FAX: (973) 642-6222, Web Site: www.handystorefixtures.com (8)

Pine Castle Animal Hospital, Orlando, FL. Tel: (407) 855-5010 (16)

Pinelli, Marc, C., Accountants Education Group, Dallas, TX. Tel: (214) 373-3486, (800) 627-7310, FAX: (800) 627-7310, E-Mail: customerservice@accountantsed.com, Web Site: www.accountantsed.com (10)

Pines, Robert, Volt Delta, Blue Bell, PA. Tel: (610) 825-7720, FAX: (610) 567-5698, Web Site: www.voltdelta.com (22)

Pingry, Pat, Ideals Publications Inc, Nashville, TN. Tel: (615) 333-0478, FAX: (615) 781-1447, Web Site: www.idealspublications.com (17)

Pinheiro, John, FileMaker Inc, Santa Clara, CA. Tel: (408) 987-7347, Web Site: www.filemaker.com (22)

Pinkerton, Debbie, Promotional Product Professionals of Canada, Saint-Laurent, PQ. Tel: (514) 489-5359, FAX: (514) 489-7760, (800) 489-8741, E-Mail: gladys@pppc.ca, Web Site: www.pppc.ca (1)

Pinkerton III, Henry, Fluid Metering Inc, Syosset, NY. Tel: (516) 922-6050, (800) 223-3388, FAX: (516) 624-8261, E-Mail: pumps@fmipump.com, Web Site: www.fmipump.com (16)

Pinkerton Security & Investigation Services, Parsippany, NJ. Tel: (973) 397-2276, (800) 724-1616, FAX: (973) 397-2491, Web Site: www.ci-pinkerton.com (16)

Pinkin, James E., The Corporate Communications Group, West Caldwell, NJ. Tel: (973) 808-1444, FAX: (973) 808-9740, E-Mail: useccg@corpcomm.com, Web Site: www.corpcomm.com (21)

Pinkin, Jim, Central Letter Shop Inc, West Caldwell, NJ. Tel: (973) 808-9595, FAX: (973) 808-8339, E-Mail: lena@centrallettershop.com, Web Site: www.centrallettershop.com (23)

Pinkston, Susan, Stonebridge Press Ltd, Henderson, KY. Tel: (270) 826-0341, FAX: (270) 826-8325 (33)

Pinnacle Direct Response, North York, ON Canada. Tel: (416) 756-9536 (35)

Pinnacle List Co, Arlington, VA. Tel: (703) 379-4394, FAX: (703) 379-5312, E-Mail: holly@pinnlistco.com, Web Site: www.pinnlistco.com (23)

Pinnacle Orchards, Maumee, OH. Tel: (419) 893-7611, (800) 442-5671, FAX: (419) 893-0164, Web Site: www.pinnacleorchards.com (4)

Pinnell, Jon, MarketVision Research Inc, Cincinnati, OH. Tel: (513) 791-3100, FAX: (513) 794-3500, E-Mail: jpinnell@mv-research.com, Web Site: www.marketvisionresearch.com (30)

Pino, Michael, M., CACI International Inc, Arlington, VA. Tel: (703) 841-7800, FAX: (703) 841-7882, Web Site: www.caci.com (22)

Pinson, Ray, OPIN Systems Inc, Bloomington, MN. Tel: (651) 994-6555, (800) 888-1804, FAX: (651) 994-7828, E-Mail: judywy@opin.com, Web Site: www.opin.com (22)

Pintaudi-Jones, Rose, Oxford University Press Inc, New York, NY. Tel: (212) 726-6000, FAX: (212) 726-6455, Web Site: www.oup.com/us/ (17)

Pintozzi, Fran, Tri-Media Marketing Services Inc, Wilmette, IL. Tel: (800) 874-4062, Web Site: www.trimediaonline.com (23)

The Pioneer Group, Waterloo, IA. Tel: (319) 234-8969, FAX: (319) 234-8518, E-Mail: jslife@thepioneergroup.com, Web Site: www.pioneergroup.com (28)

Pioneer Hi-Bred International Inc, Johnston, IA. Tel: (515) 270-3200, FAX: (515) 270-3581, E-Mail: web.editor@pioneer.com, Web Site: www.pioneer.com (4)

PIP Printing and Marketing Services, Indianapolis, IN. Tel: (317) 849-6244, Web Site: www.pip.com/pipindy (27)

Piper Jaffray, Minneapolis, MN. Tel: (612) 303-0000, Web Site: www.pjc.com (14)

Pipkin, Karen, IAEE Annual Meeting and Exhibition, Dallas, TX. Tel: (972) 458-8002, FAX: (972) 458-8119, E-Mail: info@iaee.com, Web Site: www.iaee.com (42)

Pippen, Carole, Lippincott, Williams & Wilkins, Baltimore, MD. Tel: (410) 528-4000, (800) 638-0672, FAX: (410) 528-8597, E-Mail: customerservice@lww.com, Web Site: www.lww.com (17)

Piretra, Judy, Cornwell Data Services Inc, Paramus, NJ. Tel: (201) 261-1050, FAX: (201) 261-7569, E-Mail: jpiretra@cornwelldata.com, Web Site: www.cornwelldata.com (22)

Pirri, Sue, Autodesk Inc, San Rafael, CA. Tel: (415) 507-5000, FAX: (415) 507-5100, Web Site: www.autodesk.com (16)

Pirroni, John, Target Direct Marketing Inc, Gloucester, MA. Tel: (978) 281-5967, Web Site: www.targetdirectmarketing.com (35)

Piszel, Anthony, S., Federal Home Loan Mortgage Corp (Freddie Mac), McLean, VA. Tel: (703) 903-2000, (800) 424-5401, Web Site: www.freddiemac.com (14)

Pitney Bowes, Stamford, CT. Tel: (203) 356-5000, (800) MR-BOWES, Web Site: www.pitneybowes.com (10)

Pitney Bowes International Mail Services, Newark, NJ. Tel: (800) 521-0080, FAX: (973) 368-6301, E-Mail: marketing@pb.com, Web Site: www.intmail.com (28)

Pitney Bowes of Canada Limited, Mississauga, ON Canada. Tel: (905) 219-3000, (866) 669-6627, FAX: (905) 219-3826, Web Site: www.pitneybowes.ca (34)

Pitney Bowes Software Systems, Stamford, CT. Tel: (800) 624-5377, Web Site: www.pitneybowes.com (22)

Pitsor, Kyle, National Electrical Manufacturers Association (NEMA), Rosslyn, VA. Tel: (703) 841-3200, FAX: (703) 841-5900, E-Mail: communications@nema.org, Web Site: www.nema.org (34)

Pittenger, Karen, Black Olive Co, Chicago, IL. Tel: (312) 893-5454, FAX: (312) 276-8636, E-Mail: pittenger@blackoliveco.com, Web Site: www.blackoliveco.com (35)

Pittman, Sean, Plattform Advertising, Lenexa, KS. Tel: (913) 254-6000, (800) 279-9988, FAX: (913) 538-5078, E-Mail: info@plattformad.com, Web Site: www.plattformad.com (35)

Pittman & Davis Inc, Harlingen, TX. Tel: (956) 423-2154, (800) 289-7829, FAX: (866) 329-7829, E-Mail: fruit@pittmandavis.com, Web Site: www.pittmandavis.com (4)

Pittsburgh Mailing, Pittsburgh, PA. Tel: (412) 922-8181, FAX: (412) 937-1730, E-Mail: ksmallhoover@pittsburghmailing.com, Web Site: www.pittsburghmailing.com (28)

Pittsburgh Parks Conservancy, Pittsburgh, PA. Tel: (412) 682-7275, Web Site: www.pittsburghparks.org (1)

Piunno, Frank, Marketing Communication Resource Inc, Willoughby, OH. Tel: (440) 484-3010, FAX: (440) 484-3020 (28)

Piusz, Peter, Beckmann Converting Inc, Amsterdam, NY. Tel: (518) 842-0073, FAX: (518) 842-0282, E-Mail: ppiusz@beckmannconverting.com, Web Site: www.beckmannconverting.com (16)

Pivnick, Charles, Cable Car Clothiers/Robert Kirk Ltd, San Francisco, CA. Tel: (415) 397-4740, FAX: (415) 616-8998, E-Mail: info@cablecarclothiers.com, Web Site: www.cablecarclothiers.com (2)

Pivnick, Janice, Cable Car Clothiers/Robert Kirk Ltd, San Francisco, CA. Tel: (415) 397-4740, FAX: (415) 616-8998, E-Mail: info@cablecarclothiers.com, Web Site: www.cablecarclothiers.com (2)

Pizarro, Lorraine, Bronx Council on the Arts, Bronx, NY. Tel: (718) 931-9500, FAX: (718) 409-6445, E-Mail: info@bronxarts.org, Web Site: www.bronxarts.org (1)

Pizza Hut Inc, Plano, TX. Tel: (972) 338-7700, (866) 298-6986, FAX: (972) 338-6869, Web Site: www.pizzahut.com (16)

Pizzano, Susan, Dr Leonard's Healthcare Corp, Edison, NJ. Tel: (732) 225-0100, FAX: (732) 225-0302, Web Site: www.doctorleonard.com (7)

Pizzella, Barbara, Office Depot, Boca Raton, FL. Tel: (561) 438-4800, (800) 937-3600, FAX: (561) 438-4001, Web Site: www.officedepot.com (16)

The Plain Dealer, Cleveland, OH. Tel: (216) 999-5000, FAX: (216) 999-6356, Web Site: www.plaindealer.com (18)

Plamieniak, Mary, Crossbow Group, Westport, CT. Tel: (203) 222-2244, FAX: (203) 226-7838, E-Mail: info@crossbowgroup.com, Web Site: www.crossbowgroup.com (40)

Plan USA, Warwick, RI. Tel: (401) 737-5770, (800) 556-7918, FAX: (401) 738-5608, Web Site: www.planusa.org (1)

Planet Cotton, Gaithersburg, MD. Tel: (301) 948-0400, FAX: (301) 948-9031, Web Site: www.planetcotton.com (2)

Planned Parenthood Federation of America, New York, NY. Tel: (212) 261-4686, Web Site: www.plannedparenthood.org (1)

Planned Parenthood Mar Monte, San Jose, CA. Tel: (408) 287-7532, FAX: (408) 971-6935, Web Site: www.plannedparenthood.org (1)

Plant, Roger, Truitt Brothers Inc, Salem, OR. Tel: (503) 362-3674, (800) 547-8712, FAX: (503) 588-2868, E-Mail: truittbrothers@truittbros.com, Web Site: www.truittbros.com (16)

Bud Plant Illustrated Books, Palo Alto, CA. Tel: (650) 493-1191, FAX: (650) 493-1145, E-Mail: jim@bpib.com, Web Site: www.bpib.com (6)

Plaskett, Thomas, G., Novell Inc, Waltham, MA. Tel: (801) 861-4272, (800) 529-3400, FAX: (781) 464-8100, E-Mail: crc@novell.com, Web Site: www.novell.com (22)

PLAS-TANKS Industries Inc, Hamilton, OH. Tel: (513) 942-3800, FAX: (513) 942-3993, E-Mail: info@plastanks.com, Web Site: www.plastanks.com (9)

Plastic Graphic, Wauconda, IL. Tel: (847) 487-2030, FAX: (847) 487-2050, E-Mail: bgrimespgc@sbcglobal.net, Web Site: www.plasticgraphic.com (27)

Plastic View ATC, Simi Valley, CA. Tel: (805) 520-9390, (800) 468-6301, FAX: (805) 520-0260, E-Mail: info@pvatc.com, Web Site: www.pvatc.com (9)

Plate, John, P., The CPW Group, Ronkonkoma, NY. Tel: (888) 641-7901 (28)

Platinum Press, Killingworth, CT. Tel: (860) 663-3882, FAX: (718) 825-5065, E-Mail: herbertjcohen@aol.com (17)

Platt, George R., The Harty Press Inc, New Haven, CT. Tel: (203) 562-5112, (800) 654-0562, FAX: (203) 782-9168, E-Mail: gplatt@hartynet.com, Web Site: www.hartynet.com (21)

Platt, Joel, The Bradford Group, Niles, IL. Tel: (847) 966-2770, FAX: (847) 581-8630, Web Site: www.collectiblestoday.com (16)

Platt, Mark, Heartland America, Chaska, MN. Tel: (952) 361-3640, (800) 229-2901, FAX: (952) 368-3452, E-Mail: info@heartlandamerica.com, Web Site: www.heartlandamerica.com (3)

Platt, Michael, Plattform Advertising, Lenexa, KS. Tel: (913) 254-6000, (800) 279-9988, FAX: (913) 538-5078, E-Mail: info@plattformad.com, Web Site: www.plattformad.com (35)

Plattform Advertising, Lenexa, KS. Tel: (913) 254-6000, (800) 279-9988, FAX: (913) 538-5078, E-Mail: info@plattformad.com, Web Site: www.plattformad.com (35)

Plawin, Paul, Campaigns & Elections Magazine, Arlington, VA. Tel: (703) 778-4028, (800) 771-8252, FAX: (703) 778-4024, Web Site: www.campaignsandelections.com (17)

Play Fair Toys, Boulder, CO. Tel: (303) 444-7502, (800) 824-7255, FAX: (303) 440-3393, E-Mail: service@playfairtoys.com, Web Site: www.playfairtoys.com (11)

Playboy Enterprises Inc, Beverly Hills, CA. Tel: (310) 860-1215, Web Site: www.playboyenterprises.com (17)

Player Piano Co Inc, Wichita, KS. Tel: (316) 263-3241, FAX: (316) 263-5480, Web Site: www.playerpianocompany.com (11)

Playworld Systems, Lewisburg, PA. Tel: (570) 522-9800, Web Site: www.playworldsystems.com (34)

Pleasant Company, Middleton, WI. Tel: (608) 836-4848, (800) 845-0005, FAX: (608) 836-1999, Web Site: www.americangirl.com (11)

Plecenski, Kathy, EDC Publishing, Tulsa, OK. Tel: (918) 622-4522, (800) 475-4522, FAX: (800) 747-4509, Web Site: www.edcpub.com (17)

Pletch, Evelyn, North American Co for Life & Health Insurance, Chicago, IL. Tel: (312) 648-7600, (800) 800-3656, FAX: (614) 365-9209, Web Site: www.nacolah.com (15)

Pleva, Lavena, Princess House Inc, Taunton, MA. Tel: (508) 832-6800, (508) 823-0711, (800) 622-0039, FAX: (508) 823-5182, Web Site: www.princesshouse.com (16)

Pleva, Randy, L., Paralyzed Veterans of America, Washington, DC. Tel: (202) 416-7636, (800) 424-8200, FAX: (202) 416-7643, E-Mail: info@pva.org, Web Site: www.pva.org (1)

Plexus Marketing Group Inc, Atlanta, GA. Tel: (770) 390-9692, (800) 9-PLEXUS, FAX: (770) 390-9693, Web Site: www.plexusmarketing.com (20)

Plimpton, Thomas, PACCAR Inc, Bellevue, WA. Tel: (425) 468-7400, (425) 468-8216, Web Site: www.paccar.com (16)

Pliny Jr, John, Sobelsohn School, New York, NY. Tel: (917) 441-9740, FAX: (917) 441-9740, E-Mail: sobelsohnschool@yahoo.com, Web Site: www.sobelsohnschool.com (23)

Plockinger, Harald, KTM Sportmotorcycle USA Inc, Amherst, OH. Tel: (440) 985-3553, FAX: (440) 985-3060, Web Site: www.ktmusa.com (16)

Plotnick, Stanley, Encore Marketing International, Lanham, MD. Tel: (301) 459-8020, (800) 846-9398, FAX: (301) 731-0525, E-Mail: customerservice@encoremarketing.com, Web Site: www.encoremarketing.com (16)

The Plow & Hearth Inc, Madison, VA. Tel: (540) 948-2272, (800) 494-7544, FAX: (540) 948-2273, Web Site: www.plowhearth.com (8)

Pluckhahn, William, MFS Investment Management, Boston, MA. Tel: (617) 954-6249, Web Site: www.mfs.com (14)

Pluris, Framingham, MA. Tel: (508) 663-1100, Web Site: www.plurisinc.com (22)

PlusMedia LLC, Danbury, CT. Tel: (203) 748-6500, FAX: (203) 748-6600, E-Mail: contact@plusme.com, Web Site: www.plusme.com (35)

PlusNetMarketing Inc, Exton, PA. Tel: (610) 458-0707, Web Site: www.pnmarketing.com (21)

Plusterer, Donald, Grower's Supply Co, Dexter, MI. Tel: (734) 426-5852, FAX: (734) 426-5750, E-Mail: growers@grower-supply.com, Web Site: www.growerssupplycompany.com (8)

Pluzynski, Ed, Pluzynski & Associates Inc, Fresh Meadows, NY. Tel: (212) 645-1414, FAX: (212) 645-2013, E-Mail: ed@pluzynski.com, Web Site: www.pluzynski.com (35)

Pluzynski & Associates Inc, Fresh Meadows, NY. Tel: (212) 645-1414, FAX: (212) 645-2013, E-Mail: ed@pluzynski.com, Web Site: www.pluzynski.com (35)

Pneuma Books, Elkton, MD. Tel: (410) 441-8200, FAX: (410) 441-8201, E-Mail: gettingstarted@pneumabooks.com, Web Site: www.pneumabooks.com (17)

Pocket Nurse Enterprises Inc, Monaca, PA. Tel: (800) 225-1600, FAX: (800) 763-0237, E-Mail: info@pocketnurse.com, Web Site: www.pocketnurse.com (7)

Pocock, J, Michael, Polaroid Corp, Minnetonka, MN. Tel: (781) 386-2000, (800) 765-2764, FAX: (781) 386-3263, Web Site: www.polaroid.com (16)

Podolec, Anna, National Crime Prevention Council, Amsterdam, NY. Tel: (518) 842-4388, (888) 776-7763, FAX: (800) 995-5121, E-Mail: mcgruff@spocentral.com, Web Site: www.mcgruffspo.com (17)

Poe, Karin, Cisco Systems Inc, San Jose, CA. Tel: (408) 526-4000, (800) 553-NETS, FAX: (408) 526-4100, Web Site: www.cisco.com (22)

Poehling, John, Torcom Inbound Telemarketing, Madison, WI. Tel: (800) 832-4939, FAX: (608) 275-6557, E-Mail: torcom@torcom.com, Web Site: www.torcom.com (29)

Poffenberger, Chase, Academic Travel Abroad Inc, Washington, DC. Tel: (202) 785-9000, (800) 556-7896, FAX: (202) 342-0317, Web Site: www.academictravel.com (19)

Pogell, Suzanne, Womanship, Annapolis, MD. Tel: (410) 267-6661, FAX: (410) 263-2036, E-Mail: sail@womanship.com, Web Site: www.womanship.com (14)

Pohaku Inc, Kailua, HI. Tel: (319) 653-2569, Web Site: www.gopohaku.com (20)

Pohly, Diana, The Pohly Co, Boston, MA. Tel: (617) 451-1700, (800) 383-0888, FAX: (617) 338-7767, E-Mail: info@pohlyco.com, Web Site: www.pohlyco.com (17)

The Pohly Co, Boston, MA. Tel: (617) 451-1700, (800) 383-0888, FAX: (617) 338-7767, E-Mail: info@pohlyco.com, Web Site: www.pohlyco.com (17)

Point To Point Marketing Inc, Fort Collins, CO. Tel: (970) 472-0131, Web Site: www.ptpmarketing.com (35)

PointOne Graphics Inc, Toronto, ON Canada. Tel: (416) 255-8202, Web Site: www.point-one.com (27)

Poker Player, Sherman Oaks, CA. Tel: (310) 674-3365, FAX: (310) 674-3205, E-Mail: ard@gamblingtimes.com, Web Site: www.gamblingtimes.com (17)

Pokrzyk, Steve, Vector Marketing Corp, Olean, NY. Tel: (716) 373-6141, FAX: (716) 373-6145, Web Site: www.cutco.com (5)

Polaris Direct, Hooksett, NH. Tel: (603) 626-5800, E-Mail: info@polarisdirect.net, Web Site: www.polarisdirect.net (28)

Polaroid Corp, Minnetonka, MN. Tel: (781) 386-2000, (800) 765-2764, FAX: (781) 386-3263, Web Site: www.polaroid.com (16)

Polatseck, David, DPC Computers, Monsey, NY. Tel: (845) 426-3790, (866) 513-CORP, FAX: (845) 426-6275, E-Mail: learnmore@salestax.com, Web Site: www.salestax.com (16)

Polcha, Jon, Blue Cross & Blue Shield of Oklahoma, Tulsa, OK. Tel: (918) 560-3500, (800) 942-5837, E-Mail: info@bcbsok.com, Web Site: www.bcbsok.com (15)

Poler, Noel, LatinLists, Miami, FL. Tel: (954) 302-1795, Web Site: www.latinlists.net (23)

Poles, Dave, McBee, Lancaster, CA. Tel: (973) 263-3225, (800) 878-9443, (800) 662-2331, FAX: (973) 263-8165, E-Mail: info@mcbeeinc.com, Web Site: www.mcbeeweb.com (10)

Polestar Group, West Simsbury, CT. Tel: (860) 658-4992 (20)

Polfliet, David, Apothecary Products Inc, Burnsville, MN. Tel: (952) 890-1940, (800) 328-2742, FAX: (800) 328-1584, Web Site: www.apothecaryproducts.com (7)

Policay, Barbara, Claritas Express, Ithaca, NY. Tel: (607) 257-5757, (866) 737-7429, FAX: (607) 266-0425, E-Mail: info@claritas.com, Web Site: www.claritas.com/express (30)

Policinski, Chris, Land O' Lakes Inc, Arden Hills, MN. Tel: (651) 481-2222, (800) 328-9680, FAX: (651) 481-2000, Web Site: www.landolakes.com (16)

Polinak, Peter, Hobart & William Smith Colleges, Geneva, NY. Tel: (315) 781-3000, (800) 852-2256, FAX: (315) 781-3655, Web Site: www.hws.edu (19)

Political Resources, Lake Worth, FL. Tel: (800) 423-2677, FAX: (561) 533-0104, E-Mail: info@politicalresources.com, Web Site: www.politicalresources.com (23)

Politti, Alicia, Clay Creative Direct, Lewis Center, OH. Tel: (740) 548-0307, FAX: (740) 548-0898, E-Mail: frank@claycreativegroup.com, marketing@claycreativegroup.com, Web Site: www.claydm.com (35)

Polizzi, Suzanne, REMEDY Magazine, New York, NY. Tel: (212) 695-2223, FAX: (212) 695-2936, E-Mail: info@rmedizine.com, Web Site: www.medizine.com (17)

Polk, Michael, Unilever Best Foods, Englewood Cliffs, NJ. Tel: (201) 567-8000, FAX: (201) 871-8257, E-Mail: comments@unilever.com, Web Site: www.unilever.com (16)

Polk, Stephen, RL Polk & Co, Southfield, MI. Tel: (248) 728-7100, (800) GO-4-POLK, FAX: (248) 728-4444, Web Site: www.polk.com (23)

Polkosky, Douglas, Thomas Computer Corp, Orlando, FL. Tel: (407) 855-2020, (800) 621-3906, FAX: (407) 426-2805, E-Mail: hildap@thomascompute.com, Web Site: www.thomascomputer.com (16)

Polkosky, Hilda, Thomas Computer Corp, Orlando, FL. Tel: (407) 855-2020, (800) 621-3906, FAX: (407) 426-2805, E-Mail: hildap@thomascompute.com, Web Site: www.thomascomputer.com (16)

Pollack, Daniel, Stock Yards Packing Co Inc, Chicago, IL. Tel: (312) 733-6050, (877) STK-YARD, FAX: (312) 733-1746, E-Mail: customerservice@stockyards.com, Web Site: www.stockyards.com (4)

Pollack, Jeffrey N., Harrah's Entertainment Inc, Las Vegas, NV. Tel: (702) 407-6000, FAX: (702) 407-6499, (702) 407-6500, Web Site: www.harrahs.com (19)

Pollack, Kathy, Christian Broadcasting Network Inc, Virginia Beach, VA. Tel: (757) 226-3542, FAX: (757) 226-2017, Web Site: www.cbn.org (1)

Pollack Graphics Inc, Lynbrook, NY. Tel: (800) 884-9140, FAX: (516) 599-8422, E-Mail: sales@pollack.com, Web Site: www.pollack.com (27)

Pollak, Isaac, LGP GEM LTD, New York, NY. Tel: (212) 840-2510, FAX: (212) 302-6182, E-Mail: sales@lgpltd.com, Web Site: www.lgpltd.com (16)

Pollitt, Ken, Woodworker's Supply Inc, Casper, WY. Tel: (307) 237-5528, (800) 645-9292, FAX: (307) 57-5272, E-Mail: kenp@woodworker.com, Web Site: www.woodworker.com (11)

Pollock, Brenda, School Annual Publishing Co, State College, PA. Tel: (800) 436-6030, E-Mail: yearbook@schoolannual.com, Web Site: www.schoolannual.com (17)

Pollock, Rob, Assurant Group, New York, NY. Tel: (305) 253-2244, FAX: (305) 252-6987, Web Site: www.assurant.com (15)

Pollyea, Steven, Roto-Rooter Services Co, Cincinnati, OH. Tel: (513) 762-6690, FAX: (513) 762-6590, Web Site: www.rotorooter.com (16)

Polo Ralph Lauren, Lyndhurst, NJ. Tel: (212) 531-6537, (800) 377-7656, FAX: (212) 318-7690, Web Site: www.ralphlauren.com (2)

Polomo, Nino, Blue Coral Slick 50, Houston, TX. Tel: (713) 241-6161, (800) 416-1600, FAX: (713) 241-4044, E-Mail: SCD-ConsumerSolutions@Shell.com, Web Site: www.bluecoral.com (16)

Poltrone, Kristi, Vita-Mix Corp, Cleveland, OH. Tel: (440) 235-4840, (800) VITA-MIX, FAX: (440) 235-3726, E-Mail: service@vitamix.com, Web Site: www.vitamix.com (16)

Polucci, Mike, TempoGraphics Inc, Carol Stream, IL. Tel: (630) 462-8200, FAX: (630) 462-0350 (27)

Poly-Flex Corp, Edgewood, NY. Tel: (631) 586-9500, FAX: (631) 586-6031, E-Mail: info@poly-flexcorp.com, Web Site: www.poly-flexcorp.com (26)

Poly One Corp, Avon Lake, OH. Tel: (440) 930-1000, (866) POLY-ONE, FAX: (440) 930-1428, Web Site: www.polyone.com (16)

Polyair Packaging, Chicago, IL. Tel: (773) 995-1818, (888) POLYAIR X444, FAX: (773) 995-7725, E-Mail: marketing@polyair.com, Web Site: www.polyair.com (9)

Polyline LLC, Elmhurst, IL. Tel: (630) 993-2700, (800) 701-3865, FAX: (800) 816-3330, Web Site: www.polylinecorp.com (3)

Polynesian Cultural Center, Honolulu, HI. Tel: (808) 293-3333, (800) 367-7060, FAX: (888) 722-7339, E-Mail: internetrez@polynesia.com, Web Site: www.polynesia.com (16)

Pomerantz, Michael H., F1rstmark Inc, Campton, NH. Tel: (603) 726-4800, (800) 729-2600, FAX: (603) 726-4840, E-Mail: info@firstmark.com, Web Site: www.firstmark.com (23)

Pomeroy, William G., Cablexpress Technologies, Syracuse, NY. Tel: (315) 476-3000, (800) 913-9467, FAX: (315) 455-1800, E-Mail: info@cablexpress.com, Web Site: www.CXTec.com (10)

Pompano, Carol, Anthem Blue Cross Blue Shield, North Haven, CT. Tel: (203) 239-8381, (800) 545-0948, FAX: (203) 985-7918, Web Site: www.anthem.com (15)

Pond, Dale, C., Lowe's Companies Inc, Mooresville, NC. Tel: (704) 758-1000, FAX: (336) 651-4766, Web Site: www.lowes.com (8)

Pond, Sara, Nightingale-Conant Corp, Niles, IL. Tel: (847) 647-0300, (800) 557-1660, FAX: (847) 647-7145, Web Site: www.nightingale.com (17)

The Pond-Ekberg Co, Chicopee, MA. Tel: (413) 594-7511, (800) 225-7511, FAX: (413) 594-2179, E-Mail: sales@pond-ekberg.com, Web Site: www.pondekberg.com (27)

Ponder, Dave, James Medical Rents & Sales Inc, Fort Wayne, IN. Tel: (260) 423-9571, E-Mail: sales@jamesmedical.com, Web Site: www.jamesmedical.net (7)

Poneta, Jim, Wilkes Direct Mail Co, Saint Louis, MO. Tel: (314) 776-5555, (800) 331-6441, FAX: (314) 776-0913, E-Mail: sales@wilkesdirect.com, Web Site: www.wilkesdirect.com (21)

Pont, Stefanie, Pont Media Direct, Norwalk, CT. Tel: (203) 354-8074, FAX: (203) 956-9227, E-Mail: stefanie@listgoddess.com, Web Site: www.pontmediadirect.com (23)

Pont Media Direct, Norwalk, CT. Tel: (203) 354-8074, FAX: (203) 956-9227, E-Mail: stefanie@listgoddess.com, Web Site: www.pontmediadirect.com (23)

Pontifical Mission Societies in the US, New York, NY. Tel: (212) 563-8700, Web Site: www.onefamilyinmission.org (1)

Pontis Group, Grosse Pointe, MI. Tel: (614) 764-1274, FAX: (614) 210-0598, E-Mail: cbirchfield@pontisgroup.com, Web Site: www.pontisgroup.com (35)

WS Ponton Inc, Pittsburgh, PA. Tel: (412) 782-2360, (800) 628-7806, FAX: (412) 782-1109, E-Mail: joseph@wsponton.com, Web Site: www.wsponton.com (23)

Ponzoni, Jaci, Pace Communications Inc, Greensboro, NC. Tel: (336) 378-6065, FAX: (336) 275-2864, Web Site: www.pacecommunications.com (17)

Pook, Barbara, Nutritional Research Associates Inc, South Whitley, IN. Tel: (260) 723-4931, (800) 456-4931, FAX: (260) 723-6297, E-Mail: info@nrfeeds.com, Web Site: www.nrfeeds.com (16)

Poole, Mark, M., Marsh US Consumer, Urbandale, IA. Tel: (515) 365-6102 (15)

Poole, Robert, Dome Printing, Sacramento, CA. Tel: (800) 343-3139 (27)

Pop Labs Inc, Houston, TX. Tel: (713) 243-4500, Web Site: www.poplabs.com (35)

Popalardo, Mike, Western Fulfillment Management Association Inc, North Hollywood, CA. Tel: (310) 323-7220, FAX: (310) 323-7231, E-Mail: mjordan@espcomp.com, Web Site: www.wfma.org (40)

The Popcorn Factory, Lake Forest, IL. Tel: (847) 362-0028, (888) 216-0235, FAX: (888) 333-4595, E-Mail: service@thepopcornfactory.com, Web Site: www.thepopcornfactory.com (4)

Pope, Alan, Finelight Inc, Louisville, KY. Tel: (502) 589-5896, E-Mail: info@finelight.com, Web Site: www.finelight.com (35)

Pope, Alice, Photographer's Market, Blue Ash, OH. Tel: (513) 531-2690, FAX: (513) 531-2686, E-Mail: photomarket@fwpubs.com, Web Site: www.photographersmarket.com (43)

Pope, Kate, North American Membership Group Inc, Minnetonka, MN. Tel: (952) 936-9333, FAX: (952) 936-9755, Web Site: www.namginc.com (13)

Pope, Richard, Win Craft Inc, Winona, MN. Tel: (507) 454-5510, (800) 533-8100, FAX: (507) 454-6403, Web Site: www.wincraftschool.com (5)

Pope, Wendell, Richartz Fliss Clark & Pope Inc, New York, NY. Tel: (212) 286-9339, FAX: (212) 682-4748, E-Mail: pope@rfcp.com (35)

Popkin Ph.D., Michael H., Active Parenting, Marietta, GA. Tel: (770) 429-0565, (800) 825-0060, (800) 235-7755, FAX: (770) 429-0334, E-Mail: cservice@activeparenting.com, Web Site: www.activeparenting.com (17)

Popovich, Deidre, NFIB - National Federation of Independent Business, Nashville, TN. Tel: (615) 872-5800, Web Site: www.nfib.com (1)

Popovich, Jeff, Microvideo Learning Systems, Inc, New York, NY. Tel: (403) 233-9411, (800) 231-4021, FAX: (800) 879-6857, E-Mail: info@microvideo.com, Web Site: www.microvideo.com (3)

Poppie, Sandy, ThreeSource Fulfillment, Manteno, IL. Tel: (815) 936-1094 x4179, (888) 673-4650, FAX: (815) 936-9743, E-Mail: sandyp@threesource.tv, Web Site: www.threesource.tv (28)

Popular Front Interactive Communications, Minneapolis, MN. Tel: (612) 362-0900, FAX: (612) 362-0999, E-Mail: guestlist@popularfront.com, Web Site: www.popularfront.com (35)

Population Connection, Washington, DC. Tel: (202) 332-2200, Web Site: www.populationconnection.net (1)

Porco, Carmela, Doubleday Direct, Scarborough, ON Canada. Tel: (416) 977-7891, FAX: (416) 977-8707 (13)

Pordes, Richard, Richard M Pordes LLC, Stamford, CT. Tel: (203) 316-9190 (1)

Richard M Pordes LLC, Stamford, CT. Tel: (203) 316-9190 (1)

Porepp, Cathy, Successful Farming, Des Moines, IA. Tel: (515) 284-2143, (800) 678-2711, FAX: (515) 284-3127 (17)

Porray, Dale, Amateur Electronic Supply LLC, Milwaukee, WI. Tel: (414) 558-0333, (800) 558-0411, FAX: (414) 358-3337, Web Site: www.aesham.com (16)

Porta-Bote International, Mountain View, CA. Tel: (650) 961-5334, (800) 227-8882, Web Site: www.porta-bote.com (11)

Portale, Carol, March of Dimes Birth Defects Foundation, White Plains, NY. Tel: (914) 428-7100, FAX: (914) 428-8203, Web Site: www.modimes.org (1)

Portelli, Alan, United Marketing Group LLC, Schaumburg, IL. Tel: (847) 240-2005, FAX: (847) 240-2177, E-Mail: info@unitedmarket.com, Web Site: www.unitedmarket.com (21)

Porter, Amy, National Osteoporosis Foundation, Washington, DC. Tel: (202) 721-6346, Web Site: www.nof.org (1)

Porter, Chris, JazzTimes Magazine Inc, Quincy, MA. Tel: (617) 706-9110, FAX: (617) 536-0102, E-Mail: info@jazztimes.com, Web Site: www.jazztimes.com (17)

Porter, Diane, NTL Institute, Arlington, VA. Tel: (703) 548-8840, (800) 277-4685, FAX: (703) 684-1256, E-Mail: info@ntl.org, Web Site: www.ntl.org (16)

Porter, Karen, Society for Healthcare Strategy & Market Development, Chicago, IL. Tel: (312) 422-3888, FAX: (312) 422-4579, E-Mail: stratsoc@aha.org, Web Site: www.stratsociety.org (42)

Porter Wallace Corp, Toms River, NJ. Tel: (732) 505-1675, FAX: (201) 505-1632, E-Mail: inquiries@ porterwallace.com, Web Site: www.porterwallace. com (33)

Porter's Camera Store Inc, Cedar Falls, IA. Tel: (319) 266-0303, (800) 553-2001, FAX: (800) 221-5329, E-Mail: bcondra@porters.com, Web Site: www. porters.com (3)

Porteus, Anna, Americatel Corp, Derwood, MD. Tel: (301) 610-4354, Web Site: www.startec.com (32)

Porteus, Anna, STARTEC, Rockville, MD. Tel: (310) 610-4300, Web Site: www.startec.com (32)

Portillo, Rhina, Liguori Publications, Liguori, MO. Tel: (636) 464-2500, (800) 325-9521, FAX: (800) 325-9526, E-Mail: liguori@liguori.org, Web Site: www.liguori.org (17)

Portland Cement Association, Skokie, IL. Tel: (847) 966-6200, FAX: (847) 966-9781, Web Site: www. cement.org (1)

Portland Rescue Mission, Portland, OR. Tel: (503) 906-7605, Web Site: www.portlandrescuemission. org (1)

Portman, Jeff, AMC Inc, Atlanta, GA. Tel: (404) 220-2000, FAX: (404) 220-3030 (2)

Porto-Lenza, Gia, CIT, Livingston, NJ. Tel: (973) 422-6040, FAX: (973) 740-5383, Web Site: www.cit. com (14)

Portrait International Inc, Boston, MA. Tel: (617) 457-5223, Web Site: www.portraitsoftware.com (22)

Posh Papers, Riverside, RI. Tel: (401) 331-9873, FAX: (401) 331-2229, E-Mail: info@poshpapersonline. com, Web Site: www.poshpapersonline.com (6)

Position Technologies Inc, Saint Charles, IL. Tel: (630) 262-5300, FAX: (630) 232-2998, Web Site: www.positiontech.com (16)

PossibleNOW Inc, Duluth, GA. Tel: (770) 255-1020, Web Site: www.dncsolution.com (22)

Post, Jeff, CUNA Mutual Group, Madison, WI. Tel: (608) 238-5851, (800) 356-2644, FAX: (608) 231-8839, Web Site: www.cunamutual.com (15)

Post, Jerry, Orchard Supply Hardware, San Jose, CA. Tel: (408) 281-3500, FAX: (408) 225-0388, Web Site: www.osh.com (16)

Post, Jim, Chattanooga Shooting Supplies Inc, Chatta-nooga, TN. Tel: (423) 894-3007, (800) 251-4808, FAX: (423) 855-5513, Web Site: www. chattanoogashooting.com (16)

Post Linx Corp, Scarborough, ON Canada. Tel: (416) 752-8100, FAX: (416) 752-8239, Web Site: www. postlinx.com (28)

Post University, Waterbury, CT. Tel: (203) 596-4520, (800) 345-2562, E-Mail: admissions@post.edu, Web Site: www.post.edu (41)

Postal En Espanol Inc, Tampa, FL. Tel: (813) 885-8888, Web Site: www.postalenespanol.com (20)

Posti, Steven, Periodical Publisher's Service Bureau Inc, Sandusky, OH. Tel: (419) 626-0623, (800) 220-1247, FAX: (419) 626-4576, Web Site: www. ppsb.com (18)

Postmatic Inc, Minneapolis, MN. Tel: (763) 784-6046, (888) 784-6046, FAX: (763) 784-9433, E-Mail: info@postmatic.net, Web Site: www.postmatic.com (34)

Postrel, Richard, Matrix, Miami Beach, FL. Tel: (305) 865-7000, FAX: (305) 864-3114 (30)

Posty Cards Inc, Kansas City, MO. Tel: (816) 231-2323, (800) 554-5018, FAX: (888) 577-3800, E-Mail: customerservice@postycards.com, Web Site: www.postycards.com (16)

Potawatomi Bingo Casino, Milwaukee, WI. Tel: (800) PAYS-BIG, Web Site: www.paysbig.com (19)

Potente, Ralph, CyberData, Hicksville, NY. Tel: (516) 942-8000, FAX: (516) 942-0800, E-Mail: info@ cyberdata.com, Web Site: www.cyberdata.com (22)

Potier, Bernard, Christian Dior Perfumes, New York, NY. Tel: (212) 931-2200, FAX: (212) 931-2954, Web Site: www.dior.com (7)

Potpourri Group Inc, Chelmsford, MA. Tel: (978) 256-4100, FAX: (978) 256-1961/0344, Web Site: www. potpourrigroup.com (6)

Potter, Duncan, Westcon, Tarrytown, NY. Tel: (914) 829-7000, FAX: (914) 829-7137, Web Site: www. westcon.com (16)

Potter, Vivanne, Amnesty International USA, New York, NY. Tel: (212) 807-8400, FAX: (212) 989-5478, E-Mail: vpotter@aiusa.org, Web Site: www. amnestyusa.org (1)

Pottle, Martin, K., Martin Thomas International, Bar-rington, RI. Tel: (401) 245-8500, FAX: (401) 245-0694, E-Mail: contact@martinthomas.com, Web Site: www.martinthomas.com (35)

Potts, Erwin, McClatchy Co, Sacramento, CA. Tel: (916) 321-1855, FAX: (916) 321-1869, Web Site: www.mcclatchy.com (17)

Potts, Jeffrey, C., The Company Store Inc, La Crosse, WI. Tel: (608) 785-1400, FAX: (608) 791-5790, Web Site: www.thecompanystore.com (16)

Potts, Jim, Clear Visions Inc, San Antonio, TX. Tel: (210) 496-6006, FAX: (210) 496-9225, E-Mail: bidrequest@clearvisionsinc.com, Web Site: www. clearvisionsinc.com (27)

Poulin, Pamela, Alfa Aesar-A Johnson Matthey Co, Ward Hill, MA. Tel: (800) 343-0660, FAX: (800) 322-4757, E-Mail: info@alfa.com, Web Site: www. alfa.com (9)

Poulsen, Susan, Papa John's International, Louisville, KY. Tel: (502) 261-7272, Web Site: www. papajohns.com (4)

Pound Sr., Alan, Epson America, Long Beach, CA. Tel: (562) 981-3840, (800) 873-7766, FAX: (562) 290-5220, Web Site: www.epson.com (10)

Pounders, Ambrosia, DataMentors LLC, Wesley Chapel, FL. Tel: (813) 960-7800, FAX: (813) 960-7811, E-Mail: 1bedgood@datamentors.com, Web Site: www.datamentors.com (22)

Poupard, Dennis, Gale Research Inc, Farmington Hills, MI. Tel: (248) 699-4253, (800) 877-GALE, FAX: (313) 961-6083, Web Site: www.gale.com (17)

Pow, Gordon, DeLorme Mapping, Yarmouth, ME. Tel: (207) 846-7000, (800) 561-5105, FAX: (207) 846-7051, E-Mail: caleb.mason@delorme.com, Web Site: www.delorme.com (3)

Powell III, Earl, A., National Gallery of Art Gift Shop, Washington, DC. Tel: (202) 842-6466, (800) 697-9350, FAX: (202) 842-4043, Web Site: www.nga. gov (16)

Powell Jr, Boone, Baylor Health Care System, Dallas, TX. Tel: (214) 820-4901, (800) 4Baylor, FAX: (214) 820-7499, Web Site: www.baylorhealth.com (16)

Powell, Bonnie, P., Telenational Marketing, Omaha, NE. Tel: (800) 333-6106 X132, FAX: (402) 391-2044, Web Site: www.telenational.com (29)

Powell, Cynthia, US News & World Report, New York, NY. Tel: (212) 916-7360, FAX: (212) 643-7842, Web Site: www.usnews.com (17)

Powell, Dave, Harris Infosource International Inc, In-dependence, OH. Tel: (330) 425-9000, (877) 359-6308, (800) 888-5900, (800) 748-5482, FAX: (800) 643-5997, E-Mail: customerservice@harrisinfo. com, Web Site: www.harrisinfo.com (17)

Powell, Jenny, US Bancorp, Minneapolis, MN. Tel: (651) 466-3000, (800) 872-2657, FAX: (612) 303-0782, Web Site: www.usbank.com (14)

Powell, Kendall, J., General Mills Inc, Minneapolis, MN. Tel: (763) 764-7600, FAX: (763) 764-7384, Web Site: www.generalmills.com (17)

Powell, Kendall, J., The Pillsbury Co, Minneapolis, MN. Tel: (763) 764-7600, (800) 775-4777, FAX: (763) 764-8330, Web Site: www.pillsbury.com (16)

Powell, Rick, PMG, Columbia, MD. Tel: (410) 290-0667, Web Site: www.pmgdirect.net (20)

Powell, Scott, M., DirectBuy Inc, Merrillville, IN. Tel: (219) 736-1100, FAX: (219) 755-6208, Web Site: www.ucctotalhome.com (1)

Powell, Shirley, The Weather Channel, New York, NY. Tel: (212) 856-5200, FAX: (212) 856-5215, Web Site: www.weather.com (32)

Powell, Susan, American Management Association International, New York, NY. Tel: (212) 586-8100, (800) 262-9699, FAX: (212) 903-8168 (41)

Powell, Wes, The Mail Room Inc, Colorado Springs, CO. Tel: (719) 636-1303, (888) 686-1303, FAX: (719) 636-1814, E-Mail: wpowell@ themailroominc.com, Web Site: www. themailroominc.com (28)

Power & Tel Supply, Randolph, VT. Tel: (800) 451-4381, FAX: (802) 234-5006, E-Mail: cablesales@ ptsupply.com, Web Site: www.ptsupply.com/ enterprise (16)

JD Power Associates, Westlake Village, CA. Tel: (805) 418-8000, (888) 537-6937, FAX: (805) 418-8900, E-Mail: information@jdpa.com, Web Site: www. jdpower.com (30)

Power Music, Salt Lake City, UT. Tel: (801) 292-2418, (800) 777-BEAT, FAX: (801) 292-2462, Web Site: www.powermusic.com (16)

Power Seminars, Swampscott, MA. Tel: (781) 595-9990, FAX: (781) 595-0770, Web Site: www. gailcohen.com (29)

PowerDirect, Newport Beach, CA. Tel: (949) 253-3440, Web Site: www.powerdirect.net (35)

PowerPay, Portland, ME. Tel: (207) 775-6900, (877) 877-3737, FAX: (888) 204-4040, Web Site: www. powerpay.biz (14)

Powers, Elizabeth, Cold Spring Harbor Lab Press, Woodbury, NY. Tel: (516) 422-4100, (800) 843-4388, FAX: (516) 422-4097, E-Mail: cshpress@ cshl.edu, Web Site: www.cshlpress.com (17)

Powers, Joe, L., Thomas Nelson, Inc, Nashville, TN. Tel: (615) 889-9000, (800) 251-4000, FAX: (615) 889-5940, Web Site: www.thomasnelson.com (17)

Powers, Melissa, Pro CD Inc, Omaha, NE. Tel: (800) 992-3766, FAX: (402) 750-0020 (17)

Powers, Melvin, Powers Television Marketing, Chat-sworth, CA. Tel: (818) 700-1522, FAX: (818) 700-1527, E-Mail: mpowers@mpowers.com, Web Site: www.mpowers.com (17)

Powers, Melvin, Wilshire Book Co, Chatsworth, CA. Tel: (818) 700-1522, FAX: (818) 700-1527, E-Mail: mpowers@mpowers.com, Web Site: www. mpowers.com (43)

Powers, Mike, Butler Schein Animal Health, Dublin, OH. Tel: (614) 761-9095, (888) 691-2724, FAX: (888) 329-3861, Web Site: www.butlerschein.com (16)

Powers, Suzanne, TBWA/Chiat/Day Inc, New York, NY. Tel: (212) 804-1000, FAX: (212) 804-1200, E-Mail: jamie.gallo@tbwachiat.com, Web Site: www.tbwachiat.com (35)

Powers, Tom, Sunshine Minting Inc, Coeur D'Alene, ID. Tel: (208) 772-9592, (800) 274-5837, FAX: (208) 772-9739, E-Mail: sunshine@sunshinemint. com, Web Site: www.sunshinemint.com (14)

Powers, Tonya, HP Indigo & Inkjet Press Solutions, Scottsdale, AZ. Tel: (404) 427-7418 (16)

Powers, Tonya, OCE North America Inc, Boca Raton, FL. Tel: (561) 997-3100, (800) 523-5444, FAX: (561) 998-9160, Web Site: www. oceproductionprinting.com (34)

Powers Television Marketing, Chatsworth, CA. Tel: (818) 700-1522, FAX: (818) 700-1527, E-Mail: mpowers@mpowers.com, Web Site: www. mpowers.com (17)

Powr-Flite, a Tacony Co, Fort Worth, TX. Tel: (800) 880-2913, Web Site: www.powrflite.com (9)

Poyner, William K., Hansen Corp, Princeton, IN. Tel: (812) 385-3415, FAX: (812) 385-3013, E-Mail: sales@hansen-motor.com, Web Site: www.hansen-motor.com (16)

Poynter, Dan, Book Publishing Information Kit, Santa Barbara, CA. Tel: (805) 968-7277, (800) PARA-PUB. FAX: (805) 968-1379, E-Mail: danpoynter@ parapublishing.com, Web Site: www. parapublishing.com (17)

Poynter, Dan, Para Publishing, Santa Barbara, CA. Tel: (805) 968-7277, (800) PARAPUB, FAX: (805) 986-1379, E-Mail: danpoynter@parapublishing. com, Web Site: www.parapublishing.com (17)

Pozzo, Heidi, Longview Fibre Co, Longview, WA. Tel: (360) 425-1550, FAX: (360) 230-5135, E-Mail: info@longviewfibre.com, Web Site: www. longfibre.com (25)

Practical Computer Solutions, South Orange, NJ. Tel: (973) 761-6099, FAX: (215) 243-8283, E-Mail: dbsteig@alum.mit.edu, Web Site: www.donsteig. com (20)

Practice Builders, Irvine, CA. Tel: (714) 751-7960, (800) 679-1262, FAX: (714) 751-7801, E-Mail: info@practicebuilders.com, Web Site: www. practicebuilders.com (35)

Practicing Law Institute, New York, NY. Tel: (212) 824-5700, (800) 260 4PLI, FAX: (800) 321-0093, E-Mail: info@pli.edu, Web Site: www.pli.edu (16)

Pragalz Metro Graphx Inc, Twin Lakes, WI. Tel: (708) 449-2700, FAX: (708) 449-2711 (21)

Prahm, Leah, Goodman Marketing Partners Inc, San Rafael, CA. Tel: (415) 507-9060, FAX: (415) 507-9067, E-Mail: info@goodmanmarketing.com, Web Site: www.goodmanmarketing.com (35)

Prairie Nursery, Westfield, WI. Tel: (608) 296-3679, (800) 476-9453, FAX: (608) 296-2741, E-Mail: webcs@prairienursery.com, Web Site: www. prairienursery.com (8)

Praises, Prizes & Presents, Grand Rapids, MI. Tel: (361) 851-9663, FAX: (361) 851-9663, Web Site: www.praisesprizespresents.com (5)

Prakken Publications Inc, Ann Arbor, MI. Tel: (734) 975-2800, (800) 530-9673, FAX: (734) 975-2787, E-Mail: vanessa@techdirections.com, Web Site: www.eddigest.com; www.techdirections.com (17)

Prange, Kraig, ACTON Group Ltd, Lincoln, NE. Tel: (402) 742-2820, FAX: (402) 470-2673, E-Mail: info@acton.com, Web Site: www.acton.com (23)

Pratt Jr, Daniel, D., Pratt Corp, Indianapolis, IN. Tel: (317) 924-3201, (800) 428-7728, FAX: (317) 927-0653, Web Site: www.prattcorp.com (16)

Pratt, Eric, New Mexico State University, Las Cruces, NM. Tel: (575) 646-0111, (505) 646-3341, FAX: (505) 646-1498, Web Site: www.nmsu.edu (41)

Pratt, Thomas, Pratt Corp, Indianapolis, IN. Tel: (317) 924-3201, (800) 428-7728, FAX: (317) 927-0653, Web Site: www.prattcorp.com (16)

Pratt Corp, Indianapolis, IN. Tel: (317) 924-3201, (800) 428-7728, FAX: (317) 927-0653, Web Site: www.prattcorp.com (16)

Precechtil, David, IPD Co Inc, Portland, OR. Tel: (503) 257-7500, (800) 444-6473, FAX: (503) 257-7596, E-Mail: info@ipdusa.com, Web Site: www. ipdusa.com (12)

Precept Press, Chicago, IL. Tel: (312) 467-0580, FAX: (312) 467-9271, E-Mail: bb@bonusbooks.com, Web Site: www.bonusbooks.com (17)

Precision Arts Advertising Inc, Ashburnham, MA. Tel: (978) 855-7648, E-Mail: sales@precisionarts.com, Web Site: www.precisionarts.com (17)

Precision Mailing Solutions, Huntsville, AL. Tel: (256) 852-1963, FAX: (256) 852-1963, E-Mail: precisionmailing@mchsi.com (23)

Precision Play Media / MarketLeverage, Lake Mary, FL. Tel: (407) 805-8800, Web Site: www. precisionplaymedia.com (22)

Precision Response Corp, Plantation, FL. Tel: (954) 693-3700, FAX: (954) 693-3767, Web Site: www. prcnet.com (21)

Preferred Advertising Inc, Ballwin, MO. Tel: (314) 298-8555, (800) 289-7858, FAX: (314) 298-8557, E-Mail: websales@preferredadvertising.com, Web Site: www.preferredadvertising.com (33)

Preferred Communications, Butner, NC. Tel: (919) 575-4600, (877) 589-9800, Web Site: www.satstar. com (24)

Preferred Premium & Fulfillment Corp, Deerfield, IL. Tel: (847) 677-3080, FAX: (847) 564-5738 (33)

Preiss, Steve, J., C&H Distributors LLC, Milwaukee, WI. Tel: (414) 443-1700, (888) 316-2223, FAX: (414) 443-9213, E-Mail: customerservice@chdist. com, Web Site: www.chdist.com (9)

Premera Blue Cross, Spokane, WA. Tel: (425) 670-4000, (800) 422-0032, FAX: (425) 670-5853, Web Site: www.premera.com (15)

Premier Data Group, Camarillo, CA. Tel: (805) 445-7522, FAX: (805) 445-8876, Web Site: www. premierdatagroup.com (23)

Premier Data Solution, Camarillo, CA. Tel: (805) 987-2789, (800) 537-3282, (800) 333-DATA, FAX: (800) 333-6974, E-Mail: info@premierdatasolution. com, Web Site: www.premierdatasolution.com (23)

Premier Direct Marketing Inc, Louisville, KY. Tel: (502) 367-6441, (800) 737-0205, FAX: (502) 361-2961, E-Mail: rmeredith@premierdm.net, Web Site: www.premierdm.net (28)

Premier Farnell Corp, Richfield, OH. Tel: (216) 525-4300, (800) 458-3222, FAX: (216) 525-4509, E-Mail: information@premierfarnell.com, Web Site: www.premierfarnell.com (16)

Premier IMS, Houston, TX. Tel: (713) 222-8871, FAX: (713) 222-0334, E-Mail: norm2@mailplex. com, Web Site: www.premiercompany.com (21)

Premier Messaging LP, Houston, TX. Tel: (888) 405-7000, E-Mail: sales@premiermessaging.com, Web Site: www.premiermessaging.com (29)

Premier Packaging Corp, Victor, NY. Tel: (877) 924-8460, FAX: (585) 924-8753, E-Mail: info@ premiercustompkg.com, Web Site: www. premiercustompkg.com (16)

Premier Print and Service Group Inc, Chicago, IL. Tel: (312) 648-2266, (800) 648-3677, FAX: (312) 648-1361, E-Mail: blabin@premierprint.com, Web Site: www.premierprint.com (21)

Premier World Marketing, Miami, FL. Tel: (305) 445-1077, Web Site: www.karismahotels.com (35)

Premiere Global Services Inc, Atlanta, GA. Tel: (404) 262-8400, (800) 546-1541, FAX: (913) 661-9042, Web Site: www.PGiConnect.com (22)

The Premium Connection, Las Vegas, NV. Tel: (702) 434-6900, (800) 683-0933, FAX: (702) 434-9715, Web Site: www.premiumconnection.net (33)

Premium Incentives, Ontario, CA. Tel: (951) 599-8220, (800) 950-5131, FAX: (949) 599-8244, E-Mail: mhidalgo@promotebusiness.com, Web Site: http://premiumincentives.awardselection.com/ index.icrt (33)

Prenatt, Susan, CAIG Laboratories Inc, Poway, CA. Tel: (858) 486-8388, FAX: (858) 486-8398, E-Mail: caig123@caig.com, Web Site: www.caig. com (9)

Prendergast, Jim, Mailing and Fulfillment Service Association of New York, New York, NY. Tel: (212) 217-6824, (800) 394-5106, FAX: (212) 217-6824, E-Mail: info@mfsany.com, Web Site: www. mfsany.com (34)

Prentice, Debby, Bucks County Coffee Co, Conshohocken, PA. Tel: (215) 741-1855, (800) 523-6163, FAX: (215) 741-1799, Web Site: www. buckscountycoffee.com (16)

Prentice, John, Forethought Financial Services Inc, Batesville, IN Canada. Tel: (812) 934-7139, (800) 331-8853, FAX: (812) 934-8564, Web Site: www. forethought.com (15)

Prentiss, Winnie, Creative Publishing International, Minneapolis, MN. Tel: (612) 344-8100, FAX: (612) 344-8691, E-Mail: sales@creativepub.com, Web Site: www.creativepub.com (17)

Prescott, Bruce, Talbots, Hingham, MA. Tel: (781) 749-7600, (800) 825-2687, FAX: (781) 741-4369, Web Site: www.talbots.com (2)

Prescott, Charles, Oak Knoll Limited Liability Co, South Salem, NY. Tel: (914) 533-0208 (20)

Prescott, Janice, Institute of Management & Administration (IOMA), Peterborough, NH. Tel: (800) 401-5937, FAX: (973) 622-0595 (17)

Presence II Productions, Bloomfield Hills, MI. Tel: (248) 763-8581, Web Site: www. presenceiiproductions.com (36)

Presentation Packaging, Minneapolis, MN. Tel: (763) 540-9544, (800) 818-2698, FAX: (763) 540-9522, Web Site: www.presentationpackaging.com (35)

Presque Isle Wine Cellars Inc, North East, PA. Tel: (814) 725-1314, (800) 488-7492, FAX: (814) 725-2092, E-Mail: info@piwine.com, Web Site: www. piwine.com (4)

Press, Jason, G2 Promotional Marketing, New York, NY. Tel: (212) 537-3700, FAX: (203) 352-0798, Web Site: www.g2pm.com (16)

Press, Jeff, JWT Inside, Santa Monica, CA. Tel: (310) 309-8282, (877) 665-8768, FAX: (310) 309-8283, E-Mail: conversations@jwtinside.com, Web Site: www.jwtworks.com (35)

The Press & Standard, Walterboro, SC. Tel: (843) 549-2586, Web Site: colletontoday.com (31)

Press-Enterprise Co, Riverside, CA. Tel: (951) 684-1200, FAX: (951) 368-9022, Web Site: www.pe. com (17)

Theodore Presser Co, King Of Prussia, PA. Tel: (610) 592-1222, FAX: (610) 592-1229, E-Mail: webmaster@presser.com, Web Site: www.presser. com (17)

Presskits, East Walpole, MA. Tel: (781) 762-3003, (800) 472-3497, FAX: (781) 255-7791, Web Site: www.presskits.com (27)

Pressley, Debra, L., AAFES, Dallas, TX. Tel: (214) 312-6700, (800) 527-6790, FAX: (214) 312-3000, Web Site: www.aafes.com (5)

Presstek Inc, Hudson, NH. Tel: (800) 422-3616 (34)

Presten, Valerie S., Word Dynamics of St Helena, Saint Helena, CA. Tel: (707) 963-8000, FAX: (707) 963-8000 (24)

Prestige Mailing Lists Inc, Van Nuys, CA. Tel: (818) 374-1320, FAX: (818) 374-1344, E-Mail: Debbie@ prestigemaillists.com, Web Site: www. prestigemailinglists.com (24)

Preston, Charles, Wells Fargo, San Francisco, CA. Tel: (866) 878-5865, (800) 869-3557, FAX: (626) 312-3015, Web Site: www.wellsfargo.com (14)

Preston, Joseph, Network Tel Services Inc, Woodland Hills, CA. Tel: (818) 992-4300, (800) 727-6874, FAX: (818) 992-8415, Web Site: www.nts.net (16)

Preston, Leslie, Fashion Institute of Technology Library, New York, NY. Tel: (212) 217-4346, Web Site: www.fitnyc.edu (1)

Preston, Melvin, Nelson Crab Inc, Tokeland, WA. Tel: (360) 267-2911, (800) 262-0069, FAX: (360) 267-2921, E-Mail: seatreats@techline.com, Web Site: www.nelsoncrab.com (4)

ST Preston & Son Inc, Greenport, NY. Tel: (631) 477-1990, (800) 836-1165, FAX: (631) 477-8541, E-Mail: andrew@prestons.com, Web Site: www. prestons.com (8)

Prestone Printing Co Inc, Long Island City, NY. Tel: (347) 468-7900, FAX: (347) 468-7885, Web Site: www.prestoneprinting.com (25)

Prestwick House Inc, Clayton, DE. Tel: (302) 659-2070, Web Site: www.prestwickhouse.com (17)

Prevent Blindness America, Chicago, IL. Tel: (800) 331-2020, Web Site: www.preventblindness.org (1)

Previo/Alteris, Lindon, UT. Tel: (801) 226-8500, (888) 252-5551, FAX: (801) 226-8506, Web Site: www. previo.com (1)

Price, Bernadette, Orbis Books, Maryknoll, NY. Tel: (914) 941-7636 X2576, (800) 258-5838, FAX: (914) 941-7005, E-Mail: orbisbooks@maryknoll. org, Web Site: www.orbisbooks.com (17)

Price, Elizabeth, Saks Fifth Avenue, New York, NY. Tel: (212) 940-5195, FAX: (212) 940-5339, Web Site: www.saksfifthavenue.com (16)

Price, Jeff, The Sporting News Publishing Co, Charlotte, NC. Tel: (704) 973-1546, (800) 443-1886, FAX: (704) 973-1552, Web Site: www. sportingnews.com (17)

Price, Joe, Bank of America, Charlotte, NC. Tel: (704) 386-5681, (800) 841-4000, FAX: (704) 386-6699, Web Site: www.bankofamerica.com (14)

Price, Larry, Newroads Inc, Chattanooga, TN. Tel: (423) 867-9081, FAX: (423) 867-8508 (28)

Price, Michael, Post Linx Corp, Scarborough, ON. Tel: (416) 752-8100, FAX: (416) 752-8239, Web Site: www.postlinx.com (28)

Price, Richard, W., Crane Duplicating Service Inc, Naples, FL. Tel: (305) 280-6742, FAX: (239) 732-8415, Web Site: www.craneduplicating.com (28)

Price, William, Your Man Tours, El Segundo, CA. Tel: (310) 649-3820, FAX: (310) 649-2118, E-Mail: ymt@earthlink.net, Web Site: www.ymtvacations. com (19)

Price Target Media, Carson City, NV. Tel: (775) 434-4451, FAX: (206) 888-2403, E-Mail: info@ pricetargetmedia.com, Web Site: pricetargetmedia. com (32)

Price Weber Marketing Communications Inc, Louisville, KY. Tel: (502) 499-9220, FAX: (502) 491-5593, Web Site: www.priceweber.com (17)

PricewaterhouseCoopers LLP, New York, NY. Tel: (646) 471-4000, FAX: (646) 471-4444, Web Site: www.pwc.com (14)

Priester, Rick, Tower Hobbies/Hobbico, Champaign, IL. Tel: (217) 398-3636, (800) 637-6050, FAX: (217) 398-1104, Web Site: www.towerhobbies.com (11)

Priester Pecan Co Inc, Fort Deposit, AL. Tel: (334) 227-4301, Web Site: www.priesters.com (4)

Priests of the Sacred Heart, Hales Corners, WI. Tel: (414) 425-3383, FAX: (414) 425-5719, Web Site: www.poshusa.org (1)

Prieur, C. James, Conseco Inc, Carmel, IN. Tel: (317) 817-6100, FAX: (317) 817-2847, Web Site: www. conseco.com (15)

Prieur, C., James, Bankers Life & Casualty Co, Chicago, IL. Tel: (312) 396-6000, (800) 231-9150, Web Site: www.bankerslife.com (15)

Prifitera, Aurelio, The Psychological Corp, San Antonio, TX. Tel: (800) 211-8378, FAX: (800) 232-1223, Web Site: www.psychcorp.com (17)

Prima-Nelson Printing Inc, Glenview, IL. Tel: (847) 729-8401, FAX: (847) 244-1421 (21)

Primalani, Varsha, Marshall Cavendish Corp, Tarrytown, NY. Tel: (914) 332-8888, (800) 821-9881, FAX: (914) 332-1888, Web Site: www. marshallcavendish.com (17)

Prime, Bridgeport, CT. Tel: (203) 331-9100, (800) 873-7746, FAX: (203) 330-0123, Web Site: www. primeline.com (16)

Prime Access Inc, New York, NY. Tel: (212) 868-6800, FAX: (212) 868-9495, E-Mail: contact@ primeaccess.net, Web Site: www.primeaccess.net (21)

Prime Graphics Inc, Wood Dale, IL. Tel: (630) 227-1300, FAX: (630) 227-1823, E-Mail: moreinfo@ primegraphicsinc.com, Web Site: www. primegraphicsinc.com (27)

Prime Media Equine Group, Gaithersburg, MD. Tel: (301) 977-3900, FAX: (301) 990-9015, Web Site: www.equisearch.com (17)

Prime Target Direct LLC, Mason, OH. Tel: (513) 234-8977, E-Mail: tom@primetargetdirect.com (23)

Primedia Inc, Norcross, GA. Tel: (678) 421-3000, (800) 216-1423, Web Site: www.primedia.com (31)

PrimeNet, Clearwater, FL. Tel: (651) 405-4000, FAX: (651) 405-4100, Web Site: www.pnms.com (22)

Primo, Diane, CDW Corp, Vernon Hills, IL. Tel: (847) 465-6000, (800) 800-4239 (16)

Prinaris, Alex, Meylan Corp, Montclair, NJ. Tel: (973) 744-6400, (888) 769-9667, FAX: (973) 744-1011, E-Mail: meylan1@aol.com, Web Site: www. meylan.com/home.html (9)

Prince, Charles, American Health & Life Insurance Co, Fort Worth, TX. Tel: (817) 348-7500, (800) 995-2274, FAX: (817) 348-7553, Web Site: www. citifinancial.com (15)

Prince, Robert, Richardson Electronics Ltd, Lafox, IL. Tel: (630) 208-2200, FAX: (630) 208-2550, E-Mail: edg@rell.com, Web Site: www.rell.com (16)

Princess Cruises (HQ), Santa Clarita, CA. Tel: (661) 753-0000, (800) Princess, FAX: (661) 284-4765, Web Site: www.princesscruises.com (19)

Princess House Inc, Taunton, MA. Tel: (508) 832-6800, (508) 823-0711, (800) 622-0039, FAX: (508) 823-5182, Web Site: www.princesshouse.com (16)

Princeton Book Co Publishers, Hightstown, NJ. Tel: (609) 426-0602, (800) 220-7149, FAX: (609) 426-1344, E-Mail: pbc@dancehorizons.com, Web Site: www.dancehorizons.com (17)

Princeton Marketech, Princeton Junction, NJ. Tel: (609) 936-0021, FAX: (609) 936-0015, E-Mail: bzyontz@princetonmarketech.com, Web Site: www.princetonmarketech.com (35)

Princeton Partners Inc, Princeton, NJ. Tel: (609) 452-8500, FAX: (609) 452-7212, E-Mail: mlandis@ princetonpartners.com, Web Site: www. princetonpartners.com (35)

The Princeton Review, Scranton, PA. Tel: (212) 874-8282, FAX: (212) 874-0775, E-Mail: helpme@ review.com, Web Site: www.review.com (16)

Princing, Janet, Amigo Mobility International Inc, Bridgeport, MI. Tel: (989) 777-0910, (800) 692-6446, FAX: (989) 777-8184, E-Mail: info@ myamigo.com, Web Site: www.myamigo.com (16)

The Principal Financial Group, Des Moines, IA. Tel: (515) 247-5111, (800) 986-3343, FAX: (515) 246-5475, Web Site: www.principal.com (15)

Print Arts, Broadview, IL. Tel: (708) 938-1600, Web Site: www.printarts.com (21)

The Print Box Inc, Brooklyn, NY. Tel: (212) 741-1381, (800) 546-4011, FAX: (212) 463-9071, E-Mail: info@promobrands.com, Web Site: www. promobrands.com (33)

Print Mailers Inc, Houston, TX. Tel: (832) 201-2000, (800) 656-8883, FAX: (832) 201-2001, E-Mail: steve@pminet.com, Web Site: www.pminet.com (21)

Print Management Partners, Des Plaines, IL. Tel: (847) 699-2999, Web Site: www.ourpartners.com (27)

Print Products International, Annapolis Junction, MD. Tel: (910) 695-7223, FAX: (910) 944-1724, Web Site: www.paceworldwide.com (9)

Print Services Distribution Association, Chicago, IL. Tel: (703) 836-6232, (800) 336-4641, FAX: (703) 836-2241, E-Mail: psda@psda.org, Web Site: www.psda.org (1)

PrintCom Consulting Group, Waxhaw, NC. Tel: (704) 843-5350, FAX: (704) 843-5352, E-Mail: printcom@aol.com (20)

Printed Communications Inc, Tucker, GA. Tel: (770) 934-4732, Web Site: www.printpci.com (27)

The Printer Inc, Des Moines, IA. Tel: (515) 288-7241, FAX: (515) 288-9234, E-Mail: info@the-printer. com, Web Site: www.the-printer.com (27)

Printing + Quick Copy, Philadelphia, PA. Tel: (215) 331-5999 (27)

Printing Corp of the Americas Inc (PCA), Pompano Beach, FL. Tel: (954) 781-8100, (866) 721-1PCA, FAX: (954) 781-8421, Web Site: www.pcaprinting. com (27)

Printing for Systems Inc, Carrollton, TX. Tel: (203) 245-4200, FAX: (203) 245-0349, Web Site: www. printingforsystems.com (27)

Printing Spectrum, East Setauket, NY. Tel: (631) 689-1010, Web Site: www.printingspectrum.com (27)

Printmark, East Montpelier, VT. Tel: (802) 229-9743, FAX: (802) 229-9746, E-Mail: alex@printmark. net, Web Site: www.printmark.net (20)

PrintWest Communications Ltd, Regina, SK Canada. Tel: (306) 525-2304, (800) 236-6438, FAX: (306) 757-2439, E-Mail: info@printwest.com, Web Site: www.printwest.com (27)

Prior, Christopher, General Wig Manufacturers Inc, Pompano Beach, FL. Tel: (305) 823-0600, (800) 268-7210, FAX: (314) 785-0224, E-Mail: 4service@beautytrends.com, Web Site: www. beautytrends.com (7)

PRIORITY Data Systems Inc, Omaha, NE. Tel: (402) 592-2550, (877) 273-7774, FAX: (402) 592-5052, E-Mail: sales@pdomaha.com, Web Site: www. priority-data.com (22)

Priority Systems Inc, Grayslake, IL. Tel: (773) 539-1884, (800) 330-3448, FAX: (773) 539-1755, E-Mail: sbender@priority.com, Web Site: www. priority.com (21)

Prism Data Services Ltd, Mississauga, ON Canada. Tel: (905) 278-5556, FAX: (905) 278-6603, E-Mail: bill.cram@prism-data.com; sales@prism-data.com, Web Site: www.prism-data.com (21)

Prism Marketing Group, Schaller, IA. Tel: (800) 862-4827, FAX: (712) 275-4855, E-Mail: cjgrothe@ schallertel.net, Web Site: www.prismktg.com (29)

Pritchett & Hull Associates Inc, Atlanta, GA. Tel: (770) 451-0602, (800) 241-4925, FAX: (770) 454-7130, E-Mail: sales@p-h.com, Web Site: www.p-h. com (17)

Privacy & Information Practices Advisory, Saddle River, NJ. Tel: (201) 887-2157 (20)

Privacy Journal, Providence, RI. Tel: (401) 274-7861, FAX: (401) 274-4747, E-Mail: orders@ privacyjournal.net, Web Site: www.privacyjournal. net (17)

Prizer, Joshua, American Historic Inns Inc, Dana Point, CA. Tel: (949) 497-2232, (800) 397-4667, FAX: (949) 497-9228, E-Mail: comments@ iloveinns.com, Web Site: www.iloveinns.com (17)

Pro CD Inc, Omaha, NE. Tel: (800) 992-3766, FAX: (402) 750-0020 (17)

PRO Chemical & Dye Inc, Fall River, MA. Tel: (508) 676-3838, FAX: (508) 676-3980, Web Site: www. prochemicalanddye.com (10)

Pro Media-Streff Marketing Group, Menomonee Falls, WI. Tel: (262) 532-2600, (800) 328-0439, FAX: (800) 951-5955, E-Mail: info@promediaus.com, Web Site: www.promediaus.com (35)

Pro/Phase Marketing Inc, Eden Prairie, MN. Tel: (952) 974-1100, (866) 876-2737, FAX: (952) 974-7874, E-Mail: inquiry@repeatrewards.com, Web Site: www.ppmi.com (21)

Probert, Gregory, Herbalife International of America Inc, Los Angeles, CA. Tel: (310) 410-9600, (866) 617-4273, FAX: (310) 258-7019, Web Site: www. herbalife.com (7)

Probst, Sandy, Innotrac Corp, Duluth, GA. Tel: (678) 584-4000, FAX: (678) 475-5840, Web Site: www. innotrac.com (28)

Prochaska, Gail, IMV, Des Plaines, IL. Tel: (847) 297-1404, FAX: (847) 297-5010, E-Mail: sales@ imvinfo.com, Web Site: www.imvlimited.com (20)

Prockow, Eric, Solarcom, Norcross, GA. Tel: (770) 449-6116, (888) SUN-DATA, FAX: (770) 448-7726, Web Site: www.solarcom.net (16)

The Procter & Gamble Co, Cincinnati, OH. Tel: (513) 983-4224, (800) 742-6253, FAX: (513) 983-9369, Web Site: www.pg.com (16)

Proctor, Elizabeth, International Academy - Compounding Pharmacists, Missouri City, TX. Tel: (281) 933-8400, Web Site: www.iacprx.org (1)

Proctzer, Abram, School of Management, Old Westbury, NY. Tel: (516) 686-1000, (800) 345-NYIT, (800) 345-6948, Web Site: www.nyit.edu (41)

Prodigy Mailing Services, Bolingbrook, IL. Tel: (630) 783-9070, Web Site: www.prodigymailing.com (28)

Product Information Network, Englewood, CO. Tel: (303) 792-3111, (800) 525-7002, FAX: (303) 784-8549, Web Site: www.pinnet.com (32)

Product Marketplace, Stratford, CT. Tel: (203) 375-8371, (800) 286-4768, FAX: (203) 386-1203, E-Mail: rita@sabinc.com (33)

Product to Market LLC, Cokato, MN. Tel: (320) 286-9997 (20)

The Production Partners, Toronto, ON Canada. Tel: (416) 504-5071, FAX: (416) 504-7390, Web Site: www.cfacommunications.com (32)

Production Solutions, Vienna, VA. Tel: (703) 734-5700 (20)

Productive Strategies Inc, Northfield, IL. Tel: (847) 446-0008, FAX: (847) 446-0211, E-Mail: pkrone@productivestrategies.com, Web Site: www.productivestrategies.com (20)

Productivity Development Group Inc, Westford, MA. Tel: (978) 692-1818, FAX: (978) 692-5080, E-Mail: info@martinstankard.com (20)

ProFaiser, Linda, L., Woodall Publishing Co LP, Ventura, CA. Tel: (805) 667-4100, (800) 323-9076, FAX: (805) 667-4468, Web Site: www.woodalls.com (17)

Professional Advertising Systems Inc, Armonk, NY. Tel: (914) 765-0500, FAX: (914) 765-0503, E-Mail: info@paslists.com, Web Site: www.paslists.com (22)

Professional Binding Products Inc, Thousand Oaks, CA. Tel: (800) 545-9413, (800) 443-7557, E-Mail: sales@probinding.com, Web Site: www.probinding.com (16)

Professional Creations, New Castle, IN. Tel: (765) 529-1590, (800) 428-8855, E-Mail: sales@professional-creations.com, Web Site: www.professional-creations.com (5)

Professional Cutlery Direct, North Branford, CT. Tel: (203) 871-1000, FAX: (203) 871-1010, E-Mail: terri@cutlery.com, Web Site: www.cutlery.com (4)

Professional Direct Marketing & Mailing List Inc, Boca Raton, FL. Tel: (561) 241-4414, (800) 777-5478, FAX: (561) 241-5878, E-Mail: pdm@pdmm.info, Web Site: www.pdmm.us (23)

The Professional Golfers' Association of America, Palm Beach Gardens, FL. Tel: (561) 624-8400, Web Site: www.pga.com (1)

Professional Mailing Services Inc, Springfield, NJ. Tel: (973) 376-0607, (800) 238-1316, FAX: (973) 376-0949, E-Mail: jschobel@profmail.com, Web Site: www.profmail.com (28)

Professional Marketing Associates, Mount Pleasant, SC. Tel: (843) 971-8150, FAX: (843) 971-8159 (33)

Professional Marketing Associates, Tempe, AZ. Tel: (480) 829-0131, FAX: (480) 829-9202, Web Site: www.pmafulfillment.com (22)

Professional Photographer Magazine, Atlanta, GA. Tel: (404) 522-8600, (800) 786-6277, FAX: (404) 614-6405, E-Mail: csc@ppa.com, Web Site: www.ppa.com (17)

Professional Print & Mail Inc, Fresno, CA. Tel: (559) 237-7468, (800) 654-7468, FAX: (559) 237-4929, E-Mail: dcarlile@printfresno.com, Web Site: www.printfresno.com (21)

The Professional Putters Association, Winston Salem, NC. Tel: (336) 714-3950, (866) PUTT-PUTT, FAX: (336) 714-3955, Web Site: www.putt-putt.com (1)

Professional Training Associates Inc, Duquesne, PA. Tel: (412) 460-0266, FAX: (412) 460-0269, E-Mail: info@ptainc.com, Web Site: www.ptainc.com (17)

Profile America List Co Inc, Englewood Cliffs, NJ. Tel: (201) 569-7272, FAX: (201) 569-5552, E-Mail: annt@profileamerica.com, Web Site: www.profileamerica.com (24)

Profile Coverage Corp, Melville, NY. Tel: (631) 981-7600, FAX: (631) 981-7681, E-Mail: info@profileinsure.com, Web Site: www.profileinsure.com (15)

Profile Mailing Service Inc, Syosset, NY. Tel: (516) 802-3974 (16)

Profit Boosters Copywriting, Aurora, OH. Tel: (330) 963-0330, FAX: (330) 562-2446, E-Mail: mikepavlish@profitboosterscopy.com, Web Site: www.profitboosterscopy.com (39)

Profit Center Software Inc, Port Washington, NY. Tel: (516) 414-6300, (888) 446-6240, FAX: (516) 414-6304, E-Mail: jmarrah@profitcenter.com, Web Site: www.profitcenter.com (22)

Profit Potentials Inc, Hull, IA. Tel: (712) 439-1496, (800) 543-5480, FAX: (712) 439-1434, Web Site: www.profitpotentials.com (1)

Programmers Investment Corp, Arlington Heights, IL. Tel: (847) 227-4500, FAX: (847) 299-8286, E-Mail: pic@pic-online.com, Web Site: www.pic-online.com (21)

Progress Printing Co, Lynchburg, VA. Tel: (434) 239-9213, (800) 527-7804, FAX: (434) 237-1618, Web Site: www.progressprinting.net (27)

Progress Software Corp, Bedford, MA. Tel: (781) 280-4000, (800) 477-6473, FAX: (781) 280-4095, Web Site: www.progress.com (16)

Progressive Business Publications, Malvern, PA. Tel: (610) 695-8600, (800) 220-5000, FAX: (610) 647-8089, E-Mail: customer_service@pbp.com, Web Site: www.pbp.com (17)

Progressive Communications, Lake Mary, FL. Tel: (407) 333-9500, FAX: (407) 333-7979, E-Mail: info@progressivecommunications.com, Web Site: www.progressivecommunications.com (21)

The Progressive Corp, Mayfield Village, OH. Tel: (440) 461-5000, (800) PROGRESSIVE, (800) 776-4737, FAX: (800) 456-6590, Web Site: www.progressive.com (15)

Progressive Direct Marketing, Depew, NY. Tel: (716) 681-6848, (800) 344-7593, FAX: (716) 681-9173, Web Site: www.pdmny.com (35)

Progressive Distribution Services Inc, Grand Rapids, MI. Tel: (616) 957-5900, (800) 304-3699, FAX: (616) 957-2990, E-Mail: sales@progressive-commerce.com, Web Site: www.prodist.com (28)

Progressive Energy Corp, San Marcos, CA. Tel: (760) 727-2906, (800) 525-8624, FAX: (760) 727-0947, E-Mail: patrickkilleen@cox.net (5)

Progressive Impressions International, Bloomington, IL. Tel: (309) 664-0444, Web Site: www.whateverittakes.com (35)

Project HOPE, Millwood, VA. Tel: (540) 837-2100, Web Site: www.projecthope.org (1)

Projection Video Services, Springfield, VA. Tel: (703) 912-1334, (800) 377-7650, FAX: (703) 912-1350, Web Site: www.projection.com (16)

Projector-Recorder Belt Corp, Oceanside, NY. Tel: (516) 536-5000, (800) 645-2202, FAX: (516) 764-5747, (800) 645-2200, E-Mail: sales@russellind.com, Web Site: www.russellind.com (3)

ProjectSense, Gaithersburg, MD. Tel: (240) 476-1677, Web Site: www.projectsense.com (20)

Proleika, Ron, Windstream Communications Inc, Little Rock, AR. Tel: (501) 748-7000 (32)

Promark Direct Marketing Concepts Inc, Hackensack, NJ. Tel: (201) 489-0532, (800) 776-6275, FAX: (201) 489-2680, E-Mail: jdunetz@promarkdirectmarketing.com (21)

Promissor, Bala Cynwyd, PA. Tel: (610) 617-9300, FAX: (610) 617-9301, Web Site: www.promissor.com (24)

Promo Magazine, New York, NY. Tel: (203) 358-9900, (800) 927-5007, FAX: (203) 358-5816, E-Mail: larry.jaffee@penton.com, Web Site: www.promomagazine.com (17)

Promotion Fulfillment Ctr, Camanche, IA. Tel: (563) 259-0105, (800) 493-7063, FAX: (563) 259-0110, E-Mail: info@pfcfulfills.com, Web Site: www.pfcfulfills.com (28)

Promotion Marketing Association (PMA) Inc, New York, NY. Tel: (212) 420-1100, FAX: (212) 533-7622, E-Mail: pma@pmalink.org, Web Site: www.pmalink.org (1)

Promotion Support Services Inc, Rock Island, IL. Tel: (309) 788-4400, FAX: (309) 788-4465, E-Mail: dbender@pss-inc.net, Web Site: www.pss-inc.net (28)

Promotional Media Inc, Orange, CA. Tel: (714) 639-6590, (800) 346-5348, FAX: (714) 639-6270, E-Mail: contactus@promotionalmedia.com, Web Site: www.promotionalmedia.com (33)

Promotional Product Professionals of Canada, Saint-Laurent, PQ Canada. Tel: (514) 489-5359, FAX: (514) 489-7760, (800) 489-8741, E-Mail: gladys@pppc.ca, Web Site: www.pppc.ca (1)

Promotional Products Association International, Irving, TX. Tel: (972) 252-0404, FAX: (800) I-AM-PPAI, (972) 258-3004, E-Mail: membership@ppa.org, Web Site: www.ppa.org (40)

Promotional Products Fulfillment & Distribution Ltd, Whitby, ON Canada. Tel: (905) 668-5060, (800) 263-4678, FAX: (800) 993-0543, E-Mail: sales@ppfd.com, Web Site: www.ppfd.com (22)

The Promotional Resources Group of Companies, Inc, Topeka, KS. Tel: (785) 862-3707, (800) 467-4712, FAX: (785) 862-1424, E-Mail: info@kidstuff.com, Web Site: www.kidstuffnet.com (33)

PromoWriting, Trumbull, CT. Tel: (203) 371-0654, E-Mail: shira@promowriting.com, Web Site: www.promowriting.com (35)

Prompt Mailers Inc, Staten Island, NY. Tel: (718) 447-6206, FAX: (718) 981-7333, E-Mail: info@promptmailers.com, Web Site: www.promptmailers.com (28)

Prondzinski, Laurie, Vemma Nutrition Co, Scottsdale, AZ. Tel: (800) 577-0777, FAX: (888) 314-9827, E-Mail: ms@vemma.com, Web Site: www.vemma.com (7)

Proni, Barbara, Americansource Bergan, Chesterbrook, PA. Tel: (610) 727-7000, (800) 829-3132, E-Mail: info@amerisourcebergan.com, Web Site: www.amerisourcebergan.com (7)

Pronto Post, Hialeah, FL. Tel: (305) 621-7900 (21)

Propay, Lehi, UT. Tel: (801) 341-5647, Web Site: www.propay.com (14)

Propco Promotional Marketing, Lincolnwood, IL. Tel: (773) 463-9193, FAX: (773) 463-6673, E-Mail: propco@propco.com, Web Site: www.propco.com (35)

Propp, Dennis, Propco Promotional Marketing, Lincolnwood, IL. Tel: (773) 463-9193, FAX: (773) 463-6673, E-Mail: propco@propco.com, Web Site: www.propco.com (35)

ProSing Karaoke, Nederland, CO. Tel: (800) 776-7464, FAX: (888) 388-9741, E-Mail: jack@prosing.com, Web Site: www.prosing.com (5)

Prosodie Interactive, Plantation, FL. Tel: (954) 671-6500, (866) 776-7634, FAX: (954) 915-0567, E-Mail: info@prosodiemail.com, Web Site: www.ivrinc.com (29)

ProSource, Houston, TX. Tel: (713) 667-3690, FAX: (713) 660-9629, Web Site: www.prosourcedev.com (20)

Prospect Direct Inc, Milwaukee, WI. Tel: (414) 271-3313, (800) 624-9050, FAX: (414) 271-4244, E-Mail: info@prospect-direct.com, Web Site: www.prospect-direct.com (21)

Prosper Inc, Provo, UT. Tel: (801) 371-0755, (800) 748-5799, FAX: (801) 374-2358, Web Site: www.prospering.com (32)

Prosperity And Profits Unlimited Distribution Services, Denver, CO. Tel: (303) 575-5676, FAX: (303) 575-1187, E-Mail: emailstreet@gmail.com, Web Site: www.prosperityandprofitsunlimited.com (16)

Prosser, Buz, Consolidated Mailing Corp, Shawnee Mission, KS. Tel: (913) 262-4400, (800) 706-6245, FAX: (913) 262-7801, E-Mail: cmcmail@swbell.net, Web Site: www.consolidatedmailing.com (28)

Prossick, Nancy, Thermo Pro, Duluth, GA. Tel: (678) 475-1647, (800) 523-5542, FAX: (678) 475-1747, Web Site: www.thermopro.com (16)

Protano, Mario, Ross-Simons, Cranston, RI. Tel: (401) 463-3100, (800) 835-0919, FAX: (401) 463-8599, Web Site: www.ross-simons.com (6)

Protection One Inc, Lawrence, KS. Tel: (785) 856-5500, (800) GET-HELP, Web Site: www.protectionone.com (16)

Protective Life Corp, Deerfield, IL. Tel: (847) 948-8988, (800) 323-5771, FAX: (847) 948-1156, Web Site: www.protective.com (15)

Protective Life Insurance Co, Birmingham, AL. Tel: (205) 268-1000, (800) 866-3555, FAX: (205) 868-3086, Web Site: www.protective.com (15)

Protheroe, Wesley, Gerber Life Insurance Co, White Plains, NY. Tel: (914) 272-4000, (800) 704-2180, FAX: (914) 272-4099, Web Site: www.gerberlife.com (15)

Protocol, Sarasota, FL. Tel: (800) 800-8627, FAX: (203) 271-4970, Web Site: www.protocolmarketing.com (29)

Protocol Integrated Direct Marketing, Sarasota, FL. Tel: (800) 677-2001, (800) 351-3774, FAX: (941) 906-9099, Web Site: www.protocolmarketing.com (21)

Protocol Services Acquisitions Corp, Sarasota, FL. Tel: (941) 906-9000, Web Site: www.protocolusa.com (20)

Protus, Ottawa, ON Canada. Tel: (888) 733-0000, Web Site: www.protus.com (32)

Proudfoot, Mark, Majestic Products Co, Mississauga, ON Canada. Tel: (905) 858-8010, (800) 668-5323, FAX: (905) 670-7915, Web Site: www.cfmcorp.com (16)

Prouty Esq., Allison, Simmons, New York Landmarks Conservancy, New York, NY. Tel: (212) 995-5260, FAX: (212) 995-5268, Web Site: www.nylandmarks.org (1)

Proven Prospects Inc, Hermosa Beach, CA. Tel: (805) 448-6253, Web Site: www.provemprospects.com (20)

Provencher, Scott, Cloutier Direct Inc, Scarborough, ME. Tel: (207) 883-9599, Web Site: www.cloutierdirect.com (28)

Provenza, Salvatore, EOS International Inc, Carlsbad, CA. Tel: (760) 431-8400, (800) 876-5484, FAX: (760) 431-8448, Web Site: www.eosintl.com (5)

Providence Journal Telemarketing, Providence, RI. Tel: (401) 277-7000, FAX: (401) 277-8046, E-Mail: bnauman@projo.com, Web Site: www.projo.com (29)

Provost, Jeff, Staples Industrial, Framingham, MA. Tel: (978) 443-9592, (800) 638-9899, FAX: (978) 443-2678 (28)

Proxicom, Reston, VA. Tel: (703) 262-3200, FAX: (703) 262-3201, Web Site: www.proxicom.com (32)

Prozes, Andrew, Lexis Nexis Matthew Bender, Albany, NY. Tel: (518) 487-3000, (800) 424-4200, E-Mail: lexisnexis@matthewbender, Web Site: www.bender.lexisnexis.com (17)

Prozes, Andrew, LexisNexis, Miamisburg, OH. Tel: (937) 865-6800, (800) 227-9597, (800) 227-4908, FAX: (800) 348-2609, E-Mail: pr@lexisnexis.com, Web Site: www.lexisnexis.com (16)

Prudent Publishing Co, Ridgefield Park, NJ. Tel: (201) 641-7900, FAX: (800) 772-1144 (16)

Prudential Financial, Newark, NJ. Tel: (973) 802-2195, Web Site: www.prudential.com (14)

Prugger, Patrick, KTM Sportmotorcycle USA Inc, Amherst, OH. Tel: (440) 985-3553, FAX: (440) 985-3060, Web Site: www.ktmusa.com (16)

Pruiniks, Robert, H., University of Minnesota Alumni Association, Minneapolis, MN. Tel: (612) 624-2323, (800) UM-ALUMS, FAX: (612) 626-8167, E-Mail: umalumni@umn.edu, Web Site: www.umaa.umn.edu (1)

Pruitt, Gary, McClatchy Co, Sacramento, CA. Tel: (916) 321-1855, FAX: (916) 321-1869, Web Site: www.mcclatchy.com (17)

Pruitt, Steve, Teraco Inc, Midland, TX. Tel: (888) 837-2261, Web Site: www.teraco.com (27)

Pruitt, Suzanne, Boston Gift Show, Kennesaw, GA. Tel: (678) 285-3976, (800) 272-SHOW, FAX: (678) 285-7469, Web Site: www.bostongiftshow.com (42)

Prunier, John, Petsky Prunier LLC, New York, NY. Tel: (212) 842-6001, FAX: (212) 842-6039, Web Site: www.petskyprunier.com (14)

Prvitt, David, Bike Nashbar, Crab Orchard, WV. Tel: (800) NAS-HBAR, FAX: (877) 778-9456, E-Mail: custserv@nashbar.com, Web Site: www.bikenashbar.com (11)

Pryor, Douglas, Sport Supply Group, Dallas, TX. Tel: (972) 484-9484, FAX: (972) 247-0650, Web Site: www.sportsupplygroup.com (11)

Pryor, Ray, Gamma Photo Labs LLC, Chicago, IL. Tel: (312) 337-0022, FAX: (312) 337-3753, Web Site: www.photobition.com (16)

Fred Pryor Seminars, Mission, KS. Tel: (913) 967-8518, (800) 780-8476, FAX: (913) 967-8849, E-Mail: customerservice@pryor.com, Web Site: www.pryor.com (16)

Psion Teklogix Inc, Mississauga, ON Canada. Tel: (905) 813-9900, (800) 322-3437, E-Mail: ptinfo@psion.com, Web Site: www.psionteklogix.com (3)

The Psychological Corp, San Antonio, TX. Tel: (800) 211-8378, FAX: (800) 232-1223, Web Site: www.psychcorp.com (17)

Ptak, Frank, S., The Marmon Group LLC, Chicago, IL. Tel: (312) 372-9500, FAX: (312) 845-5305, Web Site: www.marmon.com (16)

PTM Communications, New York, NY. Tel: (212) 643-5458, FAX: (212) 643-5486, E-Mail: info@ptmcomm.com, Web Site: www.ptmcomm.com (29)

Public Interest Communications Inc, Falls Church, VA. Tel: (703) 847-8300, FAX: (703) 734-9620, Web Site: www.pubintcom.com (29)

Public Issues Management, Piedmont, CA. Tel: (510) 654-9114, FAX: (510) 654-0196 (20)

Publication Fulfillment Svcs, Cypress, CA. Tel: (714) 226-9785, FAX: (714) 226-9733, E-Mail: janpullin@pfsmag.com, Web Site: www.pfsmag.com (20)

Publications Groupe RR International Inc, Montreal, PQ Canada. Tel: (514) 521-8148 (20)

Publications International Ltd, Lincolnwood, IL. Tel: (847) 745-9299, (800) 595-8484, FAX: (847) 676-3671, Web Site: www.pubint.com (17)

Publicis, Plano, TX. Tel: (972) 628-7500, FAX: (972) 628-7671, Web Site: www.publicis-usa.com (35)

Publicity Inc, Mansfield, MA. Tel: (617) 367-3555, FAX: (617) 367-3557 (35)

Publishers Circulation Fulfillment Inc, Pensacola, FL. Tel: (850) 475-2000 (32)

Publishers Clearing House, Port Washington, NY. Tel: (516) 883-5432, FAX: (516) 767-4567, E-Mail: cirving@pch.com, Web Site: www.pch.com (18)

Publishers Computer Corp, New Milford, NJ. Tel: (201) 261-3700, FAX: (201) 261-9110, E-Mail: mail@publisherscomputer.com, Web Site: www.publisherscomputer.com (22)

Publishers Diversified Mail Service Inc, Milwaukee, WI. Tel: (414) 354-1423, FAX: (414) 354-9338, E-Mail: webmaster@publishersmail.com, Web Site: www.publishersmail.com (21)

Publishers Marketing Association (PMA), Manhattan Beach, CA. Tel: (310) 372-2732, FAX: (310) 374-3342, E-Mail: info@pma-online.org, Web Site: www.pma-online.org (40)

Publisher's Media, El Cajon, CA. Tel: (619) 588-2155, FAX: (619) 588-9103, E-Mail: rvhmedia@aol.com (31)

Publishers Press Inc, Shepherdsville, KY. Tel: (502) 955-6526, Web Site: www.pubpress.com (27)

Publishing Fulfillment Consulting LLC, Brewster, NY. Tel: (845) 278-2800, Web Site: www.fulfillmentconsulting.com (20)

Pucci, Felecia, Estee Marketing Group Inc, New Rochelle, NY. Tel: (914) 235-7080, FAX: (914) 235-6518, E-Mail: info@esteemarketing.com, Web Site: www.esteemarketing.com (24)

Puccio, Dina, Microbiz Corp, Fountain Valley, CA. Tel: (201) 785-1311, (800) 726-3282, FAX: (201) 758-1568, E-Mail: info@microbiz.com, Web Site: www.microbiz.com (3)

Pucker, Ken, Timberland.com, Stratham, NH. Tel: (603) 772-9500, Web Site: www.Timberland.com (16)

Puckett, Betsy, Droll Yankees Inc, Foster, RI. Tel: (860) 799-8980, (800) 352-9164, FAX: (860) 779-8938, E-Mail: jen@drollyyankees.com, Web Site: www.drollyankees.com (8)

Puckett, Duane, Sportime International, Norcross, GA. Tel: (770) 449-5700, (800) 283-5700, FAX: (770) 510-7290, E-Mail: orders@sportime.com, Web Site: www.sportime.com (11)

Puckett-Dunn, Nancy, The Davis Center, Succasunna, NJ. Tel: (862) 251-4637, FAX: (862) 251-4642, E-Mail: info@thedaviscenter.com, Web Site: www.thedaviscenter.com (16)

Pudles, Gary, AnswerNet Network, Willow Grove, PA. Tel: (800) 411-5777, FAX: (215) 659-6486, Web Site: www.answernetnetwork.com (29)

Pudlowski, Mary Lou, VisiPak, Saint Louis, MO. Tel: (636) 282-6800, (800) 922-9391, FAX: (636) 282-6888, E-Mail: visipak@sinclair-rush.com, Web Site: www.visipak.com (34)

Puffer, Timothy, Development Resources, Saint Paul, MN. Tel: (651) 695-5558, FAX: (888) 805-1070, E-Mail: info@developmentresources.com, Web Site: www.developmentresources.com (21)

Puhala, Jim, A-T Surgical Manufacturing Co, Holyoke, MA. Tel: (413) 532-4551, (800) 225-2023, FAX: (413) 532-0826, E-Mail: atsmci@a-surgical.com, Web Site: www.atsurgical.com (2)

Puisis, Frank, Finishing Plus, Inc, Chicago, IL. Tel: (773) 523-5510, FAX: (773) 523-9155, E-Mail: info@finishingplus.com, Web Site: www.finishingplus.com (28)

Puleo, Bob, Globe Ticket & Label Co, Lombard, IL. Tel: (404) 762-9711, (800) 523-5968, FAX: (404) 762-7019, Web Site: www.globeticket.com (16)

Puleo, Steve, Bull HN Information Systems, Chelmsford, MA. Tel: (978) 294-6000, FAX: (978) 294-7999, Web Site: www.bull.com/us (16)

Pulite, William, J., Del Webb, Bloomfield Hills, MI. Tel: (248) 644-7300, (888) 717-9777, FAX: (248) 433-4598, Web Site: www.delwebb.com (16)

Pullano, Paul, Omega Direct Response Inc, Richmond Hill, ON. Tel: (905) 482-2340, FAX: (905) 482-9721, E-Mail: odrsales@omegadirect.com, Web Site: www.omegadirect.com (29)

Pullen, Curt, Herman Miller Inc, Zeeland, MI. Tel: (616) 654-3000, FAX: (616) 654-5234, E-Mail: investor@hermanmiller.com, Web Site: www.hermanmiller.com (16)

Pullen, Pam, Native American Heritage Associations, Front Royal, VA. Tel: (540) 636-1020, Web Site: www.naha-inc.org (1)

Pulliam, Larry, AGCO Inc, Norcross, GA. Tel: (770) 447-6990, FAX: (770) 446-2102, Web Site: www.agcomarble.com (9)

Pulliam, Myrta, Indianapolis Newspapers Inc, Indianapolis, IN. Tel: (317) 444-4444, FAX: (317) 633-9414, Web Site: www.indystar.com (17)

Pullin, Ericka, Frost Bank, San Antonio, TX. Tel: (210) 220-5155, Web Site: www.frostbank.com (14)

Pumphrey, Kristen, Pharmaceutical Care Management Association, Washington, DC. Tel: (202) 207-3610, FAX: (202) 207-3623, E-Mail: info@pcmanet.org, Web Site: www.pcmanet.org (1)

Punter, Dylan, InfoSource Inc, Oviedo, FL. Tel: (407) 796-5200, (800) 393-4636, FAX: (407) 796-5190, E-Mail: isisale@howtomaster.com, Web Site: www.infosourcelearning.com (3)

Puopolo, Ernest, S., ESP Printing & Mailing Inc, Boise, ID. Tel: (800) 338-6789, FAX: (208) 345-4765, E-Mail: data@espmap.com (28)

Purcell, Jack, Links Magazine, Hilton Head Island, SC. Tel: (843) 842-6200, FAX: (843) 842-6233, Web Site: www.linksmagazine.com (17)

Purelis, Eileen, Martindale-Hubbell, New Providence, NJ. Tel: (908) 464-6800, (800) 526-4902, FAX: (908) 771-7740 (17)

Puritan's Pride, Ronkonkoma, NY. Tel: (631) 567-9500, FAX: (631) 471-5693, E-Mail: info@puritan. com, Web Site: www.puritan.com (7)

Purse, Craig, Video Jet Technologies Inc, Wood Dale, IL. Tel: (630) 860-7300, (800) 654-4663, FAX: (630) 616-3657, E-Mail: info@videojet.com, Web Site: www.videojet.com (34)

Pursuant Group, Dallas, TX. Tel: (214) 866-7700, Web Site: pursuant.net (20)

Puryear, Paul, Heller Financial, Chicago, IL. Tel: (312) 441-7000, FAX: (312) 441-7367, Web Site: www.hellerfin.com (14)

Pusatera, Anthony, Royal Envelope Corp, Chicago, IL. Tel: (773) 376-1212, (800) 279-0142, FAX: (773) 376-0011, E-Mail: mattp@royalenv.com, Web Site: www.royalenv.com (26)

Pusatera, Matt, Royal Envelope Corp, Chicago, IL. Tel: (773) 376-1212, (800) 279-0142, FAX: (773) 376-0011, E-Mail: mattp@royalenv.com, Web Site: www.royalenv.com (26)

Putala, Randall, Strategic Direct Marketing Inc, Pleasant View, TN. Tel: (615) 834-9555, (800) 843-8861, FAX: (615) 834-6698, E-Mail: sales@sdmi3. com, Web Site: www.sdmi3.com (21)

Putnam, Sarah, Sarah Putnam, Cambridge, MA. Tel: (617) 547-3758, E-Mail: sarah@sarahputnam.com, Web Site: www.sarahputnam.com (37)

Putnam Group Ltd, Trumbull, CT. Tel: (203) 452-7270, FAX: (203) 268-8071, E-Mail: info@ putnamgroup.net, Web Site: putnamgroup.net (33)

Putnam Investments, Canton, MA. Tel: (617) 292-1000, (800) 225-1581, FAX: (617) 292-1683, Web Site: www.putnam.com (14)

Putnam Rolling Ladder Co Inc, New York, NY. Tel: (212) 226-5147, FAX: (212) 941-1836, E-Mail: putnam1905@aol.com, Web Site: www. putnamrollingladder.com (5)

Putt Putt Fun Centers, Winston-Salem, NC. Tel: (336) 714-3950, (866) PUTT-PUTT, FAX: (336) 714-3955, Web Site: www.puttputt.com (16)

Pych, Joseph, NextMark Inc, Hanover, NH. Tel: (603) 643-1307, Web Site: www.nextmark.com (22)

Pyle, Charlie, Starchtech, Golden Valley, MN. Tel: (763) 545-5400, (800) 597-7225, FAX: (763) 545-9450, Web Site: www.starchtech.com (16)

Pyles, Patrick, Odell, Simms & Associates Inc, Falls Church, VA. Tel: (703) 903-9797, FAX: (703) 903-8850, E-Mail: webmaster@odellsimms.com, Web Site: www.odellsimms.com (35)

Pyne, Elaine, The Gallery Shop, Buffalo, NY. Tel: (716) 882-8700 X258, FAX: (716) 882-1958, E-Mail: gallshop@albrightknox.org, Web Site: www.albrightknox.org (6)

Pyott, David, Allergan Inc, Irvine, CA. Tel: (714) 246-4500, (800) 433-8871, FAX: (714) 246-4971, Web Site: www.allergan.com (16)

Q

Q Fact Marketing Research Inc & Videoconferencing Center, Cincinnati, OH. Tel: (513) 891-2271, FAX: (513) 984-7464, E-Mail: info@qfact.com, Web Site: www.qfact.com (30)

Q Interactive, Chicago, IL. Tel: (312) 977-0390, (888) 729-6465, FAX: (312) 224-5001, E-Mail: solutions@qinteractive.com, Web Site: www. qinteractive.com (40)

QC Supply LLC, Schuyler, NE. Tel: (402) 352-3167, Web Site: www.qcsupply.com (16)

QDirect, West Chester, PA. Tel: (484) 701-1000, FAX: (484) 701-1599, Web Site: www.qdirect.com (32)

QED Marketing Inc, Central Islip, NY. Tel: (631) 851-4254 (22)

QMSI, Montague, CA. Tel: (530) 459-0910, Web Site: www.quintmail.com (22)

QUAXAR, Miami, FL. Tel: (305) 350-1919, Web Site: www.quaxar.com (35)

QVC Inc, West Chester, PA. Tel: (484) 701-1000, FAX: (484) 701-8500, Web Site: www.qvc.com (32)

Quad/Graphics, Sussex, WI. Tel: (414) 566-6000, E-Mail: qgraphics@qg.com, Web Site: www.QG. com (28)

Quade, Nathan, Heaven & Earth, Virginia Beach, VA. Tel: (757) 420-3576, E-Mail: teamkr8@ heavenandearth.hrcoxmail.com, Web Site: www. heavenandearth.com (5)

Quadra Graphics Inc, Cherry Hill, NJ. Tel: (856) 665-4060, FAX: (856) 665-7324, E-Mail: richard. nixon@qgi.com (27)

Quadracci, Joel, Quad/Graphics, Sussex, WI. Tel: (414) 566-6000, E-Mail: qgraphics@qg.com, Web Site: www.QG.com (28)

Quadrant Engineering Plastic Products, Reading, PA. Tel: (610) 320-6600, (800) 366-0300, FAX: (610) 320-6868, Web Site: www.quadrantepp.com (16)

Quadriga Art Inc, New York, NY. Tel: (212) 685-0751 (10)

Quaero Corp, Charlotte, NC. Tel: (877) 570-2199, Web Site: www.quaero.com (22)

The Quaker Oats Co, Chicago, IL. Tel: (312) 821-1000, (800) 367-6287, FAX: (312) 222-8323, Web Site: www.quakeroats.com (16)

Qualco, Inc, Passaic, NJ. Tel: (973) 473-1222, (800) 289-2567, FAX: (973) 473-0535, E-Mail: feedback@qualco.com, Web Site: www.qualco.com (8)

Qualey, Thomas, Maine Potato Board, Presque Isle, ME. Tel: (207) 769-5061, FAX: (207) 764-4148, E-Mail: mainepotatoes@mainepotatoes.com, Web Site: www.mainepotatoes.com (1)

Quality Contact Solutions Inc, Aurora, NE. Tel: (402) 210-2692, (866) 963-2889, FAX: (402) 210-2692, E-Mail: info@qualitycontactsolutions.com, Web Site: www.qualitycontactsolutions.com (29)

Quality Education Data (QED), Shelton, CT. Tel: (203) 926-4800, (800) 333-8802, E-Mail: mdrinfor@dnb.com, Web Site: www.schooldata. com (23)

Quality Letter Service Inc, New York, NY. Tel: (212) 268-3400, FAX: (212) 268-3401, E-Mail: info@ qletter.com, Web Site: www.qletter.com (21)

Quality Park Products, Minneapolis, MN. Tel: (651) 645-0251, (800) 547-4252, (800) 328-2990, FAX: (800) 637-5770, (800) 701-3291, E-Mail: mktg@ qualitypark.com, Web Site: www.qualitypark.com (26)

Quality Products Inc, Columbus, MS. Tel: (662) 328-1477, (800) 647-1057, FAX: (800) 824-8510, E-Mail: kshep@classroomsupply.com, Web Site: www.classroomsupply.com (10)

Qualkenbush, Eric, Veritas Analytics Inc, Sterling, VA. Tel: (703) 707-5620, Web Site: www.veritas-analytics.com (30)

Quandt, Peter J., Oakstone Publishing LLC, Birmingham, AL. Tel: (205) 991-5188, (800) 952-0690, FAX: (205) 995-4656, Web Site: www. oakstonepublishing.com (17)

Quantum Color, Morton Grove, IL. Tel: (847) 967-3600, FAX: (847) 967-3610, Web Site: www. cpipress.com (27)

Quantum Group, Morton Grove, IL. Tel: (847) 967-3600, Web Site: www.quantumgroup.com (35)

QuantumDigital, Austin, TX. Tel: (800) 637-7373, Web Site: www.quantumdigital.com (28)

Quark Inc, Denver, CO. Tel: (303) 894-3832, Web Site: www.quark.com (34)

Quartermaster Uniform & Equipment Co, Cerritos, CA. Tel: (562) 304-7300, (800) 444-8643, FAX: (562) 304-7335, Web Site: www.qmuniforms.com (2)

Quast, Bob, Life Fitness, Schiller Park, IL. Tel: (847) 288-3300, (800) 735-3867, FAX: (847) 288-3703, E-Mail: webmaster@lifefitness.com, Web Site: www.lifefitness.com (11)

Quattro Direct LLC, Berwyn, PA. Tel: (610) 993-0070, Web Site: www.quattrodirect.com (35)

Quattrone, Diana, Fox Chase Cancer Center, Philadelphia, PA. Tel: (215) 728-6900, (888) FOXCHASE, FAX: (215) 728-2594, Web Site: www.fccc.edu (1)

Quayside Publishing Group/MBI Publishing, Minneapolis, MN. Tel: (715) 294-3345, (800) 826-6600, FAX: (715) 294-4448, Web Site: www.motorbooks. com (17)

Quebecor-World Infiniti, Enfield, CT. Tel: (860) 741-0150, (800) 221-6052, FAX: (860) 741-2553, E-Mail: clint.humphrey@quebecorworld.com, Web Site: www.infinitigraphics.com (27)

Quebecor World Midland, Midland, MI. Tel: (989) 496-3333, (800) 448-4288, FAX: (989) 496-1921, Web Site: www.quebecorworldinc.com (27)

Quebecor World North America, North Haven, CT. Tel: (203) 288-2468, FAX: (203) 248-6478, Web Site: www.quebecorworldinc.com (27)

Queen Bee Gardens, Lovell, WY. Tel: (307) 548-2543, (800) 225-7553, FAX: (307) 548-6721, E-Mail: queenbee@tctwest.net, Web Site: queenbeegardens. com (4)

Queens College/CUNY Professional and Continuing Studies (PCS), Flushing, NY. Tel: (718) 997-5700, FAX: (718) 997-5723, E-Mail: pcs@qc.cuny.edu, Web Site: www.qc.cuny.edu/pcs (41)

Quennoz, Diane, Frontier Communications, Stamford, CT. Tel: (203) 614-5600, Web Site: www.czn.com (29)

Querceto, Jill, Capital Design, Providence, RI. Tel: (401) 270-6777, FAX: (401) 438-9360, E-Mail: info@freemiums.com, Web Site: www.freemiums. com (33)

Queue Inc, Stratford, CT. Tel: (203) 335-0906, (800) 232-2224, FAX: (800) 775-2729, E-Mail: jdk@ queueinc.com, Web Site: www.qworkbooks.com (17)

Quick Draw Clip Systems Inc, Ventura, CA. Tel: (805) 644-6888, (888) 254-7797, FAX: (805) 644-7320, E-Mail: ron@clipsystems.com, Web Site: www.clipsystems.com (9)

Quigley, James, H., Deloitte & Touche, Boston, MA. Tel: (617) 437-2000, FAX: (617) 437-2111, Web Site: www.deloitte.com (14)

Quigley, Robert, A., Charter Communications, Saint Louis, MO. Tel: (314) 965-0555, (888) 438-2427, FAX: (314) 965-9745, Web Site: www.charteroom. com (16)

Quigley, Robert, MTS Publishing, Naperville, IL. Tel: (630) 955-9750, (800) 332-4655, FAX: (630) 955-9787, E-Mail: info@mtspbl.com, Web Site: www. mtspbl.com (17)

Quigley, Robert, Quigley Consulting Group, Lake Forest, IL. Tel: (847) 604-6773 (20)

Quigley Consulting Group, Lake Forest, IL. Tel: (847) 604-6773 (20)

Quigley Simpson, Los Angeles, CA. Tel: (310) 996-5820, Web Site: www.quigleysimpson.com (35)

Quill, John, Ecological Fibers Inc, Lunenburg, MA. Tel: (978) 537-0003, FAX: (978) 537-2238, E-Mail: jquill@ecofibers.com (25)

Quill Corp, Palatine, IL. Tel: (847) 634-4800, (800) 789-1331, FAX: (800) 789-6630, Web Site: www. quill.com (16)

Quine, Richard, D&E Pharmaceuticals Inc, Farmingdale, NJ. Tel: (973) 838-8300, (800) 221-1833, FAX: (877) 838-0560, E-Mail: customerservice@ dnepharm.com, Web Site: www.dnepharm.com (7)

Quinlan III, Thomas, J., RR Donnelley & Sons Co, Chicago, IL. Tel: (312) 326-8000, FAX: (312) 326-7156, Web Site: www.rrdonnelly.com (31)

Quinlan, D.L., CYRO Industries, Parsippany, NJ. Tel: (973) 541-8000, (800) 631-5384, FAX: (973) 442-6117, (973) 442-6135, Web Site: www.cyro.com (16)

Quinn, Dave, Prism Data Services Ltd, Mississauga, ON. Tel: (905) 278-5556, FAX: (905) 278-6603, E-Mail: bill.cram@prism-data.com; sales@prism-data.com, Web Site: www.prism-data.com (21)

Quinn, Jane, Replogle Globes Inc, Broadview, IL. Tel: (708) 343-0900, FAX: (708) 343-0923, E-Mail: info@replogleglobes.com, Web Site: www.replogleglobes.com (16)

Quinn, Jeffery C., Educational Lists Services Inc, Downers Grove, IL. Tel: (630) 968-1290, FAX: (630) 968-6010, E-Mail: jquinn@educationallist.com, Web Site: www.educationallist.com (24)

Quinn, Jesse, Solitron Devices Inc, West Palm Beach, FL. Tel: (561) 848-4311, FAX: (561) 863-5946, E-Mail: sales@solitrondevices.com, Web Site: www.solitrondevices.com (16)

Quinn, Kate, Anthem Blue Cross, Westlake Village, CA. Tel: (805) 557-6655, (800) 333-0912, FAX: (800) 557-6872, Web Site: www.bluecrossca.com (15)

Quinn, Kevin C., Newhouse School of Public Communications, Syracuse, NY. Tel: (315) 443-3611, FAX: (315) 443-4426, Web Site: newhouse.syr.edu (41)

Quinn, Larry, Omega Studios, Elgin, IL. Tel: (972) 444-8556, FAX: (972) 444-8559, E-Mail: omegastudios@rrd.com, Web Site: www.omega-studios.com (37)

Quinn, Mimi, Tender Heart Treasures, Omaha, NE. Tel: (402) 593-1313, (800) 443-1367, FAX: (402) 593-1316, E-Mail: bcamenzind@thtdesigns.com (6)

Quinn, Pat, TWL Knowledge Group, Carrollton, TX. Tel: (972) 309-4000, (800) 624-2272, FAX: (972) 309-5105, Web Site: www.twlk.com (3)

Quinnell, Bruce, A., Hot Topic Inc, City of Industry, CA. Tel: (626) 839-4681, (800) 275-9169, FAX: (626) 839-4686, Web Site: www.hottopic.com (2)

Quinnipiac College, Hamden, CT. Tel: (203) 582-8600, (203) 582-8200, (800) 462-1944, FAX: (203) 281-8664, Web Site: www.quinnipiac.edu (41)

Quinones, Marcos, MVS Mailers Inc, Bohemia, NY. Tel: (800) 641-7917, FAX: (631) 699-0101, E-Mail: muraco@mvsmailers.com, Web Site: www.mvsmailers.com (28)

Quintanilla, Lucy, Integrated Alliance Limited Partnership, Denton, TX. Tel: (940) 565-9415, FAX: (940) 383-1876, E-Mail: ryoung@integratedalliance.com, Web Site: www.integratedalliance.com (29)

Quintanilla, Valerie, Booyah Networks, Westminster, CO. Tel: (303) 426-7776, FAX: (303) 345-6700, E-Mail: support@booyahnetworks.com, Web Site: www.booyahnetworks.com (35)

Quirk, Terrence, JJ Keller & Associates Inc, Neenah, WI. Tel: (920) 722-2848, (800) 327-6868, FAX: (800) 727-7516, E-Mail: thines@jjkeller.com, Web Site: www.jjkeller.com/jjk (16)

Quish, Rob, JWT Inside, Santa Monica, CA. Tel: (310) 309-8282, (877) 665-8768, FAX: (310) 309-8283, E-Mail: conversations@jwtinside.com, Web Site: www.jwtworks.com (35)

Quist, Nikki, Smith Hanley Associates, Southport, CT. Tel: (203) 319-4300, (888) 221-2900, FAX: (203) 319-4320, Web Site: www.smithhanley.com (20)

Qwest, Denver, CO. Tel: (303) 992-1400, (800) 603-6000, FAX: (303) 896-8515, Web Site: www.qwest.com (20)

R

R&S Industries Corp, Chesterfield, MO. Tel: (314) 781-5400, FAX: (314) 781-5169, E-Mail: sendeverything@miraclepolishingcloth.com, Web Site: www.miraclepolishingcloth.com (16)

R2C Group, Portland, OR. Tel: (503) 222-0025, Web Site: www.r2cgroup.com (35)

RB Toy Design Inc, Glenview, IL. Tel: (847) 577-5683, FAX: (847) 272-4034, E-Mail: info@rbtoydesign.com, Web Site: www.rbtoy.com (33)

RBC Dain Rauscher, Boston, MA. Tel: (617) 725-2000, FAX: (617) 725-1393, Web Site: www.rbcdainrauscher.com (14)

RBC Funds, Milwaukee, WI. Tel: (800) 422-2766, Web Site: us.rbcgam.com (14)

RBS Citizens Financial Group Inc, Dedham, MA. Tel: (781) 471-1565, Web Site: www.citizensbank.com (14)

RCS Response Technologies Inc, Charlotte, NC. Tel: (704) 522-1919, FAX: (704) 522-9092, E-Mail: data@rcsdirect.com, Web Site: www.rcsdirect.com (21)

RDO Marketing LLC, Minneapolis, MN. Tel: (952) 746-7585 (20)

Redi-Data, Fairfield, NJ. Tel: (973) 808-4500, FAX: (973) 808-5511, E-Mail: sales@redimail.com, Web Site: www.redidata.com (23)

REI-Recreational Equipment Inc, Kent, WA. Tel: (253) 891-2500, (800) 426-4840, FAX: (253) 891-2523, Web Site: www.rei.com (11)

RFM Broadcasting, New Rochelle, NY. Tel: (914) 633-0725, FAX: (914) 206-4144, E-Mail: andrew@rfmitv.com (35)

RJ Olsen Inc, Natick, MA. Tel: (508) 647-3777, FAX: (508) 647-6777, E-Mail: dickolsen@aol.com (30)

RL Polk & Co, Southfield, MI. Tel: (248) 728-7100, (800) GO-4-POLK, FAX: (248) 728-4444, Web Site: www.polk.com (23)

RMA-The Risk Management Association, Philadelphia, PA. Tel: (215) 446-4000, FAX: (215) 446-4101, E-Mail: customers@rmahq.org, Web Site: www.rmahq.org (1)

RMI Direct Marketing Inc, Danbury, CT. Tel: (203) 798-0448, FAX: (203) 778-6130, E-Mail: info@rmidirect.com, Web Site: www.rmidirect.com (23)

RPM Direct LLC, Lambertville, NJ. Tel: (609) 566-7150, Web Site: www.r4pm.com (35)

RPM Industries Inc, Auburn, NY. Tel: (315) 255-1105, (800) 669-3676, FAX: (315) 252-1167, Web Site: www.rpmdisplays.com (33)

RR Donnelley Response Marketing Services, Downers Grove, IL. Tel: (800) 722-9001, FAX: (630) 322-6270, Web Site: www.rms.rrd.com (31)

RSC The Quality Measurement Co, Evansville, IN. Tel: (812) 425-4562, FAX: (812) 425-2844 (30)

RSM McGladrey Inc, Charlotte, NC. Tel: (980) 233-4700, Web Site: www.rsmmcgladrey.com (20)

RSVP Publications, Tampa, FL. Tel: (813) 960-7787, Web Site: www.MailToTheAffluent.com (31)

RTC Relationship Marketing, Washington, DC. Tel: (202) 625-2111, FAX: (202) 424-7900, Web Site: www.rtcrm.com (35)

RW Consulting, Asheville, NC. Tel: (828) 299-3645, Web Site: www.rwconsulting.net (20)

Raab, David M., Raab Associates, Chappaqua, NY. Tel: (914) 241-2117, FAX: (914) 241-0080, E-Mail: info@raabassociates.com, Web Site: www.raabassociates.com (20)

Raab Associates, Chappaqua, NY. Tel: (914) 241-2117, FAX: (914) 241-0080, E-Mail: info@raabassociates.com, Web Site: www.raabassociates.com (20)

Raap, William, Gardener's Supply Co, Burlington, VT. Tel: (802) 660-3500, (888) 833-1412, FAX: (802) 660-3501, E-Mail: info@gardeners.com, Web Site: www.gardeners.com (8)

Rabbu, Christopher, AdvanceMe Inc, Kennesaw, GA. Tel: (888) 700-8181, Web Site: www.advanceme.com (14)

Raccah, Dominique, Sourcebooks Inc, Naperville, IL. Tel: (630) 961-3900, Web Site: www.sourcebooks.com (17)

Racer Walsh Co, Jacksonville, FL. Tel: (904) 721-2289, FAX: (904) 721-2935, Web Site: www.racerwalsh.com (12)

Racer's Equipment Warehouse, Warwick, RI. Tel: (401) 348-6010, (800) 556-2864, FAX: (401) 348-6023, E-Mail: scott@racers-eq.com, Web Site: www.racers-eq.com (16)

RAD Marketing & Cable Towns, Mount Vernon, NY. Tel: (914) 668-3563, FAX: (914) 668-4247, E-Mail: cabletowns@verizon.net (24)

Radcliff, Kimberly, Graphic Arts Center, Garland, TX. Tel: (972) 271-0591, (800) 865-7086, FAX: (972) 271-8392 (27)

Rader, Dave, Frito-Lay, Plano, TX. Tel: (972) 334-7000, (800) 352-4477, FAX: (972) 334-2019, Web Site: www.fritolay.com (16)

Rader, Debra, Commerce Register Inc, Midland Park, NJ. Tel: (201) 445-3000, FAX: (201) 445-5806, E-Mail: cri@comreginc.com, Web Site: www.comreginc.com (22)

Radetich, Alex, Take 5 Solutions LLC, Boca Raton, FL. Tel: (561) 819-5555, (866) 861-8862, FAX: (561) 819-0245, E-Mail: sales@take5s.com, Web Site: www.take5solutions.com (30)

Radia, Suku, V., Meredith Corp, Des Moines, IA. Tel: (515) 284-3000, FAX: (515) 284-2700, Web Site: www.meredith.com (17)

Radio Direct Response, Media, PA. Tel: (610) 892-7300, FAX: (610) 892-1899, E-Mail: info@radiodirect.com, Web Site: www.radiodirect.com (35)

RadioShack Corp, Fort Worth, TX. Tel: (817) 415-2010, FAX: (817) 415-2647, Web Site: www.radioshack.com (3)

Radock, Leslie, Music Treasures Co, Richmond, VA. Tel: (804) 730-8800, (800) 666-7565, FAX: (888) MUSIC-TC, E-Mail: musict@musictreasures.com, Web Site: www.musictreasures.com (6)

Radzik, Kim, Sportif Mail Order Inc, Sparks, NV. Tel: (775) 359-6400, (800) 776-7843, FAX: (800) 776-3291, Web Site: www.sportif.com (2)

Raether, Kandy, Enerpac, Menomonee Falls, WI. Tel: (262) 781-6600, (800) 433-2766, FAX: (262) 781-1028, Web Site: www.enerpac.com (16)

Raff, David, MDI Lists, Weston, FL. Tel: (954) 384-1557, FAX: (954) 389-0939, Web Site: www.mdilists.com (23)

Rafferty, Noreen, Family Circle Magazine Inc, New York, NY. Tel: (212) 557-6600, Web Site: www.familycircle.com (31)

Rafipour, Mary, Fairfield Industries Inc, Sugar Land, TX. Tel: (281) 275-7500, (800) 231-9809, FAX: (281) 275-7550, E-Mail: jblattman@fairfield.com, Web Site: www.fairfield.com (16)

Rafner, John, Nice Lines Direct Mail, Norristown, PA. Tel: (610) 279-1100, (888) 815-NICE, FAX: (610) 279-7800, Web Site: www.nicelines.com (21)

Ragsdale, John, Williamson-Dickie Manufacturing Co, Fort Worth, TX. Tel: (800) 336-7201, FAX: (817) 877-5027, E-Mail: customerservice@dickies.com, Web Site: www.dickies.com (2)

Ragusa, Chris, Estee Marketing Group Inc, New Rochelle, NY. Tel: (914) 235-7080, FAX: (914) 235-6518, E-Mail: info@esteemarketing.com, Web Site: www.esteemarketing.com (20)

Ragusa, John, BNY Mellon, New York, NY. Tel: (412) 234-5000, (212) 495-1784, FAX: (412) 234-1928, Web Site: www.bnymellon.com (14)

Raguso, John, Driscoll Label Co Inc, East Hanover, NJ. Tel: (973) 575-8492, FAX: (800) 342-1195, (973) 575-8345, E-Mail: info@driscolllabel.com, Web Site: www.driscolllabel.com (27)

Rahardia, Francisca, Philip Morris USA Inc, Richmond, VA. Tel: (804) 274-2000, FAX: (804) 484-8231, Web Site: www.philipmorrisusa.com (16)

Rahja, John, Augsburg Fortress Publishers, Minneapolis, MN. Tel: (612) 330-3300, (800) 426-0115, FAX: (612) 330-3455, E-Mail: info@augsburgfortress.org, Web Site: www.augsburgfortress.org (17)

Rahr, Tim, The Taunton Press, Newtown, CT. Tel: (203) 426-8171, (800) 477-8727, FAX: (203) 426-3434, Web Site: www.taunton.com (17)

Rahvar, David, Rose Electronics, Houston, TX. Tel: (281) 933-7673, (800) 333-9343, FAX: (281) 933-0044, E-Mail: sales@rose.com, Web Site: www.rose.com (3)

Raiford, William, Memphis Net & Twine Co Inc, Memphis, TN. Tel: (901) 458-2656, (888) 674-7638, FAX: (901) 458-1601, E-Mail: fishinfo@memphisnet.net, Web Site: www.memphisnet.net (11)

Raihofer, Lynda, Lynda Raihofer & Associates LLC, Pelham, NY. Tel: (914) 738-8282 (20)

Lynda Raihofer & Associates LLC, Pelham, NY. Tel: (914) 738-8282 (20)

Raimondo, Tony, F., Behlen Manufacturing Co, Columbus, NE. Tel: (402) 564-3111, FAX: (402) 563-7405, E-Mail: behlen@megavision.com, Web Site: www.behlenmfg.com (16)

Rainbow Art Glass, Wall, NJ. Tel: (732) 681-6003, (800) 526-2356, FAX: (732) 681-4984, E-Mail: info@rainbowartglass.com, Web Site: www.rainbowartglass.com (16)

Rainbow Graphics Inc, Mundelein, IL. Tel: (847) 824-9600, Web Site: www.rainbowgraphics.com (27)

Rainbow Group LLC, Middleton, WI. Tel: (608) 824-0068, Web Site: www.beaconathletics.com (11)

Raines, Franklin, D., Fannie Mae, Washington, DC. Tel: (202) 752-7000, FAX: (202) 752-3808, Web Site: www.fanniemae.com (14)

Raines, Philip, Globe Ticket & Label Co, Lombard, IL. Tel: (404) 762-9711, (800) 523-5968, FAX: (404) 762-7019, Web Site: www.globeticket.com (16)

Rainey, J., Mike, Liberty Orchards Co Inc, Cashmere, WA. Tel: (509) 782-2191, (800) 888-5696, FAX: (509) 782-1487, E-Mail: service@libertyorchards.com, Web Site: www.libertyorchards.com (16)

Rainey, Pat, National Fundraising Lists, Bowie, MD. Tel: (410) 721-5700, FAX: (410) 721-5795, E-Mail: info@nflists.com, Web Site: www.nflists.com (23)

Rainwater Associates Inc, New York, NY. Tel: (212) 861-2856, FAX: (212) 861-1729, E-Mail: rainwine@aol.com (20)

Raitt, Eugene, AIG Marketing, New York, NY. Tel: (212) 770-7000, (212) 770-2237, Web Site: www.agac.com (15)

Rajan, Bob, Creative Automation, Hillside, IL. Tel: (708) 449-2800, (800) 773-1588, FAX: (708) 449-3282, E-Mail: busmgr@cauto.com, Web Site: www.cauto.com (22)

Rajant Corp, Malvern, PA. Tel: (484) 595-0233, FAX: (484) 595-0244, E-Mail: moreinfo@rajant.com, Web Site: www.rajant.com (32)

Rajee, Karen, Star Silkscreen Design Inc, Decatur, IL. Tel: (217) 877-0804, FAX: (217) 877-0843 (2)

Raley's Bel Air Markets, West Sacramento, CA. Tel: (916) 373-3333, FAX: (916) 373-6351, Web Site: www.raleys.com (16)

Ralph, Bill, Journal of Commerce Group, Newark, NJ. Tel: (973) 848-7000, FAX: (973) 848-7004, Web Site: www.joc.com (17)

Ralston, Jamie, Wyandotte West Communications Inc, Kansas City, KS. Tel: (913) 788-5565, FAX: (913) 788-9812, E-Mail: news@wyandottewest.com, Web Site: www.wyandottewest.com (17)

Ralston, Kate, Mapping Analytics, Rochester, NY. Tel: (585) 271-6490, (877) 893-6490, FAX: (585) 271-1132, E-Mail: sales@mappinganalytics.com, Web Site: www.mappinganalytics.com (20)

Ramasamy, Kannan, Aegis Communications, Irving, TX. Tel: (972) 830-1800, (800) 332-0266, FAX: (972) 830-1801, E-Mail: info@aegisglobal.com, Web Site: www.aegiscomgroup.com (29)

Ramburg, Sherry, Planet Cotton, Gaithersburg, MD. Tel: (301) 948-0400, FAX: (301) 948-9031, Web Site: www.planetcotton.com (2)

Ramirez, Emilio, Direct Marketing Solutions Inc, Portland, OR. Tel: (503) 281-1400, Web Site: www.teamdms.com (35)

Ramirez, Luisa, Indus-Tool, Chicago, IL. Tel: (312) 226-2473, (800) 662-5021, FAX: (312) 226-2480, E-Mail: sales@indus-tool.com, Web Site: www.indus-tool.com (12)

Ramirez, Michelle, NPI, Fort Worth, TX. Tel: (214) 634-2288, FAX: (682) 503-8214, E-Mail: sales@npisorters.com, Web Site: www.npisorters.com (16)

Ramirez, Paul, Eventful Inc, San Diego, CA. Tel: (858) 754-3004, Web Site: www.eventful.com (19)

Ramoutar, Ken, Advanced Software Applications, Bridgeville, PA. Tel: (412) 220-9300, E-Mail: asa@asacorp.com, Web Site: www.asacorp.com (22)

Ramsey Jr, Joe, F., AMVETS National Service Foundation, Lanham, MD. Tel: (301) 459-6181, (877) 726-8387, FAX: (301) 459-5578, Web Site: www.amvets.org (1)

Ramussen, Neil, E., American Power Conversion Corp, West Kingston, RI. Tel: (401) 789-5735, (800) 788-2208, FAX: (401) 789-3710, E-Mail: public.relations@apcc.com, Web Site: www.apcc.com (3)

Ranaldi, Robert, A., Far West Media Services, Long Beach, CA. Tel: (562) 496-3342, FAX: (562) 496-4329, Web Site: www.farwestmedia.com (32)

Ranch House Meat Co, Menard, TX. Tel: (800) 749-6329, FAX: (888) 917-6328, E-Mail: sales@brisket.net, Web Site: www.brisket.net (4)

Rand, Gail, Government Data Publications Inc, Washington, DC. Tel: (718) 627-0819, (800) 275-4688, FAX: (718) 998-5960, E-Mail: gdp@govdata.com, Web Site: www.govdata.com (17)

Rand Material Handling Equipment Co Inc, Janesville, WI. Tel: (401) 751-7657, (800) 366-2300, FAX: (800) 755-7263, E-Mail: cs@randmh.com, Web Site: www.randmh.com (13)

Randall, Bernadette, L., Choice Point, Alpharetta, GA. Tel: (770) 752-6000, (800) 342-5339, FAX: (770) 752-6005, Web Site: www.choicepoint.com (16)

Randall, Richard, Coach, New York, NY. Tel: (212) 594-1850, (800) 444-3611, FAX: (212) 594-1682, Web Site: www.coach.com (2)

Randall, Roger, Farm Journal Inc, Philadelphia, PA. Tel: (215) 557-8937, FAX: (215) 568-4238 (17)

Randall, Shane, aNETorder/American Mailers, Naperville, IL. Tel: (630) 579-8800, Web Site: www.anetorder.com (28)

Randall, Todd, Cable Films & Video, Mission Hills, KS. Tel: (913) 362-2804, (800) 514-2804, FAX: (913) 362-2864, E-Mail: cablefilms@kc.rr.com, Web Site: www.onlineworld.com/movies (3)

Randall, William, Hatchholdings LLC, Plano, TX. Tel: (214) 505-4697 (20)

Randolph, Timothy, Americana Sales Ventures Inc, Altamonte Springs, FL. Tel: (407) 862-8388, (800) 445-4302, FAX: (407) 862-6535, Web Site: www.americanashopper.com (35)

Random House Children's Books, New York, NY. Tel: (212) 782-9000, (800) 726-0600, Web Site: www.randomhouse.com/kids (13)

Random House Direct Marketing, New York, NY. Tel: (212) 572-4985, (800) 678-5681, FAX: (212) 572-6018, Web Site: www.randomhousedirect.com (17)

Random Lengths Publications Inc, Eugene, OR. Tel: (541) 686-9925, (888) 686-9925, FAX: (541) 686-9629, (800) 874-7979, E-Mail: rlmail@rlpi.com, Web Site: www.randomlengths.com (17)

Rangel, Lynn, Finck Cigar Co, San Antonio, TX. Tel: (210) 341-8888, (800) 221-0638, FAX: (210) 341-8890, E-Mail: info@finckcigar.com, Web Site: www.finckcigar.com (5)

Ranger Joe's International Military Supply, Columbus, GA. Tel: (706) 689-0082, (800) 247-4541, FAX: (706) 682-8840, E-Mail: customerservice@rangerjoes.com, Web Site: www.rangerjoes.com (2)

Rankers, Angie, Nevco Scoreboard Co, Greenville, IL. Tel: (618) 664-0360, (800) 851-4040, FAX: (618) 664-0398, E-Mail: sales@nevcoscoreboards.com, Web Site: www.nevcoscoreboards.com (16)

Rankin, Aaron, AD-Vantage Marketing, Santa Rosa, CA. Tel: (707) 578-8700, FAX: (707) 578-0258, Web Site: www.ad-vantagemarketing.com (23)

Rankin, Charles, E., University of Oklahoma Press, Norman, OK. Tel: (800) 627-7377, FAX: (405) 364-5798, Web Site: www.oupress.com (17)

Rankin, Glen, AD-Vantage Marketing, Santa Rosa, CA. Tel: (707) 578-8700, FAX: (707) 578-0258, Web Site: www.ad-vantagemarketing.com (23)

Ransick, Neil, Neil Ransick Marketing, San Francisco, CA. Tel: (415) 664-6728 (20)

Neil Ransick Marketing, San Francisco, CA. Tel: (415) 664-6728 (20)

Ranzini, Stephen, Lange, University Bank, Ann Arbor, MI. Tel: (734) 741-5858, FAX: (734) 741-5859, E-Mail: ranzini@university-bank.com, Web Site: www.university-bank.com (14)

Rao, Steven, Relevate, Springfield, VA. Tel: (703) 658-8300, (800) 523-7346, FAX: (703) 658-8301, E-Mail: sales@relevategroup.com, Web Site: www.relevategroup.com (22)

Rapella, Steve, Neo-Tech Publishing Co, Henderson, NV. Tel: (702) 891-0303, FAX: (702) 795-8393 (17)

Raphel, Neil, Raphel Marketing, Saint Johnsbury, VT. Tel: (802) 751-8802, FAX: (802) 751-8804, E-Mail: neil@raphel.com, Web Site: www.raphel.com (20)

Raphel Marketing, Saint Johnsbury, VT. Tel: (802) 751-8802, FAX: (802) 751-8804, E-Mail: neil@raphel.com, Web Site: www.raphel.com (20)

Rapid City Journal, Rapid City, SD. Tel: (605) 394-8300, FAX: (605) 394-8462, E-Mail: classifieds@rapidcityjournal.com, Web Site: www.rapidcityjournal.com (18)

Rapid Color Printing, Las Vegas, NV. Tel: (702) 792-6055, FAX: (702) 792-1437, Web Site: www.rapidocolor.com (27)

Rapid Insight Inc, Conway, NH. Tel: (603) 447-0240, Web Site: www.rapidinsightinc.com (20)

A Rapid Mailing Inc, Jessup, MD. Tel: (410) 792-4000, (800) US-RAPID, FAX: (301) 776-3690, E-Mail: info@rairapid.com, Web Site: www.rairapid.com (28)

Rapid Progress Marketing & Modeling LLC, Saint Petersburg, FL. Tel: (727) 528-8578, Web Site: www.rpmsquared.com (22)

Rapid Response Marketing, Las Vegas, NV. Tel: (702) 631-9714, (866) 997-7297, FAX: (702) 216-4038, Web Site: www.xy7.com (32)

Rapidforms Inc, Lancaster, CA. Tel: (856) 384-1144, (800) 257-8354, FAX: (856) 384-1697, Web Site: www.rapidforms.com (27)

Rapids Wholesale Equipment, Marion, IA. Tel: (319) 447-1670, (800) 472-7431, FAX: (319) 447-1680, (800) 858-0327, E-Mail: judys@rapidswholesale.com, Web Site: www.rapidswholesale.com (16)

Raponi, Thomas, KICU-TV, San Jose, CA. Tel: (408) 953-3636, FAX: (408) 953-3610, Web Site: www.ktvu.com (32)

Rapp, Howard, Howard Rapp Enterprises Inc, New York, NY. Tel: (212) 247-6646, FAX: (212) 247-6645, E-Mail: hrapp3678@aol.com (35)

Rapp, Ken, IC System Inc, Saint Paul, MN. Tel: (651) 483-0585, (800) 245-8875, FAX: (651) 481-6363, E-Mail: promo@icsystem.com, Web Site: www.icsystem.com (21)

Rapp, Philip J., The Saint Francis Academy Inc, Salina, KS. Tel: (785) 825-0541, (800) 423-1342, FAX: (785) 825-2940, Web Site: www.st-francis.org (1)

Rapp, William K., Kolbe Corp, Phoenix, AZ. Tel: (602) 840-9770, (800) 642-2822, FAX: (602) 952-2706, E-Mail: info@kolbe.com, Web Site: www.kolbe.com (17)

Rapp, William, Vance Industries Inc, Niles, IL. Tel: (847) 375-8900, FAX: (847) 375-6818, E-Mail: vance@vanceind.com, Web Site: www.vanceind.com (16)

Rapp Collins Worldwide, New York, NY. Tel: (212) 817-6800, FAX: (212) 686-7047, Web Site: www.rappcollins.com (35)

Howard Rapp Enterprises Inc, New York, NY. Tel: (212) 247-6646, FAX: (212) 247-6645, E-Mail: hrapp3678@aol.com (35)

Rappahannock Electric Cooperative, Fredericksburg, VA. Tel: (540) 898-8500, Web Site: www.myrec.coop (1)

Rappaport, Donn, ALC Inc, Princeton, NJ. Tel: (609) 580-2800, (800) ALC-LIST, FAX: (609) 580-2888, E-Mail: info@alc.com, Web Site: www.alc.com (23)

Rappaport, Donn, DMA (Direct Marketing Association), New York, NY. Tel: (212) 768-7277, FAX: (212) 302-6714, E-Mail: customerservice@the-dma.org, Web Site: www.the-dma.org (40)

Rappel, James, F., Portland Cement Association, Skokie, IL. Tel: (847) 966-6200, FAX: (847) 966-9781, Web Site: www.cement.org (1)

Raritan Inc, Somerset, NJ. Tel: (732) 764-8886, Web Site: www.raritan.com (22)

Rascal, Sewell, NJ. Tel: (856) 468-1000, (800) 662-4548, FAX: (856) 468-3426, Web Site: www.electricmobility.com (7)

Rasekhi, Patricia, Interval International, South Miami, FL. Tel: (305) 925-7019, Web Site: www.intervalworld.com (35)

Rasin, Deborah, Samsonite Corp, Mansfield, MA. Tel: (508) 851-1400, (800) 547-BAGS, FAX: (303) 373-8715, Web Site: www.samsonite.com (16)

Raskin, Eric, Professional Advertising Systems Inc, Armonk, NY. Tel: (914) 765-0500, FAX: (914) 765-0503, E-Mail: info@paslists.com, Web Site: www.paslists.com (22)

Raskin, Micah, List Service Direct Inc, Leonia, NJ. Tel: (201) 585-1447, (800) 371-5487, FAX: (201) 585-1732, E-Mail: info@listservicedirect.com, Web Site: www.listservicedirect.com (23)

Raspe, Bill, Office Express Inc, Evanston, IL. Tel: (888) 526-8438, FAX: (773) 341-7322, E-Mail: sales@envelopesexpress.com, Web Site: www.envelopesexpress.com (26)

Rast, Bob, TT Publishing, Arlington, VA. Tel: (703) 838-1770, FAX: (703) 838-0285, Web Site: www.ttnews.com (17)

Rastar, Salt Lake City, UT. Tel: (801) 973-6720, Web Site: www.rastek.com (35)

Ratcliff, Michael, Gummed Papers of America, Mc Cook, IL. Tel: (773) 650-2020, (800) 395-9000, FAX: (708) 485-8603, (800) 395-3581, E-Mail: info@labelexperts.com, Web Site: www.labelexperts.com (34)

Rath, Colin, D, Better Lists Inc, Stamford, CT. Tel: (203) 324-4171, FAX: (203) 358-0384, E-Mail: tim@betterlists.com, Web Site: www.betterlists.com (28)

Rath, George, S., Better Lists Inc, Stamford, CT. Tel: (203) 324-4171, FAX: (203) 358-0384, E-Mail: tim@betterlists.com, Web Site: www.betterlists.com (28)

Rath, Sam, Group Mojo, Portland, OR. Tel: (503) 493-2242, FAX: (503) 493-2246, E-Mail: sam@mojops.com, Web Site: www.groupmojo.com (32)

Ratner, Dave, Dave's Soda & Pet City, Agawam, MA. Tel: (413) 789-2259, Web Site: www.daveratner.com (5)

Ratner, Howard, Nature Publishing Group, New York, NY. Tel: (212) 726-9200, FAX: (212) 696-9006, E-Mail: nature@natureny.com, Web Site: www.nature.com (17)

Ratner, Irina, New York Daily News, Jersey City, NJ. Tel: (212) 210-1844, Web Site: www.nydailynews.com (31)

Rattmann, Thomas, E., Columbian Mutual Life Insurance Co, Binghamton, NY. Tel: (607) 724-2472, (800) 423-9765 (15)

Raube, James, C., Select Comfort Corp, Minneapolis, MN. Tel: (763) 551-7000, (888) 411-2188, FAX: (763) 551-7826, Web Site: www.selectcomfort.com (16)

Rauff, Bill, Stimpson Co Inc, Pompano Beach, FL. Tel: (954) 946-3500, (877) 765-0748, FAX: (954) 941-1921, E-Mail: customerservice@stimpson.com, Web Site: www.stimpson.com (16)

Rausch, Erwin, Didactic Systems, Cranford, NJ. Tel: (908) 276-5413, FAX: (908) 276-7174, E-Mail: didacticra@aol.com (20)

Rauxa Direct, Costa Mesa, CA. Tel: (714) 427-1271, Web Site: www.rauxa.com (35)

Raven, Abbie, Arts & Entertainment Television Network, New York, NY. Tel: (212) 210-1400, FAX: (212) 210-1326, Web Site: www.aetv.com (16)

Raven's Nest Herbals, LLC, Duluth, GA. Tel: (678) 642-6691, (678) 584-0830, E-Mail: info@ravensnestherbals.com, Web Site: www.ravensnestherbals.com (7)

Ravich, Robert, THORLO INC, Statesville, NC. Tel: (704) 872-6522, (888) 846-7567, FAX: (704) 838-7005, Web Site: www.thorlo.com (16)

Rawle, David L., Rawle-Murdy Associates Inc, Charleston, SC. Tel: (843) 577-7327, FAX: (843) 722-3960, E-Mail: contact@rawlemurdy.com, Web Site: www.rawle-murdy.com (35)

Rawle-Murdy Associates Inc, Charleston, SC. Tel: (843) 577-7327, FAX: (843) 722-3960, E-Mail: contact@rawlemurdy.com, Web Site: www.rawle-murdy.com (35)

Rawlings, Penny, Arctic Trading Co Inc, Churchill, MB Canada. Tel: (204) 675-8804, (800) 665-0431, FAX: (204) 675-2164, E-Mail: atcpenny@mts.net, Web Site: www.arctictradingco.com (6)

Rawson, Maureen, US Pharmacopeia, Rockville, MD. Tel: (301) 881-0666, FAX: (301) 816-8236 (1)

Ray, James, C., McFeely's Square Drive Screws, Madison, WI. Tel: (434) 846-2729, (800) 443-7937, FAX: (804) 847-7136, E-Mail: tech@mcfeelys.com, Web Site: www.mcfeelys.com (16)

Raybuck, Lisa, Raybuck Autobody Parts, Punxsutawney, PA. Tel: (814) 938-5248, FAX: (814) 938-4250, E-Mail: service@raybuck.com, Web Site: www.raybuck.com (12)

Raybuck, Randy, Raybuck Autobody Parts, Punxsutawney, PA. Tel: (814) 938-5248, FAX: (814) 938-4250, E-Mail: service@raybuck.com, Web Site: www.raybuck.com (12)

Raybuck Autobody Parts, Punxsutawney, PA. Tel: (814) 938-5248, FAX: (814) 938-4250, E-Mail: service@raybuck.com, Web Site: www.raybuck.com (12)

Rayburn, Todd, Fresno Oxygen, Fresno, CA. Tel: (559) 233-6684, (800) 404-9353, FAX: (559) 233-4206, E-Mail: info@fresnooxygen.com, Web Site: www.fresnooxygen.com (9)

Rayburn, William, FNC INC, Oxford, MS. Tel: (662) 236-8254, Web Site: www.fncinc.com (14)

Raycom Sports, Charlotte, NC. Tel: (704) 378-4456/4400, FAX: (704) 378-4465, E-Mail: whicks@raycomsports.com, Web Site: raycomsports.com (16)

Rayher, Jack, Enco Manufacturing Co, Fernley, NV. Tel: (775) 788-7175, (800) 873-3626, FAX: (800) 965-5857, E-Mail: milanesp@use-enco.com, Web Site: www.use-enco.com (9)

Raymer, John, Helly-Hansen, Auburn, WA. Tel: (800) 435-5901, FAX: (425) 649-3740, E-Mail: webmaster@hellyhansen.com, Web Site: www.hellyhansen.com (16)

Raymond, Kevin, Metropolitan Property & Casualty Ins, Warwick, RI. Tel: (401) 827-2104 (15)

Rayner, Darrin, Xpressdocs, Fort Worth, TX. Tel: (817) 547-9705, Web Site: www.xpressdocs.com (27)

RayPress Corp, Birmingham, AL. Tel: (205) 989-3731, Web Site: www.raypress.com (27)

Raz, Rita, Analytic Recruiting Inc, New York, NY. Tel: (212) 545-8511, FAX: (212) 545-8520, E-Mail: rita@analyticrecruiting.com, Web Site: www.analyticrecruiting.com (20)

RAZOR Transaction Building Experts, Addison, TX. Tel: (972) 663-1100, Web Site: www.razordriven.com (35)

ReachForce, Austin, TX. Tel: (512) 327-9000, FAX: (512) 327-9090, E-Mail: info@reachforce.com, Web Site: www.reachforce.com (23)

Read, Phillip, Lillian Vernon Corp, Colorado Springs, CO. Tel: (757) 427-7923, FAX: (757) 427-7819, E-Mail: publicrelations@lillianvernon.com, Web Site: www.lillianvernon.com (6)

The Reader's Digest Association Inc, New York, NY. Tel: (914) 238-3599, FAX: (914) 244-7689, Web Site: www.rd.com (17)

Reading, Katherine A., Seedburo Equipment Co, Des Plaines, IL. Tel: (312) 738-3700, (800) 284-5779, FAX: (312) 738-5329, E-Mail: sales@seedburo.com, Web Site: www.seedburo.com (8)

Reading, Kathy, The Scan Group, Waukesha, WI. Tel: (262) 521-1365, Web Site: www.scangroup.net (35)

Reading for Education, Murfreesboro, TN. Tel: (615) 896-3800 (16)

Readinger, Mark, E., P & H Mining Equipment, Milwaukee, WI. Tel: (414) 671-4400, FAX: (414) 671-7618, Web Site: www.phmining.com (1)

Reagan, Kathy, Datamann Inc, Wilder, VT. Tel: (802) 295-6600, (800) 451-4263, FAX: (802) 296-3623, Web Site: www.datamann.com (22)

Real Goods Trading Corp, San Rafael, CA. Tel: (707) 542-2600, (888) 567-6527, Web Site: www.realgoods.com (5)

Real Media Solutions, Wayne, NJ. Tel: (973) 835-7060, Web Site: www.get-realmedia.com (27)

Realburn, Paul, Transamerica Occidental Life Co, Los Angeles, CA. Tel: (213) 742-3111, FAX: (213) 741-6623, Web Site: www.transamerica.com (15)

RealData Services Inc, Glenwood Springs, CO. Tel: (970) 945-2456, FAX: (970) 945-5356, E-Mail: rick@realdataservices.com, Web Site: www.realdataservices.com (22)

Reams, Edwin C., Advantage Direct Inc, Marietta, GA. Tel: (678) 921-2134, FAX: (770) 592-4746, E-Mail: ed@advantage-direct.com, Web Site: www.advantage-direct.com (35)

Reassure America Life Insurance Co, Jacksonville, IL. Tel: (800) 637-4475, FAX: (217) 291-2398, Web Site: www.swissre.com (15)

Reavis, Vicki, Accutrend Data Corp, Greenwood Village, CO. Tel: (303) 488-0011, FAX: (303) 488-0133, E-Mail: info@accutrend.com, Web Site: www.accutrend.com (24)

Reb Storage Systems International, Chicago, IL. Tel: (773) 252-0400, (800) 252-5955, FAX: (773) 252-0303, E-Mail: sales@rebsteel.com, Web Site: www.industrialebuy.com (9)

Rebain, Jenn, Sungard Computer Services, Wayne, PA. Tel: (484) 582-5673, E-Mail: GetInfo@SunGard.com, Web Site: www.sungard.com (22)

Rebecchi, John, Disc Graphics Inc, Hauppauge, NY. Tel: (631) 234-1400, FAX: (631) 234-1460, E-Mail: info@discgraphics.com, Web Site: www.discgraphics.com (27)

Rebholz, David F., FedEx Ground, Coraopolis, PA. Tel: (412) 269-1000, (800) 762-3725, FAX: (412) 747-4295, Web Site: www.fedex.com/us/ground/main (28)

Recko, Bob, Sentry Life Insurance Co, Stevens Point, WI. Tel: (715) 346-6000, FAX: (715) 346-7028, E-Mail: infoctr@coredcs.com, Web Site: sentry.com (15)

Recognition Products International, Easton, MD. Tel: (410) 820-0022, (800) 292-7354, FAX: (410) 820-5044, E-Mail: info@recognitionproducts.com, Web Site: www.shoprecognitionproducts.com (16)

Recognition Systems (Dot Works), Port Washington, NY. Tel: (516) 625-5000, FAX: (516) 625-1507, E-Mail: wade@dotworks.com, Web Site: www. dotworks.com (16)

Recording for the Blind & Dyslexic Inc, Princeton, NJ. Tel: (609) 452-0606, (800) 221-4792, FAX: (609) 520-7996, E-Mail: info@rfbd.org, Web Site: www.rfbd.org (16)

Recreational Equipment Inc, Kent, WA. Tel: (253) 395-4803, Web Site: www.rei.com (11)

Recycled Software Inc, Palm Springs, CA. Tel: (760) 655-5666, (800) 851-2425, FAX: (702) 323-5333, E-Mail: diane@recycledsoftware.com, Web Site: www.recycledsoftware.com (3)

Red Clay Media, Bayonne, NJ. Tel: (866) Red-List, Web Site: www.redclaymedia.com (21)

Red Cooper, Mission, TX. Tel: (800) 825-8531, FAX: (956) 205-7331, Web Site: www.redcooper.com (4)

Red Edge Labs LLC, Aliso Viejo, CA. Tel: (800) 931-1055, Web Site: www.rededgelabs.com (35)

Red Hill Corp, Gettysburg, PA. Tel: (717) 337-3038, (800) 822-4003, FAX: (717) 337-0732, E-Mail: custserv@supergrit.com, Web Site: www.supergrit. com (34)

Red Rock Marketing Group LLC, Las Vegas, NV. Tel: (702) 944-9604, FAX: (702) 838-9673, E-Mail: info@redrockmarketing.net, Web Site: www. redrockmarketing.net (35)

Redbook Magazine, New York, NY. Tel: (212) 649-2000, (800) 888-0008, FAX: (212) 581-7605, Web Site: www.redbookmag.com (17)

Redcats USA, New York, NY. Tel: (212) 613-9500, Web Site: www.brylane.com (17)

Reddick, J. Rex, Crazy Crow Trading Post, Pottsboro, TX. Tel: (903) 786-2287, (800) 786-6210, FAX: (903) 786-9059, E-Mail: info@crazycrow.com, Web Site: www.crazycrow.com (11)

Reddick, Jessica, Crazy Crow Trading Post, Pottsboro, TX. Tel: (903) 786-2287, (800) 786-6210, FAX: (903) 786-9059, E-Mail: info@crazycrow.com, Web Site: www.crazycrow.com (11)

RedEngine Digital, Mc Lean, VA. Tel: (703) 556-6951, Web Site: www.redenginedigital.com (20)

RedEnvelope Inc, San Diego, CA. Tel: (619) 528-4888, (877) 733-3683, Web Site: www. redenvelope.com (6)

Redfern, Ronald, Press-Enterprise Co, Riverside, CA. Tel: (951) 684-1200, FAX: (951) 368-9022, Web Site: www.pe.com (17)

Redfield & Co Inc, Omaha, NE. Tel: (402) 341-0364, Web Site: www.redfieldandcompany.com (27)

Redford, Leslie, GE Consumer & Industrial Lighting, Cleveland, OH. Tel: (216) 266-2222, (216) 266-2121, FAX: (216) 266-2930, Web Site: www. gelighting.com/na (16)

Redger, J, Manhattan Media Services Inc, New York, NY. Tel: (212) 808-4077, FAX: (212) 808-4080, E-Mail: mmorello@manhmedia.com, Web Site: www.manhmedia.com (21)

Rediker, Dennis, L., Standard Register, Dayton, OH. Tel: (937) 221-1000, (800) 755-6405, FAX: (937) 221-1239, E-Mail: julie.mcewan@standardregister. com, Web Site: www.standardregister.com (10)

Reding, Robert, W., American Airlines, Fort Worth, TX. Tel: (817) 963-1234 (12)

JP Redington & Co, Huntington, NY. Tel: (631) 754-0111, FAX: (631) 757-0878 (16)

Redirect Relationship Marketing, Salt Lake City, UT. Tel: (801) 453-0100, Web Site: www.redirectnow. com (35)

Rediscover Music Catalogue, Naperville, IL. Tel: (630) 305-0770, (800) 232-7328, FAX: (630) 305-0782, E-Mail: rediscovermusic@rediscovermusic. com, Web Site: www.rediscovermusic.com (3)

Redleaf Press, Saint Paul, MN. Tel: (651) 641-6621, (800) 423-8309, FAX: (800) 641-0115, E-Mail: jvoltz@redleafpress.org, Web Site: www. redleafpress.org (17)

Redling, Joseph, NutriSystem Inc, Fort Washington, PA. Tel: (215) 706-5300, (800) 321-THIN, FAX: (215) 706-5388, Web Site: www.nutrisystem.com (7)

Redlon, Matt, Clario Analytics, Eden Prairie, MN. Tel: (952) 653-0980, (866) 849-3341, FAX: (952) 653-5900, E-Mail: sales@clarioanalytics.com, Web Site: www.clarioanalytics.com (20)

Redman, Arthur, Airlines Reporting Corp, Arlington, VA. Tel: (703) 816-8135, FAX: (703) 816-8104, E-Mail: corpcom@arccorp.com, Web Site: www. arccorp.com (16)

Redmond, Laura, Academic Management Services, Boston, MA. Tel: (508) 235-2900, (800) 891-4203, FAX: (508) 235-2991, E-Mail: info@amsweb.com, Web Site: www.amsweb.com (16)

Redstone, Sumner, E., Viacom Inc, New York, NY. Tel: (212) 258-6000, FAX: (212) 258-6464, Web Site: www.viacom.com (16)

Redstone Federal Credit Union, Huntsville, AL. Tel: (256) 837-6110, Web Site: www.redfcu.org (1)

Redwood City Seed Co, Redwood City, CA. Tel: (650) 325-7333, FAX: (650) 325-4056, Web Site: www.ecoseeds.com (8)

Redwood Partners Ltd, New York, NY. Tel: (212) 843-8585, FAX: (212) 843-9093, E-Mail: info@ redwoodpartners.com, Web Site: www. redwoodpartners.com (20)

Reebok International Ltd, Canton, MA. Tel: (781) 401-5000, (800) 843-4444, FAX: (781) 401-4402, Web Site: www.reebok.com (2)

Reed, Bryan D., Thousand Trails LP, Chicago, IL. Tel: (214) 618-7200, (800) 205-0606, FAX: (214) 618-7324, Web Site: www.1000trails.com (16)

Reed, Bud, Timberline Interactive, Middlebury, VT. Tel: (802) 388-8377, Web Site: www. timberlineinteractive.com (20)

Reed, Debra, L., Southern California Gas Co, Anaheim, CA. Tel: (714) 634-3054, (800) 427-2200, FAX: (714) 937-7712, E-Mail: Tjavid@socalgas. com, Web Site: www.socalgas.com (1)

Reed, Dennis, Balfour, Austin, TX. Tel: (512) 444-0571, FAX: (512) 440-1138, Web Site: www. artcarved.com (16)

Reed, Heidi, A., H&M Associates, Danbury, CT. Tel: (203) 748-8248, FAX: (203) 792-9555 (33)

Reed, Howard, VG Reed & Sons, Louisville, KY. Tel: (502) 589-3770, (800) 635-9788, FAX: (502) 560-0197, E-Mail: info@vgreed.com, Web Site: www. vgreed.com (27)

Reed, Joe, National Bulk Equipment Inc, Holland, MI. Tel: (616) 399-2220, FAX: (616) 399-7365, E-Mail: sales@nbe-inc.com, Web Site: www.nbe-inc.com (16)

Reed, Linda, DMW Worldwide LLC, Chesterbrook, PA. Tel: (610) 407-0407, (877) 744-3699, FAX: (610) 407-9201, E-Mail: whunter@dmwdirect.com, Web Site: www.dmwdirect.com (35)

Reed, Mike, Bob Barker Co Inc, Fuquay Varina, NC. Tel: (919) 552-3431, Web Site: www.bobbarker. com (5)

Reed, Phil, The Staplex Co, Brooklyn, NY. Tel: (718) 768-3333, (800) 221-0822, FAX: (718) 965-0750, E-Mail: info@staplex.com, Web Site: www.staplex. com (34)

Reed, Robert A., Physicians Mutual Insurance Co, Omaha, NE. Tel: (402) 633-1604, (888) 932-7642, FAX: (402) 633-1604, Web Site: www. physiciansmutual.com (15)

Reed, Roy, Nestle Clinical Nutrition Co, Hopkins, MN. Tel: (877) 463-7853, (800) 284-9488, FAX: (877) 563-7853, Web Site: www.nestle-nutrition. com (16)

Reed, Scott E., Branch Banking & Trust Co, Wilson, NC. Tel: (252) 399-4111, FAX: (252) 246-4030 (14)

Reed, Skip, Direct Partners, Marina Del Rey, CA. Tel: (310) 482-4200, FAX: (310) 482-4201, Web Site: www.directpartners.com (35)

Reed, Thomas, P., Huntington Bancshares, Columbus, OH. Tel: (614) 480-8300, (800) 480-BANK, FAX: (614) 480-5284, Web Site: www.huntington.com (14)

Reed, Todd, National Bulk Equipment Inc, Holland, MI. Tel: (616) 399-2220, FAX: (616) 399-7365, E-Mail: sales@nbe-inc.com, Web Site: www.nbe-inc.com (16)

Reed - Elsevier, New York, NY. Tel: (212) 309-5498, FAX: (212) 309-5480, Web Site: www.reed-elsevier.com (17)

Reed Exhibitions, Norwalk, CT. Tel: (203) 840-4800, (888) 745-7644, FAX: (203) 840-5805, E-Mail: dhalter@reedexpo.com, Web Site: www. readerexpo.com (16)

Reed/Harris, Portland, OR. Tel: (503) 224-1812, (800) 238-1812, FAX: (503) 223-8283, E-Mail: info@ reedharris.com, Web Site: www.reedharris.com (21)

Reed Smith Hall Dickler Advertising & Law Marketing Group, New York, NY. Tel: (212) 549-0377, FAX: (212) 521-5450, Web Site: www.reedsmith. com (20)

VG Reed & Sons, Louisville, KY. Tel: (502) 589-3770, (800) 635-9788, FAX: (502) 560-0197, E-Mail: info@vgreed.com, Web Site: www.vgreed. com (27)

Reeder, Marsha, USA Hosts, San Francisco, CA. Tel: (415) 695-8000, (800) 368-4678, FAX: (415) 986-3668, Web Site: www.usahosts.com (19)

Reeder, Robin, National Automated Clearing House Association, Herndon, VA. Tel: (703) 561-1100, FAX: (703) 787-0996, Web Site: www.nacha.org (1)

Rees, Hywel, ap, Telecom Inc, Oakland, CA. Tel: (510) 873-8283, (800) 243-3101, FAX: (510) 873-8293, Web Site: www.telecominc.com (29)

Rees, Steve, Schoolwise Press, San Francisco, CA. Tel: (415) 337-7971, (800) 247-8443 x 202, FAX: (415) 337-1146, E-Mail: info@schoolwisepress. com, Web Site: www.schoolwisepress.com (17)

Rees, Thomas, L., St Louis Post-Dispatch, Saint Louis, MO. Tel: (314) 340-8000, (800) 365-0820, FAX: (314) 340-3140, Web Site: www.postnet.com (17)

Rees Associates Inc, Des Moines, IA. Tel: (515) 243-2127, FAX: (515) 243-1026, Web Site: www. reesassociates.com (28)

Reese, Joyce, Schnuck Markets Inc, Saint Louis, MO. Tel: (314) 994-9900, FAX: (314) 994-4465, Web Site: www.schnucks.com (16)

Reese, Stuart, MassMutual Financial Group, Springfield, MA. Tel: (413) 788-8411, FAX: (413) 744-8889, E-Mail: name@www.massmutual.com, Web Site: www.massmutual.com (15)

Reese, Thomas, MBI Inc, Norwalk, CT. Tel: (203) 853-2000, E-Mail: webmail@mbi-inc.com, Web Site: www.mbi-inc.com (16)

Reese Bullock, Cecilia, Historical Replications Inc, Jackson, MS. Tel: (601) 981-8743, (800) 426-5628, FAX: (601) 981-8185, E-Mail: info@ historicaldesigns.com, Web Site: www. historicaldesigns.com (8)

Reese Press Inc, Pikesville, MD. Tel: (410) 467-9200, FAX: (410) 467-9520 (27)

Reeves, Bonnie, Hansen Corp, Princeton, IN. Tel: (812) 385-3415, FAX: (812) 385-3013, E-Mail: sales@hansen-motor.com, Web Site: www.hansen-motor.com (16)

Reeves, Toby, Rescott LLC Marketing & Technology, Noblesville, IN. Tel: (317) 816-0700, Web Site: www.rescott.com (20)

Referee Enterprises, Franksville, WI. Tel: (262) 632-8855, FAX: (262) 632-5460, E-Mail: questions@ referee.com, Web Site: www.referee.com (1)

Refkin, David, GreenPath Sustainability Consultants, New City, NY. Tel: (914) 980-8346 (20)

Refo, John, TMP Worldwide, Mc Lean, VA. Tel: (703) 269-0144, FAX: (703) 269-0115, E-Mail: john. refo@tmp.com, Web Site: www.tmp.com (35)

Regal, Melvyn, R., Breck's Bulbs, Lawrenceburg, IN. Tel: (309) 693-8600, FAX: (309) 691-9693 (8)

Regal Ware Inc, Kewaskum, WI. Tel: (262) 626-2121, E-Mail: pseitz@regalware.com, Web Site: www. regalware.com (16)

Regan, Harold, The HW Wilson Co, Bronx, NY. Tel: (718) 588-8400, (800) 367-6770, FAX: (800) 590-1617, E-Mail: custserv@hwwilson.com, Web Site: www.hwwilson.com (17)

Regan, Kathleen, The HoneyBaked Ham Co, Holland, OH. Tel: (419) 868-6400, E-Mail: info@ honeybaked.com, Web Site: www.honeybaked.com (4)

Reggio, Michael, The Reggio Register Co Inc, Leominster, MA. Tel: (978) 870-1020, (800) 880-3090, FAX: (978) 870-1030, E-Mail: reggio@ reggioregister.com, Web Site: www.reggioregister. com (8)

The Reggio Register Co Inc, Leominster, MA. Tel: (978) 870-1020, (800) 880-3090, FAX: (978) 870-1030, E-Mail: reggio@reggioregister.com, Web Site: www.reggioregister.com (8)

Regions, Birmingham, AL. Tel: (205) 326-5262, FAX: (205) 326-4072, Web Site: www.regions.com (14)

REGIT Inc, Glen Ellyn, IL. Tel: (630) 495-1500, (800) 537-9786, FAX: (630) 495-1611, E-Mail: regit@regitinc.com, Web Site: www.regitinc.com (15)

Regitar USA Inc, Montgomery, AL. Tel: (334) 244-1885, (877) 734-4827, FAX: (334) 244-1901, E-Mail: info@regitar.com, Web Site: www.regitar. com (9)

Regnery Publishing, Washington, DC. Tel: (202) 216-0600, FAX: (202) 216-0612, Web Site: www. regnery.com (17)

Regul, Lisa, Ten Speed Press, Emeryville, CA. Tel: (510) 559-1600, (800) 841-BOOK, FAX: (510) 559-1629, E-Mail: order@tenspeed.com, Web Site: www.tenspeed.com (17)

Rehr, David, K., National Association Broadcasters Annual Conference & Expo, Washington, DC. Tel: (202) 429-5300, (800) 622-3976, FAX: (202) 429-4199, E-Mail: nab@nab.org, Web Site: www.nab. org (42)

Reiball, Tim, Alta Resources (West Coast Office), Neenah, WI. Tel: (920) 751-5800, (877) 934-6377, Web Site: www.altaresources.com (29)

Reich, Cathy, National Wholesale Co Inc, Lexington, NC. Tel: (336) 248-5904, (800) 480-4673, FAX: (336) 248-2880, E-Mail: customerservice@ shopnational.com, Web Site: www.shopnational. com (2)

Reich, Debra, The Metropolitan Opera, New York, NY. Tel: (212) 799-3100, (212) 362-6000, FAX: (212) 870-7695, Web Site: www.metopera.org (1)

Reichenbach Jr., Clarence, BBC Direct Mktg Svcs, Shamong, NJ. Tel: (877) 786-4389, FAX: (609) 268-9939, E-Mail: csr@bbcglobal.com, Web Site: www.bbcglobal.com (20)

Reichenbach, C., Stephen, BBC Direct Mktg Svcs, Shamong, NJ. Tel: (877) 786-4389, FAX: (609) 268-9939, E-Mail: csr@bbcglobal.com, Web Site: www.bbcglobal.com (20)

Reicher, Jerome, Arrco Medical Advertising, Walpole, MA. Tel: (781) 769-7190, FAX: (781) 769-9480, E-Mail: info@arrco.com, Web Site: www.arrco. com (35)

Reichert, Leo, N., Reichert & Associates Inc, Grand Marais, MN. Tel: (218) 387-1095, E-Mail: reichertln@aol.com (20)

Reichert & Associates Inc, Grand Marais, MN. Tel: (218) 387-1095, E-Mail: reichertln@aol.com (20)

Reid, Bethany, PharmArt, Circleville, OH. Tel: (860) 932-8588, (800) 848-1633, FAX: (800) 477-2923, Web Site: www.healthcarelogistics.com/Pharmart (6)

Reid, Scott, MediaWorks Advertising & Marketing Inc, Ormond Beach, FL. Tel: (407) 909-1903, E-Mail: mmalys@cfl.rr.com, Web Site: www. mediaworksusa.com (21)

Reid Supply Co, Muskegon, MI. Tel: (231) 777-3951, (800) 253-0421, FAX: (231) 767-3882, E-Mail: mail@reidsupply.com, Web Site: www.reidsupply. com (16)

Reider, Cori, Custom List Services Inc, Cape Coral, FL. Tel: (301) 497-1858, FAX: (301) 497-1858 (23)

Reidy, Christopher R., ADP Inc, Roseland, NJ. Tel: (973) 974-5000, (800) 225-5237, FAX: (973) 974-3334, Web Site: www.adp.com (16)

Reidy, Martin, Modem Media, Stamford, CT. Tel: (203) 299-7000, FAX: (203) 299-7060, Web Site: www.modemmedia.com (35)

Reifenberg, James, Farrington Transportation, Bolingbrook, IL. Tel: (630) 783-9200 (12)

Reigle, Douglas J., Regal Ware Inc, Kewaskum, WI. Tel: (262) 626-2121, E-Mail: pseitz@regalware. com, Web Site: www.regalware.com (16)

Reigle, Jeffrey A., Regal Ware Inc, Kewaskum, WI. Tel: (262) 626-2121, E-Mail: pseitz@regalware. com, Web Site: www.regalware.com (16)

Reihm, Tracie, Campbell Ewald Co, Warren, MI. Tel: (586) 574-3400, FAX: (810) 575-9925, Web Site: www.campbell-ewald.com (35)

Reilly, John, Reilly Communications Group, Arlington Heights, IL. Tel: (847) 882-6336, FAX: (847) 519-0166, E-Mail: info@rcgpubs.com, Web Site: new. reillycomm.com (31)

Reilly, Mary, Sax Arts & Crafts, Appleton, WI. Tel: (800) 558-6696, FAX: (800) 328-4729, E-Mail: info@saxarts.com, Web Site: www.saxarts.com (10)

Reilly, Mike, Award Co of America, Tuscaloosa, AL. Tel: (205) 349-2990, FAX: (205) 752-0930, Web Site: www.randallpub.com (6)

Reilly, Mona, Paul Stuart, New York, NY. Tel: (212) 682-0320, FAX: (212) 983-5871, E-Mail: info@ paulstuart.com, Web Site: www.paulstuart.com (2)

Reilly Communications Group, Arlington Heights, IL. Tel: (847) 882-6336, FAX: (847) 519-0166, E-Mail: info@rcgpubs.com, Web Site: new. reillycomm.com (31)

Reiman, Roy, Reiman Publications, Greendale, WI. Tel: (414) 423-0100, (800) 344-6913, FAX: (414) 423-3840, Web Site: www.reimanpub.com (17)

Reiman Publications, Greendale, WI. Tel: (414) 423-0100, (800) 344-6913, FAX: (414) 423-3840, Web Site: www.reimanpub.com (17)

Rein, J.M., Rein Associates Inc, Myrtle Beach, SC. Tel: (732) 741-8111, FAX: (732) 741-6666, E-Mail: info@reinassociates.com, Web Site: www. reinassociates.com (23)

Rein, Jeffrey, A., Allstate Motor Club, Inc, Deerfield, IL. Tel: (847) 914-2972, FAX: (847) 914-2804, Web Site: www.walgreens.com (7)

Rein Associates Inc, Myrtle Beach, SC. Tel: (732) 741-8111, FAX: (732) 741-6666, E-Mail: info@ reinassociates.com, Web Site: www.reinassociates. com (23)

Reinhardt, Jeff, Direct Magazine, New York, NY. Tel: (212) 204-4228, FAX: (212) 683-3986 (43)

Reinhold, Lawrence, P., Global Computer Corp, Port Washington, NY. Tel: (516) 625-4300, (888) 845-6225, FAX: (516) 625-4072, Web Site: www. globalcomputer.com (3)

Reinholtz, Michael, Comphealth, Salt Lake City, UT. Tel: (801) 930-3000, (800) 453-3030, FAX: (801) 930-4517, E-Mail: info@comphealth.com, Web Site: www.comphealth.com (16)

Reinman, Joseph, Government Data Publications Inc, Washington, DC. Tel: (718) 627-0819, (800) 275-4688, FAX: (718) 998-5960, E-Mail: gdp@ govdata.com, Web Site: www.govdata.com (17)

Reinsfelder, Eric, American Recreation Products Inc, Saint Louis, MO. Tel: (314) 576-8000, FAX: (314) 576-8072 (11)

Reis, George, Friday Report, Garden City, NY. Tel: (516) 746-6700, FAX: (516) 294-8141 (43)

Reis, George, Fund Raising Management, Garden City, NY. Tel: (516) 746-6700, FAX: (516) 294-8141 (43)

Reis, Timothy, C., EMS Technologies, Norcross, GA. Tel: (770) 263-9200, FAX: (770) 447-4405, Web Site: www.ems-t.com (16)

Reisberg, Jerry, Leaps & Bounds LLC, Fort Lee, NJ. Tel: (201) 947-5459 (20)

Reiser, Ann, Domtar Inc, Fort Mill, SC. Tel: (803) 802-8283, FAX: (810) 982-7124, Web Site: www. domtar.com (25)

Reisfeld, Donald, Morton Advertising Inc, New York, NY. Tel: (212) 465-2250, FAX: (212) 465-1575, E-Mail: don@mortonad.com, Web Site: www. mortonad.com (35)

Reiss, Robert, New York Blood Center Inc, New York, NY. Tel: (212) 570-3000, (800) 933-2566, FAX: (212) 570-3195, Web Site: www.nybloodcenter.org (1)

Reisz-Hanson, Katherine, Bitstream Inc, Marlborough, MA. Tel: (617) 497-6222, Web Site: www. bitstream.com (22)

Reith, Kathryn, Fancy Fronds, Gold Bar, WA. Tel: (360) 793-1472, FAX: (360) 793-4243, E-Mail: judith@fancyfronds.com, Web Site: www. fancyfronds.com (8)

Relationship1, Rye, NY. Tel: (914) 921-4400, E-Mail: marketing@relationship1.com, Web Site: www. relationship1.com (21)

Relaxo-Bak Inc, Anderson, IN. Tel: (765) 643-2934, (800) 527-5496, FAX: (765) 641-7448, Web Site: www.relaxobak.com (7)

Relevant Insights LLC, Euless, TX. Tel: (817) 545-8017 (30)

Relevate, Springfield, VA. Tel: (703) 658-8300, (800) 523-7346, FAX: (703) 658-8301, E-Mail: sales@ relevategroup.com, Web Site: www.relevategroup. com (22)

Reliable Mail Service Inc, Edison, NJ. Tel: (732) 346-9779, (800) 773-6338, FAX: (732) 346-9799, E-Mail: bdobin@reliablemailservice.com, Web Site: www.reliablemailservice.com (28)

Reliable Racing Supply, Queensbury, NY. Tel: (518) 793-5677, FAX: (518) 793-6491, Web Site: www. reliableracing.com (11)

Reliable Technologies Inc, Manchester, NH. Tel: (603) 644-2528, (800) 346-7890, FAX: (603) 627-5553, Web Site: www.tei-imaging.com (16)

Reliance Electric, Fort Smith, AR. Tel: (479) 646-4711, FAX: (479) 648-5792, E-Mail: smtraylor@ powersystems.rockwell.com, Web Site: www. reliance.com (9)

Reliant Data Processing, North Aurora, IL. Tel: (630) 844-4210, FAX: (630) 844-9530, E-Mail: rdpmail@aol.com (28)

Reliant Energy, Houston, TX. Tel: (713) 497-7794, Web Site: www.reliant.com (16)

Reliapon Police Products, Las Vegas, NV. Tel: (805) 289-0145, (888) 263-4482, FAX: (805) 735-4276, E-Mail: info@reliapon.com, Web Site: www. reliapon.com (5)

Relyco, Dover, NH. Tel: (603) 516-3610, Web Site: www.relyco.com (27)

ReMark USA, Minnetonka, MN. Tel: (952) 938-4699, FAX: (952) 988-8500, E-Mail: jessica.sbragia@ remarkgroup.com, Web Site: www.remarkamericas. com (15)

REMEDY Magazine, New York, NY. Tel: (212) 695-2223, FAX: (212) 695-2936, E-Mail: info@ rmedizine.com, Web Site: www.medizine.com (17)

Remer, Jane, Capezio Ballet Makers Inc, Totowa, NJ. Tel: (973) 653-2093, (800) 533-1887, FAX: (800) 522-1222, E-Mail: info@balletmakers.com, Web Site: www.capeziodance.com (16)

Remilon LLC, Mountain View, CA. Tel: (650) 425-7511, Web Site: www.remilon.com (15)

Remington, Dr Steven J., Harold Walter Siebens School of Business, Storm Lake, IA. Tel: (712) 749-2410, (800) 383-2821, FAX: (712) 749-2037, Web Site: www2.bvu.edu/academics/business (41)

Remington, Scott, Omaha Vaccine Co, Omaha, NE. Tel: (402) 731-9600, (800) 367-4444, FAX: (800) 242-9447, E-Mail: customerservice@ OmahaVaccine.com, Web Site: www. omahavaccine.com (16)

Remington College, Heathrow, FL. Tel: (407) 562-5691, Web Site: www.remingtoncollege.edu (13)

Remnick, Dave, The New Yorker Magazine, New York, NY. Tel: (212) 286-5400, FAX: (212) 286-5735, E-Mail: alatia_bradley@newyorker.com, Web Site: www.newyorker.com (17)

Remsberg, Charles, Calibre Press Inc, San Francisco, CA. Tel: (214) 545-3060, (800) 323-0037, FAX: (866) 225-4273, Web Site: www.calibrepress.com (17)

Remtulla, Husayn, Pinnacle Direct Response, North York, ON Canada. Tel: (416) 756-9536 (35)

Renaissance Greeting Cards Inc, Springvale, ME. Tel: (207) 324-4153, (800) 688-9998, FAX: (207) 324-9564, E-Mail: rencards@rencards.com (5)

Renaissance Learning, Wisconsin Rapids, WI. Tel: (715) 424-3636, (800) 338-4204, FAX: (715) 424-4242, E-Mail: answers@renlearn.com, Web Site: www.renlearn.com (5)

Reneau, Kevin, Vidi Emi Inc, San Leandro, CA. Tel: (510) 667-9999, FAX: (510) 352-9999, E-Mail: info@vidiemi.com, Web Site: www.vidiemi.com (32)

Renfrow, Joan, Onyx Productions Inc, Los Angeles, CA. Tel: (323) 692-9830, FAX: (323) 692-9832, E-Mail: info@onyxprod.com, Web Site: www. onyxprod.com (32)

Renk, Thomas, F., Incentive Manufacturers Representatives Association (IMRA), Naperville, IL. Tel: (630) 369-7786, FAX: (630) 369-3773, E-Mail: tom@imraorg.net, Web Site: www.imraorg.net (40)

Renker, Greg, Guthy-Renker Corp, Palm Desert, CA. Tel: (760) 773-9022, (800) 274-4910, FAX: (760) 773-9016, Web Site: www.guthy-renker.com (32)

Renkim Corp, Southgate, MI. Tel: (734) 374-8300, FAX: (734) 374-8323, E-Mail: info@renkim.com, Web Site: www.renkim.com (22)

Renner, Debbie, Rapid City Journal, Rapid City, SD. Tel: (605) 394-8300, FAX: (605) 394-8462, E-Mail: classifieds@rapidcityjournal.com, Web Site: www.rapidcityjournal.com (18)

Renner, Kelly, MD Anderson Cancer Center - Children's Art Project, Houston, TX. Tel: (713) 745-2575, (800) 231-1580, FAX: (713) 794-1950, E-Mail: krenner@mdanderson.org, Web Site: www. childrensart.org (1)

Reno Gazette Journal, Reno, NV. Tel: (775) 788-6200, FAX: (775) 788-6563 (17)

The Renovator's Supply Inc, Millers Falls, MA. Tel: (413) 423-3300, (800) 659-2211, FAX: (413) 423-3800, E-Mail: customercare@rensup.com, Web Site: www.rensup.com (9)

Rent-A-Center Inc, Plano, TX. Tel: (972) 801-1100, (800) 275-2996, FAX: (972) 943-0113, Web Site: www.rentacenter.com (16)

Rent Mother Nature, Cambridge, MA. Tel: (617) 868-5059, (800) 232-4048, FAX: (617) 868-5861, Web Site: www.rentmothernature.com (4)

Renton's Inc, Centennial, CO. Tel: (303) 865-7025, (800) 365-6644, E-Mail: info@rentons.com, Web Site: www.rentons.com (10)

Renwick, Glen, M., The Progressive Corp, Mayfield Village, OH. Tel: (440) 461-5000, (800) PRO-GRESSIVE, (800) 776-4737, FAX: (800) 456-6590, Web Site: www.progressive.com (15)

Renwick, Scott, Unitrin, Chicago, IL. Tel: (312) 661-4600, (800) 733-7366, FAX: (312) 494-6995, Web Site: www.unitrin.com (15)

Renwick, Terry, Potpourri Group Inc, Chelmsford, MA. Tel: (978) 256-4100, FAX: (978) 256-1961/0344, Web Site: www.potpourrigroup.com (6)

Renz, Daniel, Summit Marketing, Saint Louis, MO. Tel: (314) 569-3737, FAX: (314) 569-0037, E-Mail: info@summitmarketing.com, Web Site: www.summitmarketing.com (35)

Repeta, Beth, Ziff Davis Media Inc, New York, NY. Tel: (212) 503-5100, FAX: (212) 503-5023, Web Site: www.ziffdavis.com (17)

Replacements Ltd, Greensboro, NC. Tel: (336) 697-3000, (800) REPLACE, FAX: (336) 697-3100, E-Mail: mark.donahue@replacements.com, Web Site: www.replacements.com (8)

Replogle Globes Inc, Broadview, IL. Tel: (708) 343-0900, FAX: (708) 343-0923, E-Mail: info@ replogleglobes.com, Web Site: www. replogleglobes.com (16)

ReputationDefender, Redwood City, CA. Tel: (650) 241-7491, (888) 720-3332, E-Mail: helpdesk@ reputation.com, Web Site: www.reputationdefender. com (32)

Rescott LLC Marketing & Technology, Noblesville, IN. Tel: (317) 816-0700, Web Site: www.rescott. com (20)

Research and Management Corporation/WSI, Mississauga, ON Canada. Tel: (888) 678-7588 (35)

Research & Response International, New York, NY. Tel: (212) 489-8610, FAX: (212) 262-3474, E-Mail: rrespe@bway.net, Web Site: www.rrespe. com (23)

Research Boston Corp, Lafayette, CA. Tel: (978) 225-8030, FAX: (267) 295-8704, Web Site: www. researchboston.com (20)

Research Communications Ltd, Canton, MA. Tel: (781) 341-1190, FAX: (781) 341-1191, E-Mail: info@researchcommunications.com (30)

Research in Motion Corp, Waterloo, ON Canada. Tel: (519) 888-7465, Web Site: www.rim.com (22)

Research Institute America, Carrollton, TX. Tel: (972) 250-7000, (800) 950-1216, Web Site: www.ria. thompson.com (14)

Research To Prevent Blindness Inc, New York, NY. Tel: (212) 752-4333, (800) 621-0026, FAX: (212) 688-6231, E-Mail: inforequest@rpbusa.org, Web Site: www.rpbusa.org (1)

Reserve National Insurance Co, Oklahoma City, OK. Tel: (405) 848-7931, Web Site: www. reservenational.com (15)

Resnick, Lynda, R., Roll International Corp, Los Angeles, CA. Tel: (310) 966-5700, FAX: (310) 914-4747, Web Site: www.roll.com (16)

Resnick, Lynda, The Franklin Mint, Exton, PA. Tel: (610) 497-4800, (800) THE-MINT, FAX: (610) 497-4956, E-Mail: info@franklinmint.com, Web Site: www.franklinmint.com (16)

Resnick, Richard, Intromark Inc, Pittsburgh, PA. Tel: (412) 288-1300, (800) 851-6030 X1368, FAX: (412) 338-0497, E-Mail: licensing@intromark.com (16)

Resnick, Stewart, Roll International Corp, Los Angeles, CA. Tel: (310) 966-5700, FAX: (310) 914-4747, Web Site: www.roll.com (16)

Resnick, Stewart, The Franklin Mint, Exton, PA. Tel: (610) 497-4800, (800) THE-MINT, FAX: (610) 497-4956, E-Mail: info@franklinmint.com, Web Site: www.franklinmint.com (16)

Rose Resnick Lighthouse for the Blind & Visually Impaired, San Francisco, CA. Tel: (415) 431-1481, FAX: (415) 863-7568, E-Mail: executive@ lighthouse-sf.org, Web Site: www.lighthouse-sf.org (1)

Resnik, David, A., Emblem & Badge Inc, Johnston, RI. Tel: (401) 365-1265, (800) 875-5444, FAX: (401) 365-1263, E-Mail: sales@recognition.com, Web Site: www.recognition.com (6)

Resnikoff, Bruce, Motown Records, New York, NY. Tel: (212) 373-0750, FAX: (212) 489-9096, Web Site: www.motown.com (3)

Resnikoff, Ronald, B., Mitchell & Resnikoff/ Weightman, Elkins Park, PA. Tel: (215) 635-1000, FAX: (215) 635-6542, E-Mail: info@mitch-res. com, Web Site: www.Mitch-Res.com (35)

Resolution Inc, Williston, VT. Tel: (802) 862-8881, (800) 862-8900, FAX: (802) 865-2308, E-Mail: schubart@resodirect.com, Web Site: www. resodirect.com (32)

Resort Condominiums International Inc, Carmel, IN. Tel: (317) 876-1692, FAX: (317) 871-9699, Web Site: www.rci.com (19)

Resorts Atlantic City, Atlantic City, NJ. Tel: (609) 334-6000, (800) 336-6378, FAX: (609) 340-6349, Web Site: www.resortsac.com (19)

Resorts Worldwide Inc, White Plains, NY. Tel: (914) 640-8100, (800) 325-3535, FAX: (914) 640-8310, Web Site: www.starwood.com (19)

Resource Marketing Inc, Columbus, OH. Tel: (614) 621-2888, (800) 550-5815, FAX: (614) 621-2873, E-Mail: inquiry@resource.com, Web Site: www. resource.com (21)

Resource Publications Inc, San Jose, CA. Tel: (408) 286-8505, (888) 273-7782, FAX: (408) 287-8748, E-Mail: info@rpinet.com, Web Site: www.rpinet. com (17)

Response ADvantage, Playa Del Rey, CA. Tel: (310) 577-0389, Web Site: www.responseadvantage.com (20)

Response Agency Inc, Sandy, UT. Tel: (801) 352-9100, Web Site: www.responseagency.com (35)

Response Design Corp, Ocean City, NJ. Tel: (609) 601-5866, (800) 366-4732, FAX: (609) 788-3619, E-Mail: rdc@responsedesign.com, Web Site: www. responsedesign.com (20)

Response Dynamics Inc, Vienna, VA. Tel: (703) 442-7595, FAX: (703) 790-8564 (35)

Response Innovations Inc, Toronto, ON Canada. Tel: (416) 368-6217 (35)

Response Insurance, Scranton, PA. Tel: (203) 634-7255, (800) 518-2984, FAX: (203) 634-7319, E-Mail: webcs@response.com, Web Site: www. response.com (15)

Response Magazine, Santa Ana, CA. Tel: (714) 513-8624, (800) 371-6897, FAX: (714) 338-6710, Web Site: www.responsemagazine.com (43)

Response Management Technologies Inc, Berkeley, CA. Tel: (510) 843-8180, FAX: (510) 843-8020, E-Mail: info@respmgt.com, Web Site: www. respmgt.com (22)

Response Marketing Inc, Eden Prairie, MN. Tel: (952) 949-4913 (35)

Response Media, Norcross, GA. Tel: (770) 451-5478, FAX: (770) 451-4929, E-Mail: babion@ responsemedia.com, Web Site: www. responsemedia.com (32)

Response Mine Interactive, Atlanta, GA. Tel: (404) 233-0370, Web Site: www.responsemine.com (35)

Response Resources, Destrehan, LA. Tel: (985) 725-0162, FAX: (504) 764-2839 (35)

The Response Shop Inc, La Jolla, CA. Tel: (858) 456-6180, FAX: (858) 456-5090, E-Mail: marla@ responseshop.com, Web Site: www.responseshop. com (35)

Response Unlimited, Waynesboro, VA. Tel: (540) 943-6721, FAX: (540) 943-0841, E-Mail: info@ru-lists. com, Web Site: www.responseunlimited.com (23)

Responsys, San Bruno, CA. Tel: (650) 745-1700, Web Site: www.responsys.com (20)

Resteghini, Matthew, Monster Worldwide, Maynard, MA. Tel: (888) MONSTER, Web Site: www. monster.com (20)

Results Advertising Inc, Hasbrouck Heights, NJ. Tel: (201) 288-7888, FAX: (201) 288-5112, E-Mail: info@resultsinc.com, Web Site: www.resultsinc. com (35)

The Results Group, Boston, MA. Tel: (617) 227-0229, Web Site: www.verdant-results-group.com (20)

Results Producers, Los Angeles, CA. Tel: (213) 481-7400, FAX: (213) 481-7474, E-Mail: info@ resultsproducers.com, Web Site: www. resultsproducers.com (32)

Resumate Inc, Ann Arbor, MI. Tel: (734) 477-9402, (800) 530-9310, FAX: (734) 477-9415, E-Mail: info@resumate.com, Web Site: www.resumate.com (3)

Retawmatic Corp, Flushing, NY. Tel: (718) 886-0502 (9)

Retrieval Masters Creditors Bureau Inc, Elmsford, NY. Tel: (914) 592-0055, (800) 666-8097, FAX: (914) 345-5023, E-Mail: info@retrievalmasters.com, Web Site: www.retrievalmasters.com (20)

Return Path Inc, New York, NY. Tel: (212) 905-5500, FAX: (212) 905-5501, Web Site: www.returnpath.biz (22)

Reumell, Paul, L., Cooper Surgical Inc, Trumbull, CT. Tel: (203) 601-5200, (800) 645-3670, FAX: (203) 601-1007, Web Site: www.coopersurgical.com (7)

Reuning, Karl, Datum Timing, Test & Measurement, Beverly, MA. Tel: (978) 927-8220, FAX: (978) 927-4099, E-Mail: wriley@datum.com, Web Site: www.datum.com (9)

Reuter Loyd, Heidi, Reiman Publications, Greendale, WI. Tel: (414) 423-0100, (800) 344-6913, FAX: (414) 423-3840, Web Site: www.reimanpub.com (17)

Revel, Matt, Robert Silverman Direct Marketing, Cleveland, OH. Tel: (216) 881-9191, (888) 884-9191, FAX: (216) 881-3442, Web Site: www.cgginc.com (35)

Revelli, Vanessa, Prakken Publications Inc, Ann Arbor, MI. Tel: (734) 975-2800, (800) 530-9673, FAX: (734) 975-2787, E-Mail: vanessa@techdirections.com, Web Site: www.eddigest.com; www.techdirections.com (17)

Reverman, Dean, Hammond Paradigm Communications Group, Cincinnati, OH. Tel: (513) 381-7100, (800) 898-4121, FAX: (513) 381-8756, Web Site: www.hammondcg.com (35)

REWAY Inc, Miramar, FL. Tel: (954) 205-1996, Web Site: www.rewayconsulting.com (22)

Rex Three Inc, Sunrise, FL. Tel: (954) 452-8301, (800) 782-6509, FAX: (954) 452-0569, E-Mail: info@rex3.com, Web Site: www.rexthree.com (27)

Rexcraft Wedding Invitations, Rexburg, ID. Tel: (208) 359-1000, (800) 635-3898, FAX: (800) 826-2712, E-Mail: cs@rexcraft.com, Web Site: www.rexcraft.com (16)

Rexon, Linda, KZS Advertising, Smithtown, NY. Tel: (651) 348-1440, FAX: (631) 348-1449, Web Site: www.kzsadvertising.com (35)

Reynes, Anthony, Tesar Reynes Inc, Chicago, IL. Tel: (312) 726-1900, E-Mail: tony@tesar-reynes.com, Web Site: www.tesar-reynes.com (20)

Reynolds, Craig, The Family Handyman, Eagan, MN. Tel: (651) 454-9200, FAX: (651) 994-2250 (17)

Reynolds, Dana, Fowler's Chocolates Inc, Buffalo, NY. Tel: (716) 877-9983, (800) 824-2263, FAX: (716) 877-9959, E-Mail: customerservice@fowlerschocolates.com, Web Site: www.fowlerschocolates.com (4)

Reynolds, Darlene, The Magni Co Inc, McKinney, TX. Tel: (972) 540-2050, (800) 645-9199, FAX: (972) 540-1057, E-Mail: sales@magnico.com, Web Site: www.magnico.com; www.magnilife.com (16)

Reynolds, Douglas W., Horace Mann Educators Corp, Springfield, IL. Tel: (217) 789-2500, FAX: (217) 788-5161, Web Site: www.horacemann.com (15)

Reynolds, Evan, The Magni Co Inc, McKinney, TX. Tel: (972) 540-2050, (800) 645-9199, FAX: (972) 540-1057, E-Mail: sales@magnico.com, Web Site: www.magnico.com; www.magnilife.com (16)

Reynolds, Harry, F P International, Redwood City, CA. Tel: (650) 261-5300, (800) 866-9946, FAX: (650) 361-1713, Web Site: www.fpintl.com (16)

Reynolds, James T., Cancer Fund of America Inc, Knoxville, TN. Tel: (865) 938-5281, (800) 578-5284, FAX: (865) 938-2968, Web Site: www.cfoa.org (1)

Reynolds, Julian, Reliable Technologies Inc, Manchester, NH. Tel: (603) 644-2528, (800) 346-7890, FAX: (603) 627-5553, Web Site: www.tei-imaging.com (16)

Reynolds, Marshall, T., Donihe Graphics Inc, Kingsport, TN. Tel: (423) 246-2800, (800) 251-0337, FAX: (423) 246-7025, Web Site: www.champion-industries.com (27)

Reynolds, Michael, Cancer Fund of America Inc, Knoxville, TN. Tel: (865) 938-5281, (800) 578-5284, FAX: (865) 938-2968, Web Site: www.cfoa.org (1)

Reynolds, Michele, BMI, Nashville, TN. Tel: (615) 401-2000, (800) 925-8451, FAX: (615) 401-2812, E-Mail: genlic@bmi.com, Web Site: www.bmi.com (1)

Reynolds, Paula, Rosput, Safeco Insurance Co, Seattle, WA. Tel: (206) 545-5000, (800) 332-3226, FAX: (206) 545-5767/5651, Web Site: www.safeco.com (15)

Reynolds, Sidney, The Signature Agency, Raleigh, NC. Tel: (919) 878-8989, (800) 870-8700, FAX: (919) 878-3939, E-Mail: info@signatureagency.com, Web Site: www.signatureagency.com (35)

Reynolds, Tom, Media Horizons Inc, Norwalk, CT. Tel: (203) 857-0770, FAX: (203) 857-0296, E-Mail: mhict@mediahorizons.com, Web Site: www.mediahorizons.com (21)

Reynolds, Vicki, KCET, Los Angeles, CA. Tel: (323) 666-6500, FAX: (323) 953-5661, E-Mail: viewerservices@kcet.org, Web Site: www.kcet.org (1)

Reynolds & Reynolds Co, Houston, TX. Tel: (713) 718-1800, (800) 231-6347, FAX: (713) 718-1471, Web Site: www.reyrey.com (22)

Reznyk, Christopher, Assurant Solutions Preneed Division, Atlanta, GA. Tel: (770) 763-1000, (800) PRE NEED, FAX: (770) 859-4325, Web Site: www.assurantpreneed.com (15)

Rhea, Darrel, Cheskin, Redwood Shores, CA. Tel: (650) 802-2100, FAX: (650) 593-1125, E-Mail: info@cheskin.com, Web Site: www.cheskin.com (30)

Rhine-Patrick, Jana, Medic Alert Foundation, Turlock, CA. Tel: (209) 668-3333, (888) 633-4298, FAX: (209) 669-2495, Web Site: www.medicalert.org (1)

Rhino Marketing Inc, Los Angeles, CA. Tel: (604) 472-3240, (877) 605-7022, FAX: (604) 637-5619, Web Site: www.rhino.ca (20)

Rhode, Naomi, Smart Practice, Phoenix, AZ. Tel: (800) 522-0800, FAX: (800) 522-8329, E-Mail: info@smartpractice.com, Web Site: www.smartpractice.com (17)

Rhode Island Novelty, Cumberland, RI. Tel: (401) 335-3300, (800) 528-5599, FAX: (800) 448-1775, E-Mail: info@rinovelty.com, Web Site: www.rinovelty.com (16)

Rhodes, Bruce, Bruce Rhodes, Sudbury, MA. Tel: (978) 443-8389 (20)

Rhodes, Kevin, Viking Pump Inc, Cedar Falls, IA. Tel: (319) 266-1741, FAX: (319) 273-8157, E-Mail: info@vikingpump.com, Web Site: www.vikingpump.com (16)

Rhodes, Thomas, National Review, New York, NY. Tel: (212) 679-7330, FAX: (212) 849-2852, Web Site: www.nationalreview.com (17)

Bruce Rhodes, Sudbury, MA. Tel: (978) 443-8389 (20)

Rhyan, Tracy, Frederick's of Hollywood Group Inc, Los Angeles, CA. Tel: (323) 466-5151, (800) 323-9525, FAX: (323) 464-5149, Web Site: www.fredericks.com (2)

Rhythm Band Inc, Fort Worth, TX. Tel: (817) 335-2561, (800) 424-4724, FAX: (800) 784-9401, E-Mail: sales@rhythmband.com, Web Site: www.rhythmband.com (16)

Riazzi, Bob, ReachForce, Austin, TX. Tel: (512) 327-9000, FAX: (512) 327-9090, E-Mail: info@reachforce.com, Web Site: www.reachforce.com (23)

Ribsam, John, DelStar Technologies, Middletown, DE. Tel: (302) 378-8888, (800) 521-6713, FAX: (302) 378-4482, Web Site: www.delstarinc.com (16)

Riccelli, Richard, Richard Ricelli Inc, Charleston, SC. Tel: (843) 727-0183, FAX: (843) 727-0184, E-Mail: richard@ricelli.com, Web Site: www.ricelli.com (35)

Ricchie, Robert, COMNET Washington, Framingham, MA. Tel: (508) 879-6700, FAX: (508) 370-4325, Web Site: www.comnetexpo.com (42)

Ricci, Paul, Nuance Speech Solutions, Burlington, MA. Tel: (781) 565-5000, FAX: (781) 565-5001, E-Mail: sales@speechworks.com, Web Site: www.nuance.com (16)

Ricci Lee Hubbart Associates Inc, Cupertino, CA. Tel: (408) 725-1242, FAX: (408) 716-2704, E-Mail: susan@riccilee.com, Web Site: www.riccilee.com (16)

Ricciardi, Marie, JP Redington & Co, Huntington, NY. Tel: (631) 754-0111, FAX: (631) 757-0878 (16)

Riccitelli, Hank, Klitzner Industries, Providence, RI. Tel: (401) 751-7500, (800) 556-6860, FAX: (800) 556-3199, E-Mail: info@klitzner.com, Web Site: www.klitzner.com; www.providenceline.com (6)

Riccitiello, John, Electronic Arts Inc, Redwood City, CA. Tel: (650) 628-1500, Web Site: www.ea.com (3)

Rice Jr., Peter, The Plow & Hearth Inc, Madison, VA. Tel: (540) 948-2272, (800) 494-7544, FAX: (540) 948-2273, Web Site: www.plowhearth.com (8)

Rice, B.P., BP Rice & Co, El Segundo, CA. Tel: (562) 926-5861, FAX: (562) 404-7130, E-Mail: info@bprco.com, Web Site: www.bprco.com (35)

Rice, John, G., GE Partnership Marketing Group, Schaumburg, IL. Tel: (847) 605-3000, FAX: (847) 605-7368, Web Site: www.gepmg.com (14)

Rice, Keith, Print Products International, Annapolis Junction, MD. Tel: (910) 695-7223, FAX: (910) 944-1724, Web Site: www.paceworldwide.com (9)

Rice, Peter, G., The Plow & Hearth Inc, Madison, VA. Tel: (540) 948-2272, (800) 494-7544, FAX: (540) 948-2273, Web Site: www.plowhearth.com (8)

Rice, Randy, Arch Telecom Inc, Austin, TX. Tel: (512) 492-0735, (800) 890-7575, FAX: (512) 495-7101, Web Site: www.archtelecom.com (16)

BP Rice & Co, El Segundo, CA. Tel: (562) 926-5861, FAX: (562) 404-7130, E-Mail: info@bprco.com, Web Site: www.bprco.com (35)

Rice-Gardiner, Karen, National Geographic Society, Washington, DC. Tel: (202) 857-7311, (800) NGS-LINE, FAX: (202) 457-8200, Web Site: www.nationalgeographic.com (17)

Rich, Bryan, Phoenix Data Processing, Westmont, IL. Tel: (630) 654-4400, FAX: (630) 654-4470, E-Mail: sales@phoenixdataprocessing.com, Web Site: www.phoenixdataprocessing.com (22)

Rich, Melinda R., Rich Products Corp, Buffalo, NY. Tel: (716) 878-8000, (800) 828-2021, FAX: (716) 878-8765, Web Site: www.richs.com (16)

Rich Brands, Phoenix, AZ. Tel: (602) 889-4800, (877) 856-1753, FAX: (602) 889-4830, E-Mail: sales@esscentualbrands.com, Web Site: esscentualbrands.com (16)

Rich Jr, Robert E., Rich Products Corp, Buffalo, NY. Tel: (716) 878-8000, (800) 828-2021, FAX: (716) 878-8765, Web Site: www.richs.com (16)

The Rich List Co, Wainscott, NY. Tel: (212) 737-8917, FAX: (212) 861-5384, E-Mail: richlistco@aol.com, Web Site: www.richlist.com (24)

Rich Products Corp, Buffalo, NY. Tel: (716) 878-8000, (800) 828-2021, FAX: (716) 878-8765, Web Site: www.richs.com (16)

Richard Ricelli Inc, Charleston, SC. Tel: (843) 727-0183, FAX: (843) 727-0184, E-Mail: richard@ricelli.com, Web Site: www.ricelli.com (35)

Richards, George S., DAMARK International Inc, La Salle, IL. Tel: (877) 326-2757, Web Site: www.damark.com (16)

Richards, Jim, Houston Direct Marketing Association, Houston, TX. Tel: (281) 931-8883, FAX: (281) 820-4023, Web Site: www.houstondma.org (40)

Richards, John, Richards Communications, Beachwood, OH. Tel: (216) 514-7800, FAX: (216) 514-7801, E-Mail: jrichards@richardsgo.com, Web Site: www.richardsgo.com (35)

Richards, Laura, Veriad, Brea, CA. Tel: (714) 990-2700, (800) 962-0658, FAX: (800) 962-0658, E-Mail: info@veriad.com, Web Site: www.veriad.com (16)

Richards, Mark, R., Appleton Papers Inc, Appleton, WI. Tel: (920) 734-9841, FAX: (920) 991-8796, Web Site: www.appletonideas.com (25)

Richards, Mike, International Bible Society, Colorado Springs, CO. Tel: (719) 488-9200, FAX: (719) 867-2812, Web Site: www.ibs.org (1)

Richards, Perrie, Mid America Designs Inc, Effingham, IL. Tel: (217) 540-4200, (800) 350-4543, FAX: (217) 540-4800, E-Mail: mail@mamotorworks.com, Web Site: www.mamotorworks.com (12)

Richards, Scott, Dial 800 LLC, Los Angeles, CA. Tel: (310) 273-9023, (800) 564-8685, Web Site: www.dial800.com (32)

Richards, Steven K., Outsourcing Solutions Inc, Chesterfield, MO. Tel: (847) 419-1790, FAX: (847) 419-1818 (20)

Richards Communications, Beachwood, OH. Tel: (216) 514-7800, FAX: (216) 514-7801, E-Mail: jrichards@richardsgo.com, Web Site: www.richardsgo.com (35)

Richards Partners, Dallas, TX. Tel: (214) 891-5700, FAX: (214) 891-3515, E-Mail: ruth_fitzgibbons@richards.com, Web Site: www.richardspartners.com (35)

Richards Tulley, Elizabeth, Tully & Holland Inc, Wellesley, MA. Tel: (781) 239-2900, FAX: (781) 239-2901, E-Mail: info@tullyandholland.com, Web Site: www.tullyandholland.com (14)

Richardson, Dr. William, S., Auburn University at Montgomery, Montgomery, AL. Tel: (334) 244-3621, (800) 227-2649, FAX: (334) 244-3826, Web Site: www.aum.edu (41)

Richardson, E.J., Richardson Electronics Ltd, Lafox, IL. Tel: (630) 208-2200, FAX: (630) 208-2550, E-Mail: edg@rell.com, Web Site: www.rell.com (16)

Richardson, J.R., Globel Direct, Calgary, AB Canada. Tel: (403) 531-6500, (800) 551-5721, FAX: (403) 531-6560, E-Mail: jr.richardson@globel.com, Web Site: www.globel.com (28)

Richardson, Kathleen, Fortent, Miami, FL. Tel: (305) 530-0500, (800) 232-3652, FAX: (305) 530-9434, Web Site: www.fortent.com (31)

Richardson, Keith, Sierra Trading Post, Cheyenne, WY. Tel: (307) 775-8050, (800) 713-4534, FAX: (307) 775-8089, Web Site: www.sierratradingpost.com (2)

Richardson, Kelli, Black Entertainment Television Inc, Washington, DC. Tel: (202) 608-2000/2006, (800) 766-0053, FAX: (202) 608-2599, Web Site: www.bet.com (16)

Richardson, Rev. John, T., DePaul University, Chicago, IL. Tel: (312) 362-8000, (800) 4-DEPAUL, FAX: (312) 362-6639, E-Mail: skelly@wppost.depaul.edu, Web Site: www.depaul.edu (41)

Richardson Electronics Ltd, Lafox, IL. Tel: (630) 208-2200, FAX: (630) 208-2550, E-Mail: edg@rell.com, Web Site: www.rell.com (16)

Richartz Fliss Clark & Pope Inc, New York, NY. Tel: (212) 286-9339, FAX: (212) 682-4748, E-Mail: pope@rfcp.com (23)

Richer, Claire, S., Fidelity Investments, Boston, MA. Tel: (617) 563-7000, (800) 343-3548, FAX: (617) 476-6150, Web Site: www.fidelity.com (14)

Richie, Kelly, A., Lands' End Inc, Dodgeville, WI. Tel: (608) 935-9341, (800) 963-4816, FAX: (680) 935-4831, Web Site: www.landsend.com (2)

Richman, Joshua, Straw Hat Cooperative Corp, San Ramon, CA. Tel: (925) 837-3400, FAX: (925) 820-1080, E-Mail: info@strawhatpizza.com, Web Site: www.strawhatpizza.com (16)

Richman, Steven P., Milwaukee Electric Tool Corp, Brookfield, WI. Tel: (262) 781-3600, (800) 414-6527, FAX: (262) 781-3611, (800) 638-9582, Web Site: www.mil-electric-tool.com (16)

Richmond, Kim, FAO Schwarz, New York, NY. Tel: (212) 644-9400, (800) 426-TOYS, FAX: (212) 688-6053, Web Site: www.fao.com (11)

Richmond, Michael, Foundation Media Group, Deerfield Beach, FL. Tel: (954) 949-9500, (800) 873-5137, FAX: (954) 337-0251, Web Site: www.foundationmediagroup.com (35)

Richmond, Russell, SCI Management, Houston, TX. Tel: (713) 525-7783, Web Site: www.sci-corp.com (16)

Richter, Alan, Marden-Kane Inc, Garden City, NY. Tel: (516) 365-3999, FAX: (516) 365-5250, E-Mail: expert@mardenkane.com, Web Site: www.mardenkane.com (35)

Richter, Don, Cintas, Cincinnati, OH. Tel: (816) 474-7000, FAX: (816) 474-1258, Web Site: www.cintas.com (16)

Richter, Glenn, R., Nuveen Investments, Chicago, IL. Tel: (312) 917-7700, (800) 257-8787, FAX: (312) 917-8049, Web Site: www.nuveen.com (14)

Richtman, Max, National Committee to Preserve Social Security & Medicare, Washington, DC. Tel: (202) 216-0420, (800) 966-1935, FAX: (202) 216-0446, E-Mail: kreard@ncpssm.org, Web Site: www.ncpssm.org (1)

Richwine, Karen, Ames-Tru-Temper, Camp Hill, PA. Tel: (304) 424-3000, FAX: (304) 424-3330 (8)

Rickard, Mark, Rickard List Marketing, Hauppauge, NY. Tel: (631) 249-8710, FAX: (631) 249-9655, E-Mail: mrickard@rickardlist.com, Web Site: www.rickardlist.com (23)

Rickard List Marketing, Hauppauge, NY. Tel: (631) 249-8710, FAX: (631) 249-9655, E-Mail: mrickard@rickardlist.com, Web Site: www.rickardlist.com (23)

Pete Rickard Inc, Cobleskill, NY. Tel: (518) 234-2731, (800) 282-5663, FAX: (518) 234-2454, E-Mail: info@peterickard.com, Web Site: www.peterickard.com (11)

Rickert, Tom, Catholic Digest, New London, CT. Tel: (800) 321-0411, E-Mail: catholicdigest@bayardinc.com, Web Site: www.catholicdigest.com (17)

Ricketts, Robert, Troy Biologicals Inc, Troy, MI. Tel: (800) 521-0445, FAX: (248) 585-2490, E-Mail: info@troybio.com, Web Site: www.troybio.com (7)

Ricketts, Tom, Troy Biologicals Inc, Troy, MI. Tel: (800) 521-0445, FAX: (248) 585-2490, E-Mail: info@troybio.com, Web Site: www.troybio.com (7)

Rickless, Edward, B., Sterling Business Services, Cary, NC. Tel: (919) 467-5062 (28)

Ricks, Dr. Donald, Michigan Apple Committee, Lansing, MI. Tel: (517) 669-8353, (800) 456-2753, FAX: (517) 669-9506, E-Mail: staff@michiganapples.com, Web Site: www.michiganapples.com (1)

Ricks, Franklin K., King's Chandelier Co, Eden, NC. Tel: (336) 623-6188, FAX: (336) 627-9935, E-Mail: crystal@chandelier.com, Web Site: www.chandelier.com (6)

Ridart, Rick, Insight Direct Inc, Tempe, AZ. Tel: (480) 333-3001, (800) 467-4448, FAX: (480) 902-1180, Web Site: www.insight.com (16)

Riddell, Elaine, GFK Custom Research North America, New York, NY. Tel: (212) 240-5300, (800) 274-3577, FAX: (212) 240-5353, E-Mail: info@gfkamerica.com, Web Site: www.gfkamerica.com (30)

Riddle, Tom, Centaur Forge LLC, Burlington, WI. Tel: (262) 763-9175, (800) 666-9175, FAX: (262) 763-8350, E-Mail: info@centaurforge.com, Web Site: www.centaurforge.com (9)

Ridenour, Suzanne, S., Ridenour & Associates, Chicago, IL. Tel: (312) 787-8228, FAX: (312) 787-8528, E-Mail: ssridenour@aol.com, Web Site: www.ridenourassociates.com (20)

Ridenour, Tony, Communication Solutions LLC, Springfield, MO. Tel: (417) 862-4567, Web Site: www.comsolllc.com (29)

Ridenour & Associates, Chicago, IL. Tel: (312) 787-8228, FAX: (312) 787-8528, E-Mail: ssridenour@aol.com, Web Site: www.ridenourassociates.com (20)

Ridge, Mike, Recognition Products International, Easton, MD. Tel: (410) 820-0022, (800) 292-7354, FAX: (410) 820-5044, E-Mail: info@recognitionproducts.com, Web Site: www.shoprecognitionproducts.com (16)

Ridgway, John, Shelburne Co, Taneytown, MD. Tel: (410) 876-5902, FAX: (410) 876-4612, Web Site: www.zoysiafarms.com (8)

Ridgway, Joseph, Bruno & Ridgway Research Associates Inc, Lawrenceville, NJ. Tel: (609) 895-9889, FAX: (609) 895-6665, E-Mail: info@brunoandridgway.com, Web Site: www.brra.com (30)

Ridner, Adrian, Remilon LLC, Mountain View, CA. Tel: (650) 425-7511, Web Site: www.remilon.com (17)

Rieck, Dean, Direct Creative, Westerville, OH. Tel: (614) 882-8823, E-Mail: dean@directcreative.com, Web Site: www.directcreative.com (39)

Riedl, George, J., Allstate Motor Club, Inc, Deerfield, IL. Tel: (847) 914-2972, FAX: (847) 914-2804, Web Site: www.walgreens.com (7)

Rielly, Mike, The Family Handyman, Eagan, MN. Tel: (651) 454-9200, FAX: (651) 994-2250 (17)

Riffkin, Ronald, Riffkin Direct Inc, Roslyn Heights, NY. Tel: (516) 621-1076, FAX: (516) 621-7127 (23)

Riffkin Direct Inc, Roslyn Heights, NY. Tel: (516) 621-1076, FAX: (516) 621-7127 (23)

Rigano, Frank, Interactive Marketing Solutions, Stamford, CT. Tel: (203) 653-2746 (22)

Rigden Inc, Boulder, CO. Tel: (303) 442-8190, FAX: (303) 442-8686, E-Mail: rigden@rigden.com, Web Site: www.rigden.com (22)

Riggio, Frank, Chicago Decal Co, Burr Ridge, IL. Tel: (630) 850-2122, (888) DECALS R US, (888) 332-2577, FAX: (630) 850-7177, E-Mail: sales@chicagodecal.com, Web Site: www.chicagodecal.com (27)

Riggio, Leonard, S., BarnesandNoble.com, New York, NY. Tel: (212) 414-6000, (800) THE-BOOK, FAX: (212) 414-6140, E-Mail: service@barnesandnoble.com, Web Site: www.barnesandnoble.com (16)

The Right Lists Ltd, Clarksville, MD. Tel: (410) 531-0467, Web Site: www.rightlists.com (23)

Right On Computer Software, Greenlawn, NY. E-Mail: riteonsoft@aol.com, Web Site: rightonprograms.com (3)

The Right Start Inc, Denver, CO. Tel: (303) 320-8312, Web Site: www.rightstart.com (5)

Rightminds, Richmond, VA. Tel: (804) 755-7000, FAX: (804) 755-7200, Web Site: www.rightminds.com (35)

Riglian, Walter, Vitasoy USA Inc, Ayer, MA. Tel: (978) 772-6880, (800) VITA-SOY, FAX: (978) 772-6881, Web Site: www.vitasoy-usa.com (16)

Riley, Kevin, Dayton Daily News, Dayton, OH. Tel: (937) 222-5700, (888) 397-6397, FAX: (937) 225-2153, E-Mail: daytondaily@coxohio.com, Web Site: www.daytondailynews.com (18)

Riley, Mark, National Community Pharmacists Association, Alexandria, VA. Tel: (703) 683-8200, (800) 544-7447, FAX: (703) 683-3619, E-Mail: info@ncpanet.org, Web Site: www.ncpanet.org (1)

Riley, Melinda, Deck the Walls Inc, Saint Peters, MO. Tel: (314) 719-8200, (866) 719-8200, FAX: (314) 719-8290, Web Site: www.deckthewalls.com (5)

Riley, Patricia, MDR, Sunrise, FL. Tel: (954) 845-9500, (800) 327-4660, FAX: (954) 845-9505, E-Mail: customerservice@mdr.org, Web Site: www.mdr.org (7)

Riley, Peter, Booth, John Wiley & Sons Inc, Hoboken, NJ. Tel: (201) 748-6000, FAX: (201) 748-6088, E-Mail: info@wiley.com, Web Site: www.wiley.com (17)

Riley, Richard T., NEBS, Groton, MA. Tel: (978) 448-6111, (888) 823-6327, (800) 225-6380, FAX: (800) 234-4324, (978) 448-3653, E-Mail: customerservice@nebs.com, Web Site: www.nebs.com (10)

Riley, Richard, Histacount & Expressions, Lancaster, CA. Tel: (800) 645-5220, FAX: (800) 332-5502, E-Mail: service@rapidforms.com, Web Site: www.rapidforms.com (10)

Rill, Linda, L., LLR/Research, Haverhill, MA. Tel: (978) 374-0931, FAX: (978) 374-1008 (38)

Rimel, John, A., Mountain Press Publishing Co, Missoula, MT. Tel: (406) 728-1900, (800) 234-5308, FAX: (406) 728-1635, E-Mail: info@mtnpress.com, Web Site: www.mountain-press.com (17)

Rinaldi, Matthew J., Arquest Inc, Millstone Twp, NJ. Tel: (609) 395-9500, (888) ARQUEST, (888) 270-8378, FAX: (609) 395-9778, Web Site: www.arquest.com (16)

Rinaldi, Molly, Robertson Mailing List Co, Leesburg, VA. Tel: (703) 726-2822, (800) 788-4564, FAX: (703) 726-9882, E-Mail: vnorman@rmlc.net, Web Site: www.rmlc.net (23)

Rinaldi, Salvatore, J., Sovereign Bank New England, Glastonbury, CT. Tel: (877) 768-2265, FAX: (860) 727-6517 (14)

Riney, Charles, Myriad Systems Inc, Oklahoma City, OK. Tel: (405) 478-9000, (866) 505-1730, FAX: (405) 478-8315, Web Site: www.myriadsystems.com (22)

Rinfret Ltd, Greenwich, CT. Tel: (203) 622-0000, Web Site: www.rinfretltd.com (8)

Ring, Julie, SWBC, San Antonio, TX. Tel: (210) 525-1241, Web Site: www.swbc.com (14)

Ringold, Debra, Business Marketing Association, Naperville, IL. Tel: (630) 544-5054, FAX: (630) 544-5055, E-Mail: info@marketing.org, Web Site: www.marketing.org (40)

Ringold, Debra, Marketing News, Chicago, IL. Tel: (312) 542-9000, (800) 262-1150, FAX: (312) 542-9001, E-Mail: news@ama.org, Web Site: www.ama.org (43)

Ringuette, Arthur, A&R Mailing Machine Inc, East Hartford, CT. Tel: (860) 290-6640 (34)

Rink, Joe, Biomerica Inc, Irvine, CA. Tel: (949) 645-2111, FAX: (949) 722-6674, E-Mail: bmra@biomerica.com, Web Site: www.biomerica.com (7)

Rinke, Barry, Golfsmith International Inc, Austin, TX. Tel: (512) 821-4050, (800) 813-6897, FAX: (512) 837-9347, E-Mail: comments@golfsmith.com, Web Site: www.golfsmith.com (11)

Rio Brands, Philadelphia, PA. Tel: (215) 632-2800, FAX: (215) 824-1172 (16)

Rio Grande, Albuquerque, NM. Tel: (505) 839-3000, (800) 545-6566, FAX: (800) 965-2329, E-Mail: info@riogrande.com, Web Site: www.riogrande.com (16)

Riofrio, Lisa, Guthy-Renker Corp, Palm Desert, CA. Tel: (760) 773-9022, (800) 274-4910, FAX: (760) 773-9016, Web Site: www.guthy-renker.com (32)

Riordan, Michael, National Mail-It Inc, Shreveport, LA. Tel: (318) 683-0093, Web Site: www.nationalmailit.com (27)

Rios, Al, Time Motion Tools, Poway, CA. Tel: (800) 779-8170, FAX: (800) 779-8171, Web Site: www.timemotion.com (9)

Riotto, Charles, M., Licensing Industry Merchandisers' Association (LIMA), New York, NY. Tel: (212) 244-1944, FAX: (212) 563-6552, E-Mail: info@licensing.org, Web Site: www.licensing.org (40)

Ripka, Jim, PGI Companies Inc, Minneapolis, MN. Tel: (952) 933-5745, FAX: (952) 933-5864, E-Mail: ddallum@pgicompanies.com, Web Site: www.pgicompanies.com (27)

Ripley, Thomas, H, ThinkDirect Marketing Group, Largo, FL. Tel: (727) 369-2700, E-Mail: info@tdmg.com, Web Site: www.tdmg.com (28)

Ripon Printers, Ripon, WI. Tel: (920) 748-3136, (800) 321-3136, FAX: (920) 748-3741, E-Mail: info@riponprinters.com, Web Site: www.riponprinters.com (27)

Rippe, Mary, Minnesota Multi Housing Association, Bloomington, MN. Tel: (952) 854-8500, FAX: (952) 854-3810, E-Mail: mha@mmha.com, Web Site: www.mmha.com (1)

Ripple, Laura, Red Hill Corp, Gettysburg, PA. Tel: (717) 337-3038, (800) 822-4003, FAX: (717) 337-0732, E-Mail: custserv@supergrit.com, Web Site: www.supergrit.com (34)

Risberg, Darrel, Vestcom International Inc, Little Rock, AR. Tel: (501) 663-0100, (800) 264-0965, FAX: (501) 663-2451, Web Site: www.vestcom.com (31)

Risdall, John, Risdall Linnihan Advertising, New Brighton, MN. Tel: (651) 286-6700, (888) RISDALL, (888) 747-3255, FAX: (651) 631-2561, E-Mail: info@risdall.com, Web Site: www.risdall.com (35)

Risdall Linnihan Advertising, New Brighton, MN. Tel: (651) 286-6700, (888) RISDALL, (888) 747-3255, FAX: (651) 631-2561, E-Mail: info@risdall.com, Web Site: www.risdall.com (35)

Riseh, Deborah, Nordis Direct, Coral Springs, FL. Tel: (954) 323-5500, (800) 208-1169, FAX: (954) 323-0100, E-Mail: sdolan@nordisdirect.com, Web Site: www.nordisdirect.com (21)

Rishagen, Nancy, KCET, Los Angeles, CA. Tel: (323) 666-6500, FAX: (323) 953-5661, E-Mail: viewerservices@kcet.org, Web Site: www.kcet.org (1)

Riske, Kris, Brandt, American Federation of Astrologers, Tempe, AZ. Tel: (480) 838-1751, (888) 301-7630, FAX: (480) 838-8293, E-Mail: afa@msn.com, Web Site: www.astrologers.com (1)

Riss, Suzanne, Working Mother, New York, NY. Tel: (212) 221-9595, FAX: (212) 219-7448, Web Site: www.workingmother.com (31)

Rist, Larry, The Marmon Group LLC, Chicago, IL. Tel: (312) 372-9500, FAX: (312) 845-5305, Web Site: www.marmon.com (16)

Risti, Nora, COMNET Washington, Framingham, MA. Tel: (508) 879-6700, FAX: (508) 370-4325, Web Site: www.comnetexpo.com (42)

Ritchie, Chester, CAM Commerce Solutions, Fountain Valley, CA. Tel: (714) 241-9241, Web Site: www.camcommerce.com (22)

Ritchie, Joe, Cenveo Commercial Envelope Group, Kent, WA. Tel: (206) 576-4300, (800) 347-6989, FAX: (206) 574-8013, E-Mail: info@cenveo.com, Web Site: www.cenveo.com (26)

Ritchie, Mac, Markwins International Corp, City of Industry, CA. Tel: (909) 595-8898, FAX: (909) 595-8820, Web Site: www.markwins.com (16)

Ritter, C. Dowd, Regions, Birmingham, AL. Tel: (205) 326-5262, FAX: (205) 326-4072, Web Site: www.regions.com (14)

Ritter, Fred, Metro Speedgear, Livingston, NJ. Tel: (908) 286-1886, (800) 777-4453, FAX: (908) 286-0002, E-Mail: info@speedgear.com, Web Site: www.speedgear.com (11)

Ritter, Robert, First Direct Corp, Hopewell Junction, NY. Tel: (845) 221-3800, (800) 935-4386, E-Mail: info@1stdirect.com, Web Site: www.1stdirect.com (35)

Rittman, Dave, The Printer Inc, Des Moines, IA. Tel: (515) 288-7241, FAX: (515) 288-9234, E-Mail: info@the-printer.com, Web Site: www.the-printer.com (27)

Rittwage, William, California Offset Printers, Glendale, CA. Tel: (818) 291-1100, (800) 280-6446, FAX: (818) 291-1190, E-Mail: info@copprints.com, Web Site: www.copprints.com (27)

River Street Sweets, Savannah, GA. Tel: (912) 234-4608, (800) 793-3876, FAX: (912) 234-1584, E-Mail: randerson@riverstreetsweets.com, Web Site: www.riverstreetsweets.com (4)

Rivera, Jose, USI Affinity, Philadelphia, PA. Tel: (610) 833-2876, (800) 625-2876, FAX: (610) 265-2876, E-Mail: info@usiaffinity.com, Web Site: www.brcorp.com (15)

Rivera, Ralph, Gates Corp, Denver, CO. Tel: (303) 744-1911, FAX: (303) 744-4000, Web Site: www.gates.com (9)

Rivera, William, AMC MMI, Fullerton, CA. Tel: (888) 304-4664, FAX: (714) 888-8855 (21)

Rivers, Andrew, Franciscan Friars of the Atonement - Graymoor, Garrison, NY. Tel: (845) 424-3671, FAX: (845) 424-2168, E-Mail: info@atonementfriars.org, Web Site: www.atonementfriars.org (1)

Rivers, Linsey, Florian Tools, Southington, CT. Tel: (860) 628-9643, (800) 275-3618, FAX: (860) 628-6036, E-Mail: sales@floriantools.com, Web Site: www.floriantools.com (8)

Rivers, MaryAnn, D., Entertainment Publications Inc, Troy, MI. Tel: (248) 404-1000, (888) 231-SAVE, FAX: (248) 404-1915, Web Site: www.entertainment.com (31)

Rivkin, Harry, W., The IDT Group, Philadelphia, PA. Tel: (215) 487-4420, FAX: (215) 487-3110, Web Site: www.idthospitality.com (22)

Rizzo, Daniel, C., UDL Laboratories Inc, Sugar Land, TX. Tel: (281) 240-1000, (800) 231-3052, FAX: (281) 240-0002, Web Site: www.udllabs.com (7)

Rizzo, Albert, A, American Lung Association, New York, NY. Tel: (212) 889-3370, (800) LUNGUSA, FAX: (212) 889-3375, E-Mail: info@alany.org, Web Site: www.lungusa.org (1)

Rizzo, Frank, J., Simplicity Pattern Co Inc/Style Patterns Ltd/New Look English Pattern Co Ltd, New York, NY. Tel: (212) 372-0500, (888) 588-2700, FAX: (212) 372-0628, E-Mail: info@simplicitypatt.com, Web Site: www.simplicitypatt.com (8)

Rizzoli International Publications Inc, New York, NY. Tel: (212) 387-3400, FAX: (212) 387-3535 (17)

RJ Reynolds Tobacco Co, Winston Salem, NC. Tel: (336) 741-5111 (16)

Road Runner Sports Inc, San Diego, CA. Tel: (858) 974-4200, (800) 636-3560, FAX: (800) 453-5443, Web Site: www.roadrunnersports.com (11)

Roark, Ed, Graham Field Health Products Inc, Atlanta, GA. Tel: (800) 347-5678, FAX: (800) 726-0601, E-Mail: ics@grahamfield.com, Web Site: www.lumiscope.net (7)

Roath, Tammy, Klockit, Lake Geneva, WI. Tel: (262) 248-7000, (800) 556-2548, FAX: (262) 248-9899, E-Mail: klockit@klockit.com, Web Site: www.klockit.com (6)

Robb, Russ, Tully & Holland Inc, Wellesley, MA. Tel: (781) 239-2900, FAX: (781) 239-2901, E-Mail: info@tullyandholland.com, Web Site: www.tullyandholland.com (14)

Robbins, Scott, Midwest Direct Marketing Inc, Spring Hill, KS. Tel: (913) 686-2220, E-Mail: info@midwestdm.com, Web Site: www.midwestdm.com (21)

Robbins, Terrie, L., St Louis Post-Dispatch, Saint Louis, MO. Tel: (314) 340-8000, (800) 365-0820, FAX: (314) 340-3140, Web Site: www.postnet.com (17)

LW Robbins Associates, Holliston, MA. Tel: (508) 893-0210, (800) 229-5972, FAX: (508) 893-0212, E-Mail: ppapsador@lwra.com, Web Site: www.lwra.com (1)

Roberson, Hal, The Guild Co, Philadelphia, PA. Tel: (201) 750-3222, FAX: (201) 750-4961, E-Mail: mmi-guild@mailmkt.com, Web Site: www.mailmkt.com (23)

Robert, Elisabeth, Vermont Teddy Bear Co, Shelburne, VT. Tel: (802) 985-3001, (800) 829-BEAR, (800) 282-3131, FAX: (802) 985-1304, E-Mail: info@vtbear.com, Web Site: www.vermontteddybear.com (6)

Robert, Jeff, Robert Marketing Inc, Northbrook, IL. Tel: (847) 564-3550, FAX: (847) 564-3551 (5)

Robert, Kevin, CCH Inc, Riverwoods, IL. Tel: (847) 267-7000, (888) 224-7377, Web Site: www.cch. com (17)

Robert, Lewis, Robert Marketing Inc, Northbrook, IL. Tel: (847) 564-3550, FAX: (847) 564-3551 (5)

Robert Burger Illustration, Stockton, NJ. Tel: (609) 397-3737, E-Mail: burgerbobz@aol.com (36)

Robert Marketing Inc, Northbrook, IL. Tel: (847) 564-3550, FAX: (847) 564-3551 (5)

Roberts, Kenneth, The Ken Roberts Co, Daphne, AL. Tel: (541) 955-2867, FAX: (541) 955-2730, Web Site: www.kenroberts.com (5)

Roberts, Kevin, Saatchi & Saatchi, New York, NY. Tel: (212) 463-2000, FAX: (212) 463-9855, Web Site: www.saatchiny.com (32)

Roberts, Lisa, ThomasArts, Farmington, UT. Tel: (801) 451-5365, Web Site: www.thomasarts.com (35)

Roberts, Margaret, Rose, Roberts & Buchanan Inc, Concordia, MO. Tel: (660) 463-2192, E-Mail: kmroberts@centurytel.net (31)

Roberts, Martin, Linguistic Systems Inc, Cambridge, MA. Tel: (877) 654-5006, FAX: (617) 528-7491, E-Mail: info@linguist.com, Web Site: www. linguist.com (27)

Roberts, Richard, Oral Roberts University, Tulsa, OK. Tel: (918) 495-6161, FAX: (918) 495-6222, E-Mail: admissions@oru.edu, Web Site: www.oru. edu (1)

Roberts, Stephen, H., Echo Data, Coatesville, PA. Tel: (610) 466-2100, (800) 511-3870, FAX: (610) 466-2110, E-Mail: sroberts@echodata.com, Web Site: www.echodata.com (22)

Roberts, Tom, National Catholic Reporter Publishing Co Inc, Kansas City, MO. Tel: (816) 531-0538, (800) 444-8910, FAX: (816) 968-2268, Web Site: www.ncronline.org (17)

Roberts, Wayne, Blue Cross & Blue Shield of South Carolina, Columbia, SC. Tel: (803) 788-0222, (800) 288-2227, FAX: (803) 736-4516, Web Site: www.bcbssc.com (15)

Roberts & Buchanan Inc, Concordia, MO. Tel: (660) 463-2192, E-Mail: kmroberts@centurytel.net (31)

Roberts Communications Inc, Rochester, NY. Tel: (716) 325-6000, FAX: (716) 325-6001, Web Site: www.robertscomm.com (35)

H Armstrong Roberts Inc, Philadelphia, PA. Tel: (212) 685-3870, (800) 786-6300, FAX: (800) 786-1920, E-Mail: info@robertstock.com, Web Site: www. robertstock.com (38)

The John Roberts Co, Minneapolis, MN. Tel: (763) 755-5500, (800) 551-1534, FAX: (763) 755-0394, E-Mail: jfoster@johnroberts.com, Web Site: www. johnroberts.com (28)

The Ken Roberts Co, Daphne, AL. Tel: (541) 955-2867, FAX: (541) 955-2730, Web Site: www. kenroberts.com (5)

Roberts Stock/Classic Stock, Philadelphia, PA. Tel: (213) 386-4600, (800) 786-6300, FAX: (213) 365-7171, E-Mail: aspstockpix@earthlink.net, Web Site: www.americanstockphotos.com (38)

Robertson, Barrie, Creative Mailing & Marketing, Gardena, CA. Tel: (310) 637-7100, FAX: (714) 998-9001, Web Site: www.creativemandm.com (28)

Robertson, Ben, Game Show Placements Ltd, Hollywood, CA. Tel: (323) 874-7818, E-Mail: gsp@ix. netcom.com, Web Site: www.gspltd.com (35)

Robertson, Dale, JLG Industries Inc, McConnellsburg, PA. Tel: (717) 485-5161, (877) JLG-SELL, FAX: (717) 485-6417, E-Mail: comments@jlg.com, Web Site: www.jlg.com (16)

Robertson, Gloria, Student Union at SJSU, San Jose, CA. Tel: (408) 924-6353, Web Site: www.union. sjsu.edu (1)

Robertson, Larry, Bear Computer Systems Inc, Dallas, TX. Tel: (818) 509-0459, (800) 252-1691, FAX: (818) 769-3055, E-Mail: info@bearcom.com, Web Site: www.bearcom.com (16)

Robertson, M., G., Christian Broadcasting Network Inc, Virginia Beach, VA. Tel: (757) 226-3542, FAX: (757) 226-2017, Web Site: www.cbn.org (1)

Robertson, Mark, UniWorld Group, Brooklyn, NY. Tel: (212) 219-1600, FAX: (212) 219-6395, E-Mail: fhicks@uniworldgroup.com, Web Site: www.uniworldgroup.com (21)

Robertson, Ms. Sigrun, C., Oomingmak Musk Ox Producers Cooperative, Anchorage, AK. Tel: (907) 272-9225, (888) 360-9665, FAX: (907) 258-4225, E-Mail: oomingmak@qiviut.com, Web Site: www. qiviut.com (6)

Robertson, Paul, Movie Central, Toronto, ON Canada. Tel: (416) 479-6784, E-Mail: info@moviecentral. ca, Web Site: www.moviecentral.ca (32)

Robertson, Randy, List Alliance Inc, Alamo, CA. Tel: (925) 820-3151, E-Mail: info@listalliance.com, Web Site: www.listalliance.com (23)

Robertson, Sharon, McNichols Co, Tampa, FL. Tel: (813) 282-3828, FAX: (813) 288-9342, E-Mail: sales@mcnichols.com, Web Site: www.mcnichols. com (16)

Robertson, Sylvia, Nourse Farms, South Deerfield, MA. Tel: (413) 665-2658, FAX: (413) 665-7888, E-Mail: info@noursefarms.com, Web Site: www. noursefarms.com (8)

Robertson Mailing List Co, Leesburg, VA. Tel: (703) 726-2822, (800) 788-4564, FAX: (703) 726-9882, E-Mail: vnorman@rmlc.net, Web Site: www.rmlc. net (23)

Robillard, Mark, Clients & Profits Worldwide, Oceanside, CA. Tel: (760) 945-4334, Web Site: www. clientsandprofits.com (14)

Robin, Lou, Doremus & Co, New York, NY. Tel: (212) 366-3000, FAX: (212) 366-3060, E-Mail: anderson@doremus.com, Web Site: www.doremus. com (35)

Robinette, Carry, R., Majestic Products Co, Mississauga, ON. Tel: (905) 858-8010, (800) 668-5323, FAX: (905) 670-7915, Web Site: www.cfmcorp. com (16)

Robins, Anna, A La Carte, Chicago, IL. Tel: (773) 745-5900, (800) 723-2370, FAX: (773) 237-3075, E-Mail: info@alacarteline.com, Web Site: www. alacarteline.com (16)

Robinson, Amy, Direct Selling Association, Washington, DC. Tel: (202) 452-8866, FAX: (202) 452-9010, E-Mail: info@dsa.org, Web Site: www.dsa. org (40)

Robinson, Anne, E., Caswell-Massey Co Ltd, Edison, NJ. Tel: (732) 225-2181, (800) 326-0500, FAX: (732) 225-2385, E-Mail: info@caswellmasseyltd. com, Web Site: www.caswellmassey.com (7)

Robinson, Carole, Robinson Direct, Center Valley, PA. Tel: (610) 838-5426, FAX: (610) 838-5589 (35)

Robinson, Craig, Black Dot Group, Chicago, IL. Tel: (815) 459-8520, FAX: (815) 459-7259, E-Mail: sales@blackdot.com, Web Site: www.blackdot.com (35)

Robinson, Dale, PetEdge, Beverly, MA. Tel: (978) 998-8100, (800) 738-3343, FAX: (978) 887-8499, E-Mail: support@petedge.com, Web Site: www. petedge.com (16)

Robinson, James, D., Bristol-Myers Squibb Co, New York, NY. Tel: (212) 546-4000, FAX: (212) 546-9544, Web Site: www.bms.com (16)

Robinson, Janet, L., The New York Times Co, New York, NY. Tel: (212) 556-3881, FAX: (212) 556-7389, Web Site: www.nytimes.com (17)

Robinson, Jim, Farm Bureau Insurance, Lansing, MI. Tel: (517) 323-7000, (800) 292-2680, FAX: (517) 327-0208, Web Site: www.farmbureauinsurance-mi. com (15)

Robinson, Joanne, Golden Rule Insurance Co, Indianapolis, IN. Tel: (317) 297-4123, FAX: (317) 297-0908, Web Site: www.goldenrule.com (15)

Robinson, Joe, Lake Group Media Inc, Armonk, NY. Tel: (914) 925-2400, FAX: (914) 925-2499, E-Mail: joerobinson@lakegroupmedia.com, Web Site: www.lakegroupmedia.com (23)

Robinson, John, Michael, MELDISCO, Mahwah, NJ. Tel: (201) 934-2000, FAX: (201) 934-2570, Web Site: www.meldisco.com (16)

Robinson, Julie, Oliver Russell & Associates, Boise, ID. Tel: (208) 344-1734, FAX: (208) 344-1211, Web Site: www.oliverrussell.com (35)

Robinson, Marian, Guilford Publications Inc, New York, NY. Tel: (212) 431-9800, (800) 365-7006, FAX: (212) 966-6708, E-Mail: info@guilford.com, Web Site: www.guilford.com (17)

Robinson, Nicholas, North American Communications, Armonk, NY. Tel: (914) 273-8620, FAX: (914) 273-3135, E-Mail: info@nacmail.com, Web Site: www.nacmail.com (21)

Robinson, Philip, D., National Stationery Show, White Plains, NY. Tel: (914) 421-3200, (800) 272-SHOW, FAX: (914) 948-6180, E-Mail: cate_doyle@ glmshows.com, Web Site: www.glmshows.com (42)

Robinson, Richard, Scholastic Inc, New York, NY. Tel: (212) 343-6100, (800) SCHOLASTIC, FAX: (212) 343-6484, Web Site: www.scholastic.com/ (17)

Robinson, Rick, AcuSport Corp, Bellefontaine, OH. Tel: (937) 593-7010, FAX: (937) 592-5625, E-Mail: mwsales@acusport.com, Web Site: www. acusport.com (11)

Robinson, Steve, Jossey-Bass Inc Publishers, San Francisco, CA. Tel: (415) 433-1740, FAX: (415) 433-0499, E-Mail: webperson@jbp.com, Web Site: www.josseybass.com (17)

Robinson, Susan, Homespun Tapes Music Instruction, Woodstock, NY. Tel: (845) 246-2550, (800) 338-2737, FAX: (845) 246-5282, E-Mail: info@ homespuntapes.com, Web Site: www. homespuntapes.com (3)

Robinson, Whitney, Clampitt Paper Co, Dallas, TX. Tel: (214) 638-3300, FAX: (214) 634-7837, E-Mail: dcrew@clampitt.com, Web Site: www. clampitt.com (16)

Robinson & Maites Inc, Chicago, IL. Tel: (312) 372-9333, FAX: (312) 372-0682, E-Mail: amaites@ robinsonmaites.com, Web Site: www. robinsonmaites.com (35)

C H Robinson Worldwide Inc, Eden Prairie, MN. Tel: (952) 937-8500, FAX: (952) 937-6740, E-Mail: info@chrobinson.com, Web Site: www.chrobinson. com (16)

Robinson Direct, Center Valley, PA. Tel: (610) 838-5426, FAX: (610) 838-5589 (35)

Robinson Home Products, Buffalo, NY. Tel: (716) 685-6300, FAX: (716) 685-4916 (16)

Robison, Shane, Hewlett-Packard Co, Palo Alto, CA. Tel: (650) 857-1501, (800) 752-0900, FAX: (650) 857-5518, Web Site: www.hp.com (16)

Robison, Ted, MailBlazer, Santa Ana, CA. Tel: (714) 662-5396, Web Site: www.mailblazer.com (27)

The Roblin Group Inc, White Plains, NY. Tel: (914) 686-7221, FAX: (914) 372-1028, E-Mail: freethingsusa@yahoo.com, Web Site: www. freethingsusa.com (17)

Robson, Don, Coldwater Creek, Coeur D Alene, ID. Tel: (800) 787-9196, FAX: (800) 262-0080, Web Site: www.coldwatercreek.com (2)

Robustelli, Richard, Robustelli Merchandise, Stamford, CT. Tel: (203) 965-0200, FAX: (203) 965-0387, Web Site: www.robustelli.com (33)

Robustelli Merchandise, Stamford, CT. Tel: (203) 965-0200, FAX: (203) 965-0387, Web Site: www. robustelli.com (33)

Rocco, Frank, CCMR Advertising/Marketing Communications, Kingston, NY. Tel: (845) 331-4620, FAX: (845) 331-3026, Web Site: www.gotoccmr. com (35)

Rocco, Keitha, DMG-Lists, Deer Park, NY. Tel: (631) 586-5800, FAX: (631) 586-6080, E-Mail: kathyb@dmgltd.org, Web Site: www.dmgltd.org (24)

Rocco, Matt, Etech Inc, Lufkin, TX. Tel: (936) 633-9333, Web Site: www.effectiveteleservices.com (29)

Rocek, Ron, Data Dallas Corp, Dallas, TX. Tel: (214) 638-2007, Web Site: www.ddci.net (22)

Rocha, Robin, King Ranch Saddle Shop, Kingsville, TX. Tel: (361) 595-1424, (800) 282-KING, FAX: (361) 595-1011, E-Mail: krsaddleshop@king-ranch.com, Web Site: www.krsaddleshop.com (8)

Roche, Kevin, Getronics, Tewksbury, MA. Tel: (978) 625-5000, Web Site: www.getronics.com (16)

Roche Diagnostics Corp, Indianapolis, IN. Tel: (317) 521-2000, Web Site: www.accu-chek.com (7)

Roche Pharmaceuticals, Nutley, NJ. Tel: (973) 235-5000, FAX: (973) 235-7605, Web Site: www.rocheusa.com (7)

Rochester, Geoff, World Wrestling Entertainment, Stamford, CT. Tel: (203) 352-8600, FAX: (203) 359-5180, E-Mail: Gary.Davis@wwecorp.com, Web Site: www.wwe.com (16)

Rochester, Shelley, Accoona Corp, Jersey City, NJ. Tel: (201) 557-9388, Web Site: www.accoona.com (16)

Rochester Institute of Technology, Rochester, NY. Tel: (585) 475-7436, Web Site: www.rit.edu (1)

Rochling Engineered Plastics, Dallas, NC. Tel: (704) 922-7814, (800) 541-4419, FAX: (704) 922-7651, E-Mail: rep@roechling-plastics.us, Web Site: www.roechling-plastics.us (34)

Rock, Bradley, E., ABA/BMA Trust Wealth Management and Marketing Conference, Washington, DC. Tel: (202) 663-5000, (800) BANKERS, FAX: (202) 828-4540, E-Mail: custserv@aba.com, Web Site: www.aba.com (42)

Rock, Bradley, E., American Bankers Association, Washington, DC. Tel: (202) 789-0300, (800) BANKERS, FAX: (202) 296-9258, Web Site: www.aba.com (1)

Rock-Tred Corp, Waukegan, IL. Tel: (847) 673-8200, (800) 762-8733, FAX: (847) 679-6665, Web Site: www.rocktred.com (9)

Rocket Direct Marketing Inc, New York, NY. Tel: (212) 689-5800, FAX: (212) 689-0635, E-Mail: info@rocketdirect.com, Web Site: www.rocketdirect.com (32)

Rockett, Brian, Rockett Communications Inc, Danvers, MA. Tel: (978) 774-1780, E-Mail: rockett.comm@verizon.net (35)

Rockett Communications Inc, Danvers, MA. Tel: (978) 774-1780, E-Mail: rockett.comm@verizon.net (35)

RocketWear, New York, NY. Tel: (212) 977-9227, Web Site: www.rocketwear.net (2)

Rockler Woodworking & Hardware, Medina, MN. Tel: (763) 478-8201, (800) 279-4441, FAX: (763) 478-8393, E-Mail: info@rockler.com, Web Site: www.rockler.com (8)

Rockmore, Bette, National Enquirer, Boca Raton, FL. Tel: (561) 989-1221, Web Site: www.nationalenquirer.com (17)

Rockwell Automation, Milwaukee, WI. Tel: (414) 382-2000, FAX: (414) 382-4444, Web Site: www.rockwellautomation.com (1)

Rocky Mountain Chocolate Factory, Durango, CO. Tel: (970) 259-0554, (888) 525-2462, FAX: (970) 259-5895, E-Mail: customerservice@rmcfusa.com, Web Site: www.rmcf.com (4)

Rocky Mountain Direct Marketing Association, Aurora, CO. Tel: (720) 922-9413, FAX: (720) 922-9414, E-Mail: rmdma-ed@rmdma.org, Web Site: www.rmdma.org (41)

Rodale, Ardath, Rodale Inc, Emmaus, PA. Tel: (610) 967-5171, FAX: (610) 967-8963, Web Site: www.rodale.com (17)

Rodale Inc, Emmaus, PA. Tel: (610) 967-5171, FAX: (610) 967-8963, Web Site: www.rodale.com (17)

Rodas, Veronica, Dial-A-Mattress, Hicksville, NY. Tel: (718) 472-1200, (800) 824-7777, FAX: (718) 482-6561, E-Mail: sales@mattress.com, Web Site: www.mattress.com (16)

Rode, Cid, Ameriprise Financial Services Inc, Minneapolis, MN. Tel: (651) 671-3434, (612) 671-3131, (800) 386-2042, Web Site: www.ameriprise.com (14)

Rodelinde Graphic Design, Lenox Dale, MA. Tel: (413) 243-4350, FAX: (413) 243-3066, E-Mail: rodelinde@earthlink.net (36)

Rodgers, Mac, World Marketing Inc, La Vista, NE. Tel: (402) 384-0800, (800) 438-8797, FAX: (402) 384-0801, E-Mail: results@worldmarkinc.com, Web Site: www.worldmarkinc.com (28)

Rodgers, Susan, Pier 1 Imports Inc, Fort Worth, TX. Tel: (817) 252-8000, Web Site: www.pier1.com (8)

Rodgers, Will, SHR Perceptual Management, Phoenix, AZ. Tel: (480) 483-3700, FAX: (480) 483-9675, E-Mail: info@shrbranding.com, Web Site: www.shrbranding.com (35)

Rodriguez, Aida, Non-Profit Management Program/Milano - The New School of Management & Urban Policy, New York, NY. Tel: (212) 229-5400, FAX: (212) 229-5354, E-Mail: milanoadmissions@newschool.edu, Web Site: www.newschool.edu/milano (41)

Rodriguez, Al, Marathon Norco Aerospace Inc, Waco, TX. Tel: (254) 776-0650, FAX: (254) 776-6558, Web Site: www.mptc.com (16)

Rodriguez, Arturo, United Farm Workers of America, AFL-CIO, Keene, CA. Tel: (661) 823-6158, FAX: (661) 823-6177, E-Mail: execoffice@ufw.org, Web Site: www.ufw.org (1)

Rodriguez, Don, Utretch Art Supplies, Cranbury, NJ. Tel: (609) 409-8001, (800) 223-9132, FAX: (800) 382-1979, Web Site: www.utrechtart.com (10)

Rodriguez, Gloria, Vanderbilt Advertising, New York, NY. Tel: (212) 907-1500, FAX: (212) 907-1914, Web Site: www.valueline.com (14)

Rodriguez, Hector, Data Direct, Morton Grove, IL. Tel: (847) 966-8327, FAX: (847) 966-8382 (28)

Rodriguez, Ilia, IEEE/Spectrum Magazine, New York, NY. Tel: (212) 419-7768, FAX: (212) 419-7589, E-Mail: i.rodriguez@ieee.org, Web Site: www.spectrum.ieee.org (24)

Rodriguez, Manon, Society of American Magicians Inc, Parker, CO. E-Mail: rmblowers@aol.com, Web Site: www.magicsam.com (1)

Rodriguez, Nancy, SCA Promotions Inc, Dallas, TX. Tel: (214) 860-3700, (888) 860-3700, FAX: (214) 860-3723, E-Mail: scainfo@scapromo.com, Web Site: www.scapromo.com (15)

Rodriguez, Raul, KWHY-TV Channel 22, Burbank, CA. Tel: (213) 344-3700, E-Mail: info@canal22.tv, Web Site: www.kwhy.com (32)

Rodriguez, Rebecca, Icon Media Direct Inc, Van Nuys, CA. Tel: (818) 995-6400, (800) 818-995-6405, E-Mail: info@iconmediadirect.com, Web Site: www.iconmediadirect.com (35)

Rodriguez, Robert, Nat Com Marketing, Miami, FL. Tel: (786) 425-0028, FAX: (786) 425-0067, E-Mail: info@natcom-marketing.com, Web Site: www.natcom-marketing.com (33)

Rod's Western Palace, Columbus, OH. Tel: (614) 268-8200, (800) 325-8508, FAX: (800) 330-7637, E-Mail: rods@rods.com, Web Site: www.rods.com (2)

Rodstein, Rich, Shakespeare Co, Columbia, SC. Tel: (803) 754-7000, (800) 347-3759, FAX: (803) 754-7342, Web Site: www.shakespeare-fishing.com (11)

Rodwell, Diane, Col Voce Consulting, Exton, PA. Tel: (215) 266-2992, Web Site: www.colvoce.com (20)

Roe, Chelsea, DDB Direct Los Angeles, Los Angeles, CA. Tel: (310) 907-1500, FAX: (310) 907-1990, Web Site: www.ddbla.com (35)

Roe, Susan, AGIA Insurance Services, Carpinteria, CA. Tel: (805) 566-9191, FAX: (805) 566-1887, Web Site: www.agia.com (15)

Roebuck, Malcom, Badge-A-Minit, Oglesby, IL. Tel: (815) 883-8822, (800) 223-4103, FAX: (815) 883-9696, Web Site: www.badgeaminit.com (16)

Roedel, Jeff, American Insurance Administrators Inc, Columbus, OH. Tel: (614) 486-5388, FAX: (614) 486-2728 (15)

Roedel, Jeff, USI Affinity Collegiate Insurance Resources, Columbus, OH. Tel: (614) 486-5388, Web Site: www.collegiateinsuranceresources.com (15)

Roehlke, Katherine, H., Howell Marketing Services, Elmira, NY. Tel: (607) 734-6291, FAX: (607) 734-6759, E-Mail: gl@howellmarketingservices.com, Web Site: www.howellmarketingservices.com (28)

Roelandts, William, Xilinx Inc, San Jose, CA. Tel: (408) 559-7778, FAX: (408) 559-7114, Web Site: www.xilinx.com (16)

Roell, Eric, The Bureau of National Affairs, Inc, Arlington, VA. Tel: (703) 341-3000, (800) 372-1033, FAX: (703) 341-1688, E-Mail: mbromley@bna.com, Web Site: www.bna.com (17)

Roels, Jan, Deloitte & Touche, Boston, MA. Tel: (617) 437-2000, FAX: (617) 437-2111, Web Site: www.deloitte.com (14)

Roeser, Prugh, The Devereux Group, Marblehead, MA. Tel: (781) 631-9213, FAX: (781) 639-3044, E-Mail: roeser@devereuxgroup.com, Web Site: www.devereuxgroup.com (20)

Roeske, Richard, Unitrin, Chicago, IL. Tel: (312) 661-4600, (800) 733-7366, FAX: (312) 494-6995, Web Site: www.unitrin.com (15)

Roeth, George, The Clorox Co, Oakland, CA. Tel: (510) 271-7000, FAX: (510) 832-1463, Web Site: www.thecloroxcompany.com (16)

Roethle, Mark, Pro Media-Streff Marketing Group, Menomonee Falls, WI. Tel: (262) 532-2600, (800) 328-0439, FAX: (800) 951-5955, E-Mail: info@promediaus.com, Web Site: www.promediaus.com (35)

Roffman, Sally, Creative Strategy Inc, Chevy Chase, MD. Tel: (301) 718-4550, FAX: (301) 718-8828, E-Mail: info@creativestrategy.com, Web Site: www.creativestrategy.com (35)

Rogers, Bob, Development Dimensions International, Bridgeville, PA. Tel: (412) 257-0600, (800) 933-4463, FAX: (412) 220-2942, E-Mail: info@ddiworld.com, Web Site: www.ddiworld.com (16)

Rogers, Dana, International Planned Parenthood Federation Western Hemisphere Region Inc, New York, NY. Tel: (212) 248-6400, (866) IPPFWHR, FAX: (212) 248-2441, E-Mail: info@ippfwhr.org, Web Site: www.ippfwhr.org (1)

Rogers, Dene, L., Sears Canada Inc, Toronto, ON. Tel: (416) 362-1711, (888) 473-2772, FAX: (613) 391-3047, E-Mail: home@sears.ca, Web Site: www.sears.ca (5)

Rogers, Donald, Demco Inc, Madison, WI. Tel: (608) 241-1201, FAX: (608) 241-1799, E-Mail: custserv@demco.com, Web Site: www.demco.com (10)

Rogers, Doug, News & Observer Direct Marketing, Raleigh, NC. Tel: (919) 836-5658 (40)

Rogers, Earl, Automod, Atlanta, GA. Tel: (770) 457-9663, (800) 241-1832, FAX: (770) 457-6089, Web Site: www.automod.net (12)

Rogers, Floyd, D., Steck-Vaughn, Austin, TX. Tel: (512) 343-8227, (877) 866-2586, (800) 531-5015, FAX: (512) 795-3617, (877) 265-2730, E-Mail: info@steck-vaughn.com, Web Site: www.steck-vaughn.com (17)

Rogers, James, E., Caraustar, Austell, GA. Tel: (770) 948-3101, E-Mail: info@caraustar.com, Web Site: www.caraustar.com (16)

Rogers, Kris, Affiliate Strategies Inc, Paola, KS. Tel: (913) 294-9093 (35)

Rogers, Kristin, M., PC Mall, Torrance, CA. Tel: (310) 225-2600, (800) 555-MALL, Web Site: www.pcmall.com (3)

Rogers, Mike, StrategicOne, Overland Park, KS. Tel: (913) 342-9100 x102, Web Site: www.strategicone.com (20)

Rogers, Richard R., Mary Kay Cosmetics Inc, Addison, TX. Tel: (972) 687-6300, (800) MARY KAY, FAX: (972) 687-1611, Web Site: www.marykay.com (16)

Rogers, Robert, D., Texas Industries Inc, Dallas, TX. Tel: (972) 647-6700, FAX: (972) 647-3878, Web Site: www.txi.com (16)

Rogers, Ron, Tri Tech Laboratories Inc, Lynchburg, VA. Tel: (434) 845-7073, FAX: (434) 847-4360, Web Site: www.tritechlabs.com (16)

Rogers, Russel, Arrowhead Mountain Spring Water, Wilkes Barre, PA. Tel: (800) 873-7775, Web Site: www.arrowheadwater.com (16)

Rogers, Sherman, Finelight Inc, Louisville, KY. Tel: (502) 589-5896, E-Mail: info@finelight.com, Web Site: www.finelight.com (35)

Rogers & Rosenthal Inc, Fort Lee, NJ. Tel: (201) 346-1862, FAX: (201) 947-5812 (6)

Rogers Publishing Ltd, Toronto, ON Canada. Tel: (416) 935-7777, FAX: (416) 935-3597, Web Site: www.rogerspublishing.ca (17)

Rogge, Pat, Response Media, Norcross, GA. Tel: (770) 451-5478, FAX: (770) 451-4929, E-Mail: babion@responsemedia.com, Web Site: www.responsemedia.com (32)

Roggenkamp, Mark, Safeguard Business Systems Inc, Dallas, TX. Tel: (214) 905-3935, (800) 523-2422, FAX: (800) 439-8423, Web Site: www.gosafeguard.com (16)

Rogin, Robert, The Sound Direct Marketing Group, Austin, TX. Tel: (512) 306-0879 (20)

Rogosin, Don, Channel 13 WNET Catalog Division, New York, NY. Tel: (212) 560-2000, FAX: (212) 582-3297, Web Site: www.thirteen.org (5)

Rogovy, Hugh, Satori Software Inc, Seattle, WA. Tel: (206) 357-2900, (800) 553-6477, FAX: (206) 357-2901, E-Mail: sales@satorisoftware.com, Web Site: www.satorisoftware.com (16)

Rohlik Specialties Co, Bloomfield Hills, MI. Tel: (248) 858-8880, FAX: (248) 858-7323 (33)

Rohm & Haas Co, Philadelphia, PA. Tel: (215) 592-3000, (877) 288-5881, FAX: (215) 592-3377, Web Site: www.rohmhess.com (16)

Rola, Fernando, E., Rola-Kimmerling Associates, New York, NY. Tel: (646) 367-4815, FAX: (646) 367-4901, E-Mail: p_kimhov@rkadv.com, Web Site: www.rkadv.com (35)

Rola-Kimmerling Associates, New York, NY. Tel: (646) 367-4815, FAX: (646) 367-4901, E-Mail: p_kimhov@rkadv.com, Web Site: www.rkadv.com (35)

Roland, Donald, Roland Advisors, Annapolis, MD. Tel: (410) 268-3648 (20)

Roland Advisors, Annapolis, MD. Tel: (410) 268-3648 (20)

Roland Products Inc, Los Angeles, CA. Tel: (323) 731-1111, FAX: (323) 731-9585, E-Mail: salesinfo@rolandinc.com, Web Site: www.rolandinc.com (16)

Roldan, Sergio, Shell Oil Products US, Houston, TX. Tel: (713) 241-6161, Web Site: www.shell.us (16)

Roll, Nancy, Protection One Inc, Lawrence, KS. Tel: (785) 856-5500, (800) GET-HELP, Web Site: www.protectionone.com (16)

Roll International Corp, Los Angeles, CA. Tel: (310) 966-5700, FAX: (310) 914-4747, Web Site: www.roll.com (16)

Rolleston, Humphry, The Economist Newspaper NA Inc, New York, NY. Tel: (212) 554-0600, FAX: (212) 586-1191, Web Site: www.economist.com (17)

Rollins, Bill, Fran's Gifts to Go, Myrtle Beach, SC. Tel: (843) 445-2625, (800) 476-6887, E-Mail: customerservice@fransgiftstogo.com, Web Site: www.fransgiftstogo.com (4)

Rollins, Dr. Nita, Resource Marketing Inc, Columbus, OH. Tel: (614) 621-2888, (800) 550-5815, FAX: (614) 621-2873, E-Mail: inquiry@resource.com, Web Site: www.resource.com (21)

Rollins, Stacy, SLR Associates, Portland, OR. Tel: (503) 645-0675 (20)

Rollins, Thomas, The Teaching Co, Chantilly, VA. Tel: (703) 502-7300, (800) 832-2412, FAX: (703) 378-3819, Web Site: www.teach12.com (17)

Rollyson, Richard, V., Rollyson Financial Group, Pasadena, MD. Tel: (410) 437-5596 (14)

Rollyson Financial Group, Pasadena, MD. Tel: (410) 437-5596 (14)

Roman, Ernan, Ernan Roman Direct Marketing Corp, Little Neck, NY. Tel: (718) 225-4151, FAX: (718) 225-4889, E-Mail: ernan@erdm.com, Web Site: www.erdm.com (16)

Roman, Paul, DineWise, Farmingdale, NY. Tel: (631) 694-1111, (800) 749-1170, FAX: (631) 694-4064, E-Mail: info@dinewise.com, Web Site: www.dinewise.com (4)

Roman, Suzanne, The Taunton Press, Newtown, CT. Tel: (203) 426-8171, (800) 477-8727, FAX: (203) 426-3434, Web Site: www.taunton.com (17)

Edith Roman Associates Inc, Pearl River, NY. Tel: (845) 620-9000, (800) 223-2194, FAX: (845) 620-9035 (23)

Roman Research Inc/Simply Whispers Earring, Hanson, MA. Tel: (781) 447-3411, (800) 451-5700, FAX: (781) 447-0995, Web Site: www.simplywhispers.com (2)

Romanello, Kelly, Holiday Travel of America, Carlsbad, CA. Tel: (760) 431-8600, (888) 732-2479, FAX: (760) 431-3131, E-Mail: sales@htoa.com, Web Site: www.htoa.com (19)

Romanello, Richard J., Holiday Travel of America, Carlsbad, CA. Tel: (760) 431-8600, (888) 732-2479, FAX: (760) 431-3131, E-Mail: sales@htoa.com, Web Site: www.htoa.com (19)

Romano, Cheryl, CCL Label, Cold Spring, KY. Tel: (859) 781-6161, (800) 422-6633, FAX: (859) 781-6339 (27)

Romano, James, V., Research To Prevent Blindness Inc, New York, NY. Tel: (212) 752-4333, (800) 621-0026, FAX: (212) 688-6231, E-Mail: inforequest@rpbusa.org, Web Site: www.rpbusa.org (1)

Romans, M., Jay, Standard Register, Dayton, OH. Tel: (937) 221-1000, (800) 755-6405, FAX: (937) 221-1239, E-Mail: julie.mcewan@standardregister.com, Web Site: www.standardregister.com (10)

Romas, Chris, W Atlee Burpee Co, Warminster, PA. Tel: (215) 674-4900, (800) 333-5808, FAX: (215) 674-4170, Web Site: www.burpee.com (8)

Romberg, Harry, Houston Direct Marketing Association, Houston, TX. Tel: (281) 931-8883, FAX: (281) 820-4023, Web Site: www.houstondma.org (40)

Romero, John, John Romero Direct Marketing, Parker, CO. Tel: (303) 805-2507, FAX: (303) 805-2509, E-Mail: romeromkt@aol.com, Web Site: www.romeromarketing.com (35)

Romero, Tommy, Fisher Investments, Woodside, CA. Tel: (650) 851-3334, Web Site: www.fi.com (14)

John Romero Direct Marketing, Parker, CO. Tel: (303) 805-2507, FAX: (303) 805-2509, E-Mail: romeromkt@aol.com, Web Site: www.romeromarketing.com (35)

Rometty, Virginia, M., IBM Corp, Armonk, NY. Tel: (914) 765-1900, FAX: (914) 765-6633, Web Site: www.ibm.com (16)

Romig, Shareen, Smith & Noble, Corona, CA. Tel: (909) 734-4444, (800) 248-8888, FAX: (800) 426-7780, E-Mail: contactus@smithnoble.com, Web Site: www.smithandnoble.com (8)

Romm, Preston, Iomega Corp, Roy, UT. Tel: (801) 332-1000, (888) 446-6342, FAX: (801) 332-3158, Web Site: www.iomega.com (16)

Ron Perrella DRS (DR Specialists), Laguna Niguel, CA. Tel: (949) 495-7661, FAX: (949) 495-7660, E-Mail: rperrdrs@aol.com, Web Site: www.ronperrelladrs.com (35)

Ronan, Brian, Hello Direct, Nashua, NH. Tel: (408) 972-1990, (800) 435-5634, FAX: (408) 972-8155, Web Site: www.hello-direct.com (16)

Ronco Corp, Austin, TX. Tel: (800) 486-1806, E-Mail: customerservice@ronco.com, Web Site: www.ronco.com (16)

Rondeau, William, B., Priests of the Sacred Heart, Hales Corners, WI. Tel: (414) 425-3383, FAX: (414) 425-5719, Web Site: www.poshusa.org (1)

RONED Printing & Reproduction Inc, East Hanover, NJ. Tel: (973) 386-1848, FAX: (973) 386-0969, E-Mail: info@roned.com, Web Site: www.roned.com (27)

Ronell Clock Co, Grants Pass, OR. Tel: (541) 471-0194, (800) 334-0135, FAX: (541) 471-0099, Web Site: www.ronellclock.com (5)

Roney, Patrick, Windsor Vineyards, Santa Rosa, CA. Tel: (800) 741-6070, (800) 289-9463, E-Mail: webmaster@windsorvineyards.com, Web Site: www.windsorvineyards.com (16)

Ronon, Lynne, HSN Inc, Saint Petersburg, FL. Tel: (727) 872-1000, (800) 284-3100, Web Site: www.hsn.com (5)

Ronstein, Larry, Source Communications, Hackensack, NJ. Tel: (201) 343-5222 (35)

Roome, Hugh, Scholastic Inc, New York, NY. Tel: (212) 343-6100, (800) SCHOLASTIC, FAX: (212) 343-6484, Web Site: www.scholastic.com/ (17)

Rooney, Diane, Grand Circle Travel, Boston, MA. Tel: (617) 350-7500, (800) 959-0405, FAX: (617) 346-6030, Web Site: www.gct.com (19)

Rooney, Jack, Campbell Mithun, Minneapolis, MN. Tel: (612) 347-1000, FAX: (612) 347-1515, Web Site: www.campbellmithun.com (35)

Roosevelt Paper Co, Mount Laurel, NJ. Tel: (856) 303-4200, (856) 303-4100, (800) 523-3470, FAX: (856) 642-1949, (856) 642-1950, Web Site: www.rooseveltpaper.com (25)

Root, Gary, San Francisco Victoriana Inc, San Francisco, CA. Tel: (415) 648-0313, FAX: (415) 648-2812, Web Site: www.sfvictoriana.com (9)

Rootblast International, Canton, OH. Tel: (330) 453-5828, FAX: (330) 453-5170, Web Site: www.rootblast.cc (32)

Roovers Inc, Hazleton, PA. Tel: (570) 455-7548, FAX: (570) 454-1477 (34)

Roper, Lisa, Astronomical Society of the Pacific, San Francisco, CA. Tel: (415) 337-1100, (800) 335-2624, FAX: (415) 337-5205, E-Mail: service@astrosociety.org, Web Site: www.astrosociety.org (1)

Rosan, Rick, ULI-The Urban Land Institute, Washington, DC. Tel: (202) 624-7000, FAX: (202) 624-7140, Web Site: www.uli.org (1)

Rosane, Edwin L., USAA, San Antonio, TX. Tel: (512) 498-6524, FAX: (512) 498-8000 (15)

Rosanvallon, John, Dassault Falcon Jet Corp, Little Ferry, NJ. Tel: (201) 440-6700, FAX: (201) 541-4515, Web Site: www.dassaultfalcon.com (16)

Rose, Beth, Lesman Instrument Co, Bensenville, IL. Tel: (630) 595-8400, (800) 953-7626, FAX: (630) 595-2386, E-Mail: sales@lesman.com, Web Site: www.lesman.com (9)

Rose, Brian, Archaeology Magazine, Long Island City, NY. Tel: (718) 472-3050, FAX: (718) 472-3051, E-Mail: production@archaeology.org, Web Site: www.archaeology.org (17)

Rose, Daniel, Metrics Marketing, Westlake, OH. Tel: (440) 331-1688, Web Site: www.precisiondialogue.com (16)

Rose, David, LCA Vision, Cincinnati, OH. Tel: (513) 792-9292, FAX: (513) 792-5620, Web Site: www.lasikplus.com (41)

Rose, Gideon, Council on Foreign Relations Inc, New York, NY. Tel: (212) 434-9400, FAX: (212) 861-2759, E-Mail: editor@foreignaffairs.com, Web Site: www.foreignaffairs.org (17)

Rose, Henry, A., Unicol Inc, Pembroke Pines, FL. Tel: (954) 431-7871, FAX: (954) 430-7227, E-Mail: customerservice@unicol-publishing.com, Web Site: www.unicol-publishing.com (17)

Rose, Jeffrey D., JDR Microdevices, Mountain View, CA. Tel: (408) 494-1400, (800) 538-5000, FAX: (800) 538-5005, E-Mail: sales@jdr.com, Web Site: www.jdr.com (3)

Rose, Matthew, K., Burlington Northern & Santa Fe Railroad, Fort Worth, TX. Tel: (817) 878-2000, (800) 795-2673, FAX: (817) 333-7593, Web Site: www.bnsf.com (16)

Rose, Maureen, DMG-Lists, Deer Park, NY. Tel: (631) 586-5800, FAX: (631) 586-6080, E-Mail: kathyb@dmgltd.org, Web Site: www.dmgltd.org (24)

Rose, R., Michael, Dominion Retail Inc, Richmond, VA. Tel: (804) 819-2268, Web Site: www.dom.com (16)

Rose, Robert, Media Link Communications, New York, NY. Tel: (212) 674-8843, FAX: (212) 260-8489, E-Mail: mlinkcom@aol.com, Web Site: www.getprinted.com (27)

Rose, Russ, Watts Radiant, Springfield, MO. Tel: (417) 864-6108, (800) 276-2419, FAX: (417) 864-8161, Web Site: www.wattsheatway.com (9)

Rose, Sarah, US Gas & Electric, Miami, FL. Tel: (305) 947-7880, Web Site: www.usgande.com (16)

Rose, Stuart, Tully & Holland Inc, Wellesley, MA. Tel: (781) 239-2900, FAX: (781) 239-2901, E-Mail: info@tullyandholland.com, Web Site: www.tullyandholland.com (14)

Rose Displays Ltd, Salem, MA. Tel: (978) 219-8100, Web Site: www.rosedisplays.com (16)

Rose Electronics, Houston, TX. Tel: (281) 933-7673, (800) 333-9343, FAX: (281) 933-0044, E-Mail: sales@rose.com, Web Site: www.rose.com (3)

Rose Printing Co Inc, Tallahassee, FL. Tel: (850) 576-4151, (800) 227-3725, FAX: (850) 576-4153, E-Mail: roseprt@roseprinting.com, Web Site: www.roseprinting.com (27)

Roseberry Direct List Management & Brokerage, Elon, NC. Tel: (336) 532-1000, Web Site: www.roseberrydirect.com (23)

Roselli, John P., DeVry Inc, Oakbrook Terrace, IL. Tel: (630) 571-7700, FAX: (602) 943-4108, Web Site: www.devry.com (16)

Roseman, Karl-Heinz, McFarland & Co Inc Publishers, Jefferson, NC. Tel: (336) 246-4460, (800) 253-2187, FAX: (336) 246-5018, E-Mail: info@mcfarlandpub.com, Web Site: www.mcfarlandpub.com (17)

Rosen, Alan, Junior's Cheesecake, Brooklyn, NY. Tel: (718) 852-5257, (800) 458-6467, FAX: (718) 260-9849, E-Mail: info@juniorscheesecake.com, Web Site: www.juniorscheesecake.com (16)

Rosen, Andrew, S., Kaplan Inc, New York, NY. Tel: (212) 492-5800, (800) 527-8378, FAX: (212) 492-5933, Web Site: www.kaplan.com (16)

Rosen, Andrew, S., Kaplan Publishing, Chicago, IL. Tel: (312) 606-8905, (800) 245-2665, FAX: (312) 606-8985, E-Mail: kaplanorders@kaplan.com, Web Site: www.kaplanpublishing.com (17)

Rosen, Arlene, ARA Media Solutions Inc, New York, NY. Tel: (212) 245-6691, Web Site: www.aramediasolutions.com (31)

Rosen, Jesse, League of American Orchestras, New York, NY. Tel: (212) 262-5161, FAX: (212) 262-5198, Web Site: www.symphony.org; www.americanorchestras.org (1)

Rosen, Marvin, Junior's Cheesecake, Brooklyn, NY. Tel: (718) 852-5257, (800) 458-6467, FAX: (718) 260-9849, E-Mail: info@juniorscheesecake.com, Web Site: www.juniorscheesecake.com (16)

Rosen, Neil, eWay Direct, Southport, CT. Tel: (888) 655-0464, Web Site: www.ewaydirect.com (32)

Rosen, Richard, Rosen Inc, Portland, OR. Tel: (503) 224-9811, E-Mail: info@rgrosen.com, Web Site: www.rgrosen.com (35)

Rosen, Walter, Junior's Cheesecake, Brooklyn, NY. Tel: (718) 852-5257, (800) 458-6467, FAX: (718) 260-9849, E-Mail: info@juniorscheesecake.com, Web Site: www.juniorscheesecake.com (16)

Rosen Inc, Portland, OR. Tel: (503) 224-9811, E-Mail: info@rgrosen.com, Web Site: www.rgrosen.com (35)

Rosenbauer, Tom, The Orvis Co Inc, Manchester, VT. Tel: (802) 362-3622, FAX: (802) 362-3525, Web Site: www.orvis.com (11)

Rosenbaum, Davey, Marketsmith Inc, Parsippany, NJ. Tel: (973) 889-0006, Web Site: www.marketsmithinc.com (20)

Rosenbaum, Jan, MCCS, Mason, OH. Tel: (513) 573-2284, FAX: (513) 573-2197, Web Site: www.federated.com (14)

Rosenberg, Allen, G., Marke Communications Inc, New York, NY. Tel: (212) 201-0600, (800) 716-2753, FAX: (212) 213-0785, Web Site: www.marke.com (33)

Rosenberg, Bill, Barterbing.com, Cranston, RI. Tel: (800) 345-6733, FAX: (401) 679-0326, Web Site: www.barterbing.com (29)

Rosenberg, Charles, Rose Printing Co Inc, Tallahassee, FL. Tel: (850) 576-4151, (800) 227-3725, FAX: (850) 576-4153, E-Mail: roseprt@roseprinting.com, Web Site: www.roseprinting.com (27)

Rosenberg, James, Midland Lithographing Co, North Kansas City, MO. Tel: (816) 842-2224, FAX: (816) 842-4530 (27)

Rosenberg, Jay, JSR Advertising Corp, New York, NY. Tel: (212) 995-1661, E-Mail: jsr@nyc.rr.com, Web Site: www.quantmethod.com (35)

Rosenberg, Robert, Sturm, Rosenburg, King & Co, Chicago, IL. Tel: (312) 943-1881, FAX: (312) 943-2346, Web Site: www.sturmads.com (35)

Rosenberg, Roberta, MGP Direct Inc, Fulton, MD. Tel: (410) 531-0383, FAX: (410) 531-8142, E-Mail: roberta@mgpdirect.com, Web Site: www.mgpdirect.com (35)

Rosenblum, Bobby, Corporate Promotions, Nashville, TN. Tel: (615) 242-0501, FAX: (615) 256-0862, Web Site: www.promoville.com (35)

Rosenfeld, Theodore, Walker Publishing Co Inc, New York, NY. Tel: (212) 727-8300, (800) 289-2553, FAX: (212) 727-0984 (17)

Rosengarten, Troy, Ruud Lighting Inc, Racine, WI. Tel: (262) 886-1900, (800) 236-7000, FAX: (800) 236-7500, E-Mail: sales@ruudlighting.com, Web Site: www.ruudlighting.com (9)

Rosenheim, Robert, Robert Rosenheim Associates, Sharon, CT. Tel: (860) 364-0050, FAX: (860) 364-5577, Web Site: rrallc.com (32)

Robert Rosenheim Associates, Sharon, CT. Tel: (860) 364-0050, FAX: (860) 364-5577, Web Site: rrallc.com (32)

Rosenspan, Alan, Alan Rosenspan & Associates, Sharon, MA. Tel: (781) 784-2228, Web Site: www.alanrosenspan.com (20)

Alan Rosenspan & Associates, Sharon, MA. Tel: (781) 784-2228, Web Site: www.alanrosenspan.com (20)

Rosenthal, Gerald, Rogers & Rosenthal Inc, Fort Lee, NJ. Tel: (201) 346-1862, FAX: (201) 947-5812 (6)

Rosenthal, Jim, Morgan Stanley, New York, NY. Tel: (212) 761-4000, FAX: (212) 761-0096 (14)

Rosenthal, Larry, Teva Pharmaceuticals USA, North Wales, PA. Tel: (215) 591-3000, (888) TEVAUSA, FAX: (215) 591-8600, Web Site: www.tevausa.com (7)

Rosenthal, Paul, TT Publishing, Arlington, VA. Tel: (703) 838-1770, FAX: (703) 838-0285, Web Site: www.ttnews.com (17)

Rosenthal, Richard, A., LaCrosse Footwear Inc, Portland, OR. Tel: (503) 262-0110, (800) 323-2668, FAX: (503) 262-0115, E-Mail: customerservice@lacrossefootwear.com, Web Site: www.lacrossefootwear.com (16)

Rosenthal, Robert, Union Pen Co, Hagaman, NY. Tel: (800) 846-6600, FAX: (518) 770-7018, Web Site: www.unionpen.com (5)

Rosenzweig, Richard, S., Playboy Enterprises Inc, Beverly Hills, CA. Tel: (310) 860-1215, Web Site: www.playboyenterprises.com (17)

Rosicrucian Order AMORC, San Jose, CA. Tel: (408) 947-3600, FAX: (408) 947-3677, E-Mail: rosicrucian@amorcmail.org, Web Site: www.rosicrucian.org (1)

Rosinger, David, Magnolia Hall, Jasper, GA. Tel: (404) 351-1910, (866) 410-2755, FAX: (404) 351-2151, E-Mail: belvedere@magnoliahall.com, Web Site: www.magnoliahall.com (8)

Roska, Jon, Roska Direct Advertising, Montgomeryville, PA. Tel: (215) 699-9200, FAX: (215) 699-9240, E-Mail: jr@roskadirect.com, Web Site: www.RoskaDirect.com (35)

Roska Direct Advertising, Montgomeryville, PA. Tel: (215) 699-9200, FAX: (215) 699-9240, E-Mail: jr@roskadirect.com, Web Site: www.RoskaDirect.com (35)

Roskos, Bob, Virco Manufacturing Corp, Conway, AR. Tel: (501) 329-2901, (800) 448-4726, FAX: (800) 258-7367, E-Mail: info@virco.com, Web Site: www.virco.com (16)

Rosland Capital LLC, Santa Monica, CA. Tel: (800) 891-2341, Web Site: www.roslandcapital.com (14)

Rosmarin, John, Saunders Manufacturing Co Inc, Readfield, ME. Tel: (207) 685-3385, (800) 341-4674, FAX: (207) 685-9918, E-Mail: jsherwood@saunders-usa.com, Web Site: www.saunders-usa.com (16)

Ross, Bruce A., The Plain Dealer, Cleveland, OH. Tel: (216) 999-5000, FAX: (216) 999-6356, Web Site: www.plaindealer.com (18)

Ross, Darrell S., Ross-Simons, Cranston, RI. Tel: (401) 463-3100, (800) 835-0919, FAX: (401) 463-8599, Web Site: www.ross-simons.com (6)

Ross, E., Rod, Equitable Life & Casualty Insurance Co, Salt Lake City, UT. Tel: (801) 579-3400, FAX: (801) 579-3789, Web Site: www.equilife.com (15)

Ross, Gary, M., Compuletter Inc, Niles, IL. Tel: (847) 647-6200, FAX: (847) 647-2309, E-Mail: directmail@compuletter.com, Web Site: www.compuletter.com (28)

Ross, Jack, Angel, Ross Metals, New York, NY. Tel: (212) 869-1407, (800) 654-ROSS (16)

Ross, John, Appraisal Institute, Chicago, IL. Tel: (312) 335-4100, FAX: (312) 335-4400, E-Mail: info@appraisalinstitute.org, Web Site: www.appraisalinstitute.org (1)

Ross, John, Torcom Inbound Telemarketing, Madison, WI. Tel: (800) 832-4939, FAX: (608) 275-6557, E-Mail: torcom@torcom.com, Web Site: www.torcom.com (29)

Ross, Marilyn, Communication Creativity, Buena Vista, CO. Tel: (720) 344-4388, (800) 331-8355, FAX: (866) 685-0307, E-Mail: steve@steveheimberg.com, Web Site: www.communicationcreativity.com (17)

Ross, Marji, Regnery Publishing, Washington, DC. Tel: (202) 216-0600, FAX: (202) 216-0612, Web Site: www.regnery.com (17)

Ross, Michael, CIGNA International, Philadelphia, PA. Tel: (215) 761-1741, FAX: (215) 761-5515, Web Site: www.cigna.com (15)

Ross, Michael, World Book Inc, Chicago, IL. Tel: (312) 729-5800, (800) 255-1750, FAX: (312) 729-5600, Web Site: www.worldbook.com (17)

Ross, Peter, Ross Culbert & Lavery, New York, NY. Tel: (212) 206-0044, Web Site: www.rclnyc.com (20)

Ross, Rhianna, Rapid Response Marketing, Las Vegas, NV. Tel: (702) 631-9714, (866) 997-7297, FAX: (702) 216-4038, Web Site: www.xy7.com (32)

Ross, Robert, Schoolwise Press, San Francisco, CA. Tel: (415) 337-7971, (800) 247-8443 x 202, FAX: (415) 337-1146, E-Mail: info@schoolwisepress.com, Web Site: www.schoolwisepress.com (17)

Ross, Sam, Woodcraft Supply Corp LLC, Parkersburg, WV. Tel: (304) 422-5412, (800) 344-3348, FAX: (304) 422-5417, Web Site: www.woodcraft.com (9)

Ross, Steven, B., Compuletter Inc, Niles, IL. Tel: (847) 647-6200, FAX: (847) 647-2309, E-Mail: directmail@compuletter.com, Web Site: www.compuletter.com (28)

Ross, Tom, About Books Inc, Colorado Springs, CO. Tel: (719) 632-8226, FAX: (719) 471-2182, E-Mail: infoabi2@about-books.com, Web Site: www.about-books.com (20)

Ross, Tom, Communication Creativity, Buena Vista, CO. Tel: (720) 344-4388, (800) 331-8355, FAX: (866) 685-0307, E-Mail: steve@steveheimberg. com, Web Site: www.communicationcreativity.com (17)

Ross Culbert & Lavery, New York, NY. Tel: (212) 206-0044, Web Site: www.rclnyc.com (20)

Ross Metals, New York, NY. Tel: (212) 869-1407, (800) 654-ROSS (16)

Ross-Simons, Cranston, RI. Tel: (401) 463-3100, (800) 835-0919, FAX: (401) 463-8599, Web Site: www.ross-simons.com (6)

Rossell, Tony, Marketing General Inc, Alexandria, VA. Tel: (703) 739-1000, (800) 644-6646, FAX: (703) 549-6057, E-Mail: info@marketinggeneral.com, Web Site: www.marketinggeneral.com (35)

Rossi, Arleen, Eastern Collection Corp, Sag Harbor, NY. Tel: (631) 563-2112, (800) 243-1204, FAX: (631) 563-2471, E-Mail: ecc1626@aol.com (20)

Rossi, Eric, Buxton, Fort Worth, TX. Tel: (817) 332-3681, Web Site: www.buxtonco.com (30)

Rossi, Franceso, American Arbitration Association, New York, NY. Tel: (212) 716-5800, (800) 778-7879, FAX: (212) 716-5905, E-Mail: kesslerw@adr.org, Web Site: www.adr.org (1)

Rossi, Paul, The Economist Newspaper NA Inc, New York, NY. Tel: (212) 554-0600, FAX: (212) 586-1191, Web Site: www.economist.com (17)

Rossi, Richard, Eagle Asset Management Inc, Saint Petersburg, FL. Tel: (727) 573-2453, FAX: (727) 573-8020, Web Site: www.eagleasset.com (14)

Rossnagel, Thomas, Sunrise Medical Inc, Boulder, CO. Tel: (303) 218-4500, (800) 333-4000, FAX: (303) 218-4949, Web Site: www.sunrisemedical.com (16)

Rossner, Kathy, 800 Response, Burlington, VT. Tel: (802) 860-0378, (800) NEW-SALES, FAX: (800) NEW-ORDER, E-Mail: sales@800response.com, Web Site: www.800response.com (32)

Rossou, Alfred, Tully & Holland Inc, Wellesley, MA. Tel: (781) 239-2900, FAX: (781) 239-2901, E-Mail: info@tullyandholland.com, Web Site: www.tullyandholland.com (14)

Rosten, Bernard, Allied Premium Co, Rockville Centre, NY. Tel: (516) 766-5300 (33)

Roswarski, Todd, Ivy Tech State College, Indianapolis, IN. Tel: (317) 921-4800, (888) IVY-LINE, FAX: (317) 921-4753, Web Site: www.ivytech.edu/indianapolis (13)

Rosyn, Chris, China Books & Periodicals Inc, South San Francisco, CA. Tel: (650) 872-7076, (800) 818-2017, FAX: (650) 872-7808, E-Mail: info@chinabooks.com, Web Site: www.chinabooks.com (17)

Rotella, Stephen, Washington Mutual Home Loan, Inc, Downers Grove, IL. Tel: (847) 549-6500, FAX: (847) 549-2975 (14)

Rotenberg, Sandy, Country Dance and Song Society, Haydenville, MA. Tel: (413) 268-7426, FAX: (413) 268-7471, E-Mail: office@cdss.org, Web Site: www.cdss.org (1)

Rotenstein, Sergio, MRV Communications, Chatsworth, CA. Tel: (818) 773-0900, FAX: (818) 773-0906, Web Site: www.mrv.com (3)

Rotermund, Ralph W., Printing for Systems Inc, Carrollton, TX. Tel: (203) 245-4200, FAX: (203) 245-0349, Web Site: www.printingforsystems.com (27)

Roth, Andy, Norwood Promotional Products, Clearwater, FL. Tel: (317) 275-2500, (800) 959-9138, FAX: (317) 275-2570, Web Site: www.norwood.com (16)

Roth, Charles, A., Roth Advertising Inc, Sea Cliff, NY. Tel: (516) 674-8603, FAX: (516) 674-8606, E-Mail: charles@rothadvertising.com, Web Site: www.rothadvertising.com (35)

Roth, Chris, Professional Marketing Associates, Tempe, AZ. Tel: (480) 829-0131, FAX: (480) 829-9202, Web Site: www.pmafulfillment.com (22)

Roth, Daniel, J., Roth Advertising Inc, Sea Cliff, NY. Tel: (516) 674-8603, FAX: (516) 674-8606, E-Mail: charles@rothadvertising.com, Web Site: www.rothadvertising.com (35)

Roth, Debbie, Japs-Olson Co, Saint Louis Park, MN. Tel: (952) 932-9393, (800) 548-2897, FAX: (612) 912-1900, Web Site: www.japsolson.com (27)

Roth, Elaine, Direct Response Marketing Inc, Palm Desert, CA. Tel: (760) 360-5900, FAX: (760) 360-7266 (32)

Roth, Ernie, M., Furman Roth Advertising, New York, NY. Tel: (212) 687-2300, FAX: (212) 687-0858, Web Site: www.furmanroth.com (35)

Roth, Irwin, Color Q Inc, Miamisburg, OH. Tel: (937) 866-4001, (800) 999-9818, FAX: (937) 866-4101, E-Mail: info@colorq.com, Web Site: www.colorqinc.com (27)

Roth, Lawrence, H., American Society of Civil Engineers, Reston, VA. Tel: (703) 295-6000, (800) 548-2723, FAX: (703) 295-6343, Web Site: www.asce.org (1)

Roth, Leah, Two Roths, Forest Hills, NY. Tel: (718) 268-1998, FAX: (718) 793-3972, E-Mail: tworoths@rcn.com (35)

Roth, Steve, Ventyx, Atlanta, GA. Tel: (770) 952-8444, (800) 868-0497, FAX: (770) 955-2977, E-Mail: support@ventyx.com, Web Site: www.ventyx.com (16)

Roth Advertising Inc, Sea Cliff, NY. Tel: (516) 674-8603, FAX: (516) 674-8606, E-Mail: charles@rothadvertising.com, Web Site: www.rothadvertising.com (35)

Rothenberg, Gilbert, Global Computer Corp, Port Washington, NY. Tel: (516) 625-4300, (888) 845-6225, FAX: (516) 625-4072, Web Site: www.globalcomputer.com (3)

Rothering, Larry, Enerpac, Menomonee Falls, WI. Tel: (262) 781-6600, (800) 433-2766, FAX: (262) 781-1028, Web Site: www.enerpac.com (16)

Rothert, Eric, NOVO1, Fort Worth, TX. Tel: (817) 355-6899, FAX: (817) 355-8505, Web Site: www.novo1.com (29)

Rothfelder, Ralph, Mapping Analytics, Rochester, NY. Tel: (585) 271-6490, (877) 893-6490, FAX: (585) 271-1132, E-Mail: sales@mappinganalytics.com, Web Site: www.mappinganalytics.com (20)

Rothman, Judith, University Press of America Inc, Lanham, MD. Tel: (301) 459-3366, (800) 462-6420, FAX: (301) 429-5748, E-Mail: custserv@rowman.com, Web Site: www.univpress.com (17)

Rothman, LaVonda, JR Tobacco/800-JR Cigar Inc, Burlington, NC. Tel: (800) 572-4427, FAX: (800) 457-3299, Web Site: www.jrcigars.com (5)

Rothman, Lew, JR Tobacco/800-JR Cigar Inc, Burlington, NC. Tel: (800) 572-4427, FAX: (800) 457-3299, Web Site: www.jrcigars.com (5)

Rothschild, David, Sunshine Discount Crafts, Largo, FL. Tel: (727) 530-9572, (800) 729-2878, FAX: (727) 531-2739, E-Mail: webmaster@sunshinecrafts.com, Web Site: www.sunshinecrafts.com (11)

Rothstein, Seth, Wunderman, New York, NY. Tel: (212) 941-3000, FAX: (212) 888-7520, Web Site: www.wunderman.com (35)

Rotnicki, Benjamin, Godiva Chocolatier, New York, NY. Tel: (212) 984-5977, Web Site: www.godiva.com (4)

Roto-Rooter Services Co, Cincinnati, OH. Tel: (513) 762-6690, FAX: (513) 762-6590, Web Site: www.rotorooter.com (16)

Round Lake Publishing Co, Trumbull, CT. Tel: (203) 459-8484, Web Site: www.letterworks.com (17)

Rounder Mail Order, Burlington, MA. Tel: (617) 354-0700, (800) 768-6337, FAX: (617) 868-8769, E-Mail: info@rounder.com, Web Site: www.rounder.com (3)

Rourke, Steve, Mardev-DM2, Lombard, IL. Tel: (800) 323-4958, FAX: (303) 265-5457, E-Mail: info@mardevdm2.com, Web Site: www.mardevdm2.com (24)

Rouse, John, Ghent Manufacturing Inc, Lebanon, OH. Tel: (513) 932-3445, (800) 543-0550, FAX: (513) 932-9252, E-Mail: customer_service@!ghent.com, Web Site: www.ghent.com (10)

Roussel, Carrie, Nevada Magazine, Carson City, NV. Tel: (775) 687-5416, FAX: (775) 687-6159, E-Mail: editor@nevadamagazine.com, Web Site: www.nevadamagazine.com (17)

Roussel, Daniel, Desjardins Financial Securities, Levis, PQ Canada. Tel: (418) 838-7870, FAX: (418) 833-5985, Web Site: www.desjardinsfinancialsecurity.com (15)

Row Resources Inc, Northport, NY. Tel: (631) 261-0525 (16)

Rowan, Dan, Rascal, Sewell, NJ. Tel: (856) 468-1000, (800) 662-4548, FAX: (856) 468-3426, Web Site: www.electricmobility.com (7)

Rowe, James, Rowe Pottery Works Inc, Cambridge, WI. Tel: (608) 423-3363, (800) 356-5003, FAX: (608) 423-4273, E-Mail: sales@rowepottery.com, Web Site: www.rowepottery.com (16)

Rowe Pottery Works Inc, Cambridge, WI. Tel: (608) 423-3363, (800) 356-5003, FAX: (608) 423-4273, E-Mail: sales@rowepottery.com, Web Site: www.rowepottery.com (16)

Rowell, Amy, Level 5 Communications Inc, Dublin, NH. Tel: (603) 563-1631, FAX: (603) 563-8912, Web Site: www.deskeng.com (32)

Rowell, Fred, Blue Cross & Blue Shield of South Carolina, Columbia, SC. Tel: (803) 788-0222, (800) 288-2227, FAX: (803) 736-4516, Web Site: www.bcbssc.com (15)

Rowell, Joseph, A., RCS Response Technologies Inc, Charlotte, NC. Tel: (704) 522-1919, FAX: (704) 522-9092, E-Mail: data@rcsdirect.com, Web Site: www.rcsdirect.com (21)

Rowell, Steve, Audio Classics Ltd, Vestal, NY. Tel: (607) 766-3501, FAX: (607) 766-3502, E-Mail: steve@audioclassics.com, Web Site: www.audioclassics.com (3)

Rowland, Jay, Sauce Co, Little Rock, AR. Tel: (501) 663-3338, (800) 43- Sauce, FAX: (501) 663-0956, Web Site: www.sauceco.net (4)

Rowland, Kenneth, Row Resources Inc, Northport, NY. Tel: (631) 261-0525 (16)

Rowland, Melissa, Sauce Co, Little Rock, AR. Tel: (501) 663-3338, (800) 43- Sauce, FAX: (501) 663-0956, Web Site: www.sauceco.net (4)

Rowles, David, Bobcat Co, West Fargo, ND. Tel: (701) 241-8700, FAX: (701) 241-8704, Web Site: www.bobcat.com (16)

Rowsom, Andrew, ST Preston & Son Inc, Greenport, NY. Tel: (631) 477-1990, (800) 836-1165, FAX: (631) 477-8541, E-Mail: andrew@prestons.com, Web Site: www.prestons.com (8)

Rowsom, George H., ST Preston & Son Inc, Greenport, NY. Tel: (631) 477-1990, (800) 836-1165, FAX: (631) 477-8541, E-Mail: andrew@prestons.com, Web Site: www.prestons.com (8)

Rowsom, Peter, ST Preston & Son Inc, Greenport, NY. Tel: (631) 477-1990, (800) 836-1165, FAX: (631) 477-8541, E-Mail: andrew@prestons.com, Web Site: www.prestons.com (8)

Roxanis, Dean, University Press of America Inc, Lanham, MD. Tel: (301) 459-3366, (800) 462-6420, FAX: (301) 429-5748, E-Mail: custserv@rowman.com, Web Site: www.univpress.com (17)

Roy, Cynthia, Stromberg Consulting, New York, NY. Tel: (646) 935-4177, (212) 812-6400, FAX: (212) 812-6300, E-Mail: info@strombergconsulting.com, Web Site: www.strombergconsulting.com (35)

Roy, Robert, CBT Direct, Tarpon Springs, FL. Tel: (727) 724-8994, (877) 872-4646, FAX: (727) 797-9143, Web Site: www.cbtdirect.com (16)

Roy, Sheila, USA Fulfillment, Chestertown, MD. Tel: (410) 810-0800, (800) 777-8872, FAX: (410) 810-0910, E-Mail: sroy@usafill.com, Web Site: www.usafill.com (28)

Royal Bank of Canada, Toronto, ON Canada. Tel: (416) 974-5151, FAX: (416) 974-0365, Web Site: www.royalbank.com (14)

Royal Canadian Mint, Ottawa, ON Canada. Tel: (613) 993-1912 (16)

Royal Canin, Saint Charles, MO. Tel: (636) 926-0003, Web Site: www.royalcanin.us (16)

Royal Envelope Corp, Chicago, IL. Tel: (773) 376-1212, (800) 279-0142, FAX: (773) 376-0011, E-Mail: mattp@royalenv.com, Web Site: www.royalenv.com (26)

Royal Performance Group, Lisle, IL. Tel: (630) 353-7900, Web Site: www.rpgiftcards.com (34)

Royall, Ro, Business Extension Bureau of Texas Inc, Houston, TX. Tel: (713) 528-5568, (800) 969-5568, FAX: (713) 528-1648, E-Mail: ronr@bebtexas.com, Web Site: www.bebtexas.com (23)

Royall, Robert L., Business Extension Bureau of Texas Inc, Houston, TX. Tel: (713) 528-5568, (800) 969-5568, FAX: (713) 528-1648, E-Mail: ronr@bebtexas.com, Web Site: www.bebtexas.com (23)

Royall, Ron, Business Extension Bureau of Texas Inc, Houston, TX. Tel: (713) 528-5568, (800) 969-5568, FAX: (713) 528-1648, E-Mail: ronr@bebtexas.com, Web Site: www.bebtexas.com (23)

Royer, Renee, U-Haul International, Phoenix, AZ. Tel: (602) 263-6011, (800) GO-UHAUL, FAX: (602) 263-6598, Web Site: www.uhaul.com (16)

Royer, Rick, 800 Response, Burlington, VT. Tel: (802) 860-0378, (800) NEW-SALES, FAX: (800) NEW-ORDER, E-Mail: sales@800response.com, Web Site: www.800response.com (32)

Royse, Connie, PLAS-TANKS Industries Inc, Hamilton, OH. Tel: (513) 942-3800, FAX: (513) 942-3993, E-Mail: info@plastanks.com, Web Site: www.plastanks.com (9)

Roza, Eric, DataLogix, Westminster, CO. Tel: (303) 327-1600, FAX: (303) 327-1650, Web Site: www.datalogix.com (23)

Rozansky, Phil, Tower Media Advertising Inc, Chicago, IL. Tel: (312) 856-9200, FAX: (312) 856-1300, E-Mail: info@towermedia.com, Web Site: www.towermedia.com (35)

Rozelle, Peggy, Sport Supply Group, Dallas, TX. Tel: (972) 484-9484, FAX: (972) 247-0650, Web Site: www.sportsupplygroup.com (11)

Rozin, Philip, W., Brookstone Co, Merrimack, NH. Tel: (603) 880-9500, (800) 846-3000, FAX: (603) 577-8005, E-Mail: customerservice@brookstone.com, Web Site: www.brookstone.com (3)

Rozzell, Scott, Centerpoint Energy, Minneapolis, MN. Tel: (612) 372-4664, FAX: (612) 321-4873, E-Mail: mgc-businessinformation@centerpointenergy.com, Web Site: www.minnegasco.centerpointenergy.com (16)

Rozzini, Nadine, Grolier Publishing, Danbury, CT. Tel: (203) 797-3500, (800) 621-1115, FAX: (203) 797-3720, Web Site: www.grolier.com (17)

Rubber Stamps of America, Dublin, NH. Tel: (800) 553-5031, FAX: (603) 563-8102, E-Mail: stampusa@verizon.net, Web Site: www.stampusa.com (6)

Rubbermaid Inc, Fairlawn, OH. Tel: (888) 895-2110, (866) 271-9249, E-Mail: info@rubbermaid.com, Web Site: www.rubbermaid.com (8)

Rubei, Andrea, BroadVision Inc, Redwood City, CA. Tel: (650) 542-5100, FAX: (650) 364-3425, E-Mail: sales@broadvision.com, Web Site: www.broadvision.com (16)

Rubendall, Jami, American Crane & Equipment Corp, Douglassville, PA. Tel: (610) 385-6061, (877) 877-6778, FAX: (610) 385-3191/4876, E-Mail: info@americancrane.com, Web Site: www.americancrane.com (16)

Rubenstein, Herb, Associated Bag Co, Milwaukee, WI. Tel: (414) 769-1000, (800) 926-6100, FAX: (800) 926-4610, E-Mail: customerservice@associatedbag.com, Web Site: www.associatedbag.com (10)

Rubenzer, Bill, Storage Battery Systems Inc, Menomonee Falls, WI. Tel: (262) 703-5800, (800) 554-2243, FAX: (262) 703-3073, E-Mail: sbs@sbsbattery.com, Web Site: www.sbsbattery.com (12)

Rubenzer, Robert, Storage Battery Systems Inc, Menomonee Falls, WI. Tel: (262) 703-5800, (800) 554-2243, FAX: (262) 703-3073, E-Mail: sbs@sbsbattery.com, Web Site: www.sbsbattery.com (12)

Rubenzer, Scott, Storage Battery Systems Inc, Menomonee Falls, WI. Tel: (262) 703-5800, (800) 554-2243, FAX: (262) 703-3073, E-Mail: sbs@sbsbattery.com, Web Site: www.sbsbattery.com (12)

Rubin, Adrea, Adrea Rubin Marketing Inc, New York, NY. Tel: (212) 983-0020, FAX: (212) 983-0107, E-Mail: sales@adrearubin.com, Web Site: www.adrearubin.com (21)

Rubin, Arlene, LGP GEM LTD, New York, NY. Tel: (212) 840-2510, FAX: (212) 302-6182, E-Mail: sales@lgpltd.com, Web Site: www.lgpltd.com (16)

Rubin, Evan, New York & Co, New York, NY. Tel: (212) 884-2169, Web Site: www.nyandcompany.com (2)

Rubin, Jeff, Movie/Entertainment Book Club, Washington, DC. Tel: (800) 879-3270, FAX: (202) 216-0614, E-Mail: meb@eaglepub.com (13)

Rubin, Ken, KCMS, Upper Marlboro, MD. Tel: (301) 853-1900, FAX: (301) 853-1390, Web Site: www.kcms.com (21)

Rubin, Mitchell, Applied Info Group, Kenilworth, NJ. Tel: (908) 241-7007, Web Site: www.appliedinfogroup.com (22)

Rubin, Scott, Great Ideas Inc/CSP, Highland Park, IL. Tel: (847) 432-9060, (800) 611-5515, FAX: (800) 956-4443, E-Mail: sales@greatideasinc.com, Web Site: www.greatideasinc.com (33)

Rubin, Shellie, Filene's Basement, Secaucus, NJ. Tel: (617) 348-7000, FAX: (617) 357-2596 (16)

Rubin, Steven, Broadway Books, New York, NY. Tel: (212) 782-9644, FAX: (212) 782-8338, E-Mail: bwaypub@randomhouse.com, Web Site: www.randomhouse.com/broadway (17)

Rubin, Steven, R&S Industries Corp, Chesterfield, MO. Tel: (314) 781-5400, FAX: (314) 781-5169, E-Mail: sendeverything@miraclepolishingcloth.com, Web Site: www.miraclepolishingcloth.com (16)

Rubin, Steven, Torqmaster International, Stamford, CT. Tel: (203) 326-5945, (888) 414-4643, FAX: (203) 326-5944, E-Mail: info@torqmaster.com, Web Site: www.torqmaster.com (9)

Rubingh, Dr. Eugene, International Bible Society, Colorado Springs, CO. Tel: (719) 488-9200, FAX: (719) 867-2812, Web Site: www.ibs.org (1)

Rubino, Bill, Jofco Inc, Jasper, IN. Tel: (812) 482-5154, (800) 23-JOFCO, FAX: (812) 634-2392, E-Mail: furniture@jofco.com, Web Site: www.jofco.com (16)

Rubino, Victor, J., Practicing Law Institute, New York, NY. Tel: (212) 824-5700, (800) 260 4PLI, FAX: (800) 321-0093, E-Mail: info@pli.edu, Web Site: www.pli.edu (16)

Rubinstein, Joel, Dentino Marketing, Princeton, NJ. Tel: (201) 332-1219, (800) 477-8372, FAX: (201) 332-4262, E-Mail: karl@dentinomarketing.com, Web Site: www.dentinomarketing.com (35)

Rubio, Gonzalo R., Jafra Cosmetics International Inc, Westlake Village, CA. Tel: (805) 557-1889, (800) 551-2345, Web Site: www.jafra.com (7)

Ruble, Holly, Pinnacle List Co, Arlington, VA. Tel: (703) 379-4394, FAX: (703) 379-5312, E-Mail: holly@pinnlistco.com, Web Site: www.pinnlistco.com (23)

Ruchman, Neal, H., A Rapid Mailing Inc, Jessup, MD. Tel: (410) 792-4000, (800) US-RAPID, FAX: (301) 776-3690, E-Mail: info@rairapid.com, Web Site: www.rairapid.com (28)

Rucker, John, P., Bethesda List Center Inc, Bethesda, MD. Tel: (301) 986-1455, FAX: (301) 907-4870, E-Mail: info@bethesda-list.com, Web Site: www.bethesda-list.com (24)

Rucker, Michael, Time Out New York, New York, NY. Tel: (646) 432-3000, FAX: (212) 677-9665, E-Mail: tnew@kable.com, Web Site: www.timeout.com/newyork/ (18)

Rudasill, Susann, Center for Professional Development, Tallahassee, FL. Tel: (850) 644-8004, (850) 487-1691, FAX: (850) 644-2589, Web Site: www.Learningforlife.fsu.edu (16)

Rudd, Leslie, Windsor Vineyards, Santa Rosa, CA. Tel: (800) 741-6070, (800) 289-9463, E-Mail: webmaster@windsorvineyards.com, Web Site: www.windsorvineyards.com (16)

Rudder, Michael, Smart Dog Products, Winchester, TN. Tel: (931) 967-7482, (800) 264-3647, FAX: (931) 967-7483, E-Mail: sales@shopsmartdog.com (11)

Ruddick, Erin, Read, Creating Results/New England, Barrington, RI. Tel: (401) 289-2500, (888) 205-8899, FAX: (401) 427-6963, E-Mail: erin@creatingresults.com, Web Site: www.creatingresults.com (35)

Ruddock, Malcolm, I., Sunoco, Inc, Philadelphia, PA. Tel: (215) 977-3000, (800) 786-6261, FAX: (215) 977-3409, E-Mail: sunoco_online@sunoil.com, Web Site: www.sunocoinc.com (16)

Ruddock, Velda, TBWA, Los Angeles, CA. Tel: (310) 305-5000 (35)

Ruddy, Christopher, Newsmax Media Inc, West Palm Beach, FL. Tel: (888) 766-7542, E-Mail: sales@newsmax.com, Web Site: www.newsmax.com/advertise (24)

Ruder Finn Inc, New York, NY. Tel: (212) 593-6400, FAX: (212) 715-1556, E-Mail: rfnewyork@ruderfinn.com, Web Site: www.ruderfinn.com (30)

Rudick, Macon, SanSegal Sportswear (HQ), Sandy, UT. Tel: (801) 566-3248, (800) 338-6048, FAX: (801) 566-3350, E-Mail: sansegal@sansegal.com, Web Site: www.sansegal.com (2)

Rudin, Max, The Library of America, New York, NY. Tel: (212) 308-3360, (800) 964-5778, FAX: (212) 750-8352, E-Mail: info@loa.org, Web Site: www.loa.org (13)

Rudnick, Bryan, Best ROI Lists, Boca Raton, FL. Tel: (561) 499-3201, Web Site: www.bestroilists.com (23)

Rudolph, Scott, NBTY Inc, Ronkonkoma, NY. Tel: (631) 200-2000, FAX: (631) 567-7148, Web Site: www.nbty.com (7)

Rudolphsen, William, A., Allstate Motor Club, Inc, Deerfield, IL. Tel: (847) 914-2972, FAX: (847) 914-2804, Web Site: www.walgreens.com (7)

Rue, Mark, M R Group Inc, Plymouth, MN. Tel: (763) 550-0760, FAX: (763) 550-0760, E-Mail: webmaster@mrgrp.com, Web Site: www.mrgrp.com (33)

Rue, Sally, Caswell-Massey Co Ltd, Edison, NJ. Tel: (732) 225-2181, (800) 326-0500, FAX: (732) 225-2385, E-Mail: info@caswellmasseyltd.com, Web Site: www.caswellmassey.com (7)

Rueckel, Jill, Lawyers Diary and Manual, Newark, NJ. Tel: (208) 762-5403, (800) 444-4041, FAX: (973) 242-1905, E-Mail: mail@lawdiary.com, Web Site: www.lawdiary.com (24)

Rueff, Andrew, TransFirst Holdings Inc, Dallas, TX. Tel: (214) 453-7700, (888) 254-4137, FAX: (214) 453-7739, Web Site: www.transfirst.com (14)

Ruf, Jake, Ruf Strategic Solutions, Olathe, KS. Tel: (800) 829-8544, Web Site: www.ruf.com (22)

Ruf, Kurtis, M., Ruf Corp, Olathe, KS. Tel: (913) 782-8544, (800) 829-8544, FAX: (913) 782-0150, E-Mail: solutions@ruf.com, Web Site: www.ruf.com (30)

Ruf Corp, Olathe, KS. Tel: (913) 782-8544, (800) 829-8544, FAX: (913) 782-0150, E-Mail: solutions@ruf.com, Web Site: www.ruf.com (30)

Ruf Strategic Solutions, Olathe, KS. Tel: (800) 829-8544, Web Site: www.ruf.com (22)

Ruffner Jr., Frederick, G., Omnigraphics Inc, Aston, PA. Tel: (610) 461-3548, (800) 234-1340, FAX: (800) 875-1340, E-Mail: info@omnigraphics.com, Web Site: www.omnigraphics.com (17)

Ruffner, Peter, E., Omnigraphics Inc, Aston, PA. Tel: (610) 461-3548, (800) 234-1340, FAX: (800) 875-1340, E-Mail: info@omnigraphics.com, Web Site: www.omnigraphics.com (17)

Rufus, Gregory, Marathon Norco Aerospace Inc, Waco, TX. Tel: (254) 776-0650, FAX: (254) 776-6558, Web Site: www.mptc.com (16)

Ruggiero, Carl, Universal Training, Lake Forest, IL. Tel: (847) 235-2170, E-Mail: information@universaltraining.com, Web Site: www.universaltraining.com (16)

Rukstales, Bradley, Customer Asset Consulting Group Inc, Schaumburg, IL. Tel: (847) 805-9800, Web Site: www.cac-group.com (22)

Ruland, Rand, John Deere Consumer Products, Moline, IL. Tel: (309) 765-8000, FAX: (309) 748-0114, Web Site: www.johndeere.com (16)

Rullo, Jim, Skies America International Publishing & Communications, Beaverton, OR. Tel: (503) 520-1955, FAX: (503) 520-1275, E-Mail: skies@skies.com, Web Site: www.skies.com (36)

Rullo, Mary, Sony Electronics Inc, Park Ridge, NJ. Tel: (201) 930-6173, FAX: (201) 930-7665, Web Site: www.sony.com (16)

Rulong, Betty, American Baseball Coaches Association, Mount Pleasant, MI. Tel: (989) 775-3300, FAX: (989) 775-3600, E-Mail: abca@abca.org, Web Site: www.abca.org (1)

Rumaner, Karen, Rediscover Music Catalogue, Naperville, IL. Tel: (630) 305-0770, (800) 232-7328, FAX: (630) 305-0782, E-Mail: rediscovermusic@rediscovermusic.com, Web Site: www.rediscovermusic.com (3)

Rumley, Fene, Bell Performance Inc, Longwood, FL. Tel: (407) 831-5021, (800) 659-2355, FAX: (407) 767-8685, E-Mail: info@bellperformance.net, Web Site: www.bellperformance.net (9)

Rundle, Christina, Goddard Manufacturing Co, Logan, KS. Tel: (785) 689-4341, (800) 536-4341, E-Mail: jerry@spiral-staircases.com, Web Site: www.spiral-staircases.com (8)

Rundle, Murray, J., Supremex Inc, Etobicoke, ON Canada. Tel: (416) 675-9370, (800) 465-7603, FAX: (416) 675-1952, (416) 848-8388, E-Mail: sales.central@supremex.com, Web Site: www.supremex.com (26)

Runice, Paul, MTS Systems Corp, Eden Prairie, MN. Tel: (952) 937-4000, (800) 328-2255, FAX: (952) 937-4515, E-Mail: info@mts.com, Web Site: www.mts.com (16)

Runinstein, Helene, F., Esquire Magazine, New York, NY. Tel: (212) 649-2000, (800) 925-0485, FAX: (212) 265-0938, E-Mail: esquire@hearst.com, Web Site: www.esquire.com (17)

Runk, John, Directory Distributing Associates Inc, Hazelwood, MO. Tel: (314) 592-8600, (800) 325-1964, FAX: (314) 592-8790, E-Mail: corporate@directrac.com, Web Site: www.ddai.com (28)

Runstrom, K., Jon, BCC Software Inc, Rochester, NY. Tel: (585) 272-9130, (800) 453-3130, FAX: (585) 340-8850, Web Site: www.bccsoftware.com (22)

Runyan, W. Tim, Oneida Ltd, Oneida, NY. Tel: (315) 361-3000, (888) 263-7195, FAX: (315) 361-3700, Web Site: www.oneida.com (16)

Runyon, Thomas E., Seedburo Equipment Co, Des Plaines, IL. Tel: (312) 738-3700, (800) 284-5779, FAX: (312) 738-5329, E-Mail: sales@seedburo.com, Web Site: www.seedburo.com (8)

Runzheimer, L. Lee, Osmonics Inc, Minnetonka, MN. Tel: (952) 264-3937, (800) 605-6698, FAX: (952) 536-3301, Web Site: www.osmonics.com (16)

Rupkey, Kevin, Bankers Warranty Group, Saint Petersburg, FL. Tel: (800) 431-5843, E-Mail: info@bankerswarrantygroup.com, Web Site: www.bankerswarrantygroup.com (16)

Rupricht, William, F., Sotheby's, New York, NY. Tel: (212) 606-7000, FAX: (212) 606-7107, Web Site: www.sothebys.com (6)

Rural Alaska Community Action Program Inc, Anchorage, AK. Tel: (907) 279-2511, FAX: (907) 278-2309, Web Site: www.ruralcap.com (1)

Rusbuldt, Robert, A., Independent Insurance Agents & Brokers of America, Alexandria, VA. Tel: (703) 683-4422, (800) 221-7917, FAX: (703) 683-7556, E-Mail: info@iiaba.org, Web Site: www.iiaba.org (1)

Rush, David, Wit Postal Logistics LLC, Chicago, IL. Tel: (815) 215-5100, Web Site: www.witpostal.com (28)

Rush Industries, Inc, Mineola, NY. Tel: (516) 741-0346, FAX: (516) 741-0348, Web Site: www.rushindustries.com (16)

Rushford, Wil, Vane & Friends, Chappaqua, NY. Tel: (914) 238-8890, E-Mail: info@vaneandfriends.com, Web Site: www.vaneandfriends.com (35)

Rushnell, Squire, American Life TV Network, Washington, DC. Tel: (202) 289-6633, FAX: (202) 289-6632, Web Site: www.goodtv.com (32)

Rusin, Paul, Dexta Corp, Napa, CA. Tel: (707) 255-2454, (800) 733-3982, FAX: (707) 255-8520, Web Site: www.dexta.com (16)

The Rusin Group, LLC, Wilton, CT. Tel: (203) 529-3257 (20)

Ruskin, Moscou, Faltischek, PC, Uniondale, NY. Tel: (516) 663-6600, FAX: (516) 663-6601, E-Mail: info@rmfpc.com, Web Site: www.rmfpc.com (16)

Rusnak, Anton, Abbey of Gethsemani, New Haven, KY. Tel: (502) 549-3117, FAX: (502) 549-4124, Web Site: www.monks.org (1)

Rusnak, Walter, ESL Federal Credit Union, Rochester, NY. Tel: (585) 336-1000, (800) 848-2265, FAX: (585) 336-1138, Web Site: www.esl.org (14)

Ruso, Tony, Four Seasons Sunrooms, Holbrook, NY. Tel: (631) 563-4000, FAX: (631) 563-4010 (8)

Russ, K., Randall, Community Coffee Co, Baton Rouge, LA. Tel: (225) 291-3900, (800) 525-5583, FAX: (800) 643-8199, E-Mail: ccc@communitycoffee.com, Web Site: www.communitycoffee.com (4)

Russ, Larry, C., Russ, August, & Kabat, Los Angeles, CA. Tel: (310) 826-7474, FAX: (310) 826-6991, E-Mail: info@raklaw.com, Web Site: www.raklaw.com (20)

Russ, August, & Kabat, Los Angeles, CA. Tel: (310) 826-7474, FAX: (310) 826-6991, E-Mail: info@raklaw.com, Web Site: www.raklaw.com (20)

Russ Reid Co, Pasadena, CA. Tel: (626) 449-6100, FAX: (626) 449-6190, E-Mail: info@russreid.com, Web Site: www.russreid.com (35)

Russel, Samuel, Davidoff of Geneva Inc, Pinellas Park, FL. Tel: (203) 323-5811, (800) 328-4365, FAX: (203) 975-0090 (6)

Russell, A.G., AG Russell Knives Inc, Rogers, AR. Tel: (479) 631-0130, (800) 255-9034, FAX: (479) 631-8493, E-Mail: ag@agrussell.com, Web Site: www.agrussell.com (11)

Russell, Adam, Projector-Recorder Belt Corp, Oceanside, NY. Tel: (516) 536-5000, (800) 645-2202, FAX: (516) 764-5747, (800) 645-2200, E-Mail: sales@russellind.com, Web Site: www.russellind.com (3)

Russell, Bill, Roman Research Inc/Simply Whispers Earring, Hanson, MA. Tel: (781) 447-3411, (800) 451-5700, FAX: (781) 447-0995, Web Site: www.simplywhispers.com (2)

Russell, Dana, C., Novell Inc, Waltham, MA. Tel: (801) 861-4272, (800) 529-3400, FAX: (781) 464-8100, E-Mail: crc@novell.com, Web Site: www.novell.com (22)

Russell, Goldie, AG Russell Knives Inc, Rogers, AR. Tel: (479) 631-0130, (800) 255-9034, FAX: (479) 631-8493, E-Mail: ag@agrussell.com, Web Site: www.agrussell.com (11)

Russell, Ken, Graphic Communications Holdings Inc, Hudson, OH. Tel: (330) 650-5522, E-Mail: info@graphiccommunications.com, Web Site: www.graphiccommunications.com (25)

Russell, Liz, Media Horizons Management LLC, Norwalk, CT. Tel: (203) 857-0770, FAX: (203) 857-0296, E-Mail: info@mediahorizons.com, Web Site: www.mediahorizons.com (31)

Russell, Richard, F., Amerisure Insurance Cos, Farmington Hills, MI. Tel: (248) 615-9000, (800) 257-1900, FAX: (248) 615-8224, Web Site: www.amerisure.com (15)

Russell, Rick, Naval Institute Press, Annapolis, MD. Tel: (410) 268-6110, (800) 233-8764, FAX: (410) 571-1703, E-Mail: webmaster@usni.org, Web Site: www.usni.org/navalinstitutepress (17)

Russell, Robert, Washington Products Inc, Massillon, OH. Tel: (330) 837-5101, FAX: (330) 837-5401 (34)

Russell, Sam, Davidoff of Geneva Inc, Pinellas Park, FL. Tel: (203) 323-5811, (800) 328-4365, FAX: (203) 975-0090 (6)

Russell, Sean, Business Mailing Center, Oxnard, CA. Tel: (805) 981-2600, (800) 882-1844, FAX: (805) 981-1180, E-Mail: answers@venturaprint.com, Web Site: www.venturaprint.com (23)

Russell, Sheila, Sierra Trading Post, Cheyenne, WY. Tel: (307) 775-8050, (800) 713-4534, FAX: (307) 775-8089, Web Site: www.sierratradingpost.com (2)

AG Russell Knives Inc, Rogers, AR. Tel: (479) 631-0130, (800) 255-9034, FAX: (479) 631-8493, E-Mail: ag@agrussell.com, Web Site: www.agrussell.com (11)

Russell Investments, Seattle, WA. Tel: (206) 505-7877, (800) 426-7969, Web Site: www.russell.com (14)

Russo, Charles, Arch Telecom Inc, Austin, TX. Tel: (512) 492-0735, (800) 890-7575, FAX: (512) 495-7101, Web Site: www.archtelecom.com (16)

Russo, Edward, Vaxserve, Scranton, PA. Tel: (800) 752-9338, Web Site: www.vaxserve.com (7)

Russo, Ken, PPS - Packaging Printing Specialists, Saint Charles, IL. Tel: (630) 513-8060, (877) 573-8060, FAX: (630) 513-8062, E-Mail: pps@ppsofil.com, Web Site: www.PPSofIL.com (27)

Russo, Ronald, N., RONED Printing & Reproduction Inc, East Hanover, NJ. Tel: (973) 386-1848, FAX: (973) 386-0969, E-Mail: info@roned.com, Web Site: www.roned.com (27)

Russo, Tim, Russo & Kelly, Colchester, VT. Tel: (802) 655-7007, FAX: (802) 655-4994, E-Mail: info@russandkelly.com (35)

Russo, Tom, Kensington Technology Group, Redwood Shores, CA. Tel: (650) 572-2700, FAX: (650) 267-2800, Web Site: www.kensington.com (16)

Russo & Kelly, Colchester, VT. Tel: (802) 655-7007, FAX: (802) 655-4994, E-Mail: info@russandkelly.com (35)

Russotti, Robert, American National Standards Institute, New York, NY. Tel: (212) 642-4900, Web Site: www.ansi.org (1)

Rust Jr., Edward, B., State Farm Insurance Cos, Bloomington, IL. Tel: (309) 766-2311, FAX: (309) 766-3621, Web Site: www.statefarm.com (15)

Rust, David, ReputationDefender, Redwood City, CA. Tel: (650) 241-7491, (888) 720-3332, E-Mail: helpdesk@reputation.com, Web Site: www.reputationdefender.com (32)

Rusten, Shelly, Shelly Rusten, Hankins, NY. Tel: (917) 421-0980, (845) 887-5662, E-Mail: srusten@msn. com, Web Site: www.shellyrusten.com (37)

Shelly Rusten, Hankins, NY. Tel: (917) 421-0980, (845) 887-5662, E-Mail: srusten@msn.com, Web Site: www.shellyrusten.com (37)

Ruth, Anne, Anne Ruth, Bronxville, NY. Tel: (914) 337-7931 (20)

Ruth, Gary, R, Philip Morris USA Inc, Richmond, VA. Tel: (804) 274-2000, FAX: (804) 484-8231, Web Site: www.philipmorrisusa.com (37)

Anne Ruth, Bronxville, NY. Tel: (914) 337-7931 (20)

Rutherford, James, P., Veronis Suhler Stevenson LLC, New York, NY. Tel: (212) 935-4990, FAX: (212) 381-8168, E-Mail: stevensonj@vss.com, Web Site: www.vss.com (14)

Ruthkosky, Frank, Taylor Gifts Inc, Paoli, PA. Tel: (610) 725-1122, FAX: (610) 725-1144, Web Site: www.taylorgifts.com (8)

Rutkowski, Donna, Joint Commission, Oakbrook Terrace, IL. Tel: (630) 792-5000, Web Site: www.jcaho.org (1)

Rutland Products, Rutland, VT. Tel: (802) 775-5519, FAX: (802) 775-5262, E-Mail: sales@rutland.com, Web Site: www.rutland.com (16)

Rutrough, James, E., State Farm Insurance Cos, Bloomington, IL. Tel: (309) 766-2311, FAX: (309) 766-3621, Web Site: www.statefarm.com (15)

Ruttan, Sandra, Leslie Shoe Co Inc, Rogers City, MI. Tel: (989) 734-4030, (800) 716-8617, E-Mail: info@sexyshoes.com, Web Site: www.sexyshoes. com (24)

Ruttenberg, Jonathan, M., American Locker Security Systems Inc, Coppell, TX. Tel: (817) 329-1600, (800) 828-9118, E-Mail: info@americanlocker. com, Web Site: www.americanlocker.com (16)

Rutter, David, Brooke Distributors Inc, Miami, FL. Tel: (305) 624-9752, (800) 275-8792, FAX: (305) 620-3988, E-Mail: sales@brookedms.com, Web Site: www.brooke.com (3)

Rutter, John, W., Vail Resorts Inc, Keystone, CO. Tel: (970) 468-2316/845-2694, FAX: (970) 453-3202, Web Site: www.keystoneresort.com (19)

Ruud, Alan, Ruud Lighting Inc, Racine, WI. Tel: (262) 886-1900, (800) 236-7000, FAX: (800) 236-7500, E-Mail: sales@ruudlighting.com, Web Site: www.ruudlighting.com (9)

Ruud Lighting Inc, Racine, WI. Tel: (262) 886-1900, (800) 236-7000, FAX: (800) 236-7500, E-Mail: sales@ruudlighting.com, Web Site: www. ruudlighting.com (9)

Ruvolo, Larry, Texwipe Co, Kernersville, NC. Tel: (201) 684-1800, (800) TEXWIPE, FAX: (201) 684-1801, E-Mail: info@texwipe.com, Web Site: www.texwipe.com (16)

Ryall, Debbie, Arnaud's, New Orleans, LA. Tel: (504) 523-0611, (866) 230-8895, FAX: (504) 581-7908, Web Site: www.arnauds.com (16)

Ryan Jr, T. Timothy, SIFMA, New York, NY. Tel: (212) 313-1200, FAX: (212) 313-1301, E-Mail: inquiry@sifma.org, Web Site: www.sifma.org (1)

Ryan, Barbara, Minitab Inc, State College, PA. Tel: (814) 238-3280, (800) 448-3555, FAX: (814) 238-4383, E-Mail: sales@minitab.com, Web Site: www. minitab.com (16)

Ryan, Barry, Four Wheel Drive Hardware LLC, Columbiana, OH. Tel: (330) 482-4733, FAX: (330) 482-5035, E-Mail: info@4wd.com, Web Site: www.4wd.com (12)

Ryan, Conall, Sunburst Technology, Elgin, IL. Tel: (914) 747-3310, FAX: (914) 747-4109, E-Mail: service@nysunburst.com, Web Site: www.sunburst. com (17)

Ryan, Dave, Ryan IDirect, Wilton, CT. Tel: (203) 210-3000, FAX: (203) 210-7926, Web Site: www. ryanpartnership.com (35)

Ryan, Donald, Jenny Products Inc, Somerset, PA. Tel: (814) 445-3400, FAX: (814) 445-2280, Web Site: www.jennyproducts.com (16)

Ryan, Frank, Enterprise Ireland, New York, NY. Tel: (212) 371-3600, FAX: (212) 371-6398, Web Site: www.enterprise-ireland.com (16)

Ryan, J., Patrick, Skystone Ryan, Cincinnati, OH. Tel: (513) 241-6778, FAX: (513) 241-0551, E-Mail: cincinnati@skystoneryan.com, Web Site: www. skystoneryan.com (20)

Ryan, James T., WW Grainger Inc, Lake Forest, IL. Tel: (847) 535-1000, (888) 361-8649, FAX: (847) 535-9122, Web Site: www.grainger.com (9)

Ryan, Jennifer, Penske Logistics, Reading, PA. Tel: (610) 775-6000, (800) 529-6531, FAX: (610) 775-6432, Web Site: www.penskelogistics.com (16)

Ryan, Jim, CitiFinancial, Baltimore, MD. Tel: (410) 332-3000, (800) 995-2274, (800) 922-6235, FAX: (410) 332-3489, Web Site: www.citifinancial.com (14)

Ryan, John, Center for Creative Leadership, Greensboro, NC. Tel: (336) 545-2810, FAX: (336) 282-3284, E-Mail: info@ccl.org, Web Site: www.ccl. org (16)

Ryan, Michael, Cactus Mailing Company, Scottsdale, AZ. Tel: (480) 443-1442, (866) 443-1442, FAX: (480) 443-2518, E-Mail: info@cactusmailing.com, Web Site: www.cactusmailing.com (21)

Ryan, Michael, Techni-Tool Inc, Worcester, PA. Tel: (610) 941-2400, (800) 832-4866, FAX: (800) 854-8665, E-Mail: sales@techni-tool.com, Web Site: www.techni-tool.com (16)

Ryan, Pat, AON Center, Chicago, IL. Tel: (312) 381-1000, FAX: (312) 381-6032, Web Site: www.aon. com (15)

Ryan, Paula, Communication Industries Corp, Grafton, VT. Tel: (802) 869-6500, FAX: (802) 869-6565, E-Mail: info@cicmail.com, Web Site: www. careersatcic.com (10)

Ryan, Thomas, M., CVS Caremark, Woonsocket, RI. Tel: (401) 765-1500, FAX: (401) 769-4488, Web Site: www.cvs.com (7)

Ryan IDirect, Wilton, CT. Tel: (203) 210-3000, FAX: (203) 210-7926, Web Site: www.ryanpartnership. com (35)

Ryder, Fred, Blue Cross & Blue Shield of Florida, Jacksonville, FL. Tel: (904) 791-6111, (800) 477-3736, FAX: (904) 905-6638, E-Mail: katie. magee@bcbsfl.com, Web Site: www.bcbsfl.com (15)

Ryerson, Randy, Penske Logistics, Reading, PA. Tel: (610) 775-6000, (800) 529-6531, FAX: (610) 775-6432, Web Site: www.penskelogistics.com (16)

Rygiel, JoAnne, Recording for the Blind & Dyslexic Inc, Princeton, NJ. Tel: (609) 452-0606, (800) 221-4792, FAX: (609) 520-7996, E-Mail: info@rfbd. org, Web Site: www.rfbd.org (16)

Rykels, Sam, Louisiana State Museum, New Orleans, LA. Tel: (504) 568-6968, (800) 568-6968, FAX: (504) 568-4995, Web Site: www.lsm.crt.state.la.us (1)

Ryken, Deborah, Goodman Marketing Partners Inc, San Rafael, CA. Tel: (415) 507-9060, FAX: (415) 507-9067, E-Mail: info@goodmanmarketing.com, Web Site: www.goodmanmarketing.com (35)

Rymes, Russ, Mother Jones Magazine, San Francisco, CA. Tel: (415) 321-1700, Web Site: www. motherjones.com (17)

Rynecki, Mary, Sue, Newsweek Inc, New York, NY. Tel: (212) 445-4000, FAX: (212) 445-5068, Web Site: www.newsweek.com (1)

Ryskamp, Bruce, Zondervan Corp, Grand Rapids, MI. Tel: (616) 698-6900, (800) 727-3060, FAX: (616) 698-3235, Web Site: www.zondervan.com (17)

The RYTEX Co, Peru, IN. Tel: (317) 872-8553, (800) 277-5458, FAX: (317) 872-8535, (800) 329-1669, Web Site: www.rytex.com (10)

S

S&G Business Associates Inc, Elkhart, IN. Tel: (574) 295-0163 (23)

S&H Solutions, Delray Beach, FL. Tel: (561) 454-7600, FAX: (561) 265-2493, E-Mail: customerservice@shsolutions.com, Web Site: www. shsolutions.com (35)

S&S Worldwide, Colchester, CT. Tel: (860) 537-3451, (800) 288-9941, FAX: (860) 537-2866, E-Mail: cservice@ssww.com, Web Site: www.ssww.com (11)

S Group Inc, Akron, OH. Tel: (330) 535-2103, (800) 686-7435, FAX: (330) 535-1723, E-Mail: info@s-groupinc.com, Web Site: www.s-groupinc.com (33)

SAE International, Warrendale, PA. Tel: (724) 776-4841, Web Site: www.sae.org (6)

SAF Financial Services Inc, Schaumburg, IL. Tel: (800) 323-3000, FAX: (847) 310-8969 (27)

SAS Group, Tarrytown, NY. Tel: (914) 332-7878, FAX: (914) 332-7859, E-Mail: ssobo@sasgroup. com, Web Site: www.sasgroup.com (32)

SAS Institute, Cary, NC. Tel: (919) 677-8000, Web Site: www.sas.com (22)

SBC Advertising, Columbus, OH. Tel: (614) 891-7070, FAX: (614) 891-3664, E-Mail: info@sbcadv. com, Web Site: www.sbcadv.com (35)

SBDP Corp, Cincinnati, OH. Tel: (513) 871-7019, FAX: (513) 871-0134, E-Mail: info@sbdp.com, Web Site: www.sbdp.com (22)

SC Direct, West Bridgewater, MA. Tel: (800) 343-9695, Web Site: www.scdirect.com (2)

SCA Direct, Fairfax, VA. Tel: (703) 293-6339, Web Site: www.scadirect.com (1)

SCA Promotions Inc, Dallas, TX. Tel: (214) 860-3700, (888) 860-3700, FAX: (214) 860-3723, E-Mail: scainfo@scapromo.com, Web Site: www.scapromo. com (15)

SCI Management, Houston, TX. Tel: (713) 525-7783, Web Site: www.sci-corp.com (16)

SCP Rapp Collins Media, New York, NY. Tel: (212) 817-6800, Web Site: www.rappcollins.com (35)

SDI Marketing, Toronto, ON Canada. Tel: (949) 718-4800, (877) SDI-TEAM, FAX: (416) 674-9011, E-Mail: info@sdicapital.com, Web Site: www. sdimarketing.com (14)

SEI, Oaks, PA. Tel: (610) 676-1000, E-Mail: webmaster@seic.com, Web Site: www.seic.com (14)

SEOinhouse, Saint Charles, MO. Tel: (650) 589-8720, Web Site: www.seoinhouse.com (32)

SER Solutions Inc, Reston, VA. Tel: (703) 948-5500, (800) 274-5676, FAX: (703) 430-7738, E-Mail: info@ser.com, Web Site: www.ser.com (34)

SF Video Inc, San Francisco, CA. Tel: (415) 288-9400, (800) 545-5865, FAX: (415) 288-9410, E-Mail: selfservice@sfvideo.com, Web Site: www. sfvideo.com (3)

SGD Golf Co, Tallmadge, OH. Tel: (330) 745-4400, (800) 321-3411, FAX: (330) 745-4420, (888) 299-4240, Web Site: www.sgdgolf.com (34)

SHR Capital Partners, Greenwich, CT. Tel: (203) 618-1110 (30)

SHR Perceptual Management, Phoenix, AZ. Tel: (480) 483-3700, FAX: (480) 483-9675, E-Mail: info@ shrbranding.com, Web Site: www.shrbranding.com (35)

SIE (Select Information Exchange), New York, NY. Tel: (212) 496-6435, FAX: (212) 787-4269, Web Site: www.siecom.com (23)

SIFMA, New York, NY. Tel: (212) 313-1200, FAX: (212) 313-1301, E-Mail: inquiry@sifma.org, Web Site: www.sifma.org (1)

SIG Pack Inc Doboy Div, New Richmond, WI. Tel: (715) 246-6511, FAX: (715) 246-6539, Web Site: www.doboy.com (34)

SIGMA Marketing Group LLC, Rochester, NY. Tel: (585) 473-7300, (888) 277-9837, FAX: (585) 473-0332, E-Mail: mbush@sigmamarketing.com, Web Site: www.sigmamarketing.com; www. jthgearanalytics.com (Blog) (20)

SK&A Information Services Inc, Irvine, CA. Tel: (949) 476-2051, (800) 752-5478, FAX: (949) 476-2168, E-Mail: skasales@skainfo.com, Web Site: www.skainfo.com (23)

SKM Group, Depew, NY. Tel: (716) 989-3200, FAX: (716) 989-3220, E-Mail: info@skmgroup.com, Web Site: www.skmgroup.com (35)

SKO-Brenner-American, Baldwin, NY. Tel: (516) 771-4400, (800) 645-3390, FAX: (516) 771-7810, E-Mail: collect@skobrenner.com, Web Site: www.skobrenner.com (20)

SLM Corp, Reston, VA. Tel: (703) 810-3000, FAX: (703) 984-5042, Web Site: www.salliemae.com (16)

SLR Associates, Portland, OR. Tel: (503) 645-0675 (20)

SMG Direct Market, Bannockburn, IL. Tel: (585) 249-6100, FAX: (585) 249-6309 (35)

SMY Media Inc, Chicago, IL. Tel: (312) 621-9600, FAX: (312) 621-0924, E-Mail: info@smymedia.com, Web Site: www.smymedia.com (32)

SNL Financial, Charlottesville, VA. Tel: (434) 977-1600, FAX: (434) 977-4466, E-Mail: support@sni.com, Web Site: www.snl.com (17)

SOS Children's Villages - USA, Washington, DC. Tel: (202) 347-7920, Web Site: www.sos-usa.org (1)

SPSS Inc, Chicago, IL. Tel: (312) 651-3000, (800) 543-2185, FAX: (312) 651-3690, E-Mail: sales@spss.com, Web Site: www.spss.com (22)

SRB Marketing Inc, New Paltz, NY. Tel: (866) 210-1183, Web Site: www.srbmarketing.com (30)

SRDS, Des Plaines, IL. Tel: (800) 851-7737, FAX: (847) 375-5001, Web Site: www.srds.com (17)

SSHC Inc/Radiant Heating Commercial Applications, Old Saybrook, CT. Tel: (860) 399-5434, (800) 544-5182, FAX: (860) 399-6460, (877) 675-4968, E-Mail: info@sshcinc.com, Web Site: www.sshcinc.com (9)

ST&P Marketing Communications Inc, Fairlawn, OH. Tel: (330) 668-1932, FAX: (330) 668-2078, Web Site: www.stpinc.com (35)

ST Media Group International, Cincinnati, OH. Tel: (513) 421-2050, (800) 925-1110, FAX: (513) 421-5144, E-Mail: customer@stmediagroup.com, Web Site: www.signweb.com (17)

SW Caging Corp, Topeka, KS. Tel: (785) 232-0061, Web Site: www.swcaging.com (14)

SWAT Marketing Team, Grove City, PA. Tel: (412) 851-9700, FAX: (412) 291-1155, Web Site: www.swatmarketingteam.com (23)

SWB & R, Bethlehem, PA. Tel: (610) 866-0611, FAX: (610) 866-8650, Web Site: www.swb.com (35)

SWBC, San Antonio, TX. Tel: (210) 525-1241, Web Site: www.swbc.com (14)

Sa-So, Arlington, TX. Tel: (972) 641-4911, (800) 752-4294, FAX: (972) 660-3684, E-Mail: info@sa-so.com, Web Site: www.sa-so.com (16)

Saad, Cecilia, Center for Science in the Public Interest, Washington, DC. Tel: (202) 332-9110, FAX: (202) 265-4954, E-Mail: circ@cspinet.org, Web Site: www.cspinet.org (1)

Saadat, Tony, EOS International Inc, Carlsbad, CA. Tel: (760) 431-8400, (800) 876-5484, FAX: (760) 431-8448, Web Site: www.eosintl.com (5)

Saatchi & Saatchi, New York, NY. Tel: (212) 463-2000, FAX: (212) 463-9855, Web Site: www.saatchiny.com (32)

Saatchi & Saatchi Canada, Toronto, ON Canada. Tel: (416) 359-9595, FAX: (416) 866-8485, Web Site: www.saatchi.ca (21)

Saathoff, Ray, AAA-Chicago Motor Club, Aurora, IL. Tel: (847) 390-9000, (866) 968-7222, FAX: (847) 390-7738, Web Site: www.aaa.com (1)

Sabater, Julio, Universal Communication Enterprise, Elizabeth, NJ. Tel: (908) 355-2299, FAX: (908) 352-2931 (13)

Sabatier, James, H., Resorts Worldwide Inc, White Plains, NY. Tel: (914) 640-8100, (800) 325-3535, FAX: (914) 640-8310, Web Site: www.starwood.com (19)

Sabbatis, Mike, CCH Inc, Riverwoods, IL. Tel: (847) 267-7000, (888) 224-7377, Web Site: www.cch.com (17)

Sabin, Glenn, JazzTimes Magazine Inc, Quincy, MA. Tel: (617) 706-9110, FAX: (617) 536-0102, E-Mail: info@jazztimes.com, Web Site: www.jazztimes.com (17)

Sabin, Jeff, JazzTimes Magazine Inc, Quincy, MA. Tel: (617) 706-9110, FAX: (617) 536-0102, E-Mail: info@jazztimes.com, Web Site: www.jazztimes.com (17)

Sabine, John, Penguin Group USA Inc, East Rutherford, NJ. Tel: (201) 909-6200, FAX: (201) 236-3381, Web Site: penguingroup.com (17)

Sabio, James, Xpandomedia, Buffalo, NY. Tel: (716) 836-9668 (21)

Sable, David, Wunderman, New York, NY. Tel: (212) 941-3000, FAX: (212) 888-7520, Web Site: www.wunderman.com (35)

Sablosky, Warren, NuNaturals, Eugene, OR. Tel: (541) 344-9785, (800) 753-4372, FAX: (541) 343-0915, E-Mail: info@nunaturals.com, Web Site: www.nunaturals.com (16)

Sabol, John, ListK, Atlanta, GA. Tel: (800) 600-3389, FAX: (800) 878-2489, Web Site: www.listk.com (32)

Sabre Holdings Inc, Southlake, TX. Tel: (682) 605-1000, Web Site: www.sabre.com (19)

Sachar, Ken, Marastar Communications, Wayne, PA. Tel: (610) 902-0080, FAX: (610) 902-0600, E-Mail: info@marastar.com, Web Site: www.marastar.com (13)

Sacher, Paul, Paul Fredrick Menstyle, Fleetwood, PA. Tel: (610) 944-0909, (800) 247-1417, FAX: (610) 944-6452, E-Mail: custserv@menstyle.com, Web Site: www.paulfredricks.com (2)

Sachs, Steve, Time Inc, New York, NY. Tel: (212) 522-1212, Web Site: www.timeinc.com/home (17)

Sackett, David, WCPE-FM, Wake Forest, NC. Tel: (919) 556-5178, Web Site: www.theclassicalstation.org (32)

Sacks, Douglas, Infocore Inc, Carlsbad, CA. Tel: (760) 607-2500, FAX: (760) 607-2505, E-Mail: bstewart@infocoreinc.com, Web Site: www.infocoreinc.com (23)

Sacred Heart League, Walls, MS. Tel: (662) 781-1360, (800) 232-9079, FAX: (662) 781-3340, E-Mail: comments@shl.org, Web Site: www.shl.org (28)

Sadh, Devyani, Data Square LLC, Wilton, CT. Tel: (203) 964-9733, E-Mail: info@datasquare.com, Web Site: www.datasquare.com (22)

Sadorf, Nedra, Hunter Business Group LLC, Milwaukee, WI. Tel: (414) 203-8060, (800) 423-4010, FAX: (414) 203-8225, E-Mail: hunter@hunterbusiness.com, Web Site: www.hunterbusiness.com (20)

Saeger, Rebecca, Charles Schwab & Co Inc, San Francisco, CA. Tel: (415) 627-7000, (800) 648-5300, FAX: (415) 421-0810, Web Site: www.schwab.com (14)

Saenz, Dave, Alarmingyou.com, Boca Raton, FL. Tel: (714) 981-2900, Web Site: www.alarmingyou.com (16)

Safe Publications Inc, Southampton, PA. Tel: (215) 357-9049, FAX: (215) 357-5202, E-Mail: sales@safepub.com, Web Site: www.safepub.com (11)

Safe Specialties, Kingston, TN. Tel: (865) 675-2815, (800) 695-2815, FAX: (865) 717-8249, E-Mail: black223@aol.com, Web Site: www.safespec.com (33)

Safeco Insurance Co, Seattle, WA. Tel: (206) 545-5000, (800) 332-3226, FAX: (206) 545-5767/5651, Web Site: www.safeco.com (15)

Safeguard Business Systems Inc, Dallas, TX. Tel: (214) 905-3935, (800) 523-2422, FAX: (800) 439-8423, Web Site: www.gosafeguard.com (16)

Safeware, The Insurance Agency Inc, Columbus, OH. Tel: (614) 781-1492, (800) 800-1492, FAX: (614) 781-0559, E-Mail: service@safeware.com, Web Site: www.safeware.com (15)

Safian, Shelley, Safian Communications Services Inc, Longwood, FL. Tel: (407) 644-6996, E-Mail: ssafian@earthlink.net (35)

Safian Communications Services Inc, Longwood, FL. Tel: (407) 644-6996, E-Mail: ssafian@earthlink.net (35)

Safran, Jeff, Antares Information Tech, Chadds Ford, PA. Tel: (631) 234-5700, (800) 330-2579, FAX: (631) 234-5472, E-Mail: steve@antares-iti.com, Web Site: www.antares-iti.com (21)

Saftchick, Jay, WinterSilks LLC, Warren, PA. Tel: (904) 645-6000, Web Site: www.wintersilks.com (2)

Safti First, San Francisco, CA. Tel: (415) 824-4900, (888) 653-3333, FAX: (415) 824-5900, (888) 653-4444, E-Mail: info@safti.com, Web Site: www.safti.com (16)

Sagami, Tony, Weiss Research Inc, Jupiter, FL. Tel: (561) 627-3300, (877) 925-4833, FAX: (561) 625-6685, E-Mail: newbusiness@weissgroupinc.com, Web Site: www.weissgroupinc.com (17)

Sage, Gary, Sage Direct Inc, Grand Rapids, MI. Tel: (616) 940-8311, (800) 729-8310, FAX: (616) 940-3383, E-Mail: sageinc@sagedirect.com, Web Site: www.sagedirect.com (22)

Sage, Pamela, Sage Direct Inc, Grand Rapids, MI. Tel: (616) 940-8311, (800) 729-8310, FAX: (616) 940-3383, E-Mail: sageinc@sagedirect.com, Web Site: www.sagedirect.com (22)

Sage Communications, Hudson, MA. Tel: (978) 567-8888, Web Site: www.sagecommunications.com (35)

Sage Direct Inc, Grand Rapids, MI. Tel: (616) 940-8311, (800) 729-8310, FAX: (616) 940-3383, E-Mail: sageinc@sagedirect.com, Web Site: www.sagedirect.com (22)

Sage Financial Group, West Conshohocken, PA. Tel: (484) 342-4400, FAX: (484) 537-0550, E-Mail: sage@sagefinancial.com, Web Site: www.sagefinancial.com (14)

Sage Software Inc, Irvine, CA. Tel: (949) 753-1222, (800) 854-3415, FAX: (949) 753-0374, Web Site: www.sagesoftware.com (16)

Sagen, Warren, AllBrands.com Sewing Machine Superstore, Baton Rouge, LA. Tel: (225) 923-1285, (866) 255-2726, FAX: (225) 923-1261, E-Mail: info@allbrands.com, Web Site: www.allbrands.com (11)

Sager, Dan, Insight Direct Inc, Tempe, AZ. Tel: (480) 333-3001, (800) 467-4448, FAX: (480) 902-1180, Web Site: www.insight.com (16)

Saggio, Joseph, PDS International Mail Service, Hauppauge, NY. Tel: (631) 815-1750, Web Site: www.pdsmail.com; www.internationalmail.com (28)

Sahadeo, Meere, Pango Pango Swimwear Corp, Pompano Beach, FL. Tel: (954) 786-0255, (800) 858-9431, FAX: (954) 786-7745, E-Mail: pango_swimwear@bellsouth.net, Web Site: www.pango-pangoswimwear.com (2)

Sahlberg, John, Boise Cascade Holdings LLC, Boise, ID. Tel: (208) 384-6451, FAX: (208) 384-7189, E-Mail: mediarelations@bc.com, Web Site: www.bc.com (16)

Sahlein, Don, Alan Gordon Enterprises, Hollywood, CA. Tel: (323) 466-3561, FAX: (323) 871-2193, E-Mail: info@alangordon.com, Web Site: www.alangordon.com (32)

Saide, Barry, United Staffing Systems, New York, NY. Tel: (212) 743-0300, (800) 972-9725, FAX: (212) 576-1569, Web Site: www.unitedstaffing.com (16)

Saiia, Donna, Potpourri Group Inc, Chelmsford, MA. Tel: (978) 256-4100, FAX: (978) 256-1961/0344, Web Site: www.potpourrigroup.com (6)

The Sailing Co, Palm Coast, FL. Tel: (866) 436-2460, FAX: (401) 848-5048, Web Site: www.sailingworld.com (17)

Sailrite Enterprises, Inc, Columbia City, IN. Tel: (260) 693-2242, (800) 348-2769, FAX: (260) 693-2246, E-Mail: sailrite@sailrite.com, Web Site: www. sailrite.com (11)

The Saint Francis Academy Inc, Salina, KS. Tel: (785) 825-0541, (800) 423-1342, FAX: (785) 825-2940, Web Site: www.st-francis.org (1)

Saint Gregory Group, Cincinnati, OH. Tel: (513) 769-8440, FAX: (513) 769-1640, E-Mail: pmartin@ stgregory.com, Web Site: www.stgregory.com (35)

The St John Associates Inc, Bronx, NY. Tel: (718) 655-2500, FAX: (718) 655-0295, E-Mail: stjmail@ aol.com, Web Site: www.stjohn1.com (21)

St Joseph's College, Brooklyn, NY. Tel: (718) 399-1223, Web Site: www.sjcny.edu (1)

St Joseph's Indian School, Chamberlain, SD. Tel: (605) 734-3300, Web Site: www.stjo.org (1)

St Labre Indian School, Ashland, MT. Tel: (406) 784-4500, Web Site: www.stlabre.org (1)

St Lawrence Island Original Ivory Cooperative, Gambell, AK. Tel: (907) 985-5707, FAX: (907) 985-5927 (6)

St Louis Post-Dispatch, Saint Louis, MO. Tel: (314) 340-8000, (800) 365-0820, FAX: (314) 340-3140, Web Site: www.postnet.com (17)

St Louis Slot Machine Co, Saint Louis, MO. Tel: (314) 432-1699, E-Mail: stlslot@earthlink.net, Web Site: www.stlouisslot.com (6)

Saint Mary's Paper Corp, Wheaton, IL. Tel: (630) 668-6279, FAX: (630) 668-6292, Web Site: www. stmarys-paper.com (25)

St Petersburg/Clearwater Area CVB, Clearwater, FL. Tel: (727) 464-7200, Web Site: www. floridasbeach.com (1)

Saint Thomas, Robert, Children International, Kansas City, MO. Tel: (816) 942-2000, FAX: (816) 942-3714, E-Mail: RobS@cikc.org, Web Site: www. children.org (1)

Sait, Suaad, ReachForce, Austin, TX. Tel: (512) 327-9000, FAX: (512) 327-9090, E-Mail: info@ reachforce.com, Web Site: www.reachforce.com (23)

Saito, Joichi, Central Pacific Bank, Honolulu, HI. Tel: (808) 544-0500, (800) 544-0500, (800) 342-8422, FAX: (808) 531-2875, Web Site: www. centralpacificbank.com (14)

Saito, Matt, Isuzu Motors America Inc, Anaheim, CA. Tel: (562) 229-5000, (800) 255-6727, FAX: (562) 229-5463, Web Site: www.isuzu.com (16)

Sakach, Stephen, American Historic Inns Inc, Dana Point, CA. Tel: (949) 497-2232, (800) 397-4667, FAX: (949) 497-9228, E-Mail: comments@ iloveinns.com, Web Site: www.iloveinns.com (17)

Sakach, Tim, American Historic Inns Inc, Dana Point, CA. Tel: (949) 497-2232, (800) 397-4667, FAX: (949) 497-9228, E-Mail: comments@iloveinns. com, Web Site: www.iloveinns.com (17)

Saks Fifth Avenue, New York, NY. Tel: (212) 940-5195, FAX: (212) 940-5339, Web Site: www. saksfifthavenue.com (16)

Sakui, Masato, Mitsubishi Digital Electronics America Inc, Irvine, CA. Tel: (949) 465-6000, FAX: (949) 859-4770, Web Site: www.mitsubishi-tv.com (3)

Sala, George, Penguin Group USA Inc, East Rutherford, NJ. Tel: (201) 909-6200, FAX: (201) 236-3381, Web Site: www.penguingroup.com (17)

Salane, Nede, Demand Telemarketing Inc, Grosse Pointe, MI. Tel: (313) 823-8598, (888) 977-2256, FAX: (313) 823-8598, E-Mail: wpatterson@create-demand.com, Web Site: www.create-demand.com (29)

Salatino, Joseph, Great North American Cos Inc, Dallas, TX. Tel: (972) 481-6100, (800) 527-2782, FAX: (972) 243-1637, Web Site: www.gnamerican. com (16)

Salaway, Kevin, Penn State Hazleton, Hazleton, PA. Tel: (570) 450-3175, Web Site: www.hn.psu.edu (1)

Saleh, Jay, Village Software Inc, Boston, MA. Tel: (617) 695-9332, (800) 724-9332, FAX: (617) 695-1935, E-Mail: requests@villagesoft.com, Web Site: www.villagesoft.com (3)

Saleh, Paul, Sprint PCS, Overland Park, KS. Tel: (800) 927-2199, Web Site: www.sprintpcs.com (16)

Saleh, Sarah, Academic Travel Abroad Inc, Washington, DC. Tel: (202) 785-9000, (800) 556-7896, FAX: (202) 342-0317, Web Site: www. academictravel.com (19)

Salem, Enrique T., Symantec, Mountain View, CA. Tel: (408) 517-8000, FAX: (408) 517-8186, Web Site: www.symantec.com (16)

Salem Web Network, Richmond, VA. Tel: (804) 205-9700, FAX: (804) 205-9648, E-Mail: info@ salemwebnetwork.com, Web Site: www. salemwebnetwork.com (24)

The Sales and Marketing Institute, Scottsdale, AZ. Tel: (480) 473-5777, (888) 714-5544, FAX: (623) 979-8843, Web Site: www.b2bmarketing.com (35)

Sales & Marketing Management Magazine, New York, NY. Tel: (800) 821-6897, FAX: (905) 470-8561, E-Mail: joyce.cooney@nielsen.com, Web Site: www.salesandmarketing.com (16)

Sales Building Systems, Mentor, OH. Tel: (800) 435-7576, FAX: (440) 639-9190, E-Mail: sales@ sbsteam.com, Web Site: www.sbsteam.com (31)

Sales Development Associates Inc, Saint Louis, MO. Tel: (314) 862-8828, FAX: (314) 862-8829, E-Mail: patb@sdasti.com (21)

Sales Leads, Jupiter, FL. Tel: (866) 725-3753, FAX: (866) 702-5558, E-Mail: info@salesleadsinc.com, Web Site: www.salesleadsinc.com (17)

Sales Magic Inc, Boynton Beach, FL. Tel: (561) 732-5263, (800) 940-7991, FAX: (561) 375-9413, Web Site: www.names.com (32)

Sales Portal, Mountain View, CA. Tel: (800) 634-3474, Web Site: www.salesportal.com (30)

Sales Service/America Inc, Alexandria, VA. Tel: (703) 813-2400 (16)

Salesian Missions, New Rochelle, NY. Tel: (914) 633-8344, FAX: (914) 633-7404, E-Mail: info@ salesianmissions.org, Web Site: www. salesianmissions.org. (1)

SalesLeadsTv (Federal Union Inc), Boca Raton, FL. Tel: (561) 981-8777, (800) 590-5323, FAX: (561) 981-8786, E-Mail: contact_us@salesleads.tv, Web Site: www.salesleads.tv (23)

Salford Systems, San Diego, CA. Tel: (619) 543-8880, Web Site: www.salford-systems.com (22)

Salgado, Marco, Homeowners Marketing Services Inc, North Hollywood, CA. Tel: (818) 506-1507, (800) 232-2134, FAX: (818) 505-9729, (818) 506-4110, E-Mail: lists@homeown.org, Web Site: www. homeown.org (23)

Salguero, Jeff, Colgate-Palmolive Co, New York, NY. Tel: (212) 310-2000, (800) 468-6502, FAX: (212) 310-2475, Web Site: www.colgate.com (16)

Salic, Jacob, Talas, Brooklyn, NY. Tel: (212) 219-0770, FAX: (212) 219-0735, E-Mail: info@ talasonline.com, Web Site: www.talasonline.com (10)

Salisbury, Franklin, C., National Foundation for Cancer Research, Bethesda, MD. Tel: (301) 654-1250, (800) 321-CURE, FAX: (301) 654-5824, E-Mail: info@nfcr.org, Web Site: www.nfcr.org (1)

Salisbury, Tamara, National Foundation for Cancer Research, Bethesda, MD. Tel: (301) 654-1250, (800) 321-CURE, FAX: (301) 654-5824, E-Mail: info@nfcr.org, Web Site: www.nfcr.org (1)

Salk, Jonathan, CCIM Institute, Chicago, IL. Tel: (312) 321-4460, (800) 621-7027, FAX: (312) 321-4530, Web Site: www.ccim.com (1)

Salkin, Jonathan, Rocket Direct Marketing Inc, New York, NY. Tel: (212) 689-5800, FAX: (212) 689-0635, E-Mail: info@rocketdirect.com, Web Site: www.rocketdirect.com (32)

Salles, Barbara, Statlistics, Danbury, CT. Tel: (203) 778-8700, Web Site: www.statlistics.com (23)

Salley Sr., Tom, WTS Media, Chattanooga, TN. Tel: (423) 894-9427, (800) 251-7228, FAX: (423) 894-7281, E-Mail: customerservice@wtsmedia.com, Web Site: www.wts-tape.com (16)

Sallorenzo, Gaetano, Calvin Klein Cosmetics Co, New York, NY. Tel: (212) 759-8888, FAX: (212) 479-4399 (7)

Sally Beauty Supply LLC, Denton, TX. Tel: (940) 898-7500, (800) 275-7255, Web Site: www. sallybeauty.com (7)

Salmans, Scott, J., WRS Group Ltd, Waco, TX. Tel: (254) 776-6461, (800) 299-3366, FAX: (888) 977-7653, E-Mail: sales@wrsgroup.com, Web Site: www.wrsgroup.com (7)

Salmon, Melissa, John Hancock Financial Services Inc, Boston, MA. Tel: (617) 572-6000, (800) 732-5543, FAX: (617) 572-6451, Web Site: www. johnhancock.com (15)

Kurt Salmon Associates Inc, Atlanta, GA. Tel: (404) 892-0321, FAX: (404) 898-9590, E-Mail: infoksaweb@kurtsalmon.com, Web Site: www. kurtsalmon.com (20)

Salmore, Charles, Marketing Works Inc, Los Angeles, CA. Tel: (323) 436-2000, FAX: (213) 382-7538, E-Mail: marketingwork@mediaone.net, Web Site: www.mworks-inc.com (32)

Salomon, Dee, Anne Klein, New York, NY. Tel: (212) 536-9000, FAX: (212) 536-9000 (16)

Salt, Matt, FDAnews, Falls Church, VA. Tel: (703) 538-7600, (888) 838-5578, FAX: (703) 538-7676, E-Mail: customerservice@fdanews.com, Web Site: www.fdanews.com (17)

Salt River Project, Tempe, AZ. Tel: (602) 236-5929, Web Site: www.srpnet.com (34)

Salta, Joseph, DirectMail.com, Prince Frederick, MD. Tel: (888) 690-2252, FAX: (301) 855-9810, Web Site: www.directmail.com (28)

Salta, Robert, DirectMail.com, Prince Frederick, MD. Tel: (888) 690-2252, FAX: (301) 855-9810, Web Site: www.directmail.com (28)

Saltel, Cameron, Movada Media Inc, Winnipeg, MB Canada. Tel: (204) 284-9000, Web Site: www. movadamedia.com (5)

Saltzman, David, Triangle Printers Inc, Skokie, IL. Tel: (847) 675-3700, FAX: (847) 674-1230, E-Mail: blevin@triangleprinters.com, Web Site: www.triangleprinters.com (27)

Saltzman, Jeffrey, Entertainment Music Marketing Corp, Baldwin, NY. Tel: (631) 243-0600, FAX: (631) 243-0605, E-Mail: emmcmusic@aol.com, Web Site: www.emmcmusic.com (16)

Saluto, Christine, Direct Mail of NY-Posthaste, Buchanan, NY. Tel: (914) 736-2239 (28)

The Salvation Army National Headquarters, Alexandria, VA. Tel: (703) 684-5500, Web Site: www. salvationarmyusa.org (1)

Salvetti, Tom, Follett Library Resources, McHenry, IL. Tel: (815) 759-1700, (800) 435-6170, FAX: (800) 852-5458, E-Mail: custserv@flr.follett.com, Web Site: www.flr.follett.com (16)

Salyers, Ms. Donna, Donna Salyers' Fabulous-Furs, Covington, KY. Tel: (859) 291-3300, (800) 848-4650, E-Mail: abell@fabulousfurs.com, Web Site: fabulousfurs.com (2)

Donna Salyers' Fabulous-Furs, Covington, KY. Tel: (859) 291-3300, (800) 848-4650, E-Mail: abell@ fabulousfurs.com, Web Site: fabulousfurs.com (2)

Salzberg, Barry, Deloitte & Touche, Boston, MA. Tel: (617) 437-2000, FAX: (617) 437-2111, Web Site: www.deloitte.com (14)

Salzinger, Mark, No Load Fund Investor, Brentwood, TN. Tel: (800) 706-6364, FAX: (800) 785-9212, E-Mail: NoLoad@mleesmith.com, Web Site: www. noloadfundinvestor.com (14)

Salzman, Russ, Institute of Real Estate Management, Chicago, IL. Tel: (312) 329-6000, (800) 837-0706, FAX: (800) 338-4736, E-Mail: custserv@irem.org, Web Site: www.irem.org (1)

Samant, Rajiv, Lester Inc, Branford, CT. Tel: (203) 488-5265, (800) 999-5265, FAX: (203) 483-0408, Web Site: www.lesterusa.com (29)

Sambrook, Andrew, IDG List Services, Framingham, MA. Tel: (888) 434-5478, FAX: (508) 370-0020, Web Site: www.idglist.com (24)

Samets, Yoram, Kelliher Samets Volk, Burlington, VT. Tel: (802) 862-8261, FAX: (802) 863-4724, E-Mail: info@ksvc.com, Web Site: www.ksvc.com (35)

Samford University, Birmingham, AL. Tel: (205) 726-2011, Web Site: www.samford.edu (41)

Samiri, Omer, IVisionMobile Inc, Chatsworth, CA. Tel: (866) 655-5302, Web Site: www.ivisionmobile.com (35)

Sammons, Lyle, First National List Service Inc, Chicago, IL. Tel: (773) 509-1266, (888) 621-5548, FAX: (773) 509-1277, E-Mail: firstnl@sbcglobal.net (23)

Samon, Helen, Academy of Marketing Science Journal, Thousand Oaks, CA. Tel: (805) 499-0721, FAX: (800) 583-2665, (805) 499-0871, Web Site: www.sagepub.com (43)

Sample, Chuck, True Value Co, Chicago, IL. Tel: (773) 695-5000, Web Site: www.truevalue.com (16)

David Sams Industries Inc/TV First, Agoura Hills, CA. Tel: (818) 707-7022, FAX: (818) 707-8130, E-Mail: customerservice@samsdirect.com, Web Site: www.tvfirst.com (35)

Samsonite American Tourister, Mansfield, MA. Tel: (508) 851-1400, (800) 821-6632, FAX: (508) 851-8715, E-Mail: samsonite@casupport.ca, Web Site: www.samsonite.com (16)

Samsonite Corp, Mansfield, MA. Tel: (508) 851-1400, (800) 547-BAGS, FAX: (303) 373-8715, Web Site: www.samsonite.com (16)

San Antonio, Randall, Warrantech Direct Inc, Bedford, TX. Tel: (817) 786-1000, (800) 833-8801, FAX: (817) 786-1020, Web Site: www.warrantech.com (29)

San Antonio Express-News, San Antonio, TX. Tel: (210) 250-2601, Web Site: www.express-news.net (35)

San Diego Direct Marketing Association, San Diego, CA. Tel: (858) 503-1471, E-Mail: webmaster@sddma.org, Web Site: www.sddma.org (40)

San Francisco Bay Area Rapid Transit District (BART), Oakland, CA. Tel: (510) 464-6000, FAX: (510) 464-7103, Web Site: www.bart.gov (16)

San Francisco Chronicle, San Francisco, CA. Tel: (415) 777-1111, FAX: (415) 536-5178, E-Mail: amatthews@sfchronicle.com, Web Site: www.sfgate.com (17)

San Francisco Herb & Natural Food Co, Fremont, CA. Tel: (510) 770-1215, (800) 227-2830, FAX: (510) 770-9021, E-Mail: customerservice@herbspicetea.com, Web Site: www.herbspicetea.com (4)

San Francisco State University, San Francisco, CA. Tel: (415) 338-1111, FAX: (415) 338-0501, Web Site: www.sfsu.edu (41)

San Francisco Victoriana Inc, San Francisco, CA. (415) 648-0313, FAX: (415) 648-2812, Web Site: www.sfvictoriana.com (9)

San Jose Mercury News, San Jose, CA. Tel: (408) 920-5000, FAX: (408) 271-3690, Web Site: www.bayarea.com (17)

San Julian, Robert, Neutron Industries, Phoenix, AZ. Tel: (602) 864-0090, (888) 712-7127, FAX: (602) 357-3996, (877) 646-7337, E-Mail: questions@neutronindustries.com, Web Site: www.neutronindustries.com (16)

Sanborn, Allen, RMA-The Risk Management Association, Philadelphia, PA. Tel: (215) 446-4000, FAX: (215) 446-4101, E-Mail: customers@rmahq.org, Web Site: www.rmahq.org (1)

Sanches Jr, Enrique, Aerovox Inc, New Bedford, MA. Tel: (508) 994-9661, (888) AEROVOX, FAX: (508) 995-3000, E-Mail: sales1@aerovox.com, Web Site: www.aerovox.com (16)

Sanchez, Arlene, American Academy of Neurology, Saint Paul, MN. Tel: (651) 695-2793, Web Site: www.aan.com (1)

Sanchez, Jaime, SIGMA Marketing Group LLC, Rochester, NY. Tel: (585) 473-7300, (888) 277-9837, FAX: (585) 473-0332, E-Mail: mbush@sigmamarketing.com, Web Site: www.sigmamarketing.com; www.jthgearanalytics.com (Blog) (2)

Sanchez, Joseph, Protection One Inc, Lawrence, KS. Tel: (785) 856-5500, (800) GET-HELP, Web Site: www.protectionone.com (16)

Sanchez, Miguel, Christian Herald Association, New York, NY. Tel: (212) 684-2800, (800) BOWERY-1, FAX: (212) 684-3740, E-Mail: info@chaonline.org, Web Site: www.bowery.org (1)

Sancoa International, Lumberton, NJ. Tel: (856) 273-0700, FAX: (856) 273-2710, E-Mail: sancoa@sancoa.com (31)

Sand, Matthew, BUYSEASONS Inc, Bothell, WA. Tel: (262) 901-2000, Web Site: www.buyseasons.com (5)

Sanders, Bruce, Micro Plastics Inc, Flippin, AR. Tel: (870) 453-2261, (800) 466-1467, FAX: (870) 453-8676, E-Mail: mpsales@microplastics.com, Web Site: www.microplastics.com (16)

Sanders, Frank, CSM Inc, Marietta, GA. Tel: (800) 849-6788, FAX: (770) 514-6799, E-Mail: info@csmresearch.com, Web Site: www.csmresearch.com (30)

Sanders, Greg, Rowe Pottery Works Inc, Cambridge, WI. Tel: (608) 423-3363, (800) 356-5003, FAX: (608) 423-4273, E-Mail: sales@rowepottery.com, Web Site: www.rowepottery.com (16)

Sanders, Herb, American Appraisal Associates, Milwaukee, WI. Tel: (414) 271-7240, (800) 558-8650, FAX: (414) 225-1271, Web Site: www.american-appraisal.com (14)

Sanders, Lewis, A., Alliance Bernstein, New York, NY. Tel: (212) 969-1000, (800) 962-2134, FAX: (212) 969-2229, Web Site: www.alliancebernstein.com (14)

Sanders, Mike, Christian Appalachian Project, Lexington, KY. Tel: (859) 792-3051, (866) 270-4CAP, FAX: (859) 792-6560, E-Mail: capinfo@chrisapp.org, Web Site: www.christianapp.org (1)

Sandgeroth, Mike, Baldwin Filters, Kearney, NE. Tel: (308) 234-1951, (800) 822-5394, FAX: (800) 828-4453, E-Mail: info@baldwinfilter.com, Web Site: www.baldwinfilter.com (16)

Sandhu, Kevin, Sales Portal, Mountain View, CA. Tel: (800) 634-3474, Web Site: www.salesportal.com (30)

Sandin, Lennart, Nowell's Inc, San Rafael, CA. Tel: (415) 332-4933, FAX: (415) 332-4936, E-Mail: contact@nowellslighting.com, Web Site: www.nowellslighting.com (8)

Sandkam, Ellen, ATP List Services, Barrington, IL. Tel: (800) 223-3423, Web Site: www.atplists.com (23)

Sandler, David, MSC Industrial Supply Co, Melville, NY. Tel: (516) 812-2000, (800) 645-7270, FAX: (800) 255-5067, E-Mail: executive@mscdirect.com, Web Site: www.mscdirect.com (9)

Sandler, Marvin, Independent Living Aids, Jericho, NY. Tel: (516) 937-1848, (800) 537-2118, FAX: (516) 937-3906, E-Mail: techsupport@independentliving.com, Web Site: www.independentliving.com (7)

Sandler, Robert, M., 21st Century Insurance, Woodland Hills, CA. Tel: (818) 704-3700, FAX: (818) 226-1198, E-Mail: executiveoffice@21st.com, Web Site: www.21st.com (15)

Sandler Techworks, New York, NY. Tel: (917) 697-9678, Web Site: www.sandlertechworks.com (20)

Sandman, Elizabeth, Tristar Products, Fairfield, NJ. Tel: (973) 575-5400, FAX: (973) 683-6708, E-Mail: infotp@tristarproductsinc.com, Web Site: www.tristarproductsinc.com (16)

Sandonato, Dan, JLG Industries Inc, McConnellsburg, PA. Tel: (717) 485-5161, (877) JLG-SELL, FAX: (717) 485-6417, E-Mail: comments@jlg.com, Web Site: www.jlg.com (16)

Sandoval, Claudia, FAO Schwarz, New York, NY. Tel: (212) 644-9400, (800) 426-TOYS, FAX: (212) 688-6053, Web Site: www.fao.com (11)

Sands, David, T., Toland Home and Garden Inc, Port Townsend, WA. Tel: (504) 893-9503, (800) 989-6287, E-Mail: info@tolandhomeandgarden.com, Web Site: www.tolandhomeandgarden.com (16)

Sands, Jill, Toland Home and Garden Inc, Port Townsend, WA. Tel: (504) 893-9503, (800) 989-6287, E-Mail: info@tolandhomeandgarden.com, Web Site: www.tolandhomeandgarden.com (16)

Sandy Corp, Troy, MI. Tel: (800) 733-4739, FAX: (248) 729-4701, E-Mail: info@sandycorp.com, Web Site: www.sandycorp.com (16)

Sandy Goldshein Associates Inc, New York, NY. Tel: (212) 366-5105, Web Site: www.sgany.com (35)

Sandy Mush Herb Nursery, Leicester, NC. Tel: (828) 683-2014, E-Mail: info@sandymushherbs.com, Web Site: www.sandymushherbs.com (8)

Sanfilippo, Tony, Pennsylvania State University Press, University Park, PA. Tel: (814) 865-1327, (800) 326-9180, FAX: (814) 863-1408, Web Site: www.psupress.org (17)

Sanford, W., Scott, KCET, Los Angeles, CA. Tel: (323) 666-6500, FAX: (323) 953-5661, E-Mail: viewerservices@kcet.org, Web Site: www.kcet.org (1)

Sanford, William, JA Sexauer, Elmsford, NY. Tel: (914) 472-7501, (800) 431-1872, FAX: (914) 472-5834, Web Site: www.jasmro.com (16)

Sanger, Stephen, W., General Mills Inc, Minneapolis, MN. Tel: (763) 764-7600, FAX: (763) 764-7384, Web Site: www.generalmills.com (8)

Sanger, Stephen, W., The Pillsbury Co, Minneapolis, MN. Tel: (763) 764-7600, (800) 775-4777, FAX: (763) 764-8330, Web Site: www.pillsbury.com (16)

Sangha, Pav, Ordenza Marketing Group Inc, Burnaby, BC Canada. Tel: (604) 451-1414, Web Site: www.odenza.com (35)

Sanguinetti, Cecilia, Carnival Cruise Lines, Miami, FL. Tel: (212) 599-2600, Web Site: www.carnival.com (19)

Sanheim, John, Wm. K. Walthers Inc, Milwaukee, WI. Tel: (414) 527-0770, FAX: (414) 527-4423, Web Site: www.walthers.com (11)

Sani Serv, Mooresville, IN. Tel: (317) 831-7030, FAX: (317) 381-7036, Web Site: www.saniserv.com (16)

Sank, David, Oneida Ltd, Oneida, NY. Tel: (315) 361-3000, (888) 263-7195, FAX: (315) 361-3700, Web Site: www.oneida.com (16)

Sanky Communications Inc, New York, NY. Tel: (212) 868-4300, Web Site: www.sankyinc.com (1)

Sanna Mattson MacLeod, Smithtown, NY. Tel: (631) 265-5160, FAX: (631) 265-5185, E-Mail: info@smmadagency.com, Web Site: www.smmadagency.com (35)

SanSegal Sportswear (HQ), Sandy, UT. Tel: (801) 566-3248, (800) 338-6048, FAX: (801) 566-3350, E-Mail: sansegal@sansegal.com, Web Site: www.sansegal.com (2)

Sansone, Daniel, F., Vulcan Materials Co, Birmingham, AL. Tel: (205) 298-3000, FAX: (205) 298-2960, Web Site: www.vulcanmaterials.com (16)

Sant, Victoria, P., National Gallery of Art Gift Shop, Washington, DC. Tel: (202) 842-6466, (800) 697-9350, FAX: (202) 842-4043, Web Site: www.nga.gov (16)

Santa Barbara Greenhouses, Oxnard, CA. Tel: (805) 483-4288, (800) 544-5276, E-Mail: robsbg@aol.com, Web Site: www.sbgreenhouse.com (8)

Santa Fe Natural Tobacco Co, Santa Fe, NM. Tel: (505) 982-4257, Web Site: www.nascigs.com (16)

Santa Fe School of Cooking, Santa Fe, NM. Tel: (505) 983-4511, FAX: (505) 983-7540, Web Site: www. santafeschoolofcooking.com (4)

Santana, Dario L., NTN Communications Inc, Carlsbad, CA. Tel: (760) 438-7400, (888) PLAY-NTN, (888) 752-9686, FAX: (760) 438-3505, Web Site: www.ntn.com (32)

Santaniello, Becky, Catalyst Direct Marketing/DNA, Pompton Lakes, NJ. Tel: (973) 831-4222, FAX: (973) 831-1933, E-Mail: info@catalystdm.com, Web Site: www.catalystdm.com (23)

Santarella, Scott, American Lung Association, New York, NY. Tel: (212) 889-3370, (800) LUNGUSA, FAX: (212) 889-3375, E-Mail: info@alany.org, Web Site: www.lungusa.org (1)

Santillan, Patricia, Avon Books, New York, NY. Tel: (212) 207-7000, FAX: (212) 207-7222 (17)

Santini, Bryant, Circle K Stores Inc, Akron, OH. Tel: (330) 630-6300, Web Site: www.cirlcek.com (16)

Santoli, Joseph, Physicians Planning Association Services, Deerfield Beach, FL. Tel: (954) 571-1877, (800) 221-2168, FAX: (954) 571-8582, E-Mail: insurance@assnservices.com, Web Site: www. physiciansplanning.com (16)

Santoni, David, M., Goldsmith Agio Helms, Minneapolis, MN. Tel: (612) 339-0500, FAX: (612) 339-0507, Web Site: www.agio.com (14)

Santoro, P.J., Nike Inc, Beaverton, OR. Tel: (503) 671-4565, (800) 344-6543, FAX: (503) 671-6300, Web Site: www.nike.com (2)

Santoro, Tony, KMA Direct Communications, Dallas, TX. Tel: (972) 244-1900, FAX: (972) 244-1901, E-Mail: sales@kma.com, Web Site: www.kma.com (1)

Santos, Begona, Vazquez, The Nature Conservancy, Arlington, VA. Tel: (703) 841-5300, (800) 628-6860, FAX: (703) 841-1283, E-Mail: magazine@tnc.org, Web Site: www.nature.org (1)

Santos, Melissa, Rose Displays Ltd, Salem, MA. Tel: (978) 219-8100, Web Site: www.rosedisplays.com (16)

Santucci, Anthony, P., Weingeroff Enterprises Inc, Cranston, RI. Tel: (401) 467-2200, FAX: (401) 785-1320, Web Site: www.weingeroff.com (16)

Sapp, Dien, AEGON Direct Marketing Services Inc, Baltimore, MD. Tel: (410) 209-5617, FAX: (410) 209-5932, Web Site: www.aegondms.com (15)

Sapp, Ellen, Tinsley Tool Supply Inc, Powell, TN. Tel: (865) 681-9633, FAX: (865) 982-1655, E-Mail: gene@tinsleytool.com, Web Site: www.tinsleytool. com (9)

Sapp, Gene, Tinsley Tool Supply Inc, Powell, TN. Tel: (865) 681-9633, FAX: (865) 982-1655, E-Mail: gene@tinsleytool.com, Web Site: www.tinsleytool. com (9)

Sapp, Michael, Tinsley Tool Supply Inc, Powell, TN. Tel: (865) 681-9633, FAX: (865) 982-1655, E-Mail: gene@tinsleytool.com, Web Site: www. tinsleytool.com (9)

Sapp, Tony, Leadership Directories Inc, New York, NY. Tel: (212) 627-4140, FAX: (212) 645-0931, E-Mail: info@leadershipdirectories.com, Web Site: www.leadershipdirectories.com (17)

Sappi Fine Paper North America, Boston, MA. Tel: (617) 423-7300, FAX: (617) 423-5494, Web Site: www.sappi.com (25)

Sara Isaac, Saint Paul, MN. Tel: (651) 482-8593, FAX: (651) 481-8077, Web Site: www.saraisaac. com (22)

Sara Lee Direct Home Shopping, Winston-Salem, NC. Tel: (336) 519-4400, (800) 671-5056, E-Mail: ohp. managor@onehanesplace.com, Web Site: www. onehanesplace.com (2)

Sara Lee Hosiery, Winston Salem, NC. Tel: (336) 519-2711/2369, FAX: (336) 519-3254, Web Site: www. leggs.com (2)

Saracco, Thomas, Direct Access Marketing Services Inc, Syosset, NY. Tel: (516) 364-2777, FAX: (516) 364-0644, E-Mail: info@daxcess.com, Web Site: www.daxcess.com (22)

Saracino, Joan, The Philadelphia Contributorship Insurance Co, Philadelphia, PA. Tel: (215) 627-1752, (800) 346-9229, E-Mail: info@contributorship. com, Web Site: www.contributorship.com (15)

Saraf, Shevach, Solitron Devices Inc, West Palm Beach, FL. Tel: (561) 848-4311, FAX: (561) 863-5946, E-Mail: sales@solitrondevices.com, Web Site: www.solitrondevices.com (16)

Sarah Putnam, Cambridge, MA. Tel: (617) 547-3758, E-Mail: sarah@sarahputnam.com, Web Site: www. sarahputnam.com (37)

Sardi, Frank, Techcom Inc, Princeton, NJ. Tel: (609) 734-0004, FAX: (609) 520-0263, E-Mail: techcom1@juno.com (35)

Sardinas, Lisa, Team Nash Inc, East Hampton, NY. Tel: (646) 497-0297, (631) 267-3385, E-Mail: results@teamnash.com, Web Site: www.teamnash. com (35)

Saretsky, Peter, International Masters Publishers Inc, Montoursville, PA. Tel: (800) 570-5718, E-Mail: customerservice@imp-usa.com, Web Site: www. imponline.com (17)

Sargant, Hugh L., Sealed Air Corp, Elmwood Park, NJ. Tel: (201) 791-7600, FAX: (201) 712-7070, Web Site: www.sealedair.com (26)

Sargeant, Julie, Mac Pac Inc, Pembroke, MA. Tel: (781) 826-6900, FAX: (781) 826-6880, E-Mail: jsargeant@macpacinc.com, Web Site: www. macpacinc.com (26)

Sargent, Frank, P., Business Services Network, San Francisco, CA. Tel: (415) 282-8161, FAX: (415) 282-8176, E-Mail: sales@bsnc.com, Web Site: www.bsnc.com (28)

Sargent, Grant, Publications International Ltd, Lincolnwood, IL. Tel: (847) 745-9299, (800) 595-8484, FAX: (847) 676-3671, Web Site: www.pubint.com (17)

Sargent, Ronald, L., Staples Business Advantage, Atlanta, GA. Tel: (770) 997-2512, (877) 826-7754, FAX: (888) 387-9592, Web Site: www.staples.com (34)

Sarka, Pat, Educational Insights, Inc, Gardena, CA. Tel: (310) 884-2000, (888) 591-9334, FAX: (310) 886-8850, E-Mail: service@edin.com, Web Site: www.educationalinsights.com (16)

Sarnitakos, Nick, LDS Group Inc, New York, NY. Tel: (646) 390-5702, FAX: (646) 390-5715, E-Mail: rvergara@ldsgroupinc.com, Web Site: www. ldsgroupinc.com (23)

Sarnoff, Ann, BBC Worldwide Americas Inc, New York, NY. Tel: (212) 705-9300, (800) 898-4921, FAX: (212) 888-0576, Web Site: www.bbcamerica. com (3)

Sarnow, Greg, Direct Response Academy, Austin, TX. Tel: (512) 301-5900, FAX: (512) 301-7900, E-Mail: info@dracademy.org, Web Site: www. dracademy.org (41)

Sartori, Carl, Graphic Arts Blue Book/AF Lewis Marketing, New York, NY. Tel: (646) 746-7429, FAX: (212) 519-7434, Web Site: www.gabb.com (24)

Sartorius, Rick, Fisher Group Inc, Hiawatha, IA. Tel: (319) 393-5405, FAX: (319) 393-2738, E-Mail: info@fishergroup.com, Web Site: www. fishergroup.com (27)

Sasaki, Tadashi, Fuji Photo Film USA, Valhalla, NY. Tel: (914) 789-8100, (800) 755-3854, FAX: (914) 789-8295, Web Site: www.fujifilmusa.com (16)

Sasinski, Karen, Interstate Printing Co, Omaha, NE. Tel: (402) 341-8028, (800) 788-4177, FAX: (402) 341-6168, E-Mail: printer@interstateprinting.com, Web Site: www.interstateprinting.com (27)

Saski, Joseph, Sancoa International, Lumberton, NJ. Tel: (856) 273-0700, FAX: (856) 273-2710, E-Mail: sancoa@sancoa.com (31)

Sass, Anita, US Monitor, New City, NY. Tel: (845) 634-1331, (800) 767-7967, FAX: (845) 634-9618, E-Mail: info@usmonitor.com, Web Site: www. usmonitor.com (28)

Sass, Brian, Champion Printing Inc, Elsmere, KY. Tel: (513) 541-1100, (800) 543-1957, FAX: (513) 541-9398, E-Mail: cpi@championprintinginc.com, Web Site: www.championprintinginc.com (27)

Sass, Brian, Double Envelope, Gainesville, FL. Tel: (800) 543-5275, Web Site: www.double-envelope. com (26)

Sassaman, Steve, Trans Union Corp, Chicago, IL. Tel: (312) 258-1717, (800) 335-9888, FAX: (312) 466-8385, Web Site: www.transunion.com (14)

Sassano, Carl E., Transcat, Rochester, NY. Tel: (585) 352-9460, (800) 800-5001, FAX: (585) 352-1486, Web Site: www.transcat.com (16)

Sasser, Fred, Chicago Decal Co, Burr Ridge, IL. Tel: (630) 850-2122, (888) DECALS R US, (888) 332-2577, FAX: (630) 850-7177, E-Mail: sales@chicagodecal.com, Web Site: www.chicagodecal. com (27)

Sastra, Mike, Audio Classics Ltd, Vestal, NY. Tel: (607) 766-3501, FAX: (607) 766-3502, E-Mail: steve@audioclassics.com, Web Site: www. audioclassics.com (3)

Satell, Ed, Progressive Business Publications, Malvern, PA. Tel: (610) 695-8600, (800) 220-5000, FAX: (610) 647-8089, E-Mail: customer_service@pbp.com, Web Site: www.pbp.com (17)

Sater, Emelie, D&B Canada, Mississauga, ON. Tel: (905) 568-6000, FAX: (905) 568-6197, Web Site: www.dnb.ca (30)

Satisfaction Software Inc, Jamaica, NY. Tel: (732) 382-8736, FAX: (732) 382-8736, E-Mail: db@biink.com (20)

Satori Software Inc, Seattle, WA. Tel: (206) 357-2900, (800) 553-6477, FAX: (206) 357-2901, E-Mail: sales@satorisoftware.com, Web Site: www. satorisoftware.com (16)

Satren, Fritz, AESU Inc, Baltimore, MD. Tel: (410) 366-5494, (800) 638-7640, FAX: (410) 366-6999, E-Mail: res@aesu.com, Web Site: www.aesu.com (19)

Saturn Corp, Hyattsville, MD. Tel: (301) 772-7000, (800) USA-0090, FAX: (301) 386-4538, E-Mail: sales@saturncorp.com, Web Site: www.saturncorp. com (22)

Sauce Co, Little Rock, AR. Tel: (501) 663-3338, (800) 43- Sauce, FAX: (501) 663-0956, Web Site: www. sauceco.net (4)

Sauceda, Sandra, Jefferson Mailing Lists, Poway, CA. Tel: (858) 679-1233, FAX: (858) 679-1279 (23)

Sauerberg, Robert, Conde Nast, New York, NY. Tel: (212) 286-2860, FAX: (212) 880-8289, Web Site: www.conde.net (17)

Sauers, Michael F., Wachovia Center, Philadelphia, PA. Tel: (215) 336-3600, FAX: (215) 389-9518, E-Mail: info@comcast-spectacor.com, Web Site: www.comcast-spectacor.com (16)

Sauers, Richard, S., Sauers Group, Inc, Stone Mountain, GA. Tel: (770) 621-8888, (866) 458-5212, FAX: (770) 621-8866, E-Mail: info@sauersgroup. com, Web Site: www.sauersgroup.com (27)

Sauers Group, Inc, Stone Mountain, GA. Tel: (770) 621-8888, (866) 458-5212, FAX: (770) 621-8866, E-Mail: info@sauersgroup.com, Web Site: www. sauersgroup.com (27)

Saul, George, Scholastic Direct Mktg, Danbury, CT. Tel: (203) 797-3500, FAX: (203) 797-3667 (29)

Saunders, Rick, Orchard Supply Hardware, San Jose, CA. Tel: (408) 281-3500, FAX: (408) 225-0388, Web Site: www.osh.com (16)

Saunders Manufacturing Co Inc, Readfield, ME. Tel: (207) 685-3385, (800) 341-4674, FAX: (207) 685-9918, E-Mail: jsherwood@saunders-usa.com, Web Site: www.saunders-usa.com (16)

Saunders Military Insignia, Naples, FL. Tel: (239) 298-8228, (800) 442-3133, FAX: (239) 774-3323, E-Mail: info@saundersinsignia.com, Web Site: www.saundersinsignia.com (6)

Richard Saunders International, Cincinnati, OH. Tel: (513) 271-9911, FAX: (513) 271-9966, E-Mail: doug@eurekaranch.com, Web Site: www. eurekaranch.com (20)

Saurage, Matthew, C., Community Coffee Co, Baton Rouge, LA. Tel: (225) 291-3900, (800) 525-5583, FAX: (800) 643-8199, E-Mail: ccc@ communitycoffee.com, Web Site: www. communitycoffee.com (4)

The Sausage Maker Inc, Buffalo, NY. Tel: (716) 824-5814, (888) 490-8525, FAX: (716) 824-6465, E-Mail: customerservice@sausagemaker.com, Web Site: www.sausagemaker.com (4)

The Sausalito Group, Sausalito, CA. Tel: (415) 332-3333, FAX: (415) 332-6571, Web Site: www. sausolitogroup.com (30)

Sauser, Todd, Nilodor Inc, Bolivar, OH. Tel: (330) 874-1017, (800) 443-4321, FAX: (330) 874-3366, E-Mail: info@nilodor.com, Web Site: www.nilodor.com (16)

Sautter, Elise, New Mexico State University, Las Cruces, NM. Tel: (575) 646-0111, (505) 646-3341, FAX: (505) 646-1498, Web Site: www.nmsu.edu (41)

Savage, Ed, Sacred Heart League, Walls, MS. Tel: (662) 781-1360, (800) 232-9079, FAX: (662) 781-3340, E-Mail: comments@shl.org, Web Site: www. shl.org (28)

Savage, Mike, Merkle Inc, Columbia, MD. Tel: (443) 542-4000, (877) 9MERKLE, Web Site: www. merkleinc.com (22)

Savasta, Bob, Spectronics Corp, Westbury, NY. Tel: (800) 274-8888, FAX: (800) 491-6868, E-Mail: vscherer@spectroline.com, Web Site: www. spectroline.com (9)

Save the Children Federation Inc, Westport, CT. Tel: (203) 221-4000, (800) 728-3843, FAX: (203) 222-1067, E-Mail: twebster@savethechildren.org, Web Site: www.savethechildren.org (1)

Savein, R, Ventriloquist Voice Solutions International Inc, Mississauga, ON. Tel: (866) 446-0860, E-Mail: info@vvsii.com, Web Site: www.vvsii.com (29)

Saveology.com, South Plainfield, NJ. Tel: (866) 755-9008, Web Site: www.elephantgroup.com (5)

Savicom, San Francisco, CA. Tel: (415) 983-0990, FAX: (415) 445-9999, E-Mail: sales@savicom.net, Web Site: www.savicom.net (22)

Savig, Patricia, Taylor Corp, North Mankato, MN. Tel: (507) 625-2828, FAX: (507) 625-3388 (16)

Saville, John, M., Nor'east Miniature Roses Inc, Arroyo Grande, CA. Tel: (805) 426-6485, (800) 426-6485, FAX: (805) 481-7374, E-Mail: noreast@ greenheartfarms.com, Web Site: www.noreast-miniroses.com (8)

Savings Bank Life Insurance Co of MA (SBLI), Woburn, MA. Tel: (781) 938-3500, Web Site: www.sbli.com (15)

Saviski, Mark, Stock Yards Packing Co Inc, Chicago, IL. Tel: (312) 733-6050, (877) STK-YARD, FAX: (312) 733-1746, E-Mail: customerservice@ stockyards.com, Web Site: www.stockyards.com (4)

Savitz, Rick, Justin Discount Boots & Cowboy Outfitters, Justin, TX. Tel: (940) 648-2797, FAX: (940) 648-3282, Web Site: www.justinboots.com (2)

Savitz, Los Angeles, CA. Tel: (310) 642-4799, FAX: (310) 642-7795, E-Mail: lmoran@ savitzfieldandfocus.com, Web Site: www. savitzfieldandfocus.com (20)

Savoca, Kate, SMG Direct Market, Bannockburn, IL. Tel: (585) 249-6100, FAX: (585) 249-6309 (35)

Savoff, Mark, T., Entergy, New Orleans, LA. Tel: (504) 576-4000, (800) ENTERGY, FAX: (504) 576-4428, Web Site: www.entergy.com (16)

Savoy, Mark, First National Information Network, Burbank, CA. Tel: (855) 909-6800, FAX: (818) 558-6663, E-Mail: info@fnin.com, Web Site: www.fnin.com (30)

Sawchuck, Arthur, R., John Hancock Financial Services Inc, Boston, MA. Tel: (617) 572-6000, (800) 732-5543, FAX: (617) 572-6451, Web Site: www. johnhancock.com (15)

Sawicki, Craig, Tricor Braun, Woodridge, IL. Tel: (708) 385-9333, FAX: (708) 385-3015, Web Site: www.tricorbraun.com (16)

Sawtooth Group, Woodbridge, NJ. Tel: (732) 636-6600, FAX: (732) 602-4212, Web Site: www. sawtoothgroup.com (35)

Sawyer, Linda, Lowe Worldwide, New York, NY. Tel: (212) 981-7600, E-Mail: info@loweworldwide. com, Web Site: www.loweworldwide.com (35)

Sawyer-Lueck, Jessica, Silliker Inc, Chicago, IL. Tel: (708) 957-7878, FAX: (708) 957-3798, E-Mail: cjx@netcom.com, Web Site: www.silliker.com (20)

Sax, Pearl, Checks by Phone/Checks by Web, Boynton Beach, FL. Tel: (561) 737-8700, FAX: (561) 737-5800, E-Mail: LarrySchwartz@checksbyphone. com, Web Site: www.checksbyphone.com (14)

Sax, Pearl, Fraud & Theft Information Bureau, Boynton Beach, FL. Tel: (561) 737-8700, FAX: (561) 737-5800, E-Mail: sales@fraudandtheft.com, Web Site: www.fraudandtheftinfo.com (43)

Sax Arts & Crafts, Appleton, WI. Tel: (800) 558-6696, FAX: (800) 328-4729, E-Mail: info@saxarts.com, Web Site: www.saxarts.com (10)

Sayin, Dan, Catalogs America, Gordonsville, VA. Tel: (540) 832-2253, (800) 283-4666, FAX: (540) 832-7253, E-Mail: dsayin@catalogsamerica.com, Web Site: www.catalogsamerica.com (27)

Sayre, Bill, Merkle Inc, Columbia, MD. Tel: (443) 542-4000, (877) 9MERKLE, Web Site: www. merkleinc.com (22)

Sbragia, Jessica, ReMark USA, Minnetonka, MN. Tel: (952) 938-4699, FAX: (952) 988-8500, E-Mail: jessica.sbragia@remarkgroup.com, Web Site: www. remarkamericas.com (15)

Scales, Earl, G&S Packing Co Inc, Weirsdale, FL. Tel: (352) 821-2251, (800) 949-9074, FAX: (352) 821-5000, Web Site: www.gspacking.com (16)

Scales, George, Florida Gift Fruit Shippers Association, Orlando, FL. Tel: (407) 295-1491, FAX: (407) 290-0918, Web Site: www.fgfsa.com (1)

Scales, George, G&S Packing Co Inc, Weirsdale, FL. Tel: (352) 821-2251, (800) 949-9074, FAX: (352) 821-5000, Web Site: www.gspacking.com (16)

Scalet, J., Chris, Merck & Co Inc, Whitehouse Station, NJ. Tel: (908) 423-1000, Web Site: www. merck.com (16)

Scalf, Jeffrey, Cinmar LP, West Chester, OH. Tel: (513) 603-1000, FAX: (513) 603-1020, Web Site: www.frontgate.com (8)

The Scan Group, Waukesha, WI. Tel: (262) 521-1365, Web Site: www.scangroup.net (35)

Scan Optics Inc, Manchester, CT. Tel: (860) 645-7878, (800) 745-6001, FAX: (860) 645-7995, E-Mail: info@scanoptics.com, Web Site: www.scanoptics. com (16)

Scanlan, T.C., Surplus Record, Chicago, IL. Tel: (312) 372-9077, (800) 622-5449, FAX: (312) 372-6537, E-Mail: surplus@surplusrecord.com, Web Site: www.surplusrecord.com (17)

Scanlon, Brian, Thieme Medical Publishers Inc, New York, NY. Tel: (212) 760-0888, (800) 782-3488, FAX: (212) 947-1112, E-Mail: info@thieme.com, Web Site: www.thieme.com (17)

Scanlon, Richard, Pensions & Investments, New York, NY. Tel: (212) 210-0100, FAX: (212) 210-0117, Web Site: www.pionline.com (17)

Scannell, Herb, BBC Worldwide Americas Inc, New York, NY. Tel: (212) 705-9300, (800) 898-4921, FAX: (212) 888-0576, Web Site: www.bbcamerica. com (3)

Scannell, Jay, SkyMall Inc, Phoenix, AZ. Tel: (602) 254-9777, (800) SKY-MALL, FAX: (602) 254-6075, Web Site: www.skymall.com (16)

Scantland, Andrew, TeleTech, Englewood, CO. Tel: (303) 397-8100, (800) TELETECH, FAX: (303) 397-8199, E-Mail: solutions@TeleTech.com, Web Site: www.teletech.com (22)

Scapperotti, Sherry, PlusMedia LLC, Danbury, CT. Tel: (203) 748-6500, FAX: (203) 748-6600, E-Mail: contact@plusme.com, Web Site: www. plusme.com (35)

Scarafile, Andrew, J., Clemente Novelties Inc, Utica, NY. Tel: (315) 732-4145, FAX: (315) 732-2251, E-Mail: clemente@6org.com (16)

Scarborough, Dean A., Avery Dennison Corp, Brea, CA. Tel: (714) 674-8500, (800) 462-8379, FAX: (714) 674-6929, Web Site: www.avery.com (10)

Scardino, Dame Marjorie M., Pearson Education, Upper Saddle River, NJ. Tel: (201) 236-7000, FAX: (201) 236-3290, E-Mail: communications@ pearsoned.com, Web Site: www.pearsoned.com (17)

Scardino, Janet, The Wedding Pages, New York, NY. Tel: (212) 219-8555, (800) 843-4983, FAX: (212) 219-1929, Web Site: www.theknot.com (16)

Scarlett, Joe, Tractor Supply Co, Brentwood, TN. Tel: (615) 366-4600, (877) 872-7721, FAX: (615) 227-4608, Web Site: www.mytscstore.com (22)

Scarpelli, Guy, J., CTC Teleservices, De Kalb, IL. Tel: (815) 748-4200, FAX: (630) 773-4765, Web Site: www.ctcteleservices.com (29)

Scartz, Don, T., EMS Technologies, Norcross, GA. Tel: (770) 263-9200, FAX: (770) 447-4405, Web Site: www.ems-t.com (16)

Scenic Photo!, Minneapolis, MN. Tel: (612) 810-0797, E-Mail: manager@scenicphoto.com, Web Site: www.scenicphoto.com (38)

Schachne, Bruce, Standard & Poor's Corp, New York, NY. Tel: (212) 438-2000, FAX: (212) 438-7375, Web Site: www.standardandpoors.com (17)

Schachte, Bob, Mitchell International, San Diego, CA. Tel: (858) 368-7000, FAX: (858) 238-9111, Web Site: www.mitchell.com (17)

Schaefer Jr, George, A., Fifth Third Bank, Cincinnati, OH. Tel: (800) 972-3030, FAX: (231) 922-4060, Web Site: www.53.com (14)

Schaefer, Deborah, ABR Employment Services, Madison, WI. Tel: (608) 244-3526, FAX: (608) 244-8279, E-Mail: info@abrjobs.com, Web Site: www. abrjobs.com (20)

Schaefer, Rita, McDougal Littell, Evanston, IL. Tel: (847) 869-2300, FAX: (847) 869-0841, Web Site: www.mcdougallittell.com (17)

Schaeffer, Anne, Grey Birch Group LLC, Irvington, NY. Tel: (914) 479-5088, Web Site: www. greybirch.com (20)

Schaeffer, John, Gaiam Inc, Boulder, CO. Tel: (877) 989-6321, Web Site: life.gaiam.com (9)

Schaeffer, John, Real Goods Trading Corp, San Rafael, CA. Tel: (707) 542-2600, (888) 567-6527, Web Site: www.realgoods.com (5)

Schaeffer, Sandor, Andell Packaging Corp, Manhasset, NY. Tel: (718) 937-6500, FAX: (718) 482-9416 (27)

Schaenzer, Chris, Wm. K. Walthers Inc, Milwaukee, WI. Tel: (414) 527-0770, FAX: (414) 527-4423, Web Site: www.walthers.com (11)

Schaerr, Gene, Accuracy in Media Inc, Washington, DC. Tel: (202) 364-4401, FAX: (202) 364-4098, E-Mail: info@aim.org, Web Site: www.aim.org (1)

Schafer, Charlie, Agri Drain Corp, Adair, IA. Tel: (641) 742-5211, (800) 232-4742, FAX: (641) 742-5222, (800) 282-3353, E-Mail: info@agridrain. com, Web Site: www.agridrain.com (9)

Schaffer, Stewart, Lazydays RV Center, Seffner, FL. Tel: (813) 246-4333, Web Site: www.lazydays.com (12)

Schaffrath, Susan, McDougal Littell, Evanston, IL. Tel: (847) 869-2300, FAX: (847) 869-0841, Web Site: www.mcdougallittell.com (17)

Schaldenbrand, C.L., Resumate Inc, Ann Arbor, MI. Tel: (734) 477-9402, (800) 530-9310, FAX: (734) 477-9415, E-Mail: info@resumate.com, Web Site: www.resumate.com (3)

Schall, Heather, Lifetime Brands Inc, Garden City, NY. Tel: (516) 683-6000, FAX: (516) 683-6161, E-Mail: postmaster@brands.com, Web Site: www. lifetimebrands.com (8)

Schalle, Bonnie, E & M Media Group Inc, New York, NY. Tel: (212) 455-0177, Web Site: www. emtvsales.com (35)

Schanen III, William, F., Wind in the Rigging, Port Washington, WI. Tel: (262) 284-3494, (800) 236-7444, FAX: (262) 284-0067, E-Mail: info@ windintherigging.com, Web Site: www. windintherigging.com (11)

Schanen, Jean, Wind in the Rigging, Port Washington, WI. Tel: (262) 284-3494, (800) 236-7444, FAX: (262) 284-0067, E-Mail: info@windintherigging. com, Web Site: www.windintherigging.com (11)

Schanfeld, Maxeen, D2: Direct, Denville, NJ. Tel: (973) 627-4410, FAX: (973) 627-3703, E-Mail: info@d2direct.com, Web Site: www.d2direct.com (35)

Schang, Scott, Environmental Law Institute, Washington, DC. Tel: (202) 939-3800, FAX: (202) 939-3868, E-Mail: law@eli.org, Web Site: www.eli.org (17)

Schanke, David, Outlook Group Corp, Neenah, WI. Tel: (920) 722-2333, FAX: (920) 727-8529, E-Mail: path@outlookgroup.com, Web Site: www. outlookgroup.com (27)

Schapiro, Jeff, CSI, Conklin, NY. Tel: (607) 775-7905, Web Site: www.cleanersupply.com (16)

Scharf, Richard, Denver Metro Convention & Visitors Bureau, Denver, CO. Tel: (303) 892-1112, FAX: (303) 892-1636, Web Site: www.denver.org (1)

Schargorodski, Leo, American Nurses' Association, Silver Spring, MD. Tel: (301) 628-5000, (800) 284-2378, (800) 274-4262, FAX: (301) 628-5001, Web Site: www.nursingworld.org (1)

Scharin, Bob, Research Institute America, Carrollton, TX. Tel: (972) 250-7000, (800) 950-1216, Web Site: www.ria.thompson.com (14)

Schatz, David G., The Saint Francis Academy Inc, Salina, KS. Tel: (785) 825-0541, (800) 423-1342, FAX: (785) 825-2940, Web Site: www.st-francis. org (1)

Schatz, Thomas, A., Citizens Against Government Waste, Washington, DC. Tel: (202) 467-5300, (800) USA-DEBT, FAX: (202) 467-4253, E-Mail: membership@cagw.org, Web Site: www.cagw.org (1)

Schauble, Julie, KPBS FM/TV, San Diego, CA. Tel: (619) 594-1515, Web Site: www.kpbs.org (1)

Schaus, Cynthia M., ING USA Annuity & Life Ins Co, Des Moines, IA. Tel: (515) 698-7100, FAX: (515) 698-2001, Web Site: www.ing-usa.com (15)

Schawk, David, A., Schawk Inc, Des Plaines, IL. Tel: (847) 827-9494, (800) 621-1909, FAX: (847) 827-1264, E-Mail: information@schawk.com, Web Site: www.schawk.com (27)

Schawk, Des Plaines, IL. Tel: (847) 827-9494, FAX: (847) 827-1264, Web Site: www.schawk.com (35)

Schawk DesPlaines, Des Plaines, IL. Tel: (847) 296-6000, (800) 629-1909, FAX: (847) 296-4694, Web Site: www.schawk.com (27)

Schawk Inc, Des Plaines, IL. Tel: (847) 827-9494, (800) 621-1909, FAX: (847) 827-1264, E-Mail: information@schawk.com, Web Site: www.schawk. com (27)

Schechne, David, Vertrue Inc, Norwalk, CT. Tel: (203) 324-7635, FAX: (203) 674-7080, Web Site: www. vertrue.com (13)

Schecter, Dan, ER Carpenter, Taylor, TX. Tel: (512) 365-5833, (800) 234-9105, FAX: (512) 352-6025, Web Site: www.carpenter.com (16)

Schecterson, Jack, Jack Schecterson visualmarketing Consultants, Little Neck, NY. Tel: (718) 225-3536 (20)

Scheele, Stephanie, Vera Bradley, Fort Wayne, IN. Tel: (800) 823-8372, Web Site: www.verabradley.com (2)

Scheer, Adam, L.A., American Bank Note Holographics Inc, Robbinsville, NJ. Tel: (609) 632-0800, FAX: (609) 632-0850, Web Site: www.abnh.com (27)

Scheevel, Michael, MultiView, Irving, TX. Tel: (972) 402-7056 (1)

Scheffer, Sarah, Reliable Technologies Inc, Manchester, NH. Tel: (603) 644-2528, (800) 346-7890, FAX: (603) 627-5553, Web Site: www.tei-imaging. com (16)

Scheffers, Todd, Goodheart-Willcox Publisher, Tinley Park, IL. Tel: (708) 687-5000, (800) 323-0440, FAX: (708) 687-3900, E-Mail: custserv@g-w.com, Web Site: www.g-w.com (17)

Scheffler, Reshelle, NAVTEQ, Chicago, IL. Tel: (312) 780-1989 (35)

Scheider, Mark, Edward Don & Co, North Riverside, IL. Tel: (708) 442-9400, (800) 777-4366, FAX: (708) 442-0436, Web Site: www.don.com (16)

Scheidt, Mark, TechniPak, Gray, TN. Tel: (800) 385-1964, Web Site: www.technipak.com (28)

Henry Schein Inc, Melville, NY. Tel: (631) 843-5500, (800) 472-4346, FAX: (631) 843-5658, E-Mail: custserv@henryschein.com, Web Site: www. henryschein.com (16)

Schell, Ernest H., Marketing Systems Analysis, Ventnor, NJ. Tel: (609) 487-9340, FAX: (866) 214-3208, E-Mail: ernie@schell.com, Web Site: www. schell.com (20)

Schell, John, Easthill Group Inc, Pottstown, PA. Tel: (610) 323-9099, (610) 323-9063, (610) 323-2200, (888) 869-4433, (800) 345-1178, FAX: (610) 323-6268, Web Site: www.eastwoodcompany.com (12)

Schell, Mark, Valdawn Watch Co, Long Island City, NY. Tel: (201) 807-1110, FAX: (201) 807-0228 (16)

Scheller, Tom, Bathroom Machineries, Murphys, CA. Tel: (209) 728-3860, FAX: (209) 728-2320, E-Mail: info@deabath.com, Web Site: www. deabath.com (8)

Schemenauer, Darin, Mason Companies Inc, Chippewa Falls, WI. Tel: (715) 723-1871, (800) 826-7030, FAX: (715) 720-4247, Web Site: www. masoncompaniesinc.com (2)

Schena, Robert, Rajant Corp, Malvern, PA. Tel: (484) 595-0233, FAX: (484) 595-0244, E-Mail: moreinfo@rajant.com, Web Site: www.rajant.com (32)

Schencker, Sylvia, The Miami Herald Media Co, Miami, FL. Tel: (305) 350-2111 (17)

Schenk, Matthew, HSP Direct, Herndon, VA. Tel: (703) 793-3220, FAX: (703) 793-3221, Web Site: www.hspdirect.com (1)

Schenk, Theresa, HighScope Educational Research Foundation, Ypsilanti, MI. Tel: (734) 485-2000, (800) 40-PRESS, FAX: (734) 485-0704, E-Mail: lschweinhart@highscope.org, Web Site: www. highscope.org (17)

Schenk, Walter, D., CDI Network Inc, Naperville, IL. Tel: (708) 409-8585, FAX: (708) 409-8589, Web Site: www.cdinet.biz (27)

Schenke, Roger, American College of Physician Executives, Tampa, FL. Tel: (813) 287-2000, (800) 562-8088, FAX: (813) 287-8993, E-Mail: acpe@ acpe.org, Web Site: www.acpe.org (1)

Schenker, Mark, Anchor Computer Inc, Farmingdale, NY. Tel: (631) 293-6100, Web Site: www. anchorcomputer.com (22)

Schepp, Robina, Pace University - Div of Enrollment Mgmt, New York, NY. Tel: (212) 346-1781, (866) 722-3338, FAX: (212) 346-1821, Web Site: www. pace.edu/pace/ (16)

Scher, Laura, Working Assets, San Francisco, CA. Tel: (800) 668-9253, FAX: (415) 371-1046, Web Site: www.workingassets.com (16)

Scherer, Bruce, Pinkerton Security & Investigation Services, Parsippany, NJ. Tel: (973) 397-2276, (800) 724-1616, FAX: (973) 397-2491, Web Site: www.ci-pinkerton.com (16)

Scherer, Gary W., Programmers Investment Corp, Arlington Heights, IL. Tel: (847) 227-4500, FAX: (847) 299-8286, E-Mail: pic@pic-online.com, Web Site: www.pic-online.com (21)

Scherer, Jerry, D., Blue Cross & Blue Shield of Oklahoma, Tulsa, OK. Tel: (918) 560-3500, (800) 942-5837, E-Mail: info@bcbsok.com, Web Site: www. bcbsok.com (15)

Scherer, Ken, Motion Picture & Television Fund Foundation, Woodland Hills, CA. Tel: (818) 876-1888, Web Site: www.mptvfund.org (1)

Scherer, Valerie, Spectronics Corp, Westbury, NY. Tel: (800) 274-8888, FAX: (800) 491-6868, E-Mail: vscherer@spectroline.com, Web Site: www. spectroline.com (9)

Schermer Pecans, Glennville, GA. Tel: (800) 841-3403, E-Mail: information@schermerpecans.com, Web Site: www.pecantreats.com (4)

Scheutele, Nancy, Hugo Dunhill Mailing Lists Inc, New Rochelle, NY. Tel: (212) 213-9300, (800) 611-0557, FAX: (212) 213-9245, E-Mail: info@ hdml.com, Web Site: www.hdml.com (23)

Schiavone, Raymond, Quark Inc, Denver, CO. Tel: (303) 894-3832, Web Site: www.quark.com (34)

Schiela, John, Phoenix Marketing International, Horsham, PA. Tel: (215) 392-0264, Web Site: www. phoenixmi.com (30)

Schier, Dale, Calico Corners, Kennett Square, PA. Tel: (610) 444-9700, FAX: (610) 444-1221, Web Site: www.calicocorners.com (16)

Jacques C Schiff Jr Inc, Ridgefield Park, NJ. Tel: (201) 641-5566, FAX: (201) 641-5705 (5)

Schiff Jr, Jacques C., Jacques C Schiff Jr Inc, Ridgefield Park, NJ. Tel: (201) 641-5566, FAX: (201) 641-5705 (5)

Schiffman, Leon, Market Discovery Group, Roslyn, NY. Tel: (516) 365-8555, E-Mail: schiffmanl@ aol.com (30)

Schild, Harold, Tillamook County Creamery Association, Tillamook, OR. Tel: (503) 842-4481, (800) 542-7290, FAX: (503) 842-6039, Web Site: www. tillamookcheese.com (4)

Schiller, Anne, Marie, Rapp Collins Worldwide, New York, NY. Tel: (212) 817-6800, FAX: (212) 686-7047, Web Site: www.rappcollins.com (35)

Schiller, Howard, Hollywood Film Archive, Los Angeles, CA. Tel: (323) 655-4968, Web Site: www. hfarchive.com (17)

Schillinger, Jerry, Spilsbury Puzzle Co, Chicago, IL. Tel: (800) 722-1760, FAX: (630) 575-0857, E-Mail: service@spilsbury.com, Web Site: www. spilsbury.com (11)

Schimberg, John, Media Management & Magnetics Inc, Menomonee Falls, WI. Tel: (262) 251-5511, (800) 242-2090, FAX: (262) 251-4737, E-Mail: medmgt@computersupplypeople.com, Web Site: www.computersupplypeople.com (3)

Schimke, David, Mother Earth News Magazine, Topeka, KS. Tel: (785) 274-4300, (800) 678-5779, FAX: (785) 274-4305, E-Mail: bwelch@ ogdenpubs.com, Web Site: www.cappers.com (17)

Schimmel, Kurt, West Virginia University, Morgantown, WV. Tel: (304) 293-3505, FAX: (304) 293-3072, E-Mail: wvuwebmaster@mail.wvu.edu, Web Site: www.wvu.edu (41)

Schinco, Jim, Affinitas Corp, Omaha, NE. Tel: (402) 397-7077, (800) 369-6495, FAX: (402) 397-7576, Web Site: www.affinitas.net (29)

Schiro, James, J., Zurich, Schaumburg, IL. Tel: (847) 605-3712, (800) 382-2150, FAX: (847) 605-6403, Web Site: www.zurichna.com (15)

Schlachter, Chris, Touch of Class Catalog, Huntingburg, IN. Tel: (812) 683-3707, (800) 457-7456, FAX: (812) 683-5921, Web Site: www. touchofclasscatalog.com (8)

Schlagerhapt, Eileen, Cushman Fruit Co Inc, West Palm Beach, FL. Tel: (561) 965-3535, (800) 776-2295, FAX: (561) 968-7263, E-Mail: info@honeybell.com, Web Site: www.honeybell.com (4)

Schlecht, Steven, Duluth Trading Co Inc, Belleville, WI. Tel: (800) 505-8888, FAX: (888) 950-3199, E-Mail: customerservice@duluthtrading.com, Web Site: www.duluthtrading.com (8)

Schlegel, Beth, Anheuser-Busch Inc Promotional Products Group, Shelton, CT. Tel: (800) 742-5283, Web Site: www.budshop.com (6)

Schleich, Paul, Taylor Corp, North Mankato, MN. Tel: (507) 625-2828, FAX: (507) 625-3388 (16)

Schleider, Ernie, Audio Classics Ltd, Vestal, NY. Tel: (607) 766-3501, FAX: (607) 766-3502, E-Mail: steve@audioclassics.com, Web Site: www.audioclassics.com (3)

Schleiter, Jim, Vance Industries Inc, Niles, IL. Tel: (847) 375-8900, FAX: (847) 375-6818, E-Mail: vance@vanceind.com, Web Site: www.vanceind.com (16)

Schlesinger, Laurie, The Jewish Publication Society, Philadelphia, PA. Tel: (215) 832-0600, (800) 234-3151, FAX: (215) 568-2017, E-Mail: jewishbook@jewishpub.org, Web Site: www.jewishpub.org (17)

Schlig, Joseph, Solitron Devices Inc, West Palm Beach, FL. Tel: (561) 848-4311, FAX: (561) 863-5946, E-Mail: sales@solitrondevices.com, Web Site: www.solitrondevices.com (16)

Schlott, Dennis, Fielder's Choice Direct, Monticello, IN. Tel: (574) 583-2741 X107, (800) 321-3177, FAX: (574) 583-CORN, Web Site: www.fielderschoicedirect.com (8)

Schluger, Allen, The Allen Schluger Co Inc, New York, NY. Tel: (212) 873-8577, FAX: (212) 873-0452 (31)

The Allen Schluger Co Inc, New York, NY. Tel: (212) 873-8577, FAX: (212) 873-0452 (31)

Schlumpf, Steve, Haband Co Inc, Oakland, NJ. Tel: (201) 651-1000, FAX: (201) 405-7777, Web Site: www.haband.com (2)

Schmazl, Thomas, 1to1 Media, Stamford, CT. Tel: (203) 642-5121, FAX: (203) 316-5121, (203) 642-5126, Web Site: www.1to1media.com (35)

Schmermund, Bill, Sawtooth Group, Woodbridge, NJ. Tel: (732) 636-6600, FAX: (732) 602-4212, Web Site: www.sawtoothgroup.com (16)

Schmid, Barbara, Terumo Cardiovascular Systems Corp, Ann Arbor, MI. Tel: (734) 663-4145, Web Site: www.terumo-cvs.com (17)

Schmid, Suzanne, Focus USA Inc, Hackensack, NJ. Tel: (201) 489-2525, FAX: (201) 489-4499, E-Mail: suzanne@focus-usa-l.com, Web Site: www.focus-usa-l.com (23)

J Schmid & Associates Inc, Mission, KS. Tel: (913) 236-8988, FAX: (913) 236-8987, E-Mail: info@jschmid.com, Web Site: www.jschmid.com (20)

Schmidleithner, Rudi, Gateway Inc, Irvine, CA. Tel: (949) 471-7000, (800) 369-1409, FAX: (949) 471-7041, Web Site: www.gateway.com (3)

Schmidt Jr., Alfred, M., The Schmidt Group International Inc, Vero Beach, FL. Tel: (772) 492-0073, FAX: (772) 492-0293, E-Mail: catalogprofit@att.net, Web Site: www.the-schmidt-group.com (20)

Schmidt, Andreas, BarnesandNoble.com, New York, NY. Tel: (212) 414-6000, (800) THE-BOOK, FAX: (212) 414-6140, E-Mail: service@barnesandnoble.com, Web Site: www.barnesandnoble.com (16)

Schmidt, Andreas, Hanley Wood LLC, Washington, DC. Tel: (202) 452-0800, FAX: (202) 785-1974, Web Site: www.hanleywood.com (16)

Schmidt, Bob, CCI Solutions, Olympia, WA. Tel: (360) 943-5378, (800) 426-8664, FAX: (360) 754-1566, (800) 339-TAPE, E-Mail: info@ccisolutions.com, Web Site: www.ccisolutions.com (16)

Schmidt, Gigi, Make-A-Wish Foundation of America, Phoenix, AZ. Tel: (602) 279-9474, FAX: (602) 279-0855, Web Site: www.wish.org (1)

Schmidt, Herbert, Con-Way Truckload, Joplin, MO. Tel: (417) 623-5229, (800) CFI-DRIVE, FAX: (417) 623-8939, E-Mail: gnichols@cfi-us.com, Web Site: www.cfi-us.com (12)

Schmidt, Kim, Escort Inc, West Chester, OH. Tel: (513) 870-8500, (800) 964-3138, FAX: (513) 870-8509, E-Mail: sales@escortradar.com, Web Site: www.escortradar.com (16)

Schmidt, Liz, Cosco Industries Inc, Chicago, IL. Tel: (708) 867-5800, (800) 323-0253, FAX: (800) 323-0275 (16)

Schmidt, Nathan, Communication Industries Corp, Grafton, VT. Tel: (802) 869-6500, FAX: (802) 869-6565, E-Mail: info@cicmail.com, Web Site: www.careersatcic.com (10)

Schmidt, Stephanie, G., Direct Success Communications Inc, Chester Springs, PA. Tel: (610) 321-0321, FAX: (610) 321-0322 (35)

Schmidt, Steven A., Renaissance Learning, Wisconsin Rapids, WI. Tel: (715) 424-3636, (800) 338-4204, FAX: (715) 424-4242, E-Mail: answers@renlearn.com, Web Site: www.renlearn.com (5)

Schmidt, Byron, MN. Tel: (507) 775-6400, FAX: (507) 775-6655, Web Site: www.schmidt.com (27)

The Schmidt Group International Inc, Vero Beach, FL. Tel: (772) 492-0073, FAX: (772) 492-0293, E-Mail: catalogprofit@att.net, Web Site: www.the-schmidt-group.com (20)

Schmidtke, John, Allstate Motor Club, Inc, Deerfield, IL. Tel: (847) 914-2972, FAX: (847) 914-2804, Web Site: www.walgreens.com (7)

Schmitt, Geri, Rapids Wholesale Equipment, Marion, IA. Tel: (319) 447-1670, (800) 472-7431, FAX: (319) 447-1680, (800) 858-0327, E-Mail: judys@rapidswholesale.com, Web Site: www.rapidswholesale.com (16)

Schmitt, Jeff, L., WS Live LLC, Dubuque, IA. Tel: (563) 582-9501, (800) 582-9501, FAX: (563) 582-2003, Web Site: www.wslive.com (29)

Schmitt, Jeff, Porter's Camera Store Inc, Cedar Falls, IA. Tel: (319) 266-0303, (800) 553-2001, FAX: (800) 221-5329, E-Mail: bcondra@porters.com, Web Site: www.porters.com (3)

Schmitt, Joe, Rapids Wholesale Equipment, Marion, IA. Tel: (319) 447-1670, (800) 472-7431, FAX: (319) 447-1680, (800) 858-0327, E-Mail: judys@rapidswholesale.com, Web Site: www.rapidswholesale.com (16)

Schmookler, Alexis, Wordright Enterprises Inc, Buffalo Grove, IL. Tel: (847) 215-5190, Web Site: www.globalsources.com (17)

Schmultz, Edward, FAO Schwarz, New York, NY. Tel: (212) 644-9400, (800) 426-TOYS, FAX: (212) 688-6053, Web Site: www.fao.com (11)

Schnabel Jr, Robert R., Fitness Quest, Canton, OH. Tel: (330) 478-0755, (800) 321-9236, FAX: (330) 479-9213, E-Mail: customersupport@fitnessquest.com, Web Site: www.fitnessquest.com (16)

Schneider, Amy, Tableau Software, Seattle, WA. Tel: (206) 633-3400, Web Site: www.tableausoftware.com (22)

Schneider, Dennis, Bobcat Co, West Fargo, ND. Tel: (701) 241-8700, FAX: (701) 241-8704, Web Site: www.bobcat.com (16)

Schneider, Donald, Schneider Saddlery, Chagrin Falls, OH. Tel: (440) 543-2700, (800) 365-1311, FAX: (440) 543-2710, Web Site: www.sstack.com (11)

Schneider, Ellen, Active Voice, San Francisco, CA. Tel: (415) 487-2000, FAX: (415) 487-2260, E-Mail: info@activevoice.net, Web Site: www.activevoice.net (21)

Schneider, Eric, Atlas Pen & Pencil Corp, Shelbyville, TN. Tel: (954) 920-4444, (800) 327-3232, FAX: (954) 920-8899, E-Mail: sales@atlaspen.com, Web Site: www.atlaspen.com (35)

Schneider, Joseph, P., LaCrosse Footwear Inc, Portland, OR. Tel: (503) 262-0110, (800) 323-2668, FAX: (503) 262-0115, E-Mail: customerservice@lacrossefootwear.com, Web Site: www.lacrossefootwear.com (16)

Schneider, Kathy, F&W Publications Inc, Blue Ash, OH. Tel: (513) 531-2690, FAX: (513) 531-0293, Web Site: www.fwpublications.com (17)

Schneider, Michael, A., Coast to Coast Inc, Englewood, CO. Tel: (303) 728-2267, Web Site: www.coastresorts.com (1)

Schneider, Michael, A., Golf Card International, Englewood, CO. Tel: (800) 321-8269, FAX: (303) 792-7332, Web Site: www.golfcard.com (1)

Schneider, Michael, Haymarket Group Ltd, New York, NY. Tel: (212) 239-0855, FAX: (212) 967-4184, Web Site: www.chocalatiermagazine.com (17)

Schneider, Mike, Affinity Group Inc, Ventura, CA. Tel: (805) 667-4100, (800) 765-1912, FAX: (805) 667-4419, E-Mail: khurd@affinitygroup.com, Web Site: www.affinitygroup.com (19)

Schneider, Norbert, The Fuller Brush Co, Great Bend, KS. Tel: (800) 522-0499, FAX: (620) 792-1906, E-Mail: info@fuller.com, Web Site: www.fuller.com (5)

Schneider, Paul, Warnaco Swimwear Inc, Los Angeles, CA. Tel: (323) 726-1262, FAX: (323) 724-6931, Web Site: www.speedo.com (16)

Schneider, Robert, The Candy Factory, Newport, KY. Tel: (859) 581-4663, FAX: (859) 581-1979 (4)

Schneider, Stan, Schneider Saddlery, Chagrin Falls, OH. Tel: (440) 543-2700, (800) 365-1311, FAX: (440) 543-2710, Web Site: www.sstack.com (11)

Schneider Saddlery, Chagrin Falls, OH. Tel: (440) 543-2700, (800) 365-1311, FAX: (440) 543-2710, Web Site: www.sstack.com (11)

Schneiderman, Larry, Corinthian Direct, New York, NY. Tel: (212) 279-5700, FAX: (212) 239-1772, E-Mail: jonz@mediabuying.com, Web Site: www.mediabuying.com (35)

Schneweiss, Victor, Bear Woods Supply Co Inc, Cornwallis, NS Canada. Tel: (902) 638-8622, (800) 565-5066, FAX: (902) 638-8637, Web Site: www.bearwood.com, www.woodparts.ca (11)

Schnuck, Scott, C., Schnuck Markets Inc, Saint Louis, MO. Tel: (314) 994-9900, FAX: (314) 994-4465, Web Site: www.schnucks.com (16)

Schnuck, Todd, Schnuck Markets Inc, Saint Louis, MO. Tel: (314) 994-9900, FAX: (314) 994-4465, Web Site: www.schnucks.com (16)

Schnuck Markets Inc, Saint Louis, MO. Tel: (314) 994-9900, FAX: (314) 994-4465, Web Site: www.schnucks.com (16)

Schnurbusch, Jim, The Hughes Group Inc, Saint Louis, MO. Tel: (314) 571-6300, FAX: (314) 862-1616, E-Mail: jschnurbusch@hughes-stl.com, Web Site: www.hughesgroup.com (35)

Schobel, Jeffrey, Professional Mailing Services Inc, Springfield, NJ. Tel: (973) 376-0607, (800) 238-1316, FAX: (973) 376-0949, E-Mail: jschobel@profmail.com, Web Site: www.profmail.com (28)

Schoedler, Michael, W., Tel Look-Up Service Co, Jamison, PA. Tel: (215) 321-0706, (800) 366-0706, FAX: (215) 321-3229, E-Mail: computer@telephonelookup.com, Web Site: www.telephonelookup.com (22)

Schoeler, Larry, Unicover Corp, Cheyenne, WY. Tel: (307) 771-3000, (800) 443-3232, FAX: (307) 771-3134, E-Mail: qands@unicover.com, Web Site: www.unicover.com (6)

Schoemann, Jerry, MKS Marketing Inc, Austin, TX. Tel: (512) 263-8017, (800) 544-8989, FAX: (402) 333-9610, E-Mail: info@telemarketingoutsource.com, Web Site: www.telemarketingoutsource.com (29)

Schoenberg, Patricia, Spectra Merchandising International Inc, Chicago, IL. Tel: (773) 202-8408, FAX: (773) 202-8409 (16)

Schoener, Lucy, Gale Research Inc, Farmington Hills, MI. Tel: (248) 699-4253, (800) 877-GALE, FAX: (313) 961-6083, Web Site: www.gale.com (17)

Schoenfield, Steven, A., The Northern Trust Co, Chicago, IL. Tel: (312) 630-6000, (888) 289-6542, FAX: (312) 630-1512, Web Site: www.ntrs.com (14)

Schoewe, Thomas, M., Wal Mart Stores, Bentonville, AR. Tel: (479) 273-4000, (800) 925-6278, FAX: (479) 277-1830, Web Site: www.walmart.com (16)

Schofer, Connie, Media Management Services Inc, Newton, PA. Tel: (215) 579-8590, (800) 523-5948, FAX: (215) 579-8589, Web Site: www. mmseducation.com (20)

Schofield Broadbent, Keith, Eric Mower & Associates, Rochester, NY. Tel: (585) 385-2000, Web Site: www.mower.com (35)

The Scholar's Bookshelf, Princeton, NJ. Tel: (609) 395-6933, FAX: (609) 395-0755, E-Mail: books@ scholarsbookshelf.com, Web Site: www. scholarsbookshelf.com (5)

Scholastic Direct Mktg, Danbury, CT. Tel: (203) 797-3500, FAX: (203) 797-3667 (29)

Scholastic Inc, New York, NY. Tel: (212) 343-6100, (800) SCHOLASTIC, FAX: (212) 343-6484, Web Site: www.scholastic.com/ (17)

Scholem, Nancy, Leadership Directories Inc, New York, NY. Tel: (212) 627-4140, FAX: (212) 645-0931, E-Mail: info@leadershipdirectories.com, Web Site: www.leadershipdirectories.com (17)

Scholes, David, Targetbase, Irving, TX. Tel: (972) 506-3400, (800) 446-6603, FAX: (972) 506-3505, E-Mail: info@targetbase.com, Web Site: www. targetbase.com (35)

Scholl, Richard J., The Scholl Group, Bryn Mawr, PA. Tel: (610) 527-7310, FAX: (610) 527-7323, E-Mail: schman1034@aol.com (35)

The Scholl Group, Bryn Mawr, PA. Tel: (610) 527-7310, FAX: (610) 527-7323, E-Mail: schman1034@aol.com (35)

School of Business & Economics, Los Angeles, CA. Tel: (323) 343-2800, FAX: (323) 343-2813, Web Site: cbe.calstatela.edu (41)

Scholtens, Jim, MISSCO Corp, Flowood, MS. Tel: (601) 948-8600, (800) 647-5333, FAX: (601) 987-3038 (16)

Schonberger Jr., M., Adams Manufacturing Co, Cleveland, OH. Tel: (216) 587-6801, FAX: (216) 587-6807, E-Mail: adamsx@att.net, Web Site: www. adamsmanufacturing.com (9)

Schonberger Sr., Marty, Adams Manufacturing Co, Cleveland, OH. Tel: (216) 587-6801, FAX: (216) 587-6807, E-Mail: adamsx@att.net, Web Site: www.adamsmanufacturing.com (9)

Schonberger, Ruth, Adams Manufacturing Co, Cleveland, OH. Tel: (216) 587-6801, FAX: (216) 587-6807, E-Mail: adamsx@att.net, Web Site: www. adamsmanufacturing.com (9)

Schonwald, Barbara, Conrad Direct Inc, Cresskill, NJ. Tel: (201) 567-3200, FAX: (201) 567-1530, Web Site: www.conraddirect.com (23)

Schonwald, Barbara, Direct Mail Strategy Group (DMSG), Cresskill, NJ. Tel: (201) 567-3200, FAX: (201) 567-1530, E-Mail: bschonwald@ conraddirect.com, Web Site: www.conraddirect. com (31)

Schooefield, Gail, Photri Images LLC, Fairfax, VA. Tel: (703) 978-0129, E-Mail: info@photriimages. com, Web Site: www.photriimages.com (38)

School Annual Publishing Co, State College, PA. Tel: (800) 436-6030, E-Mail: yearbook@schoolannual. com, Web Site: www.schoolannual.com (17)

School Market Research Institute Inc, Haddam, CT. Tel: (860) 345-8183, (800) 838-3444, FAX: (860) 345-3985, E-Mail: info@smriinc.com, Web Site: www.smriinc.com (35)

School of Business Administration, Portland, OR. Tel: (503) 725-3712, FAX: (503) 725-5850, E-Mail: info@sba.pdx.edu, Web Site: www.sba.pdx.edu (41)

School of Management, Old Westbury, NY. Tel: (516) 686-1000, (800) 345-NYIT, (800) 345-6948, Web Site: www.nyit.edu (41)

School of Management, The University of Texas at Dallas, Richardson, TX. Tel: (972) 883-4421, Web Site: www.utdallas.edu (1)

School Specialty Inc, Greenville, WI. Tel: (920) 734-5712, (888) 388-3224, FAX: (920) 734-5112, E-Mail: info@schoolspecialty.com, Web Site: www.schoolspecialty.com (16)

Schoolcraft College, Livonia, MI. Tel: (734) 462-4417, Web Site: www.schoolcraft.edu (1)

Schooley, Debbie, Creative Health Products, Plymouth, MI. Tel: (734) 996-5900, (800) 742-4478, FAX: (734) 996-4650, Web Site: www.chponline. com (16)

Schoolwise Press, San Francisco, CA. Tel: (415) 337-7971, (800) 247-8443 x 202, FAX: (415) 337-1146, E-Mail: info@schoolwisepress.com, Web Site: www.schoolwisepress.com (17)

Schopfer, Harriet, Gelderman Group Inc, Brookfield, CT. Tel: (203) 740-9000, FAX: (203) 702-7096, E-Mail: geldermangroup@earthlink.net (23)

Schorsch, Louis, ArcelorMittal, Chicago, IL. Tel: (312) 899-3440, FAX: (312) 899-3504, Web Site: www.mittalsteel.com (16)

Schoustal, Walter, Microvideo Learning Systems, Inc, New York, NY. Tel: (403) 233-9411, (800) 231-4021, FAX: (800) 879-6857, E-Mail: info@ microvideo.com, Web Site: www.microvideo.com (3)

Schramm, Joseph, F., Schramm & Associates Inc, Washington, DC. Tel: (202) 466-0555, FAX: (202) 466-0541, E-Mail: schramm@schrammadvertising. com, Web Site: www.schrammadvertising.com (35)

Schramm & Associates Inc, Washington, DC. Tel: (202) 466-0555, FAX: (202) 466-0541, E-Mail: schramm@schrammadvertising.com, Web Site: www.schrammadvertising.com (35)

Schreck, Brad S., E-Z-EM Inc, Melville, NY. Tel: (516) 333-8230, (800) 544-4624, FAX: (516) 333-8278, E-Mail: webmaster@ezem.com, Web Site: www.ezem.com (7)

Schreffler, Wendy, Feed the Children, Oklahoma City, OK. Tel: (800) 627-4556, Web Site: www. feedthechildren.org (1)

Schreibman, Cindy, Essence Communications Inc, New York, NY. Tel: (212) 522-1212, FAX: (212) 921-5173, Web Site: www.essence.com (17)

Schreibman, David, US Foodservice, Rosemont, IL. Tel: (410) 312-7100, FAX: (410) 312-7167, Web Site: www.usfoodservice.com (4)

Schreier, Bradley, J., Taylor Corp, North Mankato, MN. Tel: (507) 625-2828, FAX: (507) 625-3388 (16)

Schreurs, Mike, Strategic America, West Des Moines, IA. Tel: (515) 453-2000, (888) 898-6400, FAX: (515) 224-4181, Web Site: www.strategicamerica. com (35)

Schrier, Jack, The Copy Shoppe, Mendham, NJ. Tel: (973) 543-2679, FAX: (973) 543-2679, E-Mail: catalogistics@juno.com, Web Site: www. catalogistics.com (39)

Schriver, John, Viahealth, Rochester, NY. Tel: (585) 922-4000, (585) 922-3677, FAX: (585) 922-3929, Web Site: www.viahealth.org (16)

Schroeder Jr., Bill, Collector Books & American Quilters Society, Paducah, KY. Tel: (270) 898-6211, (800) 626-5420, FAX: (270) 898-8890, E-Mail: info@collectorbooks.com, Web Site: www. collectorbooks.com (17)

Schroeder, Barbara, Children's Hospital Foundation, Washington, DC. Tel: (202) 476-3000, (800) 884-LIFE, FAX: (202) 884-5999, Web Site: www. dcchildrens.com (1)

Schroeder, Meredith, Collector Books & American Quilters Society, Paducah, KY. Tel: (270) 898-6211, (800) 626-5420, FAX: (270) 898-8890, E-Mail: info@collectorbooks.com, Web Site: www. collectorbooks.com (17)

Schroer, William, J., W J Schroer Co, Battle Creek, MI. Tel: (269) 963-4874, FAX: (269) 963-5930, E-Mail: info@socialmarketing.org, Web Site: www.socialmarketing.org (30)

W J Schroer Co, Battle Creek, MI. Tel: (269) 963-4874, FAX: (269) 963-5930, E-Mail: info@ socialmarketing.org, Web Site: www. socialmarketing.org (30)

Schubart, Bill, Resolution Inc, Williston, VT. Tel: (802) 862-8881, (800) 862-8900, FAX: (802) 865-2308, E-Mail: schubart@resodirect.com, Web Site: www.resodirect.com (32)

Schuetz, Bill, Gale Research Inc, Farmington Hills, MI. Tel: (248) 699-4253, (800) 877-GALE, FAX: (313) 961-6083, Web Site: www.gale.com (17)

Schuetz, Mary, Groza, Dover Publications Inc, Mineola, NY. Tel: (516) 294-7000, (800) 223-3130, FAX: (516) 873-1401, Web Site: www. doverpublications.com (17)

Schufelt, John, PMH/Caramanning, Farmington Hills, MI. Tel: (248) 488-5300, FAX: (248) 488-5363, E-Mail: marketing@pmh.com, Web Site: www. pmh.com (35)

Schuh, C., Scott, LSC Marketing, Little Rock, AR. Tel: (501) 374-2332, (866) LSC-MKGT, FAX: (501) 372-6570, Web Site: www.lscmarketing.com (28)

Schuh, Dale, Sentry Life Insurance Co, Stevens Point, WI. Tel: (715) 346-6000, FAX: (715) 346-7028, E-Mail: infoctr@coredcs.com, Web Site: www. sentry.com (15)

Schuh, Mary, P., Northern Kentucky University, Highland Heights, KY. Tel: (859) 572-5220, (800) 637-9948, FAX: (859) 572-6177, Web Site: www.nku. edu (41)

Schulhof, Tom, Quadriga Art Inc, New York, NY. Tel: (212) 685-0751 (10)

Schulman, John, Frederick's of Hollywood Group Inc, Los Angeles, CA. Tel: (323) 466-5151, (800) 323-9525, FAX: (323) 464-5149, Web Site: www. fredericks.com (2)

Schulte, J., Midcontinent Financial Center Inc, Columbia, MO. Tel: (573) 443-6002, Web Site: www. americanmutualloans.com (14)

Schulte, Jennifer, AdPlex, Houston, TX. Tel: (281) 821-5522, Web Site: www.adplex.com (35)

Schulte, John D., National Mail Order Association (NMOA), Minneapolis, MN. Tel: (612) 788-1673, E-Mail: info@nmoa.org, Web Site: www.nmoa.org (40)

Schulte, John D., Schulte Associates, Minneapolis, MN. Tel: (612) 788-1673, FAX: (612) 788-1147, E-Mail: schulte@nmoa.org, Web Site: www.nmoa. org/schulte (20)

Schulte, John, Direct Marketing Digest, Minneapolis, MN. Tel: (612) 788-1673, E-Mail: info@nmoa.org, Web Site: www.nmoa.org (43)

Schulte, John, Direct Marketing Tool Kit for Small Business, Minneapolis, MN. Tel: (612) 788-1673, E-Mail: info@nmoa.org, Web Site: www.nmoa.org/ directmarketingtoolkit (43)

Schulte, John, Directory of Mail Order Catalogs, Minneapolis, MN. Tel: (612) 788-1673, E-Mail: info@ nmoa.org, Web Site: www.nmoa.org (43)

Schulte Associates, Minneapolis, MN. Tel: (612) 788-1673, FAX: (612) 788-1147, E-Mail: schulte@ nmoa.org, Web Site: www.nmoa.org/schulte (20)

Schultheis, Jack, KZS Advertising, Smithtown, NY. Tel: (651) 348-1440, FAX: (631) 348-1449, Web Site: www.kzsadvertising.com (35)

Schultz II, J.J., DaimlerChrysler Corp, Auburn Hills, MI. Tel: (248) 512-1879, Web Site: www. daimlerchrysler.com (12)

Schultz, Howard, D., Starbucks Corp, Seattle, WA. Tel: (206) 447-1575, (800) 344-1575, FAX: (206) 447-0828, Web Site: www.starbucks.com (4)

Schultz, James, R., Great Lakes Integrated, Cleveland, OH. Tel: (216) 651-1500, (800) 745-4846, FAX: (216) 651-8311, E-Mail: bbemer@glintergrated. com, Web Site: www.gll.com (27)

Schultz, Joey, AT&T Inc, San Antonio, TX. Tel: (210) 821-4105, FAX: (210) 351-2071, Web Site: www. bellsouth.com (32)

Schultz, Jonathan, D., Concordia Publishing House, Saint Louis, MO. Tel: (314) 268-1000, (800) 325-3040, FAX: (314) 268-1329, E-Mail: order@cph.org, Web Site: www.cph.org (17)

Schultz, L. Scott, Schultz & Williams Inc, Philadelphia, PA. Tel: (215) 625-9955, FAX: (215) 625-2701, E-Mail: mail@schultzwilliams.com, Web Site: www.sw-inc.com (1)

Schultz, Ray, Direct Magazine, New York, NY. Tel: (212) 204-4228, FAX: (212) 683-3986 (43)

Schultz, Rita, 21st Century Marketing, Hauppauge, NY. Tel: (631) 293-8550, FAX: (631) 293-8974, E-Mail: info@21stcm.com, Web Site: www.21stcm.com (24)

Schultz, Steven A., Protective Life Insurance Co, Birmingham, AL. Tel: (205) 268-1000, (800) 866-3555, FAX: (205) 868-3086, Web Site: www.protective.com (15)

Schultz, Trish, Uline, Pleasant Prairie, WI. Tel: (847) 473-3000, FAX: (800) 295-5571, E-Mail: ulinecs@uline.com, Web Site: www.uline.com (5)

Schultz & Williams Inc, Philadelphia, PA. Tel: (215) 625-9955, FAX: (215) 625-2701, E-Mail: mail@schultzwilliams.com, Web Site: www.sw-inc.com (1)

Schulz, Jean, Canine Companions for Independence, Santa Rosa, CA Canada. Tel: (707) 577-1700, (800) 572-2275, FAX: (707) 577-1711, E-Mail: info@cci.org, Web Site: www.caninecompanions.org (16)

Schulze, Cornelia, Thieme Medical Publishers Inc, New York, NY. Tel: (212) 760-0888, (800) 782-3488, FAX: (212) 947-1112, E-Mail: info@thieme.com, Web Site: www.thieme.com (17)

Schulze, Mark, New & Unique Videos, San Diego, CA. Tel: (619) 644-3001, (619) 644-3000, E-Mail: info@newuniquevideos.com, Web Site: www.newuniquevideos.com (3)

Schupak, Donald, Schupak Group Inc, New York, NY. Tel: (212) 582-4210 (20)

Schupak Group Inc, New York, NY. Tel: (212) 582-4210 (20)

Schuppert, Jay, Cuvaison Inc, Calistoga, CA. Tel: (707) 942-6266, FAX: (707) 942-5732, E-Mail: jschuppert@cuvaison.com, Web Site: www.cuvaison.com (4)

Schure, Teri, World Press Review, New York, NY. Tel: (212) 982-8880, Web Site: www.worldpressreview.com (18)

Schurmann, Karen, Osmonics Inc, Minnetonka, MN. Tel: (952) 264-3937, (800) 605-6698, FAX: (952) 536-3301, Web Site: www.osmonics.com (16)

Schus, Stephanie, Schus & Co, Glendale, CA. Tel: (818) 550-8100, E-Mail: sschus@aol.com (20)

Schus & Co, Glendale, CA. Tel: (818) 550-8100, E-Mail: sschus@aol.com (20)

Schuster, Mike, Nancy's Notions LLC, Beaver Dam, WI. Tel: (920) 887-0391, (800) 833-0690, FAX: (800) 255-8119, E-Mail: comments@nancysnotions.com, Web Site: www.nancysnotions.com (11)

Schuster, Pauline, Imperial Supplies, Green Bay, WI. Tel: (920) 494-5403, (800) 558-2808, FAX: (800) 553-8769, Web Site: www.imperialsupplies.com (16)

Schuyler, Henry, MarCom Technologies, Kelowna, BC Canada. Tel: (250) 868-9352, FAX: (250) 868-9362 (29)

Schwab, Richard, Carson Pirie Scott & Co, Milwaukee, WI. Tel: (414) 347-1152, FAX: (414) 278-5748 (16)

Schwab, Tom, Short Sizes Inc, Northfield, OH. Tel: (440) 605-1000, (800) 272-9000, FAX: (440) 605-1065, E-Mail: orders@shortsizesinc.com, Web Site: www.shortsizesinc.com (2)

Charles Schwab & Co Inc, San Francisco, CA. Tel: (415) 627-7000, (800) 648-5300, FAX: (415) 421-0810, Web Site: www.schwab.com (14)

Schwandt, Kandy, Sunrise Greetings, Bloomington, IN. Tel: (812) 336-4045, (800) 457-4045, FAX: (812) 336-8712, E-Mail: info@interart.com, Web Site: www.interartdistribution.com (17)

Schwan's Home Service Inc, Marshall, MN. Tel: (507) 532-3274 (5)

Schwarcz, Ronald, Indus-Tool, Chicago, IL. Tel: (312) 226-2473, (800) 662-5021, FAX: (312) 226-2480, E-Mail: sales@indus-tool.com, Web Site: www.indus-tool.com (12)

Schwartz, Adam, S&S Worldwide, Colchester, CT. Tel: (860) 537-3451, (800) 288-9941, FAX: (860) 537-2866, E-Mail: cservice@ssww.com, Web Site: www.ssww.com (11)

Schwartz, David, Infomercial Solutions Inc, Agoura Hills, CA. Tel: (818) 879-1140, FAX: (818) 879-1148, E-Mail: david@infomercialsolutions.com, Web Site: www.infomercialsolutions.com (32)

Schwartz, David, O., 21st Century Marketing, Hauppauge, NY. Tel: (631) 293-8550, FAX: (631) 293-8974, E-Mail: info@21stcm.com, Web Site: www.21stcm.com (24)

Schwartz, Dean, A., SunPorch Structures Inc, Westport, CT. Tel: (203) 454-0040, (866) 919-9620, FAX: (203) 454-0020, E-Mail: leo@sunporch.com, Web Site: www.sunporch.com (8)

Schwartz, Donald A., Recognition Products International, Easton, MD. Tel: (410) 820-0022, (800) 292-7354, FAX: (410) 820-5044, E-Mail: info@recognitionproducts.com, Web Site: www.shoprecognitionproducts.com (16)

Schwartz, Hy, S&S Worldwide, Colchester, CT. Tel: (860) 537-3451, (800) 288-9941, FAX: (860) 537-2866, E-Mail: cservice@ssww.com, Web Site: www.ssww.com (11)

Schwartz, J., Blackstone Lists, Fort Lauderdale, FL. Tel: (954) 568-6411 (23)

Schwartz, Jeff, William W Schwartz Associates Inc, Sheboygan, WI. Tel: (920) 458-4661, FAX: (920) 458-6297, E-Mail: wws1503@excel.net, Web Site: www.wschwartz.com (33)

Schwartz, Jeffrey, Artrinsic Inc, New York, NY. Tel: (212) 716-1977 X201, Web Site: www.atrinsic.com (20)

Schwartz, Jim, A-KD Mailing & Fulfillment Service, Lincolnwood, IL. Tel: (847) 673-0186, (866) 330-6245, FAX: (874) 673-0188, E-Mail: dan@kdmailing.com, Web Site: www.kdmailing.com (28)

Schwartz, John, Business Objects, Palo Alto, CA. Tel: (408) 933-6000, (888) 788-9004, Web Site: www.businessobjects.com (22)

Schwartz, Kathy, Interex, Amesbury, MA. Tel: (978) 388-8755, (800) INTEREX, FAX: (978) 388-8747, Web Site: www.interexexhibits.com (17)

Schwartz, Larry, Checks by Phone/Checks by Web, Boynton Beach, FL. Tel: (561) 737-8700, FAX: (561) 737-5800, E-Mail: LarrySchwartz@checksbyphone.com, Web Site: www.checksbyphone.com (14)

Schwartz, Larry, Fraud & Theft Information Bureau, Boynton Beach, FL. Tel: (561) 737-8700, FAX: (561) 737-5800, E-Mail: sales@fraudandtheft.com, Web Site: www.fraudandtheftinfo.com (43)

Schwartz, Larry, Schwartz & Co, Verona, NJ. Tel: (973) 571-2160, (800) 526-1440, FAX: (973) 571-2165, E-Mail: swartzandcompany@gmail.com, Web Site: www.natschwartz.com (6)

Schwartz, Lisa, ICIS Inc, Upper Black Eddy, PA. Tel: (610) 982-0429, E-Mail: icis@ptdprolog.net, Web Site: www.icisjewelry.com (2)

Schwartz, Marc, Novartis Pharmaceuticals Corp, East Hanover, NJ. Tel: (862) 778-6914, FAX: (973) 781-8119, Web Site: www.pharma.us.novartis.com (7)

Schwartz, Marilyn, Schwartz & Co, Verona, NJ. Tel: (973) 571-2160, (800) 526-1440, FAX: (973) 571-2165, E-Mail: swartzandcompany@gmail.com, Web Site: www.natschwartz.com (6)

Schwartz, Michael, Babyshoe.com, Hendersonville, NC. Tel: (828) 697-5811, (800) 543-8566, FAX: (828) 697-5815, E-Mail: info@babyshoe.com, Web Site: www.babyshoe.com (6)

Schwartz, Ronald, B., R&S Industries Corp, Chesterfield, MO. Tel: (314) 781-5400, FAX: (314) 781-5169, E-Mail: sendeverything@miraclepolishingcloth.com, Web Site: www.miraclepolishingcloth.com (16)

Schwartz, Rose, Schwartz & Co, Verona, NJ. Tel: (973) 571-2160, (800) 526-1440, FAX: (973) 571-2165, E-Mail: swartzandcompany@gmail.com, Web Site: www.natschwartz.com (6)

Schwartz, Steve, Lion Apparel, Dayton, OH. Tel: (937) 898-1949, (800) 548-6614, FAX: (937) 913-5667, Web Site: www.lionapparel.com (2)

Schwartz, Steven, A., Your Move Chess & Games, North Massapequa, NY. Tel: (516) 882-9800, (800) 645-4710, FAX: (631) 424-3405, E-Mail: icd@icdchess.com, Web Site: www.icdchess.com (11)

Schwartz, Steven, Intersections, Chantilly, VA. Tel: (703) 488-6100, Web Site: www.charteredmarketing.com (14)

Schwartz, Susan, Agate Publishing, Evanston, IL. Tel: (847) 475-4457, (800) 326-4430, FAX: (312) 751-7334, Web Site: www.surreybooks.com (17)

Schwartz, Tyler Schwartz, Schwartz & Associates Creative, Clayton, MO. Tel: (314) 531-6810, FAX: (314) 531-1448, E-Mail: info@sacreative.com, Web Site: www.sacreative.com (32)

Schwartz, William, J., Schwartz & Associates Creative, Clayton, MO. Tel: (314) 531-6810, FAX: (314) 531-1448, E-Mail: info@sacreative.com, Web Site: www.sacreative.com (32)

Schwartz & Associates Creative, Clayton, MO. Tel: (314) 531-6810, FAX: (314) 531-1448, E-Mail: info@sacreative.com, Web Site: www.sacreative.com (32)

Schwartz & Co, Verona, NJ. Tel: (973) 571-2160, (800) 526-1440, FAX: (973) 571-2165, E-Mail: swartzandcompany@gmail.com, Web Site: www.natschwartz.com (6)

William W Schwartz Associates Inc, Sheboygan, WI. Tel: (920) 458-4661, FAX: (920) 458-6297, E-Mail: wws1503@excel.net, Web Site: www.wschwartz.com (33)

Schwartzman, Michael, Lea & Perrins Inc, Fair Lawn, NJ. Tel: (201) 791-1600, FAX: (201) 791-8945, Web Site: www.leaperrins.com (16)

Schwarz, Robert, Peter Pan Bus Lines Inc, Springfield, MA. Tel: (413) 781-2900, (800) 343-9999, FAX: (413) 746-8671, E-Mail: info@peterpanbus.com, Web Site: www.peterpanbus.com (19)

Schwedelson, Jay, Worldata, Boca Raton, FL. Tel: (561) 393-8200, (800) 331-8102, FAX: (561) 368-8345, E-Mail: mail@worldata.com, Web Site: www.worldata.com (23)

Schwedock, Eric, Economy Handicrafts, Brooklyn, NY. Tel: (718) 431-9300, (800) 216-1601, FAX: (718) 431-9309, Web Site: www.vanguardcrafts.com (16)

Schweinhart, Larry, HighScope Educational Research Foundation, Ypsilanti, MI. Tel: (734) 485-2000, (800) 40-PRESS, FAX: (734) 485-0704, E-Mail: lschweinhart@highscope.org, Web Site: www.highscope.org (17)

Schweitzer, William, H., Baker & Hostetler LLP, Washington, DC. Tel: (202) 861-1500, FAX: (202) 861-1783, E-Mail: wschweitzer@bakerlaw.com, Web Site: www.bakerlaw.com (20)

Schwerin, Abby, Nostrum Inc, Long Beach, CA. Tel: (562) 437-2200, Web Site: www.nostruminc.com (35)

Schwind, Courtney, Expedia Inc, Bellevue, WA. Tel: (425) 679-7200, Web Site: www.expedia.com (19)

Schwing, Rob, Char-Broil, Columbus, GA. Tel: (706) 571-7000, Web Site: www.charbroil.com (16)

Schwisow, Jay, CPI Card Group, Littleton, CO. Tel: (303) 973-9311, FAX: (303) 973-8420, E-Mail: mbarber@cpicardgroup.com, Web Site: www.cpicardgroup.com (27)

Schwitsky, Ed, Coastal Hotel Group, Seattle, WA. Tel: (206) 388-0400, FAX: (206) 388-0401, E-Mail: info@coastalhotel.com, Web Site: www.coastalhotels.com (1)

Schwotka, Alex, VistaPrint USA Inc, Lexington, MA. Tel: (800) 961-2075, Web Site: www.vistaprint.com (27)

Sci-Fi Channel, New York, NY. Tel: (212) 413-5000, FAX: (212) 413-6509, Web Site: www.scifi.com (32)

Scialfa, Chris, Carl Fischer Music, New York, NY. Tel: (212) 777-0900, (800) 762-2328, FAX: (212) 477-6996, E-Mail: cf-info@carlfischer.com, Web Site: www.carlfischer.com (17)

Scialfa, Chris, Music Sales Corp, New York, NY. Tel: (212) 254-2100, (800) 431-7187, FAX: (212) 254-2013, E-Mail: info@musicsales.com, Web Site: www.musicsales.com (17)

Sciame Jr., Frank, J., New York Landmarks Conservancy, New York, NY. Tel: (212) 995-5260, FAX: (212) 995-5268, Web Site: www.nylandmarks.org (1)

Sciarrotta, Art, Chain Store Guide, Tampa, FL. Tel: (800) 927-9292, FAX: (813) 627-6882, E-Mail: info@csgis.com, Web Site: www.csgis.com (17)

SCICOM Data Services Ltd, Minnetonka, MN. Tel: (952) 933-4200, (800) 488-9087, FAX: (952) 936-4132, Web Site: www.scicom.com (22)

Scientific Computing Associates, Villa Park, IL. Tel: (630) 834-8512, Web Site: www.scausa.com (22)

Scientific Games Canada, Montreal, PQ Canada. Tel: (514) 254-3000, FAX: (514) 254-1411, Web Site: www.scientificgames.com (27)

Scientific Marketing Services Inc, Landisville, NJ. Tel: (856) 697-1257, FAX: (856) 697-9639, E-Mail: info@smsmktg.com, Web Site: www.smsmktg.com (35)

Scime, Joe, Conney Safety Products LLC, Madison, WI. Tel: (608) 271-3300, (800) 356-9100, FAX: (608) 271-3322, (800) 845-9095, E-Mail: safety@conney.com, Web Site: www.conney.com (7)

Scinta, Sam, Fulcrum Publishing, Golden, CO. Tel: (303) 277-1623, (800) 992-2908, FAX: (303) 279-7111, Web Site: www.fulcrum-books.com (17)

Sclaventis, Wanda, M., American Graphics Network Inc, Glenview, IL. Tel: (847) 729-7220, FAX: (847) 724-5080, E-Mail: info@agninc.com, Web Site: www.agninc.com (27)

Scobie, William, Mason Companies Inc, Chippewa Falls, WI. Tel: (715) 723-1871, (800) 826-7030, FAX: (715) 720-4247, Web Site: www.masoncompaniesinc.com (2)

Scoby, Gloria, Advertising Age, New York, NY. Tel: (212) 210-0100, FAX: (212) 210-0111, Web Site: www.crain.com (43)

Scoggin, Patrick, B., Savicom, San Francisco, CA. Tel: (415) 983-0990, FAX: (415) 445-9999, E-Mail: sales@savicom.net, Web Site: www.savicom.net (22)

Scolio, Richard, MarketerNet LLC, Chicago, IL. Tel: (312) 775-9320, (888) 443-3684, FAX: (312) 775-9328, E-Mail: info@marketernet.com, Web Site: www.marketernet.com (22)

Scolnik, Alvin, National Electrical Manufacturers Association (NEMA), Rosslyn, VA. Tel: (703) 841-3200, FAX: (703) 841-5900, E-Mail: communications@nema.org, Web Site: www.nema.org (34)

Scolpino, Janine, The Taunton Press, Newtown, CT. Tel: (203) 426-8171, (800) 477-8727, FAX: (203) 426-3434, Web Site: www.taunton.com (17)

Scoltock, Sarah, Windstar Cruises, Seattle, WA. Tel: (206) 292-9606, (800) 258-SAIL, FAX: (206) 340-0975, E-Mail: info@windstarcruises.com, Web Site: www.windstarcruises.com (19)

The Scooter Store, New Braunfels, TX. Tel: (830) 608-9200 (7)

Scope 1, Kalamazoo, MI. Tel: (269) 323-1333, Web Site: www.scope 1.com (16)

Scorecards USA, North Kingstown, RI. Tel: (401) 294-4049, (800) 553-4154, FAX: (401) 294-4076, E-Mail: sales@scorecardsusa.com, Web Site: www.scorecardsusa.com (16)

Scoringe, Tony, Windstar Cruises, Seattle, WA. Tel: (206) 292-9606, (800) 258-SAIL, FAX: (206) 340-0975, E-Mail: info@windstarcruises.com, Web Site: www.windstarcruises.com (19)

Scott III, Peter, M., Florida Power Corp, Saint Petersburg, FL. Tel: (727) 820-5151, (800) 700-8744, FAX: (727) 384-7865, Web Site: www.progressenergy.com (16)

Scott Jr., H., Lee, Wal Mart Stores, Bentonville, AR. Tel: (479) 273-4000, (800) 925-6278, FAX: (479) 277-1830, Web Site: www.walmart.com (16)

Scott Jr., Virgil, A., Fort Hays State University, Hays, KS. Tel: (785) 628-FHSU, FAX: (785) 628-4046, Web Site: www.fhsu.edu (41)

Scott, Amy, COMNET Washington, Framingham, MA. Tel: (508) 879-6700, FAX: (508) 370-4325, Web Site: www.comnetexpo.com (42)

Scott, C., Ryland, Scott Computing Systems, Atlanta, GA. Tel: (770) 432-7000, (800) 241-7576, FAX: (770) 432-7500, Web Site: www.rylandscott.com (22)

Scott, Daniel, T., Unz & Co, Middlesex, NJ. Tel: (732) 868-0706, (800) 631-3098, FAX: (732) 868-0260, E-Mail: unzco@unzco.com, Web Site: www.unzco.com (27)

Scott, David, Marketfish Inc, Seattle, WA. Tel: (206) 905-1090, FAX: (206) 694-2564, Web Site: www.marketfish.com (23)

Scott, Deirdre, Bronx Council on the Arts, Bronx, NY. Tel: (718) 931-9500, FAX: (718) 409-6445, E-Mail: info@bronxarts.org, Web Site: www.bronxarts.org (1)

Scott, Gary, Cascade Outfitters, Boise, ID. Tel: (208) 322-4411, (800) 223-7328, FAX: (208) 322-5016, E-Mail: mail@cascadeoutfitters.com, Web Site: www.cascadeoutfitters.com (11)

Scott, John, Toter Inc, Statesville, NC. Tel: (704) 872-8171, (800) 424-0422, FAX: (704) 878-0734, E-Mail: info@toter.com, Web Site: www.toter.com (16)

Scott, Julie, Rosicrucian Order AMORC, San Jose, CA. Tel: (408) 947-3600, FAX: (408) 947-3677, E-Mail: rosicrucian@amorcmail.org, Web Site: www.rosicrucian.org (1)

Scott, Lauren, P., Kilgannon, Atlanta, GA. Tel: (404) 876-2800, FAX: (404) 876-2830, E-Mail: contact@kilgannon.com, Web Site: www.kilgannon.com (35)

Scott, Michele, Ultimate Office, Farmingdale, NJ. Tel: (732) 780-6911, (800) 631-2233, FAX: (732) 780-9833, Web Site: www.ultoffice.com (16)

Scott, Nancy, Marketing Advents, Alexandria, VA. Tel: (703) 706-0387, FAX: (703) 836-2181, E-Mail: info@dmaw.org, Web Site: www.dmaw.org (43)

Scott, Pam, Clement Communications, Upper Chichester, PA. Tel: (610) 497-6800, (800) 253-6368, FAX: (610) 497-6806, E-Mail: customerservice@clement.com, Web Site: www.clement.com; www.bradycorp.com (17)

Scott, R., Jon, IBux, Chico, CA. Tel: (530) 895-0431 (23)

Scott, Richard, Edelmann Scott Inc, Richmond, VA. Tel: (804) 643-1931, FAX: (804) 643-1934, E-Mail: dickscott@edelmannscott.com, Web Site: www.edelmannscott.com (35)

Scott, Steven, Steve Scott Group LLC, Midvale, UT. Tel: (801) 277-8900, (800) 220-6481, FAX: (801) 277-8986, Web Site: www.totalgymdirect.com (32)

Scott, Timothy, Bass Pro Shops, Springfield, MO. Tel: (417) 873-5000, FAX: (417) 873-5882, Web Site: www.basspro.com (11)

Scott, W., E., National Audubon Society, New York, NY. Tel: (212) 979-3000, FAX: (212) 979-3188, Web Site: www.audubon.org (17)

Scott Computing Systems, Atlanta, GA. Tel: (770) 432-7000, (800) 241-7576, FAX: (770) 432-7500, Web Site: www.rylandscott.com (22)

Scott Publications, Inc, Muskegon, MI. Tel: (248) 477-6650, (800) 458-8237, FAX: (248) 477-6795, E-Mail: contactus@scottpublications.com, Web Site: www.scottpublications.com (17)

Scott Sign Systems Inc, Sarasota, FL. Tel: (941) 355-5171, (800) 237-9447, FAX: (941) 351-1787, E-Mail: mail@scottsigns.com, Web Site: www.scottsigns.com (16)

Scotti, Deborah, Arthritis Foundation, Atlanta, GA. Tel: (404) 872-7100, FAX: (404) 872-0457, Web Site: www.arthritis.org (1)

Scotti, Gavin, A., Klemtner Advertising Inc, New York, NY. Tel: (212) 463-3400, FAX: (212) 463-3541 (35)

Scotti, Marie, International Advertising Association, New York, NY. Tel: (212) 557-1133, FAX: (212) 983-0455, E-Mail: membership@iaaglobal.com, Web Site: www.iaaglobal.org (1)

Scotti, Phil, Body by Jake Global LLC, Los Angeles, CA. Tel: (310) 571-7101, FAX: (310) 571-7107, E-Mail: info@bodybyjake.com, Web Site: www.bodybyjake.com (16)

The Scotts Co Div of Lawn Service, Marysville, OH. Tel: (937) 644-0011, FAX: (937) 644-7261, Web Site: www.scotts.com (8)

Scott's Directories, Don Mills, ON Canada. Tel: (416) 442-2010, (800) 408-9431, FAX: (416) 442-2078, E-Mail: sales@scottsinfo.com, Web Site: www.scottsinfo.com (31)

Scott's Dog Supply Inc, Indianapolis, IN. Tel: (317) 222-5382, (800) 966-3647, FAX: (317) 298-7284, E-Mail: cmurphy154@aol.com, Web Site: www.scottsdog.com (11)

Scotts-Sierra Horticultural, Marysville, OH. Tel: (888) 270-3714, Web Site: www.scottscompany.com (16)

Scrim, David, Dotomi Inc, Chicago, IL. Tel: (312) 588-3600, Web Site: www.dotomi.com (32)

Scripps Networks, Knoxville, TN. Tel: (865) 560-2700, Web Site: scrippsnetworks.com (17)

Script to Screen Inc, Santa Ana, CA. Tel: (714) 558-3971, (800) 453-0003, FAX: (714) 558-1759, E-Mail: newbusiness@scripttoscreen.com, Web Site: www.scripttoscreen.com (32)

Scriven, Glen, Spalding Laboratories Inc, Arroyo Grande, CA. Tel: (805) 489-5946, (888) 880-1579, FAX: (866) 738-9632, Web Site: www.spalding-labs.com (7)

Scruton, Steve, Direxxis Inc, Needham, MA. Tel: (781) 444-7900, Web Site: www.direxxismarketing.com (22)

Scully, Robert, Morgan Stanley, New York, NY. Tel: (212) 761-4000, FAX: (212) 761-0096 (14)

Sculpture House Inc, Skillman, NJ. Tel: (609) 466-2986, FAX: (888) 529-1980, E-Mail: customercare@sculpturehouse.com, Web Site: www.sculpturehouse.com (16)

Sculptz, Feasterville Trevose, PA. Tel: (215) 494-2900, E-Mail: sdudek@sculptz.com, Web Site: www.silkies.com (2)

Scundi, Mary, Independent Consultant, Saint Paul, MN. Tel: (612) 239-6572 (20)

Scuoc, Casey, Iroquois Products, Chicago, IL. Tel: (773) 436-3900, (800) 453-3355, FAX: (773) 436-4908, E-Mail: sales@iroquoisproducts.com, Web Site: www.iroquoisproducts.com (10)

Sea Bear, Anacortes, WA. Tel: (360) 293-4661, (800) 645-3474, FAX: (888) 487-6427, Web Site: www.seabear.com (2)

Seabach, Karen, Shopsmith Inc, Dayton, OH. Tel: (937) 898-6070, (800) 543-7586, FAX: (937) 890-5197, Web Site: www.shopsmith.com (16)

Seager, Joann, DeVry Inc, Oakbrook Terrace, IL. Tel: (630) 571-7700, FAX: (602) 943-4108, Web Site: www.devry.com (16)

Seagle, Carole, Brooks Equipment Co, Charlotte, NC. Tel: (704) 596-9438, (800) 826-3473, FAX: (704) 596-1096, Web Site: www.brooksequipment.com (9)

Seal, Oney, Databazaar.com, Miramar, FL. Tel: (954) 843-0483, (888) 335-3282, FAX: (954) 843-0429, E-Mail: rudy@databazaar.com, Web Site: www.databazaar.com (10)

Sealed Air Corp, Elmwood Park, NJ. Tel: (201) 791-7600, FAX: (201) 712-7070, Web Site: www.sealedair.com (26)

Sealey Ph.D., Peter, The Sausalito Group, Sausalito, CA. Tel: (415) 332-3333, FAX: (415) 332-6571, Web Site: www.sausolitogroup.com (30)

Seaman, Donald, William Charles Printing, Plainview, NY. Tel: (516) 349-0900, Web Site: www.williamcharlesprinting.com (27)

Seaman, Glen, Chase Media Group, Yorktown Heights, NY. Tel: (914) 962-3871, FAX: (914) 962-2040, Web Site: www.chasemultimedia.com (27)

Searles, Michael M., Wilsons Leather, Brooklyn Park, MN. Tel: (763) 391-4000, (866) 305-4704, FAX: (763) 391-4906, Web Site: www.wilsonsleather.com (2)

Searles, Rey, Life Extension Foundation, Fort Lauderdale, FL. Tel: (954) 766-8433, (800) 678-8989, FAX: (954) 771-2827, E-Mail: info@lef.org, Web Site: www.lef.org (7)

Sears, Daniel, Harvard Business School - Executive Education, Boston, MA. Tel: (617) 496-2193, Web Site: www.exed.hbs.edu (1)

Sears, James M., James M. Sears Associates, Bergenfield, NJ. Tel: (201) 501-9977, FAX: (201) 453-0833 (30)

Sears Canada Inc, Toronto, ON Canada. Tel: (416) 362-1711, (888) 473-2772, FAX: (613) 391-3047, E-Mail: home@sears.ca, Web Site: www.sears.ca (5)

Sears Home Improvement Products Inc, Longwood, FL. Tel: (407) 767-0990, (877) 840-7126, FAX: (407) 831-1848, Web Site: www.searshomepro.com (16)

James M. Sears Associates, Bergenfield, NJ. Tel: (201) 501-9977, FAX: (201) 453-0833 (30)

Sears, Roebuck & Co, Hoffman Estates, IL. Tel: (847) 286-2500, FAX: (847) 286-7829, Web Site: www.sears.com (16)

Seashore Vacations, Hilton Head Island, SC. Tel: (843) 785-2191, (800) 845-0077, FAX: (843) 785-6450, E-Mail: seashorehhi@hargray.com, Web Site: www.seashorehhi.com (19)

Seaside Publications, Saint Simons Island, GA. Tel: (912) 634-9596, Web Site: www.southeastcoastalgeorgia.com (35)

Seastrom, Robert, A., Seastrom Manufacturing Co Inc, Twin Falls, ID. Tel: (208) 737-4300, (800) 634-2356, FAX: (208) 734-7222, E-Mail: info@seastrom-mfg.com, Web Site: www.seastrom-mfg.com (3)

Seastrom Manufacturing Co Inc, Twin Falls, ID. Tel: (208) 737-4300, (800) 634-2356, FAX: (208) 734-7222, E-Mail: info@seastrom-mfg.com, Web Site: www.seastrom-mfg.com (3)

Seattle Magazine, Seattle, WA. Tel: (206) 284-1750, (800) 637-0334, FAX: (206) 284-2550, E-Mail: customerservice@seattlemag.com, Web Site: www.seattlemag.com (17)

Seavers, Dean, S., Simplex Grinnell, Westminster, MA. Tel: (978) 731-2500, (800) SIMPLEX, FAX: (978) 731-7856, Web Site: www.simplexgrinnel.com (16)

Seavey, Ava, Avalanche Creative Services Inc, New York, NY. Tel: (212) 206-9335, FAX: (212) 206-1538, E-Mail: info@avalanchecreative.tv, Web Site: www.avalanchecreative.tv (35)

Seavy, Mark, Warren Communications News, Washington, DC. Tel: (202) 872-9200, (800) 771-9202, FAX: (202) 318-8350, E-Mail: info@warren-news.com, Web Site: www.warren-news.com (17)

Sebastian, Bob, JC Whitney, Chicago, IL. Tel: (312) 431-6000, FAX: (312) 431-5650, Web Site: www.jcwhitney.com (12)

Sebek, Ken, Universal Fidelity Corp, Houston, TX. Tel: (281) 550-1444, (800) 580-8887, FAX: (281) 647-4207, Web Site: www.ufccorp.com (14)

Seberg, Randy, Alaniz - a Dmh Marketing Partners Co, Mount Pleasant, IA. Tel: (319) 385-7259, FAX: (319) 385-2825, E-Mail: info@alanizdirect.com, Web Site: www.alanizdirect.com (28)

Seckler, Donald, New Jersey Monthly, Morristown, NJ. Tel: (973) 539-8230, FAX: (973) 538-2953, E-Mail: research@njmonthly.com, Web Site: www.njmonthly.com (17)

SECO Financial Services Inc, Mount Laurel, NJ. Tel: (856) 273-0050, (800) 898-SECO, FAX: (856) 273-9228, Web Site: www.secofinancial.com (23)

SECO-LARM USA Inc, Irvine, CA. Tel: (949) 261-2999, (800) 662-0800, FAX: (949) 261-7326, E-Mail: info@seco-larm.com, Web Site: www.seco-larm.com (16)

Second Renaissance Books, Irvine, CA. Tel: (860) 354-5448, (800) 729-6149, FAX: (860) 355-7161, Web Site: www.aynrandbookstore.com (17)

Secord, Greg, ADP Inc, Roseland, NJ. Tel: (973) 974-5000, (800) 225-5237, FAX: (973) 974-3334, Web Site: www.adp.com (16)

Securitec Publications, Germantown, WI. Tel: (262) 532-4000, (800) 783-2145, FAX: (262) 532-4001, E-Mail: securitec@securitec.com (7)

Security Micro Systems Inc, Scottsdale, AZ. Web Site: www.luckit.com (3)

Sedgwick Moran Detert & Arnold LLP, Chicago, IL. Tel: (312) 849-1985, Web Site: www.michaelbest.com (9)

Sedlak, Highland Hills, OH. Tel: (216) 206-4700, FAX: (216) 206-4840, E-Mail: info@jasedlak.com, Web Site: www.jasedlak.com (20)

Seeber, Bruce, Kurt Salmon Associates Inc, Atlanta, GA. Tel: (404) 892-0321, FAX: (404) 898-9590, E-Mail: infoksaweb@kurtsalmon.com, Web Site: www.kurtsalmon.com (20)

Seedburo Equipment Co, Des Plaines, IL. Tel: (312) 738-3700, (800) 284-5779, FAX: (312) 738-5329, E-Mail: sales@seedburo.com, Web Site: www.seedburo.com (8)

Seelig, Charles, Virgin Mobile USA LLC, Warren, NJ. Tel: (908) 607-4000, Web Site: www.virginmobileusa.com (32)

Seeliger, John, Nova Power Marketing, Phoenix, AZ. Tel: (602) 558-7540, FAX: (602) 926-8351, E-Mail: novamarkdm@cox.net, Web Site: www.novamarkdm.com (35)

See's Candies Inc, Carson, CA. Tel: (800) 347-7337, Web Site: www.sees.com (4)

Sefcik, James F., Louisiana State Museum, New Orleans, LA. Tel: (504) 568-6968, (800) 568-6968, FAX: (504) 568-4995, Web Site: www.lsm.crt.state.la.us (1)

Sefrin, John, R., American Cancer Society, Atlanta, GA. Tel: (404) 471-5852, (800) ACS-2345, FAX: (404) 982-3677, Web Site: www.cancer.org (1)

Sefton, William, Executive Buying Corp, Naperville, IL. Tel: (630) 420-6200, FAX: (630) 420-2294, Web Site: www.consumerbenefit.com (33)

Segal, Alan, Bits & Pieces Inc, Lawrenceburg, IN. Tel: (866) 503-6395, FAX: (513) 354-1290, Web Site: www.bitsandpieces.com (11)

Segal, Brian, Rogers Publishing Ltd, Toronto, ON Canada. Tel: (416) 935-7777, FAX: (416) 935-3597, Web Site: www.rogerspublishing.ca (17)

Segal, Lynda, Horticulture Magazine, Blue Ash, OH. Tel: (513) 531-2690, FAX: (513) 891-7153, Web Site: www.hortmag.com (17)

Segal, Ronald, Spectrum Systems Inc, Fairfax, VA. Tel: (703) 591-7400 X217, (800) 929-3781, FAX: (703) 591-9780, E-Mail: spectrum@spectrum-systems.com, Web Site: www.spectrum-systems.com (34)

Segerdahl, Earl, E., The Segerdahl Corp, Wheeling, IL. Tel: (847) 541-1080, FAX: (847) 541-5237, Web Site: www.segerdahl.com/frameset.html (27)

The Segerdahl Corp, Wheeling, IL. Tel: (847) 541-1080, FAX: (847) 541-5237, Web Site: www.segerdahl.com/frameset.html (27)

Segerdahl Graphics, Wheeling, IL. Tel: (847) 850-8800, FAX: (773) 477-2051 (27)

Segermark, Howard, International Prepaid Communications Association, Washington, DC. Tel: (202) 544-4448, FAX: (202) 547-7417 (40)

Segill, William, Buena Vista Home Entertainment, Burbank, CA. Tel: (818) 560-1000, FAX: (818) 845-8728, Web Site: www.bvhe.com (3)

Segovia, Cheri, America's Finest Pet Doors, San Luis Obispo, CA. Tel: (805) 781-7700 X201, (800) 826-2871, FAX: (805) 781-9734, E-Mail: alan@petdoors.com, Web Site: www.petdoors.com (16)

Seibert, Drew, Manning Materials, Birdsboro, PA. Tel: (610) 385-6797, (800) 445-1719, FAX: (610) 385-7524, E-Mail: mmsupport@manningmaterials.com, Web Site: www.manningmaterials.com (16)

Seibinico, Karen, Bentley College, Waltham, MA. Tel: (781) 891-2800, FAX: (781) 891-3449, Web Site: www.bentley.edu (13)

Seiden MD, Ph.D., Michael, V., Fox Chase Cancer Center, Philadelphia, PA. Tel: (215) 728-6900, (888) FOXCHASE, FAX: (215) 728-2594, Web Site: www.fccc.edu (1)

Seiden, Lee, Smith, Schoolwise Press, San Francisco, CA. Tel: (415) 337-7971, (800) 247-8443 x 202, FAX: (415) 337-1146, E-Mail: info@schoolwisepress.com, Web Site: www.schoolwisepress.com (17)

Seiden, Neil, Ace Communications, Garden City, NY. Tel: (718) 458-3800, (800) 468-7667, FAX: (516) 872-8156, Web Site: www.aceav.com (3)

Seidenberg, Ivan, Verizon Communications Inc, New York, NY. Tel: (212) 395-1000, (800) 621-9900, FAX: (212) 571-1897, Web Site: www.verizon.com (3)

Seider, Regina, American Healthways, Franklin, TN. Tel: (615) 665-7716, FAX: (615) 665-7697, Web Site: www.americanhealthways.com (16)

Seidl, Matthias, Volkswagen Group of America Inc, Auburn Hills, MI. Tel: (248) 754-5000, FAX: (248) 754-4930, Web Site: www.vw.com (16)

Seiko Corp of America, Mahwah, NJ. Tel: (201) 529-5730, FAX: (201) 529-1548, Web Site: www.seiko.com (16)

Seiler, Roger W., Leadership Software Corp, Nyack, NY. Tel: (845) 358-0406, (800) 872-0068, FAX: (845) 358-0359, E-Mail: info@leadersoft.com, Web Site: www.leadersoft.com (16)

Seitz, Pat, Regal Ware Inc, Kewaskum, WI. Tel: (262) 626-2121, E-Mail: pseitz@regalware.com, Web Site: www.regalware.com (16)

Seiz, Bruce, American Crane & Equipment Corp, Douglassville, PA. Tel: (610) 385-6061, (877) 877-6778, FAX: (610) 385-3191/4876, E-Mail: info@americancrane.com, Web Site: www.americancrane.com (16)

Sekel, Terrence, The Weather Channel, New York, NY. Tel: (212) 856-5200, FAX: (212) 856-5215, Web Site: www.weather.com (32)

Seklemian Newell Inc (CRMC), Miami Beach, FL. Tel: (310) 622-5405, FAX: (520) 842-7344, Web Site: www.thecrmc.com (20)

Selan, Bruce, Zotos International, Darien, CT. Tel: (203) 655-8911, (800) 242-WAVE, (800) 242-9283, FAX: (203) 656-7890, E-Mail: HumanResources@zotosintl.com, Web Site: www.zotos.com (16)

Select Comfort Corp, Minneapolis, MN. Tel: (763) 551-7000, (888) 411-2188, FAX: (763) 551-7826, Web Site: www.selectcomfort.com (16)

Select List Corp, Glen Head, NY. Tel: (516) 676-7831, FAX: (516) 676-9746 (23)

Select Press, Novato, CA. Tel: (415) 209-9838, E-Mail: selectpr@aol.com (17)

ServiceMaster Co, Memphis, TN. Tel: (901) 766-1400, (901) 597-8502, (888) 937-3783, (866) 782-6787, FAX: (901) 766-1491, Web Site: www. servicemaster.com (8)

The Services Group (TSG), Arlington, VA. Tel: (703) 528-7444, FAX: (703) 522-2329, E-Mail: tsq@ tsginc.com, Web Site: www.tsginc.com (20)

Servison, Roger, T., Fidelity Investments, Boston, MA. Tel: (617) 563-7000, (800) 343-3548, FAX: (617) 476-6150, Web Site: www.fidelity.com (14)

Sesame Workshop, New York, NY. Tel: (212) 875-6677, Web Site: www.sesameworkshop.org (1)

Sessions, John, Bellomy Research Inc, Winston Salem, NC. Tel: (336) 721-1140, FAX: (336) 721-1597, E-Mail: bellomy@interpath.com, Web Site: bellomyresearch.com (30)

Sessoms, Vicki, Partners Health, Philadelphia, PA. Tel: (215) 849-9600, (800) 553-0784, E-Mail: sroberts@healthpart.com, Web Site: www. healthpart.com (15)

Seta, Angie, Seta Corp of Boca Inc, Boca Raton, FL. Tel: (561) 994-2660, FAX: (561) 997-2881, Web Site: www.setacorporatin.com (5)

Seta, Joe, D., Seta Corp of Boca Inc, Boca Raton, FL. Tel: (561) 994-2660, FAX: (561) 997-2881, Web Site: www.setacorporatin.com (5)

Seta Corp of Boca Inc, Boca Raton, FL. Tel: (561) 994-2660, FAX: (561) 997-2881, Web Site: www. setacorporatin.com (5)

Seton Hall University, South Orange, NJ. Tel: (973) 378-2650, Web Site: www.shu.edu (1)

Seton Identification Products, Branford, CT. Tel: (203) 488-8059, (800) 243-6624, FAX: (203) 488-5973, Web Site: www.seton.com (16)

Setterlund, Tawnya, White & Partners, Herndon, VA. Tel: (703) 793-3000, FAX: (703) 793-1495, E-Mail: tawnyas@whiteandpartners.com, Web Site: www.whiteandpartners.com (35)

Settles, Art, USAA, San Antonio, TX. Tel: (512) 498-6524, FAX: (512) 498-8000 (15)

Severens, Pete, ATM Advertising, Atlanta, GA. Tel: (770) 671-0404, Web Site: www.sagpromo.com (35)

Severini Communications LLC (Mogility), New York, NY. Tel: (917) 734-3991, Web Site: mogilityny. com (20)

Sevigny, Jerry, Opryland, Nashville, TN. Tel: (615) 889-1000, FAX: (615) 871-7741, E-Mail: info@ gaylordhotels.com, Web Site: www.oprylandhotels. com (16)

Seward, Ted, Bowe Bell & Howell, Durham, NC. Tel: (919) 767-6400, (800) 220-3030, E-Mail: marketing@bowebellhowell.com, Web Site: www. bowebellhowell.com (34)

Sewell, Kenneth, Database Marketing Services, Guaynabo, PR. Tel: (787) 792-7005 (22)

Sewell, Nancy, The Wexner Companies Inc, Memphis, TN. Tel: (901) 763-3925, (800) 890-5470, FAX: (901) 763-3736, E-Mail: info@JosephStores.com, Web Site: www.josephstores.com (2)

Sewell, Yolanda, Gaco Western Inc, Seattle, WA. Tel: (206) 575-0450, (800) 456-4226, FAX: (206) 575-0587, E-Mail: info@gaco.com, Web Site: www. gaco.com (16)

JA Sexauer, Elmsford, NY. Tel: (914) 472-7501, (800) 431-1872, FAX: (914) 472-5834, Web Site: www. jasmro.com (16)

Sexton, Neil, Northern Safety Co Inc, Utica, NY. Tel: (315) 793-4900, Web Site: www.northernsafety. com (16)

Seybold Publications, Gilbertsville, PA. Tel: (610) 327-3958, (888) 544-7104, FAX: (888) 463-4814, E-Mail: molly@thejossgroup.com, Web Site: www. seyboldreports.com (17)

Seyferth, William, A., Muskegon Power Tool Corp, North Muskegon, MI. Tel: (231) 766-2194, (800) 635-5465, FAX: (231) 766-3846 (16)

Seymour, Jane, Deck the Walls Inc, Saint Peters, MO. Tel: (314) 719-8200, (866) 719-8200, FAX: (314) 719-8290, Web Site: www.deckthewalls.com (5)

Sfeir, Dany, DS & A Consulting, Lexington, KY. Tel: (973) 530-4198 (20)

Sfondouris, John, Scientific Computing Associates, Villa Park, IL. Tel: (630) 834-8512, Web Site: www.scausa.com (22)

Sganga, Matthew, Stabenfeldt Inc, Danbury, CT. Tel: (203) 730-2178 (13)

Shackleton, John, Open Text Inc, Waterloo, ON. Tel: (519) 888-9933, (800) 499-6544, FAX: (519) 888-0677, E-Mail: support@opentext.com, Web Site: www.opentext.com (16)

B Shackman & Co Inc, Galesburg, MI. Tel: (269) 484-1000, (800) 221-7656, FAX: (269) 484-1010, Web Site: www.shackman.com (6)

Shada, Mark, UAA Clearinghouse, Omaha, NE. Tel: (402) 991-2810, Web Site: www.uaaclearinghouse. com (22)

Shadding, Fred, Cyber City Teleservices Marketing Inc, Hackensack, NJ. Tel: (201) 487-1616, (800) 213-4144, E-Mail: info@cctll.com, Web Site: www.cctll.com (29)

Shadek, Ed, Wildlife Education Ltd, Park Hills, KY. Tel: (858) 513-7600, FAX: (858) 513-7660, E-Mail: animals@zoobooks.com, Web Site: www. zoobooks.com (17)

Shades of Light, Richmond, VA. Tel: (804) 288-3235, (877) 288-5029, FAX: (804) 288-5029, E-Mail: visitor@shadesoflight.com, Web Site: www. shadesoflight.com (8)

Shady Oaks Nursery, LLC, Waseca, MN. Tel: (507) 835-5033, FAX: (507) 835-8772, E-Mail: shadyoaks@shadyoaks.com, Web Site: www. shadyoaks.com (8)

Shae, Gary, Strategic Marketing & Mailing, Champaign, IL. Tel: (217) 355-2600, Web Site: www. strategicmail.com (28)

Shaffer, Jacob, W., McCormick-Armstrong Co Inc, Wichita, KS. Tel: (316) 264-1363, (800) 733-1363, FAX: (316) 263-4511, E-Mail: sales@ mccormickarmstrong.com, Web Site: www. mccormickarmstrong.com (27)

Shaffer, James, W., Angelica Image Apparel, Saint Louis, MO. Tel: (314) 854-3800, (800) 235-8410, Web Site: www.angelica.com (16)

Shaffer, Michael, L., PPN INC, Holbrook, MA. Tel: (781) 767-5776, (800) 289-4776, FAX: (781) 767-4776, E-Mail: customer.service@ppninc.com, Web Site: www.ppninc.com (7)

Shaffer, Michael, Phillips-Van Heusen Corp, New York, NY. Tel: (212) 381-3500, (800) 388-9122, FAX: (212) 381-3950, Web Site: www.pvh.com (2)

Shaffer, William, F., PPN INC, Holbrook, MA. Tel: (781) 767-5776, (800) 289-4776, FAX: (781) 767-4776, E-Mail: customer.service@ppninc.com, Web Site: www.ppninc.com (7)

Shain, Harold, Newsweek Inc, New York, NY. Tel: (212) 445-4000, FAX: (212) 445-5068, Web Site: www.newsweek.com (17)

Shaker, William, Washington Marketing Group, Arlington, VA. Tel: (703) 534-9331, FAX: (703) 534-0242, E-Mail: william.shaker@twmg.com, Web Site: www.twmg.com (1)

Shaker Workshops, Ashburnham, MA. Tel: (978) 827-9900, FAX: (978) 827-6554, E-Mail: shaker9973@ shakerworkshops.com, Web Site: www. shakerworkshops.com (8)

Shakespeare Co, Columbia, SC. Tel: (803) 754-7000, (800) 347-3759, FAX: (803) 754-7342, Web Site: www.shakespeare-fishing.com (11)

Shakespeare Mailing Service, New York, NY. Tel: (212) 560-8958, E-Mail: support@ shakespearemailing.com, Web Site: www. shakespearemailing.com (28)

Shank, Tom, Kayser-Roth Corp Inc, Greensboro, NC. Tel: (800) 575-3497, Web Site: www.nononsense. com (2)

Shankar, Subromanian, American Megatrends Inc, Norcross, GA. Tel: (770) 246-8600, (800) 828-9264, FAX: (770) 246-8790, Web Site: www.ami. com (3)

Shankewitz, Rita, Boardroom Inc, Stamford, CT. Tel: (203) 973-5900, FAX: (203) 967-3086, E-Mail: kseaborne@boardroom.com, Web Site: www. boardroom.com (17)

Shanley, Mary, TTC Marketing Solutions, Chicago, IL. Tel: (773) 545-0407, (800) 777-6348, FAX: (773) 545-4034, E-Mail: sales@ ttcmarketingsolutions.com, Web Site: www. ttcmarketingsolutions.com (29)

Shannon, Jim, National Fire Protection Association, Quincy, MA. Tel: (617) 770-3000, FAX: (617) 770-0700, Web Site: www.nfpa.org (1)

Shannon, Patty, The Wordstation, Avon By The Sea, NJ. Tel: (732) 774-4831, FAX: (732) 869-1822, E-Mail: pattyshannone@optonline.net (39)

Shape Global Technology, Sanford, ME. Tel: (207) 324-5200, (800) 627-5836, FAX: (207) 324-0875, E-Mail: info@shapeglobal.com, Web Site: www. shapenet.com (34)

Shape LLC, Addison, IL. Tel: (630) 620-8394, (800) 367-5811, FAX: (630) 620-0784, E-Mail: sales@ shapellc.com, Web Site: www.shapellc.com (3)

Shapes Marketing Inc, Highland Park, IL. Tel: (847) 291-1110, FAX: (847) 291-1308, Web Site: www. shapesmarket.com (20)

Shapin, John, L., Shapes Marketing Inc, Highland Park, IL. Tel: (847) 291-1110, FAX: (847) 291-1308, Web Site: www.shapesmarket.com (20)

Shapin, Margaret, Shapes Marketing Inc, Highland Park, IL. Tel: (847) 291-1110, FAX: (847) 291-1308, Web Site: www.shapesmarket.com (20)

Shapiro, Gary, Calumet Photographic Inc, Bensenville, IL. Tel: (630) 860-7447, (800) 453-2550, FAX: (800) 577-3686, E-Mail: custserv@calumetphoto. com, Web Site: www.calumetphoto.com (3)

Shapiro, Glenn, Executive Enterprises Inc, Hawthorne, NY. Tel: (860) 701-5900, (800) 831-8333, FAX: (800) 250-3861, (860) 701-5909, E-Mail: info@ eeiconferences.com, Web Site: www. eeiconferences.com (16)

Shapiro, Milton, David Geller Associates, New York, NY. Tel: (212) 455-0100, FAX: (212) 455-0164 (31)

Shapiro, Neal, B., Channel 13 WNET Catalog Division, New York, NY. Tel: (212) 560-2000, FAX: (212) 582-3297, Web Site: www.thirteen.org (5)

Shapiro, Sally, LIM College, New York, NY. Tel: (212) 752-1530, Web Site: www.limcollege.edu (1)

Shapiro, Steve, Kyp Systems Inc, New York, NY. Tel: (212) 551-7878, FAX: (917) 591-1514, E-Mail: steves@kyp.com, Web Site: www.ikyp.com (35)

Shapley, Rick, Cade & Associates Advertising, Tallahassee, FL. Tel: (850) 385-0300, (800) 715-CADE, FAX: (850) 385-1165, E-Mail: webmaster@cade1. com, Web Site: www.cade1.com (35)

Share Group Inc, Newton, MA. Tel: (617) 629-4500, FAX: (617) 629-4510, E-Mail: info@sharegroup. com, Web Site: www.sharegroup.com (29)

Sharf, Bernie, Sharf Woodward & Associates Inc, Sherman Oaks, CA. Tel: (818) 988-2200, (877) 482-6687, Web Site: www.swjobs.com (20)

Sharf Woodward & Associates Inc, Sherman Oaks, CA. Tel: (818) 988-2200, (877) 482-6687, Web Site: www.swjobs.com (20)

Sharif, Bea, Mrs Beasley's & Miss Grace Lemon Cake Co, Los Angeles, CA. Tel: (800) 710-7742, FAX: (310) 668-2148, E-Mail: general@ mrsbeasleys.com, Web Site: www.mrsbeasleys.com (4)

Sharif, Tariq, D&B, Parsippany, NJ. Tel: (973) 921-5500, Web Site: www.dnb.com (22)

Sharma, Deven, Standard & Poor's Corp, New York, NY. Tel: (212) 438-2000, FAX: (212) 438-7375, Web Site: www.standardandpoors.com (17)

Sharman, James A., World Kitchen Inc, Corning, NY. Tel: (607) 377-8000, (800) 999-3436, FAX: (607) 377-8946, Web Site: www.worldkitchen.com (16)

Sharman, Paul, Institute of Management Accountants Inc, Montvale, NJ. Tel: (201) 573-9000, (800) 638-4427, FAX: (201) 474-1600, E-Mail: ima@imanet. org, Web Site: www.imanet.org (1)

Sharp, Dolph, Dental Products Report, New York, NY. Tel: (847) 441-3700, FAX: (847) 441-3702, Web Site: www.dentalproducts.net (17)

Sharp, Donald, C., Navistar, Warrenville, IL. Tel: (630) 753-5804, (800) 448-7825, FAX: (630) 753-2303, Web Site: www.navistar.com (16)

Sharp, Gary, PharmArt, Circleville, OH. Tel: (860) 932-8588, (800) 848-1633, FAX: (800) 477-2923, Web Site: www.healthcarelogistics.com/Pharmart (6)

Sharp, Isadore, Four Seasons Hotels & Resorts, Toronto, ON. Tel: (416) 449-1750, (800) 819-5053, FAX: (416) 441-4374, Web Site: www.fourseasons. com (19)

Sharp, Robert, AAA Auto Club South, Tampa, FL. Tel: (813) 289-1344, FAX: (813) 289-1340, Web Site: www.aaa.com (1)

Sharp, Vickie, Recognition Products International, Easton, MD. Tel: (410) 820-0022, (800) 292-7354, FAX: (410) 820-5044, E-Mail: info@ recognitionproducts.com, Web Site: www. shoprecognitionproducts.com (16)

Sharpe III, William, Goldsmith Agio Helms, Minneapolis, MN. Tel: (612) 339-0500, FAX: (612) 339-0507, Web Site: www.agio.com (14)

Sharpe, Bill, Arnold Brand Response, Toronto, ON. Tel: (416) 355-5009, Web Site: www. arnoldworldwide.com (35)

Sharpe, David, CertainTeed Corp, Valley Forge, PA. Tel: (610) 341-7000/7739, (800) 233-8990, FAX: (610) 341-7777, Web Site: www.certainteed.com (16)

The Sharper Image, New York, NY. Tel: (415) 445-6000, (800) 344-5555, FAX: (800) 552-2525, E-Mail: info@sharperimage.com, Web Site: www. sharperimage.com (6)

Shasho Jones, Glenda, Shasho Jones Direct Inc, New York, NY. Tel: (212) 929-2300, E-Mail: glenda@ sjdirect.com, Web Site: www.sjdirect.com (20)

Shasho Jones Direct Inc, New York, NY. Tel: (212) 929-2300, E-Mail: glenda@sjdirect.com, Web Site: www.sjdirect.com (20)

Shassian, Donald R., Frontier Corp, Rochester, NY. Tel: (716) 777-1000, Web Site: www. frontieronline.com (16)

Shasteen, Rhonda, Mary Kay Cosmetics Inc, Addison, TX. Tel: (972) 687-6300, (800) MARY KAY, FAX: (972) 687-1611, Web Site: www.marykay. com (16)

Shaub, Yuko, The IEI Corp, Princeton, NJ. Tel: (609) 987-2700, FAX: (609) 987-2703 (6)

Shaver Direct Inc, Phoenix, AZ. Web Site: www. dickshaver.com (35)

Shaw, Allan, Rediscover Music Catalogue, Naperville, IL. Tel: (630) 305-0770, (800) 232-7328, FAX: (630) 305-0782, E-Mail: rediscovermusic@ rediscovermusic.com, Web Site: www. rediscovermusic.com (3)

Shaw, Carl, Fisher Scientific, Pittsburgh, PA. Tel: (800) 766-7000, FAX: (800) 772-7702, Web Site: www.fishersci.com (16)

Shaw, Colin, Aspen Interactive, Saint Petersburg, FL. Tel: (727) 823-7144, (800) 777-2255, FAX: (727) 823-6523 (35)

Shaw, David, Destination Rewards, Boca Raton, FL. Tel: (561) 997-9940, (800) 242-6260, FAX: (561) 997-9945, Web Site: www.drloyalty.com (33)

Shaw, David, E., AAAS/Science, Washington, DC. Tel: (202) 326-6400, FAX: (202) 371-9526, E-Mail: webmaster@aaas.org, Web Site: www. aaas.org (1)

Shaw, Douglas, Douglas Shaw & Associates, Naperville, IL. Tel: (630) 562-1321, Web Site: www. douglasshaw.com (1)

Shaw, Lee, Federal Envelope Co, Bensenville, IL. Tel: (630) 595-2000, FAX: (630) 595-1212, E-Mail: postmaster@federalenvelope.com, Web Site: www. federalenvelope.com (26)

Shaw, Lisa, Raycom Sports, Charlotte, NC. Tel: (704) 378-4456/4400, FAX: (704) 378-4465, E-Mail: whicks@raycomsports.com, Web Site: raycomsports.com (16)

Shaw, Michael, Federal Envelope Co, Bensenville, IL. Tel: (630) 595-2000, FAX: (630) 595-1212, E-Mail: postmaster@federalenvelope.com, Web Site: www.federalenvelope.com (26)

Shaw, Ray, Watering Inc/Hemmings Motor News, Bennington, VT. Tel: (802) 442-3101, (800) 227-4373, FAX: (802) 447-1561, E-Mail: hmnmail@ hemmings.com, Web Site: www.hemmings.com (17)

Shaw, Richard, Catalyst Computer Services Inc, Los Angeles, CA. Tel: (310) 441-4300, (800) 659-2267, FAX: (310) 441-4332, E-Mail: sales@ catalystsoftware.com, Web Site: www. catalystsoftware.com (32)

Shaw, Sarah, Phone Bank Systems Inc, East Lansing, MI. Tel: (517) 332-1500, FAX: (517) 332-1514, E-Mail: rusha@phonebanks.com, Web Site: www. phonebanks.com (1)

Shaw, Sheri, The Professional Putters Association, Winston Salem, NC. Tel: (336) 714-3950, (866) PUTT-PUTT, FAX: (336) 714-3955, Web Site: www.putt-putt.com (1)

Shaw, Sherry, Putt Putt Fun Centers, Winston-Salem, NC. Tel: (336) 714-3950, (866) PUTT-PUTT, FAX: (336) 714-3955, Web Site: www.puttputt. com (16)

Shaw, Terry, ActionPak, Scarborough, ON Canada. Tel: (416) 321-2222, FAX: (416) 321-5286, Web Site: www.openandsave.com (21)

Shaw, William, Marriott International Inc, Washington, DC. Tel: (301) 380-3000, (301) 380-1791, E-Mail: internet.customer.care@marriott.com, Web Site: www.marriott.com (19)

Shawah, Penny, Meyer Fulfillment, Stratford, CT. Tel: (203) 375-5801, (800) 873-6393, E-Mail: vdarish@ meyerfulfillment.com, Web Site: www. meyerfulfillment.com (28)

Shawyer, Kyla, Operation Smile Inc, Norfolk, VA. Tel: (757) 321-7645, Web Site: www. operationsmile.org (1)

Shaytin, Paul, Empire Coffee & Tea Co, New York, NY. Tel: (212) 268-1220, (800) 262-5908, E-Mail: owners@empirecoffeetea.com, Web Site: www. empirecoffeetea.com (4)

Shea, Christina, L., General Mills Inc, Minneapolis, MN. Tel: (763) 764-7600, FAX: (763) 764-7384, Web Site: www.generalmills.com (8)

Shea, Kevin, J., Kevin J. Shea & Associates, Arlington Heights, IL. Tel: (847) 392-2713 (39)

Shea, Mindy, 3M Post-It Direct Response Products, Saint Paul, MN. Tel: (651) 733-1110, Web Site: www.mmm.com (16)

Shea, Peter, Entrepreneur Media Inc, Irvine, CA. Tel: (949) 261-2325, (800) 274-6229, FAX: (949) 261-0234, Web Site: www.entrepreneur.com (17)

Shea, Stefani, Princess House Inc, Taunton, MA. Tel: (508) 832-6800, (508) 823-0711, (800) 622-0039, FAX: (508) 823-5182, Web Site: www. princesshouse.com (16)

Kevin J. Shea & Associates, Arlington Heights, IL. Tel: (847) 392-2713 (39)

Sheadoker, Carl, American Megatrends Inc, Norcross, GA. Tel: (770) 246-8600, (800) 828-9264, FAX: (770) 246-8790, Web Site: www.ami.com (3)

Shear, Debra, Liberty Mutual Group, Inc, Boston, MA. Tel: (617) 357-9500, (800) 837-5274, Web Site: www.libertymutual.com (15)

Sheats, Phillip F., CDMI Inc, Huntington Beach, CA. Tel: (714) 969-4064 (1)

Shebesta, Sarah, HY-KO Products Co, Northfield, OH. Tel: (330) 467-7446, Web Site: www.hy-ko.com (16)

Sheck, Steven, Infinite Media, White Plains, NY. Tel: (914) 949-1547, FAX: (914) 949-1605, E-Mail: mail@infinite-media.com, Web Site: www.infinite-media.com (23)

Sheckler, Julie, Baldwin Filters, Kearney, NE. Tel: (308) 234-1951, (800) 822-5394, FAX: (800) 828-4453, E-Mail: info@baldwinfilter.com, Web Site: www.baldwinfilter.com (16)

Sheehan Jr., Thomas, F., Tom Sheehan Advertising, Reading, PA. Tel: (610) 478-8448, FAX: (610) 478-8449, E-Mail: info@tomsheehan.com, Web Site: www.tomsheehan.com (35)

Sheehan, Brian, Team One Advertising, El Segundo, CA. Tel: (310) 615-2000, FAX: (310) 322-7565, E-Mail: b.sheehan@teamoneadv.com, Web Site: www.teamone-usa.com (35)

Sheehan, Dave, History (Reference & Preservation) Division, Annapolis, MD. Tel: (410) 268-6110, (800) 233-8764, FAX: (410) 571-7940, E-Mail: dsheehan@usni.org, Web Site: www.usni.org (38)

Sheehan, Stephen, G., Thermo Fisher Scientific I, Waltham, MA. Tel: (781) 622-1000, (800) 678-5599, FAX: (781) 622-1207, Web Site: www. thermofisher.com (9)

Tom Sheehan Advertising, Reading, PA. Tel: (610) 478-8448, FAX: (610) 478-8449, E-Mail: info@ tomsheehan.com, Web Site: www.tomsheehan.com (35)

Sheehy, Declan, J, American Institute for Economic Research, Great Barrington, MA. Tel: (413) 528-1216, (888) 528-1216, E-Mail: info@aier.org, Web Site: www.aier.org (1)

Sheehy, Kevin, Midwest Direct Marketing Association Inc, Saint Paul, MN. Tel: (651) 999-5351, FAX: (651) 917-1835, E-Mail: mdma@mdma.org, Web Site: www.mdma.org (40)

Sheeks, Jeff, S Group Inc, Akron, OH. Tel: (330) 535-2103, (800) 686-7435, FAX: (330) 535-1723, E-Mail: info@s-groupinc.com, Web Site: www.s-groupinc.com (33)

Sheeler, Sue, The Reggio Register Co Inc, Leominster, MA. Tel: (978) 870-1020, (800) 880-3090, FAX: (978) 870-1030, E-Mail: reggio@reggioregister. com, Web Site: www.reggioregister.com (8)

Sheena, Esra, Rush Industries, Inc, Mineola, NY. Tel: (516) 741-0346, FAX: (516) 741-0348, Web Site: www.rushindustries.com (16)

Sheep Shop, Bridgton, ME. Tel: (207) 647-3548, FAX: (207) 647-3172 (5)

Sheeran, Joseph J., Sheeran Direct Marketing, New Castle, DE. Tel: (302) 324-0200, (888) 325-2101, FAX: (302) 324-0213, E-Mail: jjs@jjsheeran.com, Web Site: www.jjsheeran.com (28)

Sheeran Direct Marketing, New Castle, DE. Tel: (302) 324-0200, (888) 325-2101, FAX: (302) 324-0213, E-Mail: jjs@jjsheeran.com, Web Site: www. jjsheeran.com (28)

Sheets, David, Emergency Essentials Inc, Orem, UT. Tel: (801) 222-9596, FAX: (801) 222-9598, E-Mail: webmaster@beprepared.com, Web Site: www.beprepared.com (16)

Sheets, Joseph, D., Dow Corning Corp, Midland, MI. Tel: (989) 496-4000, (800) 248-2481, FAX: (989) 496-4572, Web Site: www.dowcorning.com (16)

Sheffield, Michael, L., Multi-Level Marketing International Association (MLMIA), Irvine, CA. Tel: (949) 854-0484, FAX: (949) 854-7687, E-Mail: info@mlmia.com, Web Site: www.mlmia.com/ (1)

Sheffield, Sally, Executive Enterprises Inc, Hawthorne, NY. Tel: (860) 701-5900, (800) 831-8333, FAX: (800) 250-3861, (860) 701-5909, E-Mail: info@ eeiconferences.com, Web Site: www. eeiconferences.com (16)

Shehan, Mike, Booyah Networks, Westminster, CO. Tel: (303) 426-7776, FAX: (303) 345-6700, E-Mail: support@booyahnetworks.com, Web Site: www.booyahnetworks.com (35)

Sheinbach, Harold, Market Incentives Corp, Frazer, PA. Tel: (610) 644-5700, (800) 486-8881, FAX: (610) 889-9636, E-Mail: micpa@marketincentives. com, Web Site: www.marketincentives.com (33)

Shelburne Co, Taneytown, MD. Tel: (410) 876-5902, FAX: (410) 876-4612, Web Site: www.zoysiafarms.com (8)

Shelby Insurance Companies, Birmingham, AL. Tel: (800) 443-1573, FAX: (877) 837-8203, Web Site: www.vesta.com (15)

Sheldon, Mike, Lowe Worldwide, New York, NY. Tel: (212) 981-7600, E-Mail: info@loweworldwide. com, Web Site: www.loweworldwide.com (35)

Sheldon, Ricky, House of Eyes II, Greensboro, NC. Tel: (336) 852-7107, FAX: (336) 854-0311 (2)

Sheldon, Robin, Home Decorators Collection Inc, Ha-zelwood, MO. Tel: (314) 993-1516, FAX: (314) 521-5780, Web Site: www.homedecoratorscollection.com (8)

Shell, Gary, EMS Technologies, Norcross, GA. Tel: (770) 263-9200, FAX: (770) 447-4405, Web Site: www.ems-t.com (16)

Shell Oil Products US, Houston, TX. Tel: (713) 241-6161, Web Site: www.shell.us (16)

Shelton, Anne, The Signature Agency, Raleigh, NC. Tel: (919) 878-8989, (800) 870-8700, FAX: (919) 878-3939, E-Mail: info@signatureagency.com, Web Site: www.signatureagency.com (12)

Shelton, Brent, FatWallet, Beloit, WI. Tel: (815) 877-8992, Web Site: www.fatwallet.com (14)

Shelton, Dave, Graphik Dimensions Ltd, High Point, NC. Tel: (336) 887-3500, (800) 221-0262, FAX: (336) 887-3773, E-Mail: customercare@pictureframes.com, Web Site: www.pictureframes.com (16)

Shepard III, T.R., King Features, New York, NY. Tel: (212) 455-4000, FAX: (212) 682-8332 (17)

Shepard, David B., David Shepard Associates Inc, Melville, NY. Tel: (516) 271-5567, FAX: (516) 271-5589, E-Mail: davidshepard@dsadirect.com, Web Site: www.dsadirect.com (20)

Shepard, Donald, Aegon Corp, Louisville, KY. Tel: (502) 560-2000, FAX: (502) 560-2611, Web Site: www.aegonins.com (14)

David Shepard Associates Inc, Melville, NY. Tel: (516) 271-5567, FAX: (516) 271-5589, E-Mail: davidshepard@dsadirect.com, Web Site: www.dsadirect.com (20)

Shepard's Inc, Bethel, CT. Tel: (203) 830-8300, (800) 243-0993, FAX: (203) 830-8389, Web Site: www.shepardsinc.com (22)

Shephard, Heffret, A., MELDISCO, Mahwah, NJ. Tel: (201) 934-2000, FAX: (201) 934-2570, Web Site: www.meldisco.com (16)

Shepherd, Danny, R., Vulcan Materials Co, Birming-ham, AL. Tel: (205) 298-3000, FAX: (205) 298-2960, Web Site: www.vulcanmaterials.com (16)

Sheplers Catalog Sales Inc, Wichita, KS. Tel: (316) 946-3838, (800) 835-4004, FAX: (316) 946-3729, Web Site: www.sheplers.com (2)

Shepley, Bob, Standard Tools & Equipment Co, Greensboro, NC. Tel: (336) 697-7177, Web Site: www.toolsusa.com (9)

Sheppard, David, Swords Music Co Inc, Fort Worth, TX. Tel: (817) 53-MUSIC, (800) 522-3028, FAX: (817) 536-4293, E-Mail: daveshep4300@sbcglobal. net, Web Site: www.swordsmusicinc.com (34)

Sheppard Envelope Co, Auburn, MA. Tel: (508) 791-5588, (800) 325-6622, FAX: (508) 754-3108, E-Mail: sales@sheppardenvelope.com, Web Site: www.sheppardenvelope.com (26)

Sher, Barry, Nostradamus Advertising, New York, NY. Tel: (212) 581-1362, E-Mail: nos@nostradamus. net, Web Site: www.nostradamus.net (36)

Sher, Robert, Alvion LLC, Cape Coral, FL. Tel: (239) 574-8600, (877) 528-7800, FAX: (239) 574-8551, Web Site: www.alvion.com (22)

Sheridan, William, Sotheby's, New York, NY. Tel: (212) 606-7000, FAX: (212) 606-7107, Web Site: www.sothebys.com (6)

Sheridan Books Inc, Chelsea, MI. Tel: (734) 662-3291, (734) 475-9145, (800) 999-BOOK, FAX: (734) 475-7337, E-Mail: info@sheridanbooks.com, Web Site: www.sheridanbooks.com (27)

Sheridan Labarge, Joan, Working Mother, New York, NY. Tel: (212) 221-9595, FAX: (212) 219-7448, Web Site: www.workingmother.com (31)

Sherk, Kyle, Gaco Western Inc, Seattle, WA. Tel: (206) 575-0450, (800) 456-4226, FAX: (206) 575-0587, E-Mail: info@gaco.com, Web Site: www.gaco.com (16)

Sherlock, Gary, The Journal News, White Plains, NY. Tel: (914) 694-9300, FAX: (914) 696-8152, Web Site: www.nyjournalnews.com (17)

Sherman Esq., Robert, Paul, Hastings, Janofsky & Walker LLP, New York, NY. Tel: (212) 318-6037, FAX: (212) 319-4090, E-Mail: robertsherman@paulhastings.com, Web Site: www.paulhastings.com (20)

Sherman, Jonathan, Sherman & Associates Inc, War-ren, OH. Tel: (330) 399-4500, FAX: (330) 399-6747, E-Mail: info@shermanexperience.com, Web Site: www.shermanexperience.com (35)

Sherman, Len, Tamayo Miyares & Sherman, Bridge-port, CT. Tel: (203) 416-5718, FAX: (203) 416-5721, E-Mail: lsherman@tmsdr.com, Web Site: www.tmsdr.com (35)

Sherman, Marc, My Mailing Service, Inc, Atlanta, GA. Tel: (404) 321-6222, E-Mail: info@mymailingservice.com, Web Site: www.mymailingservice.com (23)

Sherman, Suzette, Philadelphia Museum of Art, Phila-delphia, PA. Tel: (215) 684-7840, Web Site: www.philamuseum.org (1)

Sherman & Associates Inc, Warren, OH. Tel: (330) 399-4500, FAX: (330) 399-6747, E-Mail: info@shermanexperience.com, Web Site: www.shermanexperience.com (35)

Sherman Specialty Toy Co Inc, Jericho, NY. Tel: (516) 861-6420, (516) 546-7400, (800) 645-6513, FAX: (516) 861-1033, (800) 853-8697, E-Mail: orders@shermanspecialty.com, Web Site: www.shermanspecialty.com (16)

Sheroke, Ted, Cleveland Institute of Electronics, Cleveland, OH. Tel: (216) 781-9400, FAX: (216) 781-0331, E-Mail: instruct@cie-wc.edu, Web Site: www.cie-wc.edu (13)

Sherrell, Angie, GS Marketing, Houston, TX. Tel: (713) 580-3900, FAX: (713) 580-5950, E-Mail: angie.sherrell@gsmarketing.com, Web Site: www.gsmarketing.com (21)

Sherry, Joanna, VW Credit, Herndon, VA. Tel: (703) 364-7755 (14)

Sherwood, Charles, California State University at Fresno, Fresno, CA. Tel: (559) 278-7830, FAX: (559) 278-8577, Web Site: www.csufresno.edu (41)

Sherwood, Jennifer, Saunders Manufacturing Co Inc, Readfield, ME. Tel: (207) 685-3385, (800) 341-4674, FAX: (207) 685-9918, E-Mail: jsherwood@saunders-usa.com, Web Site: www.saunders-usa.com (16)

Sherwood Design & Development Center, Carlstadt, NJ. Tel: (201) 372-3900, FAX: (201) 372-0917 (27)

Sheshunoff, Alex, Sheshunoff Management Services, Austin, TX. Tel: (512) 472-4000, (800) 477-1772, FAX: (512) 479-8189, E-Mail: info@smslp.com, Web Site: www.ashesh.com (20)

Sheshunoff, Gabrielle, Sheshunoff Information Ser-vices Inc, Austin, TX. Tel: (800) 456-2340, Web Site: www.sheshunoff.com (14)

Sheshunoff Information Services Inc, Austin, TX. Tel: (800) 456-2340, Web Site: www.sheshunoff.com (14)

Sheshunoff Management Services, Austin, TX. Tel: (512) 472-4000, (800) 477-1772, FAX: (512) 479-8189, E-Mail: info@smslp.com, Web Site: www.ashesh.com (20)

Shetler, MaryAnn, Sales Building Systems, Mentor, OH. Tel: (800) 435-7576, FAX: (440) 639-9190, E-Mail: sales@sbsteam.com, Web Site: www.sbsteam.com (31)

Sheu, Caroline, Electronic Arts Inc, Redwood City, CA. Tel: (650) 628-1500, Web Site: www.ea.com (3)

Shevers Jr., Hal, Sporty's Preferred Living, Batavia, OH. Tel: (513) 735-9000, (800) 776-7897, FAX: (800) 543-8633, Web Site: www.sportys.com (5)

Shibata, Christy, Rupert, MCA/Universal Studios Inc, Universal City, CA. Tel: (818) 777-1000, FAX: (818) 866-3330, Web Site: www.universalstudios.com (3)

Shield Healthcare, Valencia, CA. Tel: (661) 294-4200, (800) 228-7150, FAX: (661) 294-1043, Web Site: www.shieldhealthcare.com (7)

Shields, Barbara, USAA, San Antonio, TX. Tel: (512) 498-6524, FAX: (512) 498-8000 (15)

Shields, Jay, Fitzgerald + Co, Atlanta, GA. Tel: (404) 504-6900, FAX: (404) 239-0548, E-Mail: dave.fitzgerald@fitzco.com, Web Site: www.fitzco.com (35)

Shields, Peggy, Cornerstone Business Services Inc, Council Bluffs, IA. Tel: (712) 256-4987, Web Site: www.conerstonelist.com (23)

Shields, Viola, American Target Advertising Inc, Ma-nassas, VA. Tel: (703) 392-7676, FAX: (703) 392-7654 (35)

Kate Shifman Consulting, Brooklyn, NY. Tel: (917) 710-0219 (20)

Shilcock, Nick, Fairfield Industries Inc, Sugar Land, TX. Tel: (281) 275-7500, (800) 231-9809, FAX: (281) 275-7550, E-Mail: jblattman@fairfield.com, Web Site: www.fairfield.com (16)

Shillcraft Inc, Annapolis, MD. Tel: (410) 682-3060, (800) 638-1542, FAX: (410) 682-3130, Web Site: www.shillcraft.com (16)

Shindigz, South Whitley, IN. Tel: (219) 723-5171, (800) 314-8736, FAX: (219) 723-6976, E-Mail: csr@shindigz.com, Web Site: www.shindigz.com (27)

Shinn, Duane, Keyboard Workshop, Medford, OR. Tel: (541) 664-7052, FAX: (541) 664-7052, E-Mail: duane@playpiano.com, Web Site: www.playpiano.com (20)

Shinsky, Janet, American Red Cross, Washington, DC. Tel: (703) 303-5000 X5, (800) RED-CROSS, Web Site: www.redcross.org (1)

Shipkosky, Casie, Advanstar Communications Inc, North Olmstead, OH. Tel: (440) 243-8100, (800) 225-4569, FAX: (440) 891-2740, E-Mail: info@advanstar.com, Web Site: www.advanstarlists.com (17)

Shipley, David, Samford University, Birmingham, AL. Tel: (205) 726-2011, Web Site: www.samford.edu (41)

Shipping Solutions, Eagan, MN. Tel: (651) 905-1727, (888) 890-7447, FAX: (651) 905-1827, E-Mail: info@shipsolutions.com, Web Site: www.shipsolutions.com (16)

Shipps, David, Horn Packaging Corp, Lancaster, MA. Tel: (978) 772-0290, (800) 832-7020, FAX: (978) 772-4611, E-Mail: mccarthy@horncorp.com, Web Site: www.hornpackaging.com (5)

Shirley, Joan, The Saint Francis Academy Inc, Salina, KS. Tel: (785) 825-0541, (800) 423-1342, FAX: (785) 825-2940, Web Site: www.st-francis.org (1)

Shirley, John, Alfa Aesar-A Johnson Matthey Co, Ward Hill, MA. Tel: (800) 343-0660, FAX: (800) 322-4757, E-Mail: info@alfa.com, Web Site: www.alfa.com (9)

Shiseido Cosmetics America, New York, NY. Tel: (212) 805-2300, FAX: (212) 688-0109, Web Site: www.sca.shiseido.com (7)

Shisler, Arden, L., Nationwide Mutual Insurance Co, Columbus, OH. Tel: (614) 249-7111, (800) 882-2822, FAX: (614) 854-3676, Web Site: www.nationwide.com (15)

Shisler, Jack, Shisler and Associates, Dallas, TX. Tel: (972) 387-8656 (20)

Shisler and Associates, Dallas, TX. Tel: (972) 387-8656 (20)

Shiunko, Jean, The Psychological Corp, San Antonio, TX. Tel: (800) 211-8378, FAX: (800) 232-1223, Web Site: www.psychcorp.com (17)

Shkordoff, Nick, Ideal Industries (Canada) Corp, Ajax, ON Canada. Tel: (905) 683-3400, (800) 824-3325, FAX: (905) 683-0209, E-Mail: nick.shkordoff@idealindustries.com, Web Site: www.idealindustries.com (9)

Shneider, Michael, A., Woodall Publishing Co LP, Ventura, CA. Tel: (805) 667-4100, (800) 323-9076, FAX: (805) 667-4468, Web Site: www.woodalls.com (17)

Shobe, Benita, Juvenile Diabetes Research Foundation, New York, NY. Tel: (212) 785-9500, (800) 533-CURE, FAX: (212) 785-9595, E-Mail: info@jdrf.org, Web Site: www.jdrf.org (1)

Shocker, Mark W., Ad Sell Co, Saint Louis, MO. Tel: (314) 773-0500, FAX: (314) 773-0555, Web Site: www.adsell.com (21)

Shoen, Joe, U-Haul International, Phoenix, AZ. Tel: (602) 263-6011, (800) GO-UHAUL, FAX: (602) 263-6598, Web Site: www.uhaul.com (16)

Shoen, Mark, U-Haul International, Phoenix, AZ. Tel: (602) 263-6011, (800) GO-UHAUL, FAX: (602) 263-6598, Web Site: www.uhaul.com (16)

Shoen, Robert, BDirect Marketing, Saint Paul, MN. Tel: (651) 483-3260, FAX: (651) 483-3267, E-Mail: bdirectlists@comcast.net, Web Site: www.bdirectlists.com (23)

Shoff, Patricia, Florida Today, Melbourne, FL. Tel: (321) 242-3500, (877) 424-0156, FAX: (321) 242-3729, Web Site: www.floridatoday.com (17)

Shoffner, Harry L., Carolina Biological Supply Co, Burlington, NC. Tel: (800) 334-5551, (800) 222-7112, E-Mail: carolina@carolina.com, Web Site: www.carolina.com (9)

Shokoff, Iris, Iris Shokoff Associates, New York, NY. Tel: (212) 295-9191, FAX: (212) 293-3779 (31)

Iris Shokoff Associates, New York, NY. Tel: (212) 295-9191, FAX: (212) 293-3779 (31)

Sholes, Greg, All-n-One List Marketing Inc, Fishersville, VA. Tel: (703) 717-5621, Web Site: www.alln1lists.com (23)

Shone, Thomas, Cooper Vision, Fairport, NY. Tel: (585) 385-6810, (800) 341-2020, Web Site: www.coopervision.com (7)

Shonebarger, Steven, Harry Winston Inc, New York, NY. Tel: (212) 245-2000, FAX: (212) 489-0016, E-Mail: hw@harrywinston.com, Web Site: www.harry-winston.com (16)

Shooster, Frank, Global Response Corp, Margate, FL. Tel: (954) 973-7300, (800) 537-8000, FAX: (954) 968-9862, E-Mail: wendys@globalresponse.com, Web Site: www.globalresponse.com (29)

Shooster, Herman, Global Response Corp, Margate, FL. Tel: (954) 973-7300, (800) 537-8000, FAX: (954) 968-9862, E-Mail: wendys@globalresponse.com, Web Site: www.globalresponse.com (29)

Shooting Star International, Hollywood, CA. Tel: (323) 469-2020, FAX: (323) 464-0880, Web Site: www.shootingstaragency.com (38)

Shop At Home LLC, Knoxville, TN. Tel: (615) 263-8000, (866) 366-4010, E-Mail: public.relations@jtv.com, Web Site: www.shopathometv.com (32)

Shop.com, Monterey, CA. Tel: (831) 647-2489, (866) 746-7005, FAX: (831) 644-9283, Web Site: www.shop.com (16)

Shopguide.com, Amarillo, TX. Tel: (806) 351-0005, FAX: (806) 351-0059, E-Mail: info@shopguide.com, Web Site: www.shopguide.com (27)

Shopsmith Inc, Dayton, OH. Tel: (937) 898-6070, (800) 543-7586, FAX: (937) 890-5197, Web Site: www.shopsmith.com (16)

Shor, Tama, J., Directory of Major Malls, Nyack, NY. Tel: (845) 348-7000, (800) 898-6255, Web Site: www.shoppingcenters.com (23)

Shore, Laura, Mohawk, Cohoes, NY. Tel: (518) 237-1740, (800) 843-6455, FAX: (518) 237-7394, E-Mail: info@mohawkpaper.com, Web Site: www.mohawkconnects.com (25)

Shoreham, Lee, Privacy Journal, Providence, RI. Tel: (401) 274-7861, FAX: (401) 274-4747, E-Mail: orders@privacyjournal.net, Web Site: www.privacyjournal.net (17)

Shorette, Ken, Time Logistics Inc, Columbia, TN. Tel: (931) 540-2801, (866) 293-8463, FAX: (931) 540-2995, Web Site: www.timelogisticsinc.com (12)

Shorette, Laura, Time Logistics Inc, Columbia, TN. Tel: (931) 540-2801, (866) 293-8463, FAX: (931) 540-2995, Web Site: www.timelogisticsinc.com (12)

Short, Diane, Easthill Group Inc, Pottstown, PA. Tel: (610) 323-9099, (610) 323-9063, (610) 323-2200, (888) 869-4433, (800) 345-1178, FAX: (610) 323-6268, Web Site: www.eastwoodcompany.com (12)

Short, John, News Notes LLC, Middleton, WI. Tel: (608) 831-9600, Web Site: www.news-notes.com (35)

Short, William S., Rent-A-Center Inc, Plano, TX. Tel: (972) 801-1100, (800) 275-2996, FAX: (972) 943-0113, Web Site: www.rentacenter.com (16)

Short Sizes Inc, Northfield, OH. Tel: (440) 605-1000, (800) 272-9000, FAX: (440) 605-1065, E-Mail: orders@shortsizesinc.com, Web Site: www.shortsizesinc.com (2)

Shortage Control Inc & SC Video, Strongsville, OH. Tel: (440) 238-5432, (800) 332-2288, FAX: (440) 238-8687, E-Mail: sales@shortagecontrol.com, Web Site: www.shortagecontrol.com (5)

Shoup, John, Great Chefs Television Publishing, New Orleans, LA. Tel: (504) 581-5000, (800) 321-1499, FAX: (504) 581-1188, E-Mail: info@greatchefs.com, Web Site: www.greatchefs.com (6)

Shoup, Mike, Antique Rose Emporium, Brenham, TX. Tel: (800) 441-0002, FAX: (979) 836-0928, E-Mail: roses@industyinet.com, Web Site: www.weareroses.com (8)

Shouse, Clay, HighScope Educational Research Foundation, Ypsilanti, MI. Tel: (734) 485-2000, (800) 40-PRESS, FAX: (734) 485-0704, E-Mail: lschweinhart@highscope.org, Web Site: www.highscope.org (17)

Showerman, Sandy, Hess Print Solutions, Kent, OH. Tel: (330) 677-3353, FAX: (330) 677-8256, E-Mail: sshowerman@hessprintsolutions.com, Web Site: www.thepressofohio.com (27)

Showtime Networks Inc, New York, NY. Tel: (212) 708-1600, FAX: (212) 708-1450, Web Site: www.sho.com (17)

Shragal, Sara, DirectBuy Inc, Merrillville, IN. Tel: (219) 736-1100, FAX: (219) 755-6208, Web Site: www.ucctotalhome.com (1)

Shriver, Norman, Orbit Manufacturing Co, Perkasie, PA. Tel: (215) 453-9228, (888) 895-0958, FAX: (215) 257-7399, Web Site: www.orbitmfg.com (9)

Shrivers, Timothy, Special Olympics International, Washington, DC. Tel: (202) 628-3630, FAX: (202) 824-0200, Web Site: www.specialolympics.org (1)

Shroeder Sr., Bill, Collector Books & American Quilters Society, Paducah, KY. Tel: (270) 898-6211, (800) 626-5420, FAX: (270) 898-8890, E-Mail: info@collectorbooks.com, Web Site: www.collectorbooks.com (17)

Shtulman, Jill, JSA Creative Services LLC, Chicago, IL. Tel: (773) 772-3445, FAX: (773) 772-3446, E-Mail: jsacreative@comcast.net, Web Site: www.jsacreative.com (39)

Shubin, Neil, L., The Field Museum, Chicago, IL. Tel: (312) 665-7909, FAX: (312) 665-7101, Web Site: www.fieldmuseum.org (1)

Shuchman, Salem, Entrepreneur Partners, Philadelphia, PA. Tel: (267) 322-7000, Web Site: www.epfunds.com (14)

Shukers, Allen, Hoover's, Austin, TX. Tel: (512) 374-4500 (22)

Shukle, Janice, Harris Marketing Group, Birmingham, MI. Tel: (248) 723-6300, FAX: (248) 723-6301, E-Mail: info@harris-hmg.com, Web Site: www.harris-hmg.com (35)

Shull, Cecily, Pritchett & Hull Associates Inc, Atlanta, GA. Tel: (770) 451-0602, (800) 241-4925, FAX: (770) 454-7130, E-Mail: sales@p-h.com, Web Site: www.p-h.com (17)

Shully, Mary, Ameritech Services Inc, Milwaukee, WI. Tel: (800) 924-1000, Web Site: www.ameritech.com (16)

Shunk, Gary, Brokers Worldwide LLC, Folcroft, PA. Tel: (610) 461-3661, (800) MAIL-287, FAX: (610) 461-4239, E-Mail: csmith@brokersworldwide.com, Web Site: www.brokersworldwide.com (28)

Shurn, Gloria, J., Gloria Shurn Creative Services, Chicago, IL. Tel: (312) 337-0032, FAX: (312) 337-3958 (35)

Gloria Shurn Creative Services, Chicago, IL. Tel: (312) 337-0032, FAX: (312) 337-3958 (35)

Shurtleff, Jane, Market Recognition, Boxborough, MA. Tel: (978) 314-0127, Web Site: www.marketrecognition.com (20)

Shusterman, Howard, Rex Three Inc, Sunrise, FL. Tel: (954) 452-8301, (800) 782-6509, FAX: (954) 452-0569, E-Mail: info@rex3.com, Web Site: www.rexthree.com (27)

Shute, Dave, TransAmerica Retirement Services, Los Angeles, CA. Tel: (213) 742-3363, Web Site: www.ta-retirement.com (15)

Shutterbug, Titusville, FL. Tel: (321) 269-3212, FAX: (321) 255-3146, Web Site: www.shutterbug.net (17)

Shutterfly, Redwood City, CA. Tel: (650) 610-5200, Web Site: www.shutterfly.com (27)

Shutts, Anthony, Charisma Brands LLC, Laguna Hills, CA. Tel: (949) 788-8803, Web Site: www.charismabrands.com (6)

Shyam, Megha, Da Vinci Technologies LLC, Auburn, AL. Tel: (334) 502-8925, (877) 334-4731, FAX: (208) 485-7749, E-Mail: sales@davinci.aero, Web Site: www.davincitechnologies.com (3)

Siadak, Amy, House of Marketing Research, Pasadena, CA. Tel: (626) 486-1400, FAX: (626) 486-1404, Web Site: www.hmr-research.com (30)

Sias, Spencer, Varian Medical Systems, Palo Alto, CA. Tel: (650) 493-4000, FAX: (650) 842-5196, Web Site: www.varian.com (9)

Sibal, Marc, Manhattan Media Services Inc, New York, NY. Tel: (212) 808-4077, FAX: (212) 808-4080, E-Mail: mmorello@manhmedia.com, Web Site: www.manhmedia.com (21)

Siburg, Dan, US Data Corp, Omaha, NE. Tel: (402) 502-5623, (888) 578-3282, FAX: (402) 502-5623, Web Site: www.usdatacorporation.com (29)

Sichler, Ron, DM News, New York, NY. Tel: (212) 925-7300, FAX: (212) 925-8752, Web Site: www.dmnews.com (43)

Sickafus Sheepskins, Strausstown, PA. Tel: (610) 488-1782, (888) 751-1300, FAX: (610) 488-1576, E-Mail: pat@patgarrett.com, Web Site: www.sheepcoat.com (2)

SickKids Foundation, Toronto, ON Canada. Tel: (416) 813-6166, Web Site: www.sickkidsfoundation.com (1)

Side, Bruce, Phoenix Marketing Group Ltd, Georgetown, CT. Tel: (203) 762-8665, FAX: (203) 762-8285 (21)

Sidell, Bob, California Cosmetics Corp, Tarzana, CA. Tel: (818) 225-2999, (800) 366-8243, FAX: (800) 345-7763, E-Mail: calcos@silkskin.com, Web Site: www.silkskin.com (7)

Sideroff, Barry, Direct Ventures Inc, Larchmont, NY. Tel: (914) 833-9842, FAX: (914) 834-3883, E-Mail: bsideroff@directventuresmcinc.wm (20)

Sidlik, Thomas, W., Eastern Michigan University, Ypsilanti, MI. Tel: (734) 487-1849, FAX: (734) 484-1151, Web Site: www.emich.edu (16)

Sieg, Albert, Photographic Society of America Inc (PSA), Oklahoma City, OK. Tel: (405) 843-1437, FAX: (405) 843-1438, E-Mail: HQ@psa-photo.org, Web Site: www.psa-photo.org (40)

Siegel M.D., Eliot, Carestream Health Inc, Rochester, NY. Tel: (585) 627-1800, (888) 777-2072, Web Site: www.carestreamhealth.com (7)

Siegel, Jeffrey, J., TAPPI (Technical Association of the Pulp & Paper Industry), Norcross, GA. Tel: (678) 642-66, (800) 332-8686, FAX: (770) 446-6947, E-Mail: webmaster@tappi.org, Web Site: www.tappi.org (1)

Siegel, Jeffrey, Lifetime Brands Inc, Garden City, NY. Tel: (516) 683-6000, FAX: (516) 683-6161, E-Mail: postmaster@brands.com, Web Site: www.lifetimebrands.com (8)

Siegel, Mo, Celestial Seasonings, Boulder, CO. Tel: (303) 530-5300, (800) 434-4246, FAX: (303) 581-1249, Web Site: www.hain-celestial.com (16)

Siegel, Neal, Tri-Media Marketing Services Inc, Wilmette, IL. Tel: (800) 874-4062, Web Site: www.trimediaonline.com (23)

Siegel, Peri, Potpourri Group Inc, Chelmsford, MA. Tel: (978) 256-4100, FAX: (978) 256-1961/0344, Web Site: www.potpourrigroup.com (6)

Siegel, Stephen, UV Process Supply, Chicago, IL. Tel: (773) 248-0099, (800) 621-1296, FAX: (773) 880-6647, E-Mail: info@uvps.com, Web Site: www.uvprocess.com (34)

Siegel Display Products, Minneapolis, MN. Tel: (612) 340-1493, (800) 626-0322, FAX: (800) 230-5598, E-Mail: mwendel@siegeldisplay.com, Web Site: www.siegeldisplay.com (5)

Siegfried, Bradford, BLS Inc, Wilmington, DE. Tel: (302) 631-1616, (800) 545-7766, FAX: (302) 631-1619, E-Mail: bls@tutorsystems.com, Web Site: www.tutorsystems.com (17)

Siemens IT Solutions & Services Inc, Norwalk, CT. Tel: (203) 642-2300, FAX: (203) 642-2399, Web Site: www.it-solutions.usa.siemens.com (16)

Siemers, Scott, Morcon Industrial Specialty Inc, Mesquite, NV. Tel: (702) 346-3447, (888) 842-7953, Web Site: www.morcon-ind.com (9)

Sierke Jr., William, H., Gothic Arch Greenhouses Inc, Mobile, AL. Tel: (251) 432-7529, (800) 531-4769, FAX: (251) 432-2655, E-Mail: gothicarch@comcast.net, Web Site: www.GothicArchGreenhouses.com (8)

Sierke, Paul, C., Gothic Arch Greenhouses Inc, Mobile, AL. Tel: (251) 432-7529, (800) 531-4769, FAX: (251) 432-2655, E-Mail: gothicarch@comcast.net, Web Site: www.GothicArchGreenhouses.com (8)

Sierke, Zack, Gothic Arch Greenhouses Inc, Mobile, AL. Tel: (251) 432-7529, (800) 531-4769, FAX: (251) 432-2655, E-Mail: gothicarch@comcast.net, Web Site: www.GothicArchGreenhouses.com (8)

Sierra, Jeff, Budco, Highland Park, MI. Tel: (313) 957-5100, Web Site: www.budco.com (35)

Sierra Club Books, San Francisco, CA. Tel: (415) 977-5500, FAX: (415) 977-5792, E-Mail: books.publishing@sierraclub.org, Web Site: www.sierraclub.org (1)

Sierra Inc, Racine, WI. Tel: (262) 638-1851, FAX: (414) 638-1852, E-Mail: support@sierrainc.com, Web Site: www.sierra.com (3)

Sierra Scientific Inc, Phoenix, AZ. Tel: (602) 256-0540, FAX: (602) 252-1972, Web Site: www.value-tek.com (9)

Sierra Trading Post, Cheyenne, WY. Tel: (307) 775-8050, (800) 713-4534, FAX: (307) 775-8089, Web Site: www.sierratradingpost.com (2)

Siewort, Harry, Cable Car Clothiers/Robert Kirk Ltd, San Francisco, CA. Tel: (415) 397-4740, FAX: (415) 616-8998, E-Mail: info@cablecarclothiers.com, Web Site: www.cablecarclothiers.com (2)

Sight Marketing, Minneapolis, MN. Tel: (651) 379-4059, Web Site: www.sightmarketing.com (30)

Sigma Micro LLC, Indianapolis, IN. Tel: (317) 631-0907, (800) 383-4421, FAX: (317) 631-6585, Web Site: www.sigma-micro.com (21)

Sigman, Betsy, Mary Culnan, Washington, DC. Tel: (202) 687-4031, (202) 687-0100, E-Mail: www.georgetown.edu (20)

The Signature Agency, Raleigh, NC. Tel: (919) 878-8989, (800) 870-8700, FAX: (919) 878-3939, E-Mail: info@signatureagency.com, Web Site: www.signatureagency.com (35)

Signature Communications, Milton, MA. Tel: (617) 642-1300, FAX: (617) 696-2144, E-Mail: info@signaturecom.com, Web Site: www.signaturecom.com (21)

Signature Inc, Ann Arbor, MI. Tel: (734) 426-2000, FAX: (734) 426-2109, E-Mail: johnagno@signatureseries.com, Web Site: www.mentoringandcoaching.com (20)

Signature Styles LLC, New York, NY. Tel: (800) 443-4856, FAX: (902) 862-5063 (2)

Sikanas, Debra, Baudville Inc, Grand Rapids, MI. Tel: (616) 698-0889, (800) 728-0888, FAX: (616) 698-0554, E-Mail: service@baudville.com, Web Site: www.baudville.com (16)

Sikorski, John, National Mail Graphics Corp, Exton, PA. Tel: (610) 524-1600, FAX: (610) 524-7638, E-Mail: jsikorski@nmgcorp.com, Web Site: www.nmgcorp.com (27)

Silber, Tony, Audience Development, Norwalk, CT. Tel: (203) 854-6730, FAX: (203) 854-6735, E-Mail: inolan@red7media.com, Web Site: www.audiencedevelopment.com (43)

Silberman, S., American Thermoplastic Co, Pittsburgh, PA. Tel: (412) 967-0900, (800) 245-6600, FAX: (412) 967-9990, E-Mail: atc@binders.com, Web Site: www.binders.com (27)

Silbert, Jules, Brylane, Indianapolis, IN. Tel: (800) 677-0339, Web Site: www.brylanehome.com (2)

Silicato, Steve, MARCOR Remediation Inc, Halethorpe, MD. Tel: (410) 785-0001, (800) 547-0128, FAX: (410) 771-0348, E-Mail: info@marcor.com, Web Site: www.marcor.com (16)

Silicon Graphics Inc, Fremont, CA. Tel: (510) 933-8300, Web Site: www.sgi.com (16)

Silliker Inc, Chicago, IL. Tel: (708) 957-7878, FAX: (708) 957-3798, E-Mail: cjx@netcom.com, Web Site: www.silliker.com (20)

The Silo Inc, New Milford, CT. Tel: (860) 355-0300, (800) 353-SILO, FAX: (860) 350-5495, E-Mail: info@hunthillfarmtrust.org, Web Site: www.thesilo.com (8)

Silva, Erin, Eastern Bank, Lynn, MA. Tel: (800) EASTERN, Web Site: www.easternbank.com (14)

Silver, Charles, Bloomingdale's By Mail Ltd, New York, NY. Tel: (212) 224-7721, (800) 472-0788, FAX: (212) 715-2805, Web Site: www.bloomingdales.com (5)

Silver, Mike, Elite Promotions, Highland Park, IL. Tel: (773) 282-0338, FAX: (773) 282-9081, E-Mail: mike@elitepromotions.com, Web Site: www.elitepromotions.com (33)

Silver, Patricia, Silver Marketing Inc, Bethesda, MD. Tel: (301) 951-3505, FAX: (301) 652-3691, E-Mail: psilver@silvermktg.com, Web Site: www.silvermarketing.com (35)

Silver Marketing Inc, Bethesda, MD. Tel: (301) 951-3505, FAX: (301) 652-3691, E-Mail: psilver@silvermktg.com, Web Site: www.silvermarketing.com (35)

Silverdides, Ian, National Wholesale Co Inc, Lexington, NC. Tel: (336) 248-5904, (800) 480-4673, FAX: (336) 248-2880, E-Mail: customerservice@shopnational.com, Web Site: www.shopnational.com (2)

Silverman, George, The Teleconference Network, Nanuet, NY. Tel: (845) 624-0633, FAX: (845) 623-9394, E-Mail: nospam@mnav.com, Web Site: www.market-navigation.com (30)

Silverman, Ivan, TelAmerica Media Inc, Philadelphia, PA. Tel: (215) 568-7066, FAX: (215) 564-5388, Web Site: www.telamericamedia.com (31)

Silverman, Mickey, MoreMedia Direct Inc, Miami Beach, FL. Tel: (305) 672-9793, E-Mail: info@moremediadirect.com, Web Site: www.moremediadirect.com (35)

Silverman, Richard, Richard Silverman, Kew Gardens, NY. Tel: (718) 441-5358, FAX: (718) 441-5358, E-Mail: vze268ci@verizon.net (39)

Silverman, Robert, The Bil-Ray Aluminum Siding Corp of Queens Inc, New Hyde Park, NY. Tel: (516) 616-4200, (800) 474-4415, FAX: (516) 616-4030, Web Site: www.homeclub.com (16)

Richard Silverman, Kew Gardens, NY. Tel: (718) 441-5358, FAX: (718) 441-5358, E-Mail: vze268ci@verizon.net (39)

Robert Silverman Direct Marketing, Cleveland, OH. Tel: (216) 881-9191, (888) 884-9191, FAX: (216) 881-3442, Web Site: www.cgginc.com (35)

SilverPop, Atlanta, GA. Tel: (866) 745-8767, FAX: (678) 247-0501, E-Mail: info@silverpop.com, Web Site: www.silverpop.com (32)

Silvers, Robert, Nyrev Inc, New York, NY. Tel: (212) 757-8070, FAX: (212) 333-5374, E-Mail: mail@nybooks.com, Web Site: www.nybooks.com (17)

SilverState Marketing Solutions, Las Vegas, NV. Tel: (702) 489-2124, Web Site: www.silverstateprintmail.com (28)

Silverstone, Bruce T., Product Marketplace, Stratford, CT. Tel: (203) 375-8371, (800) 286-4768, FAX: (203) 386-1203, E-Mail: rita@sabinc.com (35)

Silverstone, Bruce T., Silverstone, Adkins & Breit Inc, Trumbull, CT. Tel: (203) 375-2887, FAX: (203) 386-1203, E-Mail: info@sabinc.com, Web Site: www.sabinc.com (35)

Silverstone, Adkins & Breit Inc, Trumbull, CT. Tel: (203) 375-2887, FAX: (203) 386-1203, E-Mail: info@sabinc.com, Web Site: www.sabinc.com (35)

Sim, Judith, Oracle Corp, Redwood Shores, CA. Tel: (650) 506-7000, (800) 633-0738, FAX: (650) 506-7200, Web Site: www.oracle.com (16)

Simanis, Ann, Elderhostel Inc, Boston, MA. Tel: (617) 426-7788, (800) 454-5678, FAX: (617) 426-2166, Web Site: www.elderhostel.org (1)

Simcic, Christian, Fasson Roll Div, Mentor, OH. Tel: (440) 354-7900, (440) 358-4712, (440) 358-6025, Web Site: www.fasson.com (16)

Simermeyer, Julie, Shelburne Co, Taneytown, MD. Tel: (410) 876-5902, FAX: (410) 876-4612, Web Site: www.zoysiafarms.com (8)

Simic, Mateja, International Advertising Association, New York, NY. Tel: (212) 557-1133, FAX: (212) 983-0455, E-Mail: membership@iaaglobal.com, Web Site: www.iaaglobal.org (1)

Simitz, Julieanne, The Interfaith Alliance, Washington, DC. Tel: (202) 639-6370, Web Site: www.interfaithalliance.org (1)

Simkins, Laura, Western Fulfillment Management Association Inc, North Hollywood, CA. Tel: (310) 323-7220, FAX: (310) 323-7231, E-Mail: mjordan@espcomp.com, Web Site: www.wfma.org (40)

Simmonds, David, Foremost Insurance Group, Grand Rapids, MI. Tel: (616) 956-8241, (800) 527-3905, FAX: (800) 325-1507, Web Site: www.foremost.com (15)

Simmons, Charlie, Standard Register, Dayton, OH. Tel: (937) 221-1000, (800) 755-6405, FAX: (937) 221-1239, E-Mail: julie.mcewan@standardregister.com, Web Site: www.standardregister.com (10)

Simmons, Elliot, WLNY-TV, Melville, NY. Tel: (631) 622-9420, FAX: (631) 420-4846, Web Site: www.wlnytv.com (31)

Simmons, Jean, Catholic Relief Services, Baltimore, MD. Tel: (410) 951-7491, Web Site: www.catholicrelief.org (1)

Simmons, Mark, ITW Bee Leitzke, Iron Ridge, WI. Tel: (920) 625-2342, FAX: (920) 625-2643, Web Site: www.itwbeeleitzke.com (16)

Simmons, Patricia, S., University of Minnesota Alumni Association, Minneapolis, MN. Tel: (612) 624-2323, (800) UM-ALUMS, FAX: (612) 626-8167, E-Mail: umalumni@umn.edu, Web Site: www.umaa.umn.edu (1)

Simmons, Robin, Vidi Emi Inc, San Leandro, CA. Tel: (510) 667-9999, FAX: (510) 352-9999, E-Mail: info@vidiemi.com, Web Site: www.vidiemi.com (32)

Simmons, Ron, Viatech Publishing Solutions Inc, Bay Shore, NY. Tel: (631) 968-8500, (800) 645-8558, FAX: (631) 968-0830, Web Site: www.viatechpub.com (16)

Simmons, Steve, ACCUSPLIT Inc, Livermore, CA. Tel: (925) 226-0888, (800) 935-1996, FAX: (925) 463-0147, E-Mail: sales@accusplit.com, Web Site: www.accusplit.com (16)

Simmons-Boardman Publishing Corp, New York, NY. Tel: (212) 620-7200, FAX: (212) 633-1165 (17)

Simmons College, Boston, MA. Tel: (617) 521-2027, Web Site: www.simmons.edu (1)

Simms, Derek, IVisionMobile Inc, Chatsworth, CA. Tel: (866) 655-5302, Web Site: www.ivisionmobile.com (35)

Simms, John, Odell, Simms & Associates Inc, Falls Church, VA. Tel: (703) 903-9797, FAX: (703) 903-8850, E-Mail: webmaster@odellsimms.com, Web Site: www.odellsimms.com (35)

Simon, Alan, Omaha Steaks Inc, Omaha, NE. Tel: (402) 597-3000, FAX: (402) 597-8252, E-Mail: info@omahasteaks.com, Web Site: www.omahasteaks.com (4)

Simon, Bruce, A., Omaha Steaks Inc, Omaha, NE. Tel: (402) 597-3000, FAX: (402) 597-8252, E-Mail: info@omahasteaks.com, Web Site: www.omahasteaks.com (4)

Simon, Don, Avis World Headquarters, Parsippany, NJ. Tel: (973) 496-3500, Web Site: www.avis.com (19)

Simon, Frederick, J., Omaha Steaks Inc, Omaha, NE. Tel: (402) 597-3000, FAX: (402) 597-8252, E-Mail: info@omahasteaks.com, Web Site: www.omahasteaks.com (4)

Simon, Irwin, David, Hain Celestial Group, Melville, NY. Tel: (631) 730-2200, FAX: (631) 730-2500, Web Site: www.hain-celestial.com (16)

Simon, Irwin, David, Jason Natural Personal Care Products, Boulder, CO. Tel: (877) 527-6601, Web Site: www.jason-natural.com (7)

Simon, John, A., Overseas Private Investment Corp (OPIC), Washington, DC. Tel: (202) 336-8400, FAX: (202) 336-7949, E-Mail: info@opic.gov, Web Site: www.opic.gov (14)

Simon, Marc, HALO/Lee Wayne, Sterling, IL. Tel: (815) 632-0980, (866) 840-6401, FAX: (815) 632-6900, E-Mail: moreinfo@leewayne.com, Web Site: www.leewayne.com (16)

Simon, Marc, S., Halo Branded Solutions, Sterling, IL. Tel: (877) 592-4256, (866) 840-6401, FAX: (815) 632-6900, E-Mail: moreinfo@haloleewayne.com, Web Site: www.haloleewayne.com (32)

Simon, Mark, Federal Citizen Information Center, Pueblo, CO. Tel: (888) 8-PUEBLO, FAX: (719) 948-9724, E-Mail: catalog.pueblo@gsa.gov, Web Site: www.pueblo.gsa.gov (5)

Simon, Matt, Cherry Tree Toys Inc, Beloit, WI. Tel: (608) 314-3090, (800) 848-4363, FAX: (608) 314-3097, E-Mail: sales@cherrytreetoys.com, Web Site: www.cherrytreetoys.com (11)

Simon, Shari, Simon Property Group, Indianapolis, IN. Tel: (317) 636-1600, FAX: (317) 263-7925, Web Site: www.shopsimon.com (16)

Simon, Todd, Omaha Steaks Inc, Omaha, NE. Tel: (402) 597-3000, FAX: (402) 597-8252, E-Mail: info@omahasteaks.com, Web Site: www.omahasteaks.com (4)

Simon & Schuster Inc, New York, NY. Tel: (212) 698-7000, (800) 223-2348, Web Site: www.simonsays.com (17)

Simon Property Group, Indianapolis, IN. Tel: (317) 636-1600, FAX: (317) 263-7925, Web Site: www.shopsimon.com (16)

Simonds, Terry, Universal Fidelity Corp, Houston, TX. Tel: (281) 550-1444, (800) 580-8887, FAX: (281) 647-4207, Web Site: www.ufccorp.com (14)

Simone, Jim, Norwood Promotional Products, Clearwater, FL. Tel: (317) 275-2500, (800) 959-9138, FAX: (317) 275-2570, Web Site: www.norwood.com (16)

Simone, Robert, Ross-Simons, Cranston, RI. Tel: (401) 463-3100, (800) 835-0919, FAX: (401) 463-8599, Web Site: www.ross-simons.com (6)

Simone-Holmes, Deborah, Direct Partner Solutions Inc, Flowery Branch, GA. Tel: (678) 762-9869, Web Site: www.directpartnersolutions.com (23)

Simonich, Melissa, Alliance of Nonprofit Mailers, Washington, DC. Tel: (202) 462-5132, FAX: (202) 462-0423, E-Mail: alliance@nonprofitmailers.org, Web Site: www.nonprofitmailers.org (40)

Simons, Adam, Crest Healthcare Supply, Dassel, MN. Tel: (800) 369-9207, (800) 328-8908, Web Site: www.cresthealthcare.com (16)

Simons-Michelson-Zieve Inc (SMZ), Troy, MI. Tel: (248) 362-4242, FAX: (248) 362-2014, Web Site: www.smz.com (35)

Simplex Grinnell, Westminster, MA. Tel: (978) 731-2500, (800) SIMPLEX, FAX: (978) 731-7856, Web Site: www.simplexgrinnell.com (16)

Simplicity Pattern Co Inc/Style Patterns Ltd/New Look English Pattern Co Ltd, New York, NY. Tel: (212) 372-0500, (888) 588-2700, FAX: (212) 372-0628, E-Mail: info@simplicitypatt.com, Web Site: www.simplicitypatt.com (8)

Simply Batteries Inc, Dekalb, IL. Tel: (815) 756-1473, Web Site: www.simplybatteries.com (7)

Simpson, B.E., Vesey's Seeds Ltd, Charlottetown, PE Canada. Tel: (902) 368-7333, (800) 363-7333, FAX: (800) 686-0329, E-Mail: customerservice@veseys.com, Web Site: www.veseys.com (8)

Simpson, Bill, Periscope Inc, Minneapolis, MN. Tel: (612) 339-0663, (800) 339-2103, FAX: (612) 339-0600, E-Mail: bill@ps-mpls.com, Web Site: www.periscope.com (35)

Simpson, Denise, Washington Post Digital, Washington, DC. Tel: (202) 334-9900 (17)

Simpson, Donald, Directory of American Business & Insurance Attorneys, New York, NY. Tel: (732) 458-7788, (800) 445-7995, FAX: (732) 458-7710, E-Mail: staff@abialaw.com, Web Site: www.abialaw.com (15)

Simpson, Gerry, Vesey's Seeds Ltd, Charlottetown, PE. Tel: (902) 368-7333, (800) 363-7333, FAX: (800) 686-0329, E-Mail: customerservice@veseys.com, Web Site: www.veseys.com (8)

Simpson, John, Dermac Labs Inc, Salem, OR. Tel: (503) 399-8181, (800) 547-9164, FAX: (503) 581-7439, Web Site: www.touchofmink.com (16)

Simpson, Kate, Academic Travel Abroad Inc, Washington, DC. Tel: (202) 785-9000, (800) 556-7896, FAX: (202) 342-0317, Web Site: www.academictravel.com (19)

Simpson Electric Co, Lac Du Flambeau, WI. Tel: (715) 588-3311, FAX: (715) 588-3327, E-Mail: cservice@simpsonelectric.com, Web Site: www.simpsonelectric.com (16)

Simqu, Blaise R., Academy of Marketing Science Journal, Thousand Oaks, CA. Tel: (805) 499-0721, FAX: (805) 583-2665, (805) 499-0871, Web Site: www.sagepub.com (43)

Sims, Barbara, Carol Enters List Co Inc, Fairfax, VA. Tel: (703) 425-0052, FAX: (703) 425-0056, E-Mail: listmanagement@carolenters.com, Web Site: www.carolenterslists.com (23)

Sims, J., R., American Society of Mechanical Engineers, New York, NY. Tel: (973) 882-1167, (800) 843-2763, FAX: (973) 882-1717, E-Mail: infocentral@asme.org, Web Site: www.asme.org (20)

Sims, Lenny, NADA Appraisal Guides, Costa Mesa, CA. Tel: (714) 556-8511, (800) 966-6232, FAX: (714) 957-0302, E-Mail: info@nadaguides.com, Web Site: www.nadaguides.com (17)

Sims, Mike, Atlanta Journal & Constitution, Atlanta, GA. Tel: (404) 526-5151, FAX: (404) 526-7122 (17)

Sims, Patricia, IDG List Services, Framingham, MA. Tel: (888) 434-5478, FAX: (508) 370-0020, Web Site: www.idglist.com (24)

Sims, Susie, EBSCO Reception Room Subscription Services, Birmingham, AL. Tel: (205) 991-1409, (800) 527-5901, FAX: (205) 995-1621, Web Site: www.ebsco.com/errss (18)

Sims, Tory, Britton, Cuvaison Inc, Calistoga, CA. Tel: (707) 942-6266, FAX: (707) 942-5732, E-Mail: jschuppert@cuvaison.com, Web Site: www.cuvaison.com (4)

Sims, Wyatt, Sims Stoves, Billings, MT. Tel: (406) 259-5644, (800) 736-5259, Web Site: www.simsstoves.com (11)

Sims Stoves, Billings, MT. Tel: (406) 259-5644, (800) 736-5259, Web Site: www.simsstoves.com (11)

Sincerbeaux, Scott, Crabtree & Evelyn Ltd, Woodstock, CT. Tel: (860) 928-2761, (800) CRAB-TREE, FAX: (860) 928-0452, Web Site: www.crabtree-evelyn.com (4)

Sinclair, Charles L., Goodyear Tire & Rubber Co, Akron, OH. Tel: (330) 796-3250, Web Site: www.goodyear.com (16)

Sinclair, Colby, 100% Real Estate Inc, Orlando, FL. Tel: (800) 454-3422, E-Mail: rcs@100percentflorida.com, Web Site: www.100percentflorida.com (16)

Sinclair, Jack, Return Path Inc, New York, NY. Tel: (212) 905-5500, FAX: (212) 905-5501, Web Site: www.returnpath.biz (22)

Sinclair, Robert, C., 100% Real Estate Inc, Orlando, FL. Tel: (800) 454-3422, E-Mail: rcs@100percentflorida.com, Web Site: www.100percentflorida.com (16)

Sindlinger, Nellie, H., Sindlinger & Co Inc, Wallingford, PA. Tel: (610) 565-0247, E-Mail: nelSind@aol.com (30)

Sindlinger & Co Inc, Wallingford, PA. Tel: (610) 565-0247, E-Mail: nelSind@aol.com (30)

Sinfield, Leslie, Merisel, New York, NY. Tel: (212) 594-4800, FAX: (212) 594-4488, E-Mail: corp@merisel.com, Web Site: www.merisel.com (16)

Singelais, Barry, Alfa Aesar-A Johnson Matthey Co, Ward Hill, MA. Tel: (800) 343-0660, FAX: (800) 322-4757, E-Mail: info@alfa.com, Web Site: www.alfa.com (9)

Singer, Dan, Houston Direct Marketing Association, Houston, TX. Tel: (281) 931-8883, FAX: (281) 820-4023, Web Site: www.houstondma.org (40)

Singer, Fred, Fred Singer Direct Marketing Inc, Rye Brook, NY. Tel: (914) 472-7100, FAX: (914) 472-9022, E-Mail: info@singerdirect.com, Web Site: www.singerdirect.com (23)

Singer, Kenny, Planet Cotton, Gaithersburg, MD. Tel: (301) 948-0400, FAX: (301) 948-9031, Web Site: www.planetcotton.com (2)

Singer, Leslie, The NPD Group Inc, Port Washington, NY. Tel: (516) 625-0700, FAX: (516) 625-2444, Web Site: www.npd.com (30)

Singer, Lloyd, Learning Communications LLC, Irvine, CA. Tel: (800) 622-3610, FAX: (949) 727-4323, E-Mail: sales@learncom.com, Web Site: www.learncom.com (16)

Singer, Lori, Calvin Klein Cosmetics Co, New York, NY. Tel: (212) 759-8888, FAX: (212) 479-4399 (7)

Singer, Marty, J&R Music/J&R Computer World, New York, NY. Tel: (212) 238-9000, (800) 806-1115, FAX: (212) 238-9191, Web Site: www.jandr.com (3)

Singer, Paul, Cincinnati Bell Tel, Cincinnati, OH. Tel: (513) 397-9900, FAX: (513) 241-8341, Web Site: www.cincinnatibelltelephone.com (16)

Singer, Robert M., Timberline Geodesics, Berkeley, CA. Tel: (510) 849-4481, (800) 366-3466, FAX: (510) 849-3265, E-Mail: info@domehome.com, Web Site: www.domehome.com (8)

Singer, Steve, G-Neil Direct Mail, Sunrise, FL. Tel: (800) 999-9111, FAX: (954) 851-1264, E-Mail: tcs@gneil.com, Web Site: www.gneil.com (10)

Singer, Steven R., Dana-Farber Cancer Institute, Boston, MA. Tel: (617) 632-3000, FAX: (617) 632-4070, E-Mail: suzanne_fountain@dfci.harvard.edu, Web Site: www.dana-farber.org (1)

Singer Direct, New York, NY. Tel: (212) 209-1900, Web Site: www.singerdirect.com (23)

Fred Singer Direct Marketing Inc, Rye Brook, NY. Tel: (914) 472-7100, FAX: (914) 472-9022, E-Mail: info@singerdirect.com, Web Site: www.singerdirect.com (23)

Singh, Livleen, The Fidelis Group Inc, Little Ferry, NJ. Tel: (410) 721-3450, Web Site: www.thefidelisgroup.net (22)

Singh, Ranjit, Aptara, Inc, Falls Church, VA. Tel: (703) 352-0001, E-Mail: info@aptaracorp.com, Web Site: www.aptaracorp.com (27)

Singh, Ranjit, Diamond Essence, Edison, NJ. Tel: (800) 909-2525, E-Mail: info@diamondessence.com, Web Site: www.diamond-essence.com (2)

Singh, Sally, Ross Metals, New York, NY. Tel: (212) 869-1407, (800) 654-ROSS (16)

Singh, Shri, Diamond Essence, Edison, NJ. Tel: (800) 909-2525, E-Mail: info@diamondessence.com, Web Site: www.diamond-essence.com (2)

Single Scene News, Tempe, AZ. Tel: (480) 945-6746, FAX: (480) 945-6746, E-Mail: publisher@azsinglescene.com, Web Site: www.azsinglescene.com (17)

Singleton, Bob, Communication Industries Corp, Grafton, VT. Tel: (802) 869-6500, FAX: (802) 869-6565, E-Mail: info@cicmail.com, Web Site: www.careersatcic.com (10)

Singleton, Mark, E., The Union Labor Life Insurance Co, Silver Spring, MD. Tel: (202) 962-2945, FAX: (202) 962-8429, E-Mail: info@ullico.com, Web Site: www.unioncare.com (15)

Sinish, Jon, Sinish Marketing Communications, Stratford, CT. Tel: (203) 375-1919, E-Mail: jon@sinishmarketing.com, Web Site: www.sinishmarketing.com (35)

Sinish Marketing Communications, Stratford, CT. Tel: (203) 375-1919, E-Mail: jon@sinishmarketing.com, Web Site: www.sinishmarketing.com (35)

Sinn, Melinda, Kansas State University Division of Continuing Education, Manhattan, KS. Tel: (785) 532-5888, Web Site: www.dce.ksu.edu (1)

Sins, Lisa, Arnaud's, New Orleans, LA. Tel: (504) 523-0611, (866) 230-8895, FAX: (504) 581-7908, Web Site: www.arnauds.com (16)

Sion, John, J., Sage Financial Group, West Conshohocken, PA. Tel: (484) 342-4400, FAX: (484) 537-0550, E-Mail: sage@sagefinancial.com, Web Site: www.sagefinancial.com (14)

Sipa Press, New York, NY. Tel: (212) 463-0150, FAX: (212) 463-0160, E-Mail: sipa@usa.com, Web Site: www.sipa.com (38)

SIPCAMADVAN, Durham, NC. Tel: (919) 226-1287 (5)

Siquis Ltd, Baltimore, MD. Tel: (410) 323-4800, FAX: (410) 323-4113, Web Site: www.siquis.com (35)

Sir Speedy Grand Rapids, Grand Rapids, MI. Tel: (616) 554-7777, Web Site: www.sirspeedy.com (27)

Sir Speedy - Green Bay, Green Bay, WI. Web Site: www.sirspeedygb.com (27)

Sir Speedy of Newtown, Newtown, PA. Tel: (215) 968-2080, Web Site: www.sirspeedynewtown.com (27)

Sir Speedy Printing and Marketing Services, Tacoma, WA. Tel: (253) 473-0765, Web Site: www..sirspeedy0905.com (27)

Sir Speedy Westbury, Westbury, NY. Tel: (516) 334-7400, Web Site: www.sirspeedyny.net (27)

Sirius XM Radio, Washington, DC. Tel: (212) 584-5100 (16)

Sirotkin, Pete, Omaha Fixture International, Omaha, NE. Tel: (402) 592-3720, (800) 531-6627, FAX: (402) 593-5716, (800) 531-6627, Web Site: www.omahafixture.com (8)

Sisco, Julie, Teachers Credit Union, South Bend, IN. Tel: (574) 284-6455, Web Site: www.tcunet.com (1)

Sisk, Clyde, Sisk Mailing Service, Stevensville, MD. Tel: (410) 643-7900, FAX: (410) 643-7933, E-Mail: clyde_sisk@siskmail.com, Web Site: www.siskmail.com (28)

Sisk Fulfillment Service Inc, Federalsburg, MD. Tel: (410) 754-8141, FAX: (410) 754-8223, Web Site: www.siskfulfillment.com (22)

Sisk Mailing Service, Stevensville, MD. Tel: (410) 643-7900, FAX: (410) 643-7933, E-Mail: clyde_sisk@siskmail.com, Web Site: www.siskmail.com (28)

Siskind, Windy, Burlington Coat Factory, Burlington, NJ. Tel: (609) 387-7800, FAX: (609) 387-7071, Web Site: www.coat.com (16)

Sitel, Nashville, TN. Tel: (615) 301-7100, (866) 95-SITEL, E-Mail: pr-na@sitet.com, Web Site: www.sitel.com (23)

Siteman, Frank, Frank Siteman Photography, Winchester, MA. Tel: (781) 729-3747, E-Mail: frank@franksiteman.com, Web Site: www.franksiteman.com (37)

Skaar, Cynthia, Group f/64, Winston-Salem, NC. Tel: (336) 748-8272, FAX: (336) 748-8780 (20)

Skar Advertising, Omaha, NE. Tel: (402) 330-0110, FAX: (402) 330-8791, E-Mail: skar@skar.com, Web Site: www.skar.com (35)

Skelley, Christie, Strategy Corps LLC, Brentwood, TN. Tel: (615) 221-8381, (888) 577-6933, FAX: (615) 221-8479, E-Mail: info@strategycorps.com, Web Site: www.strategycorps.com (16)

Skelton, Chad, OCE North America Inc, Boca Raton, FL. Tel: (561) 997-3100, (800) 523-5444, FAX: (561) 998-9160, Web Site: www.oceproductionprinting.com (34)

Skerker, Joan, Robinson Home Products, Buffalo, NY. Tel: (716) 685-6300, FAX: (716) 685-4916 (16)

Skerker, Larry, Robinson Home Products, Buffalo, NY. Tel: (716) 685-6300, FAX: (716) 685-4916 (16)

Skerker, Robert, Robinson Home Products, Buffalo, NY. Tel: (716) 685-6300, FAX: (716) 685-4916 (16)

Skidmore, Gary, Harte-Hanks, Austin, TX. Tel: (512) 434-1100, (800) 456-9748, FAX: (512) 244-9222, Web Site: www.harte-hanks.com (22)

Skies America International Publishing & Communications, Beaverton, OR. Tel: (503) 520-1955, FAX: (503) 520-1275, E-Mail: skies@skies.com, Web Site: www.skies.com (36)

Skilling, D., Van, Cole Information Services, Omaha, NE. Tel: (800) 403-5894, Web Site: www.coleinformation.com (23)

Skillings, Jim, DeLorme Mapping, Yarmouth, ME. Tel: (207) 846-7000, (800) 561-5105, FAX: (207) 846-7051, E-Mail: caleb.mason@delorme.com, Web Site: www.delorme.com (3)

Skillington, James, New Village Media Inc, Columbia, MD. Tel: (443) 832-4007, E-Mail: jskillington@newvillagemedia.com (35)

Skinder-Strauss Associates, Newark, NJ. Tel: (973) 642-1440, Web Site: www.elaw.com (14)

Skinner, James, E., Neiman-Marcus Group, Dallas, TX. Tel: (214) 743-7600, (888) 888-4757, FAX: (214) 573-5320, Web Site: www.neimanmarcus.com (8)

Skinner, Vayia, Iris Marketing, Bel Air, MD. Tel: (443) 742-1232 (20)

Sklarsky, Frank S., Eastman Kodak Co, Rochester, NY. Tel: (585) 724-0251, (800) 698-3324, FAX: (585) 724-1089, Web Site: www.kodak.com (27)

Sklorenko, Michael, The Alesco Data Group, Fort Myers, FL. Tel: (239) 275-5006, (800) 701-6531, FAX: (239) 275-7737, E-Mail: marketing@alescodata.com, Web Site: www.alescodata.com (23)

Skogerson, Dirk, JT International, Teaneck, NJ. Tel: (201) 871-1210, Web Site: www.jti.com (16)

Skolnick, Robert, Synovate, New York, NY. Tel: (212) 293-6100, FAX: (212) 293-6666 (30)

Skop, Joe, Satori Software Inc, Seattle, WA. Tel: (206) 357-2900, (800) 553-6477, FAX: (206) 357-2901, E-Mail: sales@satorisoftware.com, Web Site: www.satorisoftware.com (16)

Skow, Kathi, Anderson/skow, San Francisco, CA. Tel: (888) 983-0880, Web Site: www.andersonskow.com (20)

Skredsvig, Janice, PACCAR Inc, Bellevue, WA. Tel: (425) 468-7400, FAX: (425) 468-8216, Web Site: www.paccar.com (16)

Skullduggery, Anaheim, CA. Tel: (714) 777-6425, (800) 3 FOSSIL, FAX: (714) 832-1215, Web Site: www.skullduggery.com (16)

Skunza, Kristen, G&A Marketing, Milford, OH. Tel: (513) 965-6301, (800) 688-1370, E-Mail: info@gamarketing.com, Web Site: www.gamarketing.com (35)

Skydiving Magazine, DeLand, FL. Tel: (386) 736-4793, FAX: (386) 736-9786, E-Mail: admin@skydivingmagazine.com, Web Site: www.skydivingmagazine.com (17)

Skyline Displays, Saint Paul, MN. Tel: (651) 234-6634, Web Site: www.skyline.com (5)

Skylist, Austin, TX. Tel: (877) 250-2922, FAX: (512) 857-0368, E-Mail: sales@skylist.com, Web Site: www.skylist.net (32)

SkyMall Inc, Phoenix, AZ. Tel: (602) 254-9777, (800) SKY-MALL, FAX: (602) 254-6075, Web Site: www.skymall.com (16)

Skypoint Communications Inc, Loretto, MN. Tel: (763) 548-2600, FAX: (763) 548-2610, E-Mail: info@skypoint.com, Web Site: www.skypoint.com (16)

Skystone Ryan, Cincinnati, OH. Tel: (513) 241-6778, FAX: (513) 241-0551, E-Mail: cincinnati@skystoneryan.com, Web Site: www.skystoneryan.com (20)

Skytel Communications Inc, Lewisville, TX. Tel: (800) 759-8737, Web Site: www.skytel.com (29)

Slade, Colin, L., Tektronix Inc, Beaverton, OR. Tel: (503) 627-7111, (800) 833-9200, FAX: (503) 627-3247, Web Site: www.tektronix.com (16)

Slade, Stephen, A&P, Montvale, NJ. Tel: (201) 573-9700, (866) 44 FRESH, FAX: (201) 505-3054, E-Mail: apcustomerrel@aptea.com, Web Site: www.aptea.com (16)

Slagle, Steve, Promotional Products Association International, Irving, TX. Tel: (972) 252-0404, FAX: (800) I-AM-PPAI, (972) 258-3004, E-Mail: membership@ppa.org, Web Site: www.ppa.org (40)

Slamkowski, Peter, Collegiate Cap & Gown, Champaign, IL. Tel: (217) 351-9500, FAX: (217) 351-9214, Web Site: www.herff-jones.com (16)

Slate, William, K., American Arbitration Association, New York, NY. Tel: (212) 716-5800, (800) 778-7879, FAX: (212) 716-5905, E-Mail: kesslerw@adr.org, Web Site: www.adr.org (1)

Slater, Brad, Rapid City Journal, Rapid City, SD. Tel: (605) 394-8300, FAX: (605) 394-8462, E-Mail: classifieds@rapidcityjournal.com, Web Site: www.rapidcityjournal.com (18)

Slater, Chad, Integrated Direct Marketing, Reston, VA. Tel: (703) 547-4961, E-Mail: info@integrated-dm.com, Web Site: www.integrated-dm.com (23)

Slater, Jon, Plan USA, Warwick, RI. Tel: (401) 737-5770, (800) 556-7918, FAX: (401) 738-5608, Web Site: www.planusa.org (1)

Slattery, Colleen, Hofstra University, Hempstead, NY. Tel: (516) 463-7200, FAX: (516) 463-4833, E-Mail: ccepa@hofstra.edu, Web Site: ccepa.hofstra.edu (41)

Slattery, Jack, Armbrust Paper Tubes Inc, Chicago, IL. Tel: (773) 586-3232, FAX: (773) 586-8997, E-Mail: tubesrus@corecomm.net, Web Site: www.tubesrus.com (10)

Slattery, Kathleen, San Jose Mercury News, San Jose, CA. Tel: (408) 920-5000, FAX: (408) 271-3690, Web Site: www.bayarea.com (17)

Slaughter, Ken, Gazette Communications Inc, Cedar Rapids, IA. Tel: (319) 398-8211, (800) 397-8211, FAX: (319) 368-8834, Web Site: www.gazettecommunications.com (17)

Slaughter, Sheila, Parsons School of Design Human Resource Dept, New York, NY. Tel: (212) 229-5671, FAX: (212) 229-8975, E-Mail: communications@newschool.edu, Web Site: www.parsons.edu (41)

Slavick, David, American Eagle Outfitters, Pittsburgh, PA. Tel: (412) 432-3382, Web Site: www.ae.com (2)

Slavitt, Andy, Ingenix, Reston, VA. Tel: (571) 521-7661, (800) 765-6713, FAX: (571) 521-7237, E-Mail: inform@ingenix.com, Web Site: www.ingenix.com (32)

Slavonic, Gary, Incentive Manufacturers Representatives Association (IMRA), Naperville, IL. Tel: (630) 369-7786, FAX: (630) 369-3773, E-Mail: tom@imraorg.net, Web Site: www.imraorg.net (40)

Slaybaugh, Amanda, University Press of America Inc, Lanham, MD. Tel: (301) 459-3366, (800) 462-6420, FAX: (301) 429-5748, E-Mail: custserv@rowman.com, Web Site: www.univpress.com (17)

Slayton, Karalee, Trilithic, Indianapolis, IN. Tel: (317) 423-6604, Web Site: www.trilithic.com (16)

Sleepy's Inc, Hicksville, NY. Tel: (516) 844-8800, (800) sleepys, FAX: (516) 844-8847, Web Site: www.sleepys.com (16)

Slevin, Tim, Healthcare Data Solutions, Foothill Ranch, CA. Tel: (949) 421-5971, Web Site: www.healthcaredatasolutions.com (23)

Slife, James, H., The Pioneer Group, Waterloo, IA. Tel: (319) 234-8969, FAX: (319) 234-8518, E-Mail: jslife@thepioneergroup.com, Web Site: www.pioneergroup.com (28)

Slifter, New York, NY. Tel: (212) 488-2222, Web Site: www.slifter.com (16)

Slight, Jim, JS Direct Address Limited, North Vancouver, BC Canada. Tel: (604) 987-1282, FAX: (604) 987-1283 (23)

Slim, Jerry, Horn Packaging Corp, Lancaster, MA. Tel: (978) 772-0290, (800) 832-7020, FAX: (978) 772-4611, E-Mail: mccarthy@horncorp.com, Web Site: www.hornpackaging.com (7)

Slinkard, Brent, Brent Slinkard Consultant, Bloomington, IN. Tel: (812) 336-1111 (20)

Brent Slinkard Consultant, Bloomington, IN. Tel: (812) 336-1111 (20)

Slipko, Spencer, Empire Scientific, Deer Park, NY. Tel: (631) 595-9206, (800) 645-7220, FAX: (631) 595-9384, (800) 343-5733, E-Mail: sales@empirescientific.com, Web Site: www.empirescientific.com (16)

Sloan, Linda, Promotional Product Professionals of Canada, Saint-Laurent, PQ. Tel: (514) 489-5359, FAX: (514) 489-7760, (800) 489-8741, E-Mail: gladys@pppc.ca, Web Site: www.pppc.ca (1)

Slocum, Peter D., Slocum Water Gardens, Winter Haven, FL. Tel: (863) 293-7151, FAX: (800) 322-1896, Web Site: www.slocumwatergardens.com (8)

Slocum Water Gardens, Winter Haven, FL. Tel: (863) 293-7151, FAX: (800) 322-1896, Web Site: www.slocumwatergardens.com (8)

Sloofman, Jay, Marketing Visions Inc, Tarrytown, NY. Tel: (914) 631-3900, FAX: (914) 631-3003, E-Mail: marvisions@aol.com (35)

Sloss, John, E., Commercial Lithographing Co Inc, Kansas City, MO. Tel: (816) 241-2218, FAX: (816) 241-6091, E-Mail: sjohnson@commercial-lithographing.com, Web Site: www.clitho.com (31)

Slotten, Randy, Foremost Insurance Group, Grand Rapids, MI. Tel: (616) 956-8241, (800) 527-3905, FAX: (800) 325-1507, Web Site: www.foremost.com (15)

Sludikoff, Stanley, R., Poker Player, Sherman Oaks, CA. Tel: (310) 674-3365, FAX: (310) 674-3205, E-Mail: ard@gamblingtimes.com, Web Site: www.gamblingtimes.com (17)

Slyper, Ray, Ray Slyper Associates, New York, NY. Tel: (212) 439-0710 (20)

Ray Slyper Associates, New York, NY. Tel: (212) 439-0710 (20)

Small, Larry, Yellow Pages Association, Berkeley Heights, NJ. Tel: (908) 286-2380, (800) 336-0440, FAX: (908) 286-0620, Web Site: www.yellowpagesima.org (1)

Small Business Service Bureau Inc, Worcester, MA. Tel: (508) 756-3513, (800) 343-0939, FAX: (508) 770-0528, E-Mail: membership@sbsb.com, Web Site: www.sbsb.com (1)

Smalley, Jackie, Ames-Tru-Temper, Camp Hill, PA. Tel: (304) 424-3000, FAX: (304) 424-3330 (8)

Smallhoover, Kurt, Pittsburgh Mailing, Pittsburgh, PA. Tel: (412) 922-8181, FAX: (412) 937-1730, E-Mail: ksmallhoover@pittsburghmailing.com, Web Site: www.pittsburghmailing.com (28)

Smallwood, Maureen, Tender Heart Treasures, Omaha, NE. Tel: (402) 593-1313, (800) 443-1367, FAX: (402) 593-1316, E-Mail: bcamenzind@thtdesigns.com (6)

Smaron, Marilyn, REGIT Inc, Glen Ellyn, IL. Tel: (630) 495-1500, (800) 537-9786, FAX: (630) 495-1611, E-Mail: regit@regitinc.com, Web Site: www.regitinc.com (15)

Smart DM, Toronto, ON Canada. Tel: (416) 461-9271, FAX: (416) 461-9201, E-Mail: info@smartdm.ca, Web Site: www.smartdm.ca (21)

Smart Dog Products, Winchester, TN. Tel: (931) 967-7482, (800) 264-3647, FAX: (931) 967-7483, E-Mail: sales@shopsmartdog.com (11)

Smart Inventions Inc, Paramount, CA. Tel: (562) 272-1416, (800) 275-7494, FAX: (562) 272-1423, E-Mail: customerservice@smartinventions.com, Web Site: www.smartinventions.com (32)

Smart Marketing, Dix Hills, NY. Tel: (631) 254-5259, FAX: (631) 254-4814, E-Mail: info@smartmarket.com, Web Site: www.smartmarket.com (35)

Smart Practice, Phoenix, AZ. Tel: (800) 522-0800, FAX: (800) 522-8329, E-Mail: info@smartpractice.com, Web Site: www.smartpractice.com (17)

Smart Source Direct, New York, NY. Tel: (617) 375-0404, FAX: (617) 425-0115, Web Site: www.newsamerica.com (20)

Smarterville Productions LLC, Elgin, IL. Tel: (800) 861-6531, FAX: (410) 843-8318, E-Mail: tom.callahan@smartville.com, Web Site: www.hooked-on-phonics.com (3)

Smarthome, Irvine, CA. Tel: (949) 221-9200, (800) 762-7846, FAX: (949) 221-9240, E-Mail: feedback@smarthome.com, Web Site: www.smarthome.com (32)

SmartReply Inc, Irvine, CA. Tel: (949) 340-0700, Web Site: www.smartreply.com (29)

SmartSource Corp, Burlington, MA. Tel: (781) 785-3375, Web Site: www.smartsourceonline.com (32)

Smati, Zin, Suez Energy North America, Houston, TX. Tel: (713) 636-0000, FAX: (713) 636-1364, Web Site: www.tractebelpowerinc.com (16)

Smidt, Alan, Harbor Freight Tools, Camarillo, CA. Tel: (805) 445-4791, (800) 423-2567, FAX: (800) 445-4925, Web Site: www.harborfreight.com (9)

Smidt, Eric, Harbor Freight Tools, Camarillo, CA. Tel: (805) 445-4791, (800) 423-2567, FAX: (800) 445-4925, Web Site: www.harborfreight.com (9)

Smigel, Jason, The Teaching Co, Chantilly, VA. Tel: (703) 502-7300, (800) 832-2412, FAX: (703) 378-3819, Web Site: www.teach12.com (17)

The Smile Train, New York, NY. Tel: (212) 689-9199, Web Site: www.smiletrain.org (1)

Smillie, Malcolm, JR Direct Response International Inc, Delta, BC. Tel: (604) 940-0277, FAX: (604) 946-1419, E-Mail: tammythackray@jrdirect.com, Web Site: www.jrdirect.com (23)

Smit, Pierre, Direct Mail Center, San Francisco, CA. Tel: (415) 252-1600, FAX: (415) 252-9100, E-Mail: dmc@directmailctr.com, Web Site: www.directmailctr.com (21)

Smith III, L., Lyne, Fry Consultants Inc, Atlanta, GA. Tel: (770) 226-8888, FAX: (770) 226-8899, E-Mail: mail@fryconsultants.com, Web Site: www.fryconsultants.com (30)

Smith Jr., Charles, Parcel Insurance Plan Inc, Saint Louis, MO. Tel: (314) 692-0300, (800) 325-7390, FAX: (314) 692-7598, E-Mail: office@pipinsure.com, Web Site: www.pipinsure.com (15)

Smith Sr., E.C., National Wholesale Co Inc, Lexington, NC. Tel: (336) 248-5904, (800) 480-4673, FAX: (336) 248-2880, E-Mail: customerservice@shopnational.com, Web Site: www.shopnational.com (2)

Smith, Alex, Vertex Inc, Berwyn, PA. Tel: (610) 640-4200, (800) 355-3500, FAX: (610) 640-5892, Web Site: www.vertexinc.com (16)

Smith, Alison, B., Ahern Communications Corp, Quincy, MA. Tel: (617) 471-1100, (800) 451-3280, FAX: (617) 328-9070, E-Mail: info@aherncorp.com, Web Site: www.aherncorp.com (34)

Smith, Arleen, Arleen Smith Marketing Inc, Stoughton, MA. Tel: (781) 341-0882, FAX: (781) 344-0710, Web Site: www.arleensmithmarketing.com (28)

Smith, Ben, Channel 13 WNET Catalog Division, New York, NY. Tel: (212) 560-2000, FAX: (212) 582-3297, Web Site: www.thirteen.org (5)

Smith, Betsy, House of Onyx, Inc, Greenville, KY. Tel: (270) 338-2363, (800) 844-3100, FAX: (270) 338-9605, E-Mail: sales@houseofonyx.com, Web Site: www.houseofonyx.com (6)

Smith, Bettie, Direct Selling Education Foundation, Washington, DC. Tel: (202) 452-8866, FAX: (202) 452-9015, Web Site: www.dsef.org (40)

Smith, Bowen, John Alden Life Insurance Co/North Star Marketing, Duluth, GA. Tel: (678) 473-1211, (800) 768-6288, FAX: (678) 473-9573, Web Site: www.nstarmarketing.com (15)

Smith, Brad, Hal Leonard Corp, Milwaukee, WI. Tel: (414) 774-3630, FAX: (414) 774-3259, Web Site: www.halleonard.com (17)

Smith, Brad, Intuit, Mountain View, CA. Tel: (650) 944-6000, Web Site: www.inuit.com (10)

Smith, Brad, ReMark USA, Minnetonka, MN. Tel: (952) 938-4699, FAX: (952) 988-8500, E-Mail: jessica.sbragia@remarkgroup.com, Web Site: www.remarkamericas.com (15)

Smith, Brian, Audio Classics Ltd, Vestal, NY. Tel: (607) 766-3501, FAX: (607) 766-3502, E-Mail: steve@audioclassics.com, Web Site: www.audioclassics.com (3)

Smith, Carlene, Lego Direct Marketing, Enfield, CT. Tel: (860) 749-2291, FAX: (860) FAX-LEGO, Web Site: www.lego.com (11)

Smith, Catherine, United Way of Greater Toronto, Toronto, ON. Tel: (416) 777-2001, FAX: (416) 777-0962, Web Site: www.unitedwaytoronto.com (1)

Smith, Cathie, Perrygraf, Carol Stream, IL. Tel: (630) 665-3333, (800) 323-4433, FAX: (630) 665-3491, E-Mail: info2@americanperrygraf.com, Web Site: www.perrygraf.com (16)

Smith, Christopher, Jockey International Global Inc, Kenosha, WI. Tel: (262) 658-8111 (2)

Smith, Chuck, National Relief Charities, Elkwood, VA. Tel: (540) 825-5950 (1)

Smith, Clay, Speedway, Lincoln, NE. Tel: (402) 323-3100, FAX: (402) 477-7476 (12)

Smith, Colleen, M., Brokers Worldwide LLC, Folcroft, PA. Tel: (610) 461-3661, (800) MAIL-287, FAX: (610) 461-4239, E-Mail: csmith@brokersworldwide.com, Web Site: www.brokersworldwide.com (28)

Smith, Daniel, Daniel Smith Inc, Seattle, WA. Tel: (206) 223-9599, (800) 426-6740, FAX: (800) 238-4065, E-Mail: sales@danielsmith.com, Web Site: www.danielsmith.com (10)

Smith, Daniel, DeHart & Darr Associates, McLean, VA. Tel: (703) 448-1000, FAX: (703) 790-3460 (20)

Smith, Dave, Calibre Press Inc, San Francisco, CA. Tel: (214) 545-3060, (800) 323-0037, FAX: (866) 225-4273, Web Site: www.calibrepress.com (17)

Smith, David, Fidelity Security Life Insurance Co, Kansas City, MO. Tel: (816) 756-1060, (800) 648-8624, FAX: (816) 968-0580, E-Mail: info@fslins.com, Web Site: www.fslins.com (15)

Smith, David, Friedman Marketing Svcs, Harrison, NY. Tel: (914) 698-9591, FAX: (914) 698-0485, E-Mail: paula.wynne@gfk.com, Web Site: www.friedmanmktg.com (30)

Smith, David, G., Veriad, Brea, CA. Tel: (714) 990-2700, (800) 962-0658, FAX: (800) 962-0658, E-Mail: info@veriad.com, Web Site: www.veriad.com (16)

Smith, Derek, V., Choice Point, Alpharetta, GA. Tel: (770) 752-6000, (800) 342-5339, FAX: (770) 752-6005, Web Site: www.choicepoint.com (16)

Smith, Diane, Michigan Apple Committee, Lansing, MI. Tel: (517) 669-8353, (800) 456-2753, FAX: (517) 669-9506, E-Mail: staff@michiganapples.com, Web Site: www.michiganapples.com (1)

Smith, Don, Merastar Insurance Co, Chattanooga, TN. Tel: (800) 637-2782, FAX: (800) 369-1430, E-Mail: merastar.assist.team@unitrindirect.com, Web Site: www.merastar.com (15)

Smith, Ed, American Direct Marketing Resources Inc, Chesterfield, MO. Tel: (636) 532-7703, FAX: (636) 532-2427, Web Site: www.admr.com (21)

Smith, Edwin, Select List Corp, Glen Head, NY. Tel: (516) 676-7831, FAX: (516) 676-9746 (23)

Smith, Elizabeth, Smith-Browning Direct Inc, Sedona, AZ. Tel: (928) 203-9420 (20)

Smith, Elliot, General Binding Corp, Northbrook, IL. Tel: (800) 723-4000, FAX: (800) 952-1166, (847) 272-1389, Web Site: www.gbc.com (10)

Smith, Ernie, Computer Solutions Inc, Miami, FL. Tel: (305) 558-7000, FAX: (305) 557-0003, E-Mail: mail@csiflorida.com, Web Site: www.csiflorida.com (22)

Smith, Frederick, W., Federal Express, Memphis, TN. Tel: (901) 369-3600, FAX: (901) 395-5082, Web Site: www.fedex.com (16)

Smith, Gem, Houston Direct Marketing Association, Houston, TX. Tel: (281) 931-8883, FAX: (281) 820-4023, Web Site: www.houstondma.org (40)

Smith, Greg, Schoolwise Press, San Francisco, CA. Tel: (415) 337-7971, (800) 247-8443 x 202, FAX: (415) 337-1146, E-Mail: info@schoolwisepress.com, Web Site: www.schoolwisepress.com (17)

Smith, Greg, Tomahawk Live Trap Co, Tomahawk, WI. Tel: (715) 453-3550, (800) 272-8727, FAX: (715) 453-4326, E-Mail: trapem@livetrap.com, Web Site: www.livetrap.com (16)

Smith, Harold, B., Christianity Today Inc, Carol Stream, IL. Tel: (630) 260-6200, FAX: (630) 260-0114, Web Site: www.christianitytoday.com (17)

Smith, Harold, B., Today's Christian Woman, Carol Stream, IL. Tel: (630) 260-6200, FAX: (630) 260-0114, E-Mail: tcwedit@christianitytoday.com, Web Site: www.todayschristianwoman.net (31)

Smith, Jack, Empire Blue Cross & Blue Shield, New York, NY. Tel: (212) 476-1000, (877) 476-7111, FAX: (212) 476-1281, Web Site: www.empireblue.com (15)

Smith, James, C., Webster Bank, Waterbury, CT. Tel: (203) 578-2460, FAX: (203) 754-5939, Web Site: www.websterbank.com (14)

Smith, James, Hello Direct, Nashua, NH. Tel: (408) 972-1990, (800) 435-5634, FAX: (408) 972-8155, Web Site: www.hello-direct.com (16)

Smith, Jeffrey, M., DWS Investments Service Co, Kansas City, MO. Tel: (800) 543-5776, Web Site: www.dws-investments.com (14)

Smith, Jill, L., Infomercial Sales Inc, Las Vegas, NV. Tel: (702) 253-0433, FAX: (702) 871-0759, Web Site: www.infomercialsalesinc.com (32)

Smith, Joan, A., Madisonavegifts.com, Watertown, NY. Tel: (315) 779-9228, (866) 421-1744, E-Mail: magsales@madisonavegifts.com, Web Site: www.madisonavegifts.com (6)

Smith, Jody, Leon Henry Inc, Hartsdale, NY. Tel: (914) 285-3456, FAX: (914) 285-3450, E-Mail: lh@leonhenryinc.com, Web Site: www.leonhenryinc.com (23)

Smith, John, Software Assistance International Ltd (SAIL), Morris Plains, NJ. Tel: (973) 285 1400, FAX: (201) 539-3253 (3)

Smith, Joseph, InteliTarget, Winchester, VA. Tel: (540) 409-4801, Web Site: www.intelitarget.com (29)

Smith, Joy, Partners for Incentives, Cleveland, OH. Tel: (216) 881-3000, (800) 292-7371, FAX: (216) 881-7413, Web Site: www.pfi-awards.com (33)

Smith, Judy, Reed, Atlantic-ACM, Boston, MA. Tel: (617) 720-3700, FAX: (617) 720-1077, E-Mail: atlantic@atlantic-acm.com, Web Site: www.atlantic-acm.com (20)

Smith, Julie, Brown, Van Remmen, Kanuit, Inc, El Segundo, CA. Tel: (310) 536-0777, FAX: (310) 536-0606, E-Mail: info@bvksearch.com, Web Site: www.bvksearch.com (20)

Smith, Kathy, Mailmaster Corp, Jonesboro, AR. Tel: (870) 972-8845, (800) 551-7018, FAX: (870) 972-0877, E-Mail: info@mail-master.com, Web Site: www.mail-master.com (28)

Smith, Keith, E., Boyd Gaming Corp, Las Vegas, NV. Tel: (702) 792-7200, FAX: (702) 792-7313, Web Site: www.boydgaming.com (16)

Smith, Kelly, Replacements Ltd, Greensboro, NC. Tel: (336) 697-3000, (800) REPLACE, FAX: (336) 697-3100, E-Mail: mark.donahue@replacements.com, Web Site: www.replacements.com (8)

Smith, Kenneth, M., Poly One Corp, Avon Lake, OH. Tel: (440) 930-1000, (866) POLY-ONE, FAX: (440) 930-1428, Web Site: www.polyone.com (16)

Smith, Kenneth, P., Smith O'Keefe & Associates, Egg Harbor Township, NJ. Tel: (609) 653-0400, (800) 222-0461, FAX: (609) 653-6483, E-Mail: info@smithokeefe.com, Web Site: www.smithokeefe.com (20)

Smith, Kim, Cellular One Group, Oklahoma City, OK. Tel: (509) 663-2162, (800) 545-5982, FAX: (425) 586-8451, Web Site: www.cellularone.com (16)

Smith, Leonard, D., Colgate-Palmolive Co, New York, NY. Tel: (212) 310-2000, (800) 468-6502, FAX: (212) 310-2475, Web Site: www.colgate.com (16)

Smith, Leslie, S., American Preferred Reader's Service Inc, Fort Lauderdale, FL. Tel: (954) 489-2443, FAX: (954) 492-2343, E-Mail: jfarrell@amerpref.com, Web Site: www.amerpref.com (18)

Smith, Lisa, Woolrich Inc, Woolrich, PA. Tel: (570) 769-6464, Web Site: www.woolrich.com (2)

Smith, M., Lee, M Lee Smith Publishers LLC, Brentwood, TN. Tel: (615) 373-7517, (800) 274-6774, FAX: (615) 373-5183, E-Mail: custserv@mleesmith.com, Web Site: www.mleesmith.com (27)

Smith, Mark, Navitar Inc, Rochester, NY. Tel: (585) 359-4000, FAX: (585) 359-4999, E-Mail: info@navitar.com, Web Site: www.navitar.com (16)

Smith, Mark, Portrait International Inc, Boston, MA. Tel: (617) 457-5223, Web Site: www.portraitsoftware.com (22)

Smith, Martin, Newport News, New York, NY. Tel: (800) 759-3950, Web Site: www.newport-news.com (2)

Smith, Mary, S., Tomahawk Live Trap Co, Tomahawk, WI. Tel: (715) 453-3550, (800) 272-8727, FAX: (715) 453-4326, E-Mail: trapem@livetrap.com, Web Site: www.livetrap.com (16)

Smith, Mary, Oliver of Adrian Inc, Adrian, MI. Tel: (517) 263-2132, (877) 668-0885, FAX: (517) 265-8698, E-Mail: info@oliverinstrument.com, Web Site: www.oliverofadrian.com (16)

Smith, Matthew, JDR Microdevices, Mountain View, CA. Tel: (408) 494-1400, (800) 538-5000, FAX: (800) 538-5005, E-Mail: sales@jdr.com, Web Site: www.jdr.com (3)

Smith, Michelle, Daily Commercial News & Construction Record, Markham, ON. Tel: (905) 752-5408, (800) 465-6475, FAX: (888) 396-9413, (905) 752-5450, E-Mail: dcnonl@reedbusiness.com, Web Site: www.dcnonl.com (16)

Smith, Murray, Nelson-Jameson Inc, Marshfield, WI. Tel: (715) 387-1151, (800) 826-8302, FAX: (715) 387-8746, E-Mail: sales@nelsonjameson.com, Web Site: www.nelsonjameson.com (9)

Smith, Nicole, AAI, Hopkinton, MA. Tel: (508) 544-1250, (877) 866-8500, FAX: (508) 544-1253, E-Mail: info@aai-agency.com, Web Site: www.aai-agency.com (35)

Smith, Noelle, Smith & Hawken Ltd, Novato, CA. Tel: (415) 506-3700, (800) 940-1170, FAX: (415) 506-3900, Web Site: www.smithandhawken.com (8)

Smith, Pete, Specialized Products Co, Southlake, TX. Tel: (817) 329-6647, (800) 866-5353, FAX: (800) 234-8286, E-Mail: spc@specialized.net, Web Site: www.specialized.net (16)

Smith, Phil, One World Projects, Batavia, NY. Tel: (585) 343-4490, FAX: (585) 344-3551, E-Mail: sales@oneworldprojects.com, Web Site: www.oneworldprojects.com (6)

Smith, Randal, Virco Manufacturing Corp, Conway, AR. Tel: (501) 329-2901, (800) 448-4726, FAX: (800) 258-7367, E-Mail: info@virco.com, Web Site: www.virco.com (16)

Smith, Richard, F., Equifax Credit Information Services Inc, Atlanta, GA. Tel: (404) 885-8000, (800) 685-5000, FAX: (404) 885-8988, Web Site: www.equifax.com (20)

Smith, Richard, Amrigon, Bloomfield Hills, MI. Tel: (248) 332-2300, FAX: (248) 333-9710 (29)

Smith, Richard, Entergy, New Orleans, LA. Tel: (504) 576-4000, (800) ENTERGY, FAX: (504) 576-4428, Web Site: www.entergy.com (16)

Smith, Richard, M., Newsweek Inc, New York, NY. Tel: (212) 445-4000, FAX: (212) 445-5068, Web Site: www.newsweek.com (17)

Smith, Richard, P., Dairy Farmers of America Inc, Kansas City, MO. Tel: (816) 801-6455, (888) 332-6455, FAX: (816) 801-6456, E-Mail: webmail@dfamilk.com, Web Site: www.dfamilk.com (16)

Smith, Richard, Telcordia Technologies, Piscataway, NJ. Tel: (732) 699-2000, FAX: (973) 829-2458, Web Site: www.telcordia.com (16)

Smith, Robert Ellis, Privacy Journal, Providence, RI. Tel: (401) 274-7861, FAX: (401) 274-4747, E-Mail: orders@privacyjournal.net, Web Site: www.privacyjournal.net (17)

Smith, Robert, All Star Carts & Vehicles, Bay Shore, NY. Tel: (631) 666-5252, (800) 831-3166, FAX: (631) 666-1319, Web Site: www.allstarcarts.com (16)

Smith, Robert, American Management Association, New York, NY. Tel: (212) 586-8100, FAX: (212) 903-8186, Web Site: www.amanet.org (1)

Smith, Robin, B., Publishers Clearing House, Port Washington, NY. Tel: (516) 883-5432, FAX: (516) 767-4567, E-Mail: cirving@pch.com, Web Site: www.pch.com (18)

Smith, Roscoe, AMC Publishing/Agent Media Corp, Erlanger, KY. Tel: (727) 446-1100, (800) 933-9449, FAX: (727) 446-1166, E-Mail: sales@agentmediacorp.com, Web Site: www.agentmediacorp.com (31)

Smith, Stephen, R., American Institute of Chemical Engineers, New York, NY. Tel: (203) 702-7660, (800) 242-4363, FAX: (203) 775-5177, E-Mail: xpress@aiche.org, Web Site: www.aiche.org (1)

Smith, Stephen, Eilenberger's Bakery Inc, Palestine, TX. Tel: (903) 729-2253, (800) 831-2544, FAX: (903) 723-2915, Web Site: www.eilenbergerbakery. com (4)

Smith, Steve, BJU Press, Greenville, SC. Tel: (864) 242-5100, (800) 845-5731, FAX: (800) 525-8398, (864) 271-8151, E-Mail: bjupinfo@bjupress.com, Web Site: www.bjupress.com (17)

Smith, Steve, Mailmaster Corp, Jonesboro, AR. Tel: (870) 972-8845, (800) 551-7018, FAX: (870) 972-0877, E-Mail: info@mail-master.com, Web Site: www.mail-master.com (28)

Smith, Terresa, Eilenberger's Bakery Inc, Palestine, TX. Tel: (903) 729-2253, (800) 831-2544, FAX: (903) 723-2915, Web Site: www.eilenbergerbakery. com (4)

Smith, Terry, Mary Kay Cosmetics Inc, Addison, TX. Tel: (972) 687-6300, (800) MARY KAY, FAX: (972) 687-1611, Web Site: www.marykay.com (16)

Smith, Terry, Norman Rockwell Museum, Stockbridge, MA. Tel: (413) 298-4100, (800) 742-9450, FAX: (413) 298-4144, E-Mail: emazzer@nrm.org, Web Site: www.nrm.org (16)

Smith, Thomas, P., Prime Target Direct LLC, Mason, OH. Tel: (513) 234-8977, E-Mail: tom@primetargetdirect.com (23)

Smith, Timothy C., Smith-Browning Direct Inc, Sedona, AZ. Tel: (928) 203-9420 (20)

Smith, Todd, Shield Healthcare, Valencia, CA. Tel: (661) 294-4200, (800) 228-7150, FAX: (661) 294-1043, Web Site: www.shieldhealthcare.com (7)

Smith, Wayne, Greenwood Publishing Group Inc, Portsmouth, NH. Tel: (203) 226-3571, FAX: (203) 222-1502, E-Mail: sales@greenwood.com, Web Site: www.greenwood.com (17)

Smith, William D., PVC Plastics Co, Evansville, IN. Tel: (812) 476-3592, (800) 782-7527, FAX: (812) 474-4531 (16)

Smith, William, D., e-Pipeconnection, Evansville, IN. Tel: (812) 474-4529, (800) 262-4300, FAX: (812) 474-4531, E-Mail: sales@e-pipeconnection.com, Web Site: www.e-pipeconnection.com (9)

Smith, William, M, Telecom Inc, Oakland, CA. Tel: (510) 873-8283, (800) 243-3101, FAX: (510) 873-8293, Web Site: www.telecominc.com (9)

AO Smith Corp, Milwaukee, WI. Tel: (414) 359-4000, FAX: (414) 359-4064, Web Site: www.aosmith. com (16)

Smith & Hawken Ltd, Novato, CA. Tel: (415) 506-3700, (800) 940-1170, FAX: (415) 506-3900, Web Site: www.smithandhawken.com (8)

Smith & Noble, Corona, CA. Tel: (909) 734-4444, (800) 248-8888, FAX: (800) 426-7780, E-Mail: contactus@smithnoble.com, Web Site: www. smithandnoble.com (8)

Arleen Smith Marketing Inc, Stoughton, MA. Tel: (781) 341-0882, FAX: (781) 344-0710, Web Site: www.arleensmithmarketing.com (28)

Smith-Browning Direct Inc, Sedona, AZ. Tel: (928) 203-9420 (20)

Daniel Smith Inc, Seattle, WA. Tel: (206) 223-9599, (800) 426-6740, FAX: (800) 238-4065, E-Mail: sales@danielsmith.com, Web Site: www. danielsmith.com (10)

Smith Hanley Associates, Southport, CT. Tel: (203) 319-4300, (888) 221-2900, FAX: (203) 319-4320, Web Site: www.smithhanley.com (20)

M Lee Smith Publishers LLC, Brentwood, TN. Tel: (615) 373-7517, (800) 274-6774, FAX: (615) 373-5183, E-Mail: custserv@mleesmith.com, Web Site: www.mleesmith.com (27)

Smith O'Keefe & Associates, Egg Harbor Township, NJ. Tel: (609) 653-0400, (800) 222-0461, FAX: (609) 653-6483, E-Mail: info@smithokeefe.com, Web Site: www.smithokeefe.com (20)

Smith-Bove, Holly, Motherwear, Holyoke, MA. Tel: (413) 586-1978, (800) 950-2500, FAX: (413) 532-4058, E-Mail: customerservice@motherwear.com, Web Site: www.motherwear.com (2)

Smith-McKee, Maureen, Universal Training, Lake Forest, IL. Tel: (847) 235-2170, E-Mail: information@universaltraining.com, Web Site: www.universaltraining.com (16)

Smithe Jr, Edgar, FL Smithe Machine Co Inc, Duncansville, PA. Tel: (814) 695-5521, FAX: (814) 695-0860, E-Mail: info@flsmithe.com, Web Site: www.flsmithe.com (34)

FL Smithe Machine Co Inc, Duncansville, PA. Tel: (814) 695-5521, FAX: (814) 695-0860, E-Mail: info@flsmithe.com, Web Site: www.flsmithe.com (34)

Smithfield Packing Co Inc, Smithfield, VA. Tel: (757) 357-4321, FAX: (757) 357-1339, E-Mail: information@smithfieldfoods.com, Web Site: www. smithfieldfoods.com (16)

Smithsonian Enterprises, New York, NY. Tel: (212) 916-1300, (800) 766-2149, FAX: (212) 490-0058, E-Mail: email@simag.si.edu, Web Site: www. smithsonianmag.com (17)

Smithsonian Institution, Washington, DC. Tel: (202) 357-2700, Web Site: www.si.edu (6)

Smithwick, Gary, Turner Greenhouses, Goldsboro, NC. Tel: (919) 734-8345, (800) 672-4770, FAX: (919) 736-4550, E-Mail: sales@turnergreenhouses. com, Web Site: www.turnergreenhouses.com (8)

Smithwick Fleming, Duffy, Turner Greenhouses, Goldsboro, NC. Tel: (919) 734-8345, (800) 672-4770, FAX: (919) 736-4550, E-Mail: sales@turnergreenhouses.com, Web Site: www. turnergreenhouses.com (8)

Smits, Conrad, DS Waters of North America LP, Flowery Branch, GA. Tel: (800) 585-1000, (800) 669-3402, FAX: (626) 585-8563, E-Mail: customerservice@water.com, Web Site: www. water.com (4)

Smitz, Alisa, Food for the Hungry Inc, Phoenix, AZ. Tel: (480) 998-3100, (800) 248-6437, FAX: (480) 998-4806, E-Mail: hunger@fh.org, Web Site: www.fh.org (1)

Smoczynski, Matt, Perfect Plastic Printing Corp, Saint Charles, IL. Tel: (630) 584-1600, FAX: (630) 584-0648, E-Mail: ppp@perfectplastic.com, Web Site: www.perfectplastic.com (27)

Smolen, Daniel, T., Dan Smolen Direct Search LLC, Stafford, VA. Tel: (703) 835-9900, FAX: (703) 835-9966, E-Mail: dsmolen@dansmolen.com, Web Site: www.dansmolen.com (20)

Smolen, Meggie, Path to Purchase Institute, Skokie, IL. Tel: (847) 675-7400, Web Site: www.p2pi.org (17)

Smolsky, Matt, Mid America Direct Marketing Association, Omaha, NE. Tel: (402) 964-8444, FAX: (402) 964-8484, Web Site: www.madma.org (40)

Smrt, Thomas, Fox Valley Systems Inc, Cary, IL. Tel: (847) 639-5744, (800) 323-4770, FAX: (847) 639-8190, Web Site: www.foxpaint.com (9)

The JM Smucker Co, Orrville, OH. Tel: (330) 682-3000, Web Site: www.smucker.com (4)

Smyk, Paul, American Crane & Equipment Corp, Douglassville, PA. Tel: (610) 385-6061, (877) 877-6778, FAX: (610) 385-3191/4876, E-Mail: info@americancrane.com, Web Site: www.americancrane. com (16)

Smyrl, Jim, Star Sprinkler Inc, Lansdale, PA. Tel: (414) 570-5000, (800) 558-5236, FAX: (414) 570-5010, Web Site: www.starsprinkler.com (9)

Smyth, Tom, Albert S Smyth Co Inc, Timonium, MD. Tel: (410) 252-6666, (800) 638-3333, FAX: (410) 252-2355, E-Mail: smyth@albertsmyth.com, Web Site: www.albertsmyth.com (6)

Albert S Smyth Co Inc, Timonium, MD. Tel: (410) 252-6666, (800) 638-3333, FAX: (410) 252-2355, E-Mail: smyth@albertsmyth.com, Web Site: www. albertsmyth.com (6)

Brody Smythe Direct Inc, Beverly Hills, CA. Tel: (310) 360-0887, FAX: (310) 360-1078, E-Mail: rsollish@brodysmythe.com, Web Site: www. brodysmythe.com (35)

Snader, Timothy G., Seedburo Equipment Co, Des Plaines, IL. Tel: (312) 738-3700, (800) 284-5779, FAX: (312) 738-5329, E-Mail: sales@seedburo. com, Web Site: www.seedburo.com (8)

Snap-on Inc, Kenosha, WI. Tel: (262) 656-5200, (800) 866-5748, (800) 786-6600, FAX: (262) 656-5577, Web Site: www.snapon.com (9)

Snapper, Michael, Demco Inc, Madison, WI. Tel: (608) 241-1201, FAX: (608) 241-1799, E-Mail: custserv@demco.com, Web Site: www.demco.com (10)

Snead, Tom, Trigon Blue Cross/Blue Shield, Roanoke, VA. Tel: (540) 853-5000, (800) 553-3164, FAX: (540) 853-3053, Web Site: www.trigon.com (15)

Sneed, Paula, Kraft Foods/Gevalia Kaffe, Tarrytown, NY. Tel: (914) 335-4239, Web Site: www.gevalia. com (16)

Snell, Jim, Shield Healthcare, Valencia, CA. Tel: (661) 294-4200, (800) 228-7150, FAX: (661) 294-1043, Web Site: www.shieldhealthcare.com (7)

Snider, Brian, S., The GRI Marketing Group Inc, Trumbull, CT. Tel: (203) 261-3337, (800) 356-4890, FAX: (203) 261-1113, E-Mail: bsnider@gridirect.com, Web Site: www.gridirect.com (35)

Snider, John, University of Alabama, Tuscaloosa, AL. Tel: (205) 348-6010, FAX: (205) 348-0249, Web Site: www.ua.edu (13)

Snitman, Bernard, Steptoe & Wife Antiques Ltd, Toronto, ON Canada. Tel: (416) 780-1707, (800) 461-0060, FAX: (416) 780-1814, E-Mail: info@steptoewife.com, Web Site: www.steptoewife.com (8)

Snitman, Marna, Steptoe & Wife Antiques Ltd, Toronto, ON. Tel: (416) 780-1707, (800) 461-0060, FAX: (416) 780-1814, E-Mail: info@steptoewife. com, Web Site: www.steptoewife.com (8)

Snitzer, Tina, Corinthian Direct, New York, NY. Tel: (212) 279-5700, FAX: (212) 239-1772, E-Mail: jonz@mediabuying.com, Web Site: www. mediabuying.com (35)

Snook, Gary, Bike Nashbar, Crab Orchard, WV. Tel: (800) NAS-HBAR, FAX: (877) 778-9456, E-Mail: custserv@nashbar.com, Web Site: www. bikenashbar.com (11)

Snow, Chuck, University of Pennsylvania, Philadelphia, PA. Tel: (215) 898-5000, FAX: (215) 898-9659, Web Site: www.upenn.edu (1)

Snow, Cindy, Planet Cotton, Gaithersburg, MD. Tel: (301) 948-0400, FAX: (301) 948-9031, Web Site: www.planetcotton.com (2)

Snow, David, Medco Health Solutions Inc, Franklin Lakes, NJ. Tel: (201) 269-3400, FAX: (201) 269-6400, Web Site: www.medco.com (7)

Snow, Keith, B2E Direct Marketing Inc, Grimes, IA. Tel: (515) 986-1992, Web Site: www. bwbmarketing.com (22)

Snow, Keith, BWB Marketing Services, Ankeny, IA. Tel: (515) 986-1992, Web Site: www. bwbmarketing.com (22)

Snow, Terry, World Publications Inc, Winter Park, FL. Tel: (407) 628-4802, FAX: (407) 628-7061, Web Site: www.worldpub.net (17)

Snow, Therese, J&L Industrial Supply, Southfield, MI. Tel: (734) 458-7000, (800) 521-9520, FAX: (734) 261-0352, Web Site: www.jlindustrial.com (9)

Snowdon, Jonathan, National Hardware Show, Norwalk, CT. Tel: (203) 840-5622, (888) 425-9377, FAX: (203) 840-9622, E-Mail: inquiry@hardware. reedexpo.com, Web Site: www. nationalhardwareshow.com (42)

Snyder, Diane, NCP Solutions, Reston, VA. Tel: (703) 438-6000, (800) 822-9919, FAX: (703) 438-3570, Web Site: www.nwf.org (17)

Snyder, George, Direct Marketing Association of Saint Louis, Washington, MO. Tel: (866) 516-0121, FAX: (636) 239-2324, E-Mail: mparisien@mac. com, Web Site: www.dmastl.org (40)

Snyder, Glenn, J., Snyder Glenn J & Assocs, Jacksonville Beach, FL. Tel: (904) 246-6223, FAX: (904) 246-6229 (20)

Snyder, Kim, Cherry Brothers LLC/ Cherrydale, Quakertown, PA. Tel: (800) 570-6010, Web Site: www.cherrydale.com (1)

Snyder, Patrick, A., Cabela's Inc, Sidney, NE. Tel: (308) 254-5505, (800) 237-4444, FAX: (308) 254-4800, Web Site: www.cabelas.com (11)

Snyder, Paula, Tinsley Tool Supply Inc, Powell, TN. Tel: (865) 681-9633, FAX: (865) 982-1655, E-Mail: gene@tinsleytool.com, Web Site: www.tinsleytool.com (9)

Snyder, Philip, R., The Snyder Agency, Missouri City, TX. Tel: (281) 437-9200, FAX: (832) 460-3022, E-Mail: info@snyderagency.com, Web Site: www.snyderagency.com (35)

Snyder, Richard, D., Gateway Inc, Irvine, CA. Tel: (949) 471-7000, (800) 369-1409, FAX: (949) 471-7041, Web Site: www.gateway.com (3)

Snyder, Tom, Ivy Tech State College, Indianapolis, IN. Tel: (317) 921-4800, (888) IVY-LINE, FAX: (317) 921-4753, Web Site: www.ivytech.edu/indianapolis (13)

The Snyder Agency, Missouri City, TX. Tel: (281) 437-9200, FAX: (832) 460-3022, E-Mail: info@snyderagency.com, Web Site: www.snyderagency.com (35)

Snyder Glenn J & Assocs, Jacksonville Beach, FL. Tel: (904) 246-6223, FAX: (904) 246-6229 (20)

Tom Snyder Productions, Watertown, MA. Tel: (617) 926-6000, (800) 342-0236, FAX: (800) 304-1254, E-Mail: ask@tomsnyder.com, Web Site: www.tomsnyder.com (16)

SA-SO/Time Wise, Arlington, TX. Tel: (972) 641-4911, (800) 523-8060, FAX: (972) 660-5684, E-Mail: info@sa-so.com, Web Site: www.sa-so.com (33)

The Soap Factory, Bedford, MA. Tel: (781) 275-8363, E-Mail: soapfac@verizon.net, Web Site: www.alcasoft.com/soapfact/ (7)

SOAR Inflatables, Healdsburg, CA. Tel: (707) 433-5599, FAX: (707) 433-4499, E-Mail: sales@soar1.com, Web Site: www.soar1.com (11)

Sobczak, Art, Tel Selling Report, Scottsdale, AZ. Tel: (402) 895-9399, FAX: (402) 896-3353, E-Mail: arts@businessbyphone.com, Web Site: www.businessbyphone.com (43)

Sobel, Paul, Dataline, Princeton, NJ. Tel: (609) 452-6014, Web Site: www.datalinedata.com (23)

Sobelsohn, Richard, Sobelsohn School, New York, NY. Tel: (917) 441-9740, FAX: (917) 441-9740, E-Mail: sobelsohnschool@yahoo.com, Web Site: www.sobelsohnschool.com (23)

Sobelsohn School, New York, NY. Tel: (917) 441-9740, FAX: (917) 441-9740, E-Mail: sobelsohnschool@yahoo.com, Web Site: www.sobelsohnschool.com (23)

Sobieraj, Cindy, Team Cheer, Geneseo, NY. Tel: (585) 243-8400, (585) 243-0841, (877) 243-5268, FAX: (800) 350-1562, E-Mail: custserv@teamcheer.com, Web Site: www.teamcheer.com (2)

Sobo, Michael, SAS Group, Tarrytown, NY. Tel: (914) 332-7878, FAX: (914) 332-7859, E-Mail: ssobo@sasgroup.com, Web Site: www.sasgroup.com (32)

Sobol, Alex, GenerH, Inc, Torrance, CA. Tel: (888) 312-3443, E-Mail: info@generh.com, Web Site: www.generh.com (21)

Social Reality, Camarillo, CA. Tel: (415) 744-1509, Web Site: www.socialreality.com (35)

Social Studies School Service, Culver City, CA. Tel: (310) 839-2436, (800) 421-4246, FAX: (310) 839-2249, (800) 944-5432, E-Mail: access@socialstudies.com, Web Site: www.socialstudies.com (14)

Society for Healthcare Strategy & Market Development, Chicago, IL. Tel: (312) 422-3888, FAX: (312) 422-4579, E-Mail: stratsoc@aha.org, Web Site: www.stratsociety.org (42)

Society for Human Resource Management, Alexandria, VA. Tel: (703) 548-3440, (800) 283-SHRM, FAX: (703) 535-6490, E-Mail: shrmstore@shrm.org, Web Site: www.shrm.org (1)

Society for Neuroscience, Washington, DC. Tel: (202) 962-4000 (1)

Society of American Magicians Inc, Parker, CO. E-Mail: rmblowers@aol.com, Web Site: www.magicsam.com (1)

Society of Financial Service Professionals, Newtown Square, PA. Tel: (610) 526-2500, FAX: (610) 527-1499, Web Site: www.financialpro.org (1)

Society of Manufacturing Engineers, Dearborn, MI. Tel: (313) 425-3000, (800) 733-4763, FAX: (313) 425-3400, E-Mail: communications@sme.org, Web Site: www.sme.org (2)

Society of Petroleum Engineers, Richardson, TX. Tel: (972) 952-9393, Web Site: www.spe.org (1)

Society of the Divine Savior, New Holstein, WI. Tel: (920) 898-4201 (1)

Soderberg, Marcia, Trumble Greetings, Boulder, CO. Tel: (800) 525-0656, FAX: (303) 530-5124, E-Mail: info@leanintree.com, Web Site: www.leanintree.com (6)

Soderman, Christine, Artisanal LLC, Holicong, PA. Tel: (215) 862-8000, FAX: (215) 862-8008, E-Mail: info@artisanaldesign.com, Web Site: www.artisanaldesign.com (8)

Sodi, Marco, Veronis Suhler Stevenson LLC, New York, NY. Tel: (212) 935-4990, FAX: (212) 381-8168, E-Mail: stevensonj@vss.com, Web Site: www.vss.com (14)

Soenen, Michael J., FTD Group Inc, Downers Grove, IL. Tel: (630) 719-7800, (800) 788-9000, FAX: (630) 719-6170, E-Mail: ftdmemberservices@ftdi.com, Web Site: www.ftdi.com (29)

Soergel, Rich C., Pacific Sportswear Co Inc, San Diego, CA. Tel: (619) 281-6688, (800) USA-8778, FAX: (619) 281-6687, E-Mail: info@pacsport.com, Web Site: www.pacsport.com (5)

Soft Surroundings, Saint Louis, MO. Tel: (314) 812-5200, Web Site: www.softsurroundings.com (2)

SofTrek Corp, Amherst, NY. Tel: (800) 442-9211, Web Site: www.softrek.com (22)

Software AG USA, Reston, VA. Tel: (703) 860-5050, (877) 724-4965, FAX: (703) 391-6975, E-Mail: info@softwareagusa.com, Web Site: www.softwareagusa.com (3)

Software Assistance International Ltd (SAIL), Morris Plains, NJ. Tel: (973) 285 1400, FAX: (201) 539-3253 (3)

The Software Labs Inc, Bellevue, WA. Tel: (425) 653-2432, FAX: (425) 643-8090, Web Site: www.softwarelabs.com (3)

Software Marketing Associates Inc, Rocky Hill, CT. Tel: (860) 721-8929, FAX: (860) 257-9679, E-Mail: sma@sma-promail.com, Web Site: www.sma-promail.com (22)

Soitenly Stooges, Glendale, CA. Tel: (818) 543-0778, (800) 543-0778, FAX: (818) 543-0779, E-Mail: custserv@threestooges.com, Web Site: www.soitenlystooges.com (6)

Soja, Joe, The Durham Manufacturing Co, Durham, CT. Tel: (860) 349-3427, (800) 243-3774, FAX: (800) 782-5499, (860) 349-8572, E-Mail: info@durhammfg.com, Web Site: www.durhammfg.com (16)

Sok, Ming, Bridge City Tool Works Inc, Portland, OR. Tel: (503) 282-6997, (800) 253-3332, FAX: (503) 287-1085, E-Mail: jjeconomaki@comcast.net, Web Site: www.bridgecitytools.com (9)

Soken, Susan, First Hawaiian Bank, Honolulu, HI. Tel: (808) 525-6273, (888) 844-4444, FAX: (808) 525-5798, E-Mail: bfarias@fhb.com, Web Site: www.fhb.com (14)

Sokolski, Andrew, Whirley Drink Works, Warren, PA. Tel: (814) 723-7600, (800) 825-5575, FAX: (814) 723-3245, E-Mail: info@whirleydrinkworks.com, Web Site: www.whirleydrinkworks.com (5)

Sokolski, Lincoln, Whirley Drink Works, Warren, PA. Tel: (814) 723-7600, (800) 825-5575, FAX: (814) 723-3245, E-Mail: info@whirleydrinkworks.com, Web Site: www.whirleydrinkworks.com (5)

Soladay, Ed, Fujitsu Transaction Solutions Inc, Richardson, TX. Tel: (972) 963-2300, (800) 340-4425, Web Site: www.fujitsu.com (16)

Solakian, V., Santa Barbara Greenhouses, Oxnard, CA. Tel: (805) 483-4288, (800) 544-5276, E-Mail: robsbg@aol.com, Web Site: www.sbgreenhouse.com (8)

Solar Cine Products Inc, Chicago, IL. Tel: (773) 254-8310, (800) 621-8796, FAX: (773) 254-4124 (5)

Solar Communications, Wheaton, IL. Tel: (630) 983-1400, (800) 890-6906, FAX: (630) 983-6125, Web Site: www.solarcommunications.com (31)

Solar Components Corp, Manchester, NH. Tel: (603) 668-8186, FAX: (603) 668-1783, Web Site: www.solar-components.com (9)

Solarcom, Norcross, GA. Tel: (770) 449-6116, (888) SUN-DATA, FAX: (770) 448-7726, Web Site: www.solarcom.net (16)

Solbenberger, Glenn, Fry Communciations Inc, Mechanicsburg, PA. Tel: (717) 766-0211 (27)

Soli, Patrick, Novus Media Inc, Plymouth, MN. Tel: (612) 758-8600, Web Site: www.npmnetwork.com (31)

Solitron Devices Inc, West Palm Beach, FL. Tel: (561) 848-4311, FAX: (561) 863-5946, E-Mail: sales@solitrondevices.com, Web Site: www.solitrondevices.com (16)

Solla, Ed, Qualco, Inc, Passaic, NJ. Tel: (973) 473-1222, (800) 289-2567, FAX: (973) 473-0535, E-Mail: feedback@qualco.com, Web Site: www.qualco.com (8)

Sollinger, Andrew, FT Publications Inc, New York, NY. Tel: (212) 641-6500, FAX: (212) 641-6544, E-Mail: adsales@ft.com, Web Site: www.ft.com (17)

Sollish, Rochelle, Brody Smythe Direct Inc, Beverly Hills, CA. Tel: (310) 360-0887, FAX: (310) 360-1078, E-Mail: rsollish@brodysmythe.com, Web Site: www.brodysmythe.com (35)

Sollo, Eugene D., Carlyle Marketing Corp, Riverwoods, IL. Tel: (847) 948-9295, FAX: (847) 948-0465, E-Mail: carlylemi@gmail.com (29)

Solly, Bruce, Toland Home and Garden Inc, Port Townsend, WA. Tel: (504) 893-9503, (800) 989-6287, E-Mail: info@tolandhomeandgarden.com, Web Site: www.tolandhomeandgarden.com (16)

Solo Printing, Miami, FL. Tel: (305) 594-8699, Web Site: www.soloprinting.com (27)

Solomon, Ann, Fifth Avenue Committee, Brooklyn, NY. FAX: (718) 237-5366, Web Site: www.fifthave.org (1)

Solomon, David, Gall's Inc, Lexington, KY. Tel: (859) 266-7227, (800) 477-7766, FAX: (859) 268-5954, E-Mail: help-desk@galls.com, Web Site: www.galls.com (16)

Solomon, David, J., Goldsmith Agio Helms, Minneapolis, MN. Tel: (612) 339-0500, FAX: (612) 339-0507, Web Site: www.agio.com (14)

Solomon, Edward, Campus Dimensions Inc, Philadelphia, PA. Tel: (215) 568-1700, (800) 592-2121, FAX: (215) 568-1701, E-Mail: recruitment@cdicccc.com, Web Site: www.cdicccc.com (31)

Solomon, Lisa, Salford Systems, San Diego, CA. Tel: (619) 543-8880, Web Site: www.salford-systems.com (22)

Solomon, Saul, Bridgestone/Firestone North American Tire LLC, Nashville, TN. Tel: (615) 937-1000, (800) 543-7522, FAX: (615) 937-3721, Web Site: www.bridgestonetire.com (16)

Peter J Solomon Co, New York, NY. Tel: (212) 508-1600, Web Site: www.pjsc.com (14)

Solow, Alan, Prudent Publishing Co, Ridgefield Park, NJ. Tel: (201) 641-7900, FAX: (800) 772-1144 (16)

Soloway, David, Institute of Reading Development, Novato, CA. Tel: (415) 884-8100, (800) 964-8888, FAX: (415) 382-0760, E-Mail: contactus@readingprograms.org, Web Site: www.readingprograms.org (1)

Soltis, Catherine, Golf Digest Co, Wilton, CT. Tel: (203) 761-5100, FAX: (203) 371-2572, Web Site: www.golfdigest.com (17)

Soltoff, Paul, SendTec Inc, Saint Petersburg, FL. Tel: (727) 576-6630, FAX: (727) 576-4864, Web Site: www.sendtec.com (35)

Solutran, Plymouth, MN. Tel: (763) 559-2225, (888) 765-8872, FAX: (763) 559-8872, E-Mail: solutions@solutran.com, Web Site: www.solutran. com (20)

Solverud, Mark, L., NGL Insurance Group, Madison, WI. Tel: (608) 257-5611, (800) 548-2962, FAX: (608) 257-9340, Web Site: www.nationalguardian. com (15)

Somer, Norman, Blakar Inc, Englewood, CO. Tel: (201) 672-0705, FAX: (201) 673-0725, Web Site: www.blakar.com (33)

Somerkamp, Sabir, Puritan's Pride, Ronkonkoma, NY. Tel: (631) 567-9500, FAX: (631) 471-5693, E-Mail: info@puritan.com, Web Site: www.puritan. com (7)

Somers, Kristin, Eaton Corp, Raleigh, NC. Tel: (216) 523-4400, (800) 356-5794, FAX: (216) 523-4787, Web Site: www.eaton.com (16)

Sommar, Jessica, Institutional Investor Inc, New York, NY. Tel: (212) 224-3300, FAX: (212) 224-3592, Web Site: www.institutionalinvestor.com (17)

Sommella, Jaime, Enertex Marketing, New York, NY. Tel: (212) 532-3115, FAX: (212) 532-1878, E-Mail: info@enertexmarketing.com, Web Site: www.enertexmarketing.com (22)

Sommers, John G., Allied Printing Services Inc, Manchester, CT. Tel: (860) 643-1101, (800) 225-8777, (800) 224-8894, FAX: (860) 643-9723, E-Mail: allied@alliedprinting.com, Web Site: www.alliedprinting.com (27)

Sommers, Michael, KickApps Corp, New York, NY. Tel: (212) 730-4558, Web Site: www.kickapps.com (32)

Song, Adi, Longevity Network Ltd, Henderson, NV. Tel: (702) 454-7000, (800) 242-1000, FAX: (702) 435-4786, Web Site: www.longevitynetwork.com (7)

Song, Delong, Boundless Corp, Phelps, NY. Tel: (631) 962-1500, (800) 231-5445, FAX: (631) 962-1505, E-Mail: sales@boundless.com, Web Site: www. boundless.com (16)

Song, Jim, Longevity Network Ltd, Henderson, NV. Tel: (702) 454-7000, (800) 242-1000, FAX: (702) 435-4786, Web Site: www.longevitynetwork.com (7)

Songbird Hearing Inc, Princeton Junction, NJ. Tel: (732) 828-8300, Web Site: www.songbirdhearing. com (7)

Songer, Jim, Esco Corp, Portland, OR. Tel: (503) 228-2141, FAX: (503) 778-6682, Web Site: www. escocorp.com (16)

Sonheim, Eileen, ERS Direct Marketing, Thousand Oaks, CA. Tel: (805) 499-1129, FAX: (805) 499-3189, E-Mail: eileen@ersdirect.com, Web Site: www.ersdirect.com (21)

Sony DADC, New York, NY. Tel: (212) 833-8000, Web Site: www.sonydadc.com (3)

Sony Electronics Inc, Park Ridge, NJ. Tel: (201) 930-6173, FAX: (201) 930-7665, Web Site: www.sony. com (16)

Sony Media Software, Middleton, WI. Tel: (608) 256-3133 (3)

Soonagrook Jr., William, St Lawrence Island Original Ivory Cooperative, Gambell, AK. Tel: (907) 985-5707, FAX: (907) 985-5927 (6)

Debbie Sorace, Valley Stream, NY. Tel: (516) 659-5614 (20)

Sorasky, Charles, Goldline International, Santa Monica, CA. Tel: (310) 587-1420, (800) 827-4653, FAX: (310) 319-0265, E-Mail: president@ goldlinecoins.com, Web Site: www.goldlinecoins. com (14)

Sorensen, Birgitte, Elite Sportswear LP, Reading, PA. Tel: (610) 921-1469, (800) 345-4087, FAX: (610) 921-0208, E-Mail: gkelite@gkelite.com, Web Site: www.gk-elitesportswear.com (2)

Sorenson, Cindy, Crowne Plaza Chateau Le Combe, Edmonton, AB. Tel: (780) 428-6611, FAX: (780) 420-8379, E-Mail: info@chateaulecombe.com, Web Site: www.chateaulecombe.com (19)

Sorge, Anjee, M., Fire Light Group, White Plains, NY. Tel: (608) 441-3473, E-Mail: mincentive@aol.com, Web Site: www.incentivesmotivate.com (33)

Sorin, Andrei, Andsor Research Inc, Etobicoke, ON Canada. Tel: (416) 245-8073, FAX: (416) 240-8473 (22)

Sorkin, Murray, L., Sorkins Inc, Saint Louis, MO. Tel: (800) 758-3228, FAX: (800) 721-5478, E-Mail: customerservice@sorkins.com, Web Site: www. sorkins.com (23)

Sorkins Inc, Saint Louis, MO. Tel: (800) 758-3228, FAX: (800) 721-5478, E-Mail: customerservice@ sorkins.com, Web Site: www.sorkins.com (23)

Sorondo, Deborah, Sierra Club Books, San Francisco, CA. Tel: (415) 977-5500, FAX: (415) 977-5792, E-Mail: books.publishing@sierraclub.org, Web Site: www.sierraclub.org (1)

Sorrells III, Tom, Motor Coach Industries International Inc, Schaumburg, IL. Tel: (847) 285-2000, (800) 624-2622, Web Site: www.mcicoach.com (16)

Sorrentino, John, United Envelope, Long Island City, NY. Tel: (718) 707-0700, FAX: (718) 729-8671, E-Mail: marketing@unitedenvelope.com, Web Site: www.unitedenvelope.com (26)

Sosa, Adrian, CVS Caremark, Woonsocket, RI. Tel: (401) 765-1500, FAX: (401) 769-4488, Web Site: www.cvs.com (7)

Soscie, Kim, The Trumpet Club, New York, NY. Tel: (212) 343-6100, FAX: (212) 343-7709, Web Site: www.scholastic.com (17)

Sotheby's, New York, NY. Tel: (212) 606-7000, FAX: (212) 606-7107, Web Site: www.sothebys.com (6)

Sottonpanah, Alesia, North Shore Animal League America Inc, Port Washington, NY. Tel: (516) 883-7900, FAX: (516) 883-8256, E-Mail: donorservices@nsalamerica.org, Web Site: www. nsalamerica.org (1)

Soublette, Luis, Foilmania, Miami, FL. Tel: (305) 854-8525, Web Site: www.foilmania.com (27)

Soucy, Mike, Kadant Johnson Inc, Three Rivers, MI. Tel: (269) 278-1715, FAX: (269) 279-5980, Web Site: www.kadantjohnson.com (16)

Souers, Steve, Tristar Products, Fairfield, NJ. Tel: (973) 575-5400, FAX: (973) 683-6708, E-Mail: infotp@tristarproductsinc.com, Web Site: www. tristarproductsinc.com (16)

Soulliard, Eric, Gemalto Inc, Montgomeryville, PA. Tel: (215) 390-2000, E-Mail: us.sales@gemalto. com, Web Site: www.gemalto.com (16)

Sound Beach Marketing Partners LLC, Old Greenwich, CT. Tel: (203) 698-0708, FAX: (203) 698-0712, E-Mail: thudock@soundbeachmarketing. com, Web Site: www.soundbeachmarketing.com (23)

The Sound Direct Marketing Group, Austin, TX. Tel: (512) 306-0879 (20)

SoundBite Communications, Bedford, MA. Tel: (781) 359-2200, Web Site: www.soundbite.com (32)

Sounder, Rick, Crutchfield Corp, Charlottesville, VA. Tel: (434) 817-1000, (800) 955-9091, FAX: (804) 817-1010, E-Mail: administration@crutchfield.com, Web Site: www.crutchfield.com (3)

Soundprints, Norwalk, CT. Tel: (800) 228-7839, FAX: (203) 846-1776, E-Mail: soundprints@soundprints. com, Web Site: www.soundprints.com (6)

The Source, Huntsville, AL. Tel: (256) 536-7305, (800) 433-2375, FAX: (256) 539-8547, Web Site: www.thesource-wti.com (33)

Source Communications, Hackensack, NJ. Tel: (201) 343-5222 (35)

Source 4 Inc, Huntersville, NC. Tel: (704) 602-0110, (800) 541-5400, FAX: (704) 602-0119, E-Mail: source4newyork@source4.com, Web Site: www. source4.com (27)

Source Link, Miamisburg, OH. Tel: (937) 885-8000, (800) 305-9414, FAX: (937) 885-8010, E-Mail: nesbit@commdata.com, Web Site: www.sourcelink. com (28)

Source Marketing, Norwalk, CT. Tel: (203) 222-2741, FAX: (203) 291-4010, E-Mail: bardes@source-marketing.com, Web Site: www.source-marketing. com (35)

The Source Stock Footage Library Inc, Tucson, AZ. Tel: (520) 298-4810, FAX: (520) 290-8831, E-Mail: requests@sourcefootage.com, Web Site: www.sourcefootage.com (38)

Sourcebooks Inc, Naperville, IL. Tel: (630) 961-3900, Web Site: www.sourcebooks.com (17)

SourceLink, Itasca, IL. Tel: (866) 947-6872, Web Site: www.sourcelink.com (20)

South Seas Island Resort, Captiva Island, FL. Tel: (866) 565-5089, FAX: (941) 482-2470, Web Site: www.southseas.com (19)

South-Western Publishing, Madison, OH. Tel: (513) 299-1000, FAX: (513) 527-6992 (17)

Southeast Toyota Distributors LLC, Deerfield Beach, FL. Tel: (954) 429-2000, Web Site: www.jmfamily. com (16)

Southerland, William, AAA Southern New England, Providence, RI. Tel: (401) 868-2005, FAX: (401) 868-2085, Web Site: www.aaa.com (1)

Southern California Gas Co, Anaheim, CA. Tel: (714) 634-3054, (800) 427-2200, FAX: (714) 937-7712, E-Mail: Tjavid@socalgas.com, Web Site: www. socalgas.com (16)

Southern Emblem Co, Toast, NC. Tel: (336) 789-3348, (800) 927-0526, FAX: (336) 789-6547, Web Site: www.southernemblemco.com (5)

Southern Flavoring Co Inc, Bedford, VA. Tel: (540) 586-8565, (800) 765-8565, FAX: (540) 586-8568, E-Mail: tom@southernflavoring.com, Web Site: www.southernflavoring.com (16)

Southern Fulfillment Services, Vero Beach, FL. Tel: (772) 226-3321 (28)

Southern Poverty Law Center, Montgomery, AL. Tel: (334) 956-8200, FAX: (334) 956-8483, Web Site: www.splcenter.org (1)

Southern Progress Corp, Birmingham, AL. Tel: (205) 877-6000, FAX: (205) 877-6283, Web Site: www. southernprogress.com (17)

Southwell, Donald, G., Unitrin, Chicago, IL. Tel: (312) 661-4600, (800) 733-7366, FAX: (312) 494-6995, Web Site: www.unitrin.com (15)

Southwest Consultants, Granada Hills, CA. Tel: (818) 635-1777, Web Site: www.southwestbancorp.com (20)

Southwest Publishing & Mailing Corp, Topeka, KS. Tel: (785) 233-5662, Web Site: www.swpks.com (28)

Southwick, Ruth, MARKET SHARE, Bradenton, FL. Tel: (941) 794-6059, FAX: (941) 794-6059, E-Mail: rsouthwick@tampabay.rr.com (23)

Southworth, Dale, Roman Research Inc/Simply Whispers Earring, Hanson, MA. Tel: (781) 447-3411, (800) 451-5700, FAX: (781) 447-0995, Web Site: www.simplywhispers.com (2)

Sovereign Bank New England, Glastonbury, CT. Tel: (877) 768-2265, FAX: (860) 727-6517 (14)

Sovern, Michael, I., Sotheby's, New York, NY. Tel: (212) 606-7000, FAX: (212) 606-7107, Web Site: www.sothebys.com (6)

Sowell, Dr. Debbie, Oral Roberts University, Tulsa, OK. Tel: (918) 495-6161, FAX: (918) 495-6222, E-Mail: admissions@oru.edu, Web Site: www.oru. edu (1)

Sowers, Lee, Audio & Video Labs Inc, Pennsauken, NJ. Tel: (856) 663-9030, (800) 468-9353, FAX: (856) 661-3450, E-Mail: info@discmakers.com, Web Site: www.discmakers.com (16)

Spa-Finder Inc, New York, NY. Tel: (212) 924-6800, (800) ALL-SPAS, FAX: (212) 924-7240, Web Site: www.spafinder.com (7)

Spack, Mark, Central States Indemnity, Omaha, NE. Tel: (402) 997-8000, (402) 397-1111, (800) 445-6500, Web Site: www.csi-omaha.com (15)

Spaeth, Steven E., Latest Products Corp, Woodbury, NY. Tel: (516) 367-4700, (800) 288-3547, FAX: (516) 367-4714, E-Mail: info@latestprod.com, Web Site: www.latestprod.com (7)

Spagnola, Ed, A Marketing Resource, South St Paul, MN. Tel: (651) 451-1765, Web Site: www.amr-advantage.com (29)

Spaide, William, J., Spaide, Kuipers & Co, Newport, RI. Tel: (610) 668-8296, FAX: (610) 579-3844, E-Mail: spaide@spaidekuipers.com, Web Site: www.spaidekuipers.com (20)

Spaide, Kuipers & Co, Newport, RI. Tel: (610) 668-8296, FAX: (610) 579-3844, E-Mail: spaide@spaidekuipers.com, Web Site: www.spaidekuipers.com (20)

Spaight, Terry, Hoffman Mint, Fort Lauderdale, FL. Tel: (831) 625-5333, (800) 227-5813, FAX: (831) 649-3318, E-Mail: sales@hoffmanmint.com, Web Site: www.hoffmanmint.com (6)

Spain, Pamela, Com-Pak Services Inc, Moorestown, NJ. Tel: (856) 802-1900, Web Site: www.com-pak.com (28)

Spainhour, J. Patrick, ServiceMaster Co, Memphis, TN. Tel: (901) 766-1400, (901) 597-8502, (888) 937-3783, (866) 782-6787, FAX: (901) 766-1491, Web Site: www.servicemaster.com (8)

Spalding, Kristie, American Council on Exercise, San Diego, CA. Tel: (858) 279-8227, (888) 825-3636, FAX: (858) 279-8064, E-Mail: kristie.spalding@acefitness.org, Web Site: www.acefitness.org (1)

Spalding, Tom, Spalding Laboratories Inc, Arroyo Grande, CA. Tel: (805) 489-5946, (888) 880-1579, FAX: (866) 738-9632, Web Site: www.spalding-labs.com (7)

Spalding Laboratories Inc, Arroyo Grande, CA. Tel: (805) 489-5946, (888) 880-1579, FAX: (866) 738-9632, Web Site: www.spalding-labs.com (7)

Spaniel, Bill, California Society of CPA's, San Mateo, CA. Tel: (800) 922-5272, FAX: (650) 522-3009, E-Mail: info@culcpa.org, Web Site: www.calcpa.org (1)

Spano, Michael, Todaro Brothers Mail Order Co, New York, NY. Tel: (877) 472-2767, FAX: (212) 689-1679, E-Mail: eat@todarobros.com, Web Site: www.todarobros.com (4)

Sparkman, Wesley, Association of the Miraculous Medal, Perryville, MO. Tel: (573) 547-8343, (800) 264-6279, FAX: (573) 547-1389, E-Mail: amm1@amm.org, Web Site: www.amm.org (1)

Sparks, Janice, Murder by Mail, West Tisbury, MA. Tel: (617) 670-9400, (508) 693-5205, FAX: (508) 693-7997, E-Mail: info@murderbymail.com, Web Site: www.murderbymail.com (1)

Sparrow, Miriam, New York Blood Center Inc, New York, NY. Tel: (212) 570-3000, (800) 933-2566, FAX: (212) 570-3195, Web Site: www.nybloodcenter.org (1)

Spates, Douglas, Spates The Florist, Newport, VT. Tel: (802) 334-8330, (800) 473-3688, FAX: (802) 334-1751, E-Mail: spates@sover.net, Web Site: www.spatestheflorist.com (8)

Spates, Vivian, Spates The Florist, Newport, VT. Tel: (802) 334-8330, (800) 473-3688, FAX: (802) 334-1751, E-Mail: spates@sover.net, Web Site: www.spatestheflorist.com (8)

Spates The Florist, Newport, VT. Tel: (802) 334-8330, (800) 473-3688, FAX: (802) 334-1751, E-Mail: spates@sover.net, Web Site: www.spatestheflorist.com (8)

Spatz, D. Dean, Osmonics Inc, Minnetonka, MN. Tel: (952) 264-3937, (800) 605-6698, FAX: (952) 536-3301, Web Site: www.osmonics.com (16)

Spaulding, Barbara, Bush Co Inc, Fort Worth, TX. Tel: (949) 752-4210, FAX: (949) 752-4220, E-Mail: barb@bushlists.com, Web Site: www.bushlists.com (23)

Spaulding, Brook, Circinus International LLC, Boston, MA. Tel: (774) 696-3517, Web Site: www.circinusinternational.com (20)

Spaulding, Huck, Huck Spaulding Enterprises, Voorheesville, NY. Tel: (518) 768-2070, (888) 982-8866, FAX: (518) 768-2240, E-Mail: orders@spaulding-rogers.com, Web Site: www.spaulding-rogers.com (16)

Spaulding, J., Lincoln, Sheppard Envelope Co, Auburn, MA. Tel: (508) 791-5588, (800) 325-6622, FAX: (508) 754-3108, E-Mail: sales@sheppardenvelope.com, Web Site: www.sheppardenvelope.com (26)

Spaulding, Josephine, Huck Spaulding Enterprises, Voorheesville, NY. Tel: (518) 768-2070, (888) 982-8866, FAX: (518) 768-2240, E-Mail: orders@spaulding-rogers.com, Web Site: www.spaulding-rogers.com (16)

Spaulding, Karen, Lee, The Gallery Shop, Buffalo, NY. Tel: (716) 882-8700 X258, FAX: (716) 882-1958, E-Mail: gallshop@albrightknox.org, Web Site: www.albrightknox.org (6)

Spaulding, Scott, Reliable Technologies Inc, Manchester, NH. Tel: (603) 644-2528, (800) 346-7890, FAX: (603) 627-5553, Web Site: www.tei-imaging.com (16)

Huck Spaulding Enterprises, Voorheesville, NY. Tel: (518) 768-2070, (888) 982-8866, FAX: (518) 768-2240, E-Mail: orders@spaulding-rogers.com, Web Site: www.spaulding-rogers.com (16)

Speakers Guild Inc, Sandwich, MA. Tel: (508) 888-6702, (800) 343-4530, FAX: (508) 888-6771, E-Mail: info@speakersguild.com, Web Site: www.speakersguild.com (16)

Spear Engineering Co, Colorado Springs, CO. Tel: (719) 471-9850 (16)

Spears, A.W., Lorillard Tobacco Co, Greensboro, NC. Tel: (336) 335-7000, (888) 818-3304, FAX: (336) 373-6917, E-Mail: externalaffairs@lorrilard.com, Web Site: www.lorillard.net (16)

Spears, Robin, St Louis Post-Dispatch, Saint Louis, MO. Tel: (314) 340-8000, (800) 365-0820, FAX: (314) 340-3140, Web Site: www.postnet.com (17)

Spears, William, Quinnipiac College, Hamden, CT. Tel: (203) 582-8600, (203) 582-8200, (800) 462-1944, FAX: (203) 281-8664, Web Site: www.quinnipiac.edu (41)

Special Libraries Association (SLA), Alexandria, VA. Tel: (703) 647-4900, FAX: (703) 647-4901, E-Mail: sla@sla.org, Web Site: www.sla.org (40)

Special Markets Sales Co, Indianapolis, IN. Tel: (317) 595-6587, FAX: (317) 595-9853, E-Mail: info@specialmkts.com, Web Site: www.specialmkts.com (33)

Special Olympics International, Washington, DC. Tel: (202) 628-3630, FAX: (202) 824-0200, Web Site: www.specialolympics.org (1)

Specialists Marketing Services Inc, Hasbrouck Heights, NJ. Tel: (201) 865-5800, FAX: (201) 288-4295, E-Mail: listinfo@specialistsms.com, Web Site: www.specialistsms.com (23)

Specialized Association Services, Irving, TX. Tel: (469) 524-5122, E-Mail: hvincent@1sas.com, Web Site: www.1sas.com (1)

Specialized Fundraising Services, Spartanburg, SC. Tel: (864) 579-7755, Web Site: www.specializedfundraising.net (23)

Specialized Information Publishers Association (SIPA), Vienna, VA. Tel: (703) 992-9339, (800) 356-9302, FAX: (703) 610-9005, E-Mail: info@sipaonline.org, Web Site: www.sipaonline.com (1)

Specialized Mailing Services Inc, Huntington Beach, CA. Tel: (714) 274-2284, E-Mail: info@specializedmailing.com, Web Site: www.specializedmailing.com (28)

Specialized Marketing Inc, Brewster, NY. Tel: (845) 278-6100, FAX: (845) 278-6150, Web Site: www.specialized-mktg.com (31)

Specialized Products Co, Southlake, TX. Tel: (817) 329-6647, (800) 866-5353, FAX: (800) 234-8286, E-Mail: spc@specialized.net, Web Site: www.specialized.net (16)

Specialty Envelope Inc, Cincinnati, OH. Tel: (513) 542-4700, (800) 288-8884, FAX: (513) 542-5260, E-Mail: info@specialtyenevelope.com, Web Site: www.specialtyenevelope.com (26)

Specialty Equipment Market Association, Diamond Bar, CA. Tel: (909) 396-0289, Web Site: www.sema.org (1)

Specialty Print Communications, Niles, IL. Tel: (847) 588-2580, Web Site: www.specialtyprintcomm.com (27)

Specialty Store Services Inc, Des Plaines, IL. Tel: (847) 470-7000, (888) 441-4440, FAX: (847) 470-5355, Web Site: www.specialtystoreservices.com (16)

Specific Media Inc, Irvine, CA. E-Mail: info@specificmedia.com, Web Site: www.specificmedia.com (35)

Spector, Gerald, A., Tribune Co, Chicago, IL. Tel: (312) 222-9100, FAX: (312) 222-1573, Web Site: www.tribune.com (17)

Spector, Jonathan, The Conference Board, Inc, New York, NY. Tel: (212) 759-0900, FAX: (212) 980-7014, Web Site: www.conference-board.org (16)

Spector, Paul, The Spector Agency, Fair Oaks, CA. Tel: (916) 966-1605, E-Mail: spector@cwnet.com (35)

Spector, Richard, Corporate Incentive Solutions, Boston, MA. Tel: (301) 340-1600, (877) 244-4505, FAX: (301) 251-5887 (33)

The Spector Agency, Fair Oaks, CA. Tel: (916) 966-1605, E-Mail: spector@cwnet.com (35)

Spectra Merchandising International Inc, Chicago, IL. Tel: (773) 202-8408, FAX: (773) 202-8409 (16)

Spectra Products LLC, Johnson City, NY. Tel: (607) 770-1985, FAX: (607) 798-7771, E-Mail: info@spectraproducts.com, Web Site: www.spectraproducts.com (31)

Spectronics Corp, Westbury, NY. Tel: (800) 274-8888, FAX: (800) 491-6868, E-Mail: vscherer@spectroline.com, Web Site: www.spectroline.com (9)

Spectrum Chemicals & Laboratory Products, Gardena, CA. Tel: (310) 516-8000, Web Site: www.spectrumchemical.com (16)

Spectrum Communication Services Inc, Brookfield, WI. Tel: (262) 821-8400, (800) 701-3559, FAX: (262) 821-1492, E-Mail: sales@spectrumcomm.com, Web Site: www.spectrumcomm.com (29)

Spectrum Data, Oregon, IL. Tel: (815) 732-6567 (22)

Spectrum eCommerce, Mission Viejo, CA. Tel: (949) 600-7900, Web Site: elifemarketers.com (15)

Spectrum Research, Ventnor City, NJ. Tel: (609) 822-0056, E-Mail: peter@spectrumresearch.com (30)

Spectrum Retail Associates, Ardmore, PA. Tel: (610) 645-9520, (800) 570-6565, FAX: (610) 645-9524 (20)

Spectrum Systems Inc, Fairfax, VA. Tel: (703) 591-7400 X217, (800) 929-3781, FAX: (703) 591-9780, E-Mail: spectrum@spectrum-systems.com, Web Site: www.spectrum-systems.com (34)

SpeechSoft Inc, Armonk, NY. Tel: (914) 273-5560, (800) 878-8117, E-Mail: sales@speechsoft.com, Web Site: www.speechsoft.com (29)

Speed-Mat, Biddeford, ME. Tel: (207) 294-4358, (800) 882-7017, FAX: (207) 882-9279, E-Mail: info@speedmat.com, Web Site: www.speed-mat.com (16)

Speedeon Data Corp, Cleveland, OH. Tel: (440) 287-7306, Web Site: www.speedeondata.com (23)

Speedway, Lincoln, NE. Tel: (402) 323-3100, FAX: (402) 477-7476 (12)

Speers, J., Alvin, Aardvark Enterprises, Calgary, AB Canada. Tel: (360) 779-5374 (17)

Speese, Mark E., Rent-A-Center Inc, Plano, TX. Tel: (972) 801-1100, (800) 275-2996, FAX: (972) 943-0113, Web Site: www.rentacenter.com (16)

Speicher, Dan, Info USA City Directories, Omaha, NE. Tel: (402) 593-4500, (800) 925-4654, FAX: (402) 593-4671, E-Mail: customerservice@infousacity.com, Web Site: www.infousacity.com (17)

Speicher, Mitch, Streamfeeder, Minneapolis, MN. Tel: (763) 502-0000, FAX: (763) 502-0100, Web Site: www.streamfeeder.com (34)

Speinhour, J., Patrick, TruGreen/ChemLawn, Lewis Center, OH. Tel: (614) 846-1800, (800) TRUE-GREEN, FAX: (614) 431-0155, Web Site: www.trugreen.com (16)

Spellman, Cindy, Kerber, Outrider North America, Saint Louis, MO. Tel: (314) 209-1005, FAX: (314) 209-1126, Web Site: www.outrider.com (30)

Spellman, Kate, United Business Media, Manhasset, NY. Tel: (516) 562-5000, Web Site: www.ubmtechnology.com (17)

Spellman, Linda, Chiasso, Chicago, IL. Tel: (877) CHIASSO, FAX: (312) 477-3827, Web Site: www.chiasso.com (6)

Spence, Dr Betty, National Association for Female Executives (NAFE), New York, NY. Tel: (800) 927-6233, E-Mail: info@nafe.com, Web Site: www.nafe.com (1)

Spencer, Carole, Children International, Kansas City, MO. Tel: (816) 942-2000, FAX: (816) 942-3714, E-Mail: RobS@cikc.org, Web Site: www.children.org (1)

Spencer, Elaine, Harvard Business School Publishing, Boston, MA. Tel: (617) 783-7400, Web Site: www.harvardbusiness.org (17)

Spencer, Jan, B., Kimberly-Clark Corp, Neenah, WI. Tel: (920) 721-2000, (888) 525-8388, FAX: (920) 721-7722, Web Site: www.kimberly-clark.com (16)

Spencer, Nelson, Heartland Boating Magazine, Saint Louis, MO. Tel: (314) 241-4310, (800) 366-9630, FAX: (314) 241-4207, E-Mail: info@heartlandboating.com, Web Site: www.heartlandboating.com (17)

Spencer, Vicki, Zale Corp, Irving, TX. Tel: (972) 580-4376, Web Site: www.zalecorp.com (6)

Spencer Zahn & Associates, Philadelphia, PA. Tel: (215) 564-5979, FAX: (215) 564-6205 (35)

SpencerStuart, Chicago, IL. Tel: (312) 822-0088, FAX: (312) 822-0116, Web Site: www.spencerstuart.com (20)

Speranza, Ernest V., Toys "R" Us, Wayne, NJ. Tel: (973) 617-5879, FAX: (973) 617-4006, Web Site: www.toysrus.com (11)

Sperber, Miles, Sperber Direct Inc, New York, NY. Tel: (212) 459-0403, FAX: (212) 459-0249, E-Mail: miless@bway.net (35)

Sperber Direct Inc, New York, NY. Tel: (212) 459-0403, FAX: (212) 459-0249, E-Mail: miless@bway.net (35)

The Sperry & Hutchinson Co Inc, Delray Beach, FL. Tel: (561) 454-7621, FAX: (561) 265-2493, E-Mail: mediarelations@shsolutions.com, Web Site: www.greenpoints.com (6)

Speyer, Jerry, I., The Museum of Modern Art, New York, NY. Tel: (212) 708-9400, FAX: (212) 333-1123, E-Mail: info@moma.org, Web Site: www.moma.org (5)

Spiegel, Lawrence E., Laran Communications Inc, Winfield, IL. Tel: (630) 690-2141, FAX: (630) 690-2143, Web Site: www.web-ads.com (16)

Spiegel, Tom, Presskits, East Walpole, MA. Tel: (781) 762-3003, (800) 472-3497, FAX: (781) 255-7791, Web Site: www.presskits.com (27)

Spiegel, Wendy, Pearson Education, Upper Saddle River, NJ. Tel: (201) 236-7000, FAX: (201) 236-3290, E-Mail: communications@pearsoned.com, Web Site: www.pearsoned.com (17)

Spiegel Brands Inc, New York, NY. Tel: (800) 222-5680, Web Site: www.spiegel.com (2)

Spielman, Harold, MSW Research, Lake Success, NY. Tel: (516) 394-6000, FAX: (516) 394-6001, E-Mail: mail@mswresearch.com, Web Site: www.mswresearch.com (30)

Spiers, Peter, Elderhostel Inc, Boston, MA. Tel: (617) 426-7788, (800) 454-5678, FAX: (617) 426-2166, Web Site: www.elderhostel.org (11)

Spiller, Mortimer, Mortimer Spiller Co Inc, Buffalo, NY. Tel: (716) 834-0860 (33)

Spillner, Cassie, Best Western International, Phoenix, AZ. Tel: (609) 957-5809, Web Site: www.bestwestern.com (19)

Spilos, Jim, Society of Manufacturing Engineers, Dearborn, MI. Tel: (313) 425-3000, (800) 733-4763, FAX: (313) 425-3400, E-Mail: communications@sme.org, Web Site: www.sme.org (1)

Spilsbury Puzzle Co, Chicago, IL. Tel: (800) 722-1760, FAX: (630) 575-0857, E-Mail: service@spilsbury.com, Web Site: www.spilsbury.com (11)

Spinali, Rosanne, Chelsea Clock Co Inc, Chelsea, MA. Tel: (617) 884-0250, (800) 284-1778, FAX: (617) 830-0599, Web Site: www.chelseaclock.com (6)

Spindell, Lynn, Phillips-Van Heusen Corp, New York, NY. Tel: (212) 381-3500, (800) 388-9122, FAX: (212) 381-3950, Web Site: www.pvh.com (2)

Spinelli, Ozzie, Barely Nothings Lingerie, Nipomo, CA. Tel: (805) 489-5591, (800) 422-7359, FAX: (888) 489-5987, E-Mail: lingerie@barelynothings.com, Web Site: www.getpassionhere.com (2)

Spinelli, Sandi, Barely Nothings Lingerie, Nipomo, CA. Tel: (805) 489-5591, (800) 422-7359, FAX: (888) 489-5987, E-Mail: lingerie@barelynothings.com, Web Site: www.getpassionhere.com (2)

Spink, Bill, DMW Worldwide LLC, Chesterbrook, PA. Tel: (610) 407-0407, (877) 744-3699, FAX: (610) 407-9201, E-Mail: whunter@dmwdirect.com, Web Site: www.dmwdirect.com (35)

Spinneybeck Enterprises, Getzville, NY. Tel: (716) 446-2380, (800) 482-7777, FAX: (716) 446-2396, E-Mail: sales@spinneybeck.com, Web Site: www.spinneybeck.com (16)

Spinozzi, Michael, Sally Beauty Supply LLC, Denton, TX. Tel: (940) 898-7500, (800) 275-7255, Web Site: www.sallybeauty.com (7)

Spire Creative Group, New York, NY. Tel: (212) 391-0200, Web Site: www.spirecreativegroup.com (27)

SPIRE Printing & Packaging LLC, New York, NY. Tel: (212) 661-1157, Web Site: www.spireprintingandpackaging.com (27)

Spirit Direct Marketing Services, Houston, TX. Tel: (281) 496-5614 (23)

Spirit Incentives, Fort Lauderdale, FL. Tel: (800) 860-5880, Web Site: www.spirit-incentives.com (35)

Spiro, Diane, Olympia Sales Inc, Enfield, CT. Tel: (860) 749-0751, (800) 338-9992, FAX: (860) 814-4451, E-Mail: info@olympiasales.net, Web Site: www.olympiasales.us (16)

Spisany, Silvana, Brotherhood America's Oldest Winery Ltd, Washingtonville, NY. Tel: (845) 496-3661, FAX: (845) 496-8720, E-Mail: contact@brotherhoodwinery.net, Web Site: www.brotherhoodwinery.net (19)

Spitalny, Eileen, Fairytale Brownies, Phoenix, AZ. Tel: (800) 324-7982, FAX: (602) 489-5122, E-Mail: service@brownies.com, Web Site: www.brownies.com (4)

Spitzer, Jennifer, TargetMail Marketing, Clover, SC. Tel: (540) 837-9337 (35)

Spivakovsky, Ariel, Direct Marketing Market Place, Berkeley Heights, NJ. Tel: (908) 673-1000, (800) 473-7020, FAX: (908) 673-1179 (43)

Spivakovsky, Ariel, Marquis Who's Who LLC, Berkeley Heights, NJ. Tel: (908) 673-1000, (800) 473-7020, FAX: (908) 673-1179, E-Mail: info@marquiswhoswho.com, Web Site: www.marquiswhoswho.com (17)

Spivey, Will, Maxim Direct, Greensboro, NC. Tel: (336) 841-6892, FAX: (336) 886-1655, Web Site: www.maximdirect.com (35)

Spizel, Edgar, S., Spizel Marketing/Advertising/Public Relations, La Jolla, CA. Tel: (858) 455-1932, E-Mail: hootspa@aol.com (35)

Spizel Marketing/Advertising/Public Relations, La Jolla, CA. Tel: (858) 455-1932, E-Mail: hootspa@aol.com (35)

Spokane Teachers Credit Union, Liberty Lake, WA. Tel: (509) 326-1954, Web Site: www.stcu.org (14)

Spoken Arts, Holmes, NY. Tel: (845) 878-9600, (800) 326-4090, FAX: (845) 878-9009, E-Mail: sales@spokenartsmedia.com, Web Site: www.spokenartsmedia.com (17)

The Spokesman-Review, Spokane, WA. Tel: (509) 459-5060, FAX: (509) 459-5083, E-Mail: shaunh@spokesman.com, Web Site: www.spokane.net (17)

Spooren, Ellen, Marketing and Product Strategy, Peabody, MA. Tel: (978) 977-2000, (800) 825-5897, FAX: (781) 238-0986, Web Site: www.lhsl.com (16)

Sport, Laura, Virtuoso Ltd, Seattle, WA. Tel: (206) 625-0969, Web Site: www.virtuoso.com (19)

Sport Supply Group, Dallas, TX. Tel: (972) 484-9484, FAX: (972) 247-0650, Web Site: www.sportsupplygroup.com (11)

Sportif Mail Order Inc, Sparks, NV. Tel: (775) 359-6400, (800) 776-7843, FAX: (800) 776-3291, Web Site: www.sportif.com (2)

Sportime International, Norcross, GA. Tel: (770) 449-5700, (800) 283-5700, FAX: (770) 510-7290, E-Mail: orders@sportime.com, Web Site: www.sportime.com (11)

Sporting Clays Ltd, Titusville, FL. Tel: (321) 268-5010, FAX: (321) 267-7216, E-Mail: sales@sportingclays.net, Web Site: www.sportingclays.net (17)

The Sporting News Publishing Co, Charlotte, NC. Tel: (704) 973-1546, (800) 443-1886, FAX: (704) 973-1552, Web Site: www.sportingnews.com (17)

Sports Illustrated Picture Sales, New York, NY. FAX: (212) 522-0102, E-Mail: andrew_judelson@timeinc.com (38)

The Sportsman's Guide Inc, South Saint Paul, MN. Tel: (651) 451-3030, (800) 882-2962, FAX: (651) 450-6130, E-Mail: custserv@sportsmansguide.com, Web Site: www.sportsmansguide.com (11)

Sportsmith LLC, Tulsa, OK. Tel: (918) 307-2446, Web Site: www.sportsmith.net (11)

Sporty's Preferred Living, Batavia, OH. Tel: (513) 735-9000, (800) 776-7897, FAX: (800) 543-8633, Web Site: www.sportys.com (5)

Spot Behavior LLC, Deerfield Beach, FL. Tel: (888) 767-7542, Web Site: www.spotbehavior.com (35)

Sprague, Lori, American Mathematical Society, Providence, RI. Tel: (401) 455-4000, (800) 321-4267, FAX: (401) 331-3842, E-Mail: ams@ams.org, Web Site: www.ams.org (17)

Spring, Christopher, Spring O'Brien & Co, New York, NY. Tel: (212) 620-7100, FAX: (212) 620-7166, Web Site: www.spring-obrien.com (35)

Spring, Mississauga, ON Canada. Tel: (905) 678-2770, (888) 624-5327, FAX: (905) 678-9788, E-Mail: lou.laforet@springglobalmail.com, Web Site: www.springglobalmail.com (21)

Spring-Green Lawn Care Corp, Plainfield, IL. Tel: (815) 436-8777, FAX: (815) 436-9056, Web Site: www.spring-green.com (16)

Spring Hill Laser Services, Sterling, PA. Tel: (570) 689-0970, FAX: (570) 689-7915, E-Mail: kkshls@icontech.com, Web Site: www.springhilllaser.com (27)

Spring O'Brien & Co, New York, NY. Tel: (212) 620-7100, FAX: (212) 620-7166, Web Site: www.spring-obrien.com (35)

Springer Science & Business Media LLC, New York, NY. Tel: (212) 460-1500, FAX: (212) 473-6272, Web Site: www.springer-ny.com (17)

Springman, Paul J., Equifax Credit Information Services Inc, Atlanta, GA. Tel: (404) 885-8000, (800) 685-5000, FAX: (404) 885-8988, Web Site: www.equifax.com (20)

Springs Global Inc, New York, NY. Tel: (888) 926-7888, Web Site: www.springs.com (16)

Springstead, Candace, Outdoor Research, Seattle, WA. Tel: (206) 467-8197, (888) 467-4327, FAX: (206) 467-0374, Web Site: www.outdoorresearch.com (11)

Sprint Corp, Overland Park, KS. Tel: (913) 624-3313, FAX: (913) 624-5386 (29)

Sprint Nextel Corp, Reston, VA. Tel: (703) 433-4000, FAX: (703) 433-4343, Web Site: www.nextel.com (3)

Sprint PCS, Overland Park, KS. Tel: (800) 927-2199, Web Site: www.sprintpcs.com (16)

Sproul, Dr. R., C., Ligonier Ministries, Lake Mary, FL. Tel: (407) 333-4244, (800) 435-4343, FAX: (407) 333-4377, Web Site: www.ligonier.org (5)

Sproul, Vesta, Ligonier Ministries, Lake Mary, FL. Tel: (407) 333-4244, (800) 435-4343, FAX: (407) 333-4377, Web Site: www.ligonier.org (5)

Sprouse, Gordon, Natcom Inc, Bixby, OK. Tel: (918) 491-6100, (888) 554-1999, FAX: (918) 491-9410, E-Mail: cs@natcom-publications.com, Web Site: www.natcom-publications.com (17)

Sprouse, Michael, Epic Media Group, New York, NY. Tel: (212) 308-8509, Web Site: www.epicadvertising.com (30)

Sprumont, Joseph, American Thermoplastic Co, Pittsburgh, PA. Tel: (412) 967-0900, (800) 245-6600, FAX: (412) 967-9990, E-Mail: atc@binders.com, Web Site: www.binders.com (27)

Spuller, Peter, Klingspor's Woodworking Shop, Hickory, NC. Tel: (828) 326-WOOD, (800) 228-0000, FAX: (828) 327-4634, E-Mail: sales@woodworkingshop.com, Web Site: www.woodworkingshop.com (9)

Squadron Mail Order, Carrollton, TX. Tel: (972) 242-8663, (877) 414-0434, FAX: (972) 242-3775, E-Mail: mailorder@squadron.com, Web Site: www.squadron.com (16)

Squibb, Dennis, Foremost Insurance Group, Grand Rapids, MI. Tel: (616) 956-8241, (800) 527-3905, FAX: (800) 325-1507, Web Site: www.foremost.com (15)

Squicciarino, Joseph, King Pharmaceuticals, Inc, Bristol, TN. Tel: (423) 989-8000, (888) 840-5370, FAX: (423) 274-8677, Web Site: www.kingpharm.com (7)

Squires, Charles, Haymarket Group Ltd, New York, NY. Tel: (212) 239-0855, FAX: (212) 967-4184, Web Site: www.chocalatiermagazine.com (17)

Squires, Christine, US Fund for UNICEF, New York, NY. Tel: (212) 686-5522, FAX: (212) 779-1679, Web Site: www.unicefusa.org (6)

St John, Richard, Support Systems International Corp, Richmond, CA. Tel: (510) 234-9090, (800) 777-6269, FAX: (510) 233-8888, E-Mail: info@support-systems-intl.com, Web Site: www.support-systems-intl.com (3)

St Joseph Communications, Concord, ON Canada. Tel: (905) 660-3111, FAX: (905) 669-1972, Web Site: www.stjoseph.com (27)

St Joseph Print Thorn, Concord, ON Canada. Tel: (416) 441-1411, FAX: (416) 441-3158, Web Site: www.stjoseph.com (27)

St Louis, Diane, Digital Vision Resources Group - DVRG, Overland Park, KS. Tel: (913) 754-8121, Web Site: www.dvrg.com (27)

St Martin, Charlotte, Loews Hotels, New York, NY. Tel: (212) 521-2000, (866) 563-9792, FAX: (212) 545-2714, Web Site: www.loewshotels.com (19)

St. James, Sydney, Etchworld, Hawthorne, NJ. Tel: (973) 423-4002, (800) 872-3458, FAX: (973) 427-8823, Web Site: www.etchworld.com (11)

St. John, Gary, Food for the Hungry Inc, Phoenix, AZ. Tel: (480) 998-3100, (800) 248-6437, FAX: (480) 998-4806, E-Mail: hunger@fh.org, Web Site: www.fh.org (1)

Staaterman, Stacy, American Express Publishing Corp, New York, NY. Tel: (212) 382-5600, (888) 461-6180, FAX: (212) 827-6496, E-Mail: aepc@custmersvc.com, Web Site: www.amexpub.com (17)

Stabel, Marsha, Ranch House Meat Co, Menard, TX. Tel: (800) 749-6329, FAX: (888) 917-6328, E-Mail: sales@brisket.net, Web Site: www.brisket.net (4)

Stabel, Max, Ranch House Meat Co, Menard, TX. Tel: (800) 749-6329, FAX: (888) 917-6328, E-Mail: sales@brisket.net, Web Site: www.brisket.net (4)

Stabenfeldt Inc, Danbury, CT. Tel: (203) 730-2178 (13)

Stacey, Richard, Northern Response (International) Ltd, Toronto, ON Canada. Tel: (905) 737-6698, (866) 584-1694, FAX: (905) 737-0099, E-Mail: general@nresponse.com, Web Site: www.shopnorthern.com (22)

Stack, J., J Stack & Associates, Baltimore, MD. Tel: (410) 889-3327, FAX: (410) 889-9039 (39)

Stack, John, Edmund Optics Inc, Barrington, NJ. Tel: (856) 573-6250, (800) 363-1992, FAX: (856) 573-6295, E-Mail: sales@edmundoptic.com, Web Site: www.edmundoptics.com (9)

Stack, Louis, Fitter International Inc, Calgary, AB Canada. Tel: (800) 348-8371, FAX: (866) 250-8824, E-Mail: sales2@filler1.com, Web Site: www.fitter1.com (1)

Stack, Sandy, Lithia Motors Inc, Medford, OR. Tel: (541) 774-7602 (12)

Stack, Tom, Tom Stack & Associates Inc, Tavernier, FL. Tel: (305) 852-5520, E-Mail: tomstack@earthlink.net, Web Site: www.tomstackassociatesphotoshelter.com (38)

J Stack & Associates, Baltimore, MD. Tel: (410) 889-3327, FAX: (410) 889-9039 (39)

Tom Stack & Associates Inc, Tavernier, FL. Tel: (305) 852-5520, E-Mail: tomstack@earthlink.net, Web Site: www.tomstackassociatesphotoshelter.com (38)

Stacks, Ed, Airs Inc, Douglasville, GA. Tel: (770) 949-0133, FAX: (770) 949-2773, E-Mail: estacks@aol.com (22)

Stacy, Steven, Sundancer Jewelry Co Inc, Albuquerque, NM. Tel: (505) 345-7475, FAX: (505) 345-7561, E-Mail: sales@sundancer.net, Web Site: www.sundancer.net (16)

Stadin, Richard, N., Mastervision Inc, New York, NY. Tel: (212) 879-0448, (800) 876-0091, FAX: (212) 744-3560, E-Mail: stadin1@aol.com, Web Site: www.mastervision.com (16)

Staff, Scott, TSE Services, Raleigh, NC. Tel: (919) 875-3037, Web Site: www.ncemcs.com (30)

Staffieri Jr, Joe A., Business Direct Marketing Associates Inc, Cumming, GA. Tel: (770) 888-8300, FAX: (770) 888-6482, E-Mail: bdmainc@aol.com, Web Site: www.bdmainc.com (35)

Stafford, Douglass, A., Legal Defense Foundation Inc, Springfield, VA. Tel: (703) 321-8501, (800) 336-3600, FAX: (703) 321-9613, E-Mail: info@nrtw.org, Web Site: www.nrtw.org (1)

Stagestep Inc, Philadelphia, PA. Tel: (267) 672-2900, (800) 523-0961, FAX: (267) 672-2914, E-Mail: stagestep@stagestep.com, Web Site: www.stagestep.com (5)

Stagg, Greg, Influence Inc, Hamilton, OH. Tel: (513) 825-8600, FAX: (513) 825-9213, E-Mail: info@influenceinc.com, Web Site: www.influenceinc.com (35)

Stagg, Phyllis, C., Stagg Direct Marketing Inc, Scarsdale, NY. Tel: (914) 725-3990, FAX: (914) 472-7298 (20)

Stagg Direct Marketing Inc, Scarsdale, NY. Tel: (914) 725-3990, FAX: (914) 472-7298 (20)

Stagner, Ross, United Investors Life Insurance Co, Birmingham, AL. Tel: (205) 325-4300, (800) 288-2722, FAX: (205) 325-4157, Web Site: www.uilic.com (15)

Staheyeff, Nicholas, Ebay, San Jose, CA. Tel: (408) 376-7400, Web Site: www.ebay.com (16)

Stahl, Jeffrey, Parts Express, Springboro, OH. Tel: (937) 743-3000, (800) 338-0531, FAX: (937) 743-1677, E-Mail: sales@parts-express.com, Web Site: www.partsexpress.com (3)

Stallings, Tom, EasyLink Services International Corp, Piscataway, NJ. Tel: (800) 828-7115, FAX: (732) 652-3810, E-Mail: sales@easylink.com, Web Site: www.easylink.com (16)

Stam, Chris, Nancy's Notions LLC, Beaver Dam, WI. Tel: (920) 887-0391, (800) 833-0690, FAX: (800) 255-8119, E-Mail: comments@nancysnotions.com, Web Site: www.nancysnotions.com (11)

Stamey, Allen, Audio-Digest Foundation, Glendale, CA. Tel: (818) 240-7500, (800) 423-2308, FAX: (818) 240-7379, Web Site: www.audio-digest.org (1)

Stamoulis, Angelo A., Direct Advertising, Holliston, MA. Tel: (508) 429-7488, E-Mail: priority@dir-adv.com, Web Site: www.dir-adv.com (35)

Stancampiano, Lou, Sentinel Direct, Orlando, FL. Tel: (407) 420-5270, FAX: (407) 420-5282, Web Site: www.orlandosentinel.com (21)

Standard & Poor's Corp, New York, NY. Tel: (212) 438-2000, FAX: (212) 438-7375, Web Site: www.standardandpoors.com (17)

Standard Buying Service Ltd, New York, NY. Tel: (212) 686-6800, FAX: (212) 532-4102, E-Mail: info@sbspromo.com, Web Site: www.standardbuying.com (33)

Standard Communications Corp, San Diego, CA. Tel: (858) 546-5300, (800) 745-2445, FAX: (858) 546-5301, E-Mail: satcommsales@stdcom.com, Web Site: www.standardcomm.com (17)

Standard Directory of Advertising Agencies, New Providence, NJ. Tel: (800) 521-8110, FAX: (908) 790-5405 (43)

Standard Life, Montreal, PQ Canada. Tel: (514) 499-8855, (877) 499-9555, FAX: (514) 499-4908, Web Site: www.standardlife.ca (15)

Standard Publishing, Cincinnati, OH. Tel: (513) 931-4050, (800) 543-1301, FAX: (877) 867-5751, Web Site: www.standardpub.com (17)

Standard Register, Dayton, OH. Tel: (937) 221-1000, (800) 755-6405, FAX: (937) 221-1239, E-Mail: julie.mcewan@standardregister.com, Web Site: www.standardregister.com (10)

Standard Tools & Equipment Co, Greensboro, NC. Tel: (336) 697-7177, Web Site: www.toolsusa.com (9)

Standing, Mark, Deseret Book, Salt Lake City, UT. Tel: (801) 534-1515, (800) 453-4532, FAX: (801) 517-3392, Web Site: www.deseretbook.com (16)

Standish, Mike, Alco Chemical, Chattanooga, TN. Tel: (423) 629-1405, FAX: (423) 698-8723, Web Site: www.alcochemical.com (16)

Standish, Thomas, R., Centerpoint Energy, Minneapolis, MN. Tel: (612) 372-4664, FAX: (612) 321-4873, E-Mail: mgc-businessinformation@centerpointenergy.com, Web Site: www.minnegasco.centerpointenergy.com (16)

Staneff, Lynn, Magellan's Catalog, Santa Barbara, CA. Tel: (800) 962-4943, FAX: (800) 962-4940, E-Mail: sales@magellans.com, Web Site: www.magellans.com (5)

Stanford, Sheila, The Stanford Group, New York, NY. Tel: (212) 333-5514, FAX: (212) 581-4202, E-Mail: info@stanfordgroupinc.com, Web Site: www.standfordgroupinc.com (35)

The Stanford Group, New York, NY. Tel: (212) 333-5514, FAX: (212) 581-4202, E-Mail: info@stanfordgroupinc.com, Web Site: www.standfordgroupinc.com (35)

Stanga, Michael, Saunders Manufacturing Co Inc, Readfield, ME. Tel: (207) 685-3385, (800) 341-4674, FAX: (207) 685-9918, E-Mail: jsherwood@saunders-usa.com, Web Site: www.saunders-usa.com (16)

Stanger, Robert, Robert A Stanger & Co Inc, Shrewsbury, NJ. Tel: (732) 389-3600, FAX: (732) 389-1751, E-Mail: info@rastanger.com, Web Site: www.rastranger.com (14)

Robert A Stanger & Co Inc, Shrewsbury, NJ. Tel: (732) 389-3600, FAX: (732) 389-1751, E-Mail: info@rastanger.com, Web Site: www.rastranger.com (14)

Stanich, Mark, American Express Publishing Corp, New York, NY. Tel: (212) 382-5600, (888) 461-6180, FAX: (212) 827-6496, E-Mail: aepc@custmersvc.com, Web Site: www.amexpub.com (17)

Stankard, Martin F., Productivity Development Group Inc, Westford, MA. Tel: (978) 692-1818, FAX: (978) 692-5080, E-Mail: info@martinstankard.com (20)

Stanley Jr., George, F., Vagabond Creations Inc, Dayton, OH. Tel: (937) 298-1124, (800) 738-7237, FAX: (937) 298-1124, E-Mail: sales@vagabondcreations.net, Web Site: www.vagabondcreations.net (10)

Stanley, Clive, Performance Media Solutions Inc & TrueWorx Inc, Las Vegas, NV. Tel: (866) 827-7077 (16)

Stanley, Debra, DS Direct Communications, Redondo Beach, CA. Tel: (310) 540-4313 (23)

Stanley, Lori, Coastal Health Train, Virginia Beach, VA. Tel: (757) 631-3142, Web Site: www.coastalhealth.com (7)

Stanley, Richard, Lortz Direct Marketing Inc, Omaha, NE. Tel: (800) 366-7686, Web Site: www.lortzdirect.com (35)

Stanley, Tracey, Print Products International, Annapolis Junction, MD. Tel: (910) 695-7223, FAX: (910) 944-1724, Web Site: www.paceworldwide.com (9)

Stanley Home Products, Great Bend, KS. Tel: (620) 792-1711, (800) 628-9032, Web Site: www.shponline.com (8)

Stanley Supply & Services, North Andover, MA. Tel: (978) 682-9844, (800) 225-5370, FAX: (800) 743-8141, Web Site: www.stanleysupplyservices.com (16)

Stanton, Aloysius, F., Stanton Direct Marketing Inc, Elmira, NY. Tel: (607) 734-1665, (877) 734-1665, FAX: (607) 734-3708, Web Site: www.stantondirect.com (31)

Stanton, Scott, Nancy's Notions LLC, Beaver Dam, WI. Tel: (920) 887-0391, (800) 833-0690, FAX: (800) 255-8119, E-Mail: comments@nancysnotions.com, Web Site: www.nancysnotions.com (11)

Stanton Direct Marketing Inc, Elmira, NY. Tel: (607) 734-1665, (877) 734-1665, FAX: (607) 734-3708, Web Site: www.stantondirect.com (31)

Stanuscek, Kris, The Sausage Maker Inc, Buffalo, NY. Tel: (716) 824-5814, (888) 490-8525, FAX: (716) 824-6465, E-Mail: customerservice@sausagemaker.com, Web Site: www.sausagemaker.com (4)

Stanvick, Chris, Faneuil ISG, Winnipeg, MB. Tel: (866) Faneuil, Web Site: www.faneuil.com (30)

Stapelfeld, Ben, New Pig Corp, Tipton, PA. Tel: (814) 684-0101, (800) 468-4647, FAX: (814) 684-0961, E-Mail: hothogs@newpig.com, Web Site: www.newpig.com (9)

Staples, Jim, Staples Marketing Communications, Pewaukee, WI. Tel: (262) 650-9900, (800) 867-1890, FAX: (262) 650-3160, Web Site: www.staplesmarketing.com (35)

Staples, Mary, Daystar Data Group Inc, Schaumburg, IL. Tel: (847) 202-0100, FAX: (847) 202-0107, E-Mail: sales@daystardg.com, Web Site: www.daystardg.com (22)

Staples Business Advantage, Atlanta, GA. Tel: (770) 997-2512, (877) 826-7754, FAX: (888) 387-9592, Web Site: www.staples.com (34)

Staples Inc, Framingham, MA. Tel: (508) 253-5000, FAX: (508) 253-7803, Web Site: www.staples.com (10)

Staples Industrial, Framingham, MA. Tel: (978) 443-9592, (800) 638-9899, FAX: (978) 443-2678 (28)

Staples Marketing Communications, Pewaukee, WI. Tel: (262) 650-9900, (800) 867-1890, FAX: (262) 650-3160, Web Site: www.staplesmarketing.com (35)

Stapleton, Amy, Missouri Life Inc, Boonville, MO. Tel: (660) 882-9898, (800) 492-2593, FAX: (660) 882-9899, E-Mail: info@missourilife.com, Web Site: www.missourilife.com (17)

The Staplex Co, Brooklyn, NY. Tel: (718) 768-3333, (800) 221-0822, FAX: (718) 965-0750, E-Mail: info@staplex.com, Web Site: www.staplex.com (34)

Star, Doug, Potpourri Group Inc, Chelmsford, MA. Tel: (978) 256-4100, FAX: (978) 256-1961/0344, Web Site: www.potpourrigroup.com (6)

STAR Direct, Kansas City, MO. Tel: (816) 234-4203, (800) 829-0151, FAX: (816) 234-4189, E-Mail: mtully@kcstar.com, Web Site: www.kcstardirect.com (21)

Star Silkscreen Design Inc, Decatur, IL. Tel: (217) 877-0804, FAX: (217) 877-0843 (2)

Star Sprinkler Inc, Lansdale, PA. Tel: (414) 570-5000, (800) 558-5236, FAX: (414) 570-5010, Web Site: www.starsprinkler.com (9)

Star Tribune, Minneapolis, MN. Tel: (612) 673-4000, FAX: (612) 673-4359, E-Mail: charte@startribune.com, Web Site: www.startribunecompany.com (17)

Starbird, Susan, Starbird Creative, Sebastopol, CA. Tel: (707) 778-7277, E-Mail: info@starbirdcreative.com, Web Site: www.starbirdcreative.com (35)

Starbird Creative, Sebastopol, CA. Tel: (707) 778-7277, E-Mail: info@starbirdcreative.com, Web Site: www.starbirdcreative.com (35)

Starbucks Corp, Seattle, WA. Tel: (206) 447-1575, (800) 344-1575, FAX: (206) 447-0828, Web Site: www.starbucks.com (4)

Starchtech, Golden Valley, MN. Tel: (763) 545-5400, (800) 597-7225, FAX: (763) 545-9450, Web Site: www.starchtech.com (16)

Starcrest Products of California Inc, Perris, CA. Tel: (909) 943-2011, FAX: (909) 943-2971, E-Mail: tmc@tstonramp.com (16)

Stark, Ben, Faultless Starch/Bon Ami Co, Kansas City, MO. Tel: (816) 842-1230, FAX: (816) 842-3417, E-Mail: info@faultless.com, Web Site: www.faultless.com (16)

Stark, Dan, Boyd Gaming Corp, Las Vegas, NV. Tel: (702) 792-7200, FAX: (702) 792-7313, Web Site: www.boydgaming.com (16)

Stark, David, Dozier Equipment International, Milwaukee, WI. Tel: (800) 251-1234, FAX: (800) 336-6608, Web Site: www.dozierequip.com (9)

Stark, Eleanor L., Eleanor L Stark, New York, NY. Tel: (212) 879-9510, FAX: (212) 879-6252, E-Mail: elstarkco@aol.com (24)

Stark, Frank, Stark Brothers Fulfillment Services, Louisiana, MO. Tel: (573) 754-5511, (800) 325-4180, FAX: (573) 754-5290, E-Mail: info@starkbros.com, Web Site: www.starkbros.com (8)

Stark Brothers Fulfillment Services, Louisiana, MO. Tel: (573) 754-5511, (800) 325-4180, FAX: (573) 754-5290, E-Mail: info@starkbros.com, Web Site: www.starkbros.com (8)

Stark Brothers Nurseries & Orchards, Louisiana, MO. Tel: (573) 754-8800, (800) 325-4180, E-Mail: info@starkbros.com, Web Site: www.starkbros.com (8)

Eleanor L Stark, New York, NY. Tel: (212) 879-9510, FAX: (212) 879-6252, E-Mail: elstarkco@aol.com (24)

Starkey Laboratories, Eden Prairie, MN. Tel: (952) 941-6401, Web Site: www.starkey.com (16)

Starmount Life Insurance Co, Baton Rouge, LA. Tel: (225) 926-2888, (888) 729-7827, (888) 729-5433, E-Mail: info@starmountlife.com, Web Site: www.starmountlife.com (15)

Staron, Carley, Nielsen Trade Dimensions, Wilton, CT. Tel: (203) 222-5750, (800) 291-0410, FAX: (203) 222-5701, E-Mail: tradedimensions.info@nielsen.com, Web Site: www.tradedimensions.com (17)

Starr, Barry, Affinion Group, Franklin, TN. Tel: (800) 251-2148, Web Site: www.progenymarketing.com (15)

START International, Addison, TX. Tel: (972) 248-1999, (800) 259-1986, FAX: (972) 248-1991, E-Mail: info@startinternational.com, Web Site: www.startinternational.com (9)

STARTEC, Rockville, MD. Tel: (310) 610-4300, Web Site: www.startec.com (32)

Starwood Hotels & Resorts, Stamford, CT. Tel: (914) 640-8268, FAX: (914) 640-8310, Web Site: www.starwoodhotels.com (19)

Starz Entertainment Group, Englewood, CO. Tel: (720) 852-7700, Web Site: www.starz.com (16)

The Stash Tea Catalog, Tigard, OR. Tel: (800) 547-1514, FAX: (503) 684-4424, E-Mail: stash@stashtea.com, Web Site: www.stashtea.com (4)

State Farm Insurance Cos, Bloomington, IL. Tel: (309) 766-2311, FAX: (309) 766-3621, Web Site: www.statefarm.com (15)

State Line Tack Inc, Phoenix, AZ. Tel: (623) 580-6100, (800) 228-9208, FAX: (623) 580-6183, E-Mail: customerservice@statelinetack.com, Web Site: www.statelinetack.com (16)

State Mutual Insurance Co, Rome, GA. Tel: (706) 291-1054, FAX: (706) 291-9459 (15)

State Street Global Advisors, Boston, MA. Tel: (617) 664-2618, Web Site: www.ssga.com (14)

State University of New York-College of Plattsburgh, Plattsburgh, NY. Tel: (518) 564-2000, FAX: (518) 564-3183, E-Mail: nancy.church@plattsburgh.edu, Web Site: www.plattsburgh.edu (41)

Staten, Anastasia, Foundation Fighting Blindness, Columbia, MD. Tel: (410) 423-0600, Web Site: www.fightblindness.org (1)

Stateside Associates, Arlington, VA. Tel: (703) 525-7466 X228 (20)

Statile, Robert, CertainTeed Corp, Valley Forge, PA. Tel: (610) 341-7000/7739, (800) 233-8990, FAX: (610) 341-7777, Web Site: www.certainteed.com (16)

Statistical Innovations Inc, Belmont, MA. Tel: (617) 489-4490, FAX: (617) 489-4499, E-Mail: statisticalinnovations@gmail.com, Web Site: www.statisticalinnovations.com (20)

Statlistics, Danbury, CT. Tel: (203) 778-8700, Web Site: www.statlistics.com (23)

Staton, Michael, Janes Information Group, Alexandria, VA. Tel: (703) 683-3700, (800) 824-0768, FAX: (703) 836-0297, Web Site: www.janes.com (17)

StatSoft Inc, Tulsa, OK. Tel: (918) 749-1119, FAX: (918) 749-2217, E-Mail: info@statsoft.com, Web Site: www.statsoft.com (9)

Statware, Centerbrook, CT. Tel: (860) 767-9000, FAX: (860) 767-3145, E-Mail: info@statware.net, Web Site: www.powerlist.com (16)

Statz, Steve, Mersco Medical, Pierre, SD. Tel: (605) 224-6687, (800) 234-1881, FAX: (605) 322-1801 (16)

Staudt, Matthew, W., Interactive Marketing Group Inc, Allendale, NJ. Tel: (201) 327-0974, FAX: (201) 327-3596, E-Mail: info@imgusa.com, Web Site: www.imgusa.com/index.aspx (21)

Stavarz, Alexander, Synergy Direct Marketing Solutions LLC, Barberton, OH. Tel: (330) 869-5886, Web Site: www.synmar.biz (29)

Stavitski, Richard, L., Crutchfield Corp, Charlottesville, VA. Tel: (434) 817-1000, (800) 955-9091, FAX: (804) 817-1010, E-Mail: administration@crutchfield.com, Web Site: www.crutchfield.com (3)

Stay, Charles, Penn Industries Inc, Cerritos, CA. Tel: (562) 926-0455, FAX: (562) 926-8955, Web Site: www.pennlitho.com (27)

StayWell/Krames, San Bruno, CA. Tel: (650) 742-0400, FAX: (650) 244-4568, Web Site: www.staywell.com (17)

Stead, Bob, American Trim, Lima, OH. Tel: (419) 228-1145, FAX: (419) 996-4850, E-Mail: sales@amtrim.com, Web Site: www.amtrim.com (9)

Stead, Jerre, L., IHS Inc, Englewood, CO. Tel: (303) 790-0600, (800) 525-7052, FAX: (303) 754-3940, E-Mail: customer.support@ihs.com, Web Site: www.ihs.com (17)

Stead, Jerre, L., Partminer, Centennial, CO. Tel: (303) 200-5500, FAX: (303) 754-3940, Web Site: www.partminer.com (17)

Steady, Glen, Quadrant Engineering Plastic Products, Reading, PA. Tel: (610) 320-6600, (800) 366-0300, FAX: (610) 320-6868, Web Site: www.quadrantepp.com (16)

Stearns, Gary, Aspen Packaging Corp, Cicero, IL. FAX: (708) 652-6444, Web Site: www.aspenpkg.com (27)

Stearns, Mark S., Crystek Corp, Fort Myers, FL. Tel: (239) 561-3311, (800) 237-3061, FAX: (239) 561-1025, E-Mail: sales@crystek.com, Web Site: www.crystek.com (9)

Stearns, Richard, World Vision Inc, Federal Way, WA. Tel: (253) 815-1000, (888) 511-6548, FAX: (253) 815-3140, E-Mail: info@worldvision.org, Web Site: www.worldvision.org (1)

Stearns, Sue, Meister Media Worldwide, Willoughby, OH. Tel: (440) 942-2000, (800) 572-7740, FAX: (440) 975-3447, E-Mail: info@meistermedia.com, Web Site: www.meistermedia.com (17)

Steck-Vaughn, Austin, TX. Tel: (512) 343-8227, (877) 866-2586, (800) 531-5015, FAX: (512) 795-3617, (877) 265-2730, E-Mail: info@steck-vaughn.com, Web Site: www.steck-vaughn.com (17)

Steckman, Nicole, Georgetown University Law Center/Continuing Legal Education Div, Washington, DC. Tel: (202) 662-9890, FAX: (202) 662-9891, E-Mail: nds25@law.georgetown.edu, Web Site: www.georgetowncle.org (13)

Steedman, Donald, Taylor-Stiles Division, Florence, KY. Tel: (859) 525-7600, (800) 365-8555, FAX: (859) 525-1446, E-Mail: sales@littleford.com, Web Site: www.littleford.com (16)

Steel, Alan, E., National Stationery Show, White Plains, NY. Tel: (914) 421-3200, (800) 272-SHOW, FAX: (914) 948-6180, E-Mail: cate_doyle@glmshows.com, Web Site: www.glmshows.com (42)

Steel, Alan, E., New York International Gift Fair, White Plains, NY. Tel: (914) 421-3200, (800) 272-SHOW, FAX: (914) 948-6180, Web Site: www.nyigf.com (42)

Steel, Richard, STEEL MEDIA, New York, NY. Tel: (212) 920-9599, Web Site: www.steelmediainc.com (35)

STEEL MEDIA, New York, NY. Tel: (212) 920-9599, Web Site: www.steelmediainc.com (35)

Steelcase Inc, Grand Rapids, MI. Tel: (616) 247-2710, FAX: (616) 475-2270, Web Site: www.steelcase.com (16)

Steele, Elinor, Tupperware, Orlando, FL. Tel: (407) 826-5050, (800) 366-3800, FAX: (407) 826-8874, Web Site: www.tupperware.com (16)

Steele, Jenine, Hampshire Pewter Co, Wolfeboro, NH. Tel: (603) 569-4944, (800) 639-7704, FAX: (603) 569-4524, E-Mail: gifts@hampshirepewter.com, Web Site: www.hampshirepewter.com (6)

Steele, Joey, Fauntleroy Supply Co/Wing Supply, Greenville, KY. Tel: (270) 338-5866, (800) 388-9464, FAX: (270) 338-0057, Web Site: www.wingsupply.com (11)

Steele, Julie, The LadyBug Co, Berry Creek, CA. Tel: (530) 589-5227, FAX: (530) 589-4639 (8)

Steele, Robert, S., Hampshire Pewter Co, Wolfeboro, NH. Tel: (603) 569-4944, (800) 639-7704, FAX: (603) 569-4524, E-Mail: gifts@hampshirepewter.com, Web Site: www.hampshirepewter.com (6)

Steenbeke, Joseph, J., Sears Home Improvement Products Inc, Longwood, FL. Tel: (407) 767-0990, (877) 840-7126, FAX: (407) 831-1848, Web Site: www.searshomepro.com (16)

Stefanki, Luke, Multi-Media Publishing & Packaging Inc, Panorama City, CA. Tel: (818) 341-7484, (800) 982-8138, FAX: (818) 341-2807, E-Mail: sales@mmppinc.com, Web Site: www.mmppinc.com (27)

Stefano, Brian, Peter Pan Bus Lines Inc, Springfield, MA. Tel: (413) 781-2900, (800) 343-9999, FAX: (413) 746-8671, E-Mail: info@peterpanbus.com, Web Site: www.peterpanbus.com (19)

Stefano, Desiree, D., Jarden Corp, Daleville, IN. Tel: (765) 557-3000, (800) 428-8150, FAX: (765) 281-5403, Web Site: www.jarden.com (16)

Stefanowicz, Marianne, TBWA/Chiat/Day Inc, New York, NY. Tel: (212) 804-1000, FAX: (212) 804-1200, E-Mail: jamie.gallo@tbwachiat.com, Web Site: www.tbwachiat.com (35)

Steffen, Ed, Gundersen Partners LLC, New York, NY. Tel: (212) 677-7660, FAX: (212) 358-0275, Web Site: www.gundersenpartners.com (20)

Steffens, Carl, Adobe Systems Inc, San Jose, CA. Tel: (408) 536-6000, (800) 833-6687, FAX: (408) 537-6000, Web Site: www.adobe.com (22)

Steig, Donald, B., Practical Computer Solutions, South Orange, NJ. Tel: (973) 761-6099, FAX: (215) 243-8283, E-Mail: dbsteig@alum.mit.edu, Web Site: www.donsteig.com (20)

Steigler, Ernie, SWB & R, Bethlehem, PA. Tel: (610) 866-0611, FAX: (610) 866-8650, Web Site: www.swb.com (35)

Stein, Johanna, Santa Fe Natural Tobacco Co, Santa Fe, NM. Tel: (505) 982-4257, Web Site: www.nascigs.com (16)

Stein, Kevin, HAVE Inc, Hudson, NY. Tel: (518) 828-2000, (800) 999-HAVE (4283), FAX: (518) 828-2008, E-Mail: kstein@haveinc.com, Web Site: www.haveinc.com (3)

Stein, Laura, The Bombay Co, Brampton, ON. Tel: (877) 536-6229, E-Mail: customerservice@bombay.ca, Web Site: www.bombay.com (8)

Stein, Lonny, Dictionary of Marketing Terms, Hauppauge, NY. Tel: (631) 434-3311, (800) 645-3476, FAX: (631) 434-3723, E-Mail: barrons@barronseduc.com, Web Site: www.barronseduc.com (43)

Stein, Martin, RMI Direct Marketing Inc, Danbury, CT. Tel: (203) 798-0448, FAX: (203) 778-6130, E-Mail: info@rmidirect.com, Web Site: www.rmidirect.com (23)

Stein, Robert, G., American Society on Aging, San Francisco, CA. Tel: (415) 974-9600, (800) 537-9728, FAX: (415) 974-0300, E-Mail: info@asaging.org, Web Site: www.asaging.org (1)

Stein, Seymour, S., K-D Lamp Co, Andover, OH. Tel: (440) 293-4064, FAX: (440) 293-4591, E-Mail: admin@atc-lighting-plastics.com, Web Site: www.k-dlamp.com (12)

Stein, Thomas, Stein Rogan & Partners, New York, NY. Tel: (212) 213-1112, FAX: (212) 779-7305, E-Mail: tstein@steinrogan.com (35)

Stein, kay, Recognition Products International, Easton, MD. Tel: (410) 820-0022, (800) 292-7354, FAX: (410) 820-5044, E-Mail: info@recognitionproducts.com, Web Site: www.shoprecognitionproducts.com (16)

Stein Rogan & Partners, New York, NY. Tel: (212) 213-1112, FAX: (212) 779-7305, E-Mail: tstein@steinrogan.com, Web Site: www.steinrogan.com (35)

Steinbarth, David A., LaPreferida Inc, Chicago, IL. Tel: (773) 254-7200, (800) 621-5422, FAX: (773) 254-8546, Web Site: www.lapreferida.com (4)

Steinbarth, Rich, LaPreferida Inc, Chicago, IL. Tel: (773) 254-7200, (800) 621-5422, FAX: (773) 254-8546, Web Site: www.lapreferida.com (4)

Steinberg, Andrea, Gary's Perennials, LLC, Maple Glen, PA. Tel: (215) 628-4070, (800) 898-6653, FAX: (215) 628-0216, E-Mail: roots@garysperennials.com, Web Site: www.garysperennials.com; www.perennialmarket.com (8)

Steinberg, Gary, Gary's Perennials, LLC, Maple Glen, PA. Tel: (215) 628-4070, (800) 898-6653, FAX: (215) 628-0216, E-Mail: roots@garysperennials.com, Web Site: www.garysperennials.com; www.perennialmarket.com (8)

Steinberg, Howard, Source Marketing, Norwalk, CT. Tel: (203) 222-2741, FAX: (203) 291-4010, E-Mail: bardes@source-marketing.com, Web Site: www.source-marketing.com (35)

Steinberg, Joseph, S., Leucadia National Corp, New York, NY. Tel: (212) 460-1900, FAX: (212) 598-4869, Web Site: www.leucadia.com (14)

Steinberg, Lisa, Diversified Investment Advisors, Harrison, NY. Tel: (914) 697-8967, FAX: (914) 697-3743, Web Site: www.divinvest.com (14)

Steinberg, Lori, Moore Medical LLC, Farmington, CT. Tel: (860) 826-3600, FAX: (860) 223-2382, Web Site: www.mooremedical.com (7)

Steinbrunner, Carla, Associated Photo, Florence, KY. Tel: (859) 344-1460, (800) 727-2580, FAX: (859) 282-0032 (16)

Steiner, Paula, Blue Cross/Blue Shield of Illinois, Chicago, IL. Tel: (312) 938-6000, FAX: (312) 938-5722, Web Site: www.bcbsil.com (15)

Steinfeld, Jeff, Type-A-Scan Inc, New York, NY. Tel: (212) 367-8406, FAX: (212) 691-8134, E-Mail: info@typeascan.com, Web Site: www.typeascan.com (12)

Steinhardt, David, J., Idealliance, Alexandria, VA. Tel: (703) 837-1070, FAX: (703) 837-1072 (40)

Steinhardt, William, Steinhardt Direct Inc, Overland Park, KS. Tel: (913) 764-6400, FAX: (913) 780-6401, E-Mail: sdirect2@home.com (35)

Steinhardt Direct Inc, Overland Park, KS. Tel: (913) 764-6400, FAX: (913) 780-6401, E-Mail: sdirect2@home.com (35)

Steinhart, David, Service Mailers Inc, Los Angeles, CA. Tel: (323) 292-0133, FAX: (323) 292-1038, E-Mail: dgsteinhart@gmail.com, Web Site: www.servicemailersinc.com (21)

Steinhouse, Eric, Commerce Bancshares Inc, Saint Louis, MO. Tel: (800) 453-2265, Web Site: www.commercebank.com (14)

Steinman, Andy, Falcon Safety Products, Branchburg, NJ. Tel: (908) 707-4900, FAX: (908) 707-8855, Web Site: www.falconsafety.com (16)

Steinmetz, Jay, Barcoding Inc, Baltimore, MD. Tel: (410) 385-8532, (888) 860-SCAN, (888) 860-7226, FAX: (410) 385-8559, E-Mail: info@barcoding.com, Web Site: www.barcoding.com (22)

Stella, Richard, Zotos International, Darien, CT. Tel: (203) 655-8911, (800) 242-WAVE, (800) 242-9283, FAX: (203) 656-7890, E-Mail: HumanResources@zotosintl.com, Web Site: www.zotos.com (16)

Stellar Technology Inc, Amherst, NY. Tel: (800) 274-1846, FAX: (716) 250-1909, E-Mail: info@stellartech.com, Web Site: www.stellartech.com (9)

Stelmachowicz, John, Pharmaceutical Care Management Association, Washington, DC. Tel: (202) 207-3610, FAX: (202) 207-3623, E-Mail: info@pcmanet.org, Web Site: www.pcmanet.org (1)

The Stelter Co, Des Moines, IA. Tel: (800) 331-6881 (20)

Stengel, Jim, Clairol Inc, Stamford, CT. Tel: (203) 357-5000, (800) 252-4765, FAX: (203) 357-5003, Web Site: www.clairol.com (7)

Stephan, George, N., Stephan Partners Inc, New York, NY. Tel: (212) 524-8583, E-Mail: george@ stephenpartners.com, Web Site: www. stephanpartners.com (35)

Stephan & Brady Inc, Madison, WI. Tel: (608) 241-4141, FAX: (608) 241-4246, E-Mail: gwhitely@ stephanbrady.com, Web Site: www.stephanbrady. com (35)

Stephan Partners Inc, New York, NY. Tel: (212) 524-8583, E-Mail: george@stephenpartners.com, Web Site: www.stephanpartners.com (35)

Stephen-Bradford Search, New York, NY. Tel: (212) 221-6333, X346, (800) 720-0922, FAX: (212) 391-7826, E-Mail: info@stephenbradford.com, Web Site: www.stephenbradford.com (20)

Stephens II, Phillip, Stephens Direct Inc, Kettering, OH. Tel: (937) 299-4993, FAX: (937) 299-9355, E-Mail: phil.stephens@stephensdirect.com (35)

Stephens, Gregory, AM Leonard Inc, Piqua, OH. Tel: (937) 773-2694, (800) 543-8955, FAX: (800) 433-0633, (937) 773-9993, E-Mail: info@amleo.com, Web Site: www.amleo.com (8)

Stephens, J.T., EBSCO Reception Room Subscription Services, Birmingham, AL. Tel: (205) 991-1409, (800) 527-5901, FAX: (205) 995-1621, Web Site: www.ebsco.com/errss (18)

Stephens, J.T., Vulcan Information Packaging, Vincent, AL. Tel: (205) 672-2241, (800) 633-4526, FAX: (205) 672-1276, Web Site: www.vulcan-online.com (16)

Stephens, Mike, Historical Replications Inc, Jackson, MS. Tel: (601) 981-8743, (800) 426-5628, FAX: (601) 981-8185, E-Mail: info@historicaldesigns. com, Web Site: www.historicaldesigns.com (8)

Stephens, Paul, Crowne Plaza Chateau Le Combe, Edmonton, AB Canada. Tel: (780) 428-6611, FAX: (780) 420-8379, E-Mail: info@chateaulecombe. com, Web Site: www.chateaulecombe.com (19)

Stephens, William, Thomas, Boise Cascade Holdings LLC, Boise, ID. Tel: (208) 384-6451, FAX: (208) 384-7189, E-Mail: mediarelations@bc.com, Web Site: www.bc.com (18)

Stephens Direct Inc, Kettering, OH. Tel: (937) 299-4993, FAX: (937) 299-9355, E-Mail: phil. stephens@stephensdirect.com (35)

Stephens Inc, New York, NY. Tel: (212) 891-1777, Web Site: www.stephens.com (20)

Stephenson APR, Lucinda, Iowa Medical Society, West Des Moines, IA. Tel: (515) 223-1401, FAX: (515) 223-0590, Web Site: www.iowamedical.org (1)

Stephenson, George, W., Stephenson Printing Inc, Alexandria, VA. Tel: (703) 642-9000, (800) 336-4637, FAX: (703) 354-0384, E-Mail: gstephenson@stephensonprinting.com, Web Site: www.stephensonprinting.com (27)

Stephenson, Laura, Berean Christian Stores, West Chester, OH. Tel: (877) 405-7194, FAX: (513) 728-6975, E-Mail: customerservice@berean.com, Web Site: www.berean.com (5)

Stephenson, Sara, DataQuick, San Diego, CA. Tel: (856) 597-3100, (800) 950-9171, Web Site: www. primerasource.com (23)

Stephenson Printing Inc, Alexandria, VA. Tel: (703) 642-9000, (800) 336-4637, FAX: (703) 354-0384, E-Mail: gstephenson@stephensonprinting.com, Web Site: www.stephensonprinting.com (27)

Steppat, David F., Minnesota Life, Saint Paul, MN. Tel: (651) 665-3500, (888) 237-1838, FAX: (651) 665-4488, Web Site: www.minnesotalife.com; www.securian.com (15)

Steppin' Out & See America, Las Vegas, NV. Tel: (702) 798-6522, E-Mail: sales@see-america.net, Web Site: steppinoutseeamerica.com (19)

Steptoe & Wife Antiques Ltd, Toronto, ON Canada. Tel: (416) 780-1707, (800) 461-0060, FAX: (416) 780-1814, E-Mail: info@steptoewife.com, Web Site: www.steptoewife.com (8)

Sterk, Leo, Wheaton Group, Chapel Hill, NC. Tel: (919) 969-8859, FAX: (425) 675-6014, E-Mail: jim.wheaton@wheatongroup.com, Web Site: www. wheatongroup.com (22)

Sterling, George, A., Sterling Print & Mail System, Peterborough, NH. Tel: (603) 924-9401, (800) 439-9401, FAX: (603) 924-7925, E-Mail: sbc@sbc.mv. com, Web Site: www.mv.com/ipusers/sbc (27)

Sterling, Rhonda, Phoenix Learning Group Inc, Maryland Heights, MO. Tel: (314) 569-0211, (800) 221-1274, FAX: (314) 569-2834, E-Mail: dealersales@ phoenixlearninggroup.com, Web Site: www. phoenixlearninggroup.com (16)

Sterling Business Services, Cary, NC. Tel: (919) 467-5062 (28)

Sterling Fluid Systems, Indianapolis, IN. Tel: (317) 925-9661, (800) 879-0182, FAX: (317) 924-7388, Web Site: www.peerlesspump.com (16)

Sterling Jewelers Inc, Akron, OH. Tel: (330) 668-5000, FAX: (330) 668-5052, E-Mail: webmaster@ jewels.com, Web Site: www.sterlingjewelers.com (16)

Sterling Name Tape Inc, Winsted, CT. Tel: (860) 379-5142, (800) 654-5210, FAX: (860) 379-0394, E-Mail: postman@sterlingtape.com, Web Site: www.sterlingtape.com (16)

Sterling Print & Mail System, Peterborough, NH. Tel: (603) 924-9401, (800) 439-9401, FAX: (603) 924-7925, E-Mail: sbc@sbc.mv.com, Web Site: www. mv.com/ipusers/sbc (27)

Sterling Publishing Co Inc, New York, NY. Tel: (212) 532-7160, (800) 367-9692, FAX: (212) 213-2495, Web Site: www.sterlingpublishing.com (17)

Stern, David, National Basketball Association, Secaucus, NJ. Tel: (212) 407-8000, FAX: (212) 826-0579, Web Site: www.nba.com (1)

Stern, Leslie, F., Central Lewmar, Clifton, NJ. Tel: (973) 622-6377, (800) 772-7301, FAX: (973) 623-4323, E-Mail: dan.watkoske@expedx.com, Web Site: www.centrallewmar.com (25)

Stern, Norm, Norscot Group, Mequon, WI. Tel: (262) 241-3313, (800) 653-3313, FAX: (262) 241-4904, Web Site: www.norscot.com (5)

Stern, Robert, Short Sizes Inc, Northfield, OH. Tel: (440) 605-1000, (800) 272-9000, FAX: (440) 605-1065, E-Mail: orders@shortsizesinc.com, Web Site: www.shortsizesinc.com (2)

Stern, Sandre, Lions Gate Television Corp, Santa Monica, CA. Tel: (310) 449-9200, FAX: (310) 255-3870, Web Site: www.lionsgate.com (16)

Stern, Scott, Norscot Group, Mequon, WI. Tel: (262) 241-3313, (800) 653-3313, FAX: (262) 241-4904, Web Site: www.norscot.com (5)

Sternberg, Deborah, Starmount Life Insurance Co, Baton Rouge, LA. Tel: (225) 926-2888, (888) 729-7827, (888) 729-5433, E-Mail: info@starmountlife. com, Web Site: www.starmountlife.com (15)

Sternberg, Donna, Starmount Life Insurance Co, Baton Rouge, LA. Tel: (225) 926-2888, (888) 729-7827, (888) 729-5433, E-Mail: info@starmountlife.com, Web Site: www.starmountlife.com (15)

Sternberg, Erich, Starmount Life Insurance Co, Baton Rouge, LA. Tel: (225) 926-2888, (888) 729-7827, (888) 729-5433, E-Mail: info@starmountlife.com, Web Site: www.starmountlife.com (15)

Sternberg, Hans, J., Starmount Life Insurance Co, Baton Rouge, LA. Tel: (225) 926-2888, (888) 729-7827, (888) 729-5433, E-Mail: info@starmountlife. com, Web Site: www.starmountlife.com (15)

Sternbert, Todd, START International, Addison, TX. Tel: (972) 248-1999, (800) 259-1986, FAX: (972) 248-1991, E-Mail: info@startinternational.com, Web Site: www.startinternational.com (9)

George Sterne Agency Inc, Fallbrook, CA. Tel: (760) 432-6913, (800) 772-8174, FAX: (760) 432-9570, E-Mail: mim@georgesterneagency.com, Web Site: www.georgesterneagency.com (23)

Sternlicht, Barry, Resorts Worldwide Inc, White Plains, NY. Tel: (914) 640-8100, (800) 325-3535, FAX: (914) 640-8310, Web Site: www.starwood. com (19)

Stetson University, Deland, FL. Tel: (904) 822-7405/7406, FAX: (904) 822-7430, Web Site: www. stetson.edu (41)

Steuben Glass, New York, NY. Tel: (607) 974-8659, (800) STEUBEN, FAX: (607) 974-8441, E-Mail: info@steuben.com, Web Site: www.steuben.com (6)

Steurer, M.Ed. David K., Wellness Councils of America, Omaha, NE. Tel: (402) 827-3590, FAX: (402) 827-3594, E-Mail: wellworkplace@welcoa. org, Web Site: www.welcoa.org (1)

Steve Scott Group LLC, Midvale, UT. Tel: (801) 277-8900, (800) 220-6481, FAX: (801) 277-8986, Web Site: www.totalgymdirect.com (32)

Stevens Jr., George, The American Film Institute, Los Angeles, CA. Tel: (323) 856-7600, FAX: (323) 467-4578, Web Site: www.afi.com (1)

Stevens, Craig, S., Stevens Publishing Co, Sandusky, OH. Tel: (419) 626-5592, (800) 236-5592, FAX: (419) 626-9333, Web Site: www. stephenspublishing.com (17)

Stevens, Don, Cumberland Woodcraft Co Inc, Carlisle, PA. Tel: (717) 243-0063, (800) 367-1884, FAX: (717) 243-6502, E-Mail: sales@ cumberlandwoodcraft.com, Web Site: www. cumberlandwoodcraft.com (8)

Stevens, George, Visible Results USA Inc, Overland Park, KS. Tel: (913) 851-9400, FAX: (913) 851-0628, E-Mail: info@visibleresults.com, Web Site: www.visibleresults.com (32)

Stevens, Harry, Datamatx Inc, Ashland, VA. Tel: (804) 550-2513, (800) 943-5240, FAX: (804) 550-2527, Web Site: www.datamatx.com (27)

Stevens, John, Paragon Media Strategies, Denver, CO. Tel: (303) 922-5600, FAX: (303) 922-1589, E-Mail: info@paragonmediastrategies.com, Web Site: www.paragonmediastrategies.com (30)

Stevens, Linda, Mystic Stamp Co Inc, Camden, NY. Tel: (866) 660-7147, FAX: (800) 385-4919, E-Mail: info@mysticstamp.com, Web Site: www. mysticstamp.com (16)

Stevens, Mark, International Gamco Inc, Omaha, NE. Tel: (402) 571-2449, (800) 524-2626, FAX: (402) 571-7941, E-Mail: mark.stevens@intlgamco.com, Web Site: www.intlgamco.com (31)

Stevens, Mark, Opex Corp, Moorestown, NJ. Tel: (856) 727-1100, FAX: (856) 727-1955, Web Site: www.opex.com (34)

Stevens, Martin B., Forum Publishing Co, Centerport, NY. Tel: (631) 754-5000, (800) 635-7654, FAX: (631) 754-0630, E-Mail: forumpublishing@aol. com, Web Site: www.forum123.com (17)

Stevens, Richard I., Stevens International Inc, Fort Worth, TX. Tel: (817) 831-3911, FAX: (817) 222-0162, E-Mail: main@stevensintl.com (34)

Stevens, Ruth, eMarketing Strategy Group, New York, NY. Tel: (212) 679-6486, Web Site: www. ruthstevens.com (20)

Stevens, Thomas, Key Bank, Cleveland, OH. Tel: (216) 689-3000, (888) 539-2968, FAX: (207) 874-7044, Web Site: www.key.com (14)

Stevens International Inc, Fort Worth, TX. Tel: (817) 831-3911, FAX: (817) 222-0162, E-Mail: main@ stevensintl.com (34)

Stevens Publishing Co, Sandusky, OH. Tel: (419) 626-5592, (800) 236-5592, FAX: (419) 626-9333, Web Site: www.stephenspublishing.com (17)

Stevenson, Bill, Who's Who - The MFSA Buyers' Guide to Blue Ribbon Mailing Services, Alexandria, VA. Tel: (703) 836-9200, FAX: (703) 548-8204, E-Mail: masa-mail@masa.org, Web Site: www.mfsanet.org (43)

Stevenson, Dudley, DWS Associates, Saint Paul, MN. Tel: (602) 321-6512, Web Site: www.dwstevenson. com (20)

Stevenson, Eric, Price Target Media, Carson City, NV. Tel: (775) 434-4451, FAX: (206) 888-2403, E-Mail: info@pricetargetmedia.com, Web Site: pricetargetmedia.com (32)

Stevenson, J., John, North Shore Animal League America Inc, Port Washington, NY. Tel: (516) 883-7900, FAX: (516) 883-8256, E-Mail: donorservices@nsalamerica.org, Web Site: www. nsalamerica.org (1)

Stevenson, Jeffrey, T., Veronis Suhler Stevenson LLC, New York, NY. Tel: (212) 935-4990, FAX: (212) 381-8168, E-Mail: stevensonj@vss.com, Web Site: www.vss.com (14)

Stevenson, William, Mailing & Fulfillment Service Association (MFSA), Alexandria, VA. Tel: (703) 836-9200, (800) 333-6272, FAX: (703) 548-8204, E-Mail: mfsa-mail@mfsanet.org, Web Site: www. mfsanet.org (40)

Stew Leonard's, Norwalk, CT. Tel: (203) 847-7214, FAX: (203) 847-1488, Web Site: www. stewleonards.com (4)

Steward, David, Krause Publications Inc, Iola, WI. Tel: (715) 445-2214, FAX: (715) 445-4087, E-Mail: info@krause.com, Web Site: www.krause. com (17)

Stewart Jr, Richard, B., American Bible Society, New York, NY. Tel: (212) 408-1200, FAX: (212) 408-1264, Web Site: www.americanbible.org (1)

Stewart Jr., Frank, B., Stewart Enterprises Inc, Jefferson, LA. Tel: (504) 729-1400, (800) 535-6017, FAX: (504) 729-1984, Web Site: www. stewartenterprises.com (16)

Stewart, Barbara S., Conseco Inc, Carmel, IN. Tel: (317) 817-6100, FAX: (317) 817-2847, Web Site: www.conseco.com (15)

Stewart, C.E., Stewart-MacDonald, Athens, OH. Tel: (740) 592-3021, (800) 848-2273, FAX: (740) 593-7922, E-Mail: hostetler@stewmac.com, Web Site: www.stewmac.com (16)

Stewart, Dina, Kid Stuff Marketing, Inc, Topeka, KS. Tel: (785) 862-3707, (800) 677-4712, FAX: (785) 862-0070, E-Mail: info@kidstuff.com, Web Site: www.kidsstuff.com (33)

Stewart, Don, Don Stewart Association, Tulsa, OK. Tel: (602) 678-3280, FAX: (602) 678-3288, Web Site: www.donstewartassociation.com (1)

Stewart, Donald, A., Sunlife of Canada, Wellesley Hills, MA. Tel: (781) 237-6030, (800) SUNLIFE, FAX: (781) 446-1779, Web Site: www.sunlife-usa. com (15)

Stewart, Jason, Demandbase Inc, San Francisco, CA. Tel: (415) 683-2660, Web Site: www.demandbase. com (23)

Stewart, Jim, ADS Direct Media, San Antonio, TX. Tel: (210) 655-6613, Web Site: www. adsmediagroup.com (27)

Stewart, Julia, A., IHOP Corp, Glendale, CA. Tel: (818) 240-6055, FAX: (818) 553-3131, Web Site: www.ihop.com (16)

Stewart, Kimberly, Getty Images, Seattle, WA. Tel: (206) 925-5018, (800) 462-4379, Web Site: www. gettyimages.com (38)

Stewart, Lynda, Spectrum Systems Inc, Fairfax, VA. Tel: (703) 591-7400 X217, (800) 929-3781, FAX: (703) 591-9780, E-Mail: spectrum@spectrum-systems.com, Web Site: www.spectrum-systems. com (34)

Stewart, Scott, Outsource America Inc, Bradenton, FL. Tel: (800) 729-5694, FAX: (441) 746-3595, E-Mail: sales@oaiworld.com, Web Site: www. oaiworld.com (24)

Stewart, Scott, The Procter & Gamble Co, Cincinnati, OH. Tel: (513) 983-4224, (800) 742-6253, FAX: (513) 983-9369, Web Site: www.pg.com (16)

Stewart, Sue, Consumer Focus, Plano, TX. Tel: (972) 378-9697, E-Mail: sstewart@consumerfocusco. com, Web Site: www.consumerfocusco.com (30)

Don Stewart Association, Tulsa, OK. Tel: (602) 678-3280, FAX: (602) 678-3288, Web Site: www. donstewartassociation.com (1)

Stewart Enterprises Inc, Jefferson, LA. Tel: (504) 729-1400, (800) 535-6017, FAX: (504) 729-1984, Web Site: www.stewartenterprises.com (16)

Stewart-MacDonald, Athens, OH. Tel: (740) 592-3021, (800) 848-2273, FAX: (740) 593-7922, E-Mail: hostetler@stewmac.com, Web Site: www.stewmac. com (16)

Martha Stewart Living Omnimedia, New York, NY. Tel: (212) 827-8000, Web Site: www. marthastewart.com (17)

Stewart-Allen, Allyson, International Marketing Partners Ltd, Los Angeles, CA. Tel: (310) 665-1155, FAX: (310) 665-1155, E-Mail: info@ intermarketingonline.com (35)

Steyer, Scott, Homespun Tapes Music Instruction, Woodstock, NY. Tel: (845) 246-2550, (800) 338-2737, FAX: (845) 246-5282, E-Mail: info@ homespuntapes.com, Web Site: www. homespuntapes.com (3)

Stezzi, Joseph, Stezzi Direct Inc, Atlanta, GA. Tel: (770) 448-9900, (800) 954-5100, FAX: (770) 448-9480, E-Mail: info@stezzi.com, Web Site: www. stezzi.com (21)

Stezzi Direct Inc, Atlanta, GA. Tel: (770) 448-9900, (800) 954-5100, FAX: (770) 448-9480, E-Mail: info@stezzi.com, Web Site: www.stezzi.com (21)

Stiansen, Gregg, Nassau Broadcasting Co, Princeton, NJ. Tel: (609) 419-0300, (800) 248-WPST, FAX: (609) 915-9778, E-Mail: lrios@wpst.com, Web Site: www.wpst.com (32)

Stibo Systems, Kennesaw, GA. Tel: (770) 425-3282, Web Site: www.stibocatalog.com (22)

Sticco, Father Peter, Pallottine Center for Apostolic Causes Inc/St Jude Shrine, Baltimore, MD. Tel: (410) 685-6026, (877) 278-5833, FAX: (410) 234-1459, E-Mail: info@stjudeshrine.org, Web Site: www.stjudeshrine.org (1)

Stichele, Jan, Vander, Corona-Lotus Inc, San Francisco, CA. Tel: (415) 956-8956, (800) 422-2924, FAX: (415) 956-4922, E-Mail: customerservice@ biscoff.com, Web Site: www.biscoff.com (4)

Stick-Em Up Inc, Pleasanton, CA. Tel: (925) 426-1040, FAX: (925) 426-1085, E-Mail: stickemup@ trivalley.com, Web Site: www.stickemup.com (5)

Stickers 'N' Stuff Inc, Louisville, CO. Tel: (303) 661-0200, E-Mail: sales@stickersnstuff.com, Web Site: www.stickersnstuff.biz (6)

Stickertape, Nesconset, NY. Tel: (800) 811-2891, FAX: (800) 727-5577, E-Mail: CustomerService@ stickertape.com, Web Site: www.stickertape.com (27)

Kirk Stieff Co, Bristol, PA. Tel: (267) 525-7800, (800) 635-3669, Web Site: www.lenox.com (16)

Stieve, Robert, Arizona Highways Magazine, Phoenix, AZ. Tel: (602) 712-2200, FAX: (602) 254-4505, E-Mail: editor@arizonahighways.com, Web Site: www.arizonahighways.com (17)

Stile-Tile Like Metal Roofing, Sellersburg, IN. Tel: (812) 246-1866, (800) 999-7777, FAX: (800) 477-9318, (800) 944-6884, Web Site: www.mtsales.com (9)

Stiles, Dawn, J., Da-Lite Screen Co Inc, Warsaw, IN. Tel: (574) 267-8101, (800) 622-3737, FAX: (574) 267-7804, E-Mail: info@da-lite.com, Web Site: www.da-lite.com (16)

Stiles, Sandra, The Wedding Pages, New York, NY. Tel: (212) 219-8555, (800) 843-4983, FAX: (212) 219-1929, Web Site: www.theknot.com (16)

Stillwell, Paul, History (Reference & Preservation) Division, Annapolis, MD. Tel: (410) 268-6110, (800) 233-8764, FAX: (410) 571-7940, E-Mail: dsheehan@usni.org, Web Site: www.usni.org (38)

Stillwell, Rob, Boyd Gaming Corp, Las Vegas, NV. Tel: (702) 792-7200, FAX: (702) 792-7313, Web Site: www.boydgaming.com (16)

Stilson, Galen, Galen Stilson Copywriter, Trinity, FL. Tel: (727) 372-2032, E-Mail: galen@galenstilson. com, Web Site: www.galenstilson.com (39)

Galen Stilson Copywriter, Trinity, FL. Tel: (727) 372-2032, E-Mail: galen@galenstilson.com, Web Site: www.galenstilson.com (39)

Stiltz, Dick, Doane, Saint Louis, MO. Tel: (314) 569-2700, (866) 647-0918, FAX: (314) 569-1083, Web Site: www.doane.com (17)

Stilwell, Amy, L., The World Bank, Washington, DC. Tel: (202) 473-1000, FAX: (202) 477-6391, Web Site: www.worldbank.org (17)

Stilwell, Jill, Strategic America, West Des Moines, IA. Tel: (515) 453-2000, (888) 898-6400, FAX: (515) 224-4181, Web Site: www.strategicamerica.com (35)

Stimolo, Bob, School Market Research Institute Inc, Haddam, CT. Tel: (860) 345-8183, (800) 838-3444, FAX: (860) 345-3985, E-Mail: info@smriinc.com, Web Site: www.smriinc.com (35)

Stimpson Co Inc, Pompano Beach, FL. Tel: (954) 946-3500, (877) 765-0748, FAX: (954) 941-1921, E-Mail: customerservice@stimpson.com, Web Site: www.stimpson.com (16)

Stinger, Jerry, The Wisconsin Cheeseman, Sun Prairie, WI. Tel: (608) 837-5166, (800) 698-1721, FAX: (608) 837-5493, Web Site: www. wisconsincheeseman.com (4)

Stinson, David, SOS Children's Villages - USA, Washington, DC. Tel: (202) 347-7920, Web Site: www.sos-usa.org (1)

STIR, Milwaukee, WI. Tel: (414) 278-0040, FAX: (414) 278-0390, E-Mail: brianb@stirstuff.com, Web Site: www.stirstuff.com (35)

Stock, Ron, Prestige Mailing Lists Inc, Van Nuys, CA. Tel: (818) 374-1320, FAX: (818) 374-1344, E-Mail: Debbie@prestigemaillists.com, Web Site: www.prestigemailinglists.com (24)

Stock, Sandra, CMA Awards, Don Mills, ON. Tel: (416) 391-2362, FAX: (416) 441-4062, E-Mail: info@the-cma.org, Web Site: www.the-cma.org/ awards (42)

Stock Boston LLC, Brookline, MA. Tel: (617) 266-2300, FAX: (617) 277-0502, E-Mail: requests@ stockboston.com, Web Site: www.stockboston.com (38)

Stock Drive Products, New Hyde Park, NY. Tel: (516) 328-3300, FAX: (516) 326-8827, E-Mail: sdp-sisupport@sdp-si.com, Web Site: www.sdp.si.com (5)

Stock Montage Inc, Chicago, IL. Tel: (773) 637-9790, (800) 404-0425, FAX: (773) 637-9794, E-Mail: mail@stockmontage.com, Web Site: www. stockmontage.com (38)

The Stock Solution Inc, West Jordan, UT. Tel: (801) 566-8684, (888) 366-0430, FAX: (801) 961-8030, E-Mail: info@tssphoto.com, Web Site: www. tssphoto.com (38)

Stock Yards Packing Co Inc, Chicago, IL. Tel: (312) 733-6050, (877) STK-YARD, FAX: (312) 733-1746, E-Mail: customerservice@stockyards.com, Web Site: www.stockyards.com (4)

Stockham, Maria, Stockham Consulting, Eden Prairie, MN. Tel: (952) 250-2206 (20)

Stockham Consulting, Eden Prairie, MN. Tel: (952) 250-2206 (20)

Stockman, Deb, Dean & Deluca Brands Inc, Wichita, KS. Tel: (316) 683-1255, Web Site: www. deandeluca.com (4)

Stockton Inc, Gaithersburg, MD. Tel: (301) 527-1550, FAX: (301) 527-1503, E-Mail: info@stocktoninc. com, Web Site: www.stocktoninc.com (22)

Stoddard, Russ, Oliver Russell & Associates, Boise, ID. Tel: (208) 344-1734, FAX: (208) 344-1211, Web Site: www.oliverrussell.com (35)

Stoddart, Rich, Leo Burnett USA, Chicago, IL. Tel: (312) 220-5959, FAX: (312) 220-3299, Web Site: www.leoburnett.com (35)

Stoebe, Richard, Jostens, Inc, Minneapolis, MN. Tel: (952) 830-3300, FAX: (952) 830-3293, Web Site: www.jostens.com (16)

Stoebich, Cindy, Chris Hansen, New Berlin, WI. Tel: (414) 607-5700, FAX: (414) 607-5704, Web Site: www.chr-hansen.com (16)

Stoeckig, Tricia, United Community Bank, Blairsville, GA. Tel: (706) 745-0911, Web Site: www.ucbi.com (14)

Stoehr, Jeremy, Audiovox, Hauppauge, NY. Tel: (631) 231-7750, (800) 645-4994, FAX: (631) 434-3995, Web Site: www.audiovox.com (16)

Stoffers, Patrick, Holiday Vacations, Eau Claire, WI. Tel: (715) 834-5555, (800) 826-2266, FAX: (715) 834-8554, E-Mail: info@holidayvacations.net, Web Site: www.holidayvacations.net (19)

Stokes, Linda, Marshall Fields Dept Stores, Minneapolis, MN. Tel: (612) 375-3004, Web Site: www.fields.com (5)

Stokes Seeds Inc, Buffalo, NY. Tel: (716) 695-6980, (800) 396-9238, FAX: (888) 834-3334, Web Site: www.stokeseeds.com (8)

Stolberg, Phil, Grizzard Advertising, Glendale, CA. Tel: (818) 325-4892, (800) 241-9351, FAX: (818) 543-1308, Web Site: www.grizzard.com (35)

Stoll, David, AmeriComm, Chesapeake, VA. Tel: (303) 371-4400, FAX: (303) 371-2527, Web Site: www.americomm.net (28)

Stoll, Kevin, Liebert Corp, Columbus, OH. Tel: (614) 841-6700, (800) LIEBERT, FAX: (614) 841-6022, Web Site: www.liebert.com (16)

Stolle Machinery LLC, Centennial, CO. Tel: (303) 708-9044, (800) 228-4593, FAX: (303) 708-9045, E-Mail: cmd.info@stollemachinery.com, Web Site: www.stollemachinery.com (34)

Stoller, Erica, Esto Photographics Inc, Mamaroneck, NY. Tel: (914) 698-4060, FAX: (914) 698-1033, E-Mail: esto@esto.com, Web Site: www.esto.com (38)

Stoller, Kevin, LS Records, Madison, TN. Tel: (615) 868-7171, FAX: (615) 860-7665, E-Mail: ls654@home.com, Web Site: www.cristylane.com (16)

Stoller, Lee, LS Records, Madison, TN. Tel: (615) 868-7171, FAX: (615) 860-7665, E-Mail: ls654@home.com, Web Site: www.cristylane.com (16)

Stoltze, Steve, Edroy Products Co Inc, Nyack, NY. Tel: (845) 358-6600, (800) 233-8803, FAX: (845) 358-4098, E-Mail: sales@edroyproducts.com, Web Site: www.edroyproducts.com (16)

Stom MD, Mary, K., Partners Health, Philadelphia, PA. Tel: (215) 849-9600, (800) 553-0784, E-Mail: sroberts@healthpart.com, Web Site: www.healthpart.com (15)

Stonaker, Daniel, North Point Resources, Alpharetta, GA. Tel: (678) 892-5000, Web Site: www.northpointstore.org (1)

Stone, Ann E.W., The Stone Group Inc, Alexandria, VA. Tel: (703) 370-8282, FAX: (703) 370-8287, E-Mail: tsgrp@aol.com, Web Site: www.tsgdirectresponse.com (35)

Stone, Bob, Bob Stone Inc, Grand Junction, CO. Tel: (970) 256-9297, E-Mail: rfstone@mymailstation.com (21)

Stone, Davey L., Butler Schein Animal Health, Dublin, OH. Tel: (614) 761-9095, (888) 691-2724, FAX: (888) 329-3861, Web Site: www.butlerschein.com (16)

Stone, Gail, PTM Communications, New York, NY. Tel: (212) 643-5458, FAX: (212) 643-5486, E-Mail: info@ptmcomm.com, Web Site: www.ptmcomm.com (29)

Stone, Jay, Infomart, Dallas, TX. Tel: (214) 800-8000, FAX: (214) 800-8100, Web Site: www.infomartusa.com (16)

Stone, John W., Artech House, Norwood, MA. Tel: (781) 769-9750, FAX: (781) 769-6334, E-Mail: artech@artechhouse.com, Web Site: www.artechhouse.com (17)

Stone, Karin, National City Bank, Cleveland, OH. Tel: (216) 222-2000, (800) 622-8100, FAX: (216) 222-9359, Web Site: www.nationalcity.com (14)

Stone, Matthew, HealthInfo Direct, Schaumburg, IL. Tel: (630) 936-9465 (20)

Stone, Mike, Butler Schein Animal Health, Dublin, OH. Tel: (614) 761-9095, (888) 691-2724, FAX: (888) 329-3861, Web Site: www.butlerschein.com (16)

Stone, Nancy, School Annual Publishing Co, State College, PA. Tel: (800) 436-6030, E-Mail: yearbook@schoolannual.com, Web Site: www.schoolannual.com (17)

Stone, Peter, M., Guideline, New York, NY. Tel: (212) 645-4500, (866) GUIDELINE, FAX: (212) 645-7681, Web Site: www.findsvp.com (30)

Stone, Will, Neighborhood Greetings, Millersville, PA. Tel: (717) 871-9053, (800) 332-9200, FAX: (717) 871-9053, E-Mail: info@neighborhoodgreetings.net, Web Site: www.neighborhoodgreetings.net (23)

Bob Stone Inc, Grand Junction, CO. Tel: (970) 256-9297, E-Mail: rfstone@mymailstation.com (21)

The Stone Group Inc, Alexandria, VA. Tel: (703) 370-8282, FAX: (703) 370-8287, E-Mail: tsgrp@aol.com, Web Site: www.tsgdirectresponse.com (35)

Stonebill Clafin, Susan, Response Insurance, Scranton, PA. Tel: (203) 634-7255, (800) 518-2984, FAX: (203) 634-7319, E-Mail: webcs@response.com, Web Site: www.response.com (15)

Stonebridge Press Ltd, Henderson, KY. Tel: (270) 826-0341, FAX: (270) 826-8325 (33)

Stoner, Greg, Aristokraft Inc, Jasper, IN. Tel: (812) 482-2527, FAX: (812) 482-9872, Web Site: www.aristokraft.com (16)

Stonwurks, Eden Prairie, MN. Tel: (785) 526-7847, (888) 884-7881, FAX: (785) 526-7841, E-Mail: stonwurks@stonwurks.com, Web Site: www.stonwurks.com (16)

Stopka, Michael, Design Toscano, Inc, Elk Grove Village, IL. Tel: (847) 952-0100, (800) 525-5141, FAX: (847) 952-8992, Web Site: www.designtoscano.com (6)

Storage Battery Systems Inc, Menomonee Falls, WI. Tel: (262) 703-5800, (800) 554-2243, FAX: (262) 703-3073, E-Mail: sbs@sbsbattery.com, Web Site: www.sbsbattery.com (12)

Storch, Gerald, L., Toys "R" Us, Wayne, NJ. Tel: (973) 617-5879, FAX: (973) 617-4006, Web Site: www.toysrus.com (11)

Store Smart Express/Visual Horizons, Rochester, NY. Tel: (585) 424-5300, (800) 424-1011, FAX: (585) 424-1064, E-Mail: cs@storesmart.com, Web Site: www.storesmart.com (16)

Storey, Ken, Patagonia, Ventura, CA. Tel: (805) 643-8616, Web Site: www.patagonia.com (2)

Storey, M., John, Berkshire Direct Inc, Williamstown, MA. Tel: (413) 458-1721, FAX: (413) 458-1727, E-Mail: info@berkshiredirect.com, Web Site: www.berkshiredirect.com (17)

Storey, Martha, Berkshire Direct Inc, Williamstown, MA. Tel: (413) 458-1721, FAX: (413) 458-1727, E-Mail: info@berkshiredirect.com, Web Site: www.berkshiredirect.com (17)

Story Jr., Robert, P., Dover Publications Inc, Mineola, NY. Tel: (516) 294-7000, (800) 223-3130, FAX: (516) 873-1401, Web Site: www.doverpublications.com (17)

Story, Mike, Physicians Mutual Insurance Co, Omaha, NE. Tel: (402) 633-1604, (888) 932-7642, FAX: (402) 633-1604, Web Site: www.physiciansmutual.com (15)

Story Time Stories That Rhyme, Denver, CO. Tel: (303) 575-5676, FAX: (303) 575-1187, E-Mail: emailstreet@gmail.com, Web Site: www.storytimestoriesthatrhyme.com (17)

Stotz, Beverly, 02Kl, Rye Brook, NY. Tel: (914) 253-4500, Web Site: www.illyusa.com (4)

Stotzer, Shelly, Highlights For Children, Columbus, OH. Tel: (614) 487-2601, (800) 848-8922, FAX: (614) 487-2700, Web Site: www.highlights.com (17)

Stowers III, James, E., American Century Investments, Kansas City, MO. Tel: (816) 531-5575, (800) 345-2021, FAX: (816) 340-7962, Web Site: www.americancentury.com (14)

Strack, Stephen, Stockton Inc, Gaithersburg, MD. Tel: (301) 527-1550, FAX: (301) 527-1503, E-Mail: info@stocktoninc.com, Web Site: www.stocktoninc.com (22)

Straczynski, Stacy, Sales & Marketing Management Magazine, New York, NY. Tel: (800) 821-6897, FAX: (905) 470-8561, E-Mail: joyce.cooney@nielsen.com, Web Site: www.salesandmarketing.com (16)

Strader, Chuck, Kappler Protective Apparel & Fabrics, Guntersville, AL. Tel: (256) 505-4005, (800) 600-4019, FAX: (256) 505-4151, E-Mail: usa@kappler.com, Web Site: www.kappler.com (2)

Stradtman, Steve, Otto Environmental Systems of North America, Charlotte, NC. Tel: (704) 588-9191, (800) 227-5885, FAX: (704) 588-5250, E-Mail: info@otto-usa.com, Web Site: www.otto-usa.com (17)

Strahan, Diane, Neustar Inc, Sterling, VA. Tel: (571) 434-5400, Web Site: www.tcpacompliance.us (29)

Strahl, Dr. Stuart D., Brookfield Zoo, Brookfield, IL. Tel: (708) 485-0263, (800) 201-0784, FAX: (708) 485-3532, Web Site: www.brookfieldzoo.org (1)

Straley, Kim, Lure-Craft, Lagrange, IN. Tel: (260) 463-2687, (800) 925-9088, FAX: (260) 463-8383, E-Mail: kimstraley@lurecraft.com, Web Site: www.lurecraft.com (11)

Straley, Shawn, Lure-Craft, Lagrange, IN. Tel: (260) 463-2687, (800) 925-9088, FAX: (260) 463-8383, E-Mail: kimstraley@lurecraft.com, Web Site: www.lurecraft.com (11)

Stranberg, Mark, PNC Global Investment Servicing, Lynnfield, MA. Tel: (781) 477-4124, Web Site: www.pnc.com (14)

Strang, Stephen, Strang Communications Co, Lake Mary, FL. Tel: (407) 333-0600, FAX: (407) 333-7100, E-Mail: magcustsvc@strang.com, Web Site: www.strang.com (17)

Strang Communications Co, Lake Mary, FL. Tel: (407) 333-0600, FAX: (407) 333-7100, E-Mail: magcustsvc@strang.com, Web Site: www.strang.com (17)

Stransky, John E., Life Fitness, Schiller Park, IL. Tel: (847) 288-3300, (800) 735-3867, FAX: (847) 288-3703, E-Mail: webmaster@lifefitness.com, Web Site: www.lifefitness.com (11)

Strasbourger, Jim, Data Management Inc, Mc Lean, VA. Tel: (703) 893-5627, (800) 334-8331, FAX: (703) 356-1698, E-Mail: info@data-management.com, Web Site: www.data-management.com (22)

Strata Marketing Inc, Chicago, IL. Tel: (312) 222-1555, FAX: (312) 222-2510, Web Site: www.stratag.com (30)

Strategic America, West Des Moines, IA. Tel: (515) 453-2000, (888) 898-6400, FAX: (515) 224-4181, Web Site: www.strategicamerica.com (35)

Strategic Data Intelligence LLC, Northbrook, IL. Tel: (847) 897-5706, FAX: (847) 897-5715, E-Mail: inquiry@sdintelligence.com, Web Site: www.sdintelligence.com (22)

Strategic Direct Marketing Inc, Pleasant View, TN. Tel: (615) 834-9555, (800) 843-8861, FAX: (615) 834-6698, E-Mail: sales@sdmi3.com, Web Site: www.sdmi3.com (21)

Strategic Fundraising Inc, Saint Paul, MN. Tel: (651) 649-0404, Web Site: www.strategicfundraising.com (1)

Strategic Marketing and Advertising Inc, Carlsbad, CA. Tel: (760) 930-6123, E-Mail: dmservices@smaresource.com, Web Site: www.responsefx.com (35)

Strategic Marketing & Mailing, Champaign, IL. Tel: (217) 355-2600, Web Site: www.strategicmail.com (28)

Strategic Marketing Services, Eagan, MN. Tel: (651) 456-0100, E-Mail: sms@fishnet.com (33)

Strategic Planning Marketing Scouting & Sales, Foxboro, MA. Tel: (781) 215-5117, (866) 638-5323, FAX: (774) 215-5117, E-Mail: cmay@dmcommunications.com, Web Site: www.dmcommunications.com (35)

Strategic Software Systems LLC, Richmond, VA. Tel: (804) 288-8827x110, Web Site: www.sss1.com (22)

StrategicOne, Overland Park, KS. Tel: (913) 342-9100 x102, Web Site: www.strategic-one.com (20)

Strategy Corps LLC, Brentwood, TN. Tel: (615) 221-8381, (888) 577-6933, FAX: (615) 221-8479, E-Mail: info@strategycorps.com, Web Site: www.strategycorps.com (16)

Strategy Network, Plymouth, MI. Tel: (734) 464-8100, FAX: (734) 464-4133, E-Mail: info@strategy-network.com, Web Site: www.strategy-network.com (35)

Stratford Hall, North Mankato, MN. Tel: (708) 496-4908, (800) 628-9028, FAX: (708) 496-8058, E-Mail: stratfordhall@myprinter.com, Web Site: www.stratfordhall.com (10)

Stratmar Systems Inc, Port Chester, NY. Tel: (914) 937-7171, (800) 866-2399, FAX: (914) 937-6045, E-Mail: info@stratmar.com, Web Site: www.stratmar.com (29)

STRATMARK, Richardson, TX. Tel: (800) 222-6070, Web Site: www.stratmark.com (1)

The Stratosphere Las Vegas, Las Vegas, NV. Tel: (702) 380-7777, (800) 998-6937, FAX: (702) 383-4755, Web Site: www.stratospherehotel.com (19)

Stratton, John, G., Verizon Communications Inc, New York, NY. Tel: (212) 395-1000, (800) 621-9900, FAX: (212) 571-1897, Web Site: www.verizon.com (3)

Stratton, Joseph, The Saint Francis Academy Inc, Salina, KS. Tel: (785) 825-0541, (800) 423-1342, FAX: (785) 825-2940, Web Site: www.st-francis.org (1)

Stratus Technologies, Maynard, MA. Tel: (978) 461-7000, (800) 787-2887, FAX: (978) 461-3670, Web Site: www.stratus.com (16)

Straub, Sarah, Communication Logistics, Inc, Plover, WI. Tel: (715) 341-6180, FAX: (715) 341-7971, Web Site: www.comloginc.com (22)

Strauser, Jack, ProSing Karaoke, Nederland, CO. Tel: (800) 776-7464, FAX: (888) 388-9741, E-Mail: jack@prosing.com, Web Site: www.prosing.com (5)

Strauss, Herschel, Hamakor Judaica Inc, Niles, IL. Tel: (847) 966-4040, (800) 426-2567, FAX: (847) 966-4033, E-Mail: service@ewishource.com, Web Site: www.jewishsource.com (5)

Strauss, M, Ventriloquist Voice Solutions International Inc, Mississauga, ON. Tel: (866) 446-0860, E-Mail: info@vvsii.com, Web Site: www.vvsii.com (29)

Strauss, Naomi, Hamakor Judaica Inc, Niles, IL. Tel: (847) 966-4040, (800) 426-2567, FAX: (847) 966-4033, E-Mail: service@ewishource.com, Web Site: www.jewishsource.com (5)

Stravitz, Russell, Brylane, Indianapolis, IN. Tel: (800) 677-0339, Web Site: www.brylanehome.com (2)

Straw Hat Cooperative Corp, San Ramon, CA. Tel: (925) 837-3400, FAX: (925) 820-1080, E-Mail: info@strawhatpizza.com, Web Site: www.strawhatpizza.com (16)

Stream International, Wellesley, MA. Tel: (781) 304-1800, (888) 264-5834, FAX: (781) 575-6999, Web Site: www.stream.com (16)

Streamfeeder, Minneapolis, MN. Tel: (763) 502-0000, FAX: (763) 502-0100, Web Site: www.streamfeeder.com (34)

Streiff, Stephenie, Potawatomi Bingo Casino, Milwaukee, WI. Tel: (800) PAYS-BIG, Web Site: www.paysbig.com (19)

Streight, Steve, Hamilton Sorter Co, Fairfield, OH. Tel: (513) 870-4400, (800) 503-9966, FAX: (800) 503-9963, E-Mail: sstreight@hamiltonsorter.com, Web Site: www.hamiltonsorter.com (34)

Streitz, Elizabeth, Elizabeth Streitz & Associates, New York, NY. Tel: (212) 749-3152 (20)

Elizabeth Streitz & Associates, New York, NY. Tel: (212) 749-3152 (20)

Stress Market, Port Angeles, WA. Tel: (360) 457-9223, (800) 578-7377, FAX: (360) 457-9466, E-Mail: info@stressmarket.com, Web Site: www.stressmarket.com (17)

Stretch, Shirley, M., School of Business & Economics, Los Angeles, CA. Tel: (323) 343-2800, FAX: (323) 343-2813, Web Site: cbe.calstatela.edu (41)

Strickland, Eleanor, Compass Bank, Birmingham, AL. Tel: (205) 933-4848, (800) 239-4357, FAX: (205) 933-3702, Web Site: www.compassbank.com (4)

Strickland, Frederic, Sandy Corp, Troy, MI. Tel: (800) 733-4739, FAX: (248) 729-4701, E-Mail: info@sandycorp.com, Web Site: www.sandycorp.com (16)

Strickland, Heidi, Lee, Scorecards USA, North Kingstown, RI. Tel: (401) 294-4049, (800) 553-4154, FAX: (401) 294-4076, E-Mail: sales@scorecardsusa.com, Web Site: www.scorecardsusa.com (16)

Strickland, Jennifer, River Street Sweets, Savannah, GA. Tel: (912) 234-4608, (800) 793-3876, FAX: (912) 234-1584, E-Mail: randerson@riverstreetsweets.com, Web Site: www.riverstreetsweets.com (4)

Strickland, Pam, River Street Sweets, Savannah, GA. Tel: (912) 234-4608, (800) 793-3876, FAX: (912) 234-1584, E-Mail: randerson@riverstreetsweets.com, Web Site: www.riverstreetsweets.com (4)

Strickland, Steven, C., Brookstone Co, Merrimack, NH. Tel: (603) 880-9500, (800) 846-3000, FAX: (603) 577-8005, E-Mail: customerservice@brookstone.com, Web Site: www.brookstone.com (3)

Strickland, Tim, River Street Sweets, Savannah, GA. Tel: (912) 234-4608, (800) 793-3876, FAX: (912) 234-1584, E-Mail: randerson@riverstreetsweets.com, Web Site: www.riverstreetsweets.com (4)

Striem, Barry, Essential Products Co Inc, New York, NY. Tel: (212) 344-4288 (7)

Strigl, Dennis, F., Verizon Communications Inc, New York, NY. Tel: (212) 395-1000, (800) 621-9900, FAX: (212) 571-1897, Web Site: www.verizon.com (3)

Stringer, Bryan, Missouri Landscape & Nursery Association, Bowling Green, MO. Tel: (636) 542-1234, E-Mail: admin@mlng.org, Web Site: www.mlna.org (1)

Striplin, Deborah, Oxbridge Communications Inc, New York, NY. Tel: (212) 741-0231, (800) 955-0231, FAX: (212) 633-2938, E-Mail: custserv@oxbridge.com, Web Site: www.mediafinder.com; www.oxbridge.com (30)

Strode, Brinton, Oxford University Press Inc, New York, NY. Tel: (212) 726-6000, FAX: (212) 726-6455, Web Site: www.oup.com/us/ (17)

Strode, Kim, Circle K Stores Inc, Akron, OH. Tel: (330) 630-6300, Web Site: www.cirlcek.com (16)

Strofina, Bainbridge Island, WA. Tel: (206) 855-9681 (20)

Strohacker, Curt, Easthill Group Inc, Pottstown, PA. Tel: (610) 323-9099, (610) 323-9063, (610) 323-2200, (888) 869-4433, (800) 345-1178, FAX: (610) 323-6268, Web Site: www.eastwoodcompany.com (12)

Stroller, John, R., Del Webb, Bloomfield Hills, MI. Tel: (248) 644-7300, (888) 717-9777, FAX: (248) 433-4598, Web Site: www.delwebb.com (16)

Strom, Tesha, CashNetUSA, Chicago, IL. Tel: (312) 676-1583, Web Site: www.cashnetusa.com (14)

Stromberg, Helen, Stromberg Brand, Peekskill, NY. Tel: (914) 739-7410, (800) 724-0996, FAX: (914) 739-8642, E-Mail: info@stromberggroup.com, Web Site: www.strombergbrand.com (33)

Stromberg, Michael, Crabtree & Evelyn Ltd, Woodstock, CT. Tel: (860) 928-2761, (800) CRABTREE, FAX: (860) 928-0452, Web Site: www.crabtree-evelyn.com (4)

Stromberg Brand, Peekskill, NY. Tel: (914) 739-7410, (800) 724-0996, FAX: (914) 739-8642, E-Mail: info@strombergbrand.com, Web Site: www.strombergbrand.com (33)

Stromberg Consulting, New York, NY. Tel: (646) 935-4177, (212) 812-6400, FAX: (212) 812-6300, E-Mail: info@strombergconsulting.com, Web Site: www.strombergconsulting.com (35)

Stroner, Bill, Demco Inc, Madison, WI. Tel: (608) 241-1201, (800) 241-1799, E-Mail: custserv@demco.com, Web Site: www.demco.com (10)

Stroner, Bill, Lab Safety Supply Inc, Janesville, WI. Tel: (608) 754-2345, (800) 356-2855, FAX: (800) 543-9910, Web Site: www.labsafety.com (5)

Strong, Ted, Strong Enterprises, Orlando, FL. Tel: (407) 859-9317, (800) 344-6319, FAX: (407) 850-6978, E-Mail: sales@strongparachutes.com, Web Site: www.strongparachutes.com (34)

Strong, Tom, Childreach US Member of Plan International, Warwick, RI. Tel: (916) 797-8707, (800) 556-7918, FAX: (916) 797-1056, Web Site: www.planusa.org (8)

Strong Enterprises, Orlando, FL. Tel: (407) 859-9317, (800) 344-6319, FAX: (407) 850-6978, E-Mail: sales@strongparachutes.com, Web Site: www.strongparachutes.com (34)

Strongmail Systems Inc, Redwood City, CA. Tel: (800) 971-0380, Web Site: www.strongmail.com (32)

Strongwell, Bristol, VA. Tel: (276) 645-8000, FAX: (276) 645-8132, E-Mail: gbarefoot@strongwell.com, Web Site: www.strongwell.com (9)

Strope, Keith, Tricor Braun, Woodridge, IL. Tel: (708) 385-9333, FAX: (708) 385-3015, Web Site: www.tricorbraun.com (16)

Strosin, Raphael, Biosciences-Amersham, Piscataway, NJ. Tel: (732) 457-8000, FAX: (732) 457-0557, Web Site: www.amersham.com (16)

Stroud, Dan, Nestle USA, Glendale, CA. Tel: (818) 549-6000, (800) 225-2270, FAX: (818) 549-6952, Web Site: www.nestleusa.com (4)

Stroud, Roland, Mays Mission for the Handicapped Inc, Heber Springs, AR. Tel: (501) 362-7526, (888) 503-7955, FAX: (501) 362-7529, E-Mail: sniehaus@maysmission.org, Web Site: www.maysmission.org (27)

Stroup Jr., Ray, Stuller, Inc, Lafayette, LA. Tel: (337) 262-7700, (800) 877-7777, FAX: (337) 981-1655, E-Mail: info@stuller.com, Web Site: www.stuller.com (2)

Stroup, Ron, Tetley USA Inc, Montvale, NJ. Tel: (203) 929-9200, (800) 728-0084, FAX: (203) 926-0876, Web Site: www.tetleyusa.com (16)

Struble, Mike, Circle K Stores Inc, Akron, OH. Tel: (330) 630-6300, Web Site: www.cirlcek.com (16)

Structural Graphics, Essex, CT. Tel: (860) 767-2661, Web Site: www.structuralgraphics.com (27)

Strum, Adam, M., Wine Enthusiast Cos, Mount Kisco, NY. Tel: (914) 345-9463, (800) 356-8466, FAX: (914) 345-3129, Web Site: www.wineenthusiast.com (4)

Strum, Sybil, N., Wine Enthusiast Cos, Mount Kisco, NY. Tel: (914) 345-9463, (800) 356-8466, FAX: (914) 345-3129, Web Site: www.wineenthusiast.com (4)

Strumillo, Donald, R., AMS Direct, Burr Ridge, IL. Tel: (630) 382-1000, FAX: (630) 325-0825, Web Site: www.amsdirect.com (13)

Strunk Jr., William, University of Chicago Press, Chicago, IL. Tel: (773) 702-7700, FAX: (773) 702-9756, Web Site: www.press.uchicago.edu (17)

Strunk, Scott, Systemax Inc, Port Washington, NY. Tel: (516) 608-7000, FAX: (516) 6208-7001, Web Site: www.systemax.com (16)

Strutzel, Dan, Nightingale-Conant Corp, Niles, IL. Tel: (847) 647-0300, (800) 557-1660, FAX: (847) 647-7145, Web Site: www.nightingale.com (17)

Stryker, Richard, Corpus Christi Museum of Science & History, Corpus Christi, TX. Tel: (361) 826-4667, FAX: (361) 884-7392, Web Site: www.ccmuseum.com (1)

Stuart, Tom, Art Instruction Schools, Minneapolis, MN. Tel: (612) 362-5075, FAX: (612) 362-5260, Web Site: www.artinstructionschools.edu (13)

Stuart Karten Design, Marina Del Rey, CA. Tel: (310) 827-8722, FAX: (310) 821-4492, Web Site: www.kartendesign.com (36)

Paul Stuart, New York, NY. Tel: (212) 682-0320, FAX: (212) 983-5871, E-Mail: info@paulstuart.com, Web Site: www.paulstuart.com (2)

Stubbs, Angela, Federal Direct, Clifton, NJ. Tel: (973) 667-9800, Web Site: www.feddirect.com (27)

Stubbs, Charles, Primedia Inc, Norcross, GA. Tel: (678) 421-3000, (800) 216-1423, Web Site: www.primedia.com (31)

Student Marketing Group Inc, Lynbrook, NY. Tel: (516) 593-8877, Web Site: www.studentmarketing.net (23)

Student Union at SJSU, San Jose, CA. Tel: (408) 924-6353, Web Site: www.union.sjsu.edu (1)

Studeo Interactive Direct, Salt Lake City, UT. Tel: (801) 993-2300, FAX: (801) 993-2301, E-Mail: info@studeo.com, Web Site: www.studeo.com (35)

Studio M Productions Unlimited, Los Angeles, CA. Tel: (213) 389-7372, (888) 389-7372 (32)

Stuebing, Laura, Simply Batteries Inc, Dekalb, IL. Tel: (815) 756-1473, Web Site: www.simplybatteries.com (7)

Stull, Elaine, Industrial Uniform Co Inc, Wichita, KS. Tel: (316) 264-2871, (800) 333-3666, FAX: (316) 264-2708, E-Mail: uniform@industrialuniform.com, Web Site: www.industrialuniform.com (2)

Stuller, Matthew, G., Stuller, Inc, Lafayette, LA. Tel: (337) 262-7700, (800) 877-7777, FAX: (337) 981-1655, E-Mail: info@stuller.com, Web Site: www.stuller.com (2)

Stuller, Inc, Lafayette, LA. Tel: (337) 262-7700, (800) 877-7777, FAX: (337) 981-1655, E-Mail: info@stuller.com, Web Site: www.stuller.com (2)

Stullman, Steve, Direct Marketing Association of Southern California, Newbury Park, CA. Tel: (818) 541-1152, FAX: (818) 541-1959, Web Site: www.ladma.org (40)

Stumm, Matthew, BBK Worldwide, Newton, MA. Tel: (617) 630-4477, Web Site: www.bbkworldwide.com (35)

Stumpf, John, Wells Fargo, San Francisco, CA. Tel: (866) 878-5865, (800) 869-3557, FAX: (626) 312-3015, Web Site: www.wellsfargo.com (14)

Stupak, Caitlin, Directory of Mail Order Catalogs, Millerton, NY. Tel: (518) 789-8700, (800) 562-2139, FAX: (518) 789-0556, E-Mail: cstupak@greyhouse.com, Web Site: www.greyhouse.com (43)

Stupak, Caitlin, Grey House Publishing, Amenia, NY. Tel: (518) 789-8700, (800) 562-2139, FAX: (518) 789-0556, E-Mail: books@greyhouse.com, Web Site: www.greyhouse.com (43)

Stupak, Caitlin, The Directory of Business Information Resources, Millerton, NY. Tel: (518) 789-8700, (800) 562-2139, FAX: (518) 789-0556, E-Mail: cstupak@greyhouse.com, Web Site: www.greyhouse.com (43)

Sturbridge Yankee Workshop Inc, Portland, ME. Tel: (207) 774-9045, (800) 343-1144, FAX: (207) 774-2561, Web Site: www.sturbridgeyankee.com (16)

Sturges, Eddie, Sturges Sportswear, Battleboro, NC. Tel: (252) 446-0096, (866) 532-6748, FAX: (252) 977-3932, E-Mail: estu73123@aol.com, Web Site: www.sturgessportswear.com (16)

Sturges, Johnny, Sturges Sportswear, Battleboro, NC. Tel: (252) 446-0096, (866) 532-6748, FAX: (252) 977-3932, E-Mail: estu73123@aol.com, Web Site: www.sturgessportswear.com (16)

Sturges Sportswear, Battleboro, NC. Tel: (252) 446-0096, (866) 532-6748, FAX: (252) 977-3932, E-Mail: estu73123@aol.com, Web Site: www.sturgessportswear.com (16)

Sturley, Wendy, Society for Neuroscience, Washington, DC. Tel: (202) 962-4000 (1)

Sturm, Arthur M., Sturm, Rosenburg, King & Co, Chicago, IL. Tel: (312) 943-1881, FAX: (312) 943-2346, Web Site: www.sturmads.com (35)

Sturm, John, Newspaper Association of America, Arlington, VA. Tel: (703) 902-1600, FAX: (571) 366-1195, Web Site: www.naa.org (1)

Sturm, Rosenburg, King & Co, Chicago, IL. Tel: (312) 943-1881, FAX: (312) 943-2346, Web Site: www.sturmads.com (35)

Sturner, Jerry, Sturner & Klein, Fort Worth, TX. Tel: (800) 678-4960, FAX: (301) 881-3745 (29)

Sturner & Klein, Fort Worth, TX. Tel: (800) 678-4960, FAX: (301) 881-3745 (29)

Stutz, Robert, Glengarry Marketing, Austin, TX. Tel: (800) 883-1924 (20)

Styes, Doug, Enco Manufacturing Co, Fernley, NV. Tel: (775) 788-7175, (800) 873-3626, FAX: (800) 965-5857, E-Mail: milanesp@use-enco.com, Web Site: www.use-enco.com (7)

Styled Packaging LLC, Philadelphia, PA. Tel: (610) 529-4122, FAX: (610) 520-9662, E-Mail: bill@styledpackaging.com, Web Site: www.styledpackaging.com (34)

Stymiest, Barbara, RBC Dain Rauscher, Boston, MA. Tel: (617) 725-2000, FAX: (617) 725-1393, Web Site: www.rbcdainrauscher.com (14)

Suarez, Benjamin, Suarez Corp Industries, North Canton, OH. Tel: (330) 494-5504, FAX: (330) 497-6837, E-Mail: suarez@suarez.com, Web Site: www.suarez.com (5)

Suarez Corp Industries, North Canton, OH. Tel: (330) 494-5504, FAX: (330) 497-6837, E-Mail: suarez@suarez.com, Web Site: www.suarez.com (5)

Subers, Mark, Grade Finders Inc, Exton, PA. Tel: (610) 524-7070, FAX: (610) 524-8912, E-Mail: info@gradefinders.com, Web Site: www.gradefinders.com (17)

Subers, W., A., Grade Finders Inc, Exton, PA. Tel: (610) 524-7070, FAX: (610) 524-8912, E-Mail: info@gradefinders.com, Web Site: www.gradefinders.com (17)

Submit Express, Burbank, CA. Tel: (818) 567-3030, Web Site: www.iclimber.com (32)

SubscriberMail LLC, Lisle, IL. Tel: (630) 303-5000, Web Site: www.subscribermail.com (22)

Subscription Agency.com Inc, Winter Haven, FL. Tel: (863) 229-2557, FAX: (508) 374-8599, E-Mail: info@subscriptionagency.com, Web Site: www.subscriptionagency.com (18)

The Suburban Chamber of Commerce, Summit, NJ. Tel: (908) 522-1700, FAX: (908) 522-9252, E-Mail: info@suburbanchambers.org, Web Site: www.suburbanchambers.org (14)

Success Magazine, Lake Dallas, TX. Tel: (800) 570-6414, Web Site: www.successmagazine.com (43)

Successful Farming, Des Moines, IA. Tel: (515) 284-2143, (800) 678-2711, FAX: (515) 284-3127 (17)

SuccessWorks Search Marketing Inc, West Linn, OR. Tel: (503) 922-3627, Web Site: www.seocopywriting.com (32)

Suchecki, Glen, UniServ Advertising Inc, Neptune City, NJ. Tel: (732) 774-1010, FAX: (732) 774-3311, Web Site: www.uniservinc.com (33)

Suesskind, Dan, Teva Pharmaceuticals USA, North Wales, PA. Tel: (215) 591-3000, (888) TEVAUSA, FAX: (215) 591-8600, Web Site: www.tevausa.com (7)

Suez Energy North America, Houston, TX. Tel: (713) 636-0000, FAX: (713) 636-1364, Web Site: www.tractebelpowerinc.com (16)

Sugarbush Farm Inc, Woodstock, VT. Tel: (802) 457-1757, (800) 281-1757, FAX: (802) 457-3269, E-Mail: contact@sugarbushfarm.com, Web Site: www.sugarbushfarm.com (4)

Sugarman, Joseph, BluBlocker Corp, Las Vegas, NV. Tel: (702) 597-2000, (800) BLUBLOCKER, FAX: (702) 597-2002, Web Site: www.blublocker.com (2)

Sugg, Ed, DataLever Corp, Boulder, CO. Tel: (303) 541-1515, Web Site: www.datalever.com (16)

Suhler, John, S., Veronis Suhler Stevenson LLC, New York, NY. Tel: (212) 935-4990, FAX: (212) 381-8168, E-Mail: stevensonj@vss.com, Web Site: www.vss.com (14)

Suk, Helen, Northern Lights Direct, Chicago, IL. Tel: (312) 263-8686, FAX: (312) 624-7701, E-Mail: contact@northernlightsdirect.com, Web Site: www.northernlightsdirect.com (32)

Sukol, Amy, Lautman Maska Neill & Co, Washington, DC. Tel: (202) 296-9660, Web Site: www.lautmandc.com (1)

Sullivan, Brian, Emerging Marketing, Columbus, OH. Tel: (614) 923-6000 X229, FAX: (614) 424-6200, E-Mail: chris@360em.com, Web Site: www.emergingmarketing.com (14)

Sullivan, Daniel, J., Direct Marketing Resources, Charlotte, NC. Tel: (704) 845-5890, (888) 644-4DMR, E-Mail: dan@dmresources.com, Web Site: www.dmresources.com (14)

Sullivan, David, Meyer Decorative Surfaces Inc, Atlanta, GA. Tel: (404) 699-3900, (800) 776-3900, FAX: (404) 699-3914, Web Site: www.meyerdeco.com (8)

Sullivan, David, National Active & Retired Federal Employees Association, Alexandria, VA. Tel: (703) 838-7760, (800) 456-8410, FAX: (703) 838-7785, Web Site: www.narfe.org (1)

Sullivan, Diane, M., Brown Shoe Co, Saint Louis, MO. Tel: (314) 854-4000, FAX: (314) 854-4274, Web Site: www.brownshoe.com (16)

Sullivan, Dianne, C., Hatton-Brown Publishers Inc, Montgomery, AL. Tel: (334) 834-1170, FAX: (334) 834-4525, E-Mail: webman@hattonbrown.com, Web Site: www.hattonbrown.com (17)

Sullivan, E., Thomas, University of Minnesota Alumni Association, Minneapolis, MN. Tel: (612) 624-2323, (800) UM-ALUMS, FAX: (612) 626-8167, E-Mail: umalumni@umn.edu, Web Site: www.umaa.umn.edu (1)

Sullivan, Floyd, Pfaltzgraff Co, York, PA. Tel: (717) 852-2211, (800) 999-2811, FAX: (800) 717-2481, E-Mail: service@pfaltzgraff.com, Web Site: www.pfaltzgraff.com (8)

Sullivan, Frank E., Sullivan-Victory Groves, Cocoa, FL. Tel: (321) 632-0550, (800) 672-6431, FAX: (321) 639-4069, E-Mail: citrus@sullivanvictorygroves.net, Web Site: www.sullivanvictorygroves.net (4)

Sullivan, Gregg, Protocol Integrated Direct Marketing, Sarasota, FL. Tel: (800) 677-2001, (800) 351-3774, FAX: (941) 906-9099, Web Site: www.protocolmarketing.com (21)

Sullivan, Jeanette, Sullivan-Victory Groves, Cocoa, FL. Tel: (321) 632-0550, (800) 672-6431, FAX: (321) 639-4069, E-Mail: citrus@sullivanvictorygroves.net, Web Site: www.sullivanvictorygroves.net (4)

Sullivan, Jim, MFE Instruments, Salem, NH. Tel: (603) 893-8778, (800) 843-8011, FAX: (603) 893-8851, Web Site: www.stockeryale.com (9)

Sullivan, John, Fox, The Atlantic Monthly, Washington, DC. Tel: (202) 266-6000, (800) 234-2411, FAX: (202) 266-7280, Web Site: www.theatlantic.com (17)

Sullivan, Lou, Newmark Laboratories, Edison, NJ. Tel: (732) 417-1870, (800) 338-8079, FAX: (732) 225-0066, E-Mail: newmark@injersey.com (7)

Sullivan, Martin, J., AIG Accident & Health, New York, NY. Tel: (212) 770-7000, (877) 638-4244, FAX: (212) 509-9705, Web Site: www.aig.com (15)

Sullivan, Martin, J., American International Group, New York, NY. Tel: (212) 770-7000, (877) 638-4244, FAX: (212) 742-8692, Web Site: www.aig.com (15)

Sullivan, Michael, Carefirst Blue Cross Blue Shield, Washington, DC. Tel: (202) 479-8000, FAX: (301) 470-8049, Web Site: www.carefirst.com (15)

Sullivan, Michael, J., IHS Inc, Englewood, CO. Tel: (303) 790-0600, (800) 525-7052, FAX: (303) 754-3940, E-Mail: customer.support@ihs.com, Web Site: www.ihs.com (17)

Sullivan, Mike, Electric Insurance Co, Beverly, MA. Tel: (978) 921-2080, (800) 227-2757, FAX: (978) 524-5583, E-Mail: sales@electricinsurance.com, Web Site: www.electricinsurance.com (15)

Sullivan, Myrna, Hogard Business Services Inc, Bradley, IL. Tel: (815) 932-1835, FAX: (815) 932-4793, E-Mail: hogards@att.net, Web Site: www.hogardbusinessservices.com (28)

Sullivan, Nick, Esquire Magazine, New York, NY. Tel: (212) 649-2000, (800) 925-0485, FAX: (212) 265-0938, E-Mail: esquire@hearst.com, Web Site: www.esquire.com (17)

Sullivan, Thomas, Princeton Partners Inc, Princeton, NJ. Tel: (609) 452-8500, FAX: (609) 452-7212, E-Mail: mlandis@princetonpartners.com, Web Site: www.princetonpartners.com (35)

Sullivan, Trudy, Talbots, Hingham, MA. Tel: (781) 749-7600, (800) 825-2687, FAX: (781) 741-4369, Web Site: www.talbots.com (2)

Sullivan, William, F., Union Federal Savings Bank, North Providence, RI. Tel: (401) 353-8900, (800) 992-0278, FAX: (401) 353-8938, Web Site: www.unionfsb.com (14)

Sullivan-Victory Groves, Cocoa, FL. Tel: (321) 632-0550, (800) 672-6431, FAX: (321) 639-4069, E-Mail: citrus@sullivanvictorygroves.net, Web Site: www.sullivanvictorygroves.net (4)

Sultz, Tara, Medical Economics Magazine, North Olmsted, OH. Tel: (440) 243-8100, FAX: (440) 891-2735, Web Site: medicaleconomics.modernmedicine.com/about (17)

Sulzberger Jr., Arthur, O., The New York Times Co, New York, NY. Tel: (212) 556-3881, FAX: (212) 556-7389, Web Site: www.nytimes.com (17)

Suman Inc, Potomac, MD. Tel: (301) 461-7625, E-Mail: sales@sumaninc.com, Web Site: www.sumaninc.com (21)

Sumi, Michael, Sumi Printing, Carson, CA. Tel: (310) 769-1600, Web Site: www.getsumi.com (27)

Sumi Printing, Carson, CA. Tel: (310) 769-1600, Web Site: www.getsumi.com (27)

Summit Direct Mail Inc, Dallas, TX. Tel: (469) 916-5170, Web Site: www.summitdm.com (28)

Summit Industries Inc, Marietta, GA. Tel: (770) 590-0600, (800) 241-6996, FAX: (770) 590-0714, E-Mail: info@summitinds.com, Web Site: www.summitinds.com (5)

Summit Marketing, Saint Louis, MO. Tel: (314) 569-3737, FAX: (314) 569-0037, E-Mail: info@summitmarketing.com, Web Site: www.summitmarketing.com (35)

Summit Racing Equipment, Tallmadge, OH. Tel: (330) 630-0270, FAX: (330) 630-5330, Web Site: www.summitracing.com (12)

SummitQwest, Dayton, OH. Tel: (937) 291-4333, Web Site: www.sqinteractive.com (30)

Sumner, Tiffany, Carl Fischer Music, New York, NY. Tel: (212) 777-0900, (800) 762-2328, FAX: (212) 477-6996, E-Mail: cf-web@carlfischer.com, Web Site: www.carlfischer.com (17)

Sumotext, Inc, Little Rock, AR. Tel: (800) 480-1248, Web Site: www.sumotext.com (21)

Sun Harvest Citrus, Fort Myers, FL. Tel: (239) 768-2686, (800) 743-1480, FAX: (239) 768-9255, E-Mail: info@sunharvestcitrus.com, Web Site: www.SunHarvestCitrus.com (6)

Sun Hope Nutritional Health, Santa Monica, CA. Tel: (888) 553-5476, Web Site: www.sunhope.net (7)

Sunbeam, Boca Raton, FL. Tel: (561) 912-4100, FAX: (561) 912-4567, Web Site: www.sunbeam.com (16)

Sunbelt Media Service, Chapel Hill, NC. Tel: (919) 967-7174, FAX: (919) 967-6050 (32)

Sunbilt Creative Sunrooms, Jamaica, NY. Tel: (718) 297-6040, FAX: (718) 297-3090, E-Mail: info@sunbilt.com, Web Site: www.sunbilt.com (8)

Sunburst Technology, Elgin, IL. Tel: (914) 747-3310, FAX: (914) 747-4109, E-Mail: service@nysunburst.com, Web Site: www.sunburst.com (17)

Sundance Catalog Co, Salt Lake City, UT. Tel: (801) 973-2711, (800) 422-2770, FAX: (801) 973-4989, E-Mail: jessica.bassin@sundance.net, Web Site: www.sundancecatalog.com (6)

Sundancer Jewelry Co Inc, Albuquerque, NM. Tel: (505) 345-7475, FAX: (505) 345-7561, E-Mail: sales@sundancer.net, Web Site: www.sundancer.net (16)

Sundman, David, Littleton Coin Co Inc, Littleton, NH. Tel: (603) 444-5386, FAX: (603) 444-0121, E-Mail: jhennessey@littletoncoin.com, Web Site: www.littletoncoin.com (6)

Sundman, Don, International Collectors Society, Camden, NY. Tel: (800) 606-3490, FAX: (410) 998-9707, E-Mail: info@mysticstamp.com, Web Site: www.icsnow.com (16)

Sundman, Donald, J., Mystic Stamp Co Inc, Camden, NY. Tel: (866) 660-7147, FAX: (800) 385-4919, E-Mail: info@mysticstamp.com, Web Site: www.mysticstamp.com (16)

Sundman, Peter, Neuberger & Berman Management, New York, NY. Tel: (212) 476-8800, (800) 877-9700, FAX: (212) 476-9090, Web Site: www.nb.com (14)

SUNDOG, Fargo, ND. Tel: (701) 235-5525, (888) 9-SUNDOG, FAX: (701) 235-8941, Web Site: www.sundog.net (35)

Sung, Tina, American Society for Training & Development, Alexandria, VA. Tel: (703) 683-8100, (800) NAT-ASTD, FAX: (703) 683-8103, Web Site: www.astd.org (1)

Sungard Computer Services, Wayne, PA. Tel: (484) 582-5673, E-Mail: GetInfo@SunGard.com, Web Site: www.sungard.com (22)

Sunlife of Canada, Wellesley Hills, MA. Tel: (781) 237-6030, (800) SUNLIFE, FAX: (781) 446-1779, Web Site: www.sunlife-usa.com (15)

Sunnyland Farms Inc, Albany, GA. Tel: (229) 436-5654, (800) 999-2488, FAX: (229) 888-8332, Web Site: www.sunnylandfarms.com (4)

Sunoco, Inc, Philadelphia, PA. Tel: (215) 977-3000, (800) 786-6261, FAX: (215) 977-3409, E-Mail: sunoco_online@sunoil.com, Web Site: www.sunocoinc.com (16)

SunPorch Structures Inc, Westport, CT. Tel: (203) 454-0040, (866) 919-9620, FAX: (203) 454-0020, E-Mail: leo@sunporch.com, Web Site: www.sunporch.com (8)

Sunrise Business Products, Mineola, NY. Tel: (800) 222-7367, FAX: (631) 588-3900 (10)

Sunrise Greetings, Bloomington, IN. Tel: (812) 336-4045, (800) 457-4045, FAX: (812) 336-8712, E-Mail: info@interart.com, Web Site: www.interartdistribution.com (17)

Sunrise Medical Inc, Boulder, CO. Tel: (303) 218-4500, (800) 333-4000, FAX: (303) 218-4949, Web Site: www.sunrisemedical.com (16)

Sunset Magazine, Menlo Park, CA. Tel: (650) 321-3600, FAX: (650) 328-6215 (17)

Sunshine, Eugene, S., Northwestern University, Evanston, IL. Tel: (847) 491-3741, FAX: (847) 491-8406, E-Mail: webmaster@northwestern.edu, Web Site: www.northwestern.edu (41)

Sunshine Discount Crafts, Largo, FL. Tel: (727) 530-9572, (800) 729-2878, FAX: (727) 531-2799, E-Mail: webmaster@sunshinecrafts.com, Web Site: www.sunshinecrafts.com (11)

Sunshine Farm & Gardens, Renick, WV. Tel: (304) 497-2208, FAX: (304) 497-2698, E-Mail: barry@sunfarm.com, Web Site: www.sunfarm.com (8)

Sunshine Glassworks Ltd, Buffalo, NY. Tel: (716) 668-2918, (800) 828-7159, FAX: (716) 668-2932, E-Mail: info23@sunshineglass.com, Web Site: www.sunshineglass.com (11)

Sunshine Minting Inc, Coeur D'Alene, ID. Tel: (208) 772-9592, (800) 274-5837, FAX: (208) 772-9739, E-Mail: sunshine@sunshinemint.com, Web Site: www.sunshinemint.com (14)

Sunshine Unlimited Inc, Lindsborg, KS. Tel: (785) 227-3880, FAX: (785) 227-3880, E-Mail: cpeterjr@aol.com, Web Site: www.sunshine-unlimited.com (9)

Sunstar, Chicago, IL. Tel: (773) 777-4000, FAX: (773) 777-1417, E-Mail: dominico@sunstar.com, Web Site: www.sunstar.com (16)

Suntel Inc, Hamden, CT. Tel: (203) 287-9114, FAX: (203) 248-3883, E-Mail: info@suntelinc.com, Web Site: www.suntelinc.com (22)

Suntrust Banks Inc, Atlanta, GA. Tel: (404) 588-7914, (800) 786-8787, FAX: (404) 532-0550, E-Mail: emmett.harmon@suntrust.com, Web Site: www.suntrust.com (14)

Sunvest Resorts, Hallandale, FL. Tel: (954) 239-4200 (23)

Supelco Inc, Bellefonte, PA. Tel: (814) 359-3441, (800) 359-3041, FAX: (814) 359-3044, E-Mail: supelco@sial.com, Web Site: www.sigma-aldrich.com (16)

Super, Philip, American Insurance Administrators Inc, Columbus, OH. Tel: (614) 486-5388, FAX: (614) 486-2728 (15)

Super Coups, East Taunton, MA. Tel: (508) 977-2000, (800) 626-2620, FAX: (508) 977-0644, Web Site: www.supercoups.com (26)

Super Disk, Ann Arbor, MI. Tel: (734) 996-8888 (22)

Super 8 Hotels Worldwide, Parsippany, NJ. Tel: (973) 428-9700, (800) 800-8000, FAX: (973) 496-7307, Web Site: www.super8.com (19)

Superior Real Estate Supply, Phoenix, AZ. Tel: (623) 516-9202, (800) 234-0095, FAX: (623) 516-9209, E-Mail: sales@superiorrealestatesupply.com, Web Site: www.superiorrealestate.com (10)

SuperMedia LLC, Dallas, TX. Tel: (972) 453-7797 (31)

Superstock Inc, Jacksonville, FL. Tel: (904) 565-0066, (800) 828-4545, FAX: (904) 641-4480, E-Mail: yourfriends@superstock.com, Web Site: www.superstockimages.com (38)

The Supplies Guys, Midland Park, NJ. Tel: (201) 493-8433, Web Site: www.suppliesguys.com (3)

Support Plus, Hudson, OH. Tel: (508) 359-2910, (800) 229-2910, FAX: (508) 359-0139, E-Mail: cs@supportplus.com, Web Site: www.supportplus.com (7)

Support Services Corp, Fort Myers, FL. Tel: (239) 332-5300, FAX: (239) 332-4555, E-Mail: steve@ss-corp.com, Web Site: www.ss-corp.com (22)

Support Systems International Corp, Richmond, CA. Tel: (510) 234-9090, (800) 777-6269, FAX: (510) 233-8888, E-Mail: info@support-systems-intl.com, Web Site: www.support-systems-intl.com (3)

Supreme Specialty Advertising, Mount Arlington, NJ. Tel: (973) 770-8700, FAX: (973) 770-0808 (33)

Supremex Inc, Etobicoke, ON Canada. Tel: (416) 675-9370, (800) 465-7603, FAX: (416) 675-1952, (416) 848-8388, E-Mail: sales.central@supremex.com, Web Site: www.supremex.com (26)

Supremex Inc, La Salle, PQ Canada. Tel: (514) 595-0555, Web Site: www.supremex.com (26)

Sur La Table, Seattle, WA. Tel: (206) 682-7175, FAX: (206) 682-1026 (8)

Surchin, Hyman, M., Surchin Advanced Mailing Technologies, Deer Park, NY. Tel: (631) 667-0200, (800) 645-5240, FAX: (631) 667-0242, E-Mail: info@surchin.com, Web Site: www.surchin.com (34)

Surchin Advanced Mailing Technologies, Deer Park, NY. Tel: (631) 667-0200, (800) 645-5240, FAX: (631) 667-0242, E-Mail: info@surchin.com, Web Site: www.surchin.com (34)

Surdell, Daniel, L., Surdell & Partners, Omaha, NE. Tel: (402) 501-7488, (800) 733-7765, FAX: (402) 733-2083, E-Mail: dsurdell@surdellpartners.com, Web Site: www.surdellpartners.com (27)

Surdell & Partners, Omaha, NE. Tel: (402) 501-7488, (800) 733-7765, FAX: (402) 733-2083, E-Mail: dsurdell@surdellpartners.com, Web Site: www.surdellpartners.com (27)

Sure-Fire Business Success Catalog, Cambridge, MA. Tel: (617) 547-6372, FAX: (617) 547-0061, E-Mail: drjlant@worldprofit.com, Web Site: www.worldprofit.com (17)

Sure Fit Inc, Alburtis, PA. Tel: (610) 264-7300, Web Site: www.surefit.com (8)

Surfass, Ken, Equitable Life & Casualty Insurance Co, Salt Lake City, UT. Tel: (801) 579-3400, FAX: (801) 579-3789, Web Site: www.equilife.com (15)

Surmani, Andrew, Alfred Publishing Co Inc, Van Nuys, CA. Tel: (818) 891-5999, (800) 292-6122, FAX: (818) 895-5301, E-Mail: sales@alfred.com, Web Site: www.alfred.com (17)

Surplus Center, Lincoln, NE. Tel: (402) 474-4055, (800) 488-3407, FAX: (402) 474-5198, E-Mail: customerservice1@surpluscenter.com, Web Site: www.surpluscenter.com (9)

Surplus Record, Chicago, IL. Tel: (312) 372-9077, (800) 622-5449, FAX: (312) 372-6537, E-Mail: surplus@surplusrecord.com, Web Site: www.surplusrecord.com (17)

Sussex Publishers Inc, New York, NY. Tel: (212) 260-7210, FAX: (212) 260-7445, Web Site: www.bluesbuster.com (17)

Sussman, David, Sunbilt Creative Sunrooms, Jamaica, NY. Tel: (718) 297-6040, FAX: (718) 297-3090, E-Mail: info@sunbilt.com, Web Site: www.sunbilt.com (8)

Sussman, Marsha, The Jewish Federation of Greater Washington, Rockville, MD. Tel: (301) 230-7261, Web Site: www.shalomdc.org (1)

Sussman, Steve, Sunbilt Creative Sunrooms, Jamaica, NY. Tel: (718) 297-6040, FAX: (718) 297-3090, E-Mail: info@sunbilt.com, Web Site: www.sunbilt.com (8)

Sustainable Forestry Initiative Inc, Washington, DC. Tel: (202) 596-3450, FAX: (202) 596-3451, E-Mail: info@sfiprogram.org, Web Site: www.sfiprogram.org (1)

Sutcliffe, Scott, Cornell Lab of Ornithology, Ithaca, NY. Tel: (607) 254-2157, (800) 843-BIRD, FAX: (607) 254-2415, E-Mail: birdslides@cornell.edu, Web Site: www.birds.cornell.edu (1)

Sutherland PhD, John, UF College of Advertising, Journalism, & Communications, Gainesville, FL. Tel: (352) 392-4046, FAX: (352) 392-3919, Web Site: www.jou.ufl.edu (41)

Sutherland, Alden, Jostens, Inc, Minneapolis, MN. Tel: (952) 830-3300, FAX: (952) 830-3293, Web Site: www.jostens.com (16)

Sutherland, George, Brookstone Co, Merrimack, NH. Tel: (603) 880-9500, (800) 846-3000, FAX: (603) 577-8005, E-Mail: customerservice@brookstone.com, Web Site: www.brookstone.com (3)

Sutherland, Smokey, John Sutherland & Associates, San Diego, CA. Tel: (858) 535-1139, (800) 545-9591, FAX: (858) 535-9124 (15)

Sutherland Global Services, Pittsford, NY. Tel: (585) 586-5757, (800) 388-4557, FAX: (585) 419-2418, E-Mail: katie-laird@suth.com, Web Site: www.suth.com (35)

John Sutherland & Associates, San Diego, CA. Tel: (858) 535-1139, (800) 545-9591, FAX: (858) 535-9124 (15)

Sutherlin, Michael, W., P & H Mining Equipment, Milwaukee, WI. Tel: (414) 671-4400, FAX: (414) 671-7618, Web Site: www.phmining.com (16)

Sutter, Chris, Hewlett-Packard Co, Palo Alto, CA. Tel: (650) 857-1501, (800) 752-0900, FAX: (650) 857-5518, Web Site: www.hp.com (16)

Sutter, Conrad, Landscape Forms Inc, Kalamazoo, MI. Tel: (616) 381-0490, (800) 430-6209, FAX: (616) 381-3455, E-Mail: specify@landscapeforms.com, Web Site: www.landscapeforms.com (16)

Sutter, Lynn, R., Sutter Marketing Inc, Palatine, IL. Tel: (847) 358-3100, FAX: (847) 705-7900, Web Site: www.suttermarketing.com (35)

Sutter, Richard, Marketing Resources Network Inc, Marina Del Rey, CA. Tel: (310) 459-2271, FAX: (310) 459-2287 (32)

Sutter Marketing Inc, Palatine, IL. Tel: (847) 358-3100, FAX: (847) 705-7900, Web Site: www.suttermarketing.com (35)

Sutton, Cindy, Sara Lee Direct Home Shopping, Winston-Salem, NC. Tel: (336) 519-4400, (800) 671-5056, E-Mail: ohp.managor@onehanesplace.com, Web Site: www.onehanesplace.com (2)

Sutton, Jeff, MSI List Marketing, Palatine, IL. Tel: (847) 934-1111, FAX: (847) 890-6700, E-Mail: jeff@msilist.com, Web Site: www.msilist.com (23)

Sutton, W. Ron, ACCUSPLIT Inc, Livermore, CA. Tel: (925) 226-0888, (800) 935-1996, FAX: (925) 463-0147, E-Mail: sales@accusplit.com, Web Site: www.accusplit.com (16)

Svenningsen, Glen, Mardev-DM2, Lombard, IL. Tel: (800) 323-4958, FAX: (303) 265-5457, E-Mail: info@mardevdm2.com, Web Site: www.mardevdm2.com (24)

Svenson, Jodie, Meister Media Worldwide, Willoughby, OH. Tel: (440) 942-2000, (800) 572-7740, FAX: (440) 975-3447, E-Mail: info@meistermedia.com, Web Site: www.meistermedia.com (17)

Svetik, Steve, Aristokraft Inc, Jasper, IN. Tel: (812) 482-2527, FAX: (812) 482-9872, Web Site: www.aristokraft.com (16)

Svinicki, Jane, Wisconsin Direct Marketing Association, Milwaukee, WI. Tel: (414) 760-9362, FAX: (414) 431-4195, E-Mail: info@wdma.org, Web Site: www.wdma.org (40)

Svoboda, Jim, Mid America Direct Marketing Association, Omaha, NE. Tel: (402) 964-8444, FAX: (402) 964-8484, Web Site: www.madma.org (40)

Svoboda, John, A., Svoboda Collins LLC, Chicago, IL. Tel: (312) 267-8750, FAX: (312) 267-6025, E-Mail: info@svoco.com, Web Site: www.svoco.com (5)

Svoboda Collins LLC, Chicago, IL. Tel: (312) 267-8750, FAX: (312) 267-6025, E-Mail: info@svoco.com, Web Site: www.svoco.com (5)

Swab, Mark, Con-Way Truckload, Joplin, MO. Tel: (417) 623-5229, (800) CFI-DRIVE, FAX: (417) 623-8939, E-Mail: gnichols@cfi-us.com, Web Site: www.cfi-us.com (12)

Swag Inc, Wichita, KS. Tel: (316) 685-3811, FAX: (316) 685-4422, E-Mail: swag@cox.net, Web Site: www.swagpromos.com (33)

Swaggart, Rev Jimmy, Jimmy Swaggart Ministries, Baton Rouge, LA. Tel: (225) 768-8300, (800) 288-8350, FAX: (225) 769-2244, Web Site: www.jsm.org (1)

Jimmy Swaggart Ministries, Baton Rouge, LA. Tel: (225) 768-8300, (800) 288-8350, FAX: (225) 769-2244, Web Site: www.jsm.org (1)

Swain, Kirk, L., DirectMail.com, Prince Frederick, MD. Tel: (888) 690-2252, FAX: (301) 855-9810, Web Site: www.directmail.com (28)

Swain, Tom, The Toro Consumer Div, Bloomington, MN. Tel: (952) 888-8801, (888) 384-9939, FAX: (952) 887-8258, Web Site: www.thetorocompany.com (16)

Swainson, John A., CA Inc, Islandia, NY. Tel: (800) 225-5224, FAX: (631) 342-3300, E-Mail: info@ca.com, Web Site: www.ca.com (16)

Swales, Bob, International Bible Society, Colorado Springs, CO. Tel: (719) 488-9200, FAX: (719) 867-2812, Web Site: www.ibs.org (1)

Swallow, G., Winn Technology Group Inc, Palm Harbor, FL. Tel: (727) 789-0006, (800) 444-5622, FAX: (727) 789-0638, E-Mail: winn@winntech.net, Web Site: www.winntech.net (29)

Swan, Craig, University of Minnesota Alumni Association, Minneapolis, MN. Tel: (612) 624-2323, (800) UM-ALUMS, FAX: (612) 626-8167, E-Mail: umalumni@umn.edu, Web Site: www.umaa.umn.edu (1)

Swan Packaging Fulfillment, Wayne, NJ. Tel: (973) 790-8417, FAX: (973) 790-0216, E-Mail: info@swanpkg.com, Web Site: www.swanpackaging.com (28)

Swanger, William, Diakon Lutheran Social Ministries, Allentown, PA. Tel: (610) 682-2145, (888) 582-2230, FAX: (610) 682-1055, E-Mail: swangerb@diakon.org, Web Site: www.diakon.org (1)

Swann, Joe, Reliance Electric, Fort Smith, AR. Tel: (479) 646-4711, FAX: (479) 648-5792, E-Mail: smtraylor@powersystems.rockwell.com, Web Site: www.reliance.com (9)

Swanson, Art, Health O Meter, Alsip, IL. Tel: (708) 377-0600, (800) 815-6615, FAX: (708) 377-0601, E-Mail: HomProCS@homscales.com, Web Site: www.homscales.com (16)

Swanson, Bob, Seiko Corp of America, Mahwah, NJ. Tel: (201) 529-5730, FAX: (201) 529-1548, Web Site: www.seiko.com (16)

Swanson, Byron, Back to the Bible, Lincoln, NE. Tel: (402) 464-7200, (800) 811-2397, FAX: (402) 464-7474, E-Mail: info@backtothebible.org, Web Site: www.backtothebible.org (5)

Swanson, Mark, Tele Resources Inc, Duluth, MN. Tel: (888) 698-8787 X114, FAX: (218) 724-2466, E-Mail: mark.swanson@teleresources.net, Web Site: www.teleresources.net (29)

Swanson Health Products, Fargo, ND. Tel: (701) 356-2800, (800) 824-4491, FAX: (800) 726-7691, E-Mail: customercare@swansonvitamins.com, Web Site: www.swansonvitamins.com (35)

Swart, Mary, Q Fact Marketing Research Inc & Videoconferencing Center, Cincinnati, OH. Tel: (513) 891-2271, FAX: (513) 984-7464, E-Mail: info@qfact.com, Web Site: www.qfact.com (30)

Swartley, Ed, Rocky Mountain Direct Marketing Association, Aurora, CO. Tel: (720) 922-9413, FAX: (720) 922-9414, E-Mail: rmdma-ed@rmdma.org, Web Site: www.rmdma.org (41)

Swartz, Elaine, Blaine Window Hardware Inc, Hagerstown, MD. Tel: (301) 797-6500, (800) 678-1919, FAX: (888) 250-3960, E-Mail: info@blainewindow.com, Web Site: www.blainewindow.com (9)

Swartz, Jan, Princess Cruises (HQ), Santa Clarita, CA. Tel: (661) 753-0000, (800) Princess, FAX: (661) 284-4765, Web Site: www.princesscruises.com (19)

Swartz, Jeffrey, Timberland.com, Stratham, NH. Tel: (603) 772-9500, Web Site: www.Timberland.com (16)

Swartz, Kress, Quadrant Engineering Plastic Products, Reading, PA. Tel: (610) 320-6600, (800) 366-0300, FAX: (610) 320-6868, Web Site: www.quadrantepp.com (16)

Swartz, Randy, Stagestep Inc, Philadelphia, PA. Tel: (267) 672-2900, (800) 523-0961, FAX: (267) 672-2914, E-Mail: stagestep@stagestep.com, Web Site: www.stagestep.com (5)

Swartzentruber, John S., Gohn Brothers, Middlebury, IN. Tel: (219) 825-2400, (800) 595-0031, Web Site: www.gohnbrothers.com (5)

Swayne, Doug, Uncharted Country Publishing, Madison, WI. Tel: (575) 776-3470, E-Mail: ucp@taichihealth.com, Web Site: www.taichihealth.com (17)

Sweat, Bob, Meyer Decorative Surfaces Inc, Atlanta, GA. Tel: (404) 699-3900, (800) 776-3900, FAX: (404) 699-3914, Web Site: www.meyerdeco.com (8)

Swedenburg, R. Scott, Mail Enterprises LLC, Birmingham, AL. Tel: (205) 595-4945, (800) 595-4945, FAX: (205) 595-4943, Web Site: www. mailent.com (21)

Sweeney, Anne, The Disney ABC Cable Network Group, Burbank, CA. Tel: (818) 569-7500, FAX: (818) 848-6925, Web Site: www.disneyabctv.com (32)

Sweeney, Ariane, E., Citizens Against Government Waste, Washington, DC. Tel: (202) 467-5300, (800) USA-DEBT, FAX: (202) 467-4253, E-Mail: membership@cagw.org, Web Site: www.cagw.org (1)

Sweeney, Daniel, F., Ikon Communications Consultants Inc, Wellesley, MA. Tel: (781) 237-6060, FAX: (781) 235-3504 (35)

Sweeney, Edward, National Semiconductor Corp, Santa Clara, CA. Tel: (408) 721-5000, (800) 272-9959, FAX: (408) 245-0671, E-Mail: new. feedback@nsc.com, Web Site: www.national.com (16)

Sweeney, Greg, Gardener's Eden, Merrimack, NH. Tel: (603) 888-9500, (800) 822-9600, FAX: (603) 577-8005, E-Mail: gsweeney@brookstone.com (8)

Sweeney, Gregory, Brookstone Co, Merrimack, NH. Tel: (603) 880-9500, (800) 846-3000, FAX: (603) 577-8005, E-Mail: customerservice@brookstone. com, Web Site: www.brookstone.com (3)

Sweeney, Judy, Disabled American Veterans, Cincinnati, OH. Tel: (859) 441-7300, FAX: (859) 442-2084, E-Mail: feedback@davmail.org, Web Site: www.dav.org (1)

Sweeney, Matthew, Computerworld DataBase Div, Framingham, MA. Tel: (508) 879-0700, (800) 343-6474, FAX: (508) 875-4394, Web Site: www. computerworld.com (22)

Sweeney, Ric, College of Business, Cincinnati, OH. Tel: (513) 556-7002, FAX: (513) 556-4891, E-Mail: business@uc.edu, Web Site: www. business.uc.edu (41)

Sweeney, William, GG Direct, Portland, ME. Tel: (207) 772-0414, FAX: (207) 871-1444, E-Mail: info@ggdirect.com, Web Site: www.ggdirect.com (21)

Sweepstakes Clearinghouse, Dallas, TX. Tel: (214) 915-7100, FAX: (214) 915-7458, E-Mail: customersupport@sweepstakesclearinghouse.com, Web Site: www.sweepstakesclearinghouse.com (16)

Sweet, Bob, Dow Theory Forecasts, Hammond, IN. Tel: (219) 931-6480, (800) 233-5922, FAX: (219) 931-6487, E-Mail: custserv@horizonpublishing. com, Web Site: www.dowtheory.com (17)

Sweetgrass, Seattle, WA. Tel: (206) 343-9000, FAX: (206) 447-2663, E-Mail: bill.toliver@ sweetgrassadvertising.com, Web Site: www. sweetgrassadvertising.com (35)

Sweetland, Helen, Sierra Club Books, San Francisco, CA. Tel: (415) 977-5500, FAX: (415) 977-5792, E-Mail: books.publishing@sierraclub.org, Web Site: www.sierraclub.org (1)

Swenson, John, C, Tri-State Envelope Corp, Ashland, PA. Tel: (570) 875-0433, (800) 233-3102, FAX: (570) 875-0125, E-Mail: tsecny@attglobal.net, Web Site: www.tristateenvelope.com (26)

Swenson, Judith J., Response Marketing Inc, Eden Prairie, MN. Tel: (952) 949-4913 (35)

Swent, Greg, Marketry Inc, Bellevue, WA. Tel: (425) 451-1262, (800) 346-2013, FAX: (425) 451-1941, E-Mail: greg@marketry.com, Web Site: www. marketry.com (23)

Swidarski, Thomas, W., Diebold Inc, Uniontown, OH. Tel: (330) 899-2510, (800) DIEBOLD, FAX: (330) 490-3794, E-Mail: barronp@diebold.com, Web Site: www.diebold.com (16)

Swift, Amber, Vierk National Supply, North Chicago, IL. Tel: (847) 869-4318, (800) 428-7548, FAX: (847) 689-4412, Web Site: www.vierk.com (16)

Swift, Diane, S., Research To Prevent Blindness Inc, New York, NY. Tel: (212) 752-4333, (800) 621-0026, FAX: (212) 688-6231, E-Mail: inforequest@ rpbusa.org, Web Site: www.rpbusa.org (1)

Swimmer, Mark, Swimmer Design Associates, Prospect Heights, IL. Tel: (847) 215-0900, FAX: (847) 215-9821, E-Mail: mail@swimmerdesign.com, Web Site: www.swimmerdesign.com (36)

Swimmer Design Associates, Prospect Heights, IL. Tel: (847) 215-0900, FAX: (847) 215-9821, E-Mail: mail@swimmerdesign.com, Web Site: www.swimmerdesign.com (36)

Swindal, Robert, Carqueville Graphics Inc, Streamwood, IL. Tel: (630) 837-4500, FAX: (630) 837-4510, Web Site: www.carqueville.com (27)

Swindell, Mitch, NOVO1, Fort Worth, TX. Tel: (817) 355-6899, FAX: (817) 355-8505, Web Site: www. novo1.com (29)

Swink, James, Young Pecan Co, Florence, SC. Tel: (843) 662-8591, (800) 829-6864, FAX: (843) 664-2344, E-Mail: sales@youngpecan.com, Web Site: www.youngpecan.com (4)

Swinwood, Craig, Harlequin Enterprises Ltd, Don Mills, ON. Tel: (416) 445-5860, FAX: (416) 445-8655, E-Mail: customer_ecare@harlequin.ca, Web Site: www.eharlequin.com (17)

The Swiss Colony Inc, Monroe, WI. Tel: (608) 328-8400, FAX: (608) 328-8457, Web Site: www. swisscolony.com (4)

Sword, Sue, Christian Appalachian Project, Lexington, KY. Tel: (859) 792-3051, (866) 270-4CAP, FAX: (859) 792-6560, E-Mail: capinfo@chrisapp.org, Web Site: www.christianapp.org (1)

Swords, Logan, Swords Music Co Inc, Fort Worth, TX. Tel: (817) 53-MUSIC, (800) 522-3028, FAX: (817) 536-4293, E-Mail: daveshep4300@sbcglobal. net, Web Site: www.swordsmusicinc.com (34)

Swords Music Co Inc, Fort Worth, TX. Tel: (817) 53-MUSIC, (800) 522-3028, FAX: (817) 536-4293, E-Mail: daveshep4300@sbcglobal.net, Web Site: www.swordsmusicinc.com (34)

Swormstedt, Tedd, ST Media Group International, Cincinnati, OH. Tel: (513) 421-2050, (800) 925-1110, FAX: (513) 421-5144, E-Mail: customer@ stmediagroup.com, Web Site: www.signweb.com (17)

Swormstedt, Wade, ST Media Group International, Cincinnati, OH. Tel: (513) 421-2050, (800) 925-1110, FAX: (513) 421-5144, E-Mail: customer@ stmediagroup.com, Web Site: www.signweb.com (17)

Sybase Inc, Dublin, CA. Tel: (925) 236-5000, Web Site: www.sybase.com/product/datawarehousing (22)

Sycoff, Jerry, Innovative Concepts, Hicksville, NY. Tel: (516) 479-2200, (800) 631-0209, FAX: (516) 479-2215, E-Mail: info@ic-mr.com, Web Site: www.ic-mr.com (30)

Sykes, Charles, ICT Group Inc, Tampa, FL. Tel: (215) 757-0200, (800) 799-6880, Web Site: www. ictgroup.com (29)

Sykes, Chris, Miracle of Aloe, Dallas, TX. Tel: (800) 966-2563, FAX: (800) 859-9881, E-Mail: LJohnson@miracleofaloe.com, Web Site: www. miracleofaloe.com (7)

Sykes, Chris, Winning Solutions Inc, Fort Worth, TX. Tel: (972) 986-5355, (866) 494-6765, E-Mail: winninginc@aol.com (7)

Sykes Acquisition, Newtown, PA. Tel: (800) 799-6880, Web Site: www.ictgroup.com (29)

Sykstus, John, NOVO1, Fort Worth, TX. Tel: (817) 355-6899, FAX: (817) 355-8505, Web Site: www. novo1.com (29)

Sylvan Learning Centers, Baltimore, MD. Tel: (410) 843-8000, FAX: (410) 843-8057, Web Site: www. educate.com (16)

Sylvester, David, C., Steelcase Inc, Grand Rapids, MI. Tel: (616) 247-2710, FAX: (616) 475-2270, Web Site: www.steelcase.com (16)

Sylvester, Marcia, Princeton Book Co Publishers, Hightstown, NJ. Tel: (609) 426-0602, (800) 220-7149, FAX: (609) 426-1344, E-Mail: pbc@ dancehorizons.com, Web Site: www.dancehorizons. com (17)

Sylvia, Mike, Reliable Racing Supply, Queensbury, NY. Tel: (518) 793-5677, (518) 793-6491, Web Site: www.reliableracing.com (11)

Symantec, Mountain View, CA. Tel: (408) 517-8000, FAX: (408) 517-8186, Web Site: www.symantec. com (16)

Symetra Financial, Bellevue, WA. Tel: (425) 256-8000, (800) 426-7355, FAX: (425) 256-5737, Web Site: www.symetra.com (15)

Symington Jr., Charles, E., Independent Insurance Agents & Brokers of America, Alexandria, VA. Tel: (703) 683-4422, (800) 221-7917, FAX: (703) 683-7556, E-Mail: info@iiaba.org, Web Site: www. iiaba.org (1)

Synapse Group Inc, Stamford, CT. Tel: (203) 595-8255, FAX: (203) 329-8237, E-Mail: webmaster@ synapsemail.com, Web Site: www.synapsegroupinc. com (18)

Synder, Gail, G., Nationwide Mutual Insurance Co, Columbus, OH. Tel: (614) 249-7111, (800) 882-2822, FAX: (614) 854-3676, Web Site: www. nationwide.com (15)

Synergy Arts Interactive, Asheville, NC. Tel: (914) 997-7222, FAX: (914) 997-8893, E-Mail: bgeorge@synergyarts.com, Web Site: www. synergyarts.com (36)

Synergy Direct Marketing Solutions LLC, Barberton, OH. Tel: (330) 869-5886, Web Site: www.synmar. biz (29)

Syngenta, Greensboro, NC. Tel: (336) 632-6000, FAX: (336) 632-7065 (16)

Synovate, New York, NY. Tel: (212) 293-6100, FAX: (212) 293-6666 (30)

Syntellect, Phoenix, AZ. Tel: (602) 789-2800, (800) 788-9733, FAX: (602) 789-2899, Web Site: www. syntellect.com (16)

Syracuse University, Syracuse, NY. Tel: (315) 443-4944, Web Site: syr.edu (1)

Syroka, Cynthia, Avaya Communication, Temecula, CA. Web Site: www.avaya.com (34)

Syron, Richard, F., Federal Home Loan Mortgage Corp (Freddie Mac), McLean, VA. Tel: (703) 903-2000, (800) 424-5401, Web Site: www.freddiemac. com (14)

Syrowiik, Joseph, American Institute of CPAs, New York, NY. Tel: (212) 596-6200, (888) 777-7077, FAX: (212) 596-6213, Web Site: www.aicpa.org (1)

System Pavers, Newport Beach, CA. Tel: (949) 263-8300, Web Site: www.systempavers.com (16)

Systemax Inc, Port Washington, NY. Tel: (516) 608-7000, FAX: (516) 6208-7001, Web Site: www. systemax.com (16)

Systems Analytics Inc, Needham, MA. Tel: (781) 444-4837, E-Mail: info@systemsanalytics.com, Web Site: www.systemsanalytics.com (20)

Szanger, Michael, V3, Oxnard, CA. Tel: (800) 882-1844, Web Site: www.v3corporation.com (27)

Szefc, Richard, The Wedding Pages, New York, NY. Tel: (212) 219-8555, (800) 843-4983, FAX: (212) 219-1929, Web Site: www.theknot.com (16)

Szeftel, Ivan, Alliance Data, Plano, TX. Tel: (972) 348-5100, Web Site: www.alliancedata.com (28)

Szilagyi, Steve, Elderly Instruments, Lansing, MI. Tel: (517) 372-7890, (888) 473-5810, FAX: (517) 372-5155, E-Mail: elderly@elderly.com, Web Site: www.elderly.com (5)

Szkody, Paula, Astronomical Society of the Pacific, San Francisco, CA. Tel: (415) 337-1100, (800) 335-2624, FAX: (415) 337-5205, E-Mail: service@ astrosociety.org, Web Site: www.astrosociety.org (1)

Sznewajs, John, G., Masco Corp, Taylor, MI. Tel: (313) 274-7400, FAX: (313) 792-6135, E-Mail: webmaster@mascohq.com, Web Site: www.masco. com (16)

Szot, Colleen, Colleen Szot - Wonderful Writer Inc, Minneapolis, MN. Tel: (763) 557-7116, (888) 557-7116, FAX: (763) 551-4831, E-Mail: colleen@ wonderfulwriter.com, Web Site: www. wonderfulwriter.com (39)

Colleen Szot - Wonderful Writer Inc, Minneapolis, MN. Tel: (763) 557-7116, (888) 557-7116, FAX: (763) 551-4831, E-Mail: colleen@wonderfulwriter. com, Web Site: www.wonderfulwriter.com (39)

Szott, Christina, BIC Graphic USA, Clearwater, FL. Tel: (727) 536-7895, FAX: (800) 753-5890, Web Site: www.bicgraphic.com (33)

Szygenda, Ralph, J., Buick Division General Motors Corp, Detroit, MI. Tel: (313) 556-5000, (800) 521-7300, FAX: (313) 556-5108, Web Site: www. buick.com (16)

Szymaczyk, Michael, E., Philip Morris USA Inc, Richmond, VA. Tel: (804) 274-2000, FAX: (804) 484-8231, Web Site: www.philipmorrisusa.com (16)

Szymanski, Greg, Metropolitan Graphic Arts, Mundelein, IL. Tel: (847) 566-9502, FAX: (847) 566-9519, Web Site: www.mgaprinting.com (27)

Szymanski, Joseph, Metropolitan Graphic Arts, Mundelein, IL. Tel: (847) 566-9502, FAX: (847) 566-9519, Web Site: www.mgaprinting.com (27)

T

T-Mobile, Bellevue, WA. Tel: (425) 999-2084, Web Site: www.t-mobile.com (29)

T Rowe Price Associates Inc, Baltimore, MD. Tel: (410) 345-2000, (800) 638-7890, FAX: (410) 986-3618, E-Mail: info@troweprice.com, Web Site: www.troweprice.com (14)

T O Printing & Mailing Services, Westlake Village, CA. Tel: (818) 991-0068 (23)

TAB Boards International Inc, Westminster, CO. Tel: (303) 839-1200, FAX: (303) 839-0012, Web Site: www.tabboards.com (14)

TALX Corp, Dallas, TX. Tel: (972) 755-2100, FAX: (972) 755-2080, E-Mail: consulting@ managementinsights.com, Web Site: www. managementinsights.com (20)

TAPPI (Technical Association of the Pulp & Paper Industry), Norcross, GA. Tel: (678) 642-66, (800) 332-8686, FAX: (770) 446-6947, E-Mail: webmaster@tappi.org, Web Site: www.tappi.org (1)

TBC Direct Inc, Baltimore, MD. Tel: (410) 347-7500, FAX: (410) 986-1299, E-Mail: direct@tbc.us, Web Site: www.tbcadv.us (35)

TBWA, Los Angeles, CA. Tel: (310) 305-5000 (35)

TBWA/Chiat/Day Inc, New York, NY. Tel: (212) 804-1000, FAX: (212) 804-1200, E-Mail: jamie.gallo@ tbwachiat.com, Web Site: www.tbwachiat.com (35)

TCI Direct, Stateline, NV. Tel: (818) 752-1800, FAX: (818) 752-1808 (24)

TCJC, New York, NY. Tel: (212) 268-4100, FAX: (212) 268-4209 (2)

TD Ameritrade Holding Corp, Omaha, NE. Tel: (402) 331-7856, (800) 237-8692, FAX: (402) 597-7789, Web Site: www.amtd.com (35)

TD Bank NA, Falmouth, ME. Tel: (207) 770-2196, Web Site: www.tdbanknorth.com (14)

TDC Direct, Mississauga, ON Canada. Tel: (905) 564-6616, FAX: (905) 564-6621, E-Mail: nam@ tdcdirect.com, Web Site: www.tdcdirect.com (21)

TDS Telecom, Madison, WI. Tel: (608) 664-4119, Web Site: www.tdstelecom.com (16)

TEC Mailing Solutions, LLC, Sun Prairie, WI. Tel: (608) 825-8525 (22)

TechBA - Fumec, San Jose, CA. Tel: (408) 821-6297, Web Site: www.techba.com (1)

TFC Inc, Napa, CA. Tel: (707) 224-6161, Web Site: www.tfcinc.com (27)

THD Inc, Lexington, MA. Tel: (781) 859-1400), Web Site: www.thdinc.com (1)

Thomson Reuters, New York, NY. Tel: (212) 367-6300, (800) 950-1216, FAX: (212) 367-6301, Web Site: www.riahome.com (17)

TIAA-CREF, New York, NY. Tel: (212) 490-9000, FAX: (212) 916-6505, Web Site: www.tiaa-cref.org (15)

TKL Interactive, The Colony, TX. Tel: (972) 370-7878, (800) 789-3893, FAX: (972) 370-7879, Web Site: www.tklinteractive.com (23)

TL Enterprises Inc, Ventura, CA. Tel: (805) 667-4100, FAX: (805) 667-4419 (17)

TMA Direct, Reston, VA. Tel: (703) 547-4940, Web Site: www.tmalist.com (23)

TMP Direct, Budd Lake, NJ. Tel: (973) 347-9400, (800) 328-2439, FAX: (973) 347-8773, E-Mail: ron.pearl@tmpwdirect.com, Web Site: www. tmpwdirect.com (29)

TMP Directional Marketing, Waukesha, WI. Tel: (212) 351-7595, Web Site: www.tmpdm.com (30)

TMP Worldwide, Mc Lean, VA. Tel: (703) 269-0144, FAX: (703) 269-0115, E-Mail: john.refo@tmp. com, Web Site: www.tmp.com (35)

TN Marketing, Wayzata, MN. Tel: (763) 577-1216, Web Site: www.tnmarketing.com (35)

TNF, Toronto, ON Canada. Tel: (416) 924-5751, FAX: (416) 923-7085, Web Site: www.tnf-cf.com (30)

TNS Intersearch, White Plains, NY. Tel: (914) 684-6100, FAX: (914) 684-6078, Web Site: www.tns-global.com (30)

TNS Media Intelligence, New York, NY. Tel: (212) 991-6000, FAX: (212) 991-6010, Web Site: www. tns-mi.com (32)

TNT International Express, Melville, NY. Tel: (800) 558-5555 (28)

TNT Packaging Inc, Miami, FL. Tel: (305) 769-0616, (305) 633-2556, (800) 327-6085, FAX: (305) 769-0619, E-Mail: tntpackaging@bellsouth.net, Web Site: www.tntpackaging.com (16)

TNT (Turner Network Television LP), Atlanta, GA. Tel: (404) 827-1700, E-Mail: tnt@turner.com, Web Site: www.tnt.tv (32)

TPG Direct Inc, Philadelphia, PA. Tel: (215) 592-8303, Web Site: www.tpgadvertising.com (35)

TRG World, Washington, DC. Tel: (202) 289-9898 (29)

TSE Services, Raleigh, NC. Tel: (919) 875-3037, Web Site: www.ncemcs.com (30)

TSI, Albany, NY. Tel: (518) 463-5555, FAX: (518) 463-4504, E-Mail: tsi@capital.net, Web Site: www. tsidrivers.com (20)

TT Publishing, Arlington, VA. Tel: (703) 838-1770, FAX: (703) 838-0285, Web Site: www.ttnews.com (17)

TTC Marketing Solutions, Chicago, IL. Tel: (773) 545-0407, (800) 777-6348, FAX: (773) 545-4034, E-Mail: sales@ttcmarketingsolutions.com, Web Site: www.ttcmarketingsolutions.com (29)

TV Guide, Tulsa, OK. Tel: (918) 488-4000, FAX: (918) 488-4200, Web Site: www.tvguideinc.com (32)

TV Guide Magazine, New York, NY. Tel: (212) 852-7500, (800) 866-1400, Web Site: www.tvguide.com (31)

TVA Productions Inc (The Video Agency), Studio City, CA. Tel: (818) 505-8300, (888) 322-4296, FAX: (818) 505-8370, E-Mail: info@ tvaproductions.com, Web Site: www. tvaproductions.com (35)

TVC Enterprises and the TV Collector Magazine, Las Vegas, NV. Tel: (760) 495-7956, E-Mail: tvcinquiries@happyretrogirl.com, Web Site: www. angelfire.com/ma/tvcollector/home.html (6)

TWL Knowledge Group, Carrollton, TX. Tel: (972) 309-4000, (800) 624-2272, FAX: (972) 309-5105, Web Site: www.twlk.com (3)

TXU Energy, Irving, TX. Tel: (972) 868-8345, Web Site: www.txu.com (16)

Tabacinic, Jose, Arnet Pharmaceutical, Davie, FL. Tel: (954) 236-9053, (800) 968-6673, FAX: (954) 370-2508, E-Mail: arnet@arnetusa.com, Web Site: www.arnetusa.com (7)

Tabacinic, Manuel, Arnet Pharmaceutical, Davie, FL. Tel: (954) 236-9053, (800) 968-6673, FAX: (954) 370-2508, E-Mail: arnet@arnetusa.com, Web Site: www.arnetusa.com (7)

Tabacinic, Mark, Arnet Pharmaceutical, Davie, FL. Tel: (954) 236-9053, (800) 968-6673, FAX: (954) 370-2508, E-Mail: arnet@arnetusa.com, Web Site: www.arnetusa.com (7)

Tabaco, Alex, Itochu Chemicals America Inc, White Plains, NY. Tel: (914) 333-7800, (800) 423-6870, FAX: (914) 333-7848, Web Site: www.itochu-sc. com (16)

Tableau Software, Seattle, WA. Tel: (206) 633-3400, Web Site: www.tableausoftware.com (22)

Tabler, William Biggs, Tabler Communications, Louisville, KY. Tel: (502) 585-2299, FAX: (502) 585-3574, E-Mail: biggs@tablercommunications.com, Web Site: www.tablercommunications.com (35)

Tabler Communications, Louisville, KY. Tel: (502) 585-2299, FAX: (502) 585-3574, E-Mail: biggs@ tablercommunications.com, Web Site: www. tablercommunications.com (35)

Tabline Data Services Inc, New York, NY. Tel: (212) 695-4873, FAX: (212) 629-4423 (30)

TABS Direct, Irving, TX. Tel: (281) 499-0417, (800) 231-0697, FAX: (281) 208-6081, E-Mail: tabsdirect@tabsdirect.com, Web Site: www. tabsdirect.com (21)

Tabsharani, Fred, F., Vidi Emi Inc, San Leandro, CA. Tel: (510) 667-9999, FAX: (510) 352-9999, E-Mail: info@vidiemi.com, Web Site: www. vidiemi.com (32)

Tacinelli, Ernie, The Other List Co Inc, Matawan, NJ. Tel: (732) 591-1180, FAX: (732) 591-8472 (23)

Tacito, Anthony J., Tacito Direct Marketing, Dallas, TX. Tel: (972) 458-2026, (800) 621-2225, FAX: (972) 490-6520, Web Site: www.tacito.com (35)

Tacito Direct Marketing, Dallas, TX. Tel: (972) 458-2026, (800) 621-2225, FAX: (972) 490-6520, Web Site: www.tacito.com (35)

Tackle Craft, Ellsworth, WI. Tel: (715) 273-5300, E-Mail: tacklecr@aol.com (11)

Tactara, Los Angeles, CA. Tel: (213) 221-3200, Web Site: www.tactara.com (32)

Taeusch, Ben, Amateur Electronic Supply LLC, Milwaukee, WI. Tel: (414) 558-0333, (800) 558-0411, FAX: (414) 358-3337, Web Site: www.aesham.com (16)

Tafarella, Jonathan, Institute of Business Forecasting, Great Neck, NY. Tel: (516) 504-7576, Web Site: www.ibf.org (1)

Tafford Uniforms, Montgomeryville, PA. Tel: (215) 643-9666, E-Mail: customerservice@tafford.com, Web Site: www.tafford.com (2)

Tailwinds Inc, Mill Valley, CA. Tel: (415) 927-4242, (800) TAILWIND, FAX: (415) 927-0199, E-Mail: service@tailwinds.com, Web Site: www.tailwinds. com (6)

Takahashi, Toshio, Fuji Photo Film USA, Valhalla, NY. Tel: (914) 789-8100, (800) 755-3854, FAX: (914) 789-8295, Web Site: www.fujifilmusa.com (16)

Takashima, Christine, Daily Commercial News & Construction Record, Markham, ON. Tel: (905) 752-5408, (800) 465-6475, FAX: (888) 396-9413, (905) 752-5450, E-Mail: dcnonl@reedbusiness. com, Web Site: www.dcnonl.com (17)

Take 5 Solutions LLC, Boca Raton, FL. Tel: (561) 819-5555, (866) 861-8862, FAX: (561) 819-0245, E-Mail: sales@take5s.com, Web Site: www. take5solutions.com (30)

Talabisco, Barbara, Wakefield Talabisco International, New York, NY. Tel: (212) 661-8600, FAX: (212) 661-8832, Web Site: www.wtali.com (20)

Talar, Maciej, Marian Helpers Center, Stockbridge, MA. Tel: (413) 298-3691, (800) 462-7426, FAX: (413) 298-3583, Web Site: www.marian.org (1)

Talarico, Greg, Mardev-DM2, Lombard, IL. Tel: (800) 323-4958, FAX: (303) 265-5457, E-Mail: info@mardevdm2.com, Web Site: www.mardevdm2.com (24)

Talas, Brooklyn, NY. Tel: (212) 219-0770, FAX: (212) 219-0735, E-Mail: info@talasonline.com, Web Site: www.talasonline.com (10)

Talbert, Nancy, King's Chandelier Co, Eden, NC. Tel: (336) 623-6188, FAX: (336) 627-9935, E-Mail: crystal@chandelier.com, Web Site: www.chandelier.com (6)

Talbot, John, Postmatic Inc, Minneapolis, MN. Tel: (763) 784-6046, (888) 784-6046, FAX: (763) 784-9433, E-Mail: info@postmatic.net, Web Site: www.postmatic.com (34)

Talbot, Keith, Form House Inc, Skokie, IL. Tel: (708) 594-7300, FAX: (708) 594-7390, E-Mail: ktalbot@theformhouse.com, Web Site: www.theformhouse.com (28)

Talbot, Patty, Melaniphy & Associates, Inc, Chicago, IL. Tel: (773) 467-1212, FAX: (773) 774-0454, E-Mail: jmelaniphy@melaniphy.com, Web Site: www.melaniphy.com (8)

Talbot, Randall, H., Symetra Financial, Bellevue, WA. Tel: (425) 256-8000, (800) 426-7355, FAX: (425) 256-5737, Web Site: www.symetra.com (15)

Talbots, Hingham, MA. Tel: (781) 749-7600, (800) 825-2687, FAX: (781) 741-4369, Web Site: www.talbots.com (2)

Talbott, Karen, B&W Press Inc, Georgetown, MA. Tel: (978) 352-6100, (877) 246-3467, FAX: (978) 352-5955, E-Mail: csr@bwpress.com, Web Site: www.bwpress.com (21)

Taliaferro, Susan, Tolliver Inc, New York, NY. Tel: (212) 758-7344, FAX: (212) 750-8617, E-Mail: tolliver12@aol.com (20)

Talian, Elizabeth, Communication Managers, LLC, Brookfield, CT. Tel: (203) 775-4213, FAX: (203) 775-6413, E-Mail: etalian@communicationmanagers.com, Web Site: www.communicationmanagers.com (20)

Talin, Patricia, A., Amica Insurance, Lincoln, RI. Tel: (401) 334-6000, (800) 652-6422, FAX: (401) 334-4241, Web Site: www.amica.com (15)

Tallal, Scott, V., Advanced Research Services, Malibu, CA. Tel: (310) 589-0223, Web Site: www.tvsurveys.com (30)

Tamarkin, Stan, Tamarkin & Co, Woodbridge, CT. Tel: (203) 397-9191, (800) 289-5342, FAX: (203) 397-9393, E-Mail: info@tamarkin.com, Web Site: www.tamarkin.com (34)

Tamarkin & Co, Woodbridge, CT. Tel: (203) 397-9191, (800) 289-5342, FAX: (203) 397-9393, E-Mail: info@tamarkin.com, Web Site: www.tamarkin.com (34)

Tamayo Miyares & Sherman, Bridgeport, CT. Tel: (203) 416-5718, FAX: (203) 416-5721, E-Mail: lsherman@tmsdr.com, Web Site: www.tmsdr.com (35)

Tamke, George W., ServiceMaster Co, Memphis, TN. Tel: (901) 766-1400, (901) 597-8502, (888) 937-3783, (866) 782-6787, FAX: (901) 766-1491, Web Site: www.servicemaster.com (16)

Tamke, George, W., TruGreen/ChemLawn, Lewis Center, OH. Tel: (614) 846-1800, (800) TRUEGREEN, FAX: (614) 431-0155, Web Site: www.trugreen.com (16)

Tamney, Joseph, Boyd Tamney Cross Inc, Wayne, PA. Tel: (610) 293-0500, FAX: (610) 687-8199, E-Mail: info@btcmarketing.com, Web Site: www.boydtamneycross.com (35)

Tamrac Inc, Chatsworth, CA. Tel: (818) 407-9500, Web Site: www.tamrac.com (2)

Tanaka, Hidezaku, Roland Products Inc, Los Angeles, CA. Tel: (323) 731-1111, FAX: (323) 731-9585, E-Mail: salesinfo@rolandinc.com, Web Site: www.rolandinc.com (16)

Tancredi, Christina, Music Choice, Horsham, PA. Tel: (215) 784-5840, Web Site: www.musicchoice.com (16)

Tandem, Bryan, Creative Publishing International, Minneapolis, MN. Tel: (612) 344-8100, FAX: (612) 344-8691, E-Mail: sales@creativepub.com, Web Site: www.creativepub.com (17)

Tandy Leather Co, Fort Worth, TX. Tel: (817) 872-3200, FAX: (817) 496-7859, E-Mail: tlfhelp@tandyleather.com, Web Site: www.tandyleatherfactory.com (11)

Tanen, Ilene, Cohn, Tanen Directed Advertising, Norwalk, CT. Tel: (203) 855-5855, FAX: (203) 855-5865, Web Site: www.tanendirected.com (35)

Tanen Directed Advertising, Norwalk, CT. Tel: (203) 855-5855, FAX: (203) 855-5865, Web Site: www.tanendirected.com (35)

Tangent Media LLC, Atlanta, GA. Tel: (404) 444-2357, Web Site: www.tangentmedia.us (30)

tangerine direct - a service of archer malmo, Memphis, TN. Tel: (901) 523-2000, Web Site: www.archermalmo.com (35)

Tanguay, Diane, Publications Groupe RR International Inc, Montreal, PQ Canada. Tel: (514) 521-8148 (20)

Tann Selective Communications Inc, Richmond Hill, ON Canada. Tel: (905) 881-1030, FAX: (416) 881-1035 (21)

Tanner, Christy, TV Guide Magazine, New York, NY. Tel: (212) 852-7500, (800) 866-1400, Web Site: www.tvguide.com (31)

Tanner, Glen, E., ITT Educational Services Inc, Carmel, IN. Tel: (317) 706-9200, E-Mail: gtanner@itt-tech.edu, Web Site: www.itt-tech.edu (16)

Tanner, Josephine, Dante University Press, Wellesley, MA. Tel: (781) 790-1059, FAX: (781) 790-1056, E-Mail: dante@danteuniversity.org, Web Site: www.danteuniversity.com (17)

Tansky, Burton, M., Neiman-Marcus Group, Dallas, TX. Tel: (214) 743-7600, (888) 888-4757, FAX: (214) 573-5320, Web Site: www.neimanmarcus.com (8)

Tanton, Tom, Collegiate Cap & Gown, Champaign, IL. Tel: (217) 351-9500, FAX: (217) 351-9214, Web Site: www.herff-jones.com (16)

Tapajna, Ray, W., Arkline Computers & Supply, Cleveland, OH. Tel: (216) 252-6560, (800) 695-1441, FAX: (216) 671-2037, Web Site: www.geocities.com (3)

Tapp, Lynell L., Ronell Clock Co, Grants Pass, OR. Tel: (541) 471-0194, (800) 334-0135, FAX: (541) 471-0099, Web Site: www.ronellclock.com (5)

Tapp, Roland V., Ronell Clock Co, Grants Pass, OR. Tel: (541) 471-0194, (800) 334-0135, FAX: (541) 471-0099, Web Site: www.ronellclock.com (5)

Tappan, Robert, A., Arrow Mailing Service II Inc, Hawthorne, CA. Tel: (310) 219-7740, FAX: (310) 219-3335 (28)

Taradel LLC, Glen Allen, VA. Tel: (804) 364-8444, Web Site: www.taradel.com (31)

Taravella, Tony, Industrial Uniform Co Inc, Wichita, KS. Tel: (316) 264-2871, (800) 333-3666, FAX: (316) 264-2708, E-Mail: uniform@industrialuniform.com, Web Site: www.industrialuniform.com (2)

Tardi, Joseph, Joseph Tardi Associates, Niskayuna, NY. Tel: (518) 782-1211, FAX: (518) 782-9488, Web Site: www.tardiassociates.com (35)

Joseph Tardi Associates, Niskayuna, NY. Tel: (518) 782-1211, FAX: (518) 782-9488, Web Site: www.tardiassociates.com (35)

Target & Response Inc, Chicago, IL. Tel: (312) 321-0500, FAX: (312) 321-0051, Web Site: www.target-response.com (35)

Target Direct Marketing Inc, Gloucester, MA. Tel: (978) 281-5967, Web Site: www.targetdirectmarketing.com (35)

Target MarkeTeam, Atlanta, GA. Tel: (770) 274-3700, FAX: (770) 274-3730, Web Site: www.tmtinc.com (35)

Target Marketing Group, Philadelphia, PA. Tel: (215) 238-5300, Web Site: www.targetonline.com (31)

Target Marketing Magazine, Philadelphia, PA. Tel: (215) 238-5300, (800) 777-8074, FAX: (215) 238-5270, Web Site: www.targetmarketingmag.com (43)

Targetbase, Irving, TX. Tel: (972) 506-3400, (800) 446-6603, FAX: (972) 506-3505, E-Mail: info@targetbase.com, Web Site: www.targetbase.com (35)

Target.com, Minneapolis, MN. Tel: (612) 304-6545, Web Site: www.target.com (16)

TargetCom Inc, Chicago, IL. Tel: (312) 822-1100, FAX: (312) 822-9628, E-Mail: tcomcontact@targetcom.com, Web Site: www.targetcom.com (35)

TargetMail Marketing, Clover, SC. Tel: (540) 837-9337 (35)

TARGUSinfo, Mc Lean, VA. Tel: (703) 272-6200, Web Site: www.TARGUSinfo.com (22)

Tarr, Jeffrey, R., IHS Inc, Englewood, CO. Tel: (303) 790-0600, (800) 525-7052, FAX: (303) 754-3940, E-Mail: customer.support@ihs.com, Web Site: www.ihs.com (17)

Tarrant, David, SmartSource Corp, Burlington, MA. Tel: (781) 785-3375, Web Site: www.smartsourceonline.com (32)

Tarricone, Anthony, American Association for Justice, Washington, DC. Tel: (202) 965-3500, (800) 424-2725, FAX: (202) 625-7313, Web Site: www.justice.org (1)

Tartamella, Samuel, Integrated Business Services Inc, Lake Forest, IL. Tel: (847) 735-1690, Web Site: www.medbase200.com (22)

Tartarsky, Amy, Dozier Equipment International, Milwaukee, WI. Tel: (800) 251-1234, FAX: (800) 336-6608, Web Site: www.dozierequip.com (9)

Tarvin, Paul, Cinmar LP, West Chester, OH. Tel: (513) 603-1000, FAX: (513) 603-1020, Web Site: www.frontgate.com (8)

Tassini, Marie, Parade Publications, New York, NY. Tel: (212) 450-7000, FAX: (212) 450-7284, Web Site: www.parade.com (31)

Tatarka, Kim, Government Technology Services Inc, Herndon, VA. Tel: (703) 502-2000, (800) 234-GTSI, FAX: (703) 222-5218, Web Site: www.gtsi.com (16)

Tate, Eric, Astro Air, LP, Jacksonville, TX. Tel: (903) 586-3691, FAX: (903) 589-8094, E-Mail: sales@astroair.com, Web Site: www.astroair.com (9)

Tate, Mike, National Wholesale Co Inc, Lexington, NC. Tel: (336) 248-5904, (800) 480-4673, FAX: (336) 248-2880, E-Mail: customerservice@shopnational.com, Web Site: www.shopnational.com (2)

Tater, Jerome, Mead Westvaco Consumer & Office Products, Dayton, OH. Tel: (937) 222-6323, (800) 345-6323, FAX: (937) 495-3192, Web Site: www.mead.com (10)

Tatko, Raymond, J., Summit Racing Equipment, Tallmadge, OH. Tel: (330) 630-0270, FAX: (330) 630-5330, Web Site: www.summitracing.com (12)

Tatsch, Gregory, Vintage Wood Works, Quinlan, TX. Tel: (903) 356-2158, FAX: (903) 356-3023, E-Mail: mail@vintagewoodworks.com, Web Site: www.vintagewoodworks.com (8)

Tatsch, Holly, Vintage Wood Works, Quinlan, TX. Tel: (903) 356-2158, FAX: (903) 356-3023, E-Mail: mail@vintagewoodworks.com, Web Site: www.vintagewoodworks.com (8)

Tattum, Lyn, Chemical Week, New York, NY. Tel: (212) 621-4900, FAX: (212) 621-4800, E-Mail: clientservices@chemweek.com, Web Site: www.chemweek.com (17)

Tatum, Steve, Baylor Health Care System, Dallas, TX. Tel: (214) 820-4901, (800) 4Baylor, FAX: (214) 820-7499, Web Site: www.baylorhealth.com (16)

Taub, Brian, Unitron Ltd, Commack, NY. Tel: (631) 589-6666, FAX: (631) 589-6795, E-Mail: johnc@unitronusa.com, Web Site: www.unitronusa.com (9)

Taube, Dace, University of Southern California, Los Angeles, CA. Tel: (213) 821-2366, FAX: (213) 740-2343, E-Mail: taube@usc.edu, Web Site: www.usc.edu (38)

Taubenpost Inc, Lake Forest, CA. Tel: (949) 770-3233, FAX: (949) 380-3940, E-Mail: info@taubenpost.com, Web Site: www.taubenpost.com (28)

Taubes, Sheri, Bronson Nutritionals LLC, Hauppauge, NY. Tel: (631) 750-0000, Web Site: www.bronsonnutritionals.com (7)

Tauck World Discovery, Norwalk, CT. Tel: (203) 899-6760, Web Site: www.tauck.com (19)

The Taunton Press, Newtown, CT. Tel: (203) 426-8171, (800) 477-8727, FAX: (203) 426-3434, Web Site: www.taunton.com (17)

Tauscher, William, Y., Vertical Communications Inc, Santa Clara, CA. Tel: (617) 354-0600, (800) COMDIAL, FAX: (617) 452-9159, Web Site: www.comdial.com (34)

Tautz, Nicole, Tecra Tools Inc, Englewood, CO. Tel: (303) 338-9224, (800) 284-0808, FAX: (303) 338-9289, E-Mail: info@tecratools.com, Web Site: www.tecratools.com (9)

Tautz, Terry, Tecra Tools Inc, Englewood, CO. Tel: (303) 338-9224, (800) 284-0808, FAX: (303) 338-9289, E-Mail: info@tecratools.com, Web Site: www.tecratools.com (9)

Tavares, Ramiro, SK&A Information Services Inc, Irvine, CA. Tel: (949) 476-2051, (800) 752-5478, FAX: (949) 476-2168, E-Mail: skasales@skainfo.com, Web Site: www.skainfo.com (23)

Tax Management Inc, Bethesda, MD. Tel: (202) 452-4200, FAX: (202) 496-6013 (17)

Tax Reduction Institute, Germantown, MD. Tel: (301) 972-3600, (800) TRI-0-TAX, FAX: (301) 972-0819, E-Mail: info@taxreductioninstitute.com, Web Site: www.taxreductioninstitute.com (14)

Taybi, Paul, GreatLists.com, Dulles, VA. Tel: (703) 821-8130, (800) 296-0888, FAX: (703) 821-8243, E-Mail: info@greatlists.com, Web Site: www.greatlists.com (23)

Taylor MD, Patrick, A., Holy Cross Hospital, Fort Lauderdale, FL. Tel: (954) 771-8000, FAX: (954) 229-8597, Web Site: www.holy-cross.com (16)

Taylor, Ann, Publications International Ltd, Lincolnwood, IL. Tel: (847) 745-9299, (800) 595-8484, FAX: (847) 676-3671, Web Site: www.pubint.com (17)

Taylor, Audrey, Chabin Concepts, Chico, CA. Tel: (530) 345-0364, FAX: (530) 345-6417, E-Mail: chabininc@aol.com (16)

Taylor, Benjamin, Star Tribune, Minneapolis, MN. Tel: (612) 673-4000, FAX: (612) 673-4359, E-Mail: charte@startribune.com, Web Site: www.startribunecompany.com (17)

Taylor, Bill, Bunn-O-Matic Corp, Springfield, IL. Tel: (217) 529-6601, FAX: (217) 529-6622, E-Mail: bunn@bunn.com, Web Site: www.bunn.com (16)

Taylor, Blair, Rexcraft Wedding Invitations, Rexburg, ID. Tel: (208) 359-1000, (800) 635-3898, FAX: (800) 826-2712, E-Mail: cs@rexcraft.com, Web Site: www.rexcraft.com (16)

Taylor, Bruce W., Taylor Capital Group, Inc, Rosemont, IL. Tel: (847) 653-7978, FAX: (847) 653-7890, E-Mail: investor.relations@coletaylor.com, Web Site: www.taylorcapitalgroup.com (14)

Taylor, Carter, S.D., Performance Direct Inc, Atlanta, GA. Tel: (678) 608-2820, (800) 869-2300, FAX: (404) 869-2547, E-Mail: info@performancede.com (22)

Taylor, Cynthia, L., National Humane Education Society, Charles Town, W.V. Tel: (304) 725-0506, FAX: (304) 725-1523, E-Mail: nhesinformation@nhes.org, Web Site: www.nhes.org (1)

Taylor, Dale, Abelson-Taylor Inc, Chicago, IL. Tel: (312) 894-5500, FAX: (312) 894-5526, E-Mail: info@abelsontaylor.com, Web Site: www.abelson-taylor.com (35)

Taylor, Diane, American Bronzing Co, Columbus, OH. Tel: (614) 252-7388, (800) 423-5678, FAX: (614) 252-4602, E-Mail: bronzeinfo@bronshoe.com, Web Site: www.abcbronze.com (16)

Taylor, Diane, Health Care Logistics, Circleville, OH. Tel: (800) 848-1633, Web Site: www.healthcarelogistics.com (16)

Taylor, Don, DCA, West Chester, PA. Tel: (610) 344-7488, (800) 638-6684, FAX: (610) 431-6500, E-Mail: ortho@dentalcorp.com, Web Site: www.dentalcorp.com (16)

Taylor, Earl, Marketing Science Institute Review, Cambridge, MA. Tel: (617) 491-2060, FAX: (617) 491-2065, E-Mail: msi@msi.org, Web Site: www.msi.org (43)

Taylor, Frank, GC Services, Houston, TX. Tel: (713) 777-4441, FAX: (713) 776-6535, E-Mail: marketing.communications@gcserv.com, Web Site: www.gcserv.com (20)

Taylor, Gary, InfoCision Management Corp, Akron, OH. Tel: (330) 668-1400, FAX: (330) 668-1401, E-Mail: infocision@infocision.com, Web Site: www.infocision.com (29)

Taylor, Glenn, Amsterdam Printing, Amsterdam, NY. Tel: (518) 842-6000, (800) 203-9917, FAX: (518) 843-5204, E-Mail: customerservice@amsterdamprinting.com, Web Site: www.amsterdamprinting.com (16)

Taylor, Greg, Liberty Orchards Co Inc, Cashmere, WA. Tel: (509) 782-2191, (800) 888-5696, FAX: (509) 782-1487, E-Mail: service@libertyorchards.com, Web Site: www.libertyorchards.com (16)

Taylor, J. Reed, Taylor Gifts Inc, Paoli, PA. Tel: (610) 725-1122, FAX: (610) 725-1144, Web Site: www.taylorgifts.com (8)

Taylor, James, D., National Humane Education Society, Charles Town, W.V. Tel: (304) 725-0506, FAX: (304) 725-1523, E-Mail: nhesinformation@nhes.org, Web Site: www.nhes.org (1)

Taylor, James, Loeb & Loeb Inc, New York, NY. Tel: (212) 407-4000, Web Site: www.loeb.com (20)

Taylor, James, U-Haul International, Phoenix, AZ. Tel: (602) 263-6011, (800) GO-UHAUL, FAX: (602) 263-6598, Web Site: www.uhaul.com (16)

Taylor, Jeanine, Mediamark Research Inc, New York, NY. Tel: (212) 884-9200, (800) 310-3305, FAX: (212) 884-9339, Web Site: www.mediamark.com (30)

Taylor, Jeffrey W., Taylor Capital Group, Inc, Rosemont, IL. Tel: (847) 653-7978, FAX: (847) 653-7890, E-Mail: investor.relations@coletaylor.com, Web Site: www.taylorcapitalgroup.com (14)

Taylor, John, C., Envelope Products Group, Springfield, MA. Tel: (413) 736-7211, (888) 715-6641, (800) 628-9265, FAX: (413) 787-9749, E-Mail: envelopes@meadwestvaco.com, Web Site: www.meadwestvaco.com/envelopeprod.nsf (26)

Taylor, Judy, Mike Murach & Associates Inc, Fresno, CA. Tel: (559) 440-9071, (800) 221-5528, FAX: (559) 440-0963, E-Mail: murachbooks@murach.com, Web Site: www.murach.com (17)

Taylor, Kathleen, Four Seasons Hotels & Resorts, Toronto, ON. Tel: (416) 449-1750, (800) 819-5053, FAX: (416) 441-4374, Web Site: www.fourseasons.com (19)

Taylor, Kathy, Oklahoma Dept of Commerce, Oklahoma City, OK. Tel: (405) 815-6552, (800) 879-6552, FAX: (405) 815-5344, Web Site: www.okcommerce.com (1)

Taylor, Kevin, U-Bild, Oceanside, CA. Tel: (818) 785-6368, (800) 828-2453, FAX: (818) 785-3229, Web Site: www.ubild.com (8)

Taylor, Kimberly, Metropolis Magazine, New York, NY. Tel: (212) 627-9977, (800) 334-3046, FAX: (212) 627-9988, E-Mail: edit@metropolismag.com, Web Site: www.metropolismag.com (2)

Taylor, Larry, D., Travelex America Inc, Washington, DC. Tel: (202) 408-1200, FAX: (202) 513-5215, Web Site: business.travelex.com/us (14)

Taylor, Leo, J., Del Webb, Bloomfield Hills, MI. Tel: (248) 644-7300, (888) 717-9777, FAX: (248) 433-4598, Web Site: www.delwebb.com (16)

Taylor, Lynn, Keiler & Co, Farmington, CT. Tel: (860) 677-8821, FAX: (860) 676-8164, E-Mail: newbiz@keiler.com, Web Site: www.keiler.com (35)

Taylor, Mark, Tyndale House Publishers, Carol Stream, IL. Tel: (630) 668-8300, FAX: (630) 668-3245 (17)

Taylor, Mark, Wunderman, New York, NY. Tel: (212) 941-3000, FAX: (212) 888-7520, Web Site: www.wunderman.com (35)

Taylor, Michael, Continuing Education of the Bar (CEB), Oakland, CA. Tel: (510) 302-2000, (800) 232-3444, FAX: (510) 302-2001, Web Site: www.ceb.com (1)

Taylor, Patricia, MAX Federal Credit Union, Montgomery, AL. Tel: (334) 260-2600, (800) 776-6776, FAX: (334) 270-0921, Web Site: www.mymax.com (14)

Taylor, Paul, Le Jardin Du Gourmet, Saint Johnsbury Center, VT. Tel: (802) 748-1446, FAX: (802) 748-9592, E-Mail: orderdesk@artisticgardens.com, Web Site: www.artisticgardens.com (8)

Taylor, Peter, Road Runner Sports Inc, San Diego, CA. Tel: (858) 974-4200, (800) 636-3560, FAX: (800) 453-5443, Web Site: www.roadrunnersports.com (11)

Taylor, Renee, Spokane Teachers Credit Union, Liberty Lake, WA. Tel: (509) 326-1954, Web Site: www.stcu.org (14)

Taylor, Robert, The Colonial Williamsburg Foundation, Williamsburg, VA. Tel: (757) 229-1000, (757) 220-7275, (800) 761-8331, Web Site: www.williamsburgmarketplace.com (1)

Taylor, T., Robert, The Creative Alliance Inc, Lafayette, CO. Tel: (303) 665-8101, (888) 293-8101, FAX: (303) 665-3136, E-Mail: t@thecreativealliance.com, Web Site: www.creativealliance.com (35)

Taylor, Victor, Laven & Loeb Inc, Beachwood, OH. Tel: (623) 217-2101, (216) 291-3483, E-Mail: alaven@lavenandloeb.com; vtaylor@lavenandloeb.com, Web Site: www.lavenandloeb.com (20)

Taylor, William, Lark in the Morning, Mendocino, CA. Tel: (707) 964-5569, FAX: (707) 964-1979, E-Mail: info@larkinam.com, Web Site: www.larkinthemorning.com (5)

Ann Taylor Inc, New York, NY. Tel: (212) 457-2075, (800) FAX-ANN, FAX: (800) DIAL-ANN, Web Site: www.anninc.com (2)

Taylor Capital Group, Inc, Rosemont, IL. Tel: (847) 653-7978, FAX: (847) 653-7890, E-Mail: investor.relations@coletaylor.com, Web Site: taylorcapitalgroup.com (14)

Taylor Corp, North Mankato, MN. Tel: (507) 625-2828, FAX: (507) 625-3388 (16)

Taylor Gifts Inc, Paoli, PA. Tel: (610) 725-1122, FAX: (610) 725-1144, Web Site: www.taylorgifts.com (8)

Taylor Jr, B. Loyall, Taylor Gifts Inc, Paoli, PA. Tel: (610) 725-1122, FAX: (610) 725-1144, Web Site: www.taylorgifts.com (8)

Taylor Nelson Sofres Intersearch, Horsham, PA. Tel: (419) 725-8560, E-Mail: info@intersearch.tnsofres.com, Web Site: www.intersearch.tnsofres.com (30)

Taylor-Stiles Division, Florence, KY. Tel: (859) 525-7600, (800) 365-8555, FAX: (859) 525-1446, E-Mail: sales@littleford.com, Web Site: www.littleford.com (16)

Taymark Inc, White Bear Lake, MN. Tel: (651) 426-1667, (800) 479-2043, FAX: (651) 426-0275, Web Site: www.mninternational.com (1)

Teachers Credit Union, South Bend, IN. Tel: (574) 284-6455, Web Site: www.tcunet.com (1)

Teachers' Discovery, Auburn Hills, MI. Tel: (248) 340-7220, FAX: (248) 340-7212 (5)

The Teaching Co, Chantilly, VA. Tel: (703) 502-7300, (800) 832-2412, FAX: (703) 378-3819, Web Site: www.teach12.com (17)

Teahon, Nathan, Quality Contact Solutions Inc, Aurora, NE. Tel: (402) 210-2692, (866) 963-2889, FAX: (402) 210-2692, E-Mail: info@qualitycontactsolutions.com, Web Site: www.qualitycontactsolutions.com (29)

Team Cheer, Geneseo, NY. Tel: (585) 243-8400, (585) 243-0841, (877) 243-5268, FAX: (800) 350-1562, E-Mail: custserv@teamcheer.com, Web Site: www.teamcheer.com (2)

Team Nash Inc, East Hampton, NY. Tel: (646) 497-0297, (631) 267-3385, E-Mail: results@teamnash.com, Web Site: www.teamnash.com (35)

Team One Advertising, El Segundo, CA. Tel: (310) 615-2000, FAX: (310) 322-7565, E-Mail: b.sheehan@teamoneadv.com, Web Site: www.teamone-usa.com (35)

Teblum, Ron, Mars Research, Fort Lauderdale, FL. Tel: (954) 771-7725, (877) 755-2805, FAX: (954) 771-8824, E-Mail: ron@marsresearch.com, Web Site: www.marsresearch.com (30)

Tech Image, Buffalo Grove, IL. Tel: (847) 279-0022, (888) 4-TECH-PR, FAX: (847) 279-8922, E-mail: info@techimage.com, Web Site: www.techimage.com (35)

Techcom Inc, Princeton, NJ. Tel: (609) 734-0004, FAX: (609) 520-0263, E-Mail: techcom1@juno.com (35)

Technekes LLC, Charlotte, NC. Tel: (704) 342-2900, FAX: (704) 342-2975, Web Site: www.technekes.com (22)

Techni-Tool Inc, Worcester, PA. Tel: (610) 941-2400, (800) 832-4866, FAX: (800) 854-8665, E-Mail: sales@techni-tool.com, Web Site: www.techni-tool.com (16)

Technical Assistance Research Programs (TARP), Arlington, VA. Tel: (703) 524-1456, FAX: (703) 524-6374, Web Site: www.tarp.com (20)

Technical Marketing Group, West Caldwell, NJ. Tel: (856) 751-9585, FAX: (856) 751-9729, E-Mail: tldirenzo@aol.com, Web Site: www2.techmktgrp.com (35)

Technicolor, Camarillo, CA. Tel: (805) 445-1122, (800) 732-4555, FAX: (805) 445-4280, E-Mail: info@technicolor.com, Web Site: www.technicolor.com (21)

TechniPak, Gray, TN. Tel: (800) 385-1964, Web Site: www.technipak.com (28)

TechniServe Inc, Troy, MI. Tel: (248) 989-0100, FAX: (248) 989-0111, E-Mail: info@techni-serve.com, Web Site: www.techni-serve.com (22)

Technology Marketing Corp/TMC, Norwalk, CT. Tel: (203) 852-6800, (800) 243-6002, FAX: (203) 953-2845, E-Mail: tmc@tmcnet.com, Web Site: www.tmcnet.com (29)

Technology Review, Cambridge, MA. Tel: (617) 475-8000, FAX: (617) 258-5850, Web Site: www.technologyreview.com (17)

Tecra Tools Inc, Englewood, CO. Tel: (303) 338-9224, (800) 284-0808, FAX: (303) 338-9289, E-Mail: info@tecratools.com, Web Site: www.tecratools.com (9)

Tedeschi, Robert, J., Citizens Against Government Waste, Washington, DC. Tel: (202) 467-5300, (800) USA-DEBT, FAX: (202) 467-4253, E-Mail: membership@cagw.org, Web Site: www.cagw.org (1)

Tedesco, Mike, Viahealth, Rochester, NY. Tel: (585) 922-4000, (585) 922-3677, FAX: (585) 922-3929, Web Site: www.viahealth.org (16)

Ted's Promotions Inc, Baldwin, GA. Tel: (770) 972-8081, FAX: (770) 573-3141, E-Mail: ted@tedspromotions.com, Web Site: www.tedspromotions.com (33)

Tegt, Robert, Hormel Foods Corp, Austin, MN. Tel: (507) 437-5611, (800) 523-4635, FAX: (507) 437-5158, Web Site: www.hormel.com (16)

Tehrani, Nadji, Communications Solutions Expo, Norwalk, CT Canada. Tel: (203) 852-6800, (877) 243-6002, FAX: (203) 853-2845, E-Mail: info@tmcnet.com, Web Site: www.tmcnet.com (42)

Tehrani, Nadji, Technology Marketing Corp/TMC, Norwalk, CT. Tel: (203) 852-6800, (800) 243-6002, FAX: (203) 953-2845, E-Mail: tmc@tmcnet.com, Web Site: www.tmcnet.com (29)

Tehrani, Rich, Communications Solutions Expo, Norwalk, CT. Tel: (203) 852-6800, (877) 243-6002, FAX: (203) 853-2845, E-Mail: info@tmcnet.com, Web Site: www.tmcnet.com (42)

Teikoku Databank America Inc, New York, NY. Tel: (212) 421-9805, FAX: (212) 421-9806, E-Mail: info@teikoku.com, Web Site: www.teikoku.com (24)

Teitler, David, Guideposts, Danbury, CT. Tel: (845) 225-3681, FAX: (845) 228-2056, Web Site: www.guideposts.org (1)

Teixeira, Gail, Connex International, Danbury, CT. Tel: (800) 426-6639, FAX: (203) 731-5425, E-Mail: marketing@connexintl.com, Web Site: www.connexintl.com (22)

Tektronix Inc, Beaverton, OR. Tel: (503) 627-7111, (800) 833-9200, FAX: (503) 627-3247, Web Site: www.tektronix.com (16)

TelAmerica Media Inc, Philadelphia, PA. Tel: (215) 568-7066, FAX: (215) 564-5388, Web Site: www.telamericamedia.com (31)

Telcordia Technologies, Piscataway, NJ. Tel: (732) 699-2000, FAX: (973) 829-2458, Web Site: www.telcordia.com (16)

Tele Business USA, Northbrook, IL. Tel: (847) 480-1560, FAX: (847) 897-4120, Web Site: www.tbiz.com (29)

Tele Resources Inc, Duluth, MN. Tel: (888) 698-8787 X114, FAX: (218) 724-2466, E-Mail: mark.swanson@teleresources.net, Web Site: www.teleresources.net (29)

Telebrands Corp, Fairfield, NJ. Tel: (973) 244-0300, FAX: (973) 244-0233, Web Site: www.telebrands.com (21)

Telecom Inc, Oakland, CA. Tel: (510) 873-8283, (800) 243-3101, FAX: (510) 873-8293, Web Site: www.telecominc.com (29)

Telecommunications Reports International Inc, Washington, DC. Tel: (202) 312-6060, (800) 234-1660, FAX: (202) 312-6111, E-Mail: bhammond@tr.com, Web Site: www.tr.com (17)

The Teleconference Network, Nanuet, NY. Tel: (845) 624-0633, FAX: (845) 623-9394, E-Mail: nospam@mnav.com, Web Site: www.market-navigation.com (30)

Telect Inc, Liberty Lake, WA. Tel: (509) 926-6000, FAX: (509) 926-8915, E-Mail: getinfo@telect.com, Web Site: www.telect.com (16)

TeleDevelopment Services Inc, Richfield, OH. Tel: (330) 659-4441, FAX: (330) 659-4442, E-Mail: jkaplan@teledevelopment.com, Web Site: www.teledevelopment.com (20)

TeleDirect International Inc, Scottsdale, AZ. Tel: (480) 585-6464, (800) 531-6440, FAX: (480) 585-3373, Web Site: www.tdirect.com (29)

Teleflora, Los Angeles, CA. Tel: (310) 966-3586, Web Site: www.teleflora.com (16)

Telefonix Inc, Waukegan, IL. Tel: (847) 244-4500, Web Site: www.telefonixinc.com (16)

TeleManagement Search, Port Washington, NY. Tel: (516) 767-6990, FAX: (516) 767-6980, E-Mail: connie@tmrecruiters.com, Web Site: www.tmrecruiters.com (20)

Telemedia Communications US, North York, ON Canada. Tel: (416) 733-7600, (888) 290-1466 Can., (800) 461-3773 U.S., FAX: (416) 733-3563, E-Mail: info@transcontinental.ca, Web Site: www.transcontinental.com (17)

Telenational Marketing, Omaha, NE. Tel: (800) 333-6106 X132, FAX: (402) 391-2044, Web Site: www.telenational.com (29)

Teleperformance Canada, Toronto, ON Canada. Tel: (416) 922-3519, Web Site: www.teleperformance.ca (35)

Teleperformance Interactive, Miami Beach, FL. Tel: (786) 437-3300, FAX: (786) 276-8452, Web Site: www.teleperformance.com (29)

Tel Look-Up Service Co, Jamison, PA. Tel: (215) 321-0706, (800) 366-0706, FAX: (215) 321-3229, E-Mail: computer@telephonelookup.com, Web Site: www.telephonelookup.com (22)

Tel Selling Report, Scottsdale, AZ. Tel: (402) 895-9399, FAX: (402) 896-3353, E-Mail: arts@businessbyphone.com, Web Site: www.businessbyphone.com (43)

Telephony, Chicago, IL. Tel: (312) 595-1080, (800) 458-0479, FAX: (312) 595-0295, Web Site: www.internettelephony.com (17)

TeleRep, Glen Burnie, MD. Tel: (800) 638-2000, FAX: (410) 761-3357, Web Site: www.telerep.com (29)

Telerx, Horsham, PA. Tel: (800) 2TELERX, Web Site: www.telerx.com (29)

TeleServices Direct, Indianapolis, IN. Tel: (888) 646-6626, Web Site: www.teleservicesdirect.com (29)

Telestar Media, Cincinnati, OH. Tel: (513) 699-3300, Web Site: www.telestarmedia.com (35)

Telesystems Marketing Inc, Houston, TX. Tel: (713) 784-3439, (800) 622-0190, FAX: (713) 780-5974, E-Mail: kimberly@nwpros.com, Web Site: www.telesystemsmarketing.com (29)

TeleTech, Englewood, CO. Tel: (303) 397-8100, (800) TELETECH, FAX: (303) 397-8199, E-Mail: solutions@TeleTech.com, Web Site: www.teletech.com (22)

Teletrack Inc, Norcross, GA. Tel: (770) 449-8809 (29)

Telpro Inc, Grand Forks, ND. Tel: (701) 775-0551, FAX: (701) 775-0629 (9)

Temkin, Steve, Temkin & Temkin, Highland Park, IL. Tel: (847) 831-0237, FAX: (847) 851-0409, Web Site: www.temkin.com (35)

Temkin & Temkin, Highland Park, IL. Tel: (847) 831-0237, FAX: (847) 851-0409, Web Site: www.temkin.com (35)

Tempco Electric Heater Corp, Wood Dale, IL. Tel: (630) 350-2252, (800) 323-6859, FAX: (630) 350-0232, E-Mail: dpadlo@tempco.com, Web Site: www.tempco.com (9)

Temple, Lavon, Delivra, Indianapolis, IN. Tel: (317) 915-9400, Web Site: www.delivra.com (32)

Temple University, Philadelphia, PA. Tel: (215) 204-7282, FAX: (215) 204-4554, Web Site: www.sbm.temple.edu (41)

TempoGraphics Inc, Carol Stream, IL. Tel: (630) 462-8200, FAX: (630) 462-0350 (27)

Ten Speed Press, Emeryville, CA. Tel: (510) 559-1600, (800) 841-BOOK, FAX: (510) 559-1629, E-Mail: order@tenspeed.com, Web Site: www.tenspeed.com (17)

Tender Heart Treasures, Omaha, NE. Tel: (402) 593-1313, (800) 443-1367, FAX: (402) 593-1316, E-Mail: bcamenzind@thtdesigns.com (6)

Tennant, J. Keith, Intermap Technologies, Englewood, CO. Tel: (303) 708-0955, FAX: (303) 708-0952, Web Site: www.intermap.com (32)

TENNANT Co, Minneapolis, MN. Tel: (763) 540-1200, (800) 553-8033, FAX: (763) 513-2142, E-Mail: info@tennantco.com, Web Site: www.tennantco.com (34)

Tennessee Valley Authority, Knoxville, TN. Tel: (865) 632-2101, Web Site: www.tva.gov (16)

Tennyson, Brian, Direct Marketing International Ltd, Huntington Beach, CA. Tel: (877) 596-1919 (41)

Tensar International Corporation, Alpharetta, GA. Tel: (404) 250-1290, Web Site: www.tensarcorp.com (16)

Tension Envelope Corp, Kansas City, MO. Tel: (816) 471-3800, FAX: (816) 283-1498, Web Site: www.tension.com (26)

Teplitz, Paul, Research Boston Corp, Lafayette, CA. Tel: (978) 225-8030, FAX: (267) 295-8704, Web Site: www.researchboston.com (20)

Tepper, Ann, Profile America List Co Inc, Englewood Cliffs, NJ. Tel: (201) 569-7272, FAX: (201) 569-5552, E-Mail: annt@profileamerica.com, Web Site: www.profileamerica.com (24)

Teraco Inc, Midland, TX. Tel: (888) 837-2261, Web Site: www.teraco.com (27)

Teradata Corp, Miamisburg, OH. Tel: (937) 242-4800, Web Site: www.teradata.com (22)

Teramoto, Masao, Fujitsu Transaction Solutions Inc, Richardson, TX. Tel: (972) 963-2300, (800) 340-4425, Web Site: www.fujitsu.com (16)

Teran, Vivian, Alliance Direct Marketing Solutions LLC, Jersey City, NJ. Tel: (201) 863-1360, (888) 455-2367, FAX: (201) 863-3910, E-Mail: vteran@alliancedirectleads.com, Web Site: www.alliancedirectleads.com (20)

TerBlanche, Craig, Axia, Jacksonville, FL. Tel: (904) 425-6652, (866) 999-AXIA, FAX: (904) 425-6653, E-Mail: tellmemore@axia.net, Web Site: www.axia.net (35)

Teres, Wayne, Teres Consulting Inc, Framingham, MA. Tel: (508) 872-4922, FAX: (253) 595-6748, E-Mail: info@teresconsulting.com, Web Site: www.teresconsulting.com (20)

Teres Consulting Inc, Framingham, MA. Tel: (508) 872-4922, FAX: (253) 595-6748, E-Mail: info@teresconsulting.com, Web Site: www.teresconsulting.com (20)

Terlizzi, Donald, Capezio Ballet Makers Inc, Totowa, NJ. Tel: (973) 653-2093, (800) 533-1887, FAX: (800) 522-1222, E-Mail: info@balletmakers.com, Web Site: www.capeziodance.com (16)

Terlizzi, Marc, Capezio Ballet Makers Inc, Totowa, NJ. Tel: (973) 653-2093, (800) 533-1887, FAX: (800) 522-1222, E-Mail: info@balletmakers.com, Web Site: www.capeziodance.com (16)

Terlizzi, Michael, Capezio Ballet Makers Inc, Totowa, NJ. Tel: (973) 653-2093, (800) 533-1887, FAX: (800) 522-1222, E-Mail: info@balletmakers.com, Web Site: www.capeziodance.com (16)

Terlizzi, Paul, Capezio Ballet Makers Inc, Totowa, NJ. Tel: (973) 653-2093, (800) 533-1887, FAX: (800) 522-1222, E-Mail: info@balletmakers.com, Web Site: www.capeziodance.com (16)

Termini, Bill, Hinda Incentives, Chicago, IL. Tel: (773) 890-5900, (800) 621-4412, FAX: (773) 890-4606, E-Mail: contact@hinda.com, Web Site: www.hinda.com (33)

Terminix International, The Trugreen Companies, Memphis, TN. Tel: (901) 766-1105, Web Site: www.trugreenchemlawn.com (16)

Terner, Moni, Bijoux Terner, Miami, FL. Tel: (305) 500-7500, (800) 262-3614, FAX: (305) 262-9286, E-Mail: customerservice@bijouxterner.com, Web Site: www.bijouxterner.com (16)

Terner, Rosa, Bijoux Terner, Miami, FL. Tel: (305) 500-7500, (800) 262-3614, FAX: (305) 262-9286, E-Mail: customerservice@bijouxterner.com, Web Site: www.bijouxterner.com (16)

Ternes, Don, Thetford Corp, Ann Arbor, MI. Tel: (734) 769-6000, (800) 543-1219, FAX: (734) 769-2023, Web Site: www.thetford.com (16)

Ternoban, Barbara, Calloway House Inc, Lancaster, PA. Tel: (717) 299-5703, (800) 233-0290, FAX: (717) 299-6754, Web Site: www.callowayhouse.com (34)

Terranova, Sandy, Institutional Real Estate Inc, San Ramon, CA. Tel: (925) 244-0500, FAX: (925) 244-0520, Web Site: www.irei.com (17)

Terrazas, Al, Hugo Dunhill Mailing Lists Inc, New Rochelle, NY. Tel: (212) 213-9300, (800) 611-0557, FAX: (212) 213-9245, E-Mail: info@hdml.com, Web Site: www.hdml.com (23)

Territorial Newspapers, Tucson, AZ. Tel: (520) 294-1200, FAX: (520) 294-4040, Web Site: www.azbiz.com (17)

Terry, Barb, JIST Publishing, Saint Paul, MN. Tel: (800) 648-5478, FAX: (800) 547-8329, E-Mail: info@jist.com, Web Site: www.jist.com (17)

Terry, Merriott, Educational First Steps, Dallas, TX. Tel: (214) 824-7940), Web Site: educationalfirststeps.org (1)

Terry, Paul, Convertible Service, San Gabriel, CA. Tel: (626) 285-2255, (800) 333-1140, FAX: (626) 285-9004, Web Site: www.convertibleparts.com (16)

Terry, Scott, Rapid Progress Marketing & Modeling LLC, Saint Petersburg, FL. Tel: (727) 528-8578, Web Site: www.rpmsquared.com (22)

Terumo Cardiovascular Systems Corp, Ann Arbor, MI. Tel: (734) 663-4145, Web Site: www.terumo-cvs.com (5)

Tervo, Kirstan, Mailing Services of Pittsburgh Inc, Freedom, PA. Tel: (724) 774-3244, (800) 876-3211, FAX: (724) 774-6996, Web Site: www.msp-pgh.com (21)

Terzariol, Giulio, Allianz Life Insurance Co of North America, Minneapolis, MN. Tel: (763) 765-6500, (800) 950-5872, Web Site: www.allianzlife.com (15)

Tesar Reynes Inc, Chicago, IL. Tel: (312) 726-1900, E-Mail: tony@tesar-reynes.com, Web Site: www.tesar-reynes.com (20)

Teschner Jr., Charles, L., The McGraw-Hill Cos, New York, NY. Tel: (212) 904-2000, (866) 436-8502, FAX: (212) 512-3840, Web Site: www.mcgraw-hill.com (17)

Tesoriero, Tony, EBA Wholesale Corp, Brooklyn, NY. Tel: (718) 253-4700, (866) 2 ASK EBA, FAX: (718) 253-9232, Web Site: www.shopeba.com (3)

Tessco Inc, Hunt Valley, MD. Tel: (410) 229-1000, (800) 508-5444, FAX: (410) 527-0005, E-Mail: webhelp@tessco.com, Web Site: www.tessco.com (16)

Tessier, Patrick, Northwest Laboratories, Seattle, WA. Tel: (206) 763-6252, FAX: (206) 763-3949, Web Site: www.nwlabs.net (9)

The Testimonial Wrangler, La Jolla, CA. Tel: (858) 735-7646 (35)

Tether, Deb, Sound Beach Marketing Partners LLC, Old Greenwich, CT. Tel: (203) 698-0708, FAX: (203) 698-0712, E-Mail: thudock@soundbeachmarketing.com, Web Site: www.soundbeachmarketing.com (23)

Tetley USA Inc, Montvale, NJ. Tel: (203) 929-9200, (800) 728-0084, FAX: (203) 926-0876, Web Site: www.tetleyusa.com (16)

Teutsch, Stanley, Medibadge Inc, Omaha, NE. Tel: (402) 571-1800, (800) 228-0040, FAX: (800) 546-1072, E-Mail: stan@medibadge.com, Web Site: www.medibadge.com (5)

Teutsch, Teri, A., Medibadge Inc, Omaha, NE. Tel: (402) 571-1800, (800) 228-0040, FAX: (800) 546-1072, E-Mail: stan@medibadge.com, Web Site: www.medibadge.com (5)

Teva Pharmaceuticals USA, North Wales, PA. Tel: (215) 591-3000, (888) TEVAUSA, FAX: (215) 591-8600, Web Site: www.tevausa.com (7)

Tewes, Patty, Agilis Co, Albert Lea, MN. Tel: (507) 377-5028 (14)

Tewmey, Jim, VF Imagewear, Nashville, TN. Tel: (615) 565-5000, (800) 733-5271, Web Site: www.vfimagewear.com (2)

Texada Capital Corp, Grasonville, MD. Tel: (866) 595-6224, Web Site: www.texada.com (14)

Texas Children's Hospital, Houston, TX. Tel: (832) 824-2936, Web Site: www.texaschildrenshospital.org (1)

Texas Farm Bureau Insurance Companies, Waxahachie, TX. Tel: (972) 825-4842, Web Site: www.sagu.edu (1)

Texas Farm Bureau Insurance Cos, Waco, TX. Tel: (254) 751-2688, Web Site: www.txfb-ins.com (15)

Texas Graphic Resource, Dallas, TX. Tel: (214) 630-2800, FAX: (214) 630-0713 (27)

Texas Industries Inc, Dallas, TX. Tel: (972) 647-6700, FAX: (972) 647-3878, Web Site: www.txi.com (16)

Texas Monthly, Austin, TX. Tel: (512) 320-6900, (800) 759-2000, FAX: (512) 476-9007, E-Mail: info@texasmonthly.com, Web Site: www.texasmonthly.com (17)

Texas Parks & Wildlife Dept, Austin, TX. Tel: (512) 389-4800, (800) 792-1112, FAX: (512) 389-8029, Web Site: www.tpwd.state.tx.us (1)

Texas Refinery Corp, Fort Worth, TX. Tel: (817) 332-1161, FAX: (817) 336-8441, E-Mail: jhopkins@texasrefinery.com, Web Site: www.texasrefinery.com (9)

Texwipe Co, Kernersville, NC. Tel: (201) 684-1800, (800) TEXWIPE, FAX: (201) 684-1801, E-Mail: info@texwipe.com, Web Site: www.texwipe.com (16)

Teynor, Tom, Wolters Kluwer Financial Services, Minneapolis, MN. Tel: (612) 656-7724, Web Site: www.wolterskluwerfs.com (35)

Thackray, Tammy, JR Direct Response International Inc, Delta, BC Canada. Tel: (604) 940-0277, FAX: (604) 946-1419, E-Mail: tammythackray@jrdirect.com, Web Site: www.jrdirect.com (23)

Thain, John, A., Merrill Lynch, New York, NY. Tel: (212) 449-1000, (800) 637-7455, FAX: (212) 449-9418, Web Site: www.ml.com (14)

Thalheimer, Richard, The Sharper Image, New York, NY. Tel: (415) 445-6000, (800) 344-5555, FAX: (800) 552-2525, E-Mail: info@sharperimage.com, Web Site: www.sharperimage.com (6)

Thane International Inc, La Quinta, CA. Tel: (760) 777-0217, FAX: (760) 777-0214, Web Site: www.thane.com (35)

Tharler, Steven, R., THARLER DIRECTs, Wayland, MA. Tel: (508) 358-3554, Web Site: www.tharlerdirects.com (35)

THARLER DIRECTs, Wayland, MA. Tel: (508) 358-3554, Web Site: www.tharlerdirects.com (35)

Tharp, Michele, Paragon Media Strategies, Denver, CO. Tel: (303) 922-5600, FAX: (303) 922-1589, E-Mail: info@paragonmediastrategies.com, Web Site: www.paragonmediastrategies.com (30)

Thatcher, Michele, Frito-Lay, Plano, TX. Tel: (972) 334-7000, (800) 352-4477, FAX: (972) 334-2019, Web Site: www.fritolay.com (16)

Theatre Development Fund Inc, New York, NY. Tel: (212) 912-9770, E-Mail: info@tdf.org, Web Site: www.tdf.org (1)

Thebault, Brian, L.P. THEBAULT CO., Parsippany, NJ. Tel: (973) 884-1300, FAX: (973) 952-8296, Web Site: www.earthcolor.com (27)

Theiler, Thomas, Lancer Insurance Co, Long Beach, NY. Tel: (516) 431-4441, (800) 782-8902, FAX: (516) 889-5111, E-Mail: roneill@lancer-ins.com, Web Site: www.lancer-ins.com (15)

Theis, Peter, F., Conversational Voice Technologies Corp, Fox Lake, IL. Tel: (847) 265-4901, (800) 994-4400, FAX: (847) 265-4915, E-Mail: sales@conservit.com, Web Site: www.conservit.com (29)

TheLaw.net Corp, San Diego, CA. Tel: (858) 554-0583, Web Site: www.thelaw.net (22)

Thelen, Kris, Eclipse Direct Marketing, Mineola, NY. Tel: (212) 931-8344, FAX: (212) 931-8377, E-Mail: jkaiser@eclipsedm.com, Web Site: www.eclipsedm.com (23)

Theobald, Stanley, C., ASM International, Materials Park, OH. Tel: (440) 338-5151, (800) 336-5152, FAX: (440) 338-4634, E-Mail: customerservice@asminternational.org, Web Site: www.asminternational.org (1)

Theodore, Phil, John Harland Co, Decatur, GA. Tel: (770) 981-5580, (800) 723-3690, FAX: (770) 593-5367, E-Mail: jhhwebmaster@harland.net, Web Site: www.harland.net (17)

Theos, Charles, W., Micron Corp, Norwood, MA. Tel: (781) 769-5771, (800) 456-0734, FAX: (781) 762-3531, E-Mail: info@microncorp.com, Web Site: www.microncorp.com (16)

Theos, John, Micron Corp, Norwood, MA. Tel: (781) 769-5771, (800) 456-0734, FAX: (781) 762-3531, E-Mail: info@microncorp.com, Web Site: www.microncorp.com (16)

Theos, William, Micron Corp, Norwood, MA. Tel: (781) 769-5771, (800) 456-0734, FAX: (781) 762-3531, E-Mail: info@microncorp.com, Web Site: www.microncorp.com (16)

ThePort Network, Atlanta, GA. Tel: (703) 431-2208 (32)

Thermal Product Solutions, White Deer, PA. Tel: (570) 538-7200, (800) 586-2473 (16)

Thermo Fisher Scientific I, Waltham, MA. Tel: (781) 622-1000, (800) 678-5599, FAX: (781) 622-1207, Web Site: www.thermofisher.com (9)

Thermo Fisher Scientific SID, Madison, WI. Tel: (608) 276-6100, Web Site: www.thermo.com (9)

Thermo Pro, Duluth, GA. Tel: (678) 475-1647, (800) 523-5542, FAX: (678) 475-1747, Web Site: www.thermopro.com (16)

Theroux, David, J., Liberty Tree Network, Oakland, CA. Tel: (510) 568-6047, (800) 927-8733, FAX: (510) 568-6040, E-Mail: info@liberty-tree.com, Web Site: www.liberty-tree.org (5)

Thetford Corp, Ann Arbor, MI. Tel: (734) 769-6000, (800) 543-1219, FAX: (734) 769-2023, Web Site: www.thetford.com (16)

Thibadeau, Richard, AW Direct Inc, Madison, WI. Tel: (860) 828-7800, (800) 243-3194, FAX: (800) 828-9678, E-Mail: contactus@awdirect.com, Web Site: www.awdirect.com (12)

Thibeau, Matthew, Standard Publishing, Cincinnati, OH. Tel: (513) 931-4050, (800) 543-1301, FAX: (877) 867-5751, Web Site: www.standardpub.com (17)

Thieme, Alan, Amigo Mobility International Inc, Bridgeport, MI. Tel: (989) 777-0910, (800) 692-6446, FAX: (989) 777-8184, E-Mail: info@myamigo.com, Web Site: www.myamigo.com (16)

Thieme, Beth, Amigo Mobility International Inc, Bridgeport, MI. Tel: (989) 777-0910, (800) 692-6446, FAX: (989) 777-8184, E-Mail: info@myamigo.com, Web Site: www.myamigo.com (16)

Thieme Medical Publishers Inc, New York, NY. Tel: (212) 760-0888, (800) 782-3488, FAX: (212) 947-1112, E-Mail: info@thieme.com, Web Site: www.thieme.com (17)

Thies, Jeff, World Marketing, Inc (HQ), La Mirada, CA. Tel: (714) 994-6245, (800) 244-3003, FAX: (714) 776-2590, E-Mail: results@worldmarkinc.com, Web Site: www.worldmarkinc.com (21)

Thimband, Denver, CO. Tel: (303) 575-5676, FAX: (303) 575-1187, E-Mail: email@contentprovidermedia.info (17)

Things Deco, New York, NY. Tel: (212) 362-8961, E-Mail: thingsdeco@hotmail.com, Web Site: www.thingsdeco.com (6)

Things Remembered, Highland Heights, OH. Tel: (440) 473-2000, (866) 902-4438, FAX: (440) 473-2018, E-Mail: customerservice@thingsremembered.com, Web Site: www.thingsremembered.com (6)

Think Ink, Bothell, WA. Tel: (425) 778-1935, (800) 778-1935, E-Mail: jean.lewis1@comcast.net, Web Site: www.thinkink.net (10)

Think Shapes Mail, Tampa, FL. Tel: (813) 885-2225, (800) 889-4406, Web Site: www.jigsawprinting.com (27)

Thinkalytics, Millburn, NJ. Tel: (973) 671-1590, Web Site: www.thinkalytics.com (20)

ThinkDirect Marketing Group, Largo, FL. Tel: (727) 369-2700, E-Mail: info@tdmg.com, Web Site: www.tdmg.com (28)

Thirteen/WNET, New York, NY. FAX: (212) 560-1314, Web Site: www.thirteen.org (1)

Thoma, Carl, Thoma Cressey Bravo, Chicago, IL. Tel: (312) 777-4444, FAX: (312) 777-4445, Web Site: www.tcb.com (14)

Thoma Cressey Bravo, Chicago, IL. Tel: (312) 777-4444, FAX: (312) 777-4445, Web Site: www.tcb.com (14)

Thomas, Amy, Our Sunday Visitor Publishing, Huntington, IN. Tel: (260) 356-8400, (800) 348-2440, FAX: (260) 356-8472, E-Mail: athomas@osv.com, Web Site: www.osv.com (17)

Thomas, Andy, Marketfish Inc, Seattle, WA. Tel: (206) 905-1090, FAX: (206) 694-2564, Web Site: www.marketfish.com (23)

Thomas, Arleen R., American Institute of CPAs, New York, NY. Tel: (212) 596-6200, (888) 777-7077, FAX: (212) 596-6213, Web Site: www.aicpa.org (1)

Thomas, Brad, Liberty Orchards Co Inc, Cashmere, WA. Tel: (509) 782-2191, (800) 888-5696, FAX: (509) 782-1487, E-Mail: service@libertyorchards.com, Web Site: www.libertyorchards.com (16)

Thomas, Brad, The Guardian Life Insurance Co, New York, NY. Tel: (212) 598-8000, Web Site: www.guardianlife.com (15)

Thomas, Bret, Peter Li Education Group, Dayton, OH. Tel: (937) 293-1415, (800) 523-4625, FAX: (937) 293-1310, Web Site: www.peterli.com (17)

Thomas, Brian, Western Psychological Services, Torrance, CA. Tel: (310) 478-2061, (800) 648-8857, FAX: (310)) 478-7838, E-Mail: marketing@wpspublish.com, Web Site: www.wpspublish.com (16)

Thomas, Caroline, Resource Publications Inc, San Jose, CA. Tel: (408) 286-8505, (888) 273-7782, FAX: (408) 287-8748, E-Mail: info@rpinet.com, Web Site: www.rpinet.com (17)

Thomas, Cindy, Bank of Hawaii, Honolulu, HI. Tel: (808) 537-8398, FAX: (808) 536-9433, Web Site: www.boh.com (14)

Thomas, Darryl, K., Nautilus Inc, Vancouver, WA. Tel: (360) 859-2900, (800) 675-0171, FAX: (360) 694-2755, Web Site: www.nautilus.com (11)

Thomas, Daryl, Herr Foods Inc, Nottingham, PA. Tel: (610) 932-9330, (800) 344-3777, FAX: (610) 932-2137, E-Mail: info@herrs.com, Web Site: www.herrfoods.com (16)

Thomas, Dave, Market Force Corp, Newtown Square, PA. Tel: (610) 356-5220, FAX: (610) 356-5110, E-Mail: davethomas@marketforcecorp.com, Web Site: www.marketforcecorporation.com (23)

Thomas, David, Loyaltyworks Inc, Atlanta, GA. Tel: (678) 539-5000, (800) 844-5000, FAX: (678) 539-5173, Web Site: www.loyaltyworks.com (21)

Thomas, Dori, Jordan Direct, Phoenix, AZ. Tel: (623) 551-2728, FAX: (623) 551-2730, E-Mail: dori@jordandirect.net (23)

Thomas, James, ASTM International, West Conshohocken, PA. Tel: (610) 832-9500, FAX: (610) 832-9555, E-Mail: service@astm.org, Web Site: www.astm.org (1)

Thomas, Jerry W., Decision Analyst Inc, Arlington, TX. Tel: (817) 640-6166, (800) 262-5974, FAX: (817) 640-6567, E-Mail: jthomas@decisionanalyst.com, Web Site: www.decisionanalyst.com (30)

Thomas, Jerry, Greater Fort Worth Builders Association, Fort Worth, TX. Tel: (817) 284-3566, FAX: (817) 284-6465, E-Mail: info@fortworthbuilders.org, Web Site: www.forthworthbuilders.org (1)

Thomas, John, Children's Hospital Foundation, Washington, DC. Tel: (202) 476-3000, (800) 884-LIFE, FAX: (202) 884-5999, Web Site: www.dcchildrens.com (1)

Thomas, John, Wildseed Farms, Fredericksburg, TX. Tel: (830) 990-8080, (800) 848-0078, FAX: (830) 990-8090, E-Mail: orders1@wildseedfarms.com, Web Site: www.wildseedfarms.com (8)

Thomas, Jonathan, American Century Investments, Kansas City, MO. Tel: (816) 531-5575, (800) 345-2021, FAX: (816) 340-7962, Web Site: www.americancentury.com (14)

Thomas, Larry, Equitable Life & Casualty Insurance Co, Salt Lake City, UT. Tel: (801) 579-3400, FAX: (801) 579-3789, Web Site: www.equilife.com (15)

Thomas, Linda, Pennwell Publishing, Tulsa, OK. Tel: (918) 835-3161, (800) 331-4463, E-Mail: headquarters@pennwell.com, Web Site: www.pennwell.com (17)

Thomas, Lisa, Chase Media Group, Yorktown Heights, NY. Tel: (914) 962-3871, FAX: (914) 962-2040, Web Site: www.chasemultimedia.com (27)

Thomas, Lucille, Mitchell & Resnikoff/Weightman, Elkins Park, PA. Tel: (215) 635-1000, FAX: (215) 635-6542, E-Mail: info@mitch-res.com, Web Site: www.Mitch-Res.com (35)

Thomas, Matthew, Manning Materials, Birdsboro, PA. Tel: (610) 385-6797, (800) 445-1719, FAX: (610) 385-7524, E-Mail: mmsupport@manningmaterials.com, Web Site: www.manningmaterials.com (16)

Thomas, Michelle, Zappos.com, Henderson, NV. Tel: (702) 943-7832, Web Site: www.zappos.com (2)

Thomas, Nancy, PMDS Inc, Annapolis Junction, MD. Tel: (301) 604-3305 (28)

Thomas, Russell, Data Services Direct, Parsippany, NJ. Tel: (973) 331-8101, FAX: (973) 331-8108, Web Site: www.dataservicesdirect.com (29)

Thomas, Steve, Stephen Thomas, Toronto, ON Canada. Tel: (416) 690-8801, FAX: (416) 690-7256, E-Mail: mail@stephenthomas.ca, Web Site: www.stephenthomas.ca (1)

Thomas, Tara, Cobalt, Seattle, WA. Tel: (206) 269-6363, Web Site: www.cobalt.com (16)

Thomas Business Lists, New York, NY. Tel: (212) 695-0500, FAX: (212) 290-7362, E-Mail: contact@thomaspublishing.com, Web Site: www.thomaspublishing.com (24)

Thomas Computer Corp, Orlando, FL. Tel: (407) 855-2020, (800) 621-3906, FAX: (407) 426-2805, E-Mail: hildap@thomascompute.com, Web Site: www.thomascomputer.com (16)

Thomas Klise/Crimson Multimedia, Mystic, CT. Tel: (800) 937-0092, FAX: (860) 536-5141, E-Mail: info@crimsoninc.com, Web Site: www.crimsoninc.com (16)

Thomas Marketing Information Center, New York, NY. Tel: (212) 695-0500, FAX: (212) 290-7362, E-Mail: contact@thomaspublishing.com, Web Site: www.thomaspublishing.com (30)

Thomas Scientific, Swedesboro, NJ. Tel: (800) 345-2100, FAX: (856) 467-3087, E-Mail: value@thomassci.com, Web Site: www.thomassci.com (9)

Stephen Thomas, Toronto, ON Canada. Tel: (416) 690-8801, FAX: (416) 690-7256, E-Mail: mail@stephenthomas.ca, Web Site: www.stephenthomas.ca (1)

ThomasArts, Farmington, UT. Tel: (801) 451-5365, Web Site: www.thomasarts.com (35)

Thomez, Brittany, Brown Printing Co, New York, NY. Tel: (212) 782-7800, FAX: (212) 782-7878, E-Mail: contact.us@bpc.com, Web Site: www.bpc.com (27)

Thompsen, John, Brush Fire, Cedar Knolls, NJ. Tel: (973) 871-1700, FAX: (973) 871-1717, Web Site: www.brushfireinc.com (35)

Thompsen, Ken, ER Carpenter, Taylor, TX. Tel: (512) 365-5833, (800) 234-9105, FAX: (512) 352-6025, Web Site: www.carpenter.com (16)

Thompson, Barbara, International Crystal Manufacturing Co, Oklahoma City, OK. Tel: (405) 236-3741, (800) 252-6780, FAX: (405) 235-1904, E-Mail: info@icmfg.com, Web Site: www.icmfg.com (16)

Thompson, Bradley, L., Inland Press, Detroit, MI. Tel: (313) 961-6000, FAX: (313) 961-7817, Web Site: www.inlandpress.com (27)

Thompson, Cale, Oakley Inc, Foothill Ranch, CA. Tel: (949) 829-0991, Web Site: www.oakley.com (2)

Thompson, Carol, Christianity Today Inc, Carol Stream, IL. Tel: (630) 260-6200, FAX: (630) 260-0114, Web Site: www.christianitytoday.com (17)

Thompson, Charles, ACE Marketing Service, Smyrna, GA. Tel: (770) 431-2500, (800) 962-4514, FAX: (770) 431-2517, E-Mail: mail@ace-marketing.com, Web Site: www.ace-marketing.com (21)

Thompson, Edmund, A., Inter-Media Marketing Solutions, West Chester, PA. Tel: (800) 835-3466, FAX: (610) 429-5137, Web Site: www. intermediamarketing.com (29)

Thompson, Erica, PetSmart Inc, Phoenix, AZ. Tel: (623) 587-2009, (800) 738-1385, FAX: (623) 580-6183, Web Site: www.petsmart.com (5)

Thompson, Ernie, CPAC Inc, Leicester, NY. Tel: (585) 382-3223, (800) 828-6011, FAX: (585) 382-3031, E-Mail: cpacinfo@cpac.com, Web Site: www.cpac.com (16)

Thompson, Everton, Omega Direct Response Inc, Richmond Hill, ON. Tel: (905) 482-2340, FAX: (905) 482-9721, E-Mail: odrsales@omegadirect. com, Web Site: www.omegadirect.com (29)

Thompson, Janie, Carnegie Marketing Associates, Torrance, CA. Tel: (310) 540-4757, FAX: (310) 540-7407 (23)

Thompson, Jim, AAA-Chicago Motor Club, Aurora, IL. Tel: (847) 390-9000, (866) 968-7222, FAX: (847) 390-7738, Web Site: www.aaa.com (1)

Thompson, Jim, Ipsos-ASI Inc, Norwalk, CT. Tel: (203) 840-3400, FAX: (203) 840-3450, E-Mail: info@ipsos-asi.com, Web Site: www.ipsos-asi.com (30)

Thompson, Joan, E., David J Thompson Mailing Corp, Bloomsburg, PA. Tel: (570) 759-6690, FAX: (570) 759-7160, E-Mail: sales@thompsonmailing.com, Web Site: www.thompsonmailing.com (28)

Thompson, Karen, E., Josiah R Coppersmythe, Harwich, MA. Tel: (508) 432-8590, (800) 426-8249, FAX: (508) 432-8587, E-Mail: kethompson@ jrcoppersmythe.com, Web Site: www. jrcoppersmythe.com (8)

Thompson, Ken, Wachovia Bank, National Association, Charlotte, NC. Tel: (704) 590-0000, (800) WACHOVIA, FAX: (704) 427-6748 (14)

Thompson, Kevin, Buhrs Americas Inc, Minneapolis, MN. Tel: (763) 557-9100, FAX: (763) 557-9700, Web Site: www.buhrs.com (34)

Thompson, Larry, Martindale-Hubbell, New Providence, NJ. Tel: (908) 464-6800, (800) 526-4902, FAX: (908) 771-7740 (17)

Thompson, Laura, Goodyear Tire & Rubber Co, Akron, OH. Tel: (330) 796-3250, Web Site: www. goodyear.com (16)

Thompson, Lee, The Wexner Companies Inc, Memphis, TN. Tel: (901) 763-3925, (800) 890-5470, FAX: (901) 763-3736, E-Mail: info@JosephStores. com, Web Site: www.josephstores.com (2)

Thompson, Mace, Pachmayr Ltd, Middletown, CT. Tel: (800) 225-9626, FAX: (860) 632-1699, Web Site: www.lymanproducts.com (11)

Thompson, Martha, Ventyx, Atlanta, GA. Tel: (770) 952-8444, (800) 868-0497, FAX: (770) 955-2977, E-Mail: support@ventyx.com, Web Site: www. ventyx.com (16)

Thompson, Mike, Suez Energy North America, Houston, TX. Tel: (713) 636-0000, FAX: (713) 636-1364, Web Site: www.tractebelpowerinc.com (16)

Thompson, Richard, J., American Power Conversion Corp, West Kingston, RI. Tel: (401) 789-5735, (800) 788-2208, FAX: (401) 789-3710, E-Mail: public.relations@apcc.com, Web Site: www.apcc. com (3)

Thompson, Robert, AMVETS National Service Foundation, Lanham, MD. Tel: (301) 459-6181, (877) 726-8387, FAX: (301) 459-5578, Web Site: www. amvets.org (1)

Thompson, Robert, Dwyer Instruments Inc, Michigan City, IN. Tel: (219) 879-8868, Web Site: www. dwyer-inst.com (16)

Thompson, Roger, Group Mojo, Portland, OR. Tel: (503) 493-2242, FAX: (503) 493-2246, E-Mail: sam@mojops.com, Web Site: www.groupmojo.com (32)

Thompson, Scott, Cision US Inc, Chicago, IL. Tel: (312) 922-2400, (866) 639-5087, FAX: (312) 922-3126, E-Mail: info.us@cision.com, Web Site: us. cision.com (43)

Thompson, Sheldon, L., Sunoco, Inc, Philadelphia, PA. Tel: (215) 977-3000, (800) 786-6261, FAX: (215) 977-3409, E-Mail: sunoco_online@sunoil. com, Web Site: www.sunocoinc.com (16)

Thompson, Simon, ESRI, Redlands, CA. Tel: (909) 793-2853, Web Site: www.esri.com (22)

Thompson, Ted, Doner Direct, Baltimore, MD. Tel: (248) 354-9700, FAX: (248) 827-0880 (21)

Thompson & Co Marketing Communications, Memphis, TN. Tel: (901) 527-8000, FAX: (901) 527-3697, E-Mail: info@thompson-co.com, Web Site: www.thompson-co.com (21)

Thompson & Morgan Inc, Tipp City, OH. Tel: (732) 363-2225, (800) 274-7333, FAX: (888) 466-4769, E-Mail: tminc@thompson-morgan.com, Web Site: www.tmseeds.com (8)

Thompson Cigar Co, Tampa, FL. Tel: (813) 884-6344, (800) 237-2559, FAX: (813) 882-4605, Web Site: www.thompsoncigar.com (6)

David J Thompson Mailing Corp, Bloomsburg, PA. Tel: (570) 759-6690, FAX: (570) 759-7160, E-Mail: sales@thompsonmailing.com, Web Site: www.thompsonmailing.com (28)

Norm Thompson Outfitters Inc, Hillsboro, OR. Tel: (503) 614-4600, (800) 547-1160, FAX: (503) 614-4599, Web Site: www.normthompson.com (2)

Thompson Publishing Group Inc, Washington, DC. Tel: (202) 872-4000, (800) 677-3789, FAX: (800) 999-5661, E-Mail: service@thompson.com, Web Site: www.thompson.com (17)

Thompson-Hass, Ann, Larkwood Group LLC, Oakland, CA. Tel: (510) 444-7766 (1)

Thomson, Debbie, Weston Distance Learning, Fort Collins, CO. Tel: (970) 282-6322 (13)

Thomson, James, J&H Berge/The Lab Mart, South Plainfield, NJ. Tel: (908) 561-1234, FAX: (908) 561-3002, E-Mail: rgardner@labmart.com, Web Site: www.labmart.com (7)

Thomson, Joe, Sheridan Books Inc, Chelsea, MI. Tel: (734) 662-3291, (734) 475-9145, (800) 999-BOOK, FAX: (734) 475-7337, E-Mail: info@ sheridanbooks.com, Web Site: www.sheridanbooks. com (27)

Thomson, Carrollton, TX. Tel: (972) 250-7000, Web Site: www.thomson.com (34)

Thomson Financial, New York, NY. Tel: (212) 803-8200, FAX: (212) 843-9608 (17)

Thomson-Gale, Farmington Hills, MI. Tel: (800) 877-4253, FAX: (877) 363-4253, Web Site: www. galegroup.com (17)

Thomson Research, Boston, MA. Tel: (617) 856-2000, Web Site: www.thomson.com/solutions/financial (14)

Thomson Reuters LPC, New York, NY. Tel: (646) 223-6890, E-Mail: lpc.americas@reuters.com, Web Site: www.loanpricing.com (14)

Thomson Tax & Accounting, Dexter, MI. Tel: (800) 968-8900, FAX: (734) 426-3750, E-Mail: jack. larue@thomson.com, Web Site: www.cs.thomson. com (22)

Thomson West, Eagan, MN. Tel: (651) 687-7000, (800) 328-9378, FAX: (651) 687-7849, E-Mail: jeff.patrios@thomsonreuters.com, Web Site: www. thomson.com (17)

Thor Information Services Inc, Old Forge, NY. Tel: (315) 369-3872, FAX: (315) 369-2330, E-Mail: sales@thorinfo.com (23)

Thoren-Peden, Deborah, Pillsbury Winthrop Shaw Pittman LLP, Los Angeles, CA. Tel: (213) 488-7100, Web Site: www.pillsburywinthrop.com (20)

Thoreson, John, Sax Arts & Crafts, Appleton, WI. Tel: (800) 558-6696, FAX: (800) 328-4729, E-Mail: info@saxarts.com, Web Site: www.saxarts.com (10)

Thoreson, John, Walch Publishing, Portland, ME. Tel: (207) 772-2846, (800) 558-2846, FAX: (207) 772-3105, E-Mail: customerservice@walch.com, Web Site: www.walch.com (17)

THORLO INC, Statesville, NC. Tel: (704) 872-6522, (888) 846-7567, FAX: (704) 838-7005, Web Site: www.thorlo.com (16)

Thorndike Press, Waterville, ME. Tel: (207) 859-1000, (800) 223-1244, E-Mail: gale.salesassistance@ cengage.com, Web Site: www.galegroup.com (17)

Thorne, Philip, Goolara LLC, Alameda, CA. Tel: (510) 522-800, Web Site: www.goolara.com (32)

Thornhill Joynes, Barbara, The Martin Agency, Richmond, VA. Tel: (804) 698-8000, FAX: (804) 698-8001, Web Site: www.martinagency.com (35)

Thornley, Fred, General Printers, Oshawa, ON Canada. Tel: (416) 490-6000, (888) 718-6600, FAX: (905) 436-0813, E-Mail: thornley@ generalprinters.com, Web Site: www. generalprinters.com (27)

Thornsbury, Mike, DM Data Solutions LLC, Alexandria, VA. Tel: (703) 415-6222, Web Site: www. dmdatasolutions.com (22)

Thornton, Mike, Progress Printing Co, Lynchburg, VA. Tel: (434) 239-9213, (800) 527-7804, FAX: (434) 237-1618, Web Site: www.progressprinting.net (27)

Thornton, Richard, Key Mail Group of Companies, Buffalo, NY. Tel: (800) 863-3128, Web Site: www. key-mail.com (28)

Grant Thornton LLP, Philadelphia, PA. Tel: (215) 561-4200, FAX: (215) 561-1066, Web Site: www. grantthornton.com (20)

Thought Technology Ltd, Montreal, PQ Canada. Tel: (514) 489-8251, (800) 361-3651, FAX: (514) 489-8255, E-Mail: lawrence@thoughttechnology.com, Web Site: www.thoughttechnology.com (16)

Thousand Trails LP, Chicago, IL. Tel: (214) 618-7200, (800) 205-0606, FAX: (214) 618-7324, Web Site: www.1000trails.com (16)

Thouvenot, Janis, A., Universal Printing, Saint Louis, MO. Tel: (314) 771-6900, FAX: (314) 771-7987, E-Mail: info@universalprintingco.com, Web Site: www.universalprintingco.com (27)

3Com Corp, Littleton, MA. Tel: (508) 323-5000, FAX: (508) 323-1111 (22)

3D Mail Results, Kent, WA. FAX: (853) 859-7300 (5)

3 Gen Co, Brooklyn, NY. Tel: (718) 773-3388, FAX: (718) 467-0843 (23)

Three Georges and the Nuthouse, Mobile, AL. Tel: (334) 433-1689, FAX: (334) 433-3364, E-Mail: sales@threegeorges.com, Web Site: www. threegeorges.com (16)

3M Post-It Direct Response Products, Saint Paul, MN. Tel: (651) 733-1110, Web Site: www.mmm.com (16)

3PL Worldwide Inc, Milford, CT. Tel: (203) 567-1099, Web Site: www.3plworldwide.com (28)

Three Sixty Inc, Chicago, IL. Tel: (312) 255-0360, FAX: (312) 255-1932, E-Mail: 360@360-communications.com, Web Site: www.360-communications.com (35)

Threefold, Indianapolis, IN. Tel: (317) 607-1995, Web Site: www.certaindy.com (9)

ThreeSource Fulfillment, Manteno, IL. Tel: (815) 936-1094 x4179, (888) 673-4650, FAX: (815) 936-9743, E-Mail: sandyp@threesource.tv, Web Site: www.threesource.tv (28)

Thrivent Financial for Lutherans, Appleton, WI. Tel: (920) 734-5721, (800) 847-4836, FAX: (920) 730-4781, E-Mail: mail@thrivent.com, Web Site: www. thrivent.com (14)

Thulin, James, E., TCI Direct, Stateline, NV. Tel: (818) 752-1800, FAX: (818) 752-1808 (24)

Thum, Dennis, Kansas City Chiefs, Kansas City, MO. Tel: (816) 920-9300, (888) 99-CHIEFS, FAX: (816) 923-4719, Web Site: www.kcchiefs.com (16)

Thurston, Chris, Rightminds, Richmond, VA. Tel: (804) 755-7000, FAX: (804) 755-7200, Web Site: www.rightminds.com (35)

Thurton, Andra, CMA Awards, Don Mills, ON. Tel: (416) 391-2362, FAX: (416) 441-4062, E-Mail: info@the-cma.org, Web Site: www.the-cma.org/ awards (42)

Tian, Shawn, Thought Technology Ltd, Montreal, PQ. Tel: (514) 489-8251, (800) 361-3651, FAX: (514) 489-8255, E-Mail: lawrence@thoughttechnology. com, Web Site: www.thoughttechnology.com (16)

Tiburzio, Nancy, American Insurance Administrators Inc, Columbus, OH. Tel: (614) 486-5388, FAX: (614) 486-2728 (15)

Tickle, John, Strongwell, Bristol, VA. Tel: (276) 645-8000, FAX: (276) 645-8132, E-Mail: gbarefoot@ strongwell.com, Web Site: www.strongwell.com (9)

Tidbits Media, Montgomery, AL. Tel: (334) 290-0225, (800) 523-3096, FAX: (334) 386-0302, E-Mail: editors@tidbitsweekly.com, Web Site: www. tidbitsweekly.com (17)

Tidewater Direct LLC, Centreville, MD. Tel: (410) 758-1500, FAX: (410) 758-2478, Web Site: www. tidewaterdirect.com (27)

Tidewater Workshop, Egg Harbor City, NJ. Tel: (609) 965-4000, (800) 666-8433, FAX: (609) 965-8212, Web Site: www.tidewaterworkshop.com (8)

Tier, Robert, Smart DM, Toronto, ON Canada. Tel: (416) 461-9271, FAX: (416) 461-9201, E-Mail: info@smartdm.ca, Web Site: www.smartdm.ca (21)

Tiernan, Frank, Anritsu Co, Morgan Hill, CA. Tel: (408) 778-2000, (800) 267-4878, FAX: (408) 776-1744, Web Site: www.us.anritsu.com (16)

Tiernan, J.S., Brokers/Consultants Inc, Flossmoor, IL. Tel: (708) 957-2900, FAX: (708) 957-4155 (15)

Tiernan, Michael, W., The Mark Group, Boca Raton, FL. Tel: (561) 241-1700, (800) 637-0152, FAX: (561) 241-1055, Web Site: www.bostonproper.com (2)

Tierney Communications, Philadelphia, PA. Tel: (215) 790-4100, FAX: (215) 545-0188, Web Site: www. tierneyagency.com (35)

Tiffany & Co, New York, NY. Tel: (212) 755-8000, FAX: (212) 320-7550, Web Site: www.tiffany.com (6)

Tiger Direct Inc, Miami, FL. Tel: (305) 415-2200, (800) 800-8300, FAX: (305) 415-2202, Web Site: biz.tigerdirect.com (3)

TigerDirect.ca, Richmond Hill, ON Canada. Tel: (888) 771-9999, (800) 800-8300, FAX: (905) 482-3134, Web Site: www.tigerdirect.ca (3)

Tigert, Bob, Tigert Communications, Nashville, TN. Tel: (615) 298-9957, Web Site: www. tigertcommunications.com (35)

Tigert Communications, Nashville, TN. Tel: (615) 298-9957, Web Site: www.tigertcommunications. com (35)

Tighe, C.J., Aim Marketing, Fremont, NE. Tel: (402) 721-2077, FAX: (402) 721-9171, E-Mail: aim@ solution-group.com (28)

Tighe, Elizabeth, Fairchild Books, New York, NY. Tel: (212) 630-4171, (800) 932-4724, FAX: (212) 630-3868, Web Site: www.fairchildbooks.com (17)

Tignanelli, Bill, Admore Inc, Macomb, MI. Tel: (810) 949-8200, (800) 523-6673, FAX: (800) 215-2664, Web Site: www.admoreonline.com (10)

Tigner, Terry, Ronco Corp, Austin, TX. Tel: (800) 486-1806, E-Mail: customerservice@ronco.com, Web Site: www.ronco.com (16)

Tilghman, Robert, G., The Colonial Williamsburg Foundation, Williamsburg, VA. Tel: (757) 229-1000, (757) 220-7275, (800) 761-8331, Web Site: www.williamsburgmarketplace.com (1)

Till, Kimberly, Harris Interactive, New York, NY. Tel: (585) 272-8400, (800) 866-7655, FAX: (585) 272-8680, E-Mail: info@harrisinteractive.com, Web Site: www.harrisinteractive.com (30)

Tillamook County Creamery Association, Tillamook, OR. Tel: (503) 842-4481, (800) 542-7290, FAX: (503) 842-6039, Web Site: www.tillamookcheese. com (4)

Tilles, Kathy, Callaway Gardens, Pine Mountain, GA. Tel: (706) 663-2281, (800) CALLAWAY, FAX: (706) 663-6812, E-Mail: info@callawaygardens. com, Web Site: www.callawaygardens.com (19)

Tilley, Liz, Williamsburg Blacksmiths Inc, Williamsburg, MA. Tel: (413) 268-7341, (800) 248-1776, FAX: (413) 268-9317, Web Site: www. williamsburgblacksmiths.com (8)

Tilley, Matthew, CMS Inc, Winston Salem, NC. Tel: (336) 631-2524, Web Site: www. promotionslogistics.com (14)

Tilley, Matthew, Inmar, Winston-Salem, NC. Tel: (336) 631-2524, FAX: (336) 770-3470, E-Mail: ibizdev@inmar.com, Web Site: www. promotionslogistics.com (14)

Tillman M.D., David, Motion Picture & Television Fund Foundation, Woodland Hills, CA. Tel: (818) 876-1888, Web Site: www.mptvfund.org (1)

Tillman, Robert, Lowe's Companies Inc, Mooresville, NC. Tel: (704) 758-1000, FAX: (336) 651-4766, Web Site: www.lowes.com (8)

Tillman, Vickie A., Standard & Poor's Corp, New York, NY. Tel: (212) 438-2000, FAX: (212) 438-7375, Web Site: www.standardandpoors.com (17)

Tilmant, Michael, ING, Minneapolis, MN. Tel: (612) 342-7061, (800) 333-6965, FAX: (612) 372-5339, Web Site: www.ing.com (15)

Timber Crest Farms, Healdsburg, CA. Tel: (707) 433-8251, FAX: (707) 433-8255, E-Mail: tcf@sonic. net, Web Site: www.sonic.net/tcf (16)

Timberland.com, Stratham, NH. Tel: (603) 772-9500, Web Site: www.Timberland.com (16)

Timberline Geodesics, Berkeley, CA. Tel: (510) 849-4481, (800) 366-3466, FAX: (510) 849-3265, E-Mail: info@domehome.com, Web Site: www. domehome.com (8)

Timberline Interactive, Middlebury, VT. Tel: (802) 388-8377, Web Site: www.timberlineinteractive. com (20)

Timberline Total Solutions LLC, Omaha, NE. Tel: (402) 397-6945, (877) 575-2255, FAX: (402) 255-5045, E-Mail: rleavitt@timberlinesolutions.com (29)

Time Communications, Saint Paul, MN. Tel: (800) 486-8581, FAX: (612) 298-1945, E-Mail: info@ timecommunications.biz, Web Site: www. timecommunications.biz (29)

Time Customer Service Inc, Tampa, FL. Tel: (813) 878-6100, (800) 723-NCOA, FAX: (813) 878-6452, Web Site: www.timecustomerservice.com (22)

Time Inc, New York, NY. Tel: (212) 522-1212, Web Site: www.timeinc.com/home (17)

Time Logistics Inc, Columbia, TN. Tel: (931) 540-2801, (866) 293-8463, FAX: (931) 540-2995, Web Site: www.timelogisticsinc.com (12)

Time Motion Tools, Poway, CA. Tel: (800) 779-8170, FAX: (800) 779-8171, Web Site: www.timemotion. com (9)

Time Out New York, New York, NY. Tel: (646) 432-3000, FAX: (212) 677-9665, E-Mail: tnew@kable. com, Web Site: www.timeout.com/newyork/ (14)

Time Products International, Del Rio, TX. Tel: (847) 459-8885, FAX: (847) 459-8111, E-Mail: cttpi@ aol.com, Web Site: www.tpi2000.com (16)

Time/System, Chicopee, MA. Tel: (800) 637-9942, FAX: (800) 269-3075, E-Mail: customerservice@ timesystem.us, Web Site: www.timesystem.us (16)

Time Warner Inc, New York, NY. Tel: (212) 484-8000, Web Site: www.timewarner.com (16)

Times Publishing Co, Erie, PA. Tel: (814) 870-1600, FAX: (814) 870-1808, E-Mail: terry.cascioli@ timesnews.com (18)

Times Union, Albany, NY. Tel: (518) 454-5694, FAX: (518) 454-5628, Web Site: www.timesunion.com (18)

Timm, Gerry, Timm Medical Technologies, Inc, Eden Prairie, MN. Tel: (952) 947-9410, (800) 438-8592, FAX: (952) 947-9411, Web Site: www. timmmedical.com (16)

Timm Medical Technologies, Inc, Eden Prairie, MN. Tel: (952) 947-9410, (800) 438-8592, FAX: (952) 947-9411, Web Site: www.timmmedical.com (16)

Timothy, Mary, Anne, TRUSTe, San Francisco, CA. Tel: (415) 520-3490, Web Site: www.truste.org (22)

Tinberg, Rich, The Bradford Group, Niles, IL. Tel: (847) 966-2770, FAX: (847) 581-8630, Web Site: www.collectiblestoday.com (16)

Tinberg, Richard W., Collectibles Today Network, Ltd, Niles, IL. Tel: (800) 323-5577 #6, Web Site: www. collectiblestoday.com (16)

Tinberg, Richard, W., Hammacher Schlemmer, New York, NY. Tel: (847) 581-8600, (800) 233-4800, FAX: (847) 581-8616, Web Site: www.hammacher. com (16)

Tindall, Joe, Kid Stuff Marketing, Inc, Topeka, KS. Tel: (785) 862-3707, (800) 677-4712, FAX: (785) 862-0070, E-Mail: info@kidstuff.com, Web Site: www.kidsstuff.com (33)

Tinnon, John, Graphic Converting Inc, Elmhurst, IL. Tel: (630) 758-4100, (800) 447-1935, FAX: (630) 833-1058, E-Mail: sales@graphicconverting.com, Web Site: www.graphicconverting.com (36)

Tinsley III, Tuck, American Printing House for the Blind, Louisville, KY. Tel: (502) 895-2405, (800) 223-1839, FAX: (502) 899-2274, E-Mail: info@ aph.org, Web Site: www.aph.org (7)

Tinsley Tool Supply Inc, Powell, TN. Tel: (865) 681-9633, FAX: (865) 982-1655, E-Mail: gene@ tinsleytool.com, Web Site: www.tinsleytool.com (9)

Tippin Jr, Ross, S., Sunoco, Inc, Philadelphia, PA. Tel: (215) 977-3000, (800) 786-6261, FAX: (215) 977-3409, E-Mail: sunoco_online@sunoil.com, Web Site: www.sunocoinc.com (16)

Tipsord, Michael, L., State Farm Insurance Cos, Bloomington, IL. Tel: (309) 766-2311, FAX: (309) 766-3621, Web Site: www.statefarm.com (15)

Tira, Peter, McClatchy Co, Sacramento, CA. Tel: (916) 321-1855, FAX: (916) 321-1869, Web Site: www.mcclatchy.com (17)

Tirocchi, Bob, Bizzaro Rubber Stamps, Greenville, RI. Tel: (401) 231-8777, FAX: (401) 231-4770, E-Mail: bizzaroinc@earthlink.net, Web Site: www. bizzaro.com (6)

Tirocchi, Doreen, Bizzaro Rubber Stamps, Greenville, RI. Tel: (401) 231-8777, FAX: (401) 231-4770, E-Mail: bizzaroinc@earthlink.net, Web Site: www. bizzaro.com (6)

Tisch, Jonathan, Loews Hotels, New York, NY. Tel: (212) 521-2000, (866) 563-9792, FAX: (212) 545-2714, Web Site: www.loewshotels.com (19)

Tischler, Diane, Assisted Access- NFSS, Lake Villa, IL. Tel: (847) 265-8022, (800) 950-9655, FAX: (888) 552-1708, E-Mail: sales@nfss.com, Web Site: www.nfss.com (3)

Titan Manufacturing, Holbrook, MA. Tel: (781) 767-1963, Web Site: www.americantitan.com (34)

TitanTV Media, Cedar Rapids, IA. Tel: (319) 365-5597, (800) 365-7629, FAX: (319) 365-5694, E-Mail: mktg@titantv.com, Web Site: www.titantv. com (20)

Tittsworth, Barry, The Source, Huntsville, AL. Tel: (256) 536-7305, (800) 433-2375, FAX: (256) 539-8547, Web Site: www.thesource-wti.com (33)

Tiziani, Robert, Tiziani Whitmyre, Sharon, MA. Tel: (781) 793-9380, FAX: (781) 793-9395, E-Mail: info@tizinc.com, Web Site: www.tizinc.com (21)

Tiziani Whitmyre, Sharon, MA. Tel: (781) 793-9380, FAX: (781) 793-9395, E-Mail: info@tizinc.com, Web Site: www.tizinc.com (21)

TMone, Iowa City, IA. Tel: (868) 577-2461, E-Mail: srteam@tmone.com, Web Site: www.tmone.com (29)

Tobe, John, Tobe Direct, Louisville, KY. Tel: (502) 423-9898, Web Site: www.tobedirect.com (35)

Tobe Direct, Louisville, KY. Tel: (502) 423-9898, Web Site: www.tobedirect.com (35)

Toben, Doreen, F., Verizon Communications Inc, New York, NY. Tel: (212) 395-1000, (800) 621-9900, FAX: (212) 571-1897, Web Site: www.verizon.com (3)

Tobias, Christopher, Dudnyk Advertising & Public Relations, Horsham, PA. Tel: (215) 443-9406, (800) 438-3695, E-Mail: fpowers@dudnyk.com, Web Site: www.dudnyk.com (35)

The Peter A Tobin College of Business, Jamaica, NY. Tel: (718) 990-2600, FAX: (718) 990-1868, Web Site: www.stjohns.edu (41)

Tobol, Mitch, Tobol Group Inc, Amityville, NY. Tel: (516) 767-8182, FAX: (516) 767-8185, E-Mail: mt@tobolgroup.com, Web Site: www.tobolgroup.com (35)

Tobol Group Inc, Amityville, NY. Tel: (516) 767-8182, FAX: (516) 767-8185, E-Mail: mt@tobolgroup.com, Web Site: www.tobolgroup.com (35)

Tocquigny, Austin, TX. Tel: (512) 532-2800, Web Site: www.tocquigny.com (35)

Toda, Yuzo, Fuji Photo Film USA, Valhalla, NY. Tel: (914) 789-8100, (800) 755-3854, FAX: (914) 789-8295, Web Site: www.fujifilmusa.com (16)

Todaka, Toyoji, Seiko Corp of America, Mahwah, NJ. Tel: (201) 529-5730, FAX: (201) 529-1548, Web Site: www.seiko.com (16)

Todaro, Luciano, Todaro Brothers Mail Order Co, New York, NY. Tel: (877) 472-2767, FAX: (212) 689-1679, E-Mail: eat@todarobros.com, Web Site: www.todarobros.com (4)

Todaro Brothers Mail Order Co, New York, NY. Tel: (877) 472-2767, FAX: (212) 689-1679, E-Mail: eat@todarobros.com, Web Site: www.todarobros.com (4)

Today's Christian Woman, Carol Stream, IL. Tel: (630) 260-6200, FAX: (630) 260-0114, E-Mail: tcwedit@christianitytoday.com, Web Site: www.todayschristianwoman.net (31)

Todd, Kevin, Finelight Inc, Louisville, KY. Tel: (502) 589-5896, E-Mail: info@finelight.com, Web Site: www.finelight.com (35)

Todd, Michael, Mustek Inc, Tustin, CA. Tel: (949) 790-3800, FAX: (949) 788-3670, Web Site: www.mustek.com (3)

Todd, Patrick, The Travelers Insurance Cos, Hartford, CT. Tel: (860) 277-8252, (651) 317-2685, FAX: (860) 954-7691, Web Site: www.travelers.com (15)

Toennies, Melissa, Anheuser-Busch Inc Promotional Products Group, Shelton, CT. Tel: (800) 742-5283, Web Site: www.budshop.com (6)

Toepfer, Andy, Rubber Stamps of America, Dublin, NH. Tel: (800) 553-5031, FAX: (603) 563-8102, E-Mail: stampusa@verizon.net, Web Site: www.stampusa.com (6)

Toffler, Betsy-Ann, Dictionary of Marketing Terms, Hauppauge, NY. Tel: (631) 434-3311, (800) 645-3476, FAX: (631) 434-3723, E-Mail: barrons@barronseduc.com, Web Site: www.barronseduc.com (43)

The Tog Shop Inc, Beverly, MA. Tel: (800) 342-6789, FAX: (800) 755-7557, Web Site: www.togshop.com (2)

Together, Dallas, TX. Tel: (972) 407-1609, (800) 678-DATE, FAX: (972) 407-0082, Web Site: www.togetherdating.com (16)

Tognoli, Dawn, SF Video Inc, San Francisco, CA. Tel: (415) 288-9400, (800) 545-5865, FAX: (415) 288-9410, E-Mail: selfservice@sfvideo.com, Web Site: www.sfvideo.com (3)

Tokar, Bob, Wolverine Mailing & Packaging Warehouse, Detroit, MI. Tel: (313) 873-6800, FAX: (313) 873-8730, Web Site: www.wolverinemail.com (28)

Tokayer, Barry, TNT Packaging Inc, Miami, FL. Tel: (305) 769-0616, (305) 633-2556, (800) 327-6085, FAX: (305) 769-0619, E-Mail: tntpackaging@bellsouth.net, Web Site: www.tntpackaging.com (16)

Tokayer, Jeffrey, TNT Packaging Inc, Miami, FL. Tel: (305) 769-0616, (305) 633-2556, (800) 327-6085, FAX: (305) 769-0619, E-Mail: tntpackaging@bellsouth.net, Web Site: www.tntpackaging.com (16)

Tokheim, Sara, Brokers International Ltd, Panora, IA. Tel: (641) 755-2775 (20)

Toland, Laura, California Society of CPA's, San Mateo, CA. Tel: (800) 922-5272, FAX: (650) 522-3009, E-Mail: info@culcpa.org, Web Site: www.calcpa.org (1)

Toland Home and Garden Inc, Port Townsend, WA. Tel: (504) 893-9503, (800) 989-6287, E-Mail: info@tolandhomeandgarden.com, Web Site: www.tolandhomeandgarden.com (16)

Toledano, Sidney, Christian Dior Perfumes, New York, NY. Tel: (212) 931-2200, FAX: (212) 931-2954, Web Site: www.dior.com (7)

Tolf, Leslie, Union Privilege, AFL-CIO, Washington, DC. Tel: (202) 293-5330, FAX: (202) 293-5311, Web Site: www.unionplus.org (1)

Toliver, Bill, Sweetgrass, Seattle, WA. Tel: (206) 343-9000, FAX: (206) 447-2663, E-Mail: bill.toliver@sweetgrassadvertising.com, Web Site: www.sweetgrassadvertising.com (35)

TollFreeForwarding.com, Los Angeles, CA. Tel: (213) 452-1505, Web Site: www.tollfreeforwarding.com (29)

Tolliver Inc, New York, NY. Tel: (212) 758-7344, FAX: (212) 750-8617, E-Mail: tolliver12@aol.com (20)

Tolosa, Carlos, Caesars Palace, Las Vegas, NV. Tel: (702) 407-6000, (800) 634-6001, FAX: (702) 407-6037, Web Site: www.caesars.com (16)

Tolosa, Carlos, Harrah's Marketing, Reno, NV. Tel: (775) 786-3232, FAX: (775) 722-2815, Web Site: www.harrahsreno.com (16)

Tomahawk Live Trap Co, Tomahawk, WI. Tel: (715) 453-3550, (800) 272-8727, FAX: (715) 453-4326, E-Mail: trapem@livetrap.com, Web Site: www.livetrap.com (16)

Toman, John, American Institute of CPAs, New York, NY. Tel: (212) 596-6200, (888) 777-7077, FAX: (212) 596-6213, Web Site: www.aicpa.org (1)

Tomasone, Marina, Toronto Hydro-Electric System, Toronto, ON Canada. Tel: (416) 542-2743, Web Site: www.torontohydro.com (1)

Tome, Carol, B., The Home Depot Inc, Atlanta, GA. Tel: (770) 433-8211, (800) 430-3376, FAX: (770) 384-2356, Web Site: www.homedepot.com (16)

Tomilson, Mark, Society of Manufacturing Engineers, Dearborn, MI. Tel: (313) 425-3000, (800) 733-4763, FAX: (313) 425-3400, E-Mail: communications@sme.org, Web Site: www.sme.org (1)

Tomlinson, Kate, S., New Jersey Monthly, Morristown, NJ. Tel: (973) 539-8230, FAX: (973) 538-2953, E-Mail: research@njmonthly.com, Web Site: www.njmonthly.com (17)

Tomlinson, William, J., Compass Communications Inc, Excelsior, MN. Tel: (952) 470-2017, Web Site: www.compasscommunications.com (35)

Tomlinson, William, Professional Training Associates Inc, Duquesne, PA. Tel: (412) 460-0266, FAX: (412) 460-0269, E-Mail: info@ptainc.com, Web Site: www.ptainc.com (17)

Tompkins, Hope, Bedford/St Martin's, Boston, MA. Tel: (617) 426-7440, FAX: (617) 426-8582, Web Site: www.bedfordstmartins.com (17)

TomTom North American, Lebanon, NH. Tel: (603) 643-0330, (800) 331-7881, FAX: (603) 653-0249, Web Site: www.tomtom.com (22)

Toner, Frank, Newsday, Melville, NY. Tel: (631) 843-2020, FAX: (631) 843-5424, Web Site: www.newsday.com (17)

Tong, Amy, UNICEF Canada, Toronto, ON. Tel: (416) 482-4444, (800) 567-4483, FAX: (416) 487-8875, E-Mail: on.secretary@unicef.ca, Web Site: www.unicef.ca (1)

Tong, Peter, Abbey of Gethsemani, New Haven, KY. Tel: (502) 549-3117, FAX: (502) 549-4124, Web Site: www.monks.org (1)

Tonge, Charles, R., Harris Bancorp Inc, Chicago, IL. Tel: (312) 461-7961, (888) 340-BANK, FAX: (312) 461-7869, E-Mail: onlineservices@harrisbank.com, Web Site: www.harrisbank.com (14)

Tongue, Tom, Sheplers Catalog Sales Inc, Wichita, KS. Tel: (316) 946-3838, (800) 835-4004, FAX: (316) 946-3729, Web Site: www.sheplers.com (2)

Tony Stone Images, Chicago, IL. Tel: (800) 234-7880, FAX: (312) 922-9075, Web Site: www.gettyimages.com (38)

Tools for Wellness, Oak Park, CA. Tel: (800) 456-9887, FAX: (818) 532-1775, E-Mail: info@toolsforwellness.com, Web Site: www.toolsforwellness.com (7)

Top USA Corp, Worthington, OH. Tel: (614) 431-1601, (800) 843-3381, FAX: (614) 431-1239, E-Mail: info@topusa.com, Web Site: www.topusa.com (27)

Top Year International Inc, Yorba Linda, CA. Tel: (714) 692-6688, (800) 942-8722, FAX: (714) 692-8691, E-Mail: sales@akirausa.com, Web Site: www.akirausa.com (33)

Topak Marketing Inc, Philadelphia, PA. Tel: (215) 574-8307, FAX: (215) 574-8316 (35)

Topec, Marsha, Cytec Industries Inc, Olean, NY. Tel: (716) 372-9650, FAX: (716) 372-1594, Web Site: www.conap.com (16)

Topitzes, Nick, PC/Nametag Inc, Verona, WI. Tel: (608) 845-1850, (800) 233-9767, E-Mail: sales@pcnametag.com, Web Site: www.pcnametag.com (16)

Topol, Bruce, Eyeglass Service Industries, Lynbrook, NY. Tel: (516) 599-1135, FAX: (516) 599-4825 (2)

Topp, John, W., Topp Direct Marketing, Harlingen, TX. Tel: (956) 421-5750, FAX: (956) 421-5721, E-Mail: info@toppmarketing.com (21)

Topp Direct Marketing, Harlingen, TX. Tel: (956) 421-5750, FAX: (956) 421-5721, E-Mail: info@toppmarketing.com (21)

TopRank Online Marketing, Mound, MN. Tel: (952) 400-0194, Web Site: www.toprankresults.com (32)

Torago, Joe, Irresistible Ink Inc, Duluth, MN. Tel: (218) 336-4200, (800) 543-8396, Web Site: www.irresistibleink.com (28)

Torah Umesorah Publications, Brooklyn, NY. Tel: (212) 227-1000, E-Mail: umesorah@aol.com, Web Site: torah-umesorah.com (5)

Toran, Daniel, J., Penn Mutual, Horsham, PA. Tel: (215) 956-8083, FAX: (215) 956-8368, Web Site: www.pennmutual.com (15)

Torcom Inbound Telemarketing, Madison, WI. Tel: (800) 832-4939, FAX: (608) 275-6557, E-Mail: torcom@torcom.com, Web Site: www.torcom.com (29)

Tordella, Stephen, J., Decision Demographics, Arlington, VA. Tel: (703) 931-9200, FAX: (703) 527-1448, E-Mail: tordella@decision-demographics.com, Web Site: www.decision-demographics.com (30)

Torgerson, Dell, Replogle Globes Inc, Broadview, IL. Tel: (708) 343-0900, FAX: (708) 343-0923, E-Mail: info@replogleglobes.com, Web Site: www.replogleglobes.com (16)

Toriello, Richard, Americalist, North Canton, OH. Tel: (330) 494-9111, (888) 219-LIST, FAX: (330) 494-0226, Web Site: www.americalist.com (21)

Torio, Michael, National Journal Group, Washington, DC. Tel: (202) 266-7541 (17)

The Toro Consumer Div, Bloomington, MN. Tel: (952) 888-8801, (888) 384-9939, FAX: (952) 887-8258, Web Site: www.thetorocompany.com (16)

Toronto Hydro-Electric System, Toronto, ON Canada. Tel: (416) 542-2743, Web Site: www.torontohydro.com (1)

Torqmaster International, Stamford, CT. Tel: (203) 326-5945, (888) 414-4643, FAX: (203) 326-5944, E-Mail: info@torqmaster.com, Web Site: www.torqmaster.com (9)

Torvik, Elin, Torcom Inbound Telemarketing, Madison, WI. Tel: (800) 832-4939, FAX: (608) 275-6557, E-Mail: torcom@torcom.com, Web Site: www.torcom.com (29)

Toschak, Barb, GlaserDirect Inc, Glen Ellyn, IL. Tel: (630) 469-2075, FAX: (630) 790-5244, E-Mail: jglaser@glaserdirect.com, Web Site: www.glaserdirect.com (23)

Total Care, Rockville, MD. Tel: (301) 251-2061, (800) 334-3802, FAX: (301) 251-5891, E-Mail: totalcare@sprintmail.com, Web Site: www.totalmedinc.com (7)

Total Data Solutions, North Andover, MA. Tel: (978) 686-2311, Web Site: www.ttldatasolutions.com (23)

The Total Mailing System, West Deptford, NJ. Tel: (856) 628-8800, FAX: (856) 628-8810, Web Site: www.ttms.com (22)

Total Training Solutions LLC, Waunakee, WI. Tel: (608) 849-5563, (800) 831-0678, FAX: (608) 849-5605, (800) 831-3776, E-Mail: kbennett@ttstrain.com, Web Site: www.ttstrain.com (5)

Toter Inc, Statesville, NC. Tel: (704) 872-8171, (800) 424-0422, FAX: (704) 878-0734, E-Mail: info@toter.com, Web Site: www.toter.com (16)

Tott, Carl, AB Lambdin Inc, Hampton, VA. Tel: (800) 528-9817, FAX: (800) 221-9231, E-Mail: service@ablambdin.com (2)

Totton, Patricia, TeleServices Direct, Indianapolis, IN. Tel: (888) 646-6626, Web Site: www.teleservicesdirect.com (29)

Touch-Base Computing, Silver Creek, GA. Tel: (706) 378-0964, E-Mail: sales@touchbase.com, Web Site: www.touchbase.com (22)

Touch of Class Catalog, Huntingburg, IN. Tel: (812) 683-3707, (800) 457-7456, FAX: (812) 683-5921, Web Site: www.touchofclasscatalog.com (8)

Touchpoint Data Solutions, Cumming, GA. Tel: (770) 886-8611, Web Site: www.touchpointdata.com (23)

Toulantis, Marie, J., BarnesandNoble.com, New York, NY. Tel: (212) 414-6000, (800) THE-BOOK, FAX: (212) 414-6140, E-Mail: service@barnesandnoble.com, Web Site: www.barnesandnoble.com (16)

Tova Corp, West Chester, PA. Tel: (484) 701-1000, Web Site: www.beautybytova.com (7)

Towell, Leonor, Amanet, Canoga Park, CA. Tel: (818) 786-1113, FAX: (818) 786-5736, E-Mail: info@amanet-usa.com, Web Site: www.amanet.com (16)

Tower Hobbies/Hobbico, Champaign, IL. Tel: (217) 398-3636, (800) 637-6050, FAX: (217) 398-1104, Web Site: www.towerhobbies.com (11)

Tower Media Advertising Inc, Chicago, IL. Tel: (312) 856-9200, FAX: (312) 856-1300, E-Mail: info@towermedia.com, Web Site: www.towermedia.com (35)

TowerData, New York, NY. Tel: (646) 742-1771, Web Site: www.towerdata.com (32)

Towers Watson, New York, NY. Tel: (212) 725-7550, FAX: (212) 644-7432, Web Site: www.towerswatson.com (20)

Towle, Steve, DST Output, South Windsor, CT. Tel: (860) 290-7337, (800) 441-7587, Web Site: www.dstoutput.com (28)

Town Money Saver, Lucas, OH. Tel: (419) 892-1913, Web Site: www.townmoneysaver.com (31)

Towne Allpoints Communications, Santa Ana, CA. Tel: (714) 540-3095, (800) 243-8099, FAX: (714) 540-4192, E-Mail: info@towne.com, Web Site: www.towne.com (21)

Towner, Joyce, Alexian Brothers Bonaventure House, Chicago, IL. Tel: (773) 327-9921, FAX: (773) 327-9113, E-Mail: info@abam.org, Web Site: www.bonaventurehouse.org (1)

Towns, Faye, Mountain West Supply Co, Scottsdale, AZ. Tel: (602) 971-1200, (800) 528-6169, FAX: (602) 996-5077 (3)

Townsend III, H. Guyon, Townsend Communications LLC, Kansas City, MO. Tel: (816) 361-0616, (800) 274-8867, FAX: (816) 361-6164, Web Site: www.townsendprint.com (17)

Townsend Jr., H.G., Townsend Communications LLC, Kansas City, MO. Tel: (816) 361-0616, (800) 274-8867, FAX: (816) 361-6164, Web Site: www.townsendprint.com (17)

Townsend, Michael J., New York Power Authority, Albany, NY. Tel: (518) 433-6700, Web Site: www.nypa.gov (16)

Townsend Communications LLC, Kansas City, MO. Tel: (816) 361-0616, (800) 274-8867, FAX: (816) 361-6164, Web Site: www.townsendprint.com (17)

The Townsend Group, New York, NY. Tel: (212) 304-9069, Web Site: livemusicguide.com (3)

Toyota Motor Sales USA Inc, Torrance, CA. Tel: (310) 468-4000, (800) 331-4331, FAX: (310) 468-7841, Web Site: www.toyota.com (16)

Toyota Racing Development USA Inc, Costa Mesa, CA. Tel: (714) 444-1188, FAX: (714) 444-0339, Web Site: www.trdusa.com (34)

Toys "R" Us, Wayne, NJ. Tel: (973) 617-5879, FAX: (973) 617-4006, Web Site: www.toysrus.com (11)

Toys To Grow On, Carson, CA. Tel: (310) 537-8600, (800) 874-4242, FAX: (800) 537-5403, E-Mail: toyinfo@toystogrowon.com, Web Site: www.ttgo.com (11)

Trabucco, Robert, Sterling Jewelers Inc, Akron, OH. Tel: (330) 668-5000, FAX: (330) 668-5052, E-Mail: webmaster@jewels.com, Web Site: www.sterlingjewelers.com (16)

Tractor Supply Co, Brentwood, TN. Tel: (615) 366-4600, (877) 872-7721, FAX: (615) 227-4608, Web Site: www.mytscstore.com (5)

Tracy, Richard, Optronics Inc, Muskogee, OK. Tel: (918) 683-9514, (800) 364-5483, FAX: (918) 683-9517, E-Mail: sales@optronicsinc.com, Web Site: www.optronicsinc.com (11)

Tracy Locke Partnership, Dallas, TX. Tel: (214) 969-9000, FAX: (214) 259-3550, E-Mail: tlpinfo@tlp.com, Web Site: www.tlp.com (35)

Trade Show Exhibitors Association, Chicago, IL. Tel: (312) 842-8732, FAX: (312) 842-8744, Web Site: www.tsea.org (42)

TradeNet Publishing Inc, Gardner, KS. Tel: (800) 884-7301, Web Site: www.tradenetonline.com (35)

Trahan, Connie, Biomerica Inc, Irvine, CA. Tel: (949) 645-2111, FAX: (949) 722-6674, E-Mail: bmra@biomerica.com, Web Site: www.biomerica.com (7)

Traina, Sharon, Conrad Direct Inc, Cresskill, NJ. Tel: (201) 567-3200, FAX: (201) 567-1530, Web Site: www.conraddirect.com (23)

Training Consultants Inc, Highland Park, IL. Tel: (847) 432-9428, FAX: (847) 432-9318, E-Mail: wetrain2@home.com (20)

Trainor, Chris, Direct Mail Depot Inc, Piscataway, NJ. Tel: (732) 469-5900, FAX: (732) 469-8414, E-Mail: sales@directmaildepot.com, Web Site: www.directmaildepot.com (28)

Traister, Scott, Arquest Inc, Millstone Twp, NJ. Tel: (609) 395-9500, (888) ARQUEST, (888) 270-8378, FAX: (609) 395-9778, Web Site: www.arquest.com (16)

Tram, Michael, Arthur D Little Inc, Boston, MA. Tel: (617) 532-9550, FAX: (617) 261-6630, Web Site: www.adlittle-us.com (20)

Trancos Inc, Pleasanton, CA. Tel: (650) 364-3110, Web Site: www.trancos.com (16)

Trandem, Don, Win Craft Inc, Winona, MN. Tel: (507) 454-5510, (800) 533-8100, FAX: (507) 454-6403, Web Site: www.wincraftschool.com (5)

Trani, Louis, Equitable Life & Casualty Insurance Co, Salt Lake City, UT. Tel: (801) 579-3400, FAX: (801) 579-3789, Web Site: www.equilife.com (15)

Trans Continental Inc, Montreal, PQ Canada. Tel: (514) 954-4000, FAX: (514) 954-4016, Web Site: www.transcontinental-gtc.com (31)

Trans Union Corp, Chicago, IL. Tel: (312) 258-1717, (800) 335-9888, FAX: (312) 466-8385, Web Site: www.transunion.com (14)

Transaction Publishers, Piscataway, NJ. Tel: (732) 445-1245, FAX: (732) 748-9801, E-Mail: trans@transactionpub.com, Web Site: www.transactionpub.com (17)

Transamerica Life & Protection, Baltimore, MD. Tel: (410) 209-5617, Web Site: www.aegondms.com (15)

Transamerica Life Insurance Co, Cedar Rapids, IA. Tel: (319) 398-8511, (800) 558-9011, FAX: (319) 369-2825, Web Site: www.transamerica.com (15)

Transamerica Occidental Life Co, Los Angeles, CA. Tel: (213) 742-3111, FAX: (213) 741-6623, Web Site: www.transamerica.com (15)

TransAmerica Retirement Services, Los Angeles, CA. Tel: (213) 742-3363, Web Site: www.ta-retirement.com (15)

Transamerican Mailing, Escondido, CA. Tel: (760) 745-5343, Web Site: www.transdirect.com (20)

Transcat, Rochester, NY. Tel: (585) 352-9460, (800) 800-5001, FAX: (585) 352-1486, Web Site: www.transcat.com (16)

Transcontinental Interactive, Montreal, PQ Canada. Tel: (514) 954-4000, FAX: (514) 954-4016 (35)

TransContinental Yorkville - O'Keefe, Etobicoke, ON Canada. Tel: (416) 741-1900, (800) 361-9690, FAX: (416) 401-2220, Web Site: www.transcontinentalprinting.com (27)

Transemantics Inc, Washington, DC. Tel: (202) 362-2505, FAX: (202) 686-5603, E-Mail: ili@transemantics.com, Web Site: www.transemantics.com (16)

TransFirst ePayment Services, Omaha, NE. Tel: (888) 541-9800, Web Site: epay.transfirst.com (14)

TransFirst Holdings Inc, Dallas, TX. Tel: (214) 453-7700, (888) 254-4137, FAX: (214) 453-7739, Web Site: www.transfirst.com (14)

Transglobal Consultants Inc, Canton, OH. Tel: (330) 477-6450, E-Mail: transglobal@earthlink.net (20)

Transit Treasure Inc, New York, NY. Tel: (646) 706-1001, Web Site: www.transittreasure.com (12)

TransitCenter Inc, New York, NY. Tel: (212) 329-2000, Web Site: www.transitcenter.com (1)

TRANZACT, Fort Lee, NJ. Tel: (201) 461-5665, Web Site: www.tranzact.net (35)

Traola, John, Bobley-Harmann Corp/GiftValues.Com, Westbury, NY. Tel: (516) 364-1800, (800) 323-1692, FAX: (516) 364-1899, E-Mail: info@bobley.com, Web Site: www.bobley.com; www.montefiorepens.com (5)

Traum, Happy, Homespun Tapes Music Instruction, Woodstock, NY. Tel: (845) 246-2550, (800) 338-2737, FAX: (845) 246-5282, E-Mail: info@homespuntapes.com, Web Site: www.homespuntapes.com (3)

Traum, Jane, Homespun Tapes Music Instruction, Woodstock, NY. Tel: (845) 246-2550, (800) 338-2737, FAX: (845) 246-5282, E-Mail: info@homespuntapes.com, Web Site: www.homespuntapes.com (3)

Trautmann, Kathleen, Zurich, Schaumburg, IL. Tel: (847) 605-3712, (800) 382-2150, FAX: (847) 605-6403, Web Site: www.zurichna.com (15)

Travel Industry Association, Washington, DC. Tel: (202) 408-8422, FAX: (202) 408-1255, E-Mail: feedback@tia.org, Web Site: www.tia.org (1)

Travel Planners Inc, New York, NY. Tel: (212) 532-1660, (800) 221-3531, FAX: (212) 779-6102, Web Site: www.tphousing.com (19)

Travelclick, Schaumburg, IL. Tel: (847) 585-5016 (19)

The Travelers Insurance Cos, Hartford, CT. Tel: (860) 277-8252, (651) 317-2685, FAX: (860) 954-7691, Web Site: www.travelers.com (15)

Travelex America Inc, Washington, DC. Tel: (202) 408-1200, FAX: (202) 513-5215, Web Site: business.travelex.com/us (14)

Travers, Will, Born Free USA, Sacramento, CA. Tel: (916) 447-3085, FAX: (916) 447-3070, E-Mail: info@bornfreeusa.org, Web Site: www.bornfreeusa.org (1)

Traverso, Mark, Lighthouse List Co, Pompano Beach, FL. Tel: (954) 489-3008, (800) 684-2180, FAX: (954) 489-0850, E-Mail: mtlistdude@aol.com, Web Site: www.lighthouselist.com (24)

Travis Jr., Richard, L., Ennis Inc, Midlothian, TX. Tel: (972) 775-9801, (800) 962-0944, FAX: (800) 645-8339, Web Site: www.ennis.com (16)

Travis, Mark, TransFirst Holdings Inc, Dallas, TX. Tel: (214) 453-7700, (888) 254-4137, FAX: (214) 453-7739, Web Site: www.transfirst.com (14)

Traylor, Shawn, Reliance Electric, Fort Smith, AR. Tel: (479) 646-4711, FAX: (479) 648-5792, E-Mail: smtraylor@powersystems.rockwell.com, Web Site: www.reliance.com (9)

Treasure Chest, New York, NY. Tel: (212) 590-2332, Web Site: treasurechestonline.com (19)

Treis, James, Arandell Corp, Menomonee Falls, WI. Tel: (262) 255-4400, (800) 558-8724, FAX: (262) 253-3162, E-Mail: jft@arandell.com, Web Site: www.arandell.com (27)

Treizman, Eddie, Dial 800 LLC, Los Angeles, CA. Tel: (310) 273-9023, (800) 564-8685, Web Site: www.dial800.com (32)

Treland, Terrie, Boelter + Lincoln Marketing Communications, Milwaukee, WI. Tel: (414) 271-0101, FAX: (414) 271-1436, Web Site: www.boelterlincoln.com (35)

Trellist Marketing and Technology, Wilmington, DE. Tel: (302) 778-1300, Web Site: www.trellist.com (30)

Tremblay, Lorene, Amanet, Canoga Park, CA. Tel: (818) 786-1113, FAX: (818) 786-5736, E-Mail: info@amanet-usa.com, Web Site: www.amanet.com (16)

Trend Magazines Inc, Saint Petersburg, FL. Tel: (727) 821-5800, (800) 821-5800, FAX: (727) 822-5083, E-Mail: feedback@fltrend.com, Web Site: www.floridatrend.com (17)

Trends International LLC, Indianapolis, IN. Tel: (317) 388-1212, (800) 354-4639, FAX: (317) 388-1414, E-Mail: info@trendsinternational.com, Web Site: www.trendsinternational.com (38)

Trent, Fred, Lundmark Advertising & Design Inc, Kansas City, MO. Tel: (816) 842-5236, FAX: (816) 221-7175, Web Site: www.lundonline.net (35)

Treul, Nancy, Foremost Insurance Group, Grand Rapids, MI. Tel: (616) 956-8241, (800) 527-3905, FAX: (800) 325-1507, Web Site: www.foremost.com (15)

Trevalyan, Jan, A., Direct Data Capture Ltd, Huntington Station, NY. Tel: (631) 547-5500, FAX: (631) 547-6800, E-Mail: jan@datacapture.com, Web Site: www.datacapture.com (22)

Trevaskis, Judith, Progressive Energy Corp, San Marcos, CA. Tel: (760) 727-2906, (800) 525-8624, FAX: (760) 727-0947, E-Mail: patrickkilleen@cox.net (5)

Trevvett, Herbert, E., Commercial Travelers Mutual Insurance Co, Utica, NY. Tel: (315) 797-5200, (800) 422-6200, FAX: (315) 797-3198, E-Mail: comtravl@commercialtravelers.com, Web Site: www.commercialtravelers.com (15)

Trevvett, Paul H., Commercial Travelers Mutual Insurance Co, Utica, NY. Tel: (315) 797-5200, (800) 422-6200, FAX: (315) 797-3198, E-Mail: comtravl@commercialtravelers.com, Web Site: www.commercialtravelers.com (15)

Tri-Chem Inc, Belleville, NJ. Tel: (973) 751-9200, FAX: (973) 450-1057, (973) 450-1260, E-Mail: paints@trichem.com, Web Site: www.trichem.com (16)

Tri-Media Marketing Services Inc, Wilmette, IL. Tel: (800) 874-4062, Web Site: www.trimediaonline.com (23)

Tri-State Advertising Co Inc, Warsaw, IN. Tel: (574) 267-5178, FAX: (574) 267-2965, E-Mail: info@tri-stateadv.com, Web Site: www.tri-stateadv.com (35)

Tri-State Envelope Corp, Ashland, PA. Tel: (570) 875-0433, (800) 233-3102, FAX: (570) 875-0125, E-Mail: tsecny@attglobal.net, Web Site: www.tristateenvelope.com (26)

Tri Tech Laboratories Inc, Lynchburg, VA. Tel: (434) 845-7073, FAX: (434) 847-4360, Web Site: www.tritechlabs.com (16)

Triangle Marketing Services Inc, New York, NY. Tel: (212) 242-4040, FAX: (212) 242-1344, Web Site: www.tms-ny.com (23)

Triangle Printers Inc, Skokie, IL. Tel: (847) 675-3700, FAX: (847) 674-1230, E-Mail: blevin@triangleprinters.com, Web Site: www.triangleprinters.com (27)

Triax Data, Knoxville, TN. Tel: (865) 971-4333, Web Site: www.triaxdata.com (23)

Tribley, Mary, Ellen, Weiss Research Inc, Jupiter, FL. Tel: (561) 627-3300, (877) 925-4833, FAX: (561) 625-6685, E-Mail: newbusiness@weissgroupinc.com, Web Site: www.weissgroupinc.com (17)

Tribune Co, Chicago, IL. Tel: (312) 222-9100, FAX: (312) 222-1573, Web Site: www.tribune.com (17)

Tribune Direct Marketing, Northlake, IL. Tel: (708) 836-2712, Web Site: www.tribunedirect.com (28)

Trice, Robert, Lockheed Martin Corp, Bethesda, MD. Tel: (301) 897-6000 (16)

Tricor Braun, Woodridge, IL. Tel: (708) 385-9333, FAX: (708) 385-3015, Web Site: www.tricorbraun.com (16)

Tricor Direct Inc/Seton, Branford, CT. Tel: (800) 243-6624, E-Mail: custsvc_setonus@seton.com, Web Site: www.seton.com (9)

Tridium Inc, Richmond, VA. Tel: (804) 525-1648, Web Site: www.tridium.com (9)

Triggerfish Marketing, San Francisco, CA. Tel: (415) 671-4699, Web Site: www.triggerfish.com (30)

Trigon Blue Cross/Blue Shield, Roanoke, VA. Tel: (540) 853-5000, (800) 553-3164, FAX: (540) 853-3053, Web Site: www.trigon.com (15)

Trilithic, Indianapolis, IN. Tel: (317) 423-6604, Web Site: www.trilithic.com (16)

Trimberger, John, Stephen Fossler Co Inc, Des Plaines, IL. Tel: (800) 762-0030, FAX: (800) 424-9292, E-Mail: customerservice@fossler.com, Web Site: sfc.stephen-fossler.com (27)

Trimensions Inc, Englewood, NJ. Tel: (212) 254-5554, FAX: (212) 473-6524 (21)

Trine, David, E., Choice Point, Alpharetta, GA. Tel: (770) 752-6000, (800) 342-5339, FAX: (770) 752-6005, Web Site: www.choicepoint.com (16)

Trinity Communications Inc, Boston, MA. Tel: (617) 292-7300, FAX: (617) 292-7400, E-Mail: info@trinitynet.com, Web Site: www.trinitynet.com (35)

Trinity Direct, Butler, NJ. Tel: (973) 283-3600, Web Site: www.trinitydirect.net (23)

Trinity Road LLC, Charlotte, NC. Tel: (704) 940-2240 (28)

Trinity Technical Group, Inc, Grand Prairie, TX. Tel: (817) 879-7907, E-Mail: info@trinitytechnicalgroup.com, Web Site: www.trinitytechnicalgroup.com (22)

Triola RN, Ph D, Nora, Holy Cross Hospital, Fort Lauderdale, FL. Tel: (954) 771-8000, FAX: (954) 229-8597, Web Site: www.holy-cross.com (16)

Tripar International Inc, Roselle, IL. Tel: (630) 980-5100, (800) 222-1142, FAX: (800) 648-9015, E-Mail: sales@tripar.com, Web Site: www.tripar.com (28)

Tripi, Karen, Karen Tripi Associates, New York, NY. Tel: (212) 972-5258, FAX: (212) 599-3809, E-Mail: karen@karentripi.com, Web Site: www.karentripi.com (20)

Karen Tripi Associates, New York, NY. Tel: (212) 972-5258, FAX: (212) 599-3809, E-Mail: karen@karentripi.com, Web Site: www.karentripi.com (20)

Triplex, Washington, DC. Tel: (202) 887-8001, (866) 872-8099, FAX: (202) 887-8008, E-Mail: info@tdmc.com, Web Site: www.tdmc.com (22)

Tripodi, Joseph V., The Coca-Cola Co, Atlanta, GA. Tel: (404) 676-2121, FAX: (404) 676-6792, Web Site: www.cocacola.com (16)

Tristar Products, Fairfield, NJ. Tel: (973) 575-5400, FAX: (973) 683-6708, E-Mail: infotp@tristarproductsinc.com, Web Site: www.tristarproductsinc.com (16)

Triton College, River Grove, IL. Tel: (708) 456-0300, FAX: (708) 583-3121, Web Site: www.triton.edu (16)

Tritsch, Shane, Chicago Magazine, Chicago, IL. Tel: (312) 222-8999, FAX: (312) 222-0287, Web Site: www.chicagomag.com (17)

Triumph Learning, New York, NY. Tel: (212) 652-0200, Web Site: http://triumphlearning.com (17)

Trivino, Ezequiel, Wikreate, San Francisco, CA. Tel: (415) 362-0440, Web Site: www.wikreate.com (35)

Troiano, Kenneth, Modernage Custom Digital Imaging Labs, New York, NY. Tel: (212) 997-1800, (800) 997-2510, FAX: (212) 869-4796, E-Mail: info@modernage.com, Web Site: www.modernage.com (16)

Troiano, Richard, Modernage Custom Digital Imaging Labs, New York, NY. Tel: (212) 997-1800, (800) 997-2510, FAX: (212) 869-4796, E-Mail: info@modernage.com, Web Site: www.modernage.com (16)

Troja, Rick, W Atlee Burpee Co, Warminster, PA. Tel: (215) 674-4900, (800) 333-5808, FAX: (215) 674-4170, Web Site: www.burpee.com (8)

Trollope, Rowan, Symantec, Mountain View, CA. Tel: (408) 517-8000, FAX: (408) 517-8186, Web Site: www.symantec.com (16)

Tromblee, Lorinda, F., Air Force Sergeants Association, Suitland, MD. Tel: (301) 899-3500, (800) 638-0594, FAX: (301) 899-8136, E-Mail: staff@hqafsa.org, Web Site: www.hqafsa.org (1)

Tromiczak, Tina, Berlin Industries Inc, Carol Stream, IL. Tel: (630) 682-0600, FAX: (630) 682-3093, E-Mail: info@berlinindustries.com, Web Site: www.berlinindustries.com (27)

Trophyland USA Inc, Hialeah, FL. Tel: (305) 823-4830, (800) 327-5820, FAX: (305) 823-4836, E-Mail: info@trophyland.com, Web Site: www.trophyland.com (5)

Trotman, Stephan, D., The CompTEL Annual Convention & Trade Exposition, Washington, DC. Tel: (202) 296-6650, FAX: (202) 296-7585, Web Site: www.comptel.org (42)

Trotta, Melissa, NCRI List Management, Englewood Cliffs, NJ. Tel: (201) 541-9500, FAX: (201) 541-1944, E-Mail: info@ncrilists.com, Web Site: www.ncrilists.com (23)

Trottere, Patricia, Hertz Corp, Park Ridge, NJ. Tel: (201) 307-2000, FAX: (201) 307-2644, Web Site: www.hertz.com (19)

Troup, Wilson, Clarin by Hussey Seating, North Berwick, ME. Tel: (207) 676-2271, Web Site: www.husseyseating.com (5)

Trout Unlimited, Arlington, VA. Tel: (703) 522-0200, Web Site: www.tu.org (1)

Trovarelli, Joe, Nielsen Trade Dimensions, Wilton, CT. Tel: (203) 222-5750, (800) 291-0410, FAX: (203) 222-5701, E-Mail: tradedimensions.info@nielsen.com, Web Site: www.tradedimensions.com (17)

Trowbridge, C., Robertson, Yankee Publishing Inc, Dublin, NH. Tel: (603) 563-8111, FAX: (603) 563-8732, Web Site: www.yankeemagazine.com (17)

Trowbridge, Keith, ActivStyle, Minneapolis, MN. Tel: (612) 520-9333, (800) 651-6223, FAX: (612) 520-9300, Web Site: www.activstyle.com (16)

Troy Biologicals Inc, Troy, MI. Tel: (800) 521-0445, FAX: (248) 585-2490, E-Mail: info@troybio.com, Web Site: www.troybio.com (7)

Troyanos, Dennis, The Troyanos Group Ltd, Irvington, NY. Tel: (914) 479-1801, FAX: (914) 993-9554, E-Mail: dennis@troyanosgroup.com, Web Site: www.troyanosgroup.com (20)

The Troyanos Group Ltd, Irvington, NY. Tel: (914) 479-1801, FAX: (914) 993-9554, E-Mail: dennis@ troyanosgroup.com, Web Site: www.troyanosgroup. com (20)

Trubey, Paulette, National Jewish Health, Denver, CO. Tel: (303) 398-1070, (800) 222-LUNG, (800) 423, FAX: (303) 398-1663, E-Mail: trubeyp@njhealth. org, Web Site: www.njhealth.org (1)

Truby, Martha, Wisconsin Historical Foundation, Sun Prairie, WI. Tel: (608) 318-1044 (1)

True North Inc, New York, NY. Tel: (212) 557-4202, Web Site: www.truenorthinc.com (35)

True Value Co, Chicago, IL. Tel: (773) 695-5000, Web Site: www.truevalue.com (16)

Truesdell, Melanie, Subscription Agency.com Inc, Winter Haven, FL. Tel: (863) 229-2557, FAX: (508) 374-8599, E-Mail: info@subscriptionagency. com, Web Site: www.subscriptionagency.com (18)

TrueSense Marketing, Freedom, PA. Tel: (877) 878-6584, Web Site: www.truesense.com (35)

Truffer, Michael, F., AeroGraphics, DeLand, FL. Tel: (386) 736-4793, FAX: (386) 736-9786, Web Site: www.skydivingmagazine.com (3)

Truffer, Michael, Skydiving Magazine, DeLand, FL. Tel: (386) 736-4793, FAX: (386) 736-9786, E-Mail: admin@skydivingmagazine.com, Web Site: www.skydivingmagazine.com (17)

TruGreen/ChemLawn, Lewis Center, OH. Tel: (614) 846-1800, (800) TRUE-GREEN, FAX: (614) 431-0155, Web Site: www.trugreen.com (16)

Truitt, David, Truitt Brothers Inc, Salem, OR. Tel: (503) 362-3674, (800) 547-8712, FAX: (503) 588-2868, E-Mail: truittbrothers@truittbros.com, Web Site: www.truittbros.com (16)

Truitt, Dean, Workflow One, Dayton, OH. Tel: (877) 735-4966, E-Mail: clientservices@workflowone. com, Web Site: www.sfinet.com (21)

Truitt, Mark, National Seminars Group, Shawnee Mission, KS. Tel: (913) 432-7755, (800) 258-7246, FAX: (913) 432-0824, E-Mail: cstserv@natsem. com, Web Site: www.natsem.com (16)

Truitt, Peter, Truitt Brothers Inc, Salem, OR. Tel: (503) 362-3674, (800) 547-8712, FAX: (503) 588-2868, E-Mail: truittbrothers@truittbros.com, Web Site: www.truittbros.com (16)

Truitt Brothers Inc, Salem, OR. Tel: (503) 362-3674, (800) 547-8712, FAX: (503) 588-2868, E-Mail: truittbrothers@truittbros.com, Web Site: www. truittbros.com (16)

Trullenque, Alfredo, No Fault Sports Products, Houston, TX. Tel: (713) 683-7101, (800) 462-7766, FAX: (713) 683-7103, E-Mail: nofaultsports@ comcast.net, Web Site: www.nofaultsports.com (11)

Trumble, Ed, Leanin' Tree Inc, Boulder, CO. Tel: (303) 530-7768, (800) 525-0656, FAX: (303) 530-5124, E-Mail: info@leanintree.com, Web Site: www.leanintree.com (6)

Trumble, Jane, Leanin' Tree Inc, Boulder, CO. Tel: (303) 530-7768, (800) 525-0656, FAX: (303) 530-5124, E-Mail: info@leanintree.com, Web Site: www.leanintree.com (6)

Trumble, Tim, Leanin' Tree Inc, Boulder, CO. Tel: (303) 530-7768, (800) 525-0656, FAX: (303) 530-5124, E-Mail: info@leanintree.com, Web Site: www.leanintree.com (6)

Trumble, Tom, Leanin' Tree Inc, Boulder, CO. Tel: (303) 530-7768, (800) 525-0656, FAX: (303) 530-5124, E-Mail: info@leanintree.com, Web Site: www.leanintree.com (6)

Trumble Greetings, Boulder, CO. Tel: (800) 525-0656, FAX: (303) 530-5124, E-Mail: info@leanintree. com, Web Site: www.leanintree.com (6)

Trumbull, Shawn, IntelliQuote Insurance Services, El Dorado Hills, CA. Tel: (800) 543-3467, Web Site: www.intelliquote.com (15)

Trumka, Richard, AFL-CIO, Washington, DC. Tel: (202) 637-5000, FAX: (202) 637-5058, (202) 637-5323, Web Site: www.aflcio.org (1)

Trumka, Richard, L., Union Privilege, AFL-CIO, Washington, DC. Tel: (202) 293-5330, FAX: (202) 293-5311, Web Site: www.unionplus.org (1)

Trump Marina Hotel & Casino, Atlantic City, NJ. Tel: (609) 441-2000, FAX: (609) 340-5107, Web Site: www.trumpmarina.com (19)

Trump Plaza Hotel & Casino, Atlantic City, NJ. Tel: (609) 441-6000, FAX: (609) 441-7727, Web Site: www.trumpplaza.com (19)

Trump University, New York, NY. Web Site: www. trumpuniversity.com (13)

The Trumpet Club, New York, NY. Tel: (212) 343-6100, FAX: (212) 343-7709, Web Site: www. scholastic.com (17)

Truncali, Joseph, National Association for Printing Leadership, East Rutherford, NJ. Tel: (201) 634-9600, (800) 642-6275, FAX: (201) 634-0324, Web Site: www.napl.org (1)

Trust, David, Professional Photographer Magazine, Atlanta, GA. Tel: (404) 522-8600, (800) 786-6277, FAX: (404) 614-6405, E-Mail: csc@ppa.com, Web Site: www.ppa.com (17)

TRUSTe, San Francisco, CA. Tel: (415) 520-3490, Web Site: www.truste.org (22)

truTV, New York, NY. Tel: (212) 973-2800, FAX: (212) 973-3210, Web Site: www.trutv.com (17)

Tsai, Amy, Fry Inc, Ann Arbor, MI. Tel: (415) 896-5300 X221, FAX: (741) 741-0906, E-Mail: mbriggs@frymulti.com, Web Site: www.fry.com (3)

Tsai, Marcel, Imagine Fulfillment Services, Torrance, CA. Tel: (310) 217-4610, FAX: (310) 217-9632, E-Mail: andya@imaginefulfillment.com, Web Site: www.imaginefulfillment.com (28)

Tsai, Susan, Top Year International Inc, Yorba Linda, CA. Tel: (714) 692-6688, (800) 942-8722, FAX: (714) 692-8691, E-Mail: sales@akirausa.com, Web Site: www.akirausa.com (33)

Tsai, Y.T., Regitar USA Inc, Montgomery, AL. Tel: (334) 244-1885, (877) 734-4827, FAX: (334) 244-1901, E-Mail: info@regitar.com, Web Site: www. regitar.com (9)

Tschiffely, Donna, Direct Marketing Association of Washington, Reston, VA. Tel: (703) 689-DMAW, FAX: (703) 481-DMAW, E-Mail: info@dmaw.org, Web Site: www.dmaw.org (40)

Tsernal, Matt, Delta Tech Industries, Ontario, CA. Tel: (714) 577-8028, FAX: (714) 577-0140, E-Mail: sales@deltatechindustries.com, Web Site: www. deltatechindustries.com (12)

Tshibangu, Judith, Liberty Life Insurance Co, Greenville, SC. Tel: (864) 609-8111, (800) 344-5834 (Mktg), FAX: (864) 609-4411, Web Site: www. libertycorp.com (15)

Tsourides, Holly, Stanley Supply & Services, North Andover, MA. Tel: (978) 682-9844, (800) 225-5370, FAX: (800) 743-8141, Web Site: www. stanleysupplyservices.com (16)

Tsukichi, Steven G., Digi-Key Corp, Thief River Falls, MN. Tel: (218) 681-6674, (800) 344-4539, FAX: (218) 681-3380, Web Site: www.digikey.com (3)

Tucci, Adrian, D&B Canada, Mississauga, ON Canada. Tel: (905) 568-6000, FAX: (905) 568-6197, Web Site: www.dnb.ca (30)

Tuchman, Kenneth, TeleTech, Englewood, CO. Tel: (303) 397-8100, (800) TELETECH, FAX: (303) 397-8199, E-Mail: solutions@TeleTech.com, Web Site: www.teletech.com (22)

Tuchman, Murray, Printing Corp of the Americas Inc (PCA), Pompano Beach, FL. Tel: (954) 781-8100, (866) 721-1PCA, FAX: (954) 781-8421, Web Site: www.pcaprinting.com (27)

Tucker, Bill, Williams Printing Co/an RR Donnelley Co, Atlanta, GA. Tel: (404) 875-6611, (800) 950-7588, FAX: (404) 872-4025, Web Site: www. rrdonnelley.com (27)

Tucker, James, Integrated Marketing Technology Inc, San Francisco, CA. Tel: (415) 699-2280, FAX: (917) 591-5333, E-Mail: information@imtnetwork. com, Web Site: www.imtnetwork.com (22)

Tucker, James, Tucker Electronics Co, Garland, TX. Tel: (214) 348-8800, (887) 667-6044, FAX: (214) 348-0367, E-Mail: sales@tucker.com, Web Site: www.tucker.com (3)

Tucker, Kathleen, Suntrust Banks Inc, Atlanta, GA. Tel: (404) 588-7914, (800) 786-8787, FAX: (404) 532-0550, E-Mail: emmett.harmon@suntrust.com, Web Site: www.suntrust.com (14)

Tucker, Larry, Hays International Mailing Services, Edgewater, NJ. Tel: (201) 307-8888, E-Mail: ltucker@haysmailing.com, Web Site: www. haysmailing.com (28)

Tucker, Larry, We Deliver America Inc, Englewood Cliffs, NJ. Tel: (201) 307-8888, FAX: (201) 307-1200, E-Mail: info@we-deliver-america.com, Web Site: www.we-deliver-america.com (31)

Tucker, Patrick, World Future Society, Bethesda, MD. Tel: (301) 656-8274, (800) 989-8274, FAX: (301) 951-0394, E-Mail: info@wfs.org, Web Site: www. wfs.org (1)

Tucker, Robert, Beacon Shoe Co Inc, Maryland Heights, MO. Tel: (636) 488-5444, FAX: (636) 488-3103 (16)

Tucker, Tom, Travelex America Inc, Washington, DC. Tel: (202) 408-1200, FAX: (202) 513-5215, Web Site: business.travelex.com/us (14)

Tucker Capital Corp, Princeton, NJ. Tel: (609) 924-5710, FAX: (609) 924-5027, E-Mail: info@ tuckercapital.com, Web Site: www.tuckercapital. com (20)

Tucker Electronics Co, Garland, TX. Tel: (214) 348-8800, (887) 667-6044, FAX: (214) 348-0367, E-Mail: sales@tucker.com, Web Site: www.tucker. com (3)

Tucker Printers, Henrietta, NY. Tel: (585) 359-3030, Web Site: www.tuckerprinters.com (27)

Tuckman, Howard, Fordham University Graduate School of Business Administration, New York, NY. Tel: (212) 636-6200, (800) 825-4422, FAX: (212) 636-7076, Web Site: www.fordham.edu (41)

Tudanger, Phil, J&R Music/J&R Computer World, New York, NY. Tel: (212) 238-9000, (800) 806-1115, FAX: (212) 238-9191, Web Site: www.jandr. com (3)

Tudor, Dr. Keith, Kennesaw State University, Kennesaw, GA. Tel: (770) 423-6060, FAX: (770) 499-3261, Web Site: www.kennesaw.edu (41)

Tuerberg, Janice, Bobley-Harmann Corp/GiftValues. Com, Westbury, NY. Tel: (516) 364-1800, (800) 323-1692, FAX: (516) 364-1899, E-Mail: info@ bobley.com, Web Site: www.bobley.com; www. montefiorepens.com (5)

Tuff, Tim, John Harland Co, Decatur, GA. Tel: (770) 981-5580, (800) 723-3690, FAX: (770) 593-5367, E-Mail: jhhwebmaster@harland.net, Web Site: www.harland.net (16)

Tukes, Terry, G-Neil Direct Mail, Sunrise, FL. Tel: (800) 999-9111, FAX: (954) 851-1264, E-Mail: tcs@gneil.com, Web Site: www.gneil.com (10)

Tukulj, Amir, Thane International Inc, La Quinta, CA. Tel: (760) 777-0217, FAX: (760) 777-0214, Web Site: www.thane.com (35)

Tulipane, Barbara, Electronic Retailing Association, Washington, DC. Tel: (703) 841-1751, FAX: (703) 841-1860, E-Mail: askera@retailing.org, Web Site: www.retailing.org (42)

Tullis, Walt, Campbell Soup Co, Camden, NJ. Tel: (856) 342-4800, (800) 257-8443, FAX: (856) 342-3878, Web Site: www.campbellsoup.com (16)

Tully, Timothy, Tully & Holland Inc, Wellesley, MA. Tel: (781) 239-2900, FAX: (781) 239-2901, E-Mail: info@tullyandholland.com, Web Site: www.tullyandholland.com (14)

Tully & Holland Inc, Wellesley, MA. Tel: (781) 239-2900, FAX: (781) 239-2901, E-Mail: info@ tullyandholland.com, Web Site: www. tullyandholland.com (14)

Tulp, Peter, SC Direct, West Bridgewater, MA. Tel: (800) 343-9695, Web Site: www.scdirect.com (2)

Tunick, Barry, Estes Industries, Penrose, CO. Tel: (719) 372-6565, FAX: (719) 372-3419, www.estesrockets.com (11)

Tunioli, Carlo, Benetton USA, New York, NY. Tel: (212) 593-0290, (800) 274-7192, FAX: (212) 371-1438, E-Mail: mtaylor@bennettonusa.com, Web Site: www.benetton.com (2)

Tunney, Greg, A., RG Barry Corp, Pickerington, OH. FAX: (614) 866-9787, E-Mail: sales@rgbarry.com, Web Site: www.rgbarry.com (2)

Tupperware, Orlando, FL. Tel: (407) 826-5050, (800) 366-3800, FAX: (407) 826-8874, Web Site: www.tupperware.com (16)

Turcot, Cindy, Gardener's Supply Co, Burlington, VT. Tel: (802) 660-3500, (888) 833-1412, FAX: (802) 660-3501, E-Mail: info@gardeners.com, Web Site: www.gardeners.com (8)

Turek, Kenneth, J., Neuberger & Berman Management, New York, NY. Tel: (212) 476-8800, (800) 877-9700, FAX: (212) 476-9090, Web Site: www.nb.com (14)

Turetzky, Julie, Home Planners, Tucson, AZ. Tel: (520) 297-8200, FAX: (520) 297-6219, E-Mail: sales@homeplanners.com, Web Site: www.homeplanners.com (17)

Turkel, Bruce, Turkel, Coconut Grove, FL. Tel: (305) 445-9111, FAX: (305) 448-6691, Web Site: www.braindarts.com (35)

Turkel, Coconut Grove, FL. Tel: (305) 445-9111, FAX: (305) 448-6691, Web Site: www.braindarts.com (35)

Turley, Amy, American Identity, Overland Park, KS. Tel: (913) 319-3100, (800) 848-8028 (33)

Turley, Brian, C., Brian Turley & Co, Melrose, MA. Tel: (781) 662-8538, FAX: (781) 662-5590, E-Mail: turley@shore.net (39)

Turley, Gavin, The Kidney Foundation of Canada/Greater Ontario Branch, Hamilton, ON. Tel: (800) 414-3484, FAX: (905) 318-8491, E-Mail: kidneyfoundation@bellnet.ca, Web Site: www.kidney.on.ca (1)

Turley, James, R., Boy Scouts of America/National Supply Group, Charlotte, NC. Tel: (972) 580-2161, (800) 323-0736, E-Mail: customerservice@scoutstuff.org, Web Site: www.scoutstuff.org (1)

Brian Turley & Co, Melrose, MA. Tel: (781) 662-8538, FAX: (781) 662-5590, E-Mail: turley@shore.net (39)

Turnbull, Mike, AMC Inc, Atlanta, GA. Tel: (404) 220-2000, FAX: (404) 220-3030 (2)

Turncraft Clocks Inc, Spring Park, MN. Tel: (952) 471-9573, (800) 544-1711, FAX: (952) 471-8579, E-Mail: office@meiselwoodhobby.com, Web Site: www.meiselwoodhobby.com (6)

Turner, Alan, Magnets USA, Roanoke, VA. Tel: (540) 857-3045, Web Site: www.magnetsusa.com (30)

Turner, Allen, M., Columbia College Chicago, Chicago, IL. Tel: (312) 663-1600, FAX: (312) 344-0869, Web Site: www.colum.edu (41)

Turner, Bill, Whirley Drink Works, Warren, PA. Tel: (814) 723-7600, (800) 825-5575, FAX: (814) 723-3245, E-Mail: info@whirleydrinkworks.com, Web Site: www.whirleydrinkworks.com (5)

Turner, Brant, American Database Marketing Inc, Jacksonville, FL. Tel: (904) 886-0744, (888) 565-7724, FAX: (888) 270-4338, E-Mail: admdun@cs.com, Web Site: www.admdun.com (23)

Turner, Frank, Valassis Canada, Toronto, ON. Tel: (416) 259-3600, Web Site: www.valassis.com (35)

Turner, Janet, Fred Pryor Seminars, Mission, KS. Tel: (913) 967-8518, (800) 780-8476, FAX: (913) 967-8849, E-Mail: customerservice@pryor.com, Web Site: www.pryor.com (14)

Turner, Linda, D., Caterpillar Insurance Services Corp, Nashville, TN. Tel: (615) 386-5800, Web Site: www.cat.com (15)

Turner, Sherran, Hanover Direct Inc, Weehawken, NJ. Tel: (201) 863-7300, FAX: (201) 272-3280, Web Site: www.hanoverdirect.com (5)

Turner, Willis, Huntsinger & Jeffer Inc, Richmond, VA. Tel: (804) 266-2499, FAX: (804) 266-8563, E-Mail: vickil@huntsinger-jeffer.com, Web Site: www.huntsinger-jeffer.com (21)

Turner Broadcasting System Inc, Atlanta, GA. Tel: (404) 827-1700, FAX: (404) 827-1575, Web Site: www.turner.com (32)

Turner Greenhouses, Goldsboro, NC. Tel: (919) 734-8345, (800) 672-4770, FAX: (919) 736-4550, E-Mail: sales@turnergreenhouses.com, Web Site: www.turnergreenhouses.com (8)

Turney, Doug, MacLaren McCann, Toronto, ON Canada. Tel: (416) 594-6000, FAX: (416) 643-7026, Web Site: www.maclaren.com (35)

Turnmire, Margie, McFarland & Co Inc Publishers, Jefferson, NC. Tel: (336) 246-4460, (800) 253-2187, FAX: (336) 246-5018, E-Mail: info@mcfarlandpub.com, Web Site: www.mcfarlandpub.com (17)

Turpin, Michael, Oxford Health Plans, Inc, Trumbull, CT. Tel: (800) 889-7658, FAX: (203) 459-6464, E-Mail: info@speedmat.com, Web Site: www.oxhp.com (15)

Turtle Bay Management Co Inc, Virginia Beach, VA. Tel: (757) 422-2760, FAX: (757) 422-1434, E-Mail: jimlant@turtlebaymanagement.com, Web Site: www.turtlebaymanagement.com (20)

Tuszynski Jr., Daniel, J., Music Treasures Co, Richmond, VA. Tel: (804) 730-8800, (800) 666-7565, FAX: (888) MUSIC-TC, E-Mail: musict@musictreasures.com, Web Site: www.musictreasures.com (6)

Tutoki, Jane, Zurich, Schaumburg, IL. Tel: (847) 605-3712, (800) 382-2150, FAX: (847) 605-6403, Web Site: www.zurichna.com (15)

Tuttle, Gene, Affinity Group Inc, Ventura, CA. Tel: (805) 667-4100, (800) 765-1912, FAX: (805) 667-4419, E-Mail: khurd@affinitygroup.com, Web Site: www.affinitygroup.com (19)

Tuttle, Wallingford, CT. Tel: (203) 949-4290, (800) 882-7511, FAX: (203) 949-4288, Web Site: www.tuttlecatalog.com (2)

Tuttle Printing & Engraving, Rutland, VT. Tel: (802) 773-9171, (800) 776-7682, FAX: (802) 773-5785, E-Mail: info@tuttleprinting.com, Web Site: www.tuttleprinting.com (10)

Tuxhorn, William, J., McNichols Co, Tampa, FL. Tel: (813) 282-3828, FAX: (813) 288-9342, E-Mail: sales@mcnichols.com, Web Site: www.mcnichols.com (16)

Tveit, Elizabeth, Seattle Magazine, Seattle, WA. Tel: (206) 284-1750, (800) 637-0334, FAX: (206) 284-2550, E-Mail: customerservice@seattlemag.com, Web Site: www.seattlemag.com (17)

Tweed, Janet, Gilbert Tweed Associates, New York, NY. Tel: (212) 758-3000, FAX: (212) 832-1040, E-Mail: hrdptgt@gmail.com, Web Site: www.gilberttweed.com (20)

Tweed, Krista, LDS Test & Measurement, Marlborough, MA. Tel: (608) 821-6600, FAX: (608) 821-6691, E-Mail: info-us@lds.spx.com, Web Site: www.lds-group.com (3)

Gilbert Tweed Associates, New York, NY. Tel: (212) 758-3000, FAX: (212) 832-1040, E-Mail: hrdptgt@gmail.com, Web Site: www.gilberttweed.com (20)

20th Century Fox Television, Los Angeles, CA. Tel: (310) 444-8100, FAX: (310) 444-8101 (16)

21st Century Insurance, Woodland Hills, CA. Tel: (818) 704-3700, FAX: (818) 226-1198, E-Mail: executiveoffice@21st.com, Web Site: www.21st.com (15)

21st Century Marketing, Hauppauge, NY. Tel: (631) 293-8550, FAX: (631) 293-8974, E-Mail: info@21stcm.com, Web Site: www.21stcm.com (24)

Twichell-O'Neal, Wedy, Moon Shine Trading Co, Woodland, CA. Tel: (530) 668-0660, (800) 678-1226, FAX: (530) 668-6061, E-Mail: store@moonshinetrading.com, Web Site: www.moonshinetrading.com (4)

Twin City Engraving/Premier Promotions, Saint Joseph, MI. Tel: (616) 983-0601, (800) 222-7752, FAX: (616) 983-3571, Web Site: www.premierpromos.com (33)

Twin Peaks Press, Vancouver, WA. Tel: (360) 694-2462, (800) 637-2256, FAX: (360) 696-3210, E-Mail: info@twinpeakspress.com, Web Site: www.twinpeakspress.com (24)

Twining, Steve, officefurniture.com, Milwaukee, WI. Tel: (414) 272-6080, (800) 933-0053, FAX: (414) 272-0248, (800) 468-1526, Web Site: www.officefurniture.com (8)

2ergo, Arlington, VA. Tel: (703) 879-3400, Web Site: www.2ergo.com (30)

Two Roths, Forest Hills, NY. Tel: (718) 268-1998, FAX: (718) 793-3972, E-Mail: tworoths@rcn.com (35)

2-10 Home Buyers Warranty, Denver, CO. Tel: (720) 747-6000, Web Site: www.2-10.com (15)

22squared Inc, Atlanta, GA. Tel: (404) 347-8700, FAX: (404) 347-8800, Web Site: www.22squared.com (35)

Ty Pac, Baldwinsville, NY. Tel: (315) 638-9431, (800) 356-8964, FAX: (315) 638-9433, E-Mail: ty-pac@hotmail.com (34)

Tyco Electronics Corp, Menlo Park, CA. Tel: (650) 361-3333, (800) 272-9243, FAX: (800) 361-5579, Web Site: www.tycoelectronics.com (16)

Tyco Valves & Controls, Houston, TX. Tel: (713) 986-4665, (800) 343-0990, FAX: (713) 937-5466, Web Site: www.tycovalves.com (16)

Tyler, Dave, Kappa Publishing Group, Blue Bell, PA. Tel: (215) 643-6385, FAX: (215) 628-3571, Web Site: www.kappapublishing.com (16)

Tyler, Shana, Sally Beauty Supply LLC, Denton, TX. Tel: (940) 898-7500, (800) 275-7255, Web Site: www.sallybeauty.com (7)

Tyler, Tiffany, Sensory Effects Powder System, Bridgeton, MO. Tel: (314) 291-5444, (800) 422-5444, FAX: (314) 291-3289, E-Mail: info@sensoryeffects.com (16)

Tyme Direct Mail Service, Long Island City, NY. Tel: (212) 691-4444, FAX: (212) 691-6747, E-Mail: info@tymedirect.com, Web Site: www.tymedirect.com (21)

Tynan, Vincent, J., Small Business Service Bureau Inc, Worcester, MA. Tel: (508) 756-3513, (800) 343-0939, FAX: (508) 770-0528, E-Mail: membership@sbsb.com, Web Site: www.sbsb.com (1)

Tyndale House Publishers, Carol Stream, IL. Tel: (630) 668-8300, FAX: (630) 668-3245 (17)

Type-A-Scan Inc, New York, NY. Tel: (212) 367-8406, FAX: (212) 691-8134, E-Mail: info@typeascan.com, Web Site: www.typeascan.com (22)

Typed Letters Corp, Mount Pleasant, IA. Tel: (316) 729-9093, FAX: (316) 729-9933, E-Mail: janet@typeletters.com, Web Site: www.typedletters.com (21)

Tyson, Elaine, Tyson Associates Inc, Brookfield, CT. Tel: (203) 775-9465, FAX: (203) 775-0563, E-Mail: elaine@tysonassociates.com, Web Site: www.tysonassociates.com (17)

Tyson, Karen, Trend Magazines Inc, Saint Petersburg, FL. Tel: (727) 821-5800, (800) 821-5800, FAX: (727) 822-5083, E-Mail: feedback@fltrend.com, Web Site: www.floridatrend.com (17)

Tyson Associates Inc, Brookfield, CT. Tel: (203) 775-9465, FAX: (203) 775-0563, E-Mail: elaine@tysonassociates.com, Web Site: www.tysonassociates.com (17)

Tzou, Shin-Yuan, BroadVision Inc, Redwood City, CA. Tel: (650) 542-5100, FAX: (650) 364-3425, E-Mail: sales@broadvision.com, Web Site: www.broadvision.com (16)

U

U-Bild, Oceanside, CA. Tel: (818) 785-6368, (800) 828-2453, FAX: (818) 785-3229, Web Site: www. ubild.com (8)

U-Haul International, Phoenix, AZ. Tel: (602) 263-6011, (800) GO-UHAUL, FAX: (602) 263-6598, Web Site: www.uhaul.com (16)

UAA Clearinghouse, Omaha, NE. Tel: (402) 991-2810, Web Site: www.uaaclearinghouse.com (22)

UBS Wealth Management US, Weehawken, NJ. Tel: (201) 352-3000, (888) 279-3343, FAX: (201) 617-8589, Web Site: www.ubs.com/financialservicesinc (14)

UCEA, Boston, MA. Tel: (617) 738-6410, FAX: (617) 734-1452, Web Site: www.revike.org (1)

UCI/Dream Giveaways, Clearwater, FL. Tel: (727) 536-2777, Web Site: www.dreamgiveaways.com (20)

UDL Laboratories Inc, Sugar Land, TX. Tel: (281) 240-1000, (800) 231-3052, FAX: (281) 240-0002, Web Site: www.udllabs.com (7)

UF College of Advertising, Journalism, & Communications, Gainesville, FL. Tel: (352) 392-4046, FAX: (352) 392-3919, Web Site: www.jou.ufl.edu (41)

UGL Equis Corp, Chicago, IL. Tel: (312) 424-8000, FAX: (312) 424-8080, Web Site: www.equiscorp.com (16)

UJA/Federation of New York, New York, NY. Tel: (212) 980-1000, FAX: (212) 785-9321, Web Site: www.ujafedny.org (1)

ULI-The Urban Land Institute, Washington, DC. Tel: (202) 624-7000, FAX: (202) 624-7140, Web Site: www.uli.org (1)

ULTA Salon Cosmetics Fragrance, Romeoville, IL. Tel: (630) 226-0020 (7)

UMI Publications Inc, Charlotte, NC. Tel: (800) 747-9287, FAX: (704) 374-0729, E-Mail: info@umipub.com, Web Site: www.umipub.com (17)

UNICEF, New York, NY. Tel: (212) 326-7000, Web Site: www.unicef.org (1)

UNICEF Canada, Toronto, ON Canada. Tel: (416) 482-4444, (800) 567-4483, FAX: (416) 487-8875, E-Mail: on.secretary@unicef.ca, Web Site: www. unicef.ca (1)

UPM North America, Westmont, IL. Tel: (630) 850-3310, (866) 300-4175, FAX: (630) 850-3510, Web Site: www.upm-kymmene.com (25)

UPMC Health Plan, Pittsburgh, PA. Tel: (412) 454-3469, Web Site: www.upmchealthplan.com (1)

USAA, San Antonio, TX. Tel: (512) 498-6524, FAX: (512) 498-8000 (15)

USAA Alliance Services Marketing, San Antonio, TX. Tel: (210) 456-9857, FAX: (210) 498-4542, Web Site: www.usaa.com (14)

USC Viterbi School of Engineering, Los Angeles, CA. Tel: (213) 740-2502, Web Site: http://viterbi.usc.edu/ (1)

USG Corp, Chicago, IL. Tel: (312) 436-4000, (800) 621-9622, FAX: (312) 672-4093, Web Site: www.usg.com (34)

USI Affinity, Philadelphia, PA. Tel: (610) 833-2876, (800) 625-2876, FAX: (610) 265-2876, E-Mail: info@usiaffinity.com, Web Site: www.brcorp.com (15)

USI Affinity Collegiate Insurance Resources, Columbus, OH. Tel: (614) 486-5388, Web Site: www. collegiateinsuranceresources.com (15)

USO Inc, Arlington, VA. Tel: (703) 908-6400, Web Site: www.usa.org (1)

USX, Pittsburgh, PA. Tel: (412) 433-1121, E-Mail: webmaster@usx.com, Web Site: www.usx.com (16)

USY Consulting Inc, Dumont, NJ. Tel: (201) 585-7402, FAX: (201) 585-2754, E-Mail: usyconsulting@hotmail.com (20)

UV Process Supply, Chicago, IL. Tel: (773) 248-0099, (800) 621-1296, FAX: (773) 880-6647, E-Mail: info@uvps.com, Web Site: www.uvprocess.com (34)

Udell, Lawrence, Horn Packaging Corp, Lancaster, MA. Tel: (978) 772-0290, (800) 832-7020, FAX: (978) 772-4611, E-Mail: mccarthy@horncorp.com, Web Site: www.hornpackaging.com (5)

Udell, Sandra, Winnipeg Art Gallery, Winnipeg, MB. Tel: (204) 786-6641, FAX: (204) 788-4998, E-Mail: inquiries@wag.mb.ca, Web Site: www. wag.mb.ca (1)

Ueberroth, Joseph, J., Windstar Cruises, Seattle, WA. Tel: (206) 292-9606, (800) 258-SAIL, FAX: (206) 340-0975, E-Mail: info@windstarcruises.com, Web Site: www.windstarcruises.com (19)

Ugalde, Carlos, WebMetro, San Dimas, CA. Tel: (909) 599-8885, Web Site: www.webmetro.com (35)

Uhl, Robin, Chief Executive Magazine, Greenwich, CT. Tel: (203) 930-2700, Web Site: www. chiefexecutive.net (17)

Uhrich, Marie A., Thrivent Financial for Lutherans, Appleton, WI. Tel: (920) 734-5721, (800) 847-4836, FAX: (920) 730-4781, E-Mail: mail@thrivent.com, Web Site: www.thrivent.com (14)

Uhrynowski, Peter, Queue Inc, Stratford, CT. Tel: (203) 335-0906, (800) 232-2224, FAX: (800) 775-2729, E-Mail: jdk@queueinc.com, Web Site: www. qworkbooks.com (17)

Uihlein, Elizabeth, Uline, Pleasant Prairie, WI. Tel: (847) 473-3000, FAX: (800) 295-5571, E-Mail: ulinecs@uline.com, Web Site: www.uline.com (5)

Uihlein, Richard, Uline, Pleasant Prairie, WI. Tel: (847) 473-3000, FAX: (800) 295-5571, E-Mail: ulinecs@uline.com, Web Site: www.uline.com (5)

Ulano Corp, Brooklyn, NY. Tel: (718) 237-4700, (800) 221-0616, FAX: (718) 802-1119, E-Mail: ulano@ulano.com, Web Site: www.ulano.com (34)

Ulian, Mark, Data Marketing Solutions Inc, Marblehead, MA. Tel: (781) 639-3270, Web Site: www. businesswatchnetwork.com (35)

Uline, Pleasant Prairie, WI. Tel: (847) 473-3000, FAX: (800) 295-5571, E-Mail: ulinecs@uline.com, Web Site: www.uline.com (5)

Ullery, Cathryn, Mentor Corp, Santa Barbara, CA. Tel: (805) 879-6000, (800) 525-0245, FAX: (805) 964-2712, Web Site: www.mentorcorp.com (16)

Ullman III, Myron, JC Penney Inc, Plano, TX. Tel: (972) 431-1000, FAX: (972) 431-1977, Web Site: www.jcpenney.com (1)

Ullman, Dave, Joseph A Bank Clothiers Inc, Hampstead, MD. Tel: (410) 239-2700, (800) 285-2265, FAX: (410) 239-5911, E-Mail: service@jos-a-bank.com, Web Site: www.josbank.com (2)

Ulrich, Dave, IPS - Sendero Corp, Norcross, GA. Tel: (770) 409-0047, (800) 879-1996, FAX: (770) 409-1735, E-Mail: sales@ips-sendero.com, Web Site: www.ips-sendero.com (14)

Ulrich, Joan, The Merchandise Mart, Chicago, IL. Tel: (312) 527-4141, (800) 677-6278, Web Site: www. merchandisemart.com (42)

Ultimate Office, Farmingdale, NJ. Tel: (732) 780-6911, (800) 631-2233, FAX: (732) 780-9833, Web Site: www.ultoffice.com (16)

Ultimate Products Inc, Chula Vista, CA. Tel: (813) 881-1575, (800) 477-4287, FAX: (813) 881-1831, E-Mail: office@ultimatehat.com, Web Site: www. ultimatehat.com (16)

Ultra Direct Marketing Inc, Jackson, NJ. Tel: (732) 364-8337, (800) 365-8587, FAX: (732) 364-9598, E-Mail: contact@ultradirect.com, Web Site: www. ultradirect.com (16)

Ultradent Products Inc, South Jordan, UT. Tel: (801) 572-4200, Web Site: www.ultradent.com (7)

UMarketing LLC, New York, NY. Tel: (630) 916-1717, Web Site: www.umarketing.com (35)

Umass Dartmouth, North Dartmouth, MA. Tel: (508) 999-8403, Web Site: www.umassd.edu (1)

Umbrell, Trish, Wesley, Massachusetts Horticultural Society, Wellesley, MA. Tel: (617) 933-4929, (617) 933-4900, FAX: (617) 933-4901, E-Mail: hort_line@masshort.org, Web Site: www.masshort. org (1)

Unadilla Laminated Products, Unadilla, NY. Tel: (607) 369-9341, FAX: (607) 369-3608, E-Mail: info@unalam.com, Web Site: www.unalam.com (16)

Uncharted Country Publishing, Madison, WI. Tel: (575) 776-3470, E-Mail: ucp@taichihealth.com, Web Site: www.taichihealth.com (17)

Uncle Ben's Inc, Greenville, MS. Tel: (662) 335-8000, (800) 548-6253, (800) 54-UNCLE, FAX: (662) 378-4370, E-Mail: info@unclebens.com, Web Site: www.unclebens.com (4)

UndercoverWear Inc, Tewksbury, MA. Tel: (978) 851-8580, FAX: (978) 640-2882, E-Mail: jamiej@undercoverwear.com, Web Site: www. undercoverwear.com (2)

Undergear.com, La Crosse, WI. Tel: (717) 633-3413, (800) 853-8555, FAX: (717) 633-3214, Web Site: www.undergear.com (2)

Underhill, Charles, Council of Better Business Bureaus - BBBOnline, Arlington, VA. Tel: (703) 276-0100, FAX: (703) 525-8277, Web Site: www.bbb. org (1)

Underhill, Robert, Channing L Bete Co Inc, South Deerfield, MA. Tel: (800) 477-4776, FAX: (800) 499-6464, E-Mail: custscvs@channing.bete.com, Web Site: www.channing-bete.com (17)

Underline Communications LLC, New York, NY. Tel: (212) 994-4340, Web Site: www.underlinecom.com (35)

Underwood, John, Behlen Manufacturing Co, Columbus, NE. Tel: (402) 564-3111, FAX: (402) 563-7405, E-Mail: behlen@megavision.com, Web Site: www.behlenmfg.com (16)

Underwood Photo Archives Inc, Woodside, CA. Tel: (650) 851-5190, FAX: (650) 851-5193, E-Mail: ray@underwoodarchives.com, Web Site: www. underwoodarchives.com (38)

Unger, Steven, Howard-Sloan-Koller Group, New York, NY. Tel: (212) 661-5250, FAX: (212) 557-9178, E-Mail: ekoller@hsksearch.com, Web Site: www.hsksearch.com (20)

Unica Corp, Waltham, MA. Tel: (781) 839-8000, Web Site: www.unicacorp.com (22)

Unicall International Inc, Fairlawn, OH. Tel: (330) 864-9364, FAX: (330) 864-9367, E-Mail: harrisb@unicallinc.com, Web Site: www.unicallinc.com (29)

Unicol Inc, Pembroke Pines, FL. Tel: (954) 431-7871, FAX: (954) 430-7227, E-Mail: customerservice@unicol-publishing.com, Web Site: www.unicol-publishing.com (17)

Unicom Electric Inc, Walnut, CA. Tel: (626) 964-7873, (800) 346-6668, FAX: (626) 964-7880, E-Mail: info@unicomlink.com, Web Site: www. unicomlink.com (16)

Unicom Marketing Group Inc, Broadview, IL. Tel: (312) 738-1404, FAX: (312) 738-1405, E-Mail: info@unicommarketing.com, Web Site: www. unicommarketing.com (35)

UNICOR- Services Business Group, Washington, DC. Tel: (202) 305-3500, Web Site: www.unicor.gov/services (28)

Unicover Corp, Cheyenne, WY. Tel: (307) 771-3000, (800) 443-3232, FAX: (307) 771-3134, E-Mail: qands@unicover.com, Web Site: www.unicover. com (6)

Unified Precious Metals Inc, Canoga Park, CA. Tel: (818) 889-7797, FAX: (818) 735-8878 (32)

UniFirst Corp, Owensboro, KY. Tel: (270) 683-5250 X523, Web Site: www.unifirst.com (2)

Uniformed Services Benefit Association, Overland Park, KS. Tel: (800) 368-7021, Web Site: www. usba.com (15)

Uniforms & Scrubs.com, Ballwin, MO. Tel: (636) 391-9200, FAX: (636) 391-9205, E-Mail: questions@uniformsandscrubs.com, Web Site: www.whiteswanscrubs.com (7)

UniGraphic Inc, Woburn, MA. Tel: (781) 231-7200, FAX: (781) 938-7727, E-Mail: info@uni-graphic.com, Web Site: www.uni-graphic.com (27)

Unilever Best Foods, Englewood Cliffs, NJ. Tel: (201) 567-8000, FAX: (201) 871-8257, E-Mail: comments@unilever.com, Web Site: www.unilever.com (16)

Unimail Corp, Rochester, NY. Tel: (585) 254-7510, (800) 688-6878, FAX: (585) 254-2367 (28)

Union Federal Savings Bank, North Providence, RI. Tel: (401) 353-8900, (800) 992-0278, FAX: (401) 353-8938, Web Site: www.unionfsb.com (14)

The Union Labor Life Insurance Co, Silver Spring, MD. Tel: (202) 962-2945, FAX: (202) 962-8429, E-Mail: info@ullico.com, Web Site: www.unioncare.com (15)

Union Pen Co, Hagaman, NY. Tel: (800) 846-6600, FAX: (518) 770-7018, Web Site: www.unionpen.com (5)

Union Privilege, AFL-CIO, Washington, DC. Tel: (202) 293-5330, FAX: (202) 293-5311, Web Site: www.unionplus.org (1)

Union Switch & Signal Inc, Pittsburgh, PA. Tel: (412) 688-2400, (800) 351-1520, FAX: (412) 688-2399, Web Site: www.switch.com (16)

Unique Data Services Inc, Downers Grove, IL. Tel: (630) 968-6000, Web Site: www.uniquedata.com (28)

Unique Embossing Services Inc & Global Cards, Downers Grove, IL. Tel: (630) 960-3337 X23, FAX: (630) 960-3618, Web Site: www.globalcrd.com (27)

Unique Mailing Services Inc, Bolingbrook, IL. Tel: (630) 739-4848, FAX: (630) 783-1838, E-Mail: info@uniqmail.com, Web Site: www.uniqmail.com (28)

UniServ Advertising Inc, Neptune City, NJ. Tel: (732) 774-1010, FAX: (732) 774-3311, Web Site: www.uniservinc.com (33)

Unisfair, Menlo Park, CA. Tel: (866) 354-4030, Web Site: www.unisfair.com (20)

Unisource Worldwide, Inc, Norcross, GA. Tel: (770) 447-9000, (800) 864-7687, FAX: (770) 729-0385, Web Site: www.unisourcelink.com (25)

Unisys, Blue Bell, PA. Tel: (215) 986-4011, (800) 874-8647, FAX: (215) 986-2312, Web Site: www.unisys.com (16)

Unit 7, New York, NY. Tel: (212) 209-1600, FAX: (212) 209-1800, E-Mail: lbabcock@unit7.com, Web Site: www.unit7.com (35)

United Air Specialists Inc, Cincinnati, OH. Tel: (513) 891-0400, (800) 992-4422, FAX: (513) 891-4882, E-Mail: uas@uasinc.com, Web Site: www.uasinc.com (16)

United America Advertising Inc, Enid, OK. Tel: (580) 233-7200, FAX: (580) 548-8432 (29)

United Business Media, Manhasset, NY. Tel: (516) 562-5000, Web Site: www.ubmtechnology.com (17)

United Church Homes, Marion, OH. Tel: (740) 382-4885, (800) 750-0750, FAX: (740) 382-4884, Web Site: www.unitedchurchhomes.org (1)

United Communications Group, Gaithersburg, MD. Tel: (301) 287-2700, FAX: (301) 816-8945, E-Mail: webmaster@ucg.com, Web Site: www.ucg.com (17)

United Community Bank, Blairsville, GA. Tel: (706) 745-0911, Web Site: www.ucbi.com (14)

United Envelope, Long Island City, NY. Tel: (718) 707-0700, FAX: (718) 729-8671, E-Mail: marketing@unitedenvelope.com, Web Site: www.unitedenvelope.com (26)

United Farm Workers of America, AFL-CIO, Keene, CA. Tel: (661) 823-6158, FAX: (661) 823-6177, E-Mail: execoffice@ufw.org, Web Site: www.ufw.org (1)

United Investors Life Insurance Co, Birmingham, AL. Tel: (205) 325-4300, (800) 288-2722, FAX: (205) 325-4157, Web Site: www.uilic.com (15)

United Jewish Communities, New York, NY. Tel: (212) 284-6500, Web Site: www.ujc.org (1)

United Marketing Group LLC, Schaumburg, IL. Tel: (847) 240-2005, FAX: (847) 240-2177, E-Mail: info@unitedmarket.com, Web Site: www.unitedmarket.com (21)

The United Methodist Publishing House, Nashville, TN. Tel: (615) 749-6000, (800) 672-1789, FAX: (615) 749-6417, E-Mail: productsandservices@umpublishing.com, Web Site: www.umpublishing.com (17)

United Nations Federal Credit Union, Long Island City, NY. Tel: (347) 686-6000, Web Site: www.unfcu.org (1)

United Nations Foundation, Washington, DC. Tel: (202) 778-3539, Web Site: www.unfoundation.org (1)

United Parcel Service, Atlanta, GA. Tel: (404) 828-6000, (800) 874-5877, FAX: (404) 828-6562, Web Site: www.ups.com (28)

United Retail Inc, Rochelle Park, NJ. Tel: (201) 845-0880, Web Site: www.avenue.com (2)

United Security Products Inc, Poway, CA. Tel: (858) 413-0149, (800) 227-1592, FAX: (858) 413-0124, E-Mail: usp@unitedsecurity.com, Web Site: www.unitedsecurity.com (16)

United Spinal Association, East Elmhurst, NY. Tel: (718) 803-3782, Web Site: www.unitedspinal.org (1)

United Staffing Systems, New York, NY. Tel: (212) 743-0300, (800) 972-9725, FAX: (212) 576-1569, Web Site: www.unitedstaffing.com (16)

US Bancorp, Minneapolis, MN. Tel: (651) 466-3000, (800) 872-2657, FAX: (612) 303-0782, Web Site: www.usbank.com (14)

US Bank, Minneapolis, MN. Tel: (612) 973-1111, Web Site: www.usbank.com (14)

US BRANDING GROUP, LLC, Lake Worth, FL. Tel: (561) 966-8090 (16)

United States Bronze Sign Co Inc, New Hyde Park, NY. Tel: (516) 352-5155, FAX: (516) 352-1761, Web Site: www.usbronze.com (1)

US Cavalry, Radcliff, KY. Tel: (270) 351-1164, FAX: (270) 352-0266, E-Mail: hq@uscavalry.com, Web Site: www.uscavalry.com (6)

US Cellular, Chicago, IL. Tel: (773) 339-8900, Web Site: www.uscellular.com (32)

US Chamber Institute for Legal Reform, Washington, DC. Tel: (202) 778-6063, Web Site: www.uschamber.com (40)

US Chamber of Commerce, Washington, DC. Tel: (202) 778-6063, (800) 638-6582, FAX: (202) 887-3430, Web Site: www.uschamber.com (1)

US Data Corp, Omaha, NE. Tel: (402) 502-5623, (888) 578-3282, FAX: (402) 502-5623, Web Site: www.usdatacorporation.com (29)

US Data Corp, Agoura Hills, CA. Tel: (818) 444-4590, Web Site: www.usdatacorp.net (23)

US Department of Commerce, Washington, DC. Tel: (202) 482-4582 (1)

US Digital Transactions Corporation, New York, NY. Tel: (800) 728-1190, Web Site: www.usdtcorp.com (14)

US Foodservice, Rosemont, IL. Tel: (410) 312-7100, FAX: (410) 312-7167, Web Site: www.usfoodservice.com (4)

US Fund for UNICEF, New York, NY. Tel: (212) 686-5522, FAX: (212) 779-1679, Web Site: www.unicefusa.org (6)

US Games Systems Inc, Stamford, CT. Tel: (203) 353-8400, (800) 544-2637, FAX: (203) 353-8431, Web Site: www.usgamesinc.com (11)

US Gas & Electric, Miami, FL. Tel: (305) 947-7880, Web Site: www.usgande.com (16)

US Historical Society, Richmond, VA. Tel: (800) 788-4478, FAX: (804) 648-0002, E-Mail: administrator@ushs.org, Web Site: www.ushs.org (16)

US Monitor, New City, NY. Tel: (845) 634-1331, (800) 767-7967, FAX: (845) 634-9618, E-Mail: info@usmonitor.com, Web Site: www.usmonitor.com (28)

US News & World Report, New York, NY. Tel: (212) 916-7360, FAX: (212) 643-7842, Web Site: www.usnews.com (17)

USA Direct Inc, York, PA. Tel: (717) 852-1000, (800) 441-1850, FAX: (717) 852-1030, Web Site: www.usamailnow.com (21)

USA 800 Inc, Raytown, MO. Tel: (816) 358-1303, (800) 821-7539, FAX: (816) 358-8845, E-Mail: dlabatt@usa-800.com, Web Site: www.usa-800.com (29)

USA Fulfillment, Chestertown, MD. Tel: (410) 810-0800, (800) 777-8872, FAX: (410) 810-0910, E-Mail: sroy@usafill.com, Web Site: www.usafill.com (28)

USA Hosts, San Francisco, CA. Tel: (415) 695-8000, (800) 368-4678, FAX: (415) 986-3668, Web Site: www.usahosts.com (19)

USA Network, New York, NY. Tel: (212) 664-4444, FAX: (212) 664-6365, Web Site: www.usanetwork.com (32)

USA TODAY, Mc Lean, VA. Tel: (703) 854-3400, (800) 872-0001, E-Mail: accuracy@usatoday.com, Web Site: www.usatoday.com (17)

USA Weekend, New York, NY. Tel: (800) 487-4956, FAX: (703) 854-2122, Web Site: www.usaweekend.com (31)

US Pharmacopeia, Rockville, MD. Tel: (301) 881-0666, FAX: (301) 816-8236 (1)

US Playing Card Co, Erlanger, KY. Tel: (513) 396-5700, (800) 542-7430, FAX: (513) 392-5879 (16)

US Postal Service-Library, Washington, DC. Tel: (202) 268-2904, FAX: (202) 268-6436, Web Site: www.usps.com (28)

US Tape & Label Corp, Saint Louis, MO. Tel: (314) 824-4444, (800) 569-1906, FAX: (314) 824-4400, E-Mail: harrisonc@ustl.com, Web Site: www.ustl.com (27)

US Tax Shield, Encino, CA. Tel: (877) 929-3535, Web Site: www.ustaxshield.com (14)

United States Tennis Association, White Plains, NY. Tel: (914) 696-7156, Web Site: www.usta.com (1)

United Stationers, Deerfield, IL. Tel: (847) 627-7000, Web Site: www.unitedstationers.com (25)

United Systems c/o Biomed, Concord, CA. Tel: (925) 609-2820 (7)

United Way of Greater Toronto, Toronto, ON Canada. Tel: (416) 777-2001, FAX: (416) 777-0962, Web Site: www.unitedwaytoronto.com (1)

United Way Store, Alexandria, VA. Tel: (703) 212-6300, (800) 772-0008, FAX: (703) 212-6319, E-Mail: customerservice@unitedwaystore.com, Web Site: www.unitedwaystore.com (34)

United Way Worldwide, Alexandria, VA. Tel: (703) 836-7100, Web Site: www.liveunited.org (1)

United Wire Service, Peoria, IL. Tel: (309) 689-6160, FAX: (309) 689-6488, E-Mail: julie.finney@choicepoint.com, Web Site: www.unitedwire.net (28)

Unitrin, Chicago, IL. Tel: (312) 661-4600, (800) 733-7366, FAX: (312) 494-6995, Web Site: www.unitrin.com (15)

Unitron Ltd, Commack, NY. Tel: (631) 589-6666, FAX: (631) 589-6795, E-Mail: johnc@unitronusa.com, Web Site: www.unitronusa.com (9)

Unity School of Christianity, Unity Village, MO. Tel: (816) 254-3550, FAX: (816) 251-3554, E-Mail: unity@unityonline.org, Web Site: www.unityonline.org (17)

Univenture Inc, Marysville, OH. Tel: (937) 645-4600, Web Site: www.univenture.com (27)

Universal Communication Enterprise, Elizabeth, NJ. Tel: (908) 355-2299, FAX: (908) 352-2931 (13)

Universal Corp, Richmond, VA. Tel: (804) 359-9311, FAX: (804) 254-3582, Web Site: www.universalcorp.com (16)

Universal Distribution Services, Reno, NV. Tel: (775) 332-5700, FAX: (775) 332-5715, E-Mail: sales@udsi.com, Web Site: www.udsi.com (28)

Universal Engineering Corp, Cedar Rapids, IA. Tel: (319) 365-0441, (800) 366-2051, FAX: (319) 369-5440, E-Mail: info@universalcrusher.com, Web Site: www.universalcrusher.com (16)

Universal Fidelity Corp, Houston, TX. Tel: (281) 550-1444, (800) 580-8887, FAX: (281) 647-4207, Web Site: www.ufccorp.com (14)

Universal Hovercraft, Cordova, IL. Tel: (309) 654-2588, FAX: (309) 654-2588, Web Site: www.hovercraft.com (11)

Universal Media Syndicate Inc, Canton, OH. Tel: (330) 966-9000, Web Site: www.uni-syn.com (35)

Universal Printing, Saint Louis, MO. Tel: (314) 771-6900, FAX: (314) 771-7987, E-Mail: info@universalprintingco.com, Web Site: www.universalprintingco.com (27)

Universal Security Instruments Inc, Owings Mills, MD. Tel: (410) 363-3000, FAX: (410) 363-2218, E-Mail: sales@universalsecurity.com, Web Site: www.universalsecurity.com (16)

Universal Training, Lake Forest, IL. Tel: (847) 235-2170, E-Mail: information@universaltraining.com, Web Site: www.universaltraining.com (16)

Universal Vintage Tire Co, Hershey, PA. Tel: (717) 534-0175, (800) 233-3827, FAX: (717) 534-0719, E-Mail: sales@universaltire.com, Web Site: www.universaltire.com (11)

University at Buffalo Center for Entrepreneurial Leadership, Buffalo, NY. Tel: (716) 885-5715, Web Site: http://mgt.buffalo.edu/entrepreneurship/cel (5)

University Bank, Ann Arbor, MI. Tel: (734) 741-5858, FAX: (734) 741-5859, E-Mail: ranzini@university-bank.com, Web Site: www.university-bank.com (14)

University of Akron, Akron, OH. Tel: (330) 972-5758 (1)

University of Alabama, Tuscaloosa, AL. Tel: (205) 348-6010, FAX: (205) 348-0249, Web Site: www.ua.edu (13)

University of California Irvine Extension, Irvine, CA. Tel: (949) 824-5413, Web Site: extension.uci.edu (1)

University of Chicago GSB, Chicago, IL. Tel: (312) 464-8733, Web Site: www.chicagoexec.net (1)

University of Chicago Press, Chicago, IL. Tel: (773) 702-7700, FAX: (773) 702-9756, Web Site: www.press.uchicago.edu (17)

University of Illinois College of LAS, Office of Advancement, Champaign, IL. Tel: (217) 333-7108, Web Site: www.las.uiuc.edu (1)

University of Illinois Foundation, Urbana, IL. Tel: (217) 333-0810, FAX: (217) 333-5577, E-Mail: uif@uillinois.edu, Web Site: www.uif.uillinois.edu (1)

University of Minnesota, Saint Paul, MN. Tel: (612) 625-0256, Web Site: www.cce.umn.edu (1)

University of Minnesota Alumni Association, Minneapolis, MN. Tel: (612) 624-2323, (800) UM-ALUMS, FAX: (612) 626-8167, E-Mail: umalumni@umn.edu, Web Site: www.umaa.umn.edu (1)

University of Missouri, Columbia, MO. Tel: (573) 882-6333, (800) 856-2181, FAX: (573) 882-2721, E-Mail: visitus@missouri.edu, Web Site: www.missouri.edu (41)

University of Missouri/Kansas City, Kansas City, MO. Tel: (816) 235-2215, FAX: (816) 235-2312, Web Site: www.umkc.edu (41)

University of North Texas, Denton, TX. Tel: (940) 565-2205, Web Site: www.unt.edu/journalism (1)

University of Oklahoma Press, Norman, OK. Tel: (800) 627-7377, FAX: (405) 364-5798, Web Site: www.oupress.com (17)

University of Pennsylvania, Philadelphia, PA. Tel: (215) 898-5000, FAX: (215) 898-9659, Web Site: www.upenn.edu (1)

University of Pennsylvania - Veterinary Medicine (Development), Philadelphia, PA. Tel: (215) 898-1480, Web Site: www.vet.upenn.edu (1)

University of Phoenix, Phoenix, AZ. Tel: (480) 557-1662, Web Site: www.phoenix.edu (13)

University of Pittsburgh at Bradford, Bradford, PA. Tel: (814) 362-7500, FAX: (814) 362-5150, E-Mail: admissions@www.upb.pitt.edu, Web Site: www.upd.pitt.edu (41)

University of Southern California, Los Angeles, CA. Tel: (213) 821-2366, FAX: (213) 740-2343, E-Mail: taube@usc.edu, Web Site: www.usc.edu (38)

University of Southern Mississippi, Hattiesburg, MS. Tel: (601) 266-4734, Web Site: www.usm.edu (1)

University of Texas School of Law, Austin, TX. Tel: (512) 232-1174, Web Site: www.utcle.org (1)

University of Washington Educational Outreach, Seattle, WA. Tel: (206) 685-6566, Web Site: www.pce.uw.edu (1)

University of Wisconsin-Madison School of Business Executive Education, Madison, WI. Tel: (608) 441-7357 (1)

University Press of America Inc, Lanham, MD. Tel: (301) 459-3366, (800) 462-6420, FAX: (301) 429-5748, E-Mail: custserv@rowman.com, Web Site: www.univpress.com (17)

University Subscription Service, Downers Grove, IL. Tel: (630) 960-3233, FAX: (630) 960-3246, Web Site: www.ussmag.com (18)

Uniway Management Corp, Forest Park, GA. Tel: (404) 363-6200, (888) 386-4929, FAX: (404) 363-8848, E-Mail: uniway@bellsouth.net, Web Site: www.uniway.com (16)

UniWorld Group, Brooklyn, NY. Tel: (212) 219-1600, FAX: (212) 219-6395, E-Mail: fhicks@uniworldgroup.com, Web Site: www.uniworldgroup.com (21)

Unsur, Annette, Washington University, Saint Louis, MO. Tel: (314) 935-4623, (800) 638-0700, FAX: (314) 935-7088, Web Site: www.wustl.edu (1)

Untiedt, Allison Webb, Webb Designs Inc, El Cajon, CA. Tel: (619) 596-6400, (800) 262-9322, FAX: (619) 596-4511, E-Mail: awebb@webbshade.com, Web Site: www.webbshade.com (16)

Unum Corp, Portland, ME. Tel: (207) 770-2211, (800) 421-0344, FAX: (207) 770-4510, Web Site: www.unum.com (15)

Unverzagt, Steve, Art Instruction Schools, Minneapolis, MN. Tel: (612) 362-5075, FAX: (612) 362-5260, Web Site: www.artinstructionschools.edu (13)

Unz & Co, Middlesex, NJ. Tel: (732) 868-0706, (800) 631-3098, FAX: (732) 868-0260, E-Mail: unzco@unzco.com, Web Site: www.unzco.com (27)

Upbeat Inc, Saint Louis, MO. Tel: (314) 535-5005, (800) 325-3047, FAX: (314) 535-4419, E-Mail: custservice@upbeat.com, Web Site: www.upbeat.com (10)

Upbin, Hal, American Recreation Products Inc, Saint Louis, MO. Tel: (314) 576-8000, FAX: (314) 576-8072 (11)

Upchurch, Howard, Sara Lee Hosiery, Winston Salem, NC. Tel: (336) 519-2711/2369, FAX: (336) 519-3254, Web Site: www.leggs.com (2)

Updegoss, Cathy, Carroll Publishing, Bethesda, MD. Tel: (301) 263-9800, (800) 336-4240, FAX: (301) 263-9801, Web Site: www.carrollpub.com (17)

Updike, Vicki, Miles Kimball Co, Oshkosh, WI. Tel: (920) 231-3800, FAX: (920) 231-0422, Web Site: www.mileskimball.com (6)

Updyke, David, C., The Mailbox of Ithaca Inc, Ithaca, NY. Tel: (607) 257-3865, (800) 382-6348, FAX: (607) 266-0508, E-Mail: mailbox@lightlink.com, Web Site: www.mailboxofithaca.com (28)

Uppercue, Crystal, EU Services, Rockville, MD. Tel: (301) 424-3300, (800) 230-3362, FAX: (301) 424-3696, Web Site: www.euservices.com (21)

Upstart, Madison, WI. Tel: (920) 563-9571, FAX: (800) 448-5828, Web Site: www.highsmith.com (16)

Urbach, Ronald, R., Davis & Gilbert, New York, NY. Tel: (212) 468-4800, FAX: (212) 468-4888, Web Site: www.dglaw.com (20)

Urban, Tracy, Parenting Concepts Inc, Murrieta, CA. Tel: (951) 672-1131, (800) 727-3683, E-Mail: babyslings@aol.com, Web Site: www.parentingconcepts.com (2)

Urban Mapping Inc, San Francisco, CA. Tel: (415) 946-8170, Web Site: www.urbanmapping.com (16)

Urban Response LLC, Hartville, OH. Tel: (330) 877-0800, (866) 550-3501, FAX: (330) 877-0802 (17)

Urban Science Applications Inc, Detroit, MI. Tel: (313) 259-9900, Web Site: www.urbanscience.com (20)

Urbani, Paul, A., Urbani Truffles USA Corp, New York, NY. Tel: (212) 247-8800, FAX: (212) 247-8900, E-Mail: info@urbani.com, Web Site: www.urbanitartufi.com (4)

Urbani Truffles USA Corp, New York, NY. Tel: (212) 247-8800, FAX: (212) 247-8900, E-Mail: info@urbani.com, Web Site: www.urbanitartufi.com (4)

Urbania, Carl, Cengage Learning, Independence, KY. Tel: (800) 354-9706, FAX: (800) 487-8488, Web Site: www.delmar.com (17)

Urbin, Norman, Parenting Concepts Inc, Murrieta, CA. Tel: (951) 672-1131, (800) 727-3683, E-Mail: babyslings@aol.com, Web Site: www.parentingconcepts.com (2)

USADATA Inc, New York, NY. Tel: (212) 679-1411, Web Site: www.usadata.com (23)

USC Marshall School of Business Dept of Marketing, Los Angeles, CA. Tel: (213) 740-5033, FAX: (213) 740-7828, E-Mail: dennis.rook@marshall.usc.edu (41)

USDiscs, Duarte, CA. Tel: (626) 359-9955, Web Site: www.usdiscs.com (27)

Usher, Thomas, J., USX, Pittsburgh, PA. Tel: (412) 433-1121, E-Mail: webmaster@usx.com, Web Site: www.usx.com (16)

Ustian, Daniel, Navistar, Warrenville, IL. Tel: (630) 753-5804, (800) 448-7825, FAX: (630) 753-2303, Web Site: www.navistar.com (16)

Utaka, Yoshimoto, Isuzu Motors America Inc, Anaheim, CA. Tel: (562) 229-5000, (800) 255-6727, FAX: (562) 229-5463, Web Site: www.isuzu.com (16)

Utilities Supply Corp, Woburn, MA. Tel: (781) 395-9023, (800) 343-7555, FAX: (781) 395-2329, (800) 232-8726, E-Mail: jge@fwwebb.com, Web Site: www.uscosupply.com (16)

Utley, Valerie, Morpace Inc, Farmington Hills, MI. Tel: (248) 737-5300, FAX: (248) 737-5326, E-Mail: information@morpace.com, Web Site: www.morpace.com (30)

Utretch Art Supplies, Cranbury, NJ. Tel: (609) 409-8001, (800) 223-9132, FAX: (800) 382-1979, Web Site: www.utrechtart.com (10)

Uwharrie Capital Corp, Albemarle, NC. Tel: (704) 991-1181, Web Site: www.uwharriecapitalcorp.com (14)

V

V12 Group, Red Bank, NJ. Tel: (732) 842-1001, Web Site: www.v12group.com (23)

V3, Oxnard, CA. Tel: (800) 882-1844, Web Site: www.v3corporation.com (27)

VAGA (Visual Artists & Galleries Associations Inc), New York, NY. Tel: (212) 736-6666, FAX: (212) 736-6767, E-Mail: rpanzer@vaga.erols.com (38)

VF Imagewear, Nashville, TN. Tel: (615) 565-5000, (800) 733-5271, Web Site: www.vfimagewear.com (2)

VGH Solutions, Markham, ON Canada. Tel: (905) 471-4735, FAX: (905) 471-2608 (7)

VMF Inc, Washington, DC. Tel: (202) 966-3361, FAX: (202) 362-8409, E-Mail: veflei@aol.com (20)

VW Credit, Herndon, VA. Tel: (703) 364-7755 (14)

VWR International, Radnor, PA. Tel: (610) 386-1700, (800) 932-5000, FAX: (866) 329-2897, Web Site: www.vwrsp.com (34)

Vacanti, Russ, Armento Inc, Buffalo, NY. Tel: (716) 875-2423, (866) 276-3686, FAX: (716) 875-8011, E-Mail: armento@aol.com, Web Site: www.armento-columbarium.com (5)

Vaccarella, Chris, Bucks County Coffee Co, Conshohocken, PA. Tel: (215) 741-1855, (800) 523-6163, FAX: (215) 741-1799, Web Site: www.buckscountycoffee.com (16)

Vaccaro, Thomas, The Orvis Co Inc, Manchester, VT. Tel: (802) 362-3622, FAX: (802) 362-3525, Web Site: www.orvis.com (11)

Vache, Noel, Ward's Natural Science, Rochester, NY. Tel: (585) 359-2502, (800) 962-2660, FAX: (585) 334-6174, E-Mail: customer_service@wardsci.com, Web Site: www.wardsci.com (34)

Vadar, Umut, LeadCreations.Com LLC, Coral Gables, FL. Tel: (305) 851-8110, Web Site: www.leadcreations.com (23)

Vadeboncoeur Jr., Jim, Bud Plant Illustrated Books, Palo Alto, CA. Tel: (650) 493-1191, FAX: (650) 493-1145, E-Mail: jim@bpib.com, Web Site: www.bpib.com (6)

Vagabond Creations Inc, Dayton, OH. Tel: (937) 298-1124, (800) 738-7237, FAX: (937) 298-1124, E-Mail: sales@vagabondcreations.net, Web Site: www.vagabondcreations.net (10)

Vail, Walter, Saint Mary's Paper Corp, Wheaton, IL. Tel: (630) 668-6279, FAX: (630) 668-6292, Web Site: www.stmarys-paper.com (25)

Vail Associates Inc, Broomfield, CO. Tel: (303) 404-1800, (800) 842-8062, FAX: (303) 404-6415, Web Site: www.snow.com (19)

Vail Resorts Inc, Keystone, CO. Tel: (970) 468-2316/845-2694, FAX: (970) 453-3202, Web Site: www.keystoneresort.com (19)

Vaillancourt, Brian, Level 5 Communications Inc, Dublin, NH. Tel: (603) 563-1631, FAX: (603) 563-8912, Web Site: www.deskeng.com (32)

Vakili, Fred, Info USA City Directories, Omaha, NE. Tel: (402) 593-4500, (800) 925-4654, FAX: (402) 593-4671, E-Mail: customerservice@infousacity.com, Web Site: www.infousacity.com (17)

Valassis, Windsor, CT. Tel: (860) 285-6100, FAX: (203) 845-5338, Web Site: www.valassis.com (31)

Valassis Canada, Toronto, ON Canada. Tel: (416) 259-3600, Web Site: www.valassis.com (35)

ValCom Inc, Indian Rocks Beach, FL. Tel: (702) 385-9000, FAX: (702) 382-2802, Web Site: www.valcom.tv (32)

Valdawn Watch Co, Long Island City, NY. Tel: (201) 807-1110, FAX: (201) 807-0228 (16)

Vale, Tom, DeLuxe Laboratories Inc, Hollywood, CA. Tel: (323) 462-6171, FAX: (323) 960-7016, E-Mail: steven.vananda@bydeluxe.com, Web Site: www.bydeluxe.com (16)

Valenta, Lee, Ingenix, Reston, VA. Tel: (571) 521-7661, (800) 765-6713, FAX: (571) 521-7237, E-Mail: inform@ingenix.com, Web Site: www.ingenix.com (32)

Valenta, Tommy, A., Texas Industries Inc, Dallas, TX. Tel: (972) 647-6700, FAX: (972) 647-3878, Web Site: www.txi.com (16)

Valente, Dennis, J., APSCO, Davenport Center, NY. Tel: (607) 278-6218, FAX: (607) 278-6218, E-Mail: webmaster@antiquephono.com, Web Site: www.antiquephono.com (11)

Valente, Patricia, F., APSCO, Davenport Center, NY. Tel: (607) 278-6218, FAX: (607) 278-6218, E-Mail: webmaster@antiquephono.com, Web Site: www.antiquephono.com (11)

Valenti, Steve, Valenti Classics, Caledonia, WI. Tel: (262) 835-2070, FAX: (262) 835-2575, Web Site: www.valenticlassics.com (16)

Valenti Classics, Caledonia, WI. Tel: (262) 835-2070, FAX: (262) 835-2575, Web Site: www.valenticlassics.com (16)

Valentine, Lisa, PowerPay, Portland, ME. Tel: (207) 775-6900, (877) 877-3737, FAX: (888) 204-4040, Web Site: www.powerpay.biz (14)

Valentine, Michael, D., Valentine Research Inc, Cincinnati, OH. Tel: (513) 984-8900, (800) 331-3030, FAX: (513) 984-8976, E-Mail: sales@valentine1.com, Web Site: www.valentine1.com (16)

Valentine, Vilia, Real Goods Trading Corp, San Rafael, CA. Tel: (707) 542-2600, (888) 567-6527, Web Site: www.realgoods.com (5)

Valentine Research Inc, Cincinnati, OH. Tel: (513) 984-8900, (800) 331-3030, FAX: (513) 984-8976, E-Mail: sales@valentine1.com, Web Site: www.valentine1.com (16)

Valentino, Gina, Hemisphere Marketing, Kansas City, MO. Tel: (816) 444-5439, Web Site: www.hemispheremarketing.com (20)

Valentino, Joanne, Medical Letter Inc, New Rochelle, NY. Tel: (914) 235-0500, Web Site: www.medicalletter.org (1)

Valeriani, Nicolas, J., Johnson & Johnson, New Brunswick, NJ. Tel: (732) 524-0400, FAX: (732) 214-0332, Web Site: www.jnj.com (16)

Valetta, John, Super 8 Hotels Worldwide, Parsippany, NJ. Tel: (973) 428-9700, (800) 800-8000, FAX: (973) 496-7307, Web Site: www.super8.com (19)

Valette, Jean-Michel, Peet's Coffee & Tea Inc, Berkeley, CA. Tel: (510) 594-2100, (800) 999-2132, FAX: (510) 594-2180, E-Mail: mailorder@peets.com, Web Site: www.peets.com (4)

Valkenburgh, Van, Torqmaster International, Stamford, CT. Tel: (203) 326-5945, (888) 414-4643, FAX: (203) 326-5944, E-Mail: info@torqmaster.com, Web Site: www.torqmaster.com (9)

Valleaux, Christine, Marimac Inc, Montreal, PQ. Tel: (514) 725-7600, FAX: (514) 376-0801, Web Site: www.marimac.com (8)

Vallee, Roy, Avnet Inc, Phoenix, AZ. Tel: (480) 643-2000, FAX: (480) 643-7240, Web Site: www.avnet.com (16)

Vallely Jr, W.F., AT Clayton & Co Inc, Stamford, CT. Tel: (203) 658-1200, E-Mail: webmaster@atclayton.com, Web Site: www.atclayton.com (25)

Valles, Beatrix, Cliggott Publishing Co, Norwalk, CT. Tel: (203) 662-6400, (203) 661-0600, FAX: (203) 662-6420, Web Site: www.cmp.com (17)

Valley Forge Tape & Label Co Inc, Exton, PA. Tel: (610) 524-8900, (800) 345-1323, FAX: (610) 524-8906, E-Mail: vfsales@vftl.com, Web Site: www.vftl.com (27)

Vallone-Raffaele, Helene, US Fund for UNICEF, New York, NY. Tel: (212) 686-5522, FAX: (212) 779-1679, Web Site: www.unicefusa.org (6)

Valmark Associates LLC, Buffalo, NY. Tel: (716) 893-1494, Web Site: www.valmarkassociates.com (35)

Valpak Direct Marketing Systems Inc, Largo, FL. Tel: (727) 399-3000, Web Site: www.valpak.com (31)

Valpak of New York, New York, NY. Tel: (212) 560-9400, Web Site: www.valpaknewyork.com (41)

Value Line Publishing Inc, New York, NY. Tel: (212) 907-1500, FAX: (212) 818-9747, Web Site: www.valueline.com (17)

ValueVision Media Inc, Eden Prairie, MN. Tel: (952) 943-6000, FAX: (952) 943-6711, Web Site: www.valuevisionmedia.com (32)

Valvo, Karen, Q., Eastern Michigan University, Ypsilanti, MI. Tel: (734) 487-1849, FAX: (734) 484-1151, Web Site: www.emich.edu (16)

Valvo, Vincent, Banker & Tradesman, Boston, MA. Tel: (617) 428-5100, FAX: (617) 428-5119, E-Mail: dmoore@thewarrengroup.com, Web Site: www.thewarrengroup.com (17)

Valvoda, Paul, Cleveland Institute of Electronics, Cleveland, OH. Tel: (216) 781-9400, FAX: (216) 781-0331, E-Mail: instruct@cie-wc.edu, Web Site: www.cie-wc.edu (13)

van Amstel, Hans, Ploos, Levi Strauss & Co, San Francisco, CA. Tel: (415) 501-6000, FAX: (415) 501-7112, Web Site: www.levistrauss.com (16)

Van Arsdel, Heather, American Society of Journalists & Authors Directory, New York, NY. Tel: (212) 997-0947, FAX: (212) 768-7414, E-Mail: asjany@ibm.net (43)

Van Bourgondien, Fred, Van Bourgondien Bros, Virginia Beach, VA. Tel: (800) 327-4268, E-Mail: blooms@dutchbulbs.com, Web Site: www.dutchbulbs.com (8)

Van Bourgondien Bros, Virginia Beach, VA. Tel: (800) 327-4268, E-Mail: blooms@dutchbulbs.com, Web Site: www.dutchbulbs.com (8)

Van Castle, Robin, Taylor Capital Group, Inc, Rosemont, IL. Tel: (847) 653-7978, FAX: (847) 653-7890, E-Mail: investor.relations@coletaylor.com, Web Site: www.taylorcapitalgroup.com (14)

Van Cleave, Robb, E., Society for Human Resource Management, Alexandria, VA. Tel: (703) 548-3440, (800) 283-SHRM, FAX: (703) 535-6490, E-Mail: shrmstore@shrm.org, Web Site: www.shrm.org (1)

Van Cott, Craig, H., Unadilla Laminated Products, Unadilla, NY. Tel: (607) 369-9341, FAX: (607) 369-3608, E-Mail: info@unalam.com, Web Site: www.unalam.com (16)

Van Dam Inc, New York, NY. Tel: (212) 929-0416, (800) UNFOLDS, FAX: (212) 929-0426, E-Mail: info@vandam.com, Web Site: www.vandam.com (17)

Van de Aast, Gerard, Reed - Elsevier, New York, NY. Tel: (212) 309-5498, FAX: (212) 309-5480, Web Site: www.reed-elsevier.com (17)

Van De Voorde, Mathew, Orion, Federal Way, WA. Tel: (253) 661-7805, Web Site: www.orionworks.org (1)

van der Horst, Carl, Upbeat Inc, Saint Louis, MO. Tel: (314) 535-5005, (800) 325-3047, FAX: (314) 535-4419, E-Mail: custservice@upbeat.com, Web Site: www.upbeat.com (9)

Van Der Veer, Gina, Dr Leonard's Healthcare Corp, Edison, NJ. Tel: (732) 225-0100, FAX: (732) 225-0302, Web Site: www.doctorleonard.com (7)

Van der Walt, Christina, Haymarket Group Ltd, New York, NY. Tel: (212) 239-0855, FAX: (212) 967-4184, Web Site: www.chocalatiermagazine.com (17)

Van Doren, Cathy, Fort Hays State University, Hays, KS. Tel: (785) 628-FHSU, FAX: (785) 628-4046, Web Site: www.fhsu.edu (41)

Van Ert, Mark, FG Companies, Wayzata, MN. Tel: (952) 540-4901, Web Site: www.fgcompanies.com (22)

van Galen, Laura, Bleu Marketing Solutions Inc, San Francisco, CA. Tel: (415) 345-3300, FAX: (415) 353-0299, E-Mail: helpdesk@bleumarketing.com, Web Site: www.bleumarketing.com (35)

Van Gelder, Kim E., Eastman Kodak Co, Rochester, NY. Tel: (585) 724-0251, (800) 698-3324, FAX: (585) 724-1089, Web Site: www.kodak.com (27)

Van Gilse, Rob, Alloyd Brands, Dekalb, IL. Tel: (815) 756-8451, (800) 756-7639, FAX: (815) 756-5187/9192, Web Site: www.alloyd.com (16)

Van Graafeiland, Gary P., ESL Federal Credit Union, Rochester, NY. Tel: (585) 336-1000, (800) 848-2265, FAX: (585) 336-1138, Web Site: www.esl.org (14)

Van Gundy, Rick, American Bar Association, Chicago, IL. Tel: (312) 988-5435, FAX: (312) 988-5455, Web Site: www.abanet.org (1)

Van Hollen, Chris, Democratic Congressional Campaign Committee, Washington, DC. Tel: (202) 863-1500, FAX: (202) 485-3436, Web Site: www.dccc.com (1)

Van Hyfte, Robert, J., Pragalz Metro Graphx Inc, Twin Lakes, WI. Tel: (708) 449-2700, FAX: (708) 449-2711 (21)

Van Kirk, Phil, The Taunton Press, Newtown, CT. Tel: (203) 426-8171, (800) 477-8727, FAX: (203) 426-3434, Web Site: www.taunton.com (17)

Van Meter, Leila, Making It Big, Cotati, CA. Tel: (707) 795-1995, (877) 644-1995, FAX: (707) 795-4874, E-Mail: mib@makingitbig.com, Web Site: www.makingitbig.com (2)

Van Milligen, Michael, C., International City/County Management Association, Washington, DC. Tel: (202) 289-ICMA, FAX: (202) 962-3500, E-Mail: customerservice@icma.org, Web Site: www.icma.org (1)

Van Oss, Stephen, A., WESCO, Pittsburgh, PA. Tel: (412) 454-2200, (800) 343-1201, E-Mail: info@wesco.com, Web Site: www.wescodist.com (16)

Van Rees, Linda, F., The HoneyBaked Ham Co, Holland, OH. Tel: (419) 868-6400, E-Mail: info@honeybaked.com, Web Site: www.honeybaked.com (4)

Van Remmen, Roger, Brown, Van Remmen, Kanuit, Inc, El Segundo, CA. Tel: (310) 536-0777, FAX: (310) 536-0606, E-Mail: info@bvksearch.com, Web Site: www.bvksearch.com (20)

Van Rockel, Gary, Melissa Data Corp, Rancho Santa Margarita, CA. Tel: (949) 589-5200, (800) 800-6245, FAX: (949) 589-5211, E-Mail: sales@melissadata.com, Web Site: www.melissadata.com (22)

van Rooyen, Guy, Donna Salyers' Fabulous-Furs, Covington, KY. Tel: (859) 291-3300, (800) 848-4650, E-Mail: abell@fabulousfurs.com, Web Site: fabulousfurs.com (2)

Van Ryzin, Wade, Elemental Scientific LLC, Appleton, WI. Tel: (920) 882-1277, E-Mail: info@elementalscientific.net (9)

Van Someren, Barbara, Beltone, Glenview, IL. Tel: (800) 235-8663, FAX: (847) 832-3300, E-Mail: info@beltone.com, Web Site: www.beltone.com (3)

Van Veen, Tony, Disc Makers, Pennsauken, NJ. Tel: (800) 237-6666, Web Site: www.discmakers.com (3)

Van Vliet, Alan, Unified Precious Metals Inc, Canoga Park, CA. Tel: (818) 889-7797, FAX: (818) 735-8878 (32)

Van Vliet, Dave, Hasco First Photo, Saint Charles, MO. Tel: (636) 946-5115, FAX: (636) 946-7148, Web Site: www.growingfamily.com (16)

van Wagenen, Jay, JVW Direct, Pittsburgh, PA. Tel: (412) 241-5920, FAX: (412) 241-5850, E-Mail: john@jvwdirect.com (35)

Van Wyck, E. Hawley, DirectMail.com, Prince Frederick, MD. Tel: (888) 690-2252, FAX: (301) 855-9810, Web Site: www.directmail.com (28)

Van Wyck, Hawley, All American List Corp, Prince Frederick, MD. Tel: (301) 420-5760, (800) 690-2252, FAX: (301) 420-5765, E-Mail: info@allamericanlist.com, Web Site: www.allamericanlist.com (23)

Van Wyk, Chris, Village Weavers, San Antonio, TX. Tel: (210) 222-0776, E-Mail: shop@villageweavers.com, Web Site: www.villageweavers.com (16)

Vance, Adam, Travel Industry Association, Washington, DC. Tel: (202) 408-8422, FAX: (202) 408-1255, E-Mail: feedback@tia.org, Web Site: www.tia.org (1)

Vance, Bob, Decko Products Inc, Sandusky, OH. Tel: (419) 626-5757, FAX: (419) 626-3135 (4)

Vance, Cindy, DirectMail.com, Prince Frederick, MD. Tel: (888) 690-2252, FAX: (301) 855-9810, Web Site: www.directmail.com (28)

Vance Industries Inc, Niles, IL. Tel: (847) 375-8900, FAX: (847) 375-6818, E-Mail: vance@vanceind.com, Web Site: www.vanceind.com (16)

VanDam, Stephan, C., Van Dam Inc, New York, NY. Tel: (212) 929-0416, (800) UNFOLDS, FAX: (212) 929-0426, E-Mail: info@vandam.com, Web Site: www.vandam.com (17)

VandenBos, Gary, American Psychological Association, Washington, DC. Tel: (202) 336-5500, (800) 374-2721, FAX: (202) 336-5568, E-Mail: order@apa.org, Web Site: www.apa.org (1)

Vander Ploeg, David, School Specialty Inc, Greenville, WI. Tel: (920) 734-5712, (888) 388-3224, FAX: (920) 734-5112, E-Mail: info@schoolspecialty.com, Web Site: www.schoolspecialty.com (16)

Vander Zanden, David J., School Specialty Inc, Greenville, WI. Tel: (920) 734-5712, (888) 388-3224, FAX: (920) 734-5112, E-Mail: info@schoolspecialty.com, Web Site: www.schoolspecialty.com (16)

Vanderbilt Advertising, New York, NY. Tel: (212) 907-1500, FAX: (212) 907-1914, Web Site: www.valueline.com (14)

VanderVeen, Ken, ABS Graphics, Addison, IL. Tel: (630) 495-2400, FAX: (630) 495-0728, E-Mail: info@absinet.com, Web Site: www.absinet.com (27)

Vandervliet, Mike, Breck's Bulbs, Lawrenceburg, IN. Tel: (309) 693-8600, FAX: (309) 691-9693 (8)

vanDongen, Henk, Mid America Motorworks, Effingham, IL. Tel: (217) 347-5591, (800) 500-1500, FAX: (217) 347-2952, E-Mail: mail@mamotorworks.com, Web Site: www.mamotorworks.com (12)

Vane, Penny, Vane & Friends, Chappaqua, NY. Tel: (914) 238-8890, E-Mail: info@vaneandfriends.com, Web Site: www.vaneandfriends.com (35)

Vane & Friends, Chappaqua, NY. Tel: (914) 238-8890, E-Mail: info@vaneandfriends.com, Web Site: www.vaneandfriends.com (35)

The Vane Brothers Co, Baltimore, MD. Tel: (410) 631-5096, FAX: (410) 631-7781, E-Mail: webmaster@vanebros.com, Web Site: www.vanebros.com (16)

Vanelli, Cynthia, ALSAC - St. Jude, Memphis, TN. Tel: (901) 495-3300, FAX: (901) 495-3103, Web Site: www.stjude.org (1)

Vanguard, Valley Forge, PA. Tel: (610) 648-6000, Web Site: www.vanguard.com (14)

Vanguard Direct, New York, NY. Tel: (212) 736-0770, FAX: (212) 736-8305, Web Site: www.vanguarddirect.com (35)

Vanhorn, Greg, ModernAd Media LLC, Deerfield Beach, FL. Tel: (561) 750-5131 X206, Web Site: www.modernad.com (40)

Vanness, Paula, Make-A-Wish Foundation of America, Phoenix, AZ. Tel: (602) 279-9474, FAX: (602) 279-0855, Web Site: www.wish.org (1)

Vannett, Paul, Dovetail, Littleton, CO. Tel: (303) 904-4771, FAX: (303) 904-4776, E-Mail: welcome@dovetailnet.com, Web Site: www.dovetailnet.com (22)

Vanorman, Dan, Prosper Inc, Provo, UT. Tel: (801) 371-0755, (800) 748-5799, FAX: (801) 374-2358, Web Site: www.prospering.com (32)

VanPatten, Mark, NCP Solutions, Reston, VA. Tel: (703) 438-6000, (800) 822-9919, FAX: (703) 438-3570, Web Site: www.nwf.org (17)

The Vantage Group Inc, Boston, MA. Tel: (617) 878-6000, FAX: (617) 878-6156, Web Site: www.vantagetravel.com (14)

Varela, Victoria, Cartel Creativo, San Antonio, TX. Tel: (210) 892-0700, FAX: (210) 696-4299, Web Site: www.thecartel.com (35)

Varey, Richard, Financial Times, New York, NY. Tel: (212) 641-6500, Web Site: www.ft.com (1)

Vargas, Alejandro, Dialogue Marketing, Auburn Hills, MI. Tel: (734) 374-8400, (800) 523-5867, FAX: (248) 836-2601, Web Site: www.dialogue-marketing.com (29)

Vargas, Jane, JR Tobacco/800-JR Cigar Inc, Burlington, NC. Tel: (800) 572-4427, FAX: (800) 457-3299, Web Site: www.jrcigars.com (5)

Varian Medical Systems, Palo Alto, CA. Tel: (650) 493-4000, FAX: (650) 842-5196, Web Site: www.varian.com (9)

Varmland, Brad, Academy of Psychic Arts & Sciences, Dallas, TX. Tel: (214) 219-2020, FAX: (214) 599-0040, E-Mail: academy@psychic2020.com (5)

Varner, Barbara, ACBL, Horn Lake, MS. Tel: (901) 332-5586, FAX: (901) 398-7754, E-Mail: service@acbl.org, Web Site: www.acbl.org (1)

Varner, Jean, Cuvaison Inc, Calistoga, CA. Tel: (707) 942-6266, FAX: (707) 942-5732, E-Mail: jschuppert@cuvaison.com, Web Site: www.cuvaison.com (4)

Varner, Maribett, BKV Inc, Atlanta, GA. Tel: (404) 233-0332, FAX: (404) 233-0302, E-Mail: sylviam@bkv.com, Web Site: www.bkv.com (35)

Vartorella, William, F., Craig/Vartorella International Marketing & Advertising Inc, Camden, SC. Tel: (803) 432-4353, FAX: (803) 432-4353, E-Mail: globebiz@juno.com, Web Site: www.colasc.com/Marketing_&_Fundraising (1)

Vasile, Joseph, Viahealth, Rochester, NY. Tel: (585) 922-4000, (585) 922-3677, FAX: (585) 922-3929, Web Site: www.viahealth.org (16)

Vasquez, Cyndi, Mike Murach & Associates Inc, Fresno, CA. Tel: (559) 440-9071, (800) 221-5528, FAX: (559) 440-0963, E-Mail: murachbooks@murach.com, Web Site: www.murach.com (17)

Vasquez, Kevin, Butler Schein Animal Health, Dublin, OH. Tel: (614) 761-9095, (888) 691-2724, FAX: (888) 329-3861, Web Site: www.butlerschein.com (16)

Vasquez-Perez, Carmen, Chain Store Guide, Tampa, FL. Tel: (800) 927-9292, FAX: (813) 627-6882, E-Mail: info@csgis.com, Web Site: www.csgis.com (17)

Vassalatti, Michael, Pitney Bowes International Mail Services, Newark, NJ. Tel: (800) 521-0080, FAX: (973) 368-6301, E-Mail: marketing@pb.com, Web Site: www.intmail.com (28)

Vassallo, Vincent, The Results Group, Boston, MA. Tel: (617) 227-0229, Web Site: www.verdant-results-group.com (20)

VastCast Media, Las Vegas, NV. Tel: (702) 221-8261, Web Site: www.vastcastmedia.com (35)

Vastola, Ray, Travel Planners Inc, New York, NY. Tel: (212) 532-1660, (800) 221-3531, FAX: (212) 779-6102, Web Site: www.tphousing.com (19)

Vatuone, Timothy, V., Syntellect, Phoenix, AZ. Tel: (602) 789-2800, (800) 788-9733, FAX: (602) 789-2899, Web Site: www.syntellect.com (16)

Vaughan, Scott, United Business Media, Manhasset, NY. Tel: (516) 562-5000, Web Site: www.ubmtechnology.com (17)

Vaughn Jr., Percy, Alabama State University/College of Business Administration, Montgomery, AL. Tel: (334) 229-4124, FAX: (334) 229-4870, E-Mail: pvaughn@alasu.edu, Web Site: www.cobanetworks.com (41)

Vavra, John, Hasler Mailing Systems and Solutions, Milford, CT. Tel: (203) 301-3400, (800) 995-2035, FAX: (203) 301-2600, E-Mail: info@haslerinc.com, Web Site: www.haslerinc.com (34)

Vaxserve, Scranton, PA. Tel: (800) 752-9338, Web Site: www.vaxserve.com (7)

Vayan Marketing Group LLC, Boynton Beach, FL. Tel: (561) 955-9660, Web Site: www.vayan.com (23)

Vcelik, Mike, Father Flanagan's Boy's Home, Boys Town, NE. Tel: (402) 498-1934, FAX: (402) 498-1969, Web Site: www.boystown.org (1)

Vcom International Multi-Media Corp, South Hackensack, NJ. Tel: (201) 229-9800, (800) 425-4268, FAX: (800) 453-6338, E-Mail: sales@800VALIANT.com, Web Site: www.800VALIANT.com (3)

Veach, Margaret, Beau Graphics Ltd Inc, Lexington, KY. Tel: (859) 277-2328, (877) 279-2328, FAX: (859) 278-6193, Web Site: www.beaugraphics.com (36)

Veale, Paula, The Advertising Council Inc, New York, NY. Tel: (212) 922-1500, FAX: (212) 922-1676, E-Mail: info@adcouncil.org, Web Site: www.adcouncil.org (1)

Vector Marketing Corp, Olean, NY. Tel: (716) 373-6141, FAX: (716) 373-6145, Web Site: www.cutco.com (5)

Vedder, Bret, Creative Learning Systems Inc, Longmont, CO. Tel: (800) 458-2880, FAX: (760) 546-1490, Web Site: www.clsinc.com (9)

Veer, Calgary, AB Canada. Tel: (403) 234-7901, Web Site: www.veer.com (16)

Vegetarian Awareness Network/VEGANET, Washington, DC. Tel: (800) USA-VEGE, (800) 872-8343, FAX: (877) 329-8343 (1)

Vegetarian Times, El Segundo, CA. Tel: (310) 356-4100, FAX: (310) 356-4110, Web Site: www.vegetariantimes.com (31)

Vehicle Assurance, Saint Charles, MO. Tel: (636) 925-7800 (5)

Vejar, Alma, ICS Audio Video Supply Inc, Phoenix, AZ. Tel: (602) 242-9207 (3)

Vejar, Ruben, ICS Audio Video Supply Inc, Phoenix, AZ. Tel: (602) 242-9207 (3)

Vella, Nino, New Pig Corp, Tipton, PA. Tel: (814) 684-0101, (800) 468-4647, FAX: (814) 684-0961, E-Mail: hothogs@newpig.com, Web Site: www.newpig.com (9)

Vellardita, Vince, ValCom Inc, Indian Rocks Beach, FL. Tel: (702) 385-9000, FAX: (702) 382-2802, Web Site: www.valcom.tv (32)

Velletri, Christopher, L., Market Street Lists Inc, Exeter, NH. Tel: (603) 772-6666, (888) 675-LIST, FAX: (603) 772-0184, E-Mail: info@market-street.com, Web Site: www.market-street.com (23)

Vellucci, Bethany, Media Two, Baltimore, MD. Tel: (410) 828-0120, FAX: (410) 825-1002, Web Site: www.mediatwo.com (17)

Veltri, Eugene, A&E Promotions LLC, Atlantic Highlands, NJ. Tel: (732) 275-1520, Web Site: www.aepromo.com (27)

Velu, Param, University Subscription Service, Downers Grove, IL. Tel: (630) 960-3233, FAX: (630) 960-3246, Web Site: www.ussmag.com (18)

Velu, Pethi, Unique Embossing Services Inc & Global Cards, Downers Grove, IL. Tel: (630) 960-3337 X23, FAX: (630) 960-3618, Web Site: www.globalcrd.com (27)

Velu, Pethi, University Subscription Service, Downers Grove, IL. Tel: (630) 960-3233, FAX: (630) 960-3246, Web Site: www.ussmag.com (18)

Veluchamy, Pethinaidu, Versatile Card Technology Inc, Downers Grove, IL. Tel: (630) 852-5600, FAX: (630) 852-5817, Web Site: www.versacard.com (27)

Vemma Nutrition Co, Scottsdale, AZ. Tel: (800) 577-0777, FAX: (888) 314-9827, E-Mail: ms@vemma.com, Web Site: www.vemma.com (9)

Venable LLP Conference Center, Washington, DC. Tel: (202) 344-4860, (202) 344-4000, (888) VENABLE, FAX: (202) 344-8300, E-Mail: info@venable.com, Web Site: www.venable.com (20)

Venables, Jeffrey, American Running Association, Bethesda, MD. Tel: (301) 913-9517, (800) 776-2732, FAX: (301) 913-9520, E-Mail: run@americanrunning.org, Web Site: www.americanrunning.org (1)

Venator Group, New York, NY. Tel: (212) 720-3700, FAX: (212) 720-4689 (2)

Vente Inc, Omaha, NE. Tel: (402) 898-6800, (877) 899-9691, FAX: (402) 334-4829, Web Site: www.venteinc.com (30)

Ventresca Jr., Benjamin, J., Brandywine Consulting Group Inc, West Chester, PA. Tel: (610) 696-5872, FAX: (610) 429-1954, Web Site: www.brandywineconsulting.com (20)

Ventriloquist Voice Solutions International Inc, Mississauga, ON Canada. Tel: (866) 446-0860, E-Mail: info@vvsii.com, Web Site: www.vvsii.com (29)

Ventura Associates International LLC, New York, NY. Tel: (212) 302-8277, FAX: (212) 302-2587, E-Mail: info@sweepspros.com, Web Site: www.sweepspros.com (35)

Venture Encoding Service Inc, Fort Worth, TX. Tel: (817) 283-9500, FAX: (817) 868-1705, E-Mail: sales@venture-encoding.com, Web Site: www.venture-encoding.com (27)

Venture Entertainment Group, Sherman Oaks, CA. Tel: (800) 981-8433, FAX: (818) 981-3466, E-Mail: venture818@aol.com, Web Site: www.venture818.com (3)

Venturella, Frank, J., Magna Visual Inc, Saint Louis, MO. Tel: (314) 843-9000, (800) 843-3399, FAX: (314) 843-0000, E-Mail: magna@magnavisual.com, Web Site: www.magnavisual.com (9)

Venturini, Patti, Cosmetique, Inc, Vernon Hills, IL. Tel: (847) 913-9099, (800) 621-8822, Web Site: www.cosmetique.com (13)

Ventyx, Atlanta, GA. Tel: (770) 952-8444, (800) 868-0497, FAX: (770) 955-2977, E-Mail: support@ventyx.com, Web Site: www.ventyx.com (16)

Venus Fashion, Inc, Jacksonville, FL. Tel: (904) 645-6000, Web Site: www.venus.com (2)

Veratad Technologies LLC, Teaneck, NJ. Tel: (201) 510-6000, FAX: (201) 510-6036 (22)

The Verdi Group Inc, Pittsford, NY. Tel: (585) 381-4275, FAX: (585) 381-4293, E-Mail: info@theverdigroup.com, Web Site: www.theverdigroup.com (35)

Vere, Brenda, Philips Lifeline, Framingham, MA. Tel: (508) 988-1533, Web Site: www.lifelinesys.com (7)

Verey, Andrew, MSC Metalworking, Melville, NY. Tel: (516) 812-2000, (800) 521-9520, E-Mail: inquiry@rutlandtool.com, Web Site: www.rutlandtool.com (34)

Vergara, Richard, LDS Group Inc, New York, NY. Tel: (646) 390-5702, FAX: (646) 390-5715, E-Mail: rvergara@ldsgroupinc.com, Web Site: www.ldsgroupinc.com (23)

Verger, Judy, American Association of Critical-Care Nurses, Aliso Viejo, CA. Tel: (949) 362-2000, (800) 809-CARE, FAX: (949) 362-2020, E-Mail: info@aacn.com, Web Site: www.aacn.org (1)

Vergolino, Joseph, Professional Direct Marketing & Mailing List Inc, Boca Raton, FL. Tel: (561) 241-4414, (800) 777-5478, FAX: (561) 241-5878, E-Mail: pdm@pdmm.info, Web Site: www.pdmm.us (23)

Veriad, Brea, CA. Tel: (714) 990-2700, (800) 962-0658, FAX: (800) 962-0658, E-Mail: info@veriad.com, Web Site: www.veriad.com (16)

Veridian Credit Union, Waterloo, IA. Tel: (319) 236-5692, (800) 235-3228, FAX: (319) 833-1185, E-Mail: sarahma@veridiancu.org, Web Site: www.veridiancu.org (1)

Veritas Analytics Inc, Sterling, VA. Tel: (703) 707-5620, Web Site: www.veritas-analytics.com (30)

Verizon, Arlington, VA. Tel: (703) 351-3156, FAX: (703) 708-4297 (16)

Verizon Communications Inc, New York, NY. Tel: (212) 395-1000, (800) 621-9900, FAX: (212) 571-1897, Web Site: www.verizon.com (3)

Vermette, David, MassMutual Financial Group, Springfield, MA. Tel: (413) 788-8411, FAX: (413) 744-8889, E-Mail: name@www.massmutual.com, Web Site: www.massmutual.com (15)

Vermie, Craig, D., Transamerica Occidental Life Co, Los Angeles, CA. Tel: (213) 742-3111, FAX: (213) 741-6623, Web Site: www.transamerica.com (15)

The Vermont Country Store, Manchester Center, VT. Tel: (802) 362-8200, Web Site: www.vermontcountrystore.com (5)

Vermont Media, West Dover, VT. Tel: (802) 464-3388, FAX: (802) 464-7255, E-Mail: vickic@vermontmedia.com, Web Site: www.dvalnews.com (35)

Vermont/New Hampshire Direct Marketing Group, Woodstock, VT. Tel: (802) 457-2807, FAX: (802) 457-2807, E-Mail: vtnhmg@vtnhmg, Web Site: www.vtnhmg.org (40)

Vermont Ski Areas Association, Montpelier, VT. Tel: (802) 223-2439, FAX: (802) 229-6917, E-Mail: info@skivermont.com, Web Site: www.skivermont.com (1)

Vermont Teddy Bear Co, Shelburne, VT. Tel: (802) 985-3001, (800) 829-BEAR, (800) 282-3131, FAX: (802) 985-1304, E-Mail: info@vtbear.com, Web Site: www.vermontteddybear.com (6)

Vermont Tubbs, Whitefield, NH. Tel: (603) 837-2547, E-Mail: dogurkis@vermonttubbs.com, Web Site: www.vermonttubbs.com (8)

Verney, Richard, G., Monadnock Paper Mills Inc, Bennington, NH. Tel: (603) 588-3311, (800) 221-2159, FAX: (603) 588-3158, Web Site: www.monadnockpaper.com (25)

Veronis, John, J., Veronis Suhler Stevenson LLC, New York, NY. Tel: (212) 935-4990, FAX: (212) 381-8168, E-Mail: stevensonj@vss.com, Web Site: www.vss.com (14)

Veronis Suhler Stevenson LLC, New York, NY. Tel: (212) 935-4990, FAX: (212) 381-8168, E-Mail: stevensonj@vss.com, Web Site: www.vss.com (14)

Verrecchia, Alfred, Hasbro Inc, Pawtucket, RI. Tel: (401) 727-5000, (800) 242-7276, FAX: (401) 727-5121, Web Site: www.hasbro.com (11)

Verrill, Frank, Advanced Image Direct, Fullerton, CA. Tel: (714) 502-3900, (800) 540-3848, FAX: (714) 502-3901, Web Site: www.advancedimagedirect.com (28)

Versatile Card Technology Inc, Downers Grove, IL. Tel: (630) 852-5600, FAX: (630) 852-5817, Web Site: www.versacard.com (27)

Verso Paper, Memphis, TN. Tel: (901) 369-4241, Web Site: www.versopaper.com (25)

Versoy Jr., Irving, R., Faire Harbour Limited, Scituate, MA. Tel: (781) 545-2465, FAX: (781) 545-2465 (5)

Versoy, Mary J., Faire Harbour Limited, Scituate, MA. Tel: (781) 545-2465, FAX: (781) 545-2465 (5)

Vertex Inc, Berwyn, PA. Tel: (610) 640-4200, (800) 355-3500, FAX: (610) 640-5892, Web Site: www.vertexinc.com (16)

Vertical Communications Inc, Santa Clara, CA. Tel: (617) 354-0600, (800) COMDIAL, FAX: (617) 452-9159, Web Site: www.comdial.com (34)

Vertical Media Group, Fort Lee, NJ. Tel: (201) 245-7935 (20)

Vertis Media & Marketing Services, Baltimore, MD. Tel: (410) 528-9800, (800) 577-8371, E-Mail: Info@VertisInc.com, Web Site: www.vertisinc.com (28)

Vertrue Inc, Norwalk, CT. Tel: (203) 324-7635, FAX: (203) 674-7080, Web Site: www.vertrue.com (13)

Vesdia Corp, Atlanta, GA. Tel: (678) 405-9208, Web Site: www.vesdia.com (35)

Vesey's Seeds Ltd, Charlottetown, PE Canada. Tel: (902) 368-7333, (800) 363-7333, FAX: (800) 686-0329, E-Mail: customerservice@veseys.com, Web Site: www.veseys.com (8)

Vest, Dr. Lamar, American Bible Society, New York, NY. Tel: (212) 408-1200, FAX: (212) 408-1264, Web Site: www.americanbible.org (1)

The Vestal Press Ltd, Lanham, MD. Tel: (301) 459-3366, (800) 462-6420, FAX: (301) 429-5746, E-Mail: sburnett@rowman.com, Web Site: www.nbnbooks.com (17)

Vestcom International Inc, Little Rock, AR. Tel: (501) 663-0100, (800) 264-0965, FAX: (501) 663-2451, Web Site: www.vestcom.com (31)

Vestcom Saint Louis, Earth City, MO. Tel: (314) 209-8443, (800) 264-0965, FAX: (314) 291-2195, E-Mail: sreinis@vestcom.com, Web Site: www.vestcom.com (21)

Vet Vax, Tonganoxie, KS. Tel: (913) 845-3760, (800) 369-8297, FAX: (913) 845-9472, E-Mail: sales@vetvax.com (11)

Veterans of Foreign Wars (VFW) of the US-National Headquarters, Kansas City, MO. Tel: (816) 756-3390, FAX: (816) 968-1149, E-Mail: info@vfw.org, Web Site: www.vfw.org (1)

Vetter, Linda, Alterian, Chicago, IL. Tel: (312) 704-1700, Web Site: www.alterian.com (22)

Vezza, Vincent, Films Media Group, New York, NY. Tel: (609) 671-1000, (800) 257-5126, FAX: (609) 671-0266, E-Mail: custserv@films.com, Web Site: www.filmsmediagroup.com (3)

Via, Wendy, Southern Poverty Law Center, Montgomery, AL. Tel: (334) 956-8200, FAX: (334) 956-8483, Web Site: www.splcenter.org (1)

Viacom Inc, New York, NY. Tel: (212) 258-6000, FAX: (212) 258-6464, Web Site: www.viacom.com (16)

Viahealth, Rochester, NY. Tel: (585) 922-4000, (585) 922-3677, FAX: (585) 922-3929, Web Site: www.viahealth.org (16)

Viall, Gregg, Petra Industries, Edmond, OK. Tel: (405) 216-2100, Web Site: www.patra.com (34)

Viatech Publishing Solutions Inc, Bay Shore, NY. Tel: (631) 968-8500, (800) 645-8558, FAX: (631) 968-0830, Web Site: www.viatechpub.com (16)

Vicarra, Mike, Safti First, San Francisco, CA. Tel: (415) 824-4900, (888) 653-3333, FAX: (415) 824-5900, (888) 653-4444, E-Mail: info@safti.com, Web Site: www.safti.com (16)

Vicens, Joe, Dial-A-Mattress, Hicksville, NY. Tel: (718) 472-1200, (800) 824-7777, FAX: (718) 482-6561, E-Mail: sales@mattress.com, Web Site: www.mattress.com (16)

Vickers, Linda, Loving Promises & More, Longview, WA. Tel: (360) 425-8466, (800) 999-6909 (16)

Victor Envelope Co, Bensenville, IL. Tel: (630) 616-2750, Web Site: www.victorenvelope.com (26)

Victor Machinery Exchange, Brooklyn, NY. Tel: (800) 723-5359, E-Mail: sales@victornet.com, Web Site: www.victornet.com (9)

Victores, Ric, Parcel Insurance Plan Inc, Saint Louis, MO. Tel: (314) 692-0300, (800) 325-7390, FAX: (314) 692-7598, E-Mail: office@pipinsure.com, Web Site: www.pipinsure.com (16)

Victoria's Secret Catalogue, Columbus, OH. FAX: (614) 337-5075, Web Site: www.victoriassecret.com (2)

Victory Corps, New Hope, MN. Tel: (763) 561-5600, (800) 328-6120, FAX: (763) 561-8523, E-Mail: cs@victorycorps.com, Web Site: www.victorycorps.com (16)

Vidal, Manny, The Vidal Partnership, New York, NY. Tel: (646) 356-6600, FAX: (212) 661-7650, Web Site: www.vidalpartnership.com (35)

The Vidal Partnership, New York, NY. Tel: (646) 356-6600, FAX: (212) 661-7650, Web Site: www.vidalpartnership.com (35)

Video Artists International, Pleasantville, NY. Tel: (914) 769-3691, (800) 477-7146, FAX: (914) 769-5407, E-Mail: orders@vaimusic.com, Web Site: www.vaimusic.com (3)

Video Jet Technologies Inc, Wood Dale, IL. Tel: (630) 860-7300, (800) 654-4663, FAX: (630) 616-3657, E-Mail: info@videojet.com, Web Site: www.videojet.com (34)

Video Ordnance Inc, New York, NY. Tel: (212) 334-3939, (800) 377-7773, FAX: (212) 219-1969, E-Mail: info@videoordnance.com, Web Site: www.videoordnance.com (32)

Video Plus Inc, Lake Dallas, TX. Tel: (940) 497-9700, (800) 752-2030, FAX: (940) 497-9987, E-Mail: support@videoplus.com, Web Site: www.videoplus.com (32)

Videoware Corp, Rye Brook, NY. Tel: (914) 937-6007, FAX: (914) 937-6414, E-Mail: info@videoware.com, Web Site: www.videoware.com (35)

Vidi Emi Inc, San Leandro, CA. Tel: (510) 667-9999, FAX: (510) 352-9999, E-Mail: info@vidiemi.com, Web Site: www.vidiemi.com (32)

Vidoni, Karen, Perrygraf, Carol Stream, IL. Tel: (630) 665-3333, (800) 323-4433, FAX: (630) 665-3491, E-Mail: info2@americanperrygraf.com, Web Site: www.perrygraf.com (16)

Vie, Richard, C., Unitrin, Chicago, IL. Tel: (312) 661-4600, (800) 733-7366, FAX: (312) 494-6995, Web Site: www.unitrin.com (15)

Vierk National Supply, North Chicago, IL. Tel: (847) 869-4318, (800) 428-7548, FAX: (847) 689-4412, Web Site: www.vierk.com (16)

Vierzba, Nicole, Employers Group, El Segundo, CA. Tel: (800) 748-8484, Web Site: www.employesgroup.com (20)

Viesti, Joe, Viesti Associates Inc, Durango, CO. Tel: (970) 382-2600, FAX: (970) 382-2700, E-Mail: photos@viestiphoto.com, Web Site: www.viestiassociates.com (38)

Viesti Associates Inc, Durango, CO. Tel: (970) 382-2600, FAX: (970) 382-2700, E-Mail: photos@viestiphoto.com, Web Site: www.viestiassociates.com (38)

Vietnam Veterans of America, Silver Spring, MD. Tel: (301) 585-4000, Web Site: www.clothingdonations.org (1)

Vietri, Charles, Direct Magazine, New York, NY. Tel: (212) 204-4228, FAX: (212) 683-3986 (43)

Viets, Brenda, MCH Strategic Data, Sweet Springs, MO. Tel: (660) 335-6373, (800) 776-6373, FAX: (660) 335-4157, E-Mail: tonyab@mchdata.com, Web Site: www.mchdata.com (23)

VIEW Video Inc/Arcadia Entertainment Corp, Saugerties, NY. Tel: (845) 246-9955, FAX: (845) 246-9966, E-Mail: sales@view.com, Web Site: www.view.com (16)

Vig, Chris, WinterSilks LLC, Warren, PA. Tel: (904) 645-6000, Web Site: www.wintersilks.com (2)

Vigil, Greg, Gates Corp, Denver, CO. Tel: (303) 744-1911, FAX: (303) 744-4000, Web Site: www.gates.com (9)

Vignola, Michael, Mailmen Inc, Hauppauge, NY. Tel: (631) 582-6900, FAX: (631) 582-6948, E-Mail: getresults@mailmeninc.com, Web Site: www.mailmeninc.com (28)

Viguerie, Richard, A., American Target Advertising Inc, Manassas, VA. Tel: (703) 392-7676, FAX: (703) 392-7654 (35)

Viking Pump Inc, Cedar Falls, IA. Tel: (319) 266-1741, FAX: (319) 273-8157, E-Mail: info@vikingpump.com, Web Site: www.vikingpump.com (16)

Vilaret, Victoria, New York Life Insurance Co/AARP, Tampa, FL. Tel: (813) 288-5500, FAX: (813) 288-5256, Web Site: www.nylaarp.com (15)

Vilbrin, Lori, The Vermont Country Store, Manchester Center, VT. Tel: (802) 362-8200, Web Site: www.vermontcountrystore.com (5)

Vile, Joel, D., Greystone Graphics, Kansas City, MO. Tel: (913) 342-1393, (800) 458-7407, FAX: (913) 621-4856, E-Mail: info@greystonegraphics.com, Web Site: www.greystonegraphics.com (27)

Vill, Neil, Gelco Information Network, Eden Prairie, MN. Tel: (952) 947-1500, (800) 444-6588, FAX: (952) 947-1525, Web Site: www.gelco.com (16)

Villa, Danny, GMAC Insurance, Atlanta, GA. Tel: (314) 493-8000, (800) GMAC-123, FAX: (314) 493-8114, Web Site: www.gmacinsurance.com (15)

Village Coin Shop, Plaistow, NH. Tel: (603) 382-5492/7151, FAX: (603) 382-5682, E-Mail: don@villagecoin.com, Web Site: www.villagecoin.com (6)

Village Interiors Carpet One, Newton, NC. Tel: (828) 465-6818, FAX: (828) 465-1864, E-Mail: sales@carpet-one.net, Web Site: www.carpetone.com/village (8)

Village Software Inc, Boston, MA. Tel: (617) 695-9332, (800) 724-9332, FAX: (617) 695-1935, E-Mail: requests@villagesoft.com, Web Site: www.villagesoft.com (3)

Village Weavers, San Antonio, TX. Tel: (210) 222-0776, E-Mail: shop@villageweavers.com, Web Site: www.villageweavers.com (16)

Villalobos, Gabriella, Comp USA, Inc, Miami, FL. Tel: (972) 982-4000, (800) COMP-USA, FAX: (972) 982-4030, Web Site: www.compusa.com (3)

Villanueva, Josephine, Manulife Financial Inc, Toronto, ON Canada. Tel: (416) 229-4515, (800) 387-0990, FAX: (416) 229-3028, Web Site: www.manulife.com (15)

Villeneuve, Edward, W., Goldsmith Agio Helms, Minneapolis, MN. Tel: (612) 339-0500, FAX: (612) 339-0507, Web Site: www.agio.com (14)

Vincelette, Bill, Gems Sensors & Controls, Plainville, CT. Tel: (860) 747-3000, (800) 378-1600, FAX: (860) 747-4244, E-Mail: info@gemssensors.com, Web Site: www.gemssensors.com (9)

Vincent, Geoff, D&B Canada, Mississauga, ON. Tel: (905) 568-6000, FAX: (905) 568-6197, Web Site: www.dnb.ca (30)

Vincent, Heidi, Specialized Association Services, Irving, TX. Tel: (469) 524-5122, E-Mail: hvincent@1sas.com, Web Site: www.1sas.com (1)

Vincent, Ty, Vincent Graphics, LLC, Hilliard, OH. Tel: (614) 771-5440, (800) 331-0517, FAX: (614) 771-5449 (28)

Vincent Graphics, LLC, Hilliard, OH. Tel: (614) 771-5440, (800) 331-0517, FAX: (614) 771-5449 (28)

Vinson, Harry, Cadmus Communications Corp, Richmond, VA. Tel: (804) 264-2711, FAX: (804) 262-6419, Web Site: www.cenveo.com (35)

Vintage Wood Works, Quinlan, TX. Tel: (903) 356-2158, FAX: (903) 356-3023, E-Mail: mail@vintagewoodworks.com, Web Site: www.vintagewoodworks.com (8)

Violet, Cindy, Thomas Moser Cabinetmakers, Freeport, ME. Tel: (207) 865-4519, (800) 708-9041, FAX: (207) 865-6539, E-Mail: freeportshowroom@thosmoser.com, Web Site: www.thosmoser.com (16)

Virco Manufacturing Corp, Conway, AR. Tel: (501) 329-2901, (800) 448-4726, FAX: (800) 258-7367, E-Mail: info@virco.com, Web Site: www.virco.com (16)

Viren, Daniel, D., RG Barry Corp, Pickerington, OH. FAX: (614) 866-9787, E-Mail: sales@rgbarry.com, Web Site: www.rgbarry.com (2)

Virgin Mobile USA LLC, Warren, NJ. Tel: (908) 607-4000, Web Site: www.virginmobileusa.com (32)

The Virginia Diner Inc, Wakefield, VA. Tel: (757) 899-6213, (888) 823-4637, FAX: (757) 899-2281, E-Mail: vadiner@vadiner.com, Web Site: www.vadiner.com (4)

Virginia Home For Boys, Richmond, VA. Tel: (804) 270-6566, FAX: (804) 270-6574, Web Site: www.boyshome.org (1)

Virginia Port Authority, Norfolk, VA. Tel: (757) 683-8000, (800) 446-8098, FAX: (757) 683-2897, Web Site: www.portofvirginia.com (16)

Virido LLC, Scottsdale, AZ. Tel: (480) 419-9063, Web Site: www.virido.com (29)

Virtuoso Ltd, Seattle, WA. Tel: (206) 625-0969, Web Site: www.virtuoso.com (19)

Virvo, Alexander, ADV Marketing Group Inc, Stamford, CT. Tel: (203) 356-9621, FAX: (203) 324-4680 (35)

Visa USA, Foster City, CA. Tel: (650) 432-3200, FAX: (650) 432-2875, Web Site: www.visa.com (14)

Visconti, John, Printing Spectrum, East Setauket, NY. Tel: (631) 689-1010, Web Site: www.printingspectrum.com (27)

Visible Computer Supply Corp, Saint Charles, IL. Tel: (630) 377-2586, (800) 323-0628, FAX: (800) 233-2016, Web Site: www.wallace.com (16)

Visible Results USA Inc, Overland Park, KS. Tel: (913) 851-9400, FAX: (913) 851-0628, E-Mail: info@visibleresults.com, Web Site: www.visibleresults.com (32)

Visible World, New York, NY. Tel: (212) 739-1914 (32)

Vision Marketing Inc, Englewood Cliffs, NJ. Tel: (201) 816-1560, FAX: (201) 816-1610, Web Site: www.visionmarketing.com (23)

Vision Media, Modesto, CA. Tel: (209) 526-6500, FAX: (209) 522-2100, E-Mail: info@visionmediatv.com, Web Site: www.visionmediatv.com (35)

Vision Solutions, Irvine, CA. Tel: (949) 253-6500, (800) 683-4667, FAX: (949) 253-6501, E-Mail: info@visionsolutions.com, Web Site: www.visionsolutions.com (22)

Visions Marketing Services, Lancaster, PA. Tel: (717) 381-2100, (800) 222-1577, FAX: (717) 295-8020, Web Site: www.wecloseloans.com (29)

VisiPak, Saint Louis, MO. Tel: (636) 282-6800, (800) 922-9391, FAX: (636) 282-6888, E-Mail: visipak@sinclair-rush.com, Web Site: www.visipak.com (34)

VistaPrint USA Inc, Lexington, MA. Tel: (800) 961-2075, Web Site: www.vistaprint.com (27)

Visual Horizons, Rochester, NY. Tel: (585) 424-5300, (800) 424-1011, FAX: (800) 424-5411, E-Mail: cs@visualhorizons.com, Web Site: www.visualhorizons.com (16)

Visual Reference Publications, New York, NY. Tel: (212) 279-7000, (800) 251-4545, FAX: (212) 279-7014 (17)

Visual Response Marketing Group, Marietta, GA. Tel: (678) 881-9400 (35)

Vita, Joseph, World Villages for Children, Annapolis, MD. Tel: (301) 779-4141, Web Site: www.worldvillages.org (1)

Vita-Mix Corp, Cleveland, OH. Tel: (440) 235-4840, (800) VITA-MIX, FAX: (440) 235-3726, E-Mail: service@vitamix.com, Web Site: www.vitamix.com (16)

Vitale, Salvatore, J., The Conference Board, Inc, New York, NY. Tel: (212) 759-0900, FAX: (212) 980-7014, Web Site: www.conference-board.org (16)

Vitamin Power Inc, Hauppauge, NY. Tel: (516) 378-0900, (800) 645-6567, FAX: (516) 378-0919, E-Mail: vitpower@aol.com, Web Site: www.vitaminpower.com (7)

Vitamin Research Products, Carson City, NV. Tel: (775) 884-8205, Web Site: www.vrp.com (7)

Vitamin Specialties Co, Freehold, NJ. Tel: (732) 308-3000, FAX: (732) 683-1622, Web Site: www.ivcinc.com (7)

Vitasoy USA Inc, Ayer, MA. Tel: (978) 772-6880, (800) VITA-SOY, FAX: (978) 772-6881, Web Site: www.vitasoy-usa.com (16)

Vitch, Michael, L., Compu-Mail, Niagara Falls, NY. Tel: (716) 297-0553, (800) 255-0670, FAX: (716) 297-0822, Web Site: www.compu-mail.com (35)

Vivendi, New York, NY. Tel: (212) 572-7000, FAX: (212) 572-1080, Web Site: www.vivendi.com (16)

Vivitar Corp, Tempe, AZ. Tel: (800) 592-9541, FAX: (909) 348-6390, Web Site: www.vivitar.com (16)

Vlachos, John, Bookspan, Garden City, NY. Tel: (516) 490-4561, FAX: (516) 490-4856 (13)

Vlok, Nicholaas, Vision Solutions, Irvine, CA. Tel: (949) 253-6500, (800) 683-4667, FAX: (949) 253-6501, E-Mail: info@visionsolutions.com, Web Site: www.visionsolutions.com (22)

Vlossak, Frank, The FX Matt Brewing Co, Utica, NY. Tel: (315) 732-0022, (800) 765-6288, FAX: (315) 624-2401, E-Mail: info@saranac.com, Web Site: www.saranac.com (4)

Vo, Troy, Autobytel Inc, Irvine, CA. Tel: (949) 225-4500, Web Site: www.autobytel.com (16)

Vocational Biographies Inc, Sauk Centre, MN. Tel: (320) 352-6516, (800) 255-0752, FAX: (320) 352-5546, E-Mail: careers@vocbios.com, Web Site: www.vocbio.com (31)

Vocus, Beltsville, MD. Tel: (301) 459-2590, Web Site: www.vocus.com (22)

Voelker, Raymond, M., The Progressive Corp, Mayfield Village, OH. Tel: (440) 461-5000, (800) PROGRESSIVE, (800) 776-4737, FAX: (800) 456-6590, Web Site: www.progressive.com (15)

Vogel, Dan, Destination Maternity Corp, Philadelphia, PA. Tel: (215) 873-2200, Web Site: www.motherswork.com (2)

Vogel, Eileen, Spectrum Retail Associates, Ardmore, PA. Tel: (610) 645-9520, (800) 570-6565, FAX: (610) 645-9524 (20)

Vogel, Paul, Planned Parenthood Federation of America, New York, NY. Tel: (212) 261-4686, Web Site: www.plannedparenthood.org (1)

Vogel, W., Viking Pump Inc, Cedar Falls, IA. Tel: (319) 266-1741, (319) 273-8157, E-Mail: info@vikingpump.com, Web Site: www.vikingpump.com (16)

Voges, Chris, Plastic View ATC, Simi Valley, CA. Tel: (805) 520-9390, (800) 468-6301, FAX: (805) 520-0260, E-Mail: info@pvatc.com, Web Site: www.pvatc.com (9)

Voges, Ryan, Plastic View ATC, Simi Valley, CA. Tel: (805) 520-9390, (800) 468-6301, FAX: (805) 520-0260, E-Mail: info@pvatc.com, Web Site: www.pvatc.com (9)

Voges, Sonny, Plastic View ATC, Simi Valley, CA. Tel: (805) 520-9390, (800) 468-6301, FAX: (805) 520-0260, E-Mail: info@pvatc.com, Web Site: www.pvatc.com (9)

Vogt, Ed, GM Customer Relationship Management, Detroit, MI. Tel: (313) 667-2621 (35)

Vogt, Jennifer, Food for the Poor Inc, Coconut Creek, FL. Tel: (954) 427-2222, Web Site: www.foodforthepoor.com (1)

Voice Message Broadcasting Corp, Irvine, CA. Tel: (714) 437-0600, FAX: (714) 242-1989, Web Site: www.vmbc.com (32)

Voice Systems Engineering Inc, Langhorne, PA. Tel: (215) 953-8568, Web Site: www.vseinc.com (32)

Voicelogic, Toronto, ON Canada. Tel: (888) 552-8858, Web Site: www.voicelogic.com (29)

Voight, Gary, Software AG USA, Reston, VA. Tel: (703) 860-5050, (877) 724-4965, FAX: (703) 391-6975, E-Mail: info@softwareagusa.com, Web Site: www.softwareagusa.com (3)

Volini, Edward, Premiere Global Services Inc, Atlanta, GA. Tel: (404) 262-8400, (800) 546-1541, FAX: (913) 661-9042, Web Site: www.PGiConnect.com (22)

Volk, Stephen R., Citigroup Inc, New York, NY. Tel: (212) 559-1000, (800) 285-3000, FAX: (212) 793-3946, Web Site: www.citigroup.com (14)

Volkema, Michael, A., Herman Miller Inc, Zeeland, MI. Tel: (616) 654-3000, FAX: (616) 654-5234, E-Mail: investor@hermanmiller.com, Web Site: www.hermanmiller.com (16)

Volkswagen Group of America Inc, Auburn Hills, MI. Tel: (248) 754-5000, FAX: (248) 754-4930, Web Site: www.vw.com (16)

Vollowitz, Eileen, Back Designs Inc, Novato, CA. Tel: (415) 883-4683, FAX: (510) 549-0837, E-Mail: info@backdesigns.com, Web Site: www.backdesigns.com (7)

Volner, Ian, Venable LLP Conference Center, Washington, DC. Tel: (202) 344-4860, (202) 344-4000, (888) VENABLE, FAX: (202) 344-8300, E-Mail: info@venable.com, Web Site: www.venable.com (20)

Volpe, Barbara, McBee, Lancaster, CA. Tel: (973) 263-3225, (800) 878-9443, (800) 662-2331, FAX: (973) 263-8165, E-Mail: info@mcbeeinc.com, Web Site: www.mcbeeweb.com (10)

Volpe, Nancy, L., Society for Human Resource Management, Alexandria, VA. Tel: (703) 548-3440, (800) 283-SHRM, FAX: (703) 535-6490, E-Mail: shrmstore@shrm.org, Web Site: www.shrm.org (1)

Volt Delta, Blue Bell, PA. Tel: (610) 825-7720, FAX: (610) 567-5698, Web Site: www.voltdelta.com (22)

Voltz, Joanne, Redleaf Press, Saint Paul, MN. Tel: (651) 641-6621, (800) 423-8309, FAX: (800) 641-0115, E-Mail: jvoltz@redleafpress.org, Web Site: www.redleafpress.org (17)

Volunteers of America, Alexandria, VA. Tel: (703) 341-5000, Web Site: www.volunteersofamerica.org (1)

Volvo Cars of North America, Northvale, NJ. Tel: (201) 768-7300, (800) 458-1552, E-Mail: customercare@volvocars.com, Web Site: www.volvocars.com (16)

Von Birgelen, Catherine, The Center for eBusiness & Advanced IT, Erie, PA. Tel: (814) 898-6500, Web Site: www.ebizitpa.org (1)

Von Hertsenberg, Kurt, Wildlife Education Ltd, Park Hills, KY. Tel: (858) 513-7600, FAX: (858) 513-7660, E-Mail: animals@zoobooks.com, Web Site: www.zoobooks.com (17)

von Hoelscher, Russ, Publisher's Media, El Cajon, CA. Tel: (619) 588-2155, FAX: (619) 588-9103, E-Mail: rvhmedia@aol.com (31)

Von Kennel, Gary, Tracy Locke Partnership, Dallas, TX. Tel: (214) 969-9000, FAX: (214) 259-3550, E-Mail: tlpinfo@tlp.com, Web Site: www.tlp.com (35)

Von Weller, Lindsey, Event 360 Inc, Chicago, IL. Tel: (773) 247-5360, Web Site: www.event360.com (1)

Vonage, Holmdel, NJ. Tel: (732) 528-2600, Web Site: www.vonage.com (32)

Vook, Barbara, Health O Meter, Alsip, IL. Tel: (708) 377-0600, (800) 815-6615, FAX: (708) 377-0601, E-Mail: HomProCS@homscales.com, Web Site: www.homscales.com (16)

Voorhees, Janice, Ranger Joe's International Military Supply, Columbus, GA. Tel: (706) 689-0082, (800) 247-4541, FAX: (706) 682-8840, E-Mail: customerservice@rangerjoes.com, Web Site: www.rangerjoes.com (2)

Voorhees, Paul, Ranger Joe's International Military Supply, Columbus, GA. Tel: (706) 689-0082, (800) 247-4541, FAX: (706) 682-8840, E-Mail: customerservice@rangerjoes.com, Web Site: www.rangerjoes.com (2)

Voors, Jerry, Arrow Companies, LLC, Elkhorn, WI. Tel: (262) 741-1660, FAX: (262) 723-6750, Web Site: www.arrowcompanies.com (22)

Vorhaus, Mike, Frank N Magid Associates Inc, Marion, IA. Tel: (319) 377-7345, FAX: (319) 377-5861, E-Mail: mailIA@magid.com, Web Site: www.magid.com (30)

Vorthmann, Mary, Mid America Direct Marketing Association, Omaha, NE. Tel: (402) 964-8444, FAX: (402) 964-8484, Web Site: www.madma.org (40)

Vosseler, Janine, 21st Century Marketing, Hauppauge, NY. Tel: (631) 293-8550, FAX: (631) 293-8974, E-Mail: info@21stcm.com, Web Site: www.21stcm.com (24)

Votel, Richard, H., Direct Response Insurance Administrative Services Inc (DRIASI), Chanhassen, MN. Tel: (952) 556-5600, (800) 688-0760, FAX: (952) 556-8200, E-Mail: tpa@driasi.com, Web Site: www.driasi.com (21)

Votruha, Dr. James, C., Northern Kentucky University, Highland Heights, KY. Tel: (859) 572-5220, (800) 637-9948, FAX: (859) 572-6177, Web Site: www.nku.edu (41)

Voxdata Telecom, Montreal, PQ Canada. Tel: (514) 871-1920, (800) 861-9599, FAX: (514) 871-0445, E-Mail: fcouture@voxdata.com, Web Site: www.voxdata.com (29)

Voyageur Inc, Easley, SC. Tel: (802) 496-3127, (800) 311-7245, FAX: (802) 496-6247 (11)

Voyles, Charles, Edwin, Ed Voyles Hyundai Inc, Smyrna, GA. Tel: (770) 952-8881, (877) 579-0642, FAX: (770) 612-9396, Web Site: www.edvoyleshyundai.com (16)

Ed Voyles Hyundai Inc, Smyrna, GA. Tel: (770) 952-8881, (877) 579-0642, FAX: (770) 612-9396, Web Site: www.edvoyleshyundai.com (16)

Vozzo, Thomas, Gall's Inc, Lexington, KY. Tel: (859) 266-7227, (800) 477-7766, FAX: (859) 268-5954, E-Mail: help-desk@galls.com, Web Site: www.galls.com (16)

Vross, Frank, J., Jaff Marketing Group Inc, Spring, TX. Tel: (281) 353-0004, FAX: (281) 288-0970 (16)

Vu, Kathy, USA TODAY, Mc Lean, VA. Tel: (703) 854-3400, (800) 872-0001, E-Mail: accuracy@ usatoday.com, Web Site: www.usatoday.com (17)

Vukelich, Ty, EMPLOYERS Insurance, Reno, NV. Tel: (775) 327-2677, Web Site: www.employers. com (15)

Vulcan Information Packaging, Vincent, AL. Tel: (205) 672-2241, (800) 633-4526, FAX: (205) 672-1276, Web Site: www.vulcan-online.com (16)

Vulcan Materials Co, Birmingham, AL. Tel: (205) 298-3000, FAX: (205) 298-2960, Web Site: www. vulcanmaterials.com (16)

W

WCPE-FM, Wake Forest, NC. Tel: (919) 556-5178, Web Site: www.theclassicalstation.org (32)

WDS Marketing & Public Relations, Overland Park, KS. Tel: (913) 362-4541, FAX: (913) 362-7342, E-Mail: bwilson@wdspr.com, Web Site: www. wdspr.com (20)

WFF'N PROOF Learning Games Associates, Fairfield, IA. Tel: (641) 472-0149, (800) 289-2377, FAX: (641) 472-0693, Web Site: www.wffnproof.com (17)

WGBH Educational Foundation, Brighton, MA. Tel: (617) 300-5400, FAX: (617) 300-1026, Web Site: www.wgbh.org (1)

WLA Inc, New York, NY. Tel: (212) 584-1810 (20)

WLNY-TV, Melville, NY. Tel: (631) 622-9420, FAX: (631) 420-4846, Web Site: www.wlnytv.com (32)

WMG USA Inc, New York, NY. Tel: (212) 278-0066, E-Mail: business@wmg-group.com, Web Site: www.wmg-group.com (28)

WNR Direct Response Consultants, Agoura Hills, CA. Tel: (818) 865-6300, FAX: (818) 865-8559, E-Mail: gwetter@wnrtv.com, Web Site: www. wnrtv.com (35)

WOL Direct Inc, Scranton, PA. Tel: (570) 961-4043, Web Site: www.pennfoster.edu (35)

WPI Group Inc, Colts Neck, NJ. FAX: (212) 202-3742, E-Mail: info@wpinj.com, Web Site: www. wpinj.com (20)

WRS Group Ltd, Waco, TX. Tel: (254) 776-6461, (800) 299-3366, FAX: (888) 977-7653, E-Mail: sales@wrsgroup.com, Web Site: www.wrsgroup. com (7)

WS Live LLC, Dubuque, IA. Tel: (563) 582-9501, (800) 582-9501, FAX: (563) 582-2003, Web Site: www.wslive.com (29)

WTB Associates Inc, Wilmette, IL. Tel: (847) 251-4188 (20)

WTS Media, Chattanooga, TN. Tel: (423) 894-9427, (800) 251-7228, FAX: (423) 894-7281, E-Mail: customerservice@wtsmedia.com, Web Site: www. wts-tape.com (16)

Wachob, George, Hearthside Quilts & Supplies, Hinesburg, VT. Tel: (802) 482-7800, (800) 451-3533, FAX: (802) 482-7803, E-Mail: hearthsidequilts@att.net, Web Site: www. hearthsidequilts.com (11)

Wachovia Bank, National Association, Charlotte, NC. Tel: (704) 590-0000, (800) WACHOVIA, FAX: (704) 427-6748 (14)

Wachovia Center, Philadelphia, PA. Tel: (215) 336-3600, FAX: (215) 389-9518, E-Mail: info@ comcast-spectacor.com, Web Site: www.comcast-spectacor.com (16)

Wachowiak, Rodney, Replogle Globes Inc, Broadview, IL. Tel: (708) 343-0900, FAX: (708) 343-0923, E-Mail: info@replogleglobes.com, Web Site: www. replogleglobes.com (16)

Wachsstock, Mel, Sunbilt Creative Sunrooms, Jamaica, NY. Tel: (718) 297-6040, FAX: (718) 297-3090, E-Mail: info@sunbilt.com, Web Site: www. sunbilt.com (8)

Wachtel, Christopher, WordCom Inc, Ellington, CT. Tel: (860) 875-7373, (800) 875-7373, (800) 822-

0622, FAX: (860) 872-2713, E-Mail: sales@ wordcom-inc.com, Web Site: www.wordcom-inc. com (21)

Wachtel, George, WordCom Inc, Ellington, CT. Tel: (860) 875-7373, (800) 875-7373, (800) 822-0622, FAX: (860) 872-2713, E-Mail: sales@wordcom-inc.com, Web Site: www.wordcom-inc.com (21)

Waddell, Frederick, H., The Northern Trust Co, Chicago, IL. Tel: (312) 630-6000, (888) 289-6542, FAX: (312) 630-1512, Web Site: www.ntrs.com (14)

Waddles, Omer, E., ITT Educational Services Inc, Carmel, IN. Tel: (317) 706-9200, E-Mail: gtanner@itt-tech.edu, Web Site: www.itt-tech.edu (16)

Wade, Chip, Legal Sea Foods Inc, Boston, MA. Tel: (617) 530-9000, (800) 343-5804, FAX: (617) 530-9649, Web Site: www.legalseafoods.com (4)

Wade, Dan, Sporting Clays Ltd, Titusville, FL. Tel: (321) 268-5010, FAX: (321) 267-7216, E-Mail: sales@sportingclays.net, Web Site: www. sportingclays.net (17)

Wade, Joyce, Church Pension Fund, New York, NY. Tel: (866) 802-6333, Web Site: www.cpg.org (1)

Wade, Kevin, P., Wade Paper Corp, Deerfield, IL. Tel: (847) 940-9777, (800) 828-8318, FAX: (847) 940-1077, E-Mail: info@wadepaper.com, Web Site: www.wadepaper.com (25)

Wade, Peter C., Ad Pro Services Inc, Blauvelt, NY. Tel: (845) 359-8332, FAX: (914) 359-3843 (35)

Wade, Sandra, SER Solutions Inc, Reston, VA. Tel: (703) 948-5500, (800) 274-5676, FAX: (703) 430-7738, E-Mail: info@ser.com, Web Site: www.ser. com (34)

Wade, Wyatt, Davis Art Images, Worcester, MA. Tel: (508) 754-7201, (800) 533-2847, FAX: (508) 753-3834, (508) 831-9260, E-Mail: lkeenekendrick@ davisart.com, Web Site: www.davisartimages.com (38)

Wade, Wyatt, Davis Publications Inc, Worcester, MA. Tel: (508) 754-7201, (800) 533-2847, FAX: (508) 753-3834, E-Mail: contactus@davisart.com, Web Site: www.davis-art.com (17)

Wade Paper Corp, Deerfield, IL. Tel: (847) 940-9777, (800) 828-8318, FAX: (847) 940-1077, E-Mail: info@wadepaper.com, Web Site: www.wadepaper. com (25)

Wadhams, Timothy, Masco Corp, Taylor, MI. Tel: (313) 274-7400, FAX: (313) 792-6135, E-Mail: webmaster@mascohq.com, Web Site: www.masco. com (16)

Wadhwani, Romesh, Information Resources Inc, Chicago, IL. Tel: (312) 726-1221, Web Site: www. infores.com (30)

Wadleigh, Maya, MCCS, Mason, OH. Tel: (513) 573-2284, FAX: (513) 573-2197, Web Site: www. federated.com (14)

Wadler, Jason, Leapfrog Online, Evanston, IL. Tel: (847) 492-1968, Web Site: www.leapfrogonline. com (35)

Wadsworth II, Eliot, White Flower Farm, Torrington, CT. Tel: (860) 496-9624, (800) 503-9624, FAX: (860) 496-1418, Web Site: www. whiteflowerfarm.com (8)

Waechter, Joseph, W., Photoworks, Cleveland, OH. Tel: (206) 281-1390, (800) PHOTOWORKS, FAX: (206) 284-5357, E-Mail: info@photoworks.com, Web Site: www.photoworks.com (16)

Wag/Aero Group, Lyons, WI. Tel: (262) 763-9586, (800) 558-6868, FAX: (262) 763-7595, E-Mail: wagaero-sales@wagaero.com, Web Site: www. wagaero.com (16)

Wagaheim, Art, Modular Mailing Systems, Tampa, FL. Tel: (305) 826-9077, (800) 881-MAIL, E-Mail: sales@modularmailing.com, Web Site: www. modularmailing.com (34)

Wagenfeld, Sandra, J., National Committee to Preserve Social Security & Medicare, Washington, DC. Tel: (202) 216-0420, (800) 966-1935, FAX:

(202) 216-0446, E-Mail: kreard@ncpssm.org, Web Site: www.ncpssm.org (1)

Wagley, Ron, Transamerica Occidental Life Co, Los Angeles, CA. Tel: (213) 742-3111, FAX: (213) 741-6623, Web Site: www.transamerica.com (15)

Wagley, Ronald F., Life Investors Insurance Co of America, Cedar Rapids, IA. Tel: (319) 398-8511, (800) 231-7220, FAX: (319) 369-2188, Web Site: www.lifeinvestors.com (14)

Wagner Jr., G., Richard, Buick Division General Motors Corp, Detroit, MI. Tel: (313) 556-5000, (800) 521-7300, FAX: (313) 556-5108, Web Site: www. buick.com (16)

Wagner, A., Richard, Domtar Inc, Fort Mill, SC. Tel: (803) 802-8283, FAX: (810) 982-7124, Web Site: www.domtar.com (25)

Wagner, Andrew, American Craft Council, Minneapolis, MN. Tel: (212) 274-0630, FAX: (212) 274-0650, E-Mail: council@craftcouncil.org, Web Site: www.craftcouncil.org (17)

Wagner, Charlotte, Direct Sports Supply, Pearisburg, VA. Tel: (540) 921-1243, (800) 456-0072, FAX: (540) 921-1475, Web Site: www.directsports.com (11)

Wagner, Dan, Blue Cross Blue Shield of Louisiana, Baton Rouge, LA. Tel: (225) 295-3307, (800) 599-2583, FAX: (225) 295-2054, E-Mail: help@bcbsla. com, Web Site: www.bcbsla.com (15)

Wagner, Eileen, Minnetonka By Mail, Bronx, NY. FAX: (718) 885-3500, E-Mail: eileenlwagner@ email.msn.com (2)

Wagner, Ellen, Minnetonka By Mail, Bronx, NY. FAX: (718) 885-3500, E-Mail: eileenlwagner@ email.msn.com (2)

Wagner, Ira, J., American Capital, Bethesda, MD. Tel: (301) 951-6122, FAX: (301) 654-6714, E-Mail: info@americancapital.com, Web Site: www. americancapital.com (15)

Wagner, Jack, Forest Envelope Co, Lisle, IL. Tel: (630) 515-1200 (26)

Wagner, Jim, Mattel Inc, El Segundo, CA. Tel: (310) 252-2000, FAX: (310) 252-2180, Web Site: www. mattel.com (16)

Wagner, Judy, Bart's Watersports, North Webster, IN. Tel: (574) 834-7666, (800) 348-5016, FAX: (574) 834-4246, E-Mail: info@barts.com, Web Site: www.bartswatersports.com (11)

Wagner, Kae, Groshong, John Alden Life Insurance Co/North Star Marketing, Duluth, GA. Tel: (678) 473-1211, (800) 768-6288, FAX: (678) 473-9573, Web Site: www.nstarmarketing.com (15)

Wagner, Kris, Neopost, Carrollton, TX. Tel: (510) 489-6800, (800) 636-7678, FAX: (510) 475-6317, (510) 487-6704, Web Site: www.neopostinc.com (9)

Wagner, Lori, Talbots, Hingham, MA. Tel: (781) 749-7600, (800) 825-2687, FAX: (781) 741-4369, Web Site: www.talbots.com (2)

Wagner, Mark, Empire Blue Cross & Blue Shield, New York, NY. Tel: (212) 476-1000, (877) 476-7111, FAX: (212) 476-1281, Web Site: www. empireblue.com (15)

Wagner, Mark, J., Hickory Farms, Maumee, OH. Tel: (419) 893-7611, (800) 822-4438, FAX: (419) 893-0164, Web Site: www.hickoryfarms.com (4)

Wagner, Mark, Pfaelzer Brothers, Maumee, OH. Tel: (419) 893-7611, (800) 345-9290, FAX: (419) 893-0164, Web Site: www.phaelzerbrothers.com (16)

Wagner, Mark, Pinnacle Orchards, Maumee, OH. Tel: (419) 893-7611, (800) 442-5671, FAX: (419) 893-0164, Web Site: www.pinnacleorchards.com (4)

Wagner, Paul, V., Direct Sports Supply, Pearisburg, VA. Tel: (540) 921-1243, (800) 456-0072, FAX: (540) 921-1475, Web Site: www.directsports.com (11)

Wagner, Tammy, American Breast Cancer Foundation, Baltimore, MD. Tel: (410) 825-9388, Web Site: www.abcf.org (1)

Wagner Hines & Avary Inc, Alexandria, VA. Tel: (703) 684-7740, FAX: (703) 548-3721 (20)

Wagnitz, Steve, Lakewood Products LLC, Suamico, WI. Tel: (920) 361-7717, (800) 872-8458, FAX: (920) 361-7719, E-Mail: info@lakewoodproducts. com, Web Site: www.lakewoodproducts.com (11)

Wagstaff, Ted, SDI Marketing, Toronto, ON. Tel: (949) 718-4800, (877) SDI-TEAM, FAX: (416) 674-9011, E-Mail: info@sdicapital.com, Web Site: www.sdimarketing.com (14)

Wait, Rick, CPM Delta 1, Inc, Dallas, TX. Tel: (214) 349-6886, (800) 627-0252, FAX: (214) 503-1557, Web Site: www.cpmdelta1.com (11)

Waite, Greg, Diamond Marketing Solutions, Bloomingdale, IL. Tel: (630) 523-5250, FAX: (630) 523-0403, Web Site: www.dmsolutions.com (35)

Waite, Katherine, Peck Rock Associates, Bristol, RI. Tel: (401) 253-9307, FAX: (401) 254-0424, E-Mail: pra@aol.com, Web Site: www.peckrock. com (33)

Waiter, Eric, EWA & Miniature Cars USA Inc, Berkeley Heights, NJ. Tel: (732) 424-7811, (800) 392-4454, FAX: (732) 424-7814, E-Mail: ewa@ ewacars.com (11)

Waizer, Mindy, Transaction Publishers, Piscataway, NJ. Tel: (732) 445-1245, FAX: (732) 748-9801, E-Mail: trans@transactionpub.com, Web Site: www.transactionpub.com (17)

Wake Forest University Baptist Medical Center, Winston Salem, NC. Tel: (336) 716-4665, Web Site: www.wfubmc.edu (1)

Wakefield Peanut Co, Wakefield, VA. Tel: (757) 899-5481, (800) 803-1309, FAX: (757) 899-7604, Web Site: www.wakefieldpeanutco.com (4)

Wakefield Talabisco International, New York, NY. Tel: (212) 661-8600, FAX: (212) 661-8832, Web Site: www.wtali.com (20)

Wal Mart Stores, Bentonville, AR. Tel: (479) 273-4000, (800) 925-6278, FAX: (479) 277-1830, Web Site: www.walmart.com (16)

Walch Publishing, Portland, ME. Tel: (207) 772-2846, (800) 558-2846, FAX: (207) 772-3105, E-Mail: customerservice@walch.com, Web Site: www. walch.com (17)

Waldbillig & Besteman, Madison, WI. Tel: (608) 829-0900, (800) 395-4767, FAX: (608) 829-0901, E-Mail: info@waldbest.com, Web Site: www. waldbest.com (35)

Walde, Dave, Johnny Appleseed's Inc, Beverly, MA. Tel: (978) 922-2040, (800) 767-6666, FAX: (978) 922-7001, Web Site: www.appleseeds.com (2)

Waldie, Greg, Farm Bureau Insurance, Lansing, MI. Tel: (517) 323-7000, (800) 292-2680, FAX: (517) 327-0208, Web Site: www.farmbureauinsurance-mi. com (15)

Walding, Jim, Disabled American Veterans, Cincinnati, OH. Tel: (859) 441-7300, FAX: (859) 442-2084, E-Mail: feedback@davmail.org, Web Site: www. dav.org (1)

Waldman, David, Eclipse Direct Marketing, Mineola, NY. Tel: (212) 931-8344, FAX: (212) 931-8377, E-Mail: jkaiser@eclipsedm.com, Web Site: www. eclipsedm.com (23)

Waldman, David, LIST Inc, Danbury, CT. Tel: (914) 765-0700, FAX: (914) 765-0046, E-Mail: info@l-i-s-t.com, Web Site: www.l-i-s-t.com (24)

Waldman, Karin, The Dreyfus Corp, New York, NY. Tel: (212) 922-6000, FAX: (212) 922-8165 (14)

Walgren, Amy, Brookfield Zoo, Brookfield, IL. Tel: (708) 485-0263, (800) 201-0784, FAX: (708) 485-3532, Web Site: www.brookfieldzoo.org (1)

Walk, Steve, Com-Pak, Berlin, CT. Tel: (856) 802-1900, (856) 802-3097, E-Mail: info@com-pak. com, Web Site: www.marketpointdirect.com (28)

Walk Thru The Bible Ministries Inc, Atlanta, GA. Tel: (770) 458-9300, Web Site: www.walkthru.org (1)

Walke, David, M., Guideline, New York, NY. Tel: (212) 645-4500, (866) GUIDELINE, FAX: (212) 645-7681, Web Site: www.findsvp.com (30)

Walker, Barclay, BC & Associates Representatives Inc, Fate, TX. Tel: (972) 722-7365, (800) 275-1298, FAX: (972) 722-7714, E-Mail: terri@bcincentives. com, Web Site: www.bcincentives.com (33)

Walker, Bob, The Dwyer Group, Waco, TX. Tel: (254) 759-5850, Web Site: www.dwyergroup.com (16)

Walker, Brian, C., Herman Miller Inc, Zeeland, MI. Tel: (616) 654-3000, FAX: (616) 654-5234, E-Mail: investor@hermanmiller.com, Web Site: www.hermanmiller.com (16)

Walker, Clay, Forestry Suppliers Inc, Jackson, MS. Tel: (601) 354-3565, (800) 543-4203, FAX: (601) 292-0165, E-Mail: fsi@forestry-suppliers.com, Web Site: www.forestry-suppliers.com (9)

Walker, Darren, PC/Nametag Inc, Verona, WI. Tel: (608) 845-1850, (800) 233-9767, E-Mail: sales@ pcnametag.com, Web Site: www.pcnametag.com (16)

Walker, Ellana, A La Mode Inc, Oklahoma City, OK. Tel: (405) 359-6587, Web Site: www.alamode.com (22)

Walker, Jeff, Renaissance Learning, Wisconsin Rapids, WI. Tel: (715) 424-3636, (800) 338-4204, FAX: (715) 424-4242, E-Mail: answers@renlearn.com, Web Site: www.renlearn.com (5)

Walker, Jim, Walch Publishing, Portland, ME. Tel: (207) 772-2846, (800) 558-2846, FAX: (207) 772-3105, E-Mail: customerservice@walch.com, Web Site: www.walch.com (17)

Walker, Joanne, EMS Technologies, Norcross, GA. Tel: (770) 263-9200, FAX: (770) 447-4405, Web Site: www.ems-t.com (16)

Walker, Joe, RL Polk & Co, Southfield, MI. Tel: (248) 728-7100, (800) GO-4-POLK, FAX: (248) 728-4444, Web Site: www.polk.com (23)

Walker, John, Sport Supply Group, Dallas, TX. Tel: (972) 484-9484, FAX: (972) 247-0650, Web Site: www.sportsupplygroup.com (11)

Walker, Ken, TKL Interactive, The Colony, TX. Tel: (972) 370-7878, (800) 789-3893, FAX: (972) 370-7879, Web Site: www.tklinteractive.com (23)

Walker, Kevin, Magnaflux, Glenview, IL. Tel: (847) 657-5300, FAX: (847) 657-5388, Web Site: www. magnaflux.com (16)

Walker, Kim, Memorial Sloan Kettering Cancer Center, New York, NY. Tel: (646) 227-3528, Web Site: www.mskcc.org (1)

Walker, Lee, Mervyn's, Pleasanton, CA. Tel: (510) 727-3000, (800) 480-5014, FAX: (510) 727-5851, Web Site: www.mervyns.com (16)

Walker, Lisa, Vance Industries Inc, Niles, IL. Tel: (847) 375-8900, FAX: (847) 375-6818, E-Mail: vance@vanceind.com, Web Site: www.vanceind. com (16)

Walker, Michael, C., International City/County Management Association, Washington, DC. Tel: (202) 289-ICMA, FAX: (202) 962-3500, E-Mail: customerservice@icma.org, Web Site: www.icma. org (1)

Walker, Peggy, The National Underwriter Co, Erlanger, KY. Tel: (800) 543-0874, FAX: (856) 692-2246, E-Mail: customerservice@nuco.com, Web Site: www.nuco.com (17)

Walker, Renee, RC Bigelow Inc, Fairfield, CT. Tel: (203) 334-1212, Web Site: www.bigelowtea.com (4)

Walker, Rod, International Specialized Book Services Inc, Portland, OR. Tel: (503) 287-3093, (800) 944-6190, FAX: (503) 280-8832, E-Mail: isbs_sales@ isbs.com, Web Site: www.isbscatalog.com (16)

Walker, Rosemary, Peter Li Education Group, Dayton, OH. Tel: (937) 293-1415, (800) 523-4625, FAX: (937) 293-1310, Web Site: www.peterli.com (17)

Walker, Theresa, The Catholic University of America Press, Washington, DC. Tel: (202) 319-5052, FAX: (202) 319-4985, E-Mail: cua-press@cua.edu, Web Site: www.cuapress.cua.edu (17)

Walker, Virginia, Walker & Associates, Welcome, NC. Tel: (336) 731-6391, (800) WALKER-1, FAX: (336) 731-7253/6973, E-Mail: info@walkerfirst. com, Web Site: www.walkerfirst.com (29)

Walker & Associates, Welcome, NC. Tel: (336) 731-6391, (800) WALKER-1, FAX: (336) 731-7253/ 6973, E-Mail: info@walkerfirst.com, Web Site: www.walkerfirst.com (29)

Walker/Fitzgibbon TV & Film Productions, Los Angeles, CA. Tel: (323) 469-6800, FAX: (323) 878-0600, E-Mail: mo@walkerfitzgibbon.com, Web Site: www.walkerfitzgibbon.com (32)

Walker Publishing Co Inc, New York, NY. Tel: (212) 727-8300, (800) 289-2553, FAX: (212) 727-0984 (17)

Walkes, Amy, Professional Photographer Magazine, Atlanta, GA. Tel: (404) 522-8600, (800) 786-6277, FAX: (404) 614-6405, E-Mail: csc@ppa.com, Web Site: www.ppa.com (17)

Walkley, Jim, Cohorts, Denver, CO. Tel: (303) 893-8600, FAX: (303) 893-8611, E-Mail: info@ cohorts.com, Web Site: www.cohorts.com (35)

Walkowiak, Tom, Newark Electronics, Chicago, IL. Tel: (773) 784-5100, (800) 4-Newark, FAX: (888) 551-4801, E-Mail: webmaster@newark.com, Web Site: www.newark.com (3)

Wall, Barbara, Lions Gate Television Corp, Santa Monica, CA. Tel: (310) 449-9200, FAX: (310) 255-3870, Web Site: www.lionsgate.com (16)

Wall, Janet, E., JIST Publishing, Saint Paul, MN. Tel: (800) 648-5478, FAX: (800) 547-8329, E-Mail: info@jist.com, Web Site: www.jist.com (17)

Wall, Joann, Spear Engineering Co, Colorado Springs, CO. Tel: (719) 471-9850 (16)

Wall, John, Demco Inc, Madison, WI. Tel: (608) 241-1201, FAX: (608) 241-1799, E-Mail: custserv@ demco.com, Web Site: www.demco.com (10)

Wall, Mary, KBM Group, Richardson, TX. Tel: (972) 664-3600, FAX: (972) 664-3656, E-Mail: info@ knowledgebasemarketing.com, Web Site: www. kbm1.com (22)

Wall, Roger, Spinneybeck Enterprises, Getzville, NY. Tel: (716) 446-2380, (800) 482-7777, FAX: (716) 446-2396, E-Mail: sales@spinneybeck.com, Web Site: www.spinneybeck.com (16)

Wallace, Beth, Conservation International, Arlington, VA. Tel: (202) 912-1285 (1)

Wallace, Brian, Coin Laundry Association, Oakbrook Terrace, IL. Tel: (630) 963-5547, FAX: (630) 963-5864, Web Site: www.coinlaundry.org (1)

Wallace, Gary, Multiple Sclerosis Association of America, Cherry Hill, NJ. Tel: (856) 488-4500, Web Site: www.msaa.com (1)

Wallace, Kendall, The NH Broadcaster, Lowell, MA. Tel: (978) 458-7100, Web Site: www. nhbroadcaster.com (31)

Wallace, Nyoto, Ace Communications, Garden City, NY. Tel: (718) 458-3800, (800) 468-7667, FAX: (516) 872-8156, Web Site: www.aceav.com (3)

Wallace, Pat, Leanin' Tree Inc, Boulder, CO. Tel: (303) 530-7768, (800) 525-0656, FAX: (303) 530-5124, E-Mail: info@leanintree.com, Web Site: www.leanintree.com (6)

Wallace, Ray, Gold Medal Hair Products Inc, Farmingdale, NY. Tel: (516) 378-6900, (800) 324-7136, FAX: (516) 378-0168, E-Mail: customerservice@ goldmedalhair.com, Web Site: www.goldmedalhair. com (7)

Wallace Targeted Communications, Saint Charles, IL. Tel: (630) 313-7000, FAX: (630) 377-4622, Web Site: www.wallace.com (27)

Wallach, Kenneth, L., Central National-Gottesman Inc, Purchase, NY. Tel: (914) 696-9000, FAX: (914) 696-1066, E-Mail: purchase@cng-inc.com, Web Site: www.cng-inc.com (25)

Wallake, Randy F., Minnesota Life, Saint Paul, MN. Tel: (651) 665-3500, (888) 237-1838, FAX: (651) 665-4488, Web Site: www.minnesotalife.com; www.securian.com (15)

Waller, Craig, Pace Communications Inc, Greensboro, NC. Tel: (336) 378-6065, FAX: (336) 275-2864, Web Site: www.pacecommunications.com (17)

Wallin, Ian, TV Guide Magazine, New York, NY. Tel: (212) 852-7500, (800) 866-1400, Web Site: www. tvguide.com (31)

Walling, Mamie, Coastal Living, Birmingham, AL. Tel: (205) 877-6007, FAX: (205) 445-8655, E-Mail: coastalliving@customersvc.com, Web Site: www.coastalliving.com (43)

Wallis, Matthew, Quark Inc, Denver, CO. Tel: (303) 894-3832, Web Site: www.quark.com (34)

Wallis, W. Budge, F&W Publications Inc, Blue Ash, OH. Tel: (513) 531-2690, FAX: (513) 531-0293, Web Site: www.fwpublications.com (17)

Wallis, William Budge, Writer's Digest Books, Blue Ash, OH. Tel: (513) 531-2690, (800) 666-0963, Web Site: www.fwpublications.com (17)

Walls, Randy, Credicorp, Dallas, TX. Tel: (214) 915-7200, FAX: (214) 915-7415, E-Mail: support@credicorp.net, Web Site: www.credicorp.net (1)

Walsh, Cheryl, Protocol, Sarasota, FL. Tel: (800) 800-8627, FAX: (203) 271-4970, Web Site: www.protocolmarketing.com (29)

Walsh, Daryl, MackayMitchell Envelope Co, Minneapolis, MN. Tel: (800) 622-5299, Web Site: www.mackayenvelope.com (26)

Walsh, Jerry, Decal Shop, Jacksonville, FL. Tel: (904) 721-3177, (800) 634-1889 (10)

Walsh, Jerry, Racer Walsh Co, Jacksonville, FL. Tel: (904) 721-2289, FAX: (904) 721-2935, Web Site: www.racerwalsh.com (12)

Walsh, Jim, EasyLink Services International Corp, Piscataway, NJ. Tel: (800) 828-7115, FAX: (732) 652-3810, E-Mail: sales@easylink.com, Web Site: www.easylink.com (16)

Walsh, Joe, The Great Amarillo Directory, Amarillo, TX. Tel: (806) 353-5155, FAX: (806) 359-2974, Web Site: www.worldpages.com (17)

Walsh, John, DataQuick, San Diego, CA. Tel: (856) 597-3100, (800) 950-9171, Web Site: www.primerasource.com (23)

Walsh, Maureen, Institute of Management Accountants Inc, Montvale, NJ. Tel: (201) 573-9000, (800) 638-4427, FAX: (201) 474-1600, E-Mail: ima@imanet.org, Web Site: www.imanet.org (1)

Walsh, Tim, Harvard Pilgrim Health Care, Wellesley, MA. Tel: (617) 509-1000, FAX: (617) 509-7590, Web Site: www.harvardpilgrim.org (7)

Walshe, Michael, The Historical Research Center International Inc, Boynton Beach, FL. Tel: (561) 732-5263, (800) 985-9956, FAX: (561) 940-7991, E-Mail: custsvc@names.com, Web Site: www.historicalresearchcenter.net (16)

Walsifer, Frederick J., Delicious Orchards, Colts Neck, NJ. Tel: (732) 462-1989, FAX: (732) 542-2111, E-Mail: info@deliciousorchardsnj.com, Web Site: www.deliciousorchardsnj.com (4)

Waltenspiel, Ronald E., Timber Crest Farms, Healdsburg, CA. Tel: (707) 433-8251, FAX: (707) 433-8255, E-Mail: tcf@sonic.net, Web Site: www.sonic.net/tcf (4)

Waltenspiel, Ruth, Timber Crest Farms, Healdsburg, CA. Tel: (707) 433-8251, FAX: (707) 433-8255, E-Mail: tcf@sonic.net, Web Site: www.sonic.net/tcf (16)

Walter, Charles, Industrial Instruments & Supplies Inc, Southampton, PA. Tel: (215) 396-0822, (800) 523-6079, FAX: (215) 396-0833, E-Mail: customerservice@iisusa.com, Web Site: www.iisusa.com (9)

Walter, Christine, Industrial Instruments & Supplies Inc, Southampton, PA. Tel: (215) 396-0822, (800) 523-6079, FAX: (215) 396-0833, E-Mail: customerservice@iisusa.com, Web Site: www.iisusa.com (9)

Walter, Gary, Infutor Data Solutions, Minooka, IL. Tel: (815) 467-0601, Web Site: www.infutor.com (23)

Walter, Ken, Sierra Trading Post, Cheyenne, WY. Tel: (307) 775-8050, (800) 713-4534, FAX: (307) 775-8089, Web Site: www.sierratradingpost.com (2)

Walter, Rob, Smith & Hawken Ltd, Novato, CA. Tel: (415) 506-3700, (800) 940-1170, FAX: (415) 506-3900, Web Site: www.smithandhawken.com (8)

Walter, W Todd, Elizabeth Arden Spas LLC, Stamford, CT. Tel: (203) 905-1700, FAX: (203) 905-1716, Web Site: www.reddoorspas.com (19)

Walter, William, G., FMC Corp, Philadelphia, PA. Tel: (215) 299-6000, FAX: (215) 299-5998, Web Site: www.fmc.com (16)

Walter Weissman Photo Studio, New York, NY. Tel: (212) 989-9694, FAX: (212) 989-9694, E-Mail: wweissmanphoto@nyc.rr.com, Web Site: www.weissmanphoto.com (37)

Walters, Darlene, American Institute of Physics, Melville, NY. Tel: (516) 576-2200, (800) 892-8259, FAX: (516) 576-2374, E-Mail: aipinfo@aip.org, Web Site: www.aip.org (17)

Walters, John, C., John Harland Co, Decatur, GA. Tel: (770) 981-5580, (800) 723-3690, FAX: (770) 593-5367, E-Mail: jhhwebmaster@harland.net, Web Site: www.harland.net (16)

Walters, Judith, Data Square LLC, Wilton, CT. Tel: (203) 964-9733, E-Mail: info@datasquare.com, Web Site: www.datasquare.com (22)

Walters, Keith, S., Ennis Inc, Midlothian, TX. Tel: (972) 775-9801, (800) 962-0944, FAX: (800) 645-8339, Web Site: www.ennis.com (16)

Walters, Michelle, Luzier Personalized Cosmetics, Kansas City, MO. Tel: (816) 531-8338, (800) 821-6632, FAX: (816) 531-6979, Web Site: www.luzier.com (7)

Walthers, Phil, Wm. K. Walthers Inc, Milwaukee, WI. Tel: (414) 527-0770, FAX: (414) 527-4423, Web Site: www.walthers.com (11)

Wm. K. Walthers Inc, Milwaukee, WI. Tel: (414) 527-0770, FAX: (414) 527-4423, Web Site: www.walthers.com (11)

Walton, S., Robson, Wal Mart Stores, Bentonville, AR. Tel: (479) 273-4000, (800) 925-6278, FAX: (479) 277-1830, Web Site: www.walmart.com (16)

Waltzer, Carl, Carl Waltzer Digital Service Bureau, New York, NY. Tel: (212) 475-8748, FAX: (212) 475-9359, E-Mail: cwdigital@aol.com, Web Site: www.waltzer.com (36)

Carl Waltzer Digital Service Bureau, New York, NY. Tel: (212) 475-8748, FAX: (212) 475-9359, E-Mail: cwdigital@aol.com, Web Site: www.waltzer.com (36)

Wambold, Richard L., Pactiv Corp, Lake Forest, IL. Tel: (847) 482-2000, (800) 828-2850, FAX: (847) 482-4738, Web Site: www.pactiv.com (26)

Wan, Tracy, The Sharper Image, New York, NY. Tel: (415) 445-6000, (800) 344-5555, FAX: (800) 552-2525, E-Mail: info@sharperimage.com, Web Site: www.sharperimage.com (6)

Wanamaker, Mary Ellen, Christian Brands, Phoenix, AZ. Tel: (602) 243-5200, (800) 521-2914, FAX: (602) 232-1855, Web Site: www.christian-brands.com (16)

Wandell, Andrew, National Fire Protection Association, Quincy, MA. Tel: (617) 770-3000, FAX: (617) 770-0700, Web Site: www.nfpa.org (1)

Wang, Dale, The Fuller Theological Seminary, Pasadena, CA. Tel: (626) 584-5200, (800) 2-FULLER, FAX: (626) 584-5449, Web Site: www.fuller.edu/cll (16)

Wang, Xitian, Boundless Corp, Phelps, NY. Tel: (631) 962-1500, (800) 231-5445, FAX: (631) 962-1505, E-Mail: sales@boundless.com, Web Site: www.boundless.com (16)

Wank, Vincent, Innovative Marketing Solutions LLC, Bangor, ME. Tel: (207) 262-6233, Web Site: www.imsmaine.net (29)

Wanning, Jeffrey, J., Central States Health & Life Co of Omaha, Omaha, NE. Tel: (402) 397-1111, (800) 826-6587, FAX: (402) 391-3772, Web Site: www.cso.com (15)

Ward, Anthony, DPC Computers, Monsey, NY. Tel: (845) 426-3790, (866) 513-CORP, FAX: (845) 426-6275, E-Mail: learnmore@salestax.com, Web Site: www.salestax.com (16)

Ward, Daniel, Foote-Jones/Illinois Gear, Aberdeen, SD. Tel: (605) 225-0360, FAX: (605) 225-0567, Web Site: www.footejones.com (16)

Ward, Deb, AcuSport Corp, Bellefontaine, OH. Tel: (937) 593-7010, FAX: (937) 592-5625, E-Mail: mwsales@acusport.com, Web Site: www.acusport.com (11)

Ward, Jerry, Successful Farming, Des Moines, IA. Tel: (515) 284-2143, (800) 678-2711, FAX: (515) 284-3127 (17)

Ward, Natasha, Global Computer Corp, Port Washington, NY. Tel: (516) 625-4300, (888) 845-6225, FAX: (516) 625-4072, Web Site: www.globalcomputer.com (3)

Ward, Richard, 22squared Inc, Atlanta, GA. Tel: (404) 347-8700, FAX: (404) 347-8800, Web Site: www.22squared.com (35)

Ward, Stephen, Support Services Corp, Fort Myers, FL. Tel: (239) 332-5300, FAX: (239) 332-4555, E-Mail: steve@ss-corp.com, Web Site: www.ss-corp.com (22)

Ward, Ted, GEICO Direct, Washington, DC. Tel: (301) 986-2842, (800) 841-3000, FAX: (301) 986-2068, Web Site: www.geico.com (15)

Ward, Terry, DMB Financial, Beverly, MA. Tel: (866) 810-3210, Web Site: www.dmbfinancial.com (14)

Bill Ward Inc, Wilmington, DE. Tel: (302) 762-6600, FAX: (302) 397-2153, E-Mail: billward@billwardinc.com (30)

Ward Jr, William, F., Bill Ward Inc, Wilmington, DE. Tel: (302) 762-6600, FAX: (302) 397-2153, E-Mail: billward@billwardinc.com (30)

Ward-Burns, J. Robert, Beauticontrol Cosmetics Inc, Carrollton, TX. Tel: (972) 458-0601, (800) BEAUTI-1, FAX: (972) 458-6904, E-Mail: clientservices@beauticontrol.com, Web Site: www.beauticontrol.com (16)

Ward-Llewellyn, Terry, Quick Draw Clip Systems Inc, Ventura, CA. Tel: (805) 644-6888, (888) 254-7797, FAX: (805) 644-7320, E-Mail: ron@clipsystems.com, Web Site: www.clipsystems.com (9)

Wardell, Keith, Marketing1by1 LLC, Fairfax, VA. Tel: (703) 934-6020, Web Site: marketing1by1.com (22)

Warden, Cynthia, K., AMA Insurance Agency Inc, Chicago, IL. Tel: (312) 464-2425, (800) 458-5736, FAX: (312) 419-5096, Web Site: www.amainsure.com (15)

Wardlow, Dan, San Francisco State University, San Francisco, CA. Tel: (415) 338-1111, FAX: (415) 338-0501, Web Site: www.sfsu.edu (41)

Wardour, Scott, EMED Co Inc, Buffalo, NY. Tel: (716) 626-1616, (800) 442-3633, FAX: (716) 626-1630, E-Mail: customerservice@emedco.com, Web Site: www.emedco.com (16)

Ward's Natural Science, Rochester, NY. Tel: (585) 359-2502, (800) 962-2660, FAX: (585) 334-6174, E-Mail: customer_service@wardsci.com, Web Site: www.wardsci.com (34)

Wareham, John, Vitasoy USA Inc, Ayer, MA. Tel: (978) 772-6880, (800) VITA-SOY, FAX: (978) 772-6881, Web Site: www.vitasoy-usa.com (16)

Warermann, David, USA Hosts, San Francisco, CA. Tel: (415) 695-8000, (800) 368-4678, FAX: (415) 986-3668, Web Site: www.usahosts.com (19)

Warman, Ann, Jensen, brandUNITY Inc, Rollingbay, WA. Tel: (206) 842-4948, E-Mail: admin@brandunity.com, Web Site: www.brandunity.com (20)

Warman, David, brandUNITY Inc, Rollingbay, WA. Tel: (206) 842-4948, E-Mail: admin@brandunity.com, Web Site: www.brandunity.com (20)

Warnaco, New York, NY. Tel: (212) 287-8207, FAX: (212) 682-7368, E-Mail: contactus@warnaco.com, Web Site: www.warnaco.com (2)

Warnaco Swimwear Inc, Los Angeles, CA. Tel: (323) 726-1262, FAX: (323) 724-6931, Web Site: www. speedo.com (16)

Warner, Brooks, Web Graphics, Glens Falls, NY. Tel: (518) 792-6501, (800) 833-8863, FAX: (518) 792-9353, (800) 833-8861, E-Mail: marketing@ printatweb.com, Web Site: www.printatweb.com (27)

Warner, Connie, Bradley Direct, Columbus, GA. Tel: (706) 565-2100, (866) 239-6774, (800) 241-8981, FAX: (706) 565-2132, (888) 224-7455, E-Mail: customerservice@grilllovers.com, Web Site: www. grilllovers.com (8)

Warner, Connie, Char-Broil Grill Lover's Catalog, Louisville, KY. Tel: (706) 565-2100, (800) 241-8981, FAX: (706) 565-2121, Web Site: www. grilllovers.com (8)

Warner, Herb, Fluid Metering Inc, Syosset, NY. Tel: (516) 922-6050, (800) 223-3388, FAX: (516) 624-8261, E-Mail: pumps@fmipump.com, Web Site: www.fmipump.com (16)

Warner, Nancy, Reliable Technologies Inc, Manchester, NH. Tel: (603) 644-2528, (800) 346-7890, FAX: (603) 627-5553, Web Site: www.tei-imaging. com (16)

Warner, Valerie, Brush Fire, Cedar Knolls, NJ. Tel: (973) 871-1700, FAX: (973) 871-1717, Web Site: www.brushfireinc.com (35)

Warner Books, New York, NY. Tel: (212) 364-1200, FAX: (212) 522-7989, Web Site: www. twbookmark.com (17)

Warner Bros, Burbank, CA. Tel: (818) 954-6000, Web Site: www.warnerbros.com (3)

Warner Press, Anderson, IN. Tel: (765) 644-7721, (800) 741-7721, FAX: (765) 640-8005, E-Mail: wporders@warnerpress.org, Web Site: www. warnerpress.com (17)

Warrantech Direct Inc, Bedford, TX. Tel: (817) 786-1000, (800) 833-8801, FAX: (817) 786-1020, Web Site: www.warrantech.com (29)

Warren Jr., Timothy, M., Banker & Tradesman, Boston, MA. Tel: (617) 428-5100, FAX: (617) 428-5119, E-Mail: dmoore@thewarrengroup.com, Web Site: www.thewarrengroup.com (17)

Warren, Albert, Warren Communications News, Washington, DC. Tel: (202) 872-9200, (800) 771-9202, FAX: (202) 318-8350, E-Mail: info@warren-news. com, Web Site: www.warren-news.com (17)

Warren, Dan, Warren Communications News, Washington, DC. Tel: (202) 872-9200, (800) 771-9202, FAX: (202) 318-8350, E-Mail: info@warren-news. com, Web Site: www.warren-news.com (17)

Warren, Dee, MarketAide Services Inc, Salina, KS. Tel: (785) 825-7161, (800) 204-2433, FAX: (785) 825-4697, E-Mail: kcarlgren@marketaide.com, Web Site: www.marketaide.com (21)

Warren, Mark, Esquire Magazine, New York, NY. Tel: (212) 649-2000, (800) 925-0485, FAX: (212) 265-0938, E-Mail: esquire@hearst.com, Web Site: www.esquire.com (17)

Warren, Paul, Warren Communications News, Washington, DC. Tel: (202) 872-9200, (800) 771-9202, FAX: (202) 318-8350, E-Mail: info@warren-news. com, Web Site: www.warren-news.com (17)

Warren Communications News, Washington, DC. Tel: (202) 872-9200, (800) 771-9202, FAX: (202) 318-8350, E-Mail: info@warren-news.com, Web Site: www.warren-news.com (17)

Warren, Gorham & Lamont Inc, New York, NY. Tel: (617) 423-2020, Web Site: ria.thomsonreuters.com (17)

Warrick, Ed, KEH.com, Smyrna, GA. Tel: (770) 333-4200, (800) 342-5534, FAX: (770) 333-4242, E-Mail: sales@keh.com, Web Site: www.keh.com (16)

Warrior Custom Golf Inc, Irvine, CA. Tel: (949) 699-2499, Web Site: www.warriorcustomgolf.com (11)

Warrner, Thomas, InfoSource Inc, Oviedo, FL. Tel: (407) 796-5200, (800) 393-4636, FAX: (407) 796-5190, E-Mail: isisale@howtomaster.com, Web Site: www.infosourcelearning.com (3)

Warsaw, Stephen, R., CDMC/Carefree Direct Marketing Corp, Carefree, AZ. Tel: (480) 488-4227, FAX: (480) 488-2841 (20)

Warwick, Peter, Thomson West, Eagan, MN. Tel: (651) 687-7000, (800) 328-9378, FAX: (651) 687-7849, E-Mail: jeff.patrios@thomsonreuters.com, Web Site: www.thomson.com (17)

Mal Warwick Associates, Berkeley, CA. Tel: (510) 843-8888, FAX: (510) 843-0142, E-Mail: info@ malwarwick.com, Web Site: www.malwarwick.com (1)

Wasco, Sonia Shaner, Grant Heilman Photography Inc, Lititz, PA. Tel: (717) 626-0296, (800) 622-2046, FAX: (717) 626-0971, E-Mail: info@ heilmanphoto.com, Web Site: www.heilmanphoto. com (38)

Washburn, David, Times Union, Albany, NY. Tel: (518) 454-5694, FAX: (518) 454-5628, Web Site: www.timesunion.com (18)

Washchilla Jr., Edward, Fairfield Marketing Group Inc, Easton, CT. Tel: (203) 261-5585 X205, (203) 261-5568, FAX: (203) 261-0884, E-Mail: ed@ fairfieldmarketing.com, Web Site: www. fairfieldmarketing.com (22)

Washington Gas Energy Services, Herndon, VA. Tel: (703) 793-7500, Web Site: www.wges.com (16)

Washington Lists Inc, McLean, VA. Tel: (703) 749-3110, FAX: (703) 749-0960, E-Mail: emahoney@ washingtonlists.com, Web Site: www. washingtonlists.com (23)

Washington Marketing Group, Arlington, VA. Tel: (703) 534-9331, FAX: (703) 534-0242, E-Mail: william.shaker@twmg.com, Web Site: www.twmg. com (1)

The Washington Monthly Co, Washington, DC. Tel: (202) 393-5155, FAX: (202) 393-2444, E-Mail: editors@washingtonmonthly.com, Web Site: www. washingtonmonthly.com (17)

Washington Mutual Home Loan, Inc, Downers Grove, IL. Tel: (847) 549-6500, FAX: (847) 549-2975 (14)

Washington National Opera, Washington, DC. Tel: (202) 295-2400, (800) US-OPERA, FAX: (202) 295-2460, E-Mail: mail@dc-opera.org, Web Site: www.dc-opera.org (16)

The Washington Post, Washington, DC. Tel: (202) 334-6000, (800) 627-1150, E-Mail: letters@ washpost.com, Web Site: www.washingtonpost. com (17)

Washington Post Digital, Washington, DC. Tel: (202) 334-9900 (17)

Washington Products Inc, Massillon, OH. Tel: (330) 837-5101, FAX: (330) 837-5401 (34)

Washington University, Saint Louis, MO. Tel: (314) 935-4623, (800) 638-0700, FAX: (314) 935-7088, Web Site: www.wustl.edu (1)

The Washingtonian, Washington, DC. Tel: (202) 296-3600, E-Mail: editorial@washingtonian.com, Web Site: www.washingtonian.com (17)

Washko, John, Broadmoor Hotel Inc, Colorado Springs, CO. Tel: (719) 634-7711, (866) 837-9520, FAX: (719) 577-5779, Web Site: www.broadmoor. com (19)

Washton, Andrew, Andrew D Washton Books On the Fine Arts, Port Chester, NY. Tel: (914) 933-0479, E-Mail: andrew@washtonbooks.com, Web Site: www.washtonbooks.com (16)

Washton, Ruth, Andrew D Washton Books On the Fine Arts, Port Chester, NY. Tel: (914) 933-0479, E-Mail: andrew@washtonbooks.com, Web Site: www.washtonbooks.com (16)

Andrew D Washton Books On the Fine Arts, Port Chester, NY. Tel: (914) 933-0479, E-Mail: andrew@washtonbooks.com, Web Site: www. washtonbooks.com (16)

Wasik, Ken, Stephens Inc, New York, NY. Tel: (212) 891-1777, Web Site: www.stephens.com (20)

Waskover, Michael, Automatic Mail Services Inc, Long Island City, NY. Tel: (718) 361-3091, FAX: (718) 937-8568, E-Mail: data@automatic-mail. com, Web Site: www.automatic-mail.com (28)

Wasser, Marcia, Source Communications, Hackensack, NJ. Tel: (201) 343-5222 (35)

Wasserberg, Edie, Christian Broadcasting Network Inc, Virginia Beach, VA. Tel: (757) 226-3542, FAX: (757) 226-2017, Web Site: www.cbn.org (1)

Wasserman Uniform Co, Fort Lauderdale, FL. Tel: (614) 279-8888, (614) 279-7000, (800) 848-3576, FAX: (614) 464-0416, (800) 204-0416, E-Mail: custserv@wassermanuniform.com, Web Site: www. wassermanuniform.com (2)

Wasson, Anthony, Advanced Medical Nutrition Inc, Pittsburgh, PA. Tel: (412) 494-0100, (800) 879-2664, (800) 437-8888, FAX: (888) 245-4440, Web Site: www.douglaslabs.com (7)

Wasson, Dawn, Nielsen, New York, NY. Tel: (703) 488-2700, (800) 765-7615, FAX: (703) 488-2800, E-Mail: bmcomm@nielsen.com, Web Site: www. nielsenbusinessmedia.com (42)

Wasson, Gregory, D., Allstate Motor Club, Inc, Deerfield, IL. Tel: (847) 914-2972, FAX: (847) 914-2804, Web Site: www.walgreens.com (7)

Watchorn, Ryan, Cabela's Inc, Sidney, NE. Tel: (308) 254-5505, (800) 237-4444, FAX: (308) 254-4800, Web Site: www.cabelas.com (11)

Watering Inc/Hemmings Motor News, Bennington, VT. Tel: (802) 442-3101, (800) 227-4373, FAX: (802) 447-1561, E-Mail: hmnmail@hemmings. com, Web Site: www.hemmings.com (17)

Waterlow, Simon, Ideals Publications Inc, Nashville, TN. Tel: (615) 333-0478, FAX: (615) 781-1447, Web Site: www.idealspublications.com (17)

Waterman, John, P., Nuveen Investments, Chicago, IL. Tel: (312) 917-7700, (800) 257-8787, FAX: (312) 917-8049, Web Site: www.nuveen.com (14)

Waters, Craig, Fitness Quest, Canton, OH. Tel: (330) 478-0755, (800) 321-9236, FAX: (330) 479-9213, E-Mail: customersupport@fitnessquest.com, Web Site: www.fitnessquest.com (16)

Waters Corp, Milford, MA. Tel: (508) 482-2000, (800) 252-4752, FAX: (508) 872-1990, Web Site: www. waters.com (16)

Water's Edge Resort & Spa, Westbrook, CT. Tel: (860) 399-5901, (800) 222-5901, FAX: (860) 399-8644, Web Site: www.watersedgeresort.com (19)

Waterson, Caroline, Coremetrics, San Mateo, CA. Tel: (877) 721-2673, Web Site: www.coremetrics.com (32)

Waterson, Sherry, Warnaco Swimwear Inc, Los Angeles, CA. Tel: (323) 726-1262, FAX: (323) 724-6931, Web Site: www.speedo.com (16)

Wathne Ltd, New York, NY. Tel: (212) 757-3001, FAX: (212) 757-2448 (2)

Watjen, Thomas, R., Unum Corp, Portland, ME. Tel: (207) 770-2211, (800) 421-0344, FAX: (207) 770-4510, Web Site: www.unum.com (15)

Watkins, Gena, Davis, Institute for Student Achievement, Carle Place, NY. Tel: (516) 812-6700, Web Site: www.studentachievement.org (1)

Watkins, Katherine, Eastman Chemical Co, Kingsport, TN. Tel: (800) 695-4322, Web Site: www.eatman. com (16)

Watkins, Richard, Cellular One Group, Oklahoma City, OK. Tel: (509) 663-2162, (800) 545-5982, FAX: (425) 586-8451, Web Site: www.cellularone. com (16)

Watkins, Richard, Frog Tool Co Ltd, Dixon, IL. Tel: (815) 288-3811, E-Mail: info@frogwoodtools.com, Web Site: www.frogwoodtools.com (11)

Watkins, Robert, A. Dean Watkins, Okemos, MI. Tel: (517) 349-7700, FAX: (517) 349-7748, E-Mail: adeanwatkins@aol.com, Web Site: www. adeanwatkins.com (33)

A. Dean Watkins, Okemos, MI. Tel: (517) 349-7700, FAX: (517) 349-7748, E-Mail: adeanwatkins@aol. com, Web Site: www.adeanwatkins.com (33)

Watkinson, Kevin, Gifts Corp, Barrie, ON Canada. Tel: (905) 670-1126, (800) 565-3130, FAX: (905) 670-1127, E-Mail: customerservice@regal.ca, Web Site: www.regalgreetings.com (6)

Watley, Dennis, Kansas City Chiefs, Kansas City, MO. Tel: (816) 920-9300, (888) 99-CHIEFS, FAX: (816) 923-4719, Web Site: www.kcchiefs.com (16)

Watson III, Robert, C., Lo Ink Specialties, Kennebunkport, ME. Tel: (207) 967-9110, (800) 777-6471, FAX: (800) 895-6465, E-Mail: rwatson@loink. com, Web Site: www.loink.com (16)

Watson, Claire, Thompson & Morgan Inc, Tipp City, OH. Tel: (732) 363-2225, (800) 274-7333, FAX: (888) 466-4769, E-Mail: tminc@thompson-morgan. com, Web Site: www.tmseeds.com (8)

Watson, Colon, Keyspan Energy Corp, Brooklyn, NY. Tel: (718) 403-2000, (888) 222-7359, Web Site: www.keyspanenergy.com (16)

Watson, Duncan, Sherwood Design & Development Center, Carlstadt, NJ. Tel: (201) 372-3900, FAX: (201) 372-0917 (27)

Watson, Greg, Florida Today, Melbourne, FL. Tel: (321) 242-3500, (877) 424-0156, FAX: (321) 242-3729, Web Site: www.floridatoday.com (17)

Watson, Jerry, Direct Response Consulting, McLean, VA. Tel: (703) 749-0010, FAX: (703) 749-0967, Web Site: www.drcs.com (17)

Watson, Karen, The Nielsen Co, New York, NY. Tel: (646) 654-5000, E-Mail: contactcommunications@ nielsen.com, Web Site: www.nielsen.com (17)

Watson, Mark, The Marketing Store, Lombard, IL. Tel: (630) 693-1400, Web Site: www. themarketingstore.com (35)

Watson, Randy, Justin Discount Boots & Cowboy Outfitters, Justin, TX. Tel: (940) 648-2797, FAX: (940) 648-3282, Web Site: www.justinboots.com (2)

Watson, Richard, SSHC Inc/Radiant Heating Commercial Applications, Old Saybrook, CT. Tel: (860) 399-5434, (800) 544-5182, FAX: (860) 399-6460, (877) 675-4968, E-Mail: info@sshcinc.com, Web Site: www.sshcinc.com (9)

Watson, Rob, MediaTree, Parsippany, NJ. Tel: (800) 475-8703, FAX: (973) 781-1071, E-Mail: sales@ mediatreegroup.com, Web Site: www. mediatreegroup.com (27)

Watt, David, American Running Association, Bethesda, MD. Tel: (301) 913-9517, (800) 776-2732, FAX: (301) 913-9520, E-Mail: run@ americanrunning.org, Web Site: www. americanrunning.org (1)

Watt, Peter, InterMedia Outdoors Inc, New York, NY. Tel: (212) 852-6600 (31)

Watts, Edwin, Edwin Watts Golf, Fort Walton Beach, FL. Tel: (850) 244-2066, (800) 874-0146, FAX: (850) 244-5217, Web Site: www.edwinwatts.com (11)

Watts, Helen, Young Pecan Co, Florence, SC. Tel: (843) 662-8591, (800) 829-6864, FAX: (843) 664-2344, E-Mail: sales@youngpecan.com, Web Site: www.youngpecan.com (4)

Watts, John, Edwin Watts Golf, Fort Walton Beach, FL. Tel: (850) 244-2066, (800) 874-0146, FAX: (850) 244-5217, Web Site: www.edwinwatts.com (11)

Watts Radiant, Springfield, MO. Tel: (417) 864-6108, (800) 276-2419, FAX: (417) 864-8161, Web Site: www.wattsheatway.com (9)

Watzka, Peter, Marriott Ownership Resorts Sales & Marketing, Orlando, FL. Tel: (407) 206-6000, (800) 850-6674, FAX: (407) 851-1304 (19)

Waugh, Seth, Deutsche Bank Alex Brown Inc, New York, NY. Tel: (212) 250-2500, FAX: (212) 469-5315, Web Site: www.db.com (14)

Wausau Paper Mills Co, Brokaw, WI. Tel: (715) 675-3361, FAX: (715) 675-5181, Web Site: www. wausaupaper.com (25)

Wax, Marie-Laurence, Transemantics Inc, Washington, DC. Tel: (202) 362-2505, FAX: (202) 686-5603, E-Mail: ili@transemantics.com, Web Site: www. transemantics.com (16)

Waxman, Armond, JA Sexauer, Elmsford, NY. Tel: (914) 472-7501, (800) 431-1872, FAX: (914) 472-5834, Web Site: www.jasmro.com (16)

Way, Kim, The Database Centre, Fairfax, VA. Tel: (703) 359-2400, Web Site: www.databasecentre. co.uk (22)

Waymire, Linda, Fielder's Choice Direct, Monticello, IN. Tel: (574) 583-2741 X107, (800) 321-3177, FAX: (574) 583-CORN, Web Site: www. fielderschoicedirect.com (8)

Wayne, Arthur, Brooks Brothers, New York, NY. Tel: (212) 682-8800, (800) 274-1815, FAX: (212) 309-7273, Web Site: www.brooksbrothers.com (2)

Wayne, Jack, The American Vintage Library, Los Angeles, CA. Tel: (310) 552-3176, (800) 235-1919, Web Site: www.vintagelibrary.com (17)

Waytek, Chanhassen, MN. Tel: (952) 465-0431, Web Site: www.waytekwire.com (16)

We Deliver America Inc, Englewood Cliffs, NJ. Tel: (201) 307-8888, FAX: (201) 307-1200, E-Mail: info@we-deliver-america.com, Web Site: www.we-deliver-america.com (31)

We-No-Nah Canoe Inc, Winona, MN. Tel: (507) 454-5430, FAX: (507) 454-5448, E-Mail: info@ wenonah.com, Web Site: www.wenonah.com (11)

Weakley, Jim, American General Co, Neptune, NJ. Tel: (732) 922-7000, FAX: (732) 922-7595 (15)

Weaks, Allen, Marketing Solutions, Lathrup Village, MI. Tel: (248) 443-5252, FAX: (248) 443-5252 (20)

Weaks, Wendell, P., Steuben Glass, New York, NY. Tel: (607) 974-8659, (800) STEUBEN, FAX: (607) 974-8441, E-Mail: info@steuben.com, Web Site: www.steuben.com (6)

WearGuard Corp, Norwell, MA. Tel: (781) 871-4100, (800) 388-3300, FAX: (781) 871-2639, Web Site: www.wearguard.com (2)

The Weather Channel, New York, NY. Tel: (212) 856-5200, FAX: (212) 856-5215, Web Site: www. weather.com (32)

Weaver, Connie, K., Bearingpoint Inc, Montvale, NJ. Tel: (201) 307-7000, FAX: (201) 505-3765, Web Site: www.bearingpoint.com (14)

Weaver, Erin, Seton Hall University, South Orange, NJ. Tel: (973) 378-2650, Web Site: www.shu.edu (1)

Weaver, Jerry, Alltel Publishing Corp, Hudson, OH. Tel: (330) 650-7100, FAX: (330) 650-7883, Web Site: www.alltel.com (22)

Weaver, Kenneth, Bridgestone/Firestone North American Tire LLC, Nashville, TN. Tel: (615) 937-1000, (800) 543-7522, FAX: (615) 937-3721, Web Site: www.bridgestonetire.com (16)

Weaver, Loren, Loyaltyworks Inc, Atlanta, GA. Tel: (678) 539-5000, (800) 844-5000, FAX: (678) 539-5173, Web Site: www.loyaltyworks.com (21)

Weaver, Michael, Networking Alternatives for Publishers, Retailers & Artists, Inc, Eastsound, WA. Tel: (360) 376-2702, (800) 367-1907, FAX: (360) 376-2704, E-Mail: futureweb@rockisland.com (40)

Weaver, Philip, G., Cooper Tire & Rubber Co Inc, Findlay, OH. Tel: (419) 423-1321, (800) 854-6288, FAX: (419) 424-4212, Web Site: www.coopertire. com (16)

Weaver, Sallie, Elite Sportswear LP, Reading, PA. Tel: (610) 921-1469, (800) 345-4087, FAX: (610) 921-0208, E-Mail: gkelite@gkelite.com, Web Site: www.gk-elitesportswear.com (2)

Weaver, Shanon, Doane, Saint Louis, MO. Tel: (314) 569-2700, (866) 647-0918, FAX: (314) 569-1083, Web Site: www.doane.com (17)

Web Decisions, Greensboro, NC. Tel: (336) 545-7817 x100 (22)

Web Direct Marketing Inc, Glenview, IL. Tel: (847) 459-0800, (877) 841-2841, FAX: (847) 459-7378, E-Mail: info@webdirectmktg.com, Web Site: www.webdirectmktg.com (35)

Web Graphics, Glens Falls, NY. Tel: (518) 792-6501, (800) 833-8863, FAX: (518) 792-9353, (800) 833-8861, E-Mail: marketing@printatweb.com, Web Site: www.printatweb.com (27)

Web Graphics, Naples, FL. Tel: (239) 775-2295 (27)

Webb, Art, Barker Campbell & Farley, Virginia Beach, VA. Tel: (757) 497-4811, FAX: (757) 497-3684, Web Site: www.bc-f.com (35)

Webb, Bob, Potpourri Group Inc, Chelmsford, MA. Tel: (978) 256-4100, FAX: (978) 256-1961/0344, Web Site: www.potpourrigroup.com (6)

Webb, Eric, RSM McGladrey Inc, Charlotte, NC. Tel: (980) 233-4700, Web Site: www.rsmmcgladrey. com (20)

Webb, Robert, L., Webb & Co, Chelmsford, MA. Tel: (978) 250-9262, FAX: (978) 250-9262 (35)

Webb, Robert, W., The Marmon Group LLC, Chicago, IL. Tel: (312) 372-9500, FAX: (312) 845-5305, Web Site: www.marmon.com (16)

Webb, Steve, International Crystal Manufacturing Co, Oklahoma City, OK. Tel: (405) 236-3741, (800) 252-6780, FAX: (405) 235-1904, E-Mail: info@ icmfg.com, Web Site: www.icmfg.com (16)

Webb, Thomas, J., Consumer's Energy, Jackson, MI. Tel: (517) 788-0550, (800) 805-0490, FAX: (517) 788-1859, E-Mail: businesscenter@ consumerenergy.com, Web Site: www. consumersenergy.com (16)

Webb, Tony, Webb Designs Inc, El Cajon, CA. Tel: (619) 596-6400, (800) 262-9322, FAX: (619) 596-4511, E-Mail: awebb@webbshade.com, Web Site: www.webbshade.com (16)

Webb, William, Kraft Foods/Gevalia Kaffe, Tarrytown, NY. Tel: (914) 335-4239, Web Site: www.gevalia. com (16)

Webb & Co, Chelmsford, MA. Tel: (978) 250-9262, FAX: (978) 250-9262 (35)

Webb Designs Inc, El Cajon, CA. Tel: (619) 596-6400, (800) 262-9322, FAX: (619) 596-4511, E-Mail: awebb@webbshade.com, Web Site: www. webbshade.com (16)

Webb Mason, Hunt Valley, MD. Tel: (410) 785-1111, Web Site: www.webbmason.com (20)

Weber, Andrew, Premiere Global Services Inc, Atlanta, GA. Tel: (404) 262-8400, (800) 546-1541, FAX: (913) 661-9042, Web Site: www.PGiConnect.com (22)

Weber, Arthur, Consumers Digest Inc, Deerfield, IL. Tel: (847) 607-3000, FAX: (847) 763-0200, E-Mail: postmaster@consumersdigest.com, Web Site: www.consumersdigest.com (17)

Weber, Harley, Zeppo Marketing Inc, New York, NY. Tel: (212) 308-5734, Web Site: www. zeppomarketing.com (23)

Weber, James, M., Brooks Sports Inc, Bothell, WA. Tel: (425) 402-1632, (800) 2 BROOKS, FAX: (425) 489-1975, Web Site: www.brooksrunning. com (16)

Weber, Josh, Avalanche Creative Services Inc, New York, NY. Tel: (212) 206-9335, FAX: (212) 206-1538, E-Mail: info@avalanchecreative.tv, Web Site: www.avalanchecreative.tv (35)

Weber, Kurt, The Flinchbaugh Co Inc, Manchester, PA. Tel: (717) 266-2202, FAX: (717) 266-7055, E-Mail: flinchbaugh@blazenet.net, Web Site: www. flinchbaugh.com (16)

Weber, Mark, Phillips-Van Heusen Corp, New York, NY. Tel: (212) 381-3500, (800) 388-9122, FAX: (212) 381-3950, Web Site: www.pvh.com (2)

Weber, Randy, Consumers Digest Inc, Deerfield, IL. Tel: (847) 607-3000, FAX: (847) 763-0200, E-Mail: postmaster@consumersdigest.com, Web Site: www.consumersdigest.com (17)

Weber, Ronald, Lowrance Electronics, Tulsa, OK. Tel: (918) 437-6881, FAX: (918) 234-1707, Web Site: www.lowrance.com (11)

Weber, Wendy, Crandall Associates Inc, Port Washington, NY. Tel: (516) 767-6800, E-Mail: joyce@crandallassociates.com, Web Site: www.crandallassociates.com (20)

Weber, Wesley R., Wesley R. Weber & Associates, West Chester, PA. Tel: (610) 909-8040, E-Mail: wesweber@aol.com (20)

Wesley R. Weber & Associates, West Chester, PA. Tel: (610) 909-8040, E-Mail: wesweber@aol.com (20)

Weberg, Inga, Redleaf Press, Saint Paul, MN. Tel: (651) 641-6621, (800) 423-8309, FAX: (800) 641-0115, E-Mail: jvoltz@redleafpress.org, Web Site: www.redleafpress.org (17)

Webloyalty.com, Norwalk, CT. Tel: (203) 846-3300, Web Site: www.webloyalty.com (32)

WebMetro, San Dimas, CA. Tel: (909) 599-8885, Web Site: www.webmetro.com (35)

WebReply.com Inc, Natick, MA. Tel: (508) 318-4600, Web Site: www.webreply.com (35)

Websource & Paper Corp, Norcross, GA. Tel: (212) 255-1600, FAX: (212) 463-7095, Web Site: www.websource-paper.com (25)

Webster, Kathy, The Miller Group, Dupo, IL. Tel: (636) 343-5700, (800) 325-3350, FAX: (618) 286-6202, E-Mail: info@miller-group.com, Web Site: www.multiplexdisplays.com (5)

Webster Bank, Waterbury, CT. Tel: (203) 578-2460, FAX: (203) 754-5939, Web Site: www.websterbank.com (14)

Wechsler, Richard, Lockard & Wechsler, Irvington, NY. Tel: (914) 591-6600 (35)

Wechter, Janet, JM Wechter & Associates Inc, Monroe, CT. Tel: (203) 452-0063, FAX: (203) 452-0414, Web Site: www.wechter.com (33)

JM Wechter & Associates Inc, Monroe, CT. Tel: (203) 452-0063, FAX: (203) 452-0414, Web Site: www.wechter.com (33)

Weckesser, Sandra, Fox Chase Cancer Center, Philadelphia, PA. Tel: (215) 728-6900, (888) FOX-CHASE, FAX: (215) 728-2594, Web Site: www.fccc.edu (1)

The Wedding Pages, New York, NY. Tel: (212) 219-8555, (800) 843-4983, FAX: (212) 219-1929, Web Site: www.theknot.com (16)

Weddle, Tiffini, Directory of Major Mailers & What They Mail, Philadelphia, PA. Tel: (800) 777-8074, FAX: (215) 238-5412, E-Mail: customerservice@napco.com, Web Site: www.majormailers.com (43)

Wedel, Randy, Schnuck Markets Inc, Saint Louis, MO. Tel: (314) 994-9900, FAX: (314) 994-4465, Web Site: www.schnucks.com (16)

Wedlock, Shireen, AmeriCall Group Inc, Naperville, IL. Tel: (630) 955-9100, (800) 688-0078, FAX: (630) 955-9955, E-Mail: sales@americallgroup.com, Web Site: www.americallgroup.com (29)

Weeden, Jeffrey B., Key Bank National Association, Albany, NY. Tel: (518) 434-4871, (800) 539-2968, Web Site: www.keybank.com (14)

Weekly Reader Corp, White Plains, NY. Tel: (914) 242-4019, (914) 242-4000, (800) 446-3355, Web Site: www.weeklyreader.com (23)

Weeks, David F., Research To Prevent Blindness Inc, New York, NY. Tel: (212) 752-4333, (800) 621-0026, FAX: (212) 688-6231, E-Mail: inforequest@rpbusa.org, Web Site: www.rpbusa.org (1)

Weeks, Doug, Magnatag Visable Systems, Macedon, NY. Tel: (315) 986-3033, FAX: (315) 986-4000, Web Site: www.magnatag.com (16)

Weeks, Mark, International Direct Response Services Ltd, Delta, BC Canada. Tel: (604) 951-6855, Web Site: www.idrs.ca (28)

Wehberg, Joyce, Shillcraft Inc, Annapolis, MD. Tel: (410) 682-3060, (800) 638-1542, FAX: (410) 682-3130, Web Site: www.shillcraft.com (16)

Wehman, Bill, Horticulture Magazine, Blue Ash, OH. Tel: (513) 531-2690, FAX: (513) 891-7153, Web Site: www.hortmag.com (17)

Wehmann, George, Direct Marketing Resources Group Inc, Raleigh, NC. Tel: (919) 231-2728, (800) 517-5253, Web Site: www.improvedmarketingresults.com (20)

Wehner, Camille, ACP Interactive, San Francisco, CA. Tel: (415) 357-5100, (800) 357-5177, FAX: (415) 357-5110, E-Mail: info@acpinteractive.com, Web Site: www.callgistics.com (29)

Wehner, David, California State Polytechnic University Business Administration Dept, San Luis Obispo, CA. Tel: (805) 756-1413, FAX: (805) 756-5057, Web Site: www.calpoly.edu (41)

Wehner, Todd, Steck-Vaughn, Austin, TX. Tel: (512) 343-8227, (877) 866-2586, (800) 531-5015, FAX: (512) 795-3617, (877) 265-2730, E-Mail: info@steck-vaughn.com, Web Site: www.steck-vaughn.com (17)

Wehr, Lisa, Oneupweb, Traverse City, MI. Tel: (231) 922-9977, (877) 568-7477, FAX: (231) 922-9966, E-Mail: info@oneupweb.com, Web Site: www.oneupweb.com (35)

Wehrwein, Sven, A., Digi International, Minnetonka, MN. Tel: (952) 912-3444, (877) 912-3444, FAX: (952) 912-4953, Web Site: www.digi.com (3)

Weichert Co, Morris Plains, NJ. Tel: (973) 397-8516, Web Site: www.weichert.com (14)

Weideman, Robert, Marketing and Product Strategy, Peabody, MA. Tel: (978) 977-2000, (800) 825-5897, FAX: (781) 238-0986, Web Site: www.lhsl.com (16)

Weidenbach, Julie, Response Management Technologies Inc, Berkeley, CA. Tel: (510) 843-8180, FAX: (510) 843-8020, E-Mail: info@respmgt.com, Web Site: www.respmgt.com (22)

Weider, Joe, Weider Publications Inc, Woodland Hills, CA. Tel: (818) 884-6800, (800) 423-5590, FAX: (818) 884-0242 (17)

Weider History Group, Ridgefield, CT. Tel: (203) 273-1092 (43)

Weider Publications Inc, Woodland Hills, CA. Tel: (818) 884-6800, (800) 423-5590, FAX: (818) 884-0242 (17)

Weidman, Robert, J., Nuance Speech Solutions, Burlington, MA. Tel: (781) 565-5000, FAX: (781) 565-5001, E-Mail: sales@speechworks.com, Web Site: www.nuance.com (16)

Weigel, Angie, Humana Inc, Louisville, KY. Tel: (502) 580-5005, FAX: (502) 580-3141, Web Site: www.humana.com (7)

Weight Watchers International, New York, NY. Tel: (516) 390-1400, FAX: (516) 390-1302, Web Site: www.weight-watchers.com (16)

Weiglein, Franz, Bloomingdale's By Mail Ltd, New York, NY. Tel: (212) 224-7721, (800) 472-0788, FAX: (212) 715-2805, Web Site: www.bloomingdales.com (5)

Weiglein, Franz, Bloomingdale's Direct, New York, NY. Tel: (212) 705-2000, (866) 593-2540, FAX: (212) 705-2805, Web Site: www.bloomingdales.com (16)

Weill, Lige, Vegetarian Awareness Network/VEGANET, Washington, DC. Tel: (800) USA-VEGE, (800) 872-8343, FAX: (877) 329-8343 (1)

Wein, Alex, SIE (Select Information Exchange), New York, NY. Tel: (212) 496-6435, FAX: (212) 787-4269, Web Site: www.siecom.com (23)

Wein, George, SIE (Select Information Exchange), New York, NY. Tel: (212) 496-6435, FAX: (212) 787-4269, Web Site: www.siecom.com (23)

Weinberg, Bob, RW Consulting, Asheville, NC. Tel: (828) 299-3645, Web Site: www.rwconsulting.net (20)

Weinberg, Eileen, ClickSquared, Boston, MA. Tel: (781) 622-1611, (866) 402-5425, FAX: (857) 246-7645, E-Mail: info@clicksquared.com, Web Site: www.clicksquared.com (20)

Weinberg, Gary, National Seminars Group, Shawnee Mission, KS. Tel: (913) 432-7755, (800) 258-7246, FAX: (913) 432-0824, E-Mail: cstserv@natsem.com, Web Site: www.natsem.com (16)

Weinberg, Gary, Quality Letter Service Inc, New York, NY. Tel: (212) 268-3400, FAX: (212) 268-3401, E-Mail: info@qletter.com, Web Site: www.qletter.com (21)

Weinberg, Gerald, Muscular Dystrophy Association, Tucson, AZ. Tel: (520) 529-2000, (800) 344-4863, FAX: (520) 529-5300, Web Site: www.mdausa.org (1)

Weinberger MD, Steven, E, American College of Physicians, Washington, DC. Tel: (215) 351-2400, (800) 523-1546, FAX: (215) 351-2686, Web Site: www.acponline.org (17)

Weinberger, Gaye, @utoRevenue, Pittsfield, MA. Tel: (413) 243-4800, Web Site: www.autorevenue.com (32)

Weiner, Barry, Homeowners Marketing Services Inc, North Hollywood, CA. Tel: (818) 506-1507, (800) 232-2134, FAX: (818) 505-9729, (818) 506-4110, E-Mail: lists@homeown.org, Web Site: www.homeown.org (23)

Weiner, David, Social Studies School Service, Culver City, CA. Tel: (310) 839-2436, (800) 421-4246, FAX: (310) 839-2249, (800) 944-5432, E-Mail: access@socialstudies.com, Web Site: www.socialstudies.com (16)

Weiner, Earl, D., Theatre Development Fund Inc, New York, NY. Tel: (212) 912-9770, E-Mail: info@tdf.org, Web Site: www.tdf.org (1)

Weiner, Janis, Kappa Publishing Group, Blue Bell, PA. Tel: (215) 643-6385, FAX: (215) 628-3571, Web Site: www.kappapublishing.com (17)

Weiner, Lee, AmeriCares, Stamford, CT. Tel: (203) 658-9500, Web Site: www.americares.org (1)

Weiner, Richard, Richard Weiner Consultant, North Miami Beach, FL. Tel: (305) 441-6470 (14)

Weiner, Sanford, Social Studies School Service, Culver City, CA. Tel: (310) 839-2436, (800) 421-4246, FAX: (310) 839-2249, (800) 944-5432, E-Mail: access@socialstudies.com, Web Site: www.socialstudies.com (16)

Richard Weiner Consultant, North Miami Beach, FL. Tel: (305) 441-6470 (14)

Weineski, Bob, Huck Spaulding Enterprises, Voorheesville, NY. Tel: (518) 768-2070, (888) 982-8866, FAX: (518) 768-2240, E-Mail: orders@spaulding-rogers.com, Web Site: www.spaulding-rogers.com (16)

Weingarten, Henry, Astrologer's Fund Inc, Brooklyn, NY. Tel: (212) 949-7275, FAX: (212) 608-6964, E-Mail: books@afund.com, Web Site: www.afund.com (14)

Weingeroff, Frederick L., Weingeroff Enterprises Inc, Cranston, RI. Tel: (401) 467-2200, FAX: (401) 785-1320, Web Site: www.weingeroff.com (16)

Weingeroff, Gregg, Weingeroff Enterprises Inc, Cranston, RI. Tel: (401) 467-2200, FAX: (401) 785-1320, Web Site: www.weingeroff.com (16)

Weingeroff, Lisa, JJI International Inc, Cranston, RI. Tel: (401) 732-8668, (866) 732-8668, FAX: (401) 732-8778, E-Mail: info@jjiinternational.com, Web Site: www.jjiinternational.com (35)

Weingeroff, Lisa, Weingeroff Enterprises Inc, Cranston, RI. Tel: (401) 467-2200, FAX: (401) 785-1320, Web Site: www.weingeroff.com (16)

Weingeroff Enterprises Inc, Cranston, RI. Tel: (401) 467-2200, FAX: (401) 785-1320, Web Site: www.weingeroff.com (16)

Weinik, Mary, American Horse Products, San Juan Capistrano, CA. Tel: (949) 248-5300, (800) 500-0799, FAX: (949) 248-5305, E-Mail: zjim@sbcglobal.net, Web Site: www.americanhorseproducts.com (11)

Weinstein, Allen, National Archives & Records Administration, College Park, MD. Tel: (301) 837-0482, (86) NARA-NARA, FAX: (301) 837-0483, Web Site: www.archives.gov (17)

Weinstein, Eric, Specialty Store Services Inc, Des Plaines, IL. Tel: (847) 470-7000, (888) 441-4440, FAX: (847) 470-5355, Web Site: www.specialtystoreservices.com (16)

Weinstein, Erika, Stephen-Bradford Search, New York, NY. Tel: (212) 221-6333, X346, (800) 720-0922, FAX: (212) 391-7826, E-Mail: info@ stephenbradford.com, Web Site: www. stephenbradford.com (20)

Weinstein, Jody, Mr Wash Car Wash, Kensington, MD. Tel: (301) 933-4858, Web Site: www.mrwash. com (16)

Weintraub, Eric, Advertising Gifts Inc, Port Washington, NY. Tel: (516) 767-3577, (877) 496-8762, E-Mail: sales@adgiftsinc.com, Web Site: www. adgiftsinc.com (33)

Weintraub, Floyd, Conmio Inc, New York, NY. Tel: (917) 583-2651, Web Site: www.conmio.com (16)

Weintraub, J., University of Chicago Press, Chicago, IL. Tel: (773) 702-7700, FAX: (773) 702-9756, Web Site: www.press.uchicago.edu (17)

Weintraub, Steve, Lawyers & Judges Publishing Co Inc, Tucson, AZ. Tel: (520) 323-1500, FAX: (520) 323-0055, E-Mail: sales@lawyersandjudges.com, Web Site: www.lawyersandjudges.com (23)

Weisbrod, Les, American Association for Justice, Washington, DC. Tel: (202) 965-3500, (800) 424-2725, FAX: (202) 625-7313, Web Site: www. justice.org (1)

Weiser, Bruce, Spire Creative Group, New York, NY. Tel: (212) 391-0200, Web Site: www. spirecreativegroup.com (27)

Weiser, Irving, Dain Rauscher Inc, Minneapolis, MN. Tel: (612) 371-2711, FAX: (612) 373-1627, Web Site: www.dainrauscher.com (14)

Weisgal, Margit, B., Trade Show Exhibitors Association, Chicago, IL. Tel: (312) 842-8732, FAX: (312) 842-8744, Web Site: www.tsea.org (42)

Weishar Jr., Paul J., Accent Advertising Inc, North Kansas City, MO. Tel: (816) 842-1860, FAX: (816) 471-4836, E-Mail: ideasaccentadv@sbcglobal.net, Web Site: www.accentadv.com (33)

Weiss Ph. D., Martin, D., Weiss Research Inc, Jupiter, FL. Tel: (561) 627-3300, (877) 925-4833, FAX: (561) 625-6685, E-Mail: newbusiness@ weissgroupinc.com, Web Site: www.weissgroupinc. com (17)

Weiss Sr, Tibor, ORC Macro International, New York, NY. Tel: (212) 941-5555, FAX: (212) 941-7031, E-Mail: info@icfi.com, Web Site: www.icfi.com (30)

Weiss, Beth, Omaha Steaks Inc, Omaha, NE. Tel: (402) 597-3000, FAX: (402) 597-8252, E-Mail: info@omahasteaks.com, Web Site: www. omahasteaks.com (4)

Weiss, Jordan, P., Roll International Corp, Los Angeles, CA. Tel: (310) 966-5700, FAX: (310) 914-4747, Web Site: www.roll.com (16)

Weiss, Larry, Atlantic Business Products, New York, NY. Tel: (212) 741-6400, FAX: (212) 645-1518, E-Mail: info@tomorrowsoffice.com, Web Site: www.tomorrowsoffice.com (29)

Weiss, Mark, C.R.W. Graphics, Pennsauken, NJ. Tel: (856) 662-9111, (800) 820-3000, FAX: (856) 665-1789, E-Mail: service@crwgraphics.com, Web Site: www.crwgraphics.com (27)

Weiss, Martin, D., Weiss Publishing & Marketing Inc, Jupiter, FL. Tel: (561) 627-3300, (800) 844-1773, Web Site: www.martinweiss.com (23)

Weiss, Morry, American Greetings Corp, Cleveland, OH. Tel: (216) 252-7300, FAX: (216) 252-6777 (16)

Weiss, Paul, Techni-Tool Inc, Worcester, PA. Tel: (610) 941-2400, (800) 832-4866, FAX: (800) 854-8665, E-Mail: sales@techni-tool.com, Web Site: www.techni-tool.com (16)

Weiss, Steven, Techni-Tool Inc, Worcester, PA. Tel: (610) 941-2400, (800) 832-4866, FAX: (800) 854-8665, E-Mail: sales@techni-tool.com, Web Site: www.techni-tool.com (16)

Weiss, Stuart, Techni-Tool Inc, Worcester, PA. Tel: (610) 941-2400, (800) 832-4866, FAX: (800) 854-8665, E-Mail: sales@techni-tool.com, Web Site: www.techni-tool.com (16)

Weiss, Trudy, Lorton Data Inc, Arden Hills, MN. Tel: (651) 203-8200, FAX: (612) 362-0299, Web Site: www.lortondata.com (22)

Weiss Publishing & Marketing Inc, Jupiter, FL. Tel: (561) 627-3300, (800) 844-1773, Web Site: www. martinweiss.com (23)

Weiss Research Inc, Jupiter, FL. Tel: (561) 627-3300, (877) 925-4833, FAX: (561) 625-6685, E-Mail: newbusiness@weissgroupinc.com, Web Site: www. weissgroupinc.com (17)

Weiss-Brown, Judy, Penguin Group USA Inc, East Rutherford, NJ. Tel: (201) 909-6200, FAX: (201) 236-3381, Web Site: penguingroup.com (17)

Weiss-Pena, Kerry, Trinity Communications Inc, Boston, MA. Tel: (617) 292-7300, FAX: (617) 292-7400, E-Mail: info@trinitynet.com, Web Site: www.trinitynet.com (35)

Weissenborn, James, General Pencil Co Inc, Jersey City, NJ. Tel: (201) 653-5351, FAX: (201) 653-2298, E-Mail: info@generalpencil.com, Web Site: www.generalpencil.com (16)

Weissman, Walter, Walter Weissman Photo Studio, New York, NY. Tel: (212) 989-9694, FAX: (212) 989-9694, E-Mail: wweissmanphoto@nyc.rr.com, Web Site: www.weissmanphoto.com (37)

Weitner, David, Techni-Tool Inc, Worcester, PA. Tel: (610) 941-2400, (800) 832-4866, FAX: (800) 854-8665, E-Mail: sales@techni-tool.com, Web Site: www.techni-tool.com (16)

Weitzner, Harriet, Amacom Books, New York, NY. Tel: (212) 903-8376, FAX: (212) 903-8083, E-Mail: customerservice@amanet.org, Web Site: www.amacombooks.org (17)

Welch, Bryan, Mother Earth News Magazine, Topeka, KS. Tel: (785) 274-4300, (800) 678-5779, FAX: (785) 274-4305, E-Mail: bwelch@ogdenpubs.com, Web Site: www.cappers.com (17)

Welch, Steve, PBM Graphics, Greensboro, NC. Tel: (336) 664-5800, (800) 849-8200, FAX: (336) 931-0965, Web Site: www.pbmgraphics.com (28)

Welch Allyn, Inc, Skaneateles Falls, NY. Tel: (315) 685-4100, Web Site: www.welchallyn.com (9)

Welch Jr, John F., General Electric Co, Fairfield, CT. Tel: (203) 373-2211, FAX: (203) 373-3131, Web Site: www.ge.com (16)

Welcomemat Services Inc, Atlanta, GA. Tel: (404) 841-2226, Web Site: www.welcomematservices. com (9)

Weldon, William, C., Johnson & Johnson, New Brunswick, NJ. Tel: (732) 524-0400, FAX: (732) 214-0332, Web Site: www.jnj.com (16)

Wellen, Paul, Walter E Heller College of Business Administration, Chicago, IL. Tel: (312) 281-3293, FAX: (312) 281-3290, Web Site: www.roosevelt. edu (41)

Weller, Ann, Ancient Circles, Willits, CA. Tel: (800) 726-8032, FAX: (707) 459-0261, E-Mail: ancient@ pacific.net, Web Site: www.ancientcircles.com (6)

Weller, Ted, D&E Pharmaceuticals Inc, Farmingdale, NJ. Tel: (973) 838-8300, (800) 221-1833, FAX: (877) 838-0560, E-Mail: customerservice@ dnepharm.com, Web Site: www.dnepharm.com (7)

Weller, Todd, D&E Pharmaceuticals Inc, Farmingdale, NJ. Tel: (973) 838-8300, (800) 221-1833, FAX: (877) 838-0560, E-Mail: customerservice@ dnepharm.com, Web Site: www.dnepharm.com (7)

Wellmark Blue Cross & Blue Shield of Iowa, Des Moines, IA. Tel: (515) 245-4500, FAX: (515) 323-7722, Web Site: www.wellmark.com (15)

Wellness Councils of America, Omaha, NE. Tel: (402) 827-3590, FAX: (402) 827-3594, E-Mail: wellworkplace@welcoa.org, Web Site: www. welcoa.org (1)

Wellott, Henry, Fidelity Investments, Boston, MA. Tel: (617) 563-7000, (800) 343-3548, FAX: (617) 476-6150, Web Site: www.fidelity.com (14)

Wellpoint, Chicago, IL. Tel: (312) 533-9779, Web Site: www.wellpoint.com (7)

Wells, Debra, Direct Approach, Phoenix, AZ. Tel: (602) 955-0649, FAX: (602) 955-0654, E-Mail: tbarker@directapproachlists.com, Web Site: www. directapproachlists.com (23)

Wells, Dr. Gail, W., Northern Kentucky University, Highland Heights, KY. Tel: (859) 572-5220, (800) 637-9948, FAX: (859) 572-6177, Web Site: www. nku.edu (41)

Wells, Rick, Mohawk Lifts, Amsterdam, NY. Tel: (518) 842-1431, (800) 833-2006, FAX: (518) 842-1289, E-Mail: rwells@mohawklifts.com, Web Site: www.mohawklifts.com (9)

Wells Fargo, San Francisco, CA. Tel: (866) 878-5865, (800) 869-3557, FAX: (626) 312-3015, Web Site: www.wellsfargo.com (14)

Wells Lamont Industry Group, Niles, IL. Tel: (847) 647-8200, (800) 247-3295, FAX: (847) 470-1026, Web Site: www.wellslamontindustry.com (34)

Welp, Christopher, ING USA Annuity & Life Ins Co, Des Moines, IA. Tel: (515) 698-7100, FAX: (515) 698-2001, Web Site: www.ing-usa.com (15)

Welsch, Mark, Bushnell Corporation, Overland Park, KS. Tel: (913) 752-3400, (800) 423-3537, FAX: (913) 752-3561, Web Site: www.bushnell.com (11)

Welsh, Daniel, Spoken Arts, Holmes, NY. Tel: (845) 878-9600, (800) 326-4090, FAX: (845) 878-9009, E-Mail: sales@spokenartsmedia.com, Web Site: www.spokenartsmedia.com (17)

Welsh, Edward, Council on Foreign Relations Inc, New York, NY. Tel: (212) 434-9400, FAX: (212) 861-2759, E-Mail: editor@foreignaffairs.com, Web Site: www.foreignaffairs.org (17)

Welsh, Susan, Spoken Arts, Holmes, NY. Tel: (845) 878-9600, (800) 326-4090, FAX: (845) 878-9009, E-Mail: sales@spokenartsmedia.com, Web Site: www.spokenartsmedia.com (17)

Welter, Eric, Collette Vacations, Pawtucket, RI. Tel: (401) 727-9000, FAX: (401) 727-1000, E-Mail: czesk@collettetours.com, Web Site: www. collettevacations.com (19)

Welty, Dan, John Henry Packaging, Lansing, MI. Tel: (707) 778-1250, (800) 327-5997, FAX: (707) 762-1253, Web Site: www.jhpackaging.com (27)

Welty, John, California State University at Fresno, Fresno, CA. Tel: (559) 278-7830, FAX: (559) 278-8577, Web Site: www.csufresno.edu (41)

Wenaas, Wendy, iMarketing Solutions Group Inc, Milwaukee, WI. Tel: (414) 224-0701, (800) 879-0076, FAX: (414) 224-0943, Web Site: imarketingsolutionsgroup.com (29)

Wendel, Mary, Siegel Display Products, Minneapolis, MN. Tel: (612) 340-1493, (800) 626-0322, FAX: (800) 230-5598, E-Mail: mwendel@siegeldisplay. com, Web Site: www.siegeldisplay.com (5)

Wendel, Pia, Top USA Corp, Worthington, OH. Tel: (614) 431-1601, (800) 843-3381, FAX: (614) 431-1239, E-Mail: info@topusa.com, Web Site: www. topusa.com (27)

Wendkos, Brad, Aspen Interactive, Saint Petersburg, FL. Tel: (727) 823-7144, (800) 777-2255, FAX: (727) 823-6523 (35)

Wendover Associates Inc, Greensboro, NC. Tel: (336) 299-6611, FAX: (336) 292-4261 (35)

Wendt, Doug, Combined Insurance Co of America, Glenview, IL. Tel: (847) 953-8116, (800) 490-1322, FAX: (847) 953-8070, Web Site: www. combinedinsurance.com (15)

Wenger, Bruce, IDC, Ltd, Henderson, NV. Tel: (702) 450-1000, FAX: (702) 450-1020, E-Mail: info@ goidc.com, Web Site: www.goidc.com (1)

Weninger, Mark, The Lacek Group, Minneapolis, MN. Tel: (612) 359-3700, FAX: (612) 359-9395, E-Mail: info@lacek.com, Web Site: www.lacek. com (35)

Wenner, Jann, S., Wenner Media LLC, New York, NY. Tel: (212) 484-1616, FAX: (212) 484-1713 (17)

Wenner Media LLC, New York, NY. Tel: (212) 484-1616, FAX: (212) 484-1713 (17)

WennSoft, New Berlin, WI. Tel: (262) 317-3717, Web Site: www.wennsoft.com (22)

Wentworth-Bete, Carol W., Channing L Bete Co Inc, South Deerfield, MA. Tel: (800) 477-4776, FAX: (800) 499-6464, E-Mail: custscvs@channing.bete. com, Web Site: www.channing-bete.com (17)

Wentz, Michael, Entertainment Music Marketing Corp, Baldwin, NY. Tel: (631) 243-0600, FAX: (631) 243-0605, E-Mail: emmcmusic@aol.com, Web Site: www.emmcmusic.com (16)

Wentz, S., Jaffe Brothers Natural Foods, Valley Center, CA. Tel: (760) 749-1133, (800) 548-1886, FAX: (760) 749-1282, E-Mail: jb54@worldnet.att. net, Web Site: www.organicfruitsandnuts.com (4)

Wentzel, Robyn, MCCS, Mason, OH. Tel: (513) 573-2284, FAX: (513) 573-2197, Web Site: www. federated.com (14)

Werbalowsky, Jeffrey, Houlihan Lokey Howard & Zukin, Los Angeles, CA. Tel: (310) 553-8871, (800) 788-5300, FAX: (310) 553-2173, Web Site: www.hlhz.com (14)

WerBell IV, Mitchell L., Brigade Quartermasters Ltd, Providence, RI. Tel: (770) 428-1248, (800) 338-4327, FAX: (800) 892-2992, Web Site: www. actiongear.com (11)

WerBell, Geoffrey, Brigade Quartermasters Ltd, Providence, RI. Tel: (770) 428-1248, (800) 338-4327, FAX: (800) 892-2992, Web Site: www.actiongear. com (11)

Werbin, Stanley, R., Elderly Instruments, Lansing, MI. Tel: (517) 372-7890, (888) 473-5810, FAX: (517) 372-5155, E-Mail: elderly@elderly.com, Web Site: www.elderly.com (5)

Werder, Claude, The Dartnell Corp, Naples, FL. Tel: (585) 240-7301, (800) 447-4030, FAX: (585) 292-4392, E-Mail: customerservice@dartnellcorp.com, Web Site: www.dartnellcorp.com (17)

Werkley, Timothy, S., Swan Packaging Fulfillment, Wayne, NJ. Tel: (973) 790-8417, FAX: (973) 790-0216, E-Mail: info@swanpkg.com, Web Site: www.swanpackaging.com (28)

Werner, George, Pearson Education, Upper Saddle River, NJ. Tel: (201) 236-7000, FAX: (201) 236-3290, E-Mail: communications@pearsoned.com, Web Site: www.pearsoned.com (17)

Werner, James, Territorial Newspapers, Tucson, AZ. Tel: (520) 294-1200, FAX: (520) 294-4040, Web Site: www.azbiz.com (17)

Werner, Michael, InfoSource Inc, Oviedo, FL. Tel: (407) 796-5200, (800) 393-4636, FAX: (407) 796-5190, E-Mail: isisale@howtomaster.com, Web Site: www.infosourcelearning.com (3)

Werner, Peter, K., Winmill & Co, New York, NY. Tel: (212) 785-0900, (800) 400-MIDAS, FAX: (212) 363-1100, E-Mail: info@midasfunds.com, Web Site: www.midasfunds.com (14)

Werner, Rosemary, Post University, Waterbury, CT. Tel: (203) 596-4520, (800) 345-2562, E-Mail: admissions@post.edu, Web Site: www.post.edu (41)

Werner-Robinson, Gail, GWR Wealth Management, Omaha, NE. Tel: (402) 496-7200, FAX: (402) 496-0378, Web Site: www.gwrwealth.com (14)

Werning, Tom J., Universal Engineering Corp, Cedar Rapids, IA. Tel: (319) 365-0441, (800) 366-2051, FAX: (319) 369-5440, E-Mail: info@ universalcrusher.com, Web Site: www. universalcrusher.com (16)

Wershaw, Frederick, I., Frederick Wershaw Management Co, Stamford, CT. Tel: (203) 329-3000, FAX: (203) 329-3044 (20)

Frederick Wershaw Management Co, Stamford, CT. Tel: (203) 329-3000, FAX: (203) 329-3044 (20)

Wertheim, A.J., Abbeon Cal Inc, Santa Barbara, CA. Tel: (805) 966-0810, (800) 922-0977, FAX: (805) 966-7659, E-Mail: abbeoncal@abbeon.com, Web Site: www.abbeon.com (9)

WESCO, Pittsburgh, PA. Tel: (412) 454-2200, (800) 343-1201, E-Mail: info@wesco.com, Web Site: www.wescodist.com (16)

Wesner, G., Thomas Scientific, Swedesboro, NJ. Tel: (800) 345-2100, FAX: (856) 467-3087, E-Mail: value@thomassci.com, Web Site: www.thomassci. com (9)

Wessan, Amy, Bruce McGaw Graphics, Manchester Center, VT. Tel: (845) 353-8600, (888) 4BMC-GAW, FAX: (845) 353-3155, E-Mail: sales@ bmcgaw.com, Web Site: www.bmcgaw.com (6)

Wessner, Mike, Conney Safety Products LLC, Madison, WI. Tel: (608) 271-3300, (800) 356-9100, FAX: (608) 271-3322, (800) 845-9095, E-Mail: safety@conney.com, Web Site: www.conney.com (7)

West, Cindy, Catalyst, Rochester, NY. Tel: (585) 453-8300, (800) 836-7720, FAX: (585) 453-8360, E-Mail: info@catalystinc.com, Web Site: www. catalystinc.com (35)

West, Doreen, Midco Call Center Services, Sioux Falls, SD. Tel: (605) 330-4125, (800) 843-8800, FAX: (605) 357-5414, Web Site: www.midcocall. com (29)

West, Kim, Unity School of Christianity, Unity Village, MO. Tel: (816) 254-3550, FAX: (816) 251-3554, E-Mail: unity@unityonline.org, Web Site: www.unityonline.org (17)

West, Larry J., West Companies Inc, Seminole, FL. Tel: (212) 319-7069 (20)

West, Lori, R., Muscular Dystrophy Association, Tucson, AZ. Tel: (520) 529-2000, (800) 344-4863, FAX: (520) 529-5300, Web Site: www.mdausa.org (1)

West, Melanie, Doctors Without Borders, New York, NY. Tel: (212) 655-3767, Web Site: www. doctorswithoutborders.org (1)

West, Michelle, Winslow Publishing, Toronto, ON Canada. Tel: (416) 789-4733, E-Mail: winslow@ interlog.com, Web Site: www.winslowpublishing. com (17)

West, Mitchell, Abbott, North Chicago, IL. Tel: (847) 937-8641, FAX: (847) 937-9555, Web Site: www. abbott.com (7)

West, Nancy, Random Lengths Publications Inc, Eugene, OR. Tel: (541) 686-9925, (888) 686-9925, FAX: (541) 686-9629, (800) 874-7979, E-Mail: rlmail@rlpi.com, Web Site: www.randomlengths. com (17)

West, Patrick, Universal Distribution Services, Reno, NV. Tel: (775) 332-5700, FAX: (775) 332-5715, E-Mail: sales@udsi.com, Web Site: www.udsi.com (28)

West, Richard, Peachtree Data Inc, Duluth, GA. Tel: (678) 987-4600, Web Site: www.peachtreedata.com (22)

West, Shane, TDS Telecom, Madison, WI. Tel: (608) 664-4119, Web Site: www.tdstelecom.com (20)

West, Stacy, OCE North America Inc, Boca Raton, FL. Tel: (561) 997-3100, (800) 523-5444, FAX: (561) 998-9160, Web Site: www. oceproductionprinting.com (34)

West, Todd, Malco Products Inc, Barberton, OH. Tel: (330) 753-0361, (800) 253-2526, FAX: (330) 753-2025, Web Site: www.malcopro.com (16)

West Bend, West Bend, WI. Tel: (262) 334-5107, (866) 290-1851, FAX: (262) 334-6800, Web Site: www.focuselectrics.com (16)

West Cary Group, Richmond, VA. Tel: (804) 343-2029 (20)

West Companies Inc, Seminole, FL. Tel: (212) 319-7069 (20)

West Corp, Omaha, NE. Tel: (800) 841-9000, FAX: (402) 963-1602, E-Mail: sales@west.com, Web Site: www.west.com (20)

West End Diving Centers Inc, Bridgeton, MO. Tel: (314) 209-7200, E-Mail: info@westenddiving.com, Web Site: www.2dive.com (35)

West Farm Foods (Branch), Caldwell, ID. Tel: (208) 459-3687, FAX: (208) 459-9135, Web Site: www. westfarm.com (16)

West Marine Inc, Watsonville, CA. Tel: (831) 761-4825, (800) BOATING, (800) 262-8464, FAX: (831) 768-5000, E-Mail: customercare@ westmarine.com, Web Site: www.westmarine.com (11)

West Shore Distributors, Westlake, OH. Tel: (440) 835-5600, (800) 344-8141, FAX: (440) 835-8654, E-Mail: westshore@ameritech.net, Web Site: www. westshoreframes.com (8)

West Virginia University, Morgantown, WV. Tel: (304) 293-3505, FAX: (304) 293-3072, E-Mail: wvuwebmaster@mail.wvu.edu, Web Site: www. wvu.edu (41)

Westbeth Gallery, New York, NY. Tel: (212) 989-4650 (36)

Westcon, Tarrytown, NY. Tel: (914) 829-7000, FAX: (914) 829-7137, Web Site: www.westcon.com (16)

Westcott, Ali, Concord Litho, Concord, NH. Tel: (603) 225-3328, FAX: (603) 225-6120, E-Mail: print@ concordlitho.com, Web Site: www.concordlitho. com (27)

Westcott, Bruce, Stanley Supply & Services, North Andover, MA. Tel: (978) 682-9844, (800) 225-5370, FAX: (800) 743-8141, Web Site: www. stanleysupplyservices.com (16)

Wester III, Al, B., Ventura Associates International LLC, New York, NY. Tel: (212) 302-8277, FAX: (212) 302-2587, E-Mail: info@sweepspros.com, Web Site: www.sweepspros.com (35)

Wester, Earl, Quadrant Engineering Plastic Products, Reading, PA. Tel: (610) 320-6600, (800) 366-0300, FAX: (610) 320-6868, Web Site: www. quadrantepp.com (16)

Westerfield, Blake, A., Celtic Life Insurance Co, Chicago, IL. Tel: (312) 332-5401, FAX: (312) 441-0341, E-Mail: info@celtic-net.com, Web Site: www.celtic-net.com (15)

Westerhouse, Kevin, Comac Inc, Milpitas, CA. Tel: (408) 945-1600, (866) COMAC4U, FAX: (408) 946-1135, E-Mail: info@comac.com, Web Site: www.comac.com (28)

Western Connecticut State University, Danbury, CT. Tel: (203) 837-8200, FAX: (203) 837-8527, E-Mail: hills@wcsu.edu, Web Site: www.wcsu.edu (41)

Western Data Services Inc, Carlsbad, NM. Tel: (505) 234-2927, FAX: (505) 234-9637, E-Mail: directmail@wdsi.net, Web Site: www.wdsi.net (35)

Western Digital Corp, Irvine, CA. Tel: (949) 672-7000, FAX: (949) 672-7837, Web Site: www. westerndigital.com (22)

Western Fulfillment Management Association Inc, North Hollywood, CA. Tel: (310) 323-7220, FAX: (310) 323-7231, E-Mail: mjordan@espcomp.com, Web Site: www.wfma.org (40)

Western Graphics, Lemon Grove, CA. Tel: (619) 668-4736, FAX: (619) 668-4742, E-Mail: jim@ westerngraphics.org, Web Site: www. westerngraphics.org (21)

Western Pennsylvania Conservancy, Pittsburgh, PA. Tel: (412) 288-2777, Web Site: www.paconserve. org (1)

Western Printing Machinery (WPM), Schiller Park, IL. Tel: (847) 678-1740, FAX: (847) 678-6176, E-Mail: info@wpm.com, Web Site: www.wpm.com (34)

Western Psychological Services, Torrance, CA. Tel: (310) 478-2061, (800) 648-8857, FAX: (310) 478-7838, E-Mail: marketing@wpspublish.com, Web Site: www.wpspublish.com (16)

Western River Expeditions, Salt Lake City, UT. Tel: (801) 942-6669, (866) 904-1160, FAX: (801) 942-8514, Web Site: www.westernriver.com (19)

Western-Southern Life, Cincinnati, OH. Tel: (513) 629-1800, Web Site: www.westernsouthernlife.com (15)

Western Web Printing, Sioux Falls, SD. Tel: (605) 339-2383, (888) 855-4563, FAX: (605) 339-1523, E-Mail: info@westernwebprinting.com, Web Site: www.westernwebprinting.com (27)

Westfield, Brian, Westcon, Tarrytown, NY. Tel: (914) 829-7000, FAX: (914) 829-7137, Web Site: www. westcon.com (16)

Westgroup, Eagan, MN. Tel: (800) 344-5008, Web Site: www.westgroup.com (17)

Westhoff Machine Co, Saint Louis, MO. Tel: (314) 963-7130, (800) 364-0280, FAX: (800) 324-1942, E-Mail: mail@westhoffinc.com, Web Site: www. westhoffinc.com (9)

Westhorpe, Barbara, Bamboo Cricket Service, Titusville, FL. Tel: (888) 634-7097, FAX: (646) 390-6313, E-Mail: info@bamboocricket.com, Web Site: www.bamboocricket.com (22)

Westhorpe, Barbara, Bamboo Cricket, West Palm Beach, FL. Tel: (561) 768-7968, (800) 260-8050, FAX: (561) 653-3990, Web Site: www. bamboocricket.com (32)

Westhorpe, Paul, Bamboo Cricket, West Palm Beach, FL. Tel: (561) 768-7968, (800) 260-8050, FAX: (561) 653-3990, Web Site: www.bamboocricket. com (32)

Westlake Plastics Co, Lenni, PA. Tel: (610) 459-1000, (800) 999-1700, FAX: (610) 459-1084, Web Site: www.westlakeplastics.com (16)

Westland, Stewart, Bike Nashbar, Crab Orchard, WV. Tel: (800) NAS-HBAR, FAX: (877) 778-9456, E-Mail: custserv@nashbar.com, Web Site: www. bikenashbar.com (11)

Westman, Penny, Standard Life, Montreal, PQ. Tel: (514) 499-8855, (877) 499-9555, FAX: (514) 499-4908, Web Site: www.standardlife.ca (15)

Westminster International, Richmond Hill, ON Canada. Tel: (416) 494-6245, FAX: (905) 771-9349 (21)

Westmoreland, Betty, Pritchett & Hull Associates Inc, Atlanta, GA. Tel: (770) 451-0602, (800) 241-4925, FAX: (770) 454-7130, E-Mail: sales@p-h.com, Web Site: www.p-h.com (17)

Weston, Ann, Edward Weston Fine Art & Photography, Chatsworth, CA. Tel: (818) 885-1044, FAX: (818) 885-1021, E-Mail: edwardweston@ westoncollection.com, Web Site: edward-weston. com (36)

Weston, Carolyn, H., Massachusetts Horticultural Society, Wellesley, MA. Tel: (617) 933-4929, (617) 933-4900, FAX: (617) 933-4901, E-Mail: hort_line@masshort.org, Web Site: www.masshort. org (1)

Weston, Stacey, League of American Orchestras, New York, NY. Tel: (212) 262-5161, FAX: (212) 262-5198, Web Site: www.symphony.org; www. americanorchestras.org (1)

Weston Distance Learning, Fort Collins, CO. Tel: (970) 282-6322 (13)

Edward Weston Fine Art & Photography, Chatsworth, CA. Tel: (818) 885-1044, FAX: (818) 885-1021, E-Mail: edwardweston@westoncollection.com, Web Site: edward-weston.com (36)

Westphal, Jeff, Vertex Inc, Berwyn, PA. Tel: (610) 640-4200, (800) 355-3500, FAX: (610) 640-5892, Web Site: www.vertexinc.com (16)

Westpro Inc, Provo, UT. Tel: (801) 373-2525, (800) 533-3885, FAX: (801) 373-8778, E-Mail: sales@ westpro.net, Web Site: westpro.net (27)

Westwood Publishing Co, Glendale, CA. Tel: (818) 242-1159, FAX: (818) 247-9379 (17)

Wetekam, Donald, J., AAFES, Dallas, TX. Tel: (214) 312-6700, (800) 527-6790, FAX: (214) 312-3000, Web Site: www.aafes.com (5)

Wetter, Gary, L., WNR Direct Response Consultants, Agoura Hills, CA. Tel: (818) 865-6300, FAX: (818) 865-8559, E-Mail: gwetter@wnrtv.com, Web Site: www.wnrtv.com (35)

Wetzel, Cheryl, M., Anglicans United & Latimer Press, Cedar Hill, TX. Tel: (972) 293-7443, (800) 553-3645, FAX: (972) 293-7559, E-Mail: anglicansunited@sbcglobal.net, Web Site: www. anglicansunited.com, www.latimerpress.com (1)

Wetzel, Rev Todd, H., Anglicans United & Latimer Press, Cedar Hill, TX. Tel: (972) 293-7443, (800) 553-3645, FAX: (972) 293-7559, E-Mail: anglicansunited@sbcglobal.net, Web Site: www. anglicansunited.com, www.latimerpress.com (1)

Wetzler, Andrew, MoreVisibility, Boca Raton, FL. Tel: (561) 620-9682, Web Site: www.morevisibility.com (32)

Wexler, David, Lerner Publishing Group, Minneapolis, MN. Tel: (612) 332-3344, (800) 328-4929, FAX: (800) 332-1132, E-Mail: info@lernerbooks.com, Web Site: www.lernerbooks.com (17)

Wexler, Sheila, Wexler Marketing Group Inc, Alexandria, VA. Tel: (703) 548-4336, FAX: (703) 548-4393, E-Mail: wexler@compuserve.com (35)

Wexler, Steve, Steve Wexler Creative Group, Farmingville, NY. Tel: (631) 736-6565, Web Site: www. wexdirect.com (20)

Wexler, Suellen, Shades of Light, Richmond, VA. Tel: (804) 288-3235, (877) 288-5029, FAX: (804) 288-5029, E-Mail: visitor@shadesoflight.com, Web Site: www.shadesoflight.com (8)

Wexler Marketing Group Inc, Alexandria, VA. Tel: (703) 548-4336, FAX: (703) 548-4393, E-Mail: wexler@compuserve.com (35)

Steve Wexler Creative Group, Farmingville, NY. Tel: (631) 736-6565, Web Site: www.wexdirect.com (20)

Wexner, Alfred B., The Wexner Companies Inc, Memphis, TN. Tel: (901) 763-3925, (800) 890-5470, FAX: (901) 763-3736, E-Mail: info@JosephStores. com, Web Site: www.josephstores.com (2)

Wexner, Leslie, H., LimitedBrands Inc, Reynoldsburg, OH. Tel: (614) 577-5902, FAX: (614) 415-7440, Web Site: www.limitedbrands.com (16)

The Wexner Companies Inc, Memphis, TN. Tel: (901) 763-3925, (800) 890-5470, FAX: (901) 763-3736, E-Mail: info@JosephStores.com, Web Site: www. josephstores.com (2)

Weyerhaeuser Co, Federal Way, WA. Tel: (253) 924-2345, (800) 525-5440, FAX: (253) 924-2685, Web Site: www.wy.com (25)

Weyers, Cherie, Tower Media Advertising Inc, Chicago, IL. Tel: (312) 856-9200, FAX: (312) 856-1300, E-Mail: info@towermedia.com, Web Site: www.towermedia.com (35)

Whalen, Chris, Embassy Digital, Oakville, ON Canada. Tel: (905) 829-9969, (888) 477-8629, FAX: (905) 829-9429, E-Mail: info@ embassydigital.com, Web Site: www. embassydigital.com (27)

Whalen, David, A T Cross Co, Lincoln, RI. Tel: (401) 333-1200, (800) 282-7677, FAX: (401) 334-2861, Web Site: www.cross.com (16)

Whalen, George, J., GJ Whalen & Co Inc, Tarrytown, NY. Tel: (914) 333-0085, E-Mail: george@ gjwhalen.com, Web Site: www.whalen.cc (39)

Whalen, Lou, Peoples Benefit Life Insurance Co, Exton, PA. Tel: (610) 648-5000, FAX: (610) 648-5348 (15)

Whalen, T. J., Green Mountain Coffee Roasters, Inc, Waterbury, VT. Tel: (802) 244-5621, (800) 545-2326, FAX: (802) 244-5436, Web Site: www.gmcr. com (4)

GJ Whalen & Co Inc, Tarrytown, NY. Tel: (914) 333-0085, E-Mail: george@gjwhalen.com, Web Site: www.whalen.cc (39)

Wham, Carol, Sullivan-Victory Groves, Cocoa, FL. Tel: (321) 632-0550, (800) 672-6431, FAX: (321) 639-4069, E-Mail: citrus@sullivanvictorygroves. net, Web Site: www.sullivanvictorygroves.net (4)

Wharton, Dennis, National Association Broadcasters Annual Conference & Expo, Washington, DC. Tel: (202) 429-5300, (800) 622-3976, FAX: (202) 429-4199, E-Mail: nab@nab.org, Web Site: www.nab. org (42)

Wharton, Peter, Iomega Corp, Roy, UT. Tel: (801) 332-1000, (888) 446-6342, FAX: (801) 332-3158, Web Site: www.iomega.com (16)

What on Earth, Hudson, OH. Tel: (330) 963-6554, (800) 945-2552, FAX: (800) 950-9569, Web Site: www.whatonearthcatalog.com (5)

Whatley, Randall, P., Cypress Media Group, Roswell, GA. Tel: (770) 640-9918, E-Mail: info@ cypressmedia.net, Web Site: www.cypressmedia.net (35)

Wheatley, Joan, Special Olympics International, Washington, DC. Tel: (202) 628-3630, FAX: (202) 824-0200, Web Site: www.specialolympics.org (1)

Wheaton, Cynthia, Wheaton Group, Chapel Hill, NC. Tel: (919) 969-8859, FAX: (425) 675-6014, E-Mail: jim.wheaton@wheatongroup.com, Web Site: www.wheatongroup.com (22)

Wheaton, Jim, Wheaton Group, Chapel Hill, NC. Tel: (919) 969-8859, FAX: (425) 675-6014, E-Mail: jim.wheaton@wheatongroup.com, Web Site: www. wheatongroup.com (22)

Wheaton Group, Chapel Hill, NC. Tel: (919) 969-8859, FAX: (425) 675-6014, E-Mail: jim. wheaton@wheatongroup.com, Web Site: www. wheatongroup.com (22)

Wheeler, M., Cass, American Heart Association, Dallas, TX. Tel: (214) 373-6300, (800) AHA-USA-1, FAX: (214) 373-3406, Web Site: www. americanheart.org (1)

Wheeler, Mark, Pacific Botanicals LLC, Grants Pass, OR. Tel: (541) 479-7777, FAX: (541) 479-7780, E-Mail: pacbot1@earthlink.net, Web Site: www. pacificbotanicals.com (7)

Whelan, Claire, Winnipeg Art Gallery, Winnipeg, MB. Tel: (204) 786-6641, FAX: (204) 788-4998, E-Mail: inquiries@wag.mb.ca, Web Site: www. wag.mb.ca (1)

Whelan, George, Carl Bloom Associates Inc, White Plains, NY. Tel: (914) 761-2800, FAX: (914) 761-2744, E-Mail: info@carlbloom.com, Web Site: www.carlbloom.com (35)

Whelan, Raymond, F., Globe Photos Inc, West Islip, NY. Tel: (212) 645-9292, FAX: (212) 627-8932 (38)

Whelan, Robert, Promissor, Bala Cynwyd, PA. Tel: (610) 617-9300, FAX: (610) 617-9301, Web Site: www.promissor.com (24)

Where 2 Get It Inc, Anaheim, CA. Tel: (888) 377-2767, Web Site: www.where2getit.com (30)

Wherry, Charles, Crush Creative, Burbank, CA. Tel: (818) 842-1121, (800) 300-3686, FAX: (818) 840-0185, E-Mail: john.davies@crushcreative.com, Web Site: www.crushcreative.com (27)

Whimpey, Jay, American Civil Defense Association, Draper, UT. Tel: (800) 501-0077, FAX: (800) 403-1369, E-Mail: info@tacda.org, Web Site: www. tacda.org (16)

Whippie, Christine, General Tours/TBI Tours, Keene, NH. Tel: (603) 357-5033, (800) 221-2216, FAX: (603) 357-4548, E-Mail: info@generaltours.com, Web Site: www.generaltours.com (19)

Whipple, Lance, Lathem Time Corp, Atlanta, GA. Tel: (404) 691-0400, (800) 241-4990, FAX: (404) 696-6048, Web Site: www.lathem.com (16)

Whirley Drink Works, Warren, PA. Tel: (814) 723-7600, (800) 825-5575, FAX: (814) 723-3245, E-Mail: info@whirleydrinkworks.com, Web Site: www.whirleydrinkworks.com (5)

Whirlpool Corp, Benton Harbor, MI. Tel: (616) 923-5000, FAX: (616) 923-2759, Web Site: www. whirlpoolcorp.com (16)

Whitaker Jr., John, C., Inmar, Winston-Salem, NC. Tel: (336) 631-2524, FAX: (336) 770-3470, E-Mail: ibizdev@inmar.com, Web Site: www. promotionslogistics.com (14)

Whitaker, Kenneth, Public Interest Communications Inc, Falls Church, VA. Tel: (703) 847-8300, FAX: (703) 734-9620, Web Site: www.pubintcom.com (29)

Whitaker National, Huntington, WV. Tel: (304) 525-0852, (800) 377-8721, FAX: (304) 525-0874, Web Site: www.neshold.com (16)

Whitcomb, Paula, Recording for the Blind & Dyslexic Inc, Princeton, NJ. Tel: (609) 452-0606, (800) 221-4792, FAX: (609) 520-7996, E-Mail: info@rfbd.org, Web Site: www.rfbd.org (16)

White, Bill, Sprint Nextel Corp, Reston, VA. Tel: (703) 433-4000, FAX: (703) 433-4343, Web Site: www.nextel.com (3)

White, Byron, Lifetips, Boston, MA. Tel: (617) 886-9001, Web Site: www.lifetips.com (16)

White, C.R., Essence Communications Inc, New York, NY. Tel: (212) 522-1212, FAX: (212) 921-5173, Web Site: www.essence.com (17)

White, Carole, Advertising Research Foundation, New York, NY. Tel: (212) 751-5656, FAX: (212) 319-5265, E-Mail: info@thearf.org, Web Site: www.thearf.org (40)

White, Charlie, Chico's FAS Inc, Fort Myers, FL. Tel: (239) 277-6200, Web Site: www.chicos.com (2)

White, Dave, Quark Inc, Denver, CO. Tel: (303) 894-3832, Web Site: www.quark.com (34)

White, David, Choice Hotels International, Silver Spring, MD. Tel: (301) 592-6636, (888) 770-6800, FAX: (301) 592-6157, E-Mail: ihelp@choicehotels.com, Web Site: www.choicebuys.com (16)

White, Denise, Viacom Inc, New York, NY. Tel: (212) 258-6000, FAX: (212) 258-6464, Web Site: www.viacom.com (16)

White, Diane, The Field Museum, Chicago, IL. Tel: (312) 665-7909, FAX: (312) 665-7101, Web Site: www.fieldmuseum.org (1)

White, Eldon, National Agri Marketing Conference & Exposition, Overland Park, KS. Tel: (913) 491-6500, FAX: (913) 491-6502, E-Mail: agrimktg@nama.org, Web Site: www.nama.org (42)

White, Ian, Urban Mapping Inc, San Francisco, CA. Tel: (415) 946-8170, Web Site: www.urbanmapping.com (16)

White, Jeff, Incept Corp, Canton, OH. Tel: (330) 649-8000, Web Site: www.inceptcorp.com (29)

White, John, Global Computer Supplies, Port Washington, NY. Tel: (732) 264-8200, (800) 446-9662, FAX: (732) 888-8316, Web Site: www.globalcomputer.com (34)

White, Julie, Rodale Inc, Emmaus, PA. Tel: (610) 967-5171, FAX: (610) 967-8963, Web Site: www.rodale.com (17)

White, Lorraine, Executive Connections LLC, Sarasota, FL. Tel: (941) 323-8300, Web Site: www.executiveconnectionsllc.com (20)

White, Matthew, C., White & Partners, Herndon, VA. Tel: (703) 793-3000, FAX: (703) 793-1495, E-Mail: tawnyas@whiteandpartners.com, Web Site: www.whiteandpartners.com (35)

White, Miles, Abbott, North Chicago, IL. Tel: (847) 937-8641, FAX: (847) 937-9555, Web Site: www.abbott.com (7)

White, Miles, D., The Field Museum, Chicago, IL. Tel: (312) 665-7909, FAX: (312) 665-7101, Web Site: www.fieldmuseum.org (1)

White, Patricia, JC Direct Mail Inc, Groveport, OH. Tel: (614) 836-4848, FAX: (614) 836-4847, E-Mail: pwhite@wcnjcd.com (28)

White, Patricia, Sales Building Systems, Mentor, OH. Tel: (800) 435-7576, FAX: (440) 639-9190, E-Mail: sales@sbsteam.com, Web Site: www.sbsteam.com (31)

White, Randall, EDC Publishing, Tulsa, OK. Tel: (918) 622-4522, (800) 475-4522, FAX: (800) 747-4509, Web Site: www.edcpub.com (17)

White, Richard, Herr Foods Inc, Nottingham, PA. Tel: (610) 932-9330, (800) 344-3777, FAX: (610) 932-2137, E-Mail: info@herrs.com, Web Site: www.herrfoods.com (16)

White, Sari, Vermont/New Hampshire Direct Marketing Group, Woodstock, VT. Tel: (802) 457-2807, FAX: (802) 457-2807, E-Mail: vtnhmg@vtnhmg, Web Site: www.vtnhmg.org (40)

White, Tonya, Prakken Publications Inc, Ann Arbor, MI. Tel: (734) 975-2800, (800) 530-9673, FAX: (734) 975-2787, E-Mail: vanessa@techdirections.com, Web Site: www.eddigest.com; www.techdirections.com (17)

White & Partners, Herndon, VA. Tel: (703) 793-3000, FAX: (703) 793-1495, E-Mail: tawnyas@whiteandpartners.com, Web Site: www.whiteandpartners.com (35)

White Cap Wholesale Contractors Supplies, Costa Mesa, CA. Tel: (800) 944-8322, FAX: (866) 791-8396, E-Mail: customerservice@whitecap.com, Web Site: www.whitecapdirect.com (16)

White Electronic Designs, Phoenix, AZ. Tel: (614) 279-6326, Web Site: www.whiteedc.com (27)

White Flower Farm, Torrington, CT. Tel: (860) 496-9624, (800) 503-9624, FAX: (860) 496-1418, Web Site: www.whiteflowerfarm.com (8)

White Mane Publishing Co Inc, Shippensburg, PA. Tel: (717) 532-2237, (888) 948-6263, FAX: (717) 532-6110, E-Mail: marketing@whitemane.com, Web Site: www.whitemane.com (17)

White Point Leads Group LLC, Gulf Breeze, FL. Tel: (850) 934-5577, Web Site: www.whitepointleads.com (29)

White Post Media Group Inc, Nashville, TN. Tel: (615) 730-7566 (35)

Whited, Lisa, National Rifle Association of America, Fairfax, VA. Tel: (703) 267-1000, (800) 672-3888, FAX: (703) 267-3957, E-Mail: nra.contact@nra.org, Web Site: www.nra.org (1)

Whitehat Inc, Tempe, AZ. Tel: (480) 858-9000, FAX: (480) 858-9001, Web Site: www.whitehat.com (32)

Whitehorse Gear, Center Conway, NH. Tel: (603) 356-6556, FAX: (603) 356-6590, E-Mail: customerservice@whitehorsepress.com, Web Site: www.whitehorsepress.com (11)

Whitely, George, Stephan & Brady Inc, Madison, WI. Tel: (608) 241-4141, FAX: (608) 241-4246, E-Mail: gwhitely@stephanbrady.com, Web Site: www.stephanbrady.com (35)

Whiteman, Tim, Condolink, Omaha, NE. Tel: (402) 592-3525, (800) 877-9600, FAX: (402) 592-4122, E-Mail: info@condolink.com, Web Site: www.condolink.com (16)

Whiter, Dana, R., Bissinger French Confections, Saint Louis, MO. Tel: (314) 534-2401, (800) 325-8881, FAX: (314) 534-2419, Web Site: www.bissingers.com (4)

Whiteway, Jerry, MetaResponse Group Inc, Deerfield Beach, FL. Tel: (954) 360-0644, FAX: (954) 360-7712, Web Site: www.metaresponse.com (23)

Whitewing Labs, Granada Hills, CA. Tel: (800) 950-3030, FAX: (818) 240-2785, E-Mail: service@whitewing.com, Web Site: www.whitewing.com (20)

Whitfield, Ross, UDL Laboratories Inc, Sugar Land, TX. Tel: (281) 240-1000, (800) 231-3052, FAX: (281) 240-0002, Web Site: www.udllabs.com (7)

Whithaus, Jerry, Hormel Foods Corp, Austin, MN. Tel: (507) 437-5611, (800) 523-4635, FAX: (507) 437-5158, Web Site: www.hormel.com (16)

Whiting, Ian, Brocade Communications Systems Inc, San Jose, CA. Tel: (408) 333-4300, FAX: (408) 333-8101, Web Site: www.brocade.com (16)

Whiting, Susan, D, Nielsen Business Media, New York, NY. Tel: (646) 654-4500, FAX: (646) 654-7212, E-Mail: bmcomm@nielsen.com, Web Site: www.nielsenbusinessmedia.com (16)

Whiting & Davis, Attleboro Falls, MA. Tel: (508) 699-4412, (800) 876-MESH, FAX: (508) 695-7606, E-Mail: info@whitinganddavis.com, Web Site: www.whitinganddavis.com (16)

Whitley, Jack, Replacements Ltd, Greensboro, NC. Tel: (336) 697-3000, (800) REPLACE, FAX: (336) 697-3100, E-Mail: mark.donahue@replacements.com, Web Site: www.replacements.com (8)

Whitlock, Gary, L., Centerpoint Energy, Minneapolis, MN. Tel: (612) 372-4664, FAX: (612) 321-4873, E-Mail: mgc-businessinformation@centerpointenergy.com, Web Site: www.minnegasco.centerpointenergy.com (16)

Whitman Publishing LLC, Atlanta, GA. Tel: (800) 546-2995, FAX: (256) 246-1116, E-Mail: info@whitmanbooks.com, Web Site: www.whitmanbooks.com (16)

Whitmore, Gary, Genium Publishing, Amsterdam, NY. Tel: (518) 842-4111, FAX: (518) 842-1843, E-Mail: sales@genium.com, Web Site: www.genium.com (17)

Whitmyre, Rick, Tiziani Whitmyre, Sharon, MA. Tel: (781) 793-9380, FAX: (781) 793-9395, E-Mail: info@tizinc.com, Web Site: www.tizinc.com (21)

Whitney, Bill, Hooleon Corp, Melrose, NM. Tel: (928) 634-7515, (800) 937-1337, E-Mail: sales@hooleon.com, Web Site: www.hooleon.com (3)

Whitney, Dennis, Institute of Management Accountants Inc, Montvale, NJ. Tel: (201) 573-9000, (800) 638-4427, FAX: (201) 474-1600, E-Mail: ima@imanet.org, Web Site: www.imanet.org (1)

Whitney, Jim, Educational Insights, Inc, Gardena, CA. Tel: (310) 884-2000, (888) 591-9334, FAX: (310) 886-8850, E-Mail: service@edin.com, Web Site: www.educationalinsights.com (16)

Whitney, Mark, TheLaw.net Corp, San Diego, CA. Tel: (858) 554-0583, Web Site: www.thelaw.net (22)

Jordan Whitney Inc, Tustin, CA. Tel: (714) 832-3353, FAX: (714) 832-4422, E-Mail: info@jwgreensheet.com, Web Site: www.jwgreensheet.com (32)

Whitney Worldwide Inc, Saint Paul, MN. Tel: (651) 748-5000, (800) 597-0227, FAX: (651) 748-4000, Web Site: www.whitneyworld.com (20)

Whitten, Kedran, Comdata Corp, Brentwood, TN. Tel: (615) 370-7000, (800) 266-3282, Web Site: www.comdata.com (14)

Whitters, Joseph, E., Mentor Corp, Santa Barbara, CA. Tel: (805) 879-6000, (800) 525-0245, FAX: (805) 964-2712, Web Site: www.mentorcorp.com (16)

Whittier, Richard, Majestic Marketing Inc, Corona, CA. Tel: (951) 280-2400, Web Site: www.bagmasters.com (35)

Whittington, Charles, L., American Trucking Association, Arlington, VA. Tel: (703) 838-1700, FAX: (800) 254-2571, E-Mail: atamembership@trucking.org, Web Site: www.truckline.com (1)

Whole Foods Market Inc, Austin, TX. Tel: (512) 477-4455, FAX: (512) 482-7000, Web Site: www.wholefoodsmarket.com (4)

Wholesale Tool Co, Warren, MI. Tel: (800) 521-3420, FAX: (800) 521-3661, E-Mail: wtmich@aol.com, Web Site: www.wttool.com (9)

Who's Calling, College Station, TX. Tel: (866) 688-9300, FAX: (888) 821-4260, E-Mail: contact@whoscalling.com, Web Site: www.whoscalling.com (30)

Who's Who - The MFSA Buyers' Guide to Blue Ribbon Mailing Services, Alexandria, VA. Tel: (703) 836-9200, FAX: (703) 548-8204, E-Mail: masa-mail@masa.org, Web Site: www.mfsanet.org (43)

Wick, Sharon, Miller Harness Co, Westford, MA. Tel: (800) 784-5831, E-Mail: customerservice@millerharness.com, Web Site: www.millerharness.com (11)

Wicka, Tom, IWCO Direct, Chanhassen, MN. Tel: (952) 474-0961, FAX: (952) 474-6467 (21)

Wicker, Gary, Zondervan Corp, Grand Rapids, MI. Tel: (616) 698-6900, (800) 727-3060, FAX: (616) 698-3235, Web Site: www.zondervan.com (17)

Wicker, Ron, LinkWorth, Lewisville, TX. Tel: (214) 440-3901, Web Site: www.linkworth.com (32)

Wickhander, Sandy, Sprint Corp, Overland Park, KS. Tel: (913) 624-3313, FAX: (913) 624-5386 (29)

Wickizer, Chris, Premera Blue Cross, Spokane, WA. Tel: (425) 670-4000, (800) 422-0032, FAX: (425) 670-5853, Web Site: www.premera.com (15)

Wideband by Kars, New Rochelle, NY. Tel: (212) 691-9000, FAX: (212) 691-9835, E-Mail: info@ widebandjewelry.com, Web Site: www. widebandjewelry.com (16)

Widess, Jim, The Caning Shop, Berkeley, CA. Tel: (510) 527-5010, (800) 544-3373, FAX: (510) 527-7718, Web Site: www.caning.com (11)

Widing, Laura, Kerr-Hays Co, Ligonier, PA. Tel: (724) 238-6694, FAX: (724) 238-7440 (16)

Widman, Paul, National Cable Communications, New York, NY. Tel: (212) 548-3300, FAX: (212) 519-0099, Web Site: www.spotcable.com (32)

Wiebe, Richard, Creative Teaching Associates, Clovis, CA. Tel: (559) 291-6626, (800) 767-4282, FAX: (559) 291-2953, Web Site: www.mastercta.com (16)

Wiedemann, George, UMarketing LLC, New York, NY. Tel: (630) 916-1717, Web Site: www. umarketing.com (35)

Wiedemer, Kathleen, National Parkinson Foundation, Miami, FL. Tel: (800) 937-4545, Web Site: www. parkinson.org (1)

Wiedman, Stephen, Mid America Designs Inc, Effingham, IL. Tel: (217) 540-4200, (800) 350-4543, FAX: (217) 540-4800, E-Mail: mail@ mamotorworks.com, Web Site: www. mamotorworks.com (12)

Wiehoff, John, P., C H Robinson Worldwide Inc, Eden Prairie, MN. Tel: (952) 937-8500, FAX: (952) 937-6740, E-Mail: info@chrobinson.com, Web Site: www.chrobinson.com (16)

Wielgus, Wayne, Choice Hotels International, Silver Spring, MD. Tel: (301) 592-6636, (888) 770-6800, FAX: (301) 592-6157, E-Mail: ihelp@choicehotels. com, Web Site: www.choicebuys.com (16)

Wiener, Adelle S., PRO Chemical & Dye Inc, Fall River, MA. Tel: (508) 676-3838, FAX: (508) 676-3980, Web Site: www.prochemicalanddye.com (10)

Wiener, Donald, PRO Chemical & Dye Inc, Fall River, MA. Tel: (508) 676-3838, FAX: (508) 676-3980, Web Site: www.prochemicalanddye.com (10)

Wiercinski, Sara, National Catholic Reporter Publishing Co Inc, Kansas City, MO. Tel: (816) 531-0538, (800) 444-8910, FAX: (816) 968-2268, Web Site: www.ncronline.org (17)

Wiese, Michael, Michael Wiese Productions, Studio City, CA. Tel: (818) 379-8799, (800) 833-5738, FAX: (818) 986-3408, Web Site: www.mwp.com (17)

Michael Wiese Productions, Studio City, CA. Tel: (818) 379-8799, (800) 833-5738, FAX: (818) 986-3408, Web Site: www.mwp.com (17)

Simon Wiesenthal Center, Los Angeles, CA. Tel: (310) 553-9036, Web Site: wiesenthal.com (1)

Wietecha, Mark, Kurt Salmon Associates Inc, Atlanta, GA. Tel: (404) 892-0321, FAX: (404) 898-9590, E-Mail: infoksaweb@kurtsalmon.com, Web Site: www.kurtsalmon.com (20)

Wiezalis, Peter, Four Directions Media, Oneida, NY. Tel: (315) 829-8316, Web Site: www. fourdirectionsinc.com (17)

The Wig Co, Pittsburgh, PA. Tel: (412) 221-4790, (800) 456-1788, FAX: (412) 257-8181, E-Mail: custserv@twcwigs.com (2)

Wight, Katy, Edward Elgar Publishing Inc, Northampton, MA. Tel: (413) 584-5551, FAX: (413) 584-9933, E-Mail: sales@e-elgar.com, Web Site: www. e-elgar.com (17)

Wight, Nelson, Cooper Wight Associates Inc, Francestown, NH. Tel: (603) 547-2144 (35)

Wikco Industries Inc, Casa Grande, AZ. Tel: (520) 316-0446, FAX: (520) 316-0446, E-Mail: sales@ wikco.com, Web Site: www.wikco.com (5)

Wikreate, San Francisco, CA. Tel: (415) 362-0440, Web Site: www.wikreate.com (35)

Wikstrom, Robert, L., Jerden Records/SpeechWorks, Redmond, WA. Tel: (425) 882-3344, (888) 401-4487, FAX: (425) 882-3494, E-Mail: jerden@aol. com, Web Site: www.soundworks.net (16)

Wiland, Phillip, Wiland Direct, Niwot, CO. Tel: (303) 485-8686, Web Site: www.wilanddirect.com (22)

Wiland Direct, Niwot, CO. Tel: (303) 485-8686, Web Site: www.wilanddirect.com (22)

Wilber, Elaine, VF Imagewear, Nashville, TN. Tel: (615) 565-5000, (800) 733-5271, Web Site: www. vfimagewear.com (2)

Wilbur, Michael, MBI Inc, Norwalk, CT. Tel: (203) 853-2000, E-Mail: webmail@mbi-inc.com, Web Site: www.mbi-inc.com (16)

Wilcher, Thomas, Soft Surroundings, Saint Louis, MO. Tel: (314) 812-5200, Web Site: www. softsurroundings.com (2)

Wilcox, Jack, Wilcox & Associates, Longwood, FL. Tel: (407) 830-4808, FAX: (407) 830-5265 (33)

Wilcox, John, Sheplers Catalog Sales Inc, Wichita, KS. Tel: (316) 946-3838, (800) 835-4004, FAX: (316) 946-3729, Web Site: www.sheplers.com (2)

Wilcox, Marjorie, DelStar Technologies, Middletown, DE. Tel: (302) 378-8888, (800) 521-6713, FAX: (302) 378-4482, Web Site: www.delstarinc.com (16)

Wilcox, Mark, DB Consulting, Harrison, NY. Tel: (914) 698-2008, E-Mail: darcybev@yahoo.com (20)

Wilcox, Ryan, Atlantic Publication Group LLC, Charleston, SC. Tel: (843) 747-0025, FAX: (843) 744-0816, E-Mail: info@atlanticpublicationgrp. com, Web Site: www.atlanticpublicationgrp.com (17)

Wilcox & Associates, Longwood, FL. Tel: (407) 830-4808, FAX: (407) 830-5265 (33)

Wild, Bill, Jaypro Sports, Waterford, CT. Tel: (860) 447-3001, (800) 243-0533, FAX: (800) 988-3363, E-Mail: info@jaypro.com, Web Site: www.jaypro. com (11)

Wild, Valerie, Power & Tel Supply, Randolph, VT. Tel: (800) 451-4381, FAX: (802) 234-5006, E-Mail: cablesales@ptsupply.com, Web Site: www. ptsupply.com/enterprise (16)

WILD Flavors Inc, Erlanger, KY. Tel: (859) 342-3600, Web Site: www.wildflavors.com (4)

Gilbert H Wild & Son Inc, Reeds, MO. Tel: (417) 548-3514, FAX: (417) 548-6831, Web Site: www. gilberthwild.com (8)

Wilde, Thomas, A., W.A. Wilde Co, Holliston, MA. Tel: (508) 429-5515, FAX: (508) 893-0399, E-Mail: info@wilde.com, Web Site: www.wilde. com (21)

W.A. Wilde Co, Holliston, MA. Tel: (508) 429-5515, FAX: (508) 893-0399, E-Mail: info@wilde.com, Web Site: www.wilde.com (21)

Wilder, Zibby, Born Free USA, Sacramento, CA. Tel: (916) 447-3085, FAX: (916) 447-3070, E-Mail: info@bornfreeusa.org, Web Site: www.bornfreeusa. org (1)

The Wilderness Society, Washington, DC. Tel: (202) 429-2609, Web Site: www.wilderness.org (40)

Wilderottes, Mary, Agnes, Frontier Corp, Rochester, NY. Tel: (716) 777-1000, Web Site: www. frontieronline.com (16)

Wildlife Education Ltd, Park Hills, KY. Tel: (858) 513-7600, FAX: (858) 513-7660, E-Mail: animals@zoobooks.com, Web Site: www.zoobooks. com (17)

Wildrick, Robert, N., Joseph A Bank Clothiers Inc, Hampstead, MD. Tel: (410) 239-2700, (800) 285-2265, FAX: (410) 239-5911, E-Mail: service@jos-a-bank.com, Web Site: www.josbank.com (2)

Wildseed Farms, Fredericksburg, TX. Tel: (830) 990-8080, (800) 848-0078, FAX: (830) 990-8090, E-Mail: orders1@wildseedfarms.com, Web Site: www.wildseedfarms.com (8)

Wilen, Darrin, Wilen Group, Farmingdale, NY. Tel: (631) 439-5000, Web Site: www.wilengroup.com (27)

Wilen Group, Farmingdale, NY. Tel: (631) 439-5000, Web Site: www.wilengroup.com (27)

Wiles, Perry, Inmar, Winston-Salem, NC. Tel: (336) 631-2524, FAX: (336) 770-3470, E-Mail: ibizdev@inmar.com, Web Site: www. promotionslogistics.com (14)

Wiles, Susan, Leisure Arts Inc, Little Rock, AR. Tel: (501) 868-8800, Web Site: www.leisurearts.com (17)

Wiley II, Bradford, Do It Yourself Direct Marketing, Hoboken, NJ. Tel: (201) 748-6000, FAX: (201) 748-6088, E-Mail: info@wiley.com, Web Site: www.wiley.com (43)

Wiley II, Bradford, John Wiley & Sons Inc, Hoboken, NJ. Tel: (201) 748-6000, FAX: (201) 748-6088, E-Mail: info@wiley.com, Web Site: www.wiley. com (17)

Wiley, Deborah E., Do It Yourself Direct Marketing, Hoboken, NJ. Tel: (201) 748-6000, FAX: (201) 748-6088, E-Mail: info@wiley.com, Web Site: www.wiley.com (43)

Wiley, Deborah, E., John Wiley & Sons Inc, Hoboken, NJ. Tel: (201) 748-6000, FAX: (201) 748-6088, E-Mail: info@wiley.com, Web Site: www.wiley. com (17)

Wiley, Mason, Hydra Group LLC, Los Angeles, CA. Tel: (310) 526-6680, FAX: (310) 526-6682, Web Site: www.hydragroup.com (9)

Wiley, Pat, Compact Information Systems Inc, Redmond, WA. Tel: (425) 869-1379, Web Site: www. cisdirect.com (22)

Wiley, Peter, Booth, Do It Yourself Direct Marketing, Hoboken, NJ. Tel: (201) 748-6000, FAX: (201) 748-6088, E-Mail: info@wiley.com, Web Site: www.wiley.com (43)

Wiley, Richard, H., Samsonite American Tourister, Mansfield, MA. Tel: (508) 851-1400, (800) 821-6632, FAX: (508) 851-8715, E-Mail: samsonite@ casupport.ca, Web Site: www.samsonite.com (16)

Wiley, Richard, H., Samsonite Corp, Mansfield, MA. Tel: (508) 851-1400, (800) 547-BAGS, FAX: (303) 373-8715, Web Site: www.samsonite.com (16)

John Wiley & Sons Canada Ltd, Etobicoke, ON Canada. Tel: (416) 236-4433, FAX: (416) 236-4448, Web Site: www.wiley.com (17)

John Wiley & Sons Inc, Hoboken, NJ. Tel: (201) 748-6000, FAX: (201) 748-6088, E-Mail: info@wiley. com, Web Site: www.wiley.com (17)

Wilgus, Carol, BJ's Wholesale Club Inc, Westborough, MA. Tel: (508) 651-7400, FAX: (508) 651-6167, Web Site: www.bjs.com (13)

Wilhelm, Markus, AKS Marketing & Media, Chapel Hill, NC. Tel: (919) 240-5496 (20)

Wilhelm, Markus, Bookspan, Garden City, NY. Tel: (516) 490-4561, FAX: (516) 490-4856 (13)

Wilhide, Douglas, Carino Nurseries, Indiana, PA. Tel: (800) 223-7075, FAX: (724) 463-3050, E-Mail: carino@carinonurseries.com, Web Site: www. carinonurseries.com (8)

Wilhite, Gerald, Abbey Press, Saint Meinrad, IN. Tel: (812) 357-8011, FAX: (812) 357-8388, Web Site: www.abbeypress.com (6)

Wilhoit, Zachary, Ethnic Technologies LLC, South Hackensack, NJ. Tel: (201) 440-8923, (866) 333-8324, FAX: (201) 440-2168, E-Mail: candace@ ethnictechnologies.com, Web Site: www. ethnictechnologies.com (23)

Wilke, Marty, St Louis Slot Machine Co, Saint Louis, MO. Tel: (314) 432-1699, E-Mail: stlslot@ earthlink.net, Web Site: www.stlouisslot.com (6)

Wilke, Robert, Nexus Direct, Virginia Beach, VA. Tel: (757) 340-5960, (800) 965-0577, FAX: (757) 340-5980, E-Mail: info@nexusdirect.com, Web Site: www.nexusdirect.com (35)

Wilkens, Monica, Helzberg Diamonds, North Kansas City, MO. Tel: (816) 842-7780, (800) HELZBURG, FAX: (816) 480-0294, Web Site: www.helzberg.com (16)

Wilkes, Corbin, M., The Kiplinger Washington Editors Inc, Washington, DC. Tel: (202) 887-6400, (800) 544-0155, FAX: (202) 496-1817, Web Site: www. kiplinger.com (17)

Wilkes, Mark, Corporate Graphics Direct Marketing Solutions, Arden Hills, MN. Tel: (651) 494-1740, Web Site: www.cgids.com (22)

Wilkes Direct Mail Co, Saint Louis, MO. Tel: (314) 776-5555, (800) 331-6441, FAX: (314) 776-0913, E-Mail: sales@wilkesdirect.com, Web Site: www.wilkesdirect.com (21)

Wilkie, Jack, NOVO1, Fort Worth, TX. Tel: (817) 355-6899, FAX: (817) 355-8505, Web Site: www.novo1.com (29)

Wilkie, Michael, DoAll Co, Wheeling, IL. Tel: (847) 824-1122, (800) 92-DOALL, FAX: (847) 699-7524, E-Mail: info@doall.com, Web Site: www.doall.com (16)

Wilkin, Gene, Bunn-O-Matic Corp, Springfield, IL. Tel: (217) 529-6601, FAX: (217) 529-6622, E-Mail: bunn@bunn.com, Web Site: www.bunn.com (16)

Wilkins, Donna, Charity Dynamics, Austin, TX. Tel: (512) 241-0561, Web Site: www.charitydynamics.com (1)

Wilkins, Jane, Mystic Seaport Museum Stores, Mystic, CT. Tel: (860) 572-5315, (860) 572-0711, FAX: (860) 572-5324, Web Site: www.mysticseaport.org (6)

Wilkinson, Harvie, Keeneland Association Inc, Lexington, KY. Tel: (859) 254-3412, (800) 456-3412, FAX: (859) 255-2484, Web Site: www.keeneland.com (16)

Wilkof, David, Harris Infosource International Inc, Independence, OH. Tel: (330) 425-9000, (877) 359-6308, (800) 888-5900, (800) 748-5482, FAX: (800) 643-5997, E-Mail: customerservice@harrisinfo.com, Web Site: www.harrisinfo.com (17)

Wilkus, Malon, American Capital, Bethesda, MD. Tel: (301) 951-6122, FAX: (301) 654-6714, E-Mail: info@americancapital.com, Web Site: www.americancapital.com (15)

Willard, Bruce, Sundance Catalog Co, Salt Lake City, UT. Tel: (801) 973-2711, (800) 422-2770, FAX: (801) 973-4989, E-Mail: jessica.bassin@sundance.net, Web Site: www.sundancecatalog.com (6)

Lt Moses Willard Inc, Milford, OH. Tel: (513) 248-5500, (800) 621-8956, FAX: (513) 831-0548, E-Mail: info@ltmoses.com, Web Site: www.ltmoses.com (16)

Willet, Bill, Lifeboat Distribution, Shrewsbury, NJ. Tel: (732) 389-8950, FAX: (732) 389-9227, Web Site: www.programmersparadise.com (16)

William, Bryan, Premier Packaging Corp, Victor, NY. Tel: (877) 924-8460, FAX: (585) 924-8753, E-Mail: info@premiercustompkg.com, Web Site: www.premiercustompkg.com (16)

William Charles Printing, Plainview, NY. Tel: (516) 349-0900, Web Site: www.williamcharlesprinting.com (27)

William-Neil Associates, Sidney, NE. Tel: (800) 216-2214, FAX: (308) 254-6102, Web Site: www.william-neil.com (24)

Williams Jr., Bill, Telect Inc, Liberty Lake, WA. Tel: (509) 926-6000, FAX: (509) 926-8915, E-Mail: getinfo@telect.com, Web Site: www.telect.com (16)

Williams, Barry, American Management Association, New York, NY. Tel: (212) 586-8100, FAX: (212) 903-8186, Web Site: www.amanet.org (1)

Williams, Betsy, Nielsen Media Research, Inc, New York, NY. Tel: (646) 654-8300, Web Site: en-us.nielsen.com (1)

Williams, Bill, Harry & David Holdings Inc, Medford, OR. Tel: (541) 864-2500, (800) 345-5655, FAX: (541) 864-2742 (4)

Williams, Bill, Medcom Inc, Cypress, CA. Tel: (800) 877-1443, FAX: (714) 891-3140, E-Mail: lhammonds@medcominc.com, Web Site: www.medcominc.com (17)

Williams, Caroline, Williams Direct Inc, Burlington, KS. Tel: (620) 364-8431, FAX: (620) 364-8432 (23)

Williams, Chip, Parise Marketing Group, Millwood, NY. Tel: (914) 941-7467, FAX: (914) 941-7931, Web Site: www.parise.com (35)

Williams, Cindy, Passport International Ltd, North Charleston, SC. Tel: (843) 881-8690, (800) 606-1383, FAX: (843) 881-6247, E-Mail: csv@passportintl.com, Web Site: www.passportintl.com (2)

Williams, Connie, Deck the Walls Inc, Saint Peters, MO. Tel: (314) 719-8200, (866) 719-8200, FAX: (314) 719-8290, Web Site: www.deckthewalls.com (5)

Williams, David, E., Citizens Against Government Waste, Washington, DC. Tel: (202) 467-5300, (800) USA-DEBT, FAX: (202) 467-4253, E-Mail: membership@cagw.org, Web Site: www.cagw.org (1)

Williams, David, Make-A-Wish Foundation of America, Phoenix, AZ. Tel: (602) 279-9474, FAX: (602) 279-0855, Web Site: www.wish.org (1)

Williams, David, Merkle Inc, Columbia, MD. Tel: (443) 542-4000, (877) 9MERKLE, Web Site: www.merkleinc.com (22)

Williams, E., Michael, Florida Power Corp, Saint Petersburg, FL. Tel: (727) 820-5151, (800) 700-8744, FAX: (727) 384-7865, Web Site: www.progressenergy.com (16)

Williams, Galen, Galen Williams Landscaping & Garden Design, East Hampton, NY. Tel: (631) 324-6220, FAX: (631) 329-3684 (16)

Williams, Glenn, Bell Performance Inc, Longwood, FL. Tel: (407) 831-5021, (800) 659-2355, FAX: (407) 767-8685, E-Mail: info@bellperformance.net, Web Site: www.bellperformance.net (17)

Williams, James, Cluett Peabody, New York, NY. Tel: (212) 984-8900, FAX: (212) 984-8910, Web Site: www.arrowshirt.com (16)

Williams, Janette, Redd, California State University at Fresno, Fresno, CA. Tel: (559) 278-7830, FAX: (559) 278-8577, Web Site: www.csufresno.edu (41)

Williams, Jeff, ArrowMail Canada, Windsor, ON Canada. Tel: (313) 961-8334, FAX: (313) 961-7849, E-Mail: info@mailingcanada.com, Web Site: www.mailingcanada.com (28)

Williams, Joe, Luggage Base, Nipomo, CA. Tel: (805) 929-8191, (888) 832-1201, FAX: (805) 929-8192, E-Mail: service@luggagebase.com, Web Site: www.luggagebase.com (16)

Williams, Landa, LandaJob, Kansas City, MO. Tel: (816) 523-1881, (800) 931-8806, FAX: (816) 523-1876, E-Mail: adstaff@landajobnow.com, Web Site: www.landajobnow.com (20)

Williams, Linda, Planned Parenthood Mar Monte, San Jose, CA. Tel: (408) 287-7532, FAX: (408) 971-6935, Web Site: www.plannedparenthood.org (1)

Williams, M. Jane, Schultz & Williams Inc, Philadelphia, PA. Tel: (215) 625-9955, FAX: (215) 625-2701, E-Mail: mail@schultzwilliams.com, Web Site: www.sw-inc.com (1)

Williams, Michael, J., National Association Broadcasters Annual Conference & Expo, Washington, DC. Tel: (202) 429-5300, (800) 622-3976, FAX: (202) 429-4199, E-Mail: nab@nab.org, Web Site: www.nab.org (42)

Williams, Nan, Topak Marketing Inc, Philadelphia, PA. Tel: (215) 574-8307, FAX: (215) 574-8316 (35)

Williams, Patricia, Optimum Group, Cincinnati, OH. Tel: (513) 577-7000, FAX: (513) 577-7099, E-Mail: info@coactivemarketing.com, Web Site: www.getcoactive.com (21)

Williams, Pete, Alderman Co, High Point, NC. Tel: (336) 889-6121, FAX: (336) 889-7717, E-Mail: sales@aldermancompany.com, Web Site: www.aldermancompany.com (37)

Williams, R. James, Keeneland Association Inc, Lexington, KY. Tel: (859) 254-3412, (800) 456-3412, FAX: (859) 255-2484, Web Site: www.keeneland.com (16)

Williams, Renee, KCET, Los Angeles, CA. Tel: (323) 666-6500, FAX: (323) 953-5661, E-Mail: viewerservices@kcet.org, Web Site: www.kcet.org (1)

Williams, Rob, Mountain Press Publishing Co, Missoula, MT. Tel: (406) 728-1900, (800) 234-5308, FAX: (406) 728-1635, E-Mail: info@mtnpress.com, Web Site: www.mountain-press.com (17)

Williams, Ronald, A., AETNA - Marketing Product & Communication, Hartford, CT. Tel: (860) 273-0123, (800) 872-3862, FAX: (860) 273-3971, Web Site: www.aetna.com (14)

Williams, Scott, Emisare, Greensboro, NC. Tel: (336) 378-0510, Web Site: www.emisare.com (32)

Williams, Shane, Hagie Manufacturing Co, Clarion, IA. Tel: (515) 532-2861, (800) 247-4885, FAX: (515) 532-3553, E-Mail: info@hagie.com, Web Site: www.hagie.com (9)

Williams, Sheryl, Amplify Federal Credit Union, Austin, TX. Tel: (512) 834-6519, Web Site: www.goamplify.com (1)

Williams, Sonia, Cables to Go, Moraine, OH. Tel: (937) 224-8646, (800) 506-9607, FAX: (800) 331-2841, (937) 496-2666, Web Site: www.cablestogo.com (3)

Williams, Susan, D., American Airlines Inc, Dallas, TX. Tel: (817) 967-1910, FAX: (817) 967-2841 (19)

Williams, Susan, Luggage Base, Nipomo, CA. Tel: (805) 929-8191, (888) 832-1201, FAX: (805) 929-8192, E-Mail: service@luggagebase.com, Web Site: www.luggagebase.com (16)

Williams, Tiffany, Group O Inc, Milan, IL. Tel: (309) 736-8300, Web Site: www.groupo.com (30)

Williams, Tony, Sunshine Minting Inc, Coeur D'Alene, ID. Tel: (208) 772-9592, (800) 274-5837, FAX: (208) 772-9739, E-Mail: sunshine@sunshinemint.com, Web Site: www.sunshinemint.com (14)

Williams, Wayne, E., Telect Inc, Liberty Lake, WA. Tel: (509) 926-6000, FAX: (509) 926-8915, E-Mail: getinfo@telect.com, Web Site: www.telect.com (16)

Williams, Caliri, Miller & Otley, Wayne, NJ. Tel: (973) 694-0800, FAX: (973) 694-0302, Web Site: www.wcmolaw.com (20)

Williams Direct Inc, Burlington, KS. Tel: (620) 364-8431, FAX: (620) 364-8432 (23)

Williams III, W. Grant, Home Decorators Collection Inc, Hazelwood, MO. Tel: (314) 993-1516, FAX: (314) 521-5780, Web Site: www.homedecoratorscollection.com (8)

Williams Printing Co/an RR Donnelley Co, Atlanta, GA. Tel: (404) 875-6611, (800) 950-7588, FAX: (404) 872-4025, Web Site: www.rrdonnelley.com (27)

Williams-Sonoma Inc, San Francisco, CA. Tel: (415) 421-7900, FAX: (415) 983-9887, Web Site: www.williams-sonomainc.com (8)

Williams Worldwide Television, Santa Monica, CA. Tel: (310) 449-4506, FAX: (310) 449-4556, E-Mail: curious@williamsworldwidetv.com, Web Site: www.williamsworldwidetv.com (35)

Williamsburg Blacksmiths Inc, Williamsburg, MA. Tel: (413) 268-7341, (800) 248-1776, FAX: (413) 268-9317, Web Site: www.williamsburgblacksmiths.com (8)

Williamson, Jerry, Williamson Printing, Dallas, TX. Tel: (214) 904-2100, (800) 843-5423, FAX: (214) 352-1842, E-Mail: jandagu@twpc.com, Web Site: www.wpcnet.com (27)

Williamson, Matt, O., Brady Corp, Milwaukee, WI. Tel: (414) 358-6600, (800) 541-1686, FAX: (800) 292-2289, Web Site: www.bradycorp.com (16)

Williamson, Phillip, C., Williamson-Dickie Manufacturing Co, Fort Worth, TX. Tel: (800) 336-7201, FAX: (817) 877-5027, E-Mail: customerservice@dickies.com, Web Site: www.dickies.com (2)

Williamson, Susan, CTRAC Information Solutions, Strongsville, OH. Tel: (440) 572-1000, FAX: (440) 572-3330, E-Mail: ctrac@ctrac.com, Web Site: www.ctrac.com (22)

Williamson-Dickie Manufacturing Co, Fort Worth, TX. Tel: (800) 336-7201, FAX: (817) 877-5027, E-Mail: customerservice@dickies.com, Web Site: www.dickies.com (2)

Williamson Jr, Henry G., Branch Banking & Trust Co, Wilson, NC. Tel: (252) 399-4111, FAX: (252) 246-4030 (14)

Williamson Printing, Dallas, TX. Tel: (214) 904-2100, (800) 843-5423, FAX: (214) 352-1842, E-Mail: jandagu@twpc.com, Web Site: www.wpcnet.com (27)

Willins, Stanton, Covalent Marketing, Denver, CO. Tel: (303) 588-7754, Web Site: www.covalentmarketing.com (22)

Willis, Aaron, Social Studies School Service, Culver City, CA. Tel: (310) 839-2436, (800) 421-4246, FAX: (310) 839-2249, (800) 944-5432, E-Mail: access@socialstudies.com, Web Site: www.socialstudies.com (16)

Willis, Bernice, Matt Brown & Associates Inc, Dayton, OH. Tel: (937) 434-3949, (800) 233-3949, FAX: (937) 434-6272, E-Mail: mba@mbalists.com, Web Site: www.mbalists.com (23)

Willis, Mike, Kappler Protective Apparel & Fabrics, Guntersville, AL. Tel: (256) 505-4005, (800) 600-4019, FAX: (256) 505-4151, E-Mail: usa@kappler.com, Web Site: www.kappler.com (2)

Willis Music Co, Florence, KY. Tel: (859) 283-2050, (800) 354-9799, FAX: (859) 283-1784, E-Mail: ordpt@willis-music.com, Web Site: www.willismusic.com (17)

Willison, Elizabeth, The Signature Agency, Raleigh, NC. Tel: (919) 878-8989, (800) 870-8700, FAX: (919) 878-3939, E-Mail: info@signatureagency.com, Web Site: www.signatureagency.com (35)

Willits Ed. D., Paula, P., The Dartnell Corp, Naples, FL. Tel: (585) 240-7301, (800) 447-4030, FAX: (585) 292-4392, E-Mail: customerservice@dartnellcorp.com, Web Site: www.dartnellcorp.com (17)

Williumstad, Robert, American Health & Life Insurance Co, Fort Worth, TX. Tel: (817) 348-7500, (800) 995-2274, FAX: (817) 348-7553, Web Site: www.citifinancial.com (15)

Willms, James, A., Unicover Corp, Cheyenne, WY. Tel: (307) 771-3000, (800) 443-3232, FAX: (307) 771-3134, E-Mail: qands@unicover.com, Web Site: www.unicover.com (6)

Willms, Jesse, JustThinkIncorporated, Sherwood Park, AB Canada. Tel: (780) 416-0244 (16)

Willock, David, The Mailing House Inc, Bell, CA. Tel: (323) 262-6000, FAX: (323) 262-6622, E-Mail: tmh4mail@themailinghouse.com, Web Site: www.themailinghouse.com (28)

Wills, Richard, Baker & Taylor Inc, Charlotte, NC. Tel: (704) 998-3100, (800) 775-1800, FAX: (704) 998-3316, E-Mail: btinfo@btol.com, Web Site: www.btol.com (16)

Wills, Rick, Tektronix Inc, Beaverton, OR. Tel: (503) 627-7111, (800) 833-9200, FAX: (503) 627-3247, Web Site: www.tektronix.com (16)

Willson, Jane, Sunnyland Farms Inc, Albany, GA. Tel: (229) 436-5654, (800) 999-2488, FAX: (229) 888-8332, Web Site: www.sunnylandfarms.com (4)

Willson, Larry, Sunnyland Farms Inc, Albany, GA. Tel: (229) 436-5654, (800) 999-2488, FAX: (229) 888-8332, Web Site: www.sunnylandfarms.com (4)

Willumstad, Rob, B., AIG Accident & Health, New York, NY. Tel: (212) 770-7000, (877) 638-4244, FAX: (212) 509-9705, Web Site: www.aig.com (15)

Willy, Mark, World Book Inc, Chicago, IL. Tel: (312) 729-5800, (800) 255-1750, FAX: (312) 729-5600, Web Site: www.worldbook.com (17)

Wilmerding, John, National Gallery of Art Gift Shop, Washington, DC. Tel: (202) 842-6466, (800) 697-9350, FAX: (202) 842-4043, Web Site: www.nga.gov (16)

Wilmet, Michael J., FMP Direct Inc, Scottsdale, AZ. Tel: (847) 816-1919, (800) 995-3343, FAX: (847) 816-1969, E-Mail: info@fmpdirect.com, Web Site: www.fmpdirect.com (21)

Wilmet, Rachel A., FMP Direct Inc, Scottsdale, AZ. Tel: (847) 816-1919, (800) 995-3343, FAX: (847) 816-1969, E-Mail: info@fmpdirect.com, Web Site: www.fmpdirect.com (21)

Wilmonth, Mark, C., Pennwell Publishing, Tulsa, OK. Tel: (918) 835-3161, (800) 331-4463, E-Mail: headquarters@pennwell.com, Web Site: www.pennwell.com (17)

Wilmsen, Jamie, Garden Botanika Inc, Saint Louis, MO. Tel: (425) 881-9603, (800) 968-7842, FAX: (425) 869-6235, Web Site: www.gardenbotanika.com (7)

Wilschek, Art, New England Journal of Medicine, Waltham, MA. Tel: (781) 893-3800, FAX: (781) 893-7729, Web Site: www.nejm.org (17)

Wilshire Book Co, Chatsworth, CA. Tel: (818) 700-1522, FAX: (818) 700-1527, E-Mail: mpowers@mpowers.com, Web Site: www.mpowers.com (43)

Wilson Jr, Jackson, D., Excalibur Enterprises Inc, Winston Salem, NC. Tel: (336) 744-5000, (800) 441-4193, FAX: (336) 767-8257, E-Mail: info@excaliburmail.com, Web Site: www.excaliburmail.com (28)

Wilson, Becky, S., WDS Marketing & Public Relations, Overland Park, KS. Tel: (913) 362-4541, FAX: (913) 362-7342, E-Mail: bwilson@wdspr.com, Web Site: www.wdspr.com (20)

Wilson, Bud, Photographer's Formulary Inc, Condon, MT. Tel: (406) 754-2891, (800) 922-5255, FAX: (406) 754-2896, E-Mail: formulary@blackfoot.net, Web Site: www.photoformulary.com (9)

Wilson, Cairine, Canadian Institute of Chartered Accountants, Toronto, ON Canada. Tel: (416) 977-3222, Web Site: www.cica.ca (1)

Wilson, Chris, Experian Simmons, New York, NY. Tel: (212) 471-2850, FAX: (212) 471-2940, E-Mail: ellenr@smrb.com, Web Site: www.smrb.com (30)

Wilson, Christine, Fox Chase Cancer Center, Philadelphia, PA. Tel: (215) 728-6900, (888) FOXCHASE, FAX: (215) 728-2594, Web Site: www.fccc.edu (1)

Wilson, David, Business Mailing Center, Oxnard, CA. Tel: (805) 981-2600, (800) 882-1844, FAX: (805) 981-1180, E-Mail: answers@venturaprint.com, Web Site: www.venturaprint.com (23)

Wilson, David, Potpourri Group Inc, Chelmsford, MA. Tel: (978) 256-4100, FAX: (978) 256-1961/0344, Web Site: www.potpourrigroup.com (6)

Wilson, David, Sells Printing Co, New Berlin, WI. Tel: (262) 784-9500, (800) 728-9501, FAX: (262) 784-7876, Web Site: www.sells.com (27)

Wilson, David, Wilson Relationship Marketing Services, New York, NY. Tel: (212) 473-6900, Web Site: www.wilsonrms.com (35)

Wilson, George, Directory of American Business & Insurance Attorneys, New York, NY. Tel: (732) 458-7788, (800) 445-7995, FAX: (732) 458-7710, E-Mail: staff@abialaw.com, Web Site: www.abialaw.com (15)

Wilson, Grant, Southeast Toyota Distributors LLC, Deerfield Beach, FL. Tel: (954) 429-2000, Web Site: www.jmfamily.com (16)

Wilsen, Hugh, Wilson, Hugh & Associate Consultants Ltd, Thornhill, ON Canada. Tel: (905) 764-5312 (22)

Wilson, Jack, Cuisinart, Stamford, CT. Tel: (203) 975-4600, FAX: (203) 975-4660, Web Site: www.cuisinart.com (16)

Wilson, Jack, ECHO - Electronic Clearing House Inc, Woodland Hills, CA. Tel: (805) 419-8700, Web Site: www.echo-inc.com (14)

Wilson, Jan, American Business Directories, Omaha, NE. Tel: (402) 593-4600, (800) 555-6124, FAX: (402) 596-0475, Web Site: www.infousa.com (43)

Wilson, John, Landmark Graphics Corp, Houston, TX. Tel: (713) 839-2000, FAX: (713) 839-2015, E-Mail: solutions@lgc.com, Web Site: www.lgc.com (16)

Wilson, Lance, Labels West Inc, Woodinville, WA. Tel: (425) 486-8484, (800) 540-3009, FAX: (425) 486-8488, Web Site: www.labelswest.com (27)

Wilson, Lisa, LG Wilson & Associates, Somers, NY. Tel: (914) 649-5928, Web Site: www.lgwilson.com (22)

Wilson, Lynn, Photographer's Formulary Inc, Condon, MT. Tel: (406) 754-2891, (800) 922-5255, FAX: (406) 754-2896, E-Mail: formulary@blackfoot.net, Web Site: www.photoformulary.com (9)

Wilson, Marc, International Newspaper Network, Moline, IL. Tel: (309) 743-0800, (800) 293-9576, FAX: (309) 743-0830, E-Mail: info@TownNews.com, Web Site: www.townnews.com (32)

Wilson, Michael, Bart's Watersports, North Webster, IN. Tel: (574) 834-7666, (800) 348-5016, FAX: (574) 834-4246, E-Mail: info@barts.com, Web Site: www.bartswatersports.com (11)

Wilson, Michael, International Foundation of Employee Benefit Plans, Brookfield, WI. Tel: (262) 373-7758, FAX: (262) 786-8670, Web Site: www.ifebp.org (1)

Wilson, Mike, Michael Wilson Photographer, Cincinnati, OH. Tel: (513) 289-3855, E-Mail: michaelwilson@fuse.net, Web Site: www.michaelwilsonphotographer.com (37)

Wilson, Mike, Wilson Marketing Group, Los Angeles, CA. Tel: (800) 445-2089, FAX: (310) 397-4980, E-Mail: wilsonmg@earthlink.net (23)

Wilson, Paul, Strategic Fundraising Inc, Saint Paul, MN. Tel: (651) 649-0404, Web Site: www.strategicfundraising.com (1)

Wilson, Perry, Advanced Image Direct, Fullerton, CA. Tel: (714) 502-3900, (800) 540-3848, FAX: (714) 502-3901, Web Site: www.advancedimagedirect.com (28)

Wilson, Shirley, Gump's By Mail Inc, San Francisco, CA. Tel: (415) 982-1616, (800) 882-8055, FAX: (800) 984-9361, Web Site: www.gumpsbymail.com (6)

Wilson, Stacy, A., Humana Inc, Louisville, KY. Tel: (502) 580-5005, FAX: (502) 580-3141, Web Site: www.humana.com (7)

Wilson, Steve, McFarland & Co Inc Publishers, Jefferson, NC. Tel: (336) 246-4460, (800) 253-2187, FAX: (336) 246-5018, E-Mail: info@mcfarlandpub.com, Web Site: www.mcfarlandpub.com (17)

Wilson, Steven A., Music Sales Corp, New York, NY. Tel: (212) 254-2100, (800) 431-7187, FAX: (212) 254-2013, E-Mail: info@musicsales.com, Web Site: www.musicsales.com (17)

Wilson, Tom G., Phoenix Poke Boats Inc, McKee, KY. Tel: (606) 965-2803, E-Mail: pokeboat@pokeboat.com, Web Site: www.pokeboat.com (16)

Wilson, Tony, Micro Plastics Inc, Flippin, AR. Tel: (870) 453-2261, (800) 466-1467, FAX: (870) 453-8676, E-Mail: mpsales@microplastics.com, Web Site: www.microplastics.com (16)

Wilson, W. Weldon, Reassure America Life Insurance Co, Jacksonville, IL. Tel: (800) 637-4475, FAX: (217) 291-2398, Web Site: www.swissre.com (15)

Wilson, W., David, Poly One Corp, Avon Lake, OH. Tel: (440) 930-1000, (866) POLY-ONE, FAX: (440) 930-1428, Web Site: www.polyone.com (16)

The HW Wilson Co, Bronx, NY. Tel: (718) 588-8400, (800) 367-6770, FAX: (800) 590-1617, E-Mail: custserv@hwwilson.com, Web Site: www.hwwilson.com (17)

Wilson, Hugh & Associate Consultants Ltd, Thornhill, ON Canada. Tel: (905) 764-5312 (22)

Wilson Jr, John F., Hygienic Fabrics & Filters Inc, Sheboygan, WI. Tel: (920) 457-7383, (800) 876-2009, FAX: (920) 457-2558, Web Site: www.hyfab.com (16)

LG Wilson & Associates, Somers, NY. Tel: (914) 649-5928, Web Site: www.lgwilson.com (22)

Wilson Marketing Group, Los Angeles, CA. Tel: (800) 445-2089, FAX: (310) 397-4980, E-Mail: wilsonmg@earthlink.net (23)

Michael Wilson Photographer, Cincinnati, OH. Tel: (513) 289-3855, E-Mail: michaelwilson@fuse.net, Web Site: www.michaelwilsonphotographer.com (37)

Wilson Relationship Marketing Services, New York, NY. Tel: (212) 473-6900, Web Site: www.wilsonrms.com (35)

Wilson Thorington, Liz, The Weather Channel, New York, NY. Tel: (212) 856-5200, FAX: (212) 856-5215, Web Site: www.weather.com (32)

Wilsons Leather, Brooklyn Park, MN. Tel: (763) 391-4000, (866) 305-4704, FAX: (763) 391-4906, Web Site: www.wilsonsleather.com (2)

Wilton, Fred, Wilton Armetale, Mount Joy, PA. Tel: (717) 653-4444, (800) 553-2048, FAX: (717) 653-6573, E-Mail: cservice@armetale.com, Web Site: www.armetale.com (16)

Wilton Armetale, Mount Joy, PA. Tel: (717) 653-4444, (800) 553-2048, FAX: (717) 653-6573, E-Mail: cservice@armetale.com, Web Site: www.armetale.com (16)

Wilton Industries Inc, Woodridge, IL. Tel: (630) 963-1818, (800) 794-5866, FAX: (630) 963-7196, E-Mail: info@wilton.com, Web Site: www.wilton.com (16)

Wiltz, James, W., Patterson Dental, Saint Paul, MN. Tel: (651) 686-1600, (800) 328-5536, FAX: (651) 686-9331, Web Site: www.pattersondental.com (10)

Wilver, Peter, M., Thermo Fisher Scientific I, Waltham, MA. Tel: (781) 622-1000, (800) 678-5599, FAX: (781) 622-1207, Web Site: www.thermofisher.com (9)

Wimbley, Ronald, Relyco, Dover, NH. Tel: (603) 516-3610, Web Site: www.relyco.com (27)

Wimmer, Dave, Wimmer's Meat Products Inc, West Point, NE. Tel: (402) 372-2437, (800) 358-0761, FAX: (402) 372-5659, Web Site: www.wimmersmeats.com (4)

Wimmer's Meat Products Inc, West Point, NE. Tel: (402) 372-2437, (800) 358-0761, FAX: (402) 372-5659, Web Site: www.wimmersmeats.com (4)

Win Craft Inc, Winona, MN. Tel: (507) 454-5510, (800) 533-8100, FAX: (507) 454-6403, Web Site: www.wincraftschool.com (5)

Win-Win Giving, West Newton, MA. Tel: (617) 645-5479 (1)

Wind in the Rigging, Port Washington, WI. Tel: (262) 284-3494, (800) 236-7444, FAX: (262) 284-0067, E-Mail: info@windintherigging.com, Web Site: www.windintherigging.com (11)

Wind River Group, Akron, OH. Tel: (330) 644-7774, FAX: (330) 645-2045 (20)

Windlass, Pradeep, Atlanta Cutlery Corp, Conyers, GA. Tel: (770) 922-3700, (800) 833-8838, FAX: (770) 760-8993, E-Mail: webmaster@atlantacutlery.com, Web Site: www.atlantacutlery.com (11)

Windlass, Sudhir, Atlanta Cutlery Corp, Conyers, GA. Tel: (770) 922-3700, (800) 833-8838, FAX: (770) 760-8993, E-Mail: webmaster@atlantacutlery.com, Web Site: www.atlantacutlery.com (11)

Windolph, John, JWT Inside, Santa Monica, CA. Tel: (310) 309-8282, (877) 665-8768, FAX: (310) 309-8283, E-Mail: conversations@jwtinside.com, Web Site: www.jwtworks.com (35)

Window Book Inc, Cambridge, MA. Tel: (617) 441-3500, Web Site: www.windowbook.com (22)

Window Coverings Exchange, North Plainfield, NJ. Tel: (908) 755-4700 (8)

Windsor, Barbara, American Trucking Association, Arlington, VA. Tel: (703) 838-1700, FAX: (800) 254-2571, E-Mail: atamembership@trucking.org, Web Site: www.truckline.com (1)

Windsor House, Windsor Locks, CT. Tel: (860) 627-5927, FAX: (860) 627-0252, E-Mail: ahalley@windsormarketing.com, Web Site: windsormarketing.com (20)

Windsor Vineyards, Santa Rosa, CA. Tel: (800) 741-6070, (800) 289-9463, E-Mail: webmaster@windsorvineyards.com, Web Site: www.windsorvineyards.com (16)

Windstar Cruises, Seattle, WA. Tel: (206) 292-9606, (800) 258-SAIL, FAX: (206) 340-0975, E-Mail: info@windstarcruises.com, Web Site: www.windstarcruises.com (19)

Windstream Communications Inc, Little Rock, AR. Tel: (501) 748-7000 (32)

Windt, R.J., Universal Hovercraft, Cordova, IL. Tel: (309) 654-2588, FAX: (309) 654-2588, Web Site: www.hovercraft.com (11)

Windward Group, Shelburne, VT. Tel: (802) 985-3631, Web Site: www.windwardgroup.us (20)

Windway Capital Corp, Sheboygan, WI. Tel: (920) 457-8600 (34)

Wine, Randi, Creative Compliance, Chicago, IL. Tel: (916) 216-3379, E-Mail: info@creativecompliance.com, Web Site: www.creativecompliance.com (29)

Wine, Randi, The Direct Marketing Specialists Inc, Chicago, IL. Tel: (312) 266-7906, FAX: (312) 266-9230, E-Mail: rwinedms@winestarmail.com (35)

Wine Enthusiast Cos, Mount Kisco, NY. Tel: (914) 345-9463, (800) 356-8466, FAX: (914) 345-3129, Web Site: www.wineenthusiast.com (4)

Winer, Cynthia, Texas Monthly, Austin, TX. Tel: (512) 320-6900, (800) 759-2000, FAX: (512) 476-9007, E-Mail: info@texasmonthly.com, Web Site: www.texasmonthly.com (17)

Winer, Russell, Marketing Science Institute Review, Cambridge, MA. Tel: (617) 491-2060, FAX: (617) 491-2065, E-Mail: msi@msi.org, Web Site: www.msi.org (43)

Winetasting.com, Napa, CA. Tel: (800) 435-2225, FAX: (707) 252-0268, Web Site: www.geerwade.com (4)

Winfield Marketing Corp, Chicago, IL. Tel: (773) 743-8784, FAX: (440) 764-4871 (31)

Wing, Rian, Higher Power Marketing, Phoenix, AZ. Tel: (480) 837-3580, (888) 922-3580, FAX: (480) 837-3589, E-Mail: info@hpowermarketing.com, Web Site: www.hpowermarketing.com (30)

Wingate, Paul J., BeaconFey LLC, Towson, MD. Tel: (410) 583-1203, Fax: (410) 583-1506, E-Mail: info@beaconfey.com, Web Site: www.beaconfey.com (35)

Winger, Michael, Fitness USA Super Centers, West Bloomfield, MI. Tel: (248) 737-7200, (800) GET-FIT-1, FAX: (248) 932-3300, Web Site: www.fitnessusa.com (16)

Winites, Eleanor, National Cable & Telecommunications Association, Washington, DC. Tel: (202) 222-2300, FAX: (202) 775-3675, Web Site: www.ncta.com (40)

Winking, Kim, Broadcast Electronics Inc, Quincy, IL. Tel: (217) 224-9600, FAX: (217) 224-9607, E-Mail: bdcast@bdcast.com, Web Site: www.bdcast.com (3)

Winkler, Wayne, WorldVu LLC, Baltimore, MD. Tel: (410) 522-4223, FAX: (410) 522-4233, E-Mail: info@worldvu.com, Web Site: www.worldvu.com (17)

Winkoff, Steve, MVS Mailers Inc, Bohemia, NY. Tel: (800) 641-7917, Fax: (631) 699-0101, E-Mail: muraco@mvsmailers.com, Web Site: www.mvsmailers.com (28)

Winmill, Thomas, Winmill & Co, New York, NY. Tel: (212) 785-0900, (800) 400-MIDAS, FAX: (212) 363-1100, E-Mail: info@midasfunds.com, Web Site: www.midasfunds.com (14)

Winmill & Co, New York, NY. Tel: (212) 785-0900, (800) 400-MIDAS, FAX: (212) 363-1100, E-Mail: info@midasfunds.com, Web Site: www.midasfunds.com (14)

Winn MD, Daniel, Carefirst Blue Cross Blue Shield, Washington, DC. Tel: (202) 479-8000, FAX: (301) 470-8049, Web Site: www.carefirst.com (15)

Winn, Carol, R., Ames Taping Tool System Inc, Stone Mountain, GA. Tel: (770) 243-2647, FAX: (770) 243-2658, Web Site: www.amestools.com (9)

Winn Devon, Richmond, BC Canada. Tel: (206) 763-9544, (800) 875-4150, FAX: (206) 762-1389, Web Site: www.winndevon.com (17)

Winn Technology Group Inc, Palm Harbor, FL. Tel: (727) 789-0006, (800) 444-5622, FAX: (727) 789-0638, E-Mail: winn@winntech.net, Web Site: www.winntech.net (29)

Winning Solutions Inc, Fort Worth, TX. Tel: (972) 986-5355, (866) 494-6765, E-Mail: winninginc@aol.com (7)

Winningham, Mark, Aloft Group, Westlake Village, CA. Tel: (805) 494-3700, Web Site: www.aloftgroup.com (33)

Winnipeg Art Gallery, Winnipeg, MB Canada. Tel: (204) 786-6641, FAX: (204) 788-4998, E-Mail: inquiries@wag.mb.ca, Web Site: www.wag.mb.ca (1)

Winograd, Charles, M., RBC Dain Rauscher, Boston, MA. Tel: (617) 725-2000, FAX: (617) 725-1393, Web Site: www.rbcdainrauscher.com (14)

Winslett, Stephen, S., Golden Bear Golf Inc, North Palm Beach, FL. Tel: (561) 626-3900, FAX: (561) 626-4104, Web Site: www.nicklaus.com (16)

Winslow, Bill, International Sign Association International Convention, Alexandria, VA. Tel: (703) 836-4012, (866) WHY-SIGN, FAX: (703) 836-8353, Web Site: www.signs.org (42)

Winslow Publishing, Toronto, ON Canada. Tel: (416) 789-4733, E-Mail: winslow@interlog.com, Web Site: www.winslowpublishing.com (17)

Winston, Arthur, Winston & Winston PC, New York, NY. Tel: (212) 922-9483, FAX: (212) 532-2722, Web Site: www.winstonandwinston.com (20)

Winston, Jen, Sage Communications, Hudson, MA. Tel: (978) 567-8888, Web Site: www.sagecommunications.com (35)

Winston & Winston PC, New York, NY. Tel: (212) 922-9483, FAX: (212) 532-2722, Web Site: www.winstonandwinston.com (20)

Harry Winston Inc, New York, NY. Tel: (212) 245-2000, FAX: (212) 489-0016, E-Mail: hw@harrywinston.com, Web Site: www.harry-winston.com (16)

Winston Marketing Group, Elk Grove Village, IL. Tel: (847) 350-5800 (8)

Winter, George, Profit Center Software Inc, Port Washington, NY. Tel: (516) 414-6300, (888) 446-6240, FAX: (516) 414-6304, E-Mail: jmarrah@profitcenter.com, Web Site: www.profitcenter.com (22)

Winter, Matthew, American General Life & Accident Insurance, Nashville, TN. Tel: (615) 749-1000, (800) 888-2452, Web Site: www.agla.com (15)

Winter, Matthew, E., American General Life Insurance Co, Houston, TX. Tel: (713) 522-1111, FAX: (713) 522-8531, Web Site: www.aglife.com (15)

Winter, Richard, POPAI-The Global Association for Marketing at-Retail, Chicago, IL. Tel: (312)-863-2900, FAX: (312) 229-1152, Web Site: www.popai.com (40)

Winter, Tara, LoyaltyOne, Toronto, ON. Tel: (416) 228-6500, Web Site: www.loyalty.com; www.airmiles.ca (22)

Winter Marketing Educators' Conference, Chicago, IL. Tel: (312) 542-9000, (800) 262-1150, FAX: (312) 542-9001, E-Mail: info@ama.org, Web Site: www.ama.org (42)

Winterberry Group, New York, NY. Tel: (212) 842-6000, FAX: (212) 842-6010, E-Mail: info@ winterberrygroup.com, Web Site: www. winterberrygroup.com (20)

Winterhaltee, Gary, Sally Beauty Supply LLC, Denton, TX. Tel: (940) 898-7500, (800) 275-7255, Web Site: www.sallybeauty.com (7)

Winterrose, Douglas, M., CCH Inc, Riverwoods, IL. Tel: (847) 267-7000, (888) 224-7377, Web Site: www.cch.com (17)

Winters, Bart, Alexian Brothers Bonaventure House, Chicago, IL. Tel: (773) 327-9921, FAX: (773) 327-9113, E-Mail: info@abam.org, Web Site: www. bonaventurehouse.org (1)

Winters, Kimberly, Nordskog Publishing Co, Ventura, CA. Tel: (805) 642-2070, FAX: (805) 642-1862, E-Mail: pwrboatmag@aol.com, Web Site: www. nordskogpublishing.com (17)

WinterSilks LLC, Warren, PA. Tel: (904) 645-6000, Web Site: www.wintersilks.com (7)

Winterthur Museum & Country Estate, Wilmington, DE. Tel: (302) 888-4600, (800) 448-3883, FAX: (302) 888-4730, E-Mail: tourinfo@winterthur.org, Web Site: www.winterthur.org (6)

Wintrub, Charles, Catalyst Marketing Communications Inc, Stamford, CT. Tel: (203) 348-7541, FAX: (203) 348-5688, E-Mail: b2b@catalystmc.com, Web Site: www.catalystmc.com (35)

Wintz, Julie, Websource & Paper Corp, Norcross, GA. Tel: (212) 255-1600, FAX: (212) 463-7095, Web Site: www.websource-paper.com (25)

Wipesyenski, Mindy, Fox River Paper Co, Appleton, WI. Tel: (920) 733-7341, (800) 558-8327, FAX: (920) 733-2975, E-Mail: info@foxriverpaper.com, Web Site: www.foxriverpaper.com (27)

Wire Works, Chester, PA. Tel: (610) 485-1981, (800) 292-1940, Web Site: www.wire-works.com (9)

Wired Assets Data Corp, Greenwich, CT. Tel: (203) 340-2316, Web Site: www.wiredassets.com (22)

Wireless Idea, San Juan, PR. Tel: (787) 925-7000 (5)

Wirth Jr, John, Woodworker's Supply Inc, Casper, WY. Tel: (307) 237-5528, (800) 645-9292, FAX: (307) 57-5272, E-Mail: kenp@woodworker.com, Web Site: www.woodworker.com (11)

Wirth, Gray, Rohm & Haas Co, Philadelphia, PA. Tel: (215) 592-3000, (877) 288-5881, FAX: (215) 592-3377, Web Site: www.rohmhess.com (16)

Wirthwein, Chris, 5Metacom, Carmel, IN. Tel: (317) 580-7540, FAX: (317) 580-7550, E-Mail: mail@ 5metacom.com, Web Site: www.5metacom.com (35)

Wischnia, Janet, ATD American Co, Wyncote, PA. Tel: (215) 576-1380, (866) 283-9327, FAX: (215) 576-1827, E-Mail: janet@atd.com, Web Site: www. atdamerican.com (34)

The Wisconsin Cheeseman, Sun Prairie, WI. Tel: (608) 837-5166, (800) 698-1721, FAX: (608) 837-5493, Web Site: www.wisconsincheeseman.com (4)

Wisconsin Converting Inc, Green Bay, WI. Tel: (920) 437-64000, (800) 544-1935, FAX: (920) 436-4964, E-Mail: wci@wisconsinconverting.com, Web Site: www.wisconsinconverting.com (26)

Wisconsin Direct Marketing Association, Milwaukee, WI. Tel: (414) 760-9362, FAX: (414) 431-4195, E-Mail: info@wdma.org, Web Site: www.wdma. org (40)

Wisconsin Historical Foundation, Sun Prairie, WI. Tel: (608) 318-1044 (1)

Wise, Judy, OPIN Systems Inc, Bloomington, MN. Tel: (651) 994-6555, (800) 888-1804, FAX: (651) 994-7828, E-Mail: judywy@opin.com, Web Site: www.opin.com (22)

Wise, Lisa, Data-Dynamix Inc, Castle Rock, CO. Tel: (720) 855-9282, (888) 314-0078, FAX: (720) 855-9099, Web Site: www.data-dynamix.com (23)

Wise, Matt, Q Interactive, Chicago, IL. Tel: (312) 977-0390, (888) 729-6465, FAX: (312) 224-5001, E-Mail: solutions@qinteractive.com, Web Site: www.qinteractive.com (40)

Wise, R., Halsey, Intergraph Corp, Madison, AL. Tel: (256) 730-2000, (800) 345-4856, FAX: (256) 730-2048, Web Site: www.intergraph.com (16)

Wise, Terri, Amos Press, Inc, Sidney, OH. Tel: (937) 498-2111, FAX: (937) 498-0876, Web Site: www. amospress.com (17)

Wise, Terri, Coin World, Sidney, OH. Tel: (937) 498-0800, (800) 253-4555, FAX: (937) 498-0812, E-Mail: cwcustomerservice@coinworld.com, Web Site: www.coinworld.com (17)

Wise, Alpharetta, GA. Tel: (770) 442-1060 (27)

Wiseman, Irwin, Mercury International Trading, North Attleboro, MA. Tel: (508) 699-9000, FAX: (508) 699-9088, Web Site: www.mercuryfootwear.com (2)

Wisemen, Howard, Mercury International Trading, North Attleboro, MA. Tel: (508) 699-9000, FAX: (508) 699-9088, Web Site: www.mercuryfootwear. com (2)

Wisley, Carol, Harrington's of Vermont Inc, Richmond, VT. Tel: (802) 434-7500, FAX: (802) 434-3166, E-Mail: info@harringtonham.com, Web Site: www.harringtonham.com (4)

Wit Postal Logistics LLC, Chicago, IL. Tel: (815) 215-5100, Web Site: www.witpostal.com (28)

Witham, Lyn, United Way of Greater Toronto, Toronto, ON. Tel: (416) 777-2001, FAX: (416) 777-0962, Web Site: www.unitedwaytoronto.com (1)

Withiam Jr, Jack, National Stationery Show, White Plains, NY. Tel: (914) 421-3200, (800) 272-SHOW, FAX: (914) 948-6180, E-Mail: cate_doyle@ glmshows.com, Web Site: www.glmshows.com (42)

Witt, Doug, Newark Electronics, Chicago, IL. Tel: (773) 784-5100, (800) 4-Newark, FAX: (888) 551-4801, E-Mail: webmaster@newark.com, Web Site: www.newark.com (3)

Witt, Dr Robert, E., University of Alabama, Tuscaloosa, AL. Tel: (205) 348-6010, FAX: (205) 348-0249, Web Site: www.ua.edu (13)

Witte, Bill, Fujitsu Transaction Solutions Inc, Richardson, TX. Tel: (972) 963-2300, (800) 340-4425, Web Site: www.fujitsu.com (16)

Witty, Jonathan, Media Two, Baltimore, MD. Tel: (410) 828-0120, FAX: (410) 825-1002, Web Site: www.mediatwo.com (17)

Witwer, Mike, American General Co, Neptune, NJ. Tel: (732) 922-7000, FAX: (732) 922-7595 (15)

Wnorowski, Doug, Surplus Record, Chicago, IL. Tel: (312) 372-9077, (800) 622-5449, FAX: (312) 372-6537, E-Mail: surplus@surplusrecord.com, Web Site: www.surplusrecord.com (17)

Woerner, Bill, Solarcom, Norcross, GA. Tel: (770) 449-6116, (888) SUN-DATA, FAX: (770) 448-7726, Web Site: www.solarcom.net (16)

Wofford, Alison, Music Sales Corp, New York, NY. Tel: (212) 254-2100, (800) 431-7187, FAX: (212) 254-2013, E-Mail: info@musicsales.com, Web Site: www.musicsales.com (17)

Wogan, Thomas, Edge Teleservices, Inc, Oak Lawn, IL. Tel: (708) 857-5000, (800) 394-2323, FAX: (708) 857-5029, E-Mail: contactme@ edgeteleservices.com, Web Site: www. edgeteleservices.com (29)

Wogoman, Jeff, Patagonia Mail Order Inc, Reno, NV. Tel: (775) 747-1992, (800) 638-6464, FAX: (775) 747-6159, Web Site: www.patagonia.com (2)

Wohlfahrt, Jeff, Advanced Concepts Inc, Milwaukee, WI. Tel: (414) 362-9640, FAX: (414) 362-9646, E-Mail: info@advanced-concepts.com, Web Site: www.advanced-concepts.com (22)

Wojcik, Pashea, The Hartford Courant, Hartford, CT. Tel: (860) 241-6200, FAX: (860) 241-3865, Web Site: www.courant.com (31)

Wojcik, Paul, The Bureau of National Affairs, Inc, Arlington, VA. Tel: (703) 341-3000, (800) 372-1033, FAX: (703) 341-1688, E-Mail: mbromley@ bna.com, Web Site: www.bna.com (17)

Wojtkiewicz, George, H., GHW Associates, Lake Suzy, FL. Tel: (941) 625-4293, E-Mail: ghw@ ghw-associates.com, Web Site: www.ghw-associates.com (35)

Wojtus, Catherine, DirectConnect Group Ltd, Cleveland, OH. Tel: (216) 634-8481, Web Site: www. directgroup.com (35)

Wolcott, Cliff, Thermo Fisher Scientific SID, Madison, WI. Tel: (608) 276-6100, Web Site: www.thermo. com (9)

Wolf, Allen, E., ORC ProTel LLC, Lansing, IL. Tel: (708) 418-7413, FAX: (708) 418-7457, Web Site: www.orcprotel.com (29)

Wolf, Carol, Steck-Vaughn, Austin, TX. Tel: (512) 343-8227, (877) 866-2586, (800) 531-5015, FAX: (512) 795-3617, (877) 265-2730, E-Mail: info@ steck-vaughn.com, Web Site: www.steck-vaughn. com (17)

Wolf, Jack, Spinneybeck Enterprises, Getzville, NY. Tel: (716) 446-2380, (800) 482-7777, FAX: (716) 446-2396, E-Mail: sales@spinneybeck.com, Web Site: www.spinneybeck.com (16)

Wolf, Marty, Marty Wolf Game Co, Las Vegas, NV. Tel: (702) 385-2963, FAX: (702) 385-6963, E-Mail: info@gamblersjunkyard.com, Web Site: www.gamblersjunkyard.com (33)

Wolf, Ruth, R., ORC ProTel LLC, Lansing, IL. Tel: (708) 418-7413, FAX: (708) 418-7457, Web Site: www.orcprotel.com (29)

Wolf, Timothy, V., Molson Coors Brewing Co, Denver, CO. Tel: (303) 279-6565, (800) 642-6116, FAX: (303) 277-5415, Web Site: www. molsoncoors.com (16)

Wolf Blumberg Krody Inc, Cincinnati, OH. Tel: (513) 784-0066, FAX: (513) 784-0986, E-Mail: sklein@ wbk.com, Web Site: www.wbk.com (35)

Wolf Envelope Co, Birmingham, MI. Tel: (248) 687-2745, (800) 466-WOLF, FAX: (248) 687-2751, Web Site: www.wolfenvelope.com (26)

Marty Wolf Game Co, Las Vegas, NV. Tel: (702) 385-2963, FAX: (702) 385-6963, E-Mail: info@ gamblersjunkyard.com, Web Site: www. gamblersjunkyard.com (33)

Wolfe, Eric, American Trucking Association, Arlington, VA. Tel: (703) 838-1700, FAX: (800) 254-2571, E-Mail: atamembership@trucking.org, Web Site: www.truckline.com (1)

Wolfe, Greg, Circulation Specialists Inc, Shelton, CT. Tel: (888) 315-2472, FAX: (888) 315-2507 (20)

Wolfe, Howard, A., Crawford Advertising Associates LTD, New City, NY. Tel: (914) 946-2444, FAX: (914) 946-9236, E-Mail: crawads@aol.com, Web Site: www.crawfordadv.com (35)

Wolfe, John, F., The Columbus Dispatch, Columbus, OH. Tel: (614) 461-5000, FAX: (614) 461-7551, E-Mail: csmith@the.dispatch.com, Web Site: www. dispatch.com (17)

Wolfe, Peggy, Micro Center, Hilliard, OH. Tel: (800) 634-3478, FAX: (614) 777-2620, E-Mail: csrs@ microcenterorder.com, Web Site: www.microcenter. com (3)

Wolfe, Stephen, P., The Toro Consumer Div, Bloomington, MN. Tel: (952) 888-8801, (888) 384-9939, FAX: (952) 887-8258, Web Site: www. thetorocompany.com (16)

Wolfe, Thomas, F., Coast to Coast Inc, Englewood, CO. Tel: (303) 728-2267, Web Site: www. coastresorts.com (1)

Wolfe, Thomas, F., Golf Card International, Englewood, CO. Tel: (800) 321-8269, FAX: (303) 792-7332, Web Site: www.golfcard.com (1)

Wolfe, Thomas, F., Woodall Publishing Co LP, Ventura, CA. Tel: (805) 667-4100, (800) 323-9076, FAX: (805) 667-4468, Web Site: www.woodalls. com (17)

Wolfe, Tom, Affinity Group Inc, Ventura, CA. Tel: (805) 667-4100, (800) 765-1912, FAX: (805) 667-4419, E-Mail: khurd@affinitygroup.com, Web Site: www.affinitygroup.com (19)

Brian Wolfe, New York, NY. Tel: (516) 840-3748 (20)

Wolfe Publishing Co Inc, Prescott, AZ. Tel: (928) 445-7810, (800) 899-7810, FAX: (928) 778-5124, E-Mail: wolfepub@riflemag.com, Web Site: www. riflemagazine.com (17)

Wolfenson, Stewart, Ansafone Communications, Santa Ana, CA. Tel: (714) 560-1000, Web Site: www. ansafone.com (29)

Wolfer, R., Dreis & Krump Manufacturing Co, Peotone, IL. Tel: (708) 258-1200, FAX: (708) 258-9682, E-Mail: chicago@dreis-krump.com, Web Site: www.dreis-krump.com (16)

Wolff, Brian, Edison Electric Institute, Washington, DC. Tel: (202) 508-5000, FAX: (202) 508-5096, Web Site: www.eei.org (1)

Wolff/SMG, Macedon, NY. Tel: (315) 986-1155, FAX: (315) 986-1161, E-Mail: rdelmonte@wolff-smg. com, Web Site: www.wolff-smg.com (28)

Wolfowitz, Paul, The World Bank, Washington, DC. Tel: (202) 473-1000, FAX: (202) 477-6391, Web Site: www.worldbank.org (17)

Wolk, Beryl, IMC - Multi Media Marketing, Jenkintown, PA. Tel: (215) 887-5700 X107, FAX: (215) 887-7076, E-Mail: berylwolk@aol.com, Web Site: berylsworld.com (31)

Wolk, David, Goodway Group, Jenkintown, PA. Tel: (215) 887-5700, FAX: (215) 881-2239, E-Mail: david@goodwaygroup.com, Web Site: www. goodwaygroup.com (35)

Wolk, Jeffrey, The Cross Country Group LLC, Medford, MA. Tel: (781) 396-3700, Web Site: www. ccgroup.com (13)

Woll, Alan, M., Tackle Craft, Ellsworth, WI. Tel: (715) 273-5300, E-Mail: tacklecr@aol.com (11)

Woll, Linda, J., Tackle Craft, Ellsworth, WI. Tel: (715) 273-5300, E-Mail: tacklecr@aol.com (11)

Wollin, Edith, DHL Global Mail, Weston, FL. Tel: (954) 903-6300, (866) 616-MAIL, FAX: (954) 903-6310, E-Mail: contact@dhlglobalmail.com, Web Site: www.dhlglobalmail.com (28)

Wolters Kluwer Financial Services, Minneapolis, MN. Tel: (612) 656-7724, Web Site: www. wolterskluwerfs.com (35)

Wolverine Mailing & Packaging Warehouse, Detroit, MI. Tel: (313) 873-6800, FAX: (313) 873-8730, Web Site: www.wolverinemail.com (28)

Womack, Wes, YELLOWPAGES.COM/ Ingenio, San Francisco, CA. Tel: (415) 248-4000, Web Site: www.ingenio.com (32)

Woman's Missionary Union, Birmingham, AL. Tel: (205) 991-8100, FAX: (205) 991-4990, E-Mail: email@wmu.org, Web Site: www.wmu.org (17)

Womanship, Annapolis, MD. Tel: (410) 267-6661, FAX: (410) 263-2036, E-Mail: sail@womanship. com, Web Site: www.womanship.com (16)

Women for Women International, Washington, DC. Tel: (202) 737-7705, Web Site: www. womenforwomen.org (40)

Women in Direct Marketing International, New York, NY. Tel: (516) 746-6700, FAX: (516) 294-8141, Web Site: www.wdmi.org (40)

Woman's Day Special Interest Publications, New York, NY. Tel: (212) 767-6000, FAX: (212) 767-5612, Web Site: www.womensday.com (17)

Women's Sports Foundation, East Meadow, NY. Tel: (516) 542-4700, Web Site: www. womenssportsfoundation.org (1)

Wong, Denise, K., Allstate Motor Club, Inc, Deerfield, IL. Tel: (847) 914-2972, FAX: (847) 914-2804, Web Site: www.walgreens.com (7)

Wong, Frederick, K., Beauty Naturally, Burlingame, CA. Tel: (650) 697-1845, (800) 432-4323, FAX: (650) 697-1970, E-Mail: sales@beautynaturally. com, Web Site: www.beautynaturally.com (7)

Wong, Janet, Beauty Naturally, Burlingame, CA. Tel: (650) 697-1845, (800) 432-4323, FAX: (650) 697-1970, E-Mail: sales@beautynaturally.com, Web Site: www.beautynaturally.com (7)

Wong, Leader, Bell & Howell Ltd, North York, ON Canada. Tel: (416) 746-2200, FAX: (416) 228-2439, Web Site: www.bellhowell.com (9)

Wood, Andy, L., Photoworks, Cleveland, OH. Tel: (206) 281-1390, (800) PHOTOWORKS, FAX: (206) 284-5357, E-Mail: info@photoworks.com, Web Site: www.photoworks.com (16)

Wood, Annabelle, Wood & Associates Direct Marketing Services Ltd, Scarborough, ON Canada. Tel: (416) 293-2511, FAX: (416) 293-2594, E-Mail: clientservices@wood-and-associates.com, Web Site: www.wood-and-associates.com (28)

Wood, Bill, Access International, Cambridge, MA. Tel: (617) 218+5000, (877) 433-9097, FAX: (617) 494-8404, E-Mail: info@accessint.com, Web Site: www.accessint.com (22)

Wood, Bob, Specialized Marketing Inc, Brewster, NY. Tel: (845) 278-6100, FAX: (845) 278-6150, Web Site: www.specialized-mktg.com (31)

Wood, Cliff, Trimensions Inc, Englewood, NJ. Tel: (212) 254-5554, FAX: (212) 473-6524 (21)

Wood, Craig, Clarity Group LLC, Chapel Hill, NC. Tel: (919) 932-6036, Web Site: www. claritygroupinc.com (20)

Wood, Dave, Historic Aviation, Minneapolis, MN. Tel: (651) 635-0100, (800) 225-5575, FAX: (651) 635-0700, E-Mail: info@historicaviation.com, Web Site: www.historicaviation.com (12)

Wood, David, Association of Bridal Consultants, New Milford, CT. Tel: (860) 355-0464, FAX: (860) 354-1404, E-Mail: office@bridalassn.com, Web Site: www.bridalassn.com (1)

Wood, David, Network Tel Services Inc, Woodland Hills, CA. Tel: (818) 992-4300, (800) 727-6874, FAX: (818) 992-8415, Web Site: www.nts.net (16)

Wood, Diane, John Wiley & Sons Canada Ltd, Etobicoke, ON Canada. Tel: (416) 236-4433, FAX: (416) 236-4448, Web Site: www.wiley.com (17)

Wood, Donald, W., Arrowhead Mountain Spring Water, Wilkes Barre, PA. Tel: (800) 873-7775, Web Site: www.arrowheadwater.com (17)

Wood, Doris, Multi-Level Marketing International Association (MLMIA), Irvine, CA. Tel: (949) 854-0484, FAX: (949) 854-7687, E-Mail: info@mlmia. com, Web Site: www.mlmia.com/ (1)

Wood, Douglas, Reed Smith Hall Dickler Advertising & Law Marketing Group, New York, NY. Tel: (212) 549-0377, FAX: (212) 521-5450, Web Site: www.reedsmith.com (20)

Wood, Ed, Cygnus Business Media, Fort Atkinson, WI. Tel: (203) 227-4037, (800) 547-7377, FAX: (203) 227-4245, Web Site: www.cygnusb2b.com (17)

Wood, Greg, Missouri Life Inc, Boonville, MO. Tel: (660) 882-9898, (800) 492-2593, FAX: (660) 882-9899, E-Mail: info@missourilife.com, Web Site: www.missourilife.com (17)

Wood, J., David, Majestic Products Co, Mississauga, ON. Tel: (905) 858-8010, (800) 668-5323, FAX: (905) 670-7915, Web Site: www.cfmcorp.com (16)

Wood, Joy, PacNet Services Ltd, Vancouver, BC. Tel: (604) 689-0399, FAX: (604) 689-0313, E-Mail: info@pacnetservices.com, Web Site: www. pacnetservices.com (14)

Wood, Ken, List Connection Inc, Simpsonville, SC. Tel: (864) 962-0761, Web Site: www. listconnection.net (23)

Wood, Kevin, Byowner.com, Shoreham, NY. Tel: (800) BY-OWNER, FAX: (866) BY-OWNER, Web Site: www.byowner.com (35)

Wood, Krishne, Litle & Co, Lowell, MA. Tel: (978) 275-6500, Web Site: www.litle.com (14)

Wood, Meeta, Vonage, Holmdel, NJ. Tel: (732) 528-2600, Web Site: www.vonage.com (7)

Wood, Phillip, R., Ten Speed Press, Emeryville, CA. Tel: (510) 559-1600, (800) 841-BOOK, FAX: (510) 559-1629, E-Mail: order@tenspeed.com, Web Site: www.tenspeed.com (17)

Wood, Sally, Penguin Group USA Inc, East Rutherford, NJ. Tel: (201) 909-6200, FAX: (201) 236-3381, Web Site: penguingroup.com (17)

Wood, Scott, Shape LLC, Addison, IL. Tel: (630) 620-8394, (800) 367-5811, FAX: (630) 620-0784, E-Mail: sales@shapellc.com, Web Site: www. shapellc.com (3)

Wood, Wayne, Farm Bureau Insurance, Lansing, MI. Tel: (517) 323-7000, (800) 292-2680, FAX: (517) 327-0208, Web Site: www.farmbureauinsurance-mi. com (15)

Wood & Associates Direct Marketing Services Ltd, Scarborough, ON Canada. Tel: (416) 293-2511, FAX: (416) 293-2594, E-Mail: clientservices@ wood-and-associates.com, Web Site: www.wood-and-associates.com (28)

Wood Carvers Supply Inc, Englewood, FL. Tel: (941) 698-0123, (800) 284-6229, FAX: (941) 698-0329, E-Mail: info@woodcarverssupply.com, Web Site: www.woodcarverssupply.com (9)

Woodall Publishing Co LP, Ventura, CA. Tel: (805) 667-4100, (800) 323-9076, FAX: (805) 667-4468, Web Site: www.woodalls.com (17)

Woodard Jr, M., Rufus, Brookstone Co, Merrimack, NH. Tel: (603) 880-9500, (800) 846-3000, FAX: (603) 577-8005, E-Mail: customerservice@ brookstone.com, Web Site: www.brookstone.com (3)

Woodard, Kathleen, M., HighScope Educational Research Foundation, Ypsilanti, MI. Tel: (734) 485-2000, (800) 40-PRESS, FAX: (734) 485-0704, E-Mail: lschweinhart@highscope.org, Web Site: www.highscope.org (17)

Woodard, Lois, MAX Federal Credit Union, Montgomery, AL. Tel: (334) 260-2600, (800) 776-6776, FAX: (334) 270-0921, Web Site: www.mymax.com (14)

Woodard, Robert, Tupperware, Orlando, FL. Tel: (407) 826-5050, (800) 366-3800, FAX: (407) 826-8874, Web Site: www.tupperware.com (16)

Woodbury, Ward, UMI Publications Inc, Charlotte, NC. Tel: (800) 747-9287, FAX: (704) 374-0729, E-Mail: info@umipub.com, Web Site: www. umipub.com (17)

Woodcock, Chris, Simplex Grinnell, Westminster, MA. Tel: (978) 731-2500, (800) SIMPLEX, FAX: (978) 731-7856, Web Site: www.simplexgrinnel.com (16)

Woodcraft Supply Corp LLC, Parkersburg, WV. Tel: (304) 422-5412, (800) 344-3348, FAX: (304) 422-5417, Web Site: www.woodcraft.com (9)

Woodcrafters Lumber Sales Inc, Portland, OR. Tel: (503) 231-0226, (800) 777-3709, FAX: (503) 232-0511, E-Mail: spen@worldnet.att.net, Web Site: www.woodcrafters.us (9)

Wooden, Roger, Wooden Information Services, Saint Louis, MO. Tel: (314) 576-1124 (22)

Wooden Information Services, Saint Louis, MO. Tel: (314) 576-1124 (22)

Woodford, Charles, H., Princeton Book Co Publishers, Hightstown, NJ. Tel: (609) 426-0602, (800) 220-7149, FAX: (609) 426-1344, E-Mail: pbc@ dancehorizons.com, Web Site: www.dancehorizons. com (17)

Woodhead, Robin, G., Sotheby's, New York, NY. Tel: (212) 606-7000, FAX: (212) 606-7107, Web Site: www.sothebys.com (6)

Woodis, Ginny, The Boston Consulting Group, New York, NY. Tel: (212) 446-2800 (20)

Woodrooffe, Allyson, Interwood Direct, Toronto, ON. Tel: (888) 275-5205, Web Site: www.interwood. com (8)

Woodrooffe, Robert, G., Interwood Direct, Toronto, ON Canada. Tel: (888) 275-5205, Web Site: www. interwood.com (8)

Woodrow, Mark, Hubert Co, Harrison, OH. Tel: (513) 367-8767, (800) 543-7374, FAX: (513) 367-8823, Web Site: www.hubert.com (16)

Woods, Brian, Comp USA, Inc, Miami, FL. Tel: (972) 982-4000, (800) COMP-USA, FAX: (972) 982-4030, Web Site: www.compusa.com (3)

Woods, Dana, American Association of Critical-Care Nurses, Aliso Viejo, CA. Tel: (949) 362-2000, (800) 809-CARE, FAX: (949) 362-2020, E-Mail: info@aacn.com, Web Site: www.aacn.org (1)

Woods, Joe, Gulf Publishing Co, Houston, TX. Tel: (713) 529-4301, FAX: (713) 520-4433, E-Mail: publications@gulfpub.com, Web Site: www.gulfpub.com (17)

Woods, Phyllis, Marriott International Inc, Washington, DC. Tel: (301) 380-3000, (301) 380-1791, E-Mail: internet.customer.care@marriott.com, Web Site: www.marriott.com (19)

Woods, Sylvia, Sylvia Woods Harp Center, Montrose, CA. Tel: (800) 272-4277, FAX: (818) 247-5212, E-Mail: info@harpcenter.com, Web Site: www.harpcenter.com (11)

Sylvia Woods Harp Center, Montrose, CA. Tel: (800) 272-4277, FAX: (818) 247-5212, E-Mail: info@harpcenter.com, Web Site: www.harpcenter.com (11)

Woodward Jr., James, H., P & H Mining Equipment, Milwaukee, WI. Tel: (414) 671-4400, FAX: (414) 671-7618, Web Site: www.phmining.com (16)

Woodward, Craig, Kappler Protective Apparel & Fabrics, Guntersville, AL. Tel: (256) 505-4005, (800) 600-4019, FAX: (256) 505-4151, E-Mail: usa@kappler.com, Web Site: www.kappler.com (2)

Woodward, Judith, Winn Technology Group Inc, Palm Harbor, FL. Tel: (727) 789-0006, (800) 444-5622, FAX: (727) 789-0638, E-Mail: winn@winntech.net, Web Site: www.winntech.net (29)

Woodward, Ken, Tidbits Media, Montgomery, AL. Tel: (334) 290-0225, (800) 523-3096, FAX: (334) 386-0302, E-Mail: editors@tidbitsweekly.com, Web Site: www.tidbitsweekly.com (17)

Woodwind & Brasswind Inc, Indianapolis, IN. Tel: (574) 251-3500, (800) 348-5003, FAX: (574) 251-3501, Web Site: www.wwbw.com (5)

Woodworker's Supply Inc, Casper, WY. Tel: (307) 237-5528, (800) 645-9292, FAX: (307) 57-5272, E-Mail: kenp@woodworker.com, Web Site: www.woodworker.com (11)

Woodworth, Lindsay, 2ergo, Arlington, VA. Tel: (703) 879-3400, Web Site: www.2ergo.com (30)

Woodworth, Stephen, Masterworks, Poulsbo, WA. Tel: (360) 394-4300, Web Site: www.masterworks.com (1)

Wooldridge, Dave, Babcox Publications LLC, Akron, OH. Tel: (330) 670-1234, FAX: (330) 670-0874, E-Mail: bbabcox@babcox.com, Web Site: www.babcox.com (17)

Woolf, Fred, Fred Woolf List Co Inc, Somers, NY. Tel: (914) 694-4466, (800) 431-1557, FAX: (914) 694-1710, E-Mail: info@woolflist.com, Web Site: www.woolflist.com (23)

Woolf, Sheila, Fred Woolf List Co Inc, Somers, NY. Tel: (914) 694-4466, (800) 431-1557, FAX: (914) 694-1710, E-Mail: info@woolflist.com, Web Site: www.woolflist.com (23)

Fred Woolf List Co Inc, Somers, NY. Tel: (914) 694-4466, (800) 431-1557, FAX: (914) 694-1710, E-Mail: info@woolflist.com, Web Site: www.woolflist.com (23)

Woolrich Inc, Woolrich, PA. Tel: (570) 769-6464, Web Site: www.woolrich.com (2)

Wooten, Mike, NCS, Danbury, CT. Tel: (562) 946-6900, (800) 975-6804, FAX: (800) 527-2488, Web Site: www.shopncs.com; www.ncs-apparel.com (16)

Wooten, Norman, D., National School Boards Association Inc, Alexandria, VA. Tel: (703) 838-6722, FAX: (703) 683-7590, E-Mail: info@nsba.org, Web Site: www.nsba.org (1)

Worcester Envelope, Auburn, MA. Tel: (800) 343-1398, FAX: (508) 832-3796, Web Site: www.worcester-envelope.com (26)

Word Dynamics of St Helena, Saint Helena, CA. Tel: (707) 963-8000, FAX: (707) 963-8000 (24)

WordCom Inc, Ellington, CT. Tel: (860) 875-7373, (800) 875-7373, (800) 822-0622, FAX: (860) 872-2713, E-Mail: sales@wordcom-inc.com, Web Site: www.wordcom-inc.com (21)

Wordright Enterprises Inc, Buffalo Grove, IL. Tel: (847) 215-5190, Web Site: www.globalsources.com (17)

Wordsman, Elizabeth (Betsy), Macy's Marketing, New York, NY. Tel: (212) 695-4400, FAX: (212) 494-1517, Web Site: www.macys.com (16)

The Wordstation, Avon By The Sea, NJ. Tel: (732) 774-4831, FAX: (732) 869-1822, E-Mail: pattyshannone@optonline.net (39)

Worick, Dick, The MSR Group, Omaha, NE. Tel: (402) 392-0755, (800) 737-0755, FAX: (402) 392-1068, E-Mail: info@theMSRgroup.com, Web Site: www.theMSRgroup.com (30)

Work, Bill, Cytec Industries Inc, Olean, NY. Tel: (716) 372-9650, FAX: (716) 372-1594, Web Site: www.conap.com (16)

Workflow One, Dayton, OH. Tel: (877) 735-4966, E-Mail: clientservices@workflowone.com, Web Site: www.sfinet.com (21)

Working Assets, San Francisco, CA. Tel: (800) 668-9253, FAX: (415) 371-1046, Web Site: www.workingassets.com (16)

Working Mother, New York, NY. Tel: (212) 221-9595, FAX: (212) 219-7448, Web Site: www.workingmother.com (31)

Workman, Eric, Polynesian Cultural Center, Honolulu, HI. Tel: (808) 293-3333, (800) 367-7060, FAX: (888) 722-7339, E-Mail: internetrez@polynesia.com, Web Site: www.polynesia.com (16)

Worland, David, Gannett Direct Marketing Services Inc, Louisville, KY. Tel: (502) 454-6660, (800) 345-5654, FAX: (502) 459-7479, Web Site: www.gdms.com (21)

The World Bank, Washington, DC. Tel: (202) 473-1000, FAX: (202) 477-6391, Web Site: www.worldbank.org (17)

World Book Inc, Chicago, IL. Tel: (312) 729-5800, (800) 255-1750, FAX: (312) 729-5600, Web Site: www.worldbook.com (17)

World Future Society, Bethesda, MD. Tel: (301) 656-8274, (800) 989-8274, FAX: (301) 951-0394, E-Mail: info@wfs.org, Web Site: www.wfs.org (1)

World Innovators Inc, Roxbury, CT. Tel: (860) 210-8088, FAX: (860) 210-7829, E-Mail: apeterson@worldinnovators.com, Web Site: www.worldinnovators.com (24)

World Kitchen Inc, Corning, NY. Tel: (607) 377-8000, (800) 999-3436, FAX: (607) 377-8946, Web Site: www.worldkitchen.com (16)

World Marketing Inc, La Vista, NE. Tel: (402) 384-0800, (800) 438-8797, FAX: (402) 384-0801, E-Mail: results@worldmarkinc.com, Web Site: www.worldmarkinc.com (28)

World Marketing, Inc (HQ), La Mirada, CA. Tel: (714) 994-6245, (800) 244-3003, FAX: (714) 776-2590, E-Mail: results@worldmarkinc.com, Web Site: www.worldmarkinc.com (21)

World Press Review, New York, NY. Tel: (212) 982-8880, Web Site: www.worldpressreview.com (18)

World Publications Inc, Winter Park, FL. Tel: (407) 628-4802, FAX: (407) 628-7061, Web Site: www.worldpub.net (17)

World Villages for Children, Annapolis, MD. Tel: (301) 779-4141, Web Site: www.worldvillages.org (1)

World Vision Canada, Mississauga, ON Canada. Tel: (905) 565-6200 X2173, Web Site: www.worldvision.ca (1)

World Vision Inc, Federal Way, WA. Tel: (253) 815-1000, (888) 511-6548, FAX: (253) 815-3140, E-Mail: info@worldvision.org, Web Site: www.worldvision.org (1)

World Wide Mailers, Windsor, ON Canada. Tel: (519) 254-6245, FAX: (519) 254-2608, E-Mail: tab@worldwidemailers.com, Web Site: www.worldwidemailers.com (28)

World Wildlife Fund, Washington, DC. Tel: (202) 293-4800, Web Site: www.worldwildlife.org (1)

World Wrestling Entertainment, Stamford, CT. Tel: (203) 352-8600, FAX: (203) 359-5180, E-Mail: Gary.Davis@wwecorp.com, Web Site: www.wwe.com (16)

Worldata, Boca Raton, FL. Tel: (561) 393-8200, (800) 331-8102, FAX: (561) 368-8345, E-Mail: mail@worldata.com, Web Site: www.worldata.com (23)

Worldcolor, Atlanta, GA. Tel: (770) 936-7100, Web Site: www.worldcolor.com (27)

WorldVu LLC, Baltimore, MD. Tel: (410) 522-4223, FAX: (410) 522-4233, E-Mail: info@worldvu.com, Web Site: www.worldvu.com (17)

WorleyParsons, Reading, PA. Tel: (610) 855-2000, FAX: (610) 885-2001, Web Site: www.worleyparsons.com (16)

Worman, Lori, Mid America Designs Inc, Effingham, IL. Tel: (217) 540-4200, (800) 350-4543, FAX: (217) 540-4800, E-Mail: mail@mamotorworks.com, Web Site: www.mamotorworks.com (12)

Worman, Lori, Mid America Motorworks, Effingham, IL. Tel: (217) 347-5591, (800) 500-1500, FAX: (217) 347-2952, E-Mail: mail@mamotorworks.com, Web Site: www.mamotorworks.com (12)

Worrell, Greg, Scholastic Inc, New York, NY. Tel: (212) 343-6100, (800) SCHOLASTIC, FAX: (212) 343-6484, Web Site: www.scholastic.com/ (17)

Worth, David, E., Doubletree Suites by Hilton, Boston, MA. Tel: (617) 783-0090, (800) 222-TREE, FAX: (617) 783-0897, E-Mail: doubletree1@hilton.com (19)

Worth, Ron, The Premium Connection, Las Vegas, NV. Tel: (702) 434-6900, (800) 683-0933, FAX: (702) 434-9715, Web Site: www.premiumconnection.net (33)

Worthington, Nancy, Quinnipiac College, Hamden, CT. Tel: (203) 582-8600, (203) 582-8200, (800) 462-1944, FAX: (203) 281-8664, Web Site: www.quinnipiac.edu (17)

Worthington-Levy, Carol, LENSER, San Rafael, CA. Tel: (415) 446-2500, E-Mail: carol@lenser.com, Web Site: www.lenser.com (35)

Wortsman, Marc, Marden-Kane Inc, Garden City, NY. Tel: (516) 365-3999, FAX: (516) 365-5250, E-Mail: expert@mardenkane.com, Web Site: www.mardenkane.com (35)

Woychick, Jay F., Transcat, Rochester, NY. Tel: (585) 352-9460, (800) 800-5001, FAX: (585) 352-1486, Web Site: www.transcat.com (16)

Woytke, Linda, Informal Education Products, Milwaukie, OR. Tel: (503) 794-7100, (888) 444-5500, FAX: (503) 794-7111, E-Mail: sales@museumtour.com, Web Site: www.museumtour.com (11)

Woznicki, Clark, Mason Companies Inc, Chippewa Falls, WI. Tel: (715) 723-1871, (800) 826-7030, FAX: (715) 720-4247, Web Site: www.masoncompaniesinc.com (2)

Wpromote Inc, El Segundo, CA. Tel: (310) 421-4844, Web Site: www.wpromote.com (30)

Wrenn, A.R., International Direct Media Co & Information Publishing Co, San Francisco, CA. Tel: (415) 661-4730, E-Mail: infopubsf@aol.com, Web Site: www.bookwormproductions.com (17)

Wright, Becky, Dorothy's Ruffled Originals Inc, Wilmington, NC. Tel: (910) 686-8087, (800) 367-6849, FAX: (910) 686-2958, E-Mail: curtains@dorothysoriginals.com, Web Site: www.dorothysoriginals.com (8)

Wright, David, Dow Theory Forecasts, Hammond, IN. Tel: (219) 931-6480, (800) 233-5922, FAX: (219) 931-6487, E-Mail: custserv@horizonpublishing.com, Web Site: www.dowtheory.com (17)

Wright, Don, Cushman Fruit Co Inc, West Palm Beach, FL. Tel: (561) 965-3535, (800) 776-2295, FAX: (561) 968-7263, E-Mail: info@honeybell.com, Web Site: www.honeybell.com (4)

Wright, Don, Florida Gift Fruit Shippers Association, Orlando, FL. Tel: (407) 295-1491, FAX: (407) 290-0918, Web Site: www.fgfsa.com (1)

Wright, Don, Gracewood Fruit Co, Vero Beach, FL. Tel: (772) 567-1154, E-Mail: info@gracewoodgroves.com, Web Site: www.gracewoodgroves.com (4)

Wright, Elizabeth, L., Citizens Against Government Waste, Washington, DC. Tel: (202) 467-5300, (800) USA-DEBT, FAX: (202) 467-4253, E-Mail: membership@cagw.org, Web Site: www.cagw.org (1)

Wright, Emily, Pace Communications Inc, Greensboro, NC. Tel: (336) 378-6065, FAX: (336) 275-2864, Web Site: www.pacecommunications.com (17)

Wright, Gary, A, G.A. Wright Direct Marketing, Denver, CO. Tel: (303) 333-4453, FAX: (303) 333-4660, E-Mail: gaming@gawright.com, Web Site: www.gawrightcasinomarketing.com (21)

Wright, James, Express LLC, Columbus, OH. Tel: (614) 415-4282, Web Site: www.expressfashion.com (2)

Wright, Jodi, Motherwear, Holyoke, MA. Tel: (413) 586-1978, (800) 950-2500, FAX: (413) 532-4058, E-Mail: customerservice@motherwear.com, Web Site: www.motherwear.com (2)

Wright, Kasie, Mid West Floor Co Inc, Saint Louis, MO. Tel: (314) 647-6060, FAX: (314) 647-9189, E-Mail: sales@mid-westfloor.com, Web Site: www.mid-westfloor.com (16)

Wright, Lauren, Fred Pryor Seminars, Mission, KS. Tel: (913) 967-8518, (800) 780-8476, FAX: (913) 967-8849, E-Mail: customerservice@pryor.com, Web Site: www.pryor.com (16)

Wright, Lynn, Char-Broil Grill Lover's Catalog, Louisville, KY. Tel: (706) 565-2100, (800) 241-8981, FAX: (706) 565-2121, Web Site: www.grilllovers.com (8)

Wright, Marshall, A., Baker & Taylor Inc, Charlotte, NC. Tel: (704) 998-3100, (800) 775-1800, FAX: (704) 998-3316, E-Mail: btinfo@btol.com, Web Site: www.btol.com (16)

Wright, Victor, R., Muscular Dystrophy Association, Tucson, AZ. Tel: (520) 529-2000, (800) 344-4863, FAX: (520) 529-5300, Web Site: www.mdausa.org (1)

G.A. Wright Direct Marketing, Denver, CO. Tel: (303) 333-4453, FAX: (303) 333-4660, E-Mail: gaming@gawright.com, Web Site: www.gawrightcasinomarketing.com (21)

Wright State University, Dayton, OH. Tel: (937) 775-3047, FAX: (513) 775-3952, E-Mail: teresa.stelmat@wright.edu, Web Site: www.wright.edu/business/acad/marketing (41)

Wrighton, Mark, S., Washington University, Saint Louis, MO. Tel: (314) 935-4623, (800) 638-0700, FAX: (314) 935-7088, Web Site: www.wustl.edu (1)

Wrisco Industries Inc, Palm Beach Gardens, FL. Tel: (561) 626-5700, (800) 627-2646, FAX: (561) 627-3574, E-Mail: sales.staff@wrisco.com, Web Site: www.wrisco.com (8)

The Write Answers Copywriting & Consulting, Blaine, WA. Tel: (888) 331-0322, Web Site: www.thewriteanswers.com (20)

The Write Direction, Boulder, CO. Tel: (808) 635-8031, E-Mail: debra@writedirection.com, Web Site: www.writedirection.com (39)

Writer's Digest Books, Blue Ash, OH. Tel: (513) 531-2690, (800) 666-0963, Web Site: www.fwpublications.com (17)

Wroblewski, Peter, MarketSense, Burr Ridge, IL. Tel: (630) 654-0170, Web Site: www.market-sense.com (35)

Wry, Paul, Vanguard Direct, New York, NY. Tel: (212) 736-0770, FAX: (212) 736-8305, Web Site: www.vanguarddirect.com (35)

Wu, Jeffrey, TBWA/Chiat/Day Inc, New York, NY. Tel: (212) 804-1000, FAX: (212) 804-1200, E-Mail: jamie.gallo@tbwachiat.com, Web Site: www.tbwachiat.com (35)

Wuller, Grant, Peak Computer Systems, Belleville, IL. Tel: (618) 398-5612, E-Mail: info@peaknet.net, Web Site: www.peaknet.net (22)

Wunderlich, Margaret, Lerner Publishing Group, Minneapolis, MN. Tel: (612) 332-3344, (800) 328-4929, FAX: (800) 332-1132, E-Mail: info@lernerbooks.com, Web Site: www.lernerbooks.com (17)

Wunderman, Lester, Wunderman, New York, NY. Tel: (212) 941-3000, FAX: (212) 888-7520, Web Site: www.wunderman.com (35)

Wunderman, New York, NY. Tel: (212) 941-3000, FAX: (212) 888-7520, Web Site: www.wunderman.com (35)

Wurst, Michael, S., Henry Wurst Inc, North Kansas City, MO. Tel: (816) 842-3113, FAX: (816) 472-6221, E-Mail: info@henrywurst.com, Web Site: www.henrywurst.com (27)

Henry Wurst Inc, North Kansas City, MO. Tel: (816) 842-3113, FAX: (816) 472-6221, E-Mail: info@henrywurst.com, Web Site: www.henrywurst.com (27)

Wurtz, Thomas, J., Wachovia Bank, National Association, Charlotte, NC. Tel: (704) 590-0000, (800) WACHOVIA, FAX: (704) 427-6748 (14)

Wurzelbacher, Kerry, Nostrum Inc, Long Beach, CA. Tel: (562) 437-2200, Web Site: www.nostruminc.com (35)

Wyandotte West Communications Inc, Kansas City, KS. Tel: (913) 788-5565, FAX: (913) 788-9812, E-Mail: news@wyandottewest.com, Web Site: www.wyandottewest.com (17)

Wyant, Andrew, LifeLock, Tempe, AZ. Tel: (480) 457-2007, Web Site: www.lifelock.com (16)

Wyatt, Mary, AAA Southern New England, Providence, RI. Tel: (401) 868-2005, FAX: (401) 868-2085, Web Site: www.aaa.com (1)

Wyckoff, Steve, Born Free USA, Sacramento, CA. Tel: (916) 447-3085, FAX: (916) 447-3070, E-Mail: info@bornfreeusa.org, Web Site: www.bornfreeusa.org (1)

Wycliffe Bible Translators, Dallas, TX. Tel: (972) 708-7522, Web Site: www.wycliffe.org (17)

Wylie, Devon, Seklemian Newell Inc (CRMC), Miami Beach, FL. Tel: (310) 622-5405, FAX: (520) 842-7344, Web Site: www.thecrmc.com (20)

Wyman, David, Fund for Public Interest Research, Washington, DC. Tel: (202) 546-3965, Web Site: www.ffpir.org (1)

Wyndham Hotel Group, Parsippany, NJ. Tel: (973) 753-8925, Web Site: www.cendant.com (19)

Wynn, Lisa, OTM Partners, Arlington, VA. Tel: (800) 759-2244, Web Site: www.otmpartners.biz (35)

Wyrostok, Chuck, AppaLight, Spencer, WV. Tel: (304) 927-2978, E-Mail: wyro@appalight.com, Web Site: www.appalight.com (38)

Wyse Direct, Cleveland, OH. Tel: (216) 696-2427, FAX: (216) 736-4440, Web Site: www.wysedirect.com (34)

Wysong, Randy, L., Wysong Corp, Midland, MI. Tel: (989) 631-0009, (800) 748-0188, FAX: (989) 631-8801, E-Mail: wysong@wysong.net, Web Site: www.wysong.net (7)

Wysong Corp, Midland, MI. Tel: (989) 631-0009, (800) 748-0188, FAX: (989) 631-8801, E-Mail: wysong@wysong.net, Web Site: www.wysong.net (7)

X

XDM Corp, San Francisco, CA. Tel: (415) 989-3000, FAX: (925) 934-0599, E-Mail: info@xdm.com, Web Site: www.xdm.com (21)

XL Environmental, Exton, PA. Tel: (610) 968-9500, (800) 327-1414, FAX: (610) 458-9109, E-Mail: webinfo.xli@xlgroup.com, Web Site: www.xlenvironmental.com (15)

XMPIE Inc, New York, NY. Tel: (212) 479-5166, Web Site: www.xmpie.com (22)

xpedx, Loveland, OH. Tel: (513) 965-2900, FAX: (513) 965-2849, Web Site: www.xpedx.com (25)

xpedx Stores Division, Chicago, IL. Tel: (773) 442-6200, (800) 600-0064, FAX: (630) 628-6310, Web Site: www.epedxstores.com (25)

XPO, Torrance, CA. Tel: (310) 784-8485, Web Site: www.xpomail.com (28)

Xcel Energy, Minneapolis, MN. Tel: (612) 330-6783, Web Site: xcelenergy.com (5)

Xcelerated Investments Inc, Hebron, KY. Tel: (877) 489-3347, Web Site: www.xcelerated.com (14)

Xerox Corp, Rochester, NY. Tel: (716) 423-5090, FAX: (716) 423-5479, Web Site: www.xerox.com (16)

Xilinx Inc, San Jose, CA. Tel: (408) 559-7778, FAX: (408) 559-7114, Web Site: www.xilinx.com (16)

Ximenes, Pat, Sheshunoff Information Services Inc, Austin, TX. Tel: (800) 456-2340, Web Site: www.sheshunoff.com (14)

Xpandomedia, Buffalo, NY. Tel: (716) 836-9668 (21)

Xpectrum Marketing Group, San Diego, CA. Tel: (858) 277-0079, FAX: (858) 277-0076, E-Mail: info@xpectrummg.com, Web Site: www.xpectrummg.com (35)

Xpressdocs, Fort Worth, TX. Tel: (817) 547-9705, Web Site: www.xpressdocs.com (27)

Xu, Ting, Evergreen Enterprises Inc, Richmond, VA. Tel: (804) 231-1800, Web Site: www.myevergreen.com (8)

Y

YP Talk, Pittsburg, KS. Tel: (620) 308-6434, E-Mail: info@yptalk.com, Web Site: www.yptalk.com (31)

YWCA of the USA, Washington, DC. Tel: (202) 467-0801, FAX: (202) 467-0802, E-Mail: info@ywca.org, Web Site: www.ywca.org (1)

Yaffa, Lee, Greystone Services Inc, Beverly, MA. Tel: (978) 535-9185, FAX: (978) 535-7826, E-Mail: greystone@gstone.biz (35)

Yager, Michael, Mid America Designs Inc, Effingham, IL. Tel: (217) 540-4200, (800) 350-4543, FAX: (217) 540-4800, E-Mail: mail@mamotorworks.com, Web Site: www.mamotorworks.com (12)

Yager, Mike, Mid America Motorworks, Effingham, IL. Tel: (217) 347-5591, (800) 500-1500, FAX: (217) 347-2952, E-Mail: mail@mamotorworks.com, Web Site: www.mamotorworks.com (12)

Yahoo Inc, New York, NY. Tel: (212) 381-6829 (32)

Yallen, Robert, InterMedia Advertising, Encino, CA. Tel: (818) 995-1455, FAX: (818) 995-7115, Web Site: www.intermedia-advertising.com (35)

Yamagishi, Tomoko, Shiseido Cosmetics America, New York, NY. Tel: (212) 805-2300, FAX: (212) 688-0109, Web Site: www.sca.shiseido.com (7)

Yamashita, Bob, Itochu Chemicals America Inc, White Plains, NY. Tel: (914) 333-7800, (800) 423-6870, FAX: (914) 333-7848, Web Site: www.itochu-sc.com (16)

Yang, Jonathan, Salem Web Network, Richmond, VA. Tel: (804) 205-9700, FAX: (804) 205-9648, E-Mail: info@salemwebnetwork.com, Web Site: www.salemwebnetwork.com (24)

Yang, Thomas, New England Life Insurance Co, Boston, MA. Tel: (617) 578-2000, FAX: (617) 536-2393, Web Site: www.nefn.metlife.com (15)

The Yankee Group, Boston, MA. Tel: (617) 598-7200, E-Mail: info@yankeegroup.com, Web Site: www.yankeegroup.com (20)

Yankee Publishing Inc, Dublin, NH. Tel: (603) 563-8111, FAX: (603) 563-8732, Web Site: www.yankeemagazine.com (17)

Yankelovich Inc, Chapel Hill, NC. Tel: (919) 932-8600, Web Site: www.yankelovich.com (22)

Yanovitch, Susan, CXO Media Inc, Framingham, MA. Tel: (508) 872-0080, (800) 859-5478, FAX: (508) 872-0618, Web Site: www.cxo.com (17)

Yarborough, Kathy, Pittman & Davis Inc, Harlingen, TX. Tel: (956) 423-2154, (800) 289-7829, FAX:

(866) 329-7829, E-Mail: fruit@pittmandavis.com, Web Site: www.pittmandavis.com (4)

Yardis, Alan, Ligonier Ministries, Lake Mary, FL. Tel: (407) 333-4244, (800) 435-4343, FAX: (407) 333-4377, Web Site: www.ligonier.org (5)

Yarnold, David, San Jose Mercury News, San Jose, CA. Tel: (408) 920-5000, FAX: (408) 271-3690, Web Site: www.bayarea.com (17)

Yarrington, John, Response Magazine, Santa Ana, CA. Tel: (714) 513-8624, (800) 371-6897, FAX: (714) 338-6710, Web Site: www.responsemagazine.com (43)

Yasuoka, Shigeto, Sunstar, Chicago, IL. Tel: (773) 777-4000, FAX: (773) 777-1417, E-Mail: dominico@sunstar.com, Web Site: www.sunstar.com (16)

Yates, Barry, Blue Raven Technology, Wilmington, MA. Tel: (781) 778-4600, (800) 274-5343, (800) 20RAVEN, FAX: (781) 778-4848, E-Mail: sales@blueraven.com, Web Site: www.blueraven.com (3)

Yates, Karen, National Court Reporters Association, Vienna, VA. Tel: (703) 556-6272, (800) 272-6272, FAX: (703) 556-6291, E-Mail: msic@ncrahg.org, Web Site: www.ncraonline.org (1)

Yates, Randy, Harling Marketing Inc, Kirkland, PQ Canada. Tel: (514) 695-1430, FAX: (514) 695-0530, E-Mail: info@harlingdirect.com, Web Site: www.harlingdirect.com (21)

Yates, Susan, Yates Advertising, Sausalito, CA. Tel: (415) 887-9545, FAX: (415) 887-9549 (35)

Yates Advertising, Sausalito, CA. Tel: (415) 887-9545, FAX: (415) 887-9549 (35)

Yeakle, Kate, American Writers & Artists Inc, Delray Beach, FL. Tel: (561) 278-5557, Web Site: www.awaionline.com (36)

Year One Inc, Braselton, GA. Tel: (706) 658-2140, FAX: (706) 654-5355, E-Mail: info@yearone.com, Web Site: www.yearone.com (16)

Yechezkell, Eyal, NextWeb Media, New York, NY. Tel: (212) 588-1180, Web Site: www.nextwebmedia.com (35)

Yeck, Robert, Yeck Brothers Co, Dayton, OH. Tel: (937) 294-4000, (800) 417-2767, FAX: (937) 294-6985, E-Mail: byeck@yeck.com, Web Site: www.yeck.com (35)

Yeck Brothers Co, Dayton, OH. Tel: (937) 294-4000, (800) 417-2767, FAX: (937) 294-6985, E-Mail: byeck@yeck.com, Web Site: www.yeck.com (35)

Yedinak, John, Mardev-DM2, Lombard, IL. Tel: (800) 323-4958, FAX: (303) 265-5457, E-Mail: info@mardevdm2.com, Web Site: www.mardevdm2.com (24)

Yee, Amanda, Air Power USA, Los Angeles, CA. Tel: (310) 641-0830, (888) 888-8231, FAX: (310) 641-8515, Web Site: www.airpowerusa.com (12)

Yehle, Monica, Pontifical Mission Societies in the US, New York, NY. Tel: (212) 563-8700, Web Site: www.onefamilyinmission.org (1)

Yellow Book USA, Uniondale, NY. Tel: (516) 730-1900, (800) 666-8230, FAX: (845) 278-3299, Web Site: www.yellowbook.com (17)

Yellow Pages Association, Berkeley Heights, NJ. Tel: (908) 286-2380, (800) 336-0440, FAX: (908) 286-0620, Web Site: www.yellowpagesima.org (1)

Yellowbook, King of Prussia, PA. Tel: (610) 731-2335, Web Site: www.yellowbook.com (29)

YELLOWPAGES.COM/ Ingenio, San Francisco, CA. Tel: (415) 248-4000, Web Site: www.ingenio.com (32)

Yena, John, A., Johnson & Wales University, Providence, RI. Tel: (401) 598-1000, (800) DIAL-JWU, FAX: (401) 598-1833, E-Mail: admissions.pvd@jwu.edu, Web Site: www.jwu.edu (41)

Yenkin-Majestic, Columbus, OH. Tel: (614) 253-8511, FAX: (614) 253-6327 (16)

Yep, Richard, American Counseling Association, Broken Arrow, OK. Tel: (703) 823-6862, FAX: (703) 823-0252, E-Mail: webmaster@counseling.org, Web Site: www.counseling.org (1)

Yingling, Edward, L., American Bankers Association, Washington, DC. Tel: (202) 789-0300, (800) BANKERS, FAX: (202) 296-9258, Web Site: www.aba.com (1)

Yoelin, Andrew, Andrew Yoelin & Co, Scottsdale, AZ. Tel: (602) 482-6214, E-Mail: corpdating@aol.com (20)

Andrew Yoelin & Co, Scottsdale, AZ. Tel: (602) 482-6214, E-Mail: corpdating@aol.com (20)

Yoga Journal / Active Interest Media, San Francisco, CA. Tel: (415) 591-0555, Web Site: www.yogajournal.com (17)

York, Jennifer, Bamboo Sourcery, Sebastopol, CA. Tel: (707) 823-5866, FAX: (707) 829-8106, E-Mail: bamboosource@earthlink.net, Web Site: www.bamboosourcery.com (8)

York, Susan E., The Silo Inc, New Milford, CT. Tel: (860) 355-0300, (800) 353-SILO, FAX: (860) 350-5495, E-Mail: info@hunthillfarmtrust.org, Web Site: www.thesilo.com (8)

York Label, Omaha, NE. Tel: (402) 829-4594, FAX: (402) 445-4282, Web Site: www.yorklabel.com (27)

York Label, York, PA. Tel: (717) 266-9675, FAX: (717) 266-9834, Web Site: www.yorklabel.com (27)

Yortsos, Yannis, C, USC Viterbi School of Engineering, Los Angeles, CA. Tel: (213) 740-2502, Web Site: http://viterbi.usc.edu/ (1)

Yoshida, Reizo, USY Consulting Inc, Dumont, NJ. Tel: (201) 585-7402, FAX: (201) 585-2754, E-Mail: usyconsulting@hotmail.com (20)

Yost, Fielding, Saturn Corp, Hyattsville, MD. Tel: (301) 772-7000, (800) USA-0090, FAX: (301) 386-4538, E-Mail: sales@saturncorp.com, Web Site: www.saturncorp.com (22)

Yother, Alton E., Regions, Birmingham, AL. Tel: (205) 326-5262, FAX: (205) 326-4072, Web Site: www.regions.com (14)

Young, Curt, Golfsmith International Inc, Austin, TX. Tel: (512) 821-4050, (800) 813-6897, FAX: (512) 837-9347, E-Mail: comments@golfsmith.com, Web Site: www.golfsmith.com (11)

Young, Dale, Kansas City Chiefs, Kansas City, MO. Tel: (816) 920-9300, (888) 99-CHIEFS, FAX: (816) 923-4719, Web Site: www.kcchiefs.com (16)

Young, Dana, Telpro Inc, Grand Forks, ND. Tel: (701) 775-0551, FAX: (701) 775-0629 (9)

Young, David, Covidien International, Mansfield, MA. Tel: (508) 261-8000, (800) 962-9888, FAX: (508) 261-8105, Web Site: www.covidien.com (7)

Young, Dendy, Government Technology Services Inc, Herndon, VA. Tel: (703) 502-2000, (800) 234-GTSI, FAX: (703) 222-5218, Web Site: www.gtsi.com (16)

Young, Dennis, Jenny Products Inc, Somerset, PA. Tel: (814) 445-3400, FAX: (814) 445-2280, Web Site: www.jennyproducts.com (16)

Young, Donald, Information Command Inc, Chicago, IL. Tel: (312) 245-1111, (800) 376-6654, FAX: (312) 245-1128, E-Mail: gon@phonebiz2000.com, Web Site: www.info2u.com (22)

Young, Gene, Colorworks Graphics Inc, Chicago, IL. Tel: (312) 666-7642, FAX: (312) 666-0473, E-Mail: colorworks@ameritech.net, Web Site: www.colorworksgraphics.com (34)

Young, Gregg, Argent Trading LLC, New York, NY. Tel: (212) 697-8800, FAX: (212) 697-8606, Web Site: www.Argenttrading.com (16)

Young, J., Morgan, Dassault Falcon Jet Corp, Little Ferry, NJ. Tel: (201) 440-6700, FAX: (201) 541-4515, Web Site: www.dassaultfalcon.com (16)

Young, James, A., USI Affinity, Philadelphia, PA. Tel: (610) 833-2876, (800) 625-2876, FAX: (610) 265-2876, E-Mail: info@usiaffinity.com, Web Site: www.brcorp.com (15)

Young, Jason, Ziff Davis Media Inc, New York, NY. Tel: (212) 503-5100, FAX: (212) 503-5023, Web Site: www.ziffdavis.com (17)

Young, Jeff, Mitsubishi Motor Sales of America Inc, Cypress, CA. Tel: (714) 372-6000, FAX: (714) 373-1736, Web Site: www.mitsubishicars.com (1)

Young, Joanne, Baker & Taylor Inc, Charlotte, NC. Tel: (704) 998-3100, (800) 775-1800, FAX: (704) 998-3316, E-Mail: btinfo@btol.com, Web Site: www.btol.com (16)

Young, John, R., Oles Envelope Corp, Baltimore, MD. Tel: (410) 243-1520, (800) 822-6537, FAX: (410) 366-7022, Web Site: www.olesenvelope.com (26)

Young, Joseph, Shortage Control Inc & SC Video, Strongsville, OH. Tel: (440) 238-5432, (800) 332-2288, FAX: (440) 238-8687, E-Mail: sales@shortagecontrol.com, Web Site: www.shortagecontrol.com (5)

Young, Marion, Laerdal Medical, Wappingers Falls, NY. Tel: (877) 523-7325, Web Site: www.laerdal.com (34)

Young, Mark, Shortage Control Inc & SC Video, Strongsville, OH. Tel: (440) 238-5432, (800) 332-2288, FAX: (440) 238-8687, E-Mail: sales@shortagecontrol.com, Web Site: www.shortagecontrol.com (5)

Young, Michael, Vision Marketing Inc, Englewood Cliffs, NJ. Tel: (201) 816-1560, FAX: (201) 816-1610, Web Site: www.visionmarketing.com (23)

Young, Rolland, Telpro Inc, Grand Forks, ND. Tel: (701) 775-0551, FAX: (701) 775-0629 (9)

Young, Stacy, Oriental Trading Co Inc, Omaha, NE. Tel: (402) 596-1200, (800) 875-8480, FAX: (402) 331-3873, Web Site: www.oriental.com (5)

Young America Corp, Young America, MN. Tel: (952) 467-1100, FAX: (952) 467-3895, Web Site: www.young-america.com (28)

Young America's Foundation, Herndon, VA. Tel: (800) USA-1776, Web Site: www.yaf.org (1)

Young Pecan Co, Florence, SC. Tel: (843) 662-8591, (800) 829-6864, FAX: (843) 664-2344, E-Mail: sales@youngpecan.com, Web Site: www.youngpecan.com (4)

Youngberg, Rebecca, Journal of Marketing Research, Chicago, IL. Tel: (312) 542-9000, (800) AMA-1150, FAX: (312) 542-9001, E-Mail: info@ama.org, Web Site: www.marketingpower.org (43)

Youngblood, Mike, Sportif Mail Order Inc, Sparks, NV. Tel: (775) 359-6400, (800) 776-7843, FAX: (800) 776-3291, Web Site: www.sportif.com (2)

Youngerman, David, Whiting & Davis, Attleboro Falls, MA. Tel: (508) 699-4412, (800) 876-MESH, FAX: (508) 695-7606, E-Mail: info@whitinganddavis.com, Web Site: www.whitinganddavis.com (16)

Youngo, Leonard, Wendell August Forge Inc, Grove City, PA. Tel: (724) 458-8360, (800) 923-1390, FAX: (724) 458-0906, E-Mail: info@wendell.com, Web Site: www.wendellaugust.com (16)

Youngs, Tillie, 1000 Islands International Tourism Council, Alexandria Bay, NY. Tel: (315) 482-2520, (800) 847-5263, (800) 456-2267, FAX: (315) 482-5906, Web Site: www.visit1000islands.com/visitorinfo/ (19)

Youngstown State University, Youngstown, OH. Tel: (330) 742-3064, Web Site: www.ysu.edu (41)

Younquist, Jon, Westwood Publishing Co, Glendale, CA. Tel: (818) 242-1159, FAX: (818) 247-9379 (17)

Your Choice Or Mine, San Mateo, CA. Tel: (650) 340-7959, FAX: (650) 340-0449 (16)

Your Man Tours, El Segundo, CA. Tel: (310) 649-3820, FAX: (310) 649-2118, E-Mail: ymt@earthlink.net, Web Site: www.ymtvacations.com (19)

Your Move Chess & Games, North Massapequa, NY. Tel: (516) 882-9800, (800) 645-4710, FAX: (631) 424-3405, E-Mail: icd@icdchess.com, Web Site: www.icdchess.com (11)

Yousendit Inc, Campbell, CA. Tel: (408) 879-9118, Web Site: www.yousendit.com (22)

Yu, Tricia, Uncharted Country Publishing, Madison, WI. Tel: (575) 776-3470, E-Mail: ucp@taichihealth.com, Web Site: www.taichihealth.com (17)

Yuan, Walter, Enterprex International Corp, Arcadia, CA. Tel: (626) 256-1444, FAX: (626) 256-1404, E-Mail: premium@enterprex.com, Web Site: www.enterprex.com (16)

Yudin, Stephanie, InterContinental Hotels Group, Atlanta, GA. Tel: (770) 604-2000, (877) 424-2449, FAX: (770) 604-8639, Web Site: www.ichotelsgroup.com (19)

Yuhn, Mark, Urban Science Applications Inc, Detroit, MI. Tel: (313) 259-9900, Web Site: www.urbanscience.com (20)

Yukevich, Stan, ER Carpenter, Taylor, TX. Tel: (512) 365-5833, (800) 234-9105, FAX: (512) 352-6025, Web Site: www.carpenter.com (16)

Yung, William, J., Montbleu Resort Casino and Spa, Stateline, NV. Tel: (775) 588-3515, (888) 829-7630, FAX: (775) 586-2030, Web Site: www.montbleuresort.com (19)

Yurko, Chuck, Newark Electronics, Chicago, IL. Tel: (773) 784-5100, (800) 4-Newark, FAX: (888) 551-4801, E-Mail: webmaster@newark.com, Web Site: www.newark.com (3)

David Yurman, New York, NY. Tel: (212) 896-1550, Web Site: davidyurman.com (5)

Yves Rocher North America Inc, Longueuil, PQ Canada. Tel: (450) 442-9555, Web Site: www.yvesrocherusa.com (7)

Z

ZLR Ignition, Des Moines, IA. Tel: (515) 244-4456, FAX: (515) 244-5749, Web Site: www.zlr.com (35)

ZS Associates, Evanston, IL. Tel: (847) 492-3600, FAX: (847) 864-6280, E-Mail: inquiry@zsassociates.com, Web Site: www.zsassociates.com (20)

Ztek Co, Lexington, KY. Tel: (859) 281-1611, (800) 247-1603, FAX: (859) 281-1521, E-Mail: cs@ztek.com, Web Site: www.ztek.com (3)

Zabel, Cynthia, Brant Publications Inc, New York, NY. Tel: (212) 941-2800, FAX: (212) 941-2885, Web Site: www.interviewmagazine.com (17)

Zacharewicz, Gene, CoverClicks LLC, New York, NY. Tel: (888) 624-1340, FAX: (212) 239-2850, E-Mail: info@coverclicksmail.com, Web Site: www.coverclicks.com (23)

Zacharius, Steven, Kensington Publishing Corp, New York, NY. Tel: (212) 407-1500, (800) 221-2647, FAX: (212) 407-1590, Web Site: www.kensingtonbooks.com (17)

Zachry Associates Inc, Abilene, TX. Tel: (325) 677-1342, E-Mail: pfulham@zachryinc.com, Web Site: www.zachryinc.com (20)

Zack, Robert, Horn Packaging Corp, Lancaster, MA. Tel: (978) 772-0290, (800) 832-7020, FAX: (978) 772-4611, E-Mail: mccarthy@horncorp.com, Web Site: www.hornpackaging.com (5)

Zadins, Paul, M., American Locker Security Systems Inc, Coppell, TX. Tel: (817) 329-1600, (800) 828-9118, E-Mail: info@americanlocker.com, Web Site: www.americanlocker.com (16)

Zagami, Robert, W., AIIM International, Silver Spring, MD. Tel: (301) 587-8202, (800) 477-2446, FAX: (301) 587-2711, E-Mail: aiim@aiim.org, Web Site: www.aiim.org (1)

Zahka, George, George Zahka, Needham, MA. Tel: (617) 332-6797 (35)

George Zahka, Needham, MA. Tel: (617) 332-6797 (35)

Zahn, Spencer, Spencer Zahn & Associates, Philadelphia, PA. Tel: (215) 564-5979, FAX: (215) 564-6205 (35)

Zahniser, Dulce, A., Overseas Private Investment Corp (OPIC), Washington, DC. Tel: (202) 336-8400,

FAX: (202) 336-7949, E-Mail: info@opic.gov, Web Site: www.opic.gov (14)

Zaitsu, Narumi, Bridgestone/Firestone North American Tire LLC, Nashville, TN. Tel: (615) 937-1000, (800) 543-7522, FAX: (615) 937-3721, Web Site: www.bridgestonetire.com (16)

Zajac, Raymond, CJ Hummul Co, Nescapeck, PA. Tel: (570) 752-0936, (800) 762-0235, FAX: (570) 752-0938, E-Mail: mail@hummul.com, Web Site: www.hummul.com (11)

Zakarian, Karin, Ross Metals, New York, NY. Tel: (212) 869-1407, (800) 654-ROSS (16)

Zaky, Sherif, JonCas PostExperts Inc, Ville Saint Laurent, PQ Canada. Tel: (514) 333-7480, FAX: (514) 332-6915, E-Mail: sherif.zaky@quebecorworld.com, Web Site: www.postexperts.com (23)

Zale Corp, Irving, TX. Tel: (972) 580-4376, Web Site: www.zalecorp.com (6)

Zamchick, Alan, R., Hachette Filipacchi List Management, New York, NY. Tel: (212) 767-6677, FAX: (212) 767-5605, Web Site: www.hfmuslists.com (17)

Zander, Edward, J., Motorola Inc, Montvale, NJ. Tel: (201) 949-5500, (800) 262-8509, Web Site: www.motorola.com (16)

Zang, Bill, Universal Hovercraft, Cordova, IL. Tel: (309) 654-2588, FAX: (309) 654-2588, Web Site: www.hovercraft.com (11)

Zank, Gregg, A., Dow Corning Corp, Midland, MI. Tel: (989) 496-4000, (800) 248-2481, FAX: (989) 496-4572, Web Site: www.dowcorning.com (16)

Zapin, Roni, L., RL Zapin Associates Inc, New York, NY. Tel: (212) 297-6248, E-Mail: roni@rlzapinassociates.com, Web Site: www.rlzapinassociates.com (20)

RL Zapin Associates Inc, New York, NY. Tel: (212) 297-6248, E-Mail: roni@rlzapinassociates.com, Web Site: www.rlzapinassociates.com (20)

Zappariello, David, Scientific Marketing Services Inc, Landisville, NJ. Tel: (856) 697-1257, FAX: (856) 697-9639, E-Mail: info@smsmktg.com, Web Site: www.smsmktg.com (35)

Zappos.com, Henderson, NV. Tel: (702) 943-7832, Web Site: www.zappos.com (2)

Zardin, John, Mel Bay Publications Inc, Pacific, MO. Tel: (800) 8-MELBAY, FAX: (636) 257-5062, E-Mail: email@melbay.com, Web Site: www.melbay.com (17)

Zaretsky, Arthur, Famous Smoke Shop Inc, Easton, PA. Tel: (610) 559-7000, (800) 672-5544, FAX: (610) 559-7170, E-Mail: info@famous-smoke.com, Web Site: www.famous-smoke.com (16)

Zaslav, David, Discovery Communications LLC, Silver Spring, MD. Tel: (240) 662-2000, FAX: (240) 662-1868, Web Site: corporate.discovery.com (11)

Zatz, Cheryl, The Popcorn Factory, Lake Forest, IL. Tel: (847) 362-0028, (888) 216-0235, FAX: (888) 333-4595, E-Mail: service@thepopcornfactory.com, Web Site: www.thepopcornfactory.com (4)

Zavatter, Suzanne, Marian Helpers Center, Stockbridge, MA. Tel: (413) 298-3691, (800) 462-7426, FAX: (413) 298-3583, Web Site: www.marian.org (1)

Zawalski, Jo Ann, Rinfret Ltd, Greenwich, CT. Tel: (203) 622-0000, Web Site: www.rinfretltd.com (8)

Zawaski, John, K., Dependable Business Forms, Villa Park, IL. Tel: (630) 530-1734, FAX: (630) 530-1789, E-Mail: j.zawaski@comcast.net, Web Site: www.dependablebusinessforms.com (27)

Zawoysky, Mike, Eastbay Running Store Inc, Wausau, WI. Tel: (715) 845-5538, (800) 826-2205, FAX: (715) 261-9500, Web Site: www.eastbay.com (2)

ZCard North America, New York, NY. Tel: (212) 797-3450, Web Site: www.zcard.com (31)

Zdancewicz, Jack, ACBL, Horn Lake, MS. Tel: (901) 332-5586, FAX: (901) 398-7754, E-Mail: service@acbl.org, Web Site: www.acbl.org (1)

Zdravecky, Robert, G., Ames Taping Tool System Inc, Stone Mountain, GA. Tel: (770) 243-2647, FAX: (770) 243-2658, Web Site: www.amestools.com (9)

Zeanah, Eric, American Accessories International, Knoxville, TN. Tel: (865) 525-9100, FAX: (865) 525-0889 (33)

Zebroski, Dan, Bethesda List Center Inc, Bethesda, MD. Tel: (301) 986-1455, FAX: (301) 907-4870, E-Mail: info@bethesda-list.com, Web Site: www.bethesda-list.com (24)

Zechman Jr., Edwin, K., Children's Hospital Foundation, Washington, DC. Tel: (202) 476-3000, (800) 884-LIFE, FAX: (202) 884-5999, Web Site: www.dcchildrens.com (1)

Zed Marketing Group, Edmond, OK. Tel: (405) 348-8145, FAX: (405) 348-5541, E-Mail: zed@zedmktg.com, Web Site: www.zedmktg.com (27)

Zefkin, Daniel, Zephyr Media Group Inc, Evanston, IL. Tel: (847) 328-1519, Web Site: www.zephyr-media.com (35)

Zeh, Tim, Fisher Scientific, Pittsburgh, PA. Tel: (800) 766-7000, FAX: (800) 772-7702, Web Site: www.fishersci.com (16)

Zeidler, Donald, W Atlee Burpee Co, Warminster, PA. Tel: (215) 674-4900, (800) 333-5808, FAX: (215) 674-4170, Web Site: www.burpee.com (8)

Zeitz, Joshua, American Heritage Picture Library, New York, NY. Tel: (212) 206-5107, (800) 777-1222, FAX: (212) 367-3151, Web Site: www.americanheritage.com (38)

Zekiel, Gretchen, Tax Management Inc, Bethesda, MD. Tel: (202) 452-4200, FAX: (202) 496-6013 (17)

Zeldner, Ishai, Moon Shine Trading Co, Woodland, CA. Tel: (530) 668-0660, (800) 678-1226, FAX: (530) 668-6061, E-Mail: store@moonshinetrading.com, Web Site: www.moonshinetrading.com (4)

Zelenetz, Neil, Neil Zelenetz & Associates, Garden City, NY. Tel: (516) 746-2981, E-Mail: nzelenetz@aol.com (20)

Neil Zelenetz & Associates, Garden City, NY. Tel: (516) 746-2981, E-Mail: nzelenetz@aol.com (20)

Zelinskas, Mike, Halsom Home Care Inc, Centerville, OH. Tel: (937) 438-6600, (800) 345-5438, FAX: (937) 438-6620, E-Mail: main@halsom.com, Web Site: www.halsom.com (16)

Zell, Samuel, Tribune Co, Chicago, IL. Tel: (312) 222-9100, FAX: (312) 222-1573, Web Site: www.tribune.com (17)

Zeller, Ben, Queen Bee Gardens, Lovell, WY. Tel: (307) 548-2543, (800) 225-7553, FAX: (307) 548-6721, E-Mail: queenbee@tctwest.net, Web Site: queenbeegardens.com (4)

Zeller, Bessie, Queen Bee Gardens, Lovell, WY. Tel: (307) 548-2543, (800) 225-7553, FAX: (307) 548-6721, E-Mail: queenbee@tctwest.net, Web Site: queenbeegardens.com (4)

Zeller, John, H., University of Pennsylvania, Philadelphia, PA. Tel: (215) 898-5000, FAX: (215) 898-9659, Web Site: www.upenn.edu (1)

Zellmer, Gary, Taylor Corp, North Mankato, MN. Tel: (507) 625-2828, FAX: (507) 625-3388 (16)

Zelstar, Craig, NNE Marketing, Concord, MA. Tel: (617) 429-7999, Web Site: www.nnemarketing.com (1)

Zemrak, Gary, Blethen Maine Newspapers Inc, Portland, ME. Tel: (207) 791-6650, FAX: (207) 791-6925, Web Site: www.mainetoday.com (17)

Zengel, William, Association of National Advertisers Inc, New York, NY. Tel: (212) 697-5950, FAX: (212) 687-7310, Web Site: www.ana.net (40)

Zengerle, Michael, Lufthansa German Airlines, East Meadow, NY. Tel: (516) 296-9416, FAX: (516) 296-9386, Web Site: www.lufthansa-usa.com (19)

Zenith Direct, New York, NY. Tel: (212) 859-5100, Web Site: www.zodirect.com (35)

Zenos, George, JDR Microdevices, Mountain View, CA. Tel: (408) 494-1400, (800) 538-5000, FAX: (800) 538-5005, E-Mail: sales@jdr.com, Web Site: www.jdr.com (3)

Zentmaier, Robert, L., Photo Researchers Inc, New York, NY. Tel: (212) 758-3420, (800) 833-9033, FAX: (212) 355-0731, E-Mail: info@

photoresearchers.com, Web Site: www.
photoresearchers.com (38)

Zephyr Media Group Inc, Evanston, IL. Tel: (847)
328-1519, Web Site: www.zephyr-media.com (35)

Zeppo Marketing Inc, New York, NY. Tel: (212) 308-
5734, Web Site: www.zeppomarketing.com (23)

02K1, Rye Brook, NY. Tel: (914) 253-4500, Web Site:
www.illyusa.com (4)

Zerovnik, Greg, Greg Zerovnik, Upland, CA. Tel:
(909) 982-3787, FAX: (909) 931-2402 (36)

Greg Zerovnik, Upland, CA. Tel: (909) 982-3787,
FAX: (909) 931-2402 (36)

Zeta Interactive, New York, NY. Tel: (646) 834-9400,
Web Site: www.zustek.com (32)

Zhang, Hao, Area Electronics Systems Inc, Anaheim,
CA. Tel: (714) 993-0300, (800) 796-1580, FAX:
(714) 993-0987, E-Mail: areasales@areasys.com,
Web Site: www.areasys.com (3)

Zhang, John, Systems Analytics Inc, Needham, MA.
Tel: (781) 444-4837, E-Mail: info@
systemsanalytics.com, Web Site: www.
systemsanalytics.com (20)

Ziebarth, Lori, Aimia, Minneapolis, MN. Tel: (763)
445-3453, FAX: (763) 496-3453, Web Site: www.
carlsonmarketing.com (35)

Ziemer, James L., Harley-Davidson Inc, Milwaukee,
WI. Tel: (414) 343-7286, FAX: (414) 343-4806,
Web Site: www.harley-davidson.com (12)

Ziemski, Nancy, Gale Research Inc, Farmington Hills,
MI. Tel: (248) 699-4253, (800) 877-GALE, FAX:
(313) 961-6083, Web Site: www.gale.com (17)

Zier, Dawn, The Reader's Digest Association Inc,
New York, NY. Tel: (914) 238-3599, FAX: (914)
244-7689, Web Site: www.rd.com (17)

Zieser, John, S., Meredith Corp, Des Moines, IA. Tel:
(515) 284-3000, FAX: (515) 284-2700, Web Site:
www.meredith.com (17)

Ziff Davis Media Inc, New York, NY. Tel: (212) 503-
5100, FAX: (212) 503-5023, Web Site: www.
ziffdavis.com (17)

Ziglar, Tom, Zig Ziglar Corp, Plano, TX. Tel: (972)
233-9191, (800) 527-0306, FAX: (469) 321-7556,
E-Mail: info@ziglar.com, Web Site: www.zigziglar.
com (16)

Ziglar, Zig, Zig Ziglar Corp, Plano, TX. Tel: (972)
233-9191, (800) 527-0306, FAX: (469) 321-7556,
E-Mail: info@ziglar.com, Web Site: www.zigziglar.
com (16)

Zig Ziglar Corp, Plano, TX. Tel: (972) 233-9191,
(800) 527-0306, FAX: (469) 321-7556, E-Mail:
info@ziglar.com, Web Site: www.zigziglar.com
(16)

Zillner Marketing Communications Inc, Lenexa, KS.
Tel: (913) 599-3230, Web Site: www.zillner.com
(35)

Zim-American Israeli Shipping Co Inc, Staten Island,
NY. Tel: (718) 313-1950, Web Site: www.zim.com
(16)

Zimbalist, Michael, The New York Times Co, New
York, NY. Tel: (212) 556-3881, FAX: (212) 556-
7389, Web Site: www.nytimes.com (17)

Zimmer, John J., Transcat, Rochester, NY. Tel: (585)
352-9460, (800) 800-5001, FAX: (585) 352-1486,
Web Site: www.transcat.com (16)

Zimmer, Mark, A., The Keystone Equities Group,
Oaks, PA. Tel: (610) 415-6300, (800) 715-9905,
FAX: (610) 415-6328, Web Site: www.
keystoneequities.com (20)

Zimmerer, Cindy, Wunderman, New York, NY. Tel:
(212) 941-3000, FAX: (212) 888-7520, Web Site:
www.wunderman.com (35)

Zimmerling, Judy, Blue Valley Tele-Marketing Inc,
Home, KS. Tel: (785) 799-3500, (800) 882-0803,
FAX: (785) 799-3504 (29)

Zimmerman, Brad, Zimmerman-McDonald Machinery
Inc, Saint Louis, MO. Tel: (314) 291-9360, FAX:
(314) 291-2981, E-Mail: zimsales@
zimmermanmcdonald.com, Web Site: www.
zimmermanmcdonald.com (16)

Zimmerman, Clayton, Stratmar Systems Inc, Port
Chester, NY. Tel: (914) 937-7171, (800) 866-2399,
FAX: (914) 937-6045, E-Mail: info@stratmar.com,
Web Site: www.stratmar.com (29)

Zimmerman, Dan, Photoworks, Cleveland, OH. Tel:
(206) 281-1390, (800) PHOTOWORKS, FAX:
(206) 284-5357, E-Mail: info@photoworks.com,
Web Site: www.photoworks.com (16)

Zimmerman, Eric, Dover Publications Inc, Mineola,
NY. Tel: (516) 294-7000, (800) 223-3130, FAX:
(516) 873-1401, Web Site: www.doverpublications.
com (17)

Zimmerman, Jordan, Zimmerman & Partners, Fort
Lauderdale, FL. Tel: (954) 731-2900, FAX: (954)
731-2977, Web Site: www.zadv.com (35)

Zimmerman, Leonard, J., Zimmerman Business Con-
sulting Inc, New York, NY. Tel: (212) 860-3107,
FAX: (212) 860-7730, E-Mail: ljzzbci@aol.com,
Web Site: www.zbcinc.com (20)

Zimmerman, P.R., Kano Laboratories, Nashville, TN.
Tel: (615) 833-4101, (800) 311-3374, FAX: (615)
833-5790, Web Site: www.kanolabs.com (16)

Zimmerman, Peter, Kano Laboratories, Nashville, TN.
Tel: (615) 833-4101, (800) 311-3374, FAX: (615)
833-5790, Web Site: www.kanolabs.com (16)

Zimmerman, Stan, Zimmerman-McDonald Machinery
Inc, Saint Louis, MO. Tel: (314) 291-9360, FAX:
(314) 291-2981, E-Mail: zimsales@
zimmermanmcdonald.com, Web Site: www.
zimmermanmcdonald.com (16)

Zimmerman, Tom, Pharmavite Corp LLC (HQ),
Northridge, CA. Tel: (818) 221-6200, (800) 423-
2405, FAX: (818) 221-6618, Web Site: www.
pharmavite.com (16)

Zimmerman & Partners, Fort Lauderdale, FL. Tel:
(954) 731-2900, FAX: (954) 731-2977, Web Site:
www.zadv.com (35)

Zimmerman Business Consulting Inc, New York, NY.
Tel: (212) 860-3107, FAX: (212) 860-7730,
E-Mail: ljzzbci@aol.com, Web Site: www.zbcinc.
com (20)

Zimmerman Irrigation Inc, Biglerville, PA. Tel: (717)
337-2727, (800) 452-5699, FAX: (717) 337-1785,
E-Mail: info@trikl-eez.com, Web Site: www.trickl-
eez.com (16)

Zimmerman-McDonald Machinery Inc, Saint Louis,
MO. Tel: (314) 291-9360, FAX: (314) 291-2981,
E-Mail: zimsales@zimmermanmcdonald.com, Web
Site: www.zimmermanmcdonald.com (16)

Zimpleman, Larry, D., The Principal Financial Group,
Des Moines, IA. Tel: (515) 247-5111, (800) 986-
3343, FAX: (515) 246-5475, Web Site: www.
principal.com (15)

Zinio Systems Inc, San Francisco, CA. Tel: (415) 494-
2700, FAX: (415) 494-2701, Web Site: www.zinio.
com (31)

Zink, Alan, E., American Insurance Administrators
Inc, Columbus, OH. Tel: (614) 486-5388, FAX:
(614) 486-2728 (15)

Zink, Alan, USI Affinity, Philadelphia, PA. Tel: (610)
833-2876, (800) 625-2876, FAX: (610) 265-2876,
E-Mail: info@usiaffinity.com, Web Site: www.
brcorp.com (15)

Zink, Stephen, J., Gorham's Inc, Springfield, IL. Tel:
(217) 544-1727, (800) 500-3949, FAX: (217) 544-
1623, E-Mail: gorhams@gorhams.com, Web Site:
www.gorhams.com (33)

Zinkel, James, R., Camelot Enterprises, Bristol, WI.
Tel: (262) 857-2695 (9)

Zinkel, Sandra L., Camelot Enterprises, Bristol, WI.
Tel: (262) 857-2695 (9)

ZIP Mailing Services Inc, Landover, MD. Tel: (301)
386-3633, FAX: (301) 386-3637, E-Mail:
zipmail@zipmailing.com, Web Site: www.
zipmailing.com (28)

Zircon Co Inc, Salem, MA. Tel: (978) 741-7000,
FAX: (978) 532-0012 (22)

Zirzow, William, Town Money Saver, Lucas, OH. Tel:
(419) 892-1913, Web Site: www.townmoneysaver.
com (31)

Zitz, Jay T., Newspapers First, Norwalk, CT. Tel:
(212) 692-7100, FAX: (212) 286-9004, E-Mail:
adunstan@newspapersfirst.com, Web Site: www.
newspapersfirst.com (31)

Zlateff, Kristina, Columbia Sportswear, Portland, OR.
Tel: (503) 985-4203, Web Site: www.columbia.com
(2)

Zlotnik, A., Air-Scent International, Pittsburgh, PA.
Tel: (800) 247-0770, FAX: (412) 252-2000,
E-Mail: laura@aromaresource.com, Web Site:
www.airscent.com (16)

Zodhiates, Philip, Response Unlimited, Waynesboro,
VA. Tel: (540) 943-6721, FAX: (540) 943-0841,
E-Mail: info@ru-lists.com, Web Site: www.
responseunlimited.com (23)

Zoe Marketing, San Diego, CA. Tel: (858) 408-1700
(20)

Zoks, Lisa, Drug Information Association, Horsham,
PA. Tel: (215) 442-6124, Web Site: www.diahome.
org (1)

Zoltners, Andris, ZS Associates, Evanston, IL. Tel:
(847) 492-3600, FAX: (847) 864-6280, E-Mail:
inquiry@zsassociates.com, Web Site: www.
zsassociates.com (20)

Zondag, Richard, JW Jung Seed Co, Randolph, WI.
Tel: (920) 326-3121, (800) 297-3123, FAX: (920)
326-5769, E-Mail: info@jungseed.com, Web Site:
www.jungseed.com (8)

Zondag, Richard, McClure & Zimmerman, Randolph,
WI. Tel: (800) 883-6998, FAX: (800) 374-6120,
Web Site: www.mzbulb.com (8)

Zondervan Corp, Grand Rapids, MI. Tel: (616) 698-
6900, (800) 727-3060, FAX: (616) 698-3235, Web
Site: www.zondervan.com (17)

Zones Inc, Auburn, WA. Tel: (253) 205-3000, (800)
408-9663, FAX: (425) 430-3626, E-Mail:
corpsales@zones.com, Web Site: www.zones.com
(3)

Zonin, Richard, Simplicity Pattern Co Inc/Style Patterns Ltd/New Look English Pattern Co Ltd, New
York, NY. Tel: (212) 372-0500, (888) 588-2700,
FAX: (212) 372-0628, E-Mail: info@
simplicitypatt.com, Web Site: www.simplicitypatt.
com (8)

Zoological Society of San Diego, San Diego, CA. Tel:
(619) 231-1515, FAX: (619) 557-3937, Web Site:
www.sandiegozoo.org (1)

Zoominfo Inc, Waltham, MA. Tel: (781) 693-7500,
Web Site: www.zoominfo.com (22)

Zoradi, Michael, Medcom Inc, Cypress, CA. Tel:
(800) 877-1443, FAX: (714) 891-3140, E-Mail:
lhammonds@medcominc.com, Web Site: www.
medcominc.com (17)

Zorn, Scott, Direct Resources Group, Seattle, WA. Tel:
(206) 749-0001, E-Mail: results@drg.com, Web
Site: www.drg.com (35)

Zoro Tools Inc, Mundelein, IL. Web Site: www.
zorotools.com (9)

Zotos International, Darien, CT. Tel: (203) 655-8911,
(800) 242-WAVE, (800) 242-9283, FAX: (203)
656-7890, E-Mail: HumanResources@zotosintl.
com, Web Site: www.zotos.com (16)

Zouire, Overland Park, KS. Tel: (913) 384-6888, (800)
346-8991, FAX: (913) 384-5757, E-Mail: info@
zouire.com, Web Site: www.zouire.com (33)

Zucchero, Vincent, Reliapon Police Products, Las Ve-
gas, NV. Tel: (805) 289-0145, (888) 263-4482,
FAX: (805) 735-4276, E-Mail: info@reliapon.com,
Web Site: www.reliapon.com (5)

Zucker, Janice, Jaz Holdings LLC, Liberty Corner, NJ.
Tel: (973) 574-7600, (800) 999-9554, FAX: (973)
944-5073, E-Mail: webmaster@regentbook.com,
Web Site: www.regentbook.com (16)

Zucker, Joshua, Jaz Holdings LLC, Liberty Corner,
NJ. Tel: (973) 574-7600, (800) 999-9554, FAX:
(973) 944-5073, E-Mail: webmaster@regentbook.
com, Web Site: www.regentbook.com (16)

Zuckerberg, Lloyd, P., New York Landmarks Conservancy, New York, NY. Tel: (212) 995-5260, FAX: (212) 995-5268, Web Site: www.nylandmarks.org (1)

Zuckerman, Mitchell, Sotheby's, New York, NY. Tel: (212) 606-7000, FAX: (212) 606-7107, Web Site: www.sothebys.com (6)

Zuckerman, Mortimer, B., US News & World Report, New York, NY. Tel: (212) 916-7360, FAX: (212) 643-7842, Web Site: www.usnews.com (17)

Zuckerman, Steven, Clipper Magazine, Mountville, PA. Tel: (717) 569-5100, Web Site: www.clippermagazine.com (31)

Zuckermandel, Jim, Zed Marketing Group, Edmond, OK. Tel: (405) 348-8145, FAX: (405) 348-5541, E-Mail: zed@zedmktg.com, Web Site: www.zedmktg.com (27)

Zukowski, Paul, The Hibbert Group, Trenton, NJ. Tel: (609) 394-7500, (800) 545-4747, FAX: (609) 695-6553, Web Site: www.hibbertco.com (28)

Zullo, Eda, Smith Hanley Associates, Southport, CT. Tel: (203) 319-4300, (888) 221-2900, FAX: (203) 319-4320, Web Site: www.smithhanley.com (20)

Zumbox, Westlake Village, CA. Tel: (818) 707-7400, Web Site: www.zumbox.com (21)

Zuniga, Anna, Magic Seasonings Mail Order, New Orleans, LA. Tel: (504) 731-3590, (800) 457-2857, FAX: (504) 731-3576, E-Mail: jlm@chefpaul.com, Web Site: www.chefpaul.com (4)

Zunk, Charles, US Playing Card Co, Erlanger, KY. Tel: (513) 396-5700, (800) 542-7430, FAX: (513) 392-5879 (16)

Zunker, Bob, Direct Mail Solutions LLC, Carol Stream, IL. Tel: (630) 653-6863, FAX: (630) 653-7144, E-Mail: support@dmspostal.com, Web Site: www.dmspostal.com (28)

Zupan, Leo, Discover Publications, Worthington, OH. Tel: (614) 785-1111, Web Site: www.discover.pubs.com (17)

Zurich, Schaumburg, IL. Tel: (847) 605-3712, (800) 382-2150, FAX: (847) 605-6403, Web Site: www.zurichna.com (15)

Zusman, Lawrence, XMPIE Inc, New York, NY. Tel: (212) 479-5166, Web Site: www.xmpie.com (22)

Zvesper, Joseph, American Appraisal Associates, Milwaukee, WI. Tel: (414) 271-7240, (800) 558-8650, FAX: (414) 225-1271, Web Site: www.american-appraisal.com (14)

Zwart, Fred, Datum Timing, Test & Measurement, Beverly, MA. Tel: (978) 927-8220, FAX: (978) 927-4099, E-Mail: wriley@datum.com, Web Site: www.datum.com (9)

Zweiger, Philip, Farrar Straus & Giroux Inc, New York, NY. Tel: (212) 741-6900, (800) 330-8477, FAX: (212) 633-2427, E-Mail: childrens_editorial@fsgbooks.com, Web Site: www.fsgbooks.com (17)

Zwemke, Thomas, Cessna Aircraft Co, Wichita, KS. Tel: (316) 517-6000, FAX: (316) 517-6640, E-Mail: pmichael@cessna.textron.com, Web Site: www.cessna.com (16)

Zyontz, Robert, Princeton Marketech, Princeton Junction, NJ. Tel: (609) 936-0021, FAX: (609) 936-0015, E-Mail: bzyontz@princetonmarketech.com, Web Site: www.princetonmarketech.com (35)

Zysman, Dennis, The Du-Rite Group Inc, Englewood, NJ. Tel: (201) 387-7000, FAX: (201) 385-8513, E-Mail: information@duriteconstruction.com, Web Site: www.duriteconstruction.com (16)

Zysman, Gary, The Du-Rite Group Inc, Englewood, NJ. Tel: (201) 387-7000, FAX: (201) 385-8513, E-Mail: information@duriteconstruction.com, Web Site: www.duriteconstruction.com (16)